W9-AQW-126

READERS' GUIDE TO PERIODICAL LITERATURE

An Author and Subject Index

MARCH 1966—FEBRUARY 1967

Edited by
ZADA LIMERICK

Indexers
ANNE W. FURNESS
LINDA LACK HOY
LOVISA J. JENKINS
MURIEL M. PHILLIPS
BARBARA STANLEY WELCH

THE H. W. WILSON COMPANY
NEW YORK   1967

PRINTED IN THE UNITED STATES OF AMERICA

Library of Congress Catalog Card No. (6-8232)

VERMONT ... COLLEGE
MONTPELIER, VT.

KEY TO ABBREVIATIONS

+	continued on later pages of same issue	jr	junior
		jt auth	joint author
abp	archbishop		
abr	abridged	ltd	limited
Ag	August		
Ap	April	m	monthly
arch	architect	Mr	March
assn	association	My	May
Aut	Autumn	N	November
av	avenue	no	number
bart	baronet	O	October
bibliog	bibliography	por	portrait
bibliog f	bibliographical foot-notes	pseud	pseudonym
		pt	part
bi-m	bimonthly	pub	published, publisher, publishing
bi-w	biweekly		
bldg	building		
bp	bishop	q	quarterly
co	company	rev	revised
comp	compiled, compiler	S	September
cond	condensed	semi-m	semimonthly
cont	continued	soc	society
corp	corporation	Spr	Spring
D	December	sq	square
dept	department	sr	senior
ed	edited, edition, editor	st	street
		Sum	Summer
F	February	sup	supplement
Hon	Honorable	supt	superintendent
il	illustrated, illustration, illustrator	tr	translated, translation, translator
inc	incorporated		
introd	introduction, introductory	v	volume
		w	weekly
Ja	January	Wint	Winter
Je	June		
Jl	July	yr	year

Sample entry: **MARINE painting**
Frederick Waugh, America's most popular marine painter. G. R. Havens. il Am Artist 31:30-7+ Ja '67

Explanation: An illustrated article on the subject **MARINE painting** entitled "Frederick Waugh, America's most popular marine painter," by G. R. Havens, will be found in volume 31 of American Artist, pages 30-7 (continued on later pages of the same issue) the January 1967 number

Readers' Guide to
Periodical Literature

MARCH 1966—FEBRUARY 1967

READERS' GUIDE TO
PERIODICAL LITERATURE

Cumulated Volumes

ACKNOWLEDGMENTS

In addition to the staff members whose names appear on the title page we wish to acknowledge the contributions of Virginia Turrell who indexed for this volume.

Z. L.

19428

ABBREVIATIONS OF PERIODICALS INDEXED

March 1966—February 1967

FOR FULL INFORMATION, CONSULT PAGES IX-XI

ALA Bul—ALA Bulletin
Am Artist—American Artist
Am City—American City
Am Ed—American Education
Am For—American Forests
*Am Heritage—American Heritage
Am Hist R—American Historical Review
Am Home—American Home
Am Rec G—American Record Guide
America—America
Américas—Américas
Ann Am Acad—Annals of the American Acad
  emy of Political and Social Science
Antiques—Antiques
Arch Forum—Architectural Forum
Arch Rec—Architectural Record
Art N—Art News
*Atlan—Atlantic
Audubon—Audubon
Aviation W—Aviation Week & Space Tech-
  nology

Bet Hom & Gard—Better Homes and Gardens
Bsns W—Business Week
Bul Atomic Sci—Bulletin of the Atomic Sci-
  entists

Cath World—Catholic World
*Changing T—Changing Times
Christian Cent—Christian Century
Commentary—Commentary
Commonweal—Commonweal
Cong Digest—Congressional Digest
*Consumer Bul—Consumer Bulletin
Consumer Rep—Consumer Reports
Craft Horiz—Craft Horizons
Cur Hist—Current History

Dance Mag—Dance Magazine
Dept State Bul—Department of State Bulletin
Design—Design
Duns R—Dun's Review
  Formerly Dun's Review and Modern
  Industry

Ebony—Ebony
Electr World—Electronics World
Esquire—Esquire

*Farm J—Farm Journal (Central edition)
Field & S—Field & Stream
Flower Grower—Flower Grower, The Home
  Garden
  Continued as Home Garden & Flower
  Grower Feb '67
Flying—Flying
Focus—Focus
*For Affairs—Foreign Affairs
Fortune—Fortune

*Good H—Good Housekeeping

*Harper—Harper's Magazine
Harvard Bsns R—Harvard Business Review
*Hi Fi—High Fidelity incorporating Musical
  America
Hobbies—Hobbies
*Holiday—Holiday
Home Gard—Home Garden & Flower Grower
*Horizon—Horizon
Horn Bk—Horn Book Magazine
Horticulture—Horticulture
Hot Rod—Hot Rod
House & Gard—House & Garden incorporating
  Living for Young Homemakers
House B—House Beautiful

Int Concil—International Conciliation

*Ladiess Home J—Ladies' Home Journal
Library J—Library Journal
Life—Life
Liv Wildn—Living Wilderness
*Look—Look (Middle Atlantic edition)

McCalls—McCall's
Miss & Roc—Missiles and Rockets
  Continued as Technology Week Je 6 '66
Mlle—Mademoiselle
Mo Labor R—Monthly Labor Review
Mod Phot—Modern Photography
Motor B—Motor Boating
Motor T—Motor Trend

NEA J—NEA Journal
N Y Times Mag—New York Times Magazine
*Nat Geog Mag—National Geographic Magazine
Nat Parks Mag—National Parks Magazine
Nat R—National Review (44p issue only, pub.
  in alternate weeks)
Nation—Nation
Nations Bsns—Nation's Business
*Natur Hist—Natural History incorporating
  Nature Magazine
Negro Hist Bul—Negro History Bulletin
New Repub—New Republic
New Yorker—New Yorker
*Newsweek—Newsweek

Opera N—Opera News
Outdoor Life—Outdoor Life

PTA Mag—PTA Magazine
Parents Mag—Parents' Magazine and Better
  Homemaking
Parks & Rec—Parks & Recreation
Plays—Plays
Poetry—Poetry
Pop Electr—Popular Electronics
Pop Gard—Popular Gardening & Living Out-
  doors
Pop Mech—Popular Mechanics
Pop Phot—Popular Photography
Pop Sci—Popular Science Monthly
Pub W—Publishers' Weekly

*Read Digest—Reader's Digest (Great Lakes
  edition)
Redbook—Redbook
Reporter—The Reporter

Sat Eve Post—Saturday Evening Post
Sat R—Saturday Review
Sch & Soc—School and Society
Sch Arts—School Arts
Sci Am—Scientific American
Sci Digest—Science Digest
Sci N—Science News
  Formerly Science News Letter
Sci N L—Science News Letter
  Continued as Science News Mr 12 '66
Science—Science
*Seventeen—Seventeen
Sky & Tel—Sky and Telescope
*Sports Illus—Sports Illustrated
Sr Schol—Senior Scholastic (Teacher edition)
Suc Farm—Successful Farming (Eastern edi-
  tion)
Sunset—Sunset (Central edition)

Tech W—Technology Week including Missiles
  and Rockets
  Formerly Missiles and Rockets
Time—Time
Todays Health—Today's Health
Travel—Travel

UN Mo Chron—UN Monthly Chronicle
UNESCO Courier—UNESCO Courier
U S Camera—U.S. Camera & Travel
U S News—U.S. News & World Report

Vital Speeches—Vital Speeches of the Day
Vogue—Vogue

Wilson Lib Bul—Wilson Library Bulletin
*Writer—Writer

Yachting—Yachting
Yale R—Yale Review

* Available for blind and other physically handicapped readers on talking books, in braille, or on magnetic tape. For information address Division for the Blind and Physically Handicapped, Library of Congress, Washington, D.C. 20542

LIST OF PERIODICALS INDEXED

All data as of latest issue received

ALA Bulletin—available only to members. m (bi-m Jl-Ag) American Library Association, 50 E Huron St, Chicago 60611

America—$9. w (bi-w year-end issue) America Press, 106 W 56th St, New York 10019

The American Academy of Political and Social Science Annals—$10. free to members. bi-m American Academy of Political and Social Science, 3937 Chestnut St, Philadelphia 19104

American Artist—$8. m (S-Je) American Artist, 2160 Patterson St, Cincinnati, Ohio 45214

The American City—$7. m Buttenheim Pub. Corp, 757 3d Av, New York 10017

American Education—$3.75. m (bi-m D, Jl) American Education, Superintendent of Documents, U.S. Government Printing Office, Washington, D.C. 20402

American Forests—$6. m American Forestry Association, 919 17th St, NW, Washington, D.C. 20006

*****American Heritage**—$15. bi-m American Heritage, 383 W Center St, Marion, Ohio 43302

The American Historical Review—$15. free to members of the American Historical Association, q The Macmillan Co, 866 3d Av, New York 10022

The American Home—$3. m (bi-m Ja, Jl) The American Home, Independence Sq, Philadelphia 19105

The American Record Guide—$4.50. m American Record Guide, P.O. Box 319, Radio City Station, New York 10019

Américas—$4. m Pan American Union, Washington, D.C. 20006

Antiques—$12. m Straight Enterprises, Inc, 551 5th Av, New York 10017

The Architectural Forum—$10. m (bi-m Ja, Jl) The Architectural Forum, 111 W 57th St, New York 10019

Architectural Record—$5.50. m (semi-m My) Architectural Record, P.O. Box 430, Hightstown, N.J. 08520

Art News—$11.50. m (S-Je) Art News, 444 Madison Av, New York 10022

*****The Atlantic**—$8.50. m Atlantic Monthly Co, 8 Arlington St, Boston 02116

Audubon—$7. bi-m National Audubon Society, 1130 5th Av, New York 10028

Aviation Week & Space Technology—$10. w Aviation Week, P.O. Box 430, Hightstown, N.J. 08520

Better Homes and Gardens—$3. m Better Homes and Gardens, 1716 Locust St, Des Moines, Ia. 50303

Bulletin of the Atomic Scientists—$7. m (S-Je) Bulletin of the Atomic Scientists, 935 E 60th St, Chicago 60637

Business Week—$8. w Business Week, P.O. Box 430, Hightstown, N.J. 08520

The Catholic World—$6. m Catholic World, Harristown Road, Glen Rock, N.J. 07452

*****Changing Times**—$6. m Changing Times, The Kiplinger Magazine, Editors Park, Md. 20782

The Christian Century—$8.50. w Christian Century Foundation, 407 S Dearborn St, Chicago 60605

Commentary—$8. m American Jewish Committee, 165 E 56th St. New York 10022

Commonweal—$9. w (bi-w year-end issue, mid-Jl-mid-S) Commonweal Pub. Co, Inc, 232 Madison Av, New York 10016

Congressional Digest—$10. m (S-Je) Congressional Digest Corp, 3231 P St, NW, Washington, D.C. 20007

*****Consumer Bulletin**—$5. m Consumers' Research, Inc, Washington, N.J. 07882

Consumer Reports—$6. m Consumers Union of U.S, Inc, 256 Washington St, Mount Vernon, N.Y. 10550

Craft Horizons—$8. bi-m American Craftsmen's Council, 44 W 53d St, New York 10019

Current History—$8.50. m Current History, Inc, 1822 Ludlow St, Philadelphia 19103

Dance Magazine—$8. m Dance Magazine, 268 W 47th St, New York 10036

The Department of State Bulletin—$10. w Department of State Bulletin, Superintendent of Documents, U.S. Government Printing Office, Washington, D.C. 20402

Design—$4.50. bi-m (S-Je) Design Magazine, 1100 Waterway Blvd, Indianapolis, Ind. 46207

Dun's Review—$5. m P.O. Box 3088, Grand Central Station, New York 10017
    Formerly Dun's Review and Modern Industry

Ebony—$5. m Johnson Pub. Co, Inc, 1820 S Michigan Av, Chicago 60616

Electronics World—$6. m Electronics World, Portland Pl, Boulder, Colo. 80301

Esquire—$7.50. m Esquire, Portland Pl, Boulder, Colo. 80301

*****Farm Journal (Central edition)**—$1. m Farm Journal, Inc, 230 W Washington Sq, Philadelphia 19105

Field & Stream—$4. m Holt, Rinehart and Winston, Inc, 383 Madison Av, New York 10017

Flower Grower, The Home Garden—$3.50. m Flower Grower, 1031 Broadway, Albany, N.Y. 12201
    Continued as Home Garden & Flower Grower Feb '67

Flying—$6. m Flying, Portland Pl, Boulder, Colo. 80301

Focus—$2. m (S-Je) American Geographical Society, Broadway at 156th St, New York 10032

*Foreign Affairs—$8. q Council on Foreign Relations, Inc, 58 E 68th St, New York 10021

Fortune—$14. m (semi-m Je, S) Fortune 540 N Michigan Av, Chicago 60611

*Good Housekeeping—$5. m Good Housekeeping, Box 517, New York 10019

*Harper's Magazine—$8.50. m Harper's Magazine, 381 W Center St, Marion, Ohio 43302

Harvard Business Review—$10. bi-m Harvard Business Review, 108 10th St, Des Moines, Ia. 50305

*High Fidelity incorporating Musical America—$7. m High Fidelity, 2160 Patterson St, Cincinnati, Ohio 45214

Hobbies—$4. m Lightner Pub. Corp, 1006 S Michigan Av, Chicago 60605

*Holiday—$5.95. m Holiday, Independence Sq, Philadelphia 19105

Home Garden & Flower Grower—$3.50. m Home Garden, 1031 Broadway, Albany, N.Y. 12201

*Horizon—$16. q Horizon, 379 W Center St, Marion, Ohio 43302

The Horn Book Magazine—$6. bi-m Horn Book, Inc, 585 Boylston St, Boston 02116

Horticulture—$4. m Horticulture, 300 Massachusetts Av, Boston 02115

Hot Rod—$5. m Petersen Pub. Co, 5959 Hollywood Blvd, Los Angeles 90028

House & Garden incorporating Living for Young Homemakers—$6. m House & Garden, Boulder, Colo. 80301

House Beautiful—$6. m House Beautiful, 250 W 55th St, New York 10019

International Conciliation—$2.25. 5 times a yr (S-My) Carnegie Endowment for International Peace, 345 E 46th St, New York 10017

*Ladies' Home Journal—$3. m Ladies' Home Journal, Independence Sq, Philadelphia 19105

Library Journal—$10. semi-m (m Jl-Ag) R. R. Bowker Co, 1180 Avenue of the Americas, New York 10036

Life—$7.75. w (except one issue at year-end) Life, 540 N Michigan Av, Chicago 60611

The Living Wilderness—$5. q The Wilderness Society, 729 15th St, NW, Washington, D.C. 20005

*Look (Middle Atlantic edition)—$4. bi-w Look, Look Bldg, Des Moines, Ia. 50304

McCall's—$3. m McCall's, McCall St, Dayton, Ohio 45401

Mademoiselle—$5. m Mademoiselle, Boulder, Colo. 80301

Missiles and Rockets—$5. w (bi-w year-end issue) Missiles and Rockets, 1001 Vermont Av, NW, Washington, D.C. 20005
Continued as Technology Week, Je 6 '66

Modern Photography—$6. m Modern Photography, 2160 Patterson St, Cincinnati, Ohio 45214

Monthly Labor Review—$7.50. m Superintendent of Documents, U.S. Government Printing Office, Washington, D.C. 20402

Motor Boating—$6. m Motor Boating, P.O. Box 544, New York 10019

Motor Trend—$5. m Petersen Pub. Co, 5959 Hollywood Blvd, Los Angeles 90028

NEA Journal—available only to members. m (S-My) National Education Association of the United States, 1201 16th St, NW, Washington, D.C. 20036

The Nation—$10. w (bi-w Jl-Ag) Nation Associates, Inc, 333 6th Av, New York 10014

*National Geographic Magazine—$8. m The Secretary, National Geographic Society, Washington, D.C. 20036

National Parks Magazine—$5. m National Parks Association, 1300 New Hampshire Av, NW, Washington, D.C. 20036

National Review—$9. bi-w (44p issue) National Review, Box 1601, Des Moines, Ia. 50306

Nation's Business—$19.75. (3 yrs) m Chamber of Commerce of the U.S, 1615 H St, NW, Washington, D.C. 20006

*Natural History incorporating Nature Magazine—$7. m (bi-m Je-S) American Museum of Natural History, Central Park W at 79th St, New York 10024

The Negro History Bulletin—$3. m (O-My) Association for the Study of Negro Life and History, Inc, 1538 9th St, NW, Washington, D.C. 20001

The New Republic—$9. w (bi-w Jl-Ag) New Republic, 381 W Center St, Marion, Ohio 43302

The New York Times Magazine—$28.50. w (complete Sunday ed; not sold separately) New York Times, Times Bldg, 229 W 43d St, New York 10036

The New Yorker—$8. w New Yorker Magazine, Inc, 25 W 43d St, New York 10036

*Newsweek—$9. w Newsweek, 117 E 3d St, Dayton, Ohio 45402

Opera News—$8. w (27 issues S 10-Je 10) The Metropolitan Opera Guild, Inc, 1865 Broadway, New York 10023

Outdoor Life—$4. m Outdoor Life, Boulder, Colo. 80313

The PTA Magazine—$2. m (S-Je) The PTA Magazine, 700 N Rush St, Chicago 60611

Parents' Magazine and Better Homemaking—$4. m Parents' Magazine, Bergenfield, N.J. 07621

Parks & Recreation—$5. m National Recreation and Park Association, 1700 Pennsylvania Av, NW, Washington, D.C. 20006

Plays—$6. m (O-My) Plays, Inc, 8 Arlington St, Boston 02116

Poetry—$10. m (bi-m Ap-My) Modern Poetry Association, 1018 N State St, Chicago 60610

Popular Electronics—$5. m Popular Electronics, Portland Pl, Boulder, Colo. 80302

* Available for blind and other physically handicapped readers on talking books, in braille, or on magnetic tape. For information address Division for the Blind and Physically Handicapped, Library of Congress, Washington, D.C. 20542

KEY TO ABBREVIATIONS

+	continued on later pages of same issue	jr	junior
		jt auth	joint author
abp	archbishop	ltd	limited
abr	abridged		
Ag	August	m	monthly
Ap	April	Mr	March
arch	architect	My	May
assn	association	N	November
Aut	Autumn	no	number
av	avenue	O	October
bart	baronet		
bibliog	bibliography	por	portrait
bibliog f	bibliographical foot-notes	pseud	pseudonym
		pt	part
bi-m	bimonthly	pub	published, publisher, publishing
bi-w	biweekly		
bldg	building	q	quarterly
bp	bishop		
co	company	rev	revised
comp	compiled, compiler	S	September
cond	condensed	semi-m	semimonthly
cont	continued	soc	society
corp	corporation	Spr	Spring
D	December	sq	square
dept	department	sr	senior
ed	edited, edition, editor	st	street
		Sum	Summer
F	February	sup	supplement
Hon	Honorable	supt	superintendent
il	illustrated, illustration, illustrator	tr	translated, translation, translator
inc	incorporated		
introd	introduction, introductory	v	volume
		w	weekly
Ja	January	Wint	Winter
Je	June		
Jl	July	yr	year

Sample entry: MARINE painting
Frederick Waugh, America's most popular marine painter. G. R. Havens. il Am Artist 31:30-7+ Ja '67

Explanation: An illustrated article on the subject MARINE painting entitled "Frederick Waugh, America's most popular marine painter," by G. R. Havens, will be found in volume 31 of American Artist, pages 30-7 (continued on later pages of the same issue) the January 1967 number

READERS' GUIDE TO
PERIODICAL LITERATURE

March 1966 — February 1967

AAA. See American automobile association
AADC. See Association of American dance
  companies
AAFSS (advanced aerial fire support system)
  See Airplanes, Military—Armaments
AALL. See American association of law li-
  braries
AASA. See American association of school ad-
  ministrators
AAU. See Amateur athletic union of the
  United States
AAUP. See Association of American university
  presses
ABA. See American bar association; American
  booksellers association
ABC. See American broadcasting company
ABM (anti-ballistic missile) See Guided mis-
  siles—Defenses
ABPC. See American book publishers council
A. C. Nielsen company. See Nielsen, A. C. com-
  pany
ACDA. See United States—Arms control and
  disarmament agency
ACEI. See Association for childhood educa-
  tion international
ACF industries
  Booms, rails and ACF. J. Weingarten. Duns
  R 87:49-50 Mr '66
ACLU. See American civil liberties union
ACP. See Associated church press (organiza-
  tion)
ACPA. See American college personnel associa-
  tion
ACRL. See Association of college and research
  libraries
ACTH
  Adrenocorticotrophin-releasing hormone in
  peripheral blood: increase during stress. E.
  Anderson. bibliog il Science 152:379-80 Ap
  15 '66
  Puromycin analogs: action of adrenocortico-
  tropic hormone and the role of glycogen.
  L. D. Garren and others. bibliog il Science
  152:1386-8 Je 3 '66
ADA. See American dental association; Ameri-
  cans for democratic action
ADL. See B'nai-b'rith—Anti-defamation league
ADP (automatic data processing) See Elec-
  tronic data processing
AEC. See United States—Atomic energy com-
  mission
AESCON. See Aerospace and electronic sys-
  tems convention
AEW. See American education week
AFIPS. See American federation of information
  processing societies
AFL. See American football league
AFL-CIO. See American federation of labor
  and Congress of industrial organizations
AFPRO. See Action for food production
AFSCME. See American federation of state,
  county and municipal employees
AFT. See American federation of teachers
AGMA. See American guild of musical artists
AI. See Artificial insemination
AIA. See Aerospace industries association of
  America, incorporated; American institute
  of architects
AIBS. See American institute of biological sci-
  ences
AID. See United States—Agency for inter-
  national development
AIFLD. See American institute for free labor
  development
AIGA. See American institute of graphic arts
AIL. See Association of international libraries
ALA. See American library association

ALPA. See Air line pilots association interna-
  tional
ALS (anti-lymphocyte serum) See Serum
ALSEP (Apollo lunar surface experiment pack-
  age) See Moon—Surface
ALTA. See American library trustee associa-
  tion
AMA. See American management association;
  American medical association
AMC. See American motors corporation
AOPA. See Aircraft owners and pilots as-
  sociation
AP. See Associated press
APA. See Allied pilots association; American
  psychological association; Association of
  producing artists
APGA. See American personnel and guidance
  association
ARD (acute respiratory disease) See Respira-
  tory organs—Diseases
ARINC. See Aeronautical radio, incorporated
ARL. See Agricultural research laboratory, Oak
  Ridge, Tenn; Association of research li-
  braries
ARPA. See United States—Defense, Depart-
  ment of—Advanced research projects
  agency
ASCD. See Association for supervision and
  curriculum development
ASIS. See American society for industrial se-
  curity
ASNLH. See Association for the study of Ne-
  gro life and history
ASOL. See American symphony orchestra
  league
ASPAC. See Asian and Pacific council
ASW (anti-submarine warfare) See Submarine
  warfare
AT and T. See American telephone and tele-
  graph company
ATA. See Air transport association of Amer-
  ica; American teachers association
ATPI. See American textbook publishers in-
  stitute
ATS (applications technology satellites) See
  Artificial satellites
AUPS. See American university press services,
  incorporated
AUTEC. See Atlantic undersea test and eval-
  uation center
AWACS (airborne warning and control sys-
  tem) See Radar defense network
AALTO, Alvar
  Aalto revisited; with account by B. Spring.
  il Arch Forum 124:70-80 Ap '66
AARON, Benjamin
  Double arbitration standard; excerpt from
  paper presented at American assembly. Mo
  Labor R 89:1387-8 D '66
AARON, Henry
  Danger with a double A. J. Mann. il por
  Sports Illus 25:22-7 Ag 1 '66
AARON, I. E.
  How to teach reading skills in social studies
  classes. Sr Schol 87:sup 15 Ja 21 '66
AARON, Jan, and Salom, G. S.
  Art of Mexican cooking; excerpt. Ladies
  Home J 83:78-9+ Jl '66
AARON, Sam
  Buying wine on a budget. House & Gard 129:
  196+ My '66
AASEN farm, Norway. See Farms
ABANDONED towns
  Ghost town on the Kona coast: Hookena,
  Hawaii. il Sunset 136:60 Ap '66
  Going places, finding ghosts in Colorado's
  nostalgic mining towns. W. Houseman. il
  House & Gard 129:40-2+ Je '66

ABASHIDZE, Iraklii
Rustaveli and the knight in the tiger's skin. UNESCO Courier 19:28-30 O '66
ABBE, George
Where the stakes are real. C. L. Sanford. Nation 203:426-7 O 24 '66
ABBEY, Edward
West's land of surprises, some terrible. Harper 233:98-9+ D '66
ABBEY theatre. See Dublin—Theater
ABBEYS
See also
Mont Saint Michel, France
Tresco abbey
ABBOT, Charles Greeley
Abbot: cycles and sub-cycles. F. Sartwell. por Sci N 90:496 D 10 '66
Profiles; Smithsonian institution. G. T. Hellman. New Yorker 42:60-2+ D 17 '66
ABBREVIATIONS
Periodical abbreviation center initiated by ASA Z39 committee. Library J 91:3891+ S 1 '66
ABDEL-GHANI, Abdel Hamid
Great international venture. UNESCO Courier 19:5-6 My '66
ABDUCTION. See Kidnapping
ABDUCTION from the Seraglio: opera. See Mozart, J. C. W. A.
ABEL, Don R.
Light-sensor diodes. Electr World 76:40 Jl '66
ABEL, I. W.
Abel finds a broader role for the USW. il pors Bsns W p57-8+ My 28 '66
Abel gives governors the labor view. por Bsns W p50 Jl 16 '66
Steel contract puts Abel on spot. por Bsns W p97-8 Ja 22 '66
ABEL, Lionel
Sartre vs. Lévi-Strauss. Commonweal 84:364-8 Je 17 '66
ABEL, Reuben
Four possibilities of being. Sat R 49:35 Ja 29 '66
ABÉLARD, Pierre
Héloïse, by E. Hamilton. Review
Sat R il 50:83 Ja 14 '67. O. Prescott
ABELL, Elizabeth Clements
Entertaining people. il pors McCalls 94:24+ N '66
ABELL, Richard P.
Challenging the gifted. NEA J 55:48-9 F '66
ABERCROMBIE and Fitch company
Abercrombie & Fitch enters book publishing; facsimilies and reprints of classics in the field of sports and adventure. Pub W 189:96-7 Je 13 '66
Notes and comment; store's catalogue. New Yorker 42:41 Ap 16 '66
ABERFAN, Wales
Aberfan's farewell to its children; with report by J. Hicks. il Life 61:105-6 N 11 '66
Murderous mountain. il Time 88:41 O 28 '66
Never one like this; avalanche of coal slag. il Newsweek 68:54+ O 31 '66
Sea of sludge upon green Aberfan. il Life 61:68-73 N 4 '66
Stirring of new life under the menacing coal tips of Aberfan; with report by J. Hicks. il Life 62:18-27 Ja 6 '67
Vulnerable eyes in coal-dusted faces. J. Hicks. Life 61:3 N 4 '66
ABERNETHY, Roy
Double shuffle at AMC. il por Newsweek 69:77-8 Ja 23 '67
ABILITIES, incorporated
Library for the handicapped; school at the Human resources center. R. Vellman. bibliog il Library J 91:4200-4 S 15 '66
ABILITY
Balancing ability with humility; interview. S. J. Weinberg. il Nations Bsns 53:44-6+ D '65
Examination of transfer of learning by nucleic acid. M. Luttges and others. bibliog il Science 151:834-7 F 18 '66
Instant access to students' reading levels; University of Chicago laboratory school. E. L. Thomas. il Library J 91:2165-8 Ap 15 '66
School success and satisfaction. Sch & Soc 94:442 D 10 '66
See also
Intelligence
ABILITY, Influence of age on
Visually evoked potentials: amplitude changes with age. R. E. Dustman and E. C. Beck. bibliog il Science 151:1013-15 F 25 '66
ABILITY grouping in education
Ability grouping: pros and cons; with study-discussion program, by D. Harris and E. Harris. W C. Olson. bibliog il PTA Mag 60:24-6, 33 Ap '66
Editor's bookshelf. P. Woodring. Sat R 49:86+ S 17 '66

South's revenge. S. Alsop. il Sat Eve Post 239:18 S 24 '66; Same abr. Read Digest 89:79-81 D '66
Tracking: what it means, how it works; with discussion group program, by S. H. Strait. bibliog il Parents Mag 41:29-30+, 64-5+ S '66
ABILITY tests
Diagnosis, retarded. P. Deutsch and R. Deutsch. il Parents Mag 41:56-7+ Mr '66
See also
Intelligence tests
Maze tests
ABLATION shielding. See Shielding (heat)
ABNORMAL psychology. See Psychology, Pathological
ABNORMALITIES (animals)
Drug-induced teratogenesis in vitro: inhibition of calcification by different tetracyclines. L. Saxén. bibliog il Science 153:1384-7 S 16 '66
Intravenous injection of thalidomide in pregnant rabbits. R. R. Fox and others. bibliog il Science 153:310-11 Jl 15 '66; Discussion. 154:1362 D 9 '66
ABNORMALITIES (man) See Deformities
ABNORMALITIES (plants)
Trees that twist; excerpt from Fantastic tree. E. A. Menninger. il Am For 72:30-3+ Jl '66
ABORTION
Abortion, by L. Lader. Review
Nation 203:492-3 N 7 '66. E. M. Schur
New Repub 155:38-40 N 26 '66. J. Ridgeway
Abortion epidemic; summary of report at meeting of the American public health association. R. E. Hall. il Newsweek 68:92 N 14 '66
Abortion issue: U.S.A. and Britain. America 115:406 O 8 '66
Abortion laws. Commonweal 83:685 Mr 18 '66
Abortion laws. N. St John-Stevas. Commonweal 85:163-6 N 11 '66
Abortion laws condemned. Sci N 90:320 O 22 '66
Arguing abortions. Commonweal 85:312 D 16 '66
Can abortion be justified? C. Northcott. Christian Cent 83:1530 D 14 '66
Catholic church and abortion. W. F. Buckley, jr. Nat R 18:308 Ap 5 '66; Discussion. 18:390, 643 My 3, Je 28 '66
Doctor Szasz on abortion. America 115:476 O 22 '66
Doctor's dilemma. Dr X. il Ladies Home J 83:98-9+ My '66
Growing consensus on abortion. America 114:219 F 12 '66
History repeats itself. F. Canavan. America 114:738-42 My 21 '66; Reply with rejoinder. L. Sprietsma. 115:1 Jl 2 '66
Illnesses in the unborn; fetology unrecognized as a medical specialty. America 116:76 Ja 21 '67
Legalized abortion urged. F. Marley. Sci N 90:19 Jl 9 '66
Let's speak out on abortion; excerpt from Abortion. L. Lader. Read Digest 88:82-5+ My '66
Right to abortion. Nation 203:373-4 O 17 '66
Speaking out: we should legalize abortion. W. B. Ober. Sat Eve Post 239:14+ O 8 '66
Test case; charges against San Francisco doctors Seymour P. Smith and J. Paul Shively. Newsweek 67:58 Je 6 '66
ABRAHAM, the patriarch
Abraham, the friend of God. K. MacLeish. il Nat Geog Mag 130:739-89 D '66
ABRAHAM, George
Care of bulbs in winter. Horticulture 44:35-7 O '66
ABRAHAM, Willard
Do you see your children as they really are? with quiz. PTA Mag 60:28-30 Je '66
Get ready for college now. bibliog Todays Health 44:72-4+ S; 64-5+ O '66
Our children, our problem. Todays Health 44:58-64 F '66
Outlook for special education. NEA J 55:50-1 D '66
Unlearning parental gobbledegook. Todays Health 44:12-13+ Jl '66
ABRAM, Morris
United Nations and human rights; statement; March 21, 1966. Dept State Bul 54:636-40 Ap 18 '66
United States favors creation of a U.N. high commissioner for human rights; statements, 25, 28, 30, 1966. Dept State Bul 54:1029-33 Je 27 '66

ABRAMS, Albert
Doctor Abrams, dean of machine quacks. J.
Kaplan. il por Todays Health 44:20-1+ Ap
'66
ABRAMS, Harry N. incorporated
Times Mirror acquires Harry N. Abrams,
inc. Pub W 189:28 Ap 11 '66
ABRAMS, Harry Nathan
New collector. il por Newsweek 68:84-5 Jl 11
'66
ABRAMSON, Harold A.
Will the legal supply of LSD to the private
medical practitioner be stopped indefinite-
ly? Mlle 64:52+ Ja '67
ABRAMSON, Lois
Bored housewife. L. Tornabene. Il pors
Ladies Home J 83:97-9+ N '66
ABRASIVES
See also
Sandpaper
ABSCISSION (botany)
Naphthaleneacetic acid: localization in the
abscission zone of the bean. H. P. Ras-
mussen and M. J. Bukovac bibliog il Sci-
ence 152:217-18 Ap 8 '66
ABSENCE; story. See Spencer, E.
ABSENTEEISM
Workers who get sick. Sci Digest 59:19 F '66
ABSORPTION spectra
Radiation absorption between the ultra-violet
and X-ray bands. bibliog il Science 153:
522-5 Jl 29 '66
Studies of alloys by X-ray absorption spec-
troscopy. L. V. Azároff. bibliog il Science
151:785-9 F 18 '66
ABSTINENCE. See Fasting; Temperance
ABSTRACT art. See Art, Abstract
ABSTRACTING
See also
Biological abstracts (periodical)
ABSURD, Theater of the. See Theater
ABSURDITY in literature. See Literature—
Themes
ABT, Clark
Games businessmen play. il por Time 88:111
S 16 '66
ABU DHABI
Demise of a midas. Time 88:28 Ag 19 '66
ABU SIMBEL, Temples of
Abu Simbel now lifted to new site. Sci N
89:317 Ap 30 '66
Books in review; salvaging Egypt's past. H.
G. Fischer. Natur Hist 75:4+ Ap '66
End of a monumental salvage. il Life 60:36
Ap 1 '66
Race to save Abu Simbel is won; with report
by G. De Carvalho. il Life 61:32-9 D 2 '66
Saving the ancient temples at Abu Simbel.
G. Gerster. il Nat Geog Mag 129:694-742
My '66
ABU ZABI. See Abu Dhabi
ABUNDANCE. See Prosperity
ABYSSINIAN church. See Ethiopic church
ACACIAS
Crying tree; God's tree, La Feria, Tex. il
Time 88:78+ S 16 '66
It simply thrives on neglect; bush acacias.
il Sunset 138:140 Ja '67
ACADEMIC degrees. See Degrees, Academic
ACADEMIC evaluation. See Grading and mark-
ing (students)
ACADEMIC freedom
Academic freedom; address, June 5, 1966.
R. M. Nixon. Vital Speeches 32:550-2 Jl 1
'66; Same with title Academic freedom
today. Sch & Soc 94:451-4 D 10 '66
Academic freedom and political liberty. A.
Lepawsky; discussion. Science 151:1034;
152:1567 Mr 4, Je 17 '66
Academic freedom and St John's. America
115:795 D 17 '66; Discussion. 116:68+ Ja
21 '67
Academic freedom; Catholic higher educa-
tion. P. Gleason. America 115:60-3 Jl 16
'66; Discussion. 115:285-7 S 17 '66
Academic freedom for historians; text of
announcement, July 22, 1966. Sch & Soc
94:461-3 D 10 '66
Academic freedom in new colleges. Sch &
Soc 94:144 Mr 19 '66
Academic freedom: lessons from the crisis
at St John's. L. J. Carter. Science 154:
1428-30 D 16 '66
Autonomy of the university. G. I. Sanchez.
Sch & Soc 94:147-9 Mr 19 '66
Battle for your child's mind. R. D.
Batchelder. Parents Mag 41:40+ Mr '66
Certifying priests' credentials; ecclesiastical
regulation by archdiocese of Chicago.
America 115:477-8 O 22 '66
Church and the university. America 114:230-
1 F 12 '66

Freedom and restraint in the Christian col-
lege. W. B. Martin. Christian Cent 83:
1372-4 N 9 '66
Join the picket line! concerning letter from
union to librarians to boycott annual con-
gress at St John's. J. N. Berry. 3d il Li-
brary J 91:1782-7 Ap 1 '66
Neutrality's implications for education. J.
Van Patten. bibliog f Sch & Soc 94:352-4
O 29 '66
St John's university: the issues. F. Cana-
van; discussion. America 114:241, 276-7 F
19-26 '66
Should college students grade their teachers?
L. S. Feuer. il N Y Times Mag p56-7+
S 18 '66
Should known Communists and Fascists be
permitted to speak on college campuses?
pro and con discussion. il Sr Schol 87:10-11
Ja 14 '66
Speaker-ban law still news in North Caro-
lina. W. M. Wells, jr. Christian Cent 83:783
Je 15 '66
Speaker ban: suit asserts a right to listen.
L. J. Carter. Science 152:330 Ap 15 '66
Strike at St John's. J. Leo. Commonweal
83:500+ Ja 28 '66; Reply. S. Poole. 83:705
Mr 18 '66
Strike at St John's: why the professors
picket. M. R. Berube. il Nation 202:172-4
F 14 '66
Student freedom. il Sch & Soc 94:372 N 12 '66
Student rights in higher education. M. P.
Sheridan. America 114:731-2 My 21 '66
Tale of a cat; concerning play written by San
Diego high-school teacher. il Newsweek 67:
74-5 F 7 '66
Time bomb in Catholic education; crisis at
St John's. R. Horchler. il Look 30:23-5 Ap
5 '66
University in contemporary society; adapta-
tion of address, June 1, 1965. G. Kirk. Sch
& Soc 94:63-5 F 5 '66
What do we mean by academic freedom?
R. M. Nixon; H. S. Commager. Sat R 49:
12-15+ Ag 27 '66
See also
Colleges and universities—Administration
Colleges and universities—Political control
Evolution—Laws and legislation
ACADEMIC performance. See Student achieve-
ments
ACADEMIES (schools) See Private schools
ACADEMY awards (moving pictures)
Awards quadrille. A. Knight. Sat R 49:42
Ap 23 '66
Ticky-tack. il Time 87:66 Ap 29 '66

Quotations, maxims, etc
Time of the Oscar; comp. by G. Flatley. il
N Y Times Mag p 133 Ap 17 '66
ACADEMY of political science
What's your P.S.Q.? H. L. Hurwitz. Sr
Schol 89:sup26 S 23 '66
ACADEMY of religion and mental health
Morality and psychiatry. S. J. Rowland, jr.
Christian Cent 83:689 My 25 '66
Religion and mental health. America 114:766
My 28 '66
ACADEMY of television arts and sciences
Looking backward; eighteenth annual Emmy
awards. il Newsweek 67:84-5 Je 6 '66
To: the staff; from: the chief, re: the Emmy
awards. Time 87:58 Je 3 '66
ACADIANS in Louisiana
Cajunland, Louisiana's French-speaking
coast. B. Keating. il Nat Geog Mag 129:
352-91 Mr '66
ACAPULCO, Mexico
In people discover, Acapulco. T. Meehan. Il
N Y Times Mag p38-9+ F 13 '66
New Acapulco. il Time 87:56 F 11 '66
ACARINA. See Mites
ACCELERATION of particles. See Particles
(nuclear physics)—Acceleration
ACCELERATORS (electrons, etc)
Accelerated competition; selecting the loca-
tion of world's largest particle accelerator.
Newsweek 67:64 Ap 4 '66
Atom smashing on a straight line; Stan-
ford's two-mile-long linear accelerator. il
Bsns W p 176-8+ O 8 '66
Beam storage in the Cambridge electron ac-
celerator; letter. M. S. Livingston. Science
151:936 F 25 '66
Electrons accelerated to the 10- to 20-gev
range. W. K. H. Panofsky and others. il
Science 152:1353-5 Je 3 '66
Energy measured directly; amount required
to initiate chemical reaction of splitting
a hydrogen molecule. Sci N 89:263 Ap 16
'66

ACCELERATORS (electrons, etc)—*Continued*
For the Midwest, a scientific plum; Weston, Ill. il U S News 61:6 D 26 '66
Fusion of uranium atoms seen possible in future; experiment using Van de Graaff accelerators. Sci N 90:176 S 10 '66
Gift from the AEC; Weston, Ill, selected as site for world's largest atom smasher. il Bsns W p 17-18 D 24 '66
Near the tree; site for atom-smashing accelerator, Weston, Ill. Time 88:21 D 23 '66
Particle storage rings. G. K. O'Neill. il Sci Am 215:107-16 N '66
Six accelerator sites recommended to AEC. Sci N 89:221 Ap 2 '66
Smash hits; Weston, Ill, and Stanford university. il Newsweek 68:48-9 D 26 '66
Superhighway for electrons; Stanford's linear accelerator. il Time 88:74 Jl 22 '66
200 Bev: beginning or end? Sci N 90:571 D 31 '66
200 bev: Illinois chosen in competition for new accelerator. D. S. Greenberg. il Science 154:1528 D 23 '66
200-bev: the Academy committee knew where it was going. D. S. Greenberg. Science 152: 326-9 Ap 15 '66
Two-mile beam pulsed. Sci N 89:439 Je 4 '66
See also
Synchrotron

Anecdotes, facetiae, satire, etc.
Build your own home atom-smasher. J. Slate. il Sat Eve Post 239:24 O 22 '66

ACCELEROMETERS
Accelerometer calibration simplified. Miss & Roc 18:45 F 28 '66

ACCEPTANCES
Profiles; merchant bank, Hambros bank, ltd, London. J. Wechsberg. New Yorker 41:42-6+ F 5 '66

ACCESSIONS, Library. See Libraries—Acquisitions

ACCIDENT; story. See Stuart, J.

ACCIDENT benefit plans. See Employees benefit plans

ACCIDENTS
Accident toll. Time 88:30 D 9 '66
Danger: children at play. K. D. Fishman. il N Y Times Mag p 114+ S 25 '66
Hazards of modern living. il Newsweek 68:60 Jl 4 '66
When children swallow things they shouldn't. L. W. Sauer. PTA Mag 61:29-30 D '66
See also
First aid in illness and injury
Shipwrecks
Traffic accidents
also subheads Accidents or Accidents and injuries under various subjects, e.g. Fishing—Accidents and injuries

Prevention
Make sure your child won't be a poison victim. il Consumer Bul 49:20-1 F '66
Safety-first for preschoolers. P. Zanotelli. il Parents Mag 41:34-5+ Jl '66
Stay alive! by J. Carper. Review
    Consumer Bul il 49:37 F '66
Still a tiger in your toolshed. R. P. Crossley. il Pop Mech 125:100-3+ Je '66
See also
Fire protection
Safety devices and measures
also subhead Safety devices and measures under various subjects, e.g. Automobiles—Safety devices and measures

ACCIDENTS, Industrial

Statistics
Work injuries; tables. See issues of Monthly labor review to October 1966

ACCIDENTS, Liability for. See Liability (law)

ACCOMPANIMENT, Musical. See Musical accompaniment

ACCORSI, William
Betty Thomson's puzzles. Craft Horiz 26:24-7 Ja '66

ACCOUNTABILITY (law)
See also
Criminal liability

ACCOUNTANTS
Personal business; hiring a CPA. Bsns W p 169-70 O 22 '66

ACCOUNTING
See also
Corporations—Accounting
Cost accounting

Mechanical aids
Accounting machines & punched-card DP. il Duns R 88:pt2 138-9+ S '66

Data-processing accounting in England; Weston-super-Mare. W. R. Bryant. il Am City 81:90-1 Je '66
See also
Computers—Business applications

ACCOUNTING, Household. See Budget, Household; Domestic finance

ACCOUNTING office, General. See United States—General accounting office

ACCREDITATION of library schools. See Library schools and education

ACCREDITATION of public schools. See Public schools—Accreditation

ACCULTURATION
Sell-out or the well acculturated Christian. R. E. Fitch. Christian Cent 83:202-5 F 16 '66; Discussion. 83:370-2 Mr 23 '66
See also
Americanization

ACCURACY
Errors of our ways. J. O'Hara. il Holiday 40:22+ D '66

ACE, Goodman
Book. Sat R 49:9 Je 25 '66
Top of my head. See issues of Saturday review

ACE books, incorporated
Ace books reaches agreement with Tolkien. Pub W 189:37-8 Mr 14 '66; Reply. R. Unwin. 189:31 My 9 '66

ACETABULARIA
Acetabularia: a useful giant cell. A. Gibor. il Sci Am 215:118-24 bibliog(p 160) N '66

ACETATES
Mechanism for intercalation of kaolinite by alkali acetates. D. L. Smith and others. bibliog il Science 153:741-3 Ag 12 '66

ACETYLCHOLINE
Circadian rhythms: variation in sensitivity of isolated rat atria to acetylcholine. R. P. Spoor and D. B. Jackson. bibliog il Science 154:782 N 11 '66
Crystal and molecular structure of acetylselenocholine iodide. E. Shefter and O. Kennard. bibliog il Science 153:1389-90 S 16 '66
Sleep deprivation and brain acetylcholine. M. B. Bowers, jr. and others. bibliog Science 153:1416-17 S 16 '66
Species specific effect on acetylcholine on bivalve rectums. M. J. Greenberg. bibliog il Science 154:1015-17 N 25 '66

ACETYLCHOLINESTERASE
Carbamylation and binding constants for the inhibition of acetylcholinesterase by physostigmine, eserine. A. R. Main and F. L. Hastings. bibliog il Science 154:400-2 O 21 '66

ACETYLENE
Cyanoacetylene in prebiotic synthesis. R. A. Sanchez and others. bibliog il Science 154:784-5 N 11 '66

ACETYLHISTIDINE. See Histidine

ACETYLSELENOCHOLINE. See Acetylcholine

ACHESON, Dean Gooderham
Dean Acheson's word for de Gaulle: nonsense; excerpts from interview. por U S News 60:79 Ap 18 '66
Earrings. Atlan 219:107-8 Ja '67
History as literature. por Esquire 69:99-102+ O '66
Holiday. Atlan 218:124-6 O '66
Under fire: U.S. policy on Rhodesia; excerpts from letter. por U S News 61:13 D 26 '66

about
Patrician. J. Kraft. Commentary 41:92+ F '66
T.R.B. from Washington; past roles and a new one. New Repub 154:4 My 28 '66

ACHIEVEMENT motivation. See Motivation (education)

ACHIEVEMENTS, Student. See Student achievements

ACHILLES' heel; drama. See Levi, S.

ACHTENHAGEN, Olga
Bon voyage, and fare well! Todays Health 44:28-31 Ag '66
Uganda. Travel 125:56-60 F '66

ACIDS, Fatty
Anxiety levels in dreams: relation to changes in plasma free fatty acids. L. A. Gottschalk and others. bibliog il Science 153: 654-7 Ag 5 '66
Branched-chain fatty acids in sediments. R. F. Leo and P. L. Parker. bibliog il Science 152:649-50 Ap 29 '66
Feedback inhibition of key glycolytic enzymes in liver: action of free fatty acids. G. Weber and others. bibliog il Science 154:1357-60 D 9 '66
Occurrence of isoprenoid fatty acids in the Green River shale. G. Eglinton and others. bibliog il Science 153:1133-5 S 2 '66

ACKERSON, Cornelius
Grow large chrysanthemums. il Horticulture 44:20-1+ O '66

ACKLEY, Gardner
Full employment; address, October 26, 1966. Vital Speeches 33:71-7 N 15 '66; Excerpts. U S News 61:72 N 7 '66
Where business is heading; interview. pors U S News 60:46-52 Ap 11 '66

about

Awash in affluence, but what next? il pors Newsweek 68:67-70+ Jl 18 '66
Councilor to Canute. por Time 87:22 Ap 15 '66
Full employment or stable prices? B. L. Masse. America 115:646 N 19 '66
Man in the middle: LBJ's economic aide. il por U S News 61:11 Ag 15 '66
Ominous swipe at profits. Fortune 73:103-4 Je '66

ACNE
Acne, hormones & milk. il Time 87:51 Ap 29 '66
Effective new ways to treat acne. Sci Digest 59:21-2 Ap '66
How teen-age skin problems should be treated, and how they shouldn't. D. M. Pillsbury. Ladies Home J 84:42 Ja '67

ACOCA, Miguel
Congressman plays a game of chicken at 35 knots. Life 61:102+ D 9 '66
Game the world plays. Life 61:91+ Ag 26 '66
Life music review. Life 61:16 N 18 '66

ACOUSTICS, Architectural
Architectural acoustics. M. R. Schroeder. bibliog il Science 151:1355-9 Mr 18 '66
Good acoustics. Parks & Rec 1:909 N '66
How to shop for a silent ceiling. il Bet Hom & Gard 44:133 Mr '66
New house; sound equipment of the Metropolitan opera house. F. Stevenson. il Opera N 31:14-15 D 3 '66
Reverb for your car. D. Meyer. il Pop Electr 24:50-3+ F '66
Reverberant rooms; their design and use. A. Oppenheim and S. Wasserman il Electr World 75:34-6 Ap '66
Silence at less than $35 an ounce. Fortune 74:191-2 D '66
Sound and the fury. R. W. Hall. il Opera N 30:8-13 Mr 26 '66
See also
Orchestra shells

ACQUISITIONS, Corporate. See Corporate acquisitions

ACQUISITIONS, Library. See Libraries—Acquisitions

ACREE, Harry
Stranger at the door. J. P. Blank. il Read Digest 89:60-6 S '66

ACROBATICS, Aerial. See Aviation—Stunt flying

ACROBATS and acrobatism
Fear on the high wire. B. Ballantine. il Pop Sci 189:88-91 Jl '66
See also
Circus performers

ACRONYMS
FASGROLIA; fast growing language of initialisms and acronyms. Newsweek 67:94+ Mr 14 '66

ACROSTICS
Mathematical games; Dr Matrix delivers a talk on acrostics. M. Gardner. il Sci Am 216:118-21+ Ja '67

ACRYLAMIDE
Acrylamide-gel electrophorograms by mechanical fractionation: radioactive adenovirus proteins. J. V. Maizel, jr. bibliog il Science 151:988-90 F 25 '66

ACRYLONITRILE
Acrylonitrile polymerization in a miniaturized-pressure optical cell. V. M. Zhulin and others. bibliog il Science 153:649-50 Ag 5 '66

ACTIN. See Muscle—Proteins

ACTING
Acting in opera. L. Donath. Opera N 30:6-7 Ap 16 '66
Bill Cosby talks about life, laughter and the pursuit of wonderfulness; interview. ed. by J. Long. B. Cosby. il Seventeen 26:94-5+ Ja '67
Cool character called Caine; ed. by E. Miller. M. Caine. il Seventeen 25:116-17+ D '66
Do you act your part? reprint. M. Scheerer. Read Digest 89:211-12+ N '66
Dogs and mice can be movie stars; ed. by E. Miller. O. Werner. il Seventeen 25:112-13+ Je '66
Face to face with a boy whose life was changed by a movie: Up the down staircase. L. Wallach. il Seventeen 25:143 O '66
Face to face: with a dresser with dreams. L. Sarovan. Seventeen 25:137 F '66
Face to face with a writer-producer-director-actor; ed. by C. Schwalberg. G. Harris, 3d. Seventeen 26:19 Ja '67
Reflections of a secret soldier of fortune; ed. by E. Miller. R. Redford. Seventeen 25:126-7+ F '66
Sound versus fury. E. Leinsdorf. il Atlan 217:82-4+ Ap '66
Who's Michael Parks? ed. by E. Miller. M. Parks. il Seventeen 25:174-5+ S '66
See also
College and school drama
Improvisation (acting)
Pantomime

ACTINOMYCETES
Actinomycete: isolation and identification of agent responsible for musty odors. J. D. Dougherty and others. bibliog il Science 152:1372-3 Je 3 '66

ACTINOMYCIN
Actinomycin D: inhibition of respiration and glycolysis. J. Laszlo and others. bibliog il Science 151:1007-10 F 25 '66
End-organ effects of thyroid hormones: subcellular interactions in cultured cells. E. Siegel and C. A. Tobias. bibliog il Science 153:763-5 Ag 12 '66
Incorporation of tritiated actinomycin D into drug-sensitive and drug-resistant HeLa cells. M. N. Goldstein and others. il Science 151:1555-6 Mr 25 '66

ACTINOTUS. See Flannel flowers

ACTION atonement. See Volunteer service, International

ACTION for food production (project)
Christian social action in India. America 114:866 Je 25 '66
Touching America's untouchables. Christian Cent 83:855-6 Jl 6 '66

ACTION in art
Children in motion. L. Lew. il Sch Arts 66:14-16 D '66
Design in the dark. E. J. Dorsey. il Design 68:19-21 N '66

ACTION photography. See Photography of moving objects

ACTIONS and defenses
Animal cruelty defined; New Jersey judge's ruling on high school live animal experimentation. P. McBroom. Sci N 89:261+ Ap 16 '66
Crime, confessions, and the Court; excerpt from The crime war. R. M. Cipes. Atlan 218:51-8 S '66; Discussion. 218:46-8 D '66
Two kinds of cases: civil and criminal. Sr Schol 87:7 Ja 7 '66
See also
Libel and slander

Anecdotes, facetiae, satire, etc.

Look at the spring suits. F. P. Tullius. New Yorker 42:86+ F 26 '66

ACTIVATED sludge. See Sewage disposal—Activated sludge method

ACTIVITIES, Student. See Student activities

ACTIVITY centers for the aged. See Recreation for the aged

ACTIVITY programs, School. See Projects (teaching)

ACTIVITY-recording devices. See Biological apparatus and supplies

ACTIVITY rhythms. See Periodicity

ACTIVITY vector analysis. See Personality tests

ACTOMYOSIN
Control of myocardial contraction; the sensitivity of cardiac actomyosin to calcium ion. A. M. Katz and D. I. Repke. bibliog il Science 152:1242-3 My 27 '66; Reply. B. L. Fanburg. 154:1208 D 2 '66

ACTORS and actresses
Double exposure; comp. by R. McDowall; excerpts. il McCalls 94:97-107 O '66
Imports. L. Lerman. il Mlle 62:156-9 F '66
What's happening. G. Shalit. il Ladies Home J 84:116 Ja '67
See also
Acting
Circus performers
Make-up, Theatrical
Moving picture actors and actresses
Television broadcasting—Performers
Vaudeville
also names of actors and actresses. e.g. L. Remick

Anecdotes, facetiae, satire, etc.

Night Elizabeth Taylor said so what? and Richard Burton kicked the television set in. W. Redfield. il Esquire 67:108-9+ Ja '67

ACTORS and actresses, Negro. See Negro actors and actresses
ACTOR'S workshop. See San Francisco—Theater
ACTRESSES. See Actors and actresses; Moving picture actors and actresses
ACTS of Corporal Charity; story. See Rieth, M.
ACUPUNCTURE
Acupuncture called feasible. Sci N 90:425 N 19 '66
ACUTE respiratory disease. See Respiratory organs—Diseases
ADAM, Adolphe Charles
Le diable à quatre. G. L. Mayer. il Am Rec G 32:591 Mr '66
Records:
Le postillon de Longjumeau. Opera N 31:34 D 24 '66
ADAM and Eve
Anecdotes, facetiae, satire, etc.
Secret thoughts of a first lady. W. Stanton. il Sat Eve Post 239:16 Je 4 '66
ADAMANTANAMINE
1-Adamantanamine hydrochloride: inhibition of rous and esh sarcoma viruses in cell culture. A. M. Wallbank and others. bibliog il Science 152:1760-1 Je 24 '66
ADAMO, S. J.
Five best Catholic papers. America 115:250-2 S 10 '66
Press. See occassional issues of America Yearling. America 114:336 Mr 5 '66
ADAMS, Alice. See Lindahl, T. jt. auth.
ADAMS, Bert N.
How Bert beat the bureaucrats. por Time 87:61 Mr 4 '66
ADAMS, Brooks
Education by uncles, by A. A. Homans. Review
New Repub 155:33-4 O 1 '66. F. Biddle
ADAMS, Charles J.
Statistical chaos: technical services in public libraries. por Library J 91:2278-80 My 1 '66
ADAMS, Clarence
By mutual consent. il por Time 88:20-1 Jl 15 '66
Homesick. il por Newsweek 67:44 Je 6 '66
ADAMS, Don
Would you believe Don Adams? G. Smith. il pors Sat Eve Post 239:32-3 Je 4 '66
ADAMS, Edward
Inspirational series. Sch Arts 65:29 Ja '66
Macro-drawing from nature. Sch Arts 66:22-6 N '66
ADAMS, Fred
Happy drop out. Yachting 120:41-3+ O '66
ADAMS, George W.
Highfields and its heritage. L. W. Watkins. il por Antiques 90:204-7 Ag '66
ADAMS, Henry
Education by uncles, by A. A. Homans. Review
New Repub 155:33-4 O 1 '66. F. Biddle
ADAMS, John
Verdicts of history: the Boston massacre. T. J. Fleming. il por Am Heritage 18:6-11+ D '66
ADAMS, Junius
How to start a cooperative nursery school. Parents Mag 41:58-9+ F '66
Some thoughts on the meaning of life; story. Esquire 65:90-3 F '66
ADAMS, Mildred
Cashing in on an inside tip. New Repub 155:14-16 Jl 30 '66
ADAMS, Philip R.
Fra Angelico's Virgin and child. Art N 65:34-5+ D '66
Some thoughts on the environmental arts. Antiques 89:391-408 Mr '66
ADAMS, Phoebe Lou
Finns on thin ice. Atlan 218:113-17 N '66
Potpourri. See issues of Atlantic
Purple cow. Atlan 217:109-13 Ap '66
Trondheim. Atlan 217:100-2+ F '66
ADAMS, Robert
Feeling for freedom. por Time 88:13 Jl 29 '66
ADAMS, Ruth Marie
New name on Wellesley's door. por Time 87:70 Mr 25 '66
ADAMS, Scott
Bibliographic organization in the biomedical sciences. bibliog por Wilson Lib Bul 40:714-18 Ap '66
ADAMS, Val
That Sunday twenty-five years ago I was on a tower overlooking all of Pearl Harbor. Esquire 66:252+ D '66
ADAMS, Walter
Something new in Britain. R. Rosenblatt. New Repub 155:9-10 D 17 '66

ADAMS, Willis Seaver
Deerfield rediscovers Willis Seaver Adams. A. F. Miller and others. il por Antiques 90:347-9 S '66
ADAMS family
Memoirs of a spry matriarch. il Life 61:61-2+ O 28 '66
My Adams uncles: Charles, Henry, Brooks. A. A. Momans. Yale R 55:321-46 Mr '66
ADAMSON, Joy
What animals can tell us about ourselves. McCalls 94:60-1+ Ja '67
ADANSONIA digitata. See Baobab trees
ADAPTATION (biology)
Adaptations of amphibia to arid environments. P. J. Bentley. bibliog Science 152:619-23 Ap 29 '66
Visual adaptation: increased efficiency resulting from spectrally distributed mixtures of stimuli. R. M. Boynton and S. R. Das. bibliog il Science 154:1581-3 D 23 '66
See also
Botany—Ecology
Evolution
Genetics
ADAPTATION (music) See Musical arrangement
ADAPTATION, Social. See Adjustment, Social
ADAPTATION, Visual. See Eye—Accommodation and refraction
ADAPTERS, Radio. See Radio apparatus
ADARKAR, Vivek B.
Girl as pretty as the Taj; story. Seventeen 25:124-5 F '66
Squealer; story Seventeen 25:146-7 Ap '66
ADDICTS, Drug. See Narcotic addicts
ADDITIONS, House. See Houses, Remodeled
ADDITIVES, Food. See Food additives
ADDRESS, Titles of. See Forms of address
ADE, Ginny
Pennsylvania revisited. Travel 125:42-4 Je '66
ADÉLIE penguins. See Penguins
ADELMAN, W. J. jr, and others
Internally perfused axons: effects of two different anions on ionic conductance. bibliog Science 151:1392-4 Mr 18 '66
ADEN
Will Britain's loss be Nasser's gain? il U S News 60:91-3 Mr 28 '66
See also
United Nations—Aden
ADENAUER, Konrad
Adenauer's view of a changing Europe. G. Bailey. il por Reporter 34:18-22 Je 30 '66
Der Alte replies to history. T. Prittie. New Repub 154:32-4 My 21 '66
Double switch. il por Newsweek 67:50 Ap 4 '66
He brought Berlin back to life. D. Schorr. il por Sat R 49:30-1 My 28 '66
Minerva's owl. S. J. Tonsor. por Nat R 18:631-2 Je 28 '66
New view of Russia. il por Time 87:33 Ap 1 '66
Touchy visit; Israel. il por Newsweek 67:49 My 16 '66
ADENOSINE triphosphate
Actin-myosin interaction: inhibition of the myosin adenosine triphosphatase by actin. S. Barron and others. bibliog il Science 151:1541-2 Mr 25 '66
Adenosine triphosphate: protection against radiation-induced chromosome loss in drosophila. S. Mittler and R. U. bibliog il Science 152:1087-8 My 20 '66
ADENOVIRUSES
Acrylamide-gel electrophorograms by mechanical fractionation: radioactive adenovirus proteins. J. V. Maizel, jr. bibliog il Science 151:988-90 F 25 '66
Adenovirus in blood clots from cases of infectious hepatitis. W. V. Hartwell and others. Science 152:1390 Je 3 '66
Adenovirus multiplication: inhibition by methisazone. D. J. Bauer and K. Apostolov. bibliog il Science 154:796-7 N 11 '66
Enhanced growth of human embryonic cells infected with adenovirus 12. I. V. Sultanian and G. Freeman. bibliog il Science 154:665-7 N 4 '66
Replication of adenovirus type 7 in monkey cells: a new determinant and its transfer to adenovirus type 2. J. S. Butel and others. bibliog il Science 154:671-3 N 4 '66
ADHESIVE tape
Self-adhering aluminum-foil tape, a versatile repair material. Consumer Bul 49:29 Ag '66
ADHESIVES
Glue replaces stitches. Sci N 89:507 Je 25 '66
Stick 'em up; Avery products corp. il Newsweek 68:66-7 D 26 '66
See also
Glue

ADIRONDACK forest preserve. See Forests,
State
ADIRONDACK lakes. See Lakes
ADIRONDACK MOUNTAINS
Adirondack trails; reprint. P. Schaeffer. Liv
Wildn 29:36-7 Aut '65
See also
Marcy, Mount
ADJUSTMENT (psychology)
See also
Conflict (psychology)
ADJUSTMENT, Social
Call of the wild: questions and answers. A.
Wood. il Seventeen 25:148-9+ Mr '66
Can a child be too good? H. Bernstein and
E. G. Neisser. il Parents Mag 41:33-5+
Ap '66
Changing human nature; excerpts from Step
to man. J. R. Platt. Science 152:1573 Je 17
'66
Coping with reality; with study-discussion
program by the authors. C. Smallenburg
and H. Smallenburg. PTA Mag 60:18-20
bibliog(p36-7) F '66
Emotional problems of preschoolers; with
study-discussion program, by R. Strang.
S. M. Finch. bibliog il PTA Mag 60:15-17,
32 Ap '66
Family on the move. E. F. Liese. il Parents
Mag 41:64-5+ O '66
I'm not what they think I am! questions
and answers. A. Wood. il Seventeen 25:
120-1+ Je '66
I'm tired of pretending; questions and an-
swers. A. Wood. il Seventeen 25:130-1+ F
'66
Malady of our times: alienation. A. A. Mes-
ser. il Todays Health 44:40-3+ S '66
Open generation: we want self-identity before
it's too late. Look 30:105-6+ S 20 '66
Role shock: an occupational hazard of Amer-
ican technical assistants abroad. F. C.
Byrnes. bibliog f Ann Am Acad 368:95-108
N '66
Social responsibility for youth. J. Moorhead.
PTA Mag 60:2-3 Je '66
Teen-ager and the telephone. E. J. Leshan.
McCalls 93:84+ Mr '66
Those teenage strangers. M. F. Farnham.
il Parents Mag 41:33-5+ Je '66
Uncommitted: alienated youth in American
society, by K. Keniston. Review
New Repub 154:29-32 Je 4 '66.   L.
Yablonsky
Unlikables: unlikable child. E. S. Ringold.
il N Y Times Mag p69-70+ Ja 15 '67
Which teen-agers are really in trouble, and
which aren't? J. Donnelly. Ladies Home J
84:34+ Ja '67
Who's out of step? questions and answers.
A. Wood. Seventeen 25:202+ N '66
See also
Aged—Adjustment problems
College students—Adjustment
Individual and society
Maturity
School children—Adjustment
Teachers—Adjustment
ADKINS, Marjorie R.
Using your public library's record collection.
Sr Schol 88:sup9 Ap 1 '66
ADKINS, R. J. and others
Control of somatosensory input by cerebral
cortex. bibliog Science 153:1020-2 Ag 26 '66
ADKISSON, Perry L.
Internal clocks and insect diapause. bibliog
Science 154:234-41 O 14 '66
ADLAI E. Stevenson institute of international
affairs (proposed)
Stevenson memorial. B. Ward. Sat R 49:19
Jl 9 '66
ADLAI E. Stevenson memorial fellowships. See
United Nations institute for training and
research
ADLAI E. Stevenson memorial fund
Stevenson memorial. B. Ward. Sat R 49:19
Jl 9 '66
ADLER, Bill
(comp) Collector's items; excerpts from Dear
Internal revenue. Look 30:86 Ap 5 '66
(ed) See Johnson, C. A. Jackie Kennedy and
Lady Bird Johnson: what they say about
love, marriage and faith
(ed) See Kennedy, J. Jackie Kennedy and
Lady Bird Johnson: what they say about
love, marriage and faith
(ed) See Roosevelt, E. Wise and warm
thoughts from Eleanor Roosevelt
ADLER, Irving
Prose imagination. por Library J 91:6160-1
D 15 '66
ADLER, James B.
James B. Adler forms his own book firm.
Pub W 190:42 Ag 15 '66

ADLER, Julius
Chemotaxis in bacteria. bibliog Science 153:
708-16 Ag 12 '66
ADLER, Kurt Herbert
Voice of the people. Opera N 31:8-12 Ja 14
'67
ADLER, Kurt S.
Decking the halls with imports. il por Bsns
W p 134-8 D 17 '66
ADLER, Larry
Fiery footnote. il por Newsweek 67:89 My 30
'66
ADLER, Lee
Symbiotic marketing. Harvard Bsns R 44:
59-71 N '66
ADLER, Lucile
Travelling out; poem. New Yorker 42:54 O
22 '66
ADLER, Morris
Murder of Rabbi Adler. T. V. LoCicero.
Commentary 41:49-53 Je '66; Discussion.
42:24+ O '66
ADLER, Renata
Current cinema. New Yorker 42:84+ Ag 6;
96+ Ag 13; 108+ Ag 20; 88+ Ag 27 '66
Other events. New Yorker 42:116+ N 12 '66
ADLER planetarium. See Planetariums
ADMINISTRATION, Public
See also
Bureaucracy
Government spending policy
ADMINISTRATION of justice. See Justice,
Administration of
ADMINISTRATIVE and budgetary committee.
See United Nations—Administrative and
budgetary committee
ADMINISTRATIVE and political divisions
See also
Gerrymander
ADMINISTRATIVE assistants to the president.
See Public officers
ADMINISTRATIVE communication. See Com-
munication in management
ADMINISTRATIVE counsel. See Administrative
remedies
ADMINISTRATIVE law
See also
Rule of law
ADMINISTRATIVE remedies
Authors & editors; the ombudsman concept;
interview. W. Gellhorn. Pub W 191:25 Ja
9 '67
Challenge of creative federalism; Senate sub-
committee on intergovernmental relations
survey findings; proposals. E. S. Muskie.
Sat R 49:12-14 Je 25 '66
For the ombudsman, a hearty skoal. L.
Wainwright. Life 61:26 D 16 '66
Grievance man for U.S? ombudsman; pro
and con discussion. il Sr Schol 88:14-15
My 13 '66
Little man's champion; the ombudsman.
Newsweek 68:28+ D 12 '66
Ombudsman; Danish official to protect the
private citizen from government. J. Egan.
il Holiday 40:28+ N '66
Ombudsman for religious. A. Broderick.
America 115:446-8+ O 15 '66; Discussion.
115:527+ N 5 '66
Ombudsman: tribune of the people. H. S.
Reuss and S. V. Anderson. bibliog f Ann
Am Acad 363:44-51 Ja '66
People's watchdog; arguments of W. Gell-
horn. il Time 88:58+ D 2 '66
Poverty, injustice and the welfare state;
ombudsman for the poor? R. A. Cloward
and R. M. Elman. il Nation 202:230-5 F 28
'66
Proposers of reform; concerning studies by
Walter Gellhorn. C. Hogan. Sat R 50:37-
8 Ja 7 '67
Swedes have it, an ombudsman. J. N. Eller.
America 114:377 Mr 19 '66

Anecdotes, facetiae, satire, etc.
Post-ombudsmanship. Christian Cent 83:1619
D 28 '66
ADMINISTRATORS, College. See College
officials
ADMINISTRATORS, Government. See Public
officers
ADMIRAL corporation
Show goes on, and production perks; Ad-
miral's new color tube plant. il Bsns W
p 122-4 Ap 16 '66
ADMIRALTY ISLAND, Alaska
What's all this about Admiralty?   H. E.
McLean. il Am For 72:38-41+ My '66
ADOLESCENCE
Early arrival of adolescence. America 115:
378 O 1 '66
Protest in adolescence. B. Spock. Redbook
127:8+ Ag '66

ADOLESCENCE—*Continued*
Those teenage strangers. M. F. Farnham. il Parents Mag 41:33-5+ Je '66
Your adolescent's health. L. W. Sauer. PTA Mag 60:31-2 Mr '66
See also
Boys
Girls
High school students
Youth

ADOLESCENT medicine. See Youth—Health and hygiene

ADOLESCENTS. See Youth

ADOPTED children. See Children, Adopted

ADOPTION
Bringing up Beth. Newsweek 69:30 Ja 16 '67
Deaf justice; cases of Wagner child; the Christensen fight. il Newsweek 68:37-8 O 17 '66
Drip, drip, drip; adopted mulatto infant. il Newsweek 67:30+ Ap 4 '66
Fathers and small sons; T. Piazza; first unmarried man to adopt a child. S. Alexander. Life 60:20 Mr 11 '66
Long journey to a new home. J. R. Moskin. il Look 30:80-4 Jl 26 '66
On adopting a blonde; the Liunis case. America 115:679 N 26 '66
Solomon in New Jersey; question of religion for the adoptee. America 115:472 O 22 '66
Who is fair to Beth? concerning Liuni's rejected request; New York. il Newsweek 68:33-4 N 28 '66
See also
Children, Adopted

Anecdotes, facetiae, satire, etc.
Adoption roulette. Christian Cent 83:1427 N 16 '66

ADRENAL glands
Release of catecholamines and specific protein from adrenal glands. N. Kirshner and others. bibliog il Science 154:529-31 O 28 '66

Diseases
Creeping up on hypertension; disease called aldosteronism. il Bsns W p 173-4 S 10 '66

ADRENAL hormones. See Hormones

ADRENAL necrosis. See Necrosis

ADRENALIN
Acceleration of ureteral peristalsis by adrenal compression. S. Boyarsky and others. il Science 154:669 N 4 '66
Adrenaline and noradrenaline: relation to performance in a visual vigilance task. J. F. O'Hanlon, jr; reply with rejoinder. A. H. Anton. bibliog Science 151:709-10 F 11 '66
Epinephrine: cascade reactions and glycogenolytic effect. J. M. Bowness. bibliog il Science 152:1370-1 Je 3 '66
Fight or flight trait is blocked in humans; harmful effects of epinephrine. Sci N 89: 169 Mr 12 '66
Noradrenaline and inhibition of Renshaw cells. T. J. Biscoe and D. R. Curtis. bibliog il Science 151:1230-1 Mr 11 '66
Study shows biochemical link; tolerance for pain and sensory deprivation. Sci N 90:425 N 19 '66

ADRENOCORTICOTROPIC hormones. See ACTH

ADSORPTION
Electrostatic aspects of physical adsorption: implications for molecular sieves and gaseous anesthesia. S. W. Benson and J. W. King, jr; discussion. bibliog Science 153: 555-6 Jl 29 '66

ADULT-child relationship. See Child-adult relationship

ADULT education
Adult education: daytime, nighttime, Saturday, too. J. R. Smith. il NEA J 55:40-1 Mr '66
Back to school go the grown-ups. il Changing T 20:25-8 Mr '66
College coed at seventy-six. il Ebony 22:79-80+ D '66
Educare for elders: University of Kentucky. il Time 88:44 Ag 12 '66
Federal aid to adult basic education. il Sch & Soc 94:445 D 10 '66
How to succeed in business? pre-packaged personal success and self-improvement. il Newsweek 67:84-6 Ap 4 '66
Liberal education for adults in a changing society; adaptation of address, May 7, 1966. J. E. Allen, jr. Sch & Soc 94:454-8 D 10 '66
Mom and dad study the new math; sponsored by PTA of Beaumont, Tex. J. L. Creswell. il Parents Mag 41:68-9+ S '66

No lid on learning; history of adult education. V. Warren. il Am Ed 3:25-6 D '66
One state's adult basic program; Edgemont elementary school, Durham, N.C. K. Erwin. il Am Ed 3:27-8 D '66
Patterns of adult education. by M. E. Ulich. Review
Sat R 49:90-1 O 15 '66. P. Woodring
Preparing adults for rapid change. R. H. Coates. il NEA J 55:23-5 D '66
Self-improvers. B. Davidson. il Ladies Home J 84:64-5+ Ja '67
Student's work is published; concerning sketch in Scholastic scope. M. A. Elliott. il Sr Schol 89:sup47-8 S 23 '66
Washington report; extension of public-education. J. Lloyd. Sr Schol 88:sup4 Mr 18 '66
Will success spoil a poverty program? drastic cut of federal funds for Houston's basic adult education program. W. P. Pannill. New Repub 154:10 F 26 '66
See also
Americanization
Radio in education
Service men, Discharged—Education
Trade schools
United States—Armed forces—Education
University extension

Anecdotes, facetiae, satire, etc.
Mamma mia! J. Brazis. Farm J 90:86 S '66

Library participation
Books for adults beginning to read. Wilson Lib Bul 41:83-7 S '66
Getting into the ghetto; preconference Workshop on books for adults beginning to read. J. N. Berry, 3d. il Library J 91: 3642-4 Ag '66
Library and the functionally illiterate in Cleveland; excerpts from letter. ed. by W. Woulfe. F. Long. ALA Bul 60:637-8 Je '66
Library workshop for adults; Dayton and Montgomery County public library. M. T. Stibitz. il ALA Bul 60:937-41 O '66
See also
Libraries—Readers advisory service

ADULTERY
Riddle of A.I. Prutting suit poses legal riddle. il Time 87:48 F 25 '66
When can infidelity be justified or forgiven? results of McCall's questioning 1,112 men and women. S. Blum. il McCalls 93:73+ My '66

ADULTHOOD. See Maturity

ADVANCED research projects agency. See United States—Defense, Department of— Advanced research projects agency

ADVENTISTS, Seventh day. See Seventh day Adventists

ADVENTURE and adventurers
When in doubt, do! A. Gordon. Read Digest 89:33-4+ O '66

ADVENTURE stories. See Fiction

ADVENTURES, Joint. See Joint adventures

ADVERTISEMENTS. See Advertising

ADVERTISING
Admen in orbit; NASA and the advertisers. D. Sanford. New Repub 155:13-15 D 17 '66
Advertising; address, November 4, 1966. C. T. Lipscomb, jr. Vital Speeches 33:145-8 D 15 '66
Advertising: creator of mass markets. il Sr Schol 88:14-15 Ap 1 '66
Man with the split-level head; advertising and the American consumer; address, February 21, 1966 E. A. Jones. Vital Speeches 32:359-63 Ap 1 '66
News behind the ads. See issues of Changing times
Shining up to a European market; Union carbide scores with American-type ad campaign. il Bsns W p 190+ My 14 '66
What an adman thinks about ads; questions and answers. F. M. Cone. il Changing T 20:38-42 O '66
See also
Communication (speech, writing, etc)
Mailing lists
Photography in advertising
Press agents
Public relations
Radio advertising
Television advertising
also subhead Advertising under various subjects, e.g. Drug trade—Advertising

Anecdotes, facetiae, satire, etc.
Ad(s) infinitum. Christian Cent 83:851 Je 29 '66

AERIAL reconnaissance cameras. See Cameras; Moving picture cameras

AERIAL routes. See Airways

AERIAL target practice. See Target practice, Aerial

AERIAL warfare. See European war, 1914-1918
—Aerial operations; Vietnamese war, 1957-
—Aerial operations

AERIALISTS. See Acrobats and acrobatism

AERO COMMANDER, incorporated
Aero Commander empire. R. B. Weeghman. il Flying 78:42-51 Mr '66
Aero Star. R. Blodget. il Flying 80:84-6 Ja '67
New boy in town; plant in Albany, Ga. il Flying 78:14+ Je '66

AERO spacelines, incorporated
Big Guppies seek a bigger pond. il Bsns W p76-7 S 10 '66

AEROBATICS. See Aviation—Stunt flying

AEROCLASSIC. See Aviation—Exhibitions

AERODYNAMICS
Applications of the Coanda effect. I. Reba. il Sci Am 214:84-92 Je '66
Nature still holds lessons for engineers. W. S. Beller. il Tech W 19:28-9 D 19 '66
See also
Automobiles—Aerodynamics
Wakes (aerodynamics)
Wind tunnels

AERODYNAMICS, Supersonic
Inlet progress key to development of advanced aircraft. M. L. Yaffee. il Aviation W 84:52-3+ Ap 4 '66
Lifting body flight investigation moving into transonic regime. il Tech W 19:116-17 N 28 '66

AEROFLOT (airline) See Airlines—Russia

AEROHYDROFOIL models. See Hydrofoil models

AERONAUTIC engineering. See Aviation engineering

AERONAUTIC instruments
Airborne turbulence sensor still sought. P. J. Klass. il Aviation W 84:97+ Mr 14 '66
Airlines outline equipment needs for built-in avionics self-testing. P. J. Klass. Aviation W 84:89+ Ap 4 '66
Anti-collision system obviates ground aid. P. J. Klass. il Aviation W 86:72-3+ Ja 2 '67
Attack angle device seen aid to piloting; improved techniques in corporate jet aircraft. il Aviation W 85:67-8+ S 26 '66
Autoland system tested in Heathrow fog. H. J. Coleman. il Aviation W 85:84-5+ D 12 '66
BOAC plans new navigation system test. B. Miller. il Aviation W 85:41+ O 3 '66
Collins to show new all-solid-state line. P. J. Klass. il Aviation W 85:100-1+ O 10 '66
Elliott presses for heads-up display sales. H. J. Coleman. il Aviation W 85:93+ S 5 '66
General anti-collision system use likely to require years of tests. P. J. Klass. il Aviation W 84:91-4 My 2 '66
Laser terrain avoidance sensor studied. il Aviation W 84:87-8+ Mr 21 '66
Lear jet expands varied avionics effort. P. J. Klass. il Aviation W 84:57+ F 28 '66
New anti-collision system stirs interest; eliminate range zero system. P. J. Klass. il Aviation W 84:52-3+ Ap 25 '66
New products. A. S. Fuchs. il Flying 79:31-2 D '66
Safety in the sky; electronic anti-collision systems. Bsns W p69 Je 11 '66
Small two-axis sensor has multiple uses; dual-axis rate transducers. B. Miller. il Aviation W 85:96-8 Ag 8 '66
SST avionics to combine proven systems with growth in technology. B. Miller. il Aviation W 85:190-1+ O 31 '66
Tests pave way for application of IHAS in army's AAFSS. B. Miller. il Aviation W 84:106-8+ My 16 '66
Tests set for miniature, tri-service ILS. P. J. Klass. il Aviation W 85:84-5+ N 28 '66
Wide use of F-111A Mk. 2 avionics seen. B. Miller. il Aviation W 84:93-101+ Je 6 '66
X-rays studied for secure stationkeeping. B. Miller. il Aviation W 84:74-5+ Ap 18 '66
See also
Accelerometers
Automatic pilot (airplanes)
Gyroscopic instruments
Inertial guidance systems
Radio apparatus on aircraft
Tacan

Testing
USAF readies reliability center; Rome air development center. Aviation W 84:105 Je 13 '66

AERONAUTIC laboratories
See also
Cornell aeronautical laboratory

AERONAUTIC meteorology. See Meteorology, Aeronautic

AERONAUTIC museums
Looking at Ontario's veteran aircraft; Air museum at Ontario international airport. il Sunset 137:46 S '66

AERONAUTIC research
Aero R&D to be probed. Sci N 90:517 D 17 '66
Centers combine in drive toward SST technology. il Tech W 19:139-41+ N 28 '66
Model drive developed by Cornell for study of transonic stability. R. D. Hibben. il Aviation W 84:101+ Ap 25 '66
NASA emphasizes aeronautical research. Aviation W 84:29 Ja 31 '66
NASA spending to approach $100 million. H. Taylor. Tech W 19:18 O 3 '66
Two schools to conduct army avionics studies; Princeton university and University of Pennsylvania. Aviation W 84:181 Je 20 '66
XB-70A flight research. il Aviation W 84:65+ Je 6; 60-1+ Je 13 '66
See also
Rand corporation

AERONAUTICAL radio, incoporated
Arinc studies domestic airline satellite. K. Johnsen. Aviation W 85:49 S 26 '66

AERONAUTICS
See also
Airplanes
Aviation
Balloon ascensions

Accidents
See Aviation—Accidents

History
How they flew the air mail. E. M. Miller. il Flying 79:64-80 Ag '66
It's a bird, it's a plane, it's the Riesenflugzeug of W.W.I. il Esquire 66:112-15 O '66
Magnificent Brazilian in his flying machine. P. De Paula. il Américas 18:16-22 S '66
Profiles; first flight; S. P. Langley of Smithsonian institution or Wright brothers. G. T. Hellman. New Yorker 42:100+ D 10 '66
Saga of the barnstormers. A. Trammell. il Flying 78:72-88 Je '66

Safety devices and measures
See Aviation—Safety devices and measures

Study and teaching
See also
Air pilots—Training

AERONAUTICS, Commercial
Airline management problems foreseen. Aviation W 85:43 N 28 '66
See also
Air freight service
Air travel
Airlines

Non-scheduled operations
See Local service airlines

Canada
Canada to strengthen regional carriers. R. G. O'Lone. Aviation W 85:38-9 N 14 '66
See also
Okanagan helicopters, limited

United States
See also
Airlines—United States

AERONAUTICS, Military
Quick reaction speeds spares to Vietnam; army Red ball express and USAF STAR. C. M. Plattner. il Aviation W 84:72-3+ Ap 11 '66
See also
Air pilots—Training
Airplanes, Military
Guns, Antiaircraft
Helicopters—Military applications
Target practice, Aerial

France
See also
Airplanes, Military—France

Germany (Federal Republic)
See also
Germany (Federal Republic)—Air force

Great Britain
See also
Great Britain—Royal air force

AERONAUTICS, Military—*Continued*

Japan

Japan's defense rests on U.S. technology. S. Nagashima. il Tech W 19:32-3 D 5 '66

Peru

Peru may seek Mirage 3 buy after rebuff on F-5, Lightning. D. C. Winston. Aviation W 85:20 D 26 '66

Russia

See also
Airplanes, Military—Russia

United States

Air war in Vietnam, introd. by E. D. Muhlfeld. F. Harvey. il Flying 79:38-95 N '66
Credibility gap widens; testimony before Senate foreign relations committee. R. Hotz. Aviation W 84:17 My 2 '66
DOD moves to sharpen air combat. M. Getler. Miss & Roc 18:14 My 16 '66
Marine tactical data system detailed; evaluation of air operations central. R. Pay. il Miss & Roc 18:24-6 F 21 '66

See also
Airplanes, Military—United States
Space flight—Military applications
United States—Air force
United States—Air force, Army

Vietnam (Republic)

See also
Vietnamese war, 1957- —Aerial operations

AERONAUTICS as a profession. See Aviation as a profession

AEROSOLS
For the home bar that has everything; cocktail glass chiller. il Consumer Rep 31: 370-1 Ag '66
Gift idea: the garden bombs. il Sunset 137: 168-9 D '66

AEROSPACE and electronic systems convention
Fluidic missile control system shown at AESCON gathering. C. D. LaFond. il Tech W 19:18-19 O 10 '66

AEROSPACE corporation
SPL probes solar, atmospheric features. R. Pay. il Tech W 19:24-6+ O 24 '66

AEROSPACE division of Martin-Marietta corporation. See Martin-Marietta corporation—Aerospace division

AEROSPACE industries
International aerospace market. il Aviation W 83:16-45+ mid-D '65

See also
Airplane industry and trade

Employees

Economic growth, war draining aerospace manpower. il Aviation W 84:106-7+ Ap 11 '66
Labor-for-rent war: machinists and UAW attack aerospace practice of leasing extra craftsmen from agencies. il Bsns W p 160+ N 5 '66

Finance

Continued aerospace sales rise forecast. il Aviation W 85:21 D 26 '66
Outlook for midyear. R. Hotz. Aviation W 84: 17 Je 27 '66
Vietnam financing challenges industry. W. H. Gregory. il Aviation W 84:26-8 Ap 11 '66
Vietnam vs. space. Nation 202:603 My 23 '66

Securities

Analysts urge aerospace selectivity. H. M. David. il Tech W 19:16-17 Jl 11 '66

Europe, Western

Changing European patterns. R. Hotz. Aviation W 85:21 S 5 '66
European propellant firm seeking non-NATO markets. J. F. Judge. il Tech W 19:30+ Ag 29 '66

See also
Eurospace

France

Anglo-French alliance. R. Hotz. Aviation W 85:21 O 3 '66
DOD denies navy FY 1968 money for purchase of AS-12. M. Getler. il Tech W 20: 18-19 Ja 9 '67
Export policy hampers U.S.-French pacts. L. L. Doty. Aviation W 85:39 S 26 '66
France may merge its aerospace industry. Aviation W 86:17 Ja 2 '67
French aerospace sales up; Russia reports export gain. Aviation W 85:35 N 7 '66

Germany (Federal Republic)

German industry marks best export year. W. C. Wetmore. il Aviation W 83:36-9 mid-D '65

Great Britain

British aerospace industry facing 1970s uncertainty. H. J. Coleman. il Aviation W 85: 26-9 S 5 '66
British aerospace technologists move for end to brain drain. H. J. Coleman. Aviation W 85:33 O 24 '66
British industry society urges formulation of national program. Aviation W 85:123 Jl 25 '66
British missile industry shows strength. W. C. Wetmore. il Aviation W 85:134-5+ S 26 '66
Farnborough reveals few moves to sustain U.K. industry. H. J. Coleman. il Aviation W 85:26-8 S 12 '66
Farnborough's paradox. R. Hotz. Aviation W 85:21 S 12 '66
Manpower slash set for British industry. H. J. Coleman. Aviation W 84:28-9 F 7 '66
Tale of two countries. W. J. Coughlin. Tech W 19:50 S 12 '66
U.K. aerospace indecision called detrimental by SBAC. Aviation W 85:29 O 17 '66

Italy

Italy foresees brighter export outlook. il Aviation W 83:40-2 mid-D '65

United States

Aerospace firms getting call to evaluate Chinese threat. R. Pay. Miss & Roc 18:23+ Ap 18 '66
Aerospace firms lead DOD contractors. Aviation W 85:29 D 5 '66
Aerospace optimism quickens in-house ocean effort funding. W. E. Wilks and R. Barnhart. il Tech W 19:62-4+ S 26 '66
Anglo-French alliance. R. Hotz. Aviation W 85:21 O 3 '66
Big overseas tactical missile buys seen. M. Getler. il Tech W 19:16-18 O 24 '66
Bold grasp on bent nettle; excerpts from address, ed. by W. J. Coughlin. K. Harr. Tech W 19:66 Ag 15 '66
California effort is key to growth area. H. D. Watkins. il Aviation W 84:79+ F 7 '66
Case for space; excerpts from address. E. Q. Daddario. Aviation W 84:21 Je 13 '66
Continued aerospace sales rise forecast. il Aviation W 85:21 D 26 '66
Economic growth, war draining aerospace manpower. il Aviation W 84:106-7+ Ap 11 '66
Export policy hampers U.S.-French pacts. L. L. Doty. Aviation W 85:39 S 26 '66
Firms urged to diversify while defense spending high. W. S. Beller. Miss & Roc 18:34+ My 9 '66
In our hands. W. J. Coughlin. Tech W 20: 50 Ja 16 '67
Industry heads for record year in sales, profits. R. Hotz. il Aviation W 84:62-6 Mr 7 '66
Inertial navaid business expands sharply. B. Miller. il Aviation W 85:136-7+ Ag 15 '66
Laurels for 1966. R. Hotz. Aviation W 85: 11 D 26 '66
Limited war problems challenge industry; with editorial comment. C. Brownlow. il Aviation W 84:21, 26-9 Mr 14 '66
Message from the publisher: outlook for the future. R. W. Martin, jr. Aviation W 84: 17 F 7 '66
Message from the publisher: war and peace. R. W. Martin, jr. Aviation W 85:15 mid-D '66
Metal shortages forcing delivery delays. M. L. Yaffee. Aviation W 85:31-2 S 19 '66
New aerospace products. See issues of Aviation week & space technology
Oilmen wary of aerospace promises; with editorial comment. Tech W 19:27, 78 S 26 '66
Once and future things. W. J. Coughlin. Miss & Roc 18:46 F 21 '66
Outlook for midyear. R. Hotz. Aviation W 84:17 Je 27 '66
Outlook for 1967. R. Holtz. Aviation W 86:11 Ja 2 '67
Profiles; Los Angeles. C. Rand. New Yorker 42:86-8+ O 8 '66
Research for Vietnam; excerpts from testimony, 1966. J. S. Foster, jr. Aviation W 84:21 Mr 21 '66
System engineering aids social problems. H. D. Watkins. il Aviation W 84:52-3+ Ja 31 '66
Tale of two countries. W. J. Coughlin. Tech W 19:50 S 12 '66

AEROSPACE industries—United States—*Cont.*
Trouble ahead in moon industry? il U S News 61:29-32 Ag 1 '66
U.S. firms realigning French operations; several companies seeking office space in Brussels. L. L. Doty. Aviation W 85:34 Jl 11 '66
U.S. space exports should double to $20-30 million. E. H. Kolcum. il Aviation W 83:30-1 mid-D '65
U.S. urges wider export participation. il Aviation W 83:24-5 mid-D '65
Vietnam financing challenges industry. W. H. Gregory il Aviation W 84:26-8 Ap 11 '66
Welcome mat out for aerospace industry. M. L. Yaffee. il Aviation W 84:65-6+ F 14 '66
See also
Government investigations—Aerospace industries
Lockheed aircraft corporation
McDonnell aircraft corporation
AEROSPACE industries association of America, incorporated
In our hands. W. J. Coughlin. Tech W 20:50 Ja 16 '67
AEROSPACE materials. See Materials
AEROSPACE museums. See Aeronautic museums
AEROTRAINS. See Ground effect machines
AESCHYLUS
Oresteia; tr. by R. Lattimore. Criticism
Life 61:8 Jl 29 '66
Sat R 49:24 Jl 16 '66
AESOP'S fables
Aesop revisited. K. Congdon. il Américas 18:1-8 O '66
AESTHETIC activity. See Creation (literary, artistic, etc)
AESTHETICS
Sontag sensibility. P. Velde. Commonweal 84:390-2 Je 24 '66
When good taste becomes bad taste. M. Mannes. McCalls 94:16+ Ja '67
Where is science taking us? visions and values of human experience; excerpts from addresses. G. Kepes. il Sat R 49:66-7 Mr 5 '66
Study and teaching
Aesthetic dimension of environmental responsibility; proposal for curriculum innovation in aesthetic education, grades 7-12; with project. R. A. Smith. bibliog il Sch Arts 65:20-2 Ap '66
AFFAIR of honor; story. See Nabokov, V.
AFFECTION. See Love
AFFELDER, Paul
Music on the Adriatic. Hi Fi 16:MA28-9 N '66
AFFORESTATION. See Reforestation
AFGHAN art. See Art, Afghan
AFGHAN hounds
Fastest crowd in the canine jet set. L. Simross. il Sports Illus 25:50-1 Jl 25 '66
AFGHAN wars
Fierce pawns, by P. A. Macrory. Review
Atlan 218:114-15 Ag '66. E. Weeks
AFGHANISTAN
Afghanistan. W. Hangen. Yale R 56:60-75 O '66
AFLATOXIN. See Fungi
AFRICA
Africa, 1966; symposium. bibliog f il Cur Hist 50:129-71+ Mr '66
Africa's search for identity, by V. C. Ferkiss. Review
Cath World 203:313-14 Ag '66. T. P. Melady
Black Africa: a case of mistaken priority. P. Webb. Newsweek 68:64-5 N 21 '66
On misunderstanding Africa. J. Lucal. Cath World 203:220-3+ Jl '66
Profile of Africa: continent in search of identity. il Sr Schol 89:pt2 8-9 S 23 '66
See also
Africans
Americans in Africa
Architecture—Africa
Botswana
Colonies in Africa
Communism—Africa
Economic assistance in Africa
France—Foreign relations—Africa
Journalism—Africa
Kilimanjaro
Negroes in Africa
Roads—Africa
Slavery—Africa
Socialism—Africa
South Africa
Southwest Africa
Sports—Africa
Technical assistance in Africa
Trade unions—Africa
Zoology—Africa

Civilization
African personality. D. O. Ajala. il Negro Hist Bul 29:157-8 Ap '66

Commerce
Promotion of African trade; summary of five-day meeting of African experts; Addis Ababa. UN Mo Chron 3:53-4 My '66

Cultural relations
Flow of ideas between Africa and America. W. S. Dillon. Bul Atomic Sci 22:23-6 Ap '66

Description and travel
Between Niger and Nile, by A. J. Toynbee. Review
Negro Hist Bul 29:67 D '65. I. Diggs

Economic conditions
Black Africa: free, but deep in trouble. il U S News 61:98-101 O 24 '66

Foreign relations
Afro-Asian inferiority complex; hatred towards Europeans and Americans. E. von Kuehnelt-Leddihn. Nat R 18:836 Ag 23 '66

History
Africa addio, by J. Cohen. Review
Sat R 50:88-90 Ja 14 '67. C. Miller
Ancient African kingdoms, by M. Shinnie. Review
Negro Hist Bul 29:117-19 F '66. I. Diggs
See also
Africa—Kings and rulers

Bibliography
Articles and other books received; comp. by D. E. Gardinier. See issues of American historical review
Books on African history. H. Finch. il Sr Schol 89:sup58 S 23 '66

Kings and rulers
Great rulers of the African past, by L. Dobler and W. A. Brown. Review
Negro Hist Bul 29:141 Mr '66. W. S. Robinson

Maps
Map of Africa (cont) Sr Schol 89:pt2 18 S 23 '66

Nationalism
Developing the academic spirit in East Africa. D. P. S. Wasawo. Bul Atomic Sci 22:19-21 O '66

Native races
Our only look at a lost race; scientists find the sole surviving river Bushman of Okavango swamps; with report by R. Shay. il Life 61:135-6+ D 9 '66
Washing of the spears; a history of the rise of the Zulu nation under Shaka and its fall in the Zulu war of 1879, by D. R. Morris. Review
New Yorker 41:129-34 F 5 '66. A. West
See also
Negroes in Africa
Pygmies
also subhead Native races under names of African countries, e.g. Sudan—Native races

Politics
Africa addio, by J. Cohen. Review
Sat R 50:88-90 Ja 14 '67. C. Miller
African game: who's leader of what? il U S News 60:12 Mr 14 '66
Africa's answer to Schweitzer. C. C. O'Brien. Atlan 217:68-71 Mr '66
Africa's officers take command. W. A. Lewis. Reporter 34:33-6 Mr 24 '66
And now Nkrumah; generals & the future of Africa. J. K. Sale. il Nation 202:317-22 Mr 21 '66
Black Africa: free, but deep in trouble. il U S News 61:98-101 O 24 '66
Cooperation for order in Africa. V. McKay. Cur Hist 50:129-34+ Mr '66
Drama in two acts. il Newsweek 68:54+ O 17 '66
Forecast for Africa: more plots, more coups. R. Matthews. il N Y Times Mag p 10-11+ Ap 10 '66
How democracy is working out in black Africa. il U S News 60:69-71 Ja 31 '66
Macbeth in Africa. Commonweal 83:653 Mr 11 '66
New Democrats. G. Comte. Nat R 18:1273-4 D 13 '66
Old hand's new look at seventeen countries. R. W. Howe. New Repub 155:15-17 Ag 27 '66

AFRICA—Politics—*Continued*
Second revolution; military coups. il Time 87:31-2 Mr 11 '66
Second round for Africa: independence on trial. S. Thompson. Atlan 218:79-83 O '66
Sense at the summit; Nairobi. il Time 87: 40 Ap 8 '66
View from Africa. C. Fritchey. Harper 233: 124+ N '66
What a top authority says about Africa's future; interview, ed. by J. Fromm. E. Huxley. il U S News 60:56-7 Mr 14 '66
   See also
Organization of African unity
Pan-Africanism
Tricontinental conference, Havana, 1966

Race problems
Address to Assembly; summary. November 15, 1966. K. D. Kaunda. UN Mo Chron 3: 64-6 D '66
Growing turmoil in black Africa. U S News 61:20 N 14 '66
How democracy is working out in black Africa. il U S News 60:69-71 Ja 31 '66
Rhodesia in the context of southern Africa. J. K. Nyerere. For Affairs 44:373-86 Ap '66
Southern Rhodesia: the time for action. T. P. Melady. Cath World 204:230-3 Ja '67
What a top authority says about Africa's future; interview, ed. by J. Fromm. E. Huxley. il U S News 60:56-7 Mr 14 '66
   See also subhead Race problems under names of African countries, e.g. South Africa—Race problems

Religious institutions and affairs
   See also
Catholic church in Africa
Christians in Africa

Social conditions
History
Booker T. Washington and the white man's burden. L. R. Harlan. bibliog f Am Hist R 71:441-67 Ja '66

AFRICA, CENTRAL
South of the moon, by B. Littell. Review Newsweek il 68:93B+ Jl 25 '66
   See also
Congo (capital Kinshasa)

AFRICA, EAST
South of the moon, by B. Littell. Review Newsweek il 68:93B+ Jl 25 '66
   See also
Aviation—Africa, East
Education—Africa, East
Eritrea
Geology—Africa, East
Kenya
Zoology—Africa, East

Description and travel
Maybe on Tuesdays. A. Wykes. il Sat R 49: 30+ D 31 '66
Politics
East Africa, unity and diversity. L. Cliffe. Cur Hist 50:147-52 Mr '66

Social life and customs
Maybe on Tuesdays. A. Wykes. il Sat R 49: 30+ D 31 '66

AFRICA, NORTH
   See also
Sahara Desert
Antiquities
   See also
Rome—Antiquities

Maps
Mosaic of new nations changes the face of northwestern Africa. Nat Geog Mag 130: 204-5, sup(folded map) Ag '66

Politics
Africa's Arab fringe. H. L. Hoskins. Cur Hist 50:136-41 Mr '66

AFRICA, NORTHWEST
   See also
Gambia

AFRICA, SOUTH. See South Africa

AFRICA, SOUTHEAST
Prospects for southern Africa. F. M. G. Willson. il Cur Hist 50:165-71+ Mr '66

AFRICA, SOUTHERN
Economic conditions
South of the Zambezi: white man's Africa? Rhodesia, South Africa, Angola and Mozambique. A. J. Meyers. il U S News 61:40-3 D 19 '66

Race problems
South of the Zambezi: white man's Africa? Rhodesia, South Africa, Angola and Mozambique. A. J. Meyers. il U S News 61:40-3 D 19 '66

AFRICA, WEST
   See also
French West Africa
Ivory Coast
Maps
Mosaic of new nations changes the face of northwestern Africa. Nat Geog Mag 130:204-5, sup(folded map) Ag '66

Native races
Freedom speaks French in Ouagadougou. J. Scofield. il Nat Geog Mag 130:153-203 Ag '66
Shakespeare in the bush; anthropological study of the Tiv in West Africa. L. Bohannan. Natur Hist 75:28-33 Ag '66

Politics
Shifting authority in West Africa. C. E. Welch. bibliog f Cur Hist 50:153-8+ Mr '66

AFRICA and the United States
On misunderstanding Africa. J. Lucal. Cath World 203:220-3+ Jl '66

History
Booker T. Washington and the white man's burden. L. R. Harlan. bibliog f Am Hist R 71:441-67 Ja '66

AFRICAN architecture. See Architecture, African

AFRICAN art. See Art, African

AFRICAN dancing. See Dancing, African

AFRICAN languages
Alphabet
Ancient scripts from the heart of Africa. D. A. Olderogge. il UNESCO Courier 19: 25-9 Mr '66

AFRICAN literature
Hidden force of black African art; tr. by A. Foulke. L. S. Senghor. il Vogue 148: 236-9+ D '66
Negritude, a romantic myth? M. Furay. New Repub 155:32-5 Jl 2 '66

AFRICAN lungfishes. See Lungfishes

AFRICAN sleeping sickness. See Trypanosomiasis

AFRICAN violets
African-violet; questions and answers. A. Tinari. Flower Grower 53:27+ N '66
African violets. F. A. Burton. il Horticulture 44:38-40 O '66
African-violets your own way. V. E. Tomasso. il Flower Grower 53:38-9 O '66
All the answers on African violets. H. Mason. il Bet Hom & Gard 44:84 N '66
Take a leaf. K. M. Bova. il Flower Grower 53:26+ N '66

AFRICANS
African personality. D. O. Ajala. il Negro Hist Bul 29:157-8 Ap '66
How do you like Africa, white man, is it like New York? excerpt from An African season. L. Levitt. Harper 234:82-8 Ja '67
Inner black and white. J. Grosjean. America 114:867-8 Je 25 '66

AFRIKAANERS. See South Africans

AFTERNOON waltz; story. See O'Hara, J.

AGABASHIAN, Freddy, and others
Four chargers talk safety; questions and answers. pors Motor T 18:40-1 S '66

AGAM, Yaacov
Carnival of chance; show of optical surprises at New York's Marlborough gallery. il Newsweek 67:107-8 Je 13 '66
180° boogie-woogie. il Time 87:75 My 27 '66
People are talking about . . . il por Vogue 147:195 My '66

AGATHA Sue, I love you; drama. See Einhorn, A.

AGATTU ISLAND. See Aleutian Islands

AGE
   See also
Age groups
Middle age
Old age

Anecdotes, facetiae, satire, etc.
All right, you're so smart, so how old is Harriet? L. Wyse. il Ladies Home J 83:77 My '66

AGE (plants)
   See also
Trees, Age of

AGE, School. See School age
AGE, Voting. See Suffrage—United States
AGE and employment
Grandparents for the asking; Foster grandparents program. E. Margolis. il Parents Mag 41:60-1+ D '66
AGE groups
All split up; isolation by age. J. Knowles. Seventeen 25:184+ My '66
AGE of innocence; story. See Allen, E.
AGE of trees. See Trees, Age of
AGED
Hazards of inactivity seen in nursing homes. Sci N 89:491 Je 18 '66
Help fight heartache. G. Nash. America 114: 835-6 Je 11 '66
Last sail; old man with model sailboat on Conservatory pond, Central park. New Yorker 42:51-2 N 26 '66
161 years old and going strong. P. Young. il Life 61:121+ S 16 '66; Same abr. with title Death is afraid of us. Read Digest 89:97-9 D '66
Ones who wait. N. Rosten. il Sat Eve Post 239:62-5 D 31 '66
    See also
Aging
Old age

Adjustment problems
Heading off the problems of the loner. B. Y. O'Dell. il Todays Health 44:46-9 Ag '66
Long lonely night. R. Butler. America 115: 649-51 N 19 '66
Love is being needed; Foster grandparents project of Office of economic opportunity. C. Brossard. il Look 30:67-71 Ag 23 '66

Anecdotes, facetiae, satire, etc.
Pop and the cuties. L. Rosten. il Look 30: M12 O 18 '66

Economic conditions
Facts about the aging poor. A. Ogle. America 115:651+ N 19 '66
Let's stop exploiting people over sixty-five! K. O. Gilmore. Read Digest 89:229-30+ S '66

Employment
    See Age and employment

Housing
Another east Harlem project: minimum standards vs. minimum decency; La Guardia memorial house. il Arch Rec 139:168-9 Ja '66
Life begins at fifty-two; Rossmoor leisure world. il Fortune 74:164 S '66
Retirement country club; Leisure World at Walnut Creek near San Francisco. J. Peter. il Look 30:M22+ D 13 '66

Recreation
    See Recreation for the aged
AGEE, Doris
My most unforgettable character. Read Digest 88:95-100 Je '66
AGEE, James
Buster Keaton. Life 60:63-4 F 11 '66

    about
James Agee, strange and wonderful. T. S. Matthews. por Sat R 49:22-3 Ap 16 '66
AGEE, Kate Keffer
Educational television in the art room. Sch Arts 66:24-5 D '66
AGEL, Jerome
That's show biz. il Newsweek 68:103 O 17 '66
AGENA (space vehicle) See Space vehicles
AGENCIES, Employment. See Employment agencies
AGENCIES, Federal. See United States—Executive departments
AGENCIES, Regulatory. See Independent regulatory commissions
AGENCIES, Social. See Social agencies
AGENCY for international development. See United States—Agency for international development
AGENTS. See Literary agents
AGENTS, Insurance. See Insurance agents
AGGLUTININS
Gamma-A cold agglutinin: importance of disulfide bonds in activity and structure. B. R. Andersen. bibliog il Science 154: 281-3 O 14 '66
Light-chain heterogeneity of cold agglutinins. N. Costea and others. bibliog il Science 152:1520-1 Je 10 '66

Phytohemagglutinin: inhibition of the agglutinating activity by N-acetyl-D-galactosamine. H. Borberg and others. bibliog il Science 154:1019-20 N 25 '66
Synthesis of nonribosomal RNA by lymphocytes: a response to phytohemagglutinin treatment. H. L. Cooper and A. D. Rubin. bibliog il Science 152:516-18 Ap 22 '66
Vesicular stomatitis virus replication in human leukocyte cultures: enhancement by phytochemagglutinin. R. Edelman and E. F. Wheelock. bibliog il Science 154:1053-5 N 25 '66
AGGRESSION (international law)
Open letter to Konrad Lorenz. E. Rabinowitch. Bul Atomic Sci 22:2-3 N '66
AGGRESSIVENESS (psychology) See Fighting (psychology)
AGHAJANIAN, George K. and Bloom, F. E.
Electron-microscopic autoradiography of rat hypothalamus after intraventricular H³-norepinephrine. bibliog Science 153:308-10 Jl 15 '66
—See Bloom, F. E. jt. auth.
AGING
Aging; report on biological aspects at a symposium. P. L. Krohn. Science 152:391-3 Ap 15 '66
How we can delay old age. A. Hamilton. il Sci Digest 59:45-8 F '66
Memory and aging biological cousins. P. McBroom. Sci N 90:399 N 12 '66
New look in aging; with bibliography. W. C. Fitch. il Wilson Lib Bul 40:832-7 My '66
Phony fountain of youth. R. L. Smith. il Todays Health 44:27-9+ F '66
AGING, Office of. See United States—Health, education and welfare, Department of
AGNELLI, Giovanni, 1921-
Fiat's new wheeler. il por Time 87:102 My 6 '66
AGNEW, Seth M.
Textbooks, 1964-1965: multi-media techniques for teaching. Pub W 189:86-7+ My 2 '66
AGNON, Samuel Joseph
Fable of the goat; story; tr. by B. Rubin. Commentary 42:42-3 D '66
First kiss; story; tr. by N. Kozodoy. Commentary 42:35-7 D '66
Lady and the peddler; story; tr. by R. Alter. Commentary 42:37-42 D '66

    about
Agnon's quest. B. Hochman. Commentary 42:45-51 D '66
Invisible world of S. Y. Agnon. E. Wilson. Commentary 42:31-2 D '66
Nobel laureate of Hebrew literature. C. Leviant. Nation 203:645-7 D 12 '66
Nobels for 1966. S. Maloff. por Newsweek 68:112 O 31 '66
S. Y. Agnon. R. Alter. por Sat R 49:44-5 D 10 '66
Shmuel Agnon, Nelly Sachs win Nobel literature prize. Pub W 190:56-7 O 31 '66
Stranger. il por Newsweek 69:60 Ja 2 '67
AGNOSTICISM
Dialogue with campus agnostics. R. E. Kavanaugh; discussion. America 114:504-5 Ap 9 '66
Freud saw it coming. D. Callahan. Commonweal 84:312-13 Je 3 '66; Discussion. 84: 405+, 483-4 Jl 1, 22 '66
Unbelievers, by A. O. J. Cockshut. Review Sat R 49:62 Je 11 '66. M. Peckham
AGREEMENTS, Trade. See Trade agreements
AGRICULTURAL administration
Food: postwar experience shows it was later than we thought. J. Walsh. Science 152: 896-9 My 13 '66
What the U.S. can do about world hunger. D. Norton-Taylor. il Fortune 73:110-14+ Je '66

    Canada
Socialism in Saskatchewan. A. Morrison. Yale R 56:256-70 D '66

    China (People's Republic)
Development of agriculture. J. Robinson; J. Gray. il Bul Atomic Sci 22:27-39 Je '66

    Europe, Western
At last. Eurofarm. Time 88:88 Ag 5 '66
Equally unhappy; EEC industrial tariffs and agriculture compromise. Newsweek 67:60 My 23 '66
Over the hump at last; Common market ministers agree on farm subsidies. il Bsns W p45 My 21 '66

    Underdeveloped areas
Agribusiness for developing countries. R. A. Goldberg. il Harvard Bsns R 44:81-93 S '66

AGRICULTURAL administration—*Continued*

United States

Chance to clean house. C. P. Streeter. Farm J 90:74 Ag '66

Farm subsidies: continue, cut back, or change? pro and con discussion. Sr Schol 89:16-17+ D 2 '66

Farmer's gamble; raising acreage to grow wheat. Reporter 35:16+ S 8 '66

Greenspan program. O. L. Freeman. il Parks & Rec 1:829-30 O '66

Greenspan program; phase of the federal Cropland adjustment program. J. J. Shomon. il Audubon Mag 68:414 N '66

Housewife and farmer; farm appropriation bill. H. C. Wallich. Newsweek 67:89 My 16 '66

It's time to turn the farmers loose. H. B. Meyers. il Fortune 74:140-5+ D '66

Last minute report straight from Washington. See issues of Farm journal

Possibly practical Utopia. J. Fischer. Harper 233:16+ Jl '66; Discussion. 233:13-14+ O '66

Should we take the wraps off production? O. L. Freeman; C. B. Shuman. Farm J 90: 30-1+ S '66

Stop government from meddling in hog business. R. C. Black. il Farm J 90:A6+ Ag '66

Those extra wheat acres. Farm J 90:22+ S '66

See also

Surplus products, Agricultural

Vietnam (Republic)

Red tape and broken promises; rural problems. S. Andrews. Reporter 34:14-16 My 5 '66

AGRICULTURAL blocs. See Farmers—Political activities

AGRICULTURAL chemicals

Farm chemicals, use them right. L. E. Zeman. Suc Farm 64:110 Mr '66

Keep records when using farm chemicals. Suc Farm 64:87 Mr '66

New chemical controls for your garden. il Flower Grower 53:72-3 My '66

New help in using chemicals; farm centers. G. W. Wormley. il Farm J 90:36H-36I+ Ag '66

Postemergence weed killers for corn and soybeans. E. L. Knake. il Suc Farm 64: 80+ Mr '66

Soil incorporation, how to do it. W. J. Fletcher. il Suc Farm 64:98+ Mr '66

See also

Fungicides

Herbicides

AGRICULTURAL chemistry

See also

Fertilizers and manures

AGRICULTURAL clubs

See also

Future farmers of America

AGRICULTURAL colonization

Bolivia

Bolivia: revolution in mid-passage. G. Delmas. Reporter 35:31-4 D 1 '66

Russia

How the East was won; Virgin lands development. R. J. Korengold. Newsweek 68:58-9 O 10 '66

AGRICULTURAL cooperation. See Agriculture, Cooperative

AGRICULTURAL credit

Machinery financing that fits your farm. il Farm J 90:58X My '66

Specialization vs. credit use; diary farm credit study. il Suc Farm 64:30K Ap '66

Ten commandments for wise credit use. Suc Farm 64:64 My '66

Two farmers tell bankers; addresses. R. K. Buck; H. B. Propst. Farm J 90:68W Mr '66

What's ahead in farm credit? J. R. Brake. Suc Farm 64:86 Ap '66

AGRICULTURAL economics. See Agriculture—Economic aspects

AGRICULTURAL education

Agricultural education agreement signed with Colombia. Dept State Bul 54:494-5 Mr 28 '66

Calling all villagers; Radio rural forums. il UNESCO Courier 19:25 Ap '66

Education for a new agricultural revolution; UNESCO program. il UNESCO Courier 19:23-4 Ap '66

What happens to vo-ag grads? changes that should broaden education. O. Bay. Farm J 90:64N F '66

AGRICULTURAL exhibitions

Iowa's state fair. P. Engle il Holiday 39:78-87 My '66

Let's all go to the fair! state and county fairs. il Changing T 20:24-6 Ag '66

AGRICULTURAL experiment stations

Best bloomin' day of the year. O. Bay. il Farm J 90:85 O '66

See also

Beltsville research center

AGRICULTURAL experimentation. See Agricultural research

AGRICULTURAL extension work

See also

United States—Federal extension service

AGRICULTURAL forecasts

Farmcast. See issues of Farm journal

Farming in 1976; symposium. Farm J 90:37-46 N '66

Look what others will plan this spring. C. W. Gifford. il Farm J 90:58N+ My '66

1967 farm outlook, still great! D. Hanson. Suc Farm 64:6 N '66

Your prospects for 1967. C. W. Gifford. Farm J 90:23+ D '66

AGRICULTURAL insurance. See Insurance, Agricultural

AGRICULTURAL labor. See Farm labor

AGRICULTURAL land. See Land

AGRICULTURAL laws and legislation

New rules on feed grain-wheat: cross compliance; oats and rye rules. Suc Farm 64:71 F '66

1966 wheat-feed grain programs. F. Bailey, jr. Suc Farm 64:50-1 F '66

Patchwork that pays off. il Bsns W p88-90+ S 17 '66

AGRICULTURAL machinery

Combine in comfort this fall. il Farm J 90:56P O '66

540 or 1,000-rpm PTO: how to use both. G. E. Melvin. il Suc Farm 64:52-3+ F '66

How to get the right parts every time. W. J. Fletcher. il Suc Farm 64:48 My '66

Machinery financing that fits your farm. il Farm J 90:58X My '66

Machinery parade; photographs. See issues of Farm journal

Power farming news; photographs. See issues of Farm journal to November 1966

Should you hire help or get more machinery? W. T. Messerly. il Suc Farm 64:40 Mr '66

Soil incorporation, how to do it. W. J. Fletcher. il Suc Farm 64:98+ Mr '66

What's new. See issues of Successful farming

See also

Corn planters

Fertilizer spreaders

Harvesting machinery

Motor trucks

Seeding machinery

Spraying apparatus

AGRICULTURAL machinery industry and trade

Famous firsts: U.S. seedbed of the manager's art; C. H. McCormick. Bsns W p53-4 Ag 27 '66

Prosperity scatters its seed; demand for new equipment. il Bsns W p38-9 Ap 30 '66

See also

Deere and company

AGRICULTURAL meteorology. See Meteorology, Agricultural

AGRICULTURAL pests

See also

Insects, Injurious and beneficial

AGRICULTURAL research

Asphalt agriculture; upgrading marginal land by undercoating sandy soils to retain rainfall. Sci Am 216:60 Ja '67

Asphalt may help relieve food shortage; keeping water from seeping down through the sand. Sci N 90:229 S 24 '66

Paving the way for more food; asphalt-layered soil to trap rain water. il Time 88:69 O 7 '66

See also

Beltsville research center

Radiation—Agricultural applications

AGRICULTURAL research laboratory, Oak Ridge, Tenn.

A-cows and other wonders. W. Yarbrough. il Am Ed 2:12-14 D '65

AGRICULTURAL subsidies. See Agricultural administration—United States

AGRICULTURAL surplus products. See Surplus products, Agricultural

AGRICULTURAL workers. See Farm labor

AGRICULTURE

See also

Dairying

Food and agriculture organization of the United Nations

Food supply

Livestock

Poultry industry and trade

AGRICULTURE—See also—*Continued*
Reclamation of land
Viticulture
  also headings beginning Agricultural; Farm; Soil

Economic aspects
Agriculture and the economy; a new day. il Sr Schol 89:17-18 D 9 '66
Agriculture: shadows on a sea of green. il Sr Schol 88:11-12 Ap 1 '66
And how we can make money with it; address. H. B. Propst. Farm J 90:68W Mr '66
Are U.S. farmers now getting rich? il U S News 60:51-4 My 16 '66
Farm business. See issues of Farm journal
Farmcast. See issues of Farm journal
How you rate in farming; with chart. Farm J 90:68M Mr '66
New day in farming. Farm J 90:130 Ap '66
Prosperity scatters its seed; demand for new equipment. il Bsns W p38-9 Ap 30 '66
Should we take the wraps off production? O. L. Freeman; C. B. Shuman. Farm J 90:30-1+ S '66
Spring outlook: best in years; field staff report; ed. by C. W. Gifford. Farm J 90:33+ Ap '66
Tight money ahead! how to get enough. J. Carlson. Farm J 90:29-30 O '66
What's new in money management. See issues of Successful farming
Why they're so rich on the farm. il Bsns W p78+ S 17 '66

Exhibitions
See Agricultural exhibitions

Federal aid
See Agricultural administration—United States

History
Digging up prehistoric America; discoveries of ancient cultivated corn solve prehistric mystery. R. Claiborne. il Harper 232:69-74 Ap '66
Searching for the beginnings of civilized man. G. Bylinsky. il Fortune 74:158-63+ O '66
Spread of agriculture in the North European periphery. C. A. Moberg. bibliog il Science 152:315-19 Ap 15 '66
  See also
Corn—History

Statistics
Big crop is coming. Suc Farm 64:59 My '66

Study and teaching
This farming business; Business of farming program, Montgomery County, Md. A. W. Tenney. il Am Ed 2:28-32 Jl '66
  See also
Agricultural education

Asia
Report from Asia: findings of Iowa trade mission. W. E. Swegle. il Suc Farm 64:46-7 Jl; 8+ Ag '66

Brazil
Bitter harvest. il Newsweek 67:60 My 2 '66

California
Grape pickers' strike. A. Kopkind. New Repub 154:12-15 Ja 29 '66
Monopoly in the vineyards; grapes of wrath strike. J. P. Degnan. il Nation 202:151-4 F 7 '66

Chile
Improving a wretched plain; Chilean Patagonia. B. F. Grossling. il Am For 72:26-7 N '66

China (People's Republic)
Report from Asia: letter to Dick Hanson. W. E. Swegle. Suc Farm 64:6+ Je '66

Europe, Western
On dry land; Common market achieves policy. Newsweek 68:64 Ag 8 '66

India
Asia needs cropland areas immediately. Sci N 90:405 N 12 '66
Rains that did not come. il UNESCO Courier 19:4-8 Ap '66
Why hunger still stalks India. il Newsweek 67:42+ Ap 4 '66

Iowa
Are U.S. farmers now getting rich? il U S News 60:51-4 My 16 '66
How Iowa farms are changing. il Farm J 90:38G Je '66
Small farmer, 1966 version. il Newsweek 67:22-3 My 2 '66

Latin America
Crops for the tropics. N. A. Haverstock. il Américas 18:10-17 F '66
Latin American land reform; enemies of promise. W. C. Thiesenhusen. il Nation 202:90-4 Ja 24 '66

Mexico
Mexico closes the food gap. J. Strohm. il Read Digest 88:165-8+ Je '66

Middle western states
1976 western corn belt. E. Miller. Farm J 90:44 N '66

Russia
Hopeful harvest. Newsweek 68:56 O 24 '66
Will Russia's farmers decide her future? R. B. Sayre. Farm J 90:99+ Mr '66

Taiwan
Report from Asia: letter to Dick Hanson. W. E. Swegle. Suc Farm 64:6+ Je '66

Underdeveloped areas
FAO: the imperative of altruism; adaptation of address. G. Myrdal. Nation 203:666-70 D 19 '66

United States
Agriculture's new direction; address, April 5, 1966. G L. Mehren. Vital Speeches 32:429-32 My 1 '66
Big new markets ahead for farmers. il Farm J 90:22-3 Ap '66
Farmcast. See issues of Farm journal
Last minute report straight from Washington. See issues of Farm journal
What's new in Washington. See issues of Successful farming
Why they're so rich on the farm. il Bsns W p78+ S 17 '66
  See also
Agricultural administration—United States
Agriculture—Economic aspects
Food supply—United States
United States—Agriculture, Department of

Utah
Migrants in the promised land. J. F. Conway. America 115:253-5 S 10 '66

Vietnam (Republic)
I saw a farmers' war in Vietnam. C. P. Streeter. il Farm J 90:34-5+ Ap '66
That second war in Vietnam; U.S. AID technicians and International voluntary services activities. C. P. Streeter. il Farm J 90:28-9+ My '66

AGRICULTURE, Cooperative
Can co-ops control all the milk? il Farm J 90:29+ S '66
They used their old barn in a new system. J. R. Borcherding. il Suc Farm 64:50-1 Mr '66
What your co-op sees ahead for you. O. Bay. Farm J 90:50BB S '66

AGRICULTURE as a profession
Careers in agriculture. D. Hanson. Suc Farm 64:8 S '66
Who will farm in the future? Suc Farm 64:30I Ap '66

AGROCLIMATOLOGY. See Meteorology, Agricultural

AGUIYI-IRONSI, Johnson Thomas Umunankwe
Another coup. Time 88:33 Ag 5 '66
Military governors. il Newsweek 67:48 Mr 21 '66
New Ironsides. por Newsweek 67:43 Ja 31 '66
Question of speed. Newsweek 68:34-5 Ag 8 '66

AGWAY, incorporated
Agway, the co-op that pays taxes. Fortune 74:311 Jl 15 '66

AHLBRANDT, Laird Kleine-. See Kleine-Ahlbrandt, L.

AHLERS, Eleanor E.
(ed) Arts, the humanities, and the school library. ALA Bul 60:899-908+ O '66

AHMAD, Badruddin
They said it with flowers. Horticulture 44:51 D '66

AHMED, Hocine Aït. See Aït Ahmed, H.

AHRENS, Kathleen. See Putnam, J. jt. ed.

AIDA; opera. See Verdi, G.

AIDES, Teachers. See Teachers aides

AIDIT, Dipa Nusantara
Convenient confession. il por Newsweek 67:41 F 21 '66

AIDS in teaching. See Teaching—Aids and devices

AIKMAN, Lonnelle
Living White House. Nat Geog Mag 130:593-643 N '66

AILEY, Alvin
Dance career: Alvin Ailey's. A. Fatt. il pors Dance Mag 40:52-9 O '66
AILEY, Alvin, dance theatre. See Alvin Ailey dance theatre
AIMS in education. See Education—Aims and objectives
AINUS. See Japan—Native races
AIR
See also
Aerodynamics
Atmosphere
AIR agreements. See Aviation—International aspects
AIR America, incorporated
Rice in the sky. Time 87:26-7 Je 3 '66
AIR bases
De Gaulle threatens NATO, U.S. with loss of bases in France. Aviation W 84:24 F 28 '66
U.S. relinquishes 99-year lease to Atkinson field in Guyana. Dept State Bul 54:935 Je 13 '66
War in Vietnam: U.S. air buildup spurs base construction. C. M. Plattner. il Aviation W 84:72-3+ Mr 14 '66
What Asian allies may get from U.S; South Vietnam and Thailand. il U S News 61:8 S 5 '66
With troops pulling out: loss to France, to U.S: Châteauroux, France. il U S News 61:47-9 S 19 '66
AIR brakes
Sonar beam keeps vigil in the cab: Life Gard. il Bsns W p 140 F 19 '66
AIR Canada
Air Canada cargo gain for 1966 may total 40 per cent as rise continues. J. W. Carter. il Aviation W 86:49-50 Ja 2 '67
Canadian Pacific to share in traffic growth. R. G. O'Lone. Aviation W 85:45 N 21 '66
AIR cleaners. See Air filters
AIR compressors
Build your own air compressor. H. A. Dehn. il Pop Mech 127:183-4 Ja '67
AIR conditioning
Now, central air conditioning for impossible houses. il Bet Hom & Gard 44:114+ My '66
Where comfort starts: the air around you. E. Stevens. House & Gard 131:104-5 Ja '67
See also subhead Air conditioning under various subjects, e.g. Automobiles—Air conditioning
AIR conditioning equipment
Air conditioner sales heat up. Bsns W p36 Jl 16 '66
Air conditioning. il Consumer Rep 31:117-32 D '66
All the news about home air conditioners. C. P. Gilmore. il Pop Sci 188:88-92+ My '66
Central air conditioning with a window unit. H. M. Burke, jr. il Pop Sci 189:132-4 Ag '66
Window air conditioners. il Consumer Bul 49:2+ Jl '66
See also
Humidifiers
AIR-cushion landing system. See Airplanes—Landing gear
AIR cushion vehicles. See Ground effect machines
AIR cushions
Harnessing air to do warehousing chores; Clark equipment's load glide. il Bsns W p 172+ Je 18 '66
AIR filters
Tractor air cleaner, service it right. G. E. Melvin. il Suc Farm 64:48 Jl '66
AIR filters, Airplane
Rigimesh now heavily used in cooling; application in jet and rocket engines. R. Barnhart. il Tech W 19:36+ D 19 '66
AIR filters, Automobile
Filter facts. J. McFarland. il Hot Rod 19: 165 N '66
How to keep those filters filtering. M. J. Schultz. il Pop Mech 126:217 N '66
AIR force academy. See United States air force academy, Colorado Springs
AIR force armament laboratory. See United States—Air force—Systems command
AIR force eastern test range. See Proving grounds
AIR force pilots. See Air pilots
AIR France. See Airlines—France
AIR freight handling. See Freight handling
AIR freight service
Air Canada cargo gain for 1966 may total 40 per cent as rise continues. J. W. Carter. il Aviation W 86:49-50 Ja 2 '67
Air cargo shows what it can do. il Bsns W p96-8+ Jl 16 '66
Air cargo: the ceiling lifts. il Duns R 87:pt2 120-2+ My '66

Air cargo: where the action is. il Duns R 87: pt2 123-4+ My '66
Airlines see 1967 commercial cargo gain. Aviation W 86:29-30 Ja 2 '67
Argentina seeks speeded cargo clearance; Ezeiza airport. J. W. Carter. il Aviation W 84:49+ My 30 '66
Atlantic case awards to spur opposition. L. L. Doty. Aviation W 84:34-5 F 21 '66
Brazilian growth spurs air cargo volume. J. W. Carter. il Aviation W 84:47+ My 9 '66
Brownline widening role in cargo trade. C. M. Plattner. il Aviation W 86:46-9 Ja 2 '67
Cargo facility modernization accelerating; Lufthansa's terminal at Frankfort. J. W. Carter. il Aviation W 85:43+ Jl 18 '66
Cargo system developed for Delta L-100. D. A. Brown. il Aviation W 85:29-31 Ag 29 '66
Cargo talks stress containers, handling; with editorial comment. J. W. Carter. Aviation W 84:21, 41-2 My 30 '66
Carriers plan appeal on blocked space. Aviation W 84:38 Mr 14 '66
Containerization problems seen for large-capacity cargo jets. Aviation W 85:52 D 19 '66
First class for freight. il Time 88:110 N 18 '66
Flying Dutchmen go after bigger cargoes; profitability has replaced KLM's emphasis on size. il Bsns W p 130-1+ S 17 '66
Fraud shifting to airfreight. Aviation W 85: 52 N 14 '66
Growth of air cargo spurs automation. R. O'Lone. il Aviation W 85:72-3+ O 31 '66
KLM compares air-surface freight cost; with tables. J. W. Carter. Aviation W 84:63-6 Mr 14 '66
Local carriers move to increase cargo business as demand rises. R. G. O'Lone. Aviation W 85:38 O 3 '66
Lufthansa accelerates cargo operations. J. W. Carter. il Aviation W 84:33-4 F 28 '66
New system measures air cargo density; cargo process control system. J. W. Carter. il Aviation W 84:42-3 My 16 '66
727QC shows high utilization in initial operations. E. J. Bulban. il Aviation W 85:84-6+ O 31 '66
727QC to expand airline, truck industry coordination. il Aviation W 85:52-3 Ag 8 '66
Trunkline traffic heading for new peak. J. W. Carter. il Aviation W 84:161-2+ Mr 7 '66
U.S. airlines expect new cargo record. J. R. Ashlock. Aviation W 85:40-1 Jl 11 '66
U.S. carriers adopt international numerical code for air freight; Standard international trade classification. Aviation W 84:46 Je 27 '66
Venezuela broadens air freight exports. J. W. Carter. Aviation W 84:47+ Ap 11 '66
See also
Airlift international, incorporated
Airplanes, Freight
Flying Tiger line, incorporated
Helicopter freight service
Periodicals—Transportation

Rates
Board again cuts military cargo rates. Aviation W 84:42-3 Ap 11 '66

Statistics
North Atlantic air cargo and mail data; table. Aviation W 85:62-3 O 31 '66
AIR freight terminals. See Airport buildings
AIR general, incorporated
Helicopter line seeks expansion formula. D. A. Brown. il Aviation W 86:71-2+ Ja 9 '67
AIR inter (airline) See Airlines—France
AIR ions. See Ions
AIR lanes. See Airways
AIR-launched missiles. See Guided missiles—Launching from airplanes
AIR line pilots association international
Pilot's dilemma. M. L. Kahn. Mo Labor R 89:264-7 Mr '66
Presidential unit asks revised Labor act. K. Johnsen. Aviation W 85:40-1 S 5 '66
AIR logistics. See Aeronautics, Military
AIR mail service
See also
Periodicals—Transportation

History
How they flew the air mail. E. M. Miller. il Flying 79:64-80 Ag '66
Stamps around the world. H. Herst, jr. Hobbies 71:99 N '66

AIR pollution—*Continued*
Pollution of man's environment. E. R. Fosdick. il Nat Parks Mag 40:16-20 S '66
Pollution on the mind; Public health service findings. Newsweek 69:86 Ja 23 '67
Resourceful waste management; address. June 7, 1966. A. Spilhaus. il Sci N 89:486-8+ Je 18 '66
Stench from New Jersey. J. Ridgeway. New Repub 155:13-15 Jl 16 '66
There's something in the air. L. Kavaler. il Redbook 127:52-3+ Ag '66
U.S. and Canada request IJC study on air pollution; text of letter, September 23, 1966. Dept State Bul 55:688-9 O 31 '66
What you can do to combat air pollution. Mrs C. F. Henderson. il Parents Mag 41:76-7+ O '66
See also
Plants, Effect of air pollution on
Smog
also subhead Air pollution under names of cities, e.g. New York (city)—Air pollution

Anecdotes, facetiae, satire, etc.
Notes and comment; trees as source of pollution. New Yorker 42:51 S 24 '66
AIR pollution control division. See United States—Public health service—Air pollution control division
AIR proving grounds. See Proving grounds
AIR purification
Conservation's big one-two; excerpts from addresses. February 23, 1966. L. B. Johnson; C. A. T. Johnson. il Am For 72:6-7+ Ap '66
Filter-bag research may relieve air-pollution problems. bibliog il Am City 81:170+ O '66
Fouling the air; coal industry's advertising strategy. N. Cousins. Sat R 49:32+ O 8 '66
How LBJ would clean up the water and air; summary of message. February 23, 1966. L. B. Johnson. U S News 60:14 Mr 7 '66
AIR purifiers
Fresh air with the flick of a switch. il House & Gard 130:16+ S '66
Where comfort starts; the air around you. E. Stevens. House & Gard 131:104-5 Ja '67
AIR races. See Airplane racing
AIR raids
See also
Berlin—Air raids
European war, 1914-1918—Aerial operations
Vietnamese war, 1957- —Aerial operations

Protective measures
See also
Radar defense networks
AIR refueling of airplanes. See Airplanes—Refueling
AIR rifles. See Rifles
AIR routes. See Airways
AIR safety. See Aviation—Safety devices and measures
AIR ships. See Airships
AIR shows. See Aviation—Exhibitions
AIR stewardesses. See Airlines—Hostesses
AIR strips. See Aviation landing stations
AIR taxi service
After the long flight: an air taxi is waiting. U S News 61:59 Jl 18 '66
American adds to New York taxi links. W. Wright. il Aviation W 84:50-1+ Mr 28 '66
Commuterlines urged to seek firm rules. R. G. O'Lone. Aviation W 85:116-18 D 12 '66
For love and money. T. Baxter. Flying 78:22 Je '66
New congressional interest spurs Washington helicopter analysis. il Aviation W 85:32 Ag 29 '66
Problems retard progress of helicopters and V/STOLs. D. A. Brown. il Aviation W 85:134-5+ O 31 '66
Strike swells some taxi, charter demands. Aviation W 85:37 Jl 18 '66
AIR terminals. See Airports
AIR tickets. See Airlines—Tickets
AIR traffic control
ATA backs time-frequency technique; cooperative airborne collision avoidance system. P. J. Klass. il Aviation W 85:104-5+ N 14 '66
Crossing the Atlantic; width of air traffic corridors. R. Burkhardt. New Repub 154:6-7 My 21 '66
FAA to test ocean separation avionics. P. J. Klass. Aviation W 85:47 Ag 15 '66

Fight over corridors. Newsweek 67:81 Mr 14 '66
Near-miss rate spurs European concern. L. L. Doty. Aviation W 85:44-5 D 12 '66
120-mi. aircraft lateral separation restored to ease traffic problem. Aviation W 84:35 Je 20 '66
Pilots, ATA battle on separation rulings. Aviation W 84:36-7 Ap 25 '66
Pilots win battle for wide air lanes; Atlantic corridor width 120 mi. Bsns W p 140 Je 18 '66
AIR traffic control, Military
Near-miss rate spurs European concern. L. L. Doty. Aviation W 85:44-5 D 12 '66
AIR traffic controllers (persons)
Training
See also
United States—Federal aviation administration—Aeronautical center
AIR transport agreements. See Aviation—International aspects
AIR transport association of America
ATA backs time-frequency technique; cooperative airborne collision avoidance system. P. J. Klass. il Aviation W 85:104-5+ N 14 '66
Airports urged to standardize terminal signs. il Aviation W 85:63+ N 14 '66
AIR transportation. See Aeronautics, Commercial
AIR travel
All in one lifetime: from crates to super jetliners; interview. W. W. Patterson. il U S News 60:62-6 F 7 '66
New U.S.-Russian link, by air. il U S News 61:93 N 14 '66
Notes and comment; effects of supersonic air travel. New Yorker 42:47-8 N 26 '66
Psychology of air travel. il Holiday 40:106-7 Jl '66
Survey disputes U.S. trade balance view. L. L. Doty. il Aviation W 84:61-2+ Mr 28 '66
Tomorrow's commuter. J. Eberhart. il Sci N L 89:138-9 F 26 '66
Traveler, beware! beat-up cruise ships, phony charter flights endanger your money, and your life. il Changing T 20:7-12 Ap '66
See also
Aeronautics, Commercial
Aviation
Private flying

History
Travel notes; a look backward to when this column started. R. Joseph. il Esquire 66:74+ D '66

Physiological effects
See Aviation—Physiological effects

China (People's Republic)
China services normal despite disorder. Aviation W 86:43+ Ja 16 '67

Europe, Western
Intra-European passenger traffic swells. L. L. Doty. il Aviation W 85:39-40 Jl 25 '66

France
International trends alter local services. L. L. Doty. Aviation W 86:41+ Ja 16 '67

United States
Across the U.S. in two hours: when? a look at the plane of the future. il U S News 62:40-3 Ja 2 '67
Big changes in air travel, coming fast. il Changing T 20:19-22 D '66
Fast growth of air travel; report on a nonstop boom. il U S News 61:51-3 S 5 '66
Strike swells some taxi, charter demands. Aviation W 85:37 Jl 18 '66
U.S. airlines: flying high, wide, and handsome. il Sr Schol 89:8-9 Ja 6 '67
AIR travel with children. See Travel with children
AIR turbines
Tiny air turbines drive surgical tools to 100,000 r.p.m. W. S. Bacon. il Pop Sci 189:82-3+ S '66
See also
Rotors
AIR turbulence. See Atmospheric turbulence
AIRBORNE infection. See Infection
AIRBUSES. See Airplanes, Jet propelled
AIRCRAFT
See also
Airplanes
Helicopters

AIRCRAFT carriers
Stand by to launch aircraft; operations on USS Independence; excerpt from Vietnam: the confusing war. H. Mulligan. il Read Digest 90:84-8 Ja '67
War in Vietnam: combat dictates shift in navy air tactics. C. M. Plattner. il Aviation W 84:64-72 F 7 '66
See also
Airplanes—Landing on carriers

Fires and fire protection
Agony of the Oriskany. il Time 88:30 N 4 '66
Carrier's agony, hell afloat; Oriskany fire; with report by D. Moser. il Life 61:104-8+ N 25 '66
Death in the Gulf; fire on U.S. carrier Oriskany. il Newsweek 68:49 N 7 '66

AIRCRAFT carriers, Atomic powered
A's for the E; U.S.S. Enterprise. il Time 87:27-8 Ap 29 '66
Big E at work; aerial missions off USS Enterprise. W. Tuohy. il Newsweek 67:42+ Ap 11 '66
Crucial test for atomic ships: what the Enterprise and Bainbridge proved. il U S News 60:46 Je 27 '66
Nuclear carriers: studies convince the skeptics. L. J. Carter. il Science 151:1368-71 Mr 18 '66
Quality of coming home; Enterprise in San Francisco after tour of duty in the South China Sea. L. Wainwright. Life 61:22 Jl 1 '66

AIRCRAFT computers. See Computers—Aeronautic applications

AIRCRAFT gas turbines. See Gas turbines, Aircraft

AIRCRAFT landing mats. See Aviation landing stations—Landing mats

AIRCRAFT owners and pilots association
Last weekend I learned to fly; AOPA's Pinch hitter course. J. Bryant. il Sci Digest 61:61-4 Ja '67

AIRCRAFT video tape recorders. See Video tape recorders and recording

AIRFIELDS. See Aviation landing stations

AIRFREIGHT. See Air freight service

AIRGLOW
Airglow. R. A. Young. il Sci Am 214:102-8+ bibliog(p 144) Mr '66

AIRLIFT international, incorporated
Cargo lines aim for blocked-space volume. J. W. Carter. il Aviation W 85:65 N 21 '66

AIRLINE hostesses. See Airlines—Hostesses

AIRLINE passenger clubs. See Airlines—Passenger service

AIRLINE schedules. See Airlines—Management

AIRLINE strikes (Canada) See Strikes—Canada

AIRLINES
Qantas, pilots, government deadlocked in labor dispute. Aviation W 85:37 D 12 '66
Qantas pilots reject appeal to end strike. Aviation W 85:40 D 5 '66
Qantas pilots threaten walkout; strike at Air Canada continues. Aviation W 85:41 N 28 '66
See also
Air travel
Helicopter airlines

Advertising
Real shocker; Lufthansa's ads. il Time 88:73-5 S 2 '66

Consolidations and mergers
Panagra acquisition approved. Aviation W 85:40 O 24 '66
Trend seen in merger of Ozark, Central. H. D. Watkins. Aviation W 85:41 S 26 '66

Employees
Boom in equipment, tight labor market begin squeeze on manpower. il Aviation W 85:92-3+ O 31 '66
Good jobs in the airlines. il Changing T 20:21-3 Je '66
See also
Air pilots

Fares
Airlines dicker on fares. Bsns W p31 Ja 29 '66
Airlines find youth a turbulent market; half-fare for younger generation. il Bsns W p 156+ Ap 23 '66
All's fare; round trip excursion plan. Time 87:95-6 F 25 '66
Atlantic tour fare agreement seen. J. W. Carter. Aviation W 85:35-6 D 5 '66
Board to offer option to surcharge ban. J. R. Ashlock. Aviation W 84:39-40 Ja 24 '66

Changes in Pacific fares sought. Aviation W 85:41 N 21 '66
CAB zooms in on thriving airlines. il Bsns W p 140+ F 26 '66
Conflict over youth fares intensifying. J. W. Carter. Aviation W 84:34 Ap 25 '66
Downward pressure on fares to continue. J. R. Ashlock. il Aviation W 84:173+ Mr 7 '66
Early adoption of universal card for youth tickets under study. Aviation W 84:39 F 7 '66
European fare rise trend believed ended. Aviation W 85:42 O 24 '66
Frequencies, fares emerging as European growth bars. L. L. Doty. il Aviation W 85:32-7 O 31 '66
IATA balks at basic fare cuts. R. G. O'Lone. Aviation W 85:34-7 O 17 '66
Jet-age bargain: youth air fares. il Sr Schol 88:15 F 11 '66
Kidding the carriers; youth-fare passengers. il Time 87:69-70 Ap 22 '66
Let's travel; youth fare. il Mlle 63:198 My '66
Lower fares; round-trip fare for groups. Time 88:90 D 2 '66
Maytag opposes gimmick fare ideas. W. H. Gregory. Aviation W 84:45 Ja 24 '66
New fares cover Pacific, South America. Aviation W 86:62 Ja 16 '67
New fares may end jet surcharge ban. Aviation W 84:41 F 14 '66
Pacific fare battle due at IATA meeting. J. W. Carter. Aviation W 85:39 Ag 8 '66
Pacific fare cuts are viewed as interim. Aviation W 84:41-2 Ap 11 '66
Promotional fare plan proposed at meeting of trunklines board. Aviation W 84:34 Ja 31 '66
Rate proposals key IATA issue. L. L. Doty. Aviation W 85:25-6 D 19 '66
Surcharge range of $20-50 for SST called reasonable. Aviation W 86:50 Ja 16 '67
Tariff simplification challenging IATA. L. L. Doty. Aviation W 85:27-8 D 26 '66
Teen travel talk; youth fares. il Seventeen 25:64 My '66
Threat of 1967 fare investigation looms. J. R. Ashlock. il Aviation W 84:38-9 My 16 '66
Time for a diplomat. il Time 87:75 Ap 22 '65
Unfare? youth program loophole uncovered. Newsweek 67:68+ Ap 25 '66
What if air fares were lowered? Consumer Rep 31:101-2 Mr '66
Year's respite from fare pressure seen. Aviation W 84:45 Mr 21 '66

Finance
Aid pact will fail to meet strike loss. H. D. Watkins. Aviation W 85:24-5 Ag 22 '66
Airline income and expense; tables. See issues of Aviation week & space technology
Airlines modernize on easier terms. il Bsns W p62+ Mr 19 '66
Boom in equipment, tight labor market begin squeeze on manpower. il Aviation W 85:92-3+ O 31 '66
Increases in U.S. airline operating revenues; table. Aviation W 85:50 O 3 '66
Local revenues rise as strike continues. Aviation W 85:40-1+ Ag 15 '66
Local service revenue to double by 1970. W. Wright. Aviation W 84:185-7 Mr 7 '66
Mutual aid for struck airlines. U S News 61:80 Ag 1 '66
Record profit forecast for local airlines. W. Wright. Aviation W 84:41 My 16 '66
Strike clouds airlines' economic future; with editorial comment. H. D. Watkins. Aviation W 85:11, 25-6 Ag 29 '66
Strike cost $93 million revenue in July. Aviation W 85:45 O 3 '66
Strike jolts July trunk earnings. Aviation W 85:41 S 5 '66
Subsonic, supersonic transport orders reflect blow of strike. J. W. Carter. Aviation W 85:41 S 12 '66
Trunk profits reach $290 million, more than doubling 1964 net. Aviation W 84:26-7 F 28 '66
Trunks set revenue record in first half. H. D. Watkins. Aviation W 85:43 Ag 8 '66
Turbojet, turbofan aircraft 1965 operating costs; table. Aviation W 84:53 My 9 '66
Turbojet, turbofan aircraft operating expense; table (title varies) Aviation W 84:56-7 My 2; 85:62 O 10 '66
Turboprop aircraft operating expense; table (title varies) Aviation W 84:58-9 My 23; 85:63 O 10 '66
U.K. rejects BEA capital structure plan. Aviation W 85:43 N 21 '66

AIRLINES—Finance—*Continued*
U.S. airline assets and liabilities; tables. Aviation W 84:58 My 9 '66
U.S. airline operating revenues and expenses, 1965; table. Aviation W 84:52-3 My 2 '66
U.S. airline revenues and expenses; table. Aviation W 85:49 O 3 '66
U.S. economy, expenses raise question on 1967 outlook. W. H. Gregory. il Aviation W 85: 26-30 O 31 '66
U.S. trunks head for third record year. J. R. Ashlock. Aviation W 84:36-7 My 9 '66
Year-end revival forecast by strike-impacted trunks. H. D. Watkins. il Aviation W 85: 37-8 O 17 '66
See also
Airlines—Securities

Food service
Eastward ho! flight from Honolulu to Japan. H. Sutton. il Sat R 49:49-50 Mr 26 '66

Freight service
See Air freight service

History
See Aeronautics—History

Hostesses
Fly now, play later. D. Klein. il Seventeen 25:108+ N '66
What do they have in common? good grooming. il Redbook 126:74-7+ F '66

International aspects
See Aviation—International aspects

Maintenance and repair
See also
Airplanes—Maintenance and repair
Airplanes, Jet propelled—Maintenance and repair

Management
Airline management problems foreseen. Aviation W 85:43 N 28 '66
BEA management faulty, pilots contend. H. J. Coleman. Aviation W 85:42-3 Jl 11 '66
Changing airline patterns. R. Hotz. Aviation W 84:21 Je 6 '66
New trends shaping policy for carriers; address, 1966. S. G. Tipton. il Aviation W 85: 100-1+ Jl 11 '66
Nonsked airlines get a new flight plan; CAB ruling giving supplemental airlines new charter rights. il Bsns W p72-4+ My 28 '66
Pilot behind TWA's success; E. R. Breech. il Bsns W p 102-4+ Ap 23 '66

Passenger service
Carriers improve Washington terminal. W. Wright. il Aviation W 85:39-40 Jl 11 '66
Come right in colonel, admiral, or whoever; airlines clubs for special customers. D. Sanford. New Repub 154:11-13 F 12 '66
Delta may expand early morning service. il Aviation W 84:47+ Je 13 '66
Eastern moves to solve shuttle problems. J. R. Ashlock. Aviation W 85:28-30 Jl 4 '66
Eastern will test newscasts on shuttle. Aviation W 85:41 Jl 18 '66
Eastward ho! Bangkok's airport. H. Sutton. il Sat R 49:46-8 Ap 2 '66
Excoriating the airlines; CAB reopens investigation on VIP clubs. D. Sanford. New Repub 156:12-13 Ja 7 '67
Fixed $2 movie charge opposed. Aviation W 85:37 D 26 '66
Henry Fonda's steak; private clubs; CAB enforcements bureau requests investigation. New Repub 155:8 Jl 30 '66
McKee yields on National airport, proposes hourly limit on flights. Aviation W 85:34 Ag 1 '66
Toward equality for VIPs; VIP clubs. il Time 88:72 Jl 15 '66
$2 surcharge called move to end movies, TV on domestic flights. J. W. Carter. Aviation W 85:30 Jl 4 '66
United bows to in-flight movies. Bsns W p 150 O 1 '66

Passenger traffic
See Airlines—Traffic

Public relations
See Aviation—Public relations

Rates
See Air freight service—Rates; Airlines—Fares

Reservation systems
Strike clogs airline reservations systems. Aviation W 85:41-3 Jl 25 '66

Routes
See Airways

Safety devices and measures
See Aviation—Safety devices and measures

Securities
Superlatives & shortages; airline stock at alltime peak. Time 87:88 Je 24 '66
What's behind the big TWA sale. Bsns W p 145-6+ Ap 16 '66

Statistics
Airline traffic; tables. See occasional issues of Aviation week & space technology
February traffic tops last year. Aviation W 84:38 Mr 14 '66
1965 air passengers between the United States and other countries by flag of carrier; table. Aviation W 85:162-3 O 31 '66
North Atlantic air passengers and load factors; table. Aviation W 85:40-1 O 31 '66
Survey disputes U.S. trade balance view. L. L. Doty. il Aviation W 84:61-2+ Mr 28 '66
Turbojet aircraft 1965 operations and traffic statistics; table. Aviation W 84:54-5 Mr 21 '66
Turboprop aircraft 1965 operating costs; table. Aviation W 84:63 My 9 '66
U.S. airline growth, 1965 over 1964; tables. Aviation W 84:170 Mr 7 '66
U.S. airline scheduled service traffic growth; table. Aviation W 85:47 S 19 '66
U.S. international airline North Atlantic passengers and load factors, year 1965; tables. Aviation W 84:158-9 Mr 7 '66
U.S. scheduled service load factors; table. Aviation W 85:52 S 26 '66

Terminals
See Airports

Tickets
Fraud shifting to airfreight. Aviation W 85: 52 N 14 '66
See also
Airlines—Reservation systems

Traffic
Are Atlantic flights too close? narrowed corridors unsafe. Bsns W p 106+ Mr 12 '66
Booming Pacific. R. Hotz. Aviation W 85:17 D 5 '66
Changing airline patterns. R. Hotz. Aviation W 84:21 Je 6 '66
500-mi. leg limit proposed for National. Aviation W 85:34 Jl 4 '66
Five trunks regaining traffic after strike. W. H. Gregory. Aviation W 85:27-8 Ag 29 '66
Frequencies, fares emerging as European growth bars. L. L. Doty. il Aviation W 85:32-7 O 31 '66
Holiday traffic hits peak despite snow. Aviation W 86:31 Ja 9 '67
Jam-up at airports; growing problem for travelers. il U S News 61:32-4 D 12 '66
July 4 holiday traffic reaches record level. Aviation W 85:43 Jl 11 '66
New battle over traffic priorities seen. W. H. Gregory. Aviation W 85:29-31 D 19 '66
North Atlantic air traffic surging. J. W. Carter. Aviation W 85:26-7 D 26 '66
Pacific case to set major policies. H. D. Watkins. il Aviation W 85:37-9 N 28 '66
Sketches of the skyways. P. Hennell. il Read Digest 88:201-2+ Ap '66
Soviets forecast slower traffic growth. Aviation W 86:27 Ja 2 '67
Total of marooned tourists in Europe mounts. L. L. Doty. Aviation W 85:42 Ag 8 '66
Traffic and airports; excerpts from address. G. E. Keck. Aviation W 85:21 N 21 '66
U.S. air traffic surges in late November. H. D. Watkins. Aviation W 85:38-9 D 5 '66
Year-end revival forecast by strike-impacted trunks. H. D. Watkins. il Aviation W 85: 37-8 O 17 '66
See also
Aviation—Transatlantic flights

Arab states
Conflicts hamper Arab block formation; Arab air carriers organization. L. L. Doty. Aviation W 84:35-8 My 2 '66

Australia
Airline that races, but can never win; Ansett-ANA airways. il Bsns W p 158+ F 12 '66
Australian carriers developing jet fleets; Trans-Australia airlines and Ansett-ANA. R. G. O'Lone. il Aviation W 84:37+ F 28 '66

AIRLINES—*Continued*

Canada
See also
Air Canada
Canadian Pacific airlines
Local service airlines

China (People's Republic)
China services normal despite disorder; Civil aviation administration of China, Aeroflot and a Mongolian air service serve Peking. Aviation W 86:43+ Ja 16 '67

Egypt
Egypt looks to West for long-haul jets. L. L. Doty. Aviation W 84:53-6 My 16 '66

Europe, Western
Frequencies, fares emerging as European growth bars. L. L. Doty. il Aviation W 85:32-7 O 31 '66
Intra-European passenger traffic swells. L. L. Doty. il Aviation W 85:39-40 Jl 25 '66

France
Flight of the Pelican; fashion from Paris to New York. il Vogue 147:150 Ap 15 '66
Flight 180 to Shanghai. Time 87:105 Je 10 '66
International trends alter local services; study of Paris-Lyon air route served by Air inter. L. L. Doty. Aviation W 86:41+ Ja 16 '67
Jet age precedent; Nice real estate man sues Air France. il Time 87:67 Mr 18 '66
Maverick airline bets on the Pacific; France's UTA. il Bsns W p 152-4 Ap 23 '66
Profit spurs Air France to independence. E. Walford. il Aviation W 84:57+ My 30 '66

Germany (Federal Republic)
Cargo facility modernization accelerating; Lufthansa's terminal at Frankfort. J. W. Carter. il Aviation W 85:43+ Jl 18 '66
Lufthansa expanding into east Europe. E. Walford. Aviation W 84:32 F 28 '66
Real shocker; Lufthansa's ads. il Time 88:73-5 S 2 '66

Great Britain
See also
British European airways corporation

Greece, Modern
Aristotle the airman; inaugurating transatlantic service of Olympic airways. il Time 87:102+ Je 10 '66
Olympic seeks 30 per cent of Athens-N.Y. traffic. C. Brownlow. il Aviation W 85:47+ Jl 25 '66

Greenland
Choppers change Greenland; world's longest helicopter airline. il U S News 61:107 O 31 '66

Hawaii
BAC 111, DC-9 competing in Island rivalry. R. G. O'Lone. il Aviation W 85:40-1+ N 7 '66

Japan
How Japan air lines flies far and fast; third member of exclusive around the world club. il Bsns W p 192-3+ N 12 '66

Lebanon
Art & adventure of bartering; simple sales competition: the winner to sell three jets to Lebanon's Middle East airlines. Time 87:87 Ja 28 '66
MEA sparks push to unify Arab carriers. L. L. Doty. il Aviation W 84:57-9+ My 23 '66

Netherlands
Flying Dutchmen go after bigger cargoes; profitability has replaced KLM's emphasis on size. il Bsns W p 130-1+ S 17 '66
KLM compares air-surface freight cost; with tables. J. W. Carter. Aviation W 84:63-6 Mr 14 '66
KLM speeds magazine shipments. il Aviation W 84:29 F 28 '66

New Zealand
Air New Zealand expands world services. R. G. O'Lone. il Aviation W 84:45+ F 14 '66
U.K. presses BAC 111 sale in New Zealand; preference for Boeing 737, expressed by National airways corp. R. G. O'Lone. il Aviation W 84:32-4 F 7 '66

Russia
Another poor bargain; agreements for New York-Moscow air service. R. Hotz. Aviation W 85:21 N 7 '66

Over the ocean to Russia; Russian airline and Air Canada to operate service between Montreal and Moscow. Time 88:86+ Jl 22 '66
Pan Am. Aeroflot talks begin this week. D. C. Winston. Aviation W 85:47 N 14 '66
Soviets forecast slower traffic growth. Aviation W 86:27 Ja 2 '67
Soviets groom Tu-154 as workhorse. il Aviation W 85:56-7+ O 10 '66

Saudi Arabia
Custom. technology clash in Saudi Arabia. L. L. Doty. il Aviation W 84:64-7+ My 9 '66

Spain
Iberia using Soviet fuel on flights from Havana. W. C. Wetmore. Aviation W 85:60 N 7 '66

Tunisia
Tunis air seeks improved trade balance. J. W. Carter. il Aviation W 84:45+ Ap 18 '66

United States
Aid pact will fail to meet strike loss. H. D. Watkins. Aviation W 85:24-5 Ag 22 '66
Airlines' new role; excerpts from remarks. J. T. Trippe. Aviation W 85:21 S 26 '66
Airlines see 1967 commercial cargo gain. Aviation W 86:29-30 Ja 2 '67
Board moves to speed Northwest-Southwest route case. W. Wright. il Aviation W 84:40-2 Je 13 '66
Caught at the crest. il Time 88:80-3+ Jl 22 '66
Doubts cloud future of diversification. H. D. Watkins. il Aviation W 85:178-9+ O 31 '66
Facing prosperity's problems. R. Hotz. Aviation W 84:21 My 16 '66
Five trunks regaining traffic after strike. W. H. Gregory. Aviation W 85:27-8 Ag 29 '66
Holiday traffic hits peak despite snow. Aviation W 86:31 Ja 9 '67
Major airlines eye Pacific local service. H. D. Watkins. Aviation W 85:38-9 D 12 '66
Nonsked airlines get a new flight plan; CAB ruling giving supplemental airlines new charter rights. il Bsns W p72-4+ My 28 '66
Pacific case to set major policies. H. D. Watkins. il Aviation W 85:37-9 N 28 '66
Permanent authority urged for three more supplementals; Overseas national airways, Standard airways and Vance international airways. Aviation W 85:33 D 26 '66
Strike clouds airlines' economic future; with editorial comment. H. D. Watkins. Aviation W 85:11, 25-6 Ag 29 '66
Strike cost $93 million revenue in July. Aviation W 85:45 O 3 '66
Supplementals' status questioned. H. D. Watkins. il Aviation W 85:45 O 10 '66
Trunkline traffic heading for new peak. J. W. Carter. il Aviation W 84:161-2+ Mr 7 '66
Trunks set revenue record in first half. H. D. Watkins. Aviation W 85:43 Ag 8 '66
U.S. air traffic surges in late November. H. D. Watkins. Aviation W 85:38-9 D 5 '66
U.S. airlines: flying high, wide, and handsome. il Sr Schol 89:8-9 Ja 6 '67
U.S. economy, expenses raise question on 1967 outlook. W. H. Gregory. il Aviation W 85:26-30 O 31 '66
U.S. trunks head for third record year. J. R. Ashlock. Aviation W 84:36-7 My 9 '66
See also
Air transport association of America
Local service airlines
Strikes—United States—Airlines
also names of airlines. e.g. Bonanza air lines

AIRLINES, Local service. See Local service airlines

AIRLINES strike. See Strikes—United States—Airlines

AIRPLANE accidents. See Aviation—Accidents

AIRPLANE armaments. See Airplanes, Military—Armaments

AIRPLANE building. See Airplanes—Manufacture

AIRPLANE buying. See Airplanes—Purchasing

AIRPLANE cabins
Boeing presses for standard 747 interior. il Aviation W 85:43 D 12 '66

AIRPLANE collisions. See Aviation—Accidents

AIRPLANE construction. See Airplanes—Manufacture

AIRPLANE decoration
Boeing presses for standard 747 interior. il Aviation W 85:43 D 12 '66

AIRPLANE engines
Inlet progress key to development of advanced aircraft. M. L. Yaffee. il Aviation W 84:52-3+ Ap 4 '66

U.S. reciprocating engines; specifications (cont) Aviation W 84:212-13 Mr 7 '66

What pilots want to know about engines. J. Diblin. Flying 78:58-60 Je '66

See also
Gas turbines, Aircraft
Helicopter engines
Jet airplane engines

Cooling
See also
Jet airplane engines—Cooling

Fuel
Thickened fuels may reduce crash fires. M. L. Yaffee. il Aviation W 85:36-9+ Jl 4 '66

Maintenance and repair
Engine overhaul. P. Hoffman, jr. il Flying 78:68-71 F '66

See also
Gas turbines, Aircraft—Maintenance and repair

AIRPLANE failures. See Aviation—Accidents

AIRPLANE fares. See Airlines—Fares

AIRPLANE hostesses. See Airlines—Hostesses

AIRPLANE industry and trade
Business aircraft makers primed for DOD utility jet competition. Aviation W 84:32 Ap 25 '66

Foreign accent. J. Fricker. See issues of Flying

U.S. Europe vie for Latin fighter order. C. Brownlow. Aviation W 84:26-7 My 30 '66

Consolidations and mergers
British plan to merge groups. H. J. Coleman. Aviation W 85:23-5 N 28 '66

British plane makers ready to bail out; proposed merger of Hawker Siddeley and British aircraft. il Bsns W p 126+ D 10 '66

Decision at Douglas; merger with McDonnell co. il Newsweek 69:77 Ja 23 '67

McDonnell flies low for a pass at Douglas. il Bsns W p42+ D 3 '66

Mr Mac & Messers Douglas; new firm to be called McDonnell Douglas corp. il Time 89: 73-4 Ja 20 '67

Finance
Clouds lifting for Douglas; merger still holds attraction. il Bsns W p44 Ja 7 '67

See also
Airplane industry and trade—Securities

Securities
High-flying airline stocks. il Duns R 88:61-2 Jl '66

Questions about airlines. il Fortune 73:208+ F '66

Soaring Boeing stock goes under a cloud. il Bsns W p 158 F 19 '66

Statistics
U.S. business & utility aircraft shipments; tables. See occasional issues of Aviation week & space technology

Australia
Aviation down under. G. R. Copley. il Flying 79:82-4 Ag '66

Czechoslovakia
Czech light aircraft produced for export. Aviation W 83:55 mid-D '65

Europe, Western
Europe adopting U.S. techniques to spur business aircraft sales. il Aviation W 84: 293-5+ Mr 7 '66

Europeans gain edge in South America. C. Brownlow. Aviation W 85:26-7 S 19 '66

France
British F-111 foes pushing Spey-Mirage. H. J. Coleman. Aviation W 84:87+ F 7 '66

Foreign accent; Société Wassmer. J. Fricker. il Flying 79:31 O '66

Papon to head Sud combine in French aerospace regrouping. Aviation W 86:35 Ja 16 '67

Germany (Federal Republic)
Dornier seeks Skyservant market abroad. L. L. Doty. il Aviation W 84:103+ Ja 24 '66

Hamburger deluxe. J. Fricker. il Flying 79:100-1 Jl '66

Regional carriers view YS-11 and VFW 614. il Aviation W 85:47+ O 10 '66

Target system aids German training; versatile Dornier application of Beech drone. il Miss & Roc 18:31-2 F 7 '66

Great Britain
British plan to merge groups. H. J. Coleman. Aviation W 85:23-5 N 28 '66

British plane makers ready to bail out; proposed merger of Hawker Siddeley and British aircraft. il Bsns W p 126+ D 10 '66

Changing altitude. Time 87:96+ Mr 4 '66

Foreign accent; Farnborough 1966. J. Fricker. il Flying 79:22-3 D '66

None if by sea; Britain's decision to buy F-111. W. J. Coughlin. Miss & Roc 18:50 F 28 '66

Quite a mother-in-law; Hawker Siddeley group ltd. and BAC. Time 88:94 D 2 '66

Stronger U.S.-British tie urged. Aviation W 84:32 Ap 4 '66

Upward trend seen in British aerospace; with list of British cooperative programs. H. J. Coleman. Aviation W 84:108-11 Je 13 '66

See also
British aircraft corporation
Rolls-Royce, limited

Japan
Regional carriers view YS-11 and VFW 614. il Aviation W 85:47+ O 10 '66

Netherlands
Fokker flies high by aiming low. il Bsns W p74-7 F 5 '66

Russia
Antonov urges cost accounting in USSR; excerpts from article. O. K. Antonov. il Aviation W 84:103+ Mr 21 '66

Soviets gear to challenge U.S. exports. il Aviation W 83:45+ mid-D '65

Trade blocks crimp east Europe trade. L. L. Doty. il Aviation W 83:43-4 mid-D '65

Yakovlev urges more integration of Russian research, production; excerpts from Izvestia article. A. S. Yakovlev. Aviation W 84:83+ Ap 25 '66

Sweden
Saab 305A complements shipping missile. il Aviation W 84:88-9 Ja 24 '66

United States
Aircraft production problems rise with galley delivery lag. R. E. Lee. Aviation W 85:25 Ag 22 '66

Better jet marketing procedures urged; reprint. G. M. Munsinger and A. L. O'Connor. il Aviation W 85:71+ D 26 '66

Booming jet sales growth stabilizing. D. A. Brown. il Aviation W 84:267-71 Mr 7 '66

Business aircraft sales rise forecast. E. J. Bulban. Aviation W 86:88 Ja 16 '67

Engines, landing gear, galleys still delaying aircraft delivery. il Aviation W 85:43 O 24 '66

Export demand may dictate finance shift. il Aviation W 83:21-3 mid-D '65

Industry seeks softer tax credit impact. Aviation W 85:35-6 S 19 '66

Jets for European carriers delayed by Viet war needs. Aviation W 85:37 O 31 '66

Mulley airs U.S. role in Saudi jet order. H. J. Coleman. Aviation W 84:32-3 My 23 '66

None if by sea; Britain's decision to buy F-111. W. J. Coughlin. Miss & Roc 18:50 F 28 '66

Room for all; competition between Lockheed and Boeing. il Time 87:69 Ap 22 '66

Strike spurs business aircraft interest. Aviation W 85:43+ Ag 15 '66

Stronger U.S.-British tie urged. Aviation W 84:32 Ap 4 '66

Tide still rising in light aircraft market. E. J. Bulban. il Aviation W 84:273+ Mr 7 '66

Traffic pattern; rumor mill; acquisitions and mergers. il Flying 79:15-16+ O '66

U.S. airlines; into the wild blue what? J. Mecklin. il Fortune 73:146-8+ My '66

U.S. Europe vie for executive jet sales. D. A. Brown. il Aviation W 83:26-8 mid-D '65

U.S. firms study high-capacity, mid-range jet transport. C. M. Plattner. il Aviation W 85:42-5+ O 31 '66

Viet needs, manpower shortage delay jet transport deliveries. Aviation W 84:43 My 30 '66

AIRPLANE industry and trade—United States
—*Continued*
What's new? R. B. Parke. Flying 79:38 D '66
Who's who of corporate jets. Bsns W p 122
Mr 26 '66
See also
Douglas aircraft company

AIRPLANE instruments. See Aeronautic instruments

AIRPLANE insurance. See Insurance, Aviation

AIRPLANE models
Traffic pattern; Ted Smith's Aero Star model
320. il Flying 79:17 N '66

AIRPLANE museums. See Aeronautic museums

AIRPLANE parachutes. See Parachutes

AIRPLANE parts
Jet delivery delays slowing new services. J.
W. Carter. Aviation W 84:41 Je 27 '66

AIRPLANE pilots. See Air pilots

AIRPLANE racing
Afterthoughts of a racing fan; National
championship air races in the West. A.
Trammell. il Flying 78:42-5 F '66
Air racing; revival meet; National air races.
F. Tinker. il Flying 78:36-41 F '66
Skirts flying; Michigan Small race. S.
Buegeleisen. il Flying 80:74 Ja '67
Skirts flying; Powder puff derby. S. Buegeleisen. il Flying 79:22+ S '66
Wings over Reno; National air races. il
Newsweek 68:110 O 10 '66

AIRPLANE schedules. See Airlines—Management

AIRPLANE selling. See Airplane industry and trade

AIRPLANE tails. See Airplanes—Tail surfaces

AIRPLANE taxi service. See Air taxi service

AIRPLANE transportation of animals. See Animals—Transportation

AIRPLANE travel. See Air travel

AIRPLANE wings
Pilot report: the Beech Staggerwing; queen
of the biplane relics. R. Bach. il Flying
79:70-5 O '66
Propulsive-wing craft gets air force, army
scrutiny; ADAM II. il Tech W 19:30 S 12
'66

Testing
Plane that tucks in its wings; variable-sweep-wing plane. il Sci Digest 59:40 Ap
'66

AIRPLANES
Leading international aircraft; specifications
(cont) Aviation W 84:202-5 Mr 7 '66
Return of the Tin Goose; Bushmaster 2000.
il Time 89:90 Ja 6 '67
USSR military and civil aircraft; specifications. Aviation W 84:207 Mr 7 '66
U.S. commercial transport; specifications
(cont) Aviation W 84:199 Mr 7 '66
United States in air and space; progress and
prospect; address, October 6, 1966. W. A.
Davis. Vital Speeches 33:38-42 N 1 '66
See also
Airplanes, Convertible
Helicopters
Seaplanes

Accidents
See Aviation—Accidents

Bird collisions
See Aviation—Bird hazards

Care
See also
Airplanes—Maintenance and repair

Chartering
British business jet company to sell time
in annual blocks. Aviation W 85:70 N 21
'66
Cargo carriers seek more charter rights.
H. D. Watkins. Aviation W 86:31-2 Ja 2
'67
CAB action expected to spur North Atlantic
charter surge. L. L. Doty. Aviation W 85:
37-8 N 7 '66
Nonsked airlines get a new flight plan; CAB
ruling giving supplemental airlines new
charter rights. il Bsns W p72-4+ My 28 '66
Permanent authority urged for three more
supplementals: Overseas national airways,
Standard airways and Vance international
airways. Aviation W 85:33 D 26 '66
Strike swells some taxi, charter demands.
Aviation W 85:37 Jl 18 '66
Supplementals' status questioned. H. D.
Watkins. il Aviation W 85:45 O 10 '66

Collectors and collecting
Great antiques; the Curtiss Fledgling; ed.
by B. Kieffer. G. Thomas. il Flying 80:
52-5 Ja '67

Construction
See Airplanes—Manufacture

Control
Fully automated flight predicted in ten years.
Sci N 90:229 S 24 '66
See also
Automatic pilot (airplanes)

Conversion
Conversion game. A. Trammell. il Flying 79:
47-50 O '66

Cost
See Airplanes—Prices

Cost of operation
Annual business aircraft operating costs. il
Aviation W 86:82-3 Ja 2 '67
Annual business aircraft operating costs: table. Aviation W 85:102-3 O 3 '66

Design
FAA to propose standards based on random
turbulence concept. W. Wright. Aviation W
84:97+ Ap 25 '66
Yakovlev urges more integration of Russian
research, production; excerpts from Izvestia article. A. S. Yakovlev. Aviation W 84:
83+ Ap 25 '66
See also
Airplanes, Jet propelled—Design

Electronic equipment
Airlines outline equipment needs for built-in avionics self-testing. P. J. Klass. Aviation W 84:89+ Ap 4 '66
Military, air transport lead avionic gains.
P. J. Klass. il Aviation W 84:233+ Mr 7 '66
New avionic products. See occasional issues
of Aviation week & space technology
See also
Computers—Aeronautic applications

Testing
Bendix expected to develop general-purpose
checkout unit. il Tech W 19:34-5 Jl 11 '66

Engines
See Airplane engines

Equipment
Boeing presses for standard 747 interior.
il Aviation W 85:43 D 12 '66
FAA to act on explosion suppression plans.
R. D. Hibben. il Aviation W 85:87+ N
14 '66
New products. A. S. Fuchs. il Flying 79:31-2
D '66
747 avionics to include 1970 concepts; Boeing's jumbo jet transport. il Aviation W
85:205+ O 31 '66
See also
Aeronautic instruments
Airplanes—Hydraulic equipment
Radio apparatus on aircraft
Radio telephone on aircraft

Escape devices
Tractor rocket escape system planned for
USAF, navy A-1s. il Aviation W 85:87 S 5
'66

History
See Aeronautics—History

Hydraulic equipment
Hydraulic systems keyed to power needs.
R. D. Hibben. il Aviation W 86:62-5 Ja
2 '67

Ice protection
On ice. A. Trammell. il Flying 78:57-60 Mr
'66

Instrument flying
See Aviation—Instrument flying

Instruments
See Aeronautic instruments

Insurance
See Insurance, Aviation

Landing
Approach with care. R. L. Kuhlman. Flying 78:88-90 Ap '66
Autoland system tested in Heathrow fog.
H. J. Coleman. il Aviation W 85:84-5+
D 12 '66

AIRPLANES—Landing—*Continued*
  Category 2 gear to be operating at twenty
    airports by late 1967; low weather min-
    imum landings. Aviation W 86:45 Ja 16 '67
  Elliott presses for heads-up display sales.
    H. J. Coleman. il Aviation W 85:93+ S 5 '66
  FAA evaluates final approach sequencer. F.
    J. Klass. il Aviation W 84:92-5+ My 30 '66
  How about the Wren 460? certificated to land
    in zero-zero. R. B. Weeghman. il Flying
    79:58-60 Jl '66
  Pilots given new eyes; Microvision. C. A.
    Betts. il Sci N 89:222-3 Ap 2 '66
  Tests planned for tactical landing aid; use of
    Talar miniature instrument landing system.
    il Aviation W 84:73-5+ Ap 25 '66
  Tests set for miniature, tri-service ILS.
    P. J. Klass. il Aviation W 85:84-5+ N 28
    '66
    See also
  Airplanes, Jet propelled—Landing
  Airplanes, Military—Landing
  Automatic pilot (airplanes)

  Landing gear
  Bell inflatable landing device slated for tests
    next year. il Tech W 18:38 Je 20 '66
  Interim fix ends gear vibration on DC-9.
    H. D. Watkins. il Aviation W 84:37 Ap
    '66
    See also
  Airplanes—Wheels

  Landing on carriers
  Carrier landings, no hands; all-weather au-
    tomatic carrier landing system (ACLS)
    Bsns W p58 N 26 '66

  Laws and regulations
  See Aviation—Laws and regulations

  Leasing
  Aircraft pooling gives Beckett flexibility.
    D. A. Brown. il Aviation W 84:114-15+ Ap
    11 '66

  Maintenance and repair
  Airlines stay poised for flight. il Bsns W
    p25-6 Jl 30 '66
    See also
  Airplane engines—Maintenance and repair
  Airplanes, Jet propelled—Maintenance and re-
    pair
  Airplanes, Light—Maintenance and repair

  Manufacture
  Engines, landing gear, galleys still delaying
    aircraft delivery. il Aviation W 85:43 O 24
    '66
  Old photos used in rebuilding of seaplane. il
    Aviation W 85:86-7 Ag 1 '66
    See also
  Airplanes, Military—Manufacture
  Airplanes, Supersonic—Manufacture

  Materials
  Interest grows in titanium alloy wheels. M.
    L. Yaffee. il Aviation W 84:69-71 My 23 '66
    See also
  Airplanes, Jet propelled—Materials
  Airplanes, Supersonic—Materials

  Noise
  Boom problem still clouds SST future. C. M.
    Plattner. Aviation W 86:28-9 Ja 9 '67
  Design studies urged at noise conference.
    Aviation W 85:67-8 D 12 '66
  Jet age precedent; Nice real estate man sues
    Air France. il Time 87:67 Mr 18 '66
  Noise complaints dwindle quickly as jet
    service begins at National. Aviation W 84:
    50 My 2 '66
  Port authority renews warnings on stretched
    DC-8 noise, weight. J. W. Carter. Avia-
    tion W 84:40 My 2 '66
  Pressure could spur noise breakthrough. H.
    J. Coleman. Aviation W 85:49+ D 19 '66
  Psychological reactions to aircraft noise. K.
    D. Kryter. bibliog il Science 151:1346-55
    Mr 18 '66; Reply. P. K. Holmes. 152:865
    My 13 '66
  Sonic boom tests seek forecast data. C. M.
    Plattner. Aviation W 84:55-7 Je 20 '66
  White House science unit seeks government
    attack on jet noise. Aviation W 84:44 Mr
    28 '66
    See also
  Airports—Noise
  Helicopters—Noise

  Photographs
  Pie in the sky. U S Camera 30:62-3 Ja '67

  Piloting
  Haldeman way. J. N. Haldeman. il Flying
    78:50-4 Je '66

  I learned about flying from that. See issues
    of Flying
  Perfect judgment every time. R. Blodget.
    Flying 79:96-7 O '66
  Pilot, aircraft face new problems in low-
    altitude, high-speed flight. Aviation W 84:
    37 My 30 '66
  Ten rules for mountain flying. E. M. Miller.
    il Flying 80:46-8 Ja '67
    See also
  Airplanes, Jet propelled—Piloting
  Meteorology, Aeronautic

  Prices
  Let's get down to business; airplane buyer's
    guide. il Flying 79:132 O '66

  Private ownership
  Boom in private planes; Americans take to
    the air. il U S News 61:57-9 Jl 18 '66
  Down time. R. B. Parke. Flying 78:36 Mr
    '66
  How to fly to Europe without buying a tic-
    ket. E. M. Iger. il Esquire 67:70-5 Ja '67
  Private aircraft performance evaluated. E. J.
    Bulban. il Aviation W 84:122-3+ Ap 18 '66
  Training boom swelling Cessna 150 sales.
    E. J. Bulban. il Aviation W 85:101+ Ag 8
    '66
    See also
  Airplanes in business
  Private flying

  Purchasing
  Let's get down to business; airplane buyer's
    guide. il Flying 79:132 O '66

  Racing
  See Airplane racing

  Radar equipment
  See Radar in aviation

  Radiation hazards
  See Aviation—Radiation hazards

  Radio equipment
  See Radio apparatus on aircraft

  Refueling
  El desastre; why refuel over other countries?
    Nation 202:283 Mr 14 '66
  Iberia using Soviet fuel on flights from
    Havana. W. C. Wetmore. Aviation W 85:
    60 N 7 '66
  Palomares learns to love the bomb. T. Szulc.
    il N Y Times Mag p22-3+ F 20 '66
    See also
  Helicopters—Refueling

  Safety devices and measures
  Air transport bomb sniffer to be tested. P. J.
    Klass. Aviation W 85:44 Ag 8 '66
  Closing up the gap in jet-age air safety. il
    Life 60:36-43 Ap 15 '66
  Cost, delay cited in FAA proposals. B. K.
    Thomas, jr. Aviation W 85:35-6 D 12 '66
  FAA proposes sweeping changes in safety
    standards on transports. B. K. Thomas, jr.
    Aviation W 85:34 Ag 8 '66
  FAA to act on explosion suppression plans.
    R. D. Hibben. il Aviation W 85:87+ N 14
    '66
  FAA will tighten aircraft safety rules. W.
    Wright. Aviation W 84:38-9 Ap 4 '66
  Thickened fuels may reduce crash fires. M.
    L. Yaffee. il Aviation W 85:36-9+ Jl 4 '66
  Unsafe flying; FAA's recommendations. D.
    Sanford. New Repub 155:6-7 O 29 '66
  What air transport people can do. Sci Digest
    60:47 O '66
  White House spurs safety studies. Aviation W
    84:123 Ap 18 '66
    See also
  Aeronautic instruments
  Airplanes—Escape devices
  Airplanes—Ice protection
  Aviation—Safety devices and measures

  Skidding
  Tests for skidding made; experiments with
    runway grooving. il Sci N 90:182 S 10 '66

  Speed
    See also
  Airplanes, Supersonic

  Stability and stabilizers
  Stability system in light aircraft evaluated.
    D. A. Brown. il Aviation W 86:80-3 Ja 2 '67
    See also
  Gyroscope

  Standards
  FAA to propose standards based on random
    turbulence concept. W. Wright. Aviation W
    84:97+ Ap 25 '66

AIRPLANES—*Continued*

Tail surfaces

BAC 111 loss prompts study of certification for T-tail jets. D. A. Brown. Aviation W 85:39 D 12 '66

Testing

British facility primed for Concorde tests; Structures laboratory at the Royal aircraft establishment, Farnborough, England. il Aviation W 85:92-3 Jl 11 '66

June FAA certification sought for FH-227. il Aviation W 84:41 F 7 '66

See also
Airplanes, Business—Testing

Traffic rules

See Aviation—Laws and regulations

Vibration

Interim fix ends gear vibration on DC-9. H. D. Watkins. il Aviation W 84:37 Ap 4 4 '66

Wheels

Interest grows in titanium alloy wheels. M. L. Yaffe. il Aviation W 84:69-71 My 23 '66

X ray equipment

See X rays in aviation

AIRPLANES, Amphibious

Pilot report: the Twin Bee. R. Weeghman. il Flying 78:46-7+ F '66

AIRPLANES, Business

Attack angle device seen aid to piloting; improved techniques in corporate jet aircraft. il Aviation W 85:67-8+ S 26 '66

Beech launches major expansion of line. il Aviation W 85:113 N 7 '66

Beech pushing for $160 million in sales. E. J. Bulban. il Aviation W 85:118-19+ N 14 '66

Better jet marketing procedures urged; reprint. G. M. Munsinger and A. L. O'Connor. il Aviation W 85:71+ D 26 '66

Booming jet sales growth stabilizing. D. A. Brown. il Aviation W 84:267-71 Mr 7 '66

Burns may sell BA-42 production rights. il Aviation W 84:111+ My 30 '66

Business aircraft sales rise forecast. E. J. Bulban. Aviation W 86:88 Ja 16 '67

Cessna twins based on models 320, 411. E. J. Bulban. il Aviation W 85:104-5+ N 7 '66

DH 125 and the bizjet mystique. J. Gilbert. il Flying 78:84-90 F '66

Europe adopting U.S. techniques to spur business aircraft sales. il Aviation W 84: 293-5+ Mr 7 '66

Executive jets head hopefully for wider sky; Fan jet Falcon. il Bsns W p 116-17+ Mr 26 '66

GAO report raps contractor operation of business aircraft. Aviation W 85:33 S 19 '66

Hamburger deluxe. J. Fricker. il Flying 79: 100-1 Jl '66

How one company utilizes its planes. Bsns W p 120 Mr 26 '66

Leading turbine-powered business aircraft; specifications (cont) Aviation W 84:201 Mr 7 '66

Mooney Mk. 20F Executive 21 designed for charter operations. Aviation W 85:67 S 12 '66

Mooney sees 50 per cent increase in net billings in fiscal 1967. E. J. Bulban. il Aviation W 85:108-9+ S 19 '66

Progress report; Commander 200; Navajo; Mu-2; Merlin II; Twin Otter. il Flying 79: 54-5+ O '66

Sabreliner: T39 in civvies. B. Rogers. il Flying 78:40-7 My '66

Strike spurs business aircraft interest. Aviation W 85:43+ Ag 15 '66

Ted Smith aircraft rolls out Aerostar. C. M. Plattner. il Aviation W 85:99+ O 3 '66

Twin Otter adds ease of piloting to STOL capabilities. D. A. Brown. il Aviation W 84:104-8+ F 14 '66

U.S. business, personal and utility aircraft; specifications (cont) Aviation W 84:200 Mr 7 '66

U.S. Europe vie for executive jet sales. D. A. Brown. il Aviation W 83:26-8 mid-D '65

Weight, power problems delay deliveries of Turbo Commander. Aviation W 84:36 Ja 24 '66

See also
Airplanes in business

Cost of operation

See Airplanes—Cost of operation

Design

Britten-Norman Islander in quantity production. il Aviation W 85:111-12 S 5 '66

NAA plans two new Sabreliner versions. H. D. Watkins. il Aviation W 84:32-3 Je 6 '66

Leasing

See Airplanes—Leasing

Testing

Italian PD-808 handles like light twin. H. J. Coleman. il Aviation W 85:97+ S 26 '66

Pilot report; fan jet Falcon. E. M. Miller. il Flying 79:36-41 O '66

Piper aims Navajo at medium twin field. D. A. Brown. il Aviation W 85:58-9+ S 26 '66

AIRPLANES, Convertible

727QC shows high utilization in initial operations. E. J. Bulban. il Aviation W 85:84-6+ O 31 '66

727QC to expand airline, truck industry coordination. il Aviation W 85:52-3 Ag 8 '66

This strip is necessary; passenger plane by day cargo plane at night. il Time 87:88 Je 17 '66

AIRPLANES, Drone

Ryan planning speed of Mach 1.5 for new version of Firebee drone. il Aviation W 84: 215-17+ Je 20 '66

Steady demand expected for Jindivik drone. il Miss & Roc 18:26-8 Ja 24 '66

Target system aids German training; versatile Dornier application of Beech drone. il Miss & Roc 18:31-2 F 7 '66

U.S. drones and target missiles; specifications (cont) Aviation W 84:227 Mr 7 '66

AIRPLANES, Experimental

Air force FX studies to begin in March; new analyses for CX-6A, V/STOL fighter. C. Brownlow. Aviation W 84:22-3 F 21 '66

Flying flatiron; M2-F2; flight without wings. il Time 88:75 Jl 22 '66

Testing

Bug-eyed airplane bugs pilots. Sci N 90:422 N 19 '66

NASA nears powered stage of lifting-body flight study. il Aviation W 86:68-9+ Ja 16 '67

X-15 flights providing baseline data on reusable space vehicles. B. K. Thomas, jr. il Aviation W 86:67+ Ja 9 '67

AIRPLANES, Freight

Big Guppies seek a bigger pond. il Bsns W p76-7 S 10 '66

Boeing shifts to low-wing 747 design; large passenger/cargo transport. I. Stone. il Aviation W 84:37-9 F 21 '66

Cargo system developed for Delta L-100. D. A. Brown. il Aviation W 85:29-31 Ag 29 '66

Flight of the Pelican; fashion from Paris to New York. il Vogue 147:150 Ap 15 '66

Jet converts from people plane to cargo carrier in forty-five minutes. il Pop Sci 189:82-3 Ag '66

See also
Air freight service
Airplanes, Convertible

AIRPLANES, Government

Whistle-stopping aboard the flying White House. R. B. Stolley. il Life 61:15 S 2 '66

AIRPLANES, Hijacking of. See Crimes aboard aircraft

AIRPLANES, Jet propelled

Airlines modernize on easier terms. il Bsns W p62+ Mr 19 '66

Airplanes plan for both large jets, SST. il Aviation W 84:180-1+ Mr 7 '66

British decision awaited on three-nation airbus plan. H. J. Coleman. Aviation W 85: 47 N 7 '66

BEA demand jolts Anglo-French airbus. H. J. Coleman. Aviation W 84:45 My 2 '66

BOAC nearing decision on 747; subsonic jet transport. Aviation W 84:47 Ap 25 '66

Executive jets head hopefully for wider sky; Fan jet Falcon. il Bsns W p 116-17+ Mr 26 '66

German firms push plans for commercial jet transports; airbus project. W. C. Wetmore. il Aviation W 84:26-9 My 9 '66

Improvement effort spurs F-27 changes; turboprop transport. il Aviation W 85:49-50 S 19 '66

Introduction of DC-9s smooth for Delta. D. A. Brown. il Aviation W 85:42-3+ S 12 '66

Jazz for the jumbo jets; many-splendored pleasure domes; Boeing 747. Time 88:100 D 9 '66

Jet delivery delays slowing new services. J. W. Carter. Aviation W 84:41 Je 27 '66

AIRPLANES, Jet propelled—*Continued*

Planners concerned over early 747 buy. J. R. Ashlock. Aviation W 84:38-9 Mr 28 '66

Race on the jet production line. Bsns W p 180 O 22 '66

Six 747 subcontracts total $1.3 billion; design and manufacture of 490-passenger jet transport. R. G. O'Lone. Aviation W 84:38-9 My 2 '66

Subsonic jet problems of the 1970s examined. Aviation W 85:65+ D 12 '66

Whoosh! there it goes, flying stovepipe. K. V. Brown. il Pop Mech 125:78-81+ My '66

See also
Airplanes, Business

Design

Airbus design tied to airport, traffic control developments. H. J. Coleman. il Aviation W 85:42-3 N 14 '66

Boeing designs 747 for future growth; subsonic jet transport. R. G. O'Lone. il Aviation W 84:41 Ap 18 '66

Boeing may pick single-deck model 747. I. Stone. il Aviation W 84:42-3 Mr 21 '66

Boeing 727 gets lift. Bsns W p 100 Mr 5 '66

Boeing shifts to low-wing 747 design; large passenger/cargo transport. I. Stone. il Aviation W 84:37-9 F 21 '66

Boeing tunes for production run of 747; 490-passenger jet transport. Aviation W 85:28-9 Ag 1 '66

By '69; jets carrying nearly 500. il U S News 60:16 Ap 25 '66

Carriers consider new airbus concepts; subsonic jet transports. J. R. Ashlock. Aviation W 84:33 Je 27 '66

Customers' reaction enlarges Lear liner. E. J. Bulban. il Aviation W 84:60+ My 30 '66

Douglas offering two DC-10 designs. J. R. Ashlock. il Aviation W 84:37-9 F 14 '66

Douglas rolls out first DC-8-62 for SAS. W. H. Gregory. il Aviation W 85:31-2 Jl 4 '66

Douglas rolls out first stretched DC-8. H. D. Watkins. il Aviation W 84:32-3 Ja 31 '66

Douglas studying 600-passenger DC-10; subsonic jet transport. H. D. Watkins. il Aviation W 84:47+ My 16 '66

European airbus concepts differ; German airbus design specifications. il Aviation W 85:27 Ag 22 '66

First DC-8-61 service planned for November. il Aviation W 84:36-7 F 7 '66

500 eggs in one basket; Boeing 747 and Lockheed C-5A. T. E. Stimson. il Pop Mech 126:68-9+ S '66

Flexibility in manufacturing permits wide 737 options. R. G. O'Lone. il Aviation W 84:54-7 Je 6 '66

Forecasts of swelling markets key in decision on 747. R. G. O'Lone. il Aviation W 84:40-1+ Ap 25 '66

Getting there is half the fun. W. McQuade. il Arch Forum 124:92 My '66

IATA chief sees major handling procedure changes for giant jets. Aviation W 84:44 My 30 '66

Layouts, characteristics shown for Douglas DC-10. il Aviation W 84:40-1 F 21 '66

Lockheed offering civil C-5As to carriers for early 1970s. Aviation W 84:43 My 23 '66

Lockheed proposes triple decks, 900 seats for civil C-5A version. Aviation W 84:39 F 21 '66

Lockheed pushes CL-1011 airbus study. C. M. Plattner. Aviation W 85:31 D 26 '66

Lockheed revises C-5A market approach. W. H. Gregory. il Aviation W 84:82-5 Je 13 '66

New Do-u-g-l-as; DC-8 Super 61 and Boeing's 727-200. il Newsweek 67:68 Ja 31 '66

Pan Am, Boeing set a new jet pace; Boeing 747. il Newsweek 67:67-8 Ap 25 '66

Pan American order for 747 opens new era in airline jet transport equipment; with editorial comment. W. H. Gregory. il Aviation W 84:21, 38-40 Ap 18 '66

Pan Am takes off with huge Boeing 747. Bsns W p46+ Ap 16 '66

Revolution in air travel about to start; air buses and supersonic jets. il U S News 60:55 My 9 '66

Room for all. il Time 87:69 Ap 22 '66

Russia gives details of Il-62 transport. il Aviation W 85:54-5+ O 17 '66

747, L-500 seating innovations sought. il Aviation W 85:44-5 Jl 25 '66

727 cleared. Time 88:104 O 21 '66

Soviets groom Tu-154 as workhorse. il Aviation W 85:56-7+ O 10 '66

Sud-Dassault team designs Galion airbus as Caravelle follow-on in markets outside U.S. W. C. Wetmore. il Aviation W 84:74-7+ My 9 '66

U.S. firms study high-capacity, mid-range jet transport. C. M. Plattner. il Aviation W 85:42-5+ O 31 '66

Equipment
See Airplanes—Equipment

Hydraulic equipment
See Airplanes—Hydraulic equipment

Landing

Airworthy planes; Boeing 727 crashes. H. B. Gonzales, and the FAA. New Repub 154:8 F 26 '66

Douglas plans all-weather landing tests. B. Miller. il Aviation W 86:51-2+ Ja 9 '67

Pan Am prepares for automatic landings. P. J. Klass. Aviation W 85:85-6 Jl 18 '66

Safety check; circling approach. Flying 79:102-3 Ag '66

Landing gear
See Airplanes—Landing gear

Maintenance and repair

Airframe maintenance challenge to grow. I. Stone. Aviation W 85:111-14 D 12 '66

Middle-age spread; inspection of Boeing jets for cracks in tail assemblies. Time 87:28 Ap 29 '66

Materials

Airframe maintenance challenge to grow. I. Stone. Aviation W 85:111-14 D 12 '66

Noise
See Airplanes—Noise

Piloting

FAA emphasizes training need after Boeing 727 accident talks. J. R. Ashlock. Aviation W 84:35 F 21 '66

Safety devices and measures
See Airplanes—Safety devices and measures

Testing

BAC 111 loss prompts study of certification for T-tail jets. D. A. Brown. Aviation W 85:39 D 12 '66

AIRPLANES, Light

Call me a Waco. R. Weeghman. il Flying 79:40-5 D '66

Light-plane makers finally get airborne. il Bsns W p 158-62 Ap 30 '66

Mark 22. R. Blodget. il Flying 79:34-9 Jl '66

Pilot report: the new Bellanca. A. Trammell. il Flying 78:48-52 My '66

Tide still rising in light aircraft market. E. J. Bulban. il Aviation W 84:273+ Mr 7 '66

Traffic pattern; new Mooney. il Flying 79:18 N '66

Training boom swelling Cessna 150 sales. E. J. Bulban. il Aviation W 85:101+ Ag 8 '66

U.S. business, personal and utility aircraft; specifications (cont) Aviation W 84:200 Mr 7 '66

See also
Airplanes, Business

Design

Aero star. R. Blodget. il Flying 80:84-6 Ja '67

Commuter aircraft plans tied to FAA. Aviation W 85:119+ D 12 '66

Instrument flying
See Aviation—Instrument flying

Landing
See Airplanes—Landing

Maintenance and repair

Down time. R. B. Parke. Flying 78:36 Mr '66

Safety devices and measures
See Airplanes—Safety devices and measures

Stability and stabilizers
See Airplanes—Stability and stabilizers

Testing

And in this corner, the champ; testing Champion's Citabria. J. Gilbert. il Flying 78:36-41 Ap '66

Beach bumming south of Nassau in a great new bonanza. R. B. Weeghman. il Flying 79:34-40 S '66

Bede seeks summer certification of BD-1. D. A. Brown. il Aviation W 84:95-7 Ap 4 '66

Pilot report:
Bamboo bomber. R. B. Weeghman. il Flying 79:60-3 D '66
Yak. R. A. Hoover. il Flying 80:40-1+ Ja '67
Zlin. J. Gilbert. il Flying 80:40-1+ Ja '67

AIRPLANES, Light—Testing—*Continued*
Pilot report: Aero commander 100. R. B. Weeghman. il Flying 79:60-2 Ag '66
Pilot report: Alon aircoupe. A. Trammell. il Flying 79:66-70 S '66
Pilot report: Cherokee six-300. J. Gilbert. il Flying 79:108-11 N '66
Pilot report: gone flying to Provincetown in the new Cherokee 235B. R. B. Weeghman. il Flying 79:76-80 O '66
Pilot report: Mooney Executive 21. R. Blodget. il Flying 79:102-5 N '66
Pilot report: the Beech Staggerwing; queen of the biplane relics. R. Bach. il Flying 79:70-5 O '66
Pilot report: the Cessna Super Skymaster. E. D. Muhlfeld. il Flying 79:40-4 Jl '66
Pilot report: the Cessna turbo-system Centurion. R. Blodget. il Flying 78:64-7 Je '66
Pilot report: the three Musketeers. il Flying 78:37-9 Je '66
Pilot report: the turbo twin Comanche. R. Weeghman. il Flying 79:44-8 Ag '66
Private aircraft performance evaluated. E. J. Bulban. il Aviation W 84:122-3+ Ap 18 '66

AIRPLANES, Military
British F-111 commitment report hit by conservatives and unions. H. J. Coleman. Aviation W 84:23-4 F 21 '66
Riding the Little Tiger; F-5. il Time 88:97-8 N 11 '66

See also
Airplanes, Drone
Airplanes, Target
Airplanes, Vertical take-off and landing

Accidents
See Aviation—Accidents

Armaments
Bomb hunt; B-52 bomber collides over Spain. Nation 202:141-2 F 7 '66
Case of the missing H-bomb; Palomares search. R. Oulahan. il Life 60:106A-106B F 25 '66
Dunderball; H-bomb search off Spanish coast. il Time 87:33 F 4 '66
GE developing varied aircraft weapons. D. A. Brown. il Aviation W 84:73-5+ Mr 21 '66
Lockheed names first AAFSS subcontractors; advanced aerial fire support system. Aviation W 85:87 O 3 '66
Magic Dragon; Gatling-style machine guns on C-47. J. Berthelson. il Newsweek 68:48 O 31 '66
Mystery of the missing H-bomb; bomber collision over the Spanish coast. il U S News 60:10 F 14 '66
Navy dives deep for a lost H-bomb; hunt for nuclear warhead sunk off Spanish coast. il Bsns W p32 F 5 '66
Palomares learns to love the bomb. T. Szulc. il N Y Times Mag p22-3+ F 20 '66
Real bomb; H-bomb, missing after B-52 and KC-135 collide. il Newsweek 67:50 Ja 31 '66
Still looking; H-bomb missing after the mid-air crash over Spain. Newsweek 67:33 F 7 '66

See also
Helicopters—Armaments

Control
Median signals control flight of F-111. P. J. Klass. il Aviation W 85:76-8+ D 12 '66

Design
Modification of Turbo Commander offered as USAF COIN backup. il Aviation W 84:127 My 16 '66
Navy stresses designing for environment. R. D. Hibben. il Aviation W 85:75+ Ag 22 '66
New fighters near critical decision stage. C. Brownlow. Aviation W 84:26-7 Ap 18 '66
V/STOL to be swing-wing, half titanium; prototype version of joint U.S.-Federal Republic of Germany fighter. M. Getler. Tech W 19:12 D 5 '66
Variable-geometry AMSA studied. C. M. Plattner. Aviation W 86:26 Ja 16 '67

Electronic equipment
C-5A to use gimbal-less stable platform; integrated navigation system for military jet transports. B. Miller. il Aviation W 85:52-3+ D 5 '66
Military, air transport lead avionic gains. P. J. Klass. il Aviation W 84:233+ Mr 7 '66
New system augments B-52 ECM ability. B. Miller. il Aviation W 84:48-51+ F 7 '66
TX concept to raise component reliability; military-quality semiconductors. P. J. Klass. il Aviation W 85:75+ D 19 '66

USAF evaluates Loran-inertial system. B. Miller. il Aviation W 84:83+ My 9 '66
USAF to test AWACS radars in 1966. P. J. Klass. Aviation W 84:28 F 21 '66
Wide use of F-111A Mk. 2 avionics seen. B. Miller. il Aviation W 84:93-101+ Je 6 '66

Equipment
Cable cutter studied for AAFSS; advanced aerial fire support system. Aviation W 85:87-8 O 3 '66
Limited war problems challenge industry; with editorial comment. C. Brownlow. il Aviation W 84:21, 26-9 Mr 14 '66
On-board cargo weight systems studied. R. D. Hibben. il Aviation W 85:85-6+ O 24 '66
Reconnaissance hardware gets realistic test at Eglin site. il Tech W 19:24-6 N 7 '66
Test planned for battlefield illuminator; airborne device to light area of two square miles. M. L. Yaffee. il Aviation W 85:65+ N 7 '66
USAF studies Saab miss-distance gear. W. C. Wetmore. il Aviation W 85:111+ Jl 18 '66
See also
Airplanes. Military—Electronic equipment
Radio telephone on aircraft

Escape devices
See Airplanes—Escape devices

Landing
SATS operation found similar to carrier; short-airfield-for-tactical-support. B. K. Thomas, jr. il Aviation W 85:75+ S 5 '66

Manufacture
Photos detail F-111A assembly flow as program is accelerated. il Aviation W 84:66-75 My 30 '66

Materials
Navy stresses designing for environment. R. D. Hibben. il Aviation W 85:75+ Ag 22 '66

Piloting
See Airplanes—Piloting

Refueling
See Airplanes—Refueling

Testing
F-4K rolled out, makes first test flight. B. K. Thomas, jr. il Aviation W 85:24-5 Jl 4 '66
Luftwaffe evaluating SATS with F-104; short airfield for tactical support. C. Brownlow. il Aviation W 85:66-7+ Ag 22 '66
Near-ground hover complicates piloting tasks in XV-5A tests; lift-fan research aircraft. B. K. Thomas, jr. il Aviation W 84:74-5+ Je 6 '66
Swiss mirage 3 training program advances. D. E. Fink. il Aviation W 85:58-60+ D 19 '66
XB-70A flight research. il Aviation W 84:65+ Je 6; 60-1+ Je 13 '66

Wings
See Airplane wings

France
Mystère mystery; six crashes. Newsweek 67:65 Je 13 '66
Variable-geometry fighter decision set for December. Aviation W 85:32-3 N 14 '66

Germany (Federal Republic)
Price of inexperience; Starfighter crashes. Newsweek 67:50+ Ap 4 '66
Why do they fall? Luftwaffe's 51st Starfighter crash since 1961. il Bsns W p54+ Ap 2 '66

Great Britain
F-4K rolled out, makes first test flight. B. K. Thomas, jr. il Aviation W 85:24-5 Jl 4 '66
F-4K version for RAF will carry British-made reconnaissance pod. il Aviation W 84:82-3 Je 27 '66
Variable-geometry fighter decision set for December. Aviation W 85:32-3 N 14 '66

Greece, Modern
Greek air force asks for T-38 trainers. C. Brownlow. il Aviation W 85:147+ Ag 15 '66

Jordan
Jordan's purchase of F-104 adds to jumble of Arab arms buildup. L. L. Doty. Aviation W 84:34 Ap 11 '66

Russia
MIG and Phantom: how they compare; fighter planes. il U S News 60:6 My 9 '66
USSR military and civil aircraft; specifications (cont) Aviation W 84:207 Mr 7 '66

AIRPLANES, Military—*Continued*

Switzerland

Swiss Mirage 3 training program advances. D. E. Fink. il Aviation W 85:58-60+ D 19 '66

United States

AMSA definition is seen in fiscal 1968; advanced manned strategic aircraft. C. Brownlow. Aviation W 84:28-9 My 23 '66

AMSA shelved in fiscal 1968 budget plan; advanced manned strategic aircraft. C. Brownlow. Aviation W 84:22-5 My 2 '66

Air force FX studies to begin in March; new analyses for CX-6A, V/STOL fighter. C. Brownlow. Aviation W 84:22-3 F 21 '66

Air force seeks A-7A changes to boost basic performance. Aviation W 84:29 F 21 '66

Both strategic and tactical airlift to receive high budget priorities. G. C. Wilson. Aviation W 84:87+ Mr 7 '66

Brown on bombers; excerpts from statement. H. Brown Aviation W 84:21 Ap 11 '66

Brown raps film approval in XB-70 loss; memorandum to R. S. McNamara. H. Brown. Aviation W 85:81+ Ag 29 '66

Cessna to convert USAF T-37Bs to AT-37D combat configuration. Aviation W 85:21 Ag 29 '66

Congress delays probe of F-111B. K. Johnsen. Aviation W 85:26-7 O 17 '66

E-2A controls navy North Vietnam strikes; Hawkeye twin-turboprop early-warning aircraft. C. Brownlow. il Aviation W 85:57+ Ag 1 '66

F-5 buy planned to bolster USAF, VNAF. Aviation W 85:19-20 Ag 1 '66

F-5, our Bantam supersonic jet. H. O. Johansen. il Pop Sci 188:77-81 Mr '66

F-111 programs up for re-investigation. Tech W 19:16 Ag 22 '66

F-111 runs into new head winds; Congress moves to limit funds. Bsns W p84+ S 10 '66

FB-111 procurement to be hiked by 25 per cent. Tech W 19:19 S 19 '66

Full story of the 2.8 seconds that killed the XB70. K. Wheeler. il Life 61:126-30+ N 11 '66

House unit fears tactical air studies stall production. Tech W 19:14 S 26 '66

Jet use to be urged on Logair, Quicktrans. G. C. Wilson. Aviation W 84:25 F 7 '66

McClellan to resume F-111 investigation. G. C. Wilson. Aviation W 85:16-17 Ag 22 '66

McNamara answers bomber critics; question of a follow-on strategic bomber. Miss & Roc 18:13 My 2 '66

McNamara under fire; now it's bomber issue; FB-111 not completely acceptable substitute for the B-52, or B-58. U S News 60:10 My 2 '66

Martell confirms delay in VSX program. Tech W 20:14 Ja 2 '67

MIG and Phantom; how they compare; fighter planes. il U S News 60:6 My 9 '66

More tactical aircraft sought as losses increase in Vietnam. Aviation W 85:30 Ag 15 '66

New storms around the F-111 warplane; the former TFX. U S News 60:10 F 28 '66

New weapon: a slow plane; counter-insurgency aircraft, the OV-10A Bsns W p40 O 22 '66

Photos detail F-111A assembly flow as program is accelerated. il Aviation W 84:66-75 My 30 '66

Plane for all seasons; U.S. navy's A-6 Intruder. il Time 88:38 N 25 '66

Propulsive-wing craft gets air force, army scrutiny; ADAM II. il Tech W 19:30 S 12 '66

Research outlook; XB-70 crash reopens arguments over missiles vs. bombers in U.S. defense planning. Bsns W p93 Je 18 '66

Routine mission; V-2 wreckage found in Bolivia. Newsweek 68:29 Ag 8 '66

Senate unit to urge TAC fighter increase. G. C. Wilson. Aviation W 85:19 Jl 4 '66

Specialized aircraft dilemma grows. D. A. Anderton. Miss & Roc 18:92+ Mr 28 '66

Spy plane that vanished mysteriously; U-2 lost somewhere south of Panama. il U S News 61:6 Ag 8 '66

Tactical aircraft production boost urged. C. Brownlow. Aviation W 85:28-9 S 26 '66

10-billion gamble on a plane: how it's paying off; McNamara's TFX, or, F-111. il U S News 61:42-5 Ag 15 '66

Troubled hybrid: the F-111. il Time 88:19 Ag 19 '66

USAF plans crucial AMSA bid in July; advanced manned strategic aircraft. C. Brownlow. Aviation W 84:28-9 My 16 '66

USAF surveys XB-70 program future. C. M. Plattner. il Aviation W 84:26-30 Je 20 '66

U.S. military aircraft; specifications (cont) Aviation W 84:191-2 Mr 7 '66

U.S. warplanes in Vietnam. K. Brown. il Pop Mech 126:107-11+ N '66

Variable-geometry AMSA studied. C. M. Plattner. Aviation W 86:26 Ja 16 '67

Variable-geometry F-4 proposed to navy. G. C. Wilson. Aviation W 85:30-1 Jl 11 '66

War in Vietnam; Mohawk helps confirm army air concept. C. M. Plattner. il Aviation W 84:70-2+ F 28 '66

Why do they hate Robert Strange McNamara? J. Burnham. il Nat R 18:1153-9 N 15 '66

XC-142A succeeds in varied field trials. E. J. Bulban. il Aviation W 84:28-9 My 30 '66

AIRPLANES, Military transport

Big plane: C-5A. New Yorker 41:28-9 F 19 '66

C-5A yields insights to procedure. Aviation W 85:25 mid-D '66

Controversial total package plan tested. il Aviation W 85:24+ mid-D '66

On-board cargo weight systems studied. R. D. Hibben. il Aviation W 85:85-6+ O 24 '66

Sky's the limit with the C-5. J. Mecklin. il Read Digest 88:83-6 F '66

AIRPLANES, Old

Collectors and collecting

See Airplanes—Collectors and collecting

AIRPLANES, Private. See Airplanes—Private ownership

AIRPLANES, Remodeled

Conversion game. A. Trammell. il Flying 79:47-50 O '66

South Vietnamese air force buys overhauled DC-6 from U.S. firm. Aviation W 85:71 Jl 18 '66

AIRPLANES, Restored

Great antiques; the Curtiss Fledgling; ed. by B. Kieffer. G. Thomas. il Flying 80:52-5 Ja '67

Slow recovery; Detroit-Ryan Speedster. R. Bach. il Flying 79:46-50 Jl '66

AIRPLANES, Short take-off and landing

Dornier seeks Skyservant market abroad. L. L. Doty. il Aviation W 84:103+ Ja 24 '66

NASA studies industry V/STOL report. R. G. O'Lone. Aviation W 84:39 Ap 11 '66

STOL saga: flying buses? America 114:278 F 26 '66

STOL transports seen growing with airport access problems. Aviation W 86:33 Ja 9 '67

USAF considering assault C-130. Aviation W 84:29 Mr 14 '66

U.S. and Canadian STOL aircraft; specifications (cont) Aviation W 84:214 Mr 7 '66

VTOL's proposed for Northeast corridor. J. R. Ashlock. il Aviation W 84:34-6 Ap 4 '66

Wren pushing for zero-zero certification; Wren 460 STOL aircraft. il Aviation W 84:115+ Je 13 '66

Testing

Pilot report: the Helio Stallion. J. Gilbert. il Flying 79:102-8 Jl '66

STOL utility shown in New York test; photographs. Aviation W 85:128-31 N 21 '66

AIRPLANES, Supersonic

Across the U.S. in two hours: when? a look at the plane of the future. il U S News 62:40-3 Ja 2 '67

Airlines' new role; excerpts from remarks. J. T. Trippe. Aviation W 85:21 S 26 '66

Airlines plan for both large jets, SST. il Aviation W 84:180-1+ Mr 7 '66

Airlines press for SST prototype. Aviation W 85:38-9 N 21 '66

Aviation week pilot report: Lockheed SST simulator research stresses low speeds. C. M. Plattner. il Aviation W 85:76-81+ N 21 '66

Boeing focuses on range-payload goal. R. G. O'Lone. Aviation W 86:26-7 Ja 9 '67

Boeing moves engines in SST redesign. J. R. Ashlock. il Aviation W 84:34-5 Je 20 '66

Boeing places its supersonic bet. il Bsns W p38-40+ D 24 '66

Braniff considers SST for Latin America. G. C. Wilson. Aviation W 84:45+ My 23 '66

BAC predicts Concorde market to reach 200 aircraft by 1975. Aviation W 86:49 Ja 16 '67

Buildings and the sonic boom. R. S. Lanier. il Arch Forum 125:54-5+ D '66

AIRPLANES, Supersonic—*Continued*

Case against the supersonic transport. J. E. Gibson. Harper 233:76-80+ Jl '66; Discussion. 233:4+ S '66

Centers combine in drive toward SST technology. il Tech W 19:139-41+ N 28 '66

Change in pitch: Russian competitor of the Concorde. il Time 87:91 Je 3 '66

Coming in on a wing & a pliers; XB-70 landing. il Time 87:32 My 13 '66

Concessions pressed on SST contracts. Aviation W 85:27-8 D 19 '66

Concorde production ahead of timetable. H. J. Coleman. il Aviation W 84:40-1+ Ap 4 '66

Concorde R&D costs reach $1.4 billion. Aviation W 85:39 S 19 '66

Confidence in the Concorde. il Fortune 73:74+ Ap '66

Europe's Concorde will be the first SST to fly. il Life 61:72-3 O 28 '66

FAA spurring measurements of radiation at SST altitudes. Tech W 19:38+ S 19 '66

FAA to complete SST phase 2C funding. J. R. Ashlock. il Aviation W 84:30-1 Ja 31 '66

Few medical unknowns anticipated in SST operations. il Aviation W 85:116-17+ Ag 15 '66

$4.9 billion backlog, and the SST, too. il Newsweek 69:66-8 Ja 16 '67

Frustration beneath elation. il Time 89:59-60 Ja 13 '67

Golden goose; Lockheed mockup at Burbank, Calif. il Time 88:71 Jl 1 '66

Guthrie urges SST economics scrutiny. R. G. O'Lone. Aviation W 85:38-9 S 19 '66

In-flight simulator considered for SST. B. K. Thomas, jr. il Aviation W 85:75+ N 7 '66

Industry to absorb ten per cent of SST phase 3. J. R. Ashlock. Aviation W 84:39 My 23 '66

Investment in SST might exceed $4 billion by first delivery date. Aviation W 84:45 Ap 11 '66

Lockheed aims at the airlines; Defense dept.'s leading contractor. il Bsns W p46-9+ D 24 '66

Lockheed boosts lift/drag ratio of SST. il Aviation W 84:40 Mr 28 '66

Lockheed likely to stretch SST design. il Tech W 19:34-5 Jl 4 '66

LBJ on SST: four choices. Sci N 90:530 D 24 '66

Magnuson answers Senate SST queries. W. G. Magnuson. il Aviation W 85:89+ S 12 '66

Near-field criteria give SST required transonic boom level. Aviation W 86:38-9 Ja 16 '67

Pan Am, Boeing set a new jet pace. il Newsweek 67:67-8 Ap 25 '66

Phase 2 to emphasize operational data. C. M. Plattner. il Aviation W 84:60-1+ Je 13 '66

Present problems of future planes. D. L. Flaherty. America 116:15 Ja 7 '67

Preview: Lockheed unveils full-scale mockup. il Newsweek 68:75 Jl 4 '66

Program geared to aid SST data search. C. M. Plattner. il Aviation W 84:65+ Je 6 '66

Science flies high with the SST. il Bsns W p68-9+ Je 25 '66

Supersonic aircraft, to build or not to build? R. Burkhardt. New Repub 155:12-13 D 24 '66

Supersonic decision. R. Hotz. Aviation W 86:11 Ja 9 '67

Supersonic jet makes a slow takeoff; choice of Boeing and GE didn't end the suspense. il Bsns W p31-2 Ja 7 '67

Supersonic transport. K. H. Hohenemser. Bul Atomic Sci 22:8-12 D '66

Supersonic transport and you. V. Block. il Sci Digest 60:60-7 Jl '66

SST called technically feasible; noise, boom still pose problems. Aviation W 84:43 My 2 '66

SST decision. W. J. Coughlin. Tech W 19:50 Ag 1 '66

SST engine battle: turbofan vs. turbojet; P&W vs. GE. Bsns W p 142 Ag 6 '66

SST evaluators to visit competitors' plants. Aviation W 85:52 S 12 '66

SST flyoff hinges on coming evaluation. G. C. Wilson. Aviation W 85:39-40 S 5 '66

SST is go, but wait! il Sci N 91:31 Ja 14 '67

SST may cost too much. Sci N 89:462 Je 11 '66

SST prototype contracts due in January. Aviation W 84:313 Mr 7 '66

SST research effort delayed two-three months by XB-70 loss. H. Taylor. il Tech W 18:18 Je 27 '66

SST: winners of the great race; Boeing and GE. il Newsweek 69:51 Ja 9 '67

SST's decisive moment; will contract go to Boeing, Lockheed, both, or neither? il Bsns W p35-7 D 24 '66

SSTs may create source of own destruction. Sci N 90:407 N 12 '66

Supersonic transports to heat earth's surface. Sci N 89:292 Ap 23 '66

Surcharge range of $20-50 for SST called reasonable. Aviation W 86:50 Ja 16 '67

Temperature can clip SST range. Aviation W 84:41+ My 2 '66

Troubled hybrid: the F-111. il Time 88:19 Ag 19 '66

Two for the SST race; U.S. effort to keep dominance in world's aircraft market. Time 88:100 D 9 '66

When $4-billion is up in the air; supersonic transport contest big challenge for W. F. McKee, head of FAA. il Bsns W p 190-2+ O 8 '66

Cost

Economist would postpone SST pending certainty of 10 per cent return. Aviation W 86:29-30 Ja 9 '67

Greater stress urged on economics of SST. Aviation W 86:45 Ja 16 '67

Magnuson answers Senate SST queries. W. G. Magnuson. il Aviation W 85:89+ S 12 '66

Magnuson details SST financing plans. Aviation W 85:39 S 5 '66

New agency proposed for SST financing. Tech W 20:17 Ja 16 '67

SST development cost put at $4.5 billion by Magnuson. Tech W 19:17 S 5 '66

SST price & progress; U.S. Anglo-French, Soviet projects. il Time 88:110 S 30 '66

Design

Airliner of tomorrow? new version is unveiled. il U S News 61:18 O 10 '66

Bids are in for the SST: Boeing's mock-up on display, contenders wait for FAA's decision. il Bsns W p 147-8 O 1 '66

Boeing changes bet in the SST race. il Bsns W p48 Je 18 '66

Boeing lengthens SST fuselage design. Aviation W 84:43 Je 13 '66

Boeing plans to let 60 per cent of SST work. R. Twiss. il Tech W 20:13-15 Ja 9 '67

Boeing proposes wide-fuselage version of larger SST. C. M. Plattner. il Aviation W 85:34-7 O 3 '66

Boeing SST design. C. M. Plattner. il Aviation W 85:36-9 Ag 15; 30-3 Ag 22 '66

Boeing SST stresses handling, comfort. C. M. Plattner. il Aviation W 85:39-41+ O 17 '66

Boeing's new version; design of supersonic transport. il Time 88:102 O 7 '66

Capacity increase may enlarge L-2000. C. M. Plattner. il Aviation W 85:26-7 Jl 4 '66

Design deadline; competing proposals on the designs to build America's supersonic transport. Newsweek 68:97 S 19 '66

Facts about airliner of the future. il U S News 62:41 Ja 16 '67

$50 billion battle to build the giant SST; Lockheed, Boeing, Concorde progress; with report by C. Welles. il Life 61:68-77+ O 28 '66

Great race. il Newsweek 67:70 Je 27 '66

Johnson expected to push SST. Aviation W 86:25-6 Ja 9 '67

Lockheed plans alternate SST version for domestic use. C. M. Plattner. il Aviation W 85:42-3+ S 5 '66

New Boeing SST. il Newsweek 68:89 O 10 '66

Non-U.S. airlines to evaluate SST designs. Aviation W 85:26 Ag 22 '66

Revolution in air travel about to start; air buses and supersonic jets. il U S News 60:55 My 9 '66

Sound, sun, and the SST; Boeing version. H. Sutton. il Sat R 49:66-9 N 19 '66

Supersonic plane as long as a football field. il U S News 61:8 Jl 4 '66

SST race, biggest of all; Boeing and Lockheed rivalry; designs. il Newsweek 68:48-52+ Ag 29 '66

Electronic equipment

Microcircuits aid onboard test concept. R. G. O'Lone. il Aviation W 84:100-2 Ap 18 '66

Engines

See Jet airplane engines

Equipment

SST avionics to combine proven systems with growth in technology. B. Miller. il Aviation W 85:190-1+ O 31 '66

AIRPORTS—*Continued*

Equipment

Airport, handling problems to accompany advent of 747. W. H. Gregory. il Aviation W 85:40-2 D 12 '66
Category 2 gear to be operating at twenty airports by late 1967; low weather minimum landings. Aviation W 86:45 Ja 16 '67
Device planned to move disabled aircraft R. G. O'Lone. il Aviation W 84:93-5 Ja 24 '66
FMC building QC support vans. il Aviation W 85:40 O 3 '66

Federal aid

Airport aid allocations cut $29 million. Aviation W 85:30 D 26 '66
Congress unit to urge more aid for development of civil airports. il Aviation W 86:28 Ja 2 '67

Finance
See also
Airports—Federal aid

Noise

Design studies urged at noise conference. Aviation W 85:67-8 D 12 '66
FAA fears political tug-of-war on noise abatement programs. Aviation W 85:36-7 D 5 '66
Pressure could spur noise breakthrough. H. J. Coleman. Aviation W 85:49+ D 19 '66
U.S. mapping program to alleviate noise. E. J. Bulban. Aviation W 85:45+ O 24 '66

Planning

Airline group changes position, backs fourth jetport for N.Y. Aviation W 85:25 D 26 '66
Airport, handling problems to accompany advent of 747. W. H. Gregory. il Aviation W 85:40-2 D 12 '66
Jam-up at airports; growing problem for travelers. il U S News 61:32-4 D 12 '66
Total-system planning of airports urged. Aviation W 85:48 N 14 '66
United moves to combat airport delays. J. W. Carter. il Aviation W 85:40-1 N 28 '66

Runways

Runway grooving to be tested as method to reduce skidding. Aviation W 85:57 Ag 29 '66
Tests for skidding made; experiments with runway grooving. il Sci N 90:182 S 10 '66

Safety devices and measures
See also
Radar in aviation

Surfaces

Life-proof grass sought for airports. Sci N 90:353 O 29 '66

Traffic

New battle over traffic priorities seen. W. H. Gregory. Aviation W 85:29-31 D 19 '66

Traffic control

ATC staff training with alpha-numerics; radar bright display at New York air route traffic control center. K. J. Stein. il Aviation W 85:119+ S 26 '66
Airline record on delays found mediocre in crowded Northeast. il Aviation W 86:59 Ja 16 '67
Clear and present danger. R. B. Parke. Flying 79:34 Ag '66
Common IFR room offers flexibility, swift coordination. K. J. Stein. il Aviation W 85:72-3+ O 17 '66
FAA evaluates final approach sequencer. P. J. Klass. il Aviation W 84:92-5+ My 30 '66

Transportation problems

Airport access held community problem. Aviation W 84:45 My 30 '66
Burgeoning traffic clogs airport roads. J. W. Carter. il Aviation W 85:167-9+ O 31 '66
Europe acts to combat traffic congestion. L. L. Doty. Aviation W 86:37+ Ja 9 '67
London focuses on rail links for airports; Heathrow international airport. H. J. Coleman. il Aviation W 86:39-41 Ja 2 '67
Los Angeles working to ease road jams. H. D. Watkins. il Aviation W 85:55+ N 14 '66
Miami congestion problem spurs dispute. G. Alexander. il Aviation W 85:54-5+ D 12 '66
Rail extension to speed Cleveland traffic. J. W. Carter. il Aviation W 85:54-5+ N 7 '66

Argentina
See also
Buenos Aires—Airports

Europe, Western

Europe acts to combat traffic congestion. L. L. Doty. Aviation W 86:37+ Ja 9 '67

Far East

Far East airports called inadequate by IATA chief. Aviation W 85:37-8 O 10 '66

Florida
See also
Tampa, Fla.—Airports

Georgia

Strips for action. S. Buegeleisen. il Flying 79: 85-7 Ag '66

Great Britain
See also
London—Airports

Hawaii
See also
Honolulu—Airports

New Jersey

One horse airport; Asbury Park air terminal. J. Gilbert. il Flying 78:54-7 My '66

Pakistan

Pakistan initiates airport effort. Aviation W 85:63 Jl 25 '66

Russia
See also
Moscow—Airports

Switzerland
See also
Geneva, Switzerland—Airports

Texas
See also
Dallas—Airports

United States

Airports in parks. P. M. Tilden. Nat Parks Mag 40:2 My '66
Burgeoning traffic clogs airport roads. J. W. Carter. il Aviation W 85:167-9+ O 31 '66
Contemporary airport architecture, or, Ain't you got no pride? R. B. Weeghman. il Flying 78:64-9 Ap '66
Traffic and airports; excerpts from address. G. E. Keck. Aviation W 85:21 N 21 '66
Traffic growth swamps airport facilities. il Aviation W 85:145-8+ O 31 '66
U.S. mapping program to alleviate noise. E. J. Bulban. Aviation W 85:45+ O 24 '66
See also
Airports—Federal aid

Washington, D.C.

Noise complaints dwindle quickly as jet service begins at National. Aviation W 84:50 My 2 '66

AIRPORTS, Military
See also
Aviation landing stations

AIRSHIPS
Dirigibles' great days. A. Gonzalez and G. Gonzalez. Sat R 49:46-8 O 29 '66
Zeps over Britain. P. G. Fredericks. il N Y Times Mag p76+ Ap 17 '66

AIRSHIPS, Atomic powered
Dirigibles' great days; Francis Morse's proposal. A. Gonzalez and G. Gonzalez. Sat R 49:46-8 O 29 '66
Goliath with a nuke; nuclear dirigible. il Time 87:46 My 6 '66

AIRWAY user tax. See Travel—Taxation

AIRWAYS
Big pie in the sky; Pacific Northwest and the Southwest; recommended carriers. Newsweek 67:90+ Je 20 '66
Board alters scope in route investigations. H. D. Watkins. Aviation W 85:28 D 26 '66
Board moves to speed Northwest-Southwest route case. W. Wright. il Aviation W 84:40-2 Je 13 '66
Bonanza sees DC-9 as wider market key. H. D. Watkins. il Aviation W 84:40-1+ Mr 14 '66
Booming Pacific. R. Hotz. Aviation W 85:17 D 5 '66
Crossing the Atlantic; width of air traffic corridors. R. Burkhardt. New Repub 154: 6-7 My 21 '66
Fight over corridors. Newsweek 67:81 Mr 14 '66
Focus on international routes to grow. L. L. Doty. il Aviation W 84:155-7 Mr 7 '66
Frontier bids for the richer trails; desire to race against the big trunks. il Bsns W p88-90+ S 3 '66

AIRWAYS—*Continued*
Great Pacific air race. J. F. Cunningham.
  il Sat R 49:58+ O 8 '66
Local hearings may speed route cases. Avia-
  tion W 84:51-2 Mr 21 '66
Maverick airline bets on the Pacific; France's
  UTA. il Bsns W p 152-4 Ap 23 '66
Next stop Moscow; direct commercial flights
  between Moscow and New York. il Time
  88:103-4 N 11 '66
Nonstop to Moscow; direct service between
  United States and Soviet Union. Newsweek
  68:80+ N 14 '66
Third Florida route backed. Aviation W 85:
  52 N 14 '66
U.S. and Chile conclude air service consultations; Department announcement, Oc-
  tober 14, 1966. Dept State Bul 55:722 N 7 '66
United States and Soviet Union sign civil
  air transport agreement; statement, November 4, 1966; with a Department announcement and texts of the agreement and related documents. L. E. Thompson. Dept
  State Bul 55:791-800 N 21 '66
U.S. and U.K. amend Bermuda air agreement. Dept State Bul 54:954-5 Je 13 '66
Vietnam war spurs traffic but chills tourism.
  R. G. O'Lone. Aviation W 84:157 Mr 7 '66
    See also
Aviation—Transatlantic flights

Traffic control
See Air traffic control

AISLAN, Eduardo Ritter
Inaugural message; excerpts, ed. by G. de
  Zéndegui. Américas 18:inside cover D '66

AIT AHMED, Hocine
Haik trick. il por Time 87:36 My 13 '66

AITKEN, Thomas, Jr
Latin America: the shadow of coming events.
  Harper 232:100-1 Je '66

**AITKEN, William Maxwell, 1st baron Beaver-
  brook.** See Beaverbrook. W. M. A.

AIX-EN-PROVENCE festival. See Music festivals—France

AJALA, Dennys O.
African personality. pors Negro Hist Bul 29:
  157-3 Ap '66

AKADEMGORODOK, Siberia
Science center in Siberia. V. K. McElheny.
  Science 152:1047 My 20 '66
What the French president saw: a Gallic
  view of Novosibirsk. V. K. McElheny. Sci-
  ence 153:45-6 Jl 1 '66

AKADEMIK Kurtshatov (ship)   See Ships,
  Research

AKHENATON, king of Egypt. See Amenhotep
  IV

AKHMADULINA, Bella
Bride; poem. Harper 232:50 Je '66

AKHMATOVA, Anna
Akhmatova: tragic Queen Anna. A. Werth.
  Nation 203:157-60 Ag 22 '66

AKRON, Ohio

City planning
Superblock points way to new building type;
  Akron cascade superblock. il Arch Rec 140:
  180-2 N '66

Police department
Traffic violators beware; taming Akron,
  Ohio's speeding motorists. V. A. Busson.
  il Am City 81:134+ Je '66

ALABAMA
    See also
Architecture, Domestic—Alabama
Booksellers and bookselling—Alabama
Courts—Alabama
Education—Alabama
Fishing—Alabama
Gardens—Alabama
Hunting—Alabama
Justice, Administration of—Alabama
Law—Alabama

Politics and government
Aftermath of the Alabama primary. America
  114:767-8 My 28 '66
Alabama in transition: integration issue
  declining in election campaigns. R. Moley.
  Newsweek 67:108 My 2 '66
Alabama votes: disappointing for Negroes.
  New Repub 154:7 Je 11 '66
Alabama's new era: the Negro votes. il
  Newsweek 67:25-30 My 16 '66
Alabama's restoration: sword in the heart of
  Dixie; significance of the gubernatorial
  primary. J. Beecher. il Nation 202:611-14
  My 23 '66
Analyzing the vote and its lessons: Alabama
  gubernatorial. L. Harris. il Newsweek 67:
  27 My 16 '66

Atlantic report; Negro electorate. Atlan 217:
  4+ My '66
Batman for governor! politicians change their
  pitch. Reporter 34:14 Ap 7 '66
Challenge in Alabama; W. Baker challenging
  J. Clark. Time 87:29A Mr 18 '66
Corner turned; Alabama's Negroes at the
  polls. il Time 87:23-4 My 13 '66
Despite Negro opposition, a Negro might
  make it; running for sheriff in Alabama.
  J. Beecher. New Repub 155:11-12 Jl 2 '66
Divided Negro vote; southern Negro. Time
  87:30 Ap 29 '66
Flowers in Alabama. New Repub 154:7-8
  Ap 23 '66
George's better half. il Time 87:28 Mr 4 '66
In the governor's race, Lurleen sweeps on
  toward a Wallace dynasty. il Life 60:42-
  42A My 13 '66
Lair of the Black Panther; Lowndes County
  Negroes form political party. A. Kopkind.
  New Repub 155:10-13 Ag 13 '66
Let George do it. Time 87:24 My 13 '66
Letter from Alabama. P. Witonski. Nat R
  18:1040+ O 18 '66
Mr & Mrs Wallace run for governor of Ala-
  bama. R. Jenkins. il N Y Times Mag p28-
  9+ Ap 24 '66
Night, what of the watchman? reactions to
  H. McCaskill's filing for office. Nation 202:
  766 Je 27 '66
One black plum. il Newsweek 67:44 Je 13 '66
Pa and Ma Wallace as a dynasty. Life 60:4
  Mr 11 '66
Panther on the prowl. il Newsweek 67:20-1 F
  7 '66
Race of the thousand clowns. H. H. Martin.
  il Sat Eve Post 239:25-9 My 7 '66
Remarkable thing is happening in Wilcox
  County, Ala. Negro candidate for sheriff.
  G. Roberts. il N Y Times Mag p26-7+
  Ap 17 '66
Second reconstruction; Alabama Negroes file
  for offices around the state. il Newsweek
  67:28-9 Mr 21 '66
Selma revisited; primary contenders. il News-
  week 67:25-6 Ap 25 '66
Wallace-ism is what Alabama (white) wants.
  P. Watters. New Repub 154:7 My 14 '66
Which is the better half? Reporter 34:20
  Mr 24 '66

ALABAMA primaries. See Primaries

ALABAMA. University, Tuscaloosa
Another season for miracles and, surprise!
  Alabama; tops the twenty best teams. D.
  Jenkins. il Sports Illus 25:48-52 S 19 '66

ALAMEDA, Calif.
Convenient boating from marina motel;
  Travelodge motel. il Arch Rec 140:132-3 Ag
  '66
Use operation & administration manuals; Re-
  creation and park department organization.
  S. Silver. Parks & Rec 1:44+ Ja '66

ALANINE. See Amino acids

ALARMS
Build the ultrasonic omni-alarm. D. Meyer.
  il Pop Electr 24:41-5+ Ap '66

ALARMS, Burglar. See Burglar alarms

ALARMS, Electric. See Electric alarms

ALARMS, Fire. See Fire alarms

ALASKA
Alaska is 100 years old, too. Todays Health
  45:37 Ja '67
    See also
Admiralty Island
Aleutian Islands
Birds—Alaska
Dams—Alaska
Geology—Alaska
Gold mines and mining—Alaska
Hospitals—Alaska
Hunting—Alaska
Investments, Foreign (in Alaska)
King Island
Natural resources—Alaska
Paleontology—Alaska
Petroleum—Alaska
Pribilof Islands
Redoubt, Mount
Yukon Flats
Yukon River
    also names of cities, counties, etc. e.g.
  Sitka

Antiquities
See Indians of North America—Antiquities—Alaska

Description and travel
Alaska by jet, new boating fun! H. E.
  McLean. il Motor B 118:30-3+ Jl '66
Alaska's 100th: a century between Johnsons.
  H. Bigart. il Sat R 50:46-8+ Ja 7 '67

ALASKA—Description and travel—*Continued*
Alaska's Panhandle. J. H. Winchester. il Travel 125:38-41 Je '66
Face to face: with a girl from the forty-ninth state. D. Napoleon. Seventeen 25: 141 Mr '66
1966 in Alaska's Southeastern. il Sunset 136: 78-97 Ap '66
Ten days in the ice age. J. Dos Passos. il Holiday 39:70-5+ Ap '66

History
Alaska's 100th: a century between Johnsons. H. Bigart. il Sat R 50:46-8+ Ja 7 '67

Parks and reserves
Deep-freeze camp site; recreation site forty miles north of Nome. R. K. Alman. il Parks & Rec 1:717+ S '66

Politics and government
Winners wanted; new governor. il Time 88: 32-3 N 25 '66

Religious institutions and affairs
Poorest diocese in the U.S.A; archdiocese of Anchorage. J. Morris. America 114:549-50 Ap 16 '66

ALASKA, GULF OF
Kodiak seamount not flat-topped. E. L. Hamilton and R. E. Von Huene. bibliog il Science 154:1323-5 D 9 '66

ALASKA highway
Longest Main Street in the world. L. Elliott. il Read Digest 89:121-6 Jl '66

ALASKA, University
University of Alaska collections. Library J 91:5923 D 1 '66

ALASKANS
Jan Koslosky of Alaska: new breed of frontiersman. H. Ehrlich. il Look 31:46-9 Ja 10 '67

ALATEEN (organization)
My father is an alcoholic. Seventeen 25:134-5+ O '66

ALBA house
Religious staff publishes diversity of titles. il Pub W 190:107 S 26 '66

ALBANIA
Description and travel
Atlantic report. P. Ustinov. Atlan 218:16+ N '66

ALBATROSSES
Midway's deadly antennas. H. I. Fisher. il Audubon Mag 68:220-3 Jl '66

ALBEE, Edward
Creativity and commitment. Sat R 49:26 Je 4 '66

about
Cry of loss: dilemma come back! T. Prideaux. il por Life 61:120 O 28 '66
Delicate balance. Criticism
  America 115:432-3 O 8 '66
  Christian Cent 83:1447 N 23 '66
  Commonweal 85:55-6 O 14 '66
  Life il 61:119 O 28 '66
  Nation 203:361-3 O 10 '66
  New Repub 155:35-6 O 8 '66
  New Yorker 42:121 O 1 '66
  Newsweek il 68:98 O 3 '66
  Reporter 35:52-3 O 20 '66
  Sat R 49:90 O 8 '66
  Time 88:88 S 30 '66
  Vogue 148:150 N 1 '66
Malcolm; dramatization of novel by J. Purdy. Criticism
  Commonweal 83:584-5 F 18 '66
  New Repub 154:34+ Ja 29 '66
  New Yorker 41:74 Ja 22 '66
  Vogue 147:56 F 15 '66
Tiny Alice. Criticism
  Commonweal 84:583-5 S 16 '66

ALBENDA, Pauline
Environment of art. il Sch Arts 66:10-12 S '66

ALBERS, Josef
Albers on Albers; interview. ed. by N. Welliver. il por Art N 64:48-51+ Ja '66

ALBERS, Roberta
Return of the littlest tiger. P. Ryan. il pors Sports Illus 25:32-4+ Ag 15 '66

ALBERT, prince of Monaco
Princess Grace: how she lovingly raises her children; ed. by S. Fliegers. M. King. il pors Good H 162:74-7+ F '66

ALBERT, Carl
Excerpt from debate, July 22, 1965. Cong Digest 45:84 Mr '66
What new laws Congress will pass; interview. pors Nations Bsns 54:63-4+ Ja '66

ALBERT, Eugen d'
Records; Tiefland. Opera N 31:30 N 5 '66

ALBERT, Richard E.
In California there are two hundred and fifty six religions; poem. Harper 232:100 My '66
Malfunction; poem. Harper 232:58 F '66

ALBERT A. Michelson award. See Case institute of technology, Cleveland, Ohio

ALBERT Lasker awards
World without cancer? work of S. Farber. il Newsweek 68:74 N 28 '66

ALBERTS, Frank. See Riessman, F. jt. auth.

ALBERTZ, Heinrich
New mayor. il por Time 88:26 D 23 '66

ALBINO, Joseph
He sells his own steaks. Suc Farm 64:30H Ap '66
—and Borcherding, J. R.
Ideas from four new dairy setups. Suc Farm 64:34-5+ N '66

ALBINOS and albinism
Albino adventure nets rare Anna's. P. W. Colburn. il Audubon Mag 68:476-8 N '66

ALBOHN, Ann
Tree ferns indoors. il Horticulture 44:12-13 D '66

ALBOK, John
John Albok, tailor-photographer. J. Deschin. il por Pop Phot 58:32+ Je '66

ALBRECHT, Margaret
Stand-in for mother. Parents Mag 41:58-9+ Mr '66

ALBRIGHT, Bliss. See Albright, J. F.

ALBRIGHT, Horace M.
Huston Thompson: a memoir. por Nat Parks Mag 40:22 Je '66

ALBRIGHT, James F.
Will set the standard in its field for the next fifty years. Pub W 190:42 D 12 '66

ALBUMIN naskapi. See Blood—Proteins

ALBUQUERQUE, N.Mex.
Land-bank program creates gold course. il Am City 81:221 S '66

ALCHEMIST; drama. See Jonson, B.

ALCINDOR, Lewis
Biggest Bruin had friends. J. Jares. il Sports Illus 25:42-4 D 19 '66
Can basketball survive Lew Alcindor? R. Lardner. il pors Sat Eve Post 240:70-3 Ja 14 '67
Color it Bruin. H. L. Masin. il por Sr Schol 89:24 D 2 '66
Lew-CLA. il Newsweek 68:63-4 D 19 '66
What to do about Lew. il por Time 88:58 D 16 '66

ALCOA. See Aluminum company of America

ALCOHOL
Physiological effects
Alcohol causes pain in some cancer patients. Sci N 90:152 S 3 '66
Alcohol impairs ability. Sci N 90:167 S 3 '66
Brain sensitivity to alcohol in inbred mouse strains. R. Kakihana and others. bibliog il Science 154:1574-5 D 23 '66
Cure for hangovers; new pill, Soba. J. Reinert. Sci Digest 60:64-6 D '66
Dog day; hangover nostrums. il Newsweek 69:49 Ja 2 '67
Latest on drinking; reports from doctors. U S News 62:10 Ja 9 '67
Liquor vs. the liver. il Newsweek 69:48 Ja 9 '67
Peroxidation of liver lipids in the pathogenesis of the ethanol-induced fatty liver. G. H. Kalish and N. R. Di Luzio. bibliog il Science 152:1390-2 Je 3 '66
What kind of mixer is alcohol? L. Galton. il Pop Sci 188:95-7+ Ap '66
See also
Alcoholism
Drinking and traffic accidents

Anecdotes, facetiae, satire, etc.
Help for the stricken. N. S. Hazelton. Nat R 19:39+ Ja 10 '67

ALCOHOL, Methol. See Methanol

ALCOHOL, Physiological effects of. See Alcohol—Physiological effects

ALCOHOL, Wood. See Methanol

ALCOHOL in the body
British to establish drinking driver test. Sci N L 89:104 F 12 '66

ALCOHOLIC drinks. See Liquors

ALCOHOLICS
Alcoholic's letter to his son. Read Digest 89:101-5 N '66
My father is an alcoholic. Seventeen 25:134-5+ O '66
Victims of the law; public intoxication alone, no cause for arrest in New York city. Time 88:39 Ag 5 '66

ALCOHOLICS—*Continued*
Rehabilitation
Austin Ripley and alcoholic priests; Guest house sanatorium, Lake Orion, Mich. H. A. Hammett. America 115:831 D 24 '66
Chronic alcoholic; new approach to old problem. il U S News 60:102-3 Ap 11 '66

ALCOHOLISM
Alcoholic's letter to his son. Read Digest 89:101-5 N '66
Alcoholism; AAAS annual meeting, Washington, D.C. J. O. Cole. il Science 154:920-1 N 18 '66
Alcoholism: the unsolved problem. America 115:505 O 29 '66
Drinking women lovelorn. Sci N 90:237 S 24 '66
Easing up on alcoholics; Joe Driver case; not criminal. il Time 87:81 F 4 '66
Two million workers affected by alcoholism. Sci N L 89:70 Ja 29 '66
See also
Alateen (organization)
Alcohol—Physiological effects
Liquor problem
Research
Case for genetic drinking. P. McBroom. Sci N 90:543 D 24 '66
Therapy
Austin Ripley and alcoholic priests; Guest house sanatorium, Lake Orion, Mich. H. A. Hammett. America 115:831 D 24 '66
LSD helps alcoholics. Sci N 90:22 Jl 9 '66
No effective treatment for chronic drinkers. Sci N 89:506 Je 25 '66

ALCORN agricultural and mechanical college, Lorman, Miss.
Negro against Negro; demonstration against principal. Newsweek 67:38+ Ap 18 '66

ALCOTT, Louisa May
Little women; dramatization. See Hackett. W. Merry Christmas

ALDAN, Daisy
Frozen frames of a last meeting; Dance without touch; Sky is moving farther back, opaque; poems. Poetry 108:243-5 Jl '66

ALDCROFT, Richard
Infinity projector. il Life 61:64-6+ S 9 '66

ALDEBURGH festival. See Music festivals—England

ALDEN, John
Reproduction vs. preservation; excerpt from Care and preservation of books. por Library J 91:5319-22 N 1 '66

ALDER
White alder berries. A. MacDougall. Horticulture 44:52 O '66

ALDERMAN, Michael
Health scandal, USA. New Repub 154:30+ Mr 5 '66
Medical experiments on humans. New Repub 155:10-12 D 3 '66
Shot in the arm. New Repub 154:38-9 My 14 '66

ALDOLASE
Isozymes of aldolase. H. B. Anstall and others. bibliog il Science 154:657-8 N 4 '66

ALDOSTERONE
Creeping up on hypertension; disease called aldosteronism. il Bsns W p 173-4 S 10 '66

ALDOSTERONISM. See Adrenal glands—Diseases

ALDOUS Huxley variations; ballet. See Ballets—Criticisms

ALDRICH, Alexander
Tweedleham & Tweedlesam. il por Time 87:21 My 27 '66

ALDRICH, Thomas Bailey
Life and times of Thomas Bailey Aldrich; address, October 7, 1965. M. S. Cosgrave. bibliog il por Horn Bk 42:223-32, 350-5, 464-73 Ap-Ag '66

ALDRIDGE, Helen
Memorizing poetry: it can be fun. Sr Schol 89:sup 16 S 23 '66

ALDRIDGE, John W.
Victim & analyst. Commentary 42:131-3 O '66
Well-tempered critic. Commentary 42:72-3 Jl '66

ALDRIN, Edwin E. Jr
Aldrin shows man can work in space. G. Alexander. il Aviation W 85:30-1 N 21 '66
Rest, new gear aided Aldrin EVA; photographs. Aviation W 85:26-9 N 28 '66
See also
Space flight—Manned flights—Lovell-Aldrin flight, 1966

ALEICHEM, Shalom, pseud. See Rabinowitz, S.

ALEMANY, Joseph Sadoc, abp
California's first archbishop. by J. B. McCloin. Review
America 115:72 Jl 16 '66. H. J. Nolan

ALEUTIAN ISLANDS
Agattu next military target. C. W. Buchheister. Audubon Mag 68:392-3 N '66
See also
Amchitka Island

ALEWIVES (fishes)
Composition of combustible concretions of the alewife, alosa pseudoharengus. E. Sondheimer and others. bibliog il Science 152:221-3 Ap 8 '66

ALEXANDER, Beatrice
Meet Madame Alexander, queen of the modern doll world. C. H. Fawcett. il por Hobbies 71:40+ Ap '66
She put fashion in the dollhouse. il por Bsns W p61-3 D 24 '66

ALEXANDER, Christopher, and others
Relational complexes in architecture. Arch Rec 140:185-90 S '66

ALEXANDER, Donald B.
Close call at Lake Tahoe. por Parks & Rec 1:146-8 F '66
Green grass from grass roots. por Parks & Rec 1:902-3 N '66
Tracking down a heritage. por Parks & Rec 1:224-6 Mr '66

ALEXANDER, Eben Roy. See Alexander, R.

ALEXANDER, Holmes M.
RFK; how he's building his own party. Nations Bsns 54:38-9+ Jl '66
Three races. Nat R 18:1042-5 O 18 '66
Where they can get jobs. Nations Bsns 54:38-9+ S '66

ALEXANDER, Lloyd
Substance and fantasy. por Library J 91:6157-9 D 15 '66

ALEXANDER, M. See Schaffer, A. G. jt. auth.

ALEXANDER, Myrl E.
What life is like in today's federal prisons; interview. por U S News 61:98-102 Jl 11 '66

ALEXANDER, R. W.
Marrying kind; story. Good H 162:106-7 Mr '66
My young and truly love; story. Good H 162:102-3 My '66

ALEXANDER, Raymond Pace
Judge Raymond Pace Alexander speaks to Vietnamese law faculty; address, August 16, 1965. Negro Hist Bul 29:109+ F '66
about
For the poor. por Time 88:41-2 Ag 5 '66

ALEXANDER, Richard D.
Evolution of cricket chirps. Natur Hist 75:26-31 bibliog(p82) N '66

ALEXANDER, Rod
Rod Alexander: back where he is happy to belong; ed. by V. H. Swisher. pors Dance Mag 41:19-21 Ja '67

ALEXANDER, Roy
Letter from the publisher. B. M. Auer. por Time 88:9 Jl 8 '66

ALEXANDER, Shana
Be sure to bring home that coonskin. Life 61:26 N 4 '66

ALEXANDER, Shari
Making the scene. il pors U S Camera 30:44-5 Ja '67

ALEXANDER, Sidney
Florence after the deluge. Reporter 35:39-41 D 15 '66

ALEXANDER, Susanna
Rise and fall of a library. A. T. Hamlin. por ALA Bul 60:339-47 Ap '66

ALEXANDER, Tom
All that gas in the North Sea. Fortune 74:110-15+ Ag '66
Ocean engineering takes the plunge. Fortune 73:144-7+ Je '66

ALEXANDER, Tony
Building as a system. Arch Forum 125:90-7 Jl '66

ALEXANDER, W. M.
Death of God or God of death? Christian Cent 83:363-5 Mr 23 '66

ALEXANDER, William M.
What educational plan for the in-betweenager? NEA J 55:30-2 Mr '66

ALEXANDER defense committee
Alexander case: defense committee ordered to register. Nation 203:69 Jl 25 '66

ALEXANDER doll company
She put fashion in the dollhouse: Manhattan's Madame Alexander. il Bsns W p61-3 D 24 '66

ALEXANDRE
Second fame: good food. N. Lyon. Vogue 148:324+ S 1 '66

ALEXANDRIA, Egypt
Alexandria reborn. J. Morris. il Holiday 39:68-77 F '66

ALFA-Romeo company. See Automobile industry and trade—Italy

ALFA Romeo museum, Milan, Italy. See Automobile museums

ALFALFA

Hybrids

What's holding up hybrid alfalfa? G. Morgan. il Suc Farm 64:34-5 Je '66

ALFALFA hybrids. See Alfalfa—Hybrids

ALFALFA silage. See Silage

ALFALFA weevils

Alfalfa weevil big threat, what to do about it. B. D. Blair and L. E. Zeman. il Suc Farm 64:34-5+ My '66

Hormonal termination of diapause in the alfalfa weevil. W. S. Bowers and C. C. Blickenstaff. bibliog il Science 154:1673-4 D 30 '66

ALFANO, Franco

Unfinished symphony. R. Lawrence. il Opera N 31:24-5 D 3 '66

ALFRED, William

Hogan's goat; interview, ed. by D. L. Flaherty. America 114:378-81 Mr 19 '66

about

Hogan's goat. Criticism

Cath World 202:318-20 F '66

Life 60:17 F 4 '66

Reporter 34:47-8 F 24 '66

Time por 87:65 F 18 '66

Prof moonlights a hit. il pors Life 60:89-90 Ap 22 '66

ALFRED I. Du Pont estate, Florida. See Charitable uses, trusts, foundations

ALGAE

Blue-green algae. P. Echlin. il Sci Am 214:74-81 Je '66

Imidonitrogen in chlorella polyphosphate. D. L. Correll. bibliog il Science 151:819-21 F 18 '66

Quantum yield of oxygen evolution and the Emerson enhancement effect in deuterated chlorella. G. Bedell and Govindjee. bibliog il Science 152:1383-5 Je 3 '66

Some symbionts of the sea. H. Freudenthal and others. il Natur Hist 75:46-51 bibliog (p82) N '66

Spin label studies in chlamydomonas. E. C. Weaver and H. P. Chon. bibliog il Science 153:301-3 Jl 15 '66

Urease activity in blue-green algae. D. S. Berns and others. bibliog il Science 152:1077-8 My 20 '66

See also

Acetabularia

Diatoms

Kelp

Culture media

Laboratory culturing of a thermophilic alga at high temperature. R. Ascione and others. bibliog il Science 153:752-5 Ag 12 '66

ALGAE, Fossil

600-million-year-old algae found in crater. Sci N 90:69 Jl 30 '66

ALGERIA

Economic conditions

Rousing ho-hum. Newsweek 67:48A-48B Je 20 '66

Foreign relations

Algeria; brakes on revolution. S. Coryell. Nation 202:116-18 Ja 31 '66

Politics and government

Algeria; brakes on revolution. S. Coryell. Nation 202:116-18 Ja 31 '66

Blushing strongman. il Time 88:20 D 30 '66

Haik trick; H. Aït Ahmed escape. il Time 87:36 My 13 '66

In Algeria it's not yah, yah. Boumediene! but wait and see. P. Braestrup and D. Ottaway. il N Y Times Mag p36-7+ F 13 '66

ALGINIC acid

Strontium 90 reduced by alginate in diet. Sci N 89:371 My 14 '66

Strontium uptake in rats on alginate-supplemented diet. G. E. Harrison and others. bibliog il Science 152:655-6 Ap 29 '66

ALGODONES dunes. See Sand dunes

ALGOL. See Programming languages (computers)

ALGONQUIN PROVINCIAL PARK

Enjoying nature; on an Algonquin howlalong. B. McMaster. il Audubon Mag 68:472-5 N '66

ALGREN, Nelson

Nobody knows; poem. Sat R 49:15 S 3 '66

Ticket on Skoronski; story. Sat Eve Post 239:48-9 N 5 '66

ALI, Muhammad. See Clay, C.

ALIAPOULIOS, Menelaos A. and others

Thyrocalcitonin inhibition of bone resorption induced by parathyroid hormone in tissue culture. bibliog Science 151:330-1 Ja 21 '66

ALICE, Sister Mary. See Mary Alice, Sister

ALICE in Wonderland; drama. See Carroll, L. pseud.

ALICE SPRINGS, Australia

Alice in Australia's wonderland. A. Villiers. il Nat Geog Mag 129:230-57 F '66

ALIEN property

Treasury department to control blocked foreign assets in U.S. Dept State Bul 54:945 Je 13 '66

ALINSKY, Saul David

Alinsky and Oakland. New Repub 154:7-8 My 21 '66

Attack on Kodak. J. Ridgeway. New Repub 156:11-13 Ja 21 '67

Is there an Alinsky in your future? W. F. Buckley, jr. Nat R 18:1104 N 1 '66

Making trouble is Alinsky's business. P. Anderson. il pors N Y Times Mag p28-31+ O 9 '66; Reply. V. S. Jones. p 139 O 30 '66

Strength through misery. il por Time 87:28-9 Mr 18 '66

ALISIO. See Trade winds

ALKALI acetates. See Acetates

ALKALI metal electrochemical power systems. See Electric power production from chemical action

ALKALINE phosphatases. See Phosphatases

ALKALOIDS

Source of indole alkaloids. W. I. Taylor. bibliog il Science 153:954-6 Ag 26 '66

See also

Ibogaine

ALKAN, Charles Henri Valentin

Curiosity piece. il por Time 87:84+ F 4 '66

ALKANES. See Hydrocarbons

ALKEMA, Chester Jay

Art of making puppets. por Design 68:29-33 S '66

Christmas eve on our street. Sch Arts 66:12-13 D '66

Gothic age revisited. Design 67:22-5 My '66

ALL-America cities

All America cities. J. Shepherd. il Look 30:78-9+ My 3 '66

All-America cities for 1965. Am City 81:132+ My '66

ALL-America football team. See Football players

ALL America selections. See Plants—All America selections

ALL-American racing team. See Motor boat racing

ALL hands on deck; drama. See Boiko, C.

ALL in good time; story. See Polikoff, B.

ALL points West; drama. See Boiko, C.

ALL risk personal property insurance. See Insurance—All risk policies

ALL the little swingers; story. See Kunasz, P.

ALL year schools. See School year

ALLAGASH WILDERNESS WATERWAY. See Wilderness areas—Maine

ALLEGANY ballistics laboratory

ABL refining filament winding art. J. F. Judge. il Tech W 18:30+ Je 27 '66

ALLEGHANY corporation

More green in other pastures. Time 87:90 Ap 8 '66

ALLEGHENY Ludlum steel corporation

Why Allegheny Ludlum profits have soared. il Bsns W p 116-17+ N 12 '66

ALLEGRI, Antonio. See Correggio

ALLEGRO, John Marco

Untold story of the Dead Sea scrolls. il Harper 233:46-54 Ag '66

about

Capriccio Allegro; or, How not to learn in ten years. P. W. Skehan. Christian Cent 83:1211-13 O 5 '66

ALLEN, Elizabeth

Age of innocence; story. Good H 162:94-5 My '66

Dancer in the dark; story. Redbook 127:139 Ag '66

Hole in the library shelf. Writer 79:23-4+ Ag '66

ALLEN, Fergus

Water of life. Horizon 9:120 Wint '67

ALLEN, Gay Wilson

Criterions for criticism. Sat R 49:64+ Je 11 '66

Critic at the center. Sat R 49:91 Ap 9 '66

ALLEN, George
Last puritan; G. Halas' dispute with the Rams. W. B. Furlong. il por Sports Illus 24:12-17 Ja 31 '66
ALLEN, George V.
Foreign service institute and the academic community; excerpt from address, June 16, 1966. Dept State Bul 55:76-7 Jl 18 '66
Overseas image of American democracy; address; with questions and answers. Ann Am Acad 366:60-7 Jl '66
ALLEN, Henry. See Allen, R.
ALLEN, Irene
Five with enterprise. P. Rifield. il por Mlle 63:147 S '66
ALLEN, Ivan, 1911-
Allen of Atlanta collides with black power and white racism. R. Cleghorn. il pors N Y Times Mag p32-3+ O 16 '66
Atlanta's baptism in black power. il por U S News 61:36 S 19 '66
ALLEN, James E. jr
Liberal education for adults in a changing society; adaptation of address, May 7, 1966. Sch & Soc 94:454-8 D 10 '66
ALLEN, Jay Presson
Prime of Miss Jean Brodie. adaptation of novel by M. Spark. Criticism
New Yorker 42:85 Jl 9 '66
ALLEN, John Alexander
Admiral; poem. New Yorker 42:231 D 10 '66
Customers; poem. Reporter 34:40 My 5 '66
Hour of refection at Assisi; poem. Reporter 34:42 Je 30 '66
Mother, being partial; poem. Atlan 217:110 My '66
To a young woman, entering a formal garden; poem. Reporter 35:53 O 20 '66
ALLEN, Linda
(ed) The look you like; questions and answers. See issues of Today's health
ALLEN, Louis
Reactionary revolution. Commonweal 85:100-2 O 28 '66
ALLEN, Merton, and Soike, Kenneth
Sterilization by electrohydraulic treatment. Science 154:155-7 O 7 '66
ALLEN, Patricia Hunt, and others
(ed) Junior books appraised (cont) Library J 91:417-18+, 1057-8+, 1687-8+ Ja 15, F 15, Mr 15 '66
ALLEN, Peter Z. See Morrison, M. jt. auth.
ALLEN, Philip M.
Self-determination in the western Indian Ocean. bibliog f por(back cover) Int Concil 560:4-74 N '66
ALLEN, R. C.
Fashions in roses. 1966. Pop Gard 17:54-8 Mr '66
ALLEN, Red
Profiles. W. Balliett. il por New Yorker 42:33-6+ Je 25 '66
ALLEN, Richard B.
New Orleans jazz archive at Tulane. por Wilson Lib Bul 40:619-23 Mr '66

about
Our footloose correspondents. W. Balliett. il New Yorker 42:128+ Je 11 '66
ALLEN, Robert D. See Bajer, A. jt. auth.
ALLEN, Robert F.
Crossover for life. il por Time 87:44 Mr 11 '66
ALLEN, Robert Porter
Reporter at large. F. McNulty. New Yorker 42:35-6+ Ag 6 '66
ALLEN, Robert V.
(comp) Articles and other books received; Soviet Union. See issues of American historical review
Recent developments in the history of the Soviet Union and eastern Europe. bibliog f Ann Am Acad 365:147-60 My '66
ALLEN, Rodney F.
Great wars as living history. Sr Schol 89:sup 14-15 N 18 '66
ALLEN, Roger B.
Workshopping. NEA J 55:31 My '66
ALLEN, Ruth N.
Herbs. Horticulture 44:38-9+ My '66
ALLEN, Samuel C.
Selecting a sweep frequency generator. Electr World 76:88-92 N '66
ALLEN, Sara Van Alstyne
Winter scene; poem. America 114:262 F 19 '66
ALLEN, V. L.
Nigeria: coup on a tightrope. Nation 202:143-5 F 7 '66
ALLEN, Ward P.
U.S. joins other American republics in denouncing Havana Tricontinental conference; statement, January 24, 1966. Dept State Bul 54:383-5 Mr 7 '66

ALLEN, Wayne
(ed) See Diller, P. Serious side of Diller
ALLEN, Wendell C. See Ford, P. M. jt. auth.
ALLEN, William B. jr
Day on snake mountain. por Outdoor Life 137:40-3+ F '66
ALLEN, William M.
Boeing places its supersonic bet. il Bsns W p38-40+ D 24 '66
ALLEN, William S.
Socialist conventioneers. Commonweal 84:409-10 Jl 1 '66
ALLEN, Woody
Attention! see Europe with the king of the international set (me) por Esquire 65:55-71 F '66
Gossage-Vardebedian papers; story. New Yorker 41:26-8 Ja 22 '66
Little louder, please. New Yorker 42:39-41 My 28 '66
Tallest dwarf in the world; ed. by E. Miller. pors Seventeen 25:158-9+ My '66
Yes, but can the steam engine do this? New Yorker 42:52-3 O 8 '66

about
Don't drink the water. Criticism
America 116:26 Ja 7 '67
Commonweal 85:349 D 23 '66
Nation 203:652 D 12 '66
New Yorker 42:155 D 3 '66
Sat R 49:69 D 3 '66
Time il 88:88 N 25 '66
ALLENBY, Edmund Hynman Allenby, 1st viscount
Bull. por Time 87:87+ F 11 '66
ALLERGENS
Sneeze sleuth discovers allergy begins in your home. R. Gannon. il Pop Sci 189:74-6+ Ag '66
ALLERGY
Allergies; ecological approach; report on first annual meeting of the Society for clinical ecology. M. Spetz. Science 153:903 Ag 19 '66
Allergy, hazard of country vacations. Consumer Bul 49:30-1 My '66
Children's allergies. L. W. Sauer. PTA Mag 60:13-14 Ap '66
Facts about those shots for allergies. il Good H 162:172-3 My '66
How to control allergies. J. P. McGovern. il Parents Mag 41:68-9+ N '66
How to keep your hands out of photography. H. Shaman. il Pop Phot 58:90-1+ Ap '66
Mechanism of a reaction in vitro associated with delayed-type hypersensitivity. B. R. Bloom and B. Bennett. bibliog il Science 153:80-2 Jl 1 '66
Sneeze sleuth discovers allergy begins in your home. R. Gannon. il Pop Sci 189:74-6+ Ag '66
You and your diet; diet and mental retardation; baking for allergic children. il Good H 162:177-9 F '66
See also
Hay fever
ALLIANCE for progress
Alliance for progress: a new kind of revolution; address, August 17, 1966. L. B. Johnson. Dept State Bul 55:330-4 S 5 '66; Excerpts. Cur Hist 51:307 N '66
Alliance for progress; address, November 3, 1966. R. C. Amerson. Vital Speeches 33:133-6 D 15 '66
Alliance for progress essay. Américas 18:45 O '66
Alliance for progress: how it looks after five years. J. N. Wallace. il U S News 61:66-9 Ag 29 '66
Alliance for progress: next steps for effective action; address, March 29, 1966. L. Gordon. Dept State Bul 54:738-46 My 9 '66
Alliance for progress notes. See issues of Américas
Alliance for progress: symbol and substance. R. F. Kennedy. Bul Atomic Sci 22:28-34 N '66
Days of the round table; Alliance seminars in Mexico. M. Valverde Garcés. il Américas 18:9-14 Mr '66
Economic trends; excerpts from report. Américas 18:41 D '66
Farewell from the wise men; CIAP. Time 87:32 My 6 '66
First five years. F. Harmon. il Américas 18:1-7 Ag '66
Free textbooks for Central American schools; Alliance project financed by Agency for international development. il Sch & Soc 94:342-3 O 29 '66
Latin America: focus for U.S. aid. J. S. Tulchin. il Cur Hist 51:28-35 Jl '66

ALLIANCE for progress—*Continued*
Latin American land reform; enemies of promise. W. C. Thiesenhusen. il Nation 202:90-4 Ja 24 '66
Missing revolution. D. A. Goulet. America 114:438-40 Ap 2 '66
New aspects of the Alliance for progress; address, November 10, 1966. H. H. Humphrey. Dept State Bul 55:878-82 D 12 '66
Panorama of challenge and response in Latin America: address, September 28, 1966. L. Gordon. Dept State Bul 55:644-8 O 24 '66
President hails fifth anniversary of the Alliance for progress; statement, March 14, 1966. L. B. Johnson. Dept State Bul 54:537-8 Ap 4 '66
Private enterprise, economic integration, and the Alliance for progress; address, June 1, 1966. L. Gordon. Dept State Bul 55:18-23 Jl 4 '66
Sick alliance. Nation 202:604 My 23 '66
United States and Brazil: partners in progress; address, February 17, 1966. L. Gordon. Dept State Bul 54:620-4 Ap 18 '66
What private enterprise means to Latin America. D. Rockefeller. For Affairs 44:403-16 Ap '66

ALLIANCES
Cold war alliances (cont) Sr Schol 89:pt2 4 S 23 '66
See also
North Atlantic treaty organization

ALLIED chemical corporation
Projections in design winners announced. Design 67:28-9 Mr '66

ALLIED debts. See Debts, Public

ALLIED Impex corporation
Men behind the camera. V. Silverman. U S Camera 29:34+ Ag '66

ALLIED pilots association
Pilot's dilemma. M. L. Kahn. Mo Labor R 89:264-7 Mr '66

ALLIGATORS
Alligator; influence on Everglades' flora and fauna. P. Caulfield. il Natur Hist 75:52-5 N '66
Alligators; dragons in distress. A. Carr. il Nat Geog Mag 131:132-48 Ja '67
Crackdown on the Everglades 'gator poachers. W. B. Hartley. il Pop Mech 126:106-9+ Ag '66
Did old Joe die in vain? C. W. Buchheister. il Audubon Mag 68:392-3 N '66

ALLIS-Chalmers manufacturing company
Impasse over mutual trust issue; UAW vs. Allis-Chalmers plant in Pittsburgh. il Bsns W p86-7 D 24 '66

ALLISON, Bobby
Wild, wicked race to the big time. K. Chapin. il pors Sports Illus 25:84-6+ N 28 '66

ALLISON, Dan
Luck of Irish ridge; ed. by M. C. Gilfillan. por Outdoor Life 138:56-7+ D '66

ALLISON, Elliott S.
Opera for the birds. Opera N 31:6-7 D 17 '66

ALLISON, Hank
Two letters: GI in Viet Nam pleads condor case. C. W. Buchheister; F. L. Donoghue. Audubon Mag 68:230 Jl '66

ALLISON, John M.
Arena for Asian affairs. Sat R 49:43-4 N 5 '66
Japan: touchstone for Asian policy. Sat R 49:50 Je 11 '66
Victorian view of Honolulu. Sat R 49:33 Mr 19 '66

ALLISON, Samuel King
Samuel K. Allison, 1901-1965. A. Weinberg. Bul Atomic Sci 22:2 Ja '66

ALLMAN, Marian I.
Report on trip to Scandinavia. por(p94) Negro Hist Bul 29:96 Ja '66

ALLMANNA svenska elektriska aktiebolaget.
See Electric equipment industry

ALLOMYCES. See Fungi

ALLOTT, Gordon
Excerpt from testimony. May 21, 1965. Cong Digest 45:297+ D '66

ALLOWANCES, Childrens. See Childrens allowances

ALLOWAY, Lawrence
Background to systemic. Art N 65:30-3 O '66
Dubuffet. Vogue 148:182 N 1 '66

ALLOYS
Eutectics provide possible one-step whisker composites. J. F. Judge. il Tech W 19:32-4 D 19 '66
New alloys promising. Sci N 90:165 S 3 '66
Stress-corrosion failure. P. R. Swann. il Sci Am 214:72-81 F '66

Studies of alloys by X-ray absorption spectroscopy. L. V. Azároff. bibliog il Science 151:785-9 F 18 '66
See also
Iron alloys
Titanium alloys

ALLUVIUM
Flood history told by tree growth; yielding more knowledge of flood plains. R. S. Sigafoos and M. D. Sigafoos. il Natur Hist 75:50-5 Ag '66

ALLY, Carl, incorporated
Bite behind: Hertz advertising account. Time 88:71 Jl 15 '66
Hertz strikes back. Newsweek 68:80 N 28 '66

ALMAN, Richard K.
Deep-freeze camp site. por Parks & Rec 1:717+ S '66

ALMANACS
Old faithful goes out on a limb. il Life 61:147-8 N 18 '66
See also
World almanac and book of facts

ALMEIJEIRAS, Efigenio
Puritan in Havana. Time 87:31 Mr 25 '66

ALOHA airlines. See Airlines—Hawaii

ALONE at last; story. See Lee, M.

ALONGI, Tony
Jab that wiped out a smile. M. Kram. il Sports Illus 24:28-9 Je 6 '66

ALONSO PIÑEIRO, Armando
Books. Américas 18:40-2 My '66

ALPENFELS, Ethel J.
Status symbols of youth. PTA Mag 60:4-6 bibliog(p36) Mr '66

ALPER, Chester A. and others
Beta-IC-globulin: metabolism in glomerulonephritis. bibliog Science 153:180-2 Jl 8 '66

ALPERN, Herbert P. See McGaugh, J. L. jt. auth.

ALPERT, Herb
Horns of plenty. il por Newsweek 67:85 Ap 25 '66
Small band, big sound, the Tijuana brass. B. Rollin. il pors Look 30:104-10 Je 14 '66

ALPERT, Hollis
France is mad for... Jerry Lewis? N Y Times Mag p28-9+ F 27 '66
O'Brien of MGM. Sat R 49:17-19+ D 24 '66
SR goes to the movies. See issues of Saturday review

ALPERT, Norman
Inventor of the month. S. V. Jones. il por Sci Digest 60:32 N '66

ALPERT, Richard
Scientists, theologians, mystics swept up in a psychic revolution. B. Farrell. il por Life 60:30D-33 Mr 25 '66

ALPHA, globulin. See Serum globulins

ALPHABET
See also
African languages—Alphabet

ALPHAND, Nicole Merenda (Bunau-Varilla)
Pegleg from Paris. por Time 87:79 My 20 '66

ALPINE buttercups. See Buttercups

ALPINE climbing. See Mountaineering

ALPINE plants
See also
Lewisias

ALPINE tunnels. See Tunnels and tunneling

ALPS
See also
Eiger (mountain) Switzerland
Mont Blanc

ALSATIAN cookery. See Cookery, French

ALSOP, Joseph
Books (cont) New Yorker 42:209-14+ S 10 '66
Reporter at large. New Yorker 42:32-8+ Ag 13 '66
Washington's other monument: Alice Longworth. Vogue 147:178-9+ F 1 '66
about
Stop me if you've heard this. Nat R 18:1202+ N 29 '66

ALSOP, Stewart
Affairs of state. See issues of Saturday evening post
Face of the President 1966. Sat Eve Post 239:23-5 S 24 '66
South's revenge. Sat Eve Post 239:18 S 24 '66; Same abr. Read Digest 89:79-81 D '66

ALSTON, C. M.
Don't stop when the sun goes down. Am City 81:114-16 My '66

ALSTON, Theodosia (Burr)
Three mysterious portraits. por Am Heritage 17:8 F '66

ALSTON, Walter Emmons
Name of the man is Alston. J. Mann. il por Sports Illus 25:75-7 O 10 '66

ALTBACH, Philip G.
New left in Japan. Christian Cent 83:333-4
Mr 16 '66
ALTER, Robert
In the community (cont) Commentary 41:67-
73 Mr; 61-6 Je '66
Malamud as Jewish writer. Commentary 42:
71-6 S '66
S. Y. Agnon. Sat R 49:44-5 D 10 '66
(tr) See Agnon, S. J. Lady and the peddler
ALTHOFF, Shirley, and Weddle, Dick
Moss man from Missouri. Pop Mech 125:112-15
Je '66
ALTHOUSE, G. F.
Continuous-flow refuse collection. por Am
City 81:90-1 D '66
ALTICK, Richard D.
Education, the common reader, and the fu-
ture; address, June 1965. ALA Bul 60:275-
82 Mr '66
ALTITUDE, Influence of
Altitude no handicap; training for Olympic
games, Mexico City, 1968. Sci N 90:267 O
8 '66
Altitude test successful. il Sci N 90:222 S
24 '66
America's gritty guinea pig. G. S. Brown. il
Sports Illus 25:40-2 Jl 11 '66
Planning for 1968 Olympic games. Parks &
Rec 1:851 O '66
R for altitude. B. Fawcett. il Field & S 71:
48+ O '66
Way up high and out of breath; Little
Olympics trial run for the 1968 games. J.
Underwood. il Sports Illus 25:30-1+ O 31
'66
ALTITUDE chambers. See Altitude, Influence of
ALTITUDES
Psychologists face ethical dilemma. Sci N 89:
259 Ap 16 '66
ALTIZER, Thomas J. J.
Heresy by translation. C. R. McCormack.
Christian Cent 83:437-8 Ap 6 '66
Tilting at Altizer. J. C. Evans. Christian
Cent 83:391-2 Mr 30 '66; Discussion. 83:
720-1, 961 Je 1, Ag 3 '66
ALTMAN, China
Right from the start. LGMcV was OOTATG.
Life 60:44+ Mr 4 '66
ALTMAN, Kurt, and Greengard, Olga
Tryptophan pyrrolase induced in human
liver by hydrocortisone: effect on excretion
of kynurenine. bibliog Science 151:332-3
Ja 21 '66
ALTOMARE, Alvaro A.
Dual-purpose step-chest. Pop Mech 126:154-6
O '66
ALTSCHUL, Frank
Lessons of Yalta. Sat R 49:42 Ap 2 '66
ALTSHULLER, A. P.
Air pollution: photochemical aspects. Science
151:1105-6 Mr 4 '66
ALTUS, William D.
Birth order and its sequelae. bibliog Science
151:44-9; 152:1181-2+ Ja 7, My 27 '66
ALUMINAUT (submarine boat) See Submarine boats
ALUMINUM
Prices
More in sorrow than in anger; increases
critized by government. Time 89:78 Ja 20
'67
ALUMINUM boats. See Boats—Materials
ALUMINUM coated mirrors. See Mirrors for telescopes
ALUMINUM company of America
Century city, Los Angeles' new ultra-uptown;
Alcoa building on 20th Century-Fox's old
movie lot. il Bsns W p98-101 Jl 23 '66
Projections in design winners announced.
Design 67:28-9 Mr '66
ALUMINUM-foil tape. See Adhesive tape
ALUMINUM industry and trade
Greece, Modern
Aluminum under Parnassus; Aluminum of
Greece in business. il Time 87:94+ Mr 11
'66
Norway
Metal glint in the fjords. il Fortune 74:79-80
O '66
United States
Aluminum: the classic rollback. G. Burck.
il Fortune 73:106-11+ F '66
ALUMNI. See College graduates
**ALUMNI funds. See Colleges and universities—
Gifts, legacies, etc.**
ALVARADO, Francisco
Transport of sugars and amino acids in the
intestine: evidence for a common carrier.
bibliog Science 151:1010-13 F 25 '66

ALVARD, Julien
Paris. Art N 65:16-17 O; 18 D '66
ALVAREZ, A.
Opinion: on getting out. por Mlle 63:72+ Je
'66
ALVAREZ, Walter
How to live with your nerves. por Farm J
90:66N Ap '66
ALVES, Margaret
Apostle spoons. Hobbies 71:116 N '66
ALVIN Ailey dance theatre
Alvin Ailey dance theatre, Hunter College
playhouse. M. Marks. Dance Mag 40:24
F '66
ALWORTH, Lance
Fawn-loving rover boy. H. L. Masin. por
Sr Schol 89:24 S 16 '66
AMABILE, George
Sun shower; poem. New Yorker 42:38 Jl 23
'66
AMALGAMATED lithographers of America
Breaking labor's rules; new magazine. Lith-
opinion. il Time 87:78 Mr 18 '66
Working with capitalistic union. il Nations
Bsns 54:38-9+ Ja '66
AMARATUNGA, C. H. J.
Shipping in UNCTAD: dynamic approach.
UN Mo Chron 3:75-80 Ag '66
AMARILLO, Tex.
Guaranteed maintenance puts strength in
equipment purchases. E. Hill. il Am City
81:148+ Ap '66
AMATEUR art. See Art, Amateur
AMATEUR athletic union of the United States
Chasing girls through a park; National AAU
women's cross-country championship in
St Louis. J. Underwood. il Sports Illus 25:
30-3 D 5 '66
Now you can't, now you can; eligibility of
America's best gymnasts in World games
in Dortmund, Germany. H. Weiskopf.
Sports Illus 24:78+ My 16 '66
Soaring above snafus: AAU national indoor
championships in Albuquerque. G. S.
Brown. il Sports Illus 24:16-19 Mr 14 '66
AMATEUR baseball. See Baseball
**AMATEUR moving pictures. See Moving pic-
tures, Amateur**
**AMATEUR radio stations. See Radio stations,
Amateur**
AMATEUR theatricals
Completely off Broadway. J. L. Collier. Hol-
iday 39:32+ Mr '66
Family terrace: teen-age theatre; Virginia
country theatre. il House & Gard 130:104-
5+ Jl '66
Trade winds; companies providing acting
fare. H. R. Mayes. Sat R 49:10 O 15 '66
See also
College and school drama
AMATEURISM (sports)
Now you can't, now you can: eligibility of
America's best gymnasts in World games
in Dortmund, Germany. H. Weiskopf.
Sports Illus 24:78+ My 16 '66
See also
Amateur athletic union of the United States
AMATO, Pasquale
Collectors' records. A. Favia-Artsay. por
Hobbies 71:36 S '66
AMAZON VALLEY
Progress in the Green hell. il Time 87:35
Ap 22 '66
AMBASSADORS
Old pros. il Time 88:34 O 14 '66
Three for the seesaw; changes at State. G.
Packard. il Newsweek 68:28 O 17 '66
See also
Negro ambassadors
United States—Diplomatic and consular serv-
ice
AMBER
Amber routes of antiquity. W. Grzedzielski.
il UNESCO Courier 19:20-2 Mr '66
AMBER nine; story. See Gardner, J.
AMBERLEY, John Russell, viscount
Lord Russell and Lord Amberley. P. Toynbee.
New Repub 156:32-3+ Ja 21 '67
AMBLYOPIA. See Blindness
AMBROGGI, Robert P.
Water under the Sahara; with biographical
sketch. Sci Am 214:16, 21-9 My '66
AMBROSE, Kay
Illustrated letter from Moscow. Dance Mag
40:36-7 Ap '66
AMBROSIA beetles
Ambrosia fungi: extent of specificity to am-
brosia beetles. L. R. Batra. bibliog il Sci-
ence 153:193-5 Jl 8 '66
AMBROSIA fungi. See Fungi
AMCHITKA ISLAND
Amchitka bomb test site. Sci N 90:571 D 31
'66

AMEBIASIS
Deadly animal that adopts people; amebic dysentery. J. F. Wilkinson. Todays Health 45:8+ Ja '67

AMEBIC dysentery. See Amebiasis

AMECHE, Don
Good-bye Sam Spade, hello Stephen Foster. T. Meehan. il por Sat Eve Post 239:18 Mr 12 '66

AMELUNG glass. See Glassware

AMENDMENTS to the Constitution. See United States—Constitution—Amendments

AMENHOTEP IV, king of Egypt
Dreams of a man-God. N. Samstag. Sat R 50: 86 Ja 14 '67

AMENOPHIS IV, king of Egypt. See Amenhotep IV

AMERADA petroleum corporation
Handsomest margin of all. Fortune 74:323 Jl 15 '66

AMERICA
See also
United States
　　　　　　Antiquities
See also
Mayas
　　　Discovery and exploration
Columbus as a Spaniard; address, October 6, 1966. A. B. Duke. Dept State Bul 55:717-21 N 7 '66
Columbus sights the New World. W. S. Kals. il Motor B 118:102+ O '66
Was America the wonderful land of Fusang? R. Larson. il Am Heritage 17:42-5+ Ap '66
See also
Vikings
　　　　　　　Maps
Map flap; skeptics suspect Vinland map may be fake. Newsweek 67:68 Ap 11 '66
Vinland map and the Tartar relation; excerpts, with introd. by O. Jensen. R. Skelton and G. D. Painter; discussion. Am Heritage 17:100-1 F '66

AMERICA (periodical)
America personalities. il America 114:back cover Ap 16 '66
Number 3,000. America 116:9 Ja 7 '67

AMERICA hurrah; drama. See Van Itallie. J.-C.

AMERICAN academy of political and social science, Philadelphia
Report of the board of directors to the members of the American academy of political and social science for the year 1965. il Ann Am Acad 365:161-4 My '66

AMERICAN afternoon; story. See Fariña, R.

AMERICAN airlines, incorporated
American adds to New York taxi links. W. Wright. il Aviation W 84:50-1+ Mr 28 '66
American challenges EAL shuttle; hourly jet flights between Boston and New York. J. W. Carter. Aviation W 86:36-7 Ja 16 '67
American stressed goodwill during strike. J. W. Carter. Aviation W 85:47 S 26 '66
American-TWU contract criticized. Aviation W 85:41 O 10 '66
Riding high in a new era; interview. C. R. Smith. il Nations Bsns 54:42-4+ Mr '66
Small jets get into a dogfight; American-Mohawk squabble over Syracuse air travelers. il Bsns W p 163 My 7 '66
Wing-over-wing elevated parking studied. il Aviation W 85:41 D 5 '66

AMERICAN antelopes. See Pronghorns

AMERICAN artists. See Artists, American

AMERICAN arts council. See Arts councils of America

AMERICAN assembly
Visitors to the bargaining table: papers from the thirtieth American assembly; October 27-30, 1966; excerpts. J. T. Dunlop; A. R. Weber; B. Aaron. Mo Labor R 89:1385-8 D '66

AMERICAN association for the advancement of science
Fifty-year members. D. Wolfle. Science 154: 1507 D 23 '66
Price: an effect, not a cause. F. Sartwell. Sci N 91:17 Ja 7 '67
Roberts next. Sci N 91:12 Ja 7 '67
U.S. science in session. Sci N 91:4 Ja 7 '67
　　　　Meetings, 1965
AAAS council meeting, 1965; reports on 132d annual meetings of committees. Science 151:842-76+ F 18 '66
　　　　Meetings, 1966
Alcoholism: annual meeting, Washington, D.C. J. O. Cole. il Science 154:920-1 N 18 '66

Eighth Washington meeting; additional program notes, advance registration, housing, and a new placement service. R. L. Taylor. Science 153:437-41 Jl 22 '66
Eighth Washington meeting; preliminary announcement of programs for annual meeting, December 26-31, 1966. R. L. Taylor. il Science 152:1117-26+ My 20 '66
Election of AAAS officers. S. O. Parsons. il Science 153:1675-80 S 30 '66
Environmental pollution; 133rd AAAS meeting, Washington, D.C. H. B. Stewart, jr. il Science 154:1056-7 N 25 '66
Holography; 133rd AAAS meeting, Washington, D.C. A. DiPentima. il Science 154: 1363-4 D 9 '66
133rd AAAS annual meeting, Washington, D.C; program. Science 154:1209-40+ D 2 '66
Over-exploited animal populations. G. A. Finger. il Science 154:544-5 O 28 '66
Public understanding of science. E. Kurtz. il Science 154:800-1 N 11 '66
Science eyes man's handiwork. il Bsns W p96-8 Ja 7 '67
World weather watch; 133rd AAAS annual meeting, 26-31 December 1966, Washington, D.C. T. F. Malone. il Science 154:678-9 N 4 '66

AMERICAN association of law libraries
African law & poolside reflections; 59th conference. E. J. Bander. Library J 91: 3661-2 Ag '66

AMERICAN association of school administrators
Funds for your own funeral; attempt to outlaw financial assistance by the government to church-related colleges. America 115:87 Jl 23 '66
Meeting, 1966. il Sr Schol 88:sup 1-2 Mr 11 '66
School administrators view professional negotiation; excerpts. NEA J 56:23-5 Ja '67
Washington report; final session. J. Lloyd. Sr Schol 88:sup6 Mr 11 '66

AMERICAN association of school librarians
AASL preconference. N. Kirin. Wilson Lib Bul 41:82+ S '66
Curricular collage: AASL preconference. L. Salinger. il Library J 91:4219-22 S 15 '66
Is central processing for you? services in Montgomery County, Md. R. L. Darling. Library J 91:6153-6 D 15 '66
Libraries at mid-decade: report on the youth divisions, ALA, 1966. E. Geller. il Library J 91:4208-12 S 15 '66
List of lists: AASL bibliography. Library J 91:1618-21+ Mr 15 '66

AMERICAN association of university professors
Academic freedom: lessons from the crisis at St John's. L. J. Carter. Science 154:1428-30 D 16 '66
Speaker ban: suit asserts a right to listen. L. J. Carter. Science 152:330 Ap 15 '66

AMERICAN astronomical society
American astronomers report: highlights of some papers (cont) il Sky & Tel 31:142-3, 208-9, 344-6; 32:12-13, 206-8, 261-3 Mr-Ap, Je-Jl, O-N '66
Wide planetary effort is seen by 2000. R. D. Hibben. il Aviation W 84:64-5+ Ap 4 '66

AMERICAN athletes. See Athletes

AMERICAN authors. See Authors, American

AMERICAN automobile association
Last speed trap? Coleman, Fla. Time 88:60 D 2 '66

AMERICAN ballet theatre
Catch up with. L. Lerman. Mlle 62:77+ Mr '66
Fashion too benefits from Ballet theatre benefit. A. Fatt. il Dance Mag 40:22-5 N '66
Lucia Chase's ballet garden; New York state theater performances. D. Hering. il Dance Mag 40:48-51+ Ap '66
Music to my ears; return to the State theater. I. Kolodin. Sat R 49:34 F 5 '66
Musical events; opening of four-week engagement at the New York state theatre. W. Sargeant. New Yorker 41:92 Ja 29 '66
Ulanova talks of American ballet theatre in USSR; interview, ed. by A. Ilupina. G. Ulanova. Dance Mag 40:28-9 Ag '66

AMERICAN bankers association
Forecast for loans: tight, dear; ABA bankers see demand outrunning supply. il Bsns W p 171-2 N 5 '66

AMERICAN Baptist convention. See Baptists in the United States

AMERICAN bar association
Law as friend; A.B.A.'s annual meeting. Time 88:48 Ag 19 '66

AMERICAN craftsmen's council
Craftsmen USA '66; symposium. il Craft Horiz 26:28-36+ Mr; 72-81+ Je '66 (to be cont)
AMERICAN dance festival. See Dance festivals
AMERICAN dance theatre
If repertory comes, can strife be far behind? interview, ed. by A. Fatt. C. Reinhart. il Dance Mag 40:32-5 Ag '66
AMERICAN dental association
What keeps dentists in steady business. il Bsns W p86+ N 26 '66
X-ray safety; safety of dental X rays. il Time 88:68+ D 9 '66
AMERICAN designers. See Costume designers
AMERICAN documentation institute
American documentation institute reviews progress at Calif. meeting. J. C. Donohue. Library J 91:6050+ D 15 '66
AMERICAN drama
Completely off Broadway. J. L. Collier. Holiday 39:32+ Mr '66
AMERICAN economic assistance. See Economic assistance, American
AMERICAN education week
Looking in on our schools, learning for all. J. Moorhead. PTA Mag 61:2-3 N '66
This is the week that will be. L. E. James. PTA Mag 61:11 N '66
AMERICAN elm. See Elm
AMERICAN explorers. See Explorers, American
AMERICAN export and Isbrandtsen lines
Ship-helicopter cargo operation offered. D. A. Brown. il Aviation W 84:58-9 My 16 '66
AMERICAN federation of astrologers
In the stars; convention. Newsweek 68:25 Jl 11 '66
AMERICAN federation of information processing societies
Statistics on computer field released in AFIPS report. Library J 91:3672 Ag '66
AMERICAN federation of labor and Congress of industrial organizations
Abel finds a broader role for the USW; unifying factor in AFL-CIO. il Bsns W p57-8+ My 28 '66
AFL-CIO foreign policy. New Repub 154:7 Je 25 '66
AFL-CIO heads for Johnson clash. il Bsns W p57-8 F 26 '66
Big losers in the election; union leaders. U S News 61:102-5 N 21 '66
Boss Meany; AFL-CIO statement of policy on Vietnam. Nation 203:204-5 S 12 '66
Conflicts shake labor's house. Bsns W p 110 Je 25 '66
Family quarrel; annual executive-council meeting. Time 87:27 Mr 4 '66
GE puts unity to test. il Bsns W p94+ Je 25 '66
Hot and bothered; mid-winter meeting. il Newsweek 67:71 Mr 7 '66
Labor's political frustrations. A. H. Raskin. il Reporter 34:26-8+ Ap 7 '66
Lovestone, Meany & State: American labor overseas. H. W. Berger. il Nation 204:80-4 Ja 16 '67
Lovestone's cold war: AFL-CIO has its own CIA. D. Kurzman. New Repub 154:17-22 Je 25 '66
Meany vs. Reuther: split widens in the AFL-CIO. U S News 61:82-3 N 28 '66
Mr Reuther to Mr Meany. B. L. Masse. America 116:53 Ja 14 '67
Negro unionists try a new tack; broader cooperation with AFL-CIO. il Bsns W p 140-2 Je 4 '66
New militancy of labor; signs of unrest. il Newsweek 68:93-5 S 26 '66
Reuther: more UAW ahead, less AFL-CIO; refuses to attend AFL-CIO executive council meetings. il Bsns W p46+ N 19 '66
Sixth biennial convention of the AFL-CIO. J. W. Bloch. Mo Labor R 89:144-6 F '66
Trouble ahead. Time 88:33 D 16 '66
Unions close ranks for next year's bargaining; AFL-CIO helping to set up new coalitions for 1967. Bsns W p90+ N 12 '66
Unions' split with LBJ; what will come out of it. il U S News 60:76-8 Mr 7 '66
When Reuther crosses Meany. U S News 60: 94 Je 27 '66

Committee on political education
How COPE will cope. Time 87:23 Ap 22 '66
Labor and politics; threat to the Democrats. S. Lens. il Commonweal 84:278-80 My 27 '66
What the unions are doing to elect their friends. U S News 61:112+ O 24 '66

Industrial union department
Coalition bargaining, the acid test; labor's newest technique to be used in GE contract talks. il Bsns W p61-2 Ag 13 '66
Computer sits in on the bargaining. Bsns W p 154 S 10 '66

United farm workers organizing committee
Decision at Di Giorgio. V. Salandini. America 115:415+ O 8 '66
Farm workers choose a union, and now the Southwest. America 115:270 S 17 '66
Newcomer wins on the farm. Bsns W p 158 S 10 '66
AMERICAN federation of priests
Priests' union: what it wants. U S News 61: 78 O 31 '66
AMERICAN federation of state, county and municipal employees
Coming: unionized government; interview. J. Wurf. U S News 61:96-9 S 26 '66
Settlement of disputes in public employment. Mo Labor R 89:III-IV Ap '66
State, county, and municipal employees' biennial convention. D. C. Kay. Mo Labor R 89:736-8 Jl '66
Young militant out to unionize city and county employes. il Life 61:36-36B Ag 26 '66
AMERICAN federation of teachers
Are teachers workers? R. D. Batchelder's polemic against the AFT. New Repub 154: 7 F 19 '66; Discussion. 154:36 Mr 12 '66
Conflict issues in negotiations; excerpt from address. W. A. Wildman. Mo Labor R 89:617-20 Je '66
Focus on bargaining/negotiating. Sr Schol 89: sup2 D 2 '66
New targets for teachers' union. U S News 60:80 Ja 31 '66
Response from the AFT. P. Schnaufer. Mo Labor R 89:620 Je '66
Strike at St John's: why the professors picket. M. R. Berube. il Nation 202:172-4 F 14 '66
Unionism versus professionalism in teaching. R. D. Batchelder. NEA J 55:18-20 Ap '66
Washington report; annual convention. J. Lloyd. Sr Schol 89:sup8 S 30 '66
AMERICAN federation of women's clubs. See General federation of women's clubs
AMERICAN fiction
Apocalyptic temper. R. Alter. Commentary 41:61-6 Je '66
Modes and mutations; comment on the modern American novel. N. Mailer. Commentary 41:37-40 Mr '66
Standards for setting standards. R. E. Spiller. Sat R 49:28-9+ Je 25 '66
Time to murder and create, by J. W. Aldridge. Review
   Commentary 42:60-2 Ag '66. P. Rahv
   Life 60:8+ Ap 29 '66. W. Sheed
   Sat R 49:38 Ap 30 '66. M. Green
Truth about fiction. G. P. Elliot. Holiday 39:84-5+ Mr '66
World elsewhere, by R. Poirier. Review
   New Repub 155:35-6 N 26 '66. G. A. Wolff
Young in the thirties; concerning T. Slesinger's The unpossessed. L. Trilling. Commentary 41:43-51 My '66
   See also
Short stories
Western stories
AMERICAN field service
Teenagers make good ambassadors. B. M. Silverman. il Parents Mag 41:38-9+ Ap '66
AMERICAN film institute (proposed)
Why we need a film institute. A. Knight. Sat R 49:50+ Ag 13 '66
AMERICAN folk art. See Folk art
AMERICAN folk ballet. See Ballet companies
AMERICAN folk music. See Folk music, American
AMERICAN football league
After Foss: a hotter pro war. E. Shrake. Sports Illus 24:44-5 Ap 18 '66
Here's how it happened; ed. by T. Maule. T. Schramm. il Sports Illus 24:14-19 Je 20 '66
Merger that ends an expensive rivalry. U S News 60:10 Je 20 '66
Quid pro quo. Newsweek 67:61-2 Je 20 '66
Seven times four equals one. Time 87:68 Je 17 '66
Superend. Sports Illus 26:5 Ja 9 '67
AMERICAN forest products industries, incorporated
Industry and tomorrow's environment; report on meeting. J. B. Craig. il Am For 72:30-1+ D '66

AMERICAN forestry association
AFA honors Walt Disney. il Am For 72:10 D
'66
Guarding our outdoor heritage; ninety-first
annual meeting. J. B. Craig. il Am For 72:
14-17+ D '66
Senator Anderson receives AFA's Distin-
guished service award. il Am For 71:6+
O '65
Towell succeeds Hornaday. il Am For 72:4 D
'66
Tree detectives and ecology; AFA's social
register of big tree champions. Am For 72:
9 My '66
See also
Fernow award
Trail riders of the wilderness
AMERICAN furniture. See Furniture, American
AMERICAN geological society. See Geological
society of America
AMERICAN glass. See Glassware
AMERICAN greetings corporation
Hearts & darts for far-aparts. il Time 88:
108 N 18 '66
AMERICAN guild of musical artists
Performers, inc; with editorial comment. H.
Faine. il Opera N 30:8-11 Mr 12 '66
AMERICAN historical association
Humanities grant to American historical assn.
Pub W 190:54 O 3 '66
San Francisco meeting, 1965. B. Dyer. Am
Hist R 71:1160-3 Ap '66
AMERICAN humor. See Humor, American
AMERICAN idealism. See Idealism
AMERICAN institute for free labor develop-
ment
CIA-AFL-CIO; dissension over activities of
J. Lovestone. Nation 202:700 Je 13 '66
Labor's new weapon for democracy. E. H.
Methvin. il Read Digest 89:21-2+ O '66
AMERICAN institute of aeronautics and astro-
nautics
AIAA meeting told of ASW problems. J. F.
Judge. Tech W 19:50+ Ag 15 '66
Comments on congestion. Aviation W 85:11 D
19 '66
Man's utility in space stressed at AIAA; spe-
cial report; with editorial comment. C.
LaFond and others. il Tech W 19:18+. 54
D 5 '66
Russians seen cutting U.S. lead in unmanned
space exploration; discussion at third Aero-
space sciences meeting. M. L. Yaffee. Avia-
tion W 84:59-61 F 7 '66
AMERICAN institute of architects
A.I.A. selects annual honor awards. il Arch
Rec 140:41-3 Jl '66
Architects weigh role in new age of archi-
tecture; 98th A.I.A. convention; report. il
Arch Rec 140:35-6+ Ag '66
Three old-timers off to a fresh start; Amer-
ican institute of architects-Sunset magazine
Western home awards. il Sunset 136:78-85
Mr '66
AMERICAN institute of biological sciences
AIBS: crisis in retrospect, and the outlook.
K. V. Thimann and R. W. Krauss. il Sci-
ence 153:507 Jl 29 '66
AMERICAN institute of graphic arts
AIGA and Fifty books. S. Salter. Pub W 191:
97-8 Ja 2 '67
AIGA calls for entries in children's book
show. Pub W 191:101 Ja 2 '67
Eighteen publishers represented in AIGA
1965-66 commerce show. il Pub W 191:83
Ja 2 '67
Fifty books in retrospect; trends in design
over forty-three years; AIGA exhibition. il
Pub W 189:96-7 Ap 4 '66
French Fifty books show emphasizes tradi-
tional high-quality bookmaking. Pub W
190:93-5 N 7 '66
George Tscherny elected president of AIGA.
Pub W 190:116 N 7 '66
Offset printing, paper reviewed at AIGA
clinics. Pub W 189:126+ Mr 7 '66
Paul Rand receives medal of AIGA. P. Rand.
Pub W 189:118 My 2 '66
Some new thoughts on color printing; sum-
mary of discussion at second seminar on
Color in print, 1966. Pub W 191:92-3 Ja 2
'67
Textbooks, 1964-1965: multi-media techniques
for teaching; 1966 Textbook show. S. M.
Agnew. il Pub W 189:86-7+ My 2 '66
Versatile design in pocket books covers
shown by AIGA. il Pub W 189:102-3 Ap 4
'66

Trade book clinic
Trade book clinic hears a pitch for letterpress. Pub W 189:109 Ap 4 '66

AMERICAN intellectuals. See Intellectuals
AMERICAN international pictures (firm)
Fallen angels; American international pic-
tures revises formula. il Newsweek 68:84
Ag 15 '66
AMERICAN investments abroad. See Invest-
ments, Foreign
AMERICAN Jews in Israel. See Americans in
Israel
AMERICAN language. See English language
AMERICAN legends. See Legends, American
AMERICAN legion
Not what they used to be; convention in
Washington, D.C. il Newsweek 68:24 S 12
'66
AMERICAN liberalism. See Liberalism
AMERICAN libraries abroad
USIS library in London to close; books to
go to University of London. Library J
91:216 Ja 15 '66
Valentine's day protest; protesting the clos-
ing of the USIS library in London. Pub W
189:69 F 7 '66
What better ambassadors? USIS library in
Constantine, Algeria. ALA Bul 60:205-6 Mr
'66
AMERICAN library association
ALA awards. il Wilson Lib Bul 41:31+ S '66
ALA cites twenty-five books for young
adults. Pub W 189:70 F 28 '66
ALA organization and information, 1966-67.
ALA Bul 60:971-5+ N '66; Correction. 60:
1127 D '66
Awards, citations, scholarships, and grants.
il Library J 91:3637-9 Ag '66
Code of ethics for librarians; reprint. Li-
brary J 91:5336-7 N 1 '66
Intellectual freedom; ALA vs CDL. E. J.
Gaines. ALA Bul 60:323 Ap '66
Invitation and a plea. F. E. Mohrhardt. ALA
Bul 60:763 S '66
Masters of the raging book? address, July 15,
1966. M. V. Gaver. bibliog f il ALA Bul
60:794-9+ S '66
News from the divisions. See issues of ALA
bulletin
1966 ALA awards winners. il ALA Bul 60:
840-4 S '66
Nominations invited for ALA awards. Li-
brary J 91:6176 D 15 '66
Nominations sought for 1967 ALA awards. Li-
brary J 91:6052-3+ D 15 '66
Pornographic convention; reprint. J. R.
Coyne, jr. bibliog Library J 91:2768-73 Je
1 '66; Discussion. 91:3290+ Jl '66
Undeveloped potential of ALA. A. P. Marshall.
ALA Bul 60:1157-9 D '66

Meetings, 1966
ALA conference: a time for regrouping forces;
report of conference. il Pub W 190:24-36
Ag 8 '66
ALA conference arrangements. Library J 91:
2796-7 Je 1 '66
ALA conference briefs. Library J 91:3152+ Je
15 '66
ALA conference: New York city. K. Molz.
il Wilson Lib Bul 41:76-82 S '66
ALA convention. Sr Schol 89:sup3 S 16 '66
ALA midwinter report. K. Molz. Wilson Lib
Bul 40:634-7+ Mr '66
Bonanzas and bugaboos; highlights of the
midwinter meeting. E. Geller. Library J
91:1614-17 Mr 15 '66
Checklist for ALA youth programs. Library J
91:2616 My 15 '66
Conference scheduling. E. Moon. Library J
91:3128 Je 15 '66
Echoes from Miami Beach; report on the
council and membership meetings. E. Moon.
il Library J 91:3615-24 Ag '66
Federal concerns highlight opening of ALA
conference. Pub W 190:47 Jl 18 '66
Highlights of the midwinter meeting. il ALA
Bul 60:239-48+ Mr '66
It happened in New York; highlights of the
conference. il ALA Bul 60:813-38 S '66;
Correction. 60:883 O '66
Libraries at mid-decade; report on the youth
divisions, ALA, 1966. E. Geller. il Library
J 91:4205-17 S 15 '66
Looking for answers; division meetings in
New York. J. Berry. il Library J 91:3625-35
Ag '66; Reply. A. H. Rinee, jr. 91:4010 S
15 '66; Correction. 91:4388+ O 1 '66
LSD in New York; long, serious, delibera-
tions. S. Haven. il Library J 91:3606-14
Ag '66
New York conference program planning. ALA
Bul 60:265-9 Mr '66
New York hosts ALA. Wilson Lib Bul 40:975-
6 Je '66

AMERICANS library association—Meetings, 1966—*Continued*

Notes from the ALA midwinter meeting in Chicago. E. Moon. Library J 91:1172-80 Mr 1 '66

Of comforts and amenities. J. Shera. Wilson Lib Bul 40:859 My '66

Pre-conference potpourri. il Library J 91:3640-50 Ag '66

Tentative program of the 85th annual ALA conference; New York city, July 10-16, 1966. ALA Bul 60:427+ My '66

Meetings, 1967

ALA midwinter meeting 1967; tentative program. ALA Bul 60:1171-3 D '66

1967 ALA conference, San Francisco, June 25-July 1. il ALA Bul 61:79-82 Ja '67

1967 ALA midwinter meeting: New Orleans, January 9-14. ALA Bul 60:948 O '66

Adult services division

ALA selects 1965's notable books. Pub W 189:69-70 F 28 '66

Books for adults beginning to read. Wilson Lib Bul 41:83-7 S '66

Getting into the ghetto; preconference Workshop on books for adults beginning to read. J. N. Berry, 3d. il Library J 91:3642-4 Ag '66

Childrens services division

Books for children and young adults; report of meeting at ALA conference. il Pub W 190:27-9 Ag 8 '66

Libraries at mid-decade: report on the youth divisions, ALA, 1966. E. Geller. il Library J 91:4212-15 S 15 '66

Notable children's books of 1965. il ALA Bul 60:353-6 Ap '66; Same. Pub W 189:34+ Ap 4 '66; Library J 91:2176+ Ap 15 '66; Wilson Lib Bul 40:797 My '66

Sixty children's books cited by ALA evaluators. Pub W 189:34+ Ap 4 '66

Constitution

ALA midwinter report; membership amendment. K. Molz. Wilson Lib Bul 40:634-6 Mr '66

Constitutional crisis in the ALA? E. M. Oboler. ALA Bul 60:384-6 Ap '66

Council: hard facts of liberalism; ALA midwinter report. E. Geller. Library J 91:1614-15 Mr 15 '66

Limitations on institutional and organizational membership; midwinter conference report. il ALA Bul 60:239-42 Mr '66

Constitution and bylaws committee

Constitution and bylaws committee report. ALA Bul 60:503-5 My '66

Council

Echoes from Miami Beach; report on the council and membership meetings during the ALA conference in New York city. E. Moon. il Library J 91:3615-24 Ag '66

Institutional membership in ALA; report of a Council committee on a membership proposal that institutional membership in ALA be restricted. il ALA Bul 60:362-74 Ap '66

Finance

Treasurer's report. ALA Bul 60:1163-9 D '66

Headquarters

ALA headquarters space problem grows. K. Laich. ALA Bul 60:501-2 My '66

Keep the lines open. K. Laich. il ALA Bul 60:1161-2 D '66

Information science and automation division

ISAD: off to a flying start; letter to the editor. S. R. Salmon. ALA Bul 60:753-4 S '66

Library administration division

Ethics: the creaking code; LAD's Code revision committee. J. F. Anderson. Library J 91:5333-5 N 1 '66; Reply. R. S. Gregory. 92:29 Ja 1 '67

Membership

ALA midwinter report; membership amendment. K. Molz. Wilson Lib Bul 40:634-6 Mr '66

Conference scheduling; change to allow more representative discussion of racial issue at membership meeting. E. Moon. Library J 91:3128 Je 15 '66

Constitutional crisis in the ALA? E. M. Oboler. ALA Bul 60:384-6 Ap '66

Council: hard facts of liberalism; ALA midwinter report. E. Geller. Library J 91:1614-15 Mr 15 '66

Follow the bouncing ball, or, Fiddling while Clapp burns; midwinter conference report. E. Moon. Library J 91:1172-5 Mr 1 '66

Institutional membership in ALA; report of a Council committee on a membership proposal that institutional membership in ALA be restricted. il ALA Bul 60:362-74 Ap '66

Limitations on institutional and organizational membership; midwinter conference report. il ALA Bul 60:239-42 Mr '66

Notable books council

See American library association—Adult services division

Office for library education

Asheim to direct ALA's new Office for library education. Library J 91:3368 Jl '66

Memo to members. D. H. Clift. ALA Bul 60:694-5 Jl '66

Public library association

Getting into the ghetto; preconference Workshop on books for adults beginning to read. J. N. Berry, 3d. il Library J 91:3642-4 Ag '66

Public library standards went that-a-way; meanwhile, back at the convention. D. Curley. Library J 91:3864-5+ S 1 '66; Reply. W. L. Emerson. 91:4866+ O 15 '66

What should PLA be doing? report on an informal survey conducted by Activities committee, with comment by E. A. Ferguson. K. Molz. ALA Bul 60:595-9+ Je '66

Reference services division

Proposed revision of the interlibrary loan form; Interlibrary loan committee. il ALA Bul 61:9 Ja '67

Resources and technical services division

LC in NY: preconference institute; sponsored by the cataloging and classification section. N. C. Batts. Library J 91:3649-50 Ag '66; Reply. D. Gore. 91:4386 O 1 '66

Subscription books committee

Caveat venditor: need for investigation and if necessary reform of committee. J. Shera. Wilson Lib Bul 40:955+ Je '66; Reply. A. B. Lemke. 41:25-6 S '66

Young adult services division

[Adult books for young people, 1965] Library J 91:1624 Mr 15 '66; Same. NEA J 55:51-2 Mr '66; Pub W 189:70 F 28 '66; Wilson Lib Bul 40:664 Ap '66

Libraries at mid-decade: report on the youth divisions, ALA, 1966. E. Geller. Library J 91:4215-17 S 15 '66

Patterns of young adults' reading; report of meeting at ALA conference. G. R. Carlsen. Pub W 190:29-32 Ag 8 '66

Teenage hits and misses to theme YASD program. Library J 91:2182 Ap 15 '66

Two blocks apart; YASD preconference on the disadvantaged. E. Geller. il Library J 91:4222-9 S 15 '66

AMERICAN library trustee association

Reaching out with books; preconference workshop. D. E. Wright. Library J 91:3648-9 Ag '66

Trustees announce packed program for ALA pre-conference workshop. Library J 91:2796 Je 1 '66

AMERICAN literature

American writer and the great depression, ed. by H. Swados. Review
Sat R 49:23-4 My 21 '66. G. Hicks

See also
American fiction
American poetry
Authors, American
Negro literature
Surrealism

History

American 1890s, by L. Ziff. Review
New Repub 155:22+ D 3 '66. C. Kauffmann

Ferment of realism, by W. Berthoff. Review
Nation 202:102-3 Ja 24 '66. S. Paul

Southern states

Something of value from the South. G. Hicks. Sat R 49:43-4 D 24 '66

AMERICAN Lutheran church.   See Lutheran church in the United States

AMERICAN management association
Education technology teaches a hard lesson. il Bsns W p32-4 Ag 20 '66
Macmillan to distribute AMA book publications. Pub W 190:41 Jl 25 '66
Middle managers get a peek at their pay; annual AMA survey. il Bsns W p80-2 My 7 '66

AMERICAN medical association
Air pollution medical research; report on eighth in a series of air pollution medical research conferences. J. R. Goldsmith. Science 154:1588-91 D 23 '66
A.M.A. & medicare. il Time 88:42 Jl 8 '66
Annals of legislation; medicare. R. Harris. New Yorker 42:29-38+ Jl 2; 30-6+ Jl 9; 35-8+ Jl 16; 35-40+ Jl 23 '66
Entertainer, two researchers honored by AMA. il Todays Health 44:17 Ag '66
Health: latest in cures and research; meeting. U S News 61:16 Jl 11 '66
Medical help for Viet Nam. F. Marley. il Sci N 90:160-1 S 3 '66
New treatments for some old ailments; annual convention. U S News 61:12-13 D 12 '66
Sacred trust, by R. Harris. Review
   Nation 204:29 Ja 2 '67. R. Carter
   New Repub 156:35-6 Ja 21 '67. R. Yoakum
Science fair winners exhibit at AMA meeting. Sci N 90:24 Jl 9 '66
What doctors see as top medical advances. U S News 61:14 D 19 '66

AMERICAN men. See Men

AMERICAN merchant marine. See Merchant marine—United States

AMERICAN military assistance. See Military assistance, American

AMERICAN minorities. See Minorities

AMERICAN motorcycle association
Daytona AMA style. B. Greene. il Hot Rod 19:70-3 Je '66

AMERICAN motors corporation
Ailing American motors gets a new treatment; Mustang-type car. Bsns W p74 Mr 19 '66
American motors. J. McFarland. il Hot Rod 19:136-8+ N '66
AM drops to low gear; second shutdown in two months. Bsns W p38 F 19 '66
American motors' new gospel. il Time 87:82+ Je 17 '66
Autos, 1966: darkest thunderhead hovers. il Newsweek 67:71-2 F 14 '66
Double shuffle at AMC. il Newsweek 69:77-8 Ja 23 '67
Help for not-so-small; American motors and eight tire companies eligible for favored treatment. Bsns W p43 S 17 '66
How big is small? SBA's new list. Newsweek 68:95 S 26 '66
Job for a giant killer. il Time 87:79 Ja 28 '66
Long way to turn. Time 88:88 D 2 '66
New man at AMC. il Newsweek 67:84 Je 20 '66
Quick wash; executive changes. il Time 89:74+ Ja 20 '67
$2,000,000 vote of confidence; R. B. Evans shares. Time 87:94 F 4 '66
Whither AMC? D. MacDonald. il Motor T 18:36-7 My '66
Why a union wants its men fired. U S News 60:79 Mr 7 '66

AMERICAN museum in Britain
American museum at Bath. M. Richler. Vogue 149:25+ Ja 1 '67

AMERICAN museum of natural history, New York
Good show: exhibition from library of natural-history books and book illustrations, supplemented with specimens. New Yorker 41:27-8 F 19 '66

AMERICAN museum of photography
Whose Hall of fame? J. Deschin. Pop Phot 58:24+ Ap '66

AMERICAN music. See Music, American

AMERICAN musicians. See Musicians, American

AMERICAN Negroes. See Negroes in the United States

AMERICAN newspaper publishers association
Eye people and ear people; annual convention. R. L. Tobin. il Sat R 49:87-8 Je 11 '66
People's right to know; ANPA report with list of major conclusions. R. L. Tobin. il Sat R 50:109+ Ja 14 '67

AMERICAN newspapers. See Newspapers—United States

AMERICAN novels. See American fiction

AMERICAN opera. See Opera, American

AMERICAN opera society
Concert opera, Donizetti and Britten. G. Movshon. il Hi Fi 16:127+ Mr '66
Mefistofele returns. J. W. Freeman. il Opera N 30:28-9 Ja 29 '66
Music to my ears; concert version of Rossini's Mosè given at Carnegie Hall. H. Weinstock. Sat R 49:92 N 12 '66
Music to my ears; Medea in Carnegie Hall. I. Kolodin. Sat R 49:30 D 24 '66
Music to my ears; performance of Giovanna d'Arco. I. Kolodin. Sat R 49:28 Mr 19 '66
Music to my ears; presentation of Anna Bolena. Sat R 49:76+ D 3 '66
Music to my ears; presentation of Boito's Mefistofele in Carnegie Hall. I. Kolodin. Sat R 49:26+ F 12 '66
Musical events; concert performance of Cherubini's Medea. W. Sargeant. New Yorker 42:194 D 17 '66
Musical events; performance of Bellini's Il pirata. W. Sargeant. New Yorker 42:126+ My 7 '66
Musical events; performance of Boito's Mefistofele. W. Sargeant. New Yorker 41:89-90 F 5 '66
Musical events; performance of Donizetti's Anna Bolena. W. Sargeant. New Yorker 42:127 N 26 '66
Musical events; performance of Verdi's Joan of Arc. W. Sargeant. New Yorker 42:166+ Mr 12 '66
New York. F. Merkling. Opera N 30:29 F 19 '66
New York; Billy Budd in concert form. J. W. Freeman. Opera N 30:30 F 5 '66
New York; Donizetti's Anna Bolena at Carnegie Hall. J. W. Freeman. Opera N 31:29 D 17 '66
New York; Gwyneth Jones sings Cherubini's Medea. R. D. Daniels. Opera N 31:30 D 31 '66

AMERICAN ordnance association
AF raps research lag; annual defense preparedness meeting in Los Angeles. Tech W 19:9 O 10 '66

AMERICAN painting. See Painting, American

AMERICAN partners, incorporated
Service and profits. America 114:793-4 Je 4 '66

AMERICAN personnel and guidance association
Counselors revisited; five largest national library associations working with APGA. M. Ricking. ALA Bul 60:665-7 Je '66

AMERICAN philosophers. See Philosophers

AMERICAN philosophical society
Annals of law; Lewis and Clark case: United States government's claim to field notes. C. Tomkins. New Yorker 42:111-12+ O 29 '66
Franklin's followers. Sci N 89:347 My 7 '66

AMERICAN philosophy. See Philosophy, American

AMERICAN photocopy equipment company
Company clobbered by competition. il Fortune 74:253 N '66

AMERICAN place theatre. See New York (city)—Theater

AMERICAN poetry
American heart of darkness. B. Cutler. Poetry 107:401-3 Mr '66
California hybrid. J. Harrison. Poetry 108:198-201 Je '66
Going it alone: estrangement in American poetry. F. Murphy. Yale R 56:17-24 O '66
Idea of poetry; Leaves of grass, Reader's edition. B. Duffey. Poetry 107:397-9 Mr '66
Illusion wedded to simple need. R. Howard. Poetry 108:329-35 Ag '66
Immortal bard and others. J. Slater. Sat R 49:24-5 D 31 '66
Lamb, the clocks, the blue light. R. Huff. Poetry 109:44-8 O '66
Muse & hearth. J. Harrison. Poetry 107:330-1 F '66
Poets on poetry, ed. by H. Nemerov. Review
   Sat R 49:45 F 19 '66. L. Untermeyer
Profiles and presences. F. Stefanile. Poetry 109:198-200 D '66
Questions of travel, by E. Bishop. Review
   New Repub 154:19-21 Ap 9 '66. F. J. Warnke
Seeing Williams with fresh eyes. S. Paul. Nation 203:356-7 O 10 '66
Shoe in the shark; national poetry. M. Goldman. Nation 202:246-8 F 28 '66
Six anthologies. A. Rich. Poetry 108:343-5 Ag '66
Verse; anthology designed as a textbook. L. Bogan. New Yorker 42:221-3 O 1 '66
   See also
English poetry

AMERICAN portraits. See Portraits, American
AMERICAN pottery. See Pottery, American
AMERICAN power boat association
　APBA action report. J. D. Paris. See issues
　　of Motor boating
　More power to you. M. Crook. See issues of
　　Yachting
AMERICAN power boat association champion-
　ship. See Motor boat racing
AMERICAN president lines
　Three or four from one & one. il Time 87:
　　96 My 13 '66
AMERICAN printing house for the blind
　Touch and sound of sight. J. Morrissey. il
　　Am Ed 2:25-7 My '66
AMERICAN property in Brazil
　Claims for property losses in the state of
　　Goiás, Brazil. Dept State Bul 55:869 D
　　5 '66
AMERICAN property in Mexico
　What Mexicanization means; expropriation of
　　U.S. companies. Bsns W p 118 N 26 '66
AMERICAN psychological association
　Psychologists speak out. Sci N 90:55 Jl 23 '66
　Risky shifts; seventy-fourth annual conven-
　　tion. New Yorker 42:51-2 S 24 '66
AMERICAN public opinion. See Public opinion
　—United States
AMERICAN public power association
　Major power grid will prevent blackout.
　　Sci N L 89:98 F 12 '66
AMERICAN public works association
　Stop dissecting the urban community; an-
　　nual congress and equipment show. Am
　　City 81:106+ N '66
　Top ten; men of the year. il Am City 81:169
　　Je '66
AMERICAN quarter horse association
　High rollers of Ruidoso; All American quarter
　　horse futurity in N.Mex. P. Ryan. il Sports
　　Illus 25:36-8+ S 26 '66
AMERICAN Racer (ship) See Freight vessels
AMERICAN record guide (periodical)
　From the editor: concerning book reviews.
　　J. Lyons. Am Rec G 32:888 My '66
AMERICAN reporters. See Reporters and re-
　porting
AMERICAN republic insurance building. See
　Des Moines—Architecture
AMERICAN revolution. See United States—
　History—Revolution
AMERICAN rocket society. See American in-
　stitute of aeronautics and astronautics
AMERICAN Royal (horse show) See Horse
　shows
AMERICAN SAMOA
　Coming of the jet age in Samoa. H. Sutton.
　　il Sat R 49:56+ F 5; 41-3 F 12 '66
　For Samoa: a barefoot teacher from Okla-
　　homa. il Look 30:88+ My 31 '66
　New ways and old in the Samoas. M. Peter-
　　sen. il Motor B 119:114+ Ja '67
　Travel's picture portfolio. Travel 125:34-9 Mr
　　'66
AMERICAN scholars. See Scholars
AMERICAN sculpture. See Sculpture, American
AMERICAN Shakespeare festival theatre and
　academy, Stratford, Conn.
　Festival of Stratford. P. E. Silberstein. il
　　Sr Schol 88:sup 14 Ap 15 '66
AMERICAN silverware. See Silverware
AMERICAN slang. See Slang
AMERICAN society for engineering education
　Goals of engineering education. Sch & Soc
　　94:50 Ja 22 '66
AMERICAN society for industrial security
　Hunting industry spies; electronic protection
　　devices. il Bsns W p42-3 O 1 '66
AMERICAN society of magazine photographers
　Increase stock picture price, day rates for
　　photographers. Pub W 190:115 Ag 1 '66
AMERICAN songs. See Songs, American
AMERICAN stock exchange
　Amex hires its critic; R. Saul former director
　　of SEC. Bsns W p36 Ag 20 '66
　Can he trade up Amex's image; R. S. Saul,
　　new president. il Bsns W p 150+ O 29 '66
　Heavy volume boosts the rally. il Bsns W
　　p34-5 Ap 23 '66
　Hiring the harasser; new president. Time
　　88:68 Ag 26 '66
　Lessons of the Amex. C. Morgello. Newsweek
　　68:73 Jl 4 '66
　New man at Amex. Newsweek 68:56 Ag 29 '66
　Tamer than the image. Time 88:101 N 11 '66
AMERICAN strategy. See Strategy
AMERICAN students. See College students;
　Students

AMERICAN students in foreign countries
　American students abroad: professional ver-
　　sus personal development. J. E. Gullahorn
　　and J. T. Gullahorn. bibliog f Ann Am
　　Acad 368:43-59 N '66
　　See also
　Foreign study
AMERICAN students in Greece; American stu-
　dents in Russia; etc. See Foreign students
　in Greece; Foreign students in Russia; etc.
AMERICAN studies. See Area studies
AMERICAN symphony orchestra
　Musical events (cont) W. Sargeant. New
　　Yorker 42:107-8+ My 21 '66
　Stoky's striplings. il Time 87:54 Je 3 '66
AMERICAN symphony orchestra league
　Mephisto's musings. il Hi Fi 16:MA2-3 S '66
AMERICAN teachers association
　NEA-ATA unification. W. N. Ridley. il
　　NEA J 55:49-50 S '66
AMERICAN teachers in foreign countries
　Around the world on a sabbatical. J. B. Carr.
　　il Sr Schol 89:sup 14-15 Ja 6 '67
　Our man in Istanbul. N. Baba. il Am Ed 2:
　　26-7 Mr '66
　Professor abroad: twenty years of change.
　　E. W. Weidner. Ann Am Acad 368:60-70
　　N '66
AMERICAN technical assistance. See Technical
　assistance, American
AMERICAN telephone and telegraph company
　AT&T, Comsat clash on merger proposal. K.
　　Johnsen. Aviation W 84:28 Je 27 '66
　AT&T plans vast comsat net with 83,000-
　　circuit capacity. K. Johnsen. Aviation W
　　85:24 D 26 '66
　A.T.&T.'s double life. Fortune 74:356 Jl 15 '66
　A.T.&T.'s new boss. il Time 88:52-3 D 30 '66
　Bellsat; grand designs for U.S. space com-
　　munications network. il Newsweek 68:66
　　D 26 '66
　Comsat charges AT&T cable plan threatens
　　satellite development. Aviation W 84:26 My
　　2 '66
　Contenders chafe over FCC comsat delay. il
　　Tech W 20:13 Ja 2 '67
　Girl from B.E.L.L.; monitoring calls. il Time
　　88:27 S 23 '66
　Lot to learn; new chairman and chief ex-
　　ecutive officer. il Newsweek 69:54 Ja 2 '67
　New top man for the AT&T. U S News 62:11
　　Ja 2 '67
　Satellites: a fight at home; a hard sell abroad.
　　il Bsns W p46-7 My 21 '66
　Significant gain seen in AT&T comsat. P. J.
　　Klass. il Aviation W 86:20-1 Ja 2 '67
　Wall Street: blues for a blue chip. il News-
　　week 67:83 Ap 18 '66
　　See also
　Bell telephone laboratories
　Government investigations—American tele-
　　phone and telegraph company
AMERICAN textbook publishers institute
　ABPC-ATPI report on copyright technology.
　　Pub W 190:57-8 O 31 '66
　ATPI prepares for new changes in education;
　　report of 24th annual meeting. il Pub W
　　189:24-36 My 30 '66
　Catholic schools and educational publishing:
　　a dialog about the future. il Pub W 190:
　　18-23 D 12 '66
　College market textbook problems analyzed
　　by publishers, suppliers; report of confer-
　　ence. il Pub W 191:44-8 Ja 16 '67
　Evaluation of materials for teaching: a
　　dilemma; report of ATPI annual industry
　　conference. il Pub W 191:26-9 Ja 9 '67
　Publishers study situation on state and local
　　taxation; summary of one-day workshop
　　by the American textbook publishers in-
　　stitute. Pub W 189:55-7 F 7 '66
　Rush for the finish line seen under ESEA
　　programs; summary of ABPC-ATPI meet-
　　ing. Pub W 189:58-60 F 7 '66
AMERICAN tobacco company
　High-stakes strategy of American tobacco.
　　J. B. Weiner. il Duns R 88:43-7+ N '66
AMERICAN toy fair. See Toy industry
AMERICAN trading company, limited
　Cool life in a commercial jungle; Saigon.
　　il Bsns W p60-1 Mr 5 '66
AMERICAN tradition. See Tradition
AMERICAN type culture collection
　Microbe menagerie that benefits you. P. M.
　　Harding. il Todays Health 44:64-5 N '66
AMERICAN university of Beirut
　American outpost for recreation. D. Rugh.
　　il Parks & Rec 1:166-7 F '66
　Meeting of West and Near East. il Time 88:
　　72 Jl 8 '66
AMERICAN university press services, incor-
　porated
　AUPS elects new directors. Pub W 190:43+
　　Jl 25 '66

AMERICAN visitors in Eastern Europe; In
India; etc. See Foreign visitors in Eastern
Europe; Foreign visitors in India; etc.
AMERICAN water color society
Art galleries; two exhibitions at Metro-
politan commemorating centennial. R. M.
Coates. New Yorker 42:62+ D 24 '66
Winners; annual exhibition. Am Artist 30:
4+ Je '66
AMERICAN water works association
Water-works men want faster progress;
highlights of the AWWA conference in
Bal Harbour, Fla. il Am City 81:105-6+
Jl '66
AMERICAN wines. See Wine
AMERICAN women. See Women—United States
AMERICAN writers. See Authors, American
AMERICAN youth hostels, incorporated
Holidays are for hosteling. L. Jonckheere. il
Sr Schol 88:sup 14 F 25 '66
See also
Youth hostels
AMERICANA, Brazil
Dixie city in Brazil. il Ebony 22:89-90+ N
'66
AMERICANISM
Americanism vs. communism: a historical
document; concerning B. G. Northrop's
Schools and communism. S. E. Fraser. Sch
& Soc 94:355 O 29 '66
AMERICANIZATION
Cultural pluralism in urban education. S.
W. Itzkoff. Sch & Soc 94:383-6 N 12 '66
School that says welcome. J. T. Gallahorn, jr.
il Am Ed 2:1-3 My '66
AMERICANIZATION school, Washington, D.C.
School that says welcome. J. T. Gallahorn, jr.
il Am Ed 2:1-3 My '66
AMERICANS
America and the Americans. J. Steinbeck.
il Sat Eve Post 239:32-8+ Jl 2 '66
American primer, ed. by D. J. Boorstin.
Review
Sat R 49:35-6 N 5 '66. R. Walters, jr
Boom times, unhappy people, why? results
of a nationwide survey. il U S News 60:
64-8+ Mr 21 '66
Foreign policy and the crisis mentality. G.
McGovern. Atlan 219:55-7 Ja '67
How America lives. See issues of Ladies'
home journal
Informal history of love U.S.A. A. Schlesin-
ger, jr. il Sat Eve Post 239:30-2+ D 31 '66
May I ask you a few questions about love?
Elmo Roper's opinion poll. S. Brown. il
Sat Eve Post 239:24-7 D 31 '66
Mood of Americans at this time; interview.
G. Gallup. il U S News 61:50-4 S 19 '66
On patience as an American virtue; Time
essay. Time 87:22-3 Mr 25 '66
Science and symbol in the Turner frontier
hypothesis. W. Coleman. bibliog f Am
Hist R 72:22-49 O '66
Speaking out; psst! I love America. J. Mor-
ris. Sat Eve Post 239:12+ O 22 '66
State of the union: unfinished; state of the
union is sounder. Bsns W p 136 Ja 7 '67
This U.S.A. by B. J. Wattenberg. Review
Cath World 202:309-10 F '66. W. J. Gib-
bons
What's bothering Americans, as told to Con-
gress. il U S News 61:56-9 Ag 15 '66
Who is the American man? excerpt from
Fortnight in the wilds. A. C. H. M. C. de
Tocqueville. Sat R 49:66 Mr 12 '66
Why the Statue of Liberty looks to the east,
etc; excerpts from The third side of the
dollar. A. Laurinchukas. il N Y Times
Mag p8-9+ D 25 '66
You don't say, by B. DeMott. Review
Sat R 49:37 Ap 30 '66. E. Capouya
See also
Californians
Texans
AMERICANS abroad. See Americans in for-
eign countries
AMERICANS for democratic action
For Bobby's peace; policy statement on Viet-
nam war. K. Crawford. Newsweek 67:35
My 9 '66
Humphrey's old pals; an account of the ADA
convention. A. Kopkind. New Repub 154:
19-22 My 7 '66; Discussion. 154:45 My 14;
37-8 My 21 '66
Not so ancient history; annual meeting of
ADA. Nation 202:538 My 9 '66
AMERICANS in Africa
Reporter at large; MIT Fellows in Africa
program. J. McPhee. New Yorker 42:116-
24+ Mr 5 '66

AMERICANS in Brazil
Dixie city in Brazil: Americana. il Ebony
22:89-90+ N '66
AMERICANS in Budapest. See Americans in
Hungary
AMERICANS in Canada
Migration between Canada and the United
States. K. V. Pankhurst. bibliog f il Ann
Am Acad 367:53-62 S '66
AMERICANS in Colombia
Mike's revolution. S. Seegers and K. Seegers.
il Américas 18:30-5 Ap '66; Same abr. with
title One-man revolution on the Amazon.
Read Digest 88:185-8+ My '66
AMERICANS in Cuba
Castro's pawns. Time 88:32 S 2 '66
AMERICANS in England
Aisle K; reading room in the British mu-
seum. E. Hahn. New Yorker 42:138+ S
17 '66; Reply. G. S. Dunbar. 42:233-7 N 12
'66
Why not work in England next year? K. F.
Kister. il ALA Bul 61:72-6 Ja '67
AMERICANS in Europe
New ambassadors. W. Marchant. il Horizon
8:50-5 Wint '66
On being foreign. T. Sterling. il Holiday
39:16+ Ap '66
See also
Foreign visitors in Europe
AMERICANS in foreign countries
American executive overseas. il Newsweek
67:86-8 Mr 21 '66
American professionals overseas. I. T. San-
ders. Bul Atomic Sci 22:40-5 D '66
Americans abroad; symposium, ed. by R. D.
Lambert. Ann Am Acad 368:1-170 N '66
Cultural analysis in overseas operations. J.
A. Lee. Harvard Bsns R 44:106-14 Mr '66
Everywhere generation; Americans abroad.
il Newsweek 68:43-50 N 28 '66
Onetime opponents praise the Peace corps'
results. Bsns W p 138 O 22 '66
See also
American teachers in foreign countries
United States—Armed forces—Forces in for-
eign countries

Employment
Businessman abroad. M. Wilkins. Ann Am
Acad 368:83-94 N '66
Science overseas; jobs galore; condensation
of How to get a job overseas. C. W.
Casewit. il Sci Digest 59:71-7 F '66
Your chances for a job overseas. il Changing
T 20:15-17 O '66

Statistics
Statistical overview of Americans abroad. E.
Rubin. il Ann Am Acad 368:1-10 N '66
AMERICANS in France
Notes from a European diary: 1963-64; Paris.
E. Wilson. New Yorker 42:54-6+ My 21 '66
AMERICANS in Germany
See also
United States—Armed forces—Forces in
Europe
AMERICANS in Hungary
Notes from a European diary: 1963-64; Buda-
pest. E. Wilson. New Yorker 42:88+ Je 4 '66
AMERICANS in India
American family in India. R. H. Useem. Ann
Am Acad 368:132-45 N '66
Department of amplification; use of snake
charmers to remove snakes from United
States embassy grounds. J. K. Galbraith.
New Yorker 42:50+ Ja 14 '67
Some minor pathologies in the American
presence in India. R. D. Lambert. bibliog f
Ann Am Acad 368:157-70 N '66
Work patterns of Americans in India. J.
Useem. Ann Am Acad 368:146-56 N '66
AMERICANS in Israel
Reporter at large; American Jews in Israel.
H. R. Isaacs. New Yorker 42:37-40+ Ag
27; 73-4+ S 3 '66
AMERICANS in Italy
Libraries, lasagna, and leaning towers; Johns
Hopkins university Bologna center. J. A.
Hoffberg. il Wilson Lib Bul 40:948-52 Je
'66
Notes from a European diary: 1963-64; Rome.
E. Wilson. New Yorker 42:42-6+ My 28 '66
On being foreign. T. Sterling. il Holiday
39:16+ Ap '66
AMERICANS in Moscow. See Americans in
Russia
AMERICANS in Nepal
Our Ulleri child; death of a child in a little
Asian village. P. Hitchcock. il Redbook
127-20+ Ag '66

AMERICANS in Paris. See Americans in France

AMERICANS in Rhodesia
We and they in Rhodesia. M. Cable. New Yorker 41:36-41 F 19 '66

AMERICANS in Rome. See Americans in Italy

AMERICANS in Russia
From two Americans: a close-up look at to-day's Russians. H. Rudd; F. C. Painton. il U S News 61:66-8 Jl 11 '66
How America lives: the Malones in Moscow. L. Benjamin. il Ladies Home J 83:99-101+ S '66
Some points on living in Moscow. G. P. Hunt. Life 60:3 Ap 8 '66

AMERICANS in Saigon. See Americans in Vietnam

AMERICANS in Sudan
Reporter at large; MIT Fellows in Africa program. J. McPhee. New Yorker 42:101-2+ Mr 5 '66

AMERICANS in Switzerland
Escape from the rat race; home of E. S. Campbell. C. L. Sanders. il Ebony 22:132-4+ N '66
Problem solver for corporate giants; W. A. Rutherford. il Ebony 21:62-4+ O '66

AMERICANS in Thailand
Americans in Thailand; counterinsurgency activities of armed forces, USIS and AID. M. Parker. Atlan 218:51-8 D '66
Face to face with a Bangkok recording star. L. Kennedy. il Seventeen 25:179 S '66
Wives alone; wives of U.S. civilians in Viet-nam. L. Martin. il Newsweek 68:29-30 S 5 '66

AMERICANS in the Congo
Josie; friendship between African and white American. P. Clingerman. Mlle 64:101+ D '66
Stewart: Belgian Congo in the late nine-teen-twenties. E. Hahn. New Yorker 42:207-10+ O 22 '66

AMERICANS in the Dominican Republic
Our boys took to embassy life. F. Martin. il Parents Mag 41:68-9+ D '66

AMERICANS in the Netherlands
Education: Dutch style; experiences teaching social studies in Enschede. G. Denzene. Sr Schol 88:sup 17+ Ap 15 '66

AMERICANS in Vietnam
Captain's paradise; alleged infractions by A. C. Kuntze. il Newsweek 68:36 Ag 15 '66
Saigon: drowning in dollars. D. Smith. il Nation 203:602-5 D 5 '66
Secretary on the edge of war. il Ebony 21:27-30+ Je '66
War without guns. by G. K. Tanham. Review New Repub 155:23-5 Jl 30 '66. I. F. Stone Sat R 49:28-9 My 28 '66. K. T. Young
Women; uniformed nurses and civilians; in-terviews, ed. by F. Sully. il Newsweek 67:40-2 Mr 28 '66
See also
United States—Armed forces—Forces in Viet-nam (Republic)

AMERICA'S cup race. See Yacht racing

AMERICA'S Junior miss contests. See Beauty contests

AMERIKA; opera. See Haubenstock-Ramati, R.

AMERIKANSKY dom. See Night clubs

AMERINE, Maynard A.
Search for good wine. bibliog Science 154:1621-8 D 30 '66

AMERSON, Lucius
Despite Negro opposition, a Negro might make it. J. Beecher. New Repub 155:11-12 Jl 2 '66
One black plum. il por Newsweek 67:44 Je 13 '66
Real reconstruction. Time 87:38 Je 10 '66

AMERSON, Robert C.
Alliance for progress; address, November 3, 1966. Vital Speeches 33:133-6 D 15 '66

AMERY, Carl, pseud. See Mayer, C.

AMERY, Julian
East of Suez up for grabs. Reporter 35:16-21 D 1 '66

AMES, Bernice
Artichoke; poem. Commonweal 83:578 F 18 '66
Canary; poem. Commonweal 85:138 N 4 '66
Picture a magpie; poem. Commonweal 84:284 My 27 '66

AMES, Francis H.
Desert rainbows. pors Outdoor Life 137:64+ My '66

AMES, Louise Bates. See Ilg, F. L. jt. auth.

AMES, Ia.
Ames, Iowa, complaint system has put citi-zens in the pink. il Am City 81:192+ My '66

AMES research center. See United States—National aeronautics and space adminis-tration—Ames research center

AMETHYSTS
Color center in amethyst quartz. G. Lehmann and W. J. Moore. bibliog il Science 152:1061-2 My 20 '66

AMEX. See American stock exchange

AMFT, M. J.
Giant sex riot; story. Seventeen 25:140-1 F '66
Good-by; story. Seventeen 25:166-7 N '66
Memento, memento; story. Seventeen 25:158-9 Ap '66
Where will all the bluebirds go? story. Seventeen 25:114-15 Je '66

AMHERST college, Amherst, Mass.
Amherst fraternities. Sch & Soc 94:446 D 10 '66

AMICK, R. J.
Why the hog business isn't likely to move South. Farm J 90:38K Jl '66

AMINES
New light on how certain amines act in the brain; report of symposium on Parkinson's disease. T. L. Campbell. il Science 152:232-6+ Ap 8 '66
See also
Catecholamines

AMINO acids
Aminooxyacetic acid: interactions with gamma-aminobutyric acid and the blood-brain barrier. M. A. Fisher and others. bibliog il Science 153:1668-70 S 30 '66
Concentration of dissolved amino acids from saline waters by ligand-exchange chroma-tography. A. Siegel and E. T. Degens. bibliog Science 151:1098-101 Mr 4 '66
Effect of sugars on transport of alanine in intestine. R. A. Chez and others. bibliog il Science 153:1012-13 Ag 26 '66
Evolution of the structure of ferredoxin based on living relics of primitive amino acid sequences. R. V. Eck and M. O. Dayhoff. bibliog il Science 152:363-6 Ap 15 '66
Formylmethionyl-tRNA dependence of amino acid incorporation in extracts of trimethop-prim-treated escherichia coli. J. Eisenstadt and P. Lengyel. bibliog il Science 152:524-7 O 28 '66
Hemoglobin Freiburg: abnormal hemoglobin due to deletion of a single amino acid residue. R. T. Jones and others. bibliog il Science 154:1024-7 N 25 '66
Hemoglobins in sheep: multiple differences in amino acid sequences of three beta-chains and possible origins. S. H. Boyer and others. bibliog il Science 153:1539-43 S 23 '66
Homocystinuria: excretion of a new sulfur-containing amino acid in urine. T. L. Perry and others. bibliog il Science 152:776-8 My 6 '66
Light chains of mouse myeloma proteins: partial amino acid sequence. R. Perham and others. bibliog il Science 154:391-3 O 21 '66
Malaria infection (plasmodium lophurae) changes in free amino acids. I. W. Sher-man and J. B. Mudd. bibliog il Science 154:287-9 O 14 '66
Synthesis of amino acid residues with reac-tive side chains under simple conditions. G. Steinman. bibliog il Science 154:1344-6 D 9 '66
Transport of sugars and amino acids in the intestine: evidence for a common carrier. F. Alvarado. bibliog il Science 151:1010-13 F 25 '66
See also
Kynurenine
Phenylalanine
Tryptophan

AMINOBUTYRIC acid. See Amino acids

AMINOOXYACETIC acid. See Amino acids

AMISH Mennonites. See Mennonites

AMISTAD DAM. See Dams

AMMONIA
Ten facts that will help you understand and get more mileage from anhydrous ammonia. il Suc Farm 64:40-1+ Ap '66

AMMONS, A. R.
Seven books by eight poets. Poetry 108:191-7 Je '66
about
Muse & hearth. J. Harrison. Poetry 107:330-1 F '66

AMNESIA
Amnesia, or reversal of forgetting by anti-cholinesterase, depending simply on time of injection. J. A. Deutsch and S. F. Leibowitz. bibliog il Science 153:1017-18 Ag 26 '66

AMNESIA—*Continued*
Effects of electroshock on memory: amnesia without convulsions. J. L. McGaugh and H. P. Alpern. bibliog il Science 152:665-6 Ap 29 '66

Long temporal gradient of retrograde amnesia for a well-discriminated stimulus. R. Kopp and others. bibliog il Science 153:1547-9 S 23 '66

Pill that helps you remember; Cylert. D. E. Cameron. il Sat Eve Post 239:64-6+ S 24 '66

Recovery of memory after amnesia induced by electroconvulsive shock. S. Zinkin and A. J. Miller. bibliog il Science 155:102-4 Ja 6 '67

Retrograde amnesia: effects of handling and microwave radiation. R. N. Bryan. bibliog Science 153:897-9 Ag 19 '66

AMNESTY
Amnesty time in Italy. Time 87:114 My 20 '66

AMNESTY international (organization)
Helping prisoners of conscience. Time 87:79 Ap 15 '66

AMONG the quiet folks; story. See Moore, J.

AMOROSE, Joseph D.
Build a one-transistor autogen radio. Pop Mech 126:169-70 S '66

AMORTIZATION deductions
Fast write-off bill has builders worried; proposal to suspend accelerated depreciation on new construction. Bsns W p53 S 24 '66

Grave mistake; suspension of investment tax credit and depreciation allowances. D. Lawrence. U S News 61:136 O 24 '66

How tax-credit suspension works. U S News 61:123 O 24 '66

Industry seeks softer tax credit impact; effect of suspension of 7 per cent tax credit on airline orders. Aviation W 85:35-6 S 19 '66

Tax credit out, with exceptions. U S News 61:126 N 21 '66

AMORY, Cleveland
First of the month. See issues of Saturday review

AMOS, Harold. See Soeiro. R. jt. auth.

AMOSOV, Nikolai Mikhailovich
Diary of a Russian surgeon. por Harper 233: 79-86 D '66

AMPEX corporation
Tape makers prosper as computer sales soar. il Bsns W p 181-2 S 17 '66

AMPHETAMINES
Pep pills act on brain like heat stroke. Sci N 90:276 O 8 '66

AMPHIBIA
Adaptations of amphibia to arid environments. P. J. Bentley. bibliog Science 152: 619-23 Ap 29 '66
See also
Embryology—Amphibia
Toads

Development
How a tadpole becomes a frog. W. Etkin. il Sci Am 214:76-80+ My '66

AMPHIBIOUS motor vehicles. See Motor vehicles, Amphibious

AMPHIBOLES
Infrared study of the hydroxyl bands in clinoamphiboles. R. G. Burns and R. G. J. Strens. bibliog il Science 153:890-2 Ag 19 '66

AMPICILLIN. See Penicillin

AMPLIFIERS
Amplification using switching techniques. D. E. Lancaster. il Electr World 75:30-2+ F '66

Audio calibrator for transistor amplifiers. R. Wilson. il Electr World 76:67 Ag '66

Build a stereo headphone control unit. C. Caringella. il Pop Electr 24:71-3+ Ap '66

Build hi-fi amplifier for solid-state phono cartridge. A. Trauffer. il Pop Electr 25: 65-7 O '66

Design requirements for solid-state amplifiers. V. Brociner. il Electr World 75: 39-41+ Ja '66

Designing silicon-transistor hi-fi amplifiers. R. D. Gold and J. G. Sondermeyer. il Electr World 76:23-6+ S; 34-6+ O; 47-50+ N '66

Dynamic power. I. Berger. Sat R 49:59 My 28 '66

First integrated-circuit phonograph. A. F. Petrie. il Electr World 76:28-9+ D '66

Fuzzbox for under $3. C. Anderton. il Pop Electr 26:87+ Ja '67

Inexpensive integrated solid-state stereo record player. J. E. Rohen. il Pop Electr 25: 51-2 Jl '66

Integrated circuit amplifier you can build for under $6! D. Lancaster. il Pop Electr 25:57-9+ O '66

Integrated stereo amplifiers. il Consumer Bul 49:11-14 Ap '66

Kit makes super hi-fi solid-state amplifier. R. M. Benrey. il Pop Sci 188:121 Je '66

Linear integrated circuits: what's available? D. E. Lancaster. il Electr World 76:38-42+ N '66

Low-noise, interference-resistant amplifier suitable for biological signals. G. Schuler and others. il Science 154:1191-2 D 2 '66

New IHF standard on amplifiers. W. A. Stocklin. Electr World 75:6+ Ap '66

New models; annual New York high fidelity show. H. Fantel. Opera N 31:29 N 19 '66

New preamps. I. Berger. Sat R 49:71 Ap 30 '66

Oscilloscope preamplifier. E. N. Smith. il Electr World 75:84+ F '66

Pepper; outboard r.f. amplifier for automobile. J. J. Borzner. il Pop Electr 24:56 My '66

Phantom of the opera; voice amplification. H. C. Schonberg. il N Y Times Mag p 10-11+ F 6 '66; Discussion. p 19+ F 20 '66

Put a guitar amplifier in your pocket. L. Steckler. il Pop Mech 126:198-9+ O '66

Reverb for your car. D. Meyer. il Pop Electr 24:50-3+ F '66

Selecting a P.A. amplifier. M. S. Sumberg. il Electr World 75:39-42+ Je '66

Solid-state hi-fi equipment directory. il Electr World 75:32-5+ Ja '66

Substituting FET's for tubes in hi-fi amplifiers. W. A. Rheinfelder. il Electr World 75:42-3 Mr '66

Tape recorder echo chamber. S. E. Auyer. il Pop Electr 25:81-2 Ag '66

Update to solid state. L. E. Garner. jr. il Pop Electr 25:41-4 S '66
See also
Lasers
Man amplifiers
Transistors

Testing
Saw-tooth testing of audio amplifiers. E. N. Monacchio and A. L. Plevy. il Electr World 76:74-6 Jl '66

AMPUTATION
New for amputees: instant limbs; M. Weiss's immediate prosthesis procedure. A. T. Jordan. Todays Health 44:37-9+ D '66; Same abr. with title They walk again, at once. Read Digest 89:61-4 D '66

AMPUTEES
Amputees on skis; Amputee slalom race, Mount Hood, Ore. E. H. Matthew. il Todays Health 45:12-13 Ja '67

Student nurse with heart: double amputee studying at Mercy hospital school of nursing in Charlotte, N.C. C. Brossard. il Look 30:M16-21 D 13 '66

Rehabilitation
See Rehabilitation

AMSBERG, Claus von
Orange blossoms. il por Time 87:51-2 Mr 18 '66

Though the heavens fall; anti-German demonstrations on wedding day. il por Newsweek 67:46-7 Mr 21 '66

AMSTERDAM, Netherlands

Architecture
How to protest in Dutch; demolition of eighteenth-century warehouse. il Horizon 8:16-17 Wint '66

Description
Amsterdam. W. Sansom. il Holiday 40:82-9+ D '66

Libraries
IFLA/FIAB report. R. Vosper; K. Molz. il Wilson Lib Bul 41:276-83+ N '66

Music
Amsterdam. J. Mindszenthy. il Opera N 30: 33 Ap 9; 31:30 D 10 '66

Notes from our correspondents (cont) J. de Kruijff. Hi Fi 16:20 Ap; 18+ Ag '66

Riots
Fun on the run. il Time 87:36 Je 24 '66

AMUN, Great temple of. See Luxor

AMUNDSON, Robert H.
Breakthrough in immigration. America 114: 168-70 Ja 29 '66

AMURAO, Corazon
Headlines and checkbooks. il Newsweek 68: 76 Ag 1 '66
In an alien land, one had the quality of survival. L. Wainwright. il Life 61:26-7 Jl 29 '66
They are all dead! il por Newsweek 68:18-20 Jl 25 '66

AMUSEMENT parks
Amusement parks ride to boom, or bust; New Jersey's Palisades. il Bsns W p32-4 Ap 9 '66
Lo! le pauvre indien; Valley of the Redskins. il Newsweek 68:56-8 Ag 29 '66
Now the bankers come to Disney. J. McDonald. il Fortune 73:138-41+ My '66

AMUSEMENTS
Elephants et cetera; basic measurement of entertainment. P. Gilliatt. Vogue 147:62-3 F 1 '66
Pleasure dome '66: the world of Murray the K. R. Kotlowitz. il Harper 233:96-100 Jl6 '6
Public entertainment and the subversion of ethical standards. G. Seldes. Ann Am Acad 363:87-94 Ja '66
St Louis blues; teeny-boppers remaking America's urban entertainment districts. il Newsweek 68:109 N 7 '66
See also
Books and reading
Childrens amusements
Entertaining
Puzzles
Recreation

AMUZEGAR, Jahangir
Nationalism vs. economic growth. For Affairs 44:651-61 Jl '66

AMY Loveman national award. See Loveman award

AMYLOIDS
Purification and reconstitution of the periodic fibril and unit structure of human amyloid. G. G. Glenner and H. A. Bladen. bibliog il Science 154:271-2 O 14 '66

AMYLOSES
Crystal structure of amylose triacetate: a nonintegral helix. A. Sarko and R. H. Marchessault. bibliog il Science 154:1658-9 D 30 '66

ANABLE, Anthony
Gulf Stream saga. Yachting 119:191-2 F '66

ANACONDA copper mining company
Perilous prosperity of Anaconda. T. O'Hanlon. il Fortune 73:116-21+ My '66
Sidelines of a copper company. Fortune 73: 121 My '66

ANADARKO, Okla.
Proud demonstration at Anadarko; D. J. Greve's Sequoyah projects. E. Selby and A. Selby. Read Digest 88:229-30+ Ap '66

ANAGNOSTOPOULOS, C. E. and others
Pacemaker synchronization. Science 153:1636 S 30 '66

ANAHEIM, Calif.
Tree time in Anaheim. P. A. Deimel. il Parks & Rec 1:218-19 Mr '66

ANAHEIM Angels (baseball) See Baseball clubs

ANAHUACALLI museum. See Mexico (city)—Galleries and museums

ANALGESIA
New ways to kill pain; audio analgesia. M. Gunther. il Sat Eve Post 239:25-7 Jl 2 '66

ANALGESICS
Analgesic drugs. M. Gates. il Sci Am 215: 131-6 bibliog(p 160) N '66

ANALOGY (rhetoric) See Figures of speech

ANALYSIS (mathematics) See Harmonic analysis

ANARCHISM and anarchists
Era of anarchy. D. Lawrence. U S News 61:96 Ag 29 '66; Same abr. Read Digest 89:127-8 N '66
Word and the deed, anarchism revisited. H. M. Douty. bibliog f Mo Labor R 89:15-18 Ja '66

ANATOMICAL models
Liquid plastic used in real heart models. il(p 193) Sci N 90:198 S 17 '66

ANATOMY
See also
Anatomical models
Cadavers
also names of regions and organs of the body, e.g. Eye

ANATOMY, Artistic
See also
Human figure in photography

ANCHORAGE, Alaska
Alaska metro government. L. L. Woodman. Am City 81:212+ S '66
Municipal photoscene. il Am City 81:110-11 Ag '66

Education
Cultural arts week in Anchorage, Alaska. B. Baer. il Sch Arts 65:31-3 My '66

ANCHORAGE, Alaska, archdiocese. See Catholic church—Dioceses

ANCHORING. See Boats—Mooring

ANCHORS
Stowing the anchor rode. J. F. Jayne. il Motor B 117:152+ Mr '66
Tips and tricks for anchoring. G. Daniels. il Pop Sci 188:112-14 Je '66

ANCHOVIES
Deserts in the sea; economic expedients at price of annihilating fish; condition of California's industry. R. G. Lillard. il Nation 202:268-70 Mr 7 '66

ANDA, Luis Aveleyra Arroyo de. See Aveleyra Arroyo de Anda, L.

ANDALUSITE
Kyanite-andalusite equilibrium from 700° to 800°C. R. C. Newton. bibliog il Science 153: 170-2 Jl 8 '66

ANDERSEN, Burton R.
Gamma-A cold agglutinin: importance of disulfide bonds in activity and structure. bibliog Science 154:281-3 O 14 '66

ANDERSEN, Hans Christian
Pied Piper of Odense. R. J. Clements. il NEA J 55:50-1 O '66

ANDERSEN, Yvonne
My son, the film maker. L. Lipton. il Pop Phot 58:128-9 Ap '66

ANDERSON, Charles B.
Bibliopola: gift for booksellers. Pub W 190: 51-4 D 26 '66

ANDERSON, Clinton Presba
Surprising facts about medicare. Look 30: 78+ My 17 '66
about
Senator Anderson receives AFA's Distinguished service award. il pors Am For 71: 6+ O '65

ANDERSON, David D.
Pakistan's search for national identity. Yale R 55:552-69 Je '66

ANDERSON, Dewey
Don't tame the wild-flowing Feather. Nat Parks Mag 40:18-20 My '66

ANDERSON, Don L.
Earth's viscosity. bibliog Science 151:321-2 Ja 21 '66

ANDERSON, Donald Jack
Born to tree coon. Field & S 71:52-3+ N '66
Cold but happy years. Field & S 71:40-1+ D '66
Long Tom. Field & S 70:38-40+ F '66
Night of the bullfrog. Field & S 71:44-6+ Je '66

ANDERSON, Donny
Locks vs. Boom Boom D. Jenkins. il por Sports Illus 25:20-3 Ag 22 '66

ANDERSON, Dorothy J.
Land of Lincoln recruits librarians. ALA Bul 60:1174-6 D '66

ANDERSON, Eugenie (Moore)
Trust Territory of the Pacific Islands: statement, June 27, 1966. Dept State Bul 55: 387-8 S 12 '66

ANDERSON, Evelyn
Adrenocorticotrophin-releasing hormone in peripheral blood: increase during stress. bibliog Science 152:379-80 Ap 15 '66

ANDERSON, Gordon L.
Sequence-operated lock. Pop Electr 26:73-4+ Ja '67

ANDERSON, Jack
Children's dance is serious fun. Dance Mag 40:68-70 My '66
What happens at a happening? Dance Mag 40:44-6 Ag '66

ANDERSON, James R.
To be perfectly frank. America 115:655 N 19 '66

ANDERSON, John Bayard
Excerpt from debate, July 28, 1966. Cong Digest 45:277+ N '66

ANDERSON, John Firth
Ethics: the creaking code. por Library J 91:5333-5 N 1 '66

ANDERSON, Kristine
Curl up and read. Seventeen 25:34 S '66

ANDERSON, Norman G.
Zonal centrifuges and other separation systems. bibliog Science 154:103-12 O 7 '66

ANDERSON, Patrick
Born hero-worshiper who serves his hero. N Y Times Mag p28-9+ F 20 '66
Making trouble is Alinsky's business. N Y Times Mag p28-31+ O 9 '66
No. 2 Texan in the White House. N Y Times Mag p23+ Ap 3 '66

ANDERSON, Quentin
Nabokov in time. New Repub 154:23-8 Je 4 '66
ANDERSON, Ray K.
Ethics and Vietnam. Christian Cent 83:1120+ S 14 '66
ANDERSON, Raymond J. and others
Calcium and bromide contents of natural waters. bibliog Science 153:1637-8; 154:1473 S 30, D 16 '66
ANDERSON, Richard J. and others
Continued evaluation of veterans' careers as a function of education. Sch & Soc 94: 357-8 O 29 '66
ANDERSON, Robert
Auto executive: he has to run faster just to keep up. il pors Bsns W p96-100 Mr 12 '66
ANDERSON, Robert A.
Trouble in outer space; drama. Plays 26:1-9, 20 D '66
ANDERSON, Roger C. and Loucks, O. L.
Osmotic pressure influence in germination tests for antibiosis. bibliog Science 152:771-3 My 6 '66
ANDERSON, Stanley V. See Reuss, H. S. jt. auth.
ANDERSON, Stephen S.
Soviet relations with east Europe. Cur Hist 51:200-5 O '66
ANDERSON, Thomas P.
Books. Commonweal 84:587-8 S 16 '66
ANDERSON, W. E. Andy
Roy Rogers goes north. il pors Outdoor Life 137:52-5+ Ap '66
ANDERSON, Wallace L.
World view for undergraduates. Sat R 49: 50-1 Ag 20 '66
ANDERSON, Wayne W.
Relevance of the college experience. Sch & Soc 94:394-6 N 12 '66
ANDERTON, Craig
Fuzzbox for under $3. Pop Electr 26:87+ Ja '67
ANDERTON, David A.
New cinetheodolite enhances accuracy. Miss & Roc 18:42-5 My 9 '66
Specialized aircraft dilemma grows. Miss & Roc 18:92+ Mr 28 '66
ANDES MOUNTAINS
Blow-up in the Andes; new trouble for U.S. J. N. Wallace. il U S News 60:72-4 Ap 11 '66
ANDOVER (school) See Private schools
ANDRADE, Vicente
Death of Camilo Torres. America 114:355 Mr 12 '66
about
America personality. por America 114:back cover Ap 16 '66
ANDREA Chénier; opera. See Giordano, U.
ANDRESEN, E.
Blood groups of the I system in pigs: association with variants of serum amylase. bibliog Science 153:1660-1 S 30 '66
ANDRESS, Ursula
Ursula. por U S Camera 29:64-5 Ag '66
ANDRETTI, Mario
How good is the new Camaro? pors Pop Sci 189:108-11 O '66
Indy-style tires for your car? ed. by P. Bryan. Pop Sci 189:128-31 S '66
New Mustang: they've improved the breed. pors Pop Sci 189:86-9 N '66
about
Fastest hee-ro at Indy. B. La Fontaine. il por Sports Illus 24:36-8+ My 30 '66
ANDREW, Thomas
Warsaw. por Dance Mag 40:62-3 Ap '66
ANDREW; story. See Morgan, B.
ANDREWS, Glenn
Excerpt from individual views filed with House report, August 25, 1965. Cong Digest 45:45+ F '66
ANDREWS, Jay K.
Seagoing classroom. Motor B 118:72-3 Ag '66
ANDREWS, John H.
Beyond the individual building. il Arch Rec 140:161-72 S '66
ANDREWS, Julie
All the things I love most; ed. by G. Christy. por Good H 162:90-3+ Mr '66
Julie Andrews; interview. ed. by R. Newquist; excerpt from Showcase. por McCalls 93:83+ Mr '66
Lively arts; interview. ed. by M. Ronan. por Sr Schol 89:22 D 2 '66
about
Hawaii. J. Poppy. il pors Look 30:54-7 S 6 '66

New & future queen. il pors Time 88:53-7 D 23 '66
Some day it will all be just wonderful. G. Smith. il pors Sat Eve Post 239:34-7 Ja 29 '66
ANDREWS, Michael F.
American art education in Japan. Sch Arts 65:32-6 Mr '66
ANDREWS, Miriam Wise
Lignum crucis; poem. Am For 72:36-7 Ap '66
ANDREWS, Paul
Castle tours. Travel 125:56-7 Ap '66
ANDREWS, Siri
Children's books in Sweden, 1750-1950, by E. von Zweigbergk; review. Horn Bk 42: 328-9 Je '66
ANDREWS, Stanley
Red tape and broken promises. Reporter 34: 14-16 My 5 '66
ANDREWS, Walter
JATACS to answer joint tactical C&C requirements. Miss & Roc 18:115-16+ Mr 28 '66
ANDREWS, Wayne
Painter in a Persian palace. Sat R 49:43+ Ap 16 '66
ANDREWS, William H.
Creative hospital administrator. il pors Ebony 22:73-4+ D '66
ANDREWS, Win
Maintenance with new products. Yachting 119:73+ Ap '66
ANDRIST, Ralph K.
Ice ahead! Am Heritage 17:60-3+ Ag '66
ANDROMEDA galaxy. See Galactic systems
ANDROS ISLAND, Bahama Islands
Descending the Andros Reef. C. L. Smith. il Natur Hist 75:38-43 O '66
Journey to chickcharney country. J. Underwood. il Sports Illus 24:80-4+ My 9 '66
ANDUJAR, Claudia
Claudia Andujar. P. Caulfield. Mod Phot 30: 50 Je '66
ANECDOTES
See also subhead Anecdotes, facetiae, satire, etc. under various subjects, e.g. Subversive activities—Anecdotes, facetiae, satire, etc.
ANELLO, Michael
Trends in Italian higher education. bibliog f Sch & Soc 94:272-4 Sum '66
ANEMIA
Erythrocyte chimerism after injection of spleen cells into anemic mice of the W-series. M. J. Seller. bibliog il Science 155: 90-1 Ja 6 '67
Incurable Negro disease strikes five in family. il Ebony 21:154-6+ My '66
Molecular mechanism of red cell sickling. M. Murayama. bibliog il Science 153:145-9 Jl 8 '66
Porotic hyperostosis, anemias, malarias, and marshes in the prehistoric eastern Mediterranean. J. L. Angel. bibliog il Science 153:760-3 Ag 12 '66
Pressure unsickles cells. Sci N 91:12 Ja 7 '67
Sex-linked anemia: a hypochromic anemia of mice. R. M. Bannerman and R. G. Cooper. bibliog il Science 151:581-2 F 4 '66
ANEMONES
Late show: Japanese anemone. il Sunset 137:267 O '66
ANESTHESIA
Action of anionic and cationic nerve-blocking agents: experiment and interpretation. M. P. Blaustein and D. E. Goldman. bibliog il Science 153:429-32 Jl 22 '66
Electrostatic aspects of physical adsorption: implications for molecular sieves and gaseous anesthesia. S. W. Benson and J. W. King, jr; discussion. bibliog Science 153: 555-6 Jl 29 '66
Silicone rubber: a new diffusion property useful for general anesthesia. J. Folkman and others. bibliog il Science 154:148-9 O 7 '66
Temperature dependence of anesthesia in goldfish. A. Cherkin and J. F Catchpool; reply with rejoinder. I. R. Fenichel and S. B. Horowitz. bibliog Science 152:1110-11 My 20 '66
See also
Analgesia
Electric anesthesia
ANESTHETICS
Anesthetic to be given by veins, not lungs. Sci N 90:323 O 22 '66
See also
Electric anesthesia
Halothane
Novocaine
ANEURYSMS
Clot of metal: magnetic surgery to treat stroke victims. il Newsweek 68:70 S 26 '66

ANGEL, J. Lawrence
Porotic hyperostosis, anemias, malarias, and marshes in the prehistoric eastern Mediterranean. bibliog Science 153:760-3 Ag 12 '66
ANGELES, Victoria de los
La vida de los Angeles. R. Lawrence. Sat R 49:80-1 S 24 '66
ANGELICO, Fra
Fra Angelico's Virgin and child. P. R. Adams. il Art N 65:34-5+ D '66
ANGELL, Roger
Exegesis of St Nick. New Yorker 42:28-9 D 24 '66
Sporting scene (cont) New Yorker 42:125-6+ My 14; 76+ Jl 23; 92+ Ag 27; 184+ O 29 '66
ANGELL, memorial animal hospital, Boston. See Hospitals, Animal
ANGELO, Bonnie
Protocol in practice. Mlle 62:168-9+ F '66
ANGELOFF, Sam
As Ky bolsters his rule, an American ark sealifts a village. Life 60:30-3 Je 3 '66
Saigon: at night, war flares and road checks. Life 60:47-52A F 25 '66
Tough, punishing work, but Dawkins asked for it. Life 60:96+ Ap 8 '66
ANGELS in the air; story. See Vivante, A.
ANGER
Mrs Parkinson's law; scientific solution for those days when everything seems to go wrong. C. N. Parkinson. il McCalls 93:104-5+ F '66
Moral indignation. V. P. McCorry. America 115:496 O 22 '66
See also
Temper
ANGINA pectoris. See Heart—Diseases
ANGIOTENSIN
Increased cardiovascular reactivity to angiotensin caused by renin. G. M. C. Masson and others. bibliog il Science 153:1002-4 Ag 26 '66
ANGLER fish
Just to change the subject. K. Severin. il Outdoor Life 138:72-3 O '66
ANGLERS (fishes) See Angler fish
ANGLICAN church of Canada. See Church of England in Canada
ANGLO-AMERICAN relations (non-political) See England and the United States
ANGLUND, Joan Walsh
Christmas is love; poem. Ladies Home J 83: 8 D '66
ANGOFF, Charles
Celestial politics; poem. Christian Cent 83: 462 Ap 13 '66
Devout heresy; poem. Christian Cent 83: 1273 O 19 '66
ANGUISH, Mental. See Suffering
ANGUS, Robert
Notes from our correspondents. Hi Fi 16:18+ Ap '66
ANHEUSER-Busch, incorporated
Beer blast; dropping of action against Anheuser-Busch by Antitrust division. Newsweek 68:24+ Jl 25 '66
Busch league; contributions to President's club. Time 88:22 Jl 22 '66
ANHYDROUS ammonia. See Ammonia
ANHYDROUS uric acid. See Uric acid
ANIMAL art. See Animals in art
ANIMAL behavior. See Animals—Habits and behavior
ANIMAL bites
Watch out for animal bites. E. Maxwell. Todays Health 44:86 O '66
ANIMAL calling
Conning and killing cunning coyotes. R. Cantwell. il Sports Illus 25:61-4 N 7 '66
ANIMAL cemeteries. See Cemeteries, Animal
ANIMAL clinics. See Veterinary medicine
ANIMAL communication

Anecdotes, facetiae, satire, etc.
Grant swinger: reflections on six years of progress. D. S. Greenberg. Science 154: 1424-5 D 16 '66
Hot line; phone conversation between two dolphins. P. Cummings. il Look 30:20 Ap 19 '66
ANIMAL experimentation
Animal-care laws: the mood of Congress; letter. L. M. Greenbaum. Science 151:1329 Mr 18 '66
Animal-care legislation; letter. E. D. Jacobson; discussion. Science 149:917; 150:1536; 151:636, 776+; 152:447-8 Ag 27, D 17 '65, F 11-18, Ap 22 '66

Animal cruelty defined; New Jersey judge's ruling on high school live animal experimentation. P. McBroom. Sci N 89:261+ Ap 16 '66
Animal tests justifiable; pending federal control over animal experimentation. P. McBroom. il Sci N 89:464-5+ Je 11 '66
Congress hears animal research testimony. Sci N 89:185 Mr 19 '66
Giant-sized approach to heart research. il Ebony 21:73-6+ F '66
Kinship of animal and human diseases. R. W. Leader. il Sci Am 216:110-16 bibliog(p 148) Ja '67
Monkey business grows in Maryland. il Ebony 21:97-100 Mr '66
New Jersey chicken trial; verdict for science. E. Langer. Science 152:479-81 Ap 22 '66
Petnapping bill passed. il Sci N 90:175 S 10 '66
Question animal research; controversy around high school biology experiment. P. McBroom. Sci N 89:166 Mr 12 '66
Swine in biomedical research; report on international symposium. L. K. Bustad and R. O. McClellan. Science 152:1526-8+ Je 10 '66
Test trial on animal cruelty coming to end. Sci N 89:184 Mr 19 '66
See also
Laboratory animals
Maze tests
Stimulus and response
Vivisection
ANIMAL instinct. See Instinct
ANIMAL intelligence
Lemur social behavior and primate intelligence. A. Jolly. bibliog il Science 153:501-6 Jl 29 '66
See also
Animals—Habits and behavior
Birds—Habits and behavior
Instinct
Learning, Psychology of
Maze tests
ANIMAL inventory. See Wildlife census
ANIMAL kingdom; story. See Boles, P. D.
ANIMAL language. See Animal communication
ANIMAL locomotion
Locomotion without limbs. C. Gans. il Natur Hist 75:10-17 bibliog(p68) F; 36-41 Mr '66
Swimming speed of a Pacific bottlenose porpoise. T. G. Lang and K. S. Norris. bibliog il Science 151:588-90 F 4 '66
ANIMAL lore
See also
Unicorn
ANIMAL medical centers. See Veterinary medicine
ANIMAL moving pictures. See Animals in moving pictures
ANIMAL obesity. See Corpulence
ANIMAL painting and illustration. See Animals in art
ANIMAL pathology. See Animals—Diseases and pests
ANIMAL plays. See Animals—Drama
ANIMAL poisons. See Venom
ANIMAL populations
Correction to one of MacArthur's species-abundance formulas. E. C. Pielou and A. N. Arnason. bibliog il Science 151:592 F 4 '66
Control
Hunting in parks. P. M. Tilden. Nat Parks Mag 40:2 My '66
Over-exploited animal populations. G. A. Finger. il Science 154:544-5 O 28 '66
ANIMAL sculpture
Animals from the rough. il Natur Hist 75: 54-7 My '66
World of Louis Paul Jonas. Z. J. Merritt. il Am Artist 31:54-60 Ja '67
ANIMAL sociology. See Animals—Habits and behavior
ANIMAL sonar. See Sonar
ANIMAL sounds
See also
Insect sounds
ANIMAL stories. See Animals—Stories
ANIMAL tagging
Bulldogging the elk; wardens tag to protect New Mexico's elk. il Life 60:101-2 Mr 18 '66
ANIMAL thefts
Concentration camps for dogs; L. W. Brown's Maryland compound raided; with report by M. Silva. il Life 60:22-9 F 4 '66
Dog watch; protecting the dog against thieves. il Newsweek 68:103A+ S 12 '66

ANIMAL thefts—*Continued*

Dognapers; bill to safeguard stolen animals against research. il Newsweek 67:33-4 My 16 '66

Dognapping: more emotion than facts. E. Langer. Science 151:1516 Mr 25 '66

Hi Joe, long time no see; stolen racing greyhound returned. J. Lovesey. il Sports Illus 24:24-5 F 28 '66

Lost pets that stray to the labs; unscrupulous dognappers. C. Phinizy. Read Digest 88:131-4 Ap '66

Pet news; report of congressional hearings on pet stealing. J. Dattel. il Ladies Home J 83:20+ Je '66

Petnapping bill passed. il Sci N 90:175 S 10 '66

Petnapping bill revised. Sci N 89:287 Ap 23 '66

Three made it safely back home to their owners. il Life 60:28-9 F 4 '66

ANIMAL traps. See Traps

ANIMALS

See also

Hearing in animals

Photography of animals

Society for indecency to naked animals

also names of animals, e.g. Leopards

Capture

Capturing strange creatures in Colombia. M. Latham. il Nat Geog Mag 129:682-93 My '66

Lions loose on a lonely road; fate of lions after highway accident in France. il Life 61:99-100 O 28 '66

Reporter at large; capturing musk-ox calves. P. Matthiessen. il New Yorker 41:94+ F 5 '66

Classification

See Zoology—Classification

Diseases and pests

Diseases of laboratory animals; report on fourth annual meeting of the Gesellschaft für versuchstierkunde. R. J. Flynn. Science 153:906 Ag 19 '66

Kinship of animal and human diseases. R. W. Leader. il Sci Am 216:110-16 bibliog(p 148) Ja '67

See also

Trypanosomiasis

Veterinary medicine

also Cattle—Diseases and pests, and similar headings

Drama

Harvest moon supper. F. B. Watts. Plays 26:75-80 O '66

Food

Anolis carolinensis: effects of feeding on reaction to aposematic prey. O. J. Sexton and others. il Science 153:1140 S 2 '66

Books. M. F. K. Fisher. New Yorker 42:157-8+ Ap 30 '66

Habits and behavior

Amateur scientist; experiment in animal behavior. E. Neville. Sci Am 215:135-6 D '66

Books: two on aggression. J. Alsop. New Yorker 42:209-14+ S 10 '66

Drive for territory; excerpts from The territorial imperative. R. Ardrey. il Life 61:40-7+ Ag 26 '66

Ethology. O. Handlin. Atlan 218:138-9 S '66

Free-ranging rhesus monkeys age and sex differences in individual activity patterns. W. A. Draper. bibliog il Science 151:476-8 Ja 28 '66

How to trace a turtle and follow a deer. D. Cohen. il Sci Digest 59:28-31 Mr '66

Instincts and prophecies. G. H. T. Kimble. Reporter 35:40+ D 29 '66

Jeopardy and alibi; aggression and territorialism; theories of K. Lorenz and R. Ardrey. C. Deemer. New Repub 155:26+ O 1 '66

The lion; with report by G. B. Schaller. il Life 62:44-55+ Ja 20 '67

Man is a territorial animal; excerpts from The territorial imperative. R. Ardrey. il Life 61:50-4+ S 2 '66

On aggression by K. Lorenz. Review
Life 60:8+ Je 3 '66. F. Russell
Redbook 128:34+ N '66. M. Mead
Sci Digest 60:30-1 D '66. J. Reinert
Time il 87:104+ Je 17 '66

Rats. S. A. Barnett. il Sci Am 216:78-85 Ja '67

Reporter at large; Serengeti and Ngorongoro Crater reserve. A. Moorehead. New Yorker 42:154+ O 29 '66

Rhesus monkey bands; social patterns are studied in Puerto Rico. J. G. Vandenbergh. il Natur Hist 75:2-7 My '66

Territorial imperative. by R. Ardrey. Review
Nat R 18:1115-17 N 1 '66. G. Davenport
Newsweek il 68:108-108B S 12 '66
Sat R 49:34-5 S 17 '66. R. D. Masters
Time 88:125+ S 16 '66
Vogue 148:167 D '66. J. Stafford

That old-time aggression. J. P. Scott. Nation 204:53-4 Ja 9 '67

Tiger and its prey. G. B. Schaller. il Natur Hist 75:30-7 O '66

Tree shrews: unique reproductive mechanism of systematic importance. R. D. Martin. bibliog il Science 152:1402-4 Je 3 '66

Underwater vocalization by sea lions: social and mirror stimuli. R. J. Schusterman and others. bibliog il Science 154:540-2 O 28 '66

What animals can tell us about ourselves. J. Adamson. il McCalls 94:60-1+ Ja '67

Why do animals fight? J. George. il Audubon Mag 68:18-20 Ja '66

Woodland wonderworld. J. D. Scott. il Read Digest 89:175-7+ Jl '66

See also

Animals as artists

Hibernation

Instinct

Periodicity

Sex behavior

also Fishes—Habits and behavior, and similar headings

Language

See Animal communication

Migration

Bats blown to Iceland; hoary bats. il Sci N 90:308 O 15 '66

Cavalcade of the caribou. J. J. Shomon. il Outdoor Life 137:46-7+ Je '66

Polar bears tracked by orbiting satellite. Sci N 89:321 Ap 30 '66

Orientation

See Orientation

Photographs

Dog days for a motherless monkey; gibbon courts Great Dane. Look 30:M20+ N 29 '66

Dogs. S. A. Thompson. il U S Camera 29:56-7 Ag '66

Friends around the clock; boy and a dog. Good H 162:52+ Mr '66

Great cats of Africa. J. Dominis. Life 62:36-52 Ja 6; 48-59+ Ja 13; 44-57 Ja 20 '67

Protection

Cat's life; English women's Venetian campaign. Newsweek 68:67 O 24 '66

For sixty days and sixty nights; solving the alligator emergency, creating a problem for deer. J. O'Reilly. il Sports Illus 25:22-3 Ag 15 '66

Hide sales imperil rare species. C. W. Buchheister. il Audubon Mag 68:73 Mr '66

Splashy open season on deer; Everglades swamp rescues. il Life 61:58-9 Ag 12 '66

See also

Animals—Treatment

Reproduction

See Reproduction

Stories

Saga of Patsy and Oscar. H. Manchester. il Read Digest 89:41-2 O '66

What animals can tell us about ourselves; stories about the wisdom of wild creatures. J. Adamson. il McCalls 94:60-1+ Ja '67

See also subhead Stories under names of animals, e.g. Cats—Stories

Training

Great new circus act; tiger on a horse trained by R. Althoff. il Life 60:88B-88D+ Ap 15 '66

Heavyweight high jump; Makapuu; performing whale at Hawaii's Sea life park. il Life 61:121-2+ N 25 '66

See also

Animals in moving pictures

Transportation

Monkeys shipped by air from India well treated. Sci N L 89:57 Ja 22 '66

Treatment

Animal care legislation. D. Wolfle. Science 153:1061 S 2 '66

Animal cruelty defined. P. McBroom. Sci N 89:261+ Ap 16 '66

Concentration camps for dogs; L. W. Browns's Maryland compound raided; with report by M. Silva. il Life 60:22-9 F 4 '66

ANIMALS—Treatment—*Continued*
Dognapers; bill to safeguard stolen animals against research. il Newsweek 67:33-4 My 16 '66
Dogs and cats: humane treatment legislation nears passage. E. Langer. Science 153:846 Ag 19 '66
Ethel Kennedy: meddler or good samaritan? il U S News 62:16 Ja 23 '67
Laboratory animal law. Sci Am 215:65 N '66
Loved ones; Senate passes bill against dog-napping and research abuses. il Newsweek 68:47 Jl 18 '66
See also
Humane society of the United States
Vivisection
ANIMALS, Cruelty to. See Animals—Treatment
ANIMALS, Experiments on. See Animal experimentation
ANIMALS, Extinct
Pleistocene overkill; extinction of North America's large mammals. Sci Am 215:58 D '66
See also
Dinosaurs
Mammoths
Mastodon
Paleontology
Quaggas
ANIMALS, Food habits of. See Animals—Food
ANIMALS, Infancy of
Monkeys reared in isolation with pictures as visual input: evidence for an innate releasing mechanism. G. P. Sackett. il Science 154:1468+ D 16 '66
Weaning of young rats: effect of time on behavior. V. Nováková. bibliog il Science 151:475-6 Ja 28 '66
Zoo babies numerous. B. Tufty. il Sci N 89:440-1+ Je 4 '66
ANIMALS, Laboratory. See Laboratory animals
ANIMALS, Performing. See Animals—Training
ANIMALS, Predatory
See also
Foxes
Wolves
Bounties
Bounties going, but not gone. C. W. Buchheister. Audubon Mag 68:4 Ja '66
State vs. the Predator; case history: South Dakota. G. Charles. il Audubon Mag 68:436-42 N '66
ANIMALS, Rescue of. See Animals—Protection
ANIMALS, Treatment of. See Animals—Treatment
ANIMALS as artists
Anecdotes, facetiae, satire, etc.
Work and worries of non-sleeping Beauty; paintings by a chimpanzee. H. B. Jacobs. Look 30:53 Jl 12 '66
ANIMALS as carriers of infection
You can catch animal diseases. W. F. McCulloch and S. L. Diesch. Suc Farm 64:70 O '66
See also
Rats as carriers of infection
ANIMALS in art
Beauty and the beast; summary of Man through his art: Man and animal; ed. by P. Bentley. il UNESCO Courier 19:27-30 Ja '66
Birds and beasts in the Queen's gallery. O. Millar. il Antiques 90:824-7 D '66
Masterpieces from a lost kingdom; Marlik. E. O. Negahban. il UNESCO Courier 19:16-21 Je '66
See also
Animal sculpture
ANIMALS in captivity. See Zoological gardens
ANIMALS in fiction. See Animals in literature
ANIMALS in literature
Anne Carroll Moore urged withdrawal of Stuart Little. E. B. White reports; excerpts from article. E. B. White. Library J 91:2187 Ap 15 '66
ANIMALS in moving pictures
Born free. il Look 30:106+ Ap 19 '66
Debonair Rex now a celebrated doctor: Dolittle on film. il Life 61:122-4+ S 30 '66
King of beasts; I. Tors. il Newsweek 67:96 F 21 '66
Rights and permissions; trials of making movie based on Doctor Dolittle. P. Nathan. Pub W 189:120 Je 13 '66
ANIMALS in the house; story. See Hale, N.
ANIMALS on television programs
Prince: Daktari's scene stealer. il Look 30:118+ N 1 '66

ANIMATED cartoons. See Television broadcasting—Animated cartoons
ANISFIELD-Wolf awards
SR-Anisfield-Wolf awards: 1966. J. F. Fixx. il Sat R 49:26-7 Je 11 '66
ANISOLE
Tetrachloroanisol: a source of musty taste in eggs and broilers. C. Engel and others. Science 154:270-1 O 14 '66
ANKRAH, Joseph Arthur
And now Nkrumah: generals & the future of Africa. J. K. Sale. il Nation 202:317-22 Mr 21 '66
Exit Nkrumah, an old dreamer; enter Ankrah, a new realist. L. Garrison. il N Y Times Mag p32-3+ Ap 3 '66
Rope that hanged Nkrumah. E. Huxley. Nat R 18:268-70 Mr 22 '66
ANLIKER, James
Simultaneous changes in visual separation threshold and voltage of cortical alpha rhythm. bibliog Science 153:316-18 Jl 15 '66
ANN, Sister Patrick. See Patrick Ann, Sister
ANN ARBOR, Mich.

Education
Conservation joins the three R's. J. Swan. il Audubon Mag 68:119-20+ Mr '66
ANN-MARGRET
Attention! see Europe with the king of the international set (me) W. Allen. il pors Esquire 65:55-71 F '66
ANNAPOLIS, Md.

Historic houses, etc.
Annapolis, Maryland. il Antiques 90:530-2 O '66
ANNAPOLIS naval academy. See United States naval academy, Annapolis
ANNE, princess of Great Britain
England's teen-age princess. R. Lecler. por Seventeen 25:154-5+ S '66
ANNE Marie, consort of Constantine II, king of the Hellenes
Visit with the world's youngest queen; interview, ed. by A. T. Bruno. pors McCalls 93:72-3+ Je '66
about
Their majesties King Constantine II and Queen Anne Marie of the Hellenes with H.R.H. Crown Princess Alexia. D. Messinesi. il pors Vogue 148:116-19+ S 15 '66
ANNIE get your gun; musical comedy. See Musical comedies, revues, etc.—Criticisms, plots, etc.
ANNIVERSARIES
See also
Celebrations
ANNIVERSARY gift; story. See Sharp, M.
ANNOUNCERS, Radio. See Radio broadcasting—Announcing
ANNUAL meetings, Stockholders. See Stockholders meetings
ANNUAL reports. See Reports
ANNUALS (plants)
Better homes & gardens selections: annuals are better every year! il Bet Hom & Gard 44:54-7 Ap '66
Four low-growing annuals for Mondrian gardens. il Flower Grower 53:13 Mr '66
Growing your own in a flat. il Sunset 136:106-7 Ap '66
How Mrs Cutting stages her winter flower show; border of winter annuals. il Sunset 137:265 O '66
ANNUALS, High school. See High school annuals
ANNUITIES
Glow gets rosier for variable annuities. il Bsns W p76+ Ja 29 '66
See also
Insurance, Life
Pensions, Industrial
ANOLIS. See Chameleons
ANONYMOUS telephone calls. See Telephone calls
ANOPHELES. See Mosquitoes
ANOUILH, Jean
Medea. Criticism
Time 88:31 D 30 '66
Poor Bitos. Criticism
Sat R 49:55 Mr 5 '66
ANOXEMIA
Nitrogen- and helium-induced anoxia: different lethal effects on rye seeds. R. L. Latterell. bibliog il Science 153:69-70 Jl 1 '66
ANQUETIL, Jacques
L'affaire Anquetil. Sports Illus 24:21 My 16 '66

ANSERMET, Ernest
Lively arts; interview, ed. by R. Hemming.
  por Sr Schol 89:27+ N 18 '66
      about
  Mellowing rebel. il Time 88:56 Jl 22 '66
ANSETT-ANA airways. See Airlines—Australia
ANSTALL, Harold B. and others
  Isozymes of aldolase. bibliog Science 154:
  657-8 N 4 '66
ANTARCTIC exploration
  Hike in Antarctica; U.S. expedition. il Time
  89:74 Ja 6 '67
      See also
  United States exploring expedition, 1838-1842
ANTARCTIC REGIONS
  Foraminiferal evidence of a shallow calcium
  carbonate solution boundary, Ross Sea,
  Antarctica. J. P. Kennett. bibliog il Science
  153:191-3 Jl 8 '66
  New research stations probe Antarctica's
  ice. Sci N L 89:105 F 12 '66
      See also
  Antarctic exploration
  Geology—Antarctic Regions
  Ice—Polar Regions
  Kerguelen Islands
      Description and travel
  Enjoying Antarctica! J. A. Chisholm. il Travel
  126:48-9 Jl '66
ANTARCTIC research. See Polar research
ANTARES. See Stars, Double
ANTEK, Samuel
  This was Toscanini; excerpt. Read Digest
  89:103-7 Jl '66
ANTELOPES, American. See Pronghorns
ANTENNA rotators. See Television antennas
ANTENNAS (electronics)
  DSIF antenna to extend Pioneer life. R. Pay.
  il Tech W 18:25-6+ Je 13 '66
  FAA tests antenna with Nimbus picture.
  Aviation W 85:103-4 N 14 '66
  Frequency extension spawns improved an-
  tenna feeds. C. D. LaFond. il Tech W 19:
  30+ Ag 8 '66
  Getting a word to outer space; Goldstone
  complex. Bsns W p 168 My 7 '66
      See also
  Radar—Antenna and scanning mechanisms
  Radio telescope
  Television antennas
ANTEPENULTIMATE; story. See Fremantle.
  A.
ANTHEMS
      See also
  Hymns
ANTHOLOGIES
  World of modern fiction, ed. by S. Marcus.
  Review
  New Repub 155:17+ N 19 '66. S. Kauff-
  mann
ANTHON, Carl G.
  West Germany and Europe. Cur Hist 50:270-
  6+ My '66
ANTHONY, Daniel S.
  Graphology, science with a future. Sci Di-
  gest 59:55-66 Mr '66
ANTHONY, Irvin
  Case of the capsule cruiser. Yachting 119:
  83+ Mr '66
ANTHONY, Norman
  Rise and fall of Elmer Zilch. Atlan 217:93-6
  Mr '66
ANTHONY, Rey, pseud.
  Arbitration hearings called for promiscuity
  handbook. Pub W 189:59 My 30 '66
ANTHONY, Robert N. See Mauriel, J. J. jt.
  auth.
ANTHROPOLOGICAL expeditions
  Margaret Mead answers questions about:
  housekeeping in the field. M. Mead. Red-
  book 127:38+ O '66
ANTHROPOLOGY
  Biological nature of man. G. G. Simpson.
  bibliog Science 152:472-8 Ap 22 '66; Reply.
  V. R. Potter. 153:121 Jl 8 '66; Rejoinder.
  154:1120 D 2 '66
      See also
  Culture
  Man
  Man, Primitive
      Bibliography
  World of savages. J. H. Plumb. Sat R 49:
  19-20 D 31 '66
      Research
  Anthropologists' debate: concern over future
  of foreign research. B. Nelson. Science
  154:1525-7 D 23 '66

ANTIAIRCRAFT guns. See Guns, Antiaircraft
ANTI-AMERICANISM. See United States—For-
  eign opinion
ANTI-BALLISTIC missile system. See Guided
  missiles—Defenses
ANTIBIOSIS
  Osmotic pressure influence in germination
  tests for antibiosis. R. C. Anderson and
  O. L. Loucks. bibliog il Science 152:771-3
  My 6 '66
ANTIBIOTIC feed supplements
  Drug residues studied; dangers to man. Sci N
  90:148 S 3 '66
  Trouble-free start for feeder pigs. D. Wolf.
  il Farm J 90:68G Mr '66
ANTIBIOTICS
  Antibiotics and the genetic code. L. Gorini.
  il Sci Am 214:102-9 Ap '66
  Antimicrobial agents and chemotherapy; re-
  ports on fifth and sixth Interscience con-
  ference on antimicrobial agents and chemo-
  therapy. D. Perlman. Science 152:108-9; 154:
  1591 Ap 1, D 23 '66
  Ineffective lozenges being taken off market.
  Sci N 89:185 Mr 19 '66
  Inhibition of protein synthesis: a mechanism
  for the production of impaired iron absorption. N. J. Greenberger and R. D. Ruppert. bibliog il Science 153:315-16 Jl 15 '66
  Invincible bacteria? Newsweek 68:92 Ag 22 '66
  Italians announce new antibiotic useful in
  TB; rifaldazine, derived from the rifamy-
  cin family. Sci N 90:398 N 12 '66
  Misuse of antibiotics. Sci Am 215:44 O '66
  Naturally occurring antimetabolite antibiotic
  related to biotin. L. J. Hanka and others.
  bibliog il Science 154:1667-8 D 30 '66
  New drug families dress for a debut; resistant
  bacteria poses dilemma. il Bsns W p98+ S
  24 '66
  Puromycin and cycloheximide: different
  effects on hippocampal electrical activity.
  H. D. Cohen and others. bibliog il Science
  154:1557-8 D 23 '66
      See also
  Penicillin
ANTIBODIES. See Antigens and antibodies
ANTICHOLINESTERASES
  Amnesia or reversal of forgetting by anti-
  cholinesterase, depending simply on time
  of injection. J. A. Deutsch and S. F.
  Leibowitz. bibliog il Science 153:1017-18
  Ag 26 '66
ANTICOAGULANTS (medicine)
  Hemopoietic colony-forming units in regene-
  rating mouse liver: suppression by anti-
  coagulants. M. L. Varon and L. J. Cole.
  bibliog il Science 153:643-4 Ag 5 '66
  No help for the heart? value of anti-
  coagulant drugs. il Newsweek 68:73 N 7 '66
  Vampire saliva prevents clotting; des-
  mokynase. Sci N 90:448 N 26 '66
ANTI-COLLISION systems. See Aeronautic in-
  struments
ANTI-COMMUNIST measures in the United
  States. See Communism—United States—
  Anti-Communist measures
ANTI-COMMUNIST movements
      Indonesia
  Bali exorcises an evil spirit. D. Kirk.
  Reporter 35:42-3 D 15 '66
  Great purge in Indonesia; slaughter of In-
  donesian Communist party. S. S. King. il
  N Y Times Mag p25+ My 8 '66
      Latin America
  One war that the Communists are losing;
  defeat of Armed forces of national libera-
  tion. il U S News 61:86-8 N 14 '66
ANTI-DEFAMATION league. See B'nai b'rith
  —Anti-defamation league
ANTI-DEPRESSANTS. See Depressants
ANTIDOTES
  Poisons & antidotes. il Changing T 21:29-30
  Ja '67
ANTI-EVOLUTION legislation. See Evolution—
  Laws and legislation
ANTI-FREEZE solutions
  Antifreeze. il Consumer Bul 49:27-9 N '66
ANTIGENS and antibodies
  Allelic antigenic factor inv(a) of the light
  chains of human immunoglobulins: chem-
  ical basis. C. Baglioni and others. bibliog
  il Science 152:1517-19 Je 10 '66
  Antibodies affecting metabolism of chicken
  erythrocytes: examination of schizophrenic
  and other subjects. J. W. Ryan and others.
  bibliog il Science 154:1408-10 Mr 18 '66
  Antibodies to photoproducts of deoxyribonucleic acids irradiated with ultraviolet
  light. L. Levine and others. bibliog il Science 153:1666-7 S 30 '66

ANTIGENS and antibodies—*Continued*

Antibody active sites and immunoglobulin molecules. S. J. Singer and R. F. Doolittle. bibliog il Science 153:13-25 Jl 1 '66

Antibody formation in nonimmune mouse peritoneal cells after incubation in gum containing antigen. A. E. Bussard. bibliog il Science 153:887-8 Ag 19 '66

Antibody-forming cells: population patterns after simultaneous immunization with different isoantigens. R. A. McBride and L. W. Schierman. bibliog il Science 154:655-7 N 4 '66

Antibody molecules: discontinuous heterogeneity of heavy chains; molecules show bands on disc electrophoresis. O. A. Roholt and D. Pressman. bibliog il Science 153: 1257-9 S 9 '66

Antibody synthesis initiated in vitro by paired explants of spleen and thymus. G. C. Saunders and D. W. King. bibliog il Science 151:1390-1 Mr 18 '66

Antigenic correspondence of serum albumins among the primates. A. S. Hafleigh and C. A. Williams, jr. bibliog il Science 151: 1530-5 Mr 25 '66

Antigenic determinants common to human immunoglobulins G and M: importance of conformational antigens. M. Seligmann and others. bibliog il Science 154:790-1 N 11 '66

Antigenic differences in the surfaces of hyphae and rhizoids in allomyces. S. A. Fultz and A. S. Sussman. bibliog il Science 152:785-7 My 6 '66

Antiserum to immunoglobulin A: inhibition of cell-mediated demyelination in tissue culture. G. F. Winkler and B. G. Arnason. bibliog il Science 153:75-6 Jl 1 '66

Association between potassium concentration and serological type of sheep red blood cells. B. A. Rasmusen and J. G. Hall. il Science 151:1551 Mr 25 '66

Blood-group substances. W. M. Watkins. bibliog il Science 152:172-81 Ap 8 '66

Chloramphenicol-specific antibody. R. N. Hamburger. bibliog il Science 152:203-5 Ap 8 '66

Complement-fixing antigens in hamster tumors induced by the Bryan strain of Rous sarcoma virus. M. J. Casey and others. bibliog il Science 151:1986-8 Mr 4 '66

Electrophoretic heterogeneity of polypeptide chains of specific antibodies. R. A. Reisfeld and P. A. Small, jr. bibliog il Science 152: 1253-5 My 27 '66

Fluctuation tests with antibody-forming spleen cell populations. M. Nakano and W. Braun. bibliog il Science 151:336-40 Ja 21 '66

Fluorescent-antibody studies of haplosporidian parasites of oysters in Chesapeake and Delaware Bays. J. H. Barrow, jr. and B. C. Taylor. bibliog il Science 153:1531-3 S 23 '66

Footprints of tumor viruses. F. Rapp and J. L. Melnick. il Sci Am 214:34-41 bibliog (p 143) Mr '66

Gamma-A cold agglutinin: importance of disulfide bonds in activity and structure. B. R. Andersen. bibliog il Science 154:281-3 O 14 '66

Genetically determined antigen of the Ne subgroup of gamma-globulin: detection by precipitin analysis. H. G. Kunkel and others. bibliog il Science 154:1041-3 N 25 '66

Goodbye to infection; laboratory-made antibodies; reprint. W. Sullivan. Sci Digest 59: 71-4 Mr '66

Heat-labile serum factor required for immunofluorescence of polyoma tumor antigens. K. K. Takemoto and others. il Science 153:1122-3 S 2 '66

Homoreactant: a naturally occurring autoantibody in rabbits. W. J. Mandy and L. C. Kormeier. bibliog il Science 154:651-2 N 4 '66

Hormone antibody may make people fat. Sci N 90:25 Jl 9 '66

Immunochemical characterization of polyribonucleotides. J. Panijel and others. bibliog il Science 152:773-5 My 6 '66

Immunochemical studies of submicrosomal membranes from liver of normal and phenobarbital-treated rats. U. Lundkvist and P. Perlmann. bibliog il Science 152:780-2 My 6 '66

Immunoglobulin M allotypes of the rabbit: identification of a second specificity. S. Sell. bibliog il Science 153:641-3 Ag 5 '66

Immunologic maturation in utero: kinetics of the primary antibody response in the fetal lamb. A. M. Silverstein and others. bibliog il Science 154:1675-7 D 30 '66

Light-chain heterogeneity of cold agglutinins. N Costea and others. bibliog il Science 152:1520-1 Je 10 '66

Lipid films as transducers for detection of antigen-antibody and enzyme-substrate reactions. J. Del Castillo and others. bibliog il Science 153:185-8 Jl 8 '66

Lymphoid cells producing antibody against simple haptens: detection and enumeration. B. Merchant and T. Hraba. bibliog il Science 152:1378-9 Je 3 '66

Natural human antibodies to gram-negative bacteria immunoglobulins G. A. and M. I. R. Cohen and L. C. Norins. bibliog il Science 152:1257-9 My 27 '66

Passive sensitization in vitro: effect of antibody concentration on the lag period and velocity. G. A. Feigen and C. B. Nielsen. bibliog il Science 154:676-7 N 4 '66

Prolonged immunosuppression and tumor induction by a chemical carcinogen injected at birth. J. K. Ball and others. bibliog il Science 152:650-1 Ap 29 '66

Protein-polysaccharide loss during endochondral ossification: immunochemical evidence. A. Hirschman and D. D. Dziewiatkowski. bibliog il Science 154:393-5 O 21 '66

Radioautographic and electron-microscopic evidence of rapid uptake of antigen by lymphocytes. S. S. Han and A. G. Johnson. bibliog il Science 153:176-8 Jl 8 '66

Rh factor: prevention of isoimmunization and clinical trial on mothers. V. J. Freda and others. bibliog il Science 151:828-30 F 18 '66

Test tube antibodies resemble natural ones. Sci N 89:278 Ap 16 '66

Virus enemy: with report by R. Campbell and N. Genet. il Life 60:56-69 F 18 '66

See also

Complement fixation

ANTIGONE; drama. See Stinchecum, T.

ANTIGUA (island)

Editor's report: Antigua awakens. M. M. Davis. il Travel 125:39-41 My '66

ANTI-INFLATION measures. See Inflation (finance)

ANTILLES. See West Indies

ANTI-LYMPHOCYTE serum. See Serum

ANTIMALARIALS

Malaria drug promising; cycloguanil pamoate. F. Marley. Sci N 89:211 Ap 2 '66

See also

Chloroquine

ANTI-MATTER. See Matter

ANTIMICROBIAL substances. See Antibiotics

ANTIMISSILE defense systems. See Guided missiles—Defenses

ANTIN, David

Art & information. Art N 65:22-4+ Ap '66

Marchers; Allegory; poems. Poetry 109:18-20 O '66

Warhol: the silver tenement. Art N 65:47-9+ Sum '66

ANTI-NEGRO prejudice. See Race prejudice

ANTIOCH college, Yellow Springs, Ohio

Antioch's challenge and response in teacher education; program at Putney graduate school of education. Putney, Vt. R. P. Fairfield. Sch & Soc 94:160-2 Mr 19 '66

ANTI-POVERTY program, 1964-

Change of emphasis for the poverty war? summary of news conference, November 22, 1966. S. Shriver. il U S News 61:10 D 5 '66

Church and the poverty program. D. M. Kelley. Christian Cent 83:741-4 Je 8 '66; Reply. H. Stroup. 83:938-9 Jl 27 '66

Co-ordinating the Great society. S. K. Bailey. Reporter 34:39-41 Mr 24 '66

Dialogue in Washington; excerpts from Senate hearings. Arch Forum 125:38-40+ O '66

Federal legislation relevant to library anti-poverty efforts; 1966; comp. by P. Winnick. Library J 91:347-53 Ja 15 '66

First-hand report on poverty war; interview. R. S. Shriver. il U S News 60:64-9 F 28 '66

$486,500 in grants for anti-poverty book programs. Pub W 189:83-4 Ap 25 '66

Grand design of the poverty program. N. Glazer. il N Y Times Mag p21+ F 27 '66; Discussion. p21+ Mr 20 '66

Grilled Shriver; annual meeting of C.C.A.P. il Time 87:21 Ap 22 '66

Guaranteed income; address, May 21, 1966. R. Theobald. Vital Speeches 32:573-6 Jl 1 '66

Hard truth; Washington convention disintegrates. Newsweek 67:24 Ap 25 '66

Harlem haven; concerning Ribicoff's subcommittee hearings. K. Crawford. Newsweek 68:28 S 12 '66

How goes the poverty war? B. L. Masse. America 115:281-3 S 17 '66

ANTI-POVERTY program, 1964—*Continued*
If I get up from here and do a little bit, a little bit more's going to come to me; story of mother of six in East St Louis. F. Powledge. il Redbook 127:66-7+ S '66
Is war on poverty becoming war on business? P. Hencke. il Nations Bsns 54:40-1+ Mr '66
Let's remove politics and profit from the war on poverty; address, December 9 1965. D. H. Clausen. Vital Speeches 32:252-4 F 1 '66
Little by little, less and less of the OEO; S. Shriver protests budget cutbacks. New Repub 155:10-11 D 10 '66
Mess in poverty war: here are some cases. il U S News 60:67-9 My 16 '66
Minimum participation; voting for OEO representatives. Reporter 34:17-18+ Mr 24 '66
Mr Shriver and the savage politics of poverty. W. F. Haddad; discussion. Harper 232:6 F '66
Moral basis of the war on poverty. S. Shriver. Christian Cent 83:1531-3 D 14 '66
More glorious war; S. Shriver's aims and schemes. New Repub 154:7-9 Mr 26 '66
More trouble for the war on poverty. il U S News 60:10 Je 13 '66
Negroes tell Congress: poverty war on—. il U S News 61:31 D 19 '66
New deal for an old problem. A. Grant. il Mlle 63:133-5+ Je '66
Poor politics; financial cutbacks. A. Kopkind. New Repub 154:15-17 Je 25 '66
Present danger. il Newsweek 68:21-2 Ag 8 '66
Shriver under fire; CCAP convention. Sr Schol 88:14 Ap 29 '66
Shriver's limited war. S. Lens. Commonweal 84:412-14 Jl 1 '66; Reply. H. Bookbinder. 84:489+ Ag 5 '66
Six-star Sargent; presentation to House poverty subcommittee. il Time 87:28 Mr 18 '66
Spirit of '76; Shriver's ten-year plan. Newsweek 68:22 Jl 4 '66
This month's feature: Congress & the Johnson poverty program. Cong Digest 45:67-96 Mr '66
Time for self-renewal: a special issue on the antipoverty programs; symposium; ed. by P. Winnick. Library J 91:317-53+ Ja 15 '66
Two anti-poverty book projects undertaken; work of National book committee. Pub W 190:40-1 Ag 15 '66
Two-armed Sargent. New Repub 154:9 Ja 29 '66
War within the war. il Time 87:25-9 My 13 '66
Washington should pay taxes to the poor; advantages of a negative income tax. M. D. Reagan. il N Y Times Mag p24-5+ F 20 '66; Discussion. p 19+ Mr 13 '66
Where are the poor? Newsweek 67:21 F 28 '66
Where were the poor on election day? il U S News 60:94 Mr 21 '66
See also
California—Anti-poverty program
Laredo, Tex.—Anti-poverty program
Mississippi—Anti-poverty program
New York (city)—Anti-poverty program
United States—Youth corps

Anecdotes, facetiae, satire, etc.
Now that poverty practice has made us perfect. . . A. H. Sypher. il Nations Bsns 54:31-2 D '66
Pa and ma and LBJ; excerpts from Pa and ma and Mister Kennedy. J. Comstock. Nations Bsns 54:48-9+ Ap '66
Promise-her-anything won't work in Washington. A. H. Sypher. Nations Bsns 54:31-2 Je '66

ANTIQUE airplane association. See Airplanes—Collectors and collecting

ANTIQUE airplanes

Collectors and collecting
See Airplanes—Collectors and collecting

ANTIQUE automobile museums. See Automobile museums

ANTIQUE automobiles

Collectors and collecting
See Automobiles—Collectors and collecting

ANTIQUE wireless association
From out of the past; wireless museums preserve the early days. T. M. Hannah. il Pop Electr 25:68-9 O '66

ANTIQUES
Antique and avant-garde; home of Mr and Mrs André Emmerich. B. Plumb. il N Y Times Mag p44-5 Jl 10 '66
Antiques: questions & answers. T. H. Ormsbee. See issues of House & garden incorporating Living for young homemakers
Antiques, what are they worth? A. R. Roalman. Bet Hom & Gard 44:146-7 Mr '66
Antiquing in Florida. A. G. Peterson. il Hobbies 71:98B-98D My '66
Highfields and its heritage. L. W. Watkins. il Antiques 90:204-7 Ag '66
How to sell what you find in the attic. il Changing T 20:45-7 F '66
Letter from London. J. Stuart. il Antiques 89:272+, 346+, 478+, 652+, 808+ F-Je '66
Living with antiques:
Bryn Mawr home of Mr and Mrs Bertram Dawson Coleman. L. H. Solis-Cohen. il Antiques 89:573-7 Ap '66
David Ross house. B. B. Hyde. il Antiques 89:233-7 F '66
Millbach, the Ohio home of Mr and Mrs Harry S. Bugbee. M. F. Rogers, jr. il Antiques 90:350-3 S '66
Pennsylvania home of Mr and Mrs John W. Batdorf. L. H. Solis-Cohen. il Antiques 90:224-7 Ag '66
Pepperrell mansion, Kittery Point, Maine. J. W. P. Frost. il Antiques 89:368-73 Mr '66
Shaker adventure. C. Upton and H. Upton. il Antiques 90:84-9 Jl '66
Stony Lonesome in Kentucky. E. O. O'Rear. il Antiques 89:851-5 Je '66
Mrs Charles Wrightsman; collector's pursuit of art and perfection; with account by B. Robertson. il Vogue 148:236-41+ O 1 '66
Personal business; antiques are fetching fancier prices. Bsns W p 173-4 Mr 12 '66
See also
Display of antiques, art objects, etc.
Heirlooms

Bibliography
Books about antiques. R. Davidson. See issues of Antiques

Collectors and collecting
American decorative arts in Texas; the Bayou bend collection of the Museum of fine arts. Houston. D. B. Warren. il Antiques 90:796-815 D '66

Exhibitions
Artistic beauty of the centuries; presented by the Art and antique dealers of America. il Antiques 89:670+ My '66
Calendar of shows. See issues of Antiques
Current and coming. See issues of Antiques

Prices
Now a bull market in antiques; why. il U S News 61:62-4 S 5 '66

ANTIQUES, Reproduction of
Turning reproductions into antiques. W. I. Fischman. ily Pop Mech 126:116-20 Jl '66

ANTIQUES shops
How to save money on antiques; excerpt from Antiques you can decorate with. G. Grotz. il Ladies Home J 83:59+ N '66

ANTIQUITIES
See also
Peru—Antiquities

ANTIRADIATION vaccines. See Vaccines

ANTI-RIOT devices. See Police—Equipment and supplies

ANTISEGREGATION demonstrations. See Civil rights demonstrations

ANTI-SEMITISM
Anti-Semitic noises; Austria. Newsweek 67:46 Mr 14 '66
Anti-Semitism's taproot. C. Northcott. Christian Cent 83:1049 Ag 31 '66
Art of anti-Semitism; concerning book called The medieval Jew in the mirror of Christian art. il Time 88:92 D 9 '66
Catholic anti-Semites. J. B. Sheerin. Cath World 203:198-201 Jl '66
Christian beliefs and anti-Semitism, by C. Y. Glock and R. Stark. Review
Christian Cent 83:987-8+ Ag 10 '66. J. K. Hadden; B. Vawter; I. Mowshowitz
Commentary 42:96-9 D '66. S. Monas
Commonweal 84:558-9 S 2 '66. P. H. Furfey
Sat R 49:27 Ag 20 '66. D. S. Harrington
End to the Christian-Jewish dialogue. A. R. Eckardt. Christian Cent 83:360-3, 393-5 Mr 23-30 '66; Reply. R. C. Holtzapple, jr. 83:718 Je 1 '66
Gospels and anti-Semitism; excerpt from A Jew in Christian America. A. Gilbert. Cath World 203:157-60 Je '66

ANTI-SEMITISM—*Continued*
Jews of silence; tr. by N Kozodoy. E. Wiesel. il Sat Eve Post 239:38-40+ N 19 '66
Study proves Negroes not strongly anti-Semitic. Christian Cent 83:1265 O 19 '66
Time for a new vow at Oberammergau. Christian Cent 83:1328-9 N 2 '66
Unforgiving; concerning survey findings of Charles Y. Glock and Rodney Stark. il Newsweek 67:66 My 2 '66
See also
Jews—Persecutions

ANTISEPSIS. See Asepsis and antisepsis

ANTISEPTIC products. See Asepsis and antisepsis

ANTISEPTICS
See also
Mouthwashes

ANTI-SMOG devices. See Automobile engines—Exhaust

ANTI-STRIKE legislation. See Labor laws and legislation—United States

ANTI-SUBMARINE airplanes. See Airplanes, Military

ANTI-SUBMARINE helicopters. See Helicopters—Military applications

ANTI-SUBMARINE warfare. See Submarine warfare

ANTI-SUBMARINE warfare trainer. See Simulators

ANTITRUST division. See United States—Justice, Department of—Antitrust division

ANTITRUST legislation. See Trusts, Industrial—Law

ANTITRYPSIN. See Serum

ANTIUREASE. See Urease

ANTI-VIETNAM demonstrations. See Vietnamese war, 1957-   —Protests, demonstrations, etc. against

ANTIVIRAL proteins. See Interferon

ANTIVIVISECTION. See Vivisection

ANTOINE
C'est la hair. por Time 87:48 My 13 '66
People are talking about ... por Vogue 148:272-3 S 1 '66

ANTOINE, Tamlin C.
Industry to India, a Yank helps out. il pors Ebony 21:83-4+ Mr '66

ANTONOV, Oleg K.
Antonov urges cost accounting in USSR; excerpts from article. por Aviation W 84:103+ Mr 21 '66

ANTONY and Cleopatra; opera. See Barber, S.

ANTS
Fungus-growing ants. N. A. Weber. bibliog il Science 153:587-604 Ag 5 '66
Trails of the leafcutters. J. C. Moser. il Natur Hist 76:32-5 bibliog(p73) Ja '67

ANTUNES, Augusto Tranjano de Azevedo. See Azevedo Antunes, A. T. de

ANTWERP
Antwerp comes of age; foreign chemical plants. il Newsweek 68:72 Jl 4 '66
Antwerp's Texas touch brings in the big ones. il Bsns W p48-9+ F 12 '66
New hub. Time 87:92 Je 24 '66

Galleries and museums
See also
Plantin-Moretus museum

Music
Antwerp; Royal Flemish opera's Ring cycle. L. Mueller. Opera N 31:32 D 31 '66

ANXIETY
Anxiety levels in dreams: relation to changes in plasma free fatty acids. L. A. Gottschalk and others. bibliog il Science 153:654-7 Ag 5 '66
Anxiety slows response; learning deficit. Sci N 90:154 S 3 '66
Anxious child can learn, but what? with study-discussion program, by R. Strang. E. J. LeShan. bibliog il PTA Mag 61:8-10, 35 D '66
Tension and tensions. V. P. McCorry. America 115:234-5 S 3 '66
See also
Fear

ANZUS council
Secretary Rusk meets with Asian leaders; text of Anzus council communique. July 1, 1966. D. Rusk. Dept State Bul 55:175 Ag 1 '66

AOUELLOUL glass. See Glass

APACHE Indians
Geronimo! chief of the most dangerous Apache band: Chiricahuas. E. M. Halliday. il Am Heritage 17:56-63+ Je '66

APACHE trail
Travel notes. R. Joseph. Esquire 66:18+ O '66

APALACHICOLA RIVER
Enjoying the ancient Apalachicola. E. White. il Motor B 118:34-6+ O '66

APARTMENT houses
Bright landmarks on a changing urban scene; New York university project. C. Robinson. il Arch Forum 125:21-9 D '66
Building types study. (cont) il Arch Rec 139:155-72 Ja '66
For the single girl: a new way of life in California; South Bay club, in a Los Angeles suburb. G. Greene. il Ladies Home J 83:58-9+ Jl '66
Happy householders of Halen; housing colony near Bern, Switzerland. R. Schafer. il Arch Forum 124:80-5 Je '66
New steel framing system promises major savings in high-rise apartments. il Arch Rec 139:191-6 Je '66
Pads for singles; South Bay club apartments, Los Angeles. il Time 88:49 Ag 26 '66
Singles swing for landlords; South Bay club apartments, Torrance, Calif. il Bsns W p38+ Mr 5 '66

Condominium plan ownership
Condominium castle for weekend living; Sea Ranch, north of San Francisco in Sonoma County. il Fortune 73:135-7 My '66

Designs and plans
California apartments make skillful use of Hillside sites. il Arch Rec 139:133-40 Mr '66

Electric equipment
Total energy for five apartment groups. il Arch Rec 140:155-7 D '66

Heating and ventilation
Total energy for five apartment groups. il Arch Rec 140:155-7 D '66

APARTMENT leases. See Leases

APARTMENT-office buildings. See Office buildings

APARTMENTS
Building types study. il Arch Rec 139:155-72 Ja '66
Chez Mlle: besting the budget. B. Plumb. il Mlle 64:42-3 Ja '67
First apartment. B. Plumb. il Mlle 62:186-7 F '66
H&G colors in action in a city apartment. il House & Gard 129:130-9 Mr '66
In the grand manner; 18th century French furnishings. R. Reif. il N Y Times Mag p 116-17 S 11 '66
Is that apartment safe from thugs? these precautions will protect you. il Changing T 20:41-2 My '66
Looking for a place to rent? il Changing T 20:35-7 N '66
Midwest to mid-Manhattan. B. Plumb. il N Y Times Mag p64-5 Mr 6 '66
Only the floor plan's the same. B. Plumb. il N Y Times Mag p52-3 Je 19 '66
Space, light, and a garden; home of Mr and Mrs Joseph Olliphant Lambert jr. Dallas. il House & Gard 130:62-9 Jl '66
Two designers' apartments: the constant adventure. il House & Gard 129:110-17 F '66

Anecdotes, facetiae, satire, etc.
How to live in a palazzo. A. Menen. House & Gard 129:132-3+ Je '66

APATITE
Apatite and octa-calcium phosphate: effects of carbon dioxide and halogens on formation. D. R. Simpson. bibliog il Science 154:1660-1 D 30 '66

APCAR, Frederic
Las Vegas scene. W. Como. il por Dance Mag 40:19 S '66

APÉRITIF wines. See Wine

APERITIFS. See Liquors

APES
See also
Chimpanzees
Gorillas

APES as artists. See Animals as artists

APGAR, Virginia
New ways to save your unborn child. Ladies Home J 83:46+ Ag '66
What every mother-to-be should know (cont) Todays Health 44:12+ F; 6+ Mr; 8+ Ap; 16+ My; 16+ Je '66

APPORTIONMENT (election law)—Continued
Third time unlucky; constitutional amendment to overturn one-man, one-vote ruling. Time 87:28 Ap 29 '66
Three-time loser; Dirksen proposal for reapportioning state legislatures fails again. Newsweek 67:19 My 2 '66
See also
Gerrymander
APPRAISAL. See Assessment
APPRAISAL of books. See Book reviews
APPRAISAL of public schools. See Evaluation (education)
APPRENTICES
See also
Employees—Training
APRICOTS
Gibberellin-like substances in the developing apricot fruit. D. I. Jackson and B. G. Coomb. bibliog il Science 154:277-8 O 14 '66
APRONS
Making your own Japanese aprons. il Sunset 137:132+ N '66
Terry towels make fine aprons. C. Houck. il Parents Mag 41:38 F '66
APTECKER, George
Guy with an eye. il U S Camera 29:50-1 Mr '66
APTHEKER, Herbert
Citizen diplomacy. Nation 202:87 Ja 24 '66
APTITUDE tests
Beating the system; tutoring school for union qualifying exams. Newsweek 69:56 Ja 16 '67
Can salesmen be tested? L. Rich. il Duns R 87:40-1+ Mr '66
Job game; about psychological job tests and how to pass them. S. Birmingham. il McCalls 93:76-7+ Jl '66
Just testing, testing, test—. A. P. Eliasberg. il N Y Times Mag p 109+ Mr 20 '66
Test your science aptitude. Sci N L 89.118+ F 19 '66
What's your photo aptitude? test prepared by Famous photographers school, Westport, Conn. il U S Camera 29:48-9+ F '66
APULEIUS, Lucius
Apuleius; Golden ass. K. Rexroth. Sat R 49:15 Jl 2 '66
AQUABOXES. See Electric water coolers
AQUANAUTS
Neon gas used by aquanauts. il Sci N 89:287 Ap 23 '66
Sea lab: man's toe in the deep sea. il Todays Health 44:18-23 F '66
Working for weeks on the sea floor; Conshelf three. J. Y. Cousteau. il Nat Geog Mag 129:498-537 Ap '66
AQUAPLANING
Kick up a spray this weekend; make your own skis or sled. H. Clark. il Pop Mech 126:138-9 Jl '66
AQUARIUM heaters. See Water heaters
AQUARIUMS
New-old village at Sea Life park. il Sunset 138:42 Ja '67
Sea treasure: New York aquarium, Coney Island. R. F. Nigrelli. New Yorker 42:22-3 Ag 27 '66
She's admiring her sea horse. il Sunset 136:135-6 My '66
Taylor Pryors' ocean adventure: Sea life park and Oceanic institute for research. V. Lawford. il Vogue 148:208-11+ N 1 '66
You can't con a porpoise. C. Phinizy. il Sports Illus 24:50-2+ Mr 21 '66
AQUATIC animals. See Marine fauna
AQUATIC herbicides. See Herbicides
AQUATIC life. See Marine biology
AQUATIC plants
Licking the coontail problem; how New Orleans rid its lagoons of obnoxious aquatic plant life. E. F. Laborde. il Parks & Rec 1:174 F '66
Moss man from Missouri; specializing in aquarium plants. S. Althoff and D. Weddle. il Pop Mech 125:112-15 Je '66
See also
Cattails
Chemical control
Forty years of water-weed control; progress from bag dragging to airplane spraying. il Am City 81:102-4 Je '66
AQUATIC sports
Bobbing on the Apple River. S. James. il Pop Mech 126:92-3 Jl '66
Octopus rasslin' is hand-to-hand-to-hand-to-hand. W. L. High. il Pop Mech 125:102-3 My '66

Snorkeling in the Virgin Islands. il Sunset 137:42-3 O '66
Water fun for everyone. R. Pinney. il Parents Mag 41:44-6+ Jl '66
See also
Aquaplaning
Surf riding
Water skis and skiing
AQUEDUCTS
Across the empire, life-bearing arteries of stone. il Life 60:68-71 Je 17 '66
Aqueducts and highways followed the trail of conquest; Sextus Julius Frontinus's structures. il Life 60:62-3 Mr 18 '66
ARAB-Jewish relations. See Jewish-Arab relations
ARAB states
See also
Airlines—Arab states
Kuwait
Foreign relations
Gamble on the Jordan. J. A. Morris, jr. il Nation 204:6-8 Ja 2 '67
Leader alone; Arab unity; Nasser's aims; Faisal's actions. Newsweek 68:40-1+ Ag 8 '66
Plutonium keg; danger of war in the Middle East steadily increasing. Nation 202:170 F 14 '66
Politics
Defining the limit; aims of A. Kosygin's Cairo visit. il Newsweek 67:48 My 30 '66
ARABIAN cookery. See Cookery, Arabian
ARABIAN horses. See Horses
ARABIC civilization. See Civilization, Arabic
ARABS in Israel
Arab refugees: a Zionist view. M. Sykin; reply with rejoinder. R. S. Goldman. Commentary 41:6+ Je '66
ARACHNIDS
See also
Book scorpions
Spiders
ARANSAS national wildlife refuge, Tex. See Wildlife sanctuaries
ARANTES DO NASCIMENTO, Edson
Most famous athlete in the world. P. Axthelm. il pors Sports Illus 25:76-8+ O 24 '66
ARAPAHO Indians
Long way from the buffalo road; excerpt from The Arapaho way, ed. by A. Bass. C. Sweezy. il Am Heritage 17:22-5+ O '66
ARAUCARIA excelsa. See Norfolk Island pine
ARAYA, Enrique
Requiescat in pace; story. Américas 18:29-31 Mr '66
ARBITRAGE
Huge profits out of tiny margins. il Bsns W p 114+ My 28 '66
ARBITRATION, Industrial
Canada
Federal strikes? Canada's solution. U S News 60:88 My 23 '66
United States
Compulsory arbitration in communications. R. L. Tobin. il Sat R 49:55-6 F 12 '66
Compulsory arbitration to settle labor disputes? Sr Schol 88:12-13 F 11 '66
Double arbitration standard; excerpt from paper presented at American assembly. B. Aaron. Mo Labor R 89:1387-8 D '66
Forced arbitration? H. Hazlitt. Newsweek 68:58 Ag 29 '66
How the big strikes are settled. L. Velie. Read Digest 88:135-9 Je '66
Labor feels its oats; deadlock between airlines and machinists. il Bsns W p90-2+ My 14 '66
Only sensible way; need for compulsory arbitration in strikes in public service industries. R. L. Tobin. Sat R 49:45-6 Ag 13 '66; Reply. G. A. Smathers. 49:110 O 8 '66
Public interest rides the rails; negotiations between carriers and railroad unions may get peaceful solution. il Bsns W p 156+ N 5 '66
Why it's hard to stop strikes against the public. U S News 61:70-1 Jl 25 '66
See also
United States—National labor relations board
ARBITRATION, International
Modern international negotiation, by A. Lall. Review
Sat R 50:31-2 Ja 7 '67. A. H. Dean
See also
Peace

ARBOR day
Tree time in Anaheim; community celebrations in Anaheim, Calif. P. A. Deimel. il Parks & Rec 1:218-19 Mr '66

ARBORETUMS
See also
Washington. D.C.—National arboretum

ARBUCKLE, June
Emperor's new clothes; or, The underground is for sleeping. Mlle 63:234 S '66

ARC welding. See Electric welding

ARC welding machines. See Electric welding machines

ARCADES
Shopping streets under roofs of glass. P. Blake. il Arch Forum 124:68-75 Ja '66

ARCHAEOLOGY. See Archeology

ARCHAMBAULT, Reginald D.
(ed) See Dewey, J. Lectures in the philosophy of education: 1899

ARCHDIOCESE of Anchorage, Alaska. See Catholic church—Dioceses

ARCHDIOCESE of Chicago. See Catholic church—Dioceses

ARCHEOLOGICAL photography. See Photography in archeology

ARCHEOLOGICAL research
Archeology and its new technology. F. Rainey and E. K. Ralph. bibliog il Science 153: 1481-91 S 23 '66
Searching for the beginnings of civilized man. G. Bylinsky. il Fortune 74:158-63+ O '66

ARCHEOLOGISTS
See also
Schliemann, H.
Schliemann, S.

ARCHEOLOGY
Archeology in an emergency; inter-agency archaeological salvage program. F. Johnson. bibliog Science 152:1592-7 Je 17 '66
Quest for Camelot. il Time 88:53 Ag 12 '66
Salvage archaeology: saving the past from the present. J. O. Brew. il Nation 203: 117-20 Ag 8 '66
Science in action: choosing a site to dig. S. Gorenstein. Natur Hist 75:64-7 F '66
See also
Excavations (archeology)
Man, Prehistoric
Numismatics, Ancient
Radiation—Archeological applications
Stone age
also subhead Antiquities under names of continents, countries, states, etc. e.g.
Peru—Antiquities

ARCHEOLOGY, Biblical. See Bible—Antiquities

ARCHEOLOGY, Submarine
Ancient ship uncovered; probable Turkish warship discovered at the mouth of Acre harbor. Sci N 90:573 D 31 '66
Excavation, sea style. il Sci N 89:106-7 F 12 '66
Found in the Pacific; carved rock columns and 800-mile crack in the ocean floor. B. Tufty. il Sci N 89:239 Ap 9 '66
Sunken treasure reveals site of Danish fleet. Sci N 90:132 Ag 27 '66

ARCHER, Eugene
Welles captures Cannes. Sat R 49:62-3 Jl 23 '66

ARCHER, Joey
When Emile got his Irish up. M. Kram. il pors Sports Illus 25:14-15 Jl 25 '66

ARCHERY
On taking up archery. G. H. Gillelan. il Outdoor Life 137:18+ Mr '66
See also
Bow and arrow
Fishing with bow and arrow
Hunting with bow and arrow

Equipment
Aim to kill. G. H. Gillelan. il Outdoor Life 137:28+ Ap '66
Archer's Christmas. G. H. Gillelan. il Outdoor Life 138:10+ D '66
Tips on buying archery gear. G. H. Gillelan. il Outdoor Life 138:14+ Jl '66
Treat your gear right. G. H. Gillelan. il Outdoor Life 137:24+ F '66
See also
Bow and arrow

ARCHES of science award. See Seattle—Pacific science center

ARCHIMEDES principle. See Specific gravity

ARCHITECTS
Architect in practice. Arch Rec 139:153-6 F '66
Architecture; campus design; challenge to architects. E. Galantay. Nation 202:789-90 Je 27 '66

Changing patterns of architectural practice. W. B. Foxhall. il Arch Rec 140:241-8 Jl '66
Dancers and architects build kinetic environments; summer workshop, San Francisco. J. Anderson. il Dance Mag 40:52-6+ N '66
Designers of the Record houses of 1966. il Arch Rec 139:120 mid-My '66
Do you understand your new clients? architects in city renewal; interview, ed. by E. Goble. W. L. Slayton. Arch Rec 140:9-10 Ag '66
How to work with an architect. W. Houseman. House & Gard 130:124-5+ Ag '66
Joint-venture practice. il Arch Rec 139:99+ My '66
Man with a billion on the drawing board; E. Stone. il Bsns W p 124-6+ O 8 '66
Old World's new blueprints; American architectural firms with headquarters in Rome. il Newsweek 67:76-8 Mr 7 '66
Overlooked bargain: bright young men with designs on the future. il Fortune 74:124-6 Jl 1 '66
Practical pressures pushing the profession; excerpts from address, with reply by E. Goble. R. F. Hastings. Arch Rec 140:9 O '66
See also
Doxiadis, C. A.
Harrison, W. K.
Portman, J. C.
White, S.
Women as architects

Licenses and registration
Interstate practice: legal and accounting problems. S. Spencer; C. M. Sapers. Arch Rec 140:104-5+ N '66

Training
See Architectural education

ARCHITECTS, Landscape. See Landscape gardening

ARCHITECTURAL acoustics. See Acoustics, Architectural

ARCHITECTURAL conferences
On the calendar. See issues of Architectural record

ARCHITECTURAL criticism
Criticism is dead: long live criticism. E. Goble. il Arch Rec 140:9-10 Jl '66

ARCHITECTURAL decoration. See Decoration and ornament, Architectural

ARCHITECTURAL design. See Architecture

ARCHITECTURAL details. See Architecture—Details

ARCHITECTURAL drawing
Drawings by Louis Sullivan; from the Frank Lloyd Wright collection, Avery library, Columbia university. il Arch Rec 139:147-54 Mr '66

ARCHITECTURAL education
Final word about the future: architectural education needs to grow closer to the profession to supply the leadership required by changing times. J. Barnett. il Arch Rec 140:249-50 Jl '66
Let's make it real. B. Thompson. Arch Rec 139:107-9 Ja '66

ARCHITECTURAL firms
Affleck, Desbarats, Dimakopoulos, Lebensold & Sise. il Arch Rec 139:137-52 F '66
Architect in practice. Arch Rec 139:153-6 F '66
Associated practice: ground rules and variations. R. Roth. Arch Rec 140:101 N '66
See also
Smith, Hinchman and Grylls associates, incorporated

ARCHITECTURAL glass. See Glass, Structural

ARCHITECTURAL plans. See Architecture, Domestic—Designs and plans

ARCHITECTURAL record (periodical)
Architectural record through seventy-five years. T. Goble. il Arch Rec 140:207-14 Jl '66
Criticism is dead: long live criticism. E. Goble. il Arch Rec 140:9-10 Jl '66
Forward progress in design and printing. E. Goble. il Arch Rec 139:9-10 Ja '66
Record houses 1956-1966; decade of innovation. il Arch Rec 139:125-36 F '66
Record houses of 1966; with introd. by H. L. Smith, jr. il Arch Rec 139:39-121 mid-My '66

ARCHITECTURAL schools. See Architectural education

ARCHITECTURE
Avant-garde anachronist; L. I. Kahn's creations. il Time 87:70-1 Je 10 '66
Buildings in the news. See issues of Architectural record

ARCHITECTURE—*Continued*
Environment as design inspiration. B. Thompson. il Arch Rec 139:110-20 Ja '66
Focus; monthly review of notable buildings. See issues of Architectural forum
Inside out; P. Rudolph and J. Johansen's functioning façades. il Time 87:72 Mr 11 '66
Monthly review of events and ideas. See issues of Architectural forum
Newest projects of Gunnar Birkerts. G. Birkerts. il Arch Rec 140:93-4 Ag '66
Projects by Gunnar Birkerts. il Arch Rec 140:95-106 Ag '66
Repetition without monotony. M. Goldfinger. il Arch Forum 124:40-5 Mr '66
Structure & design; ed. by W. McQuade and P. Herrera. See issues of Fortune

See also
Airport buildings
Building
Church architecture
City planning
Clubhouses
College architecture
Courthouses
Domes
Hotels, taverns, etc.
Library architecture
Marine structures
Park buildings
Priories
Railroads—Stations
Remodeling (architecture)
Theological schools
    also subhead Architecture under various subjects, e.g. Laboratories—Architecture; *also* subhead Architecture under names of cities, e.g. Chicago—Architecture

Anecdotes, facetiae, satire, etc.
Cracks on the facade; drawings. A. Dunn. Horizon 8:116-20 Wint '66

Bibliography
Books. See issues of Architectural forum
Required reading. See issues of Architectural record

Competitions, awards, etc.
A.I.A. selects annual honor awards. il Arch Rec 140:41-3 Jl '66
Awards, etc (title varies) See issues of Architectural forum
Bureau of higher education honors twenty-nine projects in its new design awards program. il Arch Rec 140:42-3 N '66
Record houses 1956-1966; decade of innovation. il Arch Rec 139:125-36 F '66
Three old-timers off to a fresh start; American institute of architects-Sunset magazine Western home awards. il Sunset 136:78-85 Mr '66

Composition, proportion, etc.
Academic tradition: the orders, the module, and the art of the plan. il Arch Rec 140:174-5 Jl '66

Conservation and restoration
Architecture; Cavaglieri's plans for Astor library. E. Galantay. Nation 202:500-2 Ap 25 '66
Community action in the West: Chatsworth moves its church. il Sunset 136:154 Ap '66
Cultural tourism. il UNESCO Courier 19:10-12+ D '66
Eye on past and future; urban problems of the preservation of the historic. C. J. McNaspy. America 115:100-1 Jl 23 '66
Historic preservation U.S.A: some significant dates. C. E. Peterson. il Antiques 89:229-32 F '66
Must this mansion be destroyed? F. E. Church's Olana. il Life 60:64-77+ My 13 '66
New family heirloom; Federal house in Sag Harbor, L.I. B. Plumb. il N Y Times Mag p 130-1 N 20 '66
Notes and comment; proposals for saving historic buildings. New Yorker 42:31 Ap 9 '66
Our embattled landmarks. A. Balk. Sat R 49:18 Je 25 '66
Preservation 1966. B. S. Delaney. il Antiques 90:526 O '66
Preserving the significant past-current federal policy and a local example. il Arch Rec 140:202-3 Jl '66
Restoration in Independence Hall: a continuum of historic preservation. L. H. Nelson. il Antiques 90:64-8 Jl '66
Restoring the past puts life in the till; restaurants the biggest draws. il Bsns W p 190-2 S 24 '66
Stanford White, updated; classic revival house, Kings Point. B. Plumb. il N Y Times Mag p36-7 Jl 31 '66

They bring back magic yesterdays; preservationists. K. Detzer. il Read Digest 88:160-5 Mr '66
Will salvation spoil the Dodge house? D. S. Brown. il Arch Forum 125:68-71 O '66
See also
Old Sturbridge Village, Mass.

Designs and plans
Beyond the individual building. il Arch Rec 140:161-72 S '66
Last works of Le Corbusier. J. Barnett. il Arch Rec 139:187-94 Ap '66
Relational complexes in architecture. C. Alexander and others. il Arch Rec 140:185-90 S '66
Reorganization for better design; with introd. by R. F. Hastings. il Arch Rec 140:177-88 O '66
Science and technology as a design influence; with introduction by J. S. Hornbeck. il Arch Rec 140:149-70 Jl '66
Search for appropriate form. il Arch Rec 139:127-40 My '66
See also
Architecture, Domestic—Designs and plans

Details
Architectural details (cont) il Arch Rec 139:121-32 Ja '66
See also
Cupolas
Façades

Exhibitions
See also
Montreal—Worlds fair, 1967—Architecture

History
Changing job to be done. il Arch Rec 140:215-23 Jl '66

Modular design
See Modular coordination (architecture)

Philosophy
Architects on architecture; excerpts, ed. by P. Heyer. Arch Forum 125:66-9+ N '66
Grotto for meditation. F. Kiesler. il Craft Horiz 26:22-7 Jl '66
New York's attack on design mediocrity. E. Goble. Arch Rec 140:9 N '66
Packaged society and its architecture. E. Goble. Arch Rec 140:9 S '66
Seventy-five years of architectural growth. E. Goble. Arch Rec 139:9 Je '66

Social aspects
New age of architecture. Arch Rec 140:147-8 Jl '66
Real meaning of modernism. J. Barnett. il Arch Rec 140:182-8 Jl '66

Study and teaching
Architecture for junior high. C. McMillen. il Design 67:36-7 Mr '66
Battleground of the spirit. E. R. Kohlberg. il Mlle 63:162-3+ My '66
See also
Architectural education

Africa
Old World's new blueprints; American architectural firms with headquarters in Rome. il Newsweek 67:76-8 Mr 7 '66

Australia
See also
Sydney, Australia—Architecture

Canada
Beyond the individual building. il Arch Rec 140:161-72 S '66
See also
Montreal—Architecture

Cuba
Cluster of bubbles; Cuba's school of plastic arts. il Arch Forum 124:80-5 Ja '66

England
See also
Nonsuch palace, England

Finland
Printing plant for Wellin & Göös, Tapiola, Finland. il Arch Rec 140:156-7 N '66

France
See also
Paris—Architecture

India
Louis Kahn in India: an old order at a new scale; Indian institute of management, Ahmedabad. J. Bailey. il Arch Forum 125:39-47 Jl '66
See also
Temples—India

ARCHITECTURE—*Continued*

Israel

Art that history shaped. K. Kuh. il Sat R 49:17-24 Ja 29 '66

Italy

See also
Florence—Architecture

Latin America

Space, baroque, and Indians. G. Gasparini. il Américas 18:19-25 My '66

Lebanon

Fresh spring of ideas bubbling in an ancient land. D. Otis. il House & Gard 130:178-83+ D '66

Mexico

Mexico builds. F. L. Phelps. il Américas 18:26-9 My '66

Middle East

Old World's new blueprints: American architectural firms with headquarters in Rome. il Newsweek 67:76-8 Mr 7 '66

Netherlands

See also
Amsterdam, Netherlands—Architecture

New Mexico

See also
Santa Fe, N.M.—Architecture

Pakistan

Mogul modern; designs of E. D. Stone. il Time 88:56 Ag 12 '66

South Africa

Office complex gives a new scale; Carlton centre complex, Johannesburg. il Arch Rec 140:166-7 N '66
See also
Johannesburg—Architecture

Switzerland

Cluster of huts; Swiss high school. il Arch Forum 124:86-91 Ja '66

Turkey

See also
Mosques

United States

America's architectural nightmare: the motorized megalopolis. V. Scully. Holiday 39:94-5+ Mr '66
Buildings in the news. See issues of Architectural record
Neo-Egyptian style in American architecture. R. G. Carrott. il Antiques 90:482-8 O '66
Splendid world of Stanford White; with photographs by T. Frissell and account by A. Saarinen. Life 61:87-101+ S 16 '66
Ten buildings that climax an era; Fortune's current selections for the ten best buildings. D. Haskell. il Fortune 74:156-62 D '66
See also
Architecture, Domestic—United States
also subhead Architecture under names of cities, e.g. St Louis—Architecture

ARCHITECTURE, African
Africa: new U.S. design direction. J. Peter. il Look 30:54-7 Mr 8 '66
One-man village; daring three part house inspired by an African compound; East Hampton, L.I. il House & Gard 129:150-61+ Mr '66

ARCHITECTURE, American
Richardson's North Easton. L. J. Homolka. il Arch Forum 124:72-7 My '66
Search for appropriate form. il Arch Rec 139:127-40 My '66
See also
Architecture, Cape Cod

History

American architecture since 1891. il Arch Rec 140:172-3 Jl '66

ARCHITECTURE, Baroque
Space, baroque, and Indians. G. Gasparini. Américas 18:19-25 My '66

ARCHITECTURE, Cape Cod
Spirit of '76. B. Plumb. il N Y Times Mag p 104-5 My 1 '66

ARCHITECTURE, Domestic
Atrium house surrounds its outdoor living, completely private on a crowded site. R. H. Kruse. il Bet Hom & Gard 45:70-1 Ja '67
High hopes for a new house. L. Wainwright. Life 61:18 Jl 15 '66

House that Jim built: shell homes. R. Levy. Duns R 87:51-2 My '66
Pavilion house surrounds itself with outdoor living. J. A. Hufnagel. il Bet Hom & Gard 45:72-3 Ja '67
People bridge, the auto bridge, the bridge stair, the roof bridge. il Sunset 137:92-5 O '66
See also
Beach architecture
Breezeways
Country houses
Houses, Remodeled
Pavilions
Summer homes
Tenement houses
Vacation houses

Competitions

See Architecture—Competitions

Conservation and restoration

See Architecture—Conservation and restoration

Designs and plans

Award-winning home with lasting charm; colonial type home. il Parents Mag 41:104-9 S '66
Five houses with fresh ideas. il Good H 162:136-42 My '66
House in the South. il Arch Rec 139:142-3 Je '66
Houses by Breuer: laboratory for design. M. Breuer. il Arch Rec 140:125-36 N '66
How to add lasting enjoyment to your home; symposium. il Bet Hom & Gard 44:36-59 Ag '66
How to plan a home you'll always like; interview, ed. by R. Martens. B. Tarke and L. Tarke. il Farm J 90:82+ N '66
How to work with an architect. W. Houseman. House & Gard 130:124-5+ Ag '66
Ideas in houses (cont) il Life 60:70-3+ Ja 28; 84-7+ F 11; 104-7+ Ap 1; 116-19+ My 6; 108-11+ Je 24; 61:74-7+ Ag 5; 90-3+ S 23; 140-4+ D 9 '66
Lower level is up to you! N. Seney. il Bet Hom & Gard 44:60-1 F '66
Open, but private. N. Seney. il Bet Hom & Gard 44:42+ O '66
Record houses 1956-1966; decade of innovation. il Arch Rec 139:125-36 F '66
Record houses of 1966; with introd. by H. L. Smith, jr. il Arch Rec 139:39-121 mid-My '66
Simple house with magnificent style. N. Seney. il Bet Hom & Gard 44:72-5+ N '66
Six houses from abroad. il Arch Rec 139:149-54 Ja '66
Two for the size of one. N. Seney. il Bet Hom & Gard 44:66-9 Je '66
2,000 square feet of comfort and convenience. N. Seney. il Bet Hom & Gard 44:60-3 S '66
Why build high? il Sunset 136:104-7 My '66

Exhibitions

40 under 40, young designs in living; American federation of arts gallery. B. Plumb. il N Y Times Mag p96-7+ Ap 24 '66
See also
Montreal—Worlds fair, 1967—Architecture

Alabama

Daring house, emphatically contemporary; columned whiteness of the old South; Athens. il House & Gard 129:186-93 Ap '66

Arizona

Built with tile and burnt adobe at home in the desert south of Tucson. il Sunset 138:84-5 Ja '67
House for the desert; Paradise Valley. il Sunset 137:82-4 S '66
Living house and separate sleeping house built for desert comfort; Carefree. il Sunset 137:46-7 Jl '66

Arkansas

Escape house high and low; C. Goodfellow-B. Shaheen house in the Ozarks. il Life 60:108-11+ Je 24 '66
Unusual house for an unusual site. il Arch Rec 140:193-6 O '66

Austria

Viennese suburbia. B. Plumb. il N Y Times Mag p 106-7+ O 23 '66

California

Browder residence. Burbank, California. il Arch Rec 139:74-5 mid-My '66
California: second homes spare the land. J. Peter. il Look 30:84-5 Je 28 '66

ARCHITECTURE, Domestic—California—Cont.

Cavalier residence, Marin County, California. il Arch Rec 139:56-9 mid-My '66

Cool, elegant square; steel and glass used. Rosens' house, Los Angeles. il Life 60:104-7+ Ap 1 '66

Development house, Belvedere, California. il Arch Rec 139:100-1 mid-My '66

Development house, San Rafael, California. il Arch Rec 139:88-9 mid-My '66

Fine round of woodwork; the Art Espenet Carpenter's circular house. il Life 61:140-4+ D 9 '66

Great hang-out! right over a canyon. C. Gunther. il Pop Mech 125:116-17 F '66

Ingenious houses for young families; three houses. il House & Gard 129:156-65 My '66

Mountain pavilion makes use of local materials. il Arch Rec 139:161-4 My '66

Singles swing for landlords; South Bay club apartments, Torrance. il Bsns W p38+ Mr 5 '66

This old-timer in Ross gained a new family room and a matching patio. il Sunset 136:84-5 Mr '66

Villa with a built-in whimsy. il Life 61:90-3+ S 23 '66

West coast casual. B. Plumb. il N Y Times Mag p46-7 Je 26 '66

Caribbean Region

Island bounty. il House & Gard 131:120-9 Ja '67

Colorado

Dubrow residence, Golden, Colorado. il Arch Rec 139:80-3 mid-My '66

Glassman residence, Arapahoe County, Colorado. il Arch Rec 139:96-9 mid-My '66

House whose strength is in the roof. il Arch Rec 139:215-18 Ap '66

Round home moored to a hill; the Volsky house. il Life 61:74-7 Ag 5 '66

Connecticut

Comfort for a triple life. il House & Gard 131:112-19 Ja '67

Johnson residence, Old Lyme, Connecticut. il Arch Rec 139:106-9 mid-My '66

Private residence in New Canaan, Conecticut. il Arch Rec 139:114-19 mid-My '66

Stillman house. M. Breuer. il Arch Rec 140:126-9 N '66

Warehouse for weekends; warehouse in Connecticut restored. B. Plumb. il N Y Times Mag p76-7+ Mr 13 '66

Finland

House that belongs to history; E. Saarinen's Hvitträsk. A. L. Huxtable. il N Y Times Mag p64-5+ F 13 '66

Florida

How a cut-up cottage yielded space unlimited; a typical unpretentious Florida cottage. il House & Gard 130:92-5 Ag '66

Pavilions by the water; Slater vacation home in Boca Raton. il Life 60:84-7+ F 11 '66

Small gem of a house where reason and poetry meet. il House & Gard 130:166-71 D '66

Williamson residence, Ponte Vedra Beach, Florida. il Arch Rec 139:110-13 mid-My '66

Hawaii

Doris Duke's shangri-la. V. Lawford. il Vogue 148:224-9+ N 1 '66

Illinois

Romantic house of sunlit arches; H&G'S Hallmark house for 1966. il House & Gard 129:89-99 F '66

Simmen residence, Lake Forest, Illinois. il Arch Rec 139:102-5 mid-My '66

Iowa

Schramm residence, Burlington, Iowa. il Arch Rec 139:64-7 mid-My '66

Italy

How to live in a palazzo. A. Menen. House & Gard 129:132-3+ Je '66

Living like a knight; summer retreat by Beatrice Monti. B. Plumb. il N Y Times Mag p72-3 Je 12 '66

Long Island, N.Y.

Africa: new U.S. design direction. J. Peter. il Look 30:54-7 Mr 8 '66

Architect achieves drama and economy in her own house. il Arch Rec 140:189-92 O '66

Bunshaft residence, East Hampton, New York. il Arch Rec 39:40-5 mid-My '66

Cylinders and cubes for building blocks. B. Plumb. il N Y Times Mag p60-1 Ap 10 '66

Geometry by the sea. il Arch Forum 124:52-5 Ap '66

One-man village; daring three part house inspired by an African compound; East Hampton. il House & Gard 129:150-61+ Mr '66

Wide, open spaces. B. Plumb. il N Y Times Mag p 134-5+ D 4 '66

Maryland

Development house, Bethesda, Maryland. il Arch Rec 139:50-1 mid-My '66

Neuman residence, Baltimore County, Maryland. il Arch Rec 139:84-7 mid-My '66

Massachusetts

All the features a good vacation house should have. N. Seney. il Bet Hom & Gard 44:82-3 Mr '66

House that opens outward; New Seabury. il House & Gard 130:186-95 S '66

Lyman residence, Dover, Massachusetts. il Arch Rec 139:90-5 mid-My '66

1,580-square-foot house by the editors of Better homes and gardens; Cape Cod. N. Seney and R. Kruse. il Bet Hom & Gard 44:60-7+ Ap '66

Private residence, Martha's Vineyard Island, Massachusetts. il Arch Rec 139:46-9 mid-My '66

Snail house; Berkshire County. il Arch Forum 125:84-7 Jl '66

Mexico

In Acapulco: a pavilion by the sea. il House & Gard 131:98-103 Ja '67

Three tiers of Pacific vistas; vacation haven of Warren Avis, Acapulco Bay. il Life 60:116-19+ My 6 '66

Minnesota

Pillsbury residence, Wayzata, Minnesota. il Arch Rec 139:68-73 mid-My '66

Netherlands

Van Der Wal house; Amsterdam. M. Breuer. il Arch Rec 140:130-1 N '66

New Jersey

Axelrod residence, New Jersey. il Arch Rec 139:60-3 mid-My '66

Remodeling on a grand scale. B. Plumb. il N Y Times Mag p 170-2 N 13 '66

New York (state)

In a New York town house, an elegant sequence of color moods. il House & Gard 130:100-5 Ag '66

See also
Architecture, Domestic—Long Island, N.Y.

Oregon

Family planning; R. A. Campbells house in Portland, Ore. B. Plumb. il N Y Times Mag p 116-17 O 9 '66

House of seven children. il House & Gard 130:218-27 O '66

Pennsylvania

See also
Ryan homes, incorporated

Spain

Bold new style of Spain; home of Paul and Karen Radkai. J. Peter. il Look 30:63-5 N 1 '66

Switzerland

Happy householders of Halen. R. Schafer. il Arch Forum 124:80-5 Je '66

Koerfer house; Moscia, Tessin. M. Breuer. il Arch Rec 140:132-3 N '66

Texas

Bassett residence, Nassau Bay, Texas. il Arch Rec 139:52-5 mid-My '66

Cloistered house in Texas. il Arch Rec 140:191-4 S '66

Collectors' house: the De Menils' affair with art. J. J. Sweeney. il Vogue 147:184-93+ Ap 1 '66

Good living in Houston: at home beside the bayou. W. McQuade. il Fortune 74:110-15 Jl 1 '66

How to build a quiet haven on a noisy corner; suburb of River Oaks, Houston. il House & Gard 130:200-5+ S '66

Imaginative two-story spaces dramatize low-budget house. il Arch Rec 140:129-32 D '66

Texas mansion. il Ebony 21:107-10 F '66

Thailand

House of the happy spirit; Thai house of J. H. W. Thompson in Bangkok. il Vogue 147:142-7 Mr 15 '66

ARCHITECTURE, Domestic—*Continued*

United States

Domestic vernacular: comfort, convenience, and integration with landscape. il Arch Rec 140:180-1 Jl '66

Living and sleeping wing for parents! il Bet Hom & Gard 44:54-5 Ag '66

Town houses are in. il Newsweek 67:96+ My 9 '66

View of the water: American palaces by the sea. J. T. Maher. il Holiday 40:48-53+ Jl '66

See also
Architecture. Cape Cod

Virginia

Faulkner residence, McLean, Virginia. il Arch Rec 139:76-9 mid-My '66
See also
Monticello (historic house)

Washington (state)

Cedar and glass build a dramatic house in the Pacific Northwest. il House & Gard 130:258-65+ N '66

Here's a happy marriage of outdoors and indoors behind a sheltering wall; Vancouver. il Sunset 137:70-3 D '66

This Seattle remodel won an A.I.A.-Sunset honor award. il Sunset 136:80-1 Mr '66

Three-level living on a Spokane hillside. il Sunset 137:100-1 Jl '66

Wisconsin

Log houses in Wisconsin. R. W. E. Perrin. il Antiques 89:867-71 Je '66

ARCHITECTURE, Ecclesiastical. See Church architecture

ARCHITECTURE, Egyptian
Neo-Egyptian style in American architecture. R. G. Carrott. il Antiques 90:482-8 O '66

ARCHITECTURE, Fantastic
Legacy of Simon Rodia; towers in the Watts section of Los Angeles. L. Barry. il Pop Phot 59:34 O '66

ARCHITECTURE, Finnish
Aalto revisited; with account by B. Spring. il Arch Forum 124:70-80 Ap '66

ARCHITECTURE, Hotel. See Hotels, taverns, etc.

ARCHITECTURE, Italian
Palladio was not Palladian. P. Schneider. il Horizon 8:56-71 Spr '66

ARCHITECTURE, Landscape. See Landscape gardening

ARCHITECTURE, Modern
New meaning of modern architecture. J. Barnett. il Arch Rec 140:171-88 Jl '66
Pillsbury residence, Wayzata, Minnesota. il Arch Rec 139:68-73 mid-My '66

History

Real meaning of modernism. J. Barnett. il Arch Rec 140:182-8 Jl '66

ARCHITECTURE, Roman
Feats in concrete raised colossal structures; baths of Caracalla; construction technique. il Life 60:60-3 Mr 18 '66
Romans: 1300 years; great men and their deeds. il Life 60:36-9 Mr 11 '66

ARCHITECTURE, Samoan
Far Pacific: a new frontier for architecture. E. K. Thompson. il Arch Rec 140:101-10 D '66

ARCHITECTURE, Spanish
See also
Architecture, Domestic—Spain

ARCHITECTURE, Venetian. See Architecture, Italian

ARCHITECTURE, Victorian
Where Victorian still reigns: Aspen, Colo. B. Plumb. il N Y Times Mag p 116-17+ O 2 '66

ARCHITECTURE in art
Gothic age revisited. C. J. Alkema. il Design 67:22-5 My '66

ARCHIVES
Heritage of the past; the custody and preservation of cultural values. G. de Zéndegui. il Américas 18:1 Je '66
See also
Documents
Oral history

United States

Wagner to head New York library for papers to the presidents. Library J 91:3140+ Je 15 '66
See also
United States—National archives

ARCINIEGAS, Germán
Two decades in the world of culture. UNESCO Courier 19:30-1+ Jl '66

ARCTANDER, Erik
Take-along trail bikes add vacation fun. Pop Sci 188:166-9+ My '66

ARCTIC exploration
Tomorrow, which world? W. J. Coughlin. Miss & Roc 18:46 Ja 24 '66
See also
Antarctic exploration

ARCTIC foxes. See Foxes

ARCTIC OCEAN
Arctic current watched. Sci N 89:398 My 21 '66
Diatoms and the ecological conditions of their growth in sea ice in the Arctic Ocean. H. Meguro and others. bibliog Science 152:1089-90 My 20 '66

ARCTIC REGIONS
See also
Alaska—Description and travel
Aleutian Islands
Eskimos
Greenland
Hunting—Arctic Regions
Ice—Polar Regions

ARCTIC research. See Polar research

ARCTIC terns. See Terns

ARDEN, Elizabeth
Hold fast to life & youth. pors Time 88: 65-6 O 28 '66
Merchant of beauty. il por Newsweek 68: 106 O 31 '66
Obituary
Life il pors 61:40D O 28 '66

ARDEN, John
Serjeant Musgrave's dance. Criticism
America 114:605 Ap 23 '66
Commentary 41:75 Je '66
Commonweal 84:110+ Ap 15 '66
Life 60:12 Ap 1 '66
Nation 202:372-4 Mr 28 '66
New Yorker 42:162-3 Mr 19 '66
Newsweek il 67:98 Mr 21 '66
Sat R 49:45 Mr 26 '66
Sat R 49:43 Ap 23 '66
Time 87:80 Mr 18 '66

ARDOIN, John
G&S: after the carpets. Sat R 49:69+ Ap 16 '66
Gilbert and Sullivan: two views. Sat R 49: 127+ Mr 12 '66
Lucia and the LP. Sat R 49:57 My 28 '66
Purcell in Missouri. Sat R 49:49+ Je 18 '66
(ed) See Di Filippi, A. Miami milestone

ARDREY, Robert
Drive for territory; excerpts from The territorial imperative. Life 61:40-7+ Ag 26 '66
Man is a territorial animal; excerpts from The territorial imperative. Life 61:50-4+ S 2 '66
about
Provocateur in anthropology. G. P. Hunt. por Life 61:3 Ag 26 '66

ARDURA, Ernesto
Hernán Cortez and the Mexican Iliad. Américas 18:23-31 Ag '66

AREA studies
American studies abroad: culture and foreign policy; address; with questions and answers. R. E. Spiller. bibliog f Ann Am Acad 366:1-16 Jl '66

AREA vocational schools. See Trade schools

ARECES, Elena
José Toledano, Town Hall. M. Marks. Dance Mag 40:33 N '66

ARECIBO telescope. See Radio telescope

ARENA stage. See Washington, D.C.—Theater

ARENAS
See also
New York (city)—Madison Square Garden

ARENDT, Hannah
Profiles. New Yorker 42:68-70+ N 5 '66

AREQUIPA, Peru
Arequipa. E. Hosmann. il Américas 18:24-9 N '66

ARETINO, Pietro
Divine Aretino, by J. Cleugh. Review
Sat R por 49:47 Ap 16 '66. R. J. Clements

ARFONS, Art
Duel with death on the salt. B. Ottum. il por Sports Illus 25:28-31 N 28 '66
Nightmare on the Flats. il Time 88:63 N 25 '66

ARGALI hunting
I hunt Mongolia's argali. G. H. Landreth. il Outdoor Life 138:32-5+ S '66

ARIZONA state university, Tempe
Oasis in Arizona; Charles Trumbull Hayden library. K. T. Slack. il Library J 91:5883-5 D 1 '66
ARKANSAS
See also
Architecture, Domestic—Arkansas
Education—Arkansas
Fishing—Arkansas
Prisons—Arkansas

Politics and government
Another face of Orval Faubus. R. Reed. il N Y Times Mag p44-5+ O 9 '66
Arkansas: the rage of the rednecks. T. Dearmore. il Reporter 35:24-8 O 20 '66
Different kind of Johnson. il Time 88:22 Ag 19 '66
Opportunity regained. il Time 88:24-8 D 2 '66
Squealing at the lick log; gubernatorial race. Time 88:33-4 N 4 '66
Within reach; threat to Democrat rule. Time 88:23 Ag 5 '66
ARKANSAS. University, Fayetteville
College or career for dancers? University of Arkansas' answer. E. Stodelle. il Dance Mag 40:56-9 F '66
ARKIN, Alan
Alan Arkin is coming. pors Life 61:33-4+ Jl 22 '66
about
Alan Arkin: matchless maskmaker. M. Gussow. por Holiday 40:91-5+ O '66
Child of the city. il por Newsweek 68:96+ Jl 18 '66
ARLECCHINO; opera. See Busoni, F.
ARLEDGE, Roone
It's sport, it's money, it's TV; ed. by G. Rogin. Sports Illus 24:92-4+ Ap 25 '66
about
Jackelope hunter. Sports Illus 24:94 Ap 25 '66
ARLEN, Michael J.
Air. New Yorker 42:219-20 O 1; 200-2 O 15; 196-8 O 29; 196-7 N 12; 219-20+ N 26; 140+ D 10; 46+ D 24 '66; 80+ Ja 7 '67
George Wein: jazz by the sea. Holiday 40: 91-2+ Jl '66
ARLINGTON, Va.
National cemetery
Banned from Valhalla; R. G. Thompson. Nation 202:171 F 14 '66
Beyond the pale; burial of R. Thompson. il Newsweek 67:22+ F 7 '66
Blackballed from Arlington; R. G. Thompson. Time 87:30 F 4 '66
See also
Kennedy, J. F.—Tomb
ARLINGTON classic. See Horse racing
ARLINGTON national cemetery. See Arlington, Va.—National cemetery
ARM, Walter
Speaking out. por Sat Eve Post 239:12+ My 7 '66
ARM grafting. See Transplantation of organs, tissues, etc.
ARMAMENTS
Are we on the brink of another arms race? R. L. Gilpatric. il N Y Times Mag p32-3+ Ja 15 '67
Competition for new weapons; arms race in the Middle East. P. Ben. New Repub 154: 13-14 Je 4 '66
See also
Preparedness, Military
ARMAN
Gallery for young people. C. B. Johnson. il Sch Arts 66:42 S '66
ARMBRISTER, Trevor
Embattled crusader of Conway County. Sat Eve Post 239:25-9+ N 19 '66
GI's best friend. Sat Eve Post 239:93-7 Mr 12 '66
Loser makes it big. Sat Eve Post 240:26-9 Ja 14 '67
Octopus in the state house; report. Sat Eve Post 239:25-9+ F 12 '66
Search for the invisible killer. Sat Eve Post 239:92-4+ D 3 '66
Very phony profession. Sat Eve Post 239: 100-2+ O 8 '66
ARMCO steel corporation
Armco peps up service by overhauling itself. il Bsns W p96-8+ F 26 '66
ARMED forces
Officers, Retired
See Retired military officers
ARMED forces of national liberation. See Political parties—Venezuela

ARMED forces qualification test. See Intelligence tests
ARMENIA
Antiquities
From a forgotten kingdom; with photographs. S. Tomkievicz. Horizon 8:86-9 Spr '66
ARMENIAN literature
Printing monks of Venice; Armenian Catholic monks of the Mechitarian order, printers of Books in Armenian. H. R. Lottman. Pub W 190:110-11 D 5 '66
ARMENIANS
Unremembered genocide; murder of Armenians in Turkey during 1915-1916. M. Housepian. Commentary 42:55-61 S '66; Discussion. 42:7-8+ D '66
ARMENIANS in the United States
Our greatest man. W. Saroyan. il Sat Eve Post 239:80-1 Mr 12 '66
ARMIES
Officers
See also
Generals
ARMISTICE, Korean. See Korean war, 1950-1953—Peace and mediation
ARMKNECHT, Richard F.
Giant redwoods; poem. Farm J 90:124 Mr '66
ARMORED warfare. See Mechanization, Military
ARMORIES
Armory: demolition of the old 8th regiment armory, New York. New Yorker 42:37-9 My 14 '66
ARMOUR, Richard
And make it a sonnet if you don't mind. por Pub W 189:44-5 My 16 '66
Label on the package. Writer 79:25-6 N '66
Long-distance doesn't lend enchantment. Sat R 49:6+ S 10 '66
Ode to the bookseller. Pub W 190:128 S 26 '66
Picture stricture; poem. McCalls 93:196 Ap '66
Typewriter and I. Writer 79:21-2 My '66
ARMS control. See Disarmament
ARMS control and disarmament agency. See United States—Arms control and disarmament agency
ARMS sales. See Purchasing, Military
ARMS smuggling. See Smuggling
ARMSTRONG, Gregory T.
Oneness of piety. Christian Cent 83:272 Mr 2 '66
ARMSTRONG, Louis
Authentic American genius; interview, ed. by R. Meryman. il pors Life 60:92-102+ Ap 15 '66
about
Manager Joe Glaser on Louis. J Glaser. por Life 60:114 Ap 15 '66
ARMSTRONG, Marion
Affectionate objectivity. Christian Cent 83: 367 Mr 23 '66
Constant crisis; poem. Christian Cent 83:271 Mr 2 '66
Movies. Christian Cent 83:466+, 687, 810, 1243-4, 1416-17, 1540 Ap 13, My 25, Je 22, O 12, N 16, D 14 '66
ARMSTRONG, Neil A.
See also
Space flight—Manned flights—Armstrong-Scott flight, 1966
—and Scott, D. R.
Case of constructive alarm. pors Life 60:87-8 Ap 8 '66
ARMSTRONG, O. K.
Filth for profit; the big business of pornography. Read Digest 88:73-6 Mr '66
ARMSTRONG, Richard
It's great to be alive. Sat Eve Post 239:21-6 Je 4 '66; Same abr. with title Pilot is down! Read Digest 89:42-8 Ag '66
Look at tomorrow today. Sat Eve Post 239: 23-7 Mr 26 '66
ARMSTRONG-JONES, Antony Charles Robert, 1st earl of Snowdon. See Snowdon, A. C. R. A.-J.
ARMY calibration program. See Calibration
ARMY chaplains. See Chaplains, Military
ARMY field calibration technicians. See Electric workers
ARMY intelligence tests. See Intelligence tests
ARMY libraries. See United States—Army—Libraries
ARMY materiel command. See United States—Army—Materiel command
ARMY rejections. See Military service—Physical and mental fitness

ARMY reserves. See United States—Army—Reserves

ARMY slang. See Slang

ARNALL, Ellis Gibbs
Return of a moderate. Time 88:25 S 23 '66

ARNASON, A. Neil. See Pielou, E. C. jt. auth.

ARNASON, B. G. See Winkler, G. F. jt. auth.

ARNAUDI, Carlo
Cabinet reshuffle changes Italy's science minister. V. K. McElheny. Science 152:336-7 Ap 15 '66

ARNETT, Carroll
Bushmill's; Dare; Next; poems. Poetry 108:307-8 Ag '66

ARNETT, Peter
Three for AP. il por Newsweek 67:92-3 My 16 '66

ARNEZ, Nancy L.
Effect of teacher attitudes upon the culturally different. bibliog f Sch & Soc 94:149-52 Mr 19 '66

ARNOLD, Benedict
Battle at Valcour Island: Benedict Arnold as hero. T. W. Hubbard. il por Am Heritage 17:8-11+ O '66

ARNOLD, Eddy
Country Como. il pors Time 87:62+ My 27 '66

ARNOLD, Harriet
How to take better Christmas pictures. il Pop Mech 126:146-8+ D '66

ARNOLD, John
History repeats itself. Sat R 49:8 Mr 26 '66

ARNOLD, Rus
How to shoot Christmas lights. U S Camera 29:54-5+ D '66

ARNOLD, Thurman Wesley
Talk with Thurman Arnold; interview. por Duns R 88:10-11+ N '66

ARNOLD, Walter E.
Books. Commonweal 84:315-16 Je 3 '66

ARNOLD, William
Light reaction in green plant photosynthesis: a method of study. bibliog Science 154:1046-9 N 25 '66

ARNON, Ruth Soulé
Lessons of dictatorship. Mlle 62:180-1+ Ap '66

ARNSTEIN, Arnold
Copy cat. il por Time 88:53 D 23 '66

ARNTSON, R. H. and others
Stibnite (Sb₂S₃) solubility in sodium sulfide solutions. bibliog Science 153:1673-4 S 30 '66

AROMATIC hydrocarbons. See Hydrocarbons

ARONS, Arnold Boris
Profess with a passion. il por Time 87:81-2 My 6 '66

ARONSON, Elliot
How to get obedience; reprint. Sci Digest 60:54-9 Jl '66
Parent and child. N Y Times Mag p 109+ S 11 '66

ARONSON, J. R. and others
Infrared spectra from fine particulate surfaces. bibliog Science 152:345-6 Ap 15 '66

ARONSON, Lester R. and Cooper, M. L.
Seasonal variation in mating behavior in cats after desensitization of glans penis. bibliog Science 152:226-30 Ap 8 '66

AROOSTOOK COUNTY, Me.
Uncle Sam finds hot potato in beet field. il Nations Bsns 54:58-9+ N '66

AROUND the world flights. See Aviation—World flights

ARP, Halton
Are quasars the products of peculiar galaxies? il por Time 87:88+ Ap 1 '66

ARP, Hans
Love and hiccups. il por Newsweek 67:67 Je 20 '66
Obituary
Art N 65:13 S '66

ARP, Jean. See Arp, Hans

ARRABAL, Fernando
Automobile graveyard. Criticism
Sat R 49:43 Ap 23 '66
Letter from Paris; le Theatre de Poche-Montparnasse: summer program of one-act playlets. Genêt. New Yorker 42:145-6+ S 10 '66

ARRANGEMENT (music) See Musical arrangement

ARRANGEMENT of flowers. See Flowers, Arrangement of

ARRAU, Claudio
Pianist Arrau ends a marathon. J. de Kruijff. il por Hi Fi 16:18+ Ag '66

ARRINGTON, Sandra Ann
Girl on the varsity. il pors Ebony 21:71-2+ My '66

ARROWS. See Bow and arrow

ARROWSMITH, William
Shame of the graduate schools. Harper 232:51-9 Mr '66
(tr) See Aristophanes. Birds
about
Vision of madness. Time 88:60 O 28 '66

ARROYO DE ANDA, Luis Aveleyra. See Aveleyra Arroyo de Anda, L.

ARRUZA, Carlos
Homage to a peerless matador. B. Conrad. il pors Sports Illus 25:44-52 Ag 1 '66

ARSON
Mystery of St Mark's; arson investigation at St Mark's school, Southboro, Mass. il Newsweek 67:101 Ap 18 '66
Our neighbors helped us rebuild out of the ashes; Negro family's house burned; ed. by L. Shecter. B. DeCausey. il Good H 162:98-9+ Je '66

ART
See also
Advertising art
Animals in art
Bridges in art
Childrens art
Creation (literary, artistic, etc)
Drawing
Graffiti
Graphic arts
Mural painting and decoration
Performing arts
Prints
Realism in art
Romanticism
Sculpture
Sex in art
Surrealism (art)

Appreciation
Adventure in appreciation. S. Maxey. il Design 67:8-9 Mr '66
Discovering the world of art; with discussion group program. by E. G. Neisser. J. W. Fosburgh. bibliog il Parents Mag 41:44-6+, 84+ Je '66
Do you recognize this? first grade class in Centerville school, Conn. R. L. Peck. il Sch Arts 65:18-19 My '66
How to enjoy museums. A. Eliot. Seventeen 25:140+ Je '66
More than meets the eye; why we see things as we are; excerpt from The story behind the painting. L. Rosten. il Read Digest 88:213-15 Ap '66
Ouch! I love it! E. Kendall. Holiday 40:116+ Jl '66
Path to visual realization. D. Cyr. bibliog il Design 67:26-30 Ja '66
To be a human being. B. Wasserman. il Sch Arts 66:28-32 O '66
See also
Art criticism

Bibliography
Book review section. See issues of Design
Book reviews. See issues of American artist
Books. See issues of School arts
Boom in art books. L. Kronenberger. Atlan 217:76-9 My '66
Catch up with. L. Lerman. Mlle 64:18 Ja '67
Cornucopia of art books. C. J. McNaspy. America 115:812 D 17 '66
Impact in chiaroscuro and color. G. H. Hamilton. il Sat R 49:24-7 Ag 27 '66
Panorama from the palette. G. H. Hamilton. il Sat R 49:33-5 D 3 '66
See also
Art literature

Collections
See Art—Galleries and museums; Private collections

Competitions
Competitions and awards. See issues of American artist
1966 Scholastic magazines art awards. il Sr Schol 88:14-15 My 20 '66

Conservation and restoration
Conserving man's cultural heritage; examples of art saved by UNESCO's program. il UN Mo Chron 3:49-56 Jl '66
Digging out; aid after the flood. Newsweek 68:102+ N 28 '66
Disaster in Italy; damage done by flood. il Newsweek 68:110-11 N 21 '66
Italy counts the cost of its deluge; damage widespread. il Bsns W p50-2 N 26 '66
Italy's crumbling art. il Newsweek 68:110 S 26 '66
Ruin in flood's wake: treasures of Florence. il U S News 61:34+ D 5 '66

ART—Conservation and restoration—*Continued*
Salvage of Florence. il Time 88:90 N 25 '66
Terrible plight of the renaissance land; salvaging cultural treasures. il Life 61:28-35 D 16 '66

Courses of study
See also
Art—Study and teaching

Criticism
See Art criticism

Exhibitions
American artist travelogue (cont) Am Artist 30:59-67 Ap '66
AWS, 1866-1966; Metropolitan museum of art's 200 years of watercolor painting in America. il Am Artist 30:77 D '66
Americans in Venice; Biennale internazionale d'arte. F. Getlein. New Repub 155:37-8 Jl 30 '66
Argentine in Venice; J. Le Parc, winner of biennale. O. Masotta. il Américas 18:19-22 Ag '66
Art. M. Kozloff. See issues of Nation
Art galleries. R. M. Coates. See issues of New Yorker to January 7, 1967
Art over the counter; Gallery of the masters at Bamberger's in Newark. K. Kuh. Sat R 49:38-9 D 31 '66
Beating the drum for African art; first World festival of Negro arts. Dakar. F. V. Grunfeld. il Reporter 34:34-6 Je 2 '66
Benefit bonanza; show for the public education association in New York. il Art N 65:32-3+ My '66
Birds and beasts in the Queen's gallery. O. Millar. il Antiques 90:824-7 D '66
Boom-boom never flagged: Senegal's First world festival of Negro arts; Dakar. M. R. Henry. Vogue 148:329-31 S 1 '66
Bulletin board. See issues of American artist
Come to Christie's; bicentenary celebration. H. A. La Farge. il Art N 65:42-3+ D '66
Coming soon, art exhibits. See issues of Design
Community art shows; a few questions and answers. Parks & Rec 1:336-8+ Ap '66
Cornucopia; autumn shows. il Newsweek 68:107 O 24 '66
Current and coming. See issues of Antiques
Dandy at the helm; P. Guillaume collection on exhibit at the Orangerie, Paris. F. Cachin. il Art N 65:36-8+ Ap '66
Enter government, exit art; controversy over U.S. show at Venice biennale. K. Kuh. Sat R 49:28-9 Ap 2 '66
Exploring modern art; Canadian religious art today II and Seven decades. C. J. McNaspy. America 114:755-7 My 21 '66
Force of nature; Picasso exhibition by French Ministry of culture. il Newsweek 68:102 N 28 '66
Goings on about town. See issues of New Yorker
Golden age; The age of Rembrandt, at San Francisco's Palace of the Legion of honor. il Newsweek 68:90-3 N 7 '66
Golden age of Rembrandt; loan exhibition. A. Werner. il Reporter 35:34-6 D 29 '66
How New York became the capital of 19th-century Paris; excerpts from preface to the Knoedler catalogue for the Impressionist treasures show. J. Rewald. il Art N 64:34-6+ Ja '66
In many voices; J. Love's one-man show of ink paintings at Alonzo gallery. T. F. Mathews. America 116:62 Ja 14 '67
Jammed doors; Theatre and engineering show. New York. il Newsweek 68:101-2 O 31 '66
Letter from London; National trust's pictures. J. Stuart. il Antiques 89:272+ F '66
Merchants of Venice: 33rd biennale. il Newsweek 67:90 Je 27 '66
Minotaur & the maze: Picasso's retrospective. il Time 88:72 D 2 '66
Museum calendar. See issues of American artist
New York, New York, it's a backwater town. Time 88:83 N 11 '66
Opening in San Francisco in October, an astonishing exhibit of Dutch paintings. il Sunset 137:22 O '66
Peales get together; works of the Peale family of artists. E. P. Birk. il Antiques 91:18 Ja '67
People figures; exhibition at New York's Museum of contemporary crafts. R. Howard. il Craft Horiz 26:36-41 N '66
Progressive seebang; Seven decades of modernism in Manhattan. il Time 87:70-3 My 6 '66

Reviews and previews. See issues of Art news
Romance of reality; benefit show at Wildenstein gallery. il Art N 65:28-30+ Ap '66
São Paulo in Washington; American section of the eighth São Paulo biennial. M. Kozloff. Nation 202:250-2 F 28 '66
Seven decades, 1895-1965, exhibition at ten galleries in New York. New Yorker 42:37-8 My 7 '66
Stepladders to art; exhibit at high school in Midland, Ind. N. Bridwell. il Design 67:4-7 Mr '66
Two hundred years of water color painting in America; preview of an exhibition. S. P. Feld. il Antiques 90:840-5 D '66
Venice; miniskirts or miniart? 33rd biennale. M. Gendel. il Art N 65:52-4+ S '66; Reply. R. Squirru. 65:6 D '66
Venice: the biennale. il Craft Horiz 26:28-31 S '66
What it takes to put on a $50-million art exhibit; Toledo museum of art. il Bsns W p 112-14+ D 10 '66
Where and when to exhibit; exhibition calendar. See issues of Art news
Where the action is; current sampling of exhibitions; New York city. il Newsweek 68:98-9 D 5 '66
World art at São Paulo; eighth biennial. J. Gómez-Sicre. il Américas 18:31-6 Ja '66
Yankee doodlers; Garbisch collection on view at National gallery. il Newsweek 68:102-4 O 31 '66
Year of the mechanical rabbit; International biennale of art, Venice. il Time 87:64-7 Je 24 '66
Young masters of understatement; Jewish museum, N.Y. il Art N 65:42+ My '66
See also
Childrens art—Exhibitions
Exhibitions, Traveling
Museum of modern art. New York
Photography—Exhibitions
Prints—Exhibitions

Expertising
How to smell a Rubens; strange case of the Judgment of Paris. il Time 88:88-91 S 16 '66

Galleries and museums
In the museums. R. Davidson. See issues of Antiques
Letter from London. J. Stuart. il Antiques 90:36+ Jl '66
Notes on American museums. T. B. Hess. Art N 65:27 N '66
Philip Johnson explains his remarkable underground museum. P. Johnson. il Vogue 147:200-1 My '66
Small museums of southern Europe. A. Eliot. il Holiday 39:105-10 Je '66
Sort of the Svengali of pop; L. Castelli. il N Y Times Mag p34-5+ My 8 '66
Thief-proofing our art museums. R. LeBlanc. Am Artist 30:16-17+ F '66
While nobody was looking, the West has launched an art museum boom. il Sunset 137:90-2+ N '66
See also names of museums. e.g. National gallery of art, Washington, D.C.
also subhead Galleries and museums under names of cities, e.g. New York (city)—Galleries and museums

Acquisitions
In the museums: paintings; important acquisitions by some of the largest American museums. R. Davidson. il Antiques 90:700+ N '66
Museum acquisitions in silver. R. Davidson. il Antiques 90:851+ D '66

Architecture
See Museums—Architecture

Gifts, legacies, etc.
Art and taxes. J. S. Rubin. il Horizon 8:4-15 Wint '66
Dandy at the helm; P. Guillaume collection on exhibit at the Orangerie, Paris. F. Cachin. il Art N 65:36-8+ Ap '66
Where honor is due. N. Kent. Am Artist 30:3+ Mr '66
Wickes collection given to Boston. E. P. Birk. il Antiques 90:16 Jl '66

History
Art and anti-art. E. H. Gombrich. il Atlan 217:93-9 F '66
Art galleries; changing moods and mannerisms. R. M. Coates. New Yorker 42:140+ Mr 26 '66

ART—History—*Continued*

Panoptic shoehorns. R. Howard. il Art N 65: 44-5+ Ap '66

Seven decades, 1895-1965, exhibition at ten galleries in New York. New Yorker 42: 37-8 My 7 '66

Study and teaching

Art history for grade two. L. B. Garcia. il Sch Arts 66:10-12 N '66

International aspects

Asian cultural meaning for western art; universality of art. J. L. Lauver and T. Karwaki. il Sch Arts 65:9-11 Ja '66

Philosophy

Art and knowledge. F. Porter. il Art N 64:30-2+ F '66

Art and philosophy; ed. by S. Hook. Review Sat R 49:60+ Je 11 '66. G. W. Linden

Beneath the skin; interview. ed. by G. R. Swenson. Art N 65:34-5+ Ap '66

Founder reflects. E. W. Watson. Am Artist 30:3+ My '66

Notes on American museums. T. B. Hess. Art N 65:27 N '66

Polemic on one-eye formats. P. Pavia. il Art N 65:28-31+ D '66

See also

Aesthetics

Prices

Triple rediscovery of Rubens. il Life 61:103-7 O 14 '66

Private collections

Art and taxes. J. S. Rubin. il Horizon 8:4-15 Wint '66

Bachelor queen; Sweden's Christina as royal patroness. il Time 88:66-7 Ag 5 '66

Beautician's booty; H. Rubinstein. il Time 87:82-5 Ap 29 '66

Birds and beasts in the Queen's gallery. O. Millar. il Antiques 90:824-7 D '66

Celebration of masterpieces; three of the paintings lent to the National gallery of art by Mr and Mrs P. Mellon and Mrs M. Bruce. J. Walker. il Vogue 147:94-5 Mr 15 '66

Collectors' house: the De Menils' affair with art. J. J. Sweeney. il Vogue 147:184-93+ Ap 1 '66

Duncan Phillips, a guiding force. K. Kuh. Sat R 49:29 Je 11 '66

Elegant frame for masterpieces. il House & Gard 130:78-83 Jl '66

Family reunion; French pantings from collections of Andrew Mellon's children. il Newsweek 67:99-100 Mr 21 '66

4,000 paintings and 1,500 sculptures; J. Hirshhorn's mine of modern art. V. Raynor. il N Y Times Mag p52-5+ N 27 '66

French paintings from the collection of Mrs Mellon Bruce and Mr and Mrs Paul Mellon. D. Farr. il Antiques 89:556-63 Ap '66

French paintings in the English royal collection. O. Millar. Antiques 89:706-8 My '66

Friend of the Fogg: P. J. Sachs. il Time 89: 54-5 Ja 13 '67

Furrier to the art world; collection of J. Kaplan. G. Glueck. il N Y Times Mag p38-9+ O 2 '66

Garden party at the National; loans of Paul Mellon's and Mrs Ailsa Mellon Bruce. il Time 87:66-9 Mr 25 '66

Gift of love; P. Guillaume's collection given to the Louvre. Time 87:78 F 4 '66

Glory that was France; paintings loaned by Mrs Mellon Bruce and Mr and Mrs Paul Mellon for 25th anniversary of National gallery in Washington. R. Goldwater. il Art N 65:40-2+ Mr '66

Golden loans for a silver anniversary; French impressionist and post-impressionist works lent by Andrew Mellon's children. K. Kuh. il Sat R 49:45-51 Mr 19 '66

How New York became the capital of 19th-century Paris; excerpts from preface to the Knoedler catalogue for the Impressionist treasures show. J. Rewald. il Art N 64:34-6+ Ja '66

Jewel for the mall; Hirshhorn collection. il Time 87:88 My 20 '66

King's collection; exhibition of Chinese art from the collection of H.M. Gustaf VI Adolf of Sweden. F. Getlein. New Repub 155:35-6 S 17 '66

Letter from Paris; exhibition of Walter collection at Musée de l'Orangerie. Genêt. New Yorker 42:71-2 Jl 30 '66

Mrs Charles Wrightsman: collector's pursuit of art and perfection; with account by B. Robertson. il Vogue 148:236-41+ O 1 '66

Morrison collection of silver at Princeton, New Jersey. E. P. Birk. il Antiques 90:608+ N '66

National gallery: preview of an anniversary exhibition; Mellons' collections. A. Saarinen. il McCalls 93:96-103+ Ap '66

National gallery turns twenty-five; Paul Mellon and Mrs Mellon Bruce collections. F. Getlein. New Repub 154:34-5 Ap 2 '66

New collector; Abrams collection on display at New York's Jewish museum. il Newsweek 68:84-5 Jl 11 '66

Old masters at home. B. Plumb. il N Y Times Mag p 102-3+ Mr 27 '66

$1,000,000 in Dürers found in Brooklyn; E. Eliçofon acquisitions stolen from Weimar collection il Life 60:34-5 Je 3 '66

Our far-flung correspondents: exhibition called Christina, queen of Sweden, a personality of European civilization at The Nationalmuseum; Stockholm. F. Steegmuller. il New Yorker 42:160+ S 17 '66

Paintings one lives with brighten the house. A. West. House & Gard 130:84-5+ Jl '66

Profiles; R. C. Scull collector of pop art. J. Kramer. New Yorker 42:64-6+ N 26 '66

Quick as a wink; G. David Thompson collection auctioned. Newsweek 67:94 Ap 4 '66

Radioactive treasure; Hirshhorn collection given to the government. il Newsweek 67: 100 My 23 '66

Roundup time; William F. Cody collection. il Time 88:56-8 Ag 12 '66

Royal eye for the Chinese; collection of Sweden's King Gustaf. il Time 89:54 Ja 13 '67

Thirteen colorplates; French pictures in the collections of Mrs Mellon Bruce and Mr and Mrs Paul Mellon. il Art N 65:43-50 Mr '66

Vincent Price: he likes what he knows; interview. V. Price. il Design 67:18-22 Ja '66

Scholarships and fellowships

Competitions and awards. See issues of American artist

Competitions, scholarships. See issues of Art news

Social aspects

See Art and society

Study and teaching

Art for the disadvantaged. R. H. Silverman. bibliog il NEA J 55:29-31 Ap '66

Classroom documented; class studies in motivation. H. P. Raleigh. il Sch Arts 66:21-3 D '66

Colleges graduate visual illiterates; proposal for visual studies centers. A. D. Trottenberg. il Sat R 49:73-5+ F 19 '66

CBE and the fine arts. M. Smith. Sch & Soc 94:132 Mr 5 '66

Cultural arts week in Anchorage, Alaska. B. Baer. il Sch Arts 65:31-3 My '66

Design and form through photography. R. A. Burgderfer. il Sch Arts 65:31-3 Je '66

Educational television in the art room. K. K. Agee. il Sch Arts 66:24-5 D '66

Family work shops; Des Moines art center. P. Patrick. il Sch Arts 66:5-7 O '66

Happenings in and out of school; interview, ed. by D. W. Ecker. Sch Arts 65: 23-8 Mr '66

Make a brush. R. Reinholtz. il Sch Arts 65: 29-30 Je '66

Nido de Aguilas; art program in Santiago, Chile. C. Ranstead. il Sch Arts 65:5-8 F '66

Out of focus; filmstrip projector used to assist children in producing big pictures. J. Chisholm. il Sch Arts 65:14-16 F '66

Relating to Rouault. G. Haddad. il Sch Arts 65:41 Mr '65

Summer art in northern New York. R. Plumb and S. Smith. il Sch Arts 66:36-9 O '66

Thumbs down; oil painting class in a senior high school. M. Christy. il Design 67:38-40 Ja '66

Why not every child? Irvington, N.J; cultural program. E. L. Raichle. il PTA Mag 60:35-6 Je '66

See also

Design—Study and teaching

Drawing—Study and teaching

Painting—Study and teaching

Prints—Technique

Materials

Adventure in art; plastic; use of discarded containers. J. F. Woell. il Sch Arts 65: 10-12 Mr '66

Calico pictures of storybook tales. R. Grabner. il Sch Arts 66:35 D '66

ART—Study and teaching—Materials—*Cont.*
Case of the bottles. B. W. Marxhausen. il
  Sch Arts 65:18 Ja '66
Ever use a paddle in art? H. Ringgenberg. il
  Design 68:12-15 S '66
Make a stained window; organdy and starch.
  L. Olson. il Sch Arts 66:9-11 D '66
Some projects for children's art classes. D.
  Marchese. il Sch Arts 66:21-8 S '66
String along with Ring. H. Ringgenberg. il
  Design 67:26-7 Mr '66
    See also
Arts and crafts—Study and teaching—Ma-
  terials
Sculpture—Study and teaching—Materials

Projects
Adventure in appreciation. S. Maxey. il De-
  sign 67:8-9 Mr '66
Appleheaded. M. Christy. il Design 68:30-1
  N '66
Art & human planning issue: symposium.
  bibliog il Sch Arts 65:5-22 Ap '66
Art of perception; still-life and enlargement
  project for students of elementary educa-
  tion. J. G. Cecere. il Sch Arts 66:2c-5 S '66
Catterpockings. M. Kreiger. il Sch Arts 65:
  16-17 My '66
Creative art in the classroom curriculum.
  M. L. Wooten. il Sch Arts 66:4-8 D '66
Elementary art. J. W. Cataldo. il Sch Arts
  65:26-8 Ja '66
Experimenting with color and light. P.
  Greenberg. il Sch Arts 65:16-17 Mr '66
Gothic age revisited. C. J. Alkema. il De-
  sign 67:22-5 My '66
Halloween. il Sch Arts 66:8-10 O '66
Papier-mâché animals; project for primary
  grades. L. Werdegar. il Sch Arts 65:5-9
  Mr '66
Signs and symbols; mural painting. N.
  Roukes. il Sch Arts 66:15-19 O '66
Snare some space. K. R. Morrison. il Design
  68:21-2 S '66
Some projects for children's art classes. D.
  Marchese. il Sch Arts 66:21-8 S '66
Tragedy of the tombs; art assembly program;
  Alex G. Barrett junior high school in
  Louisville. R. Friedman. il Sch Arts 65:
  36-8 My '66
Wall of the winds; Wilson high school, Los
  Angeles. A. Kaelin. il Sch Arts 66:18-19
  N '66
    See also
Mural painting and decoration

Taxation
See Taxation of works of art

Themes
Brent Kington's wheeling world. il Craft
  Horiz 26:43-5 N '66
Warhol: the silver tenement. D. Antin. il Art
  N 65:47-9+ Sum '66
    See also
History in art
West in art

Germany (Democratic Republic)
Odyssey in oils; painting taken in post-World
  war I Germany, to be returned. il Time
  89:58+ Ja 20 '67

Germany (Federal Republic)
Art news from Germany. J. Claus. Art N
  65:53 Sum '66

Great Britain
Letter from London. J. Stuart. il Antiques
  89:652+, 808+; 90:36+, 164+, 308+, 440+,
  620+; 774; 91:48 My '66-Ja '67
    See also
London—Art

Israel
Art that history shaped. K. Kuh. il Sat R
  49:17-24 Ja 29 '66

Italy
Art news from Rome. M. Gendel. Art N 65:
  54 Sum '66
    See also
Florence—Art
Venice—Art

Jamaica
Art on an island. F. Getlein. New Repub
  154:34-5 Je 4 '66

Latin America
World art at São Paulo; eighth biennial.
  J. Gómez-Sicre. il Américas 18:31-6 Ja '66

Michigan
Michigan's evangelist of art. G. A. Goodwin
  and A. Rankin. il Read Digest 88:217-18+
  My '66

Puerto Rico
Museum grows in Puerto Rico. S. W. Rich.
  il Sat R 49:24-5 F 12 '66
Old masters in Puerto Rico; Museum of fine
  arts. Ponce. L. Lastra. il Américas 18:
  11-16 N '66

United States
Creating a popular image? il Sr Schol 88:10-12
  Ap 15 '66
State of the arts: a 1966 balance sheet. R. L.
  Stevens. Sat R 49:24-5+ Mr 12 '66
Uncle Sam and the arts; National gallery of
  art. il Sr Schol 88:2-3 Mr 11 '66
    See also
Art, American
Painting, American
    also subhead Art under names of cities,
  e.g. Los Angeles—Art

Western states
While nobody was looking, the West has
  launched an art museum boom. il Sunset
  137:90-2+ N '66
ART, Abstract
Abstract background; self-interview. R.
  Moynihan. il Art N 65:41+ My '66
Art: work of K. Noland and F. Stella. M.
  Kozloff. Nation 202:370-2 Mr 28 '66
Black pastures. H. Rosenstein. il Art N 65:33-
  5+ N '66
Jenkins paints an opinion; self-interview.
  P. Jenkins. il Art N 65:54-5+ N '66
John Ferren's mandorla. L. Finkelstein. il
  Art N 65:34-5+ Sum '66
Kandinsky, no great master but a great
  influence. H. Kramer. il N Y Times Mag
  p28-9+ D 18 '66
Let's paint an abstract. R. Barrio. il Sch
  Arts 66:33-4 S '66
Old master at the new frontier. S. Burton.
  il Art N 65:52-5+ D '66
Private worlds of Sal Sirugo. N. Edgar. il
  Art N 65:42-3+ N '66
São Paulo in Washington; American section
  of the eighth São Paulo biennial. M. Koz-
  loff. Nation 202:250-2 F 28 '66
Solid anti-geometry. E. C. Baker. il Art N
  65:56-7+ Mr '66
ART, Afghan
Kabul confluence; treasures lent by the
  Afghanistan museums to Asia house. N.Y.
  M. Neff. il Art N 64:26-7+ F '66
Meeting of East & West; show at Manhat-
  tan's Asia house gallery. il Time 87:74-5 F
  18 '66
ART, African
African art in American collections. by W.
  M. Robbins. Review
    Negro Hist Bul 29:141 Mr '66. W. F.
    Woods
Behind the mask of Africa; artistic heri-
  tage; dancing, music, literature, sculpture.
  A. Malraux. il N Y Times Mag p30-1+ My
  15 '66
Hidden force of black African art; tr. by
  A. Foulke. L. S. Senghor. il Vogue 148:
  236-9+ D '66
    See also
Art, Negro
Art, Senegalese
ART, Amateur
Painting the waterfront. H. Gasser. il Parks
  & Rec 1:558-60 Jl '66
Sunday painters: Churchill, Eisenhower and
  Kennedy. C. B. Luce. McCalls 94:12+ Ja
  '67
Tomorrow's amateur. F. Du Plessix. il House
  & Gard 130:106-7+ Jl '66
ART, American
American art and the Whitney museum.
  L. Goodrich. il Antiques 90:655-62 N '66
Brandywine tradition; art of Brandywine
  Valley. H. C. Pitz. il Am Artist 30:43-9+
  D '66
Neglected American treasures. M. Frome. il
  Holiday 39:129-34 My '66
New Britain museum of American art, New
  Britain, Conn. C. B. Ferguson. il Antiques
  90:668-72 N '66
São Paulo in Washington; American section
  of the eighth São Paulo biennial. M. Koz-
  loff. Nation 202:250-2 F 28 '66
What modern art says about America. M.
  Fishwick. Sat R 49:19-20+ Ap 9 '66
    See also
Artists, American
Painting, American
Sculpture, American
Whitney museum of American art, New York
ART, Baroque
    See also
Architecture, Baroque

ART, Ceylonese
  See also
  Painting, Ceylonese
ART, Chinese
  Cycle of rice; J. June engravings portray cultivation methods. il UNESCO Courier 19:18-20 Ap '66
  King's collection; exhibition from the collection of H.M. Gustaf VI Adolf of Sweden. F. Getlein. New Repub 155:35-6 S 17 '66
  Treasury of ancient China: relics of ancient Cathay at Manhattan's Metropolitan museum. il Time 87:79 F 4 '66

    Collectors and collecting
  Chinese art from the collection of the King of Sweden. F. Getlein. il Craft Horiz 26: 30-5 N '66
ART, Commercial
  Fine arts and graphic design; excerpt from Book of art. B. Myers. il Design 68:23-6 S '66
    See also
  Push pin studios

    Study and teaching
  Package design. J. C. Bott. il Design 68:27-9 N '66
ART, Dutch
  See also
  Painting, Dutch
ART, Egyptian
  Egyptian motifs in nineteenth-century American painting and sculpture. W. H. Gerdts. il Antiques 90:495-501 O '66
  Egyptian revival in the decorative arts. J. S. Johnson. il Antiques 90:489-94 O '66
  Tutankhamen: a child's treasure far west of Thebes; Junior art museum's Egyptian tomb exhibit, 1964. D. Parker. il Sch Arts 65:12-16 Je '66
ART, Flemish
  See also
  Painting, Flemish
ART, French
  George IV and the arts of France. G. De Bellaigue. il Antiques 89:700-5 My '66
    See also
  Dadaism
  Painting, French
ART, German
  Dürer and drawing; great change in German art. F. Getlein. New Repub 154:33-4 F 5 '66
ART, Hindu. See Art, Indian (East Indian)
ART, Indian (East Indian)
  Alluring art of India; sculpture and painting shows; U.S. tour; photographs by H. Groskinsky; with report on history and styles. Life 60:48-58 F 11 '66
  Nagas, their lore and legend. G. Kaler. il Hobbies 71:50 D '66
ART, Islamic
  See also
  Art, Turkish
ART, Israeli
  Art that history shaped. K. Kuh. il Sat R 49:17-24 Ja 29 '66
  Carnival of chance; Y Agam's show of optical surprises at New York's Marlborough gallery. il Newsweek 67:107-8 Je 13 '66
ART, Italian
  Italy's crumbling art. il Newsweek 68:110 S 26 '66
ART, Japanese
  Bird's-eye view; Japan's national treasures. U.S. tour. il Time 87:72-5 Mr 11 '66
  Ukiyo-ye-prints. D. Powills. il Hobbies 71: 120-1 S '66
ART, Jewish
  Grandpa Moses; paintings of Shalom of Safed. il Newsweek 67:86 My 30 '66
  Is there a Jewish art? excerpt from address. H. Rosenberg. Commentary 42:57-60 Jl '66; Discussion. 42:16+ O '66
    See also
  Art, Israeli
ART, Latin American
  Art. See issues of Américas
    See also
  Art, Pre-Columbian
  Painting, Latin American
ART, Medieval
  Medieval splendors; manuscript illuminations. A. Werner. il Am Artist 30:38-42+ D '66
ART, Mexican
  Man needs space; Siqueiros' History of humanity. il Newsweek 68:69 Ag 29 '66
ART, Minoan
  See also
  Crete—Antiquities

ART, Modern. See Modernism (art)
ART, Negro
  Beating the drum for African art; first World festival of Negro arts, Dakar. F. V. Grunfeld. il Reporter 34:34-6 Je 2 '66
  Boom-boom never flagged; Senegal's First world festival of Negro arts. M. R. Henry. Vogue 148:329-31 S 1 '66
  First world festival of black man's art; with report by B. Farrell. il Life 60:83-88B Ap 22 '66
  Negritude, a romantic myth? World festival of Negro arts, Dakar, Senegal. M. Furay. New Repub 155:32-5 Jl 2 '66
ART, Oriental
  See also
  Art, Chinese
  Art, Indian (East Indian)
ART, Peruvian
  Gold from Peru; circulating exhibition. F. Getlein. New Repub 154:29+ F 19 '66
ART, Polish
  Grand allegiance. il Time 88:84-5+ D 9 '66
  Rare view of art from Poland. E. P. Birk. il Antiques 90:744+ D '66
ART, Pre-Columbian
  Early metallurgy in the New World. D. T. Easby, jr. il Sci Am 214:72-8+ bibliog(p 140) Ap '66
    See also
  Sculpture, Pre-Columbian
ART, Primitive
  How Mr Menen taught the Dangs primitive art. A. Menen. il N Y Times Mag p20-2+ Jl 24 '66
  Rocky road to art; World of primitive art show. il Newsweek 68:90 Jl 18 '66
  Yankee doodlers; Garbisch collection on view at National gallery. il Newsweek 68:102-4 O 31 '66
    See also
  Sculpture, Primitive
ART, Puerto Rican
  Art from Puerto Rico; exhibition at the PAU. il Américas 18:40 Jl '66
ART, Religious. See Christian art and symbolism
ART, Russian
  Russia's buried treasure; art treasures on exhibit at The Hague's Gemeentemuseum. il Newsweek 68:106 O 24 '66
ART, Senegalese
  Within the show's excitement, the deeper issue of négritude. B. Farrell. il Life 60: 88A-88B Ap 22 '66
ART, Spanish
  See also
  Dali, S.
ART, Turkish
  Turkish delights; exhibition of Ottoman art touring America. N. Kotker. il Horizon 8:78-89 Aut '66
ART, Yugoslav
  Out of Yugoslavia; works by painters and sculptors to be exhibited at six U.S. museums during 1966. F. Getlein. New Repub 154:24+ F 12 '66
  Slavs without Marx. il Newsweek 67:82 F 7 '66
ART and hallucinogenic drugs. See Hallucinogenic drugs and art
ART and industry
  Abstracts for industry; Holland's Turmac tobacco co. il Time 88:109 O 21 '66
  Culture and the corporation; address, September 20, 1966. D. Rockefeller. Vital Speeches 33:14-18 O 15 '66
  Publisher's page; Esquire symposium, with the New York Board of trade. A. Gingrick. Esquire 65:8 Je '66
    See also
  Advertising art
ART and libraries. See Libraries and art
ART and literature
  Painting poetry. M. Moody. il Design 67:31 Ja '66
  Thoughts on writing and handcraft; summer program called Cross-over at Penland school of crafts. M. C. Richards. Craft Horiz 26: 32-3 Jl '66
ART and nature. See Nature (aesthetics)
ART and photography
  Design and form through photography. R. A. Burgderfer. il Sch Arts 65:31-3 Je '66
  How's that again? B. H. Hayes, jr; L. Cheek, jr; E. H. Turner. Mod Phot 30:142+ D '66
  It began with photograms. J. Deschin. il Pop Phot 60:38+ Ja '67
  Moiré pattern projections. B. Wasserman. il Sch Arts 65:17-20 Je '66
  Photo posters in junior high school. J. Lidstone. il Sch Arts 66:27-30 N '66

ART and photography—*Continued*
Photographers can learn from painters. A. Rothstein. U S Camera 29:18+ N '66
Show of color. M. R. Weiss. il Sat R 49:45-52 S 24 '66

ART and politics
Art, politics, & the Soviet writer. T. Frankel. bibliog f Commentary 41:52-9 My '66

ART and religion
Holy-card architecture. C. Heimsath. Commonweal 85:132-4 N 4 '66
New trends in liturgical art; excerpts from panel discussion at exhibition of Religious arts and crafts sponsored by the Artist-craftsmen of New York. Craft Horiz 26:34-5+ Ja '66
Recent art in a climate of change. J. W. Moody. Christian Cent 83:401-3 Mr 30 '66
Theology and the arts, by D. B. Harned. Review
    Christian Cent 83:1575 D 21 '66. P. Meinke
Wilfred Lang: artist, critic of today's church. D. Devereux. Christian Cent 83:1515-19 D 7 '66

See also
Christian art and symbolism

ART and science
Art in science; exhibit at 1965 annual meeting of the AAAS. D. G. Barry; discussion. Science 151:1170; 152:1011-12; 153:1470 Mr 11, My 20, S 23 '66
Identity of man, by J. Bronowski. Review
    Nation 202:559-61 My 9 '66. F. H. Gardner
Jammed doors; Theatre and engineering show, New York. il Newsweek 68:101-2 O 31 '66
Partners in progress; address, April 22, 1966. G. T. Seaborg. il Sci N 89:339-40+ My 7 '66
Schism in American scholarship; address, November 6, 1965. J. Higham. bibliog f Am Hist R 72:1-21 O '66
Science invades art. il Sci Digest 60:86-7 N '66
Wacky collaboration of science and art; Nine evenings: theatre and engineering. il Fortune 75:100-3 Ja '67
Where is science taking us? visions and values of human experience; excerpts from addresses. G. Kepes. il Sat R 49:66-7 Mr 5 '66
Will the real work of art please stand up? Art-in-science touring exhibition. L. Lerman. il Mlle 62:114-16 Ja '66

ART and society
Art & man. D. Hayman. il Sch Arts 65:5-8 My '66
Art, technology and education; excerpt from address, February 1966. A. I. Cox, jr. Christian Cent 83:862-4 Jl 6 '66
Artist and/in the electronic environment. D. Smith. Craft Horiz 26:42+ N '66
Culture boom. W. Murray. il Holiday 39:70-5+ Mr '66
Marshall McLuhan. R. Kostelanetz. Commonweal 85:420-6 Ja 20 '67
Mass media's gifts to the muse; report on University of Chicago's conference on The arts and the public. G. Hicks. Sat R 49:35-6+ N 19 '66
Ouch! I love it! E. Kendall. Holiday 40:116+ Jl '66
Perfect total; excerpts from Themes and episodes. I. Stravinsky and R. Craft. Seventeen 25:304+ Ag '66
Theater of commitment; excerpt from address. E. Bentley. Commentary 42:63-72 D '66
What modern art says about America. M. Fishwick. Sat R 49:19-20+ Ap 9 '66
Yes—no. art—technology; address, July 1965. J. Landau. il Wilson Lib Bul 41:42-57 S '66

See also
Art—International aspects

ART and state
Art, government and dirty books. T. B. Hess. Art N 65:25 My '66
Arts, the humanities, and the federal government; adaptation of address, July 1966. R. L. Stevens. ALA Bul 60:900-3 O '66
Culture boom. W. Murray. il Holiday 39:70-5+ Mr '66
Editor's letters; three art bills sponsored by the office of the Attorney General of the state of New York. A. S. Lane. Art N 65:6 N '66
Enter government, exit art; controversy over U.S. show at Venice biennale. K. Kuh. Sat R 49:28-9 Ap 2 '66
First steps in legislation for the arts. L. J. Lefkowitz. Art N 65:29 S '66; Reply. R. F. Colin. 65:6 O '66

Politics and the arts; excerpt from address. P. Ustinov. Atlan 218:44-8 Jl '66
Politics of art. M. Greenfield. il Reporter 35:25-30 S 22 '66

See also
Art and society
Arts councils of America
National foundation for the arts and humanities
State encouragement of science, literature, and art
United States—National council on the arts
United States—National foundation for the arts and humanities

ART auctions. See Art sales
ART books. See Art literature
ART buildings, College. See College architecture
ART centers
Family work shops; Des Moines art center. P. Patrick. il Sch Arts 66:5-7 O '66

ART clubs
See also
Sculptors guild

ART collecting. See Art—Private collections
ART collections. See Art—Galleries and museums
ART colonies. See Artists colonies
ART competitions. See Art—Competitions

ART conferences
Mass media's gifts to the muse; report on University of Chicago's conference on The arts and the public. G. Hicks. Sat R 49:35-6+ N 19 '66
Second annual Puerto Rico art education conference. P. Greenberg. il Sch Arts 65:38-40 F '66

ART criticism
Death in the afternoon. N. Kent. Am Artist 30:3+ O '66
Fine arts. K. Kuh. See occasional issues of Saturday review

ART critics
Poet as critic; C. Baudelaire. A. Werner. Reporter 34:58+ F 24 '66

ART dealers
Choice dealer's choice. il Art N 65:55+ Mr '66
Come to Christie's; bicentenary celebration. H. A. La Farge. il Art N 65:42-3+ D '66
Five with enterprise; girl gallery owner. P. Rifield. il Mlle 63:145 S '66
How to smell a Rubens; strange case of the Judgment of Paris. il Time 88:88-91 S 16 '66
Rome's gallery girls; directors and dealers. il Newsweek 68:85-6 Ag 15 '66
Status symbols for everyman. Holiday 39:144-5 Mr '66
200 years of Christie's. il Newsweek 69:77-9 Ja 16 '67

See also
Art—Galleries and museums
Parke-Bernet galleries, incorporated
Sotheby and company

ART dealers association of America
Editor's letters. Art N 65:6 D '66

ART education
Art and the emerging elementary curriculum. P. C. Pitt. il Sch Arts 65:25-6 F '66
Art experiences and divergent thinking. M. Schultze. il Sch Arts 65:37-40 Mr '66
Art judgment & social responsibility. J. J. Lovano and J. K. McFee. bibliog il Sch Arts 65:23-4 Ap '66
Beware of the bunnies. E. Mills. il Sch Arts 66:33 O '66
Discovering the world of art; with discussion group program, by E. G. Neisser. J. W. Fosburgh. bibliog il Parents Mag 41:44-6+, 84+ Je '66
Discovery. M. Y. Krider. il Design 67:36-7 Ja '66
Environment of art. P. Albenda. il Sch Arts 66:10-12 S '66
Environmental art; work done through neighborhood self-help. K. Linn. il Sch Arts 66:26-8 D '66
How to be an artist in one lesson. R. Barrio. il Design 67:8-12 My '66
Letters (cont) Sch Arts 66:36-7 N '66
Second annual Puerto Rico art education conference. P. Greenberg. il Sch Arts 65:38-40 F '66
Seminar on elementary and secondary education in the visual arts; ed. by H. Conant. Review
    Craft Horiz 26:7-8 Ja '66. F. Schwartz
To be a human being. B. Wasserman. il Sch Arts 66:28-32 O '66

ART education—*Continued*
What makes it art? A. Ehrlich. il Sch Arts
65:5-7 Je '66
See also
Art—Study and teaching
International society for education through
art
ART exhibitions. See Art—Exhibitions
ART exhibitions, Traveling. See Exhibitions,
Traveling
ART festivals. See Art—Exhibitions
ART galleries, Commercial. See Art dealers
ART galleries and museums. See Art—Galleries
and museums
ART glass. See Glass, Ornamental
ART in industry. See Art and industry
ART in motion
Art in orbit; kinetic art. il Newsweek 67:
92-4 Ap 4 '66
Sculptures in motion; with report by D.
Bourdon. il Life 61:40-7+ Ag 12 '66
ART in public buildings
What is suitable art for public buildings. E.
Goble. Arch Rec 139:9 My '66
ART in the home
Bunshaft residence, East Hampton, New York.
il Arch Rec 139:40-5 mid-My '66
House of many treasures; Beirut. il House
& Gard 130:236-41 N '66
How three collectors display their treasures.
il House & Gard 130:62-83 Jl '66
Old masters at home. B. Plumb. il N Y
Times Mag p 102-3+ Mr 27 '66
Paintings one lives with brighten the house.
A. West. House & Gard 130:84-5+ Jl '66
Schramm residence, Burlington, Iowa. il Arch
Rec 139:64-7 mid-My '66
Stamped with personality. B. Plumb. il N Y
Times Mag p64-5 F 6 '66
See also
Art—Private collections
ART institute, Chicago. See Chicago art institute
ART juries. See Juries, Art
ART literature
Books in the field: art. J. Humphry, 3d. bibliog il Wilson Lib Bul 41:296-300+ N '66
ART loans
Kabul confluence: treasures lent by the
Afghanistan museums to Asia house, N.Y.
M. Neff. il Art N 64:26-7+ F '66
That nations may know; bill signed to facilitate exchanges with foreign countries.
W. Benton. Sat R 49:95 D 3 '66
ART metal work
Early metallurgy in the New World. D. T.
Easby, jr. il Sci Am 214:72-8+ bibliog
(p 140) Ap '66
Metals; a discussion. J. Prip; R. Pearson.
Craft Horiz 26:29-31 Je '66
Metalworkers of Europe. J. Skoogfors. il
Craft Horiz 26:36-41+ S '66
See also
Enamel and enameling
Goldsmithing
ART museums. See Art—Galleries and museums
ART news (periodical)
Honor roll, 1966. il Art N 65:27 D '66
ART objects
Golden web. il Vogue 147:202-3 My '66
Holiday world bazaar. il Holiday 40:124-7 D
'66
See also
Antiques
Display of antiques, art objects, etc.
ART objects, English
Letter from London. J. Stuart. il Antiques
89:346+ Mr '66
ART sales
Art over the counter; careless merchandising
of art by department and specialty stores.
K. Kuh. Sat R 49:38-9 D 31 '66
Auction season in review; 1965-66 season.
F. Neugass. Art N 65:18-19 S '66
Come to Christie's; bicentenary celebration.
H. A. La Farge. il Art N 65:42-3+ D '66
Coming auctions. See issues of Art news
Coming auctions, New York, London. Art N
65:19+ S '66
Reshuffling the goodies; auctions at Parke-
Bernet galleries. il Esquire 65:72-5 Mr '66
Solid-gold hammer. il Time 88:88 O 21 '66
Twelve francs, plus interest; auction of
Daumier's works at Paris' Palais galliera.
il Time 87:67 Je 24 '66
200 years of Christie's. il Newsweek 69:77-9
Ja 16 '67
See also
Parke-Bernet galleries, incorporated
Sotheby and company

ART schools
Art school directory, 1966. Am Artist 30:
AD1-AD16 [75-90] Mr '66
Cluster of bubbles; Cuba's school of plastic
arts. il Arch Forum 124:80-5 Ja '66
ART shows. See Art—Exhibitions
ART societies
See also
Sculptors guild
ART surveys
Market research art; consumer-determined
sculpture by G. Laing and P. Phillips. il
Life 60:71-2+ My 20 '66
ART teachers
Art teacher speaks his mind. J. Carlin. il Am
Artist 30:24-5+ Mr '66
Artist-teacher. J. Ottiano. il Sch Arts 65:
27-32 F '66
ART tests. See Educational tests and measurements
ART thefts
Curious case of the greatest art haul; looting
of Dulwich college picture gallery. il Life
62:60-2 Ja 13 '67
Odyssey in oils; paintings taken in post-
World war I Germany, to be returned. il
Time 89:58+ Ja 20 '67
Quick recovery; theft from Dulwich gallery,
England. il Newsweek 69:44 Ja 16 '67
Thief-proofing our art museums. R. LeBlanc.
Am Artist 30:16-17+ F '66
Unprofitable robbery; Dulwich college museum. Time 89:27 Ja 13 '67
ART therapy
Arts in therapy. M. F. Thompson. il Parks
& Rec 1:858+ O '66
Therapeutic art. B. E. Davidson. il Design
68:27-8 S '66
ART trade
See also
Art dealers
Art sales
ART vandalism. See Vandalism
ART workshops. See Art—Study and teaching
ARTAUD, Antonin
Theater of cruelty. M. Esslin. il por N Y
Times Mag p22-3+ Mr 6 '66
ARTEMIA. See Shrimps
ARTERENOL. See Norepinephrine
ARTERIES
Surgery
See Blood vessels—Surgery
ARTERIOSCLEROSIS
Atherosclerosis. D. M. Spain. il Sci Am 215:
48-56 bibliog(p 114) Ag '66; Reply with rejoinder. J. Yudkin. 215:8 D '66
Atherosclerosis; report on international symposium. D. Kritchevsky and R. Paoletti.
Science 153:1023-4 Ag 26 '66
Beta-glucuronidase activity in serum increased by coronary-artery atherosclerosis.
B. F. Miller and others. bibliog Science 152:
775-6 My 6 '66
Joint assault launched on arterial ailments.
il Sci N 90:468 D 3 '66
New life for failing hearts; new surgery. J.
D. Ratcliff. il Read Digest 88:181-2+ F '66
ARTHRITIS
Arthritis & rheumatism. il Time 87:71-2 Je 17
'66
Arthritis bug? Newsweek 69:40 Ja 2 '67

Therapy
Touch of pregnancy. Sci Digest 60:16 N '66
What is arthritis? is there a cure? Sci Digest 60:93-4 Jl '66
ARTHROPODS
Defensive secretions of arthropods. T. Eisner
and J. Meinwald. bibliog il Science 153:
1341-50 S 16 '66
See also
Mites
Peripatus
ARTHUR, Jay
Sound for shows, a buyer's guide to tape.
Pop Phot 58:94+ Mr '66
ARTHUR, Kay
Mother goes modern; drama. Plays 25:1-14,
26 My '66
ARTHUR, Thomas C.
Rural renewal; poem. Christian Cent 83:327
Mr 16 '66
Some of my best friends are; poem. Christian
Cent 83:395 Mr 30 '66
ARTHUR Bones, the reading dog; drama. See
Watts, F. B.
ARTHURIAN legends. See Grail

ARTICHOKES
Beautiful blue globe artichoke. Mrs J. D. Rogers. Flower Grower 53:42 D '66
See also
Cookery—Vegetables

ARTICLES for periodicals. See Periodical literature

ARTICULATION (speech) See Diction

ARTIFACTS, Indian. See Indians of North America—Antiquities

ARTIFICIAL body parts. See Prosthesis

ARTIFICIAL features. See Prosthesis

ARTIFICIAL flowers. See Flowers, Artificial

ARTIFICIAL fog. See Fog, Artificial

ARTIFICIAL heart. See Heart, Artificial

ARTIFICIAL heart valves. See Heart—Surgery

ARTIFICIAL insemination
Big changes coming with hog A.I. D. Hagen. il Farm J 90:30-1+ D '66
These producers found ways to make beef AI work. C. Peterson, jr. and D. Malena. il Suc Farm 64:44-5+ Mr '66
They're making swine AI work! J. Harvey. Suc Farm 64:32 Jl '66
We've bought our last bull. il Farm J 90:56A-56B D '66
See also
Semen

ARTIFICIAL insemination, Human
Fatherhood in deep freeze. H. Wray-McCann. Sci Digest 60:12-14 Jl '66
Riddle of A.I. Prutting suit poses legal riddle. il Time 87:48 F 25 '66
See also
Semen

ARTIFICIAL intelligence
Artificial intelligence. M. L. Minsky. il Sci Am 215:246-52+ S '66

ARTIFICIAL islands
Tragic sequel; collapse of sea-going oil platform. il Sci Digest 59:8 Mr '66

ARTIFICIAL kidneys. See Kidneys, Artificial

ARTIFICIAL lakes. See Lakes, Artificial

ARTIFICIAL larynx. See Larynx, Artificial

ARTIFICIAL limbs
Faster step; temporary aluminum legs; procedure at Oakland research laboratory. il Newsweek 68:44-5 Ag 29 '66
Instant prostheses. il Time 87:61-2 My 6 '66
New for amputees: instant limbs; M. Weiss's immediate prosthesis procedure. A. T. Jordan. Todays Health 44:37-9+ D '66;
Same abr. with title They walk again, at once. Read Digest 89:61-4 D '66

ARTIFICIAL organs. See Prosthesis

ARTIFICIAL respiration. See Respiration, Artificial

ARTIFICIAL rubber. See Rubber, Artificial

ARTIFICIAL satellites
Ampex device to cut waste in ATS photos; applications technology satellite B. Tech W 19:34 N 7 '66
ATS: a satellite's satellite; Applications technology satellite B. Sci N 90:471 D 3 '66
ATS-B to begin meteorology, communications, control tests. il Tech W 19:16 D 5 '66
ATS ground station ready for installation in Australia. il Miss & Roc 18:36 My 2 '66
ATS-1 data point to commercial payoffs. W. S. Beller. il Tech W 20:28-30 Ja 16 '67
ATS-1 offers improvement in air safety; equipped to monitor weather. H. Taylor. il Tech W 19:20 D 19 '66
ATS photos reflect weather patterns. il Aviation W 85:19-21 D 19 '66
ATS project seeks practical payoffs; applications technology satellites. W. S. Beller. il Miss & Roc 18:22-4 Mr 7 '66
Astrolog; current status of U.S. missile and space programs. See occasional issues of Missiles and rockets
How are satellites kept from tumbling? il Sci Digest 60:83-4 O '66
It's just a game; GREMEX, Goddard research engineering management exercise. J. Eberhart. Sci N 90:256 O 1 '66
Jam in orbit; guide and statistical record. il Newsweek 68:73-5 O 17 '66
Mirrors are coming; mirror-like satellites to reflect the sun and illuminate large areas of earth at night. il Time 89:56 Ja 13 '67
NESC outlines satellite tasks; new responsibilities taken on by the National environmental satellite center. Tech W 19:20+ N 28 '66
Satellite elongation into a true Sky-Hook. J. D. Isaacs and others. bibliog il Science 151:682-3 F 11 '66; Discussion. 152:800 My 6 '66

Satellites collide. Sci N 90:333 O 22 '66
Space vehicle log (cont) Aviation W 84:73 Ap 4 '66
Unified earth-sensor orbiter considered. W. J. Normyle. Aviation W 86:28-9 Ja 16 '67
World missile/space encyclopedia 1966. il Tech W 19:42-8+ Jl 25 '66
See also
Space vehicles

Astronomical applications
Advanced large orbital telescope systems urged as astronomy goal. W. J. Normyle. Aviation W 84:61+ F 14 '66
Europe begins its own orbiting observatory; LAS. Sci N 90:274 O 8 '66
Go-Go OGO; program under a cloud. il Newsweek 68:52 Jl 4 '66
Impact of Goddard report spreads. W. J. Normyle. Aviation W 85:26-7 D 12 '66
NAS urges solar observatory work; step-up in Orbiting solar observatory and Radio astronomy explorer programs. H. M. David. Miss & Roc 18:15 F 7 '66
NASA panel sets new guidelines for observatories at Goddard center. H. Taylor. Tech W 19:16-17 D 12 '66
New orbiting geophysical observatory. R. N. Watts, jr. il Sky & Tel 32:86-7 Ag '66
Orbiting astronomical observatory. D. A. Imgram. il Electr World 75:27-30+ Mr '66
Orbiting astronomical observatory. R. N. Watts, jr. il Sky & Tel 31:275-6 My '66
OAO fails on second day in orbit; battery, short circuit suspected. G. Alexander. il Aviation W 84:31 Ap 18 '66
O.A.O; orbiting astronomical observatory, representing first attempt to put telescope in space. New Yorker 42:41-4 Ap 23 '66
OGO III begins demanding mission. il Tech W 18:18 Je 13 '66
OSO data proposals under study of NASA. Aviation W 85:78 Ag 8 '66
Science's most sophisticated task ever; orbiting solar observatory. J. Colvin. il Sci Digest 60:20-3 Jl '66
Surprise package; OAO's aim. il Newsweek 67:68 Ap 11 '66

Communication applications
See Communications satellites

Design
See Space vehicles—Design

Detection
Spying on the sky; black art of radar signature analysis. J. Eberhart. il Sci N 90:226-7 S 24 '66

Equipment
See Space vehicles—Equipment

Launching
ESSA II: satellite launch marks new departure and new management. J. Walsh. il Science 151:1202-4 Mr 11 '66
First Biosatellite launch set amid criticism. H. M. David. il Tech W 19:20+ D 12 '66
Launch site shift paces super Diamant. W. C. Wetmore. il Aviation W 84:80-2+ My 16 '66
Lunar Orbiter experiments under way following launch. Tech W 19:16 Ag 15 '66
NASA readies Pageos satellite for launch into circular orbit. il Aviation W 84:176-7+ Je 20 '66
Orbiter launched toward moon to photograph nine Apollo sites. G. Alexander. il Aviation W 85:34 Ag 15 '66
Orbiting ATS-1 set for technology tests. il Aviation W 85:32-3 D 12 '66
Roster of space activity. R. N. Watts, jr. il Sky & Tel 33:28-30 Ja '67

Launching sites
Cosmos betrays new launch site. P. J. Klass. il Aviation W 85:16-17 D 19 '66
Soviets build polar-orbit launch site. Tech W 19:20 D 19 '66

Manufacture
See Space vehicles—Manufacture

Mapping applications
Geodetic satellite photos analyzed. Aviation W 84:180 Je 20 '66
NASA readies Pageos satellite for launch into circular orbit. il Aviation W 84:176-7+ Je 20 '66
Pageos. R. N. Watts, jr. il Sky & Tel 32:87+ Ag '66

ARTIFICIAL satellites—Mapping applications—
Continued
Satellite observations make accurate maps;
satellite geophysics project. Sci N 90:247
O 1 '66
Satellites to assist study of earth's shape;
PAGEOS. Sci N 89:213 Ap 2 '66

Meteorological applications
Computer plots national lines on photos. il
Tech W 19:37 Ag 8 '66
ESSA satellite funds chopped. Aviation W
85:33 O 10 '66
ESSAs enlarge forecasters' perspective; en-
vironmental survey satellite. D. E. Fink.
il Aviation W 84:94-9 Mr 21 '66
Fairbanks pass: routine operation of Nimbus
II. New Yorker 42:27-9 Ag 20 '66
FAA tests antenna with Nimbus picture.
Aviation W 85:103-4 N 14 '66
Geodetic institute taps U.S. weather satel-
lites. Sci N 90:361 O 29 '66
New Nimbus avionics interface transmits in-
frared on APT link; automatic picture
transmission. K. J. Stein. il Aviation W
84:77+ My 2 '66
Nimbus B package is designed to talk to
weather stations; interrogation, recording
and location system. il Tech W 19:42+ Ag
15 '66
Nimbus II keeps a global eye on the weather.
il Bsns W p 118+ My 21 '66
Nimbus II will gauge cloud height. W. S.
Beller. il Miss & Roc 18:31-3+ F 21 '66
RCA outlines world watch on weather. Miss
& Roc 18:40+ F 28 '66
Soviet weather satellite photos sent to U.S.
W. J. Normyle. Aviation W 85:26-7 S 26
'66
U.S. preparing to exchange data with Russia
on weather satellites. Aviation W 85:24
Ag 29 '66
Weather patterns mapped continuously. Sci N
89:438 Je 4 '66
Weather satellites get full-time job. il Bsns
W p 145 Ja 22 '66
World's weather in one picture; photos
taken by Tiros 9. Sci Digest 59:86-7 Ap '66

Military applications
Advanced anti-satellite system in offing. M.
Getler and R. Pay. Miss & Roc 18:69-70 My
30 '66
But who needs sun at night? Project Able,
earth orbital light-reflective system for
military operations at night. Sky & Tel
32:183+ O '66
DOD orbits record seventy satellites in 1965;
report identifies many. Aviation W 84:30 F
7 '66
DOD plans multi-mission satellite RFP. Miss
& Roc 18:17 My 2 '66
New applications, techniques sought for ad-
vanced systems. C. D. LaFond and others.
il Miss & Roc 18:37-8+ My 30 '66
New USAF satellite to include infrared,
photo scanning gear. Aviation W 85:23 D
26 '66
Soviets hike reconnaissance satellite pace.
P. J. Klass. il Aviation W 85:16-18 Jl 4 '66
Spies that can't feel the cold. H. Simons. il
Esquire 65:104-5+ My '66
Trend in space is toward refinements. E. H.
Kolcum. il Aviation W 84:83+ Mr 7 '66

Navigational applications
Aeronautical satellite faces obstacles. P. J.
Klass. il Aviation W 85:223+ O 31 '66
First civilian vessel navigates by satellite.
Sci N 90:287 O 8 '66
Navigation by satellites possible from air-
planes. Sci N 89:490 Je 18 '66
Navy tests satellite for navaid updating;
using navy navigation satellite system.
P. J. Klass. Aviation W 84:103-4 Je 13
'66
Science and space; Philco plan presented to
FAA. Newsweek 67:94-5 Mr 21 '66
Sextant in the sky. J. Martenhoff. il Motor
B 117:85+ Ja '66

Power supply
See Space vehicles—Power supply

Stability and stabilizers
See Space vehicles—Stability and stabilizers

Testing
Orbiting ATS-1 set for technology tests. il
Aviation W 85:32-3 D 12 '66

Tracking
AF uprates satellite tracking center. K. Voss.
il Tech W 19:32-3 Jl 11 '66

European space station to be located in
Alaska; White House announcement; with
text of U.S. note by Charles E. Bohlen
and executive order. Dept State Bul 55:979-
82 D 26 '66
Joint NASA/DOD tracking net studied. H.
Taylor. Miss & Roc 18:12 My 16 '66
Our secret eye on space; Space defense
center at Ent AFB in Colorado Springs.
D. Robinson. il Look 30:94-6+ N 15 '66
Signatures in the sky; Radar signature anal-
ysis. il Time 88:112 O 21 '66
Spying on the sky; black art of radar signa-
ture analysis. J. Eberhart. il Sci N 90:226-7
S 24 '66

Use in research
Bios-1 orbits thirteen biological experiments.
G. Alexander. Aviation W 85:23 D 19 '66
Biosat; laboratory in orbit. J. Eberhart.
Sci N 90:511 D 17 '66
Biosatellite mission objectives detailed. R.
Pay. il Tech W 18:24-5+ Je 27 '66
Biosatellite program faces budget hurdle.
Tech W 19:13 O 17 '66
Cold-welding experiments set for ORS-2; oc-
tahedral research satellite. I. Stone. il
Aviation W 84:85-7 My 23 '66
EROS vs. ESSA. Newsweek 68:62 O 3 '66
Earth's resources to be studied from space;
Project EROS. il Sci N 90:281 O 8 '66
Exploration by satellite; Project Eros. Sci
Am 215:66 N '66
Explorer 32. R. N. Watts, jr. il Sky & Tel
31:347-8 Je '66
First Biosatellite launch set amid criticism.
H. M. David. il Tech W 19:20+ D 12 '66
High-resolution camera proposed for Eros.
il Aviation W 85:77 N 14 '66
Interstellar deuterium found; measurements
made from IMP-III. Sci N 90:119 Ag 20 '66
Multiple satellite study set for Ames. Avia-
tion W 85:63 Ag 29 '66
NASA, DOD join in planning long primate
vestibular test; two advanced biosatellite
flight experiments Tech W 19:38+ N 14 '66
Nine firms named to build German research
satellite. W. Buedeler. il Tech W 19:36 Ag
29 '66
Plants ready for space; biosatellite mission.
Sci N 90:206 S 17 '66
Radio astronomy, stellar probe among satel-
lite uses proposed. Aviation W 85:64 O 24
'66
Saturn set to lift heaviest satellite; lunar
IMP slated. il Tech W 18:19 Je 27 '66
Some doubts about the earth's dust cloud.
C. Nilsson. bibliog il Science 153:1242-6
S 9 '66
These spacecraft say ouch! W. Von Braun.
il Pop Sci 189:76-7+ Jl '66
UCLA may become first college with complete
satellite project. W. E. Wilks. Tech W
19:36 D 12 '66
UCLA to build satellite for plasma study.
Sci N 90:339 O 22 '66

ARTIFICIAL satellites, European
First ESRO satellite readied for launch;
NASA international cooperation program.
H. J. Coleman. il Aviation W 86:79-81 Ja
16 '67

ARTIFICIAL satellites, French
D-1A bolsters French space aspirations;
Diapason. W. C. Wetmore. il Aviation W
84:111+ Ap 18 '66
D-2 launch may be first for Guiana site. W.
C. Wetmore. il Aviation W 84:209+ Je 20
'66
Launch site shift paces super Diamant.
W. C. Wetmore. il Aviation W 84:80-2+
My 16 '66

ARTIFICIAL satellites, German
Nine firms named to build German research
satellite. W. Buedeler. il Tech W 19:36
Ag 29 '66

ARTIFICIAL satellites, Japanese
Two dress rehearsals slated before Japanese
scientific shot. S. Nagashima. il Tech W
19:34-5 O 17 '66

ARTIFICIAL satellites, Russian
Cosmos betrays new launch site. P. J. Klass.
il Aviation W 85:16-17 D 19 '66
Experiments aboard Cosmos satellites. R.
N. Watts, jr. Sky & Tel 31:82 F '66
Luna 10 measurements include gravitational
field of moon. il Aviation W 84:33 Ap 11
'66
Orbiting of Soviets' Luna 10 widens USSR
lead to moon. il Miss & Roc 18:13 Ap 11
'66
Soviet weather satellite photos sent to U.S.
W. J. Normyle. Aviation W 85:26-7 S 26
'66

ARTIFICIAL satellites, Russian—*Continued*
Soviets build polar-orbit launch site. Tech W 19:20 D 19 '66
Soviets disclose orbiting of atomic clock; Cosmos 97 to check Einstein's theory of relativity. Aviation W 85:36 N 21 '66
Soviets hike reconnaissance satellite pace. P. J. Klass. il Aviation W 85:16-18 Jl 4 '66
Soviets reveal new data on spacecraft; Voskhod 2 and Cosmos 110. W. C. Wetmore. Aviation W 84:26-7 My 16 '66
Soviets trim comsat orbit for most USSR coverage. P. J. Klass. Aviation W 85:34 O 24 '66

ARTIFICIAL teeth. See Teeth, Artificial

ARTIFICIAL uterus. See Uterus, Artificial

ARTISTIC ability. See Creation (literary, artistic, etc)

ARTISTIC photography. See Photography, Artistic

ARTISTS
Art history for grade two. L. B. Garcia. il Sch Arts 66:10-12 N '66
E=MC² à go-go; ten painters and sculptors of the Park Place gallery, New York. D. Bourdon. il Art N 64:22-5+ Ja '66
Henry here, Henry there, who is Henry? il Life 60:41-2+ F 18 '66
Imports. L. Lerman. il Mlle 62:156-9 F '66
Masters in the art news. il Art N 65:24-7 O; 22-5 D '66
Movement movement; kinetic artists. il Time 87:64-9 Ja 28 '66
Potpourri of protest against war in Vietnam; Los Angeles. il Newsweek 67:101 Mr 14 '66
Top thirteen; France's Connaissance des arts poll. Time 88:46 Jl 29 '66

ARTISTS, American
For bread alone; art patronage of WPA. il Time 87:78 My 13 '66
From Pollock to pop; twenty years of painting and sculpture. H. Rosenberg. il Holiday 39:96-105+ Mr '66
St Augustine: city of artists, 1883-1895. F. A. Sharf. il Antiques 90:220-3 Ag '66
Vanguard artist, by B. Rosenberg and N. Fliegel. Review
  Commentary 41:100+ F '66. G. Dennison
See also
Artists, Negro
Bridport, H.
Brussel-Smith, B.
Morris, R.
Painting, American
Riggs, R.
Sculpture, American

ARTISTS, Brazilian
Portfolio of gifted cariocas. il Holiday 39:53-9 F '66

ARTISTS, British
See also
Blampied, E.

ARTISTS, French
See also
Arp, H.

ARTISTS, German
See also
Janssen, H.

ARTISTS, Greek
See also
Samaras, L.

ARTISTS, Japanese
See also
Matsubara, N.

ARTISTS, Jewish
See also
Shalom of Safed

ARTISTS, Latin American
From the pampas to Fifth avenue; Latin American painters and painting in the 1960's Guggenheim museum show. F. Getlein. New Repub 154:33-4 Je 25 '66

ARTISTS, Negro
Why Spiral? symposium. J. Siegel. il Art N 65:48-51+ S '66

ARTISTS, Turkish
See also
Youssouf, F.

ARTISTS, Yugoslav
Out of Yugoslavia; works by painters and sculptors to be exhibited at six US museums during 1966. F. Getlein. New Repub 154:24+ F 12 '66
Slavs without Marx; exhibition at Corcoran gallery of art. il Newsweek 67:82 F 7 '66

ARTISTS colonies
Landscape at New London; American art colony at Old Lyme, Conn. F. Getlein. New Repub 154:34-5 Mr 12 '66

ARTISTS easels. See Easels

ARTISTS guild, Incorporated
Alan E. Cober: artist of the year '65. H. C. Pitz. il Am Artist 30:36-41+ Je '66

ARTISTS materials
Art mart. See issues of American artist
How it all began. .; Creative decor kit and the Mini kit. il Design 68:22 N '66
1966 buyers' guide. Sch Arts 65:46-51 F '66
Ralph Mayer's technical question & answer page. R. Mayer. See issues of American artist
Tips for artists. F. Matranga. il Design 68:38 N '66
Twelfth annual product guide. il Am Artist 31:PG1-16 Ja '67
See also
Art—Study and teaching—Materials

ARTMOBILES
Muncie's art project. il Am Ed 2:7 Jl '66

ARTS and crafts
Holiday world bazaar. il Holiday 41:106-9 Ja '67
Twenty-five years of Craft horizons; quotations from past issues. il Craft Horiz 26:69-71+ Je '66
See also
Folk art
Glass, Ornamental
Handicraft
Papier-mâché
Pottery
Stencil work
Weaving

Bibliography
Book review section. See issues of Design
Books (cont) Craft Horiz 26:57 S '66

Competitions
Craftsmen USA '66; six regional competitions sponsored by the American craftsmen's council in cooperation with major museums and art centers; symposium. il Craft Horiz 26:28-36+ Mr; 72-81+ Je '66 (to be cont)

Exhibitions
Calendar; where to show. See issues of Craft horizons
Craftsmen USA '66; six regional competitions sponsored by the American craftsmen's council in cooperation with major museums and art centers; symposium. il Craft Horiz 26:28-36+ Mr; 72-81+ Je '66 (to be cont)
Exhibitions. See issues of Craft horizons
Stuttgart: International crafts exhibition. S. Kobell. il Craft Horiz 26:22-7 S '66

Study and teaching
Clowns; delightful center-pieces. H. Rush. il Design 67:20-1 My '66
Role of crafts in education. H. Fink. Craft Horiz 26:8+ Je '66
Summer crafts. Dorfé. il Design 67:29-31 My '66

Materials
Pine cone creations. Sister Mary Eusebio. il Design 67:26-8 My '66
Tin-can flowers. Mrs R. W. Bonnewell. il Design 67:14-15 My '66

China
Chinese legend & lore, the Three friends. G. Kaler. il Hobbies 71:50-1 O '66

Hungary
Hungarian enamels. G. Kaler. il Hobbies 71:46+ Mr; 46+ Ap; 50 My; 50 Je; 50+ Jl '66

Latin America
Crisis in folk arts. G. de Zéndegui. il Américas 18:22-30 Ja '66

Lebanon
Fresh spring of ideas bubbling in an ancient land. D. Otis. il House & Gard 130:178-83+ D '66

Philippines
Going places, finding things in the Philippines. P. K. Brooks. il House & Gard 130:36-8+ N '66

Underdeveloped areas
Crafts in underdeveloped nations. M. Greene. il Craft Horiz 26:26-7 Mr '66

United States
Crafts of the Southern Highlands; portraits of craftsmen. Craft Horiz 26:35-56 Je '66
New American craftsman; first generation; symposium. il Craft Horiz 26:15-34 Je '66
Old crafts find new hands. il Life 61:34-43 Jl 29 '66
Southern Appalachians. J. Williams. il Craft Horiz 26:46-67 Je '66

ARTS councils of America, Incorporated
Councils take counsel; preview of annual conference. E. Coleman. Sat R 49:59-60 Ap 30 '66
Culture buff; interview. R. P. Hanes, jr. New Yorker 42:19-20 Je 25 '66
Mephisto's musings. il Hi Fi 16:MA2+ Ag; MA2-3 S '66
ARTSAY, Aida Favia-. See Favia-Artsay, A.
ARTZYBASHEFF, Boris
Boris Artzybasheff. L. S. Bechtel. por Horn Bk 42:176-80 Ap '66
ARUMS
See also
Sauromatum
ARUNDEL, Jocelyn
Set in Africa. Horn Bk 42:548-52 O '66
ARVIDSSON, Ture
How to stay off cigarettes; reprint. Sci Digest 59:71-4 Ap '66
ARVIN, Newton
Critic at the center. G. W. Allen. Sat R 49:91 Ap 9 '66
ARZHAK, Nikolai, pseud. See Daniel, Y.
AS if we were God's spies; story. See Brown. J.
AS the earth gets old; story. See Tyler, A.
ASAHI cameras. See Cameras
ASBELL, Bernard
Let the children teach. Redbook 126:52-3+ F '66
ASBURY PARK air terminal. See Airports— New Jersey
ASCARIS
1,2-propanediol-2-phosphate in ascaris lumbricoides. J. Kubištová and D. Seth. bibliog Science 154:1461 D 16 '66
ASCH, Moses
At our corner. por Sr Schol 89:sup22 N 11 '66
ASCHENBAUER, Mathilda
Geometric designs. Design 67:41 Ja '66
ASCIONE, Richard, and others
Laboratory culturing of a thermophilic alga at high temperature. bibliog Science 153:752-5 Ag 12 '66
ASCORBIC acid. See Vitamins—Vitamin C
ASCOT race. See Horse racing
ASEPSIS and antisepsis
Bye-bye, bacteria! T. Irwin. il Pop Mech 125:90-3+ Je '66
ASH, David
Detroit revolution. Esquire 66:86-7+ Jl '66
Encore the Avanti! Esquire 65:140-1+ Ap '66
ASH, Gordon
Drought knows no frontiers. UNESCO Courier 19:10-15 Ap '66
ASH, James E. See McCormac, B. M. jt. auth.
ASH, Lee
Book review index: a new book selection tool. por Library J 91:2013-15 Ap 15 '66
New York's other libraries. por Library J 91:3101-7 Je 15 '66
ASH, Roy Lawrence
How Litton keeps it up, the view from inside; interviews, ed. by D. Seligman and T. A. Wise. por Fortune 74:152-4+ S '66
about
View from the top at Litton. por Bsns W p 180 Ap 16 '66
ASH trays
Connoisseur's corner. il House & Gard 130:82+ O '66
ASHBAUGH, Byron L.
Federal aid boosts outdoor education. Audubon Mag 68:188-9 My '66
ASHBEE, K. H. G. and Vassamillet, L. F.
Dislocations in a Campo del Cielo meteorite. Science 151:1526-7 Mr 25 '66
ASHBERY, John
Brooms and prisms. Art N 65:58-9+ Mr '66
Fragment; poem. Poetry 107:283-98 F '66
Post-painterly quattrocento. Art N 65:40-1+ D '66
Talking of Michelangelo. Art N 65:42-3+ Sum '66
Unknown Sisley. Art N 65:44-5+ N '66
about
Games of the poet. S. Koch. Nation 203:649-50 D 12 '66
Speeding hackney cabriolet. H. Wamsley. Poetry 109:185-7 D '66
ASHBROOK, Frank G.
Wetlands: stepchild of land use. Nat Parks Mag 40:17-19 Ag '66
ASHBROOK, John Milan
Three races. H. Alexander. Nat R 18:1045 O 18 '66

ASHBROOK, Joseph
Astronomical scrapbook. See issues of Sky and telescope
ASHE, Arthur, jr
Arthur Ashe: hottest new tennis star. C. Brossard. il pors Look 30:110-14 Ap 19 '66
Arthur Ashe thing. Sports Illus 24:8 F 21 '66
Service, but first a smile. F. Deford. il Sports Illus 25:47-50 Ag 29 '66
ASHE, James
New books for junior high readers. Sr Schol 88:sup 10 Mr 25 '66
ASHEIM, Lester E.
Asheim to direct ALA's new Office for library education. Library J 91:3368 Jl '66
ASHER, Don
Far above Cayuga's waters, g-chung, g-chung; story. Sat Eve Post 239:64-8 N 5 '66
ASHFORD, Emmett
Ashford arrives. il pors Ebony 21:65-6+ Je '66
Delayed call. por Newsweek 67:62 Ap 25 '66
Emmett Ashford: ultra ump. G. Shalit. il pors Look 30:92-5+ O 4 '66
ASHKENAZY, Vladimir
Bird boy. il por Time 87:62 Ap 15 '66
Music to my ears; Carnegie Hall recital. I. Kolodin. Sat R 49:45 Ja 29 '66
ASHMAN, Guy Williams-. See Williams-Ashman, G.
ASHTON, Penny
Model's day. R. Busch. il pors Pop Phot 59:82-3+ Jl '66
ASIA
America as a Pacific nation; symposium. il Sat R 49:35-8+ O 8 '66
Dawn over Asia; address, October 6, 1966. C. P. Kim. Vital Speeches 33:42-6 N 1 '66
Free Asia; address, October 4, 1966. U. A. Johnson. Dept State Bul 55:638-43 O 24 '66; Excerpts with editorial comment. il U S News 61:98-100+, 132 O 17 '66
Future of the Pacific community; address, November 15, 1966. D. Rusk. Dept State Bul 55:838-43 D 5 '66
On understanding Asia; Time essay. Time 88:34-5 Jl 1 '66
Profile of Asia: ancient lands in troubled transition. Sr Schol 89:pt2 7-8 S 23 '66
Rallying round the river; across-the-border cooperation. Time 87:96 Mr 18 '66
See also
Agriculture—Asia
Australia—Foreign relations—Asia
Book industries and trade—Asia
Books and reading—Asia
Children—Asia
Communism—Asia
Development banks—Asia
Economic assistance in Asia
Kazakhstan
Mongolia
Nutrition problems—Asia
Poor—Asia
Public opinion—Asia

Civilization
Asian revolution and American ideology. R. S. Manglapus. bibliog f For Affairs 45:344-52 Ja '67

Description and travel
Asia. J. Durniak. il Pop Phot 58:82-5+ Ap '66

Economic conditions
Fallout; beneficial effect from U.S. involvement in Vietnam. il Time 87:84+ Ap 1 '66

Foreign relations
Afro-Asian inferiority complex; hatred towards Europeans and Americans. E. von Kuehnelt-Leddihn. Nat R 18:836 Ag 23 '66
Asian doctrine: what it's all about. il U S News 61:30-2 Ag 8 '66
Asian leader explains America's role to Americans; address, September 15, 1966. F. E. Marcos. il U S News 61:114-16+ O 3 '66
How a French authority sees U.S. role in Asia; interview, ed. by F. C. Painton. R. Dabernat. il U S News 62:93-4+ Ja 23 '67
Where U.S. stands in Asia: a first-hand report; interview. R. P. Martin. il U S News 60:40-3 Je 27 '66

History
Salem to Saigon. A. Goodfriend. il Sat R 49:37-8+ O 8 '66

Bibliography
Articles and other books received: east Asia; comp. by H. Conroy. See issues of American historical review
Articles and other books received: south Asia; comp. by C. Hobbs. See issues of American historical review

ASIA—*Continued*

Maps

Map of Asia (cont) Sr Schol 89:pt2 19 S 23 '66

Politics

Asian leader explains America's role to Americans; address, September 15, 1966. F. E. Marcos. il U S News 61:114-16+ O 3 '66; Same. Dept State Bul 55:534-47 O 10 '66; Same with title Philippines and the United States. Vital Speeches 33:2-10 O 15 '66

Asian summit, what to expect. U S News 61:35 O 10 '66

See also

Tricontinental conference, Havana, 1966

Social life and customs

Orientalization of the West. R. Hughes. il Sat R 49:47-8+ O 8 '66

ASIA, CENTRAL

See also

Iran

ASIA, SOUTHEASTERN

Presence of Marcos; reaping dividends from the American presence in Vietnam. Nat R 18:969-70 O 4 '66

Report on southeast Asia; symposium. bibliog f il Cur Hist 52:1-47+ Ja '67

Secretary Rusk's news conference of July 12, 1966. D. Rusk. Dept State Bul 55:162-8 Ag 1 '66

Southeast Asia, by T. Durdin. Review Atlan 217:132-3 F '66. O. Handlin

Vietnam and southeast Asia; symposium. bibliog f il Cur Hist 50:65-111+ F '66

See also

Communism—Asia, Southeastern

Mekong River

Bibliography

Vietnam booklist; information on China, the Vietnamese war, and problems of southeast Asia. Nation 202:525 My 2 '66

Defenses

Ho Chi Minh trail and our Thai buildup. D. Warner. il Reporter 34:26-8 Ja 27 '66

New man in Canberra; H. Holt's beliefs and policies. D. Warner. il Reporter 34:33-6 Ap 21 '66

Economic conditions

Asia: world's new frontier. il U S News 61: 34-7 O 31 '66

Foreign relations

What LBJ will find in Asia; Allies say: win the war. il U S News 61:37-40 O 24 '66

When free Asians get together. Life 61:6 O 14 '66

Neutrality

Quid without the quo; J. W. Fulbright's proposal. il Time 87:23 Mr 11 '66

Politics

Changing face of southeast Asia, by A. Vandenbosch and R. Butwell. Review Sat R 49:43-4 N 5 '66. J. M. Allison

Pictures in our minds; concerning NBC documentary The battle for Asia. New Repub 156:9-10 Ja 7 '67

Southeast Asia: how important, to whom? R. Butwell. bibliog f il Cur Hist 52:1-7 Ja '67

ASIA and Australia

Australia looks around. D. Horne. For Affairs 44:446-57 Ap '66

ASIA and the United States

America as a Pacific nation; symposium. il Sat R 49:35-8+ O 8 '66

ASIAD (games)

Asia: beneath the rising sun; Japanese athletes win 78 of 140 gold medals in Bangkok. M. Zim. il Sports Illus 26:18-19 Ja 2 '67

Spirit in Bangkok; fifth Asian games. Time 88:44-5 D 30 '66

ASIAN and Pacific council

Asia: optimism out of Seoul; first meeting. il Newsweek 67:45 Je 27 '66

New alliance, and more help for Viet Nam; gathering in Seoul. il Time 87:40 Je 24 '66

ASIAN development bank. See Development banks—Asia

ASIAN faith and order conference

Asian faith and order conference; Hong Kong. J. R. Fleming. Christian Cent 84: 24-5 Ja 4 '67

ASIAN flu. See Influenza

ASIAN games. See Asiad (games)

ASIAN literature

Bibliography

Unesco translations of literature of Asia. UNESCO Courier 19:33 Ja '66

ASIAN names. See Names, Asian

ASIMOV, Isaac

Fantastic voyage; story. Sat Eve Post 239: 40-4 F 26; 56-60+ Mr 12 '66

How was the earth's atmosphere formed? Sci Digest 60:91-2 N '66

Is the speed of light ultimate? Sci Digest 60:87-8 D '66

Pills to help us remember? N Y Times Mag p38-9+ O 9 '66

That old chemical complex, the human mind. N Y Times Mag p 12-13+ Jl 3 '66

UFO's, what I think. Sci Digest 59:44-7 Je '66

Views on science books. See issues of Horn book magazine

What is time? Sci Digest 60:93-4 S '66

Where do sunken ships go? Sci Digest 61:87-8 Ja '67

ASINOF, Eliot

Don't bunt, the gizmo says hit! Life 60:17 Ap 15 '66

Journey back to Bushville. N Y Times Mag p8-9+ Jl 24 '66

September's heroes on an August day. N Y Times Mag p46-7+ Ag 21 '66

ASLAN, Ana

Phony fountain of youth. R. L. Smith. il por Todays Health 44:27-9+ F '66

ASOLO theater, Sarasota, Fla. See Theater buildings

ASOLO theatre comedy festival. See Drama festivals

ASPAC. See Asian and Pacific council

ASPARAGINASE. See Enzymes

ASPARAGUS

For superb flavor, grow your asparagus. H. K. Branson. il Flower Grower 53:59-60 F '66

See also

Cookery—Vegetables

ASPELUND, Odd

Profiles. L. Ross. il New Yorker 42:72+ N 19 '66

ASPEN, Colo.

Motel in a mountain resort; Applejack inn. il Arch Rec 140:135 Ag '66

Will success spoil Aspen? P. G. Ernst. il Nation 203:70-3 Jl 25 '66

ASPEN international design conference. See International design conference

ASPEN music festival. See Music festivals—Colorado

ASPHALT mulch. See Mulching

ASPHALT pavements. See Pavements, Asphalt

ASPHYXIA

Cardiovascular defense against asphyxia. R. Elsner and others. bibliog il Science 153: 941-9 Ag 26 '66

ASPIC

Aspics without ado; with recipes. P. Cannon. il Ladies Home J 83:114-15+ My '66

ASPIRIN

Aspirin, liquor and LSD. H. Downs. Sci Digest 61:91-3 Ja '67

Aspirin, major menace to health in both old and young. Consumer Bul 49:2 S '66

Long acting aspirin given short life by FDA; Measurin. Sci N 90:181 S 10 '66

Timed aspirin ready. il Sci N L 89:131 F 26 '66

Trustworthy medication; concerning manufacture of St Joseph aspirin for children. M. B. Keiser. il Parents Mag 41:40+ S '66

Wonder drug nobody understands. G. A. W. Boehm. il N Y Times Mag p56-7+ S 11 '66

ASQUITH, Herbert Henry, 1st earl of Oxford and Asquith. See Oxford and Asquith, H. H. A.

ASSASSIN; story. See Marlowe, D.

ASSASSINATION

Death in the morning; Tran van Van. il Time 88:36 D 16 '66

Funeral in Saigon; Tran-van-Van. Newsweek 68:28 D 26 '66

See also

Kennedy, J. F.—Assassination

ASSEMBLY, Right of

Speech without assembly? the Court v. the demonstrators. T. I. Emerson. il Nation 203:704-8 D 26 '66

ASSEMBLY line methods

How it works on the line. S. Kelly. il Motor T 18:29-32 My '66

ASSESSMENT
100 percenter; California property-tax situation. Newsweek 68:80 N 7 '66
Property tax scandal; conditions in California. Nation 204:68-9 Ja 16 '67
Tax wonderland; California. Newsweek 67:29-30 Mr 7 '66
ASSESSORS
Perspective; U.S. need for reform in selection methods. R. Moley. Newsweek 68:96 Jl 11 '66
ASSISTANT district attorneys. See District attorneys
ASSOCIATED church press (organization)
Associated church press comes of age. Christian Cent 83:518 Ap 27 '66
ASSOCIATED colleges at Claremont, Calif.
Big schools labor to think small; cluster college. il Bsns W p 196-8+ S 17 '66
ASSOCIATED press
Rewards of routine; follow-up story on E. Negrón. Time 87:74 Ja 28 '66
ASSOCIATION for childhood education international
Meeting, 1966. il Sr Schol 88:sup2-3 My 6 '66
ASSOCIATION for supervision and curriculum development
Curriculum development by moonlight. Sr Schol 88:sup2 Ap 15 '66
ASSOCIATION for the study of Negro life and history
Atlanta in retrospect; report on 50th annual meeting. C. W. Thomas. il Negro Hist Bul 29:29-30+ N '65
Fifty years later; founding associate reminisces. J. E. Stamps. Negro Hist Bul 29:31-2 N '65
ASSOCIATION of American colleges
Meeting, 1966. W. W. Anderson. il Sch & Soc 94:394-6 N 12 '66
ASSOCIATION of American dance companies
Appetite for action, editorial. L. Joel. Dance Mag 40:33-4 Jl '66
Association of American dance companies. L. Joel. Dance Mag 40:34 D '66
ASSOCIATION of American medical colleges
AAMC: a broader leadership role in health education prescribed for Association of medical colleges. J. Walsh; discussion. Science 150:554, 1666; 151:1170+ O 29, D 24 '65, Mr 11 '66
ASSOCIATION of American universities
AAU, higher education's enigma. W. K. Selden. il Sat R 49:76-8 Mr 19 '66
ASSOCIATION of American university presses
AAUP's second show retains awareness of quality. P. A. Bennett. il Pub W 189:136-7+ Je 13 '66
University presses study the problems of growth; summary of discussion at AAUP meeting. il Pub W 190:32-51 Jl 4 '66
University publishing and the pressures of growth. C. B. Grannis. Pub W 190:61 Jl 4 '66
ASSOCIATION of Chicago priests
Chicago priests organize. D. L. Flaherty. America 115:540-3 N 5 '66
Why priests organize. Christian Cent 83:1370 N 9 '66
ASSOCIATION of college and research libraries
Look to the East; preconference of ACRL's college libraries section: Library collections for non-western studies, at Douglass college. S. Stowe. Library J 91:3645 Ag '66
ASSOCIATION of international libraries
AIL discusses problems of access to int'l organization materials. Library J 91:3373-4 Jl '66
ASSOCIATION of lunar and planetary observers
ALPO meets in Tucson. L. J. Robinson. il Sky & Tel 32:266-70 N '66
ASSOCIATION of management consultants
Treatment for business doctors. il Bsns W p 120-1+ Je 25 '66
ASSOCIATION of producing artists
Consensus theatre. R. Brustein. New Repub 156:41-2 Ja 7 '67
Theatre: APA-Phoenix theatre. H. Clurman. Nation 203:651 D 12 '66
Two by the APA. R. Gilman. il Newsweek 68:96+ D 5 '66
ASSOCIATION of research libraries
Meetings, 1966. Library J 91:1374+, 3888-9 Mr 15, S 1 '66
Numerical news: larger university libraries. E. Moon. Library J 91:2288 My 1 '66; Correction. 91:3020+ Je 15 '66
ASSOCIATIONS
See also
Meetings
ASSYRIAN antiquities. See Nimrud
ASTAIRE, Fred
Talks to teens. por Seventeen 25:154+ O '66

ASTATINE
Rare astatine probed. Sci N 89:463 Je 11 '66
ASTICOU gardens. See Gardens—Maine
ASTIN, Allen V.
He will decide when autos are safe; interview. por Nations Bsns 54:34-5+ Ag '66
ASTON family
Aston coat-of-arms. H. K. Eilers. il Hobbies 71:126-7 My '66
ASTOR, Gavin
Thomson takes the Times. Time 88:61 O 7 '66
ASTOR, William Waldorf, family
Meet me at the Astors'. il Newsweek 67:43 Je 6 '66
ASTOR family
Astors, by L. Kavaler. Review
Newsweek il 68:89 Jl 4 '66
ASTRAKHAN coat; drama. See Macaulay, P.
ASTRODOME, Houston. See Stadiums
ASTROLITE. See Explosives
ASTROLOGY
Delicious appeal to unreason. S. Alexander. Life 60:18 My 27 '66
Look at tomorrow today. R. Armstrong. il Sat Eve Post 239:23-7 Mr 26 '66
Weight-watchers' horoscope. S. Leek. il Ladies Home J 83:78+ N '66
What's your sign? J. Morris. il U S Camera 29:24+ D '66
ASTRONAUTS
Are any astronauts experienced? J. Eberhart. Sci N 90:441 N 26 '66
Astronauts named; first manned Apollo mission and Gemini II. Sci N 89:241 Ap 9 '66
Entry of nineteen candidates swells astronaut pool. Aviation W 84:32-3 Ap 11 '66
For sale: men to Mars. B. Frisch. il Sci Digest 59:67-70 Mr '66
How astronauts are doing financially. U S News 60:22 Ap 18 '66
Man on the moon; with paintings by N. Rockwell. J. A. Osmundsen. Look 31:39-42 Ja 10 '67
Men for moon & Mars: fifth group of spacemen. Time 87:24 Ap 15 '66
NASA recruits spacemen; scientists as astronauts. il Sci N 90:275 O 8 '66
Our first eighteen in space. R. P. Crossley. il Pop Mech 126:129 N '66
Perfectly paired Gemini team falls to earth; E. See and C. Bassett. R. Morse. il Life 60:34 Mr 11 '66
Safety above, risk below? deaths of E. M. See, jr, and C. A. Bassett. il Newsweek 67:68 Mr 14 '66
Scientist-astronauts: only the perspicacious need apply. L. J. Carter. Science 154:133-5 O 7 '66
See also
Space flight—Manned flights

Clothing
Advanced EVA pressure suits gain new emphasis. il Aviation W 85:106-7+ Ag 15 '66
Air force to use Gemini suit for extra-vehicular operations. H. M. David. il Miss & Roc 18:35-7 My 30 '66
Equipment devised for future flights. il Aviation W 85:74-7+ Ag 15 '66
NASA ponders Litton hard spacesuit. H. M. David. il Tech W 18:29-30 Je 20 '66
Suiting up; Hamilton unit and Litton suit. il Newsweek 68:62 O 3 '66
Suits seen inhibiting extravehicular activity. H. M. David. Tech W 19:27 N 7 '66
Top spacesuit manufacturers prepare for MOL competition. H. M. David. Tech W 19:21 N 14 '66

Recreation
Recreation in space. D. Stracke. il Parks & Rec 1:28-9+ Ja '66

Training
Apollo training stresses operations. E. H. Kolcum. il Aviation W 86:16-17 Ja 2 '67
Cosmonauts training for space assembly. Aviation W 84:32 Ap 25 '66
How to make out with EVA; Buzz Aldrin prepares for Gemini 12. il Time 88:114 S 30 '66
NASA offers to train European scientists for U.S. space missions. W. J. Normyle. Aviation W 84:23 F 28 '66
ASTRONAUTS ejection seats, capsules, etc.
See Space vehicles—Escape devices
ASTRONOMERS
See also
Astronomical observatories—Employees

ASTRONOMY—*Continued*

Observations

Area scanning. il Sky & Tel 32:262 N '66
X rays from Scorpio. il Time 88:78 S 16 '66
See also
Interferometers
Space flight—Astronomical observations
Stars—Observations
Sun—Observations

Study and teaching

Graduate training in astronomy; letter.
B. J. Bok. Science 154:590+ N 4 '66
Spectacle in the sky. T. D. Nicholson. il
Parents Mag 41:38-9+ Ag '66
Training of an astronomer; establishing tele-
scopes in good climates. J. B. Irwin. Sci-
ence 152:1597-9 Je 17 '66; Discussion. 153:
934+; 154:1275-6 Ag 26, D 9 '66

Tables, etc.

Events of 1967 in the graphic time table. Sky
& Tel 33:33-5 Ja '67

ASTRONOMY, Nautical. See Nautical astronomy

ASTRONOMY, Oriental
Ancient Oriental records of novae and
supernovae; excerpts from address, 1964,
tr. by K. S. Yang, Z. Z. Xi and S. J.
Po. bibliog il Science 154:597-603 N 4 '66

ASTRONOMY, Prehistoric
Stonehenge revisited. B. Tufty. il Sci N 90:
514-15 D 17 '66

ASTRONOMY, Spherical and practical
Graphical device for converting coordinates.
L. Heflinger. il Sky & Tel 31:92-4 F '66

ASTROPHYSICS
Scope of astrophysics today; excerpt from
report. Sky & Tel 31:272-3 My '66
See also
Magnetic field (cosmic physics)
Stars—Atmospheres

ASTROS (baseball) See Baseball clubs

ASTROSYSTEMS International, Incorporated
Test planned for battlefield illuminator; airborne device to light area of two square
miles. M. L. Yaffee. il Aviation W 85:65+
N 7 '66

ASWAN, Egypt
Homesick for Russia in Aswan. R. J. Korengold. il Newsweek 67:52-3 My 23 '66

ASWAN HIGH DAM
Egypt's hopes rise with the Aswan Dam.
il Fortune 75:128-35 Ja '67
Great dam thunders ahead. L. Griggs. il Life
60:101-2+ Je 17 '66

ASYLUM, Right of
Sixth committee consideration; right of asylum. UN Mo Chron 3:65 N '66

AT Bertam's hotel; story. See Christie, A.

AT the drop of another hat; revue. See Musical
comedies, revues, etc.—Criticisms, plots, etc.

AT-the-table cookery. See Cookery

ATAMIAN, Sarkis
Anaktuvuk mask and cultural innovation;
adaptation of address, September 1964.
bibliog Science 151:1337-45 Mr 18 '66

ATAXIA
Neurological defect: manganese in phenocopy
and prevention of a genetic abnormality
of inner ear. L. Erway and others. bibliog
il Science 152:1766-8 Je 24 '66

ATCHESON, Richard
Creating a new town. Holiday 39:121+ F '66
Sophisticated games and gadgets. Holiday
40:139-44 D '66

ATHABASCA oil sands. See Bituminous sand

ATHEISM
Dewart on belief. G. Vahanian. Commonweal
85:257-9 D 2 '66
Dialogue: Christ and Marx. il Newsweek 69:
74+ Ja 16 '67
Iron curtain lands take religion's pulse. E.
E. Turner. il Christian Cent 83:1317-20 O
26 '66
Two kinds of humanism; Christian-atheist
dialogues. il Time 88:42-3 D 30 '66

ATHENA (launch vehicle) See Space vehicles
—Propulsion systems

ATHENAGORAS I, patriarch
—See Paul VI, pope, jt. auth.

about

Ecumenical patriarch still being scapegoated.
Christian Cent 83:294 Mr 9 '66

ATHENEUM publishers
Looks of books; interview, ed. by S. Kauffmann. H. Ford. New Repub 155:15+ N
26 '66

ATHENS festival. See Music festivals—Greece,
Modern

ATHEROSCLEROSIS. See Arteriosclerosis

ATHLETES
Allez, France! with skis and water pistols;
French captured the Werner cup at the
Sun Valley lodge. D. Jenkins. Sports Illus
24:88-9 Ap 4 '66
Clear the track! H. L. Masin. il Sr Schol
89:28 O 14 '66
Long reign as king of the apes; movie
Tarzans. T. F. Moore. il Sports Illus 26:48-
54 Ja 2 '67
Pentagon's rule change for big-name athletes.
U S News 62:6 Ja 2 '67
Really the greatest; J. Jacobs. R. H. Boyle.
il Sports Illus 24:64-70+ Mr 7 '66
Road to the top. H. L. Masin. il Sr Schol
88:24 Ap 29 '66
School athletics food facts and myths. E.
Maxwell. Todays Health 44:85-6 S '66
Sportsman of the year: J. Ryun; four others
excelled. il Sports Illus 25:46-50+ D 19 '66
Stop the world, the U.S. is on; major in-
ternational sports. D. Jenkins. il Sports
Illus 24:26-9 My 2 '66
Why all the new records in sports? V.
Block. il Todays Health 44:22-5+ S '66
See also
Basketball players
Football players
Women as athletes

Nutrition

Should athletes eat protein? J. Reinert. il
Sci Digest 59:90 F '66

Recruiting

It's one point six pick up sticks; NCAA vs
Ivy League, controversy over academic
standards of athletes. D. Jenkins. Sports
Illus 24:30-1 Mr 21 '66

Salaries

Working wage for amateurs; set salary for
Davis cup players. B. Collins. il Sports
Illus 25:28-9 Jl 18 '66
See also
Baseball players—Salaries

ATHLETES, Women. See Women as athletes

ATHLETIC scholarships and fellowships. See
Scholarships and fellowships

ATHLETICS
See also
Athletes
Football
Physical education and training
Running
Sports
Sportsmanship

ATHLETICS for girls and women. See Physical
education and training of women

ATHOS, Anthony
Profess with a passion. por Time 87:80 My
6 '66

ATHOS, MOUNT
Holy mountain. H. Kubly. il Holiday 40:68-
77+ D '66

ATKIN, John
37' practical motor-sailer, Summer Place.
Motor B 117:98-101+ Ja '66
What hull shape is for you? il Motor B 117:40-
1+ My '66

ATKINS museum of fine arts. See William
Rockhill Nelson gallery of art, Kansas City,
Mo.

ATKINSON, Basil
Pantomime at Panmunjom. Sat R 49:61+ O
8 '66

ATKINSON, Brooks
Notebook on the writer. Sat R 49:33-4 N 5
'66
Those forty dirty birds. Audubon Mag 68:
231-7 Jl '66

about

Boss. J. K. Hutchens. por Sat R 49:97-9 O
8 '66

ATKINSON, Robert E.
Regional pointers: West coast. See issues of
Flower grower, the home garden

ATKINSON, Tracy
Milwaukee art center. Antiques 90:663-7 N
'66

ATKINSON field air base. See Air bases

ATLANTA
Atlanta's operatic mores; Opera guild luncheon boycott by Metropolitan opera company.
Nation 202:701-2 Je 13 '66
Home are the Braves; in Atlanta; divorce
from Milwaukee. G. Astor. il Look 30:61-
2+ My 3 '66

ATLANTA—*Continued*
Like Gone with the wind. Braves take Atlanta. il Life 60:77-8 Ap 22 '66
War fans; Affirmation Vietnam; rally. H. Zinn. Nation 202:227 F 28 '66

Architecture
John Portman; Atlanta's one man urban renewal program. J. Barnett. il Arch Rec 139:133-40 Ja '66

City planning
Atlanta, the hopeful city. il Fortune 74:155-6+ Ag '66

Education
Pride and progress; Atlanta's school integration. C. L. Weltner. il Am Ed 2:23-5 O '66

Fire department
What does a city do when firemen go on strike? il U S News 61:86+ S 19 '66

History
Who's got Button's bones? R. M. Williams. il Am Heritage 17:28-32+ F '66

Hotels, restaurants, etc.
In Atlanta, all roads lead to the Varsity; mammoth drive-in grown from simple hot dog stand into social institution. il Bsns W p 132-3+ O 8 '66

Music
Atlanta. C. White. il Opera N 30:31 Ap 9 '66

Negroes
Allen of Atlanta collides with black power and white racism. R. Cleghorn. il N Y Times Mag p32-3+ O 16 '66
Atlanta's baptism in black power. il U S News 61:36 S 19 '66
Behind the image. il Newsweek 68:32 S 19 '66
Hector Black; white power in black Atlanta. J. Shepherd. il Look 30:137-40 D 13 '66
Out to get SNCC. P. Good. il Nation 203:536-8 N 21 '66
Stokely's spark. il Time 88:37 S 16 '66
What happened in Atlanta. New Repub 155:8-9 S 24 '66; Reply. E. Stevenson. 155:27-8 O 15 '66
What I learned from Negroes. S. Bady. il Ebony 21:58-60+ S '66
White Jesus; H. Black, Vine City and SNCC. il Newsweek 68::29 Jl 25 '66

Police
Children and the badge; Atlanta board of education's school dective department. R. Hardwick. il Am Ed 2:1-4 D '65
Police brutality vs. people brutality; reprint. B. Shipp. U S News 61:43 Ag 8 '66; Same abr. Read Digest 89:111-12 O '66

Prisons and reformatories
Case of civilized penology; G. E's computer programing course. Nation 202:115 Je 31 '66

Riots
Allen of Atlanta collides with black power and white racism. R. Cleghorn. il N Y Times Mag p32-3+ O 16 '66
Atlanta's baptism in black power. il U S News 61:36 S 19 '66
Behind the image. il Newsweek 68:32 S 19 '66
Stokely's spark. il Time 88:37 S 16 '66
Urban powder kegs. Sr School 89:20 S 23 '66
What happened in Atlanta. New Repub 155:8-9 S 24 '66; Reply. E. Stevenson. 155:27-8 O 15 '66

Social life and customs
I like it here; Criss Mills' seventeenth year. J. Poppy. il Look 30:36-9 S 20 '66

Stores
Celebrities at Rich's: authors and assorted; excerpt from Dear store. C. Sibley. Pub W 191:50-1 Ja 9 '67

Street traffic
Traffic engineer must be an educator. K. A. Bevins. il Am City 81:116-18 O '66

Theater
Conquest of Peachtree street; opening of Theatre Atlanta. H. Hewes. Sat R 49:72 N 19 '66
Peachtree playhouse; Theater Atlanta. il Time 88:84 N 11 '66

ATLANTIC (periodical)
From the new editor. R. Manning. Atlan 217:53 Ap '66
New man at the Atlantic. il Newsweek 67:61 Ja 31 '66

ATLANTIC acceptance corporation
When the roof fell in at Atlantic. il Bsns W p68-72 F 5 '66
ATLANTIC alliance. *See* Atlantic community
ATLANTIC aviation corporation
DH 125 and the bizjet mystique. J. Gilbert. il Flying 78:84-90 F '66
ATLANTIC CITY

Hospitals
Growth and replacement combined on an urban site: Atlantic City hospital addition. il Arch Rec 139:174-5 Mr '66
ATLANTIC coast
Fishingest way south. Z. Taylor. il Motor B 118:30-1+ O '66
Mike Frome; saving our coastal islands. M. Frome. Am For 72:7+ Je '66
See also
Fundy, Bay of
ATLANTIC community
Adviser to two presidents looks at trends in Europe; statement. June 20, 1966. M. Bundy. U S News 61:80-3 Jl 4 '66
Building a bigger Atlantic community market. G. E. Bradley. Harvard Bsns R 44:79-90 My '66
Department presents views on Senate resolutions on closer relations among Atlantic nations; statement, March 24, 1966. J. M. Leddy. Dept State Bul 54:672-4 Ap 25 '66
Independence and freedom: a continuing struggle; address, July 4, 1966. G. W. Ball. Dept State Bul 55:194-8 Ag 8 '66
Necessary partnership. J. R. Schaetzel. For Affairs 44:417-33 Ap '66
U.S. policy and the new Europe. F. Church. For Affairs 45:49-57 O '66

Bibliography
New books for social studies teachers. R. Steel. Sr Schol 87:sup 18 Ja 21 '66
ATLANTIC continental shelf. *See* Continental shelf
ATLANTIC flights. *See* Aviation—Transatlantic flights
ATLANTIC OCEAN
Ages of horizon A and the oldest Atlantic sediments. J. Ewing and others. bibliog il Science 154:1125-32 D 2 '66
We rowed across the North Atlantic; ed. by J. Atwater. J. Ridgway. il Sat Eve Post 239:30-6+ N 5 '66
See also
Gulf Stream
ATLANTIC states
See also
Fishing—Atlantic states

Politics
Year they stayed in; election results. il Time 88:28-9 N 18 '66
ATLANTIC undersea test and evaluation center
AUTEC operations begin at test range; testing drone anti-submarine helicopter at Atlantic undersea test and evaluation center. M. Getler. il Tech W 19:16-17 O 3 '66
ATLANTIC union (proposed)
U.S. policy on Atlantic union; statement, September 20, 1966. G. W. Ball. Dept State Bul 55:613-15 O 17 '66
ATLANTIS
Volcano that shaped the western world; Santorini eruption: theories of A. Galanopoulos. J. Lear. il Sat R 49:57-60+ N 5 '66; Discussion. 49:93-4 D 3 '66
ATLAS, David, and others
Tropopause detected by radar. bibliog Science 153:1110-12 S 2 '66
ATLASES
Revised, enlarged world atlas charts our changing earth; National geographic atlas of the world. W. Chamberlin. il Nat Geog Mag 129:818-21 Je '66
ATMOSPHERE
Ammonium micas: possible sources of atmospheric ammonia and nitrogen. H. P. Eugster and J. Munoz. bibliog il Science 151:683-6 F 11 '66
Atmospheric gases and particulates in Panama. J. P. Lodge, jr. and J. B. Pate. bibliog il Science 153:408-10 Jl 22 '66
Earth's air shakes like jelly. A. Ewing. Sci N L 89:117 F 19 '66
How was the earth's atmosphere formed? il Sci Digest 60:91-2 N '66
Primeval soup poisonous; life-like substances formed from hydrogen cyanide. Sci N 90:69 Jl 30 '66
Role of the oceans. R. Revelle. il Sat R 49:39-41 My 7 '66

ATMOSPHERE—*Continued*
Some doubts about the earth's dust cloud.
C. Nilsson. bibliog il Science 153:1242-6 S
9 '66
Total mass of earth's atmosphere calculated.
Sci N 89:473 Je 11 '66
    See also
Counterglow
Fog
Meteorology
Sun—Atmosphere

ATMOSPHERE, Upper
Big gun on Barbados. P. M. Millman. il
Sky & Tel 32:64-7 Ag '66
Chemical releases at high altitudes. N. W.
Rosenberg. bibliog il Science 152:1017-27
My 20 '66
Ionospheric topside sounding. W. Calvert.
bibliog il Science 154:228-34 O 14 '66
Metallic ions detected in lower ionosphere.
Sci N 89:394 My 21 '66
Outer atmosphere emits laser-like light. Sci N
90:201 S 17 '66

ATMOSPHERIC electricity
Luminous phenomena in nocturnal tornadoes.
B. Vonnegut and J. R. Weyer. bibliog il
Science 153:1213-20 S 9 '66; Discussion. 155:
27+ Ja 6 '67
Tornado photos needed. il Sci N 90:247 O 1
'66
    See also
Lightning

ATMOSPHERIC ions. See Ions

ATMOSPHERIC pollution. See Air pollution

ATMOSPHERIC research
Big gun on Barbados; Operation HARP. P.
M. Millman. il Sky & Tel 32:64-7 Ag '66

ATMOSPHERIC temperature
Coldest spot; Antarctica. Newsweek 67:90
My 9 '66

ATMOSPHERIC turbulence
Airborne turbulence sensor still sought. P. J.
Klass. il Aviation W 84:97+ Mr 14 '66
Atmosphere seen anew; radar waves may
detect CAT. il Sci N 90:201 S 17 '66
Avoiding turbulence costs $6 each flight;
clear air turbulence. Sci N 89:184 Mr 19 '66
CAB accident investigation report: turbulence
cited in Eastern DC-8 crash; Lake Pont-
chartrain, La, February 25, 1964. Avia-
tion W 85:123+ S 12 '66
FAA to propose standards based on random
turbulence concept. W. Wright. Aviation
W 84:97+ Ap 25 '66
Pilots see value in turbulence simulation. B.
K. Thomas, jr. Aviation W 85:147+ S 26
'66
Priority urged for turbulence research; de-
veloping airborne CAT detection systems.
B. K. Thomas, jr. Aviation W 86:18 Ja 2 '67
Tropopause detected by radar. D. Atlas and
others. bibliog il Science 153:1110-12 S 2 '66
Wallops radars probe turbulence causes. il
Aviation W 85:52 Jl 11 '66

ATOLLS. See Coral reefs and islands

ATOM smashing apparatus. See Accelerators
(electrons, etc)

ATOMIC blasting
Army advisor endorses bombs for new canal;
Canal across Central America. Sci N 90:343
O 29 '66
Atom aims for role as prospector; nuclear test
shots may unlock vast oil and gas fields. il
Bsns W p83-4+ D 17 '66

ATOMIC bomb shelters
City planners to play a key role in civil-
defense preparedness. C. Goldschmidt. Am
City 81:176+ My '66
Civil defense: notes on Project Harbor; with
reply by E. Wigner. H. Margolis. Bul
Atomic Sci 22:19-23 F '66
Notes and comment: network of tunnels as
fallout shelters proposed at annual meeting of American association for the advancement of science. New Yorker 41:21 Ja 29 '66

ATOMIC bombs
China and the bomb. Nation 203:532 N 21 '66
Hiroshima: let us never forget. R. B. Fulton.
Christian Cent 83:1254-5 O 12 '66
Historical fallout; Fat man version of twen-
ty-one years ago. il Time 88:53 Ag 12 '66
Indian Christians demand atom bomb. Chris-
tian Cent 83:1024 Ag 24 '66
    See also
Hydrogen bombs

Detection
See Atomic bombs—Testing. Detection of

History
Peril, a hope, and a movement. W. A.
Higinbotham. Bul Atomic Sci 22:34-7
Ap '66

Manufacture
Atomic bomb secret, fifteen years later. Bul
Atomic Sci 22:2-3+ D '66
Authors & editors; book about the Man-
hattan project. Pub W 191:41 Ja 16 '67
Chain reactions; Igor Golovin claims Rus-
sians launched own Manhattan project in
1942. Newsweek 68:62 Ag 29 '66
Day of Trinity, by L. Lamont. Review
Bul Atomic Sci 22:35-7 F '66. B. T. Feld
Dead secret; Rosenberg and Sobell espionage
trial. Sci Am 215:43-4 O '66
Great Chinese bomb puzzle, and a solution.
A. Kramish. il Fortune 73:157-8+ Je '66
On the Chinese separation technology. B. T.
Feld. Bul Atomic Sci 22:33-4 S '66

Testing
After the bomb; French test, protests. News-
week 68:34 Jl 18 '66
Amchitka bomb test site. Sci N 90:571 D 31
'66
China nears an H-bomb test. il Bsns W p39
My 14 '66
China poses a new test; challenges Johnson
pledge to protect countries of Asia. il Bsns
W p39-41 N 5 '66
China's nuclear puzzle. Bsns W p32 Ja 7 '67
Chinese science: it's not a paper atom. J.
M. H. Lindbeck. il N Y Times Mag p38-
9+ Ja 8 '67
Communist China conducts third nuclear
test; Department statement, May 9, 1966.
Dept State Bul 54:869 My 30 '66
Disarmament, not now. N. K. Herzfeld. Com-
monweal 85:341-3 D 23 '66
France gets trigger for hydrogen bomb; test-
ing in South Pacific. il Bsns W p90+ O 1
'66
Is China thermonuclear? il Sci N 91:32 Ja
14 '67
Nuclear muscle; What the snoopers saw;
China's third test. il Newsweek 67:53-4 My
23 '66
Nuclear weapons development in China.
L. A. Frank. Bul Atomic Sci 22:12-15 Ja
'66; Discussion. 22:29-30 Ap '66
Probing the effects of a nuclear blast;
electromagnetic pulse (EMP) threat to
power and communications facilities. Bsns
W p77 My 14 '66
Red China trying to beat France in the race
for an H-bomb? U S News 60:52 My 23 '66
Red cloud at Lop Nor; China's fifth nuclear
device. Newsweek 69:28 Ja 9 '67
Stillness on Eniwetok; island life at a former
nuclear test site. M. Berrill. il Natur Hist
75:20-5 bibliog (p70) D '66
That day in Mururoa; France's first test. E.
B. Miller. il Sat R 49:62+ O 8 '66
Three years after test ban: nuclear race
speeds up. il U S News 61:50-2 Jl 18 '66
U.S. comments on Communist Chinese nu-
clear test; Department statement. Dept
State Bul 55:744 N 14 '66
U.S. expects another nuclear test by Com-
munist China soon; Department statement,
November 29, 1966. Dept State Bul 55:925
D 19 '66
    See also
Radioactive fallout

Testing, Detection of
Blasts test detector. Sci N 90:453 N 26 '66
Detection of underground explosions. E. Bul-
lard. il Sci Am 215:19-29 Jl '66
How U.S. knows about China's A-tests. il
U S News 60:6+ My 23 '66; Same abr. with
title How we unmask China's nuclear
secrets. Read Digest 89:117-18 S '66
Test detection: dispute over DOD experi-
ment settled. E. Langer. Science 154:1526
D 23 '66

Testing, Suspension of
Comprehensive test ban treaty strongly rec-
ommended by U.S; statements, November
25-26, 1965. W. C. Foster. Dept State Bul
54:99-103 Ja 17 '66
Preventing nuclear spread; experimental mo-
ratorium on underground tests? J. Finney.
New Repub 155:10-11 Jl 16 '66
Underground-test-ban debate. Sci Am 215:40
Ag '66
    See also
Nuclear test ban treaty. 1963

Testing, Underground
Elbow room for the atom; underground blast
will test theory of decoupling. Bsns W
p 119 O 22 '66
Project Sterling reveals high decoupling potential. Tech W 20:15-16 Ja 16 '67

ATOMIC clocks
Soviets disclose orbiting of atomic clock;
Cosmos 97 to check Einstein's theory of
relativity. Aviation W 85:36 N 21 '66
ATOMIC energy act of 1946. See United States
—Atomic energy commission
ATOMIC energy agency. See International
atomic energy agency
ATOMIC energy commission. See United
States—Atomic energy commission
ATOMIC nuclei
Atomic nuclei: moments of inertia and quad-
rupole moments. J. Strnad. bibliog il Sci-
ence 154:259-61 O 14 '66
Remarks on nuclear structure. A. de Shalit.
Science 153:1063-7 S 2 '66

Fusion
  See Nuclear fusion
ATOMIC power
  See also
Atomic bombs
Nuclear fusion
Nuclear reactors

Economic aspects
Atomic bomb in the land of coal; TVA's
contract for the biggest nuclear power
plant. T. O'Hanlon. Fortune 74:132-3 S '66
Atomic transition, to what? V. L. Parsegian.
Bul Atomic Sci 22:23-6 Ja '66; Discussion.
22:34 F; 20-3 Ap '66
Breakfast with Dr Teller; discussion on eco-
nomic advantages of nuclear electric power.
N. Cousins. Sat R 49:26+ Mr 19 '66
Deep seas next region for nuclear power use.
Sci N 89:101 F 12 '66
Factors favoring nuclear power. P. H. Abel-
son. Science 152:703 My 6 '66; Reply. S.
Novick. 153:1194 S 9 '66
Harnessed atom: it's a business now. il
Newsweek 67:84-6 Ap 18 '66
Nuclear peaceful uses service offered to non-
nuclear states; statement, August 9, 1966.
A. S. Fisher. Dept State Bul 55:351-3 S 5 '66
On the role of government laboratories. V. L.
Parsegian. Bul Atomic Sci 22:35-6 S '66
Power from the atom: a boom gets under
way. il U S News 60:120-1 Ap 18 '66
U.S. urges expanded safeguards over peace-
ful nuclear activity; statement, July 28,
1966. A. S. Fisher. Dept State Bul 55:281-3
Ag 22 '66
  See also
Atomic blasting
Atomic power plants

Industrial aspects
  See Atomic power—Economic aspects

International aspects
Nuclear peaceful uses service offered to non-
nuclear states; statement. August 9, 1966.
A. S. Fisher. Dept State Bul 55:351-3 S 5 '66
  See also
International atomic energy agency

International control
China and nuclear proliferation; adaptation
of address, April 21, 1966. M. H. Halperin.
bibliog Bul Atomic Sci 22:4-10 N; 18-24
D '66
Search for agreements in the cause of peace;
address, August 26, 1966. L. B. Johnson.
Dept State Bul 55:410-13 S 19 '66
U.S. discusses proposed safeguards for cutoff
and transfer of fissionable material and
nuclear weapons destruction; statement,
April 14, 1966. W. C. Foster. Dept State
Bul 54:901-6 Je 6 '66

Laws and regulations
Atom and the law; address, April 28, 1966. J.
T. Ramey. Vital Speeches 32:731-6 S 15 '66

Medical applications
  See Radiology. Medical

United States
  See Atomic power
ATOMIC power plants
Atomic bomb in the land of coal; TVA's
contract for the biggest nuclear power
plant. T. O'Hanlon. Fortune 74:132-3 S '66
AEC moves toward sale of gas plants to
industry. Tech W 20:26 Ja 9 '67
Coal power v. nuclear. Sci Am 214:50 F '66
Nuclear fueled desalting power plant planned.
Sci N 90:130 Ag 27 '66
Nuclear plant builders see a $1-billion mar-
ket. il Bsns W p 144-6+ Mr 5 '66
Power to burn; Peach Bottom, Pa. C. A.
Betts. il Sci N 89:444-5 Je 4 '66

Switching to the atom; nationwide surge. il
Time 88:100 O 14 '66
TVA chooses atom power. Bsns W p 150
Je 25 '66
ATOMIC powered aircraft carriers; Atomic
powered airships; etc. See Aircraft carriers,
Atomic powered; Airships, Atomic powered;
etc.
ATOMIC research
Where responsibility lies. J. G. Dash. Bul
Atomic Sci 22:35-7 Ja '66
  See also
Accelerators (electrons, etc)
Atomic research laboratories

China (People's Republic)
China and nuclear proliferation; adaptation
of address, April 21, 1966. M. H. Halperin.
bibliog Bul Atomic Sci 22:4-10 N; 18-24
D '66
Is China thermonuclear? il Sci N 91:32 Ja 14
'67
Nuclear weapons development in China.
L. A. Frank. Bul Atomic Sci 22:12-15 Ja
'66; Discussion. 22:29-30 Ap '66
What to do about Peking's missile. Nat R
18:1144 N 15 '66

Europe, Western
  See also
European organization for nuclear research

Russia
Chain reactions; Igor Golovin claims Rus-
sians launched own Manhattan project in
1942. Newsweek 68:62 Ag 29 '66
ATOMIC research laboratories
Great atom-smasher contest; towns bidding
for atom-research. T. G. Harris. il Look
30:37-8 Mr 8 '66
In the running now for big atom smasher.
U S News 60:10-11 Ap 4 '66
On the role of government laboratories. V.
L. Parsegian. Bul Atomic Sci 22:35-6 S '66
Why not national laboratories? B. I. Spinrad.
Bul Atomic Sci 22:20-3 Ap '66
  See also
United States—Atomic energy commission
ATOMIC test ban treaty. See Nuclear test ban
treaty. 1963
ATOMIC time. See Time measurements
ATOMIC warfare
Doctor Jekyll and Mr Kahn. J. C. Fleck.
Christian Cent 83:680-3 My 25 '66; Reply
with rejoinder. J. Fletcher. 83:935 Jl 27 '66
Escalation and the nuclear option, by B.
Brodie. Review
Reporter 36:63-4 Ja 12 '67. T. W. Wolfe
We could stockpile birds. S. Alsop. il Sat
Eve Post 239:16 F 12 '66
  See also
Civil defense

Defenses
In a nuclear attack on America; summary
of testimony, March 8, 1966. R. S. Mc-
Namara. U S News 60:14 Mr 21 '66
Sounds of escalation; Russia and U.S. il
Newsweek 69:50 Ja 2 '67
Strike from space. by P. Schlafly and C.
Ward. Review
Nat R 18:691-4 Jl 12 '66. S. T. Possony
  See also
North Atlantic treaty organization—Multi-
lateral force (proposed)

Ethical aspects
Moral decision in the nuclear age. R. L.
Holmes. Bul Atomic Sci 22:27-9 Ap '66

Social aspects
Scientists and civil defense; dialogue at
Berkeley. J. Walsh; reply. N. Rosa. Sci-
ence 152:696+ My 6 '66
ATOMIC waste. See Radioactive waste dis-
posal
ATOMIC weapons
Bomb treaty nears; U.S. and Russia pursuing
treaty to halt the spread of nuclear weapons.
il Bsns W p37-8 O 29 '66
Fire arrow; successful missile shot. il Time
88:35 N 4 '66
Fireball over Lop Nor; fueled missile carry-
ing a nuclear warhead fired by China. il
Newsweek 68:74-5 N 7 '66
Guarantees to non-nuclear nations. M. Will-
rich. For Affairs 44:683-92 Jl '66
Mushroom over Mururoa; development of
France's atomic arsenal. Time 88:31 Jl
15 '66
Nuclear treaty snags. New Repub 155:5-6 N
12 '66

ATOMIC weapons—*Continued*
On proliferation: where's the danger? J. J. Stone; discussion. Bul Atomic Sci 22:32-3 F '66
Red China with the A-missile, meaning to U.S. Russia; with interview with C. Cheng. il U S News 61:50-2+ N 14 '66
Red China's atomic shot; what it means to the world. il U S News 61:6 N 7 '66
Sounds of escalation; Russia and U.S. il Newsweek 69:50 Ja 2 '67
Strategic consequences of nuclear proliferation. J. R. Schlesinger. il Reporter 35:36-8 O 20 '66
What we can't cover with plants, we'll paint; installation of silos for nuclear missiles. P. E. Schneider. il N Y Times Mag p 18-19+ Ag 14 '66

International control
Arms control in Congress, 1966. B. G. Lall. Bul Atomic Sci 22:35-7 D '66
Assembly adopts three resolutions; with text of resolutions. UN Mo Chron 3:22-36 D '66
Citizens speak out on proliferation; with letter to President Johnson. Bul Atomic Sci 22:37-9 N '66
Ending the cold war; Vietnam need not slow the thaw. W. C. McWilliams. Commonweal 85:363-5 Ja 6 '67
Latin America: the first nuclear free zone? P. Barnes. Bul Atomic Sci 22:37-40 D '66
Nonproliferation of nuclear weapons; statement, February 23, 1966. D. Rusk. Dept State Bul 54:406-10 Mr 14 '66
Nuclear proliferation; address, November 17, 1966. H. C. Donnelly. Vital Speeches 33:166-9 Ja 1 '67
Nuclear weapons: a liability. J. Silard. il Bul Atomic Sci 22:15-20 S '66
Nuclear weapons sharing and the German problem. W. B. Bader. For Affairs 44:693-700 Jl '66
Proliferation and Soviet-American relations. R. C. Tucker. Bul Atomic Sci 22:14-18 O '66
Stopping the spread. Commonweal 85:156-7 N 11 '66
U.N. reaffirms principles for negotiating nonproliferation treaty; calls for conference of non-nuclear-weapon states; statement, November 9, 1966; with text of resolution. W. C. Foster. Dept State Bul 55:930-6 D 19 '66
United States reviews position on nonproliferation of nuclear weapons; statements October 20, and November 2, 1966; with text of resolution. A. J. Goldberg; W. C. Foster. Dept State Bul 55:896-902 D 12 '66

ATOMIC weapons and disarmament
Arms control and disarmament at the White House; summary of report. Bul Atomic Sci 22:43-5 F; 33-7 Mr '66
Arms control; non-proliferation treaty; address, November 23, 1965. W. C. Foster. Vital Speeches 32:199-202 Ja 15 '66
Assembly adopts three resolutions; with text of resolutions. UN Mo Chron 3:22-36 D '66
Atlantic report: Middle East arms race. Atlan 218:38+ S '66
China and nuclear proliferation: adaptation of address, April 21, 1966. M. H. Halperin. bibliog Bul Atomic Sci 22:4-10 N; 18-24 D '66
Denuclearization of Africa; statement, December 1, 1965. W. C. Foster. Dept State Bul 54:103-5 Ja 17 '66
Disarmament, not now. N. K. Herzfeld. Commonweal 85:341-3 D 23 '66
Discussions in First committee: consideration of disarmament items by UN. UN Mo Chron 3:35-8 N '66
From New York and Washington: talking about disarmament. H. Margolis. Bul Atomic Sci 22:38-40 F '66
Next: a proliferation ban; with comparison of the U.S. and USSR draft treaties. B. G. Lall. Bul Atomic Sci 22:42-5 Ja '66
Non-proliferation. Commonweal 83:524-5 F 4 '66
President and the arms race; questions rising over United States and the Soviet Union deadlock on the question of West Germany, and the McNamara formula. N. Cousins. Sat R 49:34 S 10 '66
Preventing nuclear spread; International assembly on nuclear weapons, Scarborough, Ontario. J. Finney. New Repub 155:10-11 Jl 16 '66
Prospects of peace; excerpts from address. Chalfont. Bul Atomic Sci 22:2-4 My '66

U.S. presents amendments to draft treaty on nonproliferation of nuclear weapons in Eighteen-nation disarmament committee statement, March 22, 1966; with text of amendments. A. S. Fisher. Dept State Bul 54:675-81 Ap 25 '66
United States reviews position on nonproliferation of nuclear weapons; statements October 20, and November 2, 1966; with text of resolution. A. J. Goldberg; W. C. Foster. Dept State Bul 55:896-902 D 12 '66
U.S. welcomes forward-looking German note of March 25; texts of notes between United States and the Federal Republic of Germany; April 2, and March 25, 1966. Dept State Bul 54:654-7 Ap 25 '66
See also
Atomic bombs—Testing, Suspension of
Conference of the Eighteen-nation committee on disarmament, Geneva, 1962-

ATOMS
Individual carbon atoms seen through microscope. il Sci N 89:335 My 7 '66
See also
Atomic nuclei
Molecules
Muonium
Neutrinos
Protons
Transmutation (chemistry)

ATONAL music. See Music
ATORON cameras. See Cameras
ATRIUM houses. See Architecture, Domestic
ATTACK and defense (military science) See Military art and science
ATTACK on Pearl Harbor, 1941. See Pearl Harbor, Attack on, 1941
ATTAWAY, Roy
Fall windfall. Outdoor Life 138:58-9+ S '66
ATTENDANCE (school) See School attendance
ATTENTION
Components of skilled performance. M. I. Posner. bibliog il Science 152:1712-18 Je 24 '66
Now hear this. il Nations Bsns 54:78-80 Ag '66
ATTENUATORS, Radio. See Radio attenuators
ATTIG, G. K. and Clay, John
Put teeth into compaction. Am City 81:88-90 Mr '66
ATTITUDE gyro. See Gyroscope
ATTITUDES
Advertising responsibility. R. A. Webber. Cath World 204:87-91 N '66
Attitude formation and public opinion. D. Katz. bibliog f il Ann Am Acad 367:150-62 S '66
Beliefs attract people. Sci N 90:314 O 15 '66
Effect of teacher attitudes upon the culturally different. N. L. Arnez. bibliog f Sch & Soc 94:149-52 Mr 19 '66
Notes from a world tour: questions asked abroad. T. C. Sorensen. Sat R 49:31 O 1 '66
Race image improved. P. McBroom. Sci N 90:318 O 22 '66
This restless generation. C. J. McNaspy. America 114:726-30 My 21 '66
This younger generation; excerpts from address, August 1965. Sister Mary Dorothy Ann. Cath World 203:175-80 Je '66
See also
Frustration
Moral attitudes
Optimism
Public opinion
Student opinion
ATTORNEY and client
Cash for cheated clients; clients' security fund. Time 88:69 S 16 '66
ATTORNEY General (United States) See United States—Justice, Department of
ATTORNEYS. See Lawyers
ATTORNEYS, District. See District attorneys
ATTRACTANTS, Insect. See Insect sex attractants
ATTWOOD, William
Lure of Look. por Time 87:43-4 My 6 '66
ATWATER, James
(ed) See Ridgway, J. We rowed across the North Atlantic
ATWATER, Maxine
Resort isles of the future. Travel 125:57-9 Mr '66
ATWOOD, C. E. See Knerer, G. jt. auth.
ATWOOD, Cap
Harder they come; ed. by B. East. Outdoor Life 138:64-7+ O '66

ATYEO, Henry C.
Letter from Jakarta. Nat R 18:458 My 17 '66

AUBURN, Wash.
Americans view the war: to get the truth, I just don't know. R. S. Johnson. il Nation 203:502-5 N 14 '66

AUCHINCLOSS, Louis
Club bedroom; text. Esquire 66:226-9 D '66
Images of elegant New York. Am Heritage 17:48-65 O '66
Sabina and the herd; story. Sat Eve Post 239:70-5 Ja 29 '66
Secret journal of Waring Stohl; story. Sat Eve Post 239:76-80 Ap 23 '66
Urbane echo of a graceful past; interview, ed. by S. Daves. il pors Life 60:53-4+ Ap 15 '66
Wagnerians; story. McCalls 93:88-9 Jl '66

AUCKLAND ISLAND rails. See Rails (birds)

AUCLAIR, Walter, and Siegel, B. W.
Cilia regeneration in the sea urchin embryo: evidence for a pool of ciliary proteins. bibliog Science 154:913-15 N 18 '66

AUCTIONS
Chez Mlle: auctions, some dos and don'ts. B. Plumb. il Mlle 63:60-1 Je '66
Florida sets itself up to rival the bluegrass; Hialeah auction of Florida-bred yearlings. il Bsns W p28-9 F 5 '66
Steamy day at an auction of engines; Christie's auction of models of locomotives, ships and steam engines. il Life 61:69-70+ D 9 '66
Where the auction is. il Newsweek 68:108 S 19 '66
Where the fur flies; international auction at Leningrad's fur palace. il Newsweek 68:64 Ag 8 '66
With a prayer, Upland goes on the block; sold to Salvation army. il Bsns W p 194-6+ N 5 '66
With the press; old car auction, excerpt from Casper star-tribune. Hobbies 71:88 Ja '67

See also
Parke-Bernet galleries, incorporated

AUCTIONS, Art. See Art sales

AUDEN, Wystan Hugh
Auden on poetry; a conversation with S. Kunitz. Atlan 218:94-102 Ag '66
Fairground; poem. New Yorker 42:32 Ag 20 '66
Partition; poem. Atlan 218:94 D '66
Twelve: anthem for the feast-day of any apostle. Christian Cent 83:1235 O 12 '66
(tr) See Voznesenskii, A. Autumn in Sigulda
(tr) See Voznesenskii, A. My Achilles heart
(tr) See Voznesenskii, A. Party

about
Austria remaining. H. Carruth. Poetry 108: 119-21 My '66

AUDIENCE surveys, incorporated
Panic buttons; previews shown to off-the-sidewalk critics. il Time 88:60 Jl 15 '66

AUDIENCES
Consider the audience. E. Wildi. U S Camera 29:68-9+ Jl '66
Front and center; relocating Metropolitan opera subscribers in Lincoln Center. Q. Eaton. Opera N 30:6-7 Je 4 '66
Line: twenty-four hour ticket line for standees and seat buyers, at new Metropolitan. New Yorker 42:21-2 Ja 14 '67
Singer vs. public; C. MacNeil and opera audience at Parma's Royal theater. A. M. Lingg. il Opera N 31:6-7 Ja 14 '67
Troubled waters; difficulties in Italy's opera houses. P. Elvins. il Opera N 31:8-11 D 10 '66

AUDIO amplifiers. See Amplifiers
AUDIO analgesia. See Analgesia
AUDIO calibrators. See Calibrators
AUDIO equipment. See Sound—Apparatus

AUDIO fairs
Audio fairs, a call for investigation. Hi Fi 16:93 O '66
Fall fashions in audio; New York high fidelity show. I. Berger. il Sat R 49:70-1+ S 24 '66
Hands across the hi-fi; British and U.S. shows in London. T. V. Heinitz. Sat R 49:85-6 Je 11 '66
New models; annual New York high fidelity show. H. Fantel. Opera N 31:29 N 19 '66
New trends at the high fidelity show; New York high fidelity and music show. J. Wesson. U S Camera 30:28-9 Ja '67

N.Y. hi fi show. I. Berger. Sat R 49:67+ O 29 '66
New York hi-fi show program. W. A. Stocklin. Electr World 76:6+ O '66
New York high fidelity music show, 1966. L. Zide. il Am Rec G 33:260-1 N '66
New York high fidelity show happens. il Hi Fi 16:34+ D '66
News & views. il Hi Fi 16:32 Jl '66

AUDIO fidelity records, incorporated
Squeeeeeeeeeeeeee! selling recorded noise. il Bsns W p67-8 Ap 9 '66

AUDIO generators. See Signal generators

AUDIO-visual aids
How to make and use effective audio-visuals. J. L. Debes. il Sr Schol 88:26-8 Ap 29 '66
Multimedia in action; symposium. Sr Schol 87:sup8+ Ja 14 '66
New A-V products. R. H. Burgert. Sr Schol 88:sup 10 Ap 29 '66
New educational materials. il Sr Schol 89: sup 16-17 O 7 '66
New educational materials. il Sr Schol 89: sup 16-17 O 7; sup8 D 9 '66
New firm proposes to index textbooks for A-V. Pub W 190:60 Ag 22 '66
New products. Sr Schol 89:sup8 N 18 '66
Notes on new A-V equipment. R. Burgert. Sr Schol 89:sup22 S 30; sup 14 O 7 '66
Obligated funds, fiscal 1966 and 1967, for instructional and A-V materials under recent federal legislation; chart. Pub W 190: 44-5 Jl 25 '66

See also
Instructional materials centers
Libraries and audiovisual materials
National audio-visual association

Bibliography
Books on audio-visuals. Sr Schol 87:sup 13 Ja 14 '66

AUDIO-visual clubs. See Student activities

AUDIO-visual instruction
CUE: an experiment in the humanities; adaptation of address, July 1966. G. Lacy. il ALA Bul 60:918-22 O '66
CUE system. G. N. Lacy. il Sr Schol 88: sup8 Ap 29 '66
Picasso=MC²; Project CUE, experiment designed to integrate the arts and humanities into school curriculum. C. S. Carleton. il Am Ed 2:13-15 Mr '66
What is Project Discovery discovering? Terrell, Tex. school system. J. A. Brill. il Sr Schol 89:sup8+ O 7 '66

See also
Computers—Educational applications
Libraries and audiovisual materials
Moving pictures in education
National audio-visual association
Television in education

AUDIOMETER. See Audiometry

AUDIOMETRY
Deaf hear sounds on single frequency. Sci N 89:220 Ap 2 '66

AUDITING
Very private world of Peat, Marwick, Mitchell. T. A. Wise. il Fortune 74:88-91+ Jl 1 '66

AUDITORIUMS
Space frame costs less than $4 a square foot; Pauley pavilion at U.C.L.A. il Arch Rec 139:181-4 Mr '66

See also
Concert halls

AUDUBON, John James
Audubon in the original; with excerpt from The original water-color paintings by John James Audubon for The birds of America. C. L. Mee, jr. Am Heritage 17:56-65 F '66
Audubon's originals; with portfolio of six reproductions. M. B. Davidson. il Audubon Mag 68:238-49 Jl '66
Frontier epic. il Newsweek 68:85 Ag 15 '66
New look at Audubon. M. B. Davidson. il Horizon 8:32-41 Spr '66
Where are Audubon's copper plates. W. Fries. il Audubon Mag 68:259-62+ Jl '66

AUDUBON nature centers
First lady of agriculture visits an Audubon center; Aullwood Audubon center; picture story. L. Line. Audubon Mag 68:347-50 S '66

AUDUBON park zoo, New Orleans
Reporter at large; captive whooping cranes. F. McNulty. New Yorker 42:31-6+ Ag 6 '66

AUDUBON prints. See Birds in art

AUDUBON societies
See also
National Audubon society

AUERBACH, Aline B.
Inborn urge to grow. Parents Mag 41:54-5+
Je '66
AUERBACH, Arnold. See Auerbach, R.
AUERBACH, Red
Beautiful ooher. Sports Illus 26:8 Ja 16 '67
Boston Celtics: pro basketball's dynasty. I.
R. McVay. il por Look 30:64-6+ F 8 '66
Last cigar for a last hurrah? M. Cope. il pors
Sat Eve Post 239:107-8+ Mr 26 '66
Last cigar for Red Auerbach. por Sports
Illus 24:32-3 My 9 '66
Some old pros refuse to die. F. Deford. il
Sports Illus 25:30-3 My 9 '66
AUGER, Pierre
Europe's growing stake in space science.
UNESCO Courier 19:24-6 My '66
AUGSTEIN, Rudolf
Criminal state and German responsibility;
tr. by W. J. Dannhauser. Commentary 41:
33-9 F '66
AUGUST, Kendall
Utilities: production's lifeline. Duns R 87:
pt2 130-3+ Mr '66
AUGUSTA national golf club course. See Golf
courses
AUGUSTUS, emperor of Rome
Subtle genius who launched the parade of
emperors. il por Life 60:58-9 Je 3 '66
AULDECAMBE, Alexander
Unsentimental report from Mexico. Harper
232:80-4 Mr '66
AULERICH, Richard J.
Wolf. Nat Parks Mag 40:10-13 N '66
AULL, George H. jr.
Current trends in recreation and parks: ad-
dress. Parks & Rec 1:553-4 Jl '66
AULLWOOD Audubon center. See Audubon
nature centers
AUNTS
Anecdotes, facetiae, satire, etc.
Planned aunthood. B. Pfizer. il McCalls 94:
94+ O '66
AURELIUS Antoninus, Marcus emperor of
Rome
Reflections of a lonely ruler; excerpts from
Marcus Aurelius meditations; tr. by M.
Staniforth. Life 60:74+ Je 3 '66
about
Marcus Aurelius, by A. Birley. Review
America 115:621-2 N 12 '66. W. H. Fitz-
gerald
Meditations of Marcus Aurelius. K. Rexroth.
Sat R 49:46 Ja 29 '66
Noblest of emperors Marcus Aurelius Stoic
martyr to duty. il por Life 60:70-3 Je 3
'66
Wisdom and fortitude of Marcus Aurelius.
W. H. Chamberlin. por Sat R 50:22-3 Ja 7
'67
AURORAS
Auroral activity increases. il Sky & Tel 32:
380-3 D '66
AURTHUR, Robert Alan
In defense of nationality. Nation 202:107-9
Ja 24 '66
AUSCHWITZ atrocities. See World war, 1939-
1945—Atrocities
AUSCHWITZ concentration camp. See Concen-
tration camps—Poland
AUSTEN, Alice
Alice Austen's Staten Island. il por Am
Heritage 17:2, 27+ Ag '66
Island in the Bay. A. Robertson. il Am
Heritage 17:79-81 Ag '66
AUSTIN, Bill
Not a perfect friendship. T. Maule. il por
Sports Illus 25:36-8+ O 10 '66
AUSTIN, Charles F.
Where bosses fail: excerpt from Manage-
ment's self-inflicted wounds: a formula
for executive self-analysis. Nations Bsns
54:60+ O '66
AUSTIN, J. Paul
Businessmen in the news. por Fortune 74:27
Jl 1 '66
AUSTIN, Pamela
Calamity Pam. por Time 89:64 Ja 13 '67
AUSTIN, Tex.
Crime
All-American boy: C. J. Whitman killings.
il Newsweek 68:24-6+ Ag 15 '66
Madman in the tower: murders at University
of Texas. il Time 88:14-19 Ag 12 '66
Mass murder on a campus: Charles J. Whit-
man case. il U S News 61:6 Ag 15 '66
Under the clock, a sniper with 31 minutes to
live: C. Whitman shootings; with report
by D. Nevin. il Life 61:24-31 Ag 12 '66

Parks and playgrounds
Job corps on the job; recreation department
W. G. Leddick. il Parks & Rec 1:839 O '66
Sophistication of the sand box; Sandcraft
tournament. il Parks & Rec 1:323 Ap '66
AUSTRALIA
Atlantic report. Atlan 218:14+ Jl '66
Australia: it's much more than kangaroos.
H. Ehrlich. il Look 30:29-43 Ag 23 '66
Letter from Down Under. E. M. von Kueh-
nelt-Leddihn. Nat R 18:310 Ap 5 '66
Lucky Australia. D. Horne. il Holiday 40:48-
63+ S '66
This is a marvelous time to be here. il News-
week 67:42-8+ F 21 '66
See also
Airlines—Australia
Airplane industry and trade—Australia
Alice Springs
Automobile industry and trade—Australia
Aviation—Australia
Education—Australia
Elections—Australia
Green Island
Immigration and emigration—Australia
Iron mines and mining—Australia
Military service, Compulsory—Australia
Money—Australia
Paleontology—Australia
Petroleum—Australia
Political campaigns—Australia
Zoology—Australia

Army
Students of survival; Australia's Jungle war-
fare center. P. Harvey. il Newsweek 68:30
Ag 29 '66
Census
Filling in the ghastly blank. Time 88:32-3
Jl 22 '66
Defenses
Australia takes a new look, and turns to-
ward U.S. il U S News 60:74+ Ap 18 '66
New man in Canberra: H. Holt's beliefs
and policies. D. Warner. il Reporter 34:33-
6 Ap 21 '66
Now Australia steps into its place in Asia.
il U S News 61:38-40 O 31 '66

Description and travel
Australia. M. Edelson. il U S Camera 29:
50-1+ My '66

Foreign relations
Australia looks around. D. Horne. For Affairs 44:446-67 Ap '66
Now Australia steps into its place in Asia.
il U S News 61:38-40 O 31 '66

Asia
Establishing an identity: first federal election
since 1963. il Time 88:39 N 25 '66

United States
Australia takes a new look, and turns to-
ward U.S. il U S News 60:74+ Ap 18 '66
Australia votes to stay in Vietnam. D.
Warner. il Reporter 35:29-31 D 29 '66
President and Australian Prime Minister con-
clude talks; text of joint communique, July
14, 1966. Dept State Bul 55:212-13 Ag 8 '66
Why Australia backs U.S. in the Vietnam
war; interview. H. Holt. U S News 62:58-61
Ja 2 '67

Vietnam (Republic)
Australia today; U.S. Asian policy; address,
July 5, 1966. H. Holt. Vital Speeches 32:
613-17 Ag 1 '66

Industries
See also
Automobile industry and trade—Australia
Coal industry—Australia

Native races
Alice in Australia's wonderland; Alice Springs.
A. Villiers. il Nat Geog Mag 129:230-57 F
'66
Australia: its white policy and the Negro.
E. B. Thompson. il Ebony 21:46-50+ Jl;
96-8+ S '66
Prehistory of the Australian aborigine. D. J.
Mulvaney. il Sci Am 214:84-91+ bibliog
(p 143) Mr '66

Politics and government
End of the Ming dynasty. il Time 87:23 Ja
28 '66
Letter from Australia. H. Weston. il Nation
203:512-13 N 14 '66

AUSTRALIA—Politics and government—*Cont.*
Man on top Down Under; H. Holt. R. Gordon. il N Y Times Mag p38-9+ O 23 '66
New man in Canberra; H. Holt's beliefs and policies. D. Warner. il Reporter 34:33-6 Ap 21 '66

Population
See also
Australia—Census

Religious institutions and affairs
World around us (cont of) News of the Christian world. Christian Cent 83:665-6, 1188-9 My 18, S 28 '66
See also
Church of England in Australia

Statistics
See also
Australia—Census

AUSTRALIA, New Zealand, and the United States treaty council. See ANZUS council
AUSTRALIA and Asia. See Asia and Australia
AUSTRALIA and the United States
Affinity with Australia. A. Moorehead. il Sat R 49:43-4 O 8 '66
United States and Australia reaffirm common goals; exchange of greetings; exchange of toasts, June 29, 1966. L. B. Johnson; H. E. Holt. Dept State Bul 55:130-7 Jl 25 '66
See also
United States—Foreign opinion—Australian
AUSTRALIAN dialect. See English language—Dialects
AUSTRALIAN dialect dictionaries. See English language—Dictionaries
AUSTRALIAN fruit bats. See Bats
AUSTRALIAN gums. See Eucalyptus
AUSTRALIAN lifeguards. See Lifeguards
AUSTRALIANS
Australia: it's much more than kangaroos. H. Ehrlich. il Look 30:29-43 Ag 23 '66
Letter from Australia. H. Weston. Nation 203:512-13 N 14 '66
Lucky Australia. D. Horne. il Holiday 40:48-63+ S '66
AUSTRIA
See also
Architecture, Domestic—Austria
Ballet—Austria
Christmas—Austria
Elections—Austria
Music festivals—Austria
Salzburg
United Nations—Austria

Economic conditions
Troubled affluence. il Time 87:99 Ap 8 '66

History
Bibliography
Articles and other books received; comp. by A. H. Price. See issues of American historical review

Allied occupation, 1945-1955
Interpreter. F. L. Keefe. New Yorker 42:178+ D 10 '66

Politics and government
Anti-Semitic noises. Newsweek 67:46 Mr 14 '66
Habsburg happening. il Time 88:36 N 11 '66
People's party wins. Time 87:48+ Mr 18 '66
Pleasant disappointment. Time 87:31 My 6 '66
Splitting up: People's party to rule alone. Newsweek 67:34 My 2 '66
AUSTRIA-HUNGARY

History
See also
European war, 1914-1918—Austria-Hungary
AUSTRIAN cookery. See Cookery, Austrian
AUTHORITY
Stop giving in to the kids. America 115:478 O 22 '66
AUTHORITY (religion)
Use of authority. J. Meany. America 114:409-11 Mr 26 '66
See also
Bible—Inspiration
Catholic church—Infallibility
AUTHORS
ABPC annual meeting: literature of the future; excerpts from address, May 25, 1966. V. Peterson. il Pub W 189:86-7 Je 13 '66
Author, stay 'way from my door; experiences with juvenile authors in the bookstore. L. Russ. Pub W 189:37-8 My 30 '66

Authors & editors. il Pub W 191:21 Ja 2; 25 Ja 9; 41 Ja 16 '67
Can I have one? complimentary copies. C. Pinckney and E. Pinckney. il Sat R 49:61-2 F 12 '66
Literary roundtables: the writer as victim; summary of discussions. il Pub W 190:36-40 Jl 18 '66
On the mixed pleasures of uncovering new talent. A. Gingrich. Esquire 65:6 F '66
RPG workshop: publisher's role in creating and developing authors; summary of discussions. Pub W 189:22-7 Ap 11 '66
When the writer comes of age; reprint. B. J. Chute. Writer 79:20-4 N '66
Wouldn't it be easier if I just wore a sign on my back? how to turn introvert author-types into extrovert promoting types. Pub W 189:43-6 Mr 21 '66
Year the writers broke the bank; high-bidding publishers desperate for big names. Fortune 73:156-8 Ap '66
Yet another interview with B. Bonnet; fiction as nonfiction. L. L. Case. Nation 202:193-4 F 14 '66
See also
Authorship
Copyright
Dramatists
Editors and editing
Historians
Librarians as authors
Novelists
PEN club
Royalties

Homes and haunts
See Literary landmarks

Photographs
In the spring picture. Sat R 49:36-7 Ap 16 '66
AUTHORS, American
Getting to know your state's literary map. B. W. Fuson. il Sr Schol 89:sup44-5 S 23 '66
Imagination and the age; contemporary scene. A. Kazin. Reporter 34:32-5 My 5 '66
See also
American literature
Clemens, S. L.
Dahlberg, E.
Dos Passos, J.
Hawthorne, N.
Hoffer, E.
Jackson, S.
Lardner, R.
Miller, H.
Salinger, J. D.
Williams, W. C.
AUTHORS, Argentine
See also
Borges, J. L.
AUTHORS, Brazilian
See also
Jesus, C. M. de
AUTHORS, Bulgarian
See also
Guliashki, A.
AUTHORS, English
Affluence after anger; English cultural generation of the 1950s. R. Williams. Nation 203:676-7 D 19 '66
See also
Eliot, G. pseud.
Greene, G.
Lofting, H.
Maugham, W. S.
Wells, H. G.
West, R.
Williams, C.
AUTHORS, European
Gruppe 47 at Princeton. C. Mayer. Nation 202:588-90 My 16 '66
AUTHORS, Filipino
See also
Filipino literature
AUTHORS, French
European literary scene: rediscovered writers. R. J. Clements. Sat R 49:51 O 1 '66
New role for French literary agents? H. R. Lottman. Pub W 190:27-9 Ag 1 '66
See also
Breton, A.
Chateaubriand, F. A. R. de
French literature
Robbe-Grillet, A.
Sartre, J. P.
AUTHORS, German
See also
Grass, G.

AUTHORS, Irish
All the Olympians. F. O'Connor. Sat R 49:
30-2+ D 10 '66
See also
Joyce, J.
AUTHORS, Italian
See also
Casanova de Seingalt, G. G.
AUTHORS, Japanese
See also
Endo, S.
Mishima, Y.
AUTHORS, Jewish
Jew as modern writer. A. Kazin. Commen-
tary 41:37-41 Ap '66
See also
Malamud, B.
Rabinowitz, S.
Singer, I. B.
Singer, I. J.
AUTHORS, Mexican
See also
Reyes, A.
AUTHORS, Middle Eastern
Iran: goodby to the nightingale. F. M. Es-
fandiary. Nation 202:468-70 Ap 18 '66
AUTHORS, Russian
Art and politics in the U.S.S.R. il Newsweek
67:38+ F 21 '66
Art, politics, & the Soviet writer. T. Frankel.
bibliog f Commentary 41:52-9 My '66; Reply.
M. Friedberg. 42:16+ S '66
Authors league protests Sinyavsky-Daniel
trial. Pub W 189:68 F 28 '66
East and West from Paris; trial of Siniavsky
and Daniel. A. Werth. Nation 202:225 F 28
'66
Right to cry; case of Sinyavsky and Daniel.
Sr Schol 88:12-13 Mr 4 '66
Tertz case. J. Fischer. Harper 232:21 F '66
Trial and error. Newsweek 67:42+ F 28 '66
Trial ends; case of A. Tertz. J. L. Laber.
New Repub 154:26-9 Mr 19 '66
Valeriy Tarsis meets the press in New York.
Pub W 189:49 My 16 '66
West registers shock at Soviet writers' pun-
ishment. Pub W 189:151 F 21 '66
See also
Dostoevskii, F. M.
Russian literature
Tarsis, V.
AUTHORS, Venezuelan
Diary of Venezuelan literature. J. Liscano.
Américas 18:6-11 My '66
AUTHORS agents. See Literary agents
AUTHORS and libraries. See Libraries and
authors
AUTHORS and politics
Art and politics in the U.S.S.R. il Newsweek
67:38+ F 21 '66
I come out of my hiding place; address,
April 25, 1966. P. Weiss. Nation 202:652+
My 30 '66
Right to cry; case of Sinyavsky and Daniel.
Sr Schol 88:12-13 Mr 4 '66
Trial and error; case of dissenting Soviet
writers. Newsweek 67:42+ F 28 '66
Trial ends; case of A. Tertz. J. L. Laber.
New Repub 154:26-9 Mr 19 '66
West registers shock at Soviet writers' pun-
ishment. Pub W 189:151 F 21 '66
AUTHORS and publishers
Book publishing, and bookkeeping. D. N.
Fischel. Science 152:871-5 My 13 '66
Macmillan's author files, 1892-1960; go to
the NYPL. il Pub W 190:21-4 O 24 '66
Publishing explosion. il Newsweek 68:118+ O
10 '66
That darn image again. D. Dempsey. Sat
R 49:32 Ap 16 '66
W. W. Norton co. gives its authors a 5
per cent bonus. Pub W 189:72 Ja 31 '66
What right has an author? address, June 13,
1966. D. Horne. il Pub W 190:26-31 Jl 4 '66
See also
Literary agents

Anecdotes, facetiae, satire, etc.
Pro senior—signing scramble; Fulcourte inks
Swinburne; Appledore nabs Bronkowski.
New Yorker 42:68-9 N 12 '66
AUTHORS colonies
Locus: Washington square. W. Bower. il
Sat R 49:23-5 Je 4 '66
AUTHORS conferences
Confessions of a summer camper (lit'ry divi-
sion) D. Wakefield. il N Y Times Mag
p 10-11+ Jl 31 '66; Reply with rejoinder.
P. S. Collins. p22 Ag 28 '66
Group 47: nation's conscience; conference at
Princeton university. il Newsweek 67:118+
My 16 '66
Gruppe 47 at Princeton. C. Mayer. Nation
202:588-90 My 16 '66

Peripatetic reviewer. E. Weeks. Atlan 218:
137-8+ O '66
View from the East. I. Boldizsar. Nation
203:55-9 Jl 11 '66
When writers talk about writing; papers
presented at the international conference in
Lahti, Finland; with notes by N. Cousins.
E. Kos; N. Cousins; J. Myrdal. Sat R 49:
11-17+ Ag 13 '66
Workshops for writers; with list of confer-
ences. G. Munson. Sat R 49:42-5+ Ap 30
'66
Writers' conferences 1966. Writer 79:29-34
Ap '66
AUTHORS in literature
Writer as hero. L. Conger. Writer 79:8-10
O '66
AUTHORS league of America, incorporated
Authors league protests Sinyavsky-Daniel
trial. Pub W 189:68 F 28 '66
Licensing system: making copies of material
from books and periodicals on royalty basis.
il Library J 91:892-3 F 15 '66; Reply. J.
Weatherford. 91:2784 Je 1 '66
AUTHORSHIP
Finding a market for your story. F. A. Rock-
well. Writer 79:21-5 Je '66
Good word for greed. L. Conger. Writer 79:
8-10 Jl '66
How to be rejected. L. Conger. Writer 79:7-8
My '66
Journalism's guerrillas; free-lancers. A. Balk.
il Sat R 49:143-4 Mr 12 '66
Leg-up for ditched centipedes; an authors
confusion over ideas. L. Conger. Writer
79:6-8 S '66
Magic sentence. B. Lang. Writer 79:20-1+
O '66
Newbery award acceptance; address, July 12,
1966. E. B. Treviño. il Horn Bk 42:406-11
Ag '66
Ten article ideas that pay off. L. McLaughlin.
Writer 79:18-20 Je '66
Ten pitfalls and how to avoid them. J. Z.
Owen. Writer 79:15-17+ Jl '66
Three common errors in article writing. S. S.
Baker. Writer 79:14-16 D '66
Ticket in the raffle. J. Christopher. Writer
79:13-15 Je '66
Typewriter and I. R. Armour. Writer 79:
21-2 My '66
When writers talk about writing; papers
presented at the international conference in
Lahti, Finland; with notes by N. Cousins.
E. Kos; N. Cousins; J. Myrdal. Sat R 49:
11-17+ Ag 13 '66
Where to sell manuscripts. See issues of
Writer
Writer as independent spirit; questions to
be explored at New York congress; sym-
posium. il Sat R 49:16-30+ Je 4 '66
Writers do not exist. J. P. Wood. Horn Bk
42:694-8 D '66
Writing in retirement. G. D. Kratz. Writer
79:26-8 Ap '66
See also
Authors conferences
Biography
Drama—Technique
Fiction—Authorship
Fiction—Technique
Literary research
Moving picture authorship
Poetics
Poetry—Authorship
Short stories
Style, Literary
Television authorship

Anecdotes, facetiae, satire, etc.
Ollie who? R. Lemon. il Sat Eve Post 239:
26 Ap 23 '66
Bibliography
Writer's library. See issues of Writer
Competitions
See Literature—Competitions
AUTISM
Autism: a medical mystery. M. J. E. Senn.
McCalls 93:40+ Ap '66
AUTOANALYZER. See Medical instruments
and apparatus
AUTOCOLLIMATOR. See Collimators
AUTOFINE. See Photography—Developing and
developers
AUTOFLUORESCENCE. See Spectrum—Fluo-
rescence spectra
AUTOGIROS
Chairs that fly; gyrocopters. il Time 87:44
My 27 '66
Is this every man's flying machine? R. Gan-
non. il Pop Sci 188:91-4+ Ap '66

AUTOGRAPHING parties. See Booksellers and
bookselling—Publicity
AUTOGRAPHS
Are autographs an investment? reprint. M.
A. Benjamin. Hobbies 71:106-7+ Ag '66
AUTOHYPNOSIS. See Hypnotism
AUTOLAND. See Airplanes—Landing
AUTOMATED restaurants. See Restaurants—
Automation
AUTOMATED teaching aids. See Teaching—
Aids and devices
AUTOMATIC airplane control. See Airplanes—
Control
AUTOMATIC alarms. See Electric alarms
AUTOMATIC automobile control. See Automo-
biles—Control
AUTOMATIC cargo handling. See Freight hand-
ling
AUTOMATIC control
Remote-controlled filtration plant; Gary, Ind.
H. D. Harman. il Am City 81:100-2 My '66
See also
Cybernetics
Freight vessels—Automatic control
Inertial guidance systems
AUTOMATIC data processing. See Electronic
data processing
AUTOMATIC flight control system. See Auto-
matic pilot (airplanes)
AUTOMATIC landing systems. See Airplanes—
Landing
AUTOMATIC mail handling. See Mail handling
AUTOMATIC pilot (airplanes)
Let George do it; airplane autopilot, from
Sperry autopilot to Mooney positive con-
trol. R. Blodget. il Flying 79:64-8 Jl '66
Median signals control flight of F-111. P. J.
Klass. il Aviation W 85:76-8+ D 12 '66
AUTOMATIC pilot (boats)
Automatic pilots. E. Robberson. il Yacht-
ing 119:79-81+ Ja '66
AUTOMATIC processor. See Photography—
Printing processes
AUTOMATIC teaching. See Teaching machines
AUTOMATIC transmission. See Automobiles—
Transmission
AUTOMATION
Abundance in perspective: should men com-
pete with machines? R. Theobald. il Nation
202:544-50 My 9 '66
As I see it. E. Hannigan. U S Camera 29:44
Ag '66
Automation & white collar unionism. T. R.
Brooks. Duns R 87:59-62 Ja '66
Machines won't take over after all; high-
lights of Labor department study, Amer-
ica's Industrial and occupational manpower
requirements 1964-75. il Bsns W p93-4+
O 8 '66
Myths of automation, by C. E. Silberman.
Review
Sat R 49:37-8 O 29 '66. J. Diebold
Program for automated future; highlights of
National commission on technology, auto-
mation, and economic progress report.
Bsns W p30 F 5 '66
Who's afraid of automation! L. Velie. Read
Digest 88:117-20 Ap '66
See also
Assembly line methods
College libraries—Automation
Computers—Industrial applications
Electronic data processing
Libraries—Automation
Systems engineering
Unemployment, Technological
United States—National commission on tech-
nology, automation and economic progress
AUTOMATONS
Man's first robot with muscles. J. Lear. il
Sat R 49:83-6 D 3 '66
Telepuppet to aid man. A. Ewing. Sci N 89:
198 Mr 26 '66
Thinker's dream; excerpts from Theory of
self-producing automata. J. Von Neumann.
Sat R 49:56 S 3 '66
Wild transistorized West; radio-controlled
mechanical calf. J. F. Boykin. il Pop
Mech 125:118-19 F '66
AUTOMOBILE accidents. See Traffic accidents
AUTOMOBILE auctions. See Auctions
AUTOMOBILE batteries. See Storage batteries
AUTOMOBILE boat trailers
Hail the humble trailer. S. Barry. il Motor B
118:27-9+ Jl '66
How to pick a trailer for your boat. G. Daniels.
il Pop Sci 188:117-19 My '66
Load-equalizing hitch; eliminating the diffi-
culties of heavy-duty towing. L. Oertle. il
Yachting 120:54-5+ S '66
1967 trailers. il Motor B 119:174-5 Ja '67
Trailers, 1966. il Motor B 117:162-3 Ja '66

AUTOMOBILE bodies. See Automobiles—Bodies
AUTOMOBILE brakes. See Brakes, Automobile
AUTOMOBILE buying. See Automobiles—Pur-
chasing
AUTOMOBILE camping. See Camping
AUTOMOBILE clubs
Bug is small, but oh my! Grand prix of
Volkswagens in Nassau. K. Chapin. il
Sports Illus 25:22-3 D 12 '66
Top ten, 1965. D. Wells. il Hot Rod 19:76-7
Mr '66
AUTOMOBILE dealers
Are supermarkets for autos next? selling
cars through franchised automobile dealers
is being questioned. Bsns W p33 My 7 '66
Confessions of a car salesman. R. G. Shafer.
il Pop Mech 126:59-61+ S '66
Dealer's dilemma. R. J. Gottlieb. Motor T 18:
78 N '66
Dodge rebellion. il Time 88:104 O 21 '66
How to outsell them all; Chevrolet's Quality
dealer action program. L. H. Averill. il Na-
tions Bsns 55:50-1+ Ja '67
How to pick a dealer. A. Marcus. Motor T
18:64 N '66
Nightlight with the nicest guy in town;
auto salesmen's techniques. M. Greenfield.
Reporter 35:35-7 Jl 14 '66
Now the cleanup starts; unloading of 1966
models, before 1967 cars arrive. il Bsns W
p30 Jl 23 '66
Obtaining warranty service on a new car.
Consumer Bul 49:22-4 Mr '66
Open season; discount-house car sales. Time
87:94 My 6 '66
That new car can wait a while. Bsns W p41-
2 My 21 '66
AUTOMOBILE drivers
Better roads, worse drivers. R. Bensted-
Smith; K. Purdy. il Atlan 218:120+ D '66
Can you talk to other drivers? E. D. Fales,
jr. Read Digest 88:177-8+ My '66
Dangerous driving is no accident; concerning
T. C. Willett's study of English offenders.
Read Digest 88:98-100 F '66
Driving right, right from the start; the teen-
age driver. il Sr Schol 88:28-9 Ap 22 '66
Flat-out on the big curved screen; with re-
port by H. Moffett. il Life 61:122-4+ O 28
'66
Hall's Chaparral; racing to the top. il News-
week 67:48-52 F 7 '66
How states are cracking down on drivers.
U S News 60:8 F 28 '66
If there's a teen-age driver on your farm. J.
LemMon. il Suc Farm 64:71+ My '66
Keys to the car; teenage driver. Sr Schol
88:26 Ap 22 '66
McCall's 1967 report on automobiles; woman's
guide to easier maintenance and more
driving pleasure. il McCalls 94:75-82 N '66
News on wheels; relationship between good
grades and safer driving. Sr Schol 89:30
N 18 '66
B for safety; fix nut behind the wheel. A. H.
Sypher. il Nations Bsns 54:31-2 Ap '66
Real causes and cures of auto accidents;
study from the Stanford research institute.
il U S News 60:44-6 My 23 '66
Research and the automobile; address, May
13, 1966. H. E. Chesebrough. Vital Speeches
32:501-4 Je 1 '66
Ten off the top. J. Scalzo. il Motor T 18:28-
9 Mr '66
This little car went to high school; with
study-discussion program, by C. Smallen-
burg and H. Smallenburg. P. Jones. bib-
liog il PTA Mag 61:4-6, 36 Ja '67
Who's in the driver's seat? G. M. Smerk.
America 115:688-9 N 26 '66
You and the battle for traffic survival. A.
Rothenberg. il Look 30:32-6+ Ap 19 '66

Anecdotes, facetiae, satire, etc.
Road to survival in Europe. G. Bocca. il
Horizon 8:106-7 Wint '66

Licenses
Deadly loopholes in driver licensing. J. Joseph.
Motor T 19:48-50 Ja '67
AUTOMOBILE driving
Better roads, worse drivers. R. Bensted-
Smith; K. Purdy. il Atlan 218:120+ D '66
Clip out these things you'd never think to
do if involved in an accident. Bet Hom
& Gard 44:38 My '66
Defensive driving. G. E. Hollister. Motor T
18:60 O '66
Drivin' with Dan; questions and answers. D.
Gurney. il Pop Mech 126:94-5 O; 98-9 N; 74-
5 D '66; 127:34+ Ja '67

AUTOMOBILE driving—*Continued*
Driving right. right from the start: the teen-age driver. il Sr Schol 88:28-9 Ap 22 '66
En route to Christmas. H. Wilson. il Travel 126:30-2+ D '66
How to avoid car accidents in driveways. Good H 162:160 F '66
Is it really necessary to break-in your new car? J. Dunne. il Pop Sci 189:116-18+ N '66
Let's teach our teens to drive at night. M. Lederer. il Todays Health 44:68-71 S '66
Personal business; driving safety. Bsns W p 167-8 Je 11 '66
Senior citizens' driving studied. Sci N 90:457 N 26 '66
Ten driving habits guaranteed to cause an accident, sooner or later. Bet Hom & Gard 44:14 F '66
These little mistakes cost car owners plenty. il Changing T 20:35-8 F '66
Twenty ways to go in snow. E. D. Fales, jr. il Pop Mech 127:87-90+ Ja '67
What to do if: common driving situations. il Bet Hom & Gard 44:58-9+ Ap '66
See also
Automobile drivers
Automobiles—Speed
Traffic regulations

Laws and regulations
See Automobile laws and regulations

Study and teaching
Automotive safety. R. Moley. Newsweek 67:90 Ja 31 '66

Europe, Western
If you think driving in the U.S. is dangerous. il U S News 60:104-6 Je 20 '66

France
Letter from Paris; suspension of license and fining for reckless driving. J. Flanner. New Yorker 42:111-12+ Ag 27 '66

AUTOMOBILE driving and drinking. See Drinking and traffic accidents

AUTOMOBILE engines
American racing engines. Motor T 18:24-5 Mr '66
Blown 'tang. E. Dahlquist. il Hot Rod 19:64-8 O '66
Blueprinting Buicks for action. E. Dahlquist. il Hot Rod 19:40-3+ Ap '66
Can this pushrod engine win Indy? J. McFarland. il Hot Rod 20:56-61 Ja '67
Engine evolution typified by Buick's new V-8? J. Ethridge. il Motor T 18:30-2 S '66
Engine that's giving Detroit Wankel fever; rotating combustion engine. D. Francis. il Pop Sci 188:98-101 Ap '66
Engines around the world. J. Ethridge. il Motor T 18:36-7 Mr '66
Engines pack more power per pound. il Pop Sci 189:90-3 O '66
Gander at the new Drake. J. McFarland. il Hot Rod 19:28-32+ Mr '66
Hemi white paper; excerpts from address. W. L. Weertman and R. J. Lechner. il Hot Rod 19:72-7+ Ag '66
How hot can a six get? J. P. Norbye. il Pop Sci 188:70-3 Je '66
It won't work! E. Rickman. il Hot Rod 19:48-50+ Ap '66
Let's torque about horsepower. J. McFarland. il Hot Rod 19:96 O '66
Monaco Grand prix. G. Borgeson. il Motor T 18:76-8 Ag '66
New revolver-like steam engine produces 4.25 hp. per cubic inch! S. S. Miner. il Pop Sci 188:84-8 F '66
News on wheels: NSU Wankel on rotating combustion engine. D. Chu. il Sr Schol 88:22 F 11 '66
1967 engines: the year of options! L. Smith. il Motor T 19:28-33+ Ja '67
Olds' stump puller. J. McFarland. il Hot Rod 19:78-9+ Jl '66
Power by the inch. J. McFarland. il Hot Rod 19:44-7 My '66
Power mods for MoPar's 273. E. Dahlquist. il Hot Rod 19:64-7+ F '66
Red-blooded American! J. Ethridge. il Motor T 18:38-40+ My '66
Session with Mickey; interview. ed. by J. McFarland. M. Thompson. il Hot Rod 19:80-1 Ag '66
Switchables. J. McFarland. il Hot Rod 19:92-4+ S '66
Tale of a Chevelle. J. McFarland. il Hot Rod 19:64+ Ap '66
Tonic for el tigre. J. McFarland. il Hot Rod 19:94-6 N '66

327 Chevy caper. J. McFarland. il Hot Rod 19:66-9+ S '66
V8 for Rambler American. J. Dunne. il Pop Mech 125:70 My '66
See also
Anti-freeze solutions
Automobiles—Cams
Carburetors
Crankcases
Manifolds
Motor truck engines
Piston rings

Air supply
Air in a box. il Hot Rod 19:106 D '66
In's and out's of air-flow. J. McFarland. il Hot Rod 19:58-60+ D '66

Bearings
Bearing basics. J. McFarland. il Hot Rod 19:58-61 My '66

Care
Secrets for getting the best engine tune-up. R. Day. il Pop Sci 189:158-63 N '66

Cooling
Heat's on. J. McFarland. il Hot Rod 19:38-41 Je '66

Exhaust
Can air pollution be stopped? M. Neiburger. Christian Cent 83:138-40 F 2 '66; Discussion. 83:307-8 Mr 9 '66
Car exhaust levels to be tighter by 1970. Sci N 89:185 Mr 19 '66
Curbing the fumes. Time 88:47 Ag 19 '66
Ice nuclei from automobile exhaust and iodine vapor. V. J. Schaefer. bibliog Science 154:1555-7 D 23 '66
Pollution alert; anti-smog devices. il Newsweek 68:66-7 D 5 '66
Stringent controls on auto emissions. Am City 81:48 My '66
What you should know about anti-smog devices. J. M. Callahan. il Pop Sci 188:120-3 Mr '66

Filters
See Air filters, Automobile

Fuel
Engine that burns anything. Sci Digest 59:16 Ap '66
See also
Liquefied petroleum gas

Fuel consumption
Behind the bedlam of the featherfoot fleet; Mobil economy run. W. Thoms il Motor T 18:60-2 Mr '66

Fuel feeding
Fuel injection Rochester style. N. Burger. il Hot Rod 19:58-61+ F '66

Ignition
Compac solid-state C-D ignition system. M. Gellman. il Pop Electr 25:53-6+ N '66
Proven transistor ignition system. C. C. Morris. il Electr World 75:47-9 Ja '66
Solid-state tachometer for CD or transistor ignition systems. M. Gellman. il Pop Electr 24:54-7 F '66
Spark of life. J. McFarland. il Hot Rod 19:56-9 Ag '66
See also
Spark plugs

Lubrication
See Automobiles—Lubrication

Mounting
Universal mounts. L. Smith. il Hot Rod 19:56-7 O '66

Mufflers
How to live with your muffler. M. J. Schultz. il Pop Mech 126:166-9 D '66

Repairing
Shop talk. J. McFarland. See issues of Hot rod

Superchargers
Indy '66: can the Offy make a comeback with supercharging? D. Phipps and J. P. Wright. il Pop Sci 188:65-8+ My '66
Turbo-tonic. J. McFarland. il Hot Rod 19:82-3 Jl '66

Testing
Punch tape Gran prix. J. McFarland. Hot Rod 19:74 Je '66
Test drive of U.S. car with a rotating combustion engine: challenge of piston engine. J. P. Norbye. il Pop Sci 188:102-7 Ap '66

AUTOMOBILE engines—*Continued*

Valves

Job for valves. J. McFarland. il Hot Rod 19: 88-91 N '66

AUTOMOBILE factories
See also
Ford motor company

Automation

How it works on the line. S. Kelly. il Motor T 18:29-32 My '66

Employees

See also
Automobile industry and trade—Wages and hours

AUTOMOBILE filters. See Air filters, Automobile

AUTOMOBILE financing. See Instalment plan

AUTOMOBILE gasoline filters. See Gasoline filters

AUTOMOBILE graveyard; drama. See Arrabal, F.

AUTOMOBILE industry and trade
See also
Automobile factories

Advertising

Rebellion that caught the mood of youth; Dodge rebellion a household word. il Bsns W p74 D 10 '66

International aspects

Auto labor goes multinational. il Bsns W p74-6 Je 11 '66
Where Kaiser's cars lead the pack; production abroad. il Bsns W p 114:16+ N 5 '66

Quality control

Quality control: fact or fiction? il Motor T 18:23-34 My '66

Securities

Wall Street's tune on autos stays sour; sales slump persists. il Bsns W p 152-3 O 1 '66

Statistics

Way we see it; 1965 and 1966 car production. D. MacDonald. il Motor T 19:6 Ja '67

Wages and hours

Auto craftsmen step up pressure; to get increases for skilled tradesmen. il Bsns W p43-4+ Ag 27 '66
Craftsmen ask more from UAW. Bsns W p 124+ Jl 23 '66
UAW's 20th constitutional convention. R. T. Selby. Mo Labor R 89:733-5 Jl '66
What a shortage of skilled workers may do to wages. U S News 61:78-9 Jl 11 '66

Australia

Slicing a rich market too thin; oversupply of manufacturers and models. il Bsns W p 103-4+ O 22 '66

Canada

Auto pact: two years old and blooming. Bsns W p 144 D 17 '66

Europe, Eastern

Communist car: an upside-down status symbol. Reporter 34:30-1 My 5 '66
Wheels behind the curtain. il Read Digest 88:128-30 Ap '66

Europe, Western

New front for the safety furor; furor on European front over federal standards. il Time 88:115-16 N 25 '66

France

France's auto makers eye a common future; Renault and Peugeot join forces. Bsns W p44 Ap 30 '66
Renaissance at Renault. il Newsweek 68:90+ O 17 '66

Germany (Federal Republic)

Foreign bugs; Volkswagen recall campaign. Newsweek 68:80 Jl 18 '66
German autos feel the pinch. Bsns W p 112 D 17 '66
Rethinking small; new Volkswagen. Time 89: 79 Ja 20 '67
Rite of spring; Volkswagen's pick-it-up-yourself program. il Newsweek 67:88 Ap 11 '66

Great Britain

Autos in a skid. il Time 88:106 O 21 '66
See also
British motor corporation
Rolls-Royce, limited

Italy

Fiat in the future; Italians move into Russia. Newsweek 67:78 My 2 '66
Fiat's new wheeler. il Time 87:102 My 6 '66
Ghia: third in a connoisseur's series. J. Lawlor. il Motor T 18:30-1 Ap '66
How Fiat sold Moscow; Italian auto maker's deal to help make cars in Russia. il Bsns W p 106+ My 14 '66
Romeo's sweet Giulia. il Time 87:100+ Mr 4 '66
Trying harder; Fiat to build in Poland. Newsweek 67:74 My 30 '66

Japan

Car craze. il Newsweek 68:94+ O 24 '66
Japanese autos move out into the world; car exports rising fast. il Bsns W p 112-14+ D 3 '66
Japanese beetles, four-wheeled. il Fortune 73: 69-70 My '66

Poland

Trying harder; Fiat to build in Poland. Newsweek 67:74 My 30 '66

Russia

Fiat in the future; Italians move into Russia. Newsweek 67:78 My 2 '66
Happiness is driving your own Moskvich. D. D. Barry and C. B. Barry. il N Y Times Mag p 16-17+ Ap 10 '66
How Fiat sold Moscow; Italian auto maker's deal to help make cars in Russia. il Bsns W p 106+ My 14 '66
Russia enters the auto age; will it remake the country? il U S News 60:62-3 Je 6 '66
Where now the Yankee trader? Nation 202: 636 My 30 '66

United States

Amber light; plea for slow down on mandatory safety features. Newsweek 69:61-2 Ja 16 '67
Auto executive: he has to run faster just to keep up. il Bsns W p96-100 Mr 12 '66
Auto safety goes into high gear. il Newsweek 67:77-8+ F 21 '66
Auto sales: the industry view. il U S News 60:34 My 30 '66
Automobile industry looks ahead to '67. il U S News 61:54 D 26 '66
Automotive safety. R. Moley. Newsweek 67: 106 F 21 '66
Autos: Detroit hits a bumpy road; sagging sales and safety callbacks. il Newsweek 68:79 D 5 '66
Autos face uphill drive for record year. il Bsns W p36 My 28 '66
Autos finish one race and head into another. il Bsns Wp52-3 S 24 '66
Autos; 1965 sales and profits. il Time 87:90 F 18 '66
Autos, 1966: no way but up. il Newsweek 67:71-2 F 14 '66
Buying up but selling down. il Time 88:107 N 25 '66
Car maker and safety; address, June 18, 1966. J. O'Connell. Vital Speeches 32:656-60 Ag 15 '66
Car sales hit a bump; Detroit remains optimistic. il Bsns W p32 My 7 '66
Comeback trail. Newsweek 67:82 Je 13 '66
Customizer and the car maker. J. Lawlor. il Motor T 18:28-9 Ap '66
Defect or driver? recalling potentially defective cars. Newsweek 69:53 Ja 2 '67
Defects of Detroit; recall campaigns. Newsweek 67:75-6 My 16 '66
Detroit listening post. See issues of Popular mechanics
Detroit murder case; R. Nader's charges in book Unsafe at any speed. D. Cort. New Repub 154:22-4 F 12 '66
Detroit revolution. D. Ash. Esquire 66:86-7+ Jl '66
Detroit shifts down. il Bsns W p43-4 N 26 '66
Detroit slows its assembly lines; big three trim production. il Bsns W p36-7 My 14 '66
Detroit tones down; outlook for '67 and beyond. il Bsns W p35 D 17 '66
Detroit tries to defang safety bill; Senate cool to industry's plan to set own safety standards. il Bsns W p30-1 Ap 9 '66
Detroit tries to grab the auto-safety wheel; accepting President Johnson's standard-setting safety bill. Bsns W p42 Ap 30 '66
Double talk from Detroit; which to believe, auto makers' ads or safety statements? J. O'Connell. America 115:507-10 O 29 '66; Discussion. 115:673-4 N 26 '66

AUTOMOBILE industry and trade—United States—*Continued*
Economy: fair but cooler; sales decline; impact on GM-Ford rivalry. il Newsweek 67:78-9 My 23 '66
GM sets off rollback in prices; Ford and Chrysler refigure price increases. il Bsns W p46 O 1 '66
Great race, Chevy vs. Ford; with report by M. Silva. il Life 61:131-2+ O 14 '66
Here's the picture in autos. il U S News 60:31 My 23 '66
Industry forecast: no end in sight to the auto boom. il U S News 60:48-9 Mr 7 '66
Investment abroad by U.S. companies; its effect on the balance of payments; address, January 26, 1966. L. A. Townsend. Vital Speeches 32:280-3 F 15 '66
Jumping the gun on 1967. Bsns W p36-7 Je 25 '66
Making automobiles safer. H. Brandon. Sat R 49:22 F 19 '66
Many are called but fewer are defective. il Time 88:87 D 2 '66
Mixed cheers in Detroit; may have to take a back seat to 1965. il Time 87:89-90 Mr 18 '66
Nader caper; GM investigation. Newsweek 67:83 Mr 21 '66
New deal for drivers; automobile-safety bill passed the House. Time 88:12 Ag 26 '66
News on wheels; automakers in stock car racing. D. Chu. il Sr Schol 89:40 S 30 '66
1967 new car buyer's guide. il Motor T 18:36-64+ N '66
1967: the showdown year. B. Kilpatrick. il Pop Mech 126:101-4+ O '66
Now the cleanup starts; unloading of 1966 models, before 1967 cars arrive. il Bsns W p30 Jl 23 '66
Now the Tiger wears a seatbelt. J. O'Connell. il N Y Times Mag p27+ O 2 '66
Other shoe; sales lag. Newsweek 67:74 Je 6 '66
Out with the old year, on with the new. Time 88:68 Ag 12 '66
Phony auto reform. New Repub 154:8 F 5 '66
Politics of auto safety; background of bill's introduction. E. B. Drew. il Atlan 218:95-102 O '66
Pressure mounts; concerning proposals for federal authority to set automobile safety standards. Sr Schol 88:12 Ap 22 '66
Putting the chips on '66. il Bsns W p27-8 Ja 22 '66
Question marks; competition from abroad. il Newsweek 68:61-2 D 26 '66
Race for safety is on; Detroit developing safer cars. il Bsns W p 178-9+ Je 11 '66
Race of the '67's is off to a good start. il Bsns W p40-1 O 22 '66
Rattles in the engine. il Time 87:100-2+ My 20 '66
Recalling six years. Time 87:95 My 13 '66
Retreat from the record. Time 89:63-4 Ja 13 '67
Rolling with the cuts; auto industry suppliers adjust by paring overtime. Bsns W p40 My 21 '66
Safety first; industry and government moves. il Newsweek 67:76+ Ap 18 '66
Safety issue no drag on auto sales. Bsns W p31-2 F 19 '66
Safety on highways. America 114:613-14 Ap 30 '66
Splash for the '67s; hopeful auto makers welcome a new year. il Bsns W p40-2 S 10 '66
Spring fever runs high in Detroit. il Bsns W p33-4 Ap 2 '66
Stock talk. B. Myers. il Motor T 18:82+ Ap; 76+ My; 80+ Ag '66
Strategic retreat; industry to endorse Title I of safety bill. Newsweek 67:80+ My 9 '66
Those automotive call-backs. il Consumer Rep 31:340-1 Jl '66
Twenty days in May; automakers and the stock market. Time 87:81-2 Je 3 '66
Unsafe at any speed; the designed-in dangers of the American automobile, by R. Nader. Review
  Sci Am 214:137-40+ My '66. D. Hawkins
When auto industry falters; the impact on U.S. il U S News 61:44-6 Jl 11 '66
Where it all starts. J. Ethridge. il Motor T 18:24-8 My '66
Who's in the driver's seat? G. M. Smerk. America 115:688-9 N 26 '66
Why cars must, and can, be made safer; Time essay. Time 87:26-7 Ap 1 '66; Same abr. with title Safer cars on the roads ahead? Read Digest 88:115-18 Je '66

Written in cold fury. E. Larrabee. Harper 232-117-19 Ap '66
See also
Automobile dealers
Automobiles—Prices
Lehmann-Peterson, incorporated
United automobile, aerospace and agricultural implement workers of America
  also names of automobile manufacturing companies, e.g. Ford motor company

History
American automobile, by J. B. Rae. Review
  Reporter 34:55-7 Ja 27 '66. H. Cohen

Yugoslavia
Where the lure of the auto is killing communism. K. Lachmann. il U S News 60:76-8 Je 20 '66
AUTOMOBILE inspection. See Automobiles—Inspection
AUTOMOBILE insurance. See Insurance, Automobile
AUTOMOBILE laws and regulations
Auto safety dispute; need for reformed legislation. R. Moley. Newsweek 67:124 My 23 '66
Cars and the law. R. J. Gottlieb. See issues of Motor trend
High cost of passing through. E. Marshall. Motor T 18:67 O '66
Our chaotic traffic laws. A. Ribicoff. Read Digest 88:101-2 Mr '66
Private war of Prefect Bruneau; France. il Time 88:30 Ag 19 '66
See also
Automobiles—Inspection
Motor vehicles—Laws and regulations
Traffic accidents
Traffic regulations
AUTOMOBILE mechanics (persons)
Four great honest mechanics. il Esquire 65:74-5+ F '66
See also
Automobiles—Repairing
AUTOMOBILE models
Road-racing sets. Consumer Rep 31:323-8 D '66
See also
Automobiles, Toy
Racing
Build your own slot-car track. A. W. Lees. il Pop Mech 126:124-5 Ag '66
Slot-car racing sets. il Consumer Rep 31:540-6 N '66
AUTOMOBILE museums
Brooks Stevens and his magnificent driving machines. D. MacDonald. il Motor T 18:36-9 Jl '66
Harrah collection; world's largest automotive museum. D. MacDonald. il Motor T 18:40-3 Ap '66
Renaissance for relics; with list of museums. T. A. Hoge. il Travel 126:56-60 Ag '66
So what's so new, a quick trip through Harrah's automobile collection in Reno, Nevada; photographs. Motor T 18:126-7 N '66
Treasure-trove of Alfas; Alfa Romeo museum in Milan. G. Borgeson. il Motor T 18:70-3 S '66
Winthrop Rockefeller collection. D. MacDonald. il Motor T 18:42-5 My '66
AUTOMOBILE oil filters. See Oil filters
AUTOMOBILE owners
Autoeroticism; car-crazy West Germans. il Time 88:31-2 Jl 22 '66
On cars and snobbism; Rolls-Royce owner. J. O'Hara. il Holiday 40:52-3 Ag '66
AUTOMOBILE parking
Joint efforts build a shoppers' lot; Middletown, Ohio. Am City 81:140 Ap '66
Just point 'er in and push the button; how the Sidler works. M. J. Pedersen. il Pop Mech 126:62-3 S '66
Notes and comment; towing away illegally parked cars in New York. New Yorker 42:47 O 8 '66
Parking decals serve overtime parkers; New Albany, Ind. G. Inman. Am City 81:134 O '66
Public vs. private ownership of off-street parking. J. W. Gottesman. il Am City 81:126+ O '66
Structure that meets two different needs; piers for parking needs and zoning requirements. il Arch Rec 140:174-5 N '66
Towaways; Pier 74, at Thirty-fourth street and the North River, N.Y. New Yorker 42:52-4 N 12 '66
Where fringe commuter parking works. Am City 81:117 D '66
See also
Garages, Municipal

AUTOMOBILE parts

Mix 'em, match 'em and blueprint 'em. J. McFarland. il Hot Rod 19:66-8 Je '66

1967 engines: the year of options! L. Smith. il Motor T 19:28-33+ Ja '67

Street roadsters. B. Lang. il Hot Rod 19:34-8+ D '66

See also

Gulf and Western industries, incorporated

Testing

Flaw finders. E. Rickman. il Hot Rod 19:102-3 D '66

AUTOMOBILE phonographs. See Automobiles—Phonograph equipment

AUTOMOBILE racing

Affair of honor; Ford victory at Le Mans. il Time 88:59 Jl 1 '66

AHRA winter blast. J. McFarland. il Hot Rod 19:62-4+ My '66

AHRA Winter nationals. S. Kelly. il Motor T 18:64 My '66

At Sebring: victory and death; triumph was Ford's but four spectators and a driver Bob McLean lost their lives. B. La Fontaine. il Sports Illus 24:36-7 Ag 4 '66

Atlanta 500. B. Myers. il Motor T 18:72-4 Je '66

Atlanta 500: E. Dahlquist. il Hot Rod 19:62-5+ Je '66

Automobile racing; with calendar of major automobile races. S. Wilkinson. il Holiday 40:89-95 Ag '66

Bakersfield: supermeet; U.S. fuel & gas championship. E. Dahlquist. il Hot Rod 19:46-50+ Je '66

Big Hoosier hurry; photographs by R. Huntzinger; with account by B. La Fontaine. Sports Illus 24:30-8+ My 30 '66

Big ones were waiting for Mario; Indy trials. B. Ottum. il Sports Illus 24:32-3 My 23 '66

Bristol bash; NHRA's 2nd annual Springnationals. E. Dahlquist. il Hot Rod 19:60-4+ Ag '66

Bug is small, but oh my! Grand prix of Volkswagens in Nassau. K. Chapin. il Sports Illus 25:22-3 D 12 '66

Cactus patch. J. McFarland. il Hot Rod 19:62-4 Jl '66

Can anyone stop Dan Gurney. il Motor T 19:88 Ja '67

Circle track, its men and machinery. J. Scalzo. il Hot Rod 19:34-40+ Jl '66

Coming in on a wing and a bankroll; Canadian-American challenge cup race. A. Wright. il Sports Illus 25:76+ O 3 '66

Crazy mixed-up 500; disputed victory. B. Ottum. il Sports Illus 24:20-3 Je 6 '66

Curse of endurance racing; Grand prix at Sebring. il Newsweek 67:66-7 Ap 11 '66

Daytona, a hemi holiday. E. Dahlquist. il Hot Rod 19:76-8+ My '66

Daytona 500! D. MacDonald. il Motor T 18:46-8 My '66

Divided it stood; the UDRA third annual go-fest. J. McFarland. il Hot Rod 19:58-60 My '66

Dodgem game; Indianapolis 500. il Time 87:92+ Je 10 '66

Does anybody here believe Jack Brabham? eighth annual U.S. Grand prix at Watkins Glen, N.Y. K. Chapin. il Sports Illus 25:82-3 O 10 '66

Doing the desert drag; Glamis dunes races. il Time 87:76 Mr 4 '66

Down by the river side; Motor trend's annual 500-miler. J. McFarland. il Hot Rod 19:34-7+ Ap '66

Draggin' south of the border, or, ole! R. Brock. il Hot Rod 20:66-7 Ja '67

Drags. W. Parks. Motor T 18:45 Mr '66

Dry crucible for the hot ones; J. Surtees wins the Canadian-American sports car title in Las Vegas. B. Ottum. il Sports Illus 25:32-4+ N 21 '66

Duel in the sun; Los Angeles times Grand prix. il Newsweek 68:66 N 14 '66

Duel with death on the salt; A. Arfons' crash on the Bonneville Salt Flats. B. Ottum. il Sports Illus 25:28-31 N 28 '66

Epic of Indy. J. McFarland. il Hot Rod 19:42-6+ Ag '66

Escalation at Indy; opening trials, 50th Indianapolis. il Newsweek 67:83-4 My 30 '66

Fantastic Surfers. E. Dahlquist. il Hot Rod 19:76-80+ S '66

Flat-out on the big curved screen; with report by H. Moffett. il Life 61:122-4+ O 28 '66

Ford, Ford, Ford; Mark II at Daytona international speedway track; twenty-four hour race. il Newsweek 67:88 F 21 '66

Foyt vs Jones. J. Scalzo. il Motor T 18:40 Jl '66

Funny car meet of the year! second annual Super stock nationals. J. Gross. il Hot Rod 19:72-7+ O '66

La *gloire* at Le Mans. il Newsweek 67:60 Je 20 '66

Glorious festival of Fords; Ferrari's long domination ended at Le Mans. J. Lovesey. il Sports Illus 24:28-9 Je 27 '66

Grand old man; J. Brabham. il Time 88:53 Ag 5 '66

Grandest Grand Prix; race in Monte Carlo. S. Wilkinson. il Holiday 39:68-75 Je '66

Half 'n half; American hot rod association summer events. J. McFarland. il Hot Rod 19:78-81+ O '66

Hall's Chaparral: racing to the top. il Newsweek 67:48-52 F 7 '66

Happiness is; Hot rod magazine championship drags. J. Gross. il Hot Rod 19:46-8+ S '66

Hawaiian. J. Thawley. il Hot Rod 20:50-2 Ja '67

Here comes racing's Cougar. B. Ottum. il Sports Illus 25:58-9 N 7 '66

Hot rod digs; Riverside raceway. D. Wells. il Hot Rod 19:78 Ap '66

Hot rod's 1966 top ten. J. Thawley. il Hot Rod 20:64-5 Ja '67

I still get goose pimples; ed. by K. Rudeen. S. McQueen. il Sports Illus 25:39-42 Ag 8 '66

In Sicily nearly everybody loves the Targa Florio. L. Bentley. il Sports Illus 24:54-6+ My 9 '66

Inji goes to Fuji for speed and art. J. Schecter. il Sports Illus 25:38-9 O 17 '66

Judgment at Indy; Indianapolis 500; with report by J. C. Jones. il Newsweek 67:96+ Je 13 '66

Long black line; '66 Bonneville meeting. E. Dahlquist. il Hot Rod 19:78-80+ N '66

McQuagg, firecracks his first! B. Myers. il Motor T 18:65-6+ S '66

Le Mans adds fuel to Ford's future. il Bsns W p34-6 Je 25 '66

Marred victory; Sebring deaths; winners. il Time 87:65 Ap 1 '66

Motor trend Riverside 500. J. Ethridge. il Motor T 18:50-3 Ap '66

Mount Fuji 200. J. Thawley. il Hot Rod 20:70-1 Ja '67

NHRA Nationals Indy '66. J. McFarland and J. Gross. il Hot Rod 19:36-44 N '66

NHRA Winternationals; Pomona, Calif, February 18-20, 1966. S. Kelly. il Motor T 18:53 My '66

National scene. See issues of Hot rod

Nightmare on the Flats; Arfons' Green Monster crashes. il Time 88:63 N 25 '66

1966 Winternationals. D. Wells. il Hot Rod 19:36-43+ My '66

Ol' Jack was nimble, ol' Jack was quick, with his Brabham machine he turned the trick. L. Levine. il Motor T 19:56-9+ Ja '67

One lap at Indy! J. Ethridge. il Motor T 18:42-6 Ag '66

Out of the ivory tower into the grease pit: National library week at Ossining, N.Y. public library; with bibliography. E. Sclar. il Library J 91:2162-4+ Ap 15 '66

Peach Blossom 500. B. Myers. il Motor T 18:70-1 Je '66

Race to the clouds; Pikes Peak race. R. Brock. il Hot Rod 19:42-5+ S '66

Rebel 400. E. Dahlquist. il Hot Rod 19:58-60+ Jl '66

Rebel 400! B. Myers. il Motor T 18:44-6 Jl '66

Reckless dash to disaster; Indy's first-lap smashups. B. Ottum. il Sports Illus 24:30-3+ Je 13 '66

Return of the exile was rich and racy; Daytona's stock car 500. T. C. Brody. il Sports Illus 24:24-5 Mr 7 '66

Roddin' at random. il Hot Rod 20:92-5 Ja '67

Rules for racing. Motor T 18:30-1+ Mr '66

Runaway at Daytona. il Time 87:68+ F 18 '66

Safe at any speed? Indianapolis 500. il Time 87:48 My 27 '66

Show & go. See issues of Hot rod

600 mph, what it's really like! ed. by C. Maher. C. Breedlove. il Motor T 18:46 Mr '66

South Pacific championship drags. R. Brock. il Hot Rod 19:71-2+ Mr '66

Southwest showdown. J. Gross. il Hot Rod 19:66-7 D '66

AUTOMOBILE racing—*Continued*
Stirling Moss on racing. S. Moss. See issues of Motor trend
Stock car racer reaches bigtime. il Ebony 21: 61-2+ My '66
Straight racin' with NASCAR. J. Gross. il Hot Rod 19:61-4+ N '66
Ten off the top. J. Scalzo. il Motor T 18: 28-9 Mr '66
Top ten, 1965. D. Wells. il Hot Rod 19:76-7 Mr '66
Tussle in Tulsa. J. McFarland. il Hot Rod 20:36-8 Ja '67
Twenty-four hours at Le Mans. il Sports Illus 24:30-5 Je 20 '66
Twenty-four hours to end them all, Le Mans. G. Borgeson. il Motor T 18:35-8+ S '66
Twenty-four hours to shake a champ; Ford vs Ferrari in Daytona; photographs. with account by B. La Fontaine. Sports Illus 24:14-17 F 14 '66
Two big D's; Dieringer wins at Darlington's Southern 500. B. Myers. il Motor T 18:58-9+ D '66
Virginia 500! B. Myers. il Motor T 18:42-3 Jl '66
Warm-up at Phoenix; Jimmy Bryan 150, annual spring championship race. J. Ethridge. il Motor T 18:60 Je '66
What it takes to win at Indianapolis. J. Clark. il Pop Sci 188:122-6+ Ap '66
When you're no. 2 you drive harder; J. Stewart of Scotland's Grand prix team. R. Daley. il Sports Illus 25:24-6+ Ag 15 '66
Who lit the fuse on Dieringer's Comet? B. Myers. il Motor T 18:68-70 O '66
Wild, wicked race to the big time; stock car racing. K. Chapin. il Sports Illus 25: 84-6+ N 28 '66
Winner again; U.S. Grand prix at Watkins Glen, N.Y. il Time 88:79 O 14 '66
Wonderful world of wheels. B. Greene. il Hot Rod 19:82-3 S '66
World challenge from an eagle's nest; D. Gurney and C. Shelby building racers to compete in Grand prix at Monaco. B. Ottum. il Sports Illus 24:54-6+ Ap 11 '66
World 600! Charlotte World 600-mile stock car race. B. Myers. il Motor T 18:60-1+ Ag '66
Year of the Ford; Le Mans, 1966. il Newsweek 68:56-9 Jl 4 '66
Yen for speed; Fuji race. il Newsweek 68: 72 O 24 '66
See also
Automobiles, Racing
Karting
Motor vehicle racing
Speedways

Study and teaching
School for speed teaches you expert car handling. J. P. Norbye. il Pop Sci 189:94-8+ Jl '66

AUTOMOBILE research
Safety car supporters press for federal, state funds. R. D. Hibben. il Aviation W 84:66-7+ F 21 '66

AUTOMOBILE service stations
British gas stations take off their gloves. il Bsns W p 130-2+ Ap 30 '66
Clinics: an answer to auto-repair problem? il U S News 60:84-5 Ap 11 '66
Curbside service. P. K. Brown. il Motor T 18:132 N '66
Playing the games; Esso's promotional game, Tigerino. New Repub 156:10 Ja 21 '67
Self-service moves in on the pump; self-service gasoline station. il Bsns W p 129-30 O 1 '66
Service stations: the needless blot. il Fortune 74:159-60 S '66
Shell shows Hungarians how to fill 'er up. il Bsns W p 102-3 Jl 9 '66
Soft sell for beauty; First lady's persuasion is adding impetus. il Bsns W p33 F 19 '66

AUTOMOBILE shows. See Automobiles—Exhibitions

AUTOMOBILE sleds. See Motor sleds

AUTOMOBILE speeding. See Automobiles—Speed

AUTOMOBILE speedways. See Speedways

AUTOMOBILE stickers. See Labels

AUTOMOBILE styling. See Automobiles—Design

AUTOMOBILE thefts. See Automobiles, Theft of

AUTOMOBILE tires. See Tires, Automobile

AUTOMOBILE touring
Cutting expenses on vacation trips by car. il Good H 162:186 Je '66
Four family-planned circle tours. N. Kuehnl and P. Lindberg. il Bet Hom & Gard 44: 70-7 Je '66

Notes for nomads (cont) il Travel 125:28 F; 13 Mr '66
Tips for touring. L. Oertle. il Motor T 18:28-30 Ag '66
Vacation special: how to be right when driving with a car-top carrier, a trailer, or a trunk full of luggage. il Bet Hom & Gard 44:49-50+ Je '66
What you can do to get a car ready for a trip; ten important tips. Bet Hom & Gard 44:40 My '66

Accommodations
See Automobile trailer camps; Motels

France
Driving through France. W. D. Boutwell. il Sr Schol 88:sup 13 F 25 '66

Great Britain
Through darkest Britain by car. M. Zolotow. Sat R 49:64-6 Jl 23 '66

United States
Summer vacations, U.S.A. il Mlle 63:193-4+ My '66
Ten for the road; trip across the country. B. Hughes. il McCalls 94:54+ N '66
Ten great automobile trips. il McCalls 94:81-2 N '66

AUTOMOBILE touring with children. See Travel with children

AUTOMOBILE touring with dogs. See Travel with pets

AUTOMOBILE traffic. See Road traffic; Street traffic

AUTOMOBILE trailer camps
How America lives; their home is wherever they like it. G. Greene. il Ladies Home J 83:74-5+ Je '66
Roughing it in high style. S. James il Pop Mech 125:112-15+ My '66
Where to park in the wide-open spaces. il Fortune 74:191+ N '66

AUTOMOBILE trailers
How America lives; their home is wherever they like it. G. Greene. il Ladies Home J 83:74-5+ Je '66
New trailers for your best vacation ever. il Parents Mag 41:129-30 Mr '66
Roughing it in high style. S. James. il Pop Mech 125:112-15+ My '66
Where housing market has lots of life; mobile homes gaining new respectability. il Bsns W p 148-50+ S 3 '66
Which type of camper should you buy? P. McCafferty. il Pop Sci 188:148-53+ My '66
See also
Automobile boat trailers

Care
Trailers and campers need servicing too! M. J. Schultz. il Pop Mech 125:162-6 Je '66

AUTOMOBILE trips. See Automobile touring

AUTOMOBILE trucks. See Motor trucks

AUTOMOBILE warranty. See Warranty

AUTOMOBILES
All new for '67; Imperial. J. Ethridge. il Motor T 18:44 O '66
Autos for 1967; racier, safer and costlier. il Ebony 22:92-4+ Ja '67
Autos 1966. il Consumer Rep 31:160-200 Ap '66
Batman's Batmobile; Lincoln Futura. H. Shuldiner. il Pop Sci 189:46-7+ Jl '66
Black stinger for the Green Hornet; latest entry into TV's funny car field. il Motor T 18:20 O '66
Breath-taking Barracuda. J. Ethridge. il Motor T 18:28-32 D '66
Cadillac owners claim you get a lot to like. B. Kilpatrick. il Pop Mech 126:78-80+ Jl '66
Camaro; new kid on the block. E. Dahlquist. il Hot Rod 20:32-5 Ja '67
Cars à la carte. See issues of Motor trend
Cars in your family. See issues of Better homes and gardens
Comet Cyclone GT, Chevelle SS 396, Dodge Charger. J. P. Norbye. il Pop Sci 189: 48-52+ Jl '66
Complete facts and color photos of the '67 cars. J. P. Norbye and J. Dunne. il Pop Sci 189:75-86 O '66
Dead horsepower; concerning disposal of abandoned cars. New Repub 154:6-7 Ap 2 '66
Driving the hot '67's; Pontiac GTO, Buick Gran Sport 400, Olds 4-4-2, Chevelle SS 396. il Motor T 18:46-53+ O '66
Falcons, a pair. R. E. McVay. il Motor T 18: 55-7 Mr '66

AUTOMOBILES—Care—*Continued*
Saltproofing your car. J. B. Colborne. il Pop Mech 127:122-5 Ja '67
Saturday mechanic. M. Schultz. See issues of Popular mechanics
Save your car from rust and rot. E. D. Fales, jr. il Pop Sci 189:110-14+ Ag '66
Spot troubles electronically. S. Kelly. il Motor T 18:36 Je '66
Spring checkup your car may need. Good H 162:183 Mr '66
These little mistakes cost car owners plenty. il Changing T 20:35-8 F '66
What you can do to get a car ready for a trip; ten important tips. Bet Hom & Gard 44:40 My '66
See also
Automobiles—Repairing

Chassis

Chasing down chassis noise. M. J. Schultz. il Pop Mech 126:182-6+ O '66
PM's sporty suburba-car. il Pop Mech 125:162-9 Ap '66

Clutches

Safety! who needs it? hydroformed bell-housing insurance for clutch or flywheel explosion. il Hot Rod 19:74-5+ Ap '66

Collectors and collecting

Briggs Cunningham's wonderful world of cars; photographs. Motor T 18:74-7 Mr '66
Flivvers are fun; annual old car festival in Greenfield Village, Dearborn, Mich. V. R. Courtenay. il Motor T 18:80-1 Mr '66
Great old cars never die; New Hope auto show. il Pop Sci 189:74-5 N '66
Investing in old cars. R. J. Gottlieb. il Motor T 18:54-6+ D '66
Mention old cars to people and the chances are they think of but two types. R. Stein. il Motor T 18:64 D '66
Mimi; Peugeot 5-CV roadster. P. W. Hatmon. il Motor T 18:8+ Jl '66
News on wheels; production of new-old cars. il Sr Schol 88:32 My 13 '66
Renaissance for relics; with list of museums. T. A. Hoge. il Travel 126:56-60 Ag '66
Wheeler-dealers; Sotheby's antique vehicles auction. il Newsweek 68:58-61 Jl 25 '66
With the press; old car auction; excerpt from Casper Star-Tribune. Hobbies 71:88 Ja '67
See also
Automobile museums

Color

Art is a '60 Buick. il Look 30:40-1 D 27 '66

Control

This 140-m.p.h. test car is driven by remote control. J. Dunne. il Pop Sci 189:104-5 N '66

Corrosion

See Corrosion and anticorrosives

Depreciation

See Depreciation

Design

Behind the styling curtain. D. MacDonald. il Motor T 18:24-7 Ap '66
Chevy's Camaro begins chasing a hot hoss; basic dimensions of Camaro and Mustang near identical. K. Chapin. il Sports Illus 25:100 S 19 '66
Chrysler Newport, Mercury Montclair, Buick LeSabre. J. P. Norbye. il Pop Sci 188:90-4+ Mr '66
Chrysler 300-X. E. Rosen. il Motor T 18:32-3 Ap '66
Coming struggle for auto safety; excerpt from Unsafe at any speed. R. Nader. Consumer Rep 31:84-91 F '66
Customizer and the car maker. J. Lawlor. il Motor T 18:28-9 Ap '66
Detroit spotlight. See issues of Motor trend
Detroit's shape of things to come. il Newsweek 67:73-4+ Mr 14 '66
Dick; investigation of author of Unsafe at any speed. J. Ridgeway. New Repub 154:11-13 Mr 12 '66
Encore the Avanti! D. Ash. il Esquire 65:140-1+ Ap '66
Fast, sporty & expensive. il Time 87:66 Ap 15 '66
Ford's Fairlane 500. E. Dahlquist. il Hot Rod 19:34-6+ Mr '66
Four swinging young Americans. il Motor T 18:46-7 S '66
Great race, Chevy vs. Ford; with report by M. Silva. il Life 61:131-2+ O 14 '66
Higher cars are safer. Sci N 90:182 S 10 '66

Homage to Pininfarina. D. Bartley. il Esquire 66:109-15 N '66
How to become a stylist. S. MacMinn. il Motor T 18:39+ Ap '66
Ideas for the taking. V. M. Exner, jr. il Motor T 18:34-5 Ap '66
Look who's in the driver's seat! for Detroit, it's the year of the American woman. il McCalls 94:78-9 N '66
LBJ and auto safety; Traffic safety act of 1966; proposals. R. Moley. Newsweek 67:112 Mr 21 '66
Op, pop and shock; Thomas Strobel's autoart. il Newsweek 68:88 O 31 '66
Real rods for show biz; automobiles of the entertainment world. J. McFarland. il Hot Rod 19:32-7 Je '66
Reincarnated classics. A. Rothenberg. il Look 30:43-5 Ag 9 '66
Safety legislation; address, October 11, 1966. H. E. Chesebrough. Vital Speeches 33:94-6 N 15 '66
Sarantos Dia Kosa. A. S. Tremulis. il Motor T 18:36-8 Ap '66
Secret snapshots of the '67 cars. J. Dunne. il Pop Mech 125:61-5+ Je '66
Shapes to come. il Newsweek 68:89 O 3 '66
Volkswagen vs. Opel vs. Simca. J. P. Norbye. il Pop Sci 188:82-6+ My '66
What the '67 cars will be like. il U S News 60:40-3 My 2 '66
What's wrong with cars? Consumer Bul 49:43+ F '66
Year of the astronaut; styling of the 1967 cars. il Time 87:82 Je 17 '66
See also
Automobiles—Bodies
Automobiles—Safety devices and measures

Doors

Hangin' doors in glass. L. Smith. il Hot Rod 19:55-7 D '66

Driveshafts

See Automobiles—Propeller shafts

Driving

See Automobile driving

Electric equipment

Headlights-on alarm. T. R. Yocom. il Pop Electr 24:81 Ja '66
Selecting the right alternator for the job. E. Szabo. Am City 81:156+ Mr '66
Time-ratio control of mobile-radio power supplies. R. S. Bunch. il Electr World 76:84-5 O '66

Electronic equipment

Pepper; outboard r.f. amplifier. J. J. Borzner. il Pop Electr 24:56 My '66

Equipment

Accessories. il Motor T 18:75-82 D '66
Antenna placement does make a difference. R. L. Ruyle. il Pop Electr 25:64-5+ N '66
Big-load carriers for beetles; top rack for VWS. A. Youngquist and R. Hoppough. il Pop Mech 126:150-3 Ag '66
Bodies give more comfort and protection. il Pop Sci 189:104-7 O '66
Car-carried boats. J. A. Emmett. il Outdoor Life 137:132-4 Mr '66
Car stereo boom! D. MacDonald. il Motor T 18:58-9 Ap '66
Cartridge tape players. il Consumer Bul 49:20-2 D '66
Hi-fi; cartridge systems for autos. I. B. Berger. Esquire 66:28+ N '66
How to install automobile stereo tape players. H. L. Davidson. il Pop Electr 25:66-7+ N '66
In a merry stereomobile; stereotape cartridge. Time 88:58+ Ag 5 '66
Load-equalizing hitch; eliminating the difficulties of heavy-duty towing. L. Oertle. il Yachting 120:54-5+ S '66
New products. See issues of Motor trend
New things for your car (cont of) New products. See issues of Motor trend
Opting for options; accessories make the difference. M. Lamm. Motor T 18:120-1 N '66
Optional performance equipment for '67 cars. il Motor T 19:34-5 Ja '67
Stereo in your car; with editorial report. L. Marcus. il Hi Fi 16:57-64 My '66
Stereo tape players for autos. il Consumer Rep 31:220-1 My '66
Tip-up ski rack. A. Macaulay. il Pop Mech 125:178+ F '66
Tips for touring. L. Oertle. il Motor T 18:28-30 Ag '66

AUTOMOBILES—Equipment—*Continued*

Vacation special: how to be right when driving with a car-top carrier, a trailer. or a trunk full of luggage. il Bet Hom & Gard 44:49-50+ Je '66

What makes a top tow car? F. M. Paulson. il Field & S 70:94-9 F '66

What's new. See issues of Hot rod

See also

Automobiles—Safety devices and measures

Exhaust

See Automobile engines—Exhaust

Exhibitions

Motorama '66. D. Wells. il Hot Rod 19:48 My '66

Racing all the harder to sell foreign cars; 10th annual International automobile show. il Bsns W p44-6 Ap 16 '66

Rolling with safety; International automobile show. il Bsns W p46 Ap 16 '66

Show & go. See issues of Hot rod

Fastenings

See Fastenings

Four wheel drive

Cars with four-wheel drive: rugged sporty, practical. il Changing T 20:13-15 Ag '66

Frames

Street roadsters. B. Lang. il Hot Rod 19: 34-8+ D '66

Front drive

See Automobiles—Front wheel drive

Front wheel drive

Caddy's new Eldorado has front-wheel drive. J. Dunne. il Pop Sci 189:109 N '66

Front drive is gaining fast in Europe. J. P. Norbye. il Pop Sci 188:108-11+ F '66

Olds puts itself back in the race; introduction of front-wheel-drive Toronado. il Bsns W p 132-3+ Mr 12 '66

Road tests of the Oldsmobile Toronado. il Consumer Rep 31:165-7 Ap '66

Gearing

Four-speed fast-draw. E. Dahlquist. il Hot Rod 19:46-9 Mr '66

Ring around the pinion. J. McFarland. il Hot Rod 19:84-6 Ag '66

Super shift for the Satellite! L. Smith. il Motor T 18:48 Ap '66

History

American automobile, by J. B. Rae. Review Reporter 34:55-7 Ja 27 '66. H. Cohen

Big, bold Bently. P. Hatmon. il Motor T 18:79-81 O '66

Poor man's classics; cars of the 1930s. J. Lawlor. il Motor T 18:78-80+ Je '66

Ralph Stein on vintage cars. R. Stein. See issues of Motor trend

Ten most influential cars. D. MacDonald. il Motor T 19:70-2+ Ja '67

Those wild, wild getaway cars! D. MacDonald. il Motor T 18:72-4 O '66

See also

Automobile museums

Ignition

See Automobile engines—Ignition

Inspection

Auto inspection spotty. Sci N 90:402 N 12 '66

Cars that kill. Sci Digest 60:33 Jl '66

Too dangerous to drive! auto inspection in District of Columbia. N. K. Dawson. il Pop Mech 127:99-101+ Ja '67

Insurance

See Insurance. Automobile

License plates

License plates for '66; photographs. Pop Sci 188:130-1 F '66

Lighting

Driving through fog; fog lamps. Consumer Bul 49:13 Mr '66

Headlights-on alarm. T. R. Yocom. il Pop Electr 24:81 Ja '66

Transistorized auto-light minder. R. G. Persing. il Pop Electr 24:65-7 Ap '66

Lubrication

Which oil is best for your engine? interview, ed. by J. Dunne. R. I. Potter. il Pop Sci 189:98-102 S '66

Manufacture

Detroit murder case: R. Nader's charges in book Unsafe at any speed. D. Cort. New Repub 154:22-4 F 12 '66

See also

Assembly line methods

Automobile industry and trade

Materials

Fiberglass magic. J. Gross. il Hot Rod 19: 44-50+ O '66

Hangin' doors in glass. L. Smith. il Hot Rod 19:55-7 D '66

Plastics mold new auto uses. il Bsns W p 180 Je 18 '66

What police cars are made of. S. Kelly. il Motor T 18:66-8 Je '66

Names

Enter the Camaro. Newsweek 68:66 Jl 11 '66

Painting

Pigments for your imagination. R. Merriam. il Hot Rod 19:68-71 F '66

Parking

See Automobile parking

Prices

Autos finish one race and head into another. il Bsns W p52-3 S 24 '66

Buyer's market; increases. Time 88:104 O 7 '66

Confessions of a car salesman. R. G. Shafer. il Pop Mech 126:59-61+ S '66

CR's recommendations of full-size cars, in three price groups. Consumer Bul 49:28 My '66

GM sets off rollback in prices; Ford and Chrysler refigure price increases. il Bsns W p46 O 1 '66

How to pay less for a new car. il Time 87: 94+ Ap 29 '66

Introductory prices of 1966 automobile models. M. S. Stotz. il Mo Labor R 89:178-81 F '66

Major specs for the '67s. il Motor T 18:130-1 N '66

Now: bargains in '66 cars. il U S News 61:33 Ag 29 '66

Price of safety; increases. Time 88:104 S 30 '66

Price skirmish. Newsweek 68:89 O 10 '66

Way we see it. D. MacDonald. Motor T 18: 8 D '66

Propeller shafts

Drive lines: winning the war on noise and vibration. il Pop Sci 189:94-5 O '66

Purchasing

Art of buying and maintaining a car. il Consumer Rep 31:168-71 Ap '66

How to buy a new car. Consumer Rep 31: 404-6 D '66

Make the demonstration ride pay off. W. Thoms. Motor T 18:69 N '66

Obtaining warranty service on a new car. Consumer Bul 49:22-4 Mr '66

Used car buyers guide; symposium. il Motor T 18:28-42 Je '66

Radio equipment

Reverb for your car. D. Meyer. il Pop Electr 24:50-3+ F '66

Time-ratio control of mobile-radio power supplies. R. S. Bunch. il Electr World 76: 84-5 O '66

See also

Radio telephone on automobiles

Rating

Ratings of the 1966 autos. il Consumer Rep 31:181-93 Ap '66

Repairing

Fifteen sure signs your car is about to need repairs. il Bet Hom & Gard 44:38+ S '66

Frequency-of-repair records: 1960-65 models. il Consumer Rep 31:178-80 Ap '66

Go ahead, do your own body work! M. Schultz. il Pop Mech 127:178-81+ Ja '67

Gus Wilson's model garage (title varies) M. Bunn. See issues of Popular science monthly

New approach in automobile repair; Mobil's diagnostic cilincs. C. Stevenson and K. W. Purdy. il Read Digest 90:123-6 Ja '67

New hope for solving your number one car problem! diagnostic-repair center. D. L. Gregg. Bet Hom & Gard 44:46 N '66

Pointers for patchin'. J. Thawley. il Hot Rod 20:84-5 Ja '67

Saturday mechanic. M. Schultz. See issues of Popular mechanics

AUTOMOBILES—Repairing—*Continued*
Say, Smokey; questions and answers. S. Yunick. See issues of Popular science monthly
Shop talk. J. McFarland. See issues of Hot rod
Tender loving care, just for autos; proper maintenance. il Bsns W p 140-2+ S 17 '66
 See also
Automobile mechanics (persons)
Automobile service stations

Riding qualities
 See also
Automobiles—Springs and suspension

Safety devices and measures
Accent on safety. A. Rothenberg. Look 30:100 O 18 '66
Amber light; plea for slow down on mandatory safety features. Newsweek 69:61-2 Ja 16 '67
Are auto standards too tough? safety standard for '68 cars. U S News 62:14 Ja 16 '67
As auto manufacturers tell about defects in cars. il U S News 60:84-5 My 16 '66
As debate grows over auto safety. il U S News 60:14-15 Ap 18 '66
Auto inspection spotty. Sci N 90:402 N 12 '66
Auto safety author spurs new congressional hearings. Pub W 189:49 Mr 21 '66
Auto safety goes into high gear. il Newsweek 67:77-8+ F 21 '66
Auto safety: latest plan of car makers. U S News 60:13 My 9 '66
Auto safety: Nader vs. General motors. E. Langer. Science 152:47-50 Ap 1 '66
Auto safety: new study criticizes manufacturers and universities. E. Langer; discussion. Science 151:277-9+, 1480+ Ja 21, Mr 25 '66
Auto safety: what Congress is considering. il U S News 60:16 F 14 '66
Auto safety: what's likely for '68 models. U S News 61:13 Ag 29 '66
Automobile smashup. R. A. Webber. America 114:851-3 Je 18 '66
Automotive safety. R. Moley. Newsweek 67:106 F 21 '66
Bargaining over auto safety. Bsns W p35 Ja 7 '67
Calling all cars. Time 87:70 Ap 22 '66
Can you withstand 30 g's? H. Downs. il Sci Digest 60:88-90 O '66
Car maker and safety; address, June 18, 1966. J. O'Connell. Vital Speeches 32:656-60 Ag 15 '66
Car safety action speeds up. Bsns W p31 F 12 '66
Car safety: another view of science; letter. H. H. Wakeland. Science 152:452 Ap 22 '66
Car safety bill passes. Bsns W p36 Ag 20 '66
Car safety; concerning auto safety legislation. New Repub 154:10 Ap 16 '66
Car with the crumpable nose; Ford motor co. announces some 1969 models will have collapsible front ends. Time 88:59-60 Jl 29 '66
Checkups on '67 cars; what's involved. U S News 61:12 D 5 '66
Collapsible steering wheels; dual brakes. New Repub 154:6 F 19 '66
Coming: new laws to make cars safer. il U S News 60:54-5 Ap 25 '66
Coming struggle for auto safety; excerpt from Unsafe at any speed. R. Nader. Consumer Rep 31:84-91 F '66
Congress gets ready to legislate safety; writing safety standards bill. Bsns W p38 My 14 '66
Death traps. H. Swados. Commentary 41:88-92 Je '66
Defects of Detroit; recall campaigns. Newsweek 67:75-6 My 16 '66
Detroit gets the word; U.S. traffic safety agency discloses new standards for 1968 models. Bsns W p44+ D 3 '66
Detroit roulette. Commonweal 83:683-4 Mr 18 '66
Detroit strikes back; answering critics of car safety. Bsns W p40 Ap 23 '66
Detroit tries to defang safety bill; Senate cool to industry's plan to set own safety standards. il Bsns W p30-1 Ap 9 '66
Detroit tries to grab the auto-safety wheel; accepting President Johnson's standardsetting safety bill. Bsns W p42 Ap 30 '66
Dick; investigation of author of Unsafe at any speed. J. Ridgeway. New Repub 154:11-13 Mr 12 '66
Double talk from Detroit; which to believe, auto makers' ads or safety statements? J. O'Connell. America 115:507-10 O 29 '66; Discussion. 115:673-4 N 26 '66

Drive for safer cars. D. Chu. Sr Schol 89:34+ O 21 '66
Ford speaks his mind. Newsweek 67:71 Ap 25 '66
Foreign bugs; Volkswagen recall campaign. Newsweek 68:80 Jl 18 '66
Furor over car safety; concerning Ribicoff hearings. R. Nader book; with report by C. Welles. il Life 60:39-40+ Mr 25 '66
GM hired the dick; investigation of author of Unsafe at any speed. New Repub 154:8 Mr 19 '66
He will decide when autos are safe; interview. A. V. Astin. il Nations Bsns 54:34-5+ Ag '66
Head-cracking assault on the problem of car safety; research programs; with report. il Life 60:34-41 My 6 '66
Here are those rules for safer cars. U S News 61:39 D 12 '66
High-pressure market in auto safety. J. Berry. il Duns R 87:43-4+ My '66
How can we stop the slaughter on our nation's highways? forum discussion; discussion. il Sr Schol 87:22-3 Ja 14 '66
How safety harnesses protect young children. Parents Mag 41:53 Je '66
How you can survive a high-speed blowout! J. Joseph. il Motor T 18:46-8+ D '66
Important features of Detroit's 1967 models. R. Huntington. il Consumer Bul 49:18-23 N '66
Making automobiles safer. H. Brandon. Sat R 49:22 F 19 '66
More car defects; call back of some new models by Chrysler and General motors. New Repub 154:8 Ap 23 '66
More light on the auto-safety story; excerpts from statements. H. Ford, 2d; H. Pyle; R. C. Buxbaum. U S News 60:44 My 2 '66
More U.S. control of auto industry? U S News 60:13 Ap 11 '66
Muckraking, 1966; R. Nader investigation admitted. Nation 202:316 Mr 21 '66
Nader caper; GM investigation. Newsweek 67:83 Mr 21 '66
National traffic safety agency; address, November 29, 1966. W. Haddon, jr. Vital Speeches 33:179-84 Ja 1 '67
Nearer: tougher safety rules for autos. U S News 61:8 Jl 4 '66
New deal for drivers; automobile-safety bill passed the House. Time 88:12 Ag 26 '66
New front for the safety furor; furor on European front over federal standards. il Time 88:115-16 N 25 '66
New York car; design for survival; E. J. Speno and the safety car project. W. D. Gardner. il Nation 202:489-92 Ap 25 '66
News on wheels; study by Republic aviation division of the Fairchild Hiller corp. il Sr Schol 88:22 Mr 18 '66
1967 and 1968 GSA standards. Consumer Rep 31:198 Ap '66
1967 cars styled for safety and family fun. B. B. Gotthold. il Parents Mag 41:74-6 N '66
1966 safety laws. Sr Schol 89:34 O 21 '66
Now the Tiger wears a seatbelt. J. O'Connell. il N Y Times Mag p27+ O 2 '66
On auto safety, etc. Commonweal 85:6-7 O 7 '66
One man who mattered. H. Brandon. Sat R 49:9-10 My 28 '66
Parents' guide to safe driving. B. B. Gotthold. il Parents Mag 41:52-3+ Je '66
Personal business; driving safety. Bsns W p 167-8 Je 11 '66
Phony auto reform. New Repub 154:8 F 5 '66
Politics of auto safety; background of bill's introduction. E. B. Drew. il Atlan 218:95-102 O '66
Pressure mounts; concerning proposals for federal authority to set automobile safety standards. Sr Schol 88:12 Ap 22 '66
Profits and safety. Commonweal 84:247 My 20 '66
Race for safety is on; Detroit developing safer cars. il Bsns W p178-9+ Je 11 '66
Recalling six years. Time 87:95 My 13 '66
Research and the automobile; address, May 13, 1966. H. E. Chesebrough. Vital Speeches 32:501-4 Je 1 '66
Restraining the snoopers; GM's invasion of the privacy of R. Nader. Christian Cent 83:452-3 Ap 13 '66
Retreat from the record. Time 89:63-4 Ja 13 '67
Rockabye, hot rods, to the federal safety lullaby. A. H. Sypher. il Nations Bsns 54:27-8 Jl '66
Rolling with safety; International automobile show. il Bsns W p46 Ap 16 '66
Safer cars: time for decision. R. Nader. il Consumer Rep 31:194-7 Ap '66

AUTOMOBILES—Safety devices and measures
—*Continued*
Safety bill with teeth. Bsns W p37 Je 25 '66
Safety car supporters press for federal, state
  funds. R. D. Hibben. il Aviation W 84:
  66-7+ F 21 '66
Safety features in the medium-priced cars. il
  Consumer Rep 31:254-5 My '66
Safety first; industry and government moves.
  il Newsweek 67:76+ Ap 18 '66
Safety first; provisions of safety bill. News-
  week 67:83 Je 20 '66
Safety in the 1967 cars. il Consumer Rep
  32:42-4 Ja '67
Safety issue no drag on auto sales. Bsns W
  p31-2 F 19 '66
Safety legislation; address, October 11, 1966.
  H. E. Chesebrough. Vital Speeches 33:94-6
  N 15 '66
Safety lines; '67 models. il Time 88:87-8 S 23
  '66
Safety on highways. America 114:613-14 Ap 30
  '66
Safety second; European cars. il Time 88:105
  O 14 '66
Safety snout? Ford's development. il News-
  week 68:63-4 Ag 1 '66
Safety standards; auto safety bill. New Repub
  154:6 My 14 '66
Safety struggle; possibility of an auto-safety
  law. il Time 87:90+ Ap 15 '66
Seat that can save your life. il Sci Digest
  60:16 O '66
Second thoughts in Detroit; auto makers
  endorse safety bill. New Repub 154:8 My 7
  '66
Set for safety; auto-safety bill. il Time 88:106
  S 16 '66
Seven safety features cars need most. R.
  Nader. Sci Digest 60:75-9 Ag '66
Seventeen GSA safety features in 1967 cars,
  but what about better brakes? il Motor T
  18:34 S '66
Shock treatment; L. B. Johnson appeal to
  automakers. Newsweek 67:89 My 2 '66
Song of safety; makers plans for 1967 and
  1968 models. Newsweek 68:75-6 S 5 '66
Step toward safety; new safety features on
  1967 models. il Time 87:90 F 18 '66
Steps toward safety. Time 87:29 Ap 8 '66
Still unsafe at any speed. J. A. Page. New
  Repub 155:32+ Jl 30 '66
Strategic retreat; industry to endorse Title I
  of safety bill. Newsweek 67:80+ My 9 '66
That new car can wait a while. Bsns W
  p41-2 My 21 '66
This is one hula hoop we hope is here to
  stay. Fortune 73:104+ Je '66
Those automotive call-backs. il Consumer
  Rep 31:340-1 Jl '66
Toward safer cars; House and Senate com-
  mittees begin hearings. Time 87:18 Mr 25
  '66
Trade winds: Unsafe at any speed and
  General motors. J. G. Fuller. il Sat R 49:
  8+ My 14 '66
Two car seats for babies. il Consumer Bul
  49:8-9 O '66
Unanimous verdict; Senate passes auto-
  safety bill. il Newsweek 68:71 Jl 4 '66
Unsafe at any speed: the designed-in dangers
  of the American automobile. by R. Nader.
  Review
    Sci Am 214:137-40+ My '66. D. Hawkins
Washington yields on standards: modification
  of Haddon proposals. Sci N 90:559 D 31 '66
Which way to safety? R. P. Crossley. il Mo-
  tor T 18:66-9 Ap '66
Who's in the driver's seat? G. M. Smerk.
  America 115:688-9 N 26 '66
Why cars are getting safer. il Nations Bsns
  54:38-9+ My '66
Why cars must, and can, be made safer;
  Time essay. Time 87:26-7 Ap 1 '66; Same
  abr. with title Safer cars on the roads
  ahead? Read Digest 88:115-18 Je '66
Will we really get safer cars? il Changing T
  20:25-9 Jl '66
Wooing U.S. drivers with safety; foreign car
  makers. il Bsns W p52-4+ Ap 23 '66
Written in cold fury. E. Larrabee. Harper
  232:117-19 Ap '66
You and the battle for traffic survival. A.
  Rothenberg. il Look 30:32-6+ Ap 19 '66
  See also
Automobiles—Testing
Automobiles, Foreign—Safety devices and
  measures
Brakes, Automobile
Safety belts
United States—National traffic safety agency

Scrapping
  See Automobiles—Wrecking

Seats
Seat that can save your life. il Sci Digest
  60:16 O '66

Service stations
  See Automobile service stations

Shows
  See Automobiles—Exhibitions

Specifications
Guide to the specifications table (cont) Consumer Rep 31:174-7 Ap '66
Major specs for the '67s. il Motor T 18:
  130-1 N '66
1966 compact and intermediate cars. Consumer Bul 49:18-28 Ap '66
1966 full-size cars. il Consumer Bul 49:19-28
  My '66

Speed
How fast is too fast? il Sr Schol 88:5 My 20
  '66

Speed governors
Correction, governor. il Hot Rod 19:113+
  Jl '66

Springs and suspension
Bad ball-joints can bury you! M. J. Schultz.
  il Pop Mech 125:179-83+ F '66
More bounce to the jounce. J. McFarland.
  il Hot Rod 19:68-71 Jl '66
Steering and suspension stress safety. il Pop
  Sci 189:96-9 O '66
What you should know about wheel align-
  ment. M. J. Schultz. il Pop Mech 125:186-90
  Mr; 180-5+ Ap '66
Wheel-alignment bunk, are you wasting
  money up front? R. Day. il Pop Sci 188:
  180-5 F '66

Steering gear
How you can survive a high-speed blowout!
  J. Joseph. il Motor T 18:46-8+ D '66
Roller coaster; key to locking rear gears.
  E. Rickman. il Hot Rod 19:100-1 D '66
Solution for a galling problem. E. Dahlquist.
  il Hot Rod 19:94-5 D '66
Steering and suspension stress safety. il Pop
  Sci 189:96-9 O '66

Terminology
News on wheels; jargon of car designers. il
  Sr Schol 89:30 N 18 '66

Testing
Caprice 427 road test. J. Ethridge. il Mo-
  tor T 18:54-5 Ap '66
Corvette 427 road test. B. McVay. il Motor T
  18:72-3 Mr '66
Cougar, a super-Mustang? Driving the new
  T-bird. J. P. Norbye. il Pop Sci 189:112-13
  O '66
Dan Gurney tests: Chevy's hot new Camaro.
  D. Gurney. il Pop Mech 126:103-5+ N '66
Dan Gurney tests Plymouth's fastback '67
  Barracuda. D. Gurney. il Pop Mech 127:92-
  4+ Ja '67
Ford road test. S. Kelly. il Motor T 18:
  56-7 Ap '66
427 wedge shot. E. Dahlquist. il Hot Rod
  19:72-5+ Jl '66
Hemi checkin'. J. McFarland. il Hot Rod 19:
  55+ My '66
How good is the new Camaro? M. Andretti.
  il Pop Sci 189:108-11 O '66
MT road test:
  Camaro by Chevrolet. S. Kelly. il Mo-
    tor T 18:37-40 D '66
  Chevy II Nova 327. S. Kelly. il Motor T
    18:66-9 Jl '66
  Cobra 427. B. Schilling. il Motor T 18:
    42-4 S '66
  Cougar. J. Ethridge. il Motor T 19:43-6
    Ja '67
  Eldorado. R. Schilling. il Motor T 19:51-4
    Ja '67
  Electra 225. L. Smith. il Motor T 18:
    56-7 My '66
  GT-350s; stock & supercharged. S. Kelly.
    il Motor T 18:48-51 Ag '66
  GTO/GTO. S. Kelly. il Motor T 18:50-2+
    My '66
  Mercury S-55. S. Kelly. il Motor T 18:
    52-5 Ag '66
  Mustang. J. Ethridge. il Motor T 18:33-6
    D '66
  Mustangs! S. Kelly. il Motor T 18:50-3
    Je '66
  Olds Dynamic 88. B. McVay. il Motor T
    18:58-9 Mr '66
  Olds 4-4-2. J. Ethridge. il Motor T 18:
    62-4 Je '66
  Sprint by Fitch. D. MacDonald. il Mo-
    tor T 18:52-4 Jl '66
  Testing two Tigers: Pontiac's '66 and '67
    GTOs. S. Kelly. il Motor T 19:39-42
    Ja '67
  Thunderbird. J. Ethridge. il Motor T
    18:82 Mr '66
  Two Skylark Gran Sports. S. Kelly. il
    Motor T 18:60-3 Jl '66
  Valiant Signet. S. Kelly. il Motor T 18:
    56-8 Ag '66

AUTOMOBILES—Testing—*Continued*
Plymouth Sport Fury. A. Markovich. il Pop Mech 125:112-13+ F '66
Professional vs. amateur. E. Dahlquist; J. McFarland. il Hot Rod 19:66-9+ Ag '66
PS tests the compact fastbacks: Rambler Marlin, Ford Mustang, Plymouth Barracuda. J. P. Norbye. il Pop Sci 188:112-16+ Ap '66
Racing cars can tour. D. MacDonald. il Motor T 18:44-7 Ap '66
Riviera, New Yorker, Thunderbird; thousand-mile triple comparison test. il Pop Mech 126:88-71+ Ag '66
Road-test report on five full-sized V8 sedans: Chevrolet, Ford, Plymouth, Pontiac, Ambassador. il Consumer Rep 32:34-41 Ja '67
Road-testing intermediate sixes: Dodge Coronet; Chevrolet Chevelle; Pontiac Tempest; Ford Fairlane; Rambler Classic. il Consumer Rep 31:78-83 F '66
Road-testing three specialty cars: Chevrolet Corvette, Dodge Charger, Ford Mustang. il Consumer Rep 31:396-402 Ag '66
Road tests of the Oldsmobile Toronado. il Consumer Rep 31:165-7 Ap '66
'67 Barracuda: superfish. E. Dahlquist. il Hot Rod 19:42-5+ D '66
Spotlight on Comet's Cyclone GT. J. Dunne. il Pop Mech 125:24+ Ap '66
Tempest overhead, cam six. J. Dunne. il Pop Mech 125:110-11+ F '66
Testing full-sized medium-priced V8s. il Consumer Rep 31:250-4 My '66
Three 1967 automobiles: Dodge Dart, Camaro, Mustang V-8. il Consumer Bul 50:15-19 Ja '67

Tires

See Tires, Automobile

Traction

Traction kits. E. Rickman. il Hot Rod 20:90 Ja '67

Trailers

See Automobile trailers

Transmission

Belt drives. R. Huntington. il Hot Rod 19: 19:60-2 Mr '66
Cruise-o-magic by Ford. J. McFarland. il Hot Rod 19:56-7 My '66
Doin' what comes automatically; GM turbo hydra-matic 400. L. T. Smith. il Hot Rod 19:52-6 N '66
Drive lines: winning the war on noise and vibration. il Pop Sci 189:94-5 O '66
Get more life out of your automatic transmission. E. D. Fales, jr. il Pop Sci 188: 176-9+ Mr '66
See also
Automobiles—Gearing

Wheels

Go-go discs. E. Rickman. il Hot Rod 20:88 Ja '67
Truth about wheel balancing. R. Day. il Pop Sci 189:140-3+ Jl '66
What you should know about wheel alignment. M. J. Schultz. il Pop Mech 125:186-90 Mr; 180-5+ Ap '66
Wheel-alignment bunk, are you wasting money up front? R. Day. il Pop Sci 188: 180-5 F '66

Windshields

Tinted-windshield danger. Sci N L 89:62 Ja 22 '66

Wrecking

Car junkyards try sophistication. il Bsns W p 108-10+ F 26 '66
Dead horsepower; concerning disposal of abandoned cars. New Repub 154:6-7 Ap 2 '66
Death in the streets; problem of disposing of abandoned cars. il Time 87:52 Je 17 '66

AUTOMOBILES, Care of. See Automobiles—Care

AUTOMOBILES, Compact
Compacts: slightly cooler. B. Hartford. il Pop Mech 126:110-13+ O '66
Compacts: the hot ones. B. Hartford. il Pop Mech 126:108-9+ O '66
Lively Lotus-Cortina. M. Priestley. il Pop Mech 126:36+ N '66
New compacts: glamour plus economy. il Ebony 22:94 Ja '67
One cylinder success car: King Midget. A. Rothenberg. il Look 30:M22+ N 15 '66
Ratings of the 1966 autos. il Consumer Rep 31:182-93 Ap '66

Testing

MT road test: Dart GT road test. L. Smith. il Motor T 18:54-5 My '66

Road-tests and ratings of compact sixes; Dodge Dart, Rambler American, Ford Falcon, Corvair. il Consumer Rep 31:128-33 Mr '66
Three subcompact imports: Toyoto Corona, Volkswagen 1300, Opel Kadett. il Consumer Rep 31:505-11 O '66

AUTOMOBILES, Electric
Back to electric cars? more federal activity urged in research. J. Ridgeway. New Repub 155:9-10 Ag 13 '66
Back to the electrics. il Time 88:112+ O 21 '66
Electric automobile. G. A. Hoffman. il Sci Am 215:34-40 bibliog(p 150) O '66; Discussion. 215:66 N; 65 D '66
Electric cars, a preview. H. Pryor. il Sci Digest 61:9-14 Ja '67
Electrically powered autos and the pollution war. Nat Parks Mag 40:21 N '66
Fallacy of the electric car. R. W. Irvin. il Motor T 19:78-81 Ja '67
Ford plugs in a mini-car; prototype electric car. Bsns W p 123 O 8 '66
Goodbye to carbon monoxide; battery-powered miniature cars tested in London. il Sci Digest 60:36-8 S '66
It clicks, it hums, it's supercar! R. Bongartz. il Sat Eve Post 240:38-40 Ja 28 '67
Man vs. auto: Tom Swift to the rescue? il Newsweek 69:46-7 Ja 9 '67
New spark for old electrics. il Life 61:74A-74B+ O 21 '66
New talk of an electric car. il U S News 61: 21 S 26 '66
Now, GM's version of an electric car. il U S News 61:10 N 7 '66
Plug-in cars will give commuters a charge. J. Eberhart. il Sci N 90:293-4 O 15 '66
Poised for a comeback; electric autos. il U S News 61:10-11 O 17 '66
Voltswagen? major breakthrough for the electric car. il Newsweek 68:88-9 S 26 '66

AUTOMOBILES, Foreign
Arthritis in the Beetle; recall campaign. il Time 88:77 Jl 15 '66
Fiat 1100-R drivescription. J. Ethridge. il Motor T 18:64-5 Jl '66
Foreign cars roll against the tide; sales of imports increasing. il Bsns W p41-2 D 10 '66
Front drive is gaining fast in Europe. J. P. Norbye. il Pop Sci 188:108-11+ F '66
Ghia: third in a connoisseur's series. J. Lawlor. il Motor T 18:30-1 Ap '66
Homage to Pininfarina. D. Bartley. il Esquire 66:109-15 N '66
In the driver's seat: the Toyota Corona; Japanese car. A. Markovich. il Pop Mech 127:38+ Ja '67
Jaguar drivescription. D. MacDonald. il Motor T 18:79 Mr '66
Lotus Cortina: sedan for sport! J. Ethridge. il Motor T 18:72-3+ Ag '66
Mercedes 200 automatic. J. Ethridge. il Motor T 18:71+ Ap '66
Mercedes 250-S drivescription. J. Ethridge. il Motor T 18:56-8 Jl '66
New and hot from overseas. il Pop Mech 125:106-8+ F '66
On cars and snobbism: Rolls-Royce owner. J. O'Hara. il Holiday 40:52-3 Ag '66
Owners report on Volkswagen's new fastback and squareback. A. Markovich. il Pop Mech 126:82-4+ Ag '66
Porsche faces life (twice) J. Ethridge il Motor T 18:68-9 Mr '66
Question marks; U.S. sales. il Newsweek 68: 61-2 D 26 '66
Racing all the harder to sell foreign cars; 10th annual International automobile show. il Bsns W p44-6 Ap 16 '66
Rover 2000-TC drivescription. D. MacDonald. il Motor T 18:68-9 Ag '66
Safety second. il Time 88:105 O 14 '66
Spotlight on the MGB-GT. A. Markovich. il Pop Mech 125:36-7 Je '66
Toyota Corona automatic. J. Ethridge. il Motor T 18:73-4 Ap '66
Treasure-trove of Alfas; Alfa Romeo museum in Milan. G. Borgeson. il Motor T 18: 70-3 S '66
Volkswagen's 1600 Squareback is a wagonesque sedan. il Consumer Rep 31:299-300 Je '66
Volvo 122-S automatic. S. Kelly. il Motor T 18:72+ Ap '66
Wooing U.S. drivers with safety; foreign car makers. il Bsns W p52-4+ Ap 23 '66

Design

European cars follow U.S. power, size trends. Sci N 90:89 Ag 6 '66
Spotlight on the Alfa Romeo Giulia TI. A. Markovich. il Pop Mech 125:48+ My '66

AUTOMOBILES, Foreign—*Continued*

Marketing

Bugs slow the boom. il Bsns W p33 Je 4 '66

Safety devices and measures

Foreign car makers race hard to be safe. il Bsns W p31 Jl 16 '66

Testing

MT road test:
Bayerische motoren werke 1800. D. Mac-Donald. il Motor T 18:58-9 My '66
Citroën DS-21. D. MacDonald. il Motor T 18:44-6 Je '66
Opel: fastback bug-chaser? J. Ethridge. il Motor T 18:71 Mr '66
Simca 1000. E. Rosen. il Motor T 18:72 My '66
Volvo and Triumph sedans. il Consumer Rep 31:457-61 S '66

AUTOMOBILES, Miniature. See Automobile models

AUTOMOBILES, Old. See Automobile museums

AUTOMOBILES, Police

What police cars are made of. S. Kelly. il Motor T 18:66-8 Je '66

Care

Don't trade that police car; Rolling Meadows, Ill. J. McFeggan. il Am City 81:100-2 F '66

AUTOMOBILES, Racing

At Sebring: victory and death; triumph was Ford's but four spectators and a driver Bob McLean lost their lives. B. La Fontaine. il Sports Illus 24:36-7 Ap 4 '66
Best driver in the whole world. T. E. Stimson. il Pop Mech 126:86-9+ Ag '66
Big ones were waiting for Mario; Indy trials. B. Ottum. il Sports Illus 24:32-3 My 23 '66
Bug is small, but oh my! Grand prix of Volkswagens in Nassau. K. Chapin. il Sports Illus 25:22-3 D 12 '66
Coming in on a wing and a bankroll; Canadian-American challenge cup race. A. Wright. il Sports Illus 25:76+ O 3 '66
Dragster in disguise. E. Dahlquist. il Hot Rod 19:52-6 Ap '66
Editorially speaking. R. Brock. Hot Rod 20:6 Ja '67
Eight-second miracle machines; development: the so-called funny cars legal on drag strips. G. Booth. il Pop Sci 189:74-8 S '66
Exploring an altered; Explorer scouts have pooled their time, efforts and money. B. Lang. il Hot Rod 20:76-9 Ja '67
Fantastic Surfers. E. Dahlquist. il Hot Rod 19:76-80+ S '66
Ford, Ford, Ford; Mark II at Daytona international speedway track; twenty-four hour race. il Newsweek 67:88 F 21 '66
Formulas for flat-out. J. Ethridge. il Motor T 18:34 Mr '66
Glorious festival of Fords; Ferrari's long domination ended at Le Mans. J. Lovesey. il Sports Illus 24:28-9 Je 27 '66
Hall's Chaparral; racing to the top. il Newsweek 67:48-52 F 7 '66
Hardware for Indy '66. C. Brawner. il Motor T 18:26-7 Mr '66
Here comes racing's Cougar. B. Ottum. il Sports Illus 25:58-9 N 7 '66
In Sicily nearly everybody loves the Targa Florio. L. Bentley. il Sports Illus 24:54-6+ My 9 '66
Jim Hall speaks out. F. X. Tolbert. il Motor T 18:32-3 Mr '66
Meet a super sleeper. J. McFarland. il Hot Rod 19:90-1 D '66
Monaco Grand prix. G. Borgeson. il Motor T 18:76-8 Ag '66
News on wheels; automakers in stock car racing. D. Chu. il Sr Schol 89:40 S 30 '66
Ol' Jack was nimble, ol' Jack was quick, with his Brabham machine he turned the trick. L. Levine. il Motor T 19:56-9+ Ja '67
Preview of Le Mans: Ford is back and Ferrari's quaking. J. P. Norbye. il Pop Sci 188:78-81 Je '66
Racing cars can tour. D. MacDonald. il Motor T 18:44-7 Ap '66
Ramming a GTO. J. Ethridge. il Motor T 18:34+ Jl '66
Ray Nichels tells how he stiffens the stockers. R. Nichels. il Motor T 18:38-41 Mr '66
Richard Petty tells how he stokes the stockers; ed. by B. Myers. R. Petty. il Motor T 18:42-4 Mr '66
Roddin' at random. il Hot Rod 20:92-5 Ja '67
Scramble for Indy! J. Ethridge. il Motor T 18:54-8 Je '66

Tonic for el tigre. J. McFarland. il Hot Rod 19:94-6 N '66
Twenty-four hours at Le Mans. il Sports Illus 24:30-5 Je 20 '66
Twenty-four hours to shake a champ; Ford vs Ferrari in Daytona; photographs, with account by B. La Fontaine. Sports Illus 24:14-17 F 14 '66
Ultimate A/GS. E. Dahlquist. il Hot Rod 19:72-4 S '66
What makes Summers run? E. Rickman. il Hot Rod 19:44-7 Ap '66
World challenge from an eagle's nest; D. Gurney and C. Shelby building racers to compete in Grand prix at Monaco. B. Ottum. il Sports Illus 24:54-6+ Ap 11 '66

Design

All deliberate speed; J. Brabham's cars. il Newsweek 68:75 Ag 8 '66
Are these stock? S. Kelly. il Motor T 18:70-2 D '66
Indy assembly line. E. Rickman. il Hot Rod 19:72-5+ My '66
Indy '66: can the Offy make a comeback with supercharging? D. Phipps and J. P. Wright. il Pop Sci 188:65-8+ My '66
1966 at Indy: big power shoot-out. P. Bryan. il Pop Mech 125:74-7+ My '66

Exhibitions

National scene. See issues of Hot rod
Oakland roadster show '66. il Hot Rod 19:54-7 Jl '66

Safety devices and measures

Safety!! who needs it? hydroformed bellhousing insurance for clutch or flywheel explosion. il Hot Rod 19:74-5+ Ap '66

Specifications

To cheat or not to cheat? specifications governing the building and preparation of race cars. B. E. Myers. il Motor T 19:60-2 Ja '67

AUTOMOBILES, Remodeled

Chevy II go. E. Dahlquist. il Hot Rod 19:40-2 Mr '66
Novel Nova; Chevy II. J. McFarland. il Hot Rod 19:34-6 Mr '66
Ultimate A/GS (cont) E. Dahlquist. il Hot Rod 19:66-8+ Ap; 72-4 S '66

AUTOMOBILES, Second-hand. See Automobiles, Used

AUTOMOBILES, Steam

New revolver-like steam engine produces 4.25 hp. per cubic inch! S. S. Miner. il Pop Sci 188:84-8 F '66

AUTOMOBILES, Theft of

Car stealing made simple! A. Ribicoff. il Pop Mech 126:57-9+ Jl '66
Protect your car from the steal-and-strippers. R. Gannon. il Pop Sci 189:104-8 S '66

AUTOMOBILES, Toy

Little big wheel in the auto industry; London's Lesney company. il Bsns W p 178-80 Mr 26 '66

AUTOMOBILES, Used

How to buy a used car. il Consumer Rep 31:407-28 D '66
Used car buyers guide; symposium. il Motor T 18:28-42 Je '66
Used cars start skid that threatens '67s; reasons: war in Vietnam, tight money, and astronomical insurance rates for drivers twenty-five and under. il Bsns W p45 N 26 '66
You gamble when you buy a used car. Consumer Bul 49:29 Ap '66
See also
Automobiles—Wrecking

Prices

How to make the most in selling your car. R. O'Brien. Read Digest 88:93-6 Ap '66

AUTOMOBILES, Winter conditioning of. See Automobiles—Care

AUTOMOBILES and roads

Automobiles & highways: getting there is twice the effort. il Sr Schol 89:4-7 Ja 6 '67

AUTOMOTIVE industry. See Automobile industry and trade

AUTOMOTIVE museums. See Automobile museums

AUTOMOTIVE safety foundation

Automotive safety (cont) R. Moley. Newsweek 67:90 Ja 31 '66

AUTOMOTIVE terminology. See Automobiles—Terminology

AUTOMOTIVE transportation. See Transportation, Automotive

AUTONOMY
See also
Self-determination, National

AUTOPILOTS. See Automatic pilot (airplanes)

AUTOPSY
Autopsy: an important medical aid; excerpts from Matter of caring. B. B. Moss. Todays Health 44:65 My '66

AUTORADIOGRAPHY
Autoradiography with tritiated methotrexate and the cellular distribution of folate reductase. Z. Darzynkiewicz and others. bibliog il Science 151:1528-30 Mr 25 '66
Bacterial growth rate in the sea: direct analysis by thymidine autoradiography; using leucothrix mucor growing epiphytically on pure cultures of marine algae. T. D. Brock. bibliog il Science 155:81-3 Ja 6 '67

AUTRY, Ewart A.
Where nothing ever happens. Audubon Mag 68:111 Mr '66

AUTUMN
Autumn is that wide-eyed feeling. R. Weber. Farm J 90:71 O '66
Fruits of autumn. L. Line. il Audubon Mag 68:328-9 S '66

AUXINS
Auxin effects on the mobility of kinetin in the plant. A. K. Seth and others. bibliog il Science 151:587-8 F 4 '66
Intracellular localization of growth hormones in plants. S. H. Liao and R. H. Hamilton. bibliog il Science 151:822-4 F 18 '66
Naphthaleneacetic acid: localization in the abscission zone of the bean. H. P. Rasmussen and M. J. Bukovac. bibliog il Science 152:217-18 Ap 8 '66
See also
Indoleacetic acid

AUYER, Stephen E.
Tape recorder echo chamber. Pop Electr 25:81-2 Ag '66

AVALANCHES
Control of snow avalanches. E. R. LaChapelle. il Sci Am 214:92-9+ F '66
See also
Landslides

AVANT-garde fiction. See Fiction

AVANT-garde literature. See Literature

AVANT-garde moving pictures. See Moving pictures

AVANT-garde music. See Music

AVANT-garde sculpture. See Sculpture

AVANT-garde theater. See Theater

AVEDON, Elliott M.
Outdoor facilities for the aged or disabled. bibliog por Parks & Rec 1:426-9+ My '66
Therapeutic recreation in a federal maze. por Parks & Rec 1:840-1 O '66

AVELEYRA ARROYO DE ANDA, Luis, and Ekholm, G. F.
Clay sculpture from Jaina. il Natur Hist 75:40-7 Ap '66

AVENI, Anthony F.
Middle Devonian lunar month. bibliog Science 151:1221-2 Mr 11 '66

AVERAGES, Stock. See Stocks—Price indexes and averages

AVERILL, L. H.
How to outsell them all. por Nations Bsns 55:50-1+ Ja '67

AVERILL, Lloyd J.
Encounter with a confidence man. Christian Cent 83:1026-8 Ag 24 '66

AVERY, Chester, and Lyman, H. H.
Libraries and the visually handicapped. Wilson Lib Bul 40:854-7 My '66

AVERY, George S.
Unusual plants of Lappland. Horticulture 44:42+ Je '66

AVERY, Milton
On the beach in Nebraska. F. Getlein. New Repub 154:33-4 Ap 16 '66

AVERY, Ralph
Watercolor page; with biographical sketch. il por Am Artist 30:26-7+ Ap '66

AVERY Brundage collection. See M. H. De Young memorial museum, San Francisco

AVERY products corporation
Stick 'em up. il Newsweek 68:66-7 D 26 '66

AVES ridge. See Ocean bottom

AVIAN malaria. See Malaria

AVIATION
Aviation jetstream. K. V. Brown. il Pop Mech 126:52 N '66; 127:14 Ja '67
Farther and faster in the air. il Sr Schol 87:5 Ja 14 '66
See also
Air pilots
Air travel
Airplanes—Piloting
Balloon ascensions
Balloons
Gliding and soaring
Meteorology. Aeronautic
Private flying

Accident investigation
Accident hearing may bring new studies. D. A. Brown. Aviation W 85:34 D 19 '66
Autopsy on an airliner: how CAB operates; government and industry investigate Braniff airways twin-engine jet crash in Nebraska. il Bsns W p 119-22+ Ag 13 '66

Accidents
AFA crash spurs look at pilot physicals. E. J. Bulban. Aviation W 84:43+ Je 6 '66
BAC 111 loss prompts study of certification for T-tail jets. D. A. Brown. Aviation W 85:39 D 12 '66
BAC 111 lost wing, tail sections before impact in Nebraska crash. Aviation W 85:45 Ag 15 '66
Best; F-104 and XB-70A mid-air collision. il Newsweek 67:38 Je 20 '66
Blessing for the 727; CAB exonerates craft. Newsweek 67:74 Mr 28 '66
Brown raps film approval in XB-70 loss; memorandum to R. S. McNamara. H. Brown. Aviation W 85:81+ Ag 29 '66
Cider Joe at sea; missing plane with J. W. Stilwell aboard. il Time 88:24-5 Ag 5 '66
CAB accident investigation report:
    Approach technique cited in DC-6A crash: Whiteman air force base, Knob Noster, Mo, My 18, 1965. Aviation W 86:107-11+ Ja 16 '67
    Optical illusion cited as cause of collision: Trans World airlines and Eastern airlines, midair collision over Carmel, N.Y. il Aviation W 86:81+ Ja 9 '67
CAB accident investigation report: Board cites excessive 727 descent rate; crash at Salt Lake City, Utah, November 11, 1965. il Aviation W 84:91-5+ Je 27 '66
CAB accident investigation report: collision-course illusion cited in accident; Eastern Douglas DC-7B crash, February 8, 1965. il Aviation W 86:84-7+ Ja 2 '67
CAB accident investigation report: course deviation cited in L-1049H crash; San Francisco international airport. Aviation W 85:89+ Ag 1 '66
CAB accident investigation report: crew monitoring cited in 727 crash, November 8, 1965. Aviation W 85:95-6+ O 24 '66
CAB accident investigation report: disk failure is cited in 707 fire; San Francisco international airport, June 28, 1965. Aviation W 85:91-5+ O 17 '66
CAB accident investigation report: engine failure on takeoff leads to crash of Allegheny Convair; July 23, 1965. Aviation W 85:123+ S 19 '66
CAB accident investigation report: fire cause is mystery in Viscount crash; July 9, 1964. Aviation W 85:108-11+ Ag 8 '66
CAB accident investigation report: Northeast mishap laid to poor approach; accident at LaGuardia airport, June 5, 1964. Aviation W 84:121+ Ap 25 '66
CAB accident investigation report: runway condition cited in 707 accident; Kansas City, Mo, July 1, 1965. il Aviation W 85:113-17+ S 5 '66
CAB accident investigation report: turbulence cited in Eastern DC-8 crash; Lake Pontchartrain, La, February 25, 1964. Aviation W 85:123+ S 12 '66
Crash hits a company; Thermo King executives and top dealers in wreck of jetliner in Japan. il Bsns W p46 Mr 12 '66
Debris of disaster sprinkled over Mont Blanc. il Life 60:38-9 F 4 '66
Dying jet falls on Fujiyama. il Life 60:36-9 Mr 18 '66
Fall of the Valkyrie: collision of F-104 Starfighter and an XB-70 Valkyrie bomber over Mojave Desert. il Time 87:29 Je 17 '66
Falling leaf; accidents going into or coming out of Tokyo. il Newsweek 67:46 Mr 14 '66
First 727 crash hearings slated: All-Nippon accident probe starts. Aviation W 84:40 F 14 '66
Flying physicians: fatal-accident rate four times as high as the average. Time 88:64 Ag 5 '66
Full story of the 2.8 seconds that killed the XB70. K. Wheeler. il Life 61:126-30+ N 11 '66
Future of X-22 program hinges on navy study of cause of crash. il Aviation W 85:31 Ag 15 '66
Hearings focus on actions of 727 crew. D. A. Brown. Aviation W 84:25-6 F 28 '66
H-bomb is missing and the hunt goes on. il Newsweek 67:55-7 Mr 7 '66
How safe is air travel? Good H 162:181 Je '66
Last seconds of the doomed superjet XB-70. il Life 60:28-35 Je 24 '66

AVIATION—Accidents—*Continued*

Lives of good brave men; death of astronauts See and Bassett. W. J. Coughlin. Miss & Roc 18:54 Mr 14 '66

Mark of a youth who flew without wings; death of Daniel Janzen. il Life 61:50 N 18 '66

NASA accident investigation report: weather cited in astronaut T-38A crash; Houston, Tex, February 28, 1966. Aviation W 84: 121-3 Je 13 '66

Odds and evens. R. B. Parke. Flying 78:36 My '66

Off the screen; All-Nippon airways crash at Tokyo's International airport. Newsweek 67:42 F 14 '66

Palomares learns to love the bomb. T. Szulc. il N Y Times Mag p22-3+ F 20 '66

Passenger fatality rate falls. Aviation W 86:55+ Ja 16 '67

Perfectly paired Gemini team falls to earth. R. Morse. il Life 60:34 Mr 11 '66

Pilot or plane? possible causes of Lear jet crashes. il Newsweek 67:76-7 My 30 '66

Piloting found 66 per cent to blame in agricultural air accidents. D. A. Brown. Aviation W 85:97+ D 19 '66

Pilots and the 727. New Repub 154:10 Mr 19 '66

Price of inexperience; Starfighter crashes; Germany. Newsweek 67:50+ Ap 4 '66

Problems with the flying lab; crashes of the Luftwaffe Starfighter. il Time 88:23 Jl 29 '66

Publisher's memo. E. D. Muhlfeld. Flying 80:6 Ja '67

Random causes cited in F-104G crashes; West German air force's investigation of twenty-six Lockheed F-104G crashes. Aviation W 84:73 F 7 '66

Rendezvous in St Louis; deaths of E. M. See and C. Bassett. il Time 87:27 Mr 11 '66

Research outlook; XB-70 crash reopens arguments over missiles vs. bombers in U.S. defense planning. Bsns W p93 Je 18 '66

Routine mission; V-2 wreckage found in Bolivia. Newsweek 68:29 Ag 8 '66

Safety above, risk below? deaths of E. M. See, jr. and C. A. Bassett. il Newsweek 67:68 Mr 14 '66

Safety in the air; no move to ground Boeing 727. New Repub 154:7 F 19 '66

Safety in the air; Time essay. Time 87:30-1 Ap 8 '66; Same abr. with title How safe is flying? Read Digest 89:117-20 Jl '66

727 cleared. Time 88:104 O 21 '66

727 investigation underscores sink rate; CAB hearing concerning Nov. 11, 1965, crash of United air lines 727, Salt Lake City. D. A. Brown. Aviation W 84:47+ Mr 14 '66

727 probe cites sink rate, altimeters; investigation of crash at Cincinnati, November 8, 1965. D. A. Brown. il Aviation W 84:41+ Mr 28 '66

727 recorder shows rapid descent rate; crash at Greater Cincinnati airport November 8, 1965. D. A. Brown. Aviation W 84:44 Mr 21 '66

$750 million clip; B-70 landing gear mishaps. il Newsweek 67:68 My 16 '66

Soviets return wreckage, mail from Pan Am 727 crash. Aviation W 85:40 N 21 '66

Thickened fuels may reduce crash fires. M. L. Yaffee. il Aviation W 85:36-9+ Jl 4 '66

Too close for safety; XB-70 and F-104 mid-air collision. Time 88:13-14 Ag 26 '66

Trouble with the 727. il Newsweek 67:84 F 28 '66

USAF surveys XB-70 program future. C. M. Plattner. il Aviation W 84:26-30 Je 20 '66

Unsafe flying; FAA's recommendations. D. Sanford. New Repub 155:6-7 O 29 '66

Why do they fall? Luftwaffe's 51st Starfighter crash since 1961. il Bsns W p54+ Ap 2 '66

Worst single day; BOAC Boeing 707; Canadian Pacific DC-8 crashes in Japan. il Time 87:33 Mr 11 '66

XB-70 crash findings reported by air force investigating board. E. H. Kolcum. Aviation W 85:18 Ag 22 '66

XB-70A No. 2 destroyed in crash. Aviation W 84:39 Je 13 '66

See also

Survival (after airplane accidents, shipwrecks, etc)

Bibliography

Book reviews. See issues of Flying

Bird hazards

Air force war on birds. Sci N 91:26 Ja 7 '67

Clubs

See Aviation clubs

Communication systems

See Radio in aviation

Competitions

Bahama treasure hunt. R. Beatty. il Flying 78:114-15 Mr '66

Good losers; fourth World aerobatic championship. Moscow, USSR. R. B. Parke. Flying 79:32 O '66

Moscow blues; fourth World aerobatic championships. J. Gilbert and R. B. Parke. il Flying 80:38-9+ Ja '67

To Russia, with luck; competing in World aerobatic championships; with editorial comment. J. Gilbert. il Flying 79:6, 36-9 Ag '66

Traffic pattern; Fourth world aerobatic contest, Moscow. R. Blodget. il Flying 79:16-17+ Jl '66

Cost

See Airplanes—Cost of operation

Crimes

See Crimes aboard aircraft

Exhibitions

Ach du lieber flugindustrie; Hanover show. J. Fricker. il Flying 78:72-7 My '66

Aeroclassic. il Flying 78:100-4 Mr '66

British show Concorde, military avionics at Farnborough. B. Miller. il Aviation W 85:94-5+ S 19 '66

Farnborough reveals few moves to sustain U.K. industry. H. J. Coleman. il Aviation W 85:26-8 S 12 '66

Foreign accent; Farnborough 1966. J. Fricker. il Flying 79:22-3 D '66

Foreign accent; fourth Generation aviation exhibition, Cannes. J. Fricker. il Flying 79:104-5 Ag '66

German firms push plans for commercial jet transports; Hanover air show. W. C. Wetmore. il Aviation W 84:26-9 My 9 '66

Good losers; fourth World aerobatic championship. Moscow, USSR. R. B. Parke. Flying 79:32 O '66

Helicopters stir interest at Turin show; Italy's second international aircraft exhibition. L. L. Doty. Aviation W 84:89 Je 27 '66

Modern, antique aircraft displayed at Reading. il Aviation W 84:86-7 Je 27 '66

Moscow blues; fourth World aerobatic championships. J. Gilbert and R. B. Parke. il Flying 80:38-9+ Ja '67

New beginning; U.S. participation in 1967 Paris air show. W. J. Coughlin. Tech W 19:50 D 12 '66

Paucity of new vehicles marks Farnborough. C. D. LaFond. il Tech W 19:17 S 12 '66

Rockford '66; EAA's annual convention. R. B. Weeghman. il Flying 79:52-3 O '66

Show and tell; Reading air show. il Flying 79:106-9 Ag '66

To Russia, with luck; competing in World aerobatic championships; with editorial comment. J. Gilbert. il Flying 79:6, 36-9 Ag '66

U.S. still debating extent of Paris show participation. Aviation W 85:33 N 28 '66

Zurabatic cartwheel; 1951 air display, Farnborough, England. P. R. Cope. il Flying 78:69 My '66

Fog problem

More flying weather signposts. H. T. Harrison. il Flying 78:73-5 Mr '66

NASA accident investigation report: weather cited in astronaut T-38A crash; Houston, Tex, February 28, 1966. Aviation W 84: 121-3 Je 13 '66

History

See Aeronautics—History

Ice problem

See Airplanes—Ice protection

Instrument flying

Picture this; pictorial instrument flying. A. S. Fuchs. il Flying 79:31-2 D '66

International aspects

Air agreements amended with Denmark, Norway, Sweden; Department announcement; with texts of Norwegian notes; June 7, 1966. Dept State Bul 55:28-30 Jl 4 '66

Air New Zealand expands world services. R. G. O'Lone. il Aviation W 84:45+ F 14 '66

Another poor bargain; agreements for New York-Moscow air service. R. Hotz. Aviation W 85:21 N 7 '66

AVIATION—International aspects—*Continued*

Atlantic case awards to spur opposition. L. L. Doty. Aviation W 84:34-5 F 21 '66

Board sets rules for transpacific case. Aviation W 84:42 Je 6 '66

China services normal despite disorder; service between Paris and Shanghai by Air France. Aviation W 86:43+ Ja 16 '67

Focus on international routes to grow. L. L. Doty. il Aviation W 84:155-7 Mr 7 '66

Major concessions mark U.S.-U.K. pact. W. Wright. Aviation W 84:41-2 Je 6 '66

New air transport agreement to be signed with Canada; joint statement, December 31, 1965. Dept State Bul 54:140 Ja 24 '66

New jets peril small flag carriers. H. D. Watkins. Aviation W 85:36-7 N 7 '66

New trends shaping policy for carriers; address, 1966. S. G. Tipton. il Aviation W 85:100-1+ Jl 11 '66

Next stop Moscow; direct commercial flights between Moscow and New York. il Time 88:103-4 N 11 '66

Nonstop to Moscow; direct service between United States and Soviet Union. Newsweek 68:80+ N 14 '66

Olympic seeks 30 per cent of Athens-N.Y. traffic. C. Brownlow. il Aviation W 85:47+ Jl 25 '66

Over the ocean to Russia; Russian airline and Air Canada to operate service between Montreal and Moscow. Time 88:86+ Jl 22 '66

Pacific activity reflects traffic growth. R. G. O'Lone. il Aviation W 84:53+ Mr 14 '66

Pan Am, Aeroflot talks begin this week. D. C. Winston. Aviation W 85:47 N 14 '66

Prospects dim for Viet civil air solution. Aviation W 86:22 Ja 9 '67

Scandinavians' overflight stand stalls Pan Am-Aeroflot talks. L. L. Doty. Aviation W 86:30 Ja 2 '67

Second air technology congress to be held in October. Dept State Bul 55:311-12 Ag 29 '66

Survey disputes U.S. trade balance view. L. L. Doty. il Aviation W 84:61-2+ Mr 28 '66

To Moscow and back; U.S.-Soviet agreement. R. Burkhardt. New Repub 155:7-8 D 3 '66

U.S. and Austria conclude air transport agreement; Department announcement; with text of agreement. Dept State Bul 55:148-52 Jl 25 '66

U.S. and Chile conclude air service consultations; Department announcement, October 14, 1966. Dept State Bul 55:722 N 7 '66

United States and Japan amend civil air transport agreement; White House announcement, December 27, 1965, with exchanges of notes. Dept State Bul 54:141-3 Ja 24 '66

United States and Peru amend air agreement; text of U.S. note. Dept State Bul 54:467-8 Mr 21 '66

United States and Soviet Union sign civil air transport agreement; statement, November 4, 1966; with a Department announcement and texts of the agreement and related documents. L. E. Thompson. Dept State Bul 55:791-800 N 21 '66

United States and the Warsaw convention; statements, February 1, 14, 1966. A. F. Lowenfeld. il Dept State Bul 54:580-8 Ap 11 '66

U.S. and U.K. amend Bermuda air agreement. Dept State Bul 54:954-5 Je 13 '66

U.S. hopes for air pact soon in Pan Am talks with Aeroflot. J. W. Carter. Aviation W 85:47 O 24 '66

U.S. international aviation policy; address, January 20, 1966. R. M. Jackson. Vital Speeches 32:398-400 Ap 15 '66

U.S., Mexico review bilateral agreement. Aviation W 85:67+ N 21 '66

U.S. to continue adherence to Warsaw convention; Department announcement; with text of United States note. Dept State Bul 54:955-7 Je 13 '66

See also
Airlines—Fares
International civil aviation organization

Laws and regulations

Complaint department. R. B. Parke. Flying 78:32 Je '66

What every U.S. pilot should know about flying in Canada. M. J. Seeley. il Flying 78:118-19 Je '66

See also
Air traffic control
United States—Federal aviation administration

Medical aspects

Few medical unknowns anticipated in SST operations. il Aviation W 85:116-17+ Ag 15 '66

Meteorological aspects
See Meteorology, Aeronautic

Mountain flying

Ten rules for mountain flying. E. M. Miller. il Flying 80:46-8 Ja '67

Periodicals

See also
Aviation week and space technology (periodical)

Physiological aspects

Jet-age blues. C. B. Hicks. il Todays Health 44:18-19+ N '66

Jet travel and body clocks. Sci Am 214:53 F '66

Keep an eye on your inner clock. L. Thomas. Read Digest 89:61-4 Ag '66

Lessons for everybody from jet travel fatigue. S. L. Englebardt. il Sci Digest 59:80-4 Mr '66

See also
Aviation—Medical aspects
Aviation—Radiation hazards

Psychological aspects

Jet-age blues. C. B. Hicks. il Todays Health 44:18-19+ N '66

Jet travel and body clocks. Sci Am 214:53 F '66

Public relations

American stressed goodwill during strike. J. W. Carter. Aviation W 85:47 S 26 '66

Radiation hazards

FAA spurring measurements of radiation at SST altitudes. Tech W 19:38+ S 19 '66

Rain hazards
See Aviation—Storm hazards

Safety devices and measures

Fewer VIPs per flight; aim: to avoid risk of major management losses. Bsns W p 128 Ap 2 '66

How safe is air travel? Good H 162:181 Je '66

Mayday. A. Trammell. Flying 78:76-8 Ap '66

Passenger fatality rate falls. Aviation W 86:55+ Ja 16 '67

Safety in the air; Time essay. Time 87:30-1 Ap 8 '66; Same abr. with title How safe is flying? Read Digest 89:117-20 Jl '66

Transatlantic guidelines prepared to assist general aviation pilots. Aviation W 84:67+ Mr 14 '66

Uncrashworthy? Boeing and FAA cooperating on redesign studies. Newsweek 67:77 Ja 31 '66

Washington clipboard; air safety. R. Burkhardt. il Flying 79:34 D '66

See also
Airplanes—Ice protection
Airplanes—Safety devices and measures
Flight safety foundation
Parachutes
Radar in aviation
Radio in aviation

Snowstorm hazards
See Aviation—Storm hazards

Statistics

Book of numbers; FAA statistical handbook. R. B. Parke. Flying 78:34 Ap '66

New trends shaping policy for carriers; address, 1966. S. G. Tipton. Aviation W 85:100-1+ Jl 11 '66

Storm hazards

Hints on flying in thunderstorms; don't. F. C. Bates. il Flying 78:56-9 F '66

NASA accident investigation report: weather cited in astronaut T-38A crash; Houston, Tex, February 28, 1966. Aviation W 84:121-3 Je 13 '66

Tornado at 12 o'clock high. M. W. Horowitz. Flying 79:93 O '66

Stunt flying

Good losers; fourth World aerobatic championship, Moscow, USSR. R. B. Parke. Flying 79:32 O '66

Lady on the wing; Terry Holm, wing rider. il Look 30:M8-9 Mr 8 '66

Moscow blues; fourth World aerobatic championships. J. Gilbert and R. B. Parke. il Flying 80:38-9+ Ja '67

Pilot report: Krier/de Havilland Chipmunk special. J. Gilbert. il Flying 79:40-3 Ag '66

Saga of the barnstormers. A. Trammell. il Flying 78:72-88 Je '66

AVOCADOS
Eat your avocado and grow it too. G.
Taloumis. il Pop Gard 17:82-3 Mr '66
See also
Cookery—Fruit
AVOIDANCE behavior. See Behavior (psychology)
AVON, Anthony Eden, 1st earl of
Toward peace in Indochina. Harper 233:36-43
Ag '66
AVON products, incorporated
Avon paying. Time 87:86 Je 17 '66
AWAKENING; story. See Vincent-Barwood, A.
AWARDS. See Rewards, prizes, etc.
AX throwing
Darts, Paul Bunyan size; ax throwing loggers
vie for world title. J. E. Boykin. il Pop
Mech 125:118-19 Mr '66
AXELBANK, Albert
Alexis Johnson's new job in Japan. New
Repub 155:19-20 Ag 27 '66
Japan: co-prosperity again. Nation 202:479-
80 Ap 25 '66
AXELROD, Herbert R.
Piranhas, anyone? il por Time 88:62 Jl 29 '66
AXELROD, Julius, and others
Light-induced changes in pineal hydroxy-
indole-O-methyltransferase: abolition by
lateral hypothalamic lesions. bibliog Sci-
ence 154:898-9 N 18 '66
AXELROD, Stanley
Treatment of the Negro in American history
school textbooks. bibliog Negro Hist Bul
29:135-6+, 167 Mr-Ap '66
AXLES
See also
Automobiles—Axles
AXONS. See Nerve cells
AXTHELM, Kenneth W.
American language and culture: a selected
discography. Library J 91:206-10 Ja 15 '66
AXTHELM, Pete
Boo made a boo-boo. Sports Illus 24:26-9+
My 23 '66
AYACUCHO, Peru
Ayacucho. E. Hosmann. il Américas 18:32-8
O '66
AYDELOTTE, John, family
Tour of duty. pors Newsweek 68:49 N 28 '66
AYDELOTTE, William O.
Quantification in history. bibliog f Am Hist R
71:803-25 Ap '66
AYER, Ethan
Promise of heat; story. New Yorker 42:30-
5 S 3 '66
AYLON, Hélène
Hélène Aylon's Ruach palimpsest. L. Camp-
bell. il por Art N 65:47-9 D '66
AYRES, Fred D.
Giants of the puna. Natur Hist 75:54-7 Mr
'66
AYRES, William H.
Excerpt from remarks, January 19, 1966. Cong
Digest 45:91+ Mr '66
AYUB KHAN, Mohammad
Address in General assembly, December 13,
1965; summary. por UN Mo Chron 3:71-3
Ja '66
AYUDAYA. See Ayutthaya
AYUTHIA. See Ayutthaya
AYUTTHAYA, Thailand
Ayutya Venice of south Asia. S. Jumsai na
Ayutya. il UNESCO Courier 19:4-11 O '66
AYUTYA, Sumet Jumsai na. See Jumsai na
Ayutya, S.
AYUTYA. See Ayutthaya
AZALEAS
Hardier azaleas. C. M. Fitch. il Flower
Grower 53:62-4 Mr '66
AZAROFF, Leonid V.
Studies of alloys by X-ray absorption spec-
troscopy. bibliog Science 151:785-9 F 18 '66
AZERBAIJAN
161 years old and going strong. P. Young.
il Life 61:121+ S 16 '66; Same abr. with
title Death is afraid of us. Read Digest
89:97-9 D '66
AZEVEDO ANTUNES, Augusto Tranjano de
Brazil's chief miner. il por Fortune 73:76
Ap '66
AZIKIWE, Nnamdi
Eulogy on William Leo Hansberry. por Negro
Hist Bul 29:63 D '65
AZOTOBACTER
Alive for 3,400 years? azotobacter bacterial
culture from wall of the Great temple of
Amun. il Sci Digest 59:48 Ap '66
AZTECS
Baraja mexicana calendarica. D. Powills.
Hobbies 71:118-19+ Mr '66
Hernán Cortez and the Mexican Iliad. E. Ar-
dura. il Américas 18:23-31 Ag '66

B

BART (Bay area rapid transit) See San
Francisco—Rapid transit
BBC. See British broadcasting corporation
BDSA. See United States—Business and de-
fense services administration
BEA. See British European airways corpora-
tion
BIA. See United States—Indian affairs, Bureau
of
BIPAD. See Bureau of independent publishers
and distributors
BIS. See Bank for international settlements
BLM. See United States—Land management,
Bureau of
BMC. See British motor corporation
BMI. See Book manufacturers' institute
BNA. See Bureau of national affairs, incor-
porated
BNB. See British national bibliography
BOR. See United States—Outdoor recreation,
Bureau of
BPR. See United States—Public roads, Bureau
of
BVD company
How BVD bought its new outfit; underwear
maker into a clothing empire. il Bsns W
p98-100 Je 4 '66
BAALBEK, Lebanon
Let's travel: Baalbek international festival.
G. Buckman. il Mlle 64:136-9 D '66
BAALBEK international music festival. See
Music festivals—Lebanon
BABA, Nuzhet
Our man in Istanbul. por Am Ed 2:26-7 Mr
'66
BABBITT, Milton
Two extremes of avant-garde music. R.
Kostelanetz. il pors N Y Times Mag p34-5+
Ja 15 '67
BABCOCK, Richard F.
Billboards, glass houses, and the law; ex-
cerpt from address. Harper 232:20+ Ap '66
BABEL, Isaac
Shabos nahamu; story. Atlan 217:79-81 Mr '66
You must know everything; tr. by M. Hay-
ward. New Yorker 42:36-8 Ap 9 '66
about
Sunset; tr. by M. Ginsburg and R. Rosen-
thal. Criticism
Commonweal 84:336-7 Je 10 '66
Nation 202:662 My 30 '66
New Yorker 42:96 My 21 '66
BABIES. See Infants
BABINGTON, Suren H.
English was my undoing. pors NEA J 55:
16-18 F '66
BABSON, Donald P.
Air traveler writes to the President; excerpts
from letter. U S News 61:70 Ag 22 '66
BABY animals. See Animals, Infancy of
BABY care. See Infants—Care and hygiene
BABY cribs. See Cribs (beds)
BABY sitter of Burgenland; story. See Wilner.
H.
BABY sitters
Idea exchange: course for baby-sitters. R. E.
Taylor. NEA J 55:60+ S '66
Stand-in for mothers. M. Albrecht. il Parents
Mag 41:58-9+ Mr '66
BABY talk. See Children—Language
BACALL, Lauren
Lauren Bacall talks about Bogart, Sinatra
and her new life. pors McCalls 93:24+ Jl
'66
Redbook readers talk with Lauren Bacall;
interview. pors Redbook 127:45+ Jl '66
We orbit around: interview by Mademoiselle's
guest editors. por Mlle 63:348 Ag '66
about
Bacall comes back, big. G. Zimmermann. il
pors Look 30:95-8+ Mr 22 '66
Command generation. il pors Time 88:50-4 Jl
29 '66; Same abr. with title Middle age: the
command generation. Read Digest 89:201-4
O '66
Nurse Bacall gets unstarched. il pors Life
60:35-6 F 11 '66
She travels by roller coaster. T. Meehan. il
pors Sat Eve Post 239:34-9 My 21 '66

BACCALAUREATE addresses
Fresh phrases; excerpts from addresses. Time 87:74+ Je 17 '66
Past the bromide barrier; stress on America's Vietnam policy. il Newsweek 67:73 Je 20 '66
Peripatetic reviewer; commencement speaker. E. Weeks. Atlan 217:128+ Je '66

BACCARAT paperweights. See Paperweights

BACH, Clarence A.
Warm tribute to a teacher. G. P. Hunt. il por Life 62:5 Ja 13 '67

BACH, Fritz H. and Voynow, N. K.
One-way stimulation in mixed leukocyte cultures. bibliog Science 153:545-7 Jl 29 '66

BACH, Johann Sebastian
Bach passions and oratorios; discography. N. Broder. il Hi Fi 16:46-7+ Jl '66
Bach's St John, a noble ideal nobly attempted. N. Broder. il Hi Fi 16:73-4 Ag '66
Demus: spirit, drive, technique, and intelligence; Goldberg variations. S. Sell. Am Rec G 32:620-1 Mr '66
First recording of the sixteen Bach-Vivaldi concerti. S. Sell. il Am Rec G 32:1037 Jl '66
From DGG, Bach not so P.D.Q. but extraordinary. H. Glass. Am Rec G 32:511 F '66
In Bach's cello suites, playing both cerebral and passionate. B. Jacobson. Hi Fi 16:87 Ap '66
Maazal, classicist; concerning recordings. E. Salzman. Sat R 49:51 D 31 '66
Records:
Christmas oratorio. Opera N 31:34 D 17 '66

BACH, Richard
Legend of Gill Robb Wilson. Flying 79:56-7 D '66
Pilot report: the Beech Staggerwing. il Flying 79:70-5 O '66
Safety by the book. Flying 79:77-9 S '66

BACHE and company
Learn to listen; President A. C. Israel resigns; H. Bache replaces. il Time 87:82 Ap 1 '66

BACHELORS. See Single men

BACHELORS degrees. See Degrees, Academic

BACHMANN, Konrad, and others
Hylid frogs; polyploid classes of DNA in liver nuclei. bibliog Science 154:650-1 N 4 '66

BACILLUS cereus
Satellite deoxyribonucleic acid from bacillus cereus strain T. H. A. Douthit and H. O. Halvorson. bibliog il Science 153:182-3 Jl 8 '66

BACILLUS coli. See Escherichia coli

BACILLUS licheniformis
Clostridium botulinum type F; seasonal inhibition by bacillus licheniformis. M. W. Wentz and others. bbliog il Science 155: 89-90 Ja 6 '67
Ornithine transcarbamylase enzymes: occurrence in bacillus licheniformis. R. W. Bernlohr. bibliog il Science 152:87-8 Ap 1 '66

BACK-to-Africa movements
Black mischief; Hassan Jeru-Ahmed's Blackman's volunteer army of liberation. J. Ridgeway. New Repub 155:14-16 D 24 '66

BACK yards
Build a shuffleboard in your backyard. il Sunset 136:137 Ap '66
Here's a care-free back yard. il Pop Gard 17:57 D '66
There's room for children and grownups. il Pop Gard 17:8 D '66

BACKACHE
I prescribe... J. D. Wassersug. il Sci Digest 61:82-6 Ja '67

BACKGROUND. See Composition (photography)

BACKGROUND in fiction. See Fiction—Technique

BACKGROUND music. See Mood music

BACKWARD children. See Slow learning children

BACON, Charles R. T.
Editing text electronically. Pub W 190:92-4 Jl 4 '66

BACON, Francis
Coroner's report. il Time 88:90-1 N 18 '66

BACON, Marion
Christmas offer mystique. Pub W 190:50-1 Ag 8 '66
In praise of stuffers. Pub W 189:22-3 Ap 4 '66
While we wait: further thoughts on the Lasser report. Pub W 189:49-50 Mr 7 '66

BACON, Martha
Elephants; poem. Atlan 218:102 O '66

BACON, Roger
Roger Bacon and the Voynich manuscript. J. Ashbrook. il Sky & Tel 31:218-19 Ap '66

BACON, W. Stevenson
Low-cost glass-bubble sub for undesea adventure. Pop Sci 189:60-4 Jl '66
Science newsfront. See issues of Popular science monthly

BACTERIA
Bacterial signatures. Sci Am 215:54 Jl '66
Natural human antibodies to gram-negative bacteria immunoglobulins G, A, and M. I. R. Cohen and L. C. Norins. bibliog il Science 152:1257-9 My 27 '66
Phospholipids of bacteria with extensive intracytoplasmic membranes. P. O. Hagen and others. bibliog il Science 151:1543-4 Mr 25 '66

See also
Actinomycetes
American type culture collection
Azotobacter
Clostridium botulinum
Escherichia coli
Genetics (bacteria)
Iron bacteria
Microorganisms

Mutation
See Mutation (bacteria)

Resistance
Chloroquine: physiological basis of drug resistance in plasmodium berghei. P. B. Macomber and others. bibliog il Science 152: 1374-5 Je 3 '66
Invincible bacteria? Newsweek 68:92 Ag 22 '66

BACTERIA, Fossil. See Micropaleontology

BACTERIA, Nitrifying
Morphogentic substance in legume nodule formation. A. G. Schaffer and M. Alexander. bibliog il Science 152:82-3 Ap 1 '66

BACTERIA, Pathogenic
Case of the dubious dye; salmonellosis caused by dye capsules. il Time 89:44 Ja 6 '67
Galactosamine glycan of chondrococcus columnaris. J. L. Johnson and W. S. Chilton. bibliog il Science 152:1247-8 My 27 '66
Intruder; traces of salmonella found in Starlac. Newsweek 68:92 N 14 '66
Keeping food safely at home; disease-causing organisms. A. C. Dean. PTA Mag 60: 14-16 Je '66
Let's talk about food; microbial food poisoning and how to avoid infection; ed. by P. L. White. Todays Health 44:10-11+ D '66
Mutagenicity of cycasin aglycone methylazoxymethanol, a naturally occurring carcinogen. D. W. E. Smith. bibliog il Science 152:1273-4 My 27 '66
Radiation-induced mutations and their repair. E. M. Witkin. bibliog il Science 152:1345-53 Je 3 '66
Salmonella & Starlac. Time 88:69 N 11 '66
Salmonella hunt spreads nationwide; drugs and candy being watched along with Borden's Starlac. il Bsns W p48+ N 12 '66
Salmonella: scope hidden. Sci N 90:404 N 12 '66
Tryptophan operon of escherichia coli: regulatory behavior in salmonella typhimurium cytoplasm. R. L. Somerville. bibliog il Science 154:1585-7 D 23 '66
See also
Staphylococci

BACTERIAL chromatograms. See Chromatographic analysis

BACTERIAL endocarditis. See Heart—Diseases

BACTERIAL viruses. See Bacteriophage

BACTERIOLOGICAL warfare. See Biological warfare

BACTERIOLOGY
See also
Bacteriophage
Staphylococci

BACTERIOPHAGE
Allomorphic forms of bacteriophage ΦX-174 replicative DNA. T. F. Roth and M. Hayashi. bibliog il Science 154:658-60 N 4 '66
Bacteriophage T5 chromosome fractionation: genetic specificity of a DNA fragment. Y. T. Lanni and others. bibliog il Science 152:208-10 Ap 8 '66
Genetic control of the shape of a virus. E. Kellenberger. il Sci Am 215:32-9 bibliog(p 154) D '66
Replication of the RNA of bacteriophage f2. H. F. Lodish and N. D. Zinder. bibliog il Science 152:372-8 Ap 15 '66

BAD breath. See Halitosis
BAD taste. See Vulgarity

BADASH, Lawrence
How the newer alchemy was received: with biographical sketch. Sci Am 215:10, 88-95 bibliog(p 116) Ag '66

BADEAU, John S.
Development and diplomacy in the Middle East; adaptation of address. Bul Atomic Sci 22:5-10 My '66

BADER, Robert S. See Tenczar, P. jt. auth.

BADER, W. B.
Nuclear weapons sharing and the German problem. For Affairs 44:693-700 Jl '66

BADGER, Evelyn M.
Teaching music in the self-contained classroom. NEA J 55:16-18 My '66

BADHAM, Michael
Marriage sailboat style. por Motor B 117:32-4+ F '66

BADMINTON
Let's play badminton. il Pop Gard 17:74-5 Ag '66

BADY, Susan
What I learned from Negroes. pors Ebony 21:58-60+ S '66

BAER, Betty
Cultural arts week in Anchorage, Alaska. Sch Arts 65:31-3 My '66

BAER, Richard A. Jr
Land misuse: a theological concern. Christian Cent 83:1239-41 O 12 '66

BAEZ, Joan
I'm really a square; interview, ed. by D. Wakefield. Redbook 128:54-5+ Ja '67
Introduction to (and conclusion of) a future hero; with quotations by R. Farina. Esquire 66:120-1 S '66

about
California: song without music. G. Zimmermann. il pors Look 30:M10-12+ Je 28 '66
Just folks at a school for nonviolence. J. Didion. il pors N Y Times Mag p24-5+ F 27 '66
Popular records. D. Watt. New Yorker 42:202+ Mr 19 '66
Which one is the Phoanie? por Time 89:47 Ja 20 '67

BAEZA, Braulio
Icy rider with the gentle hands. por il Life 60:119-20 Ap 15 '66
Looking for a triple. il Time 87:72+ F 25 '66
Tall in the saddle. F. Graham, jr. por Sports Illus 24:45-6+ Ap 11 '66

BAFFIN ISLAND
See also
Geology

BAGDAD. See Baghdad

BAGDIKIAN, Ben H.
Death in our air. Sat Eve Post 239:31-5+ O 8 '66
Houston's shackled press. Atlan 218:87-8+ Ag '66
Rape of the land. Sat Eve Post 239:25-9+ Je 18 '66
Who is sabotaging day care for our children? Ladies Home J 83:86+ N '66

BAGELS. See Bread

BAGGAGE. See Luggage

BAGHDAD
Description
City of the caliphs. A. Waugh. Nat R 18:784+ Ag 9 '66
History
Baghdad's 1,000th: forthcoming celebrations. B. Moore. Sat R 50:74 Ja 7 '67

BAGLIETTO, Christine
Costumes by Christine. L. Slater. il Sch Arts 65:9-11 My '66

BAGLIONI, C. and others
Allelic antigenic factor inv(a) of the light chains of human immunoglobulins: chemical basis. bibliog Science 152:1517-19 Je 10 '66

BAGS
See also
Handbags

BAGSHAW, Malcolm A. See Hahn, G. M. jt. auth.

BAHAMA ISLANDS
See also
Andros Island
Fishing—Bahama Islands
Grand Bahama Island
Hotels, taverns, etc.—Bahama Islands
National parks and reserves—Bahama Islands
Tourist trade—Bahama Islands

Description and travel
Fresh landfalls in the Out Islands. F. Rohr. il Motor B 118:39-42 O '66

Gone flying south to the Bahamas. E. D. Muhlfeld. il Flying 78:127-33 Je '66
Page from a Bahama log book. J. Hart. il Yachting 120:46-8+ N '66

Politics and government
See also
Elections—Bahama Islands

BAHAMAS flying treasure hunt. See Aviation—Competitions

BAHAMIAN cookery. See Cookery, Bahamian

BAHER, Constance Whitman
Robin Hood outwits the sheriff; drama. Plays 25:51-60, 96 F '66
Trial of Manfred the magician; drama. Plays 26:59-68 D '66

BAHIA (city) See Salvador, Brazil

BAHMAN, Alice Kilgore (Rodgers) Winters
Jonathan Winters' mother. B. Weinraub. pors Esquire 66:97+ N '66

BAHRT, Giles W.
Build this creeping sulky to ease grass-cutting chores. Pop Mech 126:140-4 Jl '66

BAIL
Ransom, by R. Goldfarb. Review
New Repub 154:36-7 F 26 '66. J. Featherstone
Train of clients; Manhattan summons project. H. Bowser. Sat R 49:26 Ap 16 '66

BAILE, Clifton A. and Mayer, Jean
Hyperphagia in ruminants induced by a depressant. bibliog Science 151:458-9 Ja 28 '66

BAILEY, Anthony
Fog; story. Redbook 127:59 Jl '66
Our footloose correspondents. New Yorker 42:142+ Ap 23 '66

BAILEY, Burck
All the justice money can buy. New Repub 154:8-9 Je 11 '66

BAILEY, C. Lloyd
UNICEF celebrates its 20th birthday. por Parents Mag 41:44+ D '66

BAILEY, David
David Bailey talks of women, beauty, marriage; interview, ed. by P. Devlin. il Vogue 148:166-72+ N 15 '66

BAILEY, F. Lee
Boston prodigy. il pors Time 88:52+ D 9 '66
Case for the defense. il por Newsweek 68:27-8 D 19 '66
F. Lee Bailey: renegade in the courtroom. E. Linn. il pors Sat Eve Post 239:80-2+ N 5 '66

BAILEY, Fred, Jr
How to be a good tax manager. Suc Farm 64:36+ N '66

BAILEY, George
Adenauer's view of a changing Europe. Reporter 34:18-22 Je 30 '66
Chips are down for Harold Wilson. Reporter 34:31-4 Je 2 '66
Cultural exchange as the Soviets use it. Reporter 34:20-5 Ap 7 '66
Germany between two alliances. Reporter 35:27-32 O 6 '66
Ludwig Erhard had a great fall. Reporter 35:39-40 N 17 '66
Trial of two Soviet writers. Reporter 34:34-8 F 24 '66

BAILEY, Herbert S. Jr
Book publishing and the new technologies. Sat R 49:41-3 Je 11 '66

BAILEY, Howard T.
Ludwig's world. Opera N 30:26-9 Mr 26 '66

BAILEY, J. Martyn, and others
Mutarotase in higher plants: distribution and properties. bibliog Science 152:1270-2 My 27 '66

BAILEY, James
Building a better farmhouse. Arch Forum 124:68-71 Mr '66
Station saved for art's sake. Arch Forum 125:52-7 S '66

BAILEY, James R.
Amateur scientist. Sci Am 216:128 Ja '67

BAILEY, Margaret E.
Top nurse in uniform. il pors Ebony 21:50+ S '66

BAILEY, Mildred
Mildred. R. Gehman. il por Sat R 50:104-5 Ja 14 '67

BAILEY, Norman A.
American economy: power and paradox. Yale R 55:537-48 Je '66

BAILEY, Ralph
How to work with a landscape architect. House & Gard 130:266-7+ N '66

BAILEY, Richard W. See Frost, J. B. jt. auth.

BAILEY, Robert A.
Planner for the supersonic era. por Bsns W p48 D 24 '66

BALANCE of payments—*Continued*
It's not as good as gold. F. Morley. il Nations Bsns 54:23-4 Jl '66
New trouble in the balance of payments. Bsns W p 190 My 28 '66
New York's novel export plan; interview. K. S. McHugh. Duns R 87:55-6+ F '66
1966 battle of Britain; with editorial comments. il Bsns W p 143-4, 175-8+, 200 N 19 '66
No dollar wall; proposal to reduce gold drain by restricting travel abroad. W. D. Patterson. Sat R 49:30 Je 11 '66
No end to the deficit. il Fortune 73:44+ Je '66
Payments hole may get deeper; due to Vietnam spending and the boom at home. Bsns W p40 N 19 '66
Relief is temporary; second-quarter payments balance improves. Bsns W p 120 Ag 20 '66
Shortsighted remedy; International economic policy association's study recommendations. H. Hazlitt. Newsweek 68:77 Jl 4 '66
Substantial inprovement achieved in balance of payments in 1965; statements, February 14, 1966. H. H. Fowler; J. T. Connor; J. L. Robertson. Dept State Bul 54:398-403 Mr 14 '66
Tale of two problems. H. C. Wallich. Newsweek 67:94 Je 13 '66
Trade policy: a new approach? U S News 60:99 Je 20 '66
Unbalanced balance. il Time 87:89-90 Ap 8 '66
U.S. agencies urged to help achieve balance of payments; text of memorandum to Cabinet officers. L. B. Johnson. Dept State Bul 54:495+ Mr 28 '66
U.S. balance of payments; the American Goldfinger. il Sr Schol 89:6-9+ Ja 13 '67
Vanishing prospect. il Time 87:91-2 S 25 '66
War costs blunt drive on payments deficit; outflow of dollars for Vietnam chief factor in worsening of U.S. trade balance. il Bsns W p50 My 21 '66
Washington desk. J. R. Slevin. Duns R 88:5-6 Jl '66
Wishful thinking on the balance of payments. R. W. Stevens. bibliog f il Harvard Bsns R 44:6-8+ N '66
Your stake in the balance-of-payments problem; address, April 26, 1966. D. MacArthur, 2d. Dept State Bul 54:812-17 My 23 '66

BALANCE of power
Balance of world power; where the U.S. fits in; with charts. U S News 60:48-50 Ap 4 '66
Peace comes of age. A. J. P. Taylor. il N Y Times Mag p 14-15+ Ag 14 '66

BALANCE of trade. See Balance of payments

BALANCHINE, George
Caution: choreographer at work. H. Saal. il por N Y Times Mag pt2 p 18-19+ S 11 '66
George Balanchine at work on a permanent record. L. Joel. il pors Dance Mag 40:24-7 Ag '66

BALD eagles. See Eagles

BALD MOUNTAIN recreational area, Mich. See Recreation areas

BALDESSARINI, Ross J. and Kopin, I. J.
Tritiated norepinephrine: release from brain slices by electrical stimulation. bibliog Science 152:1630-1 Je 17 '66

BALDNESS
Baldness facts. Sci Digest 61:29 Ja '67
Science tackles the baldness problem; punch graft technique. F. Warshofsky. Read Digest 88:87-91 F '66

BALDRIGE, Malcolm, 1922-
Scovill responds to classic remedies. il pors Bsns W p 190-2+ O 22 '66

BALDWIN, Hanson Weightman
Case for escalation. N Y Times Mag p22-3+ F 27 '66
Case for mobilization. Reporter 34:20-3 My 19 '66
Cupboard is bare; summary of article. Nat R 18:195 Mr 8 '66
Draft is here to stay, but it should be changed. N Y Times Mag p48-9+ N 20 '66
Fall of Corregidor; excerpts from Battles lost and won; great campaigns of World war II. Am Heritage 17:16-23+ Ag '66
Information war in Saigon. Reporter 34:29-31 F 24 '66
To end the war in Vietnam, mobilize! Read Digest 89:93-7 O '66
Vietnam: what should we do now? por Look 30:26+ Ag 9 '66
Why not blockade North Vietnam? Read Digest 88:58-62 Mr '66

BALDWIN, James
To whom it may concern: report from occupied territory. Nation 203:39-43 Jl 11 '66
about
Lesson of the master: Henry James and James Baldwin. C. Newman. Yale R 56:45-59 O '66

BALDWIN, Roger N.
Rule of law. Sat R 49:26 Ag 6 '66
about
Fight for civil liberties never stays won. G. Samuels. il por N Y Times Mag p 14-15+ Je 19 '66

BALDWIN-Lima-Hamilton corporation
Old Baldwin works gets on a new track. il Bsns W p52-3+ Ja 29 '66

BALDWIN company
Smoke rings from Baldwin. il Time 88:82 S 9 '66

BALEWA, Sir Abubakar Tafawa
New Ironsides. Newsweek 67:43 Ja 31 '66

BALFOUR, John Patrick Douglas, 3d baron Kinross. See Kinross, J. P. D. B.

BALI
Bali exorcises an evil spirit. D. Kirk. Reporter 35:42-3 D 15 '66
Morning of the world. H. Sutton. il Sat R 49:66-9 D 10; 55-7 D 17, '66

BALINESE dancing. See Dancing, Balinese

BALK, Alfred
As others see us. Sat R 49:50-1 My 21 '66
Books in communications. See issues of Saturday review
Invitation to bribery. Harper 233:18+ O '66
Journalism's guerrillas; free-lancers. Sat R 49:143-4 Mr 12 '66
Money and politics. Sat R 49:22 O 15 '66
Racial news gap. Sat R 49:53-4 Ag 13 '66
Western man at his best. Sat R 49:15 Ap 23 '66
Who said what in the survey. Sat R 49:28-9+ Mr 5 '66

BALKAN STATES
See also
Danubian countries

Description and travel
Balkan way of life. D. Binder. il N Y Times Mag p69-70+ S 18 '66

BALL, Alice D.
USBE story; continued. por Library J 91:1349-53 Mr 15 '66

BALL, Edward
Veteran fighter engages a new foe. por Bsns W p 184-6+ S 17 '66

BALL, George Wildman
Acting Secretary Ball's news conference of July 6, 1966. Dept State Bul 55:121-8 Jl 25 '66
Department supports adjustment of status of Cuban refugees; statement, August 10, 1966. Dept State Bul 55:348-9 S 5 '66
Flaming arrows to the sky; excerpt from As we knew Adlai. Atlan 217:41-5 My '66
Independence and freedom: a continuing struggle; address, July 4, 1966. Dept State Bul 55:194-8 Ag 8 '66
Issue in Viet-Nam; address, January 30, 1966. Dept State Bul 54:239-46 F 14 '66
Larger meaning of the NATO crisis; address, April 29, 1966. Dept State Bul 54:762-8 My 16 '66; Same. Vital Speeches 32:492-5 Je 1 '66
Responsibilities of peace; address, August 20, 1966. Dept State Bul 55:373-5 S 12 '66
Toward a more rational world economic order; statement, September 29, 1966. Dept State Bul 55:633-7 O 24 '66
Under Secretary Ball discusses U.S. views on Viet-Nam and NATO; interview, ed. by A. Fontaine. Dept State Bul 54:613-16 Ap 18 '66
U.S. policy on Atlantic union; statement, September 20, 1966. Dept State Bul 55:613-15 O 17 '66
U.S. policy toward NATO; statement, June 30, 1966. Dept State Bul 55:143-8 Jl 25 '66
about
George Ball's new role. Atlan 217:22+ My '66

BALL, J. K. and others
Prolonged immunosuppression and tumor induction by a chemical carcinogen injected at birth. bibliog Science 152:650-1 Ap 29 '66

BALL, Larry
Safety check. Flying 79:114+ O '66; 80:94 Ja '67

BALL, Lester B.
Collective bargaining: a primer for superintendents. Sat R 50:70-1+ Ja 21 '67

BALL, Robert
Cold-blooded guardians of the world's moneys. Fortune 74:124-9+ O '66

BALL, William B.
Book of the month. Cath World 203:48-9 Ap '66
Church and state: the absolutist crusade. Sat R 50:58-9+ Ja 21 '67
New books. Cath World 203:369 S '66

BALL bearings. See Bearings (machinery)

BALL joints. See Joints (engineering)

BALL lightning. See Lightning

BALL parks. See Stadiums

BALLAD for the shy; drama. See Dias, E. J.

BALLAD of Baby Doe; opera. See Moore, D.

BALLAD of the Green Berets. See Vietnamese war, 1957- —Songs and music

BALLAD of Tremble Dove; story. See Webb, L.

BALLADS
See also
Phonograph records—Songs

BALLADS, American
Ancient ballads traditionally sung in New England; ed. by H. H. Flanders. Review Sat R 49:53 F 12 '66. C. M. Simpson, jr

BALLANTINE, H. Thomas, jr
Medicine and chiropractic. Todays Health 44:52 D '66

BALLANTINE, William
Fear on the high wire. por Pop Sci 189:88-91 Jl '66

BALLARD, Ernesta Drinker
Unusual indoor garden. Horticulture 45:24-5 Ja '67

BALLARD, Florence
Off the record with the Supremes; ed. by E. Miller. pors Seventeen 25:280-1+ Ag '66

BALLARDO, Ricardo. See Manitas de Plata

BALLAST (boats)
Wet sweatshirts: yes or no. E. Horan. il Yachting 119:37+ My '66

BALLERINAS. See Dancers

BALLET
Edward Villella talks; ed. by O. Maynard. E. Villella. il Dance Mag 40:50-4+ My '66
Presstime news. See issues of Dance magazine
Regional ballet, USA. D. Hering. See occasional issues of Dance magazine
Regional ballet: what's it all about? D. Hering. Dance Mag 40:49-51 S '66
Reports from abroad. il Dance Mag 40:18+ Ap '66
Reviews. See issues of Dance magazine
Sleeping beauty in Atlanta. G. Beiswanger. il Dance Mag 40:46-8 O '66
See also
Choreography
Dancing
Moving pictures—Dance films

History
Caution: choreographer at work. H. Saal. il N Y Times Mag pt2 p 18-19+ S 11 '66

Study and teaching
Anatomy for the ballet teacher; ed. by W. Como. R. Gelabert. See issues of Dance magazine
Children's dance is serious fun. J. Anderson. il Dance Mag 40:68-70 My '66
Dancer prepares. J. A. Kneeland. il Dance Mag 40:51-3+ Mr; 57-9 Ap; 65-7 My; 67-9 Je '66; Reply with rejoinder. I. Youskevitch. 40:26+ S '66
Eugene Loring talks; ed. by O. Maynard. E. Loring. il Dance Mag 40:52-4+ Ag '66
Why is a ballerina? interview. ed. by O. Maynard. M. Paul. il Dance Mag 40:38-42 Ap '66

Austria
Report from Vienna; Tancredi e Cantilena. L. Zamponi. il Dance Mag 40:23+ Jl '66

Canada
Les Grands ballets canadiens, Brooklyn academy of music. D. Hering. Dance Mag 40:60-1 Mr '66

France
Letter from Paris; Maurice Bejart ballet of Romeo et Juliette performed by Ballet du XXième siècle company. Genêt. New Yorker 42:110-12 Ja 14 '67
Ring-around-the-world; Beethoven's Ninth by Béjart. il Newsweek 67:88 Je 27 '66

Great Britain
London's world of dance. M. Seif. il Sat R 49:67-8+ S 24 '66
Report from London; Sun into darkness. J. Percival. il Dance Mag 40:22 Jl '66
See also
Royal academy of dancing

Hungary
Hungarian national ballet, New York city center. J. Maskey. Dance Mag 40:58 Mr '66
Hungarian national ballet, New York city center. M. Marks. Dance Mag 40:74 Ap '66

Mexico
See also
Ballet folklórico of Mexico

Rumania
Rumanian folk ballet, Ciocirlia, New York city center. J. Maskey. Dance Mag 40:62-3 Mr '66

Russia
Illustrated letter from Moscow. K. Ambrose. il Dance Mag 40:36-7 Ap '66
Lopukhov and his Tanzsymphonia; excerpt from Era of the Russian ballet. N. Roslavleva. Dance Mag 41:72-4 Ja '67
Lopukhov dynasty. L. Yoffe. il Dance Mag 41:35-9+ Ja '67
New thoughts in the USSR. V. Krasovskaya. il Dance Mag 40:33-5+ F '66
See also
Bolshoi ballet
Kirov ballet

BALLET companies
American folk ballet; Brooklyn academy of music. M. Marks. Dance Mag 41:67-8 Ja '67
Building balletomanes by the thousands; Newark's Garden state ballet. J. Anderson. il Dance Mag 40:47-9+ Ag '66
Geneology of a company! Ballet of Los Angeles. il Dance Mag 40:29 N '66
Giselle comes to the University of Oklahoma. J. Anderson. il Dance Mag 40:57-9 N '66
Manhattan festival ballet, 92nd street Y. D. Hering. Dance Mag 40:25+ F '66
Manhattan festival ballet; Theatre 80 St Marks. J. Maskey. Dance Mag 41:64+ Ja '67
Only five great ballet companies. C. Barnes. il Harper 232:62-7 My '66
Regional ballet, USA. See occasional issues of Dance magazine
Regional ballet: what's it all about? D. Hering. Dance Mag 40:49-51 S '66
San Diego ballet, Jacob's Pillow dance festival. J. Maskey. Dance Mag 40:31-2 S '66
See also
American ballet theatre
Chicago opera ballet
City Center Joffrey ballet
Metropolitan opera ballet
National ballet
New York city ballet
Royal Danish ballet
Western theatre ballet (organization)

Finance
Nightmare of ballet finance. A. Ewing. Dance Mag 40:36-9 O '66

BALLET festivals. See Dance festivals

BALLET folklórico of Mexico
Folklórico in Acapulco. I. Kolodin. il Sat R 49:39 Jl 9 '66

BALLET of Los Angeles. See Ballet companies

BALLET theatre. See American ballet theatre

BALLETS
Alwin Nikolais' Vaudeville of the elements, Henry street playhouse. J. Maskey. il Dance Mag 40:33+ Je '66
Antony Tudor talks about his new ballets; ed. by J. Anderson. A. Tudor. il Dance Mag 40:42-5 My '66
Eugene Loring talks; ed. by O. Maynard. E. Loring. il Dance Mag 40:35-9 Jl '66

Choreographies
See Choreography

Criticisms
Aldous Huxley variations
   Sat R 49:64+ Ap 16 '66
Brahms-Schoenberg quartet
   New Yorker 42:132 Ap 30 '66
   Newsweek 67:95 My 2 '66
Don Quixote
   New Yorker 42:131-2 Ap 30 '66
   New Yorker 42:106-7 My 21 '66
   Sat R 49:85 My 7 '66
Faerie queen
   Sat R il 49:49+ Je 18 '66

BALLETS—Criticisms—_Continued_
La guirlande de Campra
Dance Mag 41:60 Ja '67
Lac des cygnes. See Swan lake, below
Midsummer nights dream
New Yorker 42:127-8 Ap 16 '66
Narkissos
Dance Mag il 41:32+ Ja '67
Les noces
Sat R 49:34 F 5 '66
Nutcracker
Dance Mag il 40:45-55+ D '66
New Yorker 42:125-6 My 7 '66
Sat R 49:26 My 14 '66
Olympics
Sat R 49:64 Ap 16 '66
Rite of spring
New Yorker 42:125-6 My 7 '66
Sat R 49:26 My 14 '66
Romeo and Juliet
New Yorker 42:110-12 Ja 14 '67
Rose Latulippe
Dance Mag il 40:58-62 D '66
Sacre du printemps. See Rite of spring, above
Sleeping beauty
Dance Mag 40:46-8 O '66
Song of the earth
Sat R il(p67) 49:87-8 S 24 '66
Sun into darkness
Dance Mag il 40:22 Jl '66
Sat R 49:68+ S 24 '66
Swan lake
New Yorker 42:130-1 Ap 30 '66
Newsweek il 67:94 My 2 '66
Sat R 49:34 F 5 '66
Sat R 49:85 My 7 '66
Variations
New Yorker 42:164 Ap 9 '66
Newsweek il 67:95 My 2 '66
Viva Vivaldi
Sat R 49:64 Ap 16 '66
Les BALLETS africains. See Dancing, African
BALLETS de Madrid. See Dancing, Spanish
BALLIETT, Whitney
Jazz concerts. New Yorker 42:78+ F 26; 210-14 O 1 '66
Jazz records. New Yorker 41:108+ Ja 15 '66
Our footloose correspondents. New Yorker 42:128+ Je 11 '66
Profiles; Red Allen. New Yorker 42:33-6+ Je 25 '66
Un BALLO in maschera; opera. See Verdi, G.
BALLOCH, A.
Canadian automation code; excerpt from address, September 1965. Mo Labor R 89:520-2 My '66
BALLOON; story. See Barthelme, D.
BALLOON ascensions
Aerial adventures of Carlotta, the lady aeronaut. P. R. Bassett. il Am Heritage 17:64-7 Ag '66
Daffy ride in a hot-air balloon. D. Francis. il Pop Sci 189:41-5+ Jl '66
Riding the wind in a balloon: with report by M. Leatherbee. il Life 61:69-70+ N 18 '66
BALLOON racing
Hot-air balloons race on silent winds. W. R. Berry. il Nat Geog Mag 129:392-407 Mr '66
BALLOONFLOWERS
Balloon flower, insect free, drought resistant, long lasting. A. Palmore. il Flower Grower 53:31 Jl '66
BALLOONS
Daffy ride in a hot-air balloon. D. Francis. il Pop Sci 189:41-5+ Jl '66
See also
Balloon ascensions

History

Aerial adventures of Carlotta, the lady aeronaut. P. R. Bassett. il Am Heritage 17:64-7 Ag '66
Gas bags. B. Finnegan. il Hobbies 71:120+ D '66
Magnificent Brazilian in his flying machine. P. De Paula. il Américas 18:16-22 S '66

Use in research

Chuting for Mars: parachute to land payload on Mars. Newsweek 68:59 S 12 '66
Exploding gas bags may aid ABM effort; Project SLEDGE. Tech W 19:19 N 14 '66
High hoist to Martian skies. il Life 61:55-6+ O 21 '66
Ultraviolet observations from a balloon; Project Polariscope. G. S. Mumford. il Sky & Tel 32:26 Jl '66
BALLOONS, Meteorological
Weather balloons aloft. il Sci N 89:213 Ap 2 '66
BALLPARKS. See Stadiums

BALLS

Manufacture

Automation scores in sports ball plant. il Bsns W p96-7 Ag 13 '66
BALLS (parties)
After this party she'll be invited everywhere. B. Day. il Sat Eve Post 239:34-9 D 3 '66
Come with Mr Capote to a masked ball; with report by J. Howard. il Life 61:107-10+ D 9 '66
Evening at the Plaza; T. Capote's party. il Newsweek 68:66-7 D 12 '66
Truman's compote. il Time 88:88+ D 9 '66
BALLYHOO (periodical)
Rise and fall of Elmer Zilch. N. Anthony. il Atlan 217:93-6 Mr '66
BALOG, Tee
Alaska portfolio. Field & S 71:46-7 O '66
BALSAM fir
Juvenile hormone; identification of an active compound from balsam fir. W. S. Bowers and others. bibliog il Science 154:1020-1 N 25 '66
BALTIC SEA
Voyage on wheels across the Baltic Sea. R. Chelminski. il Life 60:26-7 Mr 4 '66
BALTIC states
Halfway house. R. Korengold. il Newsweek 68:32-3 Ag 29 '66

Russian occupation

How the Baltic republics fare in the Soviet Union. V. S. Vardys. For Affairs 44:512-17 Ap '66
BALTIMORE

Architecture

Art moves into an old railroad station; Maryland institute, College of art, Baltimore. il Fortune 73:170 My '66
Meeting fixed design conditions; Charles center. il Arch Rec 140:178-9 N '66
Station saved for art's sake; B&O's Mt Royal station into an art school. J. Bailey. il Arch Forum 125:52-7 S '66

City planning

Baltimore might make it; progress of Greater Baltimore committee's projects. G. W. Johnson. New Repub 154:17-18 Ap 9 '66
Charles center's latest. il Arch Rec 140:173-8 S '66
Meeting fixed design conditions; Charles center. il Arch Rec 140:178-9 N '66

Crime

Welcome to the Casbah! Time 87:28 F 4 '66

Description

Let's travel. J. Bush. il Mlle 63:200-2 S '66
Wink at a homely girl; home of 1966 world series. M. Kram. il Sports Illus 25:86-8+ O 10 '66

Education

Discovering the role of art in a changing metropolitan environment; Baltimore high school summer program. G. F. Horn. il Sch Arts 65:36-8 Ap '66

Housing

Mies apartment creates its own environment in a residential neighborhood; Highfield house. il Arch Rec 139:170-2 Ja '66

Libraries

See also
Enoch Pratt free library

Music

Baltimore. G. Fitzgerald. Opera N 30:29 Ap 16 '66
See also
Baltimore civic opera company
Peabody institute, Baltimore

Negroes

Chilling shift. il Time 87:35-6 Je 10 '66
Library service in the inner city; Community action program and Enoch Pratt free library, Baltimore. E. Levy. il Wilson Lib Bul 41:470-7 Ja '67
Target city; CORE zeroes in on Baltimore. il Newsweek 67:28+ Je 6 '66

Police

Baltimore finds the Constitution. il Time 88:65 Jl 8 '66
Time to retire; retirements after report by International association of chiefs of police. New Repub 154:7 F 12 '66
Welcome to the Casbah! Time 87:28 F 4 '66

Riots

Lynch mob. il Newsweek 68:22+ Ag 8 '66

BALTIMORE—*Continued*

Theater

Baltimore, on center. H. Hewes. Sat R 49:40 My 28 '66

[Theatre across America] J. Novick. Nation 203:28-9 Jl 4 '66

BALTIMORE civic opera company

Baltimore; performance of La Bohème. F. C. Smith. Opera N 31:29 D 10 '66

Baltimore, Philadelphia. M. De Schauensee. Opera N 30:31 Mr 12 '66

BALTIMORE Colts (football club) See Football clubs

BALTIMORE COUNTY, Md.

Emergency reporting at the lift of a receiver. W. H. Wineholt. il Am City 81:116-17 Ag '66

BALTIMORE Orioles (baseball) See Baseball clubs

BALTIMORE. University

Baltimore corners its commuters; Langsdale library. H. W. Shelton. il Library J 91: 5892-4 D 1 '66

BALTIMOREANS

Wink at a homely girl; home of 1966 world series. M. Kram. il Sports Illus 25:86-8+ O 10 '66

BALTSCHEFFSKY, Herrick, and others

Inorganic pyrophosphate; formation in bacterial photophosphorylation. bibliog Science 153:1120-2 S 2 '66

BALUSTRADES

See also

Hand railings

BALZAC, Honoré de

Prometheus, by A. Maurois. Review

New Yorker 42:88-9 Jl 9 '66. A. West

Newsweek por 67:100+ Je 6 '66

Reporter 35:44+ Ag 11 '66. G. A. Craig

Sat R 49:26-7 Jl 9 '66. J. O'Brien

Time por 87:100+ My 27 '66

BAMBOO

Bamboo. il Pop Gard 17:66-9 D '66

Nature note; bamboo; giant grass. Sci N 89:404 My 21 '66

BAN, Joseph D.

Open housing; here's why. Christian Cent 83:1031 Ag 24 '66

BANANAS, Joe. See Bonanno, J.

BANANAS, Dwarf

Dwarf bananas. J. L. Martin. il Horticulture 44:28-9 My '66

BAND of angels; story. See Cousins, M.

BANDA, Hastings Kamuzu

One-man Banda. por Newsweek 68:38 Jl 18 '66

What the doctor orders. il por Time 88:34 Jl 15 '66

BANDAGES and bandaging

Bad day at Old Hollow; treating deep lacerations made by a chain saw. R. Starnes. Field & S 71:14-16+ Je '66

BANDED creamware. See Pottery

BANDER, Edward J.

African law & poolside reflections. Library J 91:3661-2 Ag '66

BANDERA, Stepan

Licensed to kill in real life. E. Lyons. il Nat R 18:259-61 Mr 22 '66

BANDITS. See Brigands and robbers

BANDS (music)

Dancing world of Coon-Sanders. H. Shultz. il Sat R 49:57+ My 14 '66

Goodman at the Rainbow grill. H. Dance. il Sat R 49:82-3 Je 11 '66

Here comes Charlie; big band music. H. Saal. il Newsweek 68:69-70 D 26 '66

I've got the band and that's all I need; teenage band; Corporate image. N. Lotz. il Seventeen 26:82-3+ Ja '67

Jazz concerts; performance at Philharmonic Hall by G. McFarland display band. W. Balliett. New Yorker 42:80+ F 26 '66

Jazz concerts; performance at the Villa Vanguard by T. Jones-M. Lewis display band. W. Balliett. New Yorker 42:83-4 F 26 '66

Moppets; college ladies of rock. J. Morschauser. il Look 30:56+ Je 14 '66

New LBJ touch; ruffles and flourishes, marine band. U S News 61:21 O 31 '66

Newstalgia; New vaudeville band. il Time 88:64 D 2 '66

Nitty-gritty sound; San Francisco sound. il Newsweek 68:102 D 19 '66

President's own; U.S. marine band. il Newsweek 68:77-8 Ag 8 '66

Small band, big sound, the Tijuana brass. B. Rollin. il Look 30:104-10 Je 14 '66

BANFIELD, Edward C.

Urban renewal; two views. Commentary 41: 93-5 Mr; 16+ My '66

BANGKOK

Description

Most beautiful word in English? Bangkok says, progress. W. Warren. il N Y Times Mag p 18-19+ Ag 7 '66

Education

Demons, monkeys, and heroes; School of dramatic art. R. Blakey. il Dance Mag 40:46-9 My '66

Hotels and restaurants

Eastward ho! H. Sutton. il Sat R 49:46-8 Ap 2 '66

BANIN, Amos

Tactoid formation in montmorillonite; effect on iron exchange kinetics. bibliog Science 155:71-2 Ja 6 '67

BANISTER, C. E.

Three jigs for cutting wood discs. Pop Mech 125:148-51+ Je '66

BANISTER, Manly

Build a tabletop printing press. Pop Mech 126:152-6+ N; 150-2+ D '66

Concrete by the bucketful. Pop Mech 126: 158-9 O '66

Multi-action paint shaker. Pop Mech 125: 174-7+ My '66

Old lawnmower provides cutter for this garden mulch making machine. Pop Mech 125: 120-4 Je '66

Sheet metal former. Pop Mech 125:190-5+ F '66

Ultimate easel. Pop Mech 126:130-3 Jl '66

BANK, John

Appalachian girl; poem. America 114:415 Mr 26 '66

Puerto Rican children; poem. America 115: 824 D 24 '66

Waiting; poem. America 115:70 Jl 16 '66

BANK acceptances. See Acceptances

BANK advertising

Banks bait the hook for deposits. il Bsns W p88+ O 22 '66

BANK architecture. See Bank buildings

BANK buildings

Boston's State Street bank building. il Arch Rec 140:115-20 Ag '66

Love that bank; Fuji bank. Newsweek 68: 86+ S 12 '66

Thompson bank at Old Sturbridge Village. J. O. Curtis. il Antiques 90:510-13 O '66

BANK capital. See Banks and banking—Finance

BANK consolidations and mergers

Bank mergers; growing dispute. U S News 61:70 Jl 4 '66

Banks win merger bill. Bsns W p36 F 12 '66

Belgium's big bank breaks out of the mold; product of three-way merger. il Bsns W p 120-2+ S 17 '66

Courts aid bank mergers. Bsns W p92 O 22 '66

How not to get married. Time 87:89-90 F 18 '66

New rules on bank mergers. U S News 60: 99 F 21 '66

BANK credit. See Credit

BANK deposits

See also

Certificates of deposit

BANK employees

Banks and the Jews. America 115:309 S 24 '66

BANK failures

Bank crisis; closing of Intra bank, Beirut, Lebanon. Sr Schol 89:19-20 N 4 '66

Bank failures; who's to blame? U S News 60:116 Ap 25 '66

Bank run in Beirut; Intra bank closes. il Newsweek 68:80 O 31 '66

Beirut banks take an unplanned holiday; shutdown of Beirut's Intra bank. il Bsns W p46+ O 22 '66

Lesson from Detroit; Public bank of Detroit. il Time 88:105 O 21 '66

Major bank failure; the reasons; Public bank of Detroit. U S News 61:16 O 24 '66

Salvaging Intra bank; the price is high. Bsns W p66+ D 10 '66

Two object lessons for bankers; Intra bank of Beirut and Public bank of Detroit. Bsns W p 186 O 29 '66

Why bank failure brought no panic; public bank of Detroit collapsed. Bsns W p 160 O 22 '66

Your bank is defunct; Public bank of Detroit. Newsweek 68:87-8 O 24 '66

BANK for international settlements

Why U.S. gold goes abroad, and stays there; BIS report. il U S News 60:87-8 Je 27 '66

BANK holding companies
Bank chain; closing the loophole of the 1956 Bank holding company act. New Repub 154: 4 Je 18 '66
Veteran fighter engages a new foe; E. Ball of du Pont estate in Florida, vs U.S. law. Bsns W p 184-6+ S 17 '66

BANK loans. See Loans, Bank

BANK of America national trust and savings association
Biggest bank's uncommon asset. il Time 88: 50-1 D 30 '66
Enlarging the charge card; BankAmericard. il Bsns W p42 My 28 '66

BANK of New York. See New York (city)—Banks

BANK rates. See Interest

BANK Street college of education, New York
Mother of childhood schooling. il Time 88:94-5 O 7 '66

BANKAMERICARDS. See Credit cards

BANKERS
Cold-blooded guardians of the world's moneys. R. Ball. il Fortune 74:124-9+ O '66
Fine art of making money. E. Streeter. Sat R 49:51-2 D 24 '66
Merchant bankers, by J. Wechsberg. Review Time il 88:114 O 28 '66

BANKERS acceptances. See Acceptances

BANKING law
Bank chain; closing the loophole of the 1956 Bank holding company act. New Repub 154: 4 Je 18 '66
Bank merger fight begins; antitrusters vs Saxon on new 1966 law. Bsns W p 136+ Ap 9 '66
Banks win merger bill. Bsns W p36 F 12 '66
Saxon races a deadline; term expires in six months. Bsns W p 170+ Mr 26 '66
Upholding the status quo; national banks wholly bound by state laws restricting branches for state-chartered banks. Time 88:64 D 23 '66
See also
Banks and banking—Regulation

BANKRUPTCY
Nation of bankrupts. America 114:284 F 26 '66
Why Westec turned to chapter X; bankruptcy petition, SEC continues investigation. Bsns W p44 O 1 '66

BANKRUPTCY, Fraudulent. See Fraudulent conveyances

BANKS, Hartley
Talk about doves; interview. por Field & S 71:56-7+ S '66

BANKS, Coin
Old mechanical banks. F. H. Griffith. See issues of Hobbies

BANKS, Semen. See Semen

BANKS and banking
See also
Credit
Interest
Savings and loan associations

Bill payment service
Coming next; push-button banking. il U S News 60:108-10 F 14 '66

Checking accounts
Should banks reprice corporate services? J. P. Furniss and P. S. Nadler. il Harvard Bsns R 44:95-105 My '66
We agreed to his and hers bank accounts. E. R. Fenn. il Suc Farm 64:63 Jl '66
See also
Checks

Consolidation
See Bank consolidations and mergers

Credit service
New proletariat; implications for society. Reporter 35:14 D 15 '66

Employees
See Bank employees

Finance
Dipping into another money pool; federal funds market. il Bsns W p 160+ S 10 '66

Foreign subsidiaries
How to succeed as a socialist banker; Russian banks in the West. il Time 88:112 N 18 '66

Holding companies
See Bank holding companies

Investments
Banks and South Africa; campaign of deposit withdrawals from Chase-Manhattan and the First national city bank. New Repub 155:6-7 D 17 '66

Laws
See Banking law

Public relations
Credit au go-go; look what's happened to bankers; First national of Norfolk, Va. T. G. Harris. il Look 30:26-9 Ap 5 '66
What's your bank up to now? il Changing T 20:35-7 Ap '66

Anecdotes, facetiae, satire, etc.
People of property; series of pamphlets with title Problems of property by Bank of New York. B. Gill. New Yorker 42:37-41 Je 11 '66

Regulation
Undoing Saxon's rules; federal courts have ruled he went too far. Bsns W p24 D 24 '66

Savings departments
See also
Savings deposits

Securities
Bank stocks and interest rates. il Duns R 87:98-9 F '66
Case for bank stocks. C. J. Loomis. il Fortune 74:209-10+ S '66
Earnings are the lure; expecting 10 per cent increase in profits. il Bsns W p 116+ Jl 16 '66
Investing in a local bank? W. R. Bowler. il Duns R 87:36-8+ My '66
Patman pulls the veil from bank trust units. Bsns W p68 D 31 '66

Service charge
Should banks reprice corporate services? J. P. Furniss and P. S. Nadler. il Harvard Bsns R 44:95-105 My '66

Trust departments
Patman pulls the veil from bank trust units. Bsns W p68 D 31 '66

Belgium
Belgium's big bank breaks out of the mold; product of three-way merger. il Bsns W p 120-2+ S 17 '66

California
See also
Bank of America national trust and savings association

Canada
Braking the bank; bill affecting U.S. owned Mercantile bank of Canada. Time 88:96 D 16 '66

Colombia
Culture in the bank; achievements sponsored by Bank of the Republic through Luis Angel Arango library, Bogota. F. De Castro. il Américas 18:14-16 Jl '66

Cuba
Liquidation of Banco territorial de Cuba; text of note to Department of state from the Ministry of foreign affairs of Cuba, March 15, 1966. Dept State Bul 54:757 My 9 '66

Europe, Western
Fine art of making money. E. Streeter. Sat R 49:51-2 D 24 '66

France
See also
Paris—Banks

Ireland
Closing the banks. il Time 87:111+ My 20 '66

Italy
Battle at the bank; Banca del Lavoro. Time 88:93 D 2 '66
Profiles; R. Mattioli of Banca commerciale italiana, or BCI. J. Wechsberg. New Yorker 42:52-4+ Ap 30 '66

Lebanon
Back toward business; Intra bank. Time 88: 69 D 23 '66
Bank crisis; closing of Intra bank, Beirut. Sr Schol 89:19-20 N 4 '66
Bank run in Beirut; Intra bank closes. il Newsweek 68:80 O 31 '66
Beirut banks take an unplanned holiday; shutdown of Beirut's Intra bank. il Bsns W p46+ O 22 '66
Beirut is where the action is. il Bsns W p68-71 Ap 30 '66

BANKS and banking—Lebanon—*Continued*
Closing of Beirut's Intra bank. il Fortune 74: 93-4+ D '66
Day the doors closed; Intra bank. il Time 88:105-6 O 28 '66
How they broke the bank. il Time 88:116 N 25 '66
Salvaging Intra bank: the price is high. Bsns W p66+ D 10 '66
To be or not to be? Intra bank. Time 89:65 Ja 13 '67

Switzerland

See also
Zurich, Switzerland—Banks

United States

At it again; J. J. Saxon. Time 87:72-3 Ap 22 '66
Banks bait the hook for deposits. il Bsns W p88+ O 22 '66
Can a bank tell anyone else about your account? Bet Hom & Gard 44:6 My '66
Cool Camp; new chief regulator of U.S. national banks. il Time 88:107 N 18 '66
Federal savings bank bill; housing and mortgage market; address, February 21, 1966. J. E. Horne. Vital Speeches 32:363-6 Ap 1 '66
How to succeed in banking in Michigan; Michigan national bank of Lansing. Fortune 74: 291 Jl 15 '66
Is the country running out of money? il U S News 61:85-7 Jl 11 '66
Living with tight money. Newsweek 68:86 N 7 '66
Money is heading to lusher pastures; S&L losing out to stiff bank competition. il Bsns W p 147-8+ My 28 '66
Outlook for '67; as investment bankers see it. il U S News 61:82-4+ D 12 '66
Personal business; look to banks for investment advice. Bsns W p 167-8 D 10 '66
Saxon's farewell. il Newsweek 68:86 N 7 '66
Scrappy, happy James J. Saxon. I. Ross. il Fortune 73:162-4+ Ap '66
Strain is on the banks. J. Davenport. il Fortune 74:96-9+ Jl 1 '66
Swank bank; branch of Franklin national bank on Fifth avenue. il Newsweek 67:88 My 2 '66
When banking gets too friendly. Bsns W p 164 F 12 '66

See also
American bankers association
Bank failures
Banking law
Investment bankers association of America
Monetary policy
Money—United States
Morgan guaranty trust company
Savings banks
United States—Federal reserve board
also subhead Banks under names of cities, e.g. Chicago—Banks

BANNERMAN, R. M. and Cooper, R. G.
Sex-linked anemia: a hypochromic anemia of mice. bibliog Science 151:581-2 F 4 '66
BANNISTER, Dwight
Should this father raise his son? J. West; P. Engle. il Ladies Home J 83:88-9+ My '66
BANNISTER, Roger Gilbert
Punishment of the long-distance runner. por N Y Times Mag p76-7+ S 18 '66
BANNON, Joseph J.
Methods of problem solving. Parks & Rec 1:917-18 N '66
Summer internship program. por Parks & Rec 1:321+ Ap '66
La BANQUE continentale. See New York (city)—Banks
BAOBAB trees
African baobab, object of awe. I. M. Wright and O. Kerfoot. il Natur Hist 75:50-3 My '66
BAPTISM
Unseen in the sign. V. P. McCorry. America 115:42-3 Jl 9 '66
BAPTIST colleges. See Denominational colleges
BAPTIST Sunday school board
Baptist Sunday school board names NLW committees; with list of books for National library week-church library emphasis. Pub W 189:76-7 Mr 7 '66
Baptist Sunday school board observes 75th anniversary. Pub W 189:134 F 14 '66
Portland Baptist store moves because of tax ruling. Pub W 189:70-1 My 9 '66
BAPTISTS
Stark-naked Baptist. R. Drake. Christian Cent 83:1382+ N 9 '66

BAPTISTS in the United States
Baptist ambivalence. K. Haselden. Christian Cent 83:705-6 Je 1 '66
Baptist education needs two-way stretch; Southern Baptist convention meeting on Baptist higher education. Christian Cent 83: 857 Jl 6 '66
Baptists in a bind; question of accepting federal funds for Baptist-related colleges; discussion. Christian Cent 83:146 F 2 '66
Eying federal money; federal grants and loans. Time 88:78+ D 2 '66
God and man in the South; church's indifference to civil rights movement. M. Frady. il Atlan 219:37-42 Ja '67
Richmond church suit dismissed; admission of Negroes to membership in First Baptist church. S. Nichols. Christian Cent 83:411-12 Mr 30 '66
Southern Baptist dilemma in higher education; resistance to federal aid to church-related colleges. B. H. Cochran. Christian Cent 83:1598-601 D 28 '66
Southern Baptist invasion. Christian Cent 83:737 Je 8 '66
Southern Baptists in annual convention. H. H. Ward. Christian Cent 83:813-16 Je 22 '66
What's in a southern name? Southern Baptist convention. Christian Cent 83:516 Ap 27 '66
BAR, Robert S. and others
Surface area of human erythrocyte lipids: reinvestigation of experiments on plasma membrane. bibliog Science 153:1010-12 Ag 26 '66
BARBA, Maria
Swing up, bird; poem. Horn Bk 42:777 D '66
BARBADOS
Goodbye to mother. il Time 88:40+ D 2 '66
See also
United Nations—Barbados

Description and travel

Dependable Barbados. Travel 126:28 N '66
BARBE, Waverly
Circuitous routes & relocations; letter to the editor. Library J 91:4047-8 S 15 '66
BARBECUE cookery
Casseroles and kabobs make hot dishes for cool days. il Pop Gard 17:32-5+ Mr '66
Cookouts that come from the sea. K. Smith. il Pop Gard 17:44-7 My '66
Finishing touches to a fine barbecue; with recipes. il McCalls 93:100-1+ Je '66
What's your barbecue pleasure? with recipes. il Sunset 137:48-53 Jl '66
Whole family cooks. il Farm J 90:70-1 S '66
BARBECUE grills
Skewered or grilled any time of year! il Bet Hom & Gard 44:62-3 N '66

Equipment

Picnic equipment: fair-weather friends. il House & Gard 130:144 Ag '66
BARBEE, Rose
Isle of Hope: the terrapin's last stand. C. Stinnett. il Holiday 40:24+ S '66
BARBER, Red
Responsibility. Sports Illus 25:17 O 10 '66
BARBER, Richard J.
Big, bigger, biggest; American business goes global. New Repub 154:14-18 Ap 30 '66
New partnership. New Repub 155:17-22 Ag 13 '66
BARBER, Samuel
Make mingle with our tambourines; interview. por Opera N 31:32+ S 17 '66

about

Antony and Cleopatra. Criticism
Atlan il 218:126+ S '66
Dance Mag 40:29 D '66
Life 61:30B S 30 '66
N Y Times Mag pors p32-3+ Ag 28 '66
New Repub 155:23+ O 22 '66
New Yorker 42:116+ S 24 '66
Newsweek il 68:98 S 26 '66
Opera N il 31:36-8 S 17 '66
Reporter 35:57 N 17 '66
Sat R 49:35 O 1 '66
Birth of an opera; Antony and Cleopatra. H. W. Heinsheimer. il por Sat R 49:49-50+ S 17 '66
In the grand tradition. J. W. Freeman. il Opera N 31:40-1 S 17 '66
BARBER of Seville; opera. See Rossini, G.
BARBERS and barber shops

Anecdotes, facetiae, satire, etc.

Letter from Stan Delaplane. S. Delaplane. il Todays Health 44:19 Jl '66
Il BARBIERE di Siviglia; opera. See Rossini, G.

BARBIROLLI, Evelyn (Rothwell) lady. See Rothwell, E.
BARBIROLLI, Sir John
Music to my ears; Carnegie Hall appearance with the Houston symphony orchestra. I. Kolodin. Sat R 49:28 Ap 9 '66
BARBITURATES
Action of anionic and cationic nerve-blocking agents: experiment and interpretation. M. P. Blaustein and D. E. Goldman. bibliog il Science 153:429-32 Jl 22 '66
Enzyme changes in neurons and glia during barbiturate sleep. A. Hamberger and others. il Science 151:1394-5 Mr 18 '66
BARBON comet. See Comets
BARCELONA
Music
Notes from our correspondents. R. Angus. Hi Fi 16:18+ Ap '66
BARCELONA. University. See Colleges and universities—Spain
BARCELOS pottery. See Pottery, Portuguese
BARCLAY, Eddie
Le roi de pop. il por Newsweek 69:56-8 Ja 9 '67
BARD, Bernard
Why dropout campaigns fail. Sat R 49:78-9+ S 17 '66
BARDACH, John E.
Life along an Arctic river; excerpt from Downstream: a natural history of the river. Liv Wildn 29:14-19 Aut '65
BARDEN, Anne Marie
Beauty life: gadget gym. Mlle 63:126-7 O '66
BARDOT, Brigitte
Fun couples. por Newsweek 68:58 Jl 25 '66
BAREFOOT soprano; story. See Stewart, E.
BAREFOOT trader; drama. See Watts, F. B.
BARENBAUM, Ruth
Will you be my daughter? por Redbook 128: 8+ Ja '67
BARENDSEN, Robert D.
Education in Mao's China. Am Ed 2:14-19 O '66
BARFORD, George
Farewell to Corbu. Sch Arts 65:25-9 Ap '66
BARGAIN sales
August white sales. C. Mitchell. il Suc Farm 64:65+ Ag '66
Do you really get what you pay for? M. Mayer. Bet Hom & Gard 44:7 N '66
How to turn discards into dollars. J. Ratcliffe. il Read Digest 89:25-6+ Ag '66
Spirit of Christmas past; post-Christmas sale season. il Newsweek 69:52 Ja 9 '67
BARGE lines
Barge lines: catching the crest. il Duns R 87:pt2 128-30+ My '66
Danger signals from a river towboat. W. Belvin and A. Klein. il Yachting 119:72-4+ Je '66
BARGHOORN, Elso S. and Schopf, J. W.
Microorganisms three billion years old from the Precambrian of South Africa. bibliog Science 152:758-63 My 6 '66
BARHAM, Eric G.
Deep scattering layer migration and composition: observations from a diving saucer. bibliog Science 151:1399-403 Mr 18 '66
BARILLET, Pierre
Cactus flower; adaptation. See Burrows, A.
BARK beetles
Pesticide program in Grand Teton National Park: control of bark beetle. A. Murie. il Nat Parks Mag 40:17-19 Je '66
Scolytid beetles associated with Douglas fir: response to terpenes. J. A. Rudinsky. bibliog il Science 152:218-19 Ap 8 '66
Sex-ratio condition: unusual mechanisms in bark beetles. G. N. Lanier and J. H. Oliver, jr. bibliog il Science 153:208-9 Jl 8 '66
BARKA, Mehdi Ben. See Ben Barka, M.
BARKAN, Al
What the unions are doing to elect their friends. por U S News 61:112+ O 24 '66
BARKENTINES. See Sailing vessels
BARKER, B. Devereux, 3d
Deep water racing. See issues of Yachting
BARKER, Elliott S.
Pecos geology. Liv Wildn 29:27 Aut '65
BARKER, George
Two British chronicles. M. Bell. Poetry 107: 412-13 Mr '66
BARKER, John W.
Finally, the race is over, three complete recordings of Musique de table. Am Rec G 32:812-15 My '66
Four fruits of the Carl Nielsen centenary. Am Rec G 32:471-5 Ja '66

From L'Oiseau-Lyre, the first recording of Rameau's Hippolyte et Aricie. Am Rec G 32:946-8 Je '66
Heinrich Schütz. Am Rec G 33:216-20+ N '66
On Decca: an appealing collection of pages from the Little clavier book for Anna Magdalena Bach. Am Rec G 32:1112-13 Ag '66
Renaissance riches: the legacy of the music-loving Marguerite. Am Rec G 32:892+ My '66
—and others
Stereotape reviews. See issues of American record guide
BARKER, M. E.
Think like a deer. Field & S 71:46-7+ O '66
BARKER, Marie Esman
Foreign language in high school. NEA J 55: 47-8 O '66
BARKER, Mildred
Evangelist; story. Reporter 35:38-40 D 1 '66
BARKERVILLE, British Columbia. See Villages, Restored
BARKIN, Martin J.
Tunnel; interview. New Yorker 42:48-51 N 26 '66
BARKING SANDS underwater test range. See Proving grounds
BARLEY
History
Distribution of wild wheats and barley. J. R. Harlan and D. Zohary. bibliog il Science 153:1074-80 S 2 '66
BARLOW, Roger
Sports car camping. Field & S 70:53-5 F '66
BARNACLES
Nature note. Sci N L 89:109 F 12 '66
BARNARD, Boyd T.
Kindest cut of all. por Fortune 74:189 N '66
BARNARD, Mary
Pleiades; poem. New Yorker 42:38 Ag 27 '66
BARNARD college, New York
Women's higher education. R. Park. Sch & Soc 94:35-9 Ja 22 '66
BARNES, Carl E.
Get inventions off the shelf. Harvard Bsns R 44:138-9 Ja '66
BARNES, Clive
Critic's critic. New Repub 154:40-2 My 14 '66
Kirov ballet's Sleeping beauty film. Dance Mag 40:44-5 Ap '66
Only five great ballet companies. Harper 232: 62-7 My '66
BARNES, Duncan
Devilish stroll in the woods. Sports Illus 24: 22-4+ F 14 '66
Fishing (cont) Sports Illus 25:56-7 Jl 11 '66
Rugged place for a picnic. Sports Illus 24: 78-80+ My 2 '66
BARNES, Harry Elmer
Mystery of Pearl Harbor. Nat R 18:1260 D 13 '66
BARNES, Keith
Memoir, at the age of six; poem. New Repub 156:26 Ja 21 '67
BARNES, Peter
Latin America: the first nuclear free zone? Bul Atomic Sci 22:37-40 D '66
New England's power politics. Reporter 33: 36-8 D 16 '65; 34:6+ F 10 '66
BARNES, Virgil E. and others
Silurian of central Texas: a first record for the region. Science 154:1007-8 N 25 '66
BARNET, Charlie
Here comes Charlie. H. Saal. il por Newsweek 68:69-70 D 26 '66
BARNETT, Arthur Doak
China after Mao; excerpts. Look 30:31-5 N 15 '66
History's logic weighs against Maoism. Life 62:32 Ja 20 '67
about
New debate on China. por Newsweek 67:25-6 Mr 21 '66
Reading the dragon's mind. por Time 87:27A Mr 18 '66
BARNETT, Charles B. Jr. and Pirone, T. P.
Stylet-borne virus: active probing by aphids not required for acquisition. bibliog Science 154:291 O 14 '66
BARNETT, Jonathan
Last works of Le Corbusier. Arch Rec 139: 187-94 Ap '66
New planning process with built-in political support Arch Rec 139:141-6 My '66
Will Rudolph's vision of the SMTI campus be fully realized? Arch Rec 140:156-7 O '66
BARNETT, Robert Warren
United States and Japan: different paths to common goals; address, March 3, 1966. Dept State Bul 54:664-8 Ap 25 '66
BARNETT, S. A.
Rats; with biographical sketch. Sci Am 216: 22, 78-85 Ja '67

BARNETT Frummer hears a familiar ring; story. See Trillin, C.

BARNETT Frummer is an unbloomed flower; story. See Trillin, C.

BARNEY, Dick
Brace yourself for the next disaster! Pop Mech 125:102-4+ Ap '66

BARNHART, Ronald G.
Isotope-fueled diving-suit claimed to function two years. il Tech W 19:39 Jl 18 '66

about
Memo for the publisher (title varies) A. C. Boughton. il por Miss & Roc 18:6 Ap 18 '66

BARNOUW, Erik
McLuhanism reconsidered. Sat R 49:19-21+ Jl 23 '66

BARNS and stables
Borrow ideas from this low-cost beef confinement barn. M. D. Hall. il Suc Farm 64: 34-5 O '66
From a tumbledown barn, a spirited house. il House & Gard 130:80-5 Ag '66
He stopped building on; now has this new system. P. B. Jones and J. R. Borcherding. il Suc Farm 64:42-3+ Ap '66
What would it cost to build a beef confinement barn? D. Malena. il Suc Farm 64:44 Jl '66

Equipment
Are those new barns really worth it? free stalls. B. Hardy and J. Russell. il Farm J 90:34-5+ My '66
Free stalls for $25. C. M. Kotter. il Farm J 90:38R Je '66
Stanchion feeding with less work. il Farm J 90:68C Mr '66

BARNSLEY, Alan Gabriel
Book of the month. L. M. Grande. Cath World 203:368 S '66

BARNSTORMING. See Aviation—Stunt flying

BARNUM and Bailey circus. See Circus

BARO, Gene
Night poem. New Yorker 41:87 Ja 22 '66
Procession; poem. New Yorker 42:122 My 14 '66
Travelling backward; poem. New Yorker 42: 122 S 10 '66

about
Tree, lake, moon; and man. R. Roseliep. Poetry 108:55 Ap '66

BARON, Stanley
Rice: mainstay of life for 1,100 million human beings. UNESCO Courier 19:16-17+ Ap '66

BARONDES, Samuel H. and Cohen, H. D.
Puromycin effect on successive phases of memory storage. bibliog Science 151:594-5 F 4 '66

BAROQUE architecture. See Architecture, Baroque

BARR, C. E. and Broyer, T. C.
Energy balancing in nitella cells treated with dinitrophenol. bibliog Science 151:1245-6 Mr 11 '66

BARR, Donald
Should your child go to a private school? Parents Mag 41:74-7+ S '66

BARR, Joseph Moran
Excerpt from letter addressed to the President of the United States. January 5, 1966. Cong Digest 45:92+ Mr '66

BARR, Richard H. and Du Von, Jay
Education and the bond market. Am Ed 2:4 F; 24 Mr; 13 Ap; 12 My; 25 Je; 20 Jl; 31 S; 27 N; 24 D '66

BARRACUDA fishing
Father's fling on the flats. E. A. Bauer. il Outdoor Life 137:56-9+ Je '66

BARRAULT, Jean Louis
With honor and insolence; tr. by J. Gutman. Opera N 30:17 Ap 9 '66

BARREN ground caribou. See Caribou

BARRETT, Edward John Boyd
Edward Boyd Barrett: shepherd in the mist; in memoriam. D. Hayne. America 115:230 S 3 '66

BARRETT, George
Detective. J. Mills. il por Read Digest 88:219-23+ F '66

BARRETT, Lincoln
In silence; poem. Mlle 64:54 D '66

BARRETT, Mary Ellin
Castle ugly; story. Ladies Home J 83:167-74 O; 147-54 N '66

BARRETT, Patricia
Nuns in the inner city. Christian Cent 83: 1050-3 Ag 31 '66

BARRETT, Peter
Summer deer hunt. Outdoor Life 138:28-31+ Jl '66

They sail to win. por Yachting 120:36-7+ Jl; 23+ Ag '66
Trout that never hear traffic. Outdoor Life 137:36-9+ Je '66

about
They sail to win; Peter Barrett and the USISA symposium. E. Horan. il pors Yachting 119:52-3+ F '66

BARRETT, William A.
Excerpt from debate, June 28, 1965. Cong Digest 45:22+ Ja '66

BARRIENTOS ORTUÑO, René
High flier. il por Newsweek 68:44 Jl 18 '66
Letter from La Paz. C. Rand. il New Yorker 42:36-40+ D 31 '66
People of the week. por U S News 61:19 Jl 18 '66
Prepared for the worst. il por Time 88:32+ Jl 15 '66

BARRIO, Raymond
Ever draw with a bristle brush and black tempera? Design 67:32-5 Ja '66
How to be an artist in one lesson. Design 67:8-12 My '66
Let's paint an abstract. Sch Arts 66:33-4 S '66
Painting the small mural. Design 68:8-12 N '66

BARRON, John
Stench at FHA. Read Digest 88:61-7 Ap '66

BARRON, S. and others
Actin-myosin interaction: inhibition of the myosin adenosine triphosphatase by actin. bibliog Science 151:1541-2 Mr 25 '66

BARROS, Adhemar Pereira de
Magnificent reprobate. por Time 87:42 Je 17 '66

BARROW, James H. Jr. and Taylor, B. C.
Fluorescent-antibody studies of haplosporidian parasites of oysters in Chesapeake and Delaware Bays. bibliog Science 153:1531-3 S 23 '66

BARROW, W. J., research laboratory
History of the Barrow lab; or. The thirty years that revolutionized paper. il Pub W 189:72-3+ Ap 4 '66

BARRS, H. D.
Root pressure and leaf water potential. bibliog Science 152:1266-8 My 27 '66

BARRY, Carol Barner. See Barry, D. D. jt. auth.

BARRY, David G.
Art in science. Science 150:1486-7; 152:1011 D 10 '65, My 20 '66

BARRY, Donald D. and Barry, C. B.
Happiness is driving your own Moskvich. N Y Times Mag p 16-17+ Ap 10 '66

BARRY, Joseph
Gardener and the king. Read Digest 89:158-63 O '66
Letter from abroad. McCalls 93:62+ Mr; 40+ Je; 94:74+ O '66; 30+ Ja '67

BARRY, Les
Picture islands. il Pop Phot 59:94-8+ N '66
Travel. See issues of Popular photography

BARRY, Naomi
Enjoying Scandinavia. Holiday 40:117-22 N '66
Going places, finding things in Kashmir. House & Gard 130:54-6+ O '66

BARRY, Richard Francis, 3d. See Barry, R.

BARRY, Rick
Basketball's newest box-office baby. J. Fincher. il pors Life 62:54-7 Ja 6 '67
Fastest gunner in the West. il por Time 88: 50-1 D 2 '66
Sore points. il por Newsweek 68:94 D 5 '66

BARRY, Stan
Hail the humble trailer. Motor B 118:27-9+ Jl '66

BARRYMAINE, Norman
Memo from Haiphong, North Vietnam; under American bombs. Look 30:62 N 29 '66; Same with title Bomb damage in North Vietnam described. Aviation W 85:47+ D 26 '66

BARS, Snack. See Snack bars

BARS and barrooms
Beatles and Bond, and now it's pubs: Britain's biggest export. il Bsns W p76-8+ Ap 23 '66
Euphoria is a pub; attempts to introduce pubs across the U.S. il Time 87:52-3 Je 3 '66
More protection for drunks; question of tavernkeepers' liability. Time 87:80 Ap 15 '66
Vive le pub; Sir Winston Churchill, Bedford arms, Paris. il Time 87:69-70 F 25 '66

BARS for the home
Be a better host with this beverage bar. D. Jordan. il Bet Hom & Gard 44:65 O '66
Build this wonderbar. il Pop Mech 126:138-43+ S '66

BARS for the home—*Continued*
Corner-hung bar, it's handy and handsome. il Pop Sci 189:170 S '66
Good parties get started here! il Bet Hom & Gard 45:37 Ja '67
Set up a spill-proof bar in short order. D. Jordan. il Bet Hom & Gard 44:62-3 O '66
To toast the New Year. B. Plumb. il N Y Times Mag p26 Ja 1 '67

BART, Peter
Supercolossalitis. Sat R 49:14-16 D 24 '66

BARTA, Karoly
Brief biography. S. Goodman. pors Dance Mag 40:60-1 My '66

BARTEL, Virginia
Is your child a reluctant reader? Parents Mag 41:38-9+ Jl '66

BARTELL, H. Robert, Jr
Pension fund investment: both sides of the coin. Mo Labor R 89:128-9 F '66

BARTER
Art & adventure of bartering: simple sales competition: the winner to sell three jets to Lebanon's Middle East airlines. Time 87:87 Ja 28 '66
Furrier to the art world: paintings traded by artists in exchange for J. Kaplan's furs. G. Glueck. il N Y Times Mag p38-9+ O 2 '66

BARTH, Alan
Lawless lawmen. New Repub 155:19-22 Jl 30 '66
We need a firearms-control law, now! Read Digest 90:17-18+ Ja '67

BARTH, John
Night-sea journey: story. Esquire 65:82-3 Je '66

about
Gods and goats. M. Klein. Reporter 35:60-2 S 22 '66
Heroic comedy. por Newsweek 68:81-81B Ag 8 '66
John Barth: long reach, near miss. P. S. Beagle. Holiday 40:131-2+ S '66
What happened to John Barth? R. Garis. Commentary 42:89-90+ O '66

BARTH, Karl
Barth on Barth. P. M. Van Buren. Christian Cent 83:1512 D 7 '66

BARTH, Markus
Church and communism in East Germany. Christian Cent 83:1440-3, 1469-72 N 23-30 '66

BARTHEL, Joan
Biggest money-making movie of all time, how come? N Y Times Mag p45-7+ N 20 '66
How to avoid TV dinners while watching TV. N Y Times Mag p30-1+ Ag 7 '66

BARTHELME, Donald
Balloon: story. New Yorker 42:46-8 Ap 16 '66
Games are the enemies of beauty, truth, and sleep, Amanda said. Mlle 64:136+ N '66
See the moon? story. New Yorker 42:46-50 Mr 12 '66
This newspaper here: story. New Yorker 41:28-9 F 12 '66
Tired terror of Graham Greene. Holiday 39:146+ Ap '66

BARTHOLDI, Frédéric Auguste
Hail Liberty! D. G. McCullough. il por Am Heritage 17:22-3+ F '66

BARTKE, Andrzej, and Wolff, G. L.
Influence of the lethal yellow A^y gene on estrous synchrony in mice. bibliog Science 153:79-80 Jl 1 '66

BARTLESVILLE, Okla.
Why we switched to cationic emulsion. D. Farrington. il Am City 81:104-5 N '66

BARTLETT, E. L.
Polar bear conservation: letter. Audubon Mag 68:425 N '66

BARTLETT, Gerald
Stock control in bookselling. Pub W 190:68-72 Jl 18; 62-6 Jl 25 '66

BARTLETT, William Henry
Scenes of America by Bartlett and others. E. P. Birk. il Antiques 90:602+ N '66

BARTLEY, Diana
Homage to Pininfarina. Esquire 66:109-15 N '66

BARTLING, Julia
Reference books of 1965. Library J 91:1987-94 Ap 15 '66

BARTÓK, Béla
Bluebeard's castle: London edition. C. J. Luten. il Am Rec G 33:100-1 O '66
New tenants for Bluebeard's castle. R. Jacobson. Sat R 49:82 S 24 '66
Records:
Bluebeard's castle. Opera N 31:34 D 3 '66

BARTOLETTI, Bruno
High key: interview, ed. by J. W. Stedman. por Opera N 31:12 D 10 '66

BARTOLINI, R. Paul
Seven for Lake County. Library J 91:5874-7 D 1 '66

BARTON, Frank
Battle over blood. Todays Health 44:46+ F '66

BARTON, John H.
How to cook a tough buck. Field & S 71:40-2+ Jl '66

BARTOS, Armand P. See Kiesler, F. J. Jt. auth.

BARTRA, Agustí
New York: two poetic impressions. Américas 18:14-22 O '66

BARTZ, Albert E.
Eye and head movements in peripheral vision: nature of compensatory eye movements. bibliog Science 152:1644-5 Je 17 '66

BARUCH, Bernard Mannes
Unforgettable Bernard Baruch. B. Bliven. por Read Digest 89:92-6 S '66

BARUCH, Sylvan
Sylvan Baruch sells last shop, retires from book business. Pub W 190:223 Jl 11 '66

BARWELL. meteorite. See Meteorites

BARWOOD, Aileen Vincent-. See Vincent-Barwood, A.

BARZEL, Ann
Looking at television. See issues of Dance magazine

BARZEL, Rainer
No. 2 man. por Time 87:35 Je 24 '66

BARZINI, Luigi
Beauty and heart. Vogue 148:183-4+ O 1 '66
Caesar and the enigma of his death. Life 60:64+ Mr 18 '66
Communism, Italian style, has nowhere to go. N Y Times Mag p30-1+ F 13 '66
Those remarkable Italians: excerpt from The Italians. Read Digest 88:143-6 Ap '66

BASALT
Genetic relations of oceanic basalts as indicated by lead isotopes. M. Tatsumoto. bibliog il Science 153:1094-101 S 2 '66
Rare earths in Hawaiian basalts. J. G. Schilling and J. W. Winchester. bibliog il Science 153:867-9 Ag 19 '66
Willowdale red rock. H. D. Brown. il Hobbies 71:117 N '66

BASCH, Peter
Behold the lowly flashcube. D. L. Miller. il Mod Phot 30:72-3 Je '66

BASCOM, Willard
Trailbreaker of the deeps. P. O'Neil. il pors Life 61:108-10+ S 30 '66

BASEBALL
Big victory in a small town: Connie Mack world series, Farmington, N.Mex. J. Jares. il Sports Illus 25:112-15 S 12 '66
Can't anyone here use Kanehl? L. Shecter. il Sports Illus 25:54-6+ Ag 8 '66
Flawed diamond. J. Jacobs. Reporter 34:57-8 Ja 27 '66
It's a long, long season. J. Brosnan. il N Y Times Mag p30-1+ Ap 17 '66
Journey back to Bushville. E. Asinof. il N Y Times Mag p8-9+ Jl 24 '66
Percentage baseball, by E. Cook. Review Life 60:17 Ap 15 '66. E. Asinof
Sandy Koufax story: what baseball means to me; excerpts from Koufax, ed. by E. Linn. S. Koufax. Look 30:33-4+ Jl 26 '66
El Saphnie de los Tigres: Mexico. M. Cope. il Sports Illus 25:26-8+ Jl 4 '66
Year of the tape measure; batting. il Time 87:92+ My 20 '66
See also
Little leagues
Radio broadcasting—Sports
World series (baseball)

Accidents and injuries
Baseball's fragile superstars. M. Gross. il Pop Sci 188:76-9 My '66
Lame but game Dodgers. il Life 61:58B-58C S 23 '66
Painful search for a pennant; Dodgers leading the race. J. Olsen. il Sports Illus 25:28-33 S 19 '66
Sandy Koufax story: my battle with arthritis; excerpts from Koufax, ed. by E. Linn. S. Koufax. il Look 30:80-6 Jl 12 '66
Troubled time for a wounded hero. B. Gilbert. il Sat Eve Post 239:76-80 S 10 '66

Anecdotes, facetiae, satire, etc.
Ben Casey at the bat. W. K. Zinsser. il Sat Eve Post 239:20 Mr 26 '66
My son the outfielder, and my major-leaguer, Dick Stuart. M. Kitman. il Sat Eve Post 239:20 S 10 '66
Roth waxes spring training. A. Roth. il Sports Illus 24:34-41 F 28 '66

BASEBALL—*Continued*

Caricatures and cartoons

Roth waxes spring training. A. Roth.
Sports Illus 24:34-41 F 28 '66

History

Glory of their times; excerpt. L. S. Ritter. il
Sat Eve Post 239:36-40+ Ag 13 '66
Yankee dynasty can never come back. L.
Koppett. il N Y Times Mag p44-5+ O 2 '66

Organization and administration

Just because your Sox are Red; Boston Red
Sox. R. Lemon. il Sat Eve Post 239:22
N 19 '66
Men who fire managers; general managers.
W. Leggett. il Sports Illus 25:44-6+ S 12
'66
Progress report on the unknown soldier;
Lieut. General W. D. Eckert, Commis-
sioner of baseball. J. Underwood. il Sports
Illus 24:40-2+ Ap 4 '66

Photographs

How the Pirates won the pennant. W. Clark.
U S Camera 29:24 N '66

Rules

Baseball needs the spitter. J. Brosnan. il
Look 30:66-9 My 31 '66
Batter up and down; pitcher throws at a
batter. Sports Illus 24:19 Je 13 '66
Gag rule: no fraternization among players on
opposing teams. Sports Illus 24:20 My 2
'66
Time for severity; concerning attacks with
bats in professional baseball. Sports Illus
24:18 My 23 '66

Study and teaching

And now, the screwbat; John Herbold's
techniques. il Life 61:73-5 Jl 29 '66
Biggest baseball clinic; Baton Rouge youths
get coaching from pro stars. il Ebony 21:
89-90+ My '66
Summer baseball school; Parma, Ohio. R.
Bergstrom. il Parks & Rec 1:31I+ Ap '66
BASEBALL accidents. *See* Baseball—Accidents
and injuries
BASEBALL clubs
All-Orioles. il Newsweek 68:78 S 26 '66
And there were the Dodgers in third place;
Giant-Dodger rivalry. J. Mann. il Sports
Illus 24:58-60 Je 27 '66
Baltimore's early birds. il Time 88:48 Jl 22 '66
Baseball and antitrust: a legal tangle; Mil-
waukee Braves move to Atlanta. il U S
News 60:8 F 7 '66
Baseball 1966: American league. il Sports Illus
24:73-90+ Ap 18 '66
Baseball 1966: National league. il Sports Illus
24:50-68 Ap 18 '66
Baseball roundup 1966: year of the holdouts.
il Ebony 21:120-2+ Je '66
Baseball's week. H. Weiskopf. *See issues*
of Sports illustrated published during base-
ball season
Batmen strike; Baltimore Orioles lead in the
American league pennant race. M. Mulvoy.
il Sports Illus 25:12-15 Ag 1 '66
Battle for a shot at the Birds; National
league pennant race. W. Leggett. il Sports
Illus 25:24-7 O 3 '66
Big Yankee turnabout. L. Koppett. il Sports
Illus 24:22-4+ Je 20 '66
Buzzie and big D go at it in L.A; result, a
revived Drysdale. J. Olsen. il Sports Illus
25:22-3 Ag 29 '66
Case dismissed; concerning the home of the
Braves. Time 88:53 Ag 5 '66
Cellar that Houk built; Yankees. il Time
88:72 S 16 '66
Charley horse race; question of how the
leaders would finish the season. il News-
week 68:68 S 19 '66
Cincinnati's brain-picker; owner, president,
general manager and treasurer of Cincinnati
Reds. R. H. Boyle. il Sports Illus 24:40-2+
Je 13 '66
Climbing into orbit; Houston Astros. il Time
88:39 Jl 8 '66
Cold wind from Wisconsin; Braves. il Time
87:66 Ap 22 '66
CBS bespeaks; president of the Yankees. il
Time 88:69 S 30 '66
Coming in from the cold. il Newsweek 67:72
My 2 '66
Dodgers and first place; pennant race, Giants
vs Dodgers. J. Mann. il Sports Illus 24:20-1
Je 20 '66
Dodgers in a daze. il Newsweek 68:64 O
17 '66
Dodgers scent a pennant. J. Mann. il Sports
Illus 25:26-8 S 26 '66

Down go the mighty; trading of players.
Time 88:58 D 16 '66
Dying team screams for help; the New
York Yankees fire manager J. Keane.
W. Leggett. il Sports Illus 24:34-7 My
16 '66
Fall of the Dodgers; trading sessions. News-
week 68:68 D 12 '66
Frank Robinson: hawk among the Orioles. il
Ebony 21:88-90+ S '66
Fun season. il Newsweek 68:53-4 Jl 18 '66
Gone with the Braves! Milwaukee Braves
prepare to open 91st season. Newsweek 67:
98-9 Ap 18 '66
Good leader slides hard and carries a big
stick; F. Robinson of Baltimore Orioles.
B. Lindeman. il Sat Eve Post 239:74-6
Ag 27 '66
Heavenly home of the Anaheim Angels.
W. Leggett. il Sports Illus 25:53-5 Jl 4 '66
Here come the Young Turks. W. Leggett. il
Sports Illus 25:26-31 Jl 11 '66
Home are the Braves; in Atlanta; divorce
from Milwaukee. G. Astor. il Look 30:61-
2+ My 3 '66
Hottest team in baseball; Cincinnati Reds.
W. Leggett. Sports Illus 25:26-7 Ag 22 '66
How can Black Maxers lose? Pittsburgh
Pirates. M. Mulvoy. Sports Illus 25:58+
Jl 18 '66
Indian sign; Cleveland Indians. il Newsweek
67:96-7 My 16 '66
It's not bad to be going good; San Francisco
Giants. J. Mann. il Sports Illus 24:30-1 My
23 '66
Jaundiced eye; New York Yankees success
after management change. il Newsweek
67:96-7 My 23 '66
Just because your Sox are Red; Boston Red
Sox. R. Lemon. il Sat Eve Post 239:22
N 19 '66
Kansas City gets a kid to build a dream on;
J. Nash. W. Leggett. Sports Illus 25:60-1 Ag
29 '66
Kentucky windage; teams at start of season.
il Time 87:73 Ap 15 '66
Kids who boom in the spring; major league
rookies. T. C. Brody. il Sports Illus 24:28-9
Ap 11 '66
King of the jungle; W. O'Malley, owner of
Los Angeles Dodgers. J. Mann. Sports Illus
24:114-16+ Ap 18 '66
Legal spitter; home of the Braves. Sr Schol
88:15 Ap 29 '66
Like Gone with the wind, Braves take Atlanta.
il Life 60:77-8 Ap 22 '66
Long, long season could be too long; unrest
among tired ballplayers. W. Leggett. Sports
Illus 25:50-1 Ag 15 '66
Name of the man is Alston. J. Mann. il
Sports Illus 25:75-7 O 10 '66
Out in the bleachers, where the action is;
Chicago Cubs' fans. W. B. Furlong. il
Harper 233:49-53 Jl '66
Painful search for a pennant; Dodgers lead-
ing the race. J. Olsen. il Sports Illus 25:
28-33 S 19 '66
Photo finish; National league pennant won
by Dodgers. il Newsweek 68:68 O 10 '66
San Francisco: this race is not over yet by
a long shot; opinion of manager Franks.
W. Leggett. il Sports Illus 25:28-31 S 26 '66
Situation normal in the good old N.L. wild
pennant scramble. J. Mann. il Sports Illus
25:20-1 Ag 8 '66
Smash new act of the season; Frank and
Brooks Robinson of Orioles. W. Leggett.
il Sports Illus 24:28-9 My 30 '66
Space shot by the ambitious Astros; twelve
days in first division. J. Mann. il Sports
Illus 24:24-7 Je 6 '66
El Spahnie of los Tigres; Mexico. M. Cope.
il Sports Illus 25:26-8+ Jl 4 '66
Sporting scene; Houston Astros in the
Astrodome. R. Angell. New Yorker 42:125-
6+ My 14 '66
Sporting scene; world series. Orioles vs.
Dodgers. R. Angell. New Yorker 42:184+
O 29 '66
Still some dying to do; Yankees. il Time 87:
54+ My 6 '66
Survivors. il Time 88:78 O 7 '66
Team that can make a man cry; New York
Mets. J. Mann. il Sports Illus 24:36-8+ Je
27 '66
Thanks, Bill; race for National league pen-
nant. il Time 88:69 S 30 '66
They ain't getting no maiden. R. Kahn. il
Sat Eve Post 239:97-101 Je 18 '66
Those happy Birds! world series victory. J.
Mann. il Sports Illus 25:30-7 O 17 '66
Tweet for the birdies; Orioles. H. L. Masin.
il Sr Schol 89:28 S 30 '66
Two headliners take over Chicago; the Lip
with Cubs, the Brat with White Sox. W.
Leggett. il Sports Illus 24:26-8+ F 28 '66

BASEBALL clubs—*Continued*
Unhappy return of the native; L. Durocher's Cubs lose five games on West coast. W. Leggett. il Sports Illus 24:26-9 Ap 25 '66
Vero; baseball by the numbers; photographs by J. Drake; with report by J. Mann. Sports Illus 24:40-9 Mr 14 '66
Voice of the Pirates; Manager H. Walker. J. Mann. il Sports Illus 25:14-17 S 5 '66
Wail of two cities; question of places for Braves to play. il Time 87:81 F 4 '66
Wham! bam! and alley oops; Pirates off to sensational start in pennant race. T. C. Brody. il Sports Illus 24:34-5 My 2 '66
Whammy with a weenie; Pittsburgh Pirates. il Time 88:54 Ag 12 '66
Whose Braves? Newsweek 67:52 F 7 '66
Willie Mays: my story; excerpts from Willie Mays: my life in and out of baseball, ed. by C. Einstein. W. Mays. il Look 30:62-3+ Mr 8; 116-17+ Mr 22; 72-4+ Ap 5 '66
Yankee dynasty can never come back. L. Koppett. il N Y Times Mag p44-5+ O 2 '66

See also
World series (baseball)
BASEBALL coaches. See Physical directors
BASEBALL fans
Sporting scene; Houston Astros in the Astrodome. R. Angell. New Yorker 42:125-6+ My 14 '66
To those who wait; Steven and Phillip Derr of Baltimore at world series. Sports Illus 25:21 O 17 '66
BASEBALL farm clubs. See Baseball
BASEBALL hall of fame. See National baseball hall of fame and museum
BASEBALL managers
I's, we's and they's of baseball. J. Brosnan. il N Y Times Mag p 14-15+ Jl 3 '66
Jaundiced eye; New York Yankees success after management change. il Newsweek 67:96-7 My 23 '66
Men who fire managers; general managers. W. Leggett. il Sports Illus 25:44-6+ S 12 '66

See also
Alston, W. E.
Bristol, D.
Durocher, L.
Keane, J.
Walker, H.
BASEBALL players
And there were the Dodgers in third place; Giant Dodger rivalry. J. Mann. il Sports Illus 24:58-60 Je 27 '66
Baseball 1966: American league. il Sports Illus 24:73-90+ Ap 18 '66
Baseball 1966: National league. il Sports Illus 24:50-68 Ap 18 '66
Baseball roundup 1966: year of the holdouts. il pors Ebony 21:120-2+ Je '66
Baseball's fragile superstars. M. Gross. il pors Pop Sci 188:76-9 My '66
Batmen strike; Baltimore Orioles lead in the American league pennant race. M. Mulvoy. il Sports Illus 25:12-15 Ag 1 '66
Batter up and down; pitcher throws at a batter. Sports Illus 24:19 Je 13 '66
Dandy Dominican: great pitchers. il pors Time 87:88-92 Je 10 '66
Danger with a double A; H. Aaron. J. Mann. il Sports Illus 25:22-7 Ag 1 '66
Farewell to .300 hitters; batting is a dying art. J. Mann. il Sports Illus 25:42-4+ S 26 '66
Glory of their times, by L. S. Ritter. Review Newsweek pors 68:120 O 24 '66. P. D. Zimmerman
Glory of their times; excerpt. L. S. Ritter. il Sat Eve Post 239:36-40+ Ag 13 '66
Good play by a first baseman. C. Goren. il Sports Illus 24:110+ Ap 18 '66
Here come the Young Turks. W. Leggett. il Sports Illus 25:26-31 Jl 11 '66
Hit records. H. L. Masin. il Sr Schol 88:32-3 My 20 '66
How specialized can you get? fine art of pinch hitting. W. B. Furlong. il N Y Times Mag p23+ Ag 14 '66
It's a long, long season. J. Brosnan. il N Y Times Mag p30-1+ Ap 17 '66
It's not bad to be going good; San Francisco Giants. J. Mann. il Sports Illus 24:30-1 My 23 '66
Joe Torre: the last of the great catchers. M. Cope. il Sat Eve Post 239:84-6+ Jl 2 '66
Journey back to Bushville. E. Asinof. il N Y Times Mag p8-9+ Jl 24 '66
Kids who boom 'r the spring; major league rookies. T. C. Brody. il Sports Illus 24:28-9 Ap 11 '66
Koufax the incomparable; Jews and high holiday games. M. Richler. Commentary 42:87-9 N '66

Lame but game Dodgers. il Life 61:58B-58C S 23 '66
Little league shoulder bothers young pitchers. Sci N 90:105 Ag 13 '66
Long, long season could be too long; unrest among tired ballplayers. W. Leggett. Sports Illus 25:50-1 Ag 15 '66
New union's million-dollar pitch; Koufax-Drysdale dispute. il Life 60:77-8 Ap 1 '66
Off to the races! H. L. Masin. il pors Sr Schol 88:26 Ap 1 '66
Painful search for a pennant; Dodgers leading the race. J. Olsen. il pors Sports Illus 25:28-33 S 19 '66
Player of the week:
Braves' Pat Jarvis. por Sports Illus 25:103 O 3 '66
Cardinals' Larry Jaster. por Sports Illus 25:80 Ag 29 '66
Cardinals' Mike Shannon. por Sports Illus 25:56 Ag 1 '66
Cubs' Randy Hundley. por Sports Illus 25:76 Ag 22 '66
Cubs' Ron Santo. por Sports Illus 25:75 Jl 4 '66
Detroit catcher Bill Freehan. por Sports Illus 24:93 My 30 '66
Detroit's Earl Wilson. por Sports Illus 25:136 S 19 '66
Dodgers' Dick Schofield. por Sports Illus 25:88 S 26 '66
Dodgers' Jim Lefebvre. por Sports Illus 24:110 Ap 25 '66
Giants' Gaylord Perry. por Sports Illus 24:84 Je 27 '66
Giants' Juan Marichal. por Sports Illus 24:93 Je 6 '66
Indians' Fred Whitfield. por Sports Illus 24:92 My 2 '66
Indians' Sonny Siebert. por Sports Illus 24:76 Je 20 '66
Orioles' Brooks Robinson. por Sports Illus 25:64 Jl 25 '66
Orioles' John Powell. por Sports Illus 25:77 Jl 18 '66
Orioles' relaxed Frank Robinson. por Sports Illus 25:153 S 12 '66
Red Sox's George Scott. Sports Illus 24:108 My 16 '66
Reds' Tommy Harper. por Sports Illus 25:68 Ag 15 '66
Senators' Fred Valentine. por Sports Illus 24:100 My 23 '66
Twins' Dave Boswell. por Sports Illus 25:69 Ag 8 '66
Twins' Jim Kaat. por Sports Illus 25:70 S 5 '66
White Sox' Jack Lamabe. por Sports Illus 24:114 Je 13 '66
Yankees' Mickey Mantle. por Sports Illus 25:79 Jl 11 '66
Player of the year; Orioles' F. Robinson. por Sports Illus 25:107 O 10 '66
Robinson boys. il Newsweek 68:56 Jl 4 '66
Rookie cookies 1966. H. L. Masin. il Sr Schol 88:15 Mr 25 '66
Sam, you make the ball too small; Cleveland southpaw. J. Mann. il Sports Illus 24:40-2+ My 23 '66
Silver-tongued southpaw; ballplayers and articulation. J. Jacobs. Reporter 35:51-2+ Jl 14 '66
Smash new act of the season; Frank and Brooks Robinson of Orioles. W. Leggett. il Sports Illus 24:28-9 My 30 '66
Space shot by the ambitious Astros; twelve days in first division. J. Mann. il Sports Illus 24:24-7 Je 6 '66
Sporting scene; world series. Orioles vs. Dodgers. R. Angell. New Yorker 42:184+ O 29 '66
Super-holdouts; Koufax-Drysdale joint contract demand. il Newsweek 67:84 Mr 28 '66
Tweet for the birdies; Orioles. H. L. Masin. il Sr Schol 89:28 S 30 '66
Willie Mays: my story; excerpts from Willie Mays: my life in and out of baseball, ed. by C. Einstein. W. Mays. il Look 30:116-17+ Mr 22 '66
See also
National baseball hall of fame and museum
also names of baseball players, e.g. J. Marichal
Recruiting
Great Mexican war of 1946; Mexican league baseball. F. Graham, jr. il Sports Illus 25:116-20+ S 19 '66

Salaries
Double play; Drysdale & Koufax. il Time 87:63 Mr 25 '66
$1,000,000 holdout; Dodger pitchers: Koufax and Drysdale. J. Mann. il Sports Illus 24:26-9 Ap 4 '66

BASEBALL players—Salaries—*Continued*
Sandy Koufax story: my salary fights; excerpts from Koufax, ed. by E. Linn. S. Koufax. il pors Look 30:90-2+ Je 14 '66
Sic transit tradition; question of raises for Koufax and Drysdale. Time 87:75 Ap 8 '66

BASEBALL players' golf tournament. *See* Golf—Tournaments

BASEBALL teams. *See* Baseball clubs

BASEBALL umpires. *See* Umpires (sports)

BASEL, Switzerland

Music
Notes from our correspondents. E. Helm. Hi Fi 16:24+ N '66

BASEMENTS and cellars
Happy ideas for a basement playroom. R. Charles. il Parents Mag 41:70-3+ Je '66
How to reclaim a basement. il Bet Hom & Gard 44:125 Mr '66
How to work wonders with a walk-out basement. il Bet Hom & Gard 44:126 Je '66
Repairing basement leaks. H. R. Pfister. il Pop Sci 189:121 Jl '66

BASES, Air. *See* Air bases

BASES, Guided missile. *See* Guided missile bases

BASES, Military. *See* Military bases

BASIC research. *See* Research

BASIDIOMYCETES
Fungicide selective for basidiomycetes. L. V. Edgington and others. il Science 153:307-8 Jl 15 '66
Schizophyllum commune: new mutations in the B incompatibility factor. Y. Koltin and J. R. Raper. bibliog il Science 154:510-11 O 28 '66

BASIL
Grow sweet basil for flavor and fragrance. H. S. Witty. il Flower Grower 53:65 Mr '66

BASILE, John X. R.
Hartford story. R. D. Daniels. por Opera N 31:20-1 O 15 '66

BASILE, Renato. *See* Pavan, C. jt. auth.

BASKERVILLE, James
First license, and before. H. E. Church. il Pop Electr 24:54-5+ Ja '66

BASKETBALL
Baron's runts; University of Kentucky's Wildcats. il Time 87:60 F 4 '66
Basketball: the graceful game. J. Larner. il Holiday 39:30+ F '66
Basketball's bright star in Indiana; R. Mount. il Sports Illus 24:28-30+ F 14 '66
Big little men; University of Kentucky. il Newsweek 67:82+ Mr 7 '66
Biggest Bruin had friends; UCLA's L. Alcindor. J. Jares. il Sports Illus 25:42-4 D 19 '66
Bit too much for Blighty; Oxford-Cambridge varsity match. J. Lovesey. il Sports Illus 24:66-7 Mr 14 '66
Bravo for the baron; A. Rupp's undefeated Kentucky Wildcats. F. Deford. il Sports Illus 24:20-3+ Mr 7 '66
Can basketball survive Lew Alcindor? R. Lardner. il Sat Eve Post 240:70-3 Ja 14 '67
Champions get after it; Texas Western Miners hustling to retain their NCAA basketball title. F. Deford. il Sports Illus 25:26-8+ D 12 '66
College basketball 1967. F. Deford. il Sports Illus 25:39-46 D 5 '66
Defense by a coyote caller; Texas Western coach D. Haskins. il Sports Illus 24:48-9 F 7 '66
Dons are dreaming of sweet revenge; West Coast athletic conference championship for USF. J. Jares. il Sports Illus 24:53-4+ F 14 '66
Duke's full house of court kings; Duke university's basketball team. il Life 60:52A Ja 28 '66
Elvin, Melvin and The Duck; Houston team. C. Kirkpatrick. il Sports Illus 26:42-3 Ja 2 '67
Jo-Jo joins the Jayhawk mob on Snob Hill; Kansas-Kansas state basketball game. F. Deford. il Sports Illus 24:42-4 Ja 31 '66
Miners' major upset; N.C.A.A. championship. il Time 87:63 Mr 25 '66
Misery on the road; problems of visiting teams. F. Deford. il Sports Illus 24:18-21 F 28 '66
Night-time basketball fights juvenile delinquency; Leonia, N.J. il Am City 81:124 Ag '66
Off-court uproar in Dixie; Atlantic coast conference rules South Carolina's basketball star ineligible. M. Mulvoy. il Sports Illus 25:26-7 N 7 '66

Pair of sparklers in poky; Idaho state university. F. Deford. il Sports Illus 24:52+ F 21 '66
Ralph Miller of Iowa: prophet of pressure; Hawkeye basketball coach. F. Deford. il Sports Illus 24:14-17 Ja 24 '66
Tall, stoned and gatoraded; Florida Gators best basketball team in the Southeastern conference. F. Deford. il Sports Illus 26:14-17 Ja 16 '67
Who's no. 2? college basketball. Time 89:73 Ja 6 '67

Economic aspects
Coming boom in pro basketball. T. J. Murray. il Duns R 88:52-3+ N '66

BASKETBALL coaches. *See* Physical directors

BASKETBALL players
All-European boy; B. Bradley. il Newsweek 67:79-80 Ja 31 '66
Basketball All America. I. R. McVay. il pors Look 30:106+ Mr 22 '66
Basketball: the graceful game. J. Larner. il Holiday 39:30+ F '66
Biggest Bruin had friends; UCLA's L. Alcindor. J. Jares. il Sports Illus 25:42-4 D 19 '66
College basketball 1967. F. Deford. il Sports Illus 25:39-46 D 5 '66
Color it Bruin; L. Alcindor of UCLA challengers. H. L. Masin. il Sr Schol 89:24 D 2 '66
Duke's full house of court kings; Duke university's basketball team. il pors Life 60:52A Ja 28 '66
Elvin, Melvin and The Duck; Houston team. C. Kirkpatrick. il Sports Illus 26:42-3 Ja 2 '67
Nightmare: how to stop the good big man. M. Hyman. il Sports Illus 25:71-3 D 5 '66
1966 All-America H.S. basketball squad. H. L. Masin. il Sr Schol 88:26 My 13 '66
Pro basketball. il Sports Illus 25:40-52+ O 24 '66
Scouting reports. il Sports Illus 25:48-52+ O 24; 47-50+ D 5 '66
Tall, stoned and gatoraded; Florida Gators best basketball team in the Southeastern conference. F. Deford. il Sports Illus 26:14-17 Ja 16 '67
Year of the guards; pro basketball. H. L. Masin. il Sr Schol 88:24 Mr 11 '66
See also names of basketball players. e.g. R. Barry

BASKETBALL scouting
Scouting reports. il Sports Illus 25:48-52+ O 24; 47-50+ D 5 '66

BASKETBALL teams
Added attraction for a season's finale; R. Baylor lead Lakers to victory over St Louis. C. Kirkpatrick. il Sports Illus 24:88-9 Ap 25 '66
Boob bows out, B. Kerner sells the St Louis Hawks. Sports Illus 26:8 Ja 16 '67
Boston Celtics: pro basketball's dynasty. I. R. McVay. il Look 30:64-6+ F 8 '66
Cable cars on a hardwood court; San Francisco Warriors. J. Jares. il Sports Illus 25:56-7 O 31 '66
Celtics stretch an era; Boston knocks out Cincinnati. C. Kirkpatrick. il Sports Illus 24:30-1 Ap 11 '66
Lame and the fat; hectic race for first-place honors in the Eastern division. Newsweek 67:83 F 28 '66
Last cigar for a last hurrah? eighth championship for Celtics' coach Red Auerbach. M. Cope. il Sat Eve Post 239:107-8+ Mr 26 '66
New role for Bill Russell. il Ebony 22:60-1+ Ja '67
Old math; Boston Celtics. il Time 87:66 Ap 22 '66
One last smoke; Celtics win N.B.A. championship. Time 87:54 My 6 '66
Pro basketball. il Sports Illus 25:40-52+ O 24 '66
Royal reversal in the East. T. C. Brody. il Sports Illus 24:16-17 F 7 '66
Sarge takes Philly to the top; A. Hannum, coach of Philadelphia 76ers. F. Deford. il Sports Illus 26:8-13 Ja 2 '67
Scouting reports. il Sports Illus 25:48-52+ O 24 '66
Some old pros refuse to die; Boston Celtics win world championship, R. Auerbach leaves coaching. F. Deford. il Sports Illus 24:30-3 My 9 '66
Spirited 76ers. il Newsweek 69:88 Ja 23 '67
Togetherness triumphs twice; second game of the Indiana-Kentucky high school series. C. Kirkpatrick. il Sports Illus 25:60+ Jl 4 '66

BASKETBALL tournaments
Eeny, meeny, miney, mo... college basketball NCAA tournament. F. DeFord. il Sports Illus 24:32-4+ Mr 14 '66
Go-go with Bobby Joe; Texas Western national basketball championship. F. Deford. il Sports Illus 24:26-9+ Mr 28 '66
Miner upset; Kentucky's Wildcats lose NCAA semifinals to Texas Western's Miners. Newsweek 67:84 Mr 28 '66
Now there are four; Duke, Kentucky, Utah and Texas Western survive. F. DeFord. il Sports Illus 24:22-5 Mr 21 '66
War between two states; basketball in Kentucky and Indiana. C. Kirkpatrick. il Sports Illus 24:30-2+ Je 27 '66
Win over northern cookin'; University of Louisville wins the Quaker City tournament in Philadelphia. J. Jares. il Sports Illus 26:22-4+ Ja 9 '67

BASKETS
Basketville. J. Peter. il Look 30:M22 Mr 22 '66
Fitted baskets make unusual gifts. R. Miller. il Farm J 90:119 Mr '66
Serving baskets in many guises. il House & Gard 130:18+ Ag '66

BASQUES in the United States
Basque sheepherders, lonely sentinels of the American West. R. Laxalt. il Nat Geog Mag 129:870-88 Je '66

BASS, Althea
(ed) See Sweezy, C. Long way from the buffalo road

BASS, Arthur C.
Helicopter warfare opens new era. Miss & Roc 18:82-4+ Mr 28 '66

BASS, David W.
LAPL and the data service bureau. por Wilson Lib Bul 41:404-8 D '66

BASS
See also
Cookery—Fish

BASS fishing
Adventure in Latin America; Honduras. E. A. Bauer. il Outdoor Life 137:56-9+ Ap '66
Angling paradise of the Apaches. R. B. Whitaker. il Outdoor Life 138:36-9+ S '66
Awesome drum. G. Heinold. il Outdoor Life 138:8+ S '66
Basic bass bugging. E. Bauer. il Field & S 71:44-7 Jl '66
Bass with a bang; Delaware River. T. Jones. il Outdoor Life 138:32-3+ Ag '66
Beautiful new Ohio. B. Thomas. il Outdoor Life 137:54-5+ Je '66
Bed fishing for bass. W. J. O'Connor. il Outdoor Life 137:40-1+ Mr '66
Best U.S. smallmouth water? G. Gresham. il Outdoor Life 138:50-1+ N '66
Black handsaws. B. East. il Outdoor Life 138:44-5+ S '66
Blueprint for big bass. A. A. Ciuffa. il Outdoor Life 137:40-3+ My '66
Boom-or-bust bass. W. Davis. il Outdoor Life 137:68+ Mr '66
Door to fishing paradise. M. Ellis. il Field & S 71:52-5+ My '66
Follow the drum beat. K. Osborne. il Outdoor Life 137:50-1+ Ap '66
Goodby, Blue Springs. W. Blassingame. il Field & S 70:8-9+ F '66
Holiday bass. A. Pione. il Field & S 71:42-3+ D '66
How to beat the summer slump. E. A. Bauer. il Outdoor Life 138:17-19+ Jl '66
How to catch a trophy bass. M. Eggleston. il Field & S 71:46-7+ Ja '67
How to catch bass at midday. J. G. Mell. il Field & S 71:30+ My '66
I'll take the bass pits. C. Elliott. il Outdoor Life 138:68-9+ O '66
Jackpotful of bass. R. Tinsley. il Outdoor Life 138:48-9+ D '66
Lake Mead whoppers. F. Dufresne. il Field & S 71:60-1 My '66
Light-tackle stripers. P. McLain. il Field & S 71:92-5+ Jl '66
Lures that caught 2,000 bass. B. Carey. il Field & S 71:10-12+ Je '66
Montana's ignored game fish. P. Czura. il Field & S 71:58-9+ My '66
Reservoir bass. T. Trueblood. il Field & S 71:16+ Ag '66
Rough water bass. J. D. Lamon. il Outdoor Life 138:36-9+ Ag '66
Sluggers of the Saco. G. Heinold. il Outdoor Life 138:46-7+ Jl '66
Strange doings on Otsego Lake. T. Janes. il Outdoor Life 137:42-3+ Mr '66
Striped bass and southern solitude. E. White. il Sports Illus 25:60-2+ O 10 '66
Sure tricks for big bass. A. A. Ciuffa. il Outdoor Life 137:42-3+ Je '66

Trail of the ten-pound bass. G. Laycock. il Outdoor Life 137:48-9+ Ap '66
When bass go bugs. A. J. McClane. il Field & S 70:98-103 Ap '66
Worms beat the drum. J. C. Ericson. il Outdoor Life 138:48-9+ Ag '66

BASSARIDS; opera. See Henze, H. Z.

BASSE-taille enameling. See Enamel and enameling

BASSETT, Charles A.
Lives of good brave men. W. J. Coughlin. Miss & Roc 18:54 Mr 14 '66
Perfectly paired Gemini team falls to earth. R. Morse. il por Life 60:34 Mr 11 '66
Rendezvous in St Louis. il por Time 87:27 Mr 11 '66
Safety above, risk below? il por Newsweek 67:68 Mr 14 '66

BASSETT, Florence Knoll
Distinguished interior architecture for CBS. il Arch Rec 139:129-34 Je '66

BASSETT, Preston R.
Aerial adventures of Carlotta, the lady aeronaut. Am Heritage 17:64-7 Ag '66

BASSITY, Matthew
Plan to use roses in new ways. Horticulture 44:30-1+ D '66

BASTAR (district) India
Old order; Adivasi tribesmen rebel. Newsweek 67:53 Ap 11 '66

BASTILLE day
Letter from Paris. Genêt. New Yorker 42:68 Jl 30 '66

BASUTOLAND
Note:
For material after September 30, 1966, see heading Lesotho
See also
United Nations—Basutoland

BAT rays. See Rays (fishes)

BATAVIA, N.Y.
Journey back to Bushville. E. Asinof. il N Y Times Mag p8-9+ Jl 24 '66

BATAZZI, Libble F.
ABA seeks aid for bookshop wrecked in Florence. il Pub W 190:43-4 D 12 '66

BATCHELDER, Richard D.
Battle for your child's mind. por Parents Mag 41:40+ Mr '66
Message to Miami Beach convention delegates. NEA J 55:32-3 My '66
Unionism versus professionalism in teaching. NEA J 55:18-20 Ap '66

BATCHELOR, Clarence Daniel
Best of Batch. il Nat R 18:990-1 O 4 '66

BATES, Barrie. See Apple, B.

BATES, Dan
New films in review. See issues of Yale review

BATES, Dolores
Bachelor girl. R. Lantz. il pors Ebony 21:102-4+ Ag '66

BATES, Fred C.
Fine art of forecasting. Flying 79:50-1 Ag '66
Hints on flying in thunderstorms; don't. Flying 78:56-9 F '66
Things upstairs. Flying 79:52-4 Jl '66

BATES, Kenneth
Going places, finding things in Vienna. House & Gard 129:18-19+ F '66

BATES, Marian M.
Funny thing happened on my way to the Aeroclassic. por Flying 78:105 Mr '66

BATES, Marston
Man the drug taker; excerpt from Gluttons and libertines, with biographical sketch. Natur Hist 76:6, 8-10+ Ja '67

BATH rooms. See Bathrooms

BATHING beaches. See Beaches

BATHROOM fixtures
Blame the outmoded U.S. bathroom; with account by M. Mok. il Life 60:84C-86 My 20 '66
Examining the unmentionables. il Time 87:79 My 20 '66
Getting set for tomorrow's bath; results of Cornell university's five-year research study. il Bsns W p 103-4+ My 21 '66
New developments for the bathroom. il Arch Rec 139:123-4 mid-My '66
See also
Plumbing
              Manufacture
Bathroom conspiracy? charges of price fixing conspiracy in the Nation's plumbing-fixture industry. Time 88:100 O 14 '66

BATHROOMS
Add storage, lighting, or a shower to your bath. D. Jordan. il Bet Hom & Gard 44:68-9 O '66
Bathroom spectacular. il House & Gard 129:172-83+ Ap '66

BATHROOMS—*Continued*
Bath's in the middle. il Sunset 137:98 Jl '66
Blame the outmoded U.S. bathroom; with
account by M. Mok. il Life 60:84C-86 My
20 '66
Both useful and good-looking. il Sunset 138:
70 Ja '67
Deluxe bathroom for a modest home. A.
Lees. il Pop Mech 126:132-7+ S '66
Getting set for tomorrow's bath; results of
Cornell university's five-year research
study. il Bsns W p 103-4+ My 21 '66
Guess what! there's an efficiency expert in
my bathroom! L. Benjamin. Ladies Home J
83:8 S '66
Two baths in the treetops. il Sunset 137:142
O '66
Why a shower is bracing: atmosphere of a
bathroom electrified whenever water runs.
il Time 87:51 My 6 '66
See also
Plumbing

BATHS
Anecdotes, facetiae, satire, etc.
Yankee knight of the bath; mysteries of
English plumbing. R. Curtis. Esquire 66:
338-42 D '66

BATHS, Vapor
Steam bath in your home? Super-sauna por-
table steam bath. il Consumer Rep 31:54-5
F '66

BATHYSCAPHE
Deep scattering layer migration and composition: observations from a diving
saucer. E. G. Barham. bibliog il Science
151:1399-403 Mr 18 '66

BATMAN (television program) See Television
broadcasting—Childrens programs

BATON ROUGE, La.
Biggest baseball clinic. il Ebony 21:89-90+
My '66
Saving a city from a cloud of death. T. Irwin.
Pop Sci 188:108-11+ Ap '66

BATOR, Victor
Geneva, 1954: the broken mold. Reporter 34:
15-18 Je 30 '66

BATRA, Lekh R.
Ambrosia fungi: extent of specificity to
ambrosia beetles. bibliog Science 153:193-5
Jl 8 '66

BATS
Auditory system of noctuid moths; excerpts
from address, April 27, 1966. K. D. Roeder.
bibliog il Science 154:1515-21 D 23 '66
Bats aren't blind as bats. il Sci N 91:25 Ja
7 '67
Bats blown to Iceland; hoary bats. il Sci N
90:308 O 15 '66
Bats used for rhythm studies. il Sci N 90:87
Ag 6 '66
Homing ability strong in some Trinidad
bats. Sci N 89:331 My 7 '66
Nightmare on wings; giant flying foxes of
Australia. il Sci N 90:373-4 N 5 '66
Optomotor responses by echolocating bats.
R. A. Suthers. bibliog il Science 152:1102-
4 My 20 '66

BATS as carriers of infection
Isolation of St Louis encephalitis virus from
bats (Tadarida b. mexicana) in Texas.
S. E. Sulkin and others. bibliog il Science
152:223-5 Ap 8 '66

BATTAGLIA, Lee E.
No boundaries to vision; photographs. Pop
Phot 58:62-3 F '66

BATTEN, James K.
Title VI disturbs the moss of Beaufort. Reporter 36:46-8 Ja 12 '67

BATTERIES, Solar. See Solar batteries
BATTERIES, Storage. See Storage batteries
BATTERIES for boats. See Storage batteries
BATTERS, Baseball. See Baseball players
BATTERSBY, Veronica F.
Traveler's choice. Travel 126:12-13 O '66
BATTERY chargers. See Storage battery
chargers
BATTERY charging. See Storage batteries—
Charging
BATTERY-operated motors. See Electric mo-
tors
BATTERY-powered tape recorders. See Mag-
netic recorders and recording
BATTING. See Baseball
BATTLE, Mark
Speaking out. por Sat Eve Post 239:10+ Ja
29 '66
BATTLE of Britain. See World war, 1939-1945
—Great Britain
BATTLE of the sexes. See Women and men
BATTLE of Valcour Island. See United States
—History—Revolution—Naval operations
BATTLESHIPS. See Warships

BATTS, Nathalie C.
LC in NY. Library J 91:3649-50 Ag '66
BATZLINGER, Hugo
Bat about ping-pong. D. Miles. il Sports
Illus 25:90-2+ O 17 '66
BAUDELAIRE, Charles Pierre
Poet as critic. A. Werner. Reporter 34:58+
F 24 '66
BAUER, D. J. and Apostolov, K.
Adenovirus multiplication: inhibition by
methisazone. bibliog Science 154:796-7 N 11
'66
BAUER, Erwin A.
Adventure in Latin America. il pors Outdoor
Life 137:29-31+ F; 32-5+ Mr; 56-9+ Ap '66
Basic bass bugging. Field & S 71:44-7 Jl '66
Challenge. il Outdoor Life 137:60-1 Mr '66
Far-out fishing camp. Outdoor Life 138:42-5+
D '66
Father's fling on the flats. il Outdoor Life
137:56-9+ Je '66
For better fishing go fly a kite. Field & S
70:64-5+ Ap '66
How to beat the summer slump. Outdoor Life
138:17-19+ Jl '66
Jackfish country. Outdoor Life 138:50-2+ Ag
'66
Mountain hospitality. por Outdoor Life 137:
44-7+ Ap '66
My heart-attack trophies. Field & S 70:43-
5+ Mr '66
My panfish-on-light-tackle kick. pors Out-
door Life 137:56-9+ My '66
Never swing at a honeybee. Field & S 70:
73+ Mr '66
New look of duck hunting. Outdoor Life 138:
42-5+ O '66
Treasure bird. Field & S 70:61+ Ap '66
We found the elephant place. Outdoor Life
138:28-31+ Ag '66
BAUER, Hank
But Mahoney stood outside. G. W. Johnson.
New Repub 155:8 O 22 '66
Toughest bird in Baltimore. J. R. McDermott.
por Life 61:48A-48B Jl 8 '66
BAUER, Harry C.
Publish and cherish. por Library J 91:2774-6
Je 1 '66
BAUER, Malcolm
Curiosity and the kitchen sink. Am Ed 2:8-
10 Jl '66
BAUER, Ralston S. See Hong, J. S. jt. auth.
BAUER, W. W.
Why today's bread is better. Todays Health
44:60-4 D '66
BAUM, Gregory
Birth control, what happened? Commonweal
83:369-71, 543, 571+ D 24 '65, F 4, 18 '66
Book of the month. Cath World 203:309-10 Ag
'66
Witness to divine reality. Christian Cent 83:
427-9 Ap 6 '66
BAUM, Lyman Frank
Wonderful Wizard of Oz; dramatization. See
Mapp, F.
about
Wizard who created Oz. D. P. Mannix. il
por Read Digest 88:104-8 Je '66
BAUM, William A.
Image tubes in astronomy. Science 154:112-
18 O 7 '66
BAUMBACH, Jonathan
Malamud's heroes. Commonweal 85:97-9 O
28 '66
BAUMGARTNER, Leona
Better life for all children. por Parents Mag
41:58 N '66
BAUMOL, William J. and Bowen, W. G.
How big is the boom in culture? summary
of Performing arts: the economic dilemma.
U S News 61:14 N 28 '66
BAUR, Ferdinand Christian
Life in the old boys yet! B. A. Reist. Chris-
tian Cent 83:1179-80 S 28 '66
BAUTZ, Ekkehard K. F. and Reilly, Eugene
Gene-specific messenger RNA: isolation by
the deletion method. bibliog Science 151:328-
30 Ja 21 '66
BAVARIA
Politics and government
No fun in Bavaria; emergence of the Na-
tional democratic party. C. Amery. Na-
tion 203:637-9 D 12 '66
BAVASI, Emil Joseph
Buzzie and big D go at it in L.A. J. Olsen.
Sports Illus 25:22-3 Ag 29 '66
Sandy Koufax story: my salary fights; ex-
cerpts from Koufax, ed. by E. Linn. S.
Koufax. il por Look 30:92+ Je 14 '66

BAVIER, Robert N. Jr
And then there were two. il Yachting 120: 58-9+ N '66
Constellation revisited. Yachting 120:36+ N '66
Sailor cruises ashore. Holiday 39:40+ My '66

BAWTREE, Michael
Oh what a lovely tsar. H. Hewes. Sat R 49: 35 Ag 6 '66

BAXTER, Samuel S.
Dialogue on water resources; interview, ed. by E. F. Spitzer. pors Am City 81:97-9+ My '66

BAXTER, Tom
For love and money. See issues of Flying
Pro's nest. por Flying 79:14 Ag; 24 S; 23 O; 34 N; 28 D '66; 80:18 Ja '67

BAY, Ian
Pennsylvania story. Nat R 18:1041-2 O 18 '66

BAY area rapid transit. See San Francisco—Rapid transit

BAY company. See Hudson's Bay company

BAY ISLANDS
See also
Tourist trade—Bay Islands

BAY OF PIGS invasion. See Cuba—History—Invasion, 1961

BAYBERRY
You can bet on the bayberry. B. C. Kilvert, jr. il Flower Grower 53:40-1 D '66

BAYER, Ann
Goddess of aisle E; story. Mlle 63:168-9 My '66
My heart belongs to: (A) (B) (C) (D) (other) story. Sat Eve Post 239:57-9 D 31 '66

BAYEUX, France
1066: the view from France. H. Sutton. il Sat R 49:43-4 Jl 9 '66

BAYEUX tapestry
Norman conquest. K. M. Setton. il Nat Geog Mag 130:206-51 Ag '66
1066. M. Bishop. il Horizon 8:4-27 Aut '66
1066: the view from France. H. Sutton. il Sat R 49:43-4 Jl 9 '66
Winning a lost battle; Battle of Hastings. N. Lunger. il Sr Schol 89:4-5 O 14 '66

BAYLIS, Cassandra
Antiques take to the airways on Cape Cod. il por Hobbies 71:96 Ag '66

BAYLIS, John
Antiques take to the airways on Cape Cod. il por Hobbies 71:96 Ag '66

BAYLOR, Elgin
Added attraction for a season's finale. il por Sports Illus 24:88-9 Ap 25 '66
Many moves of Elgin Baylor; photographs by W. Iooss, with account by F. Deford. Sports Illus 25:40-7 O 24 '66

BAYNE, E. A.
Non-crisis in Italy. For Affairs 45:353-62 Ja '67

BAYON, Edward J.
Sludge-disposal solution: thicken, filter, dry and burn. Am City 81:95-7 Je '66

BAYONNE, France
City planning
Bayonne, France: urban planning. il Arch Rec 139:172-7 Ap '66

BAYREUTH festival
Wagner by half-light. F. V. Grunfeld. Reporter 35:55-6 S 22 '66
Wagner, legends and legacy. G. Movshon. il Hi Fi 16:MA22-3+ O '66

BAYREUTH festspielhaus
Tristan und Isolde direct from the Festspielhaus. P. G. Davis. il Hi Fi 16:16+ N '66

BAYVIEW yacht club race. See Yacht racing

BAZELON, David T.
New class. Commentary 42:48-53 Ag '66

BAZELON, Irwin
Ballad of Big Bud. il por Time 87:86-7 My 20 '66

BAZZAZ, Abdul Rahman al
No time for prudence. Time 88:28 Ag 19 '66

BEACH, Bob
Men in fashion: two American designers. por Esquire 65:105 Mr '66

BEACH, Frank A.
Books. Sci Am 215:107-10+ Ag '66

BEACH architecture
Axelrod residence, New Jersey. il Arch Rec 139:60-3 mid-My '66
Beach construction in a state park: Robert Moses state park near Massena, N.Y. H. S. Conover. il Parks & Rec 1:420-1+ My '66
Geometry by the sea. il Arch Forum 124: 52-5 Ap '66
Greek cross: panoramic views. il House & Gard 129:130-1 Je '66

Look at what $5,000 bought. il Sunset 136: 94-5 Je '66
Shelters on a scalloped shore; Sea Ranch Calif. photographs with account by P. Knight. M. E. Newman. Sports Illus 24: 46-52 Mr 28 '66
Steep roofs: exhilarating spaces. il House & Gard 129:124-7 Je '66
Williamson residence, Ponte Vedra Beach, Florida. il Arch Rec 139:110-13 mid-My '66
See also
Summer homes

BEACH erosion
Beach cusps: response to Plateau's rule? P. E. Cloud, jr. bibliog il Science 154: 890-1 N 18 '66
Sands trace erosion. il Sci N L 89:101 F 12 '66
Where the beaches go. il Sci Digest 59:38-9 Ap '66

BEACH plants. See Seashore vegetation

BEACHES
Beach construction in a state park: Robert Moses state park near Massena, N.Y. H. S. Conover. il Parks & Rec 1:420-1+ My '66
Free beach; San Gregorio beach, Calif. il Time 88:50 Ag 26 '66
Pismo: long beach, the white dunes, the delicious clams. il Sunset 136:62-7 F '66
Seventy-mile beach; San Diego County. C. Stinnett. Holiday 40:32+ Jl '66
See also
Seashore

BEACONS, Radar. See Radar in aviation

BEADED flowers. See Flowers, Artificial

BEAGLE, Peter S.
John Barth: long reach, near miss. Holiday 40:131-2+ S '66
My daughter's name is Sarah; story. Ladies Home J 83:62-3 F '66
On being the man of the house. Sat Eve Post 239:70+ D 31 '66
Tolkien's magic ring. Holiday 39:128+ Je '66

BEAGLES (dogs)
Death at White House: LBJ's favorite dog. il U S News 60:10 Je 27 '66
Grandest hunting of all; cottontail. H. Bradshaw. il Field & S 71:66-7+ N '66

BEAL, Anselm L.
Keep tabs on her running trim. Motor B 118: 36-7+ N '66

BEAL, Doone
Going places, finding things in Syria and Jordan. House & Gard 130:209-11 D '66
Let's travel: collectors' items for savvy shoppers, Europe '66. Mlle 62:95-101 F '66

BEAL, M. F.
Joining up; story. Atlan 218:102 D '66

BEALE, Sir Howard
Your ball, Sam; excerpt from address. Am Heritage 17:112 O '66

BEALMEAR, J. H.
Doctor Leviticus and the wicked imp; drama. Plays 26:57-64 Ja '67

BEALS, Ralph L.
Anthropologists' debate: concern over future of foreign research. B. Nelson. Science 154:1525-7 D 23 '66

BEAMISH, Susan
Our island paradise. Redbook 127:50-1+ Ag '66; Same abr. with title We retired at age thirty. Read Digest 89:108-12 D '66

BEAMS. See Girders

BEAMS, Molecular. See Molecular beams

BEAN, Louis H.
Mathematics of consensus. Nation 203:573 N 28 '66
—and Drummond, Roscoe
LBJ and the elections: trouble ahead. Look 30:89-90 O 4 '66

BEAR, Firman E.
Soils. Horticulture 44:40-1+ Ap '66

BEAR, Fred
Africa's meanest game. pors Outdoor Life 137:32-5+ F '66
Bear that broke a jinx. pors Outdoor Life 138:35-7+ D '66
My greatest trophy. pors Outdoor Life 137: 36-9+ Ap '66

BEAR hunting
Bear that broke a jinx. F. Bear. il Outdoor Life 138:35-7+ D '66
Black bear mountain: Monongahela national forest. D. Knight. il Field & S 71:34+ N '66
Greatest hunting of all; black bear. B. Mason. il Outdoor Life 138:42-5+ N '66
Haystack bear. J. Rearden. il Outdoor Life 137:44-6+ Je '66
Old hole-in-the-head. P. D. Smith. il Outdoor Life 138:62-3 D '66

BEAR hunting—*Continued*
Old Wino's last stand. F. J. Evans. il Outdoor Life 138:44-7+ Ag '66
Roy Rogers goes north. W. E. A. Anderson. il Outdoor Life 137:52-5+ Ap '66
Two-time loser. E. Stevens. il Outdoor Life 137:36-9+ My '66

BEARD, James A.
James Beard's menus for entertaining; excerpts. Ladies Home J 83:88-9 F '66
Pâté cook book. House & Gard 130:211+ S '66

about
If I had to practice cannibalism... J. Skow. il pors Sat Eve Post 239:28-31 Jl 30 '66

BEARDED irises. See Irises

BEARDS
Hair today, gone tomorrow; excerpts from Polite Americans. G. Carson. il Am Heritage 17:42-7 F '66

BEARDSLEY, Aubrey Vincent
Letter from London; exhibition at Victoria and Albert museum. M. Panter-Downes. New Yorker 42:86-7 Jl 9 '66
London; exhibition at Victoria & Albert museum. J. Russell. il Art N 65:18-19+ O '66
Monstrous orchid. il por Time 87:72 My 27 '66

BEARING walls. See Walls

BEARINGS (machinery)
Bearings. E. A. Muyderman. il Sci Am 214:60-6+ bibliog(p 143) Mr '66
Hexagonal crystal structure will enhance bearing alloys. il Tech W 19:36 Ag 22 '66

BEARN, Alexander G. See Kueppers, F. jt. auth.

BEARS
Bear are crazy. J. Rearden. il Field & S 71:34-5+ Ag '66
Big boar brown lore. J. S. Crawford. il Outdoor Life 139:4+ Ja '67
Day the bears go to bed; Craighead brothers bio-telemetry study of pre-hibernation habits. J. George. il Read Digest 89:137-41 O '66
Fishing lesson; bear cubs being taught to fish. J. S. Crawford. il Outdoor Life 139:50-3+ Ja '67
Has the polar bear a future? il Nat Parks Mag 40:13 Mr '66
Helping the polar bear. Nat Parks Mag 40:21 S '66
On the way to Gladstone; black bears in New Jersey. New Yorker 42:17 Jl 9 '66
Plight of the ice bear; with letter from E. L. Bartlett. F. Dufresne. il Audubon Mag 68:418-25 N '66
Polar bears tracked by orbiting satellite. Sci N 89:321 Ap 30 '66
Trailing Yellowstone's grizzlies by radio. F. Craighead, jr. and J. Craighead. il Nat Geog Mag 130:252-67 Ag '66
Vanishing grizzly; Canada. Nat Parks Mag 40:21 Ap '66

Anecdotes, facetiae, satire, etc.
Ursus horribilis; grizzly's image. New Yorker 42:42-3 My 7 '66

BEARS, Photography of. See Photography of animals

BEARTOOTH primitive area. See Wilderness areas—Montana

BEASLEY, Kenneth E.
Social and political factors; address, July 1966. por ALA Bul 60:1146+ D '66

BEASLEY, Thomas M. and Palmer, H. E.
Lead-210 and polonium-210 in biological samples from Alaska. bibliog Science 152:1062-4 My 20 '66

BEAT generation. See Beatniks

BEATIE, David
Waterhole photography. il Nat Parks Mag 40:10-11 Je '66

BEATING; story. See Mountzoures, H. L.

BEATLES
According to John; remark about Christianity. il Time 88:38 Ag 12 '66
Bards of pop. il Newsweek 67:102 Mr 21 '66
Beatles under wraps in Tokyo. J. Schecter. il Life 61:72-4 Jl 15 '66
Blues for the Beatles; U.S. tour; reactions to Lennon statement. il Newsweek 68:94 Ag 22 '66
Everybody has a Beatle. E. Wikler. il Read Digest 89:72-5 O '66
From a boy's point of view. J. Wescott. pors Seventeen 25:14 S '66
Is Beatlemania dead? North American tour. il Time 88:38 S 2 '66
Monarchs of the Beatle empire. J. Morris. il pors Sat Eve Post 239:22-7 Ag 27 '66

Notes and comment; more popular, or more famous, than Jesus. New Yorker 42:21-2 Ag 27 '66
Of many things; Beatle John Lennon's statement. T. N. Davis. America 115:164 Ag 20 '66
Old Beatles, a study in paradox. M. Cleave. il pors N Y Times Mag p 10-11+ Jl 3 '66

BEATNIKS
Baedeker of Beatnik territory. H. R. Lottman. il N Y Times Mag p40-1+ Ag 7 '66
Die Gammler; West Germany. il Time 88:32 Ag 5 '66
Hot spot; evicted beats; Eilat, Israel. il Newsweek 67:34 F 7 '66
Social dropout; Tony Conrad in New York's underground. F. Eberstadt. il Look 31:70-1 Ja 10 '67

BEATON, Cecil
Many worlds of the entrancing Princess of Berar. il Vogue 147:98-101+ F 15 '66

about
Books. N. Bliven. New Yorker 41:102+ Ja 22 '66
Second fame; good food. N. Lyon. il por Vogue 147:140-2 F 15 '66

BEATRIX, princess of the Netherlands
Orange blossoms. il por Time 87:51-2 Mr 18 '66
Though the heavens fall; anti-German demonstrations on wedding day. il por Newsweek 67:46-7 Mr 21 '66

BEATTIE, Ronald H. and Kenney, J. P.
Aggressive crimes. bibliog f Ann Am Acad 364:73-85 Mr '66

BEATTY, Frank E.
Mystery of Pearl Harbor. Nat R 18:1261-5 D 13 '66

BEATTY, Jackson. See Kahneman, D. jt. auth.

BEATTY, Jerome, jr
Trade winds. See issues of Saturday review

BEATTY, Robert
Bahama treasure hunt. Flying 78:114-15 Mr '66
Pressure cooker. Flying 79:50 S '66

BEAU for Nora; drama. See Nicholson, J.

BEAUCHAMP, Robert
Paint the devil. S. Burton. il por Art N 65:26-7+ Ap '66

BEAUCHEMIN, David J.
Marine comes home from Vietnam. C. S. Wren. il pors Look 30:30-2+ Mr 8 '66

BEAUFORT, S.C.
Title VI disturbs the moss of Beaufort. J. K. Batten. il Reporter 36:46-8 Ja 12 '67

BEAUTIFICATION of cities. See Municipal improvement

BEAUTIFICATION of landscape. See Landscape improvement

BEAUTIFUL day; story. See Iglauer, E.

BEAUTIFYING of cities. See Municipal improvement

BEAUTY. See Aesthetics

BEAUTY, Personal
Be glad you're not beautiful. E. Kaplan. il Todays Health 44:22-5+ Ag '66
Be prettier than ever before! eight before and after looks. il Good H 162:104-15+ Ap '66
Beauty and heart. L. Barzini. Vogue 148:183-4+ O 1 '66
Beauty at any age. McCalls 93:56-7 Jl '66
Beauty bulletin. See issues of Vogue
Beauty checkout. See issues of Vogue
Beauty clinic. See issues of Good housekeeping
Beauty countdown; what's new, how to. S. Harney. il Ladies Home J 83:30 F '66
Beauty faces the sporting life. S. Harney. il Ladies Home J 83:82-3 Je '66
Beauty in a hurry. il Seventeen 25:160-1 S '66
Beauty tips for savvy travellers. Vogue 147:161 Ap 1 '66
Dear beauty editor. See issues of Seventeen
Dressing table talk. See issues of Seventeen
Good looks. L. D. Kirk. See issues of Parents' magazine and better homemaking
Guide to prettier hands and feet. McCalls 93:57 Ap '66
Have a beauty happening. il Seventeen 26:70-5 Ja '67
How to keep your cool this summer. il Seventeen 25:78-83 Je '66
How to look cool when you're not. il Redbook 127:60-1+ Jl '66
In August, cool equals beauty. il McCalls 93:38 Ag '66
The look you like; questions and answers; ed. by L. Allen. See issues of Today's health
Man talk; an American dream. D. Newman and R. Benton. il Mlle 64:112 N '66

BEAUTY, Personal—*Continued*
Redbook readers in fashion: beauty; current college-girl look. il Redbook 127:74-7+ S '66
She's a very pretty girl, but. Seventeen 25:128-9 F '66
Sleeping beauty: how to wake up looking lovely and well-groomed. il McCalls 93:80-1+ F '66
Suddenly you're beautiful. il Seventeen 25:98-103 O '66
There's something about a blonde. il Ladies Home J 83:94-5+ Ap '66
Women who must look beautiful and do; answers from ten women. il Redbook 128:62-70 Ja '67
Your looks are your fortune: a quiz about beauty. il Redbook 127:78-9+ Ag '66
  See also
Cosmetics
Exercise
Hairdressing
Hand
Make-up
BEAUTY and the ballot; drama. See Dias, E. J.
BEAUTY contests
Brown beauty with courage. il Ebony 21:102+ O '66
Miss America six months later. D. Chapman. il Look 30:90+ Ap 5 '66
Smile! sparkle! be yourself! teen-age beauty contests: Miss Teenage America, and America's Junior miss. il Seventeen 25:148-9+ N '66
BEAUTY culture
Pampering room. il House & Gard 131:88-93 Ja '67
Strange rapture worth billions. R. Warfield. il Mlle 63:130-3+ O '66
BEAUTY of scenery. See Landscape
BEAUTY resorts. See Health resorts, watering places, etc.
BEAUTY shops
What on earth is this? Salon Elrhodes, Paris. il Arch Forum 124:25-7 Ap '66
BEAUVOIR, Françoise (Brasseur) de
Very easy death, by S. de Beauvoir. Review
  Esquire 66:24-5 Jl '66. M. Muggeridge
  Nation 202:718-20 Je 13 '66. M. Haynes
  Newsweek il por 67:121A+ My 16 '66
  Sat R 49:30-1 Jl 16 '66. A. Pippett
BEAUVOIR, Simone de
De Beauvoir: at the deathbed. M. Haynes. Nation 202:718-20 Je 13 '66
BEAUX-arts string quartets. See String quartets
BEAVERBROOK, William Maxwell Aitken, 1st baron
How the Duke of Windsor lost his throne. Sat Eve Post 239:38-42+ Ja 29 '66
BEAVERS
Beavers dam and be damned. B. Gilbert. il Sports Illus 24:70-2+ Je 27 '66
Un-eager beaver. C. Fletcher. il Field & S 71:53+ Ag '66
BÉCAUD, Gilbert
Poetic motor. por Time 88:87-8 N 18 '66
BECH in Rumania; story. See Updike, J.
BECHDOLT, Burley V. and Flanigan, J. M.
Financial status of public schools, 1966. NEA J 55:55-6 O '66
BECHTEL, Louise Seaman
Boris Artzybasheff. Horn Bk 42:176-80 Ap '66
BECHTOLD, John A.
Bechtold formula. K. Poli. il Pop Phot 60:110-11 Ja '67
BECHUANALAND
Note:
For material after September 30, 1966, see heading Botswana
Botswana's cheerless freedom. T. Land. Reporter 34:41-2 F 10 '66
  See also
United Nations—Bechuanaland

Native races
Scottish mother for an African tribe. N. Mitchison. il Harper 233:86-8+ S '66
BECK, Edward C. See Dustman, R. E. jt. auth.
BECK, Hansjürgen Müller-. See Müller-Beck, H.
BECK, Jacob
Perceptual grouping produced by changes in orientation and shape. bibliog Science 154:538-40 O 28 '66
BECK, Ray
How to drive deer. Outdoor Life 138:40-3+ S '66
Lost dogs. Field & S 71:116-18+ D '66
BECKER, Eugene
Taxpayers' money; interview. New Yorker 42:42-3 Mr 26 '66

BECKER, Harry A.
Norwalk plan: team teaching is a privilege; interview, ed. by W. K. Richards. Sr Schol 88:sup 13-15 Mr 25 '66
BECKER, Heywood Eric, and Cone, R. A.
Light-stimulated electrical responses from skin. bibliog Science 154:1051-3 N 25 '66
BECKER, James F.
Economics of optimism. Nation 202:751-2 Je 20 '66
Mr Keynes and his age. Nation 203:329-31 3 '66
Scarred American beauty. Nation 202:366-7 Mr 28 '66
BECKER, Joseph
Communications networks for libraries. bibliog por Wilson Lib Bul 41:383-7 D '66
BECKER, Russell J.
Sin, illness and guilt. Christian Cent 83:1007-9 Ag 17 '66
BECKER, Stephen
On being a patient. Atlan 218:95-101 Jl '66
BECKER, William W.
Bedding down the budget-minded. il por Bsns W p56-8+ Ag 27 '66
BECKETT aviation corporation
Aircraft pooling gives Beckett flexibility. D. A. Brown. il Aviation W 84:114-15+ Ap 11 '66
BECLCH; drama. See Owens, R.
BED Elizabeth Taylor once slept in; story. See Jordan, E. H.
BED-sitting rooms. See Bedrooms
BED sores. See Bedsores
BED wetting. See Urine—Incontinence
BEDAS, Yusef K.
Beirut banks take an unplanned holiday. por Bsns W p46+ O 22 '66
Day the doors closed. il por Time 88:105-6 O 28 '66
Salvaging Intra bank: the price is high. por Bsns W p66+ D 10 '66
BEDDING
New look at children's bedding. il Parents Mag 41:47-50+ Jl '66
BEDE aviation corporation
Bede seeks summer certification of BD-1. D. A. Brown. il Aviation W 84:95-7 Ap 4 '66
BEDELL, Glenn, and Govindjee
Quantum yield of oxygen evolution and the Emerson enhancement effect in deuterated chlorella. bibliog Science 152:1383-5 Je 3 '66
BEDFORD, John Robert Russell, 13th duke of
Thirteenth Duke of Bedford sells shoes; exploitation of Woburn abbey. H. Lawrenson. il Esquire 66:86-8+ Ag '66
BEDFORD, Sybille
Worst that ever happened. Sat Eve Post 239:29-33+ O 22 '66
BEDROOM furnishings. See Household furnishings
BEDROOMS
Basic best buys for your bedroom. il House & Gard 130:230-7 O '66
Bedroom suites, one for parents, one for kids! il Bet Hom & Gard 44:42-3 Ag '66
Bedrooms are comfortable around the clock. il House & Gard 131:116-17 Ja '67
Color your room clever! il Seventeen 25:160-1 My '66
Dear home editor; dormitory rooms. il Seventeen 25:408-9 Ag '66
Dear home editor; questions and answers. il Seventeen 25:138 Je '66
Give your room a make-over. il Seventeen 26:100 Ja '67
How can I make pluses out of the problems? il Seventeen 25:144-7 O '66
How to make a small bedroom look larger. il Farm J 90:111 Mr '66
Make-over room. il Seventeen 25:180-1+ S '66
Plan bedrooms space efficiently. J. LemMon. il Suc Farm 64:66-7 Ag '66
Small bedrooms with big ideas. il McCalls 93:92-7 F '66
Space-making storage. il Seventeen 25:142-3 Ap '66
Three guest decorators. il Seventeen 26:76-7 Ja '67
Twenty-two ideas to give your room a studio look. il Seventeen 25:126-9+ Mr '66
What is your room like? il Seventen 25:298-9 Ag '66
What my room really needs is. . . il Seventeen 25:110-11 Je '66
Worldly retreat; P. de Rothschild's room. il Vogue 148:144-7 O 15 '66
  See also
Childrens rooms

BEDS
Beds for our time. B. Plumb. il N Y Times Mag p94-5 S 18 '66
Enchanting bedtime stories. il Seventeen 25: 242-3 S '66
Triple-deck bunks. G. Rapp. il Pop Mech 126: 122-3 Ag '66
Year of the bed. M. C. Burke. House & Gard 130:96-7 O '66
See also
Cribs (beds)

History
New York: the bed; show at the Museum of contemporary crafts, September 23–November 6, 1966. R. Howard. il Craft Horiz 26: 8-15 S '66

BEDSORES
Floating sores away; new hospital mattress. il Time 88:75 S 9 '66

BEDSPREADS. See Coverlets

BEE hives. See Beehives

BEE tree; story. See Ford, J. H.

BEE venom. See Venom

BEEBE, Lucius
Last of the big dandies. Esquire 65:104+ F '66
Rolls mystique. Horizon 8:40-8 Wint '66

about
Obituary
Pub W 189:110 F 14 '66
What to do with leftover millions. N. Samstag. Sat R 49:41-2 Ap 16 '66

BEEBE, Robert
You can cross oceans in a motorboat. Motor B 117:36-8+ My '66

BEECH, Keyes, and Hall, C. W.
Formosa: Asia's heartening success story. Read Digest 88:139-44 F '66

BEECH aircraft corporation
Beech pushing for $160 million in sales. E. J. Bulban. il Aviation W 85:118-19+ N 14 '66
What's going on at Beech? A. Trammell. il Flying 78:34-7 Je '66

BEECH-Nut packing company
Foods catered to baby's taste. M. B. Keiser. il Parents Mag 41:34+ My '66

BEECHER, Henry K.
Experiments on humans, the growing debate; documenting the abuses. por Sat R 49:45-6 Jl 2 '66
Ethics of human experiments. por Time 88: 42+ Jl 8 '66
Pain; one mystery solved. Science 151:840-1 F 18 '66

BEECHER, John
Alabama's restoration: sword in the heart of Dixie. Nation 202:611-14 My 23 '66
Despite Negro opposition, a Negro might make it. New Repub 155:11-12 Jl 2 '66

BEECHING, Roy W. Jr
Build this 14-foot canoe for $50. Pop Mech 125:145-7+ My '66

BEECHY, Atlee
Report from Vietnam. Sat R 49:26+ D 3 '66

BEEF
Some surprises from your meatman: boneless beef. il Sunset 137:194+ O '66
Two dozen ways to enjoy steak. il Bet Hom & Gard 44:81-2 F '66
See also
Cookery—Meat

Marketing
See Meat—Marketing

BEEF industry. See Meat industry and trade

BEEHIVES
Nature's most astonishing animal: the beehive. J. George. il Read Digest 88:185-8+ Je '66

BEEN here and gone again; story. See Kolb, K.

BEENE, Geoffrey
Switch in time to design. por Life 61:53-4+ S 23 '66

BEER
When beer brought the blues; cobalt salt. Time 89:50 Ja 20 '67
Wine, women & so on. P. Cannon. Ladies Home J 83:116 S '66

Marketing
Tap beer goes home for profit; promotion of packaged draft beer ups sales. il Bsns W p63-4 O 22 '66

BEER containers
Those new tab-opening cans. il Consumer Bul 49:2 Ap '66

BEERS family (folk singers) See Singers

BEES
Gibberellic acid: effects of feeding in an artificial diet for honeybees. J. L. Nation and F. A. Robinson. bibliog Science 152:1765-6 Je 24 '66
If honey bees move in with you. Sunset 136: 253 Ap '66
Never swing at a honeybee. E. A. Bauer. il Field & S 70:73+ Mr '66
Polymorphism in some nearctic halictine bees. G. Knerer and C. E. Atwood. bibliog il Science 152:1262-3 My 27 '66
Time and space in the life of the bee. M. Renner. il Natur Hist 75:52-7 O '66
See also
Beehives

Orientation
See Orientation

BEESON, Edith
Panacea. Sr Schol 88:sup 12-13 Mr 18 '66

BEESON, Irene. See Seale, P. jt. auth.

BEETHOVEN, Ludwig van
Awesome, superlative: Klemperer's Missa solemnis. G. L. Mayer. il Am Rec G 33: 8-9 S '66
Beethoven by Arrau: searching, satisfying. R. Kammerer. Am Rec G 32:1061 Jl '66
Records:
Missa solemnis. Opera N 31:32 O 15 '66
Symphony no. 9; Christ on the Mount of Olives. Opera N 31:34 D 24 '66
Schmidt-Isserstedt's Ninth, the most satisfying in ten years. M. N. Kanny. il Am Rec G 33:208-9 N '66

BEETLE, David H.
Legislatures: the 100-year lag. Nation 203: 475-8 N 7 '66

BEETLES
Beetle's spray discourages predators; study of eleodes. T. E. Eisner. il Natur Hist 75: 42-7 bibliog(p68) F '66
Sex attractants in frass produced by male ips confusus in ponderosa pine. R. M. Silverstein and others. bibliog il Science 154: 509-10 O 28 '66
See also
Ambrosia beetles
Bark beetles
Flour beetles

BEGINNING; story. See Stern, R. M.

BEGONIAS
Begonias: here's where to see spectacular displays. il Sunset 137:148-9 Jl '66
Home garden notebook. il Flower Grower 53: 37-8 F '66
Multiflora gigantea tuberous begonias. W. Brown. il Horticulture 44:18-19+ Mr '66
Three plant garden. B. Black. il Flower Grower 53:32-3+ N '66
Tuberous begonias are tempting now. Sunset 137:168 Jl '66

BEHAN, Beatrice (Salkeld)
Beatrice and Brendan Behan: love remembered. J. Robbins and J. Robbins. il pors Redbook 126:60-1+ Mr '66

BEHAN, Brendan
Beatrice and Brendan Behan: love remembered. J. Robbins and J. Robbins. il Redbook 126:60-1+ Mr '66
To Dublin in a donkey cart. S. Weintraub. por Sat R 49:47 Je 4 '66
Where the martyrs died. S. Cronin. Nation 203:486-8 N 7 '66

BEHAR, Bracha, and Stein, Gabriel
Photochemical evolution of oxygen from certain aqueous solutions. bibliog Science 154: 1012-13 N 25 '66

BEHAVIOR. See Etiquette

BEHAVIOR (psychology)
Books: two on aggression. J. Alsop. New Yorker 42:209-14+ S 10 '66
Challenge to unconcerned bystanders. L. Wainwright. Life 61:32 S 23 '66
Curiosity and exploration. D. E. Berlyne. bibliog il Science 153:25-33 Jl 1 '66; Reply. J. M. Burgers. 154:1680-1 D 30 '66
Deterioration of work standards. C. W. Graves. il Harvard Bsns R 44:117-22+ S '66
Drive for territory; excerpts from The territorial imperative. R. Ardrey. il Life 61: 40-7+ Ag 26 '66
Erotic minorities, by L. Ullerstam. Review Sat R 49:29-30 Jl 9 '66. R. J. Levin
Ethology. O. Handlin. Atlan 218:138-9 S '66
Games keeper; Transactional analysis; E. Berne's theories. il Newsweek 68:56 Ag 8 '66
Inhibitory and facilitatory effect of two related peptides on extinction of avoidance behavior. B. Bohus and D. De Wied. bibliog il Science 153:318-20 Jl 15 '66
Instincts and prophecies. G. H. T. Kimble. Reporter 35:40+ D 29 '66

BEHAVIOR (psychology)—*Continued*
Jeopardy and alibi; aggression and territorialism; theories of K. Lorenz and R. Ardrey. C. Deemer. New Repub 155:26+ O 1 '66
Man is a territorial animal; excerpts from The territorial imperative. R. Ardrey. il Life 61:50-4+ S 2 '66
Phylogeny and ontogeny of behavior. B. F. Skinner. bibliog Science 153:1205-13 S 9 '66
Pop-psych, or, Doc. I'm fed up with these boring figures; Time essay. Time 88:38-9 O 7 '66
Protest in adolescence. B. Spock. Redbook 127:8+ Ag '66
Territorial imperative, by R. Ardrey. Review Nat R 18:1115-17 N 1 '66. G. Davenport Newsweek il 68:108-108B S 12 '66
Sat R 49:34-5 S 17 '66. R. D. Masters Time 88:125+ S 16 '66
Vogue 148:167 D '66. J. Stafford
That old-time aggression. J. P. Scott. Nation 204:53-4 Ja 9 '67
What we don't know about children's behavior. B. Berelson. il PTA Mag 60:18-20 Je '66
See also
Human nature
Motivation (psychology)
Psychobiology
BEHAVIOR, Animal. See Animals—Habits and behavior
BEHAVIOR, Group. See Groups (sociology)
BEHAVIOR of animals. See Animals—Habits and behavior
BEHAVIORAL sciences
Behavioral sciences for personnel managers. C. A. Myers. bibliog f Harvard Bsns R 44: 154-6+ Jl '66
Implications of laboratory studies of aggression for the control and regulation of violence. R. H. Walters. bibliog f Ann Am Acad 364:60-72 Mr '66
Proper study of mankind... il Newsweek 68:80-2 Ag 15 '66

Terminology
Behavioral sciences: vocabulary; report on meeting. L. H. Marshall. Science 153:323-4 Jl 15 '66
BEHEADING. See Decapitation
BEHIND-the-lens meters. See Exposure meters
BEHME, Bob
Liquid handyman. Field & S 71:66+ My '66
Never underestimate a golf ball. Field & S 70:52-3+ Mr '66
Trail bike basics. Field & S 70:69-71+ F '66
You can't go wrong in San Diego. Field & S 71:102-5 Ja '67
BEHN, Harry
Books: poem. Pub W 190:137 Jl 11 '66
Poetry for children. Horn Bk 42:163-75 Ap '66
BEHNKE, O. and Forer, Arthur
Intranuclear microtubules. bibliog Science 153:1536-7 S 23 '66
BEHRENDT, John C. and others
Airborne geophysical study in the Pensacola Mountains of Antarctica. bibliog Science 153:1373-6 S 16 '66
BEHRENS, Alver W.
Catholic education today: interview. por Sr Schol 88:sup 1-3 Ap 1 '66
BEHRENS, E. William
Recent emerged beach in eastern Mexico. bibliog Science 152:642-3 Ap 29 '66
BEHRENS, Richard. See Miller, G. jt. auth.
BEHRMAN, Beatrice Alexander. See Alexander, B.
BEHRMAN, Daniel
Controversy on continental drift. UNESCO Courier 19:12-15+ O '66
Satellites and computers may measure world's water. UNESCO Courier 19:31 Ap '66
Transmigration of shoals. UNESCO Courier 19:23-4 Mr '66
BEHRMAN, S. N.
You can't release Dante's Inferno in the summertime. N Y Times Mag p6-7+ Jl 17 '66
about
Eunuchs in the harem. J. O'Hara. il Holiday 40:16+ S '66
BEICHMAN, Arnold
Opinion: why the draft? por Mlle 62:6+ Ja '66
BEIDAS, Yusef K. See Bedas, Y. K.
BEIDLEMAN, Richard G.
Edwin James, pioneer naturalist. Horticulture 44:32-4 D '66
Lewis and Clark, plant collectors for a president. Horticulture 44:28-9+ Ap '66

BEILENSON, Betsy
Cooperative ventures in children's reading. Library J 91:2170-1 Ap 15 '66
BEILISS, Mendel
Blood accusation, by M. Samuel. Review Nation 203:394-5 O 17 '66. C. Leviant Newsweek il 68:100-1 Ag 22 '66
Fact of the matter. V. Peterson. Reporter 35:57-8 O 20 '66
BEINART, Julian
Pattern of the street. Arch Forum 125:58-63 S '66
BEING. See Ontology
BEIRUT
Banks
See Banks and banking—Lebanon
BEIRUT university. See American university of Beirut
BEISER, Edward N.
God and the draft. Commonweal 83:631-3 Mr 4 '66
BEISWANGER, George
Sleeping beauty in Atlanta. Dance Mag 40: 46-8 O '66
BÉJART, Maurice
Ring-around-the-world. il Newsweek 67:88 Je 27 '66
BEKIERKUNST, A.
Nicotinamide-adenine dinucleotide in tubercle bacilli exposed to isoniazid. bibliog Science 152:525-6 Ap 22 '66
BEKKERS, Wilhelmus Marinus, bp
Mercy and the sacrament of penance; excerpt from God's people on the march. por Cath World 203:228-32 Jl '66
BEL canto. See Singing
BELAFONTE, Harry
Big-star stomp through oldtime Harlem; with report by K. Gouldthorpe. il pors Life 60: 70-4+ F 4 '66
BELAÚNDE TERRY, Fernando
Atlantic report. Atlan 217:40+ Ap '66
BELCK, Jack
Hero bullet and other related nonsense. Atlan 217:142+ Mr '66
BELFAST
Ecumenical backlash; report on rioting when Protestant extremists and Catholics clashed. E. McKiernan. America 115:31-3 Jl 9 '66
BELFORD, Barbara
Let's travel: tips for student travelers. Mlle 63:357-8 Ag '66
BEL GEDDES, Joan
U.N: one year later. Cath World 204:98-103 N '66
BELGIAN CONGO. See Congo (capital Kinshasa)
BELGIUM
See also
Antwerp
Banks and banking—Belgium
Brussels
Canals—Belgium
Casteau
Chièvres
Coal mines and mining—Beligum
Colleges and universities—Belgium
Investments, Foreign (in Belgium)
Munitions industries—Belgium
Music festivals—Belgium

Description and travel
Off-beat Belgium. R. Deardorff. il Travel 125-61-4+ Ap '66
History
Bibliography
Articles and other books received; comp. by P. Rosenfeld. See issues of American historical review
Industries
See also
Munitions industries—Belgium
Languages
Clash at Louvain. R. J. Gerber. il America 114:645-9 My 7 '66; Discussion. 115:11-14 Jl 2 '66
They're not talking; University of Louvain. il Time 87:69 Mr 4 '66
Music
See also
Antwerp—Music
Politics and government
King's choice; finding a new government or calling general elections. Newsweek 67:55 F 21 '66
New combo. il Time 87:26-7 Mr 25 '66
Of pits & pills; miners riot and threat of doctors strike. il Time 87:31-2 F 11 '66

BELGIUM—*Continued*

Race problems

Crisis in Louvain. P. Nobile. Cath World 203: 233-5 Jl '66

BELIEF and doubt

Dynamics of unfaith. L. J. Averill; reply. P. Graybeal. Christian Cent 83:240 F 23 '66

Respect and trust; address, September 14, 1966. R. M. Vogel. Vital Speeches 33:46-9 N 1 '66

See also

Agnosticism

Rationalism

BELIEF in God. See Faith

BELITT, Ben

Winter pond; poem. New Yorker 41:38 F 19 '66

BELL, Allen L. See Kaminer, B. jt. auth.

BELL, Arthur

About Ferdinand. Pub W 190:54-5 Ag 22 '66

BELL, Daniel

Writer as public figure. Sat R 49:18-19 Je 4 '66

about

Neglected college. il por Newsweek 67:85-6 Mr 28 '66

BELL, David Elliott

Quality of aid. For Affairs 44:601-7 Jl '66

Trends in administering foreign aid; address, April 15, 1966. Vital Speeches 32:454-6 My 15 '66

about

Bell's toll. Time 88:18 Jl 8 '66

BELL, Edward J.

Politics; 1966. Nat R 18:153-9 F 22 '66

BELL, Enid

Sculpture of Eugenie Shonnard. Am Artist 30:62-7+ Je '66

BELL, Ivan

Can you decipher this interplanetary message? il Sci Digest 60:37-8 Ag '66

BELL, Jenny

Case for marrying later. Mlle 64:88+ Ja '67

BELL, Joseph N.

Caution! genius at play. Pop Mech 125:120-3+ Mr '66; Same abr. with title Look out! genius at play. Read Digest 88:201-4 My '66

Hollywood interview: canonizing the superficial. Sat R 49:115-16+ O 8 '66

Now we're mining oil from mountains. Pop Mech 126:142-5+ N '66

Special report on a growing social problem: when the cry for help comes. Good H 162: 108-9+ Je '66

Suburban daily: new power in publishing. Sat R 50:118+ Ja 14 '67

BELL, Julian

Journey to a frontier, by P. Stansky and W. Abrahams. Review

New Repub 155:28+ N 12 '66. M. Straight

Sat R 49:39 S 17 '66. S. Weintraub

Meaning of the journey. P. Hatch. Nation 203:102 Jl 25 '66

BELL, Léonie, and Wilson, H. V.

Start now for indoor fragrance. Flower Grower 53:28-9+ N '66

BELL, Lyn

For theologians and other lovers; poem. Christian Cent 83:1270 O 19 '66

BELL, Marvin

Two British chronicles. Poetry 107:410-13 Mr '66

Walking thoughts; Bride in white; Time we took to travel; Affair; poems. Poetry 108: 101-6 My '66

BELL, P. R.

Vacuum welding of olivine. bibliog Science 153:410-11 Jl 22 '66

BELL aerosystems company

Bell inflatable landing device slated for tests next year. il Tech W 18:38 Je 20 '66

Flexible simulator flies varied missions. D. A. Brown. il Aviation W 84:68-75 My 2 '66

BELL helicopter company

Volume JetRanger production planned. il Aviation W 84:99+ Ja 24 '66

BELL telephone company of Canada

Canada pushing for domestic comsat net; experimental station planned at Bouchette. K. Johnsen. Aviation W 85:35 N 21 '66

BELL telephone hour (television program) See Television broadcasting—Music

BELL telephone laboratories

Bell labs: a systems approach to innovation is the main thing. J. Walsh. il Science 153: 393-6 Jl 22 '66

Bell labs: computers loom large in both research and operations. J. Walsh. Science 153:720-2 Ag 12 '66

BTL units impress signals on laser beams. il Tech W 20:40 Ja 2 '67

BELL telephone system

Films; Bell system movies; reprint. il U S Camera 29:54-5 Je '66

BELLA, Ahmed Ben. See Ben Bella, A.

BELLAMY, Walt

Pro basketball's tall men. W. J. McKean. il Look 31:86 Ja 24 '67

BELLENGER, Maria-Jesus. See Davis, C. jt. auth.

BELLINGER, Joan

Memorial to Joe Fortes. Negro Hist Bul 29:168 Ap '66

BELLINGRATH gardens, Theodore, Ala. See Gardens—Alabama

BELLINI, Vincenzo

Also, Bellini not for singing. D. Heckman. por Am Rec G 32:513-14 F '66

BELLMAN, Richard

Dynamic programming. Science 153:34-7 Jl 1 '66

BELLOW, Saul

Enemy is academe; summary of address. por Pub W 190:34 Jl 18 '66

about

Imagination and the age. A. Kazin. Reporter 34:32-5 My 5 '66

Under the weather. Criticism

Commonweal 85:199-201 N 18 '66

Nation 203:523-4 N 14 '66

New Yorker 42:127 N 5 '66

Newsweek il 68:96 N 7 '66

Sat R 49:34 N 12 '66

Time il 88:85 N 4 '66

BELLOWS, Everett H. and Gasque, M. R.

Here's a lifesaving plan for your business. Nations Bsns 54:94+ Ap '66

BELLOWS, George Wesley

Art galleries; exhibition at the Gallery of modern art. R. M. Coates. New Yorker 42:138+ Ap 23 '66

Footnotes; exhibition at Gallery of modern art, New York. il Am Artist 30:4 My '66

Patriot for beauty; show at New York's Gallery of modern art. il Newsweek 67:94 Mr 28 '66

Portrait of the artist as a person. G. H. Hamilton. il por Sat R 49:89 Ap 9 '66

BELLS

Bells are back on the King's highway; El Camino Real bells; reprint. G. P. Parmelee. il Hobbies 71:98O-98P N '66

Joyous sound of freedom; celebrating Independence day by ringing of bells. T. J. Fleming. il Read Digest 88:19-20+ Je '66

Uncle Toby story. L. E. Springer. il Hobbies 71:98P+ O '66

See also

Jaquemarts

BELLS, Garden. See Garden ornaments

BELLWARE, Frederick T. See Smith, A. E. jt. auth.

BELLY dance. See Dancing, Oriental

BELMONDO, Jean Paul

People are talking about... por Vogue 148: 216-17 O 1 '66

Power, spell and free spirit of Belmondo; with report by R. Chelminski. il pors Life 61:111-15+ N 11 '66

BELMONT, Eleanor (Robson)

Gift of enthusiasm. R. A. Tuggle. il Opera N 30:12-13 Mr 5 '66

BELMONT stakes. See Horse racing

BELOV, Evelyn

Total violinism. Am Rec G 32:903-6 My '66

BELTS, Safety. See Safety belts

BELTSVILLE research center. See United States—Agricultural research center, Beltsvill. Md.

BELVEAL, Dee

Bugs' battle against man. il Todays Health 44:48-51 F '66

—and Phillips, Don

Secret weapons. Todays Health 44:38-41 Je '66

BELVIN, William, and Klein, Arthur

Danger signals from a river towboat. Yachting 119:72-4+ Je '66

BEMISS, FitzGerald

Virginia outdoors plan. Parks & Rec 1:964-5+ D '66

BEN, Philip

Ami, go home. New Repub 154:10-11 Ap 9 '66

Competition for new weapons. New Repub 154:13-14 Je 4 '66

Conversations on the Red Riviera. New Repub 155:9 O 29 '66

De Gaulle's mission to Moscow. New Repub 154:13-14 Je 18 '66

BEN, Philip—*Continued*
Going gets rough in Yugoslavia. New Repub 155:15-16 S 3 '66
Rumanian Gaullists. New Repub 155:20 Ag 27 '66
Sense of insecurity in West Germany. New Repub 154:10 Ap 30 '66
Tragedy of errors. New Repub 154:8-10 F 19 '66
Wanted: housing for NATO headquarters. New Repub 154:8 My 14 '66
BEN BARKA, Mehdi
L'affaire Ben Barka. il por Time 87:33 Ja 28 '66
Atlantic report. Atlan 217:30+ Ap '66
Beards. New Repub 154:7 F 5 '66
Ben Barka affair. C. Sterling. il Reporter 34:22-8 Mr 10 '66
Ben Barka is dead. A. Werth. Nation 202: 350-2 Mr 28 '66
De Gaulle and l'affaire. A. Werth. Nation 202:200-4 F 21 '66
Diminished fifth. por Newsweek 67:44+ Ja 31 '66
Enter the CIA. il Newsweek 67:32 F 7 '66
Fine French scandal over a missing Moroccan. il por Life 60:30-32B F 4 '66
Meanwhile, down in Morocco. Reporter 34:26 Mr 10 '66
Silent witnesses. Time 87:32 F 4 '66
Slight oversight. il Newsweek 68:52+ O 31 '66
Surprise witness. il Time 88:38 O 28 '66
Trial begins. Newsweek 68:46+ S 19 '66
BEN BELLA, Ahmed
In Algeria it's not yah, yah, Boumediene! but wait and see. P. Braestrup and D. Ottaway. il por N Y Times Mag p36-7+ F 13 '66
BEN GURION, David
Man of Sde Boker. G. Samuels. il pors N Y Times Mag p42+ O 16 '66
BENARES, India
Well traveled camera. il Mod Phot 30:46+ F '66
BENBOW, Hugh
Waiting for Cassius. il por Time 88:86 N 4 '66
BENCE Jones proteins. See Proteins
BENCHES
Bench around an ailing oak. il Sunset 137: 102 S '66
Easy-to-build benches everyone will enjoy. il Pop Gard 17:28-33+ Ag '66
BENCHLEY, Nathaniel
Settling in; story. McCalls 94:100-1 N '66
BENCHLEY, Peter
Group embalmed. Holiday 39:155-6+ My '66
BENCHLEY, Robert, 3d
Benchley's Bushmen. R. Gehman. Sat R 49: 59+ O 15 '66
BENDA, Harry J.
Reflections on Asian communism. Yale R 56: 1-16 O '66
BENDER, J. B. pseud.
Correspondence with Theodore Draper & Commentary, appropriate & inappropriate. Nat R 18:823-7 Ag 23 '66
Dominican intervention; the facts. Nat R 18:112-14 F 8 '66
BENDER, Michael, and others
Manganese nodules: their evolution. bibliog Science 151:325-8 Ja 21 '66
BENDINER, Elmer
Outside the kingdom of the middle class. Nation 204:22-3 Ja 2 '67
BENDINER, Robert
Truth about the Pulitzer prize awards. McCalls 93:82-3+ My '66

about
Prize complaints. Newsweek 67:96-8 My 2 '66
BENDIRE, Charles Emil
Department of amplification; letter to the editor. G. T. Heilman. New Yorker 42:171-3 Ap 16 '66
BENDIX, Dorothy
(ed) Library education and the shortage of both manpower and talent. por Library J 91:4881-98 O 15 '66
BENEDICT, Nelson
Sportfishing (title varies) See issues of Yachting
BENEDIKT, Michael
Drexler's dialetical nudes. Art N 64:50-1+ F '66
Events by moonlight; Catching it all on the way back; Villain; Strained credulity; Procession; poems. Poetry 108:388-92 S '66
BENEFIT plans, Employees. See Employees benefit plans
BENEFITS for service men. See Service men, Discharged—Benefits
BENÍTEZ, Manuel. See Cordobés

BENJAMIN, Curtis G.
Computers and copyrights. Science 152:181-4 Ap 8 '66
Copyright and government. por Library J 91:881-6 F 15 '66
Shadows on the future; address, June 13, 1966. por Pub W 190:36-9 Jl 4 '66
BENJAMIN, Harry
Body to match the mind. il Time 88:52+ D 2 '66
BENJAMIN, Lois
Have you heard? See issues of Ladies' home journal to August 1966
How to be a working mother without really crying; excerpt from So you want to be a working mother. Ladies Home J 83:101-3 My '66
—and Henley, Arthur
What every mother owes her child and herself. Ladies Home J 83:69+ Je '66
BENJAMIN, Mary A.
Are autographs an investment? reprint. Hobbies 71:106-7+ Ag '66
BENJAMIN company
Macfadden-Bartell titles used for sales promotion. Pub W 189:274-5 Ja 24 '66
BENJAMIN Franklin high school. See New York (city)—Education
BENKO, Stephen
Disappointing Marian development. Christian Cent 84:79-80 Ja 18 '67
BENNATI, Flavio
On the gypsy circuit. W. Como. il Dance Mag 40:18 D '66
BENNETT, Arnold
New look at three lives. G. Hicks. Sat R 49: 27 O 15 '66
Old pro. il por Newsweek 68:89+ S 5 '66
Writer by trade: a portrait of Arnold Bennett, by D. Barker. Review Time por 88:83-4 S 2 '66
BENNETT, Boyce. See Bloom, B. R. jt. auth.
BENNETT, Edna
Men behind the camera. U S Camera 29:34+ Ag '66
BENNETT, Enoch Arnold. See Bennett, A.
BENNETT, Hank
Short-wave listening. See issues of Popular electronics
BENNETT, James V.
Gun and how to control it. N Y Times Mag p34-5+ S 25 '66
BENNETT, John C.
Christian realism in Vietnam. America 114: 616-17 Ap 30 '66
In defense of God. Look 30:69-70+ Ap 19 '66
BENNETT, Joseph
Tomb at Rimini; Marine; poems. Poetry 109:167-71 D '66
BENNETT, Leon
Insect aerodynamics: vertical sustaining force in near-hovering flight. bibliog Science 152: 1263-6 My 27 '66
BENNETT, Lerone, jr
Black power (cont) Ebony 21:127-30+ F: 121-4+ Ap; 58-60+ Jl; 152-4+ O; 22:146-8+ D '66; 114-16+ Ja '67
BENNETT, Margaret, pseud.
I remember mama nature. Atlan 217:119-20 F '66
Inglese spoken here. Sat R 49:64+ S 17 '66
Logical extreme reading method. Pub W 189:33-5 Mr 14 '66
BENNETT, Marion T.
Immigration and nationality (McCarran-Walter) act of 1952, as amended to 1965, bibliog f Ann Am Acad 367:127-36 S '66
BENNETT, Meridan
Evaluation and the question of change. Ann Am Acad 365:119-28 My '66
BENNETT, Paul A.
AAUP's second show retains awareness of quality. Pub W 189:136-7+ Je 13 '66
Diana Klemin: art for children's books. Pub W 190:88-90 N 7 '66
John Dreyfus: typographic advisor, editor, printing historian. Pub W 190:84-6+ S 5 '66
Spiral press honored with exhibit at Morgan library. Pub W 189:97-101+ F 7 '66
(ed) See Meynell, F. Sir Francis Meynell lectures in New York

about
Obituary
Pub W 191:61 Ja 2 '67. C. B. Grannis
Pub W por 190:64-5 D 26 '66
BENNETT, Richard Rodney
Bennett's premiere. Hungarians' Beethoven; London report. E. Greenfield. il por Hi Fi 16:156-7 My '66
Mines of sulfur. Criticism
Opera N 30:25-6 My 7 '66

BENNETT, Robert LaFollette
New chief for Indian bureau. il por Sr Schol
88:18 My 13 '66
BENNETT, Rowena
Child who was made of snow; dramatiza-
tion of a Russian folktale.Plays 26:72-4,
80 D '66
French doll's surprise; drama. Plays 25:72, 85-
6 My '66
BENNETT, Wallace Foster
Excerpt from address, September 15, 1966.
Cong Digest 45:267+ N '66
BENNETT, William Andrew Cecil
Surging to nationhood. il pors Time 88:30-40
S 30 '66
BENNINGTON, Vt.
Green mountain boys; home of four artists.
A. Solomon. il Vogue 148:104-9+ Ag 1 '66
BENNSTROM, Anne-Marie
How to be happy though dieting; interview.
Mlle 62:148-9 F '66
Spot-reducing chart to end all spot-reducing
charts. Vogue 147:116-20 Ap 15 '66
BENNY, Jack
Pause. por Time 88:84 N 4 '66
BENSON, Arvid F.
Hunt for the records. il Outdoor Life 138:
20-3+ Ag '66
BENSON, Janet
To explain myself—II—August 1963; poem
Mlle 63:215 Ag '66
BENSON, Mary
South Africa: daily life in a police state.
New Repub 154:11-13 Je 11 '66
BENSON, Richard D.
Letter from southeast Asia. Nat R 18:161
F 22 '66
BENSON, Roy
Here it is! the first double super 8 camera.
Pop Phot 58:118+ My '66
BENSTED-SMITH, Richard
Better roads, worse drivers. Atlan 218:120+
D '66
BENSUSAN, Howard B.
Lathyrism. Science 153:322-3 Jl 15 '66
BENTLEY, Eric
Theater of commitment; excerpt from ad-
dress. Commentary 42:63-72 D '66
(tr) See Brecht, B. Are the people infallible?
(tr) See Brecht, B. Caucasian chalk circle
BENTLEY, Logan
In Sicily nearly everybody loves the Targa
Florio. Sports Illus 24:54-6+ My 9 '66
BENTLEY, P. J.
Adaptations of amphibia to arid environ-
ments. bibliog Science 152:619-23 Ap 29 '66
—and Schmidt-Nielsen, Knut
Cutaneous water loss in reptiles. bibliog Sci-
ence 151:1547-9 Mr 25 '66
—See Schmidt-Nielsen, K. jt. auth.
BENTLEY, Pauline
(ed) Beauty and the beast; summary of Man
through his art: Man and animal. UNESCO
Courier 19:27-30 Ja '66
BENTON, Robert. See Newman, D. jt. auth.

about

De senectute or old age, as Newmanized
and Bentonated. A. Gingrich. Esquire 66:6
S '66
BENTON, Thomas Hart
Art news from nowhere. il por Esquire 67:
124 Ja '67
BENTON, William
Education as an instrument of American
foreign policy; address, April 16, 1966. Ann
Am Acad 366:33-40 Jl '66
That nations may know. Sat R 49:25+ D 3
'66

about

Sorry, general, English is the language. Life
61:4 S 9 '66
BENUAZIZI, Ali. See Irwin, S. jt. auth.
BENVENUTI, Nino
Jab from the intellectual. M. Kane. il pors
Sports Illus 24:18-21+ F 14 '66
BENZENE hexachloride. See Hexachlorocyclo-
hexane
BENZYLOXYAMINE
Histamine synthesis in man; inhibition by
4-bromo-3-hydroxybenzyloxyamine. R. J.
Levine. bibliog il Science 154:1017-19 N 25
'66
BEQUESTS. See Colleges and universities—
Gifts, legacies, etc.
BERANEK, Leo L.
Noise; with biographical sketch. Sci Am
215:16, 66-74+ D '66
BERAR, princess of
Many worlds of the entrancing Princess of
Berar. C. Beaton. il pors Vogue 147:98-
101+ F 15 '66

BERBERIAN, Cathy
Avant-garde Callas. H. Saal. por Newsweek
68:98+ N 7 '66
BERCZELLER, Richard
Morphinist. New Yorker 42:141-2+ Ap 16
'66
Revanche. New Yorker 42:200+ N 5 '66
BEREAVEMENT
Old antic. V. P. McCorry. America 115:262 S
10 '66
BEREITER, Carl
Pressure cooker for four-year-old minds. M.
Pines. il Harper 234:55-61 Ja '67
BERELSON, Bernard
What we don't know about children's be-
havior. PTA Mag 60:18-20 Je '66
BERENSON, Bernard
Forty years with Berenson, by N. Mariano.
Review
Esquire 66:106 D '66. M. Muggeridge
New Repub 155:29-32 D 24 '66. F. Biddle
Sat R 49:30 O 29 '66. B. D. Diamonstein
BERENSON, Mary (Smith)
Forty years with Berenson, by N. Mariano.
Review
New Repub 155:29-32 D 24 '66. F. Biddle
BERENSTAIN, Janice. See Berenstain, S. jt.
auth.
BERENSTAIN, Stanley, and Berenstain,
Janice
It's all in the family. See issues of McCall's
BERG, Alban
Alban Berg, by W. Reich. Review
Am Rec G por 32:901-3 My '66
Opera N 30:32 My 7 '66. L. Marker
BERG, Gertrude
Sunset. G. Ace. Sat R 49:14 O 8 '66
BERG, Harold B.
By the way. Christian Cent 83:1146 S 21 '66
BERG, Roland H.
Why hospitals overcharge patients. Look 30:
29-33 Je 14 '66
BERG, Stephen
Ollie, answer me; Going upstairs to bed;
poems. Poetry 108:107-9 My '66
BERGAMINI, David
High-level hearsay about Hirohito. Life 60:
12+ Je 17 '66
BERGEN, Candy
Goddess upstages the girls. P. Kael. il por
Life 60:118+ Ap 8 '66
BERGEN, Dan
Bibliographic organization in the social sci-
ences. bibliog por Wilson Lib Bul 40:751-8
Ap '66
Foundations of access to knowledge. Science
151:711 F 11 '66
BERGEN, Polly
Carrying the torch. il por Newsweek 67:80
Ja 31 '66
BERGEN, Norway

Historic houses, etc.

Bergen has a museum town; reconstructed
village of Gamle Bergen. il Sunset 137:8 S
'66
BERGEN-Belsen camp. See Concentration
camps
BERGEN drug company
Prescribing for the drug stores. il Bsns W
p 149-50+ S 10 '66
BERGER, Earl
Un-American Jew. Commentary 42:82-5 S '66
BERGER, Henry W.
Lovestone, Meany & State: American labor
overseas. Nation 204:80-4 Ja 16 '67
BERGER, Ivan
Dynamic power. Sat R 49:59 My 28 '66
Hi-fi. Esquire 66:28+ N '66
Looking for trouble. Sat R 49:57 F 26 '66
Music, Moscow, and transistors. Sat R 49:
56-7 Je 25 '66
Music wherever. Sat R 49:60-1 Jl 30 '66
N.Y. hi fi show. Sat R 49:67+ O 29 '66
Plus or minus 3dB. Sat R 49:55-6 D 31 '66
Tape on the turnpike. Sat R 49:64+ N 26 '66
Taping true, for less. Sat R 49:59+ Ag 27 '66
Testing, testing. Sat R 49:70-1 Mr 26 '66
Transistors and the shape of things. Sat R
49:53 Ja 29 '66
BERGER, J. E. and others
Laser as light source for optical diffractom-
eters: Fourier analysis of electron micro-
graphs. bibliog Science 153:168-70 Jl 8 '66
BERGER, John
Art. Nation 202:341-2 Mr 21 '66
Familiars of death. Nation 203:553-7 N 21 '66
BERGER, Morroe
Belly dance. Horizon 8:42-9 Spr '66
BERGER, Rainer, and others
Radiocarbon content of marine shells from
the California and Mexican West coast.
bibliog Science 153:864-6 Ag 19 '66

BERGER, Robert A. and Orentreich, Norman
Mustaches are for men. Todays Health 44:69-70+ N '66
BERGER, Samuel D.
Korea, progress and prospects; address, May 7, 1966. S. D. Berger. Dept State Bul 54:860-5 My 30 '66
BERGES, Ruth
Unanswered question. Opera N 30:6-7 Mr 26 '66
BERGESEN, Sigval
Surge to the sea. il por Time 88:102-3 N 11 '66
BERGETHON, K. Roald
Student attitudes at Lafayette, 1964-65. Sch & Soc 94:74-6 F 5 '66
BERGGRAV, Kari
Ferns in your house. il Horticulture 44:18-21+ Je '66
Plants in offices. Horticulture 44:32-5+ F '66
BERGIN, Thomas G.
In the days of knights. Sat R 49:26 Jl 2 '66
BERGMAN, Ingmar
Scandinavian screen. R. Schickel. Holiday 40:156+ N '66
BERGMAN, Jules
If Zeus fails, can Sprint save us? N Y Times Mag p26-7+ Mr 20 '66
BERGMANN, Winogene L. and Ledlie, M. E.
Children's books of 1965-66. NEA J 55:57-8+ N '66
BERGQUIST, Laura
Never before a war like this. Look 30:27-35 D 13 '66
Women of Vietnam. Look 30:17-21 D 27 '66

about

Behind the scenes; visit to Vietnam. L. Botto. il por Look 30:M1 D 13 '66
BERGSTROM, Robert
Summer baseball school. por Parks & Rec 1:311+ Ap '66
BERING SEA
Exposure of basement rock on the continental slope of the Bering Sea. D. W. Scholl and others. bibliog il Science 153:992-4 Ag 26 '66
BERING slope. See Continental shelf
BERK, William L.
Oxidation ditch. Am City 81:120-1+ S '66
BERKELEY, Norborne, Jr
Economics of recreation. por Parks & Rec 1:549-50 Jl '66
BERKELEY, Calif.

Police

Finest of the finest. il Time 87:49 F 18 '66
BERKELEY Baptist divinity school. See Theological schools
BERKNER, Lloyd V. and Marshall, L. C.
Role of oxygen. Sat R 49:30-4 My 7 '66
—and others
Footnote to the Argentine crisis: a letter from American scientists. Science 154:992 N 25 '66
BERKSHIRE community college, Pittsfield, Mass.
Junior college: social experiment. M. Fallows. Commonweal 85:9-13 O 7 '66
BERKSHIRE symphonic festival
Lenox, Mass. Tanglewood's Die zauberflöte. F. Merkling. Opera N 31:28 S 10 '66
Magic flute, almost all-American; Tanglewood music festival. W. B. Syer. il Hi Fi 16:MA15 N '66
Tanglewood tale. F. Stevenson. il Opera N 30:20-3 Je 4 '66
BERLAND, Theodore
Hidden cancer no one talks about. Todays Health 44:36-7+ Ap '66
Lifesaving fog. Todays Health 44:22-4+ D '66
Lost radium, killer at large. Pop Mech 125:100-4+ Jl '66
More spare parts for humans. Todays Health 44:42-5+ Jl '66
New gains in war on hepatitis. Todays Health 44:20-1+ Ag '66
Our dirty sky. Todays Health 44:40-5 Mr '66
Saving the brain of General Wood. Todays Health 44:28-33+ S '66
BERLE, Milton
Uncle Miltie's back. il Newsweek 68:60 S 12 '66
BERLIN, Brent, and others
Folk taxonomies and biological classification. bibliog Science 154:273-5 O 14 '66
BERLIN, Irving
At 78, Berlin gives Annie a new show-stopper, and is pleased with himself. T. Prideaux. por Life 60:47 Je 10 '66
Berlin festival. il por Time 87:86 My 6 '66
Mr American music. H. Hewes. por Sat R 49:36+ O 1 '66

BERLIN, Irving N.
Learning as therapy. Sat R 49:78-9 O 15 '66
Special learning problems of deprived children. NEA J 55:23-4 Mr '66
BERLIN

Air raids

Day I bombed Berlin. L. Rosten. Look 30:9 F 8 '66

History

Allied occupation, 1945-
See also
Berlin wall, 1961-

Music

Stuttgart in Berlin. J. H. Sutcliffe. il Opera N 31:32 D 17 '66
BERLIN (East Berlin)
Letter from Berlin. J. Wechsberg. New Yorker 42:181-4+ O 15 '66

Music

Berlin, Dresden: East Berlin's Komische oper. J. H. Sutcliffe. il Opera N 31:32-3 Ja 14 '67
Berlin; East Berlin Staatsoper's Wozzeck. J. H. Sutcliffe. Opera N 30:32 F 5 '66
Berlin; world premiere of Paul Dessau's Puntila. J. H. Sutcliffe. il Opera N 31:31 D '66
BERLIN (West Berlin)
Caught in the middle; decision which bars Berlin deputies from voting. Newsweek 68:41-2 N 28 '66
Letter from Berlin. J. Wechsberg. New Yorker 42:149-50+ O 15 '66
New mayor. il Time 88:26 D 23 '66

Architecture

One, two, three. il Arch Forum 124:76-7 Mr '66

Economic conditions

Atlantic report. Atlan 217:18+ Je '66

Music

Berlin. J. H. Sutcliffe. il Opera N 30:31 F 19 '66
BERLIN, Battle of, 1945
Last battle, by C. Ryan. Review
Life 60:8+ Ap 1 '66. T. Carmichael
New Yorker 42:122-4 Ag 27 '66. N. Bliven
Sat R il 49:30-2 Mr 26 '66. D. Schoenbrun
Time il 87:100 Ap 1 '66
Last battle; excerpt. C. Ryan. il Read Digest 88:189-92+ Mr; 241-6+ Ap; 239-42+ My '66
BERLIN film festival. See Moving picture festivals
BERLIN free university. See Colleges and universities—Germany (Federal Republic)
BERLIN question, 1945-
Berlin revisited: thoughts on unification. K. K. Loewenstein. bibliog f Cur Hist 50:263-8+ My '66
See also
Berlin wall, 1961-
BERLIN wall, 1961-
Atlantic report; wall, after five years. Atlan 217:20+ Je '66
Berlin wall: bigger, uglier, causing new tension. il U S News 61.4 Ag 15 '66
Letter from Berlin. J. Wechsberg. New Yorker 42:149-50+ O 15 '66
No handholds for freedom. il Time 88:28+ Jl 22 '66
Walter's wow; Walter Ulbricht's praises. Time 88:29 Ag 19 '66
BERLINER, Arthur
Case for Enrico. Opera N 31:21-3 D 31 '66
BERLIOZ, Hector
Berlioz or Crespin? R. Lawrence. Sat R 49:52+ Ja 29 '66
Mediterranean Götterdämmerung; Les Troyens discs. R. Gelatt. Reporter 34:50+ Mr 24 '66
On records; Les Troyens (excerpts) Opera N 30:34 Ap 9 '66
On records: Requiem. Opera N 30:30 My 7 '66
Les Troyens (Trojan men) Criticism
Opera N 31:9+ N 5 '66
BERLITZ schools of languages
Crowell Collier hits fiscal highs, buys Berlitz schools. Pub W 189:104 F 14 '66
BERLYNE, Daniel E.
Conflict and arousal; with biographical sketch. Sci Am 215:10, 82-7 bibliog (p 116) Ag '66
Curiosity and exploration. bibliog Science 153:25-33 Jl 1 '66
BERMAN, Harold J.
We can trade with the Communists. Nation 202:766-70 Je 27 '66
BERMAN, Leopold
Case for educational parks. Arch Rec 139:182 F '66

BERMUDA
Lure of Bermuda; photographs. Yachting 119: 95-8 Je '66
See also
Tourist trade—Bermuda

Description and travel

Finish line vigil; is what you make it. J. Norton. il Yachting 119:102-4+ Je '66
BERMUDA agreement. See Aviation—International aspects
BERMUDA ocean races. See Yacht racing
BERNANOS, Georges
Unfathomable human spirit. T. Molnar. Nat R 18:1333+ D 27 '66
BERNARD, Patti
Self-improvers. B. Davidson. il por Ladies Home J 84:64-5+ Ja '67
BERNARD, Tom
Self-improvers. B. Davidson. il por Ladies Home J 84:64-5+ Ja '67
BERNARD, Tomás Diego
Museum school. Américas 18:30-2 My '66
BERNAYS, Edward L.
Permission to quote. Writer 79:20-2 Ap '66
BERNE, Eric
Games people play at Christmas. McCalls 94:82-3+ D '66
about
Doctor Berne plays the celebrity game. J. Langguth. il pors N Y Times Mag p 10-11+ Jl 17 '66; Discussion. p22 Ag 28 '66
Games keeper. por Newsweek 68:56 Ag 8 '66
Psychiatrist in the chips; with report by J. Fincher. il pors Life 61:35-6+ Ag 12 '66
BERNER, Robert A.
Diagenesis of carbonate sediments: interaction of magnesium in sea water with mineral grains. bibliog Science 153:188-91 Jl 8 '66
BERNHARDT, Sarah
Madame Sarah. by C. O. Skinner. Review Life 62:12 Ja 20 '67. T. Prideaux Newsweek pors 69:90+ Ja 16 '67. S. Schmidt
Sat R 50:37 Ja 21 '67. P. Burton
Time il por 89:86-E7 Ja 20 '67
BERNINI, Giovanni Lorenzo
Great discovery; Bernini's work at the age of thirteen; with report on I. Lavin's finds. il por Life 62:66-72+ Ja 20 '67
Prodigy Bernini; I. Lavin's discoveries. por Newsweek 69:85 Ja 23 '67
Testaments to a baroque prodigy. il Time 89: 58 Ja 20 '67
BERNINI, Pietro
Who did what in the Bernini family. il Life 62:74 Ja 20 '67
BERNLOHR, Robert W.
Ornithine transcarbamylase enzymes: occurrence in bacillus licheniformis. bibliog Science 152:87-8 Ap 1 '66
BERNS, Donald S. and others
Urease activity in blue-green algae. bibliog Science 152:1077-8 My 20 '66
BERNS, Walter
Defending politics. Commentary 42:62-4 Ag; 20+ N '66
BERNSTEIN, Blanche
UNICEF. Dept State Bul 54:271-80 F 21 '66
BERNSTEIN, Burton
Just for laughs. Look 30:M8 D 27 '66
BERNSTEIN, Haskell, and Neisser, E. G.
Can a child be too good? Parents Mag 41: 33-5+ Ap '66
BERNSTEIN, Irwin S.
Naturally occurring primate hybrid. Science 154:1559 D 23 '66
BERNSTEIN, Jeremy
Books (cont) New Yorker 42:174+ Ap 16; 117-20+ My 28 '66
Our far-flung correspondents (cont) New Yorker 42:148+ Mr 26 '66
Profiles. New Yorker 42:70-2+ N 12 '66
BERNSTEIN, Leonard
Bernstein eruption, new Rosenkavalier. E. Greenfield. il Hi Fi 16:MA28-9 Jl '66
Music to my ears; performance of Haydn's Creation. I. Kolodin. il Sat R 49:38 My 28 '66
Musical events: concert of contemporary American compositions performed by Philharmonic. W. Sargeant. New Yorker 41: 134 F 19 '66
Musical events; Philharmonic concert, in Philharmonic Hall. W. Sargeant. New Yorker 41:113 F 12 '66
Ovations for Bernstein's Falstaff. W. Weaver. il por Hi Fi 16:126-7 Je '66
BERNSTEIN, Theodore M.
Beware these word-traps! excerpt from The careful writer. Read Digest 88:33+ Ap '66

BERNSTEIN, Victor H.
Private wealth and public office: high cost of campaigning. Nation 202:770-5 Je 27 '66
What church unity demands of Catholics and Protestants. Redbook 126:64-5+ Mr '66
Why Negroes are still angry. Redbook 127: 54-5+ Jl '66
BERREMAN, Gerald D.
On the role of women. Bul Atomic Sci 22: 26-8 N '66
BERRIAULT, Gina
Last firing squad. Esquire 65:88-91+ Je '66
Naked luncheon. Esquire 65:96-7+ Mr '66
Science of life; story. Redbook 126:86-7 Ap '66
Search for J. Kruper; story. Esquire 66:104-5 O '66
BERRIES
Strange berry has a flavor secret. il Pop Mech 125:107 Je '66
See also
Cookery—Fruit
also names of berries, e.g. Blueberries
BERRIGAN, Daniel
Berrigan. New Yorker 42:34-5 Ap 9 '66
Berrigan is back. Christian Cent 83:357 Mr 23 '66
Reflections on a press conference. P. K. Cuneo. America 114:414 Mr 26 '66
Three younger poets. R. J. Mills, jr. Poetry 109:116 N '66
BERRIGAN, Ted
Portrait and its double. Art N 64:30-3+ Ja '66
Red power. Art N 65:44-6 D '66
BERRILL, Michael
Stillness on Eniwetok; with biographical sketch. por Natur Hist 75:4, 20-5 bibliog(p70) D '66
BERRILL, N. J.
Roots of human nature. Atlan 217:92-6 Je '66
BERRY, Faith
Black artist, black prophet. New Repub 154: 23-5 My 28 '66
BERRY, James R.
Can you find water with a forked stick? Pop Mech 126:88-91+ Jl '66
New 007 is a computer. Pop Mech 125:84-7+ Ap '66
Rugged camps turn boys into iron men. Pop Mech 125:116-19+ My '66
BERRY, John
Comeback at Carborundum. Duns R 87:36-9+ Ap '66
Executive bookshelf. Duns R 88:139 O '66
High-pressure market in auto safety. Duns R 87:43-4+ My '66
BERRY, John M.
Rhode Island's misspent youth. Reporter 34:29+ Ja 27 '66
—and Clay, Mary
House, the home, and Title IV. Reporter 35:28-9+ S 8 '66
BERRY, Shura
Cargo cruises. Travel 125:30-4 F '66
BERRY, Virginia
Pietà; poem. Commonweal 85:228 N 25 '66
BERRY, Walter
Man and wife; interview, ed. by R. Eyer. por Opera N 31:14-15 D 17 '66
BERRY, Wendell
Before dark; poem. Commonweal 84:52 Ap 1 '66
Boatmen's paradox: consumers of the river. Nation 203:381-5 O 17 '66
Going; Porch over the river; poems. Poetry 108:237-8 Jl '66
Strip-mine morality; landscaping of hell. Nation 202:96-100 Ja 24 '66
BERRY, Wilfred
Direct seeding. Horticulture 44:30-1+ Mr '66
BERRY, William R.
Hot-air balloons race on silent winds. Nat Geog Mag 129:392-407 Mr '66
BERRY-QUERESHI, Shirin Roshan. See Moynihan, S. R. B. M.
BERSON, Debbie
Bogie really had cool. Seventeen 26:16 Ja '67
BERSON, Minnie P. and Chase, W. W.
Planning preschool facilities. pors Am Ed 2:7-11 D '65
BERSON, Solomon A. and Yalow, R. S.
Iodoinsulin used to determine specific activity of iodine-131. bibliog Science 152:205-7 Ap 8 '66
Parathyroid hormone in plasma in adenomatous hyperparathyroidism, uremia, and bronchogenic carcinoma. bibliog Science 154:907-9 N 18 '66
BERTON, Pierre
Ingenious new laborsaving devices; excerpt from My war with the 20th century. Read Digest 88:147-8 Ap '66

BERUBE, Maurice R.
    Death in the schools. Nation 203:520-1 N 14
        '66
    Strike at St John's: why the professors
        picket. Nation 202:172-4 F 14 '66
    White liberals, black schools. Commonweal
        85:71-3 O 21 '66
BERWALD, Franz Adolf
    Two Nonesuch releases provide a new look
        at Franz Berwald. A. Cohn. por Am Rec
        G 32:1038-9 Jl '66
BERYLLIUM
    Firm seeks bigger beryllum market. J. F.
        Judge. il Miss & Roc 18:22-3 Ap 11 '66
    MSFC testing beryllium for structural use.
        Miss & Roc 18:32 Ja 24 '66
BESELER enlarger. See Photography—En-
    larging
BESS, Donovan
    View from Hunters Point: no way downtown.
        Nation 203:606-9 D 5 '66
BESSE, Ralph M.
    Community service; address, April 5, 1966.
        Vital Speeches 32:466-9 My 15 '66
BESSMAN, Samuel P. See Hammel, C. L. jt.
    auth.
BESSMERTNOVA, Natalia
    Ballerina named immortal; with report by
        P. Young. il pors Life 60:81-2 Je 24 '66
    Two for tomorrow. il por Time 87:62 My
        27 '66
BEST, Jay Boyd, and Elshtain, Errol
    Unconditioned response to electric shock:
        mechanism in planarians. bibliog Science
        151:707-9 F 11 '66
BEST, Winfield
    Case for the small family. Parents Mag 41:
        38-41 Je '66
BEST books. See Books and reading—Best
    books
BEST man; story. See Maloney, R.
BEST of friends at Farmington; story. See
    Bryan, C. D. B.
BEST play awards. See New York drama
    critics circle
BEST sellers
    Best sellers in France. H. R. Lottman. Pub
        W 190:43-5 O 10 '66
    Best sellers of the week. See issues of
        Publishers' weekly
    Truth about the best-seller list. W. Good-
        man. il McCalls 94:89+ N '66
BESTER, Alfred
    Amateur astronomy. Holiday 40:113-18 S '66
    Disappearing seacoast. Holiday 40:56-69+ Jl
        '66
BETA globulins. See Serum globulins
BETANCOURT CUETO, Angel
    Captive in church. il por Time 87:34-5 Ap
        22 '66
BETAR, Samuel J.
    Two against the mob. H. Bruno. Newsweek
        67:44+ My 23 '66
BETHEL, Paul D.
    Correspondence with Theodore Draper &
        Commentary, appropriate & inappropriate.
        Nat R 18:823-17 Ag 23 '66
    Dominican intervention: the myths. Nat R
        18:107-11 F 8 '66
    Dominican Republic goes to the polls. Re-
        porter 34:18-20+ Je 2 '66
    Havana conference. Reporter 34:26-9 Mr 24
        '66
BETHLEHEM, Jordan
    Little town of Bethlehem. C. Stinnett. Holi-
        day 40:54+ D '66
BETHLEHEM, Star of. See Star of Bethlehem
BETJEMAN, John
    Anglo-Catholic congresses; poem. Christian
        Cent 84:47 Ja 11 '67
    By the ninth green St. Enodoc; poem. New
        Yorker 42:54 O 1 '66
    Cornish cliffs; poem. New Yorker 42:46 My
        21 '66
    In Willesden churchyard; poem. New Yorker
        42:54 S 10 '66
    Tregardock; poem. Atlan 217:89 F '66
BETTELHEIM, Bruno
    Dialogue with mothers. See issues of Ladies'
        home journal
    Violence: a neglected mode of behavior. bib-
        liog f Ann Am Acad 364:50-9 Mr '66
    (ed) Why working mothers feel guilty. Red-
        book 126:55+ Mr '66
BETTER business bureau
    Slick spring swindlers. Consumer Bul 49:28-9
        Je '66
BETTING. See Book making (betting); Gam-
    bling
BETTIS, Valerie
    Dancers studio; Stage 73. J. Anderson. Dance
        Mag 40:68-9+ Jl '66

BETTS, Charles A.
    Congress goading sea science. Sci N 90:418-19
        N 19 '66
    Ocean is expansive oil field. Sci N 89:372-3
        My 14 '66
    Pilots given new eyes. Sci N 89:222-3 Ap 2 '66
BEUTLER, Ernest. See Mathai, C. K. jt.
    auth.
BEV accelerators. See Accelerators (electrons,
    etc)
BEVAN, David Crumley
    Man who met the Pennsy's bills. il por Bsns
        W p62-4 Jl 16 '66
BEVERAGE industry
    Harder sell for soft drinks; U.S. soft drinks
        abroad. il Time 88:94+ N 4 '66
        See also
    Coca-Cola company

        Securities
    Soft drinks: a touch of glamour. il Fortune
        74:160+ Jl 1 '66
BEVERAGES
    Corkscrew: mineral waters and mixers. P. S.
        Brown. House & Gard 130:210+ S '66
    Drinks for everyone! recipes from The non-
        drinker's drink book. B. Rollin and L.
        Rosenfeld. il Redbook 126:78-9+ F '66
    Elixirs for the long, cool summer. Esquire
        66:108 Jl '66
    Fabulous floats! with recipes. il Bet Hom &
        Gard 44:74 Jl '66
    Hot idea drinks to serve with a flourish.
        il Bet Hom & Gard 44:80-1+ O '66
    Soft drink labels now speak softly. Consumer
        Rep 31:218-19 My '66
    Tinting supermarkets with orange and blue.
        il Bsns W p42-3+ Jl 2 '66
        See also
    Coffee
    Fruit juices
    Liquors
    Punch (beverage)
BEVINS, Karl A.
    Traffic engineer must be an educator. Am
        City 81:116-18 O '66
BEXELIUS, Alfred
    Little man's champion. Newsweek 68:28+
        D 12 '66
BEYCHOK, Sherman
    Circular dichroism of biological macro-
        molecules. bibliog Science 154:1288-99 D
        9 '66
BEYFUS, Drusilla
    Where the boys go. Mlle 62:191-2 Mr '66
BEYLE, Marie Henri
    Sentimental education. K. Rexroth. Sat R
        49:41 D 31 '66
    Stendhal's The red and the black. K. Rex-
        roth. Sat R 49:28 Je 11 '66
BEYOND the bedroom wall; story. See Woi-
    wode. L.
BEZ, Frank
    Into the sun. il U S Camera 29:44-5+ Jl '66
            about
    Diffused Jane Fonda. il U S Camera 29:
        60-1 Jl '66
BHABHA, Homi Jehangir
    Science and the problems of development;
        address. Science 151:541-8 F 4 '66
            about
    India's AEC head dies in crash. Science 151:
        430 Ja 28 '66
BHAVANANDAN, V. P. and Meyer, Karl
    Mucopolysaccharides: N-acetylglucosamine-
        and galactose-6-sulfates from keratosulfate.
        bibliog Science 151:1404-5 Mr 18 '66
BHUMIBOL Adulyadej, king of Thailand
    Holder of the kingdom, strength of the land.
        il pors Time 87:28-30+ My 27 '66
BHUTTO, Zulfikar Ali
    Medical discharge. Time 88:30 Jl 1 '66
BIANCHI, Eugene C.
    Book review. America 115:461 O 15 '66
    Censorship in the church. America 115:411-13
        O 8 '66
    Learning church in a teaching world. Cath
        World 203:287-92 Ag '66
    New books. Cath World 203:315-16 Ag '66
    Renewed priesthood. America 116:48-50+ Ja
        14 '67
BIANCOLLI, Louis
    Maestro's choice. Opera N 30:26-7 Ja 29 '66
    (ed) See Casals, M. M. Interview
    (ed) See Casals, P. Interview
            about
    Salute to a music critic. D. J. Soria. Hi Fi
        16:MA6 S '66

BIBLE

Post-biblical Christianity. D. Callahan. Commonweal 85:291-3 D 9 '66; Discussion. 85: 359+ Ja 6 '67
See also
Theology

Antiquities

Archaeological finds. H. D. Hummel. Christian Cent 83:499-500 Ap 20 '66
Masada; with introd. by N. Kotker. Y. Yadin. il Horizon 8:18-25+ Wint '66
Superior Samaritans; Jericho cave remains challenges the Bible. Time 87:42 Ap 1 '66
See also
Israel—Antiquities
Jordan—Antiquities
Ur

Bibliography

Bibles and Bible-related books for the spring gift season. il Pub W 189:91-9 F 14 '66
Bibles and related books for the holiday season. il Pub W 190:95-101 S 26 '66
Harvest of books in the biblical field. H. D. Hummel. Christian Cent 83:431-3 Ap 6 '66
Still the best seller. D. Dempsey. Sat R 49:44 D 3 '66

Concordance

Bible themes, by D. T. Maertens. Review Cath World 204:124 N '66. J. M. Connolly

Criticism, interpretation, etc.

Cambridge Bible commentary on the new English Bible, ed. by P. R. Ackroyd and others. Review
Cath World 204:125 N '66. E. H. Peters

Bibliography

Bibles and Bible-related books for the spring gift season. il Pub W 189:91-9 F 14 '66
Bibles and related books for the holiday season. il Pub W 190:101-4 S 26 '66

Theory, methods, etc.
See Bible—Hermeneutics

Dictionaries and encyclopedias

Dictionary of the Bible, by J. L. McKenzie. Review
Cath World 203:184 Je '66. J. C. Turro
Christian Cent 83:435 Ap 6 '66. F. W. Danker
Commonweal 83:674 Mr 11 '66. B. Vawter

Editions
See Bible—Versions

Evidences, authority, etc.

Untold story of the Dead Sea scrolls. J. M. Allegro. il Harper 233:46-54 Ag '66; Discussion. America 115:227-9 S 3 '66; Christian Cent 83:1211-13 O 5 '66

Hermeneutics

Hermeneutical theology. J. M. Robinson. Christian Cent 83:579-82 My 4 '66

Inspiration

Bible's timeless, and timely, insights. S. Blanton. Read Digest 89:93-6 Ag '66
Inspired word, by L. A. Schökel. Review
Commonweal 84:35-6 Mr 25 '66. R. E. Murphy
See also
Revelation

Interpretation
See Bible—Criticism, interpretation, etc.

Publication and distribution

Boom in Bibles. J. Thackray. il Duns R 88:39-40 Jl '66
See also
Bible societies
Bible society of Mexico

Quotations

Bible's timeless, and timely, insights. S. Blanton. Read Digest 89:93-6 Ag '66
Chicago tribune eisegesis; concerning out of context quotation from Deuteronomy. Christian Cent 83:856 Jl 6 '66

Stories
See Bible stories

Translations
See Bible—Versions

Versions

American Bible society publishes new, simplified Bible translation. Pub W 190:105 S 26 '66
Bible: new translations, new editions and commentaries. D. Stanley. America 115:747-54 D 3 '66

Bible translation in Japan. G. K. Chapman. Christian Cent 83:1611 D 28 '66
Bible translation in the Far East. K. R. Crim. Christian Cent 83:1320-2 O 26 '66
Common Bible and common witness. America 115:681-2 N 26 '66
Conservatives seek modern translation of the Bible. Christian Cent 83:930 Jl 27 '66
Curt, clear, complete; Jones's Jerusalem Bible. Time 88:53-4 N 4 '66
Ecumenical commentary? Commonweal 85: 215 N 25 '66
From the Hill of Fennel; Psalms I; new translation by M. Dahood in Anchor Bible. il Time 87:54+ F 4 '66
More common word; Catholics to cooperate with Protestant, Anglican and Orthodox Christians. Newsweek 68:88 N 21 '66
One for all at last; imprimatur given to Oxford annotated Bible. Time 87:62 Je 3 '66
Pope proposes common Bible. Christian Cent 83:1465 N 30 '66
RSV is a common Bible. America 114:788 Je 4 '66
Revelation in translation. H. M. Orlinsky. Sat R 49:46 D 3 '66
Still the best-seller. D. Dempsey. Sat R 49:44 D 3 '66

Old Testament

See also
David, king of Israel

Manuscripts
See also
Dead Sea scrolls

Pentateuch

State of Jewish belief; symposium; with introd. by M. Himmelfarb. Commentary 42: 71-160 Ag '66

Job

Book of God and man, by R. Gordis. Review
Commentary 41:80-6 My '66. D. Daiches
Book of Job. K. Rexroth. Sat R 49:21 Ap 23 '66

Psalms

From the Hill of Fennel; Psalms I; new translation by M. Dahood in Anchor Bible. il Time 87:54+ F 4 '66
Psalms: hymnbook of humanity. J. Daniel. il Read Digest 88:97-100 Ap '66

New Testament

Untold story of the Dead Sea scrolls. J. M. Allegro. il Harper 233:46-54 Ag '66; Discussion. America 115:227-9 S 3 '66; Christian Cent 83:1211-13 O 5 '66
See also
Jesus Christ

Epistles

Saint Paul, apostle to all men. E. O. Hauser. il Read Digest 89:146-50+ S '66

Gospels

Gospel is in the verb. P. Sanders. Christian Cent 83:400 Mr 30 '66
Gospels and anti-Semitism; excerpt from A Jew in Christian America. A. Gilbert. Cath World 203:157-60 Je '66
Synoptic problem and the contemporary theological chaos. W. R. Farmer, jr. Christian Cent 83:1204-6 O 5 '66; Discussion. 83: 1345-6 N 2 '66
See also
Jesus Christ—Teaching

Matthew

Christmas story, from the Gospels of Matthew and Luke; excerpts from the Metropolitan museum of art's current book, ed. by M. Northrup. il McCalls 94:59-65 D '66
On reading Matthew; question of a Judeo-Christian tradition. M. Himmelfarb; discussion. Commentary 41:12+ Mr '66

Luke

Christmas story, from the Gospels of Matthew and Luke; excerpts from the Metropolitan museum of art's current book, ed. by M. Northrup. il McCalls 94:59-65 D '66
Sign of the manger; St Luke's account of the Nativity. C. H. Giblin. il America 115: 826-8 D 24 '66

John

John's triumphant Christ. V. P. McCorry. America 114:677-8 My 7 '66

BIBLE societies

Bible is for all churches; UBS council resolutions. America 114:788 Je 4 '66
See also
American Bible society
Bible society of Mexico

BIBLE society of Mexico
Full-fledged Bible society. A. Zambrano. Christian Cent 83:1293-4 N 9 '66
BIBLE stories
Bestseller in Russia; new book called Biblical stories. Time 88:80 S 2 '66
BIBLIOGRAPHY
Bibliographic organization; symposium. ed. by J. Shera. bibliog il Wilson Lib Bul 40:703-20+ Ap '66; Correction. 40:911 Je '66
BIBLIOGRAPHY, International
Bibliographic organization at the international level. H. Coblans. bibliog il Wilson Lib Bul 40:733-7 Ap '66
BIBLIOMANIA. See Book collecting
BIBLIOTHÈQUE de la Pléiade. See Books—Reprints
BIBLIOTHERAPY
Reaching troubled minds through reading. C. Carner. Todays Health 44:32-3+ D '66
BIĆANIĆ, Rudolf
Economics of socialism in a developed country. For Affairs 44:633-50 Jl '66
BICARBONATE of soda. See Sodium bicarbonate
BICKEL, Alexander M.
After the arrest. New Repub 154:14-16 F 12; 37 Mr 5 '66
Civil rights' dim prospects. New Repub 155: 17-18 S 17 '66
Failure of the Warren report. Commentary 42:31-9 O '66
Forcing desegregation through Title VI. New Repub 154:8-9 Ap 9 '66
Is the Warren court too political? N Y Times Mag p30-1+ S 25 '66
Reexamining the Warren report. New Repub 156:25-8 Ja 7 '67
Rosenberg affair. Commentary 41:69-70+ Ja; 20+ Je '66
BICKFORD, Reginald G. See Scott, D. F. jt. auth.
BICKMORE, Lee S.
Problem of executive dropout. Duns R 87: 34-5+ Ap '66
BICYCLE racing
L'affaire Anquetil; Liege-to-Bastogne-to-Liege bicycle race. Sports Illus 24:21 My 16 '66
Nation's midsummer madness; sketches; with account by J. Olsen. Sports Illus 25:60-72+ Ag 22 '66
Reconnaissance by handlebar; pre-election buildup, South Vietnam. il Time 88:17 Ag 26 '66
BICYCLE trails. See Trails
BICYCLES
And now, a few kind words for the bicycle. il Horizon 8:72-7 Aut '66
Boom in bikeways. R. Hanneman. il Travel 126:26-30 Ag '66
Shopping tips: bicycles. il Changing T 20:45-6 Jl '66
Take 'em aboard to ride 'em ashore. N. Phillips. il Motor B 117:82-4 Ja '66
Wheelies and jumpies; sting ray bike. Newsweek 67:54 F 7 '66
BICYCLING. See Cycling
BIDDING, Competitive. See Contracts; Contracts, Government
BIDDLE, Francis
Adams uncles. New Repub 155:33-4 O 1 '66
Life with the Berensons. New Repub 155: 29-32 D 24 '66
BIEBER, Irving
What you should know about homosexuality. Parents Mag 41:62+ bibliog(p32) My '66
BIEMILLER, Andrew J.
Excerpt from testimony, June 15, 1965. Cong Digest 45:50+ F '66
BIENNALE, Venice. See Art—Exhibitions
BIENNIALS (plants)
Biennials make the early summer garden. P. Shedesky. il Flower Grower 53:24-5 Jl '66
BIER, Jesse
Hyde park; poem. New Repub 155:20 N 19 '66
BIERMAN, Jacquin D.
What every young father should know about taxes. Parents Mag 41:54-5+ Mr '66
BIERY, James
Corpus Christi's squad car lawyer. Reporter 36:43-5 Ja 12 '67
BIFFLE, Kent
Golden age of stein making. Hobbies 71:88 N '66
BIG BEND NATIONAL PARK
Big Bend and the botanist. E. E. Gamer. il Nat Parks Mag 40:14-17 Ap '66
Lady Bird's boat ride; White House staff's safari. S. Alexander. Life 60:34 Ap 15 '66
Let's travel: with Mrs LBJ to Big Bend. F. Koltun. il Mlle 63:26+ Jl '66

BIG business. See Corporations—Size
BIG evening; story. See Shyer, M. F.
BIG-game fishing. See Fishing
BIG man; drama. See Weinberg, L.
BIG trees. See Trees
BIGALKE, R. C.
Springbok. Natur Hist 75:20-5 Je '66
BIGART, Homer
Alaska's 100th; a century between Johnsons. Sat R 50:46-8+ Ja 7 '67
BIGGE, Morris L.
Theories of learning. NEA J 55:18-19 Mr '66
BIGGS, Ken
Darkroom for every garage? il por Pop Phot 59:110-11 O '66
BIGHORN hunting. See Mountain sheep hunting
BIGHORNS. See Mountain sheep
BIGOTRY. See Toleration
BIK, Russell J.
Lighthouse for short people. Pop Electr 25:77-8 N '66
BIKILA, Abebe
Ethiopia's modern Pheidippides. il pors Ebony 21:128-33 Mr '66
BIKINI drone. See Aerial reconnaissance—Equipment
BILBAO, Pedro
Was Columbus in Canada? Américas 18:17-28 Jl '66
BILIARY calculi. See Calculi, Biliary
BILL (song) See Songs, American
BILL collecting. See Collecting of accounts
BILL of rights (United States) See United States—Constitution—Bill of rights
BILLBOARD (periodical)
Those gangbusting gospelers. Christian Cent 83:1163 S 21 '66
BILLBOARDS
Beauty and the billboards; OAAA support Beautification act. New Repub 154:8-9 Ap 23 '66
Politics of beauty. W. F. Buckley. jr. il Esquire 66:50-3 Jl '66
BILLIARDS
Pool shark from Brooklyn; Negro to participate in professional billiard tournaments. il Ebony 21:44-6+ S '66
Six trick billiard shots you can make. R. A. Kelly. il Pop Mech 125:144-7+ F '66
Willie Mosconi comes out shooting; after ten years in retirement. J. Tobin. Sports Illus 24:74+ My 2 '66
Wimpy was a sleeping beauty; L. Lassiter, world pocket billiards champion. B. Ottum. il Sports Illus 26:18-19 Ja 9 '67
BILLING
$50 a day, and going up. E. L. Crosby. il Atlan 218:102-4+ Jl '66
Stacey speeds delivery with new billing system. G. McCorkle. il Pub W 189:46-9 Ap 18 '66
Why hospitals overcharge patients; with case history. R. H. Berg. il Look 30:29-33 Je 14 '66
BILLINGHAM, R. E.
Tissue transplantation: scope and prospect; excerpts from addresses. bibliog Science 153:266-70 Jl 15 '66
BILLINGS, Donald E.
Problems of the solar corona. Sky & Tel 33: 18-21 Ja '67
BILLINGSLEY, Hobart Sherwood
Heretic in an arty sport. H. Weiskopf. il por Sports Illus 24:85-7 Mr 21 '66
BILLINGSLEY, Sherman
Obituary
Nat R 18:1034 O 18 '66
BILLIPP, Betty
Advice for mothers on All Hallows' eve; poem. McCalls 94:174 O '66
Ballad of the brown bag; poem. McCalls 94: 115 Ja '67
Mothers are people; poem. McCalls 93:158 Mr '66
BINARY stars. See Stars, Double
BINDER, Alan B.
Mariner IV: analysis of preliminary photographs. bibliog Science 152:1053-5 My 20 '66
BINDER, David
Balkan way of life. N Y Times Mag p69-70+ S 18 '66
Belgrade report: Keeping up with the Jovanovics. N Y Times Mag p24-5+ Ap 3 '66
Man battering at the Kremlin wall. N Y Times Mag p 10-11+ My 29 '66
BINDING (books) See Bookbinding
BINET tests. See Intelligence tests
BING, Rudolf
Four-year term; interview. ed. by F. Merkling. por Opera N 31:16 Ja 14 '67

BING, Rudolf—*Continued*

about

Bing dynasty. W. Sargeant. New Yorker 42: 76+ Je 4 '66
Lord of the manor. il pors Time 88:46-54+ S 23 '66; Same abr. with title Mr Bing calls the tune. Read Digest 89:130-4 D '66
New Met and its old master. il por Newsweek 68:70-9 S 19 '66
Profiles. J. Wechsberg. por New Yorker 42: 65-6+ S 17 '66

BING Crosby national pro-amateur championship. See Golf—Tournaments

BINGAY, Roberta Gibb
Game girl in a man's game. G. S. Brown. il por Sports Illus 24:67-8+ My 2 '66
Queen of the marathon. por Time 87:104 Ap 29 '66

BINGER, James Henry
Honeywell bets on automation. il por Bsns W p60-2+ F 5 '66

BINGHAM, Hiram
Machu Picchu; an anthology, excerpts. comp. by H. Buse. il Américas 18:15-21 Ja '66
Tombs of Machu Picchu; with bibliography. C. W. Goff. il por Américas 18:8-18 Ag '66

BINGHAM, June
U Thant: the early years. Sat R 49:16-17 My 28 '66

BINGHAM, Walter
Tennis. Sports Illus 25:73-4+ N 21 '66

BINOCULARS. See Field glasses

BINSFELD, Edmund L.
Portrait; poem. Christian Cent 84:13 Ja 4 '67

BIOASTRONAUTICS. See Space flight—Physiological aspects

BIOCHEMISTRY
Form and function: biological key. B. J. Culliton. il Sci N 91:8-9 Ja 7 '67
George Wald; interview. G. Wald. New Yorker 42:42-4 Ap 16 '66
One of the great mystery stories of medicine; search for a cure for schizophrenia. L. Galton. il N Y Times Mag p34-5+ N 6 '66; Discussion. p41 N 20; 42+ N 27 '66
That old chemical complex, the human mind. I. Asimov. il N Y Times Mag p 12-13+ Jl 3 '66
Untangling biological reactions; address, December 28, 1966. H. Eyring. bibliog il Science 154:1609-13 D 30 '66
What kind of mixer is alcohol? L. Galton. il Pop Sci 188:95-7+ Ap '66
Your body chemistry; quiz. J. Daugherty and M. Daugherty. il Sci Digest 59:89-91 Ap '66
See also
Biosynthesis
Chemoreceptivity
Enzymes
Molecules
Paleobiochemistry
Proteins

BIOELECTRIC control. See Electrophysiology
BIOENGINEERING. See Human engineering
BIOGEOCHEMISTRY. See Geochemistry
BIOGRAPHIES
Useful but much maligned books: campaign biographies and their reviews. O. Collier. ALA Bul 60:609-12 Je '66

BIOGRAPHY
And then the queen died. A. M. Wells. Writer 79:12-14 S '66
Eunuchs in the harem. J. O'Hara. il Holiday 40:16+ S '66
Literary biography: art or archaeology? L. Kronenberger. Atlan 218:111-14 S '66
Permission to quote; use of original documents, letters, etc. E. L. Bernays. Writer 79:20-2 Ap '66

Bibliography

Biography (cont) F. J. Gallagher. America 114:666+; 115:704+ My 7, N 26 '66

BIOLOGICAL abstracts (periodical)
Biosciences information service of biological abstracts. P. V. Parkins. bibliog il Science 152:889-94 My 13 '66

BIOLOGICAL apparatus and supplies
Calibration of β gauges for determining leaf water status. P. G. Jarvis and R. O. Slatyer. bibliog il Science 153:78-9 Jl 1 '66
Insulated gate field effect transistor amplifier. R. L. Cechner. il Science 153:1549-50 S 23 '66
Long-term activity recording in small aquatic animals. A. A. Heusner and J. T. Enright. bibliog il Science 154:532-3 O 28 '66
Piston extractor for the Hughes press. N. Mandell and C. F. Roberts. bibliog il Science 152:799-800 My 6 '66

BIOLOGICAL balance. See Balance of nature
BIOLOGICAL chemistry. See Biochemistry
BIOLOGICAL clocks. See Periodicity
BIOLOGICAL control of insects. See Insects, Injurious and beneficial—Control
BIOLOGICAL cycles. See Periodicity
BIOLOGICAL literature
Bibliographic organization in the biomedical sciences. S. Adams. bibliog il Wilson Lib Bul 40:714-18 Ap '66
BIOLOGICAL luminescence. See Luminescence, Biological
BIOLOGICAL models
Walk-in portrait of a gene at work: W. Burtin's models. il Life 61:70-2+ Jl 8 '66
BIOLOGICAL physics
See also
Biomedical engineering
Bionics
BIOLOGICAL research
Biomedical policy: LBJ's query leads to an illuminating conference. D. S. Greenberg. Science 154:618-20 N 4 '66
By using nature as a lab. B. Commoner. Sat R 49:68-9 My 7 '66
Dehydration and rehydration in a prebiological system. A. E. Smith and F. T. Bellware. bibliog il Science 152:362-3 Ap 15 '66
How many rabbits still in the hat? concerning E. B. Chains predictions. J. L. Breeling. Todays Health 45:39-40 Ja '67
Skin. R. F. Rushmer and others. bibliog il Science 154:343-8 O 21 '66
Synthesis and survival, 1966. B. J. Culliton. Sci N 90:553 D 24 '66
Too much silence on the potentials of biology? V. K. McElheny. Science 153:283 Jl 15 '66
See also
Biotelemetry
European molecular biology organization
Fishery research
Pasteur institute, Paris
Salk institute for biological studies, San Diego, Calif.
BIOLOGICAL sciences
See also
American institute of biological sciences
BIOLOGICAL specimens

Collection and preservation

Everybody profits but the starfish. R. Rood. il NEA J 55:34-5 My '66

BIOLOGICAL telemetry. See Biotelemetry
BIOLOGICAL transport
Facilitation by carbonic anhydrase of carbon dioxide transport. T. Enns. bibliog il Science 155:44-7 Ja 6 '67
BIOLOGICAL warfare
Scientists speak out on CB weapons; letter to President Johnson, September 19, 1966. Bul Atomic Sci 22:39 N '66
United Nations and chemical warfare. H. A. Jack. Christian Cent 84:60-2 Ja 11 '67

Defenses

Army fights bio-warfare. J. Eberhart. Sci N 90:268 O 8 '66

BIOLOGICAL zoo, Jerusalem. See Zoological gardens

BIOLOGY
See also
Biological research
Cell division (biology)
Cells
Chromosomes
Death (biology)
Embryology
Evolution
Fertilization (biology)
Genetics
Heredity
Morphology
Polymorphism (biology)
Psychobiology
Space biology
Symbiosis

Nomenclature

Copyright bill: taxonomic works; letter. R. L. Usinger and W. I. Follett. Science 152:291-2 Ap 15 '66
Folk taxonomies and biological classification. B. Berlin and others. bibliog il Science 154: 273-5 O 14 '66

Periodicals

See also
Biological abstracts (periodical)

Philosophy

Phenomenon of life. by H. Jonas. Review
    Commentary 42:94-5 S '66. M. Grene

BIOLOGY—*Continued*

Study and teaching
Need live experiments. Sci N 89:166 Mr 12 '66

Terminology
Terminology of vertebrate melanin-containing cells: 1965. T. B. Fritzpatrick and others. bibliog Science 152:88-9 Ap 1 '66

BIOLUMINESCENCE. See Luminescence, Biological

BIOMECHANICS. See Human engineering

BIOMEDICAL engineering
Hospital to benefit from space work. H. M. David. il Miss & Roc 18:26+ F 28 '66
Reflections on biological engineering. G. M. Schurr. Christian Cent 83:1300-3 O 26 '66
Space cabin contaminant study spurred by environment tests. H. M. David. Tech W 19:20+ Jl 4 '66
Space engineering techniques aid medicine; report on 19th annual conference in medicine and biology. Tech W 19:30 N 21 '66

BIOMEDICAL research. See Medical research

BIONICS
Human basis studied for space systems. H. M. David. Tech W 18:41 Je 13 '66
Model organs live faster. Sci N 90:5 Jl 2 '66
Nature still holds lessons for engineers. W. S. Beller. il Tech W 19:28-9 D 19 '66
See also
Artificial intelligence
Man amplifiers

BIORHYTHM. See Periodicity

BIOSATELLITES. See Artificial satellites—Use in research

BIOSYNTHESIS
Biosynthesis of gamma globulin: studies in a cell-free system. K. H. Stenzel and A. L. Rubin. bibliog il Science 153:537-9 Jl 29 '66
Prostaglandin synthesized; dihydro-PGE 1. il Sci N 89:481 Je 18 '66

BIOTECHNOLOGY. See Bionics; Human engineering

BIOTELEMETRY
Pill gives inside view; radio transmitters giving scientists data on basic body functions. P. McBroom. il Sci N 90:131 Ag 27 '66

BIOTIN
Naturally occurring antimetabolite antibiotic related to biotin. L. J. Hanka and others. bibliog il Science 154:1667-8 D 30 '66

BIPLANE wings. See Airplane wings

BIRCH, Albert Otis
Case of the missing millionaire. J. Phelan. il pors Sat Eve Post 239:85-91 D 17 '66

BIRCH, John, society. See John Birch society

BIRCH, Thomas
Thomas Birch: America's first marine artist. W. H. Gerdts. il Antiques 89:528-34 Ap '66

BIRD, Caroline
Speaking out. por Sat Eve Post 239:10+ Je 18 '66

BIRD, John
Our dying waters. Sat Eve Post 239:29-35+ Ap 23 '66
(ed) See Bradnick, P. A. Kidnapped!

BIRD accidents. See Birds—Accidents and hazards

BIRD baths, etc.
Birdbath from a can cover. J. Mason. il Audubon Mag 68:196 My '66
Storied rock becomes a bird oasis. H. Carleton. il Audubon Mag 68:273-4 Jl '66

BIRD census
Can I count that bird? S. Keith. il Audubon Mag 68:24-6 Ja '66

BIRD doctoring. See Veterinary medicine

BIRD dogs
Dogs. D. M. Duffey. See issues of Outdoor life
Potter. R. Bailey. il Field & S 71:148-50 O '66
See also
Pointers (dogs)
Setters

Training
See Dogs—Training

BIRD feeders. See Feeders (birds)

BIRD flight. See Birds—Flight

BIRD fountains. See Glassware

BIRD houses
Dish-pan apartments for mosquito eaters; high-rise martin houses. K. W. Nightenhelser. il Pop Mech 125:170 Mr '66

BIRD market. See Brussels—Markets

BIRD populations
Initial and resultant population densities in chickens between brooding and sexual maturity. G. L. Mangan and M. G. King. bibliog il Science 154:1568-9 D 23 '66

Control
Air force war on birds. Sci N 91:26 Ja 7 '67
Control systems in bird reproduction; hypothalamus regulates avian breeding activity. D. S. Farner. il Natur Hist 75:22-7 Ag '66

BIRD prints. See Birds in art

BIRD sanctuaries
No fly-by-night operation; Stone Harbor bird sanctuary. B. Gilbert. il Sports Illus 24:36-8+ Je 20 '66
Wanderers from paradise; E. Hallstram's Nondugl sanctuary. il Life 60:68-73 Ap 15 '66
What future for birds of prey? protection of hawks at Hawk Mountain sanctuary. M. Broun. il Audubon Mag 68:330-4+ S '66
See also
Wildlife sanctuaries

BIRD shooting. See Shooting

BIRD shot. See Shot

BIRD songs. See Birds—Song

BIRD stories
Owl who was God; excerpt from Thurber carnival. J. Thurber. Read Digest 88:172C Mr '66

BIRD study
Annals of birdwatching; concerning Birds of Massachusetts and other New England states, by E. H. Forbush. E. B. White. New Yorker 42:42-6+ F 26 '66. Reply. G. T. Hellman. 42:171-3 Ap 16 '66
Bird finding. O. S. Pettingill, jr. See issues of Audubon magazine
Bird walk to Japan. A. Sprunt, jr. il Audubon Mag 68:186-7 My '66
Visit from a proud stranger; catching redtailed hawks and a golden eagle in a bow net. B. Gilbert. il Sports Illus 26:24-8 Ja 16 '67
You can take it with you. D. Shane. Audubon Mag 68:55-6 Ja '66
See also
Photography of birds

Anecdotes, facetiae, satire, etc.
Grandfather and the racquet-tailed drongo. J. Rhoades. il Sports Illus 24:60-4+ F 28 '66

BIRD watching. See Bird study

BIRDBATH; drama. See Melfi, L.

BIRDBATHS. See Bird baths

BIRDOFF, Harry
Enrico Caruso in My cousin. il Hobbies 71:36+ N; 36 D '66
First opera singer recording. Hobbies 71:37-8+ Je '66

BIRDS
Bird finding. O. S. Pettingill, jr. See issues of Audubon magazine
Birds in your garden. See issues of Popular gardening and living outdoors
Christmas card in my garden. R. E. Jennings. il Flower Grower 53:39-40 D '66
See also
Juncos

Accidents and hazards
Bright swingers stop collisions. E. Jarvis. il Audubon Mag 68:373-4 S '66
Day we almost didn't go; rescue of oil-covered loon. A. Gordon. il Read Digest 88:54-7 Mr '66
See also
Aviation—Bird hazards

Collisions with airplanes
See Aviation—Bird hazards

Flight
How high do birds fly? excerpt from Flashing wings: a story of bird flight. J. K. Terres. il Audubon Mag 68:449-53 N '66
Oxygen consumption of a flying bird. V. A. Tucker. bibliog il Science 154:150-1 O 7 '66
Parrots' muscles active. Sci N 90:338 O 22 '66
Timing will tell. W. Page. il Field & S 71:94-6+ N '66

Food and feeding
More on bird foods and habitats; excerpts. V. E. Davison. il Audubon Mag 68:58-61, 125-30 Ja-Mr '66
Our continuing list of bird foods. V. E. Davison. Audubon Mag 68:275-7 Jl '66
See also
Feeders (birds)

Habits and behavior
Annals of birdwatching; concerning Birds of Massachusetts and other New England states, by E. H. Forbush. E. B. White. New Yorker 42:42-6+ F 26 '66; Reply. G. T. Hellman. 42:171-3 Ap 16 '66

BIRDS—Habits and behavior—*Continued*
Enhanced distress vocalization through selective reinforcement; testing imprinted ducklings. H. S. Hoffmann and others. Science 151:352-4 Ja 21 '66
Freshest thing in feathers; the kingfisher. G. Heinold. il Read Digest 89:211-12+ S '66
Reporter at large: Serengeti and Ngorongoro Crater reserve. A. Moorehead. New Yorker 42:154+ O 29 '66
See also
Birds—Food and feeding
Periodicity

Hazards
See Birds—Accidents and hazards

Migration
See also
Orientation

Nests
See Nests

Odors
See Odors

Orientation
See Orientation

Photographs
Thrushes two; portrait of a robin and a bluebird. F. Matsumoto. Audubon Mag 68: 355 S '66

Physiology
Evolution of malate dehydrogenase in birds. G. B. Kitto and A. C. Wilson. bibliog il Science 153:1408-10 S 16 '66

Protection
Changing face of spring. B. Tufty. il Sci N 89:170-1+ Mr 12 '66
Pigeons everywhere, alas! reactions to San Francisco's bird purge. J. Fincher. il Life 61:149-50 D 9 '66
See also
Bird sanctuaries

Reproduction
See Reproduction

Sanctuaries
See Bird sanctuaries

Scent
See Odors

Song
Farmer Grösch and his singing birds. J. Stewart-Gordon. il Read Digest 88: 205-6+ F '66
Opera for the birds. E. S. Allison. il Opera N 31:6-7 D 17 '66

Study
See Bird Study

Alaska
Alaska is rewarding. O. S. Pettingill, jr. il Audubon Mag 68:9-13 Ja '66
Egg Island adventure. J. J. Stophlet. il Nat Parks Mag 40:9-12 Mr '66
Enjoying nature; at a Far North homestead. J. Haines. il Audubon Mag 68:370-1 S '66

Arizona
Murder with feathers. C. G. Finney. il Harper 232:112-13 Ap '66

Australia
See also
Kookaburras

Bahama Islands
See also
Flamingos

California
Convention country. O. S. Pettingill, jr. il Audubon Mag 68:271-217c Jl '66
Pigeons everywhere, alas! reactions to San Francisco's bird purge. J. Fincher. il Life 61:149-50 D 9 '66

Galápagos Islands
Strange gull (?) of the Galápagos; swallow-tailed gull. J. P. Hailman. il Audubon Mag 68:180-4 My '66

Guatemala
In the land of the Maya. D. Puleston. il Audubon Mag 68:146-50 My '66

Hawaii
See also
Nenes

Japan
Bird walk to Japan. A. Sprunt, jr. il Audubon Mag 68:186-7 My '66

Massachusetts
Bird finding in the Bay state. O. S. Bettingill, jr. il Audubon Mag 68:394+ N '66

New Guinea
Wanderers from paradise; E. Hallstram's Nondugl sanctuary il Life 60:68-73 Ap 15 '66

North America
Audubon's originals; adaptation of introd. to The original water-color paintings by J. J. Audubon from The birds of America; with portfolio of six reproductions. M. B. Davidson. il Audubon Mag 68:238-49 Jl '66
Basil Ede's birds in a New York gallery; with paintings. A. Meyer. Natur Hist 75: 32-41 O '66
New look at Audubon; with reproductions of paintings. M. B. Davidson. Horizon 8:32-41 Spr '66
Portfolio; paintings. J. F. Lansdowne. il Audubon Mag 68:454-61 N '66

South Dakota
Trailing Lewis and Clark. H. Krause. il Audubon Mag 68:78-80 Mr '66

Spain
Coto Doñana. O. S. Pettingill, jr. il Audubon Mag 68:304-306A S '66

United States
Changing face of spring. B. Tufty. il Sci N 89:170-1+ Mr 12 '66

BIRDS; drama. See Aristophanes
BIRDS, Albino. See Albinos and albinism
BIRDS, Predatory. See Birds of prey
BIRDS, Symbolism of. See Symbolism
BIRDS as carriers of infection
Birds bring disease; pulmonary histo-plasmosis. il Sci N 89:174 Mr 12 '66
BIRDS eggs
Of spring and an egg. J. George. il Read Digest 88:181-4 Ap '66
BIRDS in art
Audubon in the original; with excerpt from The original water-color paintings by John James Audubon for The birds of America. C. L. Mee, jr. Am Heritage 17:56-65 F '66
Birds and beasts in the Queen's gallery. O. Millar. il Antiques 90:824-7 D '66
Frontier epic; Audubon prints. il Newsweek 65:85 Ag 15 '66
BIRDS in music
Opera for the birds. E. S. Allison. il Opera N 31:6-7 D 17 '66
BIRDS muscles. See Muscles
BIRDS nests. See Nests
BIRDS of paradise
Wanders from paradise; E. Hallstram's Nondugl sanctuary. il Life 60:68-73 Ap 15 '66
BIRDS of prey
Plea for the birds of prey. C. W. Buchheister. Audubon Mag 68:294 S '66
What future for birds of prey? M. Broun. il Audubon Mag 68:330-4+ S '66
See also
Condors
Hawks
BIRK, Eileen P.
Books about antiques. Antiques 89:270, 580, 876 F, Ap, Je '66
Current and coming. See issues of Antiques, beginning July 1966-
BIRKERTS, Gunnar
Newest projects of Gunnar Birkerts. il Arch Rec 140:93-4 Ag '66
  about
Projects by Gunnar Birkerts. il Arch Rec 140:95-106 Ag '66
BIRKY, C. W. Jr, and Field, Bonnie
Nuclear number in the rotifer asplanchna; intraclonal variation and environmental control. bibliog Science 151:585-7 F 4 '66
BIRMINGHAM, Stephen
Job game. McCalls 93:76-7+ Jl '66
Other Barbara, the other Harris. Holiday 39:91-2+ Je '66
BIRMINGHAM, William
Round-up of recent religious books. Commonweal 83:616-21; 84:160 F 25, Ap 22 '66
BIRMINGHAM, Ala.
Hospitals
How to raise money; Eye foundation hospital. il Time 88:36 D 30 '66
BIRMINGHAM university
Building as a system; new laboratory buildings. T. Alexander. il Arch Forum 125:90-7 Jl '66

BIRNBAUM, Abe
Obituary
New Yorker 42:68 Jl 2 '66
BIRNBAUM, Hubert C.
How to find the best buy on a camera.
U S Camera 29:49+ D '66
Medium-speed color films. il U S Camera
29:44-7+ O '66
BIRNEY, Alice McLellan
Americans not everybody knows. C. W. Ferguson. il por PTA Mag 60:10-12 F '66
BIRNEY, D. Scott
Fan Mountain station of McCormick observatory. por Sky & Tel 31:210-12 Ap '66
BIRNIE, William A. H.
Where history isn't bunk. Read Digest 89:136-43 Jl '66
BIRNN, Roland
U.S. Coast guard auxiliary. See issues of Yachting
BIRSTEIN, Ann
Movies. Vogue 147:95 Mr 1; 59 Mr 15; 66 Ap 15; 56 Je; 148:30 Jl '66
Young and you're nervous; story; excerpt from Sweet birds of Gorham. Vogue 147:124-5 Mr 15 '66
BIRTH. See Childbirth
BIRTH, Multiple
See also
Quadruplets
Quintuplets
BIRTH control
About-face on birth control; government moving ahead. il Time 88:30 D 9 '66
Ahead of Washington; Gallup poll survey findings. Time 87:25 F 25 '66
As family planning gains favor in U.S. il U S News 62:48-50 Ja 9 '67
Birth control and population; Planned parenthood-world population conference in Washington. il Newsweek 67:94+ My 16 '66
Birth control going too far in the U.S? il U S News 60:44-6 My 9 '66
Birth control in high gear. M. Phelps. America 114:869 Je 25 '66
Birth control vs status. Sci N 90:374 N 5 '66
Birth limitation, Pandora's box. America 114:213 F 12 '66
Death of a taboo; House agricultural committee's worldwide program. Newsweek 67:32 My 16 '66
Every child a wanted child; M. Sanger. il Time 88:96+ S 16 '66
From exposition to advocacy; change of policy by New York state board of social welfare. America 116:4-5 Ja 7 '67
Greatest challenge of our time. J. D. Rockefeller, 3d. Read Digest 89:85-90 O '66
Kalamazoo to Calcutta; Todd amendment to food for freedom bill. K. Crawford. Newsweek 68:27 Jl 4 '66
Negro response to birth control. H. Lees. il Reporter 34:46-8 My 19 '66
Next: a sleep-in? birth control in colleges. J. Steinberg. Mlle 62:10+ Ap '66
No more seaweed. J. O'Gara. Commonweal 85:283 D 9 '66; Reply. S. H. Hutner. 85:385 Ja 6 '67
Pennsylvania and birth prevention. America 115:220-1 S 3 '66
Please have fewer babies; case for officially-supported birth-control programs in the United States. New Repub 154:6 F 5 '66
Pop!!ulation; address, November 29, 1965. D. T. Rice. bibliog Vital Speches 32:376-81 Ap 1 '66
Population tide can be turned back. Sci N 89:515 Je 25 '66
State and overpopulation; address, June 14, 1966. B. S. Brown. Vital Speeches 32:604-8 Jl 15 '66
We know what to do; Population council's report findings. Newsweek 67:63-4 Je 27 '66
See also
Abortion
Contraceptives
Malthusianism

Anecdotes, facetiae, satire, etc.
Baby, it's dark outside: Con Ed syndrome. G. Ace. Sat R 49:16 S 17 '66

History
Rebel with a cause: M. Sanger. il Newsweek 68:34+ S 19 '66

Religious aspects
Betty and Jack; concerning Pennsylvania Catholic conference pamphlet. Commonweal 84:454-5 Jl 22 '66
Birth control and coercion; the bishops' statement. W. V. D'Antonio. Commonweal 85:247-9 D 2 '66

Birth control decision; reply with rejoinder. P. Marx. Commonweal 83:517 Ja 28 '66
Birth control; letter. R. Laird. Commonweal 84:3+ Mr 25 '66
Birth control: policy of silence; slackening of Catholic opposition. America 114:575 Ap 23 '66
Birth control, talk control; American Catholic theological opinion. il Newsweek 67:62 F 14 '66
Birth control, what happened? G. Baum; discussion. Commonweal 83:542-3, 571+ F 4, 18 '66
Bishop Corson on birth control. Christian Cent 83:977 Ag 10 '66; Reply. J. W. Lord. 83:1138 S 21 '66
Bishop speaks out. America 114:718 My 21 '66
Bishops and birth. New Repub 155:4 D 3 '66
Bishops' controversial declaration. M. McGrory. America 115:769 D 10 '66
Bishops, HEW clash. Sci N 90:450 N 26 '66
Canadian bishops on law. America 115:533 N 5 '66
Catholics, marriage and contraception, by J. Marshall. Review
America 114:232 F 12 '66. G. G. Grisez
Change on birth control? pontifical commission favors a change. il Time 88:45 Jl 1 '66
Collision on contraception. Time 88:78 D 2 '66
Coming decision. Commonweal 84:407 Jl 1 '66
Consensus on birth control. J. Leo. New Repub 155:10 N 12 '66
Contraception, a history of its treatment by the Catholic theologians and canonists, by J. Noonan. Review
America 114:174+ Ja 29 '66. R. A. McCormick
Contraception and the council. J. T. Noonan, jr. Commonweal 83:657-62 Mr 11 '66
Contraception frustrates nature. W. F. Drummond. Cath World 203:202-6 Jl '66
Contraception fulfills nature. J. M. Ryan. Cath World 203:207-12 Jl '66
Contraception; interview. J. T. Noonan, jr. Cath World 203:153-6 Je '66
Contraception? not yet; Roman Catholics. Time 88:82 N 18 '66
Contraception: toward decision; possibility of a papal pronouncement on contraception. M. F. Valente. Christian Cent 84:77-9 Ja 18 '67
Deadlock on birth control; papal commission's report. Newsweek 67:74 Je 20 '66
History repeats itself. F. Canavan. America 114:738-42 My 21 '66; Reply with rejoinder. L. Sprietsma. 115:1 Jl 2 '66
Lex dubia non obligat; Roman Catholic views. Time 87:60-Ap 22 '66
More on the council and contraception. J. C. Ford. America 114:553-7 Ap 16 '66
Paul VI receives birth control studies. Christian Cent 83:856-7 Jl 6 '66
Pennsylvania bishops speak. America 115:4 Jl 2 '66
Pope and birth control. Commonweal 85:157 N 11 '66
Pope and the pill. Newsweek 68:64 N 14 '66
Pope delays his decision. America 115:576-7 N 12 '66
Pope postpones decision on birth control. Christian Cent 83:1401 N 16 '66
Pope's unsolvable problem. J. Roddy. Look 30:120+ D 13 '66; Discussion. 31:16 Ja 24 '67
Secret drama behind the Pope's momentous decision on birth control. L. R. Chevalier. Ladies Home J 83:88-9+ Mr '66
What did the council say on contraception? J. L. Thomas. America 114:294-6 F 26 '66

Egypt
Babies along the Nile; Combined service units program. P. Seale and I. Beeson. New Repub 154:10-11 My 7 '66

France
French birth control laws due for reform. Sci N 90:352 O 29 '66
Letter from Paris (cont) Genêt. New Yorker 42:165-7 N 5 '66

India
Uncertain trumpet. il Time 88:16 D 30 '66

Japan
How Japan stopped its population explosion. C. W. Hall. Read Digest 88:138-41 Mr '66

Mexico
As many as God sends? family planning in Mexico. M. Larkin. il Nation 203:508-11 N 14 '66

United States
See Birth control

BIRTH defects. See Deformities
BIRTH order
Birth order and its sequelae. W. D. Altus; discussion. bibliog Science 152:1177-8+ My 27 '66
Firstborns seem smarter. Sci N L 89:55 Ja 22 '66
Most likely to succeed. R. Kramer. il N Y Times Mag p72+ F 13 '66
BIRTH rate
See also
Birth control
Population, Increase of

Mexico

As many as God sends? family planning in Mexico. M. Larkin. il Nation 203:508-11 N 14 '66

United States

Blackout fallout; birth rate rise in New York city nine months after blackout. Time 88:40-1 Ag 19 '66
Mother & the pill. il Time 87:89-90 Je 3 '66
U.S. population stops exploding; with editorial comment. il Bsns W p 19-21, 96 Jl 2 '66
Welcome decline. il Time 87:19-20 My 6 '66
BIRTHDAY party for UNICEF; drama. See Fisher, A. and Rabe, O.
BISCAYNE BAY
Victory in Miami; a follow-up report. P. Redford. Harper 233:30 Ag '66
BISCHOFF, Ilse
Adding to a Meissen collection. Antiques 89:535-9 Ap '66
BISCOE, T. J. and Curtis, D. R.
Noradrenaline and inhibition of Renshaw cells. bibliog Science 151:1230-1 Mr 11 '66
BISCUIT ware. See Pottery
BISHKO, C. J.
(comp) Articles and other books received; Spain and Portugal. See issues of American historical review
BISHOP, Claire Huchet
Behind Jules Verne. Commonweal 85:169-71 N 11 '66
BISHOP, Edith P.
Experiment in Watts. Library J 91:338-9 Ja 15 '66
BISHOP, Elizabeth
Under the window: Ouro Preto; poem. New Yorker 42:34 D 24 '66

about
Sun the other way around. L. Mueller. Poetry 108:335-7 Ag '66
BISHOP, James
Post-painterly quattrocento. J. Ashbery. il Art N 65:40-1+ D '66
BISHOP, Jim
Bishop plans Kennedy book despite family's objection. Pub W 190:107 S 26 '66
BISHOP, Jordan
Bitter Latins. Commonweal 84:331-3 Je 10 '66
BISHOP, Katherine
Five with enterprise. P. Rifield. il por Mlle 63:145 S '66
BISHOP, Morris
French volunteer. Am Heritage 17:46-9+ Ag '66
Making of a cynic. Horizon 8:56-64 Wint '66
Perfect university. Atlan 217:66-8 My '66
1066. Horizon 8:4-27 Aut '66
(tr) See Petrarca, F. Letters of Petrarch; selection
BISHOP, Thomas
Avant-garde in retrospect. Sat R 49:43 N 19 '66
BISHOPS
Bishop Harold Perry: man of many firsts. E. B. Thompson. il Ebony 21:62-6+ F '66
Bishops and Protestant unity; episcopacy issue. America 114:684-5 My 14 '66
Election of bishops. J. D. Conway. Cath World 204:77-81 N '66
For the people; profile of a bishop. America 114:248-9 F 19 '66
NCWC: new life and vigor; meeting of Catholic bishops in Washington. America 115:643 N 19 '66
Note on schema fourteen. America 114:280 F 26 '66
Retirement for 200 bishops; resignation. il Time 88:93 S 30 '66
To bishops with love. America 114:792, 848; 115:5 Je 4, 18, Jl 2 '66
Too many volunteers? bishops resignations. Newsweek 68:106 O 24 '66
U.S. Catholic bishops after Vatican II. C. McCarthy. Christian Cent 83:1584-6 D 21 '66
Will the bishops speed up renewal? J. B. Sheerin. Cath World 204:132-3 D '66
See also
National conference of Catholic bishops

BISMARCK, N.D.
Bad marks for Bismarck; reaction to job corps center. Christian Cent 83:293-4 Mr 9 '66
Rubber tires work well on sanitary landfills. E. Booth and E. Carlson. il Am City 81:98-9 Jl '66
BISON, American. See Buffaloes
BISON, Fossil
Paleo-Indian bison kill. J. B. Wheat. il Sci Am 216:44-52 Ja '67
BISPHAM, David
Quaker singer. W. A. Del Mar. il pors Opera. N 31:30-1 Ja 14 '67
BISSELL, Richard
O Keewatin! Holiday 40:42-51+ Ag '66
BISSELL, Trim
Stone was all our thought; poem. Yale R 55:549 Je '66
BISSON, Thomas N.
Military origins of medieval representation. bibliog f Am Hist R 71:1199-218 Jl '66
BIT much; story. See Seib, K. H.
BITANCOURT, A. A.
Reversible inactivation of aged solutions of indolyl-3-acetic acid. bibliog Science 154:1327-9 D 9 '66
BITES, Venomous. See Venom
BITTER bread; story. See Ford, J. H.
BITTLE, Camilla R.
I want to know, what about writing courses? Writer 79:26-8 Je '66
BITUMINOUS sand
Tar sands and oil shales. N. De Nevers. il Sci Am 214:21-9 F '66
BIVALVES. See Mollusks
BIXLER, Ray H.
Experiments on humans, the growing debate: ostracize them! Sat R 49:47-8 Jl 2 '66
BIZET, Georges
Carmen. Criticism
Opera N il 30:32 Mr 5 '66
BJORKSTEN, Johan Augustus
Small lab has to be different. il pors Bsns W p90-2+ Ag 27 '66
BJORKSTEN research laboratories. See Research laboratories
BLACHER, Boris
Incidents in connection with a crash landing. Criticism
Opera N il 30:31-2 Mr 19 '66
BLACK Bart
Case of the plodding highwayman or the Po8 of crime. K. Kraft and P. Kraft. il por Am Heritage 18:50-3+ D '66
BLACK, A. H. See De Toledo, L. jt. auth.
BLACK, Algernon D.
Man of that board. J. Corry. il pors N Y Times Mag p32-3+ N 6 '66
BLACK, Barbara
Journey into winter. Pop Gard 17:65+ D '66
Plant patents. Horticulture 44:26-8 Ag '66
Sort out your garden now. Pop Gard 17:42-5 Mr '66
Three plant garden. Flower Grower 53:32-3+ N '66
BLACK, Eugene Robert
Eugene Black on ten-nation trip to discuss Asian development; White House announcement, October 13, 1966. Dept State Bul 55:669 O 31 '66
BLACK, Fred B. Jr
Day in Court. Newsweek 68:22 Jl 25 '66
New ruling on electronic bugging. il por U S News 61:16 N 21 '66
BLACK, Hector
Hector Black: white power in black Atlanta. J. Shepherd. il pors Look 30:137-40 D 13 '66
White Jesus. il por Newsweek 68:29 Jl 25 '66
BLACK, Hillel
Buying credit wisely. NEA J 55:23 My '66
BLACK, Hugo La Fayette
From songs to sedition. por Newsweek 67:27 Mr 7 '66
Justice Black at eighty: common sense of freedom. N. Redlich. por Nation 202:322-6 Mr 21 '66
Justice Black dissents; turning conservative? por U S News 60:26+ Mr 21 '66
BLACK, MacKnight
Strong book and library components cited in ESEA Title I by USOE spokesman; excerpts from address, March 1966. Library J 91:2180-1 Ap 15 '66
BLACK, Mary Childs
Wood: the American folk sculptor. Craft Horiz 26:18-21+ Jl '66
—and Feld, S. P.
Drawn by I. Bradley from Great Britton. Antiques 90:502-9 O '66
BLACK, Shirley (Temple) See Temple, S.
BLACK, Virginia M.
Sky sailing! Travel 125:37-40 Ap '66
Wing away! Travel 126:39-42 N '66

BLACK alder. See Alder

BLACK-and-white photography. See Photography

BLACK-and-white prints. See Photographs

BLACK bear hunting. See Bear hunting

BLACK bears. See Bears

BLACK brant. See Geese, Wild

BLACK-capped chickadees. See Chickadees

BLACK death
  See also
  Plague

BLACK flies. See Flies

BLACK Indies; drama. See Olfson, L.

BLACK magic. See Witchcraft

BLACK markets
  Along PX alley; Saigon black market. il
    Newsweek 68:68+ N 28 '66
  Another enemy in Vietnam war: corruption.
    il U S News 60:44-5 F 14 '66
  Bonfire in PX alley; Saigon. il Time 88:39 N
    25 '66
  Contagion of corruption; sale of PX supplies
    in Vietnam. Nation 203:564 N 28 '66
  Expensive caper; Americans arrested for
    violating currency regulations; Russia. il
    Newsweek 69:28 Ja 2 '67
  Ratholes; black market in South Vietnam.
    Newsweek 67:18 F 7 '66
  Saigon: at night, war flares and road checks;
    corruption and profiteering. S. Angeloff.
    il Life 60:47-52A F 25 '66
  Strayed AID; South Viet Nam. il Time 87:
    28-9 My 20 '66
  Vietnam; our economic assistance; address,
    June 23, 1966. R. P. Griffin. Vital Speeches
    32:585-9 Jl 15 '66
  Want to change dollars? American tourists
    arrested for black-market dealings in Rus-
    sia. il Time 88:22 D 30 '66

BLACK Muslim movement
  Case of conscience. J. Olsen. il Sports Illus
    24:34-6+ My 9 '66
  Learning Elijah's advanced lesson in hate.
    J. Olsen. il Sports Illus 24:36-8+ My 2 '66

BLACK Panther party. See Lowndes County
    freedom organization

BLACK power. See Negroes in the United
    States—Civil rights; Negroes in the United
    States—Politics and suffrage; Race rela-
    tions

BLACK rhinoceros. See Rhinoceros

BLACK walnut trees. See Walnut trees

BLACKBERRIES
  Cane berry year begins in February. il Sun-
    set 136:208-9 F '66

BLACKBURN, Fred A.
  Hiking high. il Liv Wildn 30:3-5 Sum '66

BLACKBURN, Paul
  Hour; Ritual VIII; Evasion; poems. Poetry
    109:153-5 D '66
  Ritual IX; poem. Poetry 108:25-6 Ap '66
  Watchers; poem. New Yorker 42:56-7 D
    10 '66

BLACKIE, William
  Blackie of Caterpillar. por Fortune 73:47 My
    '66
  Multinational diet that helps Cat thrive.
    il pors Bsns W p70-2+ Ag 13 '66

BLACKLISTING
  See also
  Boycott

BLACKMAIL. See Extortion

BLACKMAN, Abner, and Somayajulu, B. L. K.
  Pacific pleistocene cores: faunal analyses and
    geochronology. bibliog Science 154:886-9 N
    18 '66

BLACKMAN, Honor
  Honor's judo defense of honor. M. E. Smith.
    il pors Life 60:127-8 My 20 '66

BLACKMAN, M. C.
  News from home. Sat R 49:117-18 O 8 '66

BLACKOUTS (electric power) See Electric
    power

BLACKSMITHS
  Blacksmith for the horsey set. il Ebony 21:
    83-4+ S '66

BLACKSTOCK, Charity, pseud.
  How to survive childhood. M. Polner. Nation
    203:523 N 14 '66
  Playground in hell. I. Halperin. Sat R 49:42+
    N 26 '66

BLACKWOOD, Serena Belinda Rosemary (Guin-
    ness) Hamilton-Temple-, marchioness of
    Dufferin and Ava. See Dufferin and Ava, S.
    B. R. G. H.-T.-B.

BLACKWOOD, Sheridan Frederick Terence
    Hamilton-Temple-, 5th marquess of Dufferin
    and Ava. See Dufferin and Ava, S. F. T. H.-
    T.-B.

BLADDER
  Visceral reflex activity: development in post-
    natal rabbit. W. E. Bradley and F. S.
    Wright. bibliog il Science 152:216 Ap 8 '66

Diseases
  Inventor of the month; it started with an
    article; synthetic human bladder. S. V.
    Jones. Sci Digest 59:26 My '66

BLADDER stones. See Calculi, Biliary

BLADEN, Howard A. See Glenner, G. G. jt.
    auth.

BLADENSBURG, Md.

Historic houses, etc.
  Living with antiques: David Ross house.
    B. B. Hyde. il Antiques 89:233-7 F '66

BLADES, Helicopter. See Helicopters—Blades

BLAEUW, Willem Janszoon
  Blaeuw's celestial globe and three new stars.
    K. Hujer. il Sky & Tel 32:278-9 N '66

BLAGONRAVOV, Anatolii Arkad'evich
  It does not matter who reaches the moon
    first; what counts is the benefit to man.
    UNESCO Courier 19:7-12 My '66

BLAINE, Graham B. jr
  Opinion: should God die? por Mlle 63:138+
    Ag '66

BLAINE amendment. See New York (state)—
    Constitution

BLAIR, B. D. and Zeman, L. E.
  Alfalfa weevil big threat, what to do about
    it. Suc Farm 64:34-5+ My '66

BLAIR, Eric. See Orwell, G. pseud.

BLAIR, Robert N.
  Robert N. Blair believes in action; with bio-
    graphical sketch. il por Am Artist 30:40-1+
    N '66

BLAIR House. See Washington, D.C.—Historic
    houses, etc.

BLAIS, P. and Manley, R. S.
  Morphology of nascent Ziegler-Natta poly-
    mers. bibliog Science 153:539-41 Jl 29 '66

BLAISDELL, Harold F.
  Rabbits the hard way. Field & S 71:55 D '66

BLAKE, Emma L.
  Zora Neale Hurston: author and folklorist.
    por Negro Hist Bul 29:149-50+ Ap '66

BLAKE, Eugene Carson
  Should the code of ethics in public life be
    absolute or relative? Ann Am Acad 363:
    4-11 Ja '66
  Visser 't Hooft: a tribute. Christian Cent 83:
    1467-9 N 30 '66

  about
  American in Geneva. il por Time 87:80 F 18
    '66
  Blake elected W.C.C. General Secretary.
    Christian Cent 83:229 F 23 '66
  Man for all churches. il por Newsweek 67:92
    F 21 '66
  Minister who's not afraid to fight. L. Cassels.
    il pors Look 30:79-80+ My 31 '66
  New era begins in Geneva. America 114:283-
    4 F 26 '66
  New look. il por Newsweek 67:68 Je 6 '66
  One church by inclusion. Christian Cent 83:
    906 Jl 20 '66
  World council: candor and hope. C. North-
    cott. Christian Cent 83:263-4 Mr 2 '66

BLAKE, Fay
  Invisible librarian. Library J 91:3360-2 Jl '66

BLAKE, George
  Escape into the cold. por Newsweek 68:52-4 N
    7 '66
  Great escape. W. F. Buckley, jr. Nat R 18:
    1150 N 15 '66
  Question of identity. il por Time 88:38+ N
    4 '66

BLAKE, Octave
  Man in the 100,000-mile suit. G. Holland. il
    por Sports Illus 24:54+ My 2 '66

BLAKE, Peter
  Downtown in 3-D. Arch Forum 125:31-49 S '66
  How to grow a campus: Washington uni-
    versity. Arch Forum 124:62-7 Ap '66

BLAKE, Sandra
  Photograms. il Design 67:23-5 Ja '66

BLAKE plateau. See Ocean bottom

BLAKEMORE, Barbara
  When McCall's looks for stories. Writer 79:25
    F '66

BLAKER, Charles W.
  Thanatopsis. Christian Cent 83:1503-6 D 7 '66

BLAKESLEE, Alton L.
  Today's health news. See issues of Today's
    health

BLAKEY, G. Robert
  Obscenity and the Supreme court. America
    115:152-6 Ag 13 '66

BLAKEY, Roy
  Demons, monkeys, and heroes. il Dance Mag
    40:46-9 My '66

BLAMPIED, Edmund
  Isle of Jersey's venerable master; Edmund
    Blampied. F. A. Phillipps. il por Am Artist
    30:40-5+ O '66

BLANC, MONT. See Mont Blanc
BLANCH, Lesley
  Alla Turca. Vogue 148:182-4+ D '66
  Lord and Lady Iliffe's triple entente: country,
    city, and sun. Vogue 148:102-9+ Jl '66
BLANCHARD, J. Richard. See Heron, D. W.
  jt. auth.
BLANCHARD, John
  Bec thrashing in Louisiana. Field & S 71:
    146-8+ S '66
BLANK, Blanche D.
  Big city slowdown: the battle of bureau-
    cracy. Nation 203:632-7 D 12 '66
BLANK, Joseph P.
  Lost years. Look 30:71-2+ N 29 '66
  Stranger at the door. Read Digest 89:60-6
    S '66
  Subject was faith. Read Digest 88:144-7
    Je '66
BLANKET sleepers (clothing) See Clothing and
  dress—Children
BLANKETS
  Cold comfort from outer space; NRC space
    blanket. il Consumer Rep 31:322-3 Jl '66
  Reflector blanket; NRC-space blanket. C.
    Conley. il Field & S 70:141 Ap '66
    See also
  Electric blankets, coverlets, etc.
BLANQUET, Richard, and Lenhoff, H. M.
  Disulfide-linked collagenous protein of nema-
    tocyst capsules. bibliog Science 154:152-3
    O 7 '66
BLANSHARD, Paul
  Liberty within the Catholic church. por Cath
    World 203:335-40 S '66

           about
  Outside Catholicism. J. Leo. Reporter 35:48-50
    D 1 '66
BLANTON, Smiley
  Bible's timeless, and timely, insights. Read
    Digest 89:93-6 Ag '66
BLASER, Larry
  Integrated circuit for consumer products.
    Electr World 76:32-3+ O '66
BLASINGAME, Ralph, jr
  Blasingame appointed consultant to Ohio
    public library survey. Library J 91:5567+ N
    15 '66
BLASPHEMY
    See also
  Swearing
BLASSINGAME, Wyatt
  Goodby, Blue Springs. Field & S 70:8-9+ F
    '66
BLAST furnaces
  Hottest new smelter does two jobs at once;
    Imperial smelting corp, London. il Bsns W
    p 166-8 Je 4 '66
BLASTING
    See also
  Atomic blasting
BLASTING, Atomic. See Atomic blasting
BLATGÉ, Yves
  Turboprop to a glacier. F. R. Smith. il por
    Sports Illus 24:38-43 F 7 '66
BLAU, Herbert
  Bleak house. Time 89:55 Ja 20 '67
BLAUSTEIN, Linda
  Leafy turkeys. Sch Arts 66:41-2 N '66
BLAUSTEIN, M. P. and Goldman, D. E.
  Action of anionic and cationic nerve-blocking
    agents: experiment and interpretation. bib-
    liog Science 153:429-32 Jl 22 '66
BLAVAT, Jerry
  Number one cat. B. J. Friedman. il pors Sat
    Eve Post 239:36-8+ S 24 '66
BLEEDERS disease. See Hemophilia
BLEEDING. See Hemorrhage
BLEIBTREU, John N.
  LSD and the third eye. Atlan 218:64-9 S '66
BLENDERS, Electric. See Electric apparatus
  and appliances, Domestic
BLENNERHASSETT, Harman
  Three mysterious portraits. por Am Heritage
    17:8-9 F '66
BLENNERHASSETT, Margaret (Agnew)
  Three mysterious portraits. por Am Heritage
    17:8-9 F '66
BLESSED Sacrament. See Catholic church—
  Eucharist
BLESSING
  St Patrick's day; Irish blessing. Good H
    162:262 Mr '66
BLESSING; story. See Greene, G.
BLICKENSTAFF, C. C. See Bowers, W. S.
  jt. auth.
BLIMPS. See Airships
BLIND
  Blind from birth; twin girls. il Good H 162:
    12+ F '66
  Boy who found the sun; efforts of a gifted
    teacher and a blind mother. J. Robbins
    and J. Robbins. Redbook 128:48-9+ D '66

  Only one twin can see; case of Lee Ruben-
    stein; with report by M. Byers. il Life 61:
    89-92+ O 28 '66
  Visually handicapped child; address, March 15,
    1966. J. W. Jones. il Wilson Lib Bul 824-8
    My '66
    See also
  Libraries—Work with blind

          Employment
  Roland Kirk: modern one-man band. il Ebony
    21:181-4+ My '66
  Senator Randolph's blind businessmen. R. B.
    Scott. il Todays Health 44:73-6 O '66

    Printing and writing systems
    See also
  American printing house for the blind
BLIND, Apparatus for the
  Blind read by machine; Visotactor. P. Mc-
    Broom. il Sci N L 89:99 F 12 '66
  How to see through the ears; electronic de-
    vices. il Life 61:65+ S 30 '66
BLIND, Books for the
  Book week in braille: Library for the blind,
    hospital and institutions department, Cleve-
    land public library. K. Prescott. il Li-
    brary J 91:4197-9 S 15 '66
    See also
  American printing house for the blind
BLIND, Libraries for the
    See also
  Philadelphia—Free library—Library for the
    blind
BLIND, Periodicals for the
  Seventeen at my fingertips; first braille edi-
    tion. M. E. Earls. Seventeen 26:22 Ja '67
BLIND flying. See Aviation—Instrument flying
BLIND landing of airplanes. See Airplanes—
  Landing
BLINDNESS
  Threat to sight that is preventable; am-
    blyopia. il Good H 162:159 F '66
  Vision: the most valuable sense; with bibliog-
    raphy. R. E. Hoover. il Wilson Lib Bul
    40:818-23 My '66
    See also
  Blind
  Night blindness
BLINDNESS, Color. See Color blindness
BLINDS
    See also
  Shutters
BLISS, Anthony A.
  Open letter to guild members. Opera N 31:7 D
    10 '66
BLISS, Charles A.
  Flaw in the wage-price guideposts. Harvard
    Bsns R 44:73-8 My '66
BLISS, Mildred
  Washington's Byzantine empress. J. Walker.
    por Vogue 147:180-1+ F 1 '66
BLISS, Ray Charles
  Minor masterpiece of Ray C. Bliss. A. L.
    Otten and C. B. Seib. por Reporter 34:35-8
    F 10 '66
  Party pro. T. Wicker. Atlan 217:80 Ap '66
BLISTERS
  Why we blister; study of blisters on soles
    and palms. Sci Digest 59:21 Mr '66
BLITZER, Charles
  Smithsonian: more museums in slums, more
    slums in museums? B. Nelson. Science 154:
    1152-4 D 2 '66
BLITZSTEIN, Marc
  Music to my ears; L. Bernstein conducts Air-
    borne symphony. I. Kolodin. Sat R 49:50-1
    O 29 '66
BLIVEN, Bruce
  Unforgettable Bernard Baruch. Read Digest
    89:92-6 S '66
BLIVEN, Naomi
  Books (cont) New Yorker 41:100-2+ Ja 22;
    42:173-6 Mr 12; 165-8 Ap 9; 122-6 Ag 27; 242-
    7 O 22; 233-4+ D 3 '66
BLIZZARDS. See Snowstorms
BLOATING
  Cattle bloat controlled by drug. il Sci N
    89:224 Ap 2 '66
  Now: a drug to stop bloat; bloat guard. D.
    Braun and D. Hagen. il Farm J 90:75-6 Ap
    '65
BLOBEL, Günter, and Potter, V. R.
  Nuclei from rat liver: isolation method that
    combines purity with high yield. bibliog
    Science 154:1662-5 D 30 '66
BLOCK, Jean Libman
  Bullet through the window. Good H 162:72+
    Mr '66
  Gregory Peck turns crusader. Good H 162:
    70+ My '66
BLOCK, Libbie
  Fourth Sarah; story. Redbook 126:58-9 Mr '66

BLOCK, Ruth
(comp) Where has it gone? N Y Times Mag
p38 S 18 '66
BLOCK, Victor
Supersonic transport and you. Sci Digest
60:60-7 Jl '66
Why all the new records in sports? Todays
Health 44:22-5+ S '66
(ed) See Brown, L. Warning: less food for all
(ed) See Endicott, K. M. Search for a can-
cerless cigarette
(ed) See Hornig, D. F. Science in your
life
(ed) See Smith, J. Tomorrow's new foods
BLOCK ISLAND
Block Island; report on Projects to advance
creativity in education. il Am Ed 2:9 N '66
BLOCK printing
Craft news! products to make hobbies less
work. M. Garrity. il Bet Hom & Gard 44:
111-12+ Ap '66
BLOCK walls. See Walls, Concrete
BLOCKADE
Bloodless use of superior force. R. Moley.
Read Digest 88:60-1 Mr '66
Why not blockade North Vietnam? H. W.
Baldwin. Read Digest 88:58-62 Mr '66
BLOCKER, Clyde E.
Cooperation between two-year and four-year
colleges. bibliog f Sch & Soc 94:218-22 Ap 16
'66
BLOCKLEY, Theodore
Dissent. Nat R 18:1089 N 1 '66
BLODGET, Robert
Follow me through. por Flying 78:6 F; 128
Ap; 79:78 Jl; 106 S; 116 O; 124 N; 87 D '66;
80:90 Ja '67
BLOKHINE, Margery T.
One world; poem. Negro Hist Bul 29:113 F
'66
BLOOD
Blood gases: continuous in vivo recording
of partial pressures by mass spectrography.
S. Woldring and others. bibliog il Science
153:885-7 Ag 19 '66
Molecular mechanism of red cell sickling. M.
Murayama. bibliog il Science 153:145-9
Jl 8 '66
See also
Erythropoietic factor
Fibrinogen
Leucocytes

Agglutination

Hemagglutination by fava bean extract inhibited by simple sugars. C. B. Perera and
A. M. Frumin. bibliog il Science 151:821 F
18 '66
Sialic acid binding sites: role in hemagglutination by mycoplasma gallisepticum. B.
Gesner and L. Thomas. bibliog il Science
151:590-1 F 4 '66

Circulation

Blood flow in the microvasculature of the
conjunctiva of man. R. E. Wells and others.
il Science 151:995-6 F 25 '66
Expectant mother: how the blood system re-
sponds to pregnancy. G. J. Vosburgh and
B. R. Boylan. Redbook 127:40+ My '66
Gastrointestinal circulation; report on meet-
ing of investigators. E. D. Jacobson. Sci-
ence 154:1366+ D 9 '66
Red cells and rouleaux in shear flow. H. L.
Goldsmith. bibliog il Science 153:1406-7 S
16 '66
See also
Thrombosis

Coagulation

Nonthrombogenic plastic surfaces. R. I.
Leininger and others. bibliog il Science 152:
1625-6 Je 17 '66
Reduce blood clot deaths. Sci N L 89:62 Ja 22
'66
Visual excitation and blood clotting. G. Wald;
reply. W. H. Seegers. bibliog Science 151:
841 F 18 '66
See also
Anticoagulants (medicine)

Collection and preservation

Battle over blood. F. W. Barton. il Todays
Health 44:46+ F '66
Frozen blood proves itself in Vietnam; used
successfully on wounded marines. il Bsns
W p84-6+ Mr 19 '66
See also
Blood banks

Corpuscles and platelets

See also
Erythrocytes
Leucocytes

Dialysis

See Kidneys, Artificial

Diseases

See also
Anemia
Erythroblastosis
Galactosemia
Hemophilia
Leukemia

Oxygen content

Blood oxygen and ecology of porpoises of
three genera. S. H. Ridgway and D. G.
Johnston. bibliog il Science 151:456-8 Ja
28 '66; Reply. R. P. Spencer. 152:230-1 Ap 8
'66

Plasma

Parathyroid hormone in plasma in adenomatous hyperparathyroidism, uremia, and
bronchogenic carcinoma. S. A. Berson and
R. S. Yalow. bibliog il Science 154:907-9 N
18 '66
Protein conformations in the plasma membrane. A. H. Maddy and B. R. Malcolm;
reply with rejoinder. J. L. Kavanau.
Science 153:213 Jl 8 '66

Proteins

Albumin naskapi: a new variant of serum
albumin. L. Melartin and B. S. Blumberg.
bibliog il Science 153:1664-6 S 30 '66
Antigenic correspondence of serum albumins
among the primates. A. S. Hafleigh and
C. A. Williams, jr. bibliog il Science 151:
1530-5 Mr 25 '66
Mouse complement: influence of sex hormones on its activity. R. M. Weintraub
and others. bibliog il Science 152:783-5 My
6 '66
Quantitative immunochemistry and the evolution of primate albumins: micro-complement fixation. V. M. Sarich and A. C. Wilson. bibliog il Science 154:1563-6 D 23 '66
Steroids and serum complement in mice:
influence of hydrocortisone, diethylstilbestrol, and testosterone. L. D. Caren and
L. T. Rosenberg. bibliog il Science 152:
782-3 My 6 '66
See also
Gamma globulin
Serum globulins

Serum

See Serum

Testing

Automatic blood tests frees lab technicians.
il Sci N 89:368 My 14 '66
Blood test predicts effect of cancer drug;
response to PHI activity. Sci N 89:254 Ap 9
'66
Pen-line diagnosis; autoanalyzer. il Time 88:
68 O 28 '66

Transfusion

Battle over blood. F. W. Barton. il Todays
Health 44:46+ F '66
How doctors heal the unborn. A. Lake. il
Sat Eve Post 239:39-42 F 12 '66
Your blood is best. A. J. Snider. Sci Digest
60:32-3 D '66
BLOOD accusation
Blood accusation, by M. Samuel. Review
Newsweek il 68:100-1 Ag 22 '66
Malamud's heroes; fate of fixers. J. Baum-
bach. Commonweal 85:97-9 O 28 '66
BLOOD alcohol level. See Alcohol in the body
BLOOD banks
At a blood bank, precision is more than a
word, it's a whole way of life; New Eng-
land medical center hospitals. il Todays
Health 44:47 F '66
Your blood is best. A. J. Snider. Sci Digest
60:32-3 D '66
BLOOD donors
Blood donations not accepted from everyone.
Sci N 89:220 Ap 2 '66
See also
Blood—Collection and preservation
BLOOD groups
Blood-group substances. W. M. Watkins.
bibliog il Science 152:172-81 Ap 8 '66
Blood groups of the I system in pigs: as-
sociation with variants of serum amylase.
E. Andresen. bibliog il Science 153:1660-1
S 30 '66
Seroprimatology of chimpanzees: blood-group
distribution as a racial characteristic. J.
Moor-Jankowski and others. bibliog il Sci-
ence 152:219-20 Ap 8 '66
BLOOD pressure
Blood pressure responses of wild giraffes
studied by radio telemetry. R. L. Van
Citters and others. bibliog il Science 152:
384-6 Ap 15 '66
Carotid body chemoceptors: physiological role
in buffering fall in blood pressure during
sleep. M. Guazzi and others. bibliog il Sci-
ence 153:206-8 Jl 8 '66

BLOOD pump. See Heart, Artificial
BLOOD tests. See Blood—Testing
BLOOD vessels

Surgery

Artery link helps heart. Sci N 90:114 Ag 20 '66
Cleaning out coronaries; gas-jet procedure carried out by K. E. Karison and J. H. Stuckey. Newsweek 69:86+ Ja 23 '67
BLOOM, Barry R. and Bennett, Boyce
Mechanism of a reaction in vitro associated with delayed-type hypersensitivity. bibliog Science 153:80-2 Jl 1 '66
BLOOM, Floyd E. and Aghajanian, G. K.
Cytochemistry of synapses: selective staining for electron microscopy. bibliog Science 154: 1575-7 D 23 '66
—See Aghajanian, G. K. jt. auth.
BLOOM, Julius
Jeunesses musicales. S. Fleming. Hi Fi 16: MA8 Jl '66
BLOOM, Murray Teigh
How to complain, effectively. Read Digest 89:61-3 Jl '66
Mess in our probate courts. Read Digest 89: 102-5 O '66
Never mind the answer; what's the question? Pop Mech 125:132-4+ F '66
(ed) See Sklar, S. I was the world's most expectant mother
BLOOM, Stephen E. and Buss, E. G.
Triploid-diploid mosaic chicken embryo. bibliog Science 153:759-60 Ag 12 '66
BLOOM, Sydelle
(ed) See Sklar, S. I was the world's most expectant mother
BLOOMFIELD, Howard V. L.
Interim in the Everglades. Am For 72:22-4+ Jl '66
BLOOMFIELD, Lincoln P.
Peacekeeping and peacemaking. For Affairs 44:671-82 Jl '66
BLOOMINGTON, Minn.
Balance plows and routes. A. S. Michalik. il Am City 81:110-11 S '66
BLOOMINGTON, public and Monroe County library, Ind.
Paperback wearability. E. N. Howard. il Library J 91:4057-60 S 15 '66
BLOSS, Meredith
No glass boxes for New Haven. Library J 91:5869-71 D 1 '66
Take a giant step. Library J 91:323-6 Ja 15 '66
BLOTTER press. See Printing—Private presses
BLOUGH, Roger M.
Business can satisfy the young intellectual. Harvard Bsns R 44:49-57 Ja '66
Businessman's formula to head off inflation; excerpts from address, February 19, 1966. por U S News 60:87-8 Mr 7 '66
A look at the national economy; excerpts from Public interest of private enterprise, annual report. por U S News 61:82-4 S 12 '66
Wage gains and profits: does government juggle figures? excerpts from address, November 14, 1966. por U S News 61:106 N 28 '66
Why business dislikes the curbs LBJ proposes; excerpts from address, September 19, 1966. por U S News 61:22 O 3 '66
BLOUSTEIN, Edward J.
Freshman president speaks to freshman students; adaptation of address, September 20, 1965. Sch & Soc 94:128-9 Mr 5 '66
BLOWERS, Snow. See Snow blowers, throwers, etc.
BLOWFLIES
Pyruvate oxidation and the permeability of mitochondria from blowfly flight muscle. C. C. Childress and B. Sacktor. bibliog il Science 154:268-70 O 14 '66
BLOY, Myron B. Jr
Christian function in a technological culture. bibliog f Christian Cent 83:231-4 F 23 '66
BLUE Angels. See Aviation—Stunt flying
BLUE baby. See Tetralogy of Fallot
BLUE cross hospital services. See Insurance, Hospitalization
BLUE-green algae. See Algae
BLUE lawns; story. See Brodeur, P.
BLUE mist. See Caryopteris
BLUE note records, incorporated
Music on Blue note. M. Williams. Sat R 49: 58 S 17 '66
BLUEBERRIES
Blueberries for gardens. J. F. Brooks and G. J. Galletta. il Horticulture 44:26-7+ O '66

BLUEFIN tuna fishing. See Tuna fishing
BLUEFISH
Bluefish: marauder of the seas. R. H. Boyle. il Sports Illus 24:44-6+ Je 27 '66
BLUEGILL fishing. See Sunfish fishing
BLUES (music) See Negro music
BLUFF, Utah
Why Bluff is worth a stopover. il Sunset 137: 74+ O '66
BLUHDORN, Charles
It's a deal. por Newsweek 68:77-8+ Jl 18 '66
New star at Paramount. Time 87:73 Ap 22 '66
BLUM, Etta
Passing the rose garden touched what I could; Fountain, the fire; poems. Poetry 108:305-6 Ag '66
BLUM, Ralph
Movies (cont) Vogue 147:100-1 F 1; 100 Mr 1 '66
BLUM, Sam
Noise: how much more can we take? McCalls 94:48-9+ Ja '67
Ode to the cigarette code. Harper 232:60-3 Mr '66
When can infidelity be justified or forgiven? McCalls 93:73+ My '66
Why marriages fail. Redbook 126:69+ Ap '66
Why men don't listen or talk to their wives. McCalls 93:78-9+ F '66; Same abr. with title Why men don't talk to their wives. Read Digest 88:55-8 My '66
—and Soman, S. C.
How young wives can help their husbands succeed. Redbook 127:47+ My '66
BLUM, Virgil C.
This heartless business. America 115:247-9 S 10 '66
BLUMBERG, B. S. See Melartin, L. jt. auth.
BLUMENFELD, Serge. See Gersh, M. J. jt. auth.
BLUMENKRANZ, Joseph
Hospitals: trends in planning. Arch Rec 140: 197-8 O '66
BLUMENTHAL, Joseph
Ascending Spiral. R. Lynes. il Harper 232: 24+ My '66
Spiral press honored with exhibit at Morgan library; with editorial comment. P. A. Bennett. il por Pub W 189:97-101+ F 7 '66
BLUMENTHAL, Lassor A.
Conquest of inner space. Duns R 87:pt2 121-3+ Mr '66
BLUMENTHAL, Sonia Grodka. See Murphy, R. Z. jt. auth.
BLUMENTHAL, W. Michael
Kennedy round: the final phase: address, September 28, 1966. Dept State Bul 55:671-5 O 31 '66
BLUNDEN, Edmund Charles
Seating a poet. por Time 87:31 F 11 '66
BLUNDERS
Hero bullet and other related nonsense. J. Belck. Atlan 217:142+ Mr '66
Manner of speaking; mumpsimus; definition. J. Ciardi. Sat R 49:22+ My 7 '66
Right word, wrong spelling. G. Hicks. Sat R 49:21-2 Je 25 '66
Vacation is going someplace without having to! reprint. H. Dunn. il Sr Schol 89:sup 14 S 16 '66
Wrong word for it. G. Hicks. Sat R 49:87-8 My 7 '66
BLY, Robert
American dream; Written near Rome; Life of weeds; Full moon, thinking of high school girls; Journey with women; March in Washington against the Vietnam war; poems. Poetry 108:382-7 S '66
American outsider. P. Zweig. Nation 203:517-19 N 14 '66
Hatred of men with black hair; poem. Nation 203:192 S 5 '66
Three presidents; poem. Nation 202:108 Ja 24 '66
(tr) See Machado, A. Elegy for Don Francisco Giner de los Rios
(tr) See Neruda, P. Ode to my socks; Funeral in the East
BLYTH, Charles
Heroes' reward. Newsweek 68:56 S 19 '66
We rowed across the North Atlantic; ed. by J. Atwater. J. Ridgway. il pors Sat Eve Post 239:30-6+ N 5 '66
BLYTH, Myrna
Lovers; story. Redbook 128:64-5 N '66
No one but me; story. Redbook 126:66-7 Mr '66
BLYTHIN, Edward
Press v. the accused. il por Time 87:66 Je 17 '66
B'NAI b'rith

Anti-defamation league

Whose hand to shake? W. F. Buckley, jr. Nat R 18:352 Ap 19 '66

BOARD of trade, Chicago. See Chicago board
of trade
BOARDING schools. See Private schools
BOARDMAN, Gwenn R.
Run away to sea: the fun of freighter travel.
Mlle 63:185-7 O '66
BOARDMAN, Walter S.
What lies ahead for the Appalachian trail?
Liv Wildn 29:9-14 Wint '65
BOARDS of directors. See Corporations—
Directors
BOAT camping. See Camping
BOAT clubs
If one can do it; Auburn boat club. J. Mower.
il Yachting 119:186 F '66
Outboard boating club of San Diego. B.
Crabtree. il Yachting 120:62-3+ Jl '66
BOAT docks. See Docks
BOAT dollies. See Trucks
BOAT engines. See Marine engines
BOAT finishes. See Finishing materials
BOAT harbors. See Marinas
BOAT horns. See Horns (signals)
BOAT hulls. See Hulls (naval architecture)
BOAT industry. See Boatbuilding
BOAT ladders. See Motor boats—Equipment
BOAT models. See Ship and boat models
BOAT propellers. See Propellers
BOAT racing
See also
Catamaran racing
Rowing
BOAT tools. See Tools
BOAT trailers. See Automobile boat trailers
BOATBUILDING
Aluminum construction. T. Bottomley. il
Yachting 119:81-3+ Ap '66
Boat for $12? you can build it. G. Daniels.
il Pop Sci 188:164-6 Mr '66
Boating business. W. Robberson. See issues
of Yachting
Build this white-water riverboat. C. R.
Hull. il Pop Mech 126:154-7+ D '66
Building a 23-footer, family style. C. Henkel.
il Yachting 119:96-8+ Ja '66
Building the Stiletto. A. Mikesell. il Pop Mech
127:166-71+ Ja '67
Car-top boat for $20. J. Payne. il Pop Sci
189:138-40 Ag '66
Ceiling and visibility unlimited. N. E. Moore.
Yachting 119:226+ My '66
Facts and figures. J. E. Choate. il Yachting
119:60+ Ja '66
Florida boatbuilders beckon visitors; repre-
sentative list. il Motor B 118:37 O '66
From dream to reality. E. L. Parks. il
Motor B 19:94-7+ Ja '67 (to be cont)
New lightning construction in glass. B. Cobb,
jr. il Yachting 119:73-5+ Ja '66
One way to bigger, better boats. E. B.
Childs. il Motor B 117:86-9+ Ja '66
PM's platform boat. A. Mikesell. il Pop
Mech 125:148-53+ Mr '66
See also
Hulls (naval architecture)
BOATS
Air conditioning
Cool counsel for sweltering skippers. J. E.
Weber. il Motor B 118:28-31+ S '66
Care
Rout out that rot. F. W. Fleischhauer. Motor
B 117:34+ Mr '66
Yachting special report; maintenance. il
Yachting 119:72-80+ Ap '66
Bibliography
Sources of maintenance information. E.
Horan. il Yachting 119:74+ Ap '66
Design
Design showcase (cont of) Designs of note
See issues of Motor boating
Designs. W. H. DeFontaine. il Yachting 119:
120-6+ Ja '66
Designs of note (cont) il Motor B 117:48-9
F; 50-3 Mr; 48-51 Ap '66
New utilities. F. M. Paulson. il Field & S
70:114-17 Ap '66
Perfect boat for skiers; Field & stream inter-
view. W. D. Clifford. il Field & S 71:34-5+
Ja '67
Styling today's boats: the inside story. il
Motor B 118:44-5 S '66
Electric equipment
110 volt AC A-OK aboard. R. C. Roetger. il
Motor B 118:32-5+ D '66
Volts, amperes and headaches. C. F. Kelley.
il Motor B 118:39+ Jl '66

Electronic equipment
Down to the sea in gadgets. il Sports Illus
26:20-5 Ja 2 '67
Electronic maintenance. E. Robberson. il
Yachting 119:76+ Ap '66
Hi-fi and TV for your boat. L. G. Sands.
il Motor B 117:38-9+ Je '66
Joe Burk's blinking black box; electronic
gadget designed by Pennsylvania's rowing
coach. T. C. Brody. il Sports Illus 24:65-7
Je 6 '66
1967 electronics. il Motor B 119:176-83 Ja '67
Small boat electronics: what should you in-
stall yourself? J. D. Lenk. il Motor B 118:
33-5 N '66
Tip top electronics. H. C. Lawrence. il Motor
B 117:24-7+ Mr '66
Equipment
Cabin talk. M. Wiley. See issues of Yachting
Equipment & accessories, 1966. il Motor B
117:174-96+ Ja '66
Equipment you have to have. M. Penzer.
il Motor B 117:50-2+ My '66
Fresh look at galley psychology. B. Davis.
il Motor B 117:28-9+ My '66
Gadgets and gilhickies. H. deFontaine. See
issues of Yachting
How to stretch your boat. J. Martenhoff. il
Pop Sci 188:110-11 Je '66
Kitchens go to sea. il House & Gard 129:
170-1 Je '66
Made for the shade; shade canopy. R. Miller.
il Field & S 71:133-4 My '66
Maintenance with new products. W. An-
drews. il Yachting 19:73+ Ap '66
New boating accessories. Outdoor Life 139:
79 Ja '67
New gear and gadgets. F. M. Paulson. il
Field & S 70:118-20+ Mr '66
1967 equipment & accessories. il Motor B 119:
184-99+ Ja '67
Pre-cruise check-up. E. Schelin. Motor B
117:152+ Ap '66
Stow-aboard tool kit for outboards. H. B.
Notrom. il Pop Mech 125:158-60 Mr '66
Waterfront news. M. Wiley. See issues of
Yachting
What's new. J. Gribbins. See issues of Motor
boating
See also
Anchors
Horns (signals)
Ladders
Motor boats—Equipment
Rope
Anecdotes, facetiae, satire, etc.
See fever. J. D. Williamson. il Motor B 118:
41 D '66
Exhibitions
Back stage at the boat show; National boat
show, New York city. R. W. Carrick. il
Yachting 119:76-8+ Ja '66
Boat show in 1967. il Motor B 119:121-200+ Ja
'67
Candid view of the boat show. il Motor B
117:136-9+ Mr '66
Opening day on S.F. Bay; yacht parade. D.
Selby. il Motor B 117:27+ My '66
Seattle boat show. E. Crimmin. il Motor
B 117:162+ Mr '66
Yachting's boat show. il Yachting 119:127-
30+ Ja '66
Heating and ventilation
This spring, will your boat pass the coast
guard's ventilation inspection? il Pop Sci
188:179 Ap '66
Ventilate. M. Crook. il Yachting 119:80-2+
Mr '66
Ventilate; boating industry assn. recommen-
dations. il Yachting 119:78-9 My '66
What's needed is a breath of fresh air; re-
vised coast guard regulations for boat ven-
tilation. il Motor B 117:30-3+ Mr '66
Warm words for fall cruisingmen. D. Kendall.
il Motor B 118:25-7+ S '66
Hulls
See Hulls (naval architecture)
Lighting
Your navigation lights. G. H. Dickman. il
Yachting 119:77+ Ap '66
Maneuverability
Boat handling gets fish. J. A. Emmett. il
Outdoor Life 137:102-5 F '66
Materials
Aluminum construction. T. Bottomley. il
Yachting 119:81-3+ Ap '66
Aluminum maintenance. C. W. Leveau. il
Yachting 119:80+ Ap '66
Big California cat. B. Cobb, jr. il Yachting
120:65-7 Jl '66

BOATS—Materials—Continued
Design showcase. il Motor B 117:42-5 My '66
Down to the sea with DLP. G. Rounds. il Motor B 119:80+ Ja '67
Fiberglass maintenance. B. Cobb, jr. il Yachting 119:78-9+ Ap '65
Fiberglass Q and A. Motor B 117:176+ Mr '66
Instant mahogany for boats. G. Daniels. Pop Sci 188:147 F '66
1967 finishing touches. il Motor B 119:200+ Ja '67

Mooring
Rope-ladder rafting. A. P. Fort. il Yachting 119:238-9 Mr '66
Tips and tricks for anchoring. G. Daniels. il Pop Sci 188:112-14 Je '66

Names
Boat name contest. il Motor B 117:29 F; 118:104-5 S '66

Painting
1967 finishing touches. il Motor B 119:200+ Ja '67

Propellers
See Propellers

Purchasing
Selecting a family boat. J. A. Emmett. il Outdoor Life 137:166-9 Ap '66

Refrigerators
See Refrigeration on boats

Repairing
One way to repair. W. H. Koelbel. il Motor B 117:34 Mr '66
Rub 'er down right; boat refinishing sandpaper guide. N. Meiners. Motor B 117:35+ Mr '66
Yachting special report; maintenance. il Yachting 119:72-80+ Ap '66

Speed
Pangs of ICW traffic. M. A. Scott. il Motor B 118:32-3+ S '66

Storage
Bubble baths for boats. il Time 88:69-70 D 2 '66
Outside boat storage. J. A. Emmett. il Outdoor Life 138:24+ O '66
Secrets of successful winter boat storage. G. Daniels. il Pop Sci 189:136-9 S '66

Transportation
Car-carried boats. J. A. Emmett. il Outdoor Life 137:132-4 Mr '66
Car-top boat for $20. J. Payne. il Pop Sci 189:138-40 Ag '66
See also
Automobile boat trailers

Ventilation
See Boats—Heating and ventilation
BOATS, Remodeled
Customizing the stock boat. J. Megroz. il Motor B 117:45+ Mr '66
Revamping the older powerboat. C. West. il Yachting 119:92-4+ Ap '66
Whaleboat to pleasure boat. N. J. Lays. il Motor B 117:44+ Mr '66
BOATS, Submarine. See Submarine boats
BOATS, Used
How to buy a good used boat. F. Clark, jr. il Pop Mech 125:132-5+ Mr '66
What the surveyor looks for; used-boat buying tips. J. D. Lenk. il Motor B 118:52+ S '66

BOATS and boating
Alaska by jet, new boating fun! H. E. McLean. il Motor B 118:30-3+ Jl '66
Boating. J. A. Emmett. See issues of Outdoor life
Boating; ed. by E. M. Paulson. See issues of Field & stream
Boating: best way to get away; photographs. F. M. Paulson. Field & S 71:36-9 Ja '67
Boating: clear sailing ahead? F. M. Paulson. il Field & S 71:40-1+ Ja '67
Boats and motors for 1967? J. A. Emmett. il Outdoor Life 139:70-2+ Ja '67
Calendar of coming events; comp. by R. B. Smith. See issues of Motor boating
Camping with a boat. C. B. Colby. il Outdoor Life 138:92-6 Ag '66
Desert dwellers afloat. J. F. Bonneville. il Motor B 118:26-8 D '66
Highlights for '66; symposium. il Pop Sci 188:132-51 F '66
Leaving a crowded pier. il Field & S 71:73 Jl '66
Lure of boating. W. P. Bradley. il Holiday 40:38-45+ Jl '66

Marriage sailboat style. M. Badham. il Motor B 117:32-4+ F '66
More and more boats. Parks & Rec 1:560 Jl '66
News from yachting centers. See issues of Yachting
Northern Cal roundup. J. Schmale. il Motor B 118:122 O; 110 N; 100 D '66
Northwest gales. E. Crimmin. See issues of Motor boating
Notes for nomads. il Travel 126:64 O; 66 D '66
Off my chest. See issues of Yachting
Outboarding the rapids of British Columbia. F. Clark. il Yachting 120:62-3+ Jl '66
Perfect boats for hunters; safety and practicality. W. Page. il Field & S 71:30-1+ Ja '67
Photo-boating, a sport within a sport. G. K. Gould. il Motor B 118:40-1 Jl '66
Please love me in September as you did in May! il Motor B 118:23-4 S '66
PM's platform boat. A. Mikesell. il Pop Mech 125:148-53+ Mr '66
Seasoned skipper. See issues of Motor boating
'66 boats: it's a catch-up year. A. Mikesell. il Pop Mech 125:126-8 Mr '66
'66: the way it was; happenings that made news. il Motor B 119:61-75 Ja '67
Southward ho. J. Wilson. See issues of Motor boating
Take-along boats for vacation fun. A. Mikesell. il Pop Mech 126:104-7 Jl '66
Think small (boat that is) M. MacDuffie. il Yachting 120:62-4 N '66
Under the lee of the longboat. See issues of Yachting
Westward ho. B. Ruskauff. Motor B 118:102 D '66
What's new. J. Gribbins. See issues of Motor boating
Where to get information from the states; general cruising information. Motor B 117:100-2+ Ap '66
See also
Canoe trips
Children in boating
Cookery, Marine
Fishing boats
House boats
Inland navigation
Kayaks
Marinas
Motor boats
Regattas
Rowing
Sailing

Accidents
Adventure aboard a square-rigger. F. Simpson. Yachting 119:212-14 F '66
Always in the shadow; D. Campbell. il Time 89:50 Ja 13 '67
Bluebird's last run. il Life 62:87-8 Ja 13 '67
Each boat had a story. R. Robinson. il Yachting 120:37-8+ S '66
Final proof; D. Campbell. il Newsweek 69:82 Ja 16 '67
Fire is put out; tragic death of D. Campbell. Sports Illus 26:7 Ja 16 '67
Gulf Stream saga. A. Anable. Yachting 119:191-2 F '66
Happy drop out. F. Adams. il Yachting 120:41-3+ O '66
Mist+flip = a hectic Hudson. M. Penzer. il Motor B 118:81+ Ag '66
Night they rocked the boat. A. F. Loomis. Yachting 119:178+ F '66
SAR; Coast guard search and rescue service. E. Shrake. il Sports Illus 24:76-8+ My 30 '66
Shoal water shambles. J. D. Williamson. il Motor B 117:120+ Mr '66
Strands and stranding. G. P. Wakefield. Yachting 119:242-3 Mr '66
What to do if your boat sinks. E. Crimmin. il Sci Digest 59:57-9 Je '66

Anecdotes, facetiae, satire, etc.
Great rewards and great frustrations. J. F. Hunt. il Motor B 117:54-5+ F '66
Landlocked Wateree. R. Clancy. Motor B 117:144+ Mr '66
Voices in the night. J. Martenhoff. il Motor B 117:40-1+ F '66
Whar ya headin' sailor, that ain't your bow! J. Moloney. Motor B 117:108+ F '66

Bibliography
Book notes and reviews; ed. by M. S. Britter. See issues of Yachting
New books on boating. W. R. Juettner. il Motor B 118:103 O '66

Laws and regulations
Amphibious C.G. checkup on the careless boatman. Motor B 117:139-41 F '66

BOATS and boating—Laws and regulations—
Continued
Equipment you have to have. M. Penzer. il
Motor B 117:50-2+ My '66
Great pollution pickle. R. Stone and J. Na-
pier. il Motor B 119:352-3+ Ja '67
High time the boatman came into his own.
Z. Taylor. il Motor B 117:46+ Ap '66
Important legislation affecting all yachtsmen.
C. F. Sheppard; H. Williams. Yachting
119:77-9+ F '66
Ventilate. M. Crook. il Yachting 119:80-2+
Mr '66
Washington report. W. T. Stone. See issues
of Yachting
What's needed is a breath of fresh air; re-
vised coast guard regulations for boat ven-
tilation. il Motor B 117:30-3+ Mr '66

Safety devices and measures
At the boating summit; meeting of National
association of state boating law administra-
tors. Motor B 119:347-9 Ja '67
Danger signals from a river towboat. W.
Belvin and A. Klein. il Yachting 119:72-
4+ Je '66
How to bring yourself back alive. J. Roe.
il Pop Sci 188:106-9 Je '66
Rate yourself as a skipper. H. Bowman. il
Motor B 118:35+ Jl '66
Rough water savvy. J. A. Emmett. il Out-
door Life 138:98-100 Ag '66
Safety standards for small craft. F. M. Paul-
son. il Field & S 71:104-9 O '66
See also
Life saving equipment

Study and teaching
Coast guard auxiliary offers free boating
courses. E. A. Weinberg. il Motor B 118.
77 Ag '66
Seagoing classroom; Brick Township high
school, N.J. J. K. Andrews. il Motor B
118:72-3 Ag '66
Should boating be taught in public schools?
how one man introduced boating classes
at North Mercer high school, Mercer Is-
land, Wash. E. Crimmin. il Motor B 117:
32-5+ My '66
You are invited to attend U.S. power squad-
rons free instruction classes in boat op-
eration. H. M. Hutchings. Motor B 118:
74-6 Ag '66
BOATS in bottles. See Ship and boat models
BOATYARDS
Boatyards and bywaters. J. Emmett. il
Yachting 119:68-9+ Mr '66
BOAZ, Martha
More than deliberate speed. por ALA Bul
60:286-8 Mr '66
BOB Jones university, Greenville, S.C.
Bob Jones university: the buckle on the
Bible belt. L. L. King. Harper 232:51-8
Je '66; Discussion. 233:6 Ag: 10+ S '66
BOBBIN lace. See Lace and lace making
BOBCAT hunting
Fugitive of Black Mountain. D. Lawrence.
il Outdoor Life 138:50-1+ O '66
Get a good thing going. K. Hueftle. il Out-
door life 137:62-3+ My '66
BOBINO hall, Paris. See Vaudeville
BOBROWSKI, Johannes
Kaunas 1941; poem, tr. by R. Mead and M.
Mead. Nation 202:589 My 16 '66
BOBSLEDDING. See Coasting
BOBST, Elmer H.
Toward urban excellence; donation towards
NYU library. il Time 87:94 Ap 1 '66
BOBWHITE shooting. See Quail shooting
BOCA GRANDE, Fla. See Gasparilla Island
BOCCA, Geoffrey
Road to survival in Europe. Horizon 8:106-7
Wint '66
BOCCHERINI, Luigi
Boccherini con Polo. C. Farrell. por Am Rec
G 32:702-4 Ap '66
BOCKELMAN, Wilfred
Minister at mass. America 115:832-3 D 24 '66
BOCKLET, Richard J.
Land reform in Latin America. America 115:
458-60 O 15 '66
BODET, Jaime Torres. See Torres Bodet, J.
BODI, Lewis J. and Tufts, C. F.
Thermal recrystallization of precipitated zinc
sulfide. Science 153:872-3 Ag 19 '66
BODIAN, David
Electron microscopy: two major synaptic
types on spinal motoneurons. bibliog Sci-
ence 151:1093-4 Mr 4 '66
BODIES, Dead. See Cadavers
BODO, John R.
Stewardship by individious comparison. Chris-
tian Cent 83:907-8 Jl 20 '66

BODY chemistry. See Biochemistry
BODY fluids
See also
Biological transport
BODY minerals. See Minerals in the body
BODY movements. See Movement, Psychology
of
BODY weight. See Weight (physiology)
BOECKENHAUPT, Herbert
Faceless ones. por Time 88:33 N 11 '66
Sergeant's revenge. il por Newsweek 68:37-8
N 14 '66
BOEHM, George A. W.
He is shaking Food and drug well before
using. N Y Times Mag p23+ My 15 '66
Should we build Nike-X? Read Digest 88:77-
81 Mr '66
Wonder drug nobody understands. N Y Times
Mag p56-7+ S 11 '66
BOEHM, Karl. See Böhm, K.
BOEHME, Robert
Growing practice. il por Time 87:25 F 18 '66
BOEING company
Boeing at fifty. il Time 88:60+ Jl 29 '66
Boeing changes bet in the SST race. il Bsns
W p48 Je 18 '66
Boeing chosen to produce air force SRAM. il
Tech W 19:12 N 7 '66
Boeing focuses on range-payload goal. R. G.
O'Lone. Aviation W 86:26-7 Ja 9 '67
Boeing may pick single-deck model 747. I.
Stone. il Aviation W 84:42-3 Mr 21 '66
Boeing places its supersonic bet. il Bsns W
p38-40+ D 24 '66
Boeing plans to let 60 per cent of SST work.
R. Twiss. il Tech W 20:13-15 Ja 9 '67
Boeing pushes titanium airframe effort.
C. M. Plattner. il Aviation W 85:38-9+
D 26 '66
Boeing SST design. C. M. Plattner. il Avia-
tion W 85:36-9 Ag 15; 30-3 Ag 22 '66
Boeing's billions. il Time 88:108 N 25 '66
Boeing's birthday. Newsweek 68:79 Jl 25 '66
Boeing's new version; design of supersonic
transport. il Time 88:102 O 7 '66
$50 billion battle to build the giant SST;
with report by C. Welles. il Life 61:68-
77+ O 28 '66
Flexibility in manufacturing permits wide
737 options. R. G. O'Lone. il Aviation W
84:54-7 Je 6 '66
Forecasts of swelling markets key in decision
on 747. R. G. O'Lone. il Aviation W 84:40-
1+ Ap 25 '66
$4.9 billion backlog, and the SST, too. il
Newsweek 69:66-8 Ja 16 '67
Frustration beneath elation; SST. il Time
89:59-60 Ja 13 '67
Johnson expected to push SST. Aviation W
86:25-6 Ja 9 '67
New Do-u-g-l-as; DC-8 Super 61 and Boeing's
727-200 il Newsweek 67:68 Ja 31 '66
Soaring Boeing stock goes under a cloud. il
Bsns W p 158 F 19 '66
Supersonic jet makes a slow takeoff; choice
of Boeing and GE didn't end the suspense.
il Bsns W p31-2 Ja 7 '67
SST race, biggest of all. il Newsweek 68:48-
52+ Ag 29 '66
SST: winners of the great race. il Newsweek
69:51 Ja 9 '67
SST's decisive moment; will contract go to
Boeing, Lockheed, both or neither? il
Bsns W p35-7 D 24 '66
U.K. presses BAC 111 sale in New Zealand.
R. G. O'Lone. il Aviation W 84:32-4 F 7
'66

Aerospace division
Big space company stuck on what to do
next. Sci N 89:490 Je 18 '66

Vertol division
Vertol studies rotary/fixed-wing VTOL. R. D.
Hibben. il Aviation W 85:81+ Jl 25 '66
BOELLSTORFF, Ruth
It could only happen to a farm wife. Farm J
90:83 My '66
BOETH, Richard
Please hire the handicapped. Atlan 217:120-1
F '66
BOEYNANTS, Paul Vanden
New combo. il por Time 87:26-7 Mr 25 '66
BOG gardens. See Gardens, Bog
BOGAN, Louise
Verse (cont) New Yorker 42:221-3 O 1 '66
BOGARDUS, Adam H.
Bogardus glass ball. A. G. Peterson. il
Hobbies 71:88 D '66
BOGART, Humphrey
Bacall comes back, big. G. Zimmermann. il
por Look 30:95-8+ Mr 22 '66
Bogart vogue. G. Weales. Commonweal 83:
664-6 Mr 11 '66

BOGART, Humphrey—Continued
Bogie really had cool. D. Berson. il pors Seventeen 26:16 Ja '67
Lauren Bacall talks about Bogart, Sinatra and her new life. L. Bacall. il por McCalls 93:24+ Jl '66
Tough guy and the jet set. H. Frankel. il por Sat R 49:33 S 24 '66
BOGART, Ralph
Inbreeding of zoo animals. bibliog por Parks & Rec 1:254-7 Mr '66
BOGDANOVICH, Peter
Sonny & Chér: they're what's happening. baby. Sat Eve Post 239:46-50+ Ap 23 '66
Th' respawnsibility of bein' J . . . Jimmy Stewart. Gosh! Esquire 66:104-6+ Jl '66
(ed) See Bono, S. Sonny talks about Chér
BOGDEN, Arthur E. See Sarcione, E. J. jt. auth.
BOGGS, Hale
Washington: ten of its most powerful men. por Vogue 148:154 N 15 '66
BOGOTÁ, Colombia

Banks
See Banks and banking—Colombia

Libraries
See Libraries—Colombia
BOHANNAN, Laura
Shakespeare in the bush. Natur Hist 75:28-33 Ag '66
La BOHÈME; opera. See Puccini, G.
BOHEMIANISM
New Bohemia. W. J. Smith. Commonweal 85:102-3 O 28 '66
See also
Beatniks
BOHIKEE creek; drama. See Unger, R.
BÖHM, Karl
In the wrist. por Time 88:94 O 28 '66
BOHNENBLUST, Henri Frédéric
Profess with a passion. il por Time 87:82-3 My 6 '66
BOHNET, Donald F.
Middle Atlantic. por Parks & Rec 1:644 Ag '66
BOHR, Niels Henrik David
Great Dane. H. Simons. New Repub 155:28+ D 3 '66
Niels Bohr, by R. Moore. Review
  Atlan 218:161-2 N '66. O. Handlin
BOHUS, B. and De Wied, D.
Inhibitory and facilitatory effect of two related peptides on extinction of avoidance behavior. bibliog Science 153:318-20 Jl 15 '66
BOIARSKY, Carolyn
Turncoat Rockefeller. New Repub 154:9 F 26 '66
BOIES, J. J.
Oasis on Broadway. Nat R 18:739-40 Jl 26 '66
BOIGNY, Félix Houphouet-. See Houphouet-Boigny, F.
BOIKO, Claire
All hands on deck; drama. Plays 26:35-44 Ja '67
All points West; drama. Plays 26:41-6, 62 N '66
Insatiable dragon; dramatization of A Chinese folktale. Plays 25:63-8 Ap '66
Scaredy cat; drama. Plays 26:41-6, 96 O '66
BOILEAU, Helen Houston
Vegetable pies? Parents Mag 41:84-6 O '66
BOILER room; story. See Wurlitzer, R.
BOITO, Arrigo
Mefistofele. Criticism
  Newsweek 67:81 F 7 '66
Mefistofele returns. J. W. Freeman. il Opera N 30:28-9 Ja 29 '66
BOJARSKY, Czeslaw
Leonardo of forgers. por Time 87:28 Je 3 '66
BOK, Bart J.
Books and the sky. Sky & Tel 31:357-61 Je '66
Otto Struve memorial symposium. Sky & Tel 32:68-71 Ag '66
Radio astronomy and the galactic system. Sky & Tel 32:271-4, 341-3 N-D '66
BOLDIZSAR, Ivan
View from the East. Nation 203:55-9 Jl 11 '66
BOLES, Charles E. See Black Bart
BOLES, Paul Darcy
Animal kingdom; story. Seventeen 25:148-9 O '66
Swinger; story. Seventeen 25:180-1 My '66
Verray parfit gentil knight; story. Seventeen 25:182-3 S '66
BOLIVAR, Simón
Integration or disintegration. J. Ianacio Rasco. il Américas 18:29-34 Jl '66

Drama
Youth, Bolivar. S. S. Ullman. Plays 25:59-66 Mr '66

BOLIVIA
Flamboyant is the word for Bolivia. L. McIntyre. il Nat Geog Mag 129:153-95 F '66
See also
Agricultural colonization—Bolivia
Economic assistance in Bolivia
Elections—Bolivia
Mines and mineral resources—Bolivia
Natural resources—Bolivia
Potosi

Description and travel
Bargain-priced Bolivia. C. Matty. il Travel 125:45-8 Mr '66
Travel's picture portfolio. il Travel 126:50-5 S '66

Economic policy
Bolivia: revolution in mid-passage. G. Delmas. Reporter 35:31-4 D 1 '66

Foreign relations
Summit on the wing; Barrientos & Belaúnde. il Time 88:37-8 O 28 '66

History
Bolivia. R. E. Crist. bibliog il Focus 16:1-6 Mr '66

Politics and government
Constitutional way; new president. Time 88:34 Ag 19 '66
Letter from La Paz. C. Rand. il New Yorker 42:35-40+ D 31 '66

Religious institutions and affairs
World around us (cont of) News of the Christian world. Christian Cent 83:838 Je 29 '66
BOLIVIAN hemorrhagic fever. See Hemorrhagic fever
BOLIVIAN national symphony. See Orchestras
BOLLEN, W. B. See Chandra, P. jt. auth.
BOLLES, Blair
Correctives for dishonest and unfair public administrators. Ann Am Acad 363:23-7 Ja '66
BOLLING, Richard
What the new Congress needs most. Harper 234:79-81 Ja '67
BOLLWORMS, Pink
Sex attractant of the pink bollworm moth: isolation, identification, and synthesis. W. A. Jones and others. bibliog Science 152: 1516-17 Je 10 '66
BOLOGNA, J. M. and others
Absence of short-term variability of CTA 102. bibliog Science 153:294-5 Jl 15 '66
Galactic depolarization of the 21-centimeter-wavelength radiation of extragalactic sources. bibliog Science 154:1656-8 D 30 '66
BOLOGNA, Italy
Libraries, lasagna, and leaning towers; Johns Hopkins university center. J. A. Hoffberg. il Wilson Lib Bul 40:948-52 Je '66
BOLSHOI ballet
Bolshoi portfolio; four productions; four lively controversies. J. Anderson. il Dance Mag 40:44-51 Je '66
Foolish excesses of yesterday; performances at Metropolitan opera house. D. Hering. il Dance Mag 40:28-9+ Jl '66
Music to my ears; American tour. I. Kolodin. Sat R 49:85 My 7 '66
Musical events; performances of Rite of spring and Nutcracker at Metropolitan opera house. W. Sargeant. New Yorker 42:125-6 My 7 '66
Musical events; performances of Swan Lake and Don Quixote at Metropolitan opera house. W. Sargeant. New Yorker 42:130-2 Ap 30 '66
New Nutcracker and Sacre du printemps; productions at Metropolitan opera house. I. Kolodin. Sat R 49:26 My 14 '66
Toe to toe. il Newsweek 67:94-5 My 2 '66
Wing-footed feat; last visit to Manhattan's Metropolitan opera house. Time 87:88 Ap 29 '66
BOLTÉ, Mary
How to win over your children; excerpt. Good H 162:100-1 Ap '66
BOLTIN, Lee
Animals from the rough; photographs. Natur Hist 75:54-7 My '66
BOLTON, Robert H.
Crisis in mission. Christian Cent 83:647-50 My 18 '66
BOLTON, William
(ed) That's a good question. See issues of Today's health
BOLTS and nuts
Nuts & bolts. E. Rickman. il Hot Rod 19: 58-61+ Je '66
BOLTZ, Sue
Lady shows them how it's done. il pors Bsns W p 134-6+ O 15 '66

BOMB detectors. See Detectors
BOMB shelters. See Atomic bomb shelters
BOMBE. See Desserts
BOMBING planes. See Airplanes, Military
BOMBS
  Bombs, bottlenecks & baloney; debate over administration's practical prosecution of Vietnamese war. il Time 87:26 Ap 29 '66
    See also
  Guided missiles
BOMHARD, Moritz
  Blue grass winner. R. D. Daniels. il por Opera N 30:14-16 Ap 9 '66
BONANNO, Joseph
  Bananas is back. por Newsweek 67:28 My 30 '66
BONANZA air lines
  Bonanza sees DC-9 as wider market key. H. D. Watkins. il Aviation W 84:40-1+ Mr 14 '66
BONAPARTE, Napoleon. See Napoleon I, emperor of the French
BONAPARTE family
  Bonapartes, by D. Stacton. Review Newsweek il 67:96-7 My 30 '66
    Time il pors 87:108+ My 13 '66
BONATTI, Enrico
  Deep-sea authigenic calcite and dolomite. bibliog Science 153:534-7 Jl 29 '66
  —and Joensuu, Oiva
  Deep-sea iron deposit from the South Pacific. bibliog Science 154:643-5 N 4 '66
BONAVENA, Oscar Natalio
  Clover in need of a leaf. M. Kane. Sports Illus 25:72+ O 3 '66
BONAVENTURE; story. See Gallant, M.
BOND, Harold
  There can be nothing more; poem. Horn Bk 42:418 Ag '66
BOND, Horace Julian. See Bond, J.
BOND, James (literary character) See Spies in literature
BOND, Julian
  Bond issue. Time 87:24 F 18 '66
  Bond's word. por Newsweek 68:27 D 19 '66
  Furor in legislature; with press comments. il por Sr Schol 88:15-16 F 11 '66
  Georgia bans Bond. Christian Cent 83:102 Ja 26 '66
  Inflated Bond. Nat R 18:102 F 8 '66
  Julian Bond; Georgia's uppity legislator. H. Shapiro. il Nation 202:145-8 F 7 '66
  No seat for the Negro who won. R. Cleghorn. New Repub 154:11-12 Ja 29 '66
  Right to speak. por Time 88:31 D 16 '66
  Supreme court rules for Julian Bond. Christian Cent 83:1560-1 D 21 '66
BOND, Ruskin
  Day grandfather tickled a tiger. Read Digest 88:169-70+ F '66
BOND honoured; drama. See Osborne, J.
BONDE bosse enameling. See Enamel and enameling
BONDS
  All about bonds for investment; interview. G. M. Shannon. il U S News 61:64-6+ S 26 '66
  Are prices for bonds near the bottom? il Bsns W p 155-6+ Mr 12 '66
  Bond flood rouses ire of Europe. il Bsns W p 128+ Mr 5 '66
  Case for convertibles. il Duns R 87:43-4+ Ap '66
  Even a smash can have a gilt edge; Yuba industries, inc. il Bsns W p66-7 Jl 2 '66
  Experts see for '67; period of opportunity for investors. il U S News 62:36-9 Ja 9 '67
  How to handle your money now; interview. R. D. Naess. il U S News 60:58-62 Ja 31 '66
  Reviving bond market keeps eye on the Fed. il Bsns W p40 Ja 7 '67
  Wall Street: tight money. Newsweek 67:70-1 Mr 7 '66
  What bonds now offer investors. il U S News 61:83-4 Ag 29 '66
  Will new issue flood push interest rates up? il Bsns W p46 Je 18 '66
    See also
  State bonds
BONDS, Convertible
  Dent in convertibles. Fortune 74:242+ O '66
  Wall St. converts a slump to profit; convertible debentures; with editorial comment. il Bsns W p 133-4+, 153 Ap 9 '66
BONDS, Fraudulent. See Securities, Fraudulent
BONDS, Government
  Better deal on savings bonds. il U S News 60:115 F 28 '66
  Buy bonds, the man said; Lawrence O'Brien's arm-twisting sales drive. Newsweek 67:81-2 Je 13 '66

Federal bonds that yield more than five per cent. il U S News 60:113-15 Ap 25 '66
How to succeed in selling savings bonds; President Johnson's arm-twisting campaign. Life 61:4 Jl 8 '66
In the making: a bond battle. U S News 61:89 Jl 18 '66
New U.S. bond at higher rate. U S News 61:103-4 O 3 '66
Patriotism by edict; text of follow-up communication to buy federal savings bonds. New Repub 155:9 Jl 16 '66
Plan to make millions quickly; Ohio development finance commission proceeds into U.S. treasury bonds. U S News 60:88-9 Je 27 '66
Savings bond rates jump, too; higher interest on series E and H. Bsns W p32 Ja 22 '66
Too much pressure in a good cause; postal workers pressured to buy bonds. S. Landowne. America 115:27 Jl 9 '66
Treasury bills for the Philippines. il Fortune 74:99-100 D '66
U.S. bonus bond; what it will offer; with E bonds in a package. U S News 61:100-2 N 28 '66
    See also
  State bonds

    Europe, Eastern
Bonds that measure cold war heat; east European issues that date to pre-Communist days. il Bsns W p 108-10 S 10 '66

    Russia
Bonds that measure cold war heat; east European issues that date to pre-Communist days. il Bsns W p 108-10 S 10 '66

BONDS, Highway. See Roads—Finance
BONDS, Industrial development
  Companies rush for cheaper money; tax-exempt industrial development bonds. Bsns W p 114+ Je 11 '66
  Public bonds and private profit. America 115:26 Jl 9 '66
BONDS, Municipal. See Municipal bonds
BONDS, Revenue
  Why the biggest tax-exempt failed; New Jersey turnpike's record $440-million issue. il Bsns W p 143-4+ Mr 26 '66
    See also
  Bonds, Industrial development
BONDS, State. See State bonds
BONDS, United Nations. See United Nations —Finance
BONE
  Erythropoietic and reticuloendothelial function in bone marrow in dogs. M. L. Greenberg and others. bibliog il Science 152:526-8 Ap 22 '66
  Infrared analysis of rat bone: age dependency of amorphous and crystalline mineral fractions. J. D. Termine and A. S. Posner. bibliog il Science 153:1523-5 S 23 '66
  Protein-polysaccharide loss during endochondral ossification: immunochemical evidence. A. Hirschman and D. D. Dziewiatkowski. bibliog il Science 154:1393-5 O 21 '66
  Shock can damage bone. Sci N 90:99 Ag 13 '66
  Thyrocalcitonin inhibition of bone resorption induced by parathyroid hormone in tissue culture. M. A. Aliapoulios and others. bibliog il Science 151:330-1 Ja 21 '66
BONE surgery. See Orthopedia
BONEFISH fishing
  Cozumel: the island with everything. B. Brister. il Field & S 70:68-70+ Mr '66
  Fly fishing for bones. A. J. McClane. il Field & S 71:54-7 N '66
  King of the thin water. J. Brooks. il Outdoor Life 139:58-61+ Ja '67
BONES
    See also
  Skull
BONES, Fossil. See Paleontology
BONEY, Knowles
  Mugs, jugs, and chamber pots. I. N. Hume. il Antiques 90:520-2 O '66
BONFANTE, Jordan
  Is J.J. really king of the surf? Life 60:81-2 Je 10 '66
  Italian men are lousy lovers. Life 60:81-2+ F 4 '66
  Reagan vs. Brown: see how they run! Life 61:42-7 O 14 '66
BONGARTZ, Roy
  I can always stop; story. Esquire 66:201+ D '66
  It clicks, it hums, it's supercar! Sat Eve Post 240:38-40 Ja 28 '67
BONHAM, Frank
  Return to Durango street; address. July 1966. por Library J 91:4188-91 S 15 '66
  World of Rufus Henry. Horn Bk 42:34-6 F '66

BONHAM, George W.
Ivory tower crumbles. Sat R 49:66-7+ My 21 '66

BONHOEFFER, Dietrich
Dietrich Bonhoeffer, by E. H. Robertson. Review
Christian Cent 83:1603-4 D 28 '66. J. A. Phillips
Message from Bonhoeffer. J. C. Ridd. Christian Cent 83:827-9 Je 29 '66
Prison prophet. il por Time 87:58+ My 27 '66

BONN
Description
Non-city. il Newsweek 67:46+ Je 6 '66

BONNELL, John Sutherland
He couldn't say no. por Time 88:70 Ag 5 '66

BONNEVILLE, Jane F.
Desert dwellers afloat. Motor B 118:26-8 D '66

BONNEVILLE race course. See Speedways

BONNEVILLE SALT FLATS. See Great Salt Lake Desert

BONNEWELL, Mrs R. W.
Tin-can flowers. Design 67:14-15 My '66

BONNICHSEN, Bill. See Perry, E. C. jr, jt. auth.

BONO, Salvatore
Sonny talks about Chér; interview. ed. by P. Bogdanovich. Vogue 148:137-8 N 15 '66
about
Sonny & Chér: they're what's happening, baby. P. Bogdanovich. il pors Sat Eve Post 239:46-50+ Ap 23 '66

BONSAI. See Trees, Dwarf

BONSAL, Philip W.
Cuba, Castro and the United States. For Affairs 45:260-76 Ja '67

BONTEMPS, Arna
Lonesome boy theme; address, May 5, 1966. Horn Bk 42:672-80 D '66

BONWIT Teller. See New York (city)—Stores

BONYNGE, Richard
Man of instinct; interview, ed. by Q. Eaton. pors Opera N 31:16 D 31 '66
about
Music to my ears. I. Kolodin. Sat R 50:26 Ja 7 '67

BOOK advertising. See Books—Advertising

BOOK awards, National. See National book awards

BOOK binding. See Bookbinding

BOOK buying
Inordinate delays between delivery and payment; getting institutions to pay their bills. C. B. Grannis. Pub W 190:81 N 14 '66

BOOK buying, Personal. See Libraries, Private

BOOK buying for libraries. See Libraries—Acquisitions

BOOK cases. See Bookcases

BOOK catalogs. See Catalogs, Library

BOOK censorship. See Censorship

BOOK clubs
Commentary magazine forms subscriber book club. Pub W 191:36 Ja 2 '67
Merchantry of books; Book find club. F. P. Haughton. il Wilson Lib Bul 41:219-22 O '66
Xerox division creates student paperback clubs. Pub W 190:29 O 24 '66
See also
Book-of-the-month club

BOOK collecting
Books for an early American bookcase. E. Wolf, 2d. il Antiques 90:211-13 Ag '66
Confessions of a reformed bibliomaniac; summary of address. R. Scholes. Pub W 190: 30-1 Ag 1 '66
Memoirs of a merchant-scholar. W. Targ. Sat R 49:59-60 O 22 '66

BOOK covers
Award-winning design for boxed set of books: Lincoln's log cabin library. il Pub W 189: 124 Mr 7 '66
Collier paperbacks' new covers have visual and sales impact. il Pub W 190:96-7 Jl 4 '66
Cover scheme conveys content and continuity: printed textiles as jacket art. il Pub W 189:122+ Mr 7 '66
Design considerations for contemporary religious series. il Pub W 190:114-15 D 5 '66
Fine art on paperback covers is commercial and artistic success; Washington Square press series. il Pub W 190:111-12+ O 3 '66
Front-to-back cover design for Odyssey text paperbacks. il Pub W 190:118-20 S 5 '66

Trade winds; illustrators fees. H. R. Mayes. Sat R 49:7 S 3 '66
Two covers increase one paperback's appeal. il Pub W 189:124-5 Mr 7 '66
Versatile design in pocket books covers shown by AIGA. il Pub W 189:102-3 Ap 4 '66

BOOK design
Designer's corner. S. Salter. Pub W 189:113-15 My 2; 166+ Je 13; 190:109+ Jl 4; 98+ Ag 1; 111-13 S 5; 135-7 O 3; 100+ N 7; 112-13 D 5 '66
Ellis talks on design at Philadelphia clinic; summary of address, March 8, 1966. R. Ellis. il Pub W 189:119 My 2 '66
Fifty books in retrospect: trends in design over forty-three years; AIGA exhibition. il Pub W 189:96-7 Ap 4 '66
Fifty books show: balanced view of U.S. output. E. A. Hamilton. il Pub W 189:66-7+ My 2 '66
Inventive illustration and design in new edition of The divine comedy; Washington Square press. il Pub W 191:84-5 Ja 2 '67
John Dreyfus: typographic advisor, editor, printing historian. P. A. Bennett. il Pub W 190:84-6+ S 5 '66
Looks of books; interview, ed. by S. Kauffmann. H. Ford. New Repub 155:15+ N 26 '66
Redesigning British books without resetting body type. il Pub W 189:119-20+ Mr 7 '66
Simplicity in design; excerpt from Library publications. W. R. Holman. il Wilson Lib Bul 40:517-24 F '66
Unusual design and production for a play; new edition of Bald soprano by Grove press. il Pub W 189:123+ F 7 '66
We will leave no worm unturned; address at the opening of the Textbook show 1966; April 6, 1966. L. C. Deighton. Pub W 189: 26-9 My 2 '66
What is a book? J. P. Meyers. il Sch Arts 65:34-7 Ja '66

BOOK discarding. See Libraries—Book discarding

BOOK donations. See Libraries—Gifts, legacies, etc.

BOOK editors. See Editors and editing

BOOK ends and bookracks
Photograph book ends. il Sunset 137:136 N '66

BOOK exhibits
AIGA and Fifty books. S. Salter. Pub W 191: 97-8 Ja 2 '67
AIGA calls for entries in children's book show. Pub W 191:101 Ja 2 '67
AAUP's second show retains awareness of quality. P. A. Bennett. il Pub W 189:136-7+ Je 13 '66
Book as display. il Wilson Lib Bul 41:91-4, 331-3 S, N '66
Chicago book clinic's 17th show goes on tour; with list of titles. il Pub W 189: 160-5 Je 13 '66
Craftsmanship in design: 25th Western books show. il Pub W 190:104-5+ Jl 4 '66
Eighteen publishers represented in AIGA 1965-66 commerce show. il Pub W 191:83 Ja 2 '67
Fifty books show: balanced view of U.S. output. E. A. Hamilton. il Pub W 189:66-7+ My 2 '66
French Fifty books show emphasizes traditional high-quality bookmaking. Pub W 190:93-5 N 7 '66
Good show: exhibition from library of natural-history books and book illustrations, supplemented with specimens. New Yorker 41:27-8 F 19 '66
New England book show, 1965, opens in Boston. il Pub W 189:110-14+ F 7 '66
Textbooks, 1964-1965: multi-media techniques for teaching; 1966 Textbook show. S. M. Agnew. il Pub W 189:8-7+ My 2 '66
See also
Book fairs

BOOK fairs
Alabama store sponsors children's book fair: Loveman's, Birmingham. il Pub W 190:54-6 D 5 '66
Book fair. E. O'Connor. il Atlan 218:124-5 Jl '66
Book fairs and the CBC. M. C. Childs. bibliog il Library J 91:2586-8 My 15 '66
Book festival for young people; Shorebird bookstore, Palos Verdes Peninsula, Calif. A. Fink. il Pub W 189:81-3 My 30 '66
Cleveland newspaper plans Midwest book festival. Pub W 190:43 Ag 15 '66
8000 attend Baptist book fair; Baptist book store, Nashville, Tenn. il Pub W 190:80-1 D 26 '66
Fairs and CBC aids for children's book week. il Pub W 190:136-8 Jl 11 '66
Frankfurt book fair. C. Northcott. Christian Cent 83:1284+ O 19 '66

BOOK fairs—*Continued*

Jaycees' good reading project. J. D. Burris. ALA Bul 60:635-6 Je '66

NYU store holds first book fair for faculty. il Pub W 190:83-4 D 26 '66

Publisher's own exhibits were basis of Cleveland fair; Midwest fall book festival. il Pub W 190:46-7 O 10 '66

World of books at the Frankfurt fair. il Pub W 190:22-32 N 7 '66; Correction. 190:11 N 28 '66

BOOK find club. See Book clubs

BOOK illustration. See Illustration of books and periodicals

BOOK illustrators. See Illustrators

BOOK industries and trade

Bookmaking. See first issue of each month of Publishers' weekly
See also
Booksellers and bookselling
Printing
Printing industry

Advertising

See Books—Advertising

History

Bibliopola, by S. Taubert. Review Pub W il 190:51-4 D 26 '66. C. B. Anderson

International aspects

ABPC annual meeting: the international role of the book; summary of address. W. B. Wiley. il Pub W 189:80-1 Je 13 '66

Law

But can you do that? H. F. Pilpel. See occasional issues of Publishers' weekly

Statistics

Cadillacs and Chevrolets; representative of the American book publishers council queries the validity of the Library materials indexes. E. Moon. Lbrary J 91:3343-5 Jl '66

U.S. book exports, imports up 26 per cent, 1st half of 1966. il Pub W 190:60-2 D 26 '66

Asia

Asia book conference opens in Tokyo, May 25. Pub W 189:57 My 23 '66

Europe, Western

Book market research: Europe; report of international meeting in Berlin. G. R. Davies. Pub W 191:53-5 Ja 16 '67

France

French Fifty books show emphasizes traditional high-quality bookmaking. Pub W 190:93-5 N 7 '66

Lire: the French try institutional promotion; equivalent of National library week. H. R. Lottman. Pub W 190:41-3 S 19 '66
See also
Publishers and publishing—France

Pakistan

First trip to East Pakistan. F. Watts. Pub W 190:40-2 O 10 '66

United States

Book clinic speakers agree on greater standardization; American institute of graphic arts luncheon. Pub W 190:128-9 D 5 '66

Book industry needs annual planning: adaptation of address, September 29, 1966. M. K. Smith. Pub W 190:18-20 O 24 '66

Book industry plans for 1967. C. B. Grannis. Pub W 190:68 D 26 '66

Bottlenecks viewed at D. C. conference; meeting demands under the new federal aid to education laws. Pub W 190:195-8 Jl 11 '66

College market textbook problems analyzed by publishers, suppliers; report of ATPI conference. il Pub W 191:44-8 Ja 16 '67

Common need for more information. C. B. Grannis. Pub W 189:135 Je 13 '66

Continuing comments on the production crisis. C. B. Grannis. Pub W 189:89 Mr 7 '66

Delays in production and delivery. C. B. Grannis. Pub W 190:58 O 3 '66

Government-backed library buying not alone responsible for book surge; excerpts from address, September 29, 1966. M. Smith. Library J 91:4910+ O 15 '66

Is the industry prepared for the crush of school orders? R. H. Smith. Pub W 189:69 F 7 '66

Morgan Smith's plea; market needs and demands. C. B. Grannis. Pub W 190:61 O 31 '66

Notes on the 7 per cent credit for capital investment. C. B. Grannis. Pub W 190:95 O 3 '66

Production crisis: it grows worse. Pub W 190:74-6 S 5 '66

Production crisis: manufacturers differ about severity, but expand plants; responses to PW questionnaire. Pub W 189:48-50 F 7 '66

Production facilities, East and West; needed expansion in book manufacturing plants. C. B. Grannis. Pub W 190:69 N 7 '66

Recruitment for the book industry. C. B Grannis. Pub W 190:203 Jl 11 '66

Shadows on the future; address, June 13, 1966. C. G. Benjamin. il Pub W 190:36-9 Jl 4 '66

So many projects and how about money? C. B. Grannis. Pub W 191:43 Ja 9 '67
See also
Book manufacturers' institute
Booksellers and bookselling—United States
Publishers and publishing—United States

BOOK jackets. See Book covers

BOOK jobbers

Education's book boom: are wholesalers ready? PW survey. Pub W 189:18-21 Ap 11 '66

FTC approves extra discount for premiums. Pub W 190:41 Ag 15 '66

Net prices, library editions: Senate hearings reviewed. Pub W 190:26-30 Jl 25 '66

Stacey speeds delivery with new billing system. G. McCorkle. il Pub W 189:46-9 Ap 18 '66

Truce with the publishers; discussion of net pricing between a publisher, wholesaler, and a librarian. Library J 91:2579-83 My 15 '66

When is a book really o/p? D. Melcher. Library J 91:4576-8 O 1 '66

Wholesalers and the education squeeze. R. H. Smith. Pub W 189:60 Mr 7 '66
See also
Eliot books, incorporated
Raymar book company

BOOK lending, Library. See Libraries—Circulation, loans, etc.

BOOK lists. See Books and reading—Best books; Childrens literature—Bibliography; Reading lists

BOOK making (betting)

Big action in a phone booth; illegal bookmakers. B. Surface. il Sports Illus 26:28-32 Ja 9 '67

Out in the bleachers, where the action is; Chicago Cubs' fans. W. B. Furlong. il Harper 233:49-53 Jl '66

BOOK manufacturers' institute

BMI and publishers study the book market; report, with summaries of addresses at 34th annual meeting. il Pub W 190:72-4+ D 5 '66

BMI convention: theme will be book markets and methods of supply. il Pub W 190:129-30 O 3 '66

BMI tackles some pressing practical issues; recent activities. Pub W 189:71 Ap 4 '66

We need not be oppressed by prosperity; report of annual meeting. C. B. Grannis. Pub W 190:40 D 5 '66

Anecdotes, facetiae, satire, etc.

Poetic manufacturer describes the scene; BMI convention; poem. Pub W 190:71 D 5 '66

BOOK numbers

Books without number; publishers' book numbers. D. Melcher. Pub W 190:52 Jl 18 '66

Books without number; some of the history of proposals for an industry book numbering system. D. Melcher. Pub W 190:24-7 Ag 15 '66

British books to be numbered beginning this month. D. Melcher. Pub W 191:28-30 Ja 2 '67

Electronic processing in the bookstore. D. Melcher. Pub W 190:30-3 S 5 '66

Postmark: Pall Mall; idea in Britain. G. R. Davies. Pub W 190:60-2 S 12 '66

BOOK of hours of Catherine of Cleves. See Hours, Books of

BOOK of Job. See Bible—Old Testament—Job

BOOK-of-the-month club

Birthday-of-the-month; fortieth anniversary. H. Frankel. Sat R 49:31+ Ap 16 '66

Random house dictionary tested at $7.50 by B-O-M. Pub W 190:33 N 28 '66
See also
Dorothy Canfield Fisher library awards

BOOK orders, Library. See Libraries—Acquisitions

BOOK packing. See Packing for shipment

BOOK prices. See Books—Prices

BOOK processing in libraries. See Libraries—Technical processes

BOOK rarities

Books. P. W. Schmidtchen. See issues of Hobbies

BOOK rarities—*Continued*
Final metamorphosis; handwritten Caxton manuscript of Ovid's Metamorphoses. Time 89:55 Ja 13 '67
From the red pale; first book with English illustrations ever prepared for printing; Ovid's Metamorphoses. il Time 88:56 Jl 8 '66
Rare Chinese library materials returned to Taiwan by LC. Library J 91:216 Ja 15 '66
See also
Book collecting

Facsimiles
Great 18th century book produced in facsimile; The Atlantic Neptune. il Pub W 190:115-16 D 5 '66
Legacy library; facsimiles of classic children's books. il Pub W 189:100-1 F 14 '66

Prices
Book values. il Fortune 74:242 O '66
BOOK repairing. See Books—Conservation and restoration
BOOK restoration. See Books—Conservation and restoration
BOOK reviewers. See Critics
BOOK reviews
Book review index: a new book selection tool. L. Ash. il Library J 91:2013-15 Ap 15 '66
Experiment in cooperative reviewing by scientists and librarians. P. L. Moulton. Horn Bk 42:345-9 Je '66
Hypocritics: anti-reviewers. F. Lamport. Atlan 218:104-6 Ag '66
Screening books for review; selecting and reviewing childrens and teen-agers books for the N.Y. times book review. G. Woods. il Wilson Lib Bul 41:168-72 O '66
Useful but much maligned books: campaign biographies. O. Collier. ALA Bul 60:609-12 Je '66
What I did to books and vice versa; experiences of former editor of Book week. R. Kluger. Harper 233:69-74 D '66
WLB review of books; symposium. bibliog il Wilson Lib Bul 41:284-300+ N '66
See also
American library association—Subscription books committee
Literary criticism
Television broadcasting—Book programs
BOOK sales
Disposal delusions: items later needed by historians and librarians; letter to the editor. R. Higham. Library J 91:1094+ Mr 1 '66
BOOK scorpions
False scorpions. T. H. Savory. il Sci Am 214:95-100 Mr '66
Spermatophore web formation in a pseudoscorpion. P. Weygoldt. bibliog il Science 153:1647-9 S 30 '66
BOOK selection
Book review index: a new book selection tool. L. Ash. il Library J 91:2013-15 Ap 15 '66
Book selection and the democratic dialogue. O. Kirchner-Dean. il Library J 91:2765-7 Je 1 '66
Book selection in Grosse Pointe: where school librarians advise the public library. V. Leonard. ALA Bul 60:627-9 Je '66
Caught in the draft; providing materials for both conscientious objectors and service men. J. Berry. Library J 91:907+ F 15 '66
Dissent and the children's stigma. E. Geller. Library J 91:1468+ Mr 15 '66
Drapery for Diego. J. Weatherford. Library J 91:646 F 1 '66
Fallacy of balance in public library book selection; excerpts from address, October 1965. R. A. Landor. il Library J 91:629-32 F 1 '66; Discussion. 91:1952+, 2734 Ap 15, Je 1 '66
Image's history. J. Weatherford. Library J 91:3664-5 Ag '66
In, out, or neglected? books chosen in response to an Lj book selection survey. E. Moon. il Library J 91:633-7 F 1 '66
Librarian as anthologist: problem of selection rather than acquisition or accumulation. J. Shera. Wilson Lib Bul 41:89+ S '66
Literature and the liberated spirit: programs in school libraries and classrooms; adaptation of address, June 1966. D. L. Burton. il ALA Bul 60:904-8+ O '66
Making of the catalog: Elementary school library collection. M. V. Gaver. Library J 91:1606-13 Mr 15 '66
Real and the unfamiliar; children's books. D. Broderick. il Library J 91:2172-3 Ap 15 '66
Sample projects, title III, ESEA: book examination center. M. A. Heidbreder and E. Swanker. Library J 91:1031-2 F 15 '66
Search for the instant library. L. Sutton. il Sat R 49:24-5 Ap 16 '66

Total book selection process; book examination centers for school librarians. J. Rowell. il Wilson Lib Bul 41:190-6 O '66
See also
Libraries—Acquisitions
BOOK shelves. See Bookcases
BOOK stands. See Bookcases
BOOK tariff
See also
Duty free importation
BOOK thefts
Great book robbery. L. Rosten. il Look 30:12 My 3 '66
Lost book campaign at Sacramento; state college. P. D. Morrison. il Wilson Lib Bul 40:526-9 F '66
Rare 16th century book stolen in Chicago; Cosmographiae introductio. Pub W 190:42 Ag 15 '66
Your charging system: is it thiefproof? R. F. Clarke and H. G. Clarke. Library J 91:642-3 F 1 '66; Discussion. 91:1332+ Mr 15 '66
BOOK therapy. See Bibliotherapy
BOOK titles. See Titles of books, stories, etc.
BOOK trade. See Book industries and trade
BOOK week
Book week in braille; Library for the blind, hospital and institutions department, Cleveland public library. K. Prescott. il Library J 91:4197-9 S 15 '66
Books please: the slogan. il Wilson Lib Bul 41:16 S '66
Fairs and CBC aids for children's book week. il Pub W 190:136-8 Jl 11 '66
Observe National children's book week, October 30-November 5, 1966. il PTA Mag 61:31 O '66
BOOK week (periodical)
Book week publishing for Chicago. Washington. Pub W 189:31 My 2 '66
What I did to books and vice versa; experiences of former editor of Book week. R. Kluger. Harper 233:69-74 D '66
BOOKBINDER, Jack
Urban renewal, the Philadelphia story. Sch Arts 65:11-16 Ap '66
BOOKBINDING
American book-Stratford enlarges New York plant. il Pub W 189:129 Mr 7 '66
Are books overpriced? publishers' library bindings. D. Melcher. Library J 91:2542+ My 15 '66
BDSA tells trade binders about shortages; summary of meeting with PIA group. F. B. Myrick. Pub W 191:99 Ja 2 '67
Book binderies and the information explosion; excerpts from address, April 13, 1966. K. W. James. Pub W 189:97-8+ My 2 '66
Fine renaissance bindings shown at the Grolier club. P. A. Bennett. Pub W 190:125-6 D 5 '66
Manchester concept and how it paid off; Maple press. Pub W 190:86-91 Ag 1 '66
Price-fixing of library-bound books? Senate hearings in Washington. E. Geller. il Library J 91:2570-8 My 15 '66
Publishers accused of price fixing; librarians testify before senators, excessive prices for juveniles in publisher's library bindings. Library J 91:2292+ My 1 '66
Vail-Ballou has second plant in full operation. il Pub W 190:116+ O 3 '66
See also
Paperback books—Binding
BOOKCASES
For the well-being of books and readers: furniture with distinctly bookish purposes. il House & Gard 129:162-3 Mr '66
BOOKER, Christopher
New Britain. Esquire 65:84-7+ F '66
BOOKER, Emma
When to cry "enough"? Vogue 147:60-1 F 1 '66
BOOKLETS. See Pamphlets
BOOKMAKING (betting) See Book making (betting)
BOOKMOBILES
Summer storytelling in Ohio. E. S. Ross. Horn Bk 42:279-81 Je '66
BOOKS
Plea for books; summary of address, June 15, 1966. A. Hechscher. il Pub W 190:48-9 Jl 4 '66
See also
Best sellers
Book manufacturers' institute
Copyright
Textbooks

Advertising
ABA convention offers publicity opportunities. Pub W 189:75 Ja 31 '66
Ad and promotion standards set by ABPC-SLA committee. Pub W 190:198 Jl 11 '66

BOOKS—Advertising—*Continued*
Astounding changes seen from Robinson-Patman moves. Pub W 189:48-9 My 9 '66
Book as display. il Wilson Lib Bul 41:91-4, 331-3 S, N '66
Bookstores plan their Christmas promotion; reduced co-op ad allowances a big problem. il Pub W 190:96-8 Ag 22 '66
Bookstores view the Christmas season; some books that will get major promotion. Pub W 190:50-2 N 28 '66
Brentano's promotes thirty-eight books in twenty ads in N.Y. times; supplement National economic review. Pub W 189:308 Ja 24 '66
Coop ads sell 600 books: bookshop expects to sell 1000; Milwaukee, Wis. Pub W 189: 73-4 Mr 7 '66
Fall highspot books: 275 October-December campaigns. il Pub W 190:236-84 Ag 29 '66
February-May: a calendar of some 200 leading campaigns. il Pub W 189:214-52 Ja 24 '66
FTC attorneys, publishers discuss Robinson-Patman compliance; with editorial comment. Pub W 189:58-60, 75 F 28 '66
FTC examiner drops Calories charges vs. S&S. Pub W 190:49 Jl 18 '66
Major promotions for January books. il Pub W 190:34-48 O 31 '66
150 leading book promotions: June-August. il Pub W 189:50-80 Ap 25 '66
Publishers to join in New Yorker ads, catalog. il Pub W 189:190-1 Je 6 '66
September books; some early fall campaigns. il Pub W 189:103-24 Je 6 '66
    See also
Booksellers and bookselling—Publicity

Classification
    See Classification

Collectors and collecting
    See Book collecting

Conservation and restoration
Aftermath: damage to Florence's renowned art and bibliographic riches caused by flood. il Wilson Lib Bul 41:463-4 Ja '67
Book restoration group joins national body; Operation book rescue committee to help restore flood-damaged libraries in Florence. Pub W 190:34 N 28 '66
History of the Barrow lab; or, The thirty years that revolutionized paper. il Pub W 189:72-3+ Ap 4 '66
Lab will seek solution to deterioration of paper. Pub W 191:102 Ja 2 '67
Preservation of deteriorating books; excerpts from report (cont) G. R. Williams. Library J 91:189-94 Ja 15 '66; Reply to Ja 1 issue G. B. Van Schaack. 91:870+ F 15 '66
Reproduction vs. preservation; excerpt from Care and preservation of books. J. Alden. Library J 91:5319-22 N 1 '66

Exhibitions
    See Book exhibits

History
Books for an early American bookcase. E. Wolf, 2d. il Antiques 90:211-13 Ag '66

Importation
    See also
Duty free importation

Large print books
    See Printing—Legibility

Mutilation, defacement, etc.
Lost book campaign at Sacramento; state college. P. D. Morrison. il Wilson Lib Bul 40: 526-9 F '66

Out of print books
When is a book really o/p? D. Melcher. Library J 91:4576-8 O 1 '66

Paper covered books
    See Paperback books

Photographic reproduction and projection
Peril of the librain. H. Downs. il Sci Digest 60:94-6 N '66

Pirated editions
    See Copyright—Unauthorized reprints

Prices
Book publishing, and bookkeeping. D. N. Fischel. Science 152:871-5 My 13 '66
Bookseller's dilemma; increased prices but no prior notification. il Pub W 189:113 Ap 25 '66

Cadillacs and Chevrolets; representative of the American book publishers council queries the validity of the Library materials indexes. E. Moon. Library J 91:3343-5 Jl '66
Can I have one? complimentary copies. C. Pinckney and E. Pinckney. il Sat R 49: 61-2 F 12 '66
Net prices, library editions: Senate hearings reviewed. Pub W 190:26-30 Jl 25 '66
Philadelphia schools sue eleven publishers on pricing. Pub W 190:55 Jl 4 '66
Price-fixing of library-bound books? Senate hearings in Washington. E. Geller. il Library J 91:2570-8 My 15 '66
Senate committee to study library edition pricing. Pub W 189:48 Mr 21 '66
Senate ends net-price study; grand jury starts inquiry. Pub W 189:55-6 My 23 '66
Senators hear complaints on net prices to libraries. Pub W 189:26-7 Ap 4 '66
Truce with the publishers; discussion of net pricing between a publisher, wholesaler, and a librarian. Library J 91:2579-83 My 15 '66

Anecdotes, facetiae, satire, etc.
Book. G. Ace. Sat R 49:9 Je 25 '66

Repair
    See Books—Conservation and restoration

Reprints
Anthology marks 60th year of Everyman's library. Pub W 190:40-1 O 17 '66
Pléiade library. H. R. Lottman. Pub W 191: 49+ Ja 16 '67
    See also
Paperback books

Storage
    See also
Warehouses

Translations
    See Translations and translating

Transportation
Full regional distribution is a hit at McGraw-Hill. il Pub W 191:22-7 Ja 2 '67
BOOKS (publication)
That's show biz. il Newsweek 68:103 O 17 '66
BOOKS, Art. See Art literature
BOOKS, Censorship of. See Censorship
BOOKS, Illustrated. See Illustrated books
BOOKS, Paper covered. See Paperback books
BOOKS, Rare. See Book rarities
BOOKS, Theft of. See Book thefts
BOOKS, Titles of. See Titles of books, stories, etc.
BOOKS and reading
. And Napoleon said; rereading books. L. Conger. Writer 79:9-10 N '66
Book of one's own. B. Grossman. il NEA J 56:31-2 Ja '67
Books. M. Muggeridge. See issues of Esquire
Books persist. H. Borland. il Am Ed 2:8-12 Mr '66
Future of the book; address, July 10, 1966. G. N. Ray. bibliog f il ALA Bul 60:783-93 S '66
Gift of books; symposium. Holiday 40:171-2+ D '66
In, out, or neglected? books chosen in response to an Lj book selection survey. E. Moon. il Library J 91:633-7 F 1 '66
Is reading for everyone? the Ludington plan to make a slogan a reality; getting young people hooked on books. il Pub W 190:30-4 N 21 '66
Lire: the French try institutional promotion; equivalent of National library week. H. R. Lottman. Pub W 190:41-3 S 19 '66
Literature and the liberated spirit; programs in school libraries and classrooms; adaptation of address, June 1966. D. L. Burton. il ALA Bul 60:904-8+ O '66
Of books and engagement; excerpts from address, July 1965. F. Jennings. Library J 91:2149-52 Ap 15 '66
Oh for a book and a shady nook. G. Raftery. il Sr Schol 88:sup 11 My 20 '66
On lighting candles, and on blowing them out; reactions to reading. J. Ciardi. Sat R 49:18-19 Je 18 '66
Outlook tower; books of interest to high school students; comp. by M. C. Scoggin. See issues of Horn book magazine
Patterns of young adults' reading; summary of address, July 14, 1966. G. R. Carlsen. Pub W 190:29-32 Ag 8 '66
Preview of fall books. P. K. Cuneo. America 115:422-3+ O 8 '66

BOOKS and reading—*Continued*
Pushing the book; sharing love of reading with young people. M. A. Edwards. Library J 91:6166-8 D 15 '66
Reaching out with books; preconference workshop of the American library trustee association. D. E. Wright. Library J 91:3648-9 Ag '66
Reading and the American public; address, July 1966. P. S. Buck. ALA Bul 60:931-6 O '66
Wild blueberries; role of books today. K. Nyren. Library J 91:4586 O 1 '66
WLB review of books; symposium. bibliog il Wilson Lib Bul 41:284-300+ N '66
See also
Best sellers
Bibliography
College students—Reading
Immoral literature and pictures
Libraries
Libraries, Private
Libraries and readers
Moving pictures and reading
National book committee
Reading lists
Teachers—Reading

Anecdotes, facetiae, satire, etc.
New technologies, old media; excerpt from Learn with book. J. R. Heathorn. Library J 91:6170 D 15 '66

Best books
[Adult books for young people, 1965] Library J 91:1624 Mr 15 '66; Same. NEA J 55:51-2 Mr '66; Pub W 189:70 F 28 '66; Wilson Lib Bul 40:664 Ap '66
America's survey of notable fall books (cont) America 115:692-3+ N 26 '66
Book review (cont of) New books appraised; ed. by M. Cooley and K. McQuade. See issues of Library journal
Books; critics' choices for Christmas. Commonweal 85:264-75 D 2 '66
Literary sampler; excerpts from the Season's well-seasoned titles. Sat R 49:59-60 O 1 '66
Modern movement, by C. Connolly. Review Atlan 218:76-9 Jl '66. L. Kronenberger Sat R 49:35 Ap 2 '66. L. Edel
NAIS presents books awards at annual meeting. Pub W 189:43-4 Mr 14 '66
New books appraised; ed. by M. Cooley and others. See issues of Library journal
[Notable books of 1965] Pub W 189:69-70 F 28 '66; Same. Library J 91:1188 Mr 1 '66; ALA Bul 60:284-5 Mr '66; Wilson Lib Bul 40:661-2 Ap '66; NEA J 55:67-9 Ap '66
Spring survey of notable new books. America 114:659-63+ My 7 '66
Times book review selects fifty best children's books. Pub W 189:58+ My 23 '66
See also
Best sellers
Book selection

Bibliography
Book news roundup. J. Foster. Sr Schol 89:sup 16 S 30 '66
Books for adults beginning to read (cont) Wilson Lib Bul 41:83-7 S '66
Books for autumn reading. R. Girson. il Sat R 49:56-8+ O 1 '66
Books to come; ed. by J. Putnam and J. Lindheim. Library J 91:740-854 F 1 '66
Books to come; ed. by J. Putnam and K. Ahrens. Library J 91:2894-6+, 4718-24+ Je 1, O 1 '66
Cartwheels and coppers; for $5 and under. H. Frankel. Sat R 49:38-40 D 3 '66
Choice of books for young adults; comp. by L. T. Bulman. il Library J 91:6151-2 D 15 '66
Christmas books; God's plenty. G. Davenport. Nat R 18:1281-4 D 13 '66
Curl up and read. See issues of Seventeen
Every kind of reading; grades four through twelve; ed. by J. Foster. Sr Schol 88:sup21-2+ Mr 4 '66
Fall—Christmas previews. il Pub W 189:125-60 Je 6 '66
Favorite books of disadvantaged youth. il NEA J 55:48-9+ D '66
Gift books that cost plenty. il Changing T 20:13-16 D '66
New books for junior high readers. J. Ashe. Sr Schol 88:sup 10 Mr 25 '66
New products. Sr Schol 89:sup54-5 S 23 '66
New Yorker lists at this season some books by its contributors published during the year. New Yorker 42:232-3 D 10 '66
Potpourri. P. Adams. See issues of Atlantic
Potpourri of new books. J. L. Mersand; F. S. Gross; W. K. Richards. Sr Schol 89:sup 18-19+ D 2 '66

SR's check list of the week's new books; comp. by N. Soñan. See issues of Saturday review
Science fiction for the space age; how to stimulate supplementary reading among students of all ability levels. S. Solomon. il Sr Schol 87:sup20-1 Ja 21 '66
Teenage hits and misses to theme YASD program. Library J 91:2182 Ap 15 '66
This week. See issues of Christian century
Time listings. See issues of Time
Trade winds; some camp publications. J. G. Fuller. Sat R 49:7 Ap 30 '66
Wonderland of Christmas books. R. Gibson. Sat R 49:31-2+ D 3 '66
You need books at hand; roundup of new books; ed. by J. Foster. il Sr Schol 89:sup 10-14+ O 28 '66

Reading aloud
For writing out loud! L. Conger. Writer 79:7-8 Ag '66
Off the cuff; books that read themselves aloud. L. Conger. Writer 79:7-8 Ap '66
Pleasant land of counterpane. C. Lewis. il Horn Bk 42:542-7 O '66

Asia
Reading habits and book publishing in Asia; adaptation of address, May 1966. I. Insha. il UNESCO Courier 19:12-16 N '66

England
Of luvs and lights; reading public's addiction to light novels. K. F. Kister. il Wilson Lib Bul 41:510-13+ Ja '67

France
Best sellers in France. H. R. Lottman. Pub W 190:43-5 O 10 '66

United States
See Books and reading
BOOKS and reading, Influence of. See Literature, Influence of
BOOKS as gifts
For me? children's books to give adults. L. Russ. il Pub W 190:38-9 O 10 '66
Gift books that cost plenty. il Changing T 20:13-16 D '66
BOOKS for children. See Childrens literature
BOOKS for the blind. See Blind, Books for the
BOOKS of instruction. See Instruction manuals
BOOKSELLERS and bookselling
Again, an agenda for action; publisher-bookseller relationships. C. B. Grannis. Pub W 189:59 Je 20 '66
Bookselling as a career, here and abroad. Pub W 190:81 S 12 '66
Image of the bookstore as a cultural center. il Pub W 189:85 F 28 '66
NACS sounds an alert: order fall textbooks soon! C. B. Grannis. Pub W 189:37 My 2 '66
Ode to the bookseller. R. Armour. Pub W 190:128 S 26 '66
Publishing and bookselling, two worlds, or one? C. B. Grannis. Pub W 189:200 Je 6 '66
Second-hand book store: is it vanishing? E. D. Collins. il Hobbies 71:109 S '66
Selling how-to art, craft books to hobbyists and gift shoppers. J. Koefoed. il Pub W 190:49-53 Ag 22 '66
Stock control in bookselling; condensation of pamphlet. G. Bartlett. il Pub W 190:68-72 Jl 18; 62-6 Jl 25 '66
When a book hits the jackpot; selling by mail. J. Tebbel. Sat R 49:62-4 F 12 '66
See also
Books—Prices
College bookstores
International publishers representatives (firm)
Libraries and booksellers

Childrens literature
Art of selling to the individual. M. Bruggeman. il Pub W 189:176-9 F 21 '66
Author, stay 'way from my door; experiences with juvenile authors in the bookstore. L. Russ. Pub W 189:37-8 My 30 '66
Head Start program: choosing books for the pre-school, underprivileged child; with book list by the Chinook bookshop, Colorado Springs. J. Noyes. Pub W 190:220-1 Jl 11 '66
It pays to read the books you sell, especially children's books. Pub W 189:73 Mr 7 '66
Promotional opportunities for children's books; summaries of addresses, June 7, 1966. B. Beilenson; L. Russ; J. Noyes. il Pub W 189:37-9 Je 20 '66

BOOKSELLERS and **bookselling—Childrens literature**—*Continued*

Puppet shows promote classic children's books. il Pub W 189:104-6 F 21 '66

Selling in a children's department at nine years of age. il Pub W 189:88 F 28 '66

What gift of prophecy? or promising juvenile titles for bookstores; prophesying Christmas hits. L. Russ. Pub W 190:46-8 Ag 22 '66

Cookbooks

New fall cookbooks are good Christmas items. il Pub W 190:49-59 S 12 '66

History

Bibliopola, by S. Taubert. Review
Pub W il 190:51-4 D 26 '66. C. B. Anderson

Medical literature

Growth of medical, technical department in Milwaukee store laid to expert service; Harry W. Schwartz bookstore, Milwaukee. il Pub W 190:96-8 N 14 '66

Martindale's medical section doing well; Los Angeles. Pub W 190:102 N 14 '66

Paperback books

Bookseller suit challenges ID franchise on paperbacks. Pub W 190:106 S 26 '66

Kroch's & Brentano's sold more than 1.3 million paperbacks in 1965. Pub W 189:47 Ap 11 '66

Paperback section in New Jersey store expands into former swimming pool area; Womrath's-Hackensack. il Pub W 190:42-3 O 24 '66

Paperbacks in the modern bookstore; summary of panel discussion. il Pub W 189:46-9+ Je 27 '66

Suburban Detroit shop stocks paperbacks in depth; Paperbacks unlimited. il Pub W 189:94-6 Ja 31 '66

See also
Bureau of independent publishers and distributors

Publicity

Art shows, authors' days build traffic for Tech coop; MIT. Pub W 189:105 Ap 18 '66

Astounding changes seen from Robinson-Patman moves. Pub W 189:48-9 My 9 '66

Atlanta bookshop chain blanketed city with institutional advertising last fall; Elson's book stores. Pub W 189:75 Mr 7 '66

Bookshop's book award contest boon to business and school; Book nook in Santa Monica. Pub W 190:222 Jl 11 '66

Canadian bookstore promotes books and art of Japan; Evelyn De Mille books ltd, Vancouver, B.C. il Pub W 190:222 Jl 11 '66

Cleveland store chalks up sale of 2100 copies of book; Maurice Sendak is a success at Hathaway house, Wellesley. il Pub W 189:90-1 Je 27 '66

Columbus, O., store finds radio spots most successful promotion for books; Lazarus department store. Pub W 190:70-1 Jl 4 '66

FTC attorneys, publishers discuss Robinson-Patman compliance; with editorial comment. Pub W 189:58-60, 75 F 28 '66

Harnett Kane's landmark book gets off to a flying start; autographing party at the Marion Harris bookstore, New Orleans. il Pub W 190:223 Jl 11 '66

In praise of stuffers. M. Bacon. Pub W 189:22-3 Ap 4 '66

Jeane Dixon charms them at Haslam's, St Petersburg. il Pub W 189:69 Mr 21 '66

Pre-pub promotion helps shop chalk up substantial sales; Bayberry book shop, Orleans, Mass. il Pub W 190:334-6 Ag 29 '66

Promotional tour centers on Phoenix-area teen market. il Pub W 189:62-3 Mr 28 '66

Sandy Koufax draws thousands to Elson's in Atlanta shopping center. il Pub W 190:58-9 S 5 '66

Shillito's sells 14,000 copies of one local book; Cincinnati. Pub W 191:72 Ja 16 '67

Shop talk. Pub W 189:93 Ja 31 '66

Some promotions that helped rack up Christmas sales. Pub W 191:52 Ja 9 '67

Some tips on design and display. il Pub W 189:71-3 My 23 '66

Successful mail order program; summary of address, September 19, 1966. A. P. Salisbury. Pub W 190:32 O 17 '66

Two stores rack up large sales of Koufax; Calif. il Pub W 190:73-5 O 3 '66

Wouldn't it be easier if I just wore a sign on my back? how to turn introvert author-types into extrovert promoting types. Pub W 189:43-6 Mr 21 '66

See also
Display of merchandise
Show windows

Anecdotes, facetiae, satire, etc.

And make it a sonnet if you don't mind; experiences autographing books. R. Armour. Pub W 189:44-5 My 16 '66

Religious literature

Former Bible salesman runs wholesale and retail business in Midwest; Riverside book & Bible house, Iowa Falls. il Pub W 190:127-8 S 26 '66

Recent bookshop promotions for religious books. il Pub W 189:134-5 F 14 '66

Sale at Whittemore's attracts 400 theological students; store in Needham Heights. il Pub W 189:72 My 16 '66

Some newly-remodeled and expanded religious bookstores. il Pub W 189:135-8 F 14 '66

Statistics

Comments on the survey of bookstore operating ratios. D. Melcher. Pub W 190:32-5 D 26 '66

Expenses increased in book departments in 1965; average sale also rose; study by Controllers' congress of the National retail merchants association. il Pub W 190:65-6 O 10 '66

General book sales increased 10 per cent in 1965; with table. Pub W 190:37-40 Ag 15 '66

Only 70 per cent of stores reported gains for September. Pub W 190:52 N 28 '66

Profit factors in successful bookselling; summary of panel discussion. il Pub W 189:53-5+ Je 27 '66

Report on the ABA's operating ratio survey. il Pub W 190:37-44 N 21; 23-30 N 28 '66

Retail book business in May got a lift from gift buying. il Pub W 190:66-7 Jl 18 '66

Six-store book and stationery chain analyzes its operation; Book 'n card chain, greater Newport News, Va. il Pub W 190:82-3 D 26 '66

Stock

Advantages of the Anco plan of inventory control. A. L. Ledbetter. il Pub W 190:56-7 D 5 '66

Basic stock merchandising; summary of address, September 19,1966. J. Quick. Pub W 190:32-3 O 17 '66

Electronic processing in the bookstore. D. Melcher. Pub W 190:30-3 S 5 '66

Technical literature

Growth of medical, technical department in Milwaukee store laid to expert service; Harry W. Schwartz bookstore, Milwaukee. il Pub W 190:96-8 N 14 '66

Technical books are vigorously promoted year round in upstate New York store; Scrantom's book and stationery co. il Pub W 190:98-9 N 14 '66

Alabama

Alabama store sponsors children's book fair; Loveman's, Birmingham. il Pub W 190:54-6 D 5 '66

Arizona

Promotional tour centers on Phoenix-area teen market. il Pub W 189:62-3 Mr 28 '66

California

Art of selling to the individual; Magic fishbone in Carmel-by-the-Sea. M. Bruggeman. il Pub W 189:176-9 F 21 '66

Book festival for young people; Shorebird bookstore, Palos Verdes Peninsula. A. Fink. il Pub W 189:81-3 My 30 '66

Bookshop's book award contest boon to business and school; Book nook in Santa Monica. Pub W 190:222 Jl 11 '66

Browsing the bookstores along Hollywood Boulevard. il Sunset 137:26 O '66

Hunter's books opens branch in La Jolla, California. Pub W 190:67-8 S 19 '66

Judge orders Love book to be returned for sale; San Francisco booksellers. Pub W 191:58 Ja 16 '67

Martindale's medical section doing well; Los Angeles. Pub W 190:102 N 14 '66

Menace of Moe's books; proposal to open store brings wrath in San Francisco. R. H. Smith. Pub W 190:41 N 7 '66

San Francisco police arrest booksellers; sale of book of poems entitled The love book. Pub W 190:27-8 D 12 '66

Canada

Canadian bookshop puts on one-act play, attracts 200; M. G. Hurtig booksellers ltd, Edmonton, Alta. Pub W 189:71 My 9 '66

Canadian bookstore promotes books and art of Japan; Evelyn De Mille books ltd, Vancouver, B.C. il Pub W 190:222 Jl 11 '66

BOOKSELLERS and bookselling—Canada—
Continued
Duthie books reflects rising Vancouver, B.C.
prosperity. il Pub W 190:36-9 D 26 '66
See also
Canadian booksellers association

Connecticut
Bookstore co-sponsors programs on education; Brentano's and Grade teacher. Pub W 189:175 F 21 '66
New Canaan shop enlarges; author dedicates book to shop. il Pub W 190:45 D 12 '66
New New England bookshop sells books and candles; Book & candle. Simsbury, Conn. il Pub W 189:70-1 My 16 '66

Finland
Large English-language section featured in Finnish bookshop; Academic bookstore, Helsinki. il Pub W 189:50 Ap 11 '66

Florida
Bookstore sales are booming in southern Florida boom town; Gaul's book store and The bookmark; Ft Lauderdale. il Pub W 189:55-8 Ap 4 '66
Jeane Dixon charms them at Haslam's, St Petersburg. il Pub W 189:69 Mr 21 '66
More space has meant more business for Clearwater, Fla. bookstore; Sandy book store. il Pub W 189:75-7 My 23 '66
Report from Florida tornado area. Pub W 189:104 Ap 18 '66

France
French bookselling may enter the 20th century. H. R. Lottman. Pub W 190:34-6 Ag 15 '66

Georgia
Atlanta bookshop chain blanketed city with institutional advertising last fall; Elson's book stores. Pub W 189:75 Mr 7 '66
Attractive shop in a shopping center; Elson's Atlanta. il Pub W 189:84 My 30 '66
Sandy Koufax draws thousands to Elson's in Atlanta shopping center. il Pub W 190:58-9 S 5 '66
Store ties in Pooh window with showing of Disney movie; Cokesbury bookstore in Atlanta. il Pub W 189:65 Mr 14 '66

Great Britain
Jobs tax hits British booksellers. G. R. Davies. Pub W 189:39-41 My 30 '66
Post mark Pall Mall; expansion of Blackwell's bookstores, Oxford. G. R. Davies. il Pub W 190:48-50 D 26 '66
Truth about bookselling, by T. Joy. Review Pub W 189:68-9 Je 27 '66. G. Light

Hawaii
Informal boookstore in Honolulu; Crossroads book gallery. G. Schlegel. il Pub W 190:54-6 O 17 '66

Illinois
Author goes to court over store's selling policy; Carson Pirie Scott & company, Chicago. Pub W 189:51 Mr 21 '66
Book reviews, art course used to promote new shop; Amber light book shop on December 1, 1965, at 932 Spanish court in Wilmette. il Pub W 189:117 Ap 25 '66
K&B completes major expansion program in Chicago area; Kroch's & Brentano's. il Pub W 191:49-52 Ja 2 '67
K&B Old Orchard branch moves into 13.500-square-foot store; shopping center store in Chicago. il Pub W 190:68 N 21 '66
Lake Forest book store serves a wealthy community in a Chicago suburb. il Pub W 189:48-9 Ap 11 '66
VOL I serves varied clientele in Chicago's renovated Piper's alley. L. Wimmer. il Pub W 189:72-4 My 9 '66

Iowa
Bookstore promotes employee libraries for industries; Book store in Des Moines. Pub W 190:53 N 28 '66
Former Bible salesman runs wholesale and retail business in Midwest; Riverside book & Bible house. Iowa Falls. il Pub W 190:127-8 S 26 '66

Italy
ABA seeks aid for bookshop wrecked in Florence; BM libreria. il Pub W 190:43-4 D 12 '66
La dolce vita; Italian publishers discover Rome. H. R. Lottman. Pub W 191:31-2 Ja 2 '67
Florence floods ruin Feltrinelli bookstore. Pub W 190:34 N 28 '66

Louisiana
Harnett Kane's landmark book gets off to a flying start; autographing party at the Marion Harris bookstore, New Orleans. il Pub W 190:223 Jl 11 '66

Massachusetts
Maurice Sendak is a success at Hathaway house, Wellesley. il Pub W 189:91 Je 27 '66
Pre-pub promotion helps shop chalk up substantial sales; Bayberry book shop, Orleans. il Pub W 190:334-6 Ag 29 '66
Sale at Whittemore's attracts 400 theological students; store in Needham Heights. il Pub W 189:72 My 16 '66

Minnesota
B. Dalton, bookseller opens in a suburb as subsidiary of Dayton's; Edina. il Pub W 190:332-4 Ag 29 '66
Dayton's, Minneapolis stages art book promotion. Pub W 189:65 Mr 14 '66
Minneapolis department store to open string of bookshops; Dayton company. Pub W 189:70 My 9 '66

Missouri
Foreign publications are a specialty of St Louis shop; Three arts shop. R. Potter. il Pub W 189:82-4 F 7 '66

Montana
Western Americana, juveniles, stressed in Montana bookshop; Phillips book store in Bozeman. P. Johnson, jr. il Pub W 189:66-7 Mr 14 '66

New Jersey
Curtiss-Pierce book store; keynote is personal service; Cedar Grove. il Pub W 189:92-3 Je 27 '66
Paperback section in New Jersey store expands into former swimming pool area; Womrath's-Hackensack. il Pub W 190:42-3 O 24 '66
Small bookshop sells 300 copies of one book; Book house in Plainfield. Pub W 191:73 Ja 16 '67

New York (state)
Book as display; three bookstores in New York city. N. Kirin. il Wilson Lib Bul 41:91-4 S '66
Brentano's promotes thirty-eight books in twenty ads in N.Y. times; supplement National economic review. Pub W 189:308 Ja 24 '66
Indoor and outdoor sculpture; Brentano collection. T. W. McConkey. il Library J 91:5930 D 1 '66
Lower East side bookstore publishes first book; Tompkins Square books, New York city. Pub W 191:52 Ja 2 '67
New York city shop that caters to car, airplane and armored tank buffs; R. Gordon & company. il Pub W 189:114-16 Ap 25 '66
N.Y. state chronicler Carmer to tour upstate stores. Pub W 190:58-9 N 7 '66
Obscene premises bill passes N.Y. assembly. Pub W 189:49 My 9 '66
Police nail Mishkin in raid on Times square bookstore; Square books. Pub W 189:79 Ap 18 '66
Professor; interview with owner of National memorial African bookstore in New York city. L. Michaux. New Yorker 42:28-9 S 3 '66
Service, stock control, advertising; ingredients of a successful business; John Mistletoe bookshop in Albany. H. D. Greene, 3d. Pub W 189:50-1 My 2 '66
Sylvan Baruch sells last shop, retires from book business; Bus terminal book bar, inc. Pub W 190:223 Jl 11 '66
Technical books are vigorously promoted year round in upstate New York store; Scrantom's book and stationery co, in Rochester. il Pub W 190:98-9 N 14 '66
Times square book stores raided by cleanup squad. Pub W 190:47 S 19 '66

Ohio
Cincinnati paperback shop stresses poetry and art books; Mahogany Hall. R. Potter. il Pub W 189:66-8 Mr 21 '66
Cleveland bookman arrested; police fascism charged; Asphodel bookshop, Cleveland. Pub W 191:57-8 Ja 16 '67
Cleveland store chalks up sale of 2100 copies of book. il Pub W 189:90 Je 27 '66
Columbus, O., store finds radio spots most successful promotion for books; Lazarus department store. Pub W 190:70-1 Jl 4 '66
McLean's opens store in Dayton's Miracle lane. Pub W 190:61 Jl 25 '66
Pages & prints; a paperback shop that is educationally-oriented; Cincinnati. R. Potter. il Pub W 189:86-9 F 28 '66

BOOKSELLERS and bookselling—Ohio—*Cont.*
Right-wing group pickets Cleveland bookshop; National Christian conservative society vs. Book mark. Pub W 189:73 Je 27 '66
Shillito's sells 14,000 copies of one local book; Cincinnati. Pub W 191:72 Ja 16 '67

Oregon
Portland Baptist store moves because of tax ruling. Pub W 189:70-1 My 9 '66

Pennsylvania
Phila. booksellers assn. president featured in article; L. L. Brookman. Pub W 190:67-8 O 10 '66
Raven succeeds in spite of obstacles; Lancaster. il Pub W 190:52-4 Ag 1 '66

Sweden
Modular, mobile fixtures distinguish self-service Swedish bookshop; Nordiska bokhandeln, Stockholm. il Pub W 190:56-8 N 7 '66

Tennessee
Bookseller's Christmas memory; R. M. Mills bookstores, inc, Nashville. B. Schweid. Pub W 190:79 D 26 '66; Reply. 191:52 Ja 2 '67
8000 attend Baptist book fair. il Pub W 190:80-1 D 26 '66

Texas
Dallas spent a record $6 per capita for books in 1965. Pub W 190:44-5 D 12 '66
Rosengren's, a San Antonio institution for more than thirty years. P. Johnson, jr. il Pub W 189:78-81 My 30 '66
Will set the standard in its field for the next fifty years; concerning book by Bliss Albright. Pub W 190:42 D 12 '66

United States
Booksellers take bear market in stride; some slowdown in economy seen. Pub W 190:75-6 O 31 '66
Bookselling. See issues of Publishers' weekly
Bookstores are expanding, enlarging, branching out from coast to coast. il Pub W 190:39-42 O 24 '66
Bookstores plan their Christmas promotion; reduced co-op ad allowances a big problem. il Pub W 190:96-8 Ag 22 '66
Bookstores view the Christmas season; some books that will get major promotion. Pub W 190:50-2 N 28 '66
Brentano's opens 19th store in expansion program. il Pub W 191:30-5 Ja 9 '67
Chart that cuts down on time and labor in making returns; series of charts used by Doubleday book shop chain. il Pub W 189:121-2 Je 13 '66
Christmas offer mystique; booksellers orders for Christmas stock. M. Bacon. il Pub W 190:50-1 Ag 8 '66
Comments on the survey of bookstore operating ratios. D. Melcher. Pub W 190:32-5 D 26 '66
Control of expenses stressed in ABA report. C. B. Grannis. Pub W 190:61 O 31 '66
Does the bookstore benefit from national book events? Pub W 189:74-5 My 23 '66
Getting Christmas help is no problem for many booksellers. Pub W 190:95 Ag 22 '66
Good retail mechanics theme of ABA regional; report of meeting sponsored by the Pacific Northwest booksellers. il Pub W 190:30-6 O 17 '66
I'm a bookseller, not a bookkeeper; publisher-imposed paperwork. R. W. Vanderhoef. Pub W 190:42-4 O 3 '66
In praise of publishers and their Christmas offers. R. B. Campbell. Pub W 190:60-1 S 5 '66
Increased travel means a large market for travel books. il Pub W 189:49 My 2 '66
Inventory bookstore needs urged by National book committee chairman. Library J 91:219 Ja 15 '66
Night openings during Xmas mandatory for most shops. Pub W 190:98 Ag 22 '66
Problems in bookseller-publisher relations; summary of panel discussion. Pub W 189:58+ Je 27 '66
Publishers' primary market; industry-wide research and development program needed. C. B. Grannis. Bub W 191:39 Ja 2 '67
Report on the ABA's operating ratio survey. il Pub W 190:37-44 N 21; 23-30 N 28 '66
Truth about bookselling, by T. Joy. Review Pub W 189:68-9 Je 27 '66. G. Light
While we wait: further thoughts on the Lasser report; publishers' distribution methods. M. Bacon. Pub W 189:49-50 Mr 7 '66

See also
American booksellers association
Department stores—Book departments

Virginia
Bookseller suit challenges ID franchise on paperbacks. Pub W 190:106 S 26 '66
Six-store book and stationery chain analyzes its operation; Book 'n card chain, greater Newport News. il Pub W 190:82-3 D 26 '66

Washington, D.C.
Latin-American books are specialty of Savile book shop. Pub W 190:58 N 7 '66
World affairs bookshop, inc. speaks with an international accent. il Pub W 189:221-3 Je 6 '66

Wisconsin
Coop ads sell 600 books; bookshop expects to sell 1000; Milwaukee. Pub W 189:73-4 Mr 7 '66
Growth of medical, technical department in Milwaukee store laid to expert service; Harry W. Schwartz bookstore, Milwaukee. il Pub W 190:96-8 N 14 '66

BOOKSHELVES. See Bookcases

BOOKSTANDS. See Bookcases

BOOKSTORE window. See Show windows

BOOKSTORES. See Booksellers and bookselling; College bookstores

BOORE, J. P.
Old glass paperweights. Hobbies 71:98F-98G Je; 98L-98N N '66 (to be cont)

BOORSTIN, Daniel J.
More of everything, including the kitchen sink. Harper 232:149-51 Mr '66

BOOSEY and Hawkes, limited. See Music publishing

BOOSTER heart. See Heart, Artificial

BOOSTERS for space vehicles. See Space vehicles—Propulsion systems

BOOTH, Edward, J. and Carlson, E.
Rubber tires work well on sanitary landfills. Am City 81:98-99 Jl '66

BOOTH, Gene
Eight-second miracle machines. Pop Sci 189:74-8 S '66

BOOTH, John Wilkes
End of a manhunt; excerpt from lecture. ed. by B. Fleet. R. B. Garrett. il por Am Heritage 17:40-3+ Je '66

BOOTH, Philip
Field of white birds, grounded; after a frozen lunch in central New York; poem. Sat R 49:94 Ap 9 '66
Refusing the sea; poem. Poetry 107:310-11 F '66

BOOTLEGGING of commodities. See Black markets

BOOTY
How Stalin relieved Spain of $600,000,000. A. Orlov. il Read Digest 89:37-8+ N '66

BOQUIST, Wallace P.
Airborne eclipse expedition. Sky & Tel 31:282-4 My '66

BOR, General. See Komorowski, T.

BORATES
Cage structures for polyborate ions. B. L. Dunicz. bibliog il Science 153:737-9 Ag 12 '66

BORBERG, H. and others
Phytohemagglutinin: inhibition of the agglutinating activity by N-acetyl-D-galactosamine. bibliog Science 154:1019-20 N 25 '66

BORDAZ, Victoria
(tr) See Condominas, G. Incest of Tieng and Aang who had a common ancestor fifteen generations ago

BORDEN, Dick
Wankel engine goes to sea. Pop Sci 188:148-9 F '66

BORDEN company
FDA investigates instant milk; salmonella in Starlac. Bsns W p54 N 5 '66
Salmonella hunt spreads nationwide; drugs and candy being watched along with Borden's Starlac. il Bsns W p48+ N 12 '66

BORDERS, Garden. See Garden borders

BOREDOM
Sophia Loren; on women who are bored and boring. A. Menen. McCalls 94:54-5+ Ja '67
That tired feeling, its cause and cure. H. J. Johnson. Read Digest 88:142-4 Mr '66
Virtuosos of boredom. H. Rosenberg. Vogue 148:296-7+ S 1 '66

BOREL, Helen D.
Book that ends menopause. Sci Digest 59:26-8 Je '66

BOREL, Jacques
Snack v. la grande cuisine. Time 87:102 My 6 '66

BOREN, Lamar
Adventures of an underwater cameraman. W. Hartley and E. Hartley. il por Pop Mech 126:92-5 S '66

BORETZ, Benjamin
  Music. See occasional issues of Nation
  Records (cont) Nation 202:533-4, 564-6; 203:
    364+. 428-9, 557-8, 681-3 My 2-9, O 10, 24,
    N 21, D 19 '66
BORG-Warner corporation
  Overhaul at Norge speeds deliveries and
    profits. Bsns W p 126 S 24 '66
BORGES, Jorge Luis
  Benares; poem, tr. by K. Botsford. Atlan
    219:103 Ja '67
  Other tiger; poem, tr. by H. Morland. Atlan
    219:102 Ja '67
  Three stories: Biography of Tadeo Isidoro
    Cruz; Dead man; Aleph, tr. by A. Ker-
    rigan. New Yorker 42:23-33 Ja 7 '67
  Visit with Argentina's Borges. J. Gunther.
    por Atlan 219:96-8 Ja '67
  Writings of Jorge Luis Borges. K. Botsford.
    Atlan 219:99-104 Ja '67
BORGESE, Elisabeth Mann
  Vatican II: anathema upon war. Nation 202:
    415-21 Ap 11 '66
BORGESON, Griffith
  Monaco Grand prix. il Motor T 18:76-8 Ag
    '66
  Treasure-trove of Alfas. Motor T 18:70-3 S
    '66
  Twenty-four hours to end them all. Le
    Mans. il Motor T 18:35-8+ S '66
BORI, Lucrezia
  Lasting tribute: memorials to three great
    singers. il Opera N 31:30-1 O 15 '66
BORING machinery. See Drilling and boring
    machinery
BORIO, Antonio
  Bronze miniatures from ancient Sardinia.
    UNESCO Courier 19:16-21 S '66
BORIS, Brenda
  Small lesson in relative importance. por
    Redbook 127:6+ Jl '66
BORIS Godunov; opera. See Musorgskii, M. P.
BORK, Alfred M.
  Physics just before Einstein; adaptation of
    address, December 29, 1964. bibliog Sci-
    ence 152:597-603 Ap 29 '66
BORLAND, Hal
  Books persist. por Am Ed 2:8-12 Mr '66
  March is a promise. Read Digest 88:172F+
    Mr '66
BORMAN, Frank
  Astronauts Schirra and Borman make Far
    Eastern tour. Dept State Bul 54:364-5 Mr
    7 '66
BORMAN, Madeline P.
  My garden in the woods. Flower Grower 53:
    28-9 F '66
  Patio and garden pool for summer living.
    Flower Grower 53:30-1 Je '66
BORN, Max
  Blessings and evils of space travel. Bul
    Atomic Sci 22:12-14 O '66
BORNEMAN, John C.
  Return of a condor. Audubon Mag 68:154-7
    My '66
BORODIN, Aleksandr Porfir'evich
  Prince Igor premiered in stereo. R. Mc-
    Mullen. il Hi Fi 16:26+ S '66
BOROFF, David
  Little milk, a little honey. Am Heritage
    17:12-14+ O '66
BORON
  ABL refining filament winding art. J. F.
    Judge. il Tech W 18:30+ Je 27 '66
  Boron crystals. D. S. Sullenger and C.
    H. L. Kennard. il Sci Am 215:96-107 bib-
    liog(p 132) Jl '66
  Boron filament graduates to production. J.
    F. Judge. il Tech W 19:23-4 O 10 '66
  Framework rearrangement in boranes and
    carboranes. W. N. Lipscomb. bibliog il
    Science 153:373-8 Jl 22 '66
  Material that will revolutionize construction;
    reprint. il Sci Digest 59:75-9 Mr '66
  Schriever cites progress on composites. Avia-
    tion W 84:81 Je 6 '66
  Vertol to build. flight test boron filament
    rotor blade. B. K. Thomas, jr. il Avia-
    tion W 85:40-1+ Ag 29 '66
BOROS, Julius
  Boros on the wedge. por Esquire 65:118 Ap
    '66
BOROSS, Garry
  Eternal VTVM C cell. Pop Electr 24:66 My
    '66
  Multi-master. Pop Electr 26:75-6 Ja '67
BOROUGH of Manhattan community college,
    New York
  Schools make news; theme and objective.
    Sat R 49:63 My 21 '66
BORROWERS. Registration. See Libraries—
    Registration
BORROWING of money. See Credit; Loans
BORSCH. See Soups
BORTON, Elizabeth. See Treviño, E. B.

BORTON, Terry
  Reaching the culturally deprived. Sat R 49:
    77-8+ F 19 '66
BORZNER, John J.
  Pepper. Pop Electr 24:56 My '66
BOSC, Robert
  New Americans in the Kennedy image.
    America 114:321-3 Mr 5 '66
BOSCH, Juan
  Balaguer wins. Commonweal 84:350 Je 17 '66
  Breathing spell. Newsweek 67:42 F 28 '66
  Case of defamation. T. Draper. New Repub
    154:13-19 F 19; 15-18 F 26; 37 Mr 5; 35 Mr
    12 '66
  Correspondence with Theodore Draper & Com-
    mentary, appropriate & inappropriate. T.
    Draper; J. B. Bender; P. Bethel. Nat R
    18:823-7 Ag 23 '66
  Dilemma in Dominica. Nat R 18:501-2 My 31
    '66
  Dominican crisis. T. Draper; discussion. il
    Nat R 18:99-100, 107-14 F 8 '66
  Dominican election and the role of the ob-
    servers. J. Mendelsohn. Christian Cent 83:
    894-8 Jl 13 '66
  Dominican elections: is the U.S. off the hook
    now? por U S News 60:49 Je 6 '66
  Heard but not seen. por Newsweek 67:55 My
    30 '66
  Outlook for Bosch. A. Kopkind. New Repub
    154:15-18 My 21 '66
  Overtaken by events, by J. B. Martin. Re-
    view
    Nation 204:23-5 Ja 2 '67. W. A. Williams
    New Yorker 42:226+ N 26 '66. R. H.
    Rovere
  Reluctant favorite. Newsweek 67:63-4 Ap 18
    '66
  Unfinished business. Nat R 18:449 My 17
    '66
BOSKIN, Joseph
  Good-by, Mr Bones. N Y Times Mag p30-1+
    My 1 '66
BOSOM. See Breast
BOSPORUS
  See also
  Golden Horn
BOSS rule
  Embattled crusader of Conway County;
    newspaper editor E. H. Wirges charges
    corruption against political bosses. T.
    Armbrister. il Sat Eve Post 239:25-9+ N
    19 '66
BOSTAIN, James C.
  Dream world of English grammar. NEA J
    55:20-2 S '66
BOSTON
                    Architecture
  Bold start for a renewal; Roxbury branch
    YMCA. il Arch Rec 139:157-60 My '66
  Boston's citadel of architecture; Architec-
    tural center. J. M. Dixon. il Arch Forum
    125:64-71 D '66
  Boston's State Street bank building. il Arch
    Rec 140:115-20 Ag '66

                      Banks
  Proper Bostonians modernize; State Street
    bank's 34-story skyscraper. il Bsns W
    p58-60 My 7 '66

                  City planning
  Belt for Boston's waist. il Fortune 73:168
    Mr '66
  Boston's powerful model for rebuilders; Ed
    Logue administrator of housing and plan-
    ning program. il Bsns W p 152-4 N 26 '66
  Plaza development for Boston government
    service center. il Arch Rec 139:140-1 Je '66

                      Crime
  Boston strangler, by G. Frank. Review
    Newsweek 68:118+ O 31 '66. S. Schmidt
    Sat R 49:29-30 O 29 '66. R. Stout
  Boston strangler; condensation. G. Frank.
    il Ladies Home J 83:65-72+ Ag; 91-8+ S '66
  Making the violent scene. M. Lebowitz. Na-
    tion 204:58 Ja 9 '67

                    Description
  Boston. C. Walter. il U S Camera 29:60-1+
    O '66
  Boston: exciting city with a past. R. Dunlop.
    il Todays Health 44:36-41 Jl '66
  Dickens in Boston; excerpt from American
    notes. 1842. C. Dickens. Sat R 49:125 Mr 12
    '66
  Massachusetts builds for tomorrow. R. De
    Roos. il Nat Geog Mag 130:793-815 D '66
  Travel notes. R. Joseph. Esquire 66:24+
    O '66

                     Education
  Boston: education's last hurrah. P. Schrag.
    il Sat R 49:56-8+ My 21 '66

BOSTON—Education—*Continued*
Boston's Louise Day Hicks: storm center of the busing battle. I. Mothner. il Look 30:72+ F 22 '66
Cut-off in Boston; concerning withholding federal funds. J. S. Doyle. New Repub 155: 10 Ag 27 '66
White northerner's choice: Mrs Hicks. P. Lamson. Atlan 217:58-62 Je '66
Whitewash; reclassification of Chinese-American children to get state aid. il Newsweek 68:97 O 31 '66

Galleries and museums
See also
Boston children's museum

Hospitals
Charitable cheating in your hospital bill; De-Boalt case. il Look 30:31-3 Je 14 '66
Massachusetts general: a great hospital, and why. J. Star. il Look 30:31-3 Mr 22 '66

Moral conditions
Open season on dissenters. Christian Cent 83:483-4 Ap 20 '66

Music
See also
Opera company of Boston

Negroes
Boston's Louise Day Hicks: storm center of the busing battle. I. Mothner. il Look 30:72+ F 22 '66
White northerner's choice: Mrs Hicks. P. Lamson. Atlan 217:58-62 Je '66

Newspapers
Boston loses its newspapers, finds bitterness in the strike. il Bsns W p 120 Mr 12 '66
Printers rise again; shut down of Boston's five dailies. il Time 87:77 Mr 18 '66
See also
Boston herald
Strikes—United States—Newspapers

Politics and government
Boston: education's last hurrah. P. Schrag. il Sat R 49:56-8+ My 21 '66
Boston's Louise Day Hicks: storm center of the busing battle. I. Mothner. il Look 30:72+ F 22 '66

Public health
Sickly Bostonians. Harper 232:46 My '66

Street traffic
Vault-type meters stop vandals. T. F. Carty. il Am City 81:123+ Mr '66
BOSTON Celtics (basketball team) See Basketball teams
BOSTON children's medical center. See Children—Hospitals
BOSTON children's museum
MATCH Boxes; project in Boston. il Am Ed 3:9 D '66
BOSTON herald
Out of the roaring '20s; scathing last-minute editorial attack on Elliot Lee Richardson. Newsweek 68:100 D 5 '66
BOSTON marathon. See Running
BOSTON massacre, 1770
Verdicts of history. T. J. Fleming. il Am Heritage 18:6-11+ D '66
BOSTON museum of fine arts
Wickes collection given to Boston. E. P. Birk. il Antiques 90:16 Jl '66
BOSTON newspaper strike. See Strikes—United States—Newspapers
BOSTON opera company. See Opera company of Boston
BOSTON Patriots (football club) See Football clubs
BOSTON public library
Sex education: the common denominator; with bibliography. J. Manthorne. il Library J 91:319-22 Ja 15 '66
BOSTON symphony chamber players. See Chamber orchestras
BOSTON symphony orchestra
Musical events; concert in Philharmonic hall. W. Sargeant. New Yorker 42:238+ O 22 '66
Musical events; performance of Sydeman's In memoriam John F. Kennedy. W. Sargeant. New Yorker 42:128-9 N 26 '66
Pride of the BSO, its first-desk players take a chamber bow. S. Fleming. il Hi Fi 16:81-2 D '66
Rewards beyond the regimen; Boston symphony chamber players. il Time 87:65 Mr 18 '66
BOSTON university
Different kind of Methodist for Boston U. il Time 88:33 D 30 '66

Libraries
Boston centralizes; Mugar memorial library. G. A. Harper. il Library J 91:5886-8 O 1 '66
BOSTON yacht club. See Yacht clubs
BOSWELL, James
Boswell without Johnson? G. Wills. Nat R 18:790-1 Ag 9 '66
The earlier years, by F. A. Pottle. Review Reporter 35:47-8 N 3 '66. D. Littlejohn
James Boswell, by F. A. Pottle. Review
Newsweek por 67:118+ My 23 '66
Sat R por 49:30-1 Ap 30 '66. L. Edel
Time il por 88:80+ Jl 1 '66
BOSWORTH, Adrienne
Unpaid, uncomplaining, but not unappreciated. por U S Camera 29:40+ Ag '66
BOTANICAL apparatus
Gaseous-diffusion porometer for continuous measurement of diffusive resistance of leaves. R. O. Slatyer and P. G. Jarvis. bibliog il Science 151:574-6 F 4 '66
BOTANICAL gardens
Royal botanical gardens, Hamilton, Ontario. L. Laking. il Horticulture 45:34-5+ Ja '67
See also
California. University—Berkeley campus—Botanical garden
Denver botanic gardens
New York botanical garden
Royal botanic gardens, Kew
BOTANICAL illustration. See Illustration of books and periodicals
BOTANICAL research
Among the plants men live by; proposals for increasing research on food plants; excerpt from report. K. Thimann. Sat R 50:118-20 Ja 7 '67
Osmotic pressure influence in germination tests for antibiosis. R. C. Anderson and O. L. Loucks. bibliog il Science 152:771-3 My 6 '66
Relative turgidity of leaves: temperature effects in measurement. B. D. Millar. bibliog il Science 154:512-13 O 28 '66
BOTANICAL stamps. See Postage stamps
BOTANY
See also
Fruit
Paleobotany
Pollen
Species

Bibliography
Onward and upward in the garden. K. S. White. New Yorker 42:149-50+ D 10 '66

Ecology
Ambitious violet. W. Camp. il Sat R 49:65-6 Je 4 '66
See also
Vegetation

History
Portraits in science; renaissance botanist. T. Robinson. Natur Hist 75:69-73 Mr '66

Nomenclature
English names of plants. H. W. Rickett. Horticulture 44:44-5 Je '66
People and plant names. D. S. Manks. il Horticulture 44:18-21 Ag '66

Paleontology
See Paleobotany

Physiology
Pictures taken through the many lenses of a leaf. il Life 61:24-5 D 23 '66
Plant physiology in Canada; report on meeting of the Canadian society of plant physiologists. J. A. Webb. Science 155:112+ Ja 6 '67
See also
Chloroplasts
Electrophysiology of plants
Plants—Metabolism
Plants—Translocation

Australia
Bush mammalogist; interview. W. H. Butler. New Yorker 42:18-20 Ag 6 '66

Connecticut
Ambitious violet. W. Camp. il Sat R 49:65-6 Je 4 '66

Java
Rise and fall of Sir Stamford Raffles: colonialist, naturalist. R. Silverberg. il Natur Hist 76:18+ Ja '67

Lapland
Unusual plants of Lappland. G. S. Avery. Horticulture 44:42+ Je '66

BOTANY—*Continued*

Peru

Giants of the puna; bromeliad of the Peruvian highlands. F. D. Ayres. il Natur Hist 75:54-7 Mr '66

Texas

Big Bend and the botanist. E. E. Gamer. il Nat Parks Mag 40:14-17 Ap '66

Western states

Lewis and Clark, plant collectors for a president. R. G. Beidleman. il Horticulture 44:28-9+ Ap '66

BOTANY, Economic. See Plants, Food

BOTANY, Medical
Books in review; herbals, old and new. E. C. Hall. Natur Hist 75:6+ Mr '66
Medicine and plants. J. C. Krantz, jr. il Horticulture 44:34-5+ Ag '66
See also
Drugs
Herbs

BOTEIN, Bernard
Judge with disciplined indignation. G. Samuels. il pors N Y Times Mag p38-40+ Ja 15 '67

BOTERO, Fernando
Piñatas in oil. il pors Time 88:26-7 D 30 '66

BOTHE-NAPA VALLEY STATE PARK. See California—Parks and reserves

BOTSFORD, Keith
Elite proletarians all. N Y Times Mag p54-5+ N 13 '66
Günter Grass is a different drummer. N Y Times Mag p28-9+ My 8 '66
Report from a surrealist capital. N Y Times Mag p58-9+ S 11 '66
Writings of Jorge Luis Borges. Atlan 219:99-104 Ja '67
(tr) See Borges, J. L. Benares

BOTSFORD, Ward
For its 53rd spring, a superb 26th recording of Stravinsky's Rite; P. Boulez on Nonesuch. Am Rec G 32:500-3 F '66

BOTSWANA
Drama in two acts. il Newsweek 68:54+ O 17 '66
Dry days in Botswana. N. Mitchison. il Sat R 49:65-6+ O 22 '66
Our only look at a lost race; scientists find the sole surviving river Bushman of Okavango swamps; with report by R. Shay. il Life 61:135-6+ D 9 '66
Two new nations. il Sr Schol 89:18-19 O 7 '66
Two new nations. il Time 88:46 O 7 '66
Whimsy can change the world. C. D. Downes. America 115:385-6 O 1 '66
See also
United Nations—Botswana

BOTT, George
Three faces of Beatrix Potter. Sr Schol 89: sup29 O 28 '66

BOTT, John C.
Package design. Design 68:27-9 N '66

BOTTEL, Helen
Boat campers' paradise. Lake Tahoe's Emerald Bay. Motor B 118:22-4 Jl '66
Little boat that grew. Motor B 117:126+ F '66

BOTTLE brushes (shrubs)
Colorful bottlebrushes are a California answer. il Sunset 136:262-4+ My '66

BOTTLE-nose dolphins. See Dolphins (mammals)

BOTTLE ships. See Ship and boat models

BOTTLEBRUSHES (shrubs) See Bottle brushes (shrubs)

BOTTLED water. See Water

BOTTLES
Fine art of opening wine. il House & Gard 130:294-7 N '66
Throwaway containers get a lift from pop; disposable containers and nonreturnable bottles. il Bsns W p70+ Ag 6 '66
See also
Milk bottles

BOTTLES, Used
Billions & billions of bottles. il Changing T 20:48 My '66

BOTTLING Industry
Greatest franchise of all; bottlers of Coca-Cola. J. B. Weiner. il Duns R 88:31+ O '66
Straight from the spa; French firm. Source Perrier. il Time 88:114 S 16 '66

BOTTOMLEY, Tom
Aluminum construction. Yachting 119:81-3+ Ap '66

BOTTOMORE, T. B.
Scoring points in the cold war. Nation 202:623 My 23 '66

BOTTY, Ken
How to shoot eagles. Field & S 71:60-1 Ja '67

BOTULISM
See also
Clostridium botulinum

BOUCHER, Raymond C.
Designing a transformerless power supply. Electr World 75:86-8 Ap '66

BOUDIN, Eugène Louis
Boudin: the king of the skies. L. Campbell. il Art N 65:46-7+ N '66
Inventor of the seashore. il Time 88:90 N 18 '66

BOUDOIR; story. See Singer, I. B.

BOUGAINVILLEA
Bougainvillea. W. Radcliffe. il Horticulture 45:38-9 Ja '67

BOUGHTON, Alfred C.
Memo from the publisher (title varies) Miss & Roc 18:6 Ap 18 '66 (cont as) Tech W 18: 7 Je 6; 19:6 D 12 '66

about
Memo from the publisher (title varies) J. W. Claar. por Miss & Roc 18:5 Ap 11 '66

BOUHUYS, Arend
Airflow control by auditory feedback: respiratory mechanics and wind instruments. bibliog Science 154:797-9 N 11 '66

BOULAT, Pierre
Gallic blend of old and new; photographs. Sports Illus 24:46-50 Je 6 '66

BOULDER, Colo.
Are you using your most valuable asset? Junior ranger force program. D. Miller. il Parks & Rec 1:494-5 Je '66

BOULDING, Kenneth E.
Books (cont) Sci Am 214:131-2+ Ap '66
Notes on the politics of peace. Bul Atomic Sci 22:30-2 S '66

BOULEZ, Pierre
Bout with Boulez. E. Lockspeiser. por Hi Fi 16:65-8+ My '66
For its 53rd spring, a superb 26th recording of Stravinsky's Rite; P. Boulez on Nonesuch. W. Botsford. il por Am Rec G 32:500-3 F '66
Goodbye to all that. il por Time 87:62 Je 24 '66
Music of the birds and beasts. D. Oliver. Sat R 49:68-9 Mr 26 '66
Music today via Angel, a superlative HMV project. A. Cohn. por Am Rec G 32:780-1 My '66

BOULWARE, Marcus H.
Roscoe Conkling Simmons: the golden voiced politico. bibliog Negro Hist Bul 29:131-2 Mr '66
Saint-satan leader as a public speaker, the crusader: Robert Williams. por Negro Hist Bul 29:81-2 Ja '66

BOUMEDIENNE, Houari
Blushing strongman. il por Time 88:20 D 30 '66
In Algeria it's not yah, yah, Boumediene! but wait and see. P. Braestrup and D. Ottaway. il pors N Y Times Mag p36-7+ F 13 '66
Rousing ho-hum. por Newsweek 67:48A-48B Je 20 '66

BOUNTIES for animals. See Animals, Predatory—Bounties

BOURBON-BATTENBERG, Juan de, count of Barcelona. See Juan Carlos, count of Barcelona

BOURDON, David
E=MC² à go-go. Art N 64:22-5+ Ja '66
Good janitor becomes as important as a curator. Life 61:46-7+ Ag 12 '66

BOURGEOIS-PICHAT, Jean
Population growth and development. bibliog f por(back cover) Int Concil 556:5-79 Ja '66

BOURGOIS, Christian
New imprint in Paris. H. R. Lottman. Pub W 190:34-6 N 21 '66

BOURGUIBA, Habib ben Ali
Tunisian way. For Affairs 44:480-8 Ap '66
about
Shudder at the knees; banning the miniskirt. il Time 88:26+ Ag 26 '66

BOURJAILY, Vance
Corn of Coxcatlán. bibliog Horizon 8:50-5 Spr '66

BOURKE, George
From tip to top in Florida. See issues of Travel

BOURNE, Geoffrey H. See Shanthaveerappa, T. R. jt. auth.

BOUSCAREN, Anthony T.
Catholic peaceniks. Nat R 18:202 Mr 8 '66

BOUSH, G. M. See Matsumura, F. jt. auth.

BOUTANG, Pierre
Further on the China confrontation: a question and an answer from France. Nat R 18: 208-9 Mr 8 '66
BOUTEILLER, Marion
More travel, less trouble. NEA J 55:29-30 My '66
BOUTWELL, William D.
What's happening in education? See issues of PTA magazine
BOUWMEESTER, John Henry
Flying Dutchman. R. Levy. por Duns R 88: 60-1+ N '66
BOVA, Kathryn Metcalf
Take a leaf. Flower Grower 53:26+ N '66
BOVA, Louis
Inquest on a premature burial. T. Buckley. il por Esquire 65:75-81+ Je '66
BOVE, Tony
I am: poem. Sat R 49:30 Mr 5 '66
BOW and arrow
Emergency repairs. G. H. Gillelan. il Outdoor Life 139:24-7 Ja '67
Questions readers ask. G. H. Gillelan. il Outdoor Life 138:141-3 N '66
Up-dated bow fires caps and corks. R. L. Phillips. il Pop Mech 125:167 Mr '66
See also
Hunting with bow and arrow
BOW hunting. See Hunting with bow and arrow
BOWDEN, Bertram Vivian Bowden, baron
How much science can we afford? Nation 204:17-21 Ja 2 '67
BOWDOIN college, Brunswick, Me.
Bowdoin college senior program. J. S. Coles. Sch & Soc 94:182-3 Ap 2 '66
BOWEN, Catherine Drinker
Journey through the American states; excerpt from Miracle at Philadelphia. Atlan 218:94-103 N '66
BOWEN, Ezra
Favorite times, favorite places. Mlle 64:185+ N '66
BOWEN, Howard R.
Technology and employment: address. March 30, 1966. Vital Speeches 32:435-9 My 1 '66
BOWEN, Ira S. and Rule, B. H.
Palomar 60-inch photometric reflector. Sky & Tel 32:184-7 O '66
BOWEN, William, and Shook, Edgar
Why they call those soybeans golden. Fortune 74:126-9+ Ag '66
BOWEN, William G. See Baumol, W. J. jt. auth.
BOWER, T. G. R.
Slant perception and shape constancy in infants. bibliog Science 151:832-4 F 18 '66
Visual world of infants; with biographical sketch. Sci Am 215:16, 80-4+ D '66
BOWER, Warren
Locus: Washington square. Sat R 49:23-5 Je 4 '66
BOWERS, Edgar
From woodcarver to wordcarver. R. Roseliep. Poetry 107:327 F '66
BOWERS, Faubion
Late General MacArthur, warts and all. Esquire 67:90-1+ Ja '67
Looking and listening. See issues of House & garden incorporating Living for young homemakers
What makes a good pianist? House & Gard 130:35+ N '66
BOWERS, Gwendolyn
Legends of the Grail. Horn Bk 42:37-42 F '66
BOWERS, John
From TV to Tiffany's in one wild leap. Sat Eve Post 239:97-101 N 19 '66
BOWERS, Malcolm B. Jr, and others
Sleep deprivation and brain acetylcholine. bibliog Science 153:1416-17 S 16 '66
BOWERS, Raymond
Solid-state source of microwaves; with biographical sketch. Sci Am 215:10, 22-31 Ag '66
BOWERS, Sam Holloway, Jr
Malice toward some. il Newsweek 67:39-40 Ap 11 '66
BOWERS, W. S. and Blickenstaff, C. C.
Hormonal termination of diapause in the alfalfa weevil. bibliog Science 154:1673-4 D 30 '66
—and others
Juvenile hormone: identification of an active compound from balsam fir. bibliog Science 154:1020-1 N 25 '66
BOWERS, William J.
Cheating on the college campus. NEA J 55: 20-2 F '66
BOWES, H. Angus
Vent house urges! il por Time 88:116+ S 30 '66

BOWFISHING. See Fishing with bow and arrow
BOWIE, Robert Richardson
Another Dulles alumnus. Nation 203:205 S 12 '66
BOWIE knives
Double-duty hunting knife. C. Conley. il Field & S 71:125 N '66
BOWKER, Albert Hosmer
Operation SEEK. por Sch & Soc 94:374+ N 12 '66
BOWKER, R. R, company
Bowker announces format change for Lj, SLj, and PW in 1967. Library J 91:1187 Mr 1 '66
1967 format change for Lj, SLj, PW announced by the R. R. Bowker company. Library J 91:1638 Mr 15 '66
Skyrocketing US book output forces BIP into two volumes. Library J 91:5571-2 N 15 '66
See also
Carey-Thomas award
BOWL football games. See Football
BOWLER, William R.
Investing in a local bank? Duns R 87:36-8+ My '66
BOWLES, Chester
Traveler, consider my India; ed. by R. Joseph. pors Esquire 65:110-11+ Mr '66
BOWLES, Frank H.
Dual-purpose revolution; excerpts from address, 1966. NEA J 55:38-40 D '66
BOWLES, Jane Auer
Quarreling pair; a puppet play. pors Mlle 64: 116-17 D '66
about
Shriek from wasted women. W. Schott. Life 61:17 D 16 '66
Truman Capote introduces Jane Bowles; introd. from The collected works of Jane Bowles. T. Capote. il pors Mlle 64:114-17 D '66
Women out of this world. P. MacManus. Sat R 50:87-8 Ja 14 '67
BOWLES, Paul
Casablanca. Holiday 40:74-9+ S '66
BOWLES, Ronald Edward
Inventor of the month. S. V. Jones. por Sci Digest 60:15 O '66
BOWLING
Dick Weber: king of the bowlers. W. J. McKean. il Look 30:M12+ N 1 '66
It's bigger than bingo; drawings. M. Simont. Sports Illus 24:56-9 My 16 '66
100-plus comes of age; nonprofit children's bowling program. il Parks & Rec 1:557 Jl '66
BOWLS
Further comments on the lobate bowl form. J. N. Pearce. il Antiques 90:524-5 O '66
BOWMAN, David J.
Roman Catholic joins N.C.C. staff. Christian Cent 83:930 Jl 27 '66
BOWMAN, Hank
Rate yourself as a skipper. Motor B 118:35+ Jl '66
BOWMAN, Harry R. and others
Application of high-resolution semiconductor detectors in X-ray emission spectrography. bibliog Science 151:562-8; 153:321 F 4, Jl 15 '66
BOWMAN, James L.
Dollars, decisions, and diplomas. por Am Ed 2:30-2 My '66
BOWMAN, Lowry
Home in the country. il por Time 88:56 Jl 29 '66
BOWMAN, Robert L. and Alexander, Nelson
Ozone-induced chemiluminescence of organic compounds. bibliog Science 154:1454-6 D 16 '66
—See Moskowitz, G. W. jt auth.
BOWNESS, J. M.
Epinephrine: cascade reactions and glycogenolytic effect. bibliog Science 152:1370-1 Je 3 '66
BOWRA, Sir Cecil Maurice
(tr) See Sappho. Some fragments; Parting: Absent friend
about
Poets and their politics. G. Daniels. New Repub 155:29-30+ S 17 '66
BOWRA, Sir Maurice. See Bowra, C. M.
BOWRON, Albert W.
No perfect diamonds: library buildings. por Library J 91:5544-9 N 15 '66
BOWSER, Hallowell
Perils of hasty history. Sat R 49:14 D 31 '66
Train of clients. Sat R 49:26 Ap 16 '66
Work is a proper noun. Sat R 49:32 O 22 '66
BOX cars. See Railroads—Freight cars
BOX lunches. See Lunches

BOXER uprising, 1900. See China—History—
    Boxer uprising, 1900
BOXERS
    Rating the young heavies. N. Fleischer.
        Sports Illus 24:23 Mr 14 '66
    Sudden rush of new heavies. T. Maule. il
        Sports Illus 24:14-17 F 21 '66
    Youthful, aggressive and talented enough to
        revitalize boxing's no. 1 division. M. Shar-
        nik. il Sports Illus 24:16-17 F 21 '66
        See also names of boxers. e.g. C. Clay
BOXES, Music. See Music boxes
BOXES, cases, etc.
    See also
    Christmas boxes
BOXFISH
    Pahutoxin: a fish poison. D. B. Boylan and
        P. J. Scheuer. bibliog il Science 155:52-6
        Ja 6 '67
BOXING
    All of the people all of the time; Clay-Cooper
        fight. il Time 87:48+ My 27 '66
    And an Irishman takes a shellacking at Shea;
        light heavyweight champion J. Torres
        defeats W. Thornton. M. Kram. il Sports
        Illus 24:24-5 My 30 '66
    Battle of the lionhearted; Clay-Chuvalo fight.
        G. Rogin. il Sports Illus 24:32-4+ Ap 11
        '66
    Blood at the Arsenal; C. Clay-H. Cooper's
        fight. E. Shrake. il Sports Illus 24:20-3 My
        30 '66
    Bloody shame; Clay-Cooper fight. il News-
        week 67:83 My 30 '66
    Camping out with the champ; middleweight
        champion E. Griffith. M. Gross. il Sports
        Illus 25:36-8+ N 7 '66
    Case of conscience. J. Olsen. il Sports Illus
        24:94-103 Ag 18; 48-50+ Ap 25; 36-8+ My
        2; 34-6+ My 9 '66
    Challenge shortage; Clay-Williams fight.
        Newsweek 68:65 N 28 '66
    Champion; Torres-Tiger fight. il Newsweek
        68:47-8 D 26 '66
    Clover in need of a leaf; J. Frazier beat
        heavyweight Ringo Bonavena. M. Kane.
        Sports Illus 25:72+ O 3 '66
    Cops and robbers in Mexico city; Ortiz-Ramos
        championship fight. M. Kram. il Sports
        Illus 25:26-9 O 31 '66
    Cus is back aboard a big new Bus; C.
        D'Amato promotes B. Mathis as next
        heavyweight champion of the world. R. H.
        Boyle. il Sports Illus 26:18-22 Ja 16 '67
    Delayed payday for Cleve; C. Williams-C.
        Clay fight. E. Shrake and M. Sharnik. il
        Sports Illus 25:34-6 D 5 '66
    Destination unknown; concerning Clay-Terrell
        fight. Newsweek 67:93 Mr 14 '66
    Early end for early bird; Clay-London fight.
        Newsweek 68:79 Ag 15 '66
    England's posh house of pow; photographs
        by J. Alexander and J. Cooke; account by
        J. Lovesey. il Sports Illus 25:40-5 O 31
        '66
    Fight that won't stay dead; Jack Dempsey-
        Tommy Gibbons heavyweight championship
        fight. July 4, 1923. J. W. Johnson. il Sports
        Illus 25:64-70+ Jl 4 '66
    Fighter; L. Nova. M. Kram. il Sports Illus
        25:66-8+ D 12 '66
    First lady of boxing; L. Byrd. il Ebony 21:
        81-2+ Je '66
    Foul for the sake of a good fight; Chuvalo-
        Clay fight. il Life 60:43 Ap 8 '66
    Hands of Clay; defeat of K. Mildenberger.
        il Newsweek 68:68 S 19 '66
    If Cassius can't punch, then London isn't
        down; Clay-London fight. J. Lovesey. il
        Sports Illus 25:16-19 Ag 15 '66
    In defense of Cassius Clay; interview, ed. by
        G. Talese. F. Patterson. il Esquire 66:55-8
        Ag '66
    Intimate look at the champ. I. Sutton. il
        Ebony 22:148-54+ N '66
    Jab from the intellectual; Benvenuti-Fullmer
        contest in Rome. M. Kane. il Sports Illus
        24:18-21+ F 14 '66
    Jab that wiped out a smile; T. Alongi-J.
        Quarry fight. M. Kram. il Sports Illus 24:
        28-9 Je 6 '66
    Lightweight decision; Ramos-Ortiz fight. il
        Newsweek 68:94-5 N 7 '66
    Lost hero; J. Torres. P. Hamill. il Sat Eve
        Post 239:84-6+ My 21 '66
    Low blows, tax blows; Clay-Chuvalo fight.
        il Newsweek 67:64+ Ap 11 '66
    Massacre; Clay-Williams fight in Houston.
        M. Kane. il Sports Illus 25:22-5 N 21 '66
    Muslim ministers to a southpaw; Clay-Milden-
        berger fight. M. Kane. il Sports Illus 25:
        34-5+ S 19 '66
    No zip, no lip; in Miami Beach. Sports Illus
        25:10 O 31 '66

    Quarry who likes to hunt; J. Quarry-Tony
        Alongi fight. T. Maule. il Sports Illus 24:
        20-3 Mr 14 '66
    Ready for the bloodletting; C. Clay-H. Cooper
        fight. E. Shrake. Sports Illus 24:74+ My 23
        '66
    Ringing in the old; Patterson-Cooper fight.
        Sports Illus 25:18 O 10 '66
    Showdown with a punching bag; Chuvalo-
        Clay fight in Toronto. T. Maule. il Sports
        Illus 24:34-7 Mr 28 '66
    Shrinking poppy's nonbout with a reluctant
        Tiger; middleweight title changes hands;
        E. Griffith-D. Tiger fight. M. Kram. il
        Sports Illus 24:70-2 My 9 '66
    Skinning the Cat; C. Clay-C. Williams fight.
        il Time 88:64 N 25 '66
    Speaking of indignities; Clay-Chuvalo fight.
        il Time 87:75 Ap 8 '66
    Tiger and friend; Emile Griffith takes title.
        Newsweek 67:89 My 9 '66
    When Emile got his Irish up; Archer-Griffith
        fight. M. Kram. il Sports Illus 25:14-15
        Jl 25 '66
    Will and ability; D. Tiger's defeat of
        J. Torres to win light-heavyweight cham-
        pionship. Sports Illus 26:5 Ja 2 '67
    Wind that blew in Chicago; Illinois com-
        mission hearings on Clay-Terrell fight. W.
        B. Furlong. il Sports Illus 24:26-7+ Mr 7
        '66
    Winning for old Cornbread; Gonzalez-Cokes
        welterweight-title fight. M. Kram. il Sports
        Illus 25:18-19 S 5 '66
    Without honor in his own land; J. Torres
        keeps world light heavyweight champion-
        ship, but is no hero in Puerto Rico. M.
        Kram. il Sports Illus 25:30-1 O 24 '66
    You watch out, Ali! Clay-Williams heavy-
        weight title fight. M. Kane. il Sports Illus
        25:26-9 N 14 '66
BOXING fans. See Sports fans
BOXING for shipment. See Packing for ship-
    ment
BOY scouts
    Good old days. Sports Illus 25:19-20 O 24 '66
    Good turn; scouting's new look. il Time 87:37
        Je 10 '66

Anecdotes, facetiae, satire, etc.
    Letter from Stan Delaplane. S. Delaplane.
        Todays Health 44:77 O '66

Explorer scouts
    Explorer scouts; address, December 6, 1965.
        W. H. Spurgeon, 3d. Vital Speeches 32:314-
        20 Mr 1 '66
BOY who wanted to be somebody; story. See
    Gordon, E. E.
BOYARSKY, Saul, and others
    Acceleration of ureteral peristalsis by adrenal
        compression. Science 154:669 N 4 '66
BOYCE, Benjamin
    Woman of mixed emotions. il Sat R 49:58
        D 3 '66
BOYCOTT
    Arab boycott. Newsweek 68:88+ D 5 '66
    Arabs bar Coke, Ford; boycott list of com-
        panies doing business in Israel. Bsns W p52
        N 26 '66
    Behind the boycotts; why prices are high.
        il Time 88:89 N 4 '66
    Boomerang boycott; Arab world's boycott of
        Israel and foreign companies that do more
        than just sell finished goods to Israel. il
        Time 88:93-4 D 2 '66
    Boycott on ships to Hanoi? U S News 60:4
        F 28 '66
    Boycotts and prices. M. Friedman. News-
        week 68:92 N 28 '66
    Cutting off Haiphong; U.S. administration's
        blacklist. Time 87:23 F 25 '66
    Housewives skewer high food prices; or-
        ganized action against chain food stores.
        il Bsns W p42-3 O 22 '66
    Perils of HR 10027; secondary boycotts. Nat
        R 18:255 Mr 22 '66
    Power of the dollar; Operation Breadbasket
        in Chicago. Newsweek 68:62 D 26 '66
BOYD, Alan Stephenson
    Big wheel. il por Newsweek 68:94 N 21 '66
    Boyd raps objections of airlines to proposed
        transportation dept. W. H. Gregory. Avia-
        tion W 84:49 Je 6 '66
    New Cabinet member with a problem job.
        por U S News 61:23 N 21 '66
    Pro for DOT. por Time 88:33 N 18 '66
    Quick approval of Boyd by Congress seen.
        Aviation W 85:40-1 N 14 '66
    Untangling the nation's lifeline. il por
        Bsns W p 111-12+ N 26 '66
BOYD, George W.
    Precision wirewound potentiometers. Electr
        World 75:55-7 Ap '66

BOYD, Jack
Build me a story, daddy. Farm J 90:72 My '66
BOYD, James P. Jr
Private lives. il Time 88:15 Jl 1 '66
BOYD, John Dewey
Negro against Negro. Newsweek 67:38+ Ap 18 '66
BOYD, Malcolm
Movies (cont) Christian Cent 83:178+, 305-6, 590, 937-8, 1083, 1604-5 F 9, Mr 9, My 4 Jl 27, S 7, D 28 '66
Opinion: on living religion. por Mlle 64:34+ D '66
Speaking out. por Sat Eve Post 239:10+ Ag 27 '66
What's right with Christmas. McCalls 94:149 D '66
about
And now even prayers are pop. J. Duscha. il por N Y Times Mag p 184-5+ N 13 '66
Beyond the new orthodoxy. il por Time 88:85-6 O 7 '66
Entertainment; Fr Boyd at the hungry i. L. Kinsolving. Christian Cent 83:1244 O 12 '66; Reply. B. D. Napier. 83:1411 N 16 '66
Nightclub priest. S. Alexander. Life 61:29 O 28 '66
Performing arts; prayers on record. R. Kotlowitz. por Harper 233:135 O '66
Two for the show. il por Newsweek 68:68 O 3 '66
BOYD, Margaret Verna
Co-operative creativity. Sch Arts 65:14-15 My '66
BOYD, Susan Kuehn
Fortunate failures. Writer 79:13-15+ Ag '66
BOYD, Virgil E.
Changes at Chrysler. il por Time 88:98+ D 9 '66
Rise from the grass roots. il por Newsweek 68:82+ D 12 '66
BOYDEN, Frank Learoyd
Profiles. J. McPhee. por New Yorker 42:57-8+ Mr 19 '66
BOYER, David S.
Wyoming: high, wide, and windy. il Nat Geog Mag 129:554-94 Ap '66
BOYER, J. S.
Isopiestic technique: measurement of accurate leaf water potentials. bibliog Science 154:1459-60 D 16 '66
BOYER, Neil A.
Volunteers in the field: great expectations. Ann Am Acad 365:55-62 My '66
BOYER, Samuel H. and others
Hemoglobins in sheep: multiple differences in amino acid sequences of three beta-chains and possible origins. bibliog Science 153:1539-43 S 23 '66
BOYKIN, John E.
Canine charioteers. Pop Mech 126:63-5 Jl '66
Weird new world of Old MacDonald. Pop Mech 126:112-15+ Jl '66
Wild transistorized West. Pop Mech 125:118-19 F '66
BOYKIN, Louise
Forms and shapes in nature. Sch Arts 66:19-20 S '66
BOYKIN spaniels. See Spaniels
BOYKO, Anatole
(tr) See Lipsky, Y. N. What Luna 9 told us about the moon
BOYLAN, Brian Richard. See Callagan. D. A; Vosburgh, G. J; Word, B. jt. auths.
BOYLAN, David B. and Scheuer, P. J.
Pahutoxin: a fish poison. bibliog Science 155:52-6 Ja 6 '67
BOYLE. Alan
Inmates of Charenton: bald wigs for actors in Marat/Sade. il New Yorker 41:21-3 Ja 29 '66
BOYLE, Hal
What every husband ought to know. Read Digest 89:40 Jl '66
BOYLE, Kay
Fire in the vineyards: story. Sat Eve Post 239:76-7 Jl 2 '66
Wild horses; story. Sat Eve Post 239:60-5 Ap 9 '66
BOYLE, Robert H.
Conservation (cont) Sports Illus 25:80+ O 17 '66
BOYLEN, Michael
Craftsmen USA '66; Northeast Region. Craft Horiz 26:75-7+ Je '66
BOYLES, Vernon R.
Talking book: a prelude to action. por Library J 91:201-4 Ja 15 '66
BOYNTON, Robert M. and Das, S. R.
Visual adaptation: increased efficiency resulting from spectrally distributed mixtures of stimuli. bibliog Science 154:1581-3 D 23 '66

BOYS
Boy and the big fish. R. Starnes. Field & S 71:14-15+ Jl '66
From a boy's point of view. J. Wescott. See issues of Seventeen to December 1966
What does a boy really want? questions and answers. A. Wood. il Seventeen 25: 130-1+ O '66
See also
Adolescence
Gangs
Runaway boys and girls
BOYS clubs of America, incorporated
Guilt by pronunciation; confused patriots. Nation 202:317 Mr 21 '66
BOYS reading. See Childrens reading
BOYS rooms. See Rooms
BOYS schools. See Private schools
BOZARTH, David H.
Dwell meter adapter. Pop Electr 24:58+ F '66
BOZARTH, R. de Golikov
Solidizing force; poem. Commonweal 84:524 Ag 19 '66
BOZELL, L. Brent
Future's past. S. J. Adamo. America 115:120 Jl 30 '66
BRAATEN, Carl E.
Response, demur. Christian Cent 83:1011 Ag 17 '66
about
Braaten brouhaha. Christian Cent 83:1296-7 O 26 '66
Protestant hara-kiri. Christian Cent 83:794 Je 22 '66; Discussion. 83:1011 Ag 17 '66
BRABHAM, Jack
All deliberate speed. il por Newsweek 68:75 Ag 8 '66
Does anybody here believe Jack Brabham? K. Chapin. por Sports Illus 25:82-3 O 10 '66
Grand old man. il por Time 88:53 Ag 5 '66
Ol' Jack was nimble, ol' Jack was quick, with his Brabham machine he turned the trick. L. Levine. il por Motor T 19:56-9+ Ja '67
Sportsman of the year: J. Ryun; four others excelled. por Sports Illus 25:49 D 19 '66
BRACE, Gerald Warner
Classic coastal day; excerpt from Between wind and water. Yachting 120:55+ Jl '66
BRACE, W. F. and Byerlee, J. D.
Stick-slip as a mechanism for earthquakes. bibliog Science 153:990-2 Ag 26 '66
—and Orange, A. S.
Electrical resistivity changes in saturated rock under stress. bibliog Science 153: 1525-6 S 23 '66
—See Press, F. jt. auth.
BRACEGIRDLE, Cyril
Portuguese plate. Antiques 89:834-7 Je '66
BRACEROS. See Migrant labor
BRACES. See Orthopedic apparatus
BRACHIOPODS, Fossil
Permian productoid brachiopod: life history. R. E. Grant. bibliog il Science 152:660-2 Ap 29 '66
Pholidostrophiid brachiopods: origin of the nacreous luster. K. M. Towe and C. W. Harper, jr. bibliog il Science 154:153-5 O 7 '66
BRACKEN, Peg
Peg Bracken's appendix to the I hate to cook book. Ladies Home J 83:84-5 Jl; 92+ Ag; 116+ O; 128+ N; 50+ D '66 (to be cont)
BRACKMAN, Jacob
Four ways to go; the end of the trip. Esquire 66:126+ S '66
Gospel according to St Paul's. Esquire 65:92-4+ Je '66
BRADBURY, Ray
Man who tried everything. Life 60:12 F 11 '66
BRADBURY, Will
Two views; the lab, the victim. Life 61:90-107 N 18 '66
BRADDON, Russell
Richard Burton to Liz: I love thee not . . . Sat Eve Post 239:88-91 D 3 '66
BRADEMAS, John
New federal role. Sat R 49:52+ Ag 20 '66
BRADEN, Charles S.
Slightly sycophantic. Christian Cent 83:1473-4 N 30 '66
BRADERMAN, Eugene M.
United States policy on East-West trade; address, June 8, 1966. Dept State Bul 54: 1013-19 Je 27 '66; Same. Vital Speeches 32: 559-62 Jl 1 '66
BRADFORD, Gershom
Elena vs. Atlantic, 1928. Yachting 119:190 F '66

BRADFORD, Susanne
Girl you'd like to know. por Farm J 90:95
My '66
BRADLEY, Bill
All-European boy. il por Newsweek 67:79-
80 Ja 31 '66
Basketball: the graceful game. J. Larner. il
por Holiday 39:30+ F '66
Bit too much for Blighty. J. Lovesey. il por
Sports Illus 24:66-7 Mr 14 '66
Just a guy at Oxford. J. Mann. il pors
Sports Illus 24:52-8+ F 7 '66
Now it's Super Bill. por Sports Illus 25:82
S 19 '66
Super soph. por Newsweek 68:79 S 26 '66
BRADLEY, C. Paul
Rupture in Malaysia. bibliog f Cur Hist 50:
98-105 F '66
BRADLEY, Gene E.
Building a bigger Atlantic community market.
Harvard Bsns R 44:79-90 My '66
Thousand partnerships. Am Ed 2:1-4 Je '66
BRADLEY, John
Drawn by I. Bradley from Great Britton.
M. C. Black and S. P. Feld. il Antiques
90:502-9 O '66
BRADLEY, Lisa
Brief biography. S. Goodman. pors Dance
Mag 40:54-5 Mr '66
BRADLEY, Richard C.
Ruin for the Grand Canyon? Audubon Mag
68:34-41 Ja '66; Same abr. Read Digest
88:193-8 Ap '66
BRADLEY, Sam
Easter morning; poem. Christian Cent 83:423
Ap 6 '66
Springlight; poem. Commonweal 84:394 Je 24
'66
BRADLEY, Wendell P.
Lure of boating. Holiday 40:38-45+ Jl '66
BRADLEY, William Calvin, 2d. See Bradley,
B.
BRADLEY, William E. and Wright, F. S.
Visceral reflex activity: development in post-
natal rabbit. bibliog Science 152:216 Ap 8
'66
BRADLEY university, Peoria, Ill.
Bradley builds an addition; Cullom-Davis
library. R. M. Lightfoot, jr. il Library J
91:5895-6 D 1 '66
BRADNICK, Peggy Ann
Kidnapped! interview. ed. by J. Bird. pors
Sat Eve Post 239:25-9+ Jl 16 '66

about
Battle of Gobbler's Knob. il por Time 87:23
My 27 '66
Stalking the terror of Shade Gap. M. Mok. il
pors Life 60:32B-32E My 27 '66
Terror in the Tuscaroras. il pors Newsweek
67:29-30 My 30 '66
BRADSHAW, George
Champagne. Vogue 148:20 D '66
Gay hearts; story. Sat Eve Post 239:62-7
Ag 27 '66
Privileged class; story. Sat Eve Post 239:74-6
D 3 '66
Travel (cont) Vogue 147:57-8 Je '66
BRADSHAW, Hank
Come hither coyote. Field & S 71:44-5+ D
'66
Grandest hunting of all. Field & S 71:66-7+
N '66
Hitting the hot line. Outdoor Life 137:56-8+
F '66
Take a fishing trip now. Suc Farm 64:100F
Mr '66
BRADSHAW, John S. See Phleger, F. B. jt.
auth.
BRADY, Charles
Vinland Christmas 1003; poem. America 115:
825 D 24 '66
BRADY, Charles A.
In memoriam: Arthur Evelyn St John Waugh,
1903-1966. America 114:594-5 Ap 23 '66
BRADY, Ian
In ghastly transcripts, a test of our times.
P. H. Johnson. il Life 61:62+ Ag 12 '66
Maximum sentence. Time 87:42 My 13 '66
Moorland murders. por Newsweek 67:52 My
16 '66
Trial begins. il por Newsweek 67:34 My 2 '66
BRADY, Mathew B.
Americans not everybody knows. R. Sharp.
por PTA Mag 60:30-2 My '66
BRADY, Mildred Edie
Excerpt from statement, May 7, 1965. Cong
Digest 45:188-1 Je '66
BRAESTRUP, Peter, and Ottaway, David
In Algeria it's not yah, yah, Boumediene!
but wait and see. N Y Times Mag p36-7+
F 13 '66
BRAGG, Lawrence
Art of talking about science; excerpts from
address, December 28, 1966. Science 154:
1613-16 D 30 '66

BRAHMANISM
See also
Caste
BRAHMS, Johannes
Brahms string quartets, and a great Schu-
mann quintet; Serkin-Budapest and the
Wellers. H. Glass. il Am Rec G 32:603 Mr
'66
Julius Katchen finishes the complete Brahms
piano music. S. Sell. Am Rec G 32:706-9
Ap '66
Records:
Deutsche volkslieder. Opera N 31:34 Ja
21 '67
BRAHMS-Schoenberg quartet; ballet. See Bal-
lets—Criticisms
BRAILLE editions. See Blind, Books for the
BRAILLE periodicals. See Blind, Periodicals
for the
BRAILLE-reading machines. See Reading ma-
chines
BRAIN, Dennis
Brief candles. H. Goldsmith. por Hi Fi 16:
50-1 F '66
BRAIN
Aminooxyacetic acid: interactions with
gamma-aminobutyric acid and the blood-
brain barrier. M. A. Fisher and others.
bibliog il Science 153:1668-70 S 30 '66
And an upside-down look at the brain. il
Life 60:66 Mr 11 '66
Brain information service established. Sci N
89:500 Je 18 '66
Brain research; report on third visiting
seminar of the International brain research
organization. A. Lajtha and others. Sci-
ence 152:550+ Ap 22 '66
Brain sensitivity to alcohol in inbred mouse
strains. R. Kakihana and others. bibliog il
Science 154:1574-5 D 23 '66
Brain's electrochemical telegraph system. il
Fortune 74:102-3 Jl 1 '66
Cell disruptions noted; sodium-potassium
concentrations in the brain. Sci N 90:101
Ag 13 '66
Deficits in passive avoidance and fear condi-
tioning in mice with septal lesions. B. M.
Slotnick and M. E. Jarvik. bibliog il Sci-
ence 154:1207-8 D 2 '66
Inside the molecules of the mind. L. Lessing.
il Fortune 74:100-5+ Jl 1 '66
Interaction of cortex and superior colliculus
in mediation of visually guided behavior in
the cat. J. M. Sprague. bibliog il Science
153:1544-7 S 23 '66
Magnesium pemoline: enhancement of brain
RNA polymerases. A. J. Glasky and L. N.
Simon. bibliog il Science 151:702-3 F 11 '66
Man with a half-brain; implications of hemi-
spherectomy. Newsweek 68:57 Ag 1 '66
Mind, brain, and humanist values. R. W.
Sperry. Bul Atomic Sci 22:2-6 S '66
Monoamine oxidase activity in various parts
of the rat brain during the estrous cycle.
A. J. Zolovick and others. bibliog il Science
154:649 N 4 '66
Mystery of the brain. J. F. Corwith. il
Sat R 49:44-5 My 7 '66
New light on how certain amines act in the
brain: report of symposium on Parkinson's
disease. T. L. Campbell. il Science 152:232-
6+ Ap 8 '66
Non-nervous brain tissue plays caretaker
role. Sci N L 89:87 F 5 '66
Pills to help us remember? Cylert. I. Asimov.
il N Y Times Mag p38-9+ O 9 '66
Research in America; report on Delgado-
Krech research on behavioral reactions to
electronic stimulation of the brain. J. Lear.
il Sat R 49:61-4 F 5 '66
Science is finding ways to make you smarter.
T. Drury. il Nations Bsns 54:102-4+ Je '66
Sex differences in the brain. S. Levine. il
Sci Am 214:84-90 Ap '66
That old chemical complex, the human mind.
I. Asimov. il N Y Times Mag p 12-13+
Jl 3 '66
Your brain: the most complicated machine.
L. Galton. il Pop Sci 188:86-9 Mr '66
See also
Brain waves
Cerebral cortex
Hypothalamus
Memory
Nervous system
Sleep

Diseases
Cerebrovascular disease; report on fifth
Princeton conference. C. H. Millikan. Sci-
ence 152:803-5+ My 6 '66
See also
Hydrocephalus

Localization of functions
Arousal center located in core of brain;
reticular formation. Sci N 89:419 My 28 '66

BRAIN—*Continued*

Surgery

Brain surgery by computer. S. Hopkins. il Pop Mech 126:94-7 D '66

Clot of metal; magnetic surgery to treat stroke victims. il Newsweek 68:70 S 26 '66

Cool blood for brains. il Sci N 90:37 Jl 16 '66

Dominant hemispherectomy: preliminary report on neuropsychological sequelae. A. Smith and C. W. Burklund. bibliog Science 153:1280-2 S 9 '66

Life with half a brain. il Time 88:64 Ag 5 '66

New era in brain surgery. Sci Digest 59:18-19 Mr '66

Saving the brain of General Wood; Dr Cushing. T. Berland. il Todays Health 44:28-33+ S '66

Wounds and injuries

Bobby joins his world: 5 million brain-damaged children can be helped. C. Mangel. il Look 30:84-6+ N 15 '66

Child's brain cited in ills. Sci N 90:55 Jl 23 '66

Head injury: the big killer. H. G. Earl. il Todays Health 44:18-21 D '66

BRAIN acetylcholine. See Acetylcholine

BRAIN damaged children

Bobby joins his world: 5 million brain-damaged children can be helped. C. Mangel. il Look 30:84-6+ N 15 '66

Who is this child? E. F. Lehman and R. E. Hall. il Am Ed 2:10-12 Ap '66

BRAIN research

Hormonal influences on brain organization in infant rats. S. Levine and R. F. Mullins, jr. bibliog il Science 152:1585-92 Je 17 '66

Nerve cells and Parkinsonism. P. McBroom. il Sci N 90:492 D 10 '66

BRAIN stimulation. See Stimulus and response

BRAIN surgery. See Brain—Surgery

BRAIN tumors. See Tumors

BRAIN waves

Brain affects crime; no correlation between EEG abnormality and brain disorder. Sci N 90:98 Ag 13 '66

BRAINARD, Franklin

West of a child's window; poem. Horn Bk 42:671 D '66

BRAINWASHING

Mind control is good, bad. A. J. Budrys. il Esquire 65:106-9 My '66

BRAKE, Brian

Modern thrust with a Roman spear. G. P. Hunt. il por Life 60:5 Je 17 '66

BRAKE, John R.

What's ahead in farm credit? Suc Farm 64:86 Ap '66

BRAKES, Automobile

Beat the drum with discs; with photographs. T. Medley. il Hot Rod 19:42-4 F '66

Brakes get more stopping power. il Pop Sci 189:100-3 O '66

Great brake debate: disks or drums? J. Norbye; S. Yunick. il Pop Sci 189:68-73 Ag '66

Stone-age emergency brake. P. Perrett. il Pop Mech 125:161 Mr '66

Tale of whoa. J. McFarland. il Hot Rod 19:58-61 S '66

To stop a Squire! discs give wagon drivers a brake. J. Ethridge. il Motor T 18:49 Ap '66

Warning! those cheap brake repair jobs are murder. D. L. Gregg. il Bet Hom & Gard 45:12 Ja '67

Testing

Does your new car have the power to stop? J. P. Norbye. il Pop Sci 188:200-3 Ap '66

BRANCA, John M.

Specifications for a maintenance specialist. por Parks & Rec 1:39+, 390+ Ja, My '66

BRANCH factories, Foreign

Logistics for the international manufacturer. R. E. McGarrah. Harvard Bsns R 44:154+ Mr '66

Site selection: industrial gamesmanship. D. Balaban. il Duns R 87:pt2 185-6+ Mr '66

BRANCO, Humberto Castello. See Castello Branco, H.

BRAND, Donald D.

Mexico. bibliog Focus 16:1-6 Je '66

BRAND, Max, pseud. See Faust, F.

BRAND, Paul Wilson

Sahib doctor: the healing surgeon of Vellore; condensation of Ten fingers for God. D. C. Wilson. il por Read Digest 88:207-10+ Je '66

BRAND names. See Trade names

BRANDBORG, Stewart M.

Setting new patterns under a landmark law; adaptation of address. Liv Wildn 30:40-51 Spr '66

Statement for Smokies wilderness hearing. Liv Wildn 30:19-30 Spr '66

BRANDENBURGER, Barbara

Leslie Linder. Horn Bk 42:686-9 D '66

BRANDES, Gina

Architect achieves drama and economy in her own house. il Arch Rec 140:189-92 O '66

BRANDING

See also

Livestock—Branding

BRANDO, Marlon

We're having lunch today with Marlon Brando, folks; interview. pors Esquire 65:98-9 F '66

about

Charlie and his countess. J. Hamilton. il pors Look 30:96-100+ Ap 19 '66

Marlon Brando; an American hero. P. Kael. por Atlan 217:72-5 Mr '66

BRANDON, Donald

New books. Cath World 203:53-5 Ap '66

BRANDON, Henry

State of affairs. See issues of Saturday review

BRANDON, Margaret A.

Reading is for the birds. Sr Schol 89:sup22-3 O 28 '66

BRANDON, S. G. F.

Trial of Jesus. Horizon 9:4-13 Wint '67

BRANDON, William

Paris in spring. Sat R 49:4+ My 21 '66

BRANDS, Cattle. See Cattle brands

BRANDT, Karl

Peaceful social and economic change; address, August 18, 1966. Vital Speeches 32:712-17 S 15 '66

BRANDT, Thomas O.

Professor: educator, scholar, or both? Sch & Soc 94:381-2 N 12 '66

BRANDT, Willy

Bonn tries consensus. il por Bsns W p41 D 3 '66

Willy's return. il por Time 87:40 Je 17 '66

BRANDY

Cognac, the soul of wine. H. Johnson. il House & Gard 129:138+ F '66

Drink for any hour, cognac. il House & Gard 129:136-7 F '66

BRANIFF international airways

Braniff considers SST for Latin America. G. C. Wilson. Aviation W 84:45+ My 23 '66

Colors are fun. il Time 87:90 Ap 15 '66

Panagra acquisition approved. Aviation W 85:40 O 24 '66

727QC shows high utilization in initial operations. E. J. Bulban. il Aviation W 85:84-6+ O 31 '66

Transpacific routes requested by Braniff. Aviation W 84:28 F 28 '66

BRANLEY, Franklyn M.

Christmas sky. Redbook 128:45+ D '66

BRANN, James

Now, teaching by computer; reprint. Sci Digest 59:78-81 Ap '66

BRANNER, Robert

Place to hold a past. Sat R 49:34 Jl 30 '66

BRANSON, Helen K.

For superb flavor, grow your asparagus. Flower Grower 53:59-60 F '66

BRANSON, Herman

Director of pre-college centers discusses helping the disadvantaged student choose a college. NEA J 55:43-4 O '66

BRANT. See Geese, Wild

BRASILIA, Brazil

Architecture

Arithmetic in Brasília; Latin-style Rockefeller Center. il Time 87:94 My 27 '66

BRASSENS, Georges

Letter from Paris; performances at Le théâtre national populaire. Genét. New Yorker 42:151-2+ O 8 '66

BRASSES

See also

Horse brasses

BRATKOWSKI, Edward

Starr's understudy. il por Newsweek 69:48 Ja 2 '67

BRATT, Elmer C.

Recent thinking on economic growth and fluctuations. bibliog f Ann Am Acad 364:158-68 Mr '66

BRATTON, Fred Gladstone

Adventures in Ilium. Sat R 49:38 N 26 '66

BRAUN, Japnell D. See Downs, G. L. jt. auth.

BRAUN, Sigismund, freiherr von
European common market; address, November 2, 1966. Vital Speeches 33:152-5 D 15 '66
BRAUN, Werner. See Nakano, M. jt. auth.
BRAVES (baseball) See Baseball clubs
BRAWNER, Clint
Hardware for Indy '66. pors Motor T 18: 26-7 Mr '66
BRAY, Barbara
Ibn Khaldūn: man of history; excerpts from radio program. UNESCO Courier 19:4-10 Je '66
BRAY, Robert S. and Volin, L. K.
(eds) Service for everyone. bibliog Wilson Lib Bul 40:816-57 My '66
BRAYBROOKE, Neville
Across Brittany by taxi. Christian Cent 83: 712-13 Je 1 '66
BRAYER rubbings. See Rubbings
BRAYMER, Lawrence
Obituary
Mod Phot por 30:82 Mr '66
BRAZIL
See also
Agriculture—Brazil
Amazon Valley
Americana, Brazil
Elections—Brazil
Finance—Brazil
Foreign students in Brazil
Income tax—Brazil
Investments, Foreign (in Brazil)
Libraries—Brazil
Mining industry and finance—Brazil
Political campaigns—Brazil
Portuguese language in Brazil
Postal service—Brazil
Roads—Brazil
Salvador
Science—Brazil
Trade unions—Brazil
Women—Brazil

Constitution
Making it formal. Time 88:42 D 16 '66

Economic conditions
In search of a miracle. Time 88:28 Ag 12 '66
See also
Finance—Brazil

Economic policy
Brazil: some success, much to do. il Bsns W p61-2 Ja 22 '66
Sudene: Superintendência do desenvolvimento do Nordeste, or the Government development agency for the Northeast. J. G. de Souza. il Américas 18:10-16 Ap '66
See also
Finance—Brazil

Industries
Building the Nordeste. il Time 88:100 S 9 '66
In Brazil, it's breakfast at Stern's; H. Stern's jewelry business. il Bsns W p 110-12+ My 14 '66
See also
Machine tool industry and trade

Politics and government
Atlantic report. Atlan 218:36+ D '66
Brazil; government by the consent of the military. New Repub 154:17-18 Ap 16 '66
Brazil nut. Commonweal 84:247-8 My 20 '66
Brazil's future. Commonweal 84:627 S 30 '66
Brazil's new head. Sr Schol 89:18-19 O 21 '66
Brazil's revolutionary government. C. N. Ronning. Cur Hist 51:296-300+ N '66
Democracy on the shelf. Time 88:37 O 28 '66
Elections in Brazil: the revolution digs in. N. Raymond and W. P. Carty. il Reporter 35:42-4 S 8 '66
Hard man to hang. Newsweek 67:61 Ap 11 '66
Magnificent reprobate. Time 87:42 Je 17 '66
Making of a president. Time 87:40 Ap 29 '66
Making of a president-elect. il Time 88:46+ O 7 '66
Next president? Newsweek 67:54 Ja 31 '66
Not-so-sure thing; Castelo Branco reasserts authority. il Newsweek 68:49 Jl 4 '66
Report from Brazil. F. C. Dias. America 115:546-8 N 5 '66
Some unpleasant business. il Time 89:30 Ja 13 '67
Top brass in Brazil. M. J. Kubic. New Repub 155:11-13 S 10 '66
Unwilling opposition; Brazilian Democratic movement. Time 88:34 Ag 19 '66
See also
Brazil—Constitution
Elections—Brazil

Race problems
Dixie city in Brazil: Americana. il Ebony 22:89-90+ N '66

Religious institutions and affairs
World around us (cont of) News of the Christian world. Christian Cent 83:381-2, 1064+, 1549-50 Mr 23, Ag 31, D 14 '66

Social policy
Sudene: Superintendência do desenvolvimento do Nordeste, or the Government development agency for the Northeast. J. G. de Souza. il Américas 18:10-16 Ap '66
BRAZIL and the United States
United States and Brazil: partners in progress; address, February 17, 1966. L. Gordon. Dept State Bul 54:620-4 Ap 18 '66
BRAZILIAN artists. See Artists, Brazilian
BRAZILIAN musicians. See Musicians, Brazilian
BRAZILIAN philosophy. See Philosophy, Latin American
BRAZILIANS
It's in the potato; Brazilian character and Portuguese language. P. Rónai. il Américas 18:17-23 N '66
BRAZILLER, George, incorporated
How Braziller reproduced The hours of Catherine of Cleves. il Pub W 191:88+ Ja 2 '67
BRAZZIEL, William F.
Negro history in the public schools: trends and prospects. Negro Hist Bul 29:35-6+ N '65
BREAD
And, oh, the aroma! C. Claiborne. il N Y Times Mag p23 Ja 1 '67
Baker's gift: small Swedish loaves; with recipe. il Sunset 137:148 D '66
Barbecue breads! il Bet Hom & Gard 44:110 Je '66
Good morning breads. N. Nichols. il Farm J 90:104-6 Mr '66
Good to the last crumb; recipes using bread. il Redbook 126:90-2+ Mr '66
Happy marriage; apricot-walnut tea bread; with recipe. il McCalls 93:60 My '66
It's a different hamburger when you make the bun. il Sunset 136:184 My '66
It's braid bread. il Sunset 136:98-9 Ap '66
Little loaves; with recipe. il Parents Mag 41:19 N '66
Miraculous popover. C. Claiborne. il N Y Times Mag p84 Je 5 '66
Roll with a hole; bagel, with recipes. il Seventeen 25:160-1+ Mr '66
Say good morning with a Christmas breakfast bread. il Sunset 137:116-18 D '66
She's popping in some poppy seed bread. il Sunset 136:218 Ap '66
Skip-a-step holiday breads. R. Holmberg. il Bet Hom & Gard 44:66-7+ D '66
Susan makes no-knead raisin loaf. M. F. Williams. il Good H 162:140 F '66
Things to do with refrigerated rolls; with recipes. il Ladies Home J 83:120 My '66
Why today's bread is better. W. W. Bauer. il Todays Health 44:60-4 D '66
You bake these loaves in coffee cans; with recipes. il Sunset 137:231-2 O '66
Yule breads and cakes; with recipes. P. Cannon. il Ladies Home J 83:104-5+ D '66
BREAD pudding. See Puddings
BREAKFAST foods. See Cereal foods
BREAKFASTS
Early start, then breakfast on the road. il Sunset 136:188-9 My '66
Huevos for breakfast; with recipes. C. Claiborne. il N Y Times Mag p75-6 My 15 '66
I love breakfast! with recipes; symposium. il Seventeen 25:190-3 S '66
Model schools serve model breakfasts. il Seventeen 25:202 S '66
Off to school with a good breakfast. N. Toop. Parents Mag 41:36 S '66
Sweet Sunday; with recipes. Mlle 62:89 Ap '66
See also
Brunches
BREAKTHROUGH; story. See Du Maurier, D.
BREAM, Julian
Viva the no-voltage guitar! C. Harman. Life 61:12 N 4 '66
BREAST
Bosom: a few facts. il Seventeen 25:134-5 Ap '66
Expectant mother; breast changes during pregnancy and after. J. W. Huffman. Redbook 127:28+ Ag '66
BREAST feeding. See Infants—Nutrition
BREATHING. See Respiration
BREATHING apparatus. See Respiratory apparatus
BRECHER, Edward. See Brecher, R. jt. auth.

BRECHER, Ruth, and Brecher, Edward
Disgraceful facts about infant deaths in the
U.S. McCalls 93:82-3+ F '66
Every sixth teen-age girl in Connecticut—.
N Y Times Mag p6-7+ My 29 '66
Strict homes, happy children. McCalls 93:66-
7+ Jl '66
Why some mothers reject their babies. Red-
book 127:48-9+ My '66

BRECHT, Bertolt
Are the people infallible? poem; tr. by E.
Bentley. Nation 202:461 Ap 18 '66

about

Caucasian chalk circle; tr. by E. Bentley.
Criticism
America 114:603-4 Ap 23 '66
Commentary 41:76-7 Je '66
Commonweal 84:177 Ap 29 '66
Life 60:15 Ap 22 '66
Nation 202:436-7 Ap 11 '66
New Repub 154:30+ Ap 16 '66
New Yorker 42:122 Ap 2 '66
Newsweek il 67:90-1 Ap 4 '66
Sat R 49:53 Ap 9 '66
Time il 87:63 Ap 1 '66
Vogue 147:54 Je '66
Devil's prayerbook. M. Esslin. New Repub
155:24+ N 26 '66
From Folkways, Brecht by Bentley; Excep-
tion and the rule. S. Potter. Am Rec G
32:746-7 Ap '66
Good woman of Setzuan. Criticism
Sat R 49:55 Je 4 '66
Profiles. H. Arendt. New Yorker 42:68-70+
N 5 '66
Romantically anti-bourgeois. M. Hamburger.
Nation 203:458-9 O 31 '66

BRECKINRIDGE, Aida de Acosta
Americans not everybody knows. J. A. Spalding. por PTA Mag 60:11-13 Je '66

BREECH, Ernest Robert
Reviving the giants; interview. pors Nations Bsns 54:48-9+ O '66

about

Pilot behind TWA's success. il por Bsns W
p 102-4+ Ap 23 '66

BREEDER reactors. See Nuclear reactors
BREEDING
See also
Cattle breeding
Genetics
Reindeer breeding
Reproduction
Swine breeding

BREEDLOVE, Craig
600 mph, what it's really like! ed. by C.
Maher. por Motor T 18:46 Mr '66

BREELING, James L.
Medicine '66. Todays Health 45:36-40 Ja '67
Volunteer foreign aid: M.D.s' mission to
Honduras. Todays Health 44:20-4 Jl '66

BREEZEWAYS
Breezeway is really their outdoor store-
house. il Sunset 136:152 Mr '66
Pleasant entry. il Sunset 136:80-3 F '66

BREGMAN, Alexander
Communist car: an upside-down status symbol. Reporter 34:30-1 My 5 '66

BREIER, Harold A.
Asking for trouble. Christian Cent 83:1202
O 5 '66

BREL, Jacques
Jazz notes. E Larrabee. Harper 232-130 Ap
66

BRENDAN: story. See Wallace, M.

BRENER, Stephen W.
Hotels and motels reflect a changing world.
Arch Rec 140:137-8 Ag '66

BRENNAN, Francis
It's still a man's world. Sat R 49:41 N 19
'66

BRENNAN, Maeve
I see you, Bianca: story. New Yorker 42:32-6
Je 11 '66
Twelfth wedding anniversary; story. New
Yorker 42:60-6 S 24 '66

BRENNAN, Niall
Johnson visit. Commonweal 85:215-16 N 25
'66

BRENNAN, Wendy M. and others
Age differences in infants' attention to pat-
terns of different complexities. bibliog
Science 151:354-6 Ja 21 '66

BRENNAN, William Joseph, 1906-
Brennan v Tigar. A. Kopkind. New Repub
155:21-2 Ag 27 '66

BRENNECKE, Harry E.
Speak to me brother; poem. Negro Hist Bul
29:113 F '66

BRENNER, Patricia H. and Brenner, R. L.
What really happens when your obstetrician
is late. Ladies Home J 83:42+ Je '66

BRENNER, Robert L. See Brenner, P. H. jt.
auth.

BRENT, R. Spencer
What me fly with the Blue Angels? por
Flying 79:98-100 N '66

BRENTANO'S bookstores. See Booksellers and
bookselling—United States

BRENTON, Myron
When it's hard to say good-bye. Parents
Mag 41:42-3+ Ap '66

about

Trade winds. J. G. Fuller. Sat R 49:16-17 Jl
30 '66

BRESGEN, Cesar
Last months in Mittersill; excerpt from Anton von Webern. Sat R 49:60-1 My 28 '66

BRESLAU. See Wroclaw, Poland

BRESLER, Jerry
Treatment. il por Time 88:68-9 Jl 8 '66

BRESLIN, James E. See Breslin, J.

BRESLIN, Jimmy
Speaking out. Sat Eve Post 239:10+ S 24 '66
Struck paper, famous and needed, goes down.
Life 61:26-9 Ag 26 '66

BRESS, Hyman
New York concert. S. Fleming. Hi Fi 16:133
F '66

BRESSLER, Doris
Good teeth for life. Parents Mag 41:72-3+
N '66

BRESSON, Henri Cartier-. See Cartier-
Bresson, H.

BREST, Jorge Romero
Image and imagination. Américas 18:30-3 N
'66

BRETON, André
Letter from Paris. Genêt. New Yorker 42:
202-4 O 22 '66
Magician of innocent wonder. A. Balakian.
Por Sat R 49:31-2 O 29 '66
Philosophy of surrealism, by F. Alquié. Re-
view
Sat R 49:33-4 Mr 12 '66. A. Balakian

BRETONNE, Nicolas Edme Restif de la. See
Restif de la Bretonne, N. E.

BRETT, Gerard
English furniture after printed designs in
the Royal Ontario museum. Antiques 89:
386-90 Mr '66

BRETT, Robin
Cohenite in meteorites: a proposed origin.
bibliog Science 153:60-2 Jl 1 '66

BREUER, Herb
Case for close metering. il U S Camera 29:
62-3 Je '66
Handhold a 300mm lens. il U S Camera 29:
60-1 Je '66
Making the scene. il U S Camera 30:44-5 Ja
'67
Wide on women. il U S Camera 29:54-5 N '66

BREUER, Marcel
Houses by Breuer: laboratory for design.
Arch Rec 140:125-36 N '66

about

Cliffhanger on Madison avenue. il Time 88:
88-91 O 7 '66
Darts of stone; F.D.R. memorial. il Time 88:
26 D 30 '66
Most recent architecture of Marcel Breuer;
with statement by the architect. il Arch
Rec 139:171-86 Ap '66
People are talking about. . . il por Vogue
148:218-19 O 1 '66

BREUER, Robert
Bassarids in Salzburg. Sat R 49:55+ Ag 27
'66
Waltz king and his ancestors. Sat R 49:126-
7 Mr 12 '66

BREVARD COUNTY, Fla.
Today in Florida; Gannett group's new daily.
il Newsweek 67:82 Mr 28 '66

BREW, John O.
Salvage archaeology: saving the past from
the present. Nation 203:117-20 Ag 8 '66

BREWER, Ebenezer Cobham
Bounty of Brewer. G. Frazier. Holiday 40:
106+ Ag '66

BREWER, Gay, Jr
No. 2 & blue. il por Time 87:104 Ap 29 '66

BREWER, Gene C.
Business career; address. January 12, 1966.
Vital Speeches 32:297-302 Mr 1 '66

BREWER, John M.
Ghetto children know what they're talking
about. N Y Times Mag p32-5 D 25 '66

BREWER, Roy
Walt Disney, RIP. Nat R 19:17 Ja 10 '67

BREWER, Tommy
Education counts more today than it ever
did; ed. by H. F. Waters. il por Newsweek
67:69 Mr 21 '66

BREWER, William Conant, Jr
One way to Newfoundland. bibliog por Yachting 119:65-8+ My '66

BREWERIES
Disdaneful of competition; Carlsberg and Tuborg. il Time 88:79 Jl 15 '66

BREWING industries
See also
Falstaff brewing corporation
Piel brothers, incorporated

BREWSTER, Carroll W.
Reporter at large. J. McPhee. New Yorker 42:101-2+ Mr 5 '66

BREWSTER, Daniel Baugh
Collapse and chaos, unless we do something; excerpts from address, October 13, 1966. U S News 61:54 N 7 '66

BREWSTER, R. H.
Five basic steps in lawn maintenance. Pop Gard 17:76-9 Mr '66

BREZHNEV, Leonid Il'ich
Brezhnev and Kosygin: the cult of impersonality. P. Grose. il pors N Y Times Mag p34-7+ O 9 '66
Brezhnev: first among equals now? il por U S News 62:12 Ja 2 '67
Hero. il por Time 88:21-2 D 30 '66
Kremlin travelers: what they're up to. il por U S News 61:16 D 12 '66
Meeting of the board. il por Newsweek 67: 49-51 Ap 11 '66
On the road again. Nat R 18:506-7 My 31 '66
People of the week. U S News 60:22 Ap 11 '66
Russia at the crossroads. R. Sherrod. il por Sat Eve Post 239:28-33 Mr 26 '66
Soviet promises of a better life, but—. il por U S News 60:22 Ap 18 '66

BRIBERY
Invitation to bribery; corruption among zoning officials. A. Balk. Harper 233:18+ O '66
When I looked in those files, my eyes popped; California tax scandal. J. Phelan. il Sat Eve Post 239:23-9 S 10 '66

BRICE, Edward Warner
Brice named to high USOE post. por Sr Schol 88:sup6 F 11 '66

BRICE, M. A.
Sales manager's alter ego. Duns R 88:59+ N '66

BRICKMAN, William W.
Foreign books for educators. Sch & Soc 94: 359-66 O 29 '66
Historical background of international cooperation among universities. bibliog f Sch & Soc 94:227-34 Ap 16 '66
U.S. books for educators (cont) Sch & Soc 94:288+ Sum '66

BRIDAL showers. See Entertaining

BRIDES
See also
Weddings

BRIDGE (game)
Break a rule and get a break. C. Goren. il Sports Illus 25:75 O 24 '66
Bridge nuts, doubled and redoubled. J. K. Sale. il N Y Times Mag p32-3+ My 8 '66
Chance to show up the experts. C. Goren. il Sports Illus 26:48-9 Ja 16 '67
Choked by the smother play. C. Goren. il Sports Illus 24:72-3 My 16 '66
D.A.'s assistant wins the point race; P. Rank of Contra Costa County, Calif. C. Goren. il Sports Illus 24:58 F 21 '66
Good game for gamblers. C. Goren. il Sports Illus 25:90-1 N 14 '66
Good play by a first baseman. C. Goren. il Sports Illus 24:110+ Ap 18 '66
Invasion of Jeremy Flint. C. Goren. il Sports Illus 24:78-9 Je 13 '66
It happens in the best of families. C. Goren. il Sports Illus 25:60-1 D 12 '66
Mischievous bid foments a fiasco. C. Goren. il Sports Illus 25:47 Ag 15 '66
Mr Goren's Christmas quiz. C. Goren. il Sports Illus 25:98-100 D 19 '66
One way to get expert advice. C. Goren. il Sports Illus 24:50 F 7 '66
Remember, the enemy is eavesdropping. C. Goren. il Sports Illus 24:70 Mr 21 '66
Strange case of the vanishing loser. C. Goren. Sports Illus 25:66-7 Jl 18 '66
Throw MUD in their eye; opening lead from middle, up, down. C. Goren. il Sports Illus 25:69-70 N 21 '66
Trick for the wizard. C. Goren. il Sports Illus 25:73-4 S 26 '66
Unconventional convention that works. C. Goren. il Sports Illus 26:55 Ja 9 '67
You can make something out of nothing. C. Goren. il Sports Illus 24:46 Ja 24 '66
See also
American contract bridge league

BRIDGE CANYON DAM (proposed) See Dams

BRIDGE players
Bridge nuts, doubled and redoubled. J. K. Sale. il N Y Times Mag p32-3+ My 8 '66
Call for a redeal shuffled the standings; North American international team winner of Vanderbilt cup. C. Goren. il Sports Illus 24:58-9 Mr 28 '66
Chance to show up the experts. C. Goren. il Sports Illus 26:48-9 Ja 16 '67
Choked by the smother play. C. Goren. il Sports Illus 24:72-3 My 16 '66
Dogmeat was hard to swallow; richest tournament ever held. J. Olsen. il Sports Illus 25:100-2+ N 14 '66
Final win for the Blue; Italy's Blue team to disband. C. A. Perroux. il Sports Illus 24:34-6+ My 23 '66
Frenchman with finesse; won European championship in Warsaw, Poland. C. Goren. il Sports Illus 25:84-5 O 10 '66
Good game for gamblers. C. Goren. il Sports Illus 25:90-1 N 14 '66
Guests were two-time losers. C. Goren. il Sports Illus 25:94-5 D 5 '66
Invasion of Jeremy Flint. C. Goren. il Sports Illus 24:78-9 Je 13 '66
Life status for a prodigy; sixteen-year-old Kyle Larsen. C. Goren. il Sports Illus 24: 68-9 Mr 14 '66
Major bid for the Olympiad; World team championship, St Vincent, Italy. C. Goren. il Sports Illus 24:84+ Ap 11 '66
Remember, the enemy is eavesdropping. C. Goren. il Sports Illus 24:70 Mr 21 '66
You can make something out of nothing. C. Goren. il Sports Illus 24:46 Ja 24 '66
You opened with that kind of rubbish? International team trials. C. Goren. il Sports Illus 25:76+ N 28 '66

BRIDGE tables. See Tables

BRIDGE tournaments
Call for a redeal shuffled the standings; North American international team winner of Vanderbilt cup. C. Goren. il Sports Illus 24:58-9 Mr 28 '66
Caught twice by the same squeeze; European championship in Warsaw. C. Goren. il Sports Illus 25:72-3 O 17 '66
Cut by a jewel of a play; Dutch victory in World pair Olympiad in Amsterdam. C. Goren. il Sports Illus 25:47 Ag 8 '66
Dogmeat was hard to swallow; richest tournament ever held. J. Olsen. il Sports Illus 25:100-2+ N 14 '66
Final win for the Blue; Italy's Blue team to disband. C. A. Perroux. il Sports Illus 24:34-6+ My 23 '66
Frenchman with finesse; winner of European championship in Warsaw, Poland. C. Goren. il Sports Illus 25:84-5 O 10 '66
Good way to show finesse; European championships in Warsaw. C. Goren. il Sports Illus 25:119 S 12 '66
Just when our hopes were up the Italians set us down; World bridge team championship in St Vincent. C. Goren. il Sports Illus 24:72+ My 20 '66
Major bid for the Olympiad; World team championship, St Vincent, Italy. C. Goren. il Sports Illus 24:84+ Ap 11 '66
Old Mathe uses his old math; World contract bridge team championship, St Vincent, Italy. C. Goren. il Sports Illus 24: 72 My 2 '66
One time when a loser on a loser is a loser; World bridge team championship. C. Goren. il Sports Illus 25:52 Jl 25 '66
Solution of a travel problem; getting to the dummy; hand from Bermuda tournament. C. Goren. il Sports Illus 24:58 F 28 '66
Two swings to a knockout; battle for the Spingold trophy at Denver. C. Goren. il Sports Illus 25:56 S 5 '66
When Culbertson's man outsmarted himself. C. Goren. il Sports Illus 25:66 N 7 '66
You opened with that kind of rubbish? International team trials. C. Goren. il Sports Illus 25:76+ N 28 '66

BRIDGEPORT, Conn.
We put new life in emergency reporting. S. J. Tedesco. il Am City 81:112-13 Mr '66

BRIDGES, Harry
On the waterfront: gentler roar from a labor lion. por Bsns W p 109 Jl 30 '66

BRIDGES
Bridge that breathes; Europa bridge, in the Austrian Tirol. J. Wechsberg. Holiday 41: 124a-124e+ Ja '67
People bridge, the auto bridge, the bridge stair, the roof bridge. il Sunset 137:92-5 O '66

BRIDGES—*Continued*

Maintenance and repair

How to rehabilitate a bridge. A. Lichtenstein. il Am City 81:79-81 Jl '66
Pneumatic concrete saves historic Key West bridge. il Am City 81:84-5 Je '66

BRIDGES, Foot
How to bridge a gap. il Pop Gard 17:20-3 Ag '66

BRIDGES, Suspension
Suspension bridges cross a new frontier; Severn River bridge linking England and south Wales. il Bsns W p 104-5 S 10 '66

BRIDGES, Wooden
See also
Covered bridges

BRIDGES in art
Birth of a bridge; Vincent Thomas bridge, San Pedro, Calif. A. Riley. il Am Artist 30:39-41+ F '66

BRIDGWATER, William
Obituary
Pub W por 190:66-7 D 26 '66

BRIDPORT, Hugh
Hugh Bridport, Philadelphia miniaturist, engraver, and lithographer. W. Craven. il Antiques 89:548-52 Ap '66

BRIDWELL, Nathan
Stepladders to art. Design 67:4-7 Mr '66

BRIEN, Alan
One man's meat. Sat R 49:55 F 5 '66
Theatre (cont) Vogue 148:50 Ag 15; 206 S 1 '66

BRIER, Herbert S.
Amateur equipment jamboree 1966. Pop Electr 25:67-75+ Ag '66
Amateur radio. See issues of Popular electronics
Heathkit SB-100 transceiver. Pop Electr 24:85-6+ Je '66

BRIGANDS and robbers
Case of the plodding highwayman or the Po8 of crime. K. Kraft and P. Kraft. il Am Heritage 18:50-3+ D '66
Delaware's amazon outlaw. M. B. Duda. il Negro Hist Bul 29:153-4 Ap '66

BRIGGS, Raymond
House that Jack built. J. Fritz. il Horn Bk 42:681-3 D '66

BRIGGS, Ruth
Colonel & the senator. il por Time 88:15 Ag 26 '66

BRIGHAM, Robert
Changing way of life at the hammer and sickle corral. Life 60:69-71+ Ap 22 '66

BRIGHT, Barney
Model venture thrives on space. il por Bsns W p 177 Mr 19 '66

BRIGHT, Richard Louis
Back to the drawing boards. por Am Ed 2:14-17 My '66

BRIGHT young man; story. See Cohen, M.

BRIGHTBILL, Charles K.
Obituary
Parks & Rec por 1:857 O '66

BRIGHTON pavilion. See Palaces

BRILL, Daniel Herbert
Where the Fed gets its bold new ideas. por Bsns W p 101-2+ D 10 '66

BRILL, Earl H.
Sex is dead! Christian Cent 83:957-9 Ag 3 '66

BRILL, James A.
What is Project Discovery discovering? Sr Schol 89:sup8+ O 7 '66

BRIMER, John Burton
Home garden notebook. See issues of Flower grower, the home garden

BRIMMER, Andrew F.
Mediator moves into the Fed. por Bsns W p 124+ Mr 5 '66
Outlook now: tighter credit, higher interest rates. por U S News 60:113-14 Mr 14 '66
Surprise choice. por Newsweek 67:72 Mr 7 '66

BRINDLEY, G. W. and Millhollen, G. L.
Chemisorption of water at high temperatures on kaolinite: effect on dehydroxylation. bibliog Science 152:1385 Je 3 '66

BRINE shrimp. See Shrimps

BRINER, William
Miniature house started a town. Hobbies 71:110 Ja '67

BRINHART, Betty
Bulbs to lift & store now. Flower Grower 53:40-2 O '66
Poppy planting time. Flower Grower 53:24-5 Ag '66

BRINK, David
Show goes on. Parks & Rec 1:561-2 Jl '66

BRINK, Paul L.
Why web offset for books? summary of address. Pub W 190:98+ Jl 4 '66

BRINKLEY, David
Anniversary talk with Huntley & Brinkley; interview, ed. by J. F. Fixx. por McCalls 94:56+ O '66
about
Star system and TV news. R. L. Tobin. Sat R 49:59-60 Ap 9 '66

BRINTON, Crane
Time for catching up to change. Sat R 49:34+ O 15 '66

BRINTON, Harry
Jacksonville accents color. Library J 91:5852-4 D 1 '66

BRISTER, Bob
Cozumel: the island with everything. Field & S 70:68-70+ Mr '66

BRISTLECONE pine. See Pine

BRISTOL, Dave
Hottest team in baseball. W. Leggett. por Sports Illus 25:26-7 Ag 22 '66

BRISTOL, Horace
Bitter memories and cautious hopes. Sat R 49:53 Jl 23 '66
From tea to transistors. Sat R 49:44+ N 5 '66

BRISTOL, Conn.
1,500 lights at no added cost. H. J. Wojtusik. il Am City 81:123 D '66

BRISTOL Siddeley engines, limited
Flying high with Rolls. il Time 88:99-100 S 9 '66

BRITAIN. See Great Britain

BRITAIN, Battle of. See World war, 1939-1945 —Great Britain

BRITISH
Letter home: the English, more outspoken and more unshockable than anyone in Europe. J. Crosby. Esquire 65:38+ Mr '66
Youngest romantics. A. Pryce-Jones. il Vogue 148:248+ D '66

BRITISH aircraft corporation
BAC predicts Concorde market to reach 200 aircraft by 1975. Aviation W 86:49 Ja 16 '67
BAC withdraws from contest for Middle East airlines order. Aviation W 84:43 Ja 24 '66
U.K. presses BAC 111 sale in New Zealand. R. G. O'Lone. il Aviation W 84:32-4 F 7 '66

BRITISH-American tobacco company. See Tobacco industry and trade

BRITISH aviators. See Air pilots

BRITISH broadcasting corporation
Letter from London; production of Alice in Wonderland. M. Panter-Downes. New Yorker 42:103-4 Ja 14 '67
Science broadcasting in Britain; excerpts from address, February 16, 1966. A. E. Singer. Science 154:743-5 N 11 '66
Sex in the space age. il Newsweek 68:69-70 Ag 22 '66
Sinking the pirates? BBC pop music service. il Newsweek 69:41 Ja 9 '67
That's wonderland, baby! production of Cinderella and Alice in wonderland. Newsweek 69:46 Ja 2 '67

BRITISH coins. See Coins

BRITISH COLUMBIA
See also
Canoe River
Georgia, Strait of
San Juan Islands
Transportation—British Columbia
Vancouver Island

Foreign population

See also
Dukhobors

BRITISH COMMONWEALTH. See Commonwealth of nations

BRITISH company law. See Corporation law

BRITISH council of churches
Situation sex. Time 88:44 O 28 '66

BRITISH empire and Commonwealth games. See Track athletics

BRITISH European airways corporation
Bad patch. il Time 88:81 Jl 8 '66
BEA domestic routes to get Comet 4 jets. Aviation W 84:43 Ja 24 '66
BEA management faulty, pilots contend. H. J. Coleman. Aviation W 85:42-3 Jl 11 '66
BEA records $3.6-million profit despite loss on domestic routes. Aviation W 85:52 S 5 '66
BOAC, BEA planning joint cargo terminal; Heathrow international airport. H. J. Coleman. il Aviation W 85:49-50 N 21 '66
BOAC planning to buy six 747s; BEA is ordered to buy British. Aviation W 85:51 Ag 8 '66
U.K. rejects BEA capital structure plan. Aviation W 85:43 N 21 '66
What BEA really means; forced to buy made-in-Britain aircraft. Time 88:72 Ag 12 '66

BRITISH GUIANA
Note:
  For material after May 26, 1966, see heading
    Guyana
Atlantic report. Atlan 217:14+ Mr '66
Mixed welcome; royal visit. il Newsweek
  67:48 F 14 '66
    See also
Hunting—British Guiana
Kaieteur Falls

        Politics and government
Guyana is free, to go where? A. Verrier. il
  N Y Times Mag p54-5+ My 22 '66
Guyana on the eve. P. Crane. America 114:
  297-8 F 26 '66
BRITISH Labor party. See Labor party (Great
  Britain)
BRITISH military bases. See Military bases,
  British
BRITISH money. See Money—Great Britain
BRITISH motor corporation
U-turn for Jaguar; BMC to buy out Jaguar.
  il Time 88:86 Jl 22 '66
BRITISH museum
Aisle K; reading room. E. Hahn. New Yorker
  42:138+ S 17 '66; Reply. G. S. Dunbar. 42:
  233-7 N 12 '66
    See also
Elgin marbles
BRITISH museum general catalog of printed
  books
British museum catalogue completed. il Wil-
  son Lib Bul 41:255+ N '66
BRITISH national bibliography
Plans for centralized cataloging materialize;
  LC experimental cooperative arrangement
  with the BNB.   E. Hamer and A. Mc-
  Cormick. ALA Bul 60:559-60 Je '66
BRITISH Open. See Golf—Tournaments
BRITISH overseas airways corporation
BOAC, BEA planning joint cargo terminal;
  Heathrow international airport. H. J. Cole-
  man. il Aviation W 85:49-50 N 21 '66
BOAC given clear path to buy U.S. large
  subsonic transports. Aviation W 84:40 My
  16 '66
BOAC nearing decision on 747; subsonic jet
  transport. Aviation W 84:47 Ap 25 '66
BOAC planning to buy six 747s; BEA is
  ordered to buy British. Aviation W 85:51
  Ag 8 '66
BOAC plans new navigation system test. B.
  Miller. il Aviation W 85:41+ O 3 '66
Guthrie urges SST economics scrutiny. R. G.
  O'Lone. Aviation W 85:38-9 S 19 '66
BRITISH press. See Newspapers—Great Britain
BRITISH press conferences. See Press confer-
  ences
BRITISH royal collection. See Art—Private col-
  lections
BRITISH sailors. See Strikes—Great Britain
BRITISH scientists. See Scientists, British
BRITISH sculpture. See Sculpture, British
BRITISH trades union congress. See Trades
  union congress
BRITISH VIRGIN ISLANDS
Other islands, other reefs. B. Thielen. il Holi-
  day 40:60-7+ D '66
BRITISH visitors in the United States. See
  Foreign visitors in the United States
BRITTANY
Across Brittany by taxi. N. Braybrooke.
  Christian Cent 83:712-13 Je 1 '66
BRITTEN, Benjamin
Britten's Curlew River burnished bronze
  solemnity. A. Frankenstein. il Hi Fi 16:69-
  70 Je '66
Britten's Midsummer's night makes its stereo
  debut. E. Greenfield. Hi Fi 16:16+ D '66
Burning fiery furnace. Criticism
  New Yorker 42:73 Jl 23 '66
New York. J. W. Freeman. Opera N 30:30
  F 5 '66
Parable by Britten: Curlew River. J. Diether.
  il Am Rec G 32:1034-6 Jl '66
Rape of Lucretia. Criticism
  New Yorker 42:107 Ja 14 '67
  Sat R 50:34 Ja 21 '67
Records:
  Curlew River. Opera N 31:34 D 10 '66
Tippett premiere, Britten revivals. E Green-
  field. Hi Fi 16:160-1 Ap '66
Turn of the screw. Criticism
  Opera N 30:31 Mr 26 '66
BRITTEN, Roy J. See Waring, M. jt. auth.
BRITTER, Eric
Safe bridge to the future. Sat R 49:34 Ap
  23 '66
Six hundred million. Sat R 49:34-5 F 26 '66
BRITTER, Marguerite S.
(ed) Book notes and reviews. See issues of
  Yachting

BRITTON, Nan P.
Day with papa. Todays Health 44:30-3+
  F '66
BRNO, Czechoslovakia
Brno. J. Boraros. il Opera N 30:32 Ap 16 '66
        Music
Brno. J. W. Freeman. il Opera N 31:28 O 15
  '66
BROADCASTER'S nonprofit satellite service
ETV: Ford foundation calls for nonprofit
  satellite system. E. Langer. Science 153:
  962-4 Ag 26 '66
BROADCASTING, Radio. See Radio broadcast-
  ing
BROADCASTING and film commission. See
  National council of the churches of Christ
  in the United States of America—Broad-
  casting and film commission
BROADMAN press
New prize established for religious fiction
  book; Frost fiction award. Pub W 190:200
  Jl 11 '66
BROADWAY. See New York (city)—Streets
BROADWAY, New York (theater district) See
  New York (city)—Theater
BROCH, Terry
Where to get... Motor B 117:100-1 Ap '66
BROCINER, Victor
Design requirements for solid-state ampli-
  fiers. Electr World 75:39-41+ Ja '66
BROCK, Clifton
English translations of foreign social sci-
  ence materials. por Library J 91:1995-2002
  Ap 15 '66
BROCK, Paul
Europe's oddest outpost. Travel 125:36-7 Je
  '66
BROCK, Stanley E.
Cattle slayers of Shiwishi-win. Outdoor Life
  138:66-9+ N '66
Devil jaguar. pors Outdoor Life 137:44-7+
  F '66
BROCK, Thomas D.
Bacterial growth rate in the sea: direct
  analysis by thymidine autoradiography.
  bibliog Science 155:81-3 Ja 6 '67
BROCK, Van K.
Moth; poem. New Yorker 42:38 Ap 9 '66
BROCK, William Emerson, 1930–
Excerpt from debate, June 29, 1965. Cong
  Digest 45:27+ Ja '66
BROCKMAN, Christian Frank
Park for the North Cascades? por Am For
  72:8-11+ S '66
BROCKWAY, George P.
You do it because you love somebody. Sat R
  49:53-4 O 22 '66
BRODER, David S.
Consensus politics: end of an experiment.
  Atlan 218:60-5 O '66
Struggle for power. Atlan 217:64-70 Ap '66
There's no radical change in Goldwater. N Y
  Times Mag p9+ Je 19 '66
BRODER, Nathan
Bach passions and oratorios. Hi Fi 16:46-7+
  Jl '66
Bach's St John, a noble ideal nobly at-
  tempted. Hi Fi 16:73-4 Ag '66
Game of multiple choice: Boulez, Van
  Beinum, or Wenzinger. Hi Fi 16:96 N '66
BRODERICK, Albert
Ombudsman for religious. America 115:446-
  8+ O 15 '66
BRODERICK, Dorothy M.
Catalog. por Library J 90:5492-4; 91:1604-5
  D 15 '65, Mr 15 '66
Confessions of a purist. Library J 91:1599-
  600 Mr 15 '66
Real and the unfamiliar. Library J 91:2172-
  3 Ap 15 '66
Study in conflicting values; excerpts from
  address, March 1966. bibliog Library J 91:
  2557-64 My 15 '66
        about
Dissent and the children's stigma. E. Geller.
  Library J 91:1468+ Mr 15 '66
BRODERICK, John Joseph
Unforgettable Johnny Broderick. T. Shor.
  por Read Digest 90:91-5 Ja '67
World's toughest. por Time 87:40+ Ja 28 '66
BRODERICK, Vincent L.
[Address, March 8, 1966] Nat R 18:312-13 Ap
  5 '66
Two commissioners; interview. New Yorker
  42:33-5 Mr 5 '66
BRODEUR, Paul
Blue lawns; story. Seventeen 25:154-5 Mr '66
Salt marsh caper; story. Seventeen 25:300-1
  Ag '66
Way out snow spots. Mlle 64:199-201 N '66
BRODIE, John Riley
Fabulous Brodie caper. E. Shrake. il pors
  Sports Illus 25:16-21+ Ag 29 '66

BRODY, Jane Ellen
[Mademoiselle Merit award winner] il por
Mlle 64:50 Ja '67
BRODY, Thomas C.
Baseball's week. Sports Illus 24:110-11 Ap
25; 97 My 9 '66
College football (cont) Sports Illus 25:46-8+
O 31; 75-6 N 14; 58+ N 28 '66
Rowing (cont) Sports Illus 24:65-7 Je 6 '66
BROECKER, Wallace S.
Absolute dating and the astronomical theory
of glaciation. Science 151:299-304 Ja 21 '66
—and others
Strontium-90 fallout: comparison of rates
over ocean and land. bibliog Science 152:
639-40 Ap 29 '66
—See Ku, T. L. jt. auth.
BROEHL, Wayne G. jr
Insights into business & society. bibliog (p
180+) Harvard Bsns R 44:6-8+ My '66
BROGAN, Colm
Imperial Britain, RIP. Nat R 18:928-30 S 20
'66
Letter from London (cont) Nat R 18:467-8,
722-3+ My 17. Jl 26 '66
BROGAN, Sir Denis William
Life book review. Life 61:13+ N 25 '66
BROKEN bones. See Fractures
BROKERS
All roads lead to Wall Street; U.S. overseas
branches jump. Time 87:93-4 Mr 11 '66
Brokers who ring up the records, are little
known. il Bsns W p 160-2 Je 18 '66
Wall Street's precious margin; stockbroker-
age business. S. H. Brown. il Fortune 73:
136-9+ Ap '66
See also
Merrill Lynch, Pierce, Fenner and Smith,
incorporated
Stock exchange

Commissions
Curb for Wall Street? il Newsweek 68:94-6
D 19 '66
BROMELIADS
Choose bromeliads for outdoor decorating. J.
Kramer. il Flower Grower 53:8-10 Ag '66
Show stoppers. il Sunset 137:260+ O '66
See also
Puya
BROMIDES
Bromides inhibit flames. Sci N 89:462 Je 11
'66
Calcium and bromide contents of natural
waters. R. J. Anderson and others. bibliog
il Science 153:1637-8 S 30 '66; Reply with
rejoinder. P. C. Mangelsdorf, jr. 154:1473
D 16 '66
BROMINE
Pesticide residues in total-diet samples:
bromine content. B. J. Heywood. Science
152:1408 Je 3 '66; Reply. R. E. Duggan. 152:
1645 Je 17 '66
BROMODEOXYURIDINE
Radiosensitization of X chromsome of Chinese
hamster cells related to incorporation of 5-
bromodeoxyuridine. W. C. Dewey and
others. bibliog il Science 152:519-21 Ap 22
'66
BRON, Klaus M. and others
Arterial constrictor response in a diving
mammal. bibliog Science 152:540-3 Ap 22
'66
BRONCHITIS
Our fastest-growing health menace. D. Mur-
ray. Read Digest 90:111-14 Ja '67
BRONFMAN family
Bronfmans: an instinct for dynasty. P. Siek-
man. il pors Fortune 74:144-9+ N; 176-9+ D
'66
BRONK, J. Ramsey
Thyroid hormone: effects on electron trans-
port. bibliog Science 153:638-9 Ag 5 '66
BRONNER, Finn E. See Otterman, J. jt. auth.
BRONSON, F. H. and Clarke, S. H.
Adrenalectomy and coat color in deer mice.
bibliog Science 154:1349-50 D 9 '66
BRONSTON, William G.
Physician and Vietnam. Bul Atomic Sci 22:
24 N '66
BRONTË family
Brontës as teachers. M. Spark. New York-
er 41:30-3 Ja 22 '66
BRONX zoo. See New York zoological park
BRONZE
See also
Bronzes
BRONZES
Bronze miniatures from ancient Sardinia. A.
Borio. il UNESCO Courier 19:16-21 S '66
Rare bronze: Roman sculpture purchased by
the Metropolitan museum of art, New York.
Hobbies 71:96+ S '66

BROOK, Peter
Filming Marat/Sade. A. Knight. Sat R 49:
43 Jl 30 '66
Marat/Sade. J. Roddy. il por Look 30:110 F
22 '66
BROOK Farm
Brook Farm: seedbed of education. J. B.
Wilson. bibliog f Sch & Soc 94:43-7 Ja 22
'66
BROOKE, Edward William
Bay State's color-blind candidate: interview,
ed. by M. Byers. pors Life 60:57-8+ Ap
8 '66
What's wrong with the Republican party.
por Pub W 189:37-8 Mr 28 '66
Where I stand. por Atlan 217:60-5 Mr '66

about
Black man leading a G.O.P. march on Wash-
ington. J. Skow. il pors Sat Eve Post 239:
82-7 S 10 '66
Entering quietly. il por Time 89:16 Ja 20
'67
Junior senator from Massachusetts. M. F.
Nolan. Reporter 35:46+ D 1 '66
Keep the faith, baby. W. More. America 116:
80 Ja 21 '67
Long void is filled at last. S. McBee. il por
Life 62:32-32B Ja 13 '67
Massachusetts mix-up. por Newsweek 68:30-1
O 17 '66
Negro in the Senate. il por Newsweek 68:37-8
N 21 '66
Plea for positivism. por Time 87:18 Mr 25
'66
When a state tries to clean itself up. il por
U S News 60:46-8 F 7 '66
BROOKE, Marcus
Worth of a shekel. Atlan 217:126-9 Ap '66
BROOKLYN
Whatever happened to Brooklyn? il Time 87:
29 Mr 11 '66
Crime
See also
Mafia
Hospitals
What psychiatry is doing about E.S.P.; ex-
periment at Dream laboratory of Mai-
monides hospital. F. R. Schreiber and M.
Herman. il Sci Digest 59:32-6 F '66
Music
Brooklyn; Academy of music's Mozart festi-
val. F. Stevenson. Opera N 30:30 Ja 29 '66
See also
Brooklyn academy of music
Negroes
Notes and comment; prevention of possible
riot July 23 in East New York. New Yorker
42:17-18 Ag 6 '66
Poor boy's rich life; Land family. J. Whit-
bread. il Look 30:M6-8 S 6 '66
Riots
Jungle & the city; East New York section
of Brooklyn. il Time 88:11-12 Jl 29 '66
Social work
Operation Brownsville; the poor on their
own. J. Judge. Commonweal 84:193-4 My 6
'66
BROOKLYN academy of music
New York; productions of Mozart's Idomeneo
and Rossini's Mosè. R. D. Daniels. Opera N
31:26-7 D 3 '66
BROOKLYN museum
City fragments; outdoor sculpture garden
made possible by Anonymous arts recovery
society. New Yorker 42:28-30 Je 11 '66
Open house. New Yorker 42:48-50 D 10 '66
BROOKLYN public library
Brooklyn gambit: decision by professional
librarians to join AFL-CIO American fed-
eration of state, county, and municipal em-
ployees. K. Nyren. Library J 91:5905 D 1
'66
Brooklyn library union to seek better serv-
ice. Library J 92:38+ Ja 1 '67
Who's nonverbal? preschool program. S.
Glazer. il Library J 91:341-3 Ja 15 '66
BROOKMAN, Laura Lou
Laura L. Brookman, president. Phila. book-
sellers assn. il por Pub W 190:76-7 O 31 '66
Phila. booksellers assn. president featured in
article. Pub W 190:67-8 O 10 '66
BROOKS, David B.
Strip mining, reclamation, and the public
interest. Am For 72:18-19+ Mr '66
BROOKS, Iris
Savory stuffing cook book. House & Gard
130:189+ D '66

BROOKS, Joe
  Bus ride to Atlantic salmon. Outdoor Life
    138:46-9+ O '66
  King of the thin water. pors Outdoor Life
    139:58-61+ Ja '67
BROOKS, Joe F. and Galletta, G. J.
  Blueberries for gardens. Horticulture 44:26-
    7+ O '66
BROOKS, John
  Anatomy of change 1939/1966. Horizon 8:48-55
    Aut '66
  Mr White and Mr Blue; notes on the new
    middle class; excerpts from The great leap:
    from the old world of 1939 to the new era.
    Harper 232:88-91+ Je '66
  Reporter at large (cont) New Yorker 42:159-
    60+ O 8 '66
BROOKS, John Gaunt
  Lear Siegler's fast mover. J. F. Olesky. por
    Duns R 87:63-4 F '66
BROOKS, John I.
  Double feature in Byrdland. Reporter 34:25-7
    Je 16 '66
  High cost of not spending. Reporter 35:29-31
    D 1 '66
BROOKS, Milo
  Hope and help for handicapped children; ed.
    by A. Hamilton. Todays Health 44:60-3+
    N '66
BROOKS, Patricia K.
  Explorer's guide to England. Sat R 49:67-8 S
    17 '66
  Going places, finding things in the Philip-
    pines. House & Gard 130:36-8+ N '66
BROOKS, Paul
  Rhinoceros at bay. Horizon 9:14-21+ Wint
    '67
BROOKS, Phyllis
  Men like bulls; From bulfinch; poems. Poetry
    108:313-15 Ag '66
BROOKS, Thomas R.
  Finest could be finer. N Y Times Mag p28-
    9+ Ap 3 '66
  Lindsay, Quill & the transit strike. Com-
    mentary 41:50-7 Mr '66
  New York's finest. Commentary 40:29-36 Ag
    '65; 41:22+ F '66
  No! says the P.B.A. N Y Times Mag p36-
    7+ O 16 '66
BROOKS Stevens automotive museum, Mequon,
  Wis. See Automobile museums
BROOME, Harvey
  Cougar lakes excursion; report. Liv Wildn
    29:34 Aut '65
  Mountain notebook 1950. il Liv Wildn 29:3-13
    Aut '65
  Thirty years. pors Liv Wildn 29:15-26 Wint
    '65
BROPHY, Marjorie
  Every day is mother's day. See issues of
    Good housekeeping
BROSE, Olive J.
  That parochial syndrome; two views, one
    lay, one clerical. Christian Cent 83:205 F
    16 '66
BROSNAN, Jim
  Baseball needs the spitter. Look 30:66-9 My
    31 '66
  I's, we's and they's of baseball. N Y Times
    Mag p 14-15+ Jl 3 '66
  It's a long, long season. N Y Times Mag
    p30-1+ Ap 17 '66
BROTHERHOOD of locomotive firemen and
  enginemen
  Festering fight on the rails; brotherhood con-
    tinues battle for jobs that carriers and ar-
    bitrators call obsolete. il Bsns W p 144+
    Ap 9 '66
  Nothing but trouble. Time 87:23 Ap 15 '66
  Walking the rails; largest U.S. railway walk-
    out since 1946. Time 87:27 Ap 8 '66
BROTHERHOOD of man
  Is brotherhood enough? proposals to improve
    attitude towards Negroes. N. Wright. Cath
    World 204:234-8 Ja '67

        Bibliography
  Books for brotherhood (cont) il Commonweal
    83:594-5+ F 25 '66
BROTHERHOOD of painters, decorators and
  paperhangers of America
  Death no. 3; suicide of fund administrator.
    Time 87:22 My 27 '66
  Painters in blood; murder of D. Wilson. Time
    87:30-1 My 20 '66
BROTHERHOOD of teamsters. See Interna-
  tional brotherhood of teamsters, chauffeurs,
  warehousemen and helpers of America
BROTHERHOODS
      See also
  Brothers (Catholic)
  Vocation (in religion)
BROTHERS, Dwight S.
  Mexico's economy: a new stage. Cur Hist
    51:344-8+ D '66

BROTHERS, Joyce
  On being a woman. See issues of Good house-
    keeping
BROTHERS (Catholic)
  Renewing the brotherhoods. il Time 87:58 My
    27 '66
BROTHERS; story. See Woiwode, L.
BROTHERS and sisters. See Siblings
BROUGHAM, Royal
  Personal poverty program. il por Time 87:51
    Ap 15 '66
BROUGHTON, James
  Sun is shining in the egg; poem. Sat R 49:40
    S 10 '66
BROUGHTON, T. Robert S.
  (comp) Articles and other books received;
    ancient. See issues of American historical
    review
BROUN, Heywood Hale
  Full house. Am Heritage 18:64-7 D '66
BROUN, Maurice
  What future for birds of prey? Audubon Mag
    68:330-4+ S '66
BROUWER, Dirk
  Yale's pathfinder of moons, planets and stars.
    J. Ashbrook. pors Sky & Tel 31:146 Mr '66
BROWDER, Joan
  Those curious midgets. Am For 71:12+ O '66
BROWER, Brock
  Confessions of a wounded skier. Holiday 39:
    62-7+ F '66
  Dark satanic breeze. Holiday 40:32+ S '66
  Mystique of surf fishing. Holiday 40:46-7+
    Jl '66
  Roots of the Arkansas questioner. Life 60:
    92-4+ My 13 '66
BROWER, David
  No compromise on Grand Canyon Dams;
    Sierra club's reply to Goldwater plan;
    statement. por U S News 61:60-1 D 12 '66

      about
  Battle of the wilderness. il Newsweek 68:
    108 O 3 '66
  Knight errant to nature's rescue; with inter-
    view, ed. by H. Wingo. il pors Life 60:37-8+
    My 27 '66
BROWER, Nancy
  Ladies day at sea. por Motor B 119:76-9+
    Ja '67
BROWER, Sidney
  Expressive environment. Arch Forum 124:38-9
    Ap '66
BROWN, Barry
  Biography of a 120-second thriller. H. V.
    Fondiller. il pors Pop Phot 58:112-15+ My
    '66
BROWN, Betty C.
  How'd you like Life, Look, and Paris match
    to do your wedding album? il Pop Phot
    59:86+ D '66
  Third war of Horst Faas. Pop Phot 58:58-9+
    Mr '66
BROWN, Bianca S.
  Fascinating foods of the U.S.A See issues
    of Good housekeeping
BROWN, Bob
  And in this corner, the champ. J. Gilbert.
    il por Flying 78:36-41 Ap '66
BROWN, Bob W. See Buchanan, H. A. jt.
  auth.
BROWN, Brendan S.
  State and overpopulation; address, June 14,
    1966. Vital Speeches 32:604-8 Jl 15 '66
BROWN, Bruce
  Splashy, surf-soaked sleeper. R. Vaughan.
    Life 61:19 N 25 '66
BROWN, Calvin S.
  Tale of two urban areas; reprint. Horizon
    8:120 Aut '66
BROWN, Charles E.
  Everyone's keen on Keino. Ebony 21:100-2+
    My '66
BROWN, Claude
  In defense of Uncle Tom. G. Wills; reply
    with rejoinder. N. Hentoff. Commonweal 83:
    489+ Ja 28 '66
  Menchildren speak. il por Time 88:21-2 S 9
    '66
  Voices from the ghetto. il por Newsweek 68:
    25-6 S 12 '66
BROWN, Deming
  Man from S.M.O.G. N Y Times Mag p28-9+
    Mr 20 '66
  Moscow: the defense does not rest. Reporter
    35:43-5 S 22 '66
BROWN, Denise Scott
  Will salvation spoil the Dodge house? Arch
    Forum 125:68-71 O '66
BROWN, Dorothy Foster
  Button collecting. See issues of Hobbies
BROWN, Dwight A. See Jenks, G. F. jt. auth.

BROWN, Stanley H.—*Continued*
How one man can move a corporate mountain. Fortune 74:80-3+ Jl 1 '66
Jimmy Ling's wonderful growth machine. Fortune 75:136-8+ Ja '67
BROWN, Trisha
Trisha Brown and Deborah Hay, Judson memorial church. M. Marks. Dance Mag 40:62-3 My '66
BROWN, Warren
They sail to win. Yachting 120:28-9+ N '66
BROWN, Worth
Multiflora gigantea tuberous begonias. Horticulture 44:18-19+ Mr '66
BROWN and Root, incorporated
Project nohole? relationship between L. B. Johnson and firm under scrutiny. Newsweek 68:60+ Ag 29 '66
BROWN-Forman distillers corporation
Slight change of recipe. il Time 88:87 Ag 5 '66
BROWN trout fishing. See Trout fishing
BROWN university, Providence, R. I.
Brown's Yaleman; R. L. Heffner, new president. Newsweek 67:58 Ja 31 '66
Library shaped by librarians' needs: John D. Rockefeller jr. library. il Arch Rec 140: 204-7 S '66
Library tower for the sciences. il Arch Rec 140:208-9 S '66
New blood for Brown. Time 87:43 Ja 28 '66
BROWNE, Don R.
Blue world of Tunisia. Sat R 49:69-71 N 19 '66
BROWNE, Harry L.
Is the labor board biased? an authority says this. por U S News 61:72-4+ N 28 '66
BROWNE, Louise
Royal academy of dancing. por Dance Mag 40:63-4+ D '66
BROWNE, Michael Dennis
King in May; poem. New Yorker 42:40 My 28 '66
Peter; poem. New Yorker 42:91 Ap 9 '66
BROWNE, Robert S.
Vietnam; from disorder to what? New Repub 154:11-12 Ap 23 '66
BROWNE, Rosalind
Short-range astronomy. Art N 64:37-9+ Ja '66
BROWNELL, John A. See King, A. R. jr, jt. auth.
BROWNELL, Samuel Miller
Detroit's sick schools. il por Newsweek 68: 87-8 S 5 '66
BROWNING, Don
Pastoral care and public ministry. Christian Cent 83:1175-7 S 28 '66
BROWNING, Robert
Dramatic monologue by mail. B. Grebanier. por Sat R 49:48 Je 11 '66
BROWNLINE corporation
Brownline widening role in cargo trade. C. M. Plattner. il Aviation W 86:46-9 Ja 2 '67
BROWNMILLER, Susan
Jacques Tiffeau: sauvage of Seventh avenue. N Y Times Mag p36-7+ Ja 15 '67
BROWNSVILLE. See Brooklyn
BROYER, T. C. See Barr, C. E. jt. auth.
BRUBAKER, Charles William
What's new in urban school buildings? NEA J 55:26-9 D '66
BRUCE, A. D. jr
New boom for Baja. Travel 125:41-3 Ap '66
BRUCE, Ailsa (Mellon)
Celebration of masterpieces. J. Walker. il Vogue 147:94-5+ Mr 15 '66
Family reunion. il Newsweek 67:99-100 Mr 21 '66
National gallery: preview of an anniversary exhibition. A. Saarinen. il McCalls 93:96-103+ Ap '66
Throwing a party. H. Brandon. Sat R 49:20 Mr 19 '66
BRUCE, Ben F. jr
Why golf is a lifetime sport. por Parks & Rec 1:772 S '66
BRUCE, Freda M.
How important is premarital chastity? Good H 162:16+ Je '66
BRUCE, J. Campbell
Inflatable raft: to ensure survival at sea. Read Digest 89:157-8+ Ag '66
BRUCE, Lenny
Notes and comment. New Yorker 42:25 Ag 20 '66
Obituary
Nat R 18:874 S 6 '66. F. Chodorov
BRUCE, Mellon, collection. See Art—Private collections
BRUCELLOSIS in cattle
Now: a five-minute test for brucellosis. J. A. Rohlf. il Farm J 90:37 Mr '66

BRUCK, Jerry
Gustav Mahler: the Ninth was not impassable. Am Rec G 32:412-16 Ja '66
BRUCKER, Herbert
How to write an editorial. Sat R 49:58-60 F 12 '66
Should an editor edit? Sat R 50:116-17+ Ja 14 '67
about
Stanford's Niemans. Newsweek 67:72 F 7 '66
BRUCKNER, Anton
Mehta: glorious and blazing Bruckner. J. Diether, Am Rec G 32:515 F '66
BRUEGHEL, Peeter, the elder
Bruegel; excerpts from Lives of the painters. J. Canaday. il Horizon 9:22-41 Wint '67
BRUGGEMAN, Martha
Art of selling to the individual. por Pub W 189:176-9 F 21 '66
about
It pays to read the books you sell, especially children's books. Pub W 189:73 Mr 7 '66
BRUISES
First aid. C. J. Potthoff. il Todays Health 44:80 Ap '66
BRUMBERG, Abraham
Socialist legality on trial. Reporter 34:34-6 Mr 10 '66
BRUMFIELD, Don
King from wire to wire. W. Tower. il por Sports Illus 24:30-3+ My 16 '66
BRUMMELL, O. B.
Bob Dylan, a far cry from Aristotle. Hi Fi 16:125 O '66
Folk music (cont) Hi Fi 16:38+ Mr; 50+ My; 26+ Jl; 52 S; 42 N '66
BRUNCHES
After the Easter parade. C. Claiborne. il N Y Times Mag p86 Ap 3 '66
Fort Lauderdale: brunch, an American tradition. il Ladies Home J 83:94-7+ O '66
Party brunches for summer Sundays; with recipes. il McCalls 93:92-3+ Ag '66
Sunday brunch. il Time 88:80 O 21 '66
BRUNDAGE, Avery
Gateway's Oriental treasure. il por Time 87: 92 Je 17 '66
Lotus-eater. il por Newsweek 67:66-7 Je 20 '66
BRUNDAGE, James A.
Book review. America 114:673 My 7 '66
BRUNDAGE, W. D. and Kraus, J. D.
Neutral hydrogen survey of Andromeda galaxy. bibliog Science 153:411-14 Jl 22 '66
BRUNDAGE collection of Oriental art. See M. H. De Young memorial museum, San Francisco
BRUNEAU, Jacques
Letter from Paris. J. Flanner. New Yorker 42:111-12+ Ag 27 '66
Private war of Prefect Bruneau. il por Time 88:30 Ag 19 '66
BRUNER, Jerome Seymour
Education as social invention; excerpt from Toward a theory of instruction. Sat R 49: 70-2+ F 19 '66
Will to learn; excerpt from Toward a theory of instruction. bibliog f Commentary 41: 41-6 F '66
BRUNER, Louise
Toledo museum of art. Am Artist 30:33-9+ Ap '66
BRUNING, Mrs Frank
Beef specialists from cattle country. por Suc Farm 64:72 Ag '66
BRUNN, Geoffrey
Habsburg hausfrau. Sat R 49:29 Jl 16 '66
BRUNNER, Emil
Emil Brunner, the final encounter. J. R. Nelson. Christian Cent 83:486 Ap 20 '66
BRUNO, Anne Turner
(ed) See Anne Marie. Visit with the world's youngest queen
BRUNO, Hal
Chicago's scholarly cop. Reporter 34:30-3 Mr 24 '66
BRUNS, Richard
Gretchen just had to make trouble. D. Moser. Life 60:84+ Mr 4 '66
BRUNSWICK corporation
Bowled over. Fortune 74:307 Jl 15 '66
BRUSH drawing
Ever draw with a bristle brush and black tempera? R. Barrio. il Design 67:32-5 Ja '66
Ink resist technique, with variations. W. Kelly. il Am Artist 31:50-3+ Ja '67
BRUSHES
Right brush for the job. il House & Gard 129:152-3 Ap '66
See also
Paint brushes

BRUSILOW, Anshel
Music to my ears. I. Kolodin. Sat R 49:58+
N 26 '66
BRUSSEL-SMITH, Bernard
Stations of the cross. N. Kent. il Am Artist
30:40-5 Ap '66
BRUSSELS
Brussels, center of bargaining. il Esquire 66:
176-7 D '66

Markets
Traveler's choice; Bird market. D. M. Smith.
Travel 126:9 N '66

Music
Brussels: Wieland Wagner's production of
Fliegende Holländer. L. Mueller. il Opera N
31:31 D 10 '66
Notes from our correspondents. R. McMul-
len. Hi Fi 16:24+ Mr '66
BRUSTEIN, Robert
Theatre. See issues of New republic
Third theater that is superb, gay and wild.
N Y Times Mag p32-3+ S 25 '66

about
Seasons of discontent. Review
Commonweal 83:669-70+ Mr 11 '66. J.
Simon
BRUUN, Geoffrey
Toward a wider world of choice. Sat R 49:
39 F 5 '66
BRYAN, C. D. B.
Best of friends at Farmington; story. Mlle
63:136-7 O '66
Kurt Vonnegut on target. New Repub 155:
21-2+ O 8 '66
Soon to be a major motion picture. New
Repub 154:23-5 Je 11 '66
BRYAN, Diana
Notes for the hostess. See issues of House
& garden incorporating Living for young
homemakers
BRYAN, J. 3d
Inglish spocken here. Holiday 40:56-7 O '66
Little Squirt; most famous child's statue in
the world. Holiday 39:48-9 Je '66
Phileas Fogg and the jumping frog. Holiday
40:64-5+ Ag '66
Tilt! Holiday 41:80-1+ Ja '67
BRYAN, Pack
1966 at Indy: big power shoot-out. Pop Mech
125:74-7+ My '66
(ed) See Andretti, M. Indy-style tires for
your car?
BRYAN, Robert N.
Retrograde amnesia: effects of handling and
microwave radiation. bibliog Science 153:
897-9 Ag 19 '66
BRYAN, W. Ray
1966 Nobel laureates in medicine and phy-
siology. Science 154:364-5 O 21 '66
BRYANT, Cyril E.
Washington national cathedral: our nation's
spiritual landmark. Read Digest 88:147-8+
F '66
BRYANT, Deborah
Miss America six months later. D. Chap-
man. il pors Look 30:90+ Ap 5 '66
BRYANT, Farris
Two appointments. New Repub 154:9-10 Mr
26 '66
Warm spot for Farris Bryant. Nation 202:
380-1 Ap 4 '66
BRYANT, Jack W.
Greenwich reading time. Wilson Lib Bul 40:
530-1 F '66
BRYANT, Jane
Last weekend I learned to fly. Sci Digest 61:
61-4 Ja '67
New geography. Sci Digest 60:62-5 O '66
BRYANT, Paul
I'll tell you about football; ed. by J. Under-
wood. pors Sports Illus 25:52-8+ Ag 15: 28-
30+ Ag 22; 26-8+ Ag 29; 28-30+ S 5;
98-100+ S 12 '66
BRYANT, W. R.
Data-processing accounting in England. Am
City 81:90-1 Je '66
BRYN MAWR, Pa.

Historic houses, etc.
Living with antiques; Bryn Mawr home of
Mr and Mrs Bertram Dawson Coleman.
L. H. Solis-Cohen. il Antiques 89:573-7
Ap '66
BRZEZINSKI, Zbigniew
NATO crisis. Commonweal 84:309-1 Je 3 '66
Tomorrow's agenda. For Affairs 44:662-70
Jl '66
about
Switching squads. por Time 87:29-30 My 20
'66
Thinker. Newsweek 68:44 N 14 '66

BUBAS, Vic
He goes after scholars who can also shoot
well. il pors Life 60:52B Ja 28 '66
BUBBLES, Soap. See Soap bubbles and films
BUBER, Martin
Martin Buber and the Jews; his interpreta-
tion of and path to Hasidism. C. Potok.
Commentary 41:43-9 Mr '66; Discussion.
42:20+ S '66
Personal freedom and community responsi-
bility. C. R. McCarthy. Cath World 203:165-
8 Je '66
BUBONIC plague. See Plague
BUCHAN, John, 1st baron Tweedsmuir
John Buchan, by J. A. Smith. Review
Life 60:14 Mr 11 '66. C. Elliott
Nation 202:191-3 F 14 '66. M. Richler
New Repub 154:23-4 Ap 30 '66. J. D.
Scott
Reporter 34:55-7 Mr 10 '66. R. Weaver
BUCHANAN, A. Lawrence
Thy book doth live. Américas 18:15-20 Mr '66
BUCHANAN, Annette
Pot luck. Newsweek 67:36+ Je 27 '66
Problems of protecting a source. Time 87:98
Je 24 '66
Silence on sources. Time 88:49 Jl 8 '66
BUCHANAN, Henry A. and Brown, B. W.
Integration: great dilemma of the church.
pors Ebony 21:163-4+ Je '66
BUCHANAN, Ian. See Buchanan, K. jt. auth.
BUCHANAN, Keith
Visit to a fourth of mankind. Nation 203:
302-6 O 3 '66
BUCHANAN, Kirsten, and Buchanan, Ian
Family quiz game. See issues of Parents'
magazine and better homemaking
BUCHANAN, Mich.
Fill first, then compact. M. Hankila. il Am
City 81:173-4 My '66
BUCHBINDER, Rudolf
Keeping up with the Cliburns (and the
Joneses) P. Hume. il por Sat R 49:57+ O
29 '66
BUCHHEISTER, Carl W.
President reports. See issues of Audubon
magazine
about
Carl Buchheister accorded honorary degrees.
Audubon Mag 68:402 N '66
BÜCHNER, Georg
Woyzeck. Criticism
Newsweek 67:96 Ap 18 '66
Time il 87:68 Ap 15 '66
BUCHSBAUM, Walter H.
Chroma circuits in color TV: Motorola.
Electr World 76:33-5+ S '66
Chroma circuits in color TV: Sylvania. Electr
World 76:34-5+ D '66
Chroma demodulation in color sets: RCA.
Electr World 75:45-7+ My '66
Chroma synchronization in color sets: RCA.
Electr World 75:35-7+ Je '66
Convergence circuits of color sets: RCA.
Electr World 76:38-9+ Ag '66
G-E 11-inch color TV: the new look in color
receivers. Electr World 75:39-41+ Mr '66
Line-operated transistor TV sets: Emerson.
Electr World 75:40+ F '66
Line-operated transistor TV sets: G-E.
Electr World 76:29+ O '66
Line-operated transistor TV sets: Magnavox.
Electr World 76:27+ N '66
Line-operated transistor TV sets: Sylvania.
Electr World 75:38+ Ja '66
Line-operated transistor TV sets: Westing-
house. Electr World 75:34-5 Mr '66
Line-operated transitor TV sets: Zenith.
Electr World 75:90-1 Ap '66
Oscilloscope probes. Electr World 76:46-8 Ag
'66
BUCHWALD, Art
Art Buchwald's fearless forecast for 1967.
por Nations Bsns 55:40-1+ Ja '67
How fragile is your marriage? Ladies Home
J 83:68 S '66
My wife, the writer. Ladies Home J 83:58
Je '66
Unfaithful executive. Look 31:34 Ja 10 '67
Why parents can't add; excerpt from Son of
the Great society. Read Digest 89:151-2 O
'66
BUCK, Dorothy
Curacao. Dance Mag 40:23-5 Ap '66
BUCK, Pearl (Sydenstricker)
Reading and the American public; address,
July 1966. ALA Bul 60:931-6 O '66
about
Born between East and West. M. Macmillan.
Sat R 49:51 Jl 23 '66
BUCK, Robert K.
Here's the kind of credit farmers need;
address. Farm J 90:68W Mr '66

BUCK, Robert W.
  Mushrooms. Horticulture 44:22-5 S '66
BUCK, William Alvadore
  In praise of the tomato. Pop Gard 17:66-8+
    My '66
BUCK ISLAND REEF NATIONAL MONU-
    MENT
  Beneath the surface. E. L. Rothfuss. il Parks
    & Rec 1:715-16+ S '66
BUCKBEE-Mears company
  They make the mask that makes color TV.
    il Bsns W p 126-8+ N 12 '66
BUCKETS (pails)
  Drinks on a grand scale; dispensers and
    coolers for drinks. il House & Gard 129:
    218-19 Ap '66
BUCKINGHAM palace art exhibitions. See Art
    —Exhibitions
BUCKLER, Charles E and others
  Interferon: lack of detectable uptake by cells.
    bibliog Science 152:80-2 Ap 1 '66
BUCKLEW, William Henry
  Mississippi mayor fights the Klan. A. Schardt.
    Reporter 34:39-40 Ja 27 '66
BUCKLEY, Charles E.
  City art museum of Saint Louis. Antiques
    90:686-91 N '66
BUCKLEY, John P.
  We have the tools to do the job. Am City
    81:86-9 F '66
BUCKLEY, Priscilla L.
  Bringing us back alive. por Nat R 18:625-6
    Je 28 '66
  South Africa: an unsentimental journey.
    Nat R 19:18-25 Ja 10 '67
  Theater. Nat R 18:1062-5 O 18 '66
BUCKLEY, Thomas
  Herald-tribune. New Repub 155:8 Ag 27 '66
  Inquest on a premature burial. Esquire 65:
    75-81+ Je '66
  Just plain H. L. Hunt. Esquire 67:64-9+ Ja
    '67
  LSD trigger. New Repub 154:15-21 My 14 '66
  Mother is a pinball machine. Esquire 66:84-5+
    Ag '66
  Singular silk-stocking 17th. N Y Times Mag
    p52+ F 6 '66
  Three men behind Rockefeller. N Y Times
    Mag p34-5+ O 30 '66
  Traffic jam in the taxi industry. N Y Times
    Mag p8-9+ S 4 '66
  When good Birchers get together. N Y Times
    Mag p48-9+ Je 5 '66
BUCKLEY, William Frank, 1925-
  On the right. See issues of National review
  Politics of beauty. Esquire 66:50-3+ Jl '66

                about
  Bill & Bobby show. por Time 87:29 Ap 8 '66
  Drawing the libel line. Newsweek 67:92 My
    9 '66
  Even better than Batman. S. Alexander. Life
    61:22 Ag 5 '66
  Gingering man. il por Time 87:59 Je 17 '66
BUCKMAN, Gertrude
  Let's travel. Mlle 64:136-9 D '66
BUCKMAN, Peter
  Literary letter from London. Nation 202:340-1
    Mr 21 '66
BUCKOW, Ed
  Unraveling the Everglades furor. Field & S
    71:12-16+ O '66
BUCKWITZ, Harry
  New ideas for Wagner. P. Moor. il por Hi Fi
    16:142-3 Mr '66
BUDAPEST
  Budapest: ten years after the Hungarian
    revolution. L. Gross. il Look 30:106-10+
    N 1 '66
  Road back to Budapest. T. Foote. il N Y
    Times Mag p56-7+ N 20 '66

                Description
  Notes from a European diary: 1963-64. E.
    Wilson. New Yorker 42:88+ Je 4 '66

                Music
  Kodály education in action. E. Helm. Hi Fi
    16:MA30-1 Jl '66
  Notes from our correspondents. K. Blaukopf.
    Hi Fi 16:32+ My '66
BUDD railcar. See Railroads—Trains
BUDDHA and Buddhism
  Buddhists in Saigon. K. W. Morgan. Chris-
    tian Cent 83:107-10 Ja 26 '66
    See also
  Zen Buddhism
BUDDHISTS
  Buddhists vs. the generals. il Sr Schol 88:
    11-12 Ap 22 '66
  Divided Buddhists of South Vietnam. D.
    Warner. Reporter 34:22-4 Je 16 '66

  Fiery rebellion; Buddhist self immolations
    and activities to bring down government.
    il Newsweek 67:48-9 Je 13 '66
  Just who are the Buddhists? il U S News
    60:29-30 My 30 '66
  Karma of Vietnam's Buddhists. M. Clos. il
    N Y Times Mag p28-9+ Ag 21 '66
  Ky's crackdown. il Newsweek 68:28 Jl 4 '66
  Letter from South Vietnam. R. Shaplen. New
    Yorker 42:142-4+ Je 4 '66
  Light that failed; self immolations in Viet
    Nam. il Time 87:39 Je 10 '66
  Religious meditations and political power
    plays; role played by Buddhists in Vietnam.
    il Sr Schol 88:12+ Ap 29 '66
  Thich Nhat Hanh; interview. Nhat Hanh.
    New Yorker 42:21-3 Je 25 '66
  Thich Tri Quang: Buddhist mystery man. il
    Sr Schol 88:8 My 6 '66
  Vietnam's Buddhists emerge as key power;
    vital third force to determine war's course
    and future U.S. presence. il Bsns W p38-40
    Ap 23 '66
  Why Vietnam's Buddhists act the way they
    do; report from the trouble center. G. L.
    Troelstrup. il U S News 60:58-9 My 2 '66
BUDDY family
  Case for not going to college. J. Griffin and
    D. Chapman. il pors Look 30:90+ N 29 '66
BUDGE, Hamer H.
  Disclosure and insider investing; address. por
    Duns R 87:21-2+ Ja '66
BUDGET

                Canada
  Canada tries to calm its bubbling economy.
    Bsns W p40 Ap 2 '66

                Great Britain
  Britain unwraps its budget. Bsns W p36
    My 7 '66
  Callaghan's surprise. il Newsweek 67:76 My
    16 '66
  Letter from London (cont) M. Panter-Downes.
    New Yorker 42:88+ Ag 6 '66
  Mr Wilson's nostrums. A. Lejeune. Nat R
    18:879+ S 6 '66

                United States
  Bad news for taxpayers; U.S. money troubles
    close in on LBJ. il U S News 62:82-3 Ja 9
    '67
  Balance-sheet Barnum. il Newsweek 68:25-7
    D 12 '66
  Budget keeps climbing on Vietnam escalator;
    defense spending for fiscal 1967 $67-billion.
    il Bsns W p36-7 D 10 '66
  Budget message; January 24, 1966; excerpts.
    L. B. Johnson. Dept State Bul 54:247-9 F
    14 '66
  Budget of the United States government for
    the fiscal year ending June 30, 1967; ex-
    cerpts. il Dept State Bul 54:247-53 F 14 '66
  Budget that doesn't give; why there's grow-
    ing pressure for a tax increase. il U S
    News 61:100-2 O 10 '66
  Budget that's bound to bend; with editorial
    comment. il Bsns W p27-9, 142 Ja 29 '66
  Budget won't lie still. il Bsns W p27-8 My 7
    '66
  Business as usual. Reporter 34:16 F 10 '66
  Close-up; interview, ed. by J. Berry. C.
    Schultze. il Duns R 87:8-9+ Je '66
  Congress should fix a ceiling on the budget.
    D. Lawrence. U S News 61:104 N 7 '66
  Cutting the butter. Time 87:14-15 Ja 28 '66
  Deficit drops sharply. Bsns W p40+ My 28
    '66
  Delicate balance. il Fortune 74:40+ D '66
  Different kind of cuttin'. il Time 88:23 D 2 '66
  Focus on Washington. Cato. Nat R 18:503
    My 31 '66
  Guns and butter for fiscal 1967. America 114:
    189 F 5 '66
  Guns or butter, or both for the U.S? il Sr
    Schol 88:8-10 Mr 4 '66
  How honest is the U.S. budget? interview.
    M. Stans. U S News 62:66-70 Ja 16 '67
  Inside view of the new budget; interview.
    C. L. Schultze. il Nations Bsns 55:42-3+
    Ja '67
  Interest rise hurts budget. U S News 60:114
    F 28 '66
  Irresponsible budget. H. Hazlitt. Newsweek
    67:82 F 14 '66
  Jockeying the budget; laying the ground-
    work for budget and taxes. il Bsns W p37-8
    D 3 '66
  Johnson's cure for government deficits. il
    U S News 61:78-80 D 26 '66
  LBJ and Kennedys; a showdown vote? U S
    News 61:3 O 17 '66
  LBJ's fairy tale; forecast. New Repub 156:
    6 Ja 7 '67
  LBJ's plan to trim '67 budget: sell 4.2 bil-
    lions in federal loans. U S News 60:77 My
    30 '66

BUDGET—United States—*Continued*
Needed: a watchdog. W. J. Coughlin. Tech W
20:50 Ja 9 '67
New-speak budget. W. J. Coughlin. Miss &
Roc 18:46 F 7 '66
Not so red. Newsweek 68:24 Jl 11 '66
Now you see it... Nation 202:141 F 7 '66
Once and future things. W. J. Coughlin.
Miss & Roc 18:46 F 21 '66
163-billion budget: where the money will go.
il U S News 60:107-9 Ap 18 '66
112.8 billions: how it will all be spent. il
U S News 60:88-9 Ja 31 '66
Putting a dollar sign on everything; Penta-
gon's planning-programming-budgeting sys-
tem. il Bsns W p 122-4+ Jl 16 '66
Reading the budget for fun & profit; Time
essay. Time 87:36-7 F 18 '66
Record figures. il Sr Schol 88:15 F 11 '66
Right and wrong of it. America 114:435-6
Ap 2 '66
Risky budget. Fortune 73:44+ Mr '66
Runaway spending: can LBJ check it? il U S
News 61:29-30 D 19 '66
Six-year low for budget deficit. U S News
61:63 Ag 1 '66
Sleight of hand budget? how it gets that way.
U S News 60:80-1 F 7 '66
Special budget report: Asian war may under-
mine budget hopes; with editorial comment.
G. C. Wilson. il Aviation W 84:9, 14-31 Ja
31 '66
Spreading the butter. il Newsweek 67:21-2 Ja
31 '66
State of the economy. Commonweal 83:547-8
F 11 '66
Talking turkey. Newsweek 68:29-30 D 5 '66
Thin end of the wedge. W. Lippmann. News-
week 67:15 F 14 '66
Thumbs down on a capital budget; high-
lights of study by M. Comiez. il Bsns W
p70+ F 19 '66
Too buoyant budget. il Nations Bsns 54:40-1
My '66
What we can't afford. New Repub 154:5-6 F 5
'66
Will Congress learn budget's new math?
national income accounts budget. il Bsns W
p 102+ Ja 7 '67
See also
Taxation—United States
United States—Appropriations and expendi-
tures
BUDGET, Bureau of the United States. See
United States—Budget, Bureau of the
BUDGET, Household
Family money management. N. Kuehnl and
G. Bush. See issues of Better homes and
gardens
Forty-one ways to get more for your money.
il Changing T 20:25-9 O '66
Forty ways to beat the high cost of almost
everything. Ladies Home J 83:72+ N '66
Going to start a budget this year? il Chang-
ing T 21:24 Ja '67
How farmers use money for living. il Suc
Farm 64:50 Ag '66
Is there a basic spending plan that really
works? il Bet Hom & Gard 44:8+ O '66
That always broke feeling, and what to do
about it. il Changing T 20:7-11 Mr '66
Where the family money goes. il Changing T
20:7-11 Ag '66
Why young couples spend more than they
earn. S. Margolius. il Redbook 126:56-7+
F '66
BUDGET, Library. See College libraries—Fi-
nance
BUDGET, Personal
How America's wealthiest families pinch pen-
nies. G. Greene. il Ladies Home J 83:152-
4+ O '66
How they live on $20,000 a year. il Fortune
74:186-8+ D '66
How well can your youngsters handle money?
Polly. il Farm J 90:68-9 S '66
Many meanings of money; with discussion
group program, by E. J. LeShan. E. G.
Neisser. il Parents Mag 41:34+, 52-3+ F
'66
Necessities are the mother of invention;
monthly expenditures of Mrs R. Firestone.
G. Ace. Sat R 49:12 F 26 '66
Where teenage money goes; with study-
discussion program, by C. Smallenburg and
H. Smallenburg. L. Rand. bibliog il PTA
Mag 61:8-10, 37 O '66
See also
Childrens allowances
Saving and savings
BUDGET bureau (United States) See United
States—Budget, Bureau of the
BUDGETS, Library. See Libraries—Finance
BUDIN, Shayne I.
Starry night; poem. Horn Bk 42:357 Je '66

BUDRYS, A. J.
Mind control is good, bad. Esquire 65:106-9
My '66
BUDRYS, Algis
Master of the hounds; story. Sat Eve Post
239:46-7 Ag 27 '66
BUDS
Enjoy bud watching. R. S. Gilliam. il Flower
Grower 53:25-7 Mr '66
BUECHNER, Georg. See Büchner, G.
BUEDELER, Werner
Foreign equipment sales may outstrip space
product exports. Tech W 19:44 N 14 '66
Nine firms named to build German research
satellite. Tech W 19:36 Ag 29 '66
1972 Olympic games prompt German bid for
TV satellite. Tech W 19:19 S 5 '66
BUEGELEISEN, Sally
Experiment in exposure. Flying 78:84-6 Mr
'66
Skirts flying. See issues of Flying
Strips for action. Flying 79:85-7 Ag '66
BUEHR, Wendy
New designs for megalopolis. Horizon 8:56-65
Aut '66
Station closed. Am Heritage 17:33-41 F '66
World of Youssouf bey. Horizon 8:24-31 Sum
'66
BUELL, Temple Hoyne
$25 million gift. il por Time 88:98 N 18 '66
BUENA PARK, Calif.

Water supply
Water program cuts fire-insurance rates. F.
L. Yaberg and R. C. Kenmir. il Am City
81:110-11 O '66
BUENOS AIRES

Airports
Argentina seeks speeded cargo clearance;
Ezeiza airport. J. W. Carter. il Aviation W
84:49+ My 30 '66

Historic houses, etc.
Voice of the Algarrobo; estate of J. M. de
Pueyrredón. V. Ocampo. il Américas 18:
1-7 S '66

Music
Buenos Aires. G. Knepler. Opera N 31:27
O 15; 26 N 19 '66
Buenos Aires: production of Beethoven's
Fidelio. G. Knepler. Opera N 31:30+ D 17
'66

Newspapers
See Newspapers—Argentina
BUENOS AIRES. University. See Colleges and
universities—Argentina
BUERGER, Martin J. and Taxer, Karlheinz
Rhodizite: structure and composition. bibliog
Science 152:500-2 Ap 22 '66
BUESINGEN, Germany. See Büsingen, Ger-
many
BUFANO, Beniamino Benvenuto
This summer in San Francisco: a Bufano
show. il Sunset 137:26 Jl '66
BUFFALO, N.Y.

City planning
Curtain goes up on Buffalo's Main place.
il Fortune 73:172 Ap '66
BUFFALO Bills (football club) See Football
clubs
BUFFALO hunting
Africa's meanest game. F. Bear. il Outdoor
Life 137:32-5+ F '66
My heart-attack trophies; hunting Cape buf-
falo. E. A. Bauer. il Field & S 70:43-5+
Mr '66
BUFFALOES
Summer of riches: Montana's Mission Val-
ley. H. Cruickshank. il Audubon Mag 68:
86-91 Mr '66
BUFFET meals
Atlanta: a wonderful way to say welcome to
our town, and yours. il Ladies Home J
83:98-101+ O '66
Homemade delicatessen; with recipes. il Mc-
Calls 93:108-9+ F '66
Open season for entertaining; crowd-pleasing
buffet; with recipes. il McCalls 93:106-7+
My '66
Party à la cart. il Ladies Home J 83:124+
O '66
Royal welcome; menus, with recipes. il
McCalls 94:110-12+ D '66
San Francisco: buffet dinner. il Ladies Home
J 83:104-5+ O '66
BUGANDA, Kabaka of. See Mutesa II, king of
Buganda
BUGBANES
Cimicifugas. M. Kunkel. il Horticulture 44:
41+ Je '66
BUGBEE, Percy
Quenching the continuing tragedy of clothing
fires. Todays Health 44:88+ D '66

BUGS. See Insects

BUGS; drama. See White, J.

BUILDING

Building from the idea out. Sci N 91:41 Ja 14 '67

Building moves slowly; postponement of many construction projects. il Bsns W p46+ O 15 '66

High hopes for a new house. L. Wainwright. Life 61:18 Jl 15 '66

New lower-cost, mechanized building techniques and the desire for design flexibility: a chicken-and-egg relationship. il Arch Rec 140:160-2 Jl '66

Our neighbors helped us rebuild out of the ashes; Negro family's house burned; ed. by L. Shecter. B. DeCausey. il Good H 162: 98-9+ Je '66

Pinch on home building. il Fortune 73:44+ Ap '66

Structure & design; ed. by W. McQuade and P. Herrera. See issues of Fortune

Structures should have stiffness as well as strength. H. S. Woodward. il Arch Rec 139:226-7 Ap '66

See also

Home ownership

Strains and stresses

Contracts and specifications

Competitive bidding or negotiated contract: which opposes the package better? il Arch Rec 139:186-7 Je '66

Performance criteria; a system of communication for mobilizing building industry resources. R. G. Jacques. il Arch Rec 139: 191-5 My '66

Practical pressures pushing the profession; excerpts from address, with reply by E. Goble. R. F. Hastings. Arch Rec 140:9 O '66

Cost

Building construction costs. W. H. Edgerton. See issues of Architectural record

Construction technology: can new lifting systems cut construction costs? il Arch Rec 139:203-4 Je '66

Cost of Record houses of 1966. il Arch Rec 139:121 mid-My '66

Do-it-yourself homes. il Parents Mag 41: 74-5+ Je '66

Real key to cost control is knowing what you pay for. il Arch Rec 139:182-3 Je '66

Whipsaws that drive building wages up; $10-an-hour wage no fantasy. il Bsns W p 150-2+ Je 18 '66

Finance

Tight money impact spreading. G. A. Christie. il Arch Rec 140:44 N '66

See also

Mortgages

Savings and loan associations

Rapid construction

See Buildings, Prefabricated

Regulations

See Building laws and regulations

Statistics

Changing job to be done. il Arch Rec 140: 224-6 Jl '66

Current trends in construction (title varies) G. A. Christie. See issues of Architectural record

F. W. Dodge construction outlook; plans for 1967. Arch Rec 140:147-50 N '66

BUILDING blocks

Modern ways to use building blocks. il Pop Gard 17:44-7 D '66

BUILDING codes. See Building laws and regulations

BUILDING consultants, Library. See Library consultants

BUILDING exits. See Exits

BUILDING fittings

Mechanical and electrical systems are developing toward the total integration of the building as an organic unit. W. B. Foxhall. il Arch Rec 140:164-7 Jl '66

Notes on components for use by the handicapped; excerpts. il Arch Rec 140:231-2 O '66

Product reports. See issues of Architectural record

BUILDING industry

Biggest invisible builder in the world; P. Kiewit. H. B. Meyers il Fortune 73:146-51+ Ap '66

Builders squeezed by money troubles. il Bsns W p34-5 My 28 '66

Building by the billion in Vietnam. J. Mecklin. il Fortune 74:112-17+ S '66

Building like the Caesars; Italian construction companies working throughout the world. il Time 87:92 Je 24 '66

Construction technology: can new lifting systems cut construction costs? il Arch Rec 139:203-4 Je '66

Fast write-off bill has builders worried; proposal to suspend accelerated depreciation on new construction. Bsns W p53 S 24 '66

Half a remedy; Congress to the aid of the loan-starved housing industry. Time 88: 70-1 S 2 '66

Hard sledding for full work year; Administration formula rejected by contractors. Bsns W p48+ Jl 16 '66

Home building: inflation casualty. il U S News 60:27-8 Je 27 '66

Homebuilder bucks ebbing sales tide; Pittsburgh-based Ryan homes, inc. il Bsns W p68-70+ O 8 '66

Homebuilding teeters. il Bsns W p34-5 S 3 '66

House that Jim built; shell homes. R. Levy. Duns R 87:51-2 My '66

Low-cost housing market. D. K. Newman. bibliog f il Mo Labor R 89:1362-8 D '66

Rape of the land. B. H. Bagdikian. il Sat Eve Post 239:25-9+ Je 18 '66

Reducing seasonal unemployment; in construction industry. Mo Labor R 89:990-3 S '66

Scraping bottom; credit-starved housing industry. il Time 88:89 D 16 '66

Sick industry; home builders. il Time 88:84 Ag 5 '66

Three-story pinch; housing industry. Time 87:70+ Ap 22 '66

Where tight money is pinching; credit squeeze cuts into housing. il Newsweek 68:65-6+ Jl 4 '66

See also

National association of home builders

Employees

Whipsaws that drive building wages up; $10-an-hour wage no fantasy. il Bsns W p 150-2+ Je 18 '66

Wages and hours

Administration zeroes in on wages. Bsns W p86+ Ja 29 '66

Building trades and guideposts. America 114: 316 Mr 5 '66

High wages that worry President Johnson. il U S News 60:69-71 F 7 '66

Rein on construction raises. Bsns W p75 Jl 2 '66

Year-round pay in construction? U S News 61-72 Jl 25 '66

BUILDING laws and regulations

Deciphering local building codes. Bsns W p78+ S 10 '66

Government construction grants generate over-regulation of plans, New York architects protest. Arch Rec 139:155-6 F '66

What's wrong with building codes? Am City 81:26+ Ag '66

See also

Zoning

BUILDING materials

Colorful products to improve your home. il Pop Sci 188:142 Ap '66

Exciting new products for home remodeling. R. Howe. il Pop Mech 126:128-31+ S '66

House that Jim built; shell homes. R. Levy. Duns R 87:51-2 My '66

How materials react to solar energy. J. I. Yellott. il Arch Rec 139:196-8 My; 197-8 Je '66

New for home owners who do. R. W. Howe. il Pop Mech 125:116-19+ Ap '66

New products for improving your home il Pop Sci 188:166-7 Ap '66

Product reports. See issues of Architectural record

Proper use of the proper material: an integral part of the design idea. il Arch Rec 140:137 N '66

Structural rationalism: the clear expression materials and construction. il Arch Rec 140:176-7 Jl '66

See also

Glass

Glass, Structural

Plastics

Wallboard

BUILDING movement. See Strains and stresses

BUILDING research

Needed: still closer ties between architect, engineer, and manufacturer. R. E. Fischer. Arch Rec 140:163 Jl '66

BUILDING sites

Browder residence. Burbank, California. il Arch Rec 139:74-5 mid-My '66

Lyman residence. Dover, Massachusetts. il Arch Rec 139:90-5 mid-My '66

BUILDING sites—*Continued*
Neuman residence, Baltimore County, Maryland. il Arch Rec 139:84-7 mid-My '66
Scenographic design: the sequence of spaces and the association of ideas. il Arch Rec 140:178-9 Jl '66
Simmen residence, Lake Forest, Illinois. il Arch Rec 139:102-5 mid-My '66
Unusual house for an unusual site. il Arch Rec 140:193-6 O '66

BUILDING trades unions
How to rescue America from plumbers, carpenters, and people like that. J. Fischer. Harper 234:14+ Ja '67
Jim Crow in building unions. Life 60:4 F 18 '66

BUILDINGS
Focus: monthly review of notable buildings. See issues of Architectural forum
Monthly review of events and ideas. See issues of Architectural forum
See also
Airport buildings
Office buildings

BUILDINGS, Prefabricated
Packaged buildings go up fast; pre-engineering structures. il Bsns W p47-8+ Ap 9 '66

BUILDINGS, Remodeled
Breakthrough; rehabilitation of old structures by cutting through the roofs. New Yorker 42:36-7 Ap 30 '66
Renewal without the bulldozer; renovating slum dwellings without tearing them down. il Bsns W p 173-4 D 10 '66
See also
Houses, Remodeled

BUILDINGS, Restoration of. See Architecture—Conservation and restoration

BUILDINGS, Round
Capitol in the round; new state capitol. il Time 88:84 D 16 '66
Fine round of woodwork; the Art Espenet Carpenter's circular house. il Life 61:140-4+ D 9 '66

BUILDINGS, Underwater. See Underwater structures

BUILDINGS, Wrecking. See Wrecking

BUILT-up roofs. See Roofs

BUITRAGO, Fanny
West side of the island; story. Américas 18:36-8 Ap '66

BUKOVAC, M. J. See Rasmussen, H. P. jt. auth.

BULBS
All bulbs and a yard wide. il House & Gard 130:196-7+ S '66
Care for your bulbs; after the flowers fade. C. Lewis. il Horticulture 44:26-9 Je '66
Choice small bulbs. R. Murfitt. il Horticulture 44:16-17+ S '66
For a riot of color next spring. M. Reynolds. il Pop Gard 17:22-5+ D '66
For the great spring show. il Sunset 137:102-5 O '66
Plant groundcovers with bulbs. A. Sutcliffe. il Horticulture 44:32-3+ N '66
Sunset's guide to the September bulbs. il Sunset 137:190+ S '66
See also
Crocuses

Storage
Bulbs to lift & store now. B. Brinhart. il Flower Grower 53:40-2 O '66
Care of bulbs in winter. G. Abraham. Horticulture 44:35-7 O '66

BULBS, Light. See Electric lamps

BULFIN, Matthew J. and Meilach, D. Z.
Expectant mother. Redbook 128:16 Ja '67

BULGARIA
See also
Education—Bulgaria
Tourist trade—Bulgaria

Description and travel
Bulgaria's golden sands. L. Morris. il Travel 126:56-7 S '66

Economic conditions
Big beat in the Balkans. il Time 88:42 N 25 '66

Foreign relations
To Paris on business. Time 88:48+ O 21 '66

BULL, Ephraim Wales
Ephraim Bull and his Concord grape. D. S. Manks. il por Horticulture 44:30-1+ O '66

BULL fights. See Bullfights

BULLARD, Sir Edward
Detection of underground explosions; with biographical sketch. Sci Am 215:15, 19-29 Jl '66

BULLARD, Robert W. See Van Beaumont, W. jt. auth.

BULLATY, Sonja, and Lomeo, Angelo
Kafka's Prague. il Horizon 9:88-99 Wint '67

BULLETIN boards
Bulletin board art. il Design 68:18-20 S '66

BULLETIN of the atomic scientists
Rabinowitch awarded Kalinga prize. A. K. Smith. Science 153:1627 S 30 '66

BULLETS
See also
Shot

BULLFIGHTS
El Cordobés in the afternoon. P. Crumpet. il Nat R 19:33 Ja 10 '67
Homage to a peerless matador; C. Arruza. B. Conrad. il Sports Illus 25:44-52 Ag 1 '66
No blood, some tears, a sweat of money; American style bullfights, promoted by Feld brothers. L. Smith. il Sports Illus 24:42-6 Mr 7 '66
Placid corrida; a Portuguese bullfight. V. Dabney. il Sat R 49:42+ S 10 '66
Profane view of bull baiting. R. Lynes. Harper 232:40+ Ap '66

BULLFROGS. See Frogs

BULLHEAD fishing
Outdoors. T. Williams. Esquire 66:110+ D '66

BULLITT, William C.
[Foreword] excerpt from Thomas Woodrow Wilson, by S. Freud and W. C. Bullitt. por Look 30:36-8+ D 13 '66
—See Freud, S. jt. auth.

BULLOCK, Don
All we had to give was ourselves. E. Lawrence. por Redbook 127:58-9+ My '66

BULLOCK, Linda
All we had to give was ourselves. E. Lawrence. por Redbook 127:58-9+ My '66

BULLOCK'S (store) See Bullock's-Magnin company

BULLOCK'S-Magnin company
Prestige store grows without losing gloss. il Bsns W p58-60+ Ap 9 '66

BULLS
Feed bulls? not yet! D. Malena. il Suc Farm 64:42+ My '66
What to breed for. H. H. Stonaker. il Suc Farm 64:52-3 Mr '66

BULLYING. See Child study

BULMAN, Learned T.
(comp) Choice of books for young adults. Library J 91:6151-2 D 15 '66

BUMGARDNER, Mary
Farm living 1976. por Farm J 90:45-6 N '66

BUMPER stickers. See Labels

BUNCH, Raymond S.
Time-ratio control of mobile-radio power supplies. Electr World 76:84-5 O '66

BUNDY, McGeorge
Adviser to two presidents looks at trends in Europe; statement, June 20, 1966. por U S News 61:80-3 Jl 4 '66
End of either/or. For Affairs 45:189-201 Ja '67
I think we have done damned well; excerpts from address before Senate foreign relations committee. por Newsweek 68:40 Jl 4 '66
about
Exit Mr Bundy. Atlan 217:8+ F '66
Free man. Newsweek 67:26 Mr 7 '66
Washington's grant to the Ford foundation. M. Mayer. il pors N Y Times Mag p58-9+ N 13 '66
What Bundy demanded. S. Lens. Nation 203:658 D 19 '66
White House staff. New Repub 154:8-9 Ap 16 '66

BUNDY, William Putnam
Assistant Secretary Bundy interviewed on Meet the press: transcript of program, September 4, 1966. Dept State Bul 55:428-34 S 19 '66
Call for release of American prisoners held by Communist China; address, May 7, 1966. Dept State Bul 54:866-9 My 30 '66
Elements of the Philippine-American partnership; address, February 24, 1966. Dept State Bul 54:444-51 Mr 21 '66
United States and Communist China; address, February 12, 1966. Dept State Bul 54:310-18 F 28 '66
Viet-Nam and U.S. objectives in the Far East; address, May 23, 1966. Dept State Bul 54:965-70 Je 20 '66

BUNK beds. See Beds

BUNKER, Caroline Clendening (Laise) See Laise, C. C.

BUNKER, Ellsworth
Ambassador Bunker to review Israel desalination proposals; excerpt from opening statement at news conference, October 13, 1966. L. B. Johnson. Dept State Bul 55:687 O 31 '66

BUNKER, Ellsworth—*Continued*
  Entente cordiale. por Newsweek 69:23 Ja 16
    '67
  Old pros. por Time 88:34 O 14 '66
  Three for the seesaw. G. Packard. il por
    Newsweek 68:28 O 17 '66
BUNKER silos. See Silos
BUNKS. See Beds
BUNN, Martin
  Gus Wilson's model garage (title varies) See
    issues of Popular science monthly
BUNNELL, Frederick
  Indonesia's quasi-military regime. bibliog f
    Cur Hist 52:22-8+ Ja '67
BUNNIES and bonnets; drama. See Miller,
  H. L.
BUNRAKU puppet theater, Japan. See Pup-
  pets and puppet plays
BUNRAKU puppets. See Puppets and puppet
  plays
BUNS
  Happy marriage: hot cross buns. il McCalls
    93:34 Mr '66
BUNTING, Basil
  Briggflatts; poem. Poetry 107:213-36 Ja '66
    about
  New lines. T. Clark. Poetry 109:110-12 N '66
BUNTLINE, Ned, pseud. See Judson, E. Z. C.
BUNYAN, John
  Pilgrim's progress. K. Rexroth. Sat R 49:20
    Ag 13 '66
BUOYS
    See also
  Oceanographic buoys
BURBIDGE, Geoffrey
  Origin of cosmic rays; with biographical
    sketch. Sci Am 215:10, 32-8 Ag '66
—and Hoyle, Fred
  Problem of the quasi-stellar objects; with
    biographical sketches. Sci Am 215:16, 40-52
    D '66
BURCH, G. E. and others
  Endocarditis in mice infected with coxsackie
    virus B₄. bibliog Science 151:447-8 Ja 28 '66
BURCH, Thomas K.
  How many Americans will be too many? Cath
    World 203:213-19 Jl '66
BURCHFIELD, Charles Ephraim
  Art news from nowhere. il por Esquire 67:125
    Ja '67
BURCHINAL, Lee G. and Haswell, H. A.
  How to put two and a half tons of research
    into one handy little box. pors Am Ed 2:
    23-5 F '66
BURCK, Gilbert H.
  Aluminum: the classic rollback. Fortune 73:
    106-11+ F '66
  Auspicious rise of the Soviet consumer. For-
    tune 74:130-3+ Ag '66
  Must full employment mean inflation? For-
    tune 74:120-3+ O '66
  Toughest management job in the world.
    Fortune 74:72-9+ Jl 1 '66
BURDEN, Jean
  Truth and experience become one: excerpt
    from Journey toward poetry. Mlle 63:181+
    O '66
BURDON, Eric
  An Animal views America. pors Ebony 22:
    160-2+ D '66
BUREAU of commercial fisheries. See United
  States—Fish and wildlife service
BUREAU of European affairs. See United
  States—State, Department of—European
  affairs, Bureau of
BUREAU of independent publishers and dis-
  tributors
  Bipad studies profits in drug store outlets;
    report of 57th meeting. Pub W 190:45 N 21
    '66
  Paperbacks and the distributor; summary of
    address, September 19. 1966. L. Fusco.
    Pub W 190:36 O 17 '66
BUREAU of land management. See United
  States—Land management, Bureau of
BUREAU of national affairs, incorporated
  Pay raises: now at eight-year high. U S
    News 60:96 Ap 25 '66
BUREAU of outdoor recreation. See United
  States—Outdoor recreation, Bureau of
BUREAU of sport fisheries and wildlife. See
  United States—Fish and wildlife service
BUREAU of standards. See United States—
  Standards, National bureau of
BUREAUCRACY
  Big brother is here! C. Stevenson. Read Digest
    89:81-6 N '66
  Big city slowdown: the battle of bureaucracy.
    B. D. Blank. il Nation 203:632-7 D 12 '66
  Bureaucracy and freedom: N. M. Korkunov's
    theory of the state. G. L. Yaney. bibliog
    f Am Hist R 71:468-86 Ja '66

Even LBJ's right arm can't juggle every-
  thing. P. Lisagor. il Nations Bsns 55:21-2
  Ja '67
Government by totem pole. il Nations Bsns
  54:36-7+ O '66
Government tightens the red tape noose. il
  Nations Bsns 54:54-6+ Jl '66
Oceanography: interior department bids for
  a major role. L. J. Carter. Science 154:
  749-51 N 11 '66
Plea for partnership. W. C. Cramer. Todays
  Health 44:64-5 Mr '66
Therapeutic recreation in a federal maze. E.
  M. Avedon. Parks & Rec 1:840-1 O '66
Truth about the Abba Schwartz case. C.
  Fritchey. Harper 232:33-4+ Je '66
Weather modification: Senate bills stir agen-
  cy rivalries. L. J. Carter. Science 151:
  805-8 F 18 '66
Why bureaucrats rate programs above
  people. A. H. Sypher. Nations Bsns 54:
  29-30 Mr '66
BURFORD, William
  Indian; poem. Sat R 49:8 Ap 9 '66
  Lines; Cypris. Athene; poems. Poetry 108:
    322-3 Ag '66
BURG, Ellen A. See Burg, S. P. jt. auth.
BURG, Stanley P. and Burg, E. A.
  Auxin-induced ethylene formation: its rela-
    tion to flowering in the pineapple. bibliog
    Science 152:1269 My 27 '66
  Fruit storage at subatmospheric pressures.
    bibliog Science 153:314 Jl 15 '66
BURGDERFER, Ruth A.
  Design and form through photography. Sch
    Arts 65:31-3 Je '66
BURGENER, C. W.
  All that glitters. Parks & Rec 1:573 Jl '66
BURGER, Norm
  Fuel injection Rochester style. Hot Rod 19:
    58-61+ F '66
BURGERT, Robert
  Notes on new A-V equipment. Sr Schol 89:
    sup22 S 30; sup 14 O 7 '66
BURGESS, Anthony
  Language, myth and Mr Updike. Common-
    weal 83:557-9 F 11 '66
BURGESS, Crystal J.
  Plain 'n' fancy fair. Sr Schol 88:sup24 Ap
    15 '66
BURGESS, Forrest Harrill
  How specialized can you get? W. B. Furlong.
    il pors N Y Times Mag p23+ Ag 14 '66
BURGESS, Gelett
  Don't sell yourself short. Read Digest 88:
    114-16 My '66
  Wild men of Paris; les Fauves; excerpt from
    Architectural record of May 1910. Arch Rec
    140:237-40 Jl '66
BURGESS, H. F.
  In fall; poem. Christian Cent 83:1401 N 16 '66
BURGESS, Robert
  How shall librarians organize? por Library J
    91:6043-4 D 15 '66
BURGESS, Robert F.
  New billfish discovery. Field & S 71:58-9+
    S '66
BURGETT, Gordon Lee
  ST reports: Midwest meets East. Sr Schol
    89:sup 19 S 30 '66
BURGLAR alarms
  Build a hip squawk box: intercom doubles
    as a burglar and fire alarm. C. Vlahos and
    B. G. Wels. il Pop Electr 25:97-8+ O '66
  Burglar beware; today's space age, anti-
    burglar arsenal. Newsweek 69:49 Ja 2 '67
  How to lock burglars out. J. A. Morris. il
    Read Digest 89:137-40 D '66
  Phone tattles on burglars. W. R. Kingen. il
    Pop Mech 126:174-7+ D '66
  SCR auto burglar alarm. E. R. DeLoach. il
    Electr World 76:64-5 Ag '66
  $2 intrusion alarm. R. L. Winklepleck. il
    Pop Electr 25:50 Jl '66
BURGLARY and burglars
  How I'd rob your house; ed. by J. R. Moskin.
    T. Carter. il Look 30:28-9 My 31 '66
  Personal business: how to protect your home
    from intruders. Bsns W p 167-8 O 1 '66
BURGNER, Jack
  Dome. Design 67:34-7 My '66
BURGOYNE, John
  Gentleman Johnny. R. Mitchell. por Opera N
    30:6-7 Mr 5 '66
BURI, Fritz
  Basel's Buri. C. D. Hardwicke. Christian
    Cent 83:1113-14 S 14 '66
BURIAL
    See also
  Cemeteries
  Funeral rites and ceremonies
BURIAL rites. See Funeral rites and ceremonies
BURIED treasure. See Treasure trove
BURK, Joe
  Joe Burk's blinking black box. T. C. Brody.
    il Sports Illus 24:65-7 Je 6 '66

BURKE, Arleigh
Admiral Chester Nimitz, RIP. Nat R 18:256
Mr 22 '66
BURKE, Eugene
Father Theodore Petersen; eulogy, March
16, 1966. Cath World 203:236-8 Jl '66
BURKE, Howell M. jr
Central air conditioning with a window unit.
Pop Sci 189:132-4 Ag '66
BURKE, Kenneth
And here I am, fighting dandelions; Heavy,
heavy, what hangs over? poems. Poetry
107:363-4 Mr '66
about
Burke's other life. W. H. Rueckert. Nation
203:648-9 D 12 '66
BURKE, Lee, and Inselberg, R. M.
When a mother works. Todays Health 44:
3-5 N '66
BURKE, Mary C.
Year of the bed. House & Gard 130:96-7 O '66
BURKE, Michael
CBS bespeaks. por Time 88:69 S 30 '66
BURKE, R. E. and Nelson, P. G.
Synaptic activity in motoneurons during
nautral stimulation of muscle spindles. bib-
liog Science 151:1088-91 Mr 4 '66
BURKE, Robert. See Zanco, M. L. jt. auth.
BURKHARDT, G.
Science education in Africa. Bul Atomic Sci
22:46-8 F '66
BURKHARDT, Robert
Crossing the Atlantic. New Repub 154:6-7
My 21 '66
Supersonic aircraft, to build or not to build?
New Repub 155:12-13 D 24 '66
To Moscow and back. New Repub 155:7-8
D 3 '66
Washington clipboard. See issues of Flying
BURKLEY, George
Statement by President's physician; Novem-
ber 3, 1966. por U S News 61:49 N 14 '66
BURKLUND, C. W. See Smith, A. jt. auth.
BURKS, Ed
How pushbuttons control the mighty Colo-
rado. Pop Sci 188:82-5+ Mr '66
BURLESQUE. See Vaudeville
BURLINGTON, Vt.
Family of Levi Smith. B. Villet and G.
Villet. il Life 61:72-86+ N 25 '66
Levi Smith's bonus, fifteen grandchildren. B.
Villet and G. Villet. il Life 61:80-94 D 9 '66
Three sons of Levi Smith. B. Villet and G.
Villet. il Life 61:68-82 D 2 '66
Youngest of the Smiths. B. Villet and G.
Villet. il Life 61:60-71 D 16 '66
BURMA
When China spits, we swim. R. K. McCabe.
il N Y Times Mag p26-7+ F 27 '66
See also
Missions—Burma

Economic conditions
Burma: a study in how to stop progress.
R. P. Martin. il U S News 60:116+ My 16
'66
Burma doesn't want aid. R. Butwell. New
Repub 155:14-15 S 3 '66

Foreign relations
U.S. and Burma reaffirm bonds of friendship
and cooperation; exchange of greetings,
toast by President Johnson. September 8;
with text of joint communique, September
9, 1966. L. B. Johnson; Ne Win. Dept
State Bul 55:483-6 O 3 '66

Politics and government
Burma doesn't want aid. R. Butwell. New
Repub 155:14-15 S 3 '66
Freedom now for Nu. Time 88:36 N 4 '66
Military rule in Burma. J. Silverstein. Cur
Hist 52:41-7 Ja '67
Question of Burma. V. S. Kearney. America
115:421 O 8 '66
200 per cent neutral. il Time 88:41-2 S 16 '66
See also
Socialism—Burma

Religious institutions and affairs
Exit Burma's missionaries. America 114:763
My 28 '66
BURMAN, Ben Lucien
Last of the Maoris. Read Digest 89:210-12+
O '66
BURMESTER, William F.
Keeping kids out of trouble. Parents Mag
41:50-1+ F '66
BURNAM, Tom
Short-short and the gimmick. Writer 79:16-
17 Je '66

BURNETT, Carol
Gift of love. McCalls 94:73 D '66
BURNETT, Chester Arthur. See Wolf, H.
BURNHAM, Charles W.
Ferrosilite III: a triclinic pyroxenoid-type
polymorph of ferrous metasilicate. bibliog
Science 154:513-16 O 28 '66
BURNHAM, David
Commencement is only the beginning. N Y
Times Mag p 14+ Je 5 '66
BURNHAM, Forbes
Prime Minister of Guyana visits the United
States; exchange of greetings and ex-
change of toasts, July 21, 1966. Dept State
Bul 55:230-1 Ag 15 '66
about
Atlantic report. Atlan 217:14+ Mr '66
Guyana is free, to go where? A. Verrier. il
por N Y Times Mag p54-5+ My 22 '66
BURNHAM, J. Bernard
Bit-by-bit war. Nat R 19:35-7 Ja 10 '67
BURNHAM, James
Third world war. See issues of National re-
view
Why do they hate Robert Strange Mc-
Namara? Nat R 18:1152-62 N 15 '66
BURNHAM, Walter Dean
Death of the New deal. Commonweal 85:284-
7 D 9 '66
Four-year terms? Commonweal 84:79-81 Ap
8 '66
Vietnam and the voter. Commonweal 84:635-7
S 30 '66
BURNING bush; story. See Hoyer, L. G.
BURNING fiery furnace; opera. See Britten,
B.
BURNS, Arthur Edward
Past economies and present policies. Sat R
49:32+ O 15 '66
BURNS, Arthur F.
Arthur Burns looks ahead; excerpt from ad-
dress. December 2, 1966. por U S News 61:
29 D 12 '66
about
Minimum wage vs. jobs. H. Hazlitt. News-
week 67:90 Ap 11 '66
BURNS, James MacGregor
Between presidents and the press. Sat R
49:25 S 3 '66
Presidency: power & paradox. Sat R 49:30-1
F 5 '66
Way out in Vietnam. Harper 233:34-5 Ag '66
BURNS, John Anthony
Hawaii's East-West center. por Am Ed 2:16-
23 D '65
BURNS, John L.
Our era of opportunity; excerpt from address.
Sat R 50:38-9 Ja 14 '67
BURNS, John M.
Preferential mating versus mimicry; disrup-
tive selection and sex-limited dimorphism
in papilio glaucus. bibliog Science 153:551-3
Jl 29 '66
BURNS, Marvin, and Gardner, L. A.
Rotary-percussive system favored for moon
drilling. Tech W 18:33+ Je 20 '66
BURNS, Roger G. and Strens, R. G. J.
Infrared study of the hydroxyl bands in
clinoamphiboles. bibliog Science 153:890-2
Ag 19 '66
BURNS, Vincent Godfrey
Maryland, my Maryland. Newsweek 68:41-2
O 10 '66
BURNS, W. Haydon
Two mistakes too many. Time 87:18-19 Je 3
'66
BURNS, William J. International detective
agency
Dog watch; protecting the dog against
thieves. il Newsweek 68:103A+ S 12 '66
BURNS aircraft company
Burns may sell BA-42 production rights. il
Aviation W 84:111+ My 30 '66
BURNS and scalds
Balm for burns; techniques used at Sumner
L. Koch burn unit. il Newsweek 68:84 Jl
18 '66
Germs cause burn deaths. Sci N 90:300 O 15
'66
BURNS detective agency. See Burns, William
J. international detective agency
BURNSIDE, Orvin C.
Weeds in grain sorghum, how to control
them. Suc Farm 64:112 Mr '66
BURR, Aaron
Conspiracy and trial of Aaron Burr; excerpts
from Shackles of power. J. Dos Passos. il
por Am Heritage 17:4-7+ F '66; Reply
with rejoinder. S. E. Burr, jr. 17:91 Ag '66
BURR, Elizabeth
Along the migrant stream. Library J 91:335-6
Ja 15 '66

BURR, Nelson R.
Uncommon chronicle. Christian Cent 83:1148
S 21 '66
BURR, Theodosia. See Alston. T. B.
BURRAMYS possum. See Opossums
BURRELL, Fred
Arbitrary colors of Fred Burrell. V. Garbers.
il Pop Phot 59:84-5+ Ag '66
BURRILL, B. D.
Man and his boat. Star Song. Yachting 119:
95-7+ Ap '66
BURRIS, John D.
Jaycees' good reading project. ALA Bul 60:
635-6 Je '66
BURROUGHS, John
How to set up a home print shop. Pop Sci
189:124-8+ Jl '66
Toaster you build into a wall. Pop Sci 188:
172-3 F '66
BURROUGHS, William
They do not always remember; story.
Esquire 65:95 My '66

about

Images of loathing. S. Koch. Nation 203:25-6
Jl 4 '66
BURROUGHS, Wise
New ways with hormones for beef cattle.
Suc Farm 64:52-3 F '66
BURROUGHS corporation
Computing success. Time 88:65-6 D 23 '66
BURROW, J. W.
Charles Darwin. Horizon 8:40-7 Aut '66
BURROWING, insect. See Insects—Habits and
behavior
BURROWS, Abe
Cactus flower; adaptation of play by P.
Barillet and J. P. Grédy. Criticism
Life il 60:35-6 F 11 '66
Nat R 18:739-40 Jl 26 '66
Vogue 147:99 F 1 '66
BURROWS, Larry
Air war; photographs. Life 61:44-57+ S 9
'66

about

He was right up there with the pilots. G. P.
Hunt. il por Life 61:3 S 9 '66
BURROWS, Ruby
Bachelor girl. R. Lantz. il pors Ebony 21:102-
4+ Ag '66
BURSERA microphylla. See Elephant trees
BURSK, Edward C.
Case of the product priority; excerpts from
Cases in marketing management. Harvard
Bsns R 4:6-8+ Mr '66
View your customers as investments. Har-
vard Bsns R 44:91-4 My '66
BURT, C. B.
From Grenada, Mississippi, a minister warns
Christians: stand up or get out! pors Look
30:34+ D 27 '66
BURT, Sir Cyril
What makes a child prodigy; reprint. Sci
Digest 59:63-6 Ap '66
BURT, Fairis S.
Build the tickle stick. Pop Electr 24:82+
F '66
BURTIN, Will
Walk-in portrait of a gene at work. il por
Life 61:70-2+ Jl 8 '66
BURTON, Althea N. and others
Western equine encephalitis virus in Sas-
katchewan garter snakes and leopard
frogs. bibliog Science 154:1029-31 N 25 '66
BURTON, Dwight L.
Literature and the liberated spirit; adaptation
of address, June 1966. ALA Bul 60:904-8+
O '66
BURTON, Frank A.
African violets. Horticulture 44:38-40 O '66
BURTON, Paul R.
Substructure of certain cytoplasmic micro-
tubules: an electron microscopic study.
bibliog Science 154:903-5 N 18 '66
BURTON, Philip
Divine Bernhardt. Sat R 50:37 Ja 21 '67
She conquered spirit for the stage. Sat R 49:
35-6 Ap 23 '66
Speech as he pronounced it. Sat R 49:43-4
Mr 5 '66
BURTON, Richard
Bawd of Avon. por Time 87:58 Je 3 '66
Elizabeth Taylor and Richard Burton: the
night of the brawl. J. Roddy. il pors Look
30:42-8 F 8 '66
Liz launches 1,000 ships; Faustus at Oxford:
with report by M. Smith. il pors Life 60:78-
9+ Mr 4 '66
Night Elizabeth Taylor said so what? and
Richard Burton kicked the television set
in. W. Redfield. il por Esquire 67:108-9+
Ja '67

Richard Burton to Liz: I love thee not .. .
R. Braddon. il pors Sat Eve Post 239:88-91
D 3 '66
Who's afraid of Dr Faustus? T. Sage. il
Nat R 18:1319-20 D 27 '66
BURTON, Scott
Old master at the new frontier. Art N 65:52-
5+ D '66
Paint the devil. Art N 65:26-7+ Ap '66
BURTON, Walter E.
Beauty treatments for rusty tools. Pop Mech
125:158-9 Je '66
Chip shields for milling machine. Pop Mech
125:170-1 My '66
Circular bits for your lathe. Pop Mech 126:
160-2+ Jl '66
Give your lathe a brake. Pop Mech 126:188-
91 O '66
Handiest tool ever, the hand grinder. Pop
Mech 126:176-9+ O '66
Make yourself a shrink plate. Pop Mech 125:
192-3 Mr '66
Pee-wee saws make hard jobs easy. Pop
Mech 125:186-8 F '66
Self-reading O.D. shop gauge. Pop Mech 125:
196-8 Mr '66
Templates make contour filing easy. Pop
Mech 127:176-7 Ja '67
BURUNDI
See also
United States—Foreign relations—Burundi

Politics and government

Boot for the boy king. il Time 88:43 D 9 '66
Trouble with Charles. Time 88:34 Jl 15 '66
BURY, Pol
People are talking about. . . il por Vogue
147:194 My '66
BUS stop shelters. See Shelters
BUS-wagons. See Station wagons
BUSCH, August A. jr
Busch league. Time 88:21-2 Jl 22 '66
BUSCH, Katherine C. and Gaines, E. J.
How a library won an election. pors Library
J 91:5338-43 N 1 '66
BUSCH, Noel F.
Senator Russell of Georgia. Read Digest 89:
150-2+ D '66
Should we be trading with the reds? Read
Digest 89:84-8 Jl '66
BUSCH, Richard
Model's day. Pop Phot 59:82-3+ Jl '66
BUSE, Hermann
(comp) Machu Picchu; an anthology; ex-
cerpts. Américas 18:15-21 Ja '66
BUSH, Emily
Traveling with a camera. il Horticulture 44:
38-9+ Je '66
BUSH, George. See Kuehnl, N. jt. auth.
BUSH, Ian E.
Automation of steroid analysis. bibliog Sci-
ence 154:77-83 O 7 '66
BUSH, Janet
Let's travel. Mlle 63:200-2 S '66
BUSH, Monroe
Reading about resources. See issues of Amer-
ican forests

about

New executive director for Population refer-
ence bureau. Nat Parks Mag 40:19-20 Mr
'66
BUSH stadium. See Stadiums
BUSHMAN, Francis Xavier
First movie star. il pors Newsweek 68:22-3
S 5 '66
BUSHMASTER 2000. See Airplanes
BUSHMEN. See Africa—Native races
BUSHMEN (singers) See Singers
BUSHNELL, Don D.
For each student a teacher. Sat R 49:31 Jl
23 '66
BUSINESS
Business can satisfy the young intellectual.
R. M. Blough. Harvard Bsns R 44:49-57 Ja
'66
Business career; address, January 12, 1966.
G. C. Brewer. Vital Speeches 32:297-302
Mr 1 '66
Campus image of business. H. G. Taylor.
Duns R 88:21-2+ N '66
Come and get it! address, October 21, 1966.
L. B. Worthington. Vital Speeches 33:78-
81 N 15 '66
How to succeed in business? pre-packaged
personal success and self-improvement. il
Newsweek 67:84-6 Ap 4 '66
Idealism without illusions; address, June 11,
1966. L. A. Townsend. Vital Speeches 32:
626-9 Ag 1 '66

BUSINESS—*Continued*
Unrest on the campus; business careers; address, November 9, 1965. L. A. Kimpton. Vital Speeches 32:302-5 Mr 1 '66
See also
Capitalism
Christmas business
Corporations
Efficiency, Industrial
Free enterprise
Government aid to business
Imitation in business
Monopolies
Organization charts
Profit
Retail trade
Weather and business

Bibliography

Business books of 1965; comp. by S. Mechanic. Library J 91:1159-64 Mr 1 '66
Business books to come; ed. by J. Putnam. Library J 91:5433-40+ N 1 '66
Business books to come; ed. by J. Putnam and J. Lindheim (cont) Library J 91:1254-63 Mr 1 '66
Business books to come; ed. by J. Putnam and K. Ahrens. Library J 91:3474-80 Jl '66
Executive bookshelf. See issues of Dun's review and modern industry

Directories

Guide to management services 1966. Duns R 87:pt2 103+ Ja '66

Foreign expansion

As U.S. businessmen in Europe look to the future. il U S News 61:64-5 D 5 '66
Beating an old cow; concerning K Blauhorn book and resentment at U.S. takeover of German industry. Newsweek 68:84+ O 3 '66
Building the *Nordeste*; Brazil. il Time 88:100 S 9 '66
Businessman abroad. M. Wilkins. Ann Am Acad 368:83-94 N '66
Buying advice from the top; Controls co. of America's four-man European advisory board. il Bsns W p 139-40 Mr 5 '66
Capital appropriations; surge abroad. Newsweek 67:86 Ap 4 '66
Corporate diplomacy in foreign countries; address, March 11, 1966. C. A. Herter, jr. Vital Speeches 32:407-9 Ap 15 '66
FSO and business executive exchanged in pilot project. Dept State Bul 55:279 Ag 22 '66
How business fights the war by contract. il Bsns W p58+ Mr 5 '66
Oil tool specialist uses own recipes for space age metals; Cameron iron works. il Bsns W p 116-18+ F 26 '66
Saigon: a boomtown for U.S. businessmen. W. Tuohy. il Newsweek 67:70-2 Ja 31 '66
South Africa; profitable U.S. firms. New Repub 155:7-8 Ag 13 '66
U.S. business in the new Europe; winning competitive battles. il Bsns W p94-7+ My 7 '66
U.S. firms promised gains by establishing branches abroad. W. S. Beller. Tech W 19:17-18 O 17 '66
See also
Corporations—Foreign subsidiaries

Forms, blanks, etc.

Business systems and forms. il Duns R 88:pt2 151+ S '66

International aspects

Problems resulting from the internationalization of business; statement, April 21, 1966. A. M. Solomon. Dept State Bul 54:820-5 My 23 '66
Technological competition: Europe vs U.S. J. B. Quinn. il Harvard Bsns R 44:113-16+ Jl '66
Very private world of Peat, Marwick, Mitchell. T. A. Wise. il Fortune 74:88-91+ Jl 1 '66
Where business leads, the world follows. F. Morley. Nations Bsns 54:27-8 Je '66
World business: what to expect. il Nations Bsns 54:76-7 F; 92-3 My; 58-9 Ag; 104+ N '66

Periodicals

See also
Nation's business (periodical)

Political aspects

Business and the G.O.P. J. Berry; reply. B. Goldwater. Duns R 87:16 Ja '66
Declaration of interdependence. Fortune 73:103-4 Mr '66
End in sight for LBJ's honeymoon with business? what business leaders say; symposium. il U S News 61:32-5 Ag 22 '66

Financing our parties; corporate involvement in politics. N. R. Peirce. il Reporter 34:29+ F 10 '66
Mood of the capital; corporations blackmailed to advertise in parties publications. Atlan 217:10+ F '66
Playing a civic role; NICB survey. il Bsns W p 100+ Ap 3 '66
Political action thrives in California. Bsns W p 176 O 29 '66
Politics gets welcome at the company gate; companies engaging in bipartisan efforts to foster a more enlightened electorate. il Bsns W p 172-3+ O 29 '66
Setting the right example; interview. J. S. Kemper. il Nations Bsns 54:42-4+ Ja '66
Why politics needs business in '66; symposium. il Nations Bsns 54:42-5+ Je '66
Willie's big whisper; tax bill amendment; effect on fund-raising. Time 87:26 Mr 11 '66
Your election year choice: action or apathy; adaptation from Action or apathy. il Nations Bsns 54:72-4 Ja '66

Public relations

Campus and business; difficulty in hiring top students. H. C. Wallich. Newsweek 68:67 D 26 '66
Con Edison: the company you love to hate. T. O'Hanlon. il Fortune 73:122-7+ Mr '66
GM and harassment. L. L. L. Golden. Sat R 49:56 Ag 13 '66
Plant moves house. D. Balaban. il Duns R 87:pt2 114-16+ Mr '66
Some important business for business; address, September 12, 1966. L. W. Moore. Vital Speeches 33:28-32 O 15 '66
That glittering overseas investment, the executive's lady. il Fortune 73:132-9 Je '66
Wanted: sophisticated management. L. L. L. Golden. Sat R 50:130 Ja 14 '67
What Americans really think of business; and why college students are disenchanted; L. Harris survey. il Newsweek 67:84-6+ My 2 '66
Why all the confusion over profits? J. Q. Jennings. il Nations Bsns 54:106+ S '66
Wowing the ladies; housewives tour consumer-oriented companies. il Bsns W p90-1 Mr 26 '66
See also
Business and the press

Social aspects

Building the Great society; new opportunities and responsibilities for labor and management; address, January 17, 1966. W. P. Reuther. Vital Speeches 32:432-5 My 1 '66
Business, management, and creative thinking. A. H. Maremont. il Duns R 87:45-6+ My '66
Business sees new horizons. America 115:107-8 Jl 30 '66
Businessmen: partners in crimebusting. il Nations Bsns 55:58-62+ Ja '67
Challenge to business: create its own Great society; condensation of address, March 24, 1966. G. Champion. Read Digest 89:107-10 Ag '66
Conscience in the boardroom; new attitudes towards social responsibility. il Newsweek 67:77-8+ Ap 11 '66
Cultural analysis in overseas operations. J. A. Lee. Harvard Bsns R 44:106-14 Mr '66
FDA's edict: patients, not profits, come first; excerpts from address, April 6, 1966. J. L. Goddard. Science 152:332-3 Ap 15 '66
Ford on our future. America 114:722-3 My 21 '66
Great American cities; role of private industry in solving unemployment problem; address, November 14, 1966. A. J. Cervantes. Vital Speeches 33:176-9 Ja 1 '67
How businessmen have steered history's course. il Nations Bsns 54:56-8+ F '66
How private enterprise solves public problems. il Nations Bsns 54:42-3+ O '66
How to carve your niche in the economy. il Nations Bsns 54:96-8+ My '66
Insights into business & society. W. G. Broehl, jr. bibliog(p 180+) Harvard Bsns R 44:6-8+ My '66
New cities are big business. J. Ridgeway. New Repub 155:15-17 O 1 '66
New social-industrial complex; address, July 13, 1966. L. M. Spencer. Vital Speeches 32:721-5 S 15 '66
Public affairs; address, April 21, 1966. S. M. Linowitz. Vital Speeches 32:477-80 My 15 '66
Public obligations and the private corporation. T. C. Sorensen. Sat R 49:24+ My 14 '66

BUSINESS—Social aspects—*Continued*
Social values of marketing; address, October 27, 1966. C. W. Cook. Vital Speeches 33: 86-91 N 15 '66
Troubled environment: improving our cities; address, December 8, 1965. H. Donovan. Vital Speeches 32:241-4 F 1 '66
When a corporation turns toward sociology; address, April 18, 1966. B. Oldfield. Vital Speeches 32:427-9 My 1 '66

BUSINESS administration. See Business management and organization
BUSINESS airplanes. See Airplanes, Business
BUSINESS and art. See Art and industry
BUSINESS and community. See Business—Social aspects
BUSINESS and defense services administration. See United States—Business and defense services administration
BUSINESS and education
Anatomy of the creative decision; address, March 10, 1966. R. E. Williams. Vital Speeches 32:508-12 Je 1 '66
Big business & govt: new education forces. Sr Schol 88:sup2 F 4 '66
Games in fabuland. J. Ridgeway. New Repub 155:17-18 Ag 27 '66
Industry and education. D. Wolfle. Science 153:1599 S 30 '66
Letter from the publisher. B. M. Auer. Time 87:21 Ap 29 '66
Machines that can talk but have nothing to say; educational technology. R. H. Smith. Pub W 190:79 Ag 22 '66
Officers named for new G.E.-time education unit. Pub W 189:30 My 2 '66
Right young people for business. J. S. Fielden. Harvard Bsns R 44:76-83 Mr '66
Technology in the schools: educators are uneasy. L. J. Carter. il Science 153:1624-6 S 30 '66
   See also
Corporations—Charitable contributions

BUSINESS and golf. See Golf and business
BUSINESS and professional women
Bachelor girl; Negro girls in nation's capital. R. Lantz. il Ebony 21:102-4+ Ag '66
Five with enterprise: young women who struck out on their own. P. Rifield. il Mlle 63:144-7 S '66
Now is the time for all good parties to come to the aid of the girls. D. Newman and R. Benton. Mlle 63:88+ S '66
Open for business: Baedeker for the girl who wants to be her own boss. A. Grant. il Mlle 63:142-3+ S '66
Ready, steady, go! career girls; London. A. Grant. il Mlle 62:188-90 Mr '66
Unless we begin now; address, July 25, 1966. J. W. Macy, jr. Vital Speeches 32: 678-82 S 1 '66
   See also
Secretaries
Women as executives

BUSINESS and state. See Industry and state
BUSINESS and the press
Blocking off the press. L. L. L. Golden. Sat R 49:78 S 10 '66

BUSINESS and war. See War—Economic aspects
BUSINESS as a profession. See Businessmen
BUSINESS charts
   See also
Stocks—Price indexes and averages
BUSINESS communication. See Communication in management
BUSINESS conditions
Business and finance. See issues of Newsweek
Business outlook. See issues of Business week
Business roundup. S. S. Parker and others. See issues of Fortune
Business: strong but a bit jumpy. il Bsns W p29-31 Mr 5 '66
Business tides. H. Hazlitt. See issues of Newsweek
Corporate view still glows: optimism, despite rising costs, tight money, and labor troubles. Bsns W p40-1 O 15 '66
How's business? Nat R 18:1146+ N 15 '66
Plus & minus; business activity of the week. See issues of U.S. news & World report
Spotlight on business. See issues of Newsweek
Trend of American business. See issues of U.S. news & World report
Trend of business. J. Phillips. See issues of Dun's review and modern industry
Trouble signs for the boom. il U S News 61:31 D 5 '66
U.S. business. See issues of Time
Wall Street: the butter stocks; cashing in on the Great society. Newsweek 67:68 F 7 '66

When business economists take a look ahead. il U S News 61:71-2+ O 10 '66
   See also
Business depression
Business forecasting
Economic conditions
Inflation (finance)
Investments
United States—Economic conditions

BUSINESS conferences
Harvard puts its tent show on big time circuit. il Bsns W p86+ Mr 12 '66

Anecdotes, facetiae, satire, etc.
Open-window theory of executive conference. H. R. Spencer, jr. Duns R 88:34-5 O '66

BUSINESS consolidations and mergers
Anatomy of an acquisition. J. B. Weiner. Duns R 87:34+ My '66
Anchor in the past; antitrust cases. il Time 87:85 Je 24 '66
Antitrust: a tough new line; new ruling overturns merger of two California supermarket chains. il Newsweek 67:81 Je 13 '66
Big chemical merger; Montecatini and Società Edison. il Fortune 73:69-70+ Ap '66
Buying a younger generation; Philadelphia's Wellington management co. merging with Boston's Ivest, inc. il Bsns W p 149-50+ N 19 '66
Buying into a company via the tender offer. il Bsns W p38-9 F 26 '66
Europe considers industrial mergers. V. K. McElheny. Science 152:486-8+ Ap 22 '66
Finance firm completes acquisition of A. C. McClurg. il Pub W 191:59 Ja 16 '67
From pies to pickles; United Artists and Consolidated foods merger. il Newsweek 68:71 Ag 1 '66
From the trustbusters: guidelines for businessmen. il U S News 61:46+ Jl 25 '66
Growing from within may pay off faster; stockholders lose when companies merge. il Bsns W p44+ S 17 '66
High court tightens the antitrust reins; FTC can stall mergers while legality is tested. il Bsns W p40-1 Je 18 '66
How Eaton found a perfect mate; acquisition of Yale & Towne. il Bsns W p 100-1+ My 28 '66
How one man can move a corporate mountain. S. H. Brown. il Fortune 74:80-3+ Jl 1 '66
IRS says yes to Conoco: Continental oil-Consolidation coal merger. Bsns W p30 Ag 27 '66
ITT's new network: ABC. il Time 88:53 D 30 '66
Into the back seat; RCA-Hertz merger. Newsweek 68:79 O 31 '66
Justice dept. ok's merger of McGraw-Hill and S&P. Pub W 189:53 Mr 7 '66
Marriages of necessity; companies unite in bigger and more efficient combines; Great Britain. Time 88:69 D 23 '66
Merger of sorts; Renault and Peugeot. Time 87:98 Ap 29 '66
Merger wave hits Europe. Bsns W p 153-4+ F 26 '66
Mergers: everybody wants to get bigger. il Newsweek 67:72-3+ Ap 25 '66
Mutual antipathy; antitrust suit filed to stop Genesco takeover. il Time 87:82 Ap 1 '66
New gold in the Hollywood hills; movie industry. il Time 88:108+ N 25 '66
One plus one equals five; purpose of European mergers. Time 87:101 F 4 '66
Opportunity list; Litton deal to absorb Diebold. Time 87:96 Ap 29 '66
RCA in driver's seat; acquires Hertz corp. Bsns W p48 O 22 '66
Relic of the 1920s returns; convertible participating preferred stock. il Bsns W p80+ Ag 13 '66
Richard Irwin, Dow Jones propose merger plan. Pub W 190:50-1 O 10 '66
Roadblocks slow the urge to merge; falling stock prices and tight money have soured number of mergers. il Bsns W p 183-4+ S 10 '66
Stormy marriage; ITT and ABC. il Newsweek 69:54 Ja 2 '67
Surge to merge; Europe. Newsweek 67:72+ Mr 7 '66
Trouble with antitrust; excerpts from address. M. A. Wright. il Duns R 88:50-1+ N '66
Uniting for strength; interview. G. H. Love. Nations Bsns 55:44-5+ Ja '67
Wall Street: merger stocks. Newsweek 67:74 Ap 25 '66
Whirlpool moves into living room; merger with Warwick electronics, manufacturer of home entertainment equipment for Sears. Bsns W p38 Ag 20 '66

BUSINESS consolidations and mergers—*Cont.*
Why companies seek greener fields; mergers on the upswing. il Bsns W p59-60+ Mr 12 '66
Yardley in a lather; British-American tobacco co. ltd. bid for Yardley & co. ltd. Time 89:65 Ja 13 '67
See also
Airplane industry and trade—Consolidations and mergers
Bank consolidations and mergers
Corporate acquisitions
Monopolies
Philco-Ford corporation
Railroads—Consolidations and mergers

BUSINESS consultants
And now, the captive consultant. J. Weingarten. il Duns R 88:67-8+ N '66
Corporate goals & the outside expert. M. S. Osborn. il Duns R 87:pt2 108-9+ Mr '66
How to buy, sell professional services. W. J. Wittreich. Harvard Bsns R 44:127-34+ Mr '66
Linking computers to French logic; Metra international, Paris-based management and research consulting firm. il Bsns W p96-8 D 24 '66
Treatment for business doctors. il Bsns W p 120-1+ Je 25 '66
See also
Lippincott and Margulies, incorporated
Van Dyck corporation

BUSINESS council
Business likes '67, and LBJ. il Newsweek 68:79 O 31 '66
Proprietary interest; new chairman. il Time 88:92 D 16 '66

BUSINESS cycles
See also
Business conditions

BUSINESS depression
Another '29 in sight? pro and con. il U S News 60:46-8 My 16 '66
Can we stop inflation without a recession? H. C. Wallich. Newsweek 68:72-3 S 5 '66
Inflation? recession? or both? il Nations Bsns 54:38-41+ O '66
Planned recession for Britain; how it's working. il U S News 61:70 O 3 '66
Recession danger: how real? il U S News 61:41-2 S 26 '66
See also
Business conditions

BUSINESS districts
Cooperation built a market plaza; Wheeling, W.Va. J. Rody. il Am City 81:104-5 Ap '66
Framework for lower Manhattan. D. Canty. il Arch Forum 125:48-53 Jl '66
Grass-roots facelifting; Newton, N.J. D. Whitman. jr. il Am City 81:96-7 O '66
Merchants' high hope in Minneapolis. il Fortune 73:161-2 Je '66
New downtown; Fremont, Calif. L. W. Milnes. il Am City 81:86-7+ Je '66
Philadelphia's giant shopping machine; Market street east. D. Canty. il Arch Forum 125:34-43 N '66
They're catching on! Am City 81:6 Ap '66
What it takes to make great cities. E. K. Faltermayer. il Fortune 75:118-23+ Ja '67

BUSINESS economics, Office of. See United States—Business economics, Office of

BUSINESS economists. See Economists

BUSINESS education
Education for a business career. il Changing T 21:25-8 Ja '67
Getting more out of the graduate; preference for master's in business administration. Bsns W p61-2+ Je 18 '66
Hunting for action, in small business; business school student interest in the small-business jobs. il Bsns W p82-4 Ap 9 '66
Invasion of the business schools; American marketing knowhow in Europe. Bsns W 120 My 7 '66
Mentors for Britain's flagging management; London business school helping to instill professionalism in industry's managers. il Bsns W p 190-1+ O 15 '66
Modern business education; with comments. V. Dotson. NEA J 55:44-6 F '66
Teaching the Kenyans to take a letter; secretarial training sponsored by ILO. il Bsns W p 126-7 My 7 '66
See also
Executives—Training

BUSINESS enterprises, New
Vicar wanted to travel. O. Schisgall. Read Digest 89:187-8+ O '66

BUSINESS entertaining
Happy days are here again. Nation 202:765 Je 27 '66

BUSINESS ethics
Are we going to the dogs? Cardinal Heenan on the improved moral outlook of British business. America 115:796 D 17 '66

Business morality: some unanswered and perhaps unanswerable questions. A. S. Miller. bibliog f Ann Am Acad 363:95-101 Ja '66
Regulation, by business or government? J. G. Van Cise. bibliog f Harvard Bsns R 44: 53-63 Mr '66
Sharp practice in merchandising and advertising. E. T. Grether. bibliog f Ann Am Acad 363:108-16 Ja '66
See also
Advertising ethics
Better business bureau

BUSINESS exhibitions, Traveling. See Exhibitions, Traveling

BUSINESS expenses. See Expense accounts (business)

BUSINESS failures
Business failures. R. Wyant. See issues of Dun's review and modern industry
See also
Bank failures
Bankruptcy

BUSINESS flying. See Airplanes in business

BUSINESS forecasting
America's next ten years. Nations Bsns 54:42 Ap '66
Business: a look ahead. See issues of Nation's business
Businessmen's expectations. K. E. Hickey. il Duns R 87:13 Mr; 14 Je '66
Businessmen's expectations. L. Humphries. il Duns R 88:13 S '66
Economy: what next? J. Perham. il Duns R 44:30-2+ S '66
Executive investor; ten best groups this year. il Duns R 87:93-4 Ja '66
Future of the boom as business experts see it. il U S News 60:31-4 My 30 '66
How government sizes up the business outlook now. il U S News 61:62-3 O 24 '66
How much inflation ahead? what economists say. il U S News 60:42-5 Mr 14 '66
Is the boom near a turning point? il U S News 60:29-31 My 23 '66
Look ahead by business leaders. U S News 61:71 O 31 '66
LBJ prepares to ask for a tax hike; thirteenth annual business outlook conference of First national bank of Chicago. il Newsweek 68: 61 D 26 '66
Measure of the boom LBJ sees ahead. il U S News 60:32-4 F 7 '66
More expansion still gets majority vote; with editorial comment. il Bsns W p37-8, 196 O 1 '66
New gains, new worries. il Bsns W p27-8 Ag 20 '66
Next for U.S: profitless prosperity? il U S News 61:56-9 O 17 '66
Official size-up of the business outlook; excerpts from address, May 10, 1966. A. M. Okun. U S News 60:78-9 My 23 '66
Outlook for '67; as investment bankers see it. il U S News 61:82-4+ D 12 '66
Recession danger: how real? il U S News 61:41-2 S 26 '66
'67 view: growth, but... il Newsweek 69:61 Ja 16 '67
'67: what kind of a year; forecast by twelve top economists; symposium. il U S News 62:72-9 Ja 9 '67
Trend of American business. See issues of U.S. news & World report
What the war in Vietnam will do to business now. il U S News 60:42-3 F 14 '66
What the year ahead holds for business. il U S News 61:40-3 Jl 11 '66
When business economists take a look ahead. U S News 61:71-2+ O 10 '66
Where business is heading; interview. G. Ackley. il U S News 60:46-52 Ap 11 '66
Why new worry over business. il U S News 61:27-9 Ag 29 '66
See also
Forecasts (economics)

BUSINESS games. See Management games

BUSINESS gifts. See Gifts in business

BUSINESS helicopters. See Helicopters in business

BUSINESS location. See Location in business and industry

BUSINESS machines. See Office appliances

BUSINESS management and organization
Aspects of leadership; address, January 18, 1966. F. R. Kappel. Vital Speeches 32:254-6 F 1 '66
Boost for the man in the middle; middle management, a big corporate concern. il Bsns W p85-6+ Ja 22 '66
Buying advice from the top; Controls co. of America's four-man European advisory board. il Bsns W p 139-40 Mr 5 '66
Case of the convalescent corporation. J. J. Hansen. il Harvard Bsns R 44:160-2+ My '66

BUSINESS management and organization—
Continued
Change seekers; management of change. P.
H. Irwin and F. W. Langham, jr. il Harvard
Bsns R 44:81-92 Ja '66
Conditions for manager motivation; survey
of motivation at Texas instruments. M. S.
Myers. bibliog f il Harvard Bsns R 44:58-71
Ja '66
Dangerous supervisory gap. E. C. Schleh.
il Duns R 87:57-8+ F '66
Everyone wants a hand in management.
Bsns W p89 Ap 9 '66
Executive trends. See issues of Nation's
business
Fallacy of the one big brain. P. Hunt. il
Harvard Bsns R 44:84-90 Jl '66
Famous firsts: U.S. seedbed of the man-
ager's art; C. H. McCormick. Bsns W p53-
4 Ag 27 '66
First things first? C. A. Cerami. il Nations
Bsns 55:68-71 Ja '67
How BVD bought its new outfit; underwear
maker into a clothing empire. il Bsns W
p98-100 Je 4 '66
Make mistakes, make money. C. H. Cerami.
il Nations Bsns 54:78-80 Ja '66
Management of Litton industries. J. B.
Weiner. il Duns R 87:32-3+ My '66
Management's rule-breakers: the ways of the
winners. J. B Weiner. il Duns R 87:34-7+
Ja '66
Managers tighten their grip; new study
bolsters 1932 thesis of Berle and Means
about who runs companies. il Bsns W p63-
4+ N 5 '66
Managing to manage the computer; sum-
mary of survey. J. W. Taylor and N. J.
Dean. il Harvard Bsns R 44:98-110 S '66
Never mind the answer; what's the ques-
tion? M. T. Bloom. il Pop Mech 125:132-4+
F '66
President and international operations. M. L.
Mace. bibliog Harvard Bsns R **44:72-84**
N '66
Problems of a new executive; reprint from
May 1949 issue. E. P. Learned. Harvard
Bsns R 44:20-4+ Jl '66
Professionalization of management; address,
November 11, 1966. R. V. Scacchetti. Vital
Speeches 33:137-41 D 15 '66
Reorganizing for results. D. R. Daniel.
Harvard Bsns R 44:96-104 N '66
Reviving the giants; interview. E. R. Breech.
il Nations Bsns 54:48-9+ O '66
Rewriting the script for Scripto; C. N.
Singer. il Bsns W p 168+ D 17 '66
Simon says it with a broad brush. il Bsns W
p62-4+ My 14 '66
Six business lessons from the Pentagon.
D. J. Smalter and R. L. Ruggles, jr. il
Harvard Bsns R 44:64-75 Mr '66
There's a new tune at Motorola; R. W. Gal-
vin presses decentralization. il Bsns W
p 110-12+ Ap 23 '66
Tomorrow's management: a more adven-
turous life in a free-form corporation. M.
Ways. Fortune 74:84-7+ Jl 1 '66
U.S. business in the new Europe: winning
competitive battles. il Bsns W p94-7+ My
7 '66
What it takes to make the board; study by
Heidrick & Struggles, inc. il Bsns W p93-4
Mr 12 '66
What puts the whiz in Litton's fast growth;
unique blend of finance and management.
il Bsns W p 174-6+ Ap 16 '66
Whole staff has a voice in running Sentry.
il Bsns W p 112-14 Jl 30 '66
You can shape your company's future. il Na-
tions Bsns 54:118+ Ap '66
See also
American management association
Computers—Business applications
Corporate acquisitions
Cost accounting
Decision making
Diversification in industry
Executives
Industrial management and organization
Systems management

Bibliography
What the executive reads about his job. il
Bsns W p 129-30 Ag 6 '66
BUSINESS memos. See Memorandums
BUSINESS organization. See Business man-
agement and organization
BUSINESS recession. See Business depres-
sion
BUSINESS records
Government tightens the red tape noose. il
Nations Bsns 54:54-6+ Jl '66
BUSINESS schools. See Business education

BUSINESS secrets. See Trade secrets
BUSINESS statistics
Figures of the week. See issues of Business
week
See also
Business forecasting
BUSINESS success. See Success
BUSINESS uniforms. See Uniforms
BUSINESS women. See Business and pro-
fessional women
BUSINESSMEN
Businessmen in the news. See issues of For-
tune
Conscience in the boardroom; new attitudes
towards social responsibility. il Newsweek
67:77-8+ Ap 11 '66
Conversations parents never hear; business
major. il Look 30:78-9 S 20 '66
Europe takes a tip from U.S. businessmen.
il U S News 62:72-5 Ja 16 '67
Exports: the wellspring of new business em-
pires; private entrepreneurs. Bsns W p 172
My 7 '66
Golf: pitching for the green; business evolv-
ing from the course. il Newsweek 68:68-9
Ag 8 '66
Grand old men of business. il Fortune **73:**
120-7 F '66
Right young people for business. J. S.
Fielden. Harvard Bsns R 44:76-83 Mr '66
SR's businessman of the year: T. J. Watson,
jr. W. D. Patterson. Sat R 50:74+ Ja 14
'67
Schoolboys come of age; Indian businessmen.
il Time 87:74 Ap 22 '66
Scrooge and the students. T. C. Sorensen.
Sat R 50:66 Ja 14 '67
Stretch of the imagination; address, Decem-
ber 7, 1965. M. J. Warnock. Vital Speeches
32:234-7 F 1 '66
Where expense-account living is really
worthwhile; Japanese business men. il U S
News 60:111-13 F 28 '66
See also
Executives
Negro businessmen

Political activities
See Business—Political aspects

Religious life
Pulpit and market place. B. L. Masse. Amer-
ica 115:182+ Ag 20 '66
BUSINESSMENS clubs. See Clubs
BUSINESSMENS uniforms. See Uniforms
BUSINGEN, Germany
Europe's oddest outpost. P. Brock. il Travel
125:36-7 Je '66
BUSONI, Ferruccio
Arlecchino. Criticism
Opera N 30:31 Mr 19 '66
Bridge to the future; Pietro Scarpini and
the Cleveland negotiate longest piano con-
certo. il por Time 87:44 F 18 '66
Busoni centenary. B. Jacobson. por Hi Fi 16:
135 My '66
Divided man. por Newsweek 67:91B F 21 '66
Musical events; concert in commemoration
of hundredth anniversary of his birth. W.
Sargeant. New Yorker 41:90+ F 5 '66
Turandot. Criticism
Opera N 30:31 Mr 19 '66
BUSS, Edward G. See Bloom, S. E. jt. auth.
BUSSABARGER, Robert
Terra-cotta temples of India. Craft Horiz 26:
28-33 Ja '66
BUSSARD, A. E.
Antibody formation in nonimmune mouse
peritoneal cells after incubation in gum
containing antigen. bibliog Science 153:887-8
Ag 19 '66
BUSSE, James G.
How human engineering is making better
tools for you. Pop Sci 189:114-17+ O '66
BUSTAD, Leo K.
Pigs in the laboratory; with biographical
sketch. Sci Am 214:16, 94-100 bibliog (p 144)
Je '66
—and McClellan, R. O.
Swine in biomedical research. Science 152:
1526-8+ Je 10 '66
BUSTARD, H. Robert, and Hughes, R. D.
Gekkonid lizards: average ages derived from
tail-loss data. bibliog Science 153:1670-1 S
30 '66
BUTCHER, Russell D.
(ed) See Douglas, W. O. Our wilderness
rights are missing
BUTCHERS
Meat and mortality; butcher's feud with
mortician in Italy. il Newsweek 67:42 F
28 '66

BUTEL, Janet S. and others
Replication of adenovirus type 7 in monkey cells: a new determinant and its transfer to adenovirus type 2. bibliog Science 154:671-3 N 4 '66
BUTLER, Alexander R.
History from Abbe to Zworykin. New Repub 155:20-2 O 15 '66
BUTLER, Henry
Glad good-bye to the old Met. Look 30:41-2+ Ap 19 '66
Is there a soprano in the house? Harper 233:77-81 Ag '66
BUTLER, Joseph T.
Engaging souvenirs of the Grand tour. Antiques 90:96-9 Jl '66
BUTLER, Lewis H.
Overseas staff. bibliog f Ann Am Acad 365:83-92 My '66
BUTLER, Richard
Long lonely night. America 115:649-51 N 19 '66
Present position of Catholics in English universities. por Cath World 204:37-41 O '66
BUTLER, Sue
Apollo ship, aircraft elements readied. Miss & Roc 18:24-6 Ja 24 '66
Saturn V crawler trouble cleared up. Miss & Roc 18:34-5 F 7 '66
BUTLER, W. Royce
Acquisitions; excerpts from address, 1965. por Library J 91:2271-4 My 1 '66
BUTLER, William F.
Flaw in the new economics. Duns R 88:41-2+ O '66
This is a good time to buy bonds; interview. por U S News 60:58-60 Ap 4 '66
BUTLER, William Henry
Bush mammalogist; interview. New Yorker 42:18-20 Ag 6 '66
BUTLER meteorite. See Meteorites
BUTLER university, Indianapolis
Light to go to school by. A. F. Lindberg. il Am City 81:137 S '66
BUTTER
Make your own flavored butter; with recipes. il Sunset 137:213-14 O '66

Prices
Wider spread for butter trading; declines in stockpile and in dairy herds push prices upward. il Bsns W p 107-8 Ag 6 '66
BUTTER and egg man; drama. See Kaufman, G. S.
BUTTER substitutes
See also
Margarine
BUTTER trees
Nature note; Indian butter tree, or mohwa. Sci N 90:517 D 17 '66
BUTTERCUPS
Alpine buttercup. D. E. Rose. Horticulture 44:50 D '66
Are those flowers real? il Sunset 137:80-1 N '66
BUTTERFIELD, Roger
Assassination; some serious exceptions to the Warren report. Harper 233:122+ O '66
BUTTERFINGER; story. See Stanton, W.
BUTTERFLIES
Birth of a butterfly. D. G. Schleisner. il Flower Grower 53:34+ Jl '66
Chromosomes from testicular preparations of lepidoptera. L. D. Miller and S. M. Miller. bibliog il Science 152:529-30 Ap 22 '66
Nature note; fritillaries. Sci N 90:126 Ag 20 '66
Tagging the migratory monarch. E. Stobbe. il Audubon Mag 68:343-6 S '66
BUTTERFLIES, Courtship of. See Courtship of insects
BUTTERFLY tagging. See Insect tagging
BUTTON, Daniel
Rules of the game. Nat R 18:1086 N 1 '66
BUTTONS
Bay State buttons. D. F. Brown. il Hobbies 71:50-1+ Mr '66
Button collecting. D. F. Brown. See issues of Hobbies
BUTWELL, Richard
Burma doesn't want aid. New Repub 155:14-15 S 3 '66
Getting rid of Sukarno. New Repub 155:12-13 O 8 '66
Southeast Asia: how important, to whom? bibliog f Cur Hist 52:1-7 Ja '67
BUTZ, Sam
Our pilots call Hanoi Dodge City. N Y Times Mag p30-1+ O 16 '66
BUYERS guides. See Consumer education
BUYERS laboratory, incorporated. See Testing laboratories

BUYING. See Shopping and shoppers
BUYING motives. See Market research
BUZBEE, Ellen W.
Parent and child (cont) N Y Times Mag p 132+ N 27 '66
BYBLOS
Byblos: a stony history book. il Sunset 138:28+ Ja '67
BYE, Ranulph
Ranulph Bye; with biographical sketch. il por Am Artist 30:36-7+ D '66

about
Station closed; water colors. W. Buehr. Am Heritage 17:33-41 F '66
BYERLEE, J. D. See Brace. W. F. jt. auth.
BYERS, Margery
Lynda Bird's dashing Hollywood beau. Life 60:51-2+ My 13 '66
Parents' struggle to accept the reality. Life 61:94 O 28 '66
(ed) See Brooke, E. W. Bay State's colorblind candidate
BYLINSKY, Gene
Farm technology plows ahead at John Deere. Fortune 74:147-51+ D '66
Searching for the beginnings of civilized man. Fortune 74:158-63+ O '66
BYRAM, E. T. and others
Cosmic X-ray sources, galactic and extragalactic. bibliog Science 152:66-71 Ap 1 '66
BYRD, Harry Flood, 1887-1966
Byrd of Virginia. por Newsweek 68:26-7 Jl 18 '66
Cause not lost with Harry Byrd. Life 61:4 N 4 '66
Harry Flood Byrd. J. J. Kilpatrick. Nat R 18:718 Jl 26 '66
Squire of Rosemont. il por Time 88:30 O 28 '66
Stillness at Berryville. J. Fletcher. por Nat R 18:781-3+ Ag 9 '66
Symbol of economy and states' rights. por U S News 61:21 O 31 '66
BYRD, Harry Flood, 1914-
Double feature in Byrdland. J. I. Brooks. Reporter 34:25-7 Je 16 '66
Stillness at Berryville. J. Fletcher. Nat R 18:781-3+ Ag 9 '66
BYRD, Laoma
First lady of boxing. il pors Ebony 21:81-2+ Je '66
BYRD, Robert Carlyle
Preserving a forest for recreation. por Am For 72:18-20 S '66
Spruce Knob-Seneca Rocks national recreation area. Nat Parks Mag 40:8-10 D '66
BYRD, William
Massive documentation of Byrd's technique. M. Serbin. Am Rec G 33:60-1 S '66
BYRN, Edward W.
1900 account of the phonograph; excerpt from Progress of invention in the nineteenth century. Hobbies 71:38-9 Ag; 37-8+ S; 37-8 O '66
BYRNE, John V. and others
Uplift of the continental margin and possible continental accretion off Oregon. bibliog Science 154:1654-6 D 30 '66
BYRNE, William L. and others
Memory transfer. Science 153:658-9 Ag 5 '66
BYRNES, Francis C.
Role shock: an occupational hazard of American technical assistants abroad. bibliog f Ann Am Acad 368:95-102 N '66
BYRON, George Gordon Noël Byron, 6th baron
Byron & Rossini. L. A. Marchand. il Opera N 30:6-7 Mr 19 '66
Medwin's conversations of Lord Byron, by L. A. Marchand. Review
Sat R 49:49 Je 11 '66. R. Halsband
BYRON, Robert K.
How to run a peace candidate. Nation 203:469-72 N 7 '66

C

CAIP. See Catholic association for international peace
CAMROC. See Cambridge radio observatory committee
CAP. See College of American pathologists; United States—Civil air patrol
CAPEI. See Central American program of economic integration
CAT (clear air turbulence) See Atmospheric turbulence
CATV (community antenna television systems) See Television antennas

CB radio. See Citizens radio service
CBA. See Christian booksellers association
CBC. See Canadian broadcasting corporation;
 Children's book council
CBE. See Council for basic education
CBS. See Columbia broadcasting system
CBS building. See New York (city)—Architecture
CCA. See Controls company of America
CCAP. See Citizens crusade against poverty
CCD. See Confraternity of Christian doctrine
CCF. See Political parties—Canada
CCM. See Crowell Collier and Macmillan, incorporated
CCNY. See New York (city) City university
 of New York—City college
CCP. See Communist party (China [People's
 Republic])
CCRM. See Committee on civil rights in metropolitan New York
CD. See Certificates of deposit
CDC. See Control data corporation
CDL. See Citizens for decent literature and
 motion pictures, incorporated
CDU (Christian democratic union) See Political parties—Germany (Federal Republic)
CEA. See Conservation education association;
 United States—Council of economic advisers
CED. See Committee for economic development
CEF. See Citizens for educational freedom
CENTO. See Central treaty organization
CERN (Conseil européen pour la recherche nucléaire) See European organization for nuclear research
CETS (Conférence européene des télécommunications par satellite) See European conference on satellite communications
CF. See Cystic fibrosis
CIA. See United States—Central intelligence
 agency
CIAP (Inter-American committee on the Alliance for progress) See Alliance for progress
CIOS (Conseil international pour l'organization
 scientifique) See International congress for
 scientific management
CLR. See Council on library resources, incorporated
CMH. See Medal of honor (United States)
COC (combat operations center) See North
 American air defense command
COCU. See Consultation on church union
COIN. See Community organizations for the
 improvement of neighborhoods, incorporated
COMECON. See Council for mutual economic
 assistance
COMSAT. See Communications satellite corporation
CONLIS. See Committee on national library
 and information systems
COPE. See American federation of labor and
 Congress of industrial organizations—Committee on political education
COSMOS (commission on the structure of
 Methodism overseas) See Methodist church
COSPAR. See International council of scientific unions—Committee on space research
CPA. See Catholic press association
CPIF (cost plus incentive fee) See Incentives
 in industry
CPL (combined programming language) See
 Programming languages (computers)
CPM (critical path method) See Critical path
 analysis
CPSU (Congress of the Communist party of
 the Soviet Union) See Communist party
 (Russia)
CRIA. See Committee to rescue Italian art
CROP. See Christian rural overseas program
CSD. See American library association—Children's services division
CU. See Consumers union of United States
CUE (culture, understanding, and enrichment)
 See New York (state)—Education department
CUNY. See New York (city) City university
 of New York
CURV (cable-controlled underwater research
 vehicle) See Submarine boats
CUSA. See Christians united for social action
CAB drivers. See Taxicab drivers
CABALA
Cosmic religion. M. Eliade. Commentary 41:
 95-6+ Mr '66

CABALLÉ, Montserrat
Caballé as Lucrezia Borgia. H. Weinstock.
 por Sat R 49:54 D 31 '66
Caballé records her first complete opera. W.
 Weaver. il pors Hi Fi 16:99-102 O '66
Rarest quality. R. Kotlowitz. Harper 232:127
 Ap '66
CABARET; musical comedy. See Musical
 comedies, revues, etc.—Criticisms, plots,
 etc.
CABBAGE
 See also
Cookery—Vegetables
CABBAGES
 See also
Sauerkraut
CABEZA PRIETA game range. See Game preserves
CABINET
 Great Britain
 See Great Britain—Cabinet
CABINET (United States) See United States—
 Cabinet
CABINET officers
Robert C. Weaver: quiet man wins spot in
 Cabinet. S. Booker. il Ebony 21:82-4+ Ap
 '66
Robert Clifton Weaver; Secretary of housing
 and urban development. F. Parker. bibliog
 Negro Hist Bul 29:75-6 Ja '66
 See also
United States—Cabinet
CABINET work
 See also
Woodworking
CABINETMAKERS
Collectors' notes: documented examples. E.
 Gaines. il Antiques 89:838-45 Je '66
More on the Meeks cabinetmakers. J. Pearce
 and L. W. Pearce. il Antiques 90:69-73 Jl
 '66
Providence cabinetmakers, chairmakers, upholsterers, and allied craftsmen, 1756-1838;
 a check list. W. D. Garrett. il Antiques 90:
 514-19 O '66
Those Meekses; ed. by E. Gaines. il Antiques
 90:358-9 S '66
CABINETS (furniture)
Store it where you use it, that's the new
 way. il Pop Sci 188:144-8 Ap '66
 See also
Kitchen cabinets
Television cabinets
CABINS
Down the slope and up the ladder. B. Plumb.
 il N Y Times Mag p52-3 Ja 30 '66
For snowmen only; W. Meeks house in the
 Cascades of Washington. il Life 60:70-3+ Ja
 28 '66
Four a-frames: bountiful light. il House &
 Gard 129:128-9 Je '66
CABLE, Harold
Fairest pitcher of them all; drama. Plays
 25:27-41 F '66
Peace, Pilgrim; drama. Plays 26:1-14 N '66
Young forever; drama. Plays 26:1-14 O '66
CABLE, Mary
Very pearl of the realm. Horizon 8:108-15
 Wint '66
We and they in Rhodesia. New Yorker 41:
 36-41 F 19 '66
CABLE, Heating. See Electric heating
CABLE cars. See Cable railroads
CABLE railroads
Where city transit is fueled by nostalgia;
 San Francisco's colorful cable cars. il Bsns
 W p 182-4 O 22 '66
CABLES
Demand for bigger spans has brought back
 the bearing wall and also led to practical
 solutions for bold cable structures. il Arch
 Rec 140:156-7 Jl '66
CABLES, Submarine
Satellite going up, prices going down; to
 compete with Comsat, other carriers are
 proposing lower rates. il Bsns W p 116+
 C 1 '66
 See also
Telephone cables
CABLES, Telephone. See Telephone cables
CABLEWAYS
Death and suspense on an Alpine cable. il
 Life 61:28-9 Jl 22 '66
CABRILLO music festival. See Music festivals
 —California
CACCIOLA, J. A. and Carr, E. Q.
World's first single chip integrated circuit
 radio. Electr World 76:44-6 N '66
CACHIN, Françoise
Dandy at the helm. Art N 65:36-8+ Ap '66
CACTUS
They are simply spectacular. il Sunset 136:
 268-9 My '66
CACTUS flower; drama. See Burrows, A.

CADAVERS
Cadaver crisis. J. J. Curtis, jr. and G. Hohberger. America 115:515-16 O 29 '66
Dead & the quick; concerning death abroad. Time 87:71 My 13 '66
Honoring the will of the dead. Christian Cent 83:641 My 18 '66

CADBURY, William E. Jr
Cooperative relations involving the liberal arts colleges. Sch & Soc 94:213-17 Ap 16 '66
Self-scheduled examinations under an honor system. Sch & Soc 94:68-70 F 5 '66

CADDEN, Vivian
(ed) See Eisenhower, M. Mamie Eisenhower talks about fifty years of marriage
—See Caplan, G. jt. auth.

CADDIES, Garden tool. See Carts

CADIGAN, John J.
Decision at sea. Read Digest 90:50-4 Ja '67

CADMIUM
Cadmium & blood pressure. il Time 88:61-2+ N 4 '66
Killer cadmium; relationship with hypertension. il Newsweek 68:73 N 7 '66

CADMIUM oxide
Use of silver solder may be hazardous; death from cadmium oxide fumes. Sci N 89:307 Ap 30 '66

CADUFF, Sylvia
Music to my ears; lady conductor. I. Kolodin. Sat R 49:34 F 5 '66

CADWALLADER, Mervyn
Marriage as a wretched institution. Atlan 218:62-6 N '66

CADY, John F.
French colonial regime in Vietnam. Cur Hist 50:72-8+ F '66

CAEMMERER, Richard R.
Quiet reformer. Christian Cent 83:141 F 2 '66

CAESAR, Caius Julius
Caesar and the enigma of his death. L. Barzini. il pors Life 60:64+ Mr 18 '66
Julius Caesar. K. Rexroth. Sat R 49:23 Jl 30 '66
Julius Caesar. il pors Life 60:50-5 Mr 18 '66

CAESAR, Gene
Outward bound! Seventeen 25:92-3+ Jl '66

CAESAR salad. See Salads

CAESARS. See Roman emperors

CAFÉ Chauveron. See New York (city)—Hotels, restaurants, etc.

CAFETERIAS

Equipment

Changes in food service technology and how they affect design. E. G. Daniels. il Arch Rec 140:145-8 Ag '66

CAFFEINE
What coffee really does to you. I. Ross. il Sci Digest 60:79-83 Jl '66

CAGE, John
Science of saying nothing; new recordings. O. Daniel. Sat R 49:63+ Ap 30 '66
Two extremes of avant-garde music. R. Kostelanetz. il pors N Y Times Mag p34-5+ Ja 15 '67

CAGGIULA, Anthony R. and Hoebel, B. G.
Copulation-reward site in the posterior hypothalamus. bibliog Science 153:1284-5 S 9 '66

CAHILL, Carl
Note on two Va. Negro Civil war soldiers: one Union, one Confederate. Negro Hist Bul 29:39-40 N '65

CAHILL, William Thomas
Excerpt from debate, July 26, 1966. Cong Digest 45:276+ N '66

CAHN, Rhoda. See Cahn, W. jt. auth.

CAHN, Robert D. See Coon, H. G. jt. auth.

CAHN, William, and Cahn, Rhoda
From supermarket to superlibrary. Parents Mag 41:47-9+ Je '66

CAIN, Robert E.
Original print. por Library J 91:5323-6 N 1 '66

CAIN, Stanley A.
Concepts for conservation; address, September 21, 1965. Vital Speeches 32:202-6 Ja 15 '66
Spirit of the mountain. Américas 18:1-8 Mr '66

CAINE, Marcella
Black magic; poem. Negro Hist Bul 29:133 Mr '66

CAINE, Michael
Cool character called Caine; ed. by E. Miller. il pors Seventeen 25:116-17+ D '66

about

Caine file. H. Lawrenson. por Esquire 66:260-2+ D '66
Maurice Joseph Micklewhite, what's 'e got? G. Steinem. il pors N Y Times Mag p66-7+ D 4 '66

Success of a sometime spy; with report by K. Gouldthorpe. il pors Life 61:105-6+ O 21 '66

CAJAMARCA, Peru
Cajamarca. E. Hosmann. il Américas 18:31-8 S '66

CAJUNS. See Acadians in Louisiana

CAKE
Fruit picture cakes; butter kuchen; with recipes. il Sunset 137:70-1 S '66
It's candy crossed with fruitcake; with recipe. Sunset 137:154 D '66
It's Italy's famous zuppa inglese, but you make it with mixes. il Sunset 136:184 Ap '66
Let's take the cake. il Ebony 21:134+ Mr '66
Little cooks make themselves some little strawberry cakes. il Sunset 137:96-7 Ag '66
No need to bake this cooky cake; with recipe. il Sunset 137:110 Jl '66
Our best burnt-sugar chiffon cake; with recipe. il Bet Hom & Gard 44:84 My '66
Pinwheel pecan cake. V. V. Voboril. il Good H 162:170 Mr '66
Plum pudding and fruitcake, faster than ever. il Bet Hom & Gard 44:70-1+ D '66
Redbook's Christmas cookbook. il Redbook 128:92-7 D '66
Show-stopping dessert, and surprisingly simple! il Bet Hom & Gard 44:86-7 O '66
Step by step to marble chiffon cake. il Bet Hom & Gard 44:92 Ap '66
Successful recipes, pack a picnic cake. il Suc Farm 64:73-4 Jl '66
Swedish treat for holiday visitors; soft spice cake, with recipes. Sunset 137:150 D '66
Three-tier cake for daddy from Let's start to cook. N. B. Nichols. il Farm J 90:45, 60 Jl '66
'Tis the season for chocolate and mistletoe; with recipes. G. Maddox. il Todays Health 44:54-9 D '66
Two Turkish delights; potted lamb and sweet cake. M. Kaytor. il Look 30:98-9 F 22 '66
Wedding cake that's good to eat. D. Groves. il Farm J 90:52-5 Je '66
Yule breads and cakes; with recipes. P. Cannon. il Ladies Home J 83:104-5+ D '66
See also
Coffee cake
Icings

CAKE mixes. See Food mixes

CALADIUMS
Caladium. D. E. Stebbins. Horticulture 45:48 Ja '67
See what you can do with caladiums. il Pop Gard 17:14-15 My '66

CALAHAN, Harold Augustin

Obituary

Motor B 117:366 Ja '66. M. Penzer

CALCITE
Calcite: rates of dissolution in a vertical profile in the central Pacific. M. N. A. Peterson. bibliog il Science 154:1542-4 D 23 '66
Deep-sea authigenic calcite and dolomite. E. Bonatti. bibliog il Science 153:534-7 Jl 29 '66

CALCIUM
Calcium and bromide contents of natural waters. R. J. Anderson and others. bibliog il Science 153:1637-8 S 30 '66; Reply with rejoinder. P. C. Mangelsdorf, jr. 154:1473 D 16 '66
Calcium in sea water by electrode measurement. M. E. Thompson and J. W. Ross, jr. bibliog il Science 154:1643-4 D 30 '66

CALCIUM carbonate
Foraminiferal evidence of a shallow calcium carbonate solution boundary, Ross Sea, Antarctica. J. P. Kennett. bibliog il Science 153:191-3 Jl 8 '66
High-purity calcium carbonate in fresh-water clam shell. D. J. Nelson and others. bibliog il Science 152:1368-70 Je 3 '66
See also
Calcite

CALCIUM electrodes. See Electrodes

CALCIUM in the body
Control of myocardial contraction; the sensitivity of cardiac actomyosin to calcium ion. A. M. Katz and D. I. Repke. bibliog il Science 152:1242-3 My 27 '66; Reply. B. L. Fanburg. 154:1203 D 2 '66
Muscle postjunctional membrane: changes in chemosensitivity produced by calcium. W. L. Nastuk and J. H. Liu. bibliog il Science 154:266-7 O 14 '66
Periventricular cerebral impedance after intraventricular injection of calcium. H. H. Wang and others. bibliog il Science 154: 1183-5 D 2 '66

CALCIUM in the body—*Continued*
Vitamin D₃-induced calcium-binding protein in chick intestinal mucosa. R. H. Wasserman and A. N. Taylor. bibliog il Science 152:791-3 My 6 '66
See also
Hypercalcemia
CALCIUM phosphate
Apatite and octa-calcium phosphate: effects of carbon dioxide and halogens on formation. D. R. Simpson. bibliog il Science 154: 1660-1 D 30 '66
CALCULATING machines. See Computers
CALCULI, Biliary
Uric acid, uric acid dihydrate, and urates in urinary calculi, ancient and modern. K. Lonsdale and P. Mason. bibliog il Science 152:1511-12 Je 10 '66
CALCULI, Urinary
Newberyite in ancient and modern urinary calculi: identification and space group. K. Lonsdale and D. J. Sutor. bibliog il Science 154:1353-4 D 9 '66
CALCUTTA
Calcutta: city of death. E. Behr. il Newsweek 67:41 Ap 4 '66

Sanitary affairs
Calcutta sets up water and sanitation authority. il Am City 81:28 O '66
CALDECOTT medal
ALA names book award winners. Sr Schol 88:sup4 Mr 25 '66
Newbery and Caldecott medal books: 1956-1965. E. S. Ross. Horn Bk 42:186-7 Ap '66
Newbery-Caldecott winners. il Wilson Lib Bul 40:688 Ap '66
Nonny Hogrogian. A. Durell. il Library J 91: 1594-5 Mr 15 '66
Theviño, Hogrogian: Newbery and Caldecott winners. il Pub W 189:30-2 Mr 14 '66
CALDER, Alexander
Art galleries: exhibition at the Perls gallery. R. M. Coates. New Yorker 41:140 F 19 '66
Boiler-plate beauty, stabiles. il por Time 87:78 My 13 '66
CALDER, Ritchie Calder, baron
Two decades in the world of science. UNESCO Courier 19:8-14 Jl '66
CALDERONE, Mary Steichen
Goodbye to the birds and the bees; an approach; adaptation of address. Am Ed 2: 17-18 N '66
Planning for sex education. NEA J 56:26-9 Ja '67
Sex and your teen-ager. Farm J 90:90-1 F '66
Sex education and the very young child. PTA Mag 61:16-18 O '66
Sex without secrets; interview. por Seventeen 25:106-7+ Jl '66
What men can do about it. PTA Mag 61:5-6 S '66

about
Sex education comes of age. L. Gross. il pors Look 30:20-3 Mr 8 '66
CALDWELL, Joseph R. See Dougherty, R. C jt. auth.
CALDWELL, Millard F.
Responsibility of government. Vital Speeches 32:536-40 Je 15 '66
CALDWELL, Nat. See Kovach, B. jt. auth.
CALDWELL, R. L. and others
Combination neutron experiment for remote analysis. bibliog Science 152:457-65 Ap 22 '66
CALDWELL, Sarah
Rameau in Boston. H. Rogers. il por Opera N 30:6-7 Ap 9 '66
CALENDAR
Origins of the Copernican revolution. J. R. Ravetz. il Sci Am 215:88-95+ bibliog(p 152) O '66
CALENDARS
Baraja mexicana calendarica. D. Powills. Hobbies 71:118-19+ Mr '66
Button calendar. D. F. Brown. il Hobbies 71: 52 Ja '67
Calendars 1967. il House & Gard 130:36-7 D '66
CALFO, George E.
Cool life in a commercial jungle. il pors Bsns W p60-1 Mr 5 '66
CALGARY, Alberta
Lighting changes the face of a city. G. Cornish. il Am City 81:131 Mr '66
CALHOUN, Fillmore
Diplomacy of victory in Europe. Sat R 49:29 D 31 '66
CALI, Grace
Temptation of Professor Tillich. Esquire 65: 68-9 My '66

CALIAN, Carnegie Samuel
Ecumenical shift in the Middle East. Christian Cent 83:1140-2 S 21 '66
Man in the pew. por Cath World 204:170-3 D '66
CALIBRATION
Army field calibration technicians; calibrating electronic test equipment used to maintain and check missiles. C. J. Diodati. il Electr World 76:80-2 S '66
CALIBRATION technicians. See Electric workers
CALIBRATORS
Audio calibrator for transistor amplifiers. R. Wilson. il Electr World 76:67 Ag '66
Build: solid-state scope calibrator. F. Forman and E. Nawracaj. il Pop Electr 24:61-4 Je '66
CALIFORNIA
California: golden magnet. W. Graves. il Nat Geog Mag 129:595-679 My '66
California; symposium, ed. by G. B. Leonard and J. Poppy. il Look 30:28-40+ Je 28 '66
Destruction of California, by R. Dasmann. Review
    Liv Wildn 29:30-1 Wint '65. S. E. Wood
See also
Architecture, Domestic—California
Birds—California
Booksellers and bookselling—California
Camping—California
Carson Pass
Cascade Range
Clear Lake
Crime and criminals—California
Education—California
Feather River
Festivals—California
Fishing—California
Forests and forestry—California
Gardens—California
Geology—California
Housing—California
Hunting—California
Justice, Administration of—California
Kings Canyon National Park
Lassen Volcanic National Park
Law—California
Medicine Lake
Music festivals—California
Napa Valley
Orange County
Paleontology—California
Prisons—California
Roads—California
San Francisco
Shasta, Mount
Skis and skiing—California
Taxation—California
Tehachapi Mountains
Yosemite National Park

Anti-poverty program
Weird warriors in war on poverty. il Nations Bsns 54:42-3+ My '66

Description and travel
At Mammoth in the spring; California's Mammoth Mountain. il Sunset 136:86-95 Mr '66
Better homes and gardens tour: California. il Bet Hom & Gard 45:21 Ja '67
For tramping and camping in May, look into the Sespe. il Sunset 136:42-5+ My '66
Four family-planned circle tours. M. Kuehnl and P. Lindberg. il Bet Hom & Gard 44: 74-5 Je '66
Pismo; long beach, the white dunes, the delicious clams. il Sunset 136:62-7 F '66
Robust, exciting: it's called California. C. West and J. West. il Motor B 117:22-6+ My '66
Spring cruising in the Delta; Sacramento-San Joaquin Delta. il Sunset 136:94-103 My '66
Up and over the Algodones dunes. il Sunset 137:22+ N '66

Economic conditions
TRW to study land-use planning; studies on transportation, waste disposal, information systems and juvenile delinquency. Tech W 18:20 Je 6 '66

Fish and game commission
Deserts in the sea; economic expedients at price of annihilating fish; condition of California's industry. R. G. Lillard. il Nation 202:268-70 Mr 7 '66

Historic houses, etc.
See also
Los Angeles—Historic houses, etc.

CALIFORNIA—*Continued*

History

Gilded South. N. Morgan. il Sat R 49:52+ O 8 '66
See also
California—Missions

Industries

Few notes from California; failure to exploit and advertise artichokes and sourdough bread. C. W. Morton. il Atlan 218:103-4 Ag '66
Seven wine roads of California; tour of the wine country. il Sunset 137:58-69 S '66
Tour of California wineries. H. Johnson. House & Gard 130:248+ O '66
See also
Aerospace industries—United States

Maps

California; first state map in new United States atlas series. il Nat Geog Mag 129:680-1, sup(folded map) My '66

Missions

California's mission trail. J. H. Winchester. il Travel 126:37-9 D '66

Moral conditions

California; a vision of hell and heaven. J. Poppy. il Look 30:48-54 Je 28 '66
Sex spies; UCLA study of law-enforcement policies and practices. Nation 202:572-3 My 16 '66

Parks and reserves

Fine wild Forest of Nisene Marks. il Sunset 137:20+ Ag '66
House that Hearst built. il Newsweek 68:44 Ag 29 '66
Old mill and a forest park are hiding in the Napa Valley. il Sunset 137:39 Ag '66
Raising the sights for the redwoods; address, August 17, 1966. A. W. Smith. il Nat Parks Mag 40:17-19 N '66
San Simeon revisited. il Time 88:71 N 18 '66
See also
Death Valley National Monument

Politics and government

After the primary. R. Moley. Newsweek 67:98 Je 27 '66
Analyzing the swing to the right wing. il Newsweek 67:32 Je 20 '66
Anti-politics? Commonweal 85:68-9 O 21 '66
Atlantic report. Atlan 218:22+ Ag '66
Barbecues and other trivia. G. Hill. il Nation 203:377-9 O 17 '66; Discussion. 203:466+ N 7 '66
Big contest is in California; with reports by W. Rogers and J. Roddy. il Look 30:41-2+ N 1 '66
But what if Reagan becomes the governor? J. Duscha. New Repub 155:11-13 N 5 '66
California; of men and money. S. Alsop. Sat Eve Post 239:14 Je 4 '66
California; the final battle? M. Ryskind. Nat R 18:1094-7+ N 1 '66
California; the swinging voters. R. Reinhardt. il Look 30:88+ Je 28 '66
California, there she blows! analysis of primary results. Nation 202:732-3 Je 20 '66
Can Reagan win California? J. Phelan. il Sat Eve Post 239:89-93 Je 4 '66
Conservative tide. il Newsweek 67:31-2 Je 20 '66
Cut and thrust; gubernatorial primary preview. Newsweek 67:25-6 Je 6 '66
Giant rocks block road for Reagan. il Bsns W p70-1 N 26 '66
Grandpa vs. the dude. Newsweek 68:61-2 Ag 22 '66
It's the idea that offends; dinner held for Republican candidates. S. Alexander. Life 61:17 Jl 8 '66
Just folks; gubernatorial campaign. il Newsweek 68:41-2 O 31 '66
Men from CLEAN; smut trade; election issue. Newsweek 68:23-4 S 5 '66
New left; what does it mean? E. M. Keating. Sat R 49:25-7+ S 24 '66
New politics in California. Nation 203:372-3 O 17 '66; Reply. M. Burnstein. 203:466 N 7 '66
No business like it; gubernatorial campaign. Time 88:37 S 16 '66
Notes from the land of political pop. H. Gold. il N Y Times Mag p48-9+ D 11 '66
Paradise Reagan-ed; voters psychology. Nation 203:596 D 5 '66
Parkinson's law; primary race. il Time 87:20 My 27 '66
Parties in chaos; California sweepstakes. G. Hill. Nation 202:352-5 Mr 28 '66

Pat the giant killer. il Newsweek 67:27-8 F 14 '66
Pat's last putt; Brown to run for governor. Time 87:22 F 11 '66
Peace candidates. Newsweek 67:33 Je 20 '66
Political action thrives in California. Bsns W p 176 O 29 '66
Political fun and games in California. J. Langguth. il N Y Times Mag p27-9+ O 16 '66
Politics in California; primary result. New Repub 154:7-8 Je 18 '66; Reply. G. S. Mitrovich. 155:37 Jl 2 '66
Reagan campaign purring. Nat R 18:818 Ag 23 '66
Reagan in the wilderness; and other major candidates for governorship. il Newsweek 67:30-3 Mr 28 '66
Reagan vs. Brown; how to succeed with the backlash. C. McWilliams. il Nation 203:438-42 O 31 '66
Reagan vs. Brown; see how they run! J. Bonfante. il Life 61:42-7 O 14 '66
Ronald for real. il Time 88:31-5 O 7 '66
Ronald Reagan; a light in the West. F. Clinton. il Nat R 18:613-15 Je 28 '66
Ronald Reagan to the rescue! J. Murray. il Esquire 65:76-8+ F '66
Story of Ronald Reagan, governor of nation's biggest state; an appraisal. il U S News 62:30-6 Ja 2 '67
Strenuous life of California politics. R. A. Rutland. New Repub 154:11-12 Ap 16 '66; Reply. S. Zetterberg. 154:37 Ap 30 '66
Tide coming in; gubernatorial race. Time 88:32 N 4 '66
Two's a crowd; Democratic gubernatorial nomination. Time 87:29A-29B Mr 18 '66
Under way; a key battle in 1966 campaign. il U S News 60:28 Mr 21 '66
Up from Death Valley; California's Republican gubernatorial primary. il Time 87:24-5 Je 17 '66
What makes Sammy run. Newsweek 67:29-30 Mr 21 '66
Will California stand Pat? race for governor. J. Duscha. il Reporter 35:40-2 S 22 '66
See also
Race problems
Los Angeles—Riots

Religious institutions and affairs

Bishop for California. il Newsweek 68:76 S 26 '66
See also
Protestant Episcopal church

CALIFORNIA, GULF OF
In the wake of Cortez. N. Phillips. il Motor B 118:22-4+ D '66

CALIFORNIA, LOWER
Eviction of whales; threat to breeding ground of the great gray whale. W. Marx. il Atlan 217:91-5 Ap '66
Four family-planned circle tours. M. Kuehnl and P. Lindberg. il Bet Hom & Gard 44:74-5 Je '66
New boat, a new venture (cont) E. Newmark. il Yachting 119:114-16+ Ja '66
New boom for Baja. A. D. Bruce, jr. il Travel 125:41-3 Ap '66
See also
Paleontology—California, Lower

CALIFORNIA Angels (baseball) See Baseball clubs

CALIFORNIA condors. See Condors

CALIFORNIA highway patrol academy. See Police, State—Training

CALIFORNIA institute of technology, Pasadena
Caltech & M.I.T.; rivalry between the best. il Time 88:82-3 N 4 '66
Caution! genius at play. J. N. Bell. il Pop Mech 125:120-3+ Mr '66
See also
Jet propulsion laboratory

Astrophysical observatory

See Astronomical observatories

CALIFORNIA Jays. See Jays

CALIFORNIA library association
California LA resolves to fight CLEAN, inc. anti-obscenity bill. Library J 91:3368 Jl '66

CALIFORNIA packing corporation
Brand that makes Calpak a winner. Del Monte label. il Bsns W p80-1+ Mr 26 '66

CALIFORNIA pipeline. See Gas, Natural—Pipe lines

CALIFORNIA trucking association
Touch of realism; teamsters' transportation opportunity program. Nation 203:597 D 5 '66

CALIFORNIA. University
Battle over a budget. Time 89:64 Ja 20 '67
Big schools labor to think small; cluster college. il Bsns W p 196-8+ S 17 '66
Corralling the old UC? R. Reagan's budget proposals. il Newsweek 69:63 Ja 23 '67
Institute of library research. R. M. Hayes. il Library J 91:4579-85 O 1 '66
UC extension keeps the pros up to date. il Bsns W p 196-8+ Mr 12 '66

Berkeley campus
Back to work in California. J. Rieger. New Repub 155:8-9 D 17 '66
Balancing act at Berkeley; R. Heyns. il Life 61:45-6+ D 16 '66
Berkeley: new crisis breaks out on California campus. D. S. Greenberg. Science 154:1304-6 D 9 '66
Berkeley, 1966. Commonweal 85:337 D 23 '66
Berkeley now: no revolution. il Newsweek 68:117-20+ N 21 '66
Berkeley scene, 1966. E. Langer. il Science 152:1037-41, 1220-3 My 20-27 '66
Berkeleyitis: a second look. J. F. Ohles. Sch & Soc 94:66 F 5 '66
Berkeley's peacemaker. il Time 88:38-9 Jl 1 '66
Big happening in Berkeley: Wurster hall. D. Lyndon. il Arch Forum 124:56-63 Ja '66
California classic: the Berkeley girl. J. Shepherd. il Look 30:78-80+ Je 28 '66
Cooling it at Berkeley. il Time 88:110 D 16 '66
Crackdown, and a quick end to a campus strike. il U S News 61:72-4 D 19 '66
Decline of freedom at Berkeley. L. S. Feuer. Atlan 218:78-82+ S '66; Discussion. 218:105-11 O; 38+ N '66
Experiment at Berkeley. il NEA J 56:21-2+ Ja '67
Frightened intellectuals: S. Carmichael address. Reporter 35:22-3 N 17 '66
I am a U.C. student; do not fold, bend or mutilate. H. Gold. il Sat Eve Post 239:34-6+ Je 18 '66
More furor at Berkeley. Nation 203:661 D 19 '66
More leftist trouble on the campus. il U S News 61:6 D 12 '66
Neglected college; Muscatine report, proposals for undergraduate educaton. il Newsweek 67:85-6 Mr 28 '66
Politics of outrage; notes on the student left. M. Rogin. Commonweal 84:99-102 Ap 15 '66
R&D in higher education; Center for the study of higher education authorized by Office of education. Sch & Soc 94:119-20 Mr 5 '66
Sad scenes at Berkeley. il Time 88:81 D 9 '66
Smale case: NSF and Berkeley pass through a case of jitters. D. S. Greenberg. il Science 154:130-3 O 7 '66; Discussion. 154:1395-6 D 16 '66
Uncertain future of the multiversity; Muscatine report. M. Savio. Harper 233:88-90+ O '66; Discussion. 233:8+ D '66
Uneasy truce at Berkeley. il Newsweek 68:80 D 19 '66
What to do about Berkeley; report by official committee of insiders. il Time 87:70+ Mr 25 '66
Yesterday's Berkeley rebel says: I'm just here to study. A. H. Raskin. il N Y Times Mag p 12-13+ Ja 30 '66

Botanical garden
Garden walking by Strawberry creek just minutes from Berkeley's noisy streets. il Sunset 136:250-1 My '66

Davis campus
Ceramics from Davis. J. Pugliese. il Craft Horiz 26:26-9 N '66

Irvine campus
College controversy: approach to dance in college. O. Maynard. il Dance Mag 40:62-5 S '66

Libraries
Libraries West and East. il Fortune 74:160+ S '66

Los Angeles campus
Color it Bruin: L. Alcindor of UCLA challengers. H. L. Masin. il Sr Schol 89:24 D 2 '66
Graduate research library designed to expand. il Arch Rec 140:214-17 S '66
Man from U.C.L.A. il Time 88:98 O 21 '66
Space frame costs less than $4 a square foot; Pauley pavilion at U.C.L.A. il Arch Rec 139:181-4 Mr '66
Ultimate in research: Jules Stein eye institute. il Time 88:66+ N 11 '66

Libraries
Library named at UCLA for Lawrence C. Powell. Library J 92:46 Ja 1 '67

San Diego campus
La Jolla's new university; Olympus on a mesa. K. Lamott. Harper 233:82-4+ Ag '66

Santa Cruz campus
First year at Santa Cruz. il Time 87:56 My 13 '66
Reaping the rewards of service; tribute to business' contributions to society. Bsns W p88-91 Je 18 '66
Santa Cruz after one year; report on Cowell college. J. L. Jarrett. il Sat R 50:67+ Ja 21 '67
Some advice on sex, dress and manners; Cowell college, excerpts from memorandum. P. Smith. U S News 60:14-15 Je 6 '66
U.C.S.C. fieldhouse: bold solution to size, space problems. il Arch Rec 140:146-8 D '66
CALIFORNIA wines. See Wine
CALIFORNIANS
California; symposium, ed. by G. B. Leonard and J. Poppy. il Look 30:28-40+ Je 28 '66
Notes from the land of political pop. H. Gold. il N Y Times Mag p48-9+ D 11 '66
Surf, wheels & free souls. J. Siegel. il Sat Eve Post 239:32-7 N 19 '66
Turned-on and super-sincere in California. R. Todd. il Harper 234:42-7 Ja '67
CALINA. See Fog
CALKING
Easy does it with caulking gun. il Sunset 137:160+ O '66
Hot-glue gun with lukewarm talents; Thermogrip electric glue gun. il Consumer Rep 31:102-3 Mr '66
See also
Sealing compositions
CALKINS, Frank
Buck packing made easy. Field & S 71:60-1+ S '66
CALKINS, Robert De Blois
National university; excerpts from address November 13, 1965. bibliog Science 152 884-9 My 13 '66
CALL, Charles W. 1926?-
New baker adds yeast to Ward. il por Bsns W p80-2+ Jl 16 '66
CALLAGAN, Dwight A. and Boylan, B. R.
Expectant mother. Redbook 126:40+ F '66
CALLAGHAN, James
Out of the black case. il por Time 87:101 My 13 '66
CALLAHAN, Alston
How to raise money. il por Time 88:36 D 30 '66
CALLAHAN, Daniel
Comment. See issues of Commonweal
Creating a community. Commonweal 84:24-7 Mr 25 '66
Relational nature of theology. Christian Cent 83:135-7 F 2 '66
CALLAHAN, Joseph M.
What you should know about anti-smog devices. Pop Sci 188:120-3 Mr '66
CALLAS, Maria
Divorce, Greek style. il por Time 87:79 Ap 15 '66
CALLAWAY, Helen
U. of Sussex: the establishment challenged. Mlle 63:182-4+ O '66
CALLAWAY, Howard Hollis
Excerpt from debate, July 27, 1966. Cong Digest 45:285+ N '66
about
Out of the fight into the fire. Time 88:20 Jl 15 '66
Peach state snarl. Sr Schol 89:18 D 2 '66
Three races. H. Alexander. Nat R 18:1042-3 O 18 '66
CALLAWAY gardens, Pine Mountain, Ga. See Golf courses
CALLENDER, West Winslow
North of Nakina. por Outdoor Life 137:33-5+ My '66
CALLING, Animal. See Animal calling
CALLISON, Charles H.
National outlook (cont of) National capital report. See issues of Audubon magazine
CALLS for animals. See Animal calling
CALLUNA. See Heathers
CALORIMETRY conference
Calorimetry; report on 21st conference. O. J. Kleppa. Science 154:431 O 21 '66
CALPAK. See California packing corporation
CALTECH. See California institute of technology, Pasadena

CALTHA palustris. See Marsh marigolds

CALVER, George W.
Congress' doctor prescribes: how to stay healthy under pressure; interview. pors Nations Bsns*54:92+ O '66

CALVERT, Pearce Reginald Hartley
Pirate's end. il por Newsweek 68:41 Jl 4 '66

CALVERT, Robert, jr
Returning volunteer. Ann Am Acad 365:105-18 My '66

CALVERT, W.
Ionospheric topside sounding. bibliog Science 154:228-34 O 14 '66

CALVES
He calves with care. Suc Farm 64:100G Mr '66

Care

Best calf raising setup I've seen. J. R. Borcherding. il Suc Farm 64:42-3+ O '66
How I insure a healthy calf crop. J. P. Winninger. il Suc Farm 64:60 O '66
Those critical five days; dairy. M. L. Weldy. il Suc Farm 64:53+ O '66

Diseases and pests

These tips make better calves; scours L. A. Baker. Farm J 90:A12 O '66

Feeding

Boost sale weights 150 lbs. per calf. R. Ozmon. il Farm J 90:70-1 Mr '66

Marketing

They're after your dairy calves; Holsteins. O. Bay. il Farm J 90:68R Mr '66

CALVES, Mechanical. See Automatons

CALVIN, Melvin. See Eglinton, G. jt. auth.

CALWELL, Arthur Augustus
End of a fiery campaign. M. Tatlow. Nat R 18:1208 N 29 '66
Germs of violence. il por Newsweek 68:41-2 Jl 4 '66

CAMBODIA
See also
United Nations—Cambodia
United States—Foreign relations—Cambodia

Boundaries

Conflagration spreads. Nation 202:698 Je 13 '66

Foreign relations

Ave ave; U.S. relations. Time 88:28 Ag 19 '66
Cambodia beset; background to relations with China. G. D. Stark. il Nation 202:445-9 Ap 18 '66
Cambodian neutrality. W. E. Willmott. bibliog f Cur Hist 52:36-40+ Ja '67
Hitting the Sihanouk Trail; red route to Viet Nam; with report by D. Neff. il Time 87:33-4 My 13 '66
Letter from Cambodia. R. Shaplen. New Yorker 42:186+ S 17 '66
Trouble with Cambodia. O. G. Chase. Commonweal 84:552-5 S 2 '66
See also
Cambodia—Boundaries

Neutrality

As war spreads into neutral Cambodia. il U S News 60:11 My 16 '66

Politics and government

Atlantic report; reply. Norodom Sihanouk. Atlan 217:44 Je '66
Letter from Cambodia. R. Shaplen. New Yorker 42:212+ S 17 '66
Trouble with Cambodia. O. G. Chase. Commonweal 84:552-5 S 2 '66

CAMBRIAN period. See Paleontology—Cambrian

CAMBRIDGE radio observatory committee
Radio telescope of near future. il Sci N 90:561 D 31 '66

CAMELLIAS
Gibberellic acid makes the difference in camellias. J. H. Pyron. il Horticulture 44:20-1+ S '66
New way to have bigger camellias that bloom earlier. M. Noble. il Flower Grower 53:41 N '66

CAMELOT project. See Project Camelot

CAMERA cases
Is an Omnica for real? letter. H. Keppler. il Mod Phot 30:36 Je '66

CAMERA clubs
Editorial. J. Durniak. Pop Phot 59:72 O '66
Portfolio: ISFTPOBAWP shows its true colors. il Pop Phot 59:80-5 S '66

CAMERA shutters
Automation by electronic shutter. P. Stackpole. U S Camera 29:14+ N '66

Big electronic shutter muddle. H. Kepp! r. il Mod Phot 30:68-9+ Mr '66
Caulfield on color; shutter speed. P. Caulfield. il Mod Phot 30:40 Ag '66
Electronic exposure: more & better. C. W. Kennedy il Pop Phot 60:96-7 Ja '67
Electronic shutters. E. H. Ortner. il Pop Sci 188:184-5+ Ap '66
Keppler on the SLR. H. Keppler. il Mod Phot 31:34+ Ja '67
What! an automated SLR with focal plane shutter? H. Keppler. il Mod Phot 30:79+ Mr '66

CAMERA tripods
Hold still for sharper pictures. P. Wahl. il Pop Sci 189:106-9 Ag '66
Tripods. Pop Phot 59:6C-9C D '66

CAMERAS
And some are bigger than others; ultraminiatures. J. D. Cooper and D. L. Miller. il Mod Phot 30:56-8+ My '66
Automation by electronic shutter; Olympus 35 LE. P. Stackpole. U S Camera 29:14+ N '66
Back to the half-frame. P. Stackpole. U S Camera 29:20+ Ap '66
Behind the scenes. See issues of Modern photography
Behind the scenes; the Exakta real. A. Mannheim. il Mod Phot 30:14+ N '66
Better focus; German camera-making companies. Time 88:105 O 14 '66
Box cameras were never like this. L. Edson. il Pop Mech 126:66-9+ Jl '66; Same abr. with tilte Look what they do with cameras now! Read Digest 89:181-2+ Jl '66
Buying a camera? il Consumer Bul 49:39-40 Jl '66
Buying guide to forty-four top cameras. il Mod Phot 30:81-126 D '66
Buypoints: still cameras. M. D. Grennan. Pop Phot 59:140-2 N '66
Camera from Shanghai. G. Zygmund. il U S Camera 29:16+ Ap '66
Camera that thinks it's a duck. M. V. Korda. il Pop Phot 58:62-5+ Mr '66
Can lens X fit camera Y? sometimes yes, sometimes no! D. L. Miller. il Mod Phot 30:80-1+ O '66
Dielectric camera ready for space use. W. S. Beller. il Miss & Roc 18:28 Ap 18 '66
Fiber-optics camera looks around corners. il Sci N 89:439 Je 4 '66
From what we hear. il U S Camera 29:40-1+ Ap '66
Great show: what does it total up to? symposium. il Pop Phot 60:134-7 Ja '67
Great through-the-lens meter explosion; with foreword by H. Keppler. il Mod Phot 30:52-73 S '66
Hanson, Rothschild, Pierce report. N. Rothschild; W. Hanson; B. Pierce. See issues of Popular photography
How to find the best buy on a camera. H. C. Birnbaum. U S Camera 29:49+ D '66
How to get the most from the fast-loading cameras. A. Goldsmith. il Pop Phot 58:54-7+ F '66
How to get the most out of your camera. Bet Hom & Gard 44:108 N '66
Improved cooled cameras for astrophotography. E. Kreimer. il Sky & Tel 32:106-10 Ag '66
Keppler on the SLR; new, advanced cameras from Germany. H. Keppler. il Mod Phot 30:36+ F '66
Kodak instamatic cameras; what they do, and how they do it. E. Meyers. il Mod Phot 30:72-3 Jl '66
Large camera. A. Feininger. See issues of Modern photography
Look what they do with cameras now! L. Edson. Read Digest 89:181-2+ Jl '66
Low-cost color photos. yes, but... il Consumer Rep 31:320-1 Jl '66
Meyers on technique: secrets of a careful camera and lens buyer. E. Meyers. Mod Phot 30:18+ D '66
Modern photography's Photokina product guide. il Mod Phot 31:85+ Ja '67
Modern tests. See issues of Modern photography
MRP camera: pioneer or pipe dream? W. Hanson. il Pop Phot 60:112-13 Ja '67
New? Contax II cameras. H. Keppler. il Mod Phot 30:95+ O '66
New photography. il Pop Phot 58:67-71+ Je '66
New products. See issues of U.S. camera & travel
Nikon crowds into Leica's picture; discussion. Mod Phot 30:20+ Jl '66
1966, a new-product bust year? il Pop Phot 58:98-103+ Ap '66

CAMERAS—*Continued*
1966 preview. il Mod Phot 30:66-71+ Je '66
Once again, the eternal question; picking a camera, new or used. P. Stackpole. U S Camera 29:22-3 O '66
Panoramic camera designed for low-level operations; Minipan camera. R. D. Hibben. il Aviation W 84:104-5+ My 9 '66
Photography for inept sophisticates. H. Wolf. il Mod Phot 30:54-5+ Jl '66
Pictures by invisible light. N. Rothschild. il Pop Phot 58:110 Mr '66
Pocketful of quality; the Rollei 35. N. Goldberg. il Pop Phot 60:100-1 Ja '67
Sensible advice on cameras and equipment. R. Pinney. il Parents Mag 41:58-9+ My '66
Simon says; camera features fifty-seven lenses. N. Simon. Mod Phot 31:110+ Ja '67
Sneaky photographer; candid pictures of people. P. Farber. il U S Camera 29:52-3+ Ag '66
Start small, think big. M. A. Matzkin. il Mod Phot 30:74-5 F '66
Still cameras. Consumer Rep 31:263-72 D '66
Still more automation? C. W. Kennedy. il Pop Phot 59:40+ Jl '66
Subminiatures, the giant-killers? M. V. Korda. il Pop Phot 58:88-90+ My '66
Techniques tomorrow; accuracy of a camera body. B. Sherman. Mod Phot 30:48+ O '66
Test reports. See issues of Popular photography
Tiny camera puts you in the spy business; palm-size Atoron. E. H. Ortner. il Pop Sci 189:126-7 O '66
Tony Karp on 35mm. T. Karp. il Mod Phot 30:48+ S '66
Two new single-frame cameras; Olympus Pen EM and Yashica Electro-Half. il Consumer Bul 49:26-8 Mr '66
Unconditionally guaranteed, but. . . M. D. Grennan. Pop Phot 59:65+ S '66
U.S. camera & travel test reports. See issues of U.S. camera & travel
What's new: more products at Photokina. C. W. Kennedy. il Pop Phot 60:132-3 Ja '67
What's new that's good? B. Brown. il Pop Phot 58:110+ Je '66
What's new that's good? C. W. Kennedy. il Pop Phot 58:108-10 Je '66
Wide ones. D. L. Miller. il Mod Phot 30:68-9 Ap '66
See also
Electronic cameras
Moving picture cameras
Photography
Single-lens reflex cameras
Television cameras

Collectors and collecting
Great collector, Fred Mazzulla. N. C. Lipton. il Pop Phot 58:84-5+ Je '66

History
Camera that refused to die. B. V. Stones. U S Camera 29:30+ Je '66

Loading
Here it is: first instant-loading SLR. N. Rothschild. il Pop Phot 59:80-1+ O '66
Low-cost instant-load cameras. il Consumer Rep 31:222-6 My '66
Revolution in loading systems. il U S Camera 29:58-9+ Ap '66
Super 35, coming soon? H. Zucker. il Pop Phot 59:40+ S '66; Discussion. 59:4+ D '66
Tony Karp on 35mm. T. Karp. il Mod Phot 30:28+ Ap '66
What's new that's good? J. Durniak. il Pop Phot 58:102-3 Je '66
See also
Single lens reflex cameras—Loading

Repairing
Camera repairs. G. Gilbert. il U S Camera 29:60-1+ Mr '66

Testing
How wide's wide? H. Keppler. il Mod Phot 30:66-7 Ap '66
Modern tests; how? T. Karp. il Mod Phot 30:58-61+ Je '66

CAMERAS on space vehicles. See Space vehicles—Equipment

CAMERON, Cyril Barneveldt
King Kam and the Isle of love. G. Scott. Sat R 49:68-9 O 22 '66

CAMERON, Donald Ewen
Can this drug make you smarter? W. S. Bacon. il por Pop Sci 189:84-5 N '66
Memory pills. il Time 87:56 Je 24 '66
Pill that helps you remember. S. M. Spencer. por il Sat Eve Post 239:64-6+ S 24 '66

CAMERON, Eleanor
Why not for children? adaptation of address. Horn Bk 42:21-33 F '66

CAMERON, Gail
Kennedy nobody knows. Ladies Home J 83:70-1+ Je '66

CAMERON, J. M.
Evelyn Waugh, R.I.P. Commonweal 84:167-8 Ap 29 '66
From Britain. Commonweal 84:144-5, 167-8; 85:394-5, 417-19 Ap 22-29 '66, Ja 13-20 '67

CAMERON, James
Mao tse-Tung's big Chinese restaurant. Esquire 66:66+ O '66
Shadow no larger than a crooked cross. N Y Times Mag p94-5+ S 11 '66

CAMERON, Ulysses, and others
What's wrong with our library schools? reprint. Library J 91:1773-5 Ap 1 '66

CAMERON iron works, incorporated
Oil tool specialist uses own recipes for space age metals. il Bsns W p 116-18+ F 26 '66

CAMEROON REPUBLIC
See also
Natural resources—Cameroon Republic

History
Cameroon. J. I. Clarke. bibliog il Focus 16:1-6 Ap '66

CAMOUFLAGE
Camouflage detection. Sci N 89:223 Ap 2 '66

CAMP, Dalton
Dief and grief. il por Newsweek 68:56 N 28 '66

CAMP, Wendell
Ambitious violet. Sat R 49:65-6 Je 4 '66

CAMP, William B.
Camp chosen to succeed Saxon; as comptroller of the currency. Bsns W p 162 N 12 '66
Cool Camp. il por Time 88:107 N 18 '66
Man to calm down the bankers. por Bsns W p66 N 19 '66

CAMP (term)
Church and camp. J. W. Goetz. Cath World 203:297-300 Ag '66
Sontag sensibility. P. Velde. Commonweal 84:390-2 Je 24 '66

Anecdotes, facetiae, satire, etc.
Notes on stoop. L. Israel. il Esquire 66:90-1 Ag '66

CAMP cookery
Camp cooking; with recipes. il Bet Hom & Gard 44:83-4 Jl '66
Plain and fancy camp cooking; with recipes. il Sunset 137:114-15 Jl '66
Wild food for outdoor living. H. Clepper. il Am For 72:22-4+ Je '66

CAMP equipment. See Camping outfits

CAMP fire girls
Teen travel talk; Caribbean cruise. il Seventeen 25:40 O '66

CAMP lanterns. See Lanterns

CAMP Pendleton. See Military training camps

CAMP Madison-Felicia. See Camps

CAMP stoves
Camp stoves. Consumer Rep 31:302-3 D '66
New look in stoves. C. Conley. il Field & S 70:113 F '66
Single-burner camp stoves. il Consumer Bul 49:14-17 My '66
Two-burner camp stoves. il Consumer Bul 49:6-9 Ap '66

CAMP Sweeney, Gainesville, Tex. See Camps for the handicapped

CAMPAIGN funds
Beer blast; dropping of action against Anheuser-Busch by Antitrust division. Newsweek 68:24+ Jl 25 '66
Busch league; contributions to President's club. Time 88:21-2 Jl 22 '66
Campaign dollars. W. V. Shannon. Commonweal 84:385-6 Je 24 '66
Campaign fund; question of income tax financing presidential candidates. New Repub 155:6 N 5 '66
Campaign money needs a law. Life 60:4 Je 10 '66
Campaign spending. G. Lardner. New Repub 155:9-10 O 8 '66
Campaign spending; funds controlled by Federal corrupt practices act and Hatch act. Commonweal 84:326-7 Je 10 '66
Campaign tax; how it would work. U S News 61:12 O 31 '66
Dinner at the White House L. B. Johnson's fund-raising techniques. Nation 202:762-3 Je 27 '66
Distribution of membership of President's club, by state. 1964. Nation 202:773 Je 27 '66
Dodd's case: what's ethical? il Newsweek 68:22+ Ag 1 '66
Fight over money: Republican party. W. Pincus. il Atlan 217:71-5 Ap '66

CAMPAIGN funds—*Continued*

Financing our parties; corporate involvement in politics. N. R. Peirce. il Reporter 34: 29+ F 10 '66

High cost of getting elected, and how to pay for it. il U S News 60:32-4 My 9 '66

Hypocrisy in campaign finance. Life 60:4 F 18 '66

Long green; bill promises both major parties' presidential candidates public funds. Time 88:33 N 25 '66

LBJ's club, the whiff of scandal. J. Deakin. New Repub 155:13-14 O 1 '66

Money and politics. A. Balk. Sat R 49:22 O 15 '66

Mood of the capital; corporations blackmailed to advertise in parties publications. Atlan 217:10+ F '66

Mystery in the countinghouse: Democratic party. W. Pincus. il Atlan 218:71-5 O '66

Now: politicians to get a tax check-off. U S News 61:39 N 28 '66

Paying for politics. R. Moley. Newsweek 68: 116 N 14 '66

Politics has got so expensive; controversy over special-interest contributors. il Bsns W p54+ D 24 '66

Presidency; reform bill to Congress. Newsweek 67:25 Je 6 '66

President's club: what $1,000 brings. il U S News 61:6 Ag 1 '66

Price of victory; campaign expenditures of M. Shapp. Time 88:22 Ag 19 '66

Private wealth and public office: high cost of campaigning; laws and the loopholes; reform proposals. V. H. Bernstein. Nation 202:770-5 Je 27 '66

Subsidy for presidential campaigns. J. N. Eller. America 115:537 N 5 '66

Thanking Senator Robertson; question of contributions through Manufacturers-Hanover bank. Nation 203:5 Jl 4 '66

What money can buy; Raymond P. Shafer suit against M. J. Shapp. il Newsweek 68: 62-3 Ag 22 '66

Who will pay the piper? Newsweek 68:39+ O 24 '66

Willie's big whisper; amendment to Viet Nam tax bill passed. il Time 87:26 Mr 11 '66

CAMPAIGN literature

Backlash in the Percy campaign. R. C. Wade. Reporter 36:37-40 Ja 12 '67

Useful but much maligned books: campaign biographies and their reviews. O. Collier. ALA Bul 60:609-12 Je '66

CAMPAIGNS, Advertising. See Advertising campaigns

CAMPAIGNS, Political. See Political campaigns

CAMPAIGNS, Presidential. See Presidential campaigns

CAMPANA, Dino

Three Florentine girls walk; poem, tr. by I. L. Salomon. Commonweal 84:78 Ap 8 '66

CAMPANULAS

Canterbury bells. R. C. Hands. Horticulture 44:16+ Je '66

CAMPBELL, Alex

Casting the runes. New Repub 154:23-4 Ap 23 '66

Shapes of the future. New Repub 155:22+ O 15 '66

Thailand. New Repub 154:17-20 Mr 26 '66

Their world and our money. New Repub 155: 24-5 S 3 '66

Unflappable supermac. New Repub 155:30-1 O 1 '66

What did happen in Dallas? New Repub 154: 23-5 Je 25 '66

Who's afraid of China? New Repub 154:12-16 Ap 9 '66

CAMPBELL, C. B. G.

Taxonomic status of tree shrews. bibliog Science 153:436 Jl 22 '66

CAMPBELL, Donald

Always in the shadow. il Time 89:50 Ja 13 '67

Bluebird's last run. il pors Life 62:87-8 Ja 13 '67

Final proof. il por Newsweek 69:82 Ja 16 '67

Fire is put out. Sports Illus 26:7 Ja 16 '67

CAMPBELL, E. Simms

Escape from the rat race. C. L. Sanders. il pors Ebony 22:132-4+ N '66

CAMPBELL, Haldane

For richer, for poorer, for better, for faith: story. Good H 162:98-9 Mr '66

CAMPBELL, John W.

Say-it-isn't-so! syndrome. Nat R 18:412-14 My 3 '66

CAMPBELL, Lawrence

Blots, spots and silken stains. Art N 65:44-7 My '66

Boudin: the king of the skies. Art N 65:46-7+ N '66

Hélène Aylon's Ruach palimpsest. Art N 65: 47-9 D '66

Paul Georges paints a nude. Art N 64:52-5+ Ja '66

Sterne: line and likeness. Art N 64:28-9+ F '66

CAMPBELL, Roald F.

Tomorrow's teacher. Sat R 50:60+ Ja 14 '67

CAMPBELL, Robert, and Genet, Nancy

Secret weapons of survival. Life 60:62-7 F 18 '66

CAMPBELL, Robert B.

In praise of publishers and their Christmas offers. Pub W 190:60-1 S 5 '66

CAMPBELL, T. E.

Cast-in-place drainage pipe. Am City 81:100-2 D '66

CAMPBELL, T. L.

Reflections on research and the future of medicine. Science 153:442-6+ Jl 22 '66

CAMPBELL, William P.

Amateurs, Fraktus and elegant young ladies. Art N 65:50-3+ O '66

CAMPBELL soup company

Campbell's recipe for growth. J. B. Weiner. il Duns R 88:27-30+ Ag '66

Price, price, who's got the price? code embossed in top or bottom of the can. il Consumer Rep 31:474 O '66

CAMPER cabanas. See Campers and coaches, Truck—Equipment

CAMPERS and coaches, Truck

Bonus vacation. F. Morton. il Field & S 71: 41+ Je '66

Build a high-low pickup camper. il Pop Mech 125:132-7+ My '66

Camps on wheels. il Changing T 20:26-8 Ap '66

Ford van becomes turtle top camper. il Pop Sci 188:160-2 My '66

Notes for nomads. il Travel 125:20 Ap; 14 My: 65 Je; 126:62 S; 6 N '66

Perfect camper. F. McKinley. il Outdoor Life 137:48-51+ Mr '66

Roam sweet home. L. Oertle. il Motor T 18: 64-5 Ap '66

Room at the top! car+roof-top camper=mobile motel. V. L. Oertle. il Motor T 18:74-5 Jl '66

They took to the woods; family camping. R. McCluskey. il Field & S 70:62-3 Ap '66

Which type of camper should you buy? P. McCafferty. il Pop Sci 188:148-53+ My '66

Equipment

Tuckaway camper cabana. J. Stowell. il Pop Mech 126:130-1 Ag '66

CAMPING

Boat campers' paradise, Lake Tahoe's Emerald Bay. H. Bottel. il Motor B 118:22-4 Jl '66

Camping. C. B. Colby. See issues of Outdoor life

Enjoy winter's wonderland! H. Gordon. il Read Digest 88:21-2+ F '66

For your best vacation ever. R. Charles. il Parents Mag 41:82-7+ Mr '66

Growing up with family camping. J. P. Jackson. il Am For 72:48-50+ My '66

How long has it been. . .? E. P. Hanson. Am For 71:4 O '65

More room to camp; national parks sites. Holiday 39:136 My '66

North America's best camping vacations. P. Lindberg. il Bet Hom & Gard 44:141-4 My '66

Plan a boat-camping adventure. J. A. Emmett. il Outdoor Life 138:92-4 Jl '66

Preplanning pays off; camping trips. C. B. Colby. il Outdoor Life 137:20+ Je '66

Sailor cruises ashore; trip through Arizona and Utah. R. N. Bavier, jr. Holiday 39: 40+ My '66

Soloist survives on a bouillabaisse of seaweeds and fantasies of candy; testing E. Gibbons' theories. S. Davis. il Life 61:48-9 S 23 '66

Sports car camping. R. Barlow. il Field & S 70:53-5 F '66

Station wagon camping! Bet Hom & Gard 44:12+ Jl '66

Tents for automobile camping. J. B. Miller. il Consumer Bul 49:32-6 Jl '66

Try camping afloat. P. Perrett. il Pop Mech 125:124-6+ My '66

Why go camping? A. J. McClane. il Field & S 70:82-6 F '66

Winter camping; photographs. Travel 125:45-7 F '66

See also

Camp cookery
Camping outfits
Camps
Outdoor life
Sierra club

CAMPING—*Continued*

Activities

Indians are coming; program prepared by the Recreation division staff of the Milwaukee public schools. il Parks & Rec 1:228-9 Mr '66
See also
Nature camps

Safety devices and measures

Camping has its hazards. C. B. Colby. il Outdoor Life 137:18+ Ap '66
When you camp out. P. Czura. il Todays Health 44:26-30 Jl '66

California

Bonus vacation. F. Morton. il Field & S 71:41+ Je '66

Europe

Togetherness under canvas; FICC rally. il Time 88:26 Ag 26 '66

Europe, Western

Tenting across Europe. E. A. Miles. il Travel 125:48-9+ My '66

Florida

Painting among the Seminoles. J. Hutchinson. il Am Artist 30:52-7+ Ap '66
Trailer cruise in the Keys. B. Schill and B. Schill. il Yachting 120:45+ N '66

Minnesota

Minnesota's canoe country. S. Shore. il Travel 125:26-31 My '66
Outfitting the pilgrims to a western Walden; Minnesota's government-protected canoe area draws 300,000 summer campers. il Bsns W p 130-2 Ag 27 '66

Montana

Montana's drive-in wilderness. B. W. Dalrymple. il Field & S 70:122-4+ F '66

Utah

Kayak-camping Lake Powell. J. Clark. il Field & S 71:56-9 Je '66

CAMPING outfits
Camping in style, any style. il McCalls 93:94-5+ Je '66
For your best vacation ever. R. Charles. il Parents Mag 41:82-7+ Mr '66
How to outfit your family for camping. il Bet Hom & Gard 44:22+ My '66
How to stow camp gear. C. B. Colby. Outdoor Life 139:98-100 Ja '67
I'll take the high camp. K. Connes. il Flying 79:85-7 S '66
New camp gear for 1966. C. B. Colby. il Outdoor Life 137:28+ My '66
Synthetics for camping. P. Czura. il Field & S 70:60-3+ F '66
What every new camper should know. C. Conley. il Field & S 71:50-3+ Je '66
What's new for campers. S. James. il Pop Mech 125:106-10 My '66
Why learn the hard way? mistakes, forgotten or unnecessary equipment. C. B. Colby. il Outdoor Life 138:18+ N '66
Why not try camping this summer? J. Newman and B. Newman. il PTA Mag 60:15-17 My '66
See also
Automobiles—Camping equipment
Campers and coaches, Truck—Equipment
Motor boats—Camping equipment
Tents

CAMPION, Donald R.
Book review (cont) America 114:878; 115:346+ Je 25, S 24 '66

CAMPION, Nardi Reeder
Ask, don't tell. Read Digest 89:49-52 Ag '66
(ed) See Fosdick, H. E. Whose God is dead?

CAMPO del Cielo meteorite. See Meteorites

CAMPOS, Roberto de Oliveira
Brazil: some success, much to do. il por Bsns W p61-2+ Ja 22 '66

CAMPS
About summer camps. il Dance Mag 40:78-9 Ap '66
Camper, go home! C. B. Colby. Outdoor Life 137:18-20+ F '66
Day camp with a difference. M. Wolf. il Parents Mag 41:50-1+ My '66
Hoosier senior citizens camp; project in Indiana. B. McGinnis. il Parks & Rec 1:419+ My '66
If you're thinking of sending the kids to camp. il Changing T 20:19-20 Mr '66
Learn, baby, learn! training dropouts at Camp Madison-Felicia. A. Herzog. il Am Ed 2:4-6 S '66

Teen travel talk; campers take to the road: Lincoln farm, Roscoe, N.Y. il Seventeen 25:73 My '66
There's a summer camp for every child. W. Hartley and E. Hartley. il Parents Mag 41:51-3+ Ap '66

CAMPS for the handicapped
Camping fun for diabetic youngsters; Camp Sweeney, Gainesville, Tex. L. Kaye. il Todays Health 44:50-3 Je '66

CAMPUS City, Chicago. See Illinois. University —Chicago campus

CAMPUS life. See Student life

CAMPUS lighting
Light to go to school by. A. F. Lindberg. il Am City 81:137 S '66

CAMPUS planning
Architecture that gives a campus the unity of a single building; with account by J. Barnett. il Arch Rec 140:145-60 O '66
Colorado U: respect for a robust environment. J. M. Dixon. il Arch Forum 125:54-63 O '66
Handsome beginning for Southern Illinois' new Edwardsville campus. il Arch Rec 140:111-20 D '66
New campus. O. Newman. il Arch Forum 124:30-55 My '66

CAMS
See also
Automobiles—Cams

CAMUS, Albert
Artist as prophet. R. A. Nisbet. Commentary 42:76-7 Jl '66

CAN company, American. See American can company

CAN openers
Electric can openers. il Consumer Rep 31:533-6 N '66

CANADA
Join the fun as Canada celebrates her centennial. R. Dunlop. il Todays Health 45:42-5+ Ja '67
Surging to nationhood. il Time 88:30-40 S 30 '66
See also
Aeronautics, Commercial—Canada
Agricultural administration—Canada
Arbitration, Industrial—Canada
Architecture—Canada
Automobile industry and trade—Canada
Aviation—Canada
Ballet—Canada
Banks and banking—Canada
Booksellers and bookselling—Canada
Civil service—Canada
Crime and criminals—Canada
Dams—Canada
Education—Canada
Electric power—Canada
Escuminac Bay
Hunting—Canada
Immigration and emigration—Canada
Insurance, Health—Canada
Investments, Foreign (in Canada)
Jews in Canada
Labor supply—Canada
Libraries—Canada
Library schools and education—Canada
Mines and mineral resources—Canada
Natural resources—Canada
Negroes in Canada
Opera—Canada
Petroleum—Canada
Poor—Canada
Quebec (province)
Railroads—Canada
Rocky Mountains—Canadian Rockies
Strikes—Canada
Tariff—Canada
Television broadcasting—Canada
Wages—Canada
Yukon

Armed forces

Admirals' revolt; integration issue. il Newsweek 68:41-2 Ag 1 '66
Canada's bold defense experiment; Hellyer's integration program. Reporter 34:36-8 Mr 24 '66
Canadians seek flight officer retention; plan for unification of armed services into a single, integrated defense force. il Aviation W 84:103+ Mr 14 '66
Fighting hard to unify Canada's armed forces; Defense Minister P. Hellyer. Bsns W p96 N 26 '66

Commerce

Balance of payment; address, April 27, 1966. W. E. McLaughlin. Vital Speeches 32:521-4 Je 15 '66

Commercial treaties and agreements

U.S. and Canada exchange notes on automotive products agreement; Department announcement; with texts of notes. September 16, 1966. Dept State Bul 55:616 O 17 '66

CANADA—Commercial treaties and agreements
—Continued
U.S. and Canada sign agreement updating
U.S. tariff concessions; announcement, with
annex II of the agreement. il Dept State
Bul 54:106-9 Ja 17 '66

Constitution
Widening the gulf; quarrel over how to
amend the constitution. il Newsweek 67:48
F 14 '66

Defenses
See also
North American air defense command

Description and travel
Canada's centennial preview; province by
province. A. H. Hepburn. il Sr Schol 88:sup
9-11 Mr 18 '66
Canada's 100th: the birthday party upstairs.
Thomson of Fleet. il Sat R 50:60+ Ja 7
'67
Gone flying north to Canada. R. G. Halford.
il Flying 78:114-17+ Je '66

Economic conditions
Red hot economy is cooling off; outlook for
'67. il Bsns W p70-1 D 31 '66
See also
Labor and laboring classes—Canada

Economic policy
Canada considers closer U.S. ties; excerpts
from article. R. A. Matthews. bibliog f
Harvard Bsns R 44:57-64 My '66
Canada tries to calm its bubbling economy.
Bsns W p40 Ap 2 '66
Challenge ahead. A. Harrigan. Nat R 18:1163
N 15 '66
Free trade wins a new apostle; Ottawa's Fi-
nance Minister M. Sharp. Bsns W p 142+
D 17 '66
U.S. companies face guidelines in Canada.
Bsns W p34 Ap 9 '66
See also
Price regulation by government—Canada

Economic relations
United States
Canada considers closer U.S. ties; excerpts
from article. R. A. Matthews. bibliog f
Harvard Bsns R 44:57-64 My '66
Challenge ahead. A. Harrigan. Nat R 18:1163
N 15 '66
Dependent & discontented. il Time 88:64+
Jl 29 '66
See also
Joint United States-Canadian committee on
trade and economic affairs

Exploration
Was Columbus in Canada? lunar and solar
tides in Bay of Fundy. P. Bilbao. il Américas 18:17-28 Jl '66

Foreign relations
Canada; with editorial comment. H. Mac-
Lennan. il Am Heritage 17:4, 6-45+ D '65;
Correction. 17:100 Je '66
Independent foreign policy; address, January
31, 1966. P. Martin. Vital Speeches 32:311-14
Mr 1 '66
United States
Canada: test of the American conscience; dis-
cussion. J. Reston and B. Hutchison. Read
Digest 89:189-90+ Jl '66
See also
International joint commission (United States
and Canada)

History
Canada celebrates its centennial. America
116:36 Ja 14 '67
Canada; with editorial comment. H. Mac-
Lennan. il Am Heritage 17:4, 6-45+ D '65;
Correction. 17:100 Je '66
Canada's 100th: the birthday party upstairs.
Thomson of Fleet. il Sat R 50:60+ Ja 7 '67

Industries
See also
Mines and mineral resources—Canada
Steel company of Canada

Maps
Canada's West mapped anew; mighty works
help tame a wilderness. il Nat Geog Mag
130:394-5, sup(folded map) S '66

Nationalism
Challenge ahead. A. Harrigan. Nat R 18:1163
N 15 '66

Politics and government
Canada's scandal: both sides losers? Mun-
singer case. il U S News 60:12-13 Mr 28 '66
Dief and grief. il Newsweek 68:56 N 28 '66
Dief on the ropes. il Time 88:47 N 25 '66
Finding Gerda's goat; ex-Cabinet ministers
and East German woman. Newsweek 67:
50 Mr 21 '66
Gerda cooks up a Canadian stew; Lucien
Cardin's allegations. il Life 60:105-6 Mr 25
'66
Lunch at the Chateau Laurier; Munsinger
case. Time 87:28 Mr 25 '66
Mounties get their men; Munsinger affair.
Time 87:32 My 6 '66
Munsinger affair. il Time 87:54 Mr 18 '66
Not very romantic; Munsinger enquiry. il
Newsweek 67:71 My 23 '66
Politics of scandal. M. Feinsilber. Common-
weal 84:383-5 Je 24 '66
Preparing for change? Time 87:34 F 4 '66
Suspended degradation; inquiry into Mun-
singer case. Newsweek 67:58 Mr 28 '66
See also
Canada—Constitution
Elections—Canada
Political parties—Canada

Religious institutions and affairs
Maritime provinces. Christian Cent 83:151 F
2 '66
See also
Canadian council of churches
Church of England in Canada
United church of Canada

Science council
Canada: science advisors to propose priorities. L. J. Carter. il Science 153:1083-6 S 2
'66

Scientific secretariat
Canada: science advisors to propose priorities. L. J. Carter. il Science 153:1083-6 S 2
'66

Social conditions
See also
Labor and laboring classes—Canada
CANADA cup matches. See Golf—Tourna-
ments
CANADA dry corporation
Shuffle & cut. il Time 88:88+ D 2 '66
CANADA geese. See Geese, Wild
CANADAY, John
Bruegel; excerpts from Lives of the painters.
Horizon 9:22-41 Wint '67
Flowering of Flemish art. Horizon 8:84-95
Wint '66
Watteau's forbidden world; adaptation. Hori-
zon 8:60-79 Sum '66
CANADIAN aviators. See Air pilots
CANADIAN booksellers association
Canadian booksellers study ways to streng-
then book industry. il Pub W 189:40-3 Je
20 '66
CANADIAN broadcasting corporation
Television; Seven days program. P. Gzowski.
Nation 203:61-2 Jl 11 '66
CANADIAN council of churches
Canada church council acquires new shape.
D. H. Rayner. Christian Cent 83:1582-4 D
21 '66
See also
North American conference on church and
family
CANADIAN librarians. See Librarians
CANADIAN library association
No stampede in Calgary; preconference and
main conference. E. Moon. il Library J 91:
3651-60 Ag '66
CANADIAN national railways
Flying low. Time 87:93 My 27 '66
Passenger trains that can turn a profit. A.
Steinberg. il Read Digest 89:249-50+ N '66
CANADIAN national research council. See Na-
tional research council of Canada
CANADIAN NORTHWEST TERRITORIES.
See Northwest Territories, Canada
CANADIAN opera company
Toronto. R. Ubriaco. Opera N 31:27 N 19 '66
CANADIAN Pacific airlines
Canadian Pacific aiming for expanded role.
R. G. O'Lone. il Aviation W 86:42-3 Ja 2
'67
Canadian Pacific to share in traffic growth.
R. G. O'Lone. Aviation W 85:45 N 21 '66
CANADIAN poetry
Canadian chronicle. R. Howard. Poetry 108:
45-53 Ap '66
Canadian chronicle. R. Skelton. Poetry 109:
53-8 O '66
CANADIAN ROCKIES. See Rocky Mountains—
Canadian Rockies

CANADIAN technical assistance. See Technical assistance, Canadian

CANADIAN visitors in China. See Foreign visitors in China

CANADIANS
Understanding Canada and sundry other matters; interview. M. McLuhan. Mlle 64:128-30 Ja '67

CANADIANS in the United States
Migration between Canada and the United States. K. V. Pankhurst. bibliog f il Ann Am Acad 367:53-62 S '66

CANADIENS (hockey team) See Hockey teams

CANAL ZONE. See Panama Canal Zone

CANALS
See also
Locks (hydraulic engineering)

Belgium
Ships float uphill and down; hauling canal boats in water-filled tanks. D. Scott. il Pop Sci 188:128-9 Ap '66

Central America
Army advisor endorses bombs for new canal; canal across Central America. Sci N 90:343 O 29 '66
See also
United States—Interoceanic canal commission

China
Grand Canal of China. L. Harrington. il Natur Hist 75:16-21 Ag '66

Colombia
New Raspadura? il Newsweek 68:56 N 14 '66
U.S, Colombia exchange notes on sea-level canal study; joint announcement. Dept State Bul 55:755 N 14 '66

Florida
Florida running out of wild rivers; construction of Cross-Florida barge canal. Liv Wildn 30:30 Sum '66
See also
Florida Ship Canal project

Latin America
Toward a South American canal. H. Martinez-Montero. il Américas 18:23-7 S '66

South America
See Canals—Latin America

Sweden
See also
Göta Canal

United States
Corps of engineers: the pork-barrel soldiers. R. G. Sherrill. il Nation 202:180-3 F 14 '66
See also
Erie Canal

CANARY ISLANDS
See also
Tourist trade—Canary Islands

CANAVAN, Francis P.
History repeats itself. America 114:738-42; 115:1 My 21, Jl 2 '66
Mood of Catholic education. America 114:612 Ap 30 '66
Puerto Rico's future. America 115:111-15 Jl 30 '66
Reforms that priests want. America 114:582-5 Ap 23 '66
St John's university: the issues. America 114:122-4, 241 Ja 22, F 19 '66

CANAVERAL, CAPE. See Kennedy, Cape

CANCER
Adventists' advantage; few deaths due to lung cancer. Time 88:68 O 28 '66
Congenital malformations and cancer: United States-Japan cooperative science program; report from meeting in Tokyo. R. W. Miller and H. Nishimura. Science 151:357-8 Ja 21 '66
Liver cancer: neonatal estrogen enhances induction by a carcinogen. J. H. Weisburger and others. bibliog il Science 154:673-4 N 4 '66
Man who wrote his own obituary. M. Waters. Read Digest 88:81-3 Jl '66
New progress in curing skin cancers. Good H 162:187 Ap '66
Our growing knowledge about cancer in children. M. J. E. Senn. McCalls 93:40+ F '66
Pituitary tumors in mice after prolonged feeding of synthetic progestins. W. E. Poel. bibliog il Science 154:402-3 O 21 '66
Spontaneous mammary tumors: decrease of incidence in the mice infected with an enzyme-elevating virus. V. Riley. bibliog il Science 153:1657-8 S 30 '66
Story of an ex-smoker. L. F. Fieser. Read Digest 88:68-72 Ap '66

When cancer is only skin deep. S. J. Robbins and others. Todays Health 44:31+ Jl '66
See also
Cancer research
United States—President's commission on heart disease, cancer and stroke

Causes
All ninety-two victims smoked. Sci N 89:285 Ap 23 '66
Among the troubles we don't talk about: erosion of the cervix. S. T. DeLee and B. B. Smith. Todays Health 44:62-3 O '66
Cancer clue found; hydrogen bond alteration caused by gene mutation. Sci N 90:67 Jl 30 '66
Cancer, hormones linked. F. Marley. Sci N 90:225 S 24 '66
Cancer tied to bombing; cases of leukemia in Hiroshima and Nagasaki. F. Marley. Sci N 89:437 Je 4 '66
How cancer begins: a new theory. Sci Digest 59:39 My '66
Invisible particles in air cause cancer. Sci N L 89:120 F 19 '66
Search for a cancerless cigarette; interview, ed. by V. Block. K. M. Endicott. Sci Digest 60:18-23 N '66
Watch out for too much sun! over-exposure can cause skin cancer. M. Long. Farm J 90:54 Ag '66

Diagnosis
Advances against cancer. il Newsweek 67:92+ Ap 11 '66
Cancer diagnosis by mail; Hopkins irrigation method. il Newsweek 67:79 Je 20 '66
Cancer, where doctors fail. A. J. Snider. Sci Digest 60:12-13 N '66
Cervical cancer tests best in doctor's office. Sci N 90:121 Ag 20 '66
Communities at war against cancer. G. G. Greer. Bet Hom & Gard 44:42 Ap '66
Help diagnose cancer by thermography. Sci N 89:490 Je 18 '66
Hidden cancer no one talks about: colon-rectum cancer. T. Berland. Todays Health 44:36-7+ Ap '66
Law for cervical cancer tests proposed. Sci N 89:394 My 21 '66
Procto: the cancer lifesaver we don't use. P. Deutsch and R. Deutsch. Read Digest 89:106-10 O '66
Symptoms seen before tumor is located. Sci N 90:307 O 15 '66

Statistics
Smoking woman; comparison of lung cancers in men and women; Hammond study. il Time 87:54 Mr 4 '66

Therapy
Advances against cancer; transplanting tumor tissue. M. Clark. il Newsweek 67:92+ Ap 11 '66
Arrested, at least; cross-transplants of cancer tissues with other patients. Time 88:33 Jl 29 '66
Crossover for life; tissue transplants between R. F. Allen and H. T. Griffith. il Time 87:44 Mr 11 '66
Freeze tumors to death. Sci N 89:234 Ap 9 '66
Neutrons beat X-rays; more effective in treatment of cancer. Sci N 90:372 N 5 '66
New cancer treatment; use of cancer-fighting antibodies from blood of another person. Sci Digest 60:42-3 Ag '66
See also
Krebiozen

Vaccines
Cancer vaccination tried. F. Marley. Sci N 89:285 Ap 23 '66

CANCER producing substances
Interaction of the water-soluble carcinogen 4-nitroquinoline N-oxide with DNA. M. F. Malkin and A. C. Zahalsky. bibliog il Science 154:1665-7 D 30 '66
Liver carcinogenesis by diethylnitrosamine in the rat. M. F. Rajewsky and others. bibliog il Science 152:83-5 Ap 1 '66
Nucleic acid guanine: reaction with the carcinogen N-acetoxy-2-acetylaminofluorene. E. C. Miller and others. bibliog il Science 153:1125-7 S 2 '66
Prolonged immunosuppression and tumor induction by a chemical carcinogen injected at birth. J. K. Ball and others. bibliog il Science 152:650-1 Ap 29 '66
See also
Cycasin

CANCER quacks. See Quacks and quackery

CANCER research
All ninety-two victims smoked. Sci N 89:285 Ap 23 '66

CANCER research—*Continued*
All-out assault on leukemia; with reports by W. Bradbury and A. Rosenfeld. il Life 61:88–108+ N 18 '66
Another advance in hunt for anticancer material. Sci N L 89:120 F 19 '66
Bacteria dissolve cancer. Sci N L 89:69 Ja 29 '66
Blood test predicts effect of cancer drug; response to PHl actvity. Sci N 89:254 Ap 9 '66
Cancer fighters; R. Rous–C. B. Huggins discoveries. il Newsweek 68:78+ O 24 '66
Cancer, other ills linked. Sci N 90:395 N 12 '66
Cancer research: U.S.-Japan cooperative science program; report on symposium. Y. Nishizuka and others. Science 152:1524-6 Je 10 '66
Cancer riddle unlocked. Sci N 89:229 Ap 2 '66
Cancer treatment tested in hamsters. Sci N 89:395 My 21 '66
Cold enhances drug action. Sci N 90:215 S 17 '66
Do we need new rules for experiments on people? concerning injection of live cancer cells into patients at the Jewish chronic disease hospital in Brooklyn. J. Lear. il Sat R 49:64-70 F 5 '66; Discussion. 49:58-9 Ap 2 '66
Human experimentation: New York verdict affirms patient's rights. E. Langer. Science 151:663-6 F 11 '66; Discussion. 152:448+, 865 Ap 22, My 13 '66
Osteolytic sterol in human breast cancer. G. S. Gordan and others. bibliog il Science 151:1226-8 Mr 11 '66
Plant growth as a cancer clue. S. Garb. Sat R 49:50+ My 7 '66; Reply. R. D. Gozzi. 49:67 Je 4 '66
Proteins linked to cancer. P. McBroom. il Sci N 89:283 Ap 23 '66
Radioactive chromium works in cancer research. F. Marley. Sci N 90:269 O 8 '66
Research and responsibility; concerning cancer cell injections case. Nation 202:284-5 Mr 14 '66
Research in America; three physicians dismissed from Jewish chronic disease hospital, Brooklyn. J. Lear. Sat R 49:65 Mr 5 '66
Thymus extract aids cancer immunity in mice. Sci N 90:41 Jl 16 '66
CANCER tests. See Cancer—Diagnosis
CANCER viruses
Cancer of the liver blamed on viruses. Sci N 89:460 Je 11 '66
Cold vs. cancer; sendai innoculations. Newsweek 67:96 My 16 '66
Simian virus 40: replication in the presence of specific antiserum and adenovirus 4. J. M. Easton and C. W. Hiatt. bibliog il Science 151:582-3 F 4 '66
Virus: mixed infection with herpes simplex and simian virus 40. A. S. Rabson and others. bibliog il Science 151:1535-6 Mr 25 '66

CANCO. See American can company
CANDEE, Marjorie
Driftwood inn. Travel 125:63 My '66
CANDID photography. See Photography—Portraits
CANDIDATES, Political
America votes 1966: the patterns, the issues, the key races. il Sr Schol 89:8-10+ S 30 '66
Anti-Vietnam politics; peace candidates in Oregon, California. A. Kopkind. New Repub 154:15-18 Je 4 '66
As election nears how much of a two-party South this year? il U S News 61:62-3 O 31 '66
As the '66 campaign opens: time to elect a new Congress, many governors and hundreds of state and county officials. il U S News 60:41 Ap 18 '66
Atlantic report: Illinois, senatorial contenders. Atlan 218:26+ S '66
Busiest copycat of them all; S. M. Linowitz. J. Howard. il Life 61:69-70+ Jl 1 '66
Choosing up; Mississippi, South Dakota, Massachusetts. Time 87:26 Je 17 '66
Cotton state to the polls. America 114:610 Ap 30 '66
Could this Jew be President. M. Viorst. il Esquire 65:100-4+ Ap '66
Doorbells: politics of activism; need for peace candidates. W. Meyers. il Nation 202:581-3 My 16 '66
Election trends: in thirty-four states; still no signs of big change. il U S News 61:59-60 O 24 '66
F.D.R.jr. the last race. W. V. Shannon. Commonweal 84:550-1 S 2 '66
GOP backs a new kind of candidate; younger, more attractive, more positive than the old guard. il Bsns W p45-7 O 8 '66

Grand old players; New York state legislators receive coaching in vote-getting art. G. Ace. Sat R 49:8 Ag 20 '66
Host of candidates unperturbed by terrorist threats; situation in Bien Hoa, Vietnam. D. Moser. il Life 61:36-41 S 23 '66
How to run a peace candidate. R. K. Byron. Nation 203:469-72 N 7 '66
How we would vote in key elections. Life 61:2B O 28 '66
In the race. Time 87:23 Ap 22 '66
Just ahead: first real clues to the 1966 elections; new Congress and many state and local officials to be chosen. il U S News 60:31-2 My 2 '66
Kennedy candidates. il Newsweek 67:24-5 Ap 25 '66
Man vs. machine; Michigan; Idaho; Tennessee. il Newsweek 68:22-3 Ag 15 '66
Masks of politics. E. J. Hughes. Newsweek 68:25 O 31 '66
Men who. .; office holder aspirants. Newsweek 67:46 My 23 '66
More zig than zag; Democrats announce candidacies for gubernatorial race; New York. Time 87:32-3 My 20 '66
National conference for surrender: Vietnam issue Nat R 18:562-4 Je 14 '66
Off and running: the 1966 campaign. il Newsweek 68:28-30 S 19 '66
Off-year election with a difference. K. Wheeler. il Life 61:61-4+ N 4 '66
Out of the fight into the fire. Time 88:20 Jl 15 '66
Outlook in ten key races. il U S News 61:38-9 N 7 '66
Outlook in twenty-four states: little change. U S News 61:38-40 O 17 '66
Peace candidates. New Repub 155:6-7 S 10 '66
Peace candidates. Newsweek 67:33 Je 20 '66
Peace candidates: 1966. Nation 202:539-40 My 9 '66
Peace candidates; 1966 congressional elections. Commonweal 84:351 Je 17 '66
Political scene: the big winners, the famous names. il U S News 60:16 My 23 '66
Politics and the sexual image. G. Dickerson. il Mlle 63:172-3+ O '66
Politics: 1966; races for governorships. E. J. Bell. il Nat R 18:153-9 F 22 '66
R.I.P.: peace candidates. Newsweek 68:35-6 O 10 '66
Rockefeller. R. Morley. Newsweek 68:120 O 31 '66
Ronald Reagan. star. Commonweal 84:383 Je 24 '66
Run, freshmen, run; congressional candidates. il Newsweek 68:28-9 S 26 '66
Senate races. W. V. Shannon. Commonweal 85:127-8 N 4 '66
Soapy & some others. Time 87:26-7 Mr 11 '66
Voices of politics 1966: crank up for primaries, conventions and campaigns. il Newsweek 67:27-9 Mr 28 '66
Vote for peace! Nation 203:172 S 5 '66
See also
Political campaigns
CANDIED flowers. See Confectionery
CANDIED fruit. See Confectionery
CANDLES
Candles from a sand mold. il Sunset 137:139-40+ N '66
Enchanting new roles for candlelight. il House & Gard 130:208-9 S '66
Magical flicker of candles. il House & Gard 130:150-1 D '66
CANDLES; story. See Warner, S. T.
CANDLESTICKS
Autumn candle holder. Dorfé. Design 68:11 S '66
Great, great candlesticks! il Bet Hom & Gard 44:46-7 D '66
CANDY, Walter Weaver, 1905-
Prestige store grows without losing gloss. il por(cover) Bsns W p58-60+ Ap 9 '66
CANDY
Best-ever candy. il Farm J 90:72-5 N '66
Chocolates: Mondel home made chocolates. New Yorker 41:29-31 F 19 '66
Old-fashioned candy. R. Hanna. il Suc Farm 64:136-7+ Mr '66
Quick confections! il Bet Hom & Gard 44:68-9+ D '66
Redbook's Christmas cookbook. il Redbook 128:98-102 D '66
'Tis the season for chocolate and mistletoe; with recipes. G. Maddox. il Todays Health 44:54-9 D '66
CANDY industry and trade
Wages and hours
Wages in paint, candy, and southern sawmill industries. il Mo Labor R 89:881-4 Ag '66
CANINE distemper. See Distemper
CANINE medicine. See Veterinary medicine

CANNARD, R. E.
  Desalted sea water for St Thomas. Am City
    81:104-6 F '66
CANNAS
  Dwarf cannas. E. Henderson. il Horticulture
    44:34+ Ap '66
CANNED fish
  In scooped-out oranges, in ramekins, on a
    salad plate, in a pie; with a can of salmon.
    il Sunset 136:120-1 My '66
CANNED food
  Begin with a can of . . ; with recipes. il
    Ladies Home J 83:86-7+ F '66
  Quality of canned salmon; fifty-one products
    rated. Consumer Rep 31:331-3 Jl '66
    See also
  Meat, Canned
  Vegetables, Canned
CANNED fruit. See Fruit, Canned
CANNERIES
    See also
  California packing corporation
CANNES, France

      Hotels, restaurants, etc.
  Screening the festivals. M. Levin. il Travel
    125:44-6 Ap '66
CANNES international film festival
  Culture in Cannes. il Newsweek 67:84-5 My
    30 '66
  Fine art & flapdoodle. il Time 87:82 My
    20 '66
  Ninth prize. il Time 87:82 My 27 '66
  Screening the festivals. M. Levin. il Travel
    125:44-6 Ap '66
  Welles captures Cannes. E. Archer. Sat R
    49:62-3 Jl 23 '66
CANNING and preserving
  Harvest reflections. P. Leimbach. il Farm J
    90:67 S '66
CANNOLI. See Cookery, Italian
CANNON, Patty
  Delaware's amazon outlaw. M. B. Duda. il
    Negro Hist Bul 29:153-4 Ap '66
CANNON, Poppy
  Line a day. See issues of Ladies' home
    journal
  Wine, women & so on. Ladies Home J 83:
    122 Ap; 125 My; 120 Je; 112 Jl; 116 S; 68
    O '66
CANNON, Robert C.
  Pulpit v. the bench. il por Time 88:23 S 9
    '66
CANNON, Toy. See Toys
CANOE RIVER
  Riding down a dying river. R. Cantwell. il
    Sports Illus 25:78-80+ N 21 '66
CANOE trips
  Canoeing on the Russian River. il Sunset 136:
    84+ My '66
  Minnesota's canoe country. S. Shore. il
    Travel 125:26-31 My '66
  Riding down a dying river; Canoe River,
    British Columbia. R. Cantwell. il Sports
    Illus 25:78-80+ N 21 '66
  Travel far and near; Rio Grande canoe trip.
    R. W. Schery. Natur Hist 75:58+ Ap '66
CANOES and canoeing
  Basics of canoeing. J. A. Emmett. il Outdoor
    Life 137:26-7+ Je '66
  Build this 14-foot canoe for $50. R. W.
    Beeching, jr. il Pop Mech 125:145-7+ My '66
  Canoe sailing rigs. F. M. Paulson. il Field
    & S 71:88-92 Ag '66
  Eighteen years with the same canoe. T.
    Trueblood. il Field & S 71:42-3+ Ja '67
  New life for an old canoe. J. A. Emmett. il
    Outdoor Life 138:94+ D '66
  Outfitting the pilgrims to a western Walden;
    Minnesota's government-protected canoe
    area draws 300,000 summer campers. il
    Bsns W p 130-2 Ag 27 '66
CANON law. See Ecclesiastical law
CANON law society of America
  Law and spirit; effort to reform canon law.
    Commonweal 85:155-6 N 11 '66
  Reforming canon law; recommendations for
    carrying out the spirit of Vatican II. Time
    88:44+ O 28 '66
  Straws in the wind; 28th annual convention.
    Pittsburgh. America 115:530 N 5 '66
CANOPY beds. See Beds
CANTALOUPE pie. See Pie
CANTATAS
    See also
  Phonograph records—Cantatas
CANTELLI, Guido
  Brief candles. H. Goldsmith. por Hi Fi 16:51-
    2 F '66
CANTERBURY, Arthur Michael Ramsey, abp
  of. See Ramsey, A. M.

CANTERBURY bells. See Campanulas
CANTILLON, Ann J.
  Gone with the wind. Flying 78:96 My '66
CANTINFLAS
  Traveler, consider my Mexico; ed. by R.
    Joseph. pors Esquire 66:144-5+ N '66
      about
  Mexico's Little Nobody who made good. B.
    Day. por Read Digest 89:221-2+ O '66
CANTLON, J. E. See Curtis, E. J. C. jt. auth.
CANTON, Ohio
  Honoring God's heroes; Hall of fame unveiled.
    Newsweek 67:69 Ap 18 '66
CANTONI, G. L. and Monroy, A.
  Molecular basis of differentiation. Science
    151:597-8 F 4 '66
CANTOR, Donald J.
  Right of divorce. Atlan 218:67-71 N '66
CANTOR, Lon
  New low-loss coax for TV. Electr World 76:
    33 Ag '66
  Will CATV revolutionize your TV viewing
    habits? Pop Electr 25:48-52+ S '66
CANTWELL, Robert
  Fishing. Sports Illus 25:66-7 O 24 '66
  Harness racing. Sports Illus 24:72+ Je 13 '66
  Hunting. Sports Illus 25:61-4 N 7 '66
CANTY, Donald
  Curious walls of Larsen hall. Arch Forum
    124:46-53 Mr '66
  —See Moore, C. W. jt. auth.
CANUTT, Yakima
  Great general slays 'em again; with report
    by D. Zeitlin. il pors Life 60:93-5+ My
    27 '66
CANVASSING, Political. See Political cam-
    paigns
CANYONLANDS NATIONAL PARK
  Standing-up country. P. Friggens and M.
    Friggens. il Read Digest 88:145-52 My '66
CANYONS
  You squeak through the canyon; Box Can-
    yon, Ariz. il Sunset 136:72+ Mr '66
CAPACITORS. See Electric capacitors
CAPE BRETON ISLAND
  Cabot trail. J. T. Starr. il Am For 72:34-5+
    Jl '66
CAPE buffalo hunting. See Buffalo hunting
CAPE COD
  Cape Cod's fresh water lakes. C. Koehler
    and M. Koehler. il Travel 126:45-8 S '66
CAPE COD architecture. See Architecture,
    Cape Cod
CAPE COD NATIONAL SEASHORE
  Cape Cod seashore's white cedar swamp.
    C. R. Koehler. il Nat Parks Mag 40:11 D
    '66
  They're saving America's priceless seashore.
    D. Wharton. il Read Digest 89:181+ Ag '66
CAPE coloreds. See South Africa—Native
    races
CAPE KENNEDY. See Kennedy, Cape
CAPE LOOKOUT NATIONAL SEASHORE
  Mike Frome. M. Frome. Am For 72:7+ Je '66
CAPE MAY POINT, N.J.
  Case of the disappearing coastline. F. J.
    Cook. il N Y Times Mag p38-9+ S 25 '66
CAPITAL
  Utility theory, insights into risk taking. R. O.
    Swalm. bibliog f il Harvard Bsns R 44:123-
    36 N '66
CAPITAL development fund. See United Na-
    tions—Capital development fund
CAPITAL gains tax. See Income tax—Capital
    gains tax
CAPITAL investments
  Business agrees on the medicine. Bsns W
    p37 S 17 '66
  Business spends with a difference; com-
    panies plan to sink $63.8-billion into new
    plant and equipment in '67; with editorial
    comment. il Bsns W p46-8, 202 N 12 '66
  Business sticks to plans; Commerce-SEC
    survey shows faster growth. Bsns W p36 Je
    11 '66
  Capital goods makers whistle a happy tune.
    Bsns W p 16-17 D 24 '66
  Capital qualms. il Fortune 74:44+ D '66
  Companies hold close to spending schedules;
    buying new plant and equipment as
    planned. il Bsns W p39 S 10 '66
  Firing blanks? NICB study of companies re-
    action to suspension of the 7 per cent in-
    vestment tax credit. Newsweek 68:84+
    O 10 '66
  For most companies: spending as usual; in
    wake of tax credit suspension. Bsns W
    p61-2+ O 1 '66
  Full steam for spending; McGraw-Hill sur-
    vey; with editorial comment. il Bsns W
    p37-9, 196 Ap 16 '66

CAPITAL investments—*Continued*
Industry seeks softer tax credit impact; effect of suspension of 7 per cent tax credit on airline orders. Aviation W 85:35-6 S 19 '66
Liberalizing investment credit. America 115: 408 O 8 '66
Making do with the old; McGraw-Hill economics dept. survey. il Bsns W p 101-2 N 26 '66
More expansion still gets majority vote; with editorial comment. il Bsns W p37-8, 196 O 1 '66
Pouring more billions into R&D; pursuit for new products. il Bsns W p 164-6+ My 7 '66
Real squeeze goes on. il Bsns W p21-2 Ag 27 '66
Spending slows down. Newsweek 68:79-80 N 28 '66
Spending surge; too much of a good thing? il Bsns W p35-6 Mr 12 '66
Stretch-out; Quarterly survey of capital appropriations fundings. Newsweek 67:80-1 Je 6 '66
Tax credit has fans and foes; 7 per cent investment credit; with editorial comment. il Bsns W 49-50, 200 Mr 26 '66
Tax credit is the target; possibility of suspending seven per cent investment tax credit. il Bsns W p29 S 3 '66
Tax credit that business may lose. U S News 60:102+ My 9 '66
There's little restraint in plans for outlays. il Bsns W p33-4 My 28 '66
Too much capacity? il Fortune 73:40+ Je '66
Too much of a good thing? private spending for new plant and equipment; Edie estimates. il Time 87:87-8 Mr 11 '66
U.S. business trims its expansion sails; survey of business plans released by the Commerce dept. and the Securities & exchange commission. il Bsns W p38 D 10 '66
Up, up. Newsweek 67:84 Je 20 '66
Where the money is going; investment surveys. Bsns W p37-8 Je 11 '66
CAPITAL market. See Money market
CAPITAL punishment
Capital punishment; decline in the imposition. Reporter 36:14+ Ja 12 '67
Fewer executions. Time 87:48 F 25 '66
Hangman stays; vote in Canada. Time 87:40 Ap 15 '66
Psychiatrists condemn capital punishment. Sci N 89:386 My 21 '66
Taming the beast in man. Christian Cent 83:1593-4 D 28 '66
Time to kill the death penalty? pro and con discussion. il Sr Schol 88:8-9 Ap 29 '66
United Nations and the issue of capital punishment. UN Mo Chron 3:53-8 F '66
See also
Executions and executioners
CAPITAL spending. See Capital investments
CAPITALISM
Capitalism, by A. Rand and others. Review New Repub 155:27-8 D 10 '66. H. Tracy
Future of capitalism. R. L. Heilbroner. Commentary 41:23-35 Ap '66
Modern capitalism; the changing balance of public and private power, by A. Shonfield. Review
Commentary 41:95-7 Je '66. B. D. Nossiter
Nat R 18:169+ F 22 '66. W. R. Rickenbacker
New Repub 154:32-3 F 5 '66. N. McKitterick
Monopoly capital, by P. A. Baran and P. M. Sweezy. Review
Nation 202:749-50 Je 20 '66. J. O'Connor
Where is it going; NICB discuss development trends. il Newsweek 68:80-1 O 3 '66
See also
Free enterprise
CAPITALISM and communism. See Communism and democracy
CAPITALISTS and financiers
Elegant life of the business aristocrats; portfolio. il Fortune 74:162-9 N '66
See also
Businessmen
Rich, The
CAPITOL (United States) See United States—Capitol
CAPLAN, Gerald, and Cadden, Vivian
Turning points of life. McCalls 94:114-15+ O '66; Same abr. with title How to deal with a crisis. Read Digest 90:80-3 Ja '67
CAPLIN, Mortimer Maxwell
What's in a loophole? il Time 88:62+ O 7 '66
CAPOBIANCO, Tito
Persuader; interview. por Opera N 31:18 N 19 '66

CAPON, Robert F.
Stop the wedding, I want to get off. Mlle 64:87+ Ja '67
CAPONIGRO, Paul
Paul Caponigro. P. Caulfield. il Mod Phot 31:62-5 Ja '67
CAPOTE, Truman
Christmas memory; reprint. Ladies Home J 83:86-7+ D '66; Excerpts. Look 30:79-83+ N 29 '66
Truman Capote introduces Jane Bowles; introd. from The collected works of Jane Bowles. Mlle 64:114-16 D '66
Two faces and. ., a landscape. il Vogue 147: 144-9 F 1 '66
about
Books. M. Muggeridge. Esquire 65:82+ Ap '66
Capote in Kansas. S. Kauffmann; discussion. New Repub 154:35-6 F 5 '66
Capote sued for one-tenth of Cold blood royalties. Pub W 189:60 My 30 '66
Cold-blooded crossfire; critic of In cold blood. il por Time 87:48 Ap 15 '66
Come with Mr Capote to a masked ball; with report by J. Howard. il pors Life 61:107-10+ D 9 '66
Curl up and read. L. Rose. Seventeen 25:190 My '66
Evening at the Plaza. il por Newsweek 68: 66-7 D 12 '66
Films; question of producing In cold blood. D. Macdonald. Esquire 65:44+ Ap '66
Grave and reverend book. R. West. Harper 232:108+ F '66
In cold blood target of threatened law suit. Pub W 189:81 Ap 25 '66
In cold comfort; In cold fact; nonfiction novel. B. Long; P. K. Tompkins. pors Esquire 65:124-8+ Je '66
Nonfictional visit with Truman Capote. S. Alexander. Life 60:22 F 18 '66
Other voices, other rooms. por Newsweek 68:26-7 Ag 1 '66
Truman's compote. il pors Time 88:88+ D 9 '66
CAPOTOSTO, R. J.
Bargain boat horn. Pop Mech 125:156-7 Mr '66
CAPOUYA, Emile
Ailments of the spirit. Sat R 49:30-1+ Ag 13 '66
Politics, parachutes and playboys. Sat R 49: 37 Ap 30 '66
Sad of mind but glad at heart. Sat R 49:29-30 F 12 '66
CAPP, Al
Are these films offensive? Capp's opinion. Pop Phot 59:168-71 D '66
about
Which one is the Phoanie? Time 89:47 Ja 20 '67
CAPRI observatory. See Astronomical observatories—Italy
CAPRICCIO; opera. See Strauss, R.
CAPS
Youthful caprice for caps. il Life 61:83-4 Jl 15 '66
CAPSULES
Big wonders in small packages; microencapsulation. J. F. Pearson. il Pop Mech 126:132-5+ N '66
Capsule solutions for countless problems; microencapsulation. Time 87:70 Ap 8 '66
CAPTAIN Kangaroo (television program) See Television broadcasting—Childrens programs
CAPTAINS of industry. See Businessmen
CAPTIVE animals. See Zoological gardens
CAPTIVE nations week
Captive nations week, 1966; proclamation. L. B. Johnson. Dept State Bul 55:234 Ag 15 '66
CAPTURE of animals. See Animals—Capture
CAR-top carriers. See Automobiles—Equipment
CARACAS, Venezuela
Description
Caracas's 400th; Bolivar and bulldozers. T. Moscoso. il Sat R 50:94+ Ja 7 '67
History
Caracas's 400th; Bolivar and bulldozers. T. Moscoso. il Sat R 50:94+ Ja 7 '67
CARACAS Latin American music festival. See Music festivals—Venezuela
CARAMOOR festivals. See Music festivals—New York (state)
CARBAMOYL phosphate. See Carbamyl phosphate

CARBAMYL phosphate
Control of the activity of escherichia coli carbamoyl phoshate synthetase by antagonistic allosteric effectors. A. Piérard. bibliog il Science 154:1572-3 D 23 '66

CARBIDES
Cubic carbides. W. S. Williams. bibliog il Science 152:34-42 Ap 1 '66
Firm seeks greater knowledge of carbides. J. F. Judge. il Tech W 20:23-5 Ja 16 '67
See also
Titanium carbide

CARBINES. See Rifles

CARBON
Individual carbon atoms seen through microscope. il Sci N 89:335 My 7 '66

Isotopes
Anomalous carbon-isotope ratios in nonvolatile organic material; coastal plain of southern Israel. I. R. Kaplan and A. Nissenbaum. bibliog il Science 153:744-5 Ag 12 '66
Isotopic evidence on the early life history of nautilus pompilius, Linné. R. Eichler and H. Ristedt. bibliog il Science 153:734-6 Ag 12 '66
Oxidation of graphitic carbon in certain soils. E. A. Shneour. bibliog il Science 151:991-2 F 25 '66
Oxygen and carbon isotopic composition of limestones and dolomites, Bikini and Eniwetok atolls. M. G. Gross and J. I. Tracy, jr. bibliog il Science 151:1082-4 Mr 4 '66

CARBON assimilation. See Photosynthesis

CARBON dioxide
Apatite and octa-calcium phosphate: effects of carbon dioxide and halogens on formation. D. R. Simpson. bibliog il Science 154:1660-1 D 30 '66
Behavior of carbon dioxide and other volatiles on Mars. R. B. Leighton and B. C. Murray. bibliog il Science 153:136-44 Jl 8 '66
Blood gases: continuous in vivo recording of partial pressures by mass spectrography. S. Woldring and others. bibliog il Science 153:885-7 Ag 19 '66
Electrolytic reduction of CO_2 promising; changing carbon dioxide into breathable oxygen and carbon powder. Tech W 19:45 D 5 '66
Facilitation by carbonic anhydrase of carbon dioxide transport. T. Enns. bibliog il Science 155:44-7 Ja 6 '67
Respiration of a forest measured by carbon dioxide accumulation during temperature inversions. G. M. Woodwell and W. R. Dykeman. bibliog il Science 154:1031-4 N 25 '66
Role of the oceans. R. Revelle. il Sat R 49:39-41 My 7 '66
See also
Photosynthesis

CARBON monoxide
Reversible combination of carbon monoxide with a synthetic oxygen carrier complex. L. Vaska. bibliog il Science 152:769-71 My 6 '66

CARBON tetrachloride
Carbon tetrachloride: a new crystalline modification. R. Rudman and B. Post. bibliog il Science 154:1009+ N 25 '66

CARBONACEOUS rocks. See Rocks, Sedimentary

CARBONATED beverages. See Beverages

CARBONI, William
Working with Toscanini; ed. by B. H. Haggin. Atlan 218:72-5 D '66

CARBONIC anhydrase
Facilitation by carbonic anhydrase of carbon dioxide transport. T. Enns. bibliog il Science 155:44-7 Ja 6 '67

CARBONYLS
Pseudo-fivefold symmetry in carbonyl process nickel. G. L. Downs and J. D. Braun. il Science 154:1443-4 D 16 '66

CARBORUNDUM company
Carborundum grinds at faster clip; acquisition of W. T. Copeland & sons, manufacturer of Spode china. il Bsns W p58-62 Jl 23 '62
Comeback at Carborundum. J. Berry. il Duns R 87:36-9+ Ap '66

CARBOXYPEPTIDASES
Pancreatic carboxypeptidases: activities in zinc-deficient rats. J. M. Hsu and others. bibliog il Science 153:882-3 Ag 19 '66

CARBURETORS
ABCs of carburetion. R. Huntington. il Pop Mech 126:120-3+ D '66
'Bout that carburetor. J. McFarland. il Hot Rod 20:80-3 Ja '67

Instant pony power. J. McFarland. il Hot Rod 19:92-3 O '66
Power mods for MoPar's 273. E. Dahlquist. il Hot Rod 19:64-7+ F '66

CARCINOGENIC substances. See Cancer producing substances

CARCINOGENS. See Cancer producing substances

CARD, Phyllis B.
One job too many. por Redbook 126:8+ F '66

CARD catalogs (for libraries) See Catalogs, Library

CARD tables. See Tables

CARDIAC muscle. See Heart—Muscle

CARDIAC resuscitation
Max, the lifesaver; Dr. J. Noble's cart. il Life 60:31-2+ Ja 28 '66
These hearts need not die; restored to life through external cardio-pulmonary resuscitation. R. Deutsch and P. Deutsch. Read Digest 88:181-4 Je '66

CARDI-ACTIVATOR. See Respiratory apparatus

CARDIN, Lucien
Munsinger affair. il por Time 87:54 Mr 18 '66

CARDIN, Pierre
Cardin silhouette. il por Ebony 21:132-4+ My '66
Pegleg from Paris. por Time 87:79 My 20 '66

CARDINAL utility theory. See Decision making

CARDINALE, Claudia
Something of a nomad; ed. by E. Miller. por Seventeen 25:144-5+ Ap '66

about
New seven deadly sins; portfolio. pors Esquire 66:190-5 D '66
She'd rather lose money than be a cliché. il pors Life 61:52-6 Jl 8 '66

CARDINALS (football club) See Football clubs

CARDIOVASCULAR diseases. See Heart—Diseases

CARDIOVASCULAR strokes. See Heart—Diseases

CARDONA, Carlo
Elections in Malta. America 114:412-14 Mr 26 '66

CARDS
Playing cards. D. Powills. See issues of Hobbies
Some old Spanish customs in Mexico. D. Powills. il Hobbies 71:118-19 O '66
See also
Cardsharping
Poker

Anecdotes, facetiae, satire, etc.
Curious facts and fancy figures. D. Powills. il Hobbies 71:124-5+ N '66

Collectors and collecting
Antiques of tomorrow. D. Powills. Hobbies 71:118-19 Jl '66

History
Worshipful company of makers of playing cards. D. Powills. il Hobbies 71:118-19 Je '66

CARDS, Catalog. See Catalog cards

CARDS, Greeting. See Greeting cards

CARDS of identification. See Identification cards, certificates, etc.

CARDSHARPING
Poker. J. Richardson. il Esquire 66:46+ D '66

CARE, Norman S.
Is philosophy dead too? New Repub 154:23-6 My 21 '66

CAREER girls. See Business and professional women

CAREERS. See Occupations

CAREERS for women. See Woman—Employment

CAREERS in agriculture. See Agriculture as a profession

CARELS, Guy. See Cerf, J. A. jt. auth.

CAREN, Linda D. and Rosenberg, L. T.
Steroids and serum complement in mice: influence of hydrocortisone, diethylstilbestrol, and testosterone. bibliog Science 152:782-3 My 6 '66

CAREY, Bob
Lures that caught 2,000 bass. Field & S 71:10-12+ Je '66

CAREY, Joanna A.
What parents ask about corrective dentistry. Todays Health 44:28-31 Mr '66

CAREY, Michele
Ordinary American girl; portfolio. Esquire 66:68-70 Ag '66

CAREY-Thomas award
Carey-Thomas award given for Anchor Bible. Pub W 189:54 My 23 '66

CARGO airlines. See Air freight service
CARGO handling. See Container system
(freight handling); Freight handling
CARGO ships. See Freight vessels
CARGO terminals. See Airport buildings
CARGO vessels. See Freight vessels
CARGO vessels, Navy. See United States—Navy
—Boats
CARHART, Arthur H.
Island hopping by auto. Travel 125:52-6 Mr
'66
CARIBBEAN cookery. See Cookery, West
Indian
CARIBBEAN cruises. See Cruising
CARIBBEAN national forest. See National
forests
CARIBBEAN REGION
See also
Architecture, Domestic—Caribbean Region
Foreign visitors in the Caribbean Region
Sports—Caribbean Region
West Indies

Description and travel
Better homes and gardens tour: islands of
the Caribbean. il Bet Hom & Gard 45:22
Ja '67
Eight great Caribbean islands. Mlle 62:228-31
Ap '66
Going places, finding things in seven Carib-
bean islands. J. Wilson. il House & Gard
131:16+ Ja '67
Gone flying: the route of the island traders.
H. Groenhoff. il Flying 79:86-9+ Jl '66
Guide to winter sunshine vacations. il Bet
Hom & Gard 44:121-2+ O '66
Let's travel: briefing. il Mlle 62:233-43 Ap '66
Thorny path; Florida to the Caribbean.
J. C. Kozlick. il Motor B 119:81-5+ Ja '67

Economic conditions
Islands of the Caribbean: free, and in trouble.
C. Migdail. il U S News 62:52-4 Ja 2 '67
CARIBBEAN SEA
Deep-sea pleistocene biostratigraphy. L. Lidz.
bibliog il Science 154:1448-52 D 16 '66
Layer of abnormally cold bottom water over
southern Aves ridge. A. L. Gordon and
others. bibliog il Science 151:1525-6 Mr 25
'66
CARIBOU
Cavalcade of the caribou. J. J. Shomon. il
Outdoor Life 137:46-7+ Je '66
See also
Reindeer
CARICATURES and cartoons
Best of Batch; the decade 1934-1944. C. D.
Batchelor. Nat R 18:990-1 O 4 '66
Cracks on the facade. A. Dunn. Horizon 8:
116-20 Wint '66
Drawing caricatures. E. Rother. Design 67:12-
15 Mr '66
Feiffer. J. Feiffer. See issues of New republic
Peaceable kingdom. D. Levine. Newsweek 68:
14-15 D 26 '66
Rubber stamps. New Yorker 42:56-61 D 3 '66
She. M. Ffolkes. Holiday 39:62-7 Ap '66
Variations on a four-letter word. M. Ramus.
Horizon 8:98-103 Spr '66
Wordless workshop. R. Doty. See issues of
Popular science monthly
World of Youssouf bey. W. Buehr. il Horizon
8:24-31 Sum '66
See also
Comics (books, strips, etc)
also subhead Caricatures and cartoons
under various subjects, e.g. Spies—Carica-
tures and cartoons
CARIES, Dental. See Teeth—Diseases
CARINGELLA, Charles
Build a power-failure alarm. Pop Mech 126:
200-1+ O '66
Build a stereo headphone control unit. Pop
Electr 24:71-3+ Ap '66
Build time-signal-only receiver. Pop Electr
25:41-6+ O '66
Trans-vox. Pop Electr 26:57-61 Ja '67
CARL, Herbert A. See McCormick, A; Price,
P. P. jt. auths.
—See Price, P. P. jt. auth.
CARL Ally, incorporated. See Ally, Carl,
incorporated
CARLETON, Charles S.
Echoes of a scream. Am Ed 3:20-2 D '66
Head Start or false start? Am Ed 2:20-2
S '66
Job. Am Ed 2:28-32 N '66
Picasso=MC². por Am Ed 2:13-15 Mr '66
CARLETON, Helen
Storied rock becomes a bird oasis. Audubon
Mag 68:273-4 Jl '66
CARLETON, R. Milton
Facts on fertilizers. Flower Grower 53:38-
9+ Ap '66

Regional pointers: Midwest. See issues of
Flower grower, the home garden
Solving your summer lawn problem. Flower
Grower 53:29 Jl '66
CARLETON, William G.
South's many moods. Yale R 55:623-40 Je '66
CARLETON college, Northfield, Minn.
Carleton: coming of age, cum laude. R.
Hoffmann. il Mlle 62:186-8+ Ap '66
CARLI, Luigi, bp
Carli round. America 114:643 My 7 '66
Jews, again. Commonweal 84:190-1 My 6 '66
CARLIN, George
Pop of the news. por Newsweek 69:41 Ja 9
'67
CARLIN, James
Art teacher speaks his mind. il por Am
Artist 30:24-5+ Mr '66
CARLINSKY, Dan
Authors of Trivia sue Pocket books, Metro-
media. Pub W 190:32 Ag 1 '66
CARLISLE, G. R. and Harvey, John
Ten ways to cut your hog feeding costs. Suc
Farm 64:38-9 O '66
CARLISLE, Jim
Through the green lenses. por Seventeen 25:
106-7+ Je '66
CARLISLE, Lilian Baker
Oriental painting and tinsel pictures. Antiques
90:218-19 Ag '66
CARLISLE, Thomas John
Above all; poem. America 115:825 D 24 '66
Addiction; poem. Sat R 49:24 Ap 9 '66
Dream of life; poem. Christian Cent 83:887
Jl 13 '66
Great intruder; poem. Christian Cent 83:804
Je 22 '66
CARLL, W. T. See Forgacs, J. jt. auth.
CARLO, Giancarlo de
Marriage Italian style. Arch Forum 124:66-7
My '66
CARLOTTA. See Myers, M. B. H.
CARLSBAD film festival. See Moving picture
festivals
CARLSBERG brewery. See Breweries
CARLSEN, G. Robert
Patterns of young adults' reading; summary
of address, July 14, 1966. Pub W 190:29-32
Ag 8 '66
CARLSEN, Kurt
Inventor of the month. S. V. Jones. por Sci
Digest 59:23 Mr '66
CARLSON, C. O. and others
Helium-neon laser: thermal high-resolution
recording. Science 154:1550-1 D 23 '66
CARLSON, Eddo. See Booth, E. jt. auth.
CARLSON, Herbert E.
Muskies at night. Field & S 71:36-7+ Jl '66
CARLSON, Leland H.
(comp) Articles and other books received;
British Commonwealth and Ireland. See
issues of American historical review
CARLTON, Helen
Answer to laundry in outer space. Life 61:136
N 25 '66
CARLTON, Lessie, and Moore, R. H.
Culturally disadvantaged children can be
helped. NEA J 55:13-14 S '66
CARMEN; opera. See Bizet, G.
CARMER, Carl
N.Y. state chronicler Carmer to tour up-
state stores. Pub W 190:58-9 N 7 '66
Stars fell on York state. J. K. Hutchens.
Sat R 49:45-6 D 24 '66
CARMICHAEL, Earl R.
Parks plans can simplify maintenance. Am
City 81:104-6 O '66
CARMICHAEL, Stokely
Black power speech that has Congress
aroused; excerpts from address, August 5,
1966. por U S News 61:6 Ag 22 '66

about
As draft pressures mount—. por U S News
61:8 N 7 '66
At a Black Panther meeting in Harlem. U S
News 61:14-15 S 12 '66
Atlanta's baptism in black power. il por U S
News 61:36 S 19 '66
Black power! il Newsweek 67:36 Je 27 '66
Black power. F. Millspaugh. Commonweal 84:
500-3 Ag 5 '66
Black power: politics of frustration. il por
Newsweek 68:26+ Jl 11 '66
Brilliancy of black. B. Weinraub. por Esquire
67:130-5 Ja '67
Frightened intellectuals. Reporter 35:22-3 N
17 '66
From freedom high to black power. G. Rob-
erts. il pors N Y Times Mag p27-9+ S 25
'66; Reply. S. Carmichael. p98+ O 16 '66
Growl of the Panther. Newsweek 67:33+ My
30 '66

CARROLL, Lewis, pseud.—*Continued*
about
Alice in Wonderland; dramatized for BBC television. J. Miller. il Vogue 148:240-7+ D '66
At last, an Alice unspoiled; with account by H. Judson. il Life 61:96A-98 N 25 '66
CARROLL, R. L.
D.E.D. goes underground. Am City 81:96-7 Jl '66
CARROLL, Wallace
Threnody in quarter tones; poem. Reporter 35:16 Jl 14 '66
CARROTS
Carrots keep better using high humidity. Sci N L 89:63 Ja 22 '66
CARROTT, Richard G.
Neo-Egyptian style in American architecture. Antiques 90:482-8 O '66
CARRUTH, Hayden
Austria remaining. Poetry 108:119-21 My '66
Ezra Pound and the great style. Sat R 49: 21-2+ Ap 9 '66
Failure of contempt. Poetry 107:396-7 Mr '66
How not to rate a poet. Sat R 49:21+ F 12 '66
about
To a known place. R. Howard. Poetry 107: 253-8 Ja '66
CARRY Nation; opera. See Moore, D. S.
CARS (automobiles) See Automobiles
CARSON, Gerald
Hair today, gone tomorrow; excerpts from Polite Americans. Am Heritage 17:42-7 F '66
Machine that kept them honest. Am Heritage 17:50-9+ Ag '66
CARSON, Joanne Copeland
Improbable private life of Mrs Johnny Carson. G. Greene. il pors Ladies Home J 83: 50-5+ Jl '66
CARSON, Johnny
Improbable private life of Mrs Johnny Carson. G. Greene. il pors Ladies Home J 83: 50-5+ Jl '66
CARSON CITY, Nev.
Carson City houses take you back into the nineteenth century. il Sunset 137:48+ O '66
CARSON PASS
Hiking, fishing, boating in the Carson Pass lake country. il Sunset 137:26+ Ag '66
CARSTENSON, Blue
Excerpt from statement, July 16, 1965. Cong Digest 45:54 F '66
CARTELS, International. See Trusts, Industrial —International trusts
CARTER, Albert Howard
At Christmas; poem. Christian Cent 83:1569 D 21 '66
CARTER, Anne P.
Economics of technological change; with biographical sketch. Sci Am 214:20, 25-31 bibliog(p 140) Ap '66
CARTER, Barbara
Sargent Shriver and the role of the poor. Reporter 34:17-20 My 5 '66
CARTER, Byron L.
New ways to bigger profits. Nations Bsns 54: 44-5+ D '66
CARTER, Elliott, 1908-
Piano vs. orchestra. H. Saal. il por Newsweek 69:94 Ja 16 '67
Treat worth the travail. il por Time 89:44 Ja 13 '67
CARTER, George E.
Beginnings of Peace corps programming. Ann Am Acad 365:46-54 My '66
CARTER, Hodding
Old South had something worth saving. N Y Times Mag p50-1+ D 4 '66
CARTER, Jane
Willow whistle; poem. Farm J 90:121 Ap '66
CARTER, Launor F.
National document-handling systems in science and technology. bibliog Science 154: 1299-304 D 9 '66
CARTER, Manfred A.
Christ in Christmas; poem. Christian Cent 83: 1530 D 14 '66
Head of Christ; poem. Christian Cent 83:1241 O 12 '66
Inducted; poem. Christian Cent 83:1202 O 5 '66
What wood? poem. Christian Cent 83:395 Mr 30 '66
CARTER, Mary Duncan. See Hsu, O. B. jt. auth.
CARTER, Richard
Fluoroscoping the AMA. Nation 204:29 Ja 2 '67
Superswine! Esquire 66:264+ D '66

CARTER, Richard E.
Nassau to New York, non-stop. Yachting 119:98-100+ Ap '66
CARTER, Thomas
How I'd rob your house; ed. by J. R. Moskin. pors Look 30:28-9 My 31 '66
CARTER, Thomas Henry
Loco parentis. Nation 202:541-2 My 9 '66
Sex & the single FBI man. por Time 87:23 My 6 '66
CARTER, Thomas M.
Name of progressive education taken in vain. Sch & Soc 94:102-3 F 19 '66
CARTHEW, Anthony
For the Arabs Israel does not exist. N Y Times Mag p30-1+ D 18 '66
Vietnam is like an oriental western. N Y Times Mag p8-9+ Ja 23 '66
CARTIER, John O.
Found: new duck bonanza. Outdoor Life 138: 52-5+ S '66
Look to the lakes for trout. Outdoor Life 137: 40-1+ Ap '66
New way to find winter bluegills. il Outdoor Life 137:36-7+ F '66
Pike strike back. Outdoor Life 137:48-9+ Je '66
Trophy browns of the Brule. Outdoor Life 138: 40-1+ Ag '66
Whitetails in the sands. Outdoor Life 138:46-9+ N '66
(ed) See Jullie. L. L. Giant of Mission creek
CARTIER-BRESSON, Henri
Encore at the Louvre; Henri Cartier-Bresson. M. R. Weiss. il Sat R 49:23-8 N 26 '66
Letter from Paris; one-man shoe in the Louvre. Genêt. New Yorker 42:113-14 Ja 14 '67
CARTIER, incorporated
Cartier opens its door wider. il Bsns W p70-2+ O 15 '66
CARTILAGE
Protein-polysaccharide loss during endochondral ossification: immunochemical evidence. A. Hirschman and D. D. Dziewiatkowski. bibliog il Science 154:393-5 O 21 '66
CARTOGRAPHY
Early mapping of the land and sea. G. A. Rothrock. il Natur Hist 75:24-9 bibliog(p68) F '66
Measuring the earth, from space. Sr Schol 88:5 Mr 18 '66
Three-dimensional map construction. G. F. Jenks and D. A. Brown. bibliog il Science 154:857-64 N 18 '66
CARTOONISTS
See also
Campbell, E. S.
Scarfe, G.
CARTOONS. See Caricatures and cartoons
CARTRIDGE, Phonograph. See Phonograph— Pickup
CARTRIDGE loaded tape. See Magnetic tape
CARTRIDGES
Good ole thutty-thutty. J. O'Connor. il Outdoor Life 138:70+ S '66
P is for pressure; important facts for the shooter. W. Page. il Field & S 70:124-9 Mr '66
Reloader in the family. T. Trueblood. il Field & S 71:22+ S '66
Ten little loading problems. W. Page. il Field & S 71:118-22 Je '66
.30 caliber Magnums. J. O'Connor. il Outdoor Life 137:92-7 F '66
.22 varmint cartridges. J. O'Connor. il Outdoor Life 137:138+ Ap '66
CARTRIDGES, Stereo. Phonograph—Stereophonic pickup
CARTS
Garden caddy for the green thumb set. il Pop Gard 17:18 My '66
Garden tool caddy. il Pop Gard 17:11 D '66
Seven slaves on wheels; service carts all. il Pop Mech 125:149-55+ F '66
CARTWRIGHT, Marguerite
Pope's visit. por Negro Hist Bul 29:33-4 N '65
CARTY, Winthrop P. See Raymond, N. jt. auth.
CARUSO, Enrico
And still they come, forty-five years after his death: Caruso, new and otherwise. P. L. Miller. por Am Rec G 32:956-7 Je '66
Caruso on records, by A. Favia-Artsay. Review
Am Rec G por 32:1000-2 Je '66. P. L. Miller
Enrico Caruso in My cousin. H. Birdoff. il por Hobbies 71:36+ N; 36 D '66
CARUSO, John L. and Cutter, E. G.
Proliferation of cells in the central cylinder of the reduced mutant in lanceolate tomato. bibliog Science 154:1021-3 N 25 '66
CARUSO, Nino
Faenza: International ceramics competition. Craft Horiz 26:20-1 S '66

CARVER, George A. jr
Faceless Viet Cong. For Affairs 44:347-72 Ap '66

CARVER, Lorena
Diving horses, and a three-sheet on a downtown corner; interview. New Yorker 42:19-21 Jl 2 '66

CARVING (art industries)
Animals from the rough. il Natur Hist 75:54-7 My '66
Jade jaguar in ancient Maya tomb; Tikal, Guatemala. il Sci N 89:482 Je 18 '66

CARVING (meat, etc)
Alfred Hitchcock probes the American man's aversion to carving; ed. by E. Alston. A. Hitchcock. il Look 31:50-1 Ja 10 '67
Electric carving knife in action. il House & Gard 130:312-13 N '66

CARVING knives. See Knives

CARY, Bob
Ghosts of the Shawnee. Outdoor Life 138:32-7 N '66

CARY, Diana Serra
His greatest ride. Read Digest 89:166-8+ N '66

CARY, Eve
Revolt and repression in Spain's universities. Reporter 34:43-5 My 19 '66

CARY, Gene L.
Class socialization patterns and their relationship to learning. bibliog f Sch & Soc 94:349-52 O 29 '66

CARY family
Cary coat-of arms. H. K. Eilers. il Hobbies 71:118-20 N '66

CARY memorial library, Lexington, Mass.
Controversial books; excerpt from policy statement. Library J 91:4572 O 1 '66
Original print. R. E. Cain. il Library J 91:5323-6 N 1 '66

CARYOPTERIS
Blue mist for summer & winter; unusual shrub. L. Burgess. il Flower Grower 53:48 N '66

CASA del libro. See San Juan, Puerto Rico—Libraries

CASABLANCA, Morocco
Casablanca. P. Bowles. il Holiday 40:74-9+ S '66

CASALS, Marta Montanez
Interview; ed. by L. Biancolli. por McCalls 93:100-1+ My '66

CASALS, Pablo
Interview; ed. by L. Biancolli. pors McCalls 93:100-1+ My '66

about

Big world of Don Pablo. I. Kolodin. il pors Sat R 49:43-5 D 31 '66
Gift of privilege. il por Time 88:48+ Ag 12 '66
Most un-alone alone man I ever knew. G. P. Hunt. il Life 61:3 N 11 '66
Pablo Casals: a discography. Sat R 49:45-6+ D 31 '66
Serenade to ninety years of greatness. B. Farrell. il pors Life 61:34-43 N 11 '66
Vermont magic. H. Brandon. Sat R 49:8 Ag 13 '66

CASALS, Rosemary
Bright future for little Miss Bombshell. K. Chapin. il Sports Illus 25:68-70 O 24 '66
Teeny tennis bopper. il por Newsweek 69:48 Ja 2 '67

CASANOVA DE SEINGALT, Giacomo Girolamo
All Europe was his seraglio. R. J. Clements. por Sat R 50:82 Ja 14 '67
Authors & editors; memoirs. Pub W 191:41 Ja 16 '67
Casanova. K. Rexroth. Sat R 49:23 Ap 9 '66
Casanova in England. P. Quennell. il pors Horizon 8:34-7 Aut '66

CASAROLI, Agostino
Divine diplomat. por Time 88:50+ Jl 8 '66

CASAS, Bartolomé de las
Defender of the Indians; with editorial comment. R. Gallardo. il por Américas 18:inside cover. 23-31 O '66

CASCADE Crest trail. See Trails

CASCADE RANGE
New road over the Oregon Cascades. il Sunset 137:25 S '66
North Cascades report. il Liv Wildn 29:32-9 Wint '65
Park for the North Cascades? meeting the test of national park eligibility. C. F. Brockman. il Am For 72:8-11+ S '66

CASE, H. M.
Designed decay. Harvard Bsns R 44:126-31 Ja '66

CASE, L. L.
Yet another interview with B. Bonnet. Nation 202:193-4 F 14 '66

CASE for books; drama. See Hark, M. and McQueen, N.

CASE institute of technology, Cleveland, Ohio
Michelson winner named. Sci N 90:327 O 22 '66
New face of Case. il Sci Digest 59:42-7 Ap '66
U.S. seeks wider base for science; NSF's centers of excellence program in Case and WRU. il Bsns W p60-2 S 3 '66

CASEBEER, Richard S. and Hogue, C. L.
Hideaway for moths. Natur Hist 75:40-1 My '66

CASEWIT, Curtis W.
Science overseas: jobs galore; condensation of How to get a job overseas. Sci Digest 59:71-7 F '66
Sun Valley in summer. Travel 125:45-7 Je '66

CASEY, Dermot Armstrong
Oldest Australian. il por Sci Digest 59:26-7 Ap '66

CASEY, M. J. and others
Complement-fixing antigens in hamster tumors induced by the Bryan strain of Rous sarcoma virus. bibliog Science 151:1086-8 Mr 4 '66

CASEY, Margaret M.
Pressures on students. NEA J 55:29-30 S '66

CASEY, William J.
Test of the tide. il por Newsweek 67:33 Je 27 '66

CASH flow. See Corporations—Accounting

CASH register company. See National cash register company

CASH registers
Machine that kept them honest. G. Carson. il Am Heritage 17:50-9+ Ag '66

CASHEL, Ireland
In Tipperary, the Rock of Cashel. il Sunset 136:28+ Je '66

CASHMERE
Mongolia; lush product from a harsh land. J. M. Flagler and J. A. Zill. il Look 31:52-9 Ja 24 '67

CASIDA, John E. and others
Methylene-C^{14}-dioxyphenyl compounds: metabolism in relation to their synergistic action. bibliog Science 153:1130-3 S 2 '66

CASINOS
Game is skimming; money being taken off the top by Nevada casinos. il Newsweek 68:18-19 Ag 29 '66

CASLER, L. A.
Pitfalls of acquisitions. Duns R 87:34-5+ Je '66

CASPER, Billy
Casper on the putter. por Esquire 65:118-19 Ap '66

about

At Olympic: a summit of drama. A. Wright. il pors Sports Illus 24:22-7 Je 27 '66
Course for romancing. il por Newsweek 68:59 Jl 4 '66
Happiness is a hippo steak. E. Shrake. il pors Sports Illus 24:22-6+ F 7 '66
Ten-percent tournament. il por Time 88:58 Jl 1 '66

CASS, James
Education around the world. Sat R 49:47-8 Ag 20 '66
Ideas for teen-age summers. Sat R 49:81 F 19 '66
—See Ellingson, C; Woodring, P. jt. auths.

CASSATT, Mary
Greatness of Mary Cassatt. G. Newman. il pors Am Artist 30:42-9+ F '66
Portrait of a lady; exhibition in Manhattan's Knoedler gallery. il Time 87:78 F 4 '66
Proper impressionist. por Newsweek 67:86 F 14 '66

CASSELL, Frank H.
Immigration and the Department of labor. bibliog f Ann Am Acad 367:105-14 S '66

CASSELS, Louis
Minister who's not afraid to fight. Look 30:79-80+ My 31 '66

CASSEROLE cookery
Bird and bottle, summer style; casserole of chicken. C. Claiborne. il N Y Times Mag p70+ Ag 21 '66
Casseroles and kabobs make hot dishes for cool days. il Pop Gard 17:32-5+ Mr '66
Casseroles: colorful one-dish dinners; with recipes. il Ebony 21:136+ O '66
Casseroles with class. il McCalls 94:130-1+ O '66
Rice main dishes. il Bet Hom & Gard 44:101-2 F '66
Settlement cook book; excerpts. il Ladies Home J 83:112-13+ My '66

CASSIDY, Frederic Gomes
Grinders and sneeders. il por Newsweek 69:56 Ja 16 '67

CASSILL, Ronald Verlin
Lakes of Iowa. Holiday 40:18+ Ag '66
That blue-eyed darling Nathaniel. Horizon 8:
32-9 Sum '66
CASSIRER, Henry R.
Television for the pre-school child. UNESCO
Courier 19:4-11 N '66
CASSITY, Turner
Nocturne; Grace at the Atlanta fox; Song in
subtitles; Epigoni go French line; poems.
Poetry 107:238-42 Ja '66
CASSON, Lionel
Greek poem in Roman prose. Sat R 49:34-5
F 12 '66
CASTAGNA, Edwin
Involvement in federal programs; address,
1966. por Wilson Lib Bul 41:478-83 Ja '67
CASTAN, Frances Elaine
Men facing death; letter. Harper 233:14+ D
'66
CASTAN, Sam
Photographs. il Harper 233:56-7 S '66

about

Men facing death: destruction of an Amer-
ican platoon; excerpt from Battles in the
monsoon. S. L. A. Marshall. il Harper 233:
48-53 S '66; Reply with rejoinder. F. E.
Castan. 233:14+ D '66
Sam Castan 1935-1966: Look senior editor.
J. Laurence. il por Look 30:77-8 Jl 12 '66
CASTE
Namboodiri Brahmans of Kerala. J. Mencher.
il Natur Hist 75:14-21 bibliog(p64) My '66
CASTEAU, Belgium
Place in the country. il Time 88:40+ S 30
'66
CASTELLI, John P. and Straka, R. M.
AFCRL radio observations of May's eclipse.
Sky & Tel 32:84-5 Ag '66
CASTELLI, Leo
Sort of the Svengali of pop. J. Greenfeld. il
pors N Y Times Mag p34-5+ My 8 '66;
Discussion. p41+ Je 5 '66
CASTELLO BRANCO, Humberto
Democracy on the shelf. por Time 88:37
O 28 '66
Hard man to hang. Newsweek 67:61 Ap 11
'66
Making it formal. Time 88:42 D 16 '66
Not-so-sure thing. il Newsweek 68:49 Jl 4 '66
CASTING (fishing) See Fishing
CASTING (sculpture)
Casting of Ethel Scull; and husband. il Time
87:69 Ap 1 '66
CASTING, Continuous. See Continuous casting
CASTING, Die. See Die casting
CASTING molds. See Molds (for casting)
CASTING rods. See Fishing tackle
CASTLE, Barbara Anne
Czar for British freight? Bsns W p67 Ag 6
'66
She masterminds plans for British transport.
il por Bsns W p90-2+ Mr 5 '66
CASTLE, Edward S.
Light responses of phycomyces. bibliog Sci-
ence 154:1416-20 D 16 '66
CASTLE, William Bosworth
Entertainer, two researchers honored by AMA.
por Todays Health 44:17 Ag '66
CASTLE COMBE, England
Muddle in Puddleby. il Newsweek 68:40+
Jl 11 '66
19th Century Fox; filming of Story of Doctor
Dolittle. il Time 88:28 Jl 8 '66
Trouble in Puddleby-on-the-Marsh. C. Loft-
ing. Life 61:7 S 30 '66
CASTLE ugly; story. See Barrett, M. E.
CASTLES
Castle tours. P. Andrews. il Travel 125:56-7
Ap '66
Elsinore castle: to believe or not to believe.
C. Stinnett. il Holiday 40:36+ N '66
Germany's castle hotels. H. Johnson. il House
& Gard 129:52-3+ My '66
Shades of Lammermoor: ruins of castle in
Scotland; photographs. H. Lloyd. Opera
N 30:14-16 F 19 '66
Your castle awaits you, sire! castle hotels in
Europe; with report by M. Leatherbee. il
Life 61:34-42A S 2 '66
CASTRO, Fidel
After eight years: how Castro is doing. por
U S News 62:18 Ja 16 '67
Premier Castro's speech on Cuba; excerpts
from address, August 30, 1966. Cur Hist 51:
363+ D '66

about

Big mystery in Castro's Cuba. il por U S
News 61:37-8 Jl 11 '66

Caning the students. Time 87:54 Mr 18 '66
Castro gets a satellite, in Africa. il por U S
News 61:44 Ag 8 '66
Castro regime in Cuba. E. Halperin. bibliog f
il Cur Hist 51:354-9 D '66
Cuba, Castro and the United States. P. W.
Bonsal. For Affairs 45:260-76 Ja '67
Cuba goes from bad to worse; how long can
Castro last? il por U S News 60:56-7 Ap
25 '66
Down with imperialism, 12,000 miles away.
Time 87:35 F 18 '66
Fidel Castro: did he fall, or was he pushed?
por U S News 60:6 Je 27 '66
Gloomy Castro faces more economic woes.
por Bsns W p58+ Je 25 '66
Good-by, cha-cha-cha. Newsweek 67:55 Ap 4
'66
Inside look at Castro and today's Cuba. por
U S News 60:16 My 2 '66
On the spot in Cuba, our distant neighbor:
Castro's Cuba today; symposium, ed. by
W. Johnson; discussion. Sr Schol 88:14 Mr
4 '66
One war that the Communists are losing. il
U S News 61:86-8 N 14 '66
Plot to kill Castro. por Newsweek 67:50 Mr
21 '66
Semper Fidelis? Time 87:42 Je 24 '66
CASTRO, José Gil de. See Gil de Castro, J.
CASTRO-CID, Enrique
Motion is haphazard, the situation unpredict-
able; show at Richard Feigen gallery, N.Y.
il por Time 87:78-9 Mr 4 '66
CATALANO, Eduardo Fernando
M.I.T.'s student center: Eduardo Catalano
starts with systems and creates archi-
tecture. il Arch Rec 139:125-32 Mr '66
CATALINA cherry. See Islands cherry
CATALOG cards
Commercial cataloging services: Library of
Congress, Wilson, Alanar, and R. R. Bow-
ker; juvenile cards. il Library J 91:5133-5
O 15 '66
Crisis in children's cataloging; new LC card
sets. T. C. Hines. il Library J 91:4183-7
S 15 '66; Discussion. 91:5129-32, 6140+ O 15,
D 15 '66
LC centralized cataloging plans highlighted
at 67th ARL meeting; with summary of
report by L. Q. Mumford. Library J 91:
1374+ Mr 15 '66
People that walked in darkness: LC cards
and catalogers. P. S. Dunkin. il Library J
91:2267-70 My 1 '66
Reducing the cataloging backlog: Library
of Congress cards; letter to the editor.
W. E. Jorgensen; discussion. Library J 91:
458+ F 1 '66
CATALOG codes. See Cataloging
CATALOG houses. See Mail order business
CATALOGERS
People that walked in darkness: LC cards
and catalogers. P. S. Dunkin. il Library J
91:2267-70 My 1 '66
CATALOGING
Crisis in children's cataloging; new LC card
sets. T. C. Hines. il Library J 91:4183-7
S 15 '66; Discussion. 91:5129-32, 6140+ O 15,
D 15 '66
Information technology: problems and pro-
mises; excerpts from address, May 27, 1965.
M. Taube. Library J 91:1155-8 Mr 1 '66
L.C. study tests machines at sending catalog
data. Pub W 189:42 Mr 14 '66
Myth of the delicate instrument; recom-
mendations of the Nelson report for li-
braries of New York state. G. K. Schenk.
Wilson Lib Bul 41:233 O '66; Reply. B. M.
Golumb. 41:373 D '66
Nelson associates survey recommends one cat-
alog center for state of N.Y. Library J
91:3132 Je 15 '66
Plans for centralized cataloging materialize;
LC experimental cooperative arrangement
with the BNB. E. Hamer and A. Mc-
Cormick. ALA Bul 60:559-60 Je '66
Route '66: Dewey, MARC, and Title II. E.
Moon. il Library J 92:58-60 Ja 1 '67
See also
Subject headings
Cost
Dewey: necessity or luxury? practical eco-
nomics involved in continuing with Dewey
vs. converting to LC. G. E. Evans. bibliog
il Library J 91:4038-46 S 15 '66; Reply. J. J.
Murphy. 91:5506 N 15 '66
Why catalog paperbacks; letters to the edi-
tor. Library J 91:5278+ N 1 '66
CATALOGING, Cooperative
Shared cataloging; feature of LC's plan.
E. Hamer and A. McCormick. ALA Bul 60:
1127 D '66

CATALOGS
   See also
Phonograph records—Catalogs
CATALOGS, Library
   Card catalog for the blind; Arkansas school
      for the blind, Little Rock, Ark. il Wilson
      Lib Bul 40:830-1 My '66
   Computer produced book catalog. T. W.
      McConkey. il Library J 91:1864-5 Ap 1 '66
   Computers challenge cards in library catalog-
      ing study; New York public library. Pub
      W 189:71 F 28 '66
   Forgotten key: independent research a myth?
      school libraries. M. Rossoff. Library J 91:
      5126-8+ O 15 '66
   Library study reckons catalog conversion
      cheap; National union catalog at the Li-
      brary of Congress. Pub W 189:71 F 28 '66
   Myth of the delicate instrument; recom-
      mendations of the Nelson report for li-
      braries of New York state. G. K. Schenk.
      Wilson Lib Bul 41:233 O '66; Reply. B. M.
      Golumb. 41:373 D '66
      See also
   British museum general catalog of printed
      books
CATALOGS, Mail order
      See also
   Catalogs, Seed and plant
      Anecdotes, facetiae, satire, etc.
   Mother's wonderful wishing-book. M. Holmes.
      il Todays Health 44:32-3+ Mr '66
CATALOGS, Seed and plant
   What is a good mail order catalog? R. C.
      Hands. Horticulture 44:42+ D '66
CATALOGS, Star. See Stars—Catalogs
CATALYSIS
   Heterogeneous catalysis: effect of an alternat-
      ing electric field. V. J. Lee. il Science
      152:514 Ap 22 '66
CATALYSTS
   Clue believed found to catalyst mystery.
      Sci N 90:8 Jl 2 '66
CATAMARAN racing
   Two hulls make twice as much wreckage.
      H. Whall. il Sports Illus 25:32-3 O 3 '66
CATAMARANS
   Bill Cox on catamaran developments. B. Cox.
      il Yachting 120:28+ O '66
      Design
   Big California cat. B. Cobb, jr. il Yachting
      120:65-7 Jl '66
   They sail to win; excerpts from International
      book of catamarans and trimarans. E. F.
      Cotter. il Yachting 120:29+ S '66
CATARACTS. See Waterfalls
CATCH basins
   Better way to clean catch basins; Philadel-
      phia. R. E. Doyle. il Am City 81:102-3 Ap
      '66
CATCHPOLE, Terry
   Operation contempt. Nat R 18:152 F 22 '66
CATCHPOOL, J. F. See Cherkin, A. jt. auth.
CATE, Curtis
   Eugène Ionesco. Atlan 217:114-20 Ap '66
CATECHETICS
   Catechesis of revelation, by G. Moran. Re-
      view
      America 115:288 S 17 '66. A. Murphy
   Catechetics for the real world. G. Moran.
      America 115:57-9 Jl 16 '66
CATECHOLAMINES
   Catecholamine concentrations: changes in
      plasma of rats during estrous cycle and
      pregnancy. R. D. Green. 3d, and J. W.
      Miller. bibliog il Science 151:825-6 F 18 '66
   Catecholamine symposium. S. Udenfriend. Sci-
      ence 151:481-2 Ja 28 '66
   Latin American symposium on catechol-
      amines; report. R. J. Wurtman. Science
      154:680-1 N 4 '66
   Release of catecholamines and specific pro-
      tein from adrenal glands. N. Kirshner
      and others. bibliog il Science 154:529-31 O
      28 '66
CATER, Douglass
   For the record; excerpts from address. Re-
      porter 35:24-6 D 15 '66
   Interview with Douglass Cater. por Am Ed
      2:20-1 O '66
CATERERS and catering
   Capital where the caterer is king. il Bsns
      W p42-4 Je 11 '66
CATERING. See Caterers and catering
CATERPILLAR tractor company
   Multinational diet that helps Cat thrive. il
      Bsns W p70-2+ Ag 13 '66
CATERPILLARS
      See also
   Tent caterpillars

CATFISH fishing
   First you catch a catfish. W. Davis. il
      Outdoor Life 137:68+ My '66
CATHEDRAL of St John the Divine. See New
   York (city)—St John the Divine, Cathedral
   of
CATHEDRALS
      See also
   Church architecture
CATHERINE II, empress of Russia
   Catherine's boat ride. M. Durant. il Horizon
      8:98-104 Aut '66
CATHERINE of Cleves, Book of hours of. See
   Hours, Books of
CATHETERS
   Lost catheters. Time 89:44 Ja 6 '67
CATHEY, Henry M.
   Indoor planter. Horticulture 44:53 O '66
—and others
   Chemical pruning of plants. bibliog Science
      153:1382-3 S 16 '66
CATHODE ray tubes
   Cathode ray alternative. Sci N 90:505 D
      10 '66
CATHODIC protection. See Corrosion and anti-
   corrosives
CATHOLIC association for international peace
   CAIP on red China. America 114:788 Je 4 '66
   Church and peace; convention in Washing-
      ton. America 115:641 N 19 '66
CATHOLIC authors
   Shusaku Endo: a Christian voice in Japanese
      literature. W. I. Elliott. Christian Cent 83:
      1147 S 21 '66
CATHOLIC church
   Aggiornamento. See issues of Catholic world
   Asynchronosis: untimely. America 114:847 Je
      18 '66
   Cadaver crisis. J. J. Curtis, jr. and G. Hoh-
      berger. America 115:515-16 O 29 '66
   Catholic inter-American program. G. F. Hall.
      Christian Cent 83:248-50 F 23 '66
   Censorship in the church. E. C. Bianchi.
      America 115:411-13 O 8 '66
   Censorship in the church. J. V. Schall. Com-
      monweal 83:601-3 F 25 '66
   Changing the church's attitude toward
      change. R. Kirtland. America 115:274-6
      S 17 '66
   Davis case. K. L. Woodward. Commonweal
      85:393-4 Ja 13 '67
   Defection: protest or treason? F. X. Murphy.
      America 116:44-5 Ja 14 '67
   Divorce, New York style; Catholic church's
      stand. Newsweek 67:92 F 21 '66
   Don't push the panic button. J. R. Anderson.
      America 115:655 N 19 '66
   Freedom today, by H. Küng. Review
      Christian Cent 83:716-17 Je 1 '66. R. E.
      Wentz
   Future of Catholic Christianity. ed. by M.
      de la Bedoyère. Review
      America 115:461 O 15 '66. E. C. Bianchi
   Growing up Catholic. J. O'Gara. Commonweal
      83:600 F 25 '66
   Guide to Protestant ploys; American Protes-
      tant writing on Catholicism. M. Novak;
      reply. M. L. Stackhouse. Christian Cent
      83:275-6 Mr 2 '66
   Have we loved the past too long? L. Dewart.
      America 115:798-802 D 17 '66; Discussion.
      116:70-2 Ja 21 '67
   Impedimenta Romana. Christian Cent 84:70
      Ja 18 '67
   Letter from Rome; urgent doctrinal problems
      plaguing Catholicism. il Newsweek 68:99
      S 19 '66
   New thinking on divorce. il Time 87:103-4
      Mr 18 '66
   Newman in reverse; Fr C. Davis leaves
      Roman Catholic church. C. Northcott.
      Christian Cent 84:39 Ja 11 '67
   Newman, Vatican I and II, and the church
      today. E. E. Kelly. Cath World 202:291-7
      F '66
   Of many things: church's attitude toward
      truth and truthfulness. T. N. Davis.
      America 116:67+ Ja 21 '67
   Prophetic principle; counterweight to the in-
      stitutional. B. G. Murchland. Commonweal
      84:171-5 Ap 29 '66; Reply with rejoinder.
      T. S. Hanrahan. 84:381+ Je 24 '66
   Reassembling the face of Christ. America
      115:131-5 Ag 6 '66
   Slowdown in Rome; Pope Paul and reform.
      il Newsweek 69:91-2 Ja 23 '67
   Vatican II: what does the future hold? R. M.
      Brown. Cath World 202:341-7 Mr '66
   Voices in the vanguard. R. Neuhaus. Chris-
      tian Cent 83:778-80 Je 15 '66
   Weariness and doubts. J. O'Gara. Common-
      weal 84:628 S 30 '66
   Will Catholics lose their cool over Davis?
      Christian Cent 84:68 Ja 18 '67

CATHOLIC church—*Continued*
Wounded priest, wounded church. America 116:8-9 Ja 7 '67
See also
Confession
Ecumenical movement
Encyclicals
Inquisition
Jesuits
Lent
Martyrs
Opus Dei
Popes
Priests
Saints
Sisterhoods
Vatican council, 2d
Vocation (in religion)
Women as priests
Worker priests

Authority
See Church—Authority

Bibliography
New kind of Catholicism. M. Novak. Sat R 49:48-9 Je 4 '66

Canon on marriage and divorce
Ecumenical curtsy; modification of Catholic church laws on mixed marriage. Christian Cent 83:419-20 Ap 6 '66; Reply. D. Mc-Cabe. 83:807 Je 22 '66
Gracious gesture or insult? Vatican instructions on mixed marriages. Christian Cent 83:769 Je 15 '66
Mixed decision; new Vatican ruling. Newsweek 67:86 Mr 28 '66

Clergy
Bishop Gerow retires; somebody else, not me. America 115:242 S 10 '66
Bishops and theologians. America 115:407-8, 442 O 8-15 '66
Catholicism's celibacy crisis. R. Ruether. Christian Cent 83:1268-70 O 19 '66
Changing the church's attitude toward change. R. Kirtland. America 115:274-6 S 17 '66
Clerical celibacy: an unanswered question. il Time 87:80+ F 18 '66
Evolution of a rebel priest. S. Alexander. Life 60:20 Ap 1 '66
For a white-collar union: W. DuBay trying to form a Federation of priests. Time 87:86 Mr 4 '66
Those bad conservatives. America 115:405 O 8 '66
Women clergy for Rome? Holy Spirit answering affirmatively. R. Lauer. Christian Cent 83:1107-10 S 14 '66
See also
Association of Chicago priests
Bishops
Priests

Congregation of the Holy Office
Spanish inquisition, by H. Kamen. Review Commonweal 84:587-8 S 16 '66. T. P. Anderson

Dioceses
America's survey of diocesan post-conciliar programs. America 114:825-7+; 115:28-30, 136-8, 343+ Je 11, Jl 9, Ag 6, S 24 '66
Certifying priests' credentials: ecclesiastical regulation by archdiocese of Chicago. America 115:477-8 O 22 '66
Cody in Chicago. J. Leo. Commonweal 84:334-6 Je 10 '66; Reply. J. Fitzgerald. 84:452 Jl 22 '66
Crisis in the CCD: steps taken in the diocese of Pittsburgh. M. J. Clark. America 115:277-80 S 17 '66
Ecumenical publishing falters briefly in L.A; joint Protestant and Catholic publication of the Documents of Vatican II. Pub W 189:81-2 Ap 25 '66
Poorest diocese in the U.S.A; archdiocese of Anchorage. J. Morris. America 114:549-50 Ap 16 '66

Discipline
Catholic concerns. Christian Cent 83:906 Jl 20 '66
Catholicism's celibacy crisis. R. Ruether. Christian Cent 83:1268-70 O 19 '66
De Pauw's departure; openly challenged church policy. Time 87:70 Ja 28 '66
Freedom in the Catholic church. J. Kahn. Christian Cent 83:461-3 Ap 13 '66
Issue of imprimatur. il Time 88:74 Ag 19 '66
Ombudsman for religious. A. Broderick. America 115:446-8+ O 15 '66; Discussion. 115:527-8 N 5 '66

One man's meat; Friday abstinence. Newsweek 67:57 Ja 31 '66
Philadelphia story; expulsion of five seminarians from St Charles seminary, Overbrook, Pa. S. J. Adamo. America 115:756-8 D 3 '66
Priests as witnesses. R. W. Hovda. Commonweal 83:532-4 F 4 '66
Return of Father DePauw. Newsweek 67:76-7 F 7 '66
Room for obnoxious dissenters; case of Fr DePauw. Christian Cent 84:4 Ja 4 '67
Shackling the sisters; restrictions on the Glenmary sisters. Commonweal 85:5-6 O 7 '66; Reply. K. J. Alter. 85:93+ O 28 '66
Speak softly, walk humbly. V. P. McCorry. America 115:143 Ag 6 '66
See also
Fasting
Index librorum prohibitorum
Obedience (canon law)

Education
Academic freedom; Catholic higher education. P. Gleason. America 115:60-3 Jl 16 '66; Discussion. 115:285-7 S 17 '66
. . And get back a man; concerning J. Fichter's survey of Catholic high school boys. R. A. Schroth. America 115:382-4 O 1 '66
Bad report on Catholic schools. America 114:314 Mr 5 '66
Campus corner; regarding long-established compulsory retreat policies and religious changes among students. M. P. Sheridan. America 115:543 N 5 '66
Catholic campus today. J. F. Mulligan. Commonweal 83:497-9 Ja 28 '66; Reply. E. J. Foye. 83:676 Mr 11 '66
Catholic education examined. L. Michael. Sr Schol 89:sup20-1 D 9 '66
Catholic education today; interview. A. W. Behrens. il Sr Schol 88:sup 1-3 Ap 1 '66
Catholic graduate schools. P. A. FitzGerald. America 115:510-12 O 29 '66
Catholic higher education; address, April 16, 1966. F. Pellegrin. Vital Speeches 32:567-71 Jl 1 '66
Catholic school. F. P. Chamberlain. America 114:442-4 Ap 2 '66; Discussion. 114:805-7 Je 4 '66
Catholic schools and educational publishing: a dialog about the future; meeting sponsored by the New England Catholic education center and the American textbook publishers institute. il Pub W 190:18-23 D 12 '66
Catholics and their schools. J. Cogley. il Sat R 49:72-4+ O 15 '66
CCD—R.I.P? scope of religious education. J. O'Donoghue. Commonweal 84:573-4 S 16 '66
Costs of Catholic education. America 114:375 Mr 19 '66
Education of Catholic Americans, by A. M. Greeley and P. H. Rossi. Review
Cath World 204:135-42 D '66. G. Moran
Cath World 204:143-8 D '66. R. Robbins
Education of Catholic Americans; excerpts. A. Greeley and P. H. Rossi. Commonweal 83:596 F 25 '66
Future of Catholic universities. America 114:475-6 Ap 9 '66
Future of the colleges. Commonweal 83:489-90 Ja 28 '66; Reply. J. P. Leary. 83:677-9 Mr 11 '66
How Catholic are American Catholics? E. von Kuehnelt-Leddihn. Cath World 203:42-7 Ap '66
How Catholic is the Catholic college? E. Wakin. il Sat R 49:92-4+ Ap 16 '66
Identity crisis on the Catholic campus. il Newsweek 67:84-6 Je 27 '66
If Newman had been at Vatican II; excerpt. J. Coulson. Commonweal 83:596 F 25 '66
Mood of Catholic education. F. Canavan. America 114:612 Ap 30 '66
Of many things; decisions of religious superiors in assigning members of the faculty. T. N. Davis. America 115:365 O 1 '66
Of many things: lay board of trustees in Catholic universities. T. N. Davis. America 115:635 N 19 '66
Parish as educator. G. S. Sloyan. Commonweal 84:20-3 Mr 25 '66
Philosophy in the Catholic university. J. Donceel. America 115:330-1 S 24 '66; Discussion. 115:470-1; 116:99+ O 22 '66; Ja 21 '67
Place of religion; Catholic campuses. A. M. Greeley. Commonweal 84:104+ Ap 15 '66
Student rights in higher education. M. P. Sheridan. America 114:731-2 My 21 '66

CATHOLIC church—Education—*Continued*
Theology in the state university; proposal for teaching Christian and non-Christian beliefs and practices. L. Swidler. Christian Cent 83:619-20 My 11 '66
University in America. J. F. Mulligan. America 114:832-3 Je 11 '66
Vatican II and Catholic education; interview, ed. by W. K. Richards. M. J. Hurley. Sr Schol 88:sup5 My 13 '66
What is a Catholic college? W. D. Kelly. Commonweal 83:494-7 Ja 28 '66; Discussion. 83:676-9, 706; 84:93+ Mr 11-18, Ap 15 '66
Wisdom of being apart. J. P. Leary. America 115:224-7 S 3 '66
Witness to divine reality. G. Baum. Christian Cent 83:427-9 Ap 6 '66
See also
National Catholic educational association
Parochial schools. Catholic
also names of Catholic colleges and universities, e.g. St Vincent college

Eucharist
Debate on the eucharist. G. S. Sloyan. il Commonweal 84:357-61 Je 17 '66
Ecumenism and the eucharist. America 115:441 O 15 '66

Finance
Church support. G. M. Korb. America 114:440-2 Ap 2 '66
Funny, fiscal parable. V. P. McCorry. America 115:101-2 Jl 23 '66
Men and money. T. Dinell. America 115:8-10 Jl 2 '66
Using church wealth. Commonweal 84:602 S 23 '66
See also
Mass stipends

Government
Freedom in the Catholic church. J. Kahn. Christian Cent 83:461-3 Ap 13 '66
Liberty within the Catholic church. P. Blanshard. Cath World 203:335-40 S '66
Men and money. T. Dinell. America 115:8-10 Jl 2 '66

History
Changing church. G. H. Tavard. Cath World 202:267-70 F '66
New relationship of church to world; adaptation of address, August 1965. E. H. Maly. Cath World 203:104-8 My '66

Infallibility
Witness to divine reality. G. Baum. Christian Cent 83:427-9 Ap 6 '66

Liturgy and ritual
Church to die in or to live in? M. P. Ryan. Cath World 203:17-21 Ap '66
Collegians' plea to our bishops; request for a fully vernacular mass and inexpensive burial of Catholics. America 115:644 N 19 '66
Common goal. P. J. Hallinan. America 116:11-14 Ja 7 '66
Liturgy and experimentation. America 115:794 D 17 '66
Liturgy and headlines; jazz masses. America 116:79 Ja 21 '67
Liturgy for youth. America 114:436 Ap 2 '66
Openness in liturgy. America 115:314-15 S 24 '66
Psychologist views the new liturgy. A. J. Summo. Cath World 202:272-7 F '66
Renewed liturgical life in Mexico. G. F. Hall. Christian Cent 83:1256-8 O 12 '66
Two reactions to the new mass liturgy; address, March 17, 1965. Paul VI. Cath World 203:22-3 Ap '66
What makes a Catholic conservative conservative? E. F. Tyhanic. Cath World 203:11-16 Ap '66; Discussion. 203:258 Ag '66
See also
Liturgical language
Liturgical week

Bibliography
Book reviews. C. J. McNaspy. America 114:418 Mr 26 '66

Missions
Good gringos in Guatemala; North American priests. brothers and sisters. C. J. McNaspy. America 115:97 Jl 23 '66
New general for Maryknoll. America 115:269 S 17 '66
Seamy side of charity. I. Illich. America 116:88-91 Ja 21 '67
See also
Jesuits—Missions

Music
See Church music

Negroes
Catholics and the Chicago riots. M. E. Schiltz. Commonweal 85:159-63 N 11 '66; Discussion. 85:321-4 D 16 '66
See also
National Catholic conference for interracial justice

Relations
Jews
Carli round. America 114:643 My 7 '66
Catholic anti-Semites. J. B. Sheerin. Cath World 203:198-201 Jl '66
Christian beliefs and anti-Semitism, by C. Y. Glock and R. Stark. Review
Commonweal 84:558-9 S 2 '66. P. H. Furfey
Christian-Jewish relations. America 115:533 N 5 '66
Common beliefs; Catholic and Jews; address, January 25, 1966. J. B. O'Hara. Vital Speeches 32:358-9 Ap 1 '66
Declaration on the Jews. J. B. Sheerin; reply. J. M. Oesterreicher. Cath World 202:258-9 F '66
Ecumenical encounter. R. A. Schroth. America 114:552-3 Ap 16 '66
End to the Christian-Jewish dialogue. A. R. Eckardt. Christian Cent 83:360-3, 393-5 Mr 23-30 '66; Reply. R. C. Holtzapple, jr. 83:718 Je 1 '66
How the Jews changed Catholic thinking. J. Roddy. il Look 30:18-23 Ja 25 '66; Correction. 30:18 Ap 19 '66
Jews, again. Commonweal 84:190-1 My 6 '66
Statement on the Jews. J. L. Lichten. Cath World 202:357-63 Mr '66
Torah and Gospel; ed. by P. Scharper. Review
Commonweal 84:420-1 Jl 1 '66. R. L. Rubenstein

Orthodox Eastern Church
Ecumenism is no trivial thing; Greek Orthodox clergy-Laity congress of North and South America. America 115:55 Jl 16 '66
Joint declaration Rome-Istanbul. Paul VI and Athenagoras I. Cath World 202:369-70 Mr '66

Protestant churches
Absolve Queen Elizabeth? J. B. Sheerin. Cath World 203:71-5 My '66
Archbishop at the Vatican on a mission of gravest import. America 114:470 Ap 9 '66
Dash of cold water; Anglican bishop prohibited from taking part in Catholic marriage ceremony. Christian Cent 83:905-6 Jl 20 '66
Interview with Reinhold Niebuhr; ed. by P. Granfield. R. Niebuhr. il Commonweal 85:315-21 D 16 '66
Kiss of peace; Archbishop of Canterbury-Pope Paul meet. il Time 87:42 Ap 1 '66
Real meaning of talks between the Pope and the Archbishop. il U S News 60:15 Ap 4 '66
Rome and Canterbury; colloquy of pope and primate in Rome. C. Northcott. Christian Cent 83:421-2 Ap 6 '66
To genuflect or not to genuflect? distinctions between Roman Catholic and Protestant worship as expressions of churches' growth toward unity. il Time 87:95-6 My 20 '66
Unity in truth; meeting of Pope and Archbishop of Canterbury. il Newsweek 67:63 Ap 4 '66

Relations (diplomatic)
Germany
Pius XII and the Third Reich; excerpts. ed. by R. Leiber. S. Friedlander. il Look 30:36-8+ My 17 '66
Was silence the only solution? G. Lewy. Sat R 49:26-7 My 21 '66

Russia
Continuation; A. Gromyko's papal audience. Newsweek 67:46+ My 9 '66
Cross and sickle; visit of A. Gromyko to the Vatican. Nat R 18:451-2 My 17 '66

United States
Inspector general. il Newsweek 68:64+ O 31 '66

Yugoslavia
Permanent revolution; semioffical agreement signed. Newsweek 68:42+ Jl 11 '66

Rites and ceremonies
See also
Sacraments

CATHOLIC church—*Continued*

Roman curia
Letter from Vatican City. X. Rynne. New Yorker 42:140+ O 22 '66

Societies
See also
Catholic association for international peace
Crusade of the Holy Spirit
Knights of Columbus
Serra international
Theresians (organization)

Theology
See Theology
CATHOLIC church and art. *See* Art and religion
CATHOLIC church and communism
Absolute future. M. Novak. Commonweal 85:400-2 Ja 13 '67
Catholic peaceniks. A. T. Bouscaren. il Nat R 18:202 Mr 8 '66
Christian-Communist dialogue. D. L. Flaherty. America 115:805 D 17 '66
Oh, what a lovely dialogue: the Catholic Marxism of Slant. P. Steinfels. Commonweal 85:397-9 Ja 13 '67
Project Commitment. America 115:504 O 29 '66
CATHOLIC church and politics. *See* Church and politics
CATHOLIC church and psychiatry. *See* Psychiatry and religion
CATHOLIC church and race problems. *See* Church and race problems
CATHOLIC church and science. *See* Religion and science
CATHOLIC church and social problems. *See* Church and social problems
CATHOLIC church and war. *See* War and religion
CATHOLIC church in Africa
Moderation in modernization. America 115:311 S 24 '66
CATHOLIC church in Argentina
Trouble from the pulpits. il Time 88:28 Ag 26 '66
CATHOLIC church in Brazil
Bishops' reply. Time 88:31 S 2 '66
CATHOLIC church in Canada
Canadian hierarchy abolishes compulsory Friday fasts. Christian Cent 83:1328 N 2 '66
CATHOLIC church in China
Church in China; open letter to the West; reprint. T. S. L. Wei. Commonweal 85:222-5 N 25 '66
CATHOLIC church in Colombia
Colombian cardinal seeks to stem tide of reform; Luis Cardinal Concha Córdoba. Christian Cent 83:1168 S 28 '66
CATHOLIC church in England
England, 1966. J. M. Todd. Cath World 203:284-6 Ag '66
CATHOLIC church in Haiti
Church in Haiti. America 114:717 My 21 '66
CATHOLIC church in Hungary
Visit to Budapest. E. K. Culhane and T. N. Davis. America 114:446-7 Ap 2 '66; Reply. J. A. Batori. 114:573 Ap 23 '66
CATHOLIC church in Ireland
Ireland, 1966. M. Glazier. Cath World 202:354-6 Mr '66
CATHOLIC church in Italy
Italy, 1966. A. Macchi. Cath World 202:288-90 F '66
CATHOLIC church in Latin America
Canada extends a hand. America 115:312 S 24 '66
Changing role of the church. S. Hempstone. Nation 203:216-19 S 12 '66
Church support. G. M. Korb. America 114:440-2 Ap 2 '66
Different cultures but a common ideal; lay volunteers forming international bond of charity. America 114:326-8 Mr 5 '66
Latin left; rise of the social Christians. S. Lens. Commonweal 85:52-5 O 14 '66; Reply. P. E. Sigmund. 85:182-3 N 11 '66
Seamy side of charity. I. Illich. America 116:88-91 Ja 21 '67
Truth about Latin America. America 115:638-9 N 19 '66
See also
Church and state in Latin America
CATHOLIC church in Mexico
Renewed liturgical life in Mexico. G. F. Hall. Christian Cent 83:1256-8 O 12 '66
CATHOLIC church in Poland
Angry strangler. il Time 87:40-1 Je 17 '66
Cardinal and commissar; millennium celebrations; government-inspired harassments. A. Schalk. Commonweal 84:497-9 Ag 5 '66
Cardinal vs. red. il Sr Schol 88:7 My 6 '66
Comes the millennium; church-state crisis. il Newsweek 67:41-2 Ap 25 '66

Continuing quarrel. il Time 89:29-30 Ja 6 '67
Darkening mood; Communist regime attempts to sidetrack the millennial festivities. il Time 88:23 Jl 8 '66
Double anniversary; Communist-Catholic clash. il Newsweek 68:42 Jl 11 '66
How to silence a cardinal. R. J. Gerber. America 114:195-7 F 5 '66; Reply. S. J. Markiewicz. 114:340 Mr 12 '66
Poland has seen the future. D. Halberstam. il N Y Times Mag p 14-15+ F 6 '66
Poland; twenty years of resisting the reds. il U S News 61:54-6 Jl 4 '66
Toward the millennium; Communists creating every imaginable block for occasion. il Time 87:33 Ap 22 '66
We stand on Calvary; Polish national holiday. Time 87:40 My 13 '66
CATHOLIC church in South Africa
Pastoral letter of the South African bishops, July 25, 1966. Cath World 204:240-1 Ja '67
South Africa's bishops speak; conference in Pretoria July 12-15, 1966. America 115:146 Ag 13 '66
CATHOLIC church in Spain
Moment of truth; alienation between Vatican and Spanish Catholic hierarchy. Time 87:47 My 20 '66
Now the priests; protest about police brutality against imprisoned student. Newsweek 67:59-60 My 23 '66
Priests rock Franco's boat. Christian Cent 83:736 Je 8 '66
Religion in Spain. Commonweal 85:392-3 Ja 13 '67
Revolt in Spain. Commonweal 85:190-1 N 18 '66
Spanish dialectic. Commonweal 84:270-1 My 27 '66
Troubled citadel. Time 88:65 Jl 15 '66
Warning from the church. il Time 87:41 My 27 '66
CATHOLIC church in Sudan
Sudan tragedy. J. O'Connor. America 114:171-2 Ja 29 '66
CATHOLIC church in Sweden
Second spring in Sweden. V. P. McCorry. America 114:551 Ap 16 '66
CATHOLIC church in the Netherlands
Dutch bishops speak. E. Schoenmaeckers. America 115:414 O 8 '66
Holland, 1966. H. Holstein. Cath World 203:98-9 My '66
CATHOLIC church in the United States
Adolescent Catholicism? J. O'Gara. Commonweal 85:217 N 25 '66
American Catholic strides in ecumenism. J. B. Sheerin. Cath World 203:134-7 Je '66
American Catholicism; wind from Rome. G. MacEoin. il Nation 204:42-6 Ja 9 '67
Catholic chaos; problems in New York state. W. F. Buckley, jr. Nat R 18:150 F 22 '66
Catholic layman confronts his changing church. D. Norton-Taylor. il Fortune 74:172-5+ D '66
Catholicism Midwest style; symposium. America 114:221-3+ F 12 '66; Reply. K. C. Thorne. America 114:857 Je 18 '66
Church and camp. J. W. Goetz. Cath World 203:297-300 Ag '66
Church juridical. America 114:375-6 Mr 19 '66
Church of silence. Commonweal 85:126 N 4 '66
Controversy within the church; statement. W. L. Doty; with reply by J. O'Connor and rejoinder. il America 114:480-4 Ap 9 '66
Democracy for bishops; meeting of U.S. Roman Catholic bishops. il Time 88:98 N 25 '66
De-Romanization of the American Catholic church. by E. Wakin and J. F. Scheuer. Review
America 114:780 My 28 '66. J. H. Fichter
Cath World 203:369-71 S '66. J. De Loss
Christian Cent 83:685-6 My 25 '66. R. Lauer
Commonweal 84:374-5 Je 17 '66. P. Deasy
Freedom in the Catholic church. J. Kahn. Christian Cent 83:461-3 Ap 13 '66
Hope for people, priests and bishops. America 115:534 N 5 '66
Inspector general. il Newsweek 68:64+ O 31 '66
Lay trusteeism; yesterday and today. G. P. Fogarty. America 115:656-9 N 19 '66
New Americans in the Kennedy image. R. Bosc. America 114:321-3 Mr 5 '66
Of many things; Center for applied research in the apostolate. T. N. Davis. America 115:inside cover Jl 23 '66
Reforms that priests want. F. Canavan. America 114:582-5 Ap 23 '66
Servant parish. J. E. Cunneen. Commonweal 84:5-7 Mr 25 '66

CELLS—*Continued*

Antibody-forming cells: population patterns after simultaneous immunization with different isoantigens. R. A. McBride and L. W. Schierman. bibliog il Science 154:655-7 N 4 '66

At the controls of the living cell. L. Lessing. il Fortune 73:154-8+ My '66

Brain cells survive lack of oxygen. Sci N 90: 368 N 5 '66

Cytoplasmic and environmental influences on nuclear behavior; report on symposium. L. Goldstein and D. B. Platt. Science 155: 110-11 Ja 6 '67

Differentiation in vitro: effects of sephadex fractions of chick embryo extract. H. G. Coon and R. D. Cahn. bibliog il Science 153:1116-19 S 2 '66

Electron microscopic autoradiography of rabbit reticulocytes active and inactive in protein synthesis. A. Miller and A. B. Maunsbach. bibliog il Science 151:1000-1 F 25 '66

Electron microscopy: attachment sites between connective tissue cells. R. Ross and T. K. Greenlee, jr. bibliog il Science 153: 997-9 Ag 26 '66

Establishment of four functional, clonal strains of animal cells in culture. Y. Yasumura and others. bibliog il Science 154: 1186-9 D 2 '66

Glucocorticoid-induced resistance to deoxycholate lysis in HeLa cells. G. Melnykovych. bibliog il Science 152:1086-7 My 20 '66

Glucose-6-phosphatase in tubular endoplasmic reticulum of hepatocytes. S. I. Rosen and others. bibliog il Science 152:352-4 Ap 15 '66

Hylid frogs: polyploid classes of DNA in liver nuclei. K. Bachmann and others. bibliog il Science 154:650-1 N 4 '66

Hypertrophy versus hyperplasia. R. J. Goss. bibliog il Science 153:1615-20 S 30 '66

Immunization of normal mouse spleen cell suspensions in vitro. R. I. Mishell and R. W. Dutton. bibliog il Science 153:1004-6 Ag 26 '66

Incorporation of tritiated actinomycin D into drug-sensitive and drug-resistant HeLa cells. M. N. Goldstein and others. il Science 151:1555-6 Mr 25 '66

Interaction among virus, cell, and organism; address, December 11, 1965. A. Lwoff. Science 152:1216-20 My 27 '66

Interferon: lack of detectable uptake by cells. C. E. Buckler and others. bibliog il Science 152:80-2 Ap 1 '66

Isolation of nuclei from a marine dinoflagellate. L. R. Mendiola and others. bibliog il Science 153:1661-3 S 30 '66

Nuclear number in the rotifer asplanchna: intraclonal variation and environmental control. C. W. Birky, jr. and B. Field. bibliog il Science 151:585-7 F 4 '66

Nuclei from rat liver: isolation method that combines purity with high yield. G. Blobel and V. R. Potter. bibliog il Science 154: 1662-5 D 30 '66

Nucleolus: structure and function; report on international symposium. R. P. Perry. Science 153:214-15+ Jl 8 '66

Replication of adenovirus type 7 in monkey cells: a new determinant and its transfer to adenovirus type 2. J. S. Butel and others. bibliog il Science 154:671-3 N 4 '66

Ribosomal RNA synthesis and processing in a particulate site in the HeLa cell nucleus. S. Penman and others. bibliog il Science 154:786-9 N 11 '66

Separation of living and dead cells by dielectrophoresis. H. A. Pohl and I. Hawk. bibliog il Science 152:647-9 Ap 29 '66

Substructure of certain cytoplasmic microtubules: an electron microscopic study. P. R. Burton. bibliog il Science 154:903-5 N 18 '66

Synchronization of mammalian cells with tritiated thymidine. G. F. Whitmore and S. Gulyas. bibliog il Science 151:691-4 F 11 '66

See also
Cell division (biology)
Chromatin
Chromosomes
Differentiation (biology)
Embryology
Fertilization (biology)
Mast cells
Membranes (biology)
Mitochondria
Nerve cells
Plasma membranes
Tissues

CELTICS (basketball team) See Basketball teams

CEMENT

Expansive cement: a new approach to reducing concrete cracking. il Arch Rec 140:231-2 S '66

CEMENT blocks. See Building blocks

CEMETERIES

Cemetowers; Rozzano, Italy. il Newsweek 67:49-50 Mr 14 '66

Politics invades a cemetery; Forest Lawn joins right-wing chorus. A. B. Haines. Christian Cent 83:595 My 4 '66

See also
National cemeteries—United States
Service mens graves

CEMETERIES, Animal

Loved ones; American death affair with pets. il Newsweek 68:47 Jl 18 '66

CENSORSHIP

Censorship and obscenity: what's happened to taste? with press comments. D. Reische. il Sr Schol 89:12-15 O 14 '66

Censorship panel approved by N.J. legislators. Pub W 189:60 My 30 '66

Controversies about the mass communication of violence. O. N. Larsen. bibliog f Ann Am Acad 364:37-49 Mr '66

Evolution case still undecided. Sci N 89: 262 Ap 16 '66

Implications of the Ginzburg affair; address, April 20, 1966. K. Molz. il Wilson Lib Bul 40:941-7 Je '66

JFK censored? family's attitudes towards publications. il Newsweek 68:65-6 O 3 '66

Manner of speaking; taboo language. J. Ciardi. Sat R 49:14-15 Ag 20 '66

NYLA opposes anti-obscenity bill passed by New York legislature. Library J 91:3666-7 Ag '66

Problem of pornography. C. B. Luce. McCalls 94:15 O '66

Pro-censorship Prop. 16 stays on Calif. ballot. Pub W 190:53-4 O 3 '66

Progress, where is thy sting? history of book censoring. P. W. Schmidtchen. il Hobbies 71:108-9+ Mr '66

Right-wing group pickets Cleveland bookshop; National Christian conservative society vs. Book mark. Pub W 189:73 Je 27 '66

Society's lack of confidence in itself. R. H. Smith. Pub W 189:41 Ap 4 '66

Speaking out; we need more censorship. P. H. Johnson. il Sat Eve Post 240:8+ Ja 14 '67

Spring harvest festival; Mishkin, Ginzburg, and Fanny Hill. E. J. Gaines. ALA Bul 60:551-2 Je '66

U.S. Supreme court rules pro-censorship in two of three cases involving books. Pub W 189:43-4 Mr 28 '66

Vatican censor bureau said to be downgraded. Pub W 189:101-2 F 14 '66

Whose thing? publication of Valachi biography blocked. Newsweek 67:93 My 23 '66

See also
Dramatic censorship
Freedom of the press
Government and the press
Illinois freedom to read committee
Immoral literature and pictures
Index librorum prohibitorum
Information, Freedom of
Intellectual liberty
Moving picture censorship
School libraries—Censorship

France

French publishers cope with state censorship. H. R. Lottman. Pub W 189:51-4 F 7 '66

Interdit: censorship in France. H. R. Lottman. Wilson Lib Bul 40:759-63 Ap '66

Letter from Paris; threat of subsidy cut, because of Genet's Les paravents (The screens) at Théâtre de France. Genet. New Yorker 42:223-5 N 19 '66

Of nuns & censorship; movie called Suzanne Simonin, la religieuse de Diderot. il Time 87:34 Ap 15 '66

New Zealand

Social experiment: Indecent publications tribunal. E. Moon. Library J 91:1371 Mr 15 '66

Russia

Tertz case. J. Fischer. Harper 232:21 F '66

Trial ends; case of A. Tertz. J. L. Laber. New Repub 154:26-9 Mr 19 '66

Yes, they were subversive; case of Tertz and Arzhak. Christian Cent 83:262 Mr 2 '66

Spain

Monarchy sí, liberal no; new liberalized press law against Spanish newspaper. A. B. C. Time 88:24 Jl 29 '66

Pressing toward freedom; Press law. Time 87: 27-8 Mr 25 '66

CENSORSHIP—*Continued*
United States
See Censorship

Yugoslavia
More arrests in Yugoslavia; magazine in opposition to regime. Time 88:76 D 2 '66
CENSORSHIP (canon law)
Censorship in the church. E. C. Bianchi. America 115:411-13 O 8 '66
Censorship in the church. J. V. Schall. Commonweal 83:601-3 F 25 '66
CENSORSHIP, Dramatic. See Dramatic censorship
CENSORSHIP, Library. See Libraries—Censorship
CENSUS, Wildlife. See Wildlife census
CENTER for applied linguistics. See Modern language association of America
CENTER for applied research in the apostolate. See Catholic church in the United States
CENTER for cultural and technical interchange between East and West. See Hawaii. University, Honolulu—East-West center
CENTER for editions of American authors. See Modern language association of America
CENTER for the study of democratic institutions, Santa Barbara, Calif.
From pulpit to think tank; new chapter in the Pike story. J. Cogley. il N Y Times Mag p 16-17+ Ag 14 '66
CENTERPIECES. See Table decoration
CENTERS for the performing arts
See also
Saratoga performing arts center
CENTIPEDES
Nature note; worms of many legs. Sci N L 89:126 F 19 '66
CENTRAL airlines
Trend seen in merger of Ozark, Central. H. D. Watkins. Aviation W 85:41 S 26 '66
CENTRAL AMERICA
See also
Organizaton of Central American states
Textbooks—Central America

Description and travel
Gone flying to Panama. L. L. Hallman. il Flying 79:52-6 Ag '66

Economic conditions
Central American economic integration. J. D. Cochrane. Américas 18:1-5 My '66
Focus on Central America; symposium. bibliog f il Cur Hist 51:321-59+ D '66

Economic policy
Central American plans. G. Meek. Américas 18:42-3 O '66
See also
Central American program of economic integration

Politics
Focus on Central America; symposium. bibliog f il Cur Hist 51:321-59+ D '66
Maturity of Central America. G. de Zéndegui. Américas 18:inside cover Mr '66
Togetherness in Central America; urge toward reunion. G. Delmas. il Reporter 34:34-7 Ap 7 '66
CENTRAL AMERICAN and Cuban games, 1966
Spooks among the spikes. il Time 87:42 Je 24 '66
CENTRAL AMERICAN common market. See Central American program of economic integration
CENTRAL AMERICAN program of economic integration
Central American economic integration. J. D. Cochrane. il Américas 18:1-5 My '66
New kind of revolution in Central America. il U S News 60:62-4 My 30 '66
Togetherness in Central America. G. Delmas. il Reporter 34:34-7 Ap 7 '66
U.S. support for Central American common market reaffirmed; statement, June 3, 1966. L. B. Johnson. Dept State Bul 54:1004-5 Je 27 '66
CENTRAL ARIZONA project (proposed)
Dam site; fate of Grand Canyon. W. V. Shannon. Commonweal 84:329-30 Je 10 '66
Dam the Canyon? il Newsweek 67:27 My 30 '66
Damming the Grand Canyon for a thirsty Southwest. D. Sanford. New Repub 154:9 Ap 30 '66
To save the Grand Canyon: Colorado River basin bill proposals. W. Stegner. Sat R 49:20 Ag 20 '66

CENTRAL EUROPE
See also
Balkan States
Danubian countries
CENTRAL intelligence agency. See United States—Central intelligence agency
CENTRAL nervous system. See Nervous system
CENTRAL opera service
Mephisto's musings. il Hi Fi 16:MA2+ Ag '66
Opera: quo vadis? F. Merkling. il Opera N 30:29 Je 4 '66
CENTRAL park. See New York (city)—Parks and playgrounds
CENTRAL treaty organization
Central treaty organization meets at Ankara; opening statement, April 20, remarks at the dedication of the CENTO microwave telecommunications system and transcript of press conference, April 22, 1966; with text of final communique. D. Rusk. Dept State Bul 54:775-81 My 16 '66
CENTRALIZED cataloging. See Cataloging
CENTRALIZED schools. See Consolidated schools
CENTRIFUGES
Influenza virus purification with the zonal ultracentrifuge. C. B. Reimer and others. bibliog il Science 152:1379-81 Je 3 '66
Sedimentation of an initially skewed boundary. D. J. Cox. bibliog il Science 152:359-61 Ap 15 '66
Zonal centrifuges and other separation systems. N. G. Anderson. bibliog il Science 154:103-12 O 7 '66
Zonal ultracentrifuge for the separation of ribosomal subunits. E. S. Klucis and H. J. Gould. bibliog il Science 152:378 Ap 15 '66
CENTS-off labels. See Labels
CENTURY city. See Los Angeles
CENTURY 21 exposition. See Seattle—Century 21 exposition, 1962
CEPHALOPODS
See also
Embryology—Cephalopods
CEPHALOSPORIN C
Recent advances in the chemistry of natural products: address, December 11, 1965. R. B. Woodward. bibliog il Science 153:487-93 Jl 29 '66
CERAMI, Charles A.
Make mistakes, make money. Nations Bsns 54:78-80 Ja '66
Open your mind to fresh ideas. Nations Bsns 54:86+ S '66
You can argue with success. Nations Bsns 54:82-4+ F '66
CERAMIC materials
Ceramics can be made eight times stronger. Sci N 89:475 Je 11 '66
CERAMIC pickup. See Phonograph—Stereophonic pickup
CERAMIC stoves. See Stoves, Earthenware
CERAMICS. See Pottery
CERATOCYSTIS infection. See Fungi
CERCOPIDAE. See Froghoppers
CEREAL foods
Successful recipes, cereal treats. il Suc Farm 64:109-10 S '66
When Mix put the boom in Ralston. Bsns W p78 D 3 '66
CEREBRAL concussion. See Concussion
CEREBRAL cortex
Control of somatosensory input by cerebral cortex. R. J. Adkins and others. bibliog il Science 153:1020-2 Ag 26 '66
Stimulation of the proliferation of cortical neurons by prenatal treatment with growth hormone. S. Zamenhof and others. bibliog il Science 152:1396-7 Je 3 '66
CEREBRAL hemorrhage
Hidden strokes. A. J. Snider. il Sci Digest 60:36 O '66
CEREBRAL palsy. See Paralysis
CEREBROSPINAL fluid
Secretion into the cerebrospinal fluid by caudal neurosecretory neurons. G. Fridberg and R. S. Nishioka. bibliog il Science 152:90-1 Ap 1 '66
CEREBROVASCULAR diseases. See Brain—Diseases
CERENKOV detectors. See Counters (electrons, ions, etc)
CERF, Bennett Alfred
Cerfit of riches. il pors Time 88:100-2+ D 16 '66
CERF, Jean A. and Carels, Guy
Multiple sclerosis: serum factor producing reversible alterations in bioelectric responses. bibliog Science 152:1066-8 My 20 '66

CERMAK, Robert W.
Ancient bristlecone pine forest. Nat Parks Mag 40:4-8 Jl '66
CERN (Conseil européen pour la recherche nucléaire) See European organization for nuclear research
CERNAN, Eugene A.
Gemini 9 to try third-orbit rendezvous. W. J. Normyle. il Aviation W 84:32-3 My 16 '66
CERNIGLIA, V. J. and Friedland, Alan
Smile, your incinerator is on TV. Am City 81:110-12 Ap '66
CERRI, Lawrence
Team teaching: how it works in Niskayuna; Sr Schol 88:sup 16 Mr 25 '66
CERTHIIDAE. See Creepers (birds)
CERTIFICATES, Aviators. See Air pilots—Licenses
CERTIFICATES of deposit
Business and finance; Patman bill. il Newsweek 68:63 Ag 8 '66
CDs: X factor in the economy? il Duns R 87:44-6+ F '66
Fed holds a tiger by the tail. il Bsns W p62-3 Jl 9 '66
CERTIFICATION of teachers. See Teachers—Certification
CERTIFIED public accountants. See Accountants
CERVANTES, A. J.
Great American cities; address, November 14, 1966. Vital Speeches 33:176-9 Ja 1 '67
CERVICAL cancer. See Cancer
CERVIX
Among the troubles we don't talk about: erosion of the cervix. S. T. DeLee and B. B. Smith. Todays Health 44:62-3 O '66
CESAR, Ed
Photo trap lets you bring 'em back, in pictures. il por Pop Sci 189:136-7 N '66
CESIUM in the body
Cesium-137 body burdens in Alaskan Eskimos during the summer of 1965. W. C. Hanson. bibliog il Science 153:525-6 Jl 29 '66
CETACEA
See also
Dolphins (mammals)
CEYLON
See also
Sigiriya

Antiquities
Sigiriya: palace of a god-king. M. M. Brown. il Sat R 49:48+ N 26 '66

Description and travel
Ceylon. D. K. Grosvenor and G. M. Grosvenor. il Nat Geog Mag 129:447-97 Ap '66
In Ceylon: the normal way to remove a demon. M. Wilson. Vogue 147:84+ Je '66
Paradise island, entire unto itself. F. V. Grunfeld. Reporter 35:36-8 Ag 11 '66
CÉZANNE, Paul
Importance of Cézanne. G. Laderman. il Art N 65:39-41+ O '66
CHABOT college, Hayward, Calif.
Chabot rounds out resources. W. B. Hicks. il Library J 91:5897-9 D 1 '66
CHABRIER, Alexis Emmanuel
Complete, on Vox, Chabrier's piano works: the very heart of his art. C. J. Luten. il por Am Rec G 32:949+ Je '66
Discovering a French original. Discus. Harper 233:120+ S '66
CHABROL, Claude
New life for the new wave. A. Knight. Sat R 49:38 Ag 20 '66
CHACKO, C. I. and others
Chlorinated hydrocarbon pesticides: degradation by microbes. bibliog Science 154:893-5 N 18 '66
CHADWICK, Hal
Housekeeping wasn't for Aunt Gertie. Todays Health 45:60-1 Ja '67
CHADWICK, Regenia
Machines: your master or your servant. Suc Farm 64:101+ S '66
CHAGALL, Marc
Art works in the new Metropolitan. il Sat R 49:55-7 S 17 '66
CHAGALL bride: story. See Madocs. R.
CHAGNON, Napoleon A.
Yanomamö, the fierce people; with biographical sketch. Natur Hist 76:6, 22-31 Ja '67
CHAIN saws. See Saws
CHAIN stores
After the marathon: violation of Clayton act. Time 87:80+ Mr 25 '66
Housewife rebellion: Mrs West's Denver boycott. il Life 61:57-8 N 4 '66
See also
Kresge, S. S. company
Kroger company

Consolidations and mergers
Antitrust in a coonskin cap; merger between Von's grocery co. and Shopping bag food stores in Los Angeles declared illegal. Fortune 74:65-6 Jl 1 '66
CHAIRS
Best seats in the house. il McCalls 93:68-73 Jl '66
Buying chairs for comfort. Consumer Bul 49:36 S '66
Card-table sets. il Consumer Rep 31:566-9 N '66
Custom-tailored chair; support in the lower back. il Time 88:58 N 25 '66
Italian rustic. J. Peter. il Look 30:52-3 My 3 '66
Mr Cram's fan chair. C. B. Wood, 3d. il Antiques 89:262-4 F '66
New easy chair for dad. il Farm J 90:55 Ag '66
Please be seated. F. Du Plessix. il House & Gard 131:106-9 Ja '67
Twenty chairs for under $20. M. White. il Ladies Home J 84:66-7 Ja '67
CHALCACINGO reliefs. See Petroglyphs
CHALFONT, Alun Arthur Gwynne Jones, baron. See Chalfont, A. G. J.
CHALFONT, Arthur Gwynne Jones, baron
Prospects of peace; excerpts from address. Bul Atomic Sci 22:2-4 My '66
CHALK, Warren
Hardware of a New World. Arch Forum 125:46-51 O '66
CHAMBER music
Musical events; chamber music concert: Music from Marlboro; performed by artists from Marlboro music festival. W. Sargeant. New Yorker 42:74+ F 26 '66
See also
Phonograph records—Chamber music
CHAMBER orchestras
Rewards beyond the regimen: Boston symphony chamber players. il Time 87:65 Mr 18 '66
CHAMBERLAIN, Francis P.
Catholic school. America 114:442-4 Ap 2 '66
CHAMBERLAIN, John, 1553-1627
Wits, whigs, and Paul's-walkers. B. Grebanier. Sat R 49:32-3 F 12 '66
CHAMBERLAIN, John, 1903-
Dos and the underdog. Harper 234:97 Ja '67
CHAMBERLAIN, Joseph W. and McElroy, M. B.
Martian atmosphere: the Mariner occultation experiment. bibliog Science 152:21-5 Ap 1 '66
CHAMBERLAIN, Park
Has the Fifth amendment become a menace to human rights? Nat R 18:362-4 Ap 19 '66
CHAMBERLAIN, Richard
From TV to Tiffany's in one wild leap. J. Bowers. il pors Sat Eve Post 239:97-101 N 19 '66
CHAMBERLAIN, William
Now I sit me down. Writer 79:22-4 F '66
CHAMBERLAIN, Wilt
Making the giant jolly. por Time 87:64-5 Ap 1 '66
Nose to chin whiskers. il por Time 89:51 Ja 13 '67
Spirited 76ers. il por Newsweek 69:88 Ja 23 '67
Wilt talks back. il Time 87:76 F 25 '66
CHAMBERLIN, Anne
Bad day ahead for the army's greatest loser. Sat Eve Post 239:70-3 Ag 27 '66
Great undashing lover of our time. Sat Eve Post 239:81-5 Ag 13 '66
King of supershape. Esquire 67:110-13+ Ja '67
Scandinavia's secret season. Vogue 148:56+ S 15 '66
Thirteen mad days and passionate nights loose in the Antilles. por Sat Eve Post 240:30-5 Ja 28 '67
CHAMBERLIN, Wellman
Revised, enlarged world atlas charts our changing earth. Nat Geog Mag 129:818-21 Je '66
CHAMBERLIN, William Henry
Ivan Turgenev. Sat R 49:24-5+ Je 18 '66
Myths die hard. Nat R 18:734-5 Jl 26 '66
Theodor Mommsen: neglected master of Roman history. Sat R 49:18-19+ My 21 '66
Wisdom and fortitude of Marcus Aurelius. Sat R 50:22-3 Ja 7 '67
CHAMBERS, M. M.
Higher education; address, March 24, 1966. Vital Speeches 32:447-8 My 1 '66
CHAMBERS of commerce
Changing chambers: revolution on Main street. Nations Bsns 54:40-1+ Ag '66
See also
United States junior chamber of commerce

CHAMBLISS, Oyette L. and Jones, C. M.
Cucurbitacins: specific insect attractants in cucurbitaceae. bibliog Science 153:1392-3 S 16 '66

CHAMBLISS, Sam
Freckled yellow Stearman. Flying 78:90+ Mr '66

CHAMEAU treasure. See Treasure trove

CHAMELEONS
Anolis carolinensis: effects of feeding on reaction to aposematic prey. O. J. Sexton and others. il Science 153:1140 S 2 '66

CHAMETZKY, Jules
In the shtetl of Bilgoray. Nation 203:392-3 O 17 '66

CHAMLEE, Mario
Obituary
Opera N por Opera N 31:33 D 24 '66

CHAMPAGNE
Champagne. G. Bradshaw. Vogue 148:20 D '66
Germany toasts economic boom with champagne. il Bsns W p34-5 F 19 '66
Wine, women & so on. P. Cannon. Ladies Home J 83:120 Je '66

CHAMPAGNE trade. See Wine trade

CHAMPION, George
Challenge to business: create its own Great society; condensation of address, March 24, 1966. Read Digest 89:107-10 Ag '66

CHAMPION aircraft company
And in this corner, the champ. J. Gilbert. il Flying 78:36-41 Ap '66

CHAMPLIN, Charles
Can TV save the films? Sat R 49:11-13 D 24 '66

CHAMPNEY, James Wells
This is tranquil Deerfield and this is the town's artist; with paintings. il pors Am Heritage 17:22-9 Ap '66

CHANCE, B. and others
Hemes and hemoproteins. Science 152:1409-11 Je 3 '66

CHANCE, Britton, Jr
U.S. entries for the IYRU trials. Yachting 120:45 S '66

CHANCE
See also
Coincidences

CHANCELLOR, John William
America's voice swings a little. W. Rogers. il pors Look 30:46+ N 15 '66

CHANDELIERS
English brass chandeliers in American churches. C. Oman. il Antiques 90:192-4 Ag '66

CHANDLER, Lacy
Park adds an airport, subtracts maintenance costs. Am City 81:118-19 S '66

CHANDLER, Otis
How to build an empire. il pors Newsweek 69:41-5 Ja 2 '67

CHANDLER, Stephen S.
How to remove them. por Time 87:82 F 4 '66

CHANDRA, Naresh, and Hildebrandt, A. C.
Growth in microculture of single tobacco cells infected with tobacco mosaic virus. bibliog Science 152:789-91 My 6 '66

CHANDRA, P. and Bollen, W. B.
Gibrel: effect on decomposition of plant materials. bibliog Science 153:1663-4 S 30 '66

CHANEL, Gabrielle
Vogue's ready beauty. por Vogue 147:152 Mr 15 '66

CHANG, Chieh-chein
New twist in tornadoes. il por Time 87:52+ Ap 15 '66

CHANG, Min-chueh
Three men who made a revolution. L. Lader. il por N Y Times Mag p8-9+ Ap 10 '66

CHANGE
Change seekers; management of change. P. H. Irwin and F. W. Langham, jr. il Harvard Bsns R 44:81-92 Ja '66
Freedom and change; address, January 19, 1966. A. F. Douglas-Home. Vital Speeches 32:239-41 F 1 '66
Of worth and value: human spirit and the cybercultural revolution; address, February 1, 1966. A. M. Hilton. Vital Speeches 32:335-41 Mr 15 '66

CHANGE, Economic. See Economic change

CHANGE, Social. See Social change

CHANGE of life in women. See Menopause

CHANGE of sex
Body to match the mind. il Time 88:52+ D 2 '66
Change of gender. il Newsweek 68:73 D 5 '66
Sex-change operations at a U.S. hospital. U S News 61:13 D 5 '66
Sex surgery at Hopkins; transsexuals undergoing change-of-sex surgery. Sci N 90:467 D 3 '66

CHANGE of sex surgery. See Generative organs—Surgery

CHANGING times (periodical)
Chat with W. M. Kiplinger. W. M. Kiplinger. Changing T 21:inside cover Ja '67
20th anniversary issue: a special report; oh, how your life has changed! il Changing T 21:6-14 Ja '67

CHANNEL bass fishing. See Bass fishing

CHANNEL catfish fishing. See Catfish fishing

CHANNEL tunnel. See English Channel tunnel (proposed)

CHANNON, John
John Channon and brass inlay. J. Stuart. il Antiques 90:36+ Jl '66

CHANSON de Roland. See Song of Roland

CHAO, E. C. T. and others
Nickel-iron spherules from Aouelloul glass. Science 154:759-60+ N 11 '66

CHAPELLE, Dickey
Water war in Viet Nam. il Nat Geog Mag 129:272-96 F '66

about
What was a woman doing there? W. E. Garrett. il por Nat Geog Mag 129:270-1 F '66

CHAPELLE, Georgette Louise. See Chapelle, D.

CHAPELS
U.S. air force chapel. il Sch Arts 65:38-40 Ja '66

CHAPIN, Kim
Automobiles. Sports Illus 25:100 S 19 '66
Motor sports. Sports Illus 25:82-3 O 10 '66
Tennis. Sports Illus 25:68-70 O 24 '66; 26:50-1 Ja 9 '67
Wild, wicked race to the big time. Sports Illus 25:84-6+ N 28 '66

CHAPIN, Roy Dikeman, 1915-
Double shuffle at AMC. il por Newsweek 69:77-8 Ja 23 '67

CHAPLAINS, College. See Colleges and universities—Religious life

CHAPLAINS, Military
Chaplaincy vs. mission in a secular age. W. R. Miller. Christian Cent 83:1335-7 N 2 '66
Chaplain's death; army chaplain killed in South Viet Nam. Time 88:82 N 18 '66
Chopper chaplains; service in Viet Nam. Time 87:68 F 11 '66
Father Tom Confroy: church is in his combat pack; service in Vietnam. S. Castan. il Look 30:74-6 Jl 12 '66
Military chaplaincy: an apologia. A. F. Ledebuhr. Christian Cent 83:1332-5 N 2 '66; Discussion. 83:1476-8; 84:18 N 30 '66, Ja 4 '67
Navy chaplaincy: muzzled ministry; cooperation without compromise. N. MacFarlane. Christian Cent 83:1338-9 N 2 '66
President debases chaplaincy standards; Mormon clergy as chaplains despite failure to meet educational standards. Christian Cent 83:1465 N 30 '66

CHAPLIN, Charles
Charlie and his countess. J. Hamilton. il pors Look 30:96-100+ Ap 19 '66
Custard pie of creation. il pors Newsweek 67:90-2+ Je 6 '66
Genius of Chaplin. P. Gilliatt. il pors Vogue 148:94-7+ Jl '66
Passionate clown comes back; with report by D. J. Hamblin. il pors Life 60:80-6 Ap 1 '66

CHAPLIN, Geraldine
Beauty life. por Mlle 62:138-9 Mr '66
Brash Paris styles on tanbark. il pors Life 60:88-91 Mr 11 '66
Geraldine Chaplin. pors Vogue 147:136-7 F 1 '66

CHAPLIN, Red
Motorized buck buggy. Outdoor Life 138:74 N '66

CHAPMAN, Bruce K.
Selective service and national needs. Reporter 34:15-18 Je 16 '66

CHAPMAN, Henry P.
Pueblo parade. Travel 126:42-5 Ag '66

CHAPMAN college, Orange Calif.
Ship their dormitory, the world their campus; M.S. Seven Seas. il Ebony 21:108-10+ S '66

CHAPPELL, Rachael
Gift to keep. Horn Bk 42:738-48 D '66

CHAPSAL, Madeleine
Who is Robbe-Grillet? Reporter 35:54-7 Jl 14 '66

CHARACEAE
Energy balancing in nitella cells treated with dinitrophenol. C. E. Barr and T. C. Broyer. bibliog il Science 151:1245-6 Mr 11 '66

CHARACTER
See also
Individuality
Personality
CHARACTER analysis
See also
Personality tests
CHARACTER education. See Moral education
CHARACTER reading. See Graphology
CHARACTER sketches
My most unforgettable character. See issues of Reader's digest
Talk stories, by L. Ross. Review
Sat R 49:39 *Ap 30 '66. M. Gattis
CHARACTER tests
See also
Personality tests
CHARACTERIZATION
Building tension in the short story. J. C. Oates. Writer 79:11-12+ Je '66
Who is Robbe-Grillet? M. Chapsal. il Reporter 35:54-7 Jl 14 '66
CHARACTERS in literature
Case for Enrico; Lucia's brother. A. Berliner. il Opera N 31:21-3 D 31 '66
Cup of consecrated chicken soup. M. Ely. Cath World 202:298-301 F '66
Debonair Rex now a celebrated doctor; Dolittle on film. il Life 61:122-4+ S 30 '66
Don Quixote and the ambassador; with letter from former American ambassador to Cuba. A. Gardner. F. Donahue. Horn Bk 42:43-4 F '66
Elusive Mary Poppins author expansive for children's audience; statements. P. L. Travers. Library J 91:1640+ Mr 15 '66
Fu Manchu strikes again. H. Lawrenson. Holiday 39:128+ F '66
Lesson of the master: Henry James and James Baldwin. C. Newman. Yale R 56: 45-59 O '66
Rights and permissions; unfinished Hornblower story to be in Saturday evening post. P. Nathan. Pub W 189:220 Je 6 '66
Secret agent 07; A. Gulyashki's anti-Bond hero. Avakum Zakhov. Newsweek 69:55 Ja 23 '67
Sense of style; Holden Caulfield of The catcher in the rye. G. Frazier. il Esquire 66:344-6 D '66
Silas Marner diagnosed; hero's ailments. Sci N 90:410 N 12 '66
Some friends of Mary Poppins; interview by group of American children. P. L. Travers. McCalls 93:32+ My '66
Take it seriesly! Honey West, lady private investigator. S. Fickling. Writer 79:18-20 My '66
Tiggers don't like honey; Disney and A. A. Milne's stories. G. Weales. il Reporter 34:46-7 Ap 21 '66
Trade winds; inspiration for the hero, Dr Kildare. J. Beatty, jr. Sat R 49:11 My 21 '66
Visit with Mary Poppins and P. L. Travers. R. R. Lingeman. il N Y Times Mag p 12-13+ D 25 '66
Visit with the real Mary Poppins; interview, ed. by J. Roddy. P. L. Travers. il Look 30:84+ D 13 '66
Wizard who created Oz. D. P. Mannix. il Read Digest 88:104-8 Je '66
Writers do not exist. J. P. Wood. Horn Bk 42:694-8 D '66
See also
Authors in literature
Characterization
Fiction
Spies in literature
CHARACTERS in moving pictures
Mad about the boy; role of Morgan. il Time 87:80 Je 24 '66
Types & anti-types. W. Coffey. Commentary 42:54-9 Ag '66
CHARACTERS in opera
Between two worlds; the nurse in Die frau ohne schatten. I. Dalis. Opera N 31:16 D 17 '66
Case for Enrico; Lucia's brother. A. Berliner. il Opera N 31:21-3 D 31 '66
Enter the hero; Lohengrin. E. Gerken. Opera N 31:6 Ja 21 '67
First love; Manon Lescaut set pattern for Puccini heroines. H. E. Phillips. Opera N 30:24-5 Mr 12 '66
Irrepressible spirit; Rossini's carefree Barber. S. Hughes. il Opera N 30:24-5 Mr 19 '66
Sitting pretty; reasons for Faust's popularity. R. Lawrence. Opera N 30:24-5 Ap 9 '66
CHARBONNET, Grace
Magic chart. por Redbook 127:8+ My '66
CHARDIN, Pierre Teilhard de. See Teilhard de Chardin, P.

CHARGE accounts (retail trade)
Coming next: push-button banking. il U S News 60:108-10 F 14 '66
See also
Collecting of accounts
CHARGERS, Battery. See Storage battery chargers
CHARGING systems (libraries) See Libraries —Charging systems
CHARITABLE uses, trusts, foundations
Bank chain; Du Pont trust. New Repub 154: 4 Je 18 '66
Veteran fighter engages a new foe; E. Ball of du Pont estate in Florida, vs U.S. law. Bsns W p 184-6+ S 17 '66
CHARITIES
Christmas baskets and power. A. J. Eichenberger. il Christian Cent 83:1566-9 D 21 '66
See also
Foundations, Charitable and educational
Fund raising
Giving
Public welfare
CHARITY
God, man and Christian man. V. P. McCorry. America 114:841-2 Je 11 '66
CHARLATANRY. See Quacks and quackery
CHARLEMAGNE, king of the Franks
Age of Charlemagne. R. Pernoud. bibliog il Horizon 8:16-22+ Spr '66
CHARLES, prince of Wales
Born to be king. R. Lecler. il pors Seventeen 25:156-7+ N '66
Future of Prince Charles. C. B. Luce. McCalls 94:32+ N '66
CHARLES, Gordon
State vs. the Predator. Audubon Mag 68:436-42 N '66
CHARLES, Milton
Fine art on paperback covers is commercial and artistic success. il por Pub W 190:111-12+ O 3 '66
CHARLES, Ray
Music soaring in a darkened world. T. Thompson. il pors Life 61:54-6+ Jl 29 '66
CHARLES-ROUX, Edmonde
Prize pizazz. por Time 88:34+ D 2 '66
CHARLES Pfizer and company. See Pfizer, Charles, and company
CHARLESTON, S.C.

Historic houses, etc.

Charleston, South Carolina. il Antiques 90: 527-30 O '66
History in houses; Nathaniel Russell house. F. R. Edmunds. il Antiques 89:224-8 F '66
CHARLESWORTH, James C.
(ed) American civilization; its influence on our foreign policy bibliog f Ann Am Acad 366:1-148 Jl '66
(ed) Ethics in America: norms and deviations. bibliog f Ann Am Acad 363:1-136 Ja '66
CHARLIER, Roger H.
Oceanography; report of International congress in Moscow. Science 153:1421-3 S 16 '66
CHARLOTTE AND MECKLENBURG COUNTY, N.C. public library
Breaking the ice. H. Galvin. il Library J 91:345-6 Ja 15 '66
CHARMATZ, Bill
Sunday's heroes in July; paintings. Sports Illus 25:38-43 Jl 18 '66
CHARNEY, Geri
Artist & agent. M. Orovan. il U S Camera 29:54-7+ Ap '66
CHARNEY, Melvin
Rear end of the Xerox, or how I learned to love that library. Arch Forum 124:60-1 My '66
CHARROS. See Rodeos
CHARTERING of airplanes. See Airplanes—Chartering
CHARTERIS, Leslie
Saint on TV. Writer 79:19-21 F '66
CHARTS, Astronomical. See Astronomy—Charts, diagrams, etc.
CHARTS, Calculating
Capacitance measuring nomogram. M. H. Applebaum. il Electr World 75:29+ Ja '66
Popular science concrete volume calculator. il Pop Sci 188:149 Ap '66
Straight-wire inductance graph. D. W. Moffat. il Electr World 75:27 F '66
Symmetrical attenuator pad nomograms. M. H. Applebaum. Electr World 76:27 S '66
T and H attenuator pad nomograms. M. H. Applebaum. il Electr World 75:31 Mr '66
CHARTS, Stock. See Stocks—Price indexes and averages

CHASE, Edward T.
Economics and freedom. Commonweal 85: 254-6 D 2 '66
Lindsay challenges the Port authority. Reporter 34:23-6 Je 30 '66
Manpower debate. Reporter 35:54-6 O 20 '66
New economics. Commonweal 83:551-3 F 11 '66
Physician, heal thyself. New Repub 155:28+ O 8 '66
Return to the bush. Nation 203:712-13 D 26 '66

CHASE, Oscar G.
Trouble with Cambodia. Commonweal 84: 552-5 S 2 '66

CHASE, Stuart
S-curves are forming. Sat R 49:36 Ag 13 '66

CHASE, Mrs Stuart
When a county tried to cut relief bill. il U S News 60:44-7 Ja 31 '66

CHASE, William W. See Berson, M. P. jt. auth.

CHASE Manhattan bank. See New York (city)—Banks

CHASEY, William C. Jr
Pre-racing physical conditioning. Yachting 119:60-1 Ap '66

CHASIN, Helen S.
Déjà vu; poem. Atlan 217:69 Je '66
In the sea; In the stream; poems. Atlan 217: 65 My '66
Witch house at Salem: winter; Leaving, or being left; Empty bed at the asylum; poems. Poetry 108:316-17 Ag '66

CHASINS, Abram
Heifetz-Piatigorsky, unlimited. Hi Fi 16:MA7 D '66
Return of Horowitz. Sat Eve Post 239:102-4 O 22 '66
Three Latins in Manhattan. Hi Fi 16:138+ Ap '66

CHASSIS, Automobile. See Automobiles—Chassis

CHASTAIN, Joseph E.
Will Congress kill Main Street? il por Nations Bsns 54:35-6+ My '66

CHASTITY. See Sexual ethics

CHATEAUBRIAND, François Auguste René, vicomte de
Complete romantic. P. Gay. il por Horizon 8:12-15+ Spr '66

CHATEAUGAY, N.Y.
Picasso=MC². C. S. Carleton. il Am Ed 2: 13-15 Mr '66

CHATEAUROUX, France
With troops pulling out: loss to France. to U.S. il U S News 61:47-9 S 19 '66

CHATEAUROUX air base. See Air bases

CHATFIELD, Charles
Digging for peace. Christian Cent 83:963-4 Ag 3 '66

CHATFIELD, Chester
Feel free to hunt. Outdoor Life 138:70-1+ N '66
McCormick's preposterous law. il por Outdoor Life 139:42-3+ Ja '67
Our most neglected gamebird. Outdoor Life 137:52-3+ F '66

CHATMAN, Peter. See Memphis Slim

CHATSWORTH. See England—Historic houses, etc.

CHATSWORTH, Calif. See Los Angeles

CHATTANOOGA, Tenn.

Finance
Computers occupy the royal suite. W. Zachry. il Am City 81:107 O '66

Newspapers
Competition makes a comeback; merger ended; Times and the News-free press. Time 88:70 S 9 '66
Divorce Chattanooga style. il Newsweek 68:54 S 5 '66

CHATTON, Mildred V.
Important aid to teachers; San Jose high school's A-V club. Sr Schol 87:sup22-3 Ja 14 '66

CHAUTAUQUAS
Americans not everybody knows; L. Miller; founder of the Chautauqua assembly. C. W. Ferguson. PTA Mag 61:12-14 N '66

CHAVEZ, Cesar
Grape pickers' strike. A. Kopkind. New Repub. 154:12-15 Ja 29 '66
March of migrants. il por Life 60:93-4 Ap 29 '66
Monopoly in the vineyards: grapes of wrath strike. J. P. Degnan. Nation 202:151-4 F 7 '66

CHEATING at cards. See Cardsharping

CHEATING in schoolwork
Air academy's cheating scandal; ed. by J. Shepherd. W. Snead, jr. Look 31:23-5 Ja 24 '67
Cheating can be stopped; honor codes. V. Dabney. il Sat R 49:68-9+ My 21 '66
Cheating in college. R. A. Raimi. Harper 232:68-70+ My '66; Reply. S. Miller. 233:6+ Ag '66
Cheating on the college campus. W. J. Bowers. il NEA J 55:20-2 F '66
Hard way; exam cheating at Ohio state university. Newsweek 68:86 Jl 25 '66
How we encourage cheating; forum-in-print; with study-discussion program, by E. Harris and D. Harris. bibliog il PTA Mag 60: 21-3. 35-6 F '66
Larceny in everyday life; Time essay. Time 88:26-7 S 9 '66
Testing vs. your child. G. B. Leonard. il Look 30:63-4+ Mr 22 '66
What makes students cheat? N. Bowden. Farm J 90:125 Mr '66

CHECKING accounts. See Banks and banking—Checking accounts

CHECKS
Checklist on checks. il Changing T 20:36 S '66
Facts about checks that can save you money. il Good H 162:188 Ap '66
How to write a check. il Consumer Bul 49:10 My '66

CHECKUP, Medical. See Physical examinations

CHEER leaders
Conversations parents never hear. il Look 30:88 S 20 '66

CHEESE
Cheese biscuit may aid health in Asia. Sci N L 89:104 F 12 '66
Popular American cheeses. M. Gustafson. il Parents Mag 41:65 Je '66
Science in action; mold-made flavors; excerpts from Mushrooms. molds and miracles. L. Kavaler. Natur Hist 75:62+ Ap '66
See also
Cookery—Cheese

CHEESE, Dry. See Cheese

CHEETAH (club) See Night clubs

CHEETAHS
Great cats of Africa. J. Dominis. il Life 62:48-59+ Ja 13 '67
Hunting with a cheetah! A. Whitman. il Pop Mech 125:96-9 F '66

Photographs
See Animals—Photographs

CHEEVER, John
World of apples; story. Esquire 66:216-19 D '66

CHEFS. See Cooks

CHEFS salad. See Salads

CHEKHOV, Anton Pavlovich
Chekhov and his prose, by T. Winner. Review Nation 202:684-6 Je 6 '66. D. Fanger
Chekhov's dramatic strategy. B. O. States. Yale R 56:212-24 D '66
Ivanov; adapted by J. Gielgud. Criticism
America 114:812-13 Je 4 '66
Commonweal 84:283 My 27 '66
Life 60:16 My 27 '66
Nation 202:661-2 My 30 '66
New Yorker 42:114 My 14 '66
Newsweek il 67:98 My 16 '66
Sat R 49:47 My 21 '66
Time il 87:75 My 13 '66
Ivanov; autobiographical link. M. K. Argus. Sat R 49:10 My 7 '66
Time passing. man enduring. T. S. Lindstrom. por Sat R 49:49-50 F 19 '66

CHELATION
Chelation in medicine. J. Schubert. il Sci Am 214:40-50 My '66; Reply with rejoinder. F. E. Holmes. 215:6 Jl '66

CHELATION therapy
Chelation in medicine. J. Schubert. il Sci Am 214:40-50 My '66; Reply with rejoinder. F. E. Holmes. 215:6 Jl '66

CHELF, Frank
Excerpt from testimony, August 18, 1965. Cong Digest 45:149+ My '66

CHELMINSKI, Rudolph
Life music review. Life 61:12 Ag 19 '66
Voyage on wheels across the Baltic Sea. Life 60:26-7 Mr 4 '66

about
Kids want to be like him. or belt him. Life 61:118+ N 11 '66

CHEMICAL additives in food. See Food additives

CHEMICAL apparatus and supplies
See also
Centrifuges
CHEMICAL bonds
Cage structures for polyborate ions. B. L. Dunicz. bibliog il Science 153:737-9 Ag 12 '66
CHEMICAL elements
See also names of chemical elements, e.g. Carbon
CHEMICAL finishes (textiles) See Finishing, Textile
CHEMICAL geology. See Geochemistry
CHEMICAL industries
See also
Dow chemical company
Eastman chemical products, incorporated

Wages and hours
Wages in industrial chemicals and petroleum refining. il Mo Labor R 89:994-9 S '66

Italy
Big chemical merger; Montecatini and Società Edison. il Fortune 73:69-70+ Ap '66
Italy plans for a giant in chemicals. Bsns W p 154 F 26 '66

Russia
Chemical change hits the Russian Ruhr; Donets basin. il Bsns W p 186-8+ Mr 12 '66

CHEMICAL lasers. See Lasers
CHEMICAL pruning. See Pruning
CHEMICAL reactions
Bare minimum. Sci Am 214:61 My '66
Making things more exact; one-third of an electron volt needed in forming deuterium hydride. il Time 87:76 My 27 '66
Reactivity of organic crystals. H. Morawetz. bibliog il Science 152:705-11 My 6 '66
Very fast reactions in solution. G. G. Hammes. bibliog il Science 151:1507-11 Mr 25 '66
See also
Catalysis
Decomposition
CHEMICAL reduction. See Reduction, Electrolytic
CHEMICAL research
See also
Gordon research conferences
Synthesis
CHEMICAL separation. See Separation (chemistry)
CHEMICAL warfare
Against chemical warfare; petition by twenty-two American scientists. Sci Am 215:64-5 N '66
CB, entering wedge; Harvard professors protest use of chemical-biological weapons in Vietnam. Nation 204:68 Ja 16 '67
End to Hanoi's jungle sanctuary? use of defoliation chemicals. il U S News 61:21 O 3 '66
Exterminators; American scientists petition President Johnson about use of chemical weapons in Vietnam. New Repub 155:7 O 1 '66
Scientists speak out on CB weapons; letter to President Johnson, September 19, 1966. Bul Atomic Sci 22:39 N '66
United Nations and chemical warfare. H. A. Jack. Christian Cent 84:60-2 Ja 11 '67
CHEMICAL workers
See also
Chemical industries
CHEMICALS
Physiological effects
How safe are the chemicals in our food? B. L. Oser. Todays Health 44:61-4 Mr '66
CHEMICALS, Sterilizing. See Chemosterilants
CHEMILUMINESCENCE. See Luminescence
CHEMISTRY
See also
Biochemistry
Degradation (chemistry)
Geochemistry
Photographic chemistry
Radicals (chemistry)
CHEMISTRY, Analytic
See also
Separation (chemistry)
CHEMISTRY, Industrial. See Chemical industries
CHEMISTRY, Organic
Recent advances in the chemistry of natural products; address, December 11, 1965. R. B. Woodward. bibliog il Science 153:487-93 Jl 29 '66
See also
Electroorganic chemistry
Enzymes

CHEMISTRY, Physical and theoretical
Solvay conference; report on thirteenth Solvay conference. J. E. Mayer. Science 152:393 Ap 15 '66
See also
Diffusion
Surface chemistry
CHEMISTRY, Surface. See Surface chemistry
CHEMISTRY, Technical
See also
Waste, Utilization of

Research
Research and industry in Czechoslovakia; Institute of macromolecular chemistry. V. K. McElheny. Science 153:620-2 Ag 5 '66
CHEMISTS
See also
Mulliken, R. S.
CHEMOCEPTORS. See Chemoreceptivity
CHEMORECEPTIVITY
Carotid body chemoceptors: physiological role in buffering fall in blood pressure during sleep. M. Guazzi and others. bibliog il Science 153:206-8 Jl 8 '66
CHEMOSTERILANTS
Comparative mutagenicity of two chemosterilants, tepa and hempa, in sperm of bracon hebetor. J. Palmquist and L. E. LaChance. bibliog il Science 154:915-17 N 18 '66
CHEMOSURGERY
Face burners. R. L. Smith. il Todays Health 44:20-3+ Je '66
CHEMOTAXIS. See Chemotropism
CHEMOTHERAPY
Antimicrobial agents and chemotherapy: report on fifth Interscience conference on antimicrobial agents and chemotherapy-fourth International congress for chemotherapy. D. Perlman. Science 152:108-9 Ap 1 '66
Antimicrobial agents and chemotherapy; report on sixth Interscience conference on antimicrobial agents and chemotherapy. D. Perlman. Science 154:1591 D 23 '66
CHEMOTROPISM
Chemotaxis in bacteria. J. Adler. bibliog il Science 153:708-16 Ag 12 '66
CHEN, Celia C. H. See Low, B. W. jt. auth.
CHEN, Shepley S. C. and Thimann, K. V. Nature of seed dormancy in phacelia tanacetifolia. bibliog Science 153:1537-9 S 23 '66
CHEN, Tina
Beauty life: three smart girls and what they've learned about makeup. il pors Mlle 64:98-101+ Ja '67
CHENEY, Frances Neel
Current reference books. See issues of Wilson library bulletin
CHENEY, Richard L.
Excerpt from testimony, May 5, 1965. Cong Digest 45:183+ Je '66
CHENEY, William
Empathy. il U S Camera 29:50-1 S '66
CHENG, Chu-yuan
Threat to the United States in another five or six years; interview. por U S News 61:52+ N 14 '66

about
Diligent researcher born to the facts. por Bsns W p 118 F 5 '66
CHÉNIER, André Marie de
Real poet. L. Kleine-Ahlbrandt. Opera N 30:22-3 F 5 '66
CHÉR (singer) See Lapiere, C.
CHERINGTON, Paul W.
How will a dept. of transportation really work? excerpts from comments at a northwestern university seminar. Aviation W 84:21 Ap 4 '66
CHERKIN, Arthur, and Catchpool, J. F. Temperature dependence of anesthesia in goldfish. bibliog Science 144:1460-2; 152:1111 Je 19 '64, My 20 '66
CHERNOW, Burt
(ed) See Frasconi, A. Interview with Antonio Frasconi
CHERRIES
C is for cherries. il Ladies Home J 83:118 My '66
See also
Cookery—Fruit
CHERRY festival, Traverse City. See Festivals —Michigan
CHERRY trees
See also
Oriental flowering cherry
CHESAPEAKE AND OHIO CANAL NATIONAL HISTORICAL PARK. See Potomac River

CHESAPEAKE and Ohio railway-Norfolk and Western merger. See Railroads—Consolidations and mergers

CHESAPEAKE BAY
Yachting special report: symposium. il Yachting 119:64-73+ Mr '66

CHESAPEAKE BAY bridge-tunnel
High roads & low. il Time 88:106+ S 16 '66

CHESEBROUGH, Harry E.
Research and the automobile; address, May 13, 1966. Vital Speeches 32:501-4 Je 1 '66
Safety legislation; address, October 11, 1966. Vital Speeches 33:94-6 N 15 '66

CHESHIRE, David
Sanatorium, *Le grau-du-roi*; poem. Atlan 217:64 My '66

CHESS, Stella, and Thomas, Alexander
Modern view of discipline. Parents Mag 41:43-5+ F '66

CHESS
Bobby would rather fight; Chess Olympics in Havana, Cuba. L. Evans. il Sports Illus 25:91-3 D 5 '66
Chess corner. A. Horowitz. See issues of Saturday review
In chess Piatigorsky is tops; best chess tournament in the world. R. Cantwell. il Sports Illus 25:22-4+ S 5 '66

CHESS Olympics. See Chess

CHESS players
Profiles; S. Kubrick. J. Bernstein. New Yorker 42:70-2+ N 12 '66

CHEST

Diseases
New chest disease found in coal miners. Sci N 89:197 Mr 26 '66

CHESTER, Doyle
Final shot of asphalt. por Am City 81:114-15 Ag '66

CHESTER, Pa.

Music
Chester, Pa; production of Bellini's Norma. G. M. Eby. Opera N 31:30-1 D 24 '66

CHESTNUT blight
Needed; a long-range program for the American chestnut. il Nat Parks Mag 40:4-8 Mr '66

CHESTNUT trees
Needed; a long-range program for the American chestnut. il Nat Parks Mag 40:4-8 Mr '66

Diseases and pests
See also
Chestnut blight

CHESTS
Build a toddler's toy chest. il Parents Mag 41:97 Jl '66
Dual-purpose step-chest. A. A. Altomare. il Pop Mech 126:154-6 O '66

CHETKOW, B. Harold
Creative programing in commercial recreation; address, 1965. Parks & Rec 1:696-8 S '66

Le CHEVAL évanoui; drama. See Sagan, F.

CHEVALIER, Lois R.
Best months to have your baby. Ladies Home J 83:44+ Ag '66
Secret drama behind the Pope's momentous decision on birth control. Ladies Home J 83:88-9+ Mr '66

CHEVALIER, Maurice
Le véritable Maurice. H. Kupferberg. Atlan 219:111-13 Ja '67

CHEVROLET motor company. See General motors corporation—Chevrolet division

CHEYENNE-Arapaho reservation. See Indians of North America—Reservations

CHEYENNE MOUNTAIN
Early operational status expected for new Norad center; combat operations center. P. J. Klass. il Aviation W 84:74-5+ Ja 24 '66

CHEZ, Ronald A. and others
Effect of sugars on transport of alanine in intestine. bibliog Science 153:1012-13 Ag 26 '66

CHI, Yu-ching
China's Purple Mountain observatory. Sky & Tel 31:266-7 My '66

CHIANG, Ching-kuo
Why the turmoil inside red China; interview. pors U S News 61:33-4 O 10 '66

CHIANG, Kai-shek
Problems of age. Time 87:30+ Ap 1 '66

CHIANG, Kai-shek, Mme. See Chiang, M. L. S.

CHIANG, Mei-ling (Sung)
Conflicts of China; address, December 7, 1965. Vital Speeches 32:197-9 Ja 15 '66
Foot-in-mouth syndrome; public statements. Christian Cent 83:1263 O 19 '66

Notes and comment; excerpts from address, March 18, 1966. New Yorker 42:35 Ap 2 '66

about
Old characters in new roles. C. Fritchey. Harper 233:33-4 Jl '66
Where are they now? New Repub 154:8 Ap 16 '66

CHIANTI. See Wine

CHIAPPETTA, Jerry
Big steelhead are back. por Field & S 70:47-9+ Ap '66
Cottontails or snowshoes? Field & S 71:50-2+ Ja '67
First report: salmon succeed in Great Lakes. il por Field & S 71:10-15 D '66
Michigan elk, no longer sacred cows. Field & S 71:36-7+ Ag '66

CHIAPPETTA, Michael
Latin America: education: the baited trap. Nation 203:321-3 O 3 '66

CHICAGO

Architecture
Big steel; Chicago's civic center complete. il Arch Forum 125:33-7 O '66
Chicago skyline adds a new dimension; John Hancock center, combination apartment and office building. il Bsns W p36 Ap 2 '66
For love of Chicago. S. Paul. Nation 202:657-9 My 30 '66
Sheer tower in Chicago: a design develops from engineering studies by computer; Dewitt-Chestnut apartments. il Arch Rec 139:160-1 Ja '66
Tale of two towers; Brunswick building. il Arch Forum 124:28-37 Ap '66

Art
Art news from Chicago (cont) J. Kind. Art N 64:46+ F; 65:56 Sum '66
Windy city windfall; sculpture for Chicago; by Picasso. il Time 88:73 S 23 '66

Banks
Bank that made a U-turn on LaSalle street. H. Gorey. il Fortune 73:138-41+ Mr '66

Board of trade
See Chicago board of trade

Bookstores
See Booksellers and bookselling—Illinois

City planning
Passing parade along Dearborn street. J. M. Dixon. il Arch Forum 124:34-41 Ja '66
Small shops get their own renewal; Chicago's Harper court shopping center. il Bsns W p34-5 Ja 29 '66

Crime
Chicago's scholarly cop; O. W. Wilson's police reforms reduces crime. H. Bruno. il Reporter 34:30-3 Mr 24 '66
East meets West; Tiffany's holdup. Newsweek 68:44+ O 31 '66
One by one; murder of eight student nurses. il Time 88:19-21 Jl 22 '66
Panic in Chicago's Mafia. B. Davidson and S. Smith. il Sat Eve Post 239:102-5 My 21 '66
They are all dead! murder of eight student nurses. il Newsweek 68:18-20 Jl 25 '66
Two against the mob. H. Bruno. Newsweek 67:44+ My 23 '66
Who the gentle victims were; murder of eight student nurses in Chicago. L. Wainwright. il Life 61:18-27 Jl 29 '66

Description
Chicago: first wonder of the Midwest. R. Dunlop. il Todays Health 44:44-9+ My '66
Chicago, the convention city. D. Powills. Hobbies 71:118-19 Ag '66

Economic conditions
Join: coal-operatin' in uptown. T. Gitlin. Christian Cent 83:754+ Je 8 '66

Education
Change in Chicago. Newsweek 67:98 My 23 '66
New start in Chicago; new school superintendent. Time 87:72-3 My 20 '66
No strike, but where will Chicago get money to pay teachers? U S News 62:74 Ja 23 '67
See also
Illinois. University, Urbana—Chicago campus

Foreign population
World I grew up in. J. T. Farrell. Commonweal 83:606-7+ F 25 '66

CHICAGO—*Continued*

Galleries and museums

Want a planetarium? Adler planetarium and astronomical museum. R. I. Johnson. bibliog il Parks & Rec 1:831-3+ O '66
See also
Chicago art institute

Hospitals

Balm for burns; techniques used at Sumner L. Koch burn unit. il Newsweek 68:84 Jl 18 '66

Hotels, restaurants, etc.

Chicago: gourmet's delight. R. Dunlop. il Todays Health 44:38-43+ My '66
See also
Night clubs

Housing

Close to home; end the slums drive uncovers Negro Communist slum owner. Newsweek 67:35 My 16 '66
Doctor King carries fight to northern slums. il Ebony 21:94-6+ Ap '66
Gamble in the ghetto: L. King's slum clearance campaign. Newsweek 67:24-5 Ja 31 '66
Goldberg's variation on Chicago public housing; Raymond M. Hilliard center. J. M. Dixon. il Arch Forum 125:25-33 N '66
New kind of public housing; new forms from new concepts. il Arch Rec 139:158-9 Ja '66
Open city. J. Coburn. New Repub 155:9-10 S 17 '66
Render unto King; M. L. King's takeover of building's management. il Time 87:18-19 Mr 25 '66
Still King; open housing agreement between Chicago Freedom movement and Chicago political, civic and social service organizations. Christian Cent 83:1071 S 7 '66
Too much integration? Newsweek 68:32-3 S 19 '66
Touchiest target; anti-discrimination marches. il Newsweek 68:29 Ag 15 '66
Truce in Chicago: freedom march cracks the ghetto's limits. il Bsns W p36-8 S 3 '66
Victory in the North; open-housing agreement il Newsweek 68:20-1 S 5 '66
West side story: home is where the welfare check comes. D. A. Satter. New Repub 155:15-19 Jl 2 '66

Industries

Billions build Chicago into a steel titan; nation's leading steelmaker. il Bsns W p68-75 N 19 '66

Labor and laboring classes
See also
Chicago—Poor

Libraries
See also
Chicago public library

Moral conditions

Woman's work; concerning L. Wille's series on homosexual activities. il Newsweek 68:82 Jl 11 '66

Music

Martinon, an evaluation: Chicago report. R. C. Marsh. il Hi Fi 16:151 My '66
New-music journeys in the U.S.A. E. Salzman. Hi Fi 16:MA12-13+ Ag '66
Notes from our correspondents. R. C. Marsh. il Hi Fi 16:16+ Jl '66
Ravinia and Grant Park concerts. R. C. Marsh. Hi Fi 16:MA22-3 N '66
See also
Chicago symphony orchestra
Lyric opera of Chicago

Negroes

Battle of Roosevelt road. il Time 88:18-19 Jl 22 '66
Chicago riots; Freedom rally. B. Cook. Commonweal 84:492-3 Ag 5 '66
Chicago summer: bossism, racism and Dr King. P. Good. il Nation 203:237-42 S 19 '66
Cody on Negro rights. Commonweal 84:490 Ag 5 '66
Doctor King carries fight to northern slums. il Ebony 21:94-6+ Ap '66
Focus on Chicago: the new Jericho. T. B. Morgan. il Look 30:70-3+ Je 14 '66
Gamble in the ghetto. Newsweek 67:24-5 Ja 31 '66
King in Chicago. B. Cook. Commonweal 84:175-7 Ap 29 '66

One last chance; King's program for Chicago Christian Cent 83:792-3 Je 22 '66
Power of the dollar; Operation Breadbasket in Chicago. Newsweek 68:62 D 26 '66
Riot in Chicago. America 115:117-18 Jl 30 '66
West side story: home is where the welfare check comes. D. A. Satter. New Repub 155:15-19 Jl 2 '66

Newspapers

New Day in Chicago: Arlington day launch. Newsweek 67:60-1 Ja 31 '66
Spreading suburban daily. il Time 87:43-4 F 4 '66

Police

Chicago riot: venganza! il Newsweek 67:23 Je 27 '66
Chicago's scholarly cop; O. W. Wilson's police reforms reduces crime. H. Bruno. il Reporter 34:30-3 Mr 24 '66
Church and the police. Christian Cent 83:1327 N 2 '66
Crime-Stop stops crime. K. Detzer. il Read Digest 89:133-6 O '66
Division lesson; problems of Chicago's Puerto Rican community. il Time 87:30-1 Je 24 '66
Fingerprints by wire. il Am City 81:165 My '66
No hablo ingles; police blamed for Puerto Rican riots. New Repub 154:7 Je 25 '66
Policeman looks at crime; interview. O. W. Wilson. U S News 61:51-2 Ag 1 '66
Speck: handled with care. Life 61:4 Jl 29 '66

Politics and government

Atlantic report; Mayor Daley's achievements and aims. Atlan 218:26+ S '66
Battle in the ghetto. Newsweek 67:44+ Je 13 '66
Chicago: a big city meets its problems. il U S News 60:74-8 Mr 28 '66
Coattails of bigotry; backlash candidates. H. W. De Zutter. New Repub 155:8-9 N 5 '66
Daley triple. Time 87:30 Je 24 '66
Minority objects, but Daley is Chicago. H. Higdon. il N Y Times Mag p84-5+ S 11 '66
Study in black and white; Republican candidates for Congress. S. Alsop. il Sat Eve Post 239:16 N 5 '66
William Dawson calls the tune; Democratic primary. R. Cotton. Reporter 35:21-3 Ag 11 '66

Poor

Join: coal-operatin' in uptown. T. Gitlin. Christian Cent 83:754+ Je 8 '66
New jobless count ups the figure; census in three Chicago poverty areas. il Bsns W p 160+ D 10 '66

Rapid transit

Automatic train control for Chicago transit. il Am City 81:59 Ag '66

Religious institutions and affairs

Chicago Catholic asks: where does my church stand on racial justice? J. A. McDermott. il Look 30:82+ N 1 '66

Riots

Battle of Roosevelt road. il Time 88:18-19 Jl 22 '66
Catholics and the Chicago riots. M. E. Schiltz. Commonweal 85:159-63 N 11 '66; Discussion. 85:321-4 D 16 '66
Chicago riot: venganza! il Newsweek 67:23 Je 27 '66
Chicago riots. B. Cook. Commonweal 84:492-3 Ag 5 '66
It hurts to think we haven't taught them America 115:170 Ag 20 '66; Discussion. 115:237-8 S 10 '66
New problem, Puerto Rican riots. il U S News 60:8 Je 27 '66
No hablo ingles; Puerto Ricans vs. police. New Repub 154:7 Je 25 '66
Riot in Chicago. America 115:117-18 Jl 30 '66
Violence in the city; ghetto riots. New Repub 155:5-6 Jl 30 '66
West side story. il Newsweek 65:17-18 Jl 25 '66
White backlash whips up a roadblock in Chicago. il Life 61:30-30A Ag 19 '66

Sanitary affairs

How to make a landfill attractive. J. Sexton. il Am City 81:92-3 N '66

Social conditions

Chicago: a big city meets its problems. il U S News 60:74-8 Mr 28 '66
See also
Chicago—Poor

CHICAGO—*Continued*

Social work
Chicago's Indian priest; P. J. Powell of the St Augustine center for American Indians. il Newsweek 69:91 Ja 23 '67

Street traffic
Electronic expressway strikes at rush-hour traffic; Eisenhower expressway. il Am City 81:118+ N '66

Streets
Passing parade along Dearborn street. J. M. Dixon. il Arch Forum 124:34-41 Ja '66

Theater
Broadway postscript; Goodman staff and professionals collaborate. H. Hewes. Sat R 49:54-5 Mr 5 '66
Improvisation bit; Second City. J. Novick. Nation 203:613-15 D 5 '66

Water supply
Chicago's new-fashioned waterworks; photographs. Fortune 73:159-61 Ap '66
CHICAGO; drama. See Shepard, S.
CHICAGO archdiocese. See Catholic church—Dioceses
CHICAGO art institute
Chicago's picture palace. H. E. F. Donohue. Holiday 40:72-3+ S '66
CHICAGO Bears (football club) See Football clubs
CHICAGO board of trade
Action in the pits; commodities trading. Time 88:73A Jl 1 '66
Commotion in the bean pit. il Time 88:77-8 Jl 8 '66
Futures are golden in grain. il Bsns W p22-3 Jl 2 '66
$10,000 fingers; spurt in trading. Newsweek 68:74 Jl 4 '66
CHICAGO, Burlington and Quincy railroad
Casey Jones is dead. il Time 87:98 Je 10 '66
CHICAGO Cubs (baseball) See Baseball clubs
CHICAGO daily news
Love & hate in Chicago; attacks of columnist M. Royko. il Time 88:50 Jl 1 '66
Woman's work; concerning L. Wille's series on homosexual activities. il Newsweek 68:82 Jl 11 '66
CHICAGO lyric opera. See Lyric opera of Chicago
CHICAGO-Mackinac race. See Yacht racing
CHICAGO mercantile exchange. See Exchanges
CHICAGO opera ballet
Chicago opera ballet; Charles S. Colden center, Queens college. J. Maskey. Dance Mag 40:30+ Ap '66
CHICAGO public library
Chicago pl censors art exhibit; says pictures were suggestive. Library J 91:214 Ja 15 '66
Using your public library's record collection. M. R. Adkins. Sr Schol 88:sup9 Ap 1 '66
CHICAGO, Rock Island and Pacific railway
Fight for the Rock Island. D. Cordtz. il Fortune 73:140-3+ Je '66
Western railroads collide on mergers; Union Pacific and North Western make strong bids for Rock Island. il Bsns W p 130-1+ Mr 19 '66
CHICAGO social workers strikes. See Strikes—United States—Social workers
CHICAGO symphony orchestra
Musical events; concert at Carnegie Hall. W. Sargeant. New Yorker 42:230 N 19 '66
Musical events; concert in Carnegie Hall, conducted by J. Martinon. W. Sargeant. New Yorker 42:197-8 Mr 19 '66
CHICAGO theological seminary. See Chicago. University—Federated theological faculty
CHICAGO tribune
Chicago tribune eisegesis; concerning out of context quotation from Deuteronomy. Christian Cent 83:856 Jl 6 '66
McCormick of Chicago, by F. C. Waldrop. Review
  New Repub 154:39-40 F 26 '66. E. Norlander
  Newsweek il 67:60+ Mr 7 '66
CHICAGO. University
Broadway postscript; Goodman staff and professionals collaborate. H. Hewes. Sat R 49:54-5 Mr 5 '66
Instant access to students' reading levels; laboratory school. E. L. Thomas. il Library J 91:2165-8 Ap 15 '66
President who wouldn't get mad; draft protesters. il Time 87:72 My 20 '66

Divinity school
See Chicago. University—Federated theological faculty

Federated theological faculty
Chicago at 100; Chicago's divinity school. il Time 87:74+ Mr 25 '66
CHICAGO university bookstore. See College bookstores
CHICAGO university press
Chicago's Press; seventy-five years of publishing. il Pub W 190:30-5 D 5 '66; Reply. R. F. Lane. 191:14-15 Ja 2 '67
CHICAGO White Sox (baseball) See Baseball clubs
CHICAGOANS
Division street; America, by S. Terkel. Review
  Sat R 49:65 D 24 '66. R. L. Shayon
CHICHESTER, Francis Charles
With the moan of the wind and a barrel of beer. il por Time 88:41 D 16 '66
CHICHESTER festival. See Drama festivals
CHICK embryos. See Embryology—Birds
CHICKADEES
Black-capped chickadee. E. I. Fanning. il Pop Gard 17:79 Ag '66
CHICKEN! story. See Gordon, D.
CHICKEN as food. See Cookery—Poultry
CHICKEN livers. See Cookery—Poultry
CHICOREL, Marietta
Statistical ammunition. Library J 91:3363-4+ Jl '66
CHICORY
See also
Endive
CHIDESTER, Ann
Frenchwoman; story. McCalls 93:80-1 My '66
CHIEF medical examiner, New York. See New York (city)—Chief medical examiner
CHIEFS (football club) See Football clubs
CHIÈVRES, Belgium
Hunting new quarters; SHAPE. il Time 88:26-7 Ag 12 '66
CHIHUAHUA al Pacifico. See Railroads—Mexico
CHIHUAHUAN DESERT
Late Pleistocene vegetation and degree of pluvial climatic change in the Chihuahuan Desert. P. V. Wells. bibliog il Science 153:970-5 Ag 26 '66
CHILCOTE, Ronald H.
Salazar's Portugal; anniversary on thin ice. Nation 202:638-41 My 30 '66
CHILD, Julia
Julia Child, the master chef; interview, ed. by J. Howard. il pors Life 61:45-6+ O 21 '66

about
Everyone's in the kitchen. il pors Time 88:74-80+ N 25 '66
How to avoid TV dinners while watching TV. J. Barthel. il pors N Y Times Mag p30-1+ Ag 7 '66
CHILD-adult relationship
Generations. New Yorker 42:47 D 17 '66
Love is being needed; Foster grandparents project of Office of economic opportunity. C. Brossard. il Look 30:67-71 Ag 23 '66
On learning from children. W. Marchant. il Holiday 40:8+ Ag '66
Status symbols of youth; with study-discussion program, by C. Smallenburg and H. Smallenburg. E. J. Alpenfels. bibliog il PTA Mag 60:4-6, 35-6 Mr '66
What I have learned from other people's children. M. Drury. il Read Digest 88:101-4 F '66

Anecdotes, facetiae, satire, etc.
How to talk to a baby. J. Kerr. il Ladies Home J 83:56 F '66
CHILD care centers. See Foster day care
CHILD development group of Mississippi. See Project Head Start
CHILD guidance. See Child study
CHILD guidance clinics
Echoes of a scream; emotionally disturbed children; Larimer children's center, Fort Collins, Colo. C. S. Carleton. il Am Ed 3:20-2 D '66
CHILD health. See Children—Care and hygiene
CHILD molesters. See Children and strangers
CHILD obesity. See Corpulence
CHILD of delight; story. See Hochstein, R.
CHILD photography. See Photography of children

CHILD prodigies. See Children, Gifted

CHILD psychiatry
Help for troubled families; with study-discussion program, by C. W. Mattuck. H. Milt. il Parents Mag 41:20, 84-5+ N '66
When a child needs psychiatric help. B. Spock. Redbook 127:18+ My '66
See also
Child guidance clinics

CHILD psychology. See Child study

CHILD study
Can a child be too good? H. Bernstein and E. G. Neisser. il Parents Mag 41:33-5+ Ap '66
Dialogue with mothers; how your child's conscience is born. B. Bettelheim. Ladies Home J 83:26+ O '66
Dream world, real world. C. Klein. il N Y Times Mag p 102+ O 16 '66
Early separations from mother cause anxiety. Todays Health 44:67 My '66
Environment important; study and follow-up study of orphans. Sci N 90:248 O 1 '66
Fantasy games aid child's emotional growth. Sci N 90:83 Ag 6 '66
Giant steps in baby research. S. F. Yolles. il N Y Times Mag p91+ Ap 17 '66
Implicatioins of laboratory studies of aggression for the control and regulation of violence. R. H. Walters. bibliog f Ann Am Acad 364:60-72 Mr '66
Inner world of childhood, by F. G. Wickes. Review
Nation 204:91-2 Ja 16 '67. G. Dangerfield
Learning to let go; concerning booklet by Child study association. R. Kramer. il N Y Times Mag p 104+ Ap 24 '66
Parents' maladjustments reflected in children. Sci N L 89:105 F 12 '66
Parents with too much knowledge and too little confidence. E. J. LeShan. Redbook 126:49+ F '66
Preschoolers play favorites; excerpt from Growing up with children. M. W. Piers. il Parents Mag 41:64-5+ N '66
Strict homes, happy children; with quiz; findings of S. Coopersmith study. R. Brecher and E. Brecher. McCalls 93:66-7+ Jl '66
Unlikables. E. S. Ringold. il N Y Times Mag p69-70+ Ja 15 '67
Violence and human development. E. B. McNeil. Ann Am Acad 364:149-57 Mr '66
What to do for the child who has no friends. E. W. Johnson. il Parents Mag 41:56-8+ Ag '66
What we don't know about children's behavior. B. Berelson. il PTA Mag 60:18-20 Je '66
See also
Child guidance clinics
Childrens questions

CHILD study association of America
Sex becomes a brand-new problem. K. D. Fishman. il N Y Times Mag p69+ Mr 13 '66
Todays children and sex; excerpts from panel discussion. il Changing T 20:7-12 Je '66; Discussion. 20:21-3 S '66

CHILD welfare
Children at stake. K. D. Fishman. il N Y Times Mag p 146+ D 11 '66
See also
Children—Care and hygiene
Childrens villages
Foster day care
Foster grandparents program

Europe, Western
See also
Childrens villages

United States
America's forgotten children. J. H. Reid. Parents Mag 41:40+ F '66
What every mother owes her child and herself; day care problem. L. Benjamin and A. Henley. Ladies Home J 83:69+ Je '66

CHILD who was made of snow; drama. See Bennett, R.

CHILDBIRTH
Advantage of pregnancy? case of Mrs Marvin Glidden, with a transplanted kidney. il Time 88:72 O 7 '66
Expectant mother; how to deliver a baby in an emergency. D. A. Callagan and B. R. Boylan. Redbook 126:40+ F '66
Expectant mother; vocabulary of pregnancy and childbirth. R. A. Kimbrough. Redbook 126:42+ Mr '66

Happiest way to have a baby; St Mary's hospital, Evansville, Ind, family-centered maternity care unit. M. Longwell. il Farm J 90:84-5+ My '66
Hospitals update maternity care; St Mary's, Evansville, Ind, and other programs. Farm J 90:85 My '66
How will you have your baby? D. Siegel. il Parents Mag 41:46-7+ F '66
I enjoyed having my baby. B. Motry. il Parents Mag 41:36-7+ Ag '66
I had my baby in Moscow. B. Rosenfeld. il Redbook 127:52-3+ Jl '66
What really happens when your obstetrician is late. P. H. Brenner and R. L. Brenner. Ladies Hom J 83:42+ Je '66
What really matters when you're in the maternity ward. P. Wright. Ladies Home J 83:48+ Ag '66
Woman on her way to a miracle; ed. by E. Graves. M. Falk. il Life 61:48-61+ Jl 22 '66
World's smallest mother is doing just fine. Sci N 90:383 N 5 '66
See also
Obstetrics

CHILDERS, Joanne
White garment; poem. Commonweal 85:103 O 28 '66

CHILDHOOD memories. See Reminiscence

CHILDREN
See also
Cookery by children
Family, Size of
Family life
Fathers
Mothers
Moving pictures for children
Negro children
Parents
Preschool children
Problem children
Stepparents
Television broadcasting and children
Travel with children
also headings beginning Child, Childrens

Accidents
See Accidents

Adjustment
See Adjustment, Social

Anxiety
See Anxiety

Cancer
See Cancer

Care and hygiene
America's unhealthy children: an emerging scandal. R. Tunley. Harper 232:41-6 My '66; Discussion. 233:4 Jl; 8 Ag '66
Children's eyes: how to protect them from defects and disease. M. J. E. Senn. il McCalls 93:26+ Jl '66
Danger: children at play. K. D. Fishman. il N Y Times Mag p 114+ S 25 '66
Every child needs a doctor. E. H. Matthew. il Parents Mag 41:52+ N '66
Growing pains. See issues of Today's health
Why do children get sick so often in winter? L. W. Sauer. PTA Mag 61:31-2 Ja '67
Your child's health. L. W. Sauer. See issues of PTA magazine
See also
Child guidance clinics
Children—Nutrition
Infants—Care and hygiene
Poisons
Sleep

Caricatures and cartoons
Small wonders. R. Marcus. See issues of Good housekeeping

Development
See Children—Growth and development

Diseases
Adult diseases strike children, young people. Sci N 91:43 Ja 14 '67
Conquering childhood diseases. W. H. Stewart. il Am Ed 2:30-2 Mr '66
Why do children get sick so often in winter? L. W. Sauer. PTA Mag 61:31-2 Ja '67
Your child's health. L. W. Sauer. See issues of PTA magazine
See also
Children—Care and hygiene
also names of children's diseases, e.g. Phenylketonuria

CHILDREN—*Continued*

Education
See Education of children

Etiquette
See Etiquette for children and youth

Food
See Children—Nutrition

Growth and development
Children's ways of thinking; with study-discussion program, by R. Strang. E. G. Olim. bibliog il PTA Mag 61:20-2, 34 Ja '67

Child's right to dignity; excerpt from Life among the giants. L. R. Young. McCalls 94:62+ O '66

Code that controls growth. il Life 61:93-4+ O 14 '66

How boys and girls become grownups. B. Spock. il Redbook 128:22+ Ja '67

Inborn urge to grow. A. B. Auerbach. il Parents Mag 41:54-5+ Je '66

Learning to let go; concerning booklet by Child study association. R. Kramer. il N Y Times Mag p 104+ Ap 24 '66

Ontogenetic development of the human sleep-dream cycle. H. P. Roffwarg and others. bibliog il Science 152:604-19 Ap 29 '66

Our pint-size ancestors; rapid growth of children today. V. Vlastovsky. il UNESCO Courier 19:27-9 F '66

Speech and development. Sci N 90:392 N 12 '66

Three babies day by day. K. D. Fishman. il N Y Times Mag p68+ Ja 12 '66

Two ways to grow up; study of the social growth of the Hopi child contrasted with other American children. D. McNickle. Nation 202:365-6 Mr 28 '66

Watching Johnny's memory grow. F. R. Schreiber. il Todays Health 44:22-4+ O '66
See also
Child study
Infants—Growth and development

Health
See Children—Care and hygiene

Hospital care
See Hospital care

Hospitals
Pediatric outpatient department; report on conference on conceptual and methodological approaches to research in pediatric outpatient departments. R. W. Olmsted. Science 153:1026 Ag 26 '66

Redevelopment of children's center provides clinical, research and residential spaces; Children's hospital medical center, Boston. il Arch Rec 140:204-5 O '66

Jealousy
See Jealousy

Language
Learning your baby's language. C. H. Turner. il Parents Mag 41:36-7+ Je '66

Law
See also
Adoption
Juvenile courts
Parent and child (law)

Management and training
Alone and not afraid. G. Mayer and M. Hoover. il Redbook 127:58-9+ Je '66

Antecedents of self-esteem, by S. Coppersmith. Review
N Y Times Mag il p78+ Ja 8 '67. L. L. Prina

Big bedtime argument; dialogue with mothers. B. Bettelheim. Ladies Home J 83:41 F '66

Bringing up children in an age of disenchantment. B. Spock. Redbook 126:20+ F '66

Bringing up children then, and now. S. Claiborne. il Parents Mag 41:53-7+ O '66

Bringing up Hans und Gretel. A. Shabecoff. il N Y Times Mag p 179-80+ N 13 '66

Controlling young children. B. Spock. il Redbook 128:22+ N '66

Dialogue with mothers; should you give in to your child? B. Bettelheim. Ladies Home J 84:20 Ja '67

Dialogue with mothers; when your child wants to "kill". B. Bettelhem. Ladies Home J 83:40+ My '66

Discipline isn't dated; with study-discussion program. R. Strang. bibliog il PTA Mag 61:26-8, 34 N '66

Do parents cause children's emotional troubles? B. Spock. Redbook 127:20+ Je '66

Family clinic. See issues of Parents' magazine and better homemaking

Growing pains. See issues of Today's health

How children react to praise and criticism. H. G. Ginott. il Parents Mag 41:46-7+ Ap '66

How I'm raising my twins; ed. by J. Heimlich. S. Glick. il Parents Mag 41:58-9+ D '66

How preschoolers learn to give and take. M. Nicolaysen. il Parents Mag 41:48-9+ My '66

How to get obedience; reprint. E. Aronson. il Sci Digest 60:54-9 Jl '66

How to light a fire inside (not under) a boy. R. C. Davids. il Farm J 90:84-6 Ap '66

If it were my child; contributions from readers. See issues of Ladies' home journal

Kids can't be all tidy all the time. E. Elias. il Parents Mag 41:46-7+ Mr '66

Life, the inexorable teacher; excerpt from The collective family. A. S. Makarenko. il Sat R 50:117 Ja 7 '67

Living with a four-year-old and loving it. M. Nicolaysen. il Parents Mag 41:62-3+ D '66

Men, moonships, and morality; concerning theories of R. S. Morison and A. S. Makarenko. J. Lear. il Sat R 50:113-14+ Ja 7 '67

Our boys took to embassy life. F. Martin. il Parents Mag 41:68-9+ D '66

Our kids settle their own squabbles. M. Treichler. il Parents Mag 41:50-1+ Je '66

Parents with too much knowledge and too little confidence. E. J. LeShan. Redbook 126:49+ F '66

Pony with a safety message. C. S. Karch. il Todays Health 44:5+ My '66

Rainy day fun for kids. A. Schwartz. il Parents Mag 41:40-1+ Ap '66

Strict homes, happy children; with quiz; findings of S. Coopersmith study. R. Brecher and E. Brecher. McCalls 93:66-7+ Jl '66

Take a tip from Tom Sawyer; help with household chores. J. Graham. il Parents Mag 41:40-1+ Jl '66

Treating children with respect. B. Spock. Redbook 128:33-4+ D '66

Try a little dissonance. E. Aronson. il N Y Times Mag p 109+ S 11 '66

Under-deprived. E. J. LeShan. il N Y Times Mag p83-4 Ap 3 '66

Violence and human development. E. B. McNeil. Ann Am Acad 364:149-57 Mr '66

When a child should tell. S. Frank. il Good H 162:96-7+ My '66

Where have all the children gone? J. K. Lubold. il Read Digest 88:135-7 Ap '66

Why youngsters lie. V. Balaban and C. Levine. il Parents Mag 41:41-3+ My '66

Your own Project Head Start; with study-discussion program, by R. Strang. G. D. Ewing. bibliog il PTA Mag 61:20-2, 34 S '66
See also
Child study
Children and strangers
Childrens allowances
Discipline
Moral education
Parent-child relationship

Anecdotes, facetiae, satire, etc.
My life story. S. Greenwald. il Harper 233:54-5 Jl '66

Bibliography
Books for parents. P. Pinson. See issues of Parents' magazine and better homemaking

Memories
See Reminiscence

Mortality
See also
Infant mortality

Nutrition
Better life for all children. L. Baumgartner. Parents Mag 41:58 N '66

Books. M. F. K. Fisher. New Yorker 42:191-2+ My 21 '66; Reply. K. S. White. 42:112-14 Je 18 '66

Corn to feed children; CPP and CSM food supplements. Sci N 89:361 My 14 '66
See also
Lunches

Photographs
Friends around the clock; boy and a dog. Good H 162:52+ Mr '66

Psychiatry
See Child psychiatry

Psychology
See Child study

CHILDREN—*Continued*

Punishment
See Children—Management and training

Religion
See also
Sunday schools

Sayings
Edison invented the indecent lamp. H. Dunn. il Sci Digest 59:79-81 My '66
Iorn curtin: survey of children's knowledge about Russia or the Soviet Union; report. B. Appel. Library J 91:2174-5 Ap 15 '66
Out of the mouths of babes. See issues of Parents' magazine and better homemaking
Watch out for the wollypops. W. Stanton. il Sat Eve Post 239:22 F 12 '66

Sex behavior
See Sex behavior

Sleep
See Sleep

Social and economic status
Under-deprived. E. J. LeShan. il N Y Times Mag p83-4 Ap 3 '66
See also
Socially handicapped children

Training
See Children—Management and training

Asia
Born between East and West; concerning Pearl S. Buck foundations. M. Macmillan. Sat R 49:51 Jl 23 '66

Germany
Bringing up Hans und Gretel. A. Shabecoff. il N Y Times Mag p 179-80+ N 13 '66

Great Britain
Youngest romantics. A. Pryce-Jones. il Vogue 148:248+ D '66

Russia
Life, the inexorable teacher; excerpt from The collective family. A. S. Makarenko. il Sat R 50:117 Ja 7 '67

United States
Year our children discovered America; American children born in Egypt. E. W. Fernea. il Redbook 128:12+ D '66
See also
Negro children

Vietnam (Republic)
Servicemen and the children; activities in South Vietnam. il NEA J 55:47 Ap '66

CHILDREN, Adopted
Adopted children more prone to mental illness. Sci N L 89:120 F 19 '66

CHILDREN, Adoption of. See Adoption

CHILDREN, Backward. See Slow learning children

CHILDREN, Blind. See Blind

CHILDREN, Education of. See Education of children

CHILDREN, Epileptic. See Epileptics

CHILDREN, Exceptional
Exceptional children, the neglected legion. W. L. Prouty. NEA J 55:25 Mr '66
Outlook for special education. W. Abraham. NEA J 55:30-1 D '66

CHILDREN, First born
Birth order and its sequelae. W. D. Altus; discussion. bibliog Science 152:1177-8+ My 27 '66
Firstborns seem smarter. Sci N L 89:55 Ja 22 '66
Most likely to succeed. R. Kamer. il N Y Times Mag p72+ F 13 '66

CHILDREN, Gifted
Challenging the gifted. R. P. Abell. il NEA J 55:48-9 F '66
Little Gary Ferguson. il Ebony 21:39-42+ My '66
What makes a child prodigy; reprint. C. Burt. Sci Digest 59:53-6 Ap '66
See also
Children as musicians

Education
Neglected kids, the bright ones. S. Alexander. Life 60:26 Je 24 '66

CHILDREN, Handicapped
One American family in ten. W. D. Sherman. il PTA Mag 61:14-16 Ja '67
See also
Brain damaged children
Mentally handicapped children

Apparatus and appliances
Hope and help for handicapped children; UCLA child amputee prosthetics project; ed. by A. Hamilton. M. Brooks. il Todays Health 44:60-3+ N '66
See also
Walkers, Orthopedic

Education
Bobby joins his world: 5 million brain-damaged children can be helped. C. Mangel. il Look 30:84-6+ N 15 '66
Boy who found the sun; efforts of a gifted teacher and a blind mother. J. Robbins and J. Robbins. Redbook 128:48-9+ D '66
See also
Institutes for the achievement of human potential, Philadelphia

CHILDREN, Illegitimate. See Illegitimacy

CHILDREN, Mentally handicapped. See Mentally handicapped children

CHILDREN, Photography of. See Photography of children

CHILDREN, Preschool. See Preschool children

CHILDREN, Problem. See Problem children

CHILDREN, Runaway. See Runaway boys and girls

CHILDREN and adults. See Child-adult relationship

CHILDREN and death
Dialogue with mothers: when a child asks: am I going to die? B. Bettelheim. Ladies Home J 83:24+ N '66

CHILDREN and music. See Music and children

CHILDREN and parents. See Parent-child relationship

CHILDREN and strangers
Patch the pony says. C. S. Karch. il PTA Mag 60:23 My '66
Pony with a safety message. C. S. Karch. il Todays Health 44:5+ My '66

CHILDREN and television. See Television broadcasting and children

CHILDREN and theater. See Theater and children

CHILDREN are gone; story. See Cavanaugh, A.

CHILDREN as artists. See Childrens art

CHILDREN as authors
Using records to teach poetry; with poems written by seventh-graders of Middlesex junior high school, Darien, Conn. C. L. Reed. il Sr Schol 89:sup 16 N 11 '66

CHILDREN as dancers
Question and answer; stage mothers. Y. Yourlo and E. Yourlo. Dance Mag 40:24 D '66

CHILDREN as golfers. See Golfers

CHILDREN as journalists. See Childrens newspapers

CHILDREN as musicians
Little Gary Ferguson. il Ebony 21:39-42+ My '66
Mitey miss of the concert stage; E. Engrum. il Ebony 22:112-16 D '66

CHILDREN as photographers
And what were you doing at seven? H. Keppler. il Mod Phot 30:66-9 O '66
My son, the film maker. L. Lipton. il Pop Phot 58:128-9 Ap '66

CHILDREN as poets. See Children as authors

CHILDREN in boating
Junior yachting. il Yachting 120:29+ O; 27+ N; 33 D '66

CHILDRENS allowances
Give the children an allowance? il Changing T 21:41-3 Ja '67
Kids and money. J. Whitbread. il Parents Mag 41:70-2+ D '66
Many meanings of money; with discussion group program, by E. J. LeShan. E. G. Neisser. il Parents Mag 41:34+, 52-3+ F '66
Should you manage the earnings of your child? Bet Hom & Gard 44:6 Jl '66
Teaching children about money. il Good H 162:176 My '66

CHILDRENS amusements
Bored children? here are twenty-five ways to keep them busy and happy! Bet Hom & Gard 44:32-5 S '66
Kids can't be tidy all the time. E. Elias. il Parents Mag 41:46-7+ Mr '66
Rainy day fun for kids. A. Schwartz. il Parents Mag 41:40-1+ Ap '66
Treasures in tricks and treats. S. Lewis. il Motor B 117:42-5 Ap '66
See also
Games
Nature study
Playgrounds—Equipment
Television broadcasting—Childrens programs
Toys

CHILDRENS art
Children of Chijnaya and their tapestries. il
House & Gard 130:58+ N '66
Children's art 1966; work following trip to
the Aquatic bird house at the Bronx zoo.
New York. N. Vibber. il Sch Arts 66:13
S '66
Children's art U.S.A, 1966; symposium. Sch
Arts 66:4-37 D '66
Children's work. T. F. Cioeff. il Sch Arts 66:
20-1 N '66
Creating plaster sculpture; program at
Lincoln junior high, La Crosse, Wis.
R. Sherin. il Sch Arts 66:11-14 O '66
How it all began . . ; Creative decor kit and
the Mini kit. il Design 68:22 N '66
How youngsters see Unesco. il UNESCO
Courier 19:54-9 Jl '66
Ink & tempera prints. M. E. Kerns. il Sch
Arts 65:17-20 F '66
Motivations for children's art; drawing.
D. Russell. il Sch Arts 65:40 My '66
Motivations for children's art; drawing of In-
dian. E. Szuba and M. Snyder. il Sch Arts
65:39 My '66
Motivation for children's drawings and paint-
ings. R. Freeland. il Sch Arts 66:30-2 S '66
Sixth graders express themselves in pic-
tures. Sister Patrick Ann. il Sch Arts 65:
33-4 F '66
See also
Sand sculpture

Exhibitions
Earth and the fullness thereof; 20th annual
children's art exhibit, sponsored by he
Jewish education committee. T. Gezari.
il Sch Arts 65:4-8 Ja '66
CHILDREN'S book council
Book fairs and the CBC. M. C. Childs. bib-
liog il Library J 91:2586-8 My 15 '66
Books please: the slogan. il Wilson Lib Bul
41:16 S '66
CBC-NCTE to cooperate in teacher training.
Pub W 190:53 O 3 '66
Illustration discussed by Children's book
council; summary of address. Pub W 189:
83 Ap 18 '66
Seth Agnew heads Children's book council.
Pub W 189:74 Ja 31 '66
CHILDRENS book departments. See Book-
sellers and bookselling—Childrens literature
CHILDREN'S book exhibits. See Book exhibits
CHILDRENS book fairs. See Book fairs
CHILDRENS book week. See Book week
CHILDRENS books. See Childrens literature
CHILDRENS bookshops. See Booksellers and
bookselling—Childrens literature
CHILDRENS courts. See Juvenile courts
CHILDRENS diseases. See Children—Diseases
CHILDRENS dishes. See Tableware
CHILDRENS emotions. See Emotions
CHILDRENS encyclopedias. See Encyclopedias
CHILDRENS fears. See Fear
CHILDRENS friends. See Playmates
CHILDRENS furniture. See Furniture, Chil-
drens
CHILDRENS games. See Games
CHILDRENS gardens
How to set up a children's garden. il Good H
162:184 Ap '66
CHILDRENS librarians
Beyond prejudice. R. H. Viguers. Horn Bk
42:157 Ap '66
CHILDRENS libraries. See Libraries, Childrens
CHILDRENS lies. See Lying
CHILDRENS literature
About Ferdinand; concerning the book. The
story of Ferdinand. A. Bell. il Pub W 190:
54-5 Ag 22 '66
Backstage with the judges; the Herald tri-
bune children's book awards. E. Geller.
il Library J 91:2604-8 My 15 '66
Before Babel; means of communicating in
todays changing world. M. L'Engle. il
Horn Bk 42:661-70 D '66
Books please; symposium. il Wilson Lib Bul
41:160-76+ O '66
Bridge of children's books; symposium. ed.
with introd. by E. Geller. bibliog il Library J 91:5683-92 N 15 '66
Caldecott award acceptance: address. July
12, 1966. N. Hogrogian. il Horn Bk 42:419-
21 Ag '66
Children's book needs in a changing society;
summary of addresses at conference in
Tarrytown, N.Y. Pub W 190:35-8 Jl 25 '66
Children's books and the electronikers: children's books of information. Pub W 190:203
Jl 11 '66

Commercial cataloging services: Library of
Congress, Wilson, Alanar, and R. R.
Bowker. il Library J 91:5133-5 O 15 '66
Conference report; Critical approach to chil-
dren's literature, theme of Chicago graduate
library school conference. I. McCaul. Wilson
Lib Bul 41:142 O '66
Crisis in children's cataloging; new LC card
sets. T. C. Hines. il Library J 91:4183-7
S 15 '66; Discussion. 91:5129-32, 6140+ O
15, D 15 '66
Hole in the library shelf; shortage of books
for over-twelve reader. E. Allen. Writer
79:23-4+ Ag '66
Legacy library; facsimiles of classic chil-
dren's books. il Pub W 189:100-1 F 14 '66
Man who loans the tools. R. H. Viguers.
Horn Bk 42:277 Je '66
People in books. J. Little. il Horn Bk 42:
159-62 Ap '66
Pinch of this and a dash of that; require-
ments of special groups of children. R. H.
Viguers. Horn Bk 42:18-19 F '66
Pleasant land of counterpane. C. Lewis. il
Horn Bk 42:542-7 O '66
Study in conflicting values; excerpts from
address, March 1966. D. M. Broderick. bib-
liog il Library J 91:2557-64 My 15 '66; Reply.
D. S. Smith. 91:5006 O 15 '66
That pointing finger; concerning ethical
value. A. Dalgliesh. il Sat R 49:40 S '66
To the children with love, from Leo Politi.
R. Nichols. il Horn Bk 42:218-22 Ap '66
Truman Capote, Lady Bird Johnson, Robert
Kennedy, and many more remember the
books from childhood they loved best. il
Ladies Home J 83:20+ D '66
Visit with Mary Poppins and P. L. Travers.
R. R. Lingeman. il N Y Times Mag p 12-
13+ D 25 '66
Visit with the real Mary Poppins; interview.
ed. by J. Roddy. P. L. Travers. il Look
30:84+ D 13 '66
What price categories. E. M. Graves. il
Commonweal 84:285-6 My 27 '66
Why not for children? excerpt from address.
June 21, 1965. E. Cameron. Horn Bk 42:
21-33 F '66; Reply. M. L. Hunt. 42:389 Ag
'66
Wizard who created Oz. D. P. Mannix. il
Read Digest 88:104-8 Je '66
See also
Book selection
Book week
Booksellers and bookselling—Childrens litera-
ture
Children's book council
Childrens reading
Newbery medal
Picture books for children
Publishers and publishing
Scientific literature for children

Bibliography
Andersen medal. Library J 91:5718 N 15 '66
Autumn books for young people. Z. Suther-
land. il Sat R 49:43-4+ N 12 '66
Best books of the season for children.
E. Sheehan. America 115:551-7 N 5 '66
Best books of the year; selected by the edi-
tors of Junior books appraised. il Library J
91:6147-51 D 15 '66
Booklist (title varies) comp. by R. H.
Viguers and others. See issues of Horn
book magazine
Books. J. Malcolm. New Yorker 42:210+
D 17 '66
Books for beginners. H. H. McGrady. il
Library J 91:1033-5 F 15 '66
Books for boys & girls. D. E. Leland. See
issues of Parents' magazine and better
homemaking
Books for children. C. Jackson. Atlan 218:
148+ D '66
Books for young people. A. Dalgliesh. See
issues of Saturday review to September 17.
1966
Books for young people. Z. Sutherland. See
issues of Saturday review, October 22, 1966-
Children's books; a medley. C. Simonds.
Nat R 18:1284-6 D 13 '66
Children's books: goodies galore. Christian
Cent 83:1509-10 D 7 '66
Children's books of 1965-66. W. L Bergmann
and M. E. Ledlie. NEA J 55:57-8+ N '66
Children's books; personal list of possible
winners of next year's Caldecott and Newbery awards. L. Russ. Pub W 190:81 Jl 4
'66
Children's books; some leading titles for
spring. il Pub W 189:111-50 F 21 '66

CHILDRENS research. See Research
CHILDRENS rooms
Case of the messy room. E. S. Oshin. il N Y Times Mag p97-8 Mr 27 '66
Children's stamping grounds. il House & Gard 130:224-5 O '66
Four lowers and four uppers in this girls' dormitory. il Sunset 136:113-14 Mr '66
Two rooms from one. il Pop Mech 126:137-42+ D '66
Two rooms now sleep three. il Sunset 137:70 Jl '66
CHILDRENS safety seat. See Automobiles—Safety devices and measures
CHILDRENS sayings. See Children—Sayings
CHILDREN'S services division, American library association. See American library association—Children's services division
CHILDRENS squabbles. See Quarrels
CHILDRENS stories

Technique
See Childrens literature—Technique
CHILDRENS success. See Success
CHILDRENS theater. See Theater, Childrens
CHILDRENS thinking. See Thought and thinking
CHILDRENS villages
Kinderdorf kids and their professional mothers. W. Langewiesche. Read Digest 89:123-6 D '66
CHILDRENS zoo. See New York zoological park—Childrens zoo
CHILDRENS zoos. See Zoological gardens
CHILDRESS, Charles C. and Sacktor, Bertram
Pyruvate oxidation and the permeability of mitochondria from blowfly flight muscle. bibliog Science 154:268-70 O 14 '66
CHILDRESS, William
Dreamer; poem. Harper 232:93 Mr '66
For Weldon Kees; poem. Poetry 108:100 My '66
CHILDS, E. B.
One way to bigger, better boats. Motor B 117:86-9+ Ja '66
CHILDS, Marquis W.
Johnson in the big world. New Repub 155:29-30 Jl 16 '66
President and the press secretary. New Repub 155:16-17 S 10 '66
CHILDS, Mary C.
Book fairs and the CBC. bibliog Library J 91:2586-8 My 15 '66
CHILDS, Richard S.
German council-manager form was anti-dictator measure. Am City 81:156+ My '66
CHILE
Word with Amanda Labarca; with excerpts from an interview. J. Villaverde. il Américas 18:32-5 Mr '66
See also
Agriculture—Chile
Copper industry and trade—Chile
Food relief—Chile
Political parties—Chile
Portillo

Air force
Toys or pawns? to buy jet fighters from Britain. Newsweek 68:61 N 7 '66

Boundaries
Two queens to the rescue; Chile and Argentina. Time 88:22 D 30 '66

Description and travel
Travel's picture portfolio. Travel 126:50-5 N '66

Economic conditions
Chile: revolution in liberty. F. G. Gil. Cur Hist 51:291-5 N '66

Foreign relations
See also
Chile—Boundaries
Project Camelot

Industries
See also
Anaconda copper mining company

Moral conditions
See also
Prostitution

Politics and government
Belated triumph. il Time 88:42 N 4 '66
Chile: revolution in liberty. F. G. Gil. Cur Hist 51:291-5 N '66
Frei v. FRAP. il Time 87:31 Mr 25 '66
Man with a plan. il Newsweek 68:68 O 24 '66
Toys or pawns? to buy jet fighters from Britain. Newsweek 68:61 N 7 '66
See also
Political parties—Chile

CHILEAN Patagonia. See Patagonia
CHILEAN poetry
Day with Pablo Neruda. S. Rodman. Sat R 49:16-18 Jl 9 '66

Translations into English
Ode to my socks; Funeral in the East, tr. by R. Bly. Nation 203:53-4 Jl 11 '66
CHILMAN, Catherine
We take to the woods. Parents Mag 41:56-8+ Je '66
CHILTON, W. S. See Johnson, J. L. jt. auth.
CHIMPANZEES
Are chimps really animals? D. Cohen. il Sci Digest 59:58-64 F '66
Chimps that may learn to talk. il Sci Digest 59:9-11 My '66
End of the chimpanzee? use as laboratory animals. Nat Parks Mag 40:22 O '66
Seroprimatology of chimpanzees: blood-group distribution as a racial characteristic. J. Moor-Jankowski and others. bibliog il Science 152:219-20 Ap 8 '66
CHIMPANZEES as artists. See Animals as artists
CHIN, L. See Sussman, M. V. jt. auth.
CHINA
See also
Arts and crafts—China
Communism—China
Mongolia
Prisoners of war in China
Taiwan

Antiquities
Han army spectacularly unearthed in mainland China. H. N. Ho. il Art N 65:36-7 Sum '66

Geography
Mainland China: geographic strengths and weaknesses. G. E. Pearcy. il Dept State Bul 55:294-303 Ag 29 '66

History
China (is; is not) an aggressive power; debate. F. N. Trager; H. J. Morgenthau. il N Y Times Mag p28-9+ Mr 13 '66; Reply with rejoinder. K. A. Dahl. p6+ Ap 10 '66
Conflicts of China; address, December 7, 1965. M. L. Chiang. Vital Speeches 32:197-9 Ja 15 '66
Crippled tree, by H. Suyin. Review Nation 202:303-4 Mr 14 '66. E. Snow
Dynasty died and revolution swept China. il Life 61:86-101 S 30 '66
Nation imprisoned by her history. J. K. Fairbank. il Life 61:74-82+ S 23 '66
100 violent years. il Life 61:61-3 S 23 '66
Origin of the Chinese revolution. C. P. Fitz-Gerald. Cur Hist 51:129-33+ S '66
Understanding the Chinese; address, August 26, 1966. W. J. Richardson. Vital Speeches 32:717-21 S 15 '66
War that turned China into Mao's prize; with report by S. Leavitt. il Life 61:78-90B+ O 7 '66

War of 1840-1842
Opening wedge: wars for opium and privilege. il Life 61:64-5 S 23 '66

Boxer uprising, 1900
Boxer uprising: inside the besieged legations. il Life 61:66-73 S 23 '66

Civil war, 1945-
Civil war joined again as Japan capitulates; with report by S. Leavitt. il Life 61:89-90B+ O 7 '66

Religious institutions and affairs
See also
Catholic church in China
Christians in China

Social history
People's middle kingdom. J. K. Fairbank. For Affairs 44:574-86 Jl '66
CHINA (People's Republic)
Apotheosis of Mao Tse-tung; anniversary of the Communist take-over. il Newsweek 68:53 O 10 '66
China conference; the dragon: myths and realities. S. Spector and J. H. Moore. Nation 202:256-60 Mr 7 '66
China, 1966; symposium. bibliog f il Cur Hist 51:129-71+ S '66
China, through a glass darkly; science of China watching. il Bsns W p60-2+ Ap 23 '66
China today; symposium. il Bul Atomic Sci 22:2-90+ Je '66; Discussion. 22:24-5 N '66

CHINA (People's Republic)—*Continued*
Covering the Red guards; reporting by D. Oancia of the Toronto globe and mail. Newsweek 69:101 Ja 23 '67
Reporter at large; findings of the China watchers or Pekinologists in Hong Kong. R. Shaplen. New Yorker 41:41-2+ F 12 '66
Riboud's camera covers China. M. R. Weiss. il Sat R 49:89-91 D 10 '66
Sun god's anniversary; 17th anniversary of the founding of red China. Time 88:42 O 7 '66
Unchanged China; its rare splendours. il Vogue 148:230-5 D '66
War fever. Newsweek 68:50 N 14 '66
What the U.S. knows about red China; Time essay. il Time 87:34-5 My 20 '66
See also
Agricultural administration—China (People's Republic)
Agriculture—China (People's Republic)
Air travel—China (People's Republic)
Airlines—China (People's Republic)
Astronomical observatories—China (People's Republic)
Atomic research—China (People's Republic)
Communism—China (People's Republic)
Communist party (China [People's Republic])
Education—China (People's Republic)
Foreign visitors in China
Investments, Foreign (in China)
Labor and laboring classes—China (People's Republic)
Land tenure—China (People's Republic)
Macao
Medical service—China (People's Republic)
Medicine—China (People's Republic)
Newspapers—China (People's Republic)
Petroleum—China (People's Republic)
Prisoners—China (People's Republic)
Public opinion—China (People's Republic)
Research—China (People's Republic)
Science—China (People's Republic)
Sinkiang province
Steel industry and trade—China (People's Republic)
United Nations—China (People's Republic)
Youth movement—China (People's Republic)

Armed forces
Atlantic report: red China's army. Atlan 218:24+ Jl '66
China: dangers of misunderstanding. il Newsweek 67:35-8+ Mr 7 '66
Military affairs of Communist China. R. L. Powell. bibliog f Cur Hist 51:140-6+ S '66
Soviet critique of China's total strategy. R. L. Garthoff. Reporter 34:48-9 My 19 '66

Army
Hidden battle for power in red China. B. Zorza. il Look 30:25-8 Ag 23 '66
Just how dangerous is red China? interview, ed. by K. M. Chrysler. M. Esaki. il U S News 61:84-6 O 24 '66
Nude on the basketball court, and other Chinese stories; excerpts from Red Chinese army documents published by Stanford university's Hoover institution on war, revolution and peace. Time 87:29 Ap 1 '66
Politics of the Chinese red army. ed. by J. C. Cheng. Review
Sat R 49:92 My 7 '66. W. Hangen

Bibliography
Great questions about China. G. Feifer. Harper 233:93-5 Ag '66
Knowing the unknowable. Newsweek 67:37 Mr 7 '66
Reader's guide to publications on China. A. Gundersheim. Bul Atomic Sci 22:88-90+ Je '66

Boundaries
Bordering on madness; Russia and China. il Time 88:38 D 2 '66
Chinese-Soviet gap widens. H. Portisch. il Sat R 49:8-12 Jl 2 '66
Sino-Soviet border comrades up in arms. il Sr Schol 88:14-16 Mr 18 '66

Commerce
China goes west for steel mill; West Germany to build steel-finishing complex. il Bsns W p 105-6 Mr 26 '66
China traders thrive again; Westerners getting more of the business. il Bsns W p80-4+ S 24 '66

Commercial treaties and agreements
Busy boats to China; increase in deals with West; U.S. reaction. il Time 87:84 Ap 1 '66
Two Germanys and two Chinas; background to steel-processing agreement with China. J. E. Smith. il Reporter 34:36-8 My 19 '66

Culture, Popular
See China (People's Republic)—Popular culture

Defenses
Atlantic report: red China's army. Atlan 218:24+ Jl '66
China's nuclear puzzle. Bsns W p32 Ja 7 '67
How vulnerable is red China? il U S News 60:38-41 F 14 '66
Military affairs of Communist China. R. L. Powell. bibliog f Cur Hist 51:140-6+ S '66
Red China in the nuclear race; excerpts from testimony, January 25, 1966. R. S. McNamara. U S News 60:8 F 7 '66
War with China? New Repub 154:7-8 Ja 29 '66

Description and travel
Eyewitness in red China; excerpt from Red China today. H. Portisch. il Sat R 49:14-21+ Ap 30 '66; Reply with rejoinder. H. L. Keenleyside. 49:31 Je 4 '66
Journey through China. F. Sully. il Newsweek 67:54-8 Je 13 '66
Reporter at large. H. Koningsberger. New Yorker 42:57-8+ Ap 23; 87-8+ Ap 30 '66
Through darkest red China. A. R. Topping. il N Y Times Mag p26-7+ Ag 28 '66

Diplomatic and consular service
Diplomatic corpse; death of Hsu Tzu-tsai in The Hague. Time 88:31 Ag 5 '66
Diplomats in tunics; effect of Great proletarian cultural revolution on China's embassies abroad. Time 88:43-4 O 14 '66
Mystery of the locked legation: who killed Mr Hsu? R. Chelminski. il Life 61:30B Ag 19 '66

Economic conditions
Communist China's economic growth and foreign trade, by A. Eckstein. Review
Sat R 49:27+ Je 25 '66. O. Gass
Economic realities; excerpts from address, March 12, 1966. R. F. Dernberger. Bul Atomic Sci 22:6-10 Je '66
New look at red China, an authoritative size-up; interview, ed. by K. M. Chrysler. L. La Dany. il U S News 60:56-8 F 28 '66
Rice bowl blues; forecast by Economist of Britain. Newsweek 68:77 S 5 '66
Truth about red China; how much of a threat? il U S News 61:40-3 Jl 4 '66
With or without Soviet aid, a China still bogged down. il Life 60:32-3 Ap 8 '66

Economic policy
Central economic control; excerpts from China's economic system. A. Donnithorne. Bul Atomic Sci 22:11-20 Je '66
Developing economy. J. S. Duncan. il Bul Atomic Sci 22:84-7+ Je '66
Technology in China. G. Uchida. il Sci Am 215:37-45 N '66
Third five-year plan: an economic dilemma. Y. L. Wu. bibliog f Cur Hist 51:159-64 S '66

Economic relations
Communist China's economic growth and foreign trade, by A. Eckstein. Review
Sat R 49:27+ Je 25 '66. O. Gass
Steel and jasmine tea; proposed sale, by a European consortium of a steel plant to red China. il Fortune 73:73-4+ Je '66

Foreign opinion
Alone at last. il Newsweek 68:45-6 O 3 '66
Appalling & alone. Time 88:28 S 30 '66
China: a vast and ominous tumult. il Newsweek 69:40-2 Ja 23 '67
Visit to a fourth of mankind. K. Buchanan. il Nation 203:302-6 O 3 '66
Why the Red guards? explanations of the Chinese crisis. V. Zorza. New Repub 155:14-15 O 8 '66
Russian
Russia da. China nyet. G. Feifer. il N Y Times Mag p47+ D 4 '66

Foreign policy
Lin Piao on the people's war; excerpts from article. P. Lin. Cur Hist 51:172-4+ S '66

Foreign relations
Between goals and dogma: an opening for diplomacy. I. K. Chou. Nation 203:311-15 O 3 '66
China (is; is not) an aggressive power; debate. F. N. Trager; H. J. Morgenthau. il N Y Times Mag p28-9+ Mr 13 '66; Reply with rejoinder. R. A. Dahl. p6+ Ap 10 '66
China's crisis of foreign policy. D. S. Zagoria. il N Y Times Mag p22-3+ My 1 '66

CHINA (People's Republic)—Foreign relations
—*Continued*
Chinese visions & American policies. B. Schwartz. Commentary 41:53-9 Ap '66
Criminal act; Communist rift. Sr Schol 88:13 Mr 4 '66
Directions of foreign policy. C. P. Fitzgerald. Bul Atomic Sci 22:65-70 Je '66
Four against the red China lobby; symposium; ed. with introd. by T. Lit. il Nat R 18:513-28 My 31 '66; Correction. 18:598+ Je 28 '66
Frustrated & alone. il Time 87:30 F 25 '66
Hanoi's feuding friends. M. Omori. New Repub 155:9-10 O 15 '66
How dangerous is red China? the emerging answers. il U S News 60:29-31 Ap 4 '66
How firmness in Vietnam is paying off; interview. W. E. Griffith. Read Digest 88: 112-16 Ap '66
How vulnerable is red China? il U S News 60:38-41 F 14 '66
Moscow to Peking: you're one, too; Mao Tse-tung's Great cultural revolution program. il Newsweek 68:29 S 12 '66
New look at red China, an authoritative size-up; interview, ed. by K. M. Chrysler. L. La Dany. il U S News 60:56-8 F 28 '66
Once more the yellow peril. C. P. Fitzgerald. il Nation 202:606-9 My 23 '66
Orient: a problem of nonexistence; attitudes toward two Chinas. W. J. Thorbecke. Sat R 49:38-9 Mr 26 '66
Quid without the quo; influence diminishing. il Time 87:23 Mr 11 '66
Red China's plan to conquer the world; excerpts from document. P. Lin. il Nations Bsns 54:40-1 Ja '66
Truth about red China; how much of a threat? il U S News 61:40-3 Jl 4 '66
Vietnam: the war is worth winning. H. Donovan. il Life 60:27-31 F 25 '66
What's really going on inside China; with interviews with H. Portisch and L. Stucki. il U S News 61:48-56 S 12 '66
Who's afraid of China? A. Campbell. New Repub 154:12-16 Ap 9 '66
See also
China (People's Republic)—Boundaries

Africa
Peking's stake in Africa; battleground in ideological war against the USSR. P. Lessing. Nat R 18:262-4 Mr 22 '66
Red China's footholds in Africa; map. U S News 61:99 D 12 '66

Asia
China poses a new test; challenges Johnson pledge to protect countries of Asia. il Bsns W p39-41 N 5 '66
China's Asian policy. W. Levi. il Cur Hist 51:153-8 S '66
Containing China: a round-table discussion; ed. by N. Podhoretz. Commentary 41:23-41 My '66; Discussion. 42:17-18 Ag; 28+ S '66
Dissent from the dissenters; why the U.S. is in Vietnam. A. de Borchgrave. Newsweek 67:32-3 Je 6 '66

Japan
Mutual attraction. il Newsweek 68:49 N 14 '66

Pakistan
Collectors of a debt; Liu Shao-chi and Chen Yi visit. Time 87:28 Ap 1 '66

Rumania
Another flop; Chou En-lai visit. il Newsweek 68:43 Jl 4 '66

Russia
Breakthrough in R.S.V.P.ism; Chinese reply to the Russians' invitation to attend Soviet congress. L. Wainwright. Life 60:25 Ap 8 '66
Chinese-Soviet gap widens. H. Portisch. il Sat R 49:8-12 Jl 2 '66
Chinese threat seen focused on Soviets. C. Brownlow. Aviation W 85:29 N 14 '66
Dirty deal; Chinese boycott of the 23rd congress of the Soviet Communist party. il Sr Schol 88:13 Ap 22 '66
Fight of the tigers; concerning letter of Chinese central committee to Russians. Time 87:28 Ap 1 '66
How communism split: communism divided, or multiplied? Sr Schol 89:9-10 N 11 '66
Moscow-Peiping feud: rift grows wider. U S News 60:6 Ap 4 '66
Profile of the Sino-Soviet split. il Sr Schol 89:pt2 5-6 S 23 '66
Red romance that went sour; with reports. il Life 60:26-35 Ap 8 '66

Russia vs. China: the end of revolutionary communism; interview. M. Garder. U S News 61:50 N 7 '66
Sino-Soviet conflict. K. L. London. bibliog f Cur Hist 51:206-12+ O '66
Sino-Soviet rift; compilation of world reaction to dispute. Sr Schol 88:24 Ap 15 '66

Thailand
Next on Peking's hit parade? S. Topping. il N Y Times Mag p30-1+ F 20 '66
Thailand: the anatomy of a domino. il Newsweek 67:35-6+ Ja 31 '66

United States
American dealings with Peking. K. T. Young. For Affairs 45:77-87 O '66
China and Vietnam. R. Terrill. New Repub 155:16-20 O 29 '66
China: dangers of misunderstanding. il Newsweek 67:35-8+ Mr 7 '66
Our war with red China; symposium. il Nat R 18:204-9 Mr 8 '66
Sino-American confrontation: Communist Chinese perspectives. I. C. Ojha. bibliog f Cur Hist 51:147-52+ S '66
Two Chinas: Americans are ready for a new policy. H. S. Reuss. Commonweal 84:251-4 My 20 '66
U.S. starts rethinking policies on red China. Bsns W p41 Mr 12 '66
When the U.S. negotiates with Peiping, in Warsaw; interview, ed. by R. A. Haeger. J. A. Gronouski, jr. il U S News 61:44-6 Jl 4 '66
Why Peking casts us as the villain. J. K. Fairbank. il N Y Times Mag p30-1+ My 22 '66

History
War that turned China into Mao's prize; with report by S. Leavitt. il Life 61:78-90B+ O 7 '66

Industries
See also
Investments, Foreign (in China)
Munitions industries—China (People's Republic)

Intellectual life
Atlantic report: purge in China. Atlan 218: 26+ D '66
China: behind the unheaval. H. Portisch. il Sat R 49:24-9+ D 10 '66
See also
China (People's Republic)—Popular culture

Politics and government
Alone at last. il Newsweek 68:45-6 O 3 '66
Another leap? Time 88:22+ Ag 12 '66
Back to the cave! il Time 88:28-32 S 9 '66; Same abr. with title Red guard: nightmare in the streets. Read Digest 89:196+ D '66
Central economic control; excerpts from China's economic system. A. Donnithorne. Bul Atomic Sci 22:11-20 Je '66
China: a vast and ominous tumult. il Newsweek 69:40-2 Ja 23 '67
China in context. L. W. Pye. For Affairs 45:229-45 Ja '67
China leaps: where? R. S. Elegant. il Reporter 35:35-9 S 22 '66
China: sparks of revolt. il Newsweek 69:40+ Ja 16 '67
China: two views & a proposal. K. Buchanan; R. S. Elegant; I. K. Chou. il Nation 203: 302-15 O 3 '66
Chinese Communist frenzy; address, August 23, 1966. S. K. Chow. Vital Speeches 32:760-4 O 1 '66
Communist China. . .; after Mao what? il Sr Schol 88:12-14 F 4 '66
Culture riots: Mao at bay. I. Deutscher. Nation 203:442-5 O 31 '66
Dance of the scorpion. il Time 89:20-3 Ja 13 '67
Dear comrade; Lin Piao. il Time 88:16 Ag 26 '66
Drums in the night; blast at opponents of Mao. Newsweek 68:37 D 26 '66
Frustrated & alone. il Time 87:30 F 25 '66
Handwriting on the wall; purge by poster and partisan propagandizing. il Time 89:24 Ja 6 '67
Hanoi's feuding friends. M. Omori. New Repub 155:9-10 O 15 '66
Hidden battle for power in red China. V. Zorza. il Look 30:25-8 Ag 23 '66
Internal politics since 1956; excerpt from New communism. J. R. Townsend. Bul Atomic Sci 22:58-65 Je '66
Little disorder. il Time 88:26 Ag 19 '66
Mao's closest comrade: Lin. il Newsweek 68: 26+ Ag 29 '66

CHLORAMPHENICOL
  Chloramphenicol-specific antibody. R. N. Hamburger. bibliog il Science 152:203-4 Ap 8 '66

CHLORELLA. See Algae

CHLORIDES
  d-Tubocurarine chloride: effect on insects. J. R. Larsen and others. bibliog il Science 152:225-6 Ap 8 '66

CHLORINE, Liquid
  Saving a city from a cloud of death; salvaging lost chlorine barge. T. Irwin. il Pop Sci 188:108-11+ Ap '66

CHLOROPHENYL ethane. See Ethane

CHLOROPHYL
  See also
  Chloroplasts

CHLOROPLASTS
  Chloroplast DNA from tobacco leaves. K. K. Tewari and S. G. Wildman. bibliog il Science 153:1269-71 S 9 '66
  Replication of chloroplast DNA of tobacco. B. R. Green and M. P. Gordon. bibliog il Science 152:1071-4 My 20 '66

CHLOROQUINE
  Chloroquine: mode of action. J. Ciak and F. E. Hahn. bibliog il Science 151:347-9 Ja 21 '66
  Chloroquine: physiological basis of drug resistance in plasmodium berghei. P. B. Macomber and others. bibliog il Science 152:1374-5 Je 3 '66

CHLORPROMAZINE
  Tranquilizer affects eyes. P. McBroom. Sci N 89:235 Ap 9 '66

CHOATE, Joseph E.
  Facts and figures. Yachting 119:60+ Ja '66

CHOATE, Pearl
  Case of the missing millionaire. J. Phelan. il pors Sat Eve Post 239:85-91 D 17 '66

CHOCOLATE
  See also
  Cookery—Chocolate

CHOCOLATE desserts. See Desserts

CHOCOLATES. See Candy

CHODOROV, Jerome
  Three bags full; adaptation of play by C. Magnier. Criticism
  America 114:453 Ap 2 '66
  New Yorker 42:160 Mr 19 '66
  Newsweek 67:97 Mr 21 '66
  Time il 87:80 Mr 18 '66
  Vogue 147:145 My '66

CHOICE of college. See College. Choice of

CHOICE of occupation. See Occupations

CHOIRS
  See also
  Church music
  Collegiate chorale

CHOKE coils. See Electric reactors

CHOLERA
  Experimental cholera produced in man. Sci N L 89:89 F 5 '66
  Fight against cholera continues abroad; excerpts from article. Todays Health 44:43 O '66
  When cholera struck America. B. Hildenbrand. il Todays Health 44:40-2 O '66

CHOLERA, Hog. See Hog cholera

CHOLESTEROL
  Common-sense guide to cholesterol; interview. A. Grollman. Todays Health 44:3+ Ag '66
  Myotonic response induced by inhibitors of cholesterol biosynthesis. N. Winer and others. bibliog il Science 153:312-13 Jl 15 '66
  N-cyclohexyl linoleamide: metabolism and cholesterol-lowering effects in rats. H. Nakatani and others. bibliog il Science 153:1267-9 S 9 '66

CHOLINE
  Anticholinergic blockade of centrally induced thirst. R. A. Levitt and A. E. Fisher. bibliog il Science 154:520-2 O 28 '66

CHOLINESTERASE
  Ascending and descending cholinergic fibers in cat spinal cord: histochemical evidence. D. G. Gwyn and J. H. Wolstencroft. bibliog il Science 153:1543-4 S 23 '66
  Dealkylation and loss of capacity for reactivation of cholinesterase inhibited by sarin. L. W. Harris and others. bibliog il Science 154:404-7 O 21 '66

CHOLON, Vietnam (Republic)
  Cracks in the great wall. il Time 87:37-8 My 20 '66

CHON, Hyangju P. See Weaver, E. C. jt. auth.

CHONDRITES. See Meteorites

CHONDROCOCCUS columnaris. See Bacteria, Pathogenic

CHONDRULES
  Chondrules: suggestion concerning the origin. F. L. Whipple. bibliog il Science 153:54-6 Jl 1 '66
  Lightning seen as cause of puzzling chondrules. Sci N 90:39 Jl 16 '66
  Origin of chondrules. G. S. Mumford. Sky & Tel 32:27 Jl '66

CHOPIN, Frédéric François
  Absolutely hypnotic Chopin; recital by Jeanne-Marie Darré. S. Sell. Am Rec G 32:710 Ap '66
  Connoisseur society edition of Chopin's Nocturnes by Ivan Moravec. S. Sell. Am Rec G 32:954-5 Je '66
  For Chopin, the voices of poets; nocturnes played by I. Moravec and T. Vásáry. H. Goldsmith. il Hi Fi 16:85 S '66
  Frédéric Chopin: poet of the piano. C. W. Van Ausdall. il por Read Digest 89:269-72+ O '66
  Magnificent: Piatigorsky and Firskusny. A. Cohn. Am Rec G 32:1132 Ag '66

CHOPIN, Kate (O'Flaherty)
  American 1890s, by L. Ziff. Review
  New Repub 155:22+ D 3 '66. S. Kauffmann

CHOPPING blocks
  We raised our cutting board. il Sunset 138:81 Ja '67

CHORAL music
  See also
  Church music
  Phonograph records—Choral music

CHORAL societies
  See also
  Collegiate chorale

CHORDOTOMY. See Spinal cord—Surgery

CHOREOGRAPHY
  Alwin in wonderland: creations of A. Nikolais. il Time 87:86 My 20 '66
  Alwin Nikolais' Vaudeville of the elements. Henry street playhouse. J. Maskey. il Dance Mag 40:33+ Je '66
  Anna Sokolow in Japan. E. Stodelle. il Dance Mag 41:40-2+ Ja '67
  Bolshoi portfolio; four productions; four lively controversies. J. Anderson. il Dance Mag 40:44-51 Je '66
  Choreography and computers; with reply by A. Hutchinson. A. M. Noll. il Dance Mag 41:43-6+ Ja '67
  Choreography by Gretchen MacLane, Constance Sullivan, James Waring, Deborah Lee; Judson memorial church. J. Anderson. Dance Mag 40:65-6 Jl '66
  Collegiate parnassus; the joys and sorrows of the artist-in-residence. I. Fisher. il Dance Mag 40:45-8+ Mr '66
  Eighth new choreographers concert. Clark center for the performing arts. M. Marks. Dance Mag 40:32+ My '66
  Eugene Loring talks; ed. by O. Maynard. E. Loring. il Dance Mag 40:35-9 Jl; 52-4+ Ag '66
  For the Jung in heart; R. Nureyev's Tancredi. il Time 88:56 Jl 1 '66
  George Balanchine at work on a permanent record; Midsummer night's dream. L. Joel. il Dance Mag 40:24-7 Ag '66
  Gloria Contreras dance group, 92nd street Y. M. Marks. Dance Mag 40:60 Mr '66
  Las Vegas scene. W. Como. il Dance Mag 40:14-15 Ag '66
  Lopukhov and his Tanzsymphonia; excerpt from Era of the Russian ballet. N. Roslavlova. Dance Mag 41:72-5 Ja '67
  Ninth new choreographers concert; Clark Center for the performing arts. D. Hering. Dance Mag 41:66-7 Ja '67
  Regional ballet U.S.A: Northeast regional ballet festival association's sixth summer conference on the craft of making ballets. J. Anderson. il Dance Mag 40:49+ O '66
  Rod Alexander: back where he is happy to belong; ed. by V. H. Swisher. R. Alexander. il Dance Mag 41:19-21 Ja '67
  Summerspace story; how a dance came to be. M. Cunningham. il Dance Mag 40:52-4 Je '66
  To thine own self be true; interview. ed. by V. H. Swisher. P. Godkin. il Dance Mag 40:28-9 Ap '66

CHORES, Children. See Occupations for children

CHOROVER, Stephan L. See Schiller, P. H. jt. auth.

CHORUS in opera See Opera—Chorus

CHOSEN one; story. See Davies, R.

CHOU, En-lai
  Affair cools. Newsweek 68:46 Jl 11 '66

CHOU, I-kua
Between goals and dogma: an opening for diplomacy. Nation 203:311-15 O 3 '66
CHOUINARD, Yvon
California: climb beyond the possible. C. S. Wren. il pors Look 30:70-2 Je 28 '66
CHOUTEAU, Yvonne
Giselle comes to the University of Oklahoma. J. Anderson. il pors Dance Mag 40:57-9 N '66
CHOW, Shu-kai
Chinese Communist frenzy; address, August 23, 1966. Vital Speeches 32:760-4 O 1 '66
CHOWDER
Cheering chowder. C. Claiborne. il N Y Times Mag p 112 O 30 '66
CHOWINS, Christopher
Tresco Abbey gardens. Horticulture 44:32-4+ O '66
CHOWNING, Ann
Blowgun hunters of the South Pacific. il pors Nat Geog Mag 129:792-817 Je '66
CHRIS-CRAFT corporation
Rebound in spades. Motor B 119:365+ Ja '67
Styling today's boats: the inside story. il Motor B 118:44-5 S '66
CHRIST. See Jesus Christ
CHRIST-JANER, Albert
In defense of personal expression; with biographical sketch. il por Am Artist 30:38-9+ O '66
CHRIST-JANER, Arland Frederick
Different kind of Methodist for Boston U. il por Time 88:33 D 30 '66
CHRISTAKIS, George J.
Wise woman's diet. Redbook 128:37-43+ Ja '67
CHRISTENING. See Baptism
CHRISTENSEN, J. A.
Making sculptured Christmas figures. Design 68:4-7 N '66
St Trinity's abbey; poem. Cath World 204:31 O '66
CHRISTGAU, Robert
Filmotheques. Pop Phot 60:80+ Ja '67
CHRISTI Matri Rosarii. See Encyclicals
CHRISTIAN, George
Atlantic report: musical chairs. D. Kiker. Atlan 218:10 D '66
CHRISTIAN art and symbolism
Art of anti-Semitism; concerning book called The medieval Jew in the mirror of Christian art. il Time 88:92 D 9 '66
Cover: concerning Peaceable kingdom, painting by E. Hicks. T. Gilliland. il Sat R 49:20 S 3 '66
Jonah & the Shepherd; early Christian statuary at Cleveland museum of art. il Time 88:56-7 S 2 '66
Mephistopheles and the Androgyne, by M. Eliade. Review
  Commonweal 84:315-16 Je 3 '66. W. Arnold
New trends in liturgical art; excerpts from panel discussion at exhibition of Religious arts and crafts sponsored by the Artist-craftsmen of New York. Craft Horiz 26: 34-5+ Ja '66
Raphael's St Jerome punishing Sabinian. C. Gould. bibliog il Art N 65:44-6+ Sum '66
Rubens' sacrifice of Abraham. R. T. Coe. il Art N 65:36-9+ D '66
2000 years of Christian art, by E. Newton and W. Neil. Review
  Christian Cent 83:1577-8 D 21 '66. E. W. Saunders
What is Christian art? J. Dillenberger and J. Dillenberger Christian Cent 83:497-9 Ap 20 '66
  See also
Art and religion
Church architecture
Church vestments
Jesus Christ—Art
Mary, Virgin—Art
Stations of the Cross

Exhibitions
Ecumenical arts; Canadian religious art today II, exhibit at Regis college, Toronto. C. J. McNaspy. America 114:309 F 26 '66
CHRISTIAN booksellers association
CBA meets in Chicago; report of convention. A. Hustwitt. il Pub W 190:34-6 S 5 '66
CHRISTIAN century (periodical)
Apostle in print. Christian Cent 83:323-5 Mr 16 '66; Discussion. 83:592 My 4 '66
Margin for Catholic diversity. Christian Cent 83:389-90 Mr 30 '66
CHRISTIAN character. See Christian life
CHRISTIAN civilization. See Civilization, Christian

CHRISTIAN colleges. See Denominational colleges
CHRISTIAN council of South Africa
Racial good will wins a round in South Africa. Christian Cent 83:1401 N 16 '66
CHRISTIAN democrats (Chile) See Political parties—Chile
CHRISTIAN democrats (Germany) See Political parties—Germany (Federal Republic)
CHRISTIAN democrats (Latin America) See Political parties—Latin America
CHRISTIAN doctrine. See Theology
CHRISTIAN doctrine, Confraternity of. See Confraternity of Christian doctrine
CHRISTIAN education. See Religious education
CHRISTIAN ethics
Christian ethics amid pietistic culture-Protestantism. T. C. Oden. Christian Cent 83:525-6+ Ap 27 '66
Christian ethics and contemporary philosophy, ed. by I. T. Ramsey. Review
  Christian Cent 84:84 Ja 18 '67. W. Horden
Christmas; its meaning to Christian civilization. M. Ascoli. Reporter 35:10-11 D 29 '66
Christmas sermon. A. Waugh. Nat R 18:1312-14+ D 27 '66
Dogmatist in disguise; concerning J. Fletcher's Situation ethics. J. Lachs. Christian Cent 83:1402-5 N 16 '66; Reply. V. L. Weiss. 83:1542 D 14 '66
Ethics and evidence. D. Callahan. Commonweal 85:76-8 O 21 '66; Reply. D. P. Johnson. 85:305-6 D 9 '66
Evolution in moral theology. G. H. Tavard. Cath World 203:29-32 Ap '66
Law, love and politics; learning to live with tension. B. Wicker. Commonweal 85:218-21 N 25 '66
Should the code of ethics in public life be absolute or relative? E. C. Blake. Ann Am Acad 363:4-11 Ja '66
Situation ethics, by J. Fletcher. Review
  New Repub 155:22-4 S 3 '66. W. R. Miller
  See also
Church and social problems
Conscience
Guilt
Love (theology)
Social ethics
War and religion
CHRISTIAN humanism. See Humanism
CHRISTIAN life
Eternity here and now. J. Moorhead. PTA Mag 60:2-3 Ap '66
Man in the pew. C. S. Calian. Cath World 204:170-3 D '66
Memories make the future. J. J. Navone. Cath World 204:149-53 D '66
Sunday moralizing. V. P. McCorry. America 115:435 O 8 '66
Theology of poverty. A. T. Padovano. Cath World 204:19-24 Ja '67
  See also
Piety
Prayer
CHRISTIAN love. See Love (theology)
CHRISTIAN martyrs. See Martyrs
CHRISTIAN names. See Names, Personal
CHRISTIAN peace conference, Germany. See Peace conferences
CHRISTIAN rural overseas program
Building with beans; food-for-work projects in Latin America. G. Meek. il Américas 18:35-8 Jl '66
CHRISTIAN Science
Christian Science at 100. il Newsweek 67:74 Je 20 '66
Mary Baker Eddy: the years of discovery, by R. Peel. Review
  Christian Cent 83:1473-4 N 30 '66. C. S. Braden
CHRISTIAN Science monitor (newspaper)
Monitoring the Monitor; concerning ad titled Economic giant of Africa, in the Christian Science monitor. J. C. Evans. Christian Cent 83:796 Je 22 '66
CHRISTIAN sociology. See Sociology, Christian
CHRISTIAN unity. See Church unity
CHRISTIANITY
Absolute future. M. Novak. Commonweal 85:400-2 Ja 13 '67
Black power and the American Christ. V. Harding. Christian Cent 84:10-13 Ja 4 '67
Dialogue: Christ and Marx. il Newsweek 69:74+ Ja 16 '67
Oh, Henry! concerning editorial in Christianity today. J. R. Nelson. Christian Cent 83:295 Mr 9 '66
Radical theology and the death of God, by T. J. J. Altizer and W. Hamilton. Review
  Christian Cent 83:622-4 My 11 '66. F. Ferré

CHRISTIANITY—*Continued*

Sell-out or the well acculturated Christian. R. E. Fitch. Christian Cent 83:202-5 F 16 '66; Discussion. 83:370-2 Mr 23 '66

Two kinds of humanism; Christian-atheist dialogues. il Time 88:42-3 D 30 '66
> *See also*
> Bible
> Catholic church
> Christian ethics
> Civilization, Christian
> Jesus Christ
> Paul, Saint—Teaching
> Religion and science
> Theology

CHRISTIANITY, Primitive. See Church history —Primitive and early church

CHRISTIANITY and communism. See Catholic church and communism; Communism and religion

CHRISTIANITY and crisis (periodical)

Christian realism. il Newsweek 67:61 F 28 '66

Christianity & crisis. Commonweal 83:652-3 Mr 11 '66

Christianity and crisis: irony at twenty-five. V. Harding. Christiain Cent 83:408+ Mr 30 '66

Crisis continues; 25th anniversary. il Time 87:56 F 25 '66

CHRISTIANITY and economics

Converting life into living; Iowa state university conference on alternatives for balancing future world food production and needs. K. Haselden. Christian Cent 83:1435-6 N 23 '66

Lutherans support minimum income. America 115:52-3 Jl 16 '66

Moral right & economic might; churches use of economic power to further ethical goals. Time 89:60 Ja 6 '67
> *See also*
> Sociology, Christian

CHRISTIANITY and international affairs. See Church and international relations

CHRISTIANITY and other religions

Christian beliefs and anti-Semitism, by C. Y. Glock and R. Stark. Review
> Commonweal 84:558-9 S 2 '66. P. H. Furfey
> Sat R 49:27 Ag 20 '66. D. S. Harrington

Christians and Jews: encounter and mission by J. Jocz. Review
> Christian Cent 84:84 Ja 18 '67. A. R. Eckdart

Dialogue with Christians; questions among Jews. il Time 87:60 Ap 22 '66

End to the Christian-Jewish dialogue. A. R. Eckardt. Christian Cent 83:360-3, 393-5 Mr 23-30 '66; Reply. R. C. Holtzapple, jr. 83:718 Je 1 '66

Gospels and anti-Semitism; excerpt from A Jew in Christian America. A. Gilbert. Cath World 203:157-60 Je '66

Is Christianity really different? R. C. Davids. Farm J 90:69 D '66

Jew in Christian America, by A. Gilbert. Review
> Cath World 203:369 S '66. W. B. Ball

On reading Matthew; question of a Judeo-Christian tradition. M. Himmelfarb; discussion. Commentary 41:12+ Mr '66

Road between Rome and Jerusalem. S. Sandmel. Sat R 49:42-3 D 3 '66

Speaking out; don't try to sell me your religion. H. Singer. il Sat Eve Post 240:10+ Ja 28 '67

Star and the cross, ed. by Mother K. Hargrove. Review
> Commentary 42:133-5 O '66. D. Daiches

Studies in Jewish-Christian relations, ed. by K. T. Hargrove. Review
> Cath World 203:243-4 Jl '66

CHRISTIANITY and politics. See Church and politics

CHRISTIANITY and psychiatry. See Psychiatry and religion

CHRISTIANITY and science. See Religion and science

CHRISTIANITY and social problems. See Church and social problems

CHRISTIANITY and war. See War and religion

CHRISTIANS

Brothers but not identical twins; American Christians and Jews. Christian Cent 83:641 My 18 '66

Honoring God's heroes; Hall of fame unveiled at Canton, Ohio. Newsweek 67:69 Ap 18 '66

Mandate for white Christians, by K. Haselden. Review
> Christian Cent 83:1448 N 23 '66. J. M. Dabbs

Paul, apostle for our times; excerpt from Christian in the marketplace. K. Rahner. Cath World 203:331-4 S '66

Persecution
> *See* Persecution

CHRISTIANS in Africa

Challenge in Africa; Kaunda's criticism. America 115:311 S 24 '66

Laughter in Parliament; concerning death of Verwoerd. America 115:315 S 24 '66

CHRISTIANS in Asia
> *See also*
> Eastern Asia Christian conference

CHRISTIANS in China

Canadian look at the church in China. H. G. Green. Christian Cent 83:1038-40 Ag 24 '66
> *See also*
> Catholic church in China

CHRISTIANS in Germany

Church and communism in East Germany. M. Barth. Christian Cent 83:1440-3, 1469-72 N 23-30 '66

CHRISTIANS in Ghana

How Ghana's churches failed their testing. K. E. Ankrah. Christian Cent 84:25-7 Ja 4 '67

CHRISTIANS in India

Christian witness amid Indian turmoil. H. Schomer. Christian Cent 84:38-9 Ja 11 '67

Indian Christians demand atom bomb. Christian Cent 83:1024 Ag 24 '66

CHRISTIANS in Israel

Christians in the Holy Land. America 115:3 Jl 2 '66

CHRISTIANS in Rhodesia

White Rhodesian Christians denounce secession; Christian council of Rhodesia and the Roman Catholic bishops of Rhodesia. Christian Cent 83:198 F 16 '66

CHRISTIANS united for social action

Operation Brownsville; the poor on their own. J. Judge. Commonweal 84:193-4 My 6 '66

CHRISTIE, Agatha

Agatha Christie on mystery fiction; interview, ed. by F. Wyndham. Writer 79:27-8 Ag '66

At Bertram's hotel; story, excerpt from novel. Good H 162:87-9 Mr; 92-3 Ap '66

Mallowans; interview. New Yorker 42:51-2 O 29 '66

CHRISTIE, George A.

Current trends in construction (title varies) See issues of Architectural record

Urban building; hotels vs. offices. Arch Rec 140:44 Ag '66

CHRISTIE, John

Wrong man. Time 88:41 O 28 '66

CHRISTIE, Julie

Julie Christie talks about mates and morals; interview, ed. by P. Mortimer. por Ladies Home J 83:88+ Je '66

Lively arts; interview; ed. by M. Ronan. por Sr Schol 89:30-1 S 30 '66

Style and verve of an antigoddess; interview, ed. by N. Liber. pors Life 60:61-4+ Ap 29 '66

Success can feel like a razor's edge; ed. by E. Miller. pors Seventeen 25:104-5+ Jl '66

about

Beauty life. por Mlle 62:138-9 Mr '66

Julie Christie: a face made for film. B. Glanville. por Holiday 40:95-6+ S '66

Julie Christie: new international darling. J. Hamilton. il pors Look 30:93-8 Mr 8 '66

People are talking about . . . por Vogue 147:138-9 F 1 '66

CHRISTIE, Trevor L.

Lost city of the Sybarites. Sat R 49:52-3 Mr 19 '66

SR/1967 world travel calendar. Sat R 50:77-82 Ja 7 '67

CHRISTIE'S (art dealers) See Art dealers

CHRISTINA, queen of Sweden

Bachelor queen. il por Time 88:66-7 Ag 5 '66

Christina of Sweden, by S. Stolpe. Review
> Sat R por 49:29-30 Jl 16 '66. A. Gustafson

Fit for a queen; art collection on view at Stockholm's National museum of fine arts. il por Newsweek 68:79 Ag 1 '66

Our far-flung correspondents; exhibition at Nationalmuseum, Stockholm. F. Steegmuller. il New Yorker 42:160+ S 17 '66

Queen Christina of Sweden; exhibition of her treasures. J. Stuart. il por Antiques 90:164+ Ag '66

World of Queen Christina. F. Getlein. New Repub 155:33-4 Ag 13 '66

CHRISTINE, Emma Ruth

School library extension service: real or imagined? por ALA Bul 60:623-6 Je '66

Why not listen to the librarian? ALA Bul 59:1010-11; 60:211 D '65, Mr '66

CHRISTMAS

Black Christmas; holiday season in U.S. magazines. il Time 88:44 D 23 '66

Challenge of Christmas. America 115:818 D 24 '66

Christmas away from home. A. Waugh. Nat R 18:1326 D 27 '66

Christmas; its meaning to Christian civilization. M. Ascoli. Reporter 35:10-11 D 29 '66

Games people play at Christmas. E. Berne. il McCalls 94:82-3+ D '66

How long is Christmas? il House & Gard 130:139 D '66

Mothers keep all these things. M. Holmes. il Todays Health 44:34-6 D '66

My dear children of God. R. J. Cushing. McCalls 94:98-9 D '66

Stockings were hung by the chimney with care; building anticipation with care. L. Conger. Writer 79:9-10 D '66

We are the weavers of memories. J. Moorhead. PTA Mag 61:2-3 D '66

What's right with Christmas; opinions of five unconventional theologians. McCalls 94:56+ D '66

Your Christmas moods. R. Nixon and M. S. Welch. il Seventeen 25:126-7+ D '66

See also
Christmas eve
Jesus Christ—Nativity

Austria

Christmas in Austria; Wagrain. H. Ehrlich. il Look 30:51-6 D 27 '66

England

Christmas at Chatsworth. H. Macmillan. il Horizon 9:84-7 Wint '67

Real Christmas. A. West. House & Gard 130:158-9+ D '66

Great Britain

Wassail and all that bother. J. A. Gridley. Sat R 49:59-60 D 24 '66

Hawaii

Christmas eve in Honolulu; Kawaiahao church. il Sunset 137:31 D '66

India

Christian witness amid Indian turmoil. H. Schomer. Christian Cent 84:38-9 Ja 11 '67

United States

Bah, humbug, Virginia, we don't know; Christmas poses dilemma for the schools. G. Culligan. il Am Ed 3:14-17 D '66

Christmas; holidays or dollardays? pro and con discussion. il Sr Schol 89:22-3 D 9 '66

Christmas horizon. R. H. Viguers. Horn Bk 42:659 D '66

Christmas in the country; symposium. il Farm J 90:71+ D '66

Christmas in the White House. C. B. Luce. McCalls 94:48+ D '66

Christmas in Williamsburg. il Parks & Rec 1:962-3 D '66

Who cares? teens do, says Polly. il Farm J 90:91 D '66

CHRISTMAS boxes

Buckets of love; cardboard paint buckets into gift wraps. il Seventeen 25:114-15 D '66

Gift boxes with an idea! il Bet Hom & Gard 44:64-5 D '66

CHRISTMAS breads. See Bread

CHRISTMAS business

Bookstores plan their Christmas promotion; reduced co-op ad allowances a big problem. il Pub W 190:96-8 Ag 22 '66

Bookstores view the Christmas season; some books that will get major promotion. Pub W 190:50-2 N 28 '66

Christmas trade, 1966: it's good, but. il U S News 61:76-7 D 19 '66

Christmas tune is a bit off key. il Bsns W p33-5 D 3 '66

Getting Christmas help is no problem for many booksellers. Pub W 190:95 Ag 22 '66

Jingle just wasn't quite so loud. il Bsns W p 16-17 D 31 '66

Night openings during Xmas mandatory for most shops. Pub W 190:98 Ag 22 '66

Santa '66: fattest of all. il Newsweek 68:86-8 D 5 '66

Anecdotes, facetiae, satire, etc.

Bookseller's Christmas memory. B. Schweid. Pub W 190:79 D 26 '66; Reply. 191:52 Ja 2 '67

CHRISTMAS cake. See Cake

CHRISTMAS candy. See Candy

CHRISTMAS cards

Christmas card magic. M. Perry. il Flower Grower 53:22-3+ D '66

Doll collectors' Christmas cards. C. H. Fawcett. il Hobbies 71:40 D '66

Unusual Christmas cards by artists. il Am Artist 30:30-5+ D '66

Your personal Christmas cards are simple project. W. Lane. il Travel 126:68 N '66

CHRISTMAS carols

Anecdotes, facetiae, satire, etc.

Heath Christmas carol program. A. B. Heath. Nat R 18:1321-3 D 27 '66

CHRISTMAS clubs

Ho, ho, ho; banks offers. G. Ace. Sat R 49:8 D 3 '66

Making money on Christmas clubs. il Bsns W p78-9 D 24 '66

CHRISTMAS cookery. See Cookery, Ornamental

CHRISTMAS cookies. See Cookies

CHRISTMAS cribs

Crèche in the White House. il Ladies Home J 83:98-9 D '66

Letter from Paris; international exhibition of crèches at Orly airport. Genêt. New Yorker 42:65 D 31 '66

Pasta personae for a crèche. il House & Gard 130:314-17 N '66

CHRISTMAS decorations

Christmas card magic. M. Perry. il Flower Grower 53:22-3+ D '66

Christmas comes full circle; three wreaths. il McCalls 94:108-9 D '66

Christmas dangles; ceramic Christmas tree ornaments. il Seventeen 25:200 N '66

Christmas notions. il Redbook 128:72-3+ D '66

Christmas projects for tabletop decor. il Pop Mech 126:175-8 N '66

Christmas with baubles and birds; papier-mâché ornaments. il Ladies Home J 83:46+ D '66

Christmas with daisies, yarn decorations; with instructions. il Ladies Home J 83:48-9+ D '66

Clay figures in a hanging spiral. il Sunset 137:106+ D '66

Decking the halls with imports; K. S. Adler imports goods with handcrafted touch. il Bsns W p 134-8 D 17 '66

Decorations, country grown. il Farm J 90:86 D '66

Exquisite Christmas decorations with paper. E. Craster. il Bet Hom & Gard 44:70-1 N '66

Floral fantasies in felt. il House & Gard 130:142-5 D '66

For a full and joyful Christmas. E. D. Craster and M. Garrity. il Bet Hom & Gard 44:42-55 D '66

Glistening ornaments you can make with instant papier-mâché. il House & Gard 130:164-5 D '66

Hang these on your tree. il Redbook 128:74-5 D '66

Holiday lights. N. Rothschild. il Pop Phot 60:108-9 Ja '67

Holiday slick tricks. il Farm J 90:85 D '66

How to make the ornaments on our cover. L. Woodard. il Bet Hom & Gard 44:84 D '66

Imaginative glitter and glow. il House & Gard 130:146-9 D '66

It takes patience, but oh boy! wall decoration. il Sunset 137:105 D '66

Look who's hanging in the tree: child's photograph. il Sunset 137:102 D '66

Make a gumdrop tree for Christmas. il Ladies Home J 83:42+ D '66

Making your own straw stars. il Sunset 137:86+ D '66

Merry cut-ups. il Redbook 128:70-1+ D '66

No, you're not dreaming; it's already Christmastime; store decorations. il Time 88:71-2 N 18 '66

Personal masterpiece. il House & Gard 130:140-1 D '66

Search your own garden for holiday arrangement ideas. il Sunset 137:165 D '66

Start with everyday stuff! il Bet Hom & Gard 44:58-61 D '66

Where even Santa gets ideas. M. J. Schultz. il Pop Mech 126:76-9+ D '66

Xmas candies; colorful decorations. il Ebony 22:172+ D '66

Your very own handmade decorations. il Farm J 90:38-9 D '66

Yuletide spool town. il McCalls 94:84-5+ D '66

See also
Christmas greens
Christmas trees

CHRISTMAS decorations, Outdoor

Decorate your yard and home with Walt Disney's Christmas mobile. W. C. Leckey. il Pop Mech 126:69-73+ D '66

Distinctive doorways. il Flower Grower 53:24-7 D '66

How to shoot Christmas lights. R. Arnold. il U S Camera 29:54-5+ D '66

CHRISTMAS desserts. See Desserts

CHRISTMAS entertainments
Chthonian Christmas; symposium. il Esquire 66:196-9+ D '66

CHRISTMAS eve
Christmas eve. V. P. McCorry. America 115: 813-14 D 17 '66

CHRISTMAS eve in pine cone forest; drama. See Watts, F. B.

CHRISTMAS gifts
All of a sudden it's Christmas. Changing T 20:6 N '66
Archer's Christmas. G. H. Gillelan. il Outdoor Life 138:10+ D '66
Best buy gifts (cont) il Consumer Rep 31:530 2 N '66
Catch up with: tickets and books. L. Lerman. Mlle 64:46 D '66
Christmas cheer at $17,000 and under. P. Peterson. il N Y Times Mag p60-1+ D 18 '66
Christmas gift for bird lovers. M. D. Hodgins. il Horticulture 44:36 D '66
Christmas gift game. L. Lerman. il Mlle 64:137-42 N '66
Christmas gift: your instant answers when the family asks what you want. il Seventeen 25:154 D '66
Gift idea: the serious kit. il Sunset 137:95-6+ D '66
Gifts for gardeners; an open letter. il Pop Gard 17:36-7 D '66
Gifts for the people you can't think of what to give. il Seventeen 25:144+ D '66
Gifts from $5 to $5000; suggestions for gardeners. il Flower Grower 53:31+ D '66
Gifts from museums (cont) il Consumer Rep 31:556-8 N '66
Great gift ideas. il Bet Hom & Gard 44: 32+ D '66
Holiday hoard. il Time 88:117-18+ D 9 '66
Holiday world bazaar. il Holiday 40:104-7 N '66
Horoscope for gift-giving. S. Leek. il Ladies Home J 83:61-2 D '66
In Tijuana, shopping for Mexican gifts. il Sunset 137:53 D '66
Last minute! last minute! last minute! L. Lerman. Mlle 64:92-3 D '66
Magic you make with papier-mâché. il Sunset 137:74-8 D '66
101 ideas: what the beautiful people want for Christmas. Vogue 148:188-9+ N 15 '66
Santa '66; fattest of all. il Newsweek 68: 86-8 D 5 '66
Shopping editor's choice for Christmas. M. Vennum. il Bet Hom & Gard 44:143-6+ N '66
Stocking stuffers. il House & Gard 130:322-3 N '66
Sure-to-please Christmas gifts; suggestions for boating people. il Motor B 118:26-32 N '66
Surprises and delights for the Christmas tree. il Esquire 66:230-7 D '66
Sweetest story; with recipes. il McCalls 94: 76-7+ D '66
Treasure trove of gifts to make; relishes and preserves; with recipes. il Ladies Home J 83:78-9+ D '66
See also
Books as gifts
Christmas projects
Wrapping of packages

Anecdotes, facetiae, satire, etc.
Men are like that. C. Ford. il Field & S 71: 12+ Ja '67

CHRISTMAS gifts for children
Children Santa didn't forget after all; cases of seventeen children. H. Markel. il Ladies Home J 83:26+ My '66
Game gifts for young travelers. il Sunset 137:46+ D '66
Gift of personal independence. M. Mead. Redbook 128:26+ D '66
Gifts for the children. il House & Gard 130: 252-3 N '66
Non-cliché gifts for children. il House & Gard 130:24 D '66
On and off the avenue (cont) New Yorker 42:203-4+ D 10 '66
Perfect Christmas gift. A. P. Eliasberg. il N Y Times Mag p 127+ D '66
Wonderful world of play. J. R. Komaiko. il Parents Mag 41:50-3+ D '66
See also
Toys

CHRISTMAS gifts for men
Extra specials. il Seventeen 25:134 D '66
Gift ideas for a sportsman's Christmas. il Outdoor Life 138:106-10 D '66
His for Christmas. il Seventeen 25:92-3 D '66

CHRISTMAS gifts for the home
Chez Mlle: for Christmas chez vous. B. Plumb. il Mlle 64:64-5 N '66
For the home: $25 and under. B. Plumb. il N Y Times Mag p 160-1+ D 11 '66
Gift list for cooks. M. Davidson. il Ladies Home J 83:64+ D '66
Gifts for those important people for whom the sky's the limit! il House & Gard 130: 246-7 N '66
Gifts of such value you'll find it hard to guess the price? il House & Gard 130:249 N '66
Good gifts for the family. il Bet Hom & Gard 44:20+ N '66
Indispensable gadget; for the cook. il Ladies Home J 83:68+ D '66
Mysterious marvels for those who wonder: what is it? il House & Gard 130:248 N '66
Off-beat gifts for on-beat people. il House & Gard 130:20-2 D '66
On and off the avenue (cont) New Yorker 42:165-6+ D 3 '66
On stage for Christmas. il Parents Mag 41: 84-9+ D '66
Seventy-seven unhackneyed delights for under $7. il House & Gard 130:242-5 N '66
This season's in gifts. il House & Gard 130: 250-1 N '66

CHRISTMAS gifts for women
On and off the avenue (cont) New Yorker 42:193-4+ N 26 '66
Yours for Christmas; beauty aids. il Seventeen 25:90-1 D '66

CHRISTMAS greens
Wreaths are traditional. il Horticulture 44: 28-9 D '66
See also
Holly

CHRISTMAS in art
Christmas eve on our street. C. J. Alkema. il Sch Arts 66:12-13 D '66

CHRISTMAS in literature
Turning green; Playboy's and Esquire's Christmas issues. R. A. Schroth. America 115:777 D 10 '66

CHRISTMAS journey; story. See Brown, M. F.

CHRISTMAS legends
Wreath of Christmas legends; medieval legends retold; poems. P. McGinley. il Ladies Home J 83:73-7 D '66

CHRISTMAS letters. See Letters

CHRISTMAS lighting. See Christmas decorations, Outdoor

CHRISTMAS meals
Family Christmas eve supper; with recipes. il Suc Farm 64:50-1+ D '66
Open house; with recipes. il Suc Farm 64: 48-9+ D '66

CHRISTMAS music
Giving the gift of music. F. Bowers. House & Gard 130:32+ D '66
See also
Phonograph records—Christmas music

CHRISTMAS plays
Texts
Christmas eve in pine cone forest. F. B. Watts. Plays 26:75-9 D '66
Long ago in Bethlehem. D. Newman. Plays 26:44-8 D '66
Man in the red suit. B. Messenger. Plays 26:81-7 D '66
Merry Christmas; dramatization of Little women by L. M. Alcott. W. Hackett. Plays 26:88-96 D '66
Puppy love. H. L. Miller. Plays 26:11-20 D '66
Santa calls a conference. H. L. Miller. Plays 26:49-58, 80 D '66
Toys for Santa. O. J. Robertson. Plays 26: 69-71 D '66
Visions of sugar plums. A. C. Martens. Plays 26:33-43 D '66

CHRISTMAS poetry
At Christmas. A. H. Carter. Christian Cent 83:1569 D 21 '66
Christmas is love. J. W. Anglund. il Ladies Home J 83:8 D '66
Christmas lullaby. L. H. Dick. Christian Cent 83:1565 D 21 '66
Christmas pageant. A. Kenseth. Christian Cent 83:1565 D 21 '66
Dogwood in December. M. J. Irion. Christian Cent 83:1569 D 21 '66
Good shepherd of goats. W. L. Molton. Christian Cent 83:1565 D 21 '66
How the hibernators came to Bethlehem; poem. N. Farber. Horn Bk 42:684-5 D '66
Merry Christmas to the ladies society. M. J. Irion. Christian Cent 83:1565 D 21 '66
Poems. America 115:824-5 D 24 '66
Poems for Christmas. Commonweal 85:344 D 23 '66

CHRISTMAS poetry—*Continued*
Sonnet for Christmas. A. Kenseth. Christian Cent 83:1569 D 21 '66
Twelfth night. H. Enrico. Christian Cent 83:1564 D 21 '66
Two simies for Advent. P. A. Lacey. Christian Cent 83:1564 D 21 '66
Wreath of Christmas legends; medieval legends retold. P. McGinley. il Ladies Home J 83:73-7 D '66

Anecdotes, facetiae, satire, etc.

Exegesis of St Nick. R. Angell. New Yorker 42:28-9 D 24 '66

CHRISTMAS presents. See Christmas gifts

CHRISTMAS projects
Making sculptured Christmas figures. J. A. Christensen. il Design 68:4-7 N '66

Anecdotes, facetiae, satire, etc.

Big rock candy figgy pudding pitfall. J. Didion. il Sat Eve Post 239:22 D 3 '66

CHRISTMAS puddings. See Puddings

CHRISTMAS savings plans. See Christmas clubs

CHRISTMAS star. See Star of Bethlehem

CHRISTMAS stories
Band of angels. M. Cousins. il McCalls 94:78-9 D '66
Christmas books for '66. A. Currah. il Library J 91:5136-8 O 15 '66
Christmas journey. M. F. Brown. il McCalls 94:94-5 D '66
Fisherman's luck. W. Richards. il Motor B 118:30-1+ D '66
Gift to keep. R. Chappell. Horn Bk 42:738-48 D '66
Joy cometh in the morning. D. Thomas. il Redbook 128:50-1 D '66
Little Christmas. J. Fritz. il Seventeen 25:112-13 D '66
O, feast of Happy Mari. R. Llewellyn. il McCalls 94:70-1 D '66
Pain of possession. R. McInerny. il Redbook 128:46-7 D '66
To all a good night. K. Loeser. il Redbook 128:58-9 D '66
We had us some Christmas! excerpt from This stubborn soil. W. A. Owens. il Ladies Home J 83:100-1 D '66
Young girl's gift. E. S. Hill. il Read Digest 89:49-52 D '66

Bibliography

Christmas stories. C. Jackson. Atlan 218:156+ D '66
Stories for a Christmas morning. Z. Sutherland. il Sat R 49:56 D 10 '66

CHRISTMAS table decoration. See Table decoration

CHRISTMAS television programs. See Television broadcasting—Christmas programs

CHRISTMAS toys. See Toys

CHRISTMAS tree ornaments. See Christmas decorations

CHRISTMAS trees
Christmas trees you make yourself. il Sunset 137:54-9 D '66
How to preserve your Christmas tree. il House & Gard 130:38 D '66
These Christmas trees are tropical pines. il Sunset 137:68-9 D '66
What is the best Christmas tree? A. M. Sowder. il Horticulture 44:26-7+ D '66
With capsules of the unicorn plant. il Sunset 137:173 D '66

CHRISTMAS wrappings. See Wrapping of packages

CHRISTOLOGY. See Jesus Christ

CHRISTOPHER, George
Parkinson's law. il por Time 87:20 My 27 '66

CHRISTOPHER, John
Ticket in the raffle. Writer 79:13-15 Je '66

CHRISTY, George
(ed) See Andrews, J. All the things I love most

CHRISTY, Marna
Appleheaded. Design 68:30-1 N '66
Thumbs down. Design 67:38-40 Ja '66

CHROMATIN
Heterochromatin. S. W. Brown. bibliog il Science 151:417-25 Ja 28 '66

CHROMATOGRAPHIC analysis
Amateur scientist; how to build a gas chromatograph. G. V. Downing, jr. il Sci Am 214:124-8 Je '66
Automation of steroid analysis. I. E. Bush. bibliog il Science 154:77-83 O 7 '66
Concentration of dissolved amino acids from saline waters by ligand-exchange chromatography. A. Siegel and E. T. Degens. bibliog il Science 151:1098-101 Mr 4 '66

Detection and measurement of pesticide residues. D. J. Lisk. bibliog il Science 154:93-8 O 7 '66
Electrochromatography with reversing electrophoretic field. S. Raymond and J. Broome. bibliog il Science 153:1381-2 S 16 '66
Fingerprinting bacteria. il Time 88:60 Jl 1 '66
Oligoribonucleotides: improvement in chromatographic separation. H. Ishikura and others. bibliog il Science 153:300-1 Jl 15 '66
Turbulent-gas chromatography. J. C. Giddings and others. bibliog il Science 154:146-8 O 7 '66

CHROMATOID bodies. See Nucleoproteins

CHROMIUM
Plasma chromium after glucose administration. W. H. Glinsmann and others. bibliog il Science 152:1243-5 My 27 '66

Isotopes

Chromium-51 in sea water: chemistry. N. Cutshall and others. bibliog il Science 152:202-3 Ap 8 '66
Radioactive chromium works in cancer research. F. Marley. Sci N 90:269 O 8 '66

CHROMIUM plating
Plating solves headspace. E. Bogedal. il Outdoor Life 137:131 Mr '66

CHROMOSOMES
Adenosine triphosphate: protection against radiation-induced chromosome loss in drosophila. S. Mittler and R. U. bibliog il Science 152:1087-8 My 20 '66
Centromere; absence of DNA replication during chromatid separation in human fibroblasts. D. E. Comings. bibliog il Science 154:1463 D 16 '66
Chromosomal aberrations in a population of ground squirrels. C. F. Nadler and C. E. Hughes. bibliog il Science 151:579-80 F 4 '66
Chromosome aberrations: increased incidence in bone marrow of continuously irradiated rats. O. Chlebovský and others. bibliog il Science 153:195-6 Jl 8 '66
Chromosome analysis by computer. R. S. Ledley and F. H. Ruddle. il Sci Am 214:40-6 Ap '66
Chromosome changes induced by infections in tissues of rhynchosciara angelae. C. Pavan and R. Basile. bibliog il Science 151:1556-8 Mr 25 '66
Chromosome variability and geographic distribution in insects. B. John and K. R. Lewis. bibliog il Science 152:711-21 My 6 '66
Chromosomes from testicular preparations of lepidoptera. L. D. Miller and S. M. Miller. bibliog il Science 152:529-30 Ap 22 '66
Organization of DNA in dipteran polytene chromosomes as indicated by polarized fluorescence microscopy. J. W. MacInnes and R. B. Uretz. bibliog il Science 151:689-91 F 11 '66
Polyteny: a source of cryptic speciation among copepods. I. A. McLaren and others. bibliog il Science 153:1641-2 S 30 '66
Radiosensitization of X chromosome of Chinese hamster cells relate to incorporation of 5-bromodeoxyuridine. W. C. Dewey and others. bibliog il Science 152:519-21 Ap 22 '66
Scanner to examine chromosome changes. R. D. Hibben. il Aviation W 85:95+ D 5 '66
Segregation of sister chromatids in mammalian cells. K. G. Lark and others. bibliog il Science 154:1202-5 D 2 '66
Speciation in flowering plants. H. Lewis. bibliog Science 152:167-72 Ap 8 '66
Threads of life; reports at third International congress of human genetics. il Newsweek 68:100 S 19 '66
See also
Chromatin
Genetics

CHROMOSOMES (botany)
Chromosomal variation and evolution; address, December 30, 1965. G. L. Stebbins. bibliog il Science 152:1463-9 Je 10 '66
Evolutionary significance of polyploidy in the pteridophyta. E. J. Klekowski, jr. and H. G. Baker. bibliog il Science 153:305-7 Jl 15 '66

CHROMOSPHERES. See Sun—Atmosphere

CHRONIC bronchitis. See Bronchitis

CHRONISTER, Joseph
Metro Nashville starts area-wide street-sign program. Am City 81:116+ Jl '66

CHRONOLOGY
See also
Calendar

CHRONOLOGY, Historical
Three cheers for when. R. G. Price. il Atlan 217:112 My '66

CHRYSANTHEMUMS
Grow large chrysanthemums. C. Ackerson. il Horticulture 44:20-1+ O '66
Growing chrysanthemums in pots. Sunset 136:254 Mr '66

CHRYSLER corporation
Auto executive: he has to run faster just to keep up. il Bsns W p96-100 Mr 12 '66
Changes at Chrysler. il Time 88:98+ D 9 '66
Chrysler. E. Dahlquist. il Hot Rod 19:110-16 N '66
Chrysler corp. engineering for '67s. J. Ethridge. il Motor T 18:39-41 O '66
Chrysler enters boating's big league. J. Roe. il Pop Sci 188:144-6 F '66
Chrysler 300-X. E. Rosen. il Motor T 18: 32-3 Ap '66
How Chrysler restyled its top. il Bsns W p70-1+ D 10 '66
Rise from the grass roots. il Newsweek 68: 82+ D 12 '66
Way we see it. D. MacDonald. Motor T 18:8 N '66

Dodge division
Dodge rebellion. il Time 88:104 O 21 '66

CHRYSLER museum. See Provincetown, Mass. —Galleries and museums

CHRYSOPA carnea. See Lacewings

CHRYSSA, 1933-
Times square of the mind. il Time 87:100-1 Mr 18 '66

CHU, Dan
News on wheels (cont) Sr Schol 88:22 F 11; 89:40 S 30; 30 N 18 '66

CHUKAR shooting. See Partridge shooting

CHURCH, Frank
Excerpt from debate, July 27, 1966. Cong Digest 45:216+ Ag '66
Rivers, recreation, and you; interview. por Field & S 71:10-13+ Jl '66
U.S. policy and the new Europe. For Affairs 45:49-57 O '66

CHURCH, Frederick Edwin
Destiny manifest il Time 87:76-7 Ap 15 '66
Landscapes of Frederic Edwin Church, by D. C. Huntington. Review
  Sat R il 49:43+ Ap 16 '66. W. Andrews
Must this mansion be destroyed? il pors Life 60:64-77+ My 13 '66
Reviving Edward Church. F. Getlein. New Repub 154:34-5 Mr 5 '66
Romantic of Olana. H. Cohen. Reporter 34: 51-2 Ap 7 '66

CHURCH, Henry E.
First license, and before. Pop Electr 24:54-5+ Ja '66
In the days of spark, a rescue at sea. Pop Electr 25:57-8+ N '66

CHURCH, Michael Paul
Michigan's evangelist of art. G. A. Goodwin and A. Rankin. il por Read Digest 88:217-18+ My '66

CHURCH
Minister in the marketplace; Oakbrook, Ill. L. Pompian. il Read Digest 88:29-30+ Je '66
  See also
Catholic church
Christianity
Protestantism
Women in church work

Authority
Authority and fellowship. R. O. Johann. America 114:591 Ap 23 '66
Authority in the church, by J. L. McKenzie. Review
  Commonweal 84:477-8 Jl 22 '66. G. Wills
Catholic layman confronts his changing church. D. Norton-Taylor. il Fortune 74: 172-5+ D '66
Challengers on their church: Catholic priests. il Life 60:72-4+ Je 24 '66
Loyal opposition in the church. J. G. Milhaven. America 114:622-4 Ap 30 '66; Discussion. 114:760, 844 My 28, Je 18 '66
Ombudsman for religious. A. Broderick. America 115:446-8+ O 15 '66; Discussion. 115:527-8 N 5 '66
Reflections on the church's teaching authority; excerpt from Authority in the church. J. L. McKenzie. Cath World 203: 86-90 My '66
To bishops with love. America 114:792, 848; 115:5 Je 4, 18, Jl 2 '66
What can the church demand? Q. L. Quade and J. M. Rhodes. Cath World 204:162-9 D '66

Who speaks for the church on Vietnam? J. B. Sheerin. Cath World 204:72-6 N '66
Witness to divine reality. G. Baum. Christian Cent 83:427-9 Ap 6 '66
  See also
Institute for freedom in the Church

Work with the aged
Give the elderly a chance to be useful! Christian Cent 83:1234 O 12 '66

CHURCH advertising
Pop theology via TV. Christian Cent 83:229 F 23 '66

CHURCH and art. See Art and religion

CHURCH and economic problems. See Christianity and economics

CHURCH and education
God in education: a new opportunity for American schools, by N. C. Nielsen, jr. Review
  Cath World 203:48-9 Ap '66. W. B. Ball
Idea of a Christian college. C. J. Ping. il Sat R 49:90-1+ N 19 '66
Teaching the screen arts. Brother DePaul. Cath World 203:109-12 My '66
Theology in the state university; proposal for teaching Christian and non-Christian beliefs and practices. L. Swidler. Christian Cent 83:619-20 My 11 '66
  See also
Catholic church—Education
Public schools and religion
Religious education

CHURCH and international relations
Foreign policy in Christian perspective, by J. C. Bennett. Review
  Christian Cent 83:936 Jl 27 '66. H. E. Fey
Rigging the consensus; NCC in favor of admission of Communist China to United Nations. Christian Cent 83:768, 1200-1 Je 15, O 5 '66

CHURCH and labor
Protestantism and the American labor movement: the Christian spirit in the gilded age; excerpts from address, April 1965. H. G. Gutman. bibliog f Am Hist R 72:74-101 O '66

CHURCH and peace. See War and religion

CHURCH and politics
Facing outward. M. E. Schiltz. Commonweal 84:14-16 Mr 25 '66
Missouri Catholics in political arena. J. M. Swomley, jr. Christian Cent 83:1550-1 D 14 '66
Moral stance and political action. R. L. Holmes. Christian Cent 83:776-7 Je 15 '66
Soka Gakkai enters Japanese politics. G. K. Chapman. Christian Cent 83:1546-8 D 14 '66
Unrest in U.S. churches. il U S News 62:68-71 Ja 23 '67
  See also
Church and international relations

CHURCH and race problems
Berrigan is back. Christian Cent 83:357 Mr 23 '66
Candid camera: case of the Augustana Lutheran church, Omaha, Neb. Newsweek 68:76 S 26 '66
Catholic know-nothings; integrationists and the church's racial crisis in Chicago. il Newsweek 68:64 Ag 29 '66
Caution on civil rights; opposition to clerical involvement. il Time 88:58 Ag 26 '66
Challenge to our churches. il Ebony 21:112-13 Mr '66
Chicago Catholic asks: where does my church stand on racial justice? J. A. McDermott. il Look 30:82+ N 1 '66
Christian view of civil rights. America 115:167 Ag 20 '66
Church breakthrough; film produced by Augustana Lutheran church, Omaha. A. Knight. Sat R 49:65 N 19 '66
Church's teaching on race. America 115:730 D 3 '66
Curbing the Delta ministry. Time 87:84 Je 10 '66
Don't come unto me; Negro admissions cause clergy sackings in Macon, Ga. New Repub 155:9-10 N 12 '66
From Grenada, Mississippi, a minister warns Christians: stand up or get out! C. B. Burt. il Look 30:34+ D 27 '66
Gentlemen cry peace. J. M. Dabbs. Christian Cent 83:365-6 Mr 23 '66; Reply. J. R. Scotford. 83:684 My 25 '66
God and man in the South; church's indifference to civil rights movement. M. Frady. il Atlan 219:37-42 Ja '67
Graham and King as ghetto-mates. Christian Cent 83:976 Ag 10 '66

CHURCH and race problems—*Continued*
Integration; great dilemma of the church. H. A. Buchanan and B. W. Brown. il Ebony 21:163-4+ Je '66
Let no drum be muffled; John F. Kennedy award dinner; address, February 22, 1966. T. C. Sorensen. Christian Cent 83:328-31 Mr 16 '66
New commitments of religions in civil rights; John LaFarge institute report. il America 114:292-3 F 26 '66
Penalties for sins of racism. America 115:53 Jl 16 '66
Richmond church suit dismissed; admission of Negroes to membership in First Baptist church. S. Nichols. Christian Cent 83:411-12 Mr 30 '66
Two-edged sword; A time for burning. film on racial patterns in a Lutheran parish. America 115:643-4 N 19 '66
Unrest in U.S. churches. il U S News 62:68-71 Ja 23 '67
Why foster apartheid? D. W. Hornbeck and others. Christian Cent 83:1506-7 D 7 '66
See also
National Catholic conference for interracial justice
Parochial schools, Catholic—Desegregation

CHURCH and race problems in South Africa
Church's task in South Africa. E. Crowther. Christian Cent 83:933-5 Jl 27 '66
Racial good will wins a round in South Africa. Christian Cent 83:1401 N 16 '66

CHURCH and social problems
Bishop Hanns Lilje in Denver. R. Spargur. Christian Cent 83:1129-30 S 14 '66
Brooklyn message on fair housing; Archbishop McEntegart's pastoral letter. America 114:766 My 28 '66
Canadian bishop on poverty. America 115:308-9 S 24 '66
Catholic church and abortion. W. F. Buckley, jr. Nat R 18:308 Ap 5 '66; Discussion. 18:390 My 3 '66
Catholics and urban problems. America 115:168 Ag 20 '66
Christian function in a technological culture. M. B. Bloy, jr. bibliog f Christian Cent 83:231-4 F 23 '66
Christmas baskets and power. A. J. Eichenberger. il Christian Cent 83:1566-9 D 21 '66
Church and Delano. J. Wolf. Commonweal 84:168-9 Ap 29 '66
Church and society. Christian Cent 83:485 Ap 20 '66
Church and the police. Christian Cent 83:1327 N 2 '66
Church and the poverty program. D. M. Kelley. Christian Cent 83:741-4 Je 8 '66; Reply. H. Stroup. 83:938-9 Jl 27 '66
Church and the sexual crisis. Christian Cent 83:823-4 Je 29 '66; Discussion. 83:986 Ag 10 '66
Church relevant in Michigan. America 115:23-4 Jl 9 '66
Churchmen united against poverty. America 115:105 Jl 30 '66
Controversy within the church; statement. W. L. Doty; with reply by J. O'Connor and rejoinder. il America 114:480-4 Ap 9 '66
Council modifies report on sex and morality. Christian Cent 83:1369-70 N 9 '66
Ecumenical strain and stress. America 115:167 Ag 20 '66
Farm pastoral from California. America 114:642 My 7 '66
God makes the news weeklies. Nation 202:443 Ap 18 '66
Guns or oleo. Christian Cent 83:1298-9 O 26 '66
Interchurch social mission; forming Interreligious committee against poverty. America 114:246 F 19 '66
Interview with Reinhold Niebuhr; ed. by P. Granfield. R. Niebuhr. il Commonweal 85:315-21 D 16 '66
Is the world a problem? T. Merton. Commonweal 84:305-9 Je 3 '66
Leaders with vision; Catholics in Brazil's drive for social renewal. America 114:279 F 26 '66
Learning church in a teaching world. E. C. Bianchi. Cath World 203:287-92 Ag '66
Let's end the Communist-Christian vendetta; concerning the books, From anathema to dialogue, and The future of belief. H. Cox. Christian Cent 83:1375-9 N 9 '66; Discussion. 83:1508, 1542-3 D 7-14 '66
Man in the pew. C. S. Calian. Cath World 204:170-3 D '66
Moral basis of the war on poverty. S. Shriver. Christian Cent 83:1531-3 D 14 '66
Moral right & economic might; churches use of economic power to further ethical goals. Time 89:60 Ja 6 '67

MUST; project for urban service. D. M. Lindsey. Christian Cent 83:1041-2 Ag 24 '66
New and future clergy. T. C. Sorensen. Sat R 49:24-5 Ap 30 '66
Notre Dame challenges wealth. America 114:476 Ap 9 '66
Nuns in the inner city; force for freedom and creativity. P. Barrett. Christian Cent 83:1050-3 Ag 31 '66
Pastoral care and public ministry. D. Browning. Christian Cent 83:1175-7 S 28 '66
Priest as witness. M. P. Ryan. America 114:587-9 Ap 23 '66
Project Commitment. America 115:504 O 29 '66
Pulpit and market place. B. L. Masse. America 115:182+ Ag 20 '66
Religion, human rights in New York state; Kiamesha Lake conference held on interfaith basis. T. L. Conklin. Christian Cent 83:725 Je 1 '66
Sex, sin and salvation in Sweden. D. W. Ferm. Christian Cent 83:1142-6 S 21 '66
Speaking out; we must reform the church. W. H. DuBay. il Sat Eve Post 239:10+ Je 4 '66
Strip-mined landscape and impoverished souls. P. Douglas. Christian Cent 83:753-4 Je 8 '66
Victory in the vineyards; support given to farm workers in Calif. il Time 87:59 Ap 15 '66
Was it a race riot or revolution in Brooklyn? J. B. Sheerin. Cath World 203:327-30 S '66
World around us. See issues of Christian century
WCC on church and society; meeting of world conference on church and society, Geneva, July 12-26, 1966. America 115:199 Ag 27 '66
Worldly parish; Protestant ministers revitalize parishes. il Time 87:76 Mr 11 '66
See also
Birth control—Religious aspects
Christian ethics
Church and race problems
National Catholic social action conference
Sociology, Christian

Bibliography
Secular saints. D. Poling. Sat R 49:61-2 N 12 '66

CHURCH and state
Cheerfulness breaks in twice? R. Kirk. Nat R 18:578 Je 14 '66
Church and state; how high a wall? M. Himmelfarb. Commentary 42:23-9 Jl '66; Discussion. 42:7-8+ O; 79-89 D '66
Church-school challenge. Time 88:55-6 N 25 '66
Church-state dilemma in aid to education; Maryland court's stand. R. H. Smith. Pub W 190:50 N 21 '66
Church-state issue and educational materials aid; concerning constitutionality of N.Y. legislation. R. H. Smith. Pub W 190:47 Jl 25 '66
Church-state relations in ecumenical perspective, ed. by E. A. Smith. Review
Commonweal 85:430-2 Ja 20 '67. T. G. Sanders
Congress shall make no law. . . W. B. Ball; L. Pfeffer. Sat R 50:58-60+ Ja 21 '67
Constitutional confrontation in New York state. L. Pfeffer. Christian Cent 83:885-7 Jl 13 '66
ESEA funds challenged on church-state issue. Pub W 190:195 Jl 11 '66
Eying federal money; Baptists and federal grants and loans. Time 88:78+ D 2 '66
How free from doctrine? state aid to church-related colleges; Maryland. Newsweek 68:95 N 28 '66
Interfaith discussions; positions of Jews and Catholics on church-state issues. America 115:793 D 17 '66
Learning church in a teaching world. E. C. Bianchi. Cath World 203:287-92 Ag '66
N.Y. state textbook law upheld as constitutional by court. Pub W 191:36 Ja 9 '67
N.Y. textbook law in effect, pending court appeal. Pub W 190:67 S 12 '66
N.Y. textbook law voided on church-state issue. Pub W 190:308 Ag 29 '66
NYC orders textbooks for parochial schools. Pub W 190:109 S 26 '66
New York's Blaine amendment. America 114:642-3 My 7 '66
Public funds for church schools. Christian Cent 83:626-7 My 11 '66
Religion and the schools. E. Wakin. Sat R 49:85-6 Mr 19 '66
Religion and the welfare state. America 114:820 Je 11 '66

CHURCH and state—*Continued*
Should the church meddle in civil affairs?
J. H. Pew. Read Digest 88:49-54 My '66;
Same. Farm J 90:28+ Jl '66; Discussion.
Christian Cent 83:607-8, 864-5 My 11, Jl 6
'66; Farm J 90:50DD S '66
Solomon in Pittsburgh; civic celebration of
Christmas. America 115:472 O 22 '66
Speaking out; we must reform the church.
W. H. DuBay. il Sat Eve Post 239:10+
Je 4 '66
Suits challenge federal aid to private school
students; New York suits. Pub W 190:27
D 12 '66
Testing school aid; organizations challenge
constitutionality of aid. Newsweek 68:96
D 12 '66
This heartless business. V. C. Blum. Amer-
ica 115:247-9 S 10 '66; Reply. Christian Cent
83:1137-8 S 21 '66
Unto Caesar, unto God; movements to sep-
arate church and state. Christian Cent 83:
387-8 Mr 30 '66
  See also
Church property
Protestants and other Americans united for
separation of church and state
Public schools and religion
Religious liberty
CHURCH and state in Argentina
Church in Argentina. R. O'Mara. Common-
weal 84:612-14 S 23 '66
CHURCH and state in Eastern Europe
Communism and the silent church. E. V.
Kuehnelt-Leddihn. Nat R 18:1151 N 15 '66
CHURCH and state in Latin America
Church and state in Latin America, by J. L.
Mecham. Review
  Cath World 204:116+ N '66. W. Dush-
  nyck
CHURCH and state in Norway
  See also
Lutheran church in Norway
CHURCH and state in Poland
Comrades Gomulka and Peppone; govern-
ment harassment of millennium celebra-
tions. America 114:865-6 Je 25 '66
Continuing quarrel. il Time 89:29-30 Ja 6 '67
Poland's battle over seminaries. America
116.33 Ja 14 '67
  See also
Catholic church in Poland
CHURCH and state in Russia
Open letters of protest and their aftermath.
America 115:267 S 17 '66
Orthodoxy in Russia; concerning open letter
to the patriarch and the presidium of the
supreme Soviet. J. R. Nelson. Christian
Cent 83:1170-1 S 28 '66
Russian priests condemn Soviet council; con-
cerning letter to the president of the U.S.S.
R. Christian Cent 83:767 Je 15 '66
CHURCH and state in Spain
Church in Spain; Pope Paul's reform efforts
and outcome of Spanish Episcopal confer-
ence. il Newsweek 67:86-7 Mr 28 '66
Religious freedom in Spain; letter, with ed-
itorial comment. S. I. Stuber. America 115:
inside cover. 1 Jl 2 '66
Religious liberty in Spain. America 114:793
Je 4 '66
Spain finds an excuse. S. I. Stuber. Christian
Cent 83:1246 O 12 '66
What chance for religious freedom in Spain?
J. M. Swomley, jr. Christian Cent 83:663-4
My 18 '66
  See also
Catholic church in Spain
CHURCH and state in Sweden
  See also
Lutheran church in Sweden
CHURCH architecture
Christian science building, Urbana, Illinois.
il Arch Rec 139:146-7 Je '66
Dome for the Divine; Cathedral of St John
the Divine. il Time 88:78 D 2 '66
Four religious centers gain strength from
bold massing. il Arch Rec 140:107-14 Ag '66
Good news on Racine avenue; Emmanuel
Presbyterian church, Chicago. J. M. Dixon.
il Arch Forum 124:66-71 Je '66
Holy-card architecture. C. Heimsath. Com-
monweal 85:132-4 N 4 '66
Instead of a cathedral; renovating old St
Joseph church, Baton Rouge, La. C. J.
McNaspy. America 115:561-2 N 5 '66
Memorial church; West Berlin. il Arch Forum
124:78-83 Mr '66
Not a time for monuments; criticism of
church building industry. America 115:536
N 5 '66
Poverty or pretense; missionary church
building. C. J. McNaspy. America 114:632-3
Ap 30 '66
St Luke's Episcopal church. il Arch Rec
139:178-9 Ap '66

To build or not to build. Christian Cent 83:
735-6 Je 8 '66
What is Christian art? J. Dillenberger and
J. Dillenberger. Christian Cent 83:497-9
Ap 20 '66
  See also
Mosques
CHURCH buildings
Neighborhood church as focus for renewal. J.
Bailey. il Arch Forum 124:48-53 Ja '66
CHURCH colleges. See Denominational col-
leges
CHURCH conferences. See Religious confer-
ences
CHURCH cooperation. See Religious coopera-
tion
CHURCH discipline
Urge revision of abstinence code. Christian
Cent 83:1264 O 19 '66
CHURCH finance
Money and mission; Protestant churches in
the United States, 1965. Christian Cent
83:1559 D 21 '66
  See also
Catholic church—Finance
Fund raising
CHURCH goods. See Church supplies
CHURCH government
  See also
Catholic church—Government
CHURCH history
  See also
Martyrs
Protestantism
  also subhead Church history under names
of countries, e.g. England—Church history

        Primitive and early church
Crucible of Christendom. E. Kern. il Life
60:77-8+ Je 17 '66
Text from the early church; beliefs of
Nazarenes in medieval Arab manuscript. il
Time 88:64 Jl 15 '66

            Middle ages
  See also
Crusades
CHURCH law. See Ecclesiastical law
CHURCH membership
Depletion in the pew. Christian Cent 83:101
Ja 26 '66
  See also
Church statistics
CHURCH music
Congress of lost opportunities; fifth Interna-
tional church music congress. C. J.
McNaspy. America 115:360-3 S 24 '66
Fiasco in church music. R. Thibodeau. Com-
monweal 84:73-5+ Ap 8 '66;
207-8, 296-7, 301+ My 6, 27-Je 3 '66
Folk music in liturgy. C. J. McNaspy. il
America 114:529-32 Ap 9 '66
In many voices; Praise the Lord in many
voices, concert to present six contemporary
composers. C. J. McNaspy. America 116:61-2
Ja 14 '67
Jazz goes to church. il Ebony 21:76-80 Ap '66
Retrospectives, healthy and other. C. J. Mc-
Naspy. America 115:161-2 Ag 13 '66
Sacred music in change. C. J. McNaspy.
America 114:236-8 F 12 '66
Whitney, jazz and folk; E. Bonnemere's Missa
hodierna, mass in jazz. C. J. McNaspy.
America 115:465-7 O 15 '66
  See also
Hymns
Mass (music)
Phonograph records—Choral music
Phonograph records—Church music

      Anecdotes, facetiae, satire, etc.
Those gangbusting gospelers. Christian Cent
83:1163 S 21 '66
CHURCH of Abyssinia. See Ethiopic church
CHURCH of England
Cleaner of St Paul's; England's premier ca-
thedral. C. Northcott. Christian Cent 83:238
F 23 '66
Decline of the church in England. N.
Stacey. Harper 232:64-6+ Mr '66; Reply.
W. E. Hulme. 232:4+ My '66
Real meaning of talks between the Pope and
the Archbishop. il U S News 60:15 Ap 4
'66
Rome and Canterbury; colloquy of pope and
primate in Rome. C. Northcott. Christian
Cent 83:421-2 Ap 6 '66
Toward government by synod. il Time 88:85
O 7 '66
Unity in truth; meeting of Pope and Arch-
bishop of Canterbury. il Newsweek 67:63
Ap 4 '66

CHURCH of England—*Continued*

Book of common prayer

Lord's prayer updated; Australian reactions. Newsweek 68:104+ O 10 '66

Clergy

Buried treasure; Anglican vicars would like to sell church's old treasures. il Newsweek 68:70+ D 19 '66

CHURCH of England in Australia
Lord's prayer updated; public protests. Newsweek 68:104+ O 10 '66

CHURCH of England in Canada
United church of Canada biennial general council. J. R. Mutchmor. Christian Cent 83: 1223-6 O 5 '66
Western Canada and church union. G. Lane. Christian Cent 83:1349 N 2 '66

CHURCH of Ethiopia. See Ethiopic church

CHURCH of God
Profiles; H. A. Tomlinson. W. Whitworth. New Yorker 42:67-70+ S 24 '66

CHURCH of Jesus Christ of Latter-day saints. See Mormons and Mormonism

CHURCH of Norway. See Lutheran church in Norway

CHURCH of Scotland
Church of Scotland admits women to eldership. Christian Cent 83:770 Je 15 '66
Church of Scotland General assembly. I. Logan. Christian Cent 83:870-1 Jl 6 '66

CHURCH of south India
Breakaway from the C.S.I; new Independent Anglican church of Kerala. V. Koilpillai. Christian Cent 83:872 Jl 6 '66

CHURCH of Sweden. See Lutheran church in Sweden

CHURCH of the Brethren
Brethren take to the hills and the alleys; annual conference. I. Long. Christian Cent 83:916-17 Jl 20 '66; Reply. C. W. Zunkel. 83:1010 Ag 17 '66

CHURCH of the Holy Sepulcher. See Jerusalem —Church of the Holy Sepulcher

CHURCH of the Resurrection. See New York (city)—Churches

CHURCH property

Taxation
Aggressive atheist rebuffed. Time 88:56 O 21 '66
Church-abetted favoritism; tax-exempt retirement homes. A. C. Hausske. Christian Cent 83:463-4 Ap 13 '66
Church-state debate. Sr Schol 89:5 O 28 '66
Insulting judicial concession; Supreme court's refusal to declare tax exemption for church property unconstitutional. Christian Cent 83:1327-8 N 2 '66
No taxation without representation. W. More. America 115:580 N 12 '66
Rendering unto Caesar. Time 88:45 Jl 1 '66
Should religion be taxed? Madalyn Murray O'Hair files suit in Maryland. il Time 87:45 F 25 '66

CHURCH-related colleges. See Denominational colleges

CHURCH-related housing projects. See Housing projects

CHURCH schools
Ecumenical high school. O. J. Murdick. America 115:780-1 D 10 '66
See also
Catholic church—Education
Education and state
Parochial schools
Sunday schools

CHURCH services
Churches take a cue from show biz; liturgical experiments; with report by H. Cox. il Life 61:63-70+ O 21 '66
Demurrer on jazzy Lord's suppers. L. Kinsolving. Christian Cent 83:803-4 Je 22 '66; Discussion. 83:1084 S 7 '66
See also
Liturgies
Worship

CHURCH statistics
Numerolatry; 1967 Yearbook of American churches. Christian Cent 84:67-8 Ja 18 '67

CHURCH supplies
Buried treasure; Anglican vicars would like to sell church's old treasures. il Newsweek 68:70+ D 19 '66

CHURCH unity
Called to one hope; Catholic, Protestant, Anglican and Orthodox Christians to observe week of prayer for Christian unity. il Christian Cent 84:6 Ja 4 '67
No subsidy for sectarianism. Christian Cent 83:642 My 18 '66

One church by inclusion. Christian Cent 83: 906 Jl 20 '66
Plea for unity. D. Lawrence. U S News 60: 112 My 9 '66
Praying or preying? Catholic churches and Week of prayer for Christian unity. Christian Cent 83:197 F 16 '66
Protestant manifesto; cooperative ecumenical churches. Newsweek 67:86-7 Mr 7 '66
Protestant mergers. J. L. C. Ford. America 115:486-90 O 22 '66
Protestants united; Dallas meeting of Consultation on church union. il Newsweek 67:103 My 16 '66
Reformed-Lutheran conversations. T. G. Tappert. Christian Cent 83:412-14 Mr 30 '66
United Methodist church; critique and proposal. P. M. Minus, jr. and A. C. Core. Christian Cent 83:174-5+ F 9 '66
See also
Consultation on church union
Ecumenical movement
Religious cooperation
United church of Canada
World council of churches

Canada
Union agreement must include women ministers; United church of Canada and Anglican church of Canada. Christian Cent 83:609 My 11 '66

CHURCH vestments
Ireland's greatest Gothic treasures; early 15th century crosier and miter at Treasury of St John's cathedral, Limerick. J. Stuart. il Antiques 90:448+ O '66

CHURCH work
See also
Airplanes in church work
Evangelistic work
Sunday schools

CHURCH workers
See also
Women in church work

CHURCH world service
Cooperation in compassion, by H. E. Fey. Review
Christian Cent 83:914 Jl 20 '66. D. E. Trueblood
Getting in on a good thing; One great hour of sharing. Christian Cent 83:196-7 F 16 '66

CHURCHES

England
Winding stair, a fox hunt, a fulfilling situation, some sycamores, and the church at Henning. S. T. Warner. New Yorker 42:38-41 F 26 '66

United States
Message from Bonhoeffer. J. C. Ridd. Christian Cent 83:827-9 Je 29 '66
Time for tents; mobile church for a mobile age. Christian Cent 83:639-40 My 18 '66
See also subhead Churches under names of cities, e.g. Rochester, N.Y.—Churches

CHURCHES, Restored
Rebuilding St Michael's; Russian Orthodox church in Alaska. Christian Cent 83:1003 Ag 17 '66

CHURCHES of Christ
Exodus for Christ; sending entire communities of believers to urban northeast. il Time 89:66 Ja 20 '67
Exodus to New Jersey. il Newsweek 68:82 Jl 4 '66

CHURCHILL, Doyle
Small farmer, 1966 version. il pors Newsweek 67:22-3 My 2 '66

CHURCHILL, Judith
Why women act that way; reprint. Read Digest 90:68-9 Ja '67

CHURCHILL, Sir Winston Leonard Spencer
Advice to the world; concerning previously unpublished interview. por Time 87:64-5 Ap 22 '66
Churchill, by Lord Moran. Review
Atlan 217:130 Je '66. E. Weeks
Esquire 66:30+ S '66. M. Muggeridge
Nat R por 18:581-2 Je 14 '66. A. Lejeune
Reporter 34:42+ Je 16 '66. R. Mayne
Sat R por 49:29-30 My 28 '66. J. H. Plumb
Churchill's last years, by R. Howells. Review
Sat R por 49:32-3 F 26 '66. V. Wolfson
Time il por 87:111+ F 25 '66
Great patient; British and family reactions to Lord Moran's biography. il por Newsweek 67:45-6 My 9 '66
Greatest man. S. K. Oberbeck. il pors Newsweek 68:110+ N 14 '66
Inside Winston Churchill; concerning Lord Moran's biography. il Time 87:31 My 6 '66

CIMAROSA, Domenico
New York. A. M. Lingg. Opera N 31:29 D 10 '66

CIMICIFUGAS. See Bugbanes

CINCINNATI

City planning
Big step for pedestrians in Cincinnati. il Fortune 74:196 D '66
New planning process with built-in political support. J. Barnett. il Arch Rec 139:141-6 My '66

Crime
Besieged in suburbia. Time 88:35 O 21 '66
Strangler. Newsweek 68:46 O 31 '66

Education
Cincinnati's college crusade. il Ebony 21:88+ Je '66

Galleries and museums
See also
Cincinnati art museum

Music
Cincinnati. H. S. Humphreys. il Opera N 31: 26-7 S 10 '66
Opera at the zoo; Zoo opera pavilion. A. Darack. Hi Fi 16:MA18-19+ S '66

Newspapers
(Conflict of interest) [2]; newsmen on the appraisers list. Newsweek 68:66 D 19 '66
How to follow a hunch; appointments of appraisers. Time 88:48+ D 16 '66

Street traffic
Big step for pedestrians in Cincinnati. il Fortune 74:196 D '66

Theater
Theater; presentations in Eden park. H. Hewes. Sat R 49:39 Ag 13 '66

Water supply
Gigantic reservoir floats a decorous pool; Cincinnati's century-old Eden Park reservoir. T. M. Taylor. il Am City 81:87-90+ O '66

CINCINNATI art museum
Some thoughts on the environmental arts; Adams-Emery wing. P. R. Adams. il Antiques 89:391-408 Mr '66

CINCINNATI Reds (baseball) See Baseball clubs

CINCINNATI Royals (basketball team) See Basketball teams

CINCO de mayo classic. See Yacht racing

CINEMA. See Moving pictures

CINETHEODOLITE. See Theodolites

CINNABAR
Singular metal from cinnabar. P. M. Tilden. il Natur Hist 75:26-31 Je '66

CIOEFF, Thomas Francis
Children's work. Sch Arts 66:20-1 N '66

CIPES, Robert M.
Crime, confessions, and the Court; excerpt from The crime war. Atlan 218:51-8 S; 48 D '66
How they got Jimmy Hoffa, or did they? excerpt from Crime war. Atlan 218:118-22 N '66
Wiretap war. New Repub 155:16-22 D 24 '66

CIPHER and telegraph codes
How to get the most out of your key and bug. M. Lincoln. il Pop Electr 25:68-71 Jl '66

CIPHERS
Can you decipher this interplanetary message? il Sci Digest 60:37-8 Ag '66
Information theory after eighteen years. E. N. Gilbert. bibliog il Science 152:320-6 Ap 15 '66
Roger Bacon and the Voynich manuscript. J. Ashbrook. il Sky & Tel 31:218-19 Ap '66
See also
Cryptography

CIRCADIAN rhythm. See Periodicity

CIRCULAR saws. See Saws

CIRCULATION departments in libraries. See Libraries—Circulation, loans, etc.

CIRCUS
Big top goes to college; Florida state's campus circus. B. Kocivar. il Look 30:56-9 Ag 9 '66
This is old, pussycat, but it's fun; circus in Manhattan's Madison Square Garden. il Time 87:66 Ap 29 '66

CIRCUS animals
Training
See Animals—Training

CIRCUS performers
Big top goes to college; Florida state's campus circus. B. Kocivar. il Look 30:56-9 Ag 9 '66
Face to face with a circus web girl. Seventeen 25:101 Jl '66
See also
Acrobats and acrobatism

CIRRHOSIS of the liver. See Liver—Diseases

CISTERNS
Swiss and German pewter water cisterns and lavabo sets. R. M. Vetter. il Antiques 89:690-4 My '66

CITADEL press
Dylan plea for injunction against Citadel refused. Pub W 191:35 Ja 2 '67

CITIES and towns
Urban crisis, its meaning for development. E. Weissmann. bibliog f UN Mo Chron 3:48-56 Ap '66
Zeitgeistville, 1966. il Esquire 66:169-79 D '66
See also
New towns
Plazas
Slums
Sociology, Urban
Urbanization
also headings beginning City, Community, Municipal, Street

Defenses
See also
Civil defense

Federal aid
See Federal and municipal relations

Growth
Can business be lured into urban rebirth? il Bsns W p 155-6+ D 17 '66
Scratch a city planner; report on symposium. il Am City 81:108-9 My '66
Urban crisis, its meaning for development. E. Weissmann. bibliog f UN Mo Chron 3:48-56 Ap '66
Urban geography; city planning in the classroom; project map of Portsville designed by the AAT. A. I. Mayer. il Sr Schol 88: sup 12 Ap 22 '66
See also
Metropolitan areas

History
As a city upon a hill, by P. Smith. Review Nation 203:713-14 D 26 '66. S. J. Mandelbaum
Cruise into the past and a glimpse of the future; concerning the Delos symposium in Athens, summer of 1965. M. Mead. Redbook 126:30+ F '66

Planning
See City planning

Religious life
See City churches

Transportation
See Rapid transit

Zone system
See Zoning

Germany (Federal Republic)
See also
Cologne, Germany

Italy
History
At the roots of Republicanism. F. C. Lane. bibliog f Am Hist R 71:403-20 Ja '66

Netherlands
How a country lives when it's mostly city. il U S News 60:118-20 Ap 25 '66

United States
America's architectural nightmare; the motorized megalopolis. V. Scully. Holiday 39: 94-5+ Mr '66
America's cities. il Sr Schol 88:3-7 Ap 22 '66
Big-city troubles; is there an answer? il U S News 60:78-81 Mr 21 '66
Bonfire of discontent; Ribicoff's subcommittee on executive reorganization hearings. il Time 88:9-10 Ag 26 '66
City as it is. W. Von Eckardt. New Repub 155:37-9+ N 5 '66
City is the frontier, by C. Abrams. Review New Repub 154:42+ My 14 '66. W. Thabit
Dream of fair cities; beyond redemption? F. Getlein. Commonweal 85:366-8 Ja 6 '67

CITIES and towns—United States—*Continued*
Family affair; Abraham Ribicoff's subcommittee on executive reorganization investigating plight of cities. il Newsweek 68:16-17 Ag 29 '66
How much for rebirth? making U.S. big cities livable il Bsns W p 106+ S 3 '66
Main Street: a job for the church. H. Smith. America 114:689-91 My 14 '66
Mendicant cities; who will finance renewal plans? R. Moley. Newsweek 67:116 Ap 11 '66
Negro cities, white suburbs; it's the prospect for year 2000. il U S News 60:72-3 F 21 '66
Notes for a gazetteer. P. Hamburger. New Yorker 42:219-22+ N 5 '66
Troubled environment: improving our cities; address, December 8, 1965. H. Donovan. Vital Speeches 32:241-4 F 1 '66
U.S. cities improving. Sci N 90:170 S 10 '66
Weekends for two on the town. G. G. Greer. il Bet Hom & Gard 44:135-6+ Mr '66
What it takes to make great cities. E. K. Faltermayer. il Fortune 75:118-23+ Ja '67
What to do about the cities. M. McGrory. America 115:203 Ag 27 '66
  See also
All-America cities
National cleanest town achievement contest
United States—Housing and urban development, Department of
Urban renewal

    Bibliography
American city in fiction. Library J 91:3099-100 Je 15 '66

    History
As a city upon a hill, by P. Smith. Review Sat R 49:39-40 N 5 '66. M. L. Coit

CITIES and towns, Ancient
  See also
Mohenjo-daro

CITIES and towns, Ruined, extinct, etc.
Detour visit to ancient Puye. il Sunset 137:50+ S '66
  See also
Byblos
Fatehpur Sikri, India
Hebron, Palestine
Pella, Greece (ancient city)

CITIZENS associations
Metro North moves mountains; accomplishments of the Citizens committee, east Harlem. G. R. Metcalf. il Reporter 35:24-9 N 17 '66
  See also
East central citizens organization, Columbus, Ohio

CITIZENS band radio. See Citizens radio service

CITIZENS complaints. See Complaints

CITIZENS crusade against poverty
By or for the poor? annual meeting. New Repub 154:5-6 Ap 30 '66
Poor are human; morals of the protest. Nation 202:508 My 2 '66

CITIZENS for decent literature and motion pictures, incorporated
Intellectual freedom; ALA vs CDL. E. J. Gaines. ALA Bul 60:323 Ap '66

CITIZENS for educational freedom
Repealing the Blaine amendment. America 115:535 N 5 '66

CITIZENS obligations. See Citizenship

CITIZENS radio service
Annual report on CB equipment. il Pop Electr 25:51-8+ Ag '66
CB'ers are wondering about. il Pop Electr 25:47-50+ Ag '66
On the citizens band. M. P. Spinello. See issues of Popular electronics

CITIZENSHIP
Adults outscored on national test; National citizenship test. Sr Schol 87:sup2 Ja 21 '66
Can a citizen born abroad be president? U S News 61:57 S 5 '66
Reporter at large; American Jews in Israel. H. R. Isaacs. New Yorker 42:93-4+ S 3 '66
To be a citizen. H. N. Nemerovski. il Am Ed 2:21-3 Ap '66
  See also
Patriotism

CITIZENSHIP, Education for
Can Hubert Humphrey's dream come true? A. H. Sypher. il Nations Bsns 54:27-8 Ag '66
Civic education from sea to shining sea. E. F. Pflieger. il NEA J 56:56-8 Ja '67
Civic education is where you find it. D. W. Robinson. il NEA J 55:24-6 My '66
Not by talent alone; spirit of man; address, January 18, 1966. B. O. Wireman. Vital Speeches 32:370-2 Ap 1 '66

Patriotism; symposium. il NEA J 56:9-11+ Ja '67
Teaching the Bill of rights in California; Constitutional rights foundation programs. J. W. McKenney. il Sat R 49:68-9+ Mr 19 '66
To be a citizen. H. N. Nemerovski. il Am Ed 2:21-3 Ap '66
Training for citizenship; Youth and government, sponsored by the Missouri YMCA. J. Robinson. il Sr Schol 89:sup56 S 23 '66
  See also
Americanization

CITRUS fruit industry
Executive investment: citrus groves. T. J. Murray. il Duns R 88:33-4+ Ag '66

CITRUS fruits
  See also
Oranges

CITY and country
On columns and cities H. Cox. Commonweal 85:134-6 N 4 '66

CITY and town life
As a city upon a hill, by P. Smith. Review Nation 203:713-14 D 26 '66. S. J. Mandelbaum
We live in the city and love it. P. Parrish. il Parents Mag 41:52-4+ My '66
What women want in the city of the future; symposium. Mlle 63:160-1+ My '66
  See also
City and country

CITY cemeteries. See Cemeteries

CITY Center Joffrey ballet
Gamesmanship; Joffrey dancers. il Time 87:62 Ap 15 '66
Home sweet Mecca temple; review of season. D. Hering. il Dance Mag 40:43-5+ N '66
In Balanchine's footsteps? il Newsweek 68:96 O 3 '66
Joffrey ballet: small size, large vision. A. M. Kriegsman. il Reporter 35:42+ D 1 '66
Music to my ears; Robert Joffreys City Center program. I. Kolodin. Sat R 49:64+ Ap 16 '66
Musical events; performance of Robert Joffery ballet at City Center. W. Sargeant. New Yorker 42:163 Ap 9 '66
Musical events; opening of season. W. Sargeant. New Yorker 42:130+ S 17 '66
Nightmare of ballet finance. A. Ewing. Dance Mag 40:36-9 O '66
Robert Joffrey ballet, New York city center. J. Maskey. Dance Mag 40:63-4+ My '66
Theatre. H. Clurman. Nation 203:333-4 O 3 '66

CITY churches
Main Street: a job for the church. H. Smith. America 114:689-91 My 14 '66

CITY college of New York. See New York (city) City university of New York—City college

CITY colleges. See Colleges and universities, Municipal

CITY county hospital, Houston. See Houston, Tex.—Hospitals

CITY gardens
Gardening guide for city folks. il Changing T 20:43-4 Mr '66
  See also
Roof gardens

CITY growth. See Cities and towns—Growth

CITY halls
Bow-shaped civic plaza; Syracuse, N.Y. city hall. il Arch Forum 125:84-5 N '66
City hall that mirrors the city it serves; Winter Park, Fla. R. G. Simmons. il Am City 81:118-19 Ag '66
Old city hall gets a new face; Lamesa, Tex. C. A. Taylor. il Am City 81:91 My '66
Strong, modern and bold; Clearwater, Fla. center of local government. J. R. Stewart. il Am City 81:77-9 D '66

CITY improvement. See Municipal improvement

CITY manager plan
German council-manager form was anti-dictator measure. R. S. Childs. Am City 81:156+ My '66
Who really fathered the city-manager plan? S. A. MacCorkle. bibliog il Am City 81:106-7 Mr '66

CITY managers
Recent city manager appointments. See issues of American city
What is a city manager? B. Evans. Am City 81:9 Ag '66

CITY noise. See Noise

CITY of London festival. See Music festivals—England

CITY parks. See Parks

CITY planning
America's architectural nightmare: the motorized megalopolis. V. Scully. Holiday 39:94-5+ Mr '66
Architecture. E. Galantay. il Nation 203:652-4 D 12 '66
Busy remodeler of the world; interview. ed. by D. Lurie. C. Doxiadis. il Life 61:55-6+ O 7 '66
Changing job to be done. il Arch Rec 140:227-36 Jl '66
City as it is. W. Von Eckardt. New Repub 155:37-9+ N 5 '66
City of the future. Am City 81:9 Jl '66
City planning today; with editorial comment. J. Reinert. il Sci Digest 61:41-8+, 60 Ja '67
Demonstration cities: how about design? E. Goble. Arch Rec 139:9 Ap '66
Expo 67; an experiment in the development of urban space. il Arch Rec 140:169-76 O '66
Greek vision of tomorrow; ekistics. science of human settlements. P. McBroom. il Sci N 90:521 D 17 '66
Impact of the total redevelopment of cities; address, March 21, 1966. F. L. Whitney. Vital Speeches 32:14-16 Ap 15 '66
Molecular metropolis. il Parks & Rec 1:555-6 Jl '66
New ski town in the French Alps; Flaine, France. il Arch Rec 139:180-3 Ap '66
New towns: answer to urban sprawl? il U S News 60:114-16 F 14 '66
On columns and cities. H. Cox. Commonweal 85:134-6 N 4 '66
Piazza-puttering while Rome burns. E. Goble. Arch Rec 139:9 F '66
Scratch a city planner; report on symposium. il Am City 81:108-9 My '66
Shaper of things to come; C. Doxiadis. W. Von Eckhardt. Holiday 40:110+ Ag '66
Shaping the community in an era of dynamic social change; with introd. by M. F. Schmertz. il Arch Rec 140:189-206 Jl '66
Urban development part of HUD; interview. R. C. Weaver. il Am City 81:87-9+ Jl '66
What it takes to make great cities. E. K. Faltermayer. il Fortune 75:118-23+ Ja '67
What women want in the cities of the future; symposium. Mlle 63:160-1+ My '66
Where city planners come down to earth. il Bsns W p 100-2+ Ag 20 '66
Who needs new cities? E. H. Klaber. Arch Forum 124:68-9 Ap '66
    See also
Cities and towns
Industrial districts
Land—Subdivision
Municipal improvement
Suburbs
Urban renewal
Zoning
    also subhead City planning under names of cities, e.g. Wheeling, W.Va.—City planning

Anecdotes, facetiae, satire, etc.
Shape of things practically here; fable, with paintings by G. Liebmann based on those by T. Cole. O. Jensen. il Am Heritage 17:44-9 Je '66

Caricatures and cartoons
Black museum. R. Hedman. Arch Forum 125:30-3 D '66

Poland
City and regional planning in Poland. ed. by J. C. Fisher. Review
    Arch Forum il 124:84 Ap '66. W. McQuade

CITY traffic. See Street traffic
CITY transit. See Rapid transit
CITY university of New York. See New York (city) City university of New York
CIUFFA, Anthony A.
Blueprint for big bass. pors Outdoor Life 137:40-3+ My '66
Sure tricks for big bass. pors Outdoor Life 137:42-3+ Je '66
CIVIC centers. See Municipal centers
CIVIC education. See Citizenship. Education for
CIVICS. See Citizenship. Education for
CIVIL aeronautics board. See United States—Civil aeronautics board
CIVIL air patrol. See United States—Civil air patrol
CIVIL aviation administration of China. See Airlines—China (People's Republic)
CIVIL defense
Civil defense: notes on Project Harbor; with reply by E. Wigner. H. Margolis. Bul Atomic Sci 22:19-23 F '66

Hitting close to home; pointless to establish rules for protecting civilians. il Sr Schol 88:5 My 6 '66
Scientists and civil defense; dialogue at Berkeley. J. Walsh; reply. N. Rosa. Science 152:696+ My 6 '66
Worth protecting! D. P. Culp. il NEA J 55:50 Ap '66
    See also
New York (city)—Defenses

Study and teaching
Libraries and civil defense; with bibliography. J. F. Hanna. ALA Bul 60:655-6 Je '66; Reply. E. M. Oboler. 60:755-6 S '66

Transportation problems
Traffic pattern; Manhattan project, Metro air support '66. il Flying 80:13 Ja '67
CIVIL defense centers
Parking under an island; and a civil defense office, too, Cedar Rapids, Ia. C. D. Mullinex. il Am City 81:166+ S '66
CIVIL disobedience. See Passive resistance to government
CIVIL liberties. See Civil rights
CIVIL liberties union, American. See American civil liberties union
CIVIL procedure
    See also
Cost (law)
Jury
CIVIL rights
General assembly adopts four resolutions; with texts. UN Mo Chron 3:48-53 N '66
Third committee discusses draft covenant. UN Mo Chron 3:80-3 D '66
United Nations and human rights; statement; March 21, 1966. M. Abram. Dept State Bul 54:636-40 Ap 18 '66
United States favors creation of a U.N. high commissioner for human rights; statements, March 25, 28, 30, 1966. M. Abram. Dept State Bul 54:1029-33 Je 27 '66
    See also
American civil liberties union
Assembly, Right of
International human rights year (proposed)
Privacy
Right to counsel
United Nations—Commission on human rights
Woman—Equal rights

Study and teaching
Teaching a unit on civil liberties: the case study method. D. Parker and N. Economopouly. Sr Schol 89:sup40-1 S 23 '66

South Africa
We shall overcome; students anti-government demonstrations over I. Robertson's arrest. Newsweek 67:48+ My 30 '66

United States
Absenteeism: sophisticated filibuster. W. More. America 115:379 O 1 '66
Ahead of its time; civil rights measure killed. il Time 88:20-1 S 30 '66
Alas, poor Yorick! 1966 civil rights bill. Nat R 18:970 O 4 '66
Atlantic report; white backlash. D. Kiker. Atlan 218:6+ N '66
Back at the office; new bill; House furor. Newsweek 68:21-2 Ag 15 '66
Backlash and fear. America 115:376-7 O 1 '66
Backlash jitters. New Repub 155:5-6 O 22 '66
Black power; new emphasis of SNCC on self-determination. New Repub 154:5-6 Je 18 '66
Changed climate; state of civil rights bill. Time 88:30-1 S 16 '66
Deterioration; new bill. Nation 203:138-9 Ag 22 '66
Diet of worms; bill doomed. Time 88:27 S 23 '66
Expanding liberties, by M. R. Konvitz. Review
    Sat R 49:27-8 Ag 6 '66. L. M. Hacker
Freedom's daily battle. Christian Cent 83:1496 D 7 '66
Hottest potato; L. B. Johnson's bill. Newsweek 68:20-1 Ag 8 '66
Is integration irrelevent? New Repub 154:7 Je 4 '66; Discussion. 154:29-30 Je 18; 36-8 Je 25 '66
Issue is conduct; death warrant for the civil-rights bill of 1966. Newsweek 68:32 S 26 '66
Let's have justice for non-criminals, too! effect of Supreme court decision on police authority and safeguarding civil rights. E. H. Methvin. Read Digest 89:53-60 D '66

CIVIL rights—United States—*Continued*
New commitments of religions in civil rights; John LaFarge institute report. il America 114:292-3 F 26 '66
Our man at the Golliwog lounge; second annual meeting of the Philadelphia society. J. J. Kilpatrick. Nat R 18:258+ Mr 22 '66
Policing job Washington now is trying to get; with excerpts from address by W. C. Cramer. il U S News 61:38-9 Ag 22 '66
Symptom of anger; House passes new civil-rights bill. Newsweek 68:59 Ag 22 '66
This month's feature: federal open housing controversy. Cong Digest 45:257-88 N '66
Time for a hiatus? depoliticalize the civil rights movement. W. F. Buckley, jr. Nat R 18:1035 O 18 '66
Without portfolio; Civil rights act of 1964 and the new omnibus civil-rights bill. C. B. Luce. McCalls 93:26+ S '66
World society of equality and brotherhood; address, May 12, 1966. A. J. Goldberg. Dept State Bul 54:971-5 Je 20 '66
See also
Negroes in the United States—Civil rights
United States—Constitution—Bill of rights

CIVIL rights act of 1964
Education: racial controversy dogs U.S. commissioner. L. J. Carter. Science 154:242-3+ O 14 '66
Where civil rights law is going wrong; reply. F. D. Roosevelt. Nations Bsns 53:10+ D '65
White Wednesday; Senate debate on HEW's desegregation guidelines. New Repub 155:5-6 O 8 '66

CIVIL rights demonstrations
Backlash. Christian Cent 83:1232-3 O 12 '66
Big changes are coming; march through Mississippi. J. H. Meredith. il Sat Eve Post 239:23-7 Ag 13 '66
Black power! James H. Meredith march. il Newsweek 67:36 Je 27 '66
Br'er Fox; continuation of protest march begun by James Meredith. il Time 87:31 Je 24 '66
Chicago expects more than caution from Cody; demonstrations in all-white Chicago neighborhoods and suburbs. Christian Cent 83:1025 Ag 24 '66
City cracks down on demonstrations. il U S News 61:10 Ag 29 '66
Crossing the Red Sea; postpone march through Cicero, Ill. il Time 88:19 S 2 '66
Curb on protests; Supreme court decision. Sr Schol 89:27 D 9 '66
Delicate balance; deciding major case against Negro demonstrators. il Newsweek 68:29-30 N 28 '66
Delta: rich land and poor people. F. Davis. Reporter 34:41-3 Mr 24 '66
DP's in the delta; squat-in by Negro farm hands at the deactivated air force base, Greenville, Miss. il Newsweek 67:28+ F 14 '66
From race riot to sit-in: 1919 and the 1960s, by A. I. Waskow. Review
Nation 203:189-91 S 5 '66. H. Zinn
Heat on Highway 51. il Time 87:26-7 Je 17 '66
March, in step and out; Meredith march. il Newsweek 68:14-16 Jl 4 '66
March Meredith began. il Newsweek 67:27-31 Je 20 '66
Negro campout on White House doorstep. il U S News 60:12 Ap 18 '66
No easy transfers to federal courts; pursuit of civil rights, not a license to break the law. il Time 88:66+ Jl 1 '66
Nonviolence: the only road to freedom. M. L. King, jr. il Ebony 21:27-30+ O '66
Notes and comment; James Meredith march against fear and S.N.C.C.'s rallying cry of black power. New Yorker 42:21-5 Jl 16 '66
Open city; Chicago. J. Coburn. New Repub 155:9-10 S 17 '66
Planned lawlessness threatens to get out of hand; reprint. C. E. Whittaker. il U S News 61:37-8+ S 19 '66
Race issue inflamed again: aftermath of a shooting; J. Meredith, with editorial comment. il U S News 60:36-8, 112 Je 20 '66
Riots, battles, power marches: it's still a hot summer. il U S News 61:36-7 Ag 15 '66
Strange march through Mississippi. il U S News 60:48 Je 27 '66
Strike that failed; Mississippi tent city. D. R. Maxey. il Look 30:26-9 Mr 8 '66
Target city: CORE zeroes in on Baltimore. il Newsweek 67:28+ Je 6 '66
Test that wasn't a test; decision rebuffing civil rights demonstrators. il Time 88:55 N 25 '66

Too many cooks, too much spice; multi-headed Mississippi march. Christian Cent 83:880 Jl 13 '66
Touchiest target; anti-discrimination marches, Chicago. il Newsweek 68:29 Ag 15 '66
What happened to the civil rights movement? C. V. Woodward. il Harper 234:29-37 Ja '67
Which way now? Commonweal 84:430 Jl 8 '66
White backlash whips up a roadblock in Chicago. il Life 61:30-30A Ag 19 '66
White House camp-in; Mississippi Negroes demonstrate for direct anti-poverty grants. Newsweek 67:38 Ap 18 '66
See also
Negroes in the United States—Segregation, Resistance to

CIVIL rights organizations
Apartheid for America? black power. Nat R 18:716-17 Jl 26 '66
At the breaking point; struggle between moderate and radical elements. il Time 88:15-16 Jl 15 '66
Attack on Kodak; FIGHT dispute. J. Ridgeway. New Repub 156:11-13 Ja 21 '67
Black power and the American Christ. V. Harding. Christian Cent 84:10-13 Ja 4 '67
Black power for whom? ideological split in civil rights movement. Christian Cent 83:903-4 Jl 20 '66
Civil rights forecast: maybe a bit cooler; setting up organizations to avert violence. il Bsns W p31-2 Je 4 '66
Deacons go north; Deacons for defense and justice office in Chicago. Newsweek 67:20-1 My 2 '66
Line in the dust; movement split down the middle. il Newsweek 68:23-4 Jl 18 '66
Making trouble is Alinsky's business; project FIGHT. P. Anderson. il N Y Times Mag p28-31+ O 9 '66; Reply. V. S. Jones. p 139 O 30 '66
Marching where? Reporter 35:12+ Jl 14 '66
Negro leaders dividing; the effect; with excerpts from address by R. Wilkins. il U S News 61:31-4 Jl 18 '66
New white backlash? il Sat Eve Post 239:88 S 10 '66
Notes and comment; James Meredith march against fear and S.N.C.C.'s rallying cry of black power. New Yorker 42:21-5 Jl 16 '66
Pharaoh's lesson; fighting among themselves. Time 88:22 S 9 '66
Plotting a war on whitey; extremists set for violence. R. Sackett. il Life 60:100-100B+ Je 10 '66
Pseudo-power of black power. America 115:89 Jl 23 '66
See also
Lowndes County freedom organization
Student nonviolent coordinating committee

CIVIL rights workers
African queen complex; Negro resentment towards white female civil rights workers. il Newsweek 67:94-5 My 23 '66
At the breaking point; struggle between moderate and radical elements. il Time 88:15-16 Jl 15 '66
Builders of a new South; Negro heroines of Dixie. P. Garland. il Ebony 21:27-30+ Ag '66
Crisis in civil rights leadership. C. T. Rowan. il Ebony 22:27-30+ N '66
Deep in my heart, by W. M. Kuntsler. Review
Sat R 49:40-1 Mr 12 '66. J. R. Waltz
Here lies integration. Nat R 18:1305-6 D 27 '66
Indemnifying the victims. New Repub 154:6 F 26 '66
Is there an Alinsky in your future? W. F. Buckley, jr. Nat R 18:1104 N 1 '66
New teeth in the rights laws; Supreme court decisions. U S News 60:10 Ap 11 '66
Only believe. Nat R 18:1258 D 13 '66
Pattern of revolution; black power definition. R. Moley. Newsweek 68:84 Ag 8 '66
Showdown in the Delta; National council of churches report on Mississippi clergymen. il Newsweek 67:67 Je 6 '66
Solid prospect: Supreme court ruling. Newsweek 67:34+ Ap 11 '66
Toward outlawing murder; way opened for further Justice department prosecutions. Time 87:28 Ap 8 '66
Uneasy silence; lack of historical literature after 1964 Mississippi summer project. P. Cowan. Nation 202:136-9 Ja 31 '66
Urgent new reach to be equal; conference preview; biographical sketches of Negro leaders. J. K. Jessup. il Life 60:88-90+ Je 3 '66

CIVIL rights workers—*Continued*
When white girls go South as civil-rights workers. U S News 60:10 My 30 '66
Which way now? Commonwealth 84:430 Jl 8 '66
See also
Lowndes County freedom organization
Student nonviolent coordinating committee
Younge, S. jr.

CIVIL service
See also
Bureaucracy

Canada
Bargaining by civil servants in Canada. E. E. Herman. Mo Labor R 89:603-6 Je '66

United States
Civil service: people in government. il Sr Schol 88:16-17 F 18 '66
Civil service reform: letter to the editor. J. A. Ruef. Library J 92:30 Ja 1 '67
See also
Government employees
Postmasters

CIVIL service commission. See United States—Civil service commission

CIVIL service pensions
Small cities can have pension plans. H. D. McMahan. il Am City 81:200+ S '66

CIVIL war
Does intervention work? W. Pfaff. Commonweal 85:45-6 O 14 '66

CIVIL war (United States) See United States—History—Civil war

CIVILIAN defense. See Civil defense

CIVILIAN morale. See Morale, National

CIVILIAN review board. See New York (city)—Police department

CIVILIZATION
Men, moonships, and morality; concerning theories of R. S. Morison and A. S. Makarenko. J. Lear. il Sat R 50:113-14+ Ja 7 '67
Music and the statistical age; interview. I. F. Stravinsky. Commentary 42:49-52 S '66
Of worth and value; human spirit and the cybercultural revolution; address, February 1, 1966. A. M. Hilton. Vital Speeches 32:335-41 Mr 15 '66
Perfect total; excerpts from Themes and episodes. I. Stravinsky and R. Craft. Seventeen 25:304+ Ag '66
Shapes of the future; theories of Robert L. Heilbroner and Arnold J. Toynbee. A. Campbell. New Repub 155:22+ O 15 '66
There was something about the twenties. A. MacLeish. Sat R 49:10-13 D 31 '66
University and the world; address. March 9, 1966. R. S. Hoitman. Vital Speeches 32:442-7 My 1 '66
Vanishing ideologues. E. J. Hughes. Newsweek 67:22 Ap 18 '66
Violence and human development. E. B. McNeil. Ann Am Acad 364:149-57 Mr '66
See also
Culture
Man, Prehistoric
Popular culture
Religions
Social change
Technology and civilization
Twentieth century
also subhead Civilization under names of countries, e.g. United States—Civilization

Fiction
Short story. N. Cousins. Sat R 49:26 D 17 '66

History
Civilization as a phase of world history. R. Erwin. bibliog f Am Hist R 71:1181-98 Jl '66
Cruise into the past and a glimpse of the future; concerning the Delos symposium in Athens, summer of 1965. M. Mead. Redbook 126:30+ F '66
Great men, great events. UNESCO Courier 19:30-1 Mr '66
Investigating the origins of Mesopotamian civilization. F. Hole. bibliog il Science 153:605-11 Ag 5 '66

CIVILIZATION, Arabic
Ibn Khaldūn: man of history; excerpts from radio program. B. Bray. il UNESCO Courier 19:4-10 Je '66

CIVILIZATION, Christian
Christianity in world history, by A. T. van Leeuwen. Review
Commonweal 84:506-7 Ag 5 '66. R. E. McNally

CIVILIZATION, Minoan
How a civilization disappeared. Time 87:46+ My 6 '66
See also
Crete—Antiquities

CIVILIZATION, Modern. See Civilization

CIVILIZATION, Roman. See Rome—Civilization

CIVILIZATION and science. See Science and civilization

CIVILIZATION and technology. See Technology and civilization

CLAAR, James W.
Memo from the publisher (title varies) (cont) Miss & Roc 18:7 F 21; 6 Mr 28, 5 Ap 4; 5 Ap 11 '66

CLADOCERA
Amateur scientist; electrical signals produced by microscopic animals. R. F. Wheeler. il Sci Am 214:120-4+ F '66
Toxicity of aquatic herbicides to daphnia magna. D. G. Crosby and R. K. Tucker. bibliog il Science 154:289-91 O 14 '66

CLAIBORNE, Craig
(ed) Table talk with six famous chefs; interview. McCalls 93:96-7+ Je '66

CLAIBORNE, Robert
Digging up prehistoric America. Harper 232:69-74 Ap '66

CLAIBORNE, Sybil
Bringing up children then, and now. Parents Mag 41:53-7+ O '66

CLAIMS
U.S. and Canada ratify Gut Dam agreement; Department announcement, October 11, 1966. Dept State Bul 55:724 N 7 '66
Who can't have what; current examples. Time 88:81-2 D 16 '66
See also
Insurance—Adjustment of claims

CLAIMS (land) See Homesteads

CLAIRE-LOUIS, Jean
Further on the China confrontation: a question and an answer from France. Nat R 18:208 Mr 8 '66

CLAIROL, incorporated
Rinse makers glimpse gold in graying males; introduction of Great day, men's hair rinse. il Bsns W p80 Jl 23 '66

CLAIRVOYANCE
My psychic friends; excerpts from A search for the truth. R. Montgomery. Ladies Home J 84:101-6 Ja '67

CLAM chowder. See Chowder

CLAMBAKES
Real old-fashioned clambake. C. Ford. il Field & S 71:8-9+ Jl '66

CLAMPITT, Amy
Books. See issues of Audubon magazine to January 1966

CLAMS
High-purity calcium carbonate in freshwater clam shell. D. J. Nelson and others. bibliog il Science 152:1368-70 Je 3 '66
How to open, clean, and cook your Pismos. il Sunset 136:68-9 F '66
See also
Clambakes

CLANCY, Roger M.
Landlocked Wateree. Motor B 117:144+ Mr '66

CLANS and clan system
Clan tartan cards. D. Powills. il Hobbies 71:118-19 My '66

CLAPP, Verner W.
Closing the circuit: automation and data processing for libraries; address. June 24, 1965. bibliog Library J 91:1165-71 Mr 1 '66
Lack of machine-readable book data stymies automation advance, says CLR; excerpts from introduction to report. Library J 91:220 Ja 15 '67
New ALA officer. ALA Bul 60:714+ Jl '66
about
Follow the bouncing ball, or, Fiddling while Clapp burns. E. Moon. Library J 91:1172-5 Mr 1 '66
Limitations on institutional and organizational membership; midwinter conference report. por(p245) ALA Bul 60:240-2 Mr '66

CLAPPER rail shooting. See Rail shooting

CLAPPERTON, Jane
Life book review. Life 61:R4 S 9 '66

CLARE, Bruce, and others
Peroxidase and resistance to ceratocystis in sweet potato increased by volatile materials. bibliog Science 153:62-3 Jl 1 '66

CLAREMONT, Calif.
Two roads to cleanliness. W. Glickman and G. Ford. il Am City 81:110-11 My '66

CLAREMONT colleges. See Associated colleges at Claremont, Calif.

CLAREWOOD house project, Houston. See
  Housing projects
CLARION music society
  New York; performance of Le astuzie fem-
    minili, by D. Cimarosa. A. M. Lingg.
    Opera N 31:29 D 10 '66
CLARK, Alan
  Day Hitler attacked Russia. N Y Times Mag
    p 12-13+ Je 19 '66
CLARK, Blake
  Queen of the Adriatic needs our help. Read
    Digest 88:191-2+ F '66
CLARK, Cornelia
  Redbook readers in fashion: beauty. il pors
    Redbook 127:74-7+ S '66
CLARK, Deena
  Flowers that say aloha. Nat Geog Mag 131:
    120-31 Ja '67
CLARK, Dennis
  University and the city. America 114:324-6
    Mr 5 '66
CLARK, Dick
  Jeremy Tarcher, TV's Dick Clark co-pro-
    ducing books. Pub W 189:75 Ja 31 '66
CLARK, Don
  Silent song; story. McCalls 94:128-9 O '66
CLARK, Eugenie
  Lady and the sharks. C. Brossard. il pors
    Look 30:M8-9+ Jl 12 '66
CLARK, Evert
  Scientific-government-industrial machine. New
    Repub 155:32-5 Ag 27 '66
CLARK, Frank
  Commodore left two sons. Am Heritage 17:
    4-9+ Ag '66
CLARK, Fred
  Outboarding the rapids of British Columbia.
    Yachting 120:62-3+ D '66
CLARK, Fred, Jr
  How to buy a good used boat. Pop Mech
    125:132-5+ Mr '66
CLARK, Grenville
  Man for all seasons. N. Cousins. por Sat
    R 49:31+ N 26 '66
CLARK, Hank
  Give your wife a break. Pop Mech 126:120-5
    S '66
  Kick up a spray this weekend. Pop Mech
    126:136-9 Jl '66
CLARK, Jim, 1937?-
  What it takes to win at Indianapolis. pors
    Pop Sci 188:122-6+ Ap '66
      about
  Does anybody here believe Jack Brabham?
    K. Chapin. Sports Illus 25:82-3 O 10 '66
  Winner again. il Time 88:79 O 14 '66
CLARK, Jim, 1941?-
  Kayak-camping Lake Powell. Field & S 71:
    56-9 Je '66
CLARK, Joan R. and Papike, J. J.
  Eclogitic pyroxenes, ordered with P2 sym-
    metry. bibliog Science 154:1003-4 N 25 '66
CLARK, Joseph G.
  Disease prevention starts with nutrition. por
    Farm J 90:A8-9 S '66
CLARK, Joseph S.
  Senator Clark on the White House confer-
    ence. Bul Atomic Sci 22:30-3 Mr '66
  Some ethical problems of Congress. Ann Am
    Acad 363:12-22 Ja '66
CLARK, Leland C. Jr, and Gollan, Frank
  Survival of mammals breathing organic liq-
    uids equilibrated with oxygen at atmos-
    pheric pressure. bibliog Science 152:1755-6
    Je 24 '66
CLARK, Marguerite
  Health problems of adolescents. PTA Mag
    60:4-7 bibliog(p34) Ap '66
CLARK, Mary Higgins
  Five years that taught me how to live. il
    por Redbook 128:10+ N '66
CLARK, Sister M. Josepha
  Crisis in the CCD. America 115:277-80 S 17
    '66
CLARK, Matt
  Miracles and mishaps. Atlan 218:88-94 Jl '66
CLARK, Petula
  Petula Clark: little lady with a big beat.
    B. Rollin. il pors Look 30:M6-8 Ag 23 '66
CLARK, Ramsey
  Family affair. il por Newsweek 68:31 D 5 '66
  If the President picks Ramsey Clark as attor-
    ney general. por U S News 61:22 O 31 '66
CLARK, Sidney
  Equatorial Quito. Travel 126:40-4 D '66
  Sweden's atomic city. Travel 126:41-3 Jl '66
CLARK, Thomas
  Look; Flora; Poem for Tom Pickard; Red
    wild flower in North Africa; Lamp; To J;
    Poem; To simply talk is not ever; Book of
    magic; poems. Poetry 107:353-9 Mr '66
  New lines. Poetry 109:110-12 N '66
  Seven poets Poetry 108:408-15 S '66

CLARK, Thomas Campbell
  If the Nation could speak; excerpt from
    address, November 1966. por Sr Schol 89:
    sup3 D 9 '66
  Law in American society; interview. por Sr
    Schol 87:14-15 Ja 7 '66
      about
  If the President picks Ramsey Clark as at-
    torney general. por U S News 61:22 O 31
    '66
CLARK equipment company
  Harnessing air to do warehousing chores;
    load glide. il Bsns W p 172+ Je 18 '66
CLARK university, Worcester, Mass.
  Anti-academic library; new Robert Hut-
    chings Goddard library. il Library J 91:
    2286-7 My 1 '66
  John M. Johansen declares himself; library
    for Clark university. J. M. Johansen. il
    Arch Forum 124:64-7 Ja '66
      Libraries
  Rear end of the Xerox or how I learned to
    love that library. M. Charney; S. Moholy-
    Nagy. il Arch Forum 124:60-1 My '66
CLARKE, Arthur Charles
  World of the communications satellite; ad-
    dress, December 1965. bibliog UNESCO
    Courier 19:24-9 N '66
      about
  Astounding story! about a science fiction
    writer. G. Smith. il por N Y Times Mag
    p28-9+ Mr 6 '66
  Kubrick, farther out. il Newsweek 68:106+
    S 12 '66
  Profiles; S. Kubrick, director of 2001: a space
    odyssey. J. Bernstein. New Yorker 42:82+
    N 12 '66
  To prepare man for the extraordinary. il por
    Esquire 65:117 My '66
CLARKE, Austin
  Old-fashioned pilgrimage; poem. Poetry 109:
    101-9 N '66
CLARKE, Bruce C.
  Some answers to Vietnam questions; address,
    July 7, 1966. Vital Speeches 32:741-6 O 1 '66
CLARKE, Haydee G. See Clarke, R. F. jt. auth.
CLARKE, John
  At the frontier; poem. Sat R 49:44 S 17 '66
CLARKE, John I.
  Cameroon. bibliog Focus 16:1-6 Ap '66
CLARKE, Kenneth W.
  Avoiding college booby traps. NEA J 55:40
    Ap '66
CLARKE, R. W.
  Locating radio sources with the moon; with
    biographical sketch. Sci Am 214:16, 30-41
    Je '66
CLARKE, Robert F. and Clarke, H. G.
  Your charging system: is it thiefproof? pors
    Library J 91:642-3 F 1 '66
CLARKE, Ron
  Hurry-up-and-wait game. G. S. Brown. il por
    Sports Illus 24:18-19 F 21 '66
CLARKE, S. H. See Bronson, F. H. jt. auth.
CLARKE, Thomas E.
  Significance of Teilhard. America 114:779 My
    28 '66
CLARKSON, C. W.
  Many varieties of glass panels to control
    and diffuse light. Arch Rec 139:205-6 My
    '66
CLASON, Elsie D.
  Traveler's choice. Travel 125:11 Je '66
CLASS reunions. See College graduates
CLASS struggle. See Social conflict
CLASS trips. See School excursions
CLASSES, Special. See Special classes and
    special schools
CLASSICAL education
  See also
  Humanities
  Latin language—Study and teaching
CLASSICAL literature
  Classics revisited (cont) K. Rexroth. Sat R
    49:46 Ja 29; 33 F 19; 25 F 26; 25 Ap 2;
    23 Ap 9; 21 Ap 23; 22 My 21; 28 Je 11;
    17 Je 25; 15 Jl 2; 23 Jl 30; 20 Ag 13;
    41 Ag 27; 43 S 3; 62+ S 17; 57+ S 24;
    75-6 O 22; 24 D 3; 25 D 17; 41 D 31 '66;
    50:34+ Ja 14; 30 Ja 21 '67
  See also
  Latin literature
CLASSICAL music. See Music
CLASSIFICATION
  Dewey: necessity or luxury? practical eco-
    nomics involved in continuing with Dewey
    vs. converting to LC. G. E. Evans. bib-
    liog il Library J 91:4038-46 S 15 '66; Reply.
    J. J. Murphy. 91:5506 N 15 '66

CLASSIFICATION—*Continued*
LC/DC numbers; letter to the editor. B. A. Custer. Library J 91:1746 Ap 1 '66
LC in NY: preconference institute; sponsored by the cataloging and classification section of Resources and technical services division. N. C. Batts. Library J 91:3649-50 Ag '66; Reply. D. Gore. 91:4386 O 1 '66

Zoology
See Zoology—Classification

CLASSIFICATION, Decimal
Forward or backward? both 17th edition as a whole and the Index. E. Moon. Library J 91:2437 My 15 '66; Discussion. 91:4047-51 S 15 '66
Is Dewey dead? D. Taylor. il Library J 91:4035-7 S 15 '66
[Letters to the editor] Library J 91:4368+ O 15 '66
Route '66: Dewey, MARC, and Title II. E. Moon. il Library J 92:58-60 Ja 1 '67

CLASSIFICATION of animals. See Zoology—Classification

CLASSIFIED defense information. See Defense information, Classified

CLASSROOM films. See Moving pictures in education

CLASSROOM management
Classroom incident. NEA J 55:37-8 Mr; 21-2 Ap; 60-1 D '66
Letters. M. Hawes. Sch Arts 66:36-7 N '66
Of baseball and harmonicas. J. Woods. NEA J 55:57-9 Mr '66
Speculations on the child's world of learning. M. A. White. NEA J 55:20-2 Mr '66
Teaching music in the self-contained classroom. E. M. Badger; E. M. Covell. il NEA J 55:16-18 My '66

CLASSROOM teachers. See Teachers

CLAUDE, Sister Mary. See Mary Claude, Sister

CLAUS, Juergen
Art news from Germany. Art N 65:53 Sum '66

CLAUSEN, Don H.
Excerpt from address, December 9, 1965. Cong Digest 45:93+ Mr '66
Let's remove politics and profit from the war on poverty; address, December 9, 1965. Vital Speeches 32:252-4 F 1 '66
Redwoods to the sea. Am For 72:22-5+ N '66; Correction. 72:9 D '66

CLAUSEN, Jane Welday
Dahlias now and in spring. Flower Grower 53:12-13 O '66

CLAUSEN, Oliver
Sweden goes underground. N Y Times Mag p23-5+ My 22 '66
Weiss, propagandist and Weiss, playwright. N Y Times Mag p28-9+ O 2 '66

CLAY, Cassius
Ali up; eligible for military service. il por Time 87:26 F 25 '66
Battle of the lionhearted. G. Rogin. il pors Sports Illus 24:32-4+ Ap 11 '66
Big shrink. Sports Illus 24:8 Mr 21 '66
Blood at the Arsenal. E. Shrake. il por Sports Illus 24:20-3 My 30 '66
Bloody shame. por Newsweek 67:83 My 30 '66
Case of conscience. J. Olsen. il pors Sports Illus 24:88-90+ Ap 11; 94-103 Ap 18; 48-50+ Ap 25; 36-8+ My 2; 34-6+ My 9 '66
Challenge shortage. Newsweek 68:65 N 28 '66
Destination unknown. Newsweek 67:93 Mr 14 '66
Early end for early bird. Newsweek 68:79 Ag 15 '66
Feats of Clay; Clay-London fight. Time 88:54 Ag 12 '66
Group. Sports Illus 25:20 N 14 '66
Hands of Clay. il Newsweek 68:68 S 19 '66
How about that whozis? Clay-Mildenberger fight. Time 88:70+ S 16 '66
If Cassius can't punch, then London isn't down. J. Lovesey. il pors Sports Illus 25:16-19 Ag 15 '66
In defense of Cassius Clay; interview, ed. by G. Talese. F. Patterson. il por Esquire 66:55-8 Ag '66
Intimate look at the champ. I. Sutton. il pors Ebony 22:148-54+ N '66
Low blows, tax blows. il Newsweek 67:64+ Ap 11 '66
Massacre. M. Kane. il por Sports Illus 25:22-5 N 21 '66
Mouth; incident with Ernie Terrell. Time 89:73 Ja 6 '67
Muslim ministers to a southpaw. M. Kane. il Sports Illus 25:34-5+ S 19 '66
Portable pulpit. Sports Illus 25:8 S 5 '66

Ready for the bloodletting. E. Shrake. Sports Illus 24:74+ My 23 '66
Redemption of the champion. G. Parks. il pors Life 61:76-7+ S 9 '66
Showdown with a punching bag. T. Maule. il por Sports Illus 24:34-7 Mr 28 '66
Skinning the Cat. il por Time 88:64 N 25 '66
Speaking of indignities. il pors Time 87:75 Ap 8 '66
Sudden rush of new heavies. T. Maule. il Sports Illus 24:14-17 F 21 '66
Wind that blew in Chicago. W. B. Furlong. il por Sports Illus 24:26-7+ Mr 7 '66
You watch out, Ali! M. Kane. il por Sports Illus 25:26-9 N 14 '66

CLAY, George R.
Paperweight snowstorm; story. Seventeen 25:120-1 D '66

CLAY, John. See Attig, G. K. jt. auth.

CLAY, Mary. See Berry, J. M. jt. auth.

CLAY
Availability of a cationic herbicide adsorbed on clay minerals to cucumber seedlings. J. B. Weber and D. C. Scott. il Science 152:1400-2 Je 3 '66
See also
Montmorillonite

CLAY figurines. See Figurines

CLEANING
See also
Brushes
Furniture—Care
Kitchen utensils—Care

CLEANING compositions
Scouring powders. il Consumer Rep 31:502-4 O '66
See also
Detergents

CLEANING of cities
See also
National cleanest town achievement contest

CLEANING of paintings. See Paintings—Cleaning

CLEANING services
Employees
Earnings in contract cleaning services, summer 1965. F. L. Bauer. il Mo Labor R 89:656-8 Je '66

CLEAR air turbulence. See Atmospheric turbulence

CLEAR LAKE
October and the high creel count. il Sunset 137:73 O '66

CLEARWATER, Fla.
Strong, modern and bold; center of local government. J. R. Stewart. il Am City 81:77-9 D '66

CLEAVE, Maureen
Old Beatles, a study in paradox. N Y Times Mag p 10-11+ Jl 3 '66

CLEAVER, Bill. See Cleaver, V. jt. auth.

CLEAVER, Vera, and Cleaver, Bill
Quiet girl; story. McCalls 93:84-5 F '66

CLEBSCH, William A.
Foursquare faith. Christian Cent 83:208+ F 16 '66

CLEGHORN, Reese
Allen of Atlanta collides with black power and white racism. N Y Times Mag p32-3+ O 16 '66
Mr White Blacklash. N Y Times Mag p27-9+ N 6 '66
No seat for the Negro who won. New Repub 154:11-12 Ja 29 '66

CLEMATIS
This is the month to get acquainted with the many and colorful clematis. il Sunset 136:244+ Mr '66

CLEMENS, Cyril
My visit with Herbert Hoover. Hobbies 71:106-7 Ap '66

CLEMENS, Martin
Coastwatcher's diary; with introd. by S. W. Sears. Am Heritage 17:104-10 F '66

CLEMENS, Samuel Langhorne
Prince and the pauper; dramatization. See Newman, D.
about
Funniest lies; Mark Twain tonight! Time 87:63 Ap 1 '66
Hal Holbrook tonight! concerning the one-man show, Mark Twain tonight! R. Shickel. Holiday 40:103-5 Ag '66
Mark Twain tonight! T. Lewis. America 114:605 Ap 23 '66

CLEMENS, Samuel Langhorne—about—*Cont.*
Mark Twain's letters from Hawaii. ed. by
  A. G. Day. Review
    Sat R 49:33 Mr 19 '66. J. M. Allison
    Time por 87:114+ Mr 18 '66
Mr Clemens and Mark Twain, by J. Kaplan.
  Review
    Atlan por 218:61-4 Ag '66. A. Schlesinger.
      jr
    Life 60:12 Je 24 '66. J. K. Galbraith
    New Repub 155:31-4 Jl 16 '66. L. Grau-
      man, jr
    New Yorker 42:114+ S 3 '66. B. Gill
    Sat R por 49:31-3 Je 18 '66. A. G. Day
    Time 87:108+ Je 24 '66

CLEMENT, Roland C.
Use for wilderness. Audubon Mag 68:94-5
  Mr '66

CLEMENT family
Clement coat-of-arms. H. K. Eilers. il Hobbies 71:126-7 Mr '66

CLEMENTE, Roberto Walker
Aches and pains and three batting titles. M.
  Cope. il pors Sports Illus 24:30-4+ Mr 7 '66

CLEMENTS, Claire
Photo-montage murals. Sch Arts 66:25-7 O
  '66

CLEMENTS, Robert J.
All Europe was his seraglio. Sat R 50:82 Ja 14
  '67
European literary scene. See occasional issues
  of Saturday review
First signs of the humanist hope. Sat R 49:
  34-5 Mr 12 '66
Muses are herd. Sat R 49:30-1 My 21 '66
Pied Piper of Odense. NEA J 55:50-1 O '66
Poetry on the campus. Sat R 49:68-9 Je 11
  '66
Wages from other men's sins. Sat R 49:47
  Ap 16 '66

CLEMENTS, Sid
My rockpile, fishing hole. por Outdoor Life
  138:48-51+ S '66

CLEPPER, Henry
Big five. Am For 72:18-21+ Ja '66
Wild food for outdoor living. Am For 72:
  22-4+ Je '66

CLERGY
Church and its manpower. America 115:219
  S 3 '66
Clergy mobilize for peace. Christian Cent
  84:5 Ja 4 '67
Letter from the fringe: a defense of the
  nonpastoral ministry. L. R. Lindsay. Chris-
  tian Cent 83:1075-7 S 7 '66; Discussion. 83:
  1306 O 26 '66
Lutheran clergyman looks at marriage. Cath
  World 204:174-6 D '66
Managing the church's manpower; concerning
  report of NCC's department of ministry,
  vocation and pastoral services. Christian
  Cent 83:1137 S 21 '66
Minister in the marketplace; Oakbrook, Ill.
  L. Pompian. il Read Digest 88:29-30+ Je
  '66
New and future clergy; involvement in so-
  cial problems. T. C. Sorensen. Sat R 49:
  24-5 Ap 30 '66
Parochial syndrome. L. Davis; reply. O. J.
  Brose; R. G. Kemper. Christian Cent 83:
  205-6 F 16 '66
Unions for clergymen; draft constitution for
  Episcopal clergy of California. Newsweek
  67:68 My 9 '66
  See also
Catholic church—Clergy
Celibacy
Chaplains, Military
Church of England—Clergy
Parishes
Priests
Protestant Episcopal church—Clergy
Theologians
Theological students
Women as priests

Anecdotes, facetiae, satire, etc.
Games clergy play. R. E. Gibson. Christian
  Cent 83:1443-5 N 23 '66
Powell plan. Christian Cent 83:1555 D 14 '66

Salaries
Your minister and his pay. il Changing T
  20:43-4 Je '66

CLERGY conferences
South Africa's bishops speak; conference in
  Pretoria July 12-15, 1966. America 115:146
  Ag 13 '66

CLERICAL workers. See Office workers

CLERIHEWS
Trade winds; readers offerings. J. G. Fuller.
  Sat R 49:12 Ap 2 '66

CLERKS (retail trade)
My year in the five and ten; experience as a
  clerk at Duckwell'e variety store, Topeka,
  Kan. A. House. il Seventeen 25:162-3+ S
  '66

CLEVELAND, Harlan
Political phase of NATO; address, July 19,
  1966. Dept State Bul 55:339-45 S 5 '66

  about
Can the President square the circle? J.
  Burnham. Nat R 18:106 F 8 '66

CLEVELAND, James Colgate
Robber in the House. Time 87:25A Ap 1 '66

CLEVELAND, Ohio
  See also
Garden center, Cleveland

Airports
Rail extension to speed Cleveland traffic.
  J. W. Carter. il Aviation W 85:54-5+ N
  7 '66

Galleries and museums
  See also
Cleveland museum of art

Hospitals
Creative hospital administrator. il Ebony 22:
  73-4+ D '66

Housing
Bloom in the slums; paint job sponsored by a
  business-labor organization in Cleveland's
  run-down areas. il Bsns W p 178+ O 15 '66

Libraries
  See also
Cleveland public library

Music
Bright new light in Ohio; Lake Erie opera
  theatre. B. Murray. il Hi Fi 16:134-5 Mr
  '66
Music: newer American repertory program.
  B. Boretz. Nation 202:437-8 Ap 11 '66
Port of call. A. M. Lingg. il Opera N 30:26-7
  Ap 16 '66
  See also
Lake Erie opera theater

Negroes
Jungle & the city; savagery in Hough. il
  Time 88:11-12 Jl 29 '66
Why Hough got tough; the real agitators.
  R. Fischer. New Repub 155:9-10 S 10 '66

Newspapers
  See also
Cleveland plain dealer
Cleveland press

Rapid transit
Rail extension to speed Cleveland traffic.
  J. W. Carter. il Aviation W 85:54-5+ N
  7 '66

Recreation
Craftmobile for seniors. H. Goldstein. il Parks
  & Rec 1:719 S '66

Riots
And now Cleveland. Reporter 35:8+ Ag 11 '66
Diagnosis of a riot. il U S News 61:8 Ag 22
  '66
Ice, water and fire; Hough in flames. il
  Newsweek 68:18-19 Ag 1 '66
Jungle & the city; savagery in Hough. il Time
  88:11-12 Jl 29 '66
Why Hough got tough; the real agitators.
  R. Fischer. New Repub 155:9-10 S 10 '66

Social conditions
And now Cleveland; cause of Negro riots.
  Reporter 35:8+ Ag 11 '66

Theater
Art and argot at Karamu. B. Kremen. Nation 203:257-9 S 19 '66
[Theatre across America] J. Novick. Nation
  202:689-90 Je 6 '66

CLEVELAND Browns (football club) See Football clubs

CLEVELAND Indians (baseball) See Baseball
  clubs

CLEVELAND museum of art
Aristocrat. il Time 88:88 S 16 '66
Cleveland's golden anniversary acquisitions.
  W. Stechow. il Art N 65:30-44+ S '66
Cleveland's Golden show. il Newsweek 68:
  96+ S 12 '66

CLEVELAND orchestra
Bridge to the future; Busoni's piano concerto performed at Manhattan's Carnegie Hall. il Time 87:44 F 18 '66
Music to my ears; annual Carnegie Hall appearances. I. Kolodin. Sat R 49:41 F 26 '66

CLEVELAND plain dealer
Cleveland newspaper plans Midwest book festival. Pub W 190:43 Ag 15 '66

CLEVELAND playhouse. See Cleveland, Ohio—Theater

CLEVELAND press
Press on trial; S. Sheppard case before Supreme court. il Time 87:64 Mr 11 '66
Trial by headline; Sheppard trial ruled unfair by Supreme court. il Newsweek 67:64 Je 20 '66

CLEVELAND public library
Book week in braille; Library for the blind, hospital and institutions department. K. Prescott. il Library J 91:4197-9 S 15 '66
Library and the functionally illiterate in Cleveland; excerpts from letter, ed. by W. Woulfe. F. Long. ALA Bul 60:637-8 Je '66

CLIBURN, Van
Steal not away; poem. por McCalls 93:80 Je '66

CLICHÉS. See English language—Terms and phrases

CLIFFE, Lionel
East Africa, unity and diversity. Cur Hist 50:147-52 Mr '66

CLIFFORD, Clark McAdams
Man for all Caesars. il pors Newsweek 69:21-2 Ja 2 '67

CLIFFORD, John W.
Some fallacies about the Vietnam war. Cath World 203:361-4 S '66

CLIFFORD, William D.
Perfect boat for skiers. Field & S 71:34-5+ Ja '67

CLIFT, Montgomery
Winner who lost. B. Long. Vogue 148:70+ N 15 '66

CLIFTON, James W.
Reference and regulator diodes. por Electr World 76:45-8 Jl '66

CLIMATE
Heat peak coming; theory of a 900-year heat-cold cycle. Sci N 90:309 O 15 '66
See also
Man—Influence of environment
Meteorology
Weather
    also subhead Climate under names of continents, countries, etc. e.g. United States—Climate

CLIMATE and health. See Weather—Mental and physiological effects

CLIMATIC thermal adaptation. See Adaptation (biology)

CLIMATOLOGY. See Climate; Weather

CLIMBING plants
Friendly look with vines. P. Shedesky. il Flower Grower 53:32-3+ Ag '66
Vines and shrubs on trellises, arches, posts, pyramids. il Sunset 136:102-3 Ap '66
Wall spillers usually improve their walls. il Sunset 136:86-7 Je '66
See also
Columnea

CLINE, Martin J. and Melmon, K. L.
Plasma kinins and cortisol: a possible explanation of the anti-inflammatory action of cortisol. bibliog Science 153:1135-8 S 2 '66

CLINGERMAN, Polly
Josie. Mlle 64:101+ D '66

CLINICAL pharmacology. See Pharmacology

CLINICAL radiology. See Radiology, Medical

CLINICAL thermometers. See Thermometers, Clinical

CLINOAMPHIBOLES. See Amphiboles

CLINTON, Farley
Death of a craftsman. Nat R 18:416-17 My 3 '66
Maugham's bondage. Nat R 18:174-6 F 22 '66
Ronald Reagan: a light in the West. Nat R 18:613-15 Je 28 '66
Theater. Nat R 18:325-7 Ap 5 '66
(ed) See Mahoney, D. Do the big-city police have popular support?

CLINTON, Tenn.
Children of the South, by M. Anderson. Review
New Repub 155:17-19 S 24 '66. R. Coles
Sat R 49:90 S 17 '66. K. Taylor

CLIPPERS, Hedge. See Hedge clippers

CLIVEDEN (estate) See Country estates—England

CLOAR, Carroll
Summer dies as slowly. il Time 88:56-7 Ag 19 '66

CLOCK and watch makers
Lines shift in Swiss watch war; new opportunities for competition. Bsns W p 107-8+ S 24 '66
Watch industry clocks a new record. Bsns W p58-60 D 24 '66

CLOCK radios. See Radio receiving apparatus

CLOCKS
Shelf clocks. J. Mebane. il Bet Hom & Gard 44:116 Ap '66
See also
Atomic clocks
Watches
        Collectors and collecting
Collecting old time-pieces; American clocks. L. W. Slaughter. See issues of Hobbies February-November 1966
        Repairing
Philosopher's clock. New Yorker 42:39-41 My 21 '66

CLOCKS, Atomic. See Atomic clocks

CLOCKS, Electric
Cordless electric clocks. il Consumer Bul 49:6-10 N '66

CLOISONNE
Hungarian enamels. G. Kaler. il Hobbies 70:46 F '66

CLOISTERS. See Monasteries

CLOS, Max
Karma of Vietnam's Buddhists. N Y Times Mag p28-9+ Ag 21 '66

CLOSE, Frederick J.
Look back from the year 2010; address, October 5, 1966. Vital Speeches 33:53-7 N 1 '66

CLOSE by my side; story. See Sommers, F. J.

CLOSE-up lenses. See Lenses, Photographic

CLOSED circuit television. See Television, Closed circuit

CLOSED circuit television cameras. See Television cameras

CLOSED end investment companies. See Investment trusts

CLOSETS
Children's room behind the scenes. il Sunset 137:131 O '66
Closets at Blair House. il House & Gard 129:200-3 Ap '66

CLOSTRIDIUM botulinum
Clostridium botulinum type F: isolation from salmon from the Columbia River. J. M. Craig and K. S. Pilcher. bibliog Science 153:311-12 Jl 15 '66
Clostridium botulinum type F; seasonal inhibition by bacillus licheniformis. M. W. Wentz and others. bibliog il Science 155:89-90 Ja 6 '67

CLOTHES closets. See Closets

CLOTHES dryers
Clothes dryers. Consumer Rep 31:16-21 D '66
Electric and gas clothes dryers. il Consumer Rep 31:442-8 S '66
There's a better way to dry clothes. il Redbook 127:100-1+ S '66

CLOTHES washing machines. See Washing machines

CLOTHING and dress
Fashions for Puerto Rico; versatile new apparel for two. il Holiday 39:78-83 Ap '66
How to look your best in the new pants. il Redbook 127:90 Je '66
Khadejha: the girl who started it; trend to African fashions. I. Neves. il Life 61:147-8 S 16 '66
On dressing lady dolls of the late nineteenth century. C. H. Fawcett. il Hobbies 71:40-1 O '66
Pants suits: international uniform. J. A. Zill. il Look 30:61-3 Ag 9 '66
Paper capers; disposable paper dress. il Time 87:71 Mr 18 '66
Papered over. il Newsweek 68:105 O 31 '66
Regulating student dress. D. Waleski. il NEA J 55:12-14 Ap '66
Season of sparkle plenty; evening fashions. il Time 88:70 D 2 '66
Turn on, turn off; electrc clothes. il Time 89:80 Ja 20 '67
Varsity rags. il Newsweek 68:94 Ag 22 '66
Wastebasket dress has arrived; with report by H. Carlton. il Life 61:132-4+ N 25 '66
See also
Caps
Clothing industry
Coats
Costume design

CLOTHING and dress—See also—*Continued*
Dressmaking
Fashion
Fashion as a profession
Fur
Kilts
Paper textiles
Patterns (dress)
Sweaters
Uniforms

Children

Basic buying tips for children's clothing. il Good H 162:157 F '66
Children's blanket sleepers. il Consumer Rep 31:486-9 O '66

Men

American male's way of dress. il Look 30: M6-7 F 22 '66
Dapper wrinkles of seersucker. G. Frazier. il Esquire 66:92-3 Ag '66
Double-B look. il Time 87:69 F 25 '66
Guys go all-out to get gawked at; U.S., English and French styles. il Life 60:82A-84+ My 13 '66
It's modness. il Newsweek 67:96+ Mr 14 '66
Last of the big dandies. L. Beebe. il Esquire 65:104+ F '66
Men in Vogue; interview. D. Fairbanks, jr. Vogue 148:53 Ag 15 '66
Men's suits, tailor-made, just $80. il Changing T 20:37-8 Ag '66
Menswear: opening of shop at Bonwit Teller. New Yorker 42:48-9 O 15 '66
New color styles for men. C. W. Morton. il Atlan 217:109 My '66
On the Savile road; English tailor-made suits. il Time 88:25 D 30 '66
Opinion; young men's looks. A. Pryce-Jones. Mlle 62:84-5 F '66
Personal business; summer suits: cool, dark, and subdued. Bsns W p 167 My 28 '66
Styles to suit the Mustang market; high style with medium-range price tag. il Bsns W p80-3 F 19 '66
Tails you lose! J. W. Stedman. il Opera N 31:10-11 S 17 '66
Two contributions to the art of wearing clothes. A. Gingrich. Esquire 66:6 Ag '66
White tie and tails; party at the Waldorf for Princess Margaret. R. Lynes. Harper 232:28+ F '66

Sports clothes

Boating look, or is there one? M. Wiley. il Yachting 119:104-7 Ja '66
Fast off the slopes; skiers better-looking. il Time 89:62-7 Ja 6 '67
Fitted out for a blue-water race; Newport-Bermuda race. P. Stewart. il Sports Illus 24:62 Je 27 '66
High style for skiing turns into big business; E. Engel, creates sportswear. il Bsns W p 108-10+ Ja 22 '66
Nuts to fashion; what to wear when you fly. P. Shamburger. il Flying 79:88 O '66
Sporting look. See issues of Sports illustrated
To make Alps more scenic; Paris designed outfits. il Life 60:99-100+ F 18 '66
Win or lose, Doug Sanders is a pop artist's dream. D. Jenkins. il Sports Illus 24:86-7 Ap 25 '66

CLOTHING industry

Styles to suit the Mustang market; high style with medium-range price tag. il Bsns W p80-3 F 19 '66
That little dress goes over big; Helsinki-based business of Marimekko dresses and home furnishings. il Bsns W p88-90 D 10 '66

Wages and hours

Earnings in women's and misses' coat and suit industry. G. L. Stelluto. il Mo Labor R 89:769-71 Jl '66
Wages in synthetic fibers, textile finishing, and dress manufacturing. il Mo Labor R 89:1255-61 N '66

United States

Antitrust and the apparel industry; address, June 17, 1966. P. R. Dixon. Vital Speeches 32:617-21 Ag 1 '66
California shapes the style. il Bsns W p48-9+ Ag 13 '66
See also
International ladies' garment workers' union
New York (city)—Industries

CLOUD, Preston E. Jr
Beach cusps: response to Plateau's rule? bibliog Science 154:890-1 N 18 '66
—and Nelson, C. A.
Phanerozoic-cryptozoic and related transitions: new evidence. bibliog Science 154: 766-70 N 11 '66

CLOUD seeding. See Rain making
CLOUDS
High-latitude hydrogen clouds. il Sky & Tel 32:206 O '66
Pageantry in the sky, clouds and their meaning. G. Emmons. il Motor B 119:101 Ja '67
Use of cloud observations in weather forecasting. il Motor B 119:102-3 Ja '67
CLOUGH, Roy L. jr
Up-and-flying model sailboat. Pop Mech 125: 165-7 Ag '66
CLOUSTON, J. Brian
Paved surfaces and their construction; reprint. Parks & Rec 1:422-4+, 511-12+, 580-1, 752-3+ My-Jl, S '66
CLOVER ring; story. See Dixon, C.
CLOVIS points. See Stone implements and weapons
CLOWARD, Richard A. and Elman, R. M.
First congress of the poor. Nation 202:148-51 F 7 '66
Poverty, injustice and the welfare state. Nation 202:230-5, 264-8 F 28-Mr 7 '66
—and Piven, F. F.
Weight of the poor: strategy to end poverty. Nation 202:510-17 My 2 '66
—See Piven, F. F. jt. auth.
CLUB apartments. See Apartment houses
CLUB bedroom; drama. See Auchincloss, L.
CLUB houses. See Clubhouses
CLUB Méditerranée. See Vacation villages
CLUBHOUSES
Domed club that will test the god of golf; Yomiuri country club near Tokyo. A. Wright. il Sports Illus 25:54-7 N 7 '66
Private tennis club: simple, disciplined, economical; East Hampton, Long Island, N.Y. il Arch Rec 140:142-3 D '66
CLUBS
Buying an airliner instead of a ticket. il Bsns W p 160-2+ Jl 9 '66
Clubmanship: way to avoid compliance with the discrimination-banning public accommodations section of the Civil rights act of 1964. il Time 87:19 Ja 28 '66
Extraordinary feast; American branch of Confrérie des Chevaliers du Tastevin. B. Glinn. il Holiday 39:88-9 My '66
Four buildings for leisure-time activities. il Arch Rec 139:167-72 Je '66
Great clubs of the world. il Esquire 65:148-9+ Ap '66
How to tell an Elk from an Eagle; a field guide to clubs and lodges. il Changing T 20:13-15 S '66
Peripatetic reviewer; memories of We happy few in Gander club. E. Weeks. Atlan 217: 156 Mr '66
Youth: what they need is a place to go; dance club, Waterford, Conn. il Life 61: 41-3 Ag 19 '66
See also
Garden clubs
Political clubs and associations
Science clubs
also subhead Clubs under names of cities, e.g. New York (city)—Clubs
CLUBS, School. See Student activities
CLURMAN, Harold Edgar
Festivity and ritual: reflections on true theatre. Nation 202:583-7 My 16 '66
In the air of several worlds. Nation 203:421-2 O 24 '66
Theatre. See issues of Nation

about

How a playwright triumphs; interview, ed. by A. Wagner. C. Odets. Harper 233:64-70+ S '66
CLURMAN, Robert
Problems in psychotherapy: the vacation period; excerpt from Why you need analysis. N Y Times Mag p26+ Je 26 '66
CLUSTER housing. See Housing projects—Site planning
CLUTCHES for automobiles. See Automobiles—Clutches
CLUTTER, Herbert William, family
In cold blood, by T. Capote. Review
Commentary 41:77-80 My '66. W. Phillips
Commonweal 83:561-2 F 11 '66. B. McCabe
Harper 232:108+ F '66. R. West; Reply with rejoinder. T. Caldwell. 232:4 My '66
Nat R 18:226-9 Mr 8 '66. J. G. Dunne
Nation 202:158-60 F 7 '66. S. Yurick
Reporter 34:58 Mr 10 '66. J. K. Galbraith

COACHES (academic) See Tutors and tutoring
COACHES (athletics) See Physical directors
COACHING (football) See Football players—
Training
COAL
Lighting up with coal; Mohave power project.
Time 89:78 Ja 20 '67
COAL and steel community. See European coal
and steel community
COAL industry
Fouling the air; advertising strategy. N.
Cousins. Sat R 49:32+ O 8 '66

Australia
Prosperity out of the pit. Time 87:80 F 11 '66

Germany (Federal Republic)
Crisis in coal; government's revival program.
Newsweek 67:73 Mr 28 '66
COAL liquefaction
Coal fever; gasoline from coal research. New
Repub 154:7 Ap 9 '66
COAL mine rescue work. See Mine rescue
work
COAL miners
Coal miners trail back after a pact. Bsns W
p78 Ap 30 '66
Inquest on a premature burial; caved-in
mine Sheppton, Pa. T. Buckley. il Esquire
65:75-81+ Je '66
Power struggle; Europe's coal miners. il
Time 87:90 Je 17 '66
See also
Strikes—United States—Coal mines and min-
ing
United mine workers of America
COAL mines and mining
See also
Coal miners

Accidents and explosions
See also
Coal mines and mining—Safety devices and
measures

Safety devices and measures
Explosion quencher being developed for coal
mine. Sci N 90:137 Ag 27 '66

Stripping operations
Controlling the strippers; Kentucky controls.
Time 87:96 F 4 '66
Offense against America; a mountain is ravaged, a valley shattered; Big Black Mountain. H. M. Caudill. il Audubon Mag 68:356-9
S '66
Paradise is stripped. H. M. Caudill. il N Y
Times Mag p26-7+ Mr 13 '66
Strip-mine morality; landscaping of hell;
regulations proposed by the Strip mining
and reclamation division of the Kentucky
department of natural resources. W. Berry.
il Nation 202:96-100 Ja 24 '66
Strip mining, reclamation, and the public
interest. D. B. Brooks. il Am For 72:18-
19+ Mr '66

Belgium
In poor health; mine closings. il Newsweek
67:35-6 F 14 '66

Europe, Western
Europe's coal owners mine rich, new seams;
diversifying into chemicals, plastics, auto
making. il Bsns W p 122-4+ My 28 '66
Power struggle. il Time 87:90 Je 17 '66

Wales
Murderous mountain; Aberfan. il Time 88:41
O 28 '66
Never one like this; avalanche of coal slag;
Aberfan, Wales. il Newsweek 68:54+ O 31
'66
Sea of sludge upon green Aberfan. il Life
61:68-73 N 4 '66
COAL strikes (United States) See Strikes—
United States—Coal mines and mining
COALITION bargaining. See Collective bargain-
ing
COANDA, Henri
Applications of the Coanda effect. I. Reba.
il Sci Am 214:84-92 Je '66
COAST, John
Bali revisited; 1966. Dance Mag 40:46-9+
N '66
COAST changes
Case of the disappearing coastline. F. J.
Cook. il N Y Times Mag p38-9+ S 25 '66;
Reply. J. J. Fisher. p 122+ O 23 '66
Recent emerged beach in eastern Mexico.
E. W. Behrens. bibliog il Science 152:642-3
Ap 29 '66

Where the beaches go. il Sci Digest 59:38-9
Ap '66
COAST guard. See United States—Coast guard
COASTING
Deadly zig-zag; S. Zardini killed on Mount
Van Hoevenberg run, Lake Placid, N.Y.
Time 87:53 Mr 4 '66
Just short of disaster; E. Monti's ninth world
championship. il Time 87:62 F 11 '66
COASTS
See also
Seashore
COATES, Donald R.
Glaciated Appalachian plateau; till shadows
on hills. bibliog Science 152:1617-19 Je 17
'66
COATES, Robert H.
Preparing adults for rapid change. NEA J
55:23-5 D '66
COATES, Robert M.
Art galleries. See issues of New Yorker to
January 7, 1967
COATING materials. See Finishing materials
COATINGS, Protective. See Protective coat-
ings
COATS
Botany's new raincoat finish; water-repellent
topcoat. Consumer Rep 31:424 S '66
How to choose that new spring coat. Good H
162:151 Mr '66
Water-repellent topcoats. il Consumer Rep
31:200-3 Ap '66
COAXIAL cables
See also
Television cables
COBALT
Zinc and cobalt; effect on the iron metabolism
of ustilago sphaerogena. H. Komai and J.
B. Neilands. bibliog il Science 153:751-2 Ag
12 '66
COBALT salts
When beer brought the blues. Time 89:50
Ja 20 '67
COBB, Boughton
Ferns. il Horticulture 44:18-19+ My '66
COBB, Boughton, Jr
Big California cat. Yachting 120:65-7 Jl '66
Fiberglass maintenance. il Yachting 119:78-
9+ Ap '66
New lighting construction in glass Yacht-
ing 119:73-5+ Ja '66
COBB, James C.
Iron meteorites with low cosmic ray ex-
posure ages. bibliog Science 151:1524 Mr
25 '66
COBBLE, James W.
High-temperature aqueous solutions. bibliog
Science 152:1479-85 Je 10 '66
COBBLERS (desserts) See Cookery—Fruit
COBER, Alan E.
Alan E. Cober; artist of the year '65. H. C.
Pitz. il por Am Artist 30:36-41+ Je '66
COBLANS, Herbert
Bibliographic organization at the interna-
tional level. bibliog por Wilson Lib Bul
40:733-7 Ap '66
COBURN, James
People are talking about. . . por Vogue 148:
114-15 O 15 '66
COBURN, Judy
Open city. New Repub 155:9-10 S 17 '66
COCA-COLA company
Bottled up; Israeli company denied franchise.
Newsweek 67:78 Ap 18 '66
Capping the crisis; Israeli franchise. Time
87:75 Ap 22 '66
Greatest franchise of all; bottlers. J. B.
Weiner. il Duns R 88:31+ O '66
Why things go better at Coke. J. B. Weiner.
il Duns R 88:28-30+ O '66
COCARBOXYLASE
Thiamine pyrophosphate hydrochloride; stere-
ochemical aspects from an X-ray diffrac-
tion study. J. Pletcher and M. Sax. bibliog
il Science 154:1331-3 D 9 '66
COCHELL, Shirley
8 across, 3 down. Sr Schol 89:sup 13 D 2 '66
How to teach a unit on newspapers. Sr Schol
89:sup63 S 23 '66
Teaching the Bill of rights. Sr Schol 88:sup
14 Ap 1 '66
COCHLEAR. See Ear
COCHRAN, Bernard H.
Southern Baptist dilemma in higher educa-
tion. Christian Cent 83:1598-601 D 28 '66
COCHRANE, Eric
Failure in Florence. Commonweal 85:197-9
N 18 '66
COCHRANE, James D.
Central American economic integration.
Américas 18:1-5 My '66
Ecuador; a present-day portrait. bibliog f Cur
Hist 51:264-9 N '66

COCHRANE, Shirley Graves
Remember Charlie Mock? story. Ladies Home
J 83:82-3 Mr '66
COCKROACHES
Despised one, la cucaracha. R. Rood. il
Audubon Mag 68:426-9 N '66
Dieldrin: interaction with nerve components
of cockroaches. F. Matsumura and M. Hay-
ashi. bibliog il Science 153:757-9 Ag 12 '66
Intellectual and emotional world of the cock-
roach. H. E. Evans. il Harper 233:50-5 D
'66
COCKTAIL parties. See Entertaining
COCKTAILS
Bloody-Mary man. il Newsweek 69:6 Ja 2 '67
Mixmasters; bottled cocktails. il Newsweek
67:67 F 7 '66
Wine, women & so on. P. Cannon. Ladies
Home J 83:68 O '66
COCLÉ
Gold of Coclé. R. A. Cowes. bibliog il
Américas 18:18-25 F '66
COCOA
Cocoa consultations. UN Mo Chron 3:86 D '66
See also
United Nations cocoa conference

Prices
Cocoa working party; United Nations cocoa
conference. UN Mo Chron 3:16 F '66
COCONUT
See also
Cookery—Coconut
COCONUT milk
Single cells, coconut milk, and embryogenesis
in vitro. W. Halperin. bibliog il Science
153:1287-8 S 9 '66
Summer coolers, using coconut milk. il Sun-
set 136:152 Je '66
COCTEAU, Jean
Jean Cocteau, by W. Fowlie. Review
Sat R il por 49:43 N 19 '66. T. Bishop
COD fishing
Jig is up. C. Ford. il Field & S 71:8+ Ag '66
King of the bottom. G. Heinold. il Outdoor
Life 138:12+ N '66
CODDINGTON, Dean C. See Gilmore, J. S.
jt. auth.
CODE practice oscillators. See Oscillators
CODES (ciphers) See Ciphers
CODICILS; story. See Henderson, R.
CODY, John Patrick, abp
Chicago expects more than caution from
Cody. Christian Cent 83:1025 Ag 24 '66
Chicago priests organize. D. L. Flaherty.
America 115:540-3 N 5 '66
Cody in Chicago. J. Leo. Commonweal 84:
334-6 Je 10 '66; Reply. J. Fitzgerald. 84:
452 Jl 22 '66
No-nonsense archbishop. por Time 87:96 My
20 '66
CODY, William F, collection. See Art—Private
collections
COE, Darrell L.
Katmai National Monument. il Nat Parks
Mag 40:4-9 Je '66
COE, Ralph T.
Rubens' sacrifice of Abraham. Art N 65:36-
9+ D '66
COEDS. See College students, Women
COEDUCATION
Coeducation. Commonweal 84:215-16 My 13 '66
COELACANTHS
Intracranial mobility in the coelacanth; jaw
mechanism of latimeria. K. S. Thomson.
bibliog il Science 153:999-1000 Ag 26 '66
Lipids of the living coelacanth, latimeria
chalumnae. J. C. Nevenzel and others. bib-
liog il Science 152:1753-5 Je 24 '66
Portrait of a living fossil. il Life 61:64-6 Jl
22 '66
COEN, George
Tenure for librarians. Library J 91:212-13,
1744 Ja 15, Ap 1 '66
COENZYMES
Enzyme-coenzyme complexes of pyridine
nucleotide-linked dehydrogenases. H. F.
Fisher and D. G. Cross. bibliog il Science
153:414-15 Jl 22 '66
CO-EXISTENCE policy. See United States—
Foreign relations—Russia
COFFEE
Appetizing as sin. L. F. de Faro. il Américas
18:11-13 D '66
Great coffee instantly! with recipes. il Ladies
Home J 84:87 Ja '67
What coffee really does to you. I. Ross. il
Sci Digest 60:79-83 Jl '66

Prices
Bit of good news on cents-off; labels ruled
fictitious pricing. Consumer Rep 31:52 F '66
COFFEE cake
Favorite coffee cakes. il Bet Hom & Gard
44:105-6 O '66
COFFEE parties. See Entertaining
COFFEE pots, percolators, etc.
Automatic electric coffee makers. il Consumer
Bul 49:6-10 Je '66
More about coffee makers; three brands tested.
il Consumer Bul 49:32-5 N '66
Two unusual coffee-makers. il Consumer
Rep 31:287 Je '66
COFFER, Helene Lewis
Saint on earth; story. Good H 162:98-9 Ap '66
COFFEY, Warren
Double feature. Commentary 41:79-82 Ap '66
Observations. See issues of Commentary to
August 1967
COGLEY, John
Catholics and their schools. Sat R 49:72-4+
O 15 '66
From pulpit to think tank. N Y Times Mag
p 16-17+ Ag 14 '66
(ed) See Niebuhr, R. Interview with Rein-
hold Niebuhr
COGNAC. See Brandy
COGSWELL family
Correction and addition. il Antiques 90:522
O '66
COHELAN, Jeffery
Excerpt from debate, July 28, 1966. Cong
Digest 45:278+ N '66
COHEN, Abraham B.
P.A. loudspeaker principles and practice.
Electr World 75:23-6+ Je '66
COHEN, Albert G.
Drip, drip, drip. il por Newsweek 67:30+ Ap
4 '66
COHEN, Arthur Allen
Guide to Jewish journals. Commonweal 84:
639-41 S 30 '66
Rediscovering Judaism. Commonweal 83:634-
5 Mr 4 '66
COHEN, Carl
Law, speech and disobedience. Nation 202:
357-62 Mr 28 '66
COHEN, Carolyn, and Longley, William
Tropomyosin paracrystals formed by divalent
cations. bibliog Science 152:794-6 My 6 '66
COHEN, Daniel
ESP: science or delusion? Nation 202:550-3
My 9 '66
Russians faked it. Nation 203:445-7+ O 31 '66
COHEN, Edwin
Center for ITV. Am Ed 2:22-4 Je '66
COHEN, Elliot Ettelson
Young in the thirties. L. Trilling. Commen-
tary 41:45-51 My '66
COHEN, Harriet
Craftsmen USA '66; North Central region.
Craft Horiz 26:28-30+ Mr '66
COHEN, Harry B. and Dement, W. C.
Sleep: suppression of rapid eye movement
phase in the cat after electroconvulsive
shock. bibliog Science 154:396-8 O 21 '66
COHEN, Harry D. and others
Puromycin and cycloheximide: different ef-
fects on hippocampal electrical activity.
bibliog Science 154:1557-8 D 23 '66
—See Barondes, S. H. jt. auth.
COHEN, Hennig
American classic art. Reporter 35:60-2 N 17
'66
Art of the possibility. Reporter 34:51 F 10 '66
From da Vinci to Detroit. Reporter 34:55-7
Ja 27 '66
Innocent eye. Reporter 34:45-8 Mr 10 '66
Miss Wheatley's distinction. Reporter 34:46+
Je 30 '66
Romantic of Olana. Reporter 34:51-2 Ap 7 '66
Wyeth's world. Reporter 35:56-8+ D 15 '66
COHEN, Irun R. and Norins, L. C.
Natural human antibodies to gram-negative
bacteria immunoglobulins G, A, and M.
bibliog Science 152:1257-9 My 27 '66
COHEN, Jacob
What the Warren report omits; vital docu-
ments. Nation 203:43-9 Jl 11 '66
COHEN, Jerry, and Murphy, W. S.
Burn, baby, burn! excerpts. Life 61:36-8+
Jl 15 '66
COHEN, Leonard
Poem; This is for you. Mlle 64:44 Ja '67
COHEN, Lewis H. See Klement, W. jr, jt.
auth.
COHEN, Lita H. Solis-. See Solis-Cohen, L. H.
COHEN, M. H. and others
Radio sources: angular size from scintillation
studies. bibliog Science 153:745-6 Ag 12 '66

COHEN, Manuel Frederick
Critical look at the stock market; interview. pors U S News 60:36-40+ My 30 '66

about

SEC enters a period of persuasion. por Bsns W p94-6+ F 5 '65
Where Manny Cohen is leading the SEC. C. J. Loomis. por Fortune 74:163-5+ D '66 (to be cont)

COHEN, Martin
Aftermath of a tornado. Redbook 127:64-5+ O '66
Sun shines bright. Redbook 127:60-1+ My '66

COHEN, Mike
Bright young man; story. Redbook 126:155-81 F '66

COHEN, Philip P. See Janssens, P. A. jt. auth.

COHEN, Robert David
Greater the lie, the sooner is it found out; poem. New Yorker 42:32 Ag 27 '66
Street of named houses; poem. New Yorker 42:231 O 29 '66
With a missing text; Untitled poem; poems. Poetry 108:311-12 Ag '66

COHEN, Selma Jeanne
Is this the time? Dance Mag 40:26-7 F '66

COHEN, Sheldon S.
Excerpt from testimony, May 19, 1965. Cong Digest 45:306+ D '66

COHENITE
Cohenite in meteorites; a proposed origin. R. Brett. bibliog il Science 153:60-2 Jl 1 '66

COHN, Arthur
Five symphonies by Hans Werner Henze. Am Rec G 33:118-20 O '66
From CRI and Desto: on six releases, eleven Americans. Am Rec G 32:684-7 Ap '66
From RCA Victor: after sixty-eight years, the first symphony of Chas. E. Ives. Am Rec G 32:1032-3 Jl '66
How to get a joint raided, and other electronic music. Am Rec G 32:1114-15+ Ag '66
Louisville, from strength to strength. Am Rec G 32:798-803 My '66
Now, that other American giant, Carl Ruggles. Am Rec G 32:588-90 Mr '66
Postscript: that day I visited Charles Koechlin. Am Rec G 32:782-3+ My '66

COHN, Benjamin
Guidance and counseling in groups. NEA J 55:38-9 O '66

COHN, Haim Hermann
What's in a name? por Time 87:61 My 27 '66

COHN, Lawrence
Recordings reports: folk and blues LPs (cont) Sat R 49:80 N 26 '66

COHN, Norman
Myth of the Jewish world-conspiracy; excerpt from Warrant for genocide. Commentary 41:35-42 Je; 42:22+ D '66

COHN, Sherman L. See Madden, M. S. jt. auth.

COHN, Victor
(ed) See Wright, P. M. Medicine today

COINAGE. See Silver as money

COINCIDENCES
And it came unto New York city; biblical events. W. McQuade. il Arch Forum 124:96 Ja '66

COINER, Charles T.
Wild roses and Irish salmon. il Esquire 65:94-7+ F '66

COINS
British coin history. C. French. Hobbies 71:102 Ag '66
California $50 gold pieces. C. French. Hobbies 71:102 D '66
Coin quiz. C. French. See issues of Hobbies
Look at the coin shortage. U S News 60:98 F 21 '66
Mathematical games; recreational numismatics. M. Gardner. il Sci Am 214:112-14+ F '66
Spy and the coin collector; Russia's financial arrangements with other countries, furnishing gold. M. MacDougall. Nat R 18:355 Ap 19 '66; Correction. 18:591 Je 14 '66
Story of Mormon gold. C. French. Hobbies 71:102 Ja '67
See also
Silver as money

Collectors and collecting
Hoarding will not pay. C. French. Hobbies 71:102 Je '66
Money in coins. il Fortune 73:242 Ap '66
Treasure finds could affect values. C. French. Hobbies 71:102 My '66
Who's hiding all the half-dollars? il Changing T 21:33-4 Ja '67

History
Feudal era numismatics. C. French. Hobbies 71:102 Ap '66

Names
Odd coin names well known to millions. C. French. Hobbies 71:102 Jl '66

COIT, Margaret L.
Born in Boston, bred for Washington. Sat R 49:38-9 Ap 9 '66
Government for the people. Sat R 49:47-8 D 24 '66
Neighborly for the common good. Sat R 49:39-40 N 5 '66

COKES, Curtis
Winning for old Cornbread. M. Kram. il por Sports Illus 25:18-19 S 5 '66

COLBERT, R. G.
North Atlantic treaty organization; address, November 1, 1966. Vital Speeches 33:125-8 D 1 '66

COLBORNE, James B.
Saltproofing your car. Pop Mech 127:122-5 Ja '67

COLBURN, Paul W.
Albino adventure nets rare Anna's. Audubon Mag 68:476-8 N '66

COLBY, Benjamin N.
Cultural patterns in narrative. bibliog Science 151:793-8 F 18 '66

COLBY, Carroll B.
Camping. See issues of Outdoor life

COLD
See also
Low temperatures

Physiological effects
Why do children get sick so often in winter? L. W. Sauer. PTA Mag 61:31-2 Ja '67

Therapeutic applications
Freeze tumors to death. Sci N 89:234 Ap 9 '66

COLD (disease)
Cold symptoms may be caused by chemical dust. Sci N L 89:56 Ja 22 '66
Light-chain heterogeneity of cold agglutinins. N. Costea and others. bibliog il Science 152:1520-1 Je 10 '66
No drug miracles for common cold. Todays Health 44:49 Ag '66
Oh so common cold. Field & S 71:40 S '66

Vaccines
Cold vaccines. Sci Digest 61:31-2 Ja '67

COLD agglutinins. See Agglutinins

COLD cuts. See Meat

COLD heart; story. See Marks, G. A. jr

COLD remedies. See Medicines, Patent, proprietary, etc.

COLD soups. See Soups

COLD SPRING HARBOR, N.Y.
Cold Spring Harbor high school; decentralized libraries. Z. R. George. il Library J 90:5475-7 D 15 '65; Correction. 91:365 Ja 15 '66

COLD viruses
No flu yet, just colds. Sci N L 89:103 F 12 '66

COLD war. See Communism and democracy; World politics, 1945-

COLD war (United States and Russia) See United States—Foreign relations—Russia

COLD weather photography. See Photography—Cold weather conditions

COLD welding. See Welding

COLDS. See Cold (disease)

COLDWATER, Mich.
Modern lighting adds zest to downtown renewal. S. L. Garvin. il Am City 81:130 F '66

COLE, Carol
Carol Cole. il pors Ebony 21:114-16+ Jl '66
Nat King Cole's daughter Carol: new actress with talent. C. Brossard. il pors Look 30:M8-9+ Ag 9 '66

COLE, Jonathan O.
Alcoholism. Science 154:922-3 N 18 '66

COLE, LaMont C.
Protect the friendly microbes. Sat R 49:46-7 My 7 '66

COLE, Leonard J. See Varon, M. L. jt. auth.

COLE, R. David, and Dekker, C. A.
Nucleic acid and protein chemistry. Science 153:92-4 Jl 1 '66

COLE, Sandra
Five with enterprise. P. Rifield. il por Mlle 63:147 S '66

COLE, Thomas
See Liebmann, G. Shape of things practically here

COLEMAN, Emily
Councils take counsel; preview of annual conference. Sat R 49:59-60 Ap 30 '66

COLEMAN, James S.
Learning through games. NEA J 56:69-70 Ja '67

COLEMAN, Ornette
New jazz. il por Newsweek 68:101-4+ D 12 '66
Ornette Coleman in Stockholm. M. Williams. por Sat R 49:83+ Je 11 '66

COLEMAN, Patrick
Curl up and read. Seventeen 25:20 Je '66

COLEMAN, Sheldon
What sparked the fire under Coleman co. il pors Bsns W p86-8+ Ag 13 '66

COLEMAN, William
Science and symbol in the Turner frontier hypothesis. bibliog f Am Hist R 72:22-49 O '66

COLEMAN company
Going in for outing. il Time 88:60 Jl 29 '66
What sparked the fire under Coleman co: divisionalization program. il Bsns W p86-8+ Ag 13 '66

COLES, Christie Lund
When he bore the cross; poem. Farm J 90:121 Ap '66

COLES, Edward
Americans not everybody knows. C. W. Ferguson. por PTA Mag 61:10-12 Ja '67

COLES, James S.
Bowdoin college senior program. Sch & Soc 94:182-3 Ap 2 '66

COLES, Robert
American amok. New Repub 155:12-15 Ag 27 '66
Causes and cures of delinquency. New Repub 154:28-9+ Ja 29 '66
Occasion for sadness. Sat R 50:76 Ja 21 '67
Search for community. New Repub 154:12-14 F 26 '66
Sex and students. New Repub 154:21-3 My 28 '66
Some children the schools have never served. Sat R 49:58-60 Je 18 '66
Southern children. New Repub 155:17-19 S 24 '66
Two minds about Carmichael. New Repub 155:19-21 N 12 '66
What poverty does to the mind. Nation 202:746-8 Je 20 '66
When I draw the Lord he'll be a real big man; excerpt from Courage and fear in the South. Atlan 217:69-72+ My '66
White northerner: pride and prejudice. Atlan 217:53-7 Je '66

COLETTE, Sidonie Gabrielle
Colette: the many facets of love; excerpt from Earthly paradise. pors McCalls 93:114-15+ Ap '66

about

Beloved maverick. il por Newsweek 67:102 My 9 '66
Books. E. Hardwick. Vogue 147:65 Ap 15 '66
Cats and casseroles. J. O'Brien. Reporter 35:59-60 O 20 '66
Colette: a scandalous sincerity. M. Ellmann. Nation 202:720-1 Je 13 '66
Dazzlers and astounders. G. Davenport. Nat R 18:637-8 Je 28 '66
Look! por Time 87:120 My 20 '66
Reader's choice. O. Handlin. Atlan 217:125-6 My '66
Vivid portrait of Colette by Colette. J. Flanner. Life 60:8+ My 13 '66
Woman's moments of awareness. A. Balakian. il pors Sat R 49:89-90 My 7 '66

COLGATE university, Hamilton, N.Y.
Intellectual recreation at mid-year; January special studies projects. D. C. Stewart. il Sat R 49:79-80 Mr 19 '66

COLIC
Nightly crybabies; search for a cause. il Time 88:79 S 23 '66

COLIN, Ralph F.
Editor's letters. Art N 65:6 O '66

COLITIS
Colitis tied to family type; psychosomatic illness. Sci N 90:399 N 12 '66

COLLADO, Emilio Gabriel
Statesman in the boardroom. il pors Bsns W p 186-7+ N 26 '66

COLLAGE
Adventure in appreciation. S. Maxey. il Design 67:8-9 Mr '66
Ezra Jack Keats on collage as an illustrative medium. E. J. Keats. il Pub W 189:94-5 Ap 4 '66

COLLAGEN
Formation of hydroxyproline in collagen. S. Udenfriend. bibliog il Science 152:1335-40 Je 3 '66
Hydroxylation of proline and the intracellular accumulation of a polypeptide precursor of collagen. K. Juva and others. bibliog il Science 152:92-4 Ap 1 '66

COLLAGENOUS proteins. See Proteins

COLLARS
Try these collar and cuff refreshers. C. Houck. il Parents Mag 41:120 Mr '66

COLLECTING of accounts
Art of dunning. Newsweek 68:104+ S 12 '66

COLLECTING of taxes. See Tax collection

COLLECTION of blood. See Blood—Collection and preservation

COLLECTIVE bargaining
Bargaining and wages in local cartage. V. J. Sheifer. il Mo Labor R 89:1076-84 O '66
Impasse over mutual trust issue; UAW vs. Allis-Chalmers plant in Pittsburgh. il Bsns W p86-7 D 24 '66
NLRB and the duty to bargain. P. Ross. il Mo Labor R 89:1241-5 N '66
New public expectations; excerpt from paper presented at American assembly. J. T. Dunlop. Mo Labor R 89:1385-6 D '66
Public interest comes first. D. Lawrence. U S News 61:92 Ag 8 '66
Push is on for fatter pay envelopes; bargaining issues of 1967; with charts. Bsns W p72-5 D 31 '66
Representation among teachers. M. H. Moskow. il Mo Labor R 89:728-32 Jl '66
Settlement of disputes in public employment. Mo Labor R 89:III-IV Ap '66
Strategies for decentralization; excerpt from paper presented at American assembly. A. R. Weber. Mo Labor R 89:1386-7 D '66
Unions close ranks for next year's bargaining; AFL-CIO helping to set up new coalitions for 1967. Bsns W p90+ N 12 '66
What executives should know about labor. il Nations Bsns 53:58-60+ D '65
See also
Industrial relations
Trade agreements

Electric industries

Coalition bargaining, the acid test; labor's newest technique to be used in GE contract talks. il Bsns W p61-2 Ag 13 '66
Coalition to face GE; consortium of eight unions to bargain with Westinghouse and General electric. il Bsns W p 122+ Mr 12 '66
Computer sits in on the bargaining. Bsns W p 154 S 10 '66
GE puts unity to test. il Bsns W p94+ Je 25 '66
GE stands its ground; resists pressures from both government and public opinion. Bsns W p 164+ O 15 '66
Johnson draws bead on GE fight; wins two-week delay in nationwide strike. il Bsns W p 145-7 O 8 '66
On the brink of a strike at GE; union coalition and company stand firm as deadline nears. Bsns W p96+ O 1 '66
Who won in the GE settlement. il Bsns W p 149-50+ O 22 '66
Why the rank and file say no; terms fail to resolve issues of local memberships in Schenectady, N.Y. il Bsns W p59-60+ D 17 '66

Government employees

Bargaining by civil servants in Canada. E. E. Herman. Mo Labor R 89:603-6 Je '66
Collective bargaining by public employees. A. Weisenfeld. Mo Labor R 89:610-12 Je '66
Developments in federal union-management relations. C. M. Rehmus. Mo Labor R 89:613 Je '66
Representing the teachers' interests; excerpts from address. Mo Labor R 89:617-23 Je '66

Municipal employees

Public employees ask for a better shake; rethinking of rules under which essential workers bargain. il Bsns W p92+ D 3 '66
Research on municipal collective bargaining. E. Rock. Mo Labor R 89:615-16 Je '66
Union structure in municipal collective bargaining. A. H. Cook. Mo Labor R 89:606-8 Je '66

Steel industry

Steelworkers seek a bigger voice; implications for future industry bargaining. il Bsns W p 160+ S 24 '66

COLLECTIVE bargaining—*Continued*

Teachers

New directions for professional negotiation. R. O. Daly. NEA J 55:27-9 O '66
Summer school short course in teacher negotiations. G. R. Potts. Mo Labor R 89:847-50 Ag '66

COLLECTIVE bargaining, Industry wide
British incomes experience; excerpt from address. E. H. P. Brown. Mo Labor R 89:634-7 Je '66

COLLECTIVE settlements
Communistic societies of the United States, by C. Nordhoff. Review
    Nation 203:254 S 19 '66. G. Kateb
    See also
Brook Farm

Israel
In Israel, a visit to a kibbutz. il Sunset 136:56 Ap '66

COLLECTIVISM
    See also
Socialism

COLLECTOR; drama. See Roche, F.

COLLECTORS and collecting
Antiques' travel guide. See issues of Antiques
Collectors' notes. E. Gaines. See issues of Antiques
Decorated military Americana. W. H. Guthman. il Antiques 90:60-3 Jl '66
How three collectors display their treasures. il House & Gard 130:62-83 Jl '66
How to sell what you find in the attic. il Changing T 20:45-7 F '66
New York, London, Paris collect. L. Lerman. Mlle 63:102-6 Je '66
Notes from our correspondents. P. G. Davis. Hi Fi 16:30+ My '66
Treasure hunt (cont) J. Mebane. il Bet Hom & Gard 44:30+ Mr; 116 Ap; 122 My; 29+ O '66
Ways to display collections. il Sunset 136:145 My '66
What makes a well-decorated room; display of collections. P. Rumely. il Bet Hom & Gard 44:56-7 S '66
    See also
Art—Private collections
Book collecting
Display of antiques, art objects, etc.
Insects—Collection and preservation
    also subhead Collectors and collecting under various subjects, e.g. Phonograph records—Collectors and collecting

COLLEGE, Choice of
College & careers. D. Klein. See issues of Seventeen
College conundrum: how to choose. P. Janssen. il Am Ed 2:24-7 S '66
If the college of your choice says no; nonprofit admissions centers. il Good H 162:172-3 My '66
Schools make news; admissions crush is easing. Sat R 49:64 Je 18 '66
Sensible way to choose a college. il Changing T 20:15-20 N '66
Team or tug of war? your parents, guidance counselor and you. D. Klein. il Seventeen 25:146-7+ F '66
To the class of 1971. J. F. Scott. il N Y Times Mag p 119-20+ N 20 '66

COLLEGE administrators. See College officials

COLLEGE admission. See Colleges and universities—Entrance requirements

COLLEGE alumni. See College graduates

COLLEGE and school drama
Juliet on a ladder; performance at Benjamin Franklin high school. B. Waknin. Commonweal 84:96-7 Ap 15 '66
New stage on campus; cross-fertilization between colleges and professional companies. il Newsweek 68:95-6 Ag 22 '66
Voice of the silent stage; theater at Gallaudet. E. Ferber. il Am Ed 2:29-32 O '66

Texts
Junior and senior high. See issues of Plays

COLLEGE and school journalism
Black student: new semi-annual journal by Negro students at Columbia and Barnard. New Yorker 42:41-2 Mr 26 '66
College literary magazine contest. Sat R 49:38 D 31 '66
College newspapers in search of their own voice. J. Greenfield. Harper 232:87-93 My '66; Discussion. 232:6+ Je; 233:8 Ag '66
Crimson girl. Newsweek 67:73 F 7 '66
Harvard's Mother Cobra; Crimson's managing editor; with report by C. Altman. il Life 60:43-4+ Mr 4 '66

Pot luck; case of A. Buchanan, managing editor of University of Oregon newspaper. Newsweek 67:36+ Je 27 '66
Problems of protecting a source; case of managing editor of University of Oregon newspaper. Time 87:98 Je 24 '66

COLLEGE and the community. See Colleges and universities—Public relations

COLLEGE architecture
Architecture; campus design; challenge to architects. E. Galantay. Nation 202:789-90 Je 27 '66
Architecture; E. D. Stone's design of the State university of New York Albany campus. E. Galantay. il Nation 202:629-30 My 23 '66
Architecture that gives a campus the unity of a single building; with account by J. Barnett. il Arch Rec 140:145-60 O '66
Big happening in Berkeley; Wurster hall. D. Lyndon. il Arch Forum 124:56-63 Ja '66
Building types study (cont) il Arch Rec 139:165-88 My; 140:195-218 S '66
Bureau of higher education honors twenty-nine projects in its new design awards program. il Arch Rec 140:42-3 N '66
Campus landscape. J. Du Von. il Am Ed 2:18-24 My '66
Colorado U: respect for a robust environment. J. M. Dixon. il Arch Forum 125:54-63 O '66
Columns support walls; roof is suspended; Fisher administrative center at the University of Detroit. il Arch Rec 140:100-2 Ag '66
Concrete for complex forms of a lecture hall; Stony Brook campus of the State university of New York. il Arch Rec 140:142-3 N '66
Curious walls of Larsen hall; Harvard's high-powered Graduate school of education. D. Canty. il Arch Forum 124:46-53 Mr '66
Goodbye to Gothic at Georgia tech. il Sci Digest 59:60-5 My '66
Handsome beginning for Southern Illinois' new Edwardsville campus. il Arch Rec 140:111-20 D '66
How to grow a campus; Tougaloo college and Washington university. J. M. Dixon; P. Blake. il Arch Forum 124:56-67 Ap '66
Louis Kahn in India: an old order at a new scale; Indian institute of management, Ahmedabad. J. Bailey. il Arch Forum 125:39-47 Jl '66
M.I.T.'s student center: Eduardo Catalano starts with systems and creates architecture. il Arch Rec 139:125-32 Mr '66
New campus. O. Newman. il Arch Forum 124:30-55 My '66
New shapes for ivory towers. il Am Ed 2:10-13 N '66
New shapes for the ivory towers at Colorado; engineering center. il Fortune 74:123 Jl 1 '66
Oxidized metal and glass for crisp precision; Loutit hall of science, Grand Valley state college, Allendale, Mich. il Arch Rec 140:144-6 N '66
Preview; University of Michigan's repertory theater. il Arch Forum 125:93 S '66
Station saved for art's sake; B&O's Mt Royal station into an art school; Maryland institute, college of art. J. Bailey. il Arch Forum 125:52-7 S '66
Up from the Red lion inn. T. Thomas. il Am Ed 2:16-23 Mr '66
    See also
Dormitories

COLLEGE athletics
American outpost for recreation. D. Rugh. il Parks & Rec 1:166-7 F '66
How the British score on us. M. Whitney. il Sat R 49:63+ Ag 20 '66
If at first you don't succeed try thirty-three more times; UCLA beats its rival, USC. J. Tobin. il Sports Illus 24:74-6 My 16 '66
    See also
Basketball
Football
National collegiate athletic association
Rowing
Track athletics

COLLEGE bookstores
Art shows, authors' days build traffic for Tech coop; MIT. Pub W 189:105 Ap 18 '66
College store and the publisher. C. B. Grannis. Pub W 189:54 My 16 '66
Modern structure for University of Oregon co-op. J. Goldstein. il Pub W 191:70-1 Ja 16 '67
NACS discusses pilferage and how to cope with it; summary of addresses. Pub W 189:41-3 My 16 '66

COLLEGE bookstores—*Continued*
NACS panels examine problems of management; summary of discussions. il Pub W 189:51-4 My 30 '66
NACS views special problems of college store operation; summary of discussions at NACS annual meeting. il Pub W 189:42-50 My 30 '66
New look for the campus bookshop. D. Dempsey. il Sat R 50:81 Ja 14 '67
NYU store holds first book fair for faculty. il Pub W 190:83-4 D 26 '66
Pioneers and guinea pigs: NACS bookselling seminar; report. il Pub W 190:28-33 Ag 15 '66
Student market examined at NACS annual meeting; summary of addresses. il Pub W 189:35-40 My 16 '66
Survey shows the larger the college store, the smaller the net profit. il Pub W 190: 66-7 N 21 '66
Trade book department plays vital role at Seattle's university store. il Pub W 190: 40-2 D 26 '66
What U. of Chicago store customers are reading. Pub W 189:53 Ap 4 '66
See also
National associaiton of college stores
COLLEGE buildings. See College architecture
COLLEGE clubs and societies
See also
College fraternities
COLLEGE commencements. See Commencements
COLLEGE discipline
Some advice on sex, dress and manners; Cowell college, University of California at Santa Cruz; excerpts from memorandum. P. Smith. U S News 60:14-15 Je 6 '66
COLLEGE dormitories. See Dormitories
COLLEGE drama. See College and school drama
COLLEGE dropouts. See Dropouts
COLLEGE education
Cincinnati's college crusade. il Ebony 21:88+ Je '66
Dual-purpose revolution; excerpts from address, 1966. F. H. Bowles. NEA J 55:38-40 D '66
Education in the post-modern world. C. T. Rowan. NEA J 55:19 F '66
Higher education: a population flow feedback model. A. Reisman. bibliog il Science 153: 89-91 Jl 1 '66
Higher education and cybernation; with reply by R. W. Tyler. R. Theobald. NEA J 55: 26-9 Mr '66
Higher education; who should pay? address, March 24, 1966. M. M. Chambers. Vital Speeches 32:447-8 My 1 '66
Innovation in higher education. A. R. Dykes. bibliog f Sch & Soc 94:179-81 Ap 2 '66
Institutional priorities in higher education; address, March 9, 1965. L. Wilson. Sch & Soc 94:92+ F 19 '66
Invisible librarian; report on The university in America, a convocation held in Beverly Hills, Calif. F. Blake. il Library J 91:3360-2 Jl '66
Persistence of fraud in higher education. W. W. Brickman. Sch & Soc 94:171 Ap 2 '66
To the class of 1971. J. F. Scott. il N Y Times Mag p 119-20+ N 20 '66
What's going on in schools & colleges. See issues of Changing times
World panorama of higher education. UNESCO Courier 19:33 Mr '66
See also
Colleges and universities—Curriculum
Independent study
Junior colleges
Liberal education

Aims and objectives
University in contemporary society; adaptation of address, June 1, 1965. G. Kirk. Sch & Soc 94:63-5 F 5 '66
COLLEGE education, Cost of
He's gardening his way through college. H. Garrett. Farm J 90:68B Mr '66
How to beat the high cost of college. O. Schisgall. il PTA Mag 61:11-13 S '66; Same abr. Read Digest 89:141-4 S '66
Personal business; college costs. il Bsns W p 137-8 Ag 20 '66
COLLEGE education, Value of
Case for not going to college. J. Griffin and D. Chapman. il Look 30:90+ N 29 '66
Do I really have to go to college? D. Klein. Seventeen 25:36-8+ F '66

COLLEGE entrance examination board
Equality ad absurdum. F. S. Meyer. Nat R 18:1168 N 15 '66
COLLEGE faculties. See College professors and instructors
COLLEGE fees. See Colleges and universities —Finance
COLLEGE football. See Football
COLLEGE football players. See Football players
COLLEGE fraternities
Amherst fraternities. Sch & Soc 94:446 D 10 '66
Frat's in the fire. il Time 87:54 Ap 8 '66
Sororities: do they still swing? J. Contini. il Seventeen 25:296-7+ Ag '66

Desegregation
Action for fraternity non-discrimination. Sch & Soc 94:258 Sum '66
COLLEGE freshmen. See College students
COLLEGE girls. See College students, Women
COLLEGE graduates
Boom in jobs for 1966 graduates. U S News 60:123 Je 13 '66
Bright young men choose business careers. S. Schuler. il Nations Bsns 54:46-7+ Je '66
But you haven't changed a bit! class reunion. E. L. Horwitz. il McCalls 93:63+ Je '66
Campus and business; difficulty in hiring top students. H. C. Wallich. Newsweek 68:67 D 26 '66
Commencement is only the beginning; Harvard graduates after ten years. D. Burnham. il N Y Times Mag p 14+ Je 5 '66; Reply. S. Klaw. p49 Je 19 '66
Do you have what it takes to be a boss someday? il Changing T 20:24-9 My '66
Getting more out of the graduate; preference for master's in business administration. Bsns W p61-2+ Je 18 '66
Greeting; class of '66 and the draft. il Time 87:21-4 Je 3 '66
How to keep the go-getters. R. W. Walters, jr. Nations Bsns 54:47+ Je '66
How to nail Alfred; finders of lost alumni. Time 88:66 N 25 '66
Wanted: almost any warm body. Time 87:92+ Mr 18 '66
See also
College education, Value of
COLLEGE graduates, Women
After college; the real world. J. Steinberg. Mlle 63:196+ S '66
COLLEGE journalism. See College and school journalism
COLLEGE librarians. See Librarians
COLLEGE libraries
Academic librarianship: the state of the art; excerpts from address. G. Williams. il Library J 91:2413-18 My 15 '66
Library college idea: inevitable culmination of the independent study movement. L. Shores. bibliog il Library J 91:3871-5 S 1 '66
Resources for research in urban areas; address, July 12, 1966. E. G. Holley. bibliog il Wilson Lib Bul 41:502-9 Ja '67
Square miles, love, and money; Canadian libraries: academic. B. Stuart-Stubbs. il Library J 91:5529-32 N 15 '66
Ten-point program outlined for junior college libraries. Library J 91:1377+ Mr 15 '66
Writing a building program; adaptation of address. May 16, 1966. E. Mason. il Library J 91:5838-44 D 1 '66
See also
Conference of eastern college librarians

Administration
See Library administration

Architecture
See Library architecture

Automation
Data processing in an academic library; circulation and serials systems. Texas A&M university library, College Station. B. W. Stewart. il Wilson Lib Bul 41:388-95 D '66

Book selection
See Book selection

Departmental and divisional libraries
Departmental libraries and the problem of autonomy; science library, Haverford college, Pa. S. K. Newhall. ALA Bul 60:721-2 Jl '66
Science library cooperation in three colleges: Bryn Mawr, Haverford, and Swarthmore. Pa. S. Newhall. ALA Bul 60:380-1 Ap '66

COLLEGE libraries—*Continued*

Extension work
See College library extension

Federal aid
Federal legislation and programs to assist academic libraries. T. Samore. ALA Bul 60:156-9 F '66

First $10 million. J. Berry. Library J 91: 3365 Jl '66

Title II of the Higher education act: Title V-C of the Higher education act. P. P. Price and H. A. Carl. ALA Bul 60:699 Jl '66

Twenty-seven libraries included in latest listing of HEFA grants. Library J 91:2295 My 1 '66

Finance
In a glass darkly; getting along with university administrators. J. Weatherford. Library J 91:2290 My 1 '66

Instruction in use
See Libraries—Instruction in use

Oral history collections
See Libraries—Oral history collections

Standards
Standards at the grass roots; excerpts from address, July 14, 1965. J. Lombardi. bibliog f ALA Bul 60:377-80 Ap '66

Student advisory committees
Point of increasing returns; Student library committee at Oakland university, Rochester, Mich. J. Howey and E. McKenney. il Library J 91:6039-42 D 15 '66

Textbook collections
Search for the instant library. L. Sutton. il Sat R 49:24-5 Ap 16 '66

COLLEGE library architecture. See Library architecture

COLLEGE library assistants. See Library assistants

COLLEGE library extension
Guidelines for library services to extension students; with report by N. E. Tanis. ALA Bul 61:50-5 Ja '67

COLLEGE life. See Student life

COLLEGE newspapers. See College and school journalism

COLLEGE of American pathologists
Antitrust & ethics. Time 88:52 Jl 15 '66
Labs under analysis; violation of Sherman antitrust act. Newsweek 68:85 Jl 18 '66
Pathologists get a test; antitrust suit over laboratories and test fees. Bsns W p36 Jl 16 '66

COLLEGE officials
Internships for future college administrators. Sch & Soc 94:258+ Sum '66

COLLEGE operas, revues, etc.
Berkeley; U.C.L.A. opera theater presents Kurka's Good soldier Schweik. W. Aguiar, jr. il Opera N 31:24 N 19 '66
Bloomington; Indiana university celebrates twenty-fifth anniversary with Strauss' Rosenkavalier. W. Mootz. Opera N 30:26 Je 4 '66
California. Mozart's Idomeneo at Universiy of Southern California opera theater. W. Arlen. Opera N 31:31 Ja 21 '67
Doctor Moore's Carry Nation; commissioned by University of Kansas City. A. Rich. il Hi Fi 16:MA27 Jl '66
Evanston; Northwestern university's opera workshop presented Stravinsky's Renard and Purcell's Dido and Aeneas. A. M. Swanson. Opera N 31:29 D 31 '66
Hartford: Trinity college's production of As a conductor dreams, by Arnold Franchetti. W. Miranda. Opera N 31:28 D 17 '66
Michigan's harvest. D. A. Sutherland. il Opera N 30:13-15 Mr 19 '66

COLLEGE periodicals. See College and school journalism

COLLEGE personnel association, American. See American college personnel association

COLLEGE preparatory courses. See High schools—Curriculum

COLLEGE presidents
Dillard: pint-size school with a king-size job. il Ebony 21:188-90+ My '66
Extracurricular clout of powerful college presidents; with biographical sketches. pors Time 87:64-5 F 11 '66

Training
Teaching the big men on campus; college presidents learn managerial techniques in one-week course at Princeton. il Bsns W p 152-4+ Jl 9 '66

COLLEGE professors and instructors
Catholic professors on the secular campus; symposium. il America 115:318-23 S 24 '66; Discussion. 115:498 O 29 '66
Collegiate parnassus: the joys and sorrows of the artist-in-residence. I. Fisher. il Dance Mag 40:45-8+ Mr '66
Education without magic; personal qualities of teachers; address, November 19, 1965. J. M. Moudy. Vital Speeches 32:275-8 F 15 '66
Factors affecting academic standards; address, March 1, 1966. H. C. Monroe. Vital Speeches 32:562-5 Jl 1 '66
Faculty responsibility and the executive conquest of academe. D. Long. Sch & Soc 94:89-92 F 19 '66
Profess with a passion; ten great teachers. il Time 87:80-5 My 6 '66
Prof or project director? ACE meeting. Newsweek 68:75 O 24 '66
Teacher in the university; address, January 12, 1966. R. F. Goheen. Sch & Soc 94:177-9 Ap 2 '66
Unexamined life of the professor. J. C. Moore. Sat R 49:79 D 17 '66
University; excerpt from address, May 1966. W. Lippmann. New Repub 154:17-20 My 28 '66; Discussion. 154:27-8 Je 11 '66
Where they have gone; summer migrations of college faculties. il Time 88:54-5 Ag 5 '66
Who are the great teachers? P. Woodring. Sat R 49:55-6 Je 18 '66
Writers on the campus. D. Hall. Atlan 217: 87-90 Mr '66
Your ideas carry weight; Woodrow Wilson foundation's Teaching internship program. il Newsweek 67:74 F 7 '66
See also
Academic freedom
Colleges and universities—Administration
Colleges and universities—Teaching
Teachers and students
Women as college professors and instructors

Caricatures and cartoons
Four ways to go: a road map to superprof. Esquire 66:122-3 S '66

Political activities
Scholar is not a lion or a fox. R. Kirk. il N Y Times Mag p28-9+ My 1 '66
See also
Teach-ins

Publications
History, politics, and opinion; question of the interrrelation of academia and big government. H. E. Salisbury. il Sat R 49: 52 Je 11 '66
Professor: educator, scholar, or both? T. O. Brandt. Sch & Soc 94:381-2 N 12 '66
Reader beware; sub rosa financing by the CIA. Nation 202:701 Je 13 '66
Skid row of academe. H. Winthrop. Sch & Soc 94:267-9 Sum '66

Anecdotes, facetiae, satire, etc.
Publish and cherish; books in library as courses of study. H. C. Bauer. Library J 91:2774-6 Je 1 '66

Rating by students
Should college students grade their teachers? L. S. Feuer. il N Y Times Mag p56-7+ S 18 '66; Reply. J. Toby. p 156 O 9 '66
Student evaluation of professors. W. W. Brickman. Sch & Soc 94:143 Mr 19 '66
Students rate their professors. M. P. Sheridan. America 115:593-4 N 12 '66

Recruiting
Superstars; New York state experiment. il Newsweek 68:68 O 17 '66

Salaries
Greener grows the ivy. Sr Schol 88:sup4 Ap 29 '66

Selection and appointment
Greener pastures; notable men in government turn to big think. C. Fritchey. Harper 232:50 Ap '66
Of many things; decisions of religious superiors in assigning members of the faculty. T. N. Davis. America 115:365 O 1 '66

COLLEGE professors and instructors—*Cont.*

Wives

Pool of paragons: faculty wives as helpers for college librarians. J. Weatherford. Library J 91:1790 Ap 1 '66

COLLEGE recruiting. See Employment systems

COLLEGE reunions. See College graduates

COLLEGE sororities. See College fraternities

COLLEGE sports. See College athletics

COLLEGE stores association. See National association of college stores

COLLEGE student activities. See Student activities

COLLEGE students

Battling par at the table deciding intercollegiate championship for 1966. C. Goren. Sports Illus 24:76 My 9 '66

Call me by my rightful number; computers cause anonymity. E. P. Paullin. il Sat R 49:76 F 19 '66

Campus corner. M. P. Sheridan. America 116:87 Ja 21 '67

Campus image of business. H. G. Taylor. Duns R 88:21-2+ N '66

Caution! genius at play. J. N. Bell. il Pop Mech 125:120-3+ Mr '66; Same abr. with title Look out! genius at play. Read Digest 88:201-4 My '66

Civil liberties for college students; concerning ACLU and AAUP recommendations. G. R. Hawes. il Sat R 49:61-3+ Je 18 '66

Class of 1966: loss of tragedy. L. Hamalian. il Nation 202:676-9 Je 6 '66

Concerned collegians: a new wave. America 114:613 Ap 30 '66

Disenchanted campus; attitudes towards business; L. Harris poll. il Newsweek 67:85-6+ My 2 '66

Disquiet after hours; basic conflicts of undergraduates revealed in their dreams C. S. Hall. Mlle 64:77+ Ja '67

Doubts about Vietnam; letter to President Johnson from student leaders. Newsweek 69:49 Ja 9 '67

Drugs; a student report. A. Lake. Seventeen 25:170-1+ S '66

Drugs on campus: turned on & tuned out. M. B. Freedman and H. Powelson. il Nation 202:125-7 Ja 31 '66

Drugs on the campus. R. Goldstein. il Sat Eve Post 239:40-4+ My 21; 34-8+ Je 4 '66

Five college students speak out; questions and answers. ed. by L. F. McKernan. Cath World 204:198-204 Ja '67

Five freshmen at Harvard; symposium. il Seventeen 25:154-5+ My '66

Free-sex movement; growth on campuses. il Time 87:66 Mr 11 '66

Freshman myth; result of the college characteristics index questionnaire. G. G. Stern. il NEA J 55:41-3 S '66

Freshman paper on Harvard freshmen. S. Kelman. il N Y Times Mag p50-3+ D 11 '66; Discussion. p4+ D 25 '66

Good-bye to all that. D. Newman and R. Benton. il Esquire 66:127 S '66

How Bermuda defuses the revels of spring; college week. il Bsns W p72-4 Ap 16 '66

I am a U.C. student; do not fold, bend or mutilate. H. Gold. il Sat Eve Post 239:34-6+ Je 18 '66

Learn to leave your student alone! W. F. Pillsbury. Bet Hom & Gard 44:20+ O '66

Man talk; women are for weekends. D. Newman and R. Benton. Mlle 63:46+ Je '66

Moods & mores; new responsibility, dampening of protest. il Time 88:95-6+ N 18 '66

NACS discusses pilferage and how to cope with it; summary of addresses. Pub W 189:41-3 My 16 '66

New set of labels; categories set up by K. Keniston. il Time 87:71+ Ap 29 '66

New student; K. Keniston defines. Newsweek 67:92 My 2 '66

Next: a sleep-in? birth control in colleges. J. Steinberg. Mlle 62:10+ Ap '66

Of many things; concerning Fr T. R. Fitzgerald's article Coping with the new breed. T. N. Davis. America 114:inside cover Mr 26 '66

Private world of the class of '66; with editorial comment. D. Norton-Taylor. il Fortune 73:102+128-32+ F '66

Right young people for business. J. S. Fielden. Harvard Bsns R 44:76-83 Mr '66

Roman holidays for students. R. Kirk. Nat R 18:472 My 17 '66

Romantic generation. P. F. Drucker. Harper 232:12+ My '66

Safe way to rebel; taking marijuana. il Sat Eve Post 239:106 My 21 '66

Scrooge and the students. T. C. Sorensen. Sat R 50:66 Ja 14 '67

Search for the new morality. C. B. Ketcham. Christian Cent 83:1236-9 O 12 '66

Sex and the college student, by the Committee on the college student group for the advancement of psychiatry. Review
Cath World 204:182-4 D '66. R. A. Schroth
Sat R 49:71-2 My 21 '66. E. Raushenbush

Shadow schools; academic undergrounds. il Time 88:100 O 21 '66

Something to talk about on campus. J. Strasser; M. L. Goodfriend. il Mlle 63:324-7 Ag '66

Student freedom. il Sch & Soc 94:372 N 12 '66

Student market examined at NACS annual meeting; summary of addresses. il Pub W 189:35-40 My 16 '66

Student rights in higher education. M. P. Sheridan. America 114:731-2 My 21 '66

Students' rights; question of the scope and privacy of university student records. Nation 202:573 My 16 '66

Suicidal tendencies. Time 88:114 O 14 66

Taking a McNamara fellowship; army enlisters. D. Graham. Atlan 217:59-60 F '66

That new morality. R. Kirk. Nat R 18:165 F 22 '66

This restless generation. C. J. McNaspy. America 114:726-30 My 21 '66

Truth about today's college students; with interview with K. Keniston. il U S News 60:42-7 My 30 '66

2-S, too smart to fight? report from University of Michigan. M. Levitas. il N Y Times Mag p27+ Ap 24 '66

Unbugged student; communication between activists and nonactivists. M. A. Guitar. il Mlle 63:300-1+ Ag '66

Uncommitted: alienated youth in American society, by K. Keniston. Review
New Repub 154:29-32 Je 4 '66. L. Yablonsky

Unrest on the campus; address, November 9, 1965. L. A. Kimpton. Vital Speeches 32:302-5 Mr 1 '66

What about the sinful student? E. D. Eddy. il Sat R 49:70-1+ Mr 19 '66

What every girl should know; Where the boys are; guide to dating. il Time 87:83 Ap 15 '66

Youth on the college campus; rights of the university; address, November 3, 1965. G. Kirk. Vital Speeches 32:248-52 F 1 '66

Youth questions the war; excerpts from letter to President Johnson by student leaders. Time 89:22 Ja 6 '67

See also
College fraternities
College libraries—Student advisory committees
Foreign students in the United States
Foreign study
Graduate students
Law students
Self government in education
Student achievements
Student conferences
Student demonstrations
Student life
Student unions
Students, Interchange of
Teachers and students
Vietnamese students

Adjustment

Avoiding college booby traps. K. W. Clarke. NEA J 55:40 Ap '66

Big surprises. K. Goff. il Seventeen 26:28+ Ja '67

Experiment at Berkeley. il NEA J 56:21-2+ Ja '67

Freshman president speaks to freshman students; adaptation of address, September 20, 1965. E. J. Bloustein. Sch & Soc 94:128-9 Mr 5 '66

It's what's bugging them. W. C. McFadden. America 114:502-3 Ap 9 '66

Psychiatry on the campus. C. B. Luce. McCalls 93:26 S '66

Strangle of the apron strings? J. Steinberg. il Mlle 63:342+ Ag '66

Age

College coed at seventy-six. il Ebony 22:79-80+ D '66

COLLEGE students—*Continued*

Aid

See Student aid

Caricatures and cartoons

Not all your supermen are in the funnies, meet super-student! Esquire 66:118-19 S '66

Cheating

See Cheating in schoolwork

Communist activities

Behind student strike in Mexico; National university. C. Migdail. il U S News 60:55 My 16 '66

Campus revolt, Communist style; Mexico's National university. il U S News 60:10 My 9 '66

How campus reds tried to take over a country; Central university in Caracas. il U S News 62:37-8 Ja 16 '67

New left in colleges: an ex-Communist's report. il U S News 60:43 My 30 '66

Dating

See Dating

Discipline

See College discipline

Employment

Business casts bread on campus labor pool; well-paying summer jobs to college juniors. il Bsns W p84+ S 3 '66

Capitol hill classroom; summer as congressional interns. il Newsweek 68:46 Ag 29 '66

Work your way through college? il Changing T 20:36-9 Jl '66

Expenditures

See also
College education. Cost of

Failures

See Dropouts

Federal aid

Federal aid for nearly everyone. il Changing T 20:41 F '66

How to go to college on nothing a year. L. Velie. Read Digest 88:132-6 F '66

Grading

See Grading and marking (students)

Health and hygiene

Why students get sick. il Sci Digest 60:20-1 D '66

Housing

See also
Dormitories

Mental hygiene

See College students—Health and hygiene

Political activities

Berkeley scene, 1966: politics and potshots. E. Langer. il Science 152:1037-41 My 20 '66 (to be cont)

Crowded left. il Time 88:46 S 9 '66

Elite proletarians all; students in France go Communist. K. Botsford. il N Y Times Mag p54-5+ N 13 '66

History of college student unrest. Sch & Soc 94:56 F 5 '66

Is there a student conservatism? J. F. Lulves, jr. Nat R 18:530-1 My 31 '66

Letter to a new leftist, from a tired liberal. J. Fischer. Harper 232:16+ Mr 66; Same abr. with title Letter to a young leftist. Read Digest 88:137-40 My '66; Discussion. Harper 232:6 My '66

Politics of courage: notes on the student left. M. Rogin. Commonweal 84:99-102 Ap 15 '66

Pressing toward freedom: sit-in at a Capuchin monastery, Spain. Time 87:28 Mr 25 '66

Revolt and repression in Spain's universities. E. Cary. Reporter 34:43-5 My 19 '66

Speaking for the majority; Georgia students form new organization. Affirmation: Viet Nam. il Time 87:53 F 25 '66

Student support; petition of support from college and university students. Sr Schol 87:16 Ja 21 '66

Students *au pouvoir*; revolts on French campuses. il Newsweek 69:47 Ja 2 '67

Students for victory; VIVA, or, Victory in Vietnam association. R. Kirk. Nat R 18:535 My 31 '66

Students' rights; question of the scope and privacy of university student records. Nation 202:573 My 16 '66

Universities as battlegrounds; agitators in Latin America. America 114:186-7 F 5 '66

University and anti-Communist pressure. H. K. Stanford. Sch & Soc 94:123-5 Mr 5 '66

What's bugging the students. I. Kristol; discussion. Atlan 217:44 F '66

Yesterday's Berkeley rebel says: I'm just here to study. A. H. Raskin. il N Y Times Mag p 12-13+ Ja 30 '66

Reading

New look for the campus bookshop. D. Dempsey. il Sa R 50:81 Ja 14 '67

Anecdotes, facetiae, satire, etc.

Publish and cherish; books in library as courses of study. H. C. Bauer. Library J 91:2774-6 Je 1 '66

Religion

Dialogue with campus agnostics. R. E. Kavanaugh; discussion. America 114:504-5 Ap 9 '66

It's what's bugging them. W. C. McFadden. America 114:502-3 Ap 9 '66

Unbeguiled generation. J. C. Evans. Christian Cent 83:1106 S 14 '66

See also
Colleges and universities—Religious life

Volunteer service

See Volunteer service

COLLEGE students, Catholic. See Catholic students

COLLEGE students, Men

Dress

See Clothing and dress—Men

COLLEGE students, Mentally superior

Four years of 4.0; D. F. Hilse of Hunter college, New York, and others. Time 87:74 Je 24 '66

Program for the talented college student. P. S. Mousolite. Sch & Soc 94:125-6 Mr 5 '66

COLLEGE students, Negro. See Negro students

COLLEGE students, Women

Are Negro girls getting prettier? il Ebony 21:25-8+ F '66

California classic: the Berkeley girl. J. Shepherd. il Look 30:78-80+ Je 28 '66

Freshman president speaks to freshman students, adaptation of address, September 20, 1965. E. J. Bloustein. Sch & Soc 94:128-9 Mr 5 '66

Redbook readers in fashion: beauty; current college-girl look. il Redbook 127:74-7+ S '66

Student sister on the secular campus. K. T. Connor. il America 115:604-6 N 12 '66; Discussion. 115:724 D 3 '66

What sex means to college girls today. M. Lerner. il Redbook 127:51+ Je '66

See also
College fraternities
College students—Health and hygiene
Education of women

Dress

See Clothing and dress

COLLEGE students fads. See Fads

COLLEGE students libraries. See Libraries, Private

COLLEGE teachers. See College professors and instructors

COLLEGE teaching. See Colleges and universities—Teaching

COLLEGE textbooks. See Textbooks

COLLEGE theatricals. See College and school drama

COLLEGE trustees

Rich, risky life of a university trustee. R. Sheehan. il Fortune 75:124-7+ Ja '67

COLLEGE unions. See Student unions

COLLEGE verse

Undergraduate poems. America 114:500-1 Ap 9 '66

COLLEGE women (graduates) See College graduates, Women

COLLEGE year

Trimester's tribulations; Florida drops system. Time 87:66+ Mr 11 '66

COLLEGES and universities

Small college: another view; with reply by A. Wallis. H. Lowry. Atlan 217:50, 76-8 Mr '66

COLLEGES and universities—*Continued*

English departments

Writers on the campus. D. Hall. Atlan 217:
87-90 Mr '66

Entrance requirements

College admissions; symposium. il NEA J
55:40-4 O '66
Get ready for college now. W. Abraham. bib-
liog il Todays Health 44:72-4+ S; 64-5+
O '66
Outlook for college entry: not so tough this
year; what colleges say about admissions.
U S News 60:65-7 Je 6 '66
Squeeze in college admissions. H. S. Dyer.
PTA Mag 60:19-20 My '66
Tips for college-bound youngsters. A. H.
Written and G. W. Daigler. il Parents Mag
41:50-1+ Mr '66
Unfair Harvard? advanced-rating system.
il Newsweek 68:74-5 N 14 '66

Extension

See University extension

Faculties

See College professors and instructors

Federal aid

See Federal aid to education

Finance

Costs of private higher education. America
115:680 N 26 '66
Education and the bond market. See issues
of American education
Future of the private university. J. T. Ret-
taliata. Sch & Soc 94:348-9 O 29 '66
Higher education in Pennsylvania: a case of
schizophrenia; distinction between public
and private colleges. J. Welsh. il Sat R 49:
66-7+ Mr 19 '66
Private college expenses. America 115:820
D 24 '66
Private colleges in trouble. America 115:25-6
Jl 9 '66
See also
Education and state
Federal aid to education
Fund raising

Gifts, legacies, etc.

Alumni gifts for colleges. Sch & Soc 94:
444-5 D 10 '66
Appraisals and revenooers: gifts of books,
letters or manuscripts to institutions or
organizations; excerpts from address. R.
G. Newman. il Am Heritage 17:82-4 Je '66
Colleges wrap up more gifts than ever. il
Bsns W p63-4+ My 21 '66
Fine art of fund raising. Time 89:46+ Ja 13
'67
Help for small colleges. D. Wolfle. Science
153:697 Ag 12 '66
Ivory tower crumbles; what influences potential doners. G. W. Bonham. il Sat R 49:
66-7+ My 21 '66
Now for U.S. colleges, the game of grants-
manship. il U S News 61:133-4+ N 21 '66
Science studies get help. Sci N 89:458 Je 11
'66
Struck by Ford lightning; what happens to
recipient colleges. B. Wallace. il Sat R
49:86-7+ Ap 16 '66
Where alumni funds began, at Yale. Bsns W
p66 My 21 '66

Graduate work

Assessment of quality in graduate education,
by A. M. Cartter. Review
Sat R 49:75-6 Je 18 '66. E. Walters
Catholic graduate schools. P. A. FitzGerald.
America 115:510-12 O 29 '66
Class by themselves; grading the graduate
schools. il Newsweek 67:62-3 My 30 '66
Evaluation of graduate schools; opinions of
teachers and administrators. il Sch & Soc
94:312+ O 15 '66
Graduate education: ACE study rates de-
partments qualitatively. J. Walsh. il Sci-
ence 152:1226-8 My 27 '66; Discussion. 152:
1189; 153:575, 1335 My 27, Ag 5, S 16 '66
Graduate-school squeeze. il Time 87:82+ Ap
15 '66
How graduate schools are rated now. U S
News 60:66-7 Je 6 '66
Schools make news; scholarship aid, post-
baccalaureate study. Sat R 49:64 Je 18 '66
Shame of the graduate schools. W. Arrowsmith. Harper 232:51-9 Mr '66; Discussion.
232:82-4 My '66
These are the best graduate schools. Changing
T 20:22-3 Ag '66
Who's best at what? grad schools, ranked
by effectiveness. Time 87:55 My 27 '66

Health service

See also
College students—Health and hygiene

History

Perfect university; eighteenth-century Oxford
and Cambridge. M. Bishop. il Atlan 217:
66-8 My '66

International cooperation

Some aspects of university cooperation in
international education. S. E. Fraser. bibliog f Sch & Soc 94:234-8+ Ap 16 '66
U.S.-Dutch university cooperation; Cooperation among U.S. and Japanese universities;
and U.S.-Philippine university cooperation.
Sch & Soc 94:208-9+ Ap 16 '66

History

Historical background of international cooperation among universities. W. W. Brickman. bibliog f Sch & Soc 94:227-34 Ap
16 '66

Off-campus centers

Branches for opportunity; regional campuses,
commonwealth campuses, and university
centers. H. B. Wells. il Am Ed 2:5-8 F '66
University branches: solution for college
crush. N. A. Sicuro. Sch & Soc 94:458-9
D 10 '66

Political control

University and anti-Communist pressure.
H. K. Stanford. Sch & Soc 94:123-5 Mr
5 '65

Public relations

Ivory tower crumbles; what influences potential doners. G. W. Bonham. il Sat R
49:66-7+ My 21 '66
University and the city. D. Clark. America
114:324-6 Mr 5 '66

Publications

See also
University presses

Religious life

Atlanta statement; commentary. G. F.
Simons. Cath World 202:302-5 F '66
Campus community: experiment in living. A.
M. Greeley. America 115:588-91 N 12 '66
Student chaplains. P. Goodman. New Repub
156:29-31 Ja 7 '67

Research

Basic research in the university and industrial laboratory; excerpts from address,
1966. R. E. Marshak. Science 154:1521-4
D 23 '66
Chemical reaction; University of Pennsylvania's chemical-research projects for the
Pentagon. Newsweek 68:34 S 19 '66
Demand for institutional support attains the
form of legislation. J. Walsh. Science 152:
1041-3 My 20 '66
Editor's bookshelf; concerning Earl J. Mc-
Grath's observations on sacrificing under-
graduate liberal education to research in
state institutions. P. Woodring. Sat R 49:
85 D 17 '66
Federal funds and science education; adapta-
tion of statement, January 25, 1966. G. Piel.
Bul Atomic Sci 22:10-15 My '66
Federal money and university research. D. K.
Price. bibliog Science 151:285-90 Ja 21 '66;
Discussion. 152:698+; 153:816 My 6, Ag 19
'66
Government role in science education. L. A.
DuBridge. Bul Atomic Sci 22:16-20 My '66
Government, the universities, and biomedical
research; address, August 23, 1966. J. W.
Gardner. Science 153:1601-3 S 30 '66
Money for science; the community is begin-
ning to hurt. D. S. Greenberg. Science 152:
1485-7 Je 10 '66
Problems involved in cooperation between
universities and government agencies. J. W.
Shirley. bibliog f Sch & Soc 94:222-7 Ap
16 '66
Prof or project director? ACE meeting.
Newsweek 68:75 O 24 '66
Renaissance of teaching. W. L. Hickman.
Sch & Soc 94:265-7 Sum '66
Research administration: study urges uni-
versities to improve methods. D. S. Green-
berg. Science 152:624-6 Ap 29 '66; Discus-
sion. 152:1694+; 153:1057-8 Je 24, S 2 '66
R&D in higher education. Sch & Soc 94:119-
20 Mr 5 '66
Research in teacher education at University
of Texas; and at Stanford. Sch & Soc 94:
121-2 Mr 5 '66
Secret research at Penn. Time 88:62 S 16 '66

COLLEGES and universities—Research—*Cont.*
Secret research at universities. Nation 203:
267-8 S 26 '66
University policy for research contracts. il
Sch & Soc 94:438-9 D 10 '66

Social life
See Student life

Standards
Evaluation of graduate schools; opinions of
teachers and administrators. il Sch & Soc
94:312+ O 15 '66

Teaching
Faculty responsibility and the executive con-
quest of academe. D. Long. Sch & Soc
94:89-92 F 19 '66
Neglected college; Bell and Muscatine re-
ports; proposals. il Newsweek 67:85-6 Mr
28 '66
Passion in clear reason; how students can
be better served. D. Krech. il Nation 202:
362-4 Mr 28 '66
Professor: educator, scholar, or both? T. O.
Brandt. Sch & Soc 94:381-2 N 12 '66
Renaissance of teaching. W. L. Hickman.
Sch & Soc 94:265-7 Sum '66
Shaking up college teaching. L. C. Rhett;
J. M. Stokes. il Sat R 49:62-5 Jl 16 '66
What to do about Berkeley; report by of-
ficial committee of insiders. il Time 87:70+
Mr 25 '66
Who wants to teach undergraduates? A.
Hacker. il Sat R 49:80-1 D 17 '66
Your ideas carry weight; Woodrow Wilson
foundation's Teaching internship program.
il Newsweek 67:74 F 7 '66
See also
College professors and instructors
Examinations

Trustees
See College trustees

Alaska
See also
Alaska. University

Argentina
Argentina: seizure of universities leaves in-
tellectual casualties. E. Langer. Science
153:1362-4 S 16 '66; Reply. P. Siekevitz. 154:
1117 D 2 '66
Books vs. boots; students revolt against
seizure. il Newsweek 68:49 S 5 '66
Crackdown on colleges. Argentina. F. N.
Manitzas. New Repub 155:12-15 N 19 '66;
Reply. R. C. Newton. 155:37-8 D 17 '66
Footnote to the Argentine crisis: a letter
from American scientists. L. Berkner and
others. Science 154:992 N 25 '66
Not yet, not quite; University of Buenos
Aires; police raid and reactions. il News-
week 68:49 Ag 15 '66
Where it's government vs. university. il U S
News 61:48 Ag 15 '66

Arizona
See also
Arizona state university, Tempe

Arkansas
See also
Arkansas. University, Fayetteville

Belgium
Clash at Louvain. R. J. Gerber. il America
114:645-9 My 7 '66; Discussion. 115:11-14 Jl
2 '66
Crisis in Louvain. P. Nobile. Cath World 203:
233-5 Jl '66
They're not talking; language issue. il Time
87:69 Mr 4 '66

California
See also
California institute of technology, Pasadena
California. University
Chabot college, Hayward
Chapman college, Orange
Foothill college, Los Altos Hills
Harvey Mudd college, Claremont
Long Beach state college
Sacramento, Calif. state college
San Diego Mesa college
Stanford university, Palo Alto
University of the Pacific, Stockton
Upland college, Upland

Canada
Square miles, love, and money. B. Stuart-
Stubbs. il Library J 91:5529-32 N 15 '66

Colorado
See also
Colorado. University. Boulder
Colorado woman's college, Denver

Connecticut
See also
Wesleyan university, Middletown
Yale university, New Haven

England
U. of Sussex: the establishment challenged.
H. Callaway. il Mlle 63:182-4+ O '66
See also
Birmingham university
Oxford. University

Florida
Trimester's tribulations. Time 87:66+ Mr 11
'66
See also
Florida Atlantic university, Boca Raton
Florida Presbyterian college, St Petersburg
Florida state university, Tallahassee

France
Students *au pouvoir*; revolts on campuses. il
Newsweek 69:47 Ja 2 '67

Georgia
See also
DeKalb area technical school, Clarkston
DeKalb college, Clarkston

Germany (Federal Republic)
New campus. O. Newman. il Arch Forum
124:44-50 My '66
Ruhr university. Bochum library. W. M.
Ostrem. bibliog il Wilson Lib Bul 41:418-
20 D '66

Ghana
Science education in Africa. G. Burkhardt.
Bul Atomic Sci 22:46-8 F '66

Great Britain
How the British score on us; athletics organization and coaching system. M. Whitney.
il Sat R 49:63+ Ag 20 '66

Illinois
See also
Bradley university, Peoria
Illinois institute of technology, Chicago

Indiana
See also
Purdue university, Lafayette

Iowa
See also
Parsons college, Fairfield

Iran
Pahlavi university in Iran opens undergraduate library. Library J 91:2792 Je 1 '66

Italy
Trends in Italian higher education. M. Anello.
bibliog f Sch & Soc 94:272-4 Sum '66

Japan
Cooperation among U.S. and Japanese universities. Sch & Soc 94:208-9+ Ap 16 '66

Kansas
See also
Kansas. University

Kentucky
See also
Louisville. University

Latin America
Autonomy of the university. G. I. Sanchez.
Sch & Soc 94:147-9 Mr 19 '66
Latin America's classroom chaos. il Time
88:64 S 2 '66

Lebanon
See also
American university of Beirut

Louisiana
See also
Dillard university, New Orleans
Southern university and agricultural and
mechanical college, Baton Rouge
Tulane university, New Orleans

Maine
See also
Bowdoin college, Brunswick

Maryland
See also
Baltimore. University
Maryland. University, College Park
St John's college, Annapolis

Massachusetts
See also
Amherst college
Berkshire community college, Pittsfield
Boston university
Clark university, Worcester

COLLEGES and universities—Massachusetts
—*Continued*
Hampshire college
Harvard university
Massachusetts institute of technology, Cambridge
Massachusetts. University, Amherst
Williams college, Williamstown

Mexico

Behind student strike in Mexico; National university. C. Migdail. il U S News 60:55 My 16 '66
Campus revolt. Communist style; Mexico's National university. il U S News 60:10 My 9 '66
University under siege; Mexico city's national university. il Time 87:32 My 6 '66

Michigan

See also
Detroit university
Grand Valley state college, Allendale
Michigan state university of agriculture and applied science, East Lansing
Michigan. University, Ann Arbor
Oakland university, Rochester

Middle western states

Academic common market; Committee on institutional cooperation. S. F. Salwak. il Sat R 49:72-3+ Je 18 '66
Cooperative higher education in the Midwest. Sch & Soc 94:206+ Ap 16 '66

Minnesota

See also
Carleton college, Northfield
Macalester college. St Paul
Minnesota. University, Minneapolis

Mississippi

See also
Mississippi. University
Tougaloo Southern Christian college, Tougaloo

Missouri

See also
Washington university. St Louis
Webster college, Webster Groves

Netherlands

U.S.-Dutch university cooperation. Sch & Soc 94:208-9+ Ap 16 '66

Nevada

See also
Nevada. University, Reno

New Jersey

See also
Rutgers university, New Brunswick

New York (state)

See also
Barnard college, New York
Colgate university, Hamilton
Cornell university. Ithaca, N.Y.
Dutchess community college, Poughkeepsie
Hofstra university, Hempstead
New York state university
New York university
Union college and university, Schenectady
Vassar college, Poughkeepsie, N.Y.

Nigeria

Turmoil in an African university; Nigeria's University of Lagos. S. B. Yesufu. America 114:200-3 F 5 '66

North Carolina

See also
Duke university, Durham
Meredith college, Raleigh
North Carolina. University, Chapel Hill

Ohio

See also
Dayton, Ohio. University

Oklahoma

See also
Oklahoma Christian college. Oklahoma City
Oral Roberts university, Tulsa

Oregon

Setting Oregon's record straight; letter to the editor. J. P. Browne. Library J 91: 3020+ Je 15 '66
See also
Reed college. Portland

Pennsylvania

Higher education in Pennsylvania; a case of schizophrenia. J. Welsh. il Sat R 49:66-7+ Mr 19 '66
See also
Haverford college, Haverford
Lafayette college, Easton
Pittsburgh. University
Temple university, Philadelphia

Philippines

U.S.-Philippine university cooperation; science program at Mindanao state university. Sch & Soc 94:244+ Ap 16 '66

Rhode Island

See also
Brown university, Providence
Providence college

Rhodesia

College crackdown in Rhodesia; Operation Intellect at University college of Rhodesia. I. Henderson. New Repub 155:15-16 N 19 '66
Death of learning; University college of Rhodesia. Nation 204:67 Ja 16 '67

Russia

Exam fever in Russia; entrance to institutes of higher learning. il Time 88:51 Jl 15 '66

South Carolina

See also
Bob Jones university, Greenville
Furman university, Greenville

Spain

Franco strikes back; University of Barcelona closed. Newsweek 67:46 My 9 '66
Heat in Spain; new protests. G. Jackson. Commonweal 84:327-9 Je 10 '66
Libertad, libertad! students strikes. Newsweek 67:52 My 16 '66
Revolt and repression in Spain's universities. E. Cary. Reporter 34:43-5 My 19 '66

Texas

See also
Texas A&M university system, College Station—Texas A&M university, College Station

United States

America's 1966 directory of Catholic colleges. America 115:595-7 N 12 '66
Case for the small college. C. Wren. il Look 30:23-7 O 4 '66
Changing campus; a special report; symposium. Harper 232:68-70+ My '66
College conundrum: how to choose. P. Janssen. il Am Ed 2:24-7 S '66
College scene. il Sci Digest 60:22-9 O; 42-7 N; 20-9 D '66; 61:39-40 Ja '67
Colleges that still have room. il Changing T 20:15-18 My '66
Cooperative relations involving the liberal arts colleges. W. E. Cadbury, jr. Sch & Soc 94:213-17 Ap 16 '66
Fertile academic soil; problems of new institutions. P. Schrag. Sat R 49:97 N 19 '66
Future of the private university. J. T. Rettaliata. Sch & Soc 94:348-9 O 29 '66
How colleges have changed! excerpt from report by Editorial projects for education, inc. Read Digest 90:96-100 Ja '67
Integrity of the private college; summary of address, June 1966. L. Wilson. Sch & Soc 94:436-8 D 10 '66
Issues of world power; place of the university; address, November 8, 1966. P. H. Nitze. Vital Speeches 33:98-103 D 1 '66
Living-learning cluster. il Time 88:46+ S 9 '66
Small college on the big campus. P. Woodring; J. L. Jarrett; W. B. Martin. il Sat R 50:64+ Ja 21 '67
Small, private college. D. Klein. il Seventeen 25:28+ Ap '66
Student rights in higher education. M. P. Sheridan. America 114:731-2 My 21 '66
Teaching of philosophy in universities of the United States, by H. E. Davis and H. A. Durfee. Review Américas 18:40-2 N '66. S. Lipp
Tinkering-around U; ideas at ten-college Union for research and experimentation in higher education meeting. Newsweek 69:47 Ja 2 '67
To the class of 1971. J. F. Scott. il N Y Times Mag p 119-20+ N 20 '66
University and the city. D. Clark. America 114:324-6 Mr 5 '66
University campus and foreign policy; address, November 14, 1966. D. Rusk. Dept State Bul 55:914-18 D 19 '66
University in America. J. F. Mulligan. America 114:832-3 Je 11 '66
What students think about college. Changing T 20:42-3 F '66
What's going on in schools & colleges. See issues of Changing times
Worlds of reflection and action; excerpts from address, October 24, 1966. J. W. Gardner. Science 154:849 N 18 '66
See also
Association of American colleges
Colleges and universities, State
Denominational colleges

COLLEGES and universities—United States—
See also—*Continued*
Junior colleges
Land grant colleges
Summer schools
United States—National university (proposed)
also names of colleges and universities,
e.g. Boston university

Anecdotes, facetiae, satire, etc.
Perfect university. M. Bishop. il Atlan 217:
66-8 My '66

Venezuela
How campus reds tried to take over a country;
Central university in Caracas. il U S News
62:37-8 Ja 16 '67

Virginia
See also
Virginia state college, Petersburg

Washington, D.C.
Go, pony league, go: five universities. il
Newsweek 68:73-6 D 12 '66
See also
Gallaudet college

Washington (state)
See also
Washington (state) University, Seattle
Western Washington state college, Bellingham

Wisconsin
See also
Wisconsin. University, Madison
COLLEGES and universities, Municipal
City and the university; address, February
14, 1966. J. M. Hester. Vital Speeches
32:294-7 Mr 1 '66
Studying the urban revolution. il Time 89:59
Ja 6 '67
See also
New York (city) City university of New York
COLLEGES and universities, State
Look what's happening to state colleges.
Changing T 20:22-3 Ap '66
State college upstart. G. S. Dumke. Sat R 49:
62 Ag 20 '66
See also names of state colleges and
universities, e.g. Michigan. University, Ann
Arbor
COLLEGES and universities, Traveling
Ship their dormitory, the world their campus:
M.S. Seven Seas. il Ebony 21:108-10+ S '66
COLLEGES for Negroes. See Negroes in the
United States—Education
COLLEGES for women
See also names of womens colleges, e.g.
Barnard college, New York
COLLEGIATE chorale
Debuts & reappearances; concert in Carnegie
Hall. B. Jacobson. Hi Fi 16:MA7 Ag '66
COLLEGIATE chorus of New York. See Col-
legiate chorale
COLLEY, A. G. jr. See Lewis, W. D. jt. auth.
COLLIER, Barnard Law
Wacky spy caper. Sat Eve Post 239:97-101
Jl 2 '66
COLLIER, Eric
Farewell, Eric Collier. pors Outdoor Life 139:
54-5+ Ja '67
COLLIER, James Lincoln
Completely off Broadway. Holiday 39:32+ Mr
'66
How I lost four ounces in three weeks. Read
Digest 89:129-32 N '66
When a man marries. Read Digest 89:76-9
O '66
COLLIER, John
Fate of the five tribes. Sat R 49:39 Ap 2 '66
COLLIER, Oscar
Useful but much maligned books. por ALA
Bul 60:609-12 Je '66
COLLIER, P. F. and son, corporation
FTC rules sales deception for Collier's ency-
clopedia. Pub W 190:30 D 12 '66
COLLIER, Richard
Capsule history of tourists. Holiday 41:72-3
Ja '67
COLLIER trophy
Collier trophy award; winners. B. Kocivar.
il Look 30:96+ N 1 '66
COLLIMATORS
Theodolite, gyro combined for improved
guidance accuracy; instrument using
Barnes miniature electronic autocollimator.
C. D. LaFond. il Tech W 19:32-3 N 14 '66
COLLIN, Noreen
Hi Joe, long time no see. J. Lovesey. il por
Sports Illus 24:24-5 F 28 '66
COLLIN, Robert L.
Precipitate formation in the strontium-
phosphate system. bibliog Science 151:1386-8
Mr 18 '66

COLLINGS, Kyllikki
(tr) See Kekkonen, S. Reflections of a first
lady
COLLINS, Bud
Put a lion in your tank. Sports Illus 25:36-8+
Jl 25 '66
Tennis. Sports Illus 25:54-5 S 5 '66
Working wage for amateurs. Sports Illus
25:28-9 Jl 18 '66
COLLINS, Carter Compton
Evoked pressure responses in the rabbit eye.
bibliog Science 155:106-8 Ja 6 '67
COLLINS, Dean
Hardy cyclamen. Horticulture 44:36-7 F '66
COLLINS, E. D.
Second-hand book store: is it vanishing?
Hobbies 71:109 S '66
COLLINS, John R.
Non-destructive testing. Electr World 75:
33-6 F; 53-6+ Mr '66
COLLINS, LeRoy
Traveler, consider my Florida; interview, ed.
by R. Joseph. pors Esquire 66:240-1+ D
'66
COLLINS, Lester
Innisfree garden. Horticulture 44:34-5 Je '66
COLLINS, Michael
See also
Space flight—Manned flights—Young-Collins
flight, 1966
COLLINS, Ralph T.
Employing the mentally restored. por Wilson
Lib Bul 40:838-43 My '66
COLLISION indicators. See Aeronautic instru-
ments
COLLISIONS, Airplane. See Aviation—Ac-
cidents
COLLISIONS, Automobile. See Traffic accidents
COLLISIONS at sea
In the days of spark, a rescue at sea; sink-
ing of the SS Republic. H. E. Church. il
Pop Electr 25:57-8+ N '66
COLLISON, Jim
Flying photographer. il Flying 78:69 Je '66
COLLOQUIALISMS
Grinders and sneeders; American English. il
Newsweek 69:56 Ja 16 '67
COLMAN, Gould P.
Oral history at Cornell. por Wilson Lib Bul
40:624-8 Mr '66
COLMEN, Joseph G.
Discovery of commitment. bibliog f Ann Am
Acad 365:12-20 My '66
COLMER, William Meyers
Two men who are expected to move into top
spots in Congress. por U S News 61:19
Jl 25 '66
COLOGNE, Germany
Golden cities of the Rhine. R. Tregaskis. il
Travel 126:33-7 S '66

Music
Cologne. H. Koegler. Opera N 31:30 D 10 '66
COLOGNE. See Perfumery
COLOMBIA
See also
Americans in Colombia
Banks and banking—Colombia
Canals—Colombia
Guerrillas—Colombia
Land tenure—Colombia
San Agustin
San Jorge River
Zoology—Colombia

Antiquities
See Indians of South America—Antiquities—Colombia

Commercial treaties and agreements
U.S. and Colombia amend cotton textiles
agreement; Department announcement; with
texts of U.S. note and U.S. letter, June
24, 1966. Dept State Bul 55:58-9 Jl 11 '66

Description and travel
Travel's picture portfolio. il Travel 126:50-5
Ag '66

Economic conditions
Colombia: a tarnished showcase. J. M.
Hunter. bibliog f Cur Hist 51:276-83+ N
'66

Politics and government
Colombia: a tarnished showcase. J. M.
Hunter. bibliog f Cur Hist 51:276-83+ N
'66
Constitutional way; new president. Time 88:
34 Ag 19 '66
Hollow victory. il Newsweek 67:55 Ap 4 '66
Landslide for Lleras. Time 87:36+ My 13 '66

COLOMBIA—*Continued*

Religious institutions and affairs
Religious freedom in Colombia. America 115: 22 Jl 9 '66
See also
Catholic church in Colombia

COLOMBIAN visitors in the United States. See Foreign visitors in the United States

COLOMBO, Joe
America discovers Colombo. B. Plumb. il por N Y Times Mag p30-1 S 4 '66

COLOMBO plan
Canada responds to Asia's need. America 114:371 Mr 19 '66

COLON (anatomy)

Diseases
See also
Colitis

COLON, Cancer of the. See Cancer

COLONIAL administration. See Colonies—Administration

COLONIAL dependencies. See Colonies

COLONIAL furniture. See Furniture, American

COLONIAL gardens. See Gardens, Colonial

COLONIAL history (United States) See United States—History—Colonial period

COLONIAL life and customs
Journey through the American states; excerpt from Miracle at Philadelphia. C. D. Bowen. Atlan 218:94-103 N '66
See also
Old Sturbridge Village, Mass.
United States—History—Colonial period

COLONIES
Self-determination in the western Indian Ocean. P. M. Allen. bibliog f il Int Concil 560:4-74 N '66
See also
France—Colonies
United Nations—Trusteeship council

Administration
Africa addio, by J. Cohen. Review
Sat R 50:88-90 Ja 15 '67. C. Miller

COLONIES in Africa
Africa addio, by J. Cohen. Review
Sat R 50:88-90 Ja 14 '67. C. Miller
Great Britain and the African peace settlement of 1919. W. R. Louis. bibliog f Am Hist R 71:875-92 Ap '66

COLOR blindness
Color blindness. S. Lowell. Field & S 71:146+ My '66
Color blindness genes not basis for cirrhosis. Sci N 90:228 S 24 '66

COLOR film processing. See Photography—Developing and developers

COLOR films. See Photography—Films

COLOR in gardens. See Gardens—Color

COLOR in house decoration
Art of accent decorating. il Design 67:38-9 Mr '66
Color, the active ingredient. il House & Gard 129:129-49 Mr '66
In a New York town house, an elegant sequence of color moods. il House & Gard 130: 100-5 Ag '66
Inside California: the drama of western décor. il McCalls 93:98-103 S '66
Introducing H&G colors for 1967; symposium. il House & Gard 130:165-95 S '66
Twenty-nine idea color schemes! P. Rumely and E. T. Lawyer. il Bet Hom & Gard 45: 48-67 Ja '67
What makes a well-decorated room. P. Rumely. il Bet Hom & Gard 44:46-55 S '66
Wild color invades the kitchen. M. Davidson. il Ladies Home J 83:76-7 Ag '66
Winning color team: brown+white. il House & Gard 130:230-5 N '66
See also
House decoration, Exterior

COLOR in hunting clothes. See Hunting—Safety devices and measures

COLOR of animals
Adrenalectomy and coat color in deer mice. F. H. Bronson and S. H. Clarke. bibliog il Science 154:1349-50 D 9 '66

COLOR of automobiles. See Automobiles—Color

COLOR of flowers
Gardens, for looks and fragrance both. il Changing T 20:39-40 My '66
Step into summer color. il Flower Grower 53: 38-9 Je '66

COLOR of insects
Background selections of geometrid and noctuid moths. T. D. Sargent. il Science 154: 1674-5 D 30 '66

COLOR of man
Scientists discover secret of skin color. il Ebony 22:85-6+ Ja '67

COLOR of plants
See also
Color of flowers

COLOR organ
Musette color organ. D. E. Lancaster. il Pop Electr 25:56-62+ Jl '66

COLOR photography
Arbitrary colors of Fred Burrell. V. Garbers. il Pop Phot 59:84-5+ Ag '66
Caulfield on color. P. Caulfield. See issues of Modern photography
Color clinic. D. B. Eisendrath, jr. See issues of Popular photography
Color critique (cont) il U S Camera 29:62-3 Ap; 46-7+ Ag '66
Color odds are ten to one against Tom McCarthy. il Pop Phot 59:88-97+ Jl '66
Creative color. A. Rothstein. See issues of U.S. camera & travel
Girl's the thing. il U S Camera 29:44-5 Je '66
Good subject, good idea. il Pop Phot 59:102-11 D '66
He builds in color: F. Maroon's pictures. il Pop Phot 58:78-83 My '66
How to get the most out of the Ektrachromes. N. Rothschild. il Pop Phot 58:80-3+ Mr '66
Large camera technique for 35mm color; ed. by P. Caulfield. B. Randall. il Mod Phot 30: 62-5 Je '66
Looking on the bright slide. PTA Mag 61:30 Ja '67
Night colors. N. Rothschild. il Pop Phot 59: 90-3+ O '66
No place is not for color. J. Launois. il Pop Phot 58:64-7+ F '66
Pink Kodachrome disease & what to do. P. Caulfield. il Mod Phot 30:72-3+ F '66
Secrets of using flash for better color pictures. P. Wahl. il Pop Sci 188:140-3+ My '66
Underwater color now easier with modern cameras and films. A. Rothstein. U S Camera 29:30-1 Ag '66
Warm and the cool of it. il U S Camera 29: 62-3 Mr '66
Wizard of Ozachrome. P. R. Farber. il U S Camera 30:46-7+ Ja '67

Study and teaching
Color workshop: Syracuse workshop in color photography. M. Orovan. il U S Camera 29:62-5 My '66

COLOR photomicrography. See Photomicrography

COLOR prejudice. See Race prejudice

COLOR printing
Let the printer add the color. il Pop Phot 59:98-9 O '66
Printing of The Mother Goose treasury. G. Geddes. il Pub W 190:102+ O 3 '66
Some new thoughts on color printing; summary of discussion at second seminar on Color in print, 1966. Pub W 191:92-3 Ja 2 '67

COLOR sense
Color vision in the adult female two-spotted spider mite. W. D. McEnroe and K. Dronka. bibliog il Science 154:782-4 N 11 '66
Human visual acuity measured with colored test objects. C. R. Cavonus and A. W. Schumacher. bibliog il Science 152:1276-7 My 27 '66

COLOR slides. See Transparencies

COLOR television. See Television, Color

COLOR television receiving apparatus. See Television receiving apparatus—Color receivers

COLORADO
See also
Architecture, Domestic—Colorado
Fishing—Colorado
Hunting—Colorado
Music festivals—Colorado
Skis and skiing—Colorado

Description and travel
Four family-planned circle tours. N. Kuehnl and P. Lindberg. il Bet Hom & Gard 44: 72-3 Je '66
Going places, finding ghosts in Colorado's nostalgic mining towns. W. Houseman. il House & Gard 129:40-2+ Je '66

Politics and government
Where business and labor work for reform. il Nations Bsns 54:90-1+ D '66

Recreation
See Recreation—United States

COLORADO NATIONAL MONUMENT
John Otto: letter writer extraordinary. C. Foley. il Am For 72:40-2 Ap '66

COLORADO RIVER
Abundance of alternatives; Colorado River basin fund. A. W. Simth. Nat Parks Mag 40:2+ Jl '66
Arizona's Colorado. T. B. Lesure. il Travel 126:59-63 D '66
Danger facing boom in the desert; Southwest water crisis. il U S News 60:66-70 My 9 '66
Dream come true. B. M. Goldwater. il McCalls 93:64+ Mr '66
How pushbuttons control the mighty Colorado. E. Burks. il Pop Sci 188:82-5+ Mr '66
Last days of the Colorado? G. Stayeley and B. East. il Outdoor Life 138:24-7+ Jl '66
Reformation of Old Red. F. E. Dominy. il Parks & Rec 1:314-15+ Ap '66
Storm over the Grand Canyon. H. Nash; C. Hayden. il Parks & Rec 1:496-501+ Je '66; Reply. G. Woodgates. 1:610 Ag '66
Uranium mystery in the Colorado basin; concerning special PHS report. New Repub 154:9 Mr 5 '66; Discussion. 154:36-7 Ap 16 '66
See also
Central Arizona project (proposed)
Glen Canyon
Grand Canyon
Havasu Lake

COLORADO. University, Boulder
Colorado U: respect for a robust environment. J. M. Dixon. il Arch Forum 125:54-63 O '66
Condon for regent. Nation 203:269 S 26 '66
New shapes for the ivory towers at Colorado; engineering center. il Fortune 74:123 Jl 1 '66
University of Colorado: the musical panorama. A. Young. il Hi Fi 16:123+ Je '66

COLORADO woman's college, Denver
$25 million gift. il Time 88:98 N 18 '66

COLORING of metals. See Metal coloring

COLTRANE, John William
New jazz. il por Newsweek 68:103-4+ D 12 '66

COLTS (football club) See Football clubs

COLUM, Padraic
Commemorating Michael Collins; poem. Poetry 108:116-18 My '66

COLUMBIA, Md.
Architecture. E. Galantay. Nation 203:714-16 D 26 '66
Master builder with a new concept; J. Rouse, developer of nine-village community. il Bsns W p 106+ Ag 20 '66
New concepts of library service proposed for unborn Maryland city. Library J 91:648 F 1 '66

COLUMBIA, Mo, public library
Rise and fall of a library; headquarters of Daniel Boone regional library. A. T. Hamlin. il ALA Bul 60:339-47 Ap '66

COLUMBIA broadcasting system
Bad days at Black Rock. il Newsweek 67:62-3 F 28 '66
Casting at CBS: role of J. A. Schneider. por Newsweek 67:84 F 21 '66
CBS buys Murchisons' 11 per cent interest in Holt. Pub W 190:44 S 19 '66
Farewell for Mr Friendly. America 114:317 Mr 5 '66
For the record: possession of disk-TV denied by CBS. il Newsweek 67:67 Mr 14 '66
Friendly dispute. Sr Schol 88:12 Mr 4 '66
Invaders; planned invasion of Haiti. Newsweek 69:31-2 Ja 16 '67
Matter of conscience. Nation 202:225 F 28 '66
Profiles; case of O. Preminger vs CBS over TV showing of Anatomy of a murder. L. Ross. New Yorker 41:42-6+ F 19 '66
Saarinen's CBS skyscraper. D. Jacobs. Holiday 39:122+ Je '66
Sounding brass; F. Friendly quits. il Time 87:64 F 25 '66
Victorygraph: CBS election night program; interview. A. Westin. New Yorker 42:51-3 N 5 '66
What's news at CBS? R. Severo. New Repub 154:29+ Mr 12 '66
Yankee dynasty can never come back. L. Koppett. il N Y Times Mag p44-5+ O 2 '66

COLUMBIA Journalism review
Christmas list: holiday greeting. J. Fischer. Harper 233:26+ D '66

COLUMBIA pictures corporation
Coup at Columbia. Newsweek 68:88+ O 31 '66

COLUMBIA RIVER
Sediments from the lower Columbia River and origin of graywacke. J. T. Whetten. bibliog il Science 152:1057-8 My 20 '66

30 million Americans fighting over a river. il U S News 61:70-3 S 19 '66
See also
Libby Dam project (proposed)

Power utilization
See also
Grand Coulee power and reclamation project

COLUMBIA university
Costs of private higher education. America 115:680 N 26 '66
Lion's share; $200 million fund-raising drive. il Newsweek 68:74 N 14 '66
Oral history: how and why it was born. A. Nevins. Wilson Lib Bul 40:600-1 Mr '66
See also
American assembly
Vetlesen prize

School of library service
Profile of an alumni body. C. J. Frarey. il Library J 91:1776-81 Ap 1 '66

COLUMBUS, Christopher
Columbus as a Spaniard; address, October 6, 1966. A. B. Duke. Dept State Bul 55:717-21 N 7 '66
Columbus sights the New World. W. S. Kals. il Motor B 118:102+ O '66
Was Columbus in Canada? P. Bilbao. il Américas 18:17-28 Jl '66

COLUMBUS, Ga.
Women who wait; husbands in Vietnam. M. Frady. il Good H 162:100-1+ My '66

COLUMBUS, Ind.

Architecture
Circle and square for an Indiana school; Lincoln elementary school. G. Birkerts. il Arch Rec 140:95-7 Ag '66
Hooded roofs reaching for the sky. il Arch Forum 125:48-53 D '66

COLUMBUS, Ohio

Social conditions
Missionaries in darkest Ohio. J. Ridgeway. New Repub 154:9-10 F 5 '66

Street traffic
Parking under the state capitol grounds. P. L. Heineman. il Am City 81:96-7 Mr '66

COLUMBUS, Ohio, public library
Columbus' conversion to data processing. G. E. Gordon. Wilson Lib Bul 41:414-17 D '66

COLUMBUS day
Columbus day, 1966; remarks, with text of proclamation, September 22, 1966. L. B. Johnson. Dept State Bul 55:602-4 O 17 '66

COLUMNEA
Columnea: newest big winner in basket plants. il House & Gard 130:212-13 D '66

COLUMNISTS. See Newspapers—Sections, columns, etc.

COLUMNS (newspapers) See Newspapers—Sections, columns, etc.

COLVIN, Jeff
Science's most sophisticated task ever. Sci Digest 60:20-3 Jl '66

COMBINATION locks. See Locks and keys

COMBINES. See Harvesting machinery

COMBS, William W.
Ballads are for singing. Sr Schol 88:sup 10-11 Ap 1 '66

COMBUSTIBLE materials. See Inflammable materials

COMBUSTION engineering, incorporated
Planning eases firm's air unit founding. il Aviation W 85:85+ S 26 '66

COMECON. See Council for mutual economic assistance

COMEDIANS
These jokes are 205 years old; Benny, Hope and Burns. il Esquire 66:128-9 S '66
See also
Carlin, G.
Cavett, D.
Negro comedians
Rivers, J.

COMÉDIE-FRANÇAISE
King: interview. M. Escande. New Yorker 42:29-31 F 26 '66
Vintage imports and homemade baloney. R. Kotlowitz. Harper 232:112-15 My '66

COMEDY
R for comedy. N. Simon. Writer 79:23-4 My '66
See also
Humor
Moving pictures—Comedy
Television broadcasting—Humor

COMER, Mason R. Jr
Personality of the month. L. B. Taylor. il pors Sci Digest 60:40-3 Jl '66

COMETS

Comet Barbon, 1966c. G. S. Mumford. Sky & Tel 32:198 O '66

Comet Rudnicki. G. S. Mumford. Sky & Tel 32:334 D '66

Comet Tempel-Tuttle: recovery of the long-lost comet of the November meteors. J. Schubart. bibliog Science 152:1236-7 My 27 '66

Comets, studied for many years, remain an enigma to scientists. T. D. Nicholson. il Natur Hist 75:44-6 Mr '66

Do comets really break down to produce meteor showers? T. D. Nicholson. il Natur Hist 75:50-2 D '66

Giant comet grazes the sun; Ikeya-Seki. K. F. Weaver. il Nat Geog Mag 129:258-61 F '66

Great comet of 1965; Ikeya-Seki: and past observations. O. Gingerich. il Atlan 217:57-62 My '66

Lost comet showers sky comet Tempel-Tuttle. Sci N 89:459 Je 11 '66

New, brilliant Ikeya-Seki is in family of sun-grazing comets. T. D. Nicholson. il Natur Hist 75:52-4 F '66

New comet Kilston, 1966b. il Sky & Tel 32:191 O '66

Observations of the double nucleus in comet Ikeya-Seki. H. A. Pohn. il Sky & Tel 31:376 Je '66

Periodic comet Halley. G. S. Mumford. Sky & Tel 32:71 Ag '66

Sungrazing comets. Sky & Tel 32:206-7 O '66

Year's third comet low in southeastern sky. Sci N 90:162 S 3 '66

See also
Orbits

Temperature

Comet's temperature taken for first time. Sci N 90:181 S 10 '66

Taking a comet's temperature; Ikeya-Seki. il Time 88:57 S 9 '66

COMIC book heroes. See Comics (books, strips, etc)

COMIC literature. See Humor

COMIC opera. See Opera

COMIC strips. See Comics (books, strips, etc)

COMICS (books, strips, etc)

As Barry Jenkins, Ohio '69, says: a person has to have intelligence to read them. il Esquire 66:116-17 S '66

Camera comics; our comic book heroes. il U S Camera 29:54-5 Ag '66

European literary scene; penetration into precincts of art and literature. R. J. Clements. Sat R 49:23 S 3 '66

Favorites from the funnies. D. Martin. il Hobbies 70:118-19 F '66

Friend of Batman. R. Levy. il Duns R 87:51-2 Mr '66

Great comic-book heroes, comp. by J. Feiffer. Review
    Commentary 41:86-9 My '66. R. Denney

Hail the great; French comic-book hero; Astérix Le Gaulois. Time 88:27 D 23 '66

Man of bronze; Doc Savage; latest hero. il Newsweek 67:118 My 23 '66

New (sob!) trends in the comics. M. F. Nolan. il Reporter 35:32-3 D 29 '66

O.K. you passed the 2-S test; now you're smart enough for comic books. il Esquire 66:114-15 S '66

Peanuts festival; excerpts from Peanuts books. C. M. Schulz. il McCalls 93:106-11 S '66

Pop goes the war; Vietnam story. Newsweek 68:66+ S 12 '66

Return of the (whoosh! there goes one!) superhero! B. Rollin. il Look 30:113-14 Mr 22 '66

What's not so funny about the funnies. P. Pierce. il Ebony 22:48-50+ N '66

Whole country goes supermad. il Life 60:22-3+ Mr 11 '66

Woes of a Peanut manager; Charlie Brown. il Sports Illus 24:46-50 Je 20 '66

Educational applications

Classical comics; excerpts, tr. from Greek comic books. il Horizon 8:116-20 Sum '66

COMIEZ, Maynard S.

Thumbs down on a capital budget. il Bsns W p70+ F 19 '66

COMING out parties. See Debutantes

COMINGS, David E.

Centromere: absence of DNA replication during chromatid separation in human fibroblasts. bibliog Science 154:1463 D 16 '66

COMMAGER, Henry Steele

Can we control the war in Vietnam? Sat R 49:25-7 S 17 '66

Nature of academic freedom. Sat R 49:13-15+ Ag 27 '66

Should historians write contemporary history? Sat R 49:18-20+ F 12 '66

Should the historian make moral judgments? Am Heritage 17:26-7+ F '66

COMMEMORATIVE medals. See Medals

COMMEMORATIVE stamps. See Postage stamps

COMMENCEMENT addresses. See Baccalaureate addresses

COMMENCEMENTS

Etiquette of graduations. Good H 162:182 Je '66

Time to listen: protests of college students at commencement exercises. il Time 87:74 Je 17 '66

COMMENTARY (periodical)

Guide to Jewish journals: thoughts on the publication of the Commentary reader. A. A. Cohen. Commonweal 84:639-41 S 30 '66

Letter to Commentary; tendency to befuddle the day's dominant issues. J. E. Jones. il Nat R 18:983-8, 1078+ O 4, N 1 '66

Passion for ideas. Time 87:56+ My 20 '66

COMMENTARY library (book club) See Book clubs

COMMERCE

Business around the globe. See issues of Fortune

East-West exchanges of technology increase rapidly. V. K. McElheny. Science 153:156-8 Jl 8 '66

Impact of technology on world trade and economic development; addresses, November 16, 1966. J. T. Connor; H. H. Humphrey. Dept State Bul 55:956-65 D 26 '66

Kennedy round: the final phase; address, September 28, 1966. W. M. Blumenthal. Dept State Bul 55:671-5 O 31 '66

President reports to Congress on Trade agreements program; letter of transmittal, September 20, 1966. L. B. Johnson. Dept State Bul 55:675 O 31 '66

Some fundamental problems of world trade; excerpts from a statement, January 26, 1966. R. Prebisch. UN Mo Chron 3:44-52 F '66

Technological competition de-emphasized; symposium on technology and world trade sponsored by the secretary of commerce. W. S. Beller. Tech W 19:38-9 D 5 '66

U.S. signs convention on transit trade of landlocked states. Dept State Bul 54:143 Ja 24 '66

See also
Balance of payments
Free trade and protection
International relations
Restraint of trade
Tariff
    also subhead Commerce under names of countries, e.g. United States—Commerce

COMMERCE department (United States) See United States—Commerce, Department of

COMMERCIAL ethics. See Business ethics

COMMERCIAL fisheries, Bureau of. See United States—Fish and wildlife service

COMMERCIAL law

See also
Trusts, Industrial—Law

COMMERCIAL paper. See Negotiable instruments

COMMERCIAL photography. See Photography, Commercial

COMMERCIAL products

Months ahead; guide for your work and personal living. See issues of Changing times

Technology gap; Europe's fear of falling victim to American economic conquest; Time essay. Time 89:18-19 Ja 13 '67

See also
Marine resources
Products, New

Testing

See also
Consumers union of United States
Quality of products

COMMERCIAL treaties and agreements

See also
General agreement on tariffs and trade
Tariff
United States—Commercial treaties and agreements

COMMISSION against discrimination, New York (state) See New York (state)—Commission against discrimination

COMMISSION of the churches on international affairs. See World council of churches

COMMISSION on heart disease, cancer and stroke. See United States—President's commission on heart disease, cancer and stroke

COMMISSION on human rights. See United Nations—Commission on human rights
COMMISSION on human rights, New York. See New York (city)—Commission on human rights
COMMISSION on technology, automation and economic progress. See United States—National commission on technology, automation, and economic progress
COMMISSION on the assassination of President Kennedy. See United States—President's commission on the assassination of President Kennedy
COMMISSION on the patent system. See United States—President's commission on the patent system
COMMISSION on the status of women. See United Nations—Commission on the status of women
COMMISSION on the structure of Methodism overseas. See Methodist church
COMMISSIONER of baseball. See Baseball—Organization and administration
COMMISSIONER of education. See United States—Education, Office of
COMMISSIONS, independent regulatory. See Independent regulatory commissions
COMMITTEE for a sane nuclear policy. See National committee for a sane nuclear policy
COMMITTEE for economic development
Changing directions in American education; symposium. il Sat R 50:37-43+ Ja 14 '67
Keeping watch on the economy; meaning of 1946 Employment act. K. Schriftgiesser; reply with rejoinder. C. H. Madden. Sat R 49:27 F 26 '66
Lesser of the evils; tax boost better anti-inflation weapon than guideposts. il Bsns W p 160+ My 28 '66
Now the super county; CED study urges larger and stronger county units. Bsns W p 101 Jl 23 '66
Revolution in local government recommended by CED report. Library J 91:3669 Ag '66
Strong case for a new kind of tax; value added tax vs. a corporate income tax. Bsns W p 164 Ap 23 '66
COMMITTEE for industrial development. See United Nations—Committee for industrial development
COMMITTEE of one million against the admission of Communist China to the United Nations
Liebman on the burning deck; J. K. Javits resignation. Nation 204:4-5 Ja 2 '67
Senator Javits and the Committee of one million. Nat R 19:14+ Ja 10 '67
That committee again. Nation 203:565 N 28 '66
COMMITTEE of twenty-four. See United Nations—Special committee on the situation with regard to implementation of declaration on granting of independence to colonial countries and peoples
COMMITTEE on civil rights in metropolitan New York
Reporter at large. E. Iglauer. New Yorker 42:188-92+ S 24 '66
COMMITTEE on housing, building and planning. See United Nations—Economic and social council
COMMITTEE on labor-management policy. See United States—President's advisory committee on labor-management policy
COMMITTEE on libraries. See United States—Committee on libraries
COMMITTEE on national library and information systems
Six national library associations set up committee on info systems. Library J 91:3375 Jl '66
COMMITTEE on political education. See American federation of labor and Congress of industrial organizations—Committee on political education
COMMITTEE on science and astronautics. See United States—Congress—House of representatives—Science and astronautics, Committee on
COMMITTEE on space research. See International council of scientific unions—Committee on space research
COMMITTEE on the peaceful uses of outer space. See United Nations—Committee on the peaceful uses of outer space
COMMITTEE on trade. See United Nations—Economic commission for Asia and the Far East
COMMITTEE to rescue Italian art
We must help save Florence. Life 61:4 D 2 '66
COMMITTEES, Congressional. See United States—Congress—Committees

COMMON man
Making a mass élite. E. Hoffer. il Holiday 39:10+ Mr '66
Profiles; E. Hoffer. C. Tomkins. New Yorker 42:34-6+ Ja 7 '67
COMMON market in Central America. See Central American program of economic integration
COMMON market in Western Europe. See European economic community
COMMONER, Barry
By using nature as a lab. Sat R 49:68-9 My 7 '66
Is DNA really the master key to heredity? excerpt from Science and survival. por Sat R 49:71-5 O 1 '66
COMMONS, House of. See Great Britain—Parliament—House of commons
COMMONWEAL (periodical)
Bias for the new. J. P. Leary. Commonweal 83:677-9 Mr 11 '66
On accepting ads; advertisements for Protestant books in Catholic journals. Commonweal 85:7 O 7 '66
COMMONWEALTH campuses. See Colleges and universities—Off-campus centers
COMMONWEALTH Edison company
High cost of war. Newsweek 68:71 Ag 8 '66
COMMONWEALTH games. See Track athletics
COMMONWEALTH of nations
Commonwealth: Britain's dream fades. il U S News 60:102-3 My 16 '66
Day that wasn't: Commonwealth day. il Time 87:29 Je 3 '66
Imperial Britain, RIP; closing of British Colonial office. C. Brogan. Nat R 18:928-30 S 20 '66
Moment of decision; Commonwealth conference. il Newsweek 68:44 S 19 '66
New foe emerging; Zambia departure? Newsweek 68:47-8 Ag 1 '66
Question of black power; crisis over Rhodesia. Time 88:36-7 S 9 '66
Reports of Britain's death. I. Macleod. For Affairs 45:88-97 O '66
Something burning; issue of Rhodesia. Time 88:40 S 16 '66
Wilson vs. Smith: whose last chance? Commonwealth conference. il Newsweek 68:42+ S 26 '66
Yes, but how? break-up of Commonwealth conference. Time 88:37 S 23 '66
See also
Prime ministers conferences
COMMONWEALTH prime ministers conferences. See Prime ministers conferences
COMMUNAL settlements. See Collective settlements
COMMUNICABLE diseases
Family immunization schedules. E. Maxwell. Todays Health 44:83-4 My '66
Goodbye to infection; laboratory-made antibodies; reprint. W. Sullivan. Sci Digest 59:71-4 Mr '66
When a grownup gets a children's disease. R. Winter. il Parents Mag 41:60-1+ My '66
See also
Animals as carriers of infection
Rats as carriers of infection
also names of communicable diseases, e.g. Amebiasis
COMMUNICATION
Before Babel; means of communicating in todays changing world. M. L'Engle. il Horn Bk 42:661-70 D '66
Challenge of linguistic realism; dilemmas in drama and literature. M. Pei. Sat R 49:27-8+ Ap 23 '66
Communications; ed. by R. L. Tobin. See issues of Saturday review
Communications networks for libraries. J. Becker. bibliog il Wilson Lib Bul 41:383-7 D '66
How to reduce business' credibility gap; government industry relations; address, March 24, 1966. B. C. Goss. Vital Speeches 32:396-8 Ap 15 '66
How word-of-mouth advertising works. E. Dichter. Harvard Bsns R 44:147-52+ N '66
Quest for silence; address, August 17, 1966. R. M. Ralston. Vital Speeches 32:726-31 S 15 '66
Thoughts on writing and handcraft; summer program called Cross-over at Penland school of crafts. M. C. Richards. Craft Horiz 26:32-3+ Jl '66
Visual language. D. Cyr. bibliog il Sch Arts 66:32-5 N '66
Visual literacy. D. Cyr. il Design 68:24-6 N '66
See also
Communications satellites
Computers—Communication applications

COMMUNICATION—See also—*Continued*
Interplanetary communication
Mass media
Public relations
Radio broadcasting

Anecdotes, facetiae, satire, etc.

Right you are if you say you are, obscurely; Time essay. Time 88:14-15 D 30 '66

COMMUNICATION in education
Communications; address, June 5, 1966. R. W. Sarnoff. Vital Speeches 32:670-2 Ag 15 '66

COMMUNICATION in management
Communication aids. il Duns R 88:pt2 153-4 S '66
How to get through to people. R. E. Levinson. il Nations Bsns 54:92+ N '66
Improving estimates that involve uncertainty. D. H. Woods. il Harvard Bsns R 44:91-8 Jl '66
Myth of real-time management information. J. Dearden. il Harvard Bsns R 44:123-32 My '66
Telecommunication. il Duns R 88:pt2 149-50+ S '66
Understanding McLuhan. M. McLuhan. il Newsweek 67:56-7 F 28 '66

COMMUNICATION in science
Art of talking about science; excerpts from address, December 28, 1966. L. Bragg. Science 154:1613-16 D 30 '66
Do they dig you, daddio? communication between scientist and layman, adaptation of address; reprint. R. G. Lynch. Am For 72:30-1+ F '66
Flood; problem of keeping worthless material. W. J. Coughlin. Tech W 19:50 O 3 '66
Information exchange group no. 5; created by the National institutes of health; letter. S. Dray. Science 153:694-5 Ag 12 '66; Discussion. 153:332+ O 21 '66
Information exchange groups. P. H. Abelson. Science 154:727 N 11 '66
Information exchange groups to be discontinued; letter. E. A. Confrey. Science 154:843 N 18 '66
Letters to congressmen. D. Wolfle. Science 151:639 F 11 66
On being referred to; letter. D. A. Miller. Science 153:364+ Jl 22 '66
On improving communication among scientists. D. R. Swanson. Bul Atomic Sci 22:8-11 F '66; Discussion. 22:31 My '66
Science critics; excerpts from address, October 19, 1966. R. Dubos. Science 154:595 N 4 '66
Too much silence on the potentials of biology? V. K. McElheny. Science 153:283 Jl 15 '66
See also
Television broadcasting—Scientific programs

COMMUNICATION theory. See Information theory

COMMUNICATIONS, Military
See also
Communications satellites—Military applications
Radio communication, Military
United States—Air force—Communication systems

COMMUNICATIONS research
Communicating research on the poor; the problem of telling it like it is; address. L. P. Jackson, jr. bibliog Negro Hist Bul 29:151-2+ Ap '66
Sarasota mystery; plasmonics? hydronics? K. Warner. il Pop Electr 24:50-3 Mr; 48 Ap '66

COMMUNICATIONS satellite corporation
Airline communications satellite offered. Aviation W 84:37 Mr 14 '66
Amazing story of earth satellites; interview. J. McCormack. il U S News 61:58-62 D 26 '66
AT&T, Comsat clash on merger proposal. K. Johnsen. Aviation W 84:28 Je 27 '66
AT&T plans vast comsat net with 83,000-circuit capacity. K. Johnsen. Aviation W 85:24 D 26 '66
Composite satellite, cable rate studied. K. Johnsen. Aviation W 85:32 O 3 '66
Comsat charges AT&T cable plan threatens satellite development. Aviation W 84:26 My 2 '66
Comsat looks to home. Bsns W p50 D 17 '66
Comsat pushes new domestic satellite net. K. Johnsen. Aviation W 84:27-8 Ap 18 '66
Comsat question. W. J. Coughlin. Tech W 19:50 O 24 '66
Comsat reveals $110-million plan for mid-1970s domestic system. K. Johnsen. Aviation W 85:27-8 Ag 8 '66
Comsat satellite no. 2; many uses, after all. **U S News 61:9 D 5 '66**

Comsat: the pie in the sky is really there. il Newsweek 68:86-8 O 31 '66
Comsat triumph turns to failure. il Bsns W p 108 N 5 '66
Comsat unveils domestic plans; nationwide satellite communications system. Bsns W p32 Jl 30 '66
Contenders chafe over FCC comsat delay. il Tech W 20:13 Ja 2 '67
Domestic comsat decision off until 1967. Tech W 19:16 Ag 8 '66
FCC blocking direct Comsat-DOD lease. il Aviation W 85:23 Jl 4 '66
Ford foundation, Comsat corp. clash over nonprofit TV. Tech W 19:18 Ag 22 '66
Fourth network; Ford foundation's plan vs. Comsat's. J. Ridgeway. New Repub 155:13-14 S 17 '66
Global Comsat design widens bandwidth. B. Miller. il Aviation W 84:81-4 My 2 '66
Green light for expansion by Comsat. il U S News 61:10 D 19 '66
Major communications rulings imminent. K. Johnsen. Aviation W 85:28-9 D 12 '66
Move to long-tank Delta made to boost comsat capability. H. M. David. Tech W 19:19 S 12 '66
Rivals assail Comsat defense contract bid. Aviation W 85:36-7 S 19 '66
Satellite communications. N. P. Hurley. America 115:204-6 Ag 27 '66
Satellite going up, prices going down; to compete with Comsat, other carriers are proposing lower rates. il Bsns W p 116+ O 1 '66
Satellites; a fight at home; a hard sell abroad. il Bsns W p46-7 My 21 '66
Satellites will compete for major role in commercial communications traffic. K. Johnsen. il Aviation W 84:124-5 Mr 7 '66
Second Intelsat-2 is orbiting earth. Aviation W 86:34 Ja 16 '67
Senate to air controversy in communications satellite area. H. M. David. Tech W 19:18 Ag 15 '66
Setback for hopes of Comsat investors. U S News 61:23 N 14 '66
Significant gain seen in AT&T comsat. P. J. Klass. il Aviation W 86:20-1 Ja 2 '67
Speeding Comsat into a fast orbit; J. McCormack. Bsns W p 128+ Mr 26 '66
TV and telephone by space; about to become big business. il U S News 60:87-9 Je 6 '66
Whole new system for TV? il U S News 61:82 Ag 15 '66

COMMUNICATIONS satellites
Airline communications satellite offered. Aviation W 84:37 Mr 14 '66
Airline satellite effort gains momentum. Aviation W 84:43 My 9 '66
Amazing story of earth satellites; interview. J. McCormack. il U S News 61:58-62 D 26 '66
AT&T plans vast comsat net with 83,000-circuit capacity. K. Johnsen. Aviation W 85:24 D 26 '66
Arinc studies domestic airline satellite; nationwide microwave network evaluated. K. Johnsen. Aviation W 85:49 S 26 '66
Battle line shifts on satellites; Comsat, AT&T join in opposing Ford foundation's TV plan. Bsns W p34 Ag 27 '66
Bellsat; grand designs for U.S. space communications network. il Newsweek 68:66 D 26 '66
Canada pushing for domestic comsat net; experimental station planned at Bouchette. K. Johnsen. Aviation W 85:35 N 21 '66
Comsat patent claims itemized by firm. Tech W 19:41-2 Ag 1 '66
Comsat question. W. J. Coughlin. Tech W 19:50 O 24 '66
Comsat systems monopolized? Tech W 19:24+ Jl 25 '66
Comsat triumph turns to failure. il Bsns W p 108 N 5 '66
Comsat use should swell dramatically. R. Pay. il Miss & Roc 18:34-7+ Ja 31 '66
Contenders chafe over FCC comsat delay. il Tech W 20:13 Ja 2 '67
Digital links, millimeter waves studied. W. S. Beller. il Miss & Roc 18:70+ Ja 31 '66
Domestic comsat decision off until 1967. Tech W 19:16 Ag 8 '66
Educational satellites; proposed Broadcasters' non-profit satellite service. Sci Am 215:101-2 S '66
Educational TV; NSF and arts foundation speak out. L. J. Carter. Science 154:1309-10 D 9 '66
ETV communications satellites raise new copyright issues. R. H. Smith. Pub W 190:46 S 5 '66

COMMUNICATIONS satellites—*Continued*

ETV: Ford foundation calls for nonprofit satellite system. E. Langer. Science 153:962-4 Ag 26 '66

ETV via satellites? H. E. Wigren. NEA J 55:52-4 O '66

ELDO to provide Comsat launcher. W. S. Beller. il Tech W 19:20 Jl 18 '66

Enthusiasm grows for global Comsats. C. D. LaFond. il Miss & Roc 18:46-7+ Ja 31 '66

ESRO favored for European comsat, if. Miss & Roc 18:24+ My 2 '66

FCC studies Western union bids for satellite network. Aviation W 85:33 N 14 '66

Ford foundation outlines new proposal; broadcast non-profit satellite system. H. M. David. Tech W 19:18-19 D 19 '66

Ford foundation proposes plan for non-profit radio–TV satellites. R. D. Hibben. Aviation W 85:28-9 Ag 8 '66

Fourth network; Ford foundation proposal that a nonprofit corporation operate a domestic satellite system for educational TV. J. Ridgeway. New Repub 155:13-14 S 17 '66

Global Comsat design widens bandwidth. B. Miller. il Aviation W 84:81-4 My 2 '66

Global Comsat expansion delayed two years. Aviation W 84:31 My 30 '66

High-wire act; Lani Bird. Newsweek 68:74 N 7 '66

Home TV via satellite. B. B. Underhill. il Electr World 75:39-41+ My '66

Hurdles in space broadcasting. N. I. Tchistiakov. il UNESCO Courier 19:30-2 N '66

Inter-agency group drafts U.S. position on aeronautical comsat. Aviation W 85:35 Ag 15 '66

Interest growing in use of synchronous satellites. W. C. Wetmore. Aviation W 85:81+ N 14 '66

ICAO unit opposes early airline comsat. Aviation W 85:50 O 31 '66

Launching a satellite war; Comsat and AT&T vs. Ford foundation. Bsns W p38 Ag 6 '66

Move to long-tank Delta made to boost comsat capability. H. M. David. Tech W 19:19 S 12 '66

New communications satellites. R. N. Watts, jr. il Sky & Tel 32:350-2 D '66

Newest comsat will link two-thirds of world. Sci N 90:291 O 15 '66

1972 Olympic games prompt German bid for TV satellite. W. Buedeler. il Tech W 19:19 S 5 '66

NATO comsat experiment to use U.S. defense dept. space vehicle. D. E. Fink. Aviation W 85:18 D 19 '66

People's satellite; national ETV programs; opposition to Ford foundation proposals. il Newsweek 68:76-7 Ag 15 '66

President reports to Congress on Communications satellite act; text of letter, March 3, 1966. L. B. Johnson. Dept State Bul 54:503 Mr 28 '66

Satellite communications. N. P. Hurley. America 115:204-6 Ag 27 '66

Satellite launch set; commercial communications satellites. Sci N 89:402 My 21 '66

Satellite static; critics complaints of Ford scheme. Newsweek 68:79 S 5 '66

Satellites: a fight at home; a hard sell abroad. il Bsns W p46-7 My 21 '66

Satellites and computers may measure world's water; proposal to consider global water information system. D. Behrman. UNESCO Courier 19:31 Ap '66

Satellites find a receptive world. il Bsns W p 107-8 D 17 '66

Science and space; Philco plan presented to FAA. Newsweek 67:94-5 Mr 21 '66

Senate to air controversy in communications satellite area. H. M. David. Tech W 19:18 Ag 15 '66

Shortage of frequencies threatens satellite communications growth. K. Johnsen. Aviation W 84:32 My 9 '66

Significant gain seen in AT&T comsat. P. J. Klass. il Aviation W 86:20-1 Ja 2 '67

Social and educational implications of communication satellites; adaptation of address, December 6-10, 1965. W. Schramm. Sch & Soc 94:346-8 O 29 '66

TV revolution ahead! new era potentials. D. Sarnoff. Read Digest 88:66-70 My '66

Who gets satellite profits? Bsns W p45 S 10 '66

World of the communications satellite; address, December 1965. A. C. Clarke. bibliog il UNESCO Courier 19:24-9 N '66

Worldwide mail delivery within minutes predicted; using orbiting satellite as post office. Sci N 90:183 S 10 '66

See also
Communications satellite corporation
European conference for telecommunications satellites
International telecommunications satellite consortium

Launching

Eight more IDCSP's readied for launch. R. Pay. il Tech W 20:41-2 Ja 9 '67

In a single launching, a belt of satellites. il U S News 60:10 Je 27 '66

Second Intelsat-2 is orbiting earth Aviation W 86:34 Ja 16 '67

Titan III-C successfully launches IDCSP; Initial defense communications satellite program. C. D. LaFond. il Tech W 18:16-17 Je 27 '66

Military applications

Army comsat link terminal demonstrated. C. D. LaFond. il Tech W 19:37-9 N 21 '66

Defense dept. defies FCC Comsat position. Aviation W 85:38 Jl 11 '66

DOD communication satellite launch set. P. J. Klass. Aviation W 84:33 My 9 '66

Eight more IDCSP's readied for launch; initial defense communications satellite program. R. Pay. il Tech W 20:41-2 Ja 9 '67

House scores DOD ground station progress. H. M. David. Tech W 19:15 Ag 29 '66

House unit asks vast expansion of DOD comsat net, operation. Aviation W 85:29 O 24 '66

IDCSP launch rescheduled; low signal strength probed; initial defense communications satellite program. il Tech W 19:14 Ag 29 '66

Major communications rulings imminent. K. Johnsen. Aviation W 85:28-9 D 12 '66

Military comsats deploy for global cover. P. J. Klass. il Aviation W 84:25-6 Je 27 '66

Over his head; proposal to allow NATO to use U.S. system. Newsweek 68:56+ O 10 '66

Report urges broader DOD Comsat plans. H. M. David. Tech W 19:14 O 24 '66

Tactical Comsat network planned. M. Getler. il Miss & Roc 18:58-60+ Ja 31 '66

Titan failure with satellites probed. M. Getler. il Tech W 19:18 S 5 '66

Titan III-C successfully launches IDCSP; Initial defense communications satellite program. C. D. LaFond. il Tech W 18:16-17 Je 27 '66

Orbits

Soviets trim comsat orbit for most USSR coverage. P. J. Klass. Aviation W 85:34 O 24 '66

Tracking

House scores DOD ground station progress. H. M. David. Tech W 19:15 Ag 29 '66

Seminar on communication satellite earth-station technology; text of statement, May 16, 1966, with Department announcement. U. A. Johnson. Dept State Bul 54:949-52 Je 13 '66

U.K. company bids on satellite terminals. il Aviation W 85:93 N 28 '66

U.S. spurring overseas Comsat terminals. K. Johnsen. Aviation W 84:31 My 23 '66

COMMUNICATIONS satellites ground stations. See Radio stations

COMMUNION. See Catholic church—Eucharist

COMMUNISM

Changing image of communism. il U S News 60:70-1 Ap 11 '66

Communism 1966: success or failure? V. C. Ferkiss. Cath World 204:11-16 O '66

Communism: world's greatest failure. il U S News 61:59-63 D 5 '66

Growing strength of freedom; address, June 10, 1966. W. A. Harriman. Dept State Bul 55:10-14 Jl 4 '66

Marxism in the modern world. ed. by M. M. Drachkovitch Review
Nation 202:623 My 23 '66. T. B. Bottomore

Special issue: the changing face of world communism; symposium. il Sr Schol 89:3-15+ N 11 '66

See also
Anti-Communist movements
Communist parties
Socialism
World peace council

Anti-Communist measures

Buying off Ho Chi Minh. America 114:536 Ap 16 '66

See also
Anti-Communist movements
United States—Foreign relations—Anti-Communist measures

COMMUNISM—*Continued*

History

How communism grew; from Marx to Mao. il
Sr Schol 89:4-7 N 11 '66

Study and teaching

Confrontation at Latrobe. Nation 203:404-5 O
24 '66

Africa

Communist grab for African unions. L. M.
Taubinger. Nat R 18:1222 N 29 '66
Demagogues are rocked. G. Comte. Nat R 18:
832 Ag 23 '66
Reds' strategy now. U S News 61:98 D 12
'66

Asia

New appraisal of the old domino game. C.
Fritchey. Harper 232:46 Ap '66
Reflections on Asian communism. H. J.
Benda. Yale R 56:1-16 O '66
We cannot accept a Communist seizure of
Vietnam. R. A. Scalapino. il N Y Times
Mag p46-7+ D 11 '66; Reply. New Repub
155:5-7 D 24 '66

Asia, Southeastern

Next on Peking's hit parade? Thailand. S.
Topping. il N Y Times Mag p30-1+ F 20 '66
Thailand: the anatomy of a domino. il News-
week 67:35-6+ Ja 31 '66
World that waits. E. J. Hughes. Newsweek
67:28-9 Je 13 '66

China

Origin of the Chinese revolution. C. P. Fitz-
Gerald. Cur Hist 51:129-33+ S '66

China (People's Republic)

Appalling & alone. Time 88:28 S 30 '66
China after Mao; excerpts. A. D. Barnett. il
Look 30:31-5 N 15 '66
China: behind the upheaval. H. Portisch. il
Sat R 49:24-9+ D 10 '66
China's crisis of foreign policy. D. S. Zagoria.
il N Y Times Mag p22-3+ My 1 '66
China's friend, Mao's enemy. America 116:74
Ja 21 '67
Chinese puzzle. Commonweal 85:279-80 D 9
'66
Coming dilemmas for China's leaders. L. W.
Pye. For Affairs 44:387-402 Ap '66
Enormous revival meeting. R. S. Elegant.
Nation 203:307-11 O 3 '66
First-hand report on red China today; inter-
view. C. P. Miao. il U S News 61:58-61 N 7
'66
How communism grew; from Marx to Mao. il
Sr Schol 89:6-7 N 11 '66
How to be mad for Mao; Red guard. il Sr
Schol 89:17-18 S 23 '66
Ideology and organization in Communist
China, by F. Schurmann. Review
Sat R 49:51 Je 11 '66. M. H. Fried
Just how dangerous is red China? interview,
ed. by K. M. Chrysler. M. Esaki. il U S
News 61:84-6 O 24 '66
Life under communism, two first-hand re-
ports; interviews. H. Portisch; L. Stucki.
il U S News 61:50-6 S 12 '66
Little brother is watching; Red guards re-
bellion in Peking. il Newsweek 68:32 S 5
'66
Long live Chairman Mao! long live Lin Piao!
S. Topping. il N Y Times Mag p 18-19+
Jl 17 '66
Mao's last revolution. R. MacFarquhar. bib-
liog f For Affairs 45:112-24 O '66
Nightmare across the land; Great proletarian
cultural revolution. il Time 88:22-3 S 2 '66;
Same abr. with title Red guard: nightmare
in the streets. Read Digest 89:196+ D '66
Paper that spreads the cult of Mao; Jenmin
Jih Pao, the People's daily of Peking.
I. Stewart. il N Y Times Mag p26-7+ D 18
'66
Peking has a Yenan complex. M. Gayn. il
N Y Times Mag p 10-11+ Ja 30 '66
Peking's cultural revolution. S. Y. Dai. bib-
liog f Cur Hist 51:134-9+ S '66
People's middle kingdom. J. K. Fairbank.
For Affairs 44:574-86 Jl '66
Red China with the A-missile, meaning to
U.S. Russia; with interview with C. Cheng.
il U S News 61:50-2+ N 14 '66
Red China's sinking revolution. C. J. V.
Murphy. il Fortune 74:134-9+ N '66
Red guards: today, China; tomorrow, the
world. il Time 88:32-3 S 23 '66; Same abr.
with title Red guard: nightmare in the
streets. Read Digest 89:196+ D '66
Shanghai's repentant capitalists. R. Guillain.
il Reporter 34:38-41 Ap 7 '66

Tatzepao, grim news for China; with report
by A. D. Barnett. il Life 62:26-33 Ja 20 '67
Today's subtle art of China watching. S.
Leavitt. Life 61:90B+ O 7 '66
Where's Mao? il Newsweek 67:44 My 16 '66
See also
Communist party (China [People's Republic])

Cuba

Reds plan more Vietnams. il U S News 60:27
Ja 31 '66
Whatever became of Che? P. Hofmann. il
N Y Times Mag p 14-15+ Ap 10 '66

Czechoslovakia

Prague in metamorphosis. R. J. Gerber.
America 115:480-2 O 22 '66; Discussion.
115:636; 116:30-1 N 19 '66, Ja 14 '67
See also
Communist party (Czechoslovakia)

Dominican Republic

Is Dominican trouble to go on and on? il
U S News 60:12 F 21 '66

Ethiopia

Control of the Red Sea. A. Ford. il Nat R
18:314-15 Ap 5 '66

Europe, Eastern

Perforated curtain; survey of Communist
countries. G. Farmer. il Life 61:122-4+
D 9 '66
Third communism. il Time 87:34-48 Mr 18 '66

Ghana

Blueprint for subversion; how reds tried to
take Africa. il U S News 61:97-9 D 12 '66
Ghana: communism's major defeat in Africa.
D. Reed. Read Digest 88:75-80 Je '66

Great Britain

See also
Trade unions—Communist activities

Guatemala

Undeclared war in Guatemala; well-organized
Communist guerrillas. R. Rogers and T.
Yates. il Sat Eve Post 239:30-3 Je 18 '66
Where another red revolt is brewing on U.S.
doorstep. C. Migdail. il U S News 60:53-4 Mr
7 '66
With the guerrillas in Guatemala. A. Howard.
il N Y Times Mag p8-9+ Je 26 '66

Hong Kong

Reporter at large; findings of the China
watchers or Pekinologists. R. Shaplen.
New Yorker 41:41-2+ F 12 '66

Hungary

Atlantic report. Atlan 218:36+ O '66
Budapest: ten years after the Hungarian
revolution. L. Gross. il Look 30:106-10+
N 1 '66
See also
Communist party (Indonesia)

Indonesia

Latin America

Blow-up in the Andes; new trouble for U.S.
J. N. Wallace. il U S News 60:72-4 Ap 11
'66
Latin America: revolution without revolutionaries. N. Gall. il Nation 203:145-9 Ag
22 '66
Where the terrorists are. Time 88:31 S 2 '66

Mexico

Reds heating up Mexico. il U S News 61:88 N
14 '66
Under the lid in Mexico; makings of an explosion. il U S News 60:50-1 My 2 '66

Panama

See also
Communist party (Panama)

Philippines

Peking's next target? J. M. Van Der Kroef.
Nat R 18:1165-6+ N 15 '66
See also
Hukbalahaps

Poland

Comes the millennium; church-state crisis. il
Newsweek 67:41-2 Ap 25 '66
Poland has seen the future. D. Halberstam.
il N Y Times Mag p 14-15+ F 6 '66
Poland: twenty years of resisting the reds. il
U S News 61:54-6 Jl 4 '66
Two days that shook the Communist world.
F. Lewis. il N Y Times Mag p25+ Je 12
'66
See also
Communist party (Poland)

COMMUNISM—*Continued*

Rumania

Man battering at the Kremlin wall; Ceausescu of Rumania. D. Binder. il N Y Times Mag p 10-11+ My 29 '66
See also
Communist party (Rumania)

Russia

Conditioning comrades; Lenin's prohibition of private ownership. Time 88:30 S 2 '66
How communism grew: from Marx to Mao. il Sr Schol 89:4-7 N 11 '66
Rise and fall of scientific socialism. A. P. Mendel. bibliog f For Affairs 45:98-111 O '66
Russia's other peace movement. A. Parry. Nation 203:142-5 Ag 22 '66
See also
Communist party (Russia)

Thailand

Americans in Thailand; counterinsurgency activities of armed forces, USIS and AID. M. Parker. Atlan 218:51-8 D '66
Report from Thailand: Communists heating up a second front in Asia. S. W. Sanders. il U S News 61:42-4 Jl 18 '66
Squeeze play in Thailand. M. Parker. il Reporter 35:16-18 Ag 11 '66
Thailand: a second South Viet Nam? ed. by E. Sparn. il Sr Schol 88:7-10 F 25 '66
Thailand: its meaning for the U.S. B. K. Gordon. bibliog f il Cur Hist 52:16-21+ Ja '67

United States

Americanism vs. communism: a historical document; concerning B. G. Northrop's Schools and communism. S. E. Fraser. Sch & Soc 94:355 O 29 '66
Diagnosis of a riot: Cleveland. il U S News 61:8 Ag 22 '66
Who is behind the race riots? P. A. McCombs. Nat R 18:934-5 S 20 '66
See also
Communist party (United States)

Anti-communist measures

Chair for Hoover; plans for J. Edgar Hoover foundation. Nation 203:629 D 12 '66
Communism and the United States: the Communist party from zig to zag. il Sr Schol 89:11-14 N 11 '66
Communist controversy in Washington, by E. Latham. Review
  Nation 203:423-5 O 24 '66. F. J. Donner
Government by accident: the medicare disclaimer. E. Langer. Science 151:970 F 25 '66
University and anti-Communist pressure. H. K. Stanford. Sch & Soc 94:123-5 Mr 5 '66
Warning to the unwary; proceedings to force W.E.B. DuBois clubs to register as a Communist front. Time 87:28 Mr 11 '66
Weltner bill: clear and present danger. V. Countryman. il Nation 203:16-18 Jl 4 '66
See also
Constructive action, incorporated
John Birch society

Venezuela

Castro terrorists on the move again. il U S News 61:8 D 26 '66
How campus reds tried to take over a country; Central university in Caracas. il U S News 62:37-8 Ja 16 '67
Rooting out the rebels. il Newsweek 68:36 D 26 '66
War on subversion. il Time 88:29 D 23 '66

Vietnam (Democratic Republic)

Is North Vietnam weakening? interviews with red prisoners; symposium. ed. by G. C. Troelstrup. U S News 61:52-4 D 12 '66

Vietnam (Republic)

Another enemy in Vietnam war: corruption. il U S News 60:44-5 F 14 '66
Just what is the Viet Cong? questions and answers. U S News 60:38 F 28 '66
Letter from Saigon. R. Shaplen. New Yorker 42:129-34 Ag 20 '66
Other regime in South Vietnam. T. Oka. il N Y Times Mag p8-9+ Jl 31 '66

Anti-Communist measures

Vietnam: the ordeal of pacification; Revolutionary development program. D. Warner. il Reporter 35:24-8 D 1 '66

Yugoslavia

Canceling the rubber stamp. Time 88:28 D 23 '66

Going gets rough in Yugoslavia. P. Ben. New Repub 155:15-16 S 3 '66
Tito's Yugoslavia: is it communism? with report by F. Y. Blumenfeld. il Newsweek 68:49-54 O 17 '66
Where the lure of the auto is killing communism. K. Lachmann. il U S News 60:76-8 Je 20 '66

COMMUNISM and art. See Art and politics

COMMUNISM and democracy

Canada's role in East-West relations; address, March 11, 1966. P. Martin. Vital Speeches 32:409-14 Ap 15 '66
Change and challenge; address, June 12, 1966. R. Drummond. Vital Speeches 32:660-3 Ag 15 '66
Cold war myths. R. Steel. Commonweal 83:576-8 F 18 '66
Communist challenges in the '60's: keeping a delicate balance. il Sr Schol 89:14-15+ N 11 '66
Costs and consequences of the cold war. D. F. Fleming. bibliog f Ann Am Acad 366:127-38 Jl '66
Democracy's dilemma: the totalitarian party in a free society, by B. E. Lippincott. Review
  Nat R 18:540-2 My 31 '66. E. McDowell
Economic systems compared: more achievement with less Marx? il Sr Schol 88:18-19 Ap 1 '66
Free world colossus: a critique of American foreign policy in the cold war, by D. Horowitz. Review
  Nation 202:214-16 F 21 '66. A. S. Kaufman
Freedom and change; address, January 19, 1966. A. F. Douglas-Home. Vital Speeches 32:239-41 F 1 '66
Goals for American power. R. D. Masters. Yale R 55:365-88 Mr '66
Prodigal nation. M. Ascoli. Reporter 35:22-3 S 8 '66
Red China's plan to conquer the world; excerpts from document. P. Lin. il Nations Bsns 54:40-1 Ja '66
U.S. joins other American republics in denouncing Havana Tricontinental conference; statement, January 24, 1966. W. P. Allen. Dept State Bul 54:383-5 Mr 7 '66
Vietnam: after all is said and done. E. Van Den Haag. Nat R 18:1210-12+ N 29 '66

COMMUNISM and literature

Profiles: B. Brecht. H. Arendt. New Yorker 42:68-70+ N 5 '66
Trial of two Soviet writers; case of Y. Daniel and A. Tertz. G. Bailey. il Reporter 34:34-8 F 24 '66

COMMUNISM and religion

Christian-Marxist conversation, in Paris and Prague. J. M. Swomley, jr. Christian Cent 83:1160-2 S 21 '66; Reply. H. Aptheker. 83:1346 N 2 '66
Church and communism in East Germany. M. Barth. Christian Cent 83:1440-3, 1469-72 N 23-30 '66
Communism and the silent church. E. v. Kuehnelt-Leddihn. Nat R 18:1151 N 15 '66
Dialogue: Christ and Marx. il Newsweek 69:74+ Ja 16 '67
Doctor Hromadka and the will to peace; Communist peace propaganda through Christian peace conference; reply. J. C. Heidbrink. America 114:367 Mr 19 '66
Let's end the Communist-Christian vendetta: concerning the books, From anathema to dialogue, and The future of belief. H. Cox. Christian Cent 83:1375-9 N 9 '66; Discussion. 83:1508, 1542-3 D 7-14 '66
Not dead enough. S. Hiltner. Christian Cent 83:1181-2 S 28 '66
Not without tension; coexistence of Christianity with communism. Christian Cent 83:388 Mr 30 '66
Who's afraid of Roger Garaudy? Christian Cent 83:1560 D 21 '66
See also
Catholic church and communism
Catholic church in Poland
Church and state in Russia

COMMUNISM and the Catholic church. See Catholic church and communism

COMMUNIST aggression. See Aggression (international law)

COMMUNIST countries

How communism split: communism divided, or multiplied? Sr Schol 89:7-10 N 11 '66
Worrying about China in the Lenin Hills; Moscow conference of eight Communist countries. il Newsweek 68:51 O 31 '66
See also
China (People's Republic)
Europe, Eastern
Public opinion—Communist countries
Tourist trade—Communist countries
Youth—Communist countries

COMMUNIST countries—*Continued*

Commerce

Communist trade: no bonanza yet. Bsns W p68+ O 29 '66

East-West relations: shaping a stable world; address, December 11, 1966. F. D. Kohler. Dept State Bul 56:6-11 Ja 2 '67; Excerpts. U S News 61:52-3 D 26 '66

United States policy on East-West trade; address, June 8, 1966. E. M. Braderman. Dept State Bul 54:1013-19 Je 27 '66; Same. Vital Speeches 32:559-62 Jl 1 '66

We can trade with the Communists; with report on trade relations among Communist countries. H. J. Berman. il Nation 202: 766-70 Je 27 '66

Economic relations

See also
Communist countries—Commerce

Foreign relations

Great American reflex; anti-Communist neurosis. Nation 202:378 Ap 4 '66

Pax Russo-Americana? Sino-Soviet dispute. G. Lichtheim. Commentary 41:60-5 Ap '66

Religious institutions and affairs

See also
Europe, Eastern—Religious institutions and affairs

Travel regulations

See Travel regulations

COMMUNIST newspapers
More dead than read; Western Communist press. il Newsweek 68:100+ D 5 '66
See also
Morning star (newspaper)

COMMUNIST organizations
Weltner bill: clear and present danger. V. Countryman. il Nation 203:16-18 Jl 4 '66

COMMUNIST parties
Barraged balloon; proposed conference of loyal Leninists to read red China out. il Time 88:42 N 25 '66
Moscow meeting; Communist leaders from nine nations. Sr Schol 89:18 N 4 '66
Out on a limb; Brezhnev promoting Communist conference to drum Maoists out. Newsweek 68:50+ N 28 '66
Soft-sell; Brezhnev pushing what appears to be call to drum Chinese out of world movement. il por Newsweek 68:52+ D 12 '66

COMMUNIST party (China [People's Republic])
At a loss for words. il Newsweek 68:42 Jl 25 '66
Atlantic report: purge in China. Atlan 218: 26+ D '66
Can Mao keep the upper hand in China? U S News 62:13 Ja 9 '67
Catered affair: 23rd congress of the Communist party of the Soviet Union. il Newsweek 67:44+ Ap 4 '66
China has a succession struggle begun? press attack anti-Mao faction. V. Zorza. New Repub 154:10-11 My 28 '66
China: sparks of revolt. il Newsweek 69:40+ Ja 16 '67
Cities say no; Red guards opposed by urban workers. Time 89:24-6 Ja 20 '67
Clashing absurdities; Red guards. Time 88:40 S 16 '66
Cultural revolution: education system latest purge target. Newsweek 68:43-4 Jl 4 '66
Dance of the scorpion. il Time 89:20-3 Ja 13 '67
From a single spark: purge motives of Teng and Lin. Newsweek 67:46 Je 27 '66
Further on the China confrontation: a question and an answer from France. J. Claire-Louis; P. Boutang. Nat R 18:208-9 Mr 8 '66
Great proletarian cultural revolution. il Newsweek 69:29 Ja 9 '67
Handwriting on the wall; purge by poster and partisan propagandizing. il Time 89:24 Ja 6 '67
Internal politics since 1956; excerpt from New communisms. J. R. Townsend. Bul Atomic Sci 22:58-65 Je '66
Mystery of red China: a real blowup coming? il U S News 62:46-8 Ja 23 '67
No ordinary swim; new light on the great purge as Chairman Mao surfaces; reasons; victims; aims. il Newsweek 68:36-40 Ag 8 '66
One down, more to go; purge. Newsweek 67: 53 Je 13 '66
Out on a limb: Brezhnev promoting Communist conference to drum Maoists out. Newsweek 68:50+ N 28 '66
Perils of the purge. Newsweek 68:54+ S 26 '66

Punished by history; Peking mayor, victim of Mao's purge. Time 87:40 Je 10 '66
Raging storm; downfall of Peng Chen. il Newsweek 67:48-9 Je 20 '66
Upheaval in China. il Sat Eve Post 239:82 Jl 30 '66
Where teen gangs get official support. il U S News 61:11 S 5 '66
Why the Red guards? explanations of the Chinese crisis. V. Zorza. New Repub 155: 14-15 O 8 '66
Why the turmoil inside red China; interview. C. K. Chiang. il U S News 61:33-4 O 10 '66

COMMUNIST party (Czechoslovakia)
Good neighbors; thirteenth congress. Newsweek 67:65-6 Je 13 '66

COMMUNIST party (Dominican Republic)
Case of defamation; US intelligence versus Juan Bosch; alleged Bosch-Communist plot, April 14, 1965. T. Draper. New Repub 154: 13-19 F 19; 15-18 F 26; 37 Mr 5; 35 Mr 12 '66

COMMUNIST party (Finland)
Out of the wilderness; Communists in four-party coalition. Newsweek 67:44+ Je 6 '66

COMMUNIST party (France)
Marxism in modern France, by G. Lichtheim. Review
Commentary 42:102-3+ S '66. P. M. Williams

COMMUNIST party (Indonesia)
Anti-Communist crusade of Indonesia's Moslems. D. Kirk. il Reporter 34:41-2+ Ja 27 '66
Bloodbath with reds on receiving end. il U S News 60:34 Ja 31 '66
Great purge in Indonesia; slaughter of Indonesian Communist party. S. S. King. il N Y Times Mag p25+ My 8 '66
Haunted face of a red defeat; vengeance against Communists; with report by D. Moser. il Life 61:24-33 Jl 1 '66
Indonesia: night of terror, dawn of hope; September 1965 coup. C. W. Hall. il Read Digest 89:275-8+ O '66
Indonesia: the plot that failed; PKI. L. M Taubinger. Nat R 18:160 F 22 '66
Slaughter in Indonesia: when people turn on reds; PKI. il U S News 60:66-7 My 2 '66
Students boot out the Communists; PKI. H. C. Atyeo. Nat R 18:458 My 17 '66

COMMUNIST party (Italy)
Communism, Italian style, has nowhere to go. L. Barzini. il N Y Times Mag p30-1+ F 13 '66

COMMUNIST party (Korea)
Declaration of independence. Time 88:26 Ag 19 '66

COMMUNIST party (Panama)
More riots in Panama, more trouble for U.S. il U S News 60:12 Je 20 '66

COMMUNIST party (Poland)
Double anniversary; Communist-Catholic clash. il Newsweek 68:42 Jl 18 '66
Poland: on the treadmill. B. van Voorst. il Newsweek 69:32-4 Ja 9 '67

COMMUNIST party (Rumania)
Kissed but not squeezed; ministerial meeting of the nations of the Warsaw pact. Time 88:28 Jl 15 '66
Stinging attack. il Time 87:47 My 20 '66

COMMUNIST party (Russia)
Burghers in the Kremlin; the party congress. W. C. McWilliams and G. A. Lanyi. Commonweal 84:195-7 My 6 '66
Catered affair: 23rd congress of the Communist party of the Soviet Union. il Newsweek 67:44+ Ap 4 '66
Communist party is the rear guard of Russia. P. Grose. il N Y Times Mag p36-7+ Mr 27 '66
C.P.S.U. statement on China; text of statement, August 31, 1966. Cur Hist 51:237-8+ O '66
Congress of caution; 23rd Communist party congress. Time 87:34+ Ap 15 '66
Dirty deal; Chinese boycott of the 23rd congress of the Soviet Communist party. il Sr Schol 88:13 Ap 22 '66
Do-nothing congress. il Time 87:33 Ap 8 '66
Flight of the tigers; delegations to congress. Time 87:28 Ap 1 '66
Ice age; 23rd congress of the CPUSSR. Nat R 18:345-6 Ap 19 '66
Meeting of the board; 23rd congress. il Newsweek 67:49-51 Ap 11 '66
Moscow congress: old party & the young people. I. Deutscher. il Nation 202:517-20 My 2 '66
Moscow congress: prudence and semantics. A. Ulam. Reporter 34:25-7 My 5 '66
Moscow, the new party line; outcome of twenty-third congress. W. Leonhard. New Repub 154:12-14 Ap 30 '66
Russia at the crossroads. R. Sherrod. il Sat Eve Post 239:28-33 Mr 26 '66

COMMUNIST party (Russia)—*Continued*
Sino-Soviet rift; compilation of world reaction to dispute. Sr Schol 88:24 Ap 15 '66
Soviet promises of a better life, but—. il U S News 60:22 Ap 18 '66
23rd congress: no more angry shouts? A. Werth. Nation 202:621-2 My 23 '66
Two steps forward, two steps back; 23rd congress. il Newsweek 67:55 Ap 18 '66
See also
Russia—Politics and government
COMMUNIST party (United States)
Chinese communism, U.S.A. D. McReynolds. Commonweal 83:528-31 F 4 '66
Communism and the United States: the Communist party from zig to zag. il Sr Schol 89:11-14 N 11 '66
Communists in convention. M. Feinsilber. Commonweal 84:464-6 Jl 22 '66
Down with bottomless degeneracy! conference in Greenwich Village. il Time 88:17-18 Jl 1 '66
Going public; eighteenth national convention. il Newsweek 68:21-2 Jl 4 '66
Turbulence on the campus. J. E. Hoover. il PTA Mag 60:4-6 F '66
COMMUNIST party (Vietnam [Democratic Republic])
Faceless Viet Cong. G. A. Carver, jr. For Affairs 44:347-72 Ap '66
How strong is the NLF? D. Pike. il Reporter 34:20-4 F 24 '66
COMMUNIST party (Vietnam [Republic])
Faceless Viet Cong. G. A. Carver, jr. For Affairs 44:347-72 Ap '66
COMMUNIST party (Yugoslavia)
Going gets rough in Yugoslavia. P. Ben. New Repub 155:15-16 S 3 '66
Kid glove purge. Newsweek 68:36-8 Jl 18 '66
Old class; new vice president. Newsweek 68:42 Jl 25 '66
COMMUNIST party congress. See Communist party (Russia)
COMMUNIST propaganda. See Propaganda, Communist
COMMUNIST settlements. See Collective settlements
COMMUNIST spies. See Spies
COMMUNIST strategy
Chinese visions & American policies. B. Schwartz. Commentary 41:53-9 Ap '66
Defeating Communist insurgency, by R. Thompson. Review
Newsweek 67:36 Je 6 '66
Dilemmas and agonies for all. N. Cousins. Sat R 49:32 F 5 '66
Havana conference. P. D. Bethel. il Reporter 34:25-9 Mr 24 '66
Kremlin's move? Vietnam war; escalation by diversionary moves. J. Burnham. Nat R 18:822 Ag 23 '66
Opinion: why the draft? A. Beichman. Mlle 62:6+ Ja '66
Peking's next target? J. M. Van Der Kroef. Nat R 18:1165-6+ N 15 '66
Politics of struggle, by J. D. Atkinson. Review
Nat R 18:792 Ag 9 '66. W. D. Jacobs
Red China's plan to conquer the world; excerpts from document. P. Lin. il Nations Bsns 54:40-1 Ja '66
Reds plan more Vietnams; Cuba as nerve center for subversion. il U S News 60:27 Ja 31 '66
Why Russia is our biggest danger; interview. W. E. Griffith. Read Digest 89:119-23 Ag '66
COMMUNITY and business. See Business—Social aspects
COMMUNITY and the college. See Colleges and universities—Public relations
COMMUNITY antenna television systems. See Television antennas
COMMUNITY art shows. See Art—Exhibitions
COMMUNITY arts councils, incorporated. See Arts councils of America
COMMUNITY centers
Community planning in a senior high school. M. Lindquist. il Sch Arts 65:6-10 Ap '66
See also
Library buildings as social centers
Student unions
COMMUNITY churches
See also
International council of community churches
COMMUNITY colleges. See Junior colleges
COMMUNITY development
Room at the bottom; increased federal aid. il Time 87:26-7 F 4 '66
Town that refused to go away. J. Bailey. il Arch Forum 125:78-81 O '66
COMMUNITY improvement. See Rural planning

COMMUNITY mental health centers. See Health centers
COMMUNITY organizations for the improvement of neighborhoods, incorporated
Creative venture in housing. A. D. Ward. Christian Cent 83:491-3 Ap 20 '66
COMMUNITY planning. See City planning
COMMUNITY service
Community service; address, April 5, 1966. R. M. Besse. Vital Speeches 32:466-9 My 15 '66
How San Mateo got its new Japanese garden. il Sunset 137:178-9 D '66
Pre-teenagers help improve their city; Youth service corps, Fremont, Calif. L. McVicar. il Parks & Rec 1:32-3 Ja '66
School landscaping in Dublin; Nielsen school, Dublin, Calif. il Sunset 137:230 N '66
See also
East central citizens organization, Columbus, Ohio
Industrial areas foundation
Volunteer service
COMMUNITY television antennas. See Television antennas
COMMUTER airlines. See Local service airlines
COMMUTERS
Where fringe commuter parking works. Am City 81:117 D '66
COMO, William
On the gypsy circuit. See issues of Dance magazine, April 1966-
(ed) See Gelabert, R. Anatomy for the ballet teacher
COMPACT cars. See Automobiles, Compact
COMPACT for education
Conant compact; organizational meeting. Time 87:74+ Je 24 '66
COMPACTS, interstate. See Interstate compacts
COMPANIES. See Corporations
COMPANY names. See Corporations—Names
COMPANY presidents. See Executives
COMPANY towns
Company towns still on the map; no resemblance to grimy mill towns of 19th century. il Bsns W p 102-5 Ag 27 '66
COMPARATIVE literature. See Literature, Comparative
COMPARATIVE pathology. See Pathology, Comparative
COMPASS
Compass correcting range. il Motor B 117:26-8 F '66
COMPATIBILITY (marriage). See Marriage
COMPENSATION (law)
Occupational twist; award to widow of man who died after a company dinner. Time 87:81 My 13 '66
COMPENSATION, Unemployment. See Insurance, Unemployment
COMPENSATION claims. See Claims
COMPENSATION for victims of crime. See Reparation
COMPENSATION of non-combatants. See Vietnamese war, 1957- —Compensation of non-combatants
COMPETITION
Branding on trial. T. Levitt. bibliog f Harvard Bsns R 44:20-2+ Mr '66
See also
Free enterprise
Monopolies
Restraint of trade
COMPETITION in education
Creative drive. C. Himber. il N Y Times Mag p86+ Je 5 '66
COMPETITIONS
Enter Mademoiselle's college board competition '66-'67. Mlle 63:211 O '66
Game game; firms' lottery-style sweepstakes. il Newsweek 68:80 N 7 '66
Swiss add free trips to unique calendar. il Travel 126:64 N '66
See also
Beauty contests
National cleanest town achievement contest
also subhead Competitions under various subjects, e.g. Photography—Competitions
COMPETITIVE bidding. See Contracts; Contracts, Government
COMPLAINTS
Ames, Iowa, complaint system has put citizens in the pink. il Am City 81:192+ My '66
How to complain, effectively. M. T. Bloom. Read Digest 89:61-3 Jl '66
Anecdotes, facetiae, satire, etc.
Art of the bedbug letter. R. Lasson. Look 30:M8 N 29 '66

COMPLEMENT fixation
Complement-fixing antigens in hamster tumors induced by the Bryan strain of Rous sarcoma virus. M. J. Casey and others. bibliog il Science 151:1086-8 Mr 4 '66
Multiple sclerosis: serum factor producing reversible alterations in bioelectric responses. J. A. Cerf and G. Carels. bibliog il Science 152:1066-8 My 20 '66
Murine leukemia viruses: antigenic studies by quantitative complement fixation. P. Gerber and others. bibliog il Science 152: 1074-5 My 20 '66
Quantitative immunochemistry and the evolution of primate albumins: micro-complement fixation. V. M. Sarich and A. C. Wilson. bibliog il Science 154:1563-6 D 23 '66

COMPLEXES (psychology)
Inferiority. D. A. Sugarman and R. Hochstein. Seventeen 25:158-9+ S '66

COMPOSERS
Bards of pop; P. McCartney and J. Lennon. il Newsweek 67:102 Mr 21 '66
Nadar's pantheon; portraits. F. V. Grunfeld. il Opera N 30:28-31 F 26 '66
Singer's challenge; excerpt from The great singers. H. Pleasants. il Opera N 31:6-9 O 15 '66

Caricatures and cartoons
All in line. M. Thaler. Opera N 30:12-14 Je 4 '66

COMPOSERS, American
Composers on campus. A. Keller. il Hi Fi 16: 104-7 O '66
Serious music: in serious trouble. D. J. Henahan. il Holiday 39:106-9+ Mr '66
See also
Barber, S.
Bazelon, I.
Diamond, D.
Ruggles, C.
Schuller, G.
Thomson. V.

COMPOSERS, Austrian
See also
Berg. A.
Schönberg. A.
Webern, A. von

COMPOSERS, British
New sound in British music. E. Salzman. il Hi Fi 16:71-2 Mr '66

COMPOSERS, Czech
See also
Janáček. L.

COMPOSERS, English
See also
Byrd, W.
Elgar, E. W.
Purcell, H.

COMPOSERS, French
Before Broadway; musical comedy has an ancestor in opéra comique. M. Cooper. il Opera N 30:8-12 Ap 9 '66
What's going on in Paris? R. Kotlowitz. Harper 234:103 Ja '67
See also
Alkan, C. H. V.
Boulez, P.
Koechlin, C.
Messiaen, O.
Satie. E.

COMPOSERS, German
See also
Händel, G. F.
Henze. H. W.
Kaempfert, B.
Offenbach, J.
Schumann. R.
Strauss. R.
Telemann, G. P.

COMPOSERS, Hungarian
See also
Kodály, Z.

COMPOSERS, Italian
See also
Busoni. F.
Donizetti, G.
Verdi. G.

COMPOSERS, Negro. See Negro composers

COMPOSERS, Polish
New music of Poland. O. Daniel. Sat R 49: 51-2+ Jl 30 '66
See also
Chopin, F. F.
Haubenstock-Ramati. R.

COMPOSERS, Russian
Russians are coming. il Time 87:54+ Je 3 '66
See also
Prokof'ev. S. S.
Rimskiĭ-Korsakov, N. A.
Stravinsky, I. F.

COMPOSING machines. See Typesetting machines

COMPOSITE materials. See Materials
COMPOSITE photographs. See Photomontage
COMPOSITE photography. See Photomontage
COMPOSITION (art)
Questions to Stella and Judd; interview, ed. by L. R. Lippard. B. Glaser; F. Stella; D. Judd. il Art N 65:55-61 S '66

COMPOSITION (music)
Art of the second guess; interference with an original musical composition. P. H. Lang. il Sat R 49:50+ F 26 '66
Composer's life. D. Milhaud. il Opera N 30: 8-11 Je 4 '66
In the grand tradition; libretto and music for Shakespeare's Antony and Cleopatra. J. W. Freeman. il Opera N 31:40-1 S 17 '66
Musical events. W. Sargeant. New Yorker 42:116-18 Ag 27 '66
See also
Music

COMPOSITION (photography)
Controlled backgrounds. P. Caulfield. il Mod Phot 31:66-9 Ja '67
Design and form through photography. R. A. Burgderfer. il Sch Arts 65:31-3 Je '66
$4 and op. N. Rothschild. il Pop Phot 58: 70-1+ My '66
Making the scene. il U S Camera 30:44-5 Ja '67
Making things you know that ain't. H. Keppler. il Mod Phot 30:58-61 Mr '66
Shooting through. il U S Camera 29:44-5 Mr '66
With mind and heart and a magic box; how you should take pictures. C. Mydans. il Life 61:64-6+ D 23 '66
See also
Photography—Still life

COMPOUNDS, Organic. See Organic compounds
COMPRESSED air
See also
Space vehicles—Cabin atmospheres
COMPRESSION
Pressure-induced dehydration reactions and transitions in inorganic hydrates. R. R. Sood and R. A. Stager. bibliog il Science 154:388-90 O 21 '66

COMPTON, Charles Herrick
Charles Herrick Compton, 1880-1966. L. M. Nourse. por ALA Bul 60:723-6 Jl '66

COMPTON, Martha
Leaf fragrance. Horticulture 44:46-7 F '66

COMPTON, Neil
Observations. Commentary 41:82-6 Ap; 42: 60-3 Jl; 95-6+ O '66

COMPTON effect
Inverse Compton effect: some consequences for quasars. J. Pfleiderer and M. Grewing. bibliog il Science 154:1452-3 D 16 '66

COMPULSORY arbitration. See Arbitration, Industrial
COMPULSORY military service. See Military service, Compulsory
COMPULSORY non-military service. See Service, Compulsory non-military
COMPULSORY retirement from business, etc. See Retirement from business. etc.
COMPULSORY sterilization. See Sterilization of defectives, criminals, etc.
COMPUTER industry
Big eight computer spectrum. il Duns R 88: pt2 142 S '66
$5-billion world market for computers; special report. il Bsns W p 110-14+ F 19 '66
Russia bets its future on computer knowhow; Five year plan in computer development. il Bsns W p92+ Ag 13 '66
Russians are computing. A. Parry. il N Y Times Mag p24-5+ Ag 28 '66
See also
Scientific data systems, incorporated

Great Britain
British computers start adding up faster. il Bsns W p76-8+ O 22 '66

COMPUTER match-making. See Computers— Social applications
COMPUTER process control. See Computers— Industrial applications
COMPUTER processing. See Electronic data processing
COMPUTER program languages. See Programming languages (computers)
COMPUTER that sweated; story. See Downs, H.
COMPUTER workers
Computer programming, today's high-pay career. J. F. Williams. il Sci Digest 59:50-5 My '66
Data on data; jobs in automation. P. Orth. il Mlle 64:104-5+ Ja '67

COMPUTER workers—*Continued*
Software gap, a growing crisis for computers; shortage of programmers. il Bsns W p 126-8+ N 5 '66

COMPUTERS
Bermuda race reports; first computerized race. il Yachting 120:31-6+ Ag '66
Big brother computer. H. C. Wallich. Newsweek 68:80 Jl 25 '66
Challenger for small computers. il Bsns W p 114+ Ap 9 '66
Computer age; how distorted the image? il Sr Schol 89:4-7+ O 7 '66
Computer helps study waiting time in clinics. Sci N 90:104 Ag 13 '66
Computer, the eye, the soul; excerpts from Of molecules and men. F. Crick. Sat R 49:53-5 S 3 '66
Computers and copyrights. C. G. Benjamin. Science 152:181-4 Ap 8 '66
Computers forecast tidal wave dangers; Pacific tsunami warning system. il Tech W 19:24-5 S 12 '66
Copyrights for computer publication urged. Sci N 89:299 Ap 23 '66
Downgrading computers. Newsweek 68:83 Jl 25 '66
Electronic ally for the taxpayer; computerized tax preparation. il Bsns W p 167-8 Mr 26 '66
Even in the bedroom; serve varied fields. il Time 88:102 O 14 '66
$5-billion world market for computers; special report. il Bsns W p 110-14+ F 19 '66
Information; symposium. il Sci Am 215:64-96+ S '66; Reply. G. R. Stibitz. 215:8-9 N '66
I.B.M.'s $5,000,000,000 gamble; system/360 computer. T. A. Wise. il Fortune 74:118-23+ S; 139+ O '66
Is man better than computers? H. Downs. il Sci Digest 59:88-91 Mr '66
New computerized age; potentiality of automation revolution and its implications for our society; symposium. il Sat R 49:15-25+ Jl 23 '66
Notes and comment; artificial intelligence vs. the human mind. New Yorker 42:27-8 Je 11 '66
Rock Cornish hen ousted by computer; menu planning at Sara Mayo hospital, New Orleans. Sci N 89:443 Je 4 '66
They want computers; International computer exhibition in Prague. il Time 87:105-6 Je 10 '66
See also
Control data corporation
Cybernetics
Electronic data processing
English electric company
International business machines corporation
Magnetic memory (computers)
Memory devices (computers)
Programming (computers)
Programming languages (computers)
Telephone—Computer combination

Aeronautic applications
AF to test variable instruction computer. R. Barnhart. il Tech W 19:25-6 N 14 '66
Airlines plan increased functions for new computers. K. J. Stein. il Aviation W 85:210-13+ O 31 '66
C-5A to use gimbal-less stable platform; integrated navigation system for military jet transports. B. Miller. il Aviation W 85:52-3+ D 5 '66
Computed display aids guidance, control. il Tech W 19:39 O 3 '66
Hughes offers microminiature computer; easily disassembled machine for weapons fire control and navigation. B. Miller. il Aviation W 85:91+ Jl 18 '66
New window for planes; computed display systems. il(p289) Sci N 90:294 O 15 '66
Solid-state air-data computer developed. B. Miller. il Aviation W 85:96-7+ N 14 '66

Agricultural applications
New machine that measures meatiness in live animals; electrogrammetry computer. C. E. Ball. il Farm J 90:25+ Je '66

Analog computers
Erythropoietin: hypothesis of action tested by analog computer. A. L. Kretchmar. bibliog il Science 152:367-70 Ap 15 '66
See also
Computers—Hybrid computers

Anecdotes, facetiae, satire, etc.
Computer that really cares; R. Emett's creations. il Life 61:118-20+ D 2 '66

Forget-me-not. il Sci N 90:350 O 29 '66

Architectural applications
Computer revolution: how does it affect architecture? J. Barnett. il Arch Rec 140:168-70 Jl '66

Art applications
Market research art; consumer-determined sculpture by G. Laing and P. Phillips. il Life 60:71-2+ My 20 '66

Banking applications
New proletariat; implications for society. Reporter 35:14 D 15 '66

Bibliographic applications
Use of computer in libraries analyzed at joint meeting. Library J 91:2301-2 My 1 '66

Biological applications
Erythropoietin: hypothesis of action tested by analog computer. A. L. Kretchmar. bibliog il Science 152:367-70 Ap 15 '66
Information and control processes in living systems; report on second of a projected series of conferences. D. Ramsey. Science 152:1285-6 My 27 '66
Numerical taxonomy. R. R. Sokal. il Sci Am 215:106-16 bibliog(p 155) D '66

Business applications
Data systems that cross company boundaries. F. Kaufman. il Harvard Bsns R 44:141-5 Ja '66
Describing men to machines; computerized personnel system. il Bsns W p 113-14 Je 4 '66
Electronic data processing. il Duns R 88:pt2 140-1+ S '66
Europe's stores gear up for more free spenders; computers in retail merchandising. il Bsns W p80-2 Je 4 '66
Forecasters get a new crystal ball. il Bsns W p 124+ My 21 '66
How computers liven a management's ways. il Bsns W p 112-14+ Je 25 '66
Information revolution. il Duns R 88:pt2 130-1+ S '66
Linking computers to French logic; Metra international, Paris-based management and research consulting firm. il Bsns W p96-8 D 24 '66
Managing to manage the computer; summary of survey. J. W. Taylor and N. J. Dean. il Harvard Bsns R 44:98-110 S '66
Middle managers vs. the computer. G. Berkwitt. il Duns R 88:40-2+ N '66
Uses of computers in organizations. M. Greenberger. il Sci Am 215:192-6+ S '66
What the computers will be telling you. P. F. Drucker. il Nations Bsns 54:84-90 Ag '66

Communication applications
New computerized age. McLuhanism reconsidered. E. Barnouw. il Sat R 49:19-21+ Jl 23 '66
New computerized age: town meeting reborn. V. F. Miller. Sat R 49:34-5 Jl 23 '66
Telecommunication. il Duns R 8:pt2 149-50+ S '66
TV revolution ahead! new era potentials. D. Sarnoff. Read Digest 88:66-70 Mr '66
Transmission of computer data. J. R. Pierce. il Sci Am 215:144-50+ bibliog(p312) S '66

Control applications
Robot dons chef's hat to speed up burgers; new automatic system, called AMFare. il Bsns W p42 Ap 23 '66

Cooperative use
Computer for billing, stockkeeping shared. Sci N 89:168 Mr 12 '66
Data systems that cross company boundaries. F. Kaufman. il Harvard Bsns R 44-141-5 Ja '66
Public utility data services. il Duns R 88:pt2 155-6+ S '66
Time-sharing given focus at joint computer conference. R. Pay. il Tech W 19:33-6 N 21 '66
Time-sharing on computers. R. M. Fano and F. J. Corbató. il Sci Am 215:128-36+ bibliog(p312) S '66

Court applications
Computerized docket; speedup record of the Los Angeles County Superior court. il Time 88:38 Jl 29 '66
Computers put speed into the law; unclogging court calendars. il Bsns W p 184-6+ O 1 '66

Dance applications
Choreography and computers; with reply by A. Hutchinson. A. M. Noll. il Dance Mag 41:43-6+ Ja '67

COMPUTERS—*Continued*

Digital computers

Computer logic and memory. D. C. Evans. il Sci Am 215:74-85 bibliog(p312) S '66
Computers solve puzzles; digital computers. A. Ewing. Sci N L 89:132 F 26 '66
Machines cannot think. P. McBroom. Sci N 90:6 Jl 2 '66
New digital readout system. C. W. Martel. il Electr World 76:85 Jl '66
Scientific data systems aims at bigger share of market. C. D. LaFond. il Miss & Roc 18:34 Mr 21 '66
Univac thinks small, but fast. il Bsns W p 173-4 Je 25 '66
See also
Computers—Hybrid computers

Editing applications

Editing text electronically; University of Pittsburgh's Computation and data processing center. C. R. T. Bacon. il Pub W 190:92-4 Jl 4 '66

Educational applications

Apple for the computer; computerized teaching at East Palo Alto, Calif. il Time 88:61 S 16 '66
Campus computers: NAS panel calls for more federal aid. L. J. Carter. Science 151:969+ F 25 '66; Discussion. 152:591; 153:122, 814+ Ap 29, Jl 8, Ag 19 '66
Can computers teach? Bsns W p44 Je 11 '66
Computer and excellence. P. Suppes. il Sat R 50:46+ Ja 14 '67
Computer to aid long-range planning of school systems. Sch & Soc 94:122+ Mr 5 '66
Computer-tutor. J. Ridgeway. New Repub 154:19-22 Je 4 '66
EDUCOM: Interuniversity communications council. J. G. Miller. bibliog Science 154:483-8 O 28 '66
Hello, computer? I have homework for us to do; IBM 1710 computer. il Pop Electr 25:46 Ag '66
Higher education: a population flow feedback model. A. Reisman. bibliog il Science 153:89-91 Jl 1 '66
New computerized age: for each student a teacher. D. D. Bushnell. il Sat R 49:31 Jl 23 '66
New computerized age: plug-in instruction; excerpt from The computer in American education. P. Suppes. il Sat R 49:25+ Jl 23 '66
Now, teaching by computer; reprint. J. Brann. il Sci Digest 59:78-81 Ap '66
Renaissance of teaching. W. L. Hickman. Sch & Soc 94:265-7 Sum '66
Systems approach. C. H. Springer. il Sat R 50:56+ Ja 14 '67
Technology is knocking at the schoolhouse door. C. E. Silberman. il Fortune 74:120-5+ Ag '66
Uses of computers in education. P. Suppes. il Sci Am 215:206-8+ S '66

Engineering applications

How pushbuttons control the mighty Colorado. E. Burks. il Pop Sci 188:82-5 Mr '66
Uses of computers in technology. S. A. Coons. il Sci Am 215:176-84+ bibliog(p314) S '66

Government applications

Automated (and scrambled) justice. Sr Schol 87:8 Ja 7 '66
Chains of plastic; dropping of Budget bureau's plan for file of information on U.S. citizens. Newsweek 68:27 Ag 8 '66
Computerized 90th Congress. H. Hamilton. America 115:733 D 3 '66
Computers get results on taxes. U S News 60:81-2 F 7 '66
Computers, program management and foreign affairs. J. Diebold. For Affairs 45:125-34 O '66
Computers spotting false tax returns. U S News 60:99 Ap 4 '66
Don't tell it to the computer. V. Packard. il N Y Times Mag p44-5+ Ja 8 '67
Electronic eyes are watching your tax returns; revolutionary operation called automatic data processing. T. Irwin. il Pop Mech 125:94-8+ Mr '66
Government watch on 200 million Americans? il U S News 60:56-9 My 16 '66
Meet the Monster that checks your taxes. J. A. Morris. Read Digest 90:177-8+ Ja '67
National data center: computer vs. the Bill of rights; C. E. Gallagher hearings. A. Prisendorf. il Nation 203:449-52 O 31 '66
New computerized age; use of computers in Washington. J. W. Macy, jr. il Sat R 49:23-5+ Jl 23 '66

Will the new tax computer get after you? il Farm J 90:28+ F '66
Your tax return may be questioned this year. il Changing T 20:21-3 Mr '66

Hybrid computers

EAI sees fast growth in hybrid computers; systems combining analog and digital computers. R. Barnhart. il Tech W 20:34-5 Ja 2 '67

Industrial applications

Computer planning unsnarls the job shop; scheduling shop orders of Fairfield mfg, co. il Bsns W p60-1 Ap 2 '66
Uses of computers in organizations. M. Greenberger. il Sci Am 215:192-6+ S '66

Input-output equipment

Computer inputs and outputs. I. E. Sutherland. il Sci Am 215:86-96 S '66
Data acquisition and data display. il Duns R 88:pt2 143-4+ S '66

Investment applications

Heads you win? activities of the Center for research in security prices. E. J. Kahn, jr. il Reporter 35:39-42 O 20 '66
Inventor of the month; stock forecaster. S. V. Jones. il Sci Digest 60:44 D '66
Taping instant data for investors; Intinco ltd. provides computerized investment data. il Bsns W p 147-8+ N 5 '66
Wall Street's newest drudge, and genius. il Bsns W p 117-18+ Jl 9 '66

Legal applications

See also
Computers—Court applications

Literary applications

Machine Miltons. W. Cross. il N Y Times Mag p59+ D 4 '66

Medical applications

Brain surgery by computer. S. Hopkins. il Pop Mech 126 :94-7 D '66
Coming: computer test for child heart disease? S. M. Linde. il Todays Health 44:54-5+ Je '66
Computers start to study medicine. il Bsns W p 142-4+ Jl 9 '66
Early tests can prevent chronic ills; laboratory instrument computer. F. Marley. il Sci N 90:245 O 1 '66
Enter the robot M.D; Neuberger's subcommittee discusses multiphasic screening. il Newsweek 68:92 O 3 '66
Mayo-IBM system locates tumors. il Sci N 89:286 Ap 23 '66
Model organs live faster. Sci N 90:5 Jl 2 '66
Now the automated physical checkup; Permanente center, Oakland, Calif. L. A. Stevens. Read Digest 89:95-8 Jl '66
Patient programmed; computerized interview to study behavioral sciences. Sci N 89:447 Je 4 '66
Psychiatry takes to computers. F. R. Schreiber and M. Herman. il Sci Digest 61:15-19 Ja '67

Meteorological applications

Computing the weather. A. Ewing. il Sci N 90:202-3 S 17 '66
Forecasts by computer. Sci N 90:14 Jl 2 '66
Wind and waves forecast. B. J. Culliton. il Sci N 90:295 O 15 '66

Military applications

Static, dynamic displays combined in CRT; cathode ray tube construction. il Tech W 19:38+ O 10 '66

Municipal applications

Computers occupy the royal suite; Chattanooga, Tenn. W. Zachry. il Am City 81:107 O '66
Filter backwash control; Winston-Salem, N.C. il Am City 81:112 F '66
Name it, our computer can do it; Delaware County, Pa. J. F. McNichol. il Am City 81:88-9 D '66
Up-to-the-minute management information reports; Wichita Falls, Tex. R. J. Neighbors. il Am City 81:102-4 Ag '66

Photographic applications

Book publishing and the new technologies. H. S. Bailey, jr. il Sat R 49:41-3 Je 11 '66
Computer-produced movies. K. C. Knowlton; reply. G. A. McCue and J. D. O'Keefe. il Science 151:839-40 F 18 '66

Police applications

Computer catches a traffic violator. il Am City 81:128 Mr '66

COMPUTERS—Police applications—*Continued*
Latest moves against crime in streets. il
U S News 60:38-40 Ap 11 '66
New 007 is a computer. J. R. Berry. il Pop
Mech 125:84-7+ Ap '66

Printing applications
Book publishing and the new technologies.
H. S. Bailey, jr. il Sat R 49:41-3 Je 11 '66
CIS finds nearly 300 using computers for
typesetting. Pub W 191:103 Ja 2 '67
Design and technology in computer composition; report of International computer typesetting conference held in England. Pub W
190:96-7+ O 3 '66
Long-time leader in computerized type tools
up for book work il Pub W 189:90-1+ Mr 7
'66
New computerized age: book-publishers'
salvation? J. Tebbel. il Sat R 49:32-3 Jl 23
'66
Raytheon will introduce graphic arts computer. Pub W 191:103 Ja 2 '67
R&E council is briefed on new tools from
IBM. il Pub W 189:82-5 My 2 '66
R&E seminar on automation for control in
graphic arts; summary of addresses. Pub W
189:116+ Mr 7 '66
Tomorrow's printing processes and the human element; excerpts from address. J.
Kelly. Pub W 189:98-9+ Mr 7 '66
Tools of the trade; phototypesetting equipment. il Pub W 190:110 Ag 1 '66

Psychiatric applications
See Computers—Medical applications

Readout systems
New digital readout system. C. W. Martel. il
Electr World 76:85 Jl '66

Renting
Joining the ranks of the renters. il Bsns
W p86 F 26 '66
Leasing of computers takes on new glamour;
undercutting manufacturers' rental rates. il
Bsns W p70+ Ap 23 '66

Scientific applications
Bell labs: computers loom large in both re-
search and operations. J. Walsh. Science
153:720-2 Ag 12 '66
Chromosome analysis by computer. R. S.
Ledley and F. H. Ruddle. il Sci Am 214:
40-6 Ap '66
Faster Fourier analysis. Sci Am 215:46 O '66
Human use of computing machines. P. H.
Abelson. Science 153:253 Jl 15 '66
Ultracentrifuge schlieren photographs: auto-
matic analysis. R. Moore and others. il
Science 152:1509-11 Je 10 '66
Uses of computers in science. A. G. Oettinger.
il Sci Am 215:160-6+ bibliog(p312+) S '66;
Reply. T. P. Brody. 215:9-10+ N '66

Simulation programs
New computerized age: for each student a
teacher. D. D. Bushnell. il Sat R 49:31
Jl 23 '66
Simulating poverty: input and output. J.
Ridgeway. New Repub 154:9-10 Je 11 '66;
Reply with rejoinder. E. C. Wilson. 155:
35+ Jl 2 '66

Social applications
Can electronics pick your mate? J. Joseph.
il Pop Electr 24:70-3+ Mr '66
Cupid computer. D. Fass. il Sr Schol 89:7
O 7 '66
Electronically paired. America 115:406 O 8 '66
Good grief! a computer picks the partners
for a high school dance. G. Shalit. il
Seventeen 25:124-5 D '66
Marriage is not a personal matter: match-
making by computer. J. F. Scott. il N Y
Times Mag p27+ O 30 '66; Discussion.
p 12+ N 13 '66
Matchmaker, matchmaker, compute me a
match; Jane Silberstein's correspondence
with Operation match. G. Ace. Sat R 49:
14 Ap 9 '66
New dating craze sweeps the campus; boy,
girl, computer; Tarr-Morrill process. G.
Shalit. il Look 30:30-5 F 22 '66

Anecdotes, facetiae, satire, etc.
Connubially-oriented computer of Otto
Tronix. C. Kohler. il Pop Electr 25:53-5+
Jl '66

Space flight applications
Computed display aids guidance, control. il
Tech W 19:39 O 3 '66

IBM develops line of off-the-shelf airborne
computers. P. J. Klass. il Aviation W 85:
70-1+ O 24 '66
Orbital cryogenic computer seen possible in
twenty years. W. C. Wetmore. Aviation W
85:31 O 17 '66
OSO data proposals under study of NASA.
Aviation W 85:78 Ag 8 '66
Our secret eye on space. D. Robinson. il Look
30:94-6+ N 15 '66
Saturn computer size may be cut by 2/3.
K. Voss. il Tech W 19:30+ O 17 '66
Surveyor informs LEM. Sci N 90:38 Jl 16
'66
Tape memory unit awaits GT-9 test. C. D.
LaFond. il Miss & Roc 18:16-17 My 16 '66
Wyle facility will supply on-line Saturn V
analysis. R. G. Pay. il Miss & Roc 18:37+
My 16 '66

Statistics
Statistics on computer field released in AFIPS
report. Library J 91:3672 Ag '66

Traffic control applications
Computer and camera may unsnarl traffic.
il Am City 81:150 My '66
Computer-controlled traffic moves faster:
San Jose, Calif. il Am City 81:154 My '66
Computer to unsnarl London's air traffic.
Sci N 90:386 N 5 '66
Computerized traffic-control system for any
city; Syracuse, N.Y. il Am City 81:100-2
Jl '66
Electronic expressway strikes at rush-hour
traffic; Eisenhower expressway in Chicago.
il Am City 81:118+ N '66
Sperry aids traffic flow in New York. il Tech
W 18:33 Je 13 '66

Transportation applications
Automate mass-transit fare sales; computer-
controlled ticketing in London underground.
R. S. Silver. il Am City 81:83-5 F '66
Inventor of the month; his computer figures
geography. S. V. Jones. Sci Digest 60:25 S
'66

COMPUTERS on aircraft. See Computers—
Aeronautic applications
COMROE, Julius H. jr
Lung; with biographical sketch. Sci Am
214:17, 56-66+ F '66
COMSTOCK, Helen
American furniture in the collection of Mr
and Mrs Edward H. Tevriz. Antiques 89:
256-61 F '66
Southern furniture since 1952. Antiques 91:
102-19 Ja '67
COMSTOCK, Henry B.
Fastest train in America. il Pop Mech 126:89-
92+ N '66
Look what's happening to freight cars! il
Pop Mech 126:138-41+ O '66
COMSTOCK, Jim
Pa and ma and LBJ; excerpts from Pa and
ma and Mister Kennedy. Nations Bsns 54:
48-9+ Ap '66
COMTE, Gilbert
Letter from Africa (cont) Nat R 18:832,
1273-4 Ag 23, D 13 '66
CON men. See Fraud
CONAWAY, Ray
If you need me, let me know; story. Sat
Eve Post 239:64-6 Jl 16 '66
CONCENTRATION. See Attention
CONCENTRATION camps

Germany
Belsen remembered. L. S. Dawidowicz. Commentary 41:82-5 Mr '66

Poland
Worst that ever happened; with editorial
comment. S. Bedford. il Sat Eve Post 239:
29-33+, 112 O 22 '66
CONCERT halls
Architectural acoustics. M. R. Schroeder.
bibliog il Science 151:1355-9 Mr 18 '66
Debut in Houston. il Newsweek 68:108-9 O
17 '66
Houston's culture gets a new glow; perform-
ing arts center. il Bsns W p 150-2 O 8 '66
Jesse H. Jones hall, a grand slam play;
Houston, Tex. R. C. Marsh. il Hi Fi 16:
MA20-1 D '66
Keeping up with the Cliburns (and the
Joneses) Jesse H. Jones hall. P. Hume. il
Sat R 49:72 O 29 '66
New concert hall in Rotterdam. M. Seif. il
Sat R 49:45+ Jl 16 '66
New hall for London; home for London sym-
phony orchestra. T. Heinitz. Sat R 49:71
Ap 16 '66

CONCERT halls—*Continued*
Pride of Houston; Jesse H. Jones hall for the performing arts. A. Holmes. il Opera N 31:22 O 15 '66

CONCERT managers
Putting the art before the war horse; programming of J. Hoffman and G. Schutz. il Time 88:83 S 9 '66
Reports: North American artists managements. il Hi Fi 16:160-81 D 15 '66
Sound sellers; Hoffman and Schutz. Newsweek 67:88 F 28 '66

CONCERTMASTERS
Distinguished fraternity. il Time 88:92+ O 21 '66

CONCERTOS
Piano vs. orchestra: E. Carter's new piano concerto. H. Saal. il Newsweek 69:94 Ja 16 '67
Treat worth the travail; Carter & Lateiner; new piano concerto. il Time 89:44 Ja 13 '67
See also
Phonograph records—Concertos

CONCERTS
Concerts: U.S. & Canada; list of series. Hi Fi 16:200-13 D 15 '66
Prospects of recording; electronic media, a threat to the public concert? G. Gould. Hi Fi 16:46-63 Ap '66

CONCHOLOGY. See Shells (conchology)

CONCILIATION, International. See Arbitration, International

CONCORDANCES
See also
Bible—Concordance

CONCRETE
Popular science concrete volume calculator. il Pop Sci 188:149 Ap '66

Repairing
See Concrete construction—Repairing

CONCRETE, Precast
In-factory or on-site for concreting? European system combines both. G. G. Rothenstein. il Arch Rec 139:221-3 Ap '66
Knowing expression of the nature of precast concrete. il Arch Rec 140:185-7 N '66
Precasting is done on-site in California. il Arch Rec 139:224-5 Ap '66

CONCRETE block walls. See Walls, Concrete

CONCRETE construction
Concrete for complex forms of a lecture hall. il Arch Rec 140:142-3 N '66
Expansive cement: a new approach to reducing concrete cracking. il Arch Rec 140:231-2 S '66
Knowing expression of the nature of precast concrete. il Arch Rec 140:185-7 N '66

Repairing
New patching compounds for concrete. il Consumer Bul 49:43+ Je '66

CONCRETE floors. See Floors, Concrete

CONCRETE mixers
Concrete by the bucketful. M. Banister. il Pop Mech 126:158-9 O '66

CONCRETE panels. See Panels, Decorative

CONCRETE pavements. See Pavements, Concrete

CONCRETE walls. See Walls, Concrete

CONCUSSION
Cerebral concussion in the monkey: an experimental model. A. K. Ommaya and others. bibliog il Science 153:211-12 Jl 8 '66

CONDEMNATION of land. See Eminent domain

CONDEMNED of Altona; drama. See Sartre, J. P.

CONDITIONED reflexes. See Conditioned response

CONDITIONED response
Blow flow conditioned. P. McBroom. Sci N L 89:131 F 26 '66
Classical conditioning of pain-elicited aggression. W. Vernon and R. Ulrich. bibliog Science 152:668 Ap 29 '66
Deafferentation in monkeys: effect on conditioned grasp response. E. Taub and others. bibliog il Science 151:593-4 F 4 '66
Deficits in passive avoidance and fear conditioning in mice with septal lesions. B. M. Slotnick and M. E. Parvik. bibliog il Science 154:1207-8 D 2 '66
Discrimination learning and inhibition. H. S. Terrace. bibliog il Science 154:1677-80 D 30 '66
Disinhibition of visually masked stimuli. D. N. Robinson. bibliog il Science 154:157-8 O 7 '66

Electroencephalographic activation: non-specific habituation by verbal stimuli. T. Mulholland and E. Davis. bibliog il Science 152:1104-6 My 20 '66
Evoked potential correlates of generalization. D. S. Ruchkin and E. R. John. bibliog il Science 153:209-11 Jl 8 '66
Gap between sciences narrows to fine line. P. McBroom. Sci N 90:446 N 26 '66
Heart rate: changes during conditioned suppression in rats. L. De Toledo and A. H. Black. bibliog il Science 152:1404-6 Je 3 '66
Magnesium pemoline: enhancement of learning and memory of a conditioned avoidance response. N. Plotnikoff. bibliog il Science 151:703-4; F 11 '66; Reply with rejoinder. R. Bowman. 153:902 Ag 19 '66
Monkeys reared in isolation with pictures as visual input: evidence for an innate releasing mechanism. G. P. Sackett. il Science 154:1468+ D 16 '66
Opposite responding to two sense modalities. A. Moffett and G. Ettlinger. bibliog il Science 153:205-6 Jl 8 '66; Reply. G. B. Biederman. 154:677 N 4 '66; Rejoinder. 154:799 N 11 '66
Perceptual grouping produced by changes in orientation and shape. J. Beck. bibliog il Science 154:538-40 O 28 '66
Qualitative versus directional cues in two forms of differentiation. C. Dobrzecka and others. il Science 153:87-9 Jl 1 '66
Retrograde amnesia: effects of handling and microwave radiation. R. N. Bryan. bibliog il Science 153:897-9 Ag 19 '66
Stimulus control in pigeons based on proprioceptive stimuli from floor inclination. D. C. Riccio and others. bibliog il Science 153:434-6 Jl 22 '66
Visual spatial aftereffect from prolonged head-tilt. R. H. Day and N. J. Wade. bibliog il Science 154:1201-2 D 2 '66
X-ray detection by the olfactory system: ozone as a masking odorant. E. L. Gasteiger and S. A. Helling. bibliog il Science 154:1038-41 N 25 '66

CONDOMINAS, Georges
Incest of Tieng and Aang who had a common ancestor fifteen generations ago; excerpt from Nous avons mangé la forêt de la Pierer-Génie Gôo. tr. by V. Bordaz. Natur Hist 75:13-19 Je '66
Primitive life of Vietnam's mountain people. Natur Hist 75:8-13 Je '66

CONDOMINIUM plan ownership. See Apartment houses—Condominium plan ownership

CONDON, Edward U.
Can Dr Condon see it through? Nation 203:436 O 31 '66
Condon for regent. Nation 203:269 S 26 '66
Condon to head UFO study. D. S. Greenberg. por Science 154:244 O 14 '66
Research in America; Dr Condon's study outlined. J. Lear. por Sat R 49:87-9 D 3 '66
Scientist for the saucers. por Sci Digest 60:57 D '66

CONDON-Wadlin act. See Labor laws and legislation—New York (state)

CONDOR passes; story. See Grau, S. A.

CONDORS
Help for the condor. C. W. Buchheister. Audubon Mag 68:5 Ja '66
Nature note; California condor. Sci N 89:449 Je 4 '66
Return of a condor. J. C. Borneman. il Audubon Mag 68:154-7 My '66
Those forty dirty birds. B. Atkinson. il Audubon Mag 68:231-7 Jl '66
Two letters; GI in Viet Nam pleads condor case; with reply. C. W. Buchheister; F. L. Donoghue. Audubon Mag 68:230 Jl '66

CONDUCT, Disorderly. See Disorderly conduct

CONDUCT of life
Bring to it the rainbow. J. K. Lagemann. Read Digest 89:87-9 N '66
Individual in society; commitment to discipline and compassion; address, May 25, 1966. J. Howard. Vital Speeches 32:593-6 Jl 15 '66
Informal history of love U.S.A. A. Schlesinger, jr. il Sat Eve Post 239:30-2+ D 31 '66
Man's task: a union of contrasts. L. L. Whyte. Sat R 49:32 N 12 '66
No second helping of life. L. Wainwright. Life 61:33 O 21 '66
What can the church demand? Q. L. Quade and J. M. Rhodes. Cath World 204:162-9 D '66
See also
Anger
Cheating in schoolwork
Christian life
Conscience
Courage
Ethics
Leisure

CONFINEMENT feeding of swine. See Swine—
Confinement methods

CONFLICT (psychology)
Conflict and arousal. D. E. Berlyne. il Sci
Am 215:82-7 bibliog(p 116) Ag '66
Conflict basic as hunger? Sci N 90:83 Ag 6 '66

CONFLICT, Social. See Social conflict

CONFLICT of interest (public office)
(Conflict of interest)²; newsmen on the ap-
praisers list. Cincinnati. Newsweek 68:66
D 19 '66
Dodd affair endangers ethics group. J. N.
Eller. America 114:725 My 21 '66
Dodd dinners; disclosures by Drew Pearson
and Jack Anderson. il Newsweek 67:19-20
My 2 '66
Dodd's trip: how helpful to Klein? U S News
61:8 Ag 1 '66
Matter of ethics; Pearson-Anderson charges;
Dodd seeks inquiry. S. Shaffer. il Newsweek
67:29 Ap 11 '66
New controversy involving Justice Douglas;
reprint from Los Angeles times, October
16, 1966; and excerpt from address by J. J.
Williams, October 17, 1966. R. J. Ostrow.
U S News 61:66-8 O 31 '66
President's club: what $1,000 brings. il U S
News 61:6 Ag 1 '66
University microfilms head resigns Michigan
post. Pub W 189:47-8 Mr 28 '66
Weak arm of the law; case of E. B. Power.
Nation 202:350 Mr 28 '66
What new federal ethics code means to busi-
ness. J. Kluttz. il Nations Bsns 54:108+
O '66

CONFLICT of interests (business)
Insider and the SEC. R. Phalon. il Duns R
88:38-40+ S '66

CONFORMITY
Don't stifle your students' nonconformity. K.
Harris. il NEA J 55:24-6 O '66
See also
Acculturation

CONFORMITY (religion) See Dissenters, Religious

CONFRATERNITY of Christian doctrine
CCD—R.I.P? scope of religious education.
J. O'Donoghue. Commonweal 84:573-4 S 16
'66
Crisis in the CCD; steps taken in the diocese
of Pittsburgh. M. J. Clark. America 115:
277-80 S 17 '66
Of many things. T. N. Davis. America
115:44 Jl 16 '66; Discussion. 115:165-6 Ag
20 '66

CONFRÉRIE des Chevaliers du Tastevin. See
Clubs

CONFREY, Eugene A.
Information exchange groups to be discontinued; letter. Science 154:843 N 18 '66

CONFROY, Thomas J.
Father Tom Confroy: church is in his combat
pack. S. Castan. il pors Look 30:74-6 Jl
12 '66

CONFUSED flour beetles. See Flour beetles

CONGDON, Kirby
Aesop revisited. Américas 18:1-8 O '66

CONGENITAL heart disease. See Heart—Diseases

CONGENITAL malformations. See Deformities

CONGER, Ella R.
How are your medical manners? Todays
Health 44:8-10 S '66

CONGER, Lesley
Off the cuff. See issues of Writer

CONGO (capital Brazzaville)
Foreign relations
Castro gets a satellite, in Africa. il U S
News 61:44 Ag 8 '66
Politics and government
Fidel's foreign legion. Nat R 18:664-5 Jl 12
'66
Spontaneous combustion; army resentment at
imported military advisers from Havana.
Newsweek 68:46 Jl 11 '66

CONGO (capital Kinshasa)
See also
Americans in the Congo
Copper mines and mining—Congo (capital
Kinshasa)
United Nations—Congo (capital Kinshasa)
Description and travel
It's still the heart of darkness; journey up
the Congo River. E. R. F. Sheehan. il
N Y Times Mag p30-3+ O 30 '66
Economic conditions
Congo after six years and a billion in aid.
A. J. Meyers. il U S News 60:65-7 Ap 18 '66

It's still the heart of darkness: journey up
the Congo River. E. R. F. Sheehan. il N Y
Times Mag p30-3+ O 30 '66
Expropriation policy
Papa is dead; take-over of Union Minière.
Newsweek 69:46+ Ja 16 '67
Industries
Papa is dead. Newsweek 69:46+ Ja 16 '67
Native races
See also
Pygmies
Politics and government
Black hoods in the square. il Time 87:46
Je 10 '66
Congo after six years and a billion in aid.
A. J. Meyers. il U S News 60:65-7 Ap 18
'66
Crushing the Kats. il Time 88:47 O 14 '66
Death in the sun; public hangings of four
ex-ministers. il Newsweek 67:66 Je 13 '66
Last chance for Parliament; Mobutu acts
against assemblymen. Time 87:39 Ap 1 '66
Needed: new mission stance in the Congo.
C. T. Underwood. Christian Cent 83:1091+
S 7 '66
New order. il Time 88:33+ Jl 22 '66
Political rivalry in the Congo. H. R. Rudin.
Cur Hist 50:159-64+ Mr '66
Stanleyville rescue: American policy in the
Congo. K. W. Grundy. Yale R 56:242-55
D '66

CONGO (formerly Belgian Congo)
Nominal confusion; names to change July 1.
Time 87:36 My 13 '66
Army
Rising of the Kats; hatred between Katangese
and the A.N.C. troops. il Time 88:33 Ag 5
'66

CONGO massacre, 1964
Killing them definitively. P. F. Semonin.
Nation 202:129-32 Ja 31 '66

CONGO RIVER
It's still the heart of darkness: journey up
the Congo River. E. R. F. Sheehan. il N Y
Times Mag p30-3+ O 30 '66

CONGOLESE
Needed: new mission stance in the Congo.
C. T. Underwood. Christian Cent 83:1091+
S 7 '66

CONGREGATIONAL church in England and
Wales
Congregational fusion in England and Wales.
Christian Cent 83:737 Je 8 '66

CONGREGATIONAL churches
See also
International Congregational council

CONGREGATIONAL union of England and
Wales. See Congregational church in England and Wales

CONGRESS (United States) See United States
—Congress

CONGRESS for recreation and parks
Congress for parks and recreation; high-
lights. il Parks & Rec 1:966-9 D '66
Congress program digest. il Parks & Rec 1:
702-3 S '66
Congress welcome mat is out. C. Davis. il
Parks & Rec 1:547+ Jl '66
Honeymoon year. D. B. Huyck. il Am For
72:22-5+ D '66
National congress highlights. Washington, Oc-
tober 9 to 13, 1966. il Parks & Rec 1:689-
90 S '66
See also
Everly medal awards

CONGRESS of racial equality
Chilling shift. il Time 87:35-6 Je 10 '66
White reflections on black power. C. E.
Fager. Christian Cent 83:980-3 Ag 10 '66

CONGRESS of the Soviet Communist party.
See Communist party (Russia)

CONGRESS of writers. See PEN club

CONGRESS party. See Political parties—India

CONGRESSIONAL campaigns. See Political
campaigns

CONGRESSIONAL candidates. See Candidates,
Political

CONGRESSIONAL committees. See United
States—Congress—Committees

CONGRESSIONAL cup. See Yacht racing

CONGRESSIONAL elections. See Elections—
United States

CONGRESSIONAL library. See United States—
Library of Congress

CONGRESSIONAL medal of honor. See Medal
of honor (United States)

CONGRESSIONAL primaries. See Primaries
CONGRESSIONAL procedure. See United States—Congress—Rules and practice
CONGRESSMEN
Congress: old guard's leader is beaten. L. J. Carter. il Science 153:512-15 Jl 29 '66
New faces of 1967. il Newsweek 69:27-8 Ja 23 '67
Old men of Congress. Atlan 217:8+ Mr '66
Record of the House: 89th Congress. New Repub 155:20-2 O 22 '66
Washington: ten of its most powerful men. il pors Vogue 148:153-7 N 15 '66
Way Congress sizes up the war: story a survey tells. il U S News 60:28-31 Ja 31 '66
Wedge of dissent: Democratic rebels in Congress. R. G. Sherrill. Nation 203:341-6 O 10 '66
What a congressman really does. Changing T 20:37 N '66
Young men who are remaking Congress. D. M. Davis. Holiday 39:60-1+ F '66
    See also
Conflict of interests (public office)
Negro congressmen
Senators
United States—Congress

    Public relations
New way to roll out the pork barrel. il Nations Bsns 54:38-9+ Je '66

    Salaries, allowances, etc.
Cost of public office: high, says Senator Douglas; excerpts from annual report. P. H. Douglas. U S News 62:14 Ja 9 '67

    Term
Congressmen need four-year terms. Life 60:4 Ja 28 '66
Duty to defy. House judiciary committee hearings. Time 87:25 F 25 '66
Election proposal: extending the terms of members of the House. H. Hazlitt. Newsweek 67:84 Mr 14 '66
Four-year House. W. Lippmann. Newsweek 67:15 F 28 '66
Four-year term. New Repub 154:5-6 Mr 12 '66
Four-year term for House members? il U S News 60:48 Ja 31 '66
Four-year terms for congressmen? pro and con discussion. Sr Schol 88:18-19 F 18; 89: 16-17 S 30 '66
Four-year terms? reform of Congress. W. D. Burnham. Commonweal 84:79-81 Ap 8 '66
How much power? Johnson's proposal. il Time 87:17-19 Ja 28 '66
Let's make government work better! reform proposals. D. D. Eisenhower. Read Digest 90:61-7 Ja '67; Reply. D. Lawrence. U S News 62:88 Ja 9 '67
Longer terms for men of the House? J. N. Eller. America 114:191 F 5 '66
LBJ's amendment. Nat R 18:101-2 F 8 '66
No time for haste; President Johnson's proposal to extend term to four years. R. L. Tobin. Sat R 49:26 Ja 29 '66
This month's feature: question of a longer House term. Cong Digest 45:131-9+ My '66
CONGRESSMEN, Letters to. See Lobbying
CONGRESSWOMEN
Life as a brave adventure; R. Felton first woman senator. Sr Schol 89:7 S 30 '66
CONGREVE, Willard J.
Not all the disadvantaged are poor. PTA Mag 60:15-17 bibliog (p35) F '66
CONKERS (game) See Games
CONKLIN, Bill
Smasheroo, she said softly. Sat Eve Post 239:16 Ag 13 '66
CONKLIN, Paul
Peace corps around the world; photographs. Sat R 49:16-17 Ap 23 '66
CONKLIN, T. L.
New York prepares to vote on lottery. Christian Cent 83:1157-8 S 21 '66
CONKLING, Roscoe P.
Golden age memories. Opera N 30:28-9 Ap 9 '66
CONLEY, Clare
All-season shotgun. Field & S 71:38-9+ Jl '66
Best BB shooters in the world. Field & S 71:58-61 D '66
Just plane camping. Field & S 70:72-4+ F '66
Small plane and fancy fishing. Field & S 70: 62-4+ Mr '66
What every new camper should know. Field & S 71:50-3+ Je '66

CONLY, Robert Leslie
Porpoises: our friends in the sea. por Nat Geog Mag 130:396-425 S '66
St Augustine, nation's oldest city, turns 400. Nat Geog Mag 129:196-229 F '66
CONNALLY, John Bowden, 1917-
Comradely combat; President Johnson's finest friend. il por Time 87:25 Ap 15 '66
Matter of reasonable doubt. il pors Life 61: 38-48B+ N 25 '66
Politics on the king's ranch. R. Sherrill. il por N Y Times Mag p43+ Je 5 '66
CONNECTICUT
    See also
Architecture, Domestic—Connecticut
Booksellers and bookselling—Connecticut
Fishing—Connecticut
Hunting—Connecticut

    Politics and government
How to run a peace candidate. R. K. Byron. Nation 203:469-72 N 7 '66
In the ring with Dempsey. il Time 88:16 Jl 1 '66

    Water supply
What a state can do to stop water pollution. Am City 81:43 S '66
CONNECTICUT opera association
Hartford. W. D. Miranda. il Opera N 30:29 F 19; 27 Je 4 '66
Hartford; production of Bellini's Sonnambula. W. D. Miranda. Opera N 31:29 D 31 '66
Hartford; production of Carmen. W. Miranda. Opera N 30:31 Ja 29 '66
Hartford; production of Ponchielli's Gioconda. A. N. Groth. Opera N 31:28-9 D 3 '66
Hartford story. R. D. Daniels. Opera N 31: 20-1 O 15 '66
CONNECTIVE tissues. See Tissues
CONNECTORS
Gang-nails: strong grip for home jobs; multiprong connector plates. R. Treves. il Pop Sci 188:143 Ap '66
CONNECTORS, Electric. See Electric connectors
CONNELLY, Dolly
Project overcome. il Parents Mag 41:52-5+ Ag '66
Wilderness trip with the Kennedys. McCalls 93:66+ My '66
CONNELLY, Marc
Mayors, Moreno, and a marriage. Sat R 50: 54+ Ja 7 '67
CONNELLY, Troy Stix
Constant adventure. il House & Gard 129: 114-17 F '66
CONNER, Alice. See Goldman, M. I. jt. auth.
CONNER, Caryl
Pliés please. Am Ed 2:28-32 Je '66
—See De Neufville, R. jt. auth.
CONNERY, Donald S.
Scandinavian youth. Holiday 40:76-7+ N '66
CONNES, Janine, and others
Mars: new absorption bands in the spectrum. Science 153:739-40 Ag 12 '66
CONNES, Keith
Ever on Sunday. Flying 79:83 S '66
I'll take the high camp. Flying 79:85-7 S '66
CONNIFF, James C. G.
World of the unborn. N Y Times Mag p40-1+ Ja 8 '67
CONNOLLY, Cyril
Critic's choice of contemporaries. L. Edel. Sat R 49:35 Ap 2 '66
CONNOLLY, James M.
New books. Cath World 204:124 N '66
CONNOR, John Thomas
Expanding the fabric of U.S.-Japanese economic relations; address, July 8, 1966. Dept State Bul 55:215-21 Ag 8 '66
Impact of technology on world trade and economic development; address, November 16, 1966. Dept State Bul 55:956-60 D 26 '66
Substantial improvement achieved in balance of payments in 1965; statement, February 14, 1966. Dept State Bul 54: 440-2 Mr 14 '66
    about
Paradoxical predicament of John Connor. H. B. Meyers. il por Fortune 73:150-2+ F '66
CONNOR, Sister Kathleen Thérèse
Student sister on the secular campus. America 115:604-6 N 12 '66
CONNOR, Tony
Two British chronicles. R. J. Mills, jr. Poetry 107:408-9 Mr '66

CONNORS, Mrs Donald
Pioneer library system's cadet program. ALA Bul 61:86-9 Ja '67

CONOVER, H. S.
Beach construction in a state park. Parks & Rec 1:420-1+ My '66

CONOVER, William J.
How I farm today. pors Suc Farm 64:52-3 Mr '66

CONQUEST, Right of
Defender of the Indians; with editorial comment. R. Gallardo. il Américas 18:inside cover. 23-31 O '66

CONRAD, Barnaby
Good new life of Bing Crosby. Good H 162:88-93+ My '66
Homage to a peerless matador. Sports Illus 25:44-52 Ag 1 '66

CONRAD, Charles, Jr
See also
Space flight—Manned flights—Conrad-Gordon flight, 1966

CONRAD, Ivan Willard
Inventor of the month. S. V. Jones. il Sci Digest 59:20 Ap '66

CONRAD, John P.
Violence in prison. Ann Am Acad 364:113-19 Mr '66

CONRAD, Maximilien Arthur
Pair of aces. R. B. Parke. Flying 78:34 F '66

CONRAD, Pete. See Conrad, C. jr

CONROY, Frank
Hanging on. New Yorker 42:58-63 D 10 '66
Night away from home. New Yorker 42:56-66+ O 22 '66

CONROY, Hilary
(comp) Articles and other books received; east Asia. See issues of American historical review

CONROY, John M.
Big Guppies seek a bigger pond. il por Bsns W p76-7 S 10 '66

CONSCIENCE
Conscience and I. V. P. McCorry. America 115:19-20 Jl 2 '66
Dialogue with mothers: how your child's conscience is born. B. Bettelheim. Ladies Home J 83:26+ O '66
Honor bright! M. G. Baker. Seventeen 25:124+ Je '66
When a child should tell. S. Frank. il Good H 162:96-7+ My '66
See also
Guilt
Liberty of conscience

CONSCIENTIOUS objectors
Basic training; Seventh day Adventists. Newsweek 68:54 S 12 '66
Blots on the Nation's seal. Christian Cent 84:35 Ja 11 '67
Bronze stars of peace: legionnaire says no; R. Hollis's activities. D. Ford. il Nation 202:329-31 Mr 21 '66
Churches default C.O.s. Christian Cent 83:389 Mr 30 '66
Conversations parents never hear. il Look 30:67 S 20 '66
Four ways to go: Tommy Rodd went to jail. B. Weinraub. Esquire 66:124+ S '66
God and the draft; can non-believers be conscientious objectors? E. N. Beiser. Commonweal 83:631-3 Mr 4 '66
In good conscience. Christian Cent 83:791-2 Je 22 '66
Just war and the selective objector. A. Geyer. il Christian Cent 83:199-201 F 16 '66; Reply. J. C. Fleck. 83:404 Mr 30 '66
More help for C.O.s. Christian Cent 83:825 Je 29 '66
Sidelights on the war. Christian Cent 83:1170 S 28 '66
Soldiers without arms; army medics. il Time 88:31 O 28 '66
Speaking out; we're unfair to draft-card burners. R. E. Rubenstein. Sat Eve Post 239:10+ F 12 '66
Suppose they gave a war and no one came. C. E. Keyes. McCalls 94:26+ O '66
They march to different drummers. W. Goodman. il N Y Times Mag p7+ Je 26 '66
Vatican II: anathema upon war; cases of Italian conscientious objectors. E. M. Borgese. il Nation 202:415-21 Ap 11 '66
Witnesses' Spartan trials; Jehovah's Witnesses in Greece. il Time 88:84+ S 9 '66

CONSCRIPTION, Civilian. See Service, Compulsory non-military

CONSEIL européen pour la recherche nucléaire. See European organization for nuclear research

CONSERVATION as a profession. See Natural resources—Vocational guidance

CONSERVATION associations
See also
Sierra club

CONSERVATION education. See Conservation of resources—Study and teaching

CONSERVATION education association
Teaching conservation in the city. I. Moore. il Am For 72:22-5 O '66

CONSERVATION of natural resources as a profession. See Natural resources—Vocational guidance

CONSERVATION of resources
Aid destroys wetlands. Sci N 89:224 Ap 2 '66
Awakening giant: sportsmen's part in politics. T. Trueblood. il Field & S 71:26-7+ O '66
Books in review; our dwindling heritage. S. L. Udall. Natur Hist 75:6+ F '66
Confessions of a conservationist. G. Schneider. Am For 72:8+ Ap '66
Conservation and natural beauty. P. H. Abelson; discussion. Science 151:936+, 1477+ F 25, Mr 25 '66
Conservation; ed. by H. Titus. See issues of Field & stream
Conservation faces its moment of truth. H. Higdon. il Todays Health 44:50-1+ Mr '66
Conservation is good business. Audubon Mag 68:212-13 Jl '66
Crisis in the countryside. il Am For 72:26-7 Jl '66
Crowds. L. B. Johnson. Parks & Rec 1:821-2 O '66
Destroyers; conflicting policies of the Johnson administration. New Repub 154:5-6 Je 25 '66
Destruction of California, by R. Dasmann. Review
Liv Wildn 29:30-1 Wint '65. S. E. Wood
Disappearing seacoast. A. Bester. il Holiday 40:56-69+ Jl '66
Geology and the new conservation movement; address, December 6, 1965. P. T. Flawn. bibliog Science 151:409-12 Ja 28 '66; Discussion. 152:152+, 1568-9 Ap 8, Je 17 '66
Government as guardian and developer. Liv Wildn 29:45-6 Wint '65
Green grass from grass roots. D. B. Alexander. Parks & Rec 1:902-3 N '66
Heritage in peril. M. L. Grossman. il Am Heritage 17:4-15+ Ag '66
Industry and tomorrow's environment; report on meeting of American forest products industries. J. B. Craig. il Am For 72:30-1+ D '66
Keynote address: America the beautiful; with editorial comment. R. E. Train. il Am For 71:11, 16-19+ O '65
Mike Frome; creative localism, not creative federalism in conservation. M. Frome. Am For 72:3+ Jl '66
Mike Frome; trip in Alaska. M. Frome. Am For 72:5+ S '66
National outlook (cont of) National capital report. C. H. Callison. See issues of Audubon magazine
Natural beauty, the follow through. J. B. Craig. il Am For 71:12-15+ O '65
Natural resources, conservation and use. W. W. Porter, 2d. il Am For 72:28-31+ Ap '66
News and commentary. See issues of National parks magazine
Parks, plans, and people; how South America guards her green legacy. M. Rockefeller and L. Rockefeller. il Nat Geog Mag 131:74-119 Ja '67
Parkscape U.S.A; conservation for natural and human resources. G. B. Hartzog, jr. il Parks & Rec 1:616-20 Ag '66
People and the out-of-doors: crisis of natural and open areas. T. J. Rillo. il Am For 72:8+ Mr '66
Philosophy of conservation. G. Schneider. Am For 72:10+ Jl '66
Quickening tick of the conservation clock. J. B. Craig. il Am For 72:10-13+ N '66
Redwoods win protection. B. Tufty. il Sci N 89:264-6 Ap 16 '66
Report of president and general counsel to the general membership of National parks association, May 19, 1966. A. W. Smith. Nat Parks Mag 40:I-IV My '66
Resources becoming critical. Sci N 90:549-50 D 24 '66
Storm King opinion: stunning conservation victory. R. E. Train. Am For 72:10-11 Mr '66
Trees don't vote; President's special conservation message to Congress. Newsweek 67:26 Mr 7 '66
Use for wilderness. R. C. Clement. il Audubon Mag 68:94-5 Mr '66

CONSERVATION of resources—*Continued*
Whooping it up for conservation; editorial. M. B. Durning. Am For 72:15 F '66
Wild rivers or power plants? il Liv Wildn 29:40-1 Wint '65
Wilderness bill of rights, by W. O. Douglas. Review
Nat Parks Mag il 40:18-19 Mr '66. G. S. Leisure
Wildlife, rivers, shores set for Congress action. Sci N L 89:73 Ja 29 '66
You can be a conservationist. C. E. Randall. il Am For 72:17-27 Ap '66
See also
Forest conservation
National youth conference on natural beauty and conservation
Natural resources
Reclamation of land
Water conservation
Wildlife conservation

Bibliography
Scholastic teacher reviews: conservation-books for all ages. S. Simon. Sr Schol 88: sup 19 Ap 29 '66

Study and teaching
Children of the dunes; report on PACE project. il Am Ed 2:7 S '66
Conservation education for people. G. Schneider. Am For 72:12+ S '66
Conservation is unselfishness; conservation education for sixth-graders. R. E. Klinck. il Sr Schol 88:sup 17-18 Ap 29 '66
Conservation joins the three R's. J. Swan. il Audubon Mag 68:119-20+ Mr '66
Is the Job corps conservation program working? N. T. Schweitzer. il Am For 72:18-21+ Ag '66
Teaching conservation in the city. I. Moore. il Am For 72:22-5 O '66
CONSERVATION of wildlife. See Wildlife conservation
CONSERVATION of works of art. See Art—Conservation and restoration
CONSERVATISM
American dissent, by J. Hart. Review
Nat R 18:536-7 My 31 '66. M. S. Evans
Conservatism in the South; address, April 1, 1966. S. Thurmond. Vital Speeches 32:420-3 My 1 '66
Is there a student conservatism? J. F. Lulves, jr. Nat R 18:530-1 My 31 '66
Justice Black dissents; turning convervative? U S News 60:26+ Mr 21 '66
Life without prejudice and other essays, by R. Weaver. Review
Sat R 49:38-9 Ap 2 '66. B. D. Diamonstein
Little piece of America; Orange County, Calif. il Newsweek 68:32+ N 14 '66
Notes and asides: Conservative book club opinion survey. Nat R 18:974 O 4 '66
Our man at the Golliwog lounge; second annual meeting of the Philadelphia society. J. J. Kilpatrick. Nat R 18:258+ Mr 22 '66
Questions and answers about conservatives. E. Thompson. il Esquire 66:88-9 Jl '66
See also
Liberalism
Minutemen (organization)
Right and left (political science)
CONSERVATIVE Judaism. See Judaism
CONSERVATIVE party (Canada)
But unbowed; fourth attempt to unseat Diefenbaker. Newsweek 68:60+ O 10 '66
CONSERVATIVE party (Great Britain)
Establishing an alternative. Time 88:53 O 21 '66
Tories on the ropes. B. Wenham. New Repub 154:11-12 Mr 5 '66
CONSERVATIVE party (United States)
CPNY and Mr Javits. Nat R 18:1304-5 D 27 '66
CONSERVES. See Jelly, jam, etc.
CONSHELF three. See Underwater laboratories
CONSIDER the lilies; drama. See Molloy, E. A.
CONSIDINE, Bob
Could you have loved as much? Read Digest 88:73-5 Ap '66
CONSOLIDATED Edison company of New York
Air around us; Thanksgiving weekend. New Repub 155:8 D 10 '66
Con Edison: the company you love to hate. T. O'Hanlon. il Fortune 73:122-7+ Mr '66
Storm King. Liv Wildn 29:42-3 Wint '65
Storm King gets a reprieve. il Am For 72:5 F '66
CONSOLIDATED foods corporation
Architect of the autonoplex: N. Cummings of Consolidated foods corp. il Time 87: 88 Je 24 '66

From food to films. Time 88:62 Jl 29 '66
From pies to pickles; merger with United artists. il Newsweek 68:71 Ag 1 '66
Sorry about that; United artists and Consolidated foods proposed merger off. Newsweek 68:86 Ag 22 '66
CONSOLIDATED schools
Case for educational parks; discussion. M. Wolff; E. Rothman; L. Berman. il Arch Rec 139:180-2 F '66
Park way; present and proposed projects. il Newsweek 68:48 Jl 18 '66
Regional approaches to educational problems. P. F. Johnston. NEA J 55:27-8+ Ap '66
CONSOLIDATION, Railroad. See Railroads—Consolidations and mergers
CONSOLIDATION coal company
Coal fever; Continental oil and other mergers. New Repub 154:7 Ap 9 '66
Uniting for strength; interview. G. H. Love. Nations Bsns 55:44-5+ Ja '67
CONSOLIDATIONS, Business. See Business consolidations and mergers
CONSTANCE Lindsay Skinner award
Blanche W. Knopf wins WNBA's Skinner award. Pub W 189:62 My 30 '66
WNBA dinner to honor Mrs Knopf in memoriam. Pub W 190:109 S 26 '66
WNBA's Skinner award honors memory of Blanche W. Knopf. il Pub W 190:25 O 24 '66
CONSTANT caller; story. See Hudson, H.
CONSTANTINE II, king of the Hellenes
Behind the Aspida trial. K. Kyle. New Repub 156:17-18 Ja 21 '67
King with Greek gusto; with report by P. Dragadze. il pors Life 61:78-84+ O 21 '66
Their majesties King Constantine II and Queen Anne-Marie of the Hellenes with H.R.H. Crown Princess Alexia. D. Messinesi. il pors Vogue 148:116-19+ S 15 '66
CONSTELLA
Lyndon B. Johnson. Sat Eve Post 239:27 Mr 26 '66
CONSTELLATION (yacht) See Yachts and yachting
CONSTELLATIONS
Identification of the X-ray source in Scorpius. H. Gursky. il Sky & Tel 32:252-5 N '66

Anecdotes, facetiae, satire, etc.
Unidentified shining objects. W. Holbrook. il il Atlan 217:121-2 Je '66

Names
Names of constellations reflect many religions and mythologies. T. D. Nicholson. il Natur Hist 75:28-31 My '66
CONSTITUTION (United States) See United States—Constitution
CONSTITUTIONAL amendments. See United States—Constitution—Amendments
CONSTITUTIONAL conventions
Fifty dinosaurs restyling the states: constitutions: the politics of power. H. Norris. il Nation 203:472-5 N 7 '66
See also
United States—Constitutional convention, 1787
CONSTITUTIONS
See also
Trade unions—Constitutions
CONSTITUTIONS, State
Fifty dinosaurs restyling the states: constitutions: the politics of power. H. Norris. il Nation 203:472-5 N 7 '66
CONSTRUCTION. See Building
CONSTRUCTION industry. See Building industry
CONSTRUCTIVE action, Incorporated
Bigots' book shelf; campus scare campaign. W. Wingfield. Nation 203:206-9 S 12 '66
CONSULTANTS
See also
Consulting engineers
Library consultants
CONSULTANTS, Library. See Library consultants
CONSULTANTS, Tax. See Tax consultants
CONSULTANTS and designers, Incorporated
Job shops profit from technology boom. R. G. Barnhart. Tech W 19:34-5 Ag 29 '66
CONSULTATION on church union
After Dallas: deployment. M. Frakes. Christian Cent 83:642-4 My 18 '66
Brethren take to the hills and the alleys; annual conference. I. Long. Christian Cent 83:916-17 Jl 20 '66; Reply. C. W. Zunkel. 83:1010 Ag 17 '66
COCU: self defeating? V. Eller. Christian Cent 83:488-91 Ap 20 '66

CONSULTATION on church union—*Continued*
COCU: what and whence; Consultation on church union to hold its fifth plenary meeting in Dallas. Christian Cent 83:259-60 Mr 2 '66
COCU: whither and how; six churches consider possible union. Christian Cent 83:291-3 Mr 9 '66
COCU's Principles under scrutiny. J. P. Brown. Christian Cent 83:1405-9 N 16 '66
From handholding to engagement; Consultation on church union. il Time 87:86 My 13 '66
Presbyterians, U.S: union, reunion, relevancy. J. A. Womeldorf. Christian Cent 83:690-2 My 25 '66; Discussion. 83:962 Ag 3 '66

CONSULTING engineers
Technical representative. G. Smith. il Electr World 76:40-1+ Ag '66

CONSUMER buying surveys. See Consumer surveys

CONSUMER complaints. See Complaints

CONSUMER credit. See Credit

CONSUMER education
Buying guide issue (cont) il Consumer Rep 31:1-447 D '66
Pennywise teenagers. E. Peterson. il Am Ed 2:24-8 Ap '66
Things go better with consumer education; ways of teaching the young. E. Peterson. il PTA Mag 60:7-9 My '66
Wowing the ladies; housewives tour consumer-oriented companies. il Bsns W p90-1 Mr 26 '66
See also
Consumer protection

CONSUMER goods. See Commercial products

CONSUMER price index. See Price indexes

CONSUMER protection
Citizen's role in furthering consumer interests; address, April 21, 1966. L. K. Sullivan. Vital Speeches 32:498-501 Je 1 '66
Congresswoman charges: Washington consumer aid is deceptive packaging; interview. C. May. il Nations Bsns 54:54-6+ My '66
Consumer; address, December 6, 1966. L. E. Skinner. Vital Speeches 33:189-92 Ja 1 '67
Consumer wave. Nation 202:574 My 16 '66
Docket: notes on government actions taken to enforce consumer protection laws. See issues of Consumer reports
Few and the many; need for legislation. New Repub 154:7-8 F 26 '66
Giant economy or jumbo? call for stiffer laws to protect both the buyer's money and the buyer's health. il Newsweek 67:78 Ap 4 '66
Guardian of the gullible; Special presidential assistant on consumer affairs. Time 87:29 Ap 29 '66
New look in consumer protection. il Changing T 20:43-6 N '66
Personal business; getting defective merchandise during Christmas shopping. Bsns W p 169-70 N 19 '66
Prescription for the FDA: a new dose of courage. Consumer Rep 31:411-15 Ag '66
This month's feature: Congress & consumer protection moves. Cong Digest 45:163-92 Je '66
Tomorrow's consumer; address. October 19, 1966. W. Wirsig. Vital Speeches 33:81-6 N 15 '66
Uncle Sam: consumers' champion. il Bsns W p76-8+ Ap 2 '66
Year of the consumer. Consumer Bul 50:31-2 Ja '67

CONSUMER surveys
Consumer intentions: let seller beware; University of Michigan survey. il Bsns W p33 Ja 7 '67
$500,000 peek into consumer's mind. Bsns W p64 O 22 '66
Is the stampede over? il Bsns W p31-3 My 28 '66
Reading the consumer's crystal ball; findings of University of Michigan's survey research center. il Newsweek 67:69 Je 27 '66

CONSUMERS
Auspicious rise of the Soviet consumer. G. Burck. il Fortune 74:130-3+ Ag '66
Citizen's role in furthering consumer interests; address, April 21, 1966. L. K. Sullivan. Vital Speeches 32:498-501 Je 1 '66
Consumer holds the veto; excerpts from address. ed. by D. Hanson. S. K. Seaver. Suc Farm 64:6+ Ap '66
Consumer: power behind the boom. il Sr Schol 88:17 Ap 1 '66
Consumer's stake in standards. Consumer Bul 49:29-32 F '66

Fast relief; give consumer a fair look at what he is spending his money on; NET. Newsweek 67:94+ Ap 4 '66
FDA's edict: patients, not profits, come first; excerpts from address, April 6, 1966. J. L. Goddard. Science 152:332-3 Ap 15 '66
Forty ways to beat the high cost of almost everything. Ladies Home J 83:72+ N '66
In defense of waste; Time essay. Time 88:56-7 N 18 '66
Is war on poverty becoming war on business? P. Hencke. il Nations Bsns 54:40-1+ Mr '66
No letup in rush to buy. Bsns W p37-8 Mr 19 '66
Prices, taxes, credit depress the consumer; findings of survey research center. University of Michigan. il Bsns W p39 Je 18 '66
Shoppers' spree goes on unabated. il Bsns W p32-4 S 3 '66
Speaker for the house. C. Montgomery. See issues of Good housekeeping
Tomorrow's consumer; address, October 19, 1966. W. Wirsig. Vital Speeches 33:81-6 N 15 '66
Truth in packaging: supermarket caper. J. Cross. il Nation 202:208-12 F 21 '66
See also
Consumer education
Consumer protection

CONSUMERS union of United States
30th, a year to remember. Consumer Rep 31:571-3 N '66

CONSUMPTION (economics)
Edgy, but still buying; index of consumer sentiment. il Bsns W p30 Ap 9 '66
Prosperity wears an uneasy smile. il Bsns W p43-5 Mr 26 '66
Still a shopping spree. Fortune 73:40+ Mr '66
See also
Consumer surveys
Consumers

CONTACT lenses
Contact lenses get a softer touch; hydron, a soft plastic developed in Czechoslovakia. il Bsns W p 147-8 Ap 30 '66
Czech invention licensed in the U.S. V. K. McElheny. Science 153:521 Ag 5 '66
Eye damage reported in contact lens survey. Sci N 89:220 Ap 2 '66
Visual cripples in sports. il Sci Digest 59:15-16 F '66

CONTAGIOUS diseases. See Communicable diseases

CONTAINER corporation of America
Fine arts for an institutional series. il Am Artist 30:36-41+ S '66

CONTAINER system (freight handling)
Better by the box. il Time 87:95 F 25 '66
Cargo system developed for Delta L-100. D. A. Brown. il Aviation W 85:29-31 Ag 29 '66
Cargo talks stress containers, handling; with editorial comment. J. W. Carter. Aviation W 84:21, 41-2 My 30 '66
Containerization problems seen for large-capacity cargo jets. Aviation W 85:52 D 19 '66
Containers race accross Atlantic; international, door-to-door foreign service. Bsns W p76+ F 19 '66
Containers: the boom begins. il Duns R 87:pt2 113-14+ My '66
Containers widen their world; door-to-door cargo service across the Atlantic. il Bsns W p88-90 Ja 7 '67
New kind of steamboat race: door-to-door delivery of ocean freight. il U S News 60:8 F 28 '66
Port facility planned as integrated complex for trailer-ship transfer; Elizabeth, N.J. il Arch Rec 140:126-8 D '66
727QC to expand airline, truck industry coordination. il Aviation W 85:52-3 Ag 8 '66
Shipping: storm signals lowering? il Duns R 87:pt2 125-7+ My '66

CONTAINERIZATION. See Container system (freight handling)

CONTAINERS
Safety cans for flammable liquids. il Consumer Bul 49:43+ Jl '66
Throwaway containers get a lift from pop; disposable containers and nonreturnable bottles. il Bsns W p70+ Ag 6 '66
Vegetables: can and glass container sizes. il Bet Hom & Gard 44:102 Ap '66
See also
Beer containers
Capsules

CONTAINERS, Pressurized. See Aerosols

CONTAINERS for shipping
Thirty-five tons of children's books shipped in three boxes; inter-modal van containers. il Pub W 189:155 F 21 '66
See also
Container system (freight handling)
CONTAMINATION of food. See Food contamination
CONTAX II cameras. See Cameras
CONTEMPLATION. See Meditation
CONTEMPLATION, Religious. See Meditation
CONTEMPORARY music. See Music
CONTEMPORARY theological institute. See Religious conferences
CONTEMPT of court
Pot luck; case of A. Buchanan, managing editor of University of Oregon newspaper. Newsweek 67:36+ Je 27 '66
Problems of protecting a source; case of managing editor of University of Oregon newspaper. Time 87:98 Je 24 '66
Silence on sources; editor of the University of Oregon campus newspaper. Time 88:49 Jl 8 '66
CONTENTMENT
See also
Happiness
CONTESTS. See Competitions
CONTINENT, Lost. See Atlantis
CONTINENTAL airlines
Arms & men at Continental. Time 88:71-2 Jl 1 '66
Continental purchases three Boeing 747s. C. M. Plattner. il Aviation W 85:40 O 10 '66
Continental shapes Pacific growth aims. W. H. Gregory. il Aviation W 85:45+ Ag 8 '66
Six's biggest gamble. il Newsweek 68:88 N 14 '66
Traffic spurs United, Continental orders. C. M. Plattner. Aviation W 84:35 Je 27 '66
CONTINENTAL drift
Continents sprinted; continental drift theory questioned. Sci N 89:267 Ap 16 '66
Controversy on continental drift. D. Behrman. il UNESCO Courier 19:12-15+ O '66
Is Arabia drifting slowly to the north-east? il UNESCO Courier 19:15 Je '66
CONTINENTAL enterprises, incorporated
Woes of Wolfson; indictment for sale of unregistered shares. il Time 88:106+ S 30 '66
Wolfson at bay; sales of unregistered shares by L. Wolfson and E. B. Gerbert. Newsweek 68:89 O 3 '66
CONTINENTAL Illinois national bank and trust company of Chicago. See Chicago—Banks
CONTINENTAL oil company
Coal fever; Consolidation coal and other mergers. New Repub 154:7 Ap 9 '66
Uniting for strength; interview. G. H. Love. Nations Bsns 55:44-5+ Ja '67
CONTINENTAL rise. See Continental shelf
CONTINENTAL shelf
Continental margin of western Europe: slope progradation and erosion. J. R. Curray and others. bibliog il Science 154:265-6 O 14 '66
Continental shelf survey promising. R. W. Niblock. Miss & Roc 18:35 Mr 21 '66
Elephant teeth found at sea. B. Tufty. il Sci N 90:481-D 3 '66
Exposure of basement rock on the continental slope of the Bering Sea. D. W. Scholl and others. bibliog il Science 153:992-4 Ag 26 '66
Monaco: the shallow continental shelf. H. E. Edgerton and O. Leenhardt. il Science 152:1106-7 My 20 '66
New England lake, river now 500 feet under sea. Sci N L 89:53 Ja 22 '66
Our newest frontier is underwater! R. F. Crossley. il Pop Mech 125:94-8+ My '66
Sediment movement on the Continental shelf near Washington and Oregon. M. G. Gross and J. L. Nelson. bibliog il Science 154:879-80+ N 18 '66
Shaping of the continental rise by deep geostrophic contour currents. B. C. Heezen and others. bibliog il Science 152:502-8 Ap 22 '66
Uplift of the continental margin and possible continental accretion off Oregon. J. V. Byrne and others. bibliog il Science 154:1654-6 D 30 '66
CONTINENTAL slope. See Continental shelf
CONTINENTAL telephone corporation
Management's rule-breakers: the ways of the winners. J. Weiner. Duns R 87:84-5 Ja '66
CONTINENTAL telephone supply company
Everybody's got the bug. il Time 88:76 D 16 '66

CONTINENTS
Antipodal location of continents and oceans. C. G. A. Harrison. bibliog il Science 153:1246-8 S 9 '66
See also
Continental drift
CONTINI, Jeanne
For the fastest ride out of this world, take a motorbike. Seventeen 25:152-3+ N '66
Sororities. Seventeen 25:296-7+ Ag '66
CONTINUITY testers. See Testing instruments
CONTINUOUS air circulation. See Heating
CONTINUOUS casting
Continuous casting flows ahead. il Bsns W D 176-8+ D 10 '66
CONTINUOUS-progress plan in education. See Ungraded classes
CONTOSKI, Victor
(tr) See Rozewicz, T. To the heart
CONTRA COSTA COUNTY, Calif.
Design of modern asphalt pavements. V. W. Sauer. il Am City 81:113-16 Ap '66
CONTRABAND trade. See Smuggling
CONTRACEPTION. See Birth control
CONTRACEPTIVES
Acute phase protein in serum of women using hormonal contraceptives. G. F. B. Schumacher. bibliog il Science 153:901-2 Ag 19 '66
Birth control and population; Planned parenthood-world population conference in Washington. il Newsweek 67:94+ My 16 '66
Birth control drug tests halted on 340 women. Sci N L 89:137 F 26 '66
Birth control method that may replace the pill; IUCD. il Good H 162:177-9 Ap '66
Birth control pill causes jaundice; other side effects from anovlar. Sci N 89:244 Ap 9 '66
Birth control pills not proved unsafe yet. Sci N 90:136 Ag 27 '66
Can a woman be feminine forever? N. Sommers and J. Ridgeway. New Repub 154:15-16 Mr 19 '66
Coming sooner than expected: birth-control shots; ed. by V. Cohn. P. Wright. Ladies Home J 83:18 O '66
Contraception frustrates nature. W. F. Drummond. Cath World 203:202-6 Jl '66
Contraception fulfills nature. J. M. Ryan. Cath World 203:207-12 Jl '66
Contraceptive advances; three-month protection. Sci N 89:392 My 21 '66
Control of conception by hormonal steroids; address, 1965. G. Pincus. bibliog il Science 153:493-500 Jl 29 '66
FDA revises pill labeling. Sci N 90:450 N 26 '66
Giving pill a safe label; FDA findings, favorable. Bsns W p33 Ag 13 '66
Improving the pill; chlormadinone. Newsweek 67:79 F 7 '66
Is the pill deadly? Roman Catholic view. Christian Cent 83:578 My 4 '66
Legalized abortion urged. F. Marley. Sci N 90:19 Jl 9 '66
Lifetime birth control; one-shot capsule implanted under the skin. Newsweek 68:74 O 31 '66
Loop causes problem. Sci N 89:489 Je 18 '66
Loop that can shake the world. R. G. Davids. Farm J 90:84+ F '66
More about the pill. Christian Cent 83:704-5 Je 1 '66
Morning-after pill. Time 87:60 My 6 '66
Must we now ban the birth control pills? Good H 162:62-70 F '66
New and better pill. America 115:51 Jl 16 '66
Pill: how it is affecting U.S. morals, family life. il U S News 61:62-5 Jl 11 '66
Pill side effect. A. J. Snider. il Sci Digest 60:39-40 O '66
Pills as poisoner; accidental poisonings among children. Time 87:60 Mr 25 '66
Popular, effective, safe; birth-control pills. il Newsweek 68:92 Ag 22 '66
Retroactive birth control. Sci Am 214:56 Je '66
Safe and effective pills. il Time 88:59 Ag 19 '66
Safety of contraceptive pills. Consumer Rep 32:25 Ja '67
Steroid oral contraceptives. C. Djerassi. bibliog il Science 151:1055-61 Mr 4 '66
Three men who made a revolution. L. Lader. il N Y Times Mag p8-9+ Ap 10 '66
Three new drugs for easier birth control. U S News 60:14 My 16 '66
Use of oral contraception in the United States, 1965. N. B. Ryder and C. F. Westoff. il Science 153:1199-205 S 9 '66
When the law worked: scare over new birth-control pill. Time 87:49 F 11 '66
Which way to safety? birth-control pills. il Newsweek 68:69 D 19 '66

CONTRACT bridge. See Bridge (game)

CONTRACTS

Billion-dollar proposal industry; detailed presentations of bidders. T. J. Murray. il Duns R 87:40-1+ Ja '66

See also

Land contracts

Penalties, Contractual

Subcontracting

CONTRACTS, Government

Aerospace firms lead DOD contractors. Aviation W 85:29 D 5 '66

Aircraft avionics suppliers named. Aviation W 85:38 Jl 25 '66

Arms reduction impact. B. G. Lall. Bul Atomic Sci 22:41-4 S '66

Arms spiral; Nike X project; profits for industries involved. Nation 204:35 Ja 9 '67

Attack on incentive system seen in rising debate on contracting; address. J. R. Russell. Aviation W 84:119+ My 23 '66

Concessions pressed on SST contracts. Aviation W 85:27-8 D 19 '66

Contracts and procurements (title varies) See issues of Missiles and rockets

Defense dept. lists top 100 contractors for fiscal 1966. il Aviation W 85:104-6+ D 12 '66

DOD list of FY 1966 100 top prime contractors. Tech W 19:17 D 5 '66

Diversification guides for defense firms; excerpts from article. J. S. Gilmore and D. C. Coddington. bibliog f il Harvard Bsns R 44:144-50+ My '66

Experts recommend top-down approach to smaller RFP's; request for proposal bids. I. E. Cornelius and F. Greenwood. Tech W 19:30+ Ag 1 '66

In the name of science, by H. L. Nieburg. Review

Life 61:8 S 9 '66. A. Schlesinger, jr

Johnson expected to push SST. Aviation W 86:25-6 Ja 9 '67

Lockheed bets big on new controls; air force contract to design and build giant C-5As. il Bsns W p 116+ Je 4 '66

Major contracts keyed to performance. K. Johnsen. il Aviation W 84:101-2 F 21 '66

NASA awards list shows incentives push. il Aviation W 84:55+ Je 27 '66

NASA list of FY 1966 top 100 prime contractors. Tech W 19:20 O 24 '66

NASA lists top 100 contractors. il Aviation W 85:85-6+ N 7 '66

New partnership; big government and big business. R. J. Barber. New Repub 155:20-2 Ag 13 '66

New rules guide government contracting. G. C. Wilson. Aviation W 84:26 Ap 4 '66

Pentagon eases audits; fewer government controls over contracts. Bsns W p 194 Ap 16 '66

Pentagon escalates dollars for Vietnam. il Bsns W p38-9 Mr 12 '66

Phase two Poseidon contracts let. C. D. LaFond. il Miss & Roc 18:28+ Ap 11 '66

Profits of war; putsch against McNamara. H. L. Nieburg. Nation 203:696-701 D 26 '66

R&D and the contract state; throwing away the yardstick; excerpt from Science, stagnation, and the contract state. H. L. Nieburg. Bul Atomic Sci 22:20-4 Mr '66

Squeeze tightens; Pentagon orders accelerating, list of shortages growing longer. Bsns W p39 Je 11 '66

SST race, biggest of all; Boeing and Lockheed rivalry. il Newsweek 68:48-52+ Ag 29 '66

Top 100 DOD RDT&E contractors for FY 1966. Tech W 20:19 Ja 9 '67

Vietnam shuffles the list; fifty top defense contractors. Bsns W p40 D 3 '66

Where's the money going next? Defense marketing services. il Bsns W p86+ My 7 '66

Yea, team! team bidding on major defense systems. W. J. Coughlin. Miss & Roc 18:62+ My 16 '66

See also

Government spending policy

United States—National aeronautics and space administration—Procurement

Labor problems

Administration hardens stand against job bias; St Louis scene of labor walkout. il Bsns W p94+ F 12 '66

Subcontracting

Douglas lists major MOL subsystem contractors. Miss & Roc 18:15 Ap 4 '66

Lockheed names first AAFSS subcontractors; advanced aerial fire support system. Aviation W 85:87 O 3 '66

Major Saturn 1B subcontractors listed. Aviation W 84:94-6 Mr 14 '66

Six 747 subcontracts total $1.3 billion; design and manufacture of 490-passenger jet transport. R. G. O'Lone. Aviation W 84:38-9 My 2 '66

CONTRACTS, Land. See Land contracts

CONTRACTUAL penalties. See Penalties, Contractual

CONTRERA, Joseph F. and Gordon, A. S.

Erythropoietin; production by a particulate fraction of rat kidney. bibliog Science 152:653-4 Ap 29 '66

CONTROL data corporation

Control data's magnificent fumble. T. A. Wise. il Fortune 73:165-6+ Ap '66

Joining the ranks of the renters. il Bsns W p86 F 26 '66

When a whiz kid grows up; growth pangs. Bsns W p30 Jl 30 '66

CONTROL of insects. See Insects, Injurious and beneficial—Control

CONTROLLED fusion. See Nuclear fusion

CONTROLS company of America

Buying advice from the top. il Bsns W p 139-40 Mr 5 '66

CONVAIR division. See General dynamics corporation—Convair division

CONVALESCENT homes. See Nursing homes

CONVECTION of heat. See Heat—Convection

CONVENTIONS, Constitutional. See Constitutional conventions

CONVENTIONS, Political. See National conventions (political); Political conventions

CONVENTS and nunneries

Convent and home for girls; Home of the Good Shepherd. il Arch Rec 140:108 Ag '66

See also

Priories

CONVERSATION

Ask, don't tell. N. R. Campion. Read Digest 89:49-52 Ag '66

Conversation can nourish your life. J. K. Lagemann. Read Digest 88:131-4 Je '66

Vanishing art of sweet talk; women's conversation. R. Baker. Ladies Home J 83:55-6 Ap '66

Why men don't listen or talk to their wives. S. Blum. il McCalls 93:78-9+ F '66; Same abr. with title Why men don't talk to their wives. Read Digest 88:55-8 My '66

CONVERSATION radio programs. See Radio broadcasting—Conversation programs

CONVERSATION television programs. See Television broadcasting—Conversation programs

CONVERSION

Ecumenical escalation; National faith and order colloquium; first meeting. J. R. Nelson. Christian Cent 83:858 Jl 6 '66

See also

Evangelistic work

CONVERTERS. See Electric current converters

CONVERTERS, Radio. See Radio converters

CONVERTERS, Thermionic. See Thermionic converters

CONVERTIBILITY of currency. See Currency convertibility

CONVERTIBLE airplanes. See Airplanes, Convertible

CONVERTIBLE bonds. See Bonds, Convertible

CONVERTIBLE debentures. See Bonds, Convertible

CONVERTIBLE participating preferred stock. See Stocks

CONVERTIBLES (automobiles) See Automobiles

CONVERTIPLANES. See Airplanes, Convertible

CONVULSIONS

Your child's health. L. W. Sauer. PTA Mag 60:33-4 F '66

CONWAY, Elsie. and Young, E. G.

Seaweed. Science 151:358-9 Ja 21 '66

CONWAY, J. D.

Election of bishops. por Cath World 204:77-81 N '66

Rights of priests. Commonweal 84:197-200 My 6 '66

CONWAY, James F.

Migrants in the promised land. America 115:253-5 S 10 '66

CONWAY, William G.

Why have a zoo? por Parks & Rec 1:488-90 Je '66

CONWAY COUNTY, Ark.

Embattled crusader of Conway County; newspaper editor E. H. Wirges charges corruption against political bosses. T. Armbrister. il Sat Eve Post 239:25-9+ N 19 '66

COOK, Bruce
Chicago riots. Commonweal 84:492-3 Ag 5 '66
007; the gentleman in decline. Cath World 203:169-74 Je '66
King in Chicago. Commonweal 84:175-7 Ap 29 '66
Without broomsticks. Cath World 204:92-7 N '66

COOK, C. E. and others
Germination of witchweed striga lutea lour.: isolation and properties of a potent stimulant. bibliog Science 154:1189-90 D 2 '66

COOK, Chauncey William Wallace
Social values of marketing; address, October 27, 1966. Vital Speeches 33:86-91 N 15 '66

about

Tex Cook vs. the status quo. J. F. Olesky. por Duns R 87:51-2 Ja '66

COOK, Fred J.
Case of the disappearing coastline. N Y Times Mag p38-9+ S 25 '66
Larry Gallo, Crazy Joe and Kid Blast. N Y Times Mag p36-7+ O 23 '66
Warren commission report: some unanswered questions. Nation 202:705-15 Je 13 '66
Warren commission report: testimony of the eyewitnesses. Nation 202:737-46 Je 20 '66

COOK, Ida
Visit with Farrar. Opera N 30:6 Ja 29 '66
We are scarcely James Bond ladies; interview, ed. by J. Robbins and J. Robbins. por McCalls 93:104-5+ S '66

COOK, J. Lawrence
Old piano roll man. il pors Ebony 21:125-6+ My '66

COOK, James
Opening of the South Seas; excerpts from Fatal impact. A. Moorehead. il por Harper 232:39-48 F; 121-2+ Mr '66

COOK, Jerry
Wow! what a wapiti! Outdoor Life 138:56-7+ S '66

COOK, Leslie G.
How to make R&D more productive. Harvard Bsns R 44:145-50+ Jl '66

COOK, Louise
We are scarcely James Bond ladies; interview, ed. by J. Robbins and J. Robbins. por McCalls 93:104-5+ S '66

COOK, Robert
How to run a peace candidate. R. K. Byron. por Nation 203:469-72 N 7 '66

COOK, Roderick
Books in brief (cont) Harper 232:151-3 Mr; 233:113-15 S '66

COOK COUNTY hospital. See Chicago—Hospitals

COOKBOOKS
Art of cuisine, by H. de Toulouse-Lautrec and M. Joyant. Review
  Nation 203:678 D 19 '66. H. Yglesias
Chicken in every *wok*; new crop of big books. H. Yglesias. il Nation 203:678-80 D 19 '66
Cook's treasure. L. Marek. Parents Mag 41:121 O '66
How to choose a cook book. N. S. Hazelton. House & Gard 129:216-17+ Mv '66
Let's start to cook; excerpts. N. B. Nichols. il Farm J 90:51-5+ Jl '66
Two new cook books take you around the menu clock. il Sunset 136:207 Je '66
  See also
Booksellers and bookselling—Cookbooks

  Bibliography
Books. M. F. K. Fisher. New Yorker 42:180-2+ Mr 26; 226-30+ S 24; 227-8+ O 8 '66
Books; cookery for children. M. F. K. Fisher. New Yorker 42:191-2+ My 21 '66; Reply. K. S. White. 42:112-14 Je 18 '66
Books; cookery for pets. M. F. K. Fisher. New Yorker 42:157-8 +Ap 30 '66
Cookbooks on review. Parents Mag 41:65 Ag; 24 N '66
New fall cookbooks are good Christmas items. il Pub W 190:49-59 S 12 '66
Sunday cooks. M. Sheraton. Harper 233:95-7 Ag '66
Why cookbooks? N. S. Hazelton. Nat R 18:1327 D 27 '66

COOKE, Alistair
Sporting scene. New Yorker 42:171-2+ N 5 '66

COOKE, Deryck
Mahler (and Cooke's) No. 10. I. Kolodin. por Sat R 49:55 Ja 29 '66

COOKE, Eileen D. See Krettek, G. jt. auth.

COOKE, Hope. See Hope Namgyal, maharani of Sikkim

COOKE, Jack Kent
Three names and a barrel of money. B. Ottum. il pors Sports Illus 26:52-8 Ja 16 '67

COOKE, Jerry
Glorious Goodwood; photographs. Sports Illus 25:27-30 Jl 25 '66

COOKE, Pandora
War widow. por Newsweek 68:40+ N 7 '66

COOKERY
Art of Mexican cooking; with recipes and menu; excerpt. J. Aaron and G. S. Salom. il Ladies Home J 83:78-9+ Jl '66
Artists in the kitchen; favorite foods and recipes of some opera singers. P. Gravina. il Opera N 30:26-9 Mr 19 '66
Big party cook book. E. Ross. il House & Gard 129:205+ Ap '66
Blender shortcuts and recipes. il Farm J 90:99-100 F '66
Combine the roles of hostess and cook; recipes that make use of chafing dishes. il Sunset 138:114+ Ja '67
Cook book for epicures in the arts. il House & Gard 130:113+ Jl '66
Cookbook for poor poets & others. il Ladies Home J 83:82-3+ Ag '66
Date with a dish. See issues of Ebony
Delectations. N. S. Hazelton. il Nat R 18:115, 220+, 317-18 F 8, Mr 8, Ap 5 '66
Dishes to serve when you have all the time in the world. il McCalls 93:130-4+ Ap '66
Doris Duke cooks; with recipes. Vogue 148:55+ N 1 '66
Dozen simple tricks to help you cook like an expert. R. Holmberg. il Bet Hom & Gard 45:74-9+ Ja '67
Epicure reminisces. A. L. Simon. il Holiday 40:34+ D '66
Everyone's in the kitchen; gourmet trend. il Time 88:74-80+ N 25 '66
Feasts for all seasons; excerpts. R. A. De Groot. il Ladies Home J 83:104-5+ S '66
Food at Faraway; with recipes. il Vogue 147:192-5 F 1 '66
Food Q's and A's. D. Soroka. Parents Mag 41:24 Mr; 91 Je; 154 N '66
Four favorites. C. Claiborne. il N Y Times Mag p76-7 Ja 8 '67
Frenchman in the kitchen; A. Roblin; with recipes. C. Kentfield. il Holiday 40:66-8 Ag '66
Good cooking with a pressure cooker; with recipes. H. S. Sharpe. il Parents Mag 41:61-4+ Ag '66
Good food happens here! with recipes. il Bet Hom & Gard 44:92-4+ N '66
GH's 10 p.m. specials! with recipes. il Good H 162:94-111 F '66
Good to the last crumb; recipes using bread. il Redbook 126:90-2+ Mr '66
Great dishes with the greatest ease; with recipes. il Good H 162:116-31 Mr '66
High style low cost meals. il McCalls 94:130-8+ O '66
How cooks keep their cool; dishes made the blender way; with recipes. J. Hewitt. il N Y Times Mag p40 Jl 10 '66
James Beard's menus for entertaining; excerpts. J. Beard. il Ladies Home J 83:88-9 F '66
McCall's treasury of great American cooking; fifty best-loved recipes, from the Pilgrims to the present. il McCalls 94:124-34+ N '66
Make-ahead party foods. il Farm J 90:84+ D '66
Midsummer feast. H. S. Witty. il Flower Grower 53:36+ Ag '66
Mrs Johnson talks about her love for the White House; with recipes. R. F. Pomeroy. il Redbook 127:72-8+ Jl '66
[Month] menus; with recipes. See issues of Sunset
Party strategy; tips from five great hostesses. il House & Gard 130:272-82 N '66
Peg Bracken's appendix to the I hate to cook book. P. Bracken. il Ladies Home J 83:84-5 Jl; 92+ Ag; 116+ O; 128+ N; 50+ D '66 (to be cont)
Plain food hardworking men like; with recipes. il Farm J 90:98-9 My '66
Quick and easy cook book. J. A. Beard. il House & Gard 129:197+ My '66
Ranges revisited. il McCalls 93:56+ S '66
Season's fare. H. S. Witty. See issues of Flower grower, the home garden
Seven top chefs hold a summer cook-in; with recipes. M. Kaytor. il Look 30:44-7 S 6 '66
Smart cook. E. C. Zwart. Bet Hom & Gard 44:79 Jl '66
Spectacular sword tricks! il Bet Hom & Gard 44:84-9+ Je '66
Sunset's kitchen cabinet. See issues of Sunset
Teen-age party; with recipes. R. Hanna. il Suc Farm 64:46-7++ D '66

COOKERY—*Continued*
Three flavor-packed main dishes; start with canned and packaged foods; with recipes. il Bet Hom & Gard 44:86 My '66
Tips for the cook. See issues of Successful farming to August 1966
World of fine cooking. M. Field. il McCalls 93:59-60+ F; 78+ Mr; 86+ Ap; 59-60+ Je; 94:84+ O '66
See also
Appetizers
Aspic
Barbecue cookery
Bread
Breakfasts
Buffet meals
Cake
Candy
Casserole cookery
Caterers and catering
Confectionery
Cookbooks
Cookies
Desserts
Diet
Dinners and dining
Eating
Entertaining
Food
Food mixes
Gelatin
Griddle cakes
Ice cream, ices, etc.
Jelly, jam, etc.
Lunches
Mayonnaise
Meals
Meringue
Pastry
Pickles and relishes
Pie
Puddings
Salads
Sandwiches
Sauces
Seasonings
Soufflés
Soups
Steaming (cookery)
Suppers
Thanksgiving dinners
Waffles

Bibliography
See Cookbooks—Bibliography

Competitions
Bounty of the eastern shore; chicken festival: annual National cooking contest, Pocomoke City, Md. N. S. Hazelton. Nat R 18:926+ S 20 '66

Study and teaching
Hamburger university: McDonald's corporation training academy. N. Fraser. il Life 61:100 O 21 '66
If I had to practice cannibalism. . J. Beard's methods. J. Skow. il Sat Eve Post 239:28-31 Jl 30 '66

Terminology
Barrendipity game; not finding something where you most expect it. Time 87:56 Ja 28 '66

Beer
Wine, women & so on. P. Cannon. Ladies Home J 83:116 S '66

Cheese
Blue cheese, please! with recipes. il Bet Hom & Gard 44:100 My '66
Come to a cheese tasting; with recipe. il Good H 162:208 Ap '66
Eggs & cheese; with recipes. R. Hanna. il Suc Farm 64:102-3+ Ap '66
Macaroni with cheese, the ways are almost unlimited. il Sunset 136:164 Je '66
Popular American cheeses. M. Gustafson. il Parents Mag 41:65 Je '66
Swiss salad with Swiss cheese. il Sunset 136:198+ Je '66

Chocolate
Easter's eggs and rabbits molded easily in solid chocolate or hollow chocolate. il Sunset 136:180-1 Ap '66
Using chocolate buttercream. il Sunset 136:174 Je '66

Coconut
Coconut desserts. il Bet Hom & Gard 44:89-90 Ap '66

Cream, Sour
Successful recipes; yogurt and sour cream. il Suc Farm 64:111-12 F '66

Eggs
Best way to cook an egg. il Sunset 136:100-3 Mr '66
Cooking with eggs! il Bet Hom & Gard 44:84-91+ Mr '66
Each artichoke is the nest for a Hollandaise poached egg. il Sunset 136:226+ Ap '66
Egg; dishes, with recipes. M. Field. il McCalls 93:86+ Ap '66
Eggs & cheese; with recipes. R. Hanna. il Suc Farm 64:102-3+ Ap '66
For buffet brunch, basque eggs with ham. il Sunset 136:193-4 Je '66
How to cook a good egg. il Bet Hom & Gard 44:96 Mr '66
Omelets, etc. P. Cannon. il Ladies Home J 83:84-5+ Ag '66

Fish
August is the month for fresh swordfish steaks. il Sunset 137:100 Ag '66
California crab; sandwiched or saladed; with recipes. M. Kaytor. il Look 30:46-7 My 3 '66
Chilled fish you do ahead; with recipe. Sunset 137:158 S '66
Coastal seafood. S. Spitzer. il Holiday 40:70-3+ Jl '66
Cookouts that come from the sea. K. Smith. il Pop Gard 17:44-7 My '66
Festive fish; with recipes. il McCalls 93:110-11+ F '66
Fine fish dishes. B. M. Stover. il Parents Mag 41:71-4+ Mr '66
Fish sauce is the secret. il Sunset 136:171-3 Je '66
Flavor giant: Alaska king crab. il Bet Hom & Gard 44:100 Ap '66
Four superb sauces for fish. S. Sarvis. il Farm J 90:107 Mr '66
Homage to Homarus. C. Claiborne. il N Y Times Mag p56 Je 19 '66
How to bone, bake, stuff your trout; with recipes. il Sunset 137:140-1 Jl '66
In scooped-out oranges, in ramekins, on a salad plate, in a pie; with a can of salmon. il Sunset 136:120-1 My '66
It's both elegant and quick; sole, with recipes. il Sunset 137:132+ D '66
Mousse of merit. C. Claiborne. il N Y Times Mag p 122 S 11 '66
Out of the deep. C. Claiborne. il N Y Times Mag p35 S 4 '66
Porgy and bass. C. Claiborne. il N Y Times Mag p65 My 8 '66
Pretty kettle of poached fish; with recipes and menu by E. Graves. il Life 60:118-19+ My 13 '66
Salmon and trout cook book. P. S. Brown. il House & Gard 129:175+ Mr '66
Scallops; sweets from the deep. E. Alston. il Look 30:110-11 N 15 '66
Seafood classics; with recipes. il Redbook 126:88-9+ Mr '66
Shish of fish; with recipes. C. Claiborne. il N Y Times Mag p21 Jl 3 '66
Shrimp-in-the-rough. J. Hewitt. il N Y Times Mag p48 Ja 30 '66
Shrimply delicious! assorted dishes with recipes and menus. il McCalls 93:126-7+ Ap '66
Spanish Mediterranean: where simple seafood runs to greatness; with recipes. J. Peter. il Look 30:66-7 N 1 '66
Successful recipes, fish on the grill. il Suc Farm 64:73-4 Ag '66
Temptation on a hook. C. Claiborne. il N Y Times Mag p78 Ag 28 '66
To reel in compliments. C. Claiborne. il N Y Times Mag p62 F 6 '66
Worthy of a master chef; mousse of sole. C. Claiborne. il N Y Times Mag p 100+ Ap 24 '66
You can do all sorts of things with scallops. il Sunset 136:183-4 Mr '66
See also
Chowder
Clambakes

Frogs
Are you ready for frogs' legs? Sunset 136:203+ Mr '66

Fruit
Apple salads. il Bet Hom & Gard 44:95-6 S '66
Applesauce made-to-order. il Bet Hom & Gard 44:86 S '66
Cook's discovery: the exotic flavors of litchis and longans, dried or canned; with recipes. il Sunset 137:134-5 Jl '66
Everybody likes apples! with recipes. il B. L. Henry. Farm J 90:76-7+ O '66
Fancy fruits for summer. il Ebony 21:108+ Jl '66

COOKERY—Fruit—*Continued*

Fruit cocktail specials. il Bet Hom & Gard 44:103-4 Mr '66

Fruits just seem to say summer! with recipes. il Good H 162:110-26 Je '66

Fruits of autumn. il Look 30:102-3 O 18 '66

Fruit's the finale. il Sunset 136:148-50 F '66

Have an avocado; with recipes. il Bet Hom & Gard 44:108 My '66

Honeydew balls with cranberry ice, raspberry wedges and a cantaloupe ring; with recipes. il Bet Hom & Gard 44:66-7+ Ag '66

It's the berries. il Ebony 21:174+ Je '66

Jiffy recipes for the fruits of the season. H. S. Witty. il Flower Grower 53:30+ S '66

Luscious ways to fix fresh peaches. il Farm J 90:56-7 Ag '66

Make and freeze cherry purée. D. Groves. il Farm J 90:64-5 Jl '66

Orange: perfection in the round; with recipes. E. Alston. Look 31:78-9 Ja 24 '67

Real life with tropical fruit; with recipes. M. Kaytor. il Look 30:71+ Mr 22 '66

Regal rhubarb cobbler. V. V. Voboril. il Good H 162:148 My '66

Specialty of the season, strawberries; with recipes. il Redbook 127:75+ Je '66

Successful recipes; new ways with cranberries. il Suc Farm 64:67-8 N '66

Successful recipes, oranges go fancy. il Suc Farm 64:139-40 Mr '66

Summer fresh fruits mix deliciously; with recipes. il Sunset 137:108-9 Jl '66

Summertime splendors; fresh fruit and berry treats. G. Maddox. il Todays Health 44:56-7+ Je '66

Taste of the tropics: exotic fruits; with recipes. il McCalls 93:106-8 Je '66

Ways to use winter grapefruit. il Sunset 136:173-4 F '66

Wealth of fruit in wine; with menu and recipes by E. Graves. il Life 61:86-8+ Jl 15 '66

What next with applesauce? il Bet Hom & Gard 45:101-2 O '66

With juice of pineapple guava; with recipes. Sunset 137:206+ O '66

World of fine cooking: the lemon. M. Field. il McCalls 94:84+ O '66

Game

Art of game cookery. K. Smith. il Pop Gard 17:54-6 D '66

Cooking game. T. Trueblood. il Field & S 71:20+ D '66

Fairgame for dinner: rabbit; with recipes. il Look 30:116-17+ D 13 '66

How to cook a tough buck. J. H. Barton. il Field & S 71:40-2+ Jl '66

New ways to serve venison. Sunset 137:198 N '66

Wild game cookery. G. Maddox. il Todays Health 44:56-61 O '66

Leftovers

Never overlook leftovers. C. Claiborne. il N Y Times Mag p40-1 Jl 24 '66

Liquors

Liqueur cook book; with recipes. il House & Gard 130:283+ N '66

Meat

About pâtés; with recipes. N. S. Hazelton. Nat R 18:529+ My 31 '66

Beef specialties from cattle country. Mrs F. Bruning. il Suc Farm 64:72 Ag '66

Bride makes London broil; with recipes. il McCalls 94:106 Ja '67

Bride serves veal scallopini; with recipe. il McCalls 93:130 Ag '66

Budget meals from large cuts of meat; with recipes. Redbook 127:76-7+ Je '66

California food: hamburgers, hamburgers, hamburgers, hamburgers, hamburgers; with recipes. M. Kaytor. il Look 30:65-6 Je 28 '66

Canned meats, mother's big helpers. B. M. Stover. il Parents Mag 41:61-4 Ap '66

Corned beef specials. il Bet Hom & Gard 44:101-2 N '66

Family friend: the one-dish meal; with recipes. il McCalls 93:116-17+ S '66

Feast for the season; suckling pig. C. Claiborne. il N Y Times Mag p23 D 25 '66

Flavor galore. C. Claiborne. il N Y Times Mag p72 Ja 15 '67

For buffet brunch, basque eggs with ham. il Sunset 136:193-4 Je '66

Frank cut-ups! il Bet Hom & Gard 44:128 My '66

Great American steak. il Ladies Home J 83:102-3+ Je '66

Great meats in good company: lamb & veal; with recipes. il Good H 162:116-31 Ap '66

Here is hearty variety for hungry beefeaters. G. Maddox. il Todays Health 44:50-5 My '66

Home off the range; sirloin steak au Roquefort; with recipe. il McCalls 93:98-9 Je '66

Hot dog cookbook; excerpts. W. I. Kaufman. il Ladies Home J 83:100-1+ Je '66

How to cook a steak. il Bet Hom & Gard 44:91 F '66

It's a different hamburger when you make the bun. il Sunset 136:184 My '66

It's hot pork pie for supper; with recipe. il Sunset 137:204 O '66

Lamb in fall; with winter menu. C. Claiborne. il N Y Times Mag p 110+ O 23 '66

Lamb; with recipes. P. Cannon. il Ladies Home J 83:104-5+ Ap '66

Little loaf that tries; meat loaf. C. Claiborne. il N Y Times Mag p 100 Mr 27 '66

March fare. C. Claiborne. il N Y Times Mag p62 Mr 6 '66

Meat loaves. il Bet Hom & Gard 45:83-4 Ja '67

Meat loaves using vegetables; with recipes. Sunset 137:243 O '66

Meat pies; with recipes. R. Hanna. il Suc Farm 64:84-5+ O '66

Meatballs-in-sauce, as appetizers or for an open-house buffet; with recipes. il Sunset 138:90-1 Ja '67

Only way with lamb; with menu and recipes. E. Graves. il Life 60:124-5+ Mr 18 '66

Our complete guide to smoked pork. R. Holmberg. il Bet Hom & Gard 44:72-8+ S '66

Our complete guide to steak; with recipes. il Bet Hom & Gard 44:76-80+ F '66

Pâté cook book. J. A. Beard. il House & Gard 130:211+ S '66

Perfect way to serve lamb; with recipe. M. Kaytor. il Look 30:66-7+ My 17 '66

Pork, all ways. il Bet Hom & Gard 44:105-6 O '66

Pork: an old favorite in a new light; with recipes. il McCalls 93:106-7+ N '66

Pork is for feasting. C. Claiborne. il N Y Times Mag p 109 N 6 '66

Pork: it's getting better all the time; with recipes. B. L. Henry. il Farm J 90:94-7 F '66

Potted meat: terrines; with recipes. M. Kaytor. il Look 30:88-9 Ap 5 '66

Quick-cooking with flank steak; with recipes. il Sunset 137:127 Jl '66

Roast classics. il Ebony 22:162+ N '66

Simmer dinners: the cooking liquid should barely tremble, never boil. il Sunset 136:166-7 Mr '66

Some surprises from your meatman: boneless beef; with recipes. il Sunset 137:194+ O '66

Spring ways with ham. il Bet Hom & Gard 44:89-90 Ap '66

Steak that's both good and good-looking. il Sunset 136:228+ My '66

Tangy corned beef tempts everyone; with recipes. G. Maddox. il Todays Health 45:54-9 Ja '67

Things to do with canned meats. il Ladies Home J 83:88 Ag '66

To please a gourmet. C. Claiborne. il N Y Times Mag p77 F 13 '66

Two Turkish delights: potted lamb and sweet cake. M. Kaytor. il Look 30:98-9 F 22 '66

Use the fireplace for a sausage roast; with recipes. il Sunset 137:228 O '66

Vivid Latin roll of beef; with recipes and menu by E. Graves. il Life 61:144-6+ N 11 '66

Well dressed budget meats. il McCalls 94:134-5+ O '66

See also

Cookery—Game

Meat

Stew

Mushrooms

Mushroom cook book. K. S. Nelson. il House & Gard 130:131+ Ag '66

World of fine cooking. M. Field. il McCalls 93:59-60+ F '66

Nuts

Cooking with little pine nuts. il Sunset 137:170 N '66

Nut desserts; with recipes. R. Hanna. il Suc Farm 64:108-9+ F '66

Poultry

Basic steps in turkey roasting. il Sunset 137:214+ N '66

Bird for spring; stuffed squab. C. Claiborne. il N Y Times Mag p96+ Ap 17 '66

Bride serves duckling à l'orange; recipes. il McCalls 94:46 N '66

COOKERY—Poultry—*Continued*
Chicken breasts, stuffed and fried. il Sunset 137:106 Ag '66
Chicken classic. C. Claiborne. il N Y Times Mag p 130 N 27 '66
Chicken for dinner; with recipes. il Sunset 137:138-9 S '66
Chicken, hunters' style, with tomatoes, and other things. il Sunset 136:206 My '66
Chicken in a pickle. C. Claiborne. il N Y Times Mag p54 Ag 14 '66
Everyone for chicken! B. M. Stover. il Parents Mag 41:71+ F '66
Fare for fall. C. Claiborne. il N Y Times Mag p 110 O 16 '66
Holiday drama: birds baked in clay; with recipes. P. Cannon. il Ladies Home J 83: 118-19+ N '66
Like chicken livers? il Bet Hom & Gard 44: 88 F '66
Plump potted bird; with recipes and menu. E. Graves. il Life 60:100-2 F 25 '66
Savory stuffing cook book. L. Brooks. il House & Gard 130:189+ D '66
Stuffings can be different! il Bet Hom & Gard 44:86 N '66
Successful recipes, holiday stuffings. il Suc Farm 64:53-4 D '66
Things you've never done before with chicken! with recipes. R. Holmberg. il Bet Hom & Gard 44:74-7+ My '66
Turkey stuffings, French, Italian, Greek, German, Scandinavian. Sunset 137:180+ N '66
Turkey's now a bird of parts; with recipes. il Sunset 137:170 O '66
When father carves; with menu. C. Claiborne. il N Y Times Mag p 132+ N 20 '66
Why not roast chicken tonight? il Sunset 136:194-5 Ap '66

Rhubarb
May's a good month to cook with rhubarb. il Sunset 136:234-5 My '66
Rhubarb, taste of springtime. il Farm J 90: 100-1+ Ap '66

Rice
Of course it is rice; risotto. il Sunset 136:84-6 F '66
'Round the world rice recipes. G. Maddox. il Todays Health 44:56-9 Ag '66

Vegetables
Artistry with spring asparagus. il Sunset 136:108-9 My '66
Baked tomato surprise; with recipes. il Sunset 137:173 S '66
Boiled potato; with recipes. M. Kaytor. il Look 30:54-5 Ap 19 '66
Close-up on corn; with recipes. M. Kaytor. il Look 30:56 Jl 12 '66
Cooking with dow foo. il Sunset 136:190+ F '66
Cooking with shallots; with recipes. il Sunset 137:140-1 S '66
Discover the artichoke; with recipes. il Ladies Home J 83:108-9+ Ap '66
Each artichoke is the nest for a Hollandaise poached egg. il Sunset 136:226+ Ap '66
Elegant cabbage. C. Claiborne. il N Y Times Mag p90+ S 18 '66
French fries grandma never fixed. il Ladies Home J 83:106-7+ S '66
Fresh vegetables. il Ebony 21:164+ My '66
Green and golden squash. B. L. Henry. il Farm J 90:72-3+ S '66
Green garden peas; with recipes. M. Kaytor. il Look 30:84-5 Ag 23 '66
Hearty artichokes! il Bet Hom & Gard 44: 99-100 Mr '66
How to do great new things with canned vegetables. il Bet Hom & Gard 44:72-5+ Ap '66
If you bring home some eggplant; with recipes. Sunset 138:95 Ja '67
New tomato taste tempters. B. L. Henry. il Farm J 90:58-60 Ag '66
No matter what's on top, there's spinach underneath. il Sunset 136:210 Je '66
Perfect french-fried onion rings. il Bet Hom & Gard 44:86 F '66
Potato casseroles, plain or fancy. B. L. Henry. il Farm J 90:108-9 Mr '66
Potatoes, sweet and white. il Bet Hom & Gard 44:101-2 N '66
Really special ways to serve cabbage. il Bet Hom & Gard 44:103 S '66
Redbook's specialty of the season: sweet peppers; with recipes. il Redbook 127:50+ S '66
Redbook's specialty of the season: sweet potatoes; with recipes. il Redbook 128:102+ N '66
Season's fare (cont) H. S. Witty. Flower Grower 53:53 Je; 6-7 Ag; 10+ S '66

Specialty of the season, artichokes; with recipes. il Redbook 126:64+ Ap '66
Squash spells summer. C. Claiborne. N Y Times Mag p51 Ag 7 '66
Summer vegetables. il Bet Hom & Gard 44: 85-6 Ag '66
Sweet and spicy baked beans. il Sunset 136: 221 Ap '66
Tasty stuff; stuffed vegetables. C. Claiborne. il N Y Times Mag p61 F 20 '66
Tomatoes are tops; with recipes. il McCalls 93:98-9+ Ag '66
Vegetable pies? H. H. Boileau. il Parents Mag 41:84-6 O '66
Vive la vegetable! Good H 162:223 Mr '66
World of fine cooking; not-so-lowly potato. M. Field. il McCalls 93:78+ Mr '66
Your garden's first gift to the table asparagus. P. Sheppard. il Farm J 90:104-5+ Ap '66
Zucchini! with recipes. il Bet Hom & Gard 44:86 Jl '66

Yogurt
Successful recipes; yogurt and sour cream. il Suc Farm 64:111-12 F '66

COOKERY, American
Boiled in a pot Yankee style; New England boiled dinner; with recipes and menu by E. Graves. il Life 61:124-5+ O 7 '66
Fascinating foods of the U.S.A. B. S. Brown. See issues of Good housekeeping
Heirloom southern recipes go modern. L. W. Gilliam. il Farm J 90:102 Ap '66
Pennsylvania Dutch specials. R. Hanna. il Suc Farm 64:70-1 Ag '66
Southern treats. J. Hewitt. il N Y Times Mag p50 Je 26 '66
Take a handful of bugloffe: Puritan cooking; excerpt from For meate and medicine. A. Leighton. il Am Heritage 17:66-71 O '66
Try a New England Thanksgiving; with recipes and menu. G. Maddox. il Todays Health 44:54-9 N '66
Vermont year round cookbook; excerpts. L. A. Kent. il Ladies Home J 83:106-7+ Ap '66

COOKERY, Arabian
Appetizers from Araby. C. Claiborne. il N Y Times Mag p 130+ D 4 '66

COOKERY, Austrian
Christmas eve supper in Salzburg; with recipes. il Look 30:58-9 D 27 '66

COOKERY, Bahamian
Out-island galley. M. Dreyer. Yachting 119: 182 F '66

COOKERY, Chinese
Cooking with dow foo. il Sunset 136:190+ F '66
Mao tse-Tung's big Chinese restaurant. J. Cameron. Esquire 66:66+ O '66

COOKERY, Czech
Traditional Czech foods. R. Hanna. il Suc Farm 64:68-9+ Je '66

COOKERY, Dutch
Dutch treats from the Tulip festival. R. Hanna. il Suc Farm 64:76-7+ My '66

COOKERY, English
And at long last they are doing something about the food. J. Crosby. il Esquire 66: 66-7+ Jl '66

COOKERY, European
Europe's best-loved recipes. il McCalls 93: 116-26+ Mr '66
Time-honored holiday cookies of middle Europe; with recipes. il Sunset 137:156+ D '66

COOKERY, Foreign. See Cookery, International

COOKERY, French
Ballet of flames for Christmas; with recipes and menu by E. Graves. il Life 61:108-9+ D 16 '66
Everyone's in the kitchen; gourmet trend. il Time 88:74-80+ N 25 '66
Flavor of Provence. C. Claiborne. il N Y Times Mag p 110 O 2 '66
French-American Thanksgiving. il Sunset 137: 74 N '66
Modern French culinary art; cookies and petits fours; with recipes; excerpts. H. P. Pellaprat. il Ladies Home J 83:102-3+ D '66
Pâté cook book. J. A. Beard. il House & Gard 130:211+ S '66
Penn photographs the foods of France. il Vogue 148:250-5+ O 1 '66
Pinnacle for a peasant dish: choucroute garni from Alsace; with recipes and menu by E. Graves. il Life 62:88-9+ Ja 20 '67
Potted meat; terrines; with recipes. M. Kaytor. il Look 30:88-9 Ap 5 '66
Table talk with six famous chefs; interview, ed. by C. Claiborne. il McCalls 93:96-7+ Je '66

COOKERY, French—*Continued*
Three recipes from Mme Claude Serreulles. Vogue 148:270 O 1 '66
Two kitchens in Provence. M. F. K. Fisher. New Yorker 42:29-36 Ag 27 '66
Worthy of a master chef; mousse of sole. C. Claiborne. il N Y Times Mag p 100+ Ap 24 '66

COOKERY, German
German-American Thanksgiving. il Sunset 137:75 N '66

COOKERY, Greek
Always on Sunday; with recipes. il McCalls 93:104-5+ Je '66
Greek-American Thanksgiving. il Sunset 137: 77 N '66
Greek meat sauce with a pasta or vegetables; with recipes. il Sunset 137:236+ O '66
House & garden's Greek cook book. L. S. Pappas. il House & Gard 129:139+ F '66

COOKERY, Hawaiian
Hawaii cookbook & backyard luau; excerpt. E. A. Toupin. il Ladies Home J 83:122-3+ N '66
Love tat luau! A. C. Hubert. Motor B 118: 43-4+ Jl '66

COOKERY, Hungarian
Bride makes Hungarian goulash. il McCalls 94:88 O '66

COOKERY, Indian
Change-of-pace dishes in the Thanksgiving tradition; excerpts from The art of American Indian cooking. N. Nichols. il Farm J 90:70-1+ N '66

COOKERY, Indian (East Indian)
Luncheon from India. il McCalls 93:118-19+ S '66

COOKERY, International
Barrendipity game; not finding something where you most expect it. Time 87:56 Ja 28 '66
Dallas: charity supper, plus. il Ladies Home J 83:92-3+ O '66
Line a day (cont) P. Cannon. il Ladies Home J 83:92 F '66
Menus from embassy row; symposium. il McCalls 93:118-24+ S '66
Turkey stuffings, French, Italian, Greek, German, Scandinavian. Sunset 137:180+ N '66
Why it tastes different over there. N. S. Hazelton. il Nat R 18:220+ Mr 8 '66
Wise woman's diet; with recipes. G. J. Christakis. il Redbook 128:37-43+ Ja '67

Terminology
Guide to dining out in another language. Bet Hom & Gard 44:78+ Ap '66

COOKERY, Irish
Art of Irish cooking; excerpts. M. Sheridan. il Ladies Home J 83:112-13+ Mr '66

COOKERY, Italian
As American as fried ravioli. C. Claiborne. il N Y Times Mag p 100+ My 1 '66
Eating surprises in Italy. il Sunset 136:176+ Mr '66
Gnocchi is simply Italian for lumps. il Sunset 136:196+ My '66
Italian-American Thanksgiving. il Sunset 137: 73 N '66
It's *cannoli* and it's Sicilian. il Sunset 136: 180 My '66
It's Italy's famous zuppa inglese, but you make it with mixes. il Sunset 136:184 Ap '66
Of course it is rice: risotto. il Sunset 136:84-6 F '66
Pasta! with recipes; excerpts. E. Gendel. il Ladies Home J 84:78-9+ Ja '67
Pizza-plus; with recipes. il McCalls 93:94-5+ Jl '66
Sweets for San Giuseppe; zeppole. C. Claiborne. il N Y Times Mag p72 Mr 13 '66
Why not an open mind about pizza? with recipes. Sunset 137:171 S '66
See also
Macaroni

COOKERY, Jamaican
From a new Jamaica inn; old island specialties; with recipes. M. Kaytor. il Look 30: 48-50 Mr 8 '66

COOKERY, Jewish
Season's delightful Jewish traditions and food. F. K. Hirschfeld. il Bet Hom & Gard 44:74+ D '66

COOKERY, Kuwaiti
Supper at the Kuwait embassy. il McCalls 93:122-4 S '66

COOKERY, Latin American
Vivid Latin roll of beef; with recipes and menu by E. Graves. il Life 61:144-6+ N 11 '66

COOKERY, Lenten. See Lenten menus

COOKERY, Marine
Fresh look at galley psychology. B. Davis. il Motor B 117:28-9+ My '66
Fuss-free way to your skipper's heart. R. L. Williamson. il Motor B 117:97+ Ja '66
Good food from the galley; with recipes. S. M. Fertitta. il Look 30:64-8 Je 14 '66
Out-island galley. M. Dreyer. Yachting 119: 182 F '66
Stout hearts and strong stomachs; seamen's fare of 1700's and 1800's contrasted with today's. Motor B 117:96+ Ja '66

COOKERY, Mediterranean
Season's fare (cont) H. S. Witty. Flower Grower 53:8 D '66

COOKERY, Mexican
Art of Mexican cooking; with recipes and menu; excerpt. J. Aaron and G. S. Salom. il Ladies Home J 83:78-9+ Jl '66
At this easy-going Mexican picnic you eat tacos with your fingers. il Sunset 136:154-5 Je '66
Fresh corn tamales. il Sunset 136:182 Je '66
Have a Mexican torta. il Sunset 137:110 Ag '66
Hot tortilla appetizers; with recipes. il Sunset 138:101 Ja '67
Huevos for breakfast; with recipes. C. Claiborne. il N Y Times Mag p75-6 My 15 '66
Instead of doughnuts, buñuelos; with recipe. il Sunset 137:193 O '66
Mexican eating in Tucson and Nogales. il Sunset 138:60-1 Ja '67
Mexican main dishes. il Bet Hom & Gard 44: 105-6 Je '66
Mexico's topopo is a tasty main dish salad; with recipe. il Sunset 137:210 O '66
Setting a Mexican table. C. Claiborne. il N Y Times Mag p 110+ Mr 20 '66

COOKERY, Ornamental
Into the kitchen to make a tasty cream puff tree; with recipe. il Sunset 137:60-1 D '66
Merry gingerbread; cuckoo clock and a Swiss chalet; with recipes. il McCalls 94:102-3+ D '66

COOKERY, Outdoor
Cook-out. . .country style. il Bet Hom & Gard 44:73-4 Ag '66
Cookouts unlimited; with recipes. il Redbook 127:80-1+ Ag '66
Good ideas for outdoor eating. il Sunset 137: 104 Jl '66
Moveable feast. J. Hewitt. il N Y Times Mag p51 My 29 '66
Place for the cook in the garden. il Sunset 136:88-93 Je '66
Try outdoor cooking with a flair. G. Maddox. il Todays Health 44:54-7 Jl '66
See also
Barbecue cookery
Camp cookery

COOKERY, Puerto Rican
Puerto Rico: island of good tastes. B. S. Brown. Good H 162:142 F '66

COOKERY, Quantity
Cooking for a crowd; with recipes. il Ladies Home J 83:120-1+ N '66

COOKERY, Russian
Stopping at Pojarski's: Pojarski cutlet. C. Claiborne. il N Y Times Mag p 110+ S 25 '66

COOKERY, Scandinavian
Dining in Scandinavia. S. Spitzer. il Holiday 40:90-2+ N '66
Scandinavian-American Thanksgiving. il Sunset 137:76 N '66

COOKERY, Spanish
Formal dinner, Spanish style. il McCalls 93: 121+ S '66
Spanish Mediterranean: where simple seafood runs to greatness; with recipes. J. Peter. il Look 30:66-7 N 1 '66

COOKERY, Swedish
How the Swedes celebrate the longest day; midsummer. il Sunset 136:160 Je '66

COOKERY, Swiss
It's braid bread. il Sunset 136:98-9 Ap '66

COOKERY, Turkish
Two Turkish delights; potted lamb and sweet cake. M. Kaytor. il Look 30:98-9 F 22 '66

COOKERY, Venezuelan
Venezuelan tea party. il McCalls 93:120+ S '66

COOKERY, West Indian
Caribbean cook book. E. L. De Ortiz. il House & Gard 131:137+ Ja '67

COOKERY books. See Cookbooks

COOKERY by children
Easy desserts children can make. J. Hunt. il Parents Mag 41:87 O '66
Let's start to cook; excerpts. N. B. Nichols. il Farm J 90:51-5+ Jl '66
Little cooks make themselves some little strawberry cakes. il Sunset 137:96-7 Ag '66

COOKERY by children—*Continued*
Our teenage cook. M. F. Williams. See issues of Good housekeeping
Project for junior cooks; holiday salad and rolls. il Farm J 90:69 N '66
COOKERY by men
Artists in the kitchen; favorite foods and recipes of some opera singers. P. Gravina. il Opera N 30:26-9 Mr 19 '66
Chefs of the West. See issues of Sunset
Detroit: the men show off. il Ladies Home J 83:88-91+ O '66
Great American gourmet. N. S. Hazelton. Nat R 18:115 F 8 '66
He likes to cook (cont) il Bet Hom & Gard 44:70-1+ Ap; 82 My '66
If I had to practice cannibalism. . . J. Beard's methods. J. Skow. il Sat Eve Post 239:28-31 Jl 30 '66
COOKERY contests. See Cookery—Competitions
COOKERY on yachts. See Cookery, Marine
COOKIE jars
Cookie jars. J. Mebane. il Bet Hom & Gard 44:29+ O '66
COOKIES
Baking ahead for Christmas. il Sunset 137:176+ N '66
Best bar cookies. il Bet Hom & Gard 44:95-6 S '66
Christmas artist in the kitchen; with recipes. il Sunset 137:64-7 D '66
Christmas cookie fantasy; with recipes. il Parents Mag 41:76-9+ D '66
Country kitchen cookies. B. L. Henry. il Farm J 90:80-3 D '66
Modern French culinary art; with recipes; excerpts. H. P. Pellaprat. il Ladies Home J 83:102-3+ D '66
Old-fashioned bar cookies; with recipes. il Redbook 127:104-5+ S '66
Redbook's Christmas cookbook. il Redbook 128:82-91+ D '66
Simply great Christmas cookies. il Bet Hom & Gard 44:72+ D '66
Successful recipes, bar cookies. il Suc Farm 64:79-80 My '66
Sugarplum cookies; with recipes. il Seventeen 25:128-9+ D '66
Sweetest story; with recipes. il McCalls 94:76-7+ D '66
There's lots of good baking in Let's start to cook. N. B. Nichols. il Farm J 90:52-3+ Jl '66
Time-honored holiday cookies of middle Europe; with recipes. il Sunset 137:156+ D '66
'Tis the season for chocolate and mistletoe; with recipes. G. Maddox. il Todays Health 44:54-9 D '66
Two tasty cookies; with recipes. il Sunset 137:189 O '66
We have a neighborhood cookie bake. Mrs A. Grauer. il Farm J 90:78 D '66
COOKING. See Cookery
COOKING thermometers. See Thermometers, Cooking
COOKING up a storm; drama. See Feinstein, J.
COOKING utensils. See Kitchen utensils
COOKS
Frenchman in the kitchen: A. Roblin; with recipes. C. Kentfield. il Holiday 40:66-8 Ag '66
Seven top chefs hold a summer cook-in; with recipes. M. Kaytor. il Look 30:44-7 S 6 '66
Table talk with six famous chefs; interview, ed. by C. Claiborne. il McCalls 93:96-7+ Je '66
COOLED cameras. See Cameras
COOLEY, Donald G.
Hot-weather target: your heart. Read Digest 89:104-6 Ag '66
COOLEY, Harold Dunbar
Bailing out the cotton industry; research and promotion bill before Senate agricultural committee. J. Duscha. Reporter 34:28-9 My 5 '66
COOLEY, Margaret, and McQuade, Kate
(ed) Book review (cont of) New books appraised. See issues of Library journal
—and others
(ed) New books appraised. See issues of Library journal
COOLING
See also
Jet airplane engines—Cooling
COOLING of the earth. See Earth temperature.
COOLING of water
See also
Electric water coolers
COOMBE, B. G. See Jackson, D. I. jt. auth.

COON, Hayden G. and Cahn, R. D.
Differentiation in vitro: effects of sephadex fractions of chick embryo extract. bibliog Science 153:1116-19 S 2 '66
COON hunting. See Raccoon hunting
COONEY, Timothy J.
Civil service unionism; how to avert another strike. Nation 202:88-9 Ja 24 '66
about
Sense in civil defense. Nation 202:509 My 2 '66
COONS, Albert Hewett
Telltale glow. R. Campbell and N. Genet. il por Life 60:66-7 F 18 '66
COONS, Steven Anson
Uses of computers in technology; with biographical sketch. Sci Am 215:46, 176-84+ bibliog (p314) S '66
COOP, Robert
Departmental newsletters, they aren't worth it! Am City 81:157-8 Ag '66
COOPER, Arnold C.
Small companies can pioneer new products. Harvard Bsns R 44:162-4+ S '66
COOPER, Caroline Wesley
College coed at seventy-six. il pors Ebony 22:79-80+ D '66
COOPER, Douglas J.
You own $10,000,000 worth of gems. Esquire 66:181-5+ D '66
COOPER, Gloria (Vanderbilt) See Vanderbilt, G.
COOPER, Henry
Blood at the Arsenal. E. Shrake. il por Sports Illus 24:20-3 My 30 '66
Ready for the bloodletting. E. Shrake. Sports Illus 24:74+ My 23 '66
COOPER, Herbert L. and Rubin, A. D.
Synthesis of nonribosomal RNA by lymphocytes: a response to psytohemagglutinin treatment. bibliog Science 152:516-18 Ap 22 '66
COOPER, Joseph D. and Miller, D. L.
And some are bigger than others. Mod Phot 30:56-8+ My '66
COOPER, Louis Z.
German measles; with biographical sketch. Sci Am 215:15, 30-7 bibliog (p 130) Jl '66
COOPER, Madeline L. See Aronson, L. R. jt. auth.
COOPER, Martin
Before Broadway. Opera N 30:8-12 Ap 9 '66
Pierrot of Paris. Opera N 30:6-7 My 7 '66
COOPER, Max D. and others
Restoration of gamma globulin production in agammaglobulinemic chickens. bibliog Science 151:471-3 Ja 28 '66
COOPER, R. G. See Bannerman, R. M. jt. auth.
COOPER, Richard N.
Carlyle was wrong. New Repub 155:22-4 S 10 '66
COOPER, Richard T.
Hardest campaign of Paul Douglas' career. New Repub 155:9-10 O 22 '66
COOPER, Wyatt, family
Private world: Connecticut house of Mr and Mrs Wyatt Cooper. il Vogue 147:180-91 F 1 '66
COOPERATION
See also
Electric plants, Cooperative
Latin America
Five in Bogotá; Andean summit. Time 88:28 Ag 26 '66
COOPERATION, Agricultural. See Agriculture, Cooperative
COOPERATION, Inter-American. See Inter-American relations
COOPERATION in education. See Colleges and universities—Cooperation
COOPERATIVE agriculture. See Agriculture, Cooperative
COOPERATIVE associations
Giant step, by C. T. Ellis. Review
Sat R 49:35 Je 18 '66. T. C. Sorensen
See also
Agway, incorporated
National rural electric cooperative association
COOPERATIVE associations, Wholesale
Out of business, by FTC order; Robinson-Patman act invoked on Southern California jobbers, inc. J. Ridgeway. New Repub 154:13-14 F 12 '66
COOPERATIVE cataloging. See Cataloging, Cooperative
COOPERATIVE commonwealth federation. See Political parties—Canada
CO-OPERATIVE extension service. See United States—Federal extension service

COOPERATIVE living establishments. See Collective settlements

COOPERATIVE marketing. See Marketing, Cooperative

COOPERATIVE research. See Research, Cooperative

COOPERSMITH, Stanley
Strict homes, happy children. R. Brecher and E. Brecher. McCalls 93:66-7+ Jl '66

COPE, Jack
Kathy's papa; story. New Yorker 42:207-8 O 8 '66

COPE, James K.
New kind of trophy hunt. pors Outdoor Life 139:66-7+ Ja '67

COPE, Myron
Aches and pains and three batting titles. Sports Illus 24:30-4+ Mr 7 '66
Half a glass of fresh blood on Saturday morning. Sat Eve Post 239:84-6+ N 19 '66
Joe Torre: the last of the great catchers. Sat Eve Post 239:84-6+ Jl 2 '66
Last cigar for a last hurrah? Sat Eve Post 239:107-8+ Mr 26 '66
Rich, full life of a bad guy. Sat Eve Post 239:88-91 F 12 '66
El Spahnie of los Tigres. Sports Illus 25:26-8+ Jl 4 '66
Texas, football: fierce, frantic, fabulous. Sat Eve Post 239:83-7 S 24 '66

COPE, Peter R.
Zurabatic cartwheel. Flying 78:69 My '66

COPELAND, Eugene
Salt transport organelle in artemia salenis (brine shrimp) bibliog Science 151:470-1 Ja 28 '66

COPELAND, George
Impressionist; interview, ed. by W. W. Cushing. por Opera N 31:6-7 N 5 '66

COPELAND, Pamela C.
Oriental porcelain frivolities. Antiques 89: 709-17 My '66

COPENHAGEN

History

Mayors, Moreno, and a marriage. M. Connelly. il Sat R 50:54+ Ja 7 '67

Hotels, restaurants, etc.

At home with the Danes. H. Sutton. il Sat R 49:40-1 Ag 13 '66

COPEPODS
Culture of a planktonic calanoid copepod through multiple generations. E. J. Zillioux and D. F. Wilson. bibliog il Science 151: 996-8 F 25 '66
Polyteny: a source of cryptic speciation among copepods. I. A. McLaren and others. bibliog il Science 153:1641-2 S 30 '66

COPERNICUS, Nicolaus
Origins of the Copernican revolution. J. R. Ravetz. il Sci Am 215:88-95+ bibliog(p 152) O '66

COPLAND, Aaron
Contemporary scene: excerpt from address. May 1966. por Sat R 49:49 Je 25 '66

about

Records: Tender land. il por Opera N 31:34 S 10 '66

COPLANS, John
Art news from Los Angeles (cont) Art N 65:57 Sum '66
Los Angeles: object lesson. Art N 64:40+ Ja '66

COPLEN, Leonard, and Johns, Robert
Tape cartridge comes of age. Electr World 76:30-2+ N '66

COPLEY, Gregory R.
Aviation down under. Flying 79:82-4 Ag '66

COPLEY, John Singleton
Cover; reproduction of Daniel Crommelin Verplanck. Am Artist 30:4 F '66

about

John Singleton Copley: a balanced view; excerpts from introduction J. D. Prown. il Antiques 89:380-3 Mr '66

COPPER
Copper and the role of isopods in degradation of organic matter. W. Wieser. bibliog il Science 153:67-9 Jl 1 '66
Copper artifacts: correlation with source types of copper ores. A. M. Friedman and others. il Science 152:1504-6 Je 10 '66
Copper's problem. Time 88:86 Jl 22 '66
Ease the shortage. Time 87:90+ Mr 18 '66
Great copper shortage. il Newsweek 67:73 F 21 '66
Nature note. Sci N 90:361 O 29 '66
See also
Umangite

Prices

Copper camaraderie; Frei, Kaunda agreement. il Time 88:105-6 D 9 '66
Copper prices test of persuasion. il Bsns W p42-3 S 17 '66
Perilous prosperity of Anaconda. T. O'Hanlon. il Fortune 73:116-21+ My '66

Stockpiling
See Stockpiling

COPPER engraving. See Engraving

COPPER industry and trade

Chile

Chile's copper beckons once again. il Bsns W p76+ O 1 '66

United States

See also
Anaconda copper mining company

Zambia

Copper caper; plan to blow up bridge over Kafue River. il Newsweek 68:104 N 21 '66
New troubles hit African copper; trade boycott of Rhodesia reduces output in Zambia. Bsns W p 151 N 12 '66

COPPER mines and mining
Why the free world hungers for copper; production in Africa and Latin America hampered by racial conflict, political squabbles, and strikes. il Bsns W p34-5 Ja 7 '67

Congo (capital Kinshasa)

Crisis over copper; nationalized Union minière. il Time 89:31 Ja 13 '67

COPPER silicates
Shattuckite and planchéite: a crystal chemical study. H. T. Evans, jr. and M. E. Mrose. bibliog il Science 154:506-7 O 28 '66

COPPER smelting. See Smelting

COPPER thieves. See Thieves

COPPERHEAD snakes
Day on snake mountain; snake-hunting. W. B. Allen, jr. il Outdoor Life 137:40-3+ F '66

COPPOLINO, Carl Anthony
Doctor is charged with two perfect murders. il pors Life 61:34 Ag 5 '66
Neighbors in Fox Run. il por Time 88:24 Ag 5 '66
Quiet life. il por Newsweek 68:28 Ag 8 '66

COPPOLINO, Carmela M.
Neighbors in Fox Run. il por Time 88:24 Ag 5 '66

COPPOLINO trial. See Trials (murder)

COPTIC church
See also
Ethiopic church

COPYING processes
ALA issues book on copying methods for use in libraries. Pub W 190:47 S 19 '66
Carbonless paper; streamlines forms preparation; Green Bay, Wis. R. Petreat. il Am City 81:120+ Ag '66
Copying, duplicating and printing. il Duns R 88:pt2 136-7+ S '66
Hardest duplicating job Xerox ever faced. il Fortune 74:140-3+ N '66
Put all reproduction equipment in one place and save; Middleton, Ohio. D. W. Kothe. il Am City 81:106-7 Ap '66
Teaching machines: the impact of new devices on educational publishing; summary of addresses at January meeting of the Master printers section, Graphic arts institute of New England, inc. Pub W 189:103-5+ Mr 7 '66
3M's self-help plan; setting up physically handicapped in copying-service businesses. il Bsns W p62 D 3 '66
Trying to duplicate the success of Xerox; more companies putting out copying machines. il Bsns W p66+ O 22 '66
See also
Photography—Copying

COPYISTS
Copy cat; A. Arnstein. il Time 88:58 D 23 '66

COPYRIGHT
Computers and copyrights. C. G. Benjamin. Science 152:181-4 Ap 8 '66
Copyrights for computer publication urged. Sci N 89:299 Ap 23 '66
Duty and copyright problems in importing books and sheets; summary of addresses at meeting of publishers, March 29, 1966. M. Nicholson; A. I. Demoy. Pub W 189:40-3 My 9 '66

COPYRIGHT—*Continued*

Papa's troubled legacy; Hemingway-Hotchner decision leaves unresolved legal problems. J. Tebbel. il Sat R 49:30-1+ Ap 9 '66

Pique at biography: A. E. Hotchner's Papa Hemingway. il Time 87:50 F 11 '66

See also
Property, Intellectual
Royalties

Music

Sweet Sue; writer of Hello, Dolly! sued for copyright infringement. il Time 87:44 Ap 22 '66

Unauthorized reprints

Book piracy looms in Cuba. Pub W 189:79 Ap 18 '66

Ginzburg contests bootleg promiscuity handbook. Pub W 189:53 Mr 7 '66

Piracy or champerty? H. Hughes piracy law suit against Random house. il Newsweek 68:54-5 Ag 8 '66

Report accord reached on Formosa piracy issue. Pub W 189:58 My 30 '66

Sentences reported in Formosa piracy case. Pub W 189:68 F 28 '66

Solution for Taiwan book piracy proposed. Pub W 190:56-7 Jl 4 '66

Great Britain

Britain extends copyright to four territories. Pub W 189:49 My 16 '66

United States

ABPC-ATPI report on copyright technology. Pub W 190:57-8 O 31 '66

Concise guide to copyright. il Writer 79:26-9 F '66

Copying caper. il Newsweek 68:76 Ag 8 '66

Copyright and government; need for definition of publication of the United States government. C. G. Benjamin. il Library J 91:881-6 F 15 '66

Copyright law revision. Wilson Lib Bul 40:670 Ap '66

Copyright subcommittee foresees early report. il Pub W 189:27-8 Ap 4 '66

Education and the copyright law. J. Cass. Sat R 49:53-4 My 21 '66

ETV communications satellites raise new copyright issues. R. H. Smith. Pub W 190:46 S 5 '66

House judiciary committee approves copyright bill. Pub W 190:48-9 O 10 '66

House judiciary committee gets copyright bill. Pub W 190:53 O 3 '66

It depends on what kind of idea it is. H. F. Pilpel. Pub W 189:64 F 28 '66

Licensing system: making copies of material from books and periodicals on royalty basis; proposal by Authors league of America, inc. il Library J 91:892-3 F 15 '66; Reply. J. Weatherford. 91:2784 Je 1 '66

Melodramatic world of librarians and copyright; report of ALA copyright workshop. R. H. Smith. Pub W 190:40 Ag 1 '66; Discussion. 190:22-3 Ag 15 '66

One infringement or many in a network telecast. H. F. Pilpel. Pub W 190:306-7 Ag 29 '66

Our Model T copyright law. E. Knoll. Reporter 34:39-41 Mr 10 '66; Discussion. 34:8 Ap 7 '66

Problem of commercial copyright: case in Federal district court for the Vermont district. H. F. Pilpel. Pub W 190:52 O 3 '66

Release dates debated at PPA club luncheon. Pub W 189:39-40 Mr 14 '66

Rights and permissions. P. Nathan. See issues of Publishers' weekly

Stockholders' support for copyright revision. R. H. Smith. Pub W 189:36 Ap 11 '66

Toad beneath the harrow knows; Copyright revision bill and photocopying. E. Janeway. il Library J 91:887-91 F 15 '66; Correction. 91:2740 Je 1 '66

Trade winds; confusion over copyright on Superman. J. Beatty, jr. Sat R 49:6 Ap 23 '66

Anecdotes, facetiae, satire, etc.

KOPY/CHAT; manuscript found when Lincoln Center was being demolished to build a parking garage. Library J 91:6045-6 D 15 '66

CORAL reefs and islands

Descending the Andros Reef. C. L. Smith. il Natur Hist 75:38-43 O '66

Marvels of a coral realm. W. A. Starck, 2d. il Nat Geog Mag 130:710-38 N '66

Oxygen and carbon isotopic composition of limestones and dolomites, Bikini and Eniwetok atolls. M. G. Gross and J. I. Tracy, jr. bibliog il Science 151:1082-4 Mr 4 '66

What do you know about coral? W. S. Kals. il Yachting 120:49+ N '66

See also
Eniwetok

CORAL-REEFS-ISLANDIA NATIONAL MONUMENT (proposed) See National monuments

CORALS, Fossil

Corals as paleontological clocks. S. K. Runcorn. il Sci Am 215:26-33 bibliog(p 150) O '66

CORBATó, F. J. See Fano, R. M. jt. auth.

CORBETT, Scott

Dalmatian coast on the cheap. Atlan 218:125-7 D '66

CORBUSIER, Le. See Le Corbusier

CORCORAN, Barbara

Man in the bicycle cap; story. Redbook 128:92-3 N '66

CORCORAN gallery of art, Washington, D.C.

American art. Am Artist 30:6 My '66

American collection. F. Getlein. New Repub 154:34-5+ My 21 '66

CORDASCO, Frank M.

Federal challenge and peril to the American school; adaptation of address, December 17, 1965 Sch & Soc 94:263-5 Sum '66

Race: fact and feeling. Sat R 49:40 Mr 12 '66

CORDIALS. See Liqueurs

CORDIS, Sister Maria

Villanelle of the foolish virgin; poem. Cath World 202:368 Mr '66

CORDLESS electric appliances. See Electric apparatus and appliances, Cordless

CORDLESS electric clocks. See Clocks, Electric

CORDOBA observatory. See Astronomical observatories—Argentina

el CORDOBéS

El Cordobes. R. Daley. por Vogue 148:114-15+ Ag 1 '66

El Cordobés in the afternoon. P. Crumpet. il Nat R 19:33 Ja 10 '67

CORDOTOMY. See Spinal cord—Surgery

CORDTZ, Dan

Face in the mirror at General motors. Fortune 74:116-19+ Ag '66

Fight for the Rock Island. Fortune 73:140-3+ Je '66

Negro middle class is right in the middle. Fortune 74:174-80+ N '66

There's another generation of whiz kids at Ford. Fortune 75:104-9+ Ja '67

CORDUS, Valerius

Portraits in science; renaissance botanist. T. Robinson. por Natur Hist 75:69-73 Mr '66

CORDWOOD. See Wood as fuel

CORE, Arthur C. See Minus, P. M. jr. jt. auth.

CORE laboratories. See Space stations

CORELLI, Franco

Born to the breed. E. Coleman. por Opera N 30:24-5 F 5 '66

COREN, Alan

Sound of status. Atlan 217:122+ Ap '66

CORFU (island)

Return to Corfu. L. Durrell. il Holiday 40:58-65+ O '66

CORIO, Ann

Ladies' day at the burleyque. M. Smith. il pors Life 61:128-30+ S 16 '66

CORIOLIS force

Nature note. Sci N 90:179 S 10 '66

CORKE, Hilary

Starting summer; poem. New Repub 154:19 Je 11 '66

CORKERYS; story. See O'Connor, F.

CORLISS, Richard

Movies. Nat R 18:694-6 Jl 12 '66

CORMIER, Frank

Johnson and the press. Sat R 49:70-2 S 10 '66

CORN, Nelson S.

All the justice money can buy. B. Bailey. New Repub 154:8-9 Je 11 '66

CORN

Corn to feed children; CPP and CSM food supplements. Sci N 89:361 My 14 '66

Flavin mononucleotide control of glycolic acid oxidase and photorespiration in corn leaves. B. Tregunna. bibliog il Science 151:1239-41 Mr 11 '66

Good corn feeding systems. J. R. Borcherding. il Suc Farm 64:50-1+ S '66

Shelled corn, how to handle it this fall. R. L. Maddex and P. B. Jones. il Suc Farm 64:46-7 Ag '66

Starch-deficient maize mutant lacking adenosine diphosphate glucose pyrophosphorylase activity. C. Y. Tsai and O. E. Nelson. bibliog il Science 151:341-3 Ja 21 '66

CORN—*Continued*
Twin-row corn makes more silage; ed. by R. D. Wennblom. il Farm J 90:30-1+ Je '66
See also
Popcorn

Cultivation

Heat and drought put Clyde Hight's corn growing methods to the big test. C. E. Sommers. il Suc Farm 64:26-7 D '66
How and when to feed corn nitrogen. L. Robertson and L. E. Zeman. il Suc Farm 64:42-3+ F '66
How Clyde Hight plans to grow corn this year. D. Hagen. il Farm J 90:56+ Ap '66
How I farm today. W. J. Conover. il Suc Farm 64:52-3 Mr '66
Narrow row corn, how'd it do? D. Hagen. Farm J 90:28-9+ D '66
Narrow rows pay off; corn growers in Illinois. L. E. Zeman and R. J. Reiman. il Suc Farm 64:36-7+ Ap '66
Narrow rows: will it be thirty-inches or twenty-inches? D. Seim. il Farm J 90:40-1+ F '66
Pop-up fertilizer starts corn off fast. D. Hagen. il Farm J 90:66V Ap '66
Profits hit $100 per acre! il Suc Farm 64: 42-3+ Mr '66
Switch to narrow-row corn? when to change. B. Brantley and P. B. Jones. il Suc Farm 64:48-9+ F '66
They make $120 an acre profit on corn. J. Carlson. il Farm J 90:73-4 Mr '66
This month's cover story. il Suc Farm 64: 60 My '66
Trim $3,600 from corn-growing costs. il Suc Farm 64:42-3 Jl '66

Diseases and pests

How to identify and control corn insects. H. B. Petty. Suc Farm 64:71+ Mr '66
See also
Corn dwarf mosaic

Drying

Dryers that speed up harvest. il Farm J 90: 34-5+ S '66
Ideas for faster corn handling. P. B. Jones. il Suc Farm 64:40-1 O '66
Will it pay to dry corn this year? W. Uhrig. il Suc Farm 64:60 S '66

Harvesting

Fall farming: how to handle all those stalks. J. Russell. Farm J 90:55 N '66
Fewer stops for the corn picker. il Farm J 90:42-3+ O '66
How to cut field shelling losses. P. B. Jones. il Suc Farm 64:56-7 S '66

History

Corn of Coxcatlán. V. Bourjaily. bibliog il Horizon 8:50-5 Spr '66

Hybrids

Heterosis: complementation by mitochondria. R. G. McDaniel and I. V. Sarkissian. bibliog il Science 152:1640-2 Je 17 '66
New kind of corn: high-lysine corn. J. Russell. il Farm J 90:25+ Ag '66

Seeding

Extra bushel a day from planting corn early. D. Seim. Farm J 90:58D My '66
Lots of rumors about fall-planted corn; plastic-coated seed. il Farm J 90:42 Ap '66
Switch to narrow-row corn? why it pays. L. E. Zeman. il Suc Farm 64:46-7+ F '66

Shelling

See Corn—Harvesting

Storage

Corn late? try cold storage. J. C. Herman. Farm J 90:56T O '66

CORN, Sweet
See also
Cookery—Vegetables

CORN dwarf mosaic
Report on maize dwarf mosaic. M. Shurtleff. Suc Farm 64:62 F '66

CORN picking. See Corn—Harvesting

CORN planters
How to get more space between corn plants. Farm J 90:42 My '66

CORN planting. See Corn—Seeding

CORN rootworms
Timed sprays stop resistant rootworms. Farm J 90:46 Mr '66

CORN shelling. See Corn—Harvesting

CORN silage. See Silage

CORN tamales. See Cookery, Mexican

CORNEAL transplants. See Transplantation of organs, tissues, etc.

CORNED beef. See Cookery—Meat

CORNELISON, Merle. See Vaile, H. jt. auth.

CORNELIUS, Ira E. and Greenwood, Frank
Experts recommend top-down approach to smaller RFP's. Tech W 19:30+ Ag 1 '66

CORNELL, Ezra
When Wisconsin pine went to college. E. Swift. il por Am For 72:8-9+ Ja '66

CORNELL, Joseph
Compulsive cabinetmaker. il por Time 88:56-7 Jl 8 '66

CORNELL, S. Douglas
Education for the modern age; address, February 25, 1966. Vital Speeches 32:372-6 Ap 1 '66

CORNELL, Thomas C.
Peace; interview. New Yorker 42:23-5 D 24 '66

CORNELL aeronautical laboratory
Model drive developed by Cornell for study of transonic stability. R. D. Hibben. il Aviation W 84:101+ Ap 25 '66

CORNELL university, Ithaca, N.Y.
Cornell's society for the humanities. Sch & Soc 94:315-16 O 15 '66
Oral history at Cornell. G. P. Colman. il Wilson Lib Bul 40:624-8 Mr '66
Six-year Ph.D. program. Sch & Soc 94:172+ Ap 2 '66
When Wisconsin pine went to college; Morrill land-grant college act of 1862. E. Swift. il Am For 72:8-9+ Ja '66

CORNEO, Gianmarco, and others
Mitochondrial DNA in yeast and some mammalian species. bibliog Science 151:687-9 F 11 '66

CORNFELD, Bernard
Cornfeld's empire. il por Newsweek 69:68+ Ja 16 '67

CORNFORD, John
Journey to a frontier, by P. Stansky and W. Abrahams. Review
New Repub 155:28+ N 12 '66. M. Straight
Journey to the frontier: two roads to the Spanish Civil war, by P. Stansky and W. Abrahams. Review
Sat R 49:39 S 17 '66. S. Weintraub
Meaning of the journey. P. Hatch. Nation 203:102 Jl 25 '66

CORNUELLE, Richard C.
Meandering streams of plenty. Nat R 18:1232 N 29 '66

CORNWALL, Richard
Changing mood. America 114:873-5 Je 25 '66

CORNWALL, England
Bright periods in Cornwall. E. Fay. il Sat R 49:41-2 S 3 '66

CORNWELL, David John Moore
Dare I weep, dare I mourn? story. Sat Eve Post 240:54-6 Ja 28 '67

CORNWELL, George W.
On conservation, propagation, and technology; poem. Am For 72:41 Ja '66

CORONA (electricity)
Many UFOs are identified as plasmas. P. J. Klass. il Aviation W 85:54-5+ O 3 '66
Plasma theory may explain many UFOs. P. J. Klass. il Aviation W 85:48-50+ Ag 22 '66; Discussion. 85:130 O 10 '66
Scientific explanation for the UFOs? J. Lear. il Sat R 49:67-9 O 1 '66

CORONA, Solar. See Sun—Corona

CORONARY artery disease. See Arteriosclerosis

CORONARY thrombosis. See Thrombosis

CORONATION of Poppaea; opera. See Monteverdi, C.

CORONERS
Civics lesson on homicide; coroner's inquest to determine cause of Leonard Deadwyler's death in Los Angeles. S. Alexander. Life 60:29 Je 10 '66
Deadwyler verdict; shooting of Leonard Deadwyler accidental. Time 87:38 Je 10 '66
Let's X out the coroner system. O. Marden. Todays Health 44:88+ N '66
Uneasy calm; inquest verdict on Leonard Deadwyler. il Newsweek 67:43 Je 13 '66
Watts again; testimonies of police officer Jerold Bova and Mrs Barbara Deadwyler. il Time 87:19-20 Je 3 '66
See also
Medical examiners (law)

CORPORAL punishment
Arkansas employs brutal punishment; whipping at Arkansas state penitentiary. Christian Cent 83:1072 S 7 '66

CORPORATE acquisitions
Architect of the autonoplex: N. Cummings of Consolidated foods corp. il Time 87:88 Je 24 '66

CORPORATE acquisitons—*Continued*
Deal between grandchildren; W. R. Grace & co. buys controlling interest in Miller brewing co. il Time 88:108 S 30 '66
Pitfalls of acquisitions. L. A. Casler. il Duns R 87:34-5+ Je '66
P/E analysis in acquisition strategy. D. J. Smalter and R. C. Lancey. il Harvard Bsns R 44:85-95 N '66
Rockwell-Standard's jet-age management. T. J. Murray. il Duns R 87:28-31+ Je '66

CORPORATE giving. See Corporations—Charitable contributions

CORPORATE systems center. See United aircraft corporation—Corporate systems center

CORPORATION law
Managers tighten their grip; new study bolsters 1932 thesis of Berle and Means about who runs companies. il Bsns W p63-4+ N 5 '66
Opening the books; Great Britain's new companies bill. Time 87:96 F 18 '66

CORPORATION schools
Hamburger university; McDonald's corporation training academy. N. Fraser. il Life 61:100 O 21 '66

CORPORATIONS
Business morality: some unanswered and perhaps unanswerable questions. A. S. Miller. bibliog f Ann Am Acad 363:95-101 Ja '66
Corporate mistakes on Wall Street; a company's day-to-day relations with the financial community. T. J. Murray. il Duns R 88:36-8+ O '66
Country called corporate America. A. Hacker. il N Y Times Mag p8-9+ Jl 3 '66
Top of the top. il Fortune 74:226-9 Jl 15 '66
See also
Bonds
Family corporations
Monopolies

Accounting
How do you calculate return on capital? Duns R 88:30 Ag '66
Ins and outs of profits and losses. il Nations Bsns 54:64-7+ Mr '66
Masters of cash-flow management. J. B. Weiner. il Duns R 88:30-2+ Jl '66
Misevaluation of investment center performance. J. J. Mauriel and R. N. Anthony. bibliog f il Harvard Bsns R 44:98-105 Mr '66
New system for divisional control. B. D. Henderson and J. Dearden. il Harvard Bsns R 44:144-6+ S '66
Very private world of Peat, Marwick, Mitchell. T. A. Wise. il Fortune 74:88-91+ Jl 1 '66

Charitable contributions
Beauty checkout; variety of institutions get cosmetic support. Vogue 147:50 F 1 '66
Big business do-gooders; private war on poverty. T. G. Harris. il Look 30:15-19 Ag 9 '66
Corporate giving. R. Moley. Newsweek 67: 104 Je 6; 124 Je 13; 112 Je 20 '66
Preserving corporate philanthropy. L. L. L. Golden. Sat R 49:56 Jl 9 '66
Public obligations and the private corporation. T. C. Sorensen. Sat R 49:24+ My 14 '66
Without trumpet flares; charitable activities by U. S. steel. L. L. L. Golden. Sat R 49:96 D 10 '66

Directories
Fortune directory: 500 largest U.S. industrial corporations. il Fortune 74:230-64 Jl 15 '66
Fortune directory: 200 largest industrials outside the U.S. Fortune 74:147-52 Ag '66

Directors
Big year of executive change; retirement of top executives of prominent corporations. il Bsns W p76-8 Ja 7 '67
Dilemma with directors; comments of members of the president's panel. J. Thackray. il Duns R 88:48-9+ O '66
Directors in demand. il Fortune 74:71-2+ Jl 15 '66
Jersey's board opens door to outsiders. il Bsns W p34+ F 12 '66
Managers tighten their grip; new study bolsters 1932 thesis of Berle and Means about who runs companies. il Bsns W p63-4+ N 5 '66
Overseas pilot without a chart; E. B. Lovell's study of Changing role of the international executive. Bsns W p 185-6+ S 24 '66
What it takes to make the board; study by Heidrick & Struggles, inc. il Bsns W p93-4 Mr 12 '66

Finance
Another record quarter for profits, but; with chart. U S News 60:100 My 2 '66
Attack on profits; concerning Gardner Ackley's Chamber of commerce speech. H. Hazlitt. Newsweek 67:90 My 23 '66
Bear market, for sure; tailspin won't be reversed soon. il Bsns W p41-2 O 8 '66
Beleaguered profits. il Fortune 74:36+ O '66
Business borrowing surges ahead. il Bsns W p 100-2 Ja 22 '66
Corporate earnings keep on climbing. il Bsns W p88+ Ap 30 '66
Douglas aircraft's stormy flight path. J. Mecklin. il Fortune 74:166-71+ D '66
Earnings still show plenty of bounce. il Bsns W p42-3 O 15 '66
Eurodollars at work. Time 87:111 My 20 '66
Everybody's dividend; corporate profits. il Time 87:94 My 13 '66
Financial variables in international business. D. T. Smith. Harvard Bsns R 44:93-4+ Ja '66
Full quarter; reports of profits. il Time 87: 91 Ap 29 '66
Growing from within may pay off faster; stockholders lose when companies merge. il Bsns W p44+ S 17 '66
How to improve investment decisions; impact of economic and management sciences. J. E. Fanning. bibliog f il Harvard Bsns R 44:156-8+ Ja '66
Labor's just complaint; President's wage-price guideposts. Commonweal 83:573-4 F 18 '66
Lifting corporate curtains; shedding more light on financial affairs in Europe. Fortune 73:68+ Mr '66
Master of arts; M. Riklis. Newsweek 68:84+ S 12 '66
Money should be tight but not out of reach; outlook for '67. il Bsns W p42-4 D 31 '66
More growth for profits; with editorial comment. il Bsns W p25-6, 164 F 12 '66
New interest in incentive financing; study of twenty-nine life insurance companies. S. L. Hayes, 3d. il Harvard Bsns R 44:99-112 Jl '66
New issues reviving, but with a difference. il Bsns W p 120+ Ap 23 '66
Profit. H. C. Wallich. Newsweek 69:71 Ja 16 '67
Profit reports top forecasters' hopes. il Bsns W p33-4 Ap 23 '66
Profits at another record, no sign of a squeeze yet. il U S News 61:54-5 Ag 1 '66
Profits; better than ever. Time 88:100 O 28 '66
Profits go into 1966 still on the rise. il Bsns W p23-4 F 5 '66
Profits still point up. il Bsns W p21-2 Jl 30 '66
Profits up, but not all over; third-quarter reports. Bsns W p39 O 29 '66
Relative optimism. Time 88:90 N 4 '66
Rising profits; another quarter breaks records; with chart. U S News 60:70 F 14 '66
Rosy business, but a thorny market. il Newsweek 68:63 Ag 8 '66
Splits & superlatives; sales and earnings reports. il Time 87:94 F 4 '66
Squeeze showing as profits set another record; with chart. U S News 61:96 N 7 '66
Still soaring; increase in earnings of companies. Time 88:83 Ag 5 '66
Strategies for allocating funds. S. Tilles. bibliog f Harvard Bsns R 44:72-80 Ja '66
Taking & offering stock; good news. il Time 87:92 My 6 '66
Tax those profits. New Repub 155:5-6 S 24 '66
Tips you can dig out of financial reports. il Changing T 20:29-31 Mr '66
Wage gains and profits; does government juggle figures? excerpts from address, November 14, 1966. R. M. Blough. U S News 61:106 N 28 '66
Wall St. converts a slump to profit; convertible debentures; with editorial comment. il Bsns W p 133-4+, 153 Ap 9 '66
Wall Street oracles foresee earnings drop; price-earnings ratio. il Bsns W p 152+ S 24 '66
Wall Street throws out the old rule book. il Bsns W p30-1 S 3 '66
Why all the confusion over profits? J. Q. Jennings. il Nations Bsns 54:106+ S '66
See also
Bankruptcy
Capital investments
Corporations—Accounting

Foreign expansion
See Business—Foreign expansion

CORPORATIONS—*Continued*

Foreign subsidiaries

Antwerp's Texas touch brings in the big ones. il Bsns W p48-9+ F 12 '66

Big, bigger, biggest: American business goes global. R. J. Barber. New Repub 154:14-18 Ap 30 '66

Big daddy stays & grows; Unilever in Africa. il Time 87:90+ Je 24 '66

Business in Mideast walks on shifting sands. il Bsns W p26+ Jl 2 '66

Can Europe catch up with U.S. technology? lucrative opportunities for U.S. business. il Bsns W p60+ O 29 '66

Cultural analysis in overseas operations. J. A. Lee. Harvard Bsns R 44:106-14 Mr '66

Dow chemical banks on a global formula. il Bsns W p84-6+ Ap 2 '66

Exports get an assist; IRS proposal to clarify tax laws affecting U.S. companies overseas. Bsns W p38 Ag 6 '66

Financial variables in international business. D. T. Smith. Harvard Bsns R 44:93-4+ Ja '66

Fine art of raising cash abroad. J. Davenport. il Fortune 73:142-5+ My '66

Going global; growing tendency of U.S. corporations to think and act as global companies. Time 87:84+ Mr 25 '66

Growth slows just a little; U.S. business spending more overseas. McGraw-Hill economic dept. survey. il Bsns W p36+ Ag 6 '66

Hello, dollar! renewed welcome for U.S. investments. Time 87:85B-86 Ap 1 '66

If you can't lick em'; French decisions, regarding management of U.S. firms. Newsweek 67:88+ My 23 '66

Industry's new island in the sun. il Bsns W p66+ F 12 '66

Logistics for the international manufacturer. R. E. McGarrah. Harvard Bsns R 44:154+ Mr '66

New look at investments abroad; NICB survey of investment policies of leading U.S. companies. il Bsns W p92-4+ Mr 26 '66

Overseas pilot without a chart; E. B. Lovell's study of Changing role of the international executive. Bsns W p 185-6+ S 24 '66

President and international operations. M. L. Mace. bibliog Harvard Bsns R 44:72-84 N '66

U.S. companies face guidelines in Canada. Bsns W p34 Ap 9 '66

U.S. firms promised gains by establishing branches abroad. W. S. Beller. Tech W 19:17-18 O 17 '66

U.S. firms realigning French operations; several companies seeking office space in Brussels. L. L. Doty. Aviation W 85:34 Jl 11 '66

Venezuela: there's more to it than oil; ore, power, and new industry lure U.S. companies. il Bsns W p 178-80+ N 12 '66

What U.S. companies are doing abroad. See issues of U.S. news & World report

Names

Fine art of namesmanship. R. Levy. il Duns R 87:51-2 Ap '66

Great renaming game. Fortune 74:357 Jl 15 '66

Growing companies play the name game. il Bsns W p91 F 26 '66

Political activities

See Business—Political aspects

Presidents

On the odds of becoming company president. W. P. Dommermuth. il Harvard Bsns R 44:65-72 My '66

Public relations

See Business—Public relations

Real estate operations

Real estate decisions are different. A. M. Weimer. il Harvard Bsns R 44:105-12 N '66

Reports

See Reports

Size

The 500: a decade of growth. C. J. Loomis. il Fortune 74:212-15+ Jl 15 '66

How's big business doing? Fortune 74:201-2 Jl 15 '66

Social aspects

See Business —Social aspects

Taxation

How war spending is forcing a tax rise. il U S News 62:49-50 Ja 2 '67

Life without the tax credit. il Time 88:105 S 16 '66

Paradise for profits; Liechtenstein. il Newsweek 68:93-5 O 10 '66

Private pension plans in danger? new tax rules. il U S News 61:64-5 O 10 '66

Tax date puts the pinch on cash; federal quarterly tax bite. il Bsns W p 147-8+ Je 11 '66

Valuation

Cash drawdown. il Fortune 74:193 Ag '66

Looking for a new yardstick; conglomerates, worried by low P/E ratios. il Bsns W p 119-20 Ag 20 '66

P/E analysis in acquisition strategy. D. J. Smalter and R. C. Lancey. il Harvard Bsns R 44:85-95 N '66

CORPORATIONS, Government. See Government corporations

CORPORATIONS, Nonprofit
What role for the think tanks? Defense dept. launches study of nonprofit research labs doing military work. il Bsns W p71-2+ My 14 '66

CORPORATIONS and education. See Business and education

CORPS of engineers. See United States—Army —Corps of engineers

CORPSE plant. See Indian pipes (plants)

CORPSES. See Cadavers

CORPULENCE
Advice to dieters from a formerly fat psychiatrist; excerpts from The thin book. T. I. Rubin. Todays Health 44:35+ Jl '66

Are Americans too fat? results of a new survey; U.S. public health service survey. U S News 61:16 N 14 '66

Bipiperidyl mustard, a new obesifying agent in the mouse. R. J. Rutman and others. bibliog il Science 153:1000-2 Ag 26 '66

Fat talk. il Sci Digest 59:32-3 Je '66

Heed the cries of appetite and stay thin. B. Inglis. Vogue 148:146-7+ N 15 '66

Hormone antibody may make people fat. Sci N 90:25 Jl 9 '66

How I lost 180 pounds; interview. ed. by L Robinson. J. McGee. il Ebony 21:36-8+ Jl '66

How to lose weight, and stay thin; excerpt from The thin book by a formerly fat psychiatrist. T. I. Rubin. Read Digest 89:124-7 S '66

Lipolysis in homogenates of adipose tissue; an inhibitor found in fat from obese rats. H. A. Haessler and J. D. Crawford. bibliog il Science 154:909-10 N 18 '66

Sanctuary of adiposity. Time 89:46 Ja 6 '67

Sure, you can lose weight. il Changing T 20:45-7 My '66

Tell me doctor; when should my child diet? A. Lake. Ladies Home J 83:42+ F '66

Were you born to be overweight? P. Deutsch and R. Deutsch. il Ladies Home J 83:60+ S '66

What should be done about teen-age overweight, and what shouldn't. J. Mayer. Ladies Home J 84:36+ Ja '67
  See also
Weight (physiology)
Weight reducing preparations

Anecdotes, facetiae, satire, etc.

Fat power. D. Newman and R. Benton. il Esquire 66:212-15 D '66

CORPUS CHRISTI, Tex.

Police department

Corpus Christi's squad car lawyer. J. Biery. il Reporter 36:43-5 Ja 12 '67

CORREAS, Edmundo
Congress of Tucumán. Américas 18:1-10 N '66

CORRECTIONAL institutions. See Reformatories

CORREGGIO
Correggio's Virgin and Child with the infant St John. J. Maxon. il Art N 65:30-3+ Ap '66

Sensual innocent. il Time 87:78-9 Ap 8 '66

CORREGIDOR surrender. See World war, 1939-1945—Philippines

CORRELATION (education)
Children's art 1966; work following trip to the Aquatic bird house at the Bronx zoo, New York. N. Vibber. il Sch Arts 66:13 S '66

CORRELL, David L.
Imidonitrogen in chlorella polyphosphate. bibliog Science 151:819-21 F 18 '66

CORRESPONDENCE. See Letters

CORRESPONDENCE schools and courses
Project choose:
  Correspondence schools. K. Gilmore. il Pop Electr 24:41-9 F '66

CORRESPONDENTS, Foreign. See Foreign correspondents

CORRIDORS. See Halls

CORRIGAN, Dorothy
  (ed) Across the board. por Library J 91: 212-13, 908, 1372+, 2018, 2438-9, 3130 Ja 15, F 15, Mr 15, Ap 15, My 15, Je 15 '66

CORRINGTON, John William
  Three poets. P. Weiss. Poetry 108:59-62 Ap '66

CORRINGTON, Julian D.
  Nature and the microscope (cont) Natur Hist 75:59-63 My '66

CORROSION and anticorrosives
  Beauty treatments for rusty tools. W. E. Burton. il Pop Mech 125:158-9 Je '66
  Direct evidence for the cathodic depolarization theory of bacterial corrosion. W. P. Iverson. bibliog il Science 151:986-8 F 25 '66
  Save your car from rust and rot. E. D. Fales, jr. il Pop Sci 189:110-14+ Ag '66
  Stress-corrosion failure. P. R. Swann. il Sci Am 214:72-81 F '66
    See also
  International congress on metallic corrosion

CORRUPTION in politics. See Politics, Corruption in

CORRY, John
  American novelist who sometimes teaches. N Y Times Mag p54-5+ N 20 '66
  Man of that board. N Y Times Mag p32-3+ N 6 '66
  Spokesman for the new left. N Y Times Mag p 12-13+ Ja 23 '66
  Style of the Catholic left. Harper 233:58-63 S '66
  Visit to an intellectual hotel. N Y Times Mag p50-1+ My 15 '66

CORSON, Fred Pierce, bp
  Bishop Corson on birth control. Christian Cent 83:977 Ag 10 '66

CORT, David
  Barbara Powers: she married a sky spy. Nation 202:101 Ja 24 '66
  Detroit murder case. New Repub 154:22-4 F 12 '66
  Unreliability of fables; poem. Commonweal 85:372 Ja 6 '67

CORTÉS, Hernándo
  Hernán Cortez and the Mexican Iliad. E. Ardura. il pors Américas 18:23-31 Ag '66

CORTESE, Ross W.
  Life begins at fifty-two. il por Fortune 74: 164 S '66
  Retirement country club. J. Peter. il por Look 30:M22+ D 13 '66

CORTEX, Cerebral. See Cerebral cortex

CORTICOSTEROIDS
  Corticosteroid responses to limbic stimulation in man: localization of stimulus sites. R. T. Rubin and others. bibliog il Science 153: 767-8 Ag 12 '66

CORTISOL. See Hydrocortisone

CORTISONE
  See also
  Hydrocortisone

CORWITH, Jean F.
  Mystery of the brain. Sat R 49:44-5 My 7 '66

CORYELL, Schofield
  Algeria: brakes on revolution. Nation 202: 116-18 Ja 31 '66

COSA nostra. See Mafia

COSBY, Bill
  Bill Cosby talks about life, laughter and the pursuit of wonderfulness; interview. ed. by J. Long. pors Seventeen 26:94-5+ Ja '67
    about
  Color him funny. il por Newsweek 67:76 Ja 31 '66
  Life with Bill Cosby. il pors Ebony 21:34-6+ S '66
  Primarily a guy. C. H. Simonds. Nat R 18: 1007-8 O 4 '66

COSBY, Camille
  Life with Bill Cosby. il pors Ebony 21:34-6+ S '66

COSBY, John C. Jr
  LAOS: laymen in mission. Christian Cent 83: 931-3 Jl 27 '66

COSER, Lewis A.
  Some social functions of violence. bibliog f Ann Am Acad 364:8-18 Mr '66

COSGRAVE, Mary Silva
  Life and times of Thomas Bailey Aldrich; address, October 7, 1965. bibliog Horn Bk 42:223-32, 350-5, 464-73 Ap-Ag '66

COSINDAS, Marie
  Show of color. M. R. Weiss. il Sat R 49:45-52 S 24 '66

COSMETIC creams. See Cosmetics

COSMETIC Industry and trade
  Beauty checkout: variety of institutions get cosmetic support. Vogue 147:50 F 1 '66
    See also
  Revlon, incorporated
  Yardley and company

COSMETIC surgery. See Surgery, Facial; Surgery, Plastic

COSMETICS
  Bam! gams; leg make-up. il Mlle 63:78-9 Jl '66
  Beauty bulletin: new ways to manage sun takeup. il Vogue 147:204-9 My '66
  Dressing table talk; beauty masks. il Seventeen 25:10 D '66
  Fun for beauty masks. Seventeen 25:106-7 D '66
  Leg painting: how it begins. il Vogue 148:100-1 Jl '66
  Merchants of Venus. M. Gunther. il Sat Eve Post 239:74-7 D 31 '66
  Truth about magic ingredients in cosmetics; miracle creams: excerpt from Cosmetics: trick or treat. T. Stabile. il Todays Health 45:20-1+ Ja '67
    See also
  Beauty, Personal
  Make-up
  Toilet preparations

COSMETICS for men
  Bulletin for women who take their men seriously; table. Vogue 148:174-7 N 15 '66
  By George! what will they think of next? J. Devaney. il Redbook 128:91+ N '66
  Master plan to separate the men from the boys. Vogue 148:34 N 15 '66
  Putting a new face on father; Revlon's Braggi collection of men's grooming products. il Bsns W p74+ N 12 '66
  Rinse makers glimpse gold in graying males; introduction of Great day, men's hair rinse. il Bsns W p80 Jl 23 '66
  Something... D. Erickson. il Esquire 65:111-13 Je '66
  Tell us, ladies, how should a man smell? symposium. il Esquire 67:128-9 Ja '67

COSMETOLOGY. See Beauty culture

COSMIC clouds. See Matter, Interstellar

COSMIC dust. See Matter, Interstellar

COSMIC physics
    See also
  Astrophysics
  Magnetic field (cosmic physics)

COSMIC rays
  Cosmic tests helpful. Sci N 90:385 N 5 '66
  Cosmic X-ray sources, galactic and extragalactic. E. T. Byram and others. bibliog il Science 152:66-71 Ap 1 '66
  Iron meteorites with low cosmic ray exposure ages. J. C. Cobb. bibliog il Science 151:1524 Mr 25 '66
  Magnesium-28 in rain: produced by cosmic rays. L. Husain and P. K. Kuroda. bibliog il Science 154:1180-1 D 2 '66
  Origin of cosmic rays. G. Burbidge. il Sci Am 215:32-8 Ag '66
  Possibility of maser action in cosmic radio sources. R. McCray. bibliog il Science 154: 1320-3 D 9 '66

    Measurement
  Radiation measurements in space. J. H. Wujek, jr. il Electr World 76:19-21+ Ag '66
  X-ray spectra from three cosmic sources. R. J. Grader and others. bibliog il Science 152:1499-504 Je 10 '66

COSMOGONY
  Star is born; R monocerotis may be surrounded by the beginnings of planetary system. il Time 88:43 D 23 '66

COSMOLOGY
  Observational aspects of cosmology. L. C. Green. il Sky & Tel 31:199-202 Ap '66
  Observational aspects of cosmology; report on conference. T. Page. Science 151:1411-14+ Mr 18 '66
  Opposite of you is uoy; antimatter. F. Warshofsky. il Esquire 66:82-3+ Ag '66
  Where time runs backward; reverse-time universe. Time 88:57-8 S 9 '66
    See also
  Life on other planets
  Universe

COSMONAUTS. See Astronauts

COSMOPOLITAN (periodical)
  Down with pippypo. Newsweek 68:60 Jl 18 '66

COSMOS (satellites) See Artificial satellites, Russian

COSPAR. See International council of scientific unions—Committee on space research

COST
  See also
  Labor cost
    also subhead Cost uder various subjects.
    e.g. Research—Cost
COST (law)
  When you buy a house: how much for clos-
    ing costs? il Changing T 20:30 Jl '66
COST accounting
  Antonov urges cost accounting in USSR;
    excerpts from article. O. K. Antonov. il
    Aviation W 84:103+ Mr 21 '66
COST control. See Cost accounting
COST of advertising. See Advertising—Costs
COST of airplane operation. See Airplanes—
    Cost of operation
COST of college education. See College educa-
    tion, Cost of
COST of food. See Food—Prices
COST of living
  See also
  Budget, Household
  Domestic finance
  Food—Prices
  Purchasing power
  Rent
                Russia
  See also
  Purchasing power—Russia
            United States
  Consumer and wholesale prices; tables. See
    issues of Monthly labor review
  High cost of living, bring it down! Consumer
    Bul 49:30-1 Jl '66
  Mood is militant; union members press for
    wage increases. il Bsns W p47-9 S 24 '66
  Price of scarcity; household and business
    rise forecast. il Time 87:87 Mr 11 '66
  Shift in unions' demands: back to living-
    cost raises. il U S News 60:92-3 Je 27 '66
  Taste of inflation. Nation 203:341 O 10 '66
  Why cost of living keeps going up. il U S
    News 61.26-8 Ag 22 '66
  See also
  Food—Prices
  Index numbers
  Price indexes
  Prices—United States
COST of living adjustments. See Wages—
    Cost of living adjustments
COST of medical service. See Medical service,
    Cost of
COST of sickness. See Medical service, Cost
    of
COST plus incentive fee. See Incentives in
    industry
COSTA, Richard Hauer
  Wells and the cosmic despair. Nation 203:
    222-4 S 12 '66
COSTA E SILVA, Artur da. See Silva, A. da
    Costa e
COSTA RICA
  See also
  Elections—Costa Rica
  Forests and forestry—Costa Rica
        Politics and government
  Moles have it. Newsweek 67:57 F 21 '66
COSTEA, Nicolas, and others
  Light-chain heterogeneity of cold agglutinins.
    bibliog Science 152:1520-1 Je 10 '66
COSTELLO, Clare
  Elizabeth Borton de Trevino. Library J 91:
    1592-3 Mr 15 '66
COSTIGAN, Daniel M.
  Colorful history of color TV. Pop Electr
    25:45-7+ S '66
COSTIGAN, Madeleine
  When you know how, rose pruning is so
    simple. Flower Grower 53:42-4 F '66
COSTIKYAN, Edward N.
  Tammany side of the story. W. D. Ogdon.
    Sat R 49:96-7 My 7 '66
COSTUME
  See also
  Fashion
COSTUME, Theatrical
  Beaton's La Traviata. il Vogue 148:120-3 S
    15 '66
  Costumes by Christine. L. Slater. il Sch
    Arts 65:9-11 My '66
  New house; tailor shops in new Metropolitan
    opera house. F. Stevenson. il Opera N 31:
    24-5 D 31 '66
  On stage! Capezio's costume and shoe ex-
    hibit. il Dance Mag 40:56-7 Mr '66
COSTUME design
  Americans. il Time 88:60-7 S 9 '66
  Bared bodkins; nude fashions at benefit party
    for the New York Shakespeare festival. il
    Time 87:94 Je 24 '66

Bright spirit of Marimekko. il Life 60:60-9
  Je 24 '66
Cardin silhouette; Paris designer for men's
  clothes. il Ebony 21:132-4+ My '66
La dolce vista; Italy's newest spring and
  summer fashions. il Time 87:54 Ja 28 '66
Dress for non-seamstresses: glue-it-yourself.
  il Life 67:68-9 Jl 29 '66
Fine feathered autumn. il Life 61:57-8 O 28
  '66
Paris fall styles full of surprises; photo-
  graphs. J. C. Sauer. Life 61:60-3+ S 2 '66
Pieced in plastic. il Time 87:53 Ap 8 '66
Princess turns pro. il Life 61:70+ S 9
  '66
Spanish fashion's vigorous trio: Pertegaz,
  Rovira, Berhanyer. J. A. Zill. il Look 30:68-
  70+ N 1 '66
Switch in time to design; fashions of G.
  Beene. il Life 61:53-4+ S 23 '66
  See also
Costume, Theatrical
        Study and teaching
New dress form helps home economics stu-
  dents. il Sci N L 89:54 Ja 22 '66
COSTUME designers
  Americans. il Time 88:60-7 S 9 '66
  California shapes the style. il Bsns W p48-9+
    Ag 13 '66
  Dean of American designers: A. Lowe.
    G. Major. il Ebony 22:136-8+ D '66
  Pacemakers in the world of fashion; Negro
    designers. il Ebony 21:131-2+ S '66
  Paris designers blast short skirts for women,
    long hair for boys. J. Barry. il McCalls
    94:74+ O '66
  Reluctant pilgrim to Paris. S. Alexander.
    Life 61:18 Ag 19 '66
  Short, short, short skirt story. P. L. Levin.
    il N Y Times Mag p36-7+ Mr 20 '66; Same
    abr. with title Short short story of the
    skirt. Read Digest 88:112-14 Je '66
  Spanish fashion's vigorous trio: Pertegaz,
    Rovira, Berhanyer. J. A. Zill. il Look 30:68-
    70 N 1 '66
    See also
  Gernreich, R.
  Parnis, M.
  Pignatelli, L.
  Ratia, A.
  Tiffeau, J.
COSTUME jewelry. See Jewelry
COSTUME jewelry trade. See Jewelry trade
COTO DOÑANA. See Wildlife sanctuaries
COTTAGES
  How a cut-up cottage yielded space un-
    limited; a typical unpretentious Florida
    cottage. il House & Gard 130:92-5 Ag '66
COTTAGES, Prefabricated. See Houses, Pre-
    fabricated
COTTER, Edward F.
  They sail to win; excerpts from International
    book of catamarans and trimarans. Yacht-
    ing 120:29+ S '66
COTTER, Katharine C.
  Roots of failure. NEA J 55:33-5 Ap '66
COTTON, Richard
  William Dawson calls the tune. Reporter 35:
    21-3 Ag 11 '66
COTTON industry and trade
  Bailing out the cotton industry; research and
    promotion bill before Senate agricultural
    committee. J. Duscha. Reporter 34:28-9 My
    5 '66
  Cotton textile arrangement with Japan ex-
    tended; Department announcement, January
    14, 1966; exchange of notes, January 15,
    1966. Dept State Bul 54:180-1 Ja 31 '66
  Decline of cotton factorage after the Civil
    war. H. D. Woodman. bibliog f Am Hist
    R 71:1219-36 Jl '66
  Fourth annual review of the Long-term
    cotton textile arrangement; statement,
    September 27 1966. G. R. Jacobs. Dept
    State Bul 55:903-5 D 12 '66
  Third-year major review of the Long-term
    cotton textile arrangement; statement, De-
    cember 7, 1965. G. R. Jacobs. Dept State
    Bul 54:134-9 Ja 24 '66
  United States and Hong Kong sign cotton
    textiles agreement; Department announce-
    ment with texts of agreement and related
    documents. Dept State Bul 55:467-72 S 26 '66
  United States and Korea amend cotton tex-
    tile agreement; Department announce-
    ment; with texts of U.S. note and letter,
    November 22, 1966. Dept State Bul 55:982-3
    D 26 '66
  United States and Pakistan sign cotton textile
    agreement; Department announcement with
    text of U.S. note; November 21, 1966. Dept
    State Bul 55:937-41 D 19 '66

COTTON industry and trade—*Continued*
U.S. and Singapore reach cotton textiles understanding; Department announcement, August 30, 1966; with letter from government of Singapore and Singapore cotton textile industry restraint schedule. il Dept State Bul 55:509-13 O 3 '66
U.S. and Spain amend cotton textiles agreement; Department announcement; with text of U.S. note, September 14, 1966. Dept State Bul 55:509 O 3 '66

Wages and hours

Earnings in cotton textile mills, September 1965. G. L. Stelluto. il Mo Labor R 89:765-8 Jl '66
Wage chronology: Dan River mills, inc, 1943-65. A. A. Belman. il Mo Labor R 89:48-56 Ja '66

COTTON mills

Employees

Earnings in cotton textile mills, September 1965. G. L. Stelluto. il Mo Labor R 89:765-8 Jl '66
Wage chronology: Dan River mills, inc, 1943-65. A. A. Belman. il Mo Labor R 89:48-56 Ja '66

COTTON textile workers. See Cotton mills—Employees
COTTON workers
Thorntons of Mississippi: peonage on the plantation. P. Good. il Atlan 218:95-100 S '66
See also
Strikes—United States—Cotton workers
COTTONTAIL hunting. See Rabbit hunting
COTTRELL, Richard F.
Slight fund hike predicted for solids. por Miss & Roc 18:15 My 9 '66
COUCH, John A. and others
Sporulation of minchinia nelsoni, haplosporida, haplosporidiiae, in crassostrea virginica, gmelin. bibliog Science 153:1529-31 S 23 '66
COUDERT, Jo
Making a weak marriage work; excerpt from Advice from a failure. Ladies Home J 83: 106-8 My '66
COUGAR hunting. See Puma hunting
COUGARS. See Pumas
COUGH
Coughing: bad or beneficial? S. M. Farber. il Todays Health 44:58-61 Ap '66
COUGHLIN, William J.
Editorial. See issues of Missiles and rockets
COULEE DAM. See Grand Coulee power and reclamation project
COULETTE, Henri
Prizewinner, the real thing, and two others. R. Tillinghast. Poetry 109:118-20 N '66
COULSON, John
If Newman had been at Vatican II; excerpt. Commonweal 83:596 F 25 '66
COULTER, Francis C.
Are vegetables worth growing? Pop Gard 17: 85 Ag '66
Tomato. Horticulture 44:22-3 Ag '66
COULTES, Murray E.
Build the electrolock. Pop Electr 24:60-1 Ja '66
COUNCIL for basic education
Editor's bookshelf. P. Woodring. Sat R 49:98 N 19 '66
Meeting, 1965. M. Smith. Sch & Soc 94:132 Mr 5 '66
COUNCIL for mutual economic assistance
Captive customers Newsweek 68:42+ Jl 25 '66
COUNCIL-manager government. See City manager plan
COUNCIL of community churches. See International council of community churches
COUNCIL of economic advisers. See United States—Council of economic advisers
COUNCIL of Europe
Address to the Consultative assembly of the Council of Europe at Strasbourg, France, May 3, 1966. Thant. il UN Mo Chron 3:51-60 Je '66
COUNCIL of foreign ministers, Geneva, 1954
Final declaration a Geneva, 1954; text. Cur Hist 50:113-14 F '66
Geneva, 1954: the broken mold; substance of Agreements. V. Bator. il Reporter 34:15-18 Je 30 '66
1954 Geneva agreements. K. P. Landon. bibliog f Cur Hist 50:79-84+ F '66
Stacked deck against U.S. at Geneva? U S News 60:36 F 14 '66
Vietnam: peace on the 1954 terms? F. N. Trager. Nat R 18:778-81 Ag 9 '66
COUNCIL on foreign relations
Major new series on Communist China and U.S.A. Pub W 189:65 F 7 '66

COUNCIL on library resources, incorporated
CLR grants: Federal library committee; distribution of machine-readable catalog data. E. Hamer and A. McCormick. ALA Bul 60:235-6 Mr '66
Council on library resources, inc. Wilson Lib Bul 40:583 Mr '66
Lack of machine-readable book data stymies automation advance, says CLR; excerpts from introduction to report. V. W. Clapp. Library J 91:220 Ja 15 '66
Library council grants underwrite three studies. Pub W 189:48 Mr 28 '66
Three catalog-related studies receive grant support from CLR. Library J 91:4064 S 15 '66
COUNCIL on the humanities. See United States—Council on the humanities
COUNCILS and synods
See also
Vatican council. 2d
COUNSELING
Pastoral care and public ministry. D. Browning. Christian Cent 83:1175-7 S 28 '66
Young living; questions and answers. A. Wood. See issues of Seventeen
See also
Marriage counseling
Personnel service in education
Vocational guidance
COUNSELING service, School. See Educational guidance; Personnel service in education
COUNSELL, Norman
Powerboat racers; why do they do it? Motor B 117:156-8 Je '66
COUNTER intelligence. See Secret service
COUNTERESPIONAGE. See Spies
COUNTERFEIT drugs. See Drugs
COUNTERFEITS and counterfeiting
Leonardo of forgers: C. Bojarsky of France. Time 87:28 Je 3 '66
COUNTERGLOW
Photographing the gegenschein. H. G. Solberg, jr. and R. B. Minton. il Sky & Tel 31: 380 Je '66
COUNTERIRRITANTS
See also
Acupuncture
COUNTERPOINT songs. See Songs
COUNTERS (electrons, ions, etc)
Radiation measurements in space. J. H. Wujek, jr. il Electr World 76:19-21+ Ag '66
See also
Geiger-Müller counters
COUNTERS, Kitchen. See Kitchen furniture
COUNTRIES. See Nations
COUNTRY and city. See City and country
COUNTRY clubs
Four buildings for leisure-time activities. il Arch Rec 139:167-72 Je '66
COUNTRY doctors. See Medical service, Rural; Physicians
COUNTRY estates

England

Meet me at the Astors'; Cliveden, full takeover by National trust. il Newsweek 67:43 Je 6 '66
Thirteenth Duke of Bedford sells shoes; exploitation of Woburn abbey. H. Lawrenson. il Esquire 66:86-8+ Ag '66
COUNTRY girl; drama. See Odets, C.
COUNTRY houses
Private world: Connecticut house of Mr and Mrs Wyatt Cooper. il Vogue 147:182-91 F 1 '66
Wizardy of Oise; France. V. Lawford. il Vogue 148:256-9+ O 1 '66
COUNTRY life
See also
Farm life
Ranch life
COUNTRY music. See Folk music, American
COUNTRY newspapers
Home in the country; Washington County news. il Time 88:56 Jl 29 '66
COUNTRY wife; drama. See Wycherley, W.
COUNTRYMAN, Vern
Weltner bill; clear and present danger. Nation 203:16-18 Jl 4 '66
COUNTRYMAN (periodical)
Countryman. E. R. Yarham. il Am For 72:26-9+ Ja '66
COUNTS, Charles
Written for Rose on-the-plane. March 22, 1966. Craft Horiz 26:36-7 Je '66
COUNTY buildings
See also
Courthouses

COUNTY fairs. See Agricultural exhibitions

COUNTY officers
Recommends county-manager system; Pennsylvania. Am City 81:47-8 D '66

COUNTY purchasing. See Purchasing, County

COUPLE across the street; story. See Knowlton, R. A.

COUPONS
See also
Trading stamps

COURAGE
Take courage! E. Farrell. Seventeen 25:112+ Jl '66
See also
Heroes

COURIER-journal
I resign; editor and paper part ways over Viet Nam. W. James. Time 87:63-4 Ap 22 '66

COURNAND, Edward L.
Formal, traditional New Year's party, 1967. H. Kurtzman and N. Quest. il Esquire 67: 96-103 Ja '67

COURNOS, John
Obituary
Nat R 18:972+ O 4 '66. G. Davenport

COURSES of study
Curriculum development by moonlight; annual conference. Sr Schol 88:sup2 Ap 15 '66
Curriculum molder; J. Zacharias. il Time 88:110+ D 16 '66
Directions of curriculum change; excerpts from Curriculum change, direction and process. J. I. Goodlad. NEA J 55:33-7 D '66
Monolithic theories of the curriculum; excerpt from Curriculum and the disciplines of knowledge. A. R. King, jr. and J. A. Brownell. bibliog Sch & Soc 94:190-3 Ap 2 '66
What's new in the curriculum? with study-discussion program, by E. Harris and D. B. Harris. G. K. Hodenfield. bibliog il PTA Mag 61:7-9, 35 Ja '67
See also
Colleges and universities—Curriculum
Health education—Courses of study
High schools—Curriculum

COURT buildings. See Courthouses

COURT calendars
Computerized docket; speedup record of the Los Angeles County Superior court. il Time 88:38 Jl 29 '66
Computers put speed into the law; unclogging court calendars. il Bsns W p 184-6+ O 1 '66

COURT houses. See Courthouses

COURT life. See Courts and courtiers

COURT procedure. See Procedure (law)

COURT reporting (by newspapers) See Newspaper court reporting

COURTENAY, Vincent R.
Flivvers are fun. Motor T 18:80-1 Mr '66

COURTESY
Graces of yesteryear; Soviet Union. Newsweek 69:30 Ja 9 '67
How are your medical manners? E. R. Conger. il Todays Health 44:8-10 S '66
See also
Etiquette
Sportsmanship

COURTESY associates
Capital care for the businessman. il Bsns W p24-5 Jl 2 '66

COURTHOUSES
Requiem for a courthouse; Hudson County, N.J. D. G. Lowe. il Am Heritage 17:26-9+ O '66
Supreme court building for the state of Michigan. il Arch Rec 140:186-8 O '66

COURTNEY, W. R.
R.f. chokes and coils. Electr World 76:48-52 O '66

COURTS
See also
Criminal procedure
Jury
Juvenile courts
Traffic courts

Alabama
Recusation in Alabama; entire Supreme court disqualified itself from legal hassle. Time 88:81 D 16 '66

Iowa
Father and son; Iowa Supreme court decision. Newsweek 67:32 F 21 '66

Kentucky
Prisoners on principle; Kentucky counties **fiscal courts.** Time 88:74 N 18 '66

Mississippi
Yankee lawyers in Mississippi courts. R. Hammer. Harper 233:79-84+ N '66

Russia
See also
Law—Russia

United States
Doing better by themselves; Detroit's federal district trial court. il Time 87:44 Je 3 '66
U.S. courts and the law explosion; symposium, ed. by D. Reische. il Sr Schol 87: 6-21 Ja 7 '66
See also
Justice, Administration of—United States
United States—Supreme court
also subhead Courts under names of cities, e.g. Los Angeles—Courts

Virginia
See also
Justice, Administration of—Virginia

COURTS, County
See also
Los Angeles County, Calif.—Courts

COURTS, Military. See Courts martial

COURTS, Municipal
See also
New York (city)—Courts
St Louis—Courts

COURTS and courtiers
Setting of the Sun King; Louis XIV at Versailles. L. Kronenberger. il Atlan 219:58-61 Ja '67
See also
Kings and rulers

COURTS martial
Conduct unbecoming; lieutenant on the peace line; case of H. H. Howe. J. Rechy. il Nation 202:204-8 F 21 '66; Reply. J. L. Howe. 202:346+ Mr 28 '66
Lieutenant at liberty. Nation 202:413 Ap 11 '66
Right to welsh; Robert G. Wallace; Appeals court reverses conviction. Time 87:61-2 Mr 4 '66
See here, specialist Schmidt. Time 87:67 Ap 8 '66

COURTSHIP
Rocky road to remarriage; excerpts from The world of the formerly married. M. M. Hunt. il McCalls 94:126-7+ O '66
Strange courtship customs of the formerly married; excerpt from The world of the formerly married. M. M. Hunt. McCalls 93:94-5+ S '66 (to be cont)
See also
Dating
Love

COURTSHIP of insects
Courtship in spiders without prior sperm induction. J. S. Rovner. bibliog il Science 152:543-4 Ap 22 '66
Mating speed in male drosophila melanogaster: a psychogenetic analysis. D. W. Fulker. bibliog il Science 153:203-5 Jl 8 '66
Preferential mating versus mimicry: disruptive selection and sex-limited dimorphism in papilio glaucus. J. M. Burns. bibliog il Science 153:551-3 Jl 29 '66
Spermatophore web formation in a pseudoscorpion. P. Weygoldt. bibliog il Science 153:1647-9 S 30 '66

COURTYARDS
Plant a courtyard outside your window. il Pop Gard 17:48-9 D '66

COUSINS, Margaret
Band of angels; story. McCalls 94:78-9 D '66
O. J. Hazeltine; story. Ladies Home J 83: 90-1 My '66
Still waters; story. Good H 162:90-1 Ap '66

COUSINS, Norman
Short story. Sat R 49:26 D 17 '66
Writer as world citizen. Sat R 49:14+ Ag 13 '66

COUSTEAU, Jacques Yves
Working for weeks on the sea floor. pors Nat Geog Mag 129:498-537 Ap '66

COUVE DE MURVILLE, Maurice
France and NATO; address, April 14, 1966. Vital Speeches 32:450-3 My 15 '66
French foreign affairs; address, November 3, 1966. Vital Speeches 33:106-11 D 1 '66
about
Advance man. por Newsweek 68:39-40 O 3 '66

COVELL, Elsie Milotte
Teaching music in the self-contained classroom. NEA J 55:16-18 My '66

COVENT Garden. See London—Covent Garden

COVER design. See Book covers

COVER plants
Here's what groundcovers can do. il Pop Gard 17:8 My '66

COVER plants—*Continued*
Plant groundcovers with bulbs. A. Sutcliffe. il Horticulture 44:32-3+ N '66
Where you can't have a lawn. R. W. Schery. Horticulture 45:26+ Ja '67

COVERED bridges
CBs. New Yorker 42:26-8 S 3 '66
Germantown saves a covered bridge. F. B. Rhoades. il Am City 81:41 My '66

COVERED passages. See Breezeways

COVERED wagons. See Wagons

COVERLETS
Sleeping cars; pop-art bedspreads. il Look 30:55 Ag 9 '66

COVERS, Book. See Book covers

COVICI, Pascal
Covici: Steinbeck's editor, collaborator and conscience. C. A. Madison. por Sat R 49:15-16 Je 25 '66

COW stanchions. See Barns and stables—Equipment

COWAN, Gary
Beaten by a quarry quandary. A. Wright. Sports Illus 25:120+ S 12 '66

COWAN, Paul
Dying like a true rebel. Nation 203:291-2 S 26 '66
Uneasy silence. Nation 202:136-9 Ja 31 '66

COWANS, Adger
Artist & agent. M. Orovan. il U S Camera 29:54-7+ Ap '66

COWARD, Noel
Echo of laughter; story. McCalls 93:98-9 F '66

about
Song at twilight. Criticism
New Yorker 42:70 Jl 23 '66
Vogue 148:50 Ag 15 '66

COWARD award. See Thomas R. Coward memorial award

COWBOYS
Negro cowboys. P. A. Smith. bibliog Negro Hist Bul 29:107 F '66
See also
Rodeos

Education
Cowhand school. il Time 87:75-7 Je 10 '66

COWBOYS (football club) See Football clubs

COWELL, Henry
Obituary
Am Rec G 32:434 Ja '66. J. Lyons

COWELL college. See California. University—Santa Cruz campus

COWES, Roberto A.
Gold of Coclé. bibliog Américas 18:18-25 F '66

COWEY, A. See Weiskrantz, L. jt. auth.

COWLES, John, 1898-
Cowles knows how. L. L. L. Golden. Sat R 49:100 Je 11 '66

COWLES communications, incorporated
Cowles buys ten magazines and three weekly newspapers. Pub W 190:46 S 19 '66

COWLEY, Malcolm
Fresh look at Faulkner. por Sat R 49:22-6 Je 11 '66
Solitude of William Faulkner; excerpt from Faulkner-Cowley file. por Atlan 217:91-8+ Je '66
Three memories of the jazz age; Winter tenement: 1920; Ezra Pound at the Hotel Jacob: 1921; Voices from the home: 1923; poems. Sat R 49:47 Jl 30 '66

COWRIES
Cowry menagerie. A. G. Melvin. il Hobbies 71:130 S '66

COWS
All cows are mean. J. O. Harvey. il Harper 233:81-5 S '66
See also
Dairying

Care
Are those new barns really worth it? free stalls. B. Hardy and J. Russell. il Farm J 90:34-5+ My '66
Those critical five days; dairy. M. L. Weldy. il Suc Farm 64:53+ O '66
Why rest cows? Farm J 90:38Q Je '66
See also
Calves—Care

Diseases and pests
See also
Mastitis

Feeding
Are DHIA rules out of date? il Farm J 90:A8 Jl '66
Cows fed metal screws to improve diets. Sci N 90:328 O 22 '66

Feeds often; gets more milk. C. E. Ball. il Farm J 90:56X O '66
Hay that's as good as grain. N. Reeder and D. Hagen. il Farm J 90:28-30 Mr '66
High return over feed costs. J. R. Borcherding il Suc Farm 64:30L Ap '66
How I feed for high production. J. R. Borcherding. il Suc Farm 64:44+ Je '66
Milk production of cows on protein-free feed. A. I. Virtanen. bibliog il Science 153:1603-14 S 30 '66
Thyro stops a production slump. L. A. Baker. il Farm J 90:A10 Jl '66

Grading and standardization
Raising and selling dairy replacements. D. Vilstrup. il Suc Farm 64:54-5+ Mr '66

Milk production
See Milk—Production

COWS, Sacred. See Cows in religion, folklore, etc.

COWS in religion, folklore, etc.
Beef on the table; Hindu-Muslim rioting over sacred cows. America 115:639 N 19 '66
Casualty list; rally for national ban on cattle slaughter. il Time 88:48 N 18 '66
For mother cow; clash over slaughter of cows by Moslems. il Newsweek 68:66 N 21 '66
Hindus demand total ban on slaughter of cows. Christian Cent 83:1432 N 23 '66
In search of the seekers of truth; holy men of India. K. Singh. il N Y Times Mag p42-3+ Ja 8 '67
Nature note; Bos taurus. il Sci N 90:464 D 3 '66
Violence in India; cow riots. il Sr Schol 89:25-6 D 9 '66
Where cows eat and people starve. il U S News 61:111 N 21 '66

COX, Alva I, Jr
Art, technology and education; excerpt from address, February 1966. Christian Cent 83:862-4 Jl 6 '66

COX, Annis
Flow; poem. Liv Wildn 29:19 Aut '65
Mountain meadow; poem. Liv Wildn 29:31 Wint '65

COX, Arthur M.
What does U.N. peacekeeping mean? Sat R 49:19-22 My 14 '66

COX, David J.
Sedimentation of an initially skewed boundary. bibliog Science 152:359-61 Ap 15 '66

COX, Harvey
Age-old conflict in a new form. Life 61:70+ O 21 '66
Geneva, 1966. Commonweal 84:525-8 Ag 19 '66
How to kill God. Look 30:104+ O 18 '66
Let's end the Communist-Christian vendetta. Christian Cent 83:1375-9 N 9 '66
Secular city. Commonweal 85:134-6, 426-7 N 4 '66, Ja 20 '67
What's right with Christmas. McCalls 94:56+ D '66

about
Main Street; a job for the church. H. Smith. America 114:689-91 My 14 '66
Puritanism moribundus. J. Hart. Nat R 18:847-50 Ag 23 '66
Secular city revisited. R. J. O'Connell. America 114:545-8 Ap 16 '66

COX, Hugh
Shot in the dark. pors Outdoor Life 137:56-9+ Mr '66

COX, James J.
Help your child to a career. Todays Health 44:29-31+ D '66

COX, John W.
Would you have jumped? Sci Digest 59:77-81 Je '66

COX, Robert E.
(ed) Gleanings for ATM's. See issues of Sky and telescope

COX, Roger L.
Hamlet's hamartia: Aristotle or St Paul? Yale R 55:347-64 Mr '66

COX, Wally
On the fringe. H. Frankel. Sat R 49:31 Mr 19 '66

COX, William S.
Bill Cox on catamaran developments. il Yachting 120:28+ O '66
New concepts for Bermuda racers. por Motor B 117:22-3 Je '66

about
Skipper's test. il por Time 88:50+ S 9 '66
Vindication in the Mallory. H. Whall. il Sports Illus 25:116-18 S 12 '66

COX broadcasting corporation
How a broadcaster spreads its net; community antenna cable and microwave systems. il Bsns W p57-8+ D 3 '66

COXE, Louis
Suite for the equinox; poem. Poetry 108:9-10 Ap '66

about

Poetry chronicle. L. Mueller. Poetry 107:258-63 Ja '66

COXEY, Jacob Sechler
Rebel in a wing collar. G. A. Gipe. il pors Am Heritage 18:24-9+ D '66

COXSACKIE viruses
Endocarditis in mice infected with coxsackie virus B₄. G. E. Burch and others. bibliog il Science 151:447-8 Ja 28 '66

COY, Robert E.
Power inductors. Electr World 76:33-5+ N '66

COYNE, Joanne
Los amigos. il por Library J 91:329-31 Ja 15 '66

COYNE, John R. jr
Pornographic convention; reprint. bibliog por Library J 91:2768-73 Je 1 '66

COYNE, Walter
Presidential scholars, 1966. Am Ed 2:12-13 S '66

COYOTE hunting
Come hither coyote. H. Bradshaw. il Field & S 71:44-5+ D '66
Conning and killing cunning coyotes. R. Cantwell. il Sports Illus 25:61-4 N 7 '66

COZUMEL ISLAND
Cozumel: the island with everything. B. Brister. il Field & S 70:68-70+ Mr '66
Yucatan. J. Faber. il U S Camera 30:64-5+ Ja '67

CRAB apples
Dependable crab apples. D. Wyman. il Horticulture 44:20-1+ Mr '66

CRABB, A. L.
Prologue to the last day; story. PTA Mag 61:26-8 D '66

CRABB, Cecil V. jr
Should the United States aid totalitarian countries? bibliog f Cur Hist 50:346-52+ Je '66

CRABS
See also
Cookery—Fish

CRABTREE, Bruce
Outboard boating club of San Diego. Yachting 120:62-3+ Jl '66

CRABTREE, R. G.
One plant, two processes. Am City 81:118-19 My '66

CRACKS in concrete. See Concrete construction

CRACKS in floors, Concrete. See Floors, Concrete

CRADDOCK, John G. See Cromartie, W. J. jt. auth.

CRADLE song; story. See Henderson, R.

CRAFT, Robert
Selective self-portrait. Harper 233:120+ D '66
With Stravinsky in Warsaw; excerpt from Table talk. Harper 232:66-70+ F '66
—See Stravinsky, I. F. jt. auth.

CRAFT horizons (periodical)
Craft horizons: 25th anniversary. A. O. Webb. Craft Horiz 26:12 Je '66
Craft horizons: 25th anniversary. R. Slivka. Craft Horiz 26:13+ Je '66
Twenty-five years of Craft horizons; quotations from past issues. il Craft Horiz 26:68-71+ Je '66

CRAFTS, Edward C.
Our need for bicycle trails. por Parks & Rec 1:435+ My '66
Providing new dimensions. por Parks & Rec 1:826-8+ O '66

CRAFTS. See Arts and crafts

CRAGG, Thomas A.
Ford observatory in California. pors Sky & Tel 31:138-41 Mr '66

CRAIG, Edward Gordon
Obituary
Nat R 18:842 Ag 23 '66. K. P. Shorey

CRAIG, Gordon A.
Before the deluge. Reporter 34:53-4 F 10 '66
Empire of 2,000 characters. Reporter 35:44+ Ag 11 '66
Professional touch. Reporter 34:52+ Mr 10 '66
That famous love affair. Reporter 35:64-5 N 17 '66

CRAIG, H.
Isotopic composition and origin of the Red Sea and Salton Sea geothermal brines. bibliog Science 154:1544-8 D 23 '66

CRAIG, James B.
Guarding our outdoor heritage. Am For 72:14-17+ D '66
Natural beauty, the follow through. Am For 71:12-15+ O '65
Redwood pot begins to boil. Am For 72:38-9+ Ja '66

CRAIG, James M. and Pilcher, K. S.
Clostridium botulinum type F: isolation from salmon from the Columbia River. bibliog Science 153:311-12 Jl 15 '66

CRAIGHEAD, Frank, jr, and Craighead, John
Trailing Yellowstone's grizzlies by radio. il pors Nat Geog Mag 130:252-67 Ag '66

CRAIGHEAD, John. See Craighead. F. jr. jt. auth.

CRAMBE abyssinica
Nature note. Sci N 89:519 Je 25 '66

CRAMER, Francis J.
Ingram filter provides secondary treatment. Am City 81:94-5 O '66

CRAMER, Morgan Joseph, 1906-
Moves. Time 88:72+ Jl 15 '66

CRAMER, William C.
Plea for partnership. por Todays Health 44:64-5 Mr '66
Why an antiriot law was asked, August 1966. U S News 61:39 Ag 22 '66

CRANBERRIES
C is for cranberries. J. Paulson. il Ladies Home J 83:127 N '66
Old crop, new ways. il Sci N 90:434-5 N 19 '66
See also
Cookery—Fruit

CRANE, Hart
New York: two poetic impressions. A. Bartra. il por Américas 18:14-22 O '66

CRANE, Julian C. See Lipe, W. N. jt. auth.

CRANE, Paul
Fall of Nkrumah. America 114:383 Mr 19 '66
Guyana on the eve. America 114:297-8 F 26 '66

CRANES (birds)
Birds that won't die. E. Weeks. Atlan 218:140 O '66
Nesting observation. J. Hancock. il Natur Hist 75:32-3 Je '66
Reporter at large; wild and captive whooping cranes. F. McNulty. il New Yorker 42:31-6+ Ag 6 '66
Whooping crane, by F. McNulty. Review
Time il 88:126+ O 7 '66

CRANES, derricks, etc.
Big trees moved with speed and safety; by crane-and-clam technique; Philadelphia. il Am City 81:92-3 F '66

Radio control
Space-age tools bring cranemen down to earth; radio remote-control. il Bsns W p80-2 O 29 '66

CRANFORD, Raymond
Portrait of a Klansman. S. Alsop. il pors Sat Eve Post 239:23-7 Ap 9 '66

CRANK calls. See Telephone calls

CRANKCASES
That pesky PCV. M. Schultz. il Pop Mech 126:108-11+ S '66

CRANKS and crankshafts
Inchin' up on the 327. E. Rickman. il Hot Rod 20:62-3 Ja '67
Power by the inch. J. McFarland. il Hot Rod 19:44-7 My '66

CRAPPIE fishing
My panfish-on-light-tackle kick. E. A. Bauer. il Outdoor Life 137:56-9+ My '66
Newest lake in Kansas. P. Czura. il Field & S 70:140-2+ Mr '66

CRASH seats, Automobile. See Automobiles—Safety devices and measures

CRATERING explosions. See Explosions

CRATERS
Descent into the fiery pit; Niragongo crater. il UNESCO Courier 19:12-13 Je '66

CRATERS, Moon. See Moon—Surface

CRATERS OF THE MOON NATIONAL MONUMENT
Allow enough time at Idaho's moonscape. il Sunset 136:64+ My '66
Wilderness plan for Craters of the Moon National Monument and the surrounding region. A. W. Smith and W. J. Hart. il Nat Parks Mag 40:4-9 N '66

CRAVEN, Wayne
Hugh Bridport, Philadelphia miniaturist, engraver, and lithographer. Antiques 89:548-52 Ap '66

CRAW, Freeman
Freeman Craw, graphic designer. E. M. Ettenberg. il por Am Artist 30:32-7+ Mr '66

CRAWFISH. See Crayfish

CRAWFORD, Constance
  We four teens in London town; report on the making of A Man for all seasons; ed. by E. Miller. pors Seventeen 26:80-1+ Ja '67

CRAWFORD, H. D.
  British-America's birthplace. il Am For 72:14-17+ S '66
  Knights of the golden horseshoe. il Am For 72:28-31+ N '66

CRAWFORD, James Warren
  Cutter yacht Angantyr. Motor B 118:118-21 Jl '66

CRAWFORD, John D. See Haessler, H. A. jt. auth.

CRAWFORD, John S.
  Fishing lesson. il Outdoor Life 139:50-3+ Ja '67

CRAWFORD, Kenneth
  Washington. See issues of Newsweek

CRAWFORD, Michael H.
  Hemoglobin polymorphism in macaca nemestrina. bibliog Science 154:398-9 O 21 '66

CRAWFORD, Will
  My most unforgettable character. M. Kantor. il Read Digest 89:221-2+ D '66

CRAWLER tractors
  Improved crawler undergoes first trial. G. Alexander. il Aviation W 84:51+ F 21 '66

CRAYFISH
  Crayfish's computer is danger monitor. Sci N 90:136 Ag 27 '66
  Nature note. Sci N L 89:93 F 5 '66
  Release of coordinated behavior in crayfish by single central neurons. D. Kennedy and others. bibliog il Science 154:917-19 N 18 '66
  World's best bass bait; crawfish. H. G. Tapply. il Field & S 71:52 Jl '66

CRAYFISH fishing
  Don't spare the hot sauce. L. Dietz. il Field & S 70:70-2+ Ap '66

CRAZY Horse (Sioux Indian)
  Dream as big as a mountain; 563 feet high memorial to Crazy Horse in Black Hills of S.D. H. Jones. il Sat Eve Post 239:30-1 S 10 '66

CREAM
  Oceans of cream; whipped cream. il Look 30:72-3 O 4 '66

CREAM, Sour
  See also
  Cookery—Cream, Sour

CREAM masks. See Cosmetics

CREAM puffs. See Pastry

CREAMS, Masking. See Cosmetics

CREAMWARE. See Pottery

CREASEY, John
  MWA elects John Creasey as president. Pub W 189:42 Mr 14 '66

CREASING of textiles
  Alteration aid for permanent press garments; Alter-ease. il Consumer Bul 49:43 S '66
  Miracle fabrics and new equipment add up to easier laundering. R. Charles. il Parents Mag 41:89-92+ O '66
  Permanent-press shirts (cont) il Consumer Rep 31:232-3 My '66
  What's new with permanent press. J. Gillies and N. Bowden. Farm J 90:66-7 N '66

CREATION
  Life in a test tube. P. R. Gastonguay. Cath World 204:27-31 O '66
  See also
  Cosmogony

CREATION (literary, artistic, etc)
  Age of discovery. V. Wagner. il Parks & Rec 1:904-5 N '66
  Artist-teacher. J. Ottiano. il Sch Arts 65:27-32 F '66
  Artists as they see themselves; artists' own words on the creative process. K. Kuh. Sat R 49:20 My 28 '66
  Creating a climate for creativity. D. E. Day. bibliog f Sch & Soc 94:330-4 O 15 '66
  Creative art in the classroom curriculum. M. L. Wooten. il Sch Arts 66:4-8 D '66
  Creative drive. C. Himber. il N Y Times Mag p86+ Je 5 '66
  Creative spirit. il Dance Mag 40:37-41 Mr '66
  Creative weaving. B. A. Hadley. il Sch Arts 65:36-7 F '66
  Creativity and mental health: are they related? B. B. Wolman. il Dance Mag 40:42-4 Mr '66
  Creativity+junk=. . : Eastman Kodak course in imagination for executives and technicians. il Sci N 90:177 S 10 '66
  Creativity; questions and answers. A. Hurwitz. il Sch Arts 65:30-3 Ja '66
  Gettysburg; movement in photographs. il U S Camera 29:64-5 Ap '66

How you can help your child be creative. M. B. Sharkey and M. Longwell. il Farm J 90:95-6+ Ap '66
Image and imagination. J. R. Brest. il Américas 18:30-3 N '66
Let's have a tiger for dinner. G. Neff. bibliog il Sch Arts 66:5-9 N '66
Note on the universe-building business. H. Jacobs. Writer 79:17-18 Mr '66
Path to visual realization. D. Cyr. bibliog il Design 67:26-30 Ja '66
Poetry from a magic reality; Howard Nemerov's investigation of the creative process. G. Hicks. Sat R 49:39-40 Je 11 '66
They shall have music; report on Projects to advance creativity in education. C. L. Herbert. il Am Ed 2:22 O '66
Ticket in the raffle. J. Christopher. Writer 79:13-15 Je '66
Title III of ESEA offers encouragement for innovation. N. Estes. il NEA J 55:30-2 D '66
Writer as independent spirit; questions to be explored at New York congress; symposium. il Sat R 49:16-30+ Je 4 '66
  See also
  English language—Composition—Creative activities
Inspiration

CREATIVE ability. See Creation (literary, artistic, etc)

CREATIVE playthings, incorporated
  This year give baby an ego-expander. W. K. Zinsser. Life 61:10 D 16 '66

CREATIVE writing. See English language—Composition—Creative activities

CRECHES. See Christmas cribs

CREDIT
  Bankers' brakes. il Time 88:65 Ag 26 '66
  Borrowers keep up the pace. il Bsns W p46 Jl 9 '66
  Buying on credit: the changes coming. Changing T 20:6 Ag '66
  Consumer credit. il Consumer Rep 31:391-4 D '66
  Could long-term credit save you interest costs? R. G. Fowler. Farm J 90:36F Ag '66
  Credit buying: will the U.S. economy itself have to pay later? il Sr Schol 88:10-11+ Ap 29 '66
  Credit gets still tighter. U S News 61:85 S 5 '66
  End to September; relief of bankers and businessmen. Time 89:88 Ja 6 '67
  Fear of credit crisis dulls investors' spirits. il Bsns W p36-7 Mr 12 '66
  Fed flashes new signal easing tight money. Bsns W p22 D 31 '66
  Fiscal and monetary policy; address, September 12, 1966. L. H. Olsen. Vital Speeches 33:24-8 O 15 '66
  Has the credit squeeze gone away? il Bsns W p48+ N 5 '66
  High cost of money is heading downward; Fed's policymakers easing of credit as business lags. il Bsns W p 15-16 D 24 '66
  It's easier to borrow and build. il Newsweek 69:53 Ja 2 '67
  Learning to live with tight money; Fed tightens credit. il Bsns W p35-6 Je 11 '66
  Let the borrower beware! R. C. Jancauskas. il America 115:774-6 D 10 '66
  Life without the tax credit. il Time 88:105 S 16 '66
  Money to get still tighter? U S News 61:63 Ag 1 '66
  Money turns a little easier; why Fed policy is changing. il Bsns W p35-6 D 10 '66
  Nation of bankrupts. America 114:284 F 26 '66
  New interest in incentive financing; study of twenty-nine life insurance companies. S. L. Hayes, 3d. il Harvard Bsns R 44:99-112 Jl '66
  Personal business; borrowing of money. Bsns W p 133-4 Jl 16 '66
  Pinch of tight money, meaning to the U.S. il U S News 61:36-8 Ag 1 '66
  Pitfalls of credit buying. A. Poinsett. il Ebony 21:67-8+ Ap '66
  Real squeeze goes on. il Bsns W p21-2 Ag 27 '66
  So you want to borrow: here's what you're facing. il U S News 61:30-2 Ag 29 '66
  They help families who owe too much; consumer credit counseling service. il Changing T 20:41-4 Jl '66
  What the Fed wants. il Fortune 74:40+ N '66
  Why interest rates are so high, and what you can do about it. il Changing T 20:7-10 N '66

CREDIT—*Continued*
Will tight money get tighter? R. Newcomb.
Nations Bsns 54:38-9 N '66
See also
Agricultural credit
Instalment plan
Loans, Bank
Loans, Personal
Monetary policy

Rating
What makes you a good credit risk? il Chang-
ing T 20:39-40 F '66; Same abr. with title
Are you a good credit risk? Read Digest
88:85-7 Je '66
CREDIT, Agricultural. See Agricultural credit
CREDIT associations. See Credit unions
CREDIT cards
Cashless, but not classless; Rothschild
Frères cards. Time 89:94-5 Ja 6 '67
Charge, Britannia; Barclaycards. Newsweek
68:69-70 Ag 8 '66
Charge it at the bank. Bsns W p 104 O 29
'66
Credit-card premiums; insurance. Time 87:
96+ My 13 '66
Credit cards pick up a British accent. il
Bsns W p92 Jl 2 '66
Enlarging the charge card; BankAmericard.
il Bsns W p42 My 28 '66
New proletariat; implications for society.
Reporter 35:14 D 15 '66
What if you lose a credit card? Bet Hom
& Gard 44:10 Jl '66
When money's tight, just put it on the cuff;
hot test fray in bank merchandising. il
Newsweek 68:84-6 Ag 22 '66
CREDIT life insurance. See Insurance, Life—
Credit aspects
CREDIT unions
Buying credit wisely. H. Black. NEA J 55:
23 My '66
Father Dan the money man; capitalist priest
in Peru. il Time 87:75+ Ap 22 '66
CREEGAN, George
Hansel and Gretel go back to school; drama.
Plays 25:89-92 F '66
Snow White's rescue; drama. Plays 26:92-4
Ja '67

about
Puppet shows promote classic children's
books. il Pub W 189:104-6 F 21 '66
CREEKMORE, J. Howard
Big deal that got away. S. H. Brown.
Fortune 74:164-6+ O '66
Deal done in. il por Time 87:62 Je 17 '66
CREEL, Stephen M.
Our backward medical schools. Atlan 217:46-
50 My '66
CREELEY, Robert
Foot is to kick with. Poetry 109:40-3 O '66
Shame; Reason; Window; To Bobbie; Statue;
Prayer; Flower; Circle; Song: I wouldn't
embarrass you ever; poems. Poetry 107:
318-25 F '66

about
Creeley as narrator. S. Moon. Poetry 108:
341-2 Ag '66
CREELS. See Fishing—Implements and ap-
pliances
CREEPERS (birds)
Look under the bark. K. Legg. Audubon
Mag 68:193-4 My '66
CREGIER, Don M.
World and L.B.J.: President's style in for-
eign policy. Christian Cent 83:859-61 Jl 6
'66
CREMER, Jan
Angry young Dutchman. M. Wolf. Reporter
34:56 Ap 7 '66
CRENNER, James
Notes for a wedding anniversary; Reading
habits; poems. Poetry 109:83-5 N '66
CRENSHAW, Celeste
Boy and girl. il por Newsweek 67:31B F 21
'66
Death of a hooked heiress. D. Schaap. il por
Look 30:19-25 Jl 26 '66
CRÊPES Suzette. See Griddle cakes
CRESCITELLI, Frederick, and Nilsson, S. E.
C.
Electroretinogram of the frog during em-
bryonic development. bibliog Science 151:
1545-7 Mr 25 '66
CRESPI, Henry L. See Katz, J. J. jt. auth.
CRESPIN, Régine
Mediterranean. H. Rosenthal. por Opera N
30:14-15 Ap 2 '66

CRESS
Curlicress in twenty-one days B. C. Kilvert,
jr. Flower Grower 53:44 O '66
CRESWELL, John L.
Mom and dad study the new math. Parents
Mag 41:68-9+ S '66
CRETACEOUS period. See Geology, Strati-
graphic—Cretaceous
CRETE
Antiquities
Reporter at large; Kato Zakro and its re-
lationship to Knossos. J. Alsop. il New
Yorker 42:32-8+ Ag 13 '66
CREWE, Albert V.
Scanning electron microscopes: is high resolu-
tion possible? bibliog Science 154:729-38 N
11 '66
CRIB deaths. See Infant mortality
CRIBS (beds)
Toward a safer baby bed. J. E. Summers. il
Consumer Bul 49:43+ Ap '66
CRICHTON, Robert
Day Mussolini died in Santa Vittoria; story.
Sat Eve Post 239:44-6 D 17 '66
To honor the harvest; story; excerpt from
The secret of Santa Vittoria. Ladies Home
J 84:97-100 Ja '67
CRICK, Sir Francis Harry Compton
Computer, the eye, the soul; excerpts from
Of molecules and men. Sat R 49:53-5 S 3
'66
Genetic code; with biographical sketch. Sci
Am 215:16, 55-60+ bibliog(p 150) O '66
CRICKETS
Evolution of cricket chirps. R. D. Alexander.
il Natur Hist 75:26-31 bibliog(p82) N '66
CRIME and criminals
See also
Capital punishment
Criminal investigation
Criminal law
Criminal psychology
Fraud
Insane, Criminal and dangerous
Mafia
Police
Prisoners, Discharged
Prisons
Punishment
Self defense
Sex crimes
Sterilization of defectives, criminals, etc.
Trials
Woman—Crime

Economic aspects
Bigness & badness; need to be studied. Time
89:64 Ja 13 '67

Identification
See Identification

Law
See Criminal law

Statistics
See Criminal statistics

Arizona
See also
Tucson, Ariz.—Crime

Australia
Germs of violence; A. A. Calwell shooting.
il Newsweek 68:41-2 Jl 4 '66

California
Beware the jabberwock; terrible William-
sons. confidence clan. Newsweek 68:52+
N 21 '66
How can I tell them there's nothing left?
case of Lucille Marie Maxwell Miller. J.
Didion. il Sat Eve Post 239:38-42+ My 7
'66

Canada
Canadian justice; ordeal of Steven Truscott;
case to be reviewed through publication
of I. LeBourdais book. E. Stafford. il Nation 202:614-17 My 23 '66

Communist countries
Crime & Communism. Time 88:40 Ag 5 '66

Florida
Gideon's ironic impact; crime wave following
Clarence Gideon's victory in the U.S.
Supreme court. Time 87:46 Je 3 '66

Great Britain
Britain's aristocrats of crime. L. Malkin. il
Reporter 35:46-8 S 22 '66
British plan: get tough with criminals. il
U S News 61:13 Ag 29 '66

CRIME and criminals—Great Britain—*Continued*
Flourishing legend of the greatest robbery. P. O'Neil. il Life 60:102-6+ Ap 8 '66
Harry's hideaway; capture of H. Roberts. Newsweek 68:58 N 28 '66
In ghastly transcripts, a test of our times; murders by I. Brady-M. Hindley. P. H. Johnson. il Life 61:62+ Ag 12 '66
Moorland murders; verdicts. il Newsweek 67: 52 My 16 '66
Most unusual trial; trial of Ian Brady and Myra Hindley. il Time 87:36+ Ap 29 '66
Pirate's end; O. Smedley charged with murder of P. R. H. Calvert. il Newsweek 68:41 Jl 4 '66
Too late to be happy; posthumous pardon for T. J. Evans. Newsweek 68:56 O 31 '66
Trial begins; Downey-Kilbride-Evans murders. il Newsweek 67:34 My 2 '66
See also
London—Crime

Illinois
Beyond grief; murder of V. Percy. il Time 88:22-4 S 30 '66
Who could kill Valerie Percy? il Life 61:47 S 30 '66

Italy
See also
Mafia

Japan
Tanaka scandal. il Newsweek 68:28+ Ag 29 '66

Kansas
In cold blood, by T. Capote. Review
Commentary 41:77-80 My '66. W. Phillips
Nation 202:158-60 F 7 '66. S. Yurick
Reporter 34:58 Mr 10 '66. J. K. Galbraith

Maine
Blanket over homicide; death of Peter Francis. L. Spiker. il Nation 202:483-6 Ap 25 '66

Maryland
McChan's luck; released convict held on suspicion of murder. Time 88:35 D 30 '66

Massachusetts
When a state tries to clean itself up. il U S News 60:46-8 F 7 '66
See also
Boston—Crime

New Jersey
Blue Cadillac; E. W. Long confesses to killing Penny Van Orden. il Newsweek 67:41 Ap 11 '66

Pennsylvania
Battle of Gobbler's Knob; kidnapping of P. Bradnick. il Time 87:23 My 27 '66
Stalking the terror of Shade Gap; Peggy Ann Bradnick case. M. Mok. il Life 60: 32B-32E My 27 '66
Terror in the Tuscaroras; Peggy Ann Bradnick case. il Newsweek 67:29-30 My 30 '66

Philippines
Public unsafety. Time 88:34+ D 30 '66

Rhodesia
Terror? Zimbabwe African nationalist's kill white settlers. Newsweek 67:52 My 30 '66

Russia
Bourgeois taint. Newsweek 68:51 S 19 '66
Dirty business; economic crimes. Time 88: 26 Ag 26 '66
See also
Juvenile delinquency—Russia

Sardinia
Terror in the hills; triple murder. Newsweek 69:46 Ja 16 '67

Sicily
See also
Mafia

United States
Are we a nation of hoods? P. Johnson. Read Digest 89:127-9 D '66
Bananas is back. Newsweek 67:28 My 30 '66
Businessmen; partners in crimebusting. il Nations Bsns 55:58-62+ Ja '67
Case of the missing millionaire; A. O. Birch. J. Phelan. il Sat Eve Post 239:85-91 D 17 '66
Compassion for punks too much, says Bishop Sheen; excerpts from statement. F. J. Sheen. U S News 62:16 Ja 23 '67
Crime, are you guilty? B. Frisch. il Sci Digest 60:70-7 D '66
Crime in the streets. Commonweal 85:281 D 9 '66

Crime in the U.S: still climbing. il U S News 60:16 Mr 21 '66
Crime reporting; need for professionals; address, February 14, 1966. N. de B. Katzenbach. Vital Speeches 32:351-2 Mr 15 '66
Crime wave, what can be done about it? il U S News 61:46-51 Ag 1 '66
Does law make crime? Sci N 91:11 Ja 7 '67
F. Lee Bailey; renegade in the courtroom. E. Linn. il Sat Eve Post 239:80-2+ N 5 '66
FBI's war on organized crime. J. E. Hoover. U S News 60:102-4 Ap 18 '66
Five serious crimes every minute now; with chart. U S News 61:8 Ag 8 '66
Policeman looks at crime; interview. O. W. Wilson. U S News 61:51-2 Ag 1 '66
Rethinking crime. P. McBroom. il Sci N 90: 305-6 O 15 '66
Rising storm over crime and the courts; with comments. il Sr Schol 88:6-10 Mr 18 '66
Safest large city, 1965. il Am City 81:130+ Je '66
Speaking out; give drugs to addicts so we can be safe. J. J. Goldstein. il Sat Eve Post 239:12+ Jl 30 '66
Stamping out crime; anti-crime bill vetoed by L. B. Johnson. New Repub 155:4 D 10 '66
Suburbs again show biggest crime increase. il Am City 81:22 D '66
Suburbs; made to order for crime. J. R. Moskin. il Look 30:20-7 My 31 '66
To free the captive; Johnson's second annual message on crime. Time 87:29 Mr 18 '66
Victim-induced criminality. M. Fooner. bibliog Science 153:1080-3 S 2 '66
Violence and organized crime. G. Geis. bibliog f Ann Am Acad 364:86-95 Mr '66
We're taking too many liberties with freedom. A. H. Sypher. il Nations Bsns 53: 29:30 D '65
Winter months highest in violent crime. Sci N 90:170 S 10 '66
You can end crime in your city's streets. B. L. Garmire. il Nations Bsns 55:63-5 Ja '67
See also
Automobiles, Theft of
Criminal statistics
Gambling
Mafia
Negroes in the United States—Crime
United States—Federal bureau of investigation
also subhead Crime under names of cities, e.g. New York (city)—Crime

History
Secret rulers, by F. J. Cook. Review
Sat R 50:92 Ja 14 '67. J. Haas

Vietnam (Republic)
Aid to Vietnam; business corruption nurtured on US aid. New Repub 154:9 Je 18 '66

CRIME and the press
Four-letter word called news; objections to American bar association's proposals to safeguard criminal cases against prejudicial publicity. R. L. Tobin. Sat R 49:79-80 D 10 '66
Free press & fair trial; silencing the bar and the police; American bar association's report. Time 88:96+ O 7 '66
News on trial; Chicago tribune's attack on Reardon committee recommendations. Newsweek 68:100 O 17 '66
People's right to know; ANPA report with list of major conclusions. R. L. Tobin. il Sat R 50:109+ Ja 14 '67
Press on trial; Cleveland press and S. Sheppard case. il Time 87:64 Mr 11 '66
Trial by headline; Sheppard trial ruled unfair by Supreme court. il Newsweek 67:64 Je 20 '66
See also
Newspaper court reporting

CRIME commission. See United States—National crime commission

CRIME in literature
History repeats itself; E. A. Poe's Mystery of Marie Roget, forerunner to In cold blood. J. Arnold. Sat R 49:8 Mr 26 '66
See also
Detective and mystery stories

CRIME news. See Crime and the press

CRIME novels. See Detective and mystery stories

CRIME prevention
Crime problem needs soft sciences approach. Sci N 90:25 Jl 9 '66
Stamping out crime; anti-crime bill vetoed by L. B. Johnson. New Repub 155:4 D 10 '66
See also
Juvenile delinquency—Prevention
Police

CRITICISM—*Continued*
To criticize the critic, by T. S. Eliot. Review
Nat R 18:420-1 My 3 '66. H. Kenner
See also
Art criticism
Literary criticism
Moving picture plays—Criticisms, plots, etc.
CRITICS
At the movies: function of a critic. P. Kael.
McCalls 93:34+ F '66
Common scolds; preview and review. H.
Junker. Nation 202:307-9 Mr 14 '66
Dear Kerr: you, sir! W. Kerr. Time 88:68
S 9 '66
Newspapers: U.S. & Canada; music critics.
Hi Fi 16:222-31 D 15 '66
On reviewing plays. J. Richardson. Com-
mentary 42:79-82 S '66
Pair-offs with secret specialties: book re-
viewers. G. P. Hunt. Life 60:3 Je 24 '66
Pity the poor critics; difficulties of music
critics. C. J. McNaspy. America 115:755-6
D 3 '66
Supercritic: W. Kerr. Newsweek 68:94-5 S 12
'66
200 on the aisle: critics of the Broadway
plays. il Newsweek 67:92+ F 14 '66
See also
Literary criticism
CRITTENDEN, Brian S.
International meeting of educational phi-
losophers. Sch & Soc 94:396-8 N 12 '66
CRITTENDEN, Jordan
Great mail crisis of Norfolk, Illinois. Atlan
219:106+ Ja '67
Man who made his home in the Los Angeles
international airport: story. Sat Eve Post
239:60-1 S 24 '66
Three stories. New Yorker 42:177-80+ Mr
19 '66
CRITTENDEN, Pauline
Texas trails. Travel 126:35-8 N '66
CROAN, Robert
Music where the rivers meet: Pittsburgh re-
port. Hi Fi 16:152-3 My '66
CROCE, Arlene
Movies (cont) Nat R 18:480-1, 943-6 My 17,
S 20 '66
CROCHETING
Crocheted dress built of ribbon blocks; with
directions. il Good H 162:130+ F '66
CROCKETT, William James
Continuity of refugee and migration policies;
address. March 22, 1966. Dept State Bul
54:704-6 My 2 '66
Two-way communication with the education
community; excerpt from address, June
16, 1966. Dept State Bul 55:72-5 Jl 18 '66
CROCUSES
Crocus should go in the ground this month.
il Sunset 137:184 S '66
Crocus: so little, so much. A. H. William-
son. il Flower Grower 53:28-9+ S '66
Crocuses for fall color. M. M. Graff. il Flower
Grower 53:42-3 Ag '66
Fall crocus. R. D. Roe. il Horticulture 44:
30+ S '66
CROLL, James
James Croll and solar evolution. N. J. Woolf.
il pors Sky & Tel 31:150-1 Mr '66
CROMARTIE, William J. and Craddock, J. G.
Rheumatic-like cardiac lesions in mice. bibliog
Science 154:285-7 O 14 '66
CROMIE, Robert
Good-bye Bobby, good-bye Billy Joe, good-
bye Glory. Esquire 65:123+ Ap '66
CROMIE, William J.
Food for our future from pastures of the
sea; excerpt from The living world of the
sea. Todays Health 44:48-53+ N '66
CRONHEIM, Paul
Great opera houses: Holland. Opera N 30:
26-9 F 5 '66
CRONIN, Archibald Joseph
Resurrection of João Jacinto; story. Read
Digest 89:153-7 N '66
CRONIN, John W.
LC viewpoint. por Library J 91:5129-30 O 15
'66
CRONIN, Joseph M.
Negroes in Catholic schools. Commonweal 85:
13-16 O 7 '66
CRONIN, Sean
Where the martyrs died. Nation 203:486-8
N 7 '66
CRONKITE, Nancy
Nutcracker suite; poem. Mlle 64:54 D '66
CRONKITE, Walter, 1916-
Most intimate medium. il pors Time 88:56-8+
O 14 '66
Victorygraph: CBS election night program;
interview. A. Westin. New Yorker 42:51-3
N 5 '66

CRONLY-DILLON, J. R.
Spectral sensitivity of the scallop pecten
maximus. bibliog Science 151:345-6 Ja 21
'66
CROOK, George
Geronimo! E. M. Halliday. il por Am Heritage
17:56-63+ Je '66
CROOK, Mel
More power to you. See issues of Yachting
CROOKS, Laurence E.
Our senior staff member retires. Consumer
Rep 32:5 Ja '67
CROOKS, Pete. See Crooks, L. E.
CROOKS, Richard
Voice of Crooks; interview, ed. by M. J.
Matz. por Opera N 30:26-7 Ap 9 '66
about
In retrospect, Richard Crooks. J. Maclain.
por Am Rec G 32:819+ My '66
Richard Crooks. A. Favia-Artsay. pors Hob-
bies 71:36+ Ap '66
CROP forecasts. See Agricultural forecasts
CROP insurance. See Insurance, Agricultural
CROP reports. See Agriculture—Statistics
CROP residues
Don't leave crop residues in the field, feed
them instead. D. Malena. il Suc Farm 64:
32-3+ N '66
CROPLAND. See Land
CROPLAND adjustment program. See Agricul-
tural administration—United States
CROPS
America's beautiful bounty; aerial photo-
graphs. W. A. Garnett. Fortune 73:115-19 Je
'66
Look what others will plant this spring.
C. W. Gifford. il Farm J 90:58N+ My '66
News. See issues of Farm journal
That 1966 crop: it's better than we thought!
il Farm J 90:36+ N '66
What's new. See issues of Successful farming
See also
Agriculture
Milo

Statistics
See Agriculture—Statistics
CROPS, Surplus. See Food supply
CROQUET
Croquet is for everyone. il Pop Gard 17:87+
Mr '66
Sticky wicket; plans to form Connecticut club
and U.S. association. Newsweek 68:42 Ag 29
'66
CROSBY, Bing
My second family. pors Ladies Home J 83:
80-1+ My '66
about
Bing Crosby and his new movie: old dad
has a long way to slide. B. Davidson. il
pors Sat Eve Post 239:28-9 Ap 9 '66
Bing Crosby and his new movie: Stage-
coach. M. Davidson and J. Rale. il pors
Sat Eve Post 239:30-3+ Ap 9 '66
Good new life of Bing Crosby. B. Conrad.
il pors Good H 162:88-93+ My '66
CROSBY, D. G. and Tucker, R. K.
Toxicity of aquatic herbicides to daphnia
magna. bibliog Science 154:289-91 O 14 '66
CROSBY, Edwin L.
$50 a day, and going up. Atlan 218:102-4+
Jl '66
CROSBY, John
And at long last they are doing something
about the food. Esquire 66:66-7+ Jl '66
Letter home. Esquire 65:38+ Mr; 60+ Je '66
CROSS, Dallas G. See Fisher, H. F. jt. auth.
CROSS, Gilbert
Go exploring with a map. Read Digest 89:115-
18 Ag '66
CROSS, Jennifer
Report on food: prescription for a sick in-
dustry. Nation 203:245-8 S 19 '66
Truth in packaging: supermarket caper. Na-
tion 202:208-12 F 21 '66
CROSS, Lawrence
Father takes a wife. por Time 88:45 Jl 1 '66
CROSS, Mary Ann (Evans) See Eliot, G.
pseud.
CROSS, Robert D.
Books. Commonweal 83:512-14 Ja 28 '66
Greeley-Rossi report. Commonweal 84:577-9
S 16 '66
CROSS, Wilbur
Look out! Esquire 66:130-1 N '66
Machine Miltons. N Y Times Mag p59+ D
4 '66
CROSS, Way of the. See Stations of the cross

CROSS and crosses
  Canterbury cross for a relic. J. Stuart. il
    Antiques 89:660+ My '66
  Manner of speaking; world's largest crucifix.
    J. Ciardi. Sat R 49:6 Jl 2 '66
CROSS country running. See Running
CROSS FLORIDA BARGE CANAL. See Flor-
  ida Ship Canal project
CROSSLEY, Dorothy I.
  They never say die! il Yachting 119:222-3
    Mr '66
CROSSLEY, Robert F.
  Our newest frontier is underwater! Pop Mech
    125:94-8+ My '66
CROSSLEY, Robert P.
  Ship you drive with one finger. Pop Mech 126:
    92-5+ Ag '66
  Still a tiger in your toolshed. Pop Mech 125:
    100-3+ Je '66
  Which way to safety? Motor T 18:66-9 Ap
    '66
CROSSWORD puzzles
  8 across, 3 down; crossword puzzles to build
    vocabulary and improve spelling; Alexander
    Hamilton H. S. Los Angeles. S. Cocheli. Sr
    Schol 89:sup 13 D 2 '66
CROUCH; story. See Levinson, D.
CROUSE, John
  At long last. Yachting 119:75+ Je '66
CROW, John A.
  Castilian conquest. Sat R 49:36 Jl 9 '66
CROW-quill pens. See Pens
CROW shooting
  Crows in the pigpen. N. Karas. il Field & S
    71:56-7+ D '66
  Harsh-voice fever. D. Sweigard. il Outdoor
    Life 139:62-5+ Ja '67
  What do we do now? T. Trueblood. il Field
    & S 71:20+ Ja '67
CROWDS
  Mob seen: police estimates of crowds. J.
    Ferris. Sat R 49:4 Ag 13 '66
CROWELL, Russell R.
  Excerpt from statement, June 30, 1965. Cong
    Digest 45:60 F '66
CROWELL Collier and Macmillan, incor-
  porated
  Crowell Collier begins move to new head-
    quarters. il Pub W 190:54-5 O 3 '66
  Crowell Collier hits fiscal highs, buys Berlitz
    schools. Pub W 189:104 F 14 '66
  Crowell Collier launches industrial education
    unit. Pub W 189:50 My 16 '66
  Profits in continuing education: Berlitz buy.
    Time 87:90+ F 18 '66
  Publisher makes book on learning. il Bsns W
    p 124+ My 14 '66
CROWELL-Collier publishing company. See
  Crowell Collier and Macmillan, incorporated
CROWLEY, Elmer S.
  Teacher insurance: who foots the bill? NEA
    J 55:51+ S '66
CROWN-of-thorns starfish. See Starfishes
CROWN publishers, incorporated
  Crown turning out weekly printing of pro-
    bate book. il Pub W 190:117-18 Jl 4 '66
CROWTHER, Clarence Edward, bp
  Church's task in South Africa. Christian
    Cent 83:933-5 Jl 27 '66
  White man's fears in South Africa: a bishop's
    size-up; excerpts from radio interview. U S
    News 61:132 S 26 '66
CRUCIFERAE
    See also
  Crambe abyssinica
CRUCIFIXION of Christ. See Jesus Christ—
  Crucifixion
CRUELTY, Theater of. See Theater
CRUELTY to animals. See Animals—Treat-
  ment
CRUICKSHANK, Helen
  Summer of riches. Audubon Mag 68:86-91
    Mr '66
CRUISERS. See Yachts and yachting
CRUISES. See Cruising
CRUISING
  Around Florida's tip. J. Hardie. il Motor B
    118:32-3+ O '66
  Better homes and gardens tour: shipboard
    cruise to Canada for Expo '67. il Bet Hom
    & Gard 45:20 Ja '67
  Cargo cruises. S. Berry. il Travel 125:30-4 F
    '66
  Circumnavigation of Long Island. B. Robin-
    son. il Yachting 119:82-4+ Ja '66
  Cool vacation idea; Avianca airline's tour
    of islands of Antarctica. Newsweek 68:88
    Jl 11 '66
  Cruising the Karankaway country. A. W.
    Lloyd. il Motor B 118:22-5+ N '66

Cruising to the mountains; passage up the
  Hudson to Lake Champlain. J. Hart. il
  Yachting 120:42-4+ Jl '66
Deep water Chesapeake. W. T. Stone. il
  Yachting 119:64-5+ Mr '66
Escape to the not so bounding Maine; wind-
  jammer cruise on schooner Victory Chimes.
  B. La Fontaine. il Sports Illus 25:30-3 Ag 8
  '66
Experiment in sea-gone magic; maiden voy-
  age of the M. S. Europa. K. Lloyd. Vogue
  148:102-4 N 15 '66
Florida's wild west coast. J. S. Doherty. il
  Yachting 120:52-3+ N '66
From Boston to Boothbay and beyond. H.
  Winters. il Motor B 117:28-31+ Ap '66
From England to English Harbour. E.
  Hiscock. il Yachting 120:48-9+ D '66 (to be
  cont)
Getting there is more than half the fun: New
  York city and Edgartown. E. Horan. il
  Yachting 120:56-7+ Jl '66
Go west; but do it soon: cross-Florida cruise.
  W. H. Kendall. il Motor B 117:36-9+ Ap
  '66
In the wake of Cortez; Gulf of California.
  N. Phillips. il Motor B 118:22-4+ D '66
Island hopping by auto; Puget Sound area.
  A. H. Carhart. il Travel 125:52-6 Mr '66
Island-hopping holiday; San Juan Islands,
  British Columbia. C. West. il Motor B
  119:88-9+ Ja '67
Ladies day at sea. N. Brower. il Motor B
  119:76-9+ Ja '67
Mother ship will take care of you; winter
  cruises to the Caribbean. W. K. Zinsser.
  il Horizon 8:105-9 Aut '66
Never too late! two senior citizens take their
  first long cruise. R. R. Johnson. il Motor B
  118:34-5+ S '66
New boat, a new venture: Baja California
  (cont) E. Newmark. il Yachting 119:114-16+
  Ja '66
New York to Nantucket by day sailer. W.
  Roosen. il Motor B 118:34+ Jl '66
Offshore cruiser ventures inland. E. New-
  mark. il Yachting 120:41-3+ S '66
Ohio River Heritage cruise; glorious gateway
  to the West. J. Gribbins. il Motor B 118:
  38-43 S '66
One way to Newfoundland. W. C. Brewer,
  jr. bibliog il Yachting 119:65-8+ My '66
Page from a Bahama log book. J. Hart. il
  Yachting 120:46-8+ N '66
Play life on a working ship: Grace Line. D.
  Messinesi. Vogue 147:42 Ap 15 '66
Rendezvous at Little Current. J. Roe. il
  Motor B 118:44-5+ Jl '66
Robust, exciting: it's called California. C.
  West and J. West. il Motor B 117:22-6+
  My '66
Secret of a successful cruise. G. P. Manning.
  il Motor B 117:22-5+ Ap '66
Switzerland's lakes. A. R. Pastore, jr. il
  Travel 125:32-6 Ap '66
There's a water way to Mexico; from Los
  Angeles to ports of west coast of Mexico.
  il Sunset 137:43-4 D '66
Thirteen mad days and passionate nights
  loose in the Antilles; Caribbean cruise. A.
  Chamberlin. il Sat Eve Post 240:30-5 Ja 28
  '67
Thorny path; Florida to the Caribbean. J. C.
  Kozlick. il Motor B 119:81-5+ Ja '67
To Florida via the Gulf. J. L. Naumann. il
  Yachting 120:52-4+ D '66
Venerable Queen sails into a new role: Queen
  Elizabeth, of Cunard line, converted to
  cruise business. il Bsns W p52-3 Ap 2 '66
Yankee sails again. il Motor B 117:36-9 Mr
  '66
    See also
  River trips
CRUISING houseboats. See House boats
CRUMLEY, David D.
  Tips on saving income tax dollars. Suc Farm
    64:41+ F '66
CRUMPET, Peter
  Keeping up with the caballeros. Nat R 18:
    365-7 Ap 19 '66
  Letter from Spain. Nat R 19:33 Ja 10 '67
  Wrinkles on my lady. Nat R 18:827-8 Ag 23
    '66
CRUSADE of the Holy Spirit
  Crusade of the Holy Spirit; new society
    open to both priests and laymen. G. Mac-
    Eoin. il America 115:591 N 12 '66
CRUSADES
  Bird's-eye view of the Crusades, God wills it!
    P. W. Schmidtchen. il Hobbies 71:106-9 O '66
  Crusades. by Z. Oldenbourg. Review
    Sat R il 49:26 Jl 2 '66. T. G. Bergin
CRUSHERS, ice. See Ice crushers
CRUST of the earth. See Earth—Surface

CRUSTACEA
Pheromone; evidence in decapapod crustace-
an. E. P. Ryan. bibliog il Science 151:340-1
Ja 21 '66
See also
Barnacles
Cladocera
Crayfish
Isopoda
Shrimps
CRUSTACEAN meat products. See Sea food
CRYING
See also
Infants—Crying
CRYOGENIC surgery
Cryosurgery vs. cancer. il Newsweek 69:84
Ja 16 '67
CRYOGENICS. See Low temperatures
CRYOSURGERY. See Cryogenic surgery
CRYPTANALYSIS. See Cryptography
CRYPTOGRAPHY
Modern cryptology. D. Kahn. il Sci Am 215:
38-46 Jl '66
Other guy's mail; NSA. il Newsweek 67:28
Mr 14 '66
CRYPTOLOGY. See Cryptography
CRYSTAL, Minn. See Minneapolis
CRYSTAL MOUNTAIN, Washington. See Win-
ter resorts
CRYSTAL receivers. See Radio receiving ap-
paratus
CRYSTALLIZATION
Garnet zoning: an interpretation based on
the Rayleigh fractionation model. L. S.
Hollister. bibliog il Science 154:1647-51 D
30 '66
Morphology of nascent Ziegler-Natta poly-
mers. P. Blais and R. S. Manley. bibliog il
Science 153:539-41 Jl 29 '66
Surface recrystallization of polyethylene
extended-chain crystals. B. Wunderlich
and L. Melillo. bibliog il Science 154:1329-30
D 9 '66
See also
Metal crystals
CRYSTALLOGRAPHY
Crystal structure of kernite, $Na_2B_4O_6$
$(OH)_2 \cdot 3H_2O$. R. F. Giese, jr. bibliog il
Science 154:1453-4 D 16 '66
Electric currents in organic crystals. M.
Pope. il Sci Am 216:86-97 bibliog (p 146)
Ja '67
Reactivity of organic crystals. H. Mora-
wetz. bibliog il Science 152:705-11 My 6 '66
Retrograde melting in the system Mg-Fe-Si-
O. D. H. Speidel and R. H. Nafziger. bib-
liog il Science 152:1367-8 Je 3 '66
Shattuckite and planchéite: a crystal chem-
ical study. H. T. Evans, jr. and M. E.
Mrose. bibliog il Science 154:506-7 O 28 '66
Thermal recrystallization of precipitated zinc
sulfide. L. J. Bodi and C. F. Tufts. il Sci-
ence 153:872-3 Ag 19 '66
Trace element partition coefficient in ionic
crystals. H. Nagasawa. bibliog il Science
152:767-9 My 6 '66
See also
Polymorphism

X ray studies

Boron crystals. D. B. Sullenger and C. H. L.
Kennard. il Sci Am 215:96-107 bibliog (p 132)
Jl '66
Carbon tetrachloride: a new crystalline
modification. R. Rudman and B. Post. bibliog il Science 154:1009+ N 25 '66
Crystal and molecular structure of a double
complex of manganese with phthalocyanato
and pyridine ligands. L. H. Vogt, jr. and
others. bibliog il Science 151:569-70 F 4 '66
Crystal and molecular structure of acetyl-
selenocholine iodide. E. Shefter and O.
Kennard. bibliog il Science 153:1389-90 S 16
'66
Crystal structure of amylose triacetate: a
nonintegral helix. A. Sarko and R. H. Marchessault. bibliog il Science 154:1658-9 D
30 '66
Crystal structure of the zeolite paulingite.
E. K. Gordon and others. bibliog il Science
154:1004-7 N 25 '66
Deamino-oxytocin and 1-γ-mercaptobutyric
acid-oxytocin: X-ray crystallographic data
B. W. Low and C. C. H. Chen. bibliog il
Science 151:1552-3 Mr 25 '66
Distribution of uranium in some natural
minerals. E. I. Hamilton. bibliog il Science
151:570-2 F 4 '66
Eclogitic pyroxenes, ordered with P2 symmetry. J. R. Clark and J. J. Papike. bibliog
il Science 154:1003-4 N 25 '66

Precipitate formation in the strontium-
phosphate system. R. L. Collin. bibliog il
Science 151:1386-8 Mr 18 '66
Thiamine pyrophosphate hydrochloride:
stereochemical aspects from an X-ray
diffraction study. J. Pletcher and M. Sax.
bibliog il Science 154:1331-3 D 9 '66
X-ray diffraction study of minerals from
shocked iron meteorites. M. E. Lipschutz
and R. R. Jaeger. bibliog il Science 152:
1055-7 My 20 '66
CRYSTALS. See Crystallography
CRYSTALS, Gas. See Gases, Solidified
CRYSTALS, Ice. See Ice
CRYSTALS, Metal. See Metal crystals
CRYSTALS, Organic. See Crystallography
CRYSTALS, Snow. See Snow
CUA, Van-van-. See Van van-Cua
CUATRECASAS, Pedro, and Segal, Stanton
Electrophoretic heterogeneity of mammalian
galactose dehydrogenase. bibliog Science
154:533-5 O 28 '66
Galactose conversion to D-xylulose: an alter-
nate route of galactose metabolism. bibliog
Science 153:549-51 Jl 29 '66
CUBA
Captive in church. il Time 87:34-5 Ap 22 '66
Eye on Cuba, by E. Tetlow. Review
Newsweek il 67:92+ Ap 25 '66
On the spot in Cuba, our distant neighbor;
Castro's Cuba today; symposium, ed. by
W. Johnson; discussion. Sr Schol 88:14 Mr 4
'66
Recipe for crisis; capture of A. de la Cuesta
Valle. Time 87:47 Je 10 '66
See also
Americans in Cuba
Architecture—Cuba
Banks and banking—Cuba
Labor and laboring classes—Cuba
Newspapers—Cuba
Prisons—Cuba
Schools—Cuba
Trials—Cuba

Economic conditions

Big mystery in Castro's Cuba. il U S News
61:37-8 Jl 11 '66
Cuba goes from bad to worse: how long can
Castro last? il U S News 60:56-7 Ap 25 '66
Gloomy Castro faces more economic woes.
Bsns W p58+ Je 25 '66
Sugar blues. Time 87:38+ Ap 15 '66

Foreign relations

Castro gets a satellite, in Africa. il U S News
61:44 Ag 8 '66
Down with imperialism, 12,000 miles away:
Castro's split. Time 87:35 F 18 '66
Fidel vs. Mae. Newsweek 67:56 F 21 '66
Now, a pitch to Hanoi from the Castro
team. il U S News 61:28 N 14 '66
Why Castro is acting so jittery. U S News
60:20 Je 13 '66

History
Invasion, 1961

News unfit to print; New York times coverage of events leading to invasion. il Newsweek 67:101 Je 13 '66
When is news news? Nation editorial forerunner to New York times coverage of Bay
of Pigs invasion. Nation 202:730 Je 20 '66

Invasion
See Cuba—History—Invasion, 1961

Politics and government

After eight years: how Castro is doing. F.
Castro. il U S News 62:18 Ja 16 '67
Atlantic report. Atlan 218:28+ N '66
Big mystery in Castro's Cuba. il U S News
61:37-8 Jl 11 '66
Castro regime in Cuba. E. Halperin. bibliog f
il Cur Hist 51:354-9 D '66
Cuba, Castro and the United States. P. W.
Bonsal. For Affairs 45:260-76 Ja '67
Cuba goes from bad to worse: how long can
Castro last? il U S News 60:56-7 Ap 25 '66
Fidel Castro: did he fall, or was he pushed?
U S News 60:6 Je 27 '66
Good-by, cha-cha-cha; revolutionary off-
spring guilty of heavy drinking and high
living. Newsweek 67:55 Ap 4 '66
Inside look at Castro and today's Cuba. U S
News 60:16 My 2 '66
Puritan in Havana; arrest of at least twenty
playboy officials. Time 87:31 Mr 25 '66
Review of movement of Cuban refugees and
hemisphere policy toward Cuba; statement,
March 23, 1966. R. M. Sayre. Dept State
Bul 54:707-13 My 2 '66

CUBA—*Continued*

Social conditions

American in Cuba: Revolution of good cheer. E. R. John. il Nation 202:327-9 Mr 21 '66

CUBAN crisis, 1962
Footnote to history; secret letter from Khrushchev to President Kennedy during 1962 missile crisis. Newsweek 67:41 F 14 '66

Missile crisis, by E. Abel. Review
. New Repub 154:28-30 Mr 5 '66. J. J. Stone
Newsweek il 67:96+ F 14 '66
Sat R 49:43 Mr 12 '66. D. Kurzman

CUBAN refugees. See Refugees. Cuban

CUBANS
On the spot in Cuba, our distant neighbor: Castro's Cuba today; symposium, ed. by W. Johnson; discussion. Sr Schol 88:14 Mr 4

CUBANS in the United States
Department supports adjustment of status of Cuban refugees; statement. August 10, 1966. G. W. Ball. Dept State Bul 55:348-9 S 5 '66
See also
Refugees, Cuban

CUBELA SECADES, Rolando
Caning the students. Time 87:54 Mr 18 '66

CUBS, Lion. See Lions

CUCUMBER mosaic virus. See Viruses, Plant

CUCURBITACEAE. See Cucurbits

CUCURBITS
Cucurbitacins: specific insect attractants in cucurbitaceae. O. L. Chambliss and C. M. Jones. bibliog il Science 153:1392-3 S 16 '66

CUD-chewing animals. See Ruminants

CUENCA, Spain

Galleries and museums

New view on the cliff; Museum of Spanish abstract art. il Time 88:46-8 Jl 29 '66

CUESTA VALLE, Antonio de la
Recipe for crisis. Time 87:47 Je 10 '66

CUETO, Angel Betancourt. See Betancourt Cueto, A.

CUFFS
Try these collar and cuff refreshers. C. Houck. il Parents Mag 41:120 Mr '66

CULBERT, Taylor
Founding of a university press. Sat R 49:47 Je 11 '66

CULBERTSON, John Newton
Pennsylvania boyhood; memoir. Am Heritage 18:80-8 D '66

CULBERTSON, Jon R.
Cilia isolated from tetrahymena after membrane stabilization by 1,5-difluoro-2,4-dinitrobenzene. bibliog Science 153:1390-1 S 16 '66

CULKIN, John M.
I was a teen-age movie teacher. Sat R 49: 51-3+ Jl 16 '66

CULLEN, Arthur J.
Learning in two languages. Américas 18:12-18 My '66

CULLIGAN, Glendy
Bah, humbug, Virginia, we don't know. Am Ed 3:14-17 D '66
High school and the cultural illiterate. Am Ed 2:1-5 N '66
Mrs Stanley, I presume. Reporter 34:57-8 My 19 '66

CULLIGAN, Matthew J.
Culligan rides again. Newsweek 67:74 Ja 31 '66

CULLIGAN, Incorporated
How to get salesmen through the doorway; pre-selling tactics. il Bsns W p84+ Je 4 '66

CULLINANE, K. J.
All that glitters... Nat R 18:619 Je 28 '66

CULLITON, Joseph T.
Total gift. America 115:770-3 D 10 '66

CULP, D. P.
Worth protecting? NEA J 55:50 Ap '66

CULSHAW, John
New directions for the Ring. Hi Fi 16:65-8 N '66

CULTIVATION. See Tillage

CULTIVATION of corn. See Corn—Cultivation

CULTS
See also
House of David

CULTS, Negro
See also
Black Muslim movement

CULTURAL centers
Building for the arts, or, A house is not a home. T. P. De Gaetani. il Dance Mag 40:36-9+ N '66

Lincoln Center syndrome. A. H. Reiss. Esquire 66:94+ Ag '66
Speaking out: the courts must curb culture. T. Wolfe. Sat Eve Post 239:10+ D 3 '66

CULTURAL evolution. See Social change

CULTURAL exchanges. See Exchange of persons programs

CULTURAL relations
Era of educational and cultural relations; address, April 25, 1966. C. Frankel. Dept State Bul 54:889-97 Je 6 '66
See also subhead Cultural relations under names of countries, e.g. United States—Cultural relations

CULTURE
Cultural patterns in narrative: folk tales and myths. B. N. Colby. bibliog il Science 151:793-8 F 18 '66
Impact of the concept of culture on the concept of man. C. Geertz. il Bul Atomic Sci 22:2-8 Ap '66
Two decades in the world of culture. G. Arciniegas. il UNESCO Courier 19:30-1+ Jl '66
See also
Civilization
Philistinism
Popular culture

CULTURE, American. See United States—Civilization; United States—Intellectual life; United States—Popular culture

CULTURE, British. See Great Britain—Intellectual life

CULTURE, Primitive. See Indians of North America—Culture

CULTURE, Russian. See Russia—Intellectual life

CULTURE media
Culture of a planktonic calanoid copepod through multiple generations. E. J. Zillioux and D. F. Wilson. bibliog il Science 151: 996-8 F 25 '66
Deuterated organisms: cultivation and uses. J. J. Katz and H. L. Crespi. bibliog il Science 151:1187-94 Mr 11 '66
Differentiation in vitro: effects of sephadex fractions of chick embryo extract. H. G. Coon and R. D. Cahn. bibliog il Science 153:1116-19 S 2 '66
Heme stimulation of globin synthesis in a cell free system. C. L. Hammel and S. P. Bessman. bibliog il Science 152:1080-2 My 20 '66
Retention of potential to differentiate in long-term cultures of tooth germs. J. H. P. Main. bibliog il Science 152:778-80 My 6 '66
Rotifer ecology and embryological induction. J. J. Gilbert. bibliog il Science 151:1234-7 Mr 11 '66

CULWELL, Val D.
Soft cell. Newsweek 67:25-6 Ja 31 '66

CUMBERLAND GAP
Cumberland Gap. E. L. Shaub. il Travel 125: 58-60 Ap '66

CUMBERLAND MOUNTAINS. See Cumberland Plateau

CUMBERLAND national forest. See National forests

CUMBERLAND PLATEAU
Offense against America; a mountain is ravaged, a valley shattered; Big Black Mountain. H. M. Caudill. il Audubon Mag 68:356-9 S '66

CUMMING, Joseph B. Jr
Man who had everything and cried; poem. Harper 233:129 N '66
Morgan's crusade for Negro jurors. Reporter 34:39-40 F 10 '66

CUMMING, Robert
Painter! poem. Christian Cent 83:423 Ap 6 '66

CUMMINGS, Nathan
Architect of the autonoplex. il por Time 87: 88 Je 24 '66

CUMMINGS, Parke
Hot line. Look 30:20 Ap 19 '66

CUMMINGS, Sam
Planning a war? see Sam! A. Whitman. il por Pop Mech 125:90-2+ My '66

CUMMINS, J. E. and others
Anaphase delay after inhibition of protein synthesis between late prophase and prometaphase. bibliog Science 154:1343-4 D 9 '66

CUNARD steamship company
Cunard bets on a pair of Queens. T. Green. il Fortune 75:57-8+ Ja '67
Queens looking for the sun. Time 88:78 Jl 15 '66

CUNEO, Paul K.
Preview of fall books. America 115:422-3+ O 8 '66

CUNNEEN, Joseph E.
Servant parish. Commonweal 84:5-7 Mr 25 '66

CURTIS, Mina
Proust and the tartar relation. Nation 202: 160-3 F 7 '66
CURTIS, Richard
Yankee knight of the bath. Esquire 66:338-42 D '66
CURTIS, Thomas B.
Excerpt from remarks, September 20, 1965. Cong Digest 45:45 F '66
Toward improved economic policy; address, February 23, 1966. Vital Speeches 32:327-9 Mr 15 '66
CURTIS, Will C.
Trilliums. Horticulture 44:40-1+ Mr '66
CURTIS cup. See Golf
CURTIS publishing company
New look at Curtis. J. Tebbel. il Sat R 49: 94-5+ Je 11 '66
Return of Curtis publishing. Fortune 74:282 Jl 15 '66
CURTISS, Ursula
Danger; hospital zone; story. Good H 162: 85-7 My '66
CURV (cable-controlled underwater research vehicle) See Submarine boats
CUSACK, Sister Thomasine. See Thomasine Cusack, Sister
CUSHING, Harvey Williams
Saving the brain of General Wood. T. Berland. il por Todays Health 44:28-33+ S '66
CUSHING, Mary Watkins
(ed) See Copeland, G. Impressionist
(ed) See Nuotio, P.   Northern lights
(ed) See Välkki, A.   Northern lights
CUSHING, Richard James, cardinal
My dear children of God. por McCalls 94: 98-9 D '66
Thoughts to remember. Good H 162:240 My '66

about

Cushing of Boston, by J. Dever. Review Commonweal 83:512-14 Ja 28 '66. R. D. Cross
Please reconsider, Cardinal Cushing! Christian Cent 83:453-4 Ap 13 '66
Reform in the seminaries. il Time 87:60 Ap 15 '66
Revolt in the seminary. il Newsweek 67:68-9 Ap 18 '66
CUSHIONS, Air. See Air cushions
CUSHMAN, Robert
Amateur scientist. Sci Am 215:144-9 N '66
CUSPS, Beach. See Beach erosion
CUSTARDS
Bride makes pot de crème; with recipes. McCalls 93:36 S '66
CUSTER, George Armstrong
Bad day ahead for the army's greatest loser. A. Chamberlin. il Sat Eve Post 239:70-3 Ag 27 '66
Battle of the Little Big Horn, by M. Sandoz. Review Sat R 49:25+ My 21 '66. J. K. Hutchens
Last ghastly moments at the Little Bighorn; ed. with introd. by M. Liberty. John Stands in Timber. il por Am Heritage 17: 14-21+ Ap '66
CUSTIS, George Washington Parke
Son's tribute; with paintings. D. G. Lowe. por Am Heritage 17:16-21+ F '66
CUSTOMER engineers. See Consulting engineers
CUSTOMER relations
Technical representative. G. Smith. il Electr World 76:40-1+ Ag '66
Tender, loving care for the masses. il Bsns W p84-6+ Mr 5 '66
View your customers as investments. E. C. Bursk. il Harvard Bsns R 44:91-4 My '66
CUSTOMS (tariff) See Tariff
CUSTOMS service

Russia

$500 misunderstanding. M. Levin. Sat R 49: 58+ S 24 '66

United States

ABPC group suggests import form to speed customs procedure. Pub W 190:44-6 Jl 18 '66
How to breeze through customs. J. E. Frazer. il Read Digest 89:25-6+ S '66
Strange customs of the natives. H. Sutton. il Sat R 49:54+ F 19 '66
CUSTOMS service and tourists
Customs changes for travelers abroad. Sunset 136:53-4 F '66
How to breeze through customs; U.S. regulations. J. E. Frazer. il Read Digest 89: 25-6+ S '66

How to get through customs, cheap & fast. il Changing T 20:45-7 Mr '66
Let's travel; notes from the Caribbean. Mlle 62:121 Ja '66
When you send gifts home from abroad. Good H 162:174 My '66
CUTAK, Ladislaus
Succulents offer variety of color and form. Horticulture 44:14-15+ N '66
CUTLER, Bruce
American heart of darkness. Poetry 107:401-3 Mr '66
Waking; poem. Poetry 108:303-4 Ag '66
What we are, and are not. Poetry 108:269-72 Jl '66
CUTLER, M. Rupert
Here's how to get that hideaway homesite. Pop Mech 125:122-5+ Ap '66
CUTLER, Robert
Born in Boston, bred for Washington. M. L. Coit. Sat R 49:38-9 Ap 9 '66
CUTLERY
See also
Knives
CUTSHALL, Norman, and others
Chromium-51 in sea water; chemistry. bibliog Science 152:202-3 Ap 8 '66
CUTTER, Elizabeth G. See Caruso, J. L. jt. auth.
CUTTING, Glass. See Glass cutting
CUTTING blocks. See Chopping blocks
CUTTING machines
See also
Milling tools
CUTTING tools
Lady shows them how it's done; Mrs S. Boltz, president and treasurer of Goddard & Goddard co. il Bsns W p 134-6+ O 15 '66
CUTTINGS, Plant. See Plant propagation
CUZCO, Peru
Señorita Luciana; teacher in the high Andes; Quero Indian children. il UNESCO Courier 19:7-9 S '66
CYANIDE poisoning
Cyanide intoxication: protection with oxygen. J. L. Way and others. bibliog il Science 152:210-11 Ap 8 '66
CYANOACETYLENE. See Acetylene
CYBERNETICS
Computer age: how distorted the image? il Sr Schol 89:4-7+ O 7 '66
Higher education and cybernation; with reply by R. W. Tyler. R. Theobald. NEA J 55:26-9 Mr '66
Machines cannot think. P. McBroom. Sci N 90:6 Jl 2 '66
Man's first robot with muscles. J. Lear. il Sat R 49:83-6 D 3 '66
Russians are computing. A. Parry. il N Y Times Mag p24-5+ Ag 28 '66
See also
Bionics
Systems engineering
CYCASIN
Mutagenicity of cycasin aglycone methylazoxymethanol, a naturally occuring carcinogen. D. W. E. Smith. bibliog il Science 152:1273-4 My 27 '66
CYCLADES (islands)
See also
Thera (island)
CYCLAMENS
Cheerful now, cheerful later. il Sunset 137: 167 D '66
Hardy cyclamen. D. Collins. il Horticulture 44:36-7 F '66
CYCLAZOCINE
High inhibitor. il Time 87:85 Mr 18 '66
No way out? drugs and therapeutic community programs. il Newsweek 68:77-8 O 10 '66
CYCLES, Biological. See Periodicity
CYCLING
Bicycle hours; roads inside Central park. New Yorker 42:22 Jl 23 '66
Boom in bikeways. R. Hanneman. il Travel 126:26-30 Ag '66
Forgotten outdoorsmen. il Time 87:62+ Je 10 '66
Our need for bicycle trails. E. C. Crafts. il Parks & Rec 1:435+ My '66
See also
Motorcycling
CYCLOHEXIMIDE. See Antibiotics
CYLERT. See Magnesium pemoline
CYLINDER locks. See Locks and keys
CYLINDER records. See Phonograph records
CYMBIDIUMS
Cymbidiums fit into every home. R. W. Jones. il Horticulture 44:22-3 N '66

CYPRIPEDIUM. See Ladys slippers

CYPRUS
See also
United Nations—Armed forces—Forces in Cyprus

Politics and government
Toward a boiling point; Makarios-Grivas feud; threat to government. il Time 87:39 Ap 1 '66

CYR, Don
Montage as visual synthesis. Design 67:16-19 My '66
Path to visual realization. bibliog Design 67:26-30 Ja '66
Visual language. bibliog Sch Arts 66:32-5 N '66
Visual literacy. Design 68:24-6 N '66

CYRANKIEWICZ, József
Still no visa for the cardinal. America 114:369 Mr 19 '66

CYSTATHIONINE
Homocystinuria: excretion of a new sulfur-containing amino acid in urine. T. L. Perry and others. bibliog il Science 152:776-8 My 6 '66
Homolanthionine excretion in homocystinuria. T. L. Perry and others. bibliog il Science 152:1750-2 Je 24 '66

CYSTIC fibrosis
Clues to CF. il Newsweek 68:74 N 21 '66
Cystic fibrosis forecast. Sci N 90:433 N 19 '66
Mucopolysaccharide from patients with cystic fibrosis of the pancreas. C. U. Lowe and others. bibliog il Science 153:1124-5 S 2 '66

CYSTINURIA. See Intestines—Diseases
CYSTITIS. See Bladder—Diseases
CYTOKININS. See Peptides
CYTOPLASM
Substructure of certain cytoplasmic microtubules: an electron microscopic study. P. R. Burton. bibliog il Science 154:903-5 N 18 '66

CZECH dancing. See Dancing, Czech
CZECHOSLOVAK cookery. See Cookery, Czech
CZECHOSLOVAK society of arts and sciences in America, incorporated
Czechoslovak science; report on panel discussion at meeting. M. Rechcigl, jr. Science 154:924-6 N 18 '66

CZECHOSLOVAKIA
See also
Airplane industry and trade—Czechoslovakia
Astronomical observatories—Czechoslovakia
Communism—Czechoslovakia
Communist party (Czechoslovakia)
Moving picture industry—Czechoslovakia
Moving pictures—Czechoslovakia
Prague
Research—Czechoslovakia
Science—Czechoslovakia

Economic conditions
Painful cure; profit-oriented system. Newsweek 67:33-4 F 7 '66

Economic policy
Toward market economics. il Time 88:42-3 N 11 '66

Politics and government
Changes in Czechoslovakia. America 115:789 D 17 '66

CZEL, J. E. Jr
Dewatering by wells. Am City 81:80-1 Je '66

CZURA, Pete
Elastic dog prices. Field & S 70:172-4+ Ap '66
For family vacation fun: rent a houseboat. il Todays Health 44:22-4+ Ap '66
How to combat poisons. Field & S 71:176-7+ My '66
Montana's ignored game fish. Field & S 71:58-9+ My '66
New arrow for carp. Field & S 71:48-9 Je '66
Newest lake in Kansas. Field & S 70:140-2+ Mr '66
Rabies: the growing threat. Field & S 70:162-3+ Mr '66
Synthetics for camping. Field & S 70:60-3+ F '66
Truth or consequences quail. Field & S 71:47-9 S '66
When you camp out. Todays Health 44:26-30 Jl '66

D

DAC. See Organization for economic cooperation and development—Development assistance committee
DART (dual-axis rate transducers) See Aeronautic instruments
DAV. See Disabled American veterans (organization)
D.C. Heath and company. See Heath, D. C. and company
DC international
Charges of reckless driving; DC company president. il Time 88:68 Ag 12 '66
How to 'ive with trucks. D. MacDonald. il Motor T 18:134 N '66
DDC. See Classification, Decimal
DDS. See Diaminodiphenyl sulfone
DDT (insecticide)
Dechlorination of DDT by aerobacter aerogenes. G. Wedemeyer. bibliog Science 152:647 Ap 29 '66

Injurious effects
Airborne particulates in Pittsburgh: association with p,p'-DDT. P. Antommaria and others; reply. P. E. Morrow. Science 151:1410 Mr 18 '66
DDT lethal to birds forty days after eating. Sci N 189:268 Ap 16 '66
Let's not kill ourselves; threat to fishing. D. B. Peakall and B. East. il Outdoor Life 138:17-19+ Ag; 29-31+ S '66
Residues of DDT in brains and bodies of birds that died on dosage and in survivors. L. F. Stickel and others. bibliog il Science 151:1549-51 Mr 25 '66

DEW (distant early warning) See Radar defense networks
DLI. See United States—Defense language institute
DMA. See Dance masters of America
DMS, incorporated
Where's the money going next? Defense marketing services. il Bsns W p86+ My 7 '66
DMSO. See Methyl sulfoxide
DNA. See Deoxyribonucleic acid
DPT. See Dipropyltryptamine
DRI. See Denver research institute
DSA. See United States—Defense, Department of—Defense supply agency
DABBS, James McBride
Beyond justice. Christian Cent 83:1448 N 23 '66
Gentlemen cry peace. Christian Cent 83:365-6 Mr 23 '66
DABERNAT, René
How a French authority sees U.S. role in Asia; interview, ed. by F. C. Painton. por U S News 62:93-4+ Ja 23 '67
DABNEY, Virginius
Cheating can be stopped. Sat R 49:68-9+ My 21 '66
Placid corrida. Sat R 49:42+ S 10 '66
Report on the press in Spain and Portugal. Sat R 49:50-1 Jl 9 '66
DACEY, Norman F.
Probate bonanza. il por Newsweek 67:78 Je 27 '66
Probate fuss; concerning his How to avoid probate! T. B. Morgan. il pors Look 30:36-8+ N 29 '66
DACHS, David
New long-playing libraries. Sat R 49:49-51+ Ja 29 '66
DACHSHUNDS
All in a dog's life; dachshund and motherless lion cub. il Look 31:M8 Ja 24 '67
DACRON sail. See Sails
DACUS oleae. See Olive fruit flies
DADAISM
Art and anti-art. E. H. Gombrich. il Atlan 217:93-9 F '66
Art galleries; exhibition at the Jewish museum by M. Ernst. R. M. Coates. New Yorker 42:144+ Mr 26 '66
Dada's 50th. il Time 87:74 F 18 '66
Love and hiccups; death of J. Arp. il Newsweek 67:67 Je 20 '66
Mirrors for a mad world. G. H. Hamilton. il Sat R 49:36 Ap 2 '66
DADDARIO, Emilio Q.
Case for space; excerpts from address. Aviation W 84:21 Je 13 '66
Revised charter for the science foundation. Science 152:42-5 Ap 1 '66

DADDARIO, Emilio Q.—*Continued*

about

Daddario study says NSF should be in forefront of policymaking. D. S. Greenberg; discussion. Science 152:292+ Ap 15 '66

Science and technology: House subcommittee offers Capitol ideas. N. Panush. Science 154:993-4 N 25 '66

DAFFODILS. See Narcissus

DAG Hammarskjöld library. See United Nations —Library

DAGUERRE, Louis Jacques Mandé

All at once, a moment can be caught forever. il Life 61:32-50 D 23 '66

DAGUERREOTYPES

All at once, a moment can be caught for il Life 61:32-50 D 23 '66

DAHL, Barding

White slumlord confesses. por Esquire 66: 92-4+ Jl '66

DAHLBERG, Edward

Dahlberg: aphorisms & poetry. F. MacShane. Nation 203:225-6 S 12 '66

Lord of the language. S. Maloff. por Newsweek 69:97A+ Ja 23 '67

DAHLIAS

Dahlias now and in spring. J. W. Clausen. il Flower Grower 53:12-13 O '66

Dwarf Dutch dahlias. C. Lewis. il Horticulture 44:14-15 S '66

Here's what you should do to have showcase dahlias in August. il Sunset 137:126-7 Ag '66

DAHMER, Vernon

Malice toward some. il Newsweek 67:39-40 Ap 11 '66

DAI, Shen-yu

Peking's cultural revolution. bibliog f Cur Hist 51:134-9+ S '66

DAICHES, David

Dialogue? Commentary 42:133-5 O '66

Divine justice. Commentary 41:80-6 My '66

Golden age. Commentary 42:94+ N '66

DAIEN, Bernard

Urban renewal backers play rough. por Nations Bsns 54:37 Ja '66

DAIGLER, Geoffrey W. See Witten, A. H. jt. auth.

DAIGON, Arthur

Novel of adolescent romance; with bibliography. por Library J 91:2152-6 Ap 15 '66

DAILY, Jay E.

Scrimp or splurge? por Library J 91:2431-4 My 15 '66

DAILY express international offshore powerboat race. See Motor boat racing

DAILY news, Chicago. See Chicago daily news

DAILY news, New York

Telling it to Sweeney. il Newsweek 68:100 N 14 '66

DAILY pilot, Orange County. See Orange coast pilot (newspaper)

DAILY worker (newspaper) See Morning star (newspaper)

DAIRY barns. See Barns and stables

DAIRY cooperative associations. See Dairymen's associations

DAIRY cows. See Cows

DAIRY farm management

Dairy extra; outlook. il Farm J 90:A1-2 Jl; A1-2 O '66

This farming business. A. W. Tenney. il Am Ed 2:28-32 Jl '66

DAIRY farm records

New herd health record system. il Suc Farm 64:74 F '66

This farming business. A. W. Tenney. il Am Ed 2:28-32 Jl '66

DAIRY farming. See Dairying

DAIRY farms

Economist's view of future dairy farms. Suc Farm 64:100H Mr '66

Ideas from four new dairy setups. J. Albino and J. R. Borcherding. il Suc Farm 64:34-5+ N '66

See also

Dairy farm management

DAIRY industry and trade

Dairy extra; business report. C. W. Gifford. Farm J 90:A15 Jl '66

Road ahead has fewer bumps for dairymen. N. Reeder and D. Braun. il Farm J 90:A4+ Jl '66

DAIRY products

Summery dairy foods. M. Gustafson. il Parents Mag 41:62-8 Je '66

See also

Ice cream, ices, etc.

Prices

Dairy products: why prices keep rising. il U S News 60:14 Je 20 '66

See also

Butter—Prices

DAIRYING

Dairying in 1975: less labor, more management. Suc Farm 64:82 F '66

Ideas from four new dairy setups. J. Albino and J. R. Borcherding. il Suc Farm 64:34-5+ N '66

News. See issues of Farm journal

Raising and selling dairy replacements. D. Vilstrup. il Suc Farm 64:54-5+ Mr '66

We'll stick with dairying. D. Hagen. il Farm J 90:A6-8 O '66

What's new. See issues of Successful farming

Why fourteen Wisconsin dairymen quit every day. N. Reeder. il Farm J 90:67-8 My '66

See also

Cows—Feeding

Dairy farm management

Dairy farms

DAIRYMEN'S associations

Look what these co-ops do for dairymen. C. E. Ball. il Farm J 90:59 Ap '66

DAKIN, Rosina Maria Francesca (Otto)

Grand. T. Williams. por Esquire 66:136+ N '66

DAKOTA COUNTY, Minn.

Microfilm gives us 90 per cent more space. P. R. Welshons. il Am City 81:117 My '66

DALAM, Jusuf Muda

Young wives' tale. il Newsweek 67:53 Ap 11 '66

D'ALBERT, Eugen. See Albert, E. d'

DALE, E. D.

Three offshoots of astronomy. Sky & Tel 31:277-9 My '66

DALE, Edwin L. Jr

Another look at the new economics. N Y Times Mag p50-1+ S 18 '66

Can we manage prosperity? N Y Times Mag p24-5+ Mr 6 '66

Case against a tax increase. New Repub 154:11-13 Ap 2 '66

Uncle Sam's $50,000,000,000 surplus. N Y Times Mag p32-3+ N 7 '65; Nat R 18:97+ F 8 '66

DALE family

Dale coat-of-arms. H. K. Eilers. il Hobbies 71:126-7+ Ap '66

DALES, George F.

Decline of the Harappans; with biographical sketch. Sci Am 214:16+, 92-8+ bibliog(p 147) My '66

DALEY, Richard J.

Minority objects, but Daley is Chicago. H. Higdon. il pors N Y Times Mag p84-5+ S 11 '66

DALEY, Robert

El Cordobes. Vogue 148:114-15+ Ag 1 '66

This bottle of wine is 160 years old. I. drank it. Esquire 66:102-3+ N '66

When you're no. 2 you drive harder. Sports Illus 25:24-6+ Ag 15 '66

DALGLIESH, Alice

Books for young people. See issues of Saturday review to September 17, 1966

DALI, Salvador

Dali in New York. R. Squirru. il Américas 18:34-6 F '66

Happenings are happening. il por Time 87: 76-7 Mr 4 '66

DALIS, Irene

Between two worlds. Opera N 31:16 D 17 '66

DALLAS, Philip

Sardinia. Atlan 217:145-6+ Mr '66

Zagarolo. Atlan 218:145-7 N '66

DALLAS

Airports

$8-million facility at Love field scheduled by Braniff for 1968. il Aviation W 85:39 Ag 29 '66

Architecture

Multi-level concourse connects multiple uses. il Arch Rec 140:162-5 N '66

Clubs

Arthur Ashe thing; Dallas country club invitational tennis tournament canceled. Sports Illus 24:8 F 21 '66

Monuments, statues, etc.

Living with history; opposition to text on J. F. Kennedy assassination marker. Newsweek 67:48+ Ap 18 '66

Music

See also

Dallas civic opera company

DALLAS—*Continued*

Police

Late casualty; Curry resigns. Newsweek 67:31 F 28 '66

Stores

From shops to city near Dallas. il Fortune 73:162+ Je '66

Northpark regional shopping center, Dallas. il Arch Rec 139:151-9 Ap '66

Reference books: heaviest traffic at Sanger-Harris. il Pub W 189:123-4 Je 13 '66

DALLAS civic opera company

Dallas; productions of Rigoletto and La Bohème. J. Ardoin. il Opera N 31:28 D 17 '66

Dallas; Verdi's Macbeth. J. Ardoin. il Opera N 31:28 D 31 '66

High Cs in big D. il Time 88:83 D 2 '66

Kelly of Dallas. F. Stevenson. il Opera N 31: 18-19 N 5 '66

Opera after the schism; Dallas-Chicago report. R. C. Marsh. il Hi Fi 16:142-3 F '66

DALLAS Cowboys (football club) See Football clubs

DALLAS Thomas park and marina. See Jacksonville, Fla.—Parks and playgrounds

DALLEGRET, François

School of Paris dropouts. il Art N 65:56-7+ N '66

D'ALPUGET, Lou

Is this the sailcloth secret? il Yachting 119: 102-3+ Ja '66

DALRYMPLE, Byron W.

Miniature monster. Field & S 71:29+ Jl '66

Montana's drive-in wilderness. Field & S 70:122-4+ F '66

Surefire deer country. il Outdoor Life 138: 38-41+ D '66

What's tough about javelina. Outdoor Life 138:52-3+ N '66

DALRYMPLE, G. Brent. See Doell, R. R. jt. auth.

DALTON, Henry

February spell; poem. Commonweal 83:580 F 18 '66

DALTON, Margaret

At the top of the voice. Nation 202:271-2 Mr 7 '66

DALWOOD, Hubert

Gallery for young people C. B. Johnson. il Sch Arts 66:46 O '66

DALY, Ronald O.

New directions for professional negotiation. NEA J 55:27-9 O '66

DALY CITY, Calif.

Folded floor plan with a view for all patients; Mary's help hospital. il Arch Rec 139:176-7 Mr '66

DAMAGES

Cash for good samaritans; California's Good Samaritan statute. Time 87:82 My 13 '66

D'AMATO, Anthony A.

Apartheid: catalyst in the U.N. Christian Cent 83:1303-6 O 26 '66

D'AMATO, Cus

Cus is back aboard a big new Bus. R. H. Boyle. il por Sports Illus 26:18-22 Ja 16 '67

DAMON, Roger C.

Businessmen in the news. por Fortune 74: 53 S '66

DAMS

Abundance of alternatives; Colorado River basin fund. A. W. Smith. Nat Parks Mag 40:2+ Jl '66

Canyon war deepens. Bsns W p32 Jl 30 '66

Dam site; fate of Grand Canyon. W. V. Shannon. Commonweal 84:329-30 Je 10 '66

Dam the Grand Canyon? no! cries an Arizonan. J. W. Krutch. il Audubon Mag 68: 308-11 S '66

Decision on the snake; go-ahead for Northwest Pacific at Mountain Sheep. il Time 87:79-80 Ap 1 '66

Forester speaks; Grand Canyon controversy; letter. R. J. Lentz. Parks & Rec 1:675 S '66

Grand Canyon: Colorado dams debated. L. J. Carter. il Science 152:1600-5 Je 17 '66

Grand Canyon dams blocked. C. H. Callison. Aububon Mag 68:462 N '66

Grand Canyon dams: Interior to ask, are they necessary? L. J. Carter. Science 154: 134 O 7 '66; Reply. L. I. Moss. 154:961 N 25 '66

How to save the Grand Canyon and water the desert, too; proposed Hualapai (formerly Bridge Canyon) and Marble Canyon Dams; interview. B. M. Goldwater. il U S News 61:124-6 O 24 '66; Reply. D. Brower. 61:60-1 D 12 '66

Hurricane protection; Fox Point Hurricane Dam project in Providence, R.I. il Am City 81:78 Jl '66

Last days of the Colorado? G. Staveley and B. East. il Outdoor Life 138:24-7+ Jl '66

Many-headed dragon; proposed site of Echo Park Dam. J. P. Saylor. il Audubon Mag 68:52-3 Ja '66

Mike Frome: Bridge Canyon and Marble Canyon dams. M. Frome. il Am For 72:6-7+ My '66

Our wild rivers. E. S. Helfman. il Liv Wildn 30:24-9 Sum '66

President Johnson visits Mexico to inspect Amistad Dam; statement, November 29; remarks, December 3; with text of joint statement, December 3, 1966. L. B. Johnson. Dept State Bul 56:12-13 Ja 2 '67

Ruin for the Grand Canyon? R. C. Bradley. il Audubon Mag 68:34-41 Ja '66; Same abr. Read Digest 88:193-8 Ap '66

Ruin for the Grand Canyon? R. Richter. il Audubon Mag 68:216-216a Jl '66

Sespe project setback is condor's reprieve. C. H. Callison. Audubon Mag 68:160-1 My '66

Sounds of a river. K. B. Hultquist. il Nat Parks Mag 40:9-12 Ag '66

Storms over the Grand Canyon. H. Nash; C. Hayden. il Parks & Rec 1:496-501+ Je '66; Reply. G. Woodgates. 1:610 Ag '66

To save the Grand Canyon; Colorado River basin bill proposals. W. Stegner. Sat R 49: 20 Ag 20 '66

U.S. and Canada ratify Gut Dam agreement; Department announcement, October 11, 1966. Dept State Bul 55:724 N 7 '66

Water project that dried up; Colorado River project. il Bsns W p72+ S 3 '66

See also

Libby Dam project (proposed)

Alaska

Dam will harm wildlife; Rampart Dam, Alaska. Sci N 89:207 Mr 26 '66

Rampart Dam: a costly gamble. S. H. Spurr. il Audubon Mag 68:172-5+ My '66

Rampart Dam and the perpetual engineers. H. Titus. Field & S 71:34+ Je '66

Rampart Dam, ultimate in cynicism. Am For 72-11 Ap '66

Rampart project study. Liv Wildn 29:42 Wint '65

Canada

Riding down a dying river; Canoe River, British Columbia. R. Cantwell. il Sports Illus 25:78-80+ N 21 '66

U.S. agency preparing claims relating to Gut Dam. Dept State Bul 54:207 F 7 '66

Egypt

See also

Aswan High Dam

France

French harness tides for power; St Malo tidal dam. il Bsns W p 108-10 Ap 30 '66

DAMS, Beaver. See Beavers

DAN, Phan-quang-. See Phan-quang-Dan

DANA, Robert

Some versions of silence; poem. Poetry 108: 111-15 My '66

about

Seven books by eight poets. A. R. Ammons. Poetry 108:193-7 Je '66

DANA, Samuel Trask

Dana years; interview, ed. by E. R. Maunder and A. Fry. pors Am For 72:32-5+ N; 26-9+ D '66

DANCE, Helen

Goodman at the Rainbow grill. Sat R 49:82-3 Je 11 '66

DANCE, Stanley

Recordings reports: jazz LPs. See issues of Saturday review

DANCE adventures, Incorporated

Just so stories, 92nd street Y. M. Marks. Dance Mag 40:34 My '66

DANCE bands. See Bands (music)

DANCE caravan U.S.A. See Dance institutes and workshops

DANCE clubs. See Clubs

DANCE companies

Barefoot boy with cheek; Paul Taylor dance company. il Time 89:38 Ja 6 '67

Eleo Pomare dance company, 92nd street Y. J. Maskey. Dance Mag 40:72+ D '66

Les Feux-follets, Hunter college assembly hall. D. Hering. Dance Mag 40:31+ Mr '66

Judson dance theatre; Judson memorial church. J. Anderson. Dance Mag 40:87 My '66

Judson dance theater. Judson memorial church. J. Maskey. Dance Mag 40:32 N: 74-5 D '66

DAVIE, Michael
British editor's size-up of President Johnson; excerpts from LBJ. U S News 61: 40-6 Ag 29 '66
Foreigner looks at LBJ; excerpts from LBJ: a foreign observer's viewpoint. Newsweek 67:22-3 Ap 25 '66
DAVIES, C. R. and others
Auxin and kinetin interaction in apical dominance. bibliog Science 151:468-9 Ja 28 '66
DAVIES, Don
Comments on teacher certification. NEA J 55:18-19 S '66
DAVIES, Gerald R.
Book market research: Europe. Pub W 191: 53-5 Ja 16 '67
Jobs tax hits British booksellers. Pub W 189:39-41 My 30 '66
London letter. por Library J 91:2435-6, 4052-3 My 15, S 15 '66
Post mark Pall Mall. Pub W 190:48-50 D 26 '66
Postmark: Pall Mall. por Pub W 190:60-2 S 12 '66
DAVIES, John
It's Baker! going for another touchdown! with introd. by George Frazier. il Esquire 66:132-5+ S '66
Princeton; excerpts from Tiger in the ivy: the Princeton man and his university, 1900-1967. Horizon 9:57-66+ Wint '67
DAVIES, Merton E. See Murray, B. C. jt. auth.
DAVIES, Rhys
Chosen one; story. New Yorker 42:36-44 Je 4 '66
Fugitive; story. Sat Eve Post 239:94-6 Mr 26 '66
DAVIES, William Henry
Two British chronicles. R. J. Mills, jr. Poetry 107:406-8 Mr '66
DAVIS, Ben Arthur
Regional pointers: South. See issues of Flower grower, the home garden
DAVIS, Bob
Fresh look at galley psychology.   Motor B 117:28-9+ My '66
DAVIS, Britton
Geronimo! E. M. Halliday. il Am Heritage 17:56-63+ Je '66
DAVIS, Charles
Theological asides (cont) America 114:173, 445, 800; 115:157, 419-20 Ja 29, Ap 2, Je 4, Ag 13, O 8 '66

about

Cardinal Spellman, Charles Davis. J. M. Cameron. Commonweal 85:418-19 Ja 20 '67
Charles Davis, Christian. Commonweal 85: 359-60 Ja 6 '67
Davis case. K. L. Woodward. Commonweal 85:393-4 Ja 13 '67
Newman in reverse. C. Northcott. Christian Cent 84:39 Ja 11 '67
Rejecting Rome. por Newsweek 69:51 Ja 2 '67
Theologian defects. por Time 88:42 D 30 '66
Will Catholics lose their cool over Davis? Christian Cent 84:68 Ja 18 '67
Wounded priest, wounded church. America 116:8-9 Ja 7 '67
DAVIS, Charles (writer), and Bellenger, M. J.
Belly-dancer who became a lady. Ebony 21: 79-80+ Jl '66
DAVIS, Charles N.
Warriors against disease. Todays Health 44: 30-4 N '66
DAVIS, Christopher
Death in the Sun City. Esquire 66:134-7 O '66
DAVIS, Clint
Congress welcome mat is out. Parks & Rec 1:547+ Jl '66
DAVIS, David Brion
Growth of a national state of mind. Sat R 49:26-8 S 3 '66
Violence in American literature. Ann Am Acad 364:28-36 Mr '66
DAVIS, Donald D.
New skies for a new city. Sky & Tel 31:196-8 Ap '66
DAVIS, Donald Walter
Stanley tries the faster track. il por Bsns W p84-7 N 5 '66
DAVIS, Dorothy Crane
Donna Dill's victory. Todays Health 45:26-7+ Ja '67
DAVIS, Douglas M.
Digging Dudley Do-right. Holiday 39:150+ Ap '66
Young men who are remaking Congress. Holiday 39:60-1+ F '66
DAVIS, E. Louise, and others
(ed) Junior books appraised (cont) Library J 91:2197-8+, 2677-8+, 3249-64+, 4311-12+, 5212+, 5736+, 6183-4+, Ap 15, My 15, Je 15, S 15, O 15, N 15, D 15 '66

DAVIS, Edward. See Mulholland, T. jt. auth.
DAVIS, F. W.
Elk to whistle about. pors Outdoor Life 137: 62-4+ F '66
DAVIS, Foster
Delta: rich land and poor people. Reporter 34:41-3 Mr 24 '66
DAVIS, Gene
Gene Davis paints a picture. G. Nordland. il Art N 65:46-9+ Ap '66
DAVIS, George R.
President's pastor. por Time 87:54 F 4 '66
DAVIS, Geri Turner
Storm over A cat called Jesus. A. B. Haines. Christian Cent 83:250-2 F 23 '66
Tale of a cat. il por Newsweek 67:74-5 F 7 '66
DAVIS, Gladys D.
Challenge of TV teaching. por NEA J 55: 10-11+ Ap '66
DAVIS, Jefferson
American President who fought the U.S. il Sr Schol 88:3 Ap 29 '66
Dixie's difficult perfectionist. W. B. Catton. por Sat R 50:35 Ja 7 '67
DAVIS, John Warren
For the fine arts and humanities; statement, December 5, 1965. por Negro Hist Bul 29: 57-8 D '65
DAVIS, Joseph E.
Christmas list; holiday greeting. J. Fischer. Harper 233:23 D '66
DAVIS, Laura Jo
Motors are so exciting, you feel like you own the road; ed. by H. F. Waters. il por Newsweek 67:68 Mr 21 '66
DAVIS, Maggie
Ghostly Gullah country. Holiday 40:54-5+ Jl '66
DAVIS, Malcolm McTear
Regal Rome. Travel 126:56-60 Jl '66
DAVIS, Mary Gould
Story hour; poem Horn Bk 42:540-1 O '66
DAVIS, Mildred
World of strangers; story. Redbook 128:125 Ja '67
DAVIS, Millard C.
Forests of the Smokies. il Liv Wildn 30:6-9 Spr '66
DAVIS, Peter G.
Music for, and of, our century: Hans Werner Henze's five symphonies. Hi Fi 16:74-5 Ag '66
New York opera; Met production of La Gioconda. Hi Fi 16:MA14 D '66
Notes from our correspondents (cont) Hi Fi 16:18+ F; 20+ Mr; 16+ Je; 30+ S; 16+ N; 22 D '66
Operatic contrasts: Henze, Bizet, Mozart. Hi Fi 16:MA2+ O '66
Repeat performance. Hi Fi 16:106-8 My; 94-5 Je; 89-90 Jl; 99-100 Ag; 116-17 S; 166-7 O; 50+ N; 116+ D '66
Switzerland, a musical tour through the cantons. Hi Fi 16:34+ S '66
DAVIS, Ronald
Harlem tuba player. il pors Ebony 22:82+ N '66
DAVIS, Rowland H.
Neurospora. Science 153:1553-4+ S 23 '66
DAVIS, Sammy
Is my mixed marriage mixing up my kids? reprint. pors Ebony 21:124-6+ O '66

about

Make Sammy shuffle? Sat R 49:22 F 5 '66
Sammy Davis, jr. il pors Ebony 21:165-8+ Ap '66
Yes, he can. R. L. Shayon. Sat R 49:38 My 21 '66
DAVIS, Sandi
Soloist survives on a bouillabaisse of seaweeds and fantasies of candy. por Life 61: 48-9 S 23 '66
DAVIS, Sidney E.
Shopping tips from a butcher. Consumer Bul 49:17-18 Mr '66
DAVIS, Thurston N.
Viva la huelga! America 114:589-90 Ap 23 '66
DAVIS, W. A.
United States in air and space; progress and prospect; address. October 6, 1966. Vital Speeches 33:38-42 N 1 '66
DAVIS, Wynn
Angling. See issues of Outdoor life
Hottest place on ice. il pors Outdoor Life 139:46-9+ Ja '67
DAVIS cup. See Tennis
DAVISON, John
Chimeric and ex-parabiotic frogs, rana pipiens: specificity of tolerance. bibliog Science 152:1250-3 My 27 '66

DAVISON, Peter
Collector; poem. Harper 232:70 Mr '66
Destroyer; poem. Atlan 217:45 My '66
For amphibians; poem. Atlan 218:86 Jl '66
Inhabited by a cry; last poetry of Sylvia
Plath. Atlan 218:76-7 Ag '66
Magpie; poem. Atlan 217:123 Je '66
Real cultural article. Atlan 217:141-2 Mr '66
DAVISON, Peter F.
Isopycnic centrifugation for the isolation of
DNA strands coding for ribosomal RNA.
bibliog Science 152:509-12 Ap 22 '66
DAVISON, Robert L.
Everything in a low key; public libraries;
legislation and finance. por Library J 91:
5533-6 N 15 '66
DAVISON, Verne E.
More on bird foods and habitats; excerpts.
Audubon Mag 68:58-61, 125-30 Ja-Mr '66
Our continuing list of bird foods, habitats.
Audubon Mag 68:275-7 Jl '66
DAWIDOWICZ, Lucy S.
Belsen remembered. Commentary 41:82-5 Mr
'66
When reform was young. Commentary 42:63-7
Jl '66
DAWKINS, Cecil
Displaced person; dramatization of short
stories, by F. O'Connor. Criticism
Nation 204:92-4 Ja 16 '67
Newsweek 69:71 Ja 9 '67
DAWKINS, Pete
Pete Dawkins takes the field; with report by
S. Angeloff. il pors Life 60:91-4+ Ap 8 '66
DAWSON, Charles P.
Grow better roses. Horticulture 44:44-5 Ap
'66
DAWSON, Louis W.
Gardens & vacations. Flower Grower 53:39+
Jl '66
DAWSON, Noel K.
Too dangerous to drive! Pop Mech 127:99-
101+ Ja '67
DAWSON, Richard G.
Starting a natural science camp program.
bibliog por Parks & Rec 1:220-2+ Mr '66
DAWSON, William Levi
Battle in the ghetto. por Newsweek 67:44+
Je 13 '66
William Dawson calls the tune. R. Cotton.
Reporter 35:21-3 Ag 11 '66
DAY, A. Grove
He was his own best character. Sat R 49:
31-3 Je 18 '66
DAY, Beth
After this party she'll be invited everywhere.
Sat Eve Post 239:34-9 D 3 '66
Mexico's Little Nobody who made good.
Read Digest 89:221-2+ O '66
They couldn't have a baby, and then quin-
tuplets! McCalls 93:82-3+ Je '66
—See Liley, M. jt. auth.
DAY, David E.
Creating a climate for creativity. bibliog f Sch
& Soc 94:330-4 O 15 '66
DAY, Doris
Hollywood interview: canonizing the super-
ficial. J. N. Bell. il Sat R 49:115-16+ O 8
'66
DAY, Melvin S.
Information processing in NASA's library.
por Wilson Lib Bul 41:396-400+ D '66
DAY, R. H. and Wade, N. J.
Visual spatial aftereffect from prolonged
head-tilt. bibliog Science 154:1201-2 D 2 '66
DAY, Richard
Clean up your driveway. Pop Sci 188:145 Mr
'66
Secrets for getting the best engine tune-up.
Pop Sci 189:158-63 N '66
Truth about wheel balancing. Pop Sci 189:140-
3+ Jl '66
Wheel-alignment bunk, are you wasting
money up front? Pop Sci 188:180-5 F '66
You can make your own paneling. Pop Sci
188:170-3 Mr '66
DAY camps. See Camps
DAY care. See Foster day care
DAY it all happened, baby; story. See Thom,
R.
DAY lilies
Day-lilies can solve summer's color problem.
I. Dorsey. il Flower Grower 53:37+ Je '66
Day-lilies for the new garden. M. Haislip.
il Flower Grower 53:20-2 Jl '66
Daylilies make you look good. il Sunset 136:
253 Mr '66
Include daylilies in your garden. D. L. Fer-
rick. il Horticulture 44:26-7+ My '66
Three plant garden. B. Black. il Flower
Grower 53:32-3+ N '66
DAY Mussolini died in Santa Vittoria; story.
See Crichton, R.

DAY nurseries
Here's child care for every working mother;
Denmark's day care centers. J. Kobler. il
Ladies Home J 83:34+ Ag '66
Would this day-care plan work for you? J.
Kuh. Ladies Home J 83:78 O '66
See also
Foster day care
DAY of absence; drama. See Ward, D. T.
DAY schools. See Private schools
DAYAN, Moshe
100 hours. il por Time 87:111+ Je 24 '66
DAYHOFF, Margaret O. See Eck, R. V. jt.
auth.
DAYLIGHT saving
About time: House vote for all states to ob-
serve DST. Newsweek 67:36 Mr 28 '66
End to chaos in daylight-saving time? U S
News 60:10 Mr 28 '66
Toward nationwide D.S.T. Time 87:53 Ap 8
'66
DAYLILIES. See Day lilies
DAYTON, Gary, family
They knew what they wanted. il pors
Motor B 119:86-7+ Ja '67
DAYTON, Mona
Whirlwind of wonder. NEA J 55:8-10 S '66
about
Owl in the kitchen. D. Chapman. il Look
30:100+ D 13 '66
Teacher of the year. D. Chapman. il pors
Look 30:85-6+ Ap 19 '66
Washington report. J. Lloyd. Sr Schol 88:sup7
Ap 29 '66
DAYTON, Paul
Owl in the kitchen. D. Chapman. il Look 30:
100+ D 13 '66
DAYTON, Ohio
Riots
Still hot. il Newsweek 68:27 S 12 '66
DAYTON, Ohio. University
Of many things; teaching situation ethics.
T. N. Davis. America 115:672 N 26 '66
**DAYTON and Montgomery County public li-
brary**
Library workshop for adults. M. T. Stibitz.
il ALA Bul 60:937-41 O '66
DAYTON trial. See Tennessee evolution con-
troversy
DAYTONA BEACH, Fla.
Miles; fast enough to win, slow enough to
finish. B. La Fontaine. il Sports Illus 24:
16-17 F 14 '66
DEAC, Wilfred P.
Battle off Samar. Am Heritage 18:20-3+
D '66
**DEACONS for defense and justice (organiza-
tion)** See Civil rights organizations
DEAD bodies. See Cadavers
DEAD SEA
Dead Sea isn't dead anymore. G. Gaskill. il
Read Digest 89:157-8+ Jl '66
DEAD SEA scrolls
Masada and its scrolls; excerpt from Masada.
Y. Yadin. Commentary 42:41-7 O '66
Shrine of the book; excerpt from address.
A. Eban. il Sch Arts 65:43-5 Ap '66
Untold story of the Dead Sea scrolls. J. M.
Allegro. il Harper 233:46-54 Ag '66; Dis-
cussion. 233:4+ O '66; America 115:227-9 S
3 '66; Christian Cent 83:1211-13 O 5 '66
DEADLY game; drama. See Yaffe, J.
DEADWYLER, Leonard
Flashpoint in Watts? il Newsweek 67:30+ My
30 '66
DEAF
Education
See also
Gallaudet college. Washington, D.C.
Sign language
See Sign language
DEAF, Apparatus for the
See also
Hearing aids
DEAFNESS
Stubborn husband. il Good H 162:12+ Mr '66
See also
Ear
Noise—Physiological effects
Sign language
DEAKIN, James
Games Johnson plays. New Repub 156:10-11
Ja 14 '67
LBJ's club, the whiff of scandal. New Repub
155:13-14 O 1 '66
LBJ's credibility; or, What happened to no
comment? New Repub 154:23-4 Ja 29 '66
Moyers. New Repub 154:13-14 Je 25 '66

DEAL, Andrew S.
Problem of insects; address, November 1965. por Parks & Rec 1:732-3+ S '66
DEAL, Babs H.
Night-blooming cereus; story. Ladies Home J 83:80-1 Mr '66
DEALERS, Automobile. See Automobile dealers
DEAME, Carl
In living plants, the look of sculpture. House & Gard 130:126-7+ Ag '66
DEAN, Anita C.
Keeping food safely at home; with questions and answers. PTA Mag 60:14-16 Je '66
DEAN, Arthur H.
Realism is the principle. Sat R 50:31-2 Ja 7 '67
War on weapons. Sat R 49:23-5+ Mr 19 '66
What it's like to negotiate with the Chinese. N Y Times Mag p44-5+ O 30 '66
DEAN, Charles O.
Soil sterilization. Horticulture 45:47 Ja '67
DEAN, Geoffrey
Doctor's conscience in South Africa. New Repub 154:17-18 Ja 29 '66
DEAN, Neal J. See Taylor, J. W. jt. auth.
DEAN, Otto Kirchner-. See Kirchner-Dean, O.
DEAN, Wayne
Television and the mystery masterpiece. Sch Arts 65:13-15 Mr '66
DEANE, Roger E. See Tovell, W. M. jt. auth.
DEANGELO, Richard
Branches, rags and plaster. Design 67:4-7 My '66
DEARBORN, Mich.
Dearborn referendum; concerning Vietnamese war. Nation 203:659 D 19 '66
See also
Henry Ford museum and Greenfield Village
DEARBORN street. See Chicago—Streets
DEARDEN, John
Myth of real-time management information. Harvard Bsns R 44:123-32 My '66
—See Henderson, B. D. jt. auth.
DEARDORFF, Robert
Off-beat Belgium. Travel 125:61-4 Ap '66
DEARING, Bruce
Schools, styles, and systems in thinking; adaptation of address, September 25, 1965. Sch & Soc 94:317-19+ O 15 '66
DEARMORE, Tom
Arkansas: the rage of the rednecks. Reporter 35:24-8 O 20 '66
DEASY, Philip
Books. Commonweal 84:374-5; 85:231-2 Je 17, N 25 '66
DEATH
Death in Sun City. C. Davis. il Esquire 66:134-7 O '66
Let's retain the dignity of dying. W. Kitay. Todays Health 44:62-4+ My '66
Our Uleri child; death of a child in a little Asian village. P. Hitchcock. il Redbook 127:20+ Ag '66
Very easy death, by S. de Beauvoir. Review Esquire 66:24-5 Jl '66. M. Muggeridge Time il 87:124+ My 20 '66
Why bother about life beyond death? G. M. Schurr. Christian Cent 83:424-6 Ap 6 '66; Reply. E. T. Dahlberg. 83:806 Je 22 '66
See also
Bereavement
Children and death
Euthanasia
Funeral rites and ceremonies
Suicide
Causes
See also
Heat—Physiological effects
DEATH (biology)
Final freedom. E. D. Plant. Vogue 147:40 Je '66
Frozen Christian: cryogenic interment. R. C. W. Ettinger; discussion. Christian Cent 82:1550+; 83:183-4 D 15 '65, F 9 '66
Let's retain the dignity of dying. W. Kitay. Todays Health 44:62-4+ My '66
What is life? when is death? il Time 87:78 My 27 '66
DEATH and children. See Children and death
DEATH of God theology
Are the churches in trouble? with excerpts from interview with J. A. Pike. il U S News 60:54-60 Ap 18 '66
Beware the antithesis! E. W. Hollon, jr. Christian Cent 83:303-4 Mr 9 '66
Challenge of God is dead. R. L. Richard. America 115:173-6 Ag 20 '66
Dead God. Commonweal 84:429-30 Jl 8 '66
Death of God or God of death? W. M. Alexander. Christian Cent 83:363-5 Mr 23 '66; Discussion. 83:684 My 25 '66

Death of God phenomenon. B. A. Willems. Cath World 204:17-19 O '66
Death of God theology. W. Herberg. Nat R 18:771+, 839-40, 884-5 Ag 9-S 6 '66; Discussion. 18:908+, 962-3+ S 20-O 4 '66
God is dead debate. A. Whitman. il Redbook 127:62-3+ Je '66
God is not dead; interview. B. Graham. il U S News 60:74-80+ Ap 25 '66
God makes the news weeklies. Nation 202:443 Ap 18 '66
God speaks to a godless world. M. M. Shideler. Christian Cent 83:676-80 My 25 '66
Gospel of Christian atheism, by T. J. J. Altizer. Review
Christian Cent 83:715 Je 1 '66. S. Keen
In defense of God. J. C. Bennett. Look 30:69-70+ Ap 19 '66
Not all the answers; faith in the living God. V. P. McCorry. America 114:210-11 F 5 '66
Not dead enough. S. Hiltner. Christian Cent 83:1181-2 S 28 '66
Opinion: should God die? G. B. Blaine, jr. Mlle 63:138+ Ag '66
Radical theology; from honest-to-God to God-is-dead. R. P. McBrien. Commonweal 84:605-8 S 23 '66
Revolt against heaven, by K. Hamilton. Review
Christian Cent 83:1242 O 12 '66. R. Goetz
Secular city and God. J. V. Schall. Cath World 204:20-6 O '66
State of Jewish belief; symposium; with introd. by M. Himmelfarb. Commentary 42:71-160 Ag '66; Reply. Christian Cent 83:1104 S 14 '66
Synoptic problem and the contemporary theological chaos. W. R. Farmer, jr. Christian Cent 83:1204-6 O 5 '66
Tilting at Altizer; College of bishops of the Methodist church join in the death of God debate. J. C. Evans. Christian Cent 83:391-2 Mr 30 '66; Discussion. 83:720-1, 961 Je 1, Ag 3 '66
Toward a hidden God; is God dead? il Time 87:82-7 Ap 8 '66
Urban renewal of religion; the God is dead theologians and their books. D. Poling. Sat R 49:30-1+ My 14 '66; Discussion. 49:22+ Je 25 '66
Visions of God. Sat Eve Post 239:102 N 19 '66
Whose God is dead? interview, ed. by N. R. Campion. H. E. Fosdick. Read Digest 89:67-71 O '66
DEATH penalty. See Capital punishment
DEATH VALLEY NATIONAL MONUMENT
Camera-defying Death Valley. J. Franklin. il U S Camera 29:58-9+ S '66
DEATS, Richard L.
Philippines: ray of hope? Christian Cent 83:283-6 Mr 2 '66
DEAUVILLE, France
Beaches of pleasure, beaches of pain. H. Sutton. Sat R 49:38-9+ Jl 16 '66
DEBAKEY, Lois
Simplicity in scientific writing. Writer 79:25-6 S '66
DEBAKEY, Michael Ellis
Better half-heart; operation at Houston's Methodist hospital. il por Time 87:46+ Ap 29 '66
Death of a patient. Time 87:60 My 6 '66
Patient's gift to the future of heart repair; with report by R. Bailey and A. Kerr. il pors Life 60:84-92 My 6 '66
Plastic heart. il por Newsweek 67:64 My 2 '66
They're sewing plastic standby hearts in people. H. Fantel. il por Pop Mech 127:136-9+ Ja '67
DEBATES and debating
See also
Forums (discussion and debate)
DE BEER, Sir Gavin Rylands
Portrait in science; Darwin's Origin today. Natur Hist 75:62+ Ag '66
DE BELLAIGUE, Geoffrey
George IV and the arts of France. Antiques 89:700-5 My '66
DEBENTURES. See Bonds
DEBENTURES, Convertible. See Bonds, Convertible
DE BERNARDIS, Amo
Audio-visuals at your fingertips. Sr Schol 87:sup26 Ja 14 '66
DEBES, John L.
Home-grown slide sets. Sr Schol 89:sup 18 O 7 '66
How to make and use effective audiovisuals. Sr Schol 88:sup26-8 Ap 29 '66
DEBLOCK, E. T. and Thomas, J. R.
Sealed lead-acid batteries. Electr World 75:32-4 Je '66

DE BORCHGRAVE, Arnaud
Europe goes its way. Newsweek 69:48-50+
Ja 23 '67
DEBRÉ, Michel
Duumvirate. por Time 87:34 F 25 '66
Truest believer. por Newsweek 67:46 F 28 '66
DEBROSSE, Thomas J.
Vortac to remember. Flying 79:99-100 Ag '66
DEBT
Debt-financed binge, an official warning; excerpts from address, January 29, 1966. C. N.
Shepardson. U S News 60:90 F 14 '66
Overspenders: families throughout the country. J. Gunther. il Ladies Home J 83:75-
7+ Ap '66
Why young couples spend more than they
earn. S. Margolius. il Redbook 126:56-7+
F '66
See also
Collecting of accounts
Credit
Debtor and creditor
DEBTOR and creditor
When you owe money, what are your rights?
P. Lindberg. Bet Hom & Gard 45:6+ Ja
'67
DEBTS, Public
Escalator of debt. Fortune 73:76+ Je '66
Why U.S. won't dun old war debtors; foreign
government debt to the U.S. arising from
World war I. il Bsns W p83-4+ N 12 '66

United States
Debt, debt, debt, all to our credit? how much
we owe. il Newsweek 67:73 Je 6 '66
Debt phobia. H. C. Wallich. Newsweek 67:80
Mr 7 '66
Federal debt near legal limit. U S News 61:
88-9 D 5 '66
National debt: burden or benefit to the
economy? Sr Schol 88:9-10 Ap 22 '66
Soaring cost of national debt. il U S News
62:53 Ja 16 '67
DEBUSSY, Claude
Pelléas et Mélisande. Criticism
Opera N il 31:32 S 10 '66
Still incomparable: George Copeland. R.
Kammerer. Am Rec G 32:712 Ap '66
DEBUTANTES
After this party she'll be invited everywhere.
B. Day. il Sat Eve Post 239:34-9 D 3 '66
DECADENCE, Social. See Degeneration
DECAPITATION
Decapitation revisited (all tumbrils are go)
J. H. Slate. il Atlan 218:117-18 S '66
DE CARVALHO, George
In Jordan a spunky king again fights to
hold on. Life 61:50B D 9 '66
Sun rises as Pharaoh planned. Life 61:38-9
D 2 '66
DE CASTRO, Flavio
Culture in the bank. Américas 18:14-16 Jl '66
DECATHLON. See Track athletics
DECATUR, Ill.

Parks and playgrounds
Park adds an airport, subtracts maintenance
costs. L. Chandler. il Am City 81:118-19
S '66

Streets
Job-matched units spur snow-fighting. W. D.
Kirby. il Am City 81:98-9 F '66
DECATUR, Ill. public library
Decatur: pioneer in data processing; reprint.
M. K. Weidner. Wilson Lib Bul 41:409-10+
D '66
DECAUSEY, Barbara
Our neighbors helped us rebuild out of the
ashes; ed. by L. Shecter. il Good H 162:
98-9+ Je '66
DECAY, Dental. See Teeth—Diseases
DECEDENTS estates. See Estates, Decedents
DECENCY
Arms against Venus; topless waitresses. G.
Ace. Sat R 49:16 D 10 '66
Steady as she goes: dividing line between
permissible and impermissible exposure of
female breasts. il Time 87:67 Je 17 '66
DECENTRALIZING authority in business. See
Business management and organization
DECEW, Richard E.
Greater design freedom for decorative fountains. Arch Rec 140:141-4 Ag '66
DECHANT, Tony T.
New leaders for National farmers union.
O. Bay. Farm J 90:58J My '66
DECIBELS
Determining dB power ratios. C. J. Diodati.
il Electr World 76:83 S '66
What are these things called decibels? M.
Lincoln. il Pop Electr 25:75-8+ O '66

DECIMAL classification. See Classification,
Decimal
DECISION making
Analyzing overseas investments. P. Q.
Gaddis. il Harvard Bsns R 44:115-22 My '66
Anatomy of the creative decision; address,
March 10, 1966. R. E. Williams. Vital
Speeches 32:508-12 Je 1 '66
Case of the product priority; excerpts from
Cases in marketing management. E. C.
Bursk. il Harvard Bsns R 44:6-8+ Mr '66
Dynamic programming. R. Bellman. il Science 153:34-7 Jl 1 '66
Fallacy of the one big brain. P. Hunt. il
Harvard Bsns R 44:84-90 Jl '66
How to make better decisions. il Nations
Bsns 54:48-50+ Ja '66
Improving estimates that involve uncertainty. D. H. Woods. il Harvard Bsns R
44:91-8 Jl '66
Interpersonal barriers to decision making. C.
Argyris. il Harvard Bsns R 44:84-97 Mr '66
No, not another committee. J. G. Mason. il
Nations Bsns 53:80-1+ D '65
Rewards of risking it. J. K. Lagemann. Read
Digest 90:191+ Ja '67
Scholar and the alienated generation; address, May 16, 1966. A. C. Baird. Vital
Speeches 32:590-3 Jl 15 '66
Six business lessons from the Pentagon. D. J.
Smalter and R. L. Ruggles, jr. il Harvard
Bsns R 44:64-75 Mr '66
Use that sixth sense, instinct. R. Dreyfack.
il Nations Bsns 54:80-2+ D '66
Utility theory, insights into risk taking. R.
O. Swalm. bibliog f il Harvard Bsns R 44:
123-36 N '66
DECISIONS, Judicial. See Judgments
DECKS (outdoor rooms) See Outdoor rooms
DECLARATION of human rights. See Universal declaration of human rights
DECOMPOSITION
Gibrel: effect on decomposition of plant
materials. P. Chandra and W. B. Bollen.
bibliog il Science 153:1663-4 S 30 '66
DECORATION and ornament
Decorated military Americana. W. H. Guthman. il Antiques 90:60-3 Jl '66
Egyptian revival in the decorative arts. J. S.
Johnson. il Antiques 90:489-94 O '66
Fun with words and objects. il House & Gard
130:102-3+ Jl '66
How to create a big effect for a big party.
il House & Gard 128:222-4 Ap '66
DECORATION and ornament
See also
Arts and crafts
Christmas decorations
Flowers, Arrangement of
Jewelry
Moldings (architecture)
Mural painting and decoration
Paneling
Table decoration
DECORATION and ornament, Architectural
City fragments: outdoor sculpture garden
made possible by Anonymous arts recovery
society; at Brooklyn museum. New Yorker
42:28-30 Je 11 '66
What is suitable art for public buildings.
E. Goble. Arch Rec 139:9 My '66
DECORATIONS, Christmas. See Christmas
decorations
DECORATIVE design. See Design, Decorative
DECORATIVE hardware. See Hardware
DECORATIVE plants. See Plants, Ornamental
DECOYS (hunting)
Decoys of the Pacific flyway. il Sunset 137:
36+ D '66
Dogs that decoy ducks. N. Karas. il Field &
S 71:80-2+ S '66
How to make bag decoys. H. G. Tapply. il
Field & S 71:62 O '66
DE CRISTOFORO, R. J.
Double-duty-sander-setup. Pop Mech 125:
176-8 Ap '66
Get acquainted with plug cutters. Pop Sci
188:150-2 Mr '66
How to use the drinking-cup trick in woodworking. Pop Sci 189:116-20 Jl '66
Jig-of-all-work for your table saw. Pop Sci
189:180-4 O '66
Routermatic. Pop Sci 189:119 Ag '66
Two handsome new radial-arm saws. Pop Sci
189:144-9 N '66
Woodworking champ of any shop. Pop Sci
188:166-71+ F '66
DEDIJER, Stevan
Other U.S. Bul Atomic Sci 22:28-30 F '66
DEE, Elaine Evans
Books in review. Natur Hist 75:58+ O '66

DEE, Sandra
Peter Pan is out! ed. by E. Miller. pors Seventeen 25:158-9+ Mr '66

DEEMER, Charles
Jeopardy and alibi. New Repub 155:26+ O 1 '66

DEEP sea deposits
Deep-sea pleistocene biostratigraphy. L. Lidz. bibliog il Science 154:1448-52 D 16 '66
Low-energy protons: average flux in interplanetary space during the last 100,000 years. D. Lal and V. S. Venkatavaradan. bibliog il Science 151:1381-4 Mr 18 '66
Potassium-argon geochronology of deep-sea sediments. J. R. Dymond. bibliog il Science 152:1239-41 My 27 '66
Strontium isotopes in deep-sea sediments. E. J. Dasch and others. bibliog il Science 153:295-7 Jl 15 '66

DEEP sea diving. See Diving, Submarine

DEEP sea fishes. See Fishes, Deep sea

DEEP sea photography. See Photography, Submarine

DEEP-sea research vessels. See Ships, Research

DEEP-submergence rescue vehicle. See Submarine boats

DEER, Irving
Books in the field: drama. bibliog por Wilson Lib Bul 41:318-24 N '66

DEER
How to trace a turtle and follow a deer. D. Cohen. il Sci Digest 59:28-31 Mr '66
Nature note: Père David's deer. Sci N 89:500 Je 18 '66
Those curious midgets; Florida Key deer. J. Browder. il Am For 72:12+ O '66
See also
Deer hunting
Reindeer

DEER farming
Charley Varney's deer farm. N. Karas. il Field & S 71:58-9+ O '66

DEER hunting
Backyard record deer; ed. by H. Kenny. M. Johnson. il Field & S 71:50-1+ Jl '66
Buck packing made easy. F. Calkins. il Field & S 71:60-1+ S '66
Deer you hunt like rabbit. C. Robinson. il Field & S 71:52-3+ O '66
Don't shoot unless you're loaded; hunting behind the iron curtain. C. Thayer. il Sports Illus 25:96-102+ D 5 '66
Farewell, Eric Collier. E. Collier. il Outdoor Life 139:54-5+ Ja '67
Farm-fed whitetails. B. Geagan. il Field & S 71:68-9+ N '66
Forty-five experts tell where to hunt deer; symposium. il Outdoor Life 138:54-7+ O '66
Ghosts of the Shawnee; whitetail-deer hunting. B. Cary. il Outdoor Life 138:32-7 N '66
Giant of Newcomer Hollow; ed. by J. Hayes. R. E. Miller. il Outdoor Life 137:38-9+ F '66
Good and bad bowhunting. G. H. Gillelan. il Outdoor Life 138:128+ O '66
How to drive deer; with charts. R. Beck. il Outdoor Life 138:40-3+ S '66
Hunting atomic energy reserve. C. Elliott. il Outdoor Life 138:42-3+ Ag '66
Hunting's best-kept secret; Colorado postseason on deer. R. Tinsley. il Field & S 71:25-7+ Ag '66
I shot Big Red. C. W. Shelton. il Outdoor Life 139:44-5+ Ja '67
Kansas' first deer hunt; whitetails and mule deer. A. Weaver. il Outdoor Life 138:64-5+ N '66
Late hunting is great hunting. B. Milek. il Field & S 71:49-51+ N '66
Luck of Irish ridge; ed. by M. C. Gilfillan. D. Allison. il Outdoor Life 138:56-7+ D '66
More deer than hunters. G. Hornbeck. il Field & S 71:49-51+ O '66
New trophy for bowmen. G. H. Gillelan. il Outdoor Life 137:24+ My '66
One thousand yard bucks. K. C. Hinman. il Field & S 71:56-7+ O '66
Shot in the dark;; hunting with bow-and-arrow. H. Cox. il Outdoor Life 137:56-9+ Mr '66
Summer deer hunt. P. Barrett. il Outdoor Life 138:28-31+ Jl '66
Surefire deer country; west Texas' Big Bend country. B. W. Dalrymple. il Outdoor Life 138:38-41+ D '66
Thanksgiving hunt. J. McPhee. il Outdoor Life 137:60-1+ My '66
Think like a deer. M. E. Barker. il Field & S 71:46-7+ O '66
This is trophy hunting; mule deer. C. Elliott. il Outdoor Life 138:54-7+ N '66
Too many bucks. G. H. Gillelan. il Outdoor Life 138:60-1+ S '66

Trail to buck mountain. F. Dufresne. il Field & S 71:40-1+ O '66
Where hunters never fail; southwest Idaho. L. Miracle. il Outdoor Life 137:60-1+ Je '66
Whitetails in the sands. J. O. Cartier. il Outdoor Life 138:46-9+ N '66
Whitetails vs. mule deer. G. H. Gillelan. il Outdoor Life 138:26+ S '66

DEER repellents
Uncle Perk's deer lure. C. Ford. il Field & S 71:6+ N '66

DEER snatching. See Robberies and assaults

DEERE and company
Farm technology plows ahead at John Deere. G. Bylinsky. il Fortune 74:147-51+ D '66

DEERFIELD, Mass.
Profiles: F. L. Boyden, headmaster. J. McPhee. New Yorker 42:57-8+ Mr 19 '66
This is tranquil Deerfield and this is the town's artist; with paintings. il Am Heritage 17:22-9 Ap '66

Historic houses, etc.
Wells-Thorn house in Deerfield, Massachusetts. J. P. Spang, 3d. il Antiques 89:730-3 My '66

DEERFIELD academy. See Private schools

DEERING, Elmer C. and Du Von, Jay
Education and the bond market (cont) Am Ed 2:28 D '65

DEERING, Milliken and company
Give a round to Darlington; NLRB examiner finds shutdown not illegal. Bsns W p62 Ag 20 '66

DEFAMATION. See Libel and slander

DEFECTORS, Political
American defector comes home. il Look 30:72-4 F 8 '66
American defector comes home; why I quit China; ed. by R. Moskin. M. R. Wills. il Look 30:84-8+ F 22 '66
By mutual consent; case of Clarence S. Adams. il Time 88:20-1 Jl 15 '66
Homesick; C. Adams returning to U.S. il Newsweek 67:44 Je 6 '66
Spooks among the spikes; wrestler defects to the West. il Time 87:42 Je 24 '66
Thief of Baghdad; Mounir Rowfa defection. il Newsweek 68:31-2 Ag 29 '66
Why I chose China; ed. by J. R. Moskin. M. R. Wills. il Look 30:75-80+ F 8 '66

DEFENSE, Civilian. See Civil defense

DEFENSE, Department of. See United States—Defense, Department of

DEFENSE, Self. See Self defense

DEFENSE appropriations. See United States—Armed forces—Appropriations and expenditures

DEFENSE buying. See United States—Armed forces—Procurement

DEFENSE contracts. See Contracts, Government

DEFENSE economy. See War—Economic aspects

DEFENSE electronics, incorporated
DEI monitor may have myriad new uses. Tech W 19:38 Ag 1 '66

DEFENSE industries. See Munitions industries

DEFENSE information, Classified
Research and the munitions list: scientific exchange not always easy. E. Langer. Science 154:625-6 N 4 '66

DEFENSE information school. See United States—Army—Defense information school

DEFENSE laboratories. See Military research

DEFENSE language institute. See United States—Defense language institute

DEFENSE marketing services. See DMS, incorporated

DEFENSE mechanisms (biology)
Beetle's spray discourages predators; study of eleodes. T. E. Eisner. il Natur Hist 75:42-7 bibliog(p68) F '66
Defense against killers; gulls protect themselves against ground and aerial enemies. H. Kruuk. il Natur Hist 75:48-55 Ap '66
Defensive secretions of arthropods. T. Eisner and J. Meinwald. bibliog il Science 153:1341-50 S 16 '66
1,2-dialkyl-4-(3H)-quinazolinones in the defensive secretion of a millipede (glomeris marginata) Y. C. Meinwald and others. bibliog il Science 154:390-1 O 21 '66
D-Gluconic acid; isolation from the defensive secretion of the cockroach eurycotis decipiens. G. P. Dateo and L. M. Roth. bibliog il Science 155:88-9 Ja 6 '67
Insects speak in chemicals. B. Tufty. il Sci N 90:271 O 8 '66

DEFENSE research and engineering, Director of. See United States—Defense research and engineering, Director of

DEFENSE supply agency. See United States—Defense. Department of—Defense supply agency

DEFERRED payment plan. See Instalment plan

DEFFERRE, Gaston
De Gaulle and after. For Affairs 44:434-45 Ap '66

DEFICIT spending. See Government spending policy

DE FOE, James R.
This is to recommend, well . . . me. Sat Eve Post 240:18 Ja 28 '67

DEFONTAINE, Ham
Gadgets and gilhickies. See issues of Yachting

DEFONTAINE, W. H.
Designs. il Yachting 119:120-6+ Ja '66

DEFORD, Frank
Basketball (cont) Sports Illus 24:42-4 Ja 31 '66
College basketball (cont) Sports Illus 24:52+ F 21 '66
Lacrosse (cont) Sports Illus 24:88+ Je 13 '66
Tennis (cont) Sports Illus 24:58+ Je 20; 25: 105-6+ S 19 '66

DE FOREST, Lee
Verismo in the air. A. Ronnie. il por Opera N 31:6-7 D 3 '66

DEFORMITIES
Congenital malformations and cancer; United States—Japan cooperative science program; report from meeting in Tokyo. R. W. Miller and H. Nishimura. Science 151:357-8 Ja 21 '66
Fat man and his friends. il Am Heritage 17: 34-9 Je '66
Tracking down the causes of birth defects. R. L. Masland. il Todays Health 44:60-2+ Ag '66
X-rays show pouch causes infant coughs; dead-end esophagus. Sci N 89:221 Ap 2 '66
See also
Spine—Abnormities and deformities

DEFOURNEAUX, René J.
Secret encounter with Ho chi Minh; ed. by J. Flowers. por Look 30:32-3 Ag 9 '66

DEFREN, Marcia S.
Using records to teach history. Sr Schol 89:sup 18 N 11 '66

DEFRIES, J. C. and others
Open-field behavior in mice: evidence for a major gene effect mediated by the visual system. bibliog Science 154:1577-9 D 23 '66

DE GAETANI, Thomas P.
Building for the arts, or, A house is not a home. por Dance Mag 40:36-9+ N '66

DE GAULLE, Charles. See Gaulle, C. de

DEGENERATION
Opinion: on decadence. M. Redner Mlle 63: 58+ O '66

DEGENS, Egon T. See Siegel, A. jt. auth.

DEGNAN, James P.
Monopoly in the vineyards; grapes of wrath strike. Nation 202:151-4 F 7 '66
With a hep-ful exegesis. Esquire 66:243+ D '66

DEGOOD, Jeanne
Yankee, go home; poem. Negro Hist Bul 29: 91 Ja '66

DEGRADATION (chemistry)
Copper and the role of isopods in degradation of organic matter. W. Wieser. bibliog il Science 153:67-9 Jl 1 '66

DE GRAMONT, Sanche
Under Viet Cong control. Sat Eve Post 239: 27-33+ Ja 29 '66

DEGREE mills. See Diplomas, Fraudulent

DEGREES, Academic
Higher education: a population flow feedback model. A. Reisman. bibliog il Science 153:89-91 Jl 1 '66
Language requirements for the Ph.D; letter. S. Ross and C. W. Shilling. Science 153: 1595 S 30 '66; Discussion. 154:1603 D 30 '66
Matter of degree; law school degrees. Time 88:34 D 30 '66
New routes to the B.A. Sat R 49:93 N 19 '66
Ph.D. under attack. Time 87:75 Je 10 '66
Ph.D.'s: study traces their path from sheepskin to 25 years later. M. Zeiger. il Science 152:629-30 Ap 29 '66
Qualifying orals for the Ph.D: a test of the examiners; letter. M. Hildebrand. Science 154:843-4 N 18 '66
Six-year Ph.D. program. Sch & Soc 94:172+ Ap 2 '66
See also
Diplomas, Fraudulent

DEGREES, Honorary
Kudos. Time 87:77 Je 10; 77-8 Je 17; 76 Je 24 '66
Reaping the rewards of service; tribute to business' contributions to society. Bsns W p88-91 Je 18 '66

DE GROOT, Roy Andries
Feasts for all seasons; excerpts from Feasts for all seasons. Ladies Home J 83:104-5+ S '66

DEHAAN, Bryon
Enlisting community support for civil rights; address, January 20, 1966. Vital Speeches 32: 272-5 F 15 '66

DEHN, Harold A.
Build your own air compressor. Pop Mech 127:183-4 Ja '67

DEHYDRATION
Pressure-induced dehydration reactions and transitions in inorganic hydrates. R. R. Sood and R. A. Stager. bibliog il Science 154:388-90 O 21 '66

DEHYDROGENASES
Cytochemical localization of lactate dehydrogenase in muscular dystrophy of the mouse. H. D. Fahimi and P. Roy. bibliog il Science 152:1761-3 Je 24 '66
D(−)-lactate dehydrogenase in lower fungi. F. H. Gleason and others. bibliog il Science 152:1272-3 My 27 '66
Electrophoretic heterogeneity of mammalian galactose dehydrogenase. P. Cuatrecasas and S. Segal. bibliog il Science 153:533-5 O 28 '66
Enzyme-coenzyme complexes of pyridine nucleotide-linked dehydrogenases. H. F. Fisher and D. G. Cross. bibliog il Science 153:414-15 Jl 22 '66
Enzymes' tailored forms; studying multiple forms of lactate dehydrogenase. B. J. Culliton. Sci N 90:513 D 17 '66
Evolution of malate dehydrogenase in birds. G. B. Kitto and A. C. Wilson. bibliog il Science 153:1408-10 S 16 '66
Glucose-6-phasphate dehydrogenase: homologous molecules in deer mouse and man. C. R. Shaw. bibliog Science 153:1013-15 Ag 26 '66
Hexose-6-phosphate dehydrogenase found in human liver. S. Ohno and others. bibliog il Science 153:1015-16 Ag 26 '66
Lactate dehydrogenase activity: effect in vitro of some pesticidal chemicals. C. R. Sova. bibliog il Science 154:1661-2 D 30 '66
Lactate dehydrogenase isozymes of chick embryo: response to variations of ambient oxygen tension. S. Lindy and M. Rajasalmi. bibliog il Science 153:1401-3 S 16 '66
Lactate dehydrogenase of trout: hybridization in vivo and in vitro. E. Goldberg. bibliog il Science 151:1091-3 Mr 4 '66
Negro variant of glucose-6-phosphate dehydrogenase deficiency (A-) in man. A. Yoshida and others. bibliog il Science 155: 97-9 Ja 6 '67
Peafowl lactate dehydrogenase: problem of isoenzyme identification. R. G. Rose and A. C. Wilson. bibliog il Science 153:1411-13 S 16 '66
Pyruvate inhibition of lactate dehydrogenase activity in human tissue extracts. A. L. Latner and others. bibliog il Science 154: 527-9 O 28 '66

DE-ICERS. See Airplanes—Ice protection

DEIGHTON, Lee C.
Future of printing in a data-hungry society; summary of address. Pub W 189:55-60 Ja 31 '66
We will leave no worm unturned; address at the opening of the Textbook show 1966; April 6, 1966. por Pub W 189:26-9 My 2 '66

DEIGHTON, Len
Fallen soufflé. il por Newsweek 67:89 Ja 31 '66
Hot spy writer on the lam. H. Moffett. il pors Life 60:84-6+ Mr 25 '66

DEIMEL, Peter A.
Tree time in Anaheim. pors Parks & Rec 1:218-19 Mr '66

DEINDORFER, Robert G.
Fraud in international affairs. Sat R 49:41 S 10 '66

DEJECTION. See Depression, Mental

DEJONG, David Cornel
Family court ltd; North of Hackensack; Honeymoon; poems. Poetry 109:7-11 O '66
Occupant; poem. Nation 203:394 O 17 '66

DEKALB area technical school, Clarkston, Ga. See Trade schools

DEKALB college, Clarkston, Ga.
Post-high opportunity in DeKalb, Georgia. T. W. Hollingsworth. il NEA J 55:44-5 S '66

DEKKER, Charles A. See Cole, R. D. jt. auth.

DE KOSTER, Lester Ronald
DeKoster on DeKoster: a reply; letter to the editor. Nat R 18:951 S 20 '66

about

Is Robert Welch's doctrine Christian? A. Croce. Nat R 18:762 Ag 9 '66; Discussion. 18:910+ S 20 '66
DELANEY, Barbara Snow
Preservation 1966. Antiques 90:526 O '66
DELANO, James G. and Neisser, E. G.
Truth about teenage rebellion. Parents Mag 41:42-3+ Jl '66
DE LANUX, Eyre
Montegufoni. New Yorker 42:198+ S 10 '66
DELAPLANE, Stan
Letter from Stan Delaplane. See issues of Today's health
DE LAURENTIIS, Dino
Dino, the De Mille of Italy; interview, ed. by P. Dragadze. il pors Life 61:59-60+ D 9 '66
DELAWARE
See also
Gardens—Delaware
Hunting—Delaware

Industries

War on smell; Bishop processing company, Selbyville, ordered to deodorize. Newsweek 67:23-4 Ja 31 '66
DELAWARE COUNTY, Pa.
Name it, our computer can do it. J. F. Mc-Nichol. il Am City 81:88-9 D '66
DELAWARE, Lackawanna and Western railroad. See Railroads—Consolidations and mergers
DELAWARE RIVER
Delaware River maps. Field & S 71:141 Je '66
DEL CASTILLO, J. and others
Lipid films as transducers for detection of antigen-antibody and enzyme-substrate reactions. bibliog Science 153:185-8 Jl 8 '66
DELEE, Sol T. and Smith, B. B.
Among the troubles we don't talk about. Todays Health 44:62-3 O '66
DE LEON, Candido
Operation SEEK. por Sch & Soc 94:374+ N 12 '66
DELGADO, Humberto
Who murdered General Delgado? S. De Gramont. pors Sat Eve Post 239:49-51 Ja 1 '66; Correction. 239:6 F 12 '66
DELICATE balance; drama. See Albee, E.
DELINQUENT children. See Juvenile delinquency; Problem children
DELIUS, Anthony
Nothing personal; story. New Yorker 42:47-52 Mr 19 '66
South Africa gets a new warden. Reporter 35:38-40 O 6 '66
DELIUS, Frederick
Important new soloist in a belated Delius first. M. Maxwell. il Am Rec G 32:539 F '66
Music of our time. H. Kupferberg. il Atlan 217-118-20 My '66
DELL publishing company
Court allows Peyton Place name on Dell biography. Pub W 189:30 Ap 4 '66; Correction. 189:84 Ap 18 '66
DELMAN, David
Triangle; story. Redbook 127:145 Je '66
DEL MAR, William A.
Quaker singer. Opera N 31:30-1 Ja 14 '67
DELMAS, Gladys
Argentina returns to autocracy. Reporter 35:35-8 N 3 '66
Bolivia: revolution in mid-passage. Reporter 35:31-4 D 1 '66
Togetherness in Central America. Reporter 34:34-7 Ap 7 '66
DEL MONTE brand. See California packing corporation
DEL NORTE Coast Redwoods State Park. See California—Parks and reserves
DELOACH, Edwin R.
SCR auto burglar alarm. Electr World 76:64-5 Ag '66
DELONG, Stephen E. See Powell, J. L. jt. auth.
DE LORENZO, A. J. D.
Electron microscopy: tight junctions in synapses of the chick ciliary ganglion. bibliog Science 152:76-8 Ap 1 '66
DE LOSS, John
New books. Cath World 203:369-71 S '66
DELPHINIUMS
Blue-flowered best seller. il Sunset 136:224 F '66
DELTA air lines
Delta may expand early morning service. il Aviation W 84:47+ Je 13 '66

Final flight. Time 88:91-2 S 23 '66
Introduction of DC-9s smooth for Delta. D. A. Brown. il Aviation W 85:42-3+ S 12 '66
DELTA booster. See Space vehicles—Propulsion systems
DELWICHE, C. C.
Nitrogen fixation; report on informal colloquium. Science 151:1565-6 Mr 25 '66
DELZELL, Charles F.
Black hand in Sicily. Sat R 49:29 Ag 13 '66
Country to call their own. Sat R 49:40-1 Mr 5 '66
DE MACAYA, Margarita O.
IACW. pors Américas 18:37-41 Ag '66
DEMAGGIO, A. E.
Phloem differentiation: induced stimulation by gibberellic acid. bibliog Science 152:370-2 Ap 15 '66
DEMARIA, Fernando
Homage to Alberto Greco. Américas 18:37 My '66
DEMARIS, Ovid
Going to see Gary. Esquire 65:88-91+ My '66
DEMCY, Arthur I.
Duty and copyright problems in importing books and sheets; summary of address at meeting of publishers. March 29, 1966. Pub W 189:41-3 My 9 '66
DEMELLO, Alonzo
Most entrancing man in Hawaii. il pors Ebony 21:116-18+ O '66
DE MENIL, Dominique (Schlumberger)
Collectors' house: the De Menils' affair with art. J. J. Sweeney. il por Vogue 147:184-93+ Ap 1 '66
DE MENIL, John
Collectors' house: the De Menils' affair with art. J. J. Sweeney. il por Vogue 147:184-93+ Ap 1 '66
DEMENT, William C. See Cohen, H. B. jt. auth.
DEMENTIA praecox. See Schizophrenia
DE MILLE, Agnes
Whatever has become of mommy? Horizon 8:4-15 Sum '66
DEMINERALIZERS. See Water purifiers, Domestic
DEMIREL, Suleyman
Polite distance. il por Time 88:21 D 30 '66
DEMITASSE. See Cups
DEMOCRACY
Extremism; excerpts from address, June 23, 1965. E. Duff. Library J 91:619-23+ F 1 '66
Overseas image of American democracy; address; with questions and answers. G. V. Allen. Ann Am Acad 366:60-7 Jl '66
Perennial challenge to democracy. America 115:477 O 22 '66
Social origins of dictatorship and democracy, by B. Moore, jr. Review
New Repub 156:34-6+ Ja 7 '67. J. Featherstone
See also
Communism and democracy
Liberalism
Liberty
Majorities
Town meeting

Study and teaching

Democracy in a test tube. H. Graham. Sr Schol 88:sup 13-14 Ap 22 '66
DEMOCRACY and communism. See Communism and democracy
DEMOCRATIC clubs. See Political clubs and associations
DEMOCRATIC party
Death of the New deal. W. D. Burnham. Commonweal 85:284-7 D 9 '66
Democrats. Time 87:25 Ap 1 '66
Democrats who talk back; National committee's actions against College young Democrats. New Repub 155:7 D 24 '66
Hints of malaise; meetings in Washington. Time 87:29-30 Ap 29 '66
It was no monolith. R. Moley. Newsweek 69:104 Ja 23 '67
Kennedy in '68? H. H. Miller. New Repub 155:11-13 O 15 '66
Loss column; midterm upset election. K. Crawford. Newsweek 68:49 N 21 '66
LBJ and the Democrats. M. Greenfield. il Reporter 34:8-13 Je 2 '66
My hopes for the Democrats. E. J. Mc-Carthy. Sat R 49:21-3+ N 5 '66
Need for a third party. L. La Fave. Bul Atomic Sci 22:39 O '66
Party in power; LBJ's technique; interparty rivalry; finances. D. S. Broder; D. Kiker; W. Pincus. il Atlan 218:60-75 O '66
Political realignment. W. Lippmann. Newsweek 69:13 Ja 2 '67

DEMOCRATIC party—*Continued*
Sorensen looks at '68: not a single state safe for Democrats; excerpts from address, December 12, 1966. T. C. Sorensen. U S Cent 83:1598-601 D 28 '66
What party leaders think of Bobby Kennedy's future. il U S News 61:54-6 S 26 '66
Why Democrats are losing ground; size-up by nation's governors. il U S News 61:37-9 Jl 18 '66

DEMOGRAPHY. See Population

DEMOLITION of buildings. See Wrecking

DEMONSTRATION against Vietnamese war. See Vietnamese war, 1957—Protests, demonstrations, etc. against

DEMONSTRATORS; story. See Welty, E.

DEMOTT, Benjamin
Against McLuhan. Esquire 66:71-3 Ag '66

DEMPSEY, David
Events leading up to the banquet. Sat R 49:28-9 Je 4 '66
Publishing scene. See occasional issues of Saturday review
Publishing's unagonizing reappraisal. New Repub 154:23-6 My 14; 29 My 28 '66

DEMPSEY, John
In the ring with Dempsey. il Time 88:16 Jl 1 '66

DEMUS, Joerg
Demus: spirit, drive, technique, and intelligence: Goldberg variations. S. Sell por Am Rec G 32:620-1 Mr '66

DENBY, Edwin
Dance magazine's annual awards. por Dance Mag 40:34 Ap '66
Dancers, buildings and people in the streets; excerpt from address. Dance Mag 40:55-7 Je '66

about
Critic's critic. C. Barnes. New Repub 154:40-2 My 14 '66

DENEMARK, George W.
Teacher and his staff. NEA J 55:17-19+ D '66

DE NEUFVILLE, Richard, and Conner, Caryl
How good are our schools? Am Ed 2:1-7 O '66

DENEUVE, Catherine
Catherine of France; portfolio. il pors Esquire 65:142-7 Ap '66

DE NEVERS, Noel
Tar sands and oil shales; with biographical sketch. Sci Am 214:17, 21-9 F '66

DENGLER, Dieter
I escaped from a red prison. pors Sat Eve Post 239:27-33 D 3 '66

about
Great to be alive. pors Newsweek 68:65 S 26 '66
How Communists tortured an American. il pors U S News 61:26 S 26 '66
Snakes & the angel. il pors Time 88:32+ S 23 '66
U.S. navy flier's account of torture and escape in Vietnam. pors Life 61:42C S 23 '66

DENGLER, Harry William
Say it with holly. Am For 72:1-3+ D '66

DENISON, Edward Fulton
Watching the way a giant grows. il Bsns W p86-8+ O 15 '66

DENMARK
See also
Festivals—Denmark
Jews in Denmark
Medicine—Denmark

Description and travel
Denmark. V. S. Pritchett. il Holiday 40:68-75+ N '66
Smorgasbord Sunday: Denmark's Riviera coast. H. Sutton. il Sat R 49:42+ Ag 20 '66
Traveling with Mlle; *skal*, et al. E. Schoen. il Mlle 63:351+ Ag '66

Industries
Disdaneful of competition; Carlsberg and Tuborg. il Time 88:79 Jl 15 '66

DENNERT, Jürgen
There is no longer time for herons or for clouds. Life 61:46-7 O 7 '66

DENNEY, Reuel
Good old days. Commentary 41:86-9 My '66

DENNINGHOFF, Brigitte Meier-. See Meier-Denninghoff, B.

DENNIS, Jessie McNab
Art of keeping warm. Antiques 89:374-9 Mr '66

DENNIS, Landt
Capital ideas. Travel 125:40-4 Mr '66

DENNIS, Willard K.
Kansas City combo. Library J 91:5862-3 D 1 '66

DENNISON, George
Abstracted painters. Commentary 41:100+ F '66
Artist in his skin. Commentary 42:102-4 N '66

DENNISON, Stephen
For a stolen life: $115,000. il por Time 87:43 Mr 25 '66

DE NOBLE, Henry M.
Some remedies for traffic chaos. Am City 81:106-8 D '66

DE NOIE, B. J.
Malverne: integration is not enough. Nat R 18:679-81 Jl 12 '66

DENOMINATIONAL colleges
Baptist education needs two-way stretch; Southern Baptist convention meeting on Baptist higher education. Christian Cent 83:857 Jl 6 '66
Baptists in a bind; question of accepting federal funds for Baptist-related colleges; discussion. Christian Cent 83:146 F 2 '66
Church-sponsored higher education in the United States, by M. M. Parrillo, jr. and D. M. Mackenzie. Review
Sat R 50:75 Ja 21 '67. P. Woodring
Education: facilities grants forbidden to Baptist colleges. L. J. Carter. Science 152:626-9 Ap 29 '66
Freedom and restraint in the Christian college. W. B. Martin. Christian Cent 83:1372-4 N 9 '66
Idea of a Christian college. C. J. Ping. il Sat R 49:90-1+ N 19 '66
Southern Baptist dilemma in higher education; resistance to federal aid to church-related colleges. B. H. Cochran. Christian Cent 83:1598-601 D 28 '66
See also names of denominational colleges, e.g. Upland college, Upland, Calif.

Federal aid
See Federal aid to education

Finance
See also
Education and state
DENOMINATIONAL schools. See Church schools

DENSITOMETRY
Tornadoes: puzzling phenomena and photographs; isodensitometric study. Science 155:27+ Ja 6 '67

DENSITY. See Specific gravity

DENT, Albert Walter
Dillard: pint-size school with a kingsize job. il por Ebony 21:188-90+ My '66

DENTAL caries. See Teeth—Diseases

DENTAL decay. See Teeth—Diseases

DENTAL enamel. See Teeth

DENTAL hygiene. See Teeth—Care and hygiene

DENTAL insurance. See Insurance, Dental

DENTAL metallurgy
Steel tested on teeth; stainless variety for bridgework and caps. il Sci N 89:291 Ap 23 '66

DENTAL plates. See Teeth, Artificial

DENTAL research
High protein diet makes strong teeth. Sci N 89:291 Ap 23 '66
More comfort for you at the dentist's. R. Gannon. il Pop Mech 126:96-9+ Ag '66
New miracles to fight tooth decay. B. Merson. il Good H 162:80-1+ F '66

DENTAL workers
Girls in white; AMA and ADA move to set up criteria for training and certifying assistants. J. Ridgeway. New Repub 154:10-12 F 19 '66

DENTISTRY
Dentists help surgeons. Sci N 90:262 O 1 '66
If your child knocks out a tooth. F. N. Garber. il Parents Mag 41:60-1+ F '66
New miracles to fight tooth decay. B. Merson. il Good H 162:80-1+ F '66
Now, they're saving dead teeth. L. Joseph. il Todays Health 44:14-16 O '66
Occlusal rehabilitation correlates dental treatment. F. H. Wirth. Todays Health 44:30 Mr '66
Protruding teeth corrected by surgery. Sci N 90:8 Jl 2 '66

DENTISTRY—*Continued*
World's most talkative tooth. il Todays
Health 44:92 F '66
See also
American dental association
Dental research
Orthodontics
Teeth—Extraction
Ultrasonic waves in dentistry
X rays in dentistry

DENTISTS
See also
American dental association

DENTLER, Rudolf
Rudolf Dentler. D. Masuhr. il Craft Horiz
26:16-17 Mr '66

DENTON, Winfield K.
Excerpt from testimony, February 9, 1966.
Cong Digest 45:153 My '66

DENTURES, Artificial. See Teeth, Artificial
DENTURES, Partial. See Teeth, Artificial

DENVER
Anti-poverty program
Medicine for the poor: a new deal in Denver.
E. Langer. Science 153:508-12 Jl 29 '66;
Discussion. 154:68+ O 7 '66

Education
Denver's home teaching program. C. Mulford. NEA J 56:14-16 Ja '67

Galleries and museums
Case for stacking galleries; Denver art museum. il Arch Rec 139:204-6 Ap '66

Gardens
See also
Denver botanic gardens

Music
Denver; Donizetti's Lucia di Lammermoor.
A. Young. Opera N 30:30 Ja 29 '66

Sanitary affairs
Rapid transfer system speeds refuse collection. il Am City 81:46 O '66

DENVER botanic gardens
Denver botanic gardens. A. C. Hildreth. il
Horticulture 44:28-9+ Jl '66

DENVER Chicago trucking company. See DC
international

DENVER public library
Malcolm Glenn Wyer. M. W. Killinger. ALA
Bul 60:333-4 Ap '66

DENVER research institute
When arms calls lag; defense companies to
diversify into civilian work. Bsns W p 178
Mr 19 '66

DENZENE, Georges
Education: Dutch style. Sr Schol 88:sup 17+
Ap 15 '66

DEODORIZATION
Removing skunk odor. M. C. Hosmer. Outdoor Life 139:98 Ja '67
Thumb, don't hold, your nose at odor. il Am
City 81:105-6 Je '66

DE ORTIZ Elisabeth Lambert
Caribbean cook book. House & Gard 131:137+
Ja '67

DEOXYCHOLIC acid
Glucocorticoid-induced resistance to deoxycholate lysis in HeLa cells. G. Melnykovych.
bibliog il Science 152:1086-7 My 20 '66

DEOXYRIBONUCLEIC acid
Afiatoxin B_1: binding to DNA in vitro and
alteration of RNA metabolism in vivo.
M. B. Sporn and others. bibliog il Science
151:1539-41 Mr 25 '66
Allomorphic forms of bacteriophage ΦX-174
replicative DNA. T. F. Roth and M.
Hayashi. bibliog il Science 154:658-60 N 4
'66
Antibodies to photoproducts of deoxyribonucleic acids irradiated with ultraviolet light.
L. Levine and others. bibliog il Science 153:
1666-7 S 30 '66
At the controls of the living cell. L. Lessing.
il Fortune 73:154-8+ My '66
Bacteriophage T5 chromosome fractionation:
genetic specificity of a DNA fragment.
Y. T. Lanni and others. bibliog il Science
152:208-10 Ap 8 '66
Biosynthesis of DNA by isolated mitochondria: incorporation of thymidine triphosphate-2-C^{14}. P. Parsons and M. V.
Simpson. bibliog il Science 155:91-3 Ja 6 '67
Chloroplast DNA from tobacco leaves. K. K.
Tewari and S. G. Wildman. bibliog il Science 153:1269-71 S 9 '66
DNA synthesis and differentiation in embryonic kidney mesenchyme in vitro. J. S.
Sobel. bibliog il Science 153:1387-9 S 16 '66

Deoxyribonucleic acid in germinal vesicles
of oocytes of rana pipiens. A. J. Haggis.
bibliog il Science 154:670-1 N 4 '66
Elusive code of life. B. Commoner; J. Kendrew; L. L. Whyte. il Sat R 49:71-9 O 1
'66
Hylid frogs: polyploid classes of DNA in
liver nuclei. K. Bachmann and others.
bibliog il Science 154:650-1 N 4 '66
Interaction of the water-soluble carcinogen
4-nitroquinoline N-oxide with DNA. M. F.
Malkin and A. C. Zahalsky. bibliog il Science 154:1665-7 D 30 '66
Into the core of life itself. L. Lessing. il
Fortune 73:146-51+ Mr '66
Isopycnic centrifugation for the isolation of
DNA strands coding for ribosomal RNA.
P. F. Davison. bibliog il Science 152:509-12
Ap 22 '66
Mitochondrial DNA in yeast and some mammalian species. G. Corneo and others. bibliog il Science 151:687-9 F 11 '66
Nucleohistone dissociation by ganglioside
micelles. M. H. Meisler and R. H. McCluer.
bibliog il Science 154:896-7 N 18 '66
Nucleotide sequence repetition: a rapidly reassociating fraction of mouse DNA. M.
Waring and R. J. Britten. bibliog Science
154:791-4 N 11 '66
Organization of DNA in dipteran polytene
chromosomes as indicated by polarized
fluorescence microscopy. J. W. MacInnes
and R. B. Uretz. bibliog il Science 151:689-
91 F 11 '66
Pyrimidine dimers: effect of temperature on
photoinduction. R. O. Rahn. bibliog il Science 154:503-4 O 28 '66
Radiation-induced mutations and their repair. E. M. Witkin. bibliog il Science 152:
1345-53 Je 3 '66
Replication of chloroplast DNA of tobacco.
B. R. Green and M. P. Gordon. bibliog il
Science 152:1071-4 My 20 '66
Satellite deoxyribonucleic acid from bacillus
cereus strain T. H. A. Douthit and H. O.
Halvorson. bibliog il Science 153:182-3 Jl 8
'66
Synchronization of mammalian cells with
tritiated thymidine. G. F. Whitmore and S.
Gulyas. bibliog il Science 151:691-4 F 11
'66

DEPARTMENT of housing and urban development. See United States—Housing and
urban development. Department of
DEPARTMENT store decorations, Christmas.
See Christmas decorations
DEPARTMENT store mergers. See Department
stores—Consolidations and mergers
DEPARTMENT stores
Art over the counter; careless merchandising of art. K. Kuh. Sat R 49:38-9 D 31 '66
Spaniards say *si* to department stores; Galerias' chain of sixteen stores is being followed by Federated, Sears and Woolworth.
il Bsns W p 176-8 My 28 '66
See also
Bullock's-Magnin company
Federated department stores, incorporated
Retail trade
Shopping centers
also subhead Stores under names of cities,
e.g. Dallas—Stores

Book departments
Celebrities at Rich's: authors and assorted;
excerpt from Dear store. C. Sibley. Pub W
191:50-1 Ja 9 '67
Expenses increased in book departments in
1965; average sale also rose; study by Controllers' congress of the National retail
merchants association. il Pub W 190:65-6
O 10 '66
Federal reserve terminates book department
reports. il Pub W 189:29 Ap 11 '66
Reference books: heaviest traffic at Sanger-
Harris. il Pub W 189:123-4 Je 13 '66
Year-end report shows rise of 4 per cent in
book departments. il Pub W 189:58 Mr 7
'66

Computer installations
Where the computers care, too; EDP in
Washington's Woodward & Lothrop. il
Bsns W p 140-2+ Mr 12 '66

Consolidations and mergers
Giants put on more muscle. il Bsns W p72-
4+ Jl 23 '66

DEPARTMENTAL libraries. See College libraries—Departmental and divisional libraries

DE PASQUALE string quartet. See String
quartets

DEPAUL, Brother
Teaching the screen arts. Cath World 203: 109-12 My '66

DE PAULA, Paulo
Magnificent Brazilian in his flying machine. Américas 18:16-22 S '66

DE PAUW, Gommar A.
De Pauw's departure. Time 87:70 Ja 28 '66
Return of Father DePauw. por Newsweek 67:76-7 F 7 '66
Room for obnoxious dissenters. Christian Cent 84:4 Ja 4 '67
Sitting tight. Newsweek 68:44 D 26 '66
Spy saga. S. J. Adamo. America 114:236 F 12 '66
Traditionalist trouble. Commonweal 83:549 F 11 '66
Why so much ado about DePauw? Christian Cent 83:133 F 2 '66

DEPILATORIES. See Hair, Removal of

DEPOSITION (geology) See Sedimentation and deposition

DEPOTS, Railroad. See Railroads—Stations

DEPRECIATION
Depreciation for savers. H. C. Wallich. Newsweek 67:88 Ap 4 '66
Depreciation works two ways! D. MacDonald. il Motor T 18:30-1 Je '66
See also
Amortization deductions

DEPRESSANTS
Antidepressant drugs; report on international symposium. J. J. Schildkraut. Science 154: 1058+ N 25 '66

DEPRESSED areas aid. See Economic assistance, Domestic

DEPRESSION, Business. See Business depression

DEPRESSION, Mental
Beating the blues. J. Graham. il Redbook 128:71+ Ja '67
How doctors treat postpartum blues. il Good H 162:185 Mr '66
Self test for depression. il Sci Digest 60:54-6 N '66

DEPRIVATION, Maternal. See Maternal deprivation

DEPRIVATION, Sensory. See Sensory deprivation

DEPTH perception. See Space perception

DEPUGH, Robert Bolivar
Arrest Minutemen. Sr Schol 89:20-1 D 2 '66

DEPUY, William
Men who run the war. por Newsweek 68:53 D 5 '66

DE QUINCEY, Thomas
More or less plagiarized. D. J. Gordon. Nation 202:433-4 Ap 11 '66

DERDERIAN, Constance E.
Bonsai outdoors. Horticulture 44:22-3+ Je '66

DER HOVANESSIAN, Diana
Reconciliations; poem. Mlle 63:108 O '66

DERKSEN, H. E. and Verveen, A. A.
Fluctuations of resting neural membrane potential. bibliog Science 151:1388-9 Mr 18 '66

DERMATOGLYPHICS
Diagnosis by palm reading; clues to congenital heart, kidney and lung disorders. Sci N L 89:69 Ja 29 '66
Diagnostic palmistry; simple new test for birth defects. il Life 60:88+ F 25 '66
Medical palmistry. il Sci Digest 59:22 Ap '66
Telltale palm; aid to medical diagnosis. il Time 87:50 Ja 28 '66

DERMO-OPTICAL perception. See Touch

DERNMERGER, Robert F.
Economic realities; excerpts from address, March 12, 1966. Bul Atomic Sci 22:6-10 Je '66

DE ROOS, Robert
Massachusetts builds for tomorrow. Nat Geog Mag 130:790-843 D '66
Philippines: freedom's Pacific frontier. Nat Geog Mag 130:301-51 S '66

DEROUNIAN, Steven Boghos
Test of the tide. il por Newsweek 67:33 Je 27 '66

DERUDDER, Marcel L.
Better half-heart; operation at Houston's Methodist hospital. il Time 87:46+ Ap 29 '66
Death of a patient. Time 87:60 My 6 '66
Measure of a man's heart. L. Wainwright. Life 60:36 My 20 '66
Patient's gift to the future of heart repair; with report by R. Bailey and A. Kerr. il pors Life 60:84-92 My 6 '66

DESALTING of sea water. See Sea water—Desalting

DESALVO, Albert
Boston strangler. by G. Frank. Review Newsweek por 68:118+ O 31 '66. S. Schmidt

Making the violent scene. M. Lebowitz. Nation 204:58 Ja 9 '67
Uncontrollable vegetable. il por Newsweek 69:30+ Ja 23 '67
Word is out about the Boston strangler. il por Life 61:48 O 7 '66

DESCENT. See Genealogy

DE SCHAUENSEE, Max
Donizetti. Opera N 30:32 My 7 '66
Man from the Bulletin; interview. ed. by G. M. Eby. por Opera N 31:10-11 O 15 '66

DESCHIN, Jacob
[Monthly column] See issues of Popular photography

DE SCHWEINITZ, Karl, jr
Needs of underdeveloped economies. Cur Hist 51:72-7+ Ag '66

DESCRIPTION (rhetoric)
Description: to know and to feel. C. Edwards. Writer 79:19-23 Mr '66

DESCRIPTIVE writing. See Description (rhetoric)

DESEGREGATION. See Colleges and universities—Desegregation; Parochial schools, Catholic—Desegregation; Public schools—Desegregation

DESEGREGATION of libraries. See Libraries and Negroes

DESERT. See Deserts

DESERT fauna
See also
Pocket mice

DESERT flora. See Desert vegetation

DESERT sheep hunting. See Mountain sheep hunting

DESERT tortoises. See Tortoises

DESERT vegetation
Community action: desert nature drive. il Sunset 137:68+ O '66
See also
Succulent plants

DESERTION, Military
Shaping up; South Vietnamese army. Time 88:36 S 9 '66

DESERTS
Peru's coastal deserts; land of three great cultures. P. Meigs. il UNESCO Courier 19: 19-11+ Mr '66
West's land of surprises, some terrible. E. Abbey. il Harper 233:98-9+ D '66
See also
Chihuahuan Desert
Desert vegetation
Gobi Desert
Rajasthan Desert
Sahara Desert

DESIGN
Design sans peur et sans ressources. E. Kaufmann, jr. Arch Forum 125:68-70 S '66
Making the 1930s pay off, at last. il Bsns W p 128-30+ Ag 20 '66
Swiss designer Armin Hofmann on future design. il Pub W 189:82-3 Ap 4 '66
See also
International design conference

Study and teaching

Forms and shapes in nature; design in nature. L. Boykin. il Sch Arts 66:19-20 S '66
Geometric designs. M. Aschenbauer. il Design 67:41 Ja '66
Repetitive designs at the elementary school level; pattern-making. C. Greco. il Sch Arts 65:34-5 My '66
Should design principles be taught? pro and con discussion. B. Loughran. il Sch Arts 66:20-4 O '66
Transparent color design. P. Sweazey. il Sch Arts 65:18-20 Mr '66

DESIGN, Book. See Book design

DESIGN, Decorative
Doctor on buttons. D. F. Brown. il Hobbies 71:52-3+ O '66
Happy rediscovery of Romanesque. il House & Gard 129:118-23 F '66
Moiré pattern projections. B. Wasserman. il Sch Arts 65:17-20 Je '66
See also
Printing—Design

Animal forms

Chinese legend & lore: the dragon. K. Kaler. il Hobbies 71:50+ N '66
Horses. D. F. Brown. il Hobbies 71:52-3+ Ag '66
Horses & riders. D. F. Brown. il Hobbies 71:52-3+ Jl '66

Plant forms

Leaf printing with textile paint. R. Wilcox. il Design 68:38-42 S '66
Leafy turkeys. L. Blaustein. il Sch Arts 66: 41-2 N '66

DESIGN, Decorative—*Continued*

Study and teaching

See Design—Study and teaching

DESIGN, Industrial

Putting good taste in a can opener. il Bsns W p80-2 Jl 9 '66
See also
Human engineering
Systems engineering
also subhead Design under various subjects, e.g. Furniture—Design

Exhibitions

Showing their mettle; exhibit. Metal: Germany, at the Museum of contemporary crafts. B. Plumb. il N Y Times Mag p66-7 Ja 15 '67

DESIGN in photography. See Composition (photography)

DESIGN of automobiles. See Automobiles—Design

DESIGNERS
See also
Costume designers

DESK fan. See Electric fans

DESKS

Salem secretary attributed to William Appleton. H. Comstock. il Antiques 89: 553-5 Ap '66

DES MOINES

Architecture

Iowa edifice with pop art, no fat; American republic insurance building; with report by C. Welles. il Life 60:54-7+ Ap 29 '66

Art

Family work shops. P. Patrick. il Sch Arts 66:5-7 O '66

Galleries and museums

Tutankhamen: a child's treasure far west of Thebes; Junior art museum's Egyptian tomb exhibit, 1964. D. Parker. il Sch Arts 65:12-16 Je '66

Riots

Now, race riots in Nebraska and Iowa. il U S News 61:10 Jl 18 '66

DESMOKYNASE. See Anticoagulants (medicine)

DESMOND, Elizabeth

How to be a good mother without neglecting your husband. Parents Mag 41:32-3+ Jl '66

DESMOND, James

Donkey beats himself. Nation 203:379-81 O 17 '66

Parties in chaos: New York guerrillas. Nation 202:355-7 Mr 28 '66

DESOXYRIBONUCLEIC acid. See Deoxyribonucleic acid

DESPERATE choice; story. See Dorman, S.

DESQUAMATIVE interstitial pneumonia. See Pneumonia

DESSERTS

Berry desserts; with recipes. il Bet Hom & Gard 44:83-4 Jl '66
Delicious diet desserts! with recipes. il Bet Hom & Gard 44:130-1 My '66
Dessert pancakes out of the oven. il Sunset 136:185 Je '66
Desserts you'll be remembered by; with recipes. il Redbook 127:86-8+ My '66
Dowdies & dumplings; with recipes. P. Cannon. il Ladies Home J 83:90-1+ F '66
Easy desserts children can make. J. Hunt. il Parents Mag 41:87 O '66
February's fine for fancy recipes. G. Maddox. il Todays Health 44:52-7 F '66
Freeze, don't bake. C. Claiborne. il N Y Times Mag p 112 O 9 '66
Fresh-fruit spectaculars; with recipes. il McCalls 93:96-8 Jl '66
Frosty finales; bombes; with recipes. P. Cannon. il Ladies Home J 83:80-1+ Jl '66
Fruit cocktail specials. il Bet Hom & Gard 44:103-4 Mr '66
Holiday drama: starring light fruit desserts; with recipes. il Ladies Home J 83:80-1+ D '66
Ice cream desserts. Bet Hom & Gard 44: 105-6 Je '66
Look and cook; rhubarb; with recipes. il Bet Hom & Gard 44:129 My '66
Made for each other: strawberries and cream; with recipes. il McCalls 93:128-9+ Ap '66
Make and freeze cherry purée. D. Groves. il Farm J 90:64-5 Jl '66
Nut desserts; with recipes. R. Hanna. il Suc Farm 64:108-9+ F '66

Oceans of cream; whipped cream. il Look 30: 72-3 O 4 '66
Orange-marshmallow-rice confetti. V. V. Voboril. il Good H 162:166 F '66
Orange or lemon desserts. il Bet Hom & Gard 45:83-4 Ja '67
Pear desserts: now's the time; with recipes. il Sunset 137:124- D '66
Peppermint . . all ways! L. Anderson. il Bet Hom & Gard 44:94 D '66
Plural of mousse. J. Hewitt. il N Y Times Mag p41 Jl 31 '66
Refrigerator desserts. il Bet Hom & Gard 44: 85-6 Ag '66
Rich desserts for pennies. il McCalls 94:136-8+ O '66
Salads double as desserts. il Bet Hom & Gard 44:73-4 Ag '66
Season for sweets. C. Claiborne. il N Y Times Mag p 156+ Jl 11 '66
Spirits to eat with a spoon; recipes. il Vogue 148:146 D '66
Thanksgiving desserts, only the flavors are traditional. il Sunset 137:166+ N '66
Two make-ahead holiday desserts; with recipes. Sunset 137:123 D '66
Using chocolate buttercream. il Sunset 136: 174 Je '66
Valentine desserts that husbands will love! with recipes. il McCalls 93:112-14+ F '66
Work wonders with eggnog; with recipes. il Ladies Home J 83:108+ D '66
See also
Cake
Cookery—Fruit
Cookies
Ice cream, ices, etc.
Meringue
Pastry
Pie

DESTOUCHES, Louis Ferdinand

Rage against life. por Time 89:71-2+ Ja 13 '67

DESTROYER escorts. See Warships—United States

DETECTION of atomic bomb tests. See Atomic bombs—Testing, Detection of

DETECTION of submarine boats. See Submarine boats—Detection

DETECTIVE and mystery plays

Mystery at Tumble inn. E. Lello. Plays 25: 15-25 My '66
Secret of the Roman stairs. L. B. Heshmati. Plays 25:37-42. 62 Ap '66

DETECTIVE and mystery stories

Crime, violence, espionage: 1000 volumes of *Série noire.* H. R. Lottman. il Pub W 189: 44-8 Mr 7 '66
See also
Television broadcasting—Crime programs

Bibliography

Murder fancier recommends . . . J. D. Carr. Harper 233:84+ Jl '66
Mystery, detective, suspense. M. K. Grant. See first issue of each month of Library journal

Single works

At Bertram's hotel. A. Christie. il Good H 162:87-9 Mr; 92-3 Ap '66
Dare I weep, dare I mourn? J. Le Carré. il Sat Eve Post 240:54-6+ Ja 28 '67

Technique

Agatha Christie on mystery fiction; interview, ed. by F. Wyndham. A. Christie. Writer 79:27-8 Ag '66
And then the queen died. A. M. Wells. Writer 79:12-14 S '66
Clues to a medal mystery. S. Hacker. Writer 79:34 N '66
Editing the mystery and suspense novel. J. Kahn. Writer 79:18-21 Jl '66
Planning a mystery back to front. S. Ellin. Writer 79:11-13+ D '66
Saint on TV. L. Charteris. Writer 79:19-21+ F '66
Story that goes some place. M. Gordon and G. Gordon. Writer 79:11-14 N '66
Suspense short story. P. Highsmith. Writer 79:9-12 Mr '66
Take it seriously! Honey West, lady private investigator. S. Fickling. Writer 79:18-20 My '66

DETECTIVES

Exiles from the American dream: the junkie and the cop. B. Jackson. Atlan 219:44-51 Ja '67
Keen private eye. B. Surface. il N Y Times Mag p 121-2+ D 11 '66
Spying for industry; private police and detective firms. J. Ridgeway. New Repub 154:10-11 My 14 '66
See also
Burns, William J, international detective agency

DEVELOPMENT banks—Asia—*Continued*
Asian development bank; statement. February 2, 1966. W. A. Harriman. Dept State Bul 54:379-82 Mr 7 '66
New harmony; inaugurate bank. Newsweek 68:80+ D 5 '66
President urges participation in Asian development bank; message, January 18, 1966. L. B. Johnson. Dept State Bul 54:255-7 F 14 '66
Toward economic cooperation; inaugural meeting. il Time 88:93 D 2 '66
United States joins new Asian development bank; statement, August 16, 1966. A. J. Goldberg. Dept State Bul 55:347-8 S 5 '66
U.S. officials named to boards of Asian development bank. Dept State Bul 54:718 My 2 '66
U.S. to cooperate in economic and social development in Asia; remarks, March 16, 1966; with announcement of pledges to Mekong River project. L. B. Johnson. il Dept State Bul 54:521-3 Ap 4 '66

DEVELOPMENT of children. See Children—Growth and development
DEVELOPMENT program of the United Nations. See United Nations—Development program
DEVIANT behavior. See Behavior (psychology)
DEVIATION of the compass. See Compass
DEVILLERS, Philippe
Preventing the peace: report from an intermediary. Nation 203:597-602 D 5 '66
DEVLIN, John C.
Prying medical secrets from creatures of the sea. Todays Health 44:29-33+ Ap '66
DEVLIN, Polly
Instant Barbra. Vogue 147:68-73+ Mr 15 '66
(ed) See Bailey, D. David Bailey talks of women, beauty, marriage
DEVLIN, Wende
Beat poems of a beat mother. Good H 162:54 Ap '66
DEVON horse show. See Horse shows
DEVONIAN period. See Paleontology—Devonian
DEVOTIONS. See Prayer
DEW, Diana
Turn on, turn off. il por Time 89:80 Ja 20 '67
DEW line. See Radar defense network
DEWART, Leslie
Celibacy problem. Commonweal 84:146-50 Ap 22 '66
Have we loved the past too long? America 115:798-802 D 17 '66

about
Dewart on belief. G. Vahanian. Commonweal 85:257-9 D 2 '66
God as non-being. Time 88:61 D 23 '66
Let's end the Communist-Christian vendetta. H. Cox. Christian Cent 83:1375-9 N 9 '66; Discussion. 83:1508 D 7 '66
DEWATA, India
Dewata, famine village. W. Cook and R. Ramanujam. il Newsweek 67:38-40 Ap 4 '66
DEWEY, John
Lectures in the philosophy of education: 1899; excerpt. ed. by R. D. Archambault. Sch & Soc 94:155-9 Mr 19 '66

about
Relevance of Professor Dewey. J. Featherstone. New Repub 155:22+ O 29 '66
DEWEY, W. C. and others
Radiosensitization of X chromosome of Chinese hamster cells related to incorporation of 5-bromodeoxyuridine. bibliog Science 152:519-21 Ap 21 '66
DEWEY classification. See Classification, Decimal
DE WIED, D. See Bohus, B. jt. auth.
DE WINT, Peter
Letter from London. J. Stuart. il Antiques 89: 478 Ap '66
DEWITT, Jimmy
They sail to win. M. Wiley. il Yachting 120: 31+ D '66
DEWITT, William Orville
Cincinnati's brain-picker. R. H. Boyle. por Sports Illus 24:40-2+ Je 13 '66
DEWOLF, Harry
My ride on a torpedo. Read Digest 89:167-70+ Jl '66
DE WOLFE, Elsie. See Mendl, E. D.
D'EYNCOURT, Sir Eustace Tennyson-. See Tennyson-D'Eyncourt. E.
DE YOUNG memorial museum. See M. H. De Young memorial museum, San Francisco
DEZETTEL, Lou M.
Build an 80/40 meter bandswitching vertical. Pop Electr 25:73-4 O '66

DE ZUTTER, Henry W.
Coattails of bigotry. New Repub 155:8-9 N 5 '66
DIABETES
Are you a hidden diabetic. Todays Health 44:86 F '66
Brighter future for children with diabetes; ed. by D. W. Lord. H. F. Root. il Parents Mag 41:70-1+ N '66
Camping fun for diabetic youngsters; Camp Sweeney, Gainesville, Tex. L. Kaye. il Todays Health 44:50-3 Je '66
Diabetes, a new mutation in the mouse. K. P. Hummel and others. il Science 153:1127-8 S 2 '66
Of mice and men; study of diabetic mice. Newsweek 68:93 S 12 '66
Personal business; overweight sets the stage. Bsns W p 163-4 Mr 26 '66
What I have learned from diabetes. J. L. Murphy. Read Digest 88:197-200 My '66
DIABETES research
Diabetic mouse studied. il Sci N 90:197 S 17 '66
DIABETICS diet. See Diet in disease
DIAGNOSIS
Hands clue to diagnosis. Sci N 90:225 S 24 '66
Silent language tells doctors about patients' problems. Todays Health 44:12 N '66
See also
Ultrasonic waves—Medical applications

Anecdotes, facetiae, satire, etc.
Tell me where it hurts. P. M. Wright. Ladies Home J 83:165 Mr '66
DIAGNOSIS, Radioscopic
Tumor detection aided by radioactive chemical. Sci N 90:400 N 12 '66
DIALITE. See Electric switches
DIALOGUE
Writing dialogue. K. Reed. Writer 79:16-17 Ag '66
DIALOGUE (periodical)
For ruffled believers. il Time 88:59 Ag 26 '66
DIALOGUES of the Carmelites; opera. See Poulenc. F.
DIALYSIS
See also
Kidneys, Artificial
DIAMINODIPHENYL sulfone
Shooting malaria down; research effort to find and test drugs to fight it. il Bsns W p92-3 Ap 16 '66
DIAMOND, David
Musical events; performance of his compositions by New York philharmonic. W. Sargeant. New Yorker 42:128 My 7 '66
N.Y. philharmonic: Diamond premieres; Fifth symphony and piano concerto. B. Jacobson. Hi Fi 16:MA18-19 Jl '66
On Epic: the Fourth quartet of David Diamond, magnificent creativity. A. Cohn. por Am Rec G 32:507 F '66
DIAMOND, Henry L.
Politics of beauty; excerpts from addresses. por Parks & Rec 1:138-41+ F '66
DIAMOND, Jared M.
Zoological classification system of a primitive people. bibliog Science 151:1102-4 Mr 4 '66
DIAMOND, Martin
Profess with a passion. il por Time 87:84-5 My 6 '66
DIAMOND, William
Blue Moerdler. Newsweek 67:36+ Mr 28 '66
DIAMOND smuggling. See Smuggling
DIAMONDBACK terrapin. See Terrapin
DIAMONDS
Are there diamonds on the moon? quiz. J. Daugherty and M. Daugherty. il Sci Digest 59:85-7 Je '66
Diamonds are forever; J. B. Sobrinho's find in Brazil; outcome. Newsweek 68:36 Ag 29 '66
Meteorite yields diamond; Arizona meteorite crater. Sci N 89:267 Ap 16 '66
DIAMONSTEIN, Barbaralee D.
Historic return to college. Sat R 49:31-2 My 28 '66
Hopes and fears of all the years. Sat R 49: 58-9 D 10 '66
Legal road to civil rights. Sat R 49:32 Ja 29 '66
Life true to art. Sat R 49:30 O 29 '66
Turn to the right. Sat R 49:38-9 Ap 2 '66
DIANTHUS barbatus. See Sweet williams
DIAPAUSE. See Insects—Development
DIAPERS, Infants
Important layette item: the diaper. M. B. Keiser. il Parents Mag 41:10+ Jl '66

DIARIES
Art of keeping a diary. N. Nicolson. Esquire 66:28+ D '66
See also
Notebooks
El DIARIO-la Prensa
News. New Yorker 42:38-9 My 21 '66
DIAS, Earl J.
Ballad for the shy; drama. Plays 26:21-31 D '66
Beauty and the ballot; drama. Plays 26:29-39 N '66
See you in the funnies; drama. Plays 26:1-12 Ja '67
Shades of Shakespeare; drama. Plays 25:1-12 Ap '66
DIAS, Fernando Correia
Report from Brazil. America 115:546-8 N 5 '66
DIATOMS
Diatoms and the ecological conditions of their growth in sea ice in the Arctic Ocean. H. Meguro and others. bibliog Science 152: 1089-90 My 20 '66
Nature and the microscope; mounting diatom slides. J. D. Corrington. il Natur Hist 75:59-63 My '66
DIAZ, Justino
No short cut; interview, ed. by J. W. Freeman. por Opera N 31:16 D 24 '66
DIAZ ORDAZ, Gustavo, and Johnson, L. B.
President Johnson visits Mexico city; text of joint statement, April 15, 1966. Dept State Bul 54:731-3 My 9 '66
DIBLIN, Joe
What pilots want to know about engines. Flying 78:58-60 Je '66
DICHTER, Ernest
How word-of-mouth advertising works. Harvard Bsns R 44:147-52+ N '66
DICHTER, Misha
Agony of the Tchaikovsky. il por Time 88: 60 Jl 8 '66
Testing their medals. il por Time 88:39 Ag 26 '66
DICK, Lois Hoadley
Christmas lullaby. Christian Cent 83:1565 D 21 '66
DICKENS, Charles
Dickens in Boston; excerpt from American notes, 1842. Sat R 49:125 Mr 12 '66
Tale of two cities; dramatization. See Hackett, W.
DICKENS, Monica
First of the month. C. Amory. Sat R 49:3 Jl 2 '66
DICKENSON, Fred
Beware the terrible Williamsons. Read Digest 89:175-6+ S '66
DICKERSON, George
Politics and the sexual image. Mlle 63:172-3+ O '66
Single girl and the married man. Mlle 62: 154-5+ F '66
DICKEY, Charley
Gun dogs. Field & S 71:106-9 Jl; 110-12+ Ag '66
More chukar hunters needed. Field & S 71: 68-71+ S '66
DICKEY, James
Adultery; poem. Nation 202:252 F 28 '66
Bee; poem. Harper 232:80-1 Je '66
Encounter in the cage country; poem. New Yorker 42:34 Je 11 '66
False youth; winter; poem. New Yorker 42: 44 F 26 '66
For the last wolverine; poem. Atlan 217:70-1 Je '66
James Dickey on poetry and teaching. por (p31) Pub W 189:34 Mr 28 '66
Listening to foxhounds; Salt marsh; Heaven of animals; In the marble quarry; poems. Life 61:70 Jl 22 '66
Robert Frost, man and myth. Atlan 218:53-6 N '66
Sheep-child; poem. Atlan 218:86 Ag '66
about
Four authors are given National book awards. por Pub W 189:47-8 Mr 21 '66
Lamb, the clocks, the blue light. R. Huff. Poetry 109:46-8 O '66
NBA 1966. por Newsweek 67:106 Mr 28 '66
Permanent hell. D. Ignatow. Nation 202: 752-3 Je 20 '66
Unlikeliest poet; with a sampling of his poetry. P. O'Neil. il pors Life 61:68-70+ Jl 22 '66
DICKEY, R. P.
Leonardo da Vinci; poem. Sat R 49:56 Ap 30 '66
DICKEY, William
Anniversary; poem. New Yorker 42:174 Mr 19 '66

DICKINSON, Gloria Olson
Preschool personality patterns. PTA Mag 61: 21-3 bibliog(p35-6) O '66
DICKINSON COUNTY, Kan.
When a county tried to cut relief bill. il U S News 60:44-7 Ja 31 '66
DICKMAN, Gordon H.
Your navigation lights. Yachting 119:77+ Ap '66
DICKSON, John W.
Insouciance; poem. Harper 233:97 D '66
DICKSON, Paul A.
In a little Spanish town. Sat R 49:44-5 Ag 27 '66
DICTAMNUS. See Gas plants (flowers)
DICTATORSHIP
Social origins of dictatorship and democracy, by B. Moore, jr. Review
New Repub 156:34-6+ Ja 7 '67. J. Featherstone
See also
Totalitarianism
DICTION
Silver-tongue southpaw; ballplayers and articulation. J. Jacobs. Reporter 35:51-2+ Jl 14 '66
DICTIONARIES
Bounty of Brewer; Dictionary of phrase and fable. G. Frazier. Holiday 40:106+ Ag '66
Dribbling, senile fool! Insult dictionary. Time 88:51 Ag 5 '66
See also subhead Dictionaries under various subjects, e.g. History—Dictionaries
DIDION, Joan
Big rock candy figgy pudding pitfall. Sat Eve Post 239:22 D 3 '66
Farewell to the enchanted city. Sat Eve Post 240:62-7 Ja 14 '67
Hawaii; taps at Pearl Harbor. Sat Eve Post 239:22-9 D 17 '66
How can I tell them there's nothing left? Sat Eve Post 239:38-42+ My 7 '66
Just folks at a school for nonviolence. N Y Times Mag p24-5+ F 27 '66
On keeping a notebook. Holiday 40:10+ D '66
DIDO and Aeneas; opera. See Purcell, H.
DIE casting
GE tries casting a new die; die-cast the ferrous metals. il Bsns W p 175-6 My 14 '66
DIEBOLD, John
Computers, program management and foreign affairs. For Affairs 45:125-34 O '66
New world coming. Sat R 49:17-18 Jl 23 '66
Robots in society's service. Sat R 49:37-8 O 29 '66
DIEBOLD, William, jr
New horizons in foreign trade. For Affairs 45:291-303 Ja '67
DIEFENBAKER, John George
But unbowed. Newsweek 68:60+ O 10 '66
Dief and grief. il por Newsweek 68:56 N 28 '66
Dief on the ropes. il por Time 88:47 N 25 '66
Man on the spot; Munsinger affair. il Time 87:44 My 20 '66
DIEGO GARCIA (atoll)
Indian Ocean deal? center of Anglo-American military planning for the Far East. New Repub 154:7 F 5 '66
DIEGO Rivera museum. See Mexico (city)—Galleries and museums
DIELDRIN
Dieldrin; extraction of accumulations by root uptake. R. O. Mumma and others. bibliog il Science 152:530-1 Ap 22 '66
Dieldrin; interaction with nerve components of cockroaches. F. Matsumura and M. Hayashi. bibliog il Science 153:757-9 Ag 12 '66
DIELECTRIC tape cameras. See Cameras
DIELECTROPHORESIS
Separation of living and dead cells by dielectrophoresis. H. A. Pohl and I. Hawk. bibliog il Science 152:647-9 Ap 29 '66
DIENBIENPHU, Battle of. See Indochina, French—History—Civil war, 1946-1954
DIERSON, Frank T.
Excerpt from testimony, April 29, 1965. Cong Digest 45:177+ Je '66
DIESCH, Stanley L. See McCulloch, W. F. jt. auth.
DIESEL engines, Marine
Satisfaction from a diesel. J. Emmett. il Yachting 119:111-13+ Ja; 80-2+ F '66
DIET
Academy warns against major changes in diet. Sci N 90:56 Jl 23 '66
Calorie game; with recipes. J. Scott and L. Scott. il McCalls 93:94-5+ Ag '66
Delicacies for dieters; with recipes. il Ebony 21:122+ S '66
Dieters' clipboard. See issues of Seventeen

DIET—*Continued*

Eat less to be more active. Sci N 90:181 S 10 '66

Expectant mother's diet; with recipes. Redbook 127:35-42 Jl '66

Gourmet diet cook book. B. Wason. il House & Gard 129:149+ Je '66

Great Nova Scotia diet; featuring seafood; with recipes. P. Cannon. Ladies Home J 83:114-15+ Mr '66

High protein diet makes strong teeth. Sci N 89:291 Ap 23 '66

How I lost 180 pounds; interview, ed. by L. Robinson. J. McGee. il Ebony 21:36-8+ Jl '66

How to be happy though dieting; interview. A.-M. Bennstrom. il Mlle 62:148-9 F '66

How to lose weight, and stay thin; excerpt from The thin book by a formerly fat psychiatrist. T. I. Rubin. Read Digest 89: 124-7 S '66

Low-cal picnic. il Mlle 63:138-9 My '66

School athletics food facts and myths. E. Maxwell. Todays Health 44:85-6 S '66

This is a diet? creations of Helen Corbitt; with recipes and menus. il McCalls 94:84-5+ Ja '67

Those doctors who hand out diet pills. M. A. Guitar. il Ladies Home J 83:79+ My '66; Same abr. with title Diet pill menace. Read Digest 89:55-8 Jl '66

Weight-watchers' horoscope. S. Leek. il Ladies Home J 83:78+ N '66

Why your diet needs a doctor's supervision. Bet Hom & Gard 44:72 Jl '66

Wise woman's diet; with recipes. G. J. Christakis. il Redbook 128:37-43+ Ja '67

You and your diet. See issues of Good housekeeping

See also

Athletes—Nutrition
Children—Nutrition
Corpulence
Food
Nutrition
Oils and fats, Edible
Vitamins

DIET, Deficient

Night blindness. J. E. Dowling. il Sci Am 215: 78-84 O '66

Soldiers may have hidden malnutrition. Sci N 90:40 Jl 16 '66

DIET in disease

Happiness is a hippo steak; treatment for B. Casper's food allergies. E. Shrake. il Sports Illus 24:22-6+ F 7 '66

You and your diet; bland dishes, low in fat, too. il Good H 162:170+ Je '66

You and your diet; diet and mental retardation; baking for allergic children. il Good H 162:177-9 F '66

You and your diet; dishes low in fat and sodium; with recipes. il Good H 162:204-5 My '66

You and your diet; main dishes for diabetics; with recipes. il Good H 162:206-7 Mr '66

DIETARY studies. See Diet

DIETER, Nannielou H. and others

Interstellar hydroxyl radio emission. Sky & Tel 31:132-6 Mr '66

DIETHER, Jack

For the holidays. Am Rec G 33:300-4+ D '66

From Philips, an exciting new Messiah. Am Rec G 33:92-3+ O '66

Much ado about nothing. Am Rec G 32:816-18 My '66

Must for all Mahler lovers: Angel's Des knaben wunderhorn. Am Rec G 33:212-15 N '66

On Everest, Gustav Holst; some rare and beautiful music. Am Rec G 32:952-3 Je '66

Parable by Britten: Curlew River. Am Rec G 32:1034-6 Jl '66

Previn's masterly Shostakovich Fifth; and an enthralling First from Prague. Am Rec G 32:692-3 Ap '66

DIETHYLNITROSAMINE. See Cancer producing substances

DIETRICK, Ralph

Flying high in vintage Fords. Bsns W p 132-4 Ja 7 '67

DIETS. See Diet

DIETZ, Betty A.

Dance, inc. has a 3-day clinic for teachers of handicapped children. Dance Mag 40:72-3 S '66

DIETZ, Howard

Lyrics from a lived-in life Irwin Edman, classmate; poem. Sat R 49:10 D 10 '66

DIETZ, Lew

Don't spare the hot sauce. Field & S 70:70-2+ Ap '66

Fox went out on a chilly night. Field & S 71:48-50+ My '66

Maine's high country. Field & S 71:108-11+ D '66

Rubber boot Bali Ha'i. Field & S 71:62-3+ My '66

DIETZ, Robert S.

Our deep and wide ocean. Science 153:1423-4+ S 16 '66

Pacific science congress. Science 154:1365-6 D 9 '66

DIETZEL, Paul

I have never broken a contract; ed. by M. Hyman. por Sports Illus 25:44-7 S 19 '66

about

Night they learned to forget the coach. G. Ronberg. il por Sports Illus 25:56-7 S 26 '66

DIEZ DE MEDINA, Fernando

Mines in the sky. Américas 18:24-9 Ap '66

DIFFERENCES, Racial. See Racial differences

DIFFERENTIAL topology. See Topology

DIFFERENTIALS, Wage. See Wage differentials

DIFFERENTIATION (biology)

Death in embryonic systems. J. W. Saunders, jr. bibliog il Science 154:604-12 N 4 '66

DNA synthesis and differentiation in embryonic kidney mesenchyme in vitro. J. S. Sobel. bibliog il Science 153:1387-9 S 16 '66

Inactive alkaline phosphatase in duodenum of nursling mouse; immunological evidence. M. E. Etzler and F. Moog. bibliog il Science 154:1037-8 N 25 '66

Molecular basis of differentiation; report on workshop. G. L. Cantoni and A. Monroy. Science 151:597-8 F 4 '66

Multiple causes and controls in differentiation. B. E. Wright. bibliog il Science 153: 830-7 Ag 19 '66

DIFFICULT children. See Problem children

DIFFRACTION

See also

X rays—Diffraction

DIFFRACTOMETERS, Optical. See Optical instruments

DIFFUSION

Sedimentation of an initially skewed boundary. D. J. Cox. bibliog il Science 152:359-61 Ap 15 '66

See also

Biological transport

DIFFUSION techniques (photography)

Creative color; diffusion techniques for contrast control. A. Rothstein. U S Camera 29:26-7 Jl '66

Diffused Jane Fonda. il U S Camera 29:60-1 Jl '66

DI FILIPPI, Arturo

Miami milestone; interview, ed. by J. Ardoin. por Opera N 30:14-15 Ja 29 '66

DIGESTIVE system

Gastrointestinal circulation; report on meeting of investigators. E. D. Jacobson. Science 154:1366-7 D 9 '66

Diseases

Traveling waiters spread stomach ills. Sci N 90:353 O 29 '66

DIGGER wasps. See Wasps

DIGGINS, John P.

Flirtation with fascism: American pragmatic liberals and Mussolini's Italy. Am Hist R 71:487-505 Ja '66

DIGGS, Irene

Book review. Negro Hist Bul 29:67, 117-19 D '65, F '66

DI GIOIA, Frank

European sketches of Frank di Gioia. F. Johnson. il Am Artist 30:46-51+ Ap '66

DI GIOVANNI, Norman Thomas

New Hampshire out of season. Atlan 217: 114-16 My '66

DIGITAL computers. See Computers—Digital computers

DIGITAL timer. See Timing devices

DIKEMAN, May

Tour; story. Atlan 217:82-4 F '66

DIKES (engineering)

Walls for wandering farms. A. Whitman. il Pop Mech 125:95-7+ Je '66

DILL, Donna

Donna Dill's victory. D. C. Davis. il pors Todays Health 45:26-7+ Ja '67

DILL, Wally

Man to lead the pros out of the darkness. F. Deford. il por Sports Illus 24:58+ Je 20 '66

DILL

This is dill! il Bet Hom & Gard 44:130-1 Je '66

DILLARD university, New Orleans
Dillard: pint-size school with a king-size job. il Ebony 21:188-90+ My '66
DILLE, Barbara M.
Into the wild blue yonder. Parks & Rec 1: 332-3 Ap '66
DILLENBERGER, Jane, and Dillenberger, John
What is Christian art? Christian Cent 83:497-9 Ap 20 '66
DILLENBERGER, John. See Dillenberger, Jane, jt. auth.
DILLER, Phyllis
Serious side of Diller; touring the Lincoln home; excerpts from interview, ed. by W. Allen. por Hobbies 71:124 D '66

about

TV's killer Diller. J. Reddy. por Read Digest 89:90-4 N '66
DILLON, Clarence Douglas
Business-to-business exchange. Bsns W p200 My 21 '66
DILLON, J. R. Cronly-. See Cronly-Dillon, J. R.
DILLON, Jack
Tom says it's that kids have more freedom these days; story. McCalls 93:90-1 Ag '66
DILLON, Wilton S.
Flow of ideas between Africa and America. Bul Atomic Sci 22:23-6 Ap '66
DILTS, Peggy. See Hudson, P.
DI LUZIO, N. R. See Kalish, G. H. jt. auth.
DI MAGGIO, Joe
Silent season of a hero. G. Talese. il por Esquire 66:40-3+ Jl '66
See also
DIMARZO, J. M.
Aerial survey pays big dividends. Am City 81:113-14 F '66
DIME stores. See Five- and ten-cent stores
DIMETHYL benzanthracene
Prolonged immunosuppression and tumor induction by a chemical carcinogen injected at birth. J. K. Ball and others. bibliog il Science 152:650-1 Ap 29 '66
Protective action of polycyclic hydrocarbons against induction of adrenal necrosis by dimethylbenzanthracene. P. H. Jellinck and B. Goudy. bibliog il Science 152:1375-6 Je 3 '66
Rat mammary gland RNA: incorporation of C^{14}-formate and effect of hormones and 7,12-dimethylbenzanthracene. P. R. Libby and T. L. Dao. bibliog il Science 153:303-5 Jl 15 '66
DIMETHYL oxazolidinedione
Active transport of 5,5-dimethyl-2,4-oxazolidinedione. J. M. Dietschy and N. W. Carter; discussion. Science 151:1564; 152: 799 Mr 25, My 6 '66
DIMETHYL sulfoxide. See Methyl sulfoxide
DINELEY, David L.
Ancient fishes of Escuminac Bay; with biographical sketch. Natur Hist 76:7, 40-5 bibliog(p73) Ja '67
DINELL, Tom
Men and money. America 115:8-10 Jl 2 '66
DINGELL, John David, 1926-
Excerpt from testimony, June 3, 1965. Cong Digest 45:301+ D '66
DINH, Tran-van-. See Tran-van-Dinh
DINH-long-Truong
Is North Vietnam weakening? interview, ed. by G. C. Troelstrup. por U S News 61:53-4 D 12 '66
DINING. See Dinners and dining
DINING alcoves, etc.
See also
Snack bars
DINING clubs See Clubs
DINING room chairs. See Chairs
DINING rooms
Right where you eat! il Bet Hom & Gard 44:60-1 N '66
DINITROPHENOL
Energy balancing in nitella cells treated with dinitrophenol. C. E. Barr and T. C. Broyer. bibliog il Science 151:1245-6 Mr 11 '66
DINNER at eight; drama. See Kaufman, G. S. and Ferber, E.
DINNER for three; story. See Gunther, J.
DINNERS and dining
Classic menu mates; with recipes. il Redbook 127:94-8+ O '66
Company dinner with the greatest of ease; with recipes. il Bet Hom & Gard 44:94 Ap '66
Cool cooking for hot days; with recipes and menus. il McCalls 93:90-1+ Jl '66
Detroit: the men show off. il Ladies Home J 83:88-91+ O '66
Diamond Jim invites you to a holiday feast. il Esquire 66:247-51 D '66

Double-duty dinners; with recipes. il Mc Calls 94:86-8+ Ja '67
Great dinners; menu and recipes. E. Graves. See issues of Life
Great dinners. G. Schremp. il Life 61:89+ S 9 '66
Luci's first dinner for husband Pat will include familiar family favorites; recipes and menu. M. Simons and M. Kaytor. il Look 30:38-9 Ag 9 '66
Make it now, bake it later; excerpts. B. Goodfellow. il Redbook 126:100-1+ Ap '66
No time to cook; with menu. il McCalls 94: 29 Ja '67
Oven dinners make entertaining easy; with recipes. il Parents Mag 41:90-3+ N '66
Party dinner in thirty minutes; with recipes. K. Hargis. il Seventeen 26:96-7+ Ja '67
Practice dinner party; with recipes. il Seventeen 25:398+ Ag '66
Relaxed, ranch style entertaining; with recipes. R. S. Perkins. il Farm J 90:90-1+ My '66
Table for two (cont) Ladies Home J 83:26 Mr; 20 Ap; 50 My; 122 Je; 23 Jl '66
Tangy corned beef tempts everyone; with recipes. G. Maddox. il Todays Health 45: 54-9 Ja '67
Togetherness meals for your family; with recipes. G. Maddox. il Todays Health 44: 48-53 S '66
Turkey and other dinners: plain for children, elegant for adults; with recipes. il Redbook 128:100-1+ N '66
Washington: formal dinner. il Ladies Home J 83:85-7+ O '66
See also
Caterers and catering
Thanksgiving dinners
DINNERWARE. See Pottery
DINOFLAGELLATES
Isolation of nuclei from a marine dinoflagellate. L. R. Mendiola and others. bibliog il Science 153:1661-3 S 30 '66
Pigment protein complex from gonyaulax. D. J. Haidak and others. bibliog il Science 152:212-13 Ap 8 '66
Subcellular sources of luminescence in noctiluca. R. Eckert. bibliog il Science 151:349-52 Ja 21 '66
DINOSAURS
Dinosaur cells preserved. Sci N 90:127 Ag 20 '66
Missing link found? investigating Big Horn basin of Wyoming and Montana. il Sci N 89:197 Mr 26 '66
DIOCESES
See also
Catholic church—Dioceses
DIODATI, Carmen J.
Army field calibration technicians. Electr World 76:80-2 S '66
Determining dB power ratios. Electr World 76:83 S '66
Effective use of the V.O.M. Electr World 75: 82 Ap '66
DIODES
Diode meter protectors. A. A. Mangieri. il Electr World 76:56-7+ N '66
Diodes from thin film; tunnel diodes. il Sci N 89:511 Je 25 '66
Special section: solid-state diodes; symposium. Electr World 76:37-60 Jl '66
Varactor diode applications. D. E. Lancaster. il Electr World 75:43-6+ Je '66

Testing

Testing diodes. D. Ludwig. Electr World 75:95 Ja '66
DIONAEA muscipula. See Venus's flytraps
DIPALMA, Joseph R. and others
Touch receptor of Venus flytrap, dionaea muscipula. bibliog Science 152:539-40 Ap 22 '66
DIPENTIMA, Anthony
Holography. Science 154:1363-4 D 9 '66
DIPLOMACY
Importance of being civil. T. C. Sorensen. Sat R 49:30 N 26 '66
See also
Arbitration, International
International relations
also subhead Foreign relations under names of countries, e.g. Russia—Foreign relations
DIPLOMAS, Fraudulent
Persistence of fraud in higher education. W. W. Brickman. Sch & Soc 94:171 Ap 2 '66
DIPLOMATIC and consular service
See also
Ambassadors
also subhead Diplomatic and consular service under names of countries, e.g. United States—Diplomatic and consular service

DIPLOMATS
  See also
  United States—Foreign service

DIPOLE orbital belts in space
  Last of the West Ford dipoles. I. I. Shapiro. bibliog il Science 154:1445-8 D 16 '66

DIPROPYLTRYPTAMINE
  Drug acts like LSD. Sci N 89:248 Ap 9 '66

DIPTERA
  Chromosome changes induced by infections in tissues of rhynchosciara angelae. C. Pavan and R. Basile. bibliog il Science 151:1556-8 Mr 25 '66

DIRECT energy conversion
  See also
  Electric power production from chemical action

DIRECT mail advertising. See Advertising, Direct mail

DIRECTING (theater) See Theatrical directors

DIRECTION, Sense of. See Orientation

DIRECTION books. See Instruction manuals

DIRECTION finding apparatus
  See also
  Radio in navigation

DIRECTORIES
  See also subhead Directories under various subjects, e.g. Theological schools—Directories

DIRECTORS. See Theatrical directors

DIRECTORS, Corporation. See Corporations—Directors

DIREITO, F. Teixeira. See Teixeira Direito, F.

DIRIGIBLES. See Airships

DIRKSEN, Everett McKinley
  Excerpt from debate, July 20, 1966. Cong Digest 45:212+ Ag '66
  If a man die, shall he live again? Read Digest 88:23-4 My '66
  Let the people choose! por Farm J 90:37+ F '66
  Ooze from the wizard of. Christian Cent 83:1019 Ag 17 '66
  Seduction by statistics. por Nations Bsns 54:68-72 Jl '66
  State of the Union; address, January 17, 1966. Vital Speeches 32:258-9 F 15 '66; Excerpts. U S News 60:72-3 Ja 31 '66

      about
  Blades for aid. Time 88:15 Jl 29 '66
  Dirksen-Ford rumpus: a split over war mismanagement? por U S News 60:15 My 2 '66
  Dirksen's crusade; prayer amendment bill. Christian Cent 83:951 Ag 3 '66
  Everett McKinley Dirksen: a mighty minority of one. G. Shalit. il pors Look 30:26-30 Jl 26 '66
  Grand old party; accident at Walter Reed army medical center. Newsweek 67:36 My 23 '66
  GOP albatross. New Repub 154:4 Ap 30 '66
  Hero on vacation. Reporter 35:18 S 22 '66
  Honk, honk, the marigold. M. Viorst. por Esquire 66:116-19+ O '66
  Is compulsory unionism more important than Viet Nam? por Time 87:21 F 11 '66
  Issue is conduct. Newsweek 68:32 S 26 '66
  Man of the year for Republicans. por U S News 60:16 F 7 '66
  90th girds for battle. il por Newsweek 69:24-7 Ja 23 '67
  Old impresario. T. Wicker. Atlan 217:77 Ap '66
  Overdose of Dirksen. Christian Cent 83:999-1000 Ag 17 '66
  People of the week. U S News 60:22 Mr 7 '66
  Prayer ban stays. Sr Schol 89:20 O 14 '66
  R.I.P. filibuster to repeal section 14(b) of Taft-Hartley act. Time 87:22 F 18 '66
  State of the riposte. il Newsweek 67:22 Ja 31 '66
  T.R.B. from Washington; Vorster and Dirksen. New Repub 155:4 S 24 '66
  Three-time loser. Newsweek 67:19 My 2 '66
  Time out for Ev. Time 87:30 My 20 '66
  Washington: ten of its most powerful men. por Vogue 148:154 N 15 '66
  Where are the clergymen? C. E. Rice. Nat R 18:833-5 Ag 23 '66
  Who could ask for anything more? P. Lisagor. il por Nations Bsns 54:23-4 N '66
  Who's against prayer? K. Crawford. Newsweek 68:29 Ag 8 '66
  With Dirksen away from his desk. por U S News 60:14 My 23 '66
  Without a prayer. Time 88:22 S 30 '66

DISABILITY pensions. See Pensions, Industrial

DISABLED. See Handicapped

DISABLED, Employment of. See Vocational rehabilitation

DISABLED American veterans (organization)
  Million-dollar trinket. R. L. Smith. il Nation 203:354-5 O 10 '66

DISADVANTAGED children. See Socially handicapped children

DISARMAMENT
  Arms control: a serious business; address, June 20, 1966. W. C. Foster. Dept State Bul 55:50-5 Jl 11 '66
  Assembly adopts resolutions; with texts of resolutions. UN Mo Chron 3:11-23 Ja '66
  How to keep the peace in a disarmed world. A. Rich and J. R. Platt. Bul Atomic Sci 22:14-19 Ap '66; Reply. L. P. Bloomfield. 22:38-9 O '66
  Toward a world disarmament conference. H. A. Jack. Bul Atomic Sci 22:47-8 Ap '66
  United States in a disarmed world, by A. Wolfers and others. Review
    Sat R 49:37 S 17 '66. H. J. Morgenthau
  U.S. marks anniversary of Arms control act; statement, September 24, 1966. L. B. Johnson. Dept State Bul 55:687 O 31 '66
  U.S. reiterates call for freeze of nuclear delivery systems; statement, August 2, 1966. A. S. Fisher. Dept State Bul 55:317-20 Ag 29 '66
  U.S. USSR seen nearer weapons accord. M. Getler. Tech W 20:14-15 Ja 16 '67
  Without portfolio: past and present attempts to achieve international disarmament. C. B. Luce. McCalls 94:34+ N '66
  See also
  Atomic weapons and disarmament
  Conference of the Eighteen-nation committee on disarmament, Geneva, 1962-
  International security
  Peace

DISARMAMENT agency. See United States—Arms control and disarmament agency

DISASTERS
  Brace yourself for the next disaster! battling Oregon floods. D. Barney. il Pop Mech 125:102-4+ Ap '66
  Disasters in Wales and Italy. America 115:640 N 19 '66
  Murderous mountain: Aberfan. il Time 88:41 O 28 '66
  Never one like this: avalanche of coal slag; Aberfan, Wales. il Newsweek 68:54+ O 31 '66
  Sea of sludge upon green Aberfan. il Life 61:68-73 N 4 '66
  United States hit hard by floods and storms. Sci N 89:169 Mr 12 '66
  Vulnerable eyes in coal-dusted faces. J. Hicks. Life 61:3 N 4 '66
  See also
  Shipwrecks
  Tornadoes

DISC brakes. See Brakes, Automobile

DISC electrophoresis. See Electrophoresis

DISC jockeys
  Dandy Dan in Africa; visit to publicize the fifth anniversary of Peace corps. New Yorker 42:38-9 Ap 30 '66
  Number one cat: Geator with the Heater of Philadelphia. B. J. Friedman. il Sat Eve Post 239:36-8+ S 24 '66

DISCARDING of books. See Libraries—Book discarding

DISCHARGED prisoners. See Prisoners, Discharged

DISCIPLES of Christ
  Disciples change course: International convention of Christian churches. H. E. Fey. Christian Cent 83:1266-7 O 19 '66
  From churches to church. Christian Cent 83:1231-2 O 12 '66; Reply. R. W. Huston. 83:1446 N 23 '66

DISCIPLINE
  Magic chart; family acquires self-discipline. G. Charbonnet. il Redbook 127:8+ My '66
  Modern view of discipline. S. Chess and A. Thomas. il Parents Mag 41:43-5+ F '66
  Our children, our problem: parents groups for solving problem of rebellious children. W. Abraham. il Todays Health 44:58-64 F '66
  See also
  Children—Management and training
  College discipline
  School discipline

DISCIPLINE, Library. See Library administration

DISCIPLINE, Military
  See also
  Military training

DISCOTHEQUES. See Night clubs

DISCOUNT
  Discount hike starts to pinch bank loans. Bsns W p26-7 F 5 '66

DISCOUNT houses (retail trade)
$131 million books-magazines sold in discount stores. Pub W 189:89 Je 27 '66
See also
John's bargain stores corporation
Korvette, E. J, incorporated
Spartans industries, incorporated

DISCOVERIES in science. See Research

DISCOVERY house garden. See Gardens—California

DISCRIMINATION
Idea exchange: project misery: sixth grade project. W. Wood. NEA J 55:60 S '66
See also
Anti-Semitism

DISCRIMINATION, Racial. See Race discrimination

DISCRIMINATION in education
School bias toward Mexican Americans. Sch & Soc 94:378+ N 12 '66

DISCRIMINATION in employment
Administration hardens stand against job bias; St Louis scene of labor walkout. il Bsns W p94+ F 12 '66
Banks and the Jews. America 115:309 S 24 '66
Changing patterns in employment of nonwhite workers. J. L. Russell. il Mo Labor R 89:503-9 My '66
Steel giants face a blast on bias; NAACP blames USW. Bsns W p81-2 Je 11 '66
Where civil rights law is going wrong; reply. F. D. Roosevelt. Nations Bsns 53:10+ D '65
See also
Negroes in the United States—Employment

DISCRIMINATION in housing
Back at the office; House furor and Title IV. Newsweek 68:21-2 Ag 15 '66
Block-busting on the Potomac; debate on the open-housing provisions of the Civil rights act of 1966. W. More. America 115:172 Ag 20 '66
Chaos and the civil rights bill; California, Proposition 14. W. F. Buckley, jr. Nat R 18:508 My 31 '66
Civil rights' dim prospects; bill of 1966. A. M. Bickel. New Repub 155:17-18 S 17 '66
Corkscrew compromise; Title IV of 1966 civil rights bill. Time 88:18-19 Jl 8 '66
Court vs. the voters on open housing: California Supreme court declares Proposition 14 unconstitutional. L. T. King. Commonweal 84:491-2 Ag 5 '66
Court votes no; Proposition 14 in California Supreme court. Newsweek 67:47 My 23 '66
Dirksen's defection; proposal banning racial discrimination in the sale, rental or financing of housing. Time 87:31 My 13 '66
Fair housing in trouble. New Repub 155:9 Jl 2 '66
Hero on vacation; problems of passing a bill providing for open housing. Reporter 35:18 S 22 '66
Hottest potato; Title IV divides Congress. Newsweek 68:20-1 Ag 8 '66
House, the home, and Title IV. J Berry and M. Clay. il Reporter 35:28-9+ S 8 '66
Housing and urban development; address, August 1, 1966. R. C. Weaver. Vital Speeches 32:674-8 S 1 '66
Housing in the House; amended bill. New Repub 155:7 Jl 30 '66
I'll eat the chimney; fair housing measure. il Newsweek 67:32 My 16 '66
Latest push for civil rights; LBJ's big target: housing. U S News 60:35-6 My 9 '66
LBJ's civil rights bill. A. M. Bickel. New Repub 154:12-14 My 21 '66
Modest milestone; open-housing provision. il Time 88:20-1 Ag 19 '66
New game: 1966 civil rights bill, Title 4. il Time 88:18 Ag 5 '66
Open housing in Congress. America 115:167 Ag 20 '66
Policing job Washington now is trying to get. il U S News 61:38-9 Ag 22 '66
Reporter at large; work of committee on civil rights in metropolitan New York and New York city commission on human rights. E. Iglauer. New Yorker 42:188-92+ S 24 '66
Rep. Celler vs Rep. Smith. America 115:125 Ag 6 '66
Symptom of anger; House passes new civil-rights bill. Newsweek 68:59 Ag 22 '66
T.R.B. from Washington: Vorster and Dirksen: doomed vote. New Repub 155:4 S 24 '66
Temporary surgery; administration's 1966 civil rights bill. Christian Cent 83:975-6 Ag 10 '66
This month's feature: federal open housing controversy. Cong Digest 45:257-88 N '66

Upset: California law on homeowners' rights. U S News 60:13 My 23 '66
See also
Housing—Desegregation
Negroes in the United States—Housing

DISCRIMINATION learning. See Learning, Psychology of

DISCUS, pseud.
Music in the round. See issues of Harper's magazine

DISCUSSION
Theology in the living room. il Time 88:50 Jl 8 '66
See also
Conversation

DISCUSSION groups. See Forums (discussion and debate)

DISEASE carriers. See Carriers of infection

DISEASE germs. See Bacteria, Pathogenic

DISEASES
Medical news of the month. M. Fishbein. See issues of McCall's
See also
Animals as carriers of infection
Diagnosis
Immunity
Therapeutics
Venereal diseases
also names of diseases, e.g. Gout

Causes and theories of causation

Power to resist disease: the terrain of health. B. Inglis. Vogue 147:84-5+ F 15 '66

History

Porotic hyperostosis, anemias, malarias, and marshes in the prehistoric eastern Mediterranean. J. L. Angel. bibliog il Science 153:760-3 Ag 12 '66

DISEASES, Hereditary. See Heredity of disease

DISEASES, Iatrogenic. See Iatrogenic diseases

DISEASES, Psychosomatic. See Medicine, Psychosomatic

DISEASES of animals. See Animals—Diseases and pests

DISEASES of plants. See Plants—Diseases and pests

DISHES. See Pottery; Tableware

DISHWASHING and drying machines
Dishwashers. Consumer Rep 31:94-6 D '66
Getting the dishes done. il McCalls 93:29+ My '66
Is a dishwasher for your home? J. LemMon. il Suc Farm 64:132-3 Mr '66
Westinghouse dishwasher. il Consumer Bul 49:30-1 O '66

DISHWASHING compounds. See Cleaning compositions

DISINFECTION and disinfectants
Germs on the phone. il Sci Digest 59:25 Ap '66

DISK jockeys. See Disc jockeys

DISMISSAL of teachers. See Teachers—Dismissal

DISNEY, Dorothy Cameron
(ed) Can this marriage be saved? See issues of Ladies' home journal

DISNEY, Walt
AFA honors Walt Disney. il por Am For 72:10 D '66
Footnote to Walt. P. Nathan. Pub W 191:48 Ja 2 '67
Magic kingdom. il por Time 87:84 Ap 15 '66
Obituary
Time por 88:71 D 23 '66
Walt Disney dies. il por Sr Schol 89:17 Ja 6 '67
Walt Disney (1901-1966) imagineer of fun. J. Morgenstern. il por Newsweek 68:68-9 D 26 '66
Walt Disney, RIP. R. Brewer. Nat R 19:17 Ja 10 '67

DISNEY, Walt, productions
Disney's legacy. Newsweek 69:58-9 Ja 2 '67
Now the bankers come to Disney. J. McDonald. il Fortune 73:138-41+ My '66
Scholastic and Disney sign book agreement. il Pub W 189:30-1 Ap 4 '66

DISORDERLY conduct
Blackstone on gutbucket; the trials of William Brown and Charles Bandy in New York. J. D. Zirin. il Reporter 35:48-9 O 6 '66

DISPLACED person; drama. See Dawkins, C.

DISPLACED persons. See Refugees

DISPLAY of antiques, art objects, etc.
Elegant frame for masterpieces. il House & Gard 130:78-83 Jl '66
House of many treasures; Beirut. il House & Gard 130:236-41 N '66

DISPLAY of antiques, art objects, etc.—*Cont.*
If you collect them small; collections mounted on miniature blocks. il Sunset 136:156+ Mr '66
Imaginative ideas for display. il House & Gard 130:70-7 Jl '66

DISPLAY of merchandise
Proper display can sell more books; summary of address, September 19, 1966. J. Sjursen. il Pub W 190:31 O 17 '66

DISPLAYS, Library. See Library exhibits

DISPLAYS, Window. See Show windows

DISPOSABLE containers. See Containers

DISSENTERS
Patriotism of dissent. J. W. Fulbright. Redbook 128:44+ N '66

DISSENTERS, Religious
What can Catholicism learn from the free churches? D. O'Hanlon. Cath World 203: 81-5 My '66; Reply. E. Gibson. 204:225-9 Ja '67

DISTANCES
Measurement
See also
Telemeter

DISTANT early warning line. See Radar defense network

DISTEMPER
Distemper vaccinations recommended annually. Sci N 89:514 Je 25 '66

DISTILLED water. See Water, Distilled

DISTILLERS company, limited. See Distilling industries

DISTILLERS corporation-Seagrams, limited. See Seagram, Joseph E. and sons

DISTILLING, Illicit. See Moonshining

DISTILLING industries
Potable interests; Distillers co. ltd. Time 88: 75 S 2 '66
See also
Brown-Forman distillers corporation
Seagram, Joseph E. and sons

DISTRESS signals. See Signals and signaling

DISTRESS signals; story. See Fineman, M.

DISTRIBUTION of goods
New strategies to move goods; special report. Bsns W p 112-14+ S 24 '66

DISTRIBUTION of wealth. See Wealth, Distribution of

DISTRICT attorneys
Houston's compassionate assistant DA; C. G. Ward. il Ebony 21:49-50+ Mr '66

DISTRICTS, School. See School districts

DISULFIDES. See Sulfides

DIURETICS and diuresis
Crackdown on drug ads; lasix seized. B. J. Culliton. il Sci N 90:490-1 D 10 '66

DIVCO-Wayne corporation
Many houses of Newton Glekel. Fortune 74: 194 D '66

DIVELY, George Samuel
Why the ink is black at Harris-Intertype. il por Bsns W p34-6 D 31 '66

DIVERS. See Diving, Submarine

DIVERSIFICATION in industry
Belgian defense firm diversifying; S. A. Les Forges De Zeebrugge. J. F. Judge. il Miss & Roc 18:25-6+ F 7 '66
Cat and dog food, too; diversification moves of tobacco industry. il Newsweek 68:84 D 12 '66
Diversification guides for defense firms; excerpts from article. J. S. Gilmore and D. C. Coddington. bibliog f il Harvard Bsns R 44:144-50+ My '66
Doubts cloud future of diversification. H. D. Watkins. il Aviation W 85:178-9+ O 31 '66
Dow chemical banks on a global formula. il Bsns W p84-6+ Ap 2 '66
Eastern moving to diversification with Remmert-Werner acquisition. D. A. Brown. Aviation W 85:41 S 19 '66
Europe's coal owners mine rich, new seams, diversifying into chemicals, plastics, auto making. il Bsns W p 122-4+ My 28 '66
Firms urged to diversify while defense spending high. W. S. Beller. il Miss & Roc 18:34+ My 9 '66
Foes of Eastern-Remmert cloud airline diversification. Aviation W 85:33 O 17 '66
Frawley phenomenon. S. H. Brown. il Fortune 73:136-9+ F '66
How a broadcaster spreads its net; community antenna cable and microwave systems. il Bsns W p57-8+ D 3 '66
Insurance men expand their lines; holding companies being set up to broaden industry's financial services. Bsns W p70+ Mr 19 '66

Is the sky the limit for the Pennsy? denies entering the airline business, Johnson flying service. il Bsns W p 106-8+ D 10 '66
Looking for a new yardstick; conglomerates, worried by low P/E ratios. il Bsns W p 119-20 Ag 20 '66
Management of Litton industries. J. B. Weiner. il Duns R 87:32-3+ My '66
New breed of conglomerates. il Duns R 88: 127-9 N '66
Old Baldwin works gets on a new track. il Bsns W p52-3+ Ja 29 '66
Pulling the big switch; Westinghouse air brake co. il Bsns W p 182-4+ F 19 '66
Raytheon's quicker pulse. il Bsns W p72-4+ Jl 9 '66
Rockwell-Standard's jet-age management. T. J. Murray. il Duns R 87:28-31+ Je '66
Sidelines of a copper company. Fortune 73: 121 My '66
Titan makes the sidelines pay off. il Bsns W p88-90 Jl 2 '66
Warm glow at O-I; ventures in plywood, TV tubes, and plastics. il Bsns W p82-3 Ap 2 '66
Way they think at TRW. R. Sheehan. il Fortune 74:153-7+ O '66
What sparked the fire under Coleman co; divisionalization program. il Bsns W p86-8+ Ag 13 '66
When arms calls lag; defense companies to diversify into civilian work. Bsns W p 178 Mr 19 '66
Where diversity is the tie that binds; corporate schizophrenia at TRW. il Bsns W p88-90+ S 24 '66
Why companies seek greener fields; mergers on the upswing. il Bsns W p59-60+ Mr 12 '66
You can argue with success. C. A. Cerami. il Nations Bsns 54:82-4+ F '66

DIVIDENDS
Squeeze on dividends. il Fortune 74:241 N '66

DIVIDENDS; story. See O'Faolain, S.

DIVINA commedia. See Dante Alighieri

DIVINATION
See also
Prophecies

DIVINE comedy. See Dante Alighieri

DIVINE healing. See Faith cure

DIVINE love. See Love (theology)

DIVING
Cardiovascular defense against asphyxia. R. Elsner and others. bibliog Science 153:941-9 Ag 26 '66
Girl on the varsity. il Ebony 21:71-2+ My '66
Heretic in an arty sport; diving coach H. Billingsley. H. Weiskopf. il Sports Illus 24: 85-7 Mr 21 '66

Physiological effects
Arterial constrictor response in a diving mammal. K. M. Bron and others. bibliog il Science 152:540-3 Ap 22 '66

DIVING, Submarine
Beneath the surface; Virgin Islands National Park and Buck Island Reef National Monument. E. L. Rothfuss. il Parks & Rec 1: 715-16+ S '66
Coldest swim in the world; diving under Antarctica's ice field to record sounds of the Weddell seal. D. Lavallee. il Pop Mech 126:70-4 Jl '66
Enter the poodle; efforts to retrieve H-bomb. Newsweek 67:55 Ap 4 '66
How far down can he go? J. Mayol's free dive record. il Life 61:41-2+ Jl 22 '66
How to find sunken treasure, and keep it. L. Steckler. il Pop Mech 126:124-7+ N '66
Is there a gold mine out in the ocean? money in underwater engineering. il Bsns W p90-2+ Ap 9 '66
Marvels of a coral realm. W. A. Starck, 2d. il Nat Geog Mag 130:710-38 N '66
My life as a nearsighted fish; rummaging beneath surface of the sea. N. Johnson. il Sports Illus 26:42-6 Ja 9 '67
Navy presses deep-sea probes; search for H-bomb sunk off Spain. il Bsns W p72-4+ Mr 12 '66
Scuba-diving fire-eaters. B. Grant. il Pop Mech 126:102-4 Ag '66
Skin, scuba diving took lives of eighty-six in 1965. Sci N 90:151 S 3 '66
Snorkeling in the Virgin Islands. il Sunset 137:42-3 O '66
Sport diving makes a splash. il Ebony 22: 66-8+ N '66
See also
Aquanauts
Diving suits

DIVING, Submarine—*Continued*
  Safety devices and measures
New buoy for skindivers. P. Czura. il Field &
  S 71:139 S '66
DIVING apparatus
Divers' communications improved. K. K.
  Neely. Science 153:321 Jl 15 '66
DIVING saucer. See Bathyscaphe
DIVING suits
Isotope-fueled diving-suit claimed to function
  two years. R. G. Barnhart. il Tech W 19:
  39 Jl 18 '66
DIVINING rod
Can you find water with a forked stick?
  J. R. Berry. il Pop Mech 126:88-91+ Jl '66
DIVINITY (candy) See Candy
DIVINITY of Christ See Jesus Christ—Divinity
DIVINITY schools. See Theological schools
DIVISION for the blind, Library of Congress.
  See United States—Library of Congress—
  Division for the blind
DIVORCE
Early divorce warning system; Jewish com-
  munity program. America 115:642 N 19 '66
Marriage, divorce and remarriage. F. R.
  Schreiber and M. Herman. il Sci Digest
  60:24-7 N '66
New thinking on divorce; Catholic church. il
  Time 87:103-4 Mr 18 '66
Second thoughts on second marriages; views
  of Catholic theologians. Time 88:65 Jl 22 '66
Suggest new basis for divorce. Christian
  Cent 83:1023-4 Ag 24 '66
Why marriages fail. S. Blum. il Redbook 126:
  69+ Ap '66
  See also
Marriage

  Great Britain
Divorce, English style. Newsweek 68:51 Ag
  8 '66
Liabilities of being a lord; Earl of Harewood
  case. il Time 89:28 Ja 13 '67
Suggest new basis for divorce. Christian Cent
  83:1023-4 Ag 24 '66

  New York (state)
Catholic church opposes divorce reform.
  Christian Cent 83:197 F 16 '66
Catholics of New York; divorce issue. E. J.
  Hughes. Newsweek 67:23 Mr 21 '66
Century of progress; law revised. Newsweek
  67:31-2 My 9 '66
Cutting the bonds of acrimony; New York
  may get new law. Life 60:4 F 11 '66
Divorce, New York style; Catholic church's
  stand. Newsweek 67:92 F 21 '66
Help wanted; divorce counselor. M. M. Hunt.
  il N Y Times Mag p 14-17 Ja 1 '67
In New York, new rules for easier divorces.
  U S News 60:12 My 9 '66
Liberalized divorce; New York state legisla-
  ture studying 179-year-old law. Common-
  weal 83:524 F 4 '66
New York reforms divorce. Time 87:75 My 6
  '66
New York reforms divorce statute. Christian
  Cent 83:610 My 11 '66
Sorry state of divorce law; Time essay. Time
  87:26-7 F 11 '66

  United States
Children at stake. K. D. Fishman. il N Y
  Times Mag p 146+ D 11 '66
Dearly unbeloved; Unitarian divorce rite.
  Newsweek 68:105 O 24 '66
Divorce American style. R. Hoffmann. Mlle
  63:190-1+ S '66
Divorce and the family in America. C.
  Lasch. il Atlan 218:57-61 N '66
Marriage as a wretched institution. M. Cad-
  wallader. il Atlan 218:62-6 N '66
Right of divorce. D. J. Cantor. il Atlan 218:
  67-71 N '66
Stop divorces before they start. W. Hartley
  and E. Hartley. Good H 162:89+ Ap '66
Sunday daddy. B. Rollin. il Look 31:28-9 Ja
  10 '67
Who speaks for Catholics? formation of Com-
  mittee of Catholic citizens to support di-
  vorce reform. Commonweal 83:572 F 18 '66
DIVORCEES
Etiquette of divorce. A. Vanderbilt. Ladies
  Home J 83:22 S '66
Formerly married; concerning Morton Hunt's
  survey. Newsweek 68:105-6 O 31 '66
Strange courtship customs of the formerly
  married; excerpt from The world of the
  formerly married. M. M. Hunt. McCalls 93:
  94-5+ S '66 (to be cont)

World of the formerly married; excerpt. M.
  M. Hunt. il McCalls 93:53-4+ Ag '66 (to be
  cont)
  See also
SOS (organization)
DIXON, Bill
Judith Dunn and Bill Dixon, Judson me-
  morial church. J. Maskey. Dance Mag 40:
  30 S '66
DIXON, Christine
Clover ring; story. Seventeen 26:84-5 Ja '67
DIXON, David
Putting food to sleep. C. Welles. il por Life
  60:71-2 F 18 '66
DIXON, Dean
Dean Dixon: conductor without a country. E.
  B. Thompson. il pors Ebony 21:78-80+ O
  '66
DIXON, Dorothy. See Pomeroy, K. B. jt.
  auth.
DIXON, J. L.
Examination of English eighteenth-century
  porcelains by transmitted light. Antiques
  90:214-17 Ag '66
DIXON, Jeane
Gift of prophecy, by Ruth Montgomery.
  Christian Cent 83:995 Ag 10 '66
Jeane Dixon charms them at Haslam's, St
  Petersburg. il Pub W 189:69 Mr 21 '66
DIXON, John Morris
Boston's citadel of architecture. Arch Forum
  125:64-71 D '66
How to grow a campus; Tougaloo college.
  Arch Forum 124:56-61 Ap '66
Last hitch in the inner belt. Arch Forum
  124:68-71 My '66
Whitney: big for its size. Arch Forum 125:
  80-5 S '66
DIXON, Jonathan S. and Li, C. H.
Retention of the biological potency of hu-
  man pituitary growth hormone after re-
  duction and carbamidomethylation. bibliog
  Science 154:785-6 N 11 '66
DIXON, Paul Rand
Antitrust and the apparel industry; ad-
  dress, June 17, 1966. Vital Speeches 32:617-
  21 Ag 1 '66
Excerpt from testimony, April 29, 1965. Cong
  Digest 45:178+ Je '66
Talk with Paul Rand Dixon; interview, ed.
  by J. Berry. por Duns R 87:44-5+ Ja '66
DIXON, Stephen
Neighbors; story. Atlan 217:96-102 Ap '66
DIZZINESS
  See also
Ménière's disease
DJERASSI, Carl
Steroid oral contraceptives. bibliog Science
  151:1055-61 Mr 4 '66
DJERBA (island)
Island of the lotus eaters. A. Waugh. Nat R
  18:470+ My 17 '66
DJERFISHERITE
Djerfisherite, alkali copper-iron sulfide: a new
  mineral from enstatite chondrites. L. H.
  Fuchs. bibliog il Science 153:166-7 Jl 8 '66
DJILAS, Milovan
Freedom for Djilas. Newsweek 69:34 Ja 9 '67
Ordeal of Djilas. R. Moley. Newsweek 67:
  124 My 16 '66
Policy of pardons. Time 89:29 Ja 6 '67
DLIMI, Ahmed
Surprise witness. il por Time 88:38 O 28 '66
DO-it-yourself work
Ideas in action. D. Jordan. il Bet Hom &
  Gard 44:54-71 O '66
100 ideas under $100. il Bet Hom & Gard
  44:22+ Jl '66
  See also
Kit building
DOBLER, Lavinia
Your foot-long reference shelf. Sr Schol 88:
  sup 13 F 4 '66
DOBRZECKA, Czeslawa, and others
Qualitative versus directional cues in two
  forms of differentiation. Science 153:87-9
  Jl 1 '66
DOBZHANSKY, Theodosius
Equality: a geneticist's view; reprint. Cath
  World 204:104-12 N '66
DOC Savage. See Comics (books, strips, etc)
DOCK workers. See Longshoremen
DOCKETS, Trial. See Court calendars
DOCKING in space. See Orbital rendezvous
  (space flight)
DOCKS
Easy-built dock bumpers; ethafoam with
  canvas sheath. il Field & S 71:32 Je '66
  See also
Marinas
Ports
Wharves
DOCKSTADER, Tod
Drips and drabs of Dockstader. O. Daniel.
  Sat R 49:87+ N 12 '66

DOCKTER, Kenneth W. See Thomson, J. R.
jt. auth.
DOCTOR Dolittle (literary character) See
Characters in literature
DR Kildare (literary character) See Characters
in literature
DOCTOR Leviticus and the wicked imp; drama. See Bealmear, J. H.
DOCTOR Love, hero, and heroin; story. See
Leasor, J.
DOCTOR Manners; drama. See Hark, M. and
McQueen, N.
DR X, pseud. See X, Dr, pseud.
DOCTORS. See Physicians
DOCTOR'S dilemma; drama. See Shaw, G. B.
DOCTORS hospital. See New York (city)—
Hospitals
DOCTORS of philosophy. See Degrees, Academic
DOCTORS strike (Belgium) See Strikes—Belgium
DOCTRINAL theology. See Theology
DOCTRINE, Religious. See Theology
DOCUMENT disintegration, incorporated, Los
Angeles
Shredded secrets. Newsweek 67:80 F 28 '66
DOCUMENTARY films. See Moving pictures—
Documentary films
DOCUMENTARY television programs. See
Television broadcasting—Documentary programs
DOCUMENTATION
National document-handling systems in
science and technology; federal government's responsibilities. L. F. Carter. bibliog
Science 154:1299-304 D 9 '66
Policy problems of a data-rich civilization;
address, October 1965. H. D. Lasswell. bibliog il Wilson Lib Bul 41:58-65 S '66
See also
American documentation institute
DOCUMENTATION, incorporated
Computer produced book catalog. T. W. Mc-
Conkey. il Library J 91:1864-5 Ap 1 '66
DOCUMENTATION institute, American. See
American documentation institute
DOCUMENTS
Annals of law; Lewis and Clark case: United
States government's claim to field notes.
C. Tomkins. New Yorker 42:105-6+ O 29 '66
See also
Archives
United States—National archives
DOCUMENTS, Fraudulent
Agents of deceit: frauds, forgeries and political intrigue among nations, by P. W.
Blackstock. Review
Sat R 49:41 S 10 '66. R. G. Deindorfer
DODD, Thomas Joseph
Excerpt from address, March 10, 1966. Cong
Digest 45:300+ D '66
Excerpt from debate, July 15, 1965. Cong
Digest 45:18+ Ja '66
From Senator Dodd: a denial of misconduct;
summary of testimony, June 27, 1966. U S
News 61:14-15 Jl 11 '66
about
Acceptance factor; impending investigations.
il por Time 87:23-4 My 6 '66
At odds with Dodd. Newsweek 67:29 My 9 '66
Day in court. il por Newsweek 68:23-4 Jl 11 '66
Dodd affair endangers ethics group. J. N.
Eller. America 114:725 My 21 '66
Dodd case. il por Newsweek 68:17-18 Jl 4 '66
Dodd dinners. il por Newsweek 67:19-20 My 2
'66
Dodd, unfinished business; Senate Ethics
committee closed hearings. New Repub 154:
7 My 28 '66
Dodd's case: what's ethical? il por News-
week 68:22+ Ag 1 '66
Dodd's trip: how helpful to Klein? U S News
61:8 Ag 1 '66
Focus on Washington. Cato. Nat R 18:663
Jl 12 '66
Good for Dodd. Nation 202:142 F 7 '66
Inquiry into gifts to a senator. U S News 60:
12 My 2 '66
Is Dodd dead? New Repub 154:7 Ap 30 '66
Matter of ethics. S. Shaffer. il por News-
week 67:29 Ap 11 '66
Pearson's hot potato. Nation 202:410 Ap 11 '66
Private lives. il por Time 88:15 Jl 1 '66
Senate looks at a member's conduct. il por
U S News 61:6 Jl 4 '66
Senator & the lobbyist. il por Time 88:19
Jl 8 '66
Senators are different. Nation 203:36-7 Jl 11
'66

DODGE, David
American view of the Orient. Sat R 49:52
Jl 23 '66
Capsule history of jewel thievery. Holiday 39:
60-1 Ap '66
DODGE, F. W, corporations
F. W. Dodge construction outlook at mid-
year. G. C. Christie. il Arch Rec 140:44
Jl '66
F. W. Dodge construction outlook; plans for
1967. il Arch Rec 140:147-50 N '66
DODGE, Natt N.
Pecos National Monument. il Nat Parks Mag
40:14-16 N '66
DODGE division. See Chrysler corporation—
Dodge division
DODGERS (baseball) See Baseball clubs
DODGSON, Charles Lutwidge. See Carroll, L.
pseud.
DODSON, James
Guests of the VC. por Newsweek 68:36-7
Jl 11 '66
Tale of two prisoners. Time 88:27 Jl 8 '66
DOE, William
Apples of wrath; excerpts from daily notes,
ed. by F. Russell. Nat R 18:932-3 S 20 '66
DOELL, Richard R. and Dalrymple, G. B.
Geomagnetic polarity epochs: a new polarity
event and the age of the Brunhes-
Matuyama boundary. bibliog Science 152:
1060-1 My 20 '66
DOG for Rock; story. See Senesi. M.
DOG houses. See Kennels
DOG lungs. See Lungs
DOG racing
Canine charioteers. J. Boykin. il Pop Mech
126:63-5 Jl '66
Shaggy dog racing; Afghans and dachshunds
races. il Life 61:151-4 N 18 '66
DOG runs. See Kennels
DOG schools. See Dogs—Training
DOG shows
Biggest dog of all was Finn MacCool's aunt:
Irish wolfhound. R. H. Boyle. il Sports
Illus 24:42-4+ F 14 '66
It takes a lot of ham to make a show dog.
M. Sharnik. il Sports Illus 24:56 F 28 '66
DOG training. See Dogs—Training
DOGFISH
Polypeptide chains of immunoglobulins from
the smooth dogfish (mustelus canis) J.
Marchalonis and G. M. Edelman. bibliog
il Science 154:1567-8 D 23 '66
DOGNAPPING. See Animal thefts
DOGS
Concentration camps for dogs; L. W. Brown's
Maryland compound raided; with report
by M. Silva. il Life 60:22-9 F 4 '66
Desert tragedy; caught in wolf trap. R. P.
Holland. il Field & S 71:72-3+ S '66
Dogs, D. M. Duffey. See issues of Outdoor life
Down, boy, down, blast you! C. Ogburn,
jr. il Read Digest 88:121-4 Je '66
Pet news; Soviet dogs. J. Kobler. Ladies
Home J 83:44 N '66
Prince: Daktari's scene stealer. il Look 30:
118+ N 1 '66
When you choose a puppy. il Pop Gard 17:
71 Ag '66
Wilderness dog walking. B. Leasure. il To-
days Health 44:28-9 O '66
See also
Afghan hounds
Beagles (dogs)
Dachshunds
Dog shows
Hunting dogs
Irish wolf-hounds
Pointers (dogs)

Diseases and pests
How to combat poisons; major factor in
canine mortality. P. Czura. il Field & S
71:176-7+ My '66
See also
Distemper
Worms, Intestinal and parasitic

Equipment and supplies
Fit for a dog; Canine couture show. il Time
87:69 F 25 '66
Puppy pen, catwalk, dog deck, high feeder,
A-frame dog house. il Sunset 138:62-3 Ja
'67

History
Dog and the conquistador. J. J. de
Madariaga. il Américas 18:16-25 Je '66

Kennels
See Kennels

DOMESTIC architecture. See Architecture. Domestic
DOMESTIC economic assistance. See Economic assistance. Domestic
DOMESTIC employees.   See Household employees
DOMESTIC finance
Are you really making the most of your money? Bet Hom & Gard 44:6+ S '66
Family money management. N. Kuehnl and G. Bush. See issues of Better homes and gardens
Hedging against financial trouble. M. Mayer. Bet Hom & Gard 45:44 Ja '67
Just what are you worth today? il Bet Hom & Gard 44:31-2+ My '66
Next shift in population: more young adults with more to spend on themselves. il U S News 60:73-4 Je 6 '66
Spending your money; questions and answers. S. Porter. See issues of Ladies' home journal
Understanding and using economics. M. Mayer. Bet Hom & Gard 44:112 S '66
When should parents help support newlyweds? Bet Hom & Gard 44:6+ My '66
See also
Budget. Household
Debt
Saving and savings
DOMESTIC missionaries. See Missionaries
DOMESTIC peace corps. See Volunteers in service to America
DOMESTIC relations
Informal history of love U.S.A. A. Schlesinger, jr. il Sat Eve Post 239:30-2+ D 31 '66
See also
Divorce
Family life
Husbands
Marriage
Marriage counseling
DOMINGOS, Angus B. Jr
Mark Smith planetarium in Georgia. Sky & Tel 32:142-3 S '66
DOMINIC, C. J.
Reserpine: inhibition of olfactory blockage of pregnancy in mice. bibliog Science 152: 1764-5 Je 24 '66
DOMINICAN REPUBLIC
See also
Americans in the Dominican Republic
Economic assistance in the Dominican Republic
Political campaigns—Dominican Republic
United States—Armed forces—Forces in the Dominican Republic
Youth—Dominican Republic

Economic conditions
Dominican Republic: burden of the past. K. Wagenheim. il Nation 203:541-4 N 21 '66

Politics and government
Abrazos in the night. Time 87:42 Je 17 '66
Ad hoc committee reports from Dominican Republic. il Américas 18:41 F '66
Anniversary week; shooting; anti-American demonstrations. Newsweek 67:52 My 9 '66
Another U.S. problem that just will not go away. H. Handleman. il U S News 60:52+ F 28 '66
Balaguer takes over. E. L. Simons. Commonweal 84:437-40 Jl 8 '66
Breathing spell. Newsweek 67:52 F 28 '66
Case of defamation; US intelligence versus Juan Bosch; alleged Bosch-Communist plot, April 14, 1965. T. Draper. New Repub 154: 13-19 F 19; 15-18 F 26; 37 Mr 5; 35 Mr 12 '66
Correspondence with Theodore Draper & Commentary, appropriate & inappropriate. T. Draper; J. B. Bender; P. Bethel. Nat R 18:823-7 Ag 23 '66
Dilemma in Dominica. Nat R 18:501-2 My 31 '66
Dominican crisis; case study in American policy. T. Draper; discussion. il Nat R 18: 99-100, 107-14 F 8 '66; Commentary 41:18+ Ap; 6+ My '66
Dominican double-talk. Reporter 34:8 My 5 '66
Dominican elections scheduled. Américas 18: 39 Ap '66
Dominican example. G. de Zéndegui. Américas 18:inside cover Ag '66
Dominican Republic: burden of the past. K. Wagenheim. il Nation 203:541-4 N 21 '66
Dominican Republic goes to the polls. P. D. Bethel. il Reporter 34:18-20+ Je 2 '66
Dominican rewrite: revolution of April, 1965. Commonweal 85:280 D 9 '66
Dominican search for stability. H. Wells. Cur Hist 51:328-32+ D '66

Free elections? Commonweal 84:43-4 Ap 1 '66
Government by scalpel. il Time 88:24+ Jl 8 '66
Hate reborn. il Newsweek 67:57 F 21 '66
In the Dominican Republic; Ad hoc committee. Américas 18:42 Mr '66
Latest excuse. il Time 87:35 F 18 '66
Lessons of dictatorship; report of talks with Dominican youth. R. S Arnon. Mlle 62:180-1+ Ap '66
Long wait. Time 87:34 F 4 '66
Now that GI's have left Santo Domingo. U S News 61:20 O 3 '66
Outlook for Bosch. A. Kopkind. New Repub 154:15-18 My 21 '66
Overtaken by events, by J. B. Martin. Review Atlan 218:158+ N '66. O. Handlin
Nation 204:23-5 Ja 2 '67. W. A. Williams
New Repub 155:25-8 D 24 '66. S. Halper
New Yorker 42:224+ N 26 '66. R. H. Rovere
Sat R 49:48-9 D 24 '66. D. Kurzman
Time 88:30 N 11 '66
Quiet talk; Balaguer-Bosch talk. Newsweek 67:48B Je 20 '66
Santo Domingo; labyrinth of policy; perils of an international force. T. Mockler. il Nation 202:154-7 F 7 '66
Santo Domingo: unfinished revolution. S. Lens. Nation 202:520-3 My 2 '66
Success so far. Time 88:45+ S 16 '66
Truth about Santo Domingo. K. O. Gilmore. Read Digest 88:93-8 My '66
Unaccustomed calm. il Time 87:34 Ap 22 '66
Waiting game. Newsweek 67:42 F 7 '66
See also
Elections—Dominican Republic
DOMINIONS, British. See Commonwealth of nations
DOMINIS, John
Great cats of Africa. il Life 62:36-52 Ja 6; 48-59+ Ja 13; 44-57 Ja 20 '67
about
Eight months stalking the great cats. G. P. Hunt. il por Life 62:3 Ja 6 '67
Photographers of the year. M. R. Weiss. il por Sat R 49:72-3 My 14 '66
DOMINY, Floyd E.
Reformation of Old Red. Parks & Rec 1:314-15+ Ap '66
DOMMERMUTH, William P.
On the odds of becoming company president. Harvard Bsns R 44:65-72 My '66
DOMS, Keith
Rebirth in Pittsburgh. Library J 91:5871-3 D 1 '66
DON Giovanni; opera. See Mozart, J. C. W. A.
DON Pasquale; opera. See Donizetti, G.
DON Quixote (literary character) See Characters in literature
DON Quixote; ballet. See Ballets—Criticisms
DON Rodrigo; opera. See Ginastera. A.
DONAHUE, Francis
Don Quixote and the ambassador. Horn Bk 42:43-4 F '66
DONAHUE, George T.
Robert finds a friend. J. N. Miller. il PTA Mag 60:4-7 Je '66
DONAHUE, Thomas M.
Upper atmosphere and ionosphere of Mars. bibliog Science 152:763-4 My 6 '66
DONAT, John
Cumbernauld: new town in tension. il Arch Forum 125:52-9 N '66
DONATH, Ludwig
Acting in opera. Opera N 30:6-7 Ap 16 '66
DONCEEL, Joseph
Philosophy in the Catholic university. America 115:330-1 S 24 '66
DONDERI, Don Crosbie
Visual disappearances caused by form similarity. bibliog Science 152:99-100 Ap 1 '66
DONIZETTI, Gaetano
Daughter of the regiment (Fille du régiment) Criticism
Opera N il 31:31 S 10 '66
Don Pasquale. Criticism
Opera N 30:30 Ap 9 '66
Donizetti, by W. Ashbrook. Review
Opera N 30:32 My 7 '66. M. De Schauensee
Donizetti's Lucrezia Borgia. P. L. Miller. Am Rec G 33:292-3 D '66
Elixir of love (L'elisir d'amore) Criticism
Opera N il 30:18-20 Mr 5 '66
Opera N il 30:24-5 Mr 5 '66
Lucia and the LP. J. Ardoin. Sat R 49: 57 My 28 '66
Lucia di Lammermoor. Criticism
New Yorker 42:50+ D 24 '66
Opera N il 30:17-20 F 19 '66
Opera N il 30:24-5 F 19 '66
Opera N il 31:17-20 D 31 '66
Opera N il 31:21-3 D 31 '66
Sat R 50:26 Ja 7 '67

DONIZETTI, Gaetano—*Continued*
Music to my ears; American opera society's presentation of Anna Bolena. Sat R 49:76+ D 3 '66
New York: Anna Bolena at Carnegie Hall. J. W. Freeman. Opera N 31:29 D 17 '66
On records; Don Pasquale; L'elisir d'amore. Opera N 30:34 Mr 5 '66
On records; Lucia di Lammermoor. Opera N 30:34 F 19 '66
Records:
Lucrezia Borgia. Opera N 31:34 D 31 '66
Records: Lucia di Lammermoor. Opera N 31:34 S 10 '66

DONKIN, A. E.
Static-free thermistorized aquarium heater. Pop Electr 25:73-5+ S '66

DONLON, Roger H. C.
Vietnam hero salutes his teacher. D. Chapman. il pors Look 30:68+ F 22 '66

DONN, William L. and Ewing, Maurice
Theory of ice ages III. bibliog Science 152: 1706-12 Je 24 '66

DONNAY, Gabrielle, and others
Absence of neutral alkali atoms in rhodizite. bibliog Science 154:889-90 N 18 '66

DONNELLY, Harold Cooper
Nuclear proliferation; address, November 17, 1966. Vital Speeches 33:166-9 Ja 1 '67

DONNELLY, John
Which teen-agers are really in trouble and which aren't? por Ladies Home J 84:34+ Ja '67

DONNER, Frank J.
Freedom's high-water mark. Nation 203:289-90 S 26 '66
HUAC; from pillory to farce. Nation 203:174-6 S 5 '66
Leaving out the letter E. Nation 203:422-5 O 24 '66

DONNER, Frederic G.
GM's Donner looks down the road. por Bsns W p 160-2 Je 11 '66

DONNITHORNE, Audrey
Central economic control; excerpts from China's economic system. Bul Atomic Sci 22:11-20 Je '66

DONOHUE, H. E. F.
Chicago's picture palace. Holiday 40:72-3+ S '66

DONOVAN, Hedley
Troubled environment; address, December 8, 1965. Vital Speeches 32:241-4 F 1 '66
Vietnam: the war is worth winning. Life 60:27-31 F 25 '66

DON'T die, Jeff Chandler; story. See Moore, J. B.

DON'T drink the water; drama. See Allen, W.

DOOLITTLE, Jerome H.
Young man, be a space lawyer. Esquire 65: 118-19 Je '66

DOOLITTLE, Russell F. and others
Evolution of immunoglobulin polypeptide chains; carboxy-terminal of an IgM heavy chain. bibliog Science 154:1561-2 D 23 '66
—See Singer, S. J. jt. auth.

DOOR locks. See Locks and keys

DOOR steps
These steps are bricks on sand. il Sunset 137: 158 O '66

DOORS
Facelift for your front door. W. J. Ward. jr il Pop Sci 188:156-64 Ap '66
Want a new garage door? or a carport fast? il Pop Sci 188:154-5 Ap '66

DOORS, Sliding
How to hang sliding doors. il Pop Mech 127: 150-5+ Ja '67
Open or shut, using sliding screens. il Sunset 136:116+ Ap '66
What you gain from sliding glass doors. J. Hand. il Pop Sci 188:168-70+ Ap '66

DOORWAYS
Distinctive doorways. il Flower Grower 53: 24-7 D '66
How to dress up your doorway. il Pop Gard 17:36-9 Ag '66

DOPE. See Narcotics

DOPPLER effect
Doppler interpretation of quasar red shifts H. S. Zapolsky. bibliog il Science 153:635-8 Ag 5 '66

DORAND, John
Surprise party; drama. Plays 26:25-33 Ja '67

DORFÉ, pseud.
Autumn candle holder. Design 68:11 S '66
Summer crafts. Design 67:29-31 My '66

DORIOT, Georges F.
Père Doriot. il por Newsweek 67:84 My 16 '66

DORLÉAC, Françoise
Actress alone; ed. by E. Miller. pors Seventeen 25:164-5+ N '66

DORMAN, Sonya
Desperate choice; story. Redbook 127:157-67 Ag '66
Digging a well; poem. Sat R 49:22 F 12 '66
Don't think. Writer 79:25 S '66
Suicide's daughter; poem. Sat R 49:20 F 5 '66
Voyage to the stars; story. Sat Eve Post 239: 44-5 D 31 '66

DORMIN. See Growth inhibiting substances (plants)

DORMITORIES
Campus community: experiment in living. A. M. Greeley. America 115:588-91 N 12 '66
Conservative design for a New England campus; Greylock residential houses, Williams college. il Arch Rec 140:196-9 S '66
Student dorms: a university tries variety; University of Washington. D. Lyndon. il Arch Forum 124:62-7 Mr '66
Student housing: colleges line up for U.S. loans. L. J. Carter. Science 153:277-80 Jl 15 '66
University of Massachusetts. il Arch Rec 139:168-71 My '66

DORN, Alva L.
Photo sculpture. U S Camera 29:54-5+ S '66

DORNIER, Claudius
It's a bird, it's a plane, it's the Riesenflugzeug of W.W.I. il por Esquire 66:114 O '66

DOROTHY Ann, Sister Mary. See Mary Dorothy Ann, Sister

DOROTHY Canfield Fisher library awards
Book club cancels library awards; fellowship now to go to writers. Library J 91:3676 Ag '66

DORSEY, Edna J.
Design in the dark. Design 68:19-21 N '66

DORSEY, Iva
Day-lilies can solve summer's color problem. Flower Grower 53:37+ Je '66

DORSEY, James Livingston
Linoleum blocks. Design 68:4-6+ S '66

DORSON, Richard M.
Wonderful leaps of Sam Patch; with excerpts from a children's book. Am Heritage 18:12-19 D '66

DORT, Wakefield, Jr
Nebraskan and Kansan stades: complexity and importance. Science 154:771-2 N 11 '66

DORTECH, incorporated
Cargo facility modernization accelerating. J. W. Carter. il Aviation W 85:43+ Jl 18 '66

DORTMUND, Germany
Music
Dortmund. J. H. Sutcliffe. il Opera N 30:30-1 Ap 16 '66

DORTMUND opera house. See Opera houses

DOSAGE. See Drugs—Dosage

DOSCHER, Fen K.
Profile of tomorrow's salesman; address, July 6, 1966. Vital Speeches 32:764-8 O 1 '66

DOS PASSOS, John
Conspiracy and trial of Aaron Burr; excerpts from Shackles of power. Am Heritage 17:4-7+ F; 91 Ag '66
New left: a spook out of the past. Nat R 18:1037-9 O 18 '66
Ten days in the ice age. Holiday 39:70-5+ Ap '66

about
Dos and the underdog. J. Chamberlain. Harper 234:97 Ja '67
Dos Passos' Chosen country. K. S. Lynn. New Repub 155:15-18+ O 15 '66
Dos Passos' restless times. R. Sklar. Nation 204:87-8 Ja 16 '67
Hidden artist. por Time 88:127 N 18 '66
John Dos Passos reminisces. G. Hicks. Sat R 49:33-4 N 26 '66

DOSTOEVSKII, Fedor Mikhaǐlovich
Brothers Karamazov. K. Rexroth. Sat R 49: 24 D 3 '66
Dostoevsky and romantic realism, by D. Fanger. Review
Nation 203:164-5 Ag 22 '66. S. Karlinsky

DOTSON, Verner
Modern business education. NEA J 55:44-6 F '66

DOTY, Olive
HHH as I knew him. NEA J 55:16-17 S '66

DOTY, Roy
Wordless workshop. See issues of Popular science monthly

DOTY, William L.
Controversy within the church; statement. America 114:480-2, 484 Ap 9 '66

Le **DOUANIER.** See Rousseau, H.

DOUBLE bass music
See also
Phonograph records—Double bass music

DOUBLE stars. See Stars, Double
DOUBLE taxation. See Taxation, Double
DOUBLEDAY and company
  Chart that cuts down on time and labor in making returns; series of charts used by Doubleday book shop chain. il Pub W 189: 121-2 Je 13 '66
  Doubleday to acquire radio-TV station chain. Pub W 190:33 N 7 '66
DOUBT. See Belief and doubt
DOUGHERTY, John D. and others
  Actinomycete: isolation and identification of agent responsible for musty odors. bibliog Science 152:1372-3 Je 3 '66
DOUGHERTY, Ralph C. and Caldwell, J. R.
  Evidence of early pyrometallurgy in the Kerman Range in Iran. bibliog Science 153:984-5 Ag 26 '66
DOUGLAS, Cathleen (Heffernan)
  Justice Douglas' twenty-three-year-old bride talks about her marriage. S. North. por Ladies Home J 83:92+ N '66
DOUGLAS, Kirk
  Redbook readers talk with Kirk Douglas; interview. pors Redbook 126:72-3+ Ap '66
DOUGLAS, Mike
  Mike Douglas show: he turns the stars on. C. Brossard. il pors Look 30:75-9 Ag 9 '66
DOUGLAS, Paul
  Strip-mined landscape and impoverished souls. Christian Cent 83:753-4 Je 8 '66
DOUGLAS, Paul Howard
  Cost of public office: high, says Senator Douglas; excerpts from annual report. por U S News 62:14 Ja 9 '67
  Excerpt from address, February 2, 1966. Cong Digest 45:143+ My '66

about

  Backlash in the Percy campaign. R. C. Wade. Reporter 36:37-40 Ja 12 '67
  Boy wonder grows up. P. M. Deuel. por Nation 203:374-6 O 17 '66
  Douglas and the devil theory. Nation 202:315 Mr 21 '66
  Hardest campaign of Paul Douglas' career. R. T. Cooper. New Repub 155:9-10 O 22 '66
  Percy vs. Douglas; the blighted campaign. S. Alsop. il por Sat Eve Post 239:26-9 N 5 '66
  Senator Douglas. Reporter 35:12+ D 1 '66
  T.R.B. from Washington. New Repub 155:4 N 26 '66
  What Senator Paul Douglas learned. Life 60: 6 Je 17 '66
DOUGLAS, William Orville
  Our wilderness rights are missing; excerpt from A wilderness bill of rights; ed. by R. D. Butcher. Audubon Mag 68:85 Mr '66

about

  Boy meets girl. G. Ace. Sat R 49:6 Ag 13 '66
  Honeymooners. il por Newsweek 68:21 Ag 1 '66
  Justice Douglas' twenty-three-year-old bride talks about her marriage. S. North. por Ladies Home J 83:92+ N '66
  Look at Supreme court Justice William O. Douglas. P. Romero. por Negro Hist Bul 29:129-30+ Mr '66
  New controversy involving Justice Douglas; reprint from Los Angeles times, October 16, 1966; and excerpt from address by J. J. Williams, October 17, 1966. R. J. Ostrow. por U S News 61:66-8 O 31 '66
  September song. il por Time 88:17 Jl 29 '66
DOUGLAS-HOME, Sir Alexander Frederick
  Freedom and change; address, January 19. 1966. Vital Speeches 32:239-41 F 1 '66
DOUGLAS aircraft company
  Bright side of Douglas. Fortune 74:171 D '66
  Case of indigestion. il Newsweek 68:66 Jl 11 '66
  Clouds lifting for Douglas; merger still holds attraction. il Bsns W p44 Ja 7 '67
  Dollars for Douglas? Newsweek 68:88 D 19 '66
  Douglas aircraft's stormy flight path. J. Mecklin. il Fortune 74:166-71+ D '66
  Douglas bond sale goes ahead after DC-9 loss clarification. Aviation W 85:41 Jl 11 '66
  Douglas directors will study equity funding offers this week. Aviation W 86:24 Ja 9 '67
  Douglas expects gains in sales, earnings, despite delivery delays. H. D. Watkins. Aviation W 84:31 Ap 25 '66
  Douglas invites merger bids. Aviation W 85: 24 D 19 '66
  Douglas plans all-weather landing tests. B. Miller. il Aviation W 86:51-2+ Ja 9 '67
  Douglas reaching key stage in fund talks. Aviation W 85:36-7 D 12 '66
  Douglas rolls out first stretched DC-8. H. D. Watkins. il Aviation W 84:32-3 Ja 31 '66

  Douglas studying 600-passenger DC-10; subsonic jet transport. H. D. Watkins. il Aviation W 84:47+ My 16 '66
  Downcraft at Douglas. il Time 88:80 Jl 8 '66
  Mr Mac tries again: takeover effort by McDonnell co. il Time 88:90 D 16 '66
  New Do-u-g-l-as; DC-8 Super 61 and Boeing's 727-200. il Newsweek 67:68 Ja 31 '66
  Race for Douglas. Time 89:89 Ja 6 '67
  Why Douglas is in a downdraft. il Bsns W p 175-8+ O 22 '66
DOUGLAS aircraft company-McDonnell company merger. See Airplane industry and trade—Consolidations and mergers
DOUGLAS fir

Diseases and pests

  Scolytid beetles associated with Douglas fir: response to terpenes. J. A. Rudinsky. bibliog il Science 152:218-19 Ap 8 '66
DOUGLASS, Frederick
  Frederick Douglass: bridge-builder in human relations. B. Quarles. il por Negro Hist Bul 29:99-100+ F '66
DOUGLASS, George
  Reporter at large. F. McNulty. New Yorker 42:32-6+ Ag 6 '66
DOUGLASS, June Anderson
  Samuel F. Pryor Christmas exhibit of dolls at National geographic society, 1965. Hobbies 71:40+ Ja '67
DOUGLASS, Lathrop
  Elements of shopping-center design: check list and commentary. Arch Rec 139:160-3 Ap '66
DOUGLASS, Suzanne
  Glossary of nursery terms; poem. Ladies Home J 83:113 Ag '66
DOUKHOBORS. See Dukhobors
DOUTHIT, H. A. and Halvorson, H. O.
  Satellite deoxyribonucleic acid from bacillus cereus strain T. bibliog Science 153:182-3 Jl 8 '66
DOVE shooting. See Mourning dove shooting
DOVER, N.H.
  Away from Moby Dick and Jane: high school English program. M. Mainwaring. il Sr Schol 89:sup 13-15 O 14 '66
DOW, Ron
  Who needs a camera? D. L. Miller. il Mod Phot 31:70-1 Ja '67
DOW, Thomas E. jr
  Overpopulation: dilemma for U.S. aid. bibliog f Cur Hist 51:65-71+ Ag '66
DOW chemical company
  Chemicals get their oil; petrochemical makers win import quotas. Bsns W p46 S 17 '66
  Dow chemical banks on a global formula. il Bsns W p84-6+ Ap 2 '66
  Dow puts the heat on fuel gas; new product called MAPP. il Bsns W p92+ N 5 '66
  Oil woes: fight over imports at home; petrochemical makers scrambling for special feedstock allotments. Bsns W p48 O 8 '66
DOW Corning corporation
  Dow Corning silicone sealant wins annual product award. il Tech W 19:20+ N 21 '66
DOW Jones and company
  Broad tape gets a competitor; PR newswire competing against Dow Jones' news service. il Bsns W p 147-8+ My 21 '66
  Merger cancelled by Richard Irwin. Dow Jones. Pub W 190:76-7 N 14 '66
  Richard Irwin, Dow Jones propose merger plan. Pub W 190:50-1 O 10 '66
DOW-Jones averages. See Stocks—Price indexes and averages
DOW Jones news service
  Broad tape gets a competitor; PR newswire competing against Dow Jones' news service. il Bsns W p 147-8+ My 21 '66
DOW planetarium, Montreal. See Planetariums
DOWD, Merle E.
  Caulking, a guide to the new sealants. Pop Mech 126:170-5+ O '66
DOWDEN, George
  Some uses of landscape. R. Loewinsohn. Poetry 109:123-6 N '66
DOWLING, Brian John
  Merriwell is back. por Sports Illus 25:76 S 19 '66
DOWLING, Colette, and Fahey, Patricia
  Calculus of sex. Esquire 65:122-3+ My '66
DOWLING, John E.
  Night blindness; with biographical sketch. Sci Am 215:16, 78-84 O '66
—and others
  Synapses of horizontal cells in rabbit and cat retinas. bibliog Science 153:1639-41 S 30 '66
DOWN our way; story. See Wain, J.

DRAMAS—Criticisms, plots, etc.—Single works
—*Continued*
Beclch. R. Owens
Big man. L. Weinberg
Birdbath. L. Melfi
Birds. Aristophanes
Bohikee creek. R. Unger
Bond honoured. J. Osborne
Bugs. J. White
Butter and egg man. G. S. Kaufman
Cactus flower. A. Burrows
Caucasian chalk circle. B. Brecht
Le cheval évanoui. F. Sagan
Chicago. S. Shepard
Chinese wall. M. Frisch
Chips with everything. A. Wesker
Collector. See L'obsédé, below
Condemned of Altona. J. P. Sartre
Consider the lilies. E. A. Molloy
Country girl. C. Odets
Country wife. W. Wycherley
Day of absence. D. T. Ward
Deadly game. J. Yaffe
Delicate balance. E. Albee
Dinner at eight. G. S. Kaufman and E. Ferber
Displaced person. C. Dawkins
Doctor's dilemma. G. B. Shaw
Don't drink the water. W. Allen
Duet for three. L. Weinberg
Eh? H. Livings
L'été. R. Weingarten
Fainting horse. See Le cheval évanoui, above
Gnadiges fraulein. See Slapstick tragedy, below
Good woman of Setzuan. B. Brecht
Great indoors. I. Kamp
Hail Scrawdyke! D. Halliwell
Happy ending. D. T. Ward
Happy journey to Trenton and Camden. T. Wilder
Help stamp out marriage! K. Waterhouse and W. Hall
Hogan's goat. W. Alfred
Homecoming. H. Pinter
Hostile witness. J. Roffey
How's the world treating you? R. Milner
Inadmissible evidence. J. Osborne
Investigation. P. Weiss
Ivanov, A. P. Chekhov
Jonah. P. Goodman
Journey of the fifth horse. R. Ribman
Key. K. Jones
Killing of Sister George. F. Marcus
Kitchen. A. Wesker
Leslie. H. Phelps
Lion in winter. J. Goldman
Long Christmas dinner. T. Wilder
Loves of Cass McGuire. B. Friel
Ludlow fair. L. Wilson
Madness of Lady Bright. L. Wilson
Malcolm. E. Albee
Marat/Sade. P. Weiss
Match-play. L. Kalcheim
Medea. J. Anouilh
Misanthrope. J. B. P. Molière
Monopoly. J. Kass
Murder in the cathedral. T. S. Eliot
Mutilated. See Slapstick tragedy, below
My sweet Charlie. D. Westheimer
Night of the dunce. F. Gagliano
L'obsédé. F. Roche
Oresteia. Aeschylus
Les paravents. J. Genêt
Party for divorce. L. Kalcheim
Pedestrian in the air. E. Ionesco
Persecution and assassination of Marat as performed by the inmates of the asylum at Charenton under the direction of the Marquis de Sade. See Marat/Sade, above
Phèdre. J. B. Racine
Philadelphia, here I come! B. Friel
Playroom. M. Drayton
Plebeians rehearse the uprising. G. Grass
Poor Bitos. J. Anouilh
Prime of Miss Jean Brodie. J. P. Allen
Project immortality. L. Mandel
Queens of France. T. Wilder
Rainbow terrace. M. Gorelik
Recluse. P. Foster
Red cross. S. Shepard
Right you are. L. Pirandello
Rooms. S. Mann
Rose tattoo. T. Williams
Royal hunt of the sun. P. Shaffer
School for scandal. R. B. B. Sheridan
Screens. See Les paravents, above
Les séquestrés d'Altona. See Condemned of Altona, above
Serjeant Musgrave's dance. J. Arden
Slapstick tragedy. T. Williams
La soif et la faim. E. Ionesco
Song at twilight. N. Coward
Star-spangled girl. N. Simon
Summer. See Lété, above
Sunset. I. Babel
Thank you, Miss Victoria. W. Hoffman
This is the rill speaking. L. Wilson
Three bags full. J. Chodorov

Three hand reel. P. A. Mayer
Tightrope walker. M. Lee
Tiny Alice. E. Albee
Under the weather. S. Bellow
Undercover man. N. Kennelly
Veronica. J. White
Viet rock. M. Terry
Wait until dark. F. Knott
War. J. C. Van Itallie
We have always lived in the castle. S. Jackson
Where's daddy? W. Inge
Wild duck. H. Ibsen
World of Günter Grass. G. Grass
Woyzeck. G. Buechner
Yerma. F. García Lorca

Plays for children
    See Childrens plays
DRAMATIC censorship
Manner of speaking; on purifying the antiquities in Ypsilanti. J. Ciardi. Sat R 49:22 Ag 13 '66
Queen's censor; Great Britain. il Newsweek 67:86 F 28 '66
DRAMATIC criticism
Naked image, by H. Clurman. Review Life 61:18 Ag 26 '66. T. Prideaux
Seasons of discontent, by R. Brustein. Review
    Commonweal 83:669-70+ Mr 11 '66. J. Simon
    See also
Critics
DRAMATIC education. See Drama—Study and teaching
DRAMATIC festivals. See Drama festivals
DRAMATIC form. See Drama—Technique
DRAMATIC production. See Theatrical production
DRAMATIC readings
City of yes; city of no; Yevtushenko readings in U.S. Life 61:117 N 18 '66
NCTE features poetry festival; poets read works. Sr Schol 89:sup 17 D 9 '66
Off Broadway; World of Günter Grass. E. Oliver. New Yorker 42:120+ My 7 '66
Poetry of the read-in campaign; protest gesture against Vietnam war. Nation 202: 653-5 My 30 '66
Truth and experience become one; excerpt from Journey toward poetry. J. Burden. Mlle 63:181+ O '66
Warm spell of Frost; an evening's Frost. T. Prideaux. Life 60:15 Mr 4 '66
DRAMATICS in school. See College and school drama
DRAMATISTS
Hollywood screen writers: who are they and how do they work? P. R. Reynolds. il Sat R 49:52-3+ Jl 9 '66
How playwrights lose. W. Kerr. Harper 233:75-80 S '66
Modern theater, or the world as a metaphor of dread; Time essay. Time 88:34-5 Jl 8 '66
What will happen next? M. Esslin. il N Y Times Mag pt2 p20-1+ S 11 '66
    See also
Ferlinghetti, L.
DRAMATISTS, American
    See also
Gilroy, F. D.
DRAMATISTS, French
    See also
Montherlant, H. de
DRAMATISTS, German
History onstage; documentary movement. il Newsweek 67:81-2 Ja 31 '66
    See also
Brecht, B.
Weiss, P.
DRANE, James F.
Changing law. America 114:870-2 Je 25 '66
DRAPEAU, Jean
Fair winds in Montreal. il por Newsweek 68: 107+ D 5 '66
DRAPER, Paul
How an amateur thinks out his photographs! Mod Phot 30:66-71 F '66
DRAPER, Theodore
Case of defamation. New Repub 154:13-19 F 19; 15-18 F 26; 37 Mr 5; 35 Mr 12 '66
Correspondence with Theodore Draper & Commentary, appropriate & inappropriate. Nat R 18:823-7 Ag 23 '66
Dominican crisis. Commentary 40:33-68 D '65; 41:12+ My '66
    about
What Bundy demanded. S. Lens. Nation 203:658 D 19 '66
DRAPER, William A.
Free-ranging rhesus monkeys: age and sex differences in individual activity patterns. bibliog Science 151:476-8 Ja 28 '66

DRAPER, William H. Jr
Parks, or more people? Nat Parks Mag 40:10-13 Ap '66

DRAPERIES. See Curtains and draperies

DRAWERS
Plastic drawers for flexibility. il Bsns W p 186 Ap 16 '66

DRAWING
On drawing; excerpts from Drawing; a search for from. J. Mugnaini. Am Artist 30:13+ Ap '66
Pencil thinks big. C. H. Larson. il Design 68:13-15 N '66
See also
Brush drawing
Pen drawing
Portrait drawing

Study and teaching
Cheer for the teacher; draw pictures of anything they can see. J. Ferrence. il Sch Arts 65:16-17 Ja '66
Drawings and statements. E. Eller. il Sch Arts 65:24-8 Je '66
Front to back picture. E. Harrison. Sch Arts 65:12-13 My '66
Leafy turkeys. L. Blaustein. il Sch Arts 66:41-2 N '66
Macro-drawing from nature. E. Adams. il Sch Arts 66:22-6 N '66
One approach in learning to see. J. Krauser. il Design 67:38-40 My '66
Subject matter? J. Mullen. il Sch Arts 65:8-11 Je '66

DRAWING, Childrens. See Childrens arts

DRAWING easels. See Easels

DRAWINGS
European sketches of Frank di Gioia. F. Johnson. il Am Artist 30:46-51+ Ap '66
Isle of Jersey's venerable master; Edmund Blampied. F. A. Phillipps. il Am Artist 30:40-5+ O '66
Portfolio of drawings by Paul Driscoll. Am Artist 30:62-6 O '66
See also
Drawing
Graffiti

DRAYTON, Mary
Playroom. Criticism
Commonweal 83:508-10 Ja 28 '66

DRAZ, Peter
Letter from the publisher. B. M. Auer. il por Time 87:13 Mr 25 '66

DRAZEK, Stanley J.
Training 30,000 Head Start teachers. Sch & Soc 94:130-1 Mr 5 '66

DREADNOUGHTS. See Warships

DREAMING sleep. See Sleep

DREAMS
Anatomy of slumber; rapid eye movement or dream sleep. P. McBroom. il Sci N 90:254-5 O 1 '66
Anxiety levels in dreams; relation to changes in plasma free fatty acids. L. A. Gottschalk and others. bibliog il Science 153:654-7 Ag 5 '66
Dialogue with mothers: fears and bad dreams. B. Bettelheim. Ladies Home J 83:51+ Mr '66
Disquiet after hours; basic conflicts of undergraduates revealed in their dreams. C. S. Hall. Mlle 64:77+ Ja '66
Dream deprivation: effects on dream content; rapid-eye-movement sleep. T. Pivik and D. Foulkes. bibliog il Science 153:1282-4 S 9 '66
Dream world, real world. C. Klein. il N Y Times Mag p 102+ O 16 '66
Dreams related to conversation. Sci N 89:278 Ap 16 '66
Dreams tell of maturity. P. McBroom. Sci N 90:243 O 1 '66
For dreamers only; quiz. J. Daugherty and M. Daugherty. il Sci Digest 59:87-9 My '66
See also
Sleep

DREDGING
Deep water harbors, gratis! B. D. Barker. 3d. il Yachting 119:218+ Mr '66
Don't forget the dredge. il Am City 81:122-4 S '66

DREHER, Carl
Cousin David. Nation 202:332-5 Mr 21 '66
How the wasteland began; early days of radio. Atlan 217:53-8 F '66
Transit snarl: is it back to the rails? Nation 203:11-15 Jl 4 '66

DRENNAN, Henry Thomas
(ed) Federal library legislation, programs, and services. por ALA Bul 60:139-68 F '66
Little miracle on Chapel street. Am Ed 2:1-5 Jl '66

DRENNEN, D. A.
Book review (cont) America 114:264-5, 600; 115:522 F 19, Ap 23, O 29 '66

DRESDEN

Music
Berlin, Dresden; East Berlin's Komische oper. J. H. Sutcliffe. il Opera N 31:32-3 Ja 14 '67

DRESDEN pottery. See Pottery, German

DRESS. See Clothing and dress

DRESS design. See Costume design

DRESS designers. See Costume designers

DRESS patterns. See Patterns (dress)

DRESSER, Louisa. See Rich, D. C. jt. auth.

DRESSES. See Clothing and dress

DRESSING tables
And a vanity built-in designed for beauty! il Bet Hom & Gard 44:57 Ag '66
Dressing tables use minimum space. il Sunset 138:78 Ja '66
Modern vanity for a spare corner. il Pop Sci 189:162-3 O '66

DRESSMAKING
How to make a flip lining. C. Houck. il Parents Mag 41:60 Jl '66
Quick 'n' easy zipper insert. C. Houck. il Parents Mag 41:88 N '66
See also
Costume design

DREW, Elizabeth Brenner
Education's billion-dollar baby. Atlan 218:37-43 Jl '66
Gravedoggle. New Repub 155:6-7 N 26 '66
Politics of auto safety. Atlan 218:95-102 O '66
Withholding money from hospitals that segregate. New Repub 155:11-12 Jl 30 '66

DREXLER, Rosalyn
Woman's place is on the mat. pors Esquire 65:79-81+ F '66

DREXLER, Sherman
Against the cold. il por Newsweek 67:91 F 21 '66
Drexler's dialectical nudes. M. Benedikt. il por Art N 64:50-1+ F '66

DREYER, Marion
Out-island galley. Yachting 119:182 F '66

DREYFACK, Raymond
So your employees don't like you. Nations Bsns 54:74-6 Mr '66
Use that sixth sense, instinct. Nations Bsns 54:80-2+ D '66

DREYFUS, Hubert
Downgrading computers. Newsweek 68:83 Jl 25 '66

DREYFUS, Jack
Jack Dreyfus; Maverick wizard behind the Wall Street lion. M. Smith. il pors Life 60:70-2+ F 11 '66

DREYFUS, John
John Dreyfus: typographic advisor, editor, printing historian. P. A. Bennett. il por Pub W 190:84-6+ S 5 '66

DRIED cheese. See Cheese

DRIED milk. See Milk, Dried

DRIFTING of continents. See Continental drift

DRIFTWOOD inn. See Hotels, taverns, etc.—United States

DRILLING and boring (earth and rocks)
Deep core drill set for South Pole. Sci N 90:449 N 26 '66
Frozen 10,000 years ago; core of gravelly soil recovered from the bottom of polar ice cap. il Sci Digest 60:69 D '66
See also
Mohole project

DRILLING and boring (woodwork)
Get acquainted with plug cutters. R. J. De Cristoforo. il Pop Sci 188:150-2 Mr '66

DRILLING and boring machinery
Double-duty-sander-setup. R. J. De Cristoforo. il Pop Mech 125:176-8 Ap '66
Electric drills. il Consumer Rep 31:56-60 F '66
Multiple-speed drills; portable electric drills. il Consumer Rep 31:353-7 Jl '66
New accessories for your drill. il Pop Sci 189:136-7 Ag '66
New Skil drill varies speed in reverse, too. R. P. Stevenson. il Pop Sci 188:146-9 Mr '66
Portable combination power tool kit. il Consumer Bul 49:2 D '66
Portable electric drills for the home craftsman. il Consumer Bul 49:2+ O '66
Rotary-percussive system favored for moon drilling. M. Burns and L. A. Gardner. Tech W 18:33+ Je 20 '66
Three boring bars you can make. il Pop Sci 188:164 F '66

DRILLING platforms. See Artificial islands

DRILLING rigs, Oil well. See Oil well drilling rigs

DRINK question. See Alcoholism

DRINKING, Social. See Liquor problem

DRINKING and traffic accidents
British to establish drinking driver test. Sci N L 89:104 F 12 '66

DRINKING vessels
Golden age of stein making: newspaper article; excerpts. Hobbies 71:88 N '66
See also
Tankards

DRINKING water. See Water

DRINKS. See Beverages; Liquors

DRISCOLL, Alfred E.
Warner-Lambert's new math. R. Levy. por Duns R 87:49-50 Ap '66

DRISCOLL, Paul
Portfolio of drawings. por Am Artist 30:62-6 O '66

DRIVE-in and curb services
Computerburgers hit the assembly line; an automated drive-in restaurant. C. B. Hicks. il Pop Mech 126:80-3 S '66
Dining in/out with Esquire; Jay's Brookdale drive-in Brooklyn center, Minneapolis, Minn. Esquire 66:215-16 S '66
In Atlanta, all roads lead to the Varsity; mammoth drive-in grown from simple hot dog stand into social institution. il Bsns W p 132-3+ O 8 '66
Inventor of the month; everything is automated but the carhop. S. V. Jones. il Sci Digest 60:32 N '66

DRIVE line, Automobile. See Automobiles—Transmission

DRIVES (machinery) See Power transmission

DRIVES (money raising) See Fund raising

DRIVESHAFTS. See Automobiles—Propeller shafts

DRIVEWAYS
Clean up your driveway. R. Day. il Pop Sci 188:145 Mr '66
Serviceable entryway. il Flower Grower 53:45 My '66

DRIVING, Automobile. See Automobile driving

DRONE airplanes. See Airplanes, Drone

DRONKA, Kazimierz. See McEnroe, W. D. jt. auth.

DROPOUTS
Astonishing truth about girl dropouts. J. H. Pollack. il Parents Mag 41:66-7+ S '66
College folklore and fact. S. Sulkin. New Repub 154:11-13 Mr 26 '66
Conversations parents never hear: Job corps trainee. il Look 30:61 S 20 '66
Dropouts anonymous. D. Weldon. il Parents Mag 41:44-5+ My '66; Same abr. Read Digest 89:17-18+ Ag '66
Employment lab for teenagers in trouble; Youth and work project, New York. S. L. Horwitz. il Parents Mag 41:64-7+ D '66
Employment of high school graduates and dropouts in 1965. H. R. Hamel. il Mo Labor R 89:643-9 Je '66
Learn, baby, learn! training dropouts at Camp Madison-Felicia. A. Herzog. il Am Ed 2:4-6 S '66
No room at the bottom; plight of those who don't make the first rung of the ladder of success. R. L. Heilbroner. Sat R 49:29-32 F 19 '66
Out-of-school youth two years later; resurvey of graduates and dropouts. V. C. Perrella and E. Waldman. il Mo Labor R 89:860-6 Ag '66
Schools negligent in dropout problem. Sr Schol 89:sup2 D 2 '66
Technological society can use dropouts. Sci N 89:509 Je 25 '66
When dropouts are high. il Sci Digest 60:24-5 O '66
Why dropout campaigns fail. B. Bard. il Sat R 49:78-9+ S 17 '66

DROSOPHILA
Drosophila melanogaster: inheritance of a deficiency of alkaline phosphatase in larvae. F. M. Johnson. il Science 152:361-2 Ap 15 '66
Mating speed in male drosophila melanogaster: a psychogenetic analysis. D. W. Fulker. bibliog il Science 153:203-5 Jl 8 '66
Patterns of alkaline phosphatase in developing drosophila. H. Schneiderman and others. bibliog il Science 151:461-3 Ja 28 '66
Pteridines in the fat body of a mutant of drosophila melanogaster. C .P. Wright and E. W. Hanly. bibliog il Science 152:533-5 Ap 22 '66

DROTTNINGHOLM court theatre. See Theater—Sweden—History

DROUGHT resistance of plants. See Plants—Drought resistance

DROUGHTS
As drought eases in northeastern states. U S News 60:6 Je 27 '66
Big rain that eased the drought. il U S News 61:10 S 26 '66
Can the world slake its thirst? il Bsns W p 138+ Ag 13 '66
Drought knows no frontiers; Africa and India. G. Ash. il UNESCO Courier 19:10-15 Ap '66
Drought spreads: East drying up, Midwest threatened. il U S News 61:66-7 Ag 8 '66
Hope for an end to drought, but—. il U S News 60:12 Mr 7 '66
Northeast water drought, end not in sight. il Am For 71:30-1+ O '65
Rains that did not come; situation in India. il UNESCO Courier 19:4-8 Ap '66
Snows came; Northeast drought. Newsweek 67:85 Mr 7 '66
Thirsty city: Bombay. il Time 88:32 Jl 22 '66

DROWNING
Your spare tire can prevent a drowning. S. M. Gerard. il Read Digest 88:109-11 Je '66

DROWNPROOFING. See Swimming—Safety devices and measures

DRUCKER, Peter F.
How to manage your time. Harper 233:56-60 D '66
Romantic generation. Harper 232:12+ My '66
What the computers will be telling you. Nations Bsns 54:84-90 Ag '66

DRUG addicts. See Narcotic addicts

DRUG fair-Community drug company, incorporated
Union cards were phony; case of the Washington area Drug fair chain. il Nations Bsns 54:100-1+ Mr '66

DRUG habit. See Narcotic habit

DRUG labels. See Labels

DRUG laws and legislation
Congress: a new option for addicts; a look at LSD. J. Walsh. Science 152:1726+ Je 24 '66
Drugs for heart treatment seized. Sci N 89:168 Mr 12 '66
More drugs included under drug abuse law. Sci N 89:235 Ap 9 '66
New prohibition? intensified federal drugs crackdown. il Newsweek 67:21-2 F 7 '66
Public health and drug safety; address, October 14, 1965. H. S. Ingraham. Vital Speeches 32:231-4 F 1 '66
Treating addicts humanely. Christian Cent 83:131-2 F 2 '66
See also
Narcotic laws
United States—Food and drug administration

DRUG plants. See Botany, Medical

DRUG stores. See Drugstores

DRUG trade
Bit intemperate; attack by FDA. Time 87:92+ Ap 15 '66
Drug appraisal asked. Sci N 89:289 Ap 23 '66
Drug tests get the FDA needle; keeping three pain relievers: Measurin, Norgesic and Stendin off the market. Bsns W p 114+ N 19 '66
FDA's eddict: patients, not profits, come first; excerpts from address, April 6, 1966. J. L. Goddard. Science 152:332-3 Ap 15 '66
Powwows and sinners; fixing the world prices. Newsweek 67:74 F 21 '66
Razz-ma-tazz in the drug industry; lessons of the DMSO case. R. G. Sherrill. il Nation 202:425-7 Ap 11 '66; Reply with rejoinder. J. H. Brown. 202:666+ Je 6 '66
Searle mixes a new prescription. il Bsns W p 103-4+ N 5 '66
Storm breaks over drug testing; a look at FDA procedures. il Bsns W p88-90+ F 19 '66
See also
Government investigations—Drug trade
Pfizer, Charles, and company
Smith, Kline and French laboratories
Warner-Lambert pharmaceutical company

Advertising
Crackdown on drug ads. B. Culliton. il Sci N 90:490-1 D 10 '66
Drugs for heart treatment seized. Sci N 89:168 Mr 12 '66
Suffering from seizure; Peritrate seizure by FDA. il Time 87:90 Mr 11 '66

Securities
Executive investor. il Duns R 88:115-16 S '66

DRUGS

Best new drugs. Sci Digest 59:20-1 Mr '66
Crackdown on bootleg drugs; campaign to end traffic in counterfeit drugs. T. Irwin. il Todays Health 45:18-19+ Ja '67
Delayed-action drugs. F. Marley. Sci N L 89:87 F 5 '66
Du Pont writes a new Rx; drug to prevent Asian flu; amantadine hydrochloride called Symmetrel. Bsns W p44 O 29 '66
Should leftover drugs be thrown away? Consumer Rep 31:135 Mr '66
  See also
Antibiotics
Fertility drugs
Hallucinogenic drugs
Narcotics
Pharmacology
Prescriptions
United States—Food and drug administration
  also names of drugs, e.g. Caffeine

Advertising

See Drug trade—Advertising

Dosage

Facts about those new long-acting drugs. Good H 162:175-6 Mr '66

Laws and legislation

See Drug laws and legislation

Patents

FTC rules in tetracycline case; Pfizer & co. obtained patent by making false and misleading statements. Bsns W p46+ D 10 '66

Physiological effects

Abuse of drugs can cause kidney failure. Sci N 90:276 O 8 '66
Actinomycin D: inhibition of respiration and glycolysis. J. Laszlo and others. bibliog il Science 151:1007-10 F 25 '66
Birth control pill causes jaundice; other side effects from anovlar. Sci N 89:244 Ap 9 '66
Can drugs ever be safe? F. Marley. il Sci N 89:288-9 Ap 23 '66
Circadian rhythms: variation in sensitivity of isolated rat atria to acetylcholine. R. P. Spoor and D. B. Jackson. bibliog il Science 154:782 N 11 '66
Drug-induced teratogenesis in vitro: inhibition of calcification by different tetracyclines. L. Saxén. bibliog il Science 153:1384-7 S 16 '66
Drugged driving. Sci Digest 60:15-16 N '66
Drugs affecting lipid metabolism; report on second international symposium. D. Kritchevsky. Science 151:1016-17 F 25 '66
Drugs rely on rhythms; body rhythms and susceptibility to drugs. Sci N 91:10 Ja 7 '67
Drugs without shock. Sci Digest 59:24 Ap '66
Enzyme changes in neurons and glia during barbiturate sleep. A. Hamberger and others. Science 151:1394-5 Mr 18 '66
Epilepsy drugs have bad effects on some. Sci N L 89:152 Mr 5 '66
Headache drug harmful; possible relationship of Sansert to fibrosis. Sci N L 89:147 Mr 5 '66
Helpful but also harmful. Time 87:39-40 Je 3 '66
Liver carcinogenesis by diethylnitrosamine in the rat. M. F. Rajewsky and others. bibliog il Science 152:83-5 Ap 1 '66
Magnesium pemoline: enhancement of brain RNA polymerases. A. J. Glasky and L. N. Simon. bibliog il Science 151:702-3 F 11 '66
Magnesium pemoline: enhancement of learning and memory of a conditioned avoidance response. N. Plotnikoff. bibliog il Science 151:703-4 F 11 '66
Man the drug taker; excerpt from Gluttons and libertines. M. Bates. il Natur Hist 76:8-10+ Ja '67
Medicines: the growing worry over side effects. il Changing T 20:17-18 D '66
Miltown's effect on brain a mystery. Sci N 90:24 Jl 9 '66
Puromycin effect on successive phases of memory storage. S. H. Barondes and H. D. Cohen. bibliog il Science 151:594-5 F 4 '66
Radiosensitization of X chromosome of Chinese hamster cells related to incorporation of 5-bromodeoxyuridine. W. C. Dewey and others. bibliog il Science 152:519-21 Ap 22 '66
Species specific effect of acetylcholine or bivalve rectums. M. J. Greenberg. bibliog il Science 154:1015-17 N 25 '66
Steroids and serum complement in mice: influence of hydrocortisone, diethylstilbesterol, and testosterone. L. D. Caren and L. T. Rosenberg. bibliog il Science 152:782-3 My 6 '66

Thiosemicarbazide injection followed by electric shock increases resistance to stress in rats. R. W. Reynolds and M. R. Meeker. bibliog il Science 151:1101-2 Mr 4 '66
Tranquilizer affects eyes. P. McBroom. Sci N 89:235 Ap 9 '66
d-Tubocurarine chloride: effect on insects. J. R. Larsen and others. bibliog il Science 152:225-6 Ap 8 '66
What expectant mothers need to know; interview. D. Harting. il U S News 60:54-6+ F 14 '66
What kind of mixer is alcohol? L. Galton. il Pop Sci 188:95-7+ Ap '66

Prices

Drug fees attacked. Sci N 90:100 Ag 13 '66
Nothing to lose but your chain stores; medicines with patented brand names vs. those with generic names. G. Ace. Sat R 49:8 N 19 '66
Powwows and sinners; fixing the world prices. Newsweek 67:74 F 21 '66

Psychological effects

Campus drug craze; its dangers. il U S News 60:16-17 Ap 18 '66
Drugs on the campus. R. Goldstein. il Sat Eve Post 239:40-4+ My 21; 34-8+ Je 4 '66
LSD and the drugs of the mind; uses, abuses, promise and perils; ed. by M. Clark. il Newsweek 67:59-60+ My 9 '66
Memory pills; experimenting with Cylert. il Time 87:56 Je 24 '66
Memory pills work; clinical reports on Cylert. Sci Digest 60:22 S '66
Mind drugs puzzling. P. McBroom. Sci N 90:196 S 17 '66
Ours is the addicted society. L. H. Farber. il N Y Times Mag p43+ D 11 '66; Reply. F. A. Seixas. p 15 Ja 8 '67
Pentylenetetrazol enhances memory function. S. Irwin and A. Benuazizi. bibliog il Science 152:100-2 Ap 1 '66
Pill that helps you remember; Cylert. S. M. Spencer. il Sat Eve Post 239:64-6+ S 24 '66
Safety of Symmetrel. Time 88:57 D 2 '66
Spread and perils of LSD; with reports by A. Rosenfeld and B. Farrell. il Life 60:28-33 Mr 25 '66
  See also
Depressants
Magnesium pemoline

Testing

Birth control drug tests halted on 340 women. Sci N L 89:137 F 26 '66
Can drugs ever be safe? F. Marley. il Sci N 89:288-9 Ap 23 '66
Drug tests get the FDA needle; keeping three pain relievers: Measurin, Norgesic and Stendin off the market. Bsns W p 114+ N 19 '66
Drug tests: integrity and courage; letter. P. Lowinger. Science 153:121 Jl 8 '66; Reply. C. Henze. 153:688 Ag 12 '66
Goddard rebukes drug tester; birth control pills against menopause. Sci N 90:450 N 26 '66
Investigating the investigator; FDA strikes physician's name from its approved list of researchers. Time 88:65 Ag 5 '66
New firm hand at the old FDA. New Repub 154:10-11 Mr 26 '66
Public health and drug safety; address, October 14, 1965. H. S. Ingraham. Vital Speeches 32:231-4 F 1 '66
Storm breaks over drug testing; a look at FDA procedures. il Bsns W p88-90+ F 19 '66

DRUGS, Experimental

Severe face pain helped by experimental drug; trigeminal neuralgia or tic douloureux. Sci N 89:514 Je 25 '66
  See also
Magnesium pemoline

DRUGS, Resistance to

How germs learn to live; resistance-transfer process. Time 88:46 Ag 26 '66
New drug families dress for a debut; resistant bacteria poses dilemma. il Bsns W p98+ S 24 '66
Transferable drug resistance. Sci Am 214:53 F '66

DRUGSTORES

Prescribing for the drug stores. il Bsns W p 149-50+ S 10 '66

DRUM brakes. See Brakes. Automobile

DRUMLINS

Drumlin formation: a rheological model. I. J. Smalley. bibliog Science 151:1379 Mr 18 '66

DRUMMOND, John D.

Is plasmonics for the birds? Pop Electr 25:63-5 Jl '66

DRUMMOND, Roscoe
Change and challenge; address, June 12, 1966. Vital Speeches 32:660-3 Ag 15 '66
—See Bean, L. H. jt. auth.

DRUMMOND, William F.
Contraception frustrates nature. Cath World 203:202-6 Jl '66

DRUMMONDS, Henry
Student objects to his own deferment. por Life 61:48 D 9 '66

DRUNKENNESS. See Alcoholism; Liquor problem

DRUNKENNESS testing. See Alcohol in the body

DRURY, Allen
Enemy of the press. M. S. Evans. Nat R 18: 1174-6 N 15 '66

DRURY, Michael
Secret of enthusiasm. Read Digest 88:193+ Je '66
(ed) See Hughes, S. T. Woman who swore in President Johnson recalls what happened aboard Air force one, 2:38 p.m. Dallas, November 22, 1963
What I have learned from other people's children. Read Digest 88:101-4 F '66

DRY docks
Ships go ashore for repairs in new type of drydocking: combination marine elevator and transfer systems, Port Everglades, Fla. il Bsns W p60 Ap 30 '66

DRY flies. See Fishing lures, flies, etc.

DRY goods
See also
Notions (merchandise)

DRYDEN, Hugh Latimer
Collier trophy award. B. Kocivar. il por Look 30:96+ N 1 '66
Memorial fund created honoring Hugh Dryden. Sci N 90:275 O 8 '66

DRYERS, Print. See Photography—Apparatus and supplies

DRYING
See also
Photography—Drying (films and prints)

DRYING (crops)
See also
Corn—Drying

DRYING apparatus
I am a dryer. M. Davidson. il Ladies Home J 83:50+ F '66

DRYING off of cows. See Cows—Care

DRYLOT feeding. See Cows—Feeding

DRYSDALE, Don
Buzzie and big D go at it in L.A. J. Olsen. por Sports Illus 25:22-3 Ag 29 '66
Double play. il por Time 87:63 Mr 25 '66
New union's million-dollar pitch. il por Life 60:77-8 Ap 1 '66
$1,000,000 holdout. J. Mann. il por Sports Illus 24:26-9 Ap 4 '66
Sandy Koufax story: my salary fights; excerpts from Koufax, ed. by E. Linn. S. Koufax. il Look 30:90-2+ Je 14 '66
Sic transit tradition. Time 87:75 Ap 8 '66
Super-holdouts. il por Newsweek 67:84 Mr 28 '66

DU BAY, William H.
Speaking out. por Sat Eve Post 239:10+ Je 4 '66
about
Clerical trade union. Nation 202:255 Mr 7 '66
DuBay at bay. Christian Cent 83:1023 Ag 24 '66; Discussion. 83:1216, 1348 O 5, N 2 '66
Due process for DuBay and for the church. America 115:200 Ag 27 '66
Evolution of a rebel priest. S. Alexander. Life 60:20 Ap 1 '66
Mr 11 '66
Father DuBay's union. Commonweal 83:654 Mr 11 '66; Discussion. 84:244 My 20 '66
For a white-collar union. por Time 87:86 Mr 4 '66
Issue of imprimatur. por Time 88:74 Ag 19 '66
Of many things; the human church in Los Angeles. R. A. Schroth. America 115:236 S 10 '66
Priests' union: what it wants. U S News 61:78 O 31 '66

DUBBS, Clyde A.
Transverse gradient electrophoresis: protein homogeneity test and subfractionation technique. bibliog Science 151:463-4 Ja 28 '66

DUBINSKY, David
D.D. New Repub 154:10 Ap 2 '66
D.D. of the ILG. por Sr Schol 88:22-3 Ap 1 '66
Hail and farewell. por Newsweek 67:74+ Mr 28 '66
Hell raisers' adieux. il por Time 87:20 Mr 25 '66
On the heels of a giant. por Bsns W p54+ Jl 16 '66

DUBLIN
Description
Dublin is my sure thing. S. Alexander. Life 61:8 S 2 '66
Monuments
Delayed explosion; Lord Nelson's column exploded. il Newsweek 67:46 Mr 21 '66
Music
Dublin; twenty-fifth anniversary of the Dublin grand opera society. M. E. Peltz. Opera N 31:31-2 S 10 '66
Theater
Abbey. il Newsweek 68:82 Ag 1 '66

DUBLIN revolt. See Ireland—History—Sinn Fein rebellion, 1916

DU BOIS, Donald
Know your ducks? questions and answers. Outdoor Life 138:50-3+ D '66

DUBOIS clubs. See W. E. B. DuBois clubs of America

DUBOS, Rene Jules
Science critics; excerpts from address. October 19, 1966. Science 154:595 N 4 '66
about
Dubos wins science award. il por Sci N 90: 292 O 15 '66
Personality of the month. por Sci Digest 60: 37 D '66

DUBOUCHET, Denis Jean Florimond Langlois
French volunteer. M. Bishop. il Am Heritage 17:46-9+ Ag '66

DUBRIDGE, Lee A.
Government role in science education. Bul Atomic Sci 22:16-20 My '66
How the first soft landing on the moon was achieved. Read Digest 89:100-5 D '66

DUBROVNIK, Yugoslavia
Editor's report: dramatic Dubrovnik. M. M. Davis. il Travel 125:42-4 My '66
Travel. D. Messinesi. Vogue 147:68+ My '66
Wily old man of the sea and Othello on the rocks. M. Leatherbee. Life 60:62-3 My 27 '66

DUBROVNIK summer festival. See Music festivals—Yugoslavia

DUBUFFET, Jean
Dubuffet. L. Alloway. il Vogue 148:182 N 1 '66
Shock treatment. il Time 87:78-9 Ap 22 '66

DUCHAMP-VILLON, Raymond
Mechanical centaur. il por Time 88:46 Jl 29 '66

DUCHÊNE, B. Lassudrie-. See Lassudrie-Duchêne, B.

DUCHIN, Peter
Peter Duchin: how to be a success even if you're a millionaire. H. Ehrlich. il pors Look 30:30-2+ My 31 '66

DUCK as food. See Cookery—Poultry

DUCK decoys. See Decoys (hunting)

DUCK shooting
Death walked the duck marsh; ed. by B. East. E. La Fountain. il Outdoor Life 137: 60-1+ Ap '66
Ducks are flying again. V. Kraft. il Sports Illus 25:50-2+ O 3 '66
Found: new duck bonanza: Mallard Island, N.D. J. O. Cartier. il Outdoor Life 138:52-5+ S '66
Go to sea for ducks. J. B. Robinson. il Outdoor Life 138:39-41+ N '66
New look of duck hunting. E. A. Bauer. il Outdoor Life 138:42-5+ O '66
See also
Decoys (hunting)
Game laws

Anecdotes, facetiae, satire, etc.
McCormick's preposterous law. C. Chatfield. il Outdoor Life 139:42-3+ Ja '67

DUCKS, Wild
Dogs that decoy ducks. N. Karas. il Field & S 71:80-2+ S '66
Know your ducks? questions and answers. D. Du Bois. il Outdoor Life 138:50-3+ D '66
Please don't feed the waterfowl. D. Barnes. il Sports Illus 25:32-4+ O 31 '66
See also
Duck shooting

DUCREUX, Louis
Opera on the Mediterranean; Riviera report. R. McMullen. il por Hi Fi 16:154-6 My '66

DUDA, Edward J.
Are the oaks next to disappear from our forests? Horticulture 44:32-5+ Jl '66

DUDA, Margaret B.
Delaware's amazon outlaw. por Negro Hist Bul 29:153-4 Ap '66

DUDAS, Stan
#X$!¢%; or, A gentle complaint from your friendly club pro; interview. Esquire 65: 124-5+ Ap '66
DUDDY, Lyn
Treatment. il por Time 88:68-9 Jl 8 '66
DUDE ranches. See Ranches
DUDMAN, Richard
Eyes right. New Repub 155:15-16 N 5 '66
In Johnson land. New Repub 155:11-12 D 17 '66
Military policy in Vietnam. bibliog f Cur Hist 50:91-7+ F '66
DUE process of law
See also
Jury
Right to counsel
DUENBIER, Rolf
Copper caper. il por Newsweek 68:104 N 21 '66
DUERDEN, Richard
Eyes and I. Poetry 108:125-30 My '66
Medium or web; Host, March 1965; poems. Poetry 107:245-52 Ja '66
about
California hybrid. J. Harrison. Poetry 108: 198-201 Je '66
DUERRENMATT, Friedrich. See Dürrenmatt, F.
DUET for three; drama. See Weinberg, L.
DUFAULT, Peter Kane
Retrospect; poem. New Yorker 42:220 S 24 '66
Wintersong; poem. New Yorker 41:104 Ja 29 '66
DUFF, Edward
Extremism; excerpts from address, June 23, 1965. por Library J 91:619-23+ F 1 '66
DUFF, Marilyn Wade
You gain a lot in the translation; poem. Mc-Calls 94:165 O '66
DUFFERIN AND AVA, Serena Belinda Rosemary (Guinness) Hamilton-Temple-Blackwood, marchioness of
People are talking about... il pors Vogue 147:112-15+ Ap 15 '66
DUFFERIN AND AVA, Sheridan Frederick Terence Hamilton-Temple-Blackwood, 5th marquess of
People are talking about... il pors Vogue 147:112-13+ Ap 15 '66
DUFFEY, Bernard
Idea of poetry. Poetry 107:397-9 Mr '66
DUFFEY, David Michael
Dogs. See issues of Outdoor life
Ozark quail with a twist. pors Outdoor Life 139:68-9+ Ja '67
DUFRESNE, Frank
All American goose. Field & S 71:62-3+ N '66
Cabin fever. Field & S 71:62-3+ D '66
Hell's Canyon; time for a last look. Field & S 71:136-8 N '66
Lake Mead whoppers. Field & S 71:60-1 My '66
Plight of the ice bear. Audubon Mag 68: 418-24 N '66
Trail to buck mountain. Field & S 71:40-1+ O '66
DUFTY, David G.
How I use records to teach. Sr Schol 88:sup5 Ap 1 '66
DUGDALE, R. C. See Goering, J. J. jt. auth.
DUGGAN, Peter T.
Ngo Tuong, RIP. Nat R 18:610 Je 28 '66
DUGGER, Ronnie
Eye on Texas. por Newsweek 67:62 Mr 7 '66
DUGMORE, Edith
Bernard Langlais. Craft Horiz 26:22-5 Mr '66
Compages by Golda Lewis. Craft Horiz 26:46-7 N '66
Wood; two approaches to modern sculpture. Craft Horiz 26:13-15 Jl '66
DUHAMEL, Marcel
Crime, violence, espionage: 1000 volumes of Série noire. H. R. Lottman. il por Pub W 189:44-8 Mr 7 '66
DUITZ, Murray
Single 8 grows up. Pop Phot 59:172+ D '66
DUK, Preston
Rattle and the snake; excerpt from address. New Repub 155:22-3 D 24 '66
DUKE, Angier Biddle
Columbus as a Spaniard; address, October 6, 1966. Dept State Bul 55:717-21 N 7 '66
about
Our man in Madrid. J. Barry. il por McCalls 94:30+ Ja '67
DUKE, Benjamin C.
Rise of the Japanese teen-ager. Seventeen 25:406-7 Ag '66

DUKE, Doris
Doris Duke cooks. Vogue 148:55+ N 1 '66
Doris Duke's shangri-la. V. Lawford. il pors Vogue 148:224-9+ N 1 '66
DUKE, Henry K.
Insurance ethics: from the inside looking out. bibliog f Ann Am Acad 363:102-7 Ja '66
DUKE university, Durham, N.C.
Medical school
More than a nurse, less than a doctor: ex-medical corpsmen as physicians' assistants. R. H. Berg. il Look 30:58-61 S 6 '66
DUKHOBORS
Taming the spirit wrestlers. il Time 87:32 F 11 '66
DULL, Harold
Night of the Perseids; poem. Poetry 108:90-7 My '66
DULLES, Allen Welsh
Allen Dulles answers Warren-report critics; excerpts from statement, December 4, 1966. por U S News 61:20 D 19 '66
Real Woodrow Wilson. Look 30:50 D 13 '66
Secret surrender; excerpts. por Harper 233: 37-48 Jl; 61-4+ Ag '66
about
Operation Sunrise. S. K. Oberbeck. il Newsweek 68:122+ O 24 '66
DULLES, Avery
Books. Commonweal 84:591-2 S 16 '66
DULLES, Foster Rhea
Historical view of Americans abroad. Ann Am Acad 368:11-20 N '66
DU MAURIER, Daphne
Breakthrough; story. Ladies Home J 83:101-8 Mr '66
DUMBWAITERS
Painting hides a dumbwaiter. il Sunset 137: 101 S '66
DUMKE, Glenn S.
State college upstart. por Sat R 49:62 Ag 20 '66
DUMONT, Alberto Santos-. See Santos-Dumont, A.
DUMPLINGS
Littlest dumpling; Hungarian spatzle. J. Hewitt. il N Y Times Mag p56 Ja 23 '66
DUMPSON, James R.
Philosophy of social welfare; interview. ed. by C. L. Palms. por Cath World 203:91-7 My '66
DUNAS. See New Guinea—Native races
DUNAWAY, Faye
Faye Dunaway: the farmer's grand-daughter. J. Hamilton. il pors Look 30:108+ D 13 '66
Line of her back. pors Esquire 66:106-9 O '66
DUNBAR, Georgia S.
Department of amplification. New Yorker 42:233-7 N 12 '66
DUNBAR high school. See Washington, D.C.—Education
DUNCAN, David Douglas
Books. L. Ross. New Yorker 42:236-8+ D 10 '66
Man with a camera. il por Newsweek 68: 100+ N 14 '66
Violent, gentle life of D. D. Duncan. J. Durniak. il Pop Phot 59:90-7 D '66
DUNCAN, Isadora
Isadora Duncan had nothing to pass on to the future; interview. ed. by V. H. Swisher. E. Lanchester. il Dance Mag 40: 52-3 S '66; Reply. R. St Denis. por 40:26 N '66
Recalling Isadora: exhibition in the Bourdelle museum, Paris. pors Time 88:56 Ag 19 '66
DUNCAN, James Stuart
Developing economy. Bul Atomic Sci 22:84-7 Je '66
Education in Communist China. NEA J 55: 37-40 F '66
DUNCAN, John
Negro composers of opera. bibliog por Negro Hist Bul 29:79-80+ Ja '66
DUNCAN, Lois
We eat confessions. Writer 79:25-7 O '66
DUNCAN, Mrs Orin V.
Wavecrest, Kelva and Nakara elegancies. Hobbies 71:37 My '66
DUNCAN, Robert
In the place of a passage 22; Benefice passage 23; Orders passages 24; poems. Poetry 108:1-8 Ap '66
DUNCAN, Robert Blackford
At issue: Viet Nam. il por Time 87:17 Je 3 '66
Morse of a different color. Reporter 34:9 My 5 '66
Viet Nam race. il por Time 88:36 O 14 '66
DUNCAN, Thomas
Commanding your material. Writer 79:13-16+ Mr '66

DUNDY, Elaine
Tom Wolfe...but exactly, yes! Vogue 147:
124-5+ Ap 15 '66
DUNES, Sand. See Sand dunes
DUNES NATIONAL LAKESHORE. See In-
diana Dunes National Lakeshore
DUNHAM, Aileen
Who are the great teachers? P. Woodring.
Sat R 49:55-6 Je 18 '66
DUNHAM, David W.
Occultation highlights. Sky & Tel 31:186,
382; 32:242; 33:62 Mr, Je, O '66, Ja '67
DUNICZ, Bolesław Ludwik
Cage structures for polyborate ions. bibliog
Science 153:737-9 Ag 12 '66
DUNIGAN, Vincent J.
Mrs Gandhi's legacy: the starving nation of
India. Cath World 203:34-9 Ap '66
DUNITE
Weakening of dunite by serpentine dehy-
dration. R. E. Riecker and T. P. Rooney.
bibliog il Science 152:196-8 Ap 8 '66; Reply
with rejoinder. C. B. Sclar and L. C.
Carrison. 153:1285-7 S 9 '66
DUNKIN, Paul S.
People that walked in darkness. por Library J
91:2267-70 My 1 '66
Round and round we go. por Library J 91:
5132 O 15 '66
DUNLAP, John R.
Famous firsts: organ of the great reform.
Bsns W p 127-8 Mr 19 '66
DUNLEAVY, F. J.
How modern management doubled ITT's
European sales. por Bsns W p 102 My 7 '66
DUNLOP, John T.
Guideposts, wages, and collective bargaining.
Mo Labor R 89:630-3 Je '66
New public expectations; excerpt from paper
presented at American assembly. Mo Labor
R 89:1385-6 D '66
DUNLOP, Richard
Boston: exciting city with a past. Todays
Health 44:36-41 Jl '66
Chicago: first wonder of the Midwest. Todays
Health 44:44-9+ My '66
Chicago: gourmet's delight. Todays Health
44:38-43+ My '66
Join the fun as Canada celebrates her cen-
tennial. Todays Health 45:42-5+ Ja '67
Sodbuster surgeons who helped win the
West; excerpt from Doctors of the Amer-
ican frontier. Todays Health 44:32-3+ Je
'66
Through old New Orleans by banquette and
a streetcar named St Charles. Todays
Health 44:40-5+ F '66
Wildest railroad in the West. Pop Mech 126:
82-5+ Jl '66
DUNN, Alan
Cracks on the facade; drawings. Horizon 8:
116-20 Wint '66
DUNN, Carroll
Essayons! to supervise military construction
in South Vietnam. il Time 87:25 F 11 '66
DUNN, Dennis
In my opinion. por Seventeen 25:192 D '66
DUNN, Harold
Edison invented the indecent lamp. Sci Digest
59:79-81 My '66
Vacation is going someplace without having
to! reprint. Sr Schol 89:sup 14 S 16 '66
DUNN, Judith
Judith Dunn and Bill Dixon, Judson memorial
church. J. Maskey. Dance Mag 40:30 S '66
Reviews; production at East 74th street the-
atre. M. Marks. Dance Mag 40:23 F '66
DUNN, Michael J. 3d
Land of tumbling waters. Travel 126:37-42
O '66
DUNN, Phoebe
Photographs. Sat R 49:76-7 S 10 '66
            about
Gentle persuasion. M. R. Weiss. il Sat R
49:76-7 S 10 '66
DUNNE, James
Detroit listening post. See issues of Popular
mechanics to June 1966
DUNNE, John Gregory
Fictitious novel. Nat R 18:226-9 Mr 8 '66
It's a long way to 714. Sat Eve Post 239:78-81
Jl 30 '66
No taxee, no shirtee. Sat Eve Post 239:20
Ap 9 '66
Ugly mood of Watts. Sat Eve Post 239:83-7 Jl
16 '66
DUNNING, Arthur S.
Ideas for teaching poetry. por Sr Schol 88:sup
12 Mr 11 '66
DUNNING. See Collecting of accounts
DUNOVAN, Cass
Fair is for games; story. McCalls 93:112-13
Ap '66

DUNOYER DE SEGONZAC, André
Segonzac's instant vision. H. La Farge. il
Art N 65:43+ My '66
DU PLESSIX, Francine
Governess. New Yorker 42:28-38+ Ja 14 '67
Please be seated. House & Gard 131:106-9
Ja '67
Tomorrow's amateur. House & Gard 130:106-
7+ Jl '66
DUPLICATING processes. See Copying proc-
esses
DUPLICATORS. See Copying processes
DU PONT, Henry Francis
America's head gardener, Henry Francis
Dupont. V. Lawford. il pors Vogue 147:
150-3 Mr 1 '66
Portrait
Vogue 147:149 Mr 1 '66
DU PONT, Ruth (Wales)
Portrait
Vogue 147:148 Mr 1 '66
DUPREE, Anderson Hunter
History of American science, a field finds it-
self; excerpts from address, December 1964.
bibliog f Am Hist R 71:863-74 Ap '66
DUPREY, Richard A.
Play of the month (cont) Cath World 203:379-
80 S '66
Recessional; story. Cath World 203:239-42 Jl
'66
DUPUY, Jean
School of Paris dropouts. il por Art N 65:
56-7+ N '66
DUQUETTE, Tony
Gold on gold: patterns of the Orient. Vogue
147:39+ Mr 1 '66
DURANT, Mary
Catherine's boat ride. Horizon 8:98-104 Aut '66
Garland of girls' schools. Holiday 40:68-73+
O '66
Messenger, what tidings? story. Esquire 65:
72-3 F '66
DURANT, Tim
Galloping granddad of the Grand national;
with report. il pors Life 60:80A-80B+ Ap
8 '66
DURAS, Marguerite
Nothing new. S. Kauffmann. New Repub
156:26+ Ja 14 '67
People are talking about...por Vogue 147:
106-7 Ap 15 '66
DURELL, Ann
Nonny Hogrogian. Library J 91:1594-5 Mr
15 '66
DÜRER, Albrecht
$1,000,000 in Dürers found in Brooklyn. il
Life 60:34-5 Je 3 '66
DURHAM, Michael
Her child lies below. Life 61:69-70+ S 16 '66
DURHAM, N.C. childrens museum. See Chil-
drens museums
DURHAM rule. See Insanity—Jurisprudence
DURNIAK, John
Editorial. See issues of Popular photography
Picture islands. il Pop Phot 59:94+ N '66
DURNIN, Richard G.
Dear sir, please send me all you have on
Texas... Sr Schol 89:sup42 S 23 '66
DURNING, Marvin B.
Whooping it up for conservation; editorial.
Am For 72:15 F '66
DUROCHER, Leo
The Brat and The Lip. P. Hager. il por
Newsweek 67:72-3 Ap 4 '66
Return of the Lip. G. Astor. il pors Look
30:88-90+ My 17 '66
They ain't getting no maiden. R. Kahn. il
pors Sat Eve Post 239:97-101 Je 18 '66
Two headliners take over Chicago. W. Leg-
gett. il pors Sports Illus 24:26-8+ F 28 '66
Unhappy return of the native. W. Leggett.
il pors Sports Illus 24:26-9 Ap 25 '66
Willie Mays: my story; excerpts from Willie
Mays: my life in and out of baseball, ed.
by C. Einstein. W. Mays. il por Look 30:
72-4+ Ap 5 '66
DUROVIC, Stevan
Case of the cancer cure. il por Newsweek 67:
65-6 F 14 '66
Krebiozen verdict. il por Time 87:49 F 11 '66
DURR, Clifford Judkins
Conscience of a lawyer. Nation 202:199 F 21
'66; Reply. H. L. Black. 202:442 Ap 18 '66
DURRELL, Gerald
Two in the bush. Harper 233:96-8+ O '66
DURRELL, Lawrence
Acropolis: 200 drachmae; Apteros; poems. Re-
porter 34:48 Mr 10 '66
Little affair in Paris; story. Sat Eve Post
239:64-6 Je 4 '66
Paphos; poem. New Yorker 42:57 Mr 26 '66
Return to Corfu. Holiday 40:58-65+ O '66
Taking the consequence; story. Mlle 64:131
D '66

DÜRRENMATT, Friedrich
Deadly game; dramatization. See Yaffe, J.
DURSIN, Philomene
Innocents abroad. pors Seventeen 25:146-7+
Mr '66
DURY, David
(ed) See Miller, H. Henry Miller's real
woman
(ed) See Miller, H. Sex goes public
DUSCHA, Julius
And now even prayers are pop. N Y Times
Mag p 184-5+ N 13 '66
Bailing out the cotton industry. Reporter 34:
28-9 My 5 '66
Bonanza in Colorado: who gets it? Atlan
217:82-6 Mr '66
But what if Reagan becomes the governor?
New Repub 155:11-13 N 5 '66
Will California stand Pat? Reporter 35:40-2
S 22 '66
DUSE, Eleonora
Mystic in the theatre, by E. Le Gallienne.
Review
Sat R por 49:35-6 Ap 23 '66. P. Burton
DUSENBERY, Gail
I carried with me poems: Two poems: Your
citadel; I recline on a cloud couch. Poetry
108:171-4 Je '66
DUSHNYCK, Walter
New books. Cath World 204:116+ N '66
DÜSSELDORF, Germany
Golden cities of the Rhine. R. Tregaskis. il
Travel 126:33-7 S '66
DUST, interstellar. See Matter, Interstellar
DUST allergy. See Allergy
DUST cloud hypothesis. See Cosmogony
DUST jackets. See Book covers
DUST of Yuri Serafimovich; story. See Fetler,
J.
DUSTMAN, Robert E. and Beck, E. C.
Visually evoked potentials: amplitude changes
with age. bibliog Science 151:1013-15 F 25
'66
DUTCH, Pennsylvania. See Pennsylvania Ger-
mans
DUTCH cookery. See Cookery, Dutch
DUTCH dancing. See Dancing, Dutch
DUTCH elm disease. See Elm—Diseases and
pests
DUTCH GUIANA. See Surinam
DUTCH painting. See Painting, Dutch
DUTCH Reformed church in South Africa. See
Reformed church in South Africa
DUTCHESS community college, Poughkeepsie,
N.Y.
Moving the library at Dutchess community
college. B. L. Feret. il ALA Bul 61:68-71
Ja '67
DUTIES (tariff) See Tariff
DUTIES, Childrens. See Occupations for chil-
dren
DUTTON, Richard W. See Mishell, R. I.
jt. auth.
DUTTON, E. P, and company
Anthology marks 60th year of Everyman's
library. Pub W 190:40-1 O 17 '66
DUTTON, Geoffrey
(tr) See Evtushenko, E. A. Surging outcry
against repression
DUTY
See also
Conscience
Ethics
DUTY free importation
Florence agreement implemented at last. C.
B. Grannis. Pub W 190:44 O 17 '66
Florence agreement to govern scientific in-
strument imports; statement, November 10
1966. L. B. Johnson. Dept State Bul 55:895
D 12 '66
Florence bill signed; effective date to be set.
Pub W 190:54 O 31 '66
Hearings begun on Florence agreement bill.
Pub W 190:55 Jl 4 '66
House approves Florence and Beirut pacts.
Pub W 190:44 S 19 '66
House hearings June 6-7 on Florence and
Beirut pacts. Pub W 189:189 Je 6 '66
Senate approves Florence agreement bill. Pub
W 190:37 O 17 '66
That nations may know; L. B. Johnson
makes U.S. member of the Florence agree-
ment. W. Benton. Sat R 49:25+ D 3 '66
U.S. accepts Beirut agreement; implements
Florence agreement; statement, October 14,
1966. L. B. Johnson. Dept State Bul 55:894
D 12 '66
DUVAL COUNTY, Fla.
School system that failed; with discusson
group program, by M. S. Smart. W.
Hartley and E. Hartley. il Parents Mag
41:26, 52-3+ Mr '66

DUVALIER, François
Are we ready to intervene in Haiti? R. D.
Heinl, jr. il Reporter 34:26-8 Je 2 '66
Bailing out Duvalier. R. D. Heinl, jr. New
Repub 156:15-16 Ja 14 '67
Destiny to suffer. il por Time 87:39 My 13
'66
Haiti: chaotic and corrupt. G. R. Latortue.
il Nation 203:539-41 N 21 '66
Pistol-packing papa. M. J. Kubic. il por
Newsweek 67:56-7 Je 27 '66
Tyranny in Haiti. G. R. Latortue. bibliog f
il Cur Hist 51:349-53+ D '66
What Papa Doc has done to Haiti. C. Mig-
dail. il por U S News 60:47-8 My 9 '66
DU VON, Jay
Campus landscape. por Am Ed 2:18-24 My '66
—See Barr, R. H.; Deering, E. C. jt. auths.
DVORAKOVA, Ludmilla
Music to my ears. l. Kolodin. Sat R 49:70 D
10 '66
DWARF cannas. See Cannas
DWARF dahlias. See Dahlias
DWARF trees. See Trees, Dwarf
DWARFISM
Growth-hormone deficiency in man: an iso-
lated, recessively inherited defect. D. L.
Rimoin and others. bibliog il Science 152:
1635-7 Je 17 '66
DWELL meters
Dwell meter adapter. D. H. Bozarth. il Pop
Electr 24:58+ F '66
DWORKIN, Martin S.
Modes of Greek skepticism: number ten;
poem. Cath World 202:297 F '66
DWORKIN, Stan
Love experts; story. Redbook 127:56-7 Je '66
DWYER, Florence P.
Lady blocks the pork barrel. Life 61:6 S
23 '66
DWYER, J. Gerald
Conserving liberal education. Cath World
204:82-6 N '66
DWYER, James E.
Iris the more the merrier. Pop Gard 17:16-
17 Ag '66
Train trees on walls and fences. Pop Gard
17:70-4 Mr '66
DYE, Eugene N.
Travel well. See issues of Travel
DYER, Henry S.
Squeeze in college admissions. PTA Mag 60:
19-20 My '66
DYES and dyeing
Ancient art revived; nature as a source of
pigments in dyeing yarns and fabrics. J.
Wolcott. Parks & Rec 1:168-9 F '66
Case of the dubious dye; salmonellosis caused
by dye capsules. il Time 89:44 Ja 6 '67
Computers cultivate an eye for color; elec-
tronic monitors taking control of many vari-
ables in textile dyeing. il Bsns W p 106+
O 15 '66
DYKEMAN, Winston R. See Woodwell, G. M.
jt. auth.
DYKES, Archie R.
Innovation in higher education. bibliog f Sch
& Soc 94:179-81 Ap 2 '66
DYLAN, Bob
Bob Dylan, a far cry from Aristotle. O. B.
Brummell. il por Hi Fi 16:125 O '66
Dylan plea for injunction against Citadel re-
fused. Pub W 191:35 Ja 2 '67
Evolution of Bob Dylan. A. E. Gollan. Nat
R 18:638-40 Je 28 '66
Folk rock's tambourine man. S. Castin. il
pors Look 30:76+ Mr 8 '66
Popular records. D. Watt. New Yorker 42:
200-2+ Mr 19 '66
Well, what have we here? J. Siegel. il pors
Sat Ev. Post 239:32-6+ Jl 30 '66
DYMOND, Jack R.
Potassium-argon geochronology of deep-sea
sediments. bibliog Science 152:1239-41 My
27 '66
DYNACHROME 64. See Photography—Films
DYNAMIC programming. See Mathematics—
Formulae
DYOMIN, Ivan
House at 43 Gorkey street. Library J 91:5696-
8 N 15 '66
DYSAUTONOMIA. See Nervous system—
Diseases
DYSENTERY, Amebic. See Amebiasis
DYSLEXIA. See Word blindness
DYSTROPHY, Muscular
Cytochemical localization of lactate dehydro-
genase in muscular dystrophy of the mouse.
H. D. Fahimi and P. Roy. bibliog il Science
152:1761-3 Je 24 '66
Dystrophy noncarrier not 100 per cent trace-
able. Sci N 90:197 S 17 '66
DZIEWIATKOWSKI, Dominic D. See Hirsch-
man, A. jt. auth.

E

EADIE, Bonnie
Five with enterprise. P. Rifield. il por Mlle 63:146 S '66

EAGER, Patricia R. See Eager, R. P. jt. auth.

EAGER, Robert P. and Eager, P. R.
Glial responses to degenerating cerebellar cortico-nuclear pathways in the cat. bibliog Science 153:553-5 Jl 29 '66

EAGLE, Morris, and others
Imagery: effect of a concealed figure in a stimulus. bibliog Science 151:837-9 F 18 '66

EAGLES
Eagles' nests protected in safe square mile; bald eagle. il Sci N L 89:119 F 19 '66
Help for the eagle. Nat Parks Mag 40:21 Ap '66
How to shoot eagles. K. Botty. il Field & S 71:60-1 Ja '67
Treasure bird; golden eagles. E. A. Bauer. il Field & S 70:61+ Ap '66
Vanishing eagle aided by $1,000 grant. Sci N 90:315 O 15 '66
Visit from a proud stranger; catching red-tailed hawks, and a golden eagle in a bow net. B. Gilbert. il Sports Illus 26:24-8 Ja 16 '67

EAR
Anteroventral cochlear nucleus: wave forms of extracellularly recorded spike potentials. R. R. Pfeiffer. bibliog il Science 154:667-8 N 4 '66
Prompt care urged for children's ear infections. Todays Health 44:84 Mr '66
Speech: behavior of middle ear muscle during stuttering. W. M. Shearer. bibliog il Science 152:1280 My 27 '66

Surgery

New X-ray helps cure deafness in one ear. Sci N 89:241 Ap 9 '66
Research shifts to inner ear. F. Marley. il Sci N 90:477 D 3 '66

EAR (animals)
Pressure regulation in the middle ear cavity of sea lions: a possible mechanism. S. Odend'hal and T. C. Poulter. bibliog il Science 153:768-9 Ag 12 '66

EAR (fishes)
Man may owe hearing to ancient fish; eusthenopteron. il Sci N 89:483 Je 18 '66

EAR (insects)
Auditory system of noctuid moths; excerpts from address. April 27, 1966. K. D. Roeder. bibliog il Science 15b:1515-21 D 23 '66
Moth ears give clues to survival systems. Sci N 89:358 My 7 '66

EARHART, Amelia
Search for Amelia Earhart, by F. Goerner. Review
  Time il por 88:121 S 16 '66

EARL, Howard G.
Head injury: the big killer. Todays Health 44:18-21 D '66
That dirty mess: water pollution. Todays Health 44:52-6 Mr '66
Your next nurse may be a man. Todays Health 44:38-9+ F '66

EARLE, Arthur Frederick
Mentors for Britain's flagging management. il por Bsns W p 190-1+ O 15 '66

EARLS, Mary Ellen
Seventeen at my fingertips. por Seventeen 26:22 Ja '67

EARPHONES
Build a stereo headphone control unit. C. Caringella. il Pop Electr 24:71-3+ Ap '66
Private ear. H. Fantel. Opera N 30:33 Mr 5 '66

EARTH
Probing deeper, higher, farther. B. Tufty. Sci N 90:548-9 D 24 '66
  See also
Atmosphere
Geography
Isostasy

Chemical composition
  See Geochemistry

Crust
  See Earth—Surface

Internal structure
Cooler at the core; G. Kennedy's temperature findings. Time 87:52 F 18 '66
Earth's make-up shown. Sci N 90:119 Ag 20 '66
Earth's viscosity. D. L. Anderson. bibliog il Science 151:321-2 Ja 21 '66
  See also
Mohole project

Photographs
Earth from orbit. P. D. Lowman, jr. Nat Geog Mag 130:644-71 N '66

Rotation
Toward a longer day; Vladimir Kotelnikov calculations. Time 87:102 F 25 '66
  See also
Coriolis force

Surface
Earth from orbit. P. D. Lowman, jr. il Nat Geog Mag 130:644-71 N '66
Potassium:rubidium ratio in ultramafic rocks: differentiation history of the upper mantle. A. M. Stueber and V. R. Murthy. bibliog il Science 153:740-1 Ag 12 '66
Shift in crust found. A. Ewing. Sci N 89:347 My 7 '66

EARTH movements
See also
Seismology
EARTH moving machinery. See Excavating machinery
EARTH resources observation satellites. See Artificial satellites—Use in research
EARTH satellites (artificial) See Artificial satellites
EARTH science. See Geology
EARTH temperature
Earth getting colder as ice age nears. Sci N 90:449 N 26 '66
Isotopic paleotemperatures. C. Emiliani. bibliog il Science 154:851-7 N 18 '66
Supersonic transports to heat earth's surface. Sci N 89:292 Ap 23 '66
EARTHENWARE stoves. See Stoves, Earthenware
EARTHQUAKES
Detection of underground explosions. E. Bullard. il Sci Am 215:19-29 Jl '66
Earthquake information center established. Sci N 90:120 Ag 20 '66
Our trembling earth. B. Tufty. il Sci N 90:178-9 S 10 '66
Undersea earthquake. B. Tufty. Sci N 90:348 O 29 '66
What to do in an earthquake. E. Crimmin. il Sci Digest 59:67-70 Ap '66
See also
Seismic sea waves
Seismology

Prevention
Quake forecast hopeful. Sci N 90:29 Jl 9 '66

Research
Earthquake! B. Frisch. il Sci Digest 59:58-67 Ap '66
How to predict an earthquake; dual laser beam technique. il Sci Digest 60:26 S '66
Stick-slip as a mechanism for earthquakes. W. F. Brace and J. D. Byerlee. bibliog il Science 153:990-2 Ag 26 '66

Russia
Disaster in Tashkent. il Newsweek 68:46 Jl 25 '66

Turkey
Anguish in Anatolia. il Time 88:32 S 2 '66
Her child lies below. M. Durham. il Life 61:69-70+ S 16 '66

United States
Instant earthquake; Denver area tremors cause; D. Evans theory. il Time 87:93 Ap 1 '66
See also
San Francisco—Earthquake and fire, 1906

EARTHS, Rare
Dispersed and not-so-rare earths. L. A. Haskin and F. A. Frey. bibliog il Science 152:299-314 Ap 15 '66
Rare earths in European shales: a redetermination. M. A. Haskin and L. A. Haskin. bibliog il Science 154:507-9 O 28 '66
Rare earths in Hawaiian basalts. J. G. Schilling and J. W. Winchester. bibliog il Science 153:867-9 Ag 19 '66
EARTHWORMS
Always plenty of worms. H. G. Tapply. il Field & S 71:68 Je '66
EASBY, Dudley T. Jr
Early metallurgy in the New World; with biographical sketch. Sci Am 214:20, 72-8+ bibliog(p 140) Ap '66
Gold of ancient Peru. Américas 18:24-33 D '66
EASELS
Her easel has a paper roll. il Sunset 137:120 O '66
Ultimate easel. M. Banister. il Pop Mech 126:130-3 Jl '66
EASON, Al
Texas triumph. Travel 126:46-9 Ag '66
EAST, Ben
Black handsaws. Outdoor Life 138:44-5+ S '66
New tool for gun safety. Outdoor Life 138:74-5+ Jl '66
—See Peakall, D. B; Staveley, G. jt. auths.
EAST
See also
Asia
EAST (United States) See Atlantic states
EAST and West
Paradise on earth, by H. Baudet, tr. by E. Wentholt. Review
Nation 202:787-8 Je 27 '66. E. T. Gargan
EAST ASIA Christian conference. See Eastern Asia Christian conference
EAST ASIAN and Pacific affairs, Bureau of. See United States—State, Department of—East Asian and Pacific affairs, Bureau of

EAST BERLIN. See Berlin (East Berlin)
EAST central citizens organization, Columbus, Ohio
Missionaries in darkest Ohio. J. Ridgeway. New Repub 154:9-10 F 5 '66
EAST GERMANY. See Germany (Democratic Republic)
EAST INDIANS
India: too poor to be effective, too big to be ignored. E. Dunbar. il Look 30:19-32 Jl 12 '66
EAST ORANGE, N.J.

Education
New Jersey chicken trial: verdict for science. E. Langer. Science 152:479-81 Ap 22 '66
EAST PACIFIC rise. See Ocean bottom
EAST PAKISTAN. See Pakistan
EAST ST LOUIS, Ill.
If I get up from here and do a little bit, a little bit more's going to come to me: antipoverty program. F. Powledge. il Redbook 127:66-7+ S '66
EAST-West center, Honolulu. See Hawaii. University, Honolulu—East-West center
EAST-West exchange agreements. See Exchange of persons programs
EAST-West trade. See Communist countries—Commerce
EASTER
What are we celebrating at Easter? America 114:475 Ap 9 '66
With glad and grateful hearts. Christian Cent 83:419 Ap 6 '66

Drama
Bunnies and bonnets. H. L. Miller. Plays 25:43-52, 62 Ap '66

Poetry
Any Holy week. W. L. Molton. Christian Cent 83:423 Ap 6 '66
Easter morning. S. Bradley. Christian Cent 83:423 Ap 6 '66
Nails. S. R. Hopper. Christian Cent 83:422 Ap 6 '66
Painter! R. Cumming. Christian Cent 83:423 Ap 6 '66
Query from a practical Bostonian. A. Mendez. Christian Cent 83:422 Ap 6 '66
When he bore the cross. C. L. Coles. Farm J 90:121 Ap '66
EASTER eggs
Easter eggstravaganza. il Farm J 90:103 Ap '66
Easter's eggs and rabbits molded easily in solid chocolate or hollow chocolate. il Sunset 136:180-1 Ap '66
Happy art of decorating Easter eggs. il House & Gard 129:168-9 Mr '66
EASTER entertainments
Easter's Pacific parade; traditional celebrations. Travel 125:16 Ap '66
EASTER ISLAND
Isle of stone heads; medical research and revolt; with report and photographs by C. Mydans. Life 60:48-56+ F 4 '66
EASTERBROOK, D. J.
Radiocarbon chronology of late pleistocene deposits in northwest Washington. bibliog Science 152:764-7 My 6 '66
EASTERN air lines
American challenges EAL shuttle. J. W. Carter. Aviation W 86:37-8 Ja 16 '67
Eastern moves to solve shuttle problems. J. R. Ashlock. Aviation W 85:28-30 Jl 4 '66
Eastern moving to diversification with Remmert-Werner acquisition. D. A. Brown. Aviation W 85:41 S 19 '66
Eastern will test newscasts on shuttle. Aviation W 85:41 Jl 18 '66
Foes of Eastern-Remmert cloud airline diversification. Aviation W 85:33 O 17 '66
EASTERN ASIA Christian conference
Asian faith and order conference; Hong Kong. J. R. Fleming. Christian Cent 84:24-5 Ja 4 '67
EASTERN churches
See also
Orthodox Eastern church
EASTERN college librarians. See Conference of eastern college librarians
EASTERN EUROPE. See Europe, Eastern
EASTERN EUROPEAN bonds. See Bonds, Government—Europe, Eastern
EASTERN Orthodox church. See Orthodox Eastern church
EASTERN test range. See Proving grounds
EASTLAKE, William
Alone on an elephant. Nation 203:155-6 Ag 22 '66

EASTLAKE, William—*Continued*
Dragon train to Singapore. Nation 203:283-4
S 26 '66
Night we bombed Peking. Nation 203:8-11 Jl 4
'66
There's a camel in my cocktail; story. Harper 232:63-8 Ap '66
To die in Vietnam. Nation 203:418-19 O 24 '66
EASTLAND, James O.
Massa Jim in trouble. Nation 202:605-6 My
23 '66
EASTMAN chemical products, Incorporated
One-step way to turn out plastic packages;
Eastoflow process. il Bsns W p73-4+ My 7
'66
EASTMAN Kodak company
Attack on Kodak; FIGHT dispute. J. Ridgeway. New Repub 156:11-13 Ja 21 '67
Kodak stock comes into sharpest focus; earnings are 44 per cent over last year's record.
il Bsns W p 124+ Ap 30 '66
P.R. with a touch of magic. J. Deschin.
Pop Phot 59:24+ O '66
EASTON, John M. and Hiatt, C. W.
Simian virus 40: replication in the presence
of specific antiserum and adenovirus 4.
bibliog Science 151:582-3 F 4 '66
EASTON, Mass.
Richardson's North Easton. L. J. Homolka.
il Arch Forum 124:72-7 My '66
EASTON, Pa.
Street traffic
One-way streets for winter. W. Tomino. il
Am City 81:24 D '66
EASY chairs. See Chairs
EATING
Great American gourmet. N. S. Hazelton. Nat
R 18:115 F 8 '66
See also
Diet
Food
EATON, Hubert Lewright
Dead right. il Newsweek 67:44 Ap 18 '66
First step up to heaven. il por Time 88:54
S 30 '66
Living end. il Newsweek 68:95 O 3 '66
EATON, Jerome A.
Espaliers. House & Gard 130:268-71+ N '66
Home greenhouse. See issues of Flower
grower, the home garden
EATON, Quaintance
Painting with light. Opera N 30:28-31 Ap 2
'66
EATON Yale and Towne, incorporated
How Eaton found a perfect mate; acquisition
of Yale & Towne. il Bsns W p 100-1+ My
28 '66
EAU CLAIRE, Wis.
Community for Benedictine sisters; St Bedes
priory. il Arch Rec 140:112-14 Ag '66

Galleries and museums
Chippewa Valley museum. J. L. Stoutenburgh. Hobbies 71:111 S '66
EAVESDROPPING devices. See Electronics in
criminal investigation, espionage, etc.
EBAN, Abba
Shrine of the book; excerpt from address.
Sch Arts 65:43-5 Ap '66
about
Jews; visit to Poland. il Newsweek 67:59 My
23 '66
That new boy in Israel's foreign office. J.
Feron. il pors N Y Times Mag p40-1+ Ap
17 '66
EBCO manufacturing company
Old office standby freshens up its style. il
Bsns W p68+ Jl 9 '66
EBERHART, Richard
New love; poem. Sat Eve Post 239:43 D 31
'66
Vastness and indifference of the world; poem.
Sat R 49:46 F 12 '66
about
Lamb, the clocks, the blue light. R. Huff.
Poetry 109:44 O '66
EBERT, Robert H.
Prescription; excerpt from address. March 2,
1966. Atlan 217:49 My '66
EBLE, Charles E.
Eble of Consolidated Edison. por Fortune 73:
53 F '66
EBONY (periodical)
Backstage; a winner of National magazine
award competition. il Ebony 21:26 My '66
Transoceanic happy birthday. il Ebony 21:54-
60 F '66
EBY, Gordon M.
(ed) See De Schauensee, M. Man from the
Bulletin

ECCENTRICS and eccentricities
Last of the mountain men; S. Hart in Big
Five Mile Creek primitive area, Idaho.
H. Peterson. il Sports Illus 25:84-8+ O 3 '66
ECCLESIASTICAL arts. See Christian art and
symbolism
ECCLESIASTICAL law
Freedom under church law; excerpt from address. October 16, 1965. T. M. Cunningham.
Cath World 202:348-53 Mr '66
Law and spirit; effort to reform canon law.
Commonweal 85:155-6 N 11 '66
Reforming canon law; recommendations for
carrying out the spirit of Vatican II. Time
88:44+ O 28 '66
Revising canon law. Christian Cent 83:1297-8
O 26 '66
ECCLESIASTICAL vestments. See Church vestments
ECHEVERIA
Hen-and-chickens: dramatic in a well designed garden. il Sunset 137:161 Jl '66
ECHINODERMS
See also
Embryology—Echinoderms
ECHLIN, Patrick
Blue-green algae; with biographical sketch.
Sci Am 214:16, 74-81 Je '66
ECHO of laughter; story. See Coward, N.
ECHO PARK DAM (proposed) See Dams
ECHO preamplifiers. See Amplifiers
ECHO ranging. See Sonar
ECK, Richard V. and Dayhoff, M. O.
Evolution of the structure of ferredoxin based
on living relics of primitive amino acid sequences. bibliog Science 152:363-6 Ap 15 '66
—and others
Thermodynamic equilibrium and the inorganic origin of organic compounds. bibliog Science 153:628-33 Ag 5 '66
ECKARDT, A. Roy
End to the Christian-Jewish dialogue. Christian Cent 83:360-3, 393-5 Mr 23-30 '66
Misrepresentation. Christian Cent 84:84 Ja 18
'67
ECKE, Paul
Crimson for Christmas. P. Friggens. il pors
Read Digest 89:148-9 D '66
ECKER, David W.
(ed) See Kaprow, A. Happenings in and out
of school
ECKERSON, Helen F.
Immigration and national origins. bibliog f
Ann Am Acad 367:4-14 S '66
ECKERT, Ned. See Moon, J. J.
ECKERT, Roger
Subcellular sources of luminescence in noctiluca. bibliog Science 151:349-52 Ja 21 '66
ECKERT, William Dole
Progress report on the unknown soldier. J.
Underwood. il pors Sports Illus 24:40-2+ Ap
4 '66
ECKES, Walter W.
Guests of the VC. por Newsweek 68:36-7 Jl 11
'66
Tale of two prisoners. Time 88:27 Jl 8 '66
ECKLEY, Robert S.
Company action to stabilize employment.
Harvard Bsns R 44:51-61 Jl '66
ECKRICH, Catherine
Angel apprentice; poem. Cath World 203:242
Jl '66
Ballet; poem. Cath World 204:233 Ja '67
ECLIPSES
Photographs
See Astronomical photography
ECLIPSES, Solar
Airborne eclipse expedition. W. P. Boquist.
il Sky & Tel 31:282-4 My '66
Annular eclipse of May 20th. il Sky & Tel
32:80-3 Ag '66
Coming eclipse will receive unprecedented
data coverage. W. S. Beller. il Tech W
19:28+ S 19 '66
Early reports of the May eclipse. il Sky &
Tel 32:14-15 Jl '66
Eclipse offers answers. il Sci N 90:407 N 12
'66
Eclipse over the Andes. D. H. Menzel. il
Sky & Tel 33:11-15 Ja '67
Gemini crew to photograph solar eclipse.
J. Mercer. Tech W 19:18-19 O 17 '66
Maximum eclipse effort; South America. il
Sky & Tel 32:135-7 S '66
ECLIPSES, Stellar
1988 will bring unique astronomical eclipse.
Sci N L 89:66 Ja 29 '66
ECLOGITIC pyroxenes. See Pyroxenes
ECOLOGICAL society of America
Smokies an ecological asset. il Liv Wildn
30:35-7 Spr '66

ECOLOGY
By sharing knowledge; National academy of
sciences role. F. Seitz. il Sat R 49:65-7
My 7 '66
National parks and the ecology of beauty.
D. Goldman. il Am For 72:18-21+ N '66
Perspective of the Smithsonian program in
ecology; excerpt from address, March 15,
1966. S. D. Ripley. il Nat Parks Mag 40:
10-13 O '66
See also
Seashore ecology

Study and teaching
By studying nature whole. L. J. Haworth.
il Sat R 49:59-61 My 7 '66
ECOLOGY, Human. See Human ecology
ECONOMIC and social council of the United
Nations. See United Nations—Economic
and social council
ECONOMIC assistance
Blackett decries cuts; more financial and
technical aid urged. Sci N 91:11 Ja 7 '67
Escalator of debt. Fortune 73:76+ Je '66
McNamara's new design for world peace and
security; address, May 18, 1966. R. S. Mc-
Namara. il U S News 60:90-5 My 30 '66;
Same with title Security in the contem-
porary world. Dept State Bul 54:874-81 Je
6 '66
Rich and the poor: 1966. P. G. Hoffman. Sat R
49:22-5 S 17 '66
Second challenge. E. Rabinowitch. Bul
Atomic Sci 22:25-7 My '66
Trade and the war on world poverty. R. M.
Fagley. Christian Cent 83:745-8 Je 8 '66
U.S. aid in a world setting; symposium. Cur
Hist 51:65-107+ Ag '66
See also
International bank for reconstruction and de-
velopment
Organization for economic cooperation and
development—Development assistance com-
mittee

Statistics
This month's feature: Congress considers
foreign aid for FY67. Cong Digest 45:193-224
Ag '66
ECONOMIC assistance, American
Advancement of peace; remarks, January 20,
1966. L. B. Johnson. Dept State Bul 54:
186-9 F 7 '66
Bargain billions. Newsweek 67:27 F 14 '66
Blades for aid; Congress skeptical of the
aims, methods and results. Time 88:15 Jl
29 '66
Cut to the bone. New Repub 154:4 F 12 '66
Deep conviction; how the aid is earmarked.
New Repub 154:5-6 My 7 '66
Dismay on the Nile; L. Johnson changes
tactics. Atlan 217:6+ F '66
Food for freedom: paradox of foreign aid.
B. J. Oudes. il Nation 203:120-4 Ag 8 '66
Foreign aid and conscience. America 114:
762 My 28 '66
Foreign aid and politics in Nepal. by E. B.
Mihaly. Review
New Repub 154:27-8+ My 21 '66. N.
McKitterick
Foreign aid and the brain drain. J. A. Per-
kins. For Affairs 44:608-19 Jl '66
Foreign aid; message to the Congress: Feb-
ruary 1, 1966. L. B. Johnson. Dept State
Bul 54:320-7 F 28 '66
Foreign assistance act of 1966 signed by
President Johnson; statement, September
19, 1966. L. B. Johnson. Dept State Bul
55:602 O 17 '66
Foreign assistance program: address, Febru-
ary 1, 1966. L. B. Johnson. Cur Hist 50:
358-9 Je '66
Foreign assistance program for 1967: state-
ment, March 17, 1966. D. Rusk. Dept State
Bul 54:628-34 Ap 18 '66
Legacy of Franklin D. Roosevelt and John F.
Kennedy; address, June 16, 1966. W. A.
Harriman. Dept State Bul 55:137-40 Jl 25
'66
LBJ's plan to outpolitic the Communists. P.
Lisagor. il Nations Bsns 54:23-4 Ap '66
New look in foreign aid, it will be harder
to get. U S News 61:58 Jl 25 '66
New look in foreign aid: what LBJ is asking
now. il U S News 60:48 F 14 '66
New script. Time 87:20 F 11 '66
122 billions in aid; and the results for U.S.
with charts. U S News 61:46-7 Ag 15 '66
Overpopulation: dilemma for U.S. aid. T. E.
Dow, jr. bibliog f il Cur Hist 51:65-71+
Ag '66
Parsimony in foreign aid. America 114:249-
50 F 19 '66
Policeman of foreign aid; J. K. Mansfield.
Time 87:33 Je 10 '66

Population problem and economic progress;
address, February 14, 1966. D. Rockefeller.
Vital Speeches 32:366-70 Ap 1 '66
President reaffirms support for foreign aid
program; remarks, August 3, 1966. L. B.
Johnson. Dept State Bul 55:276-7 Ag 22 '66
Quality of aid. D. E. Bell. For Affairs 44:
601-7 Jl '66
Should U.S. aid be channeled through the
U.N? M. H. McVitty. Cur Hist 51:102-7+
Ag '66
State of the Union; address, January 17,
1966. E. M. Dirksen. Vital Speeches 32:
258-9 F 15 '66
Tensions in U.S.-Latin American relations.
W. J. Hinson. Christian Cent 83:1004-7 Ag
17 '66
This month's feature: Congress considers
foreign aid for FY67. Cong Digest 45:193-224
Ag '66
Too tired for aid? Commonweal 84:165 Ap
29 '66
Trends in administering foreign aid; address,
April 15, 1966. D. E. Bell. Vital Speeches
32:454-6 My 15 '66
U.S. foreign aid: an overview; symposium.
bibliog f il Cur Hist 50:321-57+ Je '66
U.S. foreign aid program: limit it to non-
military aid? pro and con discussion. il Sr
Schol 89:8-10 N 4 '66
Victimizing foreign aid; Fulbright's stand.
New Repub 154:6 Je 11 '66
Where we're a little ahead. il Time 88:22 Ag
12 '66
William the terrible; Senate cuts administra-
tion's requests. il Newsweek 68:18 Ag 8 '66
World politics of responsibility. O. Gass;
discussion. Commentary 41:12+ Ap '66
See also
Food relief
United States—Agency for international de-
velopment

Bibliography
Readings on foreign aid. K. P. Dobkin. Cur
Hist 51:50-1 Jl '66

History
Evolution of U.S. foreign aid; excerpts from
Foreign aid in international politics. J. D.
Montgomery. Cur Hist 50:321-7+ Je '66

Statistics
Economics of foreign aid. S. E. Harris. bib-
liog f il Cur Hist 50:342-5+ Je '66
Trend of economic assistance by region;
graphs. Cur Hist 51:48-9 Jl '66
U.S. aid in Africa. D. Randall. bibliog f il
Cur Hist 51:20-7 Jl '66
U.S. aid to east Europe. V. E. Mares. bib-
liog f il Cur Hist 51:36-44 Jl '66
ECONOMIC assistance, Chinese
Communist foreign aid: successes and short-
comings. M. I. Goldman. bibliog f il Cur
Hist 51:84-6 Ag '66
ECONOMIC assistance, Communist
See also
Economic assistance, Chinese
Economic assistance, Russian
ECONOMIC assistance, Domestic
Dimming of the dream; Great Society's im-
pact disappointingly slight. il Time 88:25-6
D 9 '66
Industrial growth in areas of chronic unem-
ployment. G. Iden. il Mo Labor R 89:485-90
My '66
More of everything. Time 87:20 My 6 '66
Plight of the rural poor. B. Kovach and N.
Caldwell. il Reporter 34:27+ Ap 21 '66
Recovery of depressed areas: a gazetteer.
Mo Labor R 88:III-IV D '65
Sargent Shriver and the role of the poor.
B. Carter. il Reporter 34:17-20 My 5 '66
T.R.B. from Washington; no more poor? New
Repub 155:4 O 29 '66
Washington slipped here. il Nations Bsns 54:
38-9+ Ag '66
See also
Anti-poverty program, 1964-
United States—Job corps
Volunteers in service to America
ECONOMIC assistance, European
West European foreign aid. V. L. Galbraith.
bibliog f il Cur Hist 51:88-95+ Ag '66
ECONOMIC assistance, German
Germany in the underdeveloped world. W. W.
Schmokel. Cur Hist 50:281-8+ My '66
ECONOMIC assistance, Israeli
Israel's aid to Africa. G. Gersh. Commonweal
85:226-8 N 25 '66
ECONOMIC assistance, Russian
Communist foreign aid: successes and short-
comings. M. I. Goldman. bibliog f il Cur
Hist 51:78-87+ Ag '66
Soviet aid to Vietnam. A. Parry. il Reporter
36:28,33 Ja 12 '67

ECONOMIC assistance in Africa
Israel's aid to Africa. G. Gersh. Commonweal 85:226-8 N 25 '66
U.S. aid in Africa. D. Randall. bibliog f il Cur Hist 51:20-7 Jl '66
ECONOMIC assistance in Asia
Challenge for aid in Asia. N. D. Palmer. bibliog f Cur Hist 51:7-13+ Jl '66
Charting the future course of U.S. foreign aid in the Near East and south Asia; statement, March 22, 1966. R. A. Hare. Dept State Bul 54:668-71 Ap 25 '66
East Asian spectrum. Newsweek 68:32 O 31 '66
Escalation of policy; L. B. Johnson's promises. Nation 203:530-1 N 21 '66
Lower Mekong. W. R. D. Sewell and G. F. White. bibliog f il Int Concil 558:5-63 My '66
Next: a Marshall plan for Asia? il U S News 61:29 Jl 25 '66
U.S. to cooperate in economic and social development in Asia; remarks, March 16, 1966; with announcement of pledges to Mekong River project. L. B. Johnson. il Dept State Bul 54:521-3 Ap 4 '66
See also
Colombo plan
ECONOMIC assistance in Bolivia
Bolivia: revolution in mid-passage. G. Delmas. Reporter 35:31-4 D 1 '66
ECONOMIC assistance in Europe
Aid success in west Europe. M. G. Johnson. bibliog f Cur Hist 51:1-6+ Jl '66
U.S. aid to east Europe. V. E. Mares. bibliog f il Cur Hist 51:36-44 Jl '66
ECONOMIC assistance in Haiti
Bailing out Duvalier; Inter-American development bank approves loan. R. D. Heinl, jr. New Repub 156:15-16 Ja 14 '67
ECONOMIC assistance in Honduras
Service and profits. America 114:793-4 Je 4 '66
ECONOMIC assistance in India
For India, still more aid: and for the U.S.—il U S News 60:60-1 Ap 11 '66
Frühlingsrauschen: aid from U.S. and Russia. Nat R 18:350 Ap 19 '66
India to get aid, but no blank check. il Bsns W p34-5 Ap 2 '66
Nineteen years, billions in aid; India losing ground. R. P. Martin. il U S News 60:64-8 My 23 '66
U.S. to resume aid to India and Pakistan; Department announcement. Dept State Bul 55:17 Jl 4 '66
ECONOMIC assistance in Iran
White revolution; U.S. cuts aid; reactions. il Time 87:80 F 11 '66
ECONOMIC assistance in Latin America
Foreign assistance program for Latin America in 1967; statement, May 2, 1966. L. Gordon. Dept State Bul 54:977-86 Je 20 '66
Kennedy's prescription for Latin America. New Repub 154:8-10 My 28 '66
Latin America: focus for U.S. aid. J. S. Tulchin. il Cur Hist 51:28-35 Jl '66
Latin-American summit: how much would it cost U.S? il U S News 60:48-9 My 2 '66
Litany of woe; Robert Kennedy's Senate speech. Newsweek 67:71 My 23 '66
See also
Alliance for progress
Inter-American development bank
ECONOMIC assistance in Nepal
Foreign aid and politics in Nepal, by E. B. Mihaly. Review
New Repub 154:27-8+ My 21 '66. N. McKitterick
ECONOMIC assistance in Nigeria
Cracks in Africa's show window. Bsns W p34 Ag 13 '66
ECONOMIC assistance in Pakistan
U.S. to resume aid to India and Pakistan; Department announcement. Dept State Bul 55:17 Jl 4 '66
ECONOMIC assistance in Poland
Should the United States aid totalitarian countries? C. V. Crabb, jr. bibliog f Cur Hist 50:346-52+ Je '66
ECONOMIC assistance in southeast Asia. See Economic assistance in Asia
ECONOMIC assistance in the Dominican Republic
Dominican elections: is the U.S. off the hook now? il U S News 60:49 Je 6 '66
ECONOMIC assistance in the Middle East
Aid and diplomacy in the Middle East. H. L. Hoskins. Cur Hist 51:14-19 Jl '66
Charting the future course of U.S. foreign aid in the Near East and south Asia; statement, March 22, 1966. R. A. Hare. Dept State Bul 54:668-71 Ap 25 '66
ECONOMIC assistance in underdeveloped areas
FAO: the imperative of altruism; adaptation of address. G. Myrdal. Nation 203:666-70 D 19 '66

Foreign aid under Lyndon Johnson. A. Roseman. Cur Hist 50:335-41+ Je '66
Getting tough with poor nations; growth goals fall short. B. D. Nossiter. New Repub 155: 12-14 D 3 '66
ECONOMIC assistance in Vietnam (Democratic Republic)
Soviet aid to Vietnam. A. Parry. il Reporter 36:28-33 Ja 12 '67
ECONOMIC assistance in Vietnam (Republic)
AID for whom? Senate foreign relations committee hearings. Nation 202:198 F 21 '66
Aiding the Viet Cong? handling of the U.S. aid program. il Newsweek 67:66 My 23 '66
Atlantic report; importance of economic development. Atlan 217:8+ Je '66
Bright spirit; H. Humphrey on U.S. aims. il Time 87:21-5 Ap 1 '66
Greatest drama. il Time 87:19-20 Ap 1 '66
How corruption drains U.S. aid in Vietnam. U S News 60:10-11 F 7 '66
LBJ's plan to outpolitic the Communists. P. Lisagor. il Nations Bsns 54:23-4 Ap '66
Mr Komer reports on progress in the other war in Viet-Nam; statement, November 7 1966. R. W. Komer. Dept State Bul 55: 892-4 D 12 '66
Other war in Vietnam: progress report; with text of letter of transmittal, September 13, 1966. R. W. Komer. Dept State Bul 55:549-67, 591-601 O 10-17 '66
Pacification and development programs in Viet-Nam; statement, June 16, 1966. L. B. Johnson. Dept State Bul 55:55 Jl 11 '66
Portent for the future: welfare imperialism in Vietnam. J. McDermott. il Nation 203: 76-88 Jl 25 '66
Red tape and broken promises; rural problems. S. Andrews. Reporter 34:14-16 My 5 '66
South Viet Nam; U.S. to double aid. il Time 87:28-31 F 18 '66
Strayed AID. il Time 87:28-9 My 20 '66
That second war in Vietnam; U.S. AID technicians and International voluntary services activities. C. P. Streeter. il Farm J 90:28-9+ My '66
War where U.S. supplies are getting to both sides. il U S News 60:37-9 Je 6 '66
War without guns, by G. K. Tanham. Review Sat R 49:28-9 My 28 '66. K. T. Young
ECONOMIC assistance in Yugoslavia
Should the United States aid totalitarian countries? C. V. Crabb, jr. bibliog f Cur Hist 50:346-52+ Je '66
ECONOMIC change
Changing pattern of American life; excerpts from address. D. Gray. Parks & Rec 1: 212-14+ Mr '66
Peaceful social and economic change; address, August 18, 1966. K. Brandt. Vital Speeches 32:712-17 S 15 '66
Recent thinking on economic growth and fluctuations. E. C. Bratt. bibliog f Ann Am Acad 364:158-68 Mr '66
20th anniversary issue: a special report; oh, how your life has changed! il Changing T 21:6-14 Ja '67
ECONOMIC commission for Asia and the Far East. See United Nations—Economic commission for Asia and the Far East
ECONOMIC commission for Europe. See United Nations—Economic commission for Europe
ECONOMIC conditions
Business around the world. See issues of U.S. news and World report
Rich and the poor; 1966. P. G. Hoffman. Sat R 49:22-5 S 17 '66
Trends and objectives of the world economy; statement, October 4, 1966. P. de Seynes. UN Mo Chron 3:133-46 N '66
Trends and prospects analyzed; world economic survey. UN Mo Chron 3:37-8 Jl '66
What makes inflation go and stops it. il Bsns W p 196-8 My 14 '66
See also
Business depression
also subhead Economic conditions under names of countries, states, etc. e.g. United States—Economic conditions
ECONOMIC conferences
Projections for world economy; first United Nations interregional seminar on long-term economic projections for the world economy. UN Mo Chron 3:82 Ag '66
ECONOMIC development
Aspects of development; symposium. il For Affairs 44:601-61 Jl '66
British incomes experience; excerpt from address. E. H. P. Brown. Mo Labor R 89: 634-7 Je '66
Economic growth: key to the good life for all. il Sr Schol 89:15-17 O 21 '66

ECONOMICS—*Continued*

Terminology

Economics in the news. See issues of Senior scholastic to May 13, 1966

ECONOMICS, Agricultural. See Agriculture—Economic aspects

ECONOMICS and Christianity. See Christianity and economics

ECONOMISTS
Economists battle past a milestone. il Bsns W p 138-9 F 26 '66
Experts turn against tax boosts; survey of 100 top men finds 60 per cent opposed. il Bsns W p 154-5+ My 28 '66
Memo to economists: Uncle Sam wants you; demand by different agencies. il Bsns W p 160+ Ap 9 '66
New gains, new worries. il Bsns W p27-8 Ag 20 '66

ECONOMY in government. See Government spending policy

ECONOPOULY, Nicholas. See Parker, D. jt. auth.

ECTOPIC pregnancy. See Pregnancy, Complications of

ECUADOR
See also
Quito

Antiquities

See also
Indians of South America—Antiquities—Ecuador

Politics and government

Ecuador: a present-day portrait. J. D. Cochrane. bibliog f Cur Hist 51:264-9 N '66
Mr President; junta replaced with a civilian president. il Newsweek 67:61 Ap 11 '66
People, yes! il Time 87:36+ Ap 8 '66

ECUADORIAN pottery. See Pottery, Ecuadorian

ECUMENICAL council, 2d. See Vatican council, 2d

ECUMENICAL high schools. See Church schools

ECUMENICAL movement
Absolve Queen Elizabeth? J. B. Sheerin. Cath World 203:71-5 My '66
American Catholic strides in ecumenism. J. B. Sheerin. Cath World 203:134-7 Je '66
Church for these times, by R. E. Osborn. Review
Christian Cent 83:142 F 2 '66. R. Goetz
Church women and Christian unity. C. C. Wedel. Cath World 202:278-82 F '66
Dialogue with Christians; questions among Jews. il Time 87:60 Ap 22 '66
Ecumenical escalation; National faith and order colloquium; first meeting. J. R. Nelson. Christian Cent 83:858 Jl 6 '66
Ecumenical gap; basic problem facing the ecumenical movement. W. S. Kilpatrick. Christian Cent 83:296-300 Mr 9 '66
Ecumenical spirit, Easter, 1966. Life 60:4 Ap 8 '66
Ecumenical strain and stress. America 115:167 Ag 20 '66
Ecumenism and minorities. America 115:269 S 17 '66
Ecumenism and philosophy. G. F. Kreyche. bibliog f Christian Cent 83:521-4 Ap 27 '66
Ecumenism for students. America 114:541 Ap 16 '66
Is the ecumenical movement anti-Semitic? Christian Cent 83:1048 Ag 31 '66; Reply. J. C. Rylaarsdam. 83:1306 O 26 '66
New secular ecumenism. J. B. Sheerin. Cath World 203:261-4 Ag '66
Of many things: significant breakthroughs. T. N. Davis. America 114:275 F 26 '66
One big church? il U S News 61:54-7 Jl 25 '66
Pentecostal winds blowing Christian Cent 83:609 My 11 '66; Reply. H. W. Winger. 83:866 Jl 6 '66
Reassembling the face of Christ. R. W. Gilsdorf. America 115:131-5 Ag 6 '66
Reflections of a council observer; interview, ed. by E. M. Gaffney, A. C. Outler. Cath World 203:353-60 S '66
Religion and society: the ecumenical impact, by C. Nelson. Review
Cath World 204:55-6 O '66. J. B. Sheerin
Sociology of ecumenism. M. D. Zeik. il Commonweal 84:275-8 My 27 '66
Something new and different; workshop on education for ecumenism. M. McGrory. America 114:795 Je 4 '66
Vatican II: what does the future hold? R. M. Brown. Cath World 202:341-7 Mr '66

What church unity demands of Catholics and Protestants. V. H. Bernstein. il Redbook 126:64-5+ Mr '66
See also
Church unity
Religious cooperation
World council of churches

EDDY, Edward D.
What about the sinful student? Sat R 49:70-1+ Mr 19 '66

EDDY, Mary (Baker)
Mary Baker Eddy: the years of discovery, by R. Peel. Review
Christian Cent 83:1473-4 N 30 '66. C. S. Braden; Reply. R. Peel. 83:1605 D 28 '66

EDDY, Nick
He rambles all around. H. L. Masin. por Sr Schol 89:21 N 11 '66

EDDY, Roger W.
Opinion: on staying put. por Mlle 63:108+ My '66

EDE, Basil
Basil Ede's birds in a New York gallery; with paintings. A. Meyer. Natur Hist 75:32-41 D '66

EDEL, Leon
Biographer's borrowed personality. Sat R 49:30-1 Ap 30 '66
Critic's choice of contemporaries. Sat R 49:35 Ap 2 '66
From notes to novels. Sat R 49:70 Je 11 '66
Hard journey to Treasure Island. Sat R 49:34 S 3 '66
Life without father. Sat R 49:91 My 7 '66
Portrait by the artist as crab. Sat R 50:38 Ja 21 '67
Price of peace was war. Sat R 49:53-4 D 3 '66

EDELEN, Buddy
America's gritty guinea pig. G. S. Brown. por Sports Illus 25:40-2 Jl 11 '66

EDELMAN, G. M. See Marchalonis, J. jt. auth.

EDELMAN, Robert, and Wheelock, E. F.
Vesicular stomatitis virus replication in human leukocyte cultures: enhancement by phytohemagglutinin. bibliog Science 154:1053-5 N 25 '66

EDELSON, Michael
Winter shooting. U S Camera 30:48-51+ Ja '67

EDELSTEIN, J. M.
Lincoln papers in the Stern bequest; reprint. Hobbies 70:110-12 F; 71:106-7+ Mr '66
Tongues, like governments. New Repub 155:26-8 N 26 '66

EDEN, Anthony, 1st earl of Avon. See Avon, A. E.

EDGAR, Natalie
Private worlds of Sal Sirugo. Art N 65:42-3+ N '66

EDGAR, Robert W.
Literary monstrosities; throw them out! summary of address, November 1966. Sr Schol 89:sup 16 D 9 '66

EDGAR Allan Poe awards. See Mystery writers of America

EDGERTON, Harold E.
Sonic detection of a fresh water-salt water interface. Science 154:1555 D 23 '66
—and Leenhardt, Olivier
Monaco: the shallow continental shelf. Science 152:1106-7 My 20 '66
—and others
Mexican freetail bats: photography. Science 153:201-3 Jl 8 '66

EDGERTON, William H.
Building construction costs. See issues of Architectural record

EDGING plants. See Garden borders

EDGINGS, Garden. See Garden borders

EDGINGTON, L. V. and others
Fungicide selective for basidiomycetes. Science 153:307-8 Jl 15 '66

EDIBLE oils and fats. See Oils and fats, Edible

EDIBLE plants. See Plants, Food

EDINA, Minn.
Poll with a purpose; ed. by P. D. Eimon. il Am City 81:171-2+ S '66

EDINBURGH
Music
See also
International festival of music and drama

EDINGER, Lois V.
Technology in education. bibliog por Wilson Lib Bul 41:72-5 S '66

EDISON, Thomas Alva
Edison's sound predictions. T. Schwartz. Pop Phot 59:34 Jl '66

EDISON brothers stores, incorporated
New shine for a master retailer. il Bsns W p 110+ Ap 16 '66

EDISON institute. See Henry Ford museum and Greenfield Village, Dearborn, Mich.

EDITING. See Editors and editing

EDITING amateur moving pictures. See Moving pictures, Amateur—Editing

EDITING moving pictures. See Moving pictures —Editing

EDITION bookbinders association of New York, incorporated
Edition bookbinders of N.Y. elect officers for 1966-67. Pub W 189:119 My 2 '66

EDITIONS Christian Bourgois. See Publishers and publishing—France

EDITIONS Robert Laffont. See Publishers and publishing—France

EDITORIALS
Crime to publish an editorial on Election day; Supreme court decision: Mills v. Alabama. Pub W 189:71 Je 27 '66
Distorted cry? U.S. press and projection of black power. Newsweek 68:54 Ag 8 '66
How to write an editorial. H. Brucker. il Sat R 49:58-60 F 12 '66
Man & his Times; editorial line on Viet Nam. Time 87:64-5 Mr 11 '66

EDITORS and editing
Editing the mystery and suspense novel. J. Kahn. Writer 79:18-21 Jl '66
Editor over my shoulder. L. McLaughlin. Writer 79:29-30+ My '66
How to turn an editor into a friend. B. Ullman. U S Camera 29:16+ O '66
Manner of speaking; rejected poems. J. Ciardi. Sat R 49:18 N 5 '66
Now I sit me down; pleasing the editor. W. Chamberlain. Writer 79:22-4 F '66
Should an editor edit? H. Brucker. Sat R 50:116-17+ Ja 14 '67
Trade winds. H. R. Mayes. Sat R 49:11 Ag 6 '66
Trials of an editor: E. Wirges of the Morrilton (Ark.) democrat. il Newsweek 67:91-2 F 14 '66
Using students to evaluate manuscripts; Rosary H.S. Detroit. Sister Marie Virginia. Sr Schol 89:sup 18-19 O 14 '66
Why editors use form rejection slips. Writer 79:28-33 O '66
See also
Computers—Editing applications

Anecdotes, facetiae, satire, etc.
Trade winds; eight rejections, and then a best seller. J. G. Fuller. il Sat R 49:7-8 My 28 '66

EDLER, Karl
120,000 strong. por Parks & Rec 1:233-4 Mr '66

EDMONDSON, Harold T.
Soldier is buried in Charleston. C. Brossard. il por Look 30:72-6 My 31 '66

EDMUNDS, Frances R.
History in houses. Antiques 89:224-8 F '66

EDMUNDSON, Sandra
Hold it, that's the pose! P. Gowland. il por Pop Phot 58:76-7 My '66

EDOM, Clifton Cedric
Cliff Edom: the man in Missouri. J. G. Morris. il pors Pop Phot 59:96-7+ S '66

EDSON, Lee
Box cameras were never like this. Pop Mech 126:66-9+ Jl '66; Same abr. with title Look what they do with cameras now! Read Digest 89:181-2+ Jl '66

EDUCATED horses. See Horses, Educated

EDUCATION
Diversity; excerpts from address. J. R. Platt. Science 154:1132-9 D 2 '66
Education without magic; address. November 19, 1965. J. M. Moudy. Vital Speeches 32: 275-8 F 15 '66
Educational opportunity around the world. il NEA J 55:33-7 F '66
See also
Books and reading
Catholic church—Education
College education. Value of
Communication in education
Courses of study
Foreign study
Health education
Illiteracy
Institute of international education
International education
Learning. Psychology of
Liberal education
Motivation (education)
Professional education
Teaching
Trade schools
War and education

Aims and objectives
Art, technology and education; excerpt from address, February 1966. A. I. Cox, jr. Christian Cent 83:862-4 Jl 6 '66
Challenge to our schools. J. H. Fischer. Parents Mag 41:30 Ap '66
Coming revolution against boredom in the classroom. J. N. Miller. il PTA Mag 60: 18-21 Ap '66; Same abr. with title New cure for boredom in the classroom. Read Digest 88:171-2+ My '66
Directions of curriculum change; excerpts from Curriculum change: direction and process. J. I. Goodlad. NEA J 55:33-7 D '66
Dual-purpose revolution; excerpts from address, 1966. F. H. Bowles. NEA J 55:38-40 D '66
Education and the new technology; symposium. Sr Schol 89:sup 13 O 7 '66
Education as social invention; excerpt from Toward a theory of instruction. J. S. Bruner. il Sat R 49:70-2+ F 19 '66
Educational values and goals; can morals be taught? address, January 21, 1966. J. Newsom. Vital Speeches 32:244-8 F 1 '66
Higher education and cybernation; with reply by R. W. Tyler. R. Theobald. NEA J 55:26-9 Mr '66
Impact of universal education; remarks, June 1965. D. Lacy. il Library J 91:3866-70 S 1 '66
Spirit of science. D. Wolfle. Science 152:1699 Je 24 '66
Teacher-opinion poll; a new look at the seven cardinal principles of education. NEA J 56:53-4 Ja '67
Technology in education. L. Edinger. bibliog il Wilson Lib Bul 41:72-5 S '66
Title III of ESEA offers encouragement for innovation. N. Estes. il NEA J 55:30-2 D '66
To criticize the critic, by T. S. Eliot. Review Nat R 18:420-1 My 3 '66. H. Kenner
What tasks for the schools? S. M. McMurrin. il Sat R 50:40-3 Ja 14 '67
See also
College education—Aims and objectives
Educational sociology

Bibliography
Editor's bookshelf. P. Woodring. See issues of Saturday review
Foreign books for educators. W. W. Brickman. Sch & Soc 94:359-66 O 29 '66
New books. See issues of Saturday review
Outstanding education books of 1965. NEA J 55:60+ My '66
U.S. books for educators (cont) W. W. Brickman. Sch & Soc 94:288+ Sum '66
See also
Educational literature

Curricula
See Courses of study

Economic aspects
Facts and figures of the Americas. il Américas 18:46 Mr '66
New tycoon; interplay between education and economy. L. C. McQuade. il Am Ed 2:26-7 O '66
Techniques and costs. W. G. Harley; C. H. Springer. il Sat R 50:52+ Ja 14 '67
See also
Colleges and universities—Finance

Exhibitions
Convention exhibit notes: NCSS, NCTE. F. S. Gross; H. R. Finch. Sr Schol 89:sup7 D 9 '66

Federal aid
See Federal aid to education

Finance
See School finance

History
Christian feudal education. P. W. Schmidtchen. il Hobbies 71:108-9 Ag '66
1966 as a centennial year in the history of education. F. Parker. Sch & Soc 94:67 F 5 '66

International aspects
Come in, world. See issues of PTA magazine
Education around the world. J. Cass. Sat R 49:47-8 Ag 20 '66
Era of educational and cultural relations; address, April 25, 1966. C. Frankel. Dept State Bul 54:889-97 Je 6 '66
Exporting the Great society; funds are a limiting factor. J. Walsh. Science 152:45-7 Ap 1 '66

EDUCATION—International aspects—*Continued*
Improving teachers' status world-wide. NEA
J 55:45-6 Ap '66
International education and health; message
to the Congress; February 2, 1966. L. B.
Johnson. Dept State Bul 54:328-35 F 28 '66;
Same abr. with title Proposed international
education act of 1966; excerpts. Sch & Soc
94:186-9 Ap 2 '66
International education dialogue; letter. F. B.
Riggs, jr. Science 152:1696 Je 24 '66
International Magna charta for teachers; con-
cerning the document, adopted unanimously
by delegates to Unesco. W. G. Carr. NEA
J 55:42-4 D '66
Resources for international cooperation. W. G.
Carr. NEA J 55:45 Ap '66
Twenty years of education in Unesco. il Sch
& Soc 94:415-24 N 26 '66
See also
Colleges and universities—International co-
operation
International education
International society for education through
art
United Nations educational, scientific and cul-
tural organization

International cooperation
See also
Colleges and universities—International co-
operation
Students, Interchange of

Objectives
See Education—Aims and objectives

Philosophy
Education as social invention; excerpt from
Toward a theory of instruction. J. S.
Bruner. il Sat R 49:70-2+ F 19 '66
International meeting of educational phil-
osophers; Toronto, March 23-25, 1966. B. S.
Crittenden. il Sch & Soc 94:396-8 N 12 '66
Lectures in the philosophy of education; 1899;
excerpt. ed. by R. D. Archambault. J.
Dewey. Sch & Soc 94:155-9 Mr 19 '66
Neutrality's implications for education. J. Van
Patten. bibliog f Sch & Soc 94:352-4 O
29 '66
Will to learn; excerpt from Toward a theory
of instruction. J. S. Bruner. bibliog f Com-
mentary 41:41-6 F '66

Standards
Our era of opportunity; methods for improving the quality of education; excerpt from
address. J. L. Burns. il Sat R 50:38-9 Ja 14
'67
See also
Colleges and universities—Standards

Statistics
Back-to-school statistics. Am Ed 2:23 S '66
Facts and figures of the Americas. Américas
18:46 Mr '66
Magnitude of the American educational es-
tablishment (1966-1967) il Sat R 49:75 O
15 '66
State rankings of education indicators show
similarity in performance. Am Ed 2:8-9
O '66
Statistic of the month. See issues of Amer-
ican education
Washington report; concerning the report,
Local school expenditures: 1970 projections.
J. Lloyd. Sr Schol 88:sup7 F 4; sup8 F 11
'66
See also
School attendance
Teachers—Statistics

Study and teaching
See also
Colleges and universities—Education depart-
ments
Teachers—Education

Africa, East
Developing the academic spirit in East Africa.
D. P. S. Wasawo. Bul Atomic Sci 22:19-21
O '66

Alabama
ESEA deferred in over 200 districts; Alabama
passes anti-guidelines law. Library J 91:
5142+ O 15 '66
Making it hurt; withholding funds if Alabama
refuses to integrate. Nation 203:300 O 3 '66

Alaska
See also
Alaska. University

Argentina
Amadeo Jacques: French educator on the
River Plate. A. A. Roig. il Américas 18:7-
13 Jl '66
See also
Colleges and universities—Argentina

Arkansas
Men out of monkeys, or monkeys out of
men? Susan Epperson trial. S. Murphy.
New Repub 154:9-10 My 7 '66

Asia
Second conference of Asian education ministers. Sch & Soc 94:133-4 Mr 5 '66

Australia
How I use records to teach; school in Wagga
Wagga. D. G. Dufty. Sr Schol 88:sup5 Ap 1
'66

Bulgaria
Elementary education in Bulgaria. J. George-
off. bibliog f il Sch & Soc 94:71-4 F 5 '66

California
FEAST attracts job-hungry students; Proj-
ect FEAST program in California. C. Larsson. il NEA J 55:20-2 D '66
How parents feel; survey of attitudes toward
schools, made for the Charles F. Kettering
foundation. Time 87:51 Je 3 '66
How to start with long-term subscriptions;
Oceana high school, Pacifica. G. J.
Figgins. il Library J 91:2168-9 Ap 15 '66
Sample project. Title I, ESEA; Menlo-Ather-
ton high school, Atherton, Calif. M. Heg-
land and M. Shaw. il Library J 91:1014-16
F 15 '66
School library extension service; real or
imagined? report of survey. E. R. Chris-
tine. ALA Bul 60:623-6 Je '66
Sullivan's crusade; schools without pain. J.
Poppy. il Look 30:37-40 Je 28 '66
Teaching the Bill of rights in California;
Constitutional rights foundation programs.
J. W. McKenney. il Sat R 49:68-9+ Mr 19
'66
See also
Los Angeles—Education

Canada
Education and economic growth in Canada;
excerpt from the Second annual review by
the Economic council of Canada. towards
sustained and balanced economic growth.
il Mo Labor R 89:377-80 Ap '66
Revolt in Quebec's education system. C. de
Mestral. Christian Cent 83:630-2 My 11 '66
See also
Colleges and universities—Canada

China (People's Republic)
China's new school policy. America 116:32 Ja
14 '67
Cultural revolution; system under purge.
Newsweek 68:43-4 Jl 4 '66
Education in Communist China. J. S. Duncan.
il NEA J 55:37-40 F '66
Education in Mao's China. R. D. Barendsen.
il Am Ed 2:14-19 O '66
How school keeps in China. C. T. Hu. Sat R
49:66-7+ Ag 20 '66
I was a student in red China; ed. by H.
Evans. C. P. Tung. Read Digest 89:189-90+
D '66
Science and education. C. H. G. Oldham.
Bul Atomic Sci 22:41-50 Je '66

Connecticut
See also
Darien, Conn.—Education

Cuba
See also
Schools—Cuba

England
See Education—Great Britain

Europe, Eastern
Uninfected. Time 87:54+ Ap 8 '66

Europe, Western
Europe's schools going American? il U S
News 60:77 Je 13 '66
Falling short in Europe. Time 87:73 Ap 29 '66

France
France's school debate after six years. R. M.
Healey. Christian Cent 83:632-4 My 11 '66

Georgia
English is to enjoy; Jackson H.S. J. A.
Settle. il Sr Schol 88:sup20 F 11 '66

EDUCATION—*Continued*

Ghana
See also
Colleges and universities—Ghana

Great Britain
Reform and revolution in English education; with list of educational terms. J. D. Koerner. il Sat R 50:61-3+ Ja 21 '67
U.S. vs. British; who's best? Sr Schol 89:sup2 O 7 '66
See also
Oxford. University
Public schools (endowed)—England

Greece, Ancient
Paidagogo-go-go. P. W. Schmidtchen. il Hobbies 71:106-8 S '66

Guatemala
School-to-school; a partnership in understanding. J. Vaughn. Parents Mag 41:30+ Je '66

Holland
See Education—Netherlands

Illinois
See also
Chicago—Education
Evanston, Ill.—Education

Indonesia
Literacy by decree in Indonesia. R. M. Thomas. bibliog f il Sch & Soc 94:279-83 Sum '66

Iowa
Amish controversy; temporarily settled; Gov. Hughes acts. P. B Mather. Christian Cent 83:474-6 Ap 13 '66
No worldly schools. Sr Schol 88:17-18 Mr 11 '66
State of Iowa vs. the Amish; school dispute. F. H. Littell. Christian Cent 83:234-5 F 23 '66; Discussion. 83:468-72 Ap 13 '66
That Amish thing; education dispute in Iowa. P. B. Mather. Christian Cent 83:245-7 F 23 '66; Discussion. 83:468-72 Ap 13 '66

Israel
Fighting deprivation in the promised land. M. Smilansky. il Sat R 49:82+ O 15 '66

Italy
See also
Colleges and universities—Italy

Japan
Japanese science education centers. B. Glass. Science 154:221-8 O 14 '66
See also
Colleges and universities—Japan

Kenya
Teaching the Kenyans to take a letter; secretarial training sponsored by ILO. il Bsns W p 126-7 My 7 '66

Latin America
Catholic schools in Latin America. E. K. Culhane. America 114:514 Ap 9 '66; Discussion. 114:805-7 Je 4 '66
Culture in the limelight; with declaration on education, science and culture, and excerpts from address by J. Mora. G. de Zéndegui. il Américas 18:inside cover, 5-9 F '66
Facts and figures of the Americas. il Américas 18:46-7 F '66
Latin America: education: the baited trap. M. Chiappetta. il Nation 203:321-3 O 3 '66
Latin America: the risk of education. Sch & Soc 94:164 Mr 19 '66

Massachusetts
See also
Boston—Education
Quincy, Mass.—Education

Michigan
Ding dong, the bells are gone; Chippewa Valley high school, Mount Clemens. E. Stephens. Seventeen 25:410-11 Ag '66
False start for Head Start in Michigan. R. Kirk. Nat R 18:886 S 6 '66
See also
Ann Arbor, Mich.—Education
Detroit—Education

Mississippi
Children's library in Mississippi does double duty. E. B. Zeigler. Horn Bk 42:292-7 Je '66

Netherlands
Education: Dutch style; experiences teaching social studies in Enschede. G. Denzene. Sr Schol 88:sup 17+ Ap 15 '66
See also
Colleges and universities—Netherlands

New Hampshire
Away from Moby Dick and Jane: high school English program in Dover. M. Mainwaring. il Sr Schol 89:sup 13-15 O 14 '66

New Jersey
N.J. governor vetoes antismut bill; school librarians' influence cited. il Library J 91. 1043-4 F 15 '66
Using records to teach history; Linwood jr. high school, North Brunswick. M. S. Defren. il Sr Schol 89:sup 18 N 11 '66

New Mexico
Federal funds to meet local needs. B. Fielding. il NEA J 55:23-6 S '66

New York (state)
School library program for the blind; Lakeland school district, Mohegan Lake. S. M. Mahoney and L. Z. Stokes. Wilson Lib Bul 40:829+ My '66
See also
New York (city)—Education
New York (state)—Education department

Oregon
See also
Portland, Ore.—Education

Pennsylvania
See also
Pittsburgh—Education

Peru
Señorita Luciana: teacher in the high Andes; Quero Indian children, Cuzco, Peru. il UNCESCO Courier 19:7-9 S '66

Philippines
See also
Colleges and universities—Philippines

Quebec (province)
See Education—Canada

Rome
Paidagogo-go-go. P. W. Schmidtchen. il Hobbies 71:106-8 S '66

Russia
Life, the inexorable teacher; excerpt from The collective family. A. S. Makarenko. il Sat R 50:117 Ja 7 '67
Men, moonships, and morality; concerning theories of R. S. Morison and A. S. Makarenko. J. Lear. il Sat R 50:113-14+ Ja 7 '67
Soviet education in 1965. I. Schlesinger. bibliog f Sch & Soc 94:270-2 Sum '66
Soviet teaching of history and international understanding. V. G. Trukhanovsky. Sch & Soc 94:152-5 Mr 19 '66
Teachers and the taught in the U.S.S.R. by W. Benton. Review
Sat R 49:99 Ap 16 '66. H J. Noah
Teaching Ivan a trade; training factory workers. il Bsns W p80+ Ap 30 '66
See also
Colleges and universities—Russia

Somalia
Upper Darby senior high builds a school in Africa. R. Hoopes. il Seventeen 25:98-9+ Ap '66

South America
See Education—Latin America

Southern states
Ax for the South; cutting off federal funds from segregated schools. Time 88:32 D 16 '66
Back to school, a long way. il Newsweek 68:21-2 S 12 '66
Forcing desegregation through Title VI; new guidelines. A. M. Bickel. New Repub 154: 8-9 Ap 9 '66; Reply. C. White. 154:29-30 Ap 23 '66
High schools in the South. Sch & Soc 94: 183-4 Ap 2 '66
Mixed classes: a report as schools open. il U S News 61:12 S 12 '66
Non-compliance with desegregation guidelines. Sch & Soc 94:310+ O 15 '66
Searchlight on high schools in the South. W. W. Geier. Christian Cent 83:186-8 F 9 '66

EDUCATION—Southern states—*Continued*

Segregation fence: a young mother gets involved. M. Jaynes. il Redbook 126:8+ Mr '66

South reports education gains. Sr Schol 88: sup3+ F 4 '66

We thought they meant it; actions against Negroes enrolling their children in previously all-white schools. Sat R 49:89 Ap 16 '66

Who pulled the teeth from Title VI? G. W. Foster, jr. Sat R 49:88 Ap 16 '66

See also

Negroes in the United States—Education

Southwestern states

Few Spanish-speaking children in high school in Southwest. Sch & Soc 94:376+ N 12 '66

Sweden

Paradise for planners. J. D. Koerner. il Sat R 49:59-61+ Jl 16 '66; Discussion. 49:49 Ag 20 '66

Pupils into the breach; teachers strike; with report by B. Wise. il Life 61:65+ N 25 '66

Switzerland

Recent developments in Swiss science, technology, and education. Sch & Soc 94:104-5 F 19 '66

Texas

What is Project Discovery discovering? J. A. Brill. il Sr Schol 89:sup8+ O 7 '66

Turkey

Our man in Istanbul. N. Baba. il Am Ed 2:26-7 Mr '66

Underdeveloped areas

Education as a instrument of American foreign policy; address, April 16, 1966. W. Benton. Ann Am Acad 366:33-40 Jl '66

United States

American education in the mid-sixties; excerpts from addresses. T. Sizer; M. Mayer. il PTA Mag 61:18-23 N '66

Are schools changing too much too fast? il Changing T 20:6-10 S '66

Bill of rights; address, July 1, 1966. L. F. O'Brien. Vital Speeches 32:646-9 Ag 15 '66

Changing directions in American education; symposium. il Sat R 50:37-43+ Ja 14 '67

Compact plan moves toward ratification: nationwide policy for education. Sr Schol 87: sup2 Ja 7 '66

Editor interviews John H. Fischer; ed. by M. S. Fenner. J. H. Fischer. pors NEA J 55: 10-13 D '66

Education in America; ed. by P. Woodring and J. Cass. See issues of Saturday review

Education: the racial gap; findings of James Coleman's study. C. Jencks. New Repub 155:21-6 O 1 '66; Reply. F. McKissick. 155: 33-6 D 3 '66

Europe's schools going American? il U S News 60:77 Je 13 '66

Faults and hopeful signs in education. Sch & Soc 94:171-2 Ap 2 '66

Fourth R, the rat race; schools as high-pressure learning factories. J. Holt. il N Y Times Mag p46-7+ My 1 '66; Discussion. p 12+ My 15; 21+ My 22 '66

How good are our schools? armed forces qualification test provides a clue. R. De Neufville and C. Conner. il Am Ed 2:1-7 O '66

Interview with Francis Keppel. F. Keppel il Am Ed 2:11-13 Jl '66

Is there a new establishment? P. Schrag. Sat R 49:87 O 15 '66

Magnitude of the American educational establishment (1966-1967) il Sat R 49:75 O 15 '66

Meeting our educational needs. J. H. Fischer. Parents Mag 41:52 S '66

Nation of amateurs in education; adaptation of address, July 14, 1966. H. Howe, 2d. Sch & Soc 94:448-51 D 10 '66

National assessment; Exploratory committee on assessing the progress of education. P. Woodring. Sat R 49:71-2 S 17 '66

Necessary revolution in American education, by F Keppel. Review
New Repub 154:22-3 Je 11 '66. R. Moskowitz
Reporter il 35:58-60 S 22 '66. P. Schrag

New tycoon; interplay between education and economy. L. C. McQuade. il Am Ed 2:26-7 O '66

News and trends. See issues of NEA journal

On schools; are the children in the running? J. Holt. Harper 232:102-3 My '66

Our top ten education stories of 1965. il Sr Schol 87:sup 1 Ja 7 '66

Perfect education, by K. E. Eble. Review
Time il 88:125 O 14 '66

Schools make news. Sat R 49:67 Ja 15; 74-5 Mr 19; 97 Ap 16; 63 My 21; 64 Je 18; 88-9 O 15; 92-3 N 19; 82-3 D 17 '66; 50:72-3 Ja 21 '67

Speaking out; you force kids to rebel. S. Kelman. Sat Eve Post 239:12+ N 19 '66

Spears on education; interview, ed. by W. K. Richards. H. Spears. Sr Schol 88:sup 1+ Ap 22 '66

Technology is knocking at the schoolhouse door. C. E. Silberman. il Fortune 74:120-5+ Ag '66

Toward deeper cultural relations in the hemisphere; address, January 18, 1966. C. Frankel. Dept State Bul 54:202-7 F 7 '66

USOE creates regional labs. Sr Schol 88: sup2+ Mr 25 '66

U.S. vs. British; who's best? Sr Schol 89: sup2 O 7 '66

Vision of madness; W. Arrowsmith's charges. Time 88:60 O 28 '66

What are Americans receiving in return for their heavy investment in education? excerpts of testimony. J. Gardner; H. Howe, 2d. il Am Ed 2:24-6 N '66

What better schools will cost; interviews, ed. by S. Wren. J. W. Gardner. il Look 30:100+ My 17 '66

What's happening in education? W. D. Boutwell. See issues of PTA magazine

Who's blocking educational change? excerpts from address. J. Moorhead. PTA Mag 60:2-3 Mr '66

See also

Adult education

American education week

Americanization

Colleges and universities—United States

Compact for education

Computers—Educational applications

Education—Southern states

Education and state

Education of women—United States

High schools

Junior colleges

National education association

Negroes in the United States—Education

Private schools

Public schools—United States

School laws and legislation—United States

Service men, Discharged—Education

Summer schools

United States—Education, Office of

Vocational education

Anecdotes, facetiae, satire, etc.

View from afar; Report of earth visit, September 1966. H. Howe, 2d. Am Ed 2:inside cover S '66

History

Education in modern times. P. W. Schmidtchen. il Hobbies 71:108+ Jl '66

Uruguay

Amadeo Jacques; French education on the River Plate. A. A. Roig. il Américas 18: 7-13 Jl '66

Vietnam (Republic)

Three-R war in Vietnam; US AID and other projects. R. S. Knowles. Read Digest 90: 171-4 Ja '67

U.S.-Vietnamese team to expand education. il Sch & Soc 94:316+ O 15 '66

Virginia

Lost years; when Prince Edward County closed its public schools. J. P. Blank. il Look 30:71-2+ N 29 '66

Not on the list; Hanover County. ALA Bul 60:691+ Jl '66

They closed their schools, by B. Smith. Review
Nation 203:521-2 N 14 '66. K. Jackson, jr

Virginia book ban controversy grows. Library J 91:1632+ Mr 15 '66

Virginia librarians confronted with immoral classics, sex books. il Library J 91:1044-5 F 15 '66

Wyoming

Fierce phonics war; Sheridan. R. Kirk. Nat R 18:936 S 20 '66

EDUCATION, Adult. See Adult education

EDUCATION, Agricultural. See Agricultural education

EDUCATION, College. See College education

EDUCATION, Cooperative
How to go to college on nothing a year. L. Velie. Read Digest 88:132-6 F '66
What's happening in education? interstate program for cooperation on educational problems. W. D. Boutwell. PTA Mag 60: 13-14 F '66

EDUCATION, Cost of. See Education—Economic aspects

EDUCATION, Elementary
See also
Education of children
National education association—Department of elementary school principals

Activity programs
Planning preschool facilities. M. P. Berson and W. W. Chase. il Am Ed 2:7-11 D '65
See also
Projects (teaching)

EDUCATION, Evaluation of. See Evaluation (education)

EDUCATION, Experimental
Do-it-yourself U; experimental college at San Francisco state college. il Newsweek 68: 100+ N 7 '66
Shadow schools; academic undergrounds. il Time 88:100 O 21 '66
See also
Progressive education
Schools, Experimental

EDUCATION, Graduate schools of. See Colleges and universities—Education departments

EDUCATION, Higher. See College education; Colleges and universities

EDUCATION, Individual. See Individual instruction

EDUCATION, Industrial. See Industrial education

EDUCATION, Inter-American. See Inter-American education

EDUCATION, Liberal. See Liberal education

EDUCATION, Moral. See Moral education

EDUCATION, Musical. See Musical education

EDUCATION, Office of. See United States—Education, Office of

EDUCATION, Physical. See Physical education and training

EDUCATION, Professional. See Professional education

EDUCATION, Progressive. See Progressive education

EDUCATION, Religious. See Religious education

EDUCATION, Secondary
See also
High schools

EDUCATION, Technical. See Technical education

EDUCATION, Urban
Urban education studies; series published by John Day. E. Geller. il Library J 91: 1036-7 F 15 '66

EDUCATION, Value of
Preparing adults for rapid change. R. H. Coates. il NEA J 55:23-5 D '66
See also
College education, Value of

EDUCATION, Vocational. See Vocational education

EDUCATION and business. See Business and education

EDUCATION and church. See Church and education

EDUCATION and democracy
See also
Citizenship, Education for

EDUCATION and economic problems. See School and social and economic problems

EDUCATION and industry. See Business and education

EDUCATION and politics. See Politics and education

EDUCATION and social problems. See School and social and economic problems

EDUCATION and state
Church-school challenge; state aid to church-related colleges; Maryland. Time 88:55-6 N 25 '66
Crucial school aid case; Michigan auxiliary services act. America 114:250 F 19 '66
Education for world responsibility; address, July 16, 1966. C. Frankel. Vital Speeches 32:621-5 Ag 1 '66
Funds for your own funeral; concerning AASA letter. America 115:87 Jl 23 '66
How free from doctrine? state aid to church-related colleges; Maryland. Newsweek 68:95 N 28 '66

Maryland college case; state grants to one Protestant and two Catholic colleges ruled unconstitutional. America 114:864 Je 25 '66
N.Y. state textbook law upheld as constitutional by court. Pub W 191:36 Ja 9 '67
No review now of college aid. America 115: 675 N 26 '66
Plain people vs. the common schools; efforts to improve Amish education. D. A. Erickson. il Sat R 49:85-7+ N 19 '66
Politics, propaganda, and pedagogy. W. W. Brickman. Sch & Soc 94:55 F 5 '66
Problems involved in cooperation between universities and government agencies J. W. Shirley. bibliog f Sch & Soc 94:222-7 Ap 16 '66
State funds for higher education. Sch & Soc 94:254+ Sum '66
Subtler significance of urban unrest. Am City 81:8 O '66
Technology in the schools: educators are uneasy. L. J. Carter. il Science 153:1624-6 S 30 '66
Wisdom of being apart. J. P. Leary. America 115:224-7 S 3 '66
Your government and your schools; summary of address. H. H. Humphrey. il PTA Mag 61:8-10 S '66
See also
Education commission of the states
Federal aid to education
United States—Education, Office of

EDUCATION and state in Argentina
Where it's government vs. university; University of Buenos Aires. il U S News 61: 48 Ag 15 '66

EDUCATION commission of the states
Compact for education, still in search; quarterly meeting. Sr Schol 89:sup5 Ja 6 '67
Compact for education to meet December 8-9. Sr Schol 89:sup4 D 2 '66
States and education; interview. W. H. Pierce. Sr Schol 89:sup21-2+ S 23 '66

EDUCATION departments, College. See Colleges and universities—Education departments

EDUCATION for citizenship. See Citizenship, Education for

EDUCATION of adults. See Adult education

EDUCATION of children
Anxious child can learn, but what? with study-discussion program, by R. Strang. E. J. LeShan. bibliog il PTA Mag 61:8-10, 35 D '66
Danger of teaching your baby to read. B. Bettelheim. Ladies Home J 83:38+ S '66
Game called learning; guidance at home with low-cost self-help materials. E. Sharpe. il Todays Health 44:64-7 S '66
Great literature for little folk. Samuel Marshak, 1887-1964. M. Morton. Horn Bk 42:335-44 Je '66
How you can help your child be creative. M. B. Sharkey and M. Longwell. il Farm J 90:95-6+ Ap '66
How young children learn. J. Holt. il Parents Mag 41:60-3+ S '66
Parents can help their children succeed in school. G. G. Unruh. il NEA J 55:14-16 D '66
Preschool education. L. N. Morrisett. Science 153:1197 S 9 '66
Pressure cooker for four-year-old minds; Institute for research on exceptional children of the University of Illinois. M. Pines. il Harper 235:55-61 Ja '67
School for four-year-olds? il Time 88:39 Jl 1 '66
Teaching baby to read. il Time 88:44-5 Ag 12 '66
Universal education for four-year-olds? pro and con discussion. M. M. Mitchell; J. Spaulding. NEA J 55:10-11 N '66
Universal opportunity for early childhood education; policy of Educational policies commission of the NEA and the American association of school administrators. il NEA J 55:8-10 N '66
Washington report; extension of public-education. J. Lloyd. Sr Schol 88:sup4 Mr 18 '66
See also
Children—Management and training
Childrens literature
Childrens reading
Home study
Nature study
Preschool children
Sex instruction
Special classes and special schools

EDUCATION of librarians. See Library schools and education

EDUCATION of Negroes. See Negroes in the United States—Education

EDUCATION of prisoners
Case of civilized penology; G.E's computer programing course. Nation 202:115 Ja 31 '66
Chance on the outside; MDTA project at Lorton youth center. T. R. Sard. il Am Ed 2:29-32 Ap '66

EDUCATION of women

United States
Everywoman's village stirs up the housewives. E. Perry. il Life 60:46+ Mr 25 '66; Same abr. with title Housewives' school to beat the boredom. Read Digest 88:41-2+ Je '66
Longer view of the educated woman; excerpt from Educated American women: selfportraits. E. Ginzberg and A. M. Yohalem. Sch & Soc 94:391-2+ N 12 '66
What educated women want; report; views of Vassar seniors, ed. by J. M. Russin. il Newsweek 67:68-72+ Je 13 '66
Women moving ahead. A. Y. Scates. il Am Ed 2:1-4 Mr '66
See also
Barnard college, New York

EDUCATION week. See American education week

EDUCATIONAL achievements. See Student achievements

EDUCATIONAL associations
Local associations ask about. J. H. Starie. See issues of NEA journal
Principals and professional negotiation. W. G. Carr. NEA J 55:45-6 My '66
Unionism versus professionalism in teaching. R. D. Batchelder. NEA J 55:18-20 Ap '66
See also names of educational associations. e.g. Council for basic education

EDUCATIONAL conferences
Educational research and teaching abroad. il Sch & Soc 94:460-1 D 10 '66
It's a date (cont) NEA J 55:38 My; 6+ S '66; 56:82+ Ja '67

EDUCATIONAL cooperation
Education compact becomes reality. Sr Schol 88:sup2 Mr 18 '66
William H. Pierce named to head states' Compact for education. Science 152:739 My 6 '66
See also
Colleges and universities—Cooperation
Education commission of the states
Interuniversity communications council
Theological schools—Cooperation

EDUCATIONAL discrimination. See Discrimination in education

EDUCATIONAL exchanges
American education and the developing areas; address; with questions and answers. K. W. Thompson. Ann Am Acad 366:17-32 Jl '66
Professor abroad: twenty years of change. E. W. Weidner. Ann Am Acad 368:60-70 N '66
United States and Romania agree on 1966 program of exchanges. Dept State Bul 54: 788 My 16 '66
United States and U.S.S.R. sign exchanges agreement for 1966-67; text of joint communique, March 19, 1966. Dept State Bul 54: 543-4 Ap 4 '66
U.S.-Dutch university cooperation; Cooperation among U.S. and Japanese universities; and U.S.-Philippine university cooperation. Sch & Soc 94:208-9+ Ap 16 '66
See also
International association for the exchange of students for technical experience
Teachers, Interchange of

EDUCATIONAL films. See Moving pictures—Documentary films; Moving pictures in education

EDUCATIONAL finance. See Education—Economic aspects

EDUCATIONAL foundations. See Foundations, Charitable and educational

EDUCATIONAL games. See Games

EDUCATIONAL guidance
College admissions; symposium. il NEA J 55:40-4 O '66
What is the outlook for job or college? with study-discussion program, by C. Smallenburg and H. Smallenburg, A. M. Ross; H. S. Dyer. bibliog il PTA Mag 60:18-20, 37 My '66
See also
Personnel service in education
Vocational guidance

EDUCATIONAL leadership. See Leadership

EDUCATIONAL literature
Books in the field; education. F. M. Hechinger. bibliog il Wilson Lib Bul 41:310-17 N '66

Educators paperback service; Scholastic magazines, inc. il Sr Schol 89:sup21 S 30 '66

EDUCATIONAL materials center. See United States—Education, Office of—Educational materials center

EDUCATIONAL measurements. See Educational tests and measurements

EDUCATIONAL parks. See Consolidated schools

EDUCATIONAL planning
What tasks for the schools? S. M. McMurrin. il Sat R 50:40-3 Ja 14 '67

EDUCATIONAL products information exchange. See Institute for educational development

EDUCATIONAL psychology. See Psychology, Educational

EDUCATIONAL records. See School reports and records

EDUCATIONAL research
Research clues; questions and answers. See issues of NEA journal
See also
Colleges and universities—Research
Follow up studies (education)
Institution for the development of educational activities
United States—Education, Office of—Educational research and development, Bureau of

EDUCATIONAL research information center. See United States—Education, Office of—Educational research and development, Bureau of

EDUCATIONAL segregation. See Segregation in education

EDUCATIONAL services, incorporated
Curiosity and the kitchen sink. M. Bauer. il Am Ed 2:8-10 Jl '66
New approach to teaching social studies. K. Jorgensen. il Sr Schol 89:sup9 N 4 '66

EDUCATIONAL sociology
Cultural pluralism in urban education. S. W. Itzkoff. Sch & Soc 94:383-6 N 12 '66
See also
Socially handicapped children—Education

EDUCATIONAL standards. See Education—Standards

EDUCATIONAL statistics. See Education—Statistics

EDUCATIONAL study tours. See Travel study courses

EDUCATIONAL surveys
Education; the racial gap; findings of James Coleman's study. C. Jencks. New Repub 155:21-6 O 1 '66; Reply. F. McKissick. 155: 33-6 D 3 '66
How parents feel; survey of attitudes toward schools, made for the Charles F. Kettering foundation. Time 87:51 Je 3 '66

EDUCATIONAL television. See Television in education

EDUCATIONAL television stations. See Television stations, Educational

EDUCATIONAL testing service
Upgrading. il Sch & Soc 94:441 D 10 '66

EDUCATIONAL tests and measurements
Are national tests fair? with study-discussion program by C. W. Mattuck. N. Larrick. il Parents Mag 41:12+, 54-6+ D '66
National testing begins this month; tests to chart national gains in educational progress by groups. Sr Schol 87:sup2 Ja 14 '66
Some essays on multiple-choice tests. D. Klein. Seventeen 25:24+ S '66
Test in art. K. Koch. il Art N 65:54-7 O '66
Testing; NCSS; excerpts from address, November 1965. P. L. Hanna. Sr Schol 87: sup9 Ja 7 '66
Testing vs. your child. G. B. Leonard. il Look 30:63-4+ Mr 22 '66
What's happening in education? national assessment of educational progress. W. D. Boutwell. PTA Mag 60:8-9 Ap '66
Your child and testing. G. R. Hawes. il NEA J 56:37-52 Ja '67
See also
Examinations
Grading and marking (students)
Intelligence tests
Personality tests

EDUCATIONAL theory. See Education—Philosophy

EDUCATIONAL toys. See Toys

EDUCATIONAL workshops
Teaching the Bill of rights in California: CRF sponsored, summer workshops to improve teaching of Bill of rights. J. W. McKenney. Sat R 49:69+ Mr 19 '66
Value of writers' workshops. H. Kubly. Writer 79:22-4 O '66
Workshopping. R. B. Allen. NEA J 55:31 My '66

EDUCATORS
   See also
  College professors and instructors
  Negro educators
  Teachers
EDWARD VIII, king of Great Britain (abdicated 1936)
  Abdication of King Edward VIII, by Lord Beaverbrook. Review
    McCalls 93:28+ Ag '66. C. B. Luce
    Newsweek il por 68:86-7 Ag 1 '66
    Time il por 88:90 Jl 22 '66
  How the Duke of Windsor lost his throne. W. M. A. Beaverbrook. il pors Sat Eve Post 239:38-42+ Ja 29 '66
  Man who wouldn't be king. il por Sr Schol 89: 5 D 9 '66
  That famous love affair. G. A. Craig. il Reporter 35:64-5 N 17 '66
EDWARDS, Allen F. jr
  Gone flying to Sun Valley. Flying 78:66-70 Mr '66
EDWARDS, Carlton M.
  Prefabricated housing. Consumer Bul 49:13-18 Ag '66
EDWARDS, Charlotte
  Description: to know and to feel. Writer 79: 19-23 Mr '66
EDWARDS, Elizabeth
  Will the class please come to order! NEA J 55:11-12 S '66
EDWARDS, Evan A.
  Is super 8 good enough for professionals? questions and answers. Mod Phot 30:84+ S '66
EDWARDS, Gareth
  Modern English in the mass. America 115: 483-6 O 22 '66
EDWARDS, Joel
  Three California ceramists. J. Lovoos. il por Am Artist 30:50-4 D '66
EDWARDS, Margaret A.
  Pushing the book. por Library J 91:6166-8 D 15 '66
EDWARDS, Phil
  Riding the wave of the East coast's surfing boom. B. Ottum. pors Sports Illus 25:30-2+ Jl 18 '66
EDWARDS, R. G.
  Mammalian eggs in the laboratory; with biographical sketch. Sci Am 215:10, 72-81 bibliog(p 114+) Ag '66
EDWARDS, R. J.
  Lives saved, also dollars. por Yachting 119: 346-7 Ja '66
EDWARDSON, John R.
  Cylindrical inclusions in the cytoplasm of leaf cells infected with tobacco etch virus. bibliog Science 153:883-4 Ag 19 '66
EELLS, George
  Cole Porter, my most unforgettable character. Read Digest 89:79-83 Ag '66
EELS
  Viper of the deep. J. Fix. il Motor B 117:113+ Ap '66
EELS, Electric. See Electric eels
EFF, Johannes
  Buffalo Bill is dying; poem. Nat R 18:766-70 Ag 9 '66
EFFICIENCY
  Open letter to the girl my son didn't marry. Good H 162:61-2+ My '66
EFFICIENCY, Agricultural. See Farm management
EFFICIENCY, Industrial
  Never mind the answer; what's the question? M. T. Bloom. il Pop Mech 125:132-4+ F '66
  War against inefficiency; reprint. D. Lawrence. U S News 60:128 Je 13 '66
    See also
  Work measurement
EGAN, Georgia J.
  Journalism, open to all students. NEA J 55:53-4 My '66
EGAN, James
  Bahia. Holiday 40:80-6+ S '66
  Ombudsman. Holiday 40:28+ N '66
  Wonder kid. Holiday 40:81-5 Ag '66
EGERTON, John
  Odds against the teacher corps. Sat R 49:71 D 17 '66
EGG (biology) See Embryology
EGG industry and trade
  Sunny side down. il Newsweek 67:89-90 My 16 '66
EGG production. See Poultry—Egg production
EGGER, Hermann
  Results of sundial competition. Sky & Tel 32:256 N '66
EGGHEADS. See Intellectuals
EGGLESTON, Max
  How to catch a trophy bass. Field & S 71:46-7+ Ja '67

EGGPLANT
    See also
  Cookery—Vegetables
EGGS
    See also
  Cookery—Eggs
  Easter eggs
  Embryology
  Incubation
  Poultry—Egg production

    Grading and standardization
  Are the eggs you buy making the grade? il Consumer Rep 31:62-6 F '66
EGGS of lizards. See Lizards—Eggs
EGK, Werner
  Peer Gynt. Criticism
    Opera N il por 30:32-3 F 26 '66
    Opera N il 30:30-1 Ap 9 '66
EGLIN air force base, Fla. See Proving grounds
EGLINTON, Geoffrey, and Calvin, Melvin
  Chemical fossils; with biographical sketches. Sci Am 216:21, 32-43 Ja '67
—and others
  Occurrence of isoprenoid fatty acids in the Green River shale. bibliog Science 153: 1133-5 S 2 '66
EGORYCHEV, Nikolai Grigorievich
  Meeting of the board. il por Newsweek 67: 50-1 Ap 11 '66
EGRETS
  Egrets and herons make home near oil refinery; do-it-yourself bird sanctuary in water-conservation lagoons. il Sci N 90: 147 S 3 '66
EGYPT
  Egypt and I. W. Golding il Holiday 39:32+ Ap '66
    See also
  Airlines—Egypt
  Birth control—Egypt
  Nile River
  Russians in Egypt
  Suez Canal
  Trials—Egypt

    Antiquities
    See also
  Abu Simbel, Temples of
  Luxor
  Pyramids
  Temples—Egypt

    Defenses
  How much is Nasser worth? P. Seale and I. Beeson. New Repub 154:12-13 Je 4 '66

    Economic conditions
  As troubles pile up for another dictator. J. Law. il U S News 60:70-2 Je 20 '66
  Watermelon Village races against time. H. Smith. il N Y Times Mag p30-1+ Ag 28 '66

    Foreign relations
  Back to the balcony; Nasser's Unity day. Time 87:42 Mr 4 '66
  How much is Nasser worth? P. Seale and I. Beeson. New Repub 154:12-13 Je 4 '66
  Nasser speaks out; interview. ed. by G. P. Hunt. G. Nasser. Life 60:70A+ Mr 11 '66
  Nasser's tightrope begins to fray. il Bsns W p86-7+ My 21 '66

    Saudi Arabia
  Long breath in Yemen. Time 87:35 My 13 '66

    Yemen
  Anti-colonial imperialist; Nasser's coup. Newsweek 68:45 O 3 '66
  As troubles pile up for another dictator. J. Law. il U S News 60:70-2 Je 20 '66
  Microcosm of a struggle; Yemen. Time 87:36 Ap 22 '66
  Rough week; Nasser's latest move. Newsweek 67:46 Ap 25 '66

    History
    Invasion, 1956
  Some of the truth; concerning Anglo-French-Israeli treaty. Time 88:32 Ag 5 '66

    Social conditions
  Watermelon Village races against time. H. Smith. il N Y Times Mag p30-1+ Ag 28 '66
EGYPTIAN art. See Art, Egyptian
EGYPTIAN furniture. See Furniture, Egyptian
EH? drama. See Livings, H.
EHMANN, F. A.
  Counselor; poem. Christian Cent 83:1112 S 14 '66

EHRENBURG, Il'ia Grigor'evich
Dante: the primacy of poetry; excerpts from address, October 28, 1965. UNESCO Courier 19:16-21 Ja '66
EHRLICH, Alice
What makes it art? Sch Arts 65:5-7 Je '66
EHRLICH, Richard
Aerobiology. Science 154:293-4+ O 14 '66
EICHELBERGER, Clark M.
Promise of the seas' bounty. Sat R 49:21-3 Je 18 '66
Sharing the seas' riches. Sat R 49:18 Ag 13 '66
EICHENBERG, Fritz
Two worlds of Naoko Matsubara. il Am Artist 30:34-9+ N '66
EICHENBERGER, Alan J.
Christmas baskets and power. Christian Cent 83:1566-9 D 21 '66
EICHENGREEN, Jeffrey M. and others
Visual-cliff preference by infant rats: effects of rearing and test conditions. bibliog Science 151:830-1 F 18 '66
EICHENWALD, Heinz
Mental retardation. Science 153:1290-3+ S 9 '66
EICHLER, R. and Ristedt, H.
Isotopic evidence on the early life history of nautilus pompilius. Linné. bibliog Science 153:734-6 Ag 12 '66
EICHMANN, Adolf
Case against Eichmann continues. A. L. Fein. Sat R 49:27+ Jl 2 '66
Eichmannism described. Sci N 90:318 O 22 '66
Justice in Jerusalem. by G. Hausner. Review
Newsweek 67:97 My 30 '66
Time 88:86 Jl 8 '66
EICHMANN trial
Case against Eichmann continues. A. L. Fein. Sat R 49:27+ Jl 2 '66
Justice in Jerusalem. by G. Hausner. Review
Newsweek 66:97 My 30 '66
EIDUSON, Bernice T.
Scientists as advisors and consultants in Washington. Bul Atomic Sci 22:26-31 O '66
EIFFEL tower
Jumping-off place; suicides. il Time 88:37 S 9 '66
EIFLER, Charles W.
Men who run the war. por Newsweek 68:54 D 5 '66
EIGELAND, Tor
Our man in Damascus. il Ebony 22:29-32+ D '66
EIGER (mountain) Switzerland
I'd have thought the Eiger would break before John did: J. Harlin's death after North Face conquest. il Life 60:36-7 Ap 8 '66
Thousand feet of nothing down below; infamous north wall of the Eiger. J. Harlin. Sports Illus 24:69-70+ Ap 11 '66
EIGHTEEN-nation disarmament conference. See Conference of the Eighteen-nation committee on disarmament, Geneva, 1962-
EIGNER, Larry
Seven poems: The earth you may as well; Newspaper circling; Blackbird; Penny; Dark bird white bird; Distances are shortened; Sliding down the bannister. Poetry 108:39-44 Ap '66
EILAT, Israel. See Elath, Israel
EILERS, Hazel Kraft
At the sign of the crest. See issues of Hobbies
EIMERL, Sarel
Choreography of despair. Reporter 35:45-6 N 3 '66
Compared with me. Reporter 34:60+ My 19 '66
Essential Maugham. Reporter 36:60+ Ja 12 '67
Plea for the vieille vague. Reporter 35:51-6 D 15 '66
Tammany Hall, Spain, etc. Reporter 34:46-8 Je 16 '66
EIMON, Pan Dodd
(ed) City tells its story. See issues of American city
EINARSSON, Thorleifur. See Hopkins, D. M. jt. auth.
EINEM, Gottfried von
Craftsman; interview, ed. by C. N. Welsh. por Opera N 30:29 Mr 12 '66
about
Danton's death. Criticism
New Yorker 42:196-7 Mr 19 '66
Opera N il 30:34 Ap 2 '66
Opera N il 30:32 Ap 16 '66

EINHORN, Abe
Hey, stupid, where's the glass? interview. New Yorker 42:54-5 N 12 '66
about
Agatha Sue, I love you. Criticism
New Yorker 42:45 D 24 '66
EINSTEIN, Charles
(ed) See Mays, W. Willie Mays: my story
EINSTEIN theory. See Relativity (physics)
EISELEY, Loren C.
Editor interviews; ed. by M. S. Fenner. pors NEA J 55:71-2 N '66
EISENBERG, Leon
Can human emotions be changed? adaptation of address, April 1964. Bul Atomic Sci 22:27-31 Ja '66
EISENBERG, Lucy
Genetics and the survival of the unfit. Harper 232:53-8 F; 13 Je '66
Scientists vs. animal lovers. Harper 233:101-2+ N '66; 234:6 Ja '67
EISENBERG, Norman
Home video tape: is it ready now? Mod Phot 30:41-2+ Mr '66
Loudspeakers: their choice and installation. Hi Fi 16:51-8 Je '66
EISENDRATH, David B. Jr
Color clinic. See issues of Popular photography
about
David B. Eisendrath: photography's man for all seasons. D. S. Gelatt. il pors Pop Phot 59:66-9+ S '66
EISENHOWER, Dwight David
Dwight D. Eisenhower: what I have learned; interview, ed. by R. L. Tobin. por Sat R 49-33 S 10 '66
Eisenhower speaks his mind; interview, ed. by P. Martin. por U S News 61:42-5 N 7 '66
How an ex-President views Vietnam now; excerpts from statement, January 31, 1966. U S News 60:19 F 14 '66
Ike; interview. Nat R 18:1205 N 29 '66
Ike sparks a new debate: how much force to use in Vietnam? statements. por U S News 61:23 O 17 '66
Let's make government work better! Read Digest 90:61-7 Ja '67
Our national nominating conventions are a disgrace. Read Digest 89:76-80 Jl '66
This country needs universal military training. Read Digest 89:49-55 S '66
Thoughts for young Americans. Read Digest 88:88-92 Ap '66
about
Authors & editors; The Eisenhower papers. W. Gellhorn. Pub W 191:25 Ja 9 '67
Fine college gift for Ike. Life 61:4 Jl 1 '66
Foot-in-mouth syndrome; public statements. Christian Cent 83:1263 O 19 '66
Ike in surgery. por Newsweek 68:26 D 19 '66
Sunday painters: Churchill, Eisenhower and Kennedy. C. B. Luce. McCalls 94:12+ Ja '67
EISENHOWER, Dwight David, family
Mamie Eisenhower talks about fifty years of marriage; interview, ed. by V. Cadden. M. Eisenhower. il McCalls 93:78-83 S '66
EISENHOWER, Mamie Geneva (Doud)
Mamie Eisenhower talks about fifty years of marriage; interview, ed. by V. Cadden. pors McCalls 93:78-83 S '66
EISENHOWER college, Seneca Falls, N.Y.
Fine college gift for Ike; call for donations. Life 61:4 Jl 1 '66
EISENSTADT, Jerome, and Lengyel, Peter
Formylmethionyl-tRNA dependence of amino acid incorporation in extracts of trimethorprim-treated escherichia coli. bibliog Science 154:524-7 O 28 '66
EISENSTAEDT, Alfred
Eisie does a book; interview, ed. by J. Deschin. por Pop Phot 59:28+ D '66
Kenyatta of Kenya; photographs. Life 61:36-49+ Ag 5 '66
about
Dodie, Eisie, Marlon, Charlie and Sophia. G. P. Hunt. por Life 60:3 Ap 1 '66
Eisenstaedt: faces of our time. il por Life 61:110B-114+ S 16 '66
Eisenstaedt lens. K. Poli. il Pop Phot 59:102-11 N '66
Eisenstaedt, witness to our time, by B. Holme. Review
Mod Phot il 30:62-9+ N '66. H. Keppler
Our Eisie and Kenya's Kenyatta. G. P. Hunt. pors Life 61:3 Ag 5 '66
Witness. il por Time 88:55-6 S 2 '66

EISNER, Thomas
Beetle's spray discourages predators. Natur Hist 75:42-7 bibliog(p68) F '66
—and Meinwald, Jerrold
Defensive secretions of arthropods. bibliog Science 153:1341-50 S 16 '66
—and others
Tanning of grasshopper eggs by an exocrine secretion. bibliog Science 152:95-7 Ap 1 '66

EJECTION devices (airplanes) See Airplanes—Escape devices

EJECTION devices (space vehicles) See Space vehicles—Escape devices

EKHOLM, Gordon F. See Aveleyra Arroyo de Anda, L. jt. auth.

EKTACHROME films. See Moving picture films; Photography—Films

ELAINE Marie Prevallet, Sister. See Prevallet, E. M.

ELAM, Leland
Waste timber pays for college. il Suc Farm 64:96 S '66

ELANCO products company
Who'll be the 1966 soybean champ? D. Seim. il Farm J 90:44H+ D '66

ELATH, Israel
Hot spot; evicted beats. il Newsweek 67:34 F 7 '66

ELBERT Covell college. See University of the Pacific, Stockton, Calif.

EL CAMINO REAL. See Roads—California

EL CORDOBÉS. See Cordobés

ELDER, Eldon
Soviet scene. Opera N 30:8-13 My 7 '66

EL DORADO HILLS, Calif.
Speed with dependability. il Am City 81:112-13 Ag '66

ELDORADO national forest, Calif. See National forests

ELDRIDGE, Bruce F.
Environmental control of ovarian development in mosquitoes of the culex pipiens complex. bibliog Science 151:826-8 F 18 '66

ELECTION districts
See also
Apportionment (election law)
Gerrymander

ELECTION expenses. See Campaign funds

ELECTION forecasts. See Political forecasts

ELECTION frauds. See Elections—Corrupt practices

ELECTION laws
See also
Voters, Registration of

United States
Challenge from the South; South Carolina v. N. deB. Katzenbach. il Time 87:18-19 Ja 28 '66
Electoral college goes to Court; background to Delaware vs. New York. N. R. Peirce. il Reporter 35:34-7 O 6 '66
Nine supersolons; awaiting Supreme court ruling in Georgia's disputed gubernatorial election. Reporter 35:14+ D 15 '66
What is the law? implications of Supreme court decision on Georgia's governor. New Repub 155:8 D 24 '66

ELECTION lists. See Voters, Registration of

ELECTIONEERING. See Political campaigns

ELECTIONS
See also
Political campaigns

Corrupt practices
How to steal an election. il Changing T 20:45-7 O '66

Alaska
Northern hoorah. Time 88:22 D 2 '66

Argentina
Another putsch in the Argentine? R. Peter. Nat R 18:469 My 17 '66
How much longer? il Time 87:35 F 11 '66
Red Ridinghood & the wolf; Isabel Peron's political activities. il Time 87:34 Mr 11 '66

Australia
Australia votes to stay in Vietnam. D. Warner. il Reporter 35:29-31 D 29 '66
End of a fiery campaign. M. Tatlow. Nat R 18:1208 N 29 '66
Establishing an identity; first federal election since 1963. il Time 88:39 N 25 '66
Two for Vietnam. Newsweek 68:44 D 5 '66
Vanquished Vietniks. Time 88:43 D 2 '66
Vital election. M. Tatlow. Nat R 18:837+ Ag 23 '66

Austria
People's party wins. Time 87:48+ Mr 18 '66
Red & the black; campaign. il Time 87:34 F 25 '66

Bahama Islands
Bad news for the boys; Negro government. il Time 89:32+ Ja 20 '67
Black day on Bay street; first black government. Newsweek 69:47 Ja 23 '67

Bolivia
High flier; Barrientos' victory. il Newsweek 68:44 Jl 18 '66

Brazil
Elections in Brazil; the revolution digs in. N. Raymond and W. P. Carty. il Reporter 35:42-4 S 8 '66
In the Arena. Time 88:47 N 25 '66
Quite the contrary & above all; Costa e Silva's presidential aim. Time 87:32+ F 11 '66
Sure winner. Newsweek 68:65 O 10 '66

Canada
Moving backward? Quebec's provincial elections. il Newsweek 67:48B Je 20 '66

Colombia
Liberals' choice. Newsweek 67:60 My 16 '66
Threat of daggers. il Time 87:36 Ap 1 '66

Costa Rica
Two for the seesaw. Time 87:52 Mr 18 '66

Dominican Republic
Balaguer wins. Commonweal 84:350 Je 17 '66
Dominican election. Reporter 34:11 Je 16 '66
Dominican election; a peaceful vote, a blow to reds. il U S News 60:44 Je 13 '66
Dominican election and the role of the observers. J. Mendelsohn. Christian Cent 83:894-8 Jl 13 '66
Dominican elections; is the U.S. off the hook now? il U S News 60:49 Je 6 '66
Dominican Republic goes to the polls. P. D. Bethel. il Reporter 34:18-20+ Je 2 '66
El gallo colorao ha ganao, or, What happened in Santo Domingo. S. Huck. Nat R 18:617-18 Je 28 '66
Hot moments in a dead heat; June 1 elections. Time 87:41 My 27 '66
Landslide for peace. il Time 87:46-7 Je 10 '66
One year after; a free election and a victory for Balaguer. il Newsweek 67:51-2 Je 13 '66
Outstanding act of democratic purity. il Américas 18:45 Jl '66
Reluctant favorite; candidate Bosch? Newsweek 67:63-4 Ap 18 '66
Unfinished business. Nat R 18:449 My 17 '66
Why Balaguer won; anatomy of a revolution that failed. S. Rodman. New Repub 154:17-21 Je 18 '66

Finland
Forgetting the past. Time 87:34 Ap 1 '66

France
De Gaulle wins run-off. Sr Schol 87:4 Ja 7 '66
Letter from Paris; political campaign in preparation for March elections. Genêt. New Yorker 42:66-7 D 31 '66
Tragic victory of Charles de Gaulle. E. W. Fox. Cur Hist 50:201-8+ Ap '66

Germany (Federal Republic)
Adolf Hitler redivivus; victory of right-wing radical National democratic party. Christian Cent 83:1527 D 14 '66
Erhard in trouble. U S News 61:20 Jl 25 '66
Gloom for Uncle Boom; North Rhine-Westphalia results. Newsweek 68:45 Jl 25 '66
Low on steam; North Rhine-Westphalia elections. il Time 88:31 Jl 22 '66
No fun in Bavaria; emergence of the National democratic party. C. Amery. Nation 203:637-9 D 12 '66

Great Britain
Atlantic report. Atlan 217:30+ Je '66
Big boost for Wilson; victory in a key election; by-elections. U S News 60:14 F 7 '66
Britain: labor's chance to govern. il Newsweek 67:46+ Ap 11 '66
Diminishing third; Liberal party position. Newsweek 67:47 Mr 21 '66
Final fortnight; general election. il Time 87:26 Mr 25 '66
Labor insider vs. the Tory outsider. A. Lewis. il N Y Times Mag p27+ Mr 27 '66

ELECTIONS—Great Britain—*Continued*
Labor sweep. il Time 87:32 Ap 8 '66
Labor's big sweep. Sr Schol 88:21 Ap 15 '66
Labor's victory H. Brandon. Sat R 49:11 Ap 23 '66
Letter from London. M. Panter-Downes. New Yorker 42:131-2+ Ap 16 '66
Make or break year; general election. il Newsweek 67:45 Mr 14 '66
No furs; trip to Moscow, electoral fodder. il Newsweek 67:48 Mr 7 '66
Right extraordinary Harold Wilson wins his big victory. J. Hicks. il Life 60:44-44B+ Ap 8 '66
Socialist landslide in Britain, its meaning to U.S. U S News 60:6 Ap 11 '66
Vote where U.S. policy is the issue. U S News 60:16 Mr 28 '66
We're on our way, brothers! general election to be March 31. il Time 87:37 Mr 11 '66
What does it mean? A. Lejeune. Nat R 18: 354-5 Ap 19 '66
Wilson sounds the call for all British voters. il Bsns W p35-6 Mr 5 '66
Yorkshire pudding; Labor wins Hull by-election. il Time 87:31-2 F 4 '66

Guatemala
Two for the seesaw. Time 87:52 Mr 18 '66
Where another red revolt is brewing on U.S. doorstep. C. Migdail. il U S News 60:53-4 Mr 7 '66

Ireland
Nostalgic debt; presidential election result. Newsweek 67:65 Je 13 '66

Israel
Atlantic report. Atlan 217:24+ F '66

Italy
Red reverse. Time 87:36 Je 24 '66
Toward the center; local elections. Newsweek 67:48+ Je 27 '66

Japan
First test for Sato. il Time 89:26 Ja 6 '67
See also
Political campaigns—Japan

Laos
Fragile web. il Time 89:24+ Ja 13 '67
How to win at dominoes. Newsweek 69:42 Ja 16 '67

Latin America
Two forward, one back; El Salvador, Guatemala and Colombia. Newsweek 67:58 Mr 28 '66

Malta
Elections in Malta. C. Cardona. America 114: 412-14 Mr 26 '66

New Zealand
Two for Vietnam. Newsweek 68:44 D 5 '66
Victory over shame. Time 88:43 D 2 '66

South Africa
Election in the beloved country. Nat R 18: 348+ Ap 19 '66
Forward with Verwoerd. il Newsweek 67:52 Ap 11 '66
Forward with Verwoerd. Time 87:39 Ap 8 '66
Thunder on the right. Newsweek 67:52+ Mr 14 '66

Spain
See also
Political campaigns—Spain

United States
America votes 1966; the patterns, the issues, the key races. il Sr Schol 89:8-10+ S 30 '66
Atlantic report; Vietnam issue. D. Kiker. Atlan 218:4, 8+ N '66
Back to normal. Reporter 35:12 D 1 '66
Back to the middle way. il Bsns W p39-40 N 12 '66
Confusing clutter; the referendum. Time 88: 32-3 N 18 '66
Conservatives, si. M. S. Evans. Nat R 18:1091-3+ N 1 '66
Crucial struggle for forty-five congressional seats. L. Lamont. il Fortune 74:124-7+ S '66
Death of the New deal. W. D. Burnham. Commonweal 85:284-7 D 9 '66
Effects of election. il U S News 61:35-42+ N 21 '66
Effects of November 8. H. Brandon. Sat R 49:20+ S 10 '66
Election near; mood of voters. il U S News 61:50-2+ O 24 '66
Election 1966; resentment and unreality. il Sat Eve Post 239:94 N 5 '66
Election story that keeps growing. il U S News 61:40-2 N 28 '66

Election; what did it mean? W. F. Buckley, jr. Nat R 18:1207 N 29 '66
Elections; returns. Nation 203:530 N 21 '66
Elections; the East; the South; the Midwest; the West; results. il Time 88:23-32 N 18 '66
Elephant lives. il Sat Eve Post 239:92 D 17 '66
End of Johnson's Congress? conduct of the war in Vietnam. W. V. Shannon. Commonweal 84:433-4 Jl 8 '66
Georgia happening; election nobody won; gubernatorial election. S. Meyer. il Nation 203:640-4 D 12 '66
Goodbye to all that; indications of results. A. Kopkind. New Repub 155:7-8 N 19 '66
GOP '66; back on the map; election results, with table. il Newsweek 68:31-4 N 21 '66
G.O.P. stars who came on strong. il Life 61:44-44B N 18 '66
How we would vote in key elections. Life 61:2B O 28 '66
Ins and outs; highlights from across the Nation. il Newsweek 68:43-4+ N 21 '66
Issues that will tip the '66 elections. C. B. Seib. il Nations Bsns 54:38-9+ Mr '66
Key Republicans with new stature. il U S News 61:26-7 N 21 '66
Lester leaps in; Maddox gains governorship. il Newsweek 69:29-30 Ja 23 '67
Letter from Washington. R. H. Rovere. New Yorker 42:197-201 N 19 '66
LBJ and the elections; trouble ahead. L. H. Bean and R. Drummond. Look 30:89-90 O 4 '66
National conference for surrender; Vietnam issue. Nat R 18:562-4 Je 14 '66
90th Congress; the men; the issues. il Bsns W p41-4 N 12 '66
Off & running. Time 87:32 My 20 '66
Only in Georgia; dead heat and deadlock in Gainesville. Nation 203:692 D 26 '66
Outlook for November. il Time 87:25-6 Mr 11 '66
Peace candidates; Viet Nam issue in November's elections. Time 87:25 Je 17 '66
Politics heats up; election outlook now; congressional and gubernatorial races. U S News 60:42-4 Mr 28 '66
Politics; the white backlash, 1966. il Newsweek 68:27-8 O 10 '66
Question of how big; Republican gain. Time 88:31 N 4 '66
Racialism in the elections. T. Dearmore; A. Schardt; J. A. Maxwell. il Reporter 35:24-32 O 20 '66
Reading election tea leaves; election results. Christian Cent 83:1431 N 23 '66
Republican rebound. America 115:638 N 19 '66
Republicans battle for gains in West, mood of voters; survey. il U S News 61:83-4+ O 10 '66
Republicans win key contests. il Sr Schol 89:23 N 18 '66
$64 question; the '66 election. P. Lisagor. il Nations Bsns 54:19-20 Jl '66
Soapy & some others. Time 87:26-7 Mr 11 '66
T.R.B. from Washington; Republican recovery; midterm election, 1966. New Repub 154:4 Mr 12 '66
Test run for '68. P. Good; L. H. Bean; S. Gottlieb. il Nation 203:570-8 N 28 '66
Three races; Georgia, Texas and Ohio. H. Alexander. Nat R 18:1042-5 O 18 '66
Two-party system is back. Life 61:4 N 18 '66
Unions fail to deliver the goods. Bsns W p 103+ N 19 '66
Vietnam and the voter. W. D. Burnham. Commonweal 84:635-7 S 30 '66
Vietnam election. W. V. Shannon. Commonweal 85:249-50 D 2 '66
Vote for political competition. Fortune 74: 133 D '66
Voter backlash over race issue? il U S News 61:34-6 S 19 '66
Wanted; a responsible majority; congressional elections. D. Lawrence. U S News 61:112 O 31 '66
War and the election. W. Lippmann. Newsweek 68:23 D 5 '66
Washington desk; GOP's prospects and campaign issues. J. R. Slevin. Duns R 87:5-6 My '66
What worries the voter. il Bsns W p33-4 O 29 '66
What's happening? Commonweal 85:93-4 O 28 '66
When anxiety hides beneath affluence. J. N. Eller. America 115:683 N 26 '66
Who will win on November 8? il U S News 61:35-9 N 7 '66
Who won? analysis of 1966 elections. Nat R 18:1200-2 N 29 '66
Who won the election? the Negro or white bigotry. Christian Cent 83:1369 N 9 '66

ELECTIONS—United States—*Continued*
Wide range of issues settled by the voters.
U S News 61:24 N 21 '66
See also
Candidates, Political
National conventions (political)
Presidential campaigns
Presidential candidates
Primaries
Public opinion polls
Senators—Election
Voting

Vietnam (Republic)

As election nears in Vietnam; what's at
stake. il U S News 61:32-3 S 5 '66
Beginning. il Time 88:30 S 23 '66
Campaign non-promises. il Newsweek 68:47
S 12 '66
Campaigners; preparing for the election. il
Newsweek 67:25 My 2 '66
Election. Nation 203:266-7 S 26 '66
Election for nationhood. il Time 88:38 S 16
'66
Elections in Vietnam: prelude to an honor-
able settlement? Trans-van-Dinh. New Re-
pub 155:19-22 Jl 2 '66
Heavy vote. il Newsweek 68:60 S 26 '66
Huge vote explodes a Vietcong myth; with
report by D. Moser. il Life 61:34-5 S 23 '66
Letter from Saigon. R. Shaplen. New Yorker
42:120+ Ag 20 '66
Pregnant choice; Viet Cong terror raids to
hinder voting in South Vietnam. il News-
week 68:58 S 19 '66
Reconnaissance by handlebar; pre-election
buildup. il Time 88:17 Ag 26 '66
There's a war on. Nat R 18:450 My 17 '66
To the polls. Sr Schol 89:19-20 S 23 '66
Toward the election. Time 88:35 S 9 '66
U.S. supports Viet-Nam request for U.N.
election observers; excerpt from address by
A. J. Goldberg. Dept State Bul 54:1028
Je 27 '66
Uses of power; Ky issues electoral laws. il
Newsweek 68:36 Jl 11 '66
Vietnam elections. New Repub 155:5-6+ S
17: 8 S 24 '66
Vietnam prepares for elections. D. Warner.
Reporter 35:12-15 Ag 11 '66
Vietnam voters raise hopes for the future.
il Bsns W p 155-6 S 17 '66
Vietnam's twelve elections. B. B. Fall. New
Repub 154:12-15 My 14 '66; Correction. 154:
29 My 28 '66
Viewpoints: elections in South Viet Nam;
press comments. il Sr Schol 89:21 S 30 '66
Vote in Vietnam. Commonweal 84:601-2 S 23
'66
Voting here and there. K. Crawford. News-
week 68:39 S 26 '66

ELECTORAL college
Electoral college goes to Court; background
to Delaware vs. New York. N. R. Peirce.
il Reporter 35:34-7 O 6 '66
How much power? Johnson's proposal. il
Time 87:17-18 Ja 28 '66
Should the electoral college be abolished,
retained, or reformed? three-sided discussion. il Sr Schol 88:11-13 Mr 18 '66
Will Supreme court guard these rights, too?
suit by the state of Delaware to revise the
system whereby we elect our presidents.
F. Morley. Nations Bsns 54:27-8 O '66

ELECTRIC alarms
Build a power-failure alarm. C. Caringella.
il Pop Mech 126:200-1+ O '66
Build a swimming pool splash alarm. F.
Maynard. il Pop Electr 25:48-9+ Jl '66
Don't panic, push the button! B. M. Larsen.
il Pop Electr 24:45-7 Ja '66
Temperature sentry guards against freeze-
up. H. P. Strand. il Pop Mech 126:159-60
N '66
Transistorized auto-light minder. R. G.
Persing. il Pop Electr 24:65-7 Ap '66
See also
Automobiles—Electric equipment
Burglar alarms
Fire alarms

ELECTRIC anesthesia
Sleep machine. il Sci Digest 59:9 Ap '66

ELECTRIC apparatus and appliances
See also
Electric apparatus industry
Electric motors
Induction coils

Saftey devices and measures

Look out! it's hot! C. Sheridan. il Pop Electr
24:51-5+ Je '66
See also
Insulation (electric)

ELECTRIC apparatus and appliances, Cord-
less
H&G's guide to cordless appliances. House
& Gard 129:34+ My '66

ELECTRIC apparatus and appliances, Domestic
Blenders, juicers, extractors: which ones for
you? il Redbook 127:91+ O '66
Electric food mixers. il Consumer Rep 32:26-
31 Ja '67
Grinding nuts the easy way. il Consumer
Bul 49:34 Mr '66
Home appliances: how smart can they get?
W. S. Bacon. il Pop Sci 188:96-9+ Mr '66
Ice crushers; with electric-blender attach-
ments. il Consumer Rep 31:276-9 Je '66
Machines: your master or your servant. R.
Chadwick. il Suc Farm 64:101+ S '66
Push-button grooming; electric appliances
for personal care. il Redbook 127:31+ Jl '66
Small broiler. il Consumer Bul 50:27 Ja '67
Star performer: the blender that cooks. il
House & Gard 129:50-1 Je '66
Three rivals for the whisk broom; rechar-
geable, battery-powered, electric clothes
brush. il Consumer Rep 31:559 N '66
Two new blenders with many push buttons,
one even has a built-in cooker. il Con-
sumer Bul 49:24-5 S '66
Wild color invades the kitchen. M. David-
son. il Ladies Home J 83:76-7 Ag '66
See also
Electric toasters
Heating pads, Electric
Waffle irons

Repairing

Before calling a repairman, check this list. il
Good H 162:177 Mr '66
Toaster doesn't pop? fix it yourself, mom;
Proctor-Silex new kitchen appliances. il
Bsns W p42 Ja 7 '67

Safety devices and measures

Ground appliances for electrical safety. il
Consumer Bul 49:19-21 Mr '66
Our not-quite-safe appliances. il Changing T
20:17-19 S '66

ELECTRIC apparatus industry
Italy finds a bonanza in Europe's kitchens;
dominates refrigerator market. il Bsns W
p 104-5+ O 8 '66
See also
Philco-Ford corporation
Proctor-Silex corporation

ELECTRIC automobiles. See Automobiles,
Electric

ELECTRIC batteries
Voltage-regulated battery power supply. F.
G. Stiver. il Pop Electr 25:85-6+ N '66
See also
Fuel cells
Solar batteries
Storage batteries

ELECTRIC blankets, coverlets, etc.
Electric blanket without wires. il Consumer
Bul 49:16-17 Ap '66

ELECTRIC blenders. See Electric apparatus
and appliances, Domestic

ELECTRIC broilers. See Electric apparatus and
appliances, Domestic

ELECTRIC cables
See also
Television cables

ELECTRIC cables, Underground
Underground residential distribution. il Arch
Rec 139:181-4 Ja '66

ELECTRIC can openers. See Can openers

ELECTRIC capacitance
Capacitance measuring nomogram. M. H.
Applebaum. il Electr World 75:29+ Ja '66
RC waveshaping. W. B. Ross. il Electr
World 75:78 F '66

ELECTRIC capacitors
Capacitor know-how simplifies electronic pro-
jects; selection of fixed capacitors. C. G.
Cunningham. il Pop Electr 25:41-7 Jl '66
Combination BC substitution box. C. A.
Phillips. il Pop Electr 24:82-3 Ja '66

Testing

Testing and measuring capacitors. R. C.
Lynds and D. Quimby. il Electr World 76:
39-41+ S '66

ELECTRIC cars. See Electric railroads

ELECTRIC circuits
Impossible circuit. L. Vicens. il Pop Electr
25:72 O '66
Impossible circuit made possible. il Pop Electr
25:79 O '66
Switching-mode power conversion. D. E.
Lancaster. il Electr World 76:87-90 S '66
See also
Electronic circuits
Impedance (electricity)
Printed circuits
Television circuits

ELECTRIC clothes brushes. See Electric apparatus and appliances, Domestic
ELECTRIC clothes dryers. See Clothes dryers
ELECTRIC coffee pots. See Coffee pots, percolators, etc.
ELECTRIC coils
  See also
  Electric reactors
  Induction coils
ELECTRIC combination locks. See Locks and keys
ELECTRIC conductivity
  See also
  Superconductivity
ELECTRIC conductors
  See also
  Electric resistors
  Semiconductors
ELECTRIC connectors
  Right connections; phono plug. A. Sterling. il Hi Fi 16:108-9 O '66
ELECTRIC control
  See also
  Electric switches
  Voltage regulators
ELECTRIC control, Remote. See Remote control
ELECTRIC converters. See Electric current converters
ELECTRIC current converters
  Electromechanical choppers; converting low-level d.c. to a.c. pulses. S. L. Silver. il Electr World 76:42-5+ Ag '66
  Switching-mode power conversion. D. E. Lancaster. il Electr World 76:87-90 S '66
ELECTRIC current rectifiers
  Build a handful of power; a.c.-operated d.c. power supply. E. M. Long. il Pop Electr 25:53 S '66
  Designing a transformerless power supply. R. C. Boucher. il Electr World 75:86-8 Ap '66
  SCR revolution. J. E. Mungenast. il Electr World 75:23-6 F '66
ELECTRIC currents

Grounding
Ground appliances for electrical safety. il Consumer Bul 49:19-21 Mr '66
ELECTRIC discharges through gases
  Amateur scientist; electrical discharges in a gas. N. A. Steiner. il Sci Am 215:102-4 Ag '66
  See also
  Plasma (ionized gases)
ELECTRIC distribution
  See also
  Electric lines
  Electric plants—Interconnection
ELECTRIC drills. See Drilling and boring machinery
ELECTRIC drills, Portable. See Drilling and boring machinery
ELECTRIC eels
  Nature note. Sci N 90:215 S 17 '66
  Shocking electric eel; reprint. il Sci Digest 59:75-7 Ap '66
ELECTRIC engineering

Study and teaching
Big blackout: whooping cranes & power failures; need for preserving technology of power engineering. L. J. Hollander; reply with rejoinder. J. J. Storrow. Nation 202: inside cover Ja 24 '66
ELECTRIC engines, Outboard
  All about electric outboards. F. M. Paulson. il Field & S 71:124-7 S '66
ELECTRIC equipment
  See also
  Audio-visual aids
ELECTRIC equipment industry
  Sweden's ASEA jolts electricity's future; Allmanna svenska elektriska aktiebolaget. il Bsns W p80-4 Ag 27 '66
ELECTRIC fans
  Personal desk fans. il Consumer Rep 31: 391 Ag '66
ELECTRIC farming. See Electricity on the farm
ELECTRIC field
  Amateur scientist; study of electrostatic effects. R. Hayward. il Sci Am 216:124-8 Ja '67
  Heterogeneous catalysis: effect of an alternating electric field. V. J. Lee. il Science 152:514 Ap 22 '66
  Thunderstorm electrification of hail and graupel by polar dribble. R. Gunn. il Science 151:686 F 11 '66
ELECTRIC floor washers. See Floor machines

ELECTRIC fruit juice extractors. See Fruit juice extractors
ELECTRIC generators
  Build a handful of power; a.c.-operated d.c. power supply. E. M. Long. il Pop Electr 25: 53 S '66
  Energy at the mine mouth; M. Gourdine's electrogasdynamic generator. il Time 87: 42+ Je 3 '66
  New converter does it? power your tools anywhere. C. E. Rhine. il Pop Sci 189: 167 O '66
  See also
  Pulse generators
  Thermionic converters
ELECTRIC generators, Electrostatic
  Supercharged salt shaker; making Van de Graaff electrostatic generator. E. Francis. il Pop Electr 24:57-60 My '66
ELECTRIC grills
  Teflon-coated electric griddles. il Consumer Bul 49:6-7 O '66
ELECTRIC guitar. See Guitar
ELECTRIC hair dryers. See Hair dryers
ELECTRIC heating
  Electric heat for your home? H. Manchester. Read Digest 90:157-8+ Ja '67
  Electric heating, the ifs, ands & buts. il Changing T 20:31-4 O '66
  How practical is electric heat? Bet Hom & Gard 44:119-20 N '66
  Utilities warm up the battle over electric heat. il Bsns W p 147-8 Je 25 '66
ELECTRIC heating pads. See Heating pads, Electric
ELECTRIC inductance. See Inductance
ELECTRIC industries
  See also
  Collective bargaining—Electric industries
  also names of electric industry companies, e.g. General electric company

Wages and hours
Now a pattern for wages and fringes in 1967; General electric settlement. il U S News 61:76-7 O 31 '66
ELECTRIC instruments
  See also
  Radio instruments
ELECTRIC insulation. See Insulation (electric)
ELECTRIC irons
  Spray-steam irons. il Consumer Bul 49:6-11 F '66
ELECTRIC knives. See Knives
ELECTRIC lamps
  Caveat emptor as related to the Perky-D high intensity lamp. Consumer Bul 49:14 F '66
  Extra-life light bulbs. il Consumer Rep 31: 392-4 Ag '66
  High intensity light: help or hazard? N. Pierce. il Parents Mag 41:176 N '66
  I'd rather, three way, switch than fight. P. Farber. il U S Camera 29:46-7+ Je '66
  Light bulbs. il Consumer Bul 49:19-22 O '66
  Light touch; high-intensity lamps. il Seventeen 25:308 Ag '66
  Make a low cost slave tripper; lighting for indoor shots. T. Owen. il Pop Mech 127: 173+ Ja '67
  New lights refresh their entry. il Sunset 136:147-8 Ap '66
  Selecting the proper indicating light; lamps suited to pilot-light service. W. Walker. il Electr World 76:29-32+ Ag '66
  Sports under lights; address, March 1965. R. E. Faucett. il Parks & Rec 1:726-7+ S '66
  Two heads are better than one, when one is the Omega variable-contrast head. B. Hoffman. il Pop Phot 59:112-13 D '66
  What's new in decorative light bulbs? il Sunset 136:119-20 F '66
  When power goes: light, for a price; battery-operated or plug-in. il Consumer Rep 31: 472-3 O '66
  See also
  Electric lighting
ELECTRIC lamps, Flashing
  It's the Jinniflash. L. E. Garner, jr. il Pop Electr 24:56-9 Je '66
ELECTRIC lamps, Flashlight
  AG bulbs as super-cubes. N. Rothschild. il Pop Phot 59:84-5+ Jl '66
  Behold the lowly flashcube. D. L. Miller. il Mod Phot 30:72-3 Je '66
  Blue bulbs O.K. for B&W, too. C. W. Kennedy. Pop Phot 58:44 Mr '66
  Electronic flash: a comparative study. P. R. Farber. il U S Camera 29:52-5 O '66
  Electronic flash problems exposed. D. B. Eisendrath, jr. Pop Phot 60:16+ Ja '67
  Flash equipment. il Pop Phot 59:192-201 N '66

ELECTRIC lamps, Flashlight—*Continued*
Hitch any camera to a flashcube, if you can
find one. L. Samuels. il Pop Mech 126:180-
1 O '66
How to bounce a cube. C. W. Kennedy. il
Pop Phot 58:14+ Je '66
Portable electronic flash units. il Consumer
Bul 49:23-6 O '66
Strobes as a sideline. P. Stackpole. U S
Camera 29:28+ S '66
Tony Karp on 35mm; electronic flash. T.
Karp. il Mod Phot 31:14+ Ja '67
ELECTRIC lamps, Fluorescent
Alaska grower imports Florida sun; vege-
tables grown under fluorescent lamps. il
Bsns W p58-9 Ap 30 '66
ELECTRIC lamps, Incandescent
Hi-fi à go-go lamps; incandescent lamps
controlled by audio signal. D. Lancaster. il
Pop Electr 24:64-6+ Ja '66
ELECTRIC lamps, Mercury vapor
Mercuries mean more light for less money;
Wolcott, Conn. E. Bagley, jr. il Am City
81:114 Jl '66
ELECTRIC lamps, Reflector. See Reflectors
ELECTRIC light bulbs. See Electric lamps
ELECTRIC lighting
Approach to residential lighting. D. A. Mintz.
il Arch Rec 139:7+ mid-My '66
Easy living means easy seeing. il House &
Gard 131:110-11 Ja '67
Twenty-three ways to improve your home
lighting. C. P. Gilmore. il Pop Sci 189:172-7
S '66

Control

Full moon every night; automatic light-sensi-
tive control. il Suc Farm 64:N4 S '66
Hi-fi à go-go lamps; incandescent lamps con-
trolled by audio signal. D. Lancaster. il
Pop Electr 24:64-6+ Ja '66
Improving your home wiring; how to install
light dimmers. G. Daniels. il Pop Sci 188:
174-8+ F '66
ELECTRIC lines
Major power grid will prevent blackout. Sci
N L 89:98 F 12 '66
Power-line spike absorber. R. L. Ives. il
Electr World 75:88 Mr '66
Time domain reflectometry; measuring trans-
mission-line characteristics by means of
step generator and oscilloscope. J. D. Lenk.
il Electr World 76:48-50+ S '66

Poles

Stainless steel poles gain. il Am City 81:
103-4 Jl '66

Underground

We went underground to find beauty; Forest
Grove, Ore. H. Sherman. il Am City 81:
126+ Ag '66
ELECTRIC machinery
See also
Electricity on the farm

Control

Add an electric brake to your saw. J. D.
Griffith. il Pop Mech 125:194+ Mr '66
ELECTRIC manicure sets. See Manicuring
ELECTRIC measurements
See also
Inductance
Potentiometers
Strain gages
ELECTRIC meters
Diode meter protectors. A. A. Mangieri. il
Electr World 76:56-7+ N '66
Meter-relay devices. S. L. Silver. il Electr
World 75:36-8+ Mr '66
Popular science's nine-in-one troubleshooter.
R. M. Benrey. il Pop Sci 188:114-17+ F;
138-40+ Mr; 192-4 Ap '66
See also
Voltohmmeters

Testing

Confused about S-units? M. Lincoln. il Pop
Electr 24:54-6+ Ap '66
ELECTRIC mixers. See Electric apparatus and
appliances, Domestic
ELECTRIC motor trucks. See Motor trucks,
Electric
ELECTRIC motors
Big-tractor power on single-phase current. D.
Hagen. il Farm J 90:56S O '66
Magic motor. W. B. Ford. il Pop Electr 26:
68-9 Ja '67
Not just for hurricanes; auxiliary engine
in the water plant. R. C. Mills. il Am
City 81:100-1 Ap '66
ELECTRIC mowers. See Lawn mowers

ELECTRIC plants
Lighting up with coal; Mohave power
project. Time 89:78 Ja 20 '67
See also
Atomic power plants
Hydroelectric plants

Interconnection

Big blackout: whooping cranes & power
failures; need for preserving technology
of power engineering. L. J. Hollander;
reply with rejoinder. J. J. Storrow. Nation 202:inside cover Ja 24 '66
Keeping the lights from going out again. il
Bsns W p 136+ N 5 '66
What's needed to prevent more power blackouts. il Consumer Rep 31:136-42 Mr '66
ELECTRIC plants, Cooperative
Co-op faces legal dim-out; Supreme court's
bars help to Colorado-Ute electric assn's
plant at Hayden, Colo. Bsns W p44 O 29
'66

ELECTRIC polishers. See Polishers, Electric
ELECTRIC power
Anniversary of the night; power failure of
1965. Time 88:34 N 11 '66
Blackout: can it happen in your town? C. P.
Gilmore. il Pop Sci 188:92-5+ F '66
Blackout fallout; birth rate rise in New York
city nine months after blackout. Time 88:
40-1 Ag 19 '66
Designing a transformerless power supply.
R. C. Boucher. il Electr World 75:86-8 Ap
'66
Did flying saucers cause the blackout? ex-
cerpts from Incident at Exeter. J. G. Ful-
ler. il Pop Mech 126:100-2+ N '66
Economy through air power; compressed-air
storage of electricity; H.-J. Martini plan.
il Time 87:70 F 4 '66
Fast thinking and action on NAL's blackout
quickie; Night the lights went out. il Pub
W 189:122-3 F 7 '66
Guns and butter plus; Dickey-Lincoln scheme.
R. Moley. Newsweek 67:96 F 28 '66
How to be prepared for a power failure. il
House & Gard 129:40 My '66
Keeping the lights from going out again.
il Bsns W p 136+ N 5 '66
New England's power politics; Dickey-Lincoln
school project. P. Barnes; reply with re-
joinder. J. C. Cleveland. Reporter 34:6+
F 10 '66
Planning for reliable electric power. F. J.
Walsh. il Arch Rec 139:187-92 F; 185-8
Mr '66
Power politics in New England; importing
low-cost power from Canada. V. Maerki.
New Repub 154:10 Ja 29 '66
What the blackout taught us. B. H. Frisch.
il Sci Digest 59:10-14 F '66
What's needed to prevent more power black-
outs. il Consumer Rep 31:136-42 Mr '66
See also
Electric motors
Electric plants
Tennessee Valley authority
United States—Rural electrification admin-
istration
Voltage regulators

Transmission

See Electric transmission

Canada

Canada's coming export: hydroelectric power.
il U S News 60:74-6 F 7 '66
ELECTRIC power lines. See Electric lines
ELECTRIC power plants. See Electric plants
ELECTRIC power production from chemical
action
High-energy demands press technology;
alkali metal electrochemical power systems.
W. E. Wilks. Tech W 19:14-15 O 3 '66
See also
Fuel cells
ELECTRIC railroads
Frimbo's frolic; excursion arranged by the
Electric railroaders association; interview.
E. M. Frimbo. New Yorker 42:22-5 Ja
14 '67
Goodbye to the interurban. W. D. Middleton.
il Am Heritage 17:30-41+ Ap '66
ELECTRIC razors. See Razors
ELECTRIC reactors
How to select R.F. Chokes. J. Tartas. il
Electr World 75:48-51+ My '66
ELECTRIC rectifiers. See Electric current recti-
fiers
ELECTRIC refrigerators. See Refrigerators,
Electric

ELECTRIC relays
Meter-relay devices. S. L. Silver. il Electr World 75:36-8+ Mr '66
ELECTRIC resistance
Electrical resistivity changes in saturated rock under stress. W. F Brace and A. S. Orange. bibliog il Science 153:1525-6 S 23 '66
RC waveshaping. W. B. Ross. il Electr World 75:78 F '66
See also
Impedance (electricity)
ELECTRIC resistors
Combination RC substitution box. C. A. Phillips. il Pop Electr 24:82-3 Ja '66
Variable resistors; symposium. il Electr World 75:37-60 Ap '66
See also
Rheostats
Thermistors

Testing
Testing and measuring resistors. F. Stern. il Electr World 76:44-6 S '66
ELECTRIC rheostats. See Rheostats
ELECTRIC saws. See Saws
ELECTRIC service. Rural
See also
United States—Rural electrification administration
ELECTRIC shavers. See Razors
ELECTRIC shock
Effects of electroshock on memory: amnesia without convulsions. J. L. McGaugh and H. P. Alpern. bibliog il Science 152:665-6 Ap 29 '66
Freezing dagger; Portuguese soccer players jolted by electric shock in pool. Newsweek 68:64 D 19 '66
Look out! it's hot! C. Sheridan. il Pop Electr 24:51-5 Je '66
Recovery of memory after amnesia induced by electroconvulsive shock. S. Zinkin and A. J. Miller. bibliog il Science 155:102-4 Ja 6 '67
See also
Electricity. Injuries from
ELECTRIC signs
You have a cluttered mess; NESA meeting. il Time 87:82 Mr 25 '66
ELECTRIC steam irons. See Electric irons
ELECTRIC storage battery company
Battery firm. affiliate aim for modest electric auto. L. J. Curran. il Tech W 19:36-7 N 7 '66
ELECTRIC stoves
Choose a range that's right for you. il Parents Mag 41:63-6+ My '66
Kitchen ranges. Consumer Rep 31:54-9 D '66
ELECTRIC switches
Build this amazing touch-controlled switch; toggle switch. R. F. Graf. il Pop Sci 189:114-16 S '66
Carrier-current remote-control system. R. Zarr. il Pop Electr 26:50-3 Ja '67
Electric dice game. K. Greenberg. il Pop Electr 25:78 Jl '66
Foto facts: Dialite. P. Farber. il U S Camera 29:34-5 N '66
Reluctant (or overeager) genie; Sonuswitch to turn on or off any electrical appliance. il Consumer Rep 31:267-8 Je '66
Selecting the proper switch. B. Golbeck. il Electr World 76:42-3+ S '66
Two-wire three-way switching circuit. R. C. Hitchcock and G. E. Weber. il Pop Electr 25:88 Jl '66
ELECTRIC testing
Life testing of R.F. inductors. W. D. Hauser. il Electr World 76:60 S '66
ELECTRIC toasters
Electric toasters. il Consumer Rep 31:227-31 My '66
Toaster you build into a wall. J. Burroughs. il Pop Sci 188:172-3 F '66
ELECTRIC tools, Portable
Portable combination power tool kit. il Consumer Bul 49:2 D '66
Rockwell bets on its own name. il Bsns W p85 Ap 23 '66
Roundup of new tools for the hardware show. il Pop Sci 189:198+ N '66
See also
Garden tools, equipment and supplies
ELECTRIC toothbrushes. See Toothbrushes
ELECTRIC toothpicks. See Toothpicks. Electric
ELECTRIC toys
This magic box plays a game, can you beat it? R. M. Benrey. il Pop Sci 189:100-1+ Ag '66
ELECTRIC transformers
Direct-current transformer. Sci Am 215:71 N '66

Hermetically sealed transformer cuts utility costs; Rocky Mount. N.C. C. Bateman. il Am City 81:104 Ag '66
ELECTRIC transmission
Blackout: can it happen in your town? C. P. Gilmore. il Pop Sci 188:92-5+ F '66
See also
Corona (electricity)
Electric lines
Electric power
ELECTRIC units
Comes the revolution or 40 million Frenchmen can't be wrong; changing from cycles to hertz. il Pop Electr 24:91 My '66
Old World standards breaking through; substituting hertz for cycles. Pop Electr 24:28 Ap '66
ELECTRIC voltage regulators. See Voltage regulators
ELECTRIC waffle irons. See Waffle irons
ELECTRIC washing machines. See Washing machines
ELECTRIC water coolers
Old office standby freshens up its style. il Bsns W p68+ Jl 9 '66
ELECTRIC water heaters. See Water heaters
ELECTRIC waves
See also
Electromagnetic waves
Microwaves
ELECTRIC welding
Amateur scientist; two devices for electric welding, one using a carbon arc torch and the other a rattrap. R. Cushman. il Sci Am 215:144-9 N '66
ELECTRIC welding machines
How good are those $14.95 welders? il Pop Sci 189:175-7 O '66
ELECTRIC wire and wiring
How to install 1-v wiring; low-voltage lighting. il Sunset 137:79-80+ Jl '66
Improving your home wiring (cont) G. Daniels. il Pop Sci 188:174-8+ F; 154-7+ Mr '66
Outdoor wiring that's easy and safe. J. Parker. il Pop Sci 189:146-8+ Ag '66
ELECTRIC workers
Army field calibration technicians. C. J. Diodati. il Electr World 76:80-2 S '66
Careers in electronics; job opportunities for electronics technicians. K. Gilmore. il Pop Electr 25:47-51+ O '66
Project choose:
Correspondence schools. K. Gilmore. il Pop Electr 24:41-9 F '66
See also
International brotherhood of electrical workers
Strikes—United States—Electric workers
ELECTRICAL apparatus and appliances
See also
Exercising equipment
ELECTRICAL reducing devices. See Exercising equipment
ELECTRICITY
See also
Atmospheric electricity
Corona (electricity)
Fuel cells
Magnetism

Discharges through gases
See Electric discharges through gases

Experiments
Why a shower is bracing; atmosphere of a bathroom electrified whenever water runs. il Time 87:51 My 6 '66
ELECTRICITY, Atmospheric. See Atmospheric electricity
ELECTRICITY, Injuries from
Shock can damage bone. Sci N 90:99 Ag 13 '66
See also
Electric shock
ELECTRICITY in the home
Ohm's law chart; how to figure the electrical load. il Pop Mech 126:162 S '66
See also
Apartment houses—Electric equipment
Electric lighting
ELECTRICITY on the farm
Big-tractor power on single-phase current. D. Hagen. il Farm J 90:56S O '66
Full moon every night; automatic light-sensitive control. il Suc Farm 64:N4 S '66
See also
United States—Rural electrification administration
ELECTROBIOLOGY. See Electrophysiology
ELECTROCARDIOGRAPHY
Fickle heart; electrocardiograms. il Time 87:72 My 13 '66

ELECTROCARDIOGRAPHY—*Continued*
Pacemaker synchronization. C. E. Anagnostopoulos and others. il Science 153:1636 S 30 '66
Remote ECG system transmits patterns by phone. il Todays Health 44:92 O '66
See also
Vectorcardiography

ELECTROCHEMICAL devices. See Fuel cells

ELECTROCHEMISTRY
Headaches go into the test tube. il Bsns W p54+ Ag 6 '66
See also
Electrolysis
Electroorganic chemistry
Fuel cells
Reduction, Electrolytic

ELECTRODEPOSITION of metals. See Electroforming

ELECTRODES
Calcium in sea water by electrode measurement. M. E. Thompson and J. W. Ross, jr. bibliog il Science 154:1643-4 D 30 '66
Electrode for sensing fluoride ion activity in solution. M. S. Frant and J. W. Ross, jr. bibliog il Science 154:1553-5 D 23 '66
Marking single neurons by staining with intracellular recording microelectrodes. R. C. Thomas and V. J. Wilson. bibliog il Science 151:1538-9 Mr 25 '66

ELECTRODYNAMICS, Quantum. See Quantum electrodynamics

ELECTROENCEPHALOGRAMS. See Electroencephalography

ELECTROENCEPHALOGRAPHY
Anatomy of slumber; brain wave tracing by electroencephalograph. P. McBroom. il Sci N 90:254-5 O 1 '66
Brain affects crime; no correlation between EEG abnormality and brain disorder. Sci N 90:98 Ag 13 '66
Electrodes in the brain; help for psychomotor epileptics. il Time 87:51-3 Je 10 '66
Electroencephalographic activation: nonspecific habituation by verbal stimuli. T. Mulholland and E. Davis. bibliog il Science 152:1104-6 My 20 '66
Periventricular cerebral impedance after intraventricular injection of calcium. H. H. Wang and others. bibliog il Science 154:1183-5 D 2 '66
Simultaneous changes in visual separation threshold and voltage of cortical alpha rhythm. J. Anliker. bibliog il Science 153:316-18 Jl 15 '66
What is life? when is death? il Time 87:78 My 27 '66

ELECTROFORMING
EOS expanding applications of electroforming techniques. il Tech W 19:38-9 Ag 22 '66
EOS probes electrodeposited composite structures market. J. F. Judge. il Tech W 19:26+ N 14 '66

ELECTROHYDRAULIC effect
Sterilization by electrohydraulic treatment. M. Allen and K. Soike. il Science 154:155-7 O 7 '66

ELECTROLUX corporation
Hard sell at Electrolux. Fortune 74:300 Jl 15 '66

ELECTROLYSIS
Lunar metal production plant seen feasible; mobile plant may use electrolysis to melt lunar surface material. J. F. Judge. il Tech W 19:28-9 O 17 '66
See also
Oxidation, Electrolytic

ELECTROLYTIC capacitors. See Electric capacitors

ELECTROLYTIC oxidation. See Oxidation, Electrolytic

ELECTROLYTIC reduction. See Reduction, Electrolytic

ELECTROMAGNETIC pulse. See Electromagnetic waves

ELECTROMAGNETIC theory
See also
Quantum electrodynamics

ELECTROMAGNETIC waves
Old World standards breaking through; substituting hertz for cycles. Pop Electr 24:28 Ap '66
Probing the effects of a nuclear blast; electromagnetic pulse (EMP) threat to power and communications facilities. Bsns W p77 My 14 '66
System aids RF spectrum surveillance; identifying and analyzing unknown electromagnetic signals. il Aviation W 86:61+ Ja 9 '67
See also
Radio waves

ELECTROMAGNETISM
Physics just before Einstein; adaptation of address, December 29, 1964. A. M. Bork. bibliog il Science 152:597-603 Ap 29 '66

ELECTRON accelerators. See Accelerators (electrons, etc)

ELECTRON beam welders. See Welders

ELECTRON microscope and microscopy
Cytochemistry of synapses: selective staining for electron microscopy. F. E. Bloom and G. K. Aghajanian. bibliog il Science 154:1575-7 D 23 '66
Electron-microscopic autoradiography of rat hypothalamus after intraventricular H³-norepinephrine. G. K. Aghajanian and F. E. Bloom. bibliog il Science 153:308-10 Jl 15 '66
Electron microscopy: attachment sites between connective tissue cells. R. Ross and T. K. Greenlee, jr. bibliog il Science 153:997-9 Ag 26 '66
Electron microscopy of living insects. R. F. W. Pease and others. bibliog il Science 154:1185-6 D 2 '66
Electron microscopy: tight junctions in synapses of the chick ciliary ganglion. A. J. D. De Lorenzo. bibliog il Science 152:76-8 Ap 1 '66
Electron microscopy: two major synaptic types on spinal motoneurons. D. Bodian. bibliog il Science 151:1093-4 Mr 4 '66
How does an electron microscope work? I. Asimov. Sci Digest 60:88-9 Ag '66
Laser as light source for optical diffractometers: Fourier analysis of electron micrographs. J. E. Berger and others. bibliog il Science 153:168-70 Jl 8 '66
Rotation technique in radially symmetric electron micrographs: mathematical analysis. R. S. Norman. bibliog il Science 152:1238-9 My 27 '66
Scanning electron microscopes: is high resolution possible? bibliog il Science 154:729-38 N 11 '66
Scanning microscope. il Sci N 90:522-3 D 17 '66
Survival in a vacuum; tribolium confusum, space-suited beetle. il Sci N 90:523 D 17 '66
See also
Stains and staining (microscopy)

ELECTRON optics
See also
Image converters

ELECTRON tubes
See also
Image converters

ELECTRONIC aids. See Electronics in navigation

ELECTRONIC apparatus and appliances
Build a Reflexometer. J. Fishbeck. il Pop Electr 24:47-9+ Mr '66
Build the tickle stick. F. S. Burt. il Pop Electr 24:82+ F '66
Electronic machine analyzes world's music; Melograph. Sci N L 89:88 F 5 '66
Electronics' new gee-whiz kits. L. Steckler. il Pop Mech 125:180-4 My '66
EW lab tested. See issues of Electronics world
From rags to riches; components for the hobbyist. L. E. Garner, jr. il Pop Electr 24:41-6+ Mr '66
Heterodyne vegetation meter; electronic device measures the volume of plant growth. W. B. Morse. il Pop Electr 26:72+ Ja '67
Lighthouse for short people: a flashing light. R. J. Bik. il Pop Electr 25:77-8 N '66
New avionic products. See occasional issues of Aviation week & space technology
Parts profiles. D. Lancaster. See issues of Popular electronics to May 1966
Reflexometer reflections. il Pop Electr 25:82-3 O '66
Zero-beating the news. See issues of Popular electronics
See also
Blind, Apparatus for the
Boats—Electronic equipment
Oceanographic instruments
Translating machines

ELECTRONIC apparatus industry and trade
See also
Buckbee-Mears company
Computer industry

Japan
Akihabara: Tokyo's radio row. J. Wandres. il Pop Electr 24:54-5 My '66
Japanese IC's; semiconductor manufacturers. Electr World 76:85 N '66

United States
Airlines outline equipment needs for built-in avionics self-testing. P. J. Klass. Aviation W 84:89+ Ap 4 '66

ELECTRONIC apparatus industry and trade
  —United States—*Continued*
Avionics provide major export potential. P. J. Klass. il Aviation W 83:32 mid-D '65
Electronic sales setting records. W. A. Stocklin. Electr World 76:6 Ag '66
Electronics tastes new riches; resulting from military needs and demand for color TV sets. il Bsns W p 144+ S 3 '66
In electronics, the big stakes ride on tiny chips. P. Siekman. il Fortune 73:120-5+ Je '66
In-house microcircuit capabilities expand. il Aviation W 84:253-8+ Mr 7 '66
Inductor industry. S. Zwass. Electr World 76:37 O '66
New plants sprout on Long Island. Hi Fi 16:43+ My '66
There's a new tune at Motorola; R. W. Galvin presses decentralization. il Bsns W p 110-12+ Ap 23 '66
West coast electronics industry: a special EW report. L. Zeitsoff. il Electr World 75:25-8+ Ap '66
  See also
Litton industries, incorporated

ELECTRONIC associates, incorporated
EAI sees fast growth in hybrid computers; systems combining analog and digital computers. R. Barnhart. il Tech W 20:34-5 Ja 2 '67

ELECTRONIC autocollimator. See Collimators

ELECTRONIC brains. See Artificial intelligence; Computers—Digital computers; Memory devices (computers)

ELECTRONIC cameras
Electronic camera: cheap starlight. A. Ewing. il Sci N 91:37 Ja 14 '67

ELECTRONIC circuits
Functional designing; excerpts from remarks. J. J. Suran. il Electr World 75:46-9+ Mr '66
Gulliver-size need for Lilliputian products; integrated circuits. il Time 88:40-5 S 2 '66
In appliances, companies race to think small. il Bsns W p51 Jl 2 '66
In-house microcircuit capabilities expand. il Aviation W 84:253-8+ Mr 7 '66
Industry comments due Nov. 21 on defense microcircuitry policy. Aviation W 85:101 N 7 '66
IEEE focuses on IC radiation hardening. il Tech W 19:34-6 Ag 1 '66
Integrated circuit amplifier you can build for under $6! D. Lancaster. il Pop Electr 25:57-9+ O '66
Integrated circuit for consumer products. L. Blaser. il Electr World 76:32-3+ O '66
Integrated circuit is here, are transistors obsolete? R. M. Benrey. il Pop Sci 189:90-9 Ag '66
Integrated circuits. D. Lancaster. il Pop Electr 25:52-6+ O '66
Integrated circuits for consumer products. W. A. Stocklin. Electr World 75:6 Je '66
IBM improves board laminating technique; multi-layer interconnection boards. il Aviation W 85:82-3 Jl 11 '66
Large-scale microcircuit gains reported. P. J. Klass. il Aviation W 84:91+ F 21 '66
Linear integrated circuits. B .V. Vonderschmitt and R. L. Sanquini. il Electr World 76:23-6+ N '66
Linear integrated circuits: what's available? D. E. Lancaster. il Electr World 76:38-42+ N '66
Microcircuit oriented for avionic needs. P. J. Klass. il Aviation W 85:77+ Ag 29 '66
Microcircuits aid onboard test concept. R. G. O'Lone. il Aviation W 84:100-2 Ap 18 '66
Microcircuits trim tactical avionics bulk. P. J. Klass. il Aviation W 84:87+ Ap 18 '66
New phased-array radar uses microwave microcircuitry. P. J. Klass. il Aviation W 86:92-3+ Ja 16 '67
New processes better component isolation; experiments with silicon microcircuits disclosed at the International electron devices meeting. P. J. Klass. il Aviation W 85:91+ N 7 '66
Radiation sets new microcircuit unit. Aviation W 85:67+ D 5 '66
RCA gambles on chips; microcircuits to replace transistors in color and black-and-white TV. il Bsns W p27 F 5 '66
Silicon breadboard aids design engineer: production of experimental linear-function microcircuits. P. J. Klass. il Aviation W 84:79+ F 14 '66
Sprague intensifies microcircuit efforts. P. J. Klass. il Aviation W 84:95+ Mr 28 '66
Trend seen to uncased silicon chip use. P. J. Klass. il Aviation W 84:119+ My 16 '66

Using new low-cost integrated circuits. D. E. Lancaster. il Electr World 75:50-2+ Mr '66
World's first single chip integrated circuit radio. J. A. Cacciola and E. Q. Carr. il Electr World 76:44-6 N '66
  See also
Printed circuits
Television circuits

Quality control
Microcircuit quality control is criticized. P. J. Klass. il Aviation W 85:129+ Jl 25 '66

ELECTRONIC components. See Electronic apparatus and appliances

ELECTRONIC conductors. See Semiconductors

ELECTRONIC data processing
Computer plots national lines on photos. il Tech W 19:37 Ag 8 '66
Computer sits in on the bargaining. Bsns W p 154 S 10 '66
Data-processing accounting in England; Weston-super-Mare. W. R. Bryant. il Am City 81:90-1 Je '66
Electronic data processing. il Duns R 88:pt2 140-1+ S '66
Electronic eyes are watching your tax returns; revolutionary operation called automatic data processing. T. Irwin. il Pop Mech 125:94-8+ Mr '66
Electronic processing in the bookstore. D. Melcher. Pub W 190:30-3 S 5 '66
How to succeed; Scientific data systems, Sigma 7. il Newsweek 67:73-4 Mr 28 '66
Meet the Monster that checks your taxes. J. A. Morris. Read Digest 90:177-8+ Ja '67
New computerized age; potentiality of automation revolution and its implications for our society; symposium. il Sat R 49:15-25+ Jl 23 '66
On-site processing needed for data boom. R. Pay. il Tech W 19:26+ O 3 '66
  See also
Artificial intelligence

Libraries
  See Libraries—Automation

ELECTRONIC data processing workers. See Computer workers

ELECTRONIC digital computers. See Computers—Digital computers

ELECTRONIC equipment, Miniature. See Miniature electronic equipment

ELECTRONIC flash bulbs. See Electric lamps, Flashlight

ELECTRONIC flash meters. See Exposure meters

ELECTRONIC flash photography. See Photography, Flashlight

ELECTRONIC flash units. See Electric lamps, Flashlight

ELECTRONIC listening devices. See Electronics in criminal investigation, espionage, etc.

ELECTRONIC locks. See Locks and keys

ELECTRONIC measurements
Heterodyne vegetation meter; electronic device measures the volume of plant growth. W. B. Morse. il Pop Electr 26:72+ Ja '67
  See also
Biotelemetry
Telemeter
Testing instruments

ELECTRONIC medical apparatus. See Medical instruments and apparatus

ELECTRONIC megaphones. See Megaphones

ELECTRONIC metal detectors. See Metal detectors

ELECTRONIC monitoring. See Electronics in criminal investigation, espionage, etc.

ELECTRONIC music. See Music, Electronic

ELECTRONIC musical instruments. See Musical instruments, Electronic

ELECTRONIC organ. See Organ

ELECTRONIC parts. See Electronic apparatus and appliances

ELECTRONIC photography. See Photography, Electronic

ELECTRONIC reading aids. See Blind, Apparatus for the

ELECTRONIC reading machines. See Reading machines

ELECTRONIC service shops
Radio & TV news. See issues of Electronics world

ELECTRONIC shutters. See Camera shutters

ELECTRONIC stimulators. See Electronic apparatus and appliances

ELECTRONIC switches. See Electric switches

ELECTRONIC technicians. See Electric workers

ELECTRONIC test instruments. See Testing instruments
ELECTRONIC thermometers. See Thermometers and thermometry
ELECTRONIC timers. See Timing devices
ELECTRONIC toys. See Electric toys
ELECTRONIC typesetting machines. See Typesetting machines
ELECTRONICS
Recent developments in electronics. See issues of Electronics world
See also
Cathode ray tubes
Electronics in criminal investigation, espionage, etc.
Electronics in navigation
Pulse techniques (electronics)

Bibliography
Book reviews. See occasional issues of Missiles and rockets (cont as) Technology week including Missiles and rockets
Electronics library. See issues of Popular electronics

Exhibitions
See also
Western electronics show and convention

Study and teaching
Project choose:
Correspondence schools. K. Gilmore. il Pop Electr 24:41-9 F '66
ELECTRONICS, Medical. See Medical electronics
ELECTRONICS as a profession
See also
Electric workers
ELECTRONICS capital corporation
Thinking big about small business; C. E. Salik of ECC. il Bsns W p 123-4+ Ja 7 '67
ELECTRONICS in criminal investigation, espionage, etc.
Are we all in the fishbowl? il Sr Schol 88: 9-11 F 11 '66
Battle of the bugs; Hoover and Kennedy dispute. il Time 88:19 D 23 '66
Bugging faces the exterminator; showdown on electronic eavesdropping. il Bsns W p20-1 D 24 '66
Bugging the bedroom. N. Pileggi. il Esquire 65:96-7+ My '66
Day in Court; Supreme court ruling on bugging installations. Newsweek 68:22 Jl 25 '66
Eavesdropping: an issue now in the Baker case. il U S News 61:8 N 28 '66
Everybody's got the bug; Continental telephone supply co, inc. il Time 88:76 D 16 '66
Hunting industry spies; electronic protection devices. il Bsns W p42-3 O 1 '66
I dreamt I was a spy; Senate committee on snooping opens inquiry. New Repub 154:7 Je 18 '66
Latest moves against crime in streets. il U S News 60:38-40 Ap 11 '66
Lawless lawmen; violations of eavesdropping prohibitions by FBI. A. Barth. New Repub 155:19-22 Jl 30 '66
New ruling on electronic bugging; F. B. Black case. il U S News 61:16 N 21 '66
Now, official word on bugging. il U S News 61:53 Jl 25 '66
Passing the bug; Kennedy and Hoover. Newsweek 68:19-20 D 26 '66
Plugging the big ear; FCC partial ban. Time 87:27 Mr 11 '66
Problem of oversnoop. America 115:764 D 10 '66
Snoopers; Dean Elson and others to be prosecuted for illegal eavesdropping in Nevada. il Newsweek 68:25 Jl 18 '66
Snooping electronic invasion of privacy; devices, systems, legal problems. FCC regulations; with report by J. Neary. il Life 60: 38-47 My 20 '66
Someone knows all about you; devices for anyone who cares enough to want to learn your secrets. il Esquire 65:98-101 My '66
Spies that can't feel the cold. H. Simons. il Esquire 65:104-5+ My '66
Tapper's taint; U.S. government. Newsweek 68:27 D 12 '66
Who is being bugged, and on whose orders. il U S News 61:71-3 Jl 11 '66
Who knew about bugging; RFK's story, and the FBI's. il U S News 61:32-5 D 26 '66
Why get bugged about bugging? il Sat Eve Post 240:74 Ja 14 '67
ELECTRONICS in navigation
Down to the sea in gadgets. il Sports Illus 26:20-5 Ja 2 '67
ELECTRONICS in photography. See Photography, Electronic

ELECTRONICS in sports
How electronic gadgets are changing football. W. B. Furlong. il Pop Mech 126:91-3+ O '66
ELECTRONICS in traffic control
Pushbutton expressway; electronic traffic control outside Chicago. il Sci Digest 60:17 N '66
Somebody up there watching; information provided by gadgets, hearsay evidence. il Time 88:87 O 28 '66
ELECTRONICS industry and trade. See Electronic apparatus industry and trade
ELECTRONICS research center. See United States—National aeronautics and space administration—Electronics research center
ELECTRONS
See also
Muonium
Plasma (ionized gases)
Quantum electrodynamics

Beams
Particle storage rings. G. K. O'Neill. il Sci Am 215:107-16 N '66

Diffraction
Generation of light from free electrons. W. W. Salisbury. il Science 154:386-8 O 21 '66
ELECTRO-OPTICAL systems, incorporated
EOS expanding applications of electroforming techniques. il Tech W 19:38-9 Ag 22 '66
EOS probes electrodeposited composite structures market. J. F. Judge. il Tech W 19: 26+ N 14 '66
Lightened EOS electric unit clears full flight-type test. il Tech W 19:35 O 24 '66
ELECTROORGANIC chemistry
Synthetic electroorganic chemistry. S. Wawzonek. bibliog il Science 155:39-44 Ja 6 '67
ELECTROPHORESIS
Acrylamide-gel electrophorograms by mechanical fractionation; radioactive adenovirus proteins. J. V. Maizel, jr. bibliog il Science 151:988-90 F 25 '66
Antibody molecules; discontinuous heterogeneity of heavy chains; molecules show bands on disc electrophoresis. O. A. Roholt and D. Pressman. bibliog il Science 153:1257-9 S 9 '66
Electrochromatography with reversing electrophoretic field. S. Raymond and J. Broome. bibliog il Science 153:1381-2 S 16 '66
Electrophoretic heterogeneity of mammalian galactose dehydrogenase. P. Cuatrecasas and S. Segal. bibliog il Science 154:533-5 O 28 '66
Electrophoretic heterogeneity of polypeptide chains of specific antibodies. R. A. Reisfeld and P. A. Small, jr. bibliog il Science 152:1253-5 My 27 '66
Electrophoretic heterogeneity of the polypeptide chains of human G-myeloma proteins. W. D. Terry and others. bibliog il Science 152:1628-30 Je 17 '66
Electrophoretic variation in enzymes. C. R. Shaw; reply. J. A. Beardmore. Science 152: 1107 My 20 '66
Electrophoretic variation of galactose-1-phosphate uridyltransferase. C. K. Mathai and E. Beutler. bibliog il Science 154:1179-80 D 2 '66
Lipoprotein patterns in acrylamide gel electrophoresis. S. Raymond and others. bibliog il Science 151:346-7 Ja 21 '66
Starch-gel electrophoresis of human tissue enzymes which hydrolyze L -leucyl-β-naphthylamide. E. E. Smith and A. M. Rutenburg. bibliog il Science 152:1256-7 My 27 '66
Transverse gradient electrophoresis; protein homogeneity test and subfractionation technique. C. A. Dubbs. bibliog il Science 151:463-4 Ja 28 '66
ELECTROPHORESIS apparatus and supplies
Electrophoresis; an accident and some precautions. E. W. Spencer and others. il Science 152:1722-3 Je 24 '66; Reply. S. Raymond. 153:1336 S 16 '66
ELECTROPHYSIOLOGY
Active transport of 5,5-dimethyl-2,4-oxazolidinedione. J. M. Dietschy and N. W. Carter; discussion. Science 151:1564; 152:799 Mr 25, My 6 '66
Anteroventral cochlear nucleus; wave forms of extracellularly recorded spike potentials. R. R. Pfeiffer. bibliog il Science 154:667-8 N 4 '66
Brain's electrochemical telegraph system. il Fortune 74:102-3 Jl 1 '66

ELECTROPHYSIOLOGY—*Continued*
Cell size and rate of protein synthesis in ventral horn neurones. R. P. Peterson. bibliog il Science 153:1413-14 S 16 '66
Electrophysiologic studies during scanning and passive eye movements in humans. D. F. Scott and R. G. Bickford. bibliog il Science 155:101-2 Ja 6 '67
Electrostatic aspects of physical adsorption: implications for molecular sieves and gaseous anesthesia. S. W. Benson and J. W. King, jr; discussion. bibliog Science 153:555-6 Jl 29 '66
Fluctuations of resting neural membrane potential. H. E. Derksen and A. A. Verveen. bibliog il Science 151:1388-9 Mr 18 '66
Input resistance, electrical excitability, and size of ventral horn cells in cat spinal cord. D. Kernell. bibliog il Science 152:1637-40 Je 17 '66
Internally perfused axons: effects of two different anions on ionic conductance. W. J. Adelman, jr. and others. bibliog il Science 151:1392-4 Mr 18 '66
Muscle from a wink or twitch; myoelectric control applied to artificial limbs. Sci N 90:501 D 10 '66
Neurosecretory cell: capable of conducting impulse in rats. K. Yagi and others. bibliog il Science 154:778-9 N 11 '66
Puromycin and cycloheximide: different effects on hippocampal electrical activity. H. D. Cohen and others. bibliog il Science 154:1557-8 D 23 '66
Rate of movement and redistribution of stainable neurosecretory granules in hypothalamic neurons. A. Jasinski and others. bibliog il Science 154:776-8 N 11 '66
Reversal response elicited in nonbeating cilia of paramecium by membrane depolarization. Y. Naitoh. bibliog il Science 154:660-2 N 4 '66
Tetraethylammonium and tetrodotoxin: effects on cochlear potentials. Y. Katsuki and others. bibliog il Science 151:1544-5 Mr 25 '66
Tetrodotoxin does not block excitation from inside the nerve membrane. T. Narahashi and others. bibliog il Science 153:765-7 Ag 12 '66
Thyroid hormone: effects on electron transport. J. R. Bronk. bibliog il Science 153:638-9 Ag 5 '66
Visual excitation and blood clotting. G. Wald; reply. W. H. Seegers. bibliog Science 151:841 F 18 '66

Apparatus
Low-noise, interference-resistant amplifier suitable for biological research. G. Schuler and others. il Science 154:1191-2 D 2 '66
ELECTROPHYSIOLOGY of plants
Electric currents in organic crystals. M. Pope. il Sci Am 216:86-97 bibliog(p 146) Ja '67
ELECTROPLATING
See also
Electroforming
ELECTRORETINOGRAPHY
Electroretinogram of the frog during embryonic development. F. Crescitelli and S. E. C. Nilsson. bibliog il Science 151:1545-7 Mr 25 '66
ELECTROSHOCK. See Electric shock
ELECTROSTATIC field. See Electric field
ELECTROSTATIC generators. See Electric generators, Electrostatic
ELECTROSTATIC printers. See Printing machinery
ELECTROSTATICS
See also
Electric field
ELEGANT, Robert S.
China leaps: where? Reporter 35:35-9 S 22 '66
Enormous revival meeting. Nation 203:307-11 O 3 '66
about
Instinct for the Orient. il por Time 88:68+ S 9 '66
ELEKTRA; opera. See Strauss, R.
ELEMENTARY and secondary education act of 1965. See Federal aid to education
ELEMENTARY particles. See Particles (nuclear physics)
ELEMENTARY school buildings. See School buildings
ELEMENTARY school children. See School children
ELEMENTARY school libraries. See School libraries
ELEMENTARY school teaching. See Teaching

ELEMENTS, Transmutation of. See Transmutation (chemistry)
ELEO Pomare dance company. See Dance companies
ELEODES. See Beetles
ELEPHANT hunting
We found the elephant place. E. A. Bauer. il Outdoor Life 138:28-31+ Ag '66
ELEPHANT trees
Elephant tree. O. F. Oldendorph. il Nat Parks Mag 40:11-12 My '66
ELEPHANTS
Great elephant hunt; enormous herds faced with famine in game parks of East Africa. il Time 88:44 N 4 '66
ELEPHANTS, Fossil
See also
Mammoths
Mastodon
ELEVATED railroads
BART: the trains and tracks. J. Bailey. il Arch Forum 124:44-7 Je '66
ELEVATORS, Grain. See Grain elevators
ELFBRANDT, Barbara
Teach-in in Tucson. por Newsweek 67:21 My 2 '66
ELFBRANDT, Vernon
Teach-in in Tucson. por Newsweek 67:21 My 2 '66
ELGAR, Sir Edward William, 1st bart
Dream of Gerontius. M. Maxwell. por Am Rec G 32:796-7+ My '66
Elgar's violin concerto, as played by Menuhin today and by Menuhin yesterday. B. Jacobson. il por Hi Fi 16:86-7 S '66
Menuhin's Elgar: intimacy and bravura. J. Diether. Am Rec G 33:38 S '66
Original Edwardian. Discus. Harper 233:101-2 Jl '66
ELGIN marbles
Odyssey of the Elgin marbles. P. W. Stone. il Sat R 49:34+ O 22 '66
EL HAFEZ, Amin. See Hafez, A.
ELIADE, Mircea
Cosmic religion. Commentary 41:95-6+ Mr '66
ELIAS, Eileen
Kids can't be tidy all the time. Parents Mag 41:46-7+ Mr '66
ELIASBERG, Ann Pringle
Parent and child (cont) N Y Times Mag p 109+ Mr 20; 114+ O 30; 127+ D 4 '66
ELICOFON, Edward I.
$1,000,000 in Dürers found in Brooklyn. il Life 60:34-5 Je 3 '66
ELIOT, Alexander
How to enjoy museums. Seventeen 25:140+ Je '66
Small museums of southern Europe. Holiday 39:105-10 Je '66
ELIOT, George, pseud.
Silas Marner diagnosed. Sci N 90:410 N 12 '66
ELIOT, George Fielding
Complacency in high places. Nat R 18:937-8 S 20 '66
Piercing the fog of war. Nat R 18:1277-8 D 13 '66
Unvarnished tale of the Commune. Nat R 18:319-20 Ap 5 '66
ELIOT, Jacquetta Jean Frederika (Lampson) Eliot, lady
Upswing young. V. Lawford. il pors Vogue 148:140-7+ Ag 1 '66
ELIOT, Lord Peregrine Nicholas Eliot
Upswing young. V. Lawford. il pors Vogue 148:140-7+ Ag 1 '66
ELIOT, Thomas Stearns
Eliot as playwright. C. H. Smith. Nation 203:325-8 O 3 '66
Eliot's legacy. J. Frank. Commentary 42:87-91 S '66
Murder in the cathedral. Criticism Sat R 49:41 Jl 9 '66
Only through time. W. J. Ong. Poetry 108:265-8 Jl '66
T. S. Eliot: the poet as critic. F. J. Hoffman. Nation 203:324-5 O 3 '66
ELIOT books, incorporated
Eliot books enlarges space for its distribution service. il Pub W 190:100-1 N 14 '66
L'ELISIR d'amore; opera. See Donizetti, G.
ELIXIR of love; opera. See Donizetti, G.
ELIZABETH I, queen of England
Elizabeth's copy of Canon law. P. W. Schmidtchen. il por Hobbies 71:108 Je '66
ELIZABETH II, queen of Great Britain
Mixed welcome: visit to British Guiana. il por Newsweek 67:48 F 14 '66
Queen at forty. por Newsweek 67:52+ My 2 '66
Queen Elizabeth turns forty. R. Lecler. il pors McCalls 93:76-9+ My '66
Royal revelations; ancestry. il Time 87:38 My 20 '66

ELIZABETH, N.J.
    City planning
300-year-old city plans a big face-lifting.
    il Am City 81:106B Jl '66
ELIZABETHTOWN, Pa.
Residential streets require good lighting too.
    R. E. Parsons. il Am City 81:128 Ag '66
ELK hunting
Elk to whistle about. F. W. Davis. il Out-
    door Life 137:62-4+ F '66
Michigan elk, no longer sacred cows. J.
    Chiappetta. il Field & S 71:36-7+ Ag '66
Wow! what a wapiti! J. Cook. il Outdoor
    Life 138:56-7+ S '66
ELK tagging. See Animal tagging
ELKINS, Cande
Cande in a curtain. P. Gowland. il por Pop
    Phot 59:12+ Ag '66
ELKINS, Stanley
Fatal flaw. Commentary 42:73-5 Jl '66
ELKOFF, Marvin
Collecting original art prints. Holiday 39:101-6
    F '66
ELLENDER, Allen Joseph
Excerpt from debate, July 27, 1966. Cong
    Digest 45:200+ Ag '66
ELLER, Ed
Drawings and statements. il Sch Arts 65:24-
    8 Je '66
ELLER, J. N.
Washington front. See occasional issues of
    America
ELLER, Vernard
COCU: self-defeating? Christian Cent 83:
    488-91 Ap 20 '66
Theology of nonresistance. Christian Cent
    83:1534-7 D 14 '66
ELLIN, Stanley
Planning a mystery back to front. Writer 79:
    11-13+ D '66
ELLINGSON, Careth, and Cass, James
Teaching the dyslexic child; new hope for
    non-readers. Sat R 49:82-5+ Ap 16 '66
ELLINGSON, Marnie
Mark and the rest of the world; story.
    Ladies Home J 83:56-7 Jl '66
ELLINGSON, Steve
Fun for junior mailmen. Pop Mech 125:174-
    6+ F '66
Galley spices up patio fun. Pop Mech 125:
    148-50 My '66
ELLINGTON, Duke
Jazz goes to church. il pors Ebony 21:76-80
    Ap '66
More of the Ellington era. M. Williams.
    por Sat R 49:53 Jl 30 '66
Sophistication of Duke Ellington. G. Frazier.
    por Esquire 66:244-5 D '66
ELLINGTON, Edward Kennedy. See Ellington,
    D.
ELLIOT, Bob
Comfort in cold covers. pors Outdoor Life
    139:56-7+ Ja '67
ELLIOTT, Charles
Antelope play in Florida. Outdoor Life 137:
    52-5+ My '66
Hunting atomic energy reserve. Outdoor Life
    138:42-3+ Ag '66
I'll take the bass pits. Outdoor Life 138:68-9+
    O '66
Rooftop river. Outdoor Life 138:32-3+ Jl
    '66
This is trophy hunting. Outdoor Life 138:
    54-7+ N '66
ELLIOTT, George Paul
Achievement of Noah Greenberg. Commen-
    tary 42:67-71 Jl '66
Center in search of a role. N Y Times Mag
    pt2 p 13+ S 11 '66
Truth about fiction. Holiday 39:84-5+ Mr '66
ELLIOTT, Jay Aubrey
Copper caper. il por Newsweek 68:104 N 21
    '66
ELLIOTT, Lawrence
All we had to give was ourselves. Redbook
    127:58-9+ My '66
Longest Main Street in the world. Read
    Digest 89:121-6 Jl '66
(ed) See Huntington, J. On the edge of
    nowhere
ELLIOTT, Marjorie Atkins
Student's work is published. Sr Schol 89:
    sup47-8 S 23 '66
ELLIOTT, Robert C.
Saturnalia, satire, and utopia. Yale R 55:521-
    36 Je '66
ELLIOTT, William I.
Landslide in Yamanashi prefecture, Japan,
    September 1966; poem. Christian Cent 83:
    1537 D 14 '66
Shusaku Endo: a Christian voice in Japanese
    literature. Christian Cent 83:1147 S 21 '66
Thud; poem. Christian Cent 83:173 F 9 '66

ELLIS, Gordon W.
Holomicrography: transformation of image
    during reconstruction a posteriori. bibliog
    Science 154:1195-7 D 2 '66
ELLIS, H. F.
Weary Titans. New Yorker 42:52-3 O 15 '66
ELLIS, H. S. See Jensen, E. J. jt. auth.
ELLIS, Mel
Compleat hunter. Field & S 71:117-20 S '66
Door to fishing paradise. Field & S 71:52-
    5+ My '66
Those copper-colored bones. por Field & S
    71:26+ Je '66
ELLIS, Pamela
Greece and me. pors Seventeen 26:102-3 Ja
    '67
ELLIS, Richard
Ellis talks on design at Philadelphia clinic;
    summary of address, March 8, 1966. por
    Pub W 189:119 My 2 '66
ELLIS, Ronald
Fishing; poem. Commonweal 85:201 N 18 '66
ELLIS ISLAND
How to lose money and space; proposed mon-
    ument. America 114:540 Ap 16 '66
Stabilizing the ruins; Philip Johnson's archi-
    tecture plans. il Time 87:78 Mr 4 '66
ELLISON, Ralph
American novelist who sometimes teaches. J.
    Corry. il por N Y Times Mag p54-5+ N 20
    '66
ELLMANN, Mary
Colette: a scandalous sincerity. Nation 202:
    720-1 Je 13 '66
Sensational Susan Sontag. Atlan 218:59-63 S
    '66
ELLO, J. G.
Radiological survey meters. Electr World 75:
    44-6+ Ja '66
ELLSBERG, Helen
Things are looking up in Logan Heights.
    Read Digest 89:217+ N '66
ELLSWORTH, Ralph E.
Library education and the talent shortage.
    por Library J 91:1765 Ap 1 '66
ELLSWORTH, Ray
Impresario tells all. Am Rec G 32:898+ My
    '66
Unlikely corners. Am Rec G 32:1096-7 Jl '66
ELLUL, Jacques
Do we really want to be brainwashed? F.
    Morley. Nations Bsns 54:25-6 S '66
Is technology taking over? C. E. Silberman.
    il Fortune 73:112-15+ F '66
ELLWOOD, Craig
Leaving the columns outside. il Arch Forum
    125:70-7 N '66
ELM
Rare American elms saved by pruning. il Sci
    N 89:319 Ap 30 '66
    Diseases and pests
Dutch elm disease abroad. H. M. Heybroek.
    il Am For 72:26-9+ Je '66
D.E.D. goes underground; Madison, Wis. R.
    L. Carroll. il Am City 81:96-7 Jl '66
Penny test for Dutch elm disease; Rockford,
    Ill. A. Grimm. il Am City 81:122-3 My '66
We duck the Dutch elm disaster; Lincoln,
    Neb. D. Guinan. il Am City 81:102-3 Mr '66
EL MAHDI, Sayed Sadik. See Mahdi, S. S.
ELMAN, Richard M.
Manny Gelder: slumlord; excerpt from Poor-
    house state. Atlan 218:128-30 N '66
—See Cloward, R. A. jt. auth.
EL MOROCCO. See Night clubs
ELROD, J. McRee
Staffing of technical processes. por Library
    J 91:2275-7 My 1 '66
ELSHTAIN, Errol. See Best, J. B. jt. auth.
ELSNER, Robert, and others
Cardiovascular defense against asphyxia. bib-
    liog Science 153:941-9 Ag 26 '66
ELSON, D. See Traub, W. jt. auth.
ELSON, Robert T.
In man for the Cabinet. Read Digest 88:
    107-11 F '66
ELVIN, Lionel
Two decades in the world of education.
    UNESCO Courier 19:24-7 Jl '66
ELVINS, Peter
Troubled waters. Opera N 31:8-11 D 10 '66
ELY, Mary
Cup of consecrated chicken soup. Cath World
    202:298-301 F '66
EMANCIPATION of women. See Woman—
    Equal rights
EMBARGO
Challenge at sea; how to stop Rhodesia-
    bound oil. il Time 87:38 Ap 15 '66
Hot cargoes; oil bound for Rhodesia. Time
    87:34 Ap 22 '66

EMBARGO—*Continued*
Mutual defense assistance control act. Cur Hist 51:45-6 Jl '66
Rhodesian embargo. Commonweal 84:143-4 Ap 22 '66
Rhodesia's woes mount; Britain preparing new mandatory economic sanctions. Bsns W p44 D 10 '66
Sit-ins; UN upholds British embargo on oil shipments to Rhodesia. Newsweek 67:56+ Ap 18 '66
Troubled waters; second blockade-runner flees Rhodesia. Newsweek 67:45 Ap 25 '66
U.S. shipowners formally notified of ban on Rhodesian oil shipments; letter, May 4, 1966. T. C. Mann. Dept State Bul 54:859 My 30 '66

EMBERLEY, Ed
Crow-quill pen. Horn Bk 42:553-5 O '66

about
Meteoric career of Ed Emberley. D. Waugh. il Am Artist 30:54-61 N '66

EMBEZZLEMENT
Burnice comes home. il Time 88:20 Jl 8 '66

EMBLEMS, National
See also
United States—Seals

EMBROIDERY
Bright embroidery ideas! M. Garrity. il Bet Hom & Gard 44:70 Ag '66
Hemstitching is really easy. il Sunset 137:124 N '66
Machine embroidery, Mexican style. C. Houck. il Parents Mag 41:120 O '66

EMBRYOLOGY
Death in embryonic systems. J. W. Saunders, jr. bibliog il Science 154:604-12 N 4 '66
Enhanced growth of human embryonic cells infected with adenovirus 12. I. V. Sultanian and G. Freeman. bibliog il Science 154:665-7 N 4 '66
Hemoglobins of early human embryonic development. A. Kaltsoya and others. bibliog il Science 153:1417-18 S 16 '66
Inductive processes in embryonic development. A. G. Jacobson. bibliog il Science 152:25-34 Ap 1 '66
Predominance of hemoglobin Gower 1 in early human embryonic development. F. Hecht and others. bibliog il Science 152:91-2 Ap 1 '66
See also
Cells
Fetus
Placenta

Amphibia
Electroretinogram of the frog during embryonic development. F. Crescitelli and S. E. C. Nilsson. bibliog il Science 151:1545-7 Mr 25 '66
Evidence from cultured leucocytes of blood cell chimerism in ex-parabiotic frogs. E. P. Volpe and B. M. Gebhardt. bibliog il Science 154:1197-9 D 2 '66

Birds
Amniotic contraction and embryonic motility in the chick embryo. R. W. Oppenheim. bibliog il Science 152:528-9 Ap 22 '66
Arrested protein synthesis in polysomes of cultured chick embryo cells. R. Soeiro and H. Amos. bibliog il Science 154:662-5 N 4 '66
Hypophyseal control of genetic expression during chick feather and skin differentiation. M. B. Yatvin. bibliog il Science 153:184-5 Jl 8 '66
Lactate dehydrogenase isozymes of chick embryo: response to variations of ambient oxygen tension. S. Lindy and M. Rajasalmi. bibliog il Science 153:1401-3 S 16 '66
Of spring and an egg. J. George. il Read Digest 88:181-4 Ap '66
Polysome morphology: evidence for endocrine control during chick embryogenesis. M. B. Yatvin. bibliog il Science 151:1001-3 F 25 '66
Triploid-diploid mosaic chicken embryo. S. E. Bloom and E. G. Buss. bibliog il Science 153:759-60 Ag 12 '66

Cephalopods
Isotopic evidence on the early life history of nautilus pompilius, Linné. R. Eichler and H. Ristedt. bibliog il Science 153:734-6 Ag 12 '66

Echinoderms
Protein synthesis in micromeres of the sea urchin egg. M. Spiegel and A. Tyler. bibliog il Science 151:1233-4 Mr 11 '66

Rate of protein synthesis: regulation during first division cycle of sea urchin eggs. W. H. Sofer and others. bibliog il Science 153:1644-5 S 30 '66

Insects
Insect embryogenesis: macromolecular syntheses during early development. R. A. Lockshin. bibliog il Science 154:775-6 N 11 '66

Mammals
DNA synthesis and differentiation in embryonic kidney mesenchyme in vitro. J. S. Sobel. bibliog il Science 153:1387-9 S 16 '66
Mammalian eggs in the laboratory. R. G. Edwards. il Sci Am 215:72-81 bibliog (p 114+) Ag '66
Microinjection of mouse eggs. T. P. Lin. bibliog il Science 151:333-7 Ja 21 '66
Norepinephrine methylation in fetal rat adrenals. F. L. Margolis and others. bibliog il Science 154:275-6 O 14 '66

EMERALD snail shells. See Shells (conchology)
EMERGENCIES. See First aid in illness and injury
EMERGENCY alarms. See Alarms
EMERGENCY communication systems
Emergency reporting at the lift of a receiver; Baltimore County, Md. W. H. Wineholt. il Am City 81:116-17 Ag '66
EMERGENCY exits. See Airplanes—Safety devices and measures
EMERGENCY medical service. See Medical service
EMERGENCY powers. See Presidents—United States—Powers and duties
EMERGENCY services, Hospital. See Hospitals—Emergency services
EMERSON, James G. Jr
On forgiveness. Christian Cent 83:808 Je 22 '66
EMERSON, Thomas I.
Speech without assembly? the Court v. the demonstrators. Nation 203:704-8 D 26 '66
EMERY, John C.
Hourglass figure. R. Levy. il por Duns R 88:47-8 S '66
EMETT, Rowland
Computer that really cares. il por Life 61:118-20+ D 2 '66
EMIGRATION. See Immigration and emigration
EMIGRATION and immigration law. See Immigration and emigration law
EMILIANI, Cesare
Isotopic paleotemperatures. bibliog Science 154:851-7 N 18 '66
EMINENT domain
Good-neighbor policy; opposition to plan for state park across from the President's land in Texas. il Newsweek 67:30+ Mr 21 '66
Highwaymen come to Morristown; Interstate highway system. J. Skow. il Sat Eve Post 239:68-75 Ap 9 '66
New uproar over the LBJ state park. U S News 60:10 Mr 28 '66
EMLEN, John T. and Penney, R. L.
Navigation of penguins; with biographical sketches. Sci Am 215:16, 104-13 O '66
EMMET, Christopher
Vietnam; agonizing reappraisal. America 114:349-52 Mr 12 '66
EMMETT, J. A.
Boating. See issues of Outdoor life
Boats and motors for 1967. Outdoor Life 139:70-2+ Ja '67
EMMETT, Jim
Boats we meet: Meander. Yachting 120:47-9 Ag '66
Boatyards and bywaters. Yachting 119:68-9+ Mr '66
Satisfaction from a diesel. Yachting 119:111-13+ Ja; 80-2+ F '66
Steadying sails. il Yachting 120:50+ S '66
EMMONS, Gardner
Pageantry in the sky, clouds and their meaning. Motor B 119:101 Ja '67
EMMY awards. See Academy of television arts and sciences
EMOTIONAL fatigue. See Fatigue
EMOTIONAL maturity. See Maturity
EMOTIONAL stability
Turning points of life; crises in women's lives. G. Caplan and V. Cadden. McCalls 94:114-15+ O '66; Same abr. with title How to deal with a crisis. Read Digest 90:80-3 Ja '67

EMOTIONALLY disturbed children. See
  Mentally ill children; Problem children
EMOTIONS
  Can human emotions be changed? adaptation
    of address, April 1964. L. Eisenberg. Bul
    Atomic Sci 22:27-31 Ja '66
  Chemicals may color memories with emotion.
    Sci N 89:466 Je 11 '66
  Do parents cause children's emotional trou-
    bles? B. Spock. Redbook 127:20+ Je '66
    See also
  Frustration
  Love
  Mind and body
EMOTIONS in literature
  Realm of emotion. P. S. Curry. Writer 79:
    14-18+ F '66
EMPEY, Lamar T.
  Long quest. por Outdoor Life 137:50-3+ Je
    '66
EMPHYSEMA
  Emphysema deaths exceed TB. F. Marley.
    il Sci N 89:246-7 Ap 9 '66
  Getting at the cause of an incurable ill.
    il Bsns W p61-2 Jl 30 '66
  Increasing dangers from a little-known lung
    disease. Good H 162:178 Mr '66
  Our fastest-growing health menace. D. Mur-
    ray. Read Digest 90:111-14 Ja '67
  Smoking dogs; lung disease produced in
    dogs. Sci Am 215:42 Ag '66
  What your family should know about
    emphysema. N. Kuehnl. Bet Hom & Gard
    44:28 My '66
EMPIE, Paul C.
  Can organized religion be unethical? Ann
    Am Acad 363:70-8 Ja '66
EMPIRE state building. See New York (city)
    —Empire state building
**EMPIS (engineering materials and process in-
  formation service)** See General electric com-
  pany
EMPLOYEE libraries. See Libraries, Employee
**EMPLOYEE-management relations in govern-
  ment.** See Collective bargaining—Govern-
  ment employees
EMPLOYEE morale
  Show goes on, and production perks; Admi-
    ral's new color tube plant. il Bsns W p
    122-4 Ap 16 '66
EMPLOYEES
    See also
  Job satisfaction
  Office workers
    also subhead Employees under various
    subjects, e.g. Hotels, taverns, etc.—Em-
    ployees

Length of service
See Seniority, Employee

Promotion
Anecdotes, facetiae, satire, etc.
  Peter principle. R. Hull. il Esquire 67:76-7
    Ja '67

Rating
  Hard look in employee appraisal. J. Wein-
    garten. il Duns R 88:41-2+ S '66

Selection
See Employment systems

Training
  Breakthrough in on-the-job training; Texas
    instruments, inc. E. R. Gomersall and
    M. S. Myers. il Harvard Bsns R 44:62-72
    Jl '66
  Conceptual issues in evaluating training pro-
    grams. B. A. Weisbrod. Mo Labor R 89:
    1091-7 O '66
  Design, build, operate and train; water-
    treatment plant at Saigon, South Viet Nam.
    W. T. McPhee and J. F. Lenard. il Am City
    81:100-3 O '66
  Giving American ways to foreign engineers.
    il Bsns W p 170+ O 1 '66
  Good jobs waiting for men who learn a trade.
    il Changing T 20:26-8 N '66
  How business employs the unemployable; on-
    the-job training programs. il Nations Bsns
    55:33-4+ Ja '67
  Job for Jim; training under Manpower de-
    velopment and training act. J. N. Miller. il
    Read Digest 88:72-82 F '66
  New place in life for the unskilled; Pilot
    project in North Carolina, relocating and
    training of unempoyed agricultural workers.
    il Bsns W p 110:12 Mr 26 '66
  Program proposals for manpower policy. A.
    R. Weber. Mo Labor R 80:130-1 F '66
  South Bend comes out from under; recovers
    from Studebaker shutdown. il Bsns W p58-
    60+ F 19 '66

  Training in service occupations; excerpt from
    Manpower development and training act.
    il Mo Labor R 89:523-7 My '66
  Trends in European apprenticeship. Mo Labor
    R 89:396-7 Ap '66
    See also
  Corporation schools
EMPLOYEES benfit plans
  Here's a lifesaving plan for your business.
    E. H. Bellows and M. R. Gasque. il Nations
    Bsns 54:94+ Ap '66
  Impact of economic growth on employee
    benefit planning; address, November 1965.
    T. H. Paine. Vital Speeches 32:206-10 Ja
    15 '66
  Provisions for paid sick leave in metropolitan
    areas. K. J. Hoffmann. il Mo Labor R 89:
    164-9 F '66
EMPLOYER-employee relations. See Indus-
  trial relations
EMPLOYMENT
  Cuba's new refugees get jobs fast; opportu-
    nities in the U.S. Bsns W p69 Mr 12 '66
  Economists battle past a milestone; Em-
    ployment act of 1946; with editorial com-
    ment. il Bsns W p 138-9, 174 F 26 '66
  Full employment; address, October 26, 1966.
    G. Ackley. Vital Speeches 33:71-7 N 15 '66
  Full employment or stable prices? B. L.
    Masse. America 115:646 N 19 '66
  Geographic study of employment and earn-
    ings from 1939 to 1964. C. Utter. il Mo
    Labor R 89:132-7 F '66
  Help! developing labor shortage. il Time 87:
    79 Mr 25 '66
  Keynes isn't enough; goal beyond full em-
    ployment. L. J. Walinsky. New Repub
    154:14-16 Ap 16 '66
  Labor in a year of expansion. P. Groom.
    bibliog f Mo Labor R 88:1414-22 D '65
  Must full employment mean inflation? G.
    Burck. il Fortune 74:120-3+ O '66
  Unemployment takes back seat; it's a work-
    er's market. il Bsns W p42-4 N 5 '66
  Wanted: almost any warm body; jobs for
    recent college graduates. Time 87:92+ Mr
    18 '66
  We can get anybody a job. Nations Bsns
    55:35 Ja '67
  Where they can get jobs. H. Alexander. il
    Nations Bsns 54:38-9+ S '66
  Year of harvest; the 1966 manpower report;
    excerpt, March 8, 1966. L. B. Johnson. Mo
    Labor R 89:II+ Mr '66
    See also
  Age and employment
  Seasonal industries
  Self employed
  Unemployables
  Unemployment—United States
    also subhead Employment under various
    subjects, e.g. Youth—Employment

Stability
See Employment systems—Guaranty of
  employment

Statistics
  Business markets. il Duns R 88:pt2 70-6+
    Jl '66
  Changing patterns in employment of non-
    white workers. J. L. Russell. il Mo Labor R
    89:503-9 My '66
  Effects of employment redistribution on
    earnings. C. Hodge. il Mo Labor R 89:744-
    8 Jl '66
  Estimated need for skilled workers, 1965-75.
    A. F. Salt. il Mo Labor R 89:365-71 Ap '66
  Labor force and employment (cont of) Em-
    ployment; tables. See issues of Monthly
    labor review
  Manpower projections; some conceptual prob-
    lems and research needs. S. Swerdloff. Mo
    Labor R 80:138-43 F '66
  Where job chances will be best in the years
    just ahead. U S News 62:44-5 Ja 2 '67
  Work experience of the population. S. Saben.
    Mo Labor R 89:155-63 F '66
  Work experience of the population in 1965.
    F. A. Bogan and T. E. Swanstrom. bib-
    liog f il Mo Labor R 89:1369-77 D '66
    See also
  Unemployment—Statistics
EMPLOYMENT, Agricultural. See Farm labor
EMPLOYMENT, Free choice of. See Free
  choice of employment
EMPLOYMENT, Supplementary. See Supple-
  mentary employment
EMPLOYMENT act of 1946. See Labor laws and
  legislation—United States; United States—
  Economic policy

EMPLOYMENT agencies
Job agencies sprout satellites; tight labor market. il Bsns W p52-4 Ap 9 '66
Job shops profit from technology boom. R. G. Barnhart. Tech W 19:34-5 Ag 29 '66
Office services. il Duns R 88:pt2 157-8+ S '66
    See also
United States—Employment service
EMPLOYMENT of the aged. See Age and employment
EMPLOYMENT of the mentally ill. See Mentally ill—Employment
EMPLOYMENT statistics. See Employment—Statistics
EMPLOYMENT systems
Affluent class of '67; corporations in pursuit of talent. Time 89:59 Ja 6 '67
Brain drain starts to hurt; Britain and Europeans, worried about siphoning off of scientific and technical talent to the U.S. il Bsns W p 122+ D 10 '66
Bright young men choose business careers. S. Schuler. il Nations Bsns 54:46-7+ Je '66
Business can live with the labor shortage. C. E. Silberman. Fortune 73:112-15+ My '66
Business casts bread on campus labor pool; well-paying summer jobs to college juniors. il Bsns W p84+ S 3 '66
Campus image of business. H. G. Taylor. Duns R 88:21-2+ N '66
Can salesmen be tested? L. Rich. il Duns R 87:40-1+ Mr '66
Fair practice; job fairs. il Time 87:100 Je 10 '66
Getting more out of the graduate; preference for master's in business administration. Bsns W p61-2+ Je 18 '66
Job game; about psychological job tests and how to pass them. S. Birmingham. il McCalls 93:76-7+ Jl '66
Most wanted man; the '66 grad; campus recruiting by industry and government. il Bsns W p88+ Ap 16 '66
Private world of the class of '66; with editorial comment. D. Norton-Taylor. il Fortune 73:102+, 128-32+ F '66
Quick check; Miami employees and police checks. Nation 202:413 Ap 11 '66
    See also
Employment agencies

Guaranty of employment
Abundance in perspective; should men compete with machines? R. Theobald. il Nation 202:544-50 My 9 '66
Company action to stabilize employment. R. S. Eckley. il Harvard Bsns R 44:51-61 Jl '66
Shifting concepts of worker security. A. J. Siegel. Mo Labor R 89:126 F '66
ENAMEL and enameling
Glossary of Hungarian enamels. G. Kaler. Hobbies 71:50 Ag '66
Hungarian enamels, basse-taille. G. Kaler. il Hobbies 71:46+ Mr '66
Hungarian enamels; filigree. G. Kaler. il Hobbies 71:50 My '66
Hungarian enamels; painted. G. Kaler. il Hobbies 71:50+ Jl '66
Hungarian enamels, ronde bosse. G. Kaler. il Hobbies 71:46+ Ap '66
Hungarian enamels; Transylvanian. G. Kaler. il Hobbies 71:50 Je '66
ENAMELS. See Enamel and enameling
ENCAPSULATION. See Capsules
ENCEPHALITIS
Subacute sclerosing leukoencephalitis: ultrastructure of intranuclear and intracytoplasmic inclusions. I. Tellez-Nagel and D. H. Harter. bibliog il Science 154:899-901 N 18 '66
ENCEPHALITIS, Epidemic
Encephalitis spreading; mosquitoes blamed for the epidemic in Dallas. Sci N 90:151 S 3 '66
Epidemic on the wing; Dallas; insecticide fears. il Newsweek 68:52 S 5 '66
ENCEPHALITIS virus
Isolation of St Louis encephalitis virus from bats (Tadarida b. mexicana) in Texas. S. E. Sulkin and others. bibliog il Science 152:223-5 Ap 8 '66
Virus causes excess fat. Sci N L 89:51 Ja 22 '66
Western equine encephalitis virus in Saskatchewan garter snakes and leopard frogs. A. N. Burton and others. bibliog il Science 154:1029-31 N 25 '66
Winter resort for viruses. il Time 88:62 Ag 12 '66

ENCEPHALOMYELITIS
Autoimmune encephalomyelitis and ocular lesions in monkeys sensitized during the neonatal period. S. H. Stone and others. bibliog il Science 151:473-5 Ja 28 '66
Encephalitogenic activity of bovine basic proteins. M. W. Kies and others. bibliog il Science 151:321-2 F 18 '66
ENCHANTED broom; drama. See Lahr, G. L.
ENCLOSURES, Loudspeaker. See Loud speaking apparatus—Cabinets
ENCOUNTER (periodical)
Constant flirt. Time 88:76 S 2 '66
Encounter with the CIA. Nation 202:571 My 16 '66
ENCYCLICALS
Church and social progress, by B. I. Masse. Review
    America 114:878 Je 25 '66. D. R. Campion
Disappointing Marian development; Christi Matri Rosarii (Rosaries to the Mother of Christ) Paul VI's fourth encyclical. S. Benko. Christian Cent 84:79-80 Ja 18 '67
Rerum novarum. Commonweal 84:326 Je 10 '66
ENCYCLOPAEDIA Britannica, incorporated
Britannica buys Frederick A. Praeger, inc. Pub W 189:31-2 My 2 '66
ENCYCLOPAEDIA Britannica educational company
New Britannica firm unites learning material sales. Pub W 189:64 F 7 '66
ENCYCLOPAEDIA Britannica school library awards
School library contest names ten finalists. Pub W 189:64-5 F 7 '66
ENCYCLOPEDIAS
Encyclopedias for kids. il Time 88:55 N 11 '66
Encyclopedias; roundup of new editions. R. Hayman. Sr Schol 88:sup20 F 4 '66
How Grolier created and produced the totally new Book of knowledge. il Pub W 191:64-6+ Ja 2 '67
Non-objective encyclopedia. R. Kirk. Nat R 18:273 Mr 22 '66
    See also names of encyclopedias, e.g. New Catholic encyclopedia
END of innocence; story. See Dohan, M. H.
END of the world
    See also
Eschatology
ENDICOTT, Kenneth M.
Search for a cancerless cigarette; interview, ed. by V. Block. por Sci Digest 60:18-23 N '66
ENDIVE
Instead of $1 per pound why not grow your own? il Sunset 136:256+ Ap '66
ENDŌ, Shūsaku
Japanese-Catholic novel. M. Gallagher. Commonweal 85:136-8 N 4 '66
Shusaku Endo: a Christian voice in Japanese literature. W. I. Elliott. Christian Cent 83:1147 S 21 '66
ENDOCARDITIS. See Heart—Diseases
ENDOCRINOLOGY
Adrenalectomy and coat color in deer mice. F. H. Bronson and S. H. Clarke. bibliog il Science 154:1349-50 D 9 '66
Conference on insect endocrines; report on symposium. V. K. McElheny. Science 154:248-51 O 14 '66
Polysome morphology; evidence for endocrine control during chick embryogenesis. M. B. Yatvin. bibliog il Science 151:1001-3 F 25 '66
    See also
Gonadotropin
ENDOSPERM
Structure and organization of the living mitotic spindle of haemanthus endosperm. A. Bajer and R. D. Allen. bibliog il Science 151:572-4 F 4 '66
ENDRIN
Endrin: use of concentration in blood to diagnose acute toxicity to fish. D. I. Mount and others. bibliog il Science 152:1388-90 Je 3 '66
ENERGY resources. See Power resources
ENFIELD, Conn.

Education
Truth has many faces; contemporary history classes at Enfield, Conn. high school. F. S. Gross il Sr Schol 88:sup22-3 Ap 29 '66
ENGAGEMENT rings. See Rings
ENGBRETSON, William E.
Creative programs in teacher-education. NEA J 55:45-7 D '66
ENGEL, C. and others
Tetrachloroanisol: a source of musty taste in eggs and broilers. Science 154:270-1 O 14 '66

ENGEL, Ernst
High style for skiing turns into big business. il por Bsns W p 108-10+ Ja 22 '66

ENGELHARD, Jane Reis-Brian
Energetic life. il pors Vogue 148:126-7 O 15 '66

ENGELMANN, Siegfried
Pressure cooker for four-year-old minds. M. Pines. il Harper 234:55-61 Ja '67

ENGELS, John
Drive-in movie; poem. Reporter 34:56 My 19 '66
For Philip; poem. Reporter 35:48 D 1 '66

ENGH, Jeri
Why not year-round schools? Sat R 49:82-4 S 17 '66; Same abr. with title Case for year-round schools. Read Digest 89:141-4 D '66

ENGINEERING
See also
Technology
also Aviation engineering; Industrial engineering; etc.

Study and teaching
College scene. il Sci Digest 60:22-9 O; 42-7 N; 20:9 D '66; 61:39-40 Ja '67
See also
Engineering education

ENGINEERING, Biomedical. See Biomedical engineering

ENGINEERING, Medical. See Biomedical engineering

ENGINEERING colleges
Best science/engineering schools. Sci Digest 60:27 O '66

ENGINEERING consultants. See Consulting engineers

ENGINEERING education
Continuing education for engineers; excerpts from address, October 1965. H. A. Foecke. Science 152:880-3 My 13 '66
Engineering education for what? adaptation of address, April 1, 1965. R. F. Humphreys. Sch & Soc 94:39-41 Ja 22 '66
Giving American ways to foreign engineers; Kuljian imports trainees from developing lands. il Bsns W p 170+ O 1 '66
Professors get dirty hands. Sci N 90:447 N 26 '66
See also
American society for engineering education

ENGINEERING magazine. See Factory and industrial management (periodical)

ENGINEERING materials. See Materials

ENGINEERING materials and process information service. See General electric company

ENGINEERING research
Road to glory? Sci N 90:551 D 24 '66

ENGINEERING students
Supermice of another Troy· RPI football. H. Weiskopf. Sports Illus 25:63-4 O 3 '66

ENGINEERS
See also
Consulting engineers
Engineering education

Supply and demand
Brain drain starts to hurt; Britain and Europeans, worried about siphoning off of scientific and technical talent to the U.S. il Bsns W p 122+ D 10 '66
British aerospace technologists move for end to brain drain. H. J. Coleman. Aviation W 85:33 O 24 '66
Manpower: output of scientists and engineers may exceed goals set by White House committee. L. J. Carter. il Science 151:666-8 F 11 '66; Reply. J. O. Mingle. 152:1186 My 27 '66
Personnel: talent scouts; recruiting at IEEE convention il Newsweek 67:86 Ap 4 '66
Projections of manpower supply in a specific occupation. N. Rosenthal. il Mo Labor R 89:1262-6 N '66

ENGINES
Engine cooling system care; tractors, trucks, and cars. Suc Farm 64:76 Ap '66
Trouble-free winter engine storage. P. B. Jones. il Suc Farm 64:36 D '66
See also
Gas turbines
Marine engines
Steam engines

ENGLAND
See also
Castle Combe
Christmas—England
Churches—England
Cornwall
Country estates—England
Foreign visitors in England
Gardens—England
Great Britain
Kent
Music festivals—England
Scilly Islands

Antiquities
See also
Rome—Antiquities
Stonehenge

Church history
Elizabeth's copy of Canon law. P. W. Schmidtchen. il Hobbies 71:108 Je '66

Description and travel
England, by N. Kazantzakis. Review New Repub 154:37-8 F 26 '66. H. Tracy

Anecdotes, facetiae, satire, etc.
Explorer's guide to England. P. Brooks. Sat R 49:67-8 S 17 '66

Education
See Education—Great Britain

Historic houses, etc.
Christmas at Chatsworth. H. Macmillan. il Horizon 9.84-7 Wint '67
Letter from London; Marble Hill at Twickenham. J. Stuart. il Antiques 90:440+ O '66

Intellectual life
See also
Books and reading—England

Religious institutions and affairs
Decline of the church in England. N. Stacey. Harper 232:64-6+ Mr '66; Reply. W. E. Hulme. 232:4+ My '66
Henry VIII and the Protestant triumph. L. B. Smith. bibliog f Am Hist R 71:1237-64 Jl '66
They lost religion but kept faith. M. Peckham. Sat R 49:62 Je 11 '66
World around us (cont) Christian Cent 83: 188, 380-1. 598-9, 1255-6. 1391-2, 1522; 84:27-8 F 9, Mr 23, My 4, O 12, N 9, D 7 '66; Ja 9 '67
See also
Catholic church in England
Church of England
England—Church history

Social conditions
See also
Crime and criminals—Great Britain

Social life and customs
Letter from abroad; American woman in an English-university community. D. Trilling. il McCalls 93:36+ Jl '66
See also
Christmas—England

ENGLAND, Church of. See Church of England

ENGLAND and Europe
European idea, by Lord Gladwyn. Review Reporter 34:53-4 Ap 7 '66. R. Mayne

ENGLAND and the United States
Across the Potomac on London bridge; address, April 17, 1966. M. I. Prichard. Vital Speeches 32:464-6 My 15 '66
President Johnson confers with British Prime Minister; exchange of toasts. July 29. 1966. L. B. Johnson; H. Wilson. Dept State Bul 55:265-8 Ag 22 '66
See also
Americans in England
United States—Foreign opinion—British

ENGLE, Paul
Iowa's state fair. Holiday 39:78-87 My '66
Should this father raise his son? Ladies Home J 83:89+ My '66

ENGLEBARDT, Stanley L.
Lessons for everybody from jet travel fatigue. Sci Digest 59:80-4 Mr '66
Light that bends, twists and turns. Sci Digest 59:40-3 My '66

ENGLEHORN, A. J. and Herman, J. C.
Fall farming; best way to beat the spring labor shortage. Farm J 90:40-1 O '66

ENGLERT, Evangeline
Touring the world with stamps. Horticulture 44:36-7+ Ag '66

ENGLISH, Darrel S. See Thompson, P. E. jt. auth.

ENGLISH authors. See Authors, English

ENGLISH CHANNEL tunnel (proposed)
Do we dig it? Nat R 18:717-18 Jl 26 '66

ENGLISH coins. See Coins

ENGLISH composition. See English language—Composition

ENGLISH cookery. See Cookery, English
ENGLISH drama
See also
London—Theater
Theater—Great Britain
ENGLISH electric company
English electric's leapfrog. Fortune 73:65+
Mr '66
ENGLISH fiction
Literary letter from London; winter publications. P. Buckman. Nation 202:340-1 Mr 21 '66
Of luvs and lights; reading public's addiction to light novels. K. F. Kister. il Wilson Lib Bul 41:510-13+ Ja '67
ENGLISH furniture. See Furniture, English
ENGLISH grammar. See English language—Grammar
ENGLISH holly. See Holly
ENGLISH humor. See Humor, English
ENGLISH in action (organization)
800 volunteers and an upright idiot. R. Lynes. il Harper 234:24-6 Ja '67
ENGLISH in Malay Peninsula
East of Suez; 1926, 1955. A. Waugh. Nat R 18:685+ Jl 12 '66
ENGLISH language
English was my undoing; experiences as a Russian immigrant in 1919. S. H. Babington. NEA J 65:16-18 F '66
In defense of English; publication of Modern American usage. Newsweek 68:66+ O 17 '66
Modern American usage, by W. Follett and others. Review
Nation 203:709-12 D 26 '66. M. Pei
Sorry, general, English is the language; question of the world's international tongue. Life 61:4 S 9 '66
See also
Colloquialisms
Slang
Words

Composition
Scholastic sponsors P.E. workshop; Weehawken high school, N.J. il Sr Schol 87:sup32 Ja 14 '66
Stimulating students to write. B. Goodman. Sr Schol 88:sup 14 Mr 11 '66
Teaching students to write. L. V. Payne. NEA J 55:28-30 N '66

Creative activities
Onward and upward with the arts; fiction-writing course called Daily themes at Yale. C. Trillin. New Yorker 42:118+ Je 11 '66
Poems to learn by; haiku. il Time 88:65 S 2 '66
Screenwriter in the ghetto; workshop at Watts. il Time 88:53 Jl 22 '66
Student's work is published; concerning sketch in Scholastic scope. M. A. Elliott. il Sr Schol 89:sup47-8 S 23 '66

Dialects
Digging the man's language. R. Riessman and F. Alberts. il Sat R 49:80-1+ S 17 '66
Let stalk Strine, by A. Morrison. Review Newsweek il 67:109C+ Mr 21 '66

Dictionaries
Dictionary project; leading Random house event to date; Random house dictionary of the English language. il Pub W 189:61 My 30 '66
In defense of English; Random house dictionary of the English language and Modern American usage. Newsweek 68:66+ O 17 '66
Let stalk Strine, by A. Morrison. Review Newsweek il 67:109C+ Mr 21 '66
Modern American usage, by W. Follett and others. Review
Sat R 49:29-30 N 5 '66. G. Hicks
Newest dictionary; Random house dictionary of the English language. il Time 88:77-8 S 30 '66
Random house dictionary of the English language. il Consumer Bul 49:35-6 D '66
Random house dictionary of the English language. Review
Nation 203:675-6 D 19 '66. M. Pei
Sat R 49:49-50+ O 22 '66. G. Hicks
Random house dictionary tested at $7.50 by B-O-M. Pub W 190:33 N 28 '66
Tongues, like government; concerning Random house dictionary of the English language and Modern American usage. J. M. Edelstein. New Repub 155:26-8 N 26 '66; Reply. W. L. Pretzer. 155:35-6 D 17 '66

Grammar
Be grateful for grammar. E. W. Johnson. Parents Mag 41:67-8 Mr '66

Beware these word-traps! excerpt from The careful writer. T. M. Bernstein. il Read Digest 88:33+ Ap '66
Dream world of English grammar. J. C. Bostain. il NEA J 55:20-2 S '66
Like your cigarette should; the Winston slogan. R. L. Tobin. il Sat R 49:59-60 My 14 '66
Manner of speaking; poetic guidelines. G. Ace. Sat R 49:7 Jl 23 '66
Purest English? Lord Chandos protests against abuse. il Newsweek 68:79-80 Jl 4 '66
Roberts English series, by P. Roberts. Review
Sat R 49:48-9 Ap 16 '66. A. Dalgliesh
Tale of two urban areas; reprint. C. S. Brown. Horizon 8:120 Aut '66

Pronunciation
English as a second language; system to aid Negroes. il Time 87:60 F 18 '66

Study and teaching
Age of overwrite and underthink. S. Spender. Sat R 49:21-3+ Mr 12 '66
Away from Moby Dick and Jane; high school English program in Dover, N.H. M. Mainwaring. il Sr Schol 89:sup 13-15 O 14 '66
Be grateful for grammar. E. W. Johnson. Parents Mag 41:67-8+ Mr '66
Doctor Daniel Fader: a child without books is impoverished; summary of address, June 6, 1966. D. N. Fader. il Pub W 189:33-5 Je 20 '66
8 across, 3 down; crossword puzzles to build vocabulary and improve spelling; Alexander Hamilton H. S, Los Angeles. S. Cochell. Sr Schol 89:sup 13 D 2 '66
English from the inside. E. Welty. Am Ed 2:18-19 F '66
English is to enjoy; Jackson H.S. Ga. J. A. Settle. il Sr Schol 88:sup20 F 11 '66
National study of high school English programs. J. R. Squire. il Sr Schol 88:sup16-17 F 11 '66
Sad state of English teaching. W. W. Brickman. Sch & Soc 94:84 F 19 '66
Social studies and English combine in humanities approach; Gunn high school, Palo Alto, Calif. R. Goben. Sr Schol 88:sup8 Ap 22 '66
See also
Americanization school, Washington, D.C.
English in action (organization)
English language—Composition
English language—Grammar
National council of teachers of English

Anecdotes, facetiae, satire, etc.
800 volunteers and an upright idiot; concerning a celebrated little phrase book. R. Lynes. il Harper 234:26 Ja '67

Bibliography
What's happening in English; new NCTE publications. H. R. Finch. Sr Schol 88:sup 10 F 11; 89:sup43 S 23 '66

Terms and phrases
Fast as an elephant, strong as an ant; animal cliches inaccurate and inadequate. B. Gilbert. il Sports Illus 24:68-70+ Ap 25 '66
Tale of two urban areas; reprint. C. S. Brown. Horizon 8:120 Aut '66
To speak, correctly; excerpts from Modern American usage. W. Follett. Vogue 148:58+ D '66
We have a saying... Farm J 90:81 S '66
See also
Shibboleth (term)
Words
ENGLISH language in the United States. See English language
ENGLISH literature
See also
Authors, English
English fiction

Bibliography
Books for English teachers. J. Mersand. Sr Schol 89:sup62 S 23 '66

Study and teaching
Coy mistress caper; furor over assignment to rephrase A. Marvell's 17th century love poem. il Life 61:99-102 N 11 '66
See also
English language—Study and teaching
ENGLISH money. See Money—Great Britain
ENGLISH music. See Music, English
ENGLISH novels. See English fiction

ENGLISH poetry
British chronicle. R. Howard. Poetry 108: 399-407 S '66
On English and American poetry. S. Spender. Sat R 49:19-20+ Ap 23 '66
Three English poets. M. McCloskey. Poetry 109:126-9 N '66
Two British chronicles. R. J. Mills. jr; M. Bell. Poetry 107:406-13 Mr '66
See also
American poetry
ENGLISH pottery. See Pottery, English
ENGLISH press. See Newspapers—Great Britain
ENGLISH scientists. See Scientists, British
ENGLISH sculpture. See Sculpture, British
ENGLISH sparrows. See Sparrows
ENGLISH springer spaniel national championship. See Field trials (dogs)
ENGLISH visitors in the United States. See Foreign visitors in the United States
ENGRAVING
Where are Audubon's copper plates? W. Fries. il Audubon Mag 68:259-62+ Jl '66
ENGRAVINGS, Rock. See Petroglyphs
ENGRUM, Elaine
Mitey miss of the concert stage. il pors Ebony 22:112-16 D '66
ENIWETOK
Stillness on Eniwetok; island life at a former nuclear test site. M. Berrill. il Natur Hist 75:20-5 bibliog(p70) D '66
ENIWETOK atom bomb tests. See Atomic bombs—Testing
ENLARGING meters. See Photography—Apparatus and supplies
ENLISTMENT. See United States—Army— Recruiting and enlistment
ENNS, T.
Facilitation by carbonic anhydrase of carbon dioxide transport. bibliog Science 155:44-7 Ja 6 '67
ENOCH Pratt free library, Baltimore
Involvement in federal programs; address. 1966. E. Castagna. il Wilson Lib Bul 41: 478-83 Ja '67
Library service in the inner city; Community action program. E. Levy. il Wilson Lib Bul 41:470-7 Ja '67
Outstanding education books of 1965. NEA J 55:60+ My '66
ENOVID. See Contraceptives
ENRICO, Harold
Twelfth night; poem. Christian Cent 83:1564 D 21 '66
ENRICO (literary character) See Characters in literature
ENRICO Fermi award. See Fermi award
ENRIGHT, Elizabeth
Hour in September; story. Ladies Home J 83:80-1 S '66
ENRIGHT, J. T. See Heusner, A. A. jt. auth.
ENSLIN, Theodore
For sharing. J. L. Weil. Poetry 109:195-6 D '66
Precision in two languages. Poetry 109:112-14 N '66
Third path. Poetry 108:339-41 Ag '66
Times of day; poem. Poetry 108:248-63 Jl '66
ENTEROVIRUSES. See Viruses
ENTERPRISE (aircraft carrier) See Aircraft carriers, Atomic powered
ENTERPRISE, Free. See Free enterprise
ENTERTAINERS
Borscht belt, by J. Adams and H. Tobias. Review
Newsweek il 67:120+ Je 13 '66
Middle-aged mother visits the teen scene. H. Eustis. il McCalls 93:56-61+ Ag '66
Spats and tromoblatts; the Times square two. il Newsweek 67:96-7 Ap 11 '66
See also
Beatles
ENTERTAINING
At a party; use of color. il House & Gard 129:144-5 Mr '66
Big party cook book. E. Ross. il House & Gard 129:205+ Ap '66
Bridal shower in a box. Bet Hom & Gard 44: 133 My '66
Come to a cheese tasting; with recipe. il Good H 162:208 Ap '66
December parties. B. Plumb. il Mlle 64:58-9 D '66
Entertaining people, party ideas from everywhere. il McCalls 94:20+ O; 18+ D '66; 14 Ja '67
Everytown, U.S.A: sweet sixteen party. il Ladies Home J 83:122+ O '66
Festivity in a fresh key. il House & Gard 130:152-5 D '66

Five successful showers. Bet Hom & Gard 44:141 Je '66
For a quick snack party; with recipes. il Seventeen 25:150-3+ O '66
Formal, traditional New Year's party, 1967. H. Kurtzman and N. Quest. il Esquire 67: 96-103 Ja '67
Go-go parties; with recipes. il Seventeen 25: 166-9+ Ap '66
GH's 10 p.m. specials! with recipes. il Good H 162:94-111 F '66
How America entertains. il Ladies Home J 83:85-112+ O '66
How to make a big do great: dinner and dancing party; cocktail party. il House & Gard 129:166-71 Ap '66
How to set the stage for an outdoor party. il Bet Hom & Gard 44:139 Je '66
New form of night lighting for a party in the dark. il House & Gard 130:120-3 Ag '66
Notes for the hostess. D. Bryan. See issues of House & garden incorporating Living for young homemakers
Open season for entertaining; summer party giving; with recipes. il McCalls 93:104-12+ My '66
Parties on the patio. il Bet Hom & Gard 44:136-7 Je '66
Party planning: how to put your guests at ease. ii House & Gard 131:94-7 Ja '67
Party strategy; tips from five great hostesses. il House & Gard 130:272-82 N '66
Party with pow! with recipes. il Seventeen 25:66-81+ Jl '66
Project parties; paying guests. il Time 88: 62 D 23 '66
Return to a long, cool summer. il Esquire 66:78-83 Jl '66
Shower for the bride; with recipes. C. Brock. Good H 162:152 Mr '66
Simple but elegant back-yard party. K. Smith. il Pop Gard 17:46-9+ Ag '66
Six February happenings; more fun than a party! with recipes. il Seventeen 25:156-61+ F '66
Sunday-morning coffees make hospitality a habit! with recipes. C. Brock. il Good H 162:154 Je '66
Translated from the Lebanese: piquant party touches. buoyant decoration. il House & Gard 130:184-5 D '66
When to cry "enough"? E. Booker. Vogue 147:60-1 F 1 '66
See also
Buffet meals
Caterers and catering
Dinners and dining
Government entertaining
Guests
Luncheons
Suppers
Table decoration

Anecdotes, facetiae, satire, etc.

Fifty-three ways to entertain once. C. W. Ferguson. il Read Digest 88:33-4+ F '66
Pleasure of your company is requested; engagement party. I. Kampen. McCalls 93:49 Mr '66
ENTERTAINING, Government. See Government entertaining
ENTERTAINMENT industry
Public entertainment and the subversion of ethical standards. G. Seldes. Ann Am Acad 363:87-94 Ja '66
Return of the (whoosh! there goes one!) superhero! B. Rollin. il Look 30:113-14 Mr 22 '66
Whole country goes supermad. il Life 60: 22-7 Mr 11 '66
ENTERTAINMENTS. See Amusements
ENTHUSIASM
Secret of enthusiasm. M. Drury. Read Digest 88:193+ Je '66
ENTRANCE age, School. See School age
ENTRANCE drives. See Driveways
ENTRANCE halls. See Halls
ENTRANCES (doorways) See Doorways
ENURESIS. See Urine—Incontinence
ENVELOPES (stationery)
Many happy returns; return address envelopes. il Am Heritage 17:78-81 F '66
ENVIRONMENT
Aesthetic dimension of environmental responsibility; proposal for curriculum innovation in aesthetic education, grades 7-12; with project. R. A. Smith. bibliog il Sch Arts 65:20-2 Ap '66
Environmental art; work done through neighborhood self-help. K. Linn. il Sch Arts 66: 26-8 D '66

ENVIRONMENT—*Continued*

Industry and tomorrow's environment; report on meeting of American forest products industries. J. B. Craig. il Am For 72:30-1+ D '66

Inheritance of reactivity to experimental manipulation in mice. N. D. Henderson. bibliog il Science 153:650-2 Ag 5 '66

Politics of the future; control of our environment. M. Phelps. America 114:644 My 7 '66

Pollution: everybody's adversary; symposium. il Todays Health 44:37-65 Mr '66

See also

Adjustment, Social

Botany—Ecology

Man—Influence of environment

Man—Influence on nature

ENVIRONMENTAL engineering

Expressive environment. S. Brower. il Arch Forum 124:38-9 Ap '66

Way to influence the environment. il Arch Rec 139:207-14 Ap '66

Working environment. il Duns R 88:pt2 132-3 S '66

See also

Human engineering

ENVIRONMENTAL laboratories. See Testing laboratories

ENVIRONMENTAL science services administration. See United States—Environmental science services administration

ENVIRONMENTAL survey satellite. See Artificial satellites—Meteorological applications

ENZENSBERGER, Hans Magnus

Auf das grab eines friedlichen mannes; poem, with English tr. by M. Hamburger. Harper 233:75 Jl '66

ENZYMES

Aminooxyacetic acid: interactions with gamma-aminobutyric acid and the blood-brain barrier. M. A. Fisher and others. bibliog il Science 153:1668-70 S 30 '66

Antagonism of purified asparaginase from guinea pig serum toward lymphoma. T. O. Yellin and J. C. Wriston, jr. bibliog il Science 151:998-9 F 25 '66

Control of the activity of escherichia coli carbamoyl phosphate synthetase by antagonistic allosteric effectors. A. Piérard. bibliog il Science 154:1572-3 D 23 '66

Coordinate synthesis of heme and apoenzyme in the formation of tryptophan pyrrolase H. S. Marver and others. bibliog il Science 154:501-3 O 28 '66

Correlation between location and time of expression for genes in a single operon. D. Marver and others. bibliog il Science 153:1655-6 S 30 '66

Electrophoretic variation in enzymes. C. R. Shaw; reply. J. A. Beardmore. Science 152:1107 My 20 '66

Enzyme amplifier kinetics. S. N. Levine. il Science 152:651-3 Ap 29 '66

Enzyme changes in neurons and glia during barbiturate sleep. A. Hamberger and others. il Science 151:1394-5 Mr 18 '66

Enzyme-coenzyme complexes of pyridine nucleotide-linked dehydrogenases. H. F. Fisher and D. G. Cross. bibliog il Science 153:414-15 Jl 22 '66

Enzyme regulation in mammalian tissues; international symposium. G. Weber. Science 151:479-81 Ja 28 '66

Enzyme synthesized from natural one; bacterial enzyme subtilisin. Sci N 90:448 N 26 '66

Feedback inhibition of glycerol kinase, a catabolic enzyme in escherichia coli. N. Zwaig and E. C. C. Lin. bibliog il Science 153:755-7 Ag 12 '66

Feedback inhibition of key glycolytic enzymes in liver: action of free fatty acids. G. Weber and others. bibliog il Science 154:1357-60 D 9 '66

From enzymatic adaptation to allosteric transitions; address. December 11, 1965. J. Monod. bibliog il Science 154:475-83 O 28 '66

Glucagon, starvation, and the induction of liver enzymes by hydrocortisone. O. Greengard and G. T. Baker. bibliog il Science 154:1461-2 D 16 '66

Lactoperoxidase: identification and isolation from harderian and lacrimal glands. M. Morrison and P. Z. Allen. bibliog il Science 152:1626-8 Je 17 '66

Lipid films as transducers for detection of antigen-antibody and enzyme-substrate reactions. J. Del Castillo and others. bibliog il Science 153:185-8 Jl 8 '66

Metabolism of alveolar cells; histochemical evidence and relation to pulmonary surfactant. S. I. Said and others. bibliog il Science 152:657-9 Ap 29 '66

Nicotinamide-adenine dinucleotide in tubercle bacilli exposed to isoniazid. A. Bekierkunst. bibliog il Science 152:525-6 Ap 22 '66

Ornithine transcarbamylase enzymes: occurrence in bacillus licheniformis. R. W. Bernlohr. bibliog il Science 152:87-8 Ap 1 '66

Ornithine-urea cycle enzymes in the African lungfish, protopterus aethiopicus. P. A. Janssens and P. P. Cohen. bibliog il Science 152:358-9 Ap 15 '66

Pigment protein complex from gonyaulax. D. J. Haidak and others. bibliog il Science 152:212-13 Ap 8 '66

Spontaneous mammary tumors: decrease of incidence in mice infected with an enzyme-elevating virus. V. Riley. bibliog il Science 153:1657-8 S 30 '66

Starch-gel electrophoresis of human tissue enzymes which hydrolyze L -leucyl-β-naphthylamide. E. E. Smith and A. M. Rutenburg. bibliog il Science 152:1256-7 My 27 '66

Structure-disrupting ions: detection of qualitative change in an enzyme. J. C. Warren and D. M. Peterson. bibliog il Science 152:1245-6 My 27 '66

Uricolytic enzymes in liver of the dipnoan protopterus aethiopicus. G. W. Brown, jr. and others. bibliog il Science 153:1653-4 S 30 '66

Viral neoplastic transformation of hamster pineal cells in vitro: retention of enzymatic function. S. A. Wells, jr. and others. bibliog il Science 154:278-9 O 14 '66

See also

Aldolase

Carbonic anhydrase

Carboxypeptidases

Dehydrogenases

Fumarate

Lysozyme

Mutarotase

Peroxidases

Reductases

Trehalase

Trypsin

Urease

EOCENE period. See Paleontology—Eocene

EPHEMERIDES

Lunar Orbiter ranging data: initial results; testing the significance of corrections to the lunar ephemeris. J. D. Mulholland and W. L. Sjogren. bibliog il Science 155:74-6 Ja 6 '67

EPHEMERIS time. See Time measurements

EPIC poetry

Rustaveli and the knight in the tiger's skin. I. Abashidze. il UNESCO Courier 19:28-30 O '66

EPIDEMIC encephalitis. See Encephalitis, Epidemic

EPIDEMICS

See also

Cholera

Influenza

Plague

EPIGRAMS

See also

Aphorisms and apothegms

EPILEPSY

Electrodes in the brain; help for psychomotor epileptics. il Time 87:51-3 Je 10 '66

Epilepsy drugs have bad effects on some. Sci N L 89:152 Mr 5 '66

Report on epilepsy cure misleading. Sci N 89:317 Ap 30 '66

EPILEPTICS

What the teacher can do for the student with epilepsy. S. Livingston. NEA J 55:24-6 N '66

EPIMEDIUMS

Epimediums, plants that dance with the wind. M. M. Leister. il Flower Grower 53:24+ Ap '66

EPINEPHRINE. See Adrenalin

EPISCIAS

Episcias. A. Wright. il Horticulture 44:14-15+ Jl '66

EPISCOPAL church. See Church of England; Protestant Episcopal church

EPITHALAMION; story. See Mountzoures, H. L.

EPITHELIUM

Perineural epithelium: a new concept of its role in the integrity of the peripheral nervous system. T. R. Shanthaveerappa and G. H. Bourne. bibliog il Science 154:1464-7 D 16 '66

EPOXY coatings. See Finishing materials

EPPEL, Lou

Eleven springtime steps to make your dependable outboard dependabler. Motor B 117:28-9+ Mr '66

EPSTEIN, Alan N. See Hainsworth, F. R. jt. auth.

EPSTEIN, Edward Jay
Who's afraid of the Warren report? Esquire 66:204+ D '66

about

New wave of doubt; concerning his book: Inquest. F. Knebel. il Look 30:66-72 Jl 12 '66
Warren commission: the critics and the law; theories of E. J. Epstein and M. Lane. K. Goodall; A. L. Goodhart. Reporter 35:44-8+ D 15 '66

EPSTEIN, Eugene E.
Mercury: anomalous absense from the 3.4-millimeter radio emission of variation with phase. bibliog Science 151:445-7 Ja 28 '66

EPSTEIN, Eugene V.
Education by remote control: report on DIDACTA. Pub W 190:37-8 S 5 '66

EPSTEIN, Jason
Obscenity business. Atlan 218:56-60 Ag '66; Same. Library J 91:4566-71 O 1 '66

EPSTEIN, Joseph
Enfant terrible. Commentary 42:94-6 D '66
Free-lance. Commentary 42:96-100 N '66

EPSTEIN, Klaus
Contagious sense of discovery. Harper 232: 114-17 F; 8+ My '66

EPSTEIN, Sam
Amateur scientist. Sci Am 215:277-8+ S '66

EPSTEIN, Samuel. See O'Neil, J. R; Taylor, H. P. jr, jt. auths.

EPSTEIN, Samuel S. and Taylor, F. B.
Photosensitizing compounds in extracts of drinking water. bibliog Science 154:261-3 O 14 '66

EPSTEIN, Seymour
Person and plot. Writer 79:9-12 My '66

EPTATRETUS stoutii. See Hagfish

EPTON, William
At a Black Panther meeting in Harlem. U S News 61:14-15 S 12 '66

EQUAL employment opportunity commission. See United States—President's equal employment opportunity commission

EQUAL pay. See Wages

EQUAL rights for women. See Woman—Equal rights

EQUALITY
Equality ad absurdum. F. S. Meyer. Nat R 18:1168 N 15 '66
Freedom, when? by J. Farmer. Review Sat R 49:37+ Ap 23 '66. G. Samuels
Full equality: what it really means. D. Lawrence. U S News 61:120 S 19 '66
See also
Race relations

EQUALIZER (sound) See Sound—Apparatus

EQUILIBRIUM (thermodynamic)
Thermodynamic equilibrium and the inorganic origin of organic compounds. R. V. Eck and others. bibliog il Science 153:628-33 Ag 5 '66

EQUINE encephalitis virus. See Encephalitis virus

EQUINIL. See Meprobamates

L'EQUIPE. See Paris—Newspapers

EQUIPMENT, Industrial. See Industrial equipment

EQUIPMENT, Municipal. See Municipal equipment

EQUIPMENT industries
Capital goods makers whistle a happy tune. Bsns W p 16-17 D 24 '66

EQUIPMENT renting. See Rental services

EQUITY
See also
Justice

ERDÖS, Ervin G.
Hypotensive peptides. Science 152:1284-5 My 27 '66

ERHARD, Ludwig
Exchange of toasts with President Johnson, December 20, 1965. Dept State Bul 54:48-50 Ja 10 '66
Germany; address, May 25, 1966. Vital Speeches 32:552-4 Jl 1 '66
President Johnson and Chancellor Erhard hold talks at Washington; joint communique. Dept State Bul 54:46-51 Ja 10 '66
United States and Germany reaffirm community of interest; exchange of toast, September 26; with text of joint communique, September 27, 1966. Dept State Bul 55:579-81, 583-5 O 17 '66

about

Brutuses on the Rhine. il por Time 88:38 N 4 '66
Chancellor at the brink. il por Newsweek 68:50+ N 7 '66
Erhard crisis; what led to it. por U S News 61:30 N 14 '66

Erhard in trouble. U S News 61:20 Jl 25 '66
Erhard's last stand. il Newsweek 68:40 N 14 '66
Flashing knives. il Time 88:35 N 11 '66
Germany: time for a dose of the new economics. il por Bsns W p 123-4 N 5 '66
Gloom for Uncle Boom. por Newsweek 68:45 Jl 25 '66
In spite of himself. Time 87:30 F 11 '66
Low on steam. il por Time 88:31 Jl 22 '66
Ludwig Erhard: another Bismarck? H. A. Schmitt. bibliog f il Cur Hist 50:257-62+ My '66
Ludwig Erhard had a great fall. G. Bailey. por Reporter 35:39-40 N 17 '66
Quiet is shattered on Bonn front. il Bsns W p44-5 N 19 '66
Seeking solace in Washington. Time 88:29 S 30 '66
Snipping at Erhard. Time 88:40-1 O 14 '66
Sorrows of Erhard. por Newsweek 68:40 O 3 '66
Trouble in Germany: it means trouble for U.S. il por U S News 61:75-6 N 21 '66
What price Germany, now? E. Stillman. il pors N Y Times Mag p54-7+ D 4 '66

ERIC the Red
Men before Columbus; excerpt from Westviking, the ancient Norse in Greenland and North America. F. Mowat. il Read Digest 89:200-2+ N '66

ERICKSON, Don
Something . . . Esquire 65:111-13 Je '66

ERICKSON, Donald A.
Plain people vs. the common schools. Sat R 49:85-7+ N 19 '66

ERICKSON, Margie V.
How black plastic mulch made our garden really grow Flower Grower 53:60 Je '66

ERICKSON, Russell F.
Can cash flow be turned on? interview. por Duns R 88:32 Jl '66

ERICSON, James C.
Worms beat the drum. Outdoor Life 138:48-9+ Ag '66

ERIE, LAKE
Dying lake. B. Tufty. il(p 1) Sci N 90:10-11 Jl 2 '66
Lake Erie: test case in water-pollution battle. U S News 61:12 Jl 4 '66

ERIE CANAL
Erie Canal: a record in pastels by J. Erwin Porter. N. Kent. il Am Artist 30:42-7+ Je '66
Some early American medals; commemorating the opening. C. French. Hobbies 71:102 N '66

ERIE-Lackawanna railroad
Erie toils to make a match. il Bsns W p60-2+ Ag 6 '66

ERIKSEN, Stein
Stein Eriksen: Horatio Alger on skis. T. F. Smith. il Harper 232:87-90 Mr '66

ERITREA, Africa
Control of the Red Sea. A. Ford. il Nat R 18:314-15 Ap 5 '66

ERLANDER, Tage
Modern Sweden; address, November 9, 1965. Vital Speeches 32:425-7 My 1 '66

ERLANGER, Margaret
College or career for dancers? University of Illinois' answer. E. Stodelle. il por Dance Mag 40:52-5 Ap '66

ERLING, Bernhard
Sweden: not quite that bad. Christian Cent 83:1343-4 N 2 '66

ERNEST Orlando Lawrence memorial awards
Five scientists given AEC's Lawrence award. Sci N 89:299 Ap 23 '66

ERNST, Harry W.
Two GI's in limbo. Nation 202:294-5 Mr 14 '66

ERNST, Leo
Odyssey in oils. il Time 89:58+ Ja 20 '67

ERNST, Max
Art galleries: exhibition at the Jewish museum. R. M. Coates. New Yorker 42:144+ Mr 26 '66

ERNST, P. G.
Will success spoil Aspen? Nation 203:70-3 Jl 25 '66

ERNST, Paul
Long way home; story. Redbook 126:173 Ap '66

EROSION
Nature note; river pirates. il Sci N 90:438 N 26 '66
See also
Beach erosion
Coast changes

EROTIC art. See Sex in art

ERRORS
See also
Accuracy
Blunders

ERRORS, Popular
See also
Superstition

ERSKINE, Richard W.
Justice in the courtroom, can the poor get it? G. Samuels. Sat R 49:25+ Ja 29 '66

ERVIN, Frank
Frank's way with a filly. P. Axthelm. il Sports Illus 25:42-3 S 12 '66

ERWAY, Lawrence, and others
Neurological defect: manganese in phenocopy and prevention of a genetic abnormality of inner ear. bibliog Science 152:1766-8 Je 24 '66

ERWIN, Kate
One state's adult basic program. Am Ed 3: 27-8 D '66

ERWIN, Robert
Civilization as a phase of world history. bibliog f Am Hist R 71:1181-98 Jl '66

ERYCK, Donald
On the gypsy circuit. W. Como. por Dance Mag 40:20 N '66

ERYTHROBLASTOSIS
Tests can save unborn: blood transfusion for treating an Rh-factor disease. Sci N 90: 191 S 10 '66

ERYTHROCYTES
Antibodies affecting metabolism of chicken erythrocytes: examination of schizophrenic and other subjects. J. W. Ryan and others. bibliog il Science 151:1408-10 Mr 18 '66
Erythrocyte chimerism after injection of spleen cells into anemic mice of the W-series. M. J. Seller. bibliog il Science 155: 90-1 Ja 6 '67
Molecular mechanism of red cell sickling. M. Murayama. bibliog il Science 153:145-9 Jl 8 '66
Tryptophan deficiency in rabbit reticulocytes: polyribosomes during interrupted growth of hemoglobin chains. M. Hori and others. bibliog il Science 155:83-4 Ja 6 '67

ERYTHROPOIESIS
Erythropoietic and reticuloendothelial function in bone marrow in dogs. M. L. Greenberg and others. bibliog il Science 152: 526-8 Ap 22 '66
Erythropoietin: hypothesis of action tested by analog computer. A. L. Kretchmar. bibliog il Science 152:367-70 Ap 15 '66
Erythropoietin: production by a particulate fraction of rat kidney. J. F. Contrera and A. S. Gordon. bibliog il Science 152:653-4 Ap 29 '66

ERYTHROPOIETIC factor
Virus-induced murine leukemia: its inhibition and suppression by serum containing erythropoietin. P. G. Stansly and P. E. Schlop. bibliog il Science 152:1082-3 My 20 '66

ESAKI, Masumi
Just how dangerous is red China? interview, ed. by K. M. Chrysler. por U S News 61: 84-6 O 24 '66

ESCALATOR clause (wages) See Wages—Cost of living adjustments

ESCANDE, Maurice
King; interview. New Yorker 42:29-31 F 26 '66

ESCAPE devices (space vehicles) See Space vehicles—Escape devices

ESCAPES
Away they go! conditions of British prisons. Time 88:28 D 23 '66
Escape into the cold; escape of G. Blake from London's Wormwood Scrubs prison. Newsweek 68:52-4 N 7 '66
Holiday exodus; Great Britain. il Time 89:30 Ja 6 '67
Open-door policy; British prisons. Newsweek 69:34 Ja 9 '67
Question of identity; escape of G. Blake. il Time 88:38+ N 4 '66

ESCHATOLOGY
Bright eschatology. V. P. McCorry. America 115:634 N 12 '66
Freeze-wait-reanimate. Time 88:93 S 30 '66
See also
Second advent

ESCHER, Maurits Cornelis
Escher's eerie games. il por Horizon 8:110-15 Aut '66
Mathematical games; eerie mathematical art. M. Gardner. il Sci Am 214:110-11+ Ap '66

ESCHERICHIA coli
Bacteriophage T5 chromosome fractionation: genetic specificity of a DNA fragment. Y. T. Lanni and others. bibliog il Science 152: 208-10 Ap 8 '66
Chemotaxis in bacteria. J. Adler. bibliog il Science 153:708-16 Ag 12 '66

Control of the activity of escherichia coli carbamoyl phosphate synthetase by antagonistic allosteric effectors. A. Piérard. bibliog il Science 154:1572-3 D 23 '66
Feedback inhibition of glycerol kinase, a catabolic enzyme in escherichia coli. N. Zwaig and E. C. C. Lin. bibliog il Science 153:755-7 Ag 12 '66
Formylmethionine codon AUG as an initiator of polypeptide synthesis. R. E. Thach and others. bibliog il Science 153:416-18 Jl 22 '66
Formylmethionyl-tRNA dependence of amino acid incorporation in extracts of trimethoprim-treated escherichia coli. J. Eisenstadt and P. Lengyel. bibliog il Science 154: 524-7 O 28 '66
Germs cause burn deaths. Sci N 90:300 O 15 '66
Isopycnic centrifugation for the isolation of DNA strands coding for ribosomal RNA. P. F. Davison. bibliog il Science 152:509-12 Ap 22 '66
Polysomes extracted from escherichia coli by freeze-thaw-lysozyme lysis. E. Z. Ron and others. bibliog il Science 153:1119-20 S 2 '66
Protein and nucleic acid synthesis in escherichia coli: pressure and temperature effects. J. V. Landau. bibliog il Science 153: 1273-4 S 9 '66
Proteins start here. Sci Am 215:102 S '66
Selection of sucrose-dependent escherichia coli to obtain envelope mutants and fragile cultures. G. Mangiarotti and others. bibliog il Science 153:892-4 Ag 19 '66
Tryptophan operon of escherichia coli: regulatory behavior in salmonella typhimurium cytoplasm. R. L. Somerville. bibliog il Science 154:1585-7 D 23 '66

ESCOBEDO, Danny
Chicago v. Escobedo. Time 88:35 D 30 '66
Face is familiar. Newsweek 68:37 N 14 '66
Putting theory into practice. por Time 88:77 N 11 '66

ESCORIAL
King's prayer factory. H. R. Trevor-Roper. il Horizon 8:66-75 Wint '66

ESCUMINAC BAY
Ancient fishes of Escuminac Bay. D. L. Dineley. il Natur Hist 76:40-5 bibliog(p73) Ja '67

ESERINE
Carbamylation and binding constants for the inhibition of acetylcholinesterase by physostigmine, eserine. A. R. Main and F. L. Hastings. bibliog il Science 154:400-2 O 21 '66

ESFANDIARY, F. M.
Iran: goodby to the nightingale. Nation 202: 468-70 Ap 18 '66

ESH sarcoma. See Sarcoma

ESHELMAN, William R.
Library education and the talent shortage. por Library J 91:1766-7 Ap 1 '66

ESHERICK, Wharton
Wood; a discussion. pors Craft Horiz 26:16-19 Je '66

ESHKOL, Levi
Don't panic. il por Newsweek 69:45-6 Ja 16 '67
Worried citizen. il por Time 88:37 Jl 22 '66

ESHLEMAN, Clayton
Explorations in the apolitical. Nation 203: 285-7 S 26 '66
Poem to accompany Mary. Poetry 109:75-6 N '66

ESKIMO masks. See Masks (for the face)

ESKIMOS
Alaska's greatest hunter; Peter Koonuk-noruck. C. E. Gillham. il Field & S 71:28-30+ Ag '66
Face to face: with a girl from the forty-ninth state. D. Napoleon. Seventeen 25:141 Mr '66
New people. by E. Iglauer. Review
Time il 87:102 Mr 11 '66
Our far-flung correspondents; summer's first boat to King Island. B. Roueché. New Yorker 42:98+ O 22 '66

Art
Anaktuvuk mask and cultural innovation; adaptation of address, September 1964. S. Atamian. bibliog il Science 151:1337-45 Mr 18 '66; Reply. W. S. Neff. 152:1283 My 27 '66

Culture
Anaktuvuk mask and cultural innovation; adaptation of address, September 1964. S. Atamian. bibliog il Science 151:1337-45 Mr 18 '66; Reply. W. S. Neff. 152:1283 My 27 '66

ESKIN, Arnold. See Menaker, M. jt. auth.

ESPALIERS. See Fruit trees, Training of; Trees, Training of; Plants, Training of

ESPINOSA, Robin
Delights' of disaster. Life 60:73 Mr 25 '66

ESPIONAGE
Carrot & careless George; cases involving W. Whalen and F. Mrkva. il Time 88:23 Jl 22 '66
Cultural exchange as the Soviets use it. G. Bailey. il Reporter 34:20-5 Ap 7 '66; Discussion. 34:6+ My 19 '66
How red China spies on U.S. J. E. Hoover. il Nations Bsns 54:84-8 Je '66
Master spy. O. Handlin. Atlan 217:130-1 My '66
Master spy; condensation. G. W. Prange. il Read Digest 90:209-12+ Ja '67
My spy can lick your spy; consideration of G. Lonsdale's Spy and The Penkovskiy papers. M. Frankel. il Atlan 217:103-4+ Ap '66
Soviet science aide ousted by United States. D. S. Greenberg. il Science 153:1500 S 23 '66
Spies; symposium. il Esquire 65:77-105+ My '66
See also
Electronics in criminal investigation, espionage, etc.
Spies

ESQUIRE (periodical)
Esquire's sixth annual dubios achievement awards. il Esquire 67:82-9 Ja '67
Naming day at Esquire; roster of authors. A Gingrich. Esquire 66:8+ D '66
On the mixed pleasures of uncovering new talent. A. Gingrich. Esquire 65:6 F '66
Turning green; Playboy's and Esquire's Christmas issues. R. A. Schroth. America 115:777 D 10 '66
With regards & love to the editors of Esq. R. Mion. Esquire 66:20+ D '66

ESSAYS

Competitions

1966 Scholastic magazines writing awards. il Sr Schol 88:16-20 My 20 '66

ESSER, George H. Jr
Widening the horizons of the culturally deprived; excerpts from address, July 1965. por ALA Bul 60:175-8 F '66

ESSLIN, Martin
Devil's prayerbook. New Repub 155:24+ N 26 '66
Now all artists are surrealists. N Y Times Mag p32-3+ My 22 '66
Theater of cruelty. N Y Times Mag p22-3+ Mr 6 '66
What will happen next? N Y Times Mag pt2 p20-1+ S 11 '66

ESSO Pappas complex. See Greece, Modern—Industries

The ESTABLISHMENT. See Great Britain—Politics and government

ESTAING, Valéry Giscard d'. See Giscard d'Estaing, V.

ESTATE planning
Art of avoiding probate. Time 88:65-7 Jl 8 '66
Caveats on estate planning. E. L. Schwartz. bibliog f Harvard Bsns R 44:48-50+ Mr '66
Estate planning for farmers. il Suc Farm 64:35+ Ap; 31+ My; 33+ Je; 45+ Jl; 37+ Ag; 49+ S; 33+ O '66
Estate planning for farmers. N. G. P. Krausz and B. Brantley. Suc Farm 64:35+ Ap '66
How to use life insurance in your estate. B. Brantley. il Suc Farm 64:32-3+ N '66
If you died tonight, would your family agreement stand up? symposium, ed. by C. W. Gifford. il Farm J 90:B1-2 Jl '66
Personal business. Bsns W p85-6 D 31 '66

ESTATE tax. See Inheritance tax

ESTATES, Decedents
What does it cost to settle an estate? N. Kuehnl and G. Bush. Bet Hom & Gard 44:16+ Je '66

ESTENSSORO, Victor Paz. See Paz Estenssoro, V.

ESTES, Elliott M.
Great race, Chevy vs. Ford; with report by M. Silva. il pors Life 61:131-2+ O 14 '66

ESTES, Nolan
Title III of ESEA offers encouragement for innovation. NEA J 55:30-2 D '66
Washington report; statement, October 1966, ed. by J. Lloyd. Sr Schol 89:sup 12 N 4 '66

ESTES, Raymond L.
Big perch by jiggers. Outdoor Life 138:58-61+ D '66

ESTES PARK, Colo.
One plant, two processes. R. G. Crabtree. il Am City 81:118-19 My '66

ESTROGENS
Common sense and the femininity pill. G. Naismith. Read Digest 89:99-102 S '66
Liver cancer: neonatal estrogen enhances induction by a carcinogen. J. H. Weisburger and others. bibliog il Science 154:673-4 N 4 '66
Pills to keep women young; R. A. Wilson's hormone therapy. Time 87:50+ Ap 1 '66

ESTRUATION
Catecholamine concentrations: changes in plasma of rats during estrous cycle and pregnancy. R. D. Green, 3rd. and J. W. Miller. bibliog il Science 151:825-6 F 18 '66
Estrous cycle in the rat: effects on self-stimulation behavior. R. G. W. Prescott. bibliog il Science 152:796-7 My 6 '66
Influence of the lethal yellow A^y gene on estrous synchrony in mice. A. Bartke and G. L. Wolff. bibliog il Science 153:79-80 Jl 1 '66
Monoamine oxidase activity in various parts of the rat brain during the estrous cycle. A. J. Zolovick and others. bibliog il Science 154:649 N 4 '66
Severe impairment of heat-induced saliva-spreading in rats recovered from lateral hypothalamic lesions. F. R. Hainsworth and A. N. Epstein. bibliog il Science 153:1255-7 S 9 '66

ESTUARIES
Wetlands, wildlife and the army engineers; adaptation of address, October 2, 1965. J. S. Gottschalk. il Audubon Mag 68:116-18 Mr '66

ESTY, John C. Jr
Future of the draft. Nation 203:209-13 S 12 '66

ETA meson. See Mesons

ETCHELLS, E. W.
U.S. entries for the IYRU trials. Yachting 120:44 S '66

ETCHISON, Annie Laurie
Modern army look. Library J 91:5902-4 D 1 '66

ETCHISON, Bruce
Glen-Sanders portraits of Scotia, New York. Antiques 89:245-7 F '66

L'ÉTÉ; drama. See Weingarten, R.

ETERNAL life. See Immortality

ETHANE
Conversion of p,p'-DDT to p,p'-DDD by intestinal flora of the rat. J. L. Mendel and M. S. Walton. bibliog il Science 151:1527-8 Mr 25 '66

ETHANOL
Peroxidation of liver lipids in the pathogenesis of the ethanol-induced fatty liver. G. H. Kalish and N R. Di Luzio. bibliog il Science 152:1390-2 Je 3 '66

ETHERINGTON, Edwin Deacon
From Amex to academe. por Time 88:53 Jl 22 '66
Town to gown. por Newsweek 68:68 Jl 25 '66

ETHICAL culture society
Ethical culture's maturity. il Time 87:96 My 20 '66

ETHICAL education. See Moral education

ETHICS
Academic responsibility. D. Wolfle. Science 154:219 O '66
Consensus ethics: opinions of Bishop F. Simons. Time 88:91-2 D 9 '66
Ethics in America: norms and deviations; symposium, ed. by J. C. Charlesworth. bibliog f Ann Am Acad 363:1-136 Ja '66
Ethics in an affluent society. C. McWilliams. Christian Cent 83:797-802 Je 22 '66
Master of character. R. O. Johann. America 116:95 Ja 21 '67
Morality and situation ethics, by D. Von Hildebrand and A. Von Hildebrand. Review Commonweal 85:429 Ja 20 '67. C. E. Curran
New morality. J. Fletcher; H. McCabe; discussion. Commonweal 83:566-7, 581-4, 679 F 11-18, Mr 11 '66
Psychoanalysis and morality. L. H. Farber; discussion. Commentary 41:23+ Mr; 6+ Ap '66
Search for the new morality. C. B. Ketcham. Christian Cent 83:1236-9 O 12 '66
Soft new morality. America 115:4 Jl 2 '66
What about the sinful student? E. D. Eddy. il Sat R 49:70-1+ Mr 19 '66

ETHICS—Continued
Wrong is what you think up by yourself; school children answer questions of right and wrong; Mantua, Ohio. W. Stanton. il Redbook 128:56-7+ D '66
  See also
  Advertising ethics
  Business ethics
  Cheating in schoolwork
  Christian ethics
  Christian life
  Conduct of life
  Conscience
  Forgiveness
  Integrity
  Justice
  Love
  Marriage
  Medical ethics
  Moral attitudes
  Moral education
  Political ethics
  Responsibility
  Scientists. Professional ethics for
  Sexual ethics
  Social ethics
  Television broadcasting—Moral aspects
  Truthfulness
ETHICS committee, Senate. See United States —Congress—Senate—Standards and conduct, Committee on
ETHIOPIA
Atlantic report. Atlan 217:34+ F '66
  See also
  Communism—Ethiopia

Politics and government
Ethiopia, by R. Greenfield. Review
  Nation 202:132-4 Ja 31 '66
ETHIOPIANS
Ethiopia's modern Pheidippides: A. Bikila. il Ebony 21:128-33 Mr '66
ETHIOPIC church
Ancient, serene Ethiopian church. il Time 89:60-1 Ja 6 '67
ETHNIC minorities. See Minorities
ETHNOLOGY
Biological nature of man. G. G. Simpson. bibliog Science 152:472-8 Ap 22 '66; Reply. V. R. Potter. 153:121 Jl 8 '66; Rejoinder. 154:1120 D 2 '66
  See also
  Man
  Racial differences

Latin America
Jungle journal. J. Liedloff. Esquire 65:44+ My '66
ETHNOPSYCHOLOGY
  See also
  Racial differences
ETHOLOGY. See Character
ETHYLENE
Auxin-induced ethylene formation: its relation to flowering in the pineapple. S. P. Burg and E. A. Burg. bibliog il Science 152:1269 My 27 '66
Ethylene formation in rat liver microsomes. M. Lieberman and P. Hochstein. bibliog il Science 152:213-14 Ap 8 '66
ETIQUETTE
Etiquette; questions and answers. A. Vanderbilt. See issues of Ladies' home journal
Know your crowd courtesy? Todays Health 44:12 My '66
Silver manners. il Seventeen 25:146-7+ N '66
ETIQUETTE for children and youth
Compendium of etiquette, manners, and poise for perfectly marvelous girls and boys; excerpts from The compleat child. L. Wyse and J. Javits. il Ladies Home J 84:68-9 Ja '67
Small art of manners. il Todays Health 44: 48-51 Ap '66
ETKIN, William
How a tadpole becomes a frog; with biographical sketch. Sci Am 214:16, 76-80+ My '66
ETNA, MOUNT
Volcano residents are blase but watchful. Sci N L 89:73 Ja 29 '66
ETRUSCAN language
Few words from the Etruscans. M. I. Finley. il Horizon 8:104-9 Sum '66
ETRUSCANS
Few words from the Etruscans. M. I. Finley. il Horizon 8:104-9 Sum '66
ETTENBERG, Eugene M.
Greeman Craw, graphic designer. Am Artist 30:32-7+ Mr '66
ETTINGHAUSEN, Maurice L.
Memoirs of a merchant-scholar. W. Targ. Sat R 49:59-60 O 22 '66

ETTLINGER, G. See Moffett, A. jt. auth.
ETZLER, Marilynn E. and Moog, Florence
Inactive alkaline phosphatase in duodenum of nursling mouse: immunological evidence. bibliog Science 154:1037-8 N 25 '66
EUCALYPTUS
Choosing a eucalyptus. il Sunset 136:96-104+ Je '66
How to give a eucalypt the best start in life. il Sunset 136:229 Je '66
Tree of light; eucalyptus trees in Golden Gate park, Presidio, and Sutro forest; excerpt from Natural world of San Francisco. H. Gilliam. il Natur Hist 75:54-9 D '66
EUCHARIST. See Catholic church—Eucharist; Lords Supper
EUGENE, Ore.

Monuments, statues, etc.
Old neon cross; citizens sue city for erecting neon-lit concrete cross. Newsweek 68:60 S 5 '66
Razing a cross in Oregon. America 116:77 Ja 21 '67

Sanitary affairs
Put teeth into compaction. G. K. Attig and J. Clay. il Am City 81:88-90 Mr '66
EUGENICS
Can man perfect himself? tr. by D. T. LeFort. K. Rahner. Cath World 203:138-44 Je '66
Control of unborn life. E. T. Tyler. Todays Health 44:58-62 Jl '66
Into the core of life itself. L. Lessing. il Fortune 73:146-51+ Mr '66
Life in a test tube. P. R. Gastonguay. Cath World 204:27-31 O '66
  See also
  Heredity
  Sterilization of defectives, criminals, etc.
EUGSTER, Hans P. and Munoz, James
Ammonium micas: possible sources of atmospheric ammonia and nitrogen. bibliog Science 151:683-6 F 11 '66
EULER, Robert C.
Willow figurines from Arizona. Natur Hist 75:62-7 Mr '66
EUPHORBIA marginata. See Snow-on-the-mountain
EUROCONTROL
Near-miss rate spurs European concern. L. L. Doty. Aviation W 85:44-5 D 12 '66
EUROPE
Assembly adopts resolution: relations among European states; with text of resolution. UN Mo Chron 3:34-6 Ja '66
Profile of Europe: toward a new order? il Sr Schol 89:pt2 6-7 S 23 '66
  See also
  Americans in Europe
  Camping—Europe
  Danubian countries
  Foreign students in Europe
  Jews in Europe
  Socialism—Europe

Description and travel
Instant Europe '66. il Mlle 62:87-94 F '66

Economic conditions
  See also
  United Nations—Economic commission for Europe

Foreign relations
Europe goes its way. A. De Borchgrave. il Newsweek 69:48-50+ Ja 23 '67

History
  See also
  Rome—History

Bibliography
Articles and other books received; comp. by O. J. Falnes. See issues of American historical review

Maps
Map of Europe (cont) Sr Schol 89:pt2 14 S 23 '66

Politics
Awakening of a new Europe. B. Nossiter. New Repub 155:11-13 Jl 16 '66
Continent in motion: East-West exchanges. Time 87:41-2 Je 10 '66
De Gaulle in the urals: European stability. Commonweal 84:431 Jl 8 '66
De Gaulle sets forth to change the face of Europe. C. J. V. Murphy. il Life 61:18-25 Jl 8 '66; Same abr. with title What is de Gaulle up to? Read Digest 89:134-8 S '66
Europe goes its way. A. De Borchgrave. il Newsweek 69:48-50+ Ja 23 '67

EUROPE—Politics—*Continued*
Europe on its own; East-West relations. New Repub 154:5-6 Je 11 '66
Europe? where's that? New Repub 155:5-6 D 17 '66
European right. ed. by H. Rogger and E. Weber. Review
  Nat R 18:172-3 F 22 '66. F. D. Wilhelmsen
7,601st day. Time 87:39-40 Je 17 '66
U.S. policy and the new Europe. F. Church. For Affairs 45:49-57 O '66
West edges East. il Bsns W p40 Je 25 '66
  See also
European federation
Socialism—Europe

Religious institutions and affairs
World around us. Christian Cent 83:1184 S 28 '66

Social history
Proud tower, by B. W. Tuchman. Review
  Atlan 217:130-1 F '66. O. Handlin
  Commentary 41:89-92 My '66. J. Weightman
  Harper 232:114-17 F '66. K. Epstein; Reply with rejoinder. J. Barkham. 232:6+ My '66
  Nat R 18:117-19 F 8 '66. W. S. Schlamm
  Reporter 34:53-4 F 10 '66. G. A. Craig

Union (proposed)
See European federation

EUROPE, EASTERN
Perforated curtain; survey of Communist countries. G. Farmer. il Life 61:122-4+ D 9 '66
Third communism. il Time 87:34-48 Mr 18 '66
  See also
Church and state in Eastern Europe
Economic assistance in Europe
Education—Europe, Eastern
Foreign visitors in Eastern Europe
Hunting—Europe, Eastern
Investments, Foreign (in Europe)
Jews in Europe
Publishers and publishing—Europe, Eastern
Space research—Europe, Eastern
Theater—Europe, Eastern
United States—Foreign relations—Europe, Eastern

Commerce
East Germany: the prosperous prisoner. W. Hangen. Reporter 35:30-3 Ag 11 '66

Defenses
See also
Warsaw pact, 1955

Economic policy
As Communists start to learn capitalism, the hard way. il U S News 60:68-70 My 30 '66

Foreign relations
Europe on its own; East-West relations. New Repub 154:5-6 Je 11 '66
Worrying about China in the Lenin Hills; Moscow conference of eight Communist countries. il Newsweek 68:51 O 31 '66

Historiography
Recent developments in the history of the Soviet Union and eastern Europe. R. V. Allen. bibliog f Ann Am Acad 365:147-60 My '66

History
Bibliography
Articles and other books received; comp. by C. Morley. See issues of American historical review
Recent developments in the history of the Soviet Union and eastern Europe. R. V. Allen. bibliog f Ann Am Acad 365:147-60 My '66

Intellectual life
View from the East. I. Boldizsar. Nation 203:55-9 Jl 11 '66

Maps
Germany's lost lands in the East. Cur Hist 50:269 My '66

Politics
De Gaulle in Moscow: what he did, what it means; with report by F. B. Stevens. il U S News 61:26-7 Jl 4 '66
Grandest tour: de Gaulle's visit to Russia. il Time 88:20-4+ Jl 1 '66
Perforated curtain; survey of Communist countries. G. Farmer. il Life 61:122-4+ D 9 '66

Voyage to Muscovy; significance of de Gaulle's visit to Russia and changes taking place in eastern Europe. il Time 87:34 Je 24 '66

Religious institutions and affairs
Channel opening for East-West church study. M. Bourdeaux. Christian Cent 83:1482 N 30 '66
Iron curtain lands take religion's pulse. E. E. Turner. il Christian Cent 83:1317-20 O 26 '66
Religion behind the iron curtain. Sister Dolorosa. America 114:626-7 Ap 30 '66

Treaties
See also
Warsaw pact, 1955
EUROPE, EASTERN and Russia. See Russia and Europe

EUROPE, WESTERN
State of affairs; European notebook. H. Brandon. Sat R 49:14+ O 22; 16 O 29 '66
Week to remember; Western European NATO meetings. il Newsweek 68:31 D 26 '66
  See also
Aerospace industries—Europe, Western
Agricultural administration—Europe, Western
Agriculture—Europe, Western
Air travel—Europe, Western
Airplane industry and trade—Europe, Western
Airports—Europe, Western
Banks and banking—Europe, Western
Book industries and trade—Europe, Western
Camping—Europe, Western
Coal mines and mining—Europe, Western
Economic assistance in Europe
Education—Europe, Western
Gardens—Europe, Western
Great Britain and Europe
Hotels, taverns, etc.—Europe, Western
Insurance, Health—Europe, Western
Investments, Foreign (by Europe)
Investments, Foreign (in Europe)
Labor supply—Europe, Western
Medicine—Europe, Western
Music festivals—Europe, Western
Negroes in Europe
Petroleum industry and trade—Europe, Western
Publishers and publishing—Europe, Western
Restaurants—Europe, Western
Science—Europe, Western
Shopping and shoppers—Europe, Western
Space research—Europe, Western
Steel industry and trade—Europe, Western
Stock exchange—Europe, Western
Strikes—Europe, Western
Television broadcasting—Europe, Western
Television industry—Europe, Western
Wages—Europe, Western

Armed forces
See also
United States—Armed forces—Forces in Europe

Army
See also
Supreme headquarters, Allied powers, Europe

Commerce
China traders thrive again: Westerners getting more of the business. il Bsns W p80-4+ S 24 '66
  See also
Europe, Western—Industries
European free trade association

Defenses
New NATO hardware needs seen. D. E. Fink. Aviation W 85:16-17 D 26 '66
New proposal for European security. J. Lederberg. Bul Atomic Sci 22:28-9 D '66
U.S., U.K., Germany begin talks on central Europe defense; statement, October 11, 1966. L. B. Johnson. Dept State Bul 55:670 O 31 '66
  See also
North Atlantic treaty organization

Description and travel
Attention! see Europe with the king of the international set (me) with Travel notes by Richard Joseph. W. Allen. il Esquire 65:18+ 55-71 F '66
Better homes and gardens tour: a very special three weeks in Europe. il Bet Hom & Gard 45:19 Ja '67
Better homes and gardens tour: first-timers' trip through Europe. il Bet Hom & Gard 45:30 Ja '67
Better homes and gardens tour: take-it-easy trip to England, Scotland, Paris, and Spain. il Bet Hom & Gard 45:23 Ja '67

EUROPE, WESTERN—Description and travel
—*Continued*
Castle tours. P. Andrews. il Travel 125:56-7 Ap '66
Europe for the 2-S set. R. Joseph. Esquire 66:148-9 S '66
Going places, finding things in the wine towns of Europe. H. Johnson. il House & Gard 130:56-8+ S '66
Let's travel: tips for student travelers. B. Belford. Mlle 63:357-8 Ag '66
Let's travel to Europe; with list of books il Mlle 62:194-8 Mr '66
New twists on traveling in Europe. il Changing T 20:21-2 F '66
Tenting across Europe. E. A. Miles. il Travel 125:48-9+ My '66
Travel notes. R. Joseph. Esquire 66:58+ S '66
We never got to Paris. G. Shawe. il Am Artist 30:28-32+ Ap '66
Where the boys go; Englishwoman's rundown on the habits and haunts of European men. D. Beyfus. Mlle 62:191-2 Mr '66

Economic conditions
Boom in Europe: it's still going, but. il U S News 60:110-11 Mr 28 '66
Europe's economies: a case of the British sickness. J. Ross-Skinner. il Duns R 88:33 S '66
Good business ahead for western Europe; outlook for '67. il Bsns W p54-6 D 31 '66
Some problems of maturity. Time 87:87 Ja 28 '66
Three Europes, one boom; old Europe, new Europe, emerging Europe. il Bsns W p 116-18 S 10 '66
See also
Europe, Western—Industries
United Nations—Economic commission for Europe

Economic policy
Modern capitalism, by A. Shonfield. Review Commentary 41:95-7 Je '66. B. D. Nossiter
See also
European economic commuinty

Economic relations
China (People's Republic)
China goes west for steel mill; West Germany to build steel-finishing complex. il Bsns W p 105-6 Mr 26 '66

United States
Building a bigger Atlantic community market. G. E. Bradley. Harvard Bsns R 44:79-90 My '66

Economic union
See European economic community

Foreign relations
Bygone notions. W. Lippmann. Newsweek 68:15 Ag 1 '66
De Gaulle is not alone: the view from Europe. A. De Borchgrave. il Newsweek 67:40-1 Ap 25 '66
Europe on its own; East-West relations. New Repub 154:5-6 Je 11 '66
Europe's new mood: its meaning for U.S. il U S News 60:39-41 Je 20 '66
General's pronouncement; de Gaulle's statement on freedom right to participate in non-European conflicts. E. Taylor. Reporter 34:16+ Mr 10 '66
Is Europe pulling away from America? il U S News 60:41-3 My 9 '66
Isolationism confirmed; opinion of W. Lippmann. Time 88:95 N 25 '66
Why Europe is pulling away from the United States. il U S News 61:49-51 D 26 '66
Why Vietnam war worries U.S. allies. il U S News 60:38-9 Ja 13 '66

United States
Week to remember; Western European NATO meetings. il Newsweek 68:31 D 26 '66

History
Middle class in western Europe, 1815-1848. L. O'Boyle. bibliog f Am Hist R 71:826-45 Ap '66

Industries
Can Europe catch up with U.S. technology? lucrative opportunities for U.S. business. il Bsns W p60+ O 29 '66
Europe considers industrial mergers. V. K. McElheny. Science 152:486-8+ Ap 22 '66
Europe's coal owners mine rich, new seams, diversifying into chemicals, plastics, auto making. il Bsns W p 122-4+ My 28 '66
Merger wave hits Europe. Bsns W p 153-4+ F 26 '66

Technological competition: Europe vs. U.S. J. B. Quinn. il Harvard Bsns R 44:113-16+ Jl '66
Technology gap; Europe's fear of falling victim to American economic conquest; Time essay. Time 89:18-19 Ja 13 '67
U.S. business in the new Europe: winning competitive battles. il Bsns W p94-7+ My 7 '66
See also
Steel industry and trade—Europe, Western

Nationalism
Europe's new nationalism. M. Ways. il Fortune 74:108-11+ S '66

Politics
Europe expectant. America 115:682 N 26 '66
Europe in search of a future; report from three capitals. L. Markel. il N Y Times Mag p4-5+ Jl 17 '66
For a new Atlantic alliance; address, June 1966. H. A. Kissinger. il Reporter 35:18-27 Jl 14 '66
NATO's agonizing reappraisal; French exit and European repercussions. H. Brandon. Sat R 49:12+ My 14 '66
See also
Europe, Western—Nationalism
European federation

Race problems
Black man in Europe. J. A. Williams. il Holiday 41:8+ Ja '67

Religious institutions and affairs
Abroad; in the western world, a story of religious unrest. U S News 60:60 Ap 18 '66

Social history
Middle class in western Europe, 1815-1848. L. O'Boyle. bibliog f Am Hist R 71:826-45 Ap '66

Social life and customs
New Europe. A. Menen. il Holiday 41:46-57+ Ja '67

Union (proposed)
Necessary partnership. J. R. Schaetzel. For Affairs 44:417-33 Ap '66
Our alternatives in Europe. H. Kahn and W. Pfaff. For Affairs 44:587-600 Jl '66
Restoration Europe and world politics. R. Strausz-Hupé. Yale R 55:488-99 Je '66

EUROPE and Russia. See Russia and Europe
EUROPE and the United States
See also
Debts, Public
United States—Foreign opinion—European
EUROPE in art
European sketches of Frank di Gioia. F. Johnson. il Am Artist 30:46-51+ Ap '66
EUROPEAN affairs, Bureau of. See United States—State, Department of—European affairs, Bureau of
EUROPEAN authors. See Authors, European
EUROPEAN businessmen. See Businessmen
EUROPEAN cars. See Automobiles, Foreign
EUROPEAN coal and steel community
Cartels fence in European steel; steel producers form blocs to regulate competition and fend off U.S. giants. il Bsns W p94+ S 3 '66
Community in disarray. il Time 88:106 O 28 '66
Europe finds growth can boomerang. il Bsns W p63-4+ Je 4 '66
EUROPEAN common market. See European economic community
EUROPEAN conference for telecommunications satellites
Supranational European space agency moves toward reality. W. C. Wetmore. Aviation W 85:22 D 26 '66
EUROPEAN conference on satellite communications
Nuclear power for European Comsats furthered by study. il Miss & Roc 18:43 Ap 25 '66
EUROPEAN cookery. See Cookery, European
EUROPEAN council for nuclear research. See European organization for nuclear research
EUROPEAN defense community
Adenauer's view of a changing Europe. G. Bailey. il Reporter 34:18-22 Je 30 '66
EUROPEAN economic community
Another trade wall crumbles; European Court of justice decision resulting from Grundig-Consten case. Bsns W p32 Jl 23 '66

At last, Eurofarm. Time 88:88 Ag 5 '66

EUROPEAN economic community—*Continued*
Awakening of a new Europe. B. Nossiter.
New Repub 155:11-13 Jl 16 '66
Back for another go; Britain. Newsweek
68:64 N 21 '66
Beating de Gaulle's veto; Britain's new drive
to join the Common market. K. Kyle. New
Repub 155:17-20 D 10 '66
Blow for freer competition; Common market
move to topple restraint-of-trade tradition.
Time 88:66 Jl 29 '66
Common market back on the tracks. Bsns W
p200 My 21 '66
Common market: ten year forecast and re-
view. Nations Bsns 54:104 N '66
Coup de Murville; French demands de-
nounced. Time 87:34 Ja 28 '66
Disarray in western Europe. America 114:318
Mr 5 '66
Equally unhappy; EEC industrial tariffs and
agriculture compromise. il Newsweek 67:60
My 23 '66
European common market; address, Novem-
ber 2, 1966. S. von Braun. Vital Speeches
33:152-5 D 15 '66
EEC does it; treatment of ambassadors pre-
senting credentials. Time 88:32 Jl 22 '66
Financing the farmers. Time 87:111 My 20 '66
France and the Common market. M. Jabri.
Cur Hist 50:228-31+ Ap '66
France and the five; de Gaulle's seven-month
boycott. R. Mooney. New Repub 154:11-12
F 26 '66
France keeps pressure on Common market;
demand for veto on key issues. il Bsns W
p36+ Ja 22 '66
French foreign affairs; address, November 3,
1966. M. Couve de Murville. Vital Speeches
33:106-11 D 1 '66
In Europe, economic unity becomes a fact;
tariff walls topple within the Common mar-
ket. il Bsns W p52-4 D 31 '66
Kennedy round: down the homestretch. il
Fortune 74:67-8+ Ag '66
Letter from London; Britain and Common
market. M. Panter-Downes. New Yorker
42:204+ D 3 '66
Medium-range planning. Time 87:101 My 13
'66
1966 battle of Britain; with editorial comments. il Bsns W p 143-4, 181-2+. 200 N
19 '66
No victors, no vanquished? gentlemen's
agreement ending the seven-month-old
Common market crisis. Newsweek 67:35 F
14 '66
On dry land; agricultural policy achieved.
Newsweek 68:64 Ag 8 '66
Once more to market? Britain. Time 87:38+
My 20 '66
Over the hump at last; Common market ministers agree on farm subsidies. il Bsns W
p45 My 21 '66
Progress report on Europe's Common market.
il U S News 61:54-6 Ag 8 '66
Reunion in Brussels; France's boycott ends;
outstanding issues. il Time 87:93 Mr 11 '66
Ten commandments; Common market meet-
ing. J. Blocker. Newsweek 67:49 Ja 31 '66
Testing the market; Great Britain. Time 88:
47 N 18 '66
Time grows short for freer trade; problems confronting Kennedy round tariff
negotiators in Geneva. il Bsns W p30-2
My 7 '66
View from Europe; implications of British
membership. G. Lichtheim. Commentary 42:
49-55 Jl '66

EUROPEAN federation
European idea, by Lord Gladwyn. Review
Reporter 34:53-4 Ap 7 '66. R. Mayne.
First steps on the road to Moscow; de Gaulle's
objectives and aims; with report, ed. by
J. Blocker. Newsweek 67:40+ My 9 '66
Grand design, by F. J. Strauss; tr. by B.
Connell. Review
Sat R 49:42-3 Ap 2 '66. L. L. Snyder
Independence and freedom: a continuing
struggle; address, July 4, 1966. G. W.
Ball. Dept State Bul 55:194-8 Ag 8 '66
New deal for Europe, exploring possibilities.
A. de Borchgrave. Newsweek 68:38-9 Ag 15
'66

EUROPEAN free trade association
Disarray in western Europe. America 114:318
Mr 5 '66
EFTA arrives ahead of time. America 116:75
Ja 21 '67
Gains and pains of EFTA. Time 88:94 N 4
'66

EUROPEAN kitchens. See Kitchens

EUROPEAN launcher development organization
Britain plans to end ELDO participation. H.
J. Coleman. Aviation W 84:38 Je 13 '66
Britain pressured to stay in ELDO. W. S.
Beller. il Tech W 18:20 Je 20 '66
Decision time approaches for European
rocket programs. V. K. McElheny. Science
151:1372-4 Mr 18 '66
Dissensions peril U.K. consortium plans. L.
L. Doty. Aviation W 85:29-30 S 5 '66
Drei, deux, one . . . help! Time 87:102 My
6 '66
ELDO crisis possible despite cost move. W.
C. Wetmore. Aviation W 84:73-5 Je 27 '66
ELDO management, financing tightened. W.
C. Wetmore. Aviation W 85:117-19 Jl 25 '66
ELDO nations consider body's future. W. S.
Beller. il Tech W 18:42 Je 6 '66
ELDO to provide Comsat launcher. W. S.
Beller. il Tech W 19:20 Jl 18 '66
Europe's faltering bid in space; ELDO
wracked with discord and technical prob-
lems. Bsns W p 110 Je 18 '66
Mr Mulley and the facts. W. J. Coughlin.
Tech W 19:46 Jl 4 '66
Outlook for ELDO is brightened by move to
cut Britain's costs. Aviation W 84:30 Je
20 '66
Supranational European space agency moves
toward reality. W. C. Wetmore. Aviation W
85:22 D 26 '66
U.K. engineer warns of bleak ELDO fate.
H. J. Coleman. Aviation W 84:32 My 30 '66
Where U.S. is leaving Europe far behind.
il U S News 61:69-70 Jl 18 '66

EUROPEAN literature
European literary scene. R. J. Clements.
See occasional issues of Saturday review
Gruppe 47 Princeton. C. Mayer. Nation 202:
588-90 My 16 '66

EUROPEAN molecular biology organization
EMBO gets a modest green light. V. K.
McElheny. Science 151:436-8 Ja 28 '66

EUROPEAN nuclear energy agency
Nuclear power for European Comsats furthered by study. il Miss & Roc 18:43 Ap
25 '66

EUROPEAN organization for nuclear research
Europe's expanding nuclear research center:
CERN. M. S. Wilde. il UNESCO Courier
19:4-9+ Mr '66
No bias for the positive? CERN findings.
Sci Am 215:64 N '66

EUROPEAN painting. See Painting, European
EUROPEAN pottery. See Pottery, European
EUROPEAN refugees. See Refugees, European

EUROPEAN satellite team
Five European nations form satellite team.
Sci N 90:89 Ag 6 '66

EUROPEAN space research organization
Cost problems force changes in Europe's
space plans. W. C. Wetmore. il Aviation W
84:140-3+ Mr 7 '66
ESRO favored for European comsat, if. Miss.
& Roc 18:24+ My 2 '66
European space station to be located in
Alaska; White House announcement; with
text of U.S. note by Charles E. Bohlen
and executive order. Dept State Bul 55:979-
82 D 26 '66
First ESRO satellite readied for launch;
NASA international cooperation program.
H. J. Coleman. il Aviation W 86:79-81 Ja
16 '67
Supranational European space agency moves
toward reality. W. C. Wetmore. Aviation W
85:22 D 26 '66

EUROPEAN union. See European federation
EUROPEAN war, 1914-1918

Aerial operations

Zeps over Britain. P. G. Fredericks. il N Y
Times Mag p76+ Ap 17 '66

Campaigns and battles

See also
Verdun, Battle of, 1916

Causes

Road to Sarajevo, by V. Dedijer. Review
Nat R 18:1176-8 N 15 '66. S. T. Possony
Sat R 49:47 Jl 23 '66. H. Hansen

Diplomatic history

See also
European war, 1914-1918—Causes

Economic aspects

See also
European war, 1914-1918—Finance

Finance

Why U.S. won't dun old war debtors; foreign government debt to the U.S. arising
from World war I. il Bsns W p83-4+ N
12 '66

EUROPEAN war, 1914-1918—*Continued*

Jews

Revanche; Sopron-Ödenburg. R. Berczeller. New Yorker 42:200+ N 5 '66

Naval operations

Sea devil; exploits of F. Luckner. il Newsweek 67:42+ Ap 25 '66
See also
Warships

Peace and mediation

Thomas Woodrow Wilson; excerpts; with reply by A. Dulles. S. Freud and W. C. Bullitt. il Look 30:36-8+ D 13 '66; Discussion. 30:12 D 27 '66
See also
Peace conference, 1919, Versailles

Personal narratives

Passionate prodigality, by G. Chapman. Review
Reporter 35:43-5 N 3 '66. A. Kazin

Reparations

Why U.S. won't dun old war debtors; foreign government debt to the U.S. arising from World war I. il Bsns W p83-4+ N 12 '66

Austria-Hungary

Revanche; Sopron-Ödenburg. R. Berczeller. New Yorker 42:200+ N 5 '66

EUROPEAN war, 1939-1945. See World war, 1939-1945

EUROPEAN war in literature
Heroes' twilight, by B. Bergonzi. Review
Nation 202:432-3 Ap 11 '66. F. Howe
New Repub 154:21-4 F 5 '66

EUROPEANS
Europe breeds new colonizers; Britons, Scandinavians, and Germans rush to build or invest in Bahamas, Florida, and Hawaii. il Bsns W p 155-6+ Je 4 '66

EUROPEANS in the United States. See Immigrants in the United States

EUROSPACE
Eurospace urges satellite, launcher push. L. L. Doty. Aviation W 84:37-8 Mr 21 '66
Eurospace urges spurt to reduce U.S. Russian space effort lead. L. L. Doty. il Aviation W 85:109+ Jl 11 '66

EUSEBIO, Sister Mary. See Mary Eusebio, Sister

EUSTIS, Helen
Middle-aged mother visits the teen scene. McCalls 93:56-61+ Ag '66

EUTECTICS
Eutectics provide possible one-step whisker composites. J. F. Judge. il Tech W 19:32-4 D 19 '66

EUTHANASIA
Coup de grâce. M. M. Shideler. Christian Cent 83:1499-502 D 7 '66; Discussion. 84:20, 82-3 Ja 4, 18 '67
Speaking out; let the dying die. P. Moor. Sat Eve Post 239:12+ S 10 '66
Thanatopsis. C. W. Blaker. Christian Cent 83:1503-6 D 7 '66

EVALUATION (education)
National educational assessment; pro and con discussion. F. Keppel; B. Hoffmann. NEA J 55:24-6 F '66
What makes a good school system? evaluating by using the document. Profiles of excellence. J. H. Kleinmann. NEA J 55:45 N '66

EVANGELICAL church in Germany
Church breaks a taboo. F. Lüpsen. Christian Cent 83:188-90 F 9 '66; Reply. W. C. Schmauch. 83:442-5 Ap 6 '66
German Evangelical church statement on the Eastern territories; excerpts. Cur Hist 50: 303-6 My '66

EVANGELICAL congress on worldwide mission. See Religious conferences

EVANGELICAL foreign missions association
Evangelical congress on worldwide mission; Wheaton, Ill, college campus April 9-16, 1966. M. Shelly. Christian Cent 83:695-7 My 25 '66

EVANGELICAL United Brethren church
E.U.B.-Methodist merger. M. Frakes. Christian Cent 83:1432-3 N 23 '66
Merging Methodists. Time 88:82 N 18 '66
United church of Canada biennial general council. J. R. Mutchmor. Christian Cent 83:1223-6 O 5 '66
United Methodist church; critique and proposal. P. M. Minus, jr. and A. C. Core. Christian Cent 83:174-5+ F 9 '66

EVANGELICALISM
Bible-whackers in Berlin; World congress on evangelism. il Newsweek 68:62 N 14 '66

EVANGELIST; story. See Barker, M.

EVANGELISTIC work
Billy Graham's crusade. D. Fisher. Commonweal 84:457-8 Jl 22 '66
Billy in London. Time 87:84+ Je 10 '66
Graham crusade: abdication of evangelism. C. Northcott. Christian Cent 83:673-5 My 25 '66; Discussion. 83:913 Jl 20 '66
London and conversion. America 114:847 Je 18 '66
Methodists and evangelism in Latin America; report of consultation in Cochabamba, Bolivia. J. Bishop. Christian Cent 83:1059-61 Ag 31 '66
Spree was grey; World congress on evangelism. H. O. J. Brown. Nat R 18:1324-5 D 27 '66
Swinging crusade; B. Graham's Greater London crusade. Newsweek 68:87 Jl 18 '66

EVANOFF, Vlad
Fish 'n ships. See issues of Motor boating

EVANS, Barry
What is a city manager? Am City 81:9 Ag '66

EVANS, C. D. See Hoffmann, R. L. jt. auth.

EVANS, Dan
Wedding gift; story. New Yorker 42:219-20 O 15 '66

EVANS, Daniel Jackson
Signal for the statehouse. il por Time 87: 17-18 Je 3 '66

EVANS, David C.
Computer logic and memory; with biographical sketch. Sci Am 215:45, 74-85 bibliog (p312) S '66

EVANS, David M.
Instant earthquake. il por Time 87:93 Ap 1 '66

EVANS, Fred J.
Old Wino's last stand. Outdoor Life 138:44-7+ Ag '66

EVANS, Frederick J. and others
Response during sleep with intervening waking amnesia. bibliog Science 152:666-7 Ap 29 '66

EVANS, G. Edward
Dewey; necessity or luxury? bibliog Library J 91:4038-46 S 15 '66

EVANS, George Bird
Aging gun dog. Field & S 71:146-7+ N '66

EVANS, Howard E.
Accessory burrows of digger wasps; excerpts from Comparative ethology and evolution of the sand wasps. bibliog Science 152:465-71 Ap 22 '66
Intellectual and emotional world of the cockroach. Harper 233:50-5 D '66

EVANS, Howard T. Jr. and Mrose, M. E.
Shattuckite and planchéite: a crystal chemical study. bibliog Science 154:506-7 O 28 '66

EVANS, Humphrey
(ed) See Tung, C. P. I was a student in red China

EVANS, Humphrey, 1949?-
Tomorrow's music today. Seventeen 26:38 Ja '67

EVANS, J. Claude
Germany: bridges needed. Christian Cent 83: 1561-2 D 21 '66
Holcomb's trek. Christian Cent 83:956 Ag 3 '66
Let's control riot controls! Christian Cent 83:1203 O 5 '66
Unbeguiled generation. Christian Cent 83: 1106 S 14 '66

EVANS, James H.
Service to the American people. por Parks & Rec 1:137+ F '66

EVANS, Jane
Time and time measurement. Electr World 76:25-9+ Jl '66

EVANS, Larry
Chess. Sports Illus 25:91-3 D 5 '66

EVANS, M. Stanton
Decade's harvest. Nat R 18:536-7 My 31 '66
Enemy of the press. Nat R 18:1174-6 N 15 '66
In defense of power. Nat R 18:222-3 Mr 8 '66
Orthodox rebels. Nat R 18:687-8 Jl 12 '66
Why 14(b) wasn't repealed. Nat R 18:214-15 Mr 8 '66

EVANS, Mary
Great fur caravan. Vogue 148:89-90+ O 15 '66

EVANS, Olive
Making friends with music. Opera N 31:15-17 N 5 '66

EVANS, Robert Beverley
Ailing American motors gets a new treatment. Bsns W p74 Mr 19 '66
American motors' new gospel. il por Time 87:82+ Je 17 '66

EVANS, Robert Beverley—*Continued*
Double shuffle at AMC. il por Newsweek 69:
77-8 Ja 23 '67
New man at AMC. il por Newsweek 67:84
Je 20 '66
$2,000,000 vote of confidence. Time 87:94 F 4
'66

EVANS, Rowland, and Novak, Robert
Lyndon B. Johnson: the exercise of power.
Sat Eve Post 239:26-9+ S 24; 42-6+ O 8;
40-4+ O 22 '66
about
Zealots of the middle. por Time 88:76-7 D 2
'66

EVANS, Timothy John
Too late to be happy; posthumous pardon.
Newsweek 68:56 O 31 '66
Wrong man. Time 88:41 O 28 '66

EVANS, Tony
Steamed up for a charge into the past;
photographs. Sports Illus 24:36-40 F 14 '66

EVANS, Walker
Art of seeing. New Yorker 42:26-7 D 24 '66

EVANSTON, Ill.

Education
Computerized integration; school district 65.
Christian Cent 83:1367-9 N 9 '66
ST reports: Midwest meets East; Institute
of Far Eastern studies. G. L. Burgett.
il Sr School 89:sup 19 S 30 '66

EVANSVILLE, Ind.

Hospitals
Happiest way to have a baby; St Mary's
hospital family-centered maternity care
unit. M. Longwell. il Farm J 90:84-5+ My
'66

EVARTS, Peter
Suburbia: the target area; adaptation of address, May 1966. por Wilson Lib Bul 41:173-
6+ O '66

EVENING and continuation schools
See also
Trade schools

EVENING clothes. See Clothing and dress

EVERGLADES
Crackdown on the Everglades 'gator poach-
ers. W. B. Hartley. il Pop Mech 126:106-
9+ Ag '66
Water and the Everglades. W. J. Schneider.
il Natur Hist 75:32-41 N '66
See also
Ten Thousand Islands

EVERGLADES NATIONAL PARK
Alligator. P. Caulfield. il Natur Hist 75:52-5
N '66
Animal release in Everglades National Park.
G. K. Zimmer. il Nat Parks Mag 40:22-3
Ag '66
Await funds for Everglades water. C. W.
Buchheister. il Audubon Mag 68:295 S '66
Ecological research in Everglades National
Park. M. C. Kolipinski and A. L. Higer.
il Nat Parks Mag 40:14-17 O '66
Everglades & dollars; Everglades Park water
problems. Nat Parks Mag 40:20 D '66
Everglades emergency plan. Nat Parks Mag
40:20 Ag '66
Everglades water and the separation of
functions. Nat Parks Mag 40:21 O '66
Florida: natural resources down the drain. il
Newsweek 68:111-12+ O 24 '66
For sixty days and sixty nights; solving the
alligator emergency, creating a problem for
deer. J. O'Reilly. il Sports Illus 25:22-3 Ag
15 '66
Funds needed for Everglades water. C. H.
Callison. Audubon Mag 68:160-1 My '66
Interim in the Everglades. H. V. L. Bloom-
field. il Am For 72:22-4+ Jl '66; Discussion.
72:5-7 S '66
NPA urges protection from Everglades salt-
ing. Nat Parks Mag 40:19 Jl '66
Needless crisis in a great park. Life 60:4 Mr
25 '66
Opening of Canal 111 is delayed for study.
Nat Parks Mag 40:24 Ag '66
Relief for the Everglades? C. W. Buch-
heister. Audubon Mag 68:141 My '66
Unraveling the Everglades furor. E. Buckow.
il Field & S 71:12-16+ O '66

EVERGREENS
They can take full sun. il Sunset 137:154-5
Jl '66
Uncommon evergreens. S. L. Kelsey. il Horti-
culture 45:30-1+ Ja '67
See also
Christmas trees
Holly

EVERLY medal awards
1966 Everly medal awards announced at
congress. il Parks & Rec 1:970-1+ D '66

EVERS, Charles
Boycott and ballot. H. Hurt. il Reporter 35:
23+ Ag 11 '66

EVERYMAN'S library. See Books—Reprints

EVETT, Robert
Music. New Repub 154:35-7 Mr 19 '66
Portraitist portrayed. New Repub 155:40-2
N 26 '66
What's what in modern music. New Repub
156:36+ Ja 14 '67

EVIDENCE (law)
Somebody up there watching; information
provided by gadgets, hearsay evidence in
some traffic cases. il Time 88:87 O 28 '66
See also
Confession (law)
Wire tapping
Witnesses

EVIDENCE, Expert
See also
Medical jurisprudence

EVIL. See Good and evil

EVINRUDE, Ralph
Ship and a man to match. il por Motor B
117:50-1+ F '66

EVOLUTION
Ambitious violet. W. Camp. il Sat R 49:65-6
Je 4 '66
Evolution: basic to biology. W. T. Keeton.
Christian Cent 84:71-6 Ja 18 '67
Evolution of the structure of ferredoxin based
on living relics of primitive amino acid
sequences. R. V. Eck and M. O. Dayhoff.
bibliog il Science 152:363-6 Ap 15 '66
Experimental genetics and human evolution.
J. Lederberg. Bul Atomic Sci 22:4-11 O '66
Fragile breath of life: how it came to be,
how to keep it going; symposium, ed. by
J. Lear. il Sat R 49:29-34+ My 7 '66
Lightning as a sculptor of life; E. V.
Komarek's and other theories. J. Lear. il
Sat R 49:57-62 Je 4 '66
Portrait in science; Darwin's Origin today.
G. R. De Beer. Natur Hist 75:62+ Ag '66
Thermodynamic equilibrium and the inorganic
origin of organic compounds. R. V. Eck
and others. bibliog il Science 153:628-33 Ag
5 '66
See also
Genetics
Heredity
Man—Influence of environment
Man—Origin and antiquity
Mutation (biology)
Plants—Evolution
Religion and science

Laws and legislation
Evolution case still undecided; court-case-
testing of Arkansas law. Sci N 89:262 Ap
16 '66
Men out of monkeys, or monkeys out of
men? Susan Epperson trial. S. Murphy.
New Repub 154:9-10 My 7 '66
Monkey law unconstitutional; Arkansas' anti-
evolution law. J. R. Tompkins. Sci N 89:
461 Je 11 '66
Testing Arkansas ban on teaching of evolution. Christian Cent 83:516 Ap 27 '66

EVOLUTION, Social. See Social change; Social
progress

EVOY, John J. See O'Keefe, M. jt. auth.

EVRARD, Connie. See Evrard, J. R. jt. auth.

EVRARD, John R. and Evrard, Connie
How disgraceful are the facts about infant
deaths in the United States? Todays Health
44:72+ Jl '66

EVRY, Hal
Perfect candidate. R. Wernick. il por Life 60:
41-2+ Je 3 '66

EVTUSHENKO, Evgenii Aleksandrovich
Babi Yar; poem: tr. by G. Reavey. N Y
Times Mag p44 D 11 '66
Delicate tinkle of icicles; poem, tr. by B. L.
Koten. Mlle 62:116 Mr '66
Poet against the destroyers. Sports Illus 25:
104-8+ D 19 '66
Surging outcry against repression: The city
of yes and the city of no; poem; tr. by
G. Dutton. Life 61:118 N 18 '66
about
City of yes; city of no. pors Life 61:117 N
18 '66
People are talking about . . . por Vogue 149:
90-1 Ja 1 '67
Poetry of Yevgeny Yevtushenko: 1953 to
1965, tr. by G. Reavey. Review
Nation 202:271-2 Mr 7 '66. M. Dalton

EVTUSHENKO, Evgenii Aleksandrovich—about
—*Continued*
Yes & no of a public muse. por Time 88:102+
D 2 '66
Yevtushenko and the underground poets. S.
Karlinsky. Nation 203:549-53 N 21 '66

EWIG, Mark
Oompah, oompah, sports? H. L. Masin. por
Sr Schol 88:16 Mr 4 '66

EWING, Alexander
Nightmare of ballet finance. Dance Mag 40:
36-9 O '66

EWING, Ann
Current U.S. patents. Sci N L 89:54 Ja 22 '66

EWING, Grace D.
Your own Project Head Start. PTA Mag 61:
20-2 bibliog(p34) S '66

EWING, John, and others
Ages of horizon A and the oldest Atlantic
sediments. bibliog Science 154:1125-32 D 2
'66

EWING, Maurice, and others
Lower cretaceous sediments from the North-
west Pacific. bibliog Science 152:751-5
My 6 '66
—See Donn, W. L. jt. auth.

EXAMINATIONS
In my opinion; critics of cramming should
take another look. C. Ratisher. Seventeen
25:178 O '66
Self-scheduled examinations under an honor
system. W. E. Cadbury. jr. Sch & Soc 94:
68-70 F 5 '66
See also
Educational tests and measurements
Physical examinations

EXCAVATING machinery
Man who can move mountains: R. G.
LeTourneau. S. James. il Pop Mech 126:
96-100+ Jl '66

EXCAVATIONS (archeology)
Late Pleistocene vegetation and degree of
pluvial climatic change in the Chihuahuan
Desert; midden deposits by wood rats pro-
vide chronological record. P. V. Wells.
bibliog il Science 153:970-5 Ag 26 '66
Seek and (with luck) ye shall find. S.
Tomkievicz. il Horizon 8:94-7 Aut '66
See also
Archeology
Herculaneum
Pompeii
Sybaris
also subhead Antiquities under names
of continents, countries, states, cities, etc.
e.g. Iran—Antiquities

EX-CELLO-O corporation
Traffic lights for quality control. il Bsns W
p 196+ O 22 '66

EXCELSIOR, Minn.
Old units form basis of new plant. S. A.
Friedman. il Am City 81:90-1 F '66

EXCHANGE, Foreign. See Foreign exchange

EXCHANGE of persons programs
American studies abroad: culture and foreign
policy; address; with questions and an-
swers. R. E. Spiller. bibliog f Ann Am
Acad 366:1-16 Jl '66
Cultural exchange as the Soviets use it.
G. Bailey. il Reporter 34:20-5 Ap 7 '66;
Discussion. 34:6+ My 19 '66
Exchange lifts curtain; scientific exchanges.
Sci N 89:238 Ap 9 '66
Great new experience for teens. Polly.
Farm J 90:50 Jl '66
Limnologist visits Russia; letter. C. E.
Goulden. Science 154:461 O 28 '66
New bridge of understanding and coopera-
tion. F. S. Loescher. Sch & Soc 94:126-8
Mr 5 '66
Our cultural exchanges; one-way street? R.
Marshall. Commonweal 84:150-3 Ap 22 '66
Scientific exchange: case of a French visitor.
D. S. Greenberg. Science 153:848 Ag 19 '66;
Reply. S. P. R. Rose. 154:1396+ D 16 '66
Visitors; decade of cultural exchange. M.
Mayer. il Sat R 49:53-5+ O 29 '66
See also
Students, Interchange of

EXCHANGE peace corps. See Volunteer service, International

EXCHANGE students. See Students, Interchange of

EXCHANGES
Wider spread for butter trading; declines in
stockpile and in dairy herds push prices
upward. il Bsns W p 107-8 Ag 6 '66
See also
Stock exchange

EXCHANGES, Educational. See Educational
exchanges

EXCHANGES, Literary and scientific
United States and U.S.S.R. sign exchanges
agreement for 1966-67; text of joint communique, March 19. 1966. Dept State Bul
54:543-4 Ap 4 '66
See also
United States book exchange, incorporated

EXCISE tax
Tax hike bill goes on books; Congress tacks
old-age pensions to Johnson's proposals.
Bsns W p 160+ Mr 19 '66

EXCITONIC molecule. See Molecules

EXCLUSIVE agencies
Are supermarkets for autos next? selling
cars through franchised automobile dealers
is being questioned. Bsns W p33 My 7 '66
Facts about those franchise businesses. il
Good H 162:162 F '66
Franchises; Start your own business ex-
position at Coliseum. New Yorker 41:25-7
F 12 '66
Job agencies sprout satellites; tight labor
market. il Bsns W p52:4 Ap 9 '66
Rise of franchising. il Time 87:95-6 My 13 '66
$65 billion gold mine. A. Poinsett. il Ebony
21:88-90+ Jl '66

EXCURSIONS
See also
Hudson River day lines

EXCURSIONS, School. See School excursions

EXECUTIONS and executioners
Last firing squad; executioners of Utah. G.
Berriault. il Esquire 65:88-91+ Je '66
See also
Capital punishment

EXECUTIVE departments (United States) See
United States—Executive departments

EXECUTIVE jet aviation, incorporated
Four hours from anywhere. il Time 87:86+
Je 24 '66
Is the sky the limit for the Pennsy? denies
entering the airline business. Johnson fly-
ing service. il Bsns W p 106-8+ D 10 '66

EXECUTIVE jets. See Airplanes, Business

EXECUTIVE office of the president. See United States—Executive office of the president

EXECUTIVE power
See also
Presidents—United States—Powers and duties

EXECUTIVE service corps. See International
executive service corps

EXECUTIVES
Age of the intuitive manager. J. T. Kimball.
il Duns R 87:42-3+ Ja '66
American executive overseas. il Newsweek
67:86-8 Mr 21 '66
Big three's big three. il Fortune 74:208 Ag '66
Boost for the man in the middle: middle
management, a big corporate concern. il
Bsns W p85-6+ Ja 22 '66
Crash hits a company; Thermo King execu-
tives and top dealers in wreck of jetliner
in Japan. il Bsns W p46 Mr 12 '66
Dangerous supervisory gap. E. C. Schleh. il
Duns R 87:57-8+ F '66
Executive investment: citrus groves. T. J.
Murray. il Duns R 88:33-4+ Ag '66
Executives on the go; new tribe of gypsies.
il Newsweek 68:102-4 N 21 '66
Fill executive postions with 45-50-year olds.
Sci N 89:394 My 21 '66
How Andy McGhee got a better job. W.
Shelton. il Fortune 75:116-17+ Ja '67
How to manage your time. P. F. Drucker. il
Harper 233:56-60 D '66
I was a Soviet manager. G. Ryapolov. Har-
vard Bsns R 44:117-25 Ja '66
Lessons of leadership; symposium. See is-
sues of Nation's business
Look back from the year 2010; address,
October 5, 1966. F. J. Close. Vital Speeches
33:53-7 N 1 '66
Memo from an angry business writer; how
executives handle and mishandle press in-
terviews. R. Phalon. Duns R 87:38-9+ Ja
'66
Men on the move. See issues of Dun's review
and modern industry
New turns; turn-of-the-year management
changes. Time 89:90 Ja 6 '67
Problems of a new executive; reprint from
May 1949 issue. E. P. Learned. Harvard
Bsns R 44:20-4+ Jl '66
Professionalization of management; address.
November 11, 1966. R. V. Scacchetti. Vital
Speeches 33:137-41 D 15 '66
Tips toward the top; Revlon and Coca-Cola.
Time 87:100 My 13 '66
Top ten; most active U.S. business leaders.
Time 88:94 S 9 '66
Turns at the top; recent changes. il Time 88:
71-2 Ag 26 '66

EXECUTIVES—*Continued*
Where young managers move ahead. L. Rich.
il Duns R 88:39-40+ O '66
See also
Business conferences
Corporations—Directors
Leadership
Women as executives

Anecdotes, facetiae, satire, etc.

Unfaithful executive. A. Buchwald. Look 31:
34 Ja 10 '67

Health and hygiene

See Men—Health and hygiene

Qualifications

Do you have what it takes to be a boss
someday? il Changing T 20:24-9 My '66
Interpersonal barriers to decision making.
C. Argyris. il Harvard Bsns R 44:84-97
Mr '66
Middle managers vs. the computer. G.
Berkwitt. il Duns R 88:40-2+ N '66
On the odds of becoming company president.
W. P. Dommermuth. il Harvard Bsns R
44:65-72 My '66
Plea for the abrasive personality. A. H.
Maremont. il Duns R 88:48-9+ N '66
Problem of executive dropout. L. S. Bick-
more. il Duns R 87:34-5+ Ap '66
Where bosses fail; excerpt from Manage-
ment's self-inflicted wounds; a formula
for executive self-analysis. C. F. Austin.
il Nations Bsns 54:60+ O '66
You can't succeed in business by merely
trying. E. E. Jennings. il Nations Bsns
54:110-12+ My '66

Retirement

See Retirement from business, etc.

Salaries

Big, booming executive market. P. R. Ko-
renvaes. il Duns R 87:47-50 F '66
Executive pay takes a breather. il Bsns W
p 174+ My 21 '66
How to lure executives: cash is now in
vogue. il Newsweek 67:88+ Je 20 '66
Middle managers get a peek at their pay;
annual AMA survey. il Bsns W p80-2 My 7
'66
Pay hikes at the top are leaner. il Bsns W
p77-8 Ap 9 '66
Personal business; executive fringe benefits.
Bsns W p 101-2 Jl 30 '66
Personal business; executive job contract.
Bsns W p 175-6 S 17 '66
Top executive pay: new facts & figures. A.
Patton. il Harvard Bsns R 44:94-7 S '66

Selection and appointment

Better management of managers' careers.
L. L. Ferguson. bibliog f il Harvard Bsns
R 44:139-52 Mr '66
How do you pick an executive winner? il
Bsns W p 108:10 Mr 5 '66

Supply and demand

How do you keep executives? J. Weingarten.
Duns R 88:35-6+ Jl '66
How to keep key executives. J. G. Mason.
Nations Bsns 54:75 Ag '66
Where are tomorrow's executives? J. Per-
ham. il Duns R 87:36-7+ Je '66

Training

Brass gets a quick polish; St Louis' Meas-
uregraph co.'s charm school. il Bsns W
p 182+ Je 18 '66
Executive development, new perspective.
R. K. Stolz. Harvard Bsns R 44:133-6+
My '66
How to keep the go-getters. R. W. Wal-
ters. jr. Nations Bsns 54:47+ Je '66
How to train an executive. il Newsweek
68:92-4 O 24 '66
Hunting for action, in small business: busi-
ness school student interest in the small-
business jobs. il Bsns W p82-4 Ap 9 '66
Where executives tear off the masks; NTL's
training labs. il Bsns W p76-8+ S 3 '66
See also
Harvard university—Graduate school of busi-
ness administration
Industrial management and organization—
Study and teaching

EXECUTIVES secretaries. See Secretaries
EXECUTIVES wives. See Wives
EXEMPTION from taxation. See Taxation, Ex-
emption from
EXERCISE
Beauty life: shall we dance..? il Mlle 62:144-
5 Mr '66

Better figure while you bathe. il McCalls 93:
98-9 My '66
Body-shrinkers: what they can do for you,
inside, outside, skinside. il Vogue 147:106-
8+ F 15 '66
Breathe right, and stay well. J. Frazier.
Read Digest 88:60-2 F '66
Don't be a weekend athlete! T. Irwin. il
Todays Health 44:46-9 Jl '66
Dramatic gains in youth fitness. S. Musial.
Parents Mag 41:30 Ag '66
Exercise and inxercise; the new way to look
at fitness. il Vogue 148:142-4 S 15 '66
Exercises to change your figure. il Redbook
126:93-6 Ap '66
Gams-manship. il Mlle 63:80-1 Jl '66
Hale and hearty room. il Bet Hom & Gard
44:56 Ag '66
Help them move young. P. Mansfield. il
Dance Mag 40:16-17 Ag; 82 S; 76-7 O; 78 N;
67 D '66 (to be cont)
How the American male can be fit. S. Musial.
Parks & Rec 1:695+ S '66
Is it that good for you? il Time 88:52 Jl 15
'66
Loneliness of the long-distance runner over
forty; to the swift; health. J. Medelman.
il Esquire 65:120-3 Je '66
Lovely leggy look. il Seventeen 25:168-9 S '66
Oh, for some easy exercises! il Seventeen 25:
122-3 Mr '66
Open letter: let us help them move young.
P. Mansfield. il Dance Mag 40:16-17 Ag
'66
Pre-racing physical conditioning. W. C.
Chasey, jr. il Yachting 119:60-1 Ap '66
Project: you; exercises by expert Bob Fitz-
gerald. il Ladies Home J 84:8 Ja '67
Quality of fitness: excerpt from address. C.
B. Wilkinson. Parks & Rec 1:149-50 F '66
Short skirt, the low heel and the leg be-
tween. S. Harney. il Ladies Home J 83:
110-11+ My '66
Six-minute shape-up. il McCalls 94:122-3+
N '66
Spot-reducing chart to end all spot-reducing
charts. A. M. Bennstrom. il Vogue 147:116-
20 Ap 15 '66
Surfside shape-up. il Mlle 63:136-7 My '66

EXERCISING equipment
Beauty life: gadget gym. A. M. Barden. il
Mlle 63:126-7 O '66
Electric reducing device barred from mar-
ket. Sci N 90:262 O 1 '66
Pampering room. il House & Gard 131:88-93
Ja '67
Raise a face? lower its age? drop its flaws?
electronically? Zeigler facial exerciser.
Vogue 148:164 S 1 '66
Vogue's ready beauty. Vogue 147:148 Je '66

EXERCISING machines. See Exercising equip-
ment
EXHAUST gases. See Automobile engines—Ex-
haust
EXHAUST systems
See also
Automobile engines—Exhaust
EXHIBITION cases
Twenty-five marvelous ideas for Sunday art-
ists, over half our panel, and collectors al-
most everyone. il House & Gard 130:98-101
Jl '66

EXHIBITIONS
Foreign equipment sales may outstrip space
product exports; American oceanographic
products at the World trade center, Frank-
furt, Germany. W. Buedeler. Tech W 19:
44 N 14 '66
Franchises; Start your own business exposi-
tion at Coliseum. New Yorker 41:25-7 F 12
'66
Modern Europe takes home the U.S. past;
U.S. furniture exhibits at Cologne. il Bsns
W p56-8 F 5 '66
SR/1967 world travel calender. T. L. Christie.
Sat R 50:77-82 Ja 7 '67
Taking the hard sell to eastern Europe; IBM
and Kaiser jeep exhibit in Czechoslovakia.
il Bsns W p34-6 Je 4 '66
Tools of understanding; U.S. exhibition in
Kharkov, Ukrainia. il Time 88:29 Ag 19 '66
U.S. labor launches road show in Rio. il Bsns
W p98-100 F 12 '66
See also
Food exhibits
Moving picture festivals
Seattle—Century 21 exposition, 1962
also subhead Exhibitions under various
subjects, e.g Inventions—Exhibitions

EXHIBITIONS. Traveling
Age of Lowland giants; loan show for San
Francisco, Toledo and Boston. H. K. Ger-
son. il Art N 65:28-32+ N '66

EXHIBITIONS, Traveling—*Continued*
Alluring art of India; sculpture and painting shows; U.S. tour; photographs by H. Groskinsky; with report on history and styles. Life 60:48-58 F 11 '66
Bird's-eye view; Japan's national treasures, U.S. tour. il Time 87:72-5 Mr 11 '66
Chinese art from the collection of the King of Sweden. F. Getlein. il Craft Horiz 26:30-5 N '66
Gold from Peru; circulating exhibition. F. Getlein. New Repub 154:29+ F 19 '66
Manet's mental museum. H. G. Gardiner. il Art N 65:48-50+ N '66
Marketing's mobile persuaders; traveling shows. J. Weingarten. il Duns R 87:38-9+ Je '66
Printmaking since Goya; Prints: 1800-1945 assembled by Minneapolis institute of arts. F. Getlein. New Repub 154:27-8 Ap 23 '66
Rare view of art from Poland. E. P. Birk. il Antiques 90:744+ D '66
Turkish delights; exhibition of Ottoman art touring America. N. Kotker. il Horizon 8:78-89 Aut '66
Will the real work of art please stand up? Art-in-science touring exhibition. L. Lerman. il Mlle 62:114-16 Ja '66
See also
Artmobiles
Smithsonian institution—Traveling exhibition service

EXHIBITS
See also special types of exhibits, e.g. Library exhibits

EXIT smiling; story. See Sellars, M.

EXITS
Planning building exits that work. R. E. Stevens. il Arch Rec 140:225-6 O '66

EXITS, Emergency. See Airplanes—Safety devices and measures

EXMAN, Eugene
RPG meeting; summary of address. por Pub W 189:69-71 Je 13 '66

EXNER, Virgil Max, Jr
Ideas for the taking. Motor T 18:34-5 Ap '66

EXNICIOS, John F.
Famous old street gets a new traffic look. Am City 81:107-8 N '66

EXOBIOLOGY. See Life on other planets; Space biology

EXOCRINE secretions. See Secretions

EXOTIC foods. See Food

EXPANDING universe. See Universe

EXPANSION, House. See Houses, Remodeled

EXPANSION of industry. See Industrial expansion

EXPENDITURES, Government. See Government appropriations and expenditures

EXPENDITURES, Municipal. See Municipal finance

EXPENDITURES, State. See State finance

EXPENSE accounts (business)
On your business driving; deduct 10c a mile or itemize expenses? questions and answers. Suc Farm 64:85 F '66
Where expense-account living is really worthwhile; Japanese business men. il U S News 60:111-13 F 28 '66
See also
Business entertaining

EXPERIENCE
See also
Pragmatism

EXPERIMENT in international living (organization)
Experiment that worked. B. Stretch. il Sat R 49:60-1+ Ag 20 '66

EXPERIMENT in love; story. See Kluge, A.

EXPERIMENT stations. See Agricultural experiment stations

EXPERIMENTAL aircraft association
Rockford '66; EAA's annual convention. R. B. Weeghman. il Flying 79:52-3 O '66

EXPERIMENTAL airplanes. See Airplanes, Experimental

EXPERIMENTAL animals. See Laboratory animals

EXPERIMENTAL art. See Modernism (art)

EXPERIMENTAL drugs. See Drugs, Experimental

EXPERIMENTAL education. See Education, Experimental

EXPERIMENTAL music. See Music

EXPERIMENTAL psychology. See Psychology, Experimental

EXPERIMENTAL schools. See Schools, Experimental

EXPERIMENTATION on man. See Medical research—Experimentation on man; Psychology—Experiments

EXPERIMENTS. See Physics—Experiments

EXPERIMENTS in science. See Science—Experiments

EXPERTISING in art. See Art—Expertising

EXPERTS (in business) See Business consultants

EXPLORATION, Submarine. See Diving, Submarine

EXPLORATIONS
See also
America—Discovery and exploration
Arctic exploration

EXPLORER scouts. See Boy scouts—Explorer scouts

EXPLORERS, American
Knights of the golden horseshoe. H. D. Crawford. il Am For 72:28-31+ N '66
See also
Pike, Z. M.

EXPLORERS, Chinese
See also
Hwui Shan

EXPLOSIONS
Blasted old beer cans; tests by New Mexico institute of mining and technology on the size, shape and force of an explosive fireball. il Life 61:55-6 D 16 '66
Shock-lithification of unconsolidated rock materials. N. M. Short. bibliog il Science 154:382-4 O 21 '66

EXPLOSIVE detectors. See Detectors

EXPLOSIVES
Non-nuclear explosive more powerful than TNT. il Sci N 89:463 Je 11 '66
Piezoelectricity in secondary explosives. J. N. Maycock and D. E. Grabenstein. il Science 152:508-9 Ap 22 '66

Ignition
Lasers, fiber bundles yield rfi-immune explosive initiator; laser-energized explosive device system. R. Pay. il Tech W 19:33+ N 14 '66

Transportation
High explosives on the highways; interview. ed. by T. Stimson. R. J. Madden. il Pop Mech 126:88-92+ D '66

EXPO 67. See Montreal—Worlds fair, 1967

EXPORT controls
East-West trade gets a lift; 400 items off the export control list. Bsns W p39 O 15 '66

EXPORT trade. See Mexico—Commerce; United States—Commerce

EXPOSITIONS. See Exhibitions

EXPOSURE meters
Boldest step in metering; Luna goes five-way modular. J. S. Forney. il Pop Phot 59:122-3+ D '66
Case for close metering. il U S Camera 29:62-3 Je '66
Caulfield on color; through lens meters. P. Caulfield. il Mod Phot 30:22+ My '66
Electronic flash meter. P. Farber. U S Camera 29:28+ O '66
Exposure meters, guides. il Pop Phot 59:186-91 N '66
Exposure problems. S. Needleman. il U S Camera 29:44-5+ N '66
Great through-the-lens meter explosion; with forword by H. Keppler. il Mod Phot 30:52-73 S '66
Guide to spot-meters. J. S. Forney. Pop Phot 58:74-5+ Ap '66
How to use any spot meter and how to use any integrating meter. il Mod Phot 30:52-3 Jl '66
Keppler on the SLR; behind-the-lens meter SLR cameras. H. Keppler. Mod Phot 30:18+ Je '66
Keppler on the SLR; new, advanced cameras from Germany. H. Keppler. il Mod Phot 30:36+ F '66
Meter, meter, where are you? H. Keppler. il Mod Phot 30:50-1 Jl '66
Modern's 1966 exposure meter directory. Mod Phot 30:56-7 Jl '66
Pros & cons of BTL meters. il U S Camera 29:46-7 Jl '66
Second wave of behind-the-lens meters. il U S Camera 29:64-6 Je '66
What's new that's good? L. Drukker. il Pop Phot 58:107 Je '66
Which is the best BTL metering system, spot or average? U S Camera 29:46 D '66

EX-PRESIDENTS of the United States. See Presidents—United States

EXPRESS highways
Belt for Boston's waist. il Fortune 73:168 Mr '66
Fight against the frightful freeway. il Fortune 74:160 S '66
Freeways, by L. Halprin. Review
Nation 203:357-9 O 10 '66. N. Silver

EXPRESS highways—*Continued*
Highwaymen come to Morristown; Interstate highway system. J. Skow. il Sat Eve Post 239:68-75 Ap 9'66
How expressways affect urban development. Am City 81:153-4 Ag '66
Interstate highways. R. Moley. Newsweek 68:88 Ag 1 '66
Last hitch in the Inner belt; Boston's Inner belt highway through Cambridge. J. M. Dixon. il Arch Forum 124:68-71 My '66
San Francisco still says no. Time 87:48 Ap 1 '66
Trouble ahead for freeways in cities? il U S News 60:8 Ap 4 '66
Where business longs for the good old days; Interstate highway 91 completely bypasses Hartford, Conn. il Bsns W p 156-8 Ap 9 '66

EXPRESSIONISM (art)
Abstract expressionist ceramics. H. Giambruni. il Craft Horiz 26:16-25+ N '66
Art and emotion; excerpts. B. Myers. il Design 68:35-7 N '66
Paint the devil. S. Burton. il Art N 65:26-7+ Ap '66

EXPROPRIATION
See also
Congo (capital Kinshasa)—Expropriation policy
Mexico—Expropriation policy

EXPURGATED books
See also
Index librorum prohibitorum

EXTENSION education
See also
University extension

EXTENSION service. See United States—Federal extension service

EXTER, John
Financing freedom's future; address, April 25, 1966. Vital Speeches 32:649-56 Ag 15 '66

EXTERIOR house decoration. See House decoration, Exterior

EXTERMINATION of fishes. See Fishes—Extermination

EXTERMINATION of mosquitoes. See Mosquitoes—Extermination

EXTINCT animals. See Animals, Extinct

EXTINCTION of animals. See Animals, Extinct

EXTORTION
Iniquitous depths; blackmail of homosexuals. Time 88:14 Ag 26 '66
See also
Bribery

EXTRACTORS, Fruit juice. See Fruit juice extractors

EXTRACURRICULAR activities. See Student activities

EXTRASENSORY perception
ESP enters the laboratory. F. R. Schreiber and M. Herman. il Sci Digest 60:48-54 O '66
ESP: science or delusion? D. Cohen. il Nation 202:550-3 My 9 '66
My psychic friends; excerpts from A search for the truth. R. Montgomery. Ladies Home J 84:101-6 Ja '67
What psychiatry is doing about E.S.P. F. R. Schreiber and M. Herman. il Sci Digest 59:32-6 F '66

EXTRATERRESTRIAL dust. See Matter, Interstellar

EXTRAUTERINE pregnancy. See Pregnancy, Complications of

EXTRAVAGANCE
See also
Luxury

EXTRAVEHICULAR activity. See Space flight—Manned flights—Extravehicular activity

EXTRAVEHICULAR activity flight equipment. See Life support systems (space environment)

EXTRAVEHICULAR activity suits. See Astronauts—Clothing

EXTREMISM. See Right and left (political science)

EXUMA CAYS. See Bahama Islands

EYE
Lens differentiation; report on second conference. R. W. Reyer and others. Science 154:1682-4+ D 30 '66
Versatility of the human eye. il Life 61:28-9 D 23 '66
See also
Pupil (eye)
Retina
Sight

Accommodation and refraction
View from the eyes of a wasp and a cod. il Life 61:26-7 D 23 '66
See also
Night blindness

Care and hygiene
Children's eyes: how to protect them from defects and disease. M. J. E. Senn. il McCalls 93:26+ Jl '66
Up-to-date eye care: the better to see with. Bet Hom & Gard 44:64-5 S '66

Diseases and defects
See also
Blindness
Ophthalmology

Movements
Electrophysiologic studies during scanning and passive eye movements in humans. D. F. Scott and R. G. Bickford. bibliog il Science 155:101-2 Ja 6 '67
Eye and head movements in peripheral vision: nature of compensatory eye movements. A. E. Bartz. bibliog il Science 152:1644-5 Je 17 '66

Protection
See also
Eye—Care and hygiene

Surgery
Corneal transplants. B. Rycroft. il Sci N 89:396-7 My 21 '66
Upside-down surgery; table developed at the Retina foundation, Boston. il Life 60:63-4 Mr 11 '66

EYE (animals)
Dimethyl sulfoxide: lens changes in dogs during oral administration. L. F. Rubin and P. A. Mattis. il Science 153:83-5 Jl 1 '66; Reply. L. J. Sacks. 154:543 O 28 '66
Specialized receptive fields of the cat's retina. J. Stone and M. Fabian. bibliog il Science 152:1277-9 My 27 '66

EYE (crustacea)
Mechanism of polarized light perception. T. H. Waterman and K. W. Horch. bibliog il Science 154:467-75 O 28 '66
Simple photoreceptors in limulus polyphemus. R. Millecchia and others. bibliog il Science 154:1199-201 D 2 '66

EYE (fishes)
Unit responses from commissural fibers of optic lobes of fish. R. F. Mark and T. M. Davidson. bibliog il Science 152:797-9 My 6 '66

EYE banks
Americans not everybody knows; A. de A. Breckinridge's part in establishing the Eye bank. J. A. Spalding. PTA Mag 60:11-13 Je '66

EYE make-up. See Make-up

EYEBROWS
Project: you. il Ladies Home J 83:32 Ag '66

EYEGLASSES
Beauty bulletin. il Vogue 148:124-7 Ag 1 '66
New eyes; New eyes for the needy. Parents Mag 41:110 D '66
Should eye doctors sell glasses? I. Ross. Read Digest 89:75-8 D '66
See also
Sun glasses

EYER, Ronald
Life music review (cont) Life 60:16 F 25; 23 Mr 18 '66
(ed) See Berry, W. Man and wife
(ed) See Ludwig, C. Man and wife

EYRING, Henry
Untangling biological reactions; address, December 28, 1966. bibliog Science 154:1609-13 D 30 '66

EZEIZA airport. See Buenos Aires—Airports

F

F-111. See Airplanes, Military—United States

FAA. See United States—Federal aviation administration

FALN (Armed forces of national liberation) See Political parties—Venezuela

FAO. See Food and agriculture organization of the United Nations

FASE (fundamentally analyzable simplified English) See Programming languages (computers)

FBI. See United States—Federal bureau of investigation

FCC. See United States—Federal communications commission

FDA. See United States—Food and drug administration

FDL (fast deployment logistics ships) See Warships—United States

FET (field-effect transistors) See Transistors

FFA. See Future farmers of America

FFAR (folding fin aircraft rockets) See Guided missiles—Launching from airplanes

FHA loans. See United States—Federal housing administration

FHLBB. See United States—Federal home loan bank board

FIAB (Fédération international des associations des bibliothécaires) See International federation of library associations

FICC. See International federation of campers and caravaners

FIGHT (Freedom, integration, God, honor, today) See Civil rights organizations

FISU. See International university sports federation

FM radio stations. See Radio stations. Frequency modulation

FM receivers. See Radio receiving apparatus—Frequency modulation receivers

FMC corporation
How one company utilizes its planes. Bsns W p 120 Mr 26 '66
How one firm met wildcat strikes. U S News 61:98 O 10 '66

FNMA. See Federal national mortgage association

FPC. See United States—Federal power commission

FRB. See United States—Federal reserve board

FTC. See United States—Federal trade commission

FUNY. See Free university of New York

FWPCA. See United States—Federal water pollution control administration

FAAS, Horst
Third war of Horst Faas. B. C. Brown. il por Pop Phot 58:58-9+ Mr '66

FABER, John
Yucatan. il U S Camera 30:64-5+ Ja '67

FABIAN, Miriam. See Stone, J. jt. auth.

FABLE of the goat; story. See Agnon, S. J.

FABLES
Manner of speaking. J. Ciardi. Sat R 49:24 N 12 '66
More unseemly chronicles: low comic; queen's kids. D. Newman. Esquire 66:52 Ag '66
Phoebe reviewed. S. Fried. Cath World 203: 40-1 Ap '66
See also
Aesop's fables

FABRIC finishes (spray products)
Fabric finish or spray starch. Consumer Bul 49:43+ Ag '66

FABRIC softeners. See Softening agents

FABRICANT, Solomon
Inflation isn't easy to measure. il Bsns W p54+ Je 4 '66

FABULOUS fifty; story. See Grosser, M.

FAÇADES
Inside out: P. Rudolph and J. Johansen's functioning façades. il Time 87:72 Mr 11 '66

FACE
See also
Beauty, Personal

FACE lifting. See Surgery. Facial

FACIALS. See Skin—Care and hygiene

FACKRE, Gabriel
Renewal. Christian Cent 84:50+ Ja 11 '67

FACSIMILE transmission
Seven league boots for the scholar? problems and prospects of library telefacsimile. D. W. Heron and J. R. Blanchard. il Library J 91: 3601+ Ag '66

FACSIMILES of rare books. See Book rarities—Facsimiles

FACTORIES
Expansion runs into a logjam; construction headaches; lack of men and material. il Bsns W p 169-70+ Ap 16 '66

Design
Conquest of inner space. L. A. Blumenthal. il Duns R 87:pt2 121-3+ Mr '66
Corporate goals & the outside expert. M. S. Osborn. il Duns R 87:pt2 108-9+ Mr '66

Equipment
Utilities: production's lifeline. K. August. il Duns R 87:pt2 130-3+ Mr '66
See also
Industrial equipment

Location
See Location in business and industry

Remodeling
Management's critical choice: to build or modernize. il Duns R 87:pt2 104-7+ Mr '66

FACTORIES, Automatic. See Machinery, Automatic

FACTORY and industrial management (periodical)
Famous firsts: organ of the great reform. Bsns W p 127-8 Mr 19 '66

FACTORY management
Applied math for the production manager. C. H. Jones. Harvard Bsns R 44:20-2+ bibliog(p 182) S '66
Transformation in the office. H. E. Klein. il Duns R 87:pt2 124-5+ Mr '66
See also
Assembly line methods
Foremen
Quality control

FACTORY tours. See Industrial tours

FACTORY wages. See Wages—United States

FACULTIES, College. See College professors and instructors

FACULTY meetings. See Teachers meetings

FACULTY wives. See College professors and instructors—Wives

FADER, Daniel N.
Doctor Daniel Fader: a child without books is impoverished; summary of address, June 6, 1966. Pub W 189:33-5 Je 20 '66
about
Trade winds. J. Beatty, jr. il Sat R 49:10 Je 25 '66

FADOS
Joys of suffering; A. Rodrigues, queen of fado, at Philharmonic Hall concert. il Time 87:62-3 Je 24 '66
See also
Phonograph records—Fados

FADS
Back in with black arts. il Time 88:24-5 D 30 '66
Great fad crash. R. B. Wilson. il Esquire 66: 104-5 N '66
Homicide on the campus; newest campus game. il Time 87:70 My 13 '66
It doesn't mean a thing; wearing of crosses by Russian girls. Christian Cent 83:952 Ag 3 '66
Komsomols at the crossroads; gold crosses, the latest fad in Russia. Time 88:24 Jl 29 '66
Long hair and mini-skirts; styles in the classroom. P. Woodring. Sat R 50:55-6 Ja 21 '67
Raid on braid; uniform craze in England. il Newsweek 68:72 D 19 '66
Return to manliness. J. H. Plumb. il Horizon 9:100-1 Wint '67
Sontag sensibility. P. Velde. Commonweal 84:390-2 Je 24 '66
Story of pop. P. Benchley. il Newsweek 67: 56-8+ Ap 25 '66
Surfer's cross; German iron cross. il Time 87:81 Ap 22 '66
Teen-agers: rites, styles, passwords. H. F. Waters. il Newsweek 67:74-5 Mr 21 '66
Teen scene. See issues of Seventeen
Threading the bushes; toilet-paper tribute. il Time 89:34 Ja 13 '67
Uni-sex: neuter look of teen-agers. il Newsweek 67:59-60 F 14 '66
Want to be sophisticated? here's how. J. Crist. Ladies Home J 83:16 O '66
When is it in, and when is it sick? J. Crist. Ladies Home J 83:26 S '66
With their socks off. Time 88:52 N 11 '66

FAERIE queen; ballet. See Ballets—Criticisms

FAGER, Charles E.
Dilemma for Dr King. Christian Cent 83:331-2 Mr 16 '66
White reflections on black power. Christian Cent 83:980-3 Ag 10 '66

FAGLEY, Richard M.
Trade and the war on world poverty. Christian Cent 83:745-8 Je 8 '66

FAHEY, J. L. and others
Immunoglobulin synthesis in vitro by established human cell lines. bibliog Science 152:1259-61 My 27 '66

FAHEY, Patricia. See Dowling, C. jt. auth.

FAHIMI, H. D. and Roy, P.
Cytochemical localization of lactate dehydrogenase in muscular dystrophy of the mouse. bibliog Science 152:1761-3 Je 24 '66

FAHKAHATCHEE STRAND WILDERNESS NATIONAL MONUMENT (proposed) See National monuments

FAHLSTRÖM, öyvind
Fahlstrom: a place for everything. S. Gablik. il Art N 65:38-41+ Sum '66

FAHY, Vern
Firm price for six years of service. Am City 81:106-7 My '66

FAILURE. See Success

FAILURES in business. See Bankruptcy

FAINE, Hy
Performers, inc. por Opera N 30:8-11 Mr 12 '66

FAINTER; story. See Robinson, B.

FAINTING horse; drama. See Sagan, F.

FAIR is for games; story. See Dunovan, C.

FAIR play. See Sportsmanship

FAIRBAIRN, Ann
Goliath of a book on a modern David. E. Perry. Life 62:10 Ja 6 '67

FAIRBANK, John King
Nation imprisoned by her history. Life 61:74-82+ S 23 '66
New thinking about China. Atlan 217:77-8+ Je '66
People's middle kingdom. For Affairs 44:574-86 Jl '66
Why Peking casts us as the villain. N Y Times Mag p30-1+ My 22 '66
Taiwan: myth, dream and nightmare. New Repub 154:11-13 F 5 '66

about
New debate on China. por Newsweek 67:26 Mr 21 '66
Reading the dragon's mind. por Time 87:27A Mr 18 '66

FAIRBANKS, Douglas, Jr
Men in Vogue; interview. por Vogue 148:53 Ag 15 '66

FAIRBANKS, Alaska
Notes for a gazetteer. P. Hamburger. New Yorker 42:219-22+ N 5 '66

FAIRCHILD, D. C.
Tee or me? Flying 78:85-6 Ap '66

FAIRCHILD, Sherman M.
Genius at work. J. Gilbert. il por Flying 79:42-6 O '66

FAIRCHILD camera and instrument corporation
Mighty miniatures; Semiconductor branch. il Time 87:92+ Mr 4 '66
Shocked circuits. Time 88:108 N 25 '66

FAIRCHILD Hiller corporation
Genius at work. J. Gilbert. il Flying 79:42-6 O '66
Improvement effort spurs F-27 changes. il Aviation W 85:49-50 S 19 '66
Republic pares costs for comeback flight. C. Brownlow. il Aviation W 84:115-16+ My 23 '66

FAIREST pitcher of them all; drama. See Cable, H.

FAIRFAX COUNTY, Va.

Architecture
Merrywood: tiered clusters of houses create a new kind of environment. il Arch Rec 139:156-7 Ja '66

FAIRFIELD, Roy P.
Antioch's challenge and response in teacher education. Sch & Soc 94:160-2 Mr 19 '66

FAIRFIELD manufacturing company
Computer planning unsnarls the job shop. il Bsns W p60-1 Ap 2 '66

FAIRLEY, Jean
From Athens to Rome. bibliog Yachting 119:64-6+ F; 84-5+ Mr '66

FAIRLIE, Henry
Britain seems willing to sink giggling into the sea. N Y Times Mag p28-9+ Je 12 '66
No conspiracy, but, two assassins, perhaps? N Y Times Mag p52-5+ S 11 '66

about
English lesson. il por Newsweek 67:60-2 Je 6 '66
Old realities and new myths. Reporter 34:19-21 Je 16 '66
Praise and panning from Britain. por Time 87:76 Je 3 '66

FAIRNESS. See Justice

FAIRS
See also
Book fairs
Science fairs

FAIRY penguins. See Penguins

FAIRY plays
Fisherman and his wife; dramatization of Grimms' fairy tale. L. Swortzell. Plays 25:62-8 My '66
French doll's surprise. R. Bennett. Plays 25:72, 85-6 My '66
Leprechaun shoemakers. F. B. Watts. Plays 25:43-8, 66 Mr '66
Sleeping beauty. A. Thane. Plays 25:67-74 Mr '66

Single works
Snow White's rescue. G. R. Creegan. Plays 26:92-4 Ja '67

FAIRY tales
Hobbit-forming world of J. R. R. Tolkien. H. Resnik. il Sat Eve Post 239:90-2+ Jl 2 '66

FAISAL, king of Saudi Arabia. See Feisal

FAISON, Earl
Big rookie bonuses start a battle. E. Shrake. Sports Illus 24:44 Ja 24 '66

FAITH, Sister Mary. See Mary Faith, Sister

FAITH
Christian faith. b F. W. Dillistone. Review Christian Cent 83:208+ F 16 '66 W. A. Clebsch
Cleaner of St Paul's: England's premier cathedral. C. Northcott. Christian Cent 83:238 F 23 '66
Demythologizing the new theology. W. B. Glover. Christian Cent 83:882-4 Jl 13 '66; Discussion 83:1085 S 7 '66
Dynamics of unfaith. L. J. Averill; reply, P. Graybeal. Christian Cent 83:240 F 23 '66
Faith and feeling. C. Davis. America 114:800 Je 4 '66
Freud saw it coming. D. Callahan. Commonweal 84:312-13 Je 3 '66; Discussion. 84:405+, 483-4 Jl 1, 22 '66
Future of belief. by L. Dewart. Review America 115:522 O 29 '66. D. A. Drennen
Goad of unfaith. V. P. McCorry. America 115:162 Ag 13 '66
How it is: apologies to an unbeliever. T. Merton. Harper 233:36+ N '66
Liberal Catholic thought. S. Hook. Commentary 41:94-100 Ap '66
Love, faith, hope: three attitudes in contemporary theology. J. W. Woelfel. Christian Cent 83:1570-3 D 21 '66
What is this treasure. by J. A. Pike. Review Commonweal 84:259 My 20 '66. S. S. Garmey
Whose God is dead? interview. ed. by N. R. Campion. H. E. Fosdick. Read Digest 89:67-71 O '66
Word as sacrament. E. Gibson. Christian Cent 83:1172-5 S 28 '66
See also
Apostasy
Hope

FAITH cure
Crying tree: God's tree, La Feria, Texas. il Time 88:78+ S 16 '66
See also
Christian Science

FAKERS. See Quacks and quackery

FALASHAS
Black Jews. il Newsweek 67:50 My 9 '66

FALCIPARUM malaria. See Malaria

FALCON, Marie Cornélie
Too much too soon. C. L. Osborne. por Opera N 31:6-7 D 24 '66

FALCONER, Vera M.
New films and filmstrips. See occasional issues of Senior scholastic

FALCONRY
Visit from a proud stranger; catching red-tailed hawks, and a golden eagle in a bow net. B. Gilbert. il Sports Illus 26:24-8 Ja 16 '67
With wing & claw. il Time 88:72 O 21 '66

FALES, E. D. Jr
Can you talk to other drivers? Read Digest 88:177-8+ My '66
Get more life out of your automatic transmission. por Pop Sci 188:176-9+ Mr '66
How to stay alive on the turnpikes. Pop Mech 126:63-7+ Ag '66
Save your car from rust and rot. Pop Sci 189:110-14+ Ag '66
Twenty ways to go in snow. Pop Mech 127:87-90+ Ja '67

FALK, Margareta
Woman on her way to a miracle; ed. by E. Graves. pors Life 61:48-61+ Jl 22 '66

FALK, Michael, and Kell, G. S.
Thermal properties of water: discontinuities questioned. bibliog Science 154:1013-15 N 25 '66

FALK, Peter
They kill you with silence. W. C. Heinz. il pors Sat Eve Post 239:91-5 F 26 '66

FALK, Richard A.
Revolution in peace education. Sat R 49:59-61+ My 21 '66

FALKLAND ISLANDS
Condor commandos; attempt to capture. il Newsweek 68:60 O 10 '66
Falkland caper; attempt by band of young Argentine nationalists to take possession of the islands. Time 88:48 O 7 '66
Falklands invaded; attempt to take possession by Argentine nationalists. il Sr Schol 89:19 O 21 '66

FALL, Bernard B.
Air raids, leftover puzzles. New Repub 155: 7-8 Jl 16 '66
And still the little men of the Vietcong keep coming. N Y Times Mag p20-1+ Mr 6 '66
Four views of war. Sat R 49:101-3 O 8 '66
Other side of the 17th parallel. N Y Times Mag p4-5+ Jl 10 '66
Seventeen little wars nobody talks about. Esquire 65:93 Mr '66
Viet Nam in the balance. bibliog f For Affairs 45:1-18 O '66
Vietnam: the new Korea. bibliog f Cur Hist 50:85-90+ F '66
Vietnam: the quest for stability. bibliog f Cur Hist 52:8-15+ Ja '67
Vietnam's twelve elections. New Repub 154: 12-15 My 14 '66; Correction. 154:29 My 28 '66
You can tell 'em, Buddy; report from Artillery Plateau. New Repub 156:17-20 Ja 14 '67

about

Authors & editors. por Pub W 191:21 Ja 2 '67
Vietnam witness. por Newsweek 67:98 Ap 11 '66

FALL. See Autumn
FALL CITY'S Easter passion play. See Festivals—Washington (state)
FALL of Rome. See Rome—History
FALLA, Manuel de
La vida breve; Victoria de los Angeles. P. L. Miller. Am Rec G 33:206-7 N '66
FALLACI, Oriana
(ed) See Hefner, H. I am in the center of the world
(ed) See Hemingway, M. Interview with Mary Hemingway: my husband, Ernest Hemingway
FALLING stars. See Meteors
FALLON, Edward R.
Pulpit platitudes. America 114:548 Ap 16 '66
FALLOT'S tetralogy. See Tetralogy of Fallot
FALLOUT, Radioactive. See Radioactive fallout
FALLOUT shelters. See Atomic bomb shelters
FALLOWS, Marjorie
Junior college: social experiment. Commonweal 85:9-13 O 7 '66
FALLS. See Waterfalls
FALLS CHURCH, Va, garden club. See Garden clubs
FALLS from airplanes. See Aviation—Accidents
FALNES, Oscar J.
(comp) Articles and other books received; northern Europe. See issues of American historical review
FALSE scorpions. See Book scorpions
FALSE teeth. See Teeth, Artificial
FALSTAFF; opera. See Verdi, G.
FALSTAFF brewing corporation
Guy named Joe. R. Levy. il Duns R 88:38+ Ag '66
How Falstaff brews new markets. il Bsns W p46-8 Jl 30 '66
FALTER, Mary Elizabeth
Notes of a happy housekeeper. See issues of House & garden incorporating Living for young homemakers
FALTERMAYER, Edmund K.
How to wage war on ugliness. Fortune 73: 130-4+ My '66
Rail route to a more mobile America. Fortune 74:106-9+ Jl 1 '66
Surprising assets of South Vietnam's economy. Fortune 73:110-13+ Mr '66
We can cope with the coming suburban explosion. Fortune 74:147-51+ S '66
What it takes to make great cities. Fortune 75:118-23+ Ja '67
FAMILY
Family myths may indicate pathology. Sci N 89:249 Ap 9 '66
U.S. family: how it's changed! Life 61:4 D 16 '66
See also
Birth control
Divorce
Domestic relations
Family life
Fathers
Grandparents
Marriage
Mothers
Wives
FAMILY, Holy. See Jesus Christ—Family
FAMILY, Size of
Case for the small family. W. Best. il Parents Mag 41:38-41 Je '66
Roomy roost for a big brood; twenty-one children in Lester Matthews family of Parkdale, Ore. il Ebony 22:52-4+ Ja '67

FAMILY budget. See Budget, Household
FAMILY business. See Family corporations
FAMILY camping. See Camping
FAMILY conversation. See Conversation
FAMILY corporations
Bronfmans: an instinct for dynasty. P. Siekman. il Fortune 74:144-9+ N; 176-9+ D '66
When your real job is son; seminars for executives of family-run companies. il Bsns W p98+ O 15 '66
FAMILY doctors. See Physicians
FAMILY farm operating agreements. See Father-son farm operating agreements
FAMILY finance. See Domestic finance
FAMILY income. See Income
FAMILY life
Family of Levi Smith. B. Villet and G. Villet. il Life 61:72-86+ N 25 '66
How America lives. See issues of Ladies home journal
Levi Smith's bonus, fifteen grandchildren. B. Villet and G. Villet. il Life 61:80-94 D 9 '66
Life with grandma. E. M. Stern. il Parents Mag 41:36-7+ Jl '66
Love runs in the family; photographs. D. Haun. Sat Eve Post 239:66-8 D 31 '66
Marina life in St Thomas V.I. G. Sloane. il Motor B 118:46-7+ D '66
Men, moonships, and morality; concerning theories of R. S. Morison and A. S. Makarenko. J. Lear. il Sat R 50:113-14+ Ja 7 '67
Our three-story family. L. M. Stalvey. il Read Digest 89:111-14 Ag '66
Sam Levenson recalls: when it was a privilege; excerpt from Everything but money. S. Levenson. il Nations Bsns 54:40-1 S '66
Three sons of Levi Smith. B. Villet and G. Villet. il Life 61:68-82 D 2 '66
Violence and the masculine ideal: some qualitative data; with excerpts from a tape-recorded interview with an imprisoned armed robber. J. Toby. bibliog f Ann Am Acad 364:19-27 Mr '66
Why husbands don't say what they really think; summary of survey. A. Whitman. il McCalls 93:75+ S '66
Youngest of the Smiths. B. Villet and G. Villet. il Life 61:60-71 D 16 '66
See also
Mothers-in-law
Parent-child relationship
Stepparents

Anecdotes, facetiae, satire, etc.
Heath Christmas carol program. A. B. Heath. Nat R 118:1321-3 D 27 '66

Caricatures and cartoons
It's all in the family. S. Berenstain and J. Berenstain. See issues of McCall's
FAMILY limitation. See Birth control
FAMILY names. See Names, Personal
FAMILY photographs. See Photographs
FAMILY planning. See Birth control
FAMILY portraits. See Photography—Portraits; Portraits
FAMILY rooms. See Living rooms
FAMILY talk. See Conversation
FAMILY therapy. See Mental illness—Therapy
FAMINES
Analysis of famine. B. Tufty. il Sci N 90: 74-5 Jl 30 '66
Famine: a shadow over half the world. il Sr Schol 88:9-13 Mr 25 '66
Famine menaces world. B. Tufty. il Sci N L 89:102 F 12 '66
Food and famine: winning the war against world hunger. il Sr Schol 89:12-15 D 2 '66
See also
Droughts
Food supply
Oxford committee for famine relief

Bechuanaland
Botswana's cheerless freedom. T. Land. Reporter 34:41-2 F 10 '66

India
Cornucopia limited. il Time 88:16 D 30 '66
Famine is the world's problem. America 114: 315-16 Mr 5 '66
Giveaway food is giving out, and still the world hungers. il U S News 62:38-9 Ja 2 '67
India: how can its hunger be eased? G. Murray. Christian Cent 83:811-12 Je 22 '66
Indira Gandhi's India; with a report by W. Cook and R. Ramanujam, and one by E. Behr. il Newsweek 67:36-42+ Ap 4 '66

FAMINES—India—*Continued*
  Noose of hunger. il Newsweek 68:35 D 26 '66
  Particular hunger; Kerala riots. Time 87:36
    F 11 '66
  Rice prejudice; Kerala riot. il Newsweek 67:
    42 F 14 '66
  Sales meeting. Newsweek 67:31A F 21 '66
  Sounds of hunger; Kerala riots. Time 87:37
    F 4 '66
  Village of hunger and lethargy; Basehra, In-
    dia. J. A. Lukas. il N Y Times Mag p30-1+
    O 2 '66; Reply. J. A. Bers. p 124 O 23 '66
FAMOUS men. See Great men
FAMOUS women. See Women, Famous
FAN palms. See Palms
FANCOLLI, Ted M.
  Amateur scientist. Sci Am 214:122-4+ Ap '66
FANDEL, John
  Desire; poem. America 114:808 Je 4 '66
  Flux; poem. Cath World 203:164 Je '66
  Resource; poem. Cath World 202:281 F '66
  Salt; poem. America 115:691 N 26 '66
  White things; poem. Commonweal 84:225
    My 13 '66
FANFANI, Amintore
  Fine Italian hand. Time 87:39-40 Mr 4 '66
  Mystic mayor, and Fanfani outfoxed. C. Ster-
    ling. il Reporter 34:34-6 Ja 27 '66
FANGER, Donald
  Chekhov and his poetry. Nation 202:684-6 Je
    6 '66
FANNIE Mae. See Federal national mortgage
    association
FANNING, Eleanor Ivanye
  Black-capped chickadee. Pop Gard 17:79
    Ag '66
FANNING, James
  New plants for your flower border. Pop Gard
    17:52-4 My '66
FANNING, James E.
  How to improve investment decisions. bib-
    liog f Harvard Bsns R 44:156-8+ Ja '66
FANO, R. M. and Corbató, F. J.
  Time-sharing on computers; with biograph-
    ical sketches. Sci Am 215:45, 128-36+ bib-
    liog(p312) S '66
FANO, Ugo
  Radiation absorption between the ultraviolet
    and X-ray bands. bibliog Science 153:522-5
    Jl 29 '66
FANS
  Language of the fan. il Am Heritage 17:112
    F '66
FANS, Baseball. See Baseball fans
FANS, Electric. See Electric fans
FANTASIES, Literary
  Face to face; with R. D. Plotz, founder of
    Tolkien society of America. R. D. Plotz.
    Seventeen 25:153 Ap '66
  Hobbit habit. J. Mathewson. il Esquire 66:
    130-1+ S '66
  J. R. R. Tolkien talks about the discovery
    of middle-earth, the origins of elvish; in-
    terview, ed. by R. Plotz. J. R. R. Tolkien.
    il Seventeen 26:92-3+ Ja '67
  Prevalance of hobbits. P. Norman. il N Y
    Times Mag p30-1+ Ja 15 '67
  Substance and fantasy. L. Alexander. il Li-
    brary J 91:6157-9 D 15 '66
FANTASTIC voyage; novel. See Asimov. I.
FANTEL, Hans H.
  Audio. See issues of Opera news
  Big business takes a dive in the ocean. Pop
    Mech 125:80-3+ Je '66
  Birth control for bugs. Pop Mech 126:116-19+
    Ag '66
  Heart cart may save your life. Pop Sci 189:
    54-7 Jl '66
  I rode our newest Polaris missile sub. il por
    Pop Mech 126:112-16+ N '66
  Test out your hi-fi at home. Pop Electr
    24:57-9+ Ap '66
  They're sewing plastic standby hearts in
    people. Pop Mech 127:136-9+ Ja '67
  War on skating. Pop Electr 25:66-8+ S '66
  Why are they still inventing speakers? Pop
    Electr 25:49-52+ N '66
FANTIN-LATOUR, Henri
  Music of flowers. H. A. La Farge. il Art N
    65:40-1+ N '66
FAR above Cayuga's waters, g-chung, g-chung;
    story. See Asher, D.
FAR EAST
    See also
  Airports—Far East
  Asia
  Asia, Southeastern
  Foreign visitors in the Far East

Description and travel
  Gold on gold: patterns of the Orient. T. Du-
    quette. Vogue 147:39+ Mr 1 '66
  Ten enchanted evenings; Orient and South
    Pacific. R. Joseph. il Esquire 66:96-105 Ag
    '66
  Travel notes; Orient and South Pacific tours.
    R. Joseph. Esquire 66:40-2+ Ag '66
    Social life and customs
  Orientalization of the West. R. Hughes. il
    Sat R 49:47-8+ O 8 '66
FAR EAST and the United States
  America as a Pacific nation; symposium. il
    Sat R 49:35-8+ O 8 '66
FAR right (politics) See Right and left
    (political science)
FAR WEST. See West
FARB, Peter. See Hay, J. jt. auth.
FARBER, Leslie H.
  Ours is the addicted society. N Y Times Mag
    p43+ D 11 '66
FARBER, Marjorie
  Neighbors in Fox Run. il por Time 88:24 Ag
    5 '66
  Quiet life. il por Newsweek 68:28 Ag 8 '66
FARBER, Norma
  Fringe benefit; poem. Sat R 49:35 D 3 '66
  How the hibernators came to Bethlehem;
    poem. Horn Bk 42:684-5 D '66
  In the beginning; poem. Sat R 49:54 N 26 '66
  Sun for breakfast; poem. Horn Bk 42:185 Ap
    '66
FARBER, Paul R.
  Foto facts. See issues of U.S. camera &
    travel
FARBER, Seymour M.
  Coughing: bad or beneficial? Todays Health
    44:58-61 Ap '66
FARBER, Sidney
  World without cancer? il por Newsweek 68:74
    N 28 '66
FARBER, William
  Neighbors in Fox Run. il por Time 88:24
    Ag 5 '66
FARBSTEIN, Leonard
  Excerpt from debate, June 29, 1965. Cong
    Digest 45:30 Ja '66
FARES, Airline. See Airlines—Fares
FARINA, Gian Battista. See Pininfarina, B.
FARIÑA, Richard
  American afternoon; story. Mlle 63:166-7 S '66
    about
  Introduction to (and conclusion of) a future
    hero; with quotations. J. Baez. por Es-
    quire 66:120-1+ S '66
  Notes and comment. New Yorker 42:37 My 14
    '66
FARLEY, James A.
  Great American presidents; address, February
    3, 1966. Vital Speeches 32:393-6 Ap 15 '66
FARLEY the sailor; story. See Stone, R.
FARM animals. See Livestock
FARM boys
  How to light a fire inside (not under) a
    boy. R. C. Davids. il Farm J 90:84-6 Ap '66
FARM buildings
    See also
  Barns and stables
  Swine farrowing crates and pens
FARM cooperation. See Agriculture, Coopera-
    tive
FARM costs. See Agriculture—Economic
    aspects
FARM equipment
  Commonsense feedlot ideas. il Suc Farm 64:
    74 S '66
  Home-made and handy; photographs. See
    issues of Farm journal
    See also
  Swine farms—Equipment
FARM finance
  Bonus helps buy boars, improves feeder pigs;
    Wisconsin feeder pig marketing co-opera-
    tive. D. Hagen. Farm J 90:38H Jl '66
  How to get and spend pork promotion funds.
    R. C. Black. il Farm J 90:H8-9 N '66
FARM houses. See Farmhouses
FARM income. See Agriculture—Economic
    aspects
FARM insurance. See Insurance, Agricultural
FARM labor
  Apples of wrath: results of ruling against
    foreign labor; excerpts from daily notes,
    ed. by F. Russell. W. Doe. Nat R 18:932-3
    S 20 '66
  DP's in the Delta: squat-in by Negro farm
    hands at the deactivated air force base,
    Greenville, Miss. il Newsweek 67:28+ F 14
    '66

FARM labor—*Continued*
Farm manpower; some observations on 1965. Mo Labor R 89:1II-1V F '66
Farm vote: farm workers vote on union to represent them in California. il Newsweek 68:83 S 12 '66
Farm workers choose a union, and now the Southwest. America 115:270 S 17 '66
Farm workers: target in union drive. U S News 60:124 Je 13 '66
Farm workers' transition to industry. il Mo Labor R 89:34-5 Ja '66
Fight for farm labor. G. Logsdon. Farm J 90:89 Mr '66
How farmers are meeting the labor shortage. B. Brantley. il Suc Farm 64:42-3 Ag '66
Larger herds, higher wages; central New York state. il Suc Farm 64:30J Ap '66
Marching for a ghastly recompense in Texas; Mexican farm workers. M. Maverick, jr. New Repub 155:11 S 24 '66
New place in life for the unskilled; Pilot project in North Carolina, relocating and training of unemployed agricultural workers. il Bsns W p 110-12 Mr 26 '66
Newcomer wins on the farm. Bsns W p 158 S 10 '66
Now they walk with us; Texas pickers. il Newsweek 68:54 S 12 '66
Recommendations of the California farm labor panel. Mo Labor R 88:1413 D '65
Secret crisis in the Delta; Negro farm laborers. il Newsweek 67:28-9 Mr 7 '66
Should you hire help or get more machinery? W .T. Messerly. il Suc Farm 64:40 Mr '66
See also
Cotton workers
Migrant labor
National farm workers association
Strikes—United States—Farm labor
FARM land. See Land
FARM land contracts. See Land contracts
FARM land values. See Land values
FARM life
And the fulness thereof; excerpts from The land, the people. R. Peden. Farm J 90:65 N '66
Farm living 1976. M. Bumgardner. Farm J 90:45-6 N '66
Honey, will you go get... A. Williams. il Farm J 90:51+ Ag '66
Is farm life worth it? K. Wilcher. Farm J 90:91 S '66
It could only happen to a farm wife. R. Boellstorff. il Farm J 90:83 My '66
Letters from farm women. See issues of Farm journal
Pennsylvania boyhood; memoir. J. N. Culbertson. il Am Heritage 18:80-8 D '66
Quitting the big-city rat race: it can be done; Green family's move from New York's Westchester County to Colorado. E. Havemann. il Ladies Home J 83:84-5+ F '66
Small farmer, 1966 version. il Newsweek 67:22-3 My 2 '66
Thoughts afield. J. Stuart. il Am For 72:22-5+ Ja '66
What we hope to leave our children. M. Felkner. il Farm J 90:47 Jl '66
FARM management
If you died tonight, would your family agreement stand up? symposium, ed. by G. W. Gifford. il Farm J 90:B1-2 Jl '66
Specialization vs. credit use; dairy farm credit study. il Suc Farm 64:30K Ap '66
We agreed to his and hers bank accounts. E. R. Fenn. il Suc Farm 64:63 Jl '66
What's ahead in farm credit? J. R. Brake. Suc Farm 64:86 Ap '66
See also
Dairy farm management
Dairy farm records
Farm records
FARM models
Miniature farm in Cody, Wyo. S. A. Parvin. il Hobbies 71:110-11 D '66
FARM offices. See Offices
FARM operating agreements. See Father-son farm operating agreements
FARM ownership
Is now the time to buy farmland? F. J. Reiss. il Suc Farm 64:48H Jl '66
Look a farm for sale. B. Crago. il Farm J 90:71 My '66
FARM policy. See Agricultural administration—United States
FARM ponds. See Ponds
FARM ponds, Pollution of. See Water pollution
FARM prices. See Farm produce—Prices
FARM produce
See also
Wheat

Marketing
Agriculture's new direction; address, April 5, 1966. G. L. Mehren. Vital Speeches 32:429-32 My 1 '66
What they're saying about farm bargaining. Farm J 90:66T Ap '66
See also
Agriculture, Cooperative

Prices
Facts, best ammunition. D. Hanson. Suc Farm 64:28 Jl '66
Patchwork that pays off. il Bsns W p88-90+ S 17 '66
Squabbling over what sends food costs up. il Bsns W p29-30 Ag 20 '66
See also
Agricultural administration—United States
also subhead Prices under names of farm produce, e.g. Wheat—Prices

Transportation
What lower freight rates mean to you. R. C. Black. il Farm J 90:60-1 My '66
What lower freight rates mean to you. il Farm J 90:38H+ Je '66
FARM records
How we make our money go further. L. Lane. il Farm J 90:95+ Mr '66
Now; checks that make record-keeping easy. J. Carlson. il Farm J 90:30-1+ My '66
Seven farm records that lead to success. C. W. Gifford. il Farm J 90:32-3+ Je '66
FARM services
New help in using chemicals; farm centers. G. W. Wormley. il Farm J 90:36H-36I+ Ag '66
FARM shops. See Workshops
FARM subsidies. See Agricultural administration—United States
FARM tractors. See Tractors
FARM vacations. See Vacations
FARM values. See Land values
FARM women
Farm living 1976. M. Bumgardner. Farm J 90:45-6 N '66
Honey, will you go get... A. Williams. il Farm J 90:51+ Ag '66
How we make our money go further. L. Lane. il Farm J 90:95+ Mr '66
Indomitable Mrs Portz. J. Gillies. il Farm J 90:92-3+ F '66
Letters from farm women. See issues of Farm journal
Vanishing farm wife; dying Negro tradition. il Ebony 21:76-7+ Ag '66
FARM workshops. See Workshops
FARMER, Art
Art Farmer, a natural evolution. B. Korall. por Sat R 49:68-9 Ap 16 '66
FARMER, Gene
Perforated curtain. Life 61:122-4+ D 9 '66
about
Arkansas traveler, writer, editor. G. P. Hunt. por Life 615 D 9 '66
FARMER, James
Next: a Marshall plan for Negroes? il por U S News 60:46-7 Mr 7 '66
What happened to Farmer? New Repub 154:7-8 Ap 2 '66
FARMER, William R. Jr
Synoptic problem and the contemporary theological chaos. Christian Cent 83:1204-6 O 5 '66
FARMER-hunter relations
Feel free to hunt. C. Chatfield. il Outdoor Life 138:70-1+ N '66
Mountain hospitality; West Virginia's hospitality program. E. A. Bauer. il Outdoor Life 137:44-7+ Ap '66
No fishing, hunting, trespassing; posted land. R. Starnes. Field & S 71:16+ S '66
No hunting and fishing; Pioneer Georgia project. G. H. Gillelan. il Outdoor Life 137:29-31+ Mr '66
FARMER-labor relations
Grape pickers' strike; war in California. A. Kopkind. New Repub 154:12-15 Ja 29 '66
FARMERS
See also
Farm management
Farmer-hunter relations

Anecdotes, facetiae, satire, etc.
Our cows never talk back. G. Logsdon. il Farm J 90:22 Mr '66

Political activities
Faith, hope & parity; farm vote in the November balloting. il Time 88:30 O 21 '66
How you voted; with editorial comment. il Farm J 90:33+. 98 N '66

FARMER'S almanac. See Almanacs
FARMERS' educational and co-operative union
of America
Hell raisers' adieux. il Time 87:20 Mr 25 '66
New leaders for National farmers union. O.
Bay. Farm J 90:58J My '66
FARMERS unions
   See also
National farm workers association
FARMERS wives. See Farm women
FARMHOUSES
Building a better farmhouse; demonstration
project. J. Bailey. il Arch Forum 124:68-71
Mr '66
Plan for farmers to conquer space. J.
LemMon. il Suc Farm 64:97+ Ap '66
FARMHOUSES, Remodeled. See Houses, Re-
modeled
FARMS
Loneliest farm; Aasen farm on 1,600 feet
cliff. Norway. il Travel 126:15 S '66
   See also
Agriculture
Dairy farms
Farm management
Farm ownership
Swine farms
FARMS, Prison
Arkansas prison farm: whip pays off; Cum-
mins and Tucker farms. R. Pearman. il
Nation 203:701-4 D 26 '66
FARNBOROUGH air show. See Aviation—Ex-
hibitions
FARNER, Donald S.
Control systems in bird reproduction. Natur
Hist 75:22-7 Ag '66
FARNHAM, Mary D.
Jon goes to the hospital. Parents Mag 41:80-
3+ N '66
FARNHAM, Marynia F.
Those teenage strangers. Parents Mag 41:
33-5+ Je '66
FARNSWORTH, Dana L.
Pressures on students. NEA J 55:29 S '66
FARNUM, Billie S.
Excerpt from remarks, Feburary 10, 1966.
Cong Digest 45:176+ Je '66
FARO, Luiz Flavio de
Appetizing as sin. Américas 18:11-13 D '66
FARR, Dennis
French paintings from the collection of Mrs
Mellon Bruce and Mr and Mrs Paul Mellon.
Antiques 89:556-63 Ap '66
FARRALL, Robert A.
How and why of photocells. Am City 81:
114+ N '66
FARRAR, Geraldine
Visit with Farrar. I. Cook. Opera N 30:6 Ja
29 '66
FARRAR, Straus and Giroux, incorporated
Farrar to publish first national arts anthology.
Pub W 190:63 D 26 '66
No Noonday paperbacks in Great Britain.
R. W. Straus, jr. Pub W 190:17 O 24 '66
Noonday paperbacks in the U.S. and the U.K.
R. W. Straus, jr. Pub W 190:36 O 10 '66
FARRELL, Barry
Guru comes to Kansas. Life 60:78-80+ My
27 '66
Labor leaders, tough, remote, or feuding.
Life 61:30-36B Ag 26 '66
Scientists, theologians, mystics swept up in
a psychic revolution. Life 60:30D-33 Mr 25
'66
Serenade to ninety years of greatness. Life
61:34-43 N 11 '66
Within the show's excitement, the deeper
issue of négritude. Life 60:88A-88B Ap 22
'66
FARRELL, Charles
Boccherini con Polo. Am Rec G 32:702-4
Ap '66
FARRELL, Eileen
Take courage! por Seventeen 25:112+ Jl '66
FARRELL, James T.
World I grew up in. Commonweal 83:606-7+
F 25 '66
FARRELL, Patricia
Quetzalcoatl and the lady; story. Redbook
126:74-5 Ap '66
FARRELL, Suzanne
[Mademoiselle's Merit award winner] por Mlle
62:47 Ja '66
Toe to toe. il por Newsweek 67:95 My 2 '66
FARRELL, Tommy
Miniature Snell to quicken the indoor pulse.
G. S. Brown. il pors Sports Illus 24:49-51
Ja 24 '66
FARRINGTON, David
Why we switched to cationic emulsion. Am
City 81:104-5 N '66
FARROW, Mia
Fun couples. por Newsweek 68:58 Jl 25 '66
Mia to Mrs in four minutes. il pors Life
61:46A-46B Jl 29 '66
Vogue's eye view: who's a breakaway? por
Vogue 147:71-3 Ap 15 '66

FARROWING crates and pens. See Swine far-
rowing crates and pens
FARSTA, Sweden. See Stockholm
FASCISM
Comparing the brutes. E. Grossman. New
Repub 154:20+ F 12 '66
Three faces of fascism, by E. Nolte. Review
Sat R 49:40+ F 5 '66. F. Schoenberner

Germany
German and Jew, difficult encounter. L.
Kahn. Christian Cent 83:1207-10 O 5 '66
Lingering shadow of nazism. il Sr Schol
89:10-11 O 14 '66
Nazi culture, by G. L. Mosse. Review
Sat R 49:28 My 21 '66. L. L. Snyder
Trial of the Germans: Nuremberg 1945-1946,
by E. Davidson. Review
Newsweek il 69:64+ Ja 9 '67. S. Maloff
   See also
Reichstag fire

Germany (Federal Republic)
Comeback for Nazis in Germany? National
democratic party. il U S News 61:54 N 28
'66
Germany's radical right; Nationaldemokratische partei. A. Schalk. Commonweal 84:
609-11 S 23 '66
Inventing neo-nazism; hoax of Paris match.
il Time 88:49 Jl 8 '66
New worry over possible Nazi comeback;
second election gain by National democratic party (NPD) U S News 61:12 D 5
'66
Privacy for Nazis. Time 89:80+ Ja 6 '67
Sober look at the new Germany. F. Mayer.
Christian Cent 83:710-12 Je 1 '66; Reply.
D. Barley. 83:888-9 Jl 13 '66

Italy
Flirtation with fascism: American pragma-
tic liberals and Mussolini's Italy. J. P. Dig-
gins. Am Hist R 71:487-505 Ja '66
FASHION
Brash Paris styles on tanbark; posed by G.
Chaplin. il Life 60:88-91 Mr 11 '66
British girls in their showy thigh-high skirts.
il Life 60:47-8+ Ap 22 '66
Eyes on knees. G. Plaut. il Look 30:99 My
17 '66
Fashion forecast: the feminine look. N. Bow-
den. il Farm J 90:98-100 O '66
Fur for fall; Paris; fall trends. il Newsweek
68:76 Ag 15 '66
Guys go all-out to get gawked at; U.S.
English and French styles. il Life 60:82A-
84+ My 13 '66
How America looks; a 20th reunion in Dallas.
il Ladies Home J 83:71-9+ S '66
I just stepped out of Vogue. J. Kerr. il
Ladies Home J 83:109+ My '66
Look '67. il Vogue 149:60-3 Ja 1 '67
Paris designers blast short skirts for women,
long hair for boys. J. Barry. il McCalls 94:
74+ O '66
Reluctant pilgrim to Paris. S. Alexander. Life
61:18 Ag 19 '66
Season of the knee. il Newsweek 67:95 F 21
'66
Short, short, short skirt story. P. L. Levin.
il N Y Times Mag p36-7+ Mr 20 '66;
Same abr. with title Short short story of
the skirt. Read Digest 88:112-14 Je '66
Stopping the escalation; skirt length. il Time
88:46 Ag 5 '66
Suits that suit; women's pants suits. il Time
88:87-8 O 14 '66
Undressed look. il Newsweek 67:104 Ap 11 '66
Way out fashions are in; women's clothes
present crazy-quilt styles. il Bsns W p42-3
Ap 16 '66
Wild fashions: what too many women do
wrong. il Redbook 128:72-3+ Ja '67
You can walk across it on the grass; Lon-
don styles. il Time 87:30-4 Ap 15 '66
Young will not be dictated to; excerpts from
Quant by Quant. M. Quant. il Vogue 148:
86-8 Ag 1 '66
   See also
Clothing and dress
Costume design
Fads
Hairdressing
History
Return to manliness. J. H. Plumb. il Horizon
9:100-1 Wint '67
Whatever has become of mommy? A. De
Mille. il Horizon 8:4-15 Sum '66
FASHION as a profession
Five with enterprise; girl owners of a New
York fashion boutique. P. Rifield. il Mlle
63:147 S '66

FASHION designers. See Costume designers

FASHION industry. See Clothing industry

FASHION photography. See Photography, Fashion

FASHION shows
Fashion too benefits from Ballet theatre benefit. A. Fatt. il Dance Mag 40:22-5 N '66
Local chairmen pave way for Ebony fashion fair. il Ebony 21:136-7 S '66

FASHIONABLE society. See Upper classes

FASS, Donald
Cupid computer. Sr Schol 89:7 O 7 '66

FAST, Howard
Drive your own locomotive. Esquire 65:36+ My '66

FAST deployment logistics ships. See Warships—United States

FAST draw contest. See Shooting—Competitions

FASTEAU, Marc S.
Munich and Vietnam: a valid analogy? Bul Atomic Sci 22:22-5 S '66

FASTENINGS
Hang anything on any wall. A. W. Lees. il Pop Mech 125:157-62 F '66
Hood pins. il Hot Rod 20:96-7 Ja '67
    See also
Zippers

FASTER reading. See Speed reading

FASTING
Customers slip off the fishmen's hook; Catholic church eliminates meatless Friday. il Bsns W p84+ D 10 '66
For U.S. Catholics, end of an old rule: lifting the mandatory rule of meatless Fridays. U S News 61:12 N 28 '66
Meat on Friday. America 115:575 N 12 '66
    See also
Lent

FASTS and feasts
    See also
Lent

FAT
    See also
Corpulence

FATEHPUR SIKRI, India
Well traveled camera. H. Keppler. il Mod Phot 30:24+ Ap '66

FATHER-daughter relationship. See Parent-child relationship

FATHER-son corporations. See Family corporations

FATHER-son farm operating agreements
Are U.S. farmers now getting rich? Burt farm, Clarion, Ia. il U S News 60:51-4 My 16 '66

FATHER-son relationship. See Parent-child relationship

FATHERS
Day I really became a father. P. Parrish. il Parents Mag 41:56-7+ F '66
Expectant father. Sci Digest 59:19-20 Mr '66
Father in charge. il Look 31:24-7 Ja 10 '67
No laughing matter; breakdowns due to fatherhood. Newsweek 68:53 S 5 '66

    Quotations, maxims, etc.
Daddy, 0! comp. by E. F. Murphy. il N Y Times Mag p 12+ Je 12 '66

FATHERS-in-law
Juanita was an oversolicitous mother. D. C. Disney. Ladies Home J 83:30+ Je '66

FATIGUE
Energy; advice from a panel of experts. Vogue 148:116-18+ O 15 '66
I prescribe... J. D. Wassersug. Sci Digest 60:55-60 O '66
That tired feeling, its cause and cure. H. J. Johnson. Read Digest 88:142-4 Mr '66
What happens when you get tired? L. Galton. il Pop Sci 188:67-9+ Je '66; Same abr. with title Why you get that tired feeling. Read Digest 89:265-8 O '66

    Anecdotes, facetiae, satire, etc.
Weary Titans; search for instances of surprising langour in distinguished men. H. F. Ellis. New Yorker 42:52-3 O 15 '66

FÁTIMA, Portugal
Fátima's 50th: the day the sun danced. F. J. Spellman. il Sat R 50:70+ Ja 7 '67

FATIMAS and kisses; story. See O'Hara, J.

FATS. See Oils and fats, Edible

FATT, Amelia
Dance career: Alvin Ailey's. Dance Mag 40:52-9 O '66
Fashion too benefits from Ballet theatre benefit. Dance Mag 40:22-5 N '66
Rudi of modern dance and fashion. Dance Mag 40:26-8 D '66
(ed) See Reinhart, C. If repertory comes, can strife be far behind?

FATTY acids. See Acids, Fatty

FAUBUS, Orval Eugene
Another face of Orval Faubus. R. Reed. il pors N Y Times Mag p44-5+ O 9 '66
Fade-out for Faubus. Newsweek 67:32+ My 9 '66
Ins and outs. il por Newsweek 67:30 Ap 4 '66

FAUCETT, R. E.
Sports under lights; address. March 1965. Parks & Rec 1:726-7+ S '66

FAUL, Henry
Tektites are terrestrial. bibliog Science 152:1341-5 Je 3 '66

FAULKNER, William
Solitude of William Faulkner; excerpt from Faulkner-Cowley file. por Atlan 217:97-8+ Je '66
    about
Fresh look at Faulkner. M. Cowley. il por Sat R 49:22-6 Je 11 '66
Growing myth. por Time 87:90+ F 11 '66
He made the books and he died. C. T. Samuels. Nation 203:220-2 S 12 '66
Public and private Faulkner. G. Hicks. Sat R 49:27-8 Jl 30 '66

FAULTS (geology)
Airborne geophysical study in the Pensacola Mountains of Antarctica. J. C. Behrendt and others. bibliog il Science 153:1373-6 S 16 '66
Extension of northeastern-Pacific fracture zones. H. W. Menard. bibliog il Science 155:72-4 Ja 6 '67
Molokai fracture zone: continuation west of the Hawaiian ridge. A. Malahoff and others. bibliog il Science 153:521-2 Jl 29 '66
Shallow structure of the Straits of Florida. E. Uchupi. bibliog il Science 153:529-31 Jl 29 '66

FAURÉ, Gabriel
On records: Requiem. Opera N 30:34 F 12 '66

FAUST, Frederick
Trade winds. J. Beatty, jr. Sat R 49:11 My 21 '66

FAUST; opera. See Gounod, C. F.

FAUVISM. See Painting, French

FAVIA-ARTSAY, Aida
Historical records. See issues of Hobbies

FAVORS, Party. See Party favors

FAWCETT, Buz
R for altitude. pors Field & S 71:48+ O '66

FAWCETT, Clara H.
Dollology. See issues of Hobbies

FAWCETT, Denby
Pearl of the Orient. Sat R 49:70-2 O 8 '66

FAWCETT publications
Fawcett forms British firm with Hodder & Stoughton; Hodder Fawcett, ltd. Pub W 189:273 Ja 24 '66

FAY, Elma
Bright periods in Cornwall. Sat R 49:41-2 S 3 '66

FAY, John
My daughter the model. il U S Camera 29:56-9 O '66

FAY, Paul B. Jr
John F. Kennedy: The pleasure of his company; excerpt. pors McCalls 93:62-5+ Jl; 74-5+ Ag '66

FAY, Robert J.
Excerpt from testimony, May 17, 1965. Cong Digest 45:191 Je '66

FEAR
Childhood fears are common, normal. Sci N 89:508 Je 25 '66
Dialogue with mothers: fears and bad dreams. B. Bettelheim. Ladies Home J 83:51+ Mr '66
Puppets calm a boy's fear; John Kirchner and doll given same treatment. il Life 60:79-80 Ap 15 '66
    See also
Anxiety
Phobias
Terrorism

FEATHER palms. See Palms

FEATHER RIVER
Don't tame the wild-flowing Feather. D. Anderson. il Nat Parks Mag 40:18-20 My '66

FEATHERSTONE, Joseph L.
Modern times. New Repub 156:34-6+ Ja 7 '67
Ordeal of Evelyn Waugh. New Repub 155:21-3 Jl 16 '66
Relevance of Professor Dewey. New Repub 155:22+ O 29 '66
Word for bail is ransom. New Repub 154:36-7 F 26 '66

FEATURES, Artificial. See Prosthesis

FECUNDITY. See Fertility, Human

FEDDERSEN, Bernard G.
King of cumshaw. il por Time 88:21-2 Jl 29 '66

FEDERAL aid to education—*Continued*
Proposed federal cuts in land-grant college funds; statement, February 4, 1966. Sch & Soc 94:189-90 Ap 2 '66
Proposed fund cuts stun land-grant colleges. Sci N L 89:121 F 19 '66
Public funds for church schools. Christian Cent 83:626-7 My 11 '66
Publishers study impact of U.S. school-aid funds; ABPC meeting on Changing nature and scope of the school and library market; summary of conference. il Pub W 189:28-50 My 23 '66; Correction. 189:49 Je 20 '66
Quiet revolution; Title I of the Elementary and secondary education act of 1965. Sr Schol 89:sup6 S 23 '66
Regional educational laboratories. Sch & Soc 94:260 Sum '66
Rush for the finish line seen under ESEA programs; summary of ABPC-ATPI meeting. Pub W 189:58-60 F 7 '66
Schools in the South: guidelines to frustration. R. G. Sherrill. il Nation 204:69-74 Ja 16 '67
Sea-grant colleges: idea gains adherents. L. J. Carter. Science 152:1358-60 Je 3 '66
Senate committee votes to extend school aid. Pub W 190:48 O 10 '66
Shared services and conscience: purpose of the Elementary and secondary education act of 1965. America 114:542-3 Ap 16 '66
Should rich kids get handouts? il Nations Bsns 54:36-7+ Jl '66
Southern Baptist dilemma in higher education: resistance to federal aid to church-related colleges. B. H. Cochran. Christian Cent 83:1598-601 D 28 '66
Stable federal support: aid to colleges and universities. D. Wolfle. Science 153:125 Jl 8 '66
Strength where it counts: progress under Title V of the Elementary and secondary education act of 1965. R. L. Hopper. Am Ed 2:20-1 Je '66
Student housing: colleges line up for U.S. loans. L. J. Carter. Science 153:277-80 Jl 15 '66
Suits challenge federal aid to private school students: New York suits. Pub W 190:27 D 12 '66
Teacher-opinion poll: effect of federal funds. il NEA J 55:10 S '66
Testing school aid: organizations challenge constitutionality of aid. Newsweek 68:96 D 12 '66
This heartless business. V. C. Blum. America 115:247-9 S 10 '66; Reply. Christian Cent 83:1137-8 S 21 '66
Three R's=billions. il Newsweek 68:72-4 Jl 11 '66
Title I ESEA: the way and the means. J. F. Hughes. Sr Schol 89:sup 11 N 4 '66
Title III of ESEA offers encouragement for innovation. N. Estes. il NEA J 55:30-2 D '66
USOE scores sales zeal of educational materials firms; caution urged in drafting Title I proposals. Pub W 189:152-3 F 21 '66
Washington report: ESEA expansion. J. Lloyd. Sr Schol 89:sup 18 S 23 '66
Washington report: ESEA's Title III: PACE (projects to advance creativity in education) statement. October 1966, ed. by J. Lloyd. N. Estes. il Sr Schol 89:sup 12 N 4 '66
Washington report: final session of the American association of school administrators' convention. J. Lloyd. Sr Schol 88: sup6 Mr 11 '66
Washington report: liberal outlook: education in the new Congress. J. Lloyd. Sr Schol 89:sup23 Ja 6 '67
Washington report: Titles I and II of ESEA. J. Lloyd. Sr Schol 89:sup 12 S 16 '66
What are Americans receiving in return for their heavy investment in education? excerpts from testimony. J. Gardner; H. Howe. 2d. il Am Ed 2:24-6 N '66
What's happening in education? federal aid for the improvement of our schools and libraries. W. D. Boutwell. PTA Mag 61: 19-20 O '66
Where are the clergymen? no support for Dirksen's prayer amendment for fear of losing federal aid. C. E. Rice. Nat R 18:833-5 Ag 23 '66
Who pulled the teeth from Title VI? G. W. Foster, jr. Sat R 49:88 Ap 16 '66
Wisdom of being apart. J. P. Leary. America 115:224-7 S 3 '66
Your government and your schools: summary of address. H. H. Humphrey. il PTA Mag 61:8-10 S '66
See also
Libraries and state

FEDERAL aid to libraries. See Libraries and state
FEDERAL and municipal relations
As city problems pile up: it's Washington to the rescue. il U S News 60:43-5 Mr 7 '66
Cities need social plan; federal funds for Demonstration cities program. P. McBroom. Sci N 90:416 N 19 '66
City lobbyists head for Washington. il Bsns W p88-9+ Jl 9 '66
City that said: no thanks to Washington. il Nations Bsns 54:64-7 S '66
Getting your money back; supplementing state and city funds by federal revenues. D. Lawrence. U S News 60:124 Ap 18 '66
If Washington shares tax revenue with states. il U S News 61:86-7 D 5 '66
Is more federal aid a cure-all for cities? mayors before Senate subcommittee of the Government operations committee. il U S News 61:10 S 5 '66
Letter from Washington; mayors before Subcommittee on executive reorganization of Senate committee on government operations. R. H. Rovere. New Yorker 42:108+ S 10 '66
Mayor tells how to modernize America's cities. H. W. Goldner. Nations Bsns 54:108-10+ Ap '66
New attack on city problems; how it is to work; federal grants for demonstration cities. U S News 61:47 O 31 '66
Room at the bottom; increased federal aid for community development. il Time 87: 26-7 F 4 '66
Second-front flak; shortchanging the cities. Newsweek 68:26-7 D 19 '66
South Bend comes out from under; recovers from Studebaker shutdown. il Bsns W p58-60+ F 19 '66
Taxation as discipline; sharing of federal personal-income-tax revenue. R. Moley. Newsweek 69:68 Ja 2 '67
Trillion dollars plus. Newsweek 68:21 D 26 '66
$2.3 billion start; federal aid to the cities. Newsweek 67:19 F 7 '66
Underdeveloped Manhattan; Lindsay's appeal for federal funds. Nat R 18:970-1 O 4 '66
Urban brawl; Ribicoff hearings; mayors testimonies. S. W. Yorty. il Newsweek 68: 19 S 5 '66
Urban pleas to Washington. America 115: 243-4 S 10 '66
Urban renaissance, or boondoggle? Demonstration cities program. il Bsns W p 141-2 O 29 '66
Weaver's trade; House approves Demonstration cities program. Newsweek 68:42+ O 24 '66

FEDERAL and state relations
Beauty or the bulldozer? issues involving Great Smoky Mountains National Park and Blue Ridge Parkway. M. Frome. il Am For 72:6-9+ F '66; Discussion. 72:2-3 Ap '66
Challenge of creative federalism; Senate subcommittee on intergovernmental relations survey findings; proposals. E. S. Muskie. Sat R 49:12-14 Je 25 '66
Federal tax revenue; a share for states? U S News 60:12 Ap 18 '66
Getting your money back; supplementing state and city funds by federal revenues. D. Lawrence. U S News 60:124 Ap 18 '66
Government by totem pole. il Nations Bsns 54:36-7+ O '66
Helping to shore up small business; Technical services act of 1965. il Bsns W p 146-8 Ja '66
How federal benefits figure in the election; excerpts from Congressional record. J. R. Hansen. U S News 61:13 O 31 '66
If Washington shares tax revenue with states. il U S News 61:86-7 D 5 '66
In the 13th year of the Warren revolution: how Supreme court is changing U.S; with criticisms by both law school professors and justices. il U S News 60:48-53 Je 20 '66
Marble-cake government; Washington's new partnership with the states; Time essay. Time 87:24-5 My 27 '66
Mike Frome: hearings on road plan for the Smokies. M. Frome. Am For 72:5+ Ag '66
One state vs. the U.S. in federal-aid battle; threat to Alabama's welfare program. U S News 62:11 Ja. 23 '67
Reformer at HEW; J. W. Gardner's theories on shifting of responsibilities to the states. H. Brandon. Sat R 49:16 D 17 '66
Republican plan; Laird plan of tax sharing. K. Crawford. Newsweek 68:35 N 28 '66
State legislatures: a battle for survival? Sr Schol 88:3-5 Mr 25 '66

FEDERAL and state relations—*Continued*
Tax-sharing with the states; address, November 17, 1966. M. R. Laird. Vital Speeches 33:184-9 Ja 1 '67
Taxation as discipline; sharing of federal personal-income-tax revenue. R. Moley. Newsweek 69:68 Ja 2 '67
TRW to study land-use planning; studies on transportation, waste disposal, information systems and juvenile delinquency. Tech W 18:20 Je 6 '66
Washington vs. the states; is the struggle over? il Sr Schol 89:10-12 S 16 '66
What alternate proposal? highway through Smokies; letter to the editor. E. T. Scoyen. Am For 72:4-5+ Ag '66; Reply. E. M. Dickerman. 72:5 N '66
See also
State rights
FEDERAL aviation administration academy. See United States—Federal aviation administration—Aeronautical center
FEDERAL aviation agency. See United States—Federal aviation administration
FEDERAL debt (United States) See Debts, Public—United States
FEDERAL communications commission. See United States—Federal communications commission
FEDERAL corporations. See Government corporations
FEDERAL courts. See Courts—United States
FEDERAL debt (United States) See Debts, Public—United States
FEDERAL employees. See Government employees
FEDERAL expenditures. See United States—Appropriations and expenditures
FEDERAL extension service. See United States—Federal extension service
FEDERAL government
Challenge of creative federalism; Senate subcommittee on intergovernmental relations survey findings; proposals. E. S. Muskie. Sat R 49:12-14 Je 25 '66
Creative or destructive federalism? D. Lawrence. U S News 60:108 Ap 11 '66
See also
Democracy
Federal and state relations
United States—Politics and government
FEDERAL home loan bank board. See United States—Federal home loan bank board
FEDERAL judges. See Judges
FEDERAL laboratories. See Laboratories, Government
FEDERAL national mortgage association
For home buyers and builders: help that's in the works. il U S News 61:93-6 Ag 15 '66
Half a remedy; Congress to the aid of the loan-starved housing industry. Time 88:70-1 S 2 '66
New money for home loans; will it ease pinch? il U S News 61:82 S 5 '66
FEDERAL power commission. See United States—Federal power commission
FEDERAL prisons. See Prisons—United States
FEDERAL reserve banks
Dipping into another money pool; federal funds market. il Bsns W p 160+ S 10 '66
See also
United States—Federal reserve board
FEDERAL reserve board. See United States—Federal reserve board
FEDERAL trade commission. See United States—Federal trade commission
FEDERAL urban renewal program. See Urban renewal
FEDERAL water pollution control administration. See United States—Federal water pollution control administration
FEDERALISM. See Federal government
FEDERATED department stores, incorporated
Expanding with confidence; interview. F. R. Lazarus, jr. il Nations Bsns 54:40-1+ Jl '66
FÉDÉRATION aéronautique internationale. See International aeronautic federation
FÉDÉRATION internationale des jeunesses musicales. See Musical societies
FEDERATION of American priests
Unbinding the priest. Commonweal 85:127 N 4 '66
FEDOROV, Evgenii
New outposts of science. UNESCO Courier 19:14-18+ Jl '66
FEDOROV, Konstantin
International oceanography; way scientific cooperation develops. UN Mo Chron 3:28-37 Mr '66
FEDOROVITCH, Sister Olga
Nun's story: we hate you; interview, ed. by E. Behr. Newsweek 68:52 S 19 '66

FEED handling
Some of my best customers are rats; confessions of feed salesman. R. Gogerty; reply. Mrs B. Walters. Farm J 90:68V Mr '66
FEED supplements, Antibiotic. See Antibiotic feed supplements
FEEDERS (birds)
Try a croquet ball for hanging feeder. L. G. Upton. il Audubon Mag 68:372 S '66
FEEDING, intravenous. See Injections, Intravenous
FEEDING and feeding stuffs
Don't leave crop residues in the field, feed them instead. D. Malena. il Suc Farm 64:32-3+ N '66
See also
Antibiotic feed supplements
Cattle—Feeding
Cows—Feeding
Forage plants
Milo
Ralston Purina company
Urea
FEEDING stations for birds. See Feeders (birds)
FEEDLOTS, Cattle. See Cattle self feeders
FEELEY, Dianne
Hot draft card. New Repub 155:38 Ag 27 '66
FEELEY, Paul Terence
Green mountain boys. A. Solomon. il pors Vogue 148:104-9+ Ag 1 '66
Obituary
Art N 65:13 S '66
FEES, Trade union. See Trade unions—Dues, fees, etc.
FEHRENBACH, T. R.
Query to a literary agent. Esquire 66:122+ D '66
FEIBLEMAN, James Kern
Trade winds. J. G. Fuller. il Sat R 49:16-17 Jl 16 '66
FEIFER, George
Great questions about China. Harper 233:93-5 Ag '66
Looking aghast at Soviet Russia. Nation 202:624 My 23 '66
Russia da, China nyet. N Y Times Mag p47+ D 4 '66
FEIFFER, Jules
Feiffer. See issues of New republic
Life movie review. Life 61:10+ N 11 '66
FEIGEN, George A. and Nielsen, C. B.
Passive sensitization in vitro: effect of antibody concentration on the lag period and velocity. bibliog Science 154:676-7 N 4 '66
FEIN, Arnold L.
Case against Eichmann continues. Sat R 49:27+ Jl 2 '66
JFK in Dallas. Sat R 49:36-8+ O 22 '66
Legal right to privacy. Sat R 50:26-7 Ja 21 '67
FEININGER, Andreas
Large camera. See issues of Modern photography
FEINSILBER, Myron
Communists in convention. Commonweal 84:464-6 Jl 22 '66
Politics of scandal. Commonweal 84:383-5 Je 24 '66
FEINSINGER, Nathan Paul
Mediator. New Yorker 41:21-4 Ja 22 '66
FEINSTEIN, Joe
Cooking up a storm; drama. Plays 26:13-24 Ja '67
FEIS, Herbert
Shackled historian. For Affairs 45:332-43 Ja '67
FEISAL, king of Saudi Arabia
President Johnson and King Faisal of Saudi Arabia exchange views on matters of common interest; June 21, 1966. Dept State Bul 55:39, 41 Jl 11 '66
about
Banquet of cold shoulder; New York's official rebuff. il por Time 88:13 Jl 1 '66
Call to Mecca. il por Time 88:45 S 30 '66
Desert kingdom that is beginning to stir. il por U S News 60:66-8 Je 27 '66
Hyperbole in high places; New York snub. Newsweek 68:16-17 Jl 4 '66
King Faisal: Saudi Arabia's modern monarch. G. Gaskill. il por Read Digest 90:117-22 Ja '67
King Faisal's visit: the real meaning of all the uproar. il por U S News 61:13 Jl 4 '66
King-size question. por Newsweek 67:54+ Je 27 '66
Leader alone; starts own Arab unity movement. Newsweek 68:44 Ag 8 '66
Revolution from the throne. il por Time 87:45 Je 24 '66
Rival Arabs. P. Seale and I. Beeson. New Repub 155:11 Ag 27 '66
Three kings in accord. por Time 87:37 F 4 '66

FELD, Bernard T.
Nagasaki binge. Bul Atomic Sci 22:35-7 F '66
FELD, Irvin
No blood, some tears, a sweat of money. L.
Smith. il Sports Illus 24:42-6 Mr 7 '66
FELD, Israel
No blood, some tears, a sweat of money. L.
Smith. il Sports Illus 24:42-6 Mr 7 '66
FELD, Stuart P.
Two hundred years of water color painting
in America. Antiques 90:840-5 D '66
—See Black, M. C. jt. auth.
FELDMAN, Eugene J.
Mixer and detector diodes. por Electr
World 76:57-60 Jl '66
FELDMAN, Irving
Elegy for a suicide. Poetry 109:4-6 O '66
Night; poem. Nation 202:277 Mr 7 '66
FELDMAN, Myer
Between the decision and the action. Sat R
49:32-3 Ja 29 '66
FELKNER, Myrtle
What we hope to leave our children. Farm J
90:47 Jl '66
FELLIG, Arthur
Weegee's living screen. H. V. Fondiller. il
Pop Phot 59:44 S '66
FELLIN, David
Inquest on a premature burial. T. Buckley.
il pors Esquire 65:75-81+ Je '66
FELLING of trees. See Tree felling
**FELLOWS in Africa program. See Americans
in Sudan**
**FELLOWSHIPS. See Scholarships and fellow-
ships**
FELTON, Rebecca (Latimer)
Life as a brave adventure. por Sr Schol 89:
7 S 30 '66
FEMINISM. See Woman—Social and moral
questions
FEMUR
First aid: fracture of thigh bone. C. J. Pott-
hoff. Todays Health 44:74 N '66
FENCES
Create a secluded garden. il Pop Gard 17:20-
1 D '66
Fashions in fences. il Flower Grower 53:
41-5 Je '66
How to put fences to work. il Pop Gard 17:
48:53 Mr '66
Open to breeze, closed to blast. il Sunset 137:
86 Jl '66
Sheep fences or antelope? concerning fencing
on public land in Wyo. B. Milek. il Field
& S 71:10-12+ S '66
Suburban stockade. Newsweek 68:108 N 7 '66
FENCES, Snow. See Snow fences
FENICHEL, I. Robert, and Horowitz, S. B.
Measurement of anesthetic potency. bibliog
Science 152:1110 My 20 '66
FENN, Ellen Rebecca
We agreed to his and hers bank accounts.
Suc Farm 64:63 Jl '66
FENNER, Mildred S.
(ed) Editor interviews. por NEA J 55:71-2
S; 10-13 D '66; 56:87-8 Ja '67
Editor's notebook. See issues of NEA jour-
nal to May 1966
To take and to tape. NEA J 56:62-4 Ja '67
FEOKTISTOV, Konstantin P.
Why we are outward bound. por UNESCO
Courier 19:27-30 My '66
FERBER, Edna. See Kaufman, G. S. jt. auth.
FERBER, Ellen
Voice of the silent stage. Am Ed 2:29-32 O '66
—and Sofokidis, J. H.
Goodbye to the birds and the bees; what's
happening. Am Ed 2:16+ N '66
FERDINAND, Sister M. See M. Ferdinand,
Sister
FERET, Barbara L.
Moving the library at Dutchess community
college. por ALA Bul 61:68-71 Ja '67
FERGUSON, Charles B.
New Britain museum of American art.
Antiques 90:668-72 N '66
FERGUSON, Charles W.
Americans not everybody knows. PTA Mag
60:10-12 F '66
Fifty-three ways to entertain once. Read
Digest 88:33-4+ F '66
FERGUSON, Charlotte R.
Gems among the gloxinias. Flower Grower
53:11 O '66
FERGUSON, Eleanor A.
By way of comment; reply to article by K.
Molz. ALA Bul 60:603 Je '66
Why revise public library standards now?
por ALA Bul 60:590-4 Je '66
FERGUSON, Gary
Little Gary Ferguson. il pors Ebony 21:39-
42+ My '66
FERGUSON, James
Air force research funding detailed. Aviation
W 84:117 Ap 18 '66

FERGUSON, James Edward
Me for ma, and I ain't got a dern thing
against pa. R. S. Gallagher. il por Am
Heritage 17:46-7+ O '66
FERGUSON, Lawrence L.
Better management of managers' careers.
bibliog f Harvard Bsns R 44:139-52 Mr '66
FERGUSON, Miriam Amanda (Wallace)
Me for ma, and I ain't got a dern thing
against pa. R. S. Gallagher. il por Am
Heritage 17:46-7+ O '66
FERKAUF, Eugene
Romance at Korvette. Time 87:90 Je 3 '66
FERKISS, Victor C.
Communism 1966: success or failure? Cath
World 204:11-16 O '66
FERLINGHETTI, Lawrence
Eyes and I. R. Duerden. Poetry 108:125-6
My '66
FERM, Deane William
Sex, sin and salvation in Sweden. Christian
Cent 83:1142-6 S 21 '66
FERMI award
Fermi winners named. Sci N 90:114 Ag 20 '66
FERMOR, Patrick Leigh
Danube. Holiday 40:28-39+ Ag '66
FERNEA, Elizabeth Warnock
Year our children discovered America. por
Redbook 128:12+ D '66
FERNOW award
Doctor Verne L. Harper, first recipient of
Fernow award; remarks, September 6, 1965.
P. F. Watzek. il Am For 71:7+ O '65
FERNS
Evolutionary significance of polyploidy in the
pteridophyta. E. J. Klekowski, jr. and H.
G. Baker. bibliog il Science 153:305-7 Jl 15
'66
Ferns. B. Cobb. il Horticulture 44:18-19+ My
'66
Ferns in your house. K. Berggrav. il Horti-
culture 44:18-21+ Je '66
Growing ferns in hanging wire baskets. il
Sunset 136:246 Ap '66
See also
Tree ferns
FERON, James
That new boy in Israel's foreign office. N Y
Times Mag p40-1+ Ap 17 '66
FERRARA, Al
Fact and fancy; Dodger outfielder as a con-
cert pianist. Sports Illus 25:16 S 26 '66
FERRAS, Christian
New York concert. S. Fleming. Hi Fi 16:132
F '66
FERRÉ, Frederick
Disciples of discontinuity. Christian Cent 83:
622-4 My 11 '66
FERRE, Luis A.
Peace, the modern approach; address, March
26, 1966. Vital Speeches 32:461-4 My 15 '66
FERRÉ, Nels F. S.
Quaker panorama. Christian Cent 83:964-5
Ag 3 '66
FERREDOXIN
Evolution of the structure of ferredoxin based
on living relics of primitive amino acid
sequences. R. V. Eck and M. O. Dayhoff.
bibliog il Science 152:363-6 Ap 15 '66
FERREN, John
John Ferren's mandorla. L. Finkelstein. il
por Art N 65:34-5+ Sum '66
FERRENCE, John
Cheer for the teacher. Sch Arts 65:16-17 Ja
'66
FERRER, José M. 3d
Life TV review. Life 60:22 My 6; 15 Je 3:
61:24 D 9 '66; 62:15 Ja 13 '67
FERRICK, Daisy L.
Include daylilies in your garden. Horticulture
44:26-7+ My '66
FERRIES
By boat to Alaska; Queen of Prince Rupert
car ferry. il Time 87:44 My 27 '66
Fall ferry ride from Kelsey Bay; overnight
run to Prince Rupert. il Sunset 137:28+
O '66
FERRIES, Toy
This ferry rolls into its landing on casters. il
Sunset 137:98+ N '66
FERRIGAN, Madelyn
They guard against heart attack. Todays
Health 44:10-11 Je '66
FERRILL, Arther
Herodotus and the strategy and tactics of
the invasion of Xerxes. bibliog f Am Hist
R 72:102-15 O '66
FERRIS, John
Go join Othello in Venice. Life 61:30 N 25 '66
Hemingway is the star in his own tragedy.
Life 60:10 Ap 15 '66
Mob seen. Sat R 49:4 Ag 13 '66
FERRITE
Ferrite beads. L. Solomon. il Electr World
76:42-3 O '66

FERROCARRIL Chihuahua al Pacifico. See Railroads—Mexico

FERROSILITE
Ferrosilite III; a triclinic pyroxenoid-type polymorph of ferrous metasilicate. C. W. Burnham. bibliog il Science 154:513-16 O 28 '66

FERRY, Wilbur H.
Happy heretic. V. S. Navasky. Atlan 218:53-7 Jl '66
Masscomm. Newsweek 67:98+ My 2 '66

FERRYBOATS. See Ferries

FERTILITY
Vitamin A improves cows' fertility. Sci N 89:453 Je 4 '66

FERTILITY, Human
Gonadotropin-induced anomalies of the zona pellucida of the baboon ovum. A. A. Katzberg and A. G. Hendrickx. bibliog il Science 151:1225-6 Mr 11 '66
New help for childless couples. Todays Health 44:82-3 Mr '66
Too much fertility; case of Mrs Cwikielnik points up HMG-HCG treatment. il Newsweek 68:96 O 17 '66
Urbanites less fertile. Sci N 91:27 Ja 7 '67

FERTILITY control. See Birth control

FERTILITY drugs
Fertility drug for single births; testing Clomid and Perganol. B. J. Culliton. Sci N 90:539 D 24 '66
Too much fertility; case of Mrs Cwikielnik points up HMG-HCG treatment. il Newsweek 68:96 O 17 '66

FERTILIZATION (biology)
New facts about human reproduction. J. D. Ratcliff. Read Digest 89:119-22 D '66

FERTILIZER spreaders
Fewer stops, faster refills for fertilizer. il Farm J 90:42-5 F '66
Four time-savers for fertilizer. il Farm J 90:66J Ap '66
Pop-up fertilizer starts corn off fast. D. Hagen. il Farm J 90:66V Ap '66
Sprinkle spreading; how it has worked. G. Lorang. il Farm J 90:B4+ Jl '66

FERTILIZERS and manures
Facts on fertilizers. R. M. Carleton. Flower Grower 53:38-9+ Ap '66
Fall farming; best way to beat the spring labor shortage. D. Seim. il Farm J 90:40-1+ O '66
How and when to feed corn nitrogen. L. Robertson and L. E. Zeman. il Suc Farm 64:42-3+ F '66
How to fertilize for high-yield, high-quality wheat. F. W. Smith and L. E. Zeman. il Suc Farm 64:52-3 S '66
Lawn fertilizers. il Consumer Rep 31:204-7 Ap '66
Listing of lawn fertilizers. Consumer Rep 31:188-95 D '66
Mulch or compost. P. F. Frese. il Pop Gard 17:87+ D '66
Safe and accurate dilution of garden chemicals. il Sunset 136:240 Je '66
Supplementary feeding. W. A. Rosenau. Horticulture 44:38-9+ Jl '66
See also
Ammonia
Nitrates
Soil fertility

Spray applications
Fewer stops, faster refills for fertilizer. il Farm J 90:42-5 F '66

Spreaders
See Fertilizer spreaders

FERTITTA, Sally McLaury
Will the real Huey Long please stand up. Motor B 118:88+ Ag '66

FESTA italiana. See Pageants

FESTIVAL du Marais. See Music festivals—France

FESTIVAL of Flanders. See Music festivals—Belgium

FESTIVAL of two worlds, Spoleto. See Music festivals—Italy

FESTIVALS
Artist as playwright and engineer. R. Kostelanetz. il N Y Times Mag p32-3+ O 9 '66
SR/1967 world travel calendar. T. L. Christie. Sat R 50:77-82 Ja 7 '67

Saturnalia, satire, and utopia. R. C. Elliott. Yale R 55:521-36 Je '66
Southern cruising almanac; Florida and Bahamas events. il Motor B 118:22-5 O '66
See also
Celebrations
Dance festivals
Drama festivals
Holy week
Moving picture festivals
Music festivals
Pageants

Arizona
Gold rush days in Wickenburg. il Sunset 136:36-8 F '66

California
Twentieth century music and art, at Stanford; third annual Summer festival of the arts. il Sunset 136:69-70 Je '66

Denmark
Mayors, Moreno, and a marriage; how it is going to celebrate 800th anniversary. M. Connelly. il Sat R 50:54+ Ja 7 '67

France
1966 & all that; Veauville-les-Baons vote against celebration of 1066. Time 87:35 F 18 '66

Indiana
Indiana sesquicentennial. B. Finnegan. il Hobbies 71:120-1+ Jl; 118-19+ S; 120-1 O '66

Italy
Menotti's superb new Pelléas; Spoleto report. W. Weaver. Hi Fi 16:MA23 S '66
Spoleto's choice; exhibition of Three centuries of theater design. S. Preston. il Opera N 31:20-3 S 10 '66

Maryland
Bounty of the eastern shore; chicken festival; annual National cooking contest. Pocomoke City. N. S. Hazelton. Nat R 18:926+ S 20 '66

Michigan
Cherry festival. R. Hanna. il Suc Farm 64:68-9+ Jl '66

Mississippi
Mississippi folk festival; featured African and Afro-American artists. il Ebony 21:91-2+ Mr '66

New York (state)
Whale of a time #4; Sag Harbor. Long Island Old whalers' festival. W. Juettner. il Motor B 118:87 Ag '66

Portugal
Harvesting the grape. A. Waugh. il Nat R 18:883+ S 6 '66

Senegal
Behind the mask of Africa; artistic heritage; dancing, music, literature, sculpture. A. Malraux. il N Y Times Mag p30-1+ My 15 '66
First world festival of black man's art; with report by B. Farrell. il Life 60:83-88B Ap 22 '66
World festival of Negro arts. H. W. Fuller. il Ebony 21:96-102+ Jl '66

Sweden
How the Swedes celebrate the longest day; midsummer. il Sunset 136:158-60 Je '66

Texas
Fiesta San Antonio; vs New Orleans Mard' gras. F. P. Keyes. il Travel 125:29-31+ Mr '66

Washington (state)
Fall City's Easter passion play. il Sunset 136:69-70 Mr '66

Wisconsin
Circus parade; Old Milwaukee days. il U S Camera 29:56-7+ Jl '66

FETAL erythroblastosis. See Erythroblastosis

FETLER, James
Dust of Yuri Serafimovich; story. Atlan 217:63-9 Je '66

FETOLOGY. See Fetus

FETUS
Conquest of death before birth; intrauterine transfusion. J. D. Ratcliff. Read Digest 88:107-11 Ap '66
Fascinating story of life before birth. M. Liley and B. Day. il Parents Mag 41:62-3+ O '66
How doctors heal the unborn. A. Lake. il Sat Eve Post 239:39-42 F 12 '66
Illnesses in the unborn; fetology unrecognized as a medical specialty. America 116:76 Ja 21 '67

FETUS—*Continued*

Immunologic maturation in utero: kinetics of the primary antibody response in the fetal lamb. A. M. Silverstein and others. bibliog il Science 154:1675-7 D 30 '66

New ways to save your unborn child. V. Apgar. Ladies Home J 83:46+ Ag '66

Phenylalanine: transplacental concentrations in rhesus monkeys. G. R. Kerr and H. A. Waisman. bibliog il Science 151:824-5 F 18 '66

What expectant mothers need to know; interview. D. Harting. il U S News 60:54-6+ F 14 '66

World of the unborn. J. C. G. Conniff. il N Y Times Mag p40-1+ Ja 8 '67

FEUER, Lewis Samuel

American philosophy is dead. N Y Times Mag p30-1+ Ap 24 '66

Decline of freedom at Berkeley. Atlan 218: 78-82+ S; 38+ N '66

Should college students grade their teachers? N Y Times Mag p56-7+ S 18 '66

about

Cultural exchange as the Soviets use it. G. Bailey. il Reporter 34:23-5 Ap 7 '66

Les FEUX-follets (organization) See Dance companies

FEVER

When someone in your family has a fever. Bet Hom & Gard 44:126 Ap '66

FEVER thermometers. See Thermometers, Clinical

FEW notes about the Arabian oryx; story. See Ross, K.

FEY, Harold E.

Enduring monument. Christian Cent 83:586 My 4 '66

Inconsistent application. Christian Cent 83: 936 Jl 27 '66

FEYNMAN, Richard Phillips

Development of the space-time view of quantum electrodynamics; address, December 11, 1965. Science 153:699-708 Ag 12 '66

FEZENSAC, Robert, comte de Montesquiou-. See Montesquiou-Fezensac, R.

FFOLKES, Michael

She; cartoons. Holiday 39:62-7 Ap '66

FIAT company. See Automobile industry and trade—Italy

FIBBING. See Lying

FIBER glass. See Glass fibers

FIBER optics

Fiber-optics camera looks around corners. il Sci N 89:439 Je 4 '66

Light that bends, twists and turns. S. L. Englebardt. il Sci Digest 59:40-3 My '66

Plastic fibers can transmit light. Sci N 89: 439 Je 4 '66

FIBER research

Fibers and more fibers. R. Yoshioka. il Sci N 89:389-90+ My 21 '66

FIBERGLASS. See Glass fibers

FIBERGLASS boats. See Boats—Materials

FIBERGLASS cars. See Automobiles—Materials

FIBERS

Designing strength into materials; fiber-reinforced composite materials. il Bsns W p91-2+ D 17 '66

Inner strength for man's materials; fiber technology. T. Alexander. il Fortune 73: 152-5+ Ap '66

See also

Fiber research

FIBERS, Artificial. See Fibers

FIBRIN

Stable complex of fibrinogen and fibrin. T. Sasaki and others. bibliog il Science 152: 1069-71 My 20 '66

FIBRINOGEN

Stable complex of fibrinogen and fibrin. T. Sasaki and others. bibliog il Science 152: 1069-71 My 20 '66

FIBROSIS, Cystic. See Cystic fibrosis

FICHTER, Joseph H.

Book review. America 114:780 My 28 '66

Catholic professors on the secular campus. por America 115:320 S 24 '66

That celibacy survey. America 116:92-4 Ja 21 '67

about

. . . And get back a man. R. A. Schroth. America 115:382-4 O 1 '66

FICKES, Robert O.

Can he turn on Philco? J. B. Weiner. por Duns R 88:39-40 Ag '66

FICKLING, Skip

Take it seriesly! Writer 79:18-20 My '66

FICTION

Avant-garde and contemporary literature: excerpts from address. October 28, 1965. S. Sontag. il Wilson Lib Bul 40:930-2+ Je '66

Books; concerning Robbe-Grillet's and Moravia's essays on the novel. N. Bliven. New Yorker 42:165-8 Ap 9 '66

Myth and literature; ed. by J. B. Vickery. Review

Sat R 49:28-9 Ag 20 '66. T. H. Gaster

1966: the reviewer reviews. G. Hicks. Sat R 49:17-18 D 31 '66

Nothing new. S. Kauffmann. New Repub 156: 26+ Ja 14 '67

Novel of adolescent romance; with bibliography. A. Daigon. Library J 91:2152-6 Ap 15 '66

Publication of children's books far outweighs adult fiction; with charts. Library J 91: 1048-9 F 15 '66

Yet another interview with B. Bonnet; fiction as nonfiction. L. L. Case. Nation 202:193-4 F 14 '66

See also

Christmas stories

Historical fiction

Japanese fiction

Negroes in literature

Novelists

Realism in literature

Science fiction

Sex in literature

Short stories

War in literature

Appreciation and interpretation

See also

Literature—Appreciation and interpretation

Authorship

Interview with Eudora Welty. E. Welty. Sr Schol 89:sup 18 D 9 '66

Now I sit me down; pleasing the editor. W. Chamberlain. Writer 79:22-4 F '66

Truth in fiction. J. Stafford. il Library J 91: 4557-65 O 1 '66

See also

Short stories

Bibliography

Fiction (cont) W. B. Hill. America 114: 670-2; 115:706-10 My 7, N 26 '66

Sad, sinister, and sane: some new novels. P. Pickrel. Harper 232:98-100 Je '66

Collections

See Anthologies

History

Told in letters; epistolary fiction before Richardson. by R. A. Day. Review

Sat R 49:70 Je 11 '66. L. Edel

Technique

Anatomy of a true adventure story. H. D. Steward. Writer 79:13-17 My '66

Background; the most important character. E. Ogilvie. Writer 79:11-14 Jl '66

Butter the size of a walnut; recipe for a story. I. Foster. Writer 79:23-5 D '66

Commanding your material; novel writing. T. Duncan. Writer 79:13-16+ Mr '66

Don't think. S. Dorman. Writer 79:25 S '66

Everything that rises must converge. J. M. Kann. Cath World 204:154-9 D '66

Fiction strategy; excerpts from Tricks and techniques of the selling writer. D. V. Swain. Writer 79:15-19 N '66

For a new novel. by A. Robbe-Grillet. tr. by R. Howard. Review

Sat R 49:32 Mr 12 '66. H. T. Moore

For writing out loud! L. Conger. Writer 79: 7-8 Ag '66

Fortunate failures. S. K. Boyd. Writer 79: 13-15+ Ag '66

Hand is quicker than the I; first-person viewpoint. W. Shore. Writer 79:17-19 Ap '66

I want to know, what about writing courses? C. R. Bittle. Writer 79:26-8 Je '66

Is your story different enough? D. J. Marlowe. Writer 79:17-19 D '66

Magnificent trifles. R. Somerlott. Writer 79: 16-19 O '66

Novel of the future. T. J. Fleming. America 114:654-5+ My 7 '66

One pin and a fish-hook. M. S. Foster. Writer 79:9-12+ Ap '66

Onward and upward with the arts; fiction-writing course called Daily themes at Yale. C. Trillin. New Yorker 42:118+ Je 11 '66

Person and plot. S. Epstein. Writer 79: 9-12 My '66

Realm of emotion. P. S. Curry. Writer 79: 14-18+ F '66

FICTION—Technique—*Continued*
Stockings were hung by the chimney with care; building anticipation with care, as at Christmas. L. Conger. Writer 79:9-10 D '66
Time and transition. P. S. Curry. Writer 79:18-20+ S '66
True lie-minded man. W. H. Gass. Nation 203:453-4 O 31 '66
What happens? what if? what then? B. Robinson. Writer 79:9-11+ S '66
When the writer comes of age; reprint. B. J. Chute. Writer 79:20-4 N '66
See also
Characterization
Detective and mystery stories—Technique
Dialogue
Fiction in periodicals and newspapers
Short stories
Themes
See Literature—Themes
FICTION, Fantasy. See Fantasies, Literary
FICTION, Historical. See Historical fiction
FICTION and science. See Literature and science
FICTION for children. See Childrens literature
FICTION in periodicals and newspapers
How to raise the curtain on an article. M. Gunther. Writer 79:9-12 Ag '66
When McCall's looks for stories. B. Blakemore. Writer 79:25 F '66
FIEDLER, Leslie A.
Author. P. Meras. Sat R 49:32 Jl 30 '66
FIELD, Bonnie. See Birky, C. W. jr, jt. auth.
FIELD, Edward
Two departures: Giraffes; Giants; poems. Nation 203:558 N 21 '66
FIELD, Frank
Weather; interview. New Yorker 42:50-2 S 10 '66
FIELD, Michael
All about garlic. Holiday 39:24+ Je '66
World of fine cooking. McCalls 93:59-60+ F; 78+ Mr; 86+ Ap; 59-60+ Je; 94:84+ O '66
FIELD, Magnetic. See Magnetic fields
FIELD-effect transistors. See Transistors
FIELD enterprises, incorporated
Field now full owner of newspaper syndicate. Pub W 190:199 Jl 11 '66
New Day in Chicago; Arlington day launch. Newsweek 6:60-1 Ja 31 '66
Spreading suburban daily. il Time 87:43-4 F 4 '66
FIELD glasses
Binoculars. il Consumer Rep 31:296-8 D '66
Hunter's binoculars. J. O'Connor. il Outdoor Life 137:80+ Je '66
Try these vision-stretchers. M. D. Grennan. il Pop Phot 59:98-101+ S '66
FIELD sports. See Track athletics
FIELD trials (dogs)
Comeback of the National. M. Duffey. il Outdoor Life 139:110-12+ Ja '67
Cotton fires up Little Smoky; National at Bombay Hook national wildlife refuge. D. Barnes. il Sports Illus 24:28-33 Ja 31 '66
Shooting-dog championship. D. M. Duffey. il Outdoor Life 137:136-40 Je '66
Springer championship. D. M. Duffey. il Outdoor Life 137:146+ Mr '66
To err is canine. D. M. Duffey. il Outdoor Life 137:118+ F '66
FIELD trips, Educational. See School excursions
FIELDEN, John S.
Right young people for business. Harvard Bsns R 44:76-83 Mr '66
FIELDING, Byron
Federal funds to meet local needs. NEA J 55:23-6 S '66
FIELDING, Gabriel, pseud. See Barnsley, A. G.
FIELDING publications, incorporated
Temple Fielding and Morrow establish Fielding pubns. Pub W 189:155 F 21 '66
FIELDS, C. H. and Oniki, Saburou
Sony home video recorder. Electr World 75:42-4 My '66
FIELDS, W. C.
Dark geography of W. C. Fields. W. Markfield. il pors N Y Times Mag p32-3+ Ap 24 '66
Fields-eye view of things; comp. by G. Flatley. N Y Times Mag p 117 Ap 24 '66
FIELDS, William J.
$25,000 bundle for a fat cat. il pors Ebony 22:106-8+ N '66
FIELDS medal. See International congress of mathematicians
FIESER, Louis F.
Story of an ex-smoker. Read Digest 88:68-72 Ap '66
FIFE, J. A.
European refuse-disposal. Am City 81:125-8 S '66

FIFTH avenue bank of New York. See New York (city)—Banks
FIFTH committee of the General assembly. See United Nations—Administrative and budgetary committee
FIFTH constitutional amendment. See United States—Constitution—Bill of rights
FIFTY books of the year exhibit. See Book exhibits
Le FIGARO. See Paris—Newspapers
FIGGINS, Gregg J.
How to start with long-term subscriptions. por Library J 91:2168-9 Ap 15 '66
FIGHTER planes. See Airplanes, Military
FIGHTING. See Military art and science
FIGHTING (psychology)
Books in review; instinct and aggression. T. C. Schneirla. Natur Hist 75:16+ D '66
Books: two on aggression. J. Alsop. New Yorker 42:209-14+ S 10 '66
Man has no killer instinct. G. Gorer. N Y Times Mag p47+ N 27 '66
On aggression, by K. Lorenz. Review
Life 60:8+ Je 3 '66. F. Russell
Redbook 128:34+ N '66. M. Mead
Sci Digest 60:30-1 D '66. J. Reinert
Time il 87:104+ Je 17 '66
FIGON, Georges
Ben Barka affair. C. Sterling. il Reporter 34:22-8 Mr 10 '66
Diminished fifth. por Newsweek 6:44+ Ja 31 '66
Scandal. il pors Life 60:32-32B F 4 '66
FIGURAL aftereffects
Visual spatial aftereffect from prolonged headtilt. R. H. Day and N. J. Wade. bibliog il Science 154:1201-2 D 2 '66
FIGURE drawing
Eyes of an artist. il Design 68:34-7 S '66
FIGURE skating. See Skating
FIGUREHEADS of ships
Figures and figureheads: the maritime collection at the State Streeet bank and trust company, Boston. W. D. Garrett. il Antiques 90:820-3 D '66
FIGURES of speech
It's in the potato: Brazilian character and Portuguese language. P. Rónai. il Américas 18:17-23 N '66
FIGURINES
Clay sculpture from Jaina; island burial site yields Maya treasures. L. Aveleyra Arroyo de Anda and G. F. Ekholm. il Natur Hist 75:40-7 Ap '66
Oriental porcelain frivolities. P. C. Copeland. il Antiques 89:709-17 My '66
See also
Bronzes
FIJI
Independence? Fiji isn't sure. D. Seidler. il N Y Times Mag p50-1+ N 20 '66
Travel's picture portfolio. Travel 125:50-5 Ap '66
See also
United Nations—Fiji
FIJIANS
Independence? Fiji isn't sure. D. Seidler. il N Y Times Mag p50-1+ N 20 '66
Travel's picture portfolio. Travel 125:50-5 Ap '66
FILAMENTS
ABL refining filament winding art. J. F. Judge. il Tech W 18:30+ Je 27 '66
Boron filament graduates to production. J. F. Judge. il Tech W 19:23-4 O 10 '66
Rolls Royce materials work stresses filament composites. J. F. Judge. il Miss & Roc 18:26+ Mr 7 '66
Schriever cites progress on composites. Aviation W 84:81 Je 6 '66
SAMPE blankets reinforced composites. J. F. Judge. il Tech W 19:24-5+ N 21 '66
Whisker-carrying filaments may solve alignment problem. il Tech W 19:34 D 19 '66
FILES and filing (documents, etc)
Instant indexing; system for locating past photo magazine articles. N. S. Smith. il U S Camera 29:16-18+ F '66
FILHO, Napoleao Lopes. See Lopes Filho, N.
FILIBUSTERING in legislation. See United States—Congress—Senate—Rules and practice
FILIPINO literature
New writing from the Philippines, by L. Casper. Review
Sat R 49:27-8 Ag 27 '66. D. A. Yates
FILLE du régiment; opera. See Donizetti, G.
FILLING (earthwork)
Fill first, then compact; way to protect the unreinforced rubber tires of loader; Buchanan, Mich. M. Hankila. il Am City 81:173-4 My '66
Landfill and hospital live in harmony; disposal gardens, San Pedro, Calif. il Am City 81:38 My '66

FINANCE, International—*Continued*
World monetary reform; search for a successor to the dollar. il Sr School 87:12-13 Ja 21 '66
See also
Balance of payments
Bank for international settlements
Debts, Public
Foreign exchange
Inter-American development bank
International bank for reconstruction and development
International finance corporation
Money—International aspects
United States—National advisory council on international monetary and financial policies

FINANCE, Municipal. See Municipal finance

FINANCE, Personal
Spending your money; questions and answers. S. Porter. See issues of Ladies' home journal
That always broke feeling, and what to do about it. il Changing T 20:7-11 Mr '66
Understanding and using economics. M. Mayer. Bet Hom & Gard 44:112 S '66
What's happening in education? teenagers' pocket money. W. D. Boutwell. PTA Mag 60:18 Mr '66

FINANCE, State. See State finance

FINANCE committee (Senate) See United States—Congress—Senate—Finance committee

FINANCE companies
Are changes coming in those one-sided credit laws? il Consumer Rep 31:108-12 Mr '66
Dirty deal in small loans; relations of finance and insurance companies. J. Ridgeway. New Repub 155:11-12 O 8 '66
When the roof fell in at Atlantic; Toronto-based Atlantic acceptance corp. il Bsns W p68-72 F 5 '66

FINANCIAL analysts. See Investments—Advisers

FINANCIAL news. See Television broadcasting— Financial news

FINANCIAL times, London
In the pink. Newsweek 68:106 S 19 '66

FINANCIERS. See Capitalists and financiers

FINCH, Hardy
Books on African history. Sr School 89:sup58 S 23 '66
Convention exhibit notes; NCTE. Sr School 89:sup7 D 9 '66
New reading materials for high school students. Sr School 87:sup22-3 Ja 21 '66
What's happening in English. Sr School 88: sup 10 F 11; 89:sup43 S 23 '66
What's new in reference works? Sr School 88:sup 14-15+ F 4 '66

FINCH, Robert H.
Pragmatic Republican. R. Moley. Newsweek 67:108 Mr 14 '66

FINCH, Stuart M.
Emotional problems of preschoolers. PTA Mag 60:15-17 bibliog(p32) Ap '66

FINCHER, Jack
Balancing act at Berkeley. Life 61:45-6+ D 16 '66
Basketball's newest box-office baby. Life 62: 54-7 Ja 6 '67
Keys to a happy life: yes, no, and wow! Life 61:38 Ag 12 '66
Pigeons everywhere, alas! Life 61:149-50 D 9 '66

FINCHES
See also
Indigo buntings

FINDERS, View. See View finders

FINDLEY, Paul
Impact and potential of American diplomacy; address; with questions and answers. Ann Am Acad 366:68-77 Jl '66
Sugar: a sticky mess in Congress. Read Digest 88:88-92 Je '66
about
Findley's folly. New Repub 154:7 My 7 '66

FINE, Benjamin
Why bright children get poor marks; excerpt from Underachievers: how they can be helped. Redbook 127:72-3+ S '66

FINE silk thread; story. See Schwartz, J.

FINEMAN, Morton
Distress signals; story. Sat Eve Post 239: 50-2 D 31 '66
Games that husbands play; story. Sat Eve Post 239:52-8 Ap 9 '66

FINES (penalties)
$50 billion minus $25; letter to Mayor Lindsay. G. Ace. il Sat R 49:10 S 24 '66
Fine, but not dandy; violators of M.S.U. parking rules to be prosecuted in local courts. Time 88:40 Jl 29 '66

FINGAL, Beebe Bowers
I must believe; poem. Negro Hist Bul 29: 45 N '65

FINGER, Frank W. See Goff, M. L. R. jt. auth.

FINGER, Grayce A.
Over-exploited animal populations. Science 154:544-5 O 28 '66

FINGERPRINTS
Fingerprints by wire; Chicago. il Am City 81:165 My '66
See also
Dermatoglyphics

FINISHING, Textile. See Textile finishing

FINISHING, Wood. See Wood finishing

FINISHING materials
Epoxy and epoxy-type finishes. il Consumer Bul 49:11-12 My '66
Finishing touches; finishes for boats. Motor B 117:167+ Ja '66

FINITE. See Infinite

FINK, Augusta
Book festival for young people. Pub W 189: 81-3 My 30 '66

FINK, Daniel J.
Military space program; address, April 26, 1966. Vital Speeches 32:518-21 Je 15 '66

FINK, Herbert
Role of crafts in education. Craft Horiz 26: 8+ Je '66

FINK, Peter
Place in the sun. M. R. Weiss. il Sat R 49: 16-17 Ag 27 '66

FINKEL, Donald
Three younger poets. R. J. Mills, jr. Poetry 109:117-18 N '66

FINKEL, Henry
High flyer. H. L. Masin. il por Sr Schol 87:29 Ja 7 '66

FINKEL, Miriam P. and others
Virus induction of osteosarcomas in mice. bibliog Science 151:698-701 F 11 '66

FINKELSTEIN, Louis
John Ferren's mandorla. Art N 65:34-5+ Sum '66

FINLAND
See also
Architecture—Finland
Architecture, Domestic—Finland
Booksellers and bookselling—Finland
Foreign visitors in Finland

Description and travel
Finland. S. Schoonover. il Holiday 40:62-7+ N '66
Finns and thin ice. P. L. Adams. il Atlan 218:113-17 N '66

Politics and government
Out of the wilderness; Communists in four-party coalition. Newsweek 67:44+ Je 6 '66
See also
Elections—Finland
Political parties—Finland

FINLEY, David
Letter from Vietnam. America 115:380-1 O 1 '66

FINLEY, M. I.
Few words from the Etruscans. Horizon 8: 104-9 Sum '66

FINN, James
Debate on Vietnam. por Cath World 203:76-80 My '66

FINN, Melvin A.
Humans, plants and animals in Florida's Fahkahatchee Strand. il Nat Parks Mag 40:10-13 Jl '66

FINN, Seamus
Playing with children; poem. Nation 203:589 N 28 '66

FINN, Thomas M.
Peace, war and the Vatican council. por Cath World 203:270-5 Ag '66

FINNEGAN, Bob
Picture post card. See issues of Hobbies

FINNEY, Charles G.
Murder with feathers. Harper 232:112-13 Ap '66

FINNEY, John
Preventing nuclear spread. New Repub 155: 10-11 Jl 16 '66

FINNEY, Paul B. and Tompkins, J. S.
Wall Street establishment. Esquire 65:95-7+ Je '66

FINNIGAN, Joan
Canadian chronicle. R. Howard. Poetry 108: 45-6 Ap '66

FINNISH architecture. See Architecture, Finnish

FINO, Paul A.
Excerpt from debate, June 28, 1965. Cong Digest 45:23+ Ja '66

FINSTEIN, Max
Seven poets. T. Clark. Poetry 108:410-11 S '66

FIORDS
Metal glint in the fjords. il Fortune 74:79-80 O '66

FIRE
Built-in fire fighter; burning rates reduced by weightlessness in spacecraft. Time 88:76-7 D 16 '66
When homo erectus tamed fire, he tamed himself. J. Pfeiffer. il N Y Times Mag p58-9+ D 11 '66; Discussion. p 18+ Ja 8 '67

FIRE alarms
Alarm horns cut false fire calls; Philadelphia. J. J. McCarey. il Am City 81:50 N '66
Build a hip squawk box; intercom doubles as a burglar and fire alarm. C. Vlahos and B. G. Weis. il Pop Electr 25:97-8+ O '66
For emergency calls only; fire and police emergency calls; Greensboro, N.C. S. H. Smith. il Am City 81:153-4+ O '66
Home fire alarms, any good? il Changing T 20:11-12 N '66
Home fire alarms; could save hundreds of lives each year. A. J. Pryor. il Consumer Bul 50:35-8 Ja '67
We put new life in emergency reporting; Bridgeport, Conn. S. J. Tedesco. il Am City 81:112-13 Mr '66

FIRE arms. See Firearms
FIRE balls. See Meteors
FIRE bike brigade. See Fire patrols
FIRE drills
Fun that saves lives; family fire drill. J. Carper. il Todays Health 44:36-9 O '66

FIRE extinction
Shut the windows! the fire suds are coming through the doors. P. W. Kearney. il Pop Mech 125:136-9+ F '66
See also
Fire protection

FIRE extinguishers
Kill that fire with the right extinguisher. P. W. Kearney. il Pop Mech 127:102-5+ Ja '67

FIRE fighting. See Fire protection
FIRE fighting foam. See Fire protection
FIRE flies. See Fireflies
FIRE houses
Design for a dedication; Toledo, Ohio; ed. by P. D. Eimon. il Am City 81:142+ O '66
FIRE in the vineyards; story. See Boyle, K.
FIRE inspection. See Fire protection
FIRE insurance. See Insurance, Fire
FIRE patrols
Here comes the Fire bike brigade! H. E. McLean. il Am For 72:4-5 O '66
FIRE pits. See Fireplaces, Outdoor
FIRE prevention. See Fire protection
FIRE protection
Fighting fire with fire. A. Hamilton. il Am For 72:18-21+ Jl '66
Fire-fighting foam won't hurt fireman. il Am City 81:63 My '66
Fire protection for 300,000 barrels of liquid gas. Am City 81:48 Ag '66
First aid. C. J. Potthoff. il Todays Health 44:80 My '66
High explosives on the highways; interview, ed. by T. Stimson. R. J. Madden. il Pop Mech 126:88-92+ D '66
Measure your fire department by men, not equipment. E. W. Fowler. il Am City 81:132+ D '66
Snorkel that goes on loan; Kenosha, Wis. E. Spitzer. il Am City 81:117 Ap '66
Water program cuts fire-insurance rates; Buena Park, Calif. F. L. Yaberg and R. C. Kenmir. il Am City 81:110-11 O '66
What to do in a fire. E. Crimmin. Sci Digest 59:58-9 My '66
See also
Fire alarms
Fire extinction
Fireproofing of textiles
Forest fire protection
also subhead Fires and fire protection under various subjects, e.g. Wharves—Fires and fire protection

Laws and regulations
Firetrap, U.S.A. S. Frank. il McCalls 94:48+ N '66

Research
Computer used to study the science of fires. Sci N L 89:72 Ja 29 '66
How fire spreads; research project in the Dorchester district of South Boston. il Sci Digest 59:56-7 My '66
FIRE stations. See Fire houses

FIREARMS
Firearms. See issues of Hobbies
Getting the range. J. O'Connor. See issues of Outdoor life
No sale to SMERSH; refusal to sell Gyrojet rocket handgun. il Time 87:23 Ap 22 '66
Right to bear arms, by C. Bakal. Review Time il 88:70 Jl 29 '66
Shooting. J. O'Connor. See issues of Outdoor life
Shooting; ed. by W. Page. See issues of Field & stream
See also
Cartridges
Pistols
Rifles
Shotguns

Collectors and collecting
Accumulator versus the collector. B. Sweeney. il Hobbies 71:124-5 Je '66
Guns of Dallas; J. F. Kennedy and J. D. Tippit assassination weapons to be preserved. Time 87:28 Mr 4 '66

History
General Burnside's guns. C. G. Worman. il Hobbies 71:120-1 Mr '66

Laws and regulations
Aimless; opponents of federal legislation to control firearms. il Time 88:25 S 9 '66
Big shoot; gun-restricting legislation. R. G. Sherrill. il Nation 202:260-4 Mr 7 '66
Gun and how to control it. J. V. Bennett. il N Y Times Mag p34-5+ S 25 '66
Gun-toting nation; stricter arms licensing. Time 88:15 Ag 12 '66
Handbook for arm twisters; letters to legislators. R. Starnes. Field & S 70:20+ Mr '66
Honk's life insurance; expert marksmen through growing up with guns. R. Starnes. Field & S 71:16+ N '66
No sale to SMERSH; refusal to sell Gyrojet rocket handgun. il Time 87:23 Ap 22 '66
Philadelphia! redtape nightmare. R. Starnes. il Field & S 71:11-14+ My '66
Plea for gun control. il Ebony 22:100-1 Ja '67
Right to bear arms, by C. Bakal. Review Sat R 49:23-4 Ag 27 '66. H. Lavine
Stampede; Senator Dodd's firearms bill W. F. Buckley, jr. Nat R 18:821 Ag 23 '66
This month's feature; Congress and gun control proposals. Cong Digest 45:289-314 D '66
We need a firearms-control law, now! A. Earth. Read Digest 90:17-18+ Ja '67
Who needs an antitank gun? need for control bill. Life 62:6 Ja 13 '67

Safety devices and measures
New tool for gun safety; TV firearms course. B. East. il Outdoor Life 138:74-5+ Jl '66

Sights
Choosing the right scope. J. O'Connor. il Outdoor Life 137:118+ Mr '66
Head movement trains helicopter guns. il Aviation W 85:58-9 Jl 4 '66
Mount basics. W. Page. il Field & S 71:138-44 My '66

FIREARMS industry and trade
Shots heard round the world; Remington celebrates its 150th anniversary, Winchester its 100th. J. O'Connor. il Outdoor Life 138:48-9+ Jl '66
William Glaze and the Palmette armory. C. G. Worman. il Hobbies 71:124 Ja '67
See also
International armaments corporation
Remington arms company
FIREBALLS. See Meteors
FIREFLIES
Fireflies flash in unison. Sci N 90:130 Ag 27 '66
Swamp lights; synchronous flashing; Asia. Time 88:36 Ag 26 '66
FIREMEN
Four fives; death of twelve firemen in Manhattan fire. il Newsweek 68:44 O 31 '66
Measure your fire department by men, not equipment. E. W. Fowler. il Am City 81:132+ D '66
Shock of firemen's worst fire; death of firemen in New York city fire. il Life 61:45 O 28 '66
FIREMEN, Railroad. See Railroads—Employees
FIREMEN and oilers, International brotherhood of. See International brotherhood of firemen and oilers
FIREMENS union. See International brotherhood of firemen and oilers

FIREPITS. See Fireplaces, Outdoor
FIREPLACES
Open and shut fireplace. il Sunset 137:132 O '66
They did over their fireplace. il Sunset 137: 123 S '66
Which fireplace should you choose? D. Huff. il Pop Sci 189:156-61 O '66

Fuel

See also
Yule logs
FIREPLACES, Outdoor
Firepit has a table top. il Sunset 137:74 Jl '66
Fireplaces you can make. il Pop Gard 17: 50-3 Ag '66
How to make a sun-dial fire pit. J. S. Lorr. il Pop Sci 188:132-5 Je '66
Which fireplace should you choose? D. Huff. il Pop Sci 189:156-61 O '66
FIREPROOFING of textiles
Quenching the continuing tragedy of clothing fires. P. Bugbee. Todays Health 44: 88+ D '66

FIRES
After the fire, a sifting of ashes; experience of losing all when house burned. L. Wainwright. Life 60:19 F 11 '66
Back from the ashes in only three weeks; Spencer gifts, incorporated. il Bsns W p92+ F 26 '66
Death-defying aerial act in a Tel Aviv fire. il Life 60:24D-25 Mr 4 '66
Four fives; death of twelve firemen in Manhattan fire. il Newsweek 68:44 O 31 '66
High wind was good for 1666 London fire. Sci N 90:40 Jl 16 '66
See also
Arson
Forest fires
London—Fire, 1666
also subhead Fires and fire protection under various subjects, e.g. Wharves—Fires and fire protection

Statistics
Firetrap, U.S.A. S. Frank. il McCalls 94: 48+ N '66
FIRES at sea. See Ships—Fires and fire protection
FIRES in ships. See Ships—Fires and fire protection
FIRESTONE, Mrs Russel, Jr
Necessities are the mother of invention. G. Ace. Sat R 49:12 F 26 '66
FIRETHORNS
Bright-berried shrub, firethorn. E. Jerome. Flower Grower 53:43 D '66
FIREWOOD. See Wood as fuel
FIRST aid in illness and injury
Bad day at Old Hollow; treating deep lacerations made by a chain saw. R. Starnes. Field & S 71:14-16+ Je '66
First aid. C. J. Potthoff. See issues of Today's health
How to cope with a medical emergency. Bet Hom & Gard 44:74-5+ O '66
New firsts in first aid. W. S. Bacon. il Pop Sci 188:120-1 F '66
Surprising new facts about first aid. J. Carper. il Todays Health 44:20-3 N '66; Same abr. with title Is your first aid up-to-date? Read Digest 89:116-20 N '66
See also
Resuscitation
FIRST amendment to the Constitution. See United States—Constitution—Bill of rights
FIRST committee of the General assembly. See United Nations—Political and security committee
FIRST flower; story. See Lyons, A. W.
FIRST kiss; story. See Agnon, S. J.
FIRST love, the second time; story. See Jensen, E.
FIRST national city bank of New York. See New York (city)—Banks
FIRST shlemiel; story. See Singer, I. B.
FIRST World festival of Negro arts, Dakar. See Art—Exhibitions
FIRST year; story. See Goldreich, G.
FISCAL courts. See Courts
FISCHEL, Daniel N.
Book publishing, and bookkeeping. Science 152:871-5 My 13 '66
FISCHER, Abraham
Abram Fischer: Afrikaner fights apartheid. T. Land. pors Nation 202:650-1 My 30 '66
Enemy of the state. il por Newsweek 67:54 My 23 '66
Pimpernel's exit. Time 87:42 My 20 '66
Why did Bram Fischer choose jail? N. Gordimer. il pors N Y Times Mag p30-1+ Ag 14 '66

FISCHER, Andrew J, family
And now they are three; Fischer quints. il Sat Eve Post 239:30-5 S 24 '66
FISCHER, Bobby
Bobby would rather fight. L. Evans. il por Sports Illus 25:91-3 D 5 '66
FISCHER, Henry G.
Books in review. Natur Hist 75:4+ Ap '66
FISCHER, John
Editor's easy chair. See issues of Harper's magazine
Letter to a new leftist, from a tired liberal. Harper 232:16+ Mr '66; Same abr. with title Letter to a young leftist. Read Digest 88:137-40 My '66
Substitutes for violence. Harper 232:16+ Ja '66; Same abr. with title What young men need: a substitute for violence. Read Digest 88:82-5 Mr '66
FISCHER, John H.
Challenge to our schools. por Parents Mag 41:30 Ap '66
Editor interviews John H. Fischer; ed. by M. S. Fenner. por NEA J 55:10-13 D '66
Meeting our educational needs. por Parents Mag 41:52 S '66
FISCHER, Pat
Cardinals' bantam rooster. I. R. McVay. il pors Look 30:142-3+ O 18 '66
FISCHER, Ruth
TV: no place for satire. Nation 202:470 Ap 18 '66
Why Hough got tough; the real agitators. New Repub 155:9-10 S 10 '66
FISCHER, Virlis
Formula for mediocrity. Am For 72:16-17+ Ja '66
Seesaw in the Sawtooth. Am For 72:36-9+ N '66
FISCHER quintuplets. See Quintuplets
FISCHMAN, Walter Ian
Turning reproductions into antiques. Pop Mech 126:116-20 Jl '66
FISH, Chet
Where to go fishing, vacationing, hunting. See issues of Outdoor life
FISH, Hamilton, Jr
Tweedleham & Tweedlesam. il por Time 87: 21 My 27 '66
FISH, Canned. See Canned food
FISH, Frozen
Case of the fishy no. Consumer Rep 31:456 S '66
FISH and wildlife service. See United States —Fish and wildlife service
FISH as food
Civic meeting, Anchorage; signing fish protein concentrate act, excerpts from remarks, November 2, 1966. L. B. Johnson. Dept State Bul 55:809 N 28 '66
See also
Cookery—Fish
Fish flour
FISH baskets. See Fishing—Implements and appliances
FISH chowder. See Chowder
FISH culture
Henry Hawkins' fish farm. B. Schley. il Am For 72:34-5+ Ap '66
New nurseries for pike; Fruitport, Mich. G. Laycock. il Field & S 70:10-12+ Mr '66
FISH extermination. See Fishes—Extermination
FISH flour
Fish flour could help world's food supply. Sci N 89:443 Je 4 '66
Fish flour: FDA approval likely on improved product. J. Ayres. Science 152:738-9 My 6 '66; Reply. D. M. Hadjimarkos. 152:1567 Je 17 '66
FPC: nearing approval? B. J. Culliton. il Sci N 90:474 D 3 '66
Scientific magic and economic development. R. Solo. Bul Atomic Sci 22:25-6 N '66
FISH industry and trade
Blue Fridays. Time 88:100+ D 9 '66
Customers slip off the fishmen's hook; Catholic church eliminates meatless Friday. il Bsns W p84+ D 10 '66
Deserts in the sea; economic expedients at price of annihilating fish; condition of California's industry. R. G. Lilliard. il Nation 202:268-70 Mr 7 '66
Plenty of fish in the sea? long-lining depleting world stock of tuna, marlin and swordfish. M. Kane. il Sports Illus 24:20-2+ Ja 31 '66
Raising hake; West coast industry. il Time 87:94 Mr 18 '66
Slaughter on the long line; relations between sport fishermen and commercial fishermen. il Time 87:44 Ja 28 '66

FISH mousse. See Cookery—Fish

FISH nets. See Fishing nets

FISH noises. See Sound production by fishes

FISH ponds. See Ponds

FISH products. See Marine resources

FISH protection
 Saving trout from drought; Lake Creek Water Yield Improvement project, Colo. R. Cantwell. il Sports Illus 25:66-7 O 24 '66

FISH records. See Fishing records

FISH salads. See Salads

FISH secretions. See Secretions

FISH toxins. See Toxins and antitoxins

FISHBECK, James
 Build a Reflexometer. Pop Electr 24:47-9+ Mr '66

FISHBEIN, Harry
 Trick for the wizard. C. Goren. il Sports Illus 25:73-4 S 26 '66

FISHBEIN, Morris
 Medical news of the month. See issues of McCall's

FISHER, Adrian S.
 Nuclear peaceful uses service offered to nonnuclear states; statement, August 9, 1966. Dept State Bul 55:351-3 S 5 '66
 U.S. presents amendments to draft treaty on nonproliferation of nuclear weapons in Eighteen-nation disarmament committee; statement, March 22, 1966. Dept State Bul 54:675-80 Ap 25 '66
 U.S. reiterates call for freeze of nuclear delivery systems; statement, August 2, 1966. Dept State Bul 55:317-20 Ag 29 '66
 U.S. urges expanded safeguards over peaceful nuclear activity; statement, July 28, 1966. Dept State Bul 55:281-3 Ag 22 '66

FISHER, Aileen
 Three and the dragon; drama. Plays 25:87-94 My '66
 —and Rabe, Olive
  Birthday party for UNICEF; drama. Plays 26:47-58 O '66
  Johnny on the spot; drama. Plays 25:75-80 Mr '66

FISHER, Alan E. See Levitt, R. A. jt. auth.

FISHER, Allan C. Jr
 One man's London. Nat Geog Mag 129:743-91 Je '66

FISHER, Bernard, and Fisher, E. R.
 Transmigration of lymph nodes by tumor cells. bibliog Science 152:1397-8 Je 3 '66

FISHER, Bernard Francis
 It's great to be alive. R. Armstrong. il pors Sat Eve Post 239:21-6 Je 4 '66; Same abr. with title Pilot is down! Read Digest 89:42-8 Ag '66

FISHER, Carl Graham
 My most unforgettable character. J. Fisher. il por Read Digest 88:138-42 Ap '66

FISHER, Desmond
 Billy Graham's crusade. Commonweal 84:457-8 Jl 22 '66
 Ireland's hot summer. Commonweal 84:555-6 S 2 '66

FISHER, Duke D. See Ungerleider, J. T. jt. auth.

FISHER, E. H.
 1966 dairy fly control guide. Suc Farm 64:48D Jl '66

FISHER, Ed
 Hamadryad of ragweed; poem. Horizon 8:116-17 Aut '66

FISHER, Edwin R.
 Lysosomal nature of juxtaglomerular granules. bibliog Science 152:1752 Je 24 '66
 —See Fisher, B. jt. auth.

FISHER, Elizabeth Andrews
 Neck deep in miniaturitis. por Hobbies 71:122-3 My '66

FISHER, Glen H.
 Foreign service officer. bibliog f Ann Am Acad 368:71-82 N '66

FISHER, Harvey F. and Cross, D. G.
 Enzyme-coenzyme complexes of pyridine nucleotide-linked dehydrogenases. bibliog Science 153:414-15 Jl 22 '66

FISHER, Harvey I.
 Midway's deadly antennas. il Audubon Mag 68:220-3 Jl '66

FISHER, Isabelle
 Collegiate parnassus. Dance Mag 40:45-8+ Mr '66

FISHER, J. William
 Singers' friend; interview. ed. by A. M. Lingg. por Opera N 30:18 Ap 2 '66

FISHER, Jane
 My most unforgettable character. Read Digest 88:138-42 Ap '66

FISHER, Leonard Everett
 Leonard Everett Fisher: illustrator & painter. J. H. Michel. il por Am Artist 30:42-7+ S '66

FISHER, M. F. K.
 Books (cont) New Yorker 42:180-2+ Mr 26; 157-8+ Ap 30; 191-2+ My 21; 226-30+ S 24; 227-8+ O 8 '66
 Changeover. New Yorker 42:43-5 My 14 '66
 Two kitchens in Provence. New Yorker 42:29-36 Ag 27 '66

FISHER, Morris A. and others
 Aminooxyacetic acid: interactions with gamma-aminobutyric acid and the blood-brain barrier. bibliog Science 153:1668-70 S 30 '66

FISHER, Renee B.
 Case for a new national anthem. Sat R 49:45-6+ Je 25 '66

FISHER, Welthy (Honsinger)
 India's literacy lady. por Time 88:55 Ag 5 '66

FISHERIES
 See also
 Fishery research

 International aspects
 International issues of Pacific fisheries; adaptation of address. W. C. Herrington. Dept State Bul 55:55-4 O 3 '66
 King crab fishery agreement with Japan extended; text of U.S. note, November 29, 1966. D. Rusk. Dept State Bul 55:984 D 26 '66
 U.S. and U.S.S.R. conclude fishery discussions; Department announcement. Dept State Bul 55:273-4 Ag 22 '66

FISHERIES, Bureau of. See United States—Fish and wildlife service

FISHERMAN and his wife; drama. See Swortzell, L.

FISHERMAN'S luck; story. See Richards, W.

FISHERY laws and legislation
 Dick Gregory goes fishing; fish-in on the Nisqually River. R. C. Lee. Nation 202:487-9 Ap 25 '66
 Fishing laws; United States and Canada (cont) Field & S 70:32+ Ap; 71:36-40 My '66
 Fishing seasons (cont) Outdoor Life 137:72-3 Ap; 20+ My '66

FISHERY research
 Soviet ministry speeds fishing technology. W. S. Beller. il Tech W 19:24-5+ Ag 22 '66

FISHES
 Everybody should catch a big fish. T. Trueblood. il Field & S 71:20+ Je '66
 Fishing fallacies. J. A. Knight. il Field & S 70:60-1+ Mr '66
 Piranhas, anyone? concerning H. R. Axelrod. il Time 88:62 Jl 29 '66
 Through a snorkeler's mask; marine life in Caneel Bay, St John Island. V. B. Moore. il Read Digest 89:133-8 Ag '66
 Which is the gamest fish? A. J. McClane. il Field & S 71:80-4 Ja '67
 See also
 Fish protection

 Diseases and pests
 Lymphocystis virus: isolation and propagation in centrarchid fish cell lines. K. Wolf and others. bibliog il Science 151:1004-5 F 25 '66

 Extermination
 Let's not kill ourselves; threat to fishing. D. B. Peakall and B. East. il Outdoor Life 138:17-19+ Ag '66

 Eyes
 See Eye (fishes)

 Habits and behavior
 See also
 Sound production by fishes

 Hybrids
 Lactate dehydrogenase of trout: hybridization in vivo and in vitro. E. Goldberg. bibliog il Science 151:1091-3 Mr 4 '66

 Physiology
 Oxygen dependence of retinal S-potential-producing cells. K. Negishi and G. Svaetichin. bibliog il Science 152:1621-3 Je 17 '66
 Urea synthesis in the lungfish: relative importance of purine and ornithine cycle pathways. R. P. Forster and L. Goldstein. bibliog il Science 153:1650-2 S 30 '66

 Stories
 Exit, laughing. E. Zern. See issues of Field & stream
 Legend of the Pink Lady. E. M. Smith. il Field & S 70:54-6+ Mr '66

FISHES, Deep sea
 Ocean mystery solved: sonic echoing layers. Sci N 89:219 Ap 2 '66

FISHES, Extinct
See also
Coelacanths

FISHES, Fossil
Ancient fishes of Escuminac Bay. D. L. Dineley. il Natur Hist 76:40-5 bibliog(p73) Ja '67 '67
Intermuscular bones in pholidophorus bechei from the lower lias of England. R. Lund. bibliog il Science 152:348-9 Ap 15 '66
Mountain of the stone fishes; Fossil Butte in Wyoming. G. F. Stucker. il Nat Parks Mag 40:4-9 S '66
Triassic fish found in West. il(p580) Sci N 90: 572 D 31 '66

FISHEYE lenses. See Lenses, Photographic

FISHING
Angling. W. Davis. See issues of Outdoor life
Boat handling gets fish. J. A. Emmett. il Outdoor Life 137:102-5 F '66
Boy and the big fish. R. Starnes. Field & S 71:14-15+ Jl '66
Closeup: Barbara Holt, fisherman. J. Mazurki. il Motor B 117:48-9+ My '66
Everybody should catch a big fish. T. Trueblood. il Field & S 71:20+ Je '66
Fish 'n ships. V. Evanoff. See issues of Motor boating
Fishing (cont) Sports Illus 25:56-7 Jl 11 '66
Fishing; ed. by A. J. McClane. See issues of Field & stream
Fishing fallacies. J. A. Knight. il Field & S 70:60-1+ Mr '66
For better fishing go fly a kite. E. A. Bauer. il Field & S 70:64-5+ Ap '66
Gist of it; digest of the outdoor news, ed. by H. Moore. See issues of Outdoor life
How to catch big fish and have a winning team. T. Uhr. Field & S 71:132 My '66
How to find fish in summer. W. Davis. il Outdoor Life 138:54-7 Jl '66
How to play and land fish. G. Heinold. il Outdoor Life 138:10+ Jl '66
Practice course for better casting. W. Davis. il Outdoor Life 138:102-5 D '66
Slaughter on the long line; relations between sport fishermen and commercial fishermen. il Time 87:44 Ja 28 '66
Southern cruising almanac; Florida and Bahamas events. il Motor B 118:22-5 O '66
Sportsman's notebook. H. G. Tapply. See issues of Field & stream
Tips on wading. T. Trueblood. il Field & S 70:26+ F '66
What's your fishing IQ? il Pop Mech 125: 104-5+ Mr '66
Where to go fishing, vacationing, hunting. C. Fish. See issues of Outdoor life
See also
Salt water fishing
also Bass fishing; Cod fishing; etc.

Accidents and injuries
Face of death. B. Cihak. il Outdoor Life 137: 50-1+ My '66

Anecdotes, facetiae, satire, etc.
Dilly day at Dingle. C. Gammon. il Sports Illus 24:70-6+ Mr 14 '66
Outdoors. T. Williams. Esquire 66:110+ D '66
Something was fishy about Stonehenge. E. Zern. il Sports Illus 25:44-6 Ag 22 '66

Competitions
1965 winners; Field & stream fishing contest. il Field & S 70:34+ Mr; 38+ Ap '66

Implements and appliances
Art of wading. A. J. McClane. il Field & S 71:112-16+ S '66
Build your own wading staff. il Field & S 71:89 My '66
He's always ready to go fishing. G. Laycock. il Pop Mech 126:102-5 S '66
Japanese use sound to lure fish schools; underwater acoustical equipment. Sci N 89:317 Ap 30 '66
Master fly box. A. I. Alexander. il Outdoor Life 138:106 S '66
Nets and creels. il Consumer Rep 31:239-41 My '66
See also
Fishing tackle

Law
See Fishery laws and legislation

Alabama
Best U.S. smallmouth water? G. Gresham. il Outdoor Life 138:50-1+ N '66

Argentina
Argentina: the grand tour. A. J. McClane. il Field & S 70:94-8 Mr '66

Arizona
Angling paradise of the Apaches. R. B. Whitaker. il Outdoor Life 138:36-9+ S '66

Arkansas
Jackpotful of bass. R. Tinsley. il Outdoor Life 138:48-9+ D '66

Atlantic states
King of the bottom. G. Heinold. il Outdoor Life 138:12+ N '66
Kokanee comes east. J. Hayes. il Outdoor Life 137:29-31+ Je '66

Bahama Islands
Journey to chickcharney country. J. Underwood. il Sports Illus 24:80-4+ My 9 '66

California
Creek the crowds forgot. J. Mears. il Field & S 71:154-7+ My '66
Cruising Shasta Lake. F. M. Paulson. il Field & S 70:35-7+ F '66
Line of scrimmage. C. R. Hull. il Outdoor Life 138:58-61+ O '66
Magic circle, shortcut to weekend sport. J. Freeman. il Outdoor Life 138:64-6+ D '66
October and the high creel count; Clear Lake. il Sunset 137:73 O '66
Party boat bonanza. R. S. Mikkelsen. il Outdoor Life 137:62-4+ Je '66
Rough water bass. J. D. Lamon. il Outdoor Life 138:36-9+ Ag '66
Sacramento delta cruise. F. M. Paulson. il Field & S 71:42-3+ Je '66
Spring cruising in the Delta; Sacramento-San Joaquin Delta. il Sunset 136:101-3 My '66
Summer fishing at Medicine Lake. il Sunset 137:31-2 Jl '66
Surfcasting for surfperch; Tornton Beach. il Sunset 138:33 Ja '67
You can't go wrong in San Diego. B. Behme. il Field & S 71:102-5 Ja '67

Canada
Ever try mooneyes? W. Davis. il Outdoor Life 139:94-6 Ja '67
Exploring the Kuujjua. G. Laycock. il Field & S 71:45-7 My '66
Face of death. B. Cihak. il Outdoor Life 137: 50-1+ My '66
Fly to trophy fish on schedule. J. Parry. il Field & S 71:48-9 Jl '66
Jackfish country; Manitoba's Lake Vandekerckhove. E. A. Bauer. il Outdoor Life 138:50-2+ Ag '66
Jigging for lake trout. G. Laycock. il Field & S 70:58-60+ Ap '66
New Atlantic salmon fishing; Whale River. M. G. Terziev. il Outdoor Life 137:33-5+ Ap '66
New muskie water; upper Niagara River. T. Janes. il Outdoor Life 138:36-9+ Jl '66
North of Nakina. W. W. Callender. il Outdoor Life 137:33-5+ My '66
Pike strike back. J. O. Cartier. il Outdoor Life 137:48-9+ Je '66
Spring on the Miramichi. T. Janes. il Outdoor Life 137:48-9+ My '66
Trek to treasure island. F. M. Paulson. il Field & S 70:53-5+ Ap '66

Colorado
Snowmobiles to high-lake fishing. C. C. Niehuis. il Field & S 71:37-9+ D '66
Trout that never hear traffic. P. Barrett. il Outdoor Life 137:36-9+ Je '66

Connecticut
Fishing the shad runs. G. Heinold. il Outdoor Life 137:10+ My '66
Tidal river grab-bag. G. Heinold. il Outdoor Life 137:14-16+ My '66

Florida
Drifters make good. G. Heinold. il Outdoor Life 138:72-3+ N '66
Father's fling on the flats. E. A. Bauer. il Outdoor Life 137:56-9+ Je '66
Fly fishing for bones. A. J. McClane. il Field & S 71:54-7 N '66
Goodby, Blue Springs. W. Blassingame. il Field & S 70:8-9+ F '66
I'll take the bass pits. C. Elliott. il Outdoor Life 138:68-9+ O '66
Midwinter specktacle. K. Osborne. il Outdoor Life 137:60-1+ F '66
My rockpile, fishing hole. S. Clements. il Outdoor Life 138:48-51+ S '66
Power rods for pomps. G. X. Sand. il Field & S 71:136-8 O '66
Rough-and-ready snook. G. Heinold. il Outdoor Life 137:14+ Mr '66
Small plane and fancy fishing. C. Conley. il Field & S 70:62-4+ Mr '66

FISHING—*Florida*—*Continued*

Sweet king. G. Heinold. il Outdoor Life 138: 30+ D '66

Swinging fisherman. K. Warner. il Pop Mech 125:110-11 Ap '66

Trail of the ten-pound bass. G. Laycock. il Outdoor Life 137:48-9+ Ap '66

Georgia

No hunting and fishing; Pioneer Georgia project. G. H. Gillelan. il Outdoor Life 137: 29-31+ Mr '66

Rooftop river. C. Elliott. il Outdoor Life 138: 32-3+ Jl '66

When bass go bugs. A. J. McClane. il Field & S 70:98-103 Ap '66

Great Britain

Going fishing in Britain. Sunset 136:24 F '66

Great Lakes Region

Door to fishing paradise. M. Ellis. il Field & S 71:52-5+ My '66

First report: salmon succeed in Great Lakes. J. Chiappetta. il Field & S 71:10-15 D '66

Guatemala

Adventure in Latin America. E. A. Bauer. il Outdoor Life 137:32-5+ Mr '66

Honduras

Adventure in Latin America. E. A. Bauer. il Outdoor Life 137:56-9+ Ap '66

Idaho

Where the trout sleep late in the morning; Idaho's Teton River. J. Olsen. il Sports Illus 24:86-90+ My 16 '66

Ireland

Dilly day at Dingle. C. Gammon. il Sports Illus 24:70-6+ Mr 14 '66

Wild roses and Irish salmon. C. T. Coiner. il Esquire 65:94-7+ F '66

Japan

Tokyo trout; fisherman abroad. J. J. Platt. il Outdoor Life 139:38-41+ Ja '67

Kansas

Newest lake in Kansas. P. Czura. il Field & S 70:140-2+ Mr '66

Louisiana

Belligerent bluegill. G. Gresham. il Field & S 70:73-5+ Ap '66

Don't spare the hot sauce. L. Dietz. il Field & S 70:70-2+ Ap '66

How to catch a trophy bass. M. Eggleston. il Field & S 71:46-7+ Ja '67

Maine

Black handsaws. B. East. il Outdoor Life 138:44-5+ S '66

Hellhole fishing. E. W. Smith. il Field & S 71:26-8+ Jl '66

High-flying landlock. W. Davis. il Outdoor Life 137:82+ Ap '66

Jig is up. C. Ford. il Field & S 71:8+ Ag '66

Rubber boot Bali Ha'i. L. Dietz. il Field & S 71:62-3+ My '66

Sluggers of the Saco. G. Heinold. il Outdoor Life 138:46-7+ Jl '66

Smelt fever. J. Novick. il Field & S 70:10-12 Ap '66

Maryland

Light-tackle stripers. P. McLain. il Field & S 71:92-5+ Jl '66

Mexico

Adventure in Latin America. E. A. Bauer. il Outdoor Life 137:29-31+ F '66 (to be cont)

Cozumel: the island with everything. B. Brister. il Field & S 70:68-70+ Mr '66

Mexico, Gulf of

Bottom fishing in the Gulf. G. Heinold. il Outdoor Life 137:10+ F '66

New billfish discovery. R. F. Burgess. il Field & S 71:58-9+ S '66

Michigan

Big steelhead are back. J. Chiappetta. il Field & S 70:47-9+ Ap '66

Cold but happy years. D. J. Anderson. il Field & S 71:40-1+ D '66

How to catch bass at midday. J. G. Mell. il Field & S 71:80+ My '66

How to catch the smartest trout of all. D. Wendzel. il Outdoor Life 137:54-5+ Mr '66

Look to the lakes for trout. J. O. Cartier. il Outdoor Life 137:40-1+ Ap '66

Those copper-colored bones. M. Ellis. il Field & S 71:26+ Je '66

Middle western states

350 miles of walleyes; Mississippi River. A. W. Prince. il Outdoor Life 138:40-1+ Jl '66

Mississippi

Bed fishing for bass. W. J. O'Connor. il Outdoor Life 137:40-1+ Mr '66

Missouri

Blueprint for big bass. A. A. Ciuffa. il Outdoor Life 137:40-3+ My '66

Boom-or-bust bass. W. Davis. il Outdoor Life 137:68+ Mr '66

Sure tricks for big bass. A. A. Ciuffa. il Outdoor Life 137:42-3+ Je '66

Montana

Great trout waters west of Yellowstone. il Sunset 136:64 Je '66

Montana's ignored game fish. P. Czura. il Field & S 71:58-9+ My '66

Month the Madison goes mad. N. Strung. il Field & S 71:54-5+ Je '66

New York (state)

Ancient art of dapping. W. Davis. il Outdoor Life 138:102+ N '66

How to catch snapper blues. G. Heinold. il Outdoor Life 138:10-11+ Ag '66

Muskies at night; St Lawrence River. H. E. Carlson. il Field & S 71:36-7+ Jl '66

Pack-in ponds; Little Fish pond. in Adirondacks. N. Karas. il Field & S 71:34-5+ Jl '66

Strange doings on Otsego Lake. T. Janes. il Outdoor Life 137:42-3+ Mr '66

New Zealand

Browns of New Zealand. A. R. Phipps. il Outdoor Life 138:58-61+ N '66

North Carolina

Awesome drum. G. Heinold. il Outdoor Life 138:8+ S '66

Fall windfall. R. Attaway. il Outdoor Life 138:58-9+ S '66

Northwestern states

Grande Ronde: new steelhead paradise. R. R. Gerlach. il Field & S 71:30-3+ Jl '66

Norway

Bus ride to Atlantic salmon. J. Brooks. il Outdoor Life 138:46-9+ O '66

Royal domain for kingly salmon. il Life 61: 46-57 Ag 19 '66

Anecdotes, facetiae, satire, etc.

And one more for the river. C. Gammon. il Sports Illus 25:76-84 S 26 '66

Ohio

Basic bass bugging. E. Bauer. il Field & S 71:44-7 Jl '66

Beautiful new Ohio. B. Thomas. il Outdoor Life 137:54-5+ Je '66

How to beat the summer slump. E. A. Bauer. il Outdoor Life 138:17-19+ Jl '66

Oregon

Desert rainbows. F. H. Ames. il Outdoor Life 137:64+ My '66

Misplaced salmon of Hosmer Lake; Atlantic salmon from Oregon lake. T. Trueblood. il Field & S 70:49-51+ Mr '66

Never underestimate a golf ball; steelhead fishing. B. Behme. il Field & S 70:52-3+ Mr '66

Reservoir bass. T. Trueblood. il Field & S 71:16+ Ag '66

Silver from the sea. L. Miracle. il Outdoor Life 138:50-2+ Jl '66

Pennsylvania

Bass with a bang; Delaware River. T. Janes. il Outdoor Life 138:32-3+ Ag '66

Hickory shad on the Susquehanna. N. Karas. il Field & S 70:66-7 Ap '66

Opening for a young man. D. Shiner. il Outdoor Life 137:62-4 Ap '66

Southwestern states

Take a fishing trip now. H. Bradshaw. il Suc Farm 64:100F Mr '66

Texas

Worms beat the drum. J. C. Ericson. il Outdoor Life 138:48-9+ Ag '66

United States

Forty-five experts tell where to fish; symposium. Outdoor Life 137:65-71+ Ap '66

My panfish-on-light-tackle kick. E. A. Bauer. il Outdoor Life 137:56-9+ My '66

FISHING—*Continued*

Virginia

Just plane camping. C. Conley. il Field & S 70:72-4+ F '66

Striped bass and southern solitude. E. White. il Sports Illus 25:60-2+ O 10 '66

Washington (state)

Lake Mead whoppers. F. Dufresne. il Field & S 71:60-1 My '66

Sea-run cutthroats in Puget Sound. Sunset 137:60+ N '66

Western states

Fly fishing for trout in lakes. T. Trueblood. il Field & S 71:24+ My '66

Wisconsin

Hottest place on ice. W. Davis. il Outdoor Life 139:46-9+ Ja '67

How wild the Wolf? G. Laycock. il Outdoor Life 137:48-51+ F '66

Trophy browns of the Brule. J. O. Cartier. il Outdoor Life 138:40-1+ Ag '66

Wyoming

Dream trip for fall trout. F. R. Martin. il Outdoor Life 138:24-7+ Ag '66

Fishing with Al McClane. T. Trueblood. Field & S 70:24+ Ap '66

FISHING, Deep sea. See Salt water fishing

FISHING, Winter

Big perch by jiggers; through the ice of Conesus Lake, N.Y. R. L. Estes. il Outdoor Life 138:58-61+ D '66

Cold but happy years. D. J. Anderson. il Field & S 71:40-1+ D '66

Holiday bass. A. Pione. il Field & S 71:42-3+ D '66

Hottest place on ice. W. Davis. il Outdoor Life 139:46-9+ Ja '67

New way to find winter bluegills. J. O. Cartier. il Outdoor Life 137:36-7+ F '66

Portable ice-fishing house. H. Sibley. il Field & S 71:54-5 D '66

FISHING accidents. See Fishing—Accidents and injuries

FISHING boats

Fish 'n ships. V. Evanoff. See issues of Motor boating

Perfect boats for fishermen. A. J. McClane. il Field & S 71:28-9+ Ja '67

Satisfaction from a diesel. J. Emmett. il Yachting 119:111-13+ Ja '66

Design

Sport fisherman from the Pacific coast. il Yachting 120:58-9+ D '66

Equipment

Fish 'n ships. V. Evanoff. See issues of Motor boating

Small boat and its equipment. F. M. Paulson. il Field & S 71:126-32 My '66

FISHING clubs

Your fishing club: reprint. E. F. Karner. il Parks & Rec 1:563 Jl '66

FISHING flies. See Fishing lures, flies, etc.

FISHING guides. See Guides

FISHING industry. See Fish industry and trade

FISHING lures, flies, etc.

Big trout controversy. T. Trueblood. E. Zern. il Field & S 70:68-9+ Ap '66

Body beautiful. H. G. Tapply. il Field & S 70:64 F '66

Dry flies for sundown. W. Davis. il Outdoor Life 137:66-8+ Je '66

Fly rod over the deep blue. L. Wulff. il Esquire 66:253-5+ D '66

Legend of the Pink Lady. E. W. Smith. il Field & S 70:54-6+ Mr '66

Lures that caught 2,000 bass. B. Carey. il Field & S 71:10-12+ Je '66

Master fly box. A. I. Alexander. il Outdoor Life 138:106 S '66

Matching the fly to the water. A. J. McClane. il Field & S 71:64-7 Jl '66

Never underestimate a golf ball; steelhead fishing. B. Behme. il Field & S 70:52-3+ Mr '66

New angle for an old sport. D. Barnes. Sports Illus 25:56-7 Jl 11 '66

New muddler head. J. H. Abisch. il Field & S 70:169 Ap '66

Nymph-fishing techniques. A. J. McClane. il Field & S 71:78-81 Ag '66

Plugs for the salt. G. Heinold. il Outdoor Life 138:154-6 O '66

Scooting for bass and trout. W. Davis. il Outdoor Life 137:66+ F '66

Tricks with minnow plugs. W. Davis. il Outdoor Life 138:114+ O '66

Tricks with the wobbling spoon. A. J. McClane. il Field & S 71:104-6+ My '66

FISHING nets

Nets and creels. il Consumer Rep 31:239-41 My '66

Swinging fisherman. K. Warner. il pop Mech 125:110-11 Ap '66

FISHING outfits. See Fishing—Implements and appliances

FISHING records

New world record fish. Field & S 70:76-7 Ap '66

FISHING rods. See Fishing tackle

FISHING schooner racing. See Yacht racing

FISHING tackle

Bottom-fishing rigs. G. Heinold. il Outdoor Life 137:14+ Ap '66

Fly rods. Consumer Rep 31:282-7 D '66

How to buy a fishing rod. P. McCafferty. il Pop Sci 189:148-50+ Jl '66

Manual magic. A. J. McClane. il Field & S 71:96-9 D '66

New angle for an old sport. D. Barnes. Sports Illus 25:56-7 Jl 11 '66

New tackle to hook fishermen. S. James. il Pop Mech 125:128-31+ My '66

Spinning-reel accuracy. A. J. McClane. il Field & S 71:82-8 Je '66

FISHING with bow and arrow

Archery in midsummer. G. H. Gillelan. il Outdoor Life 138:14+ Ag '66

New arrow for carp. P. Czura. il Field & S 71:48-9 Je '66

Time for bowfishing. G. H. Gillelan. il Outdoor Life 137:10-12 Je '66

FISHMAN, Katharine Davis

Parent and child (cont) N Y Times Mag p69+ Mr 13; 68+ Je 12; 114+ S 25; 114+ O 23; 146+ D 11 '66

Place-dropper's guide. Mlle 63:145-7 Je '66

FISHNETS. See Fishing nets

FISHWICK, Marshall W.

India's long hot summer. Sat R 49:19-21 Jl 16 '66

What modern art says about America. Sat R 49:19-20+ Ap 9 '66

FISHWORMS. See Earthworms

FITCH, Charles Marden

Hardier azaleas. Flower Grower 53:62-4 Mr '66

FITCH, Robert E.

Sell-out or the well acculturated Christian. Christian Cent 83:202-5 F 16 '66

FITCH, William C.

New look in aging; with bibliography. por Wilson Lib Bul 40:832-7 My '66

FITCHBURG, Mass. public library

Battle for a library. J. R. Tunis. Sat R 49:58-9 Jl 9 '66

FITHIAN, Janet H.

How reliable is teen help? Farm J 90:96+ My '66

I've learned to put first things first. Farm J 90:83 O '66

FITNESS, Physical. See Health; Military service —Physical and mental fitness

FITZ, Earle L.

Former Bible salesman runs wholesale and retail business in Midwest. il Pub W 190:127-8 S 26 '66

FITZGERALD, C. P.

Directions of foreign policy. Bul Atomic Sci 22:65-70 Je '66

Once more the yellow peril. Nation 202:606-9 My 23 '66

Origin of the Chinese revolution. Cur Hist 51:129-33+ S '66

Strategic island in dispute. Nation 202:656-7 My 30 '66

FITZGERALD, Edmund B.

Man's limitless mind; excerpts from comments. Electr World 75:6 Mr '66

FITZGERALD, Frances

Life and death of a Vietnamese village. N Y Times Mag p4-5+ S 4 '66

Long fear: fresh eyes on Viet Nam. Vogue 149:110-11+ Ja 1 '67

Tragedy of Saigon. Atlan 218:59-67 D '66

FITZGERALD, Francis Scott Key

Scott, Ernest and whoever. A. Gingrich. il Esquire 66:186-9+ D '66

FITZGERALD, John E.

Film classification: a viewpoint. Cath World 204:32-6 O '66

FITZGERALD, Paul A.

Catholic graduate schools. America 115:510-12 O 29 '66

FITZGERALD, Robert

For Epiphany; poem. New Yorker 42:77 Ja 7 '67

July in Indiana; poem. New Yorker 42:36 Jl 16 '66

FITZGERALD, William H.
Book review. America 115:621-2 N 12 '66
FITZGIBBON, Constantine
(ed) See Thomas, D. Letters: Dylan Thomas
FITZPATRICK, Honor
Letter from the publisher. G. Valk. por
Sports Illus 25:4 N 7 '66
FITZPATRICK, Joseph P.
Oscar Lewis and the Puerto Rican family.
America 115:778-9 D 10 '66
FITZPATRICK, Thomas B. and others
Terminology of vertebrate melanin-contain-
ing cells; 1965. bibliog Science 152:88-9 Ap
1 '66
FITZSIMMONS, Frank
Hell with everybody! il por Newsweek 68:80
Jl 18 '66
Hoffa seeks stand-in, in case he's needed.
Bsns W p 144 Je 4 '66
How a union can be run from prison. por
U S News 61:76+ Jl 11 '66
Man Hoffa picked. Bsns W p 129 Jl 9 '66
FIVE- and ten-cent stores
My year in the five and ten; experience as
a clerk at Duckwell's variety store,
Topeka, Kan. A. House. il Seventeen 25:
162-3+ S '66
FIVE percenters. See Gangs
FIVE year plan, Russian. See Russia—Eco-
nomic policy
FIX, John
Viper of the deep. Motor B 117:113+ Ap '66
FIXED capacitors. See Electric capacitors
FIXTURES, Bathroom. See Bathroom fixtures
FIXX, James F.
(ed) As others see us. See occasional issues
of Saturday review
Bar hopping with a hatchet. Sat R 49:53 D
24 '66
1966 Amy Loveman awards. Sat R 49:20 Jl
2 '66
SR-Anisfield-Wolf awards: 1966. Sat R 49:
26-7 Je 11 '66
FIZDALE, Robert
Two on the bench. il Newsweek 67:110+ My
23 '66
FJELDBO, Gunnar, and others
Atmosphere of Mars: Mariner IV models
compared. bibliog Science 153:1518-23 S
23 '66
FJORDS. See Fiords
FLACKS, Richard
Is the Great society just a barbecue? New
Repub 154:18-19+ Ja 29 '66
FLAD, Harvey K.
New chance in Nigeria? Commonweal 83:
525-6 F 4 '66
FLAG football. See Football
FLAG poles. See Flagstaffs
FLAGELLATES
North Atlantic deep-sea fertility. R. O. Four-
nier. bibliog il Science 153:1250-2 S 9 '66
FLAGLER, J. M.
Reporter at large New Yorker 42:137-8+ N 26
'66
FLAGS
Designing a flag; new boating groups. H. P.
Martin. Motor B 118:112A O '66

United States
American flag; flying the flag in parks and
recreation areas. H. Grabner. il Parks &
Rec 1:131-2 F '66
FLAGSTAD, Kirsten
Two sopranos: both Wagnerians, both Scan-
dinavians. P. L. Miller. por Am Rec G
32:516-17 F '66
FLAGSTAFF, Ariz.
Flagstaff's permanent Indian show; Museum
of northern Arizona. il Sunset 136:78 My
'66
FLAGSTAFFS
Five ways to fly the American flag. C. T.
Sigman. il Pop Sci 189:122-3 Jl '66
FLAHERTY, Daniel L.
Chicago priests organize. America 115:540-3
N 5 '66
Christian-Communist dialogue. America 115:
805 D 17 '66
Of many things. America 115:inside cover
O 15 '66
Present problems of future planes. America
116:15 Ja 7 '67
(ed) See Alfred, W. Hogan's goat
FLAHERTY, Robert Joseph
Art of movie making. C. F. Trevelyan. il U S
Camera 29:68-71 Ag '66
Innocent eye, by A. Calder-Marshall. Re-
view
Sat R 49:46- F 5 '66. H. G. Weinberg
Visions in an ice-blue eye. il por Time 87:
90+ Ja 28 '66

FLAHERTY, Tom
Unprecedented tactics maligned but effec-
tive. Life 61:58A-58B+ S 9 '66
FLAME-ionization detectors. See Detectors
FLAME plating. See Metal coating
FLAMENCO
La Curra ballets Flamenco, Brooklyn acad-
emy of music. J. Maskey. Dance Mag 40:
74-5 Ap '66
FLAMINGO, Las Vegas, Nev. See Night clubs
FLAMINGOS
Nature note. il(p217) Sci N 90:218 S 24 '66
New park safeguards flamingos. C. W.
Buchheister. il Audubon Mag 68:72 Mr '66
FLAMMABLE textile fabrics. See Textile fab-
rics, Flammable
FLANDERS, Florence Reiter
Flight of the moon witches; drama. Plays
26:67-71 O '66
FLANDERS, Michael
Aromatic spirits. H. Hewes. Sat R 50:98
Ja 14 '67
Light of heart. por Newsweek 69:71 Ja 9 '67
Maharajah & the cricket. por Time 89:69 Ja
6 '67
Popular records. D. Watt. New Yorker 42:
197-8 D 17 '66
Theatre. J. McCarten. New Yorker 42:78 Ja
7 '67
FLANDORF, Vera S.
(comp) Medical books for the public library.
Library J 90:4718-23 N 1 '65; Correction. 91:
464 F 1 '66
FLANIGAN, Jean M. See Bechdolt, B. V. jt.
auth.
FLANNEL flowers
Flannel flowers. A. D. Hawkes. il Horti-
culture 44:35 D '66
FLANNER, Janet
Janet Flanner on literature and de Gaulle.
por(p31) Pub W 189:33 Mr 28 '66
Letter from Paris. New Yorker 42:98+ Jl 16;
68+ Jl 30; 116+ Ag 13; 109-12+ Ag 27; 139-
40+ S 10; 179-83 O 1; 149-52+ O 8; 199-204
O 22; 158+ N 5; 218+ N 19; 214-16+ D 3;
65-7 D 31 '66; 109-14 Ja 14 '67
Life book review. Life 60:8+ My 13 '66
about
Four authors are given National book awards.
por Pub Y 189:47-8 Mr 21 '66
NBA 1966. por Newsweek 67:106 Mr 28 '66
FLARE stars. See Stars, Variable
FLARES, Solar. See Solar flares
FLASH equipment. See Electric lamps, Flash-
light
FLASHBULBS. See Electric lamps, Flashlight
FLASHCUBE cameras. See Cameras
FLASHCUBES. See Electric lamps, Flashlight
FLASHLIGHT electric lamps. See Electric
lamps, Flashlight
FLASHLIGHT photography. See Photography,
Flashlight
FLAT TOPS primitive areas. See Wilderness
areas—Colorado
FLATLEY, Guy
(comp) Any bets? N Y Times Mag p 107
Mr 27 '66
(comp) Fields-eye view of things. N Y Times
Mag p 117 pA 24 '66
(comp) Time of the Oscar. N Y Times Mag
p 133 Ap 17 '66
FLATOW, Herbert
Color critique (Cont) U S Camera 29:62-3
Ap '66
Williamsburg; photographs. U S Camera 29:
64-5 F '66
FLATWARE, Stainless steel. See Tableware,
Stainless steel
FLAUBERT, Gustave
Sentimental education. K. Rexroth. Sat R
49:41 D 31 '66
FLAVIN, Jack
All-night diner; poem. Atlan 217:64 My '66
FLAVINS
Flavin mononucleotide control of glycolic acid
oxidase and photorespiration in corn leaves.
B. Tregunna. bibliog Science 151:1239-41 Mr
11 '66
FLAVOR. See Taste
FLAVORING essences
See also
Seasonings
FLAWN, Peter T.
Geology and the new conservation movement;
address, December 6, 1965. bibliog Science
151:409-12; 152:1568-9 Ja 28, Je 17 '66
FLAX, Serene
Paintings of Serene Flax. il por Am Artist
31:44-9+ Ja '67

FLÈCHE, J. Corbel
Passing of J. Corbel Flèche. T. W. Moore.
Christian Cent 83:494-6 Ap 20 '66
FLECK, James C.
Doctor Jekyll and Mr Kahn. Christian Cent
83:680-3, 935 My 25, Jl 27 '66
FLECKE, Joyce M.
Falling in love with Spain. Sr Schol 88:sup28
Ap 15 '66
Die FLEDERMAUS; opera. See Strauss, J. jr
FLEET, Betsy
(ed) See Garrett, R. B. End of a manhunt
FLEISCHER, Nat
Rating the young heavies. por Sports Illus
24:23 Mr 14 '66
FLEISCHHAUER, F. W.
Rout out that rot. Motor B 117:34+ Mr '66
Ten years with the same tarp. Motor B 118:
45+ N '66
FLEMING, Anne Geraldine (Charteris)
How James Bond destroyed my husband;
interview, ed. by L. Hannon. Ladies
Home J 83:158+ O '66
FLEMING, D. F.
Costs and consequences of the cold war. bib-
liog f Ann Am Acad 366:127-38 Jl '66
FLEMING, Donald Harnish
Nobel's hits and errors. Atlan 218:53-9 O '66
FLEMING, Ian
How James Bond destroyed my husband;
interview, ed. by L. Hannon. A. G. C.
Fleming. il Ladies Home J 83:158+ O '66
Ian Fleming; excerpt from The life of Ian
Fleming. J. Pearson. il pors Life 61:102-4+
O 7 '66
Life of Ian Fleming, by J. Pearson. Review
Nat R 19:41+ Ja 10 '67. A. Lejeune
Life of Ian Fleming to have errata slips;
facts involving movie producer K. McClory
and his film, Thunderball. Pub W 191:36-7
Ja 9 '67
Rough rise of a dream hero; excerpt from
The life of Ian Fleming. J. Pearson. il pors
Life 61:112-14+ O 14 '66
FLEMING, Karl
[Watts casualty] il por Newsweek 67:15
My 30 '66
FLEMING, Peggy
I'm someone else when I skate. pors Seventeen
25:118-19+ D '66

about

Champions of winter. il por Sports Illus
24:14-15 F 7 '66
Delicacy at Davos. pors Time 87:70 Mr 11 '66
High-altitude triumph for a tough little miss.
G. Gross. il Sports Illus 24:58-9 Mr 7 '66
Paris fling for a teen queen. il pors Sports
Illus 24:30-3 My 2 '66
Peggy Fleming's triumph on ice. il pors
Life 60:93-4 Mr 11 '66
FLEMING, Robert H.
Atlantic report: musical chairs. D. Kiker.
Atlan 218:10 D '66
Reshuffle. por Newsweek 67:31 F 21 '66
Sweetheart of Sigma delta chi. por Time 87:
79 Ap 29 '66
Unburdening bill. por Time 87:23 F 18 '66
FLEMING, Rodney R.
Getting ready for the storm; excerpts from
addresses. bibliog Am City 81:96-9 Ag '66
How to prevent scaling. Am City 81:96-7 D '66
Seal coats and thin overlays. bibliog Am
City 81:129-31+ S '66
Solid-waste disposal (cont) bibliog Am City
81:94-6 F '66
FLEMING, Roscoe
Shale oil: the sleeping giant. Nation 204:49-
50 Ja 9 '67
FLEMING, Shirley
Carl Ruggles festival; Brunswick report. Hi
Fi 16:158 Ap '66
Fiddlers four. Hi Fi 16:132-3 F '66
Guitar on the go. Hi Fi 16:40-5 Jl '66
Jeunesses musicales. Hi Fi 16:MA8 Jl '66
Music-making Moravians. Hi Fi 16:MA16-17
S '66
Musicians at play. Hi Fi 16:MA12-13 O '66
FLEMING, Thomas J.
Bible history; poem. America 115:339 S 24
'66
Joyous sound of freedom. Read Digest 88:19-
20+ Je '66
Novel of the future. America 114:654-5+ My
7 '66
Verdicts of history. Am Heritage 18:6-11+ D
'66
FLEMING, Willie
Willie Fleming hits pay dirt. il pors Ebony
22:77-8+ Ja '67
FLEMISH painting. See Painting, Flemish
FLEMMING, Arthur Sherwood
Support Johnson's appeal to U.N. Christian
Cent 84:36 Ja 11 '67

FLETCHER, Colin
Un-eager beaver. Field & S 71:53+ Ag '66
FLETCHER, James
British support on Vietnam? Nat R 18:356-8
Ap 19 '66
Letter from Madrid. Nat R 18:1167+ N 15 '66
Stillness at Berryville. Nat R 18:781-3+ Ag 9
'66
FLETCHER, Joseph Francis, 1905-
Dogmatist in disguise. J. Lachs. Christian
Cent 83:1402-5 N 16 '66; Reply. V. L. Weiss.
83:1542 D 14 '66
FLETCHER, William J. See Hinkle, C. N. jt.
auth.
FLIEGERS, Serge
(ed) See King. M. Princess Grace: how she
lovingly raises her children
FLIES
Curse of the North. R. V. McCormick. il Field
& S 71:47+ Je '66

Extermination

Fly traps and electric grids. Consumer Bul
49:21 Ag '66
1966 dairy fly control guide. E. H. Fisher.
Suc Farm 64:48D Jl '66

Resistance to control

See Insects, Injurious and beneficial—Re-
sistance to control
FLIESS, Wilhelm
Freud's friend Wilhelm Fliess and his theory
of male and female life cycles. M. Gardner.
il Sci Am 215:108-9+ Jl '66
FLIGHT
See also
Birds—Flight
Gliding and soaring

Physiological aspects

See Aviation—Physiological aspects
FLIGHT fatigue. See Aviation—Physiological
aspects
FLIGHT instructors. See Air pilots—Training
FLIGHT of insects. See Insects—Flight
FLIGHT of the moon witches; drama. See
Flanders. F. R.
FLIGHT research center. See United States—
National aeronautics and space administra-
tion—Flight research center
FLIGHT safety foundation
Traffic pattern; Smokey Caldera's program.
il Flying 79:15-16+ S '66
FLIGHT safety, incorporated
Margin of safety. R. B. Weeghman. il Fly-
ing 79:48-9 S '66
FLIGHT simulators
Aviation week pilot report: Lockheed SST
simulator research stresses low speeds.
C. M. Plattner. il Aviation W 85:76-81+
N 21 '66
Douglas plans all-weather landing tests; low
visibility landing flight simulator facility.
B. Miller. il Aviation W 86:51-2+ Ja 9 '67
In-flight simulator considered for SST. B. K.
Thomas. jr. il Aviation W 85:75+ N 7 '66
Margin of safety. R. B. Weeghman. il Fly-
ing 79:48-9 S '66
Pilots see value in turbulence simulation.
B. K. Thomas. jr. Aviation W 85:147+
S 26 '66
Special report on airline flight crew training;
costs of training encouraging simulation.
D. A. Brown. il Aviation W 85:42-3+ Ag
1 '66
See also
Space flight simulators
FLINT, Jeremy
Invasion of Jeremy Flint. C. Goren. Sports
Illus 24:78-9 Je 13 '66
FLINT, R. W.
On Randall Jarrell. Commentary 41:79-81
F '66
FLINT implements and weapons. See Stone
implements and weapons
FLOAT planes. See Seaplanes
FLOATING bodies
Where do sunken ships go? I. Asimov. il Sci
Digest 61:87-8 Ja '67
FLOATING hospitals. See Hospital ships
FLOATING instrument platforms. See Oceano-
graphic buoys
FLOATING platforms. See Oceanographic buoys
FLOATPLANES. See Seaplanes
FLOATS (parades)
Here comes Mr Parade. A. R. Roalman. il
Pop Mech 125:4-7+ Je '66
How to frame a float. il Pop Mech 125:145-7
Je '66

FLOATS, Seaplane. See Seaplanes—Floats

FLOOD lighting. See Light projection

FLOOD plains. See Alluvium; Plains

FLOOD prevention and control

United States

Two bags of air thwart a flood; measures taken in Winona, Minn. il Am City 81:12 N '66

Unraveling the Everglades furor. E. Buckow. il Field & S 71:12-16+ O '66

See also

Mississippi River—Regulation

FLOODLIGHTING. See Light projection

FLOODS

Italy

Aftermath: damage to Florence's renowned art and bibliographic riches. il Wilson Lib Bul 41:463-4 Ja '67

Back to the Guelphs and Ghibellines. V. Velen. il Life 61:3 N 18 '66

Disaster in Italy; damage done by flood to art. il Newsweek 68:110-11 N 21 '66

Florence: a disaster area. N. Kent. Am Artist 31:3+ Ja '67

Florence after the deluge. S. Alexander. Reporter 35:39-41 D 15 '66

Florence: after the flood. V. Velen and E. Velen. il Sat R 49:26-7+ D 24 '66

Italy counts the cost of its deluge; damage widespread. il Bsns W p50-2 N 26 '66

Rains came. Newsweek 68:71 N 21 '66

Ravaged realm of art; Florence. il Life 61:121-6 N 18 '66

Royal fury. il Time 88:42+ N 18 '66

Ruin in flood's wake: treasures of Florence. il U S News 61:34+ D 5 '66

Terrible plight of the renaissance land. il Life 61:28-35 D 16 '66

United States

Brace yourself for the next disaster! battling Oregon floods. D. Barney. il Pop Mech 125:102-4+ Ap '66

Desolate beauty as the great blizzard thaws. il Life 60:34-5 Ap 22 '66

See also

Johnstown flood, 1889

FLOOR coverings

Carpeting vs. resilient floor coverings. il Consumer Bul 49:29-30 Mr '66

Facts on floor fashions. J. LemMon. il Suc Farm 64:104-5 F '66

Some bare facts about floors. M. Davidson. il Ladies Home J 83:56 Mr '66

See also

Rugs and carpets

Tiles, Floor

FLOOR machines

Floor scrubbers and polishers and rug shampooers. il Consumer Bul 50:21-5 Ja '67

Portable sander. Consumer Bul 50:25 Ja '67

FLOOR sanders. See Floor machines

FLOOR waxes. See Waxes

FLOORS

Complete guide to handsome floors. il Mc-Calls 93:36+ Ag '66

Do something different with flooring. G. V. Young. il Bet Hom & Gard 44:72-3 O '66

Floors can be fun with jigsaw puzzles underfoot. J. Peter. il Look 30:57+ N 29 '66

See also

Floor coverings

Care

Best finishes for wood; modern flooring: it's tough, but beautiful. J. Hand. il Pop Sci 189:156-9+ S '66

Complete guide to handsome floors. il Mc-Calls 93:36+ Ag '66

How to care for floors. Ladies Home J 83:61+ Mr '66

Low-down on floor wax. R. Martens. il Farm J 90:97 Ap '66

FLOORS, Concrete

Minimizing cracks in on-grade slabs. W. C. Perry. il Arch Rec 139:197-8+ F '66

FLOORS, Slate

You can't beat slate underfoot. D. Huff. il Pop Sci 189:120-2 Ag '66

FLOORS, Tile

Who should lay your floor: you or a pro? J. LemMon. il Suc Farm 64:103+ F '66

FLOORS, Wood

Now there's self-polishing for wood floors, too! E. Taylor. il Good H 162:209 My '66

FLORAL pictures. See Pictures

FLORENCE

Architecture

Ravaged realm of art. il Life 61:121-6 N 18 '66

Art

Digging out. Newsweek 68:102+ N 28 '66

Disaster in Italy; damage done by flood. il Newsweek 68:110-11 N 21 '66

Florence: a disaster area. N. Kent. Am Artist 31:3+ Ja '67

Florence after the deluge. S. Alexander. Reporter 35:39-41 D 15 '66

Florence: after the flood. V. Velen and E. Velen. il Sat R 49:26-7+ D 24 '66

People and events. il Sr Schol 89:19 D 2 '66

Ravaged realm of art. il Life 61:121-6 N 18 '66

Ruin in flood's wake: treasures of Florence. il U S News 61:34+ D 5 '66

Salvage of Florence. il Time 88:90 N 25 '66

Terrible plight of the renaissance land; salvaging cultural treasures. il Life 61:28-35 D 16 '66

See also

Committee to rescue Italian art

Libraries

Aftermath: damage to Florence's renowned art and bibliographic riches caused by flood. il Wilson Lib Bul 41:463-4 Ja '67

Book restoration group joins national body; Operation book rescue committee to help restore flood-damaged libraries. Pub W 190:34 N 28 '66

Terrible plight of the renaissance land; salvaging cultural treasures. il Life 61:28-35 D 16 '66

Music

Florence. G. Selden-Goth. Opera N 30:32 Mr 19; 31:32 S 10 '66

Florence; performance of L'incoronazione di Poppea. J. C. Adams. Opera N 31:32 D 24 '66

Religious institutions and affairs

Failure in Florence; aggiornamento comes to a halt. E. Cochrane. Commonweal 85:197-9 N 18 '66

FLORENCE agreement. See Duty free importations

FLORENCE Lasker civil liberties award

Conscience of a lawyer. Nation 202:199 F 21 '66; Reply. H. L. Black. 202:442 Ap 18 '66

FLORENTINE May festival. See Music festivals—Italy

FLORENTINES

Failure in Florence; aggiornamento comes to a halt. E. Cochrane. Commonweal 85:197-9 N 18 '66

FLORHAM PARK, N.J.

Aerial survey pays big dividends. J. M. DiMarzo. il Am City 81:113-14 F '66

FLORIA, Carlos Alberto

Latin America 1966. Cath World 204:42-5 O '66

FLORIAN, Robert

Dominick Labino. por (p7) Craft Horiz 26:28-31 Jl '66

FLORICULTURE

Direct seeding. W. Berry. il Horticulture 44:30-1+ Mr '66

Grow your own flowers from seed. il Pop Gard 17:88-9 Mr '66

How to grow flowers from seed. il Good H 162:181 Mr '66

Regional pointers. See issues of Flower grower, the home garden

See also

Plant propagation

also names of flowers, e.g. Peonies

FLORIDA

Oceanside and inland faces of Florida; with photographs. Natur Hist 75:42-3 Mr '66

Yo ho ho! Florida's give-away program of its sunken treasure. Nation 203:629 D 12 '66

See also

Architecture, Domestic—Florida

Booksellers and bookselling—Florida

Camping—Florida

Canals—Florida

Everglades

Everglades National Park

Fishing—Florida

Golf courses—Florida

Music festivals—Florida

Prisons—Florida

Roads—Florida

Ten Thousand Islands

Water supply—Florida

Description and travel

Around Florida's tip. J. Hardie. il Motor B 118:32-3+ O '66

Florida's wild West coast. J. S. Doherty. il Yachting 120:52-3+ N '66

Four family-planned circle tours. N. Kuehnl and P. Lindberg. il Bet Hom & Gard 44:76-7 Je '66

FLORIDA—Description and travel—*Continued*
From tip to top in Florida. G. Bourke. See issues of Travel
Go west; but do it soon; cross-Florida cruise. W. H. Kendall .il Motor B 117:36-9+ Ap '66
Northwest Florida. N. Love. il Travel 126:26-30 Jl '66
Orange Blossom trail. J. H. Winchester. il Travel 125:35-8 F '66
Traveler, consider my Florida; interview, ed. by R. Joseph. L. Collins. il Esquire 66:240-1+ D '66

History
See also
Florida—Missions

Missions
Our oldest mission; symbol of peace; new votive church at Nombre de Dios mission. V. P. McCorry. America 114:625 Ap 30 '66

Politics and government
Hog-pen morality; gubernatorial primary result. Nation 202:669 Je 6 '66
Wave either way; gubernatorial race. Time 88:29-30 O 28 '66

Race problems
History
Free Negro in Florida. L. W. Neyland. bibliog Negro Hist Bul 29:27-8+ N '65

FLORIDA, Straits of
Shallow structure of the Straits of Florida. E. Uchupi. bibliog il Science 153:529-31 Jl 29 '66

FLORIDA Atlantic university, Boca Raton
Undersea college lab launched. il Tech W 19:35 Jl 11 '66

FLORIDA Derby. See Horse racing

FLORIDA East Coast railway
Ruling: railroads' duty to run. U S News 60:104 Je 6 '66

FLORIDA EVERGLADES. See Everglades

FLORIDA International music festival. See Music festivals—Florida

FLORIDA Key deer. See Deer

FLORIDA KEYS
Around Florida's tip. J. Hardie. il Motor B 118:32-3+ O '66
Ladies day at sea. N. Brower. il Motor B 119:76-9+ Ja '67
Trailer cruise in the Keys. B. Schill and B. Schill. il Yachting 120:45+ N '66
Where the roads end. P. Redford. il Atlan 217:130-2+ Ap '66

FLORIDA land boom. See Real estate business

FLORIDA Presbyterian college, St Petersburg
Coming of age at six. il Time 88:82 D 9 '66

FLORIDA primary. See Primaries

FLORIDA SHIP CANAL project
River spoilers. S. Trumbull. il Audubon Mag 68:102-10 Mr '66

FLORIDA state museum. See Florida. University—Florida state museum

FLORIDA state university, Tallahassee
Big top goes to college. B. Kocivar. il Look 30:56-9 Ag 9 '66

FLORIDA. University

Florida state museum
Florida state museum; custodian of all treasure found off the coast of Florida. J. L. Stoutenburgh. Hobbies 71:111 S '66

FLORISTS telegraph delivery association
Easter flowers by wire; letter. Consumer Bul 49:15 Ap '66

FLORSHEIM, Richard Aberle
Color lithographs of Richard Florsheim; technical commentary. il Am Artist 30:29-30+ My '66

about
Color lithographs of Richard Florsheim. il Am Artist 30:25-9 My '66

FLOUR
Here are Sunset's answers to questions about all-purpose flours. Sunset 136:160 F '66

FLOUR, Fish. See Fish flour

FLOUR beetles
Survival in a vacuum; tribolium confusum, space-suited beetle. il Sci N 90:523 D 17 '66

FLOWER, Milton E.
Watch holders. Antiques 89:862-6 Je '66

FLOWER beds, Raised. See Landscape gardening

FLOWER boxes, planters, etc.
Add color with containers. il Pop Gard 17:28-31 Mr '66
Best window boxes begin in spring. il Pop Gard 17:4 My '66
Deck plant on the ground. il Sunset 137:96 Jl '66

Easy-to-build planter box. il Pop Gard 17:70-1 D '66
Gardening on a deck, terrace or even on a roof. il Sunset 136:236-8+ Ap '66
Gardens at your windows. G. Taloumis. il Horticulture 44:16-19+ Ap '66
Go togethers: petunias & pots. L. Burgess. il Flower Grower 53:32-3 Jl '66
Hutch-style planter for the wall. J. E. Reppert. il Pop Sci 189:178-9 O '66
Indoor planter. H. M. Cathey. il Horticulture 44:53 O '66

FLOWER exhibits
Big flower boom; flower people; International flower show at Coliseum. I. Taves. il Look 30:80-5+ Mr 22 '66
Flower shows; photographs. Horticulture 44:6+ Mr '66
For April visitors to southern California, the largest orchid show ever held anywhere; World orchid conference show. il Sunset 136:108-9 Ap '66
Garden events. See issues of Flower grower, the home garden
Garden events [in month] (title varies) See issues of Sunset
H&G'S almanac of flower shows. il House & Gard 129:124 Mr '66
How flower shows have changed! A. H. Nehrling. il Horticulture 44:22-5+ Mr '66
Make way for spring; New York's International flower show. il Time 87:68-71 Mr 18 '66

FLOWER pests. See Plants—Diseases and pests

FLOWER photography. See Photography of flowers, plants, trees, etc.

FLOWER pictures. See Pictures

FLOWER seed industry. See Seed trade

FLOWER shows. See Flower exhibits

FLOWERING shrubs. See Shrubs

FLOWERING stones
Flowering stones; South African plants. D. S. Hardy. il Natur Hist 75:26-9 O '66

FLOWERING trees
Beautify America forum: trees bloom on Main Street. J. R. Downie. Flower Grower 53:26 F '66
Here are flowering surprises for northern Californians. Sunset 136:250 Je '66
See also
Magnolias

FLOWERS, James
(ed) See Defourneaux, R. J. Secret encounter with Ho chi Minh

FLOWERS, Nancy
Pottery of Barcelos. Natur Hist 75:44-51 Je '66

FLOWERS, Richmond
Southern plain talk about the Ku Klux klan. pors Look 30:36+ My 3 '66

about
Flowers in Alabama. New Repub 154:7-8 Ap 23 '66

FLOWERS, Richmond, Jr
People vs. Flowers. il por Newsweek 67:83 F 28 '66
Winning son of a dedicated loser. J. Underwood. il pors Sports Illus 24:30-2+ Je 6 '66

FLOWERS
This is my favorite. See issues of Popular gardening & living outdoors
See also
Annuals (plants)
Biennials (plants)
Bulbs
Leis
Perennials
Pollen
Wild flowers
also names of flowers, e.g. Trilliums

All America selections
See Plants—All America selections

Cut flowers
See also
Flowers, Arrangement of

Odors
See Odors

FLOWERS, Arrangement of
Arrangements for spring. Mrs A. H. Smith. il Horticulture 44:28-9+ Mr '66
Enjoy spectacular color two ways. M. A. Roche. il Pop Gard 17:48-50 My '66
Flowers for your table; Philadelphia flower show arrangements. J. Havens. il Horticulture 45:32-3 Ja '67
Flowers in the wood. il McCalls 93:92-5 Mr '66
How to make the most of a half-dozen roses. il Bet Hom & Gard 44:115 Je '66

FLYING W ranch. See Ranches
FLYNN, John P. See MacDonnell, M. F. jt. auth.
FLYNN, Robert J.
Diseases of laboratory animals. Science 153: 906 Ag 19 '66
FLYTRAPS, Venus's. See Venus's flytraps
FLYWHEELS
Safety!! who needs it? hydroformed bell-housing insurance for clutch or flywheel explosion. il Hot Rod 19:74-5+ Ap '66
FOAM, Fire fighting. See Fire protection
FOAM plastic subbase material. See Roads—Foundations
FOAMS, Fire extinction. See Fire extinction
FOCARINO, Joseph
Research & development: the wondrous world of tomorrow. Duns R 87:pt2 106-9+ My '66
FODOR, Eugene
Crash production program for Fodor-Shell travel guides U.S.A. il por Pub W 189:172-4 Je 13 '66
FOECKE, Harold A.
Continuing education for engineers; excerpts from address, October 1965. Science 152: 880-3 My 13 '66
FOETUS. See Fetus
FOG
Amateur scientist; study of the salty rain of Venezuela; periodic wind called alisio blows the calina fog away. G. Zuloaga. il Sci Am 215:136-8 D '66
Four dollar fog. W. Richards. il Motor B 117:30-2+ Je '66
See also
Aviation—Fog problem
FOG; story. See Bailey, A.
FOG, Artificial
Lifesaving fog; fog machines aid respiration. T. Berland. il Todays Health 44:22-4+ D '66
FOG, Medical. See Fog, Artificial
FOG machine. See Respiratory apparatus
FOG tent. See Respiratory apparatus
FOGARTY, Gerald P.
Lay trusteeism: yesterday and today. America 115:656-9 N 19 '66
FOGARTY, John Edward
School librarians; address, July 11, 1966. Vital Speeches 32:682-4 S 1 '66
FOGELIN, Maria Bontempi
Who do you love? story. Redbook 127:155 My '66
FOKKER, Anthony Herman Gerard
World war I dogfights powered Fokker's take-off. il por Bsns W p76 F 5 '66
FOLATE reductase. See Reductases
FOLDING chairs. See Chairs
FOLDING fin aircraft rockets. See Guided missiles—Launching from airplanes
FOLDING tables. See Tables
FOLDING walls. See Walls
FOLEY, Brian
Hip star in Harvard yard. il por Life 60:110 Je 3 '66
FOLEY, Connie
John Otto: letter writer extraordinary. Am For 72:40-2 Ap '66
FOLEY, Dave
Bull with brains. por Sports Illus 25:69 S 19 '66
FOLGER Shakespeare library, Washington, D.C.
Thy book doth live. A. L. Buchanan. il Américas 18:15-20 Mr '66
FOLK art
Artless art; Girard foundation collection. il Horizon 8:72-7 Spr '66
Crisis in folk arts; conditions in Latin America. G. de Zéndegui. il Américas 18: 22-30 Ja '66
Folk art; gifts and loans; exhibitions in New York city. E. P. Birk. il Antiques 90:586+ N '66
Wood: the American folk sculptor. M. C. Black. il Craft Horiz 26:18-21+ Jl '66

Exhibitions

Amateurs, Frakturs and elegant young ladies; Garbisch collection of American watercolors and pastels at the National gallery, Washington, D.C. W. P. Campbell. il Art N 65: 50-3+ O '66
FOLK dancing
Following in the folksteps; Hungarian and Rumanian U.S. appearances. Time 87:86+ F 4 '66

FOLK literature
Cultural patterns in narrative; folk tales and myths. B. N. Colby. bibliog il Science 151: 793-8 F 18 '66
FOLK music
Folk music in liturgy. C. J. McNaspy. il America 114:529-32 Ap 9 '66
See also
Phonograph records—Folk music
FOLK music, American
Country music snaps its regional bounds; Nashville's Grand old opry, for nationwide taste. il Bsns W p96-8+ Mr 19 '66
Gold guitars; country-music. il Newsweek 67:96+ Ap 4 '66
That new sound from Nashville; country music. C. Portis. il Sat Eve Post 239:30-4+ F 12 '66
FOLK singers. See Singers
FOLK songs, Portuguese
See also
Fados
FOLKLORE
See also
Superstition

Ireland

Leprechauns and all that. R. T. Reilly. America 114:381-2 Mr 19 '66

United States

See also
Legends, American
FOLKLORE, Negro
Mississippi folk festival; featured African and Afro-American artists. il Ebony 21:91-2+ Mr '66
Zora Neale Hurston: author and folklorist. E. L. Blake. Negro Hist Bul 29:149-50+ Ap '66
FOLKLORE of trees. See Trees in religion, folklore, etc.
FOLKMAN, Judah, and others
Silicone rubber: a new diffusion property useful for general anesthesia. bibliog Science 154:148-9 O 7 '66
FOLKWAYS records and service corporation
At our corner; M. Asch, consultant for new Folkways/Scholastic records program. Sr Schol 89:sup22 N 11 '66
FOLLETT, Wilson
To speak, correctly; excerpts from Modern American usage. Vogue 148:58+ D '66
FOLLOW up studies (education)
Talent search has 25th year. il Sci N L 89: 149-50 Mr 5 '66
FOLON, Jean Michel
Laughter in the labyrinth; portfolio. Fortune 73:133-5 F '66
FOLSOM, Arnott R.
How to start a children's zoo. Parks & Rec 1:430-2 My '66
FOLSOM, Marion Bayard
New look. K. B. Pomeroy. Am For 72:7 S '66
FOLSOM, Michael Brewster
Book of poverty. Nation 202:242-5 F 28 '66
FOLSOM points. See Stone implements and weapons
FONDA, Jane
Blonde black panther. por Time 88:76 S 9 '66
Diffused Jane Fonda. pors U S Camera 29: 60-1 Jl '66
La FONDA del sol. See New York (city)—Hotels, restaurants, etc.
FONDILLER, Harvey V.
Film notes. Pop Phot 59:141 Jl; 132 Ag; 129 S '66; 60:84+ Ja '67
Focus on Bob Yung. Pop Phot 58:100-3+ F '66
FONDUES. See Cookery
FONTAINE, André
What is French policy? For Affairs 45:58-76 O '66
(ed) See Ball, G. W. Under Secretary Ball discusses U.S. views on Viet-Nam and NATO
FONTAINE, Athanas Paul
Tales of Fontaine. R. Levy. por Duns R 88: 50-2 O '66
FONTAINE, Robert
To the moon; drama. Plays 25:93-5 F '66
United spies; drama. Plays 25:106-8 My '66
FONTINELL, Eugene
Books. Commonweal 84:122-4 Ap 15 '66
FOOD
Food Q's and A's. D. Soroka. Parents Mag 41:24 Mr; 91 Je; 154 N '66
Food: the changes ahead. Changing T 20:6 Je '66
He finds food in the oddest places; with excerpts from Stalking the healthful herbs. il Life 61:45-6 S 23 '66

FOOD for children. See Children—Nutrition

FOOD for peace program. See Food relief

FOOD freezers. See Freezers

FOOD habits of animals. See Animals—Food

FOOD industry and trade
Agribusiness for developing countries. R. A. Goldberg. il Harvard Bsns R 44:81-93 S '66
Chicken colonel; Kentucky fried chicken corp. il Newsweek 68:79 Jl 25 '66
Food processing; key to economic development. G. C. Lodge. Harvard Bsns R 44:6-8+ S '66
Food report feeds controversy; results of National commission on food marketing study. il Bsns W p 173-4 My 28 '66
Getting rich on Italian appetites; Motta of Milan. il Bsns W p 132-4+ Ap 16 '66
Hidden assassins, by B. Mooney. Review
New Repub 154:29-30 Je 25 '66. J. A. Page
Mexico taps a fat U.S. food market. il Bsns W p 104-6+ Mr 19 '66
Overuse of sugary, starchy foods. Consumer Bul 49:35-6 Ag '66
Report on food: prescription for a sick industry. J. Cross. il Nation 203:245-8 S 19 '66
Shopping for food: how it's changing. il U S News 60:12 My '66
Soybeans move up on the menu. il Bsns W p82+ Jl 23 '66
Truth in packaging: supermarket caper. J. Cross. il Nation 202:208-12 F 21 '66
See also
Consolidated foods corporation
Food, Frozen
Food additives
General foods corporation

FOOD inspection. See Food adulteration and inspection

FOOD laws and legislation
Does the food business need government controls? J. Carlson. Farm J 90:39 Jl '66
See also
United States—Food and drug administration

FOOD machinery and chemicals corporation. See FMC corporation

FOOD mixers, Electric. See Electric apparatus and appliances, Domestic

FOOD mixes
Cinderella cake; with recipes. il Seventeen 25:170-1+ N '66
Food poisoning and matters of interest to all who eat out. il Consumer Bul 49:33-4 Ap '66
Quick tricks with brownie mix; with recipes. il Seventeen 25:180 Mr '66
Things to do with soup mixes. il Ladies Home J 83:114+ S '66

FOOD plants. See Plants, Food

FOOD poisoning
Food poisoning and matters of interest to all who eat out. il Consumer Bul 49:33-4 Ap '66
High risk foods and their control. PTA Mag 60:17 Je '66
How to avoid food poisoning. Parents Mag 41:67 Jl '66
Keeping food safely at home; role of bacteria in food poisoning; with questions and answers on food safety. A. C. Dean. PTA Mag 60:14-16 Je '66
Let's talk about food; microbial food poisoning and how to avoid infection; ed. by P. L. White. Todays Health 44:10-11+ D '66

FOOD preservation and preservatives
Bacilli readied for heat death by active enzyme. Sci N 90:70 Jl 30 '66
High risk foods and their control. PTA Mag 60:17 Je '66
How long foods keep, in your refrigerator, in your freezer. il Changing T 20:13-14 N '66
Keeping food safely at home; with questions and answers on food safety. A. C. Dean. PTA Mag 60:14-16 Je '66
Putting food to sleep; inert nitrogen process. C. Welles. il Life 60:71-2 F 18 '66
See also
Food, Effect of radiation on
Freezing of food
Refrigerators

FOOD production. See Food supply

FOOD relief
Corn to feed children; CPP and CSM food supplements. Sci N 89:361 My 14 '66
Food and famine: winning the war against world hunger. il Sr Schol 89:12-15 D 2 '66
Food bandwagon picks up speed. D. Hanson. Suc Farm 64:6 F '66
Food for freedom. Commonweal 83:597-8 F 25 '66
Food for freedom act of 1966; statements. March 7, 14, 1966. D. Rusk. Dept State Bul 54:496-503 Mr 28 '66

Food for freedom; message to the Congress, February 10, 1966. L. B. Johnson. Dept State Bul 54:336-41 F 28 '66
Food for freedom: paradox of foreign aid. B. J. Oudes. il Nation 203:120-4 Ag 8 '66
Food for peace act of 1966 signed into law; statement, November 12, 1966. L. B. Johnson. Dept State Bul 55:866-7 D 5 '66
Food for peace program; Agricultural trade development and assistance act, July 1954; excerpts. Cur Hist 51:46-7+ Jl '66
For freedom from hunger; campaign's progress. UNESCO Courier 19:26-30 Ap '66
From surplus to war on hunger; Food for freedom program. Life 61:8 O 7 '66
Giveaway food is giving out, and still the world hungers. il U S News 62:38-9 Ja 2 '67
Good hunger program. Farm J 90:134 Mr '66
If U.S. had to feed the world. il U S News 60:94-5 F 7 '66
Kalamazoo to Calcutta; Todd amendment to food for freedom bill. K. Crawford. Newsweek 68:27 Jl 4 '66
LBJ's plan to help feed the world. U S News 60:12 F 21 '66
New food policy; concerning new Food for peace bill. Commonweal 84:569-70 S 16 '66
Now we send food for freedom. America 114:279 F 26 '66
Preaching to the hungry; demands of the Food for peace program. New Repub 156:7-8 Ja 14 '67
President reports to Congress on Food for peace program; White House announcement; with letter of transmittal by President Johnson. Dept State Bul 55:185-7 Ag 1 '66
Should the U.S. take the brake off food production? pro and con discussion. Sr Schol 88:12-14 Mr 25 '66
Struggle to end hunger; Time essay. Time 88:32-3 Ag 12 '66
To win the fight against world starvation; Food for peace program retards food production in needy countries. N. R. Danielian. Read Digest 89:70-4 Ag '66
Traffic in hunger; strings on food-for-peace are tighter. New Repub 155:5-6 O 29 '66
Two threats to peace: hunger and aggression; address. June 30, 1966. L. B. Johnson. Dept State Bul 55:114-19 Jl 25 '66; Same with title Vietnam war. Vital Speeches 32:578-82 Jl 15 '66
U.N. extends World food program; statement, December 10, 1965. J. Roosevelt. Dept State Bul 54:130-3 Ja 24 '66
U.S. to grow more rice; response to President Johnson's message on Food for freedom. Sci N L 89:158 Mr 5 '66
War on hunger. Time 87:23 F 18 '66
What the U.S. can do about world hunger. D. Norton-Taylor. il Fortune 73:110-14+ Je '66
World food and population crisis: DAC's fifth annual high-level meeting; statement by Secretary Rusk; remarks by Vice President Humphrey, July 20; statement by O. L. Freeman and message from President Johnson; with texts of communique and recommendation on food problems of less developed countries. July 21, 1966. Dept State Bul 55:199-212 Ag 8 '66
World food programme. UN Mo Chron 3:77 Ja '66
World is heading for a collision; proposals for food aid program; excerpt from address, November 1965. G. Myrdal. il UNESCO Courier 19:21-3 F '66
World's food and population problems; address; November 12, 1966. R. W. Reuter. Dept State Bul 55:862-6 D 5 '66
Young world manifesto; Rome assembly to aid Freedom from hunger campaign. UNESCO Courier 19:26 Ap '66
See also
Christian rural overseas program
Oxford committee for famine relief

Africa

Drought knows no frontiers; Africa and India; aid measures. G. Ash. il UNESCO Courier 19:10-15 Ap '66

Chile

Building with beans; CROP food-for-work projects. G. Meek. il Américas 18:35-8 Jl '66

India

Another plus for CRS; problem of getting food to starving India. America 116:33 Ja 14 '67
Can we feed the world? il Sat Eve Post 240:86 Ja 28 '67
Constant companion; free world rallies to India's aid. il Time 87:33 F 25 '66

FOOD relief—India—*Continued*
Cornucopia limited; U.S. delay. il Time 88: 16 D 30 '66
Decision for Mr Johnson; surplus wheat to help India. America 115:762 D 10 '66
Drought knows no frontiers; Africa and India; aid measures. G. Ash. il UNESCO Courier 19:10-15 Ap '66
Foodmanship; LBJ held up approval of mercy shipments. Newsweek 68:23-4 D 19 '66
Help is on the way. Newsweek 69:37 Ja 2 '67
India: how can its hunger be eased? G. Murray. Christian Cent 83:811-12 Je 22 '66
India to get aid, but no blank check. il Bsns W p34-5 Ap 2 '66
Message to Congress on food aid to India; March 30, 1966. L. B. Johson. Dept State Bul 54:605-7 Ap 18 '66
President hails congressional support of food aid to India; statement, April 19, 1966; with text of congressional resolution. L. B. Johnson. Dept State Bul 54:747-8 My 9 '66
Rains that did not come. il UNESCO Courier 19:4-8 Ap '66
Sales meeting. Newsweek 67:31A F 21 '66
Starvation politics. Commonweal 85:360 Ja 6 '67
U.S. welcomes U.N./FAO appeal for worldwide food aid to India; statement, February 2, 1966. A. J. Goldberg. Dept State Bul 54:385 Mr 7 '66
Warning in India's famine. Life 60:4 Mr 18 '66

Latin America
Building with beans; CROP food-for-work projects. G. Meek. il Américas 18:35-8 Jl '66

Underdeveloped areas
Food: population trends move U.S. to tie aid to self help. J. Walsh. Science 152:732-4 My 6 '66

Yugoslavia
Bridge buster; Findley amendment. Time 89: 14 Ja 13 '67

FOOD research
See also
Nutrition research
FOOD service equipment. See Cafeterias—Equipment
FOOD stores
See also
Chain stores
Supermarkets
FOOD substitutes
How science tricks your taste. J. H. Winchester. il Pop Sci 189:79-81+ S '66
FOOD supply
Agribusiness for developing countries. R. A. Goldberg. il Harvard Bsns R 44:81-93 S '66
All-consuming opportunity; profound change in world's food supply. Time 88:74 Jl 1 '66
Analysis of famine. B. Tufty. il Sci N 90:74-5 Jl 30 '66
Banquet of life. J. O'Gara. Commonweal 84:170 Ap 29 '66
Can we feed the world? il Sat Eve Post 240:86 Ja 28 '67
Converting life into living; Iowa state university conference on alternatives for balancing future world food production and needs. K. Haselden. Christian Cent 83:1435-6 N 23 '66
Crops fail, food crisis mounts. Sci N 90:327 O 22 '66
Facts of life: Thomas Malthus was right, birth control is urgent. J. Nuveen. Christian Cent 83:983-6 Ag 10 '66
Famine: a shadow over half the world. il Sr Schol 88:9-13 Mr 25 '66
Food crisis heals slowly. Sci N 90:250 O 1 '66
Food crisis nears critical stages. B. Tufty. il Sci N 89:333-4 My 7 '66
Food for tomorrow; address, September 12, 1966. J. E. Swearingen. Vital Speeches 33:61-4 N 1 '66
Food: postwar experience shows it was later than we thought. J. Walsh. Science 152:896-9 My 13 '66; Reply. D. B. Van Vleck. 154:70 O 7 '66
Food surplus running out. Sci N 90:322 O 22 '66
Giveaway food is giving out, and still the world hungers. il U S News 62:38-9 Ja 2 '67
Hunger ahead. il Changing T 20:43-6 Ag '66
Land reform and the world food crisis; summary of conference. UN Mo Chron 3:45-8 Jl '66
Nationalizing the fight against famine. Christian Cent 83:357 Mr 23 '66

Plant pathology and human welfare. A. J. Riker. bibliog il Science 152:1027-32 My 20 '66
Race with hunger can be won! C. P. Streeter. Farm J 90:74 Je '66
Struggle to end hunger; Time essay. Time 88:32-3 Ag 12 '66
To be or not to be that will be the question; implications of population growth. B. R. Sen. il UNESCO Courier 19:10-15 F '66
To establish an equilibrium; excerpt from address at FAO conference, November 2, 1959. A. Toynbee. UNESCO Courier 19:12 F '66
Twin war: hunger and population. Sci N 91:18 Ja 7 '67
Warning: less food for all; interview, ed. by V. Block. L. Brown. Sci Digest 59:12-16 My '66
World food and population crisis: DAC's fifth annual high-level meeting; statement by Secretary Rusk; remarks by Vice President Humphrey, July 20; statement by O. L. Freeman and message from President Johnson; with texts of communique and recommendation on food problems of less developed countries, July 21, 1966. Dept State Bul 55:199-212 Ag 8 '66
World food: population problem; address, November 8, 1966. L. R. Brown. il Vital Speeches 33:155-60 D 15 '66
World food problem; address, April 27, 1966. R. A. Ioanes. Vital Speeches 32:533-6 Je 15 '66
World food programme. UN Mo Chron 3:14-15 F '66
World is heading for a collision; proposals for food aid program; excerpt from address, November 1965. G. Myrdal. il UNESCO Courier 19:21-3 F '66
World's food and population problems; address, November 12, 1966. R. W. Reuter. Dept State Bul 55:862-6 D 5 '66
See also
Famines
Food and agriculture organization of the United Nations
Surplus products, Agricultural

New sources
One cell protein from oil. Sci N 91:40 Ja 14 '67
Tomorrow's new foods; interview, ed. by V. Block. J. Smith. Sci Digest 61:65-9 Ja '67
Ungathered harvests in the ocean; man's vast potential food reserve. M. Laing. il UNESCO Courier 19:11-15+ S '66
World food supply: problems and prospects. L. J. Carter. Science 155:56-8 Ja 6 '67
See also
Fish flour

Political aspects
Second challenge. E. Rabinowitch. Bul Atomic Sci 22:25-7 My '66

India
Can India break its famine cycle? Bsns W p83 D 24 '66
Constant companion; free world rallies to India's aid. il Time 87:33 F 25 '66
Fertilizer to fight hunger. il Time 87:93 My 27 '66
For India, still more aid: and for the U.S.—. il U S News 60:60-1 Ap 11 '66
Papal appeal for India. America 114:641 My 7 '66
Rupees and rice. G. Woodcock. Commonweal 84:414-17 Jl 1 '66
Starvation politics. Commonweal 85:360 Ja 6 '67
Touching America's untouchables; Action for food production project. Christian Cent 83:855-6 Jl 6 '66
Where cows eat and people starve. il U S News 61:111 N 21 '66
See also
Famines—India

Mexico
Mexico closes the food gap. J. Strohm. il Read Digest 88:165-8+ Je '66

Russia
Russia's food supply: it's getting better. il U S News 61:109 Jl 18 '66

Underdeveloped areas
To win the fight against world starvation. N. R. Danielian. Read Digest 89:70-4 Ag '66
Trying harder to feed the poor; DAC to coordinate national aid policies. Bsns W p33-4 Jl 23 '66

FOOD supply—*Continued*

United States

Chance to clean house. C. P. Streeter. Farm J 90:74 Ag '66

From surplus to food crisis. R. L. Tobin. Sat R 49:18 Ag 27 '66

Should the U.S. take the brake off food production? pro and con discussion. Sr Schol 88:12-14 Mr 25 '66

FOOD values

Let's talk about food; ed. by P. L. White. See issues of Today's health

FOONER, Michael

Victim-induced criminality. bibliog Science 153:1080-3 S 2 '66

FOOT

Care and hygiene

Carry on feet! il Mlle 62:152-3 F '66

Wounds and injuries

Surfers' feet chip. Sci N 90:87 Ag 6 '66

FOOT-and-mouth disease

Cattle killer; western European livestock. il Newsweek 67:82 Mr 14 '66

Foot-&-mouth man. il Time 88:55 D 16 '66

FOOT bridges. See Bridges, Foot

FOOTBALL

All-star pro team: a prediction for '66. S. Gelman. il Esquire 66:88-90+ O '66

Another one for the Irish; Notre Dame's victory over Northwestern. il Time 88:79 O 7 '66

Babes in wonderland; Notre Dame. il Time 88:50-2+ O 28 '66

Best and worst of the bowls. D. Jenkins. il Sports Illus 26:20-1 Ja 9 '67

Bitter harvest for the Sugar-bound Huskers; Nebraska's Cornhuskers invited to New Orleans Sugar bowl. J. Jares. il Sports Illus 25:79-80 D 5 '66

Bombs & squeaks; college football. Time 88:72 O 21 '66

Bowl games and the season; Sugar, Cotton, Orange, Gator and Rose bowls. D. Jenkins. il Sports Illus 26:26-35 Ja 2 '67

Bowl of bowls? Super bowl proposal. Newsweek 69:89 Ja 23 '67

Bows before the bruises; Super bowl. il Time 89:51 Ja 13 '67

Bulldog answer to an S.O.S; Florida Gators swamped by Georgia Bulldogs. J. Underwood. il Sports Illus 25:30-5 N 14 '66

Carruthers have a fighter; J. Pittman. G. Ronberg. il Sports Illus 25:52-3 O 10 '66

College football forecast. il Look 30:112-14+ S 20 '66

College football 1966. il Sports Illus 25:36-52+ S 19 '66

Delirious instant of Ara's reprieve; with reports by A. Parseghian and D. Daugherty. il Life 61:94-8+ D 2 '66

Exercise in frustration; Notre Dame-Michigan state game ends in tie. il Time 88:63 N 25 '66

Fair Harvard. il Newsweek 68:94 N 7 '66

Flag-football. K. L. Hoeck. il Parks & Rec 1:912-13 N '66

Football. See issues of New Yorker published during football season

Football's week. M. Hyman. See issues of Sports illustrated published during football season

For Indians, it was a day to bite the dust; Harvard, the new Ivy league leader. North Dakota State. nation's no. 1 small-college team. T. C. Brody. il Sports Illus 25:46-8+ O 31 '66

Gaelic revival; Notre Dame. Newsweek 68:68 O 10 '66

Game of the century; Notre Dame-Michigan state game. il Newsweek 68:64 N 28 '66

Half a glass of fresh blood on Saturday morning; F. Little, captain and star halfback of the Syracuse team. M. Cope. il Sat Eve Post 239:84-6+ N 19 '66

Herd psychology; North Dakota State university Bison. il Newsweek 68:72-3 O 24 '66

I'll tell you about football; ed. by J. Underwood. P. Bryant. il Sports Illus 25:52-8+ Ag 15: 28-30+ Ag 22: 26-8+ Ag 29: 28-30+ S 5: 98-100+ S 12 '66

Imagination, it's wonderful; college football. il Time 88:80 S 23 '66

In and out; USC declared ineligible for the Rose bowl. Sports Illus 25:11 D 12 '66

In the Big ten. State wins the numbers game; Michigan state gets into the Western conference. J. Underwood. il Sports Illus 25:67-70 O 17 '66

Irish launch a new Ara; Notre Dame defeats Purdue. J. Underwood. il Sports Illus 25:28-31 O 3 '66

It's Baker! going for another touchdown! with introd. by George Frazier. J. Davies. il Esquire 66:132-5+ S '66

It's ragtime in the Rockies; Cowboy Joes of Wyoming defeat Brigham Young university. T. C. Brody. il Sports Illus 25:58+ N 28 '66

It's time to bring on the dogs; Georgia Tech vs University of Georgia. D. Jenkins. il Sports Illus 25:26-7 N 21 '66

Long green season. il Newsweek 68:78-9 Ag 15 '66

Mighty win for a minor with major ambitions; San Diego state beats San Jose state. G. Ronberg. il Sports Illus 25:58-9 O 24 '66

National pastime; start of season. il Time 88:70 S 16 '66

Night they learned to forget the coach; LSU defeats P. Dietzel's South Carolina football team. G. Ronberg. il Sports Illus 25:56-7 S 26 '66

Not-so-big ten. Time 88:80+ O 14 '66

On a clear day, San Diego state saw forever; defeats North Dakota state and becomes country's no. 1 small-college team. T. C. Brody. il Sports Illus 25:75-6 N 14 '66

Paper lion by G. Plimpton. Review
    Life 61:33 N 11 '66. L. Wainwright

Positive records for the predictably good; Notre Dame and Michigan state stand above all the rest. M. Hyman. il Sports Illus 25:56+ N 21 '66

Psychologist on the sidelines; Notre Dame's Parseghian. W. B. Furlong. il N Y Times Mag p56-7+ N 13 '66

Randy passes a test in his new home; Falcons' rookie quarterback stars in Coaches All-American game. D. Jenkins. il Sports Illus 25:54-6 Jl 18 '66

Sane conclusion in a cockeyed conference; Southwest conference. D. Jenkins. il Sports Illus 25:44-6 N 7 '66

Stoic's guide to pro football; compound fractures and shattered ribs are small discomforts in the credo of Kansas City linebacker S. Headrick. E. Shrake. il Sports Illus 25:30-2+ N 7 '66

Streak is here; college halfbacks. D. Jenkins. il Sports Illus 25:20-5 O 10 '66

Supermen of Troy; Southern California beats Texas. D. Jenkins. il Sports Illus 25:20-5 S 26 '66

Supermice of another Troy; RPI football. H. Weiskopf. Sports Illus 25:63-4 O 3 '66

Surge by the tide; unbeaten Alabama defeats Tennessee in a thriller. J. Underwood. il Sports Illus 25:22-7 O 24 '66

Texas football: fierce, frantic, fabulous. M. Cope. il Sat Eve Post 239:83-7 S 24 '66

That legend is loose again; Notre Dame winning in Rockne-Leahy tradition. D. Jenkins. il Sports Illus 25:70-2+ N 7 '66

They're only no. 2; J. T. Prothro of the U.C.L.A. Bruins. il Time 88:78-9 O 7 '66

True meaning of the game; Father Hesburgh warns of prolonged seasons and the increasing orgy of bowl games. T. M. Hesburgh Sports Illus 25:56-7 D 12 '66

Upside-down game; Michigan state-Notre Dame ten-ten tie game. D. Jenkins. il Sports Illus 25:22-7 N 28 '66

Way up South; Southeastern conference. Time 88:70+ N 11 '66

What a fright; Notre Dame-Michigan state game. Time 88:58 N 18 '66

When the men met the boys; National football league champions-college All-stars game. il Time 88:54-5 Ag 12 '66

Why some All Americas don't make the pros. G. Astor. Look 30:98 D 13 '66

    See also
Football players
Rugby football
Soccer

Accidents and injuries

Breaks of the game. il Newsweek 68:73 O 3 '66

Football knee. il Newsweek 68:74 N 21 '66

Football risks examined. Sci N 90:235 S 24 '66

If it can move, then tape it. B. Gilbert. il Sports Illus 25:38-40+ N 28 '66

Stoic's guide to pro football; compound fractures and shattered ribs are small discomforts in the credo of Kansas City linebacker S. Headrick. E. Shrake. il Sports Illus 25:30-2+ N 7 '66

Anecdotes, facetiae, satire, etc.

Pigskin charade; few of this season's stranger gaffes and happenings. J. Lake. il Newsweek 68:94-5 D 5 '66

FOOTBALL—*Continued*

Economic aspects

Big dollar in pro football. E. Selby. il Read Digest 89:111-15 N '66

Quarterbacking a new industry; interview. G. Halas. il Nations Bsns 54:52-4+ D '66

Terminology

Language of pro football. K. Rote. il Look 30:148 O 18 '66

FOOTBALL accidents. See Football—Accidents and injuries

FOOTBALL clubs

Ain't peace wonderful? NFL-AFL merger. Sports Illus 25:9 Ag 1 '66

Beau Jets. il Time 88:70+ S 30 '66

Bye-bye boos; Dallas Cowboys. il Time 88:50 D 2 '66

Can they pack up the Packers? Kansas City Chiefs. il Life 62:66-8+ Ja 13 '67

Curtain falls on a long run; Cleveland Browns' J. Brown retires. T. Maule. il Sports Illus 25:18-20+ Jl 25 '66

Fabulous Brodie caper; AFL plot to sign NFL quarterbacks. E. Shrake. il Sports Illus 25:16-21+ Ag 29 '66

Fire from the ashes; Boston's Patriots lead AFL Eastern race. E. Shrake. il Sports Illus 25:18-21 D 12 '66

Firewater for some fired-up Chiefs; Kansas City Chiefs AFL champions. E. Shrake. il Sports Illus 26:14-17 Ja 9 '67

Great man: V. Lombardi, head coach and general manager of the Green Bay Packers. Sports Illus 26:5-6 Ja 2 '67

Green Bay rolls high; Green Bay Packers, winners of National football league championship. T. Maule. il Sports Illus 26:8-13 Ja 9 '67

Green crusher; Packers vs Colts. T. Maule. il Sports Illus 25:26-7 S 19 '66

Heated pursuit of the Packers; Colts victory kept Baltimore on the heels of the western division leader. T. Maule. il Sports Illus 25:20-5 O 31 '66

In a word, money; merger of the rival National and American football leagues. Time 88:34 Jl 29 '66

Insiders scout the Super bowl; Packers and the Chiefs. D. Meredith; J. Kemp. il Newsweek 69:83 Ja 16 '67

Is peace wonderful? merger of NFL and AFL. Sports Illus 24:10 Je 20 '66

Joe, Joe, you're the most beautiful thing in the world! Jet quarterback. J. Skow. il Sat Eve Post 239:99-103 D 3 '66

Last year for the big bonus babies. il Ebony 22:120-2+ N '66

Legal eagle and his boy scout; president and coach of Washington Redskins. R. H. Boyle. il Sports Illus 25:54-60 Jl 25 '66

Line bucks; AFL-NFL competition in contracts. il Newsweek 67:86-7 Je 6 '66

Little leaguers. il Newsweek 68:62 S 12 '66

Most likely to succeed; Dallas Cowboys. Sports Illus 25:15 N 21 '66

My son the quarterback; Miami Dolphins. il Time 88:86 N 4 '66

Not a perfect friendship; coach for Pittsburgh Steelers. T. Maule. il Sports Illus 25:36-8+ O 10 '66

$1,000,000 fumble; Packers assured Western title after J. Unitas of the Colts loses ball. T. Maule. il Sports Illus 25:34-9 D 19 '66

Poor show by the new rich; pro football rookies vs. Green Bay Packers in All-star game. D. Jenkins. il Sports Illus 25:20-1 Ag 15 '66

Private eye on the new Rams. E. Shrake. il Sports Illus 25:36-8+ O 3 '66

Pro. il Look 30:92-7 D 13 '66

Pro football forecast '66. G. Astor. il Look 30:72-3 S 6 '66

Pro football, 1966: scouting reports: National football league; American football league. T. Maule. il Sports Illus 25:52-4+ S 12 '66

Pro pecunia sunt; Green Bay Packers. il Time 88:44 D 30 '66

Quarterbacking a new industry; interview. G. Halas. il Nations Bsns 54:52-4+ D '66

Red hot Cowboys on a rampage; Dallas moves toward the NFL's eastern title. T. Maule. il Sports Illus 25:26-9 D 5 '66

Roar of the crowd; the Giants. il Time 88:35 D 23 '66

Rumors of war; grid war, NFL vs AFL. Sports Illus 24:14 My 30 '66

September's heroes on an August day. E. Asinof. il N Y Times Mag p46-7+ Ag 21 '66

Smiles of Texas are upon Clint's Cowboys; Dallas Cowboys. J. R. McDermott. il Life 61:79-80+ D 16 '66

Stop those Chiefs! NFL champions, Green Bay Packers vs. AFL champions Kansas City Chiefs in the Super bowl. T. Maule. il Sports Illus 26:10-13 Ja 16 '67

That Kansas City beef; Kansas City Chiefs. il Time 88:66 D 9 '66

They've got a winner; St Louis Cardinals. il Time 88:70 N 11 '66

Thinking man's Cowboy: coach T. Landry of Dallas. E. Linn. il Sat Eve Post 239:76-8+ D 17 '66

Underdogs with some great big ideas; Buffalo Bills hope to win AFL championship by defeating Kansas City Chiefs. E. Shrake. il Sports Illus 26:14-17 Ja 2 '67

Vikings heat up the war; Colts and Packers are virtually tied. M. Mulvoy. il Sports Illus 25:36-8+ N 14 '66

When the booing stopped; Dallas Cowboys defeat the Giants. T. Maule. il Sports Illus 25:32-5 S 26 '66

Where the boys went: college talent now in pro football leagues: table. Sports Illus 24:20-1 F 7 '66

Wild cards tame the tempest; Dallas Cowboys vs St Louis Cardinals. E. Shrake. il Sports Illus 25:32-4+ O 24 '66

Win one for the flipper; AFL's newest team: Miami Dolphins. T. C. Brody. il Sports Illus 25:24-6+ Ag 8 '66

Year of larceny in the pros; games decided by pass interceptions. T. Maule. il Sports Illus 25:38-40+ N 21 '66

See also
American football league
National football league

FOOTBALL coaches. See Physical directors
FOOTBALL fans. See Sports fans
FOOTBALL gambling. See Gambling

FOOTBALL players

All-star pro team: a prediction for '66. S. Gelman. il Esquire 66:88-90+ O '66

As the pros see them; Time's propicked All-America. il Time 88:65-6 D 9 '66

Babes in wonderland; college football. il Time 88:50-2+ O 28 '66

Bald case in point: pro football's magical immunity; the draft; with case histories. il Life 61:44-7 D 9 '66

Banning the bomb; pressure on defense. il Newsweek 68:92-5 O 31 '66

Battle of pros, violence under control. il Life 61:76-91 O 14 '66

Best and worst of the bowls. D. Jenkins. il Sports Illus 26:20-1 Ja 9 '67

Can they pack up the Packers? Kansas City Chiefs. il Life 62:66-8+ Ja 13 '67

Coaches' best. Sports Illus 25:40 N 21 '66

Fire from the ashes; Boston's Patriots lead AFL Eastern race. E. Shrake. il Sports Illus 25:18-21 D 12 '66

Firewater for some fired-up Chiefs; Kansas City Chiefs AFL champions. E. Shrake. il Sports Illus 26:14-17 Ja 9 '67

Football's week. M. Hyman. See issues of Sports illustrated published during football season

Four-legged halfbacks and friendly wolves; the Kansas City Chiefs and fans. E. Shrake. il Sports Illus 25:74+ N 28 '66

Glory, frustration and a gamut of emotions; college football coaches; photographs. Sports Illus 25:36-52+ S 19 '66

Green Bay rolls high; Green Bay Packers, winners of National football league championship. T. Maule. il Sports Illus 26:8-13 Ja 9 '67

Green crusher; Packers vs Colts. T. Maule. il Sports Illus 25:26-7 S 19 '66

If it can move, then tape it. B. Gilbert. il Sports Illus 25:38-40+ N 28 '66

Irish launch a new Ara; Notre Dame defeats Purdue. J. Underwood. il Sports Illus 25:28-31 O 3 '66

Last year for the big bonus babies. il pors Ebony 22:120-2+ N '66

Line bucks; AFL-NFL competition in contracts. il Newsweek 67:86-7 Je 6 '66

Locks vs. Boom Boom; P. Hornung and J. Taylor challenged by NFL's highest-priced rookies. D. Jenkins. il Sports Illus 25:20-3 Ag 22 '66

Look 1966 All America. G. Astor. pors Look 30:89-91 D 13 '66

Never to be the same; 1966 Silver anniversary All-America team. R. Cantwell. il Sports Illus 25:88-90+ D 19 '66

1966: year of the quarterbacks: ten tan signal callers. R. G. Hunter. il Ebony 22:39-40+ D '66

Not-so-big ten. Time 88:80+ O 14 '66

Paper lion. by G. Plimpton. Review
    Sat R 49:60-1 D 10 '66. R. L. Tobin

FOOTBALL players—*Continued*
Pro. il Look 30:92-7 D 13 '66
Pro football, 1966: scouting reports; National
football league; American football league. T.
Maule. il Sports Illus 25:52-4+ S 12 '66
Red hot Cowboys on a rampage; Dallas moves
toward the NFL's eastern title. T. Maule.
il Sports Illus 25:26-9 D 5 '66
Scholastic magazines 1965 All-American H.S.
football squad. H. L. Masin. il Sr Schol
88:28+ F 18 '66
Scouting reports; symposium. il Sports Illus
25:55-60+ S 19 '66
Smiles of Texas are upon Clint's Cowboys;
Dallas Cowboys. J. R. McDermott. il Life
61:79-80+ D 16 '66
Speaking out; colleges short-change their
football players. M Shaara. Sat Eve Post
239:10+ N 5 '66
Starr rises in the game's dominant West;
Bart Starr vs. Johnny Unitas and Packers
vs. Colts. il Sports Illus 25:25 O 31 '66
Stop those Chiefs! NFL champions, Green
Bay Packers vs. AFL champions Kansas
City Chiefs in the Super bowl. T. Maule. il
Sports Illus 26:10-13 Ja 16 '67
Streak is here; college halfbacks. D. Jenkins.
il Sports Illus 25:20-5 O 10 '66
Super All-American. H. L. Masin. il Sr Schol
87:30 Ja 14 '66; 89:24 Ja 13 '67
Supermen of Troy; Southern California beats
Texas. D. Jenkins. il Sports Illus 25:20-5
S 26 '66
Surge by the tide; unbeaten Alabama defeats
Tennessee in a thriller. J. Underwood. il
Sports Illus 25:22-7 O 24 '66
Sweet life of swinging Joe; Jet quarterback.
D. Jenkins. il Sports Illus 25:42-4+ O 17
'66
They couldn't cut old Ollie, could they?
Philadelphia Eagles. L. L. King. il Sat Eve
Post 239:107-11 O 22 '66
Thinking man's Cowboy; coach T. Landry of
Dallas. E. Linn. il Sat Eve Post 239:76-8+
D 17 '66
Underdogs with some great big ideas; Buffalo
Bills hope to win AFL championship by
defeating Kansas City Chiefs. E. Shrake. il
Sports Illus 26:14-17 Ja 2 '67
Vikings heat up the war; Colts and Packers
are virtually tied. M. Mulvoy. il Sports
Illus 25:36-8+ N 14 '66
Where the boys went; college talent now in
pro football leagues; table. Sports Illus 24:
20-1 F 7 '66
Why some All Americas don't make the
pros. G. Astor. Look 30:98 D 13 '66
Year of larceny in the pros; games decided
by pass interceptions. T. Maule. il Sports
Illus 25:38-40+ N 21 '66
    See also
Little, F.
Spurrier, S.

Recruiting
Fabulous Brodie caper; AFL plot to sign NFL
quarterbacks. E. Shrake. il Sports Illus 25:
16-21+ Ag 29 '66

Salaries
Big rookie bonuses start a battle; two San
Diego All-stars are bidding for $1 million.
E. Shrake. Sports Illus 24:44 Ja 24 '66
In a word, money; merger of the rival Na-
tional and American football leagues. Time
88:34 Jl 29 '66
Poor show by the new rich; pro football
rookies vs. Green Bay Packers in All-star
game. D. Jenkins. il Sports Illus 25:20-1
Ag 15 '66
Quid pro quo. Newsweek 67:61-2 Je 20 '66

Training
Not a perfect friendship; coach for Pittsburgh
Steelers. T. Maule. il Sports Illus 25:36-8+
O 10 '66
September's heroes on an August day. E.
Asinof. il N Y Times Mag p46-7+ Ag
21 '66
Sunday's heroes in July; paintings. B. Char-
matz. Sports Illus 25:38-43 Jl 18 '66

FOOTBALL referees. See Umpires (sports)
FOOTBALL scouting
Hunt for strong backs and strong minds;
college football, with painting by N. Rock-
well. G. Astor. Look 30:110-11 S 20 '66
Private eye on the new Rams. E. Shrake.
Sports Illus 25:36-8+ O 3 '66
Pro football, 1966: scouting reports; National
football league; American football league.
T. Maule. il Sports Illus 25:52-4+ S 12 '66
Scouting reports; symposium. il Sports Il-
lus 25:55-60+ S 19 '66

Anecdotes, facetiae, satire, etc.
Pro senior—signing scramble: Fulcourte inks
Swinburne; Appledore nabs Bronkowski.
New Yorker 42:68-9 N 12 '66
FOOTE, Timothy
Road back to Budapest. N Y Times Mag p56-
7+ N 20 '66
FOOTE, Cone and Belding, incorporated
Up the elevator. il Time 88:102 D 9 '66
FOOTHILL college, Los Altos Hills, Calif.
Landscape idea collecting. il Sunset 137:78-
81 S '66
FOOTPRINTS
    See also
Dermatoglyphics
FOOTWEAR, Rubber, plastic, etc. See Shoes,
Rubber, plastic, etc.
FOR richer, for poorer, for better, for faith;
story. See Campbell, M.
FOR the love of Stephanie; story. See Graham,
E. W.
FORAGE crops. See Forage plants
FORAGE plants
How to choose dairy forages. Suc Farm 64:
30F Ap '66
    See also
Milo
FORAMINIFERA
Foraminiferal evidence of a shallow calcium
carbonate solution boundary, Ross Sea, An-
tarctica. J. P. Kennett. bibliog il Science
153:191-3 Jl 8 '66
FORAMINIFERA, Fossil
Prehistoric seashell examined by X-ray
il(p49) Sci N 90:50 Jl 23 '66
FORAND bill. See Insurance, Health—United
States
FORBES, Jack D.
Tactics of a truce. Nation 202:229-30 F 28
'66
Ventura County: the barbarian conquest. Na-
tion 202:128+ Ja 31 '66
FORBES-ROBERTSON, Diana
Lady Knox. Am Heritage 17:46-7+ Ap '66
FORBUSH, Edward Howe
Annals of birdwatching. E. B. White. New
Yorker 42:42-6+ F 26 '66; Reply. G. T.
Hellman. 42:171-3 Ap 16 '66
FORCE (violence) See Violence
FORCE and energy
    See also
Coriolis force
FORCED air heating. See Heating
FORD, Alan, pseud.
Letter from abroad. Nat R 18:314-15 Ap 5
'66
FORD, Ann
Beauty of open shade. il por U S Camera 29:
60-1 S '66
FORD, Anne
Steering a Ford marriage. B. Walters. Ladies
Home J 83:67 S '66
FORD, Corey
Dog named Cider. Read Digest 89:77-80 S '66
Lower forty. See issues of Field & stream
October holiday. Field & S 71:42-5+ O '66
Some things I miss. Todays Health 44:26-7 S
'66
FORD, Daniel F.
Bronze stars of peace; legionnaire says no.
Nation 202:329-31 Mr 21 '66
FORD, Edsel
Hand-me-down; poem. Good H 162:224 My '66
FORD, Ford Madox
Revival of an old Ford. F. MacShane. Holi-
day 39:160+ My '66
FORD, Gena
In the eye; Another day, another alba; Nude
on the bathroom wall; Today, the world;
poems. Poetry 108:29-32 Ap '66
FORD, George. See Glickman, W. jt. auth.
FORD, Gerald R.
Republican answer to LBJ's program; inter-
view. por U S News 62:10 Ja 23 '67
State of the Union; address, January 17, 1966.
Vital Speeches 32:259-61 F 15 '66; Excerpts.
U S News 60:72-3 Ja 31 '66
What new laws Congress will pass; interview.
pors Nations Bsns 54:62+ Ja '66
    about
Dirksen-Ford rumpus; a split over war mis-
management? por U S News 60:15 My 2 '66
Majority rule. New Repub 154:4 Ap 30 '66
90th girds for battle. il por Newsweek 69:
24-7 Ja 23 '67
People of the week. U S News 60:22 Mr 7 '66
Positive thinker. T. Wicker. Atlan 217:79
Ap '66
State of the riposte. il Newsweek 67:22 Ja
31 '66

FORD, Harry
Looks of books; interview, ed. by S. Kauffmann. New Repub 155:15+ N 26 '66
FORD, Henry, 1917-
Common thread; address, May 3, 1966. Vital Speeches 32:495-8 Je 1 '66
Government and business; must they be enemies? address, January 12, 1967. por U S News 62:82-5 Ja 23 '67
Highway system; address, July 21, 1966. Vital Speeches 32:690-4 S 1 '66
More light on the auto-safety story; excerpts from address, April 15, 1966. U S News 60: 44 My 2 '66
Reduction of human misery; address, January 15, 1966. Vital Speeches 32:278-80 F 15 '66

about

Calling all cars. por Time 87:70 Ap 22 '66
Ford on our future. America 114:722-3 My 21 '66
Ford speaks his mind. Newsweek 67:71 Ap 25 '66
Henry Ford and his electronic can of worms. P. Siekman. il Fortune 73:116-19+ F '66
FORD, James L. C.
Protestant mergers. America 115:486-90 O 22 '66
FORD, Jesse Hill
Bee tree; story. Atlan 217:60-3 Ap '66
Bitter bread; story. Reporter 34:44-7 F 24 '66
Whistlin' Dixie: the southern governors in caucus. Atlan 218:80-2+ D '66
FORD, John C.
More on the council and contraception. America 114:553-7 Ap 16 '66
FORD, Maria Cristina Vettore
Cristina Ford. pors Vogue 148:220-3 O 1 '66
FORD, Paul M. and Allen, W. C.
Assignment and misassignment of teachers. NEA J 55:41-2 F '66
FORD, Walter B.
Build the crowd stopper. Pop Electr 24:48-51+ My '66
Magic motor. Pop Electr 26:68-9 Ja '67
FORD foundation
Battle line shifts on satellites; Comsat, AT&T join in opposing Ford foundation's TV plan. Bsns W p34 Ag 27 '66
ETV: Ford foundation calls for nonprofit satellite system. E. Langer. Science 153:962-4 Ag 26 '66
Ford education fund grants $486,500 to encourage reading for pleasure. Library J 91:2448 My 15 '66
Ford foundation, Comsat corp. clash over non-profit TV. Tech W 19:18 Ag 22 '66
Ford foundation outlines new proposal; broadcast non-profit satellite system. H. M. David. Tech W 19:18-19 D 19 '66
Ford foundation proposes plan for non-profit radio-TV satellites. R. D. Hibben. Aviation W 85:28-9 Ag 8 '66
Fourth network; proposal of providing for educational TV through a nonprofit corporation. J. Ridgeway. New Repub 155: 13-14 S 17 '66
People's dividend; proposal of a company for the Early bird. il Time 88:38+ Ag 12 '66
Storefront law: anatomy of a grant; Ford backed legal aid project in New Haven, Conn. il Newsweek 67:90-1 Mr 14 '66
Struck by Ford lightning; what happens to recipient colleges. B. Wallace. il Sat R 49:86-7+ Ap 16 '66
Three California brothers; School of American ballet reports on its 1964-65 national scholarship program. M. Moseley. il Dance Mag 40:32-3 Mr '66
Washington's grant to the Ford foundation; M. Bundy. M. Mayer. il N Y Times Mag p58-9+ N 13 '66
FORD motor company
Accidents will happen; possible consequence of government interference in automotive industry. Reporter 34:9 My 5 '66
Big auto sweepstakes. H. Higdon. il N Y Times Mag p36-7+ My 1 '66
Feedback from the owners; 1966 Galaxie, Impala. il Pop Mech 125:100-3+ Mr '66
Ford. E. Dahlquist. il Hot Rod 19:102-8+ N '66
Ford plugs in a mini-car; prototype electric car. Bsns W p 123 O 8 '66
Henry Ford and his electronic can of worms. P. Siekman. il Fortune 73:116-19+ F '66
Le Mans adds fuel to Ford's future. il Bsns W p34-6 Je 25 '66
Tender loving care, just for autos; proper maintenance. il Bsns W p 140-2+ S 17 '66
There's another generation of whiz kids at Ford. D. Cordtz. il Fortune 75:104-9+ Ja '67
Twenty-four hours to end them all. Le Mans. G. Borgeson. il Motor T 18:35-8+ S '66

FORD museum. See Henry Ford museum and Greenfield Village, Dearborn, Mich.
FORD observatory. See Astronomical observatories
FORDHAM university
Across borderlines; cooperative program in graduate courses of theology. Christian Cent 83:562 Ap 27 '66
Into the mainstream. il Time 89:64-5 Ja 20 '67
McLuhan appointed to Fordham's Schweitzer chair. Pub W 191:59 Ja 16 '67
FORDING, Addison H.
Finest of the finest. il por Time 87:49 F 18 '66
FORD'S theater. See Washington, D.C.—Theater
FORECASTS
Futurists: looking toward A. D. 2000; Time essay; professionals make prophecy an organized enterprise. Time 87:28-9 F 25 '66
New year is born. America 116:4 Ja 7 '67
Newsgram. See issues of U.S. news & World report
Parish, 1980. Commonweal 84:30-1 Mr 25 '66
Predictions '67. Seventeen 26:89 Ja '67
Road to 1977. M. Ways. il Fortune 75:92-5+ Ja '67
Science forecast by HHH; excerpts from address. H. H. Humphrey. Sci N 90:52 Jl 23 '66
Science forecast for 1967. Sci N 91:20-1 Ja 7 '67
'67: what kind of a year? il U S News 62:21-30+ Ja 9 '67
Washington report; concerning the report. Local school expenditures: 1970 projections. J. Lloyd. Sr Schol 88:sup7 F 4; sup8 F 11 '66

See also
Agricultural forecasts
Business forecasting
Political forecasts
Weather forecasts

Anecdotes, facetiae, satire, etc.
Art Buchwald's fearless forecasts for 1967. A. Buchwald. il Nations Bsns 55:40-1+ Ja '67
Here it comes! Nat R 19:16-17 Ja 10 '67
Well, that's what it says in my crystal ball. B. Hope. il Ladies Home J 84:14 Ja '67
FORECASTS (economics)
Awash in affluence, but what next? il Newsweek 68:70+ Jl 18 '66
Business likes '67, and LBJ; Business council's forecast. il Newsweek 68:79 O 31 '66
Cheers for Fed strategy; survey of leading financial economists. il Bsns W p83-4+ O 8 '66
Corporate view still glows; optimism, despite rising costs, tight money, and labor troubles. Bsns W p40-1 O 15 '66
Deflating the fears of a recession. il Bsns W p 122-4+ O 22 '66
Flaw in the new economics. W. F. Butler. il Duns R 88:41-2+ O '66
For most companies: spending as usual; in wake of tax credit suspension. Bsns W p61-2+ O 1 '66
Forecast for 1967, no pause in the expansion; Wharton school's computer prediction. il Bsns W p36-7 D 3 '66
Forecasters get a new crystal ball. il Bsns W p 124+ My 21 '66
Forecasting made easy? input-output table. Sr Schol 89:8 D 9 '66
Good business ahead for western Europe; outlook for '67. il Bsns W p54-6 D 31 '66
Growth till '70; Europe's size-up. il U S News 61:90 N 21 '66
How 1966 probably will unfold. il Bsns W p 104-6 Ja 29 '66
In Orient, Americas: both ups and downs; outlook for '67. il Bsns W p56-7 D 31 '66
Japan: a brisker pace in bar and board room. il Bsns W p 198 S 10 '66
Lifting the haze from the future; Clopper Almon's input-output models. il Bsns W p 100-2 D 17 '66
1967: how it looks from here. il Newsweek 68:79-80 O 17 '66
No time for stalling on taxes. Bsns W p 180 My 7 '66
Outlook for 1967. R. Hotz. Aviation W 86:11 Ja 2 '67
Plenty of zip for the economy; Wharton school's econometric model prediction; with editorial comment. il Bsns W p53-4+, 160 S 3 '66
Prediction for 1966: more boom. Sr Schol 88:18 F 4 '66
'67 balancing trick. il Bsns W p 13-15 D 31 '66
Steam to spare in the economy. il Bsns W p39-40 My 21 '66

FORECASTS (economics)—*Continued*
Technological developments: the economic impact five years hence; address, May 11, 1966. P. Neff. Vital Speeches 32:543-4 Je 15 '66
U.S. business trims its expansion sails; survey of business plan released by the Commerce dept. and the Securities & exchange commission. il Bsns W p38 D 10 '66
Washington: a look ahead. See issues of Nation's business
See also
Business forecasting
FOREIGN aid. See Economic assistance, American
FOREIGN automobiles. See Automobiles, Foreign
FOREIGN bodies (surgery)
Forty soldiers survive missiles in the heart. Sci N 89:453 Je 4 '66
Kids will swallow anything. J. Carper. il Todays Health 45:22-5 Ja '67
FOREIGN born. See Immigrants in the United States
FOREIGN cookery. See Cookery, International
FOREIGN correspondents
Caviar and unhappenings; covering de Gaulle's tour. R. J. Korengold. il Newsweek 68:81-2 Jl 11 '66
Covering the Moscow beat. S. Ramsey. Sat R 49:72-3+ S 10 '66
Covering the Red guards; reporting by D. Oancia of the Toronto globe and mail. Newsweek 69:101 Ja 23 '67
Sardonic man in Moscow; H. Rudd. il Time 87:69 My 27 '66
FOREIGN exchange
Moscow's stores that keep Ivan out; dollar shops. il Bsns W p96-8 N 5 '66
P.L. 480 currencies available for sale to U.S. tourists; Guinea, Tunisia, Ceylon. Dept State Bul 54:975 Je 20 '66
U.S. citizens visiting Pakistan may purchase U.S.-owned rupees. Dept State Bul 55:756 N 14 '66
See also
Currency convertibility
FOREIGN expansion of business. See Business—Foreign expansion
FOREIGN investments. See Investments, Foreign
FOREIGN investments in the United States. See Investments, Foreign (in United States)
FOREIGN languages. See Languages, Modern
FOREIGN missions. See Missions
FOREIGN opinion of the United States. See United States—Foreign opinion
FOREIGN relations, Senate committee on. See United States—Congress—Senate—Foreign relations committee.
FOREIGN scholarships, Board of. See United States—State, Department of—Foreign scholarships, Board of
FOREIGN securities. See Investments, Foreign
FOREIGN service (United States) See United States—Foreign service
FOREIGN service institute. See United States—Foreign service institute
FOREIGN students in Brazil
Innocents abroad. P. Dursin. il Seventeen 25:146-7+ Mr '66
FOREIGN students in Europe
Europe for adventurous students. R. Tillinghast. il Holiday 41:133-40 Ja '67
FOREIGN students in Great Britain
See also
Rhodes scholars and scholarships
FOREIGN students in Greece
Golden year for U.S. youth in Athens. V. Voss. il Mlle 62:166-7+ F '66
FOREIGN students in Russia
American in Moscow. T. T. Hammond. il Nat Geog Mag 129:297-351 Mr '66
Comic opera of accusation and counteraccusation as schism widens; Chinese students' injuries after U.S. embassy demonstrations. il Life 60:34-5 Ap 8 '66
March on the Kremlin by Chinese kick-outs; last Chinese students evicted. il Life 61:48 N 11 '66
FOREIGN students in Scandinavia
Fiskites win travel-study scholarships to Scandinavia. il Negro Hist Bul 29:94-6 Ja '66
Going native, without culture shock: study, adventure in Scandinavia. J. Steinberg. Mlle 64:62 N '66
International vacation study course in Scandinavia; report. C. A. Lee. Negro Hist Bul 29:108 F '66

FOREIGN students in the United States
Bonjour, Midwest; account of a young French Fulbright scholar's year as an American coed. G. M. Levy. Mlle 64:143+ N '66
Problem with non-Puerto Ricans. F. A. Pico. America 115:114-15 Jl 30 '66
FOREIGN study
College study abroad; junior year D. Klein. Seventeen 25:90+ O '66
Why study abroad pays off; with lists of programs and organizations to contact. R. T. Stavig. il Sat R 49:82+ F 19 '66
FOREIGN subsidiaries. See Corporations—Foreign subsidiaries
FOREIGN teachers in the United States
Teachers from abroad take a look at America. R. W. Lykes. il Am Ed 2:14-19 S '66
FOREIGN trade. See Commerce; also subhead Commerce under names of countries, e.g. Mexico—Commerce
FOREIGN visitors in China
Canadian look at the church in China. H. G. Green. Christian Cent 83:1038-40 Ag 24 '66
Chinese-Soviet gap widens. H. Portisch. il Sat R 49:8-12 Jl 2 '66
Eyewitness in red China; excerpt from Red China today. H. Portisch. il Sat R 49:14-21+ Ap 30 '66; Reply with rejoinder. H. L. Keeenleyside. 49:31 Je 4 '66
Hanoi's feuding friends. M. Omori. New Repub 155:9-10 O 15 '66
I saw red China, by L. Hobbs. Review
Sat R il 49:39-40 Mr 26 '66. W. Hangen
Journey through China. F. Sully. il Newsweek 67:54-8 Je 13 '66
Love and hate in China, by H. Koningsberger. Review
Sat R 49:52 Jl 23 '66. D. Dodge
No fun for tired businessmen. Bsns W p84 S 24 '66
Over pots of tea; excerpts from a diary of a visit to China. M. Oliphant. Bul Atomic Sci 22:36-43 My '66
Through darkest red China. A. R. Topping. il N Y Times Mag p26-7+ Ag 28 '66
When China wakes, by R. Guillain. Review
Sat R 49:25 Ag 20 '66. W. Hangen
FOREIGN visitors in Colombia
Journey in darkness. I. Kovacs. il Reporter 35:46-9 O 20 '66
FOREIGN visitors in Cuba
American in Cuba. E. R. John. il Nation 202:296-9, 327-9 Mr 14-21 '66
FOREIGN visitors in Denmark
At home with the Danes. H. Sutton. il Sat R 49:40-1 Ag 13 '66
Cold weather, warm hearts; Negro youngsters find brotherhood in Sweden, Denmark. C. L. Sanders. il Ebony 21:27-30+ Ap '66
FOREIGN visitors in Eastern Europe
Religion behind the iron curtain. Sister Dolorosa. America 114:626-7 Ap 30 '66
FOREIGN visitors in England
Letter from abroad; American woman in an English-university community. D. Trilling. il McCalls 93:36+ Jl '66
Teen travel talk; living with a host family this summer il Seventeen 25:212+ Ap '66
We four teens in London town; report on the making of A man for all seasons; ed. by E. Miller. C. Crawford. il Seventeen 26:80-1+ Ja '67
FOREIGN visitors in Europe
Historical view of Americans abroad. F. R. Dulles. Ann Am Acad 368:11-20 N '66
No holiday for guides. Bsns W p46 Je 11 '66
FOREIGN visitors in Finland
Innocents abroad. S. Peter. il Seventeen 25:146-7+ Mr '66
FOREIGN visitors in France
France is mad for. . . Jerry Lewis? H. Alpert. il N Y Times Mag p28-9+ F 27 '66
FOREIGN visitors in Greece
Greece and me; visit to relatives by third generation Greek-American. P. Ellis. il Seventeen 26:102-3 Ja '67
Vacancies of August; letter from the Greek islands. J. Thompson. Commentary 42:41-51 N '66
FOREIGN visitors in India
Fragments from an Oriental odyssey. H. Sutton. Sat R 49:39+ My 21 '66
FOREIGN visitors in Indonesia
Breakfast with Sukarno. D. Smith. il Nation 202:553-5 My 9 '66
FOREIGN visitors in Japan
Eastward ho! H. Sutton. il Sat R 49:49-50 Mr 26 '66
FOREIGN visitors in Jordan
Incident in Jerusalem. D. Wakefield. Commentary 41:49-55 F '66
FOREIGN visitors in Mexico
In people discover, Acapulco. T. Meehan. il N Y Times Mag p38-9+ F 13 '66
Teen travel talk; living with a host family this summer. il Seventeen 25:212+ Ap '66

FOREIGN visitors in Poland
Encounter in Warsaw; help from pocketful of Kennedy half-dollars. F. Russell. Nat R 18:430-2 My 3 '66
With Stravinsky in Warsaw; excerpt from Table talk. R. Craft. Harper 232:66-70+ F '66
Young, surprised, and hungry in Warsaw; French students' tour. M. Worth. Vogue 148:162 S 1 '66

FOREIGN visitors in Rhodesia
How do you like Africa, white man, is it like New York? excerpt from An African season. L. Levitt. Harper 234:82-8 Ja '67

FOREIGN visitors in Russia
Behind the hair curtain; visitors mail. H. B. Jacobs. Sat R 49:6+ O 8 '66
Eagles of Kazakhstan. E. S. Staples. Atlan 219:92-5 Ja '67
Expensive caper; Americans arrested for violating currency regulations. il Newsweek 69:28 Ja 2 '67
$500 misunderstanding. M. Levin. Sat R 49:58+ S 24 '66
Moscow; life is easier, for visitors. Bsns W p 144 Jl 23 '66
Of many things; unofficial, fact-finding mission. T. N. Davis. America 114:inside cover F 5 '66
Religion in the Soviet Union. T. N. Davis and E. K. Culhane. America 114:252-5+ F 19 '66
Soviet tourist traps; KGB's interest in foreign tourists. L. M. Taubinger. Nat R 18:575 Je 14 '66
Want to change dollars? American tourists arrested for black-market dealings in Russia. il Time 88:22 D 30 '66

FOREIGN visitors in Scandinavia
English as spoken in Scandinavia. T. Pratt. il Atlan 217:122-3 Je '66

FOREIGN visitors in South Africa
How do you like Africa, white man, is it like New York? excerpt from An African season. L. Levitt. Harper 234:82-8 Ja '67

FOREIGN visitors in Sweden
Cold weather, warm hearts; Negro youngsters find brotherhood in Sweden, Denmark. C. L. Sanders. il Ebony 21:27-30+ Ap '66
Wonderful trip to see the king; Chicago Negro student's Swedish tour. il Life 60:18-25 Ja 28 '66

FOREIGN visitors in Taiwan
Typhoons and taxes; Sand pebbles location troubles. il Newsweek 67:98+ My 9 '66

FOREIGN visitors in the Caribbean Region
Teen travel talk; Caribbean cruise for Camp fire girls il Seventeen 25:40 O '66

FOREIGN visitors in the Far East
Eastward ho! H. Sutton. il Sat R 49:49-50 Mr 26; 46-8 Ap 2 '66

FOREIGN visitors in the United States
America and the foreign visitor; symposium. il Sat R 49:49-52+ Mr 12 '66
An Animal views America. E. Burdon. il Ebony 22:160-2+ D '66
Foreign visitors. il NEA J 55:33 Mr '66
Foreigner discovers America and vice versa; Time essay. Time 88:33 Ag 26 '66
Last word; what visitors liked and disliked; findings of a spot survey. Sat R 49:100 Mr 12 '66
Trip to wonderland; fourteen Colombian boys visit Rockville Centre, N.Y. il Am City 81:166+ Ap '66

FOREIGN visitors in Vietnam (Democratic Republic)
AFP's man in Hanoi; experiences of J. Raffaelli. il Newsweek 68:54 Ag 15 '66
Citizen diplomacy; Lynd-Hayden-Aptheker mission. Nation 202:87 Ja 24 '66
Mission of Staughton Lynd. W. F. Buckley, jr. Nat R 18:105 F 8 '66
Spokesman for the new left. J. Corry. il N Y Times Mag p 12-13+ Ja 23 '66

FOREIGN visitors in Vietnam (Republic)
Cam Ne fund; visit of Mrs Janet Stark. N. Cousins. Sat R 49:25 My 14 '66
Campaigners; U.S. pacifist's expelled. il Newsweek 67:25 My 2 '66
Rosy view; Komer report; Washington pressure, field reactions. Newsweek 68:54+ O 3 '66
Six from Saigon. W. C. Davidon. New Repub 154:39-40 My 21 '66
View of Vietnam. E. J. Hughes. Newsweek 67:22-3 My 30 '66

FOREMAN, Percy
His lifetime record, won: 700, lost: 1. M. Smith. il pors Life 60:92-4+ Ap 1 '66
Mesmerism in Miami. por Time 87:66 Mr 18 '66

FOREMEN
Which way for the foremen? L. Stessin. il Duns R 87:45+ Ap '66

FORENSIC medicine. See Medical jurisprudence

FORENSIC psychiatry
Mental health trap; R. Simpson case. T. E. Schulz. Nat R 18:510-12+ My 31 '66
Psychiatric justice, by T. S. Szasz. Review Nat R 18:323-4 Ap 5 '66. R. J. Gerstung
Psychiatric law challenged. P. McBroom. Sci N 89:385 My 21 '66
Violence not surprising. Sci N 90:68 Jl 30 '66

FORER, Arthur. See Behnke, O. jt. auth.

FOREST conservation
But it's got to come out. C. Stephens. il Am For 72:44-5+ My '66
Forestry, conservation, and ecology. N. Simmons. Am For 72:47 Jl '66
See also
Forest fire protection

Study and teaching
Workshop in the woods, 31 centuries! Trees for tomorrow camp, Eagle River, Wis. with comments of the participants. K. B. Pomeroy. il Am For 72:16-21+ O '66

FOREST fire patrol, Aerial
Alaska smokejumper. N. Newman. il Field & S 71:60-2 Je '66

FOREST fire protection
Here comes the Fire bike brigade! H. E. McLean. il Am For 72:4-5 O '66
Keeping America green. R. M. Olzendam. Am For 72:8-11 Je '66
What to do in a forest fire. E. Crimmin. il Sci Digest 60:58-61 S '66
See also
Forest fire patrol, Aerial
Southern forest fire prevention conference

FOREST fires
Carolina blow-up; Palm Sunday, 1966. K. A. Argow. il Am For 72:14-17+ Jl '66
Fiery arc; series of fires in Alaska. il Time 88:24 S 9 '66
Lightning as a sculptor of life; E. V. Komarek's and other theories on value of controlled fires. J. Lear. il Sat R 49:57-62 Je 4 '66
When the South marched! efforts of southern states to reduce timber losses caused by forest fires. J. E. Mixon and J. H. Kitchens, jr. il Am For 72:36-41 Mr '66
See also
Forest fire patrol, Aerial

FOREST genetics
See also
Institute of forest genetics

FOREST GROVE, Ore.
We went underground to find beauty. H. Sherman. il Am City 81:126+ Ag '66

FOREST Lawn memorial park. See Los Angeles—Cemeteries

FOREST management
Forest riddle of New York. H. Kernan. il Am For 72:21 S '66
Quiet revolution; Montesano tree farm program. W. B. Morse. il Am For 72:6-9+ Jl '66
Report from Montesano. A. B. Langlie. Am For 72:6 Jl '66
Time, fire, and taxes. Am For 72:4-5 +Je '66
Trees to sell? see a forester. J. E. Moore. il Am For 72:20-7 Mr '66

FOREST OF NISENE MARKS STATE PARK. See California—Parks and reserves

FOREST planting
See also
Reforestation
Tree planting

FOREST products
Expert group on forest products meets in Geneva. UN Mo Chron 3:56-7 N '66
See also
American forest products industries, incorporated

FOREST reserves. See Forestry research; National forests

FOREST service (United States) See United States—Forest service

FOREST workers. See Foresters

FORESTATION. See Reforestation

FORESTER, C. S.
Hornblower during the crisis; story. Sat Eve Post 239:50-2 Jl 16; 40-5 Jl 30 '66

about
Obituary
Pub W 189:33-4 Ap 11 '66
Rights and permissions; unfinished novel to be in Saturday evening post. P. Nathan. Pub W 189:220 Je 6 '66

FORESTERS
Dana years; interview, ed. by E. R. Maunder and A. Fry. S. T. Dana. il Am For 72:32-5+ N: 26-9+ D '66
Dear John; excerpts from address, March 5, 1966. R. C. Wible. Am For 72:15+ Je '66
Trees to sell? see a forester. J. E. Moore. il Am For 72:20-7 Mr '66

FORESTRY congress, World. See World forestry congress

FORESTRY conservation workshop. See Forest conservation—Study and teaching

FORESTRY research
Whitaker's forest. G. B. Larson. il Am For 72:22-5+ S '66
See also
Institute of forest genetics

FORESTRY schools and education
School for tomorrow; Summer forestry school workshop to be conducted at Trees for tomorrow, inc, Eagle River, Wisc. Am For 72:11 Ja '66

FORESTRY societies
See also
New York forest owners association, incorporated

FORESTS, National. See National forests

FORESTS, Petrified. See Petrified forests

FORESTS, Private. See Forest management

FORESTS, State
Battle for wilderness in New York state's forest preserve; with editorial comment. D. L. Newhouse. il Liv Wildn 30:2+, 11-19 Sum '66
New York's constitutional convention. Liv Wildn 30:31 Sum '66

FORESTS, Tropical. See Forests and forestry—Tropics

FORESTS and forestry
See also
Lumbering
Tree breeding
Trees
World forestry congress

History
Distant end; excerpts from Trail blazers. E. A. Mason. Am For 72:25+ Jl '66

International aspects
Big five: problem areas in world forestry; biennial conference of Food and agriculture organization of the United Nations. H. Clepper. il Am For 72:18-21+ Ja '66

Study and teaching
See also
Forestry schools and education

California
Whitaker's forest. G. B. Larson. il Am For 72:22-5+ S '66

Costa Rica
Wild tropical forest in Costa Rica. Liv Wildn 29:38 Aut '65

Israel
Israel, land of milk and honey. A. Hamilton. il Am For 71:20-4+ O '65

Nebraska
Forest that men made: Nebraska national forest. J. C. Hunt. il Am For 71:18-21+ N; 32-5+ D '65; Correction. 72:3 Ja '66

New York (state)
Forest riddle of New York. H. Kernan. il Am For 72:21 S '66; Reply. D. H. Hanaburgh. 72:8 D '66

Oregon
Twenty days in June, the cautious war; tussock moth. H. E. McLean. il Am For 72:28-31+ Mr '66

Portugal
Portugal's pines: pinus pinaster, or maritime pine. C. E. Randall. il Am For 71:32-5+ O '65

Tropics
Wild Tropical forest in Costa Rica. Liv Wildn 29:38 Aut '65

United States
Dana years: interview, ed. by E. R. Maunder and A. Fry. S. T. Dana. il Am For 72:32-5+ N; 26-9+ D '66
Dear John; excerpts from address, March 5, 1966. R. C. Wible. Am For 72:15+ Je '66
Forestry in the federal budget. il Am For 72:48 Mr '66
Sounding board (cont) Am For 71:40 O '65; 72:38 F; 42-3 My; 42-3 Je; 54 Jl; 36 S '66
Sounding board (cont) il Am For 71:40 O '65; 72:38 F; 42-3 My; 42-3 Je; 54 Jl; 36 S; 32-3 D '66
Washington lookout. A. G. Hall. See issues of American forests
See also
Forest conservation
National forests
United States—Forest service

FORGACS, Joseph, and Carll, W. T.
Mycotoxicoses: toxic fungi in tobaccos. Science 152:1634-5 Je 17 '66

FORGERY
See also
Counterfeits and counterfeiting
Documents, Fraudulent
Literary forgeries and mystifications

FORGETTING. See Memory

FORGIVENESS
Forgiving community. by W. Klassen. Review
Christian Cent 83:808 Je 22 '66. J. G. Emerson, jr
Office of the keys. Christian Cent 83:227 F 23 '66

FORM, Dramatic. See Drama—Technique

FORMAN, Frederick, and Nawracaj, Edward
Build: solid-state scope calibrator. Pop Electr 24:61-4 Je '66

FORMAN, Milos
Andula's dream. il Newsweek 68:110D+ S 19 '66
Watch out for the hook, my friend. A. Levy. il pors Life 62:77-8+ Ja 20 '67

FORMATES
Rat mammary gland RNA: incorporation of C^{14}-formate and effect of hormones and 7, 12-dimethylbenzanthracene. P. R. Libby and T. L. Dao. bibliog il Science 153:303-5 Jl 15 '66

FORMOSA. See Taiwan

FORMS of address
Once and future governor? Christian Cent 83:1323 O 26 '66

FORMULA Vee cars. See Automobiles, Racing

FORMYLMETHIONINE. See Methionine

FORNEY, James S.
Guide to spot-meters. Pop Phot 58:74-5+ Ap '66

FORRESTER, Donal F.
New books; Cath World 204:189-90 D '66

FORRESTER, Maureen
Singing for the sky; interview. por Opera N 31:19 O 15 '66
about
Something to go home to. il por Time 88:54 O 7 '66

FORSTER, Arnold
Birchism at the grass roots. Nation 203:73-6 Jl 25 '66
Violence on the fanatical left and right. bibliog f Ann Am Acad 364:141-8 Mr '66
about
Whose hand to shake? W. F. Buckley, jr. Nat R 18:352 Ap 19 '66

FORSTER, Edward Morgan
Cave and the mountain, by W. Stone. Review
Cath World 203:373-4 S '66. D. Leary
Reporter 34:54+ Mr 24 '66. S. Rama Rau
Sat R 49:43 Mr 5 '66. K. Natwar-Singh

FORSTER, R. P. and Goldstein, Leon
Urea synthesis in the lungfish; relative importance of purine and ornithine cycle pathways. bibliog Science 153:1650-2 S 30 '66

FORSYTHE, Charles, family
Aftermath of a tornado; Palm Sunday tornadoes, Elkhart County, Ind. M. Cohen. il Redbook 127:64-5+ O '66

FORSYTHIAS
February's forsythia time. il Sunset 136:202 F '66

FORT, Alan P.
Rope-ladder rafting. Yachting 119:238-9 Mr '66

FORT BENNING, Ga.
Helluva way to grow up fast: paratrooper. C. S. Wren. il Look 30:73-7 S 20 '66

FORT DIX. See Military training camps

FORT LAUDERDALE, Fla.

Description
Hello dere! M. M. Davis. il Travel 126: 59:62 S '66

Sanitary affairs
Change the landscape to sell the incinerator. J. Lewis. Am City 81:26 Jl '66

Water supply
Construct the critical units first. C. S. McKinney. il Am City 81:112-13 My '66

FORT LEONARD WOOD, Mo. See Military training camps

FORT POLK, La. See Military training camps

FORT WORTH, Tex.
PR behind the yes; bond referendum. il Am City 81:136+ Mr '66

FORT WORTH, Tex.—*Continued*
City planning
Headache-free subdivision review. il Am City 81:109 S '66
Galleries and museums
Great Assyrian affair; Kimbell museum feud over Nimrud reliefs with Los Angeles County museum. il Time 87:66 Mr 25 '66
Music
Fort Worth. J. Rosenfield. Opera N 30:29 Ap 16 '66
Police department
Inside the lie box; lie-detector tests for any suspect who requests one. il Time 88:70 N 4 '66
Theater
Cultural center with new ideas; William Edrington Scott theater. H. Hewes. Sat R 49:53 F 19 '66
FORT WORTH opera association
Fort Worth. J. Rosenfield. il Opera N 30:30 F 19; 31 Mr 26; 28 Je 4 '66
Fort Worth: Madama Butterfly. J. Ardoin. Opera N 31:30 D 31 '66
FORTAS, Abe
New-type liberal on the High court? por U S News 61:14 Jl 4 '66
FORTES, Joe
Memorial to Joe Fortes. J. Bellinger. il por Negro Hist Bul 29:168 Ap '66
FORTIFICATION
Fortresses of the past. E. C. Uriburu. il Américas 18:33-6 My '66
FORTRAN. See Programming languages (computers)
FORTRESSES. See Fortification
FORTS. See Fortification
FORTUNE (periodical)
Ten buildings that climax an era; current selections for the ten best buildings. D. Haskell. il Fortune 74:156-62 D '66
FORTUNE telling
Back in with the black arts. il Time 88:24-5 D 30 '66
Letter from Paris; new year predictions by some of France's female fortune-tellers. Genêt. New Yorker 42:109-10 Ja 14 '67
Your life is in the cards. D. Powills. il Hobbies 71:126-7+ Ja '67
See also
Astrology
FORUMS (discussion and debate)
Protest, a right and a responsibility; round table discussion from 1966 student burgesses at Williamsburg. il Sr Schol 88:10-13+ My 6 '66
Talk-in on Vietnam; New York intellectuals meet with Prof. Schlesinger. il N Y Times Mag p 12-13+ F 6 '66
See also
American assembly
FOSBURGH, James Whitney
Discovering the world of art. Parents Mag 40:44-6+ bibliog(p86) Je '66
FOSDICK, Ellery R.
Pollution of man's environment. Nat Parks Mag 40:16-20 S '66
Report on present status of a new simple low-cost coal sewage treatment. Nat Parks Mag 40:18-19 Ap '66
FOSDICK, Harry Emerson
Whose God is dead? interview. ed. by N. R. Campion. por Read Digest 89:67-71 O '66
FOSKETT, Daphne
Miniatures by John Smart. Antiques 90:354-7 S '66
FOSS, Joseph Jacob
Aced out. Time 87:74 Ap 15 '66
After Foss: a hotter pro war. E. Shrake. por Sports Illus 24:44-5 Ap 18 '66
FOSSIL algae. See Algae, Fossil
FOSSIL bison. See Bison, Fossil
FOSSIL bones. See Paleontology
FOSSIL brachiopods. See Brachiopods, Fossil
FOSSIL BUTTE NATIONAL MONUMENT (proposed) See National monuments
FOSSIL corals. See Corals, Fossil
FOSSIL fishes. See Fishes, Fossil
FOSSIL foraminifera. See Foraminifera, Fossil
FOSSIL man. See Man, Prehistoric
FOSSIL microorganisms. See Micropaleontology
FOSTER, G. W. Jr
Who pulled the teeth from Title VI? por Sat R 49:88 Ap 16 '66
FOSTER, Gertrude B.
Herbs. Horticulture 44:22-5 O '66

FOSTER, Irene
Butter the size of a walnut. Writer 79:23-5 D '66
FOSTER, John Stuart, 1922-
Research for Vietnam; excerpts from testimony, 1966. Aviation W 84:21 Mr 21 '66
FOSTER, Martha Standing
One pin and a fish-hook. Writer 79:9-12+ Ap '66
FOSTER, Paul
Recluse. Criticism
Nation 202:405-6 Ap 4 '66
FOSTER, Phil
With a comic to the Catskills; interview. New Yorker 42:30-1 Je 11 '66
FOSTER, William C.
Arms control: a serious business; address, June 20, 1966. Dept State Bul 55:50-5 Jl 11 '66
Arms control; address, November 23, 1965. Vital Speeches 32:199-202 Ja 15 '66
Comprehensive test ban treaty strongly recommended by U.S: statements November 25-26, 1965. Dept State Bul 54:99-103 Ja 17 '66
Denuclearization of Africa: statement, December 1, 1965. Dept State Bul 54:103-5 Ja 17 '66
U.N. reaffirms principles for negotiating nonproliferation treaty; calls for conference of non-nuclear-weapon states; statement, November 9, 1966. Dept State Bul 55:930-5 D 19 '66
U.S. discusses proposed safeguards for cutoff and transfer of fissionable material and nuclear weapons destruction; statement, April 14, 1966. Dept State Bul 54:901-6 Je 6 '66
U.S. proposes seven-point program for disarmament at Geneva; statement, January 26, 1966. Dept State Bul 54:262 F 21 '66
United States reviews position on non-proliferation of nuclear weapons; statement, November 2, 1966. Dept State Bul 55:901-2 D 12 '66
FOSTER day care
One city that cares, enough to make every mother's day care dream come true; Houston day-care centers. J. Robbins and J. Robbins. Ladies Home J 83:71+ Jl '66
One woman can make the difference: a blueprint for day care action. G. Gibson. il Ladies Home J 83:62+ S '66
Perfect day-care home for Tommy. C. Painter. il Ladies Home J 83:72+ O '66
Who is sabotaging day care for our children? B. H. Bagdikian. Ladies Home J 83:86+ N '66
FOSTER grandparents program
Grandparents for the asking. E. Margolis. il Parents Mag 41:60-1+ D '66
FOSTER home care
Man with 8000 miracles; Glenn Cunningham youth ranch, inc. V. Pizer. il Read Digest 88:112-16 F '66
FOTHERINGHAM, Hamish
International youth library. Library J 91:5704-5 N 15 '66
FOUJITA, Tsugouharu
Wild man of Wisteria. por Time 88:76 O 28 '66
FOULKE, Adrienne
(tr) See Robbe-Grillet, A. Istanbul: city tinged with blood and gold
(tr) See Senghor. L. S. Hidden force of black African art
FOULKES, David. See Pivik, T. jt. auth.
FOUNDATION garments
Thinmanship; slenderizing underwear for men. Newsweek 69:40 Ja 9 '67
FOUNDATION planting. See Shrubs
FOUNDATIONS, Charitable and educational
American way of giving. il Newsweek 67:87-92 Mr 14 '66
Attention foundations and university presses: here is a new way of getting those deletions back. D. Hall. Am Rec G 32:944-5+ Je '66
Chair for Hoover; plans for J. Edgar Hoover foundation. Nation 203:629 D 12 '66
Contemporary opera and the foundations; a plea to support recording of operas. Hi Fi 16:39 Je '66
Contests, foundations, awards, domestic and foreign. Hi Fi 16:248-51 D 15 '66
First great cheerful giver; G. Peabody. G. T. Hellman. il Am Heritage 17:28-33+ Je '66
Foundation pipe lines: the beneficent CIA; funneling money to shape foreign policy; Group research findings. R. G. Sherrill. Nation 202:542-4+ My 9 '66
Foundations in blinders: cool billions; need for wider programs. T. C. Reeves. il Nation 202:381-5 Ap 4 '66

FOUNDATIONS, Charitable and educational
    —Continued
Infinity of options; expanding fields. Time
    87:74 Mr 18 '66
Mephisto's musings; music foundations. Hi
    Fi 16:MA2+ Jl '66
        See also names of foundations, e.g. Ford
        foundation
FOUNDING fathers. See Great men
FOUNDRIES
            Wages and hours
Earnings in nonferrous foundries in June-
    July 1965. J. C. Bush. il Mo Labor R 89:
    653-5 Je '66
FOUNDRY practice
        See also
Continuous casting
Die casting
FOUNTAIN, Colo.
Rubber membrane seals leaking tanks. il Am
    City 81:33 D '66
FOUNTAIN cafe. See New York (city)—Hotels,
    restaurants, etc.
FOUNTAINS
Fountains: New York city. New Yorker 42:
    17-19 Jl 9 '66
Greater design freedom for decorative foun-
    tains. R. E. DeCew. il Arch Rec 140:141-4
    Ag '66
        See also
Garden pools
FOUR o'clocks
Four o'clocks are a perennial favorite. K.
    Geesaman. Flower Grower 53:42 D '66
FOUR wheel drive automobiles. See Automo-
    biles—Four wheel drive
FOUR-wheel-drive Grand prix. See Motor
    vehicle racing
FOURIER series. See Harmonic analysis
FOURNIER, Robert O.
North Atlantic deep-sea fertility. bibliog
    Science 153:1250-2 S 9 '66
FOURTEENTH amendment. See United States
    —Constitution—Amendments
FOURTH amendment to the Constitution. See
    United States—Constitution—Bill of rights
FOURTH committee of the General assembly.
    See United Nations—Trusteeship commit-
    tee
FOURTH of July
Joyous sound of freedom; celebrating Inde-
    pendence day by ringing of bells. T. J.
    Fleming. il Read Digest 88:19-20+ Je '66
Old-fashioned skyrocketing Fourth; Mountain
    View, Calif. D. Gale. il Parks & Rec 1:
    551-2 Jl '66
FOURTH Sarah; story. See Block, L.
FOWLER, Audree V. and Zabin, Irving
Co-linearity of β-galactosidase with its gene
    by immunological detection of incomplete
    polypeptide chains. bibliog Science 154:1027-
    9 N 25 '66
FOWLER, Dona J. and Goodnight, C. J.
Neurosecretory cells; daily rhythmicity in
    leiobunum longipes. bibliog Science 152:
    1078-80 My 20 '66
FOWLER, E. W.
Measure your fire department by men, not
    equipment. Am City 81:132+ D '66
FOWLER, Henry Hamill
Substantial improvement achieved in balance
    of payments in 1965; statement, February
    14, 1966. Dept State Bul 54:398-400 Mr 14
    '66
Toward a more rational world economic
    order; texts of statements, September 28,
    29, 1966. Dept State Bul 55:626-33 O 24 '66
        about
As the new tax picture rounds into shape.
    por U S News 61:112+ S 26 '66
Tax credit that business may lose. por U S
    News 60:102+ My 9 '66
FOWLER, Robert G.
Imitation milk gets a foothold. Farm J 90:
    64 O '66
FOWLER, T. K. and Post, R. F.
Progress toward fusion power; with bio-
    graphical sketches. Sci Am 215:16, 21-31
    bibliog(p 154) D '66
FOWLES, John
Collector; adaptation. See Roche, F. L'obsédé
Trouble with starlets. Holiday 39:12+ Je '66
FOWLIE, Wallace
French chronicle. Poetry 107:267-70 Ja '66
FOWLING
        See also
Falconry
FOX, Bernie. See McConnaughy, M. J. jt.
    auth.
FOX, Charles K.
Pure water is basic. Esquire 66:48+ O '66
FOX, Douglas A.
Sound, candid. Christian Cent 83:1342-3 N
    2 '66

FOX, Edward Whiting
Tragic victory of Charles de Gaulle. Cur Hist
    50:201-8+ Ap '66
FOX, Jonathan
Europe, under their own steam; excerpts
    from Europe à go-go: life and love abroad
    a student ship. Mlle 63:122-3+ Je '66
FOX, Marvin
Subjective faith. Commentary 41:88+ F; 26
    Je '66
FOX, R. R. and others
Intravenous injection of thalidomide in preg-
    nant rabbits. bibliog Science 153:310-11 Jl
    15 '66
FOX, Ruth
Viper's bugloss; poem. New Yorker 42:138
    Ap 16 '66
FOX, Sanford J.
Constructive look at destruction. Sat R 49:
    40-1 N 19 '66
FOX, William Price, Jr
Lost art of moonshine. Sat Eve Post 239:34-
    5 Mr 26 '66
Room 306 doesn't tip! Holiday 40:78-81+ D
    '66
FOX hunting
Fire Island fox hunt. N. Karas. il Field & S
    71:48-9 Ja '67
Fox went out on a chilly night. L. Dietz.
    il Field & S 71:48-50+ My '66
Long Tom. D. J. Anderson. il Field & S 70:38-
    40+ F '66
Merry chase; hunts in the British Isles. il
    Time 88:37-8 N 11 '66
They don't yell yoicks! in New Jersey. B.
    Lefferts. il N Y Times Mag p52-3+ D 4 '66
FOXES
Ghost of the North; Arctic fox. W. O. Pruitt,
    jr. il Audubon Mag 68:470-1 N '66
State vs. the Predator; case history; South
    Dakota. G. Charles. il Audubon Mag 68:436-
    42 N '66
        See also
Fox hunting
FOXHOUNDS
Aging gun dog. G. B. Evans. il Field & S
    71:146-7+ N '66
FOXWORTH, Jo
Our creeping idiot savantism; address, June
    12, 1966. Vital Speeches 32:596-9 Jl 15 '66
FOYERS. See Halls
FRACTIONATION. See Separation (technology)
FRACTURES
First aid. C. J. Potthoff. Todays Health 44:78
    O '66
First aid: fracture of thigh bone. C. J.
    Potthoff. Todays Health 44:74 N '66
First aid: wrist fractures. C. J. Potthoff. il
    Todays Health 45:74 Ja '67
FRACTURES (geology) See Faults (geology)
FRADY, Marshall
God and man in the South. Atlan 219:37-42
    Ja '67
If they wouldn't play Dixie so much. Mlle 63:
    333+ Ag '66
Women who wait. Good H 162:100-1+ My '66
FRAGER, Malcolm
Music to my ears; Carnegie Hall recital.
    I. Kolodin. Sat R 49:45 Ja 29 '66
FRAGRANT gardens. See Gardens, Fragrant
FRAKES, L. A. and others
Movement directions in late Paleozoic glacial
    rocks of the Horlick and Pensacola Moun-
    tains, Antarctica. bibliog Science 153:746-9
    Ag 12 '66
FRAKES, Margaret
After Dallas; deployment. Christian Cent 83:
    642-4 My 18 '66
E.U.B.-Methodist merger. Christian Cent 83:
    1432-3 N 23 '66
FRAMING (building)
New steel framing system promises major
    savings in high-rise apartments. il Arch
    Rec 139:191-6 Je '66
FRAMPTON, Mary
New breed of society photographer. P.
    Gowland. il por Pop Phot 59:6+ D '66
FRANCE, Bill
Return of the exile was rich and racy. T. C.
    Brody. il Sports Illus 24:24-5 Mr 7 '66
FRANCE
France today; symposium. bibliog f Cur Hist
    50:193-237+ Ap '66
        See also
Advertising—France
Air travel—France
Airlines—France
Airplane industry and trade—France
Americans in France
Automobile driving—France
Automobile touring—France
Ballet—France
Bastille day
Birth control—France
Book industries and trade—France

Armed forces

Duty to say no; new code of discipline. Nation 203:500 N 14 '66
French military police. E. Stabler. bibliog f Cur Hist 50:232-7+ Ap '66

Army

French army in politics 1945-1962, by J. S. Ambler. Review
    Commonweal 84:444-5 Jl 8 '66. P. Geismar
Theirs to reason why; rewriting French military code. il Time 88:37 N 11 '66

Forces in Germany (Federal Republic)

Acid test; Erhard agrees to de Gaulle's terms. il Newsweek 68:40-1 Ag 1 '66
Permanent watch? Time 88:22-3 Jl 29 '66
Sense of insecurity in West Germany: why French troops are wanted. P. Ben. New Repub 154:10 Ap 30 '66

Colonies

Backyard troubles. il Newsweek 68:53-4 S 26 '66
    See also
New Caledonia
Somaliland, French

Commerce

U.S. is prime Anglo-French export goal. H. J. Coleman. il Aviation W 83:33-5 mid-D '65

Cultural relations

French community, does it exist? B. Weinstein. bibliog f Cur Hist 50:214-20+ Ap '66

Defenses

Empty French chair in Geneva; the *force de frappe*. A. Freund. New Repub 154-15-16 My 7 '66
England, France combine for strength. H. J. Coleman. Aviation W 84:91+ Mr 7 '66
French military police. E. Stabler. bibliog f Cur Hist 50:232-7+ Ap '66
Roosevelt as friend of France. J. M. Haight, jr. bibliog f For Affairs 44:518-26 Ap '66
What we can't cover with plants, we'll paint; installation of silos for nuclear missiles. P. E. Schneider. il N Y Times Mag p 18-19+ Ag 14 '66

Economic conditions

Back of the grandeur: a close look at de Gaulle's France. il U S News 60:39-40 Ap 4 '66
French planning experiment. V. E. Mares. bibliog f il Cur Hist 50:221-7+ Ap '66
Now de Gaulle likes those Yankee dollars. il Bsns W p44+ My 14 '66
Shift in gold. Time 88:94 N 4 '66
Special report. il Bsns W p 128+ S 10 '66

Economic policy

Duumvirate; M. Debre's plans. Time 87:34 F 25 '66
France today; address, September 16, 1966. C. Lucet. Vital Speeches 32:746-9 O 1 '66
French planning experiment. V. E. Mares. bibliog f il Cur Hist 50:221-7+ Ap '66
Half leap. il Newsweek 67:44+ F 28 '66

Economic relations

Flight 180 to Shanghai. Time 87:105 Je 10 '66
France and the five; de Gaulle's seven-month boycott. R. Mooney. New Repub 154:11-12 F 26 '66
France keeps pressure on Common market; demand for veto on key issues. il Bsns W p36+ Ja 22 '66

Finance

    See also
France—Economic conditions

Foreign relations

Advance man; reasons for Couve's travels. Newsweek 68:39-40 O 3 '66
Ami, go home; history behind de Gaulle policies. P. Ben. New Repub 154:10-11 Ap 9 '66
As de Gaulle sees it. New Repub 155:7-8 N 12 '66; Reply. M. Dupont. 155:35 D 17 '66
Dean Acheson's word for de Gaulle: nonsense; excerpts from interview. D. Acheson. U S News 60:79 Ap 18 '66
De Gaulle is not alone: the view from Europe. A. De Borchgrave. il Newsweek 67:40-1 Ap 25 '66
De Gaulle: no nation has friends, only interests. U S News 61:46 S 19 '66
De Gaulle on the loose. Nat R 18:916 S 20 '66
De Gaulle sets forth to change the face of Europe. C. J. V. Murhpy. il Life 61:18-25 Jl 8 '66; Same abr. with title What is de Gaulle up to? Read Digest 89:134-8 S '66
De Gaulle threatens NATO, U.S. with loss of bases in France. Aviation W 84:24 F 28 '66
De Gaulle's stance: one French opinion. Y. Chabas. Christian Cent 83:1218 O 5 '66
Doctor de Gaulle; eviction notice to NATO. K. Crawford. Newsweek 67:39 Mr 28 '66
Elysée matinee; press conference of de Gaulle. Newsweek 68:52 N 7 '66
For a new Atlantic alliance; address, June 1966. H. A. Kissinger. il Reporter 35:18-27 Jl 14 '66
Four books on de Gaulle and the future of Europe. J. M. Gavin. Harper 232:114-17 Ap '66
France hands NATO an eviction notice. Bsns W p42+ Mr 19 '66
France today; address, September 16, 1966. C. Lucet. Vital Speeches 32:746-9 O 1 '66
French foreign affairs; address, November 3, 1966. M. Couve de Murville. Vital Speeches 33:106-11 D 1 '66
French foreign policy under de Gaulle. E. S. Furniss, jr. Cur Hist 50:209-13+ Ap '66
Letter from Paris; excerpts from news conference, November 4, 1966; ed. by Genêt. C. de Gaulle. New Yorker 42:218+ N 19 '66
Long NATO crisis. E. Taylor. il Reporter 34: 16-21 Ap 21 '66
Maître de Gaulle; reactions to détente with the Communist powers. M. Ascoli. Reporter 34:10 Je 30 '66
NATO: a question of survival; reactions to de Gaulle plan to oust foreign troops, bases, etc. il Newsweek 67:44+ Mr 28 '66
NATO seeks a new defense line; France determined to quit, but other members want to keep it going. Bsns W p40-1 Je 11 '66
NATO without France; de Gaulle forces U.S. to showdown in Europe; with analysis by M. S. Johnson. il U S News 60:44-6+ Mr 21 '66
Now that France is out of NATO. il U S News 61:46+ Jl 18 '66
Other trouble; de Gaulle's objectives. W. Lippmann. Newsweek 67:23 My 9 '66
Time to start U.S. pullback in Europe? interview; ed. by R. Haeger. F. J. Strauss. il U S News 60:68-70+ Ap 18 '66
Two sides of a miracle. A. Werth. il Sat R 49:40-1 F 19 '66
What is French policy? A. Fontaine. For Affairs 45:58-76 O '66
Who pays the bill? French messages to NATO. Time 87:33 Ap 8 '66
Word from the landlord; de Gaulle's eviction dates for NATO tenants. Newsweek 67:51-2 Ap 11 '66

Africa

French community, does it exist? B. Weinstein. bibliog f Cur Hist 50:214-20+ Ap '66

FRANCE—Foreign relations—*Continued*

Europe, Eastern

First steps on the road to Moscow; de Gaulle's objectives and aims; with report, ed. by J. Blocker. Newsweek 67:40+ My 9 '66

Europe, Western

France and the Common market. M. Jabri. Cur Hist 50:228-31+ Ap '66

Germany (Federal Republic)

Acid test; Franco-German semiannual meeting. il Newsweek 68:40-1 Ag 1 '66
Cliff-hanger: the perils of NATO; Schroeder-Couve confrontation. il Newsweek 67:32+ My 2 '66
Resurgence of the spirit; Kiesinger & de Gaule in Paris. Time 89:26+ Ja 20 '67
Still married; concerning latest of the Paris-Bonn summit conferences. il Newsweek 67:55 F 21 '66

Morocco

L'affaire Ben Barka. il Time 87:33 Ja 28 '66
Ben Barka affair. C. Sterling. il Reporter 34:22-8 Mr 10 '66
Ben Barka is dead. A. Werth. Nation 202:350-2 Mr 28 '66
Diminished fifth; l'affaire Ben Barka erupts into scandal. il Newsweek 67:44+ Ja 31 '66
Enter the CIA; Ben Barka affair. il Newsweek 67:32 F 7 '66
Fine French scandal over a missing Moroccan. il Life 60:30-32B F 4 '66
Silent witnesses; Ben Barka affair. Time 87:32 F 4 '66

Russia

De Gaulle and Russia: some closer ties ahead? U S News 61:16 D 5 '66
De Gaulle in Moscow: what he did, what it means; with report by F. B. Stevens. il U S News 61:26-7 Jl 4 '66
De Gaulle in Russia: tour de force. il Newsweek 68:34-9 Jl 4 '66
De Gaulle's mission to Moscow. P. Ben. New Repub 154:13-14 Je 18 '66
End of a stately visit; with report on European reaction. Newsweek 68:38-40 Jl 11 '66
First steps on the road to Moscow; de Gaulle's objectives and aims; with report, ed. by J. Blocker. Newsweek 67:40+ My 9 '66
French and Russian cooperation; address, June 23, 1966. C. de Gaulle. Vital Speeches 32:589-90 Jl 15 '66
French mission to Moscow; what de Gaulle is up to. F. B. Stevens. U S News 60:68 My 2 '66
Grandest tour; de Gaulle's visit to Russia. il Time 88:20-4+ Jl 1 '66
Lively robot; A. Kosygin. Time 88:38+ D 16 '66
Marxist mellowed; Kosygin's visit to France. il Newsweek 68:50 D 19 '66
Nervous host; nine-day state visit of Russian Premier. il Time 88:41 D 9 '66
Seeds of disengagement; de Gaulle's visit to Russia. il Time 88:22 Jl 8 '66
Wait until spring; Kosygin visit to France. il Newsweek 68:52 D 12 '66
West edges East. il Bsns W p40 Je 25 '66

United States

As France sees it. Time 87:37 Ap 29 '66
France opts out; intention to pull out from NATO. Newsweek 67:42+ Mr 21 '66
If you've wondered what de Gaulle is driving at— U S News 61:83 O 24 '66
Oh hateful love, oh loving hate. J. Burnham. Nat R 18:353+ Ap 19 '66
Opening duel; de Gaulle's decrees. Time 87:33 Ap 22 '66
U.S. and France. P. Steinfels. Commonweal 84:570-1 S 16 '66
United States and France exchange views on Atlantic alliance: texts of memoires of March 25, 1966 and March 10, 1966. Dept State Bul 54:617-18 Ap 18 '66
U.S. ready to consult with France and NATO on French demands; texts of aide memoire exchanged between United States and France; April 12 and March 29, 1966. Dept State Bul 54:699-703 My 2 '66
What makes de Gaulle act that way? U S News 60:36 Mr 7 '66
What U.S. has done for France. il U S News 60:36-8 Ap 4 '66
Why de Gaulle is so anti-American. U S News 60:26 Mr 21 '66
See also
France and the United States

Vietnam (Republic)

General de Gaulle and Vietnam. J. Lacouture. New Repub 154:19-21 Mr 12 '66

History

1066: the view from France. H. Sutton. il Sat R 49:43-4 Jl 9 '66
See also
World war, 1939-1945—France

Bibliography

Articles and other books received; comp. by B. F. Hyslop. See issues of American historical review

Industries

French giant shakes off feudalism; Schneider, France's no. 1 heavy equipment maker. il Bsns W p64-6+ Ja 29 '66
Merger of sorts; Renault and Peugeot. Time 87:98 Ap 29 '66
Messieurs Fixit: SOS plumbing and repair company. il Time 87:102 F 4 '66
Not so much non. il Time 88:115 N 25 '66
Toward corporate glory; Pont-à-Mousson-Compagnie financière de Suez merger step. Time 87:84+ Ja 28 '66
Trouble at Bull; Franco-American Bull-General electric computer giant. Newsweek 69:62 Ja 16 '67
Unlocking corporate secrets; Paris-based company, known as Eurofinance. il Time 87:99-100 Ap 8 '66
See also
Bottling industry
Publishers and publishing—France
Steel industry and trade—France
Wine trade

Intellectual life

See also
Books and reading—France
French literature

Politics and government

De Gaulle and after. G. Defferre. For Affairs 44:434-45 Ap '66
De Gaulle and l'affaire; Ben Barka scandal. A. Werth. Nation 202:200-4 F 21 '66
De Gaulle and the new France. P. J. Larmour. Yale R 55:500-20 Je '66
France is no longer a democracy. F. Mitterrand. il N Y Times Mag p 14-15+ My 29 '66
French foreign policy under de Gaulle. E. S. Furniss, jr. Cur Hist 50:209-13+ Ap '66
Letter from Paris; concerning interview on television with G. Pompidou. Genêt. New Yorker 42:151 O 8 '66
Letter from Paris; excerpts from news conference, November 4, 1966; ed. by Genêt. C. de Gaulle. New Yorker 42:218+ N 19 '66
New road for France, by J. Soustelle. Review Nat R 18:122+ F 8 '66. T. Molnar. Reply with rejoinder. Pyrrho. 18:343+ Ap 19 '66
Saint Charles. J. J. Kaplow. Nation 202:368-70 Mr 28 '66
Suspense in France; de Gaulle muddles through. S. Hoffmann. Commonweal 83:554-6 F 11 '66
Two faces of JFK; Lecanuet and Giscard. il Newsweek 68:63-4 N 21 '66
What is French policy? A. Fontaine. For Affairs 45:58-76 O '66
See also
Elections—France
Political parties—France

Religious institutions and affairs

World around us (cont of) News of the Christian world. Christian Cent 83:214 F 16 '66

Social conditions

New France; changes in French society and culture. H. Peyre. bibliog f Cur Hist 50:193-200+ Ap '66

Social history

De Gaulle and the new France. P. J. Larmour. Yale R 55:500-20 Je '66
Goncourt journal. K. Rexroth. Sat R 49:75-6 O 22 '66
Women incendiaries, by E. Thomas. Review Atlan 217:126 My '66. O. Handlin

Social life and customs

Love in the afternoon. il Time 88:36 N 11 '66

FRANCE and the United States

Déjà vu; anti-Americanism. E. Taylor Reporter 35:18+ O 6 '66
Not all the Yanks can go home; Normandy American cemetery. A. H. Sypher. il Nations Bsns 54:31-2 '66
See also
Americans in France
United States—Foreign opinion—French
United States—History—Revolution—French participation

FRANCE Dimanche. See Newspapers—France
FRANCEKEVICH, Al
    In the darkroom. See issues of Popular
    photography
FRANCES, Sister Marian. See Marian Frances,
    Sister
FRANCES, Mona
    Reminiscences of a dancing family. pors
    Dance Mag 40:22-5 S '66
FRANCESCHINI, Romulus
    From Folkways, Brecht by Bentley; and the
    Wolpe music. Am Rec G 32:747 Ap '66
FRANCHISE system. See Exclusive agencies
FRANCHISED automobile dealers. See Auto-
    mobile dealers
FRANCIS Ferdinand, archduke of Austria
    Road to Sarajevo, by V. Dedijer. Review
    Sat R 49:47 Jl 23 '66. H. Hansen
FRANCIS Joseph I, emperor of Austria
    Emperor's war games. F. Kormendi. il Re-
    porter 35:50-4+ N 17 '66
FRANCIS, Earl L.
    Gold mine in the sky. por Newsweek 68:19
    Ag 29 '66
FRANCIS, Ed
    Supercharged salt shaker. Pop Electr 24:57-
    60 My '66
FRANCIS, Sharon F.
    If all you want is a penguin's egg. .; ad-
    dress. June 27, 1966. Liv Wildn 30:20-1
    Sum '66
FRANCK, Thomas M.
    Left behind in Sinai. Nation 202:723-4 Je 13
    '66
FRANCO, Francisco
    After Franco, the generalissimo's plans. il
    por U S News 61:16 D 5 '66
    After him, the deluge? il por Newsweek 68:
    40+ D 5 '66
    Spain faces the future. B. van Voorst. il por
    Newsweek 67:46-8 Je 20 '66
    Spain's new constitution. il por Sr Schol
    89:13-14 Ja 13 '67
    Umbrella of monarchy. il por Time 88:32-3 D
    2 '66
FRANCOEUR, George
    Art news from Detroit (title varies) Art N
    65:56 Sum; 58+ O '66
FRANCOEUR, Robert T.
    Convergence and the biblical scholar. Com-
    monweal 84:83-4 Ap 8 '66
FRANCO-GERMAN war, 1870-1871
    See also
    Paris—History
FRANCOIS, Bill
    Living laboratory of human relations. Sat R
    49:64-5 My 21 '66
FRANCONIA Notch
    Franconia Notch. il Liv Wildn 29:44 Wint
    '65
FRANEY, Pierre
    Vive les surgelés! il por Time 88:100+ O 28
    '66
FRANK, Bill
    Bill Frank and company; Henry Street play-
    house. J. Maskey. Dance Mag 41:60 Ja '67
FRANK, Gerold
    Boston strangler; condensation. Ladies Home
    J 83:65-72+ Ag; 91-8+ S '66
FRANK, Howard A. See Lambert, P. B. jt.
    auth.
FRANK, Jerome D.
    Atrocities in Vietnam. Sat R 49:31 Je 4 '66
FRANK, Jerome P.
    Upgrading the industrial package. Duns R 88:
    145 N '66
FRANK, Joseph
    Eliot's legacy. Commentary 42:87-91 S '66
FRANK, Lewis A.
    Nuclear weapons development in China. Bul
    Atomic Sci 22:12-15 Ja; 30 Ap '66
FRANK, Philipp
    Philipp Frank dies at eighty-two; colleague
    of Einstein. Sci N 90:84 Ag 6 '66
FRANK, Stanley
    Firetrap, U.S.A. McCalls 94:48+ N '66
    Shocking shortage of nurses. Good H 162:
    96-7+ Mr '66
    When a child should tell. Good H 162:96-7+
    My '66
FRANKEL, Charles
    Education for world responsibility; address,
    July 16, 1966. Vital Speeches 32:621-5 Ag
    1 '66
    Education for world responsibility; an old
    phrase, a transformed problem; excerpt
    from address, June 16, 1966. Dept State Bul
    55:84-90 Jl 18 '66
    Era of educational and cultural relations;
    address, April 25, 1966. Dept State Bul 54:
    889-97 Je 6 '66
    International education act of 1966; state-
    ment, March 31, 1966. Dept State Bul 54:
    754-7 My 9 '66

Toward deeper cultural relations in the hemi-
    sphere; address, January 18, 1966. Dept
    State Bul 54:202-7 F 7 '66
United States commitment to UNESCO;
    statement, October 27, 1966. Dept State Bul
    55:883-9 D 12 '66
FRANKEL, Haskel
    Bernard Malamud. Sat R 49:39-40 S 10 '66
    On the fringe. Sat R 49:31+ Ap 16; 33+ S
    24; 38-40 D 3 '66
FRANKEL, Jonathan
    Communist rabbi: Moses Hess. bibliog f
    Commentary 41:77-81 Je '66
FRANKEL, Max
    My spy can lick your spy. Atlan 217:103-
    4+ Ap '66
FRANKEL, Theodore
    Art, politics, & the Soviet writer. bibliog f
    Commentary 41:52-9 My; 42:19-20 S '66
FRANKENSTEIN, Alfred
    Britten's Curlew River burnished bronze
    solemnity. Hi Fi 16:69-70 Je '66
FRANKENTHALER, Helen
    Second fame: good food. N. Lyon. il por
    Vogue 147:194-6 Ap 1 '66
    Towards the total color image. B. H. Fried-
    man. il Art N 65:31-3+ Sum '66
FRANKFORT ON THE MAIN

Description
    Frankfurt. W. Sansom. il Holiday 41:74-9+ Ja
    '67

Music
    New ideas for Wagner. P. Moor. il Hi Fi 16:
    142-3 Mr '66
FRANKFURTER, Felix
    Note on Felix Frankfurter. J. Grossman.
    Commentary 41:59-64 Mr '66
FRANKFURTERS
    Case of the overstretched hot dog; added
    water. Consumer Rep 31:475 O '66
    See also
    Cookery—Meat
FRANKLIN, Adele
    Christmas records for the young, 1966. Sat R
    49:78-80 D 3 '66
FRANKLIN, Benjamin
    Mon cher papa: Franklin and the ladies of
    Paris, by C. A. Lopez. Review
    Sat R 49:34 D 17 '66. L. Gershoy
FRANKLIN, Frederic
    Coppélius in the capital. F. Merkling. il por
    Opera N 30:16 Ja 29 '66
FRANKLIN, John Hope
    Book review. Negro Hist Bul 29:40 N '65
FRANKLIN, Joseph
    Camera-defying Death Valley. il U S Camera
    29:58-9+ S '66
FRANKLIN, Paul K.
    Microphones for public address. Electr
    World 75:50-2+ Je '66
FRANKLIN, Robert D.
    How many copies are enough? reprint. por
    Library J 91:4573-5 O 1 '66
    Library education and the talent shortage.
    por Library J 91:1762-3 Ap 1 '66
FRANKLIN award for distinguished service
    Franklin award for distinguished service;
    citation; with text of a telegram sent by
    President Johnson to the organization. Dept
    State Bul 54:198-9 F 7 '66
FRANKLIN book programs, incorporated
    Franklin book programs elects Booher
    chairman. Pub W 190:78 N 14 '66
    Franklin opens Int'l bookselling workshop.
    Pub W 189:60 My 30 '66
    Grant to Franklin for Latin American pro-
    grams; medical book publishing. Pub W
    189:46-7 My 16 '66
    Interview with Datus C. Smith, jr; ed. by
    K. Molz. D. C. Smith, jr. il Wilson Lib
    Bul 40:532-7 F '66
    Launching the new literate; Africa, Asia, the
    Americas. R. Stein. il Library J 91:5713-15
    N 15 '66
FRANKLIN Delano Roosevelt memorial. See
    Washington, D.C.—Monuments, statues,
    etc.
FRANKLIN national bank. See New York (city)
    —Banks
FRANKLIN publications, incorporated. See
    Franklin book programs, incorporated
FRANKLIN SQUARE, Long Island national
    bank. See Banks and banking—United
    States
FRANKLIN Watts, incorporated. See Watts,
    Franklin, incorporated
FRANKS, Herman
    San Francisco: this race is not over yet by
    a long shot. W. Leggett. il por Sports Illus
    25:28-31 S 26 '66
FRANT, Martin S. and Ross, J. W. Jr
    Electrode for sensing fluoride ion activity in
    solution. bibliog Science 154:1553-5 D 23 '66
FRANTZ, John C.
    Library services and construction act. ALA
    Bul 60:149-52 F '66

FRANZ Joseph I, emperor of Austria. See
Francis Joseph I
FRANZEL, Adeline
Day at a library for the blind. S. Havens.
il por Library J 91:3333-8 Jl '66
FRANZEN, Ulrich
Search for appropriate form. il Arch Rec
139:127-40 My '66
FRANZINI, Paolo
Step away from symmetry. il por Time 88:54
Jl 8 '66
FRAREY, Carlyle J.
Profile of an alumni body. Library J 91:
1776-81 Ap 1 '66
FRASCONI, Antonio
Interview with Antonio Frasconi; ed. by B.
Chernow. il pors Sch Arts 65:22-6 My '66
FRASE, Robert W.
Cadillacs and Chevrolets. E. Moon. por Li-
brary J 91:3343-5 Jl '66
FRASER, Kathleen
Baker's daughter; Grass; Poem wondering if
I'm pregnant; poems. Poetry 108:318-21 Ag
'66
Change of address; poem. New Yorker 42:40
Je 11 '66
Little joy poem. New Yorker 42:114 Ja 14 '67
Reaching out poem. Mlle 63:107 My '66
FRASER, Nancy
Art of chairman-baiting. Life 60:120+ Mr
18 '66
Hamburger university. Life 61:100 O 21 '66
FRASER, Russell
On Milton's poetry. Yale R 56:172-96 D '66
FRASER, Stewart E.
Americanism vs. communism: a historical
document. Sch & Soc 94:355 O 29 '66
Some aspects of university cooperation in in-
ternational education. bibliog f Sch & Soc
94:234-8+ Ap 16 '66
FRATER, Alexander
Matriarch; story. New Yorker 42:53-6 Ap 16
'66
FRATERNITIES. See College fraternities
Die FRAU ohne schatten; opera. See Strauss,
R.
FRAUD
Beware the jabberwock; terrible William-
sons, confidence clan. Newsweek 68:52+
N 21 '66
Beware the terrible Williamsons; confidence
tricksters. F. Dickenson. Read Digest 89:
175-6+ S '66
Crash artists. Newsweek 68:80 Ag 22 '66
Encounter with a confidence man. L. J.
Averill. Christian Cent 83:1026-8 Ag 24 '66
Fraud shifting to airfreight. Aviation W 85:
52 N 14 '66
Golden fleece; picture of California as the con
capital of the world. Newsweek 68:109A+
S 19 '66
Riddle of the vanishing insurance companies;
G. Head's indictments against companies
fraudulent manipulations. L. Velie. Read
Digest 89:109-13 S '66
Saga of the Little green pig; scheme for
selling vacuum cleaners at several times
their worth. R. L. Smith. il Reporter 35:
39-40+ N 3 '66
$65 billion gold mine. A. Poinsett. il Ebony
21:88-90+ Jl '66
Slick spring swindlers. Consumer Bul 49:28-9
Je '66
Union cards were phony; case of the Wash-
ington area Drug fair chain. il Nations
Bsns 54:100-1+ Mr '66
See also
Advertising, Fraudulent
Diplomas, Fraudulent
Documents, Fraudulent
Impostors and imposture
Insurance—Fraudulent promotion
Politics, Corruption in
Quacks and quackery
Securities, Fraudulent
FRAUDULENT conveyances
Planned bankruptcy: the racket that cheats
us all. B. Surface. Read Digest 88:125-9
My '66
FRAUDULENT voting. See Elections—Corrupt
practices
FRAWLEY, Patrick Joseph, 1923?-
Frawley phenomenon. S. H. Brown. il por
Fortune 73:136-9+ F '66
FRAZER, John E.
How to breeze through customs. Read Di-
gest 89:25-6+ S '66
Plant tours. Travel 126:31-4 Jl '66; Same abr.
Read Digest 89:19-20+ Jl '66
FRAZER, Robert L. and Schmidt, L. C.
Long-term tests on plastic pipe. Am City 81:
84-5 Jl '66
FRAZIER, Brenda Diana Duff
Girl of the year, 1938. B. Weinraub. il por
Esquire 66:72-5+ Jl '66

FRAZIER, George
Bounty of Brewer. Holiday 40:106+ Ag '66
Dapper wrinkles of seersucker. Esquire 66:
92-3 Ag '66
Memo to the Corinthians: is Zak Starr entered
for Eton? Esquire 66:191-4 O '66
Second greatest shoeshine. Esquire 66:147-52
N '66
Sense of style. Esquire 66:80+ N; 344-6 D '66
Sophistication of Duke Ellington. Esquire 66:
244-5 D '66
FRAZIER, Joe
Clover in need of a leaf. M. Kane. Sports
Illus 25:72+ O 3 '66
FRAZIER, John
Breathe right, and stay well. Read Digest
88:60-2 F '66
FREAKS. See Deformities
FRED, James. See Frey, R. jt. auth.
FREDA, Vincent J. and others
Rh factor: prevention of isoimmunization and
clinical trial on mothers. bibliog Science
151:828-30 F 18 '66
FREDERICK A. Praeger, incorporated. See
Praeger, Frederick A., incorporated
FREDERICKS, Pierce G.
Zeps over Britain. N Y Times Mag p76+
Ap 17 '66
FREDERICKSON, William, Jr
Public seashores: their administration. por
Parks & Rec 1:638-40 Ag '66
FREDLAND, John Roger
Of dollars and sense. Sat R 49:31-2 Jl 16 '66
FREE choice of employment
President Johnson urges Senate to ratify
ILO convention 122; statement. June 2, 1966.
L. B. Johnson. Debt State Bul 54:1026-7 Je
27 '66
FREE churches. See Dissenters, Religious
FREE enterprise
Advertising; address, November 4, 1966. C. T.
Lipscomb, jr. Vital Speeches 33:145-8 D
15 '66
Blessed are the work-makers; creation of jobs
providing income-tax revenues of our gov-
ernment. D. Lawrence. U S News 61:92 S 5
'66
Burying free enterprise; K. Galbraith's new
industrial state. Time 89:92 Ja 6 '67
Business, social progress and religion;
address, October 27, 1966. B. Moreell.
Vital Speeches 33:119-25 D 1 '66
Come and get it! address, October 21, 1966.
L. B. Worthington. Vital Speeches 33:78-81
N 15 '66
A look at the national economy; excerpts from
Public interest of private enterprise; annual
report. R. Blough. il U S News 61:82-4 S 12
'66
Must competitors be equalized in money and
skills? D. Lawrence. U S News 61:112 N 28
'66
Private profit and public gain; address, June
6, 1966. M. C. Whatmore. Vital Speeches
32:571-3 Jl 1 '66
Public and private enterprise, by J. Jewkes.
Review
Nat R 18:583-4 Je 14 '66. H. Hazlitt
Role of the professional manager; address,
August 22, 1966. J. T. McCarty. Vital
Speeches 32:751-4 O 1 '66
Some important business for business; ad-
dress, September 12, 1966. L. W. Moore.
Vital Speeches 33:28-32 O 15 '66
There's plenty of privacy left in private
enterprise. R. Sheehan. il Fortune 74:224-
5+ Jl 15 '66
We need a new capitalism in America. G.
Romney. Nations Bsns 54:34-5+ Jl '66
What private enterprise means to Latin
America. D. Rockefeller. For Affairs 44:
403-16 Ap '66
When it's your own money; Yugoslavia. S.
G. Slappey. il Nations Bsns 54:72-6+ N '66
See also
Profit
FREE Europe committee
See also
Radio free Europe
FREE-falling. See Parachuting
FREE lance writing. See Authorship
FREE piston engines. See Marine engines;
Motor truck engines
FREE press. See Freedom of the press
FREE radicals. See Radicals (chemistry)
FREE society association
Right think-in. Reporter 34:7 Je 2 '66
FREE Southern theater. See Theater, Negro
FREE speech
Protest, a right and a responsibility; round
table discussion from 1966 student burgesses
at Williamsburg. il Sr Schol 88:10-13+ My 6
'66

FREE speech—*Continued*
Restless generation; address, April 27, 1966. D. J. Goulding. Vital Speeches 32:506-8 Je 1 '66
Right of public to criticize. H. F. Pipel. Pub W 189:65 Ja 31 '66
Right to speak or write inciting words; Supreme court decision: Ashton v. Kentucky. H. F. Pilpel. Pub W 189:70 Je 27 '66
Should known Communists and Fascists be permitted to speak on college campuses? pro and con discussion. il Sr Schol 87: 10-11 Ja 14 '66
Smale case: NSF and Berkeley pass through a case of jitters. D. S. Greenberg. il Science 154:130-3 O 7 '66; Discussion. 154:1395-6 D 16 '66
Speaker ban: controversy is revived at U.N.C. L. J. Carter. Science 152:50-2 Ap 1 '66
Un-American un-American activities committee. J. B. Sheerin. Cath World 204:7-10 O '66
See also
Academic freedom
American civil liberties union
Assembly, Right of
Libel and slander

FREE speech; story. See Robertson, S.

FREE-spending. See Consumption (economics)

FREE textbooks. See Textbooks

FREE trade and protection
Free trade wins a new apostle; Ottawa's Finance Minister M. Sharp. Bsns W p 142+ D 17 '66

FREE universities
See also
Institute for the study of nonviolence

FREE university of Berlin. See Colleges and universities—Germany (Federal Republic)

FREE university of New York
It's a groovy thing to do. R. Vaughan. il Life 60:119-20 My 20 '66
New York's schoolhouse for the left. E. Grossman. Harper 232:75-6+ Ap '66
Society's just got to go; we all know that. R. Mathews. il Sat R 49:74-6+ S 17 '66; Discussion. 49:71 O 15 '66

FREE will and determinism
See also
Will

FREED, Richard
Piracy on the high C's. Sat R 49:55-6+ Mr 26 '66
Puccini concerto. Sat R 49:85 N 26 '66
(comp) Year's best recordings. Sat R 49: 76-9+ N 26 '66

FREEDMAN, Janet
Birch tree grows. por Library J 91:624-8 F 1 '66

FREEDMAN, Mervin B. and Powelson, Harvey
Drugs on campus; turned on & tuned out. Nation 202:125-7 Ja 31 '66

FREEDMAN, Monroe H.
Lies & lawyers. por Time 87:81 My 13 '66

FREEDMEN
Free Negro in Florida. L. W. Neyland. bibliog Negro Hist Bul 29:27-8+ N '65

FREEDOM. See Liberty

FREEDOM, Intellectual. See Intellectual liberty

FREEDOM from hunger campaign. See Food relief

FREEDOM house (organization)
On misleading the enemy. America 115:676 N 26 '66

FREEDOM, integration, God, honor, today (organization) See Civil rights organizations

FREEDOM marches. See Civil rights demonstrations

FREEDOM national bank. See New York (city) —Banks

FREEDOM of assembly. See Assembly, Right of

FREEDOM of conscience. See Liberty of conscience

FREEDOM of employment. See Free choice of employment

FREEDOM of information. See Information, Freedom of

FREEDOM of religion. See Religious liberty

FREEDOM of speech. See Free speech

FREEDOM of teaching. See Academic freedom

FREEDOM of the press
Censorship in the church. E. C. Bianchi. America 115:411-13 O 8 '66
Censorship in the church. J. V. Schall. Commonweal 83:601-3 F 25 '66
How the Constitution was violated: newspaper strike, New York city, December 1953 and interference with right to publish; reprint. D. Lawrence. U S News 61:136+ S 26 '66
Painless news control. S. J. Adamo. America 115:190-2 Ag 20 '66

People's right to know; ANPA report with list of major conclusions. R. L. Tobin. il Sat R 50:109+ Ja 14 '67
Right of public to criticize. H. F. Pipel. Pub W 189:65 Ja 31 '66
Right to speak or write inciting words; Supreme court decision: Ashton v. Kentucky. H. F. Pilpel. Pub W 189:70 Je 27 '66
See also
Government and the press
Libel and slander

FREEDOM studies center
Eyes right. R. Dudman. New Repub 155:15-16 N 5 '66

FREEDOM to know. See Information, Freedom of

FREEDOM to travel. See Travel regulations

FREEDOMITES. See Dukhobors

FREELAND, Robert
Motivation for children's drawings and paintings. Sch Arts 66:30-2 S '66

FREEMAN, A. D.
Gifts; poem. Sat R 49:70 Je 11 '66
To meet E. E. Cummings; poem. Sat R 49: 77 N 19 '66

FREEMAN, Arthur
Five poets. Poetry 109:189-95 D '66

FREEMAN, David C.
Fight at Monkey; excerpt from Battles in the monsoon. S. L. A. Marshall. il por Harper 233:112-14+ N '66

FREEMAN, G. See Sultanian, I. V. jt. auth.

FREEMAN, Jane Charlotte (Shields)
Don't miss the National arboretum. por Parks & Rec 1:566-7+ Jl '66

FREEMAN, Jean Todd
Charades; poem. Ladies Home J 83:186 Mr '66
Thirty-sixth brick; story. Redbook 128:54-5 D '66

FREEMAN, Jim
Magic circle. pors Outdoor Life 138:64-6+ D '66

FREEMAN, John W.
Edge of truth. Opera N 31:6-7 N 19 '66
Mefistofele returns. Opera N 30:28-9 Ja 29 '66
Voice in the wilderness. Opera N 30:14-15 My 7 '66
(tr) See Puccini, G. Here's your letter, asking me

FREEMAN, Neal B.
Freeman's guide to unsatisfactory people. Nat R 18:924-5 S 20 '66

FREEMAN, Orville Lothrop
Greenspan program. pors Parks & Rec 1: 829-30 O '66
Should we take the wraps off production? por Farm J 90:30+ S '66
We must eradicate animal disease. Suc Farm 64:6+ O '66
World food and population crisis: DAC's fifth annual high-level meeting; statement, July 21, 1966. Dept State Bul 55:205-9 Ag 8 '66
about
Farmer's gamble. Reporter 35:16+ S 8 '66
Patchwork that pays off. il pors Bsns W p88-90+ S 17 '66

FREEMASONS
Knights & Masons together. Time 88:74-5 Ag 19 '66

FREER, Charles Lang
Profiles; Smithsonian institution. G. T. Hellman. New Yorker 42:58-62+ D 17 '66

FREER gallery of art, Washington, D.C.
Profiles; Smithsonian institution. G. T. Hellman. New Yorker 42:58-62+ D 17 '66

FREEWAYS. See Express highways

FREEZE-branding of livestock. See Livestock —Branding

FREEZE drying
Dioramas out of the deepfreeze; new method of taxidermy. C. West. il Pop Mech 125:126-9+ F '66

FREEZERS
Coolest place in the house! il Bet Hom & Gard 44:64-5 N '66
Refrigerator-freezers. il Consumer Rep 31:476-81 O '66
Which type of home freezer for you? K. Warner. il Pop Mech 125:140-1+ F '66

FREEZING
Temperature sentry guards against freeze-up. H. P. Strand. il Pop Mech 126:159-60 N '66
Vacuum freezing effects probed. J. F. Judge. il Miss & Roc 18:22-3 Mr 21 '66
See also
Ice

FREEZING (therapy) See Cold—Therapeutic applications

FREEZING of food
Freezing points; guide to buying, preparing, wrapping, storing and thawing of foods in your freezer. McCalls 93:45+ Jl '66
How to be an organized cook. M. Davidson. il Ladies Home J 83:30+ Jl '66

FREEZING points
See also
Eutectics

FREI, Eduardo
Belated triumph. il por Time 88:42 N 4 '66
Frei v. FRAP. il por Time 87:31 Mr 25 '66
Man with a plan. il por Newsweek 68:68 O 24 '66

FREIBERG, Stanley K.
Birthright; poem. Christian Cent 83:113 Ja 26 '66

FREIBERGER, Howard, and Murphy, E. F.
Reading machines for the blind. Science 152: 679-80 Ap 29 '66

FREIDEL, Frank
System of checks and challenges. Sat R 49: 38 F 5 '66

FREIDES, Thelma
Will the real reference problem please stand up? bibliog por Library J 91:2008-12 Ap 15 '66

FREIGHT and freightage
See also
Air freight service
Trucking

FREIGHT cars. See Railroads—Freight cars

FREIGHT handling
Automation speeds cargo flow at Pan Am's new mechanized facility at Kennedy airport; photographs. Aviation W 86:44-5 Ja 9 '67
Brownline widening role in cargo trade. C. M. Plattner. il Aviation W 86:46-9 Ja 2 '67
Growth of air cargo spurs automation. R. O'Lone. il Aviation W 85:72-3+ O 31 '66
New system measures air cargo density; cargo process control system. J. W. Carter. il Aviation W 84:42-3 My 16 '66
Pan Am opens mechanized cargo facility; cargo terminal at Kennedy international airport. il Aviation W 85:49-50 D 5 '66
See also
Container system (freight handling)

FREIGHT rates. See Shipping—Rates

FREIGHT vessels
Cargo cruises. S. Berry. il Travel 125:30-4 F '66
Chesapeake Bay cargo boats. J. Frye. il Motor B 117:184-6 Ap '66
Containers race across Atlantic; international, door-to-door foreign service. Bsns W p76+ F 19 '66
Dalmatian coast on the cheap. S. Corbett. il Atlan 218:125-7 D '66
New kind of steamboat race; door-to-door delivery of ocean freight. il U S News 60:8 F 28 '66

Automatic control
Ship you drive with one finger; American Racer has built-in electronic brain and computers. R. P. Crossley. il Pop Mech 126:92-5+ Ag '66

FREIGHTER cruises. See Ocean travel

FREISER, Leonard H.
Report on the St John report. Library J 91: 5693-5 N 15 '66
Technology in the library. por Wilson Lib Bul 41:69-71 S '66

FRELINGHUYSEN, Peter H. B.
Financing the United Nations emergency force; statement, December 20, 1965. Dept State Bul 54:295-6 F 21 '66
United States announces pledge for Palestine refugees; statement, December 20, 1965. Dept State Bul 54:212 F 7 '66
United States expresses views on 1966 U.N. budget estimates; statement, October 19, 1965. Dept State Bul 54:69-74 Ja 10 '66

FREMANTLE, Anne
Antepenultimate; story. New Yorker 42:52-7 Mr 12 '66
Books. Commonweal 84:159-60 Ap 22 '66
Corridor talk. Reporter 35:42-4 D 29 '66

FREMON, Suzanne
How Uncle Sam is helping to upgrade our schools. Parents Mag 41:55-7+ S '66

FREMONT, Calif.
New downtown. L. W. Milnes. il Am City 81:86-7+ Je '66
Pre-teenagers help improve their city. L. McVicar. il Parks & Rec 1:32-3 Ja '66

FRENCH, Bevan M.
Shock metamorphism of natural materials. Science 153:903-6 Ag 19 '66

FRENCH, Charles
Coin quiz. See issues of Hobbies

FRENCH, Mary
Aileen Rowe had a thing about death. D. Moser. il Life 60:80D+ Mr 4 '66

FRENCH, Norman R. and others
Periodicity of desert rodent activity. bibliog Science 154:1194-5 D 2 '66

FRENCH, Zelia J.
On library consulting: a comment. por ALA Bul 60:711-12 Jl '66

FRENCH
The French, by J. F. Revel. Review
Sat R il 49:32-3 Ap 23 '66. D. Schoenbrun
Nation's midsummer madness; sketches; with account by J. Olsen. Sports Illus 25:60-72+ Ag 22 '66
New mood in France. N. Cousins. Sat R 49: 28+ S 24 '66

FRENCH antiques. See Antiques

FRENCH art. See Art, French

FRENCH artificial satellites. See Artificial satellites, French

FRENCH athletes. See Athletes

FRENCH atomic bomb test. See Atomic bombs —Testing

FRENCH authors. See Authors, French

FRENCH CANADA. See Quebec (province)

FRENCH CANADIANS
University of Montreal: where the two Canadas meet. L. J. Carter. il Science 154: 868-72 N 18 '66
See also
Acadians in Louisiana

FRENCH composers. See Composers, French

FRENCH cookery. See Cookery, French

FRENCH doll's surprise; drama. See Bennett. R.

FRENCH drama
Eugène Ionesco. C. Cate. Atlan 217:114-20 Ap '66

FRENCH fiction
Letter from Paris; five of seven annual December book prizes won by Grasset. Genêt. New Yorker 42:65-6 D 31 '66
My life in the new novel; concerning meetings with authors of Le nouveau roman. V. Mercier. Nation 202:434-6 Ap 11 '66
Restif de la Bretonne; concerning Rodker edition of Monsieur Nicolas. K. Rexroth. Sat R 49:25 Ap 2 '66
Stendhal's The red and the black. K. Rexroth. Sat R 49:28 Je 11 '66
See also
Goncourt prize

FRENCH furniture. See Furniture, French

FRENCH GUIANA
Three Guianas. T. Mathews. Cur Hist 51:333-7+ D '66
See also
United States—History—Revolution—French participation

FRENCH in the United States

FRENCH language question, Belgium. See Belgium—Languages

FRENCH literature
For a new novel, by A. Robbe-Grillett, tr. by R. Howard. Review
Sat R 49:32 Mr 12 '66. H. T. Moore
French literary scene. J. G. Weightman. Commentary 41:57-62 F '66
Reactionary revolution; Catholic literary revival in France. L. Allen. Commonweal 85: 100-2 O 28 '66
Sentimental education; plots and characters of Flaubert and Stendhal. K. Rexroth. Sat R 49:41 D 31 '66
See also
Authors, French
Childrens literature—France
French fiction
French poetry
Philosophy, French
Publishers and publishing—France
Surrealism

FRENCH names. See Names, French

FRENCH opera. See Opera, French

FRENCH pastry. See Pastry

FRENCH philosophy. See Philosophy, French

FRENCH poetry
French chronicle. W. Fowlie. Poetry 107: 267-70 Ja '66
Works of Rimbaud. K. Rexroth. Sat R 50:34+ Ja 14 '67

FRENCH scientists. See Scientists, French

FRENCH singers. See Singers

FRENCH SOMALILAND. See Somaliland, French

FRENCH students in the United States. See Foreign students in the United States

FRENCH WEST AFRICA
Freedom speaks French in Ouagadougou. J. Scofield. il Nat Geog Mag 130:153-203 Ag '66

FRENCH wines. See Wine

FRENCHWOMAN; story. See Chidester, A.

FRENI, Mirella
Charmer; interview, ed. by G. Fitzgerald. por Opera N 31:16 D 3 '66

FREQUENCY, Radio. See Radio frequency

FREQUENCY measurement
Frequency and frequency measurement. M. J. Willrodt. il Electr World 76:25-8+ O '66

FREQUENCY modulation receivers. See Radio receiving apparatus—Frequency modulation receivers
FREQUENCY signal generators. See Signal generators
FRESCO painting. See Frescoes
FRESCOES
Sleuthing behind the wall; frescoes hidden from sight in Badia church. il Time 88:78 S 9 '66
FRESH water biology
See also
Limnology
FRESHMEN. See College students
FRESNO, Calif.

Art

City that puts people first; Fresno plan. B. Taper. McCalls 93:186 Ap '66; Same abr. with title City remade for people. Read Digest 89:146-50 O '66

City planning

City that puts people first. B. Taper. il McCalls 93:62+ Ap '66; Same abr. with title City remade for people. Read Digest 89: 146-50 O '66

Music

Fresno; production of La Bohème. W. Aguiar, jr. Opera N 31:30 D 31 '66
FRESQUET, Rufo López-. See López-Fresquet, R.
FREUD, Sigmund
Freud's friend Wilhelm Fliess and his theory of male and female life cycles. M. Gardner. il Sci Am 215:108-9+ Jl '66
Importance of Freud. Sister Marie Michael. Cath World 204:212-18 Ja '67
—and Bullitt, W. C.
Thomas Woodrow Wilson; excerpts. pors Look 30:36-8+ D 13 '66
FREUDENTHAL, Hugo, and others
Some symbionts of the sea. Natur Hist 75:46-51 bibliog(p82) N '66
FREUDISM. See Psychoanalysis
FREUND, Andreas
Empty French chair in Geneva. New Repub 154-15-16 My 7 '66
Performance from Poland. New Repub 155:35-6 Jl 30 '66
FREY, Donald Nelson
Great race, Chevy vs. Ford; with report by M. Silva. il pors Life 61:131-2+ O 14 '66
FREY, Fred A. See Haskin, L. A. jt. auth.
FREY, Robert, and Fred, James
General-purpose wirewound potentiometers. Electr World 75:52-4 Ap '66
FREYDBERG, Margaret H.
Art of apology. McCalls 93:87+ Mr '66
FREYMAN, Leonard, and Van Sickle, B. L.
Some classroom-tested ideas. NEA J 55:39-40 N '66
FRICK, Helen Clay
Banning history: Frick vs. Stevens. E. Langer. Science 153:616 Ag 5 '66
Stevens asks court to enjoin Frick suit. Pub W 190:49-50 O 10 '66
Stevens countersues Frick, charges rights violation. Pub W 190:41-2 Ag 15 '66
Stevens loses suit in federal court. Pub W 190:26 O 24 '66
Stevens takes case to U.S. Court of appeals. Pub W 190:38 N 28 '66
FRICK, Henry Clay
Banning history: Frick vs. Stevens. E. Langer. Science 153:616 Ag 5 '66
People's right to the past. Christian Cent 83:1169 S 28 '66
FRICKER, John
Ach du lieber flugindustrie. Flying 78:72-7 My '66
Foreign accent. See issues of Flying
Gone flying USA. il Flying 78:48-52 F '66
Hamburger deluxe. il Flying 79:100-1 Jl '66
FRIDAY abstinence. See Fasting
FRIDBERG, Gunnar, and Nishioka, R. S.
Secretion into the cerebrospinal fluid by caudal neurosecretory neurons. bibliog Science 152:90-1 Ap 1 '66
FRIEBERT, Stuart
Children; poem. Cath World 203:166 Je '66
FRIED, Irving M.
New sights on stereo arms. Hi Fi 16:80-4 D '66
FRIED, Morton H.
Peking way to power. Sat R 49:51 Je 11 '66
FRIED, Sister Sharon
Phoebe reviewed. Cath World 203:40-1 Ap '66
FRIEDAN, Betty
How Mrs Gandhi shattered the feminine mystique. Ladies Home J 83:100+ My '66
FRIEDBERG, M. Paul
Landscape architect Paul Friedberg creates handsome public spaces for Lower East Side public housing. il Arch Rec 140:197 Jl '66

FRIEDE, Robert
Boy and girl. il por Newsweek 67:31B F 21 '66
Death of a hooked heiress. D. Schaap. il por Look 30:19-25 Jl 26 '66
FRIEDENBERG, Edgar Z.
Modest proposals. Commentary 42:79-80 Jl '66
FRIEDLAND, Alan. See Cerniglia, V. J. jt. auth.
FRIEDLANDER, Albert H.
Converts in the Vatican. Sat R 49:37 Je 18 '66
Rabbis, angels and demons. Sat R 49:91 My 7 '66
FRIEDLANDER, Bernard Z.
Today's innovations in teaching. NEA J 55:10-14 Mr '66
FRIEDLÄNDER, Saul
Pius XII and the Third Reich; excerpts. ed. by R. Leiber. Look 30:36-8+ My 17 '66
about
Pius' silence. il Time 87:63 Je 3 '66
FRIEDMAN, A. M. and others
Copper artifacts; correlation with source types of copper ores. Science 152:1504-6 Je 10 '66
FRIEDMAN, B. H.
Focus as physical reality. por Art N 65:47-9+ O '66
Introducing Joellen Hall. Art N 65:32-3+ D '66
Towards the total color image. Art N 65:31-3+ Sum '66
FRIEDMAN, Bernard
What are mathematicians doing? address, December 27, 1965. bibliog Science 154:357-62 O 21 '66
FRIEDMAN, Bruce Jay
Number one cat. Sat Eve Post 239:36-8+ S 24 '66
about
Domestic felicity? G. Hicks. Sat R 49:31-2 S 24 '66
Frightened writer. S. Kauffmann. New Repub 155:20+ O 8 '66
John and Bruce. por Newsweek 68:116 S 26 '66
FRIEDMAN, Bruno
Lunar international laboratory. UNESCO Courier 19:31-2+ My '66
FRIEDMAN, Emanuel A.
Expectant mother; ed. by D. Meilach. Redbook 127:35-6 S '66
FRIEDMAN, Herbert
Violent sun. Read Digest 88:167-8+ Mr '66
—and others
Spectrum and distance of source Sco XR-1. bibliog Science 153:1527-8 S 23 '66
FRIEDMAN, Maurice
Elie Wiesel: the modern Job. Commonweal 85:48-52 O 14 '66
FRIEDMAN, Melvin A.
Grouping of similar formats could help in production crisis. Pub W 189:114-15 Mr 7 '66
FRIEDMAN, Milton
Bank depositor. por Newsweek 68:88 N 7 '66
Boycotts and prices. por Newsweek 68:92 N 28 '66
Coming period of inflation won't get out of hand; interview. por U S News 60:63-4 Ap 4 '66
Current monetary policy. por Newsweek 69:59 Ja 9 '67
Inflationary recession. por Newsweek 68:92 O 17 '66
Minimum-wage rates. por Newsweek 68:96 S 26 '66
Volunteer army. por Newsweek 68:100 D 19 '66
FRIEDMAN, Ruth
Tragedy of the tombs. il Sch Arts 65:36-8 My '66
FRIEDMAN, S. Allen
Old units form basis of new plant. Am City 81:90-1 F '66
FRIEL, Brian
Loves of Cass McGuire. Criticism
Commonweal 85:106 O 28 '66
New Yorker 42:118+ O 15 '66
Newsweek 68:98 O 17 '66
Sat R 49:73 O 22 '66
Time il 88:93 O 14 '66
Philadelphia, here I come! Criticism
America 114:364 Mr 12 '66
Cath World 203:319-20 Ag '66
Commonweal 83:668-9 Mr 11 '66
Nation 202:309-10 Mr 14 '66
New Yorker 42:71 F 26 '66
Newsweek 67:87 F 28 '66
Sat R 49:54 Mr 5 '66
Time il 87:101 F 25 '66
Vogue 147:109 Ap 1 '66
FRIEND, D. J. C. and Helson V. A.
Brassica campestris L.: floral induction by one long day. bibliog Science 153:1115-16 S 2 '66

FRIENDLY, Fred W.
Bad days at Black Rock. il por Newsweek 67:62-3 F 28 '66
Farewell for Mr Friendly. America 114:317 Mr 5 '66
Friendly dispute. Sr Schol 88:12 Mr 4 '66
Friendly talk. il por Newsweek 67:97 Ap 18 '66
Matter of conscience. Nation 202:225 F 28 '66
Noble networks. New Repub 154:6 F 26 '66
Ready for Fred; new jobs. Time 87:86 Ap 15 '66
Sounding brass. il por Time 87:64 F 25 '66

FRIENDS, Society of
People called Quakers, by D. E. Trueblood.
Review
    Christian Cent 83:964-5 Ag 3 '66. N. F. S. Ferré

FRIENDSHIP
Different lands, different friendships. M. Mead. Redbook 127:38+ Ag '66
What to do for the child who has no friends. E. W. Johnson. il Parents Mag 41:56-8+ Ag '66
    See also
Love

FRIENDSHIP trees. See Trees

FRIENDSHIP wheel; drama. See Miller, H. L.

FRIES, Waldemar
Where are Audubon's copper plates? Audubon Mag 68:259-62+ Jl '66

FRIESWYK, Siebolt H.
Arts and communications in recreation and park programs. por Parks & Rec 1:976-7+ D '66
Museums-a-go-go. por Parks & Rec 1:414-15+ My '66

FRIGATE birds
Man-o'-war bird. B. Nelson. il Natur Hist 75:32-9 My '66

FRIGGENS, Myriam. See Friggens, P. jt. auth.

FRIGGENS, Paul
Crimson for Christmas. Read Digest 89:146-9 D '66
Great redwoods controversy. Read Digest 89:91-6 D '66
Is that judge fit to sit? Read Digest 89:127-31 Jl '66
Should teachers strike? Read Digest 89:95-9 N '66
—and Friggens, Myriam
Standing-up country. il Read Digest 88:145-52 My '66

FRIMBO, Ernest M.
Frimbo's frolic; interview. New Yorker 42:22-5 Ja 14 '67

FRIMKESS, Michael
Importance of being classical. Craft Horiz 26:18-21+ Mr '66

FRINGE benefits. See Non-wage payments

FRISBIE, Anne
George; poem. Horn Bk 42:475 Ag '66

FRISCH, Bruce
Can we change the weather? Sci Digest 60:76-82 S '66
Crime, are you guilty? Sci Digest 60:70-7 D '66

FRISCH, Max
Chinese wall. Criticism
    Sat R 49:40 My 28 '66

FRISSELL, Toni
Splendid world of Stanford White; photographs. Life 61:87-101 S 16 '66
    about
Patrician photographer of a vanishing age. G. P. Hunt. il por Life 61:3 S 16 '66

FRITCHEY, Clayton
Washington insight. See issues of Harper's magazine

FRITILLARY butterflies. See Butterflies

FRITTERS
Good way to get acquainted with fritters. il Sunset 136:186+ Je '66

FRITTS, Harold C.
Growth-rings of trees: their correlation with climate; excerpts from address, December 27, 1965. bibliog Science 154:973-9 N 25 '66

FRITZ, David H.
More maintenance per man-hour. Am City 81:96-8 N '66

FRITZ, Gretchen
Gretchen just had to make trouble. D. Moser. Life 60:84+ Mr 4 '66

FRITZ, Jean
House that Jack built. Horn Bk 42:681-3 D '66
Little Christmas; story. il Seventeen 25:112-13 D '66

FROBEN, Johann
More than just a businessman. P. W. Schmidtchen. Hobbies 71:104-5+ D '66

FROGHOPPERS
Spittle bug bubbles up a house. il Sci N 90:159 S 3 '66

FROGS
Capturing strange creatures in Colombia; arrow-poison frogs. M. Latham. il Nat Geog Mag 129:682-93 My '66
N-acetylhistidine isolated from frog heart. Y. Kuroda and T. Ikoma. bibliog il Science 152:1241-2 My 27 '66
Night of the bullfrog. D. J. Anderson. il Field & S 71:44-6+ Je '66
    See also
Cookery—Frogs
Embryology—Amphibia
Toads
    Development
        See Amphibia—Development

FROGS as laboratory animals. See Laboratory animals

FROME, Michael
Chimney tops; excerpt from Strangers in high places. Liv Wildn 30:3-5 Spr '66
Mike Frome. See issues of American forests
Neglected American treasures. Holiday 39:129-34 My '66
Ski report: excellent. Holiday 40:90-7+ D '66
Trees of Williamsburg; reprint. Am For 72:18-21+ D '66

FRONT doors. See Doors; Doorways

FRONT drive automobiles. See Automobiles—Front wheel drive

FRONT street theater, Memphis. See Memphis, Tenn.—Theater

FRONTIER airlines, incorporated
Frontier bids for the richer trails; desire to race against the big trunks. il Bsns W p88-90+ S 3 '66

FRONTIER and pioneer life
    Drama
All points West. C. Boiko. Plays 26:41-6, 62 N '66
    United States
Pennsylvania boyhood; memoir. J. N. Culbertson. il Am Heritage 18:84-8 D '66
Science and symbol in the Turner frontier hypothesis. W. Coleman. bibliog f Am Hist R 72:22-49 O '66
Sodbuster surgeons who helped win the West; excerpt from Doctors of the American frontier. R. Dunlop. il Todays Health 44:32-3+ Je '66
There I grew up; A. Lincoln's boyhood in Indiana. W. E. Wilson. il Am Heritage 17:30-1+ O '66
    See also
Homesteads
Pioneers

FROOK, John
At Parsons, a little learning is a profitable thing. Life 60:78+ Je 3 '66

FROST, Albert D. and Palmer, H. P.
Long-base-line interferometer at Jodrell Bank. Sky & Tel 32:21-4 Jl '66

FROST, Douglas L.
That March day; poem. Commonweal 83:642 Mr 4 '66

FROST, Douglas V.
U.S. should adopt a whole new system of measurement. por Nations Bsns 54:86+ Ja '66

FROST, John B. and Bailey, R. W.
Audible continuity and semiconductor checker. Electr World 76:86+ O '66

FROST, Joseph W. P.
Living with antiques. Antiques 89:368-73 Mr '66

FROST, Robert
Robert Frost, by L. Thompson. Review
    Newsweek por 68:112+ O 31 '66. S. Maloff
    Sat R por 49:32-3 N 5 '66
    Time por 88:114+ O 28 '66
Robert Frost, man and myth. J. Dickey. Atlan 218:53-6 N '66; Discussion. 219:30 Ja '67
Robert Frost revisited. G. Hicks. Sat R 49:23-4 Jl 9 '66
Warm spell of Frost. T. Prideaux. Life 60:15 Mr 4 '66

FROST, Tom
California: climb beyond the possible. C. S. Wren. il pors Look 30:70-2 Je 28 '66

FROST
    See also
Ice

FROST protection
Flirting with frost. G. Schultz. il Pop Gard 17:88-9+ D '66
Giving plants frost protection. il Sunset 137:242+ N '66

FROSTINGS. See Icings

FROZEN blood. See Blood—Collection and preservation

FROZEN desserts. See Desserts; Ice cream, ices, etc.

FROZEN food. See Food, Frozen
FROZEN ground
  Particle sorting by repeated freezing and thawing. A. E. Corte; discussion. Science 148:1616-17; bibliog 152:545-6 Je 18 '65, Ap 22 '66
FROZEN soufflé. See Desserts
FRUIT
  Fruits of autumn. L. Line. il Audubon Mag 68:328-9 S '66
    See also
  Cookery—Fruit
    also names of fruits, e.g. Oranges

  Laws and legislation
  Maharajah's mangoes; bar lifted in Italy. il Newsweek 67:93 Je 20 '66

  Storage
  Fruit life doubled. Sci N 90:70 Jl 30 '66
  Fruit storage at subatmospheric pressures. S. P. Burg and E. A. Burg. bibliog il Science 153:314 Jl 15 '66
  Improved fruit storage may affect farm prices; keeping peaches and nectarines in controlled atmospheres. Sci N 90:187 S 10 '66

FRUIT, Candied. See Confectionery
FRUIT, Canned
  Problem with canned fruit. il Consumer Bul 49:15 D '66
FRUIT cake. See Cake
FRUIT culture
  Fruit-truck news. See issues of Farm journal
  Fruits and vegetables. R. Gannon. il Horticulture 44:34-7+ My '66
    See also
  Blueberries

FRUIT desserts. See Desserts
FRUIT flies
    See also
  Olive fruit flies
FRUIT handling
    See also
  Motor trucks, Refrigerated
  Peaches—Handling
FRUIT in art
  Still life with tropical fruit; with painting by H. Rousseau. M. Kaytor. Look 30:70-1 Mr 22 '66
FRUIT industry
    See also
  California packing corporation
FRUIT juice extractors
  Blenders, juicers, extractors; which ones for you? il Redbook 127:91+ O '66
FRUIT juices
  Brand that makes Calpak a winner Del Monte label. il Bsns W p80-1+ Mr 26 '66
FRUIT juices, Frozen
  When advertising is truly a taste-maker. Consumer Rep 32:8 Ja '67
FRUIT trees
  Planting guide to home-grown fruits. il Flower Grower 53:31 S '66
    See also
  Apple trees
  Fruit culture

  Care
  Mice in your orchard? better feed 'em. Farm J 90:68N Mr '66
  Spring tonic for winter-damaged fruit. J. C. Snyder. il Farm J 90:58K My '66

  Pruning
    See Pruning
FRUIT trees, Training of
  Apple growing fence. H. A. Rollins, jr. il Flower Grower 53:34-5+ F '66
FRUITS. See Fruit
FRUMIN, Abraham M. See Perera, C. B. jt. auth.
FRUSTRATION
  Racial reaction pattern studied. Sci N 90: 475 D 3 '66
FRUTKIN, Arnold W.
  Joint enterprises are now a going concern in the exciting field of space research. UNESCO Courier 19:13-14+ My '66
  United States space program and its international signficance; address; with questions and answers. Ann Am Acad 366:89-98 Jl '66
FRY, Amelia
  (ed) See Dana, S. T. Dana years
FRY, B. J. See Gross, P. R. jt. auth.
FRYE, John
  Chesapeake Bay cargo boats. il Motor B 117:184-6 My '66
  Secondhand water? why not? Todays Health 44:56-61 Mr '66

FRYE, William R.
  Tax-appeal ordeal. Reporter 34:21-4 My 5 '66
FUCHS, Alice S.
  New products. Flying 79:31-2 D '66
FUCHS, Joseph
  Musical events: recital in Carnegie Hall. W. Sargeant. New Yorker 42:231 N 19 '66
  New York concert. S. Fleming. Hi Fi 16:132 F '66
FUCHS, Louis H.
  Djerfisherite, alkali copper-iron sulfide: a new mineral from enstatite chondrites. bibliog Science 153:166-7 Jl 8 '66
FUCHS, Roland J.
  Moscow. Focus 16:1-6 Ja '66
FUDGE. See Candy
FUEL
  Report pussyfoots on issues; government report on energy resources. Sci N 90:417 N 19 '66
    See also
  Coal
    also subhead Fuel under various subjects, e.g. Rockets—Fuel
FUEL cells
  Bringing the fuel cell down to earth. L. Lessing. il Fortune 74:128-31+ S '66
  Fuel cell works after 7-mi. fall. il Tech W 19:19 Jl 18 '66
  Fuel cells for future power. A. Ewing. il Sci N 89:270-1 Ap 16 '66
  Fuel cells: new way to make electricity. il Changing T 20:25-8 Je '66
  High-energy demands press technology; alkali metal electrochemical power systems. W. E. Wilks. Tech W 19:14-15 O 3 '66
  Short circuits boost fuel cell power. Sci N 89:244 Ap 9 '66
FUEL injection systems. See Automobile engines—Fuel feeding
FUEL research
    See also
  Guided missiles—Fuel
FUEL tanks
    See also
  Space vehicles—Fuel tanks
FUEL tanks, Motor boat. See Motor boats—Fuel tanks
FUGERE, Barry
  New Jersey chicken trial: verdict for science. E. Langer. Science 152:479-81 Ap 22 '66
FUGITIVE; story. See Davies, R.
FUGITIVE slaves. See Slavery—United States —Fugitive slaves
FUGUE in three voices; story. See Simon, M. L.
FUJICHROME films. See Moving picture films
FUJIMOTO, M. and others
  Electron paramagnetic resonance of methyl radicals on porous glass surface. bibliog Science 154:381-2 O 21 '66
FUJITA, Y. See Turkevich, J. jt. auth.
FUKAS, Vladimir
  Prague designer-illustrator shows work to U.S. publishers. il Pub W 190:116-18 D 5 '66
FUKUYAMA, Betty Adkins
  Comment on the un-daily bulletin; poem. Christian Cent 83:1601 D 28 '66
  Reflections in a pool; poem. Christian Cent 83:953 Ag 3 '66
FULBRIGHT, James William
  Arrogance of power: a clash over U.S. policy; address, May 5, 1966. por U S News 60: 113-21 My 23 '66
  Excerpt from address, March 1, 1966. Cong Digest 45:119-21 Ap '66
  Excerpt from debate, July 18, 27, 1966. Cong Digest 45:204+ Ag '66
  Fatal arrogance of power. por N Y Times Mag p28-9+ My 15 '66
  Patriotism of dissent. Redbook 128:44+ N '66
  Speaking out. por Sat Eve Post 239:10+ Ap 9 '66
  Why our foreign policy is failing; interview, ed. by E. Sevareid. pors Look 30:23-31 My 3 '66

    about
  Advice and dissent. il por Newsweek 67:30-1 F 21 '66
  Agony, yes: arrogance, no. America 114:767 My 28 '66
  Apologia pro verbis suis: expression of regret over recent remarks about moral conditions in Saigon. Time 87:70 My 27 '66
  Be kind to China. K. Crawford. Newsweek 67:34 Ap 4 '66
  Blunderball. por Newsweek 68:19 Ag 8 '66
  Can he be serious? concerning his Asian policy speech Nat R 18:757-8 Ag 9 '66
  CIA chief vs. Fulbright; Helms's letter irks Senate. por U S News 61:16 Ag 8 '66
  Closer ties for LBJ and Fulbright? il por U S News 60:15 Je 27 '66
  Controversial senator surrounded by controversy. il por U S News 60:26 Mr 14 '66

FULBRIGHT, James William—about—_Cont._
Courage to be wrong. K. Crawford. Newsweek 67:27 F 7 '66
Dissent & defeat. il por Time 87:24 Mr 11 '66
Duel of chairmen. Time 88:21 Jl 22 '66
Exhaustive, explicit & enough. il Time 87:21-3 F 25 '66
From Fulbright: a sweeping attack on LBJ's Asian doctrine. por U S News 61:12 Ag 1 '66
Fulbright on camera. A. Campbell. New Repub 154:19-22 My 21 '66
Fulbright pro and con. R. Reston. Atlan 218:10+ O '66
Fulbright revolt. M. J. Goldbloom. Commentary 42:64-9 S '66
Fulbright the undecider. Life 60:4 My 13 '66
Goldwater speaks out about Senator Fulbright; excerpts from address, May 5, 1966. B. M. Goldwater. U S News 60:23 My 16 '66
Grand alliance. Reporter 34:16 F 24 '66
Hawaii conference; criticism of Johnson's Vietnam approach. il Time 87:19-20 F 11 '66
Mr Dove and Mr Hawk. S. Alsop. por Sat Eve Post 239:18 Je 18 '66
Of junkets & the USIA. Time 88:43 Ag 26 '66
Old realities and new myths; difference between 1964 and 1966 views. H. Fairlie. por Reporter 34:19-21 Je 16 '66; Discussion. 35:6+ Jl 14 '66; Nat R 18:662-4 Jl 12 '66
On the subject of arrogance. Time 87:31 My 13 '66
Portrait of the chairman. il por Time 87:21-2 F 18 '66
Power akin to freedom. il por Time 87:25 Ap 29 '66
Quid without the quo. il Time 87:23 Mr 11 '66
Replacement needed. K. Crawford. Newsweek 68:44 O 10 '66
Roots of the Arkansas questioner. B. Brower. il pors Life 60:92-4+ My 13 '66
Senate rift over Vietnam widens. por Bsns W p28-9 F 12 '66
Senator Fulbright. by T. Coffin. Review New Repub 155:25-6 D 3 '66. G. W. Johnson
Spooks need course in ghostwriting. J. N. Eller. America 115:151 Ag 13 '66
Strange story of a Senate committee. il pors U S News 60:32+ Ap 4 '66
T.R.B. from Washington. New Repub 154:4 Ap 16 '66
Victory for Russell Fulbright loses CIA wrangle. U S News 61:19 Jl 25 '66

FULBRIGHT international exchange program. See Scholarships and fellowships

FULBRIGHT students. See Scholarships and fellowships

FULDHEIM, Dorothy
Cleveland store chalks up sale of 2100 copies of book. il por Pub W 189:90 Je 27 '66

FULKER, D. W.
Mating speed in male drosophila melanogaster: a psychogenetic analysis. bibliog Science 153:203-5 Jl 8 '66

FULL, Jerome K.
Sailing the inland brine. Yachting 120:42-3+ Ag '66

FULL employment. See Employment

FULLER, Buckminster. See Fuller, R. B.

FULLER, Helen
Pressure on Congress. New Repub 155:32-4 D 10 '66

FULLER, Hoyt W.
Famous writer faces challenge. Ebony 21:188-90+ Je '66
World festival of Negro arts. Ebony 21:96-102+ Jl '66

FULLER, John G.
Aboard a flying saucer; excerpt from The interrupted journey. Look 30:44-8+ O 4; 111-14+ O 18 '66
Did flying saucers cause the blackout? excerpts from Incident at Exeter. Pop Mech 126:100-2+ N '66
Outer-space ghost story; excerpt from Incident at Exeter. Look 30:36+ F 22 '66; Same abr. Read Digest 88:72-6 My '66
Report of a hypnotic episode with a UFO in New England; excerpt from Incident at Exeter. Sat R 49:44-5 Ag 6 '66
Trade winds. See issues of Saturday review

FULLER, Muriel
Youth magazines in the United States. Horn Bk 42:110+ F '66

FULLER, Richard Buckminster
How little I know. por Sat R 49:29-31+ N 12 '66

about
Amazing sun dome you can build. C. E. Rhine. il Pop Sci 188:108-12 My '66
Bucky's biggest bubble. il Arch Forum 124:74-9 Je '66

Dome. J. Burgner. il Design 67:34-7 My '66
Habitat 67. D. Jacobs. il Horizon 9:70-3 Wint 67
R. Buckminster Fuller. J. Peter. pors Look 30:56-8 Ag 23 '66

FULLER, Susan
Cornflake syndrome. Atlan 217:110-12 My '66

FULLMER, Don
Jab from the intellectual. M. Kane. il Sports Illus 24:18-21+ F 14 '66

FULTON, W. R. and Moffitt, J. C.
Characteristics of good school financing. PTA Mag 60:14 F '66

FULTZ, Sara A. and Sussman, A. S.
Antigenic differences in the surfaces of hyphae and rhizoids in allomyces. bibliog il Science 152:785-7 My 6 '66

FU MANCHU (literary character) See Characters in literature

FUMARATE
Fumarate reductase in the control of heme biosynthesis. T. Kurumada and R. F. Labbe. bibliog il Science 151:1228-9 Mr 11 '66

FUND for the advancement of education
$486,500 in grants for anti-poverty book programs. Pub W 189:83-4 Ap 25 '66
National book committee, Ford foundation bring books to VISTA, other programs. Library J 91:5721+ N 15 '66
Schools make news; grants designed to encourage the reading and owning of pleasurable books by disadvantaged children and adults. Sat R 49:63 My 21 '66

FUND raising
Charity or duplicity? Bishop Sheen's advertisement, God love you medal. Christian Cent 83:1167 S 28 '66
Colleges wrap up more gifts than ever. il Bsns W p63-4+ My 21 '66
Dallas: charity supper, plus. il Ladies Home J 83:92-3+ O '66
Fine art of fund raising; nation's institutes of higher learning. Time 89:46+ Ja 13 '67
How to start a children's zoo; zoo fever sweeps Lincoln, Neb. A. R. Folsom. il Parks & Rec 1:430-2 My '66
If you're asked to work on the fund drive; it takes know-how. il Changing T 20:41-3 Ap '66
Million-dollar trinket; Disabled American veterans activities. R. L. Smith. il Nation 203:354-5 O 10 '66
Poverty and fund-raising. America 115:128 Ag 6 '66
Stewardship by invidious comparison; fifty million dollar drive by United Presbyterian church in the U.S.A. J. R. Bodo. Christian Cent 83:907-8 Jl 20 '66
Where the auction is. il Newsweek 68:108 S 19 '66
See also
Campaign funds

Anecdotes, facetiae, satire, etc.
Make a buck. Christian Cent 83:1131 S 14 '66

FUNDAMENTAL particles. See Particles (nuclear physics)

FUNDY, BAY OF
Was Columbus in Canada? P. Bilbao. il Américas 18:17-28 Jl '66

FUNERAL rings. See Rings

FUNERAL rites and ceremonies
Aberfan's farewell to its children; with report by J. Hicks. il Life 61:105-6 N 11 '66
Funeral: vestige or value? by P. E. Irion. Review
Christian Cent 83:369 Mr 23 '66. J. D. Townsend
How dearly beloved? America 115:504-5 O 29 '66

FUNERAL services. See Funeral rites and ceremonies

FUNERALS, Cost of
Facts you should know about funerals. A. Q. Maisel. Read Digest 89:81-6 S '66

FUNGAL spores. See Spores (botany)

FUNGI
Aflatoxin B_1: binding to DNA in vitro and alteration of RNA metabolism in vivo. M. B. Sporn and others. bibliog il Science 151:1539-41 Mr 25 '66
Ambrosia fungi: extent of specificity to ambrosia beetles. L. R. Batra. bibliog il Science 153:193-5 Jl 8 '66
Antigenic differences in the surfaces of hyphae and rhizoids in allomyces. S. A. Fultz and A. S. Sussman. bibliog il Science 152:785-7 My 6 '66
D(—)-lactate dehydrogenase in lower fungi. F. H. Gleason and others. bibliog il Science 152.1272-3 My 27 '66
Fungus-growing ants. N. A. Weber. bibliog il Science 153:587-604 Ag 5 '66

FUNGI—*Continued*
Gibberellin production: genetic control in the fungus gibberella fujikuroi. C. Spector and B. O. Phinney. bibliog il Science 153:1397-8 S 16 '66

It's a moldy world; quiz. J. Daugherty and M. Daugherty. il Sci Digest 60:88-90 N '66

Morphogenesis in trichoderma: suppression of photoinduction by 5-fluorouracil. E. Galun and J. Gressel. bibliog il Science 151:696-8 F 11 '66

Mycotoxicoses: toxic fungi in tobaccos. J. Forgacs and W. T. Carll. il Science 152:1634-5 Je 17 '66

Peanut mold test devised; using marine borer eggs to detect aflatoxin. Sci N 90:451 N 26 '66

Peroxidase and resitance to ceratocystis in sweet potato increased by Volatile materials. B. Clare and others. bibliog il Science 153:62-3 Jl 1 '66

Plasmodesmata between hyphal cells of geotrichum candidum. B. T. Kirk and J. B. Sinclair. bibliog il Science 153:1646 S 30 '66

Rapid and marked inhibition of rat-liver RNA polymerase by aflatoxin B_1. H. V. Gelboin and others. bibliog Science 154:1205-6 D 2 '66

Tobacco fungus causes emphysema in animals. Sci N 90:261 O 1 '66

Zinc and cobalt: effect on the iron metabolism of ustilago sphaerogena. H. Komai and J. B. Neilands. bibliog il Science 153:751-2 Ag 12 '66
See also
Basidiomycetes
Schizophyllum commune

Translocation
See Plants—Translocation

FUNGI, Pathogenic
Systemic fungicidal activity of 1,4-oxathiin derivatives. B. Von Schmeling and M. Kulka. il Science 152:659-60 Ap 29 '66

FUNGI, Sex in
Schizophyllum commune: new mutations in the B incompatibility factor. Y. Koltin and J. R. Raper. bibliog il Science 154:510-11 O 28 '66

FUNGICIDES
Fungicidal phthalimidophosphonothionates; novel type of organophosphoramide compound. H. Tolkmith and others. bibliog l Science 155:85-6 Ja 6 '67

Fungicide selective for basidiomycetes. L. V. Edgington and others. il Science 153:307-8 Jl 15 '66

Safe and accurate dilution of garden chemicals. il Sunset 136:240 Je '66

FUNK, Peter
It pays to increase your word power. See issues of Reader's digest

FUNKE, Lewis
(ed) See Hayes, H. Queen and I

FUNNIES. See Comics (books, strips, etc)

FUNNY man; story. See MacDonald, J. D.

FUNSTON, George Keith
Funston's farewell. por Newsweek 68:87 S 26 '66

Man for everyman's capitalism. il por Time 88:88+ S 23 '66

FUR
Furrier to the art world: J. Kaplan. G. Glueck. il N Y Times Mag p38-9+ O 2 '66

Notes and comment; show sponsored by Saks Fifth avenue, in collaboration with Hudson's Bay company. New Yorker 42:43 D 17 '66

FUR auctions. See Auctions

FUR coats, wraps, etc.
Please don't feed the fun furs. W. K. Zinsser. il Horizon 9:118-19 Wint '67

What's Christmas without a mink? new shades and patterns, ranging in price up to $75,000. il Bsns W p 122-3+ N 26 '66

FUR farming
What's Christmas without a mink? new shades and patterns, ranging in price up to $75,000. il Bsns W p 122-3+ N 26 '66

FUR trade
Hide sales imperil rare species. C. W. Buchheister. il Audubon Mag 68:73 Mr '66

Ordeal in Hell's Canyon; expedition of Astor's fur traders, under W. P. Hunt, 1810-12. A. M. Josephy, jr. il Am Heritage 18:72-9+ D '66

Where the fur flies; international auction at Leningrad's fur palace. il Newsweek 68:64 Ag 8 '66
See also
Fur farming
Hudson's Bay company

FURAY, Michael
Negritude, a romantic myth? New Repub 155:32-5 Jl 2 '66

FURFEY, Paul Hanly
Books. Commonweal 84:558-9 S 2 '66

FURLONG, William Barry
How electronic gadgets are changing football. Pop Mech 126:91-3+ O '66

How specialized can you get? N Y Times Mag p23+ Ag 14 '66

It's a three-billion-dollar business. N Y Times Mag p50-1+ Je 5 '66

Last puritan. Sports Illus 24:12-17 Ja 31 '66

Out in the bleachers, where the action is. Harper 233:49-53 Jl '66

Psychologist on the sidelines. N Y Times Mag p56-7+ N 13 '66

Wind that blew in Chicago. Sports Illus 24:26-7+ Mr 7 '66

FURMAN university, Greenville, S.C.
Education: facilities grants forbidden to Baptist colleges. L. J. Carter. Science 152:626-9 Ap 29 '66

FURNACES
See also
Heating

FURNACES, Blast. See Blast furnaces

FURNAS, Clifford Cook
Coming water crisis. Nation 203:205-6 S 12 '66

FURNAS, J. C.
And sudden death; reprint. Read Digest 89:153-7 O '66

FURNISHINGS, Household. See Household furnishings

FURNISS, Edgar S. Jr
French foreign policy under de Gaulle. Cur Hist 50:209-13+ Ap '66

FURNISS, James P. and Nadler, P. S.
Should banks reprice corporate services? Harvard Bsns R 44:95-105 My '66

FURNITURE
Back to the '30s; kooky furniture. il Time 89:80 Ja 20 '67

Chez Mile: besting the budget. B. Plumb. il Mlle 64:42-3 Ja '67

Custom look, with hardware and moldings. il Bet Hom & Gard 44:42 Je '66

Furniture finds under $50. il House & Gard 129:166-7 My '66

Furniture trends for '66. R. Martens. il Farm J 90:96-8 Mr '66

Good gifts for the family. il Bet Hom & Gard 44:20+ N '66

Great news in furniture that won't scuttle your budget! P. Rumely. il Bet Hom & Gard 44:60-5 Je '66

Ideas in action. D. Jordan. il Bet Hom & Gard 44:54-71 O '66

It's easier now to build good furniture. L. D. Kreitz. il Pop Sci 189:164-6 O '66

News! summer furniture you won't put in cold storage. il Bet Hom & Gard 44:30+ Je '66

100 ideas under $100. il Bet Hom & Gard 44:22+ Jl '66

Royal pavilion, Brighton. C. Musgrave. il Antiques 90:320-5 S '66

Sculptured furniture. J. Peter. il Look 30:64-5 O 4 '66

Twelve ways to attach legs. W. C. Lammey. il Pop Mech 126:122-3 Jl '66
See also
Bookcases
Chairs
Rugs and carpets

Care
Care and safekeeping of furniture. House & Gard 129:82-4+ Ap; 228-9+ My '66

Design
America discovers Colombo B. Plumb. il N Y Times Mag p30-1 S 4 '66

Designers in a mod mood; English furniture design. B. Plumb. il N Y Times Mag p 116-17+ O 30 '66

Fantasy furniture: exhibition at New York's Museum of contemporary crafts, with comments of craftsmen. il Craft Horiz 26:10-17 Ja '66

Form follows fantasy; Fantasy furniture at Museum of contemporary crafts. B. Plumb. il N Y Times Mag p48-9 Ja 23 '66

Made in U.S.A. B. Plumb. il N Y Times Mag p70-2 My 8 '66

New dimension in comfort. il House & Gard 129:176-7 My '66

They coined modern more than thirty years ago. B. Plumb. il N Y Times Mag p78-9+ Ap 3 '66; Reply. C. Eames. p 16 Jl 17 '66

Tomorrow, Italian-style. B. Plumb. il N Y Times Mag p90-1+ Je 5 '66

FURNITURE--Design--*Continued*
Who is sitting on that man there? R. Reif. il N Y Times Mag p58-9 Ag 7 '66
Wood; a discussion. S. Maloof; W. Esherick; D. McKinley. il Craft Horiz 26:16-19 Je '66

Competitions

Projections in design winners announced. Design 67:28-9 Mr '66

Exhibitions

Back to the '30s; International home furnishings show. il Time 89:80 Ja 20 '67
Cologne collection; international furniture fair. B. Plumb. il N Y Times Mag p56-7 F 27 '66
Fantasy furniture; exhibition at New York's Museum of contemporary crafts, with comments of craftsmen. il Craft Horiz 26:10-17 Ja '66
New York: the bed; show at the Museum of contemporary crafts, September 23-November 6, 1966. R. Howard. il Craft Horiz 26:8-15 S '66

Finishing

Five simple steps to an antique finish. il House & Gard 129:48 Mr '66
How to save money on antiques; excerpt from Antiques you can decorate with. G. Grotz. il Ladies Home J 83:59+ N '66
Refinish furniture the easy way. J. LemMon. il Suc Farm 64:106-7 F '66
Step by step to a perfect mess! J. Laury. il Bet Hom & Gard 44:92 Mr '66
Turning reproductions into antiques. W. I. Fischman. il Pop Mech 126:116-20 Jl '66

History

Some thoughts on the environmental arts; Adams-Emery wing at the Cincinnati art museum. P. R. Adams. il Antiques 89:391-8 Mr '66

Refinishing

See Furniture--Finishing

FURNITURE, American
American decorative arts in Texas; the Bayou bend collection of the Museum of fine arts, Houston. D. B. Warren. il Antiques 90:796-815 D '66
Ameican furniture. il Antiques 90:538+ O '66
American furniture in the collection of Mr and Mrs Edward H. Tevriz. H. Comstock. il Antiques 89:256-61 F '66
American furniture of the Federal period, 1788-1825; Antiques book preview. C. F. Montgomery. il Antiques 90:326-33 S '66
Collectors' notes; documented examples. E. Gaines. il Antiques 89:838-45 Je '66
Finest of America's design heritage. il Good H 162:132-9 Ap '66
In the museums. R. Davidson. il Antiques 90:368+ S '66
Living with antiques; Shaker adventure. C. Upton and H. Upton. il Antiques 90:84-9 Jl '66
Modern Europe takes home the U.S. past; U.S. furniture exhibits at Cologne. il Bsns W p56-8 F 5 '66
More on the Meeks cabinetmakers. J. Pearce and L. W. Pearce. il Antiques 90:69-73 Jl '66
Museum of early southern decorative arts; the rooms and their furnishings. F. L. Horton. il Antiques 91:72-95 Ja '67
Southern furniture since 1952. H. Comstock. il Antiques 91:102-19 Ja '67

FURNITURE, Arrangement of
Comfort is a whole way of life. il House & Gard 131:80-7 Ja '67
Great news in furniture that won't scuttle your budget! P. Rumely. il Bet Home & Gard 44:60-5 Je '66
Report on residential interior design. G. O'Brien. il Arch Rec 139:29+ Mid-My '66

FURNITURE, Built in
Two rooms from one. il Pop Mech 126:137-42+ D '66

FURNITURE, Childrens
Child's chair is not just to sit. J. Peter. il Look 30:55 F 8 '66
Playpens. il Consumer Rep 31:452-5 S '66
Redbook guide to children's furniture. il Redbook 126:94-102 F '66
Revolution in the nursery. B. Plumb. il N Y Times Mag p22 D 25 '66

FURNITURE, Egyptian
Furniture in the ancient world. by H. S. Baker. Review
House & Gard il 130:56-7 N '66

FURNITURE, English
Eighteenth century, a furniture style of many moods. il House & Gard 130:214-17 O '66
English furniture after printed designs in the Royal Ontario museum. G. Brett. Antiques 89:386-90 Mr '66
In the proper English manner. J. Peter. il Look 30:48-9 Ap 5 '66

FURNITURE, French
In the grand manner; 18th-century French furnishings. R. Reif. il N Y Times Mag p 116-17 S 11 '66

FURNITURE, Italian
Italian rustic; chairs and stools with rush woven seats. J. Peter. il Look 30:52-3 My 3 '66
Tomorrow, Italian-style. B. Plumb. il N Y Times Mag p90-1+ Je 5 '66

FURNITURE, Outdoor
And the living is easy. B. Plumb. il N Y Times Mag p98-9 Ap 17 '66
Bright summer of turned-on furniture; Bill Bell inventions. il Life 61:86-7 Jl 22 '66
News! summer furniture you won't put in cold storage. il Bet Hom & Gard 44:30+ Je '66
Patio furniture for the style conscious home-owner. il Pop Gard 17:20-5 My '66
Poolside joys and comforts. il House & Gard 129:144-5 Je '66
Redbook's guide to outdoor furniture. il Redbook 127:64-72 My '66
Selecting furniture for outdoor use. Good H 162:150 My '66
Smart look in outdoor furniture. il Flower Grower 53:34-6+ My '66

See also
Benches

FURNITURE, Papier-mâché
Paper weight. il Time 87:47 Ap 1 '66

FURNITURE, Victorian
Where Victorian still reigns: Aspen, Colo. B. Plumb. il N Y Times Mag p 116-17+ O 2 '66

FURNITURE, Wicker
Wicker is wonderful. il Bet Hom & Gard 44:122 Je '66
Wonderful, whimsical wicker. il House & Gard 129:148-55 My '66
Wood is good, but wicker is kickier. B. Plumb. il Mlle 63:110-11 O '66

FURNITURE dealers. See Furniture industry and trade

FURNITURE design. See Furniture--Design

FURNITURE factories
See also
Shelby Williams industries, incorporated

Employees

See also
Furniture industry and trade--Wages and hours

FURNITURE industry and trade
Chairs across the sea; U.S. furniture industry. Newsweek 67:78+ F 14 '66
Sitting pretty in contract furniture. il Bsns W p62+ My 7 '66
Technology restyles furniture business. il Bsns W p94-6+ N 19 '66

Wages and hours

Earnings in wood household furniture, May-June 1965. F. L. Bauer. il Mo Labor R 89:398-400 Ap '66

FURNITURE makers. See Cabinetmakers

FURS. See Fur

FURST, Joseph
Cashing in on high risks abroad; Income fund of Boston, inc. il por Bsns W p 154+ N 12 '66

FURTH, Hertha
Hertha Furth advises on painting abroad; with biographical sketch. il por Am Artist 31:28-9+ Ja '67

FURY, Kathleen D.
Wonderful toys any father can make for Christmas. Redbook 28:70-7 N '66

FUSED twins. See Siamese twins

FUSES (ordnance)
2.75-in. rocket fuze production gains. C. D. LaFond. Miss & Roc 18:21 Ap 25 '66

FUSION, Nuclear. See Nuclear fusion

FUSON, Ben W.
Getting to know your state's literary map. Sr Schol 89:sup44-5 S 23 '66

FUTTIPUR SIKRI. See Fatehpur Sikri, India

FUTURE
Blueprint for the future U.S. il U S News 60:60-2 F 21 '66
Day after tomorrow. J. Curtis. Parks & Rec 1:677-8 S '66

FUTURE—*Continued*
Shapes of the future; theories of Robert L. Heilbroner and Arnold J. Toynbee. A. Campbell. New Repub 155:22+ O 15 '66
Where the California game is taking us. G. B. Leonard. il Look 30:108-12+ Je 28 '66
See also
Forecasts
Two thousand (year)
FUTURE farmers of America
Farmers of the future. H. N. Hunsicker. il Am Ed 2:20-2 F '66
FUTURE life
See also
Eschatology

FUTURES. See Exchanges; Hedging

FUZES (ordnance) See Fuses (ordnance)

G

GAMIS. See Printing industries of America, incorporated—Graphic arts marketing information service
GAO. See United States—General accounting office
GATF. See Graphic arts technical foundation
GATT. See General agreement on tariffs and trade
G. D. Searle and company. See Searle, G. D. and company
GE. See General electric company
GEM. See Ground effect machines
GFWC. See General federation of women's clubs
GI bill of rights. See Service men, Discharged —Education
G.I. Joe dolls. See Dolls
GM. See General motors
GNP. See Gross national product
GOMA. See Good outdoor manners association
GOP. See Republican party
GSA. See Geological society of America
GABLIK, Suzi
Fahlstrom: a place for everything. Art N 65:38-42+ Sum '66
GABO, Naum
Plumbing the space age. il por Time 87:78 Ap 22 '66
GABRIEL, Bill
Some observations on strutting sage grouse. il Nat Parks Mag 40:18-19 O '66
GABRIEL, Jack P.
Wonders of India. Travel 126:56-62 O '66
GADDIS, Paul O.
Analyzing overseas investments. Harvard Bsns R 44:115-22 My '66
GADGETS
Handyman how-to time-savers! il Bet Hom & Gard 44:145-6+ Je '66
Indispensable gadget; for the cook. il Ladies Home J 83:68+ D '66
Sophisticated games and gadgets. R. Atcheson. il Holiday 40:143-4 D '66
GADSDEN, Ala.
New sewer system sparks new industry. il Am City 81:66 My '66
GAFFNEY, Edward M.
(ed) See Outler, A. C. Reflections of a council observer
GAFFRON, Carole
Girl who knew everything; story. Redbook 128:171 N '66
GAGARIN, İUriĭ Alekseevich
Heart of the matter; statement. por UNESCO Courier 19:4 My '66
GAGES
Self-reading O.D. shop gauge. W. E. Burton. il Pop Mech 125:196-8 Mr '66
See also
Strain gages
GAGLIANO, Frank
Night of the dunce. Criticism New Yorker 42:78 Ja 7 '67
GAIN, Dick
Brief biography. S. Goodman. pors Dance Mag 40:62-3 Je '66
GAINES, Edith
Collectors' notes. See issues of Antiques
GAINES, Ervin J.
Intellectual freedom. See issues of ALA bulletin to June 1966
Library education and the talent shortage. por Library J 91:1770-1 Ap 1 '66

Reference librarian in an urban public library; excerpts from address, July 1965. por Library J 91:2003-7 Ap 15 '66
—See Busch, K. C. jt. auth.
GAINES, Kenneth Ward
Angel of mercy to the astronauts. il pors Ebony 21:49-50+ Je '66
GAINESVILLE, Ga.
Only in Georgia; dead heat and deadlock. Nation 203:692 D 26 '66
GAINS tax. See Income tax—Capital gains tax
GAINSBRUGH, Martin R.
Savings accounts: attractive at prevailing rates of interest; interview. por U S News 60:64-5 Ap 4 '66
GALACTIC systems
Deep-sky wonders. W. S. Houston. See issues of Sky and telescope
Faint blue objects. Sky & Tel 31:345 Je '66
Galactic depolarization of the 21-centimeter-wavelength radiation of extragalactic sources. J. M. Bologna and others. bibliog il Science 154:1656-8 D 30 '66
Galactic structure; ed. by A. Blaauw and M. Schmidt. Review
Sky & Tel il 31:357-61 Je '66. B. J. Bok
Galaxies, quasars, and the expanding universe. T. D. Nicholson. il Natur Hist 76: 36-9 Ja '67
Jekyll-Hyde life led by galaxies. Sci N 89: 379 My 14 '66
Motions in the galaxy M77. il Sky & Tel 31: 143 Mr '66
Neutral hydrogen survey of Andromeda galaxy. W. D. Brundage and J. D. Kraus. bibliog il Science 153:411-14 Jl 22 '66
Peculiar galaxies and radio sources. H. Arp. bibliog il Science 151:1214-16 Mr 11 '66; Reply. B. Hoffmann. 152:671 Ap 29 '66
Quasi-stellar objects: possible local origin. J. Terrell. bibliog Science 154:1281-8 D 9 '66
Radio astronomy and the galactic system. B. J. Bok. il Sky & Tel 32:271-4, 341-3 N-D '66

GALACTOSAMINE. See Sugars
GALACTOSAMINE glycan. See Polysaccharides
GALACTOSE
Effect of sugars on transport of alanine in intestine. R. A. Chez and others. bibliog il Science 153:1012-13 Ag 26 '66
GALACTOSE dehydrogenases. See Dehydrogenases
GALACTOSE metabolism
Galactose conversion to d-xylulose; an alternate route of galactose metabolism. P. Cuatrecasas and S. Segal. bibliog il Science 153:549-51 Jl 29 '66
Galactose metabolism and cell sociology. H. M. Kalckar; reply with rejoinder. W. E. Razzell. Science 151:478 Ja 28 '66
GALACTOSEMIA
Electrophoretic variation of galactose-1-phosphate uridyltransferase. C. K. Mathai and E. Beutler. bibliog il Science 154:1179-80 D 2 '66
GALACTOSIDASES
Co-linearity of β-galactosidase with its gene by immunological detection of incomplete polypeptide chains. A. V. Fowler and I. Zabin. bibliog il Science 154:1027-9 N 25 '66
GALANOPLOS, Ruth
Art of writing greeting cards. Sat R 49: 94-6 D 10 '66
GALANOPOULOS, A. G.
Atlantis hypothesis. Sat R 49:93 D 3 '66
GALANTAY, Ervin
Architecture. Nation 202:500-2, 629-30, 789-90; 203:292-4, 652-4, 714-16 Ap 25, My 23, Je 27, S 26, D 12, 26 '66
GALANTIÈRE, Lewis
Writer as independent spirit. Sat R 49:30+ Je 4 '66
GALANTIN, I. J.
Worlds oceans; address, August 13, 1966. Vital Speeches 32:738-41 O 1 '66
GALÁPAGOS ISLANDS
Man-o'-war bird. B. Nelson. il Natur Hist 75:32-9 My '66
See also
Birds—Galápagos Islands
GALAXY (Milky way) See Milky way
GALBRAITH, Georgie Starbuck
Short subject; poem. McCalls 94:116 Ja '67
Song of the gift-bearing husband. McCalls 93:126 Jl '66
GALBRAITH, John Kenneth
Agenda for American liberals; excerpt from address, April 1966. Commentary 41:29-34 Je; 42:16 S '66
Department of amplification. New Yorker 42: 50+ Ja 14 '67
Life book review. Life 60:12 Je 24 '66
Polipollutionists. Atlan 219:52-4 Ja '67

GALBRAITH, John Kenneth—*Continued*
Rising prices will be less of a problem in the future; interview. por U S News 60:60-2 Ap 4 '66
That book. Reporter 34:58 Mr 10 '66
Was Mrs Kennedy justified in bringing suit? Sat R 50:18-21 Ja 21 '67
World through Galbraith's eyes; interview. ed. by A. Lewis. pors N Y Times Mag p25+ D 18 '66
about
Burying free enterprise. por Time 89:92 Ja 6 '67

GALBRAITH, Virginia L.
West European foreign aid. bibliog f Cur Hist 51:88-95+ Ag '66

GALBREATH, John Wilmer
Superfan and super achiever. J. Mann. il por Sports Illus 24:52-60 Ja 24 '66

GALE, Bill
Advice to tall girls from a tall man. Seventeen 25:206-7 Mr '66

GALE, Don
Old-fashioned skyrocketing Fourth. por Parks & Rec 1:551-2 Jl '66

GALE, John Mackinnon
Shape of madness. L. Schaffer. New Repub 155:25-6 S 3 '66

GALE, Vi
Prizewinner, the real thing, and two others. R. Tillinghast. Poetry 109:120-2 N '66

GALE family
At the sign of the crest. H. K. Eilers. il Hobbies 71:120 Ja '67

GALILEI, Galileo
Galileo, science and the church, by J. J. Langford. Review
Commonweal 85:144+ N 4 '66. T. P. McTighe

GALINTIN, I. J.
Naval material support; address, January 20, 1966. Vital Speeches 32:308-11 Mr 1 '66

GALL, Norman
Latin America: revolution without revolutionaries. Nation 203:145-9 Ag 22 '66

GALLAGHER, Francis J.
Biography (cont) America 114:666+; 115:704+ My 7, N 26 '66

GALLAGHER, J. Roswell
Teen-agers need a doctor of their own. por Ladies Home J 84:32+ Ja '67

GALLAGHER, James J.
Who can afford to work for the church? America 114:192-4 F 5 '66

GALLAGHER, Joseph
State of the question. America 115:548-9 N 5 '66
about
Baltimore blues.   S. J. Adamo. America 115:837 D 24 '66

GALLAGHER, Michael
Japanese-Catholic novel. Commonweal 85:136-8 N 4 '66

GALLAGHER, Patrick
World of Levi-Strauss. New Repub 156:38-40 Ja 7 '67

GALLAGHER, Robert S.
Four score and seven hours ago. Horizon 8:38-9 Aut '66
Me for ma, and I ain't got a dern thing against pa. Am Heritage 17:46-7+ O '66

GALLAGHER, Thomas
Oona O'; story. Redbook 126:161 Mr '66

GALLAHER, Thomas M.
Excerpt from statement, June 30, 1965. Cong Digest 45:61+ F '66

GALLAHORN, James T. Jr
School that says welcome. por Am Ed 2:1-3 My '66

GALLANT, Mavis
Bonaventure; story. New Yorker 42:34-8 Jl 30 '66
Questions and answers; story. New Yorker 42:33-8 My 28 '66
Report; story. New Yorker 42:62-5 D 3 '66
Vacances pax; story. New Yorker 42:26-9 Jl 16 '66

GALLARDO, Ricardo
Defender of the Indians. Américas 18:23-31 O '66

GALLASHAW, Ernest
Case in point. Newsweek 68:46 O 24 '66
Very fine boy. il por Newsweek 68:27 Ag 8 '66

GALLAUDET college, Washington, D.C.
Voice of the silent stage. E. Ferber. il Am Ed 2:29-32 O '66

GALLER, David
Information; poem. Nation 202:334 Mr 21 '66
Partridge; Hundred years; To my lust; poems. Poetry 108:162-6 Je '66
To the swifts; poem. New Yorker 42:50 Mr 19 '66

GALLER, Sidney Roland
Science chases dust from nation's attic. the Smithsonian. il Bsns W p 110-12+ My 21 '66

GALLERIES and museums. See Art—Galleries and museums

GALLERY, D. V.
So you don't remember Pearl Harbor? Pop Mech 126:84-6+ D '66

GALLETTA, G. J. See Brooks, J. F. jt. auth.

GALLEYS (ships)
Department of correction and amplification; concerning number of banks of oars on ancient ships. T. L. Stocken. New Yorker 42:101-3 Ag 6 '66

GALLEYS, Boat. See Boats—Equipment

GALLICO, Paul William
Dropout who made it to the top. Read Digest 89:121-6 N '66

GALLIMARD (firm) See Publishers and publishing—France

GALLO brothers
Larry Gallo, Crazy Joe and Kid Blast. Robin Hoods or real tough boys? F. J. Cook. il pors N Y Times Mag p36-7+ O 23 '66

GALLSTONES. See Calculi, Biliary

GALLUP, George
Mood of Americans at this time; interview. pors U S News 61:50-4 S 19 '66

GALPHIN, Bruce
Political triumph over racism. Sat R 49:97-8 My 7 '66

GALTON, Sir Francis
What makes a child prodigy; reprint. C. Burt. por Sci Digest 59:53-6 Ap '66

GALTON, Lawrence
It's your skin. Pop Sci 188:69-71 My '66
One of the great mystery stories of medicine. N Y Times Mag p34-5+ N 6 '66
What happens when you get tired? Pop Sci 188:67-9+ Je '66; Same abr. with title Why you get that tired feeling. Read Digest 89:265-8 O '66
What kind of mixer is alcohol? Pop Sci 188:95-7+ Ap '66
Your brain: the most complicated machine. Pop Sci 188:86-9 Mr '66

GALUN, Esra, and Gressel, Jonathan
Morphogenesis in trichoderma: suppression of photoinduction by 5-fluorouracil. bibliog Science 151:696-8 F 11 '66

GALVIN, Hoyt
Breaking the ice. Library J 91:345-6 Ja 15 '66

GALVIN, Robert W.
There's a new tune at Motorola. il por Bsns W p 110-12+ Ap 23 '66

GALVIN, Thomas J.
Will the real reference problem please stand up? T. Freides. bibliog il Library J 91:2008-12 Ap 15 '66; Discussion. 91:2736+, 3018 Je 1, 15 '66

GAM, Ngugen-van-. See Nguguen-van-Gam

GAMAGE, Gay K. and Wright, M. A.
Cataloger's problem; letter to the editor. Library J 91:4050 S 15 '66

GAMBIA
Enter Gambia, laughing. B. Rice. il Harper 233:74-8+ O '66

GAMBLE, Robert R.
County park system grows up. por Parks & Rec 1:316-18 Ap '66

GAMBLERS
Nick the legend; Nick the Greek. il Newsweek 69:40 Ja 9 '67
Odds against me, by J. Scarne. Review
Atlan 217:140 Ap '66. E. Weeks
See also
Dandolos, N. A.

GAMBLING
Betting system outlined to avoid going broke. Sci N L 89:153 Mr 5 '66
Feds, sharpers and politics in Nevada. E. F. Sherman. New Repub 155:12-13 O 29 '66
Gambling. C. W. Morton. Atlan 217:118-19 F '66
Game is skimming; money being taken off the top by Nevada casinos. il Newsweek 68:18-19 Ag 29 '66
Hi-ho, silver! gaming tokens. il Time 87:51 Mr 25 '66
Las Vegas: it wins, it worries, it weeps. F. Knebel. il Look 30:75-8+ D 27 '66
Phileas Fogg and the jumping frog: collection of wild, weird bets; historical and fictional. J. Bryan, 3d. Holiday 40:64-5+ Ag '66
Shadow; betting on pro football games. Sports Illus 25:20 N 14 '66
See also
Book making (betting)
Cardsharping
Lotteries

GAMBLING—*Continued*

Psychology

Everyone in the pool. Newsweek 67:106 Ap 18 '66

Quotations, maxims, etc.

Any bets? comp. by G. Flatley. N Y Times Mag p 107 Mr 27 '66

Grand Bahama Island

Island in the sun. il Newsweek 69:22-4 Ja 9 '67

Great Britain

Dip in the pool; soccer pool winner. il Time 88:36 S 9 '66

England gambles for survival. H. Ehrlich. il Look 30:27-35 N 29 '66

Mr Right; soccer pool winner. il Newsweek 68:36 S 12 '66

GAME

See also

Cookery—Game

GAME birds

I give you the bird. C. E. Gillham. il Field & S 70:56-7+ Ap '66

See also

Shooting

GAME farm, Catskill. See Catskill game farm, Catskill, N.Y.

GAME fishes. See Fishes

GAME hijacking. See Robberies and assaults

GAME laws

Hunting seasons (cont) Outdoor Life 138:16+ S '66

Outdoors; hunting at night. T. Williams. Esquire 66:18+ S '66

Please don't feed the waterfowl. D. Barnes. il Sports Illus 25:32-4+ O 31 '66

See also

Animals, Predatory—Bounties

Poaching

GAME preserves

Charley Varney's deer farm. N. Karas. il Field & S 71:58-9+ O '66

Deep in the heart of darkest Texas; Y.O. ranch. D. Barnes. il Sports Illus 24:57-8+ My 23 '66

Great elephant hunt; enormous herds faced with famine in game parks of East Africa. il Time 88:44 N 4 '66

Immersion in life: journey to East Africa. A. M. Lindbergh. il Life 61:88-90+ O 21 '66; Same abr. with title Discovery and renewal. Read Digest 90:37-43 Ja '67

Sonoran Desert National Park; proposal to combine Organ Pipe Cactus National Monument and the Cabeza Prieta game range. W. F. Heald. il Nat Parks Mag 40:4-9 Ap '66

GAME protection

See also

Game wardens

Wildlife conservation

GAME-simulation. See Management games

GAME wardens

Most unusual warden; Tony Mazza in Manhattan. D. Shaw. il Field & S 71:77-9+ My '66

GAMER, Eleanor E.

Big Bend and the botanist. Nat Parks Mag 40:14-17 Ap '66

GAMES

Adult round; pro quarterback. il Time 87:84+ F 18 '66

Chthonian Christmas; symposium. il Esquire 66:196-9+ D '66

Fun and games. il Seventeen 25:197 F '66

Games are the enemies of beauty, truth, and sleep, Amanda said. D. Barthelme. Mlle 64:136+ N '66

Games in fabuland; teaching devices. J. Ridgeway. New Repub 155:17-18 Ag 27 '66

Games students play; games to help students get an inside feel of social and political conflict. il Time 87:51 Je 3 '66

Go join Othello in Venice; Shakespeare game. J. Ferris. Life 61:30 N 25 '66

Hail the conkering hero; Conker championship of Great Britain. Sports Illus 25:20 D 5 '66

Learning through games. J. S. Coleman. NEA J 56:69-70 Ja '67

Let's bring back the old games. P. H. Kendall. PTA Mag 60:27+ Mr '66

Pedagogical futility in fun and games? I. Kraft. NEA J 56:71-2 Ja '67

Sophisticated games and gadgets. R. Atcheson. il Holiday 40:139-43 D '66

Whatever happened to run, sheep, run? M. Holmes. il Todays Health 44:52-5 Ag '66

See also

Bridge (game)

Croquet

Horseshoe pitching

Poker

Puzzles

Shuffleboard

Anecdotes, facetiae, satire, etc.

Plead insanity and skip three turns; monopoly. N. Poirier. il Sat Eve Post 239:16 Ag 27 '66

GAMES, Promotional. See Sales promotion

GAMES of chance. See Gambling

GAMES that husbands play; story. See Fineman, M.

GAMMA globulin

Alpha globulin injections and decreased gamma globulin production in chickens. B. B. Kamrin. bibliog il Science 153:1261-2 S 9 '66

Biosynthesis of gamma globulin: studies in a cell-free system. K. H. Stenzel and A. L. Rubin. bibliog il Science 153:537-9 Jl 29 '66

Genetically determined antigen of the Ne subgroup of gamma-globulin: detection by precipitin analysis. H. G. Kunkel and others. bibliog il Science 154:1041-3 N 25 '66

Microinjection of mouse eggs. T. P. Lin. bibliog il Science 151:333-7 Ja 21 '66

Restoration of gamma globulin production in agammaglobulinemic chickens. M. D. Cooper and others. bibliog il Science 151:471-3 Ja 28 '66

GAMMA rays

Gamma ray source discovered in heavens. Sci N 89:349 My 7 '66

GAMMON, Clive

And one more for the river. Sports Illus 25:76-84 S 26 '66

Dilly day at Dingle. Sports Illus 24:70-6+ Mr 14 '66

about

Letter from the publisher. G. Valk. il por Sports Illus 25:4 S 26 '66

GAMMONS, Homer

Wise old hand at a new calling. il pors Life 61:39-40+ N 4 '66

GAMPERT, Rachel

28th International conference on public education. Sch & Soc 94:48-9 Ja 22 '66

GANDHI, Indira (Nehru)

India in perspective; address, March 29, 1966. Vital Speeches 32:423-5 My 1 '66

Interview with Indira Gandhi; ed. by A. Michaelis. pors McCalls 93:104-5+ Ap '66

President Johnson and Prime Minister Gandhi of India confer at Washington; exchange of greetings; exchange of toasts; with joint communique, March 29, 1966. Dept State Bul 54:598-605 Ap 18 '66

about

Attack from a family friend; K. Menon's attack. Time 87:32+ My 6 '66

Blow to the West; Mrs Gandhi has leftist ties. por U S News 60:16 Ja 31 '66

Congress party after Nehru. S. Rajan. il Reporter 35:33-5 O 20 '66

First duty. il Newsweek 67:37-8 F 7 '66

Frühlingsrauschen; aid from U.S. and Russia. Nat R 18:350 Ap 19 '66

Harmonizing the tensions; revisiting some of Jawaharlal Nehru's old haunts. Time 88:31 Jl 15 '66

Her father's daughter. il por Time 87:28-9 Je 3 '66

How Mrs Gandhi shattered the feminine mystique. B. Friedan. il por Ladies Home J 83:100+ My '66

India: a huge country on the verge of collapse. S. W. Sanders. il por U S News 61:68-71 N 28 '66

India elects Mrs Gandhi. Christian Cent 83:134 F 2 '66

India puts a woman at the top. por Bsns W p38 Ja 22 '66

India: too poor to be effective, too big to be ignored. E. Dunbar. il pors Look 30:20-32 Jl 12 '66

India's continuing crisis. P. Altbach. Christian Cent 83:1158-60 S 21 '66

India's first lady. Nation 202:115 Ja 31 '66

Indira Gandhi's India; with a report by W. Cook and R. Ramanujam, and one by E. Behr. il por Newsweek 67:36-42+ Ap 4 '66

Lady from India speaks her mind. America 114:542 Ap 16 '66

GANDHI, Indira (Nehru)—about—*Continued*
Lady who leads 480 million; with report by H. Moffett. il pors Life 60:75-8+ Mr 25 '66
Lady who now leads India. M. Zim. il pors Life 60:26-7 Ja 28 '66
Mrs Gandhi elected. por Sr Schol 88:17 F 4 '66
Mrs Gandhi: peaceful, Kosygin: hostile. il por U S News 61:20 Jl 25 '66
Mrs Gandhi's legacy: the starving nation of India. V. J. Dunigan. por Cath World 203:34-9 Ap '66
Mrs Gandhi's mission. A. Campbell. New Repub 154:13-17 Ap 2 '66
Mrs Indira Gandhi, prime minister of India. D. Norman. il por Vogue 147:146-7+ Mr 1 '66
Muddling through. Newsweek 68:56+ N 28 '66
Nehru will. por Newsweek 67:41-2 Ja 31 '66
New bloom. il pors Time 87:25-6 Ap 8 '66
Return of the rosebud. il pors Time 87:24-6+ Ja 28 '66; Same abr. Read Digest 88:83-7 Ap '66
Riots in India; prelude to a visit to U.S. U S News 60:16 Mr 28 '66
Sari-clad visitor from India. por Sr Schol 88:21 Ap 15 '66
Saris and petticoats; U.S. visit. por Newsweek 67:28 Ap 11 '66
She stands remarkably alone. J. A. Lukas. il pors N Y Times Mag p34-5+ Mr 27 '66
Show of independence. Time 88:40 N 25 '66
Visitor in a sari; U.S. visit. il por Time 87:29-30 Ap 1 '66
Warm visit from India's Indira. il pors Life 60:38 Ap 8 '66
GANDY, Joseph Edward
Aftermath in Seattle. R. Lynes. il Harper 232:22-+ F '66
GANGLIONIC nervous system. See Nervous system, Sympathetic
GANGLIOSIDES. See Sialic acids
GANGS
Harlem's immortal five per cent; growing band of young Negro militants. T. M. Gannon. America 115:208-10 Ag 27 '66
Life styles: the cyclist; Hell's Angels. H. S. Thompson. il Esquire 67:57-63+ Ja '67
Violent crimes in city gangs. W. B. Miller. bibliog f il Ann Am Acad 364:96-112 Mr '66
Watch out whitey; Negro youth gangs and violence. L. Yablonsky; discussion. New Repub 154:29-30 Ja 22; 37-8 F 19 '66
World of Rufus Henry; juvenile gangs of Los Angeles. F. Bonham. Horn Bk 42:34-6 F '66
GANGSTERS. See Crime and criminals—United States
GANNETT, Lewis
Obituary
Nation 202:200 F 21 '66. M. Young
Pub W 189:109 F 14 '66
War game. R. L. Tobin. Sat R 49:6+ F 26 '66
GANNETT newspaper group. See Newspapers—United States
GANNON, Michael V.
New books. Cath World 204:186-7 D '66
GANNON, Robert
Is this every man's flying machine? Pop Sci 188:91-4+ Ap '66
More comfort for you at the dentist's. Pop Mech 126:96-9+ Ag '66
New shapes make news in tents. Pop Sci 188:154-9 My '66
New skins for anything and everything. Pop Mech 125:112-15+ Ap '66
Protect your car from the steal-and-strippers. Pop Sci 189:104-8 S '66
Sick river is returned to health. Read Digest 89:29-30+ Jl '66
Sneeze sleuth discovers allergy begins in your home. Pop Sci 189:74-6+ Ag '66
GANNON, Ruth
Fruits and vegetables. Horticulture 44:34-7+ My '66
GANNON, Thomas M.
Harlem's immortal five per cent. America 115:208-10 Ag 27 '66
GANS, Carl
Locomotion without limbs. Natur Hist 75:10-17 bibliog(p68) F; 36-41 Mr '66
GANS, Herbert J.
Doing something about slums. Commonweal 83:688-93 Mr 18 '66
GANSCHOW, Roger
Glucuronidase gene expression in somatic hybrids. bibliog Science 153:84-5 Jl 1 '66
GARAGE doors. See Doors
GARAGES
Carport can lead a double life. il Pop Gard 17:30-3 My '66

Converting the garage or carport. il Sunset 136:120+ Ap '66
Look what happened to their old garage. il Sunset 136:76-7 F '66
New carport is also a party court. il Sunset 136:104-5 Ap '66
Park 'em in their own garage; motorcycle, mower or tractor. il Pop Mech 126:179-87+ N '66
Want a new garage door? or a carport fast? il Pop Sci 188:154-5 Ap '66
GARAGES, Municipal
Meet parking demands before they beat you; Montgomery County, Md. J. M. Hunnicutt. il Am City 81:113+ D '66
Parking under an island; and a civil defense office, too, Cedar Rapid, Ia. C. D. Mullinex. il Am City 81:164+ S '66
Parking under the state capitol grounds; Columbus, Ohio. P. L. Heineman. il Am City 81:96-7 Mr '66
This automatic parking has tight revenue controls; Brooklyn civic center. il Am City 81:145-6 S '66
GARAUDY, Roger
Let's end the Communist-Christian vendetta. H. Cox. Christian Cent 83:1375-9 N 9 '66
Two kinds of humanism. il por Time 88:42-3 D 30 '66
GARB, Solomon
Plant growth as a cancer clue. Sat R 49:50+ My 7 '66
GARBAGE, Utilization of. See Refuse, Utilization of
GARBAGE cans. See Refuse receptacles
GARBAGE grinders. See Refuse grinders
GARBER, Frederick N.
If your child knocks out a tooth. Parents Mag 41:60-1+ F '66
GARBERS, Virginia
Arbitrary colors of Fred Burrell. Pop Phot 59:84-5+ Ag '66
GARCEAU, Oliver
Morals of medicine. bibliog f Ann Am Acad 363:60-9 Ja '66
GARCÉS, Mario Valverde. See Valverde Garcés, M.
GARCIA, Louise B.
Art history for grade two. Sch Arts 66:10-12 N '66
GARCIA, Rolando V.
Organizing scientific research. Bul Atomic Sci 22:12-15 S '66
GARCIA LORCA, Federico
Song of the little death; tr. by R. Humphries; reprint. Nation 203:92 Jl 25 '66

about

New York: two poetic impressions. A. Bartra. il por Américas 18:14-22 O '66
Yerma. Criticism
Nation 204:30 Ja 2 '67
New Repub 156:41-2 Ja 7 '67
Newsweek 68:106 D 19 '66
Sat R 49:68 D 24 '66
Time il 88:87 D 16 '66
GARDEN, Mary
Mary the first. por Time 89:44-5 Ja 13 '67
Tigress, serpent, Eve. por Newsweek 69:94-5 Ja 16 '67
GARDEN benches. See Benches
GARDEN borders
Bring glamor to your yard with marble chips. A. Markovich. il Pop Sci 189:130-1 Ag '66
How to put an edge on your lawn. J. Hand. il Pop Sci 189:145 Ag '66
New plants for your flower border. J. Fanning. il Pop Gard 17:52-4 My '66
Trim ideas for edging. il Pop Gard 17:16 My; 4 D '66
GARDEN bridges. See Bridges, Foot
GARDEN carts. See Carts
GARDEN catalogs. See Catalogs, Seed and plant
GARDEN center, Cleveland, Ohio
Garden center of Greater Cleveland. E. F. Steffek. il Horticulture 44:30-1+ My '66
GARDEN chemicals. See Agricultural chemicals
GARDEN clubs
Flower people. I. Taves. il Look 30:87-8 Mr 22 '66
Improving the garden club's image. D. P. Watson. il Horticulture 44:14-15 D '66
They said it with flowers; Falls Church garden club ships rose bushes to Islamabad, Pakistan. B. Ahmad. il Horticulture 44:51 D '66
GARDEN design
Big ideas for small gardens. il House & Gard 130:244-7 O '66
Concentrate, don't scatter flowers. E. McClure. il Pop Gard 17:40-1 Ag '66

GARDEN design—*Continued*
Here's beauty that needs little upkeep; terrace garden. E. B. McClure. il Pop Gard 17:16 Mr '66
Mondrian designs for the garden. il Flower Grower 53:48-50 Mr '66
GARDEN equipment. See Garden tools, equipment and supplies
GARDEN fences. See Fences
GARDEN furniture. See Furniture, Outdoor
GARDEN gates. See Gates
GARDEN houses, shelters, etc.
Amazing sun dome you can build. C. E. Rhine. il Pop Sci 188:108-12 My '66
Build a cool retreat for plants and people. H. Sibley. il Pop Gard 17:12-13 Mr '66
Mower port solves storage problems. il Pop Gard 17:19 Ag '66
Old ideas for new gardens. il Pop Gard 17:76 D '66
Sun-dome fun; building geodesic dome. il Pop Sci 189:132 O '66
Take a tip from Tahiti. R. A. Henry, jr. il Pop Gard 17:24-7 Ag '66
These Sacramento gazebos are sun shelters. il Sunset 136:250 Ap '66
Two-faced storage tower. il Pop Sci 189:152-3 S '66
See also
Trellises
GARDEN labels. See Plant labels
GARDEN lanterns. See Lanterns
GARDEN lighting. See Gardens—Lighting
GARDEN ornaments
Feature a bell. il Flower Grower 53:24-5 N '66
Garden features come back. il Flower Grower 53:28-30 Ag '66
Old ideas for new gardens. il Pop Gard 17:14-15 Ag '66
Sculptured garden ornament. R. Hoppough. il Pop Mech 125:136-7 Je '66
Stoneware: an ancient art makes an exciting comeback. W. Radcliffe. il Pop Gard 17:58-61 Ag '66
Try your hand at rock sculpture. W. Radcliffe. il Pop Gard 17:90-1 My '66
See also
Lanterns
Sundials
GARDEN pests. See Plants—Diseases and pests
GARDEN pools
Floor-level garden pool. L. Rosenhouse. il Flower Grower 53:18-19 Jl '66
Home garden project for spring: how to build a terrace pool. il Flower Grower 53:30-1 F '66
Patio and garden pool for summer living. M. P. Borman. il Flower Grower 53:30-1 Je '66
Tiny pool that makes a terrace look big. il Pop Gard 17:12 My '66
See also
Water gardens
GARDEN sculpture. See Garden ornaments
GARDEN seeds. See Seeds
GARDEN shelters. See Garden houses, shelters, etc.
GARDEN sprinklers. See Sprinklers
GARDEN state ballet. See Ballet companies
GARDEN steps
Two ways with steps. il Flower Grower 53:35 N '66
Whole bank is steps. il Sunset 136:145-6 Mr '66
GARDEN supplies. See Garden tools, equipment and supplies
GARDEN therapy
Horticultural therapy achieves results. G. Taloumis. il Horticulture 44:26-7+ Jl '66
Ŗ for executive health: garden therapy. il Pop Gard 17:14-19+ D '66
GARDEN tool caddies. See Carts
GARDEN tools, equipment and supplies
Eight aids for summer gardening. il Flower Grower 53:58-9 Je '66
Guide to garden power equipment. L. C. Grove. il Bet Hom & Gard 44:20+ Je '66
Have you heard? See issues of Flower grower, the home garden
Old lawnmower provides cutter for this garden mulch making machine. M. Banister. il Pop Mech 125:120-4 Je '66
Special preview for gardeners. Changing T 20:6 F '66
Tool belts for gardeners. il Sunset 136:260+ Ap '66
See also
Hedge clippers
Spraying apparatus
Tractors

Care
Keeping electric garden tools cutting. S. J. Howard. il Pop Mech 125:126-9+ Je '66

Storage
Get your yard equipment up to par. il Pop Gard 17:62-4 D '66
See also
Garden houses, shelters, etc.
GARDEN tours
Europe's grandest gardens. G. Taloumis. il Travel 125:32-3+ Mr '66
Home & garden tours. House & Gard 129:125-6 Mr '66
Virginia blooms in spring. il Flower Grower 53:14-15 Mr '66
GARDEN tractors. See Tractors
GARDEN walks
Garden walkways up, down, around. il Sunset 137:107+ N '66
Make your own walks and paths. il Pop Gard 17:20-3 Mr '66
Underfoot; look at eleven splendid kinds of garden paving. il Sunset 136:110-13 My '66
GARDENERS
Gardener did it; Japanese gardeners of Beverly Hills. il Newsweek 67:113-13A Ja 13 '66
GARDENING
Clean sweep for fall; to ready your garden for spring. il Flower Grower 53:30-1 N '66
Fruit truck news. See issues of Farm journal
Garden timesavers. K. Robinson. Horticulture 45:44+ Ja '67
Gardens & vacations. M. M. Leister; L. W. Dawson. il Flower Grower 53:37-9+ Jl '66
He's gardening his way through college. H. Garrett. Farm J 90:68B Mr '66
H&G's gardener's month. See issues of House & garden incorporating Living for young homemakers
[Month] gardening where you live! See issues of Better homes and gardens
[Month] in your garden. See issues of Sunset
Quick and easy tips. See issues of Popular gardening & living outdoors
-Regional gardening; symposium. See issues of Popular gardening & living outdoors
Regional pointers. See issues of Flower grower, the home garden
Tips to clip. il Pop Gard 17:18 Mr; 70 Ag; 12 D '66
What to do in [month] See issues of Horticulture
See also
Bulbs
City gardens
Frost protection
Garden center, Cleveland, Ohio
Garden therapy
Gardeners
Herbs
House plants
Lanscape gardening
Plant propagation
Vegetable gardening
Window gardening

Bibliography
Latest gardening books. E. C. Hall. il Pop Gard 17:34-5+ D '66

Competitions
Rules for Garden club yearbook contest. Horticulture 44:45 O '66

Terminology
If gardeners' talk is Greek to you. il Sunset 137:268-71 O '66
GARDENING, Indoor. See Greenhouses
GARDENING, Vegetable. See Vegetable gardening
GARDENS
Big ideas for small gardens. il House & Gard 130:244-7 O '66
See also
Childrens gardens
City gardens
Gardening
Gardens, Bog
Roof gardens

Color
Choose flowers to put bright color into summer borders. M. A. Roche. il Pop Gard 17:34-5 Ag '66
Concentrate, don't scatter flowers. E. McClure. il Pop Gard 17:40-1 Ag '66
Day-lilies can solve summer's color problem. I. Dorsey. il Flower Grower 53:37+ Je '66
Enjoy spectacular color two ways. M. A. Roche. il Pop Gard 17:48-50 My '66
Flowers for your fall garden. il Pop Gard 17:32-3+ D '66

GARDENS—Color—*Continued*

For a riot of color next spring. M. Reynolds. il Pop Gard 17:22-5+ D '66

Grace of summer greens. il House & Gard 130:124-5+ Jl '66

Ideas from Australia for plant color combinations. Sunset 137:178+ S '66

In pursuit of the rainbow. M. Price. il Flower Grower 53:24-7 Je '66

Make a little color work big! H. Mason. il Bet Hom & Gard 44:76-7 O '66

More summer color for problem spots! H. Mason and L. Grove. il Bet Hom & Gard 44:54-9 Je '66

Quick summer color for problem spots. H. Mason. il Bet Home & Gard 44:70-3 My '66

Three ways with color. il Flower Grower 53:34-5 Ap '66

See also

Color of flowers

History

Look down at the plants; gardens in seventeenth-century New England. A. Leighton. il Antiques 90:200-3 Ag '66

Lighting

Garden lighting. J. L. Pennock. il Horticulture 44:32 Je '66

Garden lighting. N. Silver. il Flower Grower 53:10+ My '66

Garden lighting that's simple and safe. il Sunset 137:54-7 Jl '66

How to install 1-v wiring; low-voltage lighting. il Sunset 137:79-80+ Jl '66

Outdoor wiring that's easy and safe. J. Parker. il Pop Sci 189:146-8+ Ag '66

Paint your nighttime garden with soft color. il Flower Grower 53:32+ Je '66

See also

Lanterns

Outdoor rooms—Lighting

Alabama

Bellingrath gardens. F. W. Holder. il Horticulture 44:42-4 F '66

California

All six senses are served by a garden masterpiece. il House & Gard 130:90-1 Jl '66

Discovery house garden is now three years old. il Sunset 136:116-19 My '66

Gardener did it; Japanese gardeners of Beverly Hills. il Newsweek 67:113-13A Je 13 '66

Woodland garden in a canyon bottom. il Sunset 136:270-1 My '66

See also

Los Angeles—Gardens

Delaware

America's head gardener Henry Francis Dupont. V. Lawford. il Vogue 147:150-3 Mr 1 '66

England

Rock gardens: Windsor, Wisley, and Kew. il House & Gard 129:179-81+ My '66

Tresco Abbey gardens. C. Chowins. il Horticulture 44:32-4+ O '66

Europe, Western

Europe's grandest gardens. G. Taloumis. il Travel 125:32-3+ Mr '66

France

Gardener and the king; Louis XIV's gardens designed by A. Le Nôtre. J. Barry. il Read Digest 89:158-63 O '66

Hawaii

Home gardens in Hawaii. M. Perry. Flower Grower 53:48-9 F '66

Italy

Queen Helen's garden; grounds of Villa Sparta. V. Lawford. il Vogue 147:154-7+ Mr 1 '66

Japan

Look of Japan's gardens. L. Perry. il Flower Grower 53:30-1 Mr '66

Long Island

Big flower boom; gardens of Old Westbury. I. Taves. il Look 30:84-5 Mr 22 '66

Maine

Japanese garden, Maine-style. M. A. Roche. il Flower Grower 53:26-8 Jl '66

Massachusetts

See also

Shelburne Falls, Mass.—Gardens

New England

Look down at the plants; gardens in seventeenth-century New England. A. Leighton. il Antiques 90:200-3 Ag '66

New York (state)

Innisfree garden, Millbrook, N.Y. L. Collins. il Horticulture 44:34-5 Je '66

Pennsylvania

Longwood gardens; Kennett Square, Pa. R. J. Seibert. il Horticulture 44:46-50 Ap '66

Spain

In a Spanish garden. M. Adams. il Flower Grower 53:32-4 D '66

Sweden

Natural look of Sweden's country gardens. il Flower Grower 53:24-7 S '66

Virginia

Historic garden week in Virginia. A. H. Matthews. il Horticulture 44:46-7+ Mr '66

West Indies

Gardens of the West Indies. J. V. Watkins. il Horticulture 44:18-21+ D '66

GARDENS, Bog

Bogs; a new world of mystery for gardeners to explore. E. M. Woodford. il Horticulture 44:14-15+ Ag '66

GARDENS, Childrens. See Childrens gardens

GARDENS, Colonial

Colonial Williamsburg. D. H. Parker. il Horticulture 44:26-9+ S '66

GARDENS, Fragrant

Fragrant roses are back in style. C. Westcott. il Flower Grower 53:32-3+ F '66

Gardens, for looks and fragrance both. il Changing T 20:39-40 My '66

Leaf fragrance. M. Compton. Horticulture 44:46-7 F '66

Start now for indoor fragrance; scented plant for every month of the year. L. Bell and H. V. Wilson. il Flower Grower 53:28-9+ N '66

GARDENS, Indoor

Church with an indoor garden. M. A. Roche. il Flower Grower 53:54-5 Mr '66

How to make indoor gardening more enjoyable. Pop Gard 17:77 D '66

Invite summer to stay all year. il Pop Gard 17:54-7 Ag '66

GARDENS, Japanese

Handkerchief-size demonstration garden in San Francisco's Golden Gate park; Japanese-style garden. il Sunset 137:182-3 S '66

How San Mateo got its new Japanese garden. il Sunset 137:178-9 D '66

Japanese garden in Los Angeles. il Sunset 136:104-7 Mr '66

Japanese garden, Maine-style. M. A. Roche. il Flower Grower 53:26-8 Jl '66

See also

Gardens—Japan

GARDENS, Protection of. See Plants, Protection of

GARDENS, Rock

How to build a rock garden. il House & Gard 129:236-8+ My '66

Many styles of rock gardens. il Flower Grower 53:42-4 Ap '66

Rock garden built for bulbs. il Flower Grower 53:30-1 O '66

Rock gardens. J. B. Brimer. il Flower Grower 53:45-6 Ap '66

Rock gardens. il House & Gard 129:178-81+ My '66

GARDENS, Roof. See Roof gardens

GARDENS, Spanish

See also

Gardens—Spain

GARDENS, Vegetable. See Vegetable gardening

GARDENS, Watering of. See Watering of gardens, lawns, etc.

GARDENS, Wild

Back-yard wild-flower garden. S. Gottscho. il Flower Grower 53:35 O '66

My garden in the woods. M. P. Borman. il Flower Grower 53:28-9 F '66

GARDER, Michel

Russia vs. China: the end of revolutionary communism; interview. por U S News 61:50 N 7 '66

GARDINER, Henry G.

Manet's mental museum. Art N 65:48-50+ N '66

GARDINER, Robert David Lion

One man is an island. M. Levitas. il pors N Y Times Mag p46-7+ Je 5 '66

GARDINERS ISLAND, N.Y.

One man is an island. M. Levitas. il N Y Times Mag p46-7+ Je 5 '66

GARDINIER, David E.

(comp) Articles and other books received; Africa. See issues of American historical review

GARDNER, Albert Ten Eyck
On watercolor; excerpts from A history of watercolor painting in America. Am Artist 31:79-81 Ja '67

GARDNER, Arthur
Don Quixote and the ambassador. F. Donahue. Horn Bk 42:43-4 F '66

GARDNER, Erle Stanley
How I search for lost gold mines, and why. por Pop Sci 188:100-5 Mr '66
My stories of the wild West. Atlan 218:60-2 Jl '66

about

World of Erle Stanley Gardner. C. W. Morton. Atlan 219:79-86+ Ja '67

GARDNER, Frederick H.
Actor's workshop is dead. Nation 203:256-7 S 19 '66
Identity crisis. Nation 202:559-61 My 9 '66
Return of the Continental Op. Nation 203:454-6 O 31 '66

GARDNER, Isabella
Accomplices; poem. Poetry 109:100 N '66
Salt; poem. Nation 203:654 D 12 '66

about

Lamb, the clocks, the blue light. R. Huff. Poetry 109:45 O '66

GARDNER, John
Amber mine; novel; condensation. Mlle 63:89-120 Jl '66

GARDNER, John W.
Government, the universities, and biomedical research; address, August 23, 1966. Science 153:1601-3 S 30 '66
Need for leaders, excerpts from Antileadership vaccine. Science 151:283 Ja 21 '66
What are Americans receiving in return for their heavy investment in education? excerpts of testimony. por Am Ed 2:24-6 N '66
What better schools will cost; interviews, ed. by S. Wren. pors Look 30:100+ My 17 '66
Worlds of reflection and action; excerpts from address, October 24, 1966. Science 154:849 N 18 '66

about

Gardner hews out the Great society. il por Newsweek 67:22-4+ F 28 '66
HEW: Gardner proposes reorganization. E. Langer. Science 154:1151-2 D 2 '66
In man for the Cabinet. R. T. Elson. por Read Digest 88:107-11 F '66
Leadership and scholarship. W. W. Brickman. Sch & Soc 94:116 Mr 5 '66
Mover, a thinker, a writer. Bsns W p 132 My 21 '66
Prime mover of the Great society. il por Bsns W p 130-2+ My 21 '66
Reformer at HEW. H. Brandon. Sat R 49:16 D 17 '66
Sense of what should be. il por Time 89:16-21 Ja 29 '67

GARDNER, Lester A. See Burns, M. jt. auth.

GARDNER, Martin
Can time go backward? with biographical sketch. Sci Am 216:22, 98-102+ bibliog(p 146+) Ja '67
Dermo-optical perception; a peek down the nose. bibliog Science 151:654-7 F 11 '66
Mathematical games. See issues of Scientific American

GARDNER, Richard N.
ICY plus one: an inventory. Sat R 49:24-5+ N 5 '66

GARDNER, Robert Wallace
Frustrated minority. bibliog Negro Hist Bul 29:83-4+ Ja '66

GARDNER, W. David
New York car: design for survival. Nation 202:489-92 Ap 25 '66

GARFUNKEL, Art
Simon & Garfunkel, young poets of folk-rock. B. Rollin. il pors Look 30:M14-16 N 29 '66

GARGAN, Ann
Kennedy nobody knows. G. Cameron. il por Ladies Home J 83:70-1+ Je '66

GARGAN, Edward T.
Injustice drinkers. Nation 202:787-8 Je 27 '66

GARGOYLISM. See Lipocondrodystrophy

GARIBALDI, Carole
Movie report. See issues of Good housekeeping

GARIBALDI, Giuseppe
Garibaldi and his enemies. by C. Hibbert. Review
Sat R por 49:40-1 Mr 5 '66. C. F. Delzell
Time por 87:102+ Mr 11 '66
Glorious revolutionist. il Newsweek 67:108+ Mr 21 '66

GARIS, Howard R.
My father was Uncle Wiggily. by R. Garis. Review
Newsweek il 68:114-15 N 7 '66. S. K. Oberbeck

GARIS, Robert
What happened to John Barth? Commentary 42:89-90+ O '66

GARLAND, Phyl
Builders of a new South Ebony 21:27-30+ Ag '66
Natural look. Ebony 21:142-4+ Je '66
Revolt in the 'in' crowd. Ebony 21:82-4+ F '66

GARLANDS. See Leis

GARLIC
All about garlic; with recipes. M. Field. Holiday 39:24+ Je '66

GARMENT trades. See Clothing industry

GARMENT workers
See also
Clothing industry—Wages and hours
International ladies' garment workers' union

GARMENTS, Pressing. See Pressing of garments

GARMEY, Stephen S.
Books. Commonweal 84:259 My 20 '66

GARMIRE, Bernard L.
You can end crime in your city's streets. por Nations Bsns 55:63-5 Ja '67

GARNER, James
James Garner drives at Monte Carlo. J. P. Norbye. por Pop Sci 189:78-9 Ag '66
James Garner really races in Grand prix. D. Scott. il pors Pop Sci 189:78-81+ Ag '66

GARNER, John Nance
Garner: he couldn't be elected without our Lyndon; interview, ed. by L. W. Robert. il por U S News 62:44-5 Ja 16 '67

GARNER, Louis E. Jr
It's the Jinniflash. Pop Electr 24:56-9 Je '66
Solid state. See issues of Popular electronics
Update to solid state. Pop Electr 25:41-4 S '66

GARNET necklace; story. See Klein, N.

GARNETS
Garnet zoning: an interpretation based on the Rayleigh fractionation model. L. S. Hollister. bibliog il Science 154:1647-51 D 30 '66

GARNETT, William A.
America's beautiful bounty; aerial photographs. Fortune 73:115-19 Je '66

GARREN, Leonard D. and others
Puromycin analogs: action of adrenocorticotropic hormone and the role of glycogen. bibliog Science 152:1386-8 Je 3 '66

GARRETSON, Robert C.
Why fight? ruble-dollar road to peace. Nation 202:576-81 My 16 '66

GARRETT, Henry E.
Lesson in bias. por Newsweek 67:63 My 30 '66

GARRETT, Mike
Trouble runner. il Newsweek 68:68 D 12 '66

GARRETT, Paul
Sloan touch. L. L. L. Golden. Sat R 49:78 Ap 9 '66

GARRETT, Richard Baynham
End of a manhunt; excerpt from lecture, ed. by B. Fleet. por Am Heritage 17:40-3+ Je '66

GARRETT, Richard H.
End of a manhunt; excerpt from lecture, ed. by B. Fleet. R. B. Garrett. il por Am Heritage 17:40-3+ Je '66

GARRETT, W. E.
What was a woman doing there? Nat Geog Mag 129:270-1 F '66

GARRETT, Wendell D.
Figures and figureheads. Antiques 90:816-23 D '66
Providence cabinetmakers, chairmakers, upholsterers, and allied craftsmen, 1756-1838. Antiques 90:514-19 O '66

GARRETT-JONES, C.
Drought in London; poem. Harper 233:110 N '66

GARRIGUE, Jean
Brief letter; poem. Nation 202:597 My 16 '66
(tr) See Voznesenskii, A. Last train to Malakhovka

GARRISON, Lloyd
Africa's good guy under pressure. N Y Times Mag p 14-15+ Ag 7 '66
Africa's top nationalist, or Africa's prima donna? N Y Times Mag p 12-13+ Ja 1 '67
Exit Nkrumah, an old dreamer; enter Ankrah, a new realist. N Y Times Mag p32-3+ Ap 3 '66

GART, Murray J.
British company that found a way out. Fortune 74:104-9+ Ag '66
Labor's rebellious rank and file. Fortune 74: 150-3+ N '66

GARTH, Midi
Midi Garth 92nd street Y. M. Marks. Dance Mag 40:82 Je '66

GARTHOFF, Raymond L.
Soviet critique of China's total strategy. Reporter 34:48-9 My 19 '66

GARVIE, James B.
Rustproofing that pays for itself. por Am City 81:104-5 Mr '66

GARY, Ind.

Crime
Abandoned county. il Time 87:31 Ap 29 '66

Water supply
Remote-controlled filtration plant. H. D. Harman. il Am City 81:100-2 My '66

GAS, Natural
All that gas in the North Sea. T. Alexander. il Fortune 74:110-15+ Ag '66
Gasman cometh. il Duns R 88:60-2 N '66
North Sea bonanza. Newsweek 67:86 Ap 18 '66
What offshore gas means to Europe. il U S News 60:98 Je 13 '66

Liquefaction
Gas from Alaska: destination Tokyo; liquefied natural gas. il Bsns W p32-3 Ag 6 '66

Pipe lines
Daring floating-pipeline gamble. J. D. Ratcliff. Read Digest 88:225-6+ My '66
FPC bars new pipeline into California market; denying Tenneco's bid to send natural gas into Los Angeles. Bsns W p26-7 Jl 30 '66
Pipelines. E. J. Jensen and H. S. Ellis. il Sci Am 216:62-70+ bibliog(p 146) Ja '67

Production methods
Atom aims for role as prospector; nuclear test shots may unlock vast oil and gas fields. il Bsns W p83-4+ D 17 '66

Transportation
Liquified gas sails the seas; from Algeria to Britain. il Bsns W p 175-6+ F 19 '66
See also
Gas, Natural—Pipe lines

GAS and oil engines
First test-drive report on no-piston power for boats; Wankel-type rotating combustion engine. J. Roe. il Pop Sci 189:88-91 Ag '66
See also
Marine engines
Piston rings

GAS and oil engines, Inboard
First test-drive report on no-piston power for boats. J. Roe. il Pop Sci 189:88-91 Ag '66
Inboard engines, 1966. il Motor B 117:136-43 Ja '66
1967 inboard engines. il Motor B 119:140-4 Ja '67
Preview: inboard power for '67. E. H. Nabb. il Motor B 118:80-7 N '66

Care
Mid-season tune-up for inboard engines. L. Heiner. il Motor B 118:26-9 Ag '66

GAS and oil engines, Outboard
Antique outboards too frisky to retire. K. Warner. il Pop Mech 125:142-4+ Mr '66
First look at the 1967 outboard engines. J. Roe. il Pop Sci 189:138-41+ O '66
In's and out's of electric starting. H. B. Notrom. il Pop Mech 125:170-3 Ap '66
New outboard engines for 1967. il Yachting 120:50-2+ O '66
1967 outboard motors. il Motor B 119:170-3 Ja '67
1967 outboard preview. Outdoor Life 138:8 O '66
Now it's the waltz-me-around-again Wankel. M. J. Hodges. il Sports Illus 24:79-80 Ap 25 '66
Outboard auxiliaries. R. W. Carrick. il Yachting 119:83-4+ F '66
Outboard motors. il Consumer Bul 49:6-11 Jl '66
Outboard motors, 1966. il Motor B 117:150-3 Ja '66
'67 outboard outlook. il Motor B 118:108-10 O '66
'67 outboards: jazzed-up looks and performance. A. Mikesell. il Pop Mech 126:96-9+ O '66
Space age outboards. F. M. Paulson. il Field & S 71:90-5 D '66

Tilt pin adjustment. il Yachting 119:78-9 Je '66
Tips on buying a fishing motor. P. Richards. il Pop Mech 125:106-9+ Ap '66

Care
Doctoring a dunked motor. H. B. Notrom. il Pop Mech 126:125-8+ Jl '66
Eleven springtime steps to make your dependable outboard dependabler. L. Eppel. il Motor B 117:28-9+ Mr '66
Lowdown on lower units. H. B. Notrom. il Pop Mech 125:158-61+ My '66

Control
Troubleshooting remote controls. H. B. Notrom. il Pop Mech 125:141-4 Je '66

Fuel
What's the truth about fuel mixes? H. B. Notrom. il Pop Mech 126:156-9+ S '66

Storage
Right way to store your outboard. H. B. Notrom. il Pop Mech 126:162-5+ N '66

GAS as fuel
Saving sewage gas saves money; Danville, Ill. il Am City 81:28 D '66
See also
Gas, Natural

GAS chromatography. See Chromatographic analysis

GAS clothes dryers. See Clothes dryers

GAS detectors
FAA to act on explosion suppression plans. R. D. Hibben. il Aviation W 85:87+ N 14 '66

GAS endarterectomy. See Blood vessels—Surgery

GAS heating
Utilities warm up the battle over electric heat. il Bsns W p 147-8 Je 25 '66

GAS industry
Cooking with gas. J. F. Olesky. Duns R 87: 67+ F '66

Regulation
See also
United States—Federal power commission

Great Britain
British gas stations take off their gloves. il Bsns W p 130-2+ Ap 30 '66

GAS lasers. See Lasers

GAS pipes

Leakage
Bomb in the cellar. S. Morrison. il Nation 203:318-20 O 3 '66

GAS plants (flowers)
Perennial favorite. A. Palmore. il Flower Grower 53:35+ S '66

GAS stations. See Automobile service stations

GAS stoves
Kitchen ranges. Consumer Rep 31:58-62 D '66
New ratings for Tappan ranges. Consumer Rep 31:157-8 Ap '66

GAS surgery. See Blood vessels—Surgery

GAS tankers. See Tank ships

GAS turbine locomotives. See Locomotives, Gas turbine

GAS turbines
Sales of gas turbine engines for industrial uses grow. M. L. Yaffee. il Aviation W 85:66-7+ N 28 '66
See also
Locomotives, Gas turbine

GAS turbines, Aircraft
Allison pushes direct lift engine effort. M. L. Yaffee. il Aviation W 84:50-1+ Je 27 '66
Beta way. R. Blodget. il Flying 78:80-3 Mr '66
8:1 bypass ratio marks design of GE's C-5A engine. M. L. Yaffee. il Aviation W 84:84-6 Mr 14 '66
Foreign accent. J. Fricker. Flying 78:32-3 F '66
Improvement effort spurs F-27 changes; turboprop transport. il Aviation W 85:49-50 S 19 '66
June FAA certification sought for FH-227. il Aviation W 84:41 F 7 '66
Leading international gas turbines; specifications (cont) Aviation W 84:210-11 Mr 7 '66
Leading turbine-powered business aircraft; specifications (cont) Aviation W 84:201 Mr 7 '66
Nord 262 grounded world-wide after inflight turbine failures. Aviation W 85:26 Ag 22 '66
Performance increase sought for Convair Dart conversions. Aviation W 84:39 Mr 28 '66

GAS turbines, Aircraft—*Continued*
Pilot report: the Cessna turbo-system Centurion. R. Blodget. il Flying 78:64-7 Je '66
Pilot report: the turbo twin Comanche. R. Weeghman. il Flying 79:44-8 Ag '66
P&W unveils mockup of SST turbofan. M. L. Yaffee. il Aviation W 84:44-5+ F 28 '66
Rolls-Royce to test demonstrator of alternative 747 powerplant; turbofan for subsonic transport. Aviation W 84:45+ Ap 25 '66
Rolls shows three-spool Trent turbofan. W. C. Wetmore. il Aviation W 85:30-1 S 12 '66
Soviets groom Tu-154 as workhorse. il Aviation W 85:56-7+ O 10 '66
U.S. gas turbine engines; specifications (cont) Aviation W 84:208-9 Mr 7 '66
    See also
Helicopter engines

Maintenance and repair
Maintainability becomes engine byword. M. L. Yaffee. il Aviation W 85:106-7+ O 31 '66

Statistics
Turbojet aircraft 1965 operations and traffic statistics; table. Aviation W 84:54-5 Mr 21 '66
Turbojet, turbofan aircraft operating expense; table (title varies). Aviation W 84:56-7 My 2; 53 My 9; 85:62 O 10 '66
Turboprop aircraft operating expense; table (title varies) Aviation W 84:63 My 9; 58-9 My 23; 85:63 O 10 '66

Testing
Improved match of TF30, F-111 sought. M. L. Yaffee. il Aviation W 84:68-71+ Mr 28 '66

GAS turbines, Automotive
Way we see it. D. MacDonald. Motor T 18:8 N '66

GAS turbines, Marine
Down to the sea by jet power; gas turbine engines for ships. il Bsns W p 152+ Ja 22 '66
Inventor of the month; Captain Carlsen's jet turbine engine. S. V. Jones. Sci Digest 59:23 Mr '66
Ruckus over the turbine. J. Martenhoff. il Motor B 117:181-5 My '66
UAC planing hull craft aimed at oilmen; high-speed planing boat powered by two aircraft gas turbine engines. R. W. Niblock. il Tech W 19:12-13 Ag 1 '66

GAS turbines, Railroad. See Locomotives, Gas turbine

GAS warfare. See Gases in warfare
GAS wells. See Gas, Natural
GASCOYNE, David
British chronicle. R. Howard. Poetry 108: 404-5 S '66

GASES
    See also
Atmosphere
Electric discharges through gases
Space vehicles—Cabin atmospheres

Industrial applications
Feeding it fast to the customers; gas for industry. il Bsns W p94-5 Ag 6 '66

Liquefaction
    See also
Gas, Natural—Liquefaction

GASES, Asphyxiating and poisonous
Is poison safe? Sat Eve Post 239:102 Ap 23 '66
    See also
Carbon dioxide

GASES, Electric discharges through. See Electric discharges through gases

GASES, Rare
Atmospheric noble gases from extraterrestrial dust. D. Tilles. bibliog Science 151: 1015 F 25 '66
Solid noble gases. G. L. Pollack. il Sci Am 215:64-74 bibliog(p 150) O '66

GASES, Solidified
Solid noble gases. G. L. Pollack. il Sci Am 215:64-74 bibliog(p 150) O '66

GASES in rocks
Oxygen fugacities directly measured in magmatic gases; Makaopuhi lava lake, Kilauea volcano, Hawaii. M. Sato and T. L. Wright. bibliog il Science 153:1103-5 S 2 '66

GASES in warfare
Gas and guerrillas, a word of caution. D. Savitz. New Repub 154:13-14 Mr 19 '66
    Discussion. 154:35-6 Ap 2 '66
How gas is being used in Vietnam; tear gas. il U S News 60:8+ Ja 31 '66
Pandora's box. Sci Am 214:49-50 Ap '66
    See also
Chemical warfare

GASKILL, Dale T.
Community range development. por Parks & Rec 1:708-10 S '66

GASKILL, Gordon
Dead Sea isn't dead anymore. Read Digest 89:157-8+ Jl '66
King Faisal: Saudi Arabia's modern monarch. Read Digest 90:117-22 Ja '67

GASOLINE
Notes on gasoline. il Sr Schol 88:33-4 Ap 22 '66

Advertising
Gas station games lose their glitter; Win-a-check boosted sales for Tidewater are having second thoughts. il Bsns W p54+ N 26 '66

Contamination
Water in the gas. B. Wells. il Motor B 117: 66+ Mr '66

Manufacture
    See also
Coal liquefaction

Rating
Gasoline, myth vs. fact. il Changing T 20:29-32 N '66

GASOLINE filters
How to keep those filters filtering. M. J. Schultz. il Pop Mech 126:168-70+ N '66

GASOLINE fume detectors. See Gas detectors

GASOLINE industry
Gas & rubber war; western European and American competition. il Time 88:112+ S 16 '66

GASOLINE pumps
Self-service moves in on the pump; self-service gasoline station. il Bsns W p 129-30 O 1 '66

GASOLINE stations. See Automobile service stations

GASPARILLA ISLAND
Group; or, Us old men and the sea; Boca Grande. R. Lynes. il Harper 233:30+ S '66

GASPARINI, Graziano
Space, baroque, and Indians. Américas 18: 19-25 My '66

GASPÉ PENINSULA
Circling the Gaspe Peninsula. C. Koehler and M. Koehler. il Travel 125:56-62 Je '66

GASQUE, Mac Roy. See Bellows, E. H. jt. auth.

GASS, Oscar
Britain under socialism. bibliog f Commentary 41:65-72 F '66
Financial report on red China. Sat R 49: 27+ Je 25 '66
Literature of American government. bibliog f Commentary 41:67-72 Je '66
Tensions and conservatism in American politics. bibliog f Commentary 42:63-70 N '66

GASS, William H.
True lie-minded man. Nation 203:453-4 O 31 '66

GASSER, Henry
Henry Gasser's paintings of Newark. il por Am Artist 30:48-53+ N '66
Painting the waterfront. Parks & Rec 1: 558-60 Jl '66

GASTEIGER, Edgar L. and Helling, S. A.
X-ray detection by the olfactory system: ozine as a masking odorant. bibliog Science 154:1038-41 N 25 '66

GASTER, Theodor H.
Prometheus and Persephone reborn. Sat R 49:28-9 Ag 20 '66

GASTONGUAY, Paul R.
Life in a test tube. Cath World 204:27-31 O '66

GASTROINTESTINAL diseases. See Digestive system—Diseases

GASTROINTESTINAL tract. See Digestive system

GATES, David M.
Spectral distribution of solar radiation at the earth's surface. bibliog Science 151:523-9 F 4 '66

GATES, Gary Paul
Beginnings of salvation. Holiday 40:178+ D '66
Broadway's Prince Charming. Holiday 39:99-104+ Ap '66

GATES, Marshall
Analgesic drugs; with biographical sketch. Sci Am 215:30, 131-6 bibliog(p 160) N '66

GATES, Thomas M.
Books and the sky. Sky & Tel 32:32-4+ Jl '66

GATES
Double gates that stay fit. B. Gilmore. il Pop Sci 189:154-5 S '66
How to carve a Mexican gate. il Sunset 137:94 S '66
It's easy to be clever with gates. il Pop Gard 17:42-5 Ag '66
Make gates last longer. E. Stout. il Suc Farm 64:124 Mr '66

GATEWAY arch. See St Louis—Monuments, statues, etc.

GATSBY and the sea gull; story. See Lamott, K.

GATTIS, David A.
Pedal-plane whiz-around. Pop Mech 126:134-7+ Ag '66

GATTIS, Murrah
Woman's eye on New York. Sat R 49:39 Ap 30 '66

GAUCHER'S disease
Diagnosis of Gaucher's disease and Niemann-Pick disease with small samples of venous blood. J. P. Kampine and others. bibliog il Science 155:86-8 Ja 6 '67

GAUD, William Steen, 1907-
Review of United States foreign and military policy; transcript of press conference, August 25, 1966. Dept State Bul 55:419-20 S 19 '66

about
Bell's toll. por Time 88:18 Jl 8 '66
New look in foreign aid, it will be harder to get. por U S News 61:58 Jl 25 '66

GAUER, Charlotte E.
Inventions, teachers, and patents. NEA J 55:52-3 S '66

GAUGES. See Gages

GAUGUIN, Paul
Bridge of color; Guggenheim exhibition. il por Newsweek 68:83 Jl 25 '66
Gauguin in the South Seas, by B. Danielsson. Review
  Reporter 35:46-8 Ag 11 '66. H. B. Jacobs
  Time il 87:108 My 6 '66
Gauguin: the hidden tradition. il Art N 65:26-9 Sum '66

GAULLE, Charles de
French and Russian cooperation; address, June 23, 1966. Vital Speeches 32:589-90 Jl 15 '66
From de Gaulle's speech in Moscow; excerpts. Science 153:46 Jl 1 '66
Letter from Paris; excerpts from news conference, November 4, 1966; ed. by Genêt. New Yorker 42:218+ N 19 '66

about
Acid test. il por Newsweek 68:40-1 Ag 1 '66
Advice to U.S. on blackmail. U S News 60:105-6 My 23 '66
Alliance under fire. Sr Schol 88:18 Mr 11 '66
Ami, go home. P. Ben. New Repub 154:10-11 Ap 9 '66
As de Gaulle sees it. New Repub 155:7-8 N 12 '66; Reply. M. Dupont. 155:35 D 17 '66
Atlantic report: de Gaulle and NATO. Atlan 217:24+ My '66
Back of the grandeur: a close look at de Gaulle's France. il U S News 60:39-40 Ap 4 '66
Cost of moving; NATO. il Time 87:51 Mr 18 '66
Dean Acheson's word for de Gaulle: nonsense; excerpts from interview. D. Acheson. U S News 60:79 Ap 18 '66
De Gaulle among the Boswells. M. Viorst. New Repub 155:28-31 Ag 13 '66
De Gaulle and after. G. Defferre. For Affairs 44:434-45 Ap '66
De Gaulle and l'affaire. A. Werth. Nation 202:200-4 F 21 '66
De Gaulle and Russia; some closer ties ahead? por U S News 61:16 D 5 '66
De Gaulle and the new France. P. J. Larmour. Yale R 55:500-20 Je '66
De Gaulle, by J. Lacouture. Review
  Sat R 49:65-6 N 12 '66. S. K. Padover
De Gaulle in the Urals. Commonweal 84:431 Jl 8 '66
De Gaulle: no nation has friends, only interests. por U S News 61:46 S 19 '66
De Gaulle sets forth to change the face of Europe. C. J. V. Murphy. il por Life 61:18-25+ Jl 8 '66; Same abr. with title What is de Gaulle up to? Read Digest 89:134-8 S '66
De Gaulle, the U.S. and Russia: a look at the trends; interview, ed. by F. C. Painton. A. Grosser. U S News 60:42-3 Je 20 '66
De Gaulle; two new books. Atlan 217:134 F '66
De Gaulle wins run-off. Sr Schol 87:4 Ja 7 '66

De Gaulle's quatorzième; meets the press. Time 88:41-2 N 4 '66
De Gaulle's stance: one French opinion. Y. Chabas. Christian Cent 83:1218 O 5 '66
Doctor de Gaulle. K. Crawford. Newsweek 67:39 Mr 28 '66
Elysée matinee; press conference. por Newsweek 68:52 N 7 '66
Europe's new mood: its meaning for U.S. il U S News 60:39-41 Je 20 '66
First steps on the road to Moscow; with report, ed. by J. Blocker. Newsweek 67:40+ My 9 '66
Four books on de Gaulle and the future of Europe. J. M. Gavin. Harper 232:114-17 Ap '66
Fourflusher. K. Crawford. Newsweek 68:39 S 19 '66
France is no longer a democracy. F. Mitterrand. il por N Y Times Mag p 14-15+ My 29 '66
France: will de Gaulle change? Y. Chabas. Christian Cent 83:314-17 Mr 9 '66
Franco-Russian collaboration in science: De Gaulle's visit. V. K. McElheny. Science 153:43-5 Jl 1 '66
French foreign policy under de Gaulle. E. S. Furniss, jr. Cur Hist 50:209-13+ Ap '66
French mission to Moscow: what de Gaulle is up to. F. B. Stevens. por U S News 60:68 My 2 '66
General de Gaulle and Vietnam. J. Lacouture. New Repub 154:19-21 Mr 12 '66
General's pronouncement. E. Taylor. Reporter 34:16+ Mr 10 '66
Hail the great; French comic-book hero; Astérix Le Gaulois. Time 88:27 D 23 '66
If you've wondered what de Gaulle is driving at—. por U S News 61:83 O 24 '66
It's your ball, chum. J. Burnham. Nat R 18:457 My 17 '66
Letter from Paris (cont) Genêt. New Yorker 42:139-40 S 10; 66-7 D 31 '66
Long NATO crisis. E. Taylor. il Reporter 34:16-21 Ap 21 '66
Looking forward; NATO. Newsweek 67:50 Mr 7 '66
Maître de Gaulle. M. Ascoli. Reporter 34:10 Je 30 '66
Mischief-maker. Time 87:98 Mr 18 '66
New road for France, by J. Soustelle. Review
  Nat R 18:122+ F 8 '66. T. Molnar; Reply with rejoinder. Pyrrho. 18:343+ Ap 19 '66
New style; tour through the northern provinces. Newsweek 67:42+ My 9 '66
No laurels for de Gaulle: an appraisal of the London years, by R. Mengin. Review
  New Yorker 42:242-7 O 22 '66. N. Bliven
NATO trouble: immaturity. E. M. von Kuehnelt-Leddihn. Nat R 18:576 Je 14 '66
NATO without France: de Gaulle forces U.S. to showdown in Europe; with analysis by M. S. Johnson. il U S News 60:44-6+ Mr 21 '66
Now Europe is catching up with de Gaulle. por U S News 62:57 Ja 2 '67
Resurgence of the spirit; Kiesinger in Paris. por Time 89:26+ Ja 20 '67
Return of the native; visit to Lille. il por Time 87:30 My 6 '66
Saint Charles. J. J. Kaplow. Nation 202:368-70 Mr 28 '66
Soil, sky & sea. il por Time 87:39 Mr 4 '66
Sons of France, by J. R. Tournoux. Review
  Sat R 49:31 Ag 6 '66. D. Schoenbrun
Speaking his mind; opinion on the United States in Vietnam. Time 88:22 Jl 22 '66
Suspense in France. S. Hoffmann. Commonweal 83:554-6 F 11 '66
Three lives of Charles de Gaulle, by D. Schoenbrun. Review
  Cath World 203:53-5 Ap '66. D. Brandon
  Commonweal 83:643-5 Mr 4 '66. W. C. McWilliams
Time to start U.S. pullback in Europe? interview; ed. by R. Haeger. F. J. Strauss. il U S News 60:68-70+ Ap 18 '66
Tragic victory of Charles de Gaulle. E. W. Fox. Cur Hist 50:201-8+ Ap '66
Two sides of a miracle. A. Werth. il pors Sat R 49:40-1 F 19 '66
What is French policy? A. Fontaine. For Affairs 45:58-76 O '66
What makes de Gaulle act that way? por U S News 60:36 Mr 7 '66
What U.S. has done for France. il U S News 60:36-8 Ap 4 '66
Why de Gaulle is so anti-American. por U S News 60:26 Mr 21 '66

Bibliography
Gallic paradox. S. K. Padover. por Sat R 49:29-31 Ag 6 '66

GAULLE, Charles de—about—*Continued*

Visit to Russia, 1966

Apologies to the bull, from the china shop. Nat R 18:660+ Jl 12 '66

De Gaulle in Moscow: what he did, what it means; with report by F. B. Stevens. il por U S News 61:26-7 Jl 4 '66

De Gaulle in Russia: tour de force. il pors Newsweek 68:34-9 Jl 4 '66

De Gaulle's mission to Moscow. P. Ben. New Repub 154:13-14 Je 18 '66

End of a stately visit; with report on European reaction. Newsweek 68:38-40 Jl 11 '66

Le grand tovarish; Russia prepares. Newsweek 67:48 Je 27 '66

Grandest tour. il pors Time 88:20-4+ Jl 1 '66

Letter from Paris. Genêt. New Yorker 42:98+ Jl 16 '66

Seeds of disengagement. il por Time 88:22 Jl 8 '66

Voyage to Muscovy. il Time 87:34 Je 24 '66

Visits abroad, 1966

Atlantic report. Atlan 218:16+ S '66

Backyard troubles. il Newsweek 68:53-4 S 26 '66

Cambodia gives de Gaulle a gilded platform. il pors Life 61:44-7 S 16 '66

Le cool Charles; Djibouti; Addis Ababa; Phnom Penh visits. il por Newsweek 68:39 S 5 '66

De Gaulle on the loose. Nat R 18:916 S 20 '66

De Gaulle's grand tour; what he hopes to achieve. U S News 61:12 S 5 '66

Le grand tourist. il por Time 88:42 S 16 '66

Incident in Djibouti. il por Time 88:29 S 2 '66

Islands in the sun. il por Newsweek 68:44+ S 19 '66

Letter from Paris. Genet. New Yorker 42:139-40 S 10 '66

Message for the U.S. il Time 88:35 S 9 '66

Soul brothers. il por Newsweek 68:30 S 12 '66

GAULT, Donald E. and others
Luna 9 photographs: evidence for a fragmental surface layer. bibliog Science 153:985-8 Ag 26 '66

GAUNTT, Jefferson
Portraits by Gauntt. E. Gaines. il por Antiques 89:238-9 F '66

GAUTHIER, Eva
Eva Gauthier. A. Favia-Artsay. por Hobbies 71:36 Ag '66

GAUTIER, Felisa Rincón de
Fabulous Doña Felisa. S. Seegers and K. Seegers. il Read Digest 89:145-8+ Jl '66

GAVER, Jessyca Russell
Absence; poem. Ladies Home J 83:54 Ag '66

GAVER, Mary Virginia
Making of the catalog. Library J 91:1606-13 Mr 15 '66

Masters of the raging book? address, July 15, 1966. bibliog f por ALA Bul 60:794-9+ S '66; Excerpts. Sr Schol 89:sup3 S 16 '66

New Jersey plan; address, July 1966. por ALA Bul 60:1138-42 D '66

School libraries today; interview, ed. by W. D. Boutwell. por Sr Schol 88:sup 1-3 My 20 '66

Schools and scholarly books; summary of address, June 14, 1966. por Pub W 190:44-6 Jl 4 '66

Set up a committee. por Library J 91:5131 O 15 '66

GAVIN, James M.
Communication on Vietnam; letter. Harper 232:16+ F '66; Excerpts. por U S News 60:26-7 F 7 '66

Excerpts from testimony, February 8, 1966, before Senate committee on foreign relations. Cong Digest 45:107-8 Ap '66; U S News 60:21 F 21 '66

Four books on de Gaulle and the future of Europe. Harper 232:114-17 Ap '66

Military power: the limits of persuasion. por Sat R 49:18-22+ Jl 30 '66

Voices of dissent: Gavin and Kennan; testimony before the Senate foreign relations committee; excerpts. il Newsweek 67:28-9 F 21 '66

about

Letter from Washington. R. H. Rovere. New Yorker 41:146+ F 19 '66

Voices of dissent. Newsweek 67:34 Ja 31 '66

GAY, Carlo T. E.
Rock carvings at Chalcacingo. Natur Hist 75:56-61 Ag '66

GAY, Nelson, and others
Cheapest ways to feed a beef herd. Suc Farm 64:38-9 Ap '66

GAY, Peter
Complete romantic. Horizon 8:12-15+ Spr '66

GAY Head, pseud.
Talking it over with Gay Head; questions and answers. See issues of Senior scholastic

GAY hearts; story. See Bradshaw, G.

GAYLE, Addison, jr
Literature of protest. Negro Hist Bul 29:61-2 D '65

GAYN, Mark
China convulsed. For Affairs 45:246-59 Ja '67

Peking has a Yenan complex. N Y Times Mag p 10-11+ Ja 30 '66

GAZDAK, Joe
Out of the frying pan. il U S Camera 29:48-51+ Ag '66

GAZEBOS. See Garden houses, shelters, etc.

GEAGAN, Bill
Farm-fed whitetails. Field & S 71:68-9+ N '66

GEARING
See also
Automobiles—Gearing

GEBALLE, T. H. and others
Superconductivity of alpha-uranium and the role of 5f electrons. bibliog Science 152:755-7 My 6 '66

GEBHARDT, Bryan M. See Volpe, E. P. jt. auth.

GEBHARDT, Louis Philipp, 1905-
Winter resort for viruses. il Time 88:62 Ag 12 '66

GEDDES, Geoffrey
Printing of The Mother Goose treasury. Pub W 190:102+ O 3 '66

GEDDES, Robert L.
Rockville'e multi-level mini-core. J. Bailey. il Arch Forum 125:56-61 D '66

GEERTZ, Clifford
Impact of the concept of culture on the concept of man. Bul Atomic Sci 22:2-8 Ap '66

GEESE, Wild
All American goose; Canada goose. F. Dufresne. il Field & S 71:62-3+ N '66

Black brant, sea goose of the Pacific Coast, by A. S. Einarsen. Review
Liv Wildn 29:28 Aut '65. L. W. Swift

Nemesis of the black brant. R. Cantwell. il Sports Illus 24:44-6+ My 16 '66

War over goose-use; Horicon refuge eviction campaign. il Life 61:48-9 O 14 '66

GEGENSCHEIN. See Counterglow

GEHMAN, Richard
Benchley's Bushmen. Sat R 49:59+ O 15 '66

Mildred. Sat R 50:104-5 Ja 14 '67

GEHRINGER, V. O.
Sell the salesman on city hall. Am City 81:90-1 Jl '66

GEIBERGER, Al
Don't forget the sandwiches. il por Time 88:52 Ag 5 '66

Happy stroll for golf's smiling Gei. D. Jenkins. il por Sports Illus 25:16-19 Ag 1 '66

GEIGER, Burnice Iverson
Burnice comes home. il por Time 88:20 Jl 8 '66

GEIGER-Müller counters
Radiological survey meters. J. G. Ello. il Electr World 75:44-6+ Ja '66

GEIMAN, Quentin M. and others
Plasma replacement for in vitro culture of plasmodium knowlesi. bibliog Science 153:1129-30 S 2 '66

GEIS, Gilbert
Violence and organized crime. bibliog f Ann Am Acad 364:86-95 Mr '66

GEISMAR, Peter
Books. Commonweal 84:444-5 Jl 8 '66

GEISSLER, Ruth O'Donnell
Getting used to a new smile. Todays Health 44:66-8 D '66

GEKKONID lizards. See Lizards

GELABERT, Raoul
Anatomy for the ballet teacher; ed. by W. Como. See issues of Dance magazine

GELATIN
Off with the mold! gelatin salad or dessert! il Bet Hom & Gard 44:160 O '66

GELATIN salads. See Salads

GELATT, Esther
Old Met. striking the tent. Hi Fi 16:MA10+ Jl '66

GELATT, Roland
Brave new generation. Reporter 34:50-1 Ja 27 '66

Family album; collection of Wagner family pictures. Hi Fi 16:69-77 N '66

Handel makes the scene. Reporter 35:40-1 D 1 '66

High notes. Reporter 35:36+ D 29 '66

Long and short of short wave. Hi Fi 16:69-71 D '66

Low-price revolution. Reporter 35:52-3 O 6 '66

GELATT, Roland—*Continued*
Masterpieces galore. Reporter 34:40+ My 5 '66
Mediterranean Götterdämmerung. Reporter 34:50+ Mr 23 '66
Middling Verdi. Reporter 34:39-40 Je 16 '66
Midsummer miscellany. Reporter 35:38-40 Ag 11 '66
Murrow in London, you can hear him now. Hi Fi 16:123 O '66
New wine in new bottles. Reporter 35:57-9 N 17 '66
New York's other opera company. Reporter 34:43-4+ Ap 21 '66
Opening night at the new Met. Hi Fi 16:MA8-10 N '66
Opera notes. Reporter 35:50-2 S 8 '66
Record notes. Reporter 34:49-50 F 24 '66

GELBOIN, H. V. and others
Rapid and marked inhibition of rat-liver RNA polymerase by aflatoxin B₁. bibliog Science 154:1205-6 D 2 '66

GELDER, Manny
Manny Gelder: slumlord; excerpt from Poorhouse state. R. M. Elman. il Atlan 218:128-30 N '66

GELDZAHLER, Henry
Henry here, Henry there, who is Henry? il pors Life 60:41-2+ F 18 '66

GELFAND, Morris A.
Brazil's library law. bibliog por Library J 91:1362-4 Mr 15 '66

GELLER, S.
Pressure-induced phases of sulfur. bibliog Science 152:644-6 Ap 29 '66
—and Lind, M. D.
Pressure-induced phase of sulfur-selenium. Science 155:79-80 Ja 6 '67

GELLHORN, Martha
Animals running free: two weeks in the Serengeti. Atlan 217:70-6 F '66
Spiral to a gun. Harper 233:69-73 O '66
Suffer the little children. Ladies Home J 84:57+ Ja '67

GELLHORN, Walter
Authors & editors; interview. Pub W 191:25 Ja 9 '67

about
People's watchdog. il por Time 88:58+ D 2 '66

GELLMAN, Murray
Compac solid-state C-D ignition system. Pop Electr 25:53-6+ N '66
Electronic ignition takes to the water. Pop Mech 125:200-3 Mr '66
Solid-state tachometer for CD or transistor ignition systems. Pop Electr 24:54-7 F '66

GELMAN, Steve
All-star pro team: a prediction for '66. Esquire 66:88-90+ O '66

GELTMAN, Max
Hot hundred: a surprise. Nat R 18:894-6 S 6 '66
Jewish affirmation. Nat R 18:977-83 O 4 '66
Negro-Jewish confrontation. Nat R 18:621-3 Je 28 '66

GEM carving. See Carving (art industries)
GEM cutting. See Lapidary work
GEM stones. See Precious stones
GEMINI project. See Space flight—Manned flights

GEMS
Gems and minerals. H. D. Brown. See issues of Hobbies
You own $10,000,000 worth of gems; Hall of gems and minerals, Smithsonian institution. D. J. Cooper. il Esquire 66:181-5+ D '66
See also
Precious stones

GENAUER, Emily
What is suitable art for public buildings? E. Goble. Arch Rec 139:9 My '66

GENDEL, Evelyn
Pasta! excerpts. Ladies Home J 84:78-9+ Ja '67

GENDEL, Milton
Art news from Rome. Art N 65:22+ Mr; 54 Sum '66
Venice: miniskirts or miniart? Art N 65:52-4+ S '66

GENEALOGY
Blue blood; glorification of Norman blood. J. H. Plumb. Sat R 49:27-8 O 29 '66
What's in a name? American political families. America 114:318-19 Mr 5 '66

GENEEN, Harold Sydney
How one man can move a corporate mountain. S. H. Brown. il por Fortune 74:80-3+ Jl 1 '66

GENERAL accounting office. See United States—General accounting office

GENERAL agreement on tariffs and trade
Further steps taken to remove restrictions on U.S. exports; Department announcement, March 14, 1966; with lists of import liberalizations of Denmark; Finland; and Spain. Dept State Bul 54:624-7 Ap 18 '66
GATT contracting parties meet at Geneva. Dept State Bul 54:589-90 Ap 11 '66
New horizons in foreign trade. W. Diebold, jr. For Affairs 45:291-303 Ja '67
U.S. welcomes Yugoslav membership in GATT; Department statement, August 25, 1966. Dept State Bul 55:435 S 19 '66

GENERAL assembly of the national council. See National council of the churches of Christ in the United States of America

GENERAL assembly of the Presbyterian church in the United States (southern) See Presbyterian church in the United States (South)

GENERAL assembly of the United Nations. See United Nations—General assembly

GENERAL aviation affairs, Office of. See United States—Federal aviation administration

GENERAL dynamics corporation
Photos detail F-111A assembly flow as program is accelerated. il Aviation W 84:66-75 My 30 '66

Convair division
Convair examines closed-loop prospects. il Tech W 19:39 Ag 15 '66

Electric boat division
G/D courting research sub market. R. W. Niblock. il Miss & Roc 18:25+ My 16 '66

GENERAL education. See Liberal education

GENERAL electric company
Bargaining basement; strike threat. Newsweek 68:80 O 17 '66
Bargaining that's different: General electric makes an offer. U S News 61:102 S 26 '66
Case of civilized penology; sponsor of Georgia prisoners computer course. Nation 202:115 Ja 31 '66
GE boosts thrust in phase 3 SST engine. M. L. Yaffee. il Aviation W 85:42-3+ S 26 '66
GE divisions determine air fleet usage. D. A. Brown. il Aviation W 85:56-7+ S 12 '66
GE puts unity to test. il Bsns W p94+ Je 25 '66
GE stands its ground; resists pressures from both government and public opinion. Bsns W p 164+ O 15 '66
GE tries casting a new die; die-cast the ferrous metals. il Bsns W p 175-6 My 14 '66
GE will market its knowhow commercially; venture, known as Empis. il Bsns W p 138 F 19 '66
It takes a bigger offer now to head off a strike. U S News 61:92-3 O 17 '66
Johnson expected to push SST. Aviation W 86:25-6 Ja 9 '67
Maintainability becomes engine byword. M. L. Yaffee. il Aviation W 85:106-7+ O 31 '66
Now a pattern for wages and fringes in 1967. il U S News 61:76-7 O 31 '66
On the brink of a strike at GE; union coalition and company stand firm as deadline nears. Bsns W p96+ O 1 '66
Shared victory. Time 88:103-4 O 21 '66
Supersonic jet makes a slow takeoff; choice of Boeing and GE didn't end the suspense. il Bsns W p31-2 Ja 7 '67
SST: winners of the great race. il Newsweek 69:51 Ja 9 '67
Trouble at Bull; Franco-American Bull-General electric computer giant. Newsweek 69:62 Ja 16 '67
Up from the sidewalk; G.E.'s entry into the city-building field. Time 88:94 S 9 '66
Why the rank and file say no; terms fail to resolve issues of local memberships in Schenectady, N.Y. il Bsns W p59-60+ D 17 '66
See also
General learning corporation

Flight propulsion division
G.E.'s hard-driving jockey in the jet-engine race. J. Mecklin. il Fortune 74:116-18+ Jl 1 '66

GENERAL federation of women's clubs
Turn in the road; address, June 7, 1966. Mrs W. H. Hasebroock. Vital Speeches 32:700-4 S 1 '66

GENERAL federation of women's clubs, Washington, D.C.
Women who do things. A. R. Kimsey. il Parks & Rec 1:836-8+ O '66

GENERAL foods corporation
Tex Cook vs. the status quo. J. F. Olesky. Duns R 87:51-2 Ja '66

GENERAL GRANT NATIONAL PARK. See Kings Canyon National Park

GENETICS—*Continued*
Tampering with our genetic blueprint. W. Gilman. New Repub 155:12-13 N 12 '66
Yeast genetics; report on conference. R. C. Von Borstel. Science 152:1287-8 My 27 '66
See also
Chromosomes
Heredity

Research
See Genetic research

GENETICS (bacteria)
Genetics of the bacterial cell; address, December 11, 1965. F. Jacob. bibliog il Science 152:1470-8 Je 10 '66

GENETICS, Medical. See Heredity of disease

GENEVA, Switzerland

Airports
Satellites planned for Geneva terminal; loading stations connected to the main building by underground moving sidewalks. il Aviation W 84:61+ Je 20 '66

Music
Geneva. D. A. Mackinnon. Opera N 30:31-2 F 19; 31:29-30 S 10 '66
Geneva; production of Elektra. D. A. Mackinnon. Opera N 31:30 D 10 '66
Mines of sulphur; recital in Geneva. W. Legge. il Hi Fi 16:128-9 Je '66
Opera on three fronts; Geneva-Munich-Milan. W. Legge. Hi Fi 16:136-9 Mr '66

GENEVA-Cointrin international airport. See Geneva, Switzerland—Airports

GENEVA conference of foreign ministers. See Council of foreign ministers, Geneva, 1954

GENGRAS, Edmund Clayton
In the ring with Dempsey. il por Time 88:16 Jl 1 '66

GENNARO, Peter
Peter Gennaro works at what makes a special special; Stage 67's Rodgers and Hart today. V. H. Swisher. il por Dance Mag 40:20-1 D '66

GENNOY, Peter
Polls '66: Nixon or Romney? Nat R 18:1084 N 1 '66

GENOCIDE
Unremembered genocide; murder of Armenians in Turkey during 1915-1916. M. Housepian. Commentary 42:55-61 S '66; Discussion. 42:7-8+ D '66

GENOVESA ISLAND. See Galápagos Islands

GENOVESE, Eugene D.
Paradoxical American radical. Nation 203: 191-3 S 5 '66

GENTLE giant-killer; drama. See Miller, H. L.

GENTRY, Loyd
Boo made a boo-boo. P. Axthelm. il por Sports Illus 24:26-9+ My 23 '66

GENUINE fur eyelashes; story. See Tyler, A.

GEOCHEMISTRY
Chemical fossils. G. Eglinton and M. Calvin. il Sci Am 216:32-43 Ja '67

GEODESIC dome. See Domes

GEODESY
Level-surface profiles across the Puerto Rico Trench. W. S. Von Arx. bibliog il Science 154:1651-4 D 30 '66
Superline; 500 meters of air; first geodetic standard base line in the United States. Sci N 90:519 D 17 '66
See also
Isostasy

GEODETIC satellites. See Artificial satellites—Mapping applications

GEOFFRION, Bernard
One more boom or bust for the Boomer. P. Axthelm. il pors Sports Illus 25:42-4+ N 14 '66

GEOGRAPHICAL distribution of animals and plants
Chromosome variability of geographic distribution in insects. B. John and K. R. Lewis. bibliog il Science 152:711-21 My 6 '66
Distribution of wild wheats and barley. J. R. Harlan and D. Zohary. bibliog il Science 153:1074-80 S 2 '66

GEOGRAPHICAL names. See Names, Geographical

GEOGRAPHY
See also
Continents
Man—Influence of environment
also subhead Geography under names of regions and countries, e.g. China—Geography

Study and teaching
Geography as invention. I. L. Walker. il Sr Schol 89:sup8 O 14 '66

How do you move the mountain into the classroom? R. Gray. il NEA J 55:34-6 Mr '66
New geography; high school geography project. J Bryant. il Sci Digest 60:62-5 O '66
See also
National council for geographic education

Projects
Urban geography: city planning in the classroom; project map of Portsville designed by the AAG. A. I. Mayer. il Sr Schol 88: sup 12 Ap 22 '66

GEOGRAPHY, Historical

Maps
Early mapping of the land and sea. G. A. Rothrock. il Natur Hist 75:24-9 bibliog (p68) F '66
See also
Maps, Early

GEOLOGICAL chemistry. See Geochemistry

GEOLOGICAL research
Instant earthquake; Denver area tremors cause: D. Evans theory; grants for more study. il Time 87:93 Ap 1 '66
Probing deeper, higher, farther. B. Tufty. Sci N 90:548-9 D 24 '66
Stratigraphic sections, bedding sequences, and random processes. D. D. Carr and others. bibliog il Science 154:1162-4 D 2 '66

GEOLOGICAL society of America
Unearthing the future; GSA digging into new space-age role. Bsns W p 105-6 D 3 '66

GEOLOGICAL time
Age of the ocean floor; with discussion. E. Orowan. bibliog Science 154:413-16 O 21 '66
Geomagnetic polarity epochs: a new polarity event and the age of the Brunhes-Matuyama boundary. R. R. Doell and G. B. Dalrymple. bibliog il Science 152:1060-1 My 20 '66
James Croll and soar evolution. N. J. Woolf. il Sky & Tel 31:150-1 Mr '66
Middle Devonian lunar month. A. F. Aveni. bibliog Science 151:1221-2 Mr 11 '66; Reply. S. K. Runcorn. Science 154:292 O 14 '66
Paleomagnetic study of Antarctic deep-sea cores. N. D. Opdyke and others. bibliog il Science 154:349-57 O 21 '66
Tektites are terrestrial. H. Faul. bibliog il Science 152:1341-5 Je 3 '66

GEOLOGY
Geologist and his apple; reprint. G. Teleki. il Am For 72:6+ Ag '66
Pacific science congress; report. R. S. Dietz. Science 154:1365-6 D 9 '66
See also
Alluvium
Coast changes
Continents
Geological research
Geological society of America
Glacial geology
Ocean bottom
Oceanography
Submarine geology
Volcanoes

Africa, East
Cracks in a continent. B. H. Baker. il UNESCO Courier 19:11-15 Je '66

Alaska
Kodiak seamount not flat-topped. E. L. Hamilton and R. E. Von Huene. bibliog il Science 154:1323-5 D 9 '66
Radiocarbon dating of coastal peat, Barrow, Alaska. J. Brown and P. V. Sellmann. bibliog il Science 153:299-300 Jl 15 '66

Antarctic Regions
Airborne geophysical study in the Pensacola Mountains of Antarctica. J. C. Behrendt and others. bibliog il Science 153:1373-6 S 16 '66
Glacier ice flooded ancient Antarctica. Sci N 89:219 Ap 2 '66
Movement directions in late Paleozoic glacial rocks of the Horlick and Pensacola Mountains, Antarctica. L. A. Frakes and others. bibliog il Science 153:746-9 Ag 12 '66
Stratigraphy of the Wisconsin Range, Horlick Mountains, Antarctica. V. H. Minshew. bibliog il Science 152:637-8 Ap 29 '66

Baffin Island
Baffin Island refugia older than 54,000 years. O. H. Löken. bibliog il Science 153:1378-80 S 16 '66

California
In the track of Yosemite's glaciers. il Sunset 137:35-6 Jl '66

GEORGIA—Politics and government—*Cont.*
LBJ backlash; Lester G. Maddox's victory in primary. Nation 203:340 O 10 '66
Mr White Backlash; L. Maddox of Georgia. R. Cleghorn. il N Y Times Mag p27-9+ N 6 '66
Nine supersolons; awaiting Supreme court ruling in disputed gubernatorial election. Reporter 35:14+ D 15 '66
Out of the battle. Time 88:35 O 14 '66
Peach state snarl; no absolute majority for Maddox nor Callaway. Sr Schol 89:18 D 2 '66
Picking Maddox. Newsweek 68:20 D 26 '66
Politics: the white backlash, 1966. il Newsweek 68:27-8 O 10 '66
Pride and progress. C. L. Weltner. il Am Ed 2:23-5 O '66
Profile in courage; C. L. Weltner exit from congressional race. Newsweek 68:30 O 17 '66
Return of a moderate; Arnall wins. Time 88:25 S 23 '66
Right to speak; case of H. J. Bond. il Time 88:31 D 16 '66
Surprise from Maddox: he sounds a changed note. U S News 62:14 Ja 23 '67
Untying legal knots: Georgia governorship and Bond case. Sr Schol 89:17 Ja 6 '67
Up to the legislature. Time 88:20-1 D 23 '66
What is the law? Supreme court's decision on governor's election. New Repub 155:8 D 24 '66
Winners wanted; new governor. il Time 88:32-3 N 25 '66

GEORGIA, Russia
Georgia on their minds. Time 88:38 N 11 '66

Antiquities
Rustaveli and the knight in the tiger's skin. I. Abashidze. il UNESCO Courier 19:28-30 O '66

GEORGIA, STRAIT OF
Outboarding the rapids of British Columbia. F. Clark. il Yachting 120:62-3+ D '66

GEORGIA institute of technology, Atlanta
Goodbye to Gothic at Georgia tech. il Sci Digest 59:60-5 My '66

GEORGIA-Pacific corporation
Fair exchange? shortchanging acquired companies; SEC action. Newsweek 67:74 My 9 '66

GEOTRICHUM candidum. See Fungi

GERALD, Thetis
Vanishing farm wife. il pors Ebony 21:76-7+ Ag '66

GERANIUMS
Ivy geraniums. H. V. Wilson. il Flower Grower 53:34+ O '66

GERARD, Robert D.
Potential freshwater reservoir in the New York area. bibliog Science 153:870-1 Ag 19 '66

GERARD, Sue M.
Your spare tire can prevent a drowning. Read Digest 88:109-11 Je '66

GERASSI, John
Liberal establishment voice. Nation 202:495-6 Ap 25 '66
Third world in the real world. Nation 203:252-4 S 19 '66

GERASSI, Marysa Navarro
(comp) Recent books on Latin America. Nation 204:26 Ja 2 '67

GERBER, Merrill Joan
Invitation to the dance; story. Redbook 127:58-9 O '66
Ten cents' worth of love; story. Redbook 127:66-7 Jl '66

GERBER, Paul, and others
Murine leukemia viruses: antigenic studies by quantitative complement fixation. bibliog Science 152:1074-5 My 20 '66

GERBER, Rudolph J.
Clash at Louvain. America 114:645-9 7 '66
How to silence a cardinal. America 114:195-7 F 5 '66
Prague in metamorphosis. America 115:480-2 O 22 '66

GERBER products company
Mother & the pill. il Time 87:89-90 Je 3 '66

GERBILS
Happiness is a pocket kangaroo. il Time 87:67 Ap 15 '66
Mongolian gerbil aids circulatory disease study. Sci N L 89:57 Ja 22 '66
Nature note; gerbils make good pets. il Sci N 90:285 O 8 '66

GERDTS, William H.
Egyptian motifs in nineteenth-century American painting and sculpture. Antiques 90:495-501 O '66
Thomas Birch: America's first marine artist. Antiques 89:528-34 Ap '66

GEREN, Paul F.
Diplomatic adjustment by the maritime nations. Dept State Bul 54:78-85 Ja 17 '66

GERHOLZ, Robert Paul
Power of persuasion. Newsweek 67:67-8 Ja 31 '66

GERKEN, Eva
Enter the hero. Opera N 31:6 Ja 21 '67
Traveling salesman. Opera N 30:6 Mr 12 '66

GERLACH, Rex R.
Grande Ronde: new steelhead paradise. Field & S 71:30-3+ Jl '66

GERLING, Jacob
Instead of big bulky trees. Am City 81:105-7 Ag '66

GERM proofing. See Asepsis and antisepsis

GERM warfare. See Biological warfare

GERMAN art. See Art, German

GERMAN atrocities. See World war, 1939-1945 —Atrocities

GERMAN automobiles. See Automobiles, Foreign

GERMAN castles. See Castles

GERMAN cookery. See Cookery, German

GERMAN economic assistance. See Economic assistance, German

GERMAN literature
German tradition in literature, 1871-1945, by R. Gray. Review
Nation 202:593+ My 16 '66. R. Hauser
See also
Childrens literature—Germany

GERMAN mail order business. See Mail order business

GERMAN measles. See Rubella

GERMAN poetry

Translations into English
For the grave of a peace-loving man; tr. by M. Hamburger. H. M. Enzensberger. Harper 233:75 Jl '66
Kaunas 1941; tr. by R. Mead and M. Mead. J. Bobrowski. Nation 202:589 My 16 '66
O the chimneys; tr. by M. Roloff. N. Sachs. Sat R 49:47 D 10 '66
Young man: five a.m; poem. tr. by J. Simon. E. Kästner. Mlle 62:112 F '66

GERMAN pottery. See Pottery, German

GERMAN refugees. See Refugees, German

GERMAN reunification question. See Germany —Union (proposed)

GERMAN-Russian war, 1941-1945. See World war, 1939-1945—Campaigns and battles— Russia

GERMAN sculpture. See Sculpture, German

GERMAN shepherd dogs
Sentry dogs needed in Vietnam. Field & S 70:24 F '66

GERMAN technical assistance. See Technical assistance, German

GERMAN war criminals. See World war, 1939-1945—War criminals

GERMANIUM counters. See Radiation—Measurement

GERMANIUM diodes. See Diodes

GERMANIUM transistors. See Transistors

GERMANS
Germans feel like Germans again. R. Lowenthal. il N Y Times Mag p36-7+ Mr 6 '66
Germany: bridges needed; East vs West Germans. J. C. Evans. Christian Cent 83:1561-2 D 21 '66
Shadow no larger than a crooked cross. J. Cameron. il N Y Times Mag p94-5+ S 11 '66; Reply. P. Laukhuff p 156-7 O 9 '66
Sober look at the new Germany. F. Mayer. Christian Cent 83:710-12 Je 1 '66; Reply. D. Barley. 83:888-9 Jl 13 '66

GERMANS and Jews. See Jews and Germans

GERMANTOWN, Ohio
Germantown saves a covered bridge. F. B. Rhoades. il Am City 81:41 My '66

GERMANY
See also
Children—Germany
Fascism—Germany
Jews in Germany
Negroes in Germany

Antiquities
See also
Rome—Antiquities

Description and travel
See also
Frankfort on the Main—Description

GERMANY—*Continued*

Foreign relations

Trouble in Germany; it means trouble for U.S. il U S News 61:75-6 N 21 '66

History

Shadow no larger than a crooked cross. J. Cameron. il N Y Times Mag p94-5+ S 11 '66; Discussion. p21+ O 2; 156-7 O 9 '66

Bibliography

Articles and other books received; comp. by A. H. Price. See issues of American historical review

20th century

Germans and their modern history, by F. Ernst. Review
Atlan 217:129-30 My '66. O. Handlin

1933-1945

Nazi culture, by G. L. Mosse. Review
Sat R 49:28 My 21 '66. L. L. Snyder

Intellectual life

See also
German literature

National socialist movement

See Fascism—Germany

Politics and government

Shadow no larger than a crooked cross. J. Cameron. il N Y Times Mag p94-5+ S 11 '66; Discussion. p21+ O 2; 156-7 O 9 '66

See also
Fascism—Germany

Reichstag fire

See Reichstag fire

Union (proposed)

Adenauer's view of a changing Europe. G. Bailey. il Reporter 34:18-22 Je 30 '66
Berlin revisited; thoughts on unification. K. Loewenstein. bibliog f Cur Hist 50:263-8+ My '66
Buoyant mood. Time 87:41 My 20 '66
Germans feel like Germans again. R. Lowenthal. il N Y Times Mag p36-7+ Mr 6 '66
Strongest emotion; East Germany's desire for reunification. Time 87:37 Ap 15 '66
Talk across the wall; East-West televised debates on reunification postponed. il Newsweek 67:42 My 9 '66
Worried look at West Germany. H. C. Wolfe. Sat R 49:22-3+ Mr 26 '66

GERMANY (Democratic Republic)
Bridge on the River Saale; widened gap between East and West. il Time 88:18-19 D 30 '66
Muted revolution: East Germany's challenge to Russia and the West, by W. Hangen. Review
Sat R 49:35-6 S 17 '66. H. C. Wolfe
New perspectives behind the wall. W. Hangen. For Affairs 45:135-47 O '66
Two views of two Germanys; observations of Welles Hangen and Peter Lust. H. Pol. Nation 203:457-8 O 31 '66
We did it all ourselves. il Newsweek 67:48-9 Mr 14 '66

See also
Art—Germany (Democratic Republic)
Berlin (East Berlin)
Merchant marine—Germany (Democratic Republic)
Natural resources—Germany (Democratic Republic)
Shipbuilding

Boundaries

Country cousin of the Berlin wall. P. Shabecoff. il N Y Times Mag p8-9+ Jl 10 '66
Europe's unsettled borders; Oder-Neisse line. E. M. von Kuehnelt-Leddihn. Nat R 18: 678 Jl 12 '66

Commerce

East Germany; the prosperous prisoner. W. Hangen. Reporter 35:30-3 Ag 11 '66

Economic conditions

One red nation that's enjoying a boom. R. A. Haeger. il U S News 60:80-2 Mr 14 '66
Visit to East Germany. W. Hoffmann. America 114:486+ Ap 9 '66

Economic policy

East Germany; the prosperous prisoner. W. Hangen. Reporter 35:30-3 Ag 11 '66

Foreign relations

Atlantic report; wall, after five years. Atlan 217:20+ Je '66
Jack-boot diplomacy; Ghanaians held; retaliation for J. Krueger's imprisonment. Newsweek 67:52 My 23 '66
Still voices; speakers' exchange to debate East-West problems called off. Time 88:23 Jl 8 '66

Industries

East Germany; Soviet-occupied zone of Germany. N. J. G. Pounds. bibliog il Focus 17:1-6 O '66
Of Meissen men. il Newsweek 67:74+ Je 6 '66

Intellectual life

Letter from Berlin. H. Lohr; reply with rejoinder. E. Bentley. Nation 202:inside cover F 28 '66

Politics and government

Atlantic report; Ulbricht loosens the reins. Atlan 217:24+ Je '66

Religious institutions and affairs

Celebrating the 450th year of the reformation; in East Germany. Christian Cent 83:1370 N 9 '66
Church and communism in East Germany. M. Barth. Christian Cent 83:1440-3, 1469-72 N 23-30 '66
World around us (cont of) News of the Christian world. Christian Cent 83:280-2, 837, 1252-4; 84:92-3 Mr 2, Je 29, O 12 '66, Ja 18 '67

GERMANY (Federal Republic)
Bridge on the River Saale; widened gap between East and West. il Time 88:18-19 D 30 '66
Two views of two Germanys; observations of Welles Hangen and Peter Lust. H. Pol. Nation 203:457-8 O 31 '66
West Germany, 1966; symposium. bibliog f Cur Hist 50:257-9+ My '66

See also
Aerospace industries—Germany (Federal Republic)
Airlines—Germany (Federal Republic)
Airplane industry and trade—Germany (Federal Republic)
Airplanes, Military—Germany (Federal Republic)
Art—Germany (Federal Republic)
Automobile industry and trade—Germany (Federal Republic)
Berlin (West Berlin)
Busingen
Colleges and universities—Germany (Federal Republic)
Cologne, Germany
Dortmund, Germany—Music
Fascism—Germany (Federal Republic)
Hamburg
Hanover
Hotels, taverns, etc.—Germany (Federal Republic)
Justice, Administration of—Germany (Federal Republic)
Labor supply—Germany (Federal Republic)
Municipal government—Germany (Federal Republic)
Music festivals—Germany (Federal Republic)
National parks and reserves—Germany (Federal Republic)
Newspapers—Germany (Federal Republic)
Petroleum industry and trade—Germany (Federal Republic)
Political parties—Germany (Federal Republic)
Public officers—Germany (Federal Republic)
Public opinion—Germany (Federal Republic)
Public works—Germany (Federal Republic)
Publishers and publishing—Germany (Federal Republic)
Ruhr Valley
Space research—Germany (Federal Republic)
Steel industry and trade—Germany (Federal Republic)
Trials—Germany (Federal Republic)
Youth—Germany (Federal Republic)

Air force

Luftwaffe flies again. in Arizona skies; Luke air force base. il U S News 60:82-3 My 9 '66
Problems with flying lab; crashes of the Luftwaffe Starfighter. il Time 88:23 Jl 29 '66
Random causes cited in F-104G crashes. Aviation W 84:73 F 7 '66

GERMANY (Federal Republic)—*Continued*

Armed forces

Anger in the barracks; resignations of generals. Time 88:29 S 2 '66

Generals' revolt; resignations due to influence of civilians over military affairs. il Newsweek 68:34+ S 5 '66

Germany between two alliances; background to Ministry of defense scandal-and-crisis. G. Bailey. il Reporter 35:27-32 O 6 '66

Letter from Germany: sword too heavy? army-defense ministry crisis. C. Amery. Nation 203:346-7 O 10 '66

Army

Germany's new army: no. 1 in Europe again. il U S News 61:69-70 S 12 '66

Germany's un-German army. il Newsweek 68:38 S 12 '66

I'm all right, Hans; unionization of West German army. Time 88:40+ N 18 '66

Boundaries

Country cousin of the Berlin wall. P. Shabecoff. il N Y Times Mag p8-9+ Jl 10 '66

Cabinet

Romanized Teuton; new government. il Newsweek 68:52 D 19 '66

Civilization

Changing culture in Germany. F. E. Hirsch. Cur Hist 50:289-94+ My '66

Commerce

East Germany: the prosperous prisoner. W. Hangen. Reporter 35:30-3 Ag 11 '66

Shrewd gambit; step toward boosting trade with East Germany. Newsweek 67:49 My 16 '66

See also
Germany (Federal Republic)—Industries

Commercial treaties and agreements

Busy boats to China; U.S. reaction to steel deal. il Time 87:84 Ap 1 '66

Two Germanys and two Chinas; background to steel-processing agreement with China. J. E. Smith. il Reporter 34:36-8 My 19 '66

Constitution

Whither West Germany? C. Mayer. il Nation 203:88-90 Jl 25 '66

Defenses

Crisis in German defense. E. M. von Kuehnelt-Leddihn. Nat R 18:995 O 4 '66

F-104G dispute spurs crisis in Germany. W. C. Wetmore. Aviation W 85:23 Ag 29 '66

Sense of insecurity in West Germany: why French troops are wanted. P. Ben. New Repub 154:10 Ap 30 '66

Description and travel

Autumn wine tour in Germany. il Sunset 137: 25 O '66

Economic conditions

Busting Uncle Boom. Newsweek 68:36+ S 12 '66

Special report. il Bsns W p 123-4+ S 10 '66

Twenty-one years later: a report on today's Germany. il U S News 61:86-8 Ag 29 '66

West German economy. A. Radspieler. Cur Hist 50:295-9 My '66

West Germany minds its booming business. H. Nickel. il N Y Times Mag p54-5+ Mr 27 '66

Woe in the *wirtschaftswunder* il Time 89: 92+ Ja 6 '67

See also
Munich—Economic conditions

Economic policy

Germany: time for a dose of the new economics. il Bsns W p 123-4 N 5 '66

Germany's spending spree; government spending on public works, subsidies, and social services. il Fortune 74:72+ Ag '66

Little planning. Time 88:64 Jl 29 '66

Economic relations

Two Germanys and two Chinas; background to steel-processing agreement with China. J. E. Smith. il Reporter 34:36-8 My 19 '66

When GIs come marching home; cut in spending could have major impact on companies here. il Bsns W p43-4 O 8 '66

Foreign opinion
American

Letter from Germany; asking American liberals to forget German past. E. J. Hughes. Newsweek 68:25 N 28 '66

Foreign relations

New leaders in Germany; meaning to U.S. alliance. il U S News 61:30-1 D 12 '66

Parting of the ways? B. Van Voorst. il Newsweek 68:40-2+ N 14 '66

Still voices; speakers' exchange to debate East-West problems called off. Time 88: 23 Jl 8 '66

Time for a new look at Germany. Bsns W p 196 N 26 '66

Twenty-one years later: a report on today's Germany. il U S News 61:86-8 Ag 29 '66

What price Germany, now? E. Stillman. il N Y Times Mag p64-7+ D 4 '66

Worried look at West Germany. H. C. Wolfe. Sat R 49:22-3+ Mr 26 '66

Europe

West Germany and Europe. C. G. Anthon. Cur Hist 50:270-6+ My '66

Europe, Eastern

Double switch. il Newsweek 67:50 Ap 4 '66

Drang nach osten; efforts to improve relations. Newsweek 69:42+ Ja 16 '67

German Evangelical church statement on the Eastern territories; excerpts. Cur Hist 50: 303-6 My '66

U.S. welcomes forward-looking German note of March 25; texts of notes between United States and the Federal Republic of Germany; April 2, and March 25, 1966. Dept State Bul 54:654-7 Ap 25 '66

France

Germany; address, May 25, 1966. L. Erhard. Vital Speeches 32:552-4 Jl 1 '66

Permanent watch? French troops in Germany. Time 88:22-3 Jl 29 '66

Resurgence of the spirit; Kiesinger & de Gaulle in Paris. Time 89:26+ Ja 20 '67

Slow-motion diplomacy; Erhard-de Gaulle meeting. il Time 87:31 F 18 '66

Still married; concerning latest of the Paris-Bonn summit conferences. il Newsweek 67: 55 F 21 '66

Great Britain

Bridging the channel; Anglo-German summit conference. Newsweek 67:43-4 Je 6 '66

Germany; address, May 25, 1966. L. Erhard. Vital Speeches 32:552-4 Jl 1 '66

Poland

Church breaks a taboo. F. Lüpsen. Christian Cent 83:188-90 F 9 '66; Reply. W. C. Schmauch. 83:442-5 Ap 6 '66

Russia

New view of Russia. il Time 87:33 Ap 1 '66

United States

Can U.S. troops in Europe be cut soon? outcome of Erhard's U.S. visit. il U S News 61:23 O 10 '66

End of the affair. W. S. Schlamm. Nat R 18:1316-18 D 27 '66

President Johnson and Chancellor Erhard hold talks at Washington; exchange of toasts, December 20, 1965; with joint communique. L. Erhard; L. B. Johnson. Dept State Bul 54:46-51 Ja 10 '66

Sorrows of Erhard. Newsweek 68:40 O 3 '66

United States and Germany reaffirm community of interest; exchange of toasts, September 26; with text of joint communique, September 27, 1966. L. B. Johnson; L. Erhard. Dept State Bul 55:578-80, 583-5 O 17 '66

West Germany and the United States. H. Kohn. Cur Hist 50:277-80+ My '66

Industries

Beating an old cow; concerning K. Blauhorn book and resentment at U.S. takeover of German industry. Newsweek 68:84+ O 3 '66

Germany toasts economic boom with champagne. il Bsns W p34-5 F 19 '66

New Ruhr; Germany's industrial heartland. W. Hangen. il Sat Eve Post 239:30-4+ My 7 '66

Intellectual life

Changing culture in Germany. F. E. Hirsch. Cur Hist 50:289-94+ My '66

Letter from Berlin. H. Lohr; reply with rejoinder. E. Bentley. Nation 202:inside cover F 28 '66

Nationalism

Straws in the wind; rehabilitation of Hitlerism? A. Werth. Nation 202:442 Ap 18 '66

Ugly echoes; NDP expansion. Newsweek 67: 61-2 Ap 18 '66

Worried look at West Germany. H. C. Wolfe. Sat R 49:22-3+ Mr 26 '66

GERMANY (Federal Republic)—Continued

Politics and government

Bonn tries consensus; new coalition in West Germany, NATO its biggest problem. il Bsns W p41 D 3 '66

Brutuses on the Rhine; crisis in West German politics. il Time 88:33 N 4 '66

Caught in the middle; decision which bars Berlin deputies from voting. Newsweek 68:41-2 N 28 '66

Chancellor at the brink. il Newsweek 68:50+ N 7 '66

Criminal state and German responsibility: a dialogue; tr. by W. J. Dannhauser. K. Jaspers; R. Augstein. Commentary 41:33-9 F '66

End of the affair. W. S. Schlamm. Nat R 18:1316-18 D 27 '66

Erhard crisis; what led to it. U S News 61:30 N 14 '66

Erhard's last stand. il Newsweek 68:40 N 14 '66

F-104G dispute spurs crisis in Germany. W. C. Wetmore. Aviation W 85:23 Ag 29 '66

Flashing knives. il Time 88:35 N 11 '66

Germany between two alliances; background to Ministry of defense scandal-and-crisis. G. Bailey. il Reporter 35:27-32 O 6 '66

Germany: government by compromise. il Newsweek 68:50+ D 12 '66

Germany: the arithmetic of politics. il Newsweek 68:60+ N 21 '66

Germany: the quickest coalition. il Newsweek 68:37 D 5 '66

Germany turns the clock ahead; crisis resolved by coalition. Life 61:6 D 9 '66

Grand coalition. Sr Schol 89:14-15 Ja 13 '67

Grand coalition. il Time 88:32 D 2 '66

Grand coalition; Christian democrats and socialists in Bonn. America 115:795-6 D 17 '66

In search of coalition. il Time 88:40 N 18 '66

Ludwig Erhard: another Bismarck? H. A. Schmitt. bibliog f il Cur Hist 50:257-62+ My '66

Ludwig Erhard had a great fall. G. Bailey. Reporter 35:39-40 N 17 '66

Nationalism rises as Germany seeks leadership. il Life 61:42-42A D 2 '66

Nazi past. Newsweek 68:62+ O 24 '66

New leaders in Germany; meaning to U.S. alliance. il U S News 61:30-1 D 12 '66

On the job; new black-and-red coalition government. Time 88:38 D 16 '66

Order of the day; German equivalent of a state-of-the-union message. Newsweek 68:32 D 26 '66

Parting of the ways? B. Van Voorst. il Newsweek 68:40-2+ N 14 '66

Red meets black. il Time 88:40+ N 25 '66

Renewal on the Rhine. il Time 88:34-8 D 9 '66

Romanized Teuton. il Newsweek 68:50+ D 19 '66

Smell of change; mounting criticism of Erhard's failure. Newsweek 68:33-4 Ag 29 '66

Sniping at Erhard. Time 88:40-1 O 14 '66

Sorrows of Erhard. Newsweek 68:40 O 3 '66

Stalking the elusive coalition. il Newsweek 68:41 N 28 '66

Trouble in Germany: it means trouble for U.S. il U S News 61:75-6 N 21 '66

Whither West Germany? C. Mayer. il Nation 203:88-90 Jl 25 '66

See also
Fascism—Germany (Federal Republic)
Political parties—Germany (Federal Republic)

Rearmament

See Germany (Federal Republic)—Army

Reconstruction

West Germany minds its booming business. H. Nickel. il N Y Times Mag p54-5+ Mr 27 '66

Religious institutions and affairs

World around us (cont of) News of the Christian world. Christian Cent 83:188-90 F 9 '66

Social conditions

Journey into the past. H. J. Massaquoi. il Ebony 21:91-4+ F; 102-4+ Mr '66

Social life and customs

Ultimate status symbol; specialty foods. il Time 88:28+ Jl 8 '66

GERMANY (Federal Republic) and Israel. See Israel and Germany

GERMANY, EASTERN. See Germany (Democratic Republic)

GERMANY, WESTERN. See Germany (Federal Republic)

GERMANY and Israel. See Israel and Germany

GERMANY and Poland

Church breaks a taboo. F. Lüpsen. Christian Cent 83:188-90 F 9 '66; Reply. W. C. Schmauch. 83:442-5 Ap 6 '66

GERMANY and the United States

United States and Germany: our mutual responsibilities and our mutual dependence; address, February 18, 1966. G. C. McGhee. Dept State Bul 54:657-63 Ap 25 '66

GERMINATION

Germination of witchweed striga lutea lour.: isolation and properties of a potent stimulant. C. E. Cook and others. bibliog il Science 154:1189-90 D 2 '66

Nature of seed dormancy in phacelia tanacetifolia. S. S. C. Chen and K. V. Thimann. bibliog il Science 153:1537-9 S 23 '66

GERMS. See Microorganisms; Microorganisms, Pathogenic

GERNREICH, Rudi

Rudi of modern dance and fashion. A. Fatt. il por Dance Mag 40:26-8 D '66

GERONIMO (Apache chief)

Geronimo! E. M. Halliday. il pors Am Heritage 17:56-63+ Je '66

GEROW, Richard O. bp

Bishop Gerow retires; somebody else, not me. America 115:242 S 10 '66

GERRISH, B. A.

New Presbyterian confession. Christian Cent 83:582-5 My 4 '66

GERRYMANDER

Survival of the gerrymander. R. J. Sickels. New Repub 155:9 D 3 '66

GERSH, Gabriel

He stands for hope in Sicily. Sat R 49:86 Ap 9 '66

Israel's aid to Africa. Commonweal 85:226-8 N 25 '66

Mafia establishment. Nation 203:360-1 O 10 '66

GERSH, Marvin J. and Blumenfeld, Serge

Bedwetting; a common problem. Parents Mag 41:44-5+ Ap '66

GERSHOY, Leo

At home in the hall of mirrors. Sat R 49:34 N 5 '66

Poor Richard in Paris. Sat R 49:34 D 17 '66

GERSHWIN, George

Porgy and Bess. Criticism
Opera N il 30:33 Ap 9 '66

GERSON, Betsy

My first rose garden. Flower Grower 53:40-1+ Mr '66

GERSON, Horst K.

Age of Lowland giants. Art N 65:28-32+ N '66

GERSTENMAIER, Eugen

Sniping at Erhard. por Time 88:40-1 O 14 '66

GERSTER, Georg

Saving the ancient temples at Abu Simbel. il Nat Geog Mag 129:694-742 My '66

GERSTRUNG, Robert J.

Modern star chamber. Nat R 18:323-4 Ap 5 '66

GERTZ, Elmer

Wall-to-wall ego. Christian Cent 83:236 F 23 '66

GERWIN, Katherine Earls

Boy in a tree; poem. Am For 72:46 S '66

GESCHEIDT, Alfred

Why didn't I see that? K. Poli il Pop Phot 59:104-9 O '66

GESNER, Bertram, and Thomas, Lewis

Sialic acid binding sites: role in hemagglutination by mycoplasma gallisepticum. bibliog Science 151:590-1 F 4 '66

GESSFORD, R. K.

Modern shadow-mask color-TV tube. Electr World 76:43-5+ D '66

GESSNER, Peter

Films from the Vietcong. Nation 202:110-11 Ja 24 '66

GESTIDO, Oscar Daniel

Shake-up in Uruguay; ahead: tightening of belts? por U S News 61:16 D 12 '66

GETAWAY; story. See Savage, J.

GETLEIN, Frank

Art. See issues of New republic

Chinese art from the collection of the King of Sweden. Craft Horiz 26:30-5 N '66

Dream of fair cities. Commonweal 85:366-8 Ja 6 '67

$475 bargain. New Repub 154:27-8 Ap 30 '66

Huxley to his friends. New Repub 154:23-4 Mr 26 '66

GETTELL, Richard Glenn

Age of discretion. por Seventeen 25:162+ F '66

GEYER, Alan

Just war and the selective objector. Christian Cent 83:199-201 F 16 '66

GEYER, Georgie Anne

Cuba's press today. Sat R 49:106-7+ N 12 '66

GEZARI, Temina
Earth and the fullness thereof. Sch Arts 65:
4-8 Ja '66
GHANA
See also
Colleges and universities—Ghana
Communism—Ghana

Economic conditions

Back from the brink of communism in
Ghana. A. J. Meyers. il U S News 61:88-
9 Ag 22 '66
Year of the mandarins: air of confidence in
post-Nkrumah Ghana. R. W. Howe. New
Repub 155:13-14 D 10 '66

Foreign relations

Flight 150 to Accra. il Newsweek 68:52 N
14 '66
Hostages held: Ghana vs. Guinea. il Sr Schol
89:25-6 N 18 '66
Jack-boot diplomacy; East Germany holds
Ghanaians. Newsweek 67:52 My 23 '66
Unhappy landing of Flight 150; international
incident over a Pan American put down
at Accra airport. il Time 88:41 N 11 '66
U.S. informs OAU of position of Ghana-
Guinea dispute; text of note. Dept State
Bul 55:790-1 N 21 '66

Politics and government

African revolt that pleased the U.S. il U S
News 60:8 Mr 7 '66
Africa's officers take command. W. A. Lewis.
Reporter 34:33-6 Mr 24 '66
And now Nkrumah: generals & the future
of Africa. J. K. Sale. il Nation 202:317-
22 Mr 21 '66
Atlantic report. Atlan 217:12+ My '66
Back from the brink of communism in
Ghana. A. J. Meyers. il U S News 61:
88-9 Ag 22 '66
Cocoa curtain comes down. il Sr Schol 88:
16 Mr 11 '66
Exit Nkrumah, an old dreamer; enter Ankrah,
a new realist. L. Garrison. il N Y Times
Mag p32-3+ Ap 3 '66
Fall of Nkrumah. P. Crane. America 114:383
Mr 19 '66
Fount of honor; Commissions of inquiry into
misdeeds of Nkrumah and administration.
il Newsweek 68:44+ Jl 11 '66
Ghana gets a second chance. C. Sterling. il
Reporter 34:23-7 Ap 21 '66
Ghana without The Redeemer. R. W. Howe.
New Repub 154:9-11 Mr 12 '66; Reply with
rejoinder. A. W. Wolfe. 154:36+ Ap 2 '66
Ghana's burst of joy over a tyrant's fall. il
Life 60:28-31 Mr 11 '66
Goodbye to the aweful; K. Nkrumah over-
throw. il Time 87:34-5 Mr 4 '66
Kwame Nkrumah: fall of a messiah. C. L.
Sanders. il Ebony 21:138-40+ S '66
Longing for home. il Time 87:30 Mr 11 '66
My country is yours. il Newsweek 67:57-8
Mr 14 '66
Myth is broken. il Newsweek 67:43-4 Mr 7 '66
New neutralism. il Sr Schol 88:17-18 Mr 18
'66
Nkrumah-charisma fails. P. E. Sigmund.
Commonweal 84:50-2 Ap 1 '66
Nkrumah's friends are all in trouble. il Life
60:45 Mr 18 '66
Rope that hanged Nkrumah. E. Huxley. Nat
R 18:268-70 Mr 22 '66
Year of the mandarins: air of confidence in
post-Nkrumah Ghana. R. W. Howe. New
Repub 155:13-14 D 10 '66
See also
Communism—Ghana

Anecdotes, facetiae, satire, etc.

Fangs a lot. Time 87:40 Ap 8 '66

Religious institutions and affairs

See also
Christians in Ghana
GHANI, Abdel Hamid Abdel-. See Abdel-
Ghani. A. H.
GHIAUROV, Nicolai
Met worth waiting for. G. Movshon. il por
Hi Fi 16:126-7 F '66
Recordings. M. Mayer. Esquire 65:38 F '66
GHOST plays
Shades of Shakespeare. E. J. Dias. Plays
25:1-12 Ap '66
GHOST towns. See Abandoned towns
GHOSTS
Haunted: home of Elke Sommer. Beverly
Hills. Calif. J. Hyams. il Sat Eve Post
239:28-31 Jl 2 '66; Same abr. with title Our
haunted house. Read Digest 89:74-8 N '66
More phantoms of the opera. P. Saltzman. il
Opera N 31:6-7 D 31 '66

GIACOMETTI, Alberto
Art: Giacometti: 1901-1966. J. Berger. Nation
202:341-2 Mr 21 '66
Giacometti; career and quest of a great
sculptor; with report by M. Matter. il pors
Life 60:53-7+ Ja 28 '66
Obituary
Art N 65:35 Mr '66.   T. B. Hess
GIAMBRUNI, Helen
Abstract expressionist ceramics. Craft Horiz
26:16-25+ N '66
Craftsmen USA '66; South Central region.
Craft Horiz 26:35-6+ Mr '66
National invitational glass exhibition. Craft
Horiz 26:36-41 Ja '66
GIANCANA, Momo Salvatore
Panic in Chicago's Mafia. B. Davidson and
S. Smith. il por Sat Eve Post 239:102-5 My
21 '66
GIANNINI, Vittorio
Obituary
Opera N por 31:33 D 24 '66
Taming of the shrew. Criticism
Opera N il 30:30 Mr 5 '66
GIANT sex riot; story. See Amft. M. J.
GIANTS (baseball) See Baseball clubs
GIAP, Vo-nguyen-. See Vo-nguyen-Giap
GIBB, Walter M.
Safari. Atlan 218:140-1 N '66
GIBBERELLA fujikuroi. See Fungi
GIBBERELLIC acid
Gibberellic acid: effects of feeding in an arti-
ficial diet for honeybees. J. L. Nation and
F. A. Robinson. bibliog Science 152:1765-6
Je 24 '66
Gibberellic acid makes the difference in
camellias. J. H. Pyron. il Horticulture
44:20-1+ S '66
Gibrel: effect on decomposition of plant ma-
terials. P. Chandra and W. B. Bollen. bib-
liog il Science 153:1663-4 S 30 '66
Phloem differentiation: induced stimulation
by gibberellic acid. A. E. DeMaggio. bibliog
il Science 152:370-2 Ap 15 '66
GIBBERELLINS
Gibberellin-like substances in the developing
apricot fruit. D. I. Jackson and B. G.
Coombe. bibliog il Science 154:277-8 O 14 '66
Gibberellin production: genetic control in the
fungus gibberella fujikuroi. C. Spector and
B. O. Phinney. bibliog il Science 153:1397-8
S 16 '66
GIBBON, John
Grisly epilogue. M. Sandoz. Am Heritage 17:
73 Ap '66
GIBBONS, Euell
He finds food in the oddest places; with ex-
cerpts from Stalking the healthful herbs. il
pors Life 61:45-6 S 23 '66
GIBBONS, Sam M.
Excerpt from remarks. October 21, 1965. Cong
Digest 45:90+ Mr '66
GIBBONS, William J.
New books. Cath World 202:309-10 F '66
GIBBONS
Dog days for a motherless monkey; gibbon
courts Great Dane. il Look 30:M20+ N 29
'66
Falciparum malaria: transmission to the gib-
bon by anopheles balabacensis. D. J. Gould
and others. bibliog Science 153:1384 S 16 '66
GIBBS, Barbara
Distance: Sand-pit; poems. Poetry 109:158-
60 D '66
What you see is me; poem. New Yorker 42:
40 Je 18 '66
GIBLIN, Charles H.
Sign of the manger. America 115:826-8 D 24
'66
GIBOR, Aharon
Acetabularia: a useful giant cell; with bio-
graphical sketch. Sci Am 215:30, 118-24
bibliog(p 160) N '66
GIBRALTAR
Captain's paradise. A. Waugh. Nat R 18:272+
Mr 22 '66
Gibraltar revisited. J. White. il Sat R 49:
44-6 Jl 30 '66
Gibraltar, rock of contention. H. La Fay.
il Nat Geog Mag 130:102-21 Jl '66
Last outpost; Britain's stand. Newsweek 68:
55 N 7 '66
Of mountains, molehills and the Rock. J.
Fletcher. Nat R 18:1167+ N 15 '66
Rock that does not roll to Franco's beat.
R. W. Howe. New Repub 156:16-17 Ja 21
'67
Will Spain win out in fight for Rock? il
Bsns W p36-7 Mr 5 '66
Willing subjects. Time 88:42+ N 4 '66
World's most spectacular Rock. N. Mostert.
il Read Digest 88:39-40+ Ap '66
Writing on the Rock; Anglo-Spanish con-
ference. N. Mostert. Reporter 34:28-31 Je
30 '66

GIBSON, Elsie
 Free churches are changing. por Cath World
  204:225-9 Ja '67
 Word as sacrament. Christian Cent 83:1172-5
  S 28 '66
GIBSON, Gwen
 One woman can make the difference: a blue-
  print for day care action. Ladies Home J
  83:62+ S '66
GIBSON, Jack
 Credit au go-go: look what's happened to
  bankers. T. G. Harris. il pors Look 30:26-
  9 Ap 5 '66
GIBSON, John E.
 What you don't know about pain can hurt
  you. Todays Health 44:36-7 My '66
GIBSON, John Egan
 Case against the supersonic transport. Harper
  233:76-80+ Jl; 4+ S '66
GIBSON, John S.
 Spotlight on the social studies. por Sr Schol
  88:sup 11+ Ap 22 '66
GIBSON, Raymond E.
 Games clergy play. Christian Cent 83:1443-5
  N 23 '66
GIBSON, Rochelle
 Wonderland of Christmas books. Sat R 49:
  31-2+ D 3 '66
GIBSON, Walter Brown
 Man who cast the shadow. il por Newsweek
  69:10 Ja 16 '67
GIBSON, William M.
 First humanities grant: MLA receives
  $300,000. Pub W 190:39-40 Ag 8 '66
GIBSON refrigerator sales corporation
 Goodbye Hong Kong, hello Acapulco; Gib-
  son's free travel as sales incentive. il Time
  88:106 S 30 '66
GIDDINGS, J. Calvin, and others
 Turbulent-gas chromatography. bibliog Sci-
  ence 154:146-8 O 7 '66
GIDDINGS, J. L.
 Cross-dating the archeology of northwestern
  Alaska. bibliog Science 153:127-35 Jl 8 '66
GIDDINGS and Lewis machine tool company
 Machine tool maker with taste for expansion.
  il Bsns W p 156+ D 3 '66
GIDE, André Paul Guillaume
 Polyphony in letters. V. Lange. New Repub
  154:33-5 My 14 '66
 Rose petals among the postscripts. L. Le-
  Sage. por Sat R 49:34-5 Ap 2 '66
GIDLEY, Mick
 From passion-love: a cycle of poems. Poetry
  109:161-2 D '66
GIELGUD, Sir John
 In a strange land. por Opera N 30:8-9 F 12 '66
 Ivanov; adaptation. See Chekhov, A. P.

            about
 Night Elizabeth Taylor said so what? and
  Richard Burton kicked the television set in.
  W. Redfield. il por Esquire 67:108-9+ Ja
  '67
GIESE, Donald John
 Your pet's second best friend. Read Digest
  89:177-80 Ag '66
GIESE, R. F. Jr
 Crystal structure of kernite, $Na_2B_4O_6(OH)_2$·
  $3H_2O$. bibliog Science 154:1453-4 D 16 '66
GIFT, Frank
 Rectifier diodes. por Electr World 76:37-40
  Jl '66
GIFT; story. See Rich, B.
GIFT boxes. See Christmas boxes
GIFT every morning; story. See Wilner, H.
GIFT from Johnny Appleseed; drama. See
  Whittaker, H.
GIFT of dolphins; story. See Holland, B.
GIFT wrappings. See Wrapping of packages
GIFTED children. See Children, Gifted
GIFTED college students. See College students,
  Mentally superior
GIFTS
 Cool it, dad; Father's day gifts. il Esquire
  65:99 Je '66
 Go forth, my son; graduation gifts. il Esquire
  65:98 Je '66
   See also
 Books as gifts
 Christmas gifts
 Colleges and universities—Gifts, legacies, etc.
 Giving
 Hospitals—Gifts, legacies, etc.
 Libraries—Gifts, legacies, etc.
 Wedding gifts
            Taxation
 Appraisals and revenooers: gifts of books,
  letters or manuscripts to institutions or
  organizations; excerpts from address. R.
  G. Newman. il Am Heritage 17:82-4 Je '66

 For your family's future: how to save taxes
  on an estate. il U S News 61:48-52 Ag 8 '66
 Gift taxes, who pays & why. il Changing T
  20:11-12 S '66
 How to use gifts to save taxes. B. Brantley.
  Suc Farm 64:49+ S '66
 Making sense of transfer taxes. il Bsns W
  p98+ Jl 9 '66
 Personal business; gift-planning. Bsns W
  p 167 S 24 '66
GIFTS for children
   See also
 Christmas gifts for children
GIFTS for teachers
 Acceptance of gifts. NEA J 55:27 My '66
GIFTS in business
 Feeding the food editor; gifts from the na-
  tion's leading food manufacturers. N. S.
  Hazelton. Nat R 18:1164 N 15 '66
GIGLI, Beniamino
 Gigli across thirty years. P. L. Miller. por Am
  Rec G 32:688-9 Ap '66
GIGLI, Ormond
 What makes Gigli click? W. Rodarmor. il Pop
  Phot 59:96-7+ O '66
GIL, Federico G.
 Chile: revolution in liberty. Cur Hist 51:291-5
  N '66
 Latin America: economic integration for
  progress. Nation 203:280-3 S 26 '66
GILBERT, Al
 Tap for young children (title varies) por
  Dance Mag 40:72-5 My; 84-5 Je; 70-2 Jl;
  68-9 Ag; 84 S; 96 O; 77 N; 70-1 D '66 (to be
  cont)
GILBERT, Albert Earl
 Hawks of eastern North America; paintings.
  with biographical sketch. por Audubon Mag
  68:335-40 S '66
GILBERT, Arthur
 Gospels and anti-Semitism; excerpt from A
  Jew in Christian America. Cath World 203:
  157-60 Je '66
GILBERT, Bentley B.
 Winston Churchill versus the Webbs: the
  origins of British unemployment insurance.
  bibliog f Am Hist R 71:846-62 Ap '66
GILBERT, Bil
 Beavers dam and be dammed. Sports Illus
  24:70-2+ Je 27 '66
 No fly-by-night operation. Sports Illus 24:
  36-8+ Je 20 '66
 Pet news; excerpt from Bears in the ladies
  room. Ladies Home J 83:12 S '66
 Troubled time for a wounded hero. Sat Eve
  Post 239:76-80 S 10 '66
 Visit from a proud stranger. Sports Illus 26:
  24-8 Ja 16 '67
GILBERT, E. N.
 Information theory after eighteen years. bib-
  liog Science 152:320-6 Ap 15 '66
GILBERT, George
 Camera repairs. U S Camera 29:60-1+ Mr '66
 Movies without a projector. U S Camera
  29:70-1+ Mr '66
 One projector for two film sizes. U S Camera
  29:66-7 N '66
 Stampede of super 8. U S Camera 29:50-3 Je
  '66
GILBERT, Helen
 Swans into Larks. por Library J 91:2780-2
  Je 1 '66
GILBERT, James
 Flying photographer. il Flying 78:82-3 Ap '66
GILBERT, John J.
 Rotifer ecology and embryological induction.
  bibliog Science 151:1234-7 Mr 11 '66
GILBERT and Sullivan operas
   See also
 Phonograph records—Operas
GILBRETH, Frank B.
 Please don't steal my reporters. Sat R 49:119-
  20+ O 8 '66
GIL DE CASTRO, José
 News of art: Latin American painter-patriot.
  il Horizon 8:90-1 Aut '66
GILFILLAN, Merrill C.
 (ed) See Allison, D. Luck of Irish ridge
GILKEY, Langdon
 Parable from prison. por Time 88:78+ S 2
  '66
GILKEY, Linda
 Victory number three; story. Seventeen 26:
  90-1 Ja '67
GILL, Brendan
 Books. New Yorker 42:114+ S 3 '66
 Current cinema. See issues of New Yorker
 People of property. New Yorker 42:37-41 Je
  11 '66
GILL, Eric
 Life of Eric Gill, by R. Speaight. Review
  Cath World 204:189-90 D '66. D. F. For-
  rester

GILLELAN, G. Howard
Archery. See issues of Outdoor life
No hunting and fishing. pors Outdoor Life 137:29-31+ Mr '66
Report from the field. por Outdoor Life 138: 24+ N '66
Too many bucks. Outdoor Life 138:60-1+ S '66
GILLEN, Vincent
Keen private eye. B. Surface. il por N Y Times Mag p 121-2+ D 11 '66
GILLESPIE, John Freund
It's a miracle that we save any of them. W. R. Young. il por Life 61:102-4+ D 2 '66
GILLESSEN, Walter
Music to my ears. I. Kolodin. Sat R 49:34 F 5 '66
GILLHAM, C. E.
Alaska's greatest hunter. Field & S 71:28-30+ Ag '66
Bad luck *oogruk*. Field & S 70:46-8+ Mr '66
I give you the bird. Field & S 70:56-7+ Ap '66
Pete. Field & S 71:50-2+ S '66
GILLIAM, Harold
Tree of light; excerpt from Natural world of San Francisco. Natur Hist 75:54-9 D '66
GILLIAM, Lila Williamson
Heirloom southern recipes go modern. Farm J 90:102 Ap '66
Lacy-edged batter cakes, a southern favorite. Farm J 90:81 O '66
GILLIAM, Rebecca S.
Enjoy bud watching. Flower Grower 53:25-7 Mr '66
GILLIATT, Penelope
Decade that destroyed a stuffed flunkey. Life 60:98+ My 20 '66
Elephants et cetera. Vogue 147:62-3 F 1 '66
Genius of Chaplin. Vogue 148:94-7+ Jl '66
Living on the box; story. New Yorker 42:48-52 D 17 '66
Nabokov. Vogue 148:224-9+ D '66
GILLIGAN, John Joyce
Great-grandson race. il por Time 88:32-3 O 21 '66
GILLIGAN, Thomas R.
Another clash between fundamental principles. H. F. Pilpel. Pub W 189:64-5 F 28 '66
GILLILAND, Trudy
Cover; E. Hicks art. Sat R 49:20 S 3 '66
GILMAN, Richard
Edmund Wilson, then and now. New Repub 155:23-8 Jl 2 '66
Sorrows of Lincoln Center. Holiday 39:117-20 Je '66
Theatre: kinky, arrogant and frankly magnificent. Esquire 66:62-3+ Jl '66
about
Nize baby, et op all your Robbe-Grillet! letter to the editor. H. A. Perluck. New Repub 155:35-7 Ag 13 '66
GILMAN, William
Tampering with our genetic blueprint. New Repub 155:12-13 N 12 '66
GILMORE, Bob
Double gates that stay fit. Pop Sci 189:154-5 S '66
GILMORE, C. P.
All the news about home air conditioners. Pop Sci 188:88-92+ My '66
Are your tires safe enough? Pop Sci 188:108-12+ Mr '66
Birth and life of the universe. N Y Times Mag p26-7+ Je 12 '66
Blackout: can it happen in your town? Pop Sci 188:92-5+ F '66
Malaria wins round two. N Y Times Mag p44-5+ S 25 '66
PS buyer's guide to personal tape recorders. Pop Sci 189:124-9+ N '66
Those incredible holograms; amazing frozen light waves give first true 3D pictures. Pop Sci 189:78-82+ Jl '66
Twenty-three ways to improve your home lighting. Pop Sci 189:172-7 S '66
(ed) See Walton, R. R. Expert's blueprint for successful inventing
GILMORE, John S. and Coddington, D. C.
Diversification guides for defense firms: excerpts from article. bibliog f Harvard Bsns R 44:144-50+ My '66
GILMORE, Ken
Careers in electronics. Pop Electr 25:47-51+ O '66
Project choose (cont) Pop Electr 24:41-9 F '66
GILMORE, Kenneth O.
Laredo learns about the war on poverty. Read Digest 90:44-9 Ja '67
Let's stop exploiting people over sixty-five! Read Digest 89:229-30+ S '66

Truth about Santo Domingo. Read Digest 88:93-8 My '66
GILMORE, Thomas
Second reconstruction. il por Newsweek 67:28-9 Mr 21 '66
GILMORE, Voit
Yaks and yeti. Sat R 49:38+ Ap 23; 51-2 Ap 30 '66
GILMOUR, Craddock M.
What it costs to break rules in Russia. il por U S News 62:12 Ja 2 '67
GILPATRIC, Roswell L.
Are we on the brink of another arms race? N Y Times Mag p32-3+ Ja 15 '67
GILROY, Frank Daniel
Subject was faith. J. P. Blank. il Read Digest 88:144-7 Je '66
GILSDORF, Richard W.
Reassembling the face of Christ. America 115:131-5 Ag 6 '66
GILSON, Estelle
Is nursery school necessary? por Sat R 49:94 N 19 '66
GIMBEL, Bernard Feustman
Ruler of Greeley square. por Time 88:104-6 O 7 '66
GIMBEL, Peter R.
Shark! Sports Illus 25:68-76 Ag 29 '66
GIMENEZ, Joaquin Ruiz-. See Ruiz-Gimenez, J.
GIMPEL, René
Diary of a Paris art dealer; excerpts from Diary of an art dealer. Vogue 148:275+ O 1 '66
GINASTERA, Alberto
Composer from the pampas. E. Helm. il pors Hi Fi 16:54-6+ Mr '66
Don Rodrigo. Criticism
Life 60:23 Mr 18 '66
New Repub 154:35-7 Mr 19 '66
New Yorker 42:154-6 Mr 5 '66
Sat R 49:44+ Mr 12 '66
Time il 87:75 Mr 4 '66
South American way. R. Evett. New Repub 154:35-7 Mr 19 '66
GINGER (spice)
Cooking with ginger root. il Sunset 136:186+ Mr '66
GINGERICH, Owen
Great comet of 1965. Atlan 217:57-62 My '66
GINGRICH, Arnold
Publisher's page. See issues of Esquire
Scott, Ernest and whoever. Esquire 66:186-9+ D '66
Servants I have worked for. Esquire 66:74-5+ Ag '66
Simple confession. Esquire 65:82-3+ Mr '66
Truth as personal property. Sat R 50:22-3 Ja 21 '67
What makes the wheels go round; excerpt from Toys of a lifetime. Atlan 217:80-6 My '66
GINIGER, K. S. company
Rights and permissions. P. Nathan. Pub W 189:133 F 14 '66
GINKGO
Nature note; maidenhair tree. Sci N L 89:78 Ja 29 '66
GINOTT, Haim G.
How children react to praise and criticism. Parents Mag 41:46-7+ Ap '66
GINSBERG, Allen
Great marijuana hoax; excerpt from Marihuana papers. bibliog f Atlan 218:104+ N '66
New Ginsberg poem from Kansas; concluding passage from Wichita vortex sutra. Life 60:80 My 27 '66
Through native eyes. Library J 91:3076 Je 15 '66
about
Guru comes to Kansas. B. Farrell. il pors Life 60:78-80+ My 27 '66
Performing arts; Kaddish on record R. Kotlowitz. Harper 233:134-5 O '66
GINSBURG, Mirra
(tr) See Babel. I. Sunset
(tr) See Zamiatin, E. I. Lion
GINTER, Donald E.
Financing of the Whig party organization, 1783-1793. bibliog f Am Hist R 71:421-40 Ja '66
GINZBERG, Eli
Segregation could kill the city. Sat R 49:38-9 F 12 '66
—and Yohalem, E. M.
Longer view of the educated woman; excerpt from Educated American women: self-portraits. Sch & Soc 94:391-2+ N 12 '66
GINZBERG, Louis
Keeper of the law, by E. Ginzberg. Review
Commentary 42:91-4 S '66. M. Hadas

GINZBURG, Ralph
Arbitration hearings called for promiscuity handbook. Pub W 189:59 My 30 '66
Author-editor group hits Ginzburg conviction. Pub W 189:29-30 Ap 11 '66
Bad news for smut peddlers. il Time 87:56+ Ap 1 '66
Court declines to review two censorship convictions. Pub W 189:49 My 9 '66
Court grants stay of Ginzburg imprisonment. Pub W 190:48 Jl 18 '66
Demeaning the Court. Nation 202:379 Ap 4 '66
Dissent to the High court's harsh verdict. L. Wainwright. Life 60:26 Ap 22 '66
Ginzburg & pornography. Nat R 18:346 Ap 19 '66
Ginzburg appeal argued; awaits ruling by Court. Pub W 190:108 S 26 '66
Ginzburg appeal protests Supreme court trap. Pub W 189:82 Ap 25 '66
Ginzburg contests bootleg promiscuity handbook. Pub W 189:53 Mr 7 '66
Ginzburg petitions for rehearing; urges federal censorship board. Library J 91:2440+ My 15 '66
Implications of the Ginzburg affair; address, April 20, 1966. K. Molz. il por Wilson Lib Bul 40:941-7 Je '66
Is love, sweet love, a crime? J. Skow. il por Sat Eve Post 239:82-4+ F 12 '66
Notes and comment. New Yorker 42:31 Ap 9 '66
Obscenity business. J. Epstein. Atlan 218: 56-60 Ag '66; Same. Library J 91:4566-71 O 1 '66
Obscenity test; legal poser. il Newsweek 67: 19+ Ap 4 '66
Pornography problem. por Sat Eve Post 239: 98 My 7 '66

La GIOCONDA; opera. See Ponchielli, A.
GIORDANO, Umberto
Andrea Chénier. Criticism
Opera N 30:22-3 F 5 '66
Opera N il 30:18-20 F 5 '66
On records; Andrea Chénier. Opera N 30:34 F 5 '66

GIOTTO di Bondone
Sleuthing behind the wall. il Time 88:78 S 9 '66

GIOVANNI da Fiesole. See Angelico, Fra
GIPE, George A.
Rebel in a wing collar. Am Heritage 18: 24-9+ D '66

GIPSIES in Spain
Gypsy, gypsy, where are you? Estremadura gypsies; with photographs by I. Penn. N. Tucci. Vogue 148:114-27+ Ag 15 '66

GIRAFFES
Blood pressure responses of wild giraffes studied by radio telemetry. R. L. Van Citters and others. bibliog il Science 152:384-6 Ap 15 '66

GIRANDOLA, Anthony
When a priest marries. il por Newsweek 67: 83 Ap 25 '66

GIRARD, Alexander
Artless art. il pors Horizon 8:72-7 Spr '66

GIRDERS
Beams make news in suspended ceilings. il Pop Sci 188:165 Ap '66

GIRDLES. See Foundation garments
GIRL and the gold mine; drama. See Huff, B. T.
GIRL as pretty as the Taj; story. See Adarkar, V.
GIRL athletes. See Women as athletes
GIRL in the green hat; story. See Sire, G. and Sire, J.
GIRL on a dark road; story. See Pratt, J.
GIRL who knew everything; story. See Gaffron, C.

GIRLS
Are girls getting too aggressive? forum discussion; with study-discussion program, by C. Smallenburg and H. Smallenburg. bibliog il PTA Mag 61:4-7, 36 S '66
Everybody has a Beatle. E. Wikler. il Read Digest 89:72-5 O '66
Five freshmen at Harvard; symposium. il Seventeen 25:154-5+ My '66
How can I be me? G. Zimmermann. il Look 30:52-7 S 20 '66
Junior journal; a monthly report from, by, and for the younger journal set (title varies) M. Kadison. il Ladies Home J 83: 52 Je; 18 Jl; 20 Ag; 34 O '66; 84:4 Ja '67
News and views; excerpts from Cosmopolitan magazine article. What it's like to be a Catholic girl. J. Walsh. Commonweal 83: 682 Mr 18 '66
This girl is a winner! J. Wescott. il Seventeen 25:20 My '66

Through the green lenses; from a lifeguard's point of view. J. Carlisle. il Seventeen 25: 106-7+ Je '66
What it means to be a girl now! D. A. Sugarman and R. Hochstein. Seventeen 25:172-3+ My '66
Young living; questions and answers. A. Wood. See issues of Seventeen
See also
Adolescence
Camp fire girls
Physical education and training of women
Runaway boys and girls
Youth

Photographs
Len Steckler's girls. Pop Phot 58:84-7+ My '66

GIRLS, Tall. See Stature
GIRLS clubs
See also
Camp fire girls

GIRLS schools. See Private schools
GIRSON, Rochelle
Books for autumn reading. Sat R 49:56-8+ O 1 '66
Books to read while the grass grows green. Sat R 49:33-5+ Ap 16 '66
Vale of Kashmir won't be undersold. Atlan 217:122-4 F '66

GISCARD D'ESTAING, Valéry
Two faces of JFK. il por Newsweek 68:63-4 N 21 '66

GITLIN, Todd
Join; coal-operatin' in uptown. Christian Cent 83:754+ Je 8 '66

GIUFFRE, Jimmy
New places to go. por Newsweek 68:78+ Ag 8 '66

GIULIO Cesare; opera. See Händel, G. F.
GIVEN names. See Names, Personal
GIVENCHY, Hubert de
Vogue's ready beauty. por Vogue 147:153 Mr 15 '66

GIVING
Art of giving; Time essay. Time 88:34 D 16 '66
Reduction of human misery; address, January 15, 1966. H. Ford. 2d. Vital Speeches 32:278-80 F 15 '66
See also
Charities
Christmas gifts
Church finance

Quotations, maxims, etc.
Gift of giving; comp. by E. F. Murphy. N Y Times Mag p74+ D 11 '66

GJELSNESS, Rudolph H.
Library education and the talent shortage. por Library J 91:1769-70 Ap 1 '66

GJESDAL, Tor
What's happening to the E in UNESCO? Sr Schol 89:sup 14-15 D 2 '66

GLACIAL epochs
Absolute dating and the astronomical theory of glaciation. W. S. Broecker. il Science 151:299-304 Ja 21 '66
Earth getting colder as ice age nears. Sci N 90:449 N 26 '66
Ice cap age disputed. Sci N 90:348 O 29 '66
Theory of ice ages III. W. L. Donn and M. Ewing. bibliog il Science 152:1706-12 Je 24 '66

GLACIAL geology
Baffin Island refugia older than 54,000 years. O. H. Löken. bibliog il Science 153: 1378-80 S 16 '66
Glaciated Appalachian plateau; till shadows on hills. D. R. Coates. bibliog il Science 152:1617-19 Je 17 '66
Ice cap age disputed. Sci N 90:348 O 29 '66
Movement directions in late Paleozoic glacial rocks of the Horlick and Pensacola Mountains, Antarctica. L. A. Frakes and others. bibliog il Science 153:746-9 Ag 12 '66
Pleistocene glaciation on St George, Pribilof Islands. D. M. Hopkins and T. Einarsson. bibliog il Science 152:343-5 Ap 15 '66
Radiocarbon chronology of late pleistocene deposits in northwest Washington. D. J. Easterbrook. bibliog il Science 152:764-7 My 6 '66
Sediment transport in a Precambrian ice age; the Huronian Gowganda formation. D. A. Lindsey. bibliog il Science 154:1442-3 D 16 '66
See also
Drumlins
Geology, Stratigraphic—Pleistocene

GLACIAL lakes. See Lakes

GLACIER NATIONAL PARK
Hike to lost lake. E. J. Ronshausen. Nat Parks Mag 40:9 Jl '66

GLACIERS
Galloping glacier; Steele glacier. il Time 88:33 Ag 19 '66
Glaciers are retreating Russian survey finds; observations of ancient ice sheet on the Arctic islands. Sci N 90:88 Ag 6 '66
Turboprop to a glacier; flying to ski in the French Alps. F. R. Smith. il Sports Illus 24:36-43 F 7 '66
See also
Glacial epochs

GLACKENS, William James
Reporter of innocence. il Time 88:72-3+ D 2 '66

GLADIOLUS
Gladiolus, one plant you can't miss with. il Flower Grower 53:48+ Ap '66
How to grow glads. il Bet Hom & Gard 44:140 Je '66

GLADSTONE, Daniel
High school students have no voice. por Sat R 49:62 My 21 '66

GLAMOR. See Beauty, Personal

GLANDS
Circadian rhythm in pineal tyrosine hydroxylase. E. G. McGeer and P. L. McGeer. bibliog il Science 153:73-4 Jl 1 '66
Lactoperoxidase: identification and isolation from harderian and lacrimal glands. M. Morrison and P. Z. Allen. bibliog il Science 152:1626-8 Je 17 '66
Mystery gland; pineal gland. S. F. Yolles. il Todays Health 44:76-9 Mr '66
Viral neoplastic transformation of hamster pineal cells in vitro: retention of enzymatic function. S. A. Wells, jr. and others. bibliog il Science 154:278-9 O 14 '66
See also
Pituitary body
Thymus gland

Diseases
See also
Cystic fibrosis

GLANDS, Ductless
See also
Thymus gland

GLANDS, Lacrimal. See Lacrimal organs

GLANVILLE, Brian
Julie Christie: a face made for film. Holiday 40:95-6+ S '66

GLANVILLE-HICKS, Peggy
Music: how its built. Vogue 147:200-1+ Mr 1 '66

GLASER, Bruce
Questions to Stella and Judd; interview, ed. by L. R. Lippard. Art N 65:55-61 S '66

GLASER, Joe
Manager Joe Glaser on Louis. por Life 60:114 Ap 15 '66

GLASER, Milton
Milton Glaser of Push pin studios. D. Waugh. il Am Artist 30:56-61+ Je '66

GLASER, Vera
(ed) See Knight, F. G. Inside look at a struggle over policy

GLASIER, Fred Whitman
Big top's Mathew Brady. M. R. Weiss. il Sat R 49:146-7 Mr 12 '66

GLASKY, Alvin J. and Simon, L. N.
Magnesium pemoline: enhancement of brain RNA polymerases. bibliog Science 151:702-3 F 11 '66

GLASS, Andrew J.
Compulsive candidate. por Sat Eve Post 239:36-8+ Ap 23 '66

GLASS, Bentley
Japanese science education centers. Science 154:221-8 O 14 '66

GLASS, Bill
Shop talk; personal appearances at bookshops. il por Pub W 189:93 Ja 31 '66

GLASS, Herbert
Mozart by Rudolf, et al. Am Rec G 33:47-8 S '66
Die Walküre. Am Rec G 33:196-9 N '66

GLASS
Chemicals toughen glass. il Sci N 90:45 Jl 16 '66
Electron paramagnetic resonance of methyl radicals on porous glass surface. M. Fujimoto and others. bibliog il Science 154:381-2 O 21 '66
Glazing recommendations for tinted glass. il Arch Rec 140:151-4 D '66
How materials react to solar energy. J. I. Yellott. il Arch Rec 139:197-8 Je '66
New look at glass. R. Yoshioka. il Sci N 90:324-6 O 22 '66
Nickel-iron spherules from Aouelloul glass. E. C. T. Chao and others. Science 154:759-60+ N 11 '66

Quiz: glass that almost isn't. J. Daugherty and M. Daugherty. il Sci Digest 59:85-7 Mr '66

GLASS, Decorated. See Glass, Ornamental

GLASS, Ornamental
Art glass for everyone; exhibits. R. Grover and L. Grover. Hobbies 71:76-7 Ag '66
National invitational glass exhibition; San Jose, Calif. H. Giambruni. il Craft Horiz 26:36-41 Ja '66
Wavecrest, Kelva and Nakara elegancies. Mrs O. V. Duncan. il Hobbies 71:37 My '66

GLASS, Safety
New glass is harder to break, safer when it does. il Pop Sci 189:170-1 O '66

GLASS, Structural
Mirror, mirror, on the wall; reflecting glass costly, beautiful, saves on air conditioning. il Bsns W p 150-2+ My 7 '66

GLASS blowing and working
Dominick Labino: the color of glass dictates form. R. Florian. il Craft Horiz 26:28-31 Jl '66
National invitational glass exhibition; San Jose, Calif. H. Giambruni. il Craft Horiz 26:36-41 Ja '66

GLASS construction
Glazing recommendations for tinted glass. il Arch Rec 140:151-4 D '66

GLASS cutting
Wall rack for cutting glass. R. Treves. il Pop Sci 188:179 F '66

GLASS fiber cars. See Automobiles—Materials

GLASS fibers
Fresh spin on tires: Armstrong rubber co. using glass fiber for cords. il Bsns W p70 Mr 12 '66
Rash washing of glass-fiber fabrics. Consumer Rep 31:473-4 O '66

GLASS industry
New look at glass. R. Yoshioka. il Sci N 90:324-6 O 22 '66
Pride, wreath and R.B. glass patterns. A. G. Peterson. il Hobbies 71:90-1 Je '66
See also
Owens-Illinois, incorporated

GLASS lighting panels. See Paneling

GLASS manufacture
New England glass company marks. M. F. Rogers, jr. il Antiques 89:724-9 My '66
See also
Owens-Illinois, incorporated

GLASS painting and staining
Art galleries; Hutton galleries: first showing anywhere of Hinterglasmalerei; or, Painting on glass. R. M. Coates. New Yorker 42:62+ D 24 '66
Oriental painting and tinsel pictures. L. B. Carlisle. il Antiques 90:218-19 Ag '66

GLASS pictures. See Glass painting and staining

GLASS plates (photography) See Photography—Plates

GLASSBERG, Bert Y.
Steady dating, in or out? PTA Mag 61:13-15 bibliog(p37) D '66

GLASSWARE
Adams-Emery wing at the Cincinnati art museum. il Antiques 89:406-7 Mr '66
Glassware patents by the Daniel C. Ripleys. A. G. Peterson il Hobbies 71:98B-98C S:84+ O '66
Information wanted and supplied; Handel glass. E. Gaines. il Antiques 89:541+ Ap '66
New Amelung tumbler. K. M. Wilson. il Antiques 90:334-6 S '66
Ornamental glass bird fountains of the eighteenth century. I. Noël Hume. il Antiques 90:208-10 Ag '66
Pride, wreath and R.B. glass patterns. A. G. Peterson. il Hobbies 71:90-1 Je '66
Redbook's guide to early American china, silver and glass. il Redbook 127:66-74 Je '66

Collectors and collecting
Mill, my lady's bower, or a church? T. H. Marsh. Hobbies 70:84-5 F '66
Stars and stripes; pattern glass. C. Marston. il Hobbies 71:36 Jl '66; Correction. 71:96 S '66

Exhibitions
Corning announces new exhibit. il Hobbies 71:72 S '66
Glass from the Josef & Fritzi Mahler collection. il Hobbies 71:98 Ag '66
Making of a glass exhibition. E. P. Birk. il Antiques 90:764+ D '66

GLAUCUS atlanticus. See Mollusks

GLAZE, Eleanor
Longest time; story. Redbook 127:64-5 Je '66

GLAZE, William
William Glaze and the Palmette armory. C. G. Worman. il Hobbies 71:124 Ja '67
GLAZER, Nathan
Grand design of the poverty program. N Y Times Mag p21+ F 27 '66
GLAZER, Sidney
(comp) Articles and other books received; Near East. See issues of American historical review
GLAZER, Suzanne
Who's nonverbal? Library J 91:341-3 Ja 15 '66
GLAZES and glazing
Glazing recommendations for tinted glass. il Arch Rec 140:151-4 D '66
Workshop: the Greek black glaze; excerpts from Techniques of painted attic pottery. J. V. Noble. il Craft Horiz 26:37-9+ Mr '66
GLAZIER, Michael
Ireland, 1966. Cath World 202:354-6 Mr '66
GLEASON, Frank H. and others
D(—)-lactate dehydrogenase in lower fungi. bibliog Science 152:1272-3 My 27 '66
GLEASON, Harold Willard
Pioneer; poem. McCalls 93:116 Jl '66
GLEASON, Jackie
Gleason and Carney: a second honeymoon for The honeymooners. B. Rollin. il pors Look 30:76-80+ N 15 '66
Second honeymoon. il por Time 88:108 O 14 '66
GLEASON, Philip
Academic freedom. America 115:60-3 Jl 16 '66
Thanks to the Irish. America 114:696-8 My 14 '66
GLEASON, Thomas W.
ILA tries its hand at unclogging Saigon. il por Bsns W p53+ F 19 '66
GLEAZER, Edmund J. Jr
Technical education and society; address, May 12, 1966. Vital Speeches 32:540-3 Je 15 '66
about
Junior college and technical education. por Sch & Soc 94:340 O 29 '66
GLEKEL, Newton
Many houses of Newton Glekel. por Fortune 74:194 D '66
GLEN CANYON
Lake Powell. W. Stegner. il Holiday 39:64-9+ My '66
Visit to a drowning canyon. F. L. Griffin, jr. il Audubon Mag 68:27-33 Ja '66
GLEN CANYON DAM
Visit to a drowning canyon. F. L. Griffin, jr. il Audubon Mag 68:27-33 Ja '66
GLENDAY, Alice
Unhappy returns; story. Redbook 126:68-9 Mr '66
GLENMARY sisters. See Sisterhoods
GLENNER, George G. and Bladen, H. A.
Purification and reconstitution of the periodic fibril and unit structure of human amyloid. bibliog Science 154:271-2 O 14 '66
GLENS FALLS, N.Y.

Education
Improving the teaching of world affairs. H. M. Long. Sr Schol 89:sup 16 D 2 '66
GLICK, Sue
How I'm raising my twins; ed. by J. Heimlich. Parents Mag 41:58-9+ D '66
GLICKMAN, William, and Ford, George
Two roads to cleanliness. por Am City 81:110-11 My '66
GLIDERS (aeronautics)
Dornier tests guided integral paraglider. W. C. Wetmore. il Aviation W 84:57-8 F 7 '66
Inflatable re-entry glider may aid many technologies. W. E. Wilks. il Tech W 19:30+ Jl 18 '66
Jet-powered sailplane. il Pop Mech 125:105 Ap '66
Long ride home. H. Peterson. il Sports Illus 25:35-7 Ag 1 '66
NASA nears powered stage of lifting-body flight study. il Aviation W 86:68-9+ Ja 16 '67
New leap forward for space flight; testing of lifting body concept by M2-F2. il Bsns W p92+ My 28 '66
Sailors of the sky. G. Young. il Nat Geog Mag 131:48-73 Ja '67
See also
Gliding and soaring
GLIDING and soaring
Sailors of the shadowed skies; photographs by C. Manos; with account by H. Peterson. Sports Illus 25:28-37 Ag 1 '66
Sky sailing! V. M. Black. il Travel 125:37-40 Ap '66

Soaring. E. M. Miller. il Flying 79:52-61 S '66
Weekend fling. M. Kvaka. il Flying 79:62-4 S '66
GLINN, Burt
Extraordinary feast. il Holiday 39:88-9 My '66
GLINSMANN, Walter H. and others
Plasma chromium after glucose administration. bibliog Science 152:1243-5 My 27 '66
GLIOMAS. See Tumors
GLIXON, David M.
All the facts and where to find them. Sat R 49:34-8+ Mr 19 '66
With reference to. Sat R 49:49-52+ N 19 '66
—See Winterich, J. T. jt. ed.
GLOBAL atmospheric research program. See Weather research
GLOBAL meteorological experiment. See Weather research
GLOBAL satellite communications systems. See Communications satellites—International aspects
GLOBES, Astronomical
Blaeuw's celestial globe and three new stars. K. Hujer. il Sky & Tel 32:278-9 N '66
GLOBINS. See Proteins
GLOBULAR clusters. See Stars—Clusters
GLOMERULONEPHRITIS. See Nephritis
GLOMERULUS
Chromium-51 ethylenediaminetetraacetate for estimation of glomerular filtration rate. B. D. Stacy and G. D. Thorburn. bibliog il Science 152:1076-7 My 20 '66
GLORIA, Sister
Meditation at an altar; poem. America 114:808 Je 4 '66
GLOVER, Kenneth M. and others
Radar observations of insects in free flight. bibliog Science 154:967-72 N 25 '66
GLOVER, Willis B.
Demythologizing the new theology. Christian Cent 83:882-4 Jl 13 '66
GLOVES, Rubber
How to keep your hands out of photography. H. Shaman. il Pop Phot 58:90-1+ Ap '66
GLOXINIAS
For a thr'll glorious gloxinia. il Flower Grower 53:32-3 O '66
Gems among the gloxinias. C. R. Ferguson. il Flower Grower 53:11 O '66
GLUCAGON
Glucagon, starvation, and the induction of liver enzymes by hydrocortisone. O. Greengard and G. T. Baker. bibliog il Science 154:1461-2 D 16 '66
GLUCK, Christoph Willibald
On records; Orfeo ed Euridice. Opera N 30:30 My 7 '66
RCA Victor's Orfeo ed Euridice. P. L. Miller. il Am Rec G 32:792-4 My '66
GLUCK, Louise
Game; poem. Nation 203:229 S 12 '66
Life is a nice place; poem. Mlle 62:158 Ap '66
Monologue at nine A.M; Dead end; Anniversary: poems. Poetry 108:33-4 Ap '66
GLUCONIC acid
D-Gluconic acid: isolation from the defensive secretion of the cockroach eurycotis decipiens. G. P. Dateo and L. M. Roth. bibliog il Science 155:88-9 Ja 6 '67
GLUCOSE
Effect of sugars on transport of alanine in intestine. R. A. Chez and others. bibliog il Science 153:1012-13 Ag 26 '66
Plasma chromium after glucose administration. W. H. Glinsmann and others. bibliog il Science 152:1243-5 My 27 '66
GLUCOSE phosphatase. See Phosphatases
GLUCOSE phosphate dehydrogenase. See Dehydrogenases
GLUCURONIDASE genes. See Genes
GLUE
Which glue is best for wood? J. D. Thompson. il Pop Mech 126:138-40+ Ag '66
See also
Adhesives
GLUE guns. See Spraying apparatus
GLUE sniffing
See also
Narcotic habit
GLUECK, Grace
Furrier to the art world. N Y Times Mag p38-9+ O 2 '66
Rivers paints himself into the canvas. N Y Times Mag p34-5+ F 13 '66
GLUING. See Glue
GLUTTONS (animals) See Wolverines
GLYCERIDES
Seed lipids. I. A. Wolff. bibliog Science 154:1140-9 D 2 '66

GLYCOGEN
Epinephrine: cascade reactions and glyco-genolytic effect. J. M. Bowness. bibliog il Science 152:1370-1 Je 3 '66
Glucose-6-phosphatase in tubular endoplasmic reticulum of hepatocytes. S. I. Rosen and others. bibliog il Science 152:352-4 Ap 15 '66
Glycogen content in the wood-boring isopod, limnoria lignorum. R. Y. George. bibliog il Science 153:1262-4 S 9 '66
Phosphorylase kinase of the liver: deficiency in a girl with increased hepatic glycogen. G. Hug and others. bibliog il Science 153:1534-5 S 23 '66
Puromycin analogs: action of adrenocortico-tropic hormone and the role of glycogen. L. D. Garren and others. bibliog il Science 152:1386-8 Je 3 '66

GLYCOLIC acid
Flavin mononucleotide control of glycolic acid oxidase and photorespiration in corn leaves. B. Tregunna. bibliog il Science 151:1239-41 Mr 11 '66

GLYCOLYTIC enzymes. See Enzymes

GLYN, Caroline
Chick off the literary block. P. Huston. il pors Life 60:59-60 My 13 '66
GLYNDEBOURNE festival. See Music festivals—England

GMEINER, Hermann
Kinderdorf kids and their professional mothers. W. Langewiesche. Read Digest 89:123-6 D '66

GNADIGES fraulein; drama. See Williams, T.

GNOCCHI. See Macaroni

GNOMON. See Astronomical instruments

GO (game)
From the Orient with guile. il Time 87:82 Ap 22 '66

GO-go girls. See Dancers

GOALS, National. See United States

GOARD, Dotty
Resurrection; poem. Christian Cent 83:1077 S 7 '66

GOBBI, Tito
Open window; interview, ed. by J. W. Freeman. por Opera N 31:18 O 15 '66

GOBELIN tapestry
Warp & woof for the ages. il Time 88:80-1 S 30 '66

GOBEN, Ronald
Social studies and English combine in humanities approach. Sr Schol 88:sup8 Ap 22 '66

GOBI DESERT
Gobi's treasure of bones. il Time 88:75 Jl 22 '66

GOBIES
Tree-walking fish. A. J. McClane. Field & S 70:86 F '66

GOBLE, Emerson
Behind the record. See issues of Architectural record

GOD
American bishop's search for a space-age God. C. S. Wren. il Look 30:25-9 F 22 '66
First and last word. V. P. McCorry. America 115:787 D 10 '66
Future of belief, by L. Dewart. Review Newsweek 68:67 N 7 '66. K. L. Woodward
God as non-being; theology of L. Dewart. Time 88:61 D 23 '66
God in creation and evolution, by A. Hulsbosch. Review America 114:264-5 F 19 '66. D. A. Drennen Commonweal 84:83-4 Ap 8 '66. R. T. Francoeur
Healing fountain; excerpt from The eternal promise. T. Kelly. Christian Cent 83:323 Mr 16 '66
Heresy by translation; Service book and hymnal used by National Lutheran council churches. C. R. McCormack. Christian Cent 83:437-8 Ap 6 '66
Hidden God. C. Davis. America 114:173 Ja 29 '66
Life does care; excerpt from The magnificent defeat. F. Buechner. Christian Cent 83:259 Mr 2 '66
On judging God. D. Callahan. Commonweal 83:611-13 F 25 '66; Reply. N. J. Rigali. 84:189+ My 6 '66
Talk about God. W. A. Van Roo. America 114:691-4 My 14 '66
Theological historicism as an experiment in thought. G. D. Kaufman. Christian Cent 83:268-71 Mr 2; Discussion. 83:439-40 Ap 6 '66

See also
Atheism
Christianity
Death of God theology

Jesus Christ
Love (theology)
Metaphysics
Ontology
Religion
Trinity

GOD, Grace of. See Grace (theology)

GOD is dead (theology) See Death of God theology

GODARD, Jean Luc
Movie brutalists. P. Kael. New Repub 155:24+ S 24 '66

GODDARD, James Lee
Clampdown on the drug industry; its meaning; interview. U S News 60:76-8+ My 16 '66
FDA's edict: patients, not profits, come first; excerpts from address, April 6, 1966. Science 152:332-3 Ap 15 '66
Hard-nosed medic, policeman of all pills; interview, ed. by B. Paisner. il pors Life 61:60+ Ag 26 '66
Menace of drug abuse. por Am Ed 2:4-7 My '66

about
Drug makers get a tough, new cop. pors Bsns W p72+ Mr 26 '66
Food and drug administration: test for leadership vaccine. J. Walsh. por Science 151:801-3 F 18 '66
Goddard at FDA: new rules for the game. E. Langer. Science 152:1487-90 Je 10 '66
He is shaking Food and drug well before using. G. A. W. Boehm. il por N Y Times Mag p23+ My 15 '66
Meet Dr Goddard, new FDA chief. T. Lewis. il por Todays Health 44:6-7 Ap '66
New firm hand at the old FDA. New Repub 154:10-11 Mr 26 '66
Prescription for the FDA: a new dose of courage. Consumer Rep 31:411-15 Ag '66
Some stand up. New Repub 154:4 Ap 23 '66
Support for a shake-up. il por Time 87:55 Ap 1 '66
Vitamin crackdown. il Time 88:48+ Jl 1 '66

GODDARD and Goddard company
Lady shows them how it's done. il Bsns W p 134-6+ O 15 '66

GODDARD space flight center. See United States—National aeronautics and space administration—Goddard space flight center

GODDEN, Jon
Content in another country. G. Parthasarathi. Sat R 49:58 Jl 23 '66
Farewell to Eden. por Newsweek 68:94+ Jl 11 '66
Growing up was all the raj. E. Perry. Life 61:10 Ag 5 '66

GODDEN, Rumer
Beatrix Potter. Horn Bk 42:391-8 Ag '66
Handsome young bee, or What did the lotus want? poem. Mlle 64:94-5 D '66
Kitchen madonna; story. Ladies Home J 83:39-46 Ap '66
Prince for all seasons. Ladies Home J 83:100+ Mr '66

about
Content in another country. G. Parthasarathi. Sat R 49:58 Jl 23 '66
Farewell to Eden. por Newsweek 68:94+ Jl 11 '66
Growing up was all the raj. E. Perry. Life 61:10 Ag 5 '66

GODDESS of aisle E; story. See Bayer, A.

GODFREY, Arthur
Arthur Godfrey tells how he flew around the world in eighty-six hours; interview, ed. by D. Francis. pors Pop Sci 189:134-7+ O '66

GODFREY, John Henry
Where are they now? por Newsweek 69:10 Ja 23 '67

GODKIN, Paul
To thine own self be true; interview, ed. by V. H. Swisher. por Dance Mag 40:28-9 Ap '66

GOERING, J. J. and Dugdale, R. C.
Denitrification rates in an island bay in the equatorial Pacific Ocean. bibliog Science 154:505-6 O 28 '66

GOETHE, Charles Matthias
Obituary
Nat Parks Mag 40:21 S '66

GOETHE, Johann Wolfgang von
Goethe on private confession. H. Rueckriegel. America 115:210 Ag 27 '66

GOETZ, Joseph W.
Church and camp. Cath World 203:297-300 Ag '66

GOETZ, Ronald
Uncompromising. Christian Cent 83:1242 O 12 '66
Visionary. Christian Cent 83:142 F 2 '66

GOETZMANN, William F.
(ed) See Upton, B. Our first foreign war
GOFF, Charles W.
Tombs of Machu Picchu; with bibliography. Américas 18:8-18 Ag '66
GOFF, Kristin
Big surprises. Seventeen 26:28+ Ja '67
GOFF, M. L. Roy, and Finger, F. W.
Activity rhythms and adiurnal light-dark control. bibliog Science 154:1346-9 D 9 '66
GOFF, Regina
Promises fulfilled. por Am Ed 2:10-17 F '66
GOGARTEN, Friedrich
Prophet of the future God. por Time 88:63 D 16 '66
GOGOLAK, Charlie
Little Redskin with big medicine. W. J. McKean. il pors Look 30:113-16 N 15 '66
GOHEEN, Robert F.
Teacher in the university; address, January 12, 1966. Sch & Soc 94:177-9 Ap 2 '66
GOHL, William S.
Meet the Mini-organ. Pop Electr 24:70-1 F '66
GOLATZ, Helmut J.
Steelworkers on campus. America 114:652-4 My 7 '66
GOLAY, J. F.
Bourgeois gentleman. New Repub 154:29-31 My 7 '66
GOLBECK, Bernard
Selecting the proper switch. Electr World 76:42-3+ S '66
GOLD, Arthur
Two on the bench. il Newsweek 67:110+ My 23 '66
GOLD, Herbert
Golden Gate. Sat R 49:51-2+ O 8 '66
I am a U.C. student; do not fold, bend or mutilate. Sat Eve Post 239:34-6+ Je 18 '66
Notes from the land of political pop. N Y Times Mag p48-9+ D 11 '66
Toppling the ivory tower. Holiday 39:10+ My '66
GOLD, Ivan
Short history of a short-story writer. Commonweal 84:223-4 My 13 '66
GOLD, Michael
Book of poverty. M. B. Folsom. Nation 202: 242-5 F 28 '66
GOLD, R. D. and Sondermeyer, J. C.
Designing silicon-transistor hi-fi amplifiers. Electr World 76:23-6+ S; 34-6+ O; 47-50+ N '66
GOLD, Thomas, and Hapke, B. W.
Luna 9 pictures: implications. bibliog Science 153:290-3 Jl 15 '66

about

Research in America; Lunar surface theory. J. Lear. il Sat R 49:64-5 Mr 5 '66
GOLD
Gold of ancient Peru. D. T. Easby. jr. il Américas 18:24-33 D '66
Gold of Coclé. R. A. Cowes. bibliog il Américas 18:18-25 F '66
Golden web. il Vogue 147:202-3 My '66
Great London gold rush. il Fortune 74:92-5 Jl 1 '66
Spy and the coin collector; Russia's financial arrangement with other countries, furnishing gold. M. McDougall. Nat R 18:355 Ap 19 '66; Correction. 18:591 Je 14 '66
See also
Goldsmithing
GOLD as money
All about gold and the dollar: how experts see the future. il U S News 61:62-7 N 28 '66
Answers to your questions about gold and the dollar. il U S News 61:63-4+ O 17 '66
Contingency planning. H. C. Wallich. Newsweek 68:100 O 24 '66
Expert; concerning C. D. Stengel's address at Independent bankers association meeting. Newsweek 67:74 Je 6 '66
Grim new grab for gold threatens your dollars. T. G. Harris. il Look 30:25-7 N 1 '66
Is gold at the end of its reign? il Bsns W p 129-30+ F 26 '66
Losing bet: French suggestion to raise price of gold. il Time 89:79 Ja 20 '67
Other side of the gold and dollar story; interview. W. S. Salant. il U S News 61:76-8 O 24 '66
Piggy bank; gold constitutes 86 per cent of all French reserves. Time 88:73 Ag 19 '66
Rising risk of runaway inflation; effect on gold stock. W. L. White. Read Digest 89: 128-32 Ag '66
Shift in gold; U.S. picture looks brighter. Time 88:94 N 4 '66
Why U.S. gold goes abroad, and stays there; BIS report. il U S News 60:87-8 Je 27 '66

Anecdotes, facetiae, satire, etc.
All that glitters... K. J. Cullinane. Nat R 18:619 Je 28 '66
GOLD coating. See Metal coating
GOLD cup regatta. See Motor boat racing
GOLD dollar. See Money—United States
GOLD in submerged lands
New Alaskan gold rush. T. E. Stimson. il Pop Mech 126:148-51+ O '66
GOLD mines and mining
See also
Prospecting

Securities
Is there really gold in them thar stocks? il Bsns W p 106+ Ja 7 '67

Alaska
New Alaskan gold rush. T. E. Stimson. il Pop Mech 126:148-51+ O '66

South Africa
Less gold to come from South Africa? U S News 61:67 N 28 '66

United States
Gold from lead; Homestake mining co. il Time 87:88 Mr 11 '66
How I search for lost gold mines, and why. E. S. Gardner. il Pop Sci 188:100-5 Mr '66
Something of the utmost importance; deposits unearthed in 1848. il Sr Schol 87:3 Ja 21 '66

GOLD reserves. See Gold as money
GOLD rush days. See Festivals—Arizona
GOLD rush of 1849. See Gold mines and mining—United States
GOLD standard. See Gold as money
GOLD work. See Goldsmithing
GOLDBERG, Alfred L. and Wittes, R. E.
Genetic code: aspects of organization. bibliog Science 153:420-4 Jl 22 '66
GOLDBERG, Arthur Joseph
Ambassador Goldberg reports to President Johnson on U.N. accomplishments in the past year; text of letter, August 22, 1966. Dept State Bul 55:382-6 S 12 '66
Ambassador Goldberg reviews U.N. peace efforts with President; statement, February 11, 1966. Dept State Bul 54:309 F 28 '66
Ambassador Goldberg submits Viet-Nam question to U.N. Security council; texts of two letters of January 31, 1966 and texts of two statements, February 1, 1966. Dept State Bul 54:229-39 F 14 '66
Ambassador Goldberg visits President Johnson to report on U.N. developments; statement, November 7, 1966. Dept State Bul 55:851-5 D 5 '66
America and Britain: unity of purpose; address, March 4, 1966. Dept State Bul 54:539-43 Ap 4 '66
Barbados admitted to United Nations; statement, December 7, 1966. Dept State Bul 56: 28-9 Ja 2 '67
Coming of age of the U.N; address, September 6, 1966. Dept State Bul 55:492-6 O 3 '66
Communications from permanent representative of United States. UN Mo Chron 3:3-4 F '66
Gift of love. McCalls 94:74 D '66
Initiative for peace; statement, September 22, 1966. Dept State Bul 55:518-25 O 10 '66; Same with title Vietnam settlement. Vital Speeches 33:34-8 N 1 '66
International cooperation in outer space; statement, December 18, 1965. Dept State Bul 54:163-7 Ja 31 '66
International cooperation in space; statement, September 19, 1966. Dept State Bul 55:605-8 O 17 '66
International evening at the ABA convention; summary of address, June 6, 1966. por Pub W 189:36-7 Je 20 '66
Key questions in the United Nations; address, April 25, 1966. Vital Speeches 32: 489-92 Je 1 '66
Move to change representation of China in U.N. again rejected by the General assembly; statement, November 21, 1966. Dept State Bul 55:926-9 D 19 '66
Peace and justice among nations: the agenda of the international community; address, May 2, 1966. Dept State Bul 54:798-802 My 23 '66
Peace talks: U Thant gets go-ahead, but; summary of letter. por U S News 62:11 Ja 2 '67
Problems and challenges of the U.N. decade of development; statement, July 6, 1966. Dept State Bul 55:241-8 Ag 15 '66

GOLDBERG, Arthur Joseph—*Continued*
Quest for peace; address, March 25, 1966.
  Dept State Bul 54:608-13 Ap 18 '66
Quest for peace in Viet-Nam; address,
  January 17, 1966. Dept State Bul 54:197-201
  F 7 '66
Question of intervention in the domestic af-
  fairs of states; statement. December 10,
  1965. Dept State Bul 54:124-8 Ja 24 '66
Rule of law in an unruly world; address,
  May 18, 1966. Dept State Bul 54:936-44
  Je 13 '66
Security council authorizes U.K. to use force
  to divert oil shipments bound for Rhodesia;
  statement, April 9, 1966. Dept State Bul
  54:713-17 My 2 '66
Security council recommends Guyana's ad-
  mission to U.N; statement, June 21, 1966.
  Dept State Bul 55:188 Ag 1 '66
U.S.S.R. vetoes Security council resolution
  on Israel complaint; statements. Dept State
  Bul 55:969-74 D 26 '66
United Nations: a great chapter in man's
  pilgrimage toward peace; address, October
  25, 1966. Dept State Bul 55:739-44 N 14 '66
United Nations: a progress report; address,
  April 18, 1966. Dept State Bul 54:749-54
  My 9 '66
United Nations adopts convention on racial
  discrimination; statement; December 14,
  1965. Dept State Bul 54:212-16 F 7 '66
U.N. peace force in Cyprus extended for six
  months; statement, June 16, 1966. Dept
  State Bul 55:63-4 Jl 11 '66
U.N. security council censures Israel for
  raid against Jordan; statement, November
  25, 1966. Dept State Bul 55:974-8 D 26 '66
U.N. urges nations to refrain from interfer-
  ence in the Congo; statement, October 14,
  1966. Dept State Bul 55:759-60 N 14 '66
United States calls for treaty on exploration
  of the moon; letter, May 9, 1966. Dept
  State Bul 54:900-1 Je 6 '66
U.S. commitment to political solution in Viet-
  Nam reaffirmed; statement. October 18,
  1966. Dept State Bul 55:757-8 N 14 '66
U.S. emphasizes need to reserve outer space
  and celestial bodies for peaceful activities;
  statement, July 12, 1966. Dept State Bul
  55:249-52 Ag 15 '66
U.S. hopes U.N. will extend Secretary-
  General's term; statement. September 1,
  1966. Dept State Bul 55:434-5 S 19 '66
U.S. informs U.N. Security council of action
  on Rhodesian agent; letter to Security
  council, February 28, 1966. Dept State Bul
  54:588-9 Ap 11 '66
United States joins new Asian development
  bank; statement, August 16, 1966. Dept
  State Bul 55:347-8 S 5 '66
U.S. notes progress of negotiations on peaceful uses of outer space, the moon, and
  other celestial bodies; statement, August
  3, 1966. Dept State Bul 55:321-5 Ag 29 '66
U.S. peace efforts reported to members of
  U.N; letter, January 4, 1966. Dept State
  Bul 54:117 Ja 24 '66
U.S. presents draft treaty on exploration of
  the moon and other celestial bodies to
  U.N. committee; text of letter to the chair-
  man of the U.N. committee on the peace-
  ful uses of outer space, June 16, 1966.
  Dept State Bul 55:60-1 Jl 11 '66
United States presents views on Security
  council procedures; letter, April 21, 1966.
  Dept State Bul 54:906-8 Je 6 '66
U.S. replies to Cambodian charges on
  frontier situation; letter to U Thant,
  January 8, 1966. Dept State Bul 54:167-8
  Ja 31 '66
U.S. replies to statements on Viet-Nam pro-
  posals; statements. September 23 and 28,
  1966. Dept State Bul 55:609 O 17 '66
U.S. reports to U.N. on actions taken against
  North Viet-Nam; text of letter to president
  of the U.N. Security council, June 30, 1966.
  Dept State Bul 55:119-20 Jl 25 '66
United States reviews position on nonproli-
  feration of nuclear weapons; statement,
  October 20, 1966. Dept State Bul 55:896-
  901 D 12 '66
U.S. signs convention on racial discrimina-
  tion; statement, September 28, 1966. Dept
  State Bul 55:653 O 24 '66
U.S. urges better U.N. machinery for peace-
  ful settlement; statement. November 24,
  1965. bibliog f Dept State Bul 54:93-9 Ja 17
  '66
United States urges concrete U.N. action on
  South West Africa; statement. October 12,
  1966. Dept State Bul 55:690-1 O 31 '66
U.S. urges early action on space treaty;
  statement, September 15, 1966. Dept State
  Bul 55:508 O 3 '66

U.S. urges Security council unity on Rhode-
  sian problem; statement, May 18, 1966.
  Dept State Bul 54:986-91 Je 20 '66
U.S. welcomes Security council views on Viet-
  Nam situation; statement, February 26,
  1966. Dept State Bul 54:547-8 Ap 4 '66
U.S. welcomes U.N./FAO appeal for world-
  wide food aid to India; statement, Feb-
  ruary 2, 1966. Dept State Bul 54:385 Mr 7
  '66
We orbit around; interview by Mademoiselle's
  guest editors. por Mlle 63:347 Ag '66
What the U.S. wants; summary of address,
  September 20, 1966. il por Time 88:19-20
  S 30 '66
World society of equality and brotherhood;
  address, May 12, 1966. Dept State Bul 54:
  971-5 Je 20 '66

about

Adventures of Arthur Goldberg. A. Kopkind.
  New Repub 155:15-18 O 8 '66
Ambassador. New Yorker 41:32-3 F 5 '66
Goldberg parallel center. Nat R 18:1086+ N
  1 '66
Goldberg proposals. New Repub 155:5-6 O 1
  '66
Goldberg represents Lyndon Johnson. M.
  Mayer. il pors N Y Times Mag p 16-17+
  F 6 '66
I'm not discouraged either, got it? R. Kahn.
  il pors Sat Eve Post 239:85-9 Ja 29 '66
Mr Goldberg dissents; challenging his func-
  tion. Nation 202:668 Je 6 '66
Rule of law. R. Baldwin. Sat R 49:26 Ag 6
  '66

GOLDBERG, Bertrand
Goldberg's variation on Chicago public hous-
  ing. J. M. Dixon. il Arch Forum 125:25-33
  N '66
GOLDBERG, Dorothy
How to live with memories. Redbook 127:57+
  O '66
GOLDBERG, Erwin
Lactate dehydrogenase of trout: hybridiza-
  tion in vivo and in vitro. bibliog Science
  151:1091-3 Mr 4 '66
GOLDBERG, Leo
New Harvard director. Sky & Tel 31:195 Ap
  '66
GOLDBERG, Michelle
Selling in a children's department at nine
  years of age. il por Pub W 189:88 F 28 '66
GOLDBERG, Ray A.
Agribusiness for developing countries. Har-
  vard Bsns R 44:81-93 S '66
GOLDBERG, Rube
Don't brush off all the old rules. por Seven-
  teen 25:194+ S '66
GOLDBLOOM, Maurice J.
Fulbright revolt. Commentary 42:63-9 S '66
GOLDE, Roger A.
Sharpen your number sense. Harvard Bsns R
  44:73-83 Jl '66
GOLDEN, Harry
Jim Crow and 14-B. New Repub 155:16-18 N
  12 '66
Thoughts to remember. Good H 162:246 Je '66
GOLDEN, L. L. L.
Public relations. See second issue of each
  month of Saturday review
Republican ideals and party image. Sat R 49:
  46-7 Ap 23 '66
GOLDEN, Morton J.
Dog control by county contract. Am City 81:
  197 S '66
GOLDEN fable for St Valentine's day; story.
  See Wescott, J.
GOLDEN GATE park. See San Francisco—
  Parks and playgrounds
GOLDEN HORN
Golden Horn; photographs. A. Güler. Horizon
  8:76-83 Wint '66
GOLDEN key award. See Rewards, prizes, etc.
GOLDEN mouse. See Mice, White footed
GOLDEN press, incorporated
Golden books reports it has mastered its
  Univac computer; automated distribution
  system. il Pub W 190:45-50 O 3 '66
Keys to successful co-publishing; communi-
  cation and organization. il Pub W 189:118-
  20 F 7 '66
Thirty-five tons of children's books shipped
  in three boxes; inter-modal van containers.
  il Pub W 189:155 F 21 '66
GOLDFARB, Robert W.
Institutional public relations. Wilson Bul
  40:509-12 F '66
GOLDFARB, Ronald
No room in the jail. New Repub 154:12-14
  Mr 5 '66
GOLDFINGER, Myron
Repetition without monotony. il Arch Forum
  124:40-5 Mr '66

GOLDIN, Milton
Great Rubinstein road show. Hi Fi 16:60-2 S '66

GOLDING, William
Egypt and I. Holiday 39:32+ Ap '66
Inside a pyramid; story. Esquire 66:165-9 D '66

GOLDMAN, Albert
Books. Vogue 147:110 Ap 1; 146 My; 148:29 Jl; 51 Ag 15; 163 O 1; 152 N 1 '66

GOLDMAN, D. E. See Blaustein, M. P. jt. auth.

GOLDMAN, Danny
Watch for a kidnaped son. L. Wainwright. por Life 60:25 Je 3 '66

GOLDMAN, Don
National parks and the ecology of beauty. Am For 72:18-21+ N '66

GOLDMAN, Eric Frederick
Exit Goldman, enter Roche: can LBJ and intellectuals be friends? B. Nelson. por Science 153:1505-7 S 23 '66
Failure of a mission. Nation 203:236 S 19 '66
Professor at the White House calls it quits. por U S New 61:14 S 19 '66
Unfortunate standoff: Johnson versus the intellectuals. H. Sidey. il por Life 61:42D S 23 '66

GOLDMAN, Hannah Stern
Season's end; story. Reporter 34:50 My 19 '66

GOLDMAN, James
Lion in winter. Criticism
America 114:452 Ap 2 '66
Commonweal 84:114 Ap 15 '66
Nation 202:374 Mr 28 '66
New Repub 154:37 Mr 26 '66
New Yorker 42:110 Mr 12 '66
Newsweek il 67:94 Mr 14 '66
Sat R 49:55 Mr 19 '66
Time il 87:52 Mr 11 '66
Vogue 147:145 My '66

GOLDMAN, Marshall I.
Communist foreign aid: successes and shortcomings. bibliog f Cur Hist 51:78-87+ Ag '66
Economic revolution in the Soviet Union. For Affairs 45:319-31 Ja '67
—and Conner, Alice
Businessmen appraise East-West trade. Harvard Bsns R 44:6-8+ Ja '66

GOLDMAN, Michael
Three firsts. G. Malanga. Poetry 108:131-2 My '66

GOLDMAN, Robert
Mike fright. Newsweek 67:21 F 7 '66

GOLDNER, Herman W.
Mayor tells how to modernize America's cities. por Nations Bsns 54:108-10+ Ap '66

GOLDRATH, Bert
Liquid logging. Am For 72:34-6 F '66

GOLDREICH, Gloria
First year; story. McCalls 93:58-9 Jl '66

GOLDSCHMIDT, Carl
City planners to play a key role in civil-defense preparedness. Am City 81:176+ My '66

GOLDSMITH, Arthur
How much should you charge for a picture? Pop Phot 58:70-2+ Ap '66
How to get the most from fast-loading cameras. il Pop Phot 58:54-7+ F '66
Seeing beyond the obvious; interview. U S Camera 29:48-9+ Mr '66

GOLDSMITH, H. L.
Red cells and rouleaux in shear flow. bibliog Science 153:1406-7 S 16 '66

GOLDSMITH, Harris
Brief candles. Hi Fi 16:50-4+ F '66
For Chopin, the voices of poets. Hi Fi 16:85 S '66
Magical month of Mozart. Hi Fi 16:MA7+ N '66
Nielsen's Fourth symphony, it makes a splendid sound. Hi Fi 16:67 Jl '66
Pianists, new encounters and old; New York concerts. Hi Fi 16:126+ Mr '66
Recordings from piano rolls: valid history. rewarding artistry. Hi Fi 16:82+ D '66
Shed at Norfolk. Hi Fi 16:40-3 Je '66
World series: a budget line from Philips. Hi Fi 16:169 O '66

GOLDSMITH, John R.
Air pollution medical research. Science 154: 1588-91 D 23 '66

GOLDSMITHING
Gypsy's treasure: discovery of ancient trove of gold near Villena, Spain. B. Wason. il Horizon 9:102-4 Wint '67
Masterpieces from a lost kingdom; Marlik. E. O. Negahban. il UNESCO Courier 19: 18-21 Je '66

GOLDSTEIN, Abraham S.
Police and the law. New Repub 155:26-8 Ag 27 '66

GOLDSTEIN, Ardath Ann
Americans not everybody knows. PTA Mag 60:10-12 Ap '66

GOLDSTEIN, David
Golden age. D. Daiches. Commentary 42:94+ N '66

GOLDSTEIN, J. I.
Butler, Missouri: an unusual iron meteorite. bibliog Science 153:975-6 Ag 26 '66

GOLDSTEIN, Joel
Modern structure for University of Oregon co-op. Pub W 191:70-1 Ja 16 '67

GOLDSTEIN, Jonah J.
Speaking out. por Sat Eve Post 239:12+ Jl 30 '66

GOLDSTEIN, Laurence
Survivor's heritage. Nation 203:390-2 O 17 '66
Troublesome comfort. Nation 202:274-6 Mr 7 '66

GOLDSTEIN, Leon. See Forster, R. P. jt. auth.

GOLDSTEIN, Lester, and Platt, D. B.
Cytoplasmic and environmental influences on nuclear behavior. Science 155:110-11 Ja 6 '67

GOLDSTEIN, M. J.
Kinetic isotope effects and organic reaction mechanisms. bibliog Science 154:1616-21 D 30 '66

GOLDSTEIN, Milton N. and others
Incorporation of tritiated actinomycin D into drug-sensitive and drug-resistant HeLa cells. Science 151:1555-6 Mr 25 '66

GOLDSTEIN, Richard
Drugs on the campus. Sat Eve Post 239:40-4+ My 21; 34-8+ Je 4 '66

about
Pops and boppers. il por Newsweek 68:66 D 19 '66

GOLDSTEIN, Walter
How to win the war. New Repub 155:8-9 S 10 '66

GOLDSTONE, Richard H.
Too terrible to be told. Sat R 49:59+ Je 11 '66

GOLDWATER, Barry Morris
As Goldwater now sees the war in Vietnam; interview. por U S News 60:44-6 Ap 25 '66
Dream come true; expedition down the Colorado. pors McCalls 93:64+ Mr '66
Goldwater advises LBJ; visit riot sites; excerpts from address, July 27, 1966. por U S News 61:14 Ag 8 '66
Goldwater speaks out about Senator Fulbright; excerpts from address, May 5, 1966. por U S News 60:23 My 16 '66
Goldwater: where were you, George? letter, December 8, 1964. U S News 61:64-6 D 19 '66
How Goldwater views '68, and '64; interview. por U S News 61:22 S 12 '66
How to save the Grand Canyon and water the desert, too; interview. U S News 61: 124-6 O 24 '66
Republican party pulled itself together; interview. por U S News 61:60-1 N 21 '66
Senator Goldwater vs. the Sierra club; statement. Nat R 18:918-20 S 20 '66
Traveler, consider my Arizona; interview. ed. by R. Joseph. pors Esquire 66:124-6 O '66

about
Back to Goldwater? A. Kopkind. New Repub 155:12-13 S 17 '66
Fellow traveler; proposal for U.S.-Soviet alliance. Nation 202:478 Ap 25 '66
Letter to Barry; concerning G. Romney's letter of 1964. Newsweek 68:27 D 12 '66
Mr Goldwater talks sense. Christian Cent 83: 905 Jl 20 '66
Polar elephants. T. Wicker. Atlan 217:80 Ap '66
Romney-Goldwater clash; storm signal for '68. por U S News 61:14 D 12 '66
Romney's letter. Nat R 18:1257 D 13 '66
Story of two letters: effect on Romney changes. por U S News 61:62-5 D 19 '66
There's no radical change in Goldwater. D. S. Broder. il pors N Y Times Mag p9+ Je 19 '66
Where George was; summary of G. Romney's letter of 1964. G. Romney. por Time 88:28 D 9 '66

GOLDWATER, Robert
Glory that was France. Art N 65:40-2+ Mr '66

GOLDWYN, Samuel
Creating with enthusiasm; interview. pors Nations Bsns 54:46-8+ N '66

GOLF
Advice on weekend golf. A. Palmer. il Look 30:64-6+ Ag 9 '66

GOLF—*Continued*

Fore! J. Boros; B. Casper; J. Hebert. il Esquire 65:117-19 Ap '66

Give the target the back of your hand. J. Nicklaus. il Sports Illus 24:62 Je 6 '66

Golf (cont) C. Price. Esquire 66:44+ S '66

Happiness is a hippo steak; B. Casper's exotic diet. E. Shrake. il Sports Illus 24:22-6+ F 7 '66

Here is the shot that is toughest of all; drive off the first tee. J. Nicklaus. il Sports Illus 24:48 Mr 7 '66

Hitting a one-hopper for the short stop. J. Nicklaus. il Sports Illus 25:48 Ag 22 '66

It matters if you wiggle a toe. J. Nicklaus. il Sports Illus 24:61 Mr 14 '66

It was fun time in the thirties. D. Jenkins. il Sports Illus 24:100-6+ Ap 4 '66

It's a three-billion-dollar business. W. B. Furlong. il N Y Times Mag p50-1+ Je 5 '66

Mickey finds a game she likes; world's best woman golfer. P. Ryan. Sports Illus 24:78+ Ap 11 '66

Not the time to be half safe. J. Nicklaus. il Sports Illus 25:72 O 24 '66

Perils of paralysis; slowdown, golfers mimic the pros. P. Ryan. il Sports Illus 25:22-5+ Jl 11 '66

Two to try when coming through the rye. J. Nicklaus. il Sports Illus 25:49 Jl 25 '66

Untroubled sport for those who play VAAGG; Van Alen's answer to grief in golf. J. Van Alen. il Sports Illus 25:48-50+ N 28 '66

See also
Putting (golf)
Swing (golf)

Anecdotes, facetiae, satire, etc.

Welcome to the country club, you misfortunates. M. Siegel. il Nations Bsns 54:75 Je '66

Bibliography

Golf. C. Price. Esquire 66:48+ S '66

Equipment

Equipage of choice. il Esquire 65:184 Ap '66

Study and teaching

School for golfers; University of Houston and Dave Williams. Newsweek 68:80 Jl 11 '66

Why golf is a lifetime sport. B. F. Bruce, jr. Parks & Rec 1:772 S '66

Anecdotes, facetiae, satire, etc.

#X$!¢%; or, A gentle complaint from your friendly club pro; interview. S. Dudas. il Esquire 65:124-5+ Ap '66

Tournaments

At Olympic: a summit of drama; U.S. Open at San Francisco's Olympic country club. A. Wright. il Sports Illus 24:22-7 Je 27 '66

Awful putt showed me how to win; 1966 Masters. J. Nicklaus. il Sports Illus 24:36-8+ Ap 25 '66

Beaten by a quarry quandary; G. Cowan wins at Merion golf club outside Philadelphia. A. Wright. Sports Illus 25:120+ S 12 '66

Billy survives the face-off; A. Palmer wins Houston tournament; Casper emerges as golf's leading money-winner for 1966. A. Wright. il Sports Illus 25:32-4+ N 28 '66

Bogeys at the beach; Bing Crosby championship. il Time 87:60-1 F 4 '66

Caught on a barbless hook; British Curtis cup team. P. Ryan. il Sports Illus 25:22-3 Ag 8 '66

Course for romancing; 66th U.S. Open. il Newsweek 68:59 Jl 4 '66

Course you have to woo; U.S. Open golf championship to be played at San Francisco's Olympic country club. A. Wright. il Sports Illus 24:52-5 Je 13 '66

Domed club that will test the god of golf; Canada cup matches held at Yomiuri country club near Tokyo. A. Wright. il Sports Illus 25:54-7 N 7 '66

Don't forget the sandwiches; P.G.A. winner Geiberger. il Time 88:52 Ag 5 '66

Golfing events. Sports Illus 24:8+ Ap 18 '66

Good-bye Bobby, good-bye Billy Joe, good-bye Glory. R. Cromie. il Esquire 65:123+ Ap '66

Happy stroll for golf's smiling Gei; A. Geiberger wins PGA championship. D. Jenkins. il Sports Illus 25:16-19 Ag 1 '66

Hit it my way. G. Player. il Sports Illus 24:32-41 Mr 21 '66

How to be a golf champion. C. Price. il N Y Times Mag p34-5+ Ag 28 '66

Is the Masters fixed? Augusta national suited to golf games of Nicklaus, Palmer and Player. G. S. Brown. il Sports Illus 24:56-66 Ap 4 '66

Jack plays too good; Nicklaus wins the Masters. il Newsweek 67:62 Ap 25 '66

Missing links; British Open. il Newsweek 68:54-5 Jl 18 '66

Money is a girl's best friend; M. Wright first prizewinner of Ladies world series of golf. P. Ryan. il Sports Illus 25:36-+ S 12 '66

Name your game, baby, and I'll beat you; baseball players' golf tournament in Miami. M. Mulvoy. Sports Illus 24:63-5 Mr 14 '66

A nobody at the Open; Bellerive country club. J. Underwood. il Sports Illus 24:96-100+ Je 13 '66

On the green; prize money. Time 89:74 Ja 6 '67

Out of the woods to a title; J. G. Carner wins amateur championship. J. Jares. il Sports Illus 25:54-5 Ag 22 '66

Postures of a Peewee prodigy; Pee Wee golf tournament, Orlando, Fla. il Sports Illus 25:24-5 Ag 29 '66

Smiling Jack wins a rough one; British Open. A. Wright. il Sports Illus 25:20-3 Jl 18 '66

Some lessons from teacher; women's intercollegiate. P. Ryan. il Sports Illus 25:56-8 Jl 4 '66

Some thin tempers among friendly enemies; G. Player wins Piccadilly world match play tournament. A. Wright. il Sports Illus 25:74-6 O 17 '66

Sorry about that; World series of golf. il Time 88:80-1 S 23 '66

Sporting scene; British Open at Muirfield. H. W. Wind. New Yorker 42:100+ Ag 13 '66

Sporting scene; Masters championship. H. W. Wind. il New Yorker 42:134+ Ap 30 '66

Sporting scene; Piccadilly tournament at Wentworth. A. Cooke. New Yorker 42:171-2+ N 5 '66

Stopwatches are not the answer. J. Nicklaus. Sports Illus 25:25 Jl 11 '66

Stranger stars in a Crosby cliffhanger; 25th Bing Crosby national pro-am. A. Wright. il Sports Illus 24:40-1 Ja 31 '66

Sugoi try nearly won a trophy for Sugi; U.S. wins the Canada cup, Palmer and Nicklaus unbeatable at Tokyo. J. Schecter. il Sports Illus 25:67-8 N 21 '66

Sweet talk from Old Wool; Colonial national invitation tournament Chairman F. Rogers. D. Jenkins. Sports Illus 24:67-8 My 30 '66

Ten-percent tournament; U.S. Open. il Time 88:58 Jl 1 '66

They are almost too tired to walk to the bank. M. Mulvoy. il Sports Illus 25:62-4 S 26 '66

Three was a crowd; J. Nicklaus winner of Masters three-way playoff. A. Wright. il Sports Illus 24:36-43 Ap 18 '66

Too many Masters. il Newsweek 67:98 Ap 18 '66

Up from the basement; U.S. women's Open. il Time 88:40 Jl 15 '66

Upset from down under; Australians win the Eisenhower trophy. A. Wright. il Sports Illus 25:28-9 N 14 '66

Victory at Verdun; British Open. il Time 88:40 Jl 15 '66

When two were twice as good; Palmer and Nicklaus at PGA. A. Wright. il Sports Illus 25:40-1 D 19 '66

While the cats are away; K. Venturi wins Lucky international. il Time 87:62 F 11 '66

Young pros with careers at stake; U.S. Open at the Olympic club in San Francisco. G. S. Brown. il Sports Illus 25:94+ N 14 '66

GOLF and business

Golf: pitching for the green; business evolving from the course. il Newsweek 68:68-9 Ag 8 '66

GOLF clubs (sticks)

Don't let your golf be a dirty business. J. Nicklaus. il Sports Illus 25:72 N 14 '66

Equipage of choice. il Esquire 65:184 Ap '66

GOLF courses

Best U.S. golf resorts. T. B. Lesure. il Travel 125:24-8+ Mr '66

Course you have to woo; U.S. Open golf championship to be played at San Francisco's Olympic country club. A. Wright. il Sports Illus 24:52-5 Je 13 '66

Domed club that will test the god of golf; Canada cup matches held at Yomiuri country club near Tokyo. A. Wright. il Sports Illus 25:54-7 N 7 '66

Fabulous world of Florida; from Miami to Palm Beach, photographs by M. E. Newman, with account by G. S. Brown. Sports Illus 24:30-7 Ja 24 '66

GOLF courses—*Continued*
Four seasons of golf; a travel chart of the leading foreign golf courses. Esquire 65:122 Ap '66
Golfer, go abroad. C. Price. il Esquire 65:120-1+ Ap '66
Is the Masters fixed? Augusta national suited to golf games of Nicklaus, Palmer and Player. G. S. Brown. il Sports Illus 24: 56-66 Ap 4 '66
It is a Ben Hogan kind of course; Lakeside course at Olympic country club. K. Venturi. Sports Illus 24:56-6+ Je 13 '66
Land-bank program creates golf course; Albuquerque, N.Mex. il Am City 81:221 S '66
Open approach for a treacherous sand; Pebble Beach in California and Augusta National in Georgia. J. Nicklaus. il Sports Illus 25: 52 Ag 29 '66
Shakes in quake corner; Olympic country club course. K. Venturi. il Sports Illus 24:56-64 Je 13 '66
Some things to think about before you swing. J. Nicklaus. il Sports Illus 24:51 F 7 '66
Sporting scene; British Open at Muirfield. H. W. Wind. New Yorker 42:100+ Ag 13 '66
Treasure of a golf links for the Crosby, and the public; Spyglass hill, on Monterey Peninsula, Calif. il Sports Illus 26:34-41 Ja 9 '67
Two golf courses in record time; Callaway gardens, Pine Mountain, Ga. F. Veale. il Parks & Rec 1:410-12 My '66
Two to try when coming through the rye. J. Nicklaus. il Sports Illus 25:49 Jl 25 '66

Construction and care
Flags are flying among the palms; from Palm Beach to Miami. G. S. Brown. il Sports Illus 24:38-41 Ja 24 '66
Green elephant; grass to the homeowner. B. La Fontaine. il Sports Illus 24:68-70+ Ap 1 '66

Lighting
Don't stop when the sun goes down; Blue golf course, Nassau County. C. M. Alston. il Am City 81:114-16 My '66

GOLFERS
Billy survives the face-off; A. Palmer wins Houston tournament; Casper emerges as golf's leading money-winner for 1966. A. Wright. il Sports Illus 25:32-4+ N 28 '66
Bogey man; unintentional flubs disqualify players. Newsweek 68:62+ S 12 '66
Caught on a barbless hook; British Curtis cup team. P. Ryan. il Sports Illus 25:22-3 Ag 8 '66
Dandiest swinger on the fairway; interview, ed. by D. Fales. D. Sanders. il Life 60: 53-4+ Je 10 '66
Flags are flying among the palms; from Palm Beach to Miami. G. S. Brown. il Sports Illus 24:38-41 Ja 24 '66
Gary and his beloved country; South Africa. J. Underwood. il Sports Illus 24:82-6+ My 23 '66
Green from the greens; official winnings. il Time 88:52 S 9 '66
How to be a golf champion. C. Price. il N Y Times Mag p34-5+ Ag 28 '66
Is the Masters fixed? Augusta national suited to golf games of Nicklaus, Palmer and Player. G. S. Brown. il Sports Illus 24: 56-66 Ap 4 '66
It was fun time in the thirties. D. Jenkins. il Sports Illus 24:100-6+ Ap 4 '66
It's a three-billion-dollar business. W. B. Furlong. il N Y Times Mag p50-1+ Je 5 '66
A nobody at the Open; Bellerive country club. J. Underwood. il Sports Illus 24:96-100+ Je 13 '66
Perils of paralysis; slowdown, golfers mimic the pros. P. Ryan. il Sports Illus 25:22-5+ Jl 11 '66
Please, lady, get off my golf course. M. Smith. il Life 60:105-6+ Je 17 '66
Postures of a Peewee prodigy; Pee Wee golf tournament, Orlando, Fla. il Sports Illus 25:24-5 Ag 22 '66
Return of the littlest tiger; prodigy at twelve. R. Albers. teen-age golfer. P. Ryan. il Sports Illus 25:32-4+ Ag 15 '66
Some lessons from teacher; women's intercollegiate. P. Ryan. il Sports Illus 25:56-8 Jl 4 '66
Sugoi try nearly won a trophy for Sugi; U.S. wins the Canada cup, Palmer and Nicklaus unbeatable at Tokyo. J. Schecter. il Sports Illus 25:67-8 N 21 '66
They are almost too tired to walk to the bank. M. Mulvoy. il Sports Illus 25:62-4 S 26 '66

Three more to watch. il Sports Illus 24: 67 Ap 4 '66
Upset from down under; Australians win the Eisenhower trophy. A. Wright. il Sports Illus 25:28-9 N 7 '66
Young pros with careers at stake; U.S. Open at the Olympic club in San Francisco. G. S. Brown. il Sports Illus 25:94+ N 14 '66
GOLLAN, Antoni E.
Evolution of Bob Dylan. Nat R 18:638-40 Je 28 '66
GOLLAN, Frank. See Clark, L. C. jr, jt. auth.
GOLLER, A. P.
Senator Kennedy crosses the color line. Commonweal 84:455-6 Jl 22 '66
GOLLIN, James
Life insurance: the monolithic sect; concerning the book. Pay now, die later. Nation 203:670-4 D 19 '66
GOLOVIN, Nicholas E.
Nth country's problem in space exploration. Bul Atomic Sci 22:13-18 D '66
GOMBERG, Harold
Great Gomberg. V. N. Jackson. por Am Rec G 32:771 My '66
GOMBRICH, Ernst H.
Art and anti-art. Atlan 217:93-9 F '66
GOMERSALL, Earl R. and Myers, M. S.
Breakthrough in on-the-job training. Harvard Bsns R 44:62-72 Jl '66
GÓMEZ-SICRE, José
World art at São Paulo. Américas 18:31-6 Ja '66
GOMUŁKA, Władysław
Angry strangler. il por Time 87:40-1 Je 17 '66
No place for chitchat. Time 88:28 D 23 '66
Poland: on the treadmill. B. van Voorst. il por Newsweek 69:32-4 Ja 9 '67
Polish Catholic witness. Commonweal 84:166 Ap 29 '66
GONADOTROPIC hormones. See Hormones, Sex
GONADOTROPIN
Cancer, hormones linked. F. Marley. Sci N 90:225 S 24 '66
GONÇALVES DE SOUZA, João
Sudene. por Américas 18:10-16 Ap '66
GONCOURT, Edmond Louis Antoine Huot de
Goncourt journal. K. Rexroth. Sat R 49:75-6 O 22 '66
GONCOURT, Jules Alfred Huot de
Goncourt journal. K. Rexroth. Sat R 49: 75-6 O 22 '66
GONCOURT prize
French literary prizes confound, somewhat, their critics. H. R. Lottman. il Pub W 190:43-7 D 26 '66
Prize pizazz. Time 88:34+ D 2 '66
GONDWANALAND. See Continental drift
GONYAULAX. See Dinoflagellates
GONZALEZ, Amado
Amado Gonzalez: San Francisco artist. F. Johnson. il por Am Artist 30:56-61+ F '66
GONZALEZ, Arturo F. jr, and Gonzalez, Gloria
Dirigibles' great days. Sat R 49:46-8 O 29 '66
Youthpower! summer jobs for teens. Seventeen 25:156-7+ Mr '66
GONZALEZ, Gloria. See Gonzalez, A. F. jr. jt. auth.
GONZALEZ, Manuel
Winning for old Cornbread. M. Kram. il pors Sports Illus 25:18-19 S 5 '66
GOOD, Paul
Blue notes from Dixie. Nation 203:570-5 N 28 '66
Chicago summer: bossism, racism and Dr King. Nation 203:237-42 S 19 '66
Out to get SNCC. Nation 203:534-8 N 21 '66
Thorntons of Mississippi: peonage on the plantation. Atlan 218:95-100 S '66
White look at black power. Nation 203:112-17 Ag 8 '66
GOOD and evil
Evil and the God of love, by J. Hick. Review
Sat R 49:35 Ag 13 '66. R. C. Muska
On judging God. D. Callahan. Commonweal 83:611-13 F 25 '66; Reply. N. J. Rigali. 84: 189+ My 6 '66
GOOD and evil in literature. See Literature and morals
GOOD-by; story. See Amft, M. J.
GOOD-by, kitten; story. See Marks, G. A. jr
GOOD housekeeping (periodical)
Magazine puts seal on its own success. il Bsns W p 190-2+ Mr 19 '66
GOOD housekeeping institute
Magazine puts seal on its own success. il Bsns W p 190-2+ Mr 19 '66
GOOD outdoor manners association
Setting an example. Time 87:66 Ap 15 '66

GOOD Samaritan (parable)
  Twice-told tale. V. P. McCorry. America 115:194 Ag 20 '66
GOOD soldier Schweik; opera. See Kurka, R.
GOOD taste. See Aesthetics
GOOD woman of Setzuan; drama. See Brecht, B.
GOODALE, Jane C.
  Blowgun hunters of the South Pacific. il pors Nat Geog Mag 129:792-817 Je '66
GOODALL, Donald
  Craftsmen USA '66; Southwest region. Craft Horiz 26:33-4+ Mr '66
GOODALL, Forrest R.
  Progesterone retards postpartum involution of the rabbit myometrium. bibliog Science 152:356-8 Ap 15 '66
GOODALL, Jane. See Van Lawick, J. G.
GOODALL, Kenneth
  Beyond reasonable doubt? Reporter 35:44-6 D 15 '66
GOODARD, James L.
  Quackery in the market place. Todays Health 44:51-2+ D '66
GOODFELLOW, Barbara
  Make it now, bake it later; excerpts. Redbook 126:100-1+ Ap '66
GOODFRIEND, Arthur
  Salem to Saigon. Sat R 49:37-8+ O 8 '66
GOODFRIEND, Mary Louis
  Something to talk about on campus. Mlle 63:326-7 Ag '66
GOODGOLD, Edwin
  Authors of Trivia sue Pocket books. Metromedia. Pub W 190:32 Ag 1 '66
GOODHART, A. L.
  Legal ignorance and false logic. Reporter 35:47-8+ D 15 '66
GOODHART, William
  Some day he'll come along, the man I love. Esquire 65:124-7 My '66
GOODHEW, H. R.
  Politics took second place. por Am City 81:177+ S '66
GOODLAD, John I.
  Directions of curriculum change; excerpts from Curriculum change: direction and process. NEA J 55:33-7 D '66
GOODMAN, Benny
  Goodman at the Rainbow grill. H. Dance. il por Sat R 49:82-3 Je 11 '66
GOODMAN, Burton
  Stimulating students to write. Sr Schol 88:sup 14 Mr 11 '66
GOODMAN, Ezra
  Goodman position clarified on Howard Hughes biography. Pub W 190:49 Jl 18 '66
  Stuart wins award in Goodman, Hughes case. Pub W 190:28 D 12 '66
GOODMAN, Jeffrey
  How to be patriotic and live with yourself. Atlan 217:61-2 F '66
GOODMAN, Joel W.
  Western amateurs convene in California. Sky & Tel 32:188-90 O '66
GOODMAN, Mitchell
  Traveling through history. Redbook 127:97+ S '66
GOODMAN, Norman, and Klein, David
  What kind of man will you marry? Seventeen 25:156-7+ Ap '66
GOODMAN, Paul
  Empty society; excerpts from Massey lectures. Commentary 42:53-60 N '66
  Student chaplains. New Repub 156:29-31 Ja 7 '67
        about
  Jonah. Criticism
    Commonweal 83:699 Mr 18 '66
    New Yorker 42:71-2 F 26 '66
  Prevalence of Paul Goodman. il pors N Y Times Mag p70-1+ Ap 3 '66
GOODMAN, Percival
  Books. Arch Forum 124:78-9 My '66
GOODMAN, Robert B.
  Australia; photographs. Look 30:29-43 Ag 23 '66
GOODMAN, Saul
  Brief biographies. See issues of Dance magazine
GOODMAN, Walter
  Comic twist to an old familiar fez. Life 61:10 Jl 15 '66
  Doctor's image is sickly. N Y Times Mag p38-9+ O 16 '66
  Life book review. Life 60:20 Je 24 '66
  Man who couldn't be bought. Redbook 128:66-7+ N '66
  They march to different drummers. N Y Times Mag p7+ Je 26 '66
  Truth about the best-seller list. McCalls 94:89+ N '66

GOODMAN memorial theater. See Chicago—Theater
GOODNIGHT, Clarence J. See Fowler, D. J. jt. auth.
GOODRICH, B. F. company
  Bridging the gap; State department opens exchange program. Newsweek 68:64+ Ag 15 '66
GOODRICH, Baxter Dee
  Gasman cometh. il por Duns R 88:60-2 N '66
GOODRICH, David L.
  Bold new trend in plaything creation. Sat Eve Post 239:14 D 17 '66
GOODRICH, Laurence B.
  Little-noted aspect of Spencer's art. Antiques 90:361-3 S '66
GOODRICH, Lloyd
  American art and the Whitney museum. Antiques 90:655-62 N '66
GOODRUM, Charles A.
  Are they getting their money's worth? por Library J 91:2759-64 Je 1 '66
GOODSELL, Charles T.
  Puerto Rico moves forward. Cur Hist 51:321-6 D '66
GOODSELL, James Nelson
  Dominican dilemma. New Repub 154:29-31 F 5 '66
  South America's place in the sun. Sat R 49:35 Jl 9 '66
GOODSELL, Jane
  Love in a nutshell; excerpt from I've only got two hands and I'm busy wringing them. Read Digest 89:65-6 D '66
GOODWIN, G. A. and Rankin, Allen
  Michigan's evangelist of art. Read Digest 88:217-18+ My '66
GOODWIN, Jeanne
  Naturalist's bookshelf. Audubon Mag 68:480 N '66
GOODWIN, Richard Naradof
  Reflections on Vietnam. New Yorker 42:57-8+ Ap 16 '66
        about
  Idea man for J.F.K. and L.B.J. has idea G.O.P. could use; with excerpts from speeches. H. Sidey. il por Life 61:48 S 30 '66
GOODWOOD race track. See Race tracks
GOOKIN, Ralph Burton
  Businessmen in the news. por Fortune 73:51 Mr '66
GOOSE shooting. See Geese, Wild
GOPHERUS agassizii. See Tortoises
GORDAN, Gilbert S. and others
  Osteolytic sterol in human breast cancer. bibliog Science 151:1226-8 Mr 11 '66
GORDIMER, Nadine
  Say something African; story. New Yorker 42:34-40 Ag 20 '66
  Why did Bram Fischer choose jail? N Y Times Mag p30-1+ Ag 14 '66
  Zambia. Holiday 39:38-47+ Je '66
GORDON, Albert S. See Contrera, J. F. jt auth.
GORDON, Arnold L. and others
  Layer of abnormally cold bottom water over southern Aves ridge. bibliog Science 151:1525-6 Mr 25 '66
GORDON, Arthur
  Day we almost didn't go. Read Digest 88:54-7 Mr '66
  Foolproof formula for success. Read Digest 89:88-90 D '66
  Freedom is a two-edged sword. Read Digest 89:37-9 Jl '66
  Joy of the here-and-now. Read Digest 90:107-10 Ja '67
  When in doubt, do! Read Digest 89:33-4+ O '66
  Wonder is for sharing. Read Digest 88:159-60+ Je '66
GORDON, Bernard K.
  Thailand; its meaning for the U.S. bibliog f Cur Hist 52:16-21+ Ja '67
GORDON, Bert I.
  Shooting movies with a Nikon. por U S Camera 30:68-9+ Ja '67
GORDON, Charles
  Ameliorating hardships under the immigration laws. bibliog f Ann Am Acad 367:85-92 S '66
GORDON, Charles George
  Gordon of Khartoum, by A. Nutting. Review Newsweek il por 68:116+ O 31 '66. S. K. Oberbeck
GORDON, Cyrus H.
  Books in review. Natur Hist 76:68+ Ja '67
GORDON, Daniel
  Chicken! story. Reporter 34:33-7 Je 16 '66
  Hiding from Walter; story. New Yorker 42:159-62 My 21 '66

GORDON, David J.
Lawrence as playwright. Nation 202:686 Je 6 '66
More or less plagiarized. Nation 202:433-4 Ap 11 '66
Two anti-puritan Puritans: Bernard Shaw and D. H. Lawrence. Yale R 56:76-90 O '66
GORDON, E. Kent, and others
Crystal structure of the zeolite paulingite. bibliog Science 154:1004-7 N 25 '66
GORDON, Edmund W.
Which way Head Start? interview; ed. by T. L. Moses. Sr Schol 88:sup2+ My 13 '66
GORDON, Ethel Edison
Boy who wanted to be somebody; story. Redbook 126:54-5 F '66
Legacy; story. McCalls 93:106-7 Ap '66
GORDON, Galvy
Columbus' conversion to data processing. por Wilson Lib Bul 41:414-17 D '66
Some of my best friends. Library J 91:908 F 15 '66
GORDON, Gordon. See Gordon, M. jt. auth.
GORDON, Harry
Man on top Down Under. N Y Times Mag p38-9+ O 23 '66
What we can learn about tennis. N Y Times Mag p 185-7+ N 27 '66
GORDON, Herbert
Enjoy winter's wonderland! Read Digest 88: 21-2+ F '66
GORDON, Hilary
Lost childhood; poem. Horn Bk 42:356 Je '66
GORDON, James Stewart-. See Stewart-Gordon, J.
GORDON, Lincoln
Alliance for progress: next steps for effective action; address, March 29, 1966. Dept State Bul 54:738-46 My 9 '66
Foreign assistance program for Latin America in 1967; statement, May 2, 1966. Dept State Bul 54:977-86 Je 20 '66
Inter-American cooperation: the road ahead; address, December 1, 1966. Dept State Bul 55:946-52 D 26 '66
Panorama of challenge and response in Latin America; address, September 28, 1966. Dept State Bul 55:644-8 O 24 '66
Private enterprise, economic integration, and the Alliance for progress; address, June 1, 1966. Dept State Bul 55:18-23 Jl 4 '66
Progress of Central American regional integration hailed; statement, October 14, 1966. Dept State Bul 55:716 N 7 '66
United States and Brazil: partners in progress; address, February 17, 1966. Dept State Bul 54:620-4 Ap 18 '66

about
Adjustable Linc. por Newsweek 67:54 Ja 31 '66
GORDON, Linda S.
Films in review. Natur Hist 75:11-13 My '66
GORDON, Marvin
Marvin Gordon's ballet concepts; Theatre four. D. Hering. Dance Mag 40:87 O '66
GORDON, Mildred, and Gordon, Gordon
Story that goes some place; with biographical sketch. Writer 79:11-14 N '66
GORDON, Milton P. See Green, B. R. jt. auth.
GORDON, Richard F.
See also
Space flight—Manned flights—Conrad-Gordon flight, 1966
GORDON, William H.
Why people go to quacks. Todays Health 44: 50-1 D '66
GORDON and Breach, science publishers, incorporated
Gordon and Breach forms new publishing subsidiary; entry into microfiche field. Pub W 191:37 Ja 9 '67
GORDON research conferences
Gordon research conferences: program for 1966. W. G. Parks. Science 151:1249-64+ Mr 11 '66
Gordon research conferences: winter session. Science 154:1474-5+ D 16 '66
GORDY, Berry, Jr
Triumph of a stay-at-home. il pors Ebony 21:32-4+ F '66
GORDY, W. Frank
In Atlanta, all roads lead to the Varsity. il Bsns W p 132-3+ O 8 '66
GORDY, Walter. See Herak, J. N. jt. auth.
GORE, Daniel
Unrepentant Gore; letter to the editor. Library J 91:5792+ D 1 '66

about
Gored from within; concerning his article in March 1966 issue of AAUP bulletin; letter to the editor. M. C. M. Souza. Library J 91:3014+ Je 15 '66
Last one in bed's a librarian! concerning his article: The mismanagement of college libraries. B. E. Richardson. il Library J 91:4904-7 O 15 '66; Discussion. 91:5792+ D 1 '66
GOREAU, Thomas F.
Sponge: effect on the form of reef corals. bibliog Science 151:343-4 Ja 21 '66
GORELIK, Mordecai
Rainbow terrace. Criticism
Sat R 49:16 D 31 '66
GOREN, Charles Henry
Bridge. See issues of Sports illustrated
GORENSTEIN, Shirley
Science in action. Natur Hist 75:64-7 F '66
GORER, Geoffrey
Man has no killer instinct. N Y Times Mag p47+ N 27 '66
GORER, Edward St John
Three for the cult. G. Weales. New Repub 155:32-4 N 26 '66
GOREY, Hays
Bank that made a U-turn on LaSalle street. Fortune 73:138-41+ Mr '66
GORILLAS
Gorillas in the family; pets of Isabelle and Henri de Meyer in Gabon. il Look 30:M14-16 Mr 22 '66
GORINI, Luigi
Antibiotics and the genetic code; with biographical sketch. Sci Am 214:20, 102-9 Ap '66
GORME, Eydie
Offstage with Eydie Gorme. R. Hochstein. il por Good H 162:48+ F '66
GORSLINE, Douglas
New dimension of Douglas Gorsline. F. Whitaker. il por Am Artist 30:38-43+ My '66
GOSPELS. See Bible—New Testament—Gospels
GOSS, Bert C.
How to reduce business' credibility gap; address, March 24, 1966. Vital Speeches 32:396-8 Ap 15 '66
GOSS, Richard J.
Hypertrophy versus hyperplasia. bibliog Science 153:1615-20 S 30 '66
GOSSAGE-Vardebedian papers; story. See Allen, W.
GÖTA CANAL
Three-day cruise across Sweden. il Sunset 136:70+ Ap '66
GÖTEBORG

Music
Göteborg. O. Wallgren. Opera N 31:27 N 19 '66
GOTHAM, Robert M.
1000 Islands, then and now. il por Motor B 118:34-7 Ag '66
GOTT, Edwin Hays
Toward the top at U.S. steel. por Bsns W p52 S 10 '66
GOTT, Helen T. and Hurlburt, M. L.
Getting-involved-for-good club. NEA J 55:15-16 S '66
GOTTESMAN, Jerome W.
Public vs. private ownershp of off-street parking. Am City 81:126+ O '66
GOTTLIEB, Adolph
Gottlieb at the summit. H. Rosenstein. il Art N 65:42-3+ Ap '66
GOTTLIEB, Linda
Lizzie and me in a wagon-lit. Mlle 63:197-9 S '66
Traveling with Mlle; what makes a good honeymoon, besides a good man? Mlle 62: 117-18 Ja '66
GOTTLIEB, Robert
Magic of Martha Graham. Holiday 39:166+ My '66
GOTTLIEB, Robert J.
Cars and the law. See issues of Motor trend
Dealer's dilemma. Motor T 18:78 N '66
Financing and insurance, tips & traps. Motor T 18:40-2 Je '66
Investing in old cars. Motor T 18:54-6+ D '66
Pitfalls of financing. Motor T 18:84 N '66
GOTTLIEB, Sanford
Too soon for peace. Nation 203:575-8 N 28 '66
GOTTSCHALK, Earl C.
Suit against the unions. New Repub 154:7-8 Mr 12 '66
GOTTSCHALK, John S.
Wetlands, wildlife and the army engineers; adaptation of address, October 2, 1965. Audubon Mag 68:116-18 Mr '66
GOTTSCHALK, Louis A. and others
Anxiety levels in dreams: relation to changes in plasma free fatty acids. bibliog Science 153:654-7 Ag 5 '66

GOTTSCHO, Samuel Herman
Back-yard wild-flower garden. il Flower Grower 53:35 O '66
Take photographs in your garden. il Horticulture 44:26-7+ F '66

GOUDEY, Ray
Remember Ray Goudey? Am City 81:8 My '66

GOUDY, Barbara. See Jellinck, P. H. jt. auth.

GOUDY, Frederic
Dinner and exhibition climax Goudy centennial year. il Pub W 189:98+ Ap 4 '66

GOUDY society, incorporated
Goudy society is incorporated. Pub W 189:132 F 7 '66

GOULASH. See Stew

GOULD, Cecil
Raphael's St Jerome punishing Sabinian. bibliog Art N 65:44-6+ Sum '66

GOULD, Douglas J. and others
Falciparum malaria: transmission to the gibbon by anopheles balabacensis. bibliog Science 153:1384 S 16 '66

GOULD, George K.
Photo-boating, a sport within a sport. Motor B 118:40-1 Jl '66

GOULD, Glenn
Prospects of recording. Hi Fi 16:46-63 Ap '66
We, who are about to be disqualified salute you! Hi Fi 16:MA23-4+ D '66
Yehudi Menuhin: musician of the year. por Hi Fi 16:7-9 D 15 '66

about
Schoenberg revealed by Gould. A. Rich. il por Sat R 49:78 S 24 '66

GOULD, H. J. See Klucis, E. S. jt. auth.

GOULD, Jack
For the record. il Newsweek 67:67 Mr 14 '66
Most influential fellow. por Newsweek 67:92+ My 9 '66
Take a letter. G. Ace. Sat R 49:12 N 12 '66

GOULD, Joan
Aquarium for people. Esquire 66:46-9 Jl '66
Boating. Sports Illus 25:66+ S 26 '66
Fastest, smoothest boat yet. Esquire 65:108-9+ F '66

GOULD, Samuel Brookner
New era for the public library; address, April 1966. por ALA Bul 60:585-90 Je '66
about
How to lower the higher learning. R. Kirk. Nat R 18:686 Jl 12 '66
New York's late-blooming State university. R. Gross and J. Murphy. il Harper 233:87-90+ D '66

GOULDING, Daniel J.
Restless generation; address, April 27, 1966. Vital Speeches 32:506-8 Je 1 '66

GOULDING, Phil G.
Pentagon answer to critics of bombing; excerpts from letter. U S News 62:16 Ja 16 '67

GOULDTHORPE, Kenneth
His escape from the butter factory. Life 61:110 O 21 '66
Will you have a good time? yeah, man! Life 60:76+ F 4 '66

GOULET, Denis A.
Missing revolution. America 114:438-40 Ap 2 '66
Voluntary austerity: the necessary art: vital to welfare of underprivileged men. Christian Cent 83:748-52 Je 8 '66

GOUNOD, Charles François
Faust. Criticism
New Yorker 42:232+ O 29 '66
Opera N 30:17 Ap 9 '66
Opera N 30:24-5 Ap 9 '66
Opera N il 30:18-20 Ap 9 '66
Opera N il 31:17-20 D 24 '66
Sat R 49:51 N 5 '66
Homage to Saint Cecilia. P. L. Miller. Am Rec G 32:853 My '66
On records; Roméo et Juliette; excerpts; Faust; highlights. Opera N 30:34 Ap 9 '66
On records; St Cecilia mass. Opera N 30:34 F 12 '66

GOURDINE, Meredith
Energy at the mine mouth. il por Time 87:42+ Je 3 '66

GOURDS
You'll want gourds. M. A. Roche il Pop Gard 17:6-7 D '66
See also
Gourmet clubs. See Clubs

GOURMETS. See Eating

GOUT
Big-shot disease. Sci Digest 59:33-4 Je '66
Gout & achievement; G. Brooks and E. Mueller findings. il Time 87:57 F 18 '66
Gout and greatness. il Newsweek 67:62 F 21 '66

Gout is in. R. G. Whalen. il N Y Times Mag p66+ My 1 '66
Moonshiners get gout from lead poisoning. Sci N 90:9 Jl 2 '66

GOVERNESSES
Governess. F. Du Plessix. New Yorker 42:28-38+ Ja 14 '67

GOVERNMENT. See Nations; Political science; State, The

GOVERNMENT, Resistance to
Now Cosa nostra and the Klan; renewed discussion and debate of the McCarran act. Nation 202:413-14 Ap 11 '66
Sanity test. C. Barus. Nation 203:156 Ag 22 '66
Selective reprisal: sniping at dissent; incidents and retaliatory acts by U.S. government and private citizens. M. L. Wulf. il Nation 203:149-52 Ag 22 '66
Violence on the fanatical left and right. A. Forster. bibliog f Ann Am Acad 364:141-8 Mr '66
See also
Revolutions

GOVERNMENT agencies. See United States—Executive departments

GOVERNMENT aid to business
Helping to shore up small business; Technical services act of 1965. il Bsns W p 146-8 Ja 22 '66
See also
Government lending
Industry and state

GOVERNMENT and art. See Art and state

GOVERNMENT and labor. See Labor laws and legislation

GOVERNMENT and science. See Science and state

GOVERNMENT and the press
Back of the uproar about LBJ managing the news. il U S News 60:42-3 Ja 31 '66
Between presidents and the press. J. M. Burns. Sat R 49:25 S 3 '66
Danger of getting used to lies: managed news; address, January 19, 1966. R. M. Shaw. Vital Speeches 32:332-4 Mr 15 '66
Did you hear that? concerning A. Sylvester's alleged statement that press should be handmaiden of the government. Nation 202:668 Je 6 '66
Games Johnson plays: deeper and deeper into the credibility gap. J. Deakin. New Repub 156:10-11 Ja 14 '67
Johnson and the press. F. Cormier. il Sat R 49:70-2 S 10 '66
Leakiest winter on record. C. Fritchey. Harper 232:42+ Mr '66
LBJ meets the press . . . sort of. R. L. Strout. New Repub 154:13-14 Ap 16 '66
LBJ's credibility; or, What happened to no comment? J. Deakin. New Repub 154:23-4 Ja 29 '66
News manglement; feud between the White House and the press corps. Nation 202:699 Je 13 '66
Nosey newsmen. New Repub 155:7 O 8 '66
Operation disparagement; Washington correspondents. Nation 202:349 Mr 28 '66
President prefers a direct line. E. T. Folliard. America 114:217 F 12 '66
Press in Washington, by R. E. Hiebert. Review
Sat R 49:80 Ap 9 '66. J. F. Fixx
Press, the President and foreign policy. J. B. Reston. For Affairs 44:553-73 Jl '66; Same abr. Read Digest 89:69-73 S '66
Reshuffle: R. H. Fleming as press secretary. il Newsweek 67:31 F 21 '66
Senior scholastic interview. il Sr Schol 89:21 N 4 '66
Snow job; Administration's news distortion campaign of Vietnamese war news. Nation 203:66-7 Jl 25 '66
Times and the signs. W. J. Coughlin. Tech W 20:50 Ja 2 '67
Unburdening bill; R. H. Fleming appointed Moyers deputy. Time 87:23 F 18 '66
Unplugging the muted trumpet; Senate says, NIH, blow your horn. B. Nelson. Science 154:491+ O 28 '66
Use & misuse of politicians. Time 88:92+ N 11 '66
When is news news? White House and Bay of Pigs invasion. Nation 202:730 Je 20 '66
You can't fool all the people even some of the time. A. H. Sypher. il Nations Bsns 54:31-2 F '66
See also
Press conferences

GOVERNMENT appropriations and expenditures
Worldwide defense expenditures. il Bul Atomic Sci 22:44-8 S '66
See also
Budget
United States—Appropriations and expenditures

GOVERNMENT bonds. See Bonds. Government
GOVERNMENT budgets. See Budget
GOVERNMENT contracts. See Contracts, Government

GOVERNMENT corporations
Government use of nonprofit companies. J. L. Trainor. Harvard Bsns R 44:38-40+ My '66
Nonprofits: air force says we can't do without them. E. Langer. Science 152:734-6 My 6 '66

GOVERNMENT employees
Agencies to exchange personnel for selected training assignments. Dept State Bul 54:470 Mr 21 '66
Cooperation and arbitration in the federal service. W. W. Heimbach. Mo Labor R 89:614 Je '66
Correctives for dishonest and unfair public administrators. B. Bolles. Ann Am Acad 363:23-7 Ja '66
Grievance procedures in the federal service. O. Pragan. Mo Labor R 89:609 Je '66
How to get a science job at home. J. A. Kraft, jr. Sci Digest 59:77-9 F '66
How to succeed in selling savings bonds; President Johnson's arm-twisting campaign. Life 61:4 Jl 8 '66
Patriotism by edict; text of follow-up communication to buy federal savings bonds. New Repub 155:9 Jl 16 '66
Public payroll, up and up and up. il Nations Bsns 54:105 S '66
Science overseas: jobs galore; condensation of How to get a job overseas. C. W. Casewit. il Sci Digest 59:71-7 F '66
Under fire: race check on federal workers. il U S News 60:12 My 23 '66
 See also
Bureaucracy
Civil service
Collective bargaining—Government employees
Negro government employees
Postal employees
Public officers
Strikes—United States—Government employees
United States—Congress—Employees

Appointment, qualifications, tenure, etc.
Brass pyramid. R. G. Sherrill. il Nation 203:49-51 Jl 11 '66
New computerized age; use of computers in Washington. J. W. Macy, jr. il Sat R 49:23-5+ Jl 23 '66

Salaries, allowances, etc.
Memo to economists: Uncle Sam wants you; demand by different agencies. il Bsns W p 160+ Ap 9 '66
New round of federal pay raises. il U S News 61:108 Jl 18 '66
Now it pays to work for the government. il U S News 60:85-7 Mr 21 '66

GOVERNMENT entertaining
Doing the L.B.J.; party for Prime Minister Jens Otto Krag. il Time 87:26 My 6 '66
Entertaining people; planning, staging and presenting social functions at White House. il McCalls 94:24+ N '66
Look what's going on in Washington. il U S News 60:56-7 My 30 '66
Lyndon's set. Nation 202:637 My 30 '66
Mrs Johnson talks about her love for the White House; with recipes. R. F. Pomeroy. il Redbook 127:72-8+ Jl '66
New twist, the LBJ; dance in honor of Danish Prime Minister. il Newsweek 67:27-8 My 9 '66
Partying: Great society style; gyrating dances, peekaboo dresses; excerpts from address, May 10, 1966. H. R. Gross. il U S News 60:10 My 23 '66
Pecksniffs squeeze the fun from a joyless bunch. H. Sidey. il Life 60:40B Je 17 '66
Washington's swinging scene: Kuwaiti, Moroccan; Algerian embassies' parties and people. il Newsweek 67:34-8 Je 20 '66
When 3,400 women visited the LBJ's; Campaign conference for Democratic women. il U S News 60:14 My 2 '66
When Washington entertains in halls of government. il U S News 60:78-9 Je 27 '66
 See also
Washington, D.C.—Social life and customs
GOVERNMENT ethics. See Political ethics
GOVERNMENT information
Bureaucracy unbound. Time 88:14 Jl 1 '66
GOVERNMENT investigations
Congressional investigations: business in the spotlight. il Nations Bsns 54:38-9+ F '66

Ferreting out the spies in business; Senate subcommittee investigation of industrial espionage. il Bsns W p51 Ap 2 '66
Government watch on 200 million Americans? il U S News 60:56-9 My 16 '66
You ought to be left alone. E. V. Long. Esquire 65:102-3 My '66
 See also
United States—President's commission on the assassination of President Kennedy

Aerospace industries
Aero R&D to be probed. Sci N 90:517 D 17 '66
Changes in store for AF non-profits; with editorial comment. M. Getler. Miss & Roc 18:14-15, 54 Ap 25 '66
House unit drops non-profit investigation. K. Johnsen. Aviation W 84:29-30 Ap 25 '66
What role for the think tanks? Defense dept. launches study of nonprofit research labs doing military work. il Bsns W p71-2+ My 14 '66

American telephone and telegraph company
AT&T case: what's ahead for the company now. il U S News 61:106-7 D 5 '66
AT&T masses its forces for FCC investigation. il Bsns W p38+ Je 4 '66
AT&T shareowners win a voice; protest FCC probe of the Bell system. Bsns W p 158+ O 22 '66
AT&T takes a hard look at its past and future; with editorial comment. il U S News 60:62-4, 100 Je 27 '66
Higher earning rate for the AT&T? U S News 60:10 Je 20 '66
Ma Bell & her friends. Time 87:92 F 18 '66
Ma Bell on the stand; hearings open. Newsweek 67:93 Je 20 '66
Telephone rates; FCC may come off second best. New Repub 154:8 F 19 '66
Where AT&T inquiry is really heading. il U S News 60:64-6 F 21 '66
Wringing the Bell. il Time 87:81 Je 17 '66

Baker case
Eavesdropping: an issue now in the Baker case. il U S News 61:8 N 28 '66

Drug trade
Clampdown on the drug industry; its meaning; interview. J. L. Goddard. il U S News 60:76-8+ My 16 '66

Government contracts
GAO may press probe of federal R&D. H. M. David. Miss & Roc 18:15 F 21 '66
House space report to ask detail on fiscal 1968 advanced plans. W. J. Normyle. Aviation W 84:30 Ap 18 '66
House unit fears tactical air studies stall production. Tech W 19:14 S 26 '66
McClellan to resume F-111 investigation. G. C. Wilson. Aviation W 85:16-17 Ag 22 '66
U.S. defenses seen suffering from DOD cost reduction. H. M. David. Tech W 19:20 S 19 '66

Government funded research
Federal laboratories: are they adjusting to changing needs? L. J. Carter. Science 154:1529-30 D 23 '66

Industrial pensions
More reins on pension plans? Bsns W p 136 Ap 30 '66

Ku Klux klan
HUAC vs. the KKK; with press comments. Sr Schol 88:16-17 Mr 11 '66
Knacker knark knipperdolling; hearings ended. Time 87:28 Mr 4 '66
Operation contempt; HUAC vs. KKK. T. Catchpole. Nat R 18:152 F 22 '66

Packaging
Big package flap. R. Tunley. Sat R 49:64+ Ap 9 '66
Truth in packaging; supermarket caper. J. Cross. il Nation 202:208-12 F 21 '66
GOVERNMENT labor policy. See United States—Labor policy
GOVERNMENT laboratories. See Laboratories, Government
GOVERNMENT lending
Another Johnson gimmick; expanded loan-participation plan. Nation 202:605 My 23 '66
LBJ plan for investors; certificates of participation in pool of government-owned loans. U S News 60:94-5 My 2 '66

GOVERNMENT lending—*Continued*
New force moves into money markets; with editorial comment. il Bsns W p 160+, 190 Je 25 '66
P.C. gimmick; participating certificates. Nation 204:37 Ja 9 '67
Small business loans; part of the poverty loan program to go to SBA. New Repub 155:9-10 S 24 '66

GOVERNMENT lotteries. See Lotteries

GOVERNMENT officials. See Public officers

GOVERNMENT ownership

Great Britain

Why bureaucrats can't run a business; British road and rail operations. J. N. Sites. Nations Bsns 54:35+ O '66

United States

World's biggest property owner. il U S News 60:18 Ap 18 '66
See also
United States—Government property

GOVERNMENT property. See United States— Government property

GOVERNMENT publications
Bibliographic organization in the federal government. H. Holzbauer. bibliog il Wilson Lib Bul 40:719-20+ Ap '66
Copyright and government; need for definition of publication of the United States government. C. G. Benjamin. il Library J 91:881-6 F 15 '66
Informative reading for consumers. Consumer Rep 31:100 Mr '66

Bibliography

Congressional documents relating to foreign policy. See issues of Department of state bulletin
Publications of the Department of state. See issues of Department of state bulletin
Source material; comp. by D. Wasson. See issues of Foreign affairs

GOVERNMENT publicity
See also
Government and the press

GOVERNMENT records. See Records

GOVERNMENT regulation of industry. See Industry and state

GOVERNMENT research
Industry, institutions, universities conduct NASA bio-sciences research. Aviation W 85:98-9 Ag 15 '66
Secret research at universities. Nation 203: 267-8 S 26 '66
See also
Ordnance research

GOVERNMENT secrets. See Official secrets

GOVERNMENT service. See Civil service; Public officers

GOVERNMENT spending policy
Dispute over LBJ's spending cuts. U S News 60:18 My 16 '66
How big is the Johnson deficit? excerpts from address, January 17, 1966. J. J. Williams. U S News 60:73 Ja 31 '66
If you wonder where government spending is headed. U S News 60:51-2 F 14 '66
Is government spending getting out of hand? excerpt from address, October 25, 1966. G. H. Mahon. U S News 61:79-80 N 7 '66
Needed: a watchdog. W. J. Coughlin. Tech W 20:50 Ja 9 '67
New way to roll out the pork barrel. il Nations Bsns 54:38-9+ Je '66
Pentagon dollars tip the scale; concerning new book, Defense purchases and regional growth, by Brookings institution. il Bsns W p 166+ Ap 9 '66
Putting a dollar sign on everything; Pentagon's planning-programming-budgeting system. il Bsns W p 122-4+ Jl 16 '66
Runaway spending; can LBJ check it? il U S News 61:29-30 D 19 '66
Tax take up, deficit down, and a surplus in '67? il U S News 60:99-100 Je 6 '66
Thumbs down on a capital budget; highlights of study by M. Comiez. il Bsns W p70+ F 19 '66
What price the Great society? C. Stevenson. Read Digest 88:49-53 Mr '66
Where government can cut spending; interview. E. B. Staats. il Nations Bsns 54:42-3+ D '66
See also
United States—Economic policy

GOVERNMENT statistics. See United States— Statistics

GOVERNMENT statistics, Economic. See Economic statistics

GOVERNMENT surplus. See Surplus products

GOVERNORS
As Republican governors look over the ranks for '68. il U S News 61:37-8 D 26 '66
Big three among Republican governors, what they urge. il U S News 62:17 Ja 16 '67
Creative localism; emphasis on reform. il Time 89:21 Ja 20 '67
Governors: Republican sweep. il U S News 61:45-6 N 21 '66
Governors speak; inaugural addresses, state-of-the-state speeches and legislative-launching talks. il Time 89:14-16 Ja 13 '67
Job the Republicans asked for. Life 61:4 N 25 '66
Signal for the statehouses; Republican governors. il Time 87:17-18 Je 3 '66
Society notes; swearing in. il Newsweek 69: 30-1 Ja 16 '67
We are very human; Democratic governors meet at LBJ ranch. il Newsweek 69:19 Ja 2 '67
See also
Southern governors conference
Women as governors

GOVERNORS (machinery)
See also
Automobiles—Speed governors

GOVERNORS conference, 1966
Abel gives governors the labor view. Bsns W p50 Jl 16 '66
Auditioning for '68; G. Romney and the issue of Vietnam. il Newsweek 68:21 Jl 18 '66
GOP: it's Romney vs. Nixon; report. J. Lindsay. il Newsweek 67:23 Je 6 '66

GOVERNOR'S cup race. See Motor boat racing

GOVERNORS wives
Why I feel sorry for Lurleen Wallace and Alabama. L. I. Smylie. il Ladies Home J 83:64+ S '66

GOVINDJEE. See Bedell, G. jt. auth.

GOWEN, Charles L.
Supreme court; address, March 1, 1966. Vital Speeches 32:404-7 Ap 15 '66

GOWING, Lawrence
Painting set free. Vogue 147:166-7+ Ap 1 '66
Turner's emissary; interview. New Yorker 42:36-7 Ap 2 '66

GOWLAND, Peter
Gowland's L.A. scene. Pop Phot 59:6+ D '66 [Monthly column] See issues of Popular photography
Novelist Henry Miller. il Pop Phot 58:66-7+ Mr '66

GOWON, Yakubu
Cracks in Africa's show window. por Bsns W p34 Ag 13 '66
Grisly record. por Time 88:43 D 9 '66
Man must whack. por Time 88:45 O 7 '66
On the razor's edge. il por Newsweek 68:44 Ag 15 '66

GOYA Y LUCIENTES, Francisco José de
Printmaking since Goya. F. Getlein. New Repub 154:27-8 Ap 23 '66

GRABENSTEIN, D. E. See Maycock, J. N. jt. auth.

GRABNER, Ruth
Calico pictures of storybook tales. Sch Arts 66:35 D '66

GRABOWSKI, Jim
Locks vs. Boom Boom. D. Jenkins. il por Sports Illus 25:20-3 Ag 22 '66

GRACE Patricia, consort of Rainier III, prince of Monaco
Flower; Slumber; poems. por McCalls 93:81 Je '66
about
How now, Princess Grace? B. Walters. por Ladies Home J 83:65 N '66
Princess Grace: how she lovingly raises her children; ed. by S. Fliegers. M. King. il pors Good H 162:74-7+ F '66

GRACE, W. R, and company
Deal between grandchildren; Miller brewing co. deal. il Time 88:108 S 30 '66

GRACE (at meals)
Speaking out; our prayers are meaningless. M. Boyd. Sat Eve Post 239:10+ Ag 27 '66

GRACE (theology)
Skeptics in misery. V. P. McCorry. America 114:238-9 F 12 '66

GRACIE mansion. See New York (city)—Gracie mansion

GRADE school athletics. See School athletics

GRADER, R. J. and others
X-ray spectra from three cosmic sources. bibliog Science 152:1499-504 Je 10 '66

GRADING and marking (students)
Downgrading the grade; campuses experimenting with pass-fail system. Newsweek 68: 103-4 N 7 '66

GRADING and marking (students)—*Continued*
Life & death grades; Selective service's classification for draft deferment for students. Time 87:70 Mr 25 '66
Russian roulette in the classroom; grades and the draft. N. Cousins. Sat R 49:22 Ap 23 '66
Your child may be in the wrong grade at school; findings of Gesell institute studies. F. L. Ilg and L. B. Ames. Read Digest 89:56-60 Ag '66
See also
Ungraded classes
GRADING of eggs. See Eggs—Grading and standardization
GRADING of meat. See Meat—Grading and standardization
GRADUATE school of business administration. See Harvard university—Graduate school of business administration
GRADUATE schools. See Colleges and universities—Graduate work
GRADUATE schools of education. See Colleges and universities—Education departments
GRADUATE students
Graduate student support. D. Wolfle. Science 152:19 Ap 1 '66; Discussion. 152:1458; 153:249, 479 Je 10, Jl 15, 29 '66
Graduate training in astronomy; letter. B. J. Bok. Science 154:590+ N 4 '66; Reply. E. G. Kovach. 154:1502 D 23 '66
GRADUATE work. See Colleges and universities—Graduate work
GRADUATES, College. See College graduates; College graduates, Women
GRADUATION. See Commencements
GRADUATION addresses. See Baccalaureate addresses
GRADUATION gifts. See Gifts
GRAEBNER, Clark
Bounce-ball, anyone? il por Newsweek 68:65-6 Ag 29 '66
Lot of horses. il por Time 88:44-5 Ag 26 '66
GRAEBNER, Norman A.
Limits of military aid. Cur Hist 50:353-7+ Je '66
GRAF, Rudolf F.
Build this amazing touch-controlled switch. Pop Sci 189:114-16 S '66
GRAF Zeppelin (airship) See Airships
GRAFF, Henry F.
Teach-in on Vietnam. N Y Times Mag p25+ Mr 20 '66
Wealth of presidents. Am Heritage 17:4-5+ O '66
GRAFF, M. M.
Crocuses for fall color. il Flower Grower 53:42-3 Ag '66
Some choice miniature iris for your garden. il Horticulture 44:30-1+ F '66
GRAFFITI
Cliff-hanging drama of art censorship; Lynne Seemayer's nude figure erased from Los Angeles cliff side. il Life 61:49 N 18 '66
Washroom wit; analytic study by H. Lomas and G. Weltman. il Newsweek 68:110+ O 10 '66
GRAFFMAN, Gary
Recordings. M. Mayer. il Esquire 65:30+ My '66
GRAFTING (surgery) See Transplantation of organs, tissues, etc.
GRAFTON, Samuel
Pressures that push children into the wrong careers. McCalls 93:66-7+ Je '66
GRAHAM, A. F. See Prevec, L. jt. auth.
GRAHAM, Bessie
Obituary
Pub W 190:48 S 19 '66
GRAHAM, Billy
God is not dead; interview. por U S News 60:74-80+ Ap 25 '66
about
Billy Graham, by J. Pollock. Review
Commonweal 85:61-3 O 14 '66. D. J. O'Hanlon
Billy Graham's crusade. D. Fisher. Commonweal 84:457-8 Jl 22 '66
Billy in London. Time 87:84+ Je 10 '66
Billy's victory in London. il por Time 88:64-5 Jl 15 '66
Boycotting Billy; students and faculty of Bob Jones university, Greenville, S.C. il Time 87:103 Mr 18 '66
Case of mistaken identity. Christian Cent 83:358 Mr 23 '66
Graham and King as ghetto-mates. Christian Cent 83:976 Ag 10 '66
Graham crusade: abdication of evangelism. C. Northcott. Christian Cent 83:673-5 My 25 '66; Discussion. 83:913 Jl 20 '66

Issue (and some miscellaneous trimmings) C. Fritchey. Harper 232:32+ My '66
London and conversion. America 114:847 Je 18 '66
Swinging crusade. Newsweek 68:87 Jl 18 '66
GRAHAM, Charles H.
Pipefitting job becomes threadless snap. il Bsns W p 134+ F 19 '66
GRAHAM, Dominick
Vietnam and the crisis in war. Yale R 55:391-402 Mr '66
GRAHAM, Donald
Taking a McNamara fellowship. Atlan 217:59-60 F '66
GRAHAM, Edward Harrison
Obituary
Nat Parks Mag 40:20 Jl '66
GRAHAM, Elizabeth W.
For the love of Stephanie; story. Seventeen 25:108-9 Jl '66
GRAHAM, Frank, Jr
Great Mexican war of 1946. Sports Illus 25:116-20+ S 19 '66
Tall in the saddle. Sports Illus 24:45-6+ Ap 11 '66
GRAHAM, Helen
Democracy in a test tube. Sr Schol 88:sup 13-14 Ap 22 '66
GRAHAM, James A. Maxtone
British skybikers take to the air. Pop Mech 126:106-9 D '66
GRAHAM, James J.
Backlash in Brooklyn. Commonweal 85:287-91 D 9 '66
GRAHAM, Janet
Beating the blues. Redbook 128:71+ Ja '67
Rule of thumb for the open road. Sports Illus 24:76-80+ Je 6 '66
Take a tip from Tom Sawyer. Parents Mag 41:40-1+ Jl '66
GRAHAM, John D.
News of art. pors Horizon 9:74-5 Wint '67
GRAHAM, Katharine (Meyer)
Katharine Graham. A. Schlesinger, jr. por Vogue 149:108-9 Ja 1 '67
GRAHAM, Martha
Lonely voyager. il pors Time 88:82 D 2 '66
Magic of Martha Graham. R. Gottlieb. Holiday 39:166+ My '66
Martha Graham: portrait of the lady as an artist; excerpt. L. Leatherman. il por Dance Mag 40:60-5 N '66
GRAHAM, Otto
Legal eagle and his boy scout. R. H. Boyle. il pors Sports Illus 25:54-60 Jl 25 '66
GRAHAM, Richard
Teacher corps head speaks out; interview, ed. by J. Lloyd. por Sr Schol 89:sup2-3 Ja 13 '67
GRAHAM, Robert A.
Latest charges against Pius XII. America 114:733-6 My 21 '66
Vatican peace initiatives. America 114:416 Mr 26 '66
GRAHAM, Robert E.
International infant? Duns R 88:151-4 N '66
GRAHAM, Sheilah
(ed) See Hamilton, G. Close-up: George Hamilton
GRAHAM, W. S.
Malcolm Mooney's land; poem. Poetry 108:393-8 S '66
GRAIL
Legends of the Grail. G. Bowers. Horn Bk 42:37-42 F '66
GRAIL motive. See Music—Themes, motives, etc.
GRAIN
See also names of cereal plants, e.g. Wheat
Drying
See also
Grain driers
Moisture content
What you need to know about moisture testers. W. J. Fletcher. il Suc Farm 64:89 S '66
Prices
Action in the pits; commodities trading. Time 88:73A Jl 1 '66
$10,000 fingers; spurt in trading. Newsweek 68:74 Jl 4 '66
Protein content
Are you wasting money on protein? J. Russell. il Farm J 90:36-7+ S '66
GRAIN driers
How about grain stirring? W. J. Fletcher. il Suc Farm 64:70 S '66
GRAIN elevators
Getting better service from your elevator. B. R. Ingram. Suc Farm 64:83 S '66

GRAIN trade
 Futures are golden in grain. il Bsns W p22-3 Jl 2 '66
GRAMMAR, English. See English language— Grammar
GRAM-negative bacteria. See Bacteria
GRAMONT, Sanche de. See De Gramont, S.
GRAND BAHAMA ISLAND
 Grand Bahama: island in the sun. A. H. Hepburn. il Sr Schol 87:sup6 Ja 7 '66
  See also
 Gambling—Grand Bahama Island
GRAND CANAL, China. See Canals—China
GRAND CANYON
 Battle of the wilderness. il Newsweek 68:108 O 3 '66
 Canyon war deepens. Bsns W p32 Jl 30 '66
 Dam the Grand Canyon? no! cries an Arizonan. J. W. Krutch. il Audubon Mag 68: 308-11 S '66
 Forester speaks; Grand Canyon controversy; letter. R. J. Lentz. Parks & Rec 1:675 S '66
 Grand Canyon: Colorado dams debated. L. J. Carter. il Science 152:1600-5 Je 17 '66
 How to save the Grand Canyon and water the desert, too; interview. B. M. Goldwater. il U S News 61:124-6 O 24 '66; Reply. D. Brower. 61:60-1 D 12 '66
 People of the blue-green waters. D. Janson. il Audubon Mag 68:464-9 N '66
 Ruin for the Grand Canyon? R. C. Bradley. il Audubon Mag 68:34-41 Ja '66; Same abr. Read Digest 88:193-8 Ap '66
 Ruin for the Grand Canyon? R. Richter. il Audubon Mag 68:216-216a Jl '66
 Storm over the Grand Canyon. H. Nash; C. Hayden. il Parks & Rec 1:496-501+ Je '66; Reply. G. Woodgates. 1:610 Ag '66
 Water project that dried up; Colorado River project. il Bsns W p72+ S 3 '66
GRAND CANYON DAMS. See Dams
GRAND CANYON NATIONAL PARK
 Last days of the Colorado? G. Staveley and B. East. il Outdoor Life 138:24-7+ Jl '66
 Senator Goldwater vs. the Sierra club; statement. B. M. Goldwater. Nat R 18:918-20 S 20 '66
 Their constituents are the next generation. A. C. Ringland. il Am For 72:8 Ag '66
GRAND COULEE power and reclamation project
 Grand Coulee Dam to be monitored by computer. Sci N 90:120 Ag 20 '66
GRAND national steeplechase. See Horse racing
GRAND ole opry (radio program) See Radio broadcasting—Music
GRAND opera. See Opera
GRAND prix endurance races. See Automobile racing
GRAND prix of Le Mans. See Automobile racing
GRAND prix of Volkswagens. See Automobile racing
GRAND TETON NATIONAL PARK
 Ladybird country. H. Sutton. il Sat R 49: 40+ O 1 '66
 Pesticide program in Grand Teton National Park. A. Murie. il Nat Parks Mag 40:17-19 Je '66
GRAND VALLEY state college, Allendale, Mich.
 Oxidized metal and glass for crisp precision. il Arch Rec 140:144-6 N '66
GRANDBOIS, Alain
 Canadian chronicle. R. Howard. Poetry 108: 50 Ap '66
GRANDE, Luke M.
 Book of the month. Cath World 203:368 S '66
 Demise of a party-people; poem. Harper 232: 109 Ap '66
GRANDFATHERS. See Grandparents
GRANDMOTHERS. See Grandparents
GRANDPARENTS
 Life with grandma. E. M. Stern. il Parents Mag 41:36-7+ Jl '66
 Margaret Mead answers: changing role of grandparents in American society today. M. Mead. Redbook 127:28+ Je '66
  See also
 Foster grandparents program

  Anecdotes, facetiae, satire, etc.
 Grandfather and the racquet-tailed drongo. J. Rhoades. il Sports Illus 24:60-4+ F 28 '66
Les GRANDS ballets canadiens. See Ballet— Canada
GRANFIELD, Patrick
 (ed) See Neibuhr, R. Interview with Reinhold Niebuhr

GRANGER, Christopher
 Friendly debate between two professionals; letters. por Am For 72:30+ Ja; 12+ F '66
GRÄNGESBERG company. See Sweden—Industries
GRANITE industry and trade
 New age for the rock of ages. il Fortune 73: 142-5 Mr '66
GRANT, Allan
 When a camera gets under the skin. il Pop Phot 59:118-19 O '66
GRANT, Annette
 Dance, art, & eating. Mlle 64:168-9+ N '66
 New deal for an old problem. Mlle 63:133-5+ Je '66
 Open for business. Mlle 63:142-3+ S '66
 Ready, steady, go! Mlle 62:188-90 Mr '66
GRANT, Bob
 Scuba-diving fire-eaters. Pop Mech 126:102-4 Ag '66
 Three-D color TV. Pop Mech 125:192 Ap '66
GRANT, Cary
 Cary Grant: the perennial dreamboat in a new role. S. Gordon. il pors Look 30:70-4 Jl 26 '66
GRANT, Donald
 If he wants peace. . . Nation 203:338-9 O 10 '66
GRANT, Gerald
 Desegregation in the North. Sat R 49:75-6+ D 17 '66
 Tracking: what it means, how it works. Parents Mag 41:64-5+ bibliog(p32) S '66
GRANT, Mary Kent
 Mystery, detective, suspense. See first issue of each month of Library journal
GRANT, Richard E.
 Permian productoid brachiopod: life history. bibliog Science 152:660-2 Ap 29 '66
GRANT, Ulysses Simpson, 1822-1885
 Two porches, two parades. B. Catton. por Am Heritage 17:64-5 Je '66
GRANT, Vernon W.
 Help for troubled marriages. Parents Mag 41:25-7+ Jl '66
GRANT, William Thomas
 Grant surrenders. por Time 88:79 Jl 8 '66
GRANT, W. T, company
 Grant surrenders. Time 88:79 Jl 8 '66
GRANTS to colleges and universities. See Colleges and universities—Gifts, legacies, etc.
GRAPE industry. See Viticulture
GRAPE vines. See Grapes
GRAPEFRUIT
  See also
 Cookery—Fruit
GRAPES
 Ephraim Bull and his Concord grape. D. S. Manks. il Horticulture 44:30-1+ O '66
 Grapes for your garden. G. L. Slate. il Horticulture 44:16-17+ N '66
 In the Greek islands grape vines as leafy eyebrows. il Sunset 137:258 O '66
 Sex conversion in a male vitis vinifera L. by a kinin. S. S. Negi and H. P. Olmo. bibliog il Science 152:1624 Je 17 '66
GRAPHIC arts
 Graphic designer in a college community. B. C. Taylor. il Am Artist 30:56-61+ S '66
 New events in the world of the graphic arts; ed. by J. Levy. Am Artist 30:A-B [83-4] Ap '66
 Swiss designer Armin Hofmann on future design. il Pub W 189:82-3 Ap 4 '66
 Systems approach to automation is explained to R&E council; annual conference. Pub W 189:154-6+ Je 13 '66
  See also
 American institute of graphic arts
 Engraving
 Push pin studios

  Exhibitions
 Mixed-up medium; display at Manhattan's Museum of modern art. Time 88:80 S 30 '66
GRAPHIC arts marketing information service. See Printing industries of America, incorporated—Graphic arts marketing information service
GRAPHIC arts research and engineering council. See Research and engineering council of the graphic arts industry, incorporated
GRAPHIC arts technical foundation
 Education council merges with GATF. Pub W 190:126 D 5 '66
 GATF annual meeting report; changes are noted in staff, organization and policy. Pub W 189:105-6 My 2 '66
 GATF awarded $75,089 for dissemination work. Pub W 190:124 S 5 '66
GRAPHIC methods
  See also
 Organization charts

GRAPHIC recorders. See Recording instruments

GRAPHOLOGY
Graphology, science with a future. D. S. Anthony. il Sci Digest 59:55-66 Mr '66

GRASS, Günter
Gruppe 47 at Princeton. C. Mayer-Amery. Nation 202:588-90 My 16 '66
Günter Grass is a different drummer. K. Botsford. il pors N Y Times Mag p28-9+ My 8 '66
Off Broadway. E. Oliver. New Yorker 42: 120+ My 7 '66
Plebeians rehearse the uprising. Criticism Life 60:17 F 18 '66
World of Günter Grass. Criticism Nation 202:597 My 16 '66

GRASS airfields. See Airports—Surfaces

GRASSES
Green elephant; grass to the homeowner. B. La Fontaine. il Sports Illus 24:68-70+ Ap 4 '66
Growth-inhibiting action of tris(1-aziridinyl)-phosphine oxide in grasses. T. W. Holmsen and J. K. Leasure. bibliog il Science 153: 1659 S 30 '66
You feel the difference when you walk on zoysia! il Flower Grower 53:49 Ap '66
Your turfgrass headache; what variety? T. Grether. Parks & Rec 1:504-5 Je '66
See also
Bamboo
Harvesting
Hay
Lawns

Diseases and pests
Problem of insects; address, November 1965. A. S. Deal. il Parks & Rec 1:732-3+ S '66

GRASSHOPPER eggs. See Insects—Eggs

GRATITUDE
See also
Thanksgiving

GRAU, Shirley Ann
Condor passes; story. Atlan 219:62-7 Ja '67

GRAUMAN, Lawrence, Jr
Mark Twain beside himself. New Repub 155: 31-4 Jl 16 '66
Who should be drafted? New Repub 155:11-12 D 10 '66

GRAVELY, Samuel Lee, Jr
Negro to command destroyer. por Negro Hist Bul 29:64 D '65
Proud new victory for navy destroyer. il pors Ebony 21:25-8+ Jl '66

GRAVER, Lawrence
Commonplace book of Doris Lessing. New Repub 154:27-9 Ap 2 '66

GRAVES, Clare W.
Deterioration of work standards. Harvard Bsns R 44:117-22+ S '66

GRAVES, Eleanor
Great dinners; menu and recipes. See issues of Life
(ed) See Falk, M. Woman on her way to a miracle

GRAVES, Elizabeth Minot
Selected list of children's books (cont) Commonweal 84:287-94; 85:172-81 My 27, N 11 '66
What price categories. Commonweal 84:285-6 My 27 '66

GRAVES, Robert
Face in the mirror; Portrait; Your private way; I will write; Like snow; poems. N Y Times Mag p37, 142, 149, 156 O 30 '66
Four poems: Queen Silver and King Gold; The near eclipse; On giving; The utter rim of nowhere. New Repub 155:19 N 26 '66
Gooseflesh abbey; poem. Atlan 218:136 N '66
If love becomes a game; poem. Atlan 218:93 Ag '66
In perspective; poem. Harper 233:20 O '66
Necklace; poem. Atlan 218:106 S '66
Palm tree; poem. Opera N 31:17 D 10 '66
Tangled thread; Lure of murder; Loving true, flying blind; poems. Mlle 62:14 Ja '66
Two poems: Mist; Sun-face and moon-face. New Repub 155:23 N 12 '66
about
Robert Graves's secret vice pays off. A. S. Mehdevi. il pors N Y Times Mag p36-7+ O 30 '66

GRAVES, Walter A.
To take and to tape. NEA J 56:62-4 Ja '67

GRAVES, William
California: golden magnet. Nat Geog Mag 129:595-679 My '66

GRAVES, Soldiers. See Service mens graves

GRAVINA, Peter
Artists in the kitchen. Opera N 30:26-9 Mr 19 '66

GRAVITATION
Lunar Orbiter: tracking data indicate properties of moon's gravitational field. W. H. Michael, jr. and others. Science 153:1102 S 2 '66
Mice thrive in high gravity. il Sci N 89:237 Ap 9 '66
Orbiting potato. J. Lear; discussion. Sat R 48:92 D 4 '65; 49:72 F 5 '66
Zero-gravity makes fires put themselves out. Sci N 90:398 N 12 '66
See also
Weightlessness

GRAY, David
Changing pattern of American life; excerpts from address. por Parks & Rec 1:212-14+ Mr '66

GRAY, Donald P.
New books. Cath World 202:312-14 F '66

GRAY, Elisha, 1906-
Problems of inflation; excerpts from statement before the Joint economic committee of Congress. por Duns R 87:21-2+ Ap '66
about
Whirlpool moves into living room. por Bsns W p38 Ag 20 '66

GRAY, Francine du Plessix. See Du Plessix. F.

GRAY, Francis C. Jr
Hold back the sea. Yachting 120:54+ Jl '66

GRAY, Harry
How Litton keeps it up, the view from inside; interviews, ed. by D. Seligman and T. A. Wise. por Fortune 74:152-4+ S '66

GRAY, Jack
Agrarian policies. Bul Atomic Sci 22:32-9 Je '66

GRAY, James
Great payoff. Newsweek 68:35 D 12 '66

GRAY, Joseph H.
Miniaturia at the spring show. Hobbies 71:123 Ag '66

GRAY, L. F.
How to have instant hot water. Pop Sci 188: 142 Mr '66

GRAY, Ralph
How do you move the mountain into the classroom? NEA J 55:34-6 Mr '66

GRAY, Wood
(comp) Articles and other books received: United States. See issues of American historical review

GRAY whales. See Whales

GRAY wolves. See Wolves

GRAYBEAL, William S.
What the college faculty thinks. NEA J 55: 48-9 Ap '66

GRAYWACKE
Sediments from the lower Columbia River and origin of graywacke. J. T. Whetten. bibliog il Science 152:1057-8 My 20 '66

GREAT BASIN NATIONAL PARK (proposed)
See National parks and reserves—United States

GREAT BRITAIN
Britain seems willing to sink giggling into the sea. H. Fairlie. il N Y Times Mag p28-9+ Je 12 '66
New Britain. C. Booker. il Esquire 65:84-7+ F '66
Reports of Britain's death. I. Macleod. For Affairs 45:88-97 O '66
State of the Nation. C. Brogan. Nat R 18: 467-8 My 17 '66
What's wrong in Britain; a noted editor looks at his country; interview, ed. by J. Fromm. M. Muggeridge. il U S News 61:67-9 Jl 25 '66
See also
Advertising—Great Britain
Airplanes, Military—Great Britain
Automobile industry and trade—Great Britain
Automobile touring—Great Britain
Aviation—Great Britain
Ballet—Great Britain
Budget—Great Britain
Children—Great Britain
Colleges and universities—Great Britain
Computer industry—Great Britain
Crime and criminals—Great Britain
Divorce—Great Britain
Education—Great Britain
Finance—Great Britain
Fishing—Great Britain
Gas industry—Great Britain
Government ownership—Great Britain
Hospitals—Great Britain
Hotels, taverns, etc.—Great Britain
Immigration and emigration—Great Britain
Insurance, Unemployment—Great Britain
Jews in Great Britain
Justice, Administration of—Great Britain

GREAT BRITAIN—See also—*Continued*
  Labor and laboring classes—Great Britain
  Libraries—Great Britain
  Medical service—Great Britain
  Money—Great Britain
  Negroes in Great Britain
  Newspapers—Great Britain
  Periodicals—Great Britain
  Police—Great Britain
  Price regulation by government—Great Britain
  Prisons—Great Britain
  Publishers and publishing—Great Britain
  Science—Great Britain
  Severn River
  Space research—Great Britain
  Strikes—Great Britain
  Taxation—Great Britain
  Television broadcasting—Great Britain
  Theater—Great Britain
  Trade unions—Great Britain
  Transportation—Great Britain
  Trials—Great Britain
  Unemployment—Great Britain
  Wages—Great Britain
  World war, 1939-1945—Great Britain
  Youth—Great Britain

Antiquities
Quest for Camelot. il Time 88:53 Ag 12 '66

Appropriations and expenditures
  See also
Budget—Great Britain

Armed forces
Auld song's end; new defense program. il Newsweek 67:48+ Mr 7 '66

Appropriations and expenditures
Mr Wilson under fire: east-of-Suez defense debate. B. Wenham. New Repub 155:14 N 5 '66
U.K. sacrifices carrier for F-111A order. H. J. Coleman. il Aviation W 84:21-2 F 28 '66
Veering toward a vote; posture for the 1970s. il Time 87:36 Mr 4 '66

Forces in Germany (Federal Republic)
Massive retaliation? Newsweek 68:52 O 31 '66
Payments are the problem. Time 88:34 O 28 '66

Army
Scottish regiments
Whirl of kilts, the skirl of pipes: the Royal Highland fusiliers tour. J. Lord. Life 61:12 O 21 '66

Cabinet
Musical chairs. Newsweek 68:68 Ag 22 '66
Old and new; Wilson's new Cabinet. Newsweek 67:56 Ap 18 '66
Sideways shuffle. Time 88:30+ Ag 19 '66

Caricatures and cartoons
Come to Britain. Saxon. New Yorker 42:28-33 Jl 30 '66

Civilization
  See also
Great Britain—Intellectual life

Colonial office
Imperial Britain, RIP. C. Brogan. Nat R 18:928-30 S 20 '66
No time for tears; surrender of functions to the Commonwealth office. Time 88:26 Ag 12 '66
Striking the flag. Newsweek 68:40 Ag 15 '66

Colonies
  See also
Commonwealth of nations
Fiji
Seychelles (islands)

Commerce
Beating de Gaulle's veto; Britain's new drive to join the Common market. K. Kyle. New Repub 155:17-20 D 10 '66
Letter from London; Britain and Common market. M. Panter-Downes. New Yorker 42:204+ D 3 '66
  See also
Investments, Foreign (by Great Britain)

Commercial treaties and agreements
U.S. and U.K. sign agreement updating U.S. tariff concessions. Dept State Bul 54:719-20 My 2 '66

Defenses
Britain dons shield of auxiliary police. Bsns W p36-7 F 26 '66
England, France combine for strength. H. J. Coleman. Aviation W 84:91+ Mr 7 '66
  See also
Great Britain—Royal air force

Economic conditions
As the British drift... il U S News 61:66-7 Jl 25 '66
Atlantic report (cont) Atlan 217:16+ F '66
Belt tightener. Time 88:86 Jl 22 '66
Britain at the brink; with reports by A. Simmons and A. de Borchgrave. il Newsweek 68:32-6+ Jl 25 '66
Britain needs a second industrial revolution. A. Shonfield. il N Y Times Mag p32-3+ Ag 21 '66
Britain tries for a comeback, but ... il U S News 60:44-5 Je 6 '66
Britain under socialism. O. Gass. bibliog f Commentary 41:65-72 F '66
Britain: win some, lose some. Newsweek 68:32+ Jl 18 '66
British incomes experience; excerpt from address. E. H. P. Brown. Mo Labor R 89:634-7 Je '66
England gambles for survival. H. Ehrlich. il Look 30:27-35 N 29 '66
Never have so many done so little for so much. il Time 88:74-5 Jl 1 '66
Party will soon be over: Tom Wolfe and Time can go home again. B. Wenham. New Repub 156:14-15 Ja 7 '67
Planned recession for Britain; how it's working. il U S News 61:70 O 3 '66
Shrinking pains of mini-England. G. Farmer. il Life 61:73-4+ D 16 '66
Special report. il Bsns W p 118+ S 10 '66
Still freezing. Time 88:105 D 9 '66
Too much deflation? Time 88:97-8 N 4 '66
Two island nations: a study in contrasts. il U S News 62:58-60 Ja 16 '67
What's the matter with the British businessman? S. White. Read Digest 88:207-8+ Ap '66
Will recession save Great Britain? il Newsweek 68:86-8 N 28 '66
World through Galbraith's eyes; interview, ed. by A. Lewis. J. K. Galbraith. il N Y Times Mag p25+ D 18 '66
  See also
Budget—Great Britain
Labor and laboring classes—Great Britain
Money—Great Britain
Unemployment—Great Britain
Wages—Great Britain

Economic policy
Austerity in Britain pays its first dividend. Bsns W p50+ N 12 '66
Belt tightener. Time 88:86 Jl 22 '66
Bolder policies for British technology? V. K. McElheny. Science 152:741-4 My 6 '66
Britain gulps but takes its medicine. il Newsweek 68:37 Ag 15 '66
Britain's battle for the pound. America 115:149 Ag 13 '66
Britain's fight to save the pound. Bsns W p 158 Ag 20 '66
Britain's squeeze hurts. il Bsns W p40 S 3 '66
British economic situation; address, July 20, 1966. H. Wilson Vital Speeches 32:642-6 Ag 15 '66
Can austerity for Britain save the pound this time? il U S News 61:61-2 Ag 1 '66
Freeze & squeeze. Time 88:19 Jl 29 '66
Future of sterling. H. C. Wallich. Newsweek 68:73 Ag 8 '66
Gas and the brakes. H. C. Wallich. Newsweek 67:91 My 2 '66
Mr Wilson goes to Washington; more economics. il Newsweek 68:32 Ag 8 '66
More weight to the pound; H. Wilson's measures. Time 87:96+ F 18 '66
1966 battle of Britain; with editorial comments. il Bsns W p 143-4, 175-8+. 200 N 19 '66
Radical cures, and radical dangers. il Newsweek 68:39-40 Ag 1 '66
Settling in to stay; austerity program. il Newsweek 68:44 S 26 '66
Severest controls in peacetime history. Time 88:40 O 14 '66
Still freezing. Time 88:105 D 9 '66
Strong medicine for Britain's economic ills. C. Sterling. il Reporter 35:47-9 N 17 '66
Travel & travail. il Time 88:28+ Ag 5 '66
Victory gives Wilson strong grip on future. Bsns W p 119 Ap 9 '66
Wage freeze gets a cool reception; labor fears it will create unemployment. il Bsns W p 160+ O 15 '66
Why Britain needs Wilson's recession. Life 61:4 Ag 5 '66
Wilson clamps down on British economy; freeze on wages, prices and dividends. il Bsns W p31 Jl 23 '66
Wilson under fire. Time 88:25 Ag 12 '66
Wilson's double trouble; both political left and right oppose anti-inflationary program. il Bsns W p24 Jl 30 '66

GREAT BRITAIN—*Continued*

Economic relations

Back for another go; Common market. Newsweek 68:64 N 21 '66

Beating de Gaulle's veto; Britain's new drive to join the Common market. K. Kyle. New Repub 155:17-20 D 10 '66

Britain's choice. A. de Borchgrave. il Newsweek 68:35-6+ Jl 25 '66

Testing the market. Time 88:47 N 18 '66

Rhodesia

Masquerade at sea fails for Rhodesia; Britain scuttles oil ship to Rhodesia. il Bsns W p41-2 Ap 16 '66

South Africa

Oil of discord; African effort to force Britain to embark on crusade against South Africa. Nation 202:477-8 Ap 25 '66

Foreign relations

Britain's choice. A. de Borchgrave. il Newsweek 68:35-6+ Jl 25 '66

George Brown is too much. A. Lewis. il N Y Times Mag p6-7+ D 25 '66

View from Europe. G. Lichtheim. Commentary 42:49-55 Jl '66

Africa

Great Britain and the African peace settlement of 1919. W. R. Louis. bibliog f Am Hist R 71:875-92 Ap '66

China

See also
China—History—War of 1840-1842

Europe, Western

Once more to market? Time 87:38+ My 20 '66

Rhodesia

Admission of failure; failure of British policy. il Time 88:35-6 D 16 '66

Letter from London. M. Panter-Downes. New Yorker 42:54-5 D 24 '66

Rhodesia: the fight goes on. il Newsweek 68:33+ D 19 '66

Storm signals on Rhodesia. A. Lejeune. Nat R 18:1309-10 D 27 '66

U.S. and U.K. hold talks on Southern Rhodesia; joint statement, December 1, 1966. Dept State Bul 55:965 D 26 '66

Russia

New Mr Brown; trip to Moscow. il Newsweek 68:44 D 5 '66

Spain

Will Spain win out in fight for Rock? il Bsns W p36-7 Mr 5 '66

Writing on the Rock; Anglo-Spanish conference. N. Mostert. Reporter 34:28-31 Je 30 '66

United States

Britain brings its woes to Washington. U S News 61:25-6 Ag 8 '66

Mr Wilson goes to Washington. il Newsweek 68:32 Ag 8 '66

President Johnson confers with British Prime Minister; exchange of toasts, July 29, 1966. L. B. Johnson; H. Wilson. Dept State Bul 55:265-8 Ag 22 '66

Reasons of state: Hanoi-Haiphong raids condemned. Newsweek 68:40 Jl 11 '66

Socialist landslide in Britain, its meaning to U.S. U S News 60:6 Ap 11 '66

Vietnam puts a strain on U.S. ties to Britain; Prime Minister Wilson criticizes. Bsns W p30 Jl 16 '66

Wilson's mission: a test of U.S.-British partnership. il U S News 61:33-4 Ag 1 '66

History

See also
Hastings, Battle of, 1066

Bibliography

Articles and other books received; comp. by L. H. Carlson. See issues of American historical review

Textbooks

History is a dangerous subject: findings of Anglo-United States team survey of secondary school textbooks. R. A. Billington; discussion. Sat R 49:68+ F 19 '66

Norman period, 1066-1154

900 years and all that; British festivals. H. Sutton. il Sat R 49:52-3 Mr 5 '66

Norman conquest. K. M. Setton. il Nat Geog Mag 130:206-51 Ag '66

Tudors, 1485-1603

See also
Henry VIII, king of England

Victorian period, 1837-1901

Other Victorians, by S. Marcus. Review Commentary 42:78+ N '66. D. Jacobson New Repub 155:19-20 S 3 '66. P. Toynbee

Victorian pornography and other fallibilities. E. Moers. Harper 233:119-20+ O '66

Afghan wars

See Afghan wars

20th century

Muddling through chaos. T Roszak. Nation 202:428-31 Ap 11 '66

World war, 1939-1945

See World war, 1939-1945—Great Britain

History, Naval

Great mutiny, by J. Dugan. Review Reporter 34:53-4 Mr 24 '66. A. Ward

House of lords

See Great Britain—Parliament—House of lords

Industries

Cash on the barrelhead; government's grants to industry. Newsweek 67:72 Ja 31 '66

Hottest new smelter does two jobs at once; Imperial smelting corp, London. il Bsns W p 166-8 Je 4 '66

Little big wheel in the auto industry; London's Lesney company. il Bsns W p 178-80 Mr 26 '66

Marriages of necessity; companies unite in bigger and more efficient combines. Time 88:69 D 23 '66

Technology in Britain: new moves. V. K. McElheny. Science 153:619-20 Ag 5 '66

See also
Airplane industry and trade—Great Britain
Computer industry—Great Britain
English electric company
Imperial chemical industries, limited
Moving picture industry—Great Britain
Shipbuilding
Tobacco industry and trade

Intellectual life

Affluence after anger; English cultural generation of the 1950s. R. Williams. Nation 203:676-7 D 19 '66

British renaissance. F. Getlein. New Repub 155:27-8 S 3 '66

Kings and rulers

Norman conquest. K. M. Setton. il Nat Geog Mag 130:206-51 Ag '66

See also
Great Britain—Royal family

Moral conditions

Other Victorians, by S. Marcus. Review Commentary 42:78+ N '66. D. Jacobson New Repub 155:19-20 S 3 '66. P. Toynbee

National health service

Britain's Rx. for our drug addicts. J. Kobler. il Sat Eve Post 239:74-8 Ag 13 '66

British medicine. J. Walsh. Science 154:365-8 O 21 '66

Fugitive British doctors. R. Kirk. Nat R 18:1113 N 1 '66

New emigrés: British doctors head for U.S. in large numbers. J. Walsh. Science 154:494-6 O 28 '66

Navy

Auld song's end; new defense program. il Newsweek 67:48+ Mr 7 '66

Britannia's waning rule of the waves. Life 60:4 Mr 11 '66

Great mutiny, by J. Dugan. Review Am Heritage 17:68-9 F '66. B. Catton

None if by sea; Britain's decision to buy F-111. W. J. Coughlin. Miss & Roc 18:50 F 28 '66

U.K. sacrifices carrier for F-111A order. H. J. Coleman. il Aviation W 84:21-2 F 28 '66

See also
Warships—Great Britain

Nobility

Blue blood; glorification of Norman blood. J. H. Plumb. Sat R 49:27-8 O 29 '66

GREAT BRITAIN—*Continued*

Parliament

House of commons

From Britain; a long Parliament. J. M. Cameron. Commonweal 84:144-5 Ap 22 '66
Laborious Parliament; Commons summoned to a parliamentary session by the Queen. il Time 87:35-6 Ap 29 '66
Old mother Parliament; need for reform. il Newsweek 68:54-5 N 7 '66

House of lords

Other place. S. Hagerty. il Newsweek 67:40 F 14 '66
Sex and the lords; beginning to show effect of nonhereditary element. B. Wenham. New Repub 154:9-10 F 12 '66

Politics and government

Atlantic report (cont) Atlan 217:16+ F '66
Britain at the brink; with reports by A. Simmons and A. de Borchgrave. il Newsweek 68:32-6+ Jl 25 '66
Britain: win some, lose some; Vietnam policy and economic pressures. Newsweek 68:32+ Jl 18 '66
Dividing the critics; H. Wilson's answer to his critics. Time 87:35-6 Je 24 '66
How the Duke of Windsor lost his throne. W. M. A. Beaverbrook. il Sat Eve Post 239:38-42+ Ja 29 '66
Keeping his counsel; options open for date of general election. Newsweek 67:52+ F 21 '66
Laborious Parliament; Commons summoned to a parliamentary session by the Queen. il Time 87:35-6 Ap 29 '66
Letter from Britain. R. Williams. See issues of Nation to September 1966
Letter from London. M. Panter-Downes. New Yorker 42:68+ Jl 23 '66
Mr Wilson sees it through. il Newsweek 67:31-2 F 7 '66
Post-imperial Britain. G. Lichtheim. Commentary 42:71-80 O '66
Revolts from the left. Time 87:31 F 18 '66
Sex and the lords; liberalizing the laws on homosexuality and abortion. B. Wenham. New Repub 154:9-10 F 12 '66
Standing up to labor: unpolitical but practical. F. Morley. Nations Bsns 53:25-6 D '65
Veering toward a vote. il Time 87:36 Mr 4 '66
View from Europe. G. Lichtheim. Commentary 42:49-55 Jl '66
Wilson dispersing aviation ministry tasks. H. J. Coleman. Aviation W 84:27 Je 27 '66
Wilson, the juggler. B. Wenham. New Repub 154:9-10 Ap 23 '66
Wilson's big chance. Life 60:6 Ap 15 '66
Winds of change: 1914-39, by H. Macmillan. Review
  Atlan 218:141-3 O '66. O. Handlin
  Sat R 49:99-100 O 8 '66. E. M. Yoder, jr
See also
Conservative party (Great Britain)
Elections—Great Britain
Great Britain—Cabinet
Labor party (Great Britain)
Political campaigns—Great Britain
Political parties—Great Britain

Popular culture

Late transplant: why I left London for New York. A. Pryce-Jones. Harper 233:11-12+ Ag '66

Population

See also
Immigration and emigration—Great Britain

Prime ministers conferences

See Prime ministers conferences

Protectorates

See also
Trucial States

Race problems

Colored minorities and present British policies. E. M. Bussey. Mo Labor R 89:1111-15 O '66
See also
Negroes in Great Britain

Religious institutions and affairs

Billy Graham's crusade; religious attitudes. D. Fisher. Commonweal 84:457-8 Jl 22 '66
England; religious news. C. Northcott. Christian Cent 83:873-4 Jl 6 '66
See also
England—Religious institutions and affairs

Royal air force

U.K. sacrifices carrier for F-111A order. H. J. Coleman. il Aviation W 84:21-2 F 28 '66

Royal family

Can Britain afford its royal family? il U S News 61:16 N 28 '66
Future of Prince Charles. C. B. Luce. McCalls 94:32+ N '66

Social conditions

Behind Britain's swingers. H. Brandon. Sat R 49:12+ Jl 16 '66
Swing, Britannia. W. Pfaff. Commonweal 84:248-9 My 20 '66

Social life and customs

English madness; Weekend literary competitions. P. Rowlett. Commonweal 84:475-6 Jl 22 '66
Shrinking pains of mini-England. G. Farmer. il Life 61:73-4+ D 16 '66
Surfeit of money and honey; swinging England. il Bsns W p 148+ Jl 16 '66
See also
Christmas—Great Britain
Great Britain—Nobility

GREAT Britain and the United States. See England and the United States

GREAT Danes
Dog days for a motherless monkey; gibbon courts Great Dane. il Look 30:M20+ N 29 '66

GREAT FALLS, Mont.

Galleries and museums

Russell gallery at Great Falls. J. Meyer. il Am Artist 30:26-9+ N '66

GREAT fire of London. See London—Fire, 1666

GREAT horned owls. See Owls

GREAT indoors; drama. See Kamp, I.

GREAT LAKES
Aging Great Lakes. C. F. Powers and A. Robertson. il Sci Am 215:94-100+ bibliog (p 160) N '66
Great Lakes research: report on ninth conference. B. M. McCormac and J. E. Ash. Science 152:1773-4+ Je 24 '66
O Keewatin! trip on a real, old-fashioned passenger steamer. R. Bissell. il Holiday 40:42-51+ Ag '66
Sailing the eighth sea. J. D. Scott. Redbook 126:49 Mr '66
Three-ship navy fights Great Lakes pollution. Sci N 90:105 Ag 13 '66
See also
Erie, Lake

GREAT LAKES booksellers association
Great Lakes booksellers hold first annual meeting. Pub W 190:59 O 31 '66

GREAT LAKES REGION
See also
Fishing—Great Lakes Region
Hunting—Great Lakes Region

GREAT LAKES-St Lawrence waterway. See St Lawrence Seaway

GREAT LAKES Shakespeare festival
Theater. H. Hewes. Sat R 49:39 Ag 13 '66

GREAT LAKES shipping. See Inland water transportation

GREAT men
Americans not everybody knows. C. W. Ferguson. See issues of PTA magazine
Great men, great events. UNESCO Courier 19:30-1 Mr '66
1787, by C. Rossiter. Review
  Nat R 18:539-40 My 31 '66. J. Lobdell
  Sat R 49:38 Ap 2 '66. W. R. Jacobs
Unknockables. il Esquire 65:84-5 Je '66
See also
Celebrities
Leadership

Anecdotes, facetiae, satire, etc.

Freeman's guide to unsatisfactory people. N. B. Freeman. il Nat R 18:924-5 S 20 '66
Weary titans; search for instances of surprising languor in distinguished men. H. F. Ellis. New Yorker 42:52-3 O 15 '66

GREAT NECK, N.Y.
Negro shortage. Newsweek 67:82 F 28 '66

GREAT NECK PLAZA, N.Y.
Brighter future for shoppers. F. B. Nuss. il Am City 81:141-2 My '66

GREAT PLAINS
See also
Paleontology—Great Plains

GREAT SALT LAKE
Reaping the minerals in Great Salt Lake. il Bsns W p94-6 O 15 '66
Sailing the inland brine. J. K. Full. il Yachting 120:42-3+ Ag '66

GREAT SALT LAKE DESERT
Salt in a pinch; Bonneville Flats. J. McFarland. il Hot Rod 19:62-4+ S '66

GREAT seal of the United States. See United States—Seals

GREAT SMOKY MOUNTAINS
Forests of the Smokies. F. C. Davis. il Liv Wildn 30:6-9 Spr '66
Mountain notebook 1950. H. Broome. il Liv Wildn 29:3-13 Aut '65
See also
Great Smoky Mountains National Park

GREAT SMOKY MOUNTAINS NATIONAL PARK
Beauty or the bulldozer? issues involving Great Smoky Mountains National Park and Blue Ridge Parkway. M. Frome. il Am For 72:6-9+ F '66; Discussion. 72:2-3 Ap '66
Great Smokies park and the wilderness act. il Liv Wildn 29:20-4 Aut '65
Handbook for Smokies wilderness; with the wilderness regulations of the Departments of agriculture and interior under the Wilderness act; symposium. il Liv Wildn 30:1+ Spr '66
Hiking the Great Smokies. il Todays Health 44:46-7 Ap '66
Mike Frome; hearings on road plan for the Smokies. M. Frome. Am For 72:5+ Ag '66
North Carolina's trail riding. M. Rabb. il Travel 125:32-5 My '66
Path through the mist forest. M. B. Mellinger. il Nat Parks Mag 40:21-3 My '66
What alternate proposal? highway through Smokies; letter to the editor. E. T. Scoyen. Am For 72:4-5+ Ag '66; Reply. E. M. Dickerman. 72:5 N '66
Wilderness act: Great Smoky plan debated. L. J. Carter. Science 153:39-42 Jl 1 '66; Reply. W. A. Calder, jr. 154:1118 D 2 '66
Wilderness in the Smokies; statements. June 13, 15, 1966. A. W. Smith. Nat Parks Mag 40:1-IV Ag '66
With the national parks. Natur Hist 75:72+ O '66

GREAT spangled fritillary. See Butterflies
GREAT swamp wildlife reservation, Rhode Island. See Wildlife sanctuaries
GREAT temple of Amun. See Luxor
GREAT women. See Women, Famous
GREAVES, Percy
Mystery of Pearl Harbor. Nat R 18:1266-72 D 13 '66

GREBANIER, Bernard
Dramatic monologue by mail. Sat R 49:48 Je 11 '66
Wits, whigs, and Paul's-walkers. Sat R 49:32-3 F 12 '66

GRECO, Alberto
Obituary
Américas por 18:37 My '66. F. Demaría

GRECO, Carl
Repetitive designs at the elementary school level. Sch Arts 65:34-5 My '66

GRÉCO, Juliette
Letter from Paris: performances at Le théâtre national populaire. Genêt. New Yorker 42:151-2+ O 8 '66

GRÉDY, Jean Pierre
Cactus flower; adaptation. See Burrows, A.

GREECE. Ancient
See also
Education—Greece, Ancient
Archeology
See also
Pella, Greece (ancient city)

History
Persian wars, 500-449 B.C.
Herodotus and the strategy and tactics of the invasion of Xerxes. A. Ferrill. bibllog f Am Hist R 72:102-15 O '66

GREECE, Modern
See also
Airlines—Greece, Modern
Athos, Mount
Crete
Foreign students in Greece
Foreign visitors in Greece
Investments, Foreign (in Greece)
Music festivals—Greece, Modern
Trials—Greece, Modern

Air force
Greek air force asks for T-38 trainers. C. Brownlow. il Aviation W 85:147+ Ag 15 '66

Armed forces
See also
Military service, Compulsory—Greece, Modern

Commercial treaties and agreements
U.S. and Greece amend cotton textile agreement; Department announcement, with text of U.S. note, May 23, 1966. Dept State Bul 54:992-3 Je 20 '66

Description and travel
Greek was Greek to us! G. L. Kackley. il Sr Schol 88:sup 18 Ap 15 '66
Vacancies of August; letter from the Greek islands. J. Thompson. Commentary 42:41-51 N '66

Industries
Esso Pappas complex. il Fortune 73:69-70+ F '66

Politics and government
Behind the Aspida trial; plot to carry out a left-wing coup against the palace. K. Kyle. New Repub 156:17-18 Ja 21 '67
End of the string. Newsweek 69:27-8 Ja 2 '67
Finishing the condemned. Time 88:19 D 30 '66
One man's family; Papandreous. Newsweek 69:45 Ja 16 '67
Year of clear sailing. il Time 88:38 S 23 '66

Royal family
King with Greek gusto; with report by P. Dragadze. il Life 61:78-84+ O 21 '66

GREEK archipelago. See Aegean Islands
GREEK cookery. See Cookery, Greek
GREEK drama

Production, Modern
Grandeur in the grandstand: Ypsilanti Greek theater, Mich. il Time 88:68 Jl 8 '66
Grandeur in Ypsilanti, gaiety in Minneapolis. R. Kotlowitz. il Harper 233:116+ S '66
Manner of speaking; on purifying the antiquities in Ypsilanti. J. Ciardi. Sat R 49:22 Ag 13 '66
Pisthetairos in Ypsi; Ypsilanti, Mich, home of America's first classic Greek repertory theater. il Newsweek 68:85-6 Jl 11 '66
Stratford and Ypsilanti. J. Novick. Nation 203:261 S 19 '66
Theater; Ypsilanti Greek theatre. H. Hewes. Sat R 49:24 Jl 16 '66
Two great Greeks in a ball park: Greek theater in Ypsilanti. T. Prideaux. Life 61: 8+ Jl 29 '66

GREEK letter societies. See College fraternities
GREEK literature
Apuleius: Golden ass. K. Rexroth. Sat R 49:15 Jl 2 '66
Greek poem in Roman prose. L. Casson. Sat R 49:34-5 F 12 '66
Plato's Republic. K. Rexroth. Sat R 49:33 F 19 '66

GREEK poetry
From the Greek. G. Davenport. Poetry 108: 416-19 S '66
See also
Sappho

Translations into English
Four modes of translation. G. Davenport. Poetry 107:264-6 Ja '66
Some fragments; Parting; Absent friend; tr. by C. M. Bowra. Sappho. Horizon 8:109 Spr '66
Some fragments; Throned in splendor; Some say a host; Peer of immortal gods; tr. by P. Green. Sappho. Horizon 8:109 Spr '66

GREEK vases. See Vases, Greek
GREEKS in Germany (Federal Republic)
Alien horror; killing of Miltiades Vlachos by son in Germany to avenge family honor. Time 87:32 Ja 28 '66
Crime of the country; killing by son in Germany to restore family honor. il Newsweek 67:33 F 7 '66

GREEKS in Turkey
Ecumenical patriarch still being scapegoated. Christian Cent 83:294 Mr 9 '66

GREELEY, Andrew M.
Age of innocents. Reporter 35:52-4 S 8 '66
Campus community: experiment in living. America 115:588-91 N 12 '66
Chap in his place. Reporter 36:64 Ja 12 '67
Farewell to the new breed. America 114:801-4 Je 4 '66
Place of religion. Commonweal 84:104+ Ap 15 '66
St Matthew without passion. Reporter 34: 39-40 Je 30 '66
—and Rossi, P. H.
Education of Catholic Americans; excerpts. Commonweal 83:596 F 25 '66
about
Adolescent Catholicism? J. O'Gara. Commonweal 85:217 N 25 '66
Greeley-Rossi report. R. D. Cross. Commonweal 84:577-9 S 16 '66

GREELEY, Andrew M.—About—*Continued*
Greeley-Rossi report on Catholic schools.
America 115:128 Ag 6 '66
Using the Greeley-Rossi report. America 115:
150 Ag 13 '66

GREEN, Barbara B.
Soviet politics and interest groups. bibliog f
Cur Hist 51:213-17+ O '66

GREEN, Beverley R. and Gordon, M. P.
Replication of chloroplast DNA of tobacco.
bibliog Science 152:1071-4 My 20 '66

GREEN, Charles
Powerhouse two-tube short-wave receiver.
Pop Electr 25:59-63 Ag '66

GREEN, D. G. and Kellerth, J. O.
Postsynaptic versus presynaptic inhibition
in antagonistic stretch reflexes. bibliog Science 152:1097-9 My 20 '66

GREEN, Ely
Soul-searching in Tennessee. M. Walker. Sat
R 50:35 Ja 7 '67

GREEN, H. Gordon
Dissent on China. C. P. Tung. Christian Cent
83:1183 S 28 '66

GREEN, Hannah
Sphinx and the pyramid. New Yorker 42:
130+ Ap 2 '66

GREEN, Joshua
Nemesis of the black brant. R. Cantwell. il
por Sports Illus 24:44-6+ My 16 '66

GREEN, Joyce
Beauty life: three smart girls and what
they've learned about makeup. il pors Mlle
64:98-101+ Ja '67

GREEN, Louis C.
Observational aspects of cosmology. Sky &
Tel 31:199-202 Ap '66
Peculiar A stars. Sky & Tel 31:84-8 F '66

GREEN, Martin
Success and failure in fiction. Sat R 49:38 Ap
30 '66

GREEN, Peter
In search of Sappho. Horizon 8:104-8+ Spr
'66
(tr) See Sappho. Some fragments: Throned in
splendor; Some say a host; Peer of immortal gods

GREEN, Richard D. 3d, and Miller, J. W.
Catecholamine concentrations: changes in
plasma of rats during estrous cycle and
pregnancy. bibliog Science 151:825-6 F 18
'66

GREEN, Robert
Nigeria's new man. Nation 202:465-6 Ap 18 '66

GREEN, Theodore Francis
Boulevardier Brahmin. il por Time 87:19 My
27 '66

GREEN, Timothy
Passing of a fine front page. Life 60:23 Je 10
'66

GREEN BAY (city), Wis.
Carbonless paper. R.   Petreat. il Am City
81:120+ Ag '66

GREEN BAY Packers (football club) See Football clubs

GREEN beret forces. See United States—Army
—Special forces

GREEN-broke stud: story. See Mayer, T.

GREEN ISLAND
Under water: Down Under. M. Hemingway.
il Holiday 40:64-5+ S '66

GREEN lacewings. See Lacewings

GREEN MOUNTAIN national forest. See National forests

GREEN turtles. See Turtles. Green

GREENBERG, Joanne
Hunting season; story. McCalls 93:74-5 Je '66

GREENBERG, M. J.
Species specific effect of acetylcholine on
bivalve rectums. bibliog Science 154:1015-17
N 25 '66

GREENBERG, Martin
It's a Kafkaesque world. N Y Times Mag
p 12-13+ My 29 '66

GREENBERG, Michael L. and others
Erythropoietic and reticuloendothelial function in bone marrow in dogs. bibliog Science 152:526-8 Ap 22 '66

GREENBERG, Noah
Achievement of Noah Greenberg. G. P. El-
liott. Commentary 42:67-71 Jl '66
Obituary
Hi Fi por 16:136+ Ap '66
On Decca, Noah Greenberg's last recording.
J. W. Barker. por Am Rec G 32:795 My '66
Pro musica in retrospect. P. L. Miller. por
Sat 49:48-9 Je 25 '66
Recordings. M. Mayer. Esquire 65:28 Ap '66

GREENBERG, Pearl
Second annual Puerto Rico art education conference. Sch Arts 65:38-40 F '66

GREENBERG, Selig
Medicare bonanza. Nation 203:513-16; 204:62
N 14 '66, Ja 9 '67
Medicare: promises and pitfalls. Nation 202:
617-20 My 23 '66

GREENBERG, Syd
Gettysburg: movement in photographs. il U S
Camera 29:64-5 Ap '66

GREENBERGER, Martin
Uses of computers in organizations; with
biographical sketch. Sci Am 215:46, 192-6+
S '66

GREENBERGER, Norton J. and Ruppert, R. D.
Inhibition of protein synthesis: a mechanism
for the production of impaired iron absorption. bibliog Science 153:315-16 Jl 15 '66

GREENBRIER resort, W.Va. See Health resorts. watering places. etc.

GREENE, Bob
Up on two wheels. See issues of Hot rod

GREENE, Gael
How America's wealthiest families pinch pennies. Ladies Home J 83:152-4+ O '66
Improbable bachelor life of John D. Rockefeller IV. Ladies Home J 83:108-9+ N '66
Improbable private life of Mrs Johnny Carson. Ladies Home J 83:50-5+ Jl '66

GREENE, Graham
Blessing; story. Harper 232:91-4 Mr '66
New honor and a new novel; interview. pors
Life 60:43-4 F 4 '66
Secret; story. Vogue 149:94-5 Ja 1 '67
about
Graham Greene's comedians. D. Lodge. Com-
monweal 83:604-6 F 25 '66
Tired terror of Graham Greene. D. Barthelme.
Holiday 39:146+ Ap '66

GREENE, H. D. 3d
Service, stock control, advertising: ingredients of a successful business. Pub W 189:
50-1 My 2 '66

GREENE, James J.
Play of the month. Cath World 202:318-20
F '66
Theater in the red. Cath World 202:364-8
Mr '66

GREENE, Martin
Crafts in underdeveloped nations. Craft Horiz
26:26-7 Mr '66

GREENE, Mary Frances, and Ryan, Orletta
Normal day in P.S. 200; excerpt from Schoolchildren: growing up in the slums. McCalls
93:96-7+ Mr '66

GREENE, Nancy
Bunny from B.C. il por Time 89:68 Ja 20 '67

GREENE, Paul A.
Bedding down the budget-minded. il por
Bsns W p56-8+ Ag 27 '66

GREENE, Wallace Martin, 1907-
General Greene tells the story of Vietnam
war; interview. por U S News 61:34-40 S
5 '66; Same abr. with title Vietnam progress
and prospects. Read Digest 89:175-8+ N '66
Vietnam, top marine's size-up; excerpts
from news conference, January 17, 1966.
por U S News 60:15 Ja 31 '66
Why we will win in Viet Nam. pors Nations
Bsns 54:36-9+ Ap '66

GREENE COUNTY, Ala.
Challenging the sheriff. Newsweek 67:28-9
My 16 '66

GREENEWALT, Crawford H.
Marvelous hummingbird rediscovered. il Nat
Geog Mag 130:98-101 Jl '66

GREENFELD, Josh
Curtain going up for Wallace Harrison.
N Y Times Mag p36-7+ Ag 21 '66
Enjoy, enjoy now, we'll talk later. Life 61:
7+ N 4 '66
Sort of the Svengali of pop. N Y Times Mag
p34-5+ My 8 '66

GREENFIELD, Edward
Bernstein eruption, new Rosenkavalier. Hi
Fi 16:MA28-9 Jl '66
Britain's swinging festival. Hi Fi 16:MA31
D '66
Festival in the ancient city. Hi Fi 16:MA26-7
O '66
Festivals in England. Hi Fi 16:MA20-1 S '66
London report. Hi Fi 16:160-1 Ap; 156-7 My
'66
Notes from our correspondents. See issues of
High fidelity incorporating Musical Amer-
ica
Repeat performance at fifty. Hi Fi 16:24+
Ap '66

GREENFIELD, Jeff
College newspapers in search of their own
voice. Harper 232:87-93 My '66

GREENFIELD, Meg
Editorial disorder and early sorrow. Reporter
34:46-8 F 10 '66

GREENFIELD, Meg—*Continued*
  Nightfight with the nicest guy in town. Reporter 35:35-7 Jl 14 '66
  Senior Senator Kennedy. Reporter 35:19-24 D 15 '66
  War in Washington: the temper of the capital. Reporter 34:29+ Mr 10 '66
GREENFIELD Village. See Henry Ford museum and Greenfield Village, Dearborn, Mich.
GREENGARD, Olga, and Baker, G. T.
  Glucagon, starvation, and the induction of liver enzymes by hydrocortisone. bibliog il Science 154:1461-2 D 16 '66
  —See Altman, K. jt. auth.
GREENGLASS, David
  End of a mystery? A-bomb sketch release; M. Sobell appeal. il Newsweek 68:22 Ag 15 '66
GREENHOUSE resort, Texas. See Health resorts, watering places, etc.
GREENHOUSES
  Greenhouse you can build yourself. G. A. Springer. il Pop Gard 17:86-7 My '66
  Home greenhouse. J. Eaton. See issues of Flower grower, the home garden
  Lath house for plants. J. E. Thompson. il Flower Grower 53:75 Mr '66
  Low-cost plastic greenhouses. il Farm J 93:69 Mr '66
  This garden room is the living end! il Bet Hom & Gard 44:58-9 Ag '66

Lighting
  Alaska grower imports Florida sun: vegetables grown under fluorescent lamps. il Bsns W p58-9 Ap 30 '66
GREENLAND
  Ice on the rocks; icecap depth. Newsweek 68:53 Ag 8 '66
  See also
  Airlines—Greenland

Economic conditions
  As the modern world comes to Greenland. R. K. Brome. il U S News 61:104-7 O 31 '66

Social conditions
  As the modern world comes to Greenland. R. K. Brome. il U S News 61:104-7 O 31 '66
GREENLEE, Lyman E.
  Build the little honker. Pop Electr 25:55-8 S '66
GREENSBORO, N. C.
  For emergency calls only; fire and police emergency calls. S. H. Smith. il Am City 81:153-4+ O '66
GREENSPAN program. See Agricultural administration—United States
GREENWALD, Harold
  Forgotten visit to a flying saucer. Sat R 49:22-3 D 31 '66
GREENWALD, Joseph A.
  East-West trade policy in a balanced strategy for peace; address, October 11, 1966. Dept State Bul 55:676-80 O 31 '66
GREENWALD, Sheila
  My life story. Harper 233:54-5 Jl '66
GREENWICH, Conn.

Parks and playgrounds
  Pocket parks. R. F. Jass. il Am City 81:86-7 D '66
GREENWICH, Conn. library
  Greenwich reading time. J. W. Bryant. il Wilson Lib Bul 40:530-1 F '66
GREENWICH mean time. See Time measurements
GREENWICH VILLAGE, New York. See New York (city)—Greenwich Village
GREENWOOD, Frank. See Cornelius, I. E. jt. auth.
GREER, Barbara
  Blues for George and Henry: Judson Hall. J. Maskey. Dance Mag 40:63 Jl '66
GREER, Richard S.
  We merged city and county purchasing. Am City 81:114-15 O '66
GREETING cards
  Art of writing greeting cards. R. Galanoplos. il Sat R 49:94-6 D 10 '66
  First you gather seaweed, then you make your card. il Sunset 137:96 S '66
  See also
  American greetings corporation
  Christmas cards
  Hallmark cards, incorporated
GREGG, Duane
  Cars in your family. Bet Hom & Gard 45:12 Ja '67
  (ed) See Slutz, D. This traffic safety expert has an idea!

GREGG, James R.
  Houseboat holiday. Motor B 117:34-5+ Je '66
GREGG, Richard N.
  Fabulous Oriental rug collection. Hobbies 71:36-7 Je '66
  Persian palace rugs in Oshkosh. Antiques 89:718-23 My '66
GREGOR, Arthur
  Calm; poem. New Yorker 42:30 Ja 7 '67
  Don Carlos, Saturday afternoon; poem. Nation 203:646 D 12 '66
  Irreconcilables; poem. New Yorker 41:36 F 5 '66
  Lament for a gifted man; poem. Nation 203:622 D 5 '66
  Short poem: When eyes pass by trembling with presence; Enchanted flowers; poems. Poetry 108:225-9 Jl '66
GREGOR, Arthur S.
  River Severn again. Horn Bk 42:523-7 O '66
GREGORY, Dick
  Dick Gregory goes fishing. R. C. Lee. por Nation 202:487-9 Ap 25 '66
  Inverted racism. Christian Cent 83:575-6 My 4 '66
GREGORY, Isabella Augusta (Persse) lady
  All the Olympians. F. O'Connor. Sat R 49:30-2+ D 10 '66
GREGORY, John R.
  Movie Q's and A's. See issues of U.S. camera & travel, June 1966-
  Quick cuts & action shots. See issues of U.S. camera & travel
GREGORY, Jon
  Labanotation and me. B. Mahoney. il Dance Mag 40:56+ Ap '66
GREIFF, Victor
  Bulb for a cold window. Flower Grower 53:28 O '66
GRENADA, Miss.
  From Grenada, Mississippi, a minister warns Christians: stand up or get out! C. B. Burt. il Look 30:34+ D 27 '66
  Intruders in the dust: Negro children attacked at schools. il Time 88:26 S 23 '66
  Message from Grenada. Christian Cent 83:1199-200 O 5 '66
  What Grenadans are like; Negroes beaten on their way to school. il Newsweek 68:33-4 S 26 '66
  White venom in Grenada. Christian Cent 83:1169 S 28 '66
GRENE, Marjorie
  Organic thinking. Commentary 42:94-5 S '66
  Portmann's thought; adaptation of address, August 1965. Commentary 40:31-8 N '65; 41:10+ Mr '66
GRENNAN, Jacqueline
  Another nun defects. por Time 89:66 Ja 20 '67
  New vows. il por Newsweek 69:63-4 Ja 23 '67
GRENNAN, Michael Dennis
  Buypoints: movie cameras. Pop Phot 59:132-45 O '66
  Buypoints: still cameras. Pop Phot 59:140-2 N '66
  Try these vision-stretchers. il Pop Phot 59:98-101+ S '66
  Unconditionally guaranteed, but... Pop Phot 59:65+ S '66
GRESHAM, Grits
  Belligerent bluegill. Field & S 70:73-5+ Ap '66
  Best U.S. smallmouth water? Outdoor Life 138:50-1+ N '66
  Bighorn by the seat of my pants. por Field & S 71:37-9+ O '66
  Compleat hunter. Field & S 71:133-6 S '66
  From BB to V.C. Field & S 71:32+ S '66
  Montana mixture. pors Field & S 71:44-7 Ag '66
GRESSEL, Jonathan. See Galun, E. jt. auth.
GRETH, Roma
  Two masks; drama. Plays 25:15-26 F '66
GRETHER, E. T.
  Sharp practice in merchandising and advertising. bibliog f Ann Am Acad 363:108-16 Ja '66
GRETHER, Toby
  Your turfgrass headache: what variety? Parks & Rec 1:504-5 Je '66
GREVE, Donald J.
  Private-plus plan to ease poverty. J. P. Eddy. Christian Cent 83:1064 Ag 31 '66
  Proud demonstration at Anadarko. E. Selby and A. Selby. Read Digest 88:230+ Ap '66
GREWING, M. See Pfleiderer, J. jt. auth.
GREY, Aida
  Beauty bulletin: sound of makeup; with quotes from tape-recorded talk. Vogue 147:172-5 F 1 '66

GREY, Hugh
Compleat hunter. Field & S 71:153-6 S '66
GREY, Joel
New star on Broadway. il por Newsweek 68:106+ D 19 '66
GREYHOUNDS
Hi Joe, long time no see; stolen racing greyhound returned. J. Lovesey. il Sports Illus 24:24-5 F 28 '66
GREYLOCK, MOUNT
Mike Frome; Mount Greylock protective association. Am For 72:5+ Ap '66
Mount Greylock in peril. il Liv Wildn 29:35 Aut '65
GRIBBINS, Joseph
What's new. See issues of Motor boating
GRIDDLE cakes
Art of the Mandarin pancake. il Sunset 136:217+ My '66
Dessert pancakes out of the oven. il Sunset 136:185 Je '66
Lacy-edge batter cakes, a southern favorite. L. W. Gilliam. il Farm J 90:81 O '66
Origin unknown; crêpes Suzette. C. Claiborne. il N Y Times Mag p70 Je 12 '66
Pancake nonpareil. C. Claiborne. il N Y Times Mag p56 Ap 10 '66
Pancakes and waffles. il Bet Hom & Gard 44:103-4 Mr '66
GRIDDLES, Electric. See Electric grills
GRIDLEY, Josephine A.
Wassail and all that bother. Sat R 49:59-60 D 24 '66
GRIEF. See Bereavement
GRIERSON, Francis
Grierson: a strange fish. H. P. Simonson. Nation 203:226-7 S 12 '66
GRIESE, Bob
That Griese kid stuff. H. L. Masin. il por Sr Schol 89:24 N 4 '66
GRIESEDIECK, Joseph E.
Guy named Joe. R. Levy. il por Duns R 88:38+ Ag '66
GRIEVANCE procedures
Cooperation and arbitration in the federal service. W. W. Heimbach. Mo Labor R 89:614 Je '66
Grievance procedures in the federal service. O. Pragan. Mo Labor R 89:609 Je '66
GRIFFIN, C. W. Jr
Rise of nopanaceism. Atlan 218:76-7 S '66
GRIFFIN, Denham R.
New programs under the sun. Parks & Rec 1:550 Jl '66
GRIFFIN, Edward I.
Making friends with a killer whale. por Nat Geog Mag 129:418-46 Mr '66
GRIFFIN, Frank L. Jr
Visit to a drowning canyon. Audubon Mag 68:27-33 Ja '66
GRIFFIN, Ida Ruth
I am Mississippi fed; poem. Nation 203:522 N 14 '66
GRIFFIN, Robert P.
Speaking out. por Sat Eve Post 239:12+ F 26 '66
Vietnam; address, June 23, 1966. Vital Speeches 32:585-9 Jl 15 '66
about
Calling Saigon. por Time 87:32 My 20 '66
Faceless favorite. il por Time 88:25 S 30 '66
GRIFFIN. Stuart
Hachijojima. Travel 126:44-7 Jl '66
GRIFFIN, William D.
Beach babies. U S Camera 29:42-3+ Ap '66
GRIFFITH, David Wark
Birth of an art. W. Johnson. il Sr Schol 88:4-5+ Mr 4 '66
GRIFFITH, Emile
Camping out with the champ. M. Gross. il por Sports Illus 25:36-8+ N 7 '66
Shrinking poppy's nonbout with a reluctant Tiger. por Sports Illus 24:70-2 My 9 '66
When Emile got his Irish up. M. Kram. il pors Sports Illus 25:14-15 Jl 25 '66
GRIFFITH, F. H.
Old mechanical banks. See issues of Hobbies
GRIFFITH, Francis
St John's. Commonweal 83:647; 84:85-6 Mr 4, Ap 8 '66
GRIFFITH, Harry T.
Crossover for life. il por Time 87:44 Mr 11 '66
GRIFFITH, William E.
How firmness in Vietnam is paying off; interview. Read Digest 88:112-16 Ap '66
Why Russia is our biggest danger; interview. Read Digest 89:119-23 Ag '66
GRIFFITHS, Martha (Wright)
From the women: what about our job rights? il por U S News 61:61-2 Jl 4 '66

GRIFFITHS' gift: story. See O'Sullivan. A. D.
GRIGGS, Lee
Great dam thunders ahead. Life 60:101-2+ Je 17 '66
GRILLET, Alain Robbe-. See Robbe-Grillet, A.
GRILLS, Barbecue. See Barbecue grills
GRIMM, Arthur
Penny test for Dutch elm disease. Am City 81:122-3 My '66
GRINDING machines
Handiest tool ever, the hand grinder. W. E. Burton. il Pop Mech 126:176-9+ O '66
GRIS, Charles Édouard Jeanneret-. See Le Corbusier
GRISEZ, Germain G.
Book reviews. America 114:232 F 12 '66
GRIST, Reri
Reri; interview, ed. by H. E. Phillips. por Opera N 30:16 Mr 19 '66
Mephisto's musings. il por Hi Fi 16:120-1 F '66
GRISWOLD, Wesley S.
His bag of tricks makes physics fun. Pop Sci 188:95-9 My '66
GRIVAS, George
Behind the Aspida trial. K. Kyle. New Repub 156:17-18 Ja 21 '67
Toward a boiling point. il por Time 87:39 Ap 1 '66
GRIZZLY bear hunting. See Bear hunting
GRIZZLY bears. See Bears
GROCERY chains. See Chain stores
GROCERY stores
See also
Supermarkets
GROCERY trade
High court bars merger of rivals; in retail grocery markets. Bsns W p36 Je 4 '66
Now a little merger is ruled illegal. il U S News 60:58 Je 13 '66
GROEBLI, René
René Groebli's variations. N. Rothschild. il Pop Phot 59:94-5 O '66
GROENHOFF, Hans
Flying photographer (cont) Flying 78:27 My; 79:89 Ag; 89 S '66
Gone flying: the route of the island traders. il Flying 79:86-9+ Jl '66
about
Hans Herman Hugo Ernest Wilhelm Von Groenhoff. E. D. Muhlfield. pors Flying 80:64-9 Ja '67
GROFF, Patrick J.
Where are we going with poetry for children? Horn Bk 42:456-63 Ag '66
GROLIER, Incorporated
Grolier acquires correspondence school. Pub W 189:156 F 21 '66
Grolier diversifies with big new books. il Pub W 190:188-92 Jl 11 '66
How Grolier created and produced the totally new Book of knowledge. il Pub W 191:64-6+ Ja 2 '67
Waller to head new Grolier educational subsidiary. Pub W 189:63 F 7 '66
GROLIER club, New York
Fine renaissance bindings shown at the Grolier club. P. A. Bennett. Pub W 190:125-6 D 5 '66
GROLLMAN, Arthur
Common-sense guide to cholesterol; interview. por Todays Health 44:3+ Ag '66
GROMYKO, Andrei Andreevich
Continuation; papal audience. Newsweek 67:46+ My 9 '66
Cross and sickle. Nat R 18:451-2 My 17 '66
Red carpet for Gromyko. il por Newsweek 68:35 Ag 8 '66
Up the back stairs. il por Time 88:33-4 O 21 '66
Visitor; visit to Italy. il por Newsweek 67:54 My 2 '66
GRONOUSKI, John Austin
When the U.S. negotiates with Peiping, in Warsaw; interview, ed. by R. A. Haeger. por U S News 61:44-6 Jl 4 '66
about
Bridge builder. por Time 87:37 Ap 15 '66
GROOMING. See Beauty, Personal
GROOMS, Charles Rogers. See Grooms, R.
GROOMS, Red
News of art. il Horizon 9:78-9 Wint '67
Red power. T. Berrigan. il Art N 65:44-6 D '66
GROPPI, James Edward
Pulpit v. the bench. il por Time 88:23 S 9 '66

GROSE, Peter
Brezhnev and Kosygin: the cult of impersonality. N Y Times Mag p34-7+ O 9 '66
Communist party is the rear guard of Russia. N Y Times Mag p36-7+ Mr 27 '66

GROSJEAN, Joseph
Inner black and white. America 114:867-8 Je 25 '66

GROSKINSKY, Henry
Alluring art of India; photographs. Life 60: 48-58 F 11 '66

GROSS, Alfred A.
Sad tale, well told. Christian Cent 83:761-2 Je 8 '66
Shadows of doubt. Christian Cent 83:1178 S 28 '66

GROSS, Courtlandt Sherrington
No end in sight. il por Time 87:72-6+ F 11 '66

GROSS, Ernest A.
South West Africa case: what happened? For Affairs 45:36-48 O '66

GROSS, Franklin S.
Convention exhibit notes; NCSS. Sr Schol 89:sup7 D 9 '66
New books for teaching world history. Sr Schol 89:sup20 N 18 '66
Potpourri of new books. Sr Schol 89:sup 19+ D 2 '66
Truth has many faces. Sr Schol 88:sup22-3 Ap 29 '66

GROSS, George
Figure skating. Sports Illus 24:58-9 Mr 7 '66

GROSS, H. R.
Excerpt from debate, July 13, 1966. Cong Digest 45:220+ Ag '66
Partying: Great society style; gyrating dances, peekaboo dresses; excerpts from address, May 10, 1966. U S News 60:10 My 23 '66

GROSS, Jerry
Happiness is. Hot Rod 19:46-8+ S '66

GROSS, M. Grant, and Nelson, J. L.
Sediment movement on the Continental shelf near Washington and Oregon. bibliog Science 154:879-80+ N 18 '66
—and Tracey, J. I. Jr
Oxygen and carbon isotopic composition of limestones and dolomites, Bikini and Eniwetok atolls. bibliog Science 151:1082-4 Mr 4 '66

GROSS, Martin L.
Great debate about your family doctor; excerpt from The doctors. Good H 162:90-1+ Je '66
Hidden death threats in our hospitals; excerpts from The doctors. Look 30:27-30 Mr 22 '66; Excerpts. U S News 60:19 Mr 21 '66

GROSS, Milton
Baseball's fragile superstars. Pop Sci 188:76-9 My '66

GROSS, P. R. and Fry, B. J.
Continuity of protein synthesis through cleavage metaphase. bibliog Science 153: 749-51 Ag 12 '66

GROSS, Ronald, and Murphy, Judith
New York's late-blooming State university. Harper 233:87-90+ D '66
—See Murphy, J. jt. auth.

GROSS, S. H. and others
Mars: upper atmosphere. bibliog Science 151: 1216+ Mr 11 '66

GROSS, Sarah Chokla
And the books came tumblin' in. Sr Schol 88: sup9-10 My 6 '66

GROSS national product
Japan is one of the biggest countries in the world. E. O. Reischauer. il N Y Times Mag p34-5+ O 16 '66
New economics. E. T. Chase. Commonweal 83:551-3 F 11 '66
Poverty gap is big and growing. America 115:472 O 22 '66
Rich and poor nations. America 114:185 F 5 '66
Taking the expansion in stride; whopping first-quarter rise in GNP. il Bsns W p31-3 Ap 23 '66
Uncle Sam's $50,000,000,000 surplus. E. L. Dale, jr; discussion. Nat R 17:1151-2; 18: 97+ D 14 '65, F 8 '66
What comes after the new economics? with editorial comment. il Bsns W p 125-6, 128 F 5 '66
Where the world's real power lies. il U S News 60:76-7 Ja 31 '66
Why fight? ruble-dollar road to peace. R. C. Garretson. il Nation 202:576-81 My 16 '66

GROSSE, Aristid V.
Effect of temperature on the life of soap bubbles, and their solidification at low temperature. bibliog Science 153:894-5 Ag 19 '66

GROSSE POINTE, Mich, public library
Book selection in Grosse Pointe: where school librarians advise the public library. V. Leonard. ALA Bul 60:627-9 Je '66

La GROSSE valise; musical comedy. See Musical comedies, revues, etc.—Criticisms, plots, etc.

GROSSER, Alfred
De Gaulle, the U.S. and Russia: a look at the trends; interview, ed. by F. C. Painton. por U S News 60:42-3 Je 20 '66

GROSSER, Maurice
Art. Nation 202:531-3 My 2 '66

GROSSER, Morton
Fabulous fifty; story. Sat Eve Post 239:78-82 O 8 '66
Sand hill road; poem. Harper 232:58 Ap '66

GROSSINGER'S hotel. See Hotels, taverns, etc.—United States

GROSSLING, Bernardo F.
Improving a wretched plain. Am For 72:26-7 N '66

GROSSMAN, Allen
Seven poets. T. Clark. Poetry 108:411-12 S '66

GROSSMAN, Barney
Book of one's own. NEA J 56:31-2 Ja '67

GROSSMAN, Edward
Comparing the brutes. New Repub 154:20+ F 12 '66
Götterdämmerung, with beer and pretzels. Harper 232:106-8 My '66
New York's schoolhouse for the left. Harper 232:75-6+ Ap '66

GROSSMAN, James
Note on Felix Frankfurter. Commentary 41: 59-64 Mr '66

GROSSMAN, Mary Louise
Heritage in peril. Am Heritage 17:4-15+ Ag '66

GROSSMAN, Sylva
Throne in heaven; story. Redbook 127:94-5 My '66

GROSSMAN publishers, incorporated
Paragraphics, artists' medium in large-size quality paperback. il Pub W 190:116-17 S 5 '66

GROSSO, Mike
Off-court uproar in Dixie. M. Mulvoy. il por Sports Illus 25:26-7 N 7 '66

GROSVENOR, Donna K. and Grosvenor, G. M.
Ceylon. il por Nat Geog Mag 129:447-97 Ap '66

GROSVENOR, Gilbert Hovey
To Gilbert Grosvenor; monthly monument twenty-five miles high. F. G. Vosburgh. il pors Nat Geog Mag 130:445-87 O '66

GROSVENOR, Gilbert M. See Grosvenor, D. K. jt. auth.

GROSVENOR, Melville Bell
Special publications. Nat Geog Mag 129:408-17 Mr '66
Today and tomorrow in our national parks. por Nat Geog Mag 130:1-5 Jl '66

GROTH, F. J.
Our customers like remote-reading meters. Am City 81:78-9 Je '66

GROTZ, George
How to save money on antiques; excerpt from Antiques you can decorate with. Ladies Home J 83:59+ N '66

GROUEFF, Stéphane
Authors & editors. por Pub W 191:41 Ja 16 '67

GROUND covers. See Cover plants

GROUND effect machines
Agency delivers transportation report; study of air-cushion-vehicle technology. Tech W 19:17 O 10 '66
Air cushion craft stir industry interest. R. G. O'Lone. il Aviation W 84:75-6+ My 23 '66
Amazing hovercraft goes to work. D. Scott. il Pop Sci 189:94-7+ N '66
France set to fund Aerotrain system. W. C. Wetmore. il Aviation W 85:114-15+ O 10 '66
French company speeding development of Aerotrain. W. C. Wetmore. il Aviation W 85:78-84 O 3 '66
French put Aerotrain onto a faster track; high-speed train that rides on cushion of air, guided by a monorail. il Bsns W p50-1 D 31 '66
Government interest spurs British air cushion vehicles. H. J. Coleman. il Aviation W 85:70-3 Jl 4 '66
Hitting the beach: air cushion landing system for aircraft. il Sci N 89:445 Je 4 '66
Leading international ground effect machines; specifications (cont) Aviation W 84:213 Mr 7 '66
New designs seen for patrol boats. il Miss & Roc 18:79-81 Mr 28 '66

GROUND effect machines—*Continued*
Ninety-passenger GEM develpment under way at Bell aerosystems. Aviation W 84:41 My 9 '66
Now, hoverships. il Sci Digest 60:inside cover Jl '66
Princeton designs GEM for crop dusting. M. L. Yaffee. il Aviation W 85:104-5+ D 5 '66
Ram wing studied as transit vehicle. M. L. Yaffee. il Aviation W 86:56-8+ Ja 2 '67
Skim boats: our new weapon in Vietnam. J. H. Winchester. il Pop Sci 189:122-5+ O '66
Son of monorail: aerotrain. il Time 88:96 D 16 '66
GROUND floor (restaurant) See New York (city)—Hotels, restaurants, etc.
GROUND support equipment. See Ground support systems (space flight)
GROUND support systems (space flight)
Ground-based guidance problem stymies launch of Gemini 9A. Aviation W 84:40 Je 6 '66
GROUND temperature. See Earth temperature
GROUNDCOVERS. See Cover plants
GROUP conflict. See Social conflict
GROUP development, National training laboratory in. See National training laboratory in group development
GROUP discussion. See Discussion
GROUP 47. See Authors, European
GROUP 47 conference. See Authors conferences
GROUP insurance. See Insurance, Group
GROUP psychology. See Groups (sociology)
GROUP psychotherapy
Group therapy valuable aid to married couples. Sci N L 89:153 Mr 5 '66
Playback: new aid in the ordeal of self-discovery; tool of Drs Peter Hogan and Ian Alger. D. Monaco. il Look 31:26-9 Ja 24 '67
GROUP rivalry in education. See Competition in education
GROUP work, Social. See Social group work
GROUPER fishing
My rockpile, fishing hole. S. Clements. il Outdoor Life 138:48-51+ S '66
GROUPING, Homogeneous. See Ability grouping in education
GROUPING by ability. See Ability grouping in education
GROUPS (sociology)
You and fourteen strangers. F. R. Schreiber and M. Herman. il Sci Digest 59:28-32 Ap '66
See also
Age groups
GROUPS, Age. See Age groups
GROUSE
Some observations on strutting sage grouse. B. Gabriel. il Nat Parks Mag 40:18-19 O '66
GROUSE shooting
How to hunt prairie grouse. D. Harbour. il Field & S 71:62-3+ S '66
Potter. R. Bailey. il Field & S 71:148-50 O '66
GROVE, Gene
Army and the Negro. N Y Times Mag p4-5+ Jl 24 '66
GROVE, Kay
Turn left at the mummy, right at Van Gogh. Mlle 62:202-3+ Ap '66
GROVE, Larry C.
Guide to garden power equipment. Bet Hom & Gard 44:20+ Je '66
—See Mason, H. jt. auth.
GROVE, Sir William Robert
Bringing the fuel cell down to earth. L. Lessing. il Fortune 74:128-31+ S '66
GROVE press
Grove buys film library and Mid-Century book club. Pub W 191:57 Ja 16 '67
GROVER, Lee. See Grover, R. jt. auth.
GROVER, Ray, and Grover, Lee
Art glass for everyone; exhibits. Hobbies 71:76-7 Ag '66
GROVES, Dorothy
Wedding cake that's good to eat. Farm J 90:52-5 Je '66
GROVES, Wallace
Island in the sun. il por Newsweek 69:22-4 Ja 9 '67
GROW old along with me; story. See Livingston. D.
GROWTH
See also
Children—Growth and development
Maturity

GROWTH (plants)
Amateur scientist; stimulating plant growth with ultrasonic vibrations. E. Horowitz. il Sci Am 215:100-2 Ag '66
Auxin and kinetin interaction in apical dominance. C. R. Davies and others. bibliog il Science 151:468-9 Ja 28 '66
Compact subsoil can be harmful to plant growth. R. W. Rickman and others. il Parks & Rec 1:334-5 Ap '66
Excretion and heartwood formation in living trees. C. M. Stewart. bibliog il Science 153:1068-74 S 2 '66
Flood history told by tree growth; yielding more knowledge of flood plains. R. S. Sigafoos and M. D. Sigafoos. il Natur Hist 75:50-5 Ag '66
Gibberellin-like substances in the developing apricot fruit. D. I. Jackson and B. G. Coombe. bibliog il Science 154:277-8 O 14 '66
GROWTH, Economic. See Economic development
GROWTH hormones. See Hormones
GROWTH inhibiting substances (plants)
Chemical pruning of plants. H. M. Cathey and others. bibliog il Science 153:1382-3 S 16 '66
Dormancy regulation in peach seeds. W. N. Lipe and J. C. Crane. bibliog il Science 153:541-2 Jl 29 '66
Growth-inhibiting action of tris(1-aziridinyl)-phosphine oxide in grasses. T. W. Holmsen and J. K. Leasure. bibliog il Science 153:1659 S 30 '66
Plant growth as a cancer clue. S. Garb. Sat R 49:50+ My 7 '66; Reply. R. D. Gozzi. 49:67 Je 4 '66
Plant hormones and regulators. J. van Overbeek. bibliog il Science 152:721-31 My 6 '66
Spray speeds up pruning; chemical growth regulator helps prune plants. Sci N 90:251 O 1 '66
GROWTH inhibiting substances (protozoa)
Toxic impurities in nalgene filter units. L. Simpson. il Science 153:548 Jl 29 '66; Reply. O. Henry. 153:1551-2 S 23 '66
GROWTH of children. See Children—Growth and development
GROWTH of cities and towns. See Cities and towns—Growth
GROWTH promoting substances
New RNA chemical found. il Sci N 90:35 Jl 16 '66
Regeneration in spinal neurons: proteosynthesis following nerve growth factor administration. D. Scott, jr. and others. bibliog il Science 152:787-8 My 6 '66
GROWTH promoting substances (plants)
Hormone-induced repression of a peroxidase isozyme in plant tissue. R. Ockerse and others. bibliog il Science 151:452-3 Ja 28 '66
Plant hormones and regulators. J. van Overbeek. bibliog il Science 152:721-31 My 6 '66
See also
Gibberellic acid
GROWTH stocks. See Stocks
GROZNY, I. L.
Tape recorders today, a guide to features and performance. Hi Fi 16:49-52 Ag '66
GRUBEL, Herbert G.
Brain drain: a U.S. dilemma. bibliog Science 154:1420-4 D 16 '66
GRUBER, K. A.
Leak-free roof for underground garage. Arch Rec 140:163-4 D '66
GRUBER, Leo Fritz
L. Fritz Gruber: statesman in photography; director of Photokina. C. Reynolds. il pors Pop Phot 59:74-7+ Ag '66
GRUBS. See Larvae
GRUENBERG, Selma
Crepe paper prints. Sch Arts 65:20-1 My '66
GRUENBERG, Stefanie
Three California ceramists. J. Lovoos. il por Am Artist 30:52-5+ D '66
GRUENINGER, Walter F.
Phonograph records. See issues of Consumer bulletin
GRUMBACH, Doris
Parish organizations. Commonweal 84:11-13 Mr 25 '66
GRUMIAUX, Arthur
Music to my ears. I. Kolodin. Sat R 49:76 N 19 '66
GRUMMAN aircraft engineering corporation
Grumman refining lunar module design. M. L. Yaffee. il Aviation W 85:56-9+ O 24 '66
Ready for new strides on pathway to moon; lunar module. il Bsns W p80-1+ N 26 '66

GRUMP (periodical)
Case for Grump. C. W. Morton. il Atlan 218:
115-16 S '66
Humor in the moral middle. il Time 87:48+
Ap 15 '66
GRUNDY, Kenneth W.
Stanleyville rescue: American policy in the
Congo. Yale R 56:242-55 D '66
GRUNFELD, Frederic V.
Beating the drum for African art. Reporter
34:34-6 Je 2 '66
Paradise island, entire unto itself. Reporter
35:36-8 Ag 11 '66
Portrait of the artist as a music-lover. Opera
N 30:8-13 Ja 29 '66
Sahara song: the last legions, the first art.
Reporter 35:48-50 Jl 14 '66
Scoring the D train. Reporter 34:47-8+ Ap
7 '66
Wagner by half-light. Reporter 35:55-6 S 22
'66
GRUNITZKY, Nicolas
Togo does it again. Newsweek 69:47 Ja 23 '67
GRUNWALD, Arnold P.
Braille-reading machine. Science 154:144-6 O
7 '66
GRUPPE 47. See Authors, European
GRZEDZIELSKI, Wladislaw
Amber routes of antiquity. UNESCO Courier
19:20-2 Mr '66
GUADALAJARA, Mexico
Eating out is a pleasure in Guadalajara. il
Sunset 137:180+ O '66
Guadalajara. il Sunset 137:78-91 O '66
Rewards of Guadalajara shopping. il Sunset
137:39 O '66
GUADALCANAL, Battle of, 1942-1943
Coastwatcher's diary; with introd. by S. W.
Sears. M. Clemens. Am Heritage 17:104-10
F '66
I've served my time in hell. G. McMillan. il
Am Heritage 17:10-15 F '66
GUADALUPE MOUNTAINS NATIONAL PARK
Park system expands. Nat Parks Mag 40:18
D '66
GUAM
Guam is a surprise bonus for cross-Pacific
travelers. il Sunset 136:30-2+ Ap '66
Sunrise serenade: Guam. L. M. Rhodes. il
Travel 126:38+ S '66
GUANINE
Coding properties of 7-methylguanine. R. C.
Wilhelm and D. B. Ludlum. bibliog il Sci-
ence 153:1403-5 S 16 '66
Nucleic acid guanine: reaction with the
carcinogen N-acetoxy-2-acetylamino-fluo-
rene. E. C. Miller and others. bibliog il
Science 153:1125-7 S 2 '66
GUARANTEED income. See Income
GUARANTEED maintenance. See Municipal
equipment—Repairing
GUARANTEES. See Guaranty of goods
GUARANTY. See Warranty
GUARANTY of employment. See Employment
systems—Guaranty of employment
GUARANTY of goods
Unconditionally guaranteed, but. .; shopping
for cameras and accessories. M. D.
Grennan. Pop Phot 59:65+ S '66
GUARANTY of wages. See Wage payment
plans
GUARD, William
Magic garden. R. A. Livant. il por Opera N
30:6-7 Ap 2 '66
GUARD rails. See Roads—Safety guards
GUARDIAN (newspaper)
Guardian going down? Newsweek 69:62 Ja 9
'67
Squeeze on Fleet Street. Time 88:45 D 23 '66
GUARDS, Life. See Lifeguards
GUARESCHI, Giovanni
Family life Italian style. W. Guzzardi, jr.
Sat R 49:35 D 17 '66
GUATEMALA
Guatemala in perspective; 1944-. M. Rod-
riguez. bibliog f Cur Hist 51:338-43+ D '66
See also
Birds—Guatemala
Communism—Guatemala
Education—Guatemala
Elections—Guatemala
Fishing—Guatemala
Guerrillas—Guatemala
Mataquescuintla

Description and travel
Land of eternal spring. C. J. McNaspy.
America 115:18 Jl 2 '66

History
Guatemala in perspective; 1944-. M. Rodriguez. bibliog f Cur Hist 51:338-43+ D '66

Politics and government
Against the odds. Time 88:27 Jl 8 '66
Foretaste of trouble. Time 87:44 My 20 '66
See also
Communism—Guatemala
Elections—Guatemala
GUAVAS
See also
Cookery—Fruit
GUAZZI, Maurizio, and others
Carotid body chemoceptors: physiological role
in buffering fall in blood pressure during
sleep. bibliog Science 153:206-8 Jl 8 '66
GUBERNATORIAL campaigns. See Political
campaigns
GUBERNATORIAL candidates. See Candidates,
Political
GUBERNATORIAL primaries. See Primaries
GUERINOT, J. V.
On Peter's tears: poem. Commonweal 84:
581 S 16 '66
GUERNICA, Spain
In a little Spanish town. P. A. Dickson. il
Sat R 49:44-5 Ag 27 '66
GUÉRON, Henri M.
Reflections on international security. Bul
Atomic Sci 22:32-3 S '66
GUERRILLA warfare
Armchair guide to guerrilla warfare. il Es-
quire 65:88-93 Mr '66
Defeating Communist insurgency, by R.
Thompson. Review
Newsweek 67:36 Je 6 '66
Little boy who plays Vietcong; with report
by D. Sider. il Life 61:50B-52+ Ag 5 '66
Seventeen little wars nobody talks about.
B. B. Fall. Esquire 65:93 Mr '66
See also
Minutemen (organization)
GUERRILLAS

Colombia
Death of a rebel priest: Padre Torres. A. W.
Wilde. Commonweal 83:693-6 Mr 18 '66
Death of Camilo Torres. V. Andrade. Amer-
ica 114:355 Mr 12 '66; Discussion. 114:650-1
My 7 '66

Guatemala
Red Robin Hood. M. J. Kubie. il Newsweek
68:61 O 17 '66
Undeclared war in Guatemala; well-organized
Communist guerrillas. R. Rogers and T.
Yates. il Sat Eve Post 239:30-3 Je 18 '66
With the guerrillas in Guatemala. A. Howard.
il N Y Times Mag p8-9+ Je 26 '66

Laos
Laos report: gains in a forgotten war; team
of Americans and Meo tribesmen. S. W.
Sanders. il U S News 61:24-5 Jl 4 '66

Latin America
Latin America: revolution without revolutionaries. N. Gall. il Nation 203:145-9 Ag 22
'66
Where the terrorists are. Time 88:31 S 2 '66

Syria
Dangerous border: El Fatah. R. Chesnoff.
il Newsweek 68:40+ Ag 15 '66

Thailand
Americans in Thailand; counterinsurgency
activities of armed forces, USIS and AID.
M. Parker. Atlan 218:51-8 D '66
Down south: second front of Communist
guerrillas. Time 88:24+ S 2 '66
Fighting guerrillas from the lab; U.S.-
Thailand military research and develop-
ment center near Bangkok. il Time 88:69-
70 O 7 '66
Menace in the northeast. il Time 87:32 F 25
'66
Squeeze play in Thailand. M. Parker. il Re-
porter 35:16-18 Ag 11 '66

Venezuela
End of Lt. Hilton. Newsweek 68:49 Jl 4 '66
Gone, the bold rebels; dwindling forces of
the FALN. il Newsweek 67:42 F 7 '66

Vietnam (Democratic Republic)
See also
Vietnamese war, 1957- —Guerrillas

Vietnam (Republic)
See also
Vietnamese war, 1957- —Guerrillas
GUEST, Raymond Richard
Muddy horse of the year. W. Tower. il por
Sports Illus 25:30-2+ O 10 '66

GUEST houses
Snail house; Berkshire County, Mass. il Arch Forum 125:84-7 Jl '66

GUEST Pac corporation
Big marketing man on campus. il Time 87: 94 Mr 4 '66

GUEST rooms
Do you want an office or guest room or both? il Bet Hom & Gard 44:48-9 Ag '66

GUESTS
Care and feeding of week-end guests. N. S. Hazelton. il Nat R 18:721+ Jl 26 '66
Week ends: the saving graces. N. S. Hazelton. Nat R 18:624+ Je 28 '66

GUEVARA, Ernesto
Guevara mystery: leader of a new program of red revolution? por U S News 60:22 Mr 7 '66
Whatever became of Che? P. Hofmann. il pors N Y Times Mag p 14-15+ Ap 10 '66

GUGGENHEIM, Harry F.
Captain takes command. por Time 88:80-1 N 4 '66

GUGGENHEIMER, Minnie (Schafer)
Artist life. D. J. Soria. il por Hi Fi 16: MA4-6 Ag '66

GUIANA, BRITISH. See British Guiana
GUIANA, DUTCH. See Surinam
GUIANA, FRENCH. See French Guiana

GUIDA, Salvatore
Reviews. M. Marks. Dance Mag 40:64 F '66

GUIDANCE. See Personnel service in education; Vocational guidance

GUIDANCE, Reader. See Libraries—Readers advisory service

GUIDANCE clinics. See Child guidance clinics
GUIDE books. See Guidebooks

GUIDEBOOKS
Crash production program for Fodor-Shell travel guides U.S.A. il Pub W 189:172-4 Je 13 '66
For traveling families. Parents Mag 41:87 Jl '66
Learning U.S. geography on vacation. Consumer Bul 49:31-2 Ap '66
Notes and comment; Guide Michelin omission of Relais de Porquerolles cause of restaurant owner's suicide. New Yorker 42:47 D 3 '66
One for the road. D. Dempsey. Sat R 49: 27-8 Jl 16 '66
Rich man's Europe. Newsweek 67:110 Je 13 '66
Seeing America: eight regional guides. Holiday 39:136-7 My '66
Skeptical guide to Michelin. H. R. Lottman. Harper 232:82-5 Je '66
Star-crossed; Relais de Porquerolles, Guide Michelin omission causes owner's suicide. Newsweek 68:67-8 O 24 '66
Temple Fielding and Morrow establish Fielding pubns. Pub W 189:155 F 21 '66
Travel information. L. Jonckheere. Sr Schol 87:sup 12 Ja 7 '66
World's facsimile of an early guidebook; World publishing company's Civitates orbis terrarum. il Pub W 189:174-6 Je 13 '66
You can't tell the countries without a book; Time essay. il Time 87:32-3 Ap 29 '66

GUIDED missile bases
Bids due soon on new Nike-X radar; multifunction array radar. R. Barnhart. il Miss & Roc 18:14-15 My 30 '66
Closing out: 1 billion dollars' worth of missiles; Atlas and Titan I (ICBMS) il U S News 61:40-2 Ag 22 '66
SAMs spur changes in combat tactics, new equipment; North Vietnamese sites. C. M. Plattner. il Aviation W 84:26-31 Ja 24 '66

GUIDED missile industries
Big overseas tactical missile buys seen. M. Getler. il Tech W 19:16-18 O 24 '66
British missile industry shows strength. W. C. Wetmore. il Aviation W 85:134-5+ S 26 '66

GUIDED missile targets. See Airplanes, Target

GUIDED missiles
Astrolog; current status of U.S. missile and space programs. See occasional issues of Missiles and rockets
Balancing the terror; US plans to counter Soviet Union's anti-ballistic missile system. il Newsweek 68:50+ N 21 '66
Ballistic missiles ruled out in Vietnam. M. Getler. Miss & Roc 18:12-13 Mr 7 '66
Blowpipe missile unveiled at Farnborough; shoulder-launched anti-aircraft missile. il Aviation W 85:29 S 12 '66
Closing out: 1 billion dollars' worth of missiles; Atlas and Titan I (ICBMS) il U S News 61:40-2 Ag 22 '66

Laser-, fluid-guided army missiles planned. Tech W 19:19 N 7 '66
Leading international missiles; specifications (cont) Aviation W 84:224-5 Mr 7 '66
MAW under test for anti-tank use; medium assault weapon. il Aviation W 85:22 Ag 29 '66
Minuteman 2 reliability problems arise. Aviation W 85:19 Ag 22 '66
Missile myths exploding. R. Hotz. Aviation W 84:21 Ja 24 '66
New ICBM program taking shape. M. Getler. Miss & Roc 18:12-13 Ap 11 '66
Next, Poseidon; U.S. planning expansion of missile arsenal. Time 88:32 N 25 '66
Phase two Poseidon contracts let. C. D. LaFond. il Miss & Roc 18:28+ Ap 11 '66
Photos reveal new serb. savage details. il Aviation W 84:85-7 Je 6 '66
Russia talks of peace, builds up missiles. navy. il U S News 61:70-2 N 21 '66
Shoulder-fired missile system passes tests; Redeye. il(p281) Sci N 89:282 Ap 23 '66
Soviet May day review reveals Shaddock, Galosh, Scud details; with photographs. Aviation W 84:30-1 My 16 '66
Soviet missile efforts emphasize concealment, mobility, anti-ICBM. Aviation W 84:90 Mr 7 '66
Soviets show details of various missiles; photographs. Aviation W 85:58-9+ N 28 '66
Soviets still lack solid-fuel ICBM's. M. Getler. il Tech W 18:17 Je 6 '66
Soviets trying to close strategic gap. M. Getler. Tech W 18:14-15 Je 27 '66
Three missiles figure in DOD request. M. Getler. Miss & Roc 18:13-14 Ja 24 '66
USSR to put multiple warheads on ICBM's. M. Getler. Tech W 19:13-14 D 12 '66
U.S. drones and target missiles; specifications (cont) Aviation W 84:227 Mr 7 '66
U.S. missiles; specifications (cont) Aviation W 84:193-4 Mr 7 '66
Viet spurs tactical missile development. M. L. Yaffee. Aviation W 84:29-30 Mr 28 '66
World missile/space encyclopedia 1966. il Tech W 19:42-8+ Jl 25 '66
World's handiest guided missile; Redeye. il Life 60:69-70 Ap 29 '66

Control

Fluid missile control moves closer. il Miss & Roc 18:25-6+ Mr 28 '66
Fluidic missile control system shown at AESCON gathering. C. D. LaFond. il Tech W 19:18-19 O 10 '66
Martin missile guidance development center opening. C. D. LaFond. il Miss & Roc 18: 32-3 My 2 '66
Need for accurate missile guidance systems emphasized. R. Pay. Miss & Roc 18:101-2 Mr 28 '66
Theodolite, gyro combined for improved guidance accuracy; instrument using Barnes miniature electronic autocollimator. C. D. LaFond. il Tech W 19:32-3 N 14 '66

Defenses

AMOS may feed new ABM designs. M. Getler. Tech W 18:20 Je 13 '66
Advanced anti-satellite system in offing. M. Getler and R. Pay. Miss & Roc 18:69-70 My 30 '66
Anti-arms race; ABM deployment. Commonweal 85:392 Ja 13 '67
ABM, the next MLF? J. J. Stone. Bul Atomic Sci 22:20-1 S '66
Anti-missile defense: should Nike X be deployed? L. J. Carter; reply. G. S. Stanford. Science 151:1329-30 Mr 18 '66
Anti-missile gap? U.S. and U.S.S.R. il Newsweek 69:21-2 Ja 9 '67
AMM decision. Nation 202:114 Ja 31 '66
Anti-missile missile for export? A. Hamilton. New Repub 155:14-17 D 10 '66
Anti-missile missile: next entry in the arms race? L. J. Carter. il Science 154:985-7 N 25 '66
Anti-missiles: new twist in the arms spiral. G. C. Wilson. il Nation 204:46-9 Ja 9 '67
Anti-SAM weapon development stressed. C. Brownlow. Aviation W 84:26-8 Mr 21 '66
Anti-SLBM being developed using surplus army Redstones. Miss & Roc 18:15 Ap 4 '66
Arms race, a spiral of fear. R. D. Senter. New Repub 154:17-18 My 7 '66
Arms spiral; Nike X project; profits for industries involved. Nation 204:35 Ja 9 '67
Balancing the terror; US plans to counter Soviet Union's anti-ballistic missile system. il Newsweek 68:50+ N 21 '66
Bids due soon on new Nike-X radar; multifunction array radar. R. Barnhart. il Miss & Roc 18:14-15 My 30 '66

GUIDED missiles—Defenses—*Continued*

Can Nike X save us? B. Davidson. il Sat Eve Post 239:19-21 Ag 27 '66

Chinese missile shot forcing Nike choice. M. Getler. il Tech W 19:13-14 N 7 '66

Containing ABM; anti-ballistic missile system. Commonweal 84:271-2 My 27 '66

Decision near on future of interim ARM. Aviation W 85:28 D 5 '66

Defusing an arms race; administration persuading Russia not to deploy an antimissile system. il Bsns W p 13-14 D 24 '66

DOD asks restoration of funds for guided missile destroyers. H. M. David. Tech W 19:17 Ag 8 '66

DOD halves Nike-X cost estimate for area defense against China. Aviation W 85:77 Jl 4 '66

Fragile shelter; ABM system. Nation 204: 36 Ja 9 '67

Glimpse of the '70s. Time 87:26 F 4 '66

Hawks on the wing; ABM system. Nation 203:563-4 N 28 '66

House seen pushing Nike-X acceleration. G. C. Wilson. il Aviation W 84:30-1 Je 6 '66

If Zeus fails, can Sprint save us? J. Bergman. il N Y Times Mag p26-7+ Mr 20 '66

Inadequate defense against World war III. D. Lawrence. U S News 61:88 D 26 '66

Is Soviet arms race starting again? Russians' anti-missile system raises Pentagon fears. il Bsns W p38-40 N 19 '66

McNamara says Soviets err on ABM. M. Getler. Miss & Roc 18:12-14 My 2 '66

Mind over missile? U.S.-Soviet talks to head off escalation in missile race. Newsweek 69:16 Ja 2 '67

Missile defense: signs of another hot debate; concerning State-of-the-Union message. U S News 62:12 Ja 23 '67

Missile puzzle; U.S. mystified by new spurt of Russian missile activity. Time 88:28+ D 16 '66

Navy's standard missile gets nod as anti-radiation weapon. Tech W 19:18 D 12 '66

New heat in the missile killer race; Russia's antimissile rocket. il U S News 61:12 N 21 '66

New radar system to aid ECM design; investigating vulnerability of missile systems to electronic countermeasures. R. Pay. Miss & Roc 18:36-7 Mr 7 '66

Next: a new, costly arms race? U S News 62:18 Ja 2 '67

Nike-X: bullet that can hit a bullet; antimissile defense system. il U S News 60:50 My 23 '66

Nike-X deployment feud heightening. M. Getler. Miss & Roc 18:12 My 9 '66

Nike-X production still in doubt. C. Brownlow. Aviation W 85:26-7 N 7 '66

Nike-X: who needs it? J. J. Stone. New Repub 154:11-12 Je 18 '66

North Vietnam may seek new SAM's. Tech W 19:15 Jl 4 '66

Now it's official: missile gap narrows. il U S News 61:8 D 19 '66

Pacific test site shortcomings hamper ICBM, penaids efforts. il Tech W 19:32-3 Jl 4 '66

Senate may force new anti-missile policy. G. C. Wilson. Aviation W 84:28 My 2 '66

Should we build Nike-X? G. A. W. Boehm. Read Digest 88:77-81 Mr '66

Soviet ABM deployment expected in year. M. Getler. il Tech W 19:10-12 N 21 '66

Soviet ICBM report awesome; summary of address, June 2, 1966. F. J. Larsen. Tech W 18:10 Je 6; il Je 13 '66

Soviet ICBM strength; letter to the editor. A. Sylvester. Tech W 18:8 Je 13 '66

$30 billion vs. 70 million U.S. lives. U S News 61:30-3 N 28 '66

Troubles shadow SAM-D development nod. M. Getler. Tech W 19:14 Ag 22 '66

U.S. opting for new, low-cost ABM; anti-ballistic missile system to counter a Communist Chinese ICBM threat. M. Getler. Tech W 18:14-16 Je 20 '66

U.S. USSR seen nearer weapons accord. M. Getler. Tech W 20:14-15 Ja 16 '67

Viet action dramatizes SAM deficiencies. C. Brownlow. il Aviation W 85:26-9 Jl 11 '66

Why not an anti-missile missile? J. Burnham. Nat R 18:567 Je 14 '66

See also
Radar defense network

Electronic equipment

Electron-beam device aids ECM problems; electronic countermeasures devices for ICBM warheads. il Tech W 19:16-17 D 19 '66

Testing

Bendix expected to develop general-purpose checkout unit. il Tech W 19:34-5 Jl 11 '66

Equipment

Background contrast is key to missile targeting system; weapon getting army scrutiny; homing system for air-launched anti-tank missile. il Tech W 19:40 O 3 '66

2.75-in. rocket fuze production gains. C. D. LaFond. Miss & Roc 18:21 Ap 25 '66

Fuel

LPC moves toward practical hybrid. J. F. Judge. il Miss & Roc 18:34+ My 16 '66

Launching

Delivery of refurbished Atlas boosters begins this month. il Tech W 19:18 Jl 11 '66

Gun-launched rocket interest rejuvenated. J. F. Judge. il Tech W 19:24-5 O 3 '66

Launching from airplanes

Area correlation tracker demonstrated. il Miss & Roc 18:41 Mr 14 '66

Boeing chosen to produce air force SRAM. il Tech W 19:12 N 7 '66

Decision near on future of iterim ARM. Aviation W 85:28 D 5 '66

DOD denies navy FY 1968 money for purchase of AS-12. M. Getler. il Tech W 20: 18-19 Ja 9 '67

Mach 4 AF target to use UTC hybrid. il Tech W 19:20+ Jl 11 '66

Navy moves to add Sparrow to F-111B. il Tech W 18:19 Je 20 '66

Navy to seek Nord AS.12 missile buy; wire-guided, air-to-surface missile. Aviation W 84:34+ My 16 '66

Navy's standard missile gets nod as anti-radiation weapon. Tech W 19:18 D 12 '66

Phoenix coming in underweight; navy/DOD optimism grows. M. Getler. il Tech W 19: 26-7 S 19 '66

Saab 305A complements shipping missile. il Aviation W 84:88-9 Ja 24 '66

Shortages slow 2.75-in. rocket effort; folding fin aircraft rockets. J. F. Judge and C. D. LaFond. il Miss & Roc 18:16-17 Ap 18 '66

Thiokol builds prototype ducted rocket. il Aviation W 84:100 Je 13 '66

USAF contracts for SRAM, A-7. il Aviation W 85:30 N 7 '66

Launching from ships

Navy eyes new sea-based deterrent. M. Getler. Tech W 19:14-15 Jl 4 '66

Tactical Polaris proposed for Vietnam. R. Lindsey. il Tech W 19:31-2 Jl 4 '66

Launching from submarine boats

America's poseidon: absolutely guaranteed to breach red defenses; bigger than present Polaris. il U S News 61:30-1 N 28 '66

I rode our newest Polaris missile sub. H. Fantel. il Pop Mech 126:112-16+ N '66

Materials refinement assists Poseidon launcher designers. R. Lindsey. il Tech W 18: 32-3 Je 13 '66

Navy eyes new sea-based deterrent. M. Getler. Tech W 19:14-15 Jl 4 '66

Materials

Materials refinement assists Poseidon launcher designers. R. Lindsey. il Tech W 18: 32-3 Je 13 '66

New effort aimed at X-ray protection. R. Pay. il Tech W 20:10-12 Ja 2 '67

Propulsion

Aerojet to build alternate Phoenix motor. il Tech W 19:19 Ag 8 '66

ARC production Redeye units for army, marine corps use. J. F. Judge. il Tech W 19: 29-30 O 24 '66

Hercules, Thiokol unique in Poseidon team; rocket motor. J. F. Judge. il Tech W 19: 23-4 S 5 '66

Lockheed pulse motor seen feasible for navy missiles. il Tech W 18:36 Je 27 '66

Possible second phase studied after successful HIBEX tests; High-G boost experiment. Tech W 19:38 O 3 '66

RPI sees F-111 escape rocket proving ability. J. F. Judge. il Tech W 19:25+ Jl 18 '66

Protective measures

See also
Guided missiles—Shielding (radiation)

Repairing

Clinic for sick missiles. A. Whitman. il Pop Mech 125:120-4 F '66

GUIDED missiles—*Continued*

Shielding (radiation)

New effort aimed at X-ray protection. R. Pay. il Tech W 20:10-12 Ja 2 '67

Testing

ACT tested for air-to-surface weapon use. C. D. LaFond. il Tech W 19:33-4 O 31 '66

Clinic for sick missiles. A. Whitman. il Pop Mech 125:120-4 F '66

Fire arrow; successful missile shot. il Time 88:35 N 4 '66

Fireball over Lop Nor; fueled missile carrying a nuclear warhead fired by China. il Newsweek 68:74-5 N 7 '66

Mao's missile in Sinkiang. America 115:572 N 12 '66

Red China with the A-missile, meaning to U.S. Russia; with interview with C. Cheng. il U S News 61:50-2+ N 14 '66

Red China's atomic shot; what it means to the world. il U S News 61:6 N 7 '66

Torture rides the desert rails. J. Eberhart. Sci N 90:533 D 24 '66

What to do about Peking's missile. Nat R 18:1144 N 15 '66

Tracking

AN/FPQ-10 radar in final checkout at PMR. il Tech W 19:46 Ag 15 '66

Area correlation tracker demonstrated. il Miss & Roc 18:41 Mr 14 '66

Missile guidance simulator for tests; electro-optical guidance simulator. il Sci N 89:309 Ap 30 '66

Pacific test site shortcomings hamper ICBM, penaids efforts. il Tech W 19:32-3 Jl 4 '66

Track plans Mach 6 nose cone tests. R. Pay. il Miss & Roc 18:26+ Mr 21 '66

GUIDED missiles, Atomic powered

Testing

Chinese puzzle. W. J. Coughlin. Tech W 19:50 N 7 '66

Track plans Mach 6 nose cone tests. R. Pay. il Miss & Roc 18:26+ Mr 21 '66

GUIDES

How to hire a guide. A. J. McClane. il Field & S 71:110-12 O '66

Seize the moment! aspects of field practice for the park guide. F. Tilden. Parks & Rec 1:625+ Ag '66

See also
Mountaineering

GUILLAIN, Robert
Shanghai's repentant capitalists. Reporter 34: 38-41 Ap 7 '66

GUILLAUME, Paul
Dandy at the helm. F. Cachin. il Art N 65: 36-8+ Ap '66
Gift of love. Time 87:78 F 4 '66

GUILT
How to handle guilt. F. R. Schreiber and M. Herman. il Sci Digest 59:16-18 Je '66

GUINAN, Don
We duck the Dutch elm disaster. il Am City 81:102-3 Mr '66

GUINEA

Foreign relations

Africa's top nationalist, or Africa's prima donna? S. Touré. L. Garrison. il N Y Times Mag p 12-13+ Ja 1 '67

Flight 150 to Accra. il Newsweek 68:52 N 14 '66

Hostages held; Ghana vs. Guinea. il Sr Schol 89:25-6 N 18 '66

Unhappy landing of Flight 150; international incident over a Pan American put down at Accra airport. il Time 88:41 N 11 '66

U.S. informs OAU of position of Ghana-Guinea dispute; text of note. Dept State Bul 55:790-1 N 21 '66

Politics and government

My country is yours. il Newsweek 67:57-8 Mr 14 '66

Parlor games at the Villa Sily; no move to restore Nkrumah to power. Time 87:39 Ap 1 '66

La GUIRLANDE de campra; ballet. See Ballets—Criticisms

GUITAR, Mary Anne
Putting a push in compassion. Mlle 62:100-1+ Ja '66

Those doctors who hand out diet pills. Ladies Home J 83:79+ My '66; Same abr. with title Diet pill menace. Read Digest 89:55-8 Jl '66

Unbugged student. Mlle 63:300-1+ Ag '66

You only go around once. Mlle 63:132+ Je '66

GUITAR
Guitar on the go. S. Fleming. il Hi Fi 16: 40-5 Jl '66

Instant music; or how to play the guitar in one easy lesson. il Seventeen 25:412-13 Ag '66

Loud the twang of the guitar. V. Kelly. il Read Digest 90:143-6 Ja '67

Put a guitar amplifier in your pocket. L. Steckler. il Pop Mech 126:198-9+ O '66

Teen-age money music; combo groups. il Life 60:102-4+ Je 3 '66

There's more than one way to pick a guitar. Bet Hom & Gard 44:125 Je '66

Viva the no-voltage guitar! J. Bream's playing. C. Harman. Life 61:12 N 4 '66

GUITAR music
Guitar on the go. S. Fleming. il Hi Fi 16:40-5 Jl '66

GUITARISTS
Loud the twang of the guitar V. Kelly. il Read Digest 90:143-6 Ja '67

GÜLER, Ara
Golden Horn; photographs. Horizon 8:76-83 Wint '66

GULF and Western industries, incorporated
It's a deal; new mergers. Newsweek 68: 77-8+ Jl 18 '66

Mergers; everybody wants to get bigger. il Newsweek 67:72-3+ Ap 25 '66

GULF OF ALASKA. See Alaska, Gulf of

GULF oil corporation
How Gulf beats industry averages. il Bsns W p 100-2+ S 3 '66

GULF STREAM
Gulf Stream wall charted for ASW; Anti-submarine warfare environmental prediction service. R. W. Niblock. il Miss & Roc 18:40-1 My 9 '66

GULI, Francesca
For a letter received; poem. America 115:691 N 26 '66

GULIASHKI, Andrei
Secret agent 07. por Newsweek 69:55 Ja 23 '67

GULICK, Louise Arndt
Shakedown. Flying 79:58 D '66

GULICK, Luther
Road to unity; excerpts from address. por Parks & Rec 1:309 Ap '66

GULKIS, Samuel, and Carr, T. D.
Radio rotation period of Jupiter. bibliog Science 154:257-9 O 14 '66

GULLAHORN, Jeanne E. and Gullahorn, J. T.
American students abroad; professional versus personal development. bibliog f Ann Am Acad 368:43-59 N '66

GULLAHORN, John T. See Gullahorn, J. E. jt. auth.

GULLANDER, Werner Paul
Excerpt from statement, July 12, 1965. Cong Digest 45:47+ F '66

NAM is playing by a new set of rules. il por Bsns W p 114-16+ D 17 '66

GULLS
Defense against killers. H. Kruuk. il Natur Hist 75:48-55 Ap '66

Strange gull (?) of the Galápagos; swallow-tailed gull. J. P. Hailman. il Audubon Mag 68:180-4 My '66

GULYAS, S. See Whitmore, G. F. jt. auth.

GUM trees. See Eucalyptus

GUMBO. See Soups

GUMPERTZ, Werner H.
Building movement can damage built-up roofing systems. il Arch Rec 140:221-4 S '66

GUMS (anatomy)

Diseases

More comfort for you at the dentist's. R. Gannon. il Pop Mech 126:96-9+ Ag '66

Most common adult dental disease; periodontal disease. il Good H 162:180 Ap '66

Secret of keeping your teeth; how to avoid periodontal disease. D. Murray. Read Digest 88:63-5 Mr '66

GUN carriages
Army adopts Vulcan anti-aircraft vehicle. D. A. Brown. il Aviation W 84:88-9+ Mr 14 '66

GUN drawing. See Shooting

GUN mounts. See Gun carriages

GUN sights. See Firearms—Sights

GUN stocks. See Gunstocks

GUN turrets. See Turrets, Gun

GUNDERSHEIM, Art
Reader's guide to publications on China. Bul Atomic Sci 22:88-90+ Je '66

GUNDERSHEIMER, Werner L.
Patterns of history. Reporter 34:50-2 Ap 21 '66

GUNDERSON, Doris V.
Reading-go-round. por Am Ed 2:26-7 D '65

GUNN, Benjamin
U.S. rocketeers rip the iron curtain. Pop Mech 126:152-3 O '66

GUNN, J. B.
Solid-state source of microwaves. R. Bowers. il Sci Am 215:22-31 Ag '66

GUNN, Ross
Thunderstorm electrification of hail and graupel by polar dribble. Science 151:686 F 11 '66

GUNN, Thom
Taylor street; Old man in the Britannia; No speech from the scaffold; Snowfall; Produce district; poems. Poetry 109:69-74 N '66

GUNNERY
Beat the recoil rap! W. Page. il Field & S 71:70-3 Ja '67

GUNNERY, Aerial
See also
Target practice, Aerial

GUNNING. See Hunting

GUNS (small arms) See Firearms; Pistols; Shotguns

GUNS, Antiaircraft
Army adopts Vulcan anti-aircraft vehicle. D. A. Brown. il Aviation W 84:88-9+ Mr 14 '66

GUNS, Spray. See Spraying apparatus

GUNSMITHING
See also
Firearms industry and trade

GUNSTOCKS
Shotgun stock. J. O'Connor. il Outdoor Life 138:76-8+ N '66

GUNTHER, Curt
Great hang-out! right over a canyon. Pop Mech 125:116-17 F '66

GUNTHER, John
Dinner for three; story. Esquire 66:238-9 D '66
Inside Peru. Read Digest 90:134-40 Ja '67
Inside Venezuela. Read Digest 88:147-8+ Mr '66
Overspenders. Ladies Home J 83:75-7+ Ap '66
Trouble with Argentina. Read Digest 89:103-8 S '66
Uruguay: Utopia gone wild. Read Digest 88:187-8+ Ap '66
Visit with Argentina's Borges. Atlan 219:96-8 Ja '67

GUNTHER, Max
How to raise the curtain on an article. Writer 79:9-12 Ag '66
How to research articles by mail. Writer 79:13-16 Ap '66
Long look back to creation. Sat Eve Post 239:23-5 Mr 12 '66
Merchants of Venus. Sat Eve Post 239:74-7 D 31 '66
New ways to kill pain. Sat Eve Post 239:25-7 Jl 2 '66

GUPTON, James A. Jr
How to etch professional printed circuit boards. Pop Electr 24:54-9+ Mr '66

GUREWITZ, Esther
Trembling the inner wall; poem. Harper 232:110-11 Ap '66

GURNEY, Dan
Dan Gurney tests: Chevy's hot new Camaro. Pop Mech 126:103-5+ N '66
Dan Gurney tests Plymouth's fastback '67 Barracuda. Pop Mech 127:92-4+ Ja '67
Drivin' with Dan; questions and answers. por Pop Mech 126:94-5 O; 98-9 N; 74-5 D '66; 127:34+ Ja '67

about
Best driver in the whole world. T. E. Stimson. il por Pop Mech 126:86-9+ Ag '66
Can anyone stop Dan Gurney. il Motor T 19:88 Ja '67
Curse of endurance racing. il Newsweek 67:66-7 Ap 11 '66

GURSKY, Herbert
Identification of the X-ray source in Scorpius. Sky & Tel 32:252-5 N '66

GUSSOW, Mel
Alan Arkin: matchless maskmaker. Holiday 40:91-5+ O '66

GUSTAFSON, Alrik
From royalty to religion. Sat R 49:29-30 Jl 16 '66

GUSTAFSON, James M.
How does love reign? Christian Cent 83:654-5 My 18 '66

GUSTAFSON, Marguerite
Summery dairy foods. por Parents Mag 41:62-8 Je '66

GUSTAITIS, Rasa
Angry parents of I.S. 201. Reporter 35:30-4 N 17 '66

GUSTAVUS III, king of Sweden
Mozart, Moliere, and Cupid. M. Moseley. il Dance Mag 40:56-61 S '66

GUSTAVUS VI, king of Sweden
Chinese art from the collection of the King of Sweden. F. Getlein. il Craft Horiz 26:30-5 N '66
Royal eye for the Chinese. il Time 89:54 Ja 13 '67

GUT DAM. See Dams

GUTENBERG, Johann
Gutenberg and the Master of the playing cards, by H. Lehmann-Haupt. Review
Pub W 190:108-9 N 7 '66

GUTENSTEIN, Hanns S.
Swinging lens gives 35mm SLR the right view. D. L. Miller. il Mod Phot 30:26+ S '66

GUTERMUTH, Clinton Raymond
Excerpt from testimony, June 2, 1965. Cong Digest 45:309+ D '66

GUTHMAN, William H.
Decorated military Americana. il Antiques 90:60-3 Jl '66

GUTHRIE, Arlo
Woody's boy. il Newsweek 67:112-13 My 23 '66

GUTHRIE, William L.
Aerial garbage. L. Kent. New Repub 154:8 F 12 '66

GUTIÉRREZ, René Schick-. See Schick-Gutiérrez, R.

GUTMAN, Herbert G.
Protestantism and the American labor movement: the Christian spirit in the gilded age; excerpts from address, April 1965. bibliog f Am Hist R 72:74-101 O '66

GUTTENPLAN, Samuel
Philosopher's clock. New Yorker 42:39-41 My 21 '66

GUTTERS (roof)
Hidden gutters for a shake roof. il Sunset 137:138 O '66

GUTTMACHER, Alan F.
Yes, I'll still prescribe the pills. Good H 162:68-70 F '66

GUTTMANN, Allen
Before the great barbecue. Nation 202:272-3 Mr 7 '66
Body testing the slogans. Nation 204:90-1 Ja 16 '67

GUYANA
Independence for Guyana. T. M. Petry. America 114:854 Je 18 '66
Three Guianas. T. Mathews. Cur Hist 51:333-7+ D '66
See also
Hunting—Guyana
United Nations—Guyana

Foreign relations
Prime Minister of Guyana visits the United States; exchange of greetings and exchange of toasts, July 21, 1966. L. B. Johnson; F. Burnham. Dept State Bul 55:229-31 Ag 15 '66

Politics and government
Gay face of a new nation; independence celebrations. il Life 60:123-4 Je 10 '66
Guyana: rich potential with a space of risk. il Bsns W p 132+ My 28 '66
New nation with big troubles. il U S News 60:16 Je 6 '66
Under five colors. il Time 87:30 Je 3 '66
Uneasy freedom. il Newsweek 67:55 Je 6 '66

GUYS and dolls; musical comedy. See Musical comedies, revues, etc.—Criticisms, plots, etc.

GUZMAN, Ralph. See Moore, J. W. jt. auth.

GUZZARDI, Walter, Jr
Family life Italian style. Sat R 49:35 D 17 '66

GWINNETT, Button
Who's got Button's bones? R. M. Williams. il por Am Heritage 17:28-32+ F '66

GWYN, D. G. and Wolstencroft, J. H.
Ascending and descending cholinergic fibers in cat spinal cord: histochemical evidence. bibliog Science 153:1543-4 S 23 '66

GWYNNE JONES, Arthur, baron Chalfont. See Chalfont, A. G. J.

GYMNASIUMS
Funny thing happened on my way to the sybaritic bath. L. Botto. il Look 31:84-6 Ja 10 '67

GYNECOLOGY
See also
Woman—Diseases
GYPSUM panels. See Paneling
GYPSUM wallboard. See Wallboard
GYROCOPTERS. See Autogiros
GYROPLANES. See Autogiros
GYROSCOPE
Laser unit challenges conventional gyros. P.
J. Klass. il Aviation W 85:103+ S 12 '66
Proving Einstein right; Stanford experiment
to orbit perfect gyroscope. il Time 87:58-9
Ap 22 '66
Theodolite, gyro combined for improved
guidance accuracy; instrument using
Barnes miniature electronic autocollimator.
C. D. LaFond. Tech W 19:32-3 N 14 '66
See also
Gyroscopic instruments
GYROSCOPIC instruments
GPI's two-axis inertial gyro undergoing
service evaluation. R. Barnhart. il Tech
W 19:25 O 10 '66
See also
Automatic pilot (airplanes)
Inertial guidance systems
GZOWSKI, Peter
Television. Nation 203:61-2 Jl 11 '66

H

HAPDAR (hard-point demonstration array
radar) See Radar—Military applications
HARP (high altitude research project) See
Atmospheric research
HARYOU. See Harlem youth opportunities un-
limited, incorporated
H-bombs. See Hydrogen bombs
HSGT (high speed ground transport) systems.
See Transportation. High speed
HUAC. See United States—Congress—House of
representatives—Un-American activities
committee
HUD. See United States—Housing and urban
development, Department of
H. W. Wilson company. See Wilson, H. W.
company
HAAN, E. R.
Reproduce this prized antique on your lathe;
ed. by A. W. Lees. Pop Mech 125:176-81+
Mr '66
HAAS, Joseph
Business and politics of crime. Sat R 50:92
Ja 14 '67
HABER, Leo
School for annotators, or The case of the
multiple liner notes. Hi Fi 16:59-60+ Mr
'66
HABERER, James H.
Granular lime takes bite out of water. Am
City 81:183-4 My '66
HABITABLE worlds. See Life on other planets
HABITS of animals. See Animals—Habits and
behavior
HACHIJOJIMA (island)
Hachijojima. S. Griffin. il Travel 126:44-7 Jl
'66
HACK, Margherita
Hertzsprung-Russell diagram today. Sky &
Tel 31:260-3, 332-6 My-Je '66
HACKER, Andrew
Below the belt. Commentary 42:99-102 D '66
Country called corporate America. N Y Times
Mag p8-9+ Jl 3 '66
Who wants to teach undergraduates? Sat R
49:80-1 D 17 '66
HACKER, Louis M.
Civil rights progress. Sat R 49:27-8 Ag 6 '66
HACKER, Shyrle
Clues to a medal mystery. Writer 79:34 N '66
HACKETT, Robert A.
Harness racing (cont) Sports Illus 25:62+
Ag 29 '66
HACKETT, Walter
Merry Christmas; dramatization of Little
women by L. M. Alcott. Plays 26:88-96
D '66
Tale of two cities; dramatization of novel
by C. Dickens. Plays 26:99-111 N '66
HADAS, Moses
Portrait of a scholar. Commentary 42:91-4
S '66
about
Obituary
Pub W 190:311 Ag 29 '66

HADDAD, Gladys
Relating to Rouault. Sch Arts 65:41 Mr '65
HADDAD, William F.
Mr Shriver and the savage politics of poverty.
Harper 231:43-50 D '65; 232:6 F '66
HADDEN, Jeffrey K.
Churchly particularism and the Jews. Chris-
tian Cent 83:987 Ag 10 '66
HADDON, William, Jr
National traffic safety agency; address,
November 29, 1966. Vital Speeches 33:179-
84 Ja 1 '67
about
Are auto standards too tough? safety stand-
ard for '68 cars. por U S News 62:14 Ja 16
'67
New federal safety czar's tough views on
cars! R. W. Irvin. Motor T 18:42-4 D '66
Scientist buckles the seat belt. por Bsns W
p 120+ O 29 '66
Set for safety. por Time 88:106 S 16 '66
Twenty-three rules. il por Time 88:97-8 D 9
'66
HADLEY, Bernice Albinson
Creative weaving. Sch Arts 65:36-7 F '66
HADLEY, Leila
Practical parents' guide to touring Europe
with children. Holiday 39:179-90 Mr '66
HADLEY, Paul
Now there's even a regatta for houseboats.
Pop Sci 189:142-5 O '66
HADRIAN, emperor of Rome
Royal wanderer with a dream. il pors Life
60:66-9 Je 3 '66
HADRIAN'S wall. See Roman walls—Great
Britain
HAESSLER, Herbert A. and Crawford, J. D.
Lipolysis in homogenates of adipose tissue:
an inhibitor found in fat from obese rats.
bibliog Science 154:909-10 N 18 '66
HAFER, Alvin B.
Forester meets recreationists. Liv Wildn 29:
25-6 Aut '65
el HAFEZ, Amin
Party affair. il por Time 87:42 Mr 4 '66
HAFEZ, E. S. E.
Reproductive failure. Science 154:546+ O 28
'66
HAFLEIGH, Ann S. and Williams, C. A. Jr
Antigenic correspondence of serum albumins
among the primates. bibliog Science 151:
1530-5 Mr 25 '66
HAFLER, David
Derived center-channel stereo system. Electr
World 75:76-7 Ap '66
HAFTEL, Zvi
Waiting for Mr Right. il por Time 87:65
Je 17 '66
HAGANAH
Haganah, by M. M. Mardor, tr. by H. A. G.
Schmuckler. Review
Sat R 49:32-3 Mr 26 '66. H. Lehrman
HAGE, Elizabeth B.
Computer potential in Maryland. por Wilson
Lib Bul 41:401-3 D '66
HAGEL, Raymond Charles
Publisher makes book on learning. il por
Bsns W p 124+ My 14 '66
HAGEN, P. O. and others
Phospholipids of bacteria with extensive in-
tracytoplasmic membranes. bibliog Science
151:1543-4 Mr 25 '66
HAGFISH
Hagfish. D. Jensen. il Sci Am 214:82-90 F '66;
Reply with rejoinder. C. D. Hill. 214:8 My
'66
Multiple gene loci for the monomeric hemo-
globin of the hagfish (eptatretus stoutii).
S. Ohno and M. Morrison. bibliog il Science
154:1034-5 N 25 '66
HAGGADAH. See Passover
HAGGIN, Bernard H.
New records in review. See issues of Yale
review
Records. See issues of New republic
(ed) See Carboni, W. Working with Tosca-
nini
HAGGIS, Alex J.
Deoxyribonucleic acid in germinal vesicles
of oocytes of rana pipiens. bibliog Science
154:670-1 N 4 '66
HAGIOGRAPHY. See Saints
HAGUE, The
International court of Justice
See International court of Justice, The
Hague
HAHN, Emily
Aisle K. New Yorker 42:138+ S 17 '66
Stewart. New Yorker 42:207-10+ O 22 '66
Woman scorned. Sat R 49:38 S 24 '66

HAHN, Fred E. See Ciak, J. jt. auth.

HAHN, George M. and Bagshaw, M. A.
Serum concentration: effects on cycle and X-ray sensitivity of mammalian cells. bibliog Science 151:459-61 Ja 28 '66

HAHN, Otto
Otto the lucky. por Sat R 49:39 D 3 '66

HAIDAK, David J. and others
Pigment protein complex from gonyaulax. bibliog Science 152:212-13 Ap 8 '66

HAIGHT, John McVickar, Jr
Roosevelt as friend of France. bibliog f For Affairs 44:518-26 Ap '66

HAIKU. See Japanese poetry

HAIL
Thunderstorm electrification of hail and graupel by polar dribble. R. Gunn. il Science 151:686 F 11 '66

HAIL Scrawdyke! drama. See Halliwell, D.

HAILE Selassie I, emperor of Ethiopia
Importance of mythology. Nation 202:132-4 Ja 31 '66
Lion comes calling; visit to Trinidad-Tobago, Jamaica and Haiti. il por Time 87:38 Ap 29 '66
Lion wept; Caribbean tour. il por Newsweek 67:52 My 9 '66

HAILMAN, Jack P.
Strange gull (?) of the Galápagos. il por Audubon Mag 68:180-4 My '66

HAINES, Aubrey B.
Miss Velma descends. Christian Cent 83:992+ Ag 10 '66

HAINES, Edmund
In Spain, new music on the rise. Hi Fi 16:MA18-19 Ag '66

HAINES, Jo
Enjoying nature. Audubon Mag 68:370-1 S '66

HAINSWORTH, F. Reed, and Epstein, A. N.
Severe impairment of heat-induced saliva-spreading in rats recovered from lateral hypothalmic lesions. bibliog Science 153:1255-7 S 9 '66

HAINSWORTH, Waldo R.
New England. por Parks & Rec 1:644 Ag '66

HAIPHONG, Vietnam
Memo from Haiphong, North Vietnam; under American bombs. N. Barrymaine. Look 30:62 N 29 '66; Same with title Bomb damage in North Vietnam described. il Aviation W 85:47+ D 26 '66

HAIR
Activation analysis of ungulate hair. G. S. Kennington and C. F. T. Ching. bibliog il Science 151:1085-6 Mr 4 '66
Hairy argument; question of how man lost his body hair. Time 88:55 Ag 19 '66
Mustaches are for men; hirsutism. R. A. Berger and N. Orentreich. il Todays Health 44:69-70+ N '66
See also
Baldness
Beards
Hairdressing
Wigs

Care
Capsule guide to hair care. McCalls 93:55 Mr '66
Four hair woes and how to solve them. il Good H 162:92-3 F '66
Long-hair care. il Mlle 63:128-9 My '66
Quick clinic for problem hair. il Mlle 62:146-7 F '66

Dyeing and bleaching
Colors that bloom in the fall. il McCalls 94:124-5+ O '66
Project: you; questions and answers. Ladies Home J 83:37 Ap '66
Rinse makers glimpse gold in graying males; introduction of Great day, men's hair rinse. il Bsns W p80 Jl 23 '66
There's something about a blonde. il Ladies Home J 83:94-5+ Ap '66

HAIR, Removal of
Mustaches are for men; hirsutism. R. A. Berger and N. Orentreich. il Todays Health 44:69-70+ N '66
Not by the hair of my chinny-chin-chin! il Mlle 63:128-9 O '66
Removing unwanted hair permanently, not a do-it-yourself job. il Consumer Bul 49:34-6 O '66

HAIR dressing. See Hairdressing

HAIR dryers
New portable hair dryers; hard-top. il Consumer Bul 49:16-19 D '66

HAIR pieces. See Wigs

HAIR preparations
By the hair; men advertising hair spray. il Time 89:78 Ja 20 '67
Proof of the product; hair-setting preparations. P. Schwind. McCalls 93:131 Ag '66

HAIR sprays. See Hair preparations

HAIR transplantation. See Transplantation of organs, tissues, etc.

HAIRCUTTING
Hair: cut & dried. il Mlle 63:130-1 My '66

Anecdotes, facetiae, satire, etc.
Of hair: being a disquisition upon its abundance, maintenance, beauty, significance, and excellence. Nat R 18:1090 N 1 '66

HAIRDOS. See Hairdressing

HAIRDRESSING
A.M. and P.M; hairpieces. il McCalls 93:70-1+ Je '66
Be prettier than ever before! eight before and after looks. il Good H 162:104-15+ Ap '66
Beauty bulletin; how to know what to ask for at the hairdresser. il Vogue 147:134-7 Ap 15 '66
Beauty bulletin; 1967. Vogue 149:88 Ja 1 '67
Beauty bulletin; ten hairdressers' predictions on the way hair is going. il Vogue 148:94-6 Ag 15 '66
Beauty life: twenty-one-day dos. il Mlle 62:142-3 F '66
Center part. il Seventeen 25:199 Mr '66
Going straight. il Mlle 63:282-3+ Ag '66
Hair-brained schemes for summer. il Mlle 63:138-9 Je '66
Hairdo of the month. See issues of Seventeen
Have a beauty happening. il Seventeen 26:70-5 Ja '67
How to cope with curly hair: straightening. Seventeen 25:98-9 Jl '66
Integration comes to the beauty business. il Ebony 21:140+ Ag '66
Let it fall. P. Peterson. il N Y Times Mag p48-9 My 29 '66
Long-hair controversy. America 115:578 N 12 '66
Man for all disasters: G. Masters. J. Howard. il Life 61:57-8+ N 25 '66
Natural look. P. Garland. il Ebony 21:142-4+ Je '66
One set, a week of hairdos. il Seventeen 25:174-5+ My '66
Presto! a party hairdo. il Seventeen 25:144-5 N '66
Redbook's guide to the perfect hair style. il Redbook 126:74-82 Mr '66
Romantic long hair. il Redbook 127:74-9+ O '66
Short cuts for spring. il McCalls 93:114-15+ Mr '66
Should you wear bangs? il Seventeen 25:154-5+ F '66
Snip in the air. il Newsweek 69:58 Ja 23 '67
Step by step: Lynda Bird Johnson's Hollywood beauty treatment. V. Scott. il Ladies Home J 83:62+ Jl '66
Swingers: twenty-one carefree hairdos. il Seventeen 25:254-9+ Ag '66
Twelve long hairdos: very, very young! il Good H 162:102-5+ Mr '66

Anecdotes, facetiae, satire, etc.
Guess what! how I found happiness with my hairdresser. L. Benjamin. Ladies Home J 83:11 Ag '66

HAIRPIECES. See Wigs

HAISLIP, Martha
Day-lilies for the new garden. Flower Grower 53:20-2 Jl '66

HAITI
See also
Catholic church in Haiti
Economic assistance in Haiti
Finance—Haiti
Medical relief work—Haiti
United States—Foreign relations—Haiti

Economic conditions
Tyranny in Haiti. G. R. Latortue. bibliog f il Cur Hist 51:349-53+ D '66
What Papa Doc has done to Haiti. C. Migdail. il U S News 60:47-8 My 9 '66

Politics and government
Are we ready to intervene in Haiti? R. D. Heinl, Jr. il Reporter 34:26-8 Je 2 '66
Destiny to suffer. il Time 87:39 My 13 '66
Duvalier's Haiti. Commonweal 84:246 My 20 '66
Haiti: chaotic and corrupt. G. R. Latortue. il Nation 203:539-41 N 21 '66

HAITI—Politics and government—*Continued*
Invaders; planned invasion. Newsweek 69:
31-2 Ja 16 '67
Pistol-packing papa. M. J. Kubic. il News-
week 67:56-7 Je 27 '66
Tyranny in Haiti. G. R. Latortue. bibliog f
il Cur Hist 51:349-53+ D '66
What Papa Doc has done to Haiti. C. Mig-
dail. il U S News 60:47-8 My 9 '66
HAITI in literature
Graham Greene's comedians. D. Lodge. Com-
monweal 83:604-6 F 25 '66
HAKE
Raising hake; West coast industry. il Time
87:94 Mr 18 '66
HAKOSHIMA, Yass
Yass Hokoshima; 92nd street Y. J. Maskey.
Dance Mag 40:63 Jl '66
Yass Hakoshima, 92nd street Y. M. Marks.
Dance Mag 40:75 D '66
HALAS, George Stanley
Quarterbacking a new industry; interview.
pors Nations Bsns 54:52-4+ D '66

about

Last puritan. W. B. Furlong. il por Sports
Illus 24:12-17 Ja 31 '66
HALBACH, Edward
Equipment for timing extreme grazing occul-
tations. il Sky & Tel 33:52-6 Ja '67
HALBERSTAM, David
Poland has seen the future. N Y Times Mag
p 14-15+ F 6 '66
HALBERSTICH, David E.
Which history of photography is best? Pop
Phot 59:75+ Jl '66
HALDANE, Bernard
Focus on success instead of failure. NEA J
55:32 Ap '66
HALDEMAN, Josh N.
Haldeman way. pors Flying 78:50-4 Je '66
HALE, Dennis
Pounds of prevention. Time 88:30 D 9 '66
—See McWilliams, W. C. jt. auth.
HALE, Frank
Overhead projector progress at Willow Glen
h.s. Sr Schol 87:sup20-1 Ja 14 '66
HALE, George Ellery
Explorer of the universe, by H. Wright.
Review
Sci Am 215:153-5 N '66. H. Shapley
HALE, Nancy
Animals in the house; story. Harper 233:94-
100 S '66
Most elegant drawing room in Europe; story.
New Yorker 42:55-64 S 17 '66
HALE telescope. See Telescope
HALEAKALA observatory. See Observatories
HALES, David
Enlightenment from the East. Sat R 49:48 D
3 '66
Inside the lower East side. Sat R 49:42+
O 15 '66
HALEY, Alex
Interviewing the interviewer; ed. by H.
Frankel. Sat R 49:37-8 F 5 '66
HALEY, Joseph
Jet in my windshield. Flying 78:108 F '66
HALF dollars. See Money—United States
HALF-frame cameras. See Cameras
HALFORD, Robert G.
Gone flying north to Canada. Flying 78:
114-17+ Je '66
HALFWAY houses. See Mentally ill—Care and
treatment
HALI, Rinske
Beauty life: three smart girls and what
they've learned about makeup. il pors
Mlle 64:98-101+ Ja '67
HALICTINE bees. See Bees
HALIFAX, Edward Frederick Lindley Wood,
1st earl of
Halifax, by the Earl of Birkenhead. Review
Nat R 18:844+ Ag 23 '66. S. Leslie
Professional touch. G. A. Craig. Reporter 34:
54 Mr 10 '66
HALITOSIS
Finding the hidden causes of bad breath. D.
W. Stephens. il Todays Health 44:4-5 D
'66
HALL, Albert G.
Washington lookout. See issues of American
forests
HALL, Alice M.
Index is a mockery; letter to the editor. Li-
brary J 91:4050-1 S 15 '66
HALL, Bob
Boudoir Bob. il por Time 88:30 Jl 29 '66
HALL, Calvin S.
Disquiet after hours. Mlle 64:77+ Ja '67

HALL, Cameron P.
Those who stand at the queue's end. Chris-
tian Cent 83:1271-3 O 19 '66
HALL, Clarence W.
How Japan stopped its population explosion.
Read Digest 88:138-41 Mr '66
Indonesia: night of terror, dawn of hope.
Read Digest 89:275-8+ O '66
—See Beech, K. jt. auth.
HALL, David
Attention foundations and university presses:
here is a new way of getting those deletions
back. Am Rec G 32:944-5+ Je '66
HALL, Donald
Man in the dead machine; poem. New Yorker
42:195 N 19 '66
Writers on the campus. Atlan 217:87-90 Mr
'66
HALL, Durward Gorham
Excerpt from remarks. Cong Digest 45:150+
My '66
HALL, Edward T.
Editor interviews; ed. by M. S. Fenner. por
NEA J 56:87-8 Ja '67
HALL, Elizabeth C.
Books in review. Natur Hist 75:6+ Mr '66
Latest gardening books. Pop Gard 17:34-5+
D '66
HALL, ElvaJean
Pointers on paperbacks. Library J 91:2589-91
My 15 '66
Read now and enjoy it later. Sr Schol 88:sup
10 Mr 4 '66
HALL, Emilie T.
Make nature study a family hobby. Suc
Farm 64:63+ Je '66
HALL, Ernest M. Jr
Broadsider. por Time 88:96 S 9 '66
Trouble at Westec. por Newsweek 68:78+
S 12 '66
HALL, Frances
Continuity; poem. America 114:808 Je 4 '66
Morning in Anatolia; poem. America 115:691
N 26 '66
HALL, J. Edward, and Nelson, B. J.
Expectant mother. Redbook 128:50+ N '66
HALL, J. G. See Rasmusen, B. A. jt. auth.
HALL, J. Revis, and others
Personalizing instruction. NEA J 55:36-7 N
'66
HALL, James B.
Duel in the sun. il Newsweek 68:66 N 14 '66
Hall's Chaparral: racing to the top. il pors
Newsweek 67:48-52 F 7 '66
HALL, Joellen
Introducing Joellen Hall. B. H. Friedman. il
Art N 65:32-3+ D '66
HALL, Lee
Ian is like a wounded buffalo. Life 60:30-1
My 27 '66
Well-tamer Boots Hansen tackles the wild
inferno. Life 60:26-31 F 18 '66

about

One spark could immolate all of us. G. P.
Hunt. il por Life 60:3 F 18 '66
HALL, Marvin D.
Borrow ideas from this low-cost beef con-
finement barn. Suc Farm 64:34-5 O '66
HALL, Richard W.
Footing the bill. Opera N 31:8-12 D 17 '66
Sound and the fury. Opera N 30:8-13 Mr 26
'66
HALL, Robert E. See Lehman, E. F. jt. auth.
HALL, Robert Elliott
Abortion epidemic; summary of report at
meeting of the American public health
association. por Newsweek 68:92 N 14 '66
HALL, William M.
Many faces of Padre Island. il Am For 72:
30-2+ O '66
HALL, Willis. See Waterhouse, K. jt. auth.
HALL of science. See New York (city)—Hall
of science
HALLE, Louis J.
Halle's applied philosophy. R. Steel. New
Repub 154:28-30 My 14 '66
HALLER, Henri
Into the blender. Time 87:20 Ja 28 '66
HALLIDAY, E. M.
Geronimo! Am Heritage 17:56-63+ Je '66
I lift my lamp beside the golden door. Am
Heritage 17:97 F '66
HALLIDAY, James D.
Why security analysts run harder these days.
il pors Bsns W p 128-30+ D 17 '66
HALLINAN, Paul John, abp
Common goal. America 116:11-14 Ja 7 '67
HALLINAN, Terence
Lawyer despite himself. il por Time 89:39 Ja
13 '67

HALLIWELL, David
Hail Scrawdyke! Criticism
  Commonweal 85:348 D 23 '66
  New Repub 155:32-3+ D 17 '66
  Newsweek 68:100 D 12 '66
HALLMAN, Laura Lee
Gone flying to Panama. Flying 79:52-6 Ag '66
HALLMARK cards, incorporated
Books as display; A. Skira exhibition. F. P.
  Naughton. il Wilson Lib Bul 41:331-3 N '66
Story behind Hallmark. il Changing T 20:20
  My '66
HALLOWEEN
Halloween. il Sch Arts 66:8-10 O '66
Once again here comes Hallow's eve; chil-
  dren's party. il Sunset 137:96-7 O '66
Treats for tricksters; recipes. B. M. Stover. il
  Parents Mag 41:82-3 O '66

Drama
Enchanted broom. G. L. Lahr. Plays 26:72-4
  O '66
Flight of the moon witches. F. R. Flanders.
  Plays 26:67-71 O '66
Hound of the Maskervilles. H. L. Miller.
  Plays 26:15-27 O '66
Scaredy cat. C. Boiko. Plays 26:41-6, 96 O
  '66
HALLOWELL, John
How the angels smiled on Angela. Life 60:
  92B+ Je 17 '66
I don't want people to see me as myself.
  Life 60:60+ My 6 '66
I hate that woman! no, I love her! Life 61:
  59+ D 2 '66
HALLS
Bassett residence, Nassau Bay, Texas. il
  Arch Rec 139:52-5 mid-Mv '66
Going out in the rain and coming back in.
  il Sunset 137:167 O '66
How to live happily without an entrance hall.
  C. T. Sigman. il Pop Sci 188:154-7 F '66
Peripheral corridor provides sun control. il
  Arch Rec 140:172-3 N '66
These entries don't stop at the door! il Bet
  Hom & Gard 44:52-3 Ag '66
HALLSTORM, Sir Edward John Lees
Friend in time of trouble. por Life 60:75 Ap
  15 '66
HALLUCINATIONS. See Illusions and halluci-
  nations
HALLUCINOGENIC drugs
Chemical salvation. America 115:403 O 8 '66
Doctor Leary and Dr Pusey. America 115:
  440 O 15 '66
More light, less heat over LSD. il Bsns W
  p78+ Je 25 '66
Mysticism in the lab; drug-induced mystic-
  ism. il Time 88:62 S 23 '66
Notes and comment; effects of consciousness-
  expanding drugs. New Yorker 42:41-2 O
  1 '66
Offerings at the psychedelicatessen. R. R.
  Lingeman. il N Y Times Mag p6-7+ Jl 10
  '66; Discussion. p2 Jl 31 '66
Psychedelic game; excerpt from Psychedelic
  reader. R. Hoffmann. Mlle 62:179+ Mr '66
Turned-on way of life. il Newsweek 68:72+
  N 28 '66
  See also
Dipropyltryptamine
Ibogaine
Lysergic acid diethylamide
HALLUCINOGENIC drugs and art
Psychedelic art. il Life 61:60-6+ S 9 '66
HALOGENS
Apatite and octa-calcium phosphate: effects
  of carbon dioxide and halogens on forma-
  tion. D. R. Simpson. bibliog il Science 154:
  1660-1 D 30 '66
HALOID company. See Xerox corporation
HALOTHANE
Popular anesthetic safe. F. Marley. Sci N
  90:194 S 17 '66
HALPER, Sam
After Trujillo. New Repub 155:25-8 D 24 '66
HALPERIN, Ernst
Castro regime in Cuba. bibliog f Cur Hist
  51:354-9 D '66
HALPERIN, Irving
Playground in hell. Sat R 49:42+ N 26 '66
Reconciliation in Israel. Christian Cent 83:
  216-22 F 16 '66
HALPERIN, Morton H.
China and nuclear proliferation: adaptation
  of address, April 21, 1966. bibliog Bul
  Atomic Sci 22:4-10 N; 18-24 D '66
HALPERIN, Samuel
Halperin: government action affecting books;
  summary of address. Pub W 190:80+ D 5
  '66

HALPERIN, Walter
Single cells, coconut milk, and embryogen-
  esis in vitro. bibliog Science 153:1287-8 S
  9 '66
HALPERN, A. M.
Way red China can be stopped; interview.
  por U S News 60:56-9 Mr 21 '66
HALPERN, Irving W.
Most uncommon man. Nation 204:5 Ja 2 '67
HALPERN, Seymour
Excerpt from testimony, August 19, 1965.
  Cong Digest 45:153+ My '66
HALPRIN, Ann
Dancers and architects build kinetic environ-
  ments. J. Anderson. il Dance Mag 40:52-6+
  N '66
HALPRIN, Kenneth M.
Scientists discover secret of skin color. il por
  Ebony 22:85-6+ Ja '67
HALPRIN, Lawrence
Dancers and architects build kinetic environ-
  ments. J. Anderson. il Dance Mag 40:52-6+
  N '66
Pioneer planner in the western wilderness. P.
  Knight. por Sports Illus 24:52 Mr 28 '66
HALS, Frans
Uncle behind the laughter. il Time 88:90-1 N
  25 '66
HALSEY, Margaret
Integration has failed. Christian Cent 83:1596-
  7 D 28 '66
HALSMAN, Philippe
Halsman talks portraits; excerpts from ad-
  dress. pors Pop Phot 59:102-3+ O '66
HALSTED, William Stewart
William Halsted: tragic figure, great sur-
  geon; excerpt from The great doctors. R.
  Silverberg. il Todays Health 45:62-7 Ja '67
HALVORSON, H. O. See Douthit, H. A. jt.
  auth.
HAM
  See also
Cookery—Meat
HAM radio stations. See Radio stations, Ama-
  teur
HAMALIAN, Leo
Class of 1966: loss of tragedy. Nation 202:
  676-9 Je 6 '66
HAMAMELIS virginiana. See Witch hazel
HAMBERGER, A. and others
Enzyme changes in neurons and glia during
  barbiturate sleep. Science 151:1394-5 Mr 18
  Mr 18 '66
HAMBLETONIAN race. See Harness racing
HAMBLIN, Dora Jane
It may be funny but no laughter, please,
  we're very serious. Life 60:84-6 Ap 1 '66
They are idiot savants, wizards of the cal-
  endar. Life 60:106-8+ Mr 18 '66
Visit to mama Mussolini. Life 60:39-44 F 11
  '66
  about
Dodie, Eisie, Marlon, Charlie and Sophia.
  G. P. Hunt. por Life 60:3 Ap 1 '66
HAMBRECHT, Margaret
La casserole emaillee; poem. Mlle 63:215 Ag
  '66
HAMBRO family
Profiles. J. Wechsberg. New Yorker 41:42-6+
  F 5 '66
HAMBROS bank, limited. See London—Banks
HAMBURG
Gripe corner; Theodor Heuss Platz. il News-
  week 67:50 Mr 14 '66

Industries
West Germany's publishing powerhouse; A.
  Springer's empire. J. Tebbel. Sat R 50:125-
  6 Ja 14 '67

Music
Berlin, Hamburg. J. H. Sutcliffe. il Opera N
  31:25 N 19 '66
Ginger in the opera house. P. Moor. Hi Fi
  16:147 F '66
New wine in new bottles; premiere of G.
  Schuller's opera The visitation. R. Gelatt.
  il Reporter 35:58-9 N 17 '66

Rapid transit
  See also
Hamburg—Subways

Street traffic
One way to beat the traffic; Hamburg goes
  underground. il U S News 61:112 O 3 '66

Subways
One way to beat the traffic; Hamburg goes
  underground. il U S News 61:112 O 3 '66

HAMBURG opera festival. See Music festivals
—Germany (Federal Republic)
HAMBURGER, Michael
Romantically anti-bourgeois. Nation 203:458-9
O 31 '66
U.S. offers condolence and aid to Vietnamese
bombed in error; poem. Nation 203:711 D
26 '66
(tr) See Enzensberger, H. M. For the grave
of a peace-loving man
HAMBURGER, Philip
Notes for a gazetteer. New Yorker 42:219-
22+ N 5 '66
HAMBURGER, Robert N.
Chloramphenicol-specific antibody. bibliog Sci-
ence 152-203-5 Ap 8 '66
HAMBURGERS. See Cookery—Meat
HAMER, Elizabeth E. and McCormick, Adoreen
Washington report: from the Library of Con-
gress. See issues of ALA bulletin
HAMER, Fannie Lou
Builders of a new South. P. Garland. il pors
Ebony 21:27-30+ Ag '66
HAMILL, Pete
Lost hero. por Sat Eve Post 239:84-6+ My
21 '66
HAMILTON, Andrew
Anti-missile missile for export? New Repub
155:14-17 D 10 '66
HAMILTON, Andrew Jackson
Fighting fire with fire. Am For 72:18-21+ Jl
'66
How we can delay old age. Sci Digest 59:45-
8 F '66
Israel, land of milk and honey. Am For 71:
20-4+ O '65
Little red schoolhouse goes modern. Read
Digest 89:164-6+ O '66
New facts about fats in your diet. Sci Digest
59:53-6 Je '66
Personality of the month. Sci Digest 59:12-
17 Mr '66
Tomorrow's schools are here today. PTA
Mag 61:4-7 O '66; Same with title Little
red schoolhouse goes modern. Read Digest
89:164-6+ O '66
What science is learning about smell. Sci
Digest 60:81-4 N '66
(ed) See Brooks, M. Hope and help for handi-
capped children
HAMILTON, Bryce
Project Sam. O. Bay. il por Farm J 90:66
My '66
HAMILTON, Clive, pseud. See Lewis, C. S.
HAMILTON, Denis
Thomson takes the Times. por Time 88:61
O 7 '66
HAMILTON, Donald
Pronghorns in the pasture. por Outdoor Life
137:54-5+ F '66
HAMILTON, E. I.
Distribution of uranium in some natural
minerals. bibliog Science 151:570-2 F 4 '66
HAMILTON, E. L. and Von Huene, R. E.
Kodiak seamount not flat-topped. bibliog Sci-
ence 154:1323-5 D 9 '66
HAMILTON, Edward A.
Fifty books show: balanced view of U.S.
output. por Pub W 189:66-7+ My 2 '66
HAMILTON, George
Close-up: George Hamilton; interview. ed.
by S. Graham. por McCalls 93:42+ S '66

about

As draft pressures mount—. por U S News
61:8 N 7 '66
Charley, mv boy? il por Time 88:37 O 7 '66
First family suitors: their military status.
il por U S News 60:22 Ap 25 '66
George Hamilton: elegant young rebel. C.
Brossard. il pors Look 30:76+ Mr 22 '66
Hollywood house party. il por Newsweek 67:
36 Mr 28 '66
Lynda Bird's dashing Hollywood beau. M.
Byers. il pors Life 60:51-2+ My 13 '66
New girl in town; L. Johnson's visit. por
Time 87:21 Mr 25 '66
Number one; draft deferment. il por News-
week 68:38 N 7 '66
That Hamilton man. il pors Newsweek 67:27
Ap 4 '66
Wonderful, terrible life of the President's
daughters. il por Newsweek 67:36-8+ My
23 '66
HAMILTON, George Heard
American artist with a mission. Sat R 49:49
Je 11 '66
Impact in chiaroscuro and color. Sat R 49:24-7
Ag 27 '66
Mirrors for a mad world. Sat R 49:36 Ap 2
'66

Panorama from the palette. Sat R 49:33-5
D 3 '66
Portrait of the artist as a person. Sat R 49:
89 Ap 9 '66
HAMILTON, Harry
Washington front (cont) America 115:56,
733 Jl 16, D 3 '66
HAMILTON, James
James Hamilton rediscovered; retrospective
exhibition at the Brooklyn museum. R.
Davidson. il Antiques 89:630+ My '66
HAMILTON, Kenneth
Essentiality of tradition. Christian Cent 83:
707-10 Je 1 '66
HAMILTON, Michael
Pastor's guidelines on some tough issues; ex-
cerpts from sermon, November 20, 1966.
U S News 61:11 D 5 '66
HAMILTON, Ray
Why take the chance? il por Newsweek 68:
50 N 28 '66
HAMILTON, Robert H. See Liao, S. H. jt.
auth.
HAMILTON, William
What's right with Christmas. McCalls 94:56
D '66
HAMILTON college, Clinton, N.Y.
Struck by Ford lightning. B. Wallace. il Sat
R 49:86-7+ Ap 16 '66
HAMLET; drama. See Shakespeare W.—Plays
HAMLIN, Arthur T.
Rise and fall of a library. por ALA Bul 60:339-
47 Ap '66
HAMLYN, Paul
Paul Hamlyn discusses possible U.S. activ-
ities; interview. por Pub W 189:46-7 Je
20 '66

about

Forty million books a year from new IPC
company. Pub W 189:45 Mr 28 '66
HAMMARSKJÖLD, Dag
Dag Hammarskjöld, by S. Stolpe. Review
Christian Cent 83:367 Mr 23 '66. M. Arm-
strong
Dag Hammarskjold today. S. A. Davenport.
Cath World 203:341-6 S '66
Lonely one. por Time 87:111-12 F 4 '66
Safe bridge to the future. E. Britter. il Sat R
49:34 Ap 23 '66
What is a Secretary General? F. T. P. Plimp-
ton. il por N Y Times Mag p58-9+ N 27 '66
HAMMARSKJÖLD, Knut
New chief will modify IATA's philosophy. L.
L. Doty. por Aviation W 84:50 Ap 4 '66
HAMMEL, Claire L. and Bessman, S. P.
Heme stimulation of globin synthesis in a
cell free system. bibliog Science 152:1080-2
My 20 '66
HAMMER, Armand
Man with the golden touch. S. Klaw. il por
Sat Eve Post 239:83-5+ Mr 12 '66
You see an opportunity... il por Time 87:
82 Ja 28 '66
HAMMER, Claire
Torn pictures for Halloween. Sch Arts 66:8
O '66
HAMMER, Richard
Yankee lawyers in Mississippi courts. Harper
233:79-84+ N '66
HAMMES, Gordon G.
Very fast reactions in solution. bibliog Sci-
ence 151:1507-11 Mr 25 '66
HAMMETT, Dashiell
Reader's choice. O. Handlin. Atlan 218:137-9
Jl '66
Return of the Continental Op. F. H. Gardner.
Nation 203:454-6 O 31 '66
HAMMETT, Henry A.
Austin Ripley and alcoholic priests. America
115:831 D 24 '66
HAMMIL, Carrie Esther
What every first grader needs to know.
Parents Mag 41:44-7 Ag '66
HAMMOND, C. S. and company. See Hammond,
incorporated
HAMMOND, John Henry, family
Annals of law; Lewis and Clark case: United
States government's claim to field notes.
C. Tomkins. New Yorker 42:105-6+ O 29 '66
HAMMOND, Macsawyer
Five poets. A. Freeman. Poetry 109:194 D '66
HAMMOND, Mary Katharine
Month in review. Cur Hist 50:54-64, 120-8
Ja-F '66
HAMMOND, Philip C.
Ancient Hebron, the city of David. Natur
Hist 75:42-9 My '66
HAMMOND, Thomas T.
American in Moscow. Nat Geog Mag 129:297-
351 Mr '66
HAMMOND incorporated
C. S. Hammond becomes Hammond, incor-
porated. Pub W 189:196 Je 6 '66

HAMOWY, Ronald
  Left and right meet. New Repub 154:14-16
    Mr 12 '66
HAMPLE, Stuart. See Marshall, E. jt. comp.
HAMPSHIRE college
  Hampshire college. Sch & Soc 94:88 F 19 '66
HAMPTON, Va.
  Hampton tour. il Travel 126:67 S '66
HAMPTON institute, Hampton, Va.
  Innocent eye; F. B. Johnston photographs re-
    flect educational philosophy. H. Cohen. il
    Reporter 34:45-8 Mr 10 '66
HAN, J. See Oró, J. jt. auth.
HAN, Seong S. and Johnson, A. G.
  Radioautographic and electron-microscopic
    evidence of rapid uptake of antigen by
    lymphocytes. bibliog Science 153:176-8 Jl 8
    '66
HANAN, Joe J.
  Water conservation. Horticulture 44:26-7 N '66
HANCHEY, Penelope J. See Wheeler, H. jt.
  auth
HANCOCK, James
  Nesting observation. Natur Hist 75:32-3 Je
    '66
HANCOCK, John, mutual life insurance com-
  pany. See John Hancock mutual life insur-
  ance company
HANCOCK, Mass.

Historic houses, etc.

Movers and Shakers. R. Lynes. il Harper
  233:34+ D '66
HAND, A. J.
  Which house shutters: wood, plastic, alu-
    minum? Pop Sci 189:164-5 N '66
HAND, Jackson
  Amazing new world of silicone rubber. Pop
    Sci 188:158-61+ Je '66
  Best finishes for wood: how to use stains
    to get the color you want. Pop Sci 189:
    170-6 N '66
  Best finishes for wood: modern flooring: it's
    tough, but beautiful. Pop Sci 189:156-9+
    S '66
  Best finishes for wood: paint removal, how
    to do it right. Pop Sci 188:150-3+ Ap '66
  Best finishes for wood: penetrating resin, the
    perfect wood finish. Pop Sci 189:151-3+ Jl
    '66
  Best finishes for wood: sanding is the start
    that makes the finish. Pop Sci 189:124-8 Ag
    '66
  Best finishes for wood: the smart ways to
    use shellac. Pop Sci 189:172-4 O '66
  Common pine, eighteen ways to improve its
    beauty. Pop Sci 188:136-9+ Je '66
  Fix it before you finish it. Pop Sci 188:170-3+
    My '66
  Glazing, the expensive look, the easy way.
    Pop Sci 188:182-5+ Mr '66
  Greenest lawn for the least water. Pop Sci
    189:134-9 Jl '66
  What you gain from sliding glass doors. Pop
    Sci 188:168-70+ Ap '66
  Why the new power mowers are safer. Pop
    Sci 188:158-62+ Mr '66
HAND
  Don't neglect your busy hands. L. D. Kirk.
    il Parents Mag 41:108 F '66
  Hands across the sea. il Mlle 62:150-1 F '66
  Hands clue to diagnosis. Sci N 90:225 S 24
    '66
  What your hands tell about you. il Seventeen
    25:82-3 Jl '66
HAND bags. See Handbags
HAND ball
  It was action day in Brooklyn; J. Jacobs
    world champion of four-wall handball. T.
    Brody. il Sports Illus 25:20-1 S 5 '66
  Really the greatest; J. Jacobs. R. H. Boyle.
    il Sports Illus 24:64-70+ Mr 7 '66
HAND care. See Hand
HAND looms. See Looms
HAND luggage. See Luggage
HAND presses. See Printing presses, Hand
HAND railings
  Six easy steps to watching your step. il Pop
    Mech 126:171-2 N '66
HAND tools. See Tools
HANDBAGS
  Carry on! il Seventeen 25:396 Ag '66
  It's a tote bag, easy to make. il Sunset 137:
    98-9 S '66
HANDBALL. See Hand ball
HÄNDEL, Georg Friedrich
  Authentic Messiah. B. Jacobson. Hi Fi 16:56-9
    D '66
  For the holidays: Robert Shaw's Messiah.
    J. Diether. il Am Rec G 33:302-4+ D '66

From Philips, an exciting new Messiah.
  J. Diether. il Am Rec G 33:92-3+ O '66
Game of multiple choice: Boulez, Van Beinum,
  or Wenzinger; Water music. N. Broder. por
  Hi Fi 16:96 N '66
George Frideric Handel, by P. H. Lang.
  Review
    Opera N 31:32 D 10 '66. B. Priestman
    Sat R 49:66 O 29 '66. H. Weinstock
Handel makes the scene. R. Gelatt. Report-
  er 35:40-1 D 1 '66
Julius Caesar (Giulio Cesare) Criticism
    Hi Fi 16:MA8-10 D '66
    New Yorker 42:119-20 O 8 '66
    Newsweek il 68:100 O 10 '66
    Sat R 49:56+ O 15 '66
Music to my ears: performances of Rodelinda
  and Serse. H. Weinstock. Sat R 49:70 D
  10 '66
On records; Arias. Opera N 30:34 F 19 '66
On records; Belshazzar; Judas Maccabaeus.
  Opera N 30:34 F 19 '66
Records:
  Messiah: Dixit Dominus. Opera N 31:34
    D 10 '66
  Serse. Opera N 31:30 N 19 '66
Stokowski's Messiah. R. Jones. Am Rec G
  33:308 D '66
HANDEL glass. See Glassware
HANDEL society of New York
  Music to my ears: performances of Rodelinda
    and Serse. H. Weinstock. Sat R 49:70
    D 10 '66
  Musical events; concert performance of Han-
    del's Rodelinda at Carnegie Hall. W. Sar-
    geant. New Yorker 42:202-3 D 3 '66
  New York; performances of Xerxes and Rode-
    linda at Carnegie Hall. R. D. Daniels.
    Opera N 31:31 D 24 '66
HANDICAPPED
  Down-to-earth look at a growing problem;
    excerpts from letter. I. Palmer. U S News
    61:53 Ag 22 '66
  How to treat the handicapped. G. Ross. Good
    H 162:242 Ap '66
  Not according to the appearance. R. L.
    Tobin. Sat R 49:26 F 26 '66
    See also
  Amputees
  Children, Handicapped
  Libraries—Work with the handicapped
  Sports for the handicapped

Employment

  See Vocational rehabilitation

Rehabilitation

  See Rehabilitation
HANDICAPPED, Libraries for the
  Library for the handicapped: school at the
    Human resources center of Abilities, inc. R.
    Vellman. bibliog il Library J 91:4200-4 S 15
    '66
HANDICRAFT
  They are just cone birds. il Sunset 137:155
    O '66
    See also
  Arts and crafts
  Folk art
HANDLEY, Lucretia. See Cannon, P.
HANDLIN, Oscar
  At last: a fair deal for immigrants. Read
    Digest 88:29+ My '66
  Reader's choice (cont) Atlan 218:136-8 Jl;
    116-18 Ag; 141-3 O; 158+ N; 138+ D '66;
    219:117-20 Ja '67
HANDLING of materials. See Materials
  handling
HANDMADE paper. See Paper making and
  trade
HANDOUTS, Publicity. See Publicity
HANDPRINTS
    See also
  Dermatoglyphics
HANDRAILS. See Hand railings
HANDS. See Hand
HANDWRITING analysis. See Graphology
HANDY, John
  Man with a brain. il por Time 88:116 S 30 '66
HANDY and Harman (firm)
  Unique fabricator. T. J. Murray. il Duns R
    87:41-3+ F '66
HANES, Ralph Philip, Jr
  Culture buff; interview. New Yorker 42:
    19-20 Je 25 '66
HANGEN, Welles
  Afghanistan. Yale R 56:60-75 O '66
  East Germany: the prosperous prisoner. Re-
    porter 35:30-3 Ag 11 '66
  Failure of the great leap forward. Sat R 49:92
    My 7 '66

HANGEN, Wells—*Continued*
Giant step forward. Sat R 49:25 Ag 20 '66
New perspectives behind the wall. For Affairs 45:135-47 O '66
New Ruhr. Sat Eve Post 239:30-4 My 7 '66
Tourist in Mao's Shanghai. Sat R 49:39-40 Mr 26 '66
Unofficial voice from Asia. Sat R 49:33-4 Ap 9 '66

HANGING baskets. See Plants, Potted

HANGING lamps. See Lighting fixtures

HANGING of pictures. See Pictures, Hanging of

HANGOVERS. See Alcohol—Physiological effects

HANKA, L. J. and others
Naturally occurring antimetabolite antibiotic related to biotin. bibliog Science 154:1667-8 D 30 '66

HANKER, Jacob S. and others
Staining tissue for light and electron microscopy by bridging metals with multidentate ligands. bibliog Science 152:1631-4 Je 17 '66

HANKILA, Michael
Fill first, then compact. Am City 81:173-4 My '66

HANKINS, Junius E.
River view home. il pors Ebony 21:123-6 Mr '66

HANKS, James J. and Kube, H. D.
Industry action to combat pollution. bibliog f Harvard Bsns R 44:49-62 S '66

HANKS, Jane
Decorative stenciling the early American way. por Farm J 90:86 O '66

HANLIN, Richard L.
Where the action isn't. New Repub 155:7-8 S 3 '66

HANLY, E. W. See Wright, C. P. jt. auth.

HANNA, Jane Fiquet
Libraries and civil defense; with bibliography. ALA Bul 60:655-6 Je '66

HANNA, Paul L.
Testing: NCSS; excerpts from address, November 1965. Sr Schol 87:sup9 Ja 7 '66

HANNA, Robert M.
Be lazy about lawn sprinkling. il Pop Mech 125:108-11 Je '66

HANNAH, John Alfred
Spies beside the red cedar. R. Kirk. Nat R 18:630 Je 28 '66

HANNAH, Theodore M.
From out of the past. Pop Electr 25:68-9 O '66

HANNAN, Cecil J.
Professional negotiation for improving education. NEA J 55:56-7 D '66

HANNEMAN, Ralph
Boom in bikeways. Travel 126:26-30 Ag '66

HANNIGAN, Ed
As I see it. See issues of U.S. camera & travel

HANNON, Leslie
(ed) See Fleming, A. G. C. How James Bond destroyed my husband

HANNUM, Alex
Nose to chin whiskers. il por Time 89:51 Ja 13 '67
Sarge takes Philly to the top. F. Deford. il pors Sports Illus 26:8-13 Ja 2 '67
Spirited 76ers. il por Newsweek 69:88 Ja 23 '67

HANO, Arnold
Andy Williams. Good H 162:66+ Ap '66

HANOI, Vietnam
Civilians weren't the target, but: U.S. air raids. il Newsweek 69:17-18 Ja 9 '67
Facts in a propaganda war over U.S. bombing; civilian casualties. U S News 62:6+ Ja 9 '67
Flak from Hanoi; U.S. bombing raids as reported by H. Salisbury. il Time 89:13-14 Ja 6 '67
They seem to be waiting for the bombs. il U S News 60:30-1 F 7 '66

HANOVER, Germany

Music
Hanover. J. H. Sutcliffe. Opera N 30:36 Ap 2 '66

HANOVER air show. See Aviation—Exhibitions

HANOVER COUNTY, Va.
Not on the list. ALA Bul 60:691+ Jl '66

HANRATTY, Terrence Hugh
Babes in wonderland. il por Time 88:50-2+ O 28 '66

HANS Christian Andersen award
Andersen medal. Library J 91:5718 N 15 '66

HANSBERRY, William Leo
Eulogy on William Leo Hansberry. N. Azikiwe. por Negro Hist Bul 29:63 D '65

HANSEL and Gretel go back to school; drama. See Creegan, G.

HANSEN, Asger
Well-tamer Boots Hansen tackles the wild inferno. L. Hall. il pors Life 60:26-31 F 18 '66

HANSEN, Clifford Peter
Change on the range. il por Time 87:23 F 11 '66

HANSEN, Harry
America in transition. Sat R 49:28 S 3 '66
From expansion to secession. Sat R 48:37 F 12 '66
Killers with a cause. Sat R 49:47 Jl 23 '66
Monticello and after. Sat R 49:99 My 7 '66
Motive was economic. Sat R 49:71-2 Je 11 '66
President's first politics. Sat R 49:37-8 N 5 '66

HANSEN, James
Behind the scenes. il por Look 30:M2 F 8 '66

HANSEN, John R.
How federal benefits figure in the election; excerpts from Congressional record. U S News 61:13 O 31 '66

HANSEN, Joseph J.
Case of the convalescent corporation. Harvard Bsns R 44:160-2+ My '66

HANSEN, Kurt
Man who keeps Bayer swinging. il por Fortune 73:80 Je '66

HANSEN, Zenon Clayton Raymond
Bulldog tenacity puts truck maker on the high road. il por Bsns W p 182-4+ O 15 '66

HANSEN'S disease. See Leprosy and lepers

HANSON, Dick
Across the editor's desk. See issues of Successful farming

HANSON, Earl P.
How long has it been...? Am For 71:4 O '65

HANSON, Earl Parker
New conquistadors in the Amazon jungle. Américas 17:1-8 S '65; 18:48 F '66; Correction of September issue. 17:48 N '65

HANSON, Karen
Curl up and read. Seventeen 25:70 O '66

HANSON, Norwood Russell
Bearcat professor. J. Gilbert. il pors Flying 78:52-6 Mr '66

HANSON, Suzanne
Stick lettering. il Sch Arts 65:12-15 Ja '66

HANSON, Wallace
Great stop-bath squabble. il Pop Phot 58:84-5+ Mr '66
Hanson, Rothschild, Pierce report. See issues of Popular photography
MRP camera: pioneer or pipe dream? il Pop Phot 60:112-13 Ja '67
Pushing film speed. Pop Phot 59:98-101+ Ag '66
Why you should forget lens testing! Pop Phot 58:72-3+ Mr '66

HANSON, Wayne C.
Cesium-137 body burdens in Alaskan Eskimos during the summer of 1965. bibliog Science 153:525-6 Jl 29 '66

HA'OLAM Hazeh. See Newspapers—Israel

HAPKE, B. W. See Gold, T. jt. auth.

HAPPENING; story. See Schaeling, M.

HAPPENINGS (art)
Happening: art or jest? R. Squirru. il Américas 18:26-33 Je '66
Happening at the Hamptons. il Time 88:42+ Ag 19 '66
Happenings in and out of school; interview, ed. by D. W. Ecker. Sch Arts 65:23-8 Mr '66
New Bohemia. W. J. Smith. Commonweal 85:102-3 O 28 '66
Water light; water needle, St Mark's church-in-the-Bowery. D. Hering. Dance Mag 40:31-2 My '66
What happens at a happening? J. Anderson. il Dance Mag 40:44-6 Ag '66

HAPPINESS
Aim is joy. R. O. Johann. America 115:513 O 29 '66
I like it here: Criss Mills' seventeenth year in Atlanta. J. Poppy. il Look 30:36-9 S 20 '66
Is happy childhood the goal? with study-discussion program, by R. Strang. W. G. Hollister. bibliog il PTA Mag 60:10-12, 36 My '66
Shock of happiness. G. Kent. il Read Digest 88:97-100 Mr '66
Time out for happiness. E. S. Hill. Read Digest 88:237-8+ Ap '66

HAPPY ending; drama. See Ward, D. T.

HAPPY journey to Trenton and Camden; drama. See Wilder, T.

HARNESS racing—*Continued*
Knobby-legs becomes a star; Polaris Hamble-tonian favorite. P. Ryan. il Sports Illus 25:52-3 Ag 22 '66
Man in the 100,000-mile suit. G. Holland. il Sports Illus 24:54+ My 2 '66
Press got the message; Romeo Hanover wins pacing's Triple crown. M. R. Werner. Sports Illus 25:69 N 7 '66
Very good horse race that hoopla built; publicity for the Roosevelt international; with account by P. Ryan. il Sports Illus 25:24-27+ Jl 18 '66
Wreck from down under paces on top; ten-year-old Cardigan Bay defeats American Bret Hanover at Yonkers raceway. P. Ryan. il Sports Illus 24:70-1 My 30 '66

HAROLD II, king of England
1066: the story of a year, by D. Butler. Review
Time il 87:120+ My 20 '66

HARP, Solomon, 3d
Sitting ducks of aerial war. il por Ebony 22:58-60+ N '66

HARPER, Charles W. jr. See Towe, K. M. jt. auth.

HARPER, Harriett J. and Stallings, C. P.
Seasonally adjusted CPI components. Mo Labor R 89:887-9 Ag '66

HARPER, Mary-Angela
Woman's role in the church. America 115:91-3, 436 Jl 23, O 15 '66

HARPER, Paul C. jr
What's happening, baby? address, June 21, 1966. Vital Speeches 33:57-61 N 1 '66

HARPER, Verne Lester
Harper to new post. por Am For 72:6 S '66

HARPER and Row, publishers, incorporated
Harper & Row, Manchester file official answers. Pub W 191:57 Ja 16 '67
Mrs Kennedy and Harper & Row continue negotiations on editorial content of Death of a President. Pub W 191:33-4 Ja 2 '67
Start the presses; Manchester's The death of a President; Harper & Row clearance. il Time 89:47 Ja 20 '67

HARPSICHORD music
See also
Phonograph records—Harpsichord music

HARR, Karl Gottlieb
Bold grasp on bent nettle; excerpts from address, ed. by W. J. Coughlin. Tech W 19:66 Ag 15 '66

HARRAH automobile collection, Reno, Nev. See Automobile museums

HARRELL, George Thomas, 1908-
New medical schools: building up for tomorrow's patients. L. Prato. il pors Todays Health 44:36-41 N '66

HARRELSON, Ken
Name your game, baby, and I'll beat you; baseball players' golf tournament in Miami. M. Mulvoy. por Sports Illus 24:63-5 Mr 14 '66

HARRER, G. A.
Boston centralizes. Library J 91:5886-8 D 1 '66

HARRER, John M.
Superior people are rejecting classroom teaching. NEA J 55:20-2 N '66

HARRIGAN, Anthony
Letter from Canada. Nat R 18:1163 N 15 '66
Our war with red China. Nat R 18:204-8 Mr 8 '66

HARRIMAN, William Averell
Ambassador Harriman discusses his post-Manila trip; excerpts from press conference, November 11, 1966; with questions and answers. Dept State Bul 55:889-92 D 12 '66
Asian development bank; statement, February 2, 1966. Dept State Bul 54:379-82 Mr 7 '66
Growing strength of freedom; address, June 10 1966. Dept State Bul 55:10-4 Jl 4 '66
Legacy of Franklin D. Roosevelt and John F. Kennedy; address, June 16, 1966. Dept State Bul 55:137-40 Jl 25 '66
U.S. asks international action on passenger-ship fire safety; statement, May 3, 1966. Dept State Bul 54:952-4 Je 13 '66

about
Ave, durable servant of four presidents. H. Sidey. il por Life 61:54 N 25 '66
Durable Crocodile. por Time 88:35-6 N 25 '66
Mr Harriman to supervise U.S. actions on POW's in Viet-Nam; statement, May 18, 1966. R. J. McCloskey. Dept State Bul 54:888 Je 6 '66
Old Croc. il pors Newsweek 68:28-9 N 28 '66
Two leaders in drive for peace. por U S News 61:30 N 14 '66

HARRINGTON, Donald Szantho
Gospel poison. Sat R 49:27 Ag 20 '66

HARRINGTON, Lyn
Grand Canal of China. Natur Hist 75:16-21 Ag '66

HARRINGTON, Michael
Evading the issues. Commentary 42:91-2+ D '66
Mystical militants. New Repub 154:20-2 F 19 '66
Taking the Great society seriously. Harper 233:43-9 D '66

HARRIS, Barbara
Other Barbara, the other Harris. S. Birmingham. por Holiday 39:91-2+ Je '66
People are talking about... por Vogue 148:214 D '66
What a change in Barbara Harris; with report by M. Nichols. il pors Life 61:103-4+ D 16 '66

HARRIS, Beverly
Hundredth for the Boston yacht club. Motor B 118:46-7+ S '66

HARRIS, Fred R.
National research policy: ambuscade for the establishment. D. S. Greenberg. il por Science 153:611-15 Ag 5 '66

HARRIS, Frederick Brown
Date with a tree; reprint. Am For 72:15 O '66

HARRIS, George, 3d
Face to face with a writer-producer-director-actor; ed. by C. Schwalberg. por Seventeen 26:19 Ja '67

HARRIS, Harold
New U.H.F. TV antenna design. Electr World 75:44-5 Mr '66

HARRIS, James J.
Big marketing man on campus. il por Time 87:94 Mr 4 '66

HARRIS, Kenneth
Don't stifle your students' nonconformity. NEA J 55:24-6 O '66

HARRIS, Larrel W. and others
Dealkylation and loss of capacity for reactivation of cholinesterase inhibited by sarin. bibliog Science 154:404-7 O 21 '66

HARRIS, Leon A.
Marie Tippit and Marina Oswald: the forgotten widows of the Kennedy tragedy. Good H 162:94-7+ Ap '66

HARRIS, Louis
Analyzing the vote and its lessons. Newsweek 67:27 My 16 '66
Changing U.S. offers GOP hope. por Newsweek 68:34-5 O 10 '66
New coalition, wave of the future? Newsweek 68:24 Jl 25 '66
State of the LBJ image. Newsweek 69:18-19 Ja 9 '67

about
Politics and a poll. J. O'Gara. Commonweal 84:411 Jl 1 '66

HARRIS, MacDonald
Trepleff; story. Harper 233:61-8 D '66

HARRIS, Mark
Eye on the Peace corps. G. Hicks. Sat R 49:95-6 O 8 '66
Seal of approval. C. R. Larson. Nation 203:425-6 O 24 '66

HARRIS, Michael
Bay area rapid transit: advance into yesterday. Nation 202:679-83 Je 6 '66
Savings and loan; easy lenders. Nation 203:152-4 Ag 22 '66

HARRIS, Phyllis
Phonograph; poem. Poetry 109:165-6 D '66

HARRIS, Richard
Annals of legislation. New Yorker 42:29-38+ Jl 2; 30-6+ Jl 9; 35-8+ Jl 16; 35-40+ Jl 23 '66

HARRIS, Rosemary
Broadway finds a new first lady; with report by J. Hallowell. pors Life 60:57-8+ My 6 '66
Chameleon on a tarton. por Time 88:74+ D 9 '66

HARRIS, Seymour E.
Economics of foreign aid. bibliog f Cur Hist 50:342-5+ Je '66

HARRIS, T. George
Big business do-gooders; private war on poverty. Look 30:15-19 Ag 9 '66

HARRIS-Intertype corporation
Harris-Intertype acquires box machinery manufacturer. Pub W 190:121 Jl 4 '66
Harris-Intertype sells lithoplate subsidiary. Pub W 189:121 My 2 '66
Why the ink is black at Harris-Intertype; planning, the watchword. il Bsns W p34-6 D 31 '66

HARRISBURG, Pa.

Galleries and museums

William Penn memorial museum. J. L. Stoutenburgh. Hobbies 71:112 Ag '66

Wm. Penn memorial museum. il Design 67:40 Mr '66

HARRISON, Christopher G. A.

Antipodal location of continents and oceans. bibliog Science 153:1246-8 S 9 '66

HARRISON, Elizabeth

Front to back picture. Sch Arts 65:12-13 My '66

HARRISON, George

Old Beatles, a study in paradox. M. Cleave. il pors N Y Times Mag p 10-11+ Jl 3 '66

HARRISON, George E. and others

Strontium uptake in rats on alginate-supplemented diet. bibliog Science 152:655-6 Ap 29 '66

HARRISON, Henry T.

More flying weather signposts. Flying 78: 73-5 Mr; 79-81 Ap '66

HARRISON, J. M. and Irving R.

Visual and nonvisual auditory systems in mammals. bibliog Science 154:738-43 N 11 '66

HARRISON, Jim

California hybrid. Poetry 108:198-201 Je '66

Muse & hearth. Poetry 107:330-1 F '66

about

Five poets. M. McCloskey. Poetry 108:272-3 Jl '66

HARRISON, Noel

Singing son of 'enry 'iggins. il pors Life 60: 65-6+ F 25 '66

HARRISON, Percy

Dip in the pool. il por Time 88:36 S 9 '66

Mr Right. il por Newsweek 68:36 S 12 '66

HARRISON, Rex

Debonair Rex now a celebrated doctor. il pors Life 61:122-4+ S 30 '66

Men in Vogue. por Vogue 148:179 O 1 '66

HARRISON, Robert S.

Libya. bibliog Focus 17:1-6 N '66

HARRISON, Selig S.

America, India, and Pakistan: chance for a fresh start. Harper 233:56-60+ Jl '66

HARRISON, W.

Marine geotechnique. Science 153:326+ Jl 15 '66

HARRISON, Wallace Kirkman

Bridge to the future; interview, ed. by W. Toscanini. pors Opera N 31:26-7 S 17 '66

about

Curtain going up for Wallace Harrison. J. Greenfeld. il pors N Y Times Mag p36-7+ Ag 21 '66

New opera house, a triumph of technology. il por Newsweek 68:77 S 19 '66

HARRISS, Clement Lowell

Needed, property tax reform. Am City 81:38 D '66

HARRITY, Richard

Sixty-three years of Yanks at Oxford. Look 30:80-3+ O 4 '66

HARROWER, Rexford

Interopera. Q. Eaton. il Opera N 30:32 F 12 '66

HARRY Belten and the Mendelssohn violin concerto; story. See Targan, B.

HARRY N. Abrams, incorporated. See Abrams, Harry N. incorporated

HART, Basil Henry Liddell. See Liddell Hart, B. H.

HART, Jeffrey

Beyond the romantics. Nat R 18:371+, 547 Ap 19, My 31 '66

Puritanism moribundus. Nat R 18:847-50 Ag 23 '66

Stop the milieu, I've got to get off. Nat R 18:999+ O 4 '66

Two faces of Hemingway. Nat R 18:632+ Je 28 '66

Unexplored territory. Nat R 18:1233-4 N 29 '66

HART, Jerry

Cruising to the mountains. il Yachting 120: 42-4+ Jl '66

Locksmanship; how to cope with the ups and downs of canal linking Lake Champlain with the Hudson River. il Yachting 119:72-3 My '66

Page from a Bahama log book. il Yachting 120:46-8+ N '66

HART, Philip

For Crossroads' debut, a truce Czech Smetana. Hi Fi 16:94 N '66

HART, Philip A.

Excerpt from statement, May 1965. Cong Digest 45:172+ Je '66

Use & misuse of politicians. Time 88:92+ N 11 '66

HART, Sylvan

Last of the mountain men. H. Peterson. il pors Sports Illus 25:84-8+ O 3 '66

HART, William J. See Smith, A. W. jt. auth.

HARTE, Bret

Bret Harte, by R. O'Connor. Review
   Sat R 49:33-4 Ap 2 '66. J. K. Hutchens
   Time 87:116+ Mr 18 '66

HARTER, Donald H. See Tellez-Nagel, I. jt. auth.

HARTFORD, Huntington

Harassed Hartford. por Newsweek 67:95-6 Je 20 '66

Hunt for success. por Time 87:84+ Je 17 '66

HARTFORD, Conn.

Where business longs for the good old days. il Bsns W p 156-8 Ap 9 '66

City planning

Can our cities be saved? S. Alsop. il Sat Eve Post 239:18 Ag 13 '66

Lighting

Urban renewal leads to winter wonderland; Constitution plaza. il Am City 81:119 D '66

Music

Hartford opera season. W. B. Syer. Hi Fi 16:MA24-5 Jl '66
   See also
   Hartt opera guild

Negroes

Sharing Negro pupils with suburbs; a test. il U S News 61:49 Jl 4 '66

HARTH, Sidney

Musical events; recital in Carnegie Hall. W. Sargeant. New Yorker 42:233-4 N 5 '66

HARTING, Donald

What expectant mothers need to know; interview. por U S News 60:54-6+ F 14 '66

HARTKE, Vance

One-way street; L. Johnson-V. Hartke feud. por Newsweek 67:34-6 Mr 28 '66

Trouble in four syllables. Time 87:27B-28 Mr 18 '66

HARTLEY, Ellen. See Hartley, W. jt. auth.

HARTLEY, William

Crackdown in the Everglades 'gator poachers. Pop Mech 126:106-9+ Ag '66

—and Hartley, Ellen

Adventures of an underwater cameraman. Pop Mech 126:92-5 S '66

School system that failed. Parents Mag 41: 52-3+ Mr '66

Stop divorces before they start. Good H 162: 89+ Ap '66

There's summer camp for every child. Parents Mag 41:51-3+ Ap '66

HARTMAN, Elizabeth

Me, Biff. L. A. Schmidt. il pors Look 30: M14+ My 31 '66

HARTMANN, William K.

Lunar basins, lunar lineaments, and the moon's far side. bibliog Sky & Tel 32:128-31 S '66

HARTOG, Jan de

What money cannot buy. Atlan 218:111-15 Jl '66

HARTT opera guild

In the hall of the mountain king; Hartt college brings Egk's Peer Gynt in Ducloux translation to America. M. Paranov. il Opera N 30:32-3 F 26 '66

HARTUNG, H. O.

Before you build that water filter; address, 1965. Am City 81:89-92 Ag; 105-8 S '66

HARTUNG, Philip T.

Screen. See issues of Commonweal

HARTWELL, W. V. and others

Adenovirus in blood clots from cases of infectious hepatitis. Science 152:1390 Je 3 '66

HARTZELL, Bernie

Old oak is gone; poem. il Am For 72:25 Je '66

HARTZOG, George B. Jr

Heritage to discover. Am Ed 2:15-19 Jl '66

Looms weave by themselves; excerpts from address. por Parks & Rec 1:20-2 Ja '66

Parkscape U.S.A. por Nat Geog Mag 130:48-93 Jl '66

Parkscape U.S.A. por Parks & Rec 1:616-20 Ag '66

Welcome to Washington. por Parks & Rec 1:687-8 S '66

HARV is plowing now; story. See Updike, J.

HARVAN, George
Along the Leigh River. H. M. Kinzer. il Pop
Phot 58:80-3 Je '66
HARVARD business conference. See Business
conferences
HARVARD business school. See Harvard uni-
versity—Graduate school of business ad-
ministration
HARVARD divinity school. See Harvard uni-
versity—Divinity school
HARVARD graduates. See College graduates
HARVARD university
Aberrations at Harvard; S.D.S. members
heckle McNamara. il Time 88:95 N 18 '66
Commencement is only the beginning. Har-
vard graduates after ten years. D. Burn-
ham. il N Y Times Mag p 14+ Je 5 '66;
Reply. S. Klaw. p49 Je 19 '66
Five freshmen at Harvard; symposium. il
Seventeen 25:154-5+ My '66
Freshman paper on Harvard freshmen. S.
Keiman. il N Y Times Mag p50-3+ D 11 '66;
Discussion. p4+ D 25 '66
Signs of backlash against student mobs. il
U S News 61:14 N 21 '66
Unfair Harvard? advanced-rating system. il
Newsweek 68:74-5 N 14 '66

Divinity school

Doubts & the Divinity school; summary of
address. N. Pusey. Time 88:94 O 7 '66

Graduate school of business administration

Harvard puts its tent show on big-time circuit; highlights of National business conference, New York. il Bsns W p86+ Mr 12
'66
Making of a company president; Peter Trowbridge Cook, first year man. T. G. Harris.
il Look 31:64-7 Ja 10 '67
Pattern for success; Harvard business school's
advanced management course (cont) il Nations Bsns 53:58-60+ D '65; 54:48-50+ Ja;
56-8+ F; 64-7+ Mr; 118+ Ap; 96-8+ My '66

Graduate school of education

Curious walls of Larsen hall. D. Canty. il
Arch Forum 124:46-53 Mr '66

Graduate school of public
administration

See Harvard university—John Fitzgerald
Kennedy school of government

Harvard medical school

Independent study in medical school. Sch &
Soc 94:262+ Sum '66
Self-prescription; permission to study in-
dependently. Newsweek 67:66 F 14 '66

John Fitzgerald Kennedy school
of government

In-and-outers; renaming of graduate school
of public administration. il Newsweek 68:
96 O 31 '66
John F. Kennedy school; helping government's in-and-outers. B. Nelson. il Science 154:135-8 O 7 '66

Law school

Yales vs. the Harvards (legal division) V.
S. Navasky. il N Y Times Mag p47-9+
S 11 '66; Discussion. p42 O 2 '66
HARVEST festivals. See Festivals
HARVEST frenzy; story. See Thomas, G.
HARVEST hands. See Farm labor
HARVEST labor. See Farm labor
HARVEST moon supper; drama. See Watts,
F. B.
HARVESTING
When to cut and graze grasses and legumes.
W. A. Hayes. il Suc Farm 64:38-9 Je '66
HARVESTING machinery
Adjustment of combine affects wheat grades.
Suc Farm 64:48E Jl '66
Harvesting machines seek wider fields; de-
vices that can select as well as pick. il
Bsns W p 164-6+ D 3 '66
Weird new world of Old MacDonald. J. E.
Boykin. il Pop Mech 126·112-15+ Jl '66
HARVEY, Bartlett
World impact of American technology; ad-
dress; with questions and answers. Ann Am
Acad 366:41-50 Jl '66
HARVEY, Frank
Air war in Vietnam. introd. by E. D. Muhl-
feld. por Flying 79:38-95 N '66

about

Publisher's memo. E. D. Muhlfeld. il por
Flying 79:6 S '66

HARVEY, J. O.
All cows are mean. Harper 233:81-5 S '66
HARVEY, N. D.
Aerated sewage lagoon. O. O. Olson and J.
Klingenberg. il Am City 81:94-5 N '66
HARVEY Mudd college, Claremont, Calif.
When dropouts are high. il Sci Digest 60:
24-5 O '66
HARWOOD, Richard
Powell story; reprint from Washington post,
January 9, 1967. U S News 62:33-4+ Ja 23
'67
Sanctity of pork. New Repub 155:7-8 O 29 '66
HASEBROOCK, Mrs William H.
Turn in the road; address, June 7, 1966. Vital
Speeches 32:700-4 S 1 '66
HASELDEN, Kyle
Converting life into living. Christian Cent
83:1435-6 N 23 '66
HASHEM, Nemat
Mitosis; induction by cultures of human
peripheral lymphocytes. bibliog Science 150:
1460-2; 152:231 D 10 '65, Ap 8 '66
HASIDISM
Martin Buber and the Jews; his interpreta-
tion of and path to Hasidism. C. Potok.
Commentary 41:43-9 Mr '66; Discussion. 42:
20+ S '66
HASKELL, Douglas
New grandeur for Washington. Harper 232:84-
91 Ap '66
Ten buildings that climax an era. Fortune
74:156-62 D '66
Unity and harmony at Rockefeller Center.
Arch Forum 124:42-7 Ja '66
HASKIN, Harold H. and others
Minchinia nelsoni n. sp. (haplosporida,
haplosporidiidae) causative agent of the
Delaware Bay oyster epizoötic. bibliog Sci-
ence 153:1414-16 S 16 '66
HASKIN, Larry A. and Frey, F. A.
Dispersed and not-so-rare earths. bibliog
Science 152:299-314 Ap 15 '66
—See Haskin, M. A. jt. auth.
HASKIN, Mary A. and Haskin, L. A.
Rare earths in European shales; a redeterm-
ination. bibliog Science 154:507-9 O 28 '66
HASKINS, Caryl P.
Haskins speaks out; summary of report. Sci
N 90:528 D 24 '66
HASKINS, Charles Clarence
Patrol chief of the ski slopes. il pors Ebony
22:34-6+ D '66
HASKINS, Don
Champions get after it. F. Deford. il por
Sports Illus 25:26-8+ D 12 '66
Defense by a coyote caller. Jares. il Sports
Illus 24:48-9 F 7 '66
HASKINS, John
Celebration of Henry Purcell. Hi Fi 16:MA9
Ag '66
HASKO, Esther
Primulas. Horticulture 44:22-5+ My '66
HASLEIET, Donna
Can you reduce the noise in your kitchen?
Bet Hom & Gard 44:104+ My '66
HASS, Carl F.
Ethics and Vietnam. Christian Cent 83:1124-
5 S 14 '66
HASS, Margaret W.
Roots of failure; elementary school comment.
NEA J 55:35 Ap '66
HASSAN, Jeru-Ahmed
Black mischief. J. Ridgeway. New Repub 155:
14-16 D 24 '66
HASSEL, Kai-Uwe von
Generals' revolt. il por Newsweek 68:34+
S 5 '66
HASTIE, William Henry
Colored judges. J. H. Roy. por Negro Hist
Bul 29:37-8 N '65
HASTINGS, F. L. See Main, A. R. jt. auth.
HASTINGS, Robert F.
Practical pressures pushing the profession;
excerpts from address. Arch Rec 140:9
O '66
HASTINGS, Battle of, 1066
. . . And all that; 900th anniversary. il Time
88:53 O 21 '66
Everybody out for Hastings! 900th anniver-
sary celebrations. il Life 61:157-8 N 18 '66
900 years and all that; British festivals. H.
Sutton. il Sat R 49:52-3 Mr '66
1066. M. Bishop. il Horizon 8:4-27 Aut '66
1066; Montgomery at Senlac Hill. B. L.
Montgomery. Sat R 49:44-6 Jl 9 '66
1066; the view from France. H. Sutton. il
Sat R 49:43-4 Jl 9 '66
Winning a lost battle. N. Lunger. il Sr Schol
89:4-5 O 14 '66
HASWELL, Harold A. See Burchinal, L. G
jt. auth.

HAWKER Siddeley aviation limited-British aircraft corporation merger. See Airplane industry and trade—Consolidations and mergers

HAWKES, Alex D.
Flannel flowers. Horticulture 44:35 D '66

HAWKING. See Falconry

HAWKINS, Coleman
Forty years of Hawk's mighty honk. C. Harman. Life 61:8 Jl 22 '66

HAWKINS, David
Books. Sci Am 214:137-40+ My '66

HAWKINS, Erick
Erick Hawkins and dance company, Hunter college playhouse. M. Marks. Dance Mag 40:70 Ap '66

HAWKINS, Robert F.
Venice: controversy. Sat R 49:92+ O 8 '66

HAWKS
Hawks of eastern North America; paintings. A. E. Gilbert. Audubon Mag 68:335-40 S '66
Hawks of western North America; paintings. D. L. Malick. il Audubon Mag 68:443-8 N '66
Visit from a proud stranger; catching red-tailed hawks, and a golden eagle in a bow net. B. Gilbert. il Sports Illus 26:24-8 Ja 16 '67

HAWORTH, Leland J.
By studying nature whole. Sat R 49:59-61 My 7 '66

HAWTHORNE, Nathaniel
Hawthorne: the artist of New England. A. Kazin. por Atlan 218:109-13 D '66
Sins of the fathers, by F. C. Crews. Review Commonweal 84:504-6 Ag 5 '66. C. T. Samuels
That blue-eyed darling Nathaniel. R. V. Cassill. il pors Horizon 8:32-9 Sum '66

HAXTON, Gerald
Twisted marriage of Somerset Maugham; excerpts from A case of human bondage. B. Nichols. il por Look 30:32-7 O 18 '66

HAY, Deborah
Trisha Brown and Deborah Hay, Judson memorial church. M. Marks. Dance Mag 40:62-3 My '66

HAY, John, and Farb, Peter
Shore in human hands; excerpts from Atlantic shore. Audubon Mag 68:162-6 My '66

HAY
Four cuttings; ten and one half tons of hay. J. Russell. Farm J 90:56 N '66
Hay that's as good as grain. N. Reeder and D. Hagen. il Farm J 90:28-30 Mr '66

HAY fever
Do hay fever shots really work? J. D. Wassersug. il Sci Digest 60:57-62 Ag '66
Hay fever season is here. il Sci N 90:102 Ag 13 '66
Running debate; hay-fever injections. Newsweek 67:71 Ap 4 '66

HAY handling
Make hay and silage with less help. il Farm J 90:30-1 Jl '66
When to cut and graze grasses and legumes. W. A. Hayes. il Suc Farm 64:38-9 Je '66

HAY making. See Hay handling

HAYASHI, Akira, and others
Hemoglobins M: identification of Iwate, Boston, and Saskatoon variants. bibliog Science 152:207-8 Ap 8 '66

HAYASHI, Masaki. See Matsumura, F; Roth, T. F. jt. auths.

HAYATSU, Ryoichi
Artifacts in polarimetry and optical activity in meteorites. bibliog Science 153:859-61 Ag 19 '66

HAYCRAFT, Howard
Lighthouse. Wilson Lib Bul 40:977 Je '66
Through native eyes. Library J 91:3081 Je 15 '66

HAYDEN, Carl
Utilizing the great river. por Parks & Rec 1: 501+ Je '66

HAYDEN, Melissa
Melissa. H. Saal. por Newsweek 68:69 D 26 '66

HAYDEN, Thomas
Citizen diplomacy. Nation 202:87 Ja 24 '66

HAYDN, Franz Joseph
Haydn by two grandes dames of the keyboard. S. Sell. il Am Rec G 33:210-11 N '66
Music to my ears; The creation, as conducted by L. Bernstein. I. Kolodin. il Sat R 49:38 My 28 '66

HAYES, Geneva. See Veatch, J. jt. auth.

HAYES, Helen
Queen and I; excerpt from A gift of joy; ed. by L. Funke. por Read Digest 88:103-6 Ap '66

about
One for the road. G. Weales. Reporter 34:54-5 My 19 '66

HAYES, Jim
Kentucky's happiest hunting ground. por Field & S 71:58-61+ N '66
Kokanee comes east. pors Outdoor Life 137: 29-31+ Je '66
(ed) See Miller, R. E. Giant of Newcomer Hollow

HAYES, Robert M.
Institute of library research. por Library J 91:4579-85 O 1 '66

HAYES, Samuel L. 3d
New interest in incentive financing. Harvard Bsns R 44:99-112 Jl '66

HAYLOCK, E. F.
Atlantic with elan. Motor B 118:80 S '66
Sail trainer. Motor B 117:102 F '66
Salty centennial at Copenhagen. Motor B 118: 32-3+ Ag '66
To Wynne Ghost Rider, another offshore feather. por Motor B 118:40+ N '66
Transatlantic triumph for Ondine. Motor B 118:129-30 S '66

HAYMAN, D'Arcy
Art & man. Sch Arts 65:5-8 My '66

HAYMAN, Jane
Murdered girl is found on a bridge; poem. New Yorker 42:97 Ag 6 '66

HAYNE, Donald
Edward Boyd Barrett: shepherd in the mist. America 115:230 S 3 '66

HAYNES, C. Vance, jr
Elephant-hunting in North America; with biographical sketch. Sci Am 214:16, 104-12 bibliog(p 144) Je '66
Radiocarbon samples: chemical removal of plant contaminants. bibliog Science 151: 1391-2 Mr 18 '66

HAYNES, Lincoln
Down on the reservation. Sat R 49:48-9 Ap 9 '66

HAYNES, Muriel
De Beauvoir: at the deathbed. Nation 202: 718-20 Je 13 '66
Many ways of man. Sat R 49:59-60 Jl 23 '66

HAYNES, Trudy
TV news hens. il pors Ebony 21:44-6+ O '66

HAYS, Wayne Levere
House loses patience with HUAC. D. Rapoport. il Reporter 35:35-6 D 1 '66

HAYUM, Walter
Through Europe with a Polaroid color pack camera. U S Camera 29:18+ S '66

HAYWARD, John Tucker
Dropout who made it to the top. P. Gallico. por Read Digest 89:121-6 N '66

HAYWARD, Max
(tr) See Babel, I. You must know everything
(tr) See Voznesensky, A. Give me peace

HAYWARD, Roger
Amateur scientist. Sci Am 216:124-8 Ja '67

HAZARD, Leland
Strikes and people: a proposal. Atlan 218:116-18 D '66

HAZE filters. See Light filters

HAZELTON, Nika Standen
Delectations. See issues of National review, February 8, 1966-
How to choose a cook book. House & Gard 129:216-17+ My '66
Traveler's guide to native drinks in Germany and Switzerland. House & Gard 129: 174+ Mr '66

HAZEN, Richard
Rising tide of water pollution. Duns R 87:pt2 138-40+ Mr '66

HAZLITT, Henry
Business tides. See issues of Newsweek to Septembr 12, 1966
Fifty billion to play with? the fear of fiscal drag. Nat R 17:1151-2; 18:129 D 14 '65, F 8 '66
Free market. Nat R 18:583-4 Je 14 '6
Parting words; last regular column for Newsweek. por Newsweek 68:90 S 12 '66
Slash the spending. por Newsweek 67:76 Mr 26 '66; Same abr. Read Digest 88:129-30 Je '66

HAZZARD, Shirley
Meeting; story. New Yorker 42:26-31 Jl 23 '66
Nothing in excess; story. New Yorker 42: 48-57 Mr 26 '66

H'DOUBLER, Margaret Newell
Dance magazine's annual awards. por Dance Mag 40:33+ Ap '66

HEAD, George
Riddle of the vanishing insurance companies. L. Velie. Read Digest 89:110-13 S '66

HEAD, Matthew, pseud. See Canaday, J.

HEAD
  See also
Jaws
Skull

Wounds and injuries

Head injury: the big killer. H. G. Earl. il Todays Health 44:18-21 D '66

HEAD Start, Project. See Project Head Start

HEADACHE
British migraine trust seeks headache cure. Sci N 90:9 Jl 2 '66
Headaches go into the test tube. il Bsns W p54+ Ag 6 '66
I prescribe. . . J. D. Wassersug. Sci Digest 60:67-71 N '66
What's behind your headaches. C. Mitchell. il Suc Farm 64:131+ Mr '66

HEADPHONES. See Earphones

HEADRICK, Sherrill
Stoic's guide to pro football. il Sports Illus 25:30-2+ N 7 '66

HEADS of state
Who's who around the world (cont) il Sr Schol 89:pt2 23-6 S 23 '66

HEALD, Weldon F.
Shasta: tepee of the Great Spirit. Nat Parks Mag 40:15-18 F '66
Sonoran Desert National Park il Nat Parks Mag 40:4-9 Ap '66

HEALEY, Denis Winston
Auld song's end. il Newsweek 67:48+ Mr 7 '66

HEALEY, James S.
Automated library in New England. por Wilson Lib Bul 41:411-13+ D '66

HEALING, Divine. See Faith cure

HEALTH
Do you really follow doctors' orders? il Good H 162:169 My '66
Energy; advice from a panel of experts. Vogue 148:116-18+ O 15 '66
How to maintain good health in the summer. Good H 162:175-6 Je '66
Look out! fifty certified things to worry about. W. Cross. il Esquire 66:130-1 N '66
Making school days healthy days. C. L. Hudson. Todays Health 44:92 S '66
National health test. PTA Mag 60:24-8 My; 24-7 Je '66
Plain talk about family health. See issues of Better homes and gardens
President's goal: good health for everyone. U S News 60:46 Mr 14 '66
Quality of fitness; excerpt from address. C. B. Wilkinson. Parks & Rec 1:149-50 F '66
To your health; miscellaneous facts of interest. il Changing T 20:24 Mr '66
Today's health news. A. L. Blakeslee. See issues of Today's health
U.S. youngsters gain in physical fitness; University of Michigan study. Sr Schol 87:sup2 Ja 14 '66
  See also
Diet
Exercise
Men—Health and hygiene
Sleep
Woman—Health and hygiene

HEALTH and aviation. See Aviation—Physiological effects

HEALTH and religion. See Medicine and religion

HEALTH and weather. See Weather—Mental and physiological effects

HEALTH benefit plans. See Employees benefit plans; Insurance, Health

HEALTH centers
Centers for poor approved; neighborhood health centers. P. McBroom. Sci N 90:36 Jl 16 '66
Federal support for construction of health-related facilities. T. H. Klausmeyer. Arch Rec 139:160-3 Mr '66
Medicine for the poor: a new deal in Denver. E. Langer. Science 153:508-12 Jl 29 '66; Discussion. 154:68+ O 7 '66
Psychologists speak out; recommendations to avoid past mistakes in mental health. Sci N 90:55 Jl 23 '66
$2-billion war on mental ills; federal, state, and local money pouring into community mental health centers. il Bsns W p 178+ N 5 '66
You could die waiting; new centers supported by OEO. il Newsweek 68:76 D 12 '66

HEALTH costs. See Medical service, Cost of

HEALTH education
  See also
Moving pictures in health education

Courses of study

Shall our schools teach about venereal disease? S. Podair. il Sat R 49:72-3+ Mr 19 '66

HEALTH, education and welfare, Department of. See United States—Health, education and welfare, Department of

HEALTH examinations. See Physical examinations

HEALTH insurance. See Insurance, Health

HEALTH machines. See Quacks and quackery

HEALTH records, Childrens. See Children—Care and hygiene

HEALTH resorts, watering places, etc.
American way of aging; visit to Elizabeth Arden's Maine Chance in Arizona. J. Mitford. il McCalls 93:90-1+ Mr '66
Gone flying to Greenbrier. R. B. Parke. il Flying 78:62-4 My '66
Greenhouse for wilted women. M. W. Lear. il N Y Times Mag p 16-17+ Je 19 '66
Pampering the body to boost the spirit. il Bsns W p58-61 Jl 2 '66
Texas greenhouse: a diet-and-fitness haven for rich females. B. Rollin. il Look 30:48-53 Ag 9 '66
  See also
Vichy, France

HEALTH service. See Medical service

HEALTH superstitions. See Medical delusions

HEALTH workers
Wanted: 750,000 humanitarians. D. L. Wilbur. Todays Health 45:88+ Ja '67

Training

Health careers. il Todays Health 45:33-5 Ja '67

HEALY, Gerry
Pie in the sky. il U S Camera 30:62-3 Ja '67

HEARING
Auditory sensitivity of the monkey. W. C. Stebbins and others. bibliog il Science 153:1646-7 S 30 '66
Marine bioacoustics; report on symposium. W. N. Tavolga. Science 153:771+ Ag 12 '66
  See also
Ear
Loudness

Testing

  See also
Audiometry

HEARING aids
Hearing-aid reprint with new material. Consumer Rep 31:264-5 Je '66
Hearing aids we didn't rate. Consumer Rep 131:156-7 Ap '66
Hearing electrically. il Sci N 90:53 Jl 23 '66
More financial help for hearing aid buyers. Consumer Rep 31:103 Mr '66
Personal business; hearing loss. Bsns W p 149-50 Je 4 '66

HEARING in animals
Visual and nonvisual auditory systems in mammals. J. M. Harrison and R. Irving. bibliog il Science 154:738-43 N 11 '66

HEARING in fishes
  See also
Ear (fishes)

HEARST, James
Potencies; poem. Commonweal 84:368 Je 17 '66
Winter mood; poem. America 114:262 F 19 '66

HEARST, William Randolph
House that Hearst built. il Newsweek 68:44 Ag 29 '66

HEARST-San Simeon state historical monument. See California—Parks and reserves

HEART
Bullets in the heart. Time 87:78+ My 27 '66
Giant-sized approach to heart research. il Ebony 21:73-6+ F '66
Protein synthesis by heart muscle ribosomes: an effect of insulin independent of substrate transport. W. S. Stirewalt and I. G. Wool. bibliog il Science 154:284 O 14 '66

Abnormalities and deformities

Balloon to save a baby; Rashkind technique overcomes congenital heart defect. il Life 60:65-6 My 27 '66

Diseases

Balloon to save a baby; Rashkind technique overcomes congenital heart defect. il Life 60:65-6 My 27 '66
Blood flow conditioned. P. McBroom. Sci N L 89:131 F 26 '66
Coming: computer test for child heart disease? S. M. Linde. il Todays Health 44:54-5+ Je '66

HEART—Diseases—*Continued*

Diet reduces heart attacks. Sci N 90:433 N 19 '66

Endocarditis in mice infected with coxsackie virus B₄. G. E. Burch and others. bibliog il Science 151:447-8 Ja 28 '66

Heart attack behavior. il Sci Digest 59:23 Ap '66

Hidden strokes. A. J. Snider. il Sci Digest 60:36 O '66

How to prevent a heart attack. il Todays Health 44:9+ Ap '66

Imaginary heart disease; cardiac neurotics, vexing medical problem. W. Kitay. Sci Digest 60:53-7 S '66

In the midst of life. M. Shaara. il Sat Eve Post 239:79-83 Ag 27 '66

Loneliness of the long-distance runner over forty; to the swift; health. J. Medelman. il Esquire 65:120-3 Je '66

Mustard affects heart; Heart disease a part of general disease. Sci N 90:369 N 5 '66

No help for the heart? value of anticoagulant drugs. il Newsweek 68:73 N 7 '66

Rheumatic-like cardiac lesions in mice. W. J. Cromartie and J. G. Craddock. bibliog il Science 154:285-7 O 14 '66

Stroke causes linked to electrical change. Sci N 89:247 Ap 9 '66

Suggest cocktail for shock victims; norepinephrine and phenolamine in treatment of heart attack. Sci N 90:57 Jl 23 '66

They guard against heart attack. M. Ferrigan. il Todays Health 44:10-11 Je '66

Valsalva maneuver; aid for pain from angina pectoris. Time 88:75 S 9 '66

Work to keep young. Sci N 90:21 Jl 9 '66

See also

Chest—Diseases

United States—President's commission on heart disease, cancer and stroke

Diagnosis

Gas bubble helps spot disease. il Sci N 89:306 Ap 30 '66

Fibrillation

See Muscles—Fibrillation

Muscle

Control of myocardial contraction; the sensitivity of cardiac actomyosin to calcium ion. A. M. Katz and D. I. Repke. bibliog il Science 152:1242-3 My 27 '66; Reply. B. L. Fanburg. 154:1208 D 2 '66

Rhythm

See Heart beat

Surgery

Another aortic valve ready for heart patients. Sci N 90:367 N 5 '66

Better half-heart; operation at Houston's Methodist hospital. il Time 87:46+ Ap 29 '66

Brooklyn booster; case of Mr Louise Ceraso. il Newsweek 67:58 Je 6 '66

Bullets in the heart. Time 87:78+ My 27 '66

Death of a patient; case of Marcel L. De-Rudder. Time 87:60 My 6 '66

Diary of a Russian surgeon. N. M. Amosov. il Harper 233:79-86 D '66

Fatal heart infections are cured by surgery. Sci N 90:376 N 5 '66

First artificial heart survivor. il Sci Digest 60:37 N '66

Heart-pump success? Esperanza del Valle Vásquez. Newsweek 68:45 Ag 29 '66

Help for failing hearts; two more implants of artificial heart boosters. il Newsweek 67:78 My 30 '66

Hunt for a mechanical heart; some success in implants at Brooklyn and Houston. il Bsns W p87-8 My 28 '66

Implanted half heart; Mrs Louise Ceraso's operation. il Time 87:39 Je 3 '66

Increasing the blood flow; Vineberg technique in multiple blockages. il Time 87:57-8 F 18 '66

New life for failing hearts; new surgery to revascularize coronary-artery disease. P. D. Ratcliff. il Read Digest 88:181-2+ F '66

Outlook for the artificial heart; with photographs. J. Reinert. Sci Digest 60:46-53 Jl '66

Patients gift to the future of heart repair; pump implant on M. DeRudder; with report by R. Bailey and A. Kerr. il Life 60:84-92 My 6 '66

Plastic heart; left ventricular bypass used on M. DeRudder. il Newsweek 67:64 My 2 '66

Setbacks; Marcel DeRudder's death. Newsweek 67:64 My 9 '66

Spare hearts are already here. B. H. Frisch. il Sci Digest 59:65-70 F '66

Surgical spectacular; reporting the DeBakey operation on Marcel DeRudder. Nation 202:540 My 9 '66

Ticker triumphs; open-heart surgery; cases in Houston and off Viet Nam on U.S. navy hospital ship. il Time 88:46 Ag 26 '66

Upside-down valve; transplanted heart valve. Time 87:80 My 27 '66

HEART, Artificial

Artificial heart analyzed in survey. Sci N 89:245 Ap 9 '66

Artificial heart comes closer; use of left ventricular pump. il Bsns W p81-2+ Mr 12 '66

Artificial hearts: they're practical now; booster pumps. U S News 60:11 My 9 '66

Auxiliary ventricle proposed as aid to ailing hearts. il Todays Health 44:7 F '66

Better half-heart; operation at Houston's Methodist hospital. il Time 87:46+ Ap 29 '66

Boost in time; left ventricular pump. il Newsweek 67:78-9 F 7 '66

Brooklyn booster; case of Mrs Louise Ceraso. il Newsweek 7:58 Je '66

Death of a patient; case of Marcel L. DeRudder. Time 87:60 My 6 '66

First artificial heart survivor. il Sci Digest 60:37 N '66

Heart-pump success? Esperanza del Valle Vásquez. Newsweek 68:45 Ag 29 '66

Help for failing hearts; two more implants of artificial heart boosters. il Newsweek 67:78 My 30 '66

Hunt for a mechanical heart; some success in implants at Brooklyn and Houston. il Bsns W p87-8 My 28 '66

Mechanical aids for the heart. J. L. Breeling. il Todays Health 45:36 Ja '67

Metal implants help hip victims walk better; promising work on artificial hearts. F. Marley. il Sci N 90:321 O 22 '66

Outlook for the artificial heart; with photographs. J. Reinert. Sci Digest 60:46-53 Jl '66

Patient's gift to the future of heart repair; pump implant on M. DeRudder; with report by R. Bailey and A. Kerr. il Life 60:84-92 My 6 '66

Plastic heart; left ventricular bypass used on M. DeRudder. il Newsweek 67:64 My 2 '66

Research advances on heart substitutes. Sci N 89:348 My 7 '66

Setbacks; Marcel DeRudder's death. Newsweek 67:64 My 9 '66

Spare hearts are already here. B. H. Frisch. il Sci Digest 59:65-70 F '66

Step toward a mechanical heart. il U S News 60:61 My 2 '66

They're sewing plastic standby hearts in people. H. Fantel. il Pop Mech 127:136-9+ Ja '67

Total heart; developed by Drs Harris B. Shumacker, jr. and Winton H. Burns. Newsweek 68:96 O 17 '66

HEART beat

Heart flutter explained; action of heart fibrillation or irregular heart beats. Sci N 90:134 Ag 27 '66

Heart rate; changes during conditioned suppression in rats. L. De Toledo and A. H. Black. bibliog il Science 152:1404-6 Je 3 '66

HEART carts. See Hospitals—Emergency services

HEART disease. See Heart—Diseases

HEART massage. See Cardiac resuscitation

HEART muscle. See Heart—Muscle

HEART pump. See Heart, Artificial

HEART rate. See Heart beat

HEART research

Crash heart program cut. Sci N 90:489 D 10 '66

Work to keep young. Sci N 90:21 Jl 9 '66

HEART valves, Artificial. See Heart—Surgery

HEARTWORMS. See Worms, Intestinal and parasitic

HEAT

See also

Hot weather

Thermionic converters

Convection

Amateur scientist; convection currents in liquids. J. R. Bailey. il Sci Am 216:128 Ja '67

Physiological effects

Heat plague. il Newsweek 68:62 Jl 25 '66

Heat wave causes deaths. Sci N 90:66 Jl 30 '66

Hot-weather target; your heart. D. G. Cooley. Read Digest 89:104-6 Ag '66

HEIDBREDER, M. Ann, and Swanker, Esther
Sample projects, title III ESEA. pors Library J 91:1031-2 F 15 '66
HEIDT, Ann
Motor-oil painting. Design 68:16-17 S '66
HEIFERS
His business: bred replacement heifers. C. E. Ball. Farm J 90:66L Ap '66
Push growth, freshen sooner. N. Reeder. Farm J 90:56F D '66
HEIFETZ, Jascha
Heifetz-Piatigorsky, unlimited. A. Chasins. il por Hi Fi 16:MA7 D '66
HEIGHT of men. See Stature
HEILBRONER, Robert L.
Future of capitalism. Commentary 41:23-35 Ap '66
No room at the bottom. Sat R 49:29-32 F 19 '66
HEILER, Friedrich
Friedrich Heiler revisited. A. Winston. Christian Cent 84:56-7 Ja 11 '67
HEIMLICH, Jane
(ed) See Glick, S. How I'm raising my twins
HEIMSATH, Clovis
Holy-card architecture. Commonweal 85:132-4 N 4 '66
HEIN, Piet
King of supershape. A. Chamberlin. il pors Esquire 67:110-13+ Ja '67
Poet with a slide rule. J. Hicks. il pors Life 61:55-6+ O 14 '66
HEINE, Cornelius W.
Washington's flowering cherries. Horticulture 44:30-1+ Ap '66
HEINE, Eerik
CIA above the law. Nation 202:541 My 9 '66
Undercover slander. New Repub 154:5-6 My 14 '66
HEINEMAN, Ben Walter
More for Negroes? a price tag of billions. por U S News 60:10 Je 6 '66
New drive to fulfill these rights. il por Bsns W p38-40 My 28 '66
HEINEMAN, Paul L.
Parking under the state capitol grounds. Am City 81:96-7 Mr '66
HEINEMANN, Arthur
Magic touch; story. Redbook 127:46-7 Jl '66
Vandal; story. Sat Eve Post 239:72-9 My 21 '66
Visible surface; story. McCalls 93:106-7 Mr '66
HEINER, Lou
Check out your charging system. Motor B 117:34-5+ Ap '66
Innovations in ignition systems. Yachting 120:53-5+ O '66
Marriage of inboard and outboard. Motor B 118:92-4+ N '66
Mid-season tune-up for inboard engines. Motor B 118:26-9 Ag '66
Spark plug analysis. Yachting 120:52-3+ Ag '66
HEINITZ, Thomas
Other side. See occasional issues of Saturday review
HEINL, Robert Debs, Jr
Are we ready to intervene in Haiti? Reporter 34:26-8 Je 2 '66
Bailing out Duvalier. New Repub 156:15-16 Ja 14 '67
HEINOLD, George
Drifters make good. Outdoor Life 138:72-3+ N '66
Freshest thing in feathers. Read Digest 89:211-12+ S '66
Salt water. See issues of Outdoor life
Sluggers at the Saco. Outdoor Life 138:46-7+ Jl '66
Snow hunt for stew. Outdoor Life 138:62-4+ S '66
Tidal river grab-bag. por Outdoor Life 137:14-16+ My '66
Twin bill. Outdoor Life 137:62-4+ Mr '66
HEINSHEIMER, Hans W.
Birth of an opera. Sat R 49:49-50+ S 17 '66
Out of Ellison into Kafka. Sat R 49:86-7 N 12 '66
HEINZ, W. C.
I've been living with it a long time. Sat Eve Post 239:112-17 O 8 '66
They kill you with silence. Sat Eve Post 239:91-5 F 26 '66
HEIRLOOMS
Nobody cares about grandfather's clock but grandma. D. Van Ark. il Read Digest 89:98-101 O '66
HEIRS. See Inheritance
HEIRTZLER, J. R. See Pitman, W. C. 3d, jt. auth.
HEISERMAN, Arthur
Peaks and a valley. Nation 202:788-9 Je 27 '66

HEIZER, Robert F.
Ancient heavy transport, methods and achievements. bibliog Science 153:821-30 Ag 19 '66
HEKMAN, Edward John
Third man's theme. R. Levy. il por Duns R 88:43 Ag '66
HELA cells. See Cells
HELFER, Harold
(comp) Just average. N Y Times Mag p32 My 1 '66
(comp) Not so vital statistics. N Y Times Mag p60 N 13 '66
(comp) Recent rulings (cont) N Y Times Mag p 19 Je 12 '66
HELFMAN, Elizabeth S.
Our wild rivers. Liv Wildn 30:24-9 Sum '66
HELICOPTER airlines
Choppers change Greenland; world's longest helicopter airline. il U S News 61:107 O 31 '66
See also
Air general, incorporated
New York airways, incorporated
HELICOPTER association of America
Helicopters, fore; meeting. il Flying 78:52-3 Ap '66
HELICOPTER blades. See Helicopters—Blades
HELICOPTER engines
CH-46As get anti-sand filters. il Aviation W 85:83 Jl 18 '66
Hughes designing civil, military hot-cycle aircraft. H. D. Watkins. il Aviation W 84:48-9+ F 28 '66
Turbine helicopter planned by Filper. Aviation W 86:35 Ja 16 '67
HELICOPTER freight service
Helicopter line seeks expansion formula. D. A. Brown. il Aviation W 86:71-2+ Ja 9 '67
HELICOPTER industry and trade

United States

Big new whirl in helicopters. P. Siekman. il Fortune 73:124-31+ Ap '66
Civil helicopter total may double by 1971. il Aviation W 84:287+ Mr 7 '66
Helicopters confront production squeeze. il Aviation W 84:30-2 Mr 14 '66
Military boom expected to spur growth of commercial helicopter. E. J. Bulban. il Aviation W 84:115+ F 14 '66
West German helicopter order seen facing another long delay. L. L. Doty. Aviation W 84:33-4 Je 6 '66
See also
United aircraft corporation—Sikorsky aircraft division
HELICOPTER rotors. See Rotors (helicopters)
HELICOPTER taxi service. See Air taxi service
HELICOPTERS
Civil helicopter total may double by 1971. il Aviation W 84:287+ Mr 7 '66
For all purposes. il Time 87:82-9 Je 3 '66
Helicopter comes of age: big jobs, big sales ahead; Herding buffalo, laying pipe, what helicopters can do now. il U S News 60:71-3 Mr 7 '66
Helicopters, fore; meeting of Helicopter association of America. il Flying 78:52-3 Ap '66
Leading international rotary-wing aircraft; specifications (cont) Aviation W 84:218 Mr 7 '66
Poor man's back-yard whirlybird. K. V. Brown. il Pop Mech 126:132-3 D '66
Schramm Javelin: price chopper. J. Ethridge. il Motor T 18:70 Ag '66
U.S. rotary-wing aircraft; specifications (cont) Aviation W 84:215+ Mr 7 '66
Volume JetRanger production planned. il Aviation W 84:99+ Ja 24 '66
See also
Autogiros
Rotors (helicopters)

Agricultural applications
See Helicopters in agriculture

Armaments

GE developing varied aircraft weapons. D. A. Brown. il Aviation W 84:73-5+ Mr 21 '66
Head movement trains helicopter guns. il Aviation W 85:58-9 Jl 4 '66
RAC study pivotal for copter armament. M. Getler. Tech W 19:13 Ag 29 '66

Blades

Vertol to build, flight test boron filament rotor blade. B. K. Thomas, jr. il Aviation W 85:40-1+ Ag 29 '66

HELICOPTERS—*Continued*

Design

Hughes designing civil, military hot-cycle aircraft. H. D. Watkins. il Aviation W 84: 48-9+ F 28 '66

Equipment

Helicopter unloads on treetops: using NET landing platform. il Sci N 89:250 Ap 9 '66
Motion-picture camera mount eliminates helicopter's shakes. R. Barnhart. il Tech W 19:42-4 D 5 '66
See also
Aeronautic instruments

Military applications

Air force, army agree on roles, missions. Aviation W 84:26-7 Ap 25 '66
AUTEC operations begin at test range; testing drone anti-submarine helicopter at Atlantic undersea test and evaluation center. M. Getler. il Tech W 19:16-17 O 3 '66
Copter rescues copter. Sci N 90:95 Ag 6 '66
Early Vietnam service sought for CH-6A. C. M. Plattner. il Aviation W 85:97+ S 12 '66
Head movement trains helicopter guns. il Aviation W 85:58-9 Jl 4 '66
Hearings on LOH could cause review of military procurement; light observation helicopter. Aviation W 86:30 Ja 16 '67
Helicopter hearing aid spots machine gun fire. Sci N 90:401 N 12 '66
Helicopter unloads on treetops. il Sci N 89: 250 Ap 9 '66
Helicopter warfare opens new era. A. C. Bass. Miss & Roc 18:82-4+ Mr 28 '66
Helicopters confront production squeeze. il Aviation W 84:30-2 Mr 14 '66
Honeycomb rotor blade patching cuts Viet helicopter downtime. il Aviation W 85:57 Jl 4 '66
HueyCobra offers high maneuverability. D. A. Brown. il Aviation W 84:54-5+ Je 13 '66
Looking for a war. H. Mitgang. il N Y Times Mag p28-9+ My 22 '66
Marine control of air tested in combat. C. M. Plattner. il Aviation W 84:90-1+ F 14 '66
Our fabulous choppers; eyewitness report from Vietnam. J. H. Winchester. il Pop Sci 188:80-3+ F '66
RAC study pivotal for copter armament. M. Getler. Tech W 19:13 Ag 29 '66
Tests pave way for application of IHAS in army's AAFSS. B. Miller. il Aviation W 84: 106-8+ My 16 '66
War in Vietnam: Mohawk helps confirm army air concept. C. M. Plattner. il Aviation W 84:70-2+ F 28 '66
West German helicopter order seen facing another long delay. L. L. Doty. Aviation W 84:33-4 Je 6 '66
West Germany postpones helicopter buy. L. L. Doty. Aviation W 85:121+ Jl 25 '66
Whirlybirds get claws. Sci N 90:79 Jl 30 '66
X-rays studied for secure stationkeeping. B. Miller. il Aviation W 84:74-5+ Ap 18 '66

Noise

Anti-heliporters: meeting of those living near Pan Am building. New York. New Yorker 42:37-9 Ap 2 '66

Private ownership

For whom doth Bell toil? R. Weeghman. il Flying 78:102-7 My '66

Refueling

First mid-air fueling between plane, copter. il(p65) Sci N L 89:66 Ja 29 '66

Rotors

See Rotors (helicopters)

Testing

Egg and I. R. Blodget. il Flying 78:62-5 Mr '66

X ray equipment

See X rays in aviation

HELICOPTERS, Jet propelled
For whom doth Bell toil? R. Weeghman. il Flying 78:102-7 My '66

HELICOPTERS, Military. See Helicopters—Military applications

HELICOPTERS in agriculture
Mi-2 being pushed for foreign markets: Soviet multipurpose helicopter. Aviation W 86:73 Ja 16 '67

HELICOPTERS in business
Brantly 305 used for bank deliveries. Aviation W 85:65 Jl 11 '66

HELICOPTERS in freight service. See Helicopter freight service

HELICOPTERS in industry
Turbine, crane helicopters sought by Okanagan of Canada. R. G. O'Lone. il Aviation W 85:86-7+ D 19 '66

HELICOPTERS in rescue work
Copter rescues copter. Sci N 90:95 Ag 6 '66
Mid-air parachutist recovery may be flier rescue boon. il Tech W 19:32+ S 19 '66
That others may live; Aerospace rescue and recovery service. il Newsweek 67:58 Ap 4 '66
That others may live: Third aerospace rescue and recovery group. il Time 88:27 Jl 22 '66

HELIO aircraft corporation
Pilot report: the Helio Stallion. J. Gilbert. il Flying 79:102-8 Jl '66

HELIPORTS
Anti-heliporters; meeting of those living near Pan Am building. New York. New Yorker 42:37-9 Ap 2 '66
Helicopter line seeks expansion formula. D. A. Brown. il Aviation W 86:71-2+ Ja 9 '67
Problems retard progress of helicopters and V/STOLs. D. A. Brown. il Aviation W 85: 134-5+ O 31 '66

HELIUM
Cosmic helium abundant. Sci N 89:425 My 28 '66
Device clarifies helium speech from Sealab II. Sci N 89:482 Je 18 '66
Double hyper-nucleus; lambda helium nucleus. Sci N 89:435 Je 4 '66
Helium from a fireball. Sci Am 214:54+ My '66
Helium spotted by radio; clues to structure and composition of the Milky way. Sci N 90:54 Jl 23 '66
Nitrogen- and helium-induced anoxia; different lethal effects of rye seeds. R. L. Latterell. bibliog il Science 153:69-70 Jl 1 '66
Radio astronomers detect cosmic helium emission. Sky & Tel 32:123 S '66

HELIUM-neon lasers. See Lasers

HELIUM whistler (radio waves) See Radio waves

HELLEBORE
If you are looking for winter performers. il Sunset 137:174+ D '66

HELLEINER, Mary
Old roses for small gardens. Horticulture 45:42-3 Ja '67

HELLER, Joseph
Something happened; condensation of novel. Esquire 66:136-41 S '66

HELLER, Walter E.
Spotting the seed of success; interview. pors Nations Bsns 54:78-80+ Ap '66

HELLER, Walter Wolfgang
Dash of bitters, but no recession now in sight. Life 61:28-31 S 9 '66
Newest idea about raising taxes; summary of interview. por U S News 62:96 Ja 16 '67
Tax boost soon? adaptation of address. May 2, 1966. New Repub 154:9-11 My 21 '66

about
Minnesota puts own stamp on economics. il por Bsns W p68-70+ O 1 '66
Plan for a tax transfusion. Life 61:6 D 9 '66
Presidential instructor. L. S. Martz. por Newsweek 68:90 D 5 '66

HELLING, Sharon A. See Gasteiger, E. L. jt. auth.

HELLMAN, Geoffrey T.
Department of amplification. New Yorker 42: 171-3 Ap 16 '66
First great cheerful giver. Am Heritage 17: 28-33+ Je '66
Profiles: Smithsonian institution. New Yorker 42:66-8+ D 3; 64-6+ D 10; 58-62+ D 17 '66

HELL'S Angels. See Gangs

HELL'S CANYON
Hell's Canyon: time for a last look. F. Dufresne. il Field & S 71:136-8 N '66
Ordeal in Hell's Canyon; expedition of Astor's fur traders, under W. P. Hunt. 1810-12. A. M. Josephy, jr. il Am Heritage 18:72-9+ D '66

HELLYER, David T.
First days at home with the baby; excerpt from Your child and you. Parents Mag 41: 36-7+ Ap '66

HELLYER, Paul Theodore
Canada's bold defense experiment. F. Nossal. Reporter 34:36-8 Mr 24 '66
Fighting hard to unify Canada's armed forces. Bsns W p96 N 26 '66

HELM, Everett
And this from Wagner's grandson! N Y Times
Mag p68-9+ Je 5 '66
Composer from the pampas. Hi Fi 16:54-6+
Mr '66
Kodály education in action. Hi Fi 16:MA30-1
Jl '66
Notes from our correspondents (cont) Hi Fi
16:20+ Ap; 24+ N '66
Schat's Labyrinth; Rotterdam's new hall.
Hi Fi 16:MA22 S '66
Yehudi Menuhin's festival. Hi Fi 16:MA27+
N '66

HELMS, Harvey
How to prevent marketing losses. Farm J
90:A12 Ag '66
Keeping hogs healthy; interview. Farm J
90:H15-16 N '66

HELMS, Richard McGarrah
Blunderball. por Newsweek 68:19 Ag 8 '66
CIA chief vs. Fulbright; Helms's letter irks
Senate. por U S News 61:16 Ag 8 '66
Pro for CIA. por Time 87:24 Je 24 '66
Shake-up at CIA. il por Newsweek 67:31-2
Je 27 '66
Spooks need course in ghostwriting.   J. N.
Eller. America 115:151 Ag 13 '66
Why LBJ chose Helms to run the CIA. por
U S News 61:14 Jl 4 '66

HÉLOÏSE
Héloïse, by E. Hamilton. Review
Sat R il 50:83 Ja 14 '67. O. Prescott

HELOU, Charles
Tiger at the helm. por Time 87:30 F 11 '66

HELP stamp out marriage! drama. See Waterhouse, K. and Hall, W.

HELPER, Hinton Rowan
Hinton Rowan Helper: abolitionist-racist, by
H. C. Bailey. Review
Nation 203:191-3 S 5 '66. E. G. Genovese

HELPERN, Milton
Not whodunit, but whatdidit? M. W. Lear.
il por N Y Times Mag p48-9+ D 4 '66

HELSINGOR, Denmark
Elsinore castle: to believe or not to believe.
C. Stinnett. il Holiday 40:36+ N '66
Smorgasbord Sunday. H. Sutton. il Sat R
49:42+ Ag 20 '66

HELSON, V. A. See Friend, D. J. C. jt. auth.

HEMAGGLUTINATION. See Blood—Agglutin-
ation

HEME
Coordinate synthesis of heme and apoenzyme in the formation of tryptophan
pyrrolase. H. S. Marver and others. bibliog
il Science 154:501-3 O 28 '66
Fumarate reductase in the control of heme
biosynthesis. T. Kurumada and R. F. Labbe. bibliog il Science 151:1228-9 Mr 11 '66
Heme stimulation of globin synthesis in a cell
free system. C. L. Hammel and S. P. Bessman. bibliog il Science 152:1080-2 My 20 '66
Hemes and hemoproteins; report on colloquium. B. Chance and others. Science 152:
1409-11 Je 3 '66

HEMENWAY, Paul D.
Washington 6-inch transit circle. Sky & Tel
31:72-7 F '66

HEMI engines. See Automobile engines

HEMINGWAY, Ernest
Ernest Hemingway, by N. A. Scott, jr.
Review
Christian Cent 83:1539-40 D 14 '66. R.
Drake
Hemingway si, papa no; Hotchner's echo. W.
Sheed. Commonweal 84:221-3 My 13 '66
Interview with Mary Hemingway: my hus-
band, Ernest Hemingway; ed. by O. Fallaci.
M. Hemingway. il pors Look 30:62-8 S 6 '66
No compromise with life; comment on A. E.
Hotchner and P. Young studies. G. Hicks.
Sat R 49:29-30 Ap 9 '66
On dismembering Hemingway; concerning A.
E. Hotchner's book. P. Young. por Atlan
218:45-9 Ag '66; Discussion. 218:47-9 N '66
Papa Hemingway, by A. E. Hotchner. Review
Esquire 65:34+ Je '66. M. Muggeridge
Harper 232:101-2 Je '66. R. Hatch
Life 60:10 Ap 15 '66. J. Ferris
Nat R 18:632+ Je 28 '66. J. Hart
New Repub 154:24-7 Ap 23 '66. G. Wickes
Newsweek 67:111 Ap 11 '66
Time il 87:107 Ap 15 '66
Vogue 147:146 My '66. A. Goldman
Papa Hemingway; excerpt. A. E. Hotchner.
il pors Sat Eve Post 239:32-8+ Mr 12; 36-
40+ Mr 26; 34-40+ Ap 9 '66
Papa's troubled legacy. J. Tebbel. il por Sat
R 49:30-1+ Ap 9 '66
Peripatetic reviewer. E. Weeks. Atlan 217:
122 My '66
Scott, Ernest and whoever. A. Gingrich. il
Esquire 66:186-9+ D '66

HEMINGWAY, Mary (Welsh)
Gift of love. McCalls 94:75+ D '66
Interview with Mary Hemingway: my hus-
band, Ernest Hemingway; ed. by O. Fallaci.
Look 30:62-8 S 6 '66
Under water; Down Under. Holiday 40:64-5+
S '66
about
Hemingway's widow sues to stop new book
of memoirs. Pub W 189:274 Ja 24 '66
Mrs Hemingway denied injunction on mem-
oirs. Pub W 189:52-3 Mr 7 '66
Papa's troubled legacy. J. Tebbel. il Sat R
49:30-1+ Ap 9 '66
Pique at biography: A. E. Hotchner's Papa
Hemingway. il por Time 87:50 F 11 '66
Privacy cases versus freedom of expression.
H. F. Pilpel. Pub W 189:42 Mr 28 '66

HEMIPTERA
Iphita limbata stal.: components of neuro-
secretory material. K. R. Seshan and P. I.
Iittycheriah. bibliog il Science 153:427-8
Jl 22 '66

HEMISPHERECTOMY. See Brain—Surgery

HEMLEY, Cecil
Founding of a university press. T. Culbert.
por Sat R 49:47 Je 11 '66

HEMMING, Gary
High performance. il por Newsweek 68:40+
S 5 '66

HEMMING, Roy
DISCussions. See issues of Senior scholastic
(ed) See Winter, P.   Cool cat against the
reds' cherry bombs

HEMOCYANIN
Lobster hemocyanin: properties of the minimum functional subunit and of aggregates.
S. M. Pickett and others. bibliog il Science
151:1005-7 F 25 '66

HEMOGLOBIN
Hemoglobin Freiburg: abnormal hemoglobin
due to deletion of a single amino acid
residue. R. T. Jones and others. bibliog
il Science 154:1024-7 N 25 '66
Hemoglobin polymorphism in macaca nemestrina. M. H. Crawford. bibliog il Science
154:398-9 O 21 '66
Hemoglobin Sphakiá: a delta-chain variant
of hemoglobin A_2 from Crete. R. T. Jones
and others. bibliog il Science 151:1406-8
Mr 18 '66
Hemoglobins in sheep: multiple differences
in amino acid sequences of three beta-
chains and possible origins. S. H. Boyer
and others. bibliog il Science 153:1539-43
S 23 '66
Hemoglobins M: identification of Iwate, Boston, and Saskatoon variants. A. Hayashi
and others. bibliog il Science 152:207-8 Ap
8 '66
Hemoglobins of early human embryonic development. A. Kaltsoya and others. bibliog
il Science 153:1417-18 S 16 '66
Multiple gene loci for the monomeric hemoglobin of the hagfish (eptatretus stoutii)
S. Ohno and M. Morrison. bibliog il Science
154:1034-5 N 25 '66
Multiplicity of hemoglobins in the genus
chironomus, tendipes. P. E. Thompson and
D. S. English. bibliog il Science 152:75-6
Ap 1 '66
Predominance of hemoglobin Gower 1 in
early human embryonic development. F.
Hecht and others. bibliog il Science 152:91-
2 Ap 1 '66
Sea cucumber sibling species: polypeptide
chain types and oxygen equilibrium of
hemoglobin. C. Manwell. bibliog il Science
152:1393-6 Je 3 '66
Tryptophan deficiency in rabbit reticulocytes:
polyribosomes during interrupted growth of
hemoglobin chains. M. Hori and others.
bibliog il Science 155:83-4 Ja 6 '67

HEMOLYTIC disease. See Erythroblastosis

HEMOPHILIA
Help for hemophiliacs; safe surgery with
factor VIII. il Newsweek 67:58 F 28 '66
Morning smells best; concerning a ten-year-
old boy. S. L. Robinson. Redbook 127:8+
Je '66

HEMOPROTEINS. See Proteins

HEMORRHAGE
First aid. C. J. Potthoff. il Todays Health
44:70 Je '66

HEMORRHAGIC fever
Search for the invisible killer; Bolivian
hemorrhagic fever in the village of San
Joaquin. T. Armbrister. il Sat Eve Post
239:92-4+ D 3 '66

HEMORRHAGIC shock. See Shock

HEMORRHOIDS
Palliatives but no cures. Time 89:52 Ja 13 '67

HEMPA. See Chemosterilants

HEMPSTEAD, N.Y.

Recreation
Mobile programs; showmobile. R. A. Fitch. il
Parks & Rec 1:718 S '66

Street traffic
Signs that sell traffic safety. M. A. Pancia.
il Am City 81:122 N '66

HEMPSTONE, Smith
Changing role of the church. Nation 203:216-
19 S 12 '66

HEMSLEY, Stuart
Antiseptic lover to his love; poem. Atlan
217:135 Ap '66
Perfect pet; poem. Atlan 218:125 S '66
Who's what; poem. Atlan 217:117 My '66

HEMSTITCHING. See Embroidery

HEN-and-chickens. See Houseleeks

HENAHAN, Donal J.
Opera hits the road. Holiday 39:111-14+ My
'66
Serious music: in serious trouble. Holiday
39:106-9+ Mr '66

HENDERSON, Bruce D. and Dearden, John
New system for divisional control. Harvard
Bsns R 44:144-6+ S '66

HENDERSON, Mrs Carter F.
What you can do to combat air pollution.
Parents Mag 41:76-7+ O '66

HENDERSON, Edward
When millions demand hospital care all at
once; interview. por U S News 60:53-4 Je 6
'66

HENDERSON, Everett S.
Add some new perennial plants to your gar-
den. Horticulture 44:20-3 Jl '66
Dwarf cannas. Horticulture 44:34+ Ap '66
Fragrant mock-orange. Flower Grower 53:56+
Mr '66

HENDERSON, Girard Brown
Avon paying. Time 87:86 Je 17 '66

HENDERSON, Ian
College crackdown in Rhodesia. New Repub
155:15-16 N 19 '66

HENDERSON, Norman D.
Inheritance of reactivity to experimental
manipulation in mice. bibliog Science 153:
650-2 Ag 5 '66

HENDERSON, Robert
Codicils; story. New Yorker 42:32-6 D 24 '66
Cradle song; story. New Yorker 42:56-9 O
29 '66
Long letter; story. New Yorker 42:36-40 Je
18 '66

HENDERSON, William
Battle of words over the war. Sat R 49:32-3
D 17 '66

HENDERSON, William L.
Then and now, yachting on the Chesapeake.
Yachting 119:66-7+ Mr '66

HENDRA, Tony
Foftly, foftly, blowf the gale. por Time
88:85 N 11 '66

HENDRICH, Bob, family
Fun that saves lives: family fire drill. J.
Carper. il Todays Health 44:36-9 O '66

HENDRICKSON, Robert
Leave well enough alone? Flower Grower
53:31+ Ag '66

HENDRICKX, Andrew G. See Katzberg, A. A.
jt. auth.

HENIZE, Karl G. and Wackerling, L. R.
Stellar ultraviolet spectra from Gemini 10.
Sky & Tel 32:204-5 O '66

HENKEL, Carol
Building a 23-footer, family style. il Yachting
119:96-8+ Ja '66

HENLEY, Arthur. See Benjamin, L. jt. auth.

HENLEY royal regatta. See Regattas

HENNE, Frances
As good as librarians make them. por Library J 91:2565-9 My 15 '66

HENNELL, Pamela
Sketches of the skyways. Read Digest 88:201-
2+ Ap '66

HENNEPIN, Ill.
Small town prepares for a big change. il
Fortune 74:187+ N '66

HENNESEY, James J.
Book review. America 114:385-6 Mr 19 '66

HENRION, Marc
Rich little wine. Time 88:81 Jl 8 '66

HENRIOT, Peter J.
Reapportionment revolution. America 115:538-
40 N 5 '66

HENRIQUEZ, Joseph Stephen
Death of a navy pilot. S. Booker. il pors
Ebony 22:25-8+ Ja '67

HENRY VIII, king of England
Henry VIII and the Protestant triumph. L. B.
Smith. bibliog f Am Hist R 71:1237-64 Jl '66
King is dead, long live the king! L. B.
Smith. il pors Horizon 8:90-7 Spr '66
Very pearl of the realm. M. Cable. il por
Horizon 8:108-15 Wint '66

HENRY, Edwin R.
Selection of volunteers. Ann Am Acad 365:
21-8 My '66

HENRY, Emil William
Figures of fun. G. Ace. Sat R 49:8 My 7 '66
Quitting time. Newsweek 67:37 Ap 18 '66

HENRY, Joseph
Profiles: Smithsonian institution. G. T. Hellman. New Yorker 42:68+ D 3; 64-6+ D 10
'66

HENRY, Jules
Capital's last frontier. Nation 202:480-3 Ap
25 '66

HENRY, Mary Roblee
Boom-boom never flagged. Vogue 148:329-31
S 1 '66

HENRY, Rene A. Jr
Take a tip from Tahiti. Pop Gard 17:24-7
Ag '66

HENRY Ford museum and Greenfield Village,
Dearborn, Mich.
Where history isn't bunk. W. A. H. Birnie.
il Read Digest 89:136-43 Jl '66

HENRY VI; drama. See Shakespeare, W.—
Plays

HENTOFF, Nat
Books. Commonweal 83:511-12; 84:371-3 Ja 28,
Je 17 '66
Books (cont) New Yorker 42:237-8+ N 19
'66
Getting inside jazz country. Horn Bk 42:528-32
O '66
Inheritance comes to P.S. 83. por Am Ed 2:
28-32 F '66
New jazz. Vogue 147:177+ F 1 '66
New jazz, black, angry, and hard to under-
stand. N Y Times Mag p 10-11+ D 25 '66
Profiles (cont) New Yorker 41:39-40+ Ja 22;
42:52-4+ My 7 '66

HENTON, Wendon W. and others
Odor discrimination in pigeons. bibliog Science 153:1138-9 S 2 '66

HENZE, Hans Werner
Bassarids. Criticism
Sat R 49:55+ Ag 27 '66
Time 88:50 Ag 12 '66
Five symphonies by Hans Werner Henze.
A. Cohn. por Am Rec G 33:118-20 O '66
Germany's wonder composer: Hans Werner
Henze. P. Heyworth. il Hi Fi 16:65-8 D '66
Music for, and of, our century: Hans Werner
Henze's five symphonies. P. G. Davis. por
Hi Fi 16:74-5 Ag '66

HEPATIC glycogen. See Glycogen

HEPATITIS
New gains in the war on hepatitis. T. Berland. il Todays Health 44:20-1+ Ag '66

HEPATITIS, Infectious
Hepatitis vaccine? Sci Digest 60:15 N '66
Leukocyte mitosis: suppression in vitro as-
sociated with acute infectious hepatitis. B.
Mella and D. J. Lang. bibliog il Science
155:80-1 Ja 6 '67
Single form postulated. Sci N 91:11 Ja 7 '67

HEPATITIS virus
Adenovirus in blood clots from cases of infectious hepatitis. W. V. Hartwell and
others. Science 152:1390 Je 3 '66
Single form postulated. Sci N 91:11 Ja 7 '67

HEPATOCYTES. See Cells

HEPATOMAS. See Tumors

HEPBURN, Andrew H.
Holiday travel; with questions and answers
(cont) Sr Schol 88:sup20-1 F 25 '66

HEPBURN, Audrey
Look at Audrey Hepburn now! il pors Ladies
Home J 84:60-3+ Ja '67
Steal-scening with Hepburn & O'Toole. V.
Leduc. por Vogue 147:172-3+ Ap 1 '66

HERAK, Janko N. and Gordy, Walter
Addition radicals formed by hydroxyl radical bombardment of uracil. bibliog Science
153:1649-50 S 30 '66

HERAKLION (ship) See Shipwrecks

HERALD, Paris. See Paris herald

HERALD tribune, New York. See New York
herald tribune

HERALD tribune children's book awards. See
New York herald tribune children's spring
festival awards

HERALDRY
At the sign of the crest. H. K. Eilers. See
issues of Hobbies
Heraldry and playing cards. D. Powills. il
Hobbies 71:118-19+ Ap '66

HERBALS. See Botany, Medical

HERBERG, Will
Death of God theology. por Nat R 18:771+, 839-40, 884-5 Ag 9-S 6 '66
Post-Vatican II theology. Nat R 18:421-4 My 3 '66
What is religious freedom? Nat R 18:1228-30 N 29 '66

HERBERT, Clarke L.
They shall have music. Am Ed 2:22 O '66

HERBERT, Donald Jeffry
Return of the wizard. il por Time 88:80 O 7 '66

HERBICIDES
Herbicide mixtures, a good tool for controlling weeds. G. Miller and R. Behrens. Suc Farm 64:94+ Mr '66
Preemergence weed killers for corn and soybeans. Suc Farm 64:90+ Mr '66
Weeds to small grains, how to control them. L. W. Mitich. Suc Farm 64:97+ Mr '66

Injurious effects
Availability of a cationic herbicide adsorbed on clay minerals to cucumber seedlings. J. B. Weber and D. C. Scott. il Science 152:1400-2 Je 3 '66
Toxicity of equatic herbicides to daphnia magna. D. G. Crosby and R. K. Tucker. bibliog il Science 154:289-91 O 14 '66

HERBS
Books. M. F. K. Fisher. New Yorker 42:226-30+ S 24 '66
Herbs. G. Foster. il Horticulture 44:22-5 O '66
Herbs. R. N. Allen. il Horticulture 44:38-9+ My '66
Herbs, in your garden, in your kitchen. il Changing T 20:39-40 Ap '66
Midsummer feast. H. S. Witty. il Flower Grower 53:36+ Ag '66
Practical approach to herbs. il Flower Grower 53:34-5 Ag '66
See also
Dill
Garlic
Yarrows

HERBST, Josephine
Spain's agony: a period of exposure. Nation 203:91-4 Jl 25 '66

HERCULANEUM
Herculaneum, by J. J. Deiss. Review
Time il 88:130 N 25 '66

HERCULES, incorporated
Hercules enters tactical missile field. J. F. Judge. il Tech W 19:28-9 N 7 '66

HERDING of sheep. See Sheep herding

HEREDITY
Elusive code of life. B. Commoner; J. Kendrew; L. L. Whyte. il Sat R 49:71-9 O 1 '66
Inheritance of reactivity to experimental manipulation in mice. N. D. Henderson. bibliog il Science 153:650-2 Ag 5 '66
Inherited variations of human serum α₁-antitrypsin. F. Kueppers and A. G. Bearn. bibliog il Science 154:407-8 O 21 '66
Who should bear children? F. Marley. il Sci N 90:537 D 24 '66
See also
Chromosomes
Genetics

HEREDITY of disease
Does it run in the family? S. G. Streshinsky. il Parents Mag 41:61-3+ N '66
Genetics and the survival of the unfit. L. Eisenberg. il Harper 232:53-8 F '66; Reply with rejoinder. H. J. Muller. 232:13 Je '66
Sex-linked anemia: a hypochromic anemia of mice. R. M. Bannerman and R. G. Cooper. bibliog il Science 151:581-2 F 4 '66

HEREMANS, Joseph F. See Vaerman, J. P. jt. auth.

HERESY
Case of heresy? concerning Bishop Pike. il Newsweek 68:66 N 7 '66
In defense of heresy. A. Towne. Christian Cent 84:44-7 Ja 11 '67
See also
Apostasy
Inquisition

HERING, Doris
Regional ballet, USA. See occasional issues of Dance magazine

HERLONG, Albert Sydney, 1909-
Excerpt from debate, June 30, 1965. Cong Digest 45:21+ Ja '66

HERMAN, J. Clayton
Corn late? try cold storage. Farm J 80:56T O '66

HERMAN, Jerry
Sweet Sue. il Time 87:44 Ap 22 '66

HERMAN, Leon M.
Close-up: talk with Leon M. Herman; interview, ed. by J. Berry. pors Duns R 88:8-9+ S '66

HERMAN, Melvin. See Schreiber, F. R. jt. auth.

HERMENEUTICS, Biblical. See Bible—Hermeneutics

HERMITS
See also
Eccentrics and eccentricities

HERNIA
Polyp, hernia like LBJ's not rare. Sci N 90:393 N 12 '66
President's surgery no small matter. F. Marley. Sci N 90:443 N 26 '66

HERO worship
Hard times for heroes; D. Meredith. G. Astor. il Look 31:82-3 Ja 10 '67

HERODOTUS
Dig confirms Herodotus' tales. il Sci N 90:426 N 19 '66
Herodotus and the strategy and tactics of the invasion of Xerxes. A. Ferrill. bibliog f Am Hist R 72:102-15 O '66

HEROES
Notes and comment: Meredith, Stafford, and Cernan. New Yorker 42:27 Je 18 '66
On the difficulty of being a contemporary hero; Time essay. Time 87:32-3 Je 24 '66
Who is a hero? and why? interview with five celebrities. il Mlle 63:57-9+ Jl '66
See also
Great men
Hero worship
Television heroes

Anecdotes, facetiae, satire, etc.
Handful of heroes. L. Rosten. il Look 30:24 D 13 '66

HEROES and lovers; story. See Silverman, R.

HEROINES in literature. See Characters in literature

HERON, David W. and Blanchard, J. R.
Seven league boots for the scholar? pors Library J 91:3601+ Ag '66

HERONS
Egrets and herons make home near oil refinery; do-it-yourself bird sanctuary in water-conservation lagoons. il Sci N 90:147 S 3 '66
No fly-by-night operation; Stone Harbor bird sanctuary. B. Gilbert. il Sports Illus 24:36-8+ Je 20 '66

HERPES simplex virus
Partial purification and electron microscopy of virus in the EB-3 cell line derived from a Burkitt lymphoma. I. Toplin and G. Schidlovsky. bibliog il Science 152:1084-5 My 20 '66
Polysomes and protein synthesis in cells infected with a DNA virus. R. J. Sydiskis and B. Roizman. bibliog il Science 153:76-8 Jl 1 '66
Virus: mixed infection with herpes simplex and simian virus 40. A. S. Rabson and others. bibliog il Science 151:1535-6 Mr 25 '66

HERR, Michael
Fort Dix: the new army game. Holiday 39:68-9+ Ap '66
Museum of modern art. Holiday 40:115-18+ D '66

HERRERA, Philip
Eavesdropping in Harlem. Reporter 34:47-8 My 5 '66
—See McQuade, W. jt. ed.

HERRESHOFF, Halsey C. and Newman, J. N.
Antiope sails indoors. pors Yachting 120:55-7+ D '66
Study of sailing yachts; with biographical sketches. Sci Am 215:10, 60-8 bibliog (p 114) Ag '66

HERRINGTON, William C.
International issues of Pacific fisheries; adaptation of address. Dept State Bul 55:500-4 O 3 '66

HERRMANN, Cyril C.
Systems approach to city planning. Harvard Bsns R 44:71-80 S '66

HERSEY, M. Leonard
Control points. See issues of Yachting
Powerboats in competition. Yachting 119:67-9+ F '66

HERSH, Burton
New twin cities. Holiday 39:50-5+ Je '66

HERSHEY, Lenore
Sight and sound. See issues of McCall's

HERSHEY, Lewis Blaine
Draft: an old problem; Congress takes another look; summary of testimony, June 22, 1966. por U S News 61:28-9 Jl 4 '66
Equality does not exist; excerpts from testimony before the House armed services committee. Time 88:13-14 Jl 1 '66

HERSHEY, Lewis Blaine—*Continued*

about

Drill sergeant. il por Newsweek 67:21 F 28 '66
Hershey favors drafting women. Christian Cent 83:1561 D 21 '66
How fair is the draft? J. Star. il Look 30:26-7 Ap 19 '66
Straus scores Hershey. Christian Cent 83: 325 Mr 16 '66

HERSHON, Robert
Report to the blue guard; poem. Nation 203: 555 N 21 '66

HERST, Herman, jr
Stamps. See issues of Hobbies

HERTEL, Heinrich
Nature still holds lessons for engineers. W. S. Beller. il Tech W 19:28-9 D 19 '66

HERTER, Christian Archibald, 1895-1966
Yankee internationalist. por Time 89:16 Ja 13 '67

HERTER, Christian Archibald, 1919-
Corporate diplomacy in foreign countries; address, March 11, 1966. Vital Speeches 32:407-9 Ap 15 '66

HERTZ, Heinrich Rudolf
Old World standards breaking through. Pop Electr 24:28 Ap '66

HERTZ (electric unit) See Electric units

HERTZ corporation
Bite behind; Hertz advertising account. Time 88:71 Jl 15 '66
Hertz strikes back; Hertz ad. Newsweek 68:80 N 28 '66
Hertz, too, becomes a no. 2; merger with RCA. Time 88:99-100 O 28 '66
Into the back seat; RCA merger. Newsweek 68:79 O 31 '66
When the big guy hits back; advertising. il Time 88:65 D 23 '66

HERTZBERG, Richard
New York city shop that caters to car, airplane and armored tank buffs. Pub W 189: 115-16 Ap 25 '66

HERTZIAN waves. See Electromagnetic waves

HERTZSPRUNG-Russell diagram. See Astronomy—Charts, diagrams, etc.

HERVEY, Michael
Virtue is her own reward; drama. Plays 25: 27-35 Ap '66

HERZFELD, Norma Krause
Disarmament, not now. Commonweal 85:341-3 D 23 '66

HERZOG, Arthur
Learn, baby, learn. Am Ed 2:4-6 S '66
Suicide can't be eliminated. N Y Times Mag p32-3+ Mr 20 '66

HESBURGH, Theodore M.
College football. por Sports Illus 25:56-7 D 12 '66

HESCHEL, Abraham Joshua
What God thinks of man. por Newsweek 67:57 Ja 31 '66

HESHMATI, Leota B.
Secret of the Roman stairs; drama. Plays 25:37-42, 62 Ap '66

HESS, Arthur
If you have questions about medicare: here are the answers; interview. por U S News 60:58-63 My 9 '66

HESS, H. H. and Ladd, H. S.
Mohole: preliminary drilling. bibliog Science 152:544-5 Ap 22 '66

HESS, M. Whitcomb
Mary and the Christian. Cath World 203: 100-3 My '66
Three *haiku*; poems. Cath World 203:204 Jl '66

HESS, Moses
Communist rabbi: Moses Hess. J. Frankel. bibliog f Commentary 41:77-81 Je '66

HESS, Rudolf
Cost of incarceration. il por Time 88:48 S 16 '66
Last prisoner of Spandau. P. Shabecoff. il pors N Y Times Mag p28-9+ Ag 28 '66

HESS, Stephen
Big Bill Taft. Am Heritage 17:32-7+ O '66
Long, Long trail; excerpts from America's political dynasties: from Adams to Kennedy. Am Heritage 17:40-2+ Ag '66
People's dukes; excerpts from America's political dynasties; from Adams to Kennedy. Am Heritage 17:43-4 Ag '66

HESS, Thomas B.
In praise of reason. Art N 65:22-5+ Sum '66

HESSLER, Victor P.
On a floating island. por Science 151:1360-2 Mr 18 '66

HESTER, James M.
City and the university; address, February 14, 1966. Vital Speeches 32:294-7 Mr 1 '66

HESTON, Charlton
Graven image. il pors Time 88:43 Ag 12 '66

HETACILLIN. See Penicillin

HETEROCHROMATIN. See Chromatin

HETERODYNE vegetation meter. See Electronic apparatus and appliances

HETEROGENEOUS catalysis. See Catalysis

HETEROSIS (biology)
Heterosis: complementation by mitochondria. R. G. McDaniel and I. V. Sarkissian. bibliog il Science 152:1640-2 Je 17 '66

HETZEL, Pierre Jules
Behind Jules Verne. C. H. Bishop. il Commonweal 85:169-71 N 11 '66

HEUBLEIN, incorporated
Management's rule-breakers: the ways of the winners. J. B. Weiner. il Duns R 87:34-6 Ja '66

HEUSNER, A. A. and Enright, J. T.
Long-term activity recording in small aquatic animals. bibliog Science 154:532-3 O 28 '66

HEWES, Henry
SR goes to the movies. Sat R 49:40 Jl 9 '66
Theater (cont of) Broadway postcript. See issues of Saturday review

HEWITT, Jean
Food (cont) N Y Times Mag p56 Ja 23; 48 Ja 30; 50 Je 26; 40 Jl 10; 41 Jl 31 '66

HEWITT, John P.
Unique answer to urban sprawl problem. por Parks & Rec 1:491-2 Je '66

HEWITT-Robins, incorporated
Anatomy of an acquisition. J. B. Weiner. Duns R 87:34+ My '66

HEXACHLOROCYCLOHEXANE
Biodegradation of the gamma isomer of benzene hexachloride in submerged soils. K. Raghu and I. C. MacRae. bibliog il Science 154:263-4 O 14 '66

HEXING. See Witchcraft

HEYBROEK, Hans M.
Dutch elm disease abroad. Am For 72:26-9+ Je '66

HEYER, Diana
It's spring; poem. Horn Bk 42:234 Ap '66

HEYER, Paul
(ed) Architects on architecture; excerpts. Arch Forum 125:66-9+ N '66

HEYES, Frank C.
Blitzen leads fleet from Chicago. Yachting 120:49+ S '66

HEYNS, Roger William
Balancing act at Berkeley. J. Fincher. il pors Life 61:45-6+ D 16 '66
Berkeley's peacemaker. il por Time 88:38-9 Jl 1 '66

HEYWORTH, Peter
Germany's wonder composer: Hans Werner Henze. Hi Fi 16:65-8 D '66
New house, old problems. Hi Fi 16:146 F '66

HI-Fi systems. See High fidelity sound systems

HIATT, C. W. See Easton, J. M. jt. auth.

HIBBARD, Everett
I draw in my pocket. Am Artist 30:48-9 Je '66

HIBBEN, Frank C.
New Zealand at the crossroads. por Field & S 71:12-13+ Ag '66

HIBERNATION
Day the bears go to bed; Craighead brothers bio-telemetry study of pre-hibernation habits. J. George. il Read Digest 89:137-41 O '66
How to spend the winter; quiz. J. Daugherty and M. Daugherty. il Sci Digest 59:93-5 F '66

HIBISCUS
Hibiscus. J. V. Watkins. il Horticulture 44: 24-5+ Je '66

HIBLER, Dave
Love song. Christian Cent 83:802 Je 22 '66

HICCUPS
Don't laugh at hiccups! causes and treatments. L. M. Nash. il Todays Health 44: 26-7 Ag '66

HICKE, Donald R.
Designing an oscilloscope vertical attenuator. Electr World 76:94-6 S '66

HICKEY, K. Elaine
Businessmen's expectations (cont) Duns R 87:13 Mr; 14 Je '66

HICKMAN, Kenneth
Oases for the future; excerpts from address, August 1966. bibliog Science 154:612-17 N 4 '66

HICKMAN, W. Braddock
Economic situation; address, May 23, 1966. Vital Speeches 32:565-7 Jl 1 '66

HICKMAN, Warren L.
Renaissance of teaching. Sch & Soc 94:265-7 Sum '66

HICKOCK, Eunice
In cold blood target of threatened law suit.
Pub W 189:81 Ap 25 '66
HICKOCK, Richard Eugene
In cold blood, by T. Capote. Review
Commentary 41:77-80 My '66. W. Phillips
Harper 232:110+ F '66. R. West
Nat R 18:226-9 Mr 8 '66. J. G. Dunne
Two faces and.., a landscape. T. Capote.
il por Vogue 147:144-9 F 1 '66
HICKOK, James Butler
Western hero, by K. L. Steckmesser. Review
Nation 202:107-9 Ja 24 '66. R. A. Aurthur
HICKS, Clifford B.
Blessed is the mother of twins. Todays
Health 44:24-7 My '66
Do mosquitoes love you? Todays Health 44:
32-4 Jl '66
Jet-age blues. Todays Health 44:18-19+ N
'66
HICKS, Edward
Cover: concerning Peaceable kingdom. T. Gil-
liland. il Sat R 49:20 S 3 '66
HICKS, Granville
Literary horizons. See issues of Saturday
review
HICKS, Jim
For little Dai from his auntie. Life 61:106
N 11 '66
Poet with a slide rule. Life 61:55-6+ O 14
'66
Right extraordinary Harold Wilson wins his
big victory. Life 60:44-44B+ Ap 8 '66
Shakespearean turned sexpot. Life 61:79-80+
Jl 1 '66
Vulnerable eyes in coal-dusted faces. por
Life 61:3 N 4 '66
We Welsh are all the same, we dig our
roots deep. Life 62:24-7 Ja 6 '67
(ed) See West, R. Specialist in traitors,
spies and weeds
HICKS, Louise Day
Boston: education's last hurrah. P. Schrag.
il por Sat R 49:56-8+ My 21 '66
Boston's Louise Day Hicks: storm center
of the busing battle. I. Mothner. il pors
Look 30:72+ F 22 '66
White northerner's choice. P. Lamson. por
Atlan 217:58-62 Je '66
HICKS, Mabel
For Tim; poem. Christian Cent 84:9 Ja 4
'67
HICKS, Peggy Glanville-. See Glanville-Hicks,
P.
HICKS, Warren B.
Chabot rounds out resources. Library J 91:
5897-9 D 1 '66
HICKSVILLE, N.Y.
Pool-rink complex. il Parks & Rec 1:750+
S '66

HIDDEN language. See Jargon
HIDDEN treasure. See Treasure trove
HIDDEN VALLEY downs. See Race tracks
HIDES and skins
See also
Fur
HIDING from Walter; story. See Gordon, D.
HIERTH, Harriet
Curl up and read. Seventeen 25:13 Jl '66
HIGDON, Hal
Big auto sweepstakes. N Y Times Mag p 36-7+
My 1 '66
Conservation faces its moment of truth. To-
days Health 44:50-1+ Mr '66
Minority objects, but Daley is Chicago. N Y
Times Mag p84-5+ S 11 '66
Road runner's bonanza; or, Has anybody seen
Kelley? Sports Illus 25:58-60+ S 5 '66
HIGER, Aaron L. See Kolipinski, M. C. jt.
auth.
HIGGINS, Alice
Horse shows (cont) Sports Illus 24:90 Ap 25;
54+ Je 20; 25:52-3 Ag 8; 86+ N 14 '66
HIGGINS, George C.
Why Sedalia selected plastic. bibliog Am City
81:112-13+ S '66
HIGGINS, James
You never know who's who in Vietnam; con-
versation with ex-soldiers. New Repub 154:
12 Ap 16 '66
HIGGINS, James E.
Letter from C. S Lewis. Horn Bk 42:533-9
O '66
HIGGINS, John B.
Pioneering vidwan. il por Newsweek 68:49-50
N 28 '66
HIGGINS, Marguerite
Dedicated reporter. por Sr Schol 88:19 F 4 '66
HIGH, Robert King
Wave either way. Time 88:29-30 O 28 '66
HIGH, William L.
Octopus rasslin' is hand-to-hand-to-hand-to-
hand. Pop Mech 125:102-3 My '66

HIGH altitudes, Influence of. See Altitude, In-
fluence of
HIGH ASWAN DAM. See Aswan High Dam
HIGH blood pressure. See Hypertension
HIGH commissioner for refugees. See United
Nations—High commissioner for refugees
HIGH cost of living. See Cost of living
HIGH energy physics. See Nuclear physics
HIGH fidelity amplifiers. See Amplifiers
HIGH fidelity incorporating Musical America
(periodical)
New directions for old departments. Hi Fi
16:55 D '66
Progress report: editorial. R. Gelatt. Hi Fi
16:45 Ap '66
HIGH fidelity music shows. See Audio fairs
HIGH fidelity shows. See Audio fairs
HIGH fidelity sound systems
Equipment in the news. See issues of High
fidelity incorporating Musical America
Hi-fi and TV for your boat. L. G. Sands. il
Motor B 117:38-9+ Je '66
High fidelity equipment reports. See issues
of High fidelity incorporating Musical
America
How it all began. il Hi Fi 16:68-71 Ap '66
News & views. il Hi Fi 16:32+ Je '66
Plus or minus 3dB. I. Berger. Sat R 49:55-6
D 31 '66
Sound; tape recorders can be the nucleus of
a high fidelity system. J. Wesson. U S
Camera 29:30-1 N '66
Stereo decor, a new kind of harmony. Hi Fi
16:45 Mr '66
Stereo vs .hi fi: that eternal, irritating ques-
tion. J. Wesson. U S Camera 29:34+ Jl
'66
Why are they still inventing speakers? H.
Fantel. il Pop Electr 25:49-52+ N '66
See also
Phonograph—High fidelity sound systems
Stereophonic sound systems

Repairing
Looking for trouble. I. B. Berger. Sat R 49:
57 F 26 '66
Testing
Test out your hi-fi at home. H. Fantel. il
Pop Electr 24:57-9+ Ap '66
Testing, testing. I. Berger. Sat R 49:70-1
Mr 26 '66
HIGH fidelity speakers. See Loud speaking ap-
paratus
HIGH frequency radiation. See Radiation
HIGH-intensity lamps. See Electric lamps
HIGH pressure oxygenation. See Hyperbaric
oxygenation
HIGH-rise apartment houses. See Apartment
houses
HIGH school annuals
Pretty as a picture; will the camera be smil-
ing at you? il Seventeen 25:22 S '66
HIGH school athletes. See Athletes
HIGH school buildings. See School buildings
HIGH school counselors. See Personnel service
in education
HIGH school dropouts. See Dropouts
HIGH school education, Value of. See Educa-
tion, Value of
HIGH school football players. See Football
players
HIGH school girls. See Girls
HIGH school graduates
Employment of high school graduates and
dropouts in 1965. H. R. Hamel. il Mo Labor
R 89:643-9 Je '66
Joy has gone out of learning. A. H. Lass.
Sat R 49:65 Je 18 '66
Out-of-school youth two years later; resur-
vey of graduates and dropouts. V. C. Per-
rella and E. Waldman. il Mo Labor R 89:
860-6 Ag '66
HIGH school libraries
Coast range gem: the Los Gatos high school
library. E. Mason. il ALA Bul 60:270-4
Mr '66; Reply with rejoinder. E. T. Scho-
field. 60:529-31 Je '66
See also
Knapp school libraries project

Paperback books
See School libraries—Paperback books

Periodical collections
See School libraries—Periodical collections
HIGH school of performing arts. See New York
(city)—Education

HIGH school students
Drugs: a student report. A. Lake. Seventeen 25:170-1+ S '66
Explorer scouts; address, December 6, 1965. W. H. Spurgeon, 3d. Vital Speeches 32: 314-20 Mr 1 '66
Hair-do's, and don'ts; faculty-student squabbles over hair and dress styles. il Newsweek 68:94 O 3 '66
Pressures on students; symposium. NEA J 55:28-31 S '66
Talking it over with Gay Head: questions and answers. Gay Head. See issues of Senior scholastic
Workshop in the woods. 31 centuries! Trees for tomorrow camp, Eagle River, Wis, with comments of the participants. K. B. Pomeroy. il Am For 72:16-21+ O '66
See also
Scholastic research center
Student activities

Clothing
See Clothing and dress

Dating
See Dating

Photographs
Teach me! excerpts. C. Purcell. Sat R 49:72-3 D 17 '66

Political activities
High school students have no voice. D. Gladstone. Sat R 49:62 My 21 '66
Today's teenagers: youth in ferment, or, youth playing it safe? il Sr Schol 88:6-9 F 4 '66

HIGH school students, Married
Early to wed. B. Rollin. il Look 30:93-5 S 20 '66
Teen-age marriage. Time 87:102 Ap 29 '66

HIGH school students, Mentally superior
Presidential scholars, 1966. W. Coyne. il Am Ed 2:12-13 S '66

HIGH school students, Negro. See Negro students

HIGH school students as automobile drivers. See Automobile drivers

HIGH school teachers. See Teachers

HIGH school teaching. See Teaching

HIGH schools
High schools in the South. Sch & Soc 94: 183-4 Ap 2 '66
What's bugging you about school; letters with answers. D. Klein. Seventeen 25:66+ Je '66
What's going on in schools & colleges. See issues of Changing times

Curriculum
College readiness program of east Harlem; Benjamin Franklin high school, New York city. K. K. Waller. il Sat R 49:90-1+ Ap 16 '66
High school and the cultural illiterate. G. Culligan. il Am Ed 2:1-5 N '66
Humanities in high school. Time 88:32-3 D 30 '66

Personnel service
See Personnel service in education

Summer sessions
See Summer schools

HIGH schools, Catholic. See Catholic church—Education
HIGH schools, Ecumenical. See Church schools
HIGH schools, Private. See Private schools
HIGH schools, Technical. See Trade schools
HIGH schools, Vocational. See Trade schools
HIGH schools for Negroes. See Negroes in the United States—Education
HIGH society. See Upper classes
HIGH speed aerodynamics. See Aerodynamics, Supersonic
HIGH speed ground transport systems. See Transportation, High speed
HIGH speed railroads. See Railroads—Train speed
HIGH speed trains. See Railroads—Trains
HIGH speed transportation. See Transportation, High speed
HIGH temperature engineering
Fever in pyrogenics. G. J. Berkwitt. il Duns R 87:30-3+ Ap '66
HIGH temperatures
Chemisorption of water at high temperatures on kaolinite: effect on dehydroxylation. G. W. Brindley and G. L. Millhollen. bibliog il Science 152:1385 Je 3 '66

Chemistry at high temperatures; report on conference. M. A. Paul and J. L. Margrave. Science 152:1113-14 My 20 '66
Laboratory culturing of a thermophilic alga at high temperature. R. Ascione and others. bibliog il Science 153:752-5 Ag 12 '66
HIGH voltage transmission. See Electric transmission
HIGH wire walking. See Acrobats and acrobatism
HIGHAM, Charles
Three poems: Sisters; Hunter; Hyenas. Yale R 56:104-6 O '66
HIGHAM, John
Schism in American scholarship; address, November 6, 1965. bibliog f Am Hist R 72:1-21 O '66
HIGHER education. See College education; Colleges and universities; Junior colleges
HIGHER education act, 1965. See Federal aid to education
HIGHER education division of the United States office of education. See United States—Education, Office of—Higher education division
HIGHLAND costume. See Tartans
HIGHLAND PARK, Ill.
More maintenance per man-hour. D. H. Fritz. il Am City 81:96-8 N '66
HIGHSMITH, Patricia
Suspense short story. Writer. 79:9-12 Mr '66
HIGHT, Clyde
This month's cover story. il por Suc Farm 64:60 My '66
HIGHWAY accidents. See Traffic accidents
HIGHWAY beautification. See Roadside improvement
HIGHWAY bonds. See Roads—Finance
HIGHWAY engineering
Concrete Juggernaut. W. G. Wing. il Audubon Mag 68:266-72, 294, 360-7 Jl-S '66
Street construction and maintenance. See issues of American city
See also
Roads—Safety guards
HIGHWAY law
See also
Traffic courts
HIGHWAY location. See Roads—Location
HIGHWAY patrol. See Police, State
HIGHWAY police. See Police, State
HIGHWAY safety. See Roads—Safety devices and measures; Traffic safety
HIGHWAY transportation. See Transportation, Automotive
HIGHWAYMEN. See Brigands and robbers
HIGHWAYS. See Roads
HIGINBOTHAM, William A.
Peril, a hope, and a movement. Bul Atomic Sci 22:34-7 Ap '66
HIJACKING. See Robberies and assaults
HIJACKING of airplanes. See Crimes aboard aircraft
HIKING. See Walking
HILDEBRANDT, A. C. See Chandra, N. jt. auth.
HILDENBRAND, Barbara
When cholera struck America. Todays Health 44:40-2 O '66
HILDRETH, A. C.
Denver botanic gardens. Horticulture 44:28-9+ Jl '66
HILEMAN, Dale
Heterodyne receiver. Electr World 75:80-3 Ja '66
HILL, Barney
Aboard a flying saucer; excerpt from The interrupted journey. J. G. Fuller. il por Look 30:44-8+ O 4; 111-14+ O 18 '66
Interrupted journey, by J. G. Fuller. Review Sat R 49:22-3 D 31 '66. H. Greenwald
HILL, Betty
Aboard a flying saucer; excerpt from The interrupted journey. J. G. Fuller. il por Look 30:44-8+ O 4; 111-14+ O 18 '66
Interrupted journey, by J. G. Fuller. Review Sat R 49:22-3 D 31 '66. H. Greenwald
HILL, Bobby Joe
Go-go with Bobby Joe. F. Deford. il por Sports Illus 24:26-9+ Mr 28 '66
HILL, C. R.
Polonium-210 content of human tissues in relation to dietary habit. Science 152:1261-2 My 27 '66
HILL, Elizabeth Starr
Time out for happiness. Read Digest 88:237-8+ Ap '66
Young girl's gift. Read Digest 89:49-52 D '66

HILL, Elmo
Guaranteed maintenance puts strength in equipment purchases. Am City 81:148+ Ap '66

HILL, Gladwin
Barbecues and other trivia. Nation 203:377-9 O 17 '66
Parties in chaos: California sweepstakes. Nation 202:352-5 Mr 28 '66

HILL, Granam
Crazy mixed-up 500. B. Ottum. il Sports Illus 24:20-3 Je 6 '66

HILL, Henry H.
It will take time. Sat R 49:54-6+ Jl 16 '66

HILL, James
Privacy v. free press. il Time 87:74 My 6 '66
Vote for the press over privacy; case of James Hill and his family. il Time 89:56 Ja 20 '67

HILL, Joe
Dying like a true rebel. P. Cowan. Nation 203:291-2 S 26 '66

HILL, Lister
Hill-Burton at twenty: hospital progress and challenge. por Todays Health 44:76 Ag '66

HILL, Rochelle
Alice in Wonderland; dramatization of story by L. Carroll. Plays 26:81-91 Ja '67

HILL, Sir Rowland
Stamps around the world. H. Herst, jr. Hobbies 71:99 D '66

HILL, Samuel and company. See London—Banks

HILL, Thomas
(ed) See Wolbarst, J. 1966 film-developer roundup

HILL, Tom W.
Stay young with ions. Sci Digest 61:74-7 Ja '67

HILL, Walter E. jr, and Neuman, R. W.
Copper artifacts from prehistoric archeological sites in the Dakotas. bibliog Science 154:1171-3 D 2 '66

HILL, William B.
Fiction (cont) America 114:670-2; 115:706-10 My 7, N 26 '66

HILL-Burton act. See Hospitals—United States
HILLBILLY music. See Folk music, American

HILLEGAS, Mark R.
Other worlds to conjure. Sat R 49:33-4 Mr 26 '66

HILLER, Arthur
New faces. H. Alpert. il por Sat R 49:24 D 24 '66

HILLGEN, Marcella
Renton bridges a river. Library J 91:5864-6 D 1 '66

HILLIGAN, Earl, and Maxwell, G. E.
Ride the waves on skis. Todays Health 44:40-5 Ag '66

HILLMAN, Richard
Obituary
Nat R 18:1034 O 18 '66

HILLMAN, William S.
Photoperiodism in lemna: reversal of night-interruption depends on color of the main photoperiod. bibliog Science 154:1360-2 D 9 '66

HILLSIDE architecture
California apartments make skillful use of Hillside sites. il Arch Rec 139:133-40 Mr '66
Development house, Belvedere, California. il Arch Rec 139:100-1 mid-My '66
Dubrow residence, Golden, Colorado. il Arch Rec 139:80-3 mid-My '66
Great hang-out! right over a canyon. C. Gunther. il Pop Mech 125:116-17 F '66
Mountain pavilion makes use of local materials. il Arch Rec 139:161-4 My '66
Norwegian terrace housing; high-density on an unbuildable hillside. il Arch Rec 139:162-3 Ja '66
Schramm residence, Burlington, Iowa. il Arch Rec 139:64-7 mid-My '66

HILSE, Daisy Frances
Four years of 4.0 por Time 87:74 Je 24 '66

HILTNER, Seward
Not dead enough. Christian Cent 83:1181-2 S 28 '66

HILTON, Alice Mary
Of worth and value; address, February 1, 1966. Vital Speeches 32:335-41 Mr 15 '66

HILTON, Conrad Nicholson
Daring to build on a dream: interview. pors Nations Bsns 54:94-6+ S '66

HILTON, Hank
Automatic thermostat booster. Pop Mech 126:160-1+ D '66

HILTON hotels corporation
Daring to build on a dream: interview. C. N. Hilton. il Nations Bsns 54:94-6+ S '66
Hilton invades Paris. H. Sutton. Sat R 49:32+ Je 4 '66

Mr Hilton goes to Paris. il Newsweek 67:71 Ap 25 '66
Switch in time; concerning dismissal of suit because of plaintiff's ignorance. Time 87:67 Mr 18 '66

HIMALAYAS
See also
Nepal

HIMBER, Charlotte
Parent and child (cont) N Y Times Mag p59+ F 27; 86+ Je 5 '66

HIMMELFARB, Milton
In the community (cont) Commentary 41:66-70 Ap; 42:23-9 Jl; 83-6 O '66

HINCKLEY, Robert H.
Politics of extremism; address, May 24, 1966. Vital Speeches 32:599-604 Jl 15 '66

HINDEMITH, Paul
Mathis der maler. Criticism
Opera N il 30:24 Je 4 '66

HINDENBURG (airship) See Airships

HINDERAKER, Ivan
Political party officials: responsiveness to the public Ann Am Acad 363:28-35 Ja '66

HINDLEY, Myra
In ghastly transcripts, a test of our times. P. H. Johnson. il Life 61:62+ Ag 12 '66
Maximum sentence. Time 87:42 My 13 '66
Moorland murders. por Newsweek 67:52 My 16 '66
Trial begins. il por Newsweek 67:34 My 2 '66

HINDS, Jeanette
Fashion footnote: poem. Farm J 90:89 S '66

HINDUISM
Faith, mushrooms linked; soma, plant with hallucinogenic properties worshiped by ancient Hindus. P. McBroom. Sci N 90:398 N 12 '66
Mauna. P. Perera. New Yorker 42:205-10+ O 29 '66
Three ways of Asian wisdom, by N. W. Ross. Review
Sat R 49:48 D 3 '66. D. Hales
See also
Sadhus
Vedanta

HINDUS
Casualty list; rally for national ban on cattle slaughter. il Time 88:48 N 18 '66
Flames in Punjab; Sikhs and Hindus. il Time 87:32 Mr 25 '66
For mother cow; clash over slaughter of cows by Moslems. il Newsweek 68:66 N 21 '66
Hindus demand total ban on slaughter of cows. Christian Cent 83:1432 N 23 '66
Wonders of India. J. P. Gabriel. il Travel 126:56-62 O '66
See also
India—Hindu-Muslim relations

HINES, Earl
Fatha knows best. il por Time 88:72+ Ag 5 '66

HINES, Gerald D.
Dealer who's remaking Houston. il pors Bsns W p 170-2+ D 3 '66

HINES, James J.
Immigration act of 1965; address, December 7, 1965. Dept State Bul 54:119-23 Ja 24 '66

HINES, Theodore C.
Crisis in children's cataloging. por Library J 91:4183-7 S 15 '66

HINGES
Nine novel hinges, can you guess what they're for? il Pop Mech 126:147-9 S '66

HINGSON, Robert Andrew
Warriors against disease. C. M. Davis. il por Today Health 44:30-4 N '66

HINKLE, C. N. and Fletcher, W. J.
Know your diesel. Suc Farm 64:48 Ag; 94+ S '66

HINMAN, Charles
And now: Top. il por Time 87:58-9 F 11 '66

HINMAN, Keith C.
One thousand yard bucks. Field & S 71:56-7+ O '66

HINRICHES, Marie A. and Kaplan, Robert
Home, the school, and sex education. Todays Health 44:16+ F '66

HINSON, William J.
Tensions in U.S.-Latin American relations. Christian Cent 83:1004-7 Ag 17 '66

HIPPOLYTE et Aricie; opera. See Rameau, J. P.

HIPPOPOTAMUS
Waiting for Hugo; efforts to catch a destructive hippo in Tanzania. il Time 87:33 Je 3 '66

HIRAOKA, Kimitake. See Mishima, Y. pseud.
HIRED men. See Farm labor
HIRING. See Employment systems

HIROHITO, emperor of Japan
God-king. por Newsweek 67:96C-96D+ Je 27 '66
Hirohito, emperor of Japan, by L. Mosley. Review
Life 60:12+ Je 17 '66. D. Bergamini
Sat R 49:24-5 Je 25 '66. D. Kurzman
Time il por 88:82+ Jl 1 '66
HIROSHIMA
Hiroshima: let us never forget. R. B. Fulton. Christian Cent 83:1254-5 O 12 '66
Postscript from Hiroshima, by R. Steinberg. Review
Newsweek il 68:98 Jl 18 '66
Sat R il 49:53 Jl 23 '66. H. Bristol
HIRSCH, Ed
(ed) See Ray, M. Man Ray on the future
HIRSCH, Felix E.
Changing culture in Germany. Cur Hist 50: 289-94+ My '66
HIRSCHFELD, Florence Kerr
Season's delightful Jewish traditions and food. Bet Hom & Gard 44:74+ D '66
HIRSCHMAN, Albert, and Dziewiatkowski, D. D.
Protein-polysaccharide loss during endochondral ossification: immunochemical evidence. bibliog Science 154:393-5 O 21 '66
HIRSH, Nicole
Portugal's Gulbenkian festival. Hi Fi 16: MA23 Ag '66
HIRSHBERG, Al. See Nelson, L. jt. auth.
HIRSHHORN, Joseph Herman
4,000 paintings and 1,500 sculptures. V. Raynor. il pors N Y Times Mag p52-5+ N 27 '66
Jewel for the mall. il por Time 87:88 My 20 '66
Radioactive treasure. il por Newsweek 67:100 My 23 '66
HIRSHHORN collection. See Art—Private collections
HIRSUTISM. See Hair
HISCOCK, Eric
From England to English Harbour. il Yachting 120:48-9+ D '66 (to be cont)
HISPANIC AMERICAN history. See Latin America—History
HISPANIOLA
See also
Dominican Republic
HISTAMINE
Histamine synthesis in man: inhibition by 4-bromo-3-hydroxybenzyloxyamine. R. J. Levine. bibliog il Science 154:1017-19 N 25 '66
HISTIDINE
Correlation between location and time of expression for genes in a single operon. D. Marver and others. bibliog il Science 153: 1655-6 S 30 '66
N-acetylhistidine isolated from frog heart. Y. Kuroda and T. Ikoma. bibliog il Science 152:1241-2 My 27 '66
HISTONES
Biosynthesis and composition of histones in Novikoff hepatoma nuclei and nucleoli. L. S. Hnilica and others. bibliog il Science 152:521-3 Ap 22 '66
HISTOPLASMOSIS
Birds bring disease: pulmonary histoplasmosis. il Sci N 89:174 Mr 12 '66
HISTORIANS
Ibn Khaldūn: man of history: excerpts from radio program. B. Bray. il UNESCO Courier 19:4-10 Je '66
Shackled historian. H. Feis. For Affairs 45: 332-43 Ja '67
Should historians write contemporary history? H. S. Commager. il Sat R 49:18-20+ F 12 '66
Should the historian make moral judgments? H. S. Commager. il Am Heritage 17:26-7+ F '66
Where are Tacitus, Plutarch, Voltaire? J. H. Plumb. Sat R 49:29+ N 26 '66
See also
Negro historians
HISTORIANS, American
See also
Negro historians
HISTORIANS, English
Macaulay and his critics. J. Valenti. Sat R 49:22-3 Ap 30 '66
HISTORIANS, German
See also
Mommsen, T.
HISTORIC houses, etc.
Historic houses, landmarks, and museums. See issues of Antiques
See also subhead Historic houses, etc. under names of countries, states, cities, etc. e.g. United States—Historic houses, etc.

Conservation and restoration
See Architecture—Conservation and restoration
HISTORIC sites. See Historic houses, etc.
HISTORICAL art. See History in art
HISTORICAL chronology. See Chronology, Historical
HISTORICAL criticism. See History—Historiography
HISTORICAL fiction
Biography: the other face of the coin. R. Sprague. Horn Bk 42:282-9 Je '66
Getting into historical fiction. J. Sanders. Writer 79:18-22 Ag '66
History with its eyes wide open. G. Davenport. Nat R 18:1227-8 N 29 '66
HISTORICAL research
Quantification in history. W. O. Aydelotte. bibliog f Am Hist R 71:803-25 Ap '66
HISTORIOGRAPHY. See History—Historiography
HISTORY
Sense of history: address. R. Taft, jr. PTA Mag 60:28-9 Mr '66
See also
Current events
Historians
Historical fiction
Man
Oral history
also subheads Antiquities; Foreign relations; History; Politics and government under names of countries, states, etc. e.g. France—History; also subhead History under various subjects. e.g. Aeronautics—History

Bibliography
History (cont) J. J. O'Connor. America 114: 668-70; 115:700+ My 7, N 26 '66
Reading, writing, and history. B. Catton. See occasional issues of American heritage to April 1966

Dictionaries
Oxford companion to American history, by T. H. Johnson. Review
New Repub 155:20-2 O 15 '66. A. R. Butler

Historiography
Banning history: Frick vs. Stevens: suit to ban distribution of a recent history of Pennsylvania. E. Langer. Science 153:616 Ag 5 '66
History as literature. D. Acheson. il Esquire 66:99-102+ O '66
People's right to the past: law suit to ban Pennsylvania: birthplace of a nation, by S. K. Stevens. Christian Cent 83:1169 S 28 '66
Quantification in history. W. O. Aydelotte. bibliog f Am Hist R 71:803-25 Ap '66
Shackled historian. H. Feis. For Affairs 45: 332-43 Ja '67
Should the historian make moral judgments? H. S. Commager. il Am Heritage 17:26-7+ F '66
See also
Russia—History—Historiography
United States—History—Civil war—Historiography

Philosophy
At the roots of Republicanism. F. C. Lane. bibliog f Am Hist R 71:403-20 Ja '66
Current Soviet theory of history: new trends or old? A. P. Mendel. bibliog f Am Hist R 72:50-73 O '66
On time and history. W. C. McWilliams. Yale R 56:91-103 O '66
Patterns of history. W. L. Gundersheimer. Reporter 34:50-2 Ap 21 '66

Sources
See also
Archives
Oral history

Statistics
Quantification in history. W. O. Aydelotte. bibliog f Am Hist R 71:803-25 Ap '66

Study and teaching
History with spirit of inquiry: excerpts from address, November 1966. P. L. Ward. Sr Schol 89:sup 14 D 9 '66
Soviet teaching of history and international understanding. V. G. Trukhanovsky. Sch & Soc 94:152-5 Mr 19 '66
1066, 1492, and student 49631: letter in answer to student theme. E. R. Wilcox. il NEA J 55:22-3 O '66
Truth has many faces: contempoary history classes at Enfield, Conn. high school. F. S. Gross. il Sr Schol 88:sup22-3 Ap 29 '66
Using records to teach history; Linwood jr. high school, North Brunswick, N.J. M. S. Defren. il Sr Schol 89:sup 18 N 11 '66

HISTORY, Ancient
   Lost city of the Sybarites. T. L. Christie.
      Sat R 49:52-3 Mr 19 '66
      See also
   Numismatics, Ancient
   Rome—History
         Bibliography
   Articles and other books received; comp.
      by T. R. S. Broughton. See issues of
      American historical review
HISTORY, Modern
   Misuses of the past. W. Jovanovich. Sat R
      49:21-4 Ap 2 '66
   Should historians write contemporary his-
      tory? H. S. Commager. il Sat R 48:18-20+
      F 12 '66
   Tragedy and hope, by C. Quigley. Review
      Sat R 49:34 F 12 '66. G. Smith
HISTORY, Roman. See Rome—History
HISTORY, Universal. See World history
HISTORY and science. See Science and civiliza-
      tion
HISTORY in art
   Series of historical paintings. A. L. Ripley.
      il Am Artist 30:44-9+ My '66
   Where both sides gained; Spanish history in
      art. il Time 88:76-81 O 28 '66
HITACHI, limited. See Japan—Industries
HITCH hiking. See Hitchhiking
HITCHCOCK, Alfred Joseph
   Alfred Hitchcock probes the American man's
      aversion to carving; ed. by E. Alston. pors
      Look 31:50-1 Ja 10 '67
HITCHCOCK, James
   Reflections on the St John's case. Cath World
      203:24-8 Ap '66
HITCHCOCK, Patricia
   Our Ulleri child. Redbook 127:20+ Ag '66
HITCHES (automobile) See Automobiles—
      Equipment
HITCHHIKING
   Cars & the law. R. J. Gottlieb. Motor T 18:
      12 D '66
   Rule of thumb for the open road. J. Graham.
      il Sports Illus 24:76-80+ Je 6 '66
HITLERISM. See Fascism—Germany
HITSVILLE USA (corporation) See Motown
      record corporation
HIVES, Bee. See Beehives
HLEBINE, Yugoslavia
   Village of painters. A. Werner. Reporter 35:
      49-50 S 8 '66
HNILICA, Lubomir S. and others
   Biosynthesis and composition of histones in
      Novikoff hepatoma nuclei and nucleoli.
      bibliog Science 152:521-3 Ap 22 '66
HO, Han-nan
   Han army spectacularly unearthed in main-
      land China. Art N 65:36-7 Sum '66
HO, Yin
   Eastward Ho. il por Newsweek 68:56 O 17 '66
HOARY bats. See Bats
HOAXES
   Seminole with a hole in his head. L. Rosten.
      Look 30:20 Ag 23 '66
HOBART, George F.
   Something lost behind the ranges. Nat R
      18:166 F 22 '66
HOBBIES
   Craft news! products to make hobbies less
      work. M. Garrity. il Bet Hom & Gard 44:
      111-12+ Ap '66
   Writing in retirement. G. D. Kratz. Writer
      79:26-8 Ap '66
HOBBS, Cecil
   (comp) Articles and other books received;
      south Asia. See issues of American his-
      torical review
HOBBS, R. W. See Hollinger, J. P. jt. auth.
HOBBS, Robert M.
   Fabulous Smoky River. Field & S 71:54-5+
      O '66
   Last frontier. por Outdoor Life 137:44-7+
      Mr '66
HOBBY kits, Electronic. See Electronic ap-
      paratus and appliances
HOBBY rooms. See Rooms
HOBERMAN, Norman L.
   Way to influence the environment. il Arch
      Rec 139:207-14 Ap '66
HOBERMAN, Stuart
   Automatic TV brightness control. Electr
      World 75:38 My '66
HOBSON, Karl
   Wheat shortage is here. Farm J 90:21+ Ag
      '66

HOBSON, Laura Z.
   Single, age twenty-five; story. Good H 162:
      87-9 Je '66
HO-chi-Minh
   From Ho, with love. J. Burnham. Nat R 18:
      203 Mr 8 '66
   Hanoi's special weapons system. J. Burnham.
      Nat R 18:765 Ag 9 '66
   Ho chi Minh: poet in leg irons. J. Mirsky.
      Nation 202:302-3 Mr 14 '66
   Secret encounter with Ho chi Minh; ed. by
      J. Flowers. R. J. Defourneaux. il pors Look
      30:32-3 Ag 9 '66
HOCHMAN, Baruch
   Agnon's quest. Commentary 42:45-51 D '66
HOCHMAN, Sandra
   Alice in Vegas. Holiday 39:30+ My '66
   Directions for an act; poem. Mlle 62:112 F'
      '66
   Night harbour; poem. Nation 203:134 Ag 8 '66
   Potential prisoner; poem. Nation 203:490 N
      7 '66
   Written at Vivian court; poem. Atlan 218:80
      N '66
HOCHSTEIN, Paul. See Lieberman, M. jt.
      auth.
HOCHSTEIN, Rolaine
   Child of delight; story. Redbook 127:80-1 O '66
HOCHSTEIN, Rollie
   Offstage with Eydie Gorme. Good H 162:48+
      F '66
   —See Sugarman, D. jt. auth.
HOCKEY
   Cup play: a whole new game; Montreal
      Canadiens vs Toronto Maple Leafs in Stan-
      ley cup playoffs. M. Kane. il Sports Illus
      24:30-5 Ap 25 '66
   Huskies from Houghton; Michigan technolog-
      ical university beats Minnesota. il Time
      87:70-1 Mr 11 '66
   It's Baker! going for another touchdown!
      and another goal! with introd. by George
      Frazier. J. Davies. il Esquire 66:132-5+
      S '66
   Mayhem on ice; Canada's specialty. D. Mac-
      Donald. il Read Digest 88:17-18+ Mr '66
   Poison ivy in the ivy league; Cornell's
      hockey team. M. Mulvoy. il Sports Illus
      26:44-6 Ja 2 '67
      See also
   National hockey league
HOCKEY coaches. See Physical directors
HOCKEY players
   Boston's Bobby; Orr. il Newsweek 68:77 N
      21 '66
   Goalie is the goat; with report by J. R.
      McDermott. il Life 60:33-4+ Mr 4 '66
   Policeman's life. il Newsweek 67:79 Ja 31 '66
   You take the Punch or quit; coach Imlach
      at Toronto Maple Leaf hockey practice. P.
      Axthelm. Sports Illus 25:32-4+ D 12 '66
      See also
   Mikita, S.
HOCKEY teams
   All in the mind; Canadiens win the Stanley
      Cup. il Times 87:55 My 13 '66
   Boom booming along. il Newsweek 68:63 D
      19 '66
   Boy on Bobby's back is back; B. Watson of
      the Detroit Red Wings. G. Ronberg. il
      Sports Illus 25:71-3 N 28 '66
   Cold cash; expansion teams. Newsweek 67:
      88+ F 21 '66
   Cup play: a whole new game; Montreal Ca-
      nadiens vs Toronto Maple Leafs in Stanley
      cup playoffs. M. Kane. il Sports Illus 24:
      30-5 Ap 25 '66
   Detroit New Year's wish: one for the road;
      Red Wings cannot win out of town. G.
      Ronberg. il Sports Illus 26:46-7 Ja 16 '67
   Double the fun; N.H.L. to expand teams.
      Time 87:71 F 18 '66
   Habs hold a torch bien haut; Montreal
      Canadiens win their 13th Stanley cup. M.
      Kane. il Sports Illus 24:38-40+ My 16 '66
   Hockey's biggest moment; no. 51; B. Hull of
      Black Hawks broke the record. M. Kane.
      il Sports Illus 24:26-9 Mr 21 '66
   Look who's no. 1; the Rangers. il Time 88:
      35 D 23 '66
   Nice guy who learned to be troublesome;
      N. Ullman of Detroit Red Wings. G. Ron-
      berg. il Sports Illus 24:53-4 F 28 '66
   One more boom or bust for the Boomer;
      former Montreal Canadiens hero, now with
      New York Rangers. P. Axthelm. il Sports
      Illus 25:42-4+ N 14 '66
   Pitt penguins; names of new National hockey
      league teams. Sports Illus 25:24 S 12 '66
   Sporting scene; Montreal Canadiens and
      Detroit Red Wings. H. W. Wind. il New
      Yorker 41:116+ F 12 '66
   You take the Punch or quit; coach Imlach
      at Toronto Maple Leaf hockey practice. P.
      Axthelm. Sports Illus 25:32-4+ D 12 '66

HOCKING, William Ernest
People's philosopher. por Time 87:74 Je 24 '66
Professor Hocking: last of a golden age. Christian Cent 83:825 Je 29 '66
HODDENBACH, G. A. See McCoy, C. J. jt. auth.
HODDER and Stoughton, limited
Fawcett forms British firm with Hodder & Stoughton; Hodder Fawcett, ltd. Pub W 189:273 Ja 24 '66
HODENFIELD, G. K.
Freeing kids for learning. PTA Mag 60:8-10 Je '66
What's new in the curriculum? PTA Mag 61:7-9 bibliog(p35) Ja '67
HODGE, Russ
What price what glory? il por Time 88:52-3 Ag 5 '66
HODGENS, Richard M.
Movies in brief (cont) Nat R 18:229-30, 377-9, 850 Mr 8, Ap 19, Ag 23 '66
HODGES, Mary Jane
Boating. Sports Illus 24:79-80 Ap 25 '66
HODGES, Robert M.
Drug tests get the FDA needle. pors Bsns W p 114+ N 19 '66
HODGINS, Maibelle Dickey
Christmas gift for bird lovers. Horticulture 44:36 D '66
HODGKIN'S disease
Thymus helps in cure. Sci N 89:227 Ap 2 '66
HODGSON, Moira
Let's travel Mlle 64:121-3 Ja '67
HODKINSON, J. Raymond
Negro in Britain. bibliog Negro Hist Bul 29:77-8+ Ja '66

about

Integration: Negro college hires an impatient Briton. L. J. Carter. il por Science 152:481-5 Ap 22 '66
HOEBEL, Bartley G. See Caggiula, A. R. jt. auth.
HOECK, Ken L.
Flag-football. por Parks & Rec 1:912-13 N '66
HOEFGEN, Ruth
Ways to keep clothing looking like new. Parents Mag 41:18 O '66
HOEKENGA, Mark T.
It almost makes one cry: what a doctor sees in Vietnam; excerpts from diary. por U S News 61:74-6+ S 19 '66
HOELLEN, John J.
Study in black and white. S. Alsop. por Sat Eve Post 239:16 N 5 '66
HOELTL, Georg
Germans mate bus and hotel. il por Bsns W p 172-3 My 21 '66
HOFER, Evelyn
Washington's unknown memorials; excerpts from Evidence of Washington; photographs. W. Walton. Arch Forum 125:60-5 N '66
HOFF, Gail
Kissing disease. il pors Life 60:81-2 Mr 18 '66
HOFF, Laurie
Little fish; poem. Horn Bk 42:751 D '66
HOFF, Philip Henderson
Power politics in New England. V. Maerki. New Repub 154:10 Ja 29 '66
HOFFA, James Riddle
As Hoffa's deadline nears; a strike deadline too. il por U S News 62:85-7 Ja 16 '67
Elusive heel. Time 87:21 F 11 '66
Fighting Hoffa's blues. il por Time 88:17-18 Jl 15 '66
Hell with everybody! il por Newsweek 68:80 Jl 18 '66
Hoffa conviction: was evidence illegal? U S News 61:35 D 26 '66
Hoffa decision. Nation 204:5-6 Ja 2 '67
Hoffa seeks stand-in, in case he's needed. Bsns W p 144 Je 4 '66
Hoffa still holds the reins, for now. il por Bsns W p 128-30 Jl 9 '66
Hoffa's funeral. il por Newsweek 68:20-1 D 26 '66
How a union can be run from prison. por U S News 61:76+ Jl 11 '66
How they got Jimmy Hoffa, or did they? excerpt from Crime war. R. M. Cipes. por Atlan 218:118-22 N '66
If Jimmy Hoffa goes to jail. il por U S News 61:65-6 D 26 '66
Jimmy's boy. Newsweek 67:76 My 16 '66
Long wait starts for Hoffa; Supreme court decision could be delayed until next June. Bsns W p 154+ O 22 '66
Pragmatic view of privacy. il por Time 88:36+ D 23 '66
Will jailing Hoffa hurt the teamsters? por Bsns W p44 D 17 '66

HOFFBAUER, Charles
Fin-de-siècle. J. Ashbery. il Art N 65:43+ My '66
HOFFBERG, Judith A.
Libraries, lasagna, and leaning towers. Wilson Lib Bul 40:948-52 Je '66
HOFFER, Eric
Comments on the human condition. Harper 233:90-1 N '66
Making a mass élite. Holiday 39:10+ Mr '66
What I have learned: strategy for the war with nature. por Sat R 49:27-9+ F 5 '66

about

Blue-collar Plato. S. K. Oberbeck. il por Newsweek 69:92-92A+ Ja 16 '67
Profiles. C. Tomkins. por New Yorker 42:34-6+ Ja 7 '67
HOFFMAN, Bernard
Too thin negative: how to get the most out of it. Pop Phot 59:92-3+ Ag '66
Two heads are better than one. il Pop Phot 59:112-13 D '66
HOFFMAN, Daniel
Asylum; poem. Nation 203:364 O 10 '66
Edwin Muir: the story and the fable. Yale R 55:403-26 Mr '66
February; poem. Nation 202:242 F 28 '66
This day; Testament; Other poems; When my wiser brother; poems. Poetry 109:89-93 N '66
HOFFMAN, Frederick J.
T. S. Eliot: the poet as critic. Nation 203:324-5 O 3 '66
HOFFMAN, George A.
Electric automobile; with biographical sketch. Sci Am 215:16, 34-40 bibliog(p 150) O '66
HOFFMAN, Howard S. and others
Enhanced distress vocalization through selective reinforcement. Science 151:352-4 Ja 21 '66
HOFFMAN, Jay K.
Putting the art before the war horse. il por Time 88:83 S 9 '66
Sound sellers. Newsweek 67:88 F 28 '66
HOFFMAN, Joyce
Is surfing too tough for girls? pors Seventeen 25:88-9+ Jl '66

about

Joyce Hoffman: number one in the surf. S. Gordon. il pors Look 30:92-3+ My 3 '66
Shoo-in surf champ. il por Life 61:141-2+ O 14 '66
HOFFMAN, Marvin, and Mudd, John
Mississippi: new plantations. Nation 203:411-15 O 24 '66
HOFFMAN, Paul, jr
Engine overhaul. Flying 78:68-71 F '66
HOFFMAN, Paul G.
He helped make this small world. Sat R 49:36 Mr 5 '66
Rich and the poor: 1966. por Sat R 49:22-5 S 17 '66
HOFFMAN, Robert
Inventor of the month. S. V. Jones. por Sci Digest 61:23 Ja '67
HOFFMAN, Theodore
Florida rococo. Opera N 30:6-7 F 5 '66
HOFFMAN, William
Sea tides; story. McCalls 93:86-7 S '66

about

Thank you, Miss Victoria. Criticism
Nation 202:404 Ap 4 '66
New Yorker 42:126 Ap 23 '66
HOFFMANN, Banesh
National educational assessment. NEA J 55:25 F '66
HOFFMANN, Frederick
F. Hoffmann, Philadelphia silversmith. E. Gaines. il Antiques 89:385 Mr '66
HOFFMANN, R. L. and Evans, C. D.
Thermal conductivity effect of carrier gases on flame-ionization detector sensitivity. Science 153:172-3 Jl 8 '66
HOFFMANN, Rita
Carleton: coming of age. cum laude. Mlle 62:186-8+ Ap '66
Divorce American style. Mlle 63:190-1+ S '66
Psychedelic game; excerpt from Psychedelic reader. Mlle 62:179+ Mr '66
HOFFMANN, Stanley
Suspense in France. Commonweal 83:554-6 F 11 '66
HOFFMANN, Wolfgang
Visit to East Germany. America 114:486+ Ap 9 '66
HOFHEINZ, Roy
Sporting scene. R. Angell. New Yorker 42:132+ My 14 '66

HOFMANN, Armin
Swiss designer Armin Hofmann on future design. il Pub W 189:82-3 Ap 4 '66
HOFMANN, Hans
Art galleries; exhibition at the Kootz. R. M. Coates. New Yorker 41:140+ F 19 '66
Eulogy, February 20, 1966. H. Rosenberg. por Art N 65:21 Ap '66
Hans Hofmann: 1880-1966. por Newsweek 67: 85 F 28 '66
Hans Hoffman, 1880-1966. J. Love. America 114:396 Mr 19 '66
Schoolmaster of the abstract. il por Time 87: 78+ F 25 '66
HOFMANN, Paul
Whatever became of Che? N Y Times Mag p 14-15+ Ap 10 '66
HOFMANNSTAHL, Hugo Hofmann, edler von
Of timeless passions. R. Breuer. il Opera N 31:24-5 D 10 '66
HOFMEYR, Jan Hendrik
South African tragedy, by A. Paton. Review Christian Cent 83:586 My 4 '66. H. E. Fey
Esquire 65:44+ Mr '66
HOFSTRA university, Hempstead, N.Y.
Library becomes campus focal point. il Arch Rec 140:210-13 S '66
HOG cholera
Cholera eradication makes headway. il Farm J 90:47 Mr '66
Closing in on hog cholera. Farm J 90:39 S '66
HOG houses. See Swine houses
HOGAN, Charles
Proposers of reform. Sat R 50:37-8 Ja 7 '67
HOGAN, Sheila Mary
Fortune-teller; poem. America 115:514 O 29 '66
HOGAN, William
Author; C. O. Sauer. Sat R 49:25 Jl 2 '66
HOGAN'S goat; drama. See Alfred. W.
HOGARTH, William
Hogarth in Virginia. il Newsweek 69:82-3+ Ja 23 '67
HOGE, Dorothy
Before the dawn; poem. Horn Bk 42:693 D '66
HOGE, Thomas A.
Renaissance for relics. Travel 126:56-9 Ag '66
HOGG, Ima
American decorative arts in Texas. D. B Warren. il Antiques 90:796-815 D '66
HOGROGIAN, Nonny
Caldecott award acceptance; address, July 12, 1966. Horn Bk 42:419-21 Ag '66
Story sets the pace; an illustrator's view of design. il Pub W 189:100-3 F 21 '66
                    about
Newbery-Caldecott winners. por Wilson Lib Bul 40:688 Ap '66
Nonny Hogrogian. A. Durell. il Library J 91:1594-5 Mr 15 '66
Nonny Hogrogian. J. P. Itta. por Horn Bk 42:421-5 Ag '66
Nonny Hogrogian: decorator of books for children. D. Waugh. il por Am Artist 30: 52-7 O '66
Treviño, Hogrogian: Newbery and Caldecott winners. il por Pub W 189:30-2 Mr 14 '66
HOGS. See Swine
HOGUE, Charles L. See Casebeer, R. S. jt. auth.
HOHBERGER, George. See Curtis, J. J. jr. jt. auth.
HOHEISEL, Peter
In flesh; poem. Cath World 204:153 D '66
New books. Cath World 202:372-3 Mr '66
HOHENBERG, John
Fifty years of Pulitzer prizes. por Sat R 49: 73-4+ Mr 7 '66
HOHENEMSER, Kurt H.
Supersonic transport. Bul Atomic Sci 22:8-12 D '66
HOITMAN, Robert S.
University and the world; address, March 9, 1966. Vital Speeches 32:442-7 My 1 '66
HOKANSON, Hans
Wood: two approaches to modern sculpture. E. Dugmore. il Craft Horiz 26:13-15 Jl '66
HOKKAIDO (island)
Vanishing Ainu of north Japan. S. Takakura. il Natur Hist 75:16-25 O '66
HOLBROOK, Hal
Funniest lies: Mark Twain tonight! Time 87:63 Ap 1 '66
Hal Holbrook tonight! concerning the one-man show, Mark Twain tonight! R. Shickel. Holiday 40:103-5 Ag '66
Mark Twain on Holbrook. T. Prideaux. Life 60:16 My 13 '66

Mark Twain tonight! Hal Holbrook this morning. New Yorker 42:44-5 Ap 23 '66
Mark Twain tonight! T. Lewis. America 114:605 Ap 23 '66
HOLBROOK, Martin E.
Eight little-known ways to cut your tax bill. Nations Bsns 54:36-7+ Mr '66
HOLBROOK, Weare
Unidentified shining objects. Atlan 217:121-2 Je '66
HOLCOMB, Luther
Holcomb's trek. J. C. Evans. Christian Cent 83:956 Ag 3 '66
HOLDEN, David
Unholy row over the tomb of Christ. Sat Eve Post 239:80-5 Ap 9 '66
HOLDEN, Donald
New addition. por Am Artist 30:4 D '66
HOLDEN, Stephen
In praise of Antonioni; poem. New Yorker 42: 40 Je 4 '66
HOLDER, Albin O.
Cartier opens its door wider. il por Bsns W p70-2+ O 15 '66
HOLDER, Fred W.
Belingrath gardens. Horticulture 44:42-4 F '66
HOLDING companies
Paradise for profits; Liechtenstein. il News-week 68:93-5 O 10 '66
    See also
Bank holding companies
Mercantile financial corporation
HOLDING devices (machine work)
Make this unique work-holding vacuum plate. il Pop Mech 126:163-4+ S '66
    See also
Jigs
HOLE, Frank
Investigating the origins of Mesopotamian civilization. bibliog Science 153:605-11 Ag 5 '66
HOLIDAYS
Tisha b'Av in Moscow; Judaism's national day of mourning. R. I. Rubin. Christian Cent 83:1186-7 S 28 '66
    See also names of holidays, e.g. United Nations day
HOLIDAYS with pay. See Vacations, Employee
HOLIFIELD, Chet
Creation of a nuclear navy; address, January 17, 1966. Vital Speeches 32:261-4 F 15 '66
HOLLAND, Albert E.
Big man & the little lady. il por Time 88: 71 Jl 22 '66
HOLLAND, Barbara
Gift of dolphins; story. Redbook 126:62-3 Mr '66
Someone in the kitchen; story. McCalls 93: 64-5 Je '66
HOLLAND, D. K.
Slurry seal cures spalled-concrete ills. Am City 81:103 F '66
HOLLAND, Ray P.
Desert tragedy. Field & S 71:72-3+ S '66
HOLLAND, Robert C.
Where the Fed gets its bold new ideas. por Bsns W p 101-2+ D 10 '66
HOLLAND festival. See Music festivals—Netherlands
HOLLANDER, Gino
Enough of New York. il por Newsweek 68:48 N 28 '66
HOLLANDER, J. M. and Perlman, I.
Semiconductor revolution in nuclear radiation counting. bibliog Science 154:84-93 O 7 '66
HOLLANDER, John
Five shaped poems: Normal bell-curve; Swan and shadow; Crise de coeur; Graven image; Broken column. Poetry 109:175-80 D '66
From woodcarver to woodcarver. R. Roseliep. Poetry 107:327-8 F '66
HOLLANDER, Lawrence J.
Big blackout: whooping cranes & power fail-ures. Nation 202:33-6 Ja 10; inside cover Ja 24 '66
HOLLANDER, Robert
For my pregnant cat Grendel who's giving love another chance without a single thought; poem. Atlan 218:125 Jl '66
HOLLEIN, Hans
Keyhole shop. il Arch Forum 124:33-7 Je '66
HOLLEMAN, S. Brooks
Reformation of Bill. por Outdoor Life 137: 52-3+ Mr '66
HOLLENBAUGH, William Diller
Battle of Gobbler's Knob. il por Time 87:23 My 27 '66
Kidnapped! interview, ed. by J. Bird P A. Bradnick. il por Sat Eve Post 239:25-9+ Jl 16 '66
Stalking the terror of Shade Gap. M. Mok. il por Life 60:32B-32E My 27 '66
Terror in the Tuscaroras. il por Newsweek 67:29-30 My 30 '66

HOLLERITH, Herman
Automated government. J. W. Macy, jr. il Sat R 49:23-5+ Jl 23 '66
HOLLEY, Edward G.
Resources for research in urban areas; address. July 12, 1966. bibliog por Wilson Lib Bul 41:502-9 Ja '67
HOLLEY, L. E.
Putting payroll on a paying basis. Am City 81:154+ S '66
HOLLEY, Robert W.
Nucleotide sequence of a nucleic acid; with biographical sketch. Sci Am 214:17, 30-9 bibliog(p 138) F '66
HOLLIDAYSBURG, Pa.
Renovate or rebuild? J. M. Mitchell. il Am City 81:147-8+ O '66
HOLLINGER, J. P. and Hobbs, R. W.
Supernova remnant W-44: observations at 8350 megacycles per second. bibliog Science 153:1633-4 S 30 '66
HOLLINGSWORTH, T. W.
Post-high opportunity in DeKalb, Georgia. NEA J 55:44-5 S '66
HOLLIS, Robert
Bronze stars of peace: legionnaire says no. D. Ford. il Nation 202:329-31 Mr 21 '66
HOLLISTER, George E.
Defensive driving. Motor T 18:60 O '66
HOLLISTER, Lincoln S.
Garnet zoning: an interpretation based on the Rayleigh fractionation model. bibliog Science 154:1647-51 D 30 '66
HOLLISTER, Paul, Jr
Outstanding French and American paperweights in the Wells collection. Antiques 89:265-9 F '66
HOLLISTER, William G.
Is happy childhood the goal? PTA Mag 60: 10-12 bibliog(p36) My '66
HOLLOMON, J. Herbert
Science and engineering; address, November 2, 1966. Vital Speeches 33:111-15 D 1 '66

about

Inventors win an ally. por Sci N 90:444 N 26 '66
HOLLON, Ellis W. Jr
Beware the antithesis! Christian Cent 83: 303-4 Mr 9 '66
HOLLOWAY, Bruce K.
Atlantic alliance; southeast Asia; address, September 13, 1966. Vital Speeches 33:11-14 O 15 '66
HOLLY
Folklore and nature; the immortal holly tree. D. Jacob. il Natur Hist 75:6+ D '66
Holly in the landscape. C. E. Lewis. il Horticulture 44:24-5+ D '66
Say it with holly. H. W. Dengler. il Am For 72:1-3+ D '66
HOLLYHOCKS
Hollyhocks in the news. M. C. Ohlander. il Flower Grower 53:29 Je '66
HOLLYLEAF cherry
They are the do anything cherries. il Sunset 137:287-8 O '66
HOLLYWOOD, Calif.
Hollywood sunset. G. Swanson. il Esquire 66: 76-81 Ag '66

Anecdotes, facetiae, satire, etc.

Out of the death bag in west Hollywood. F. P. Tullius. New Yorker 42:57-8 N 5 '66

Industries

See also
Moving picture industry—United States

Riots

When rioters struck on Hollywood's historic street. il U S News 61:10 N 28 '66
HOLM, Bernard J.
(comp) Articles and others books received; medieval. See issues of American historical review
HOLMAN, Kime
Life without father. E. Dunbar. il pors Look 30:30-5 My 17 '66
HOLMAN, Thomas
Two worlds of Thomas Holman. W. Rogers. il pors Look 31:60-3 Ja 10 '67
HOLMAN, William R.
Simplicity in design; excerpt from Library publications. Wilson Lib Bul 40:517-24 F '66
HOLME, Bryan
Eisie does a book; interview, ed. by J. Deschin. Pop Phot 59:28+ D '66
HOLMES, Doris
Evan's bandaid; poem. Sat R 50:101 Ja 7 '67
Poet's workshop. Writer 79:25-8 My; 24-7+ Jl; 21-4 S; 27-30 N '66

HOLMES, Marjorie
Mothers keep all these things. Todays Health 44:34-6 D '66
Mother's wonderful wishing-book. Todays Health 44:32-3+ Mr '66
Whatever happened to run, sheep, run? Todays Health 44:52-5 Ag '66
HOLMES, Monty
Giant step for Monty. il pors Ebony 21:57-60+ Ap '66
HOLMES, Robert L.
Moral decision in the nuclear age. Bul Atomic Sci 22:27-9 Ap '66
Moral stance and political action. Christian Cent 83:776-7 Je 15 '66
HOLMQUEST, D. L. and others
Circadian rhythms in rats; effects of random lighting. bibliog Science 152:662-4; 154:159 Ap 29, O 7 '66
HOLMSEN, Theodore W. and Leasure, J. K.
Growth-inhibiting action of tris(l-aziridinyl)-phosphine oxide in grasses. bibliog Science 153:1659 S 30 '66
HOLOGRAM. See Holography
HOLOGRAPHY
Holographic microscopy as a technique for recording dynamic microscopic subjects. C. Knox. bibliog il Science 153:989-90 Ag 26 '66
Holography; 133rd AAAS meeting, Washington, D.C. A. Dipentima. il Science 154: 1363-4 D 9 '66
Holomicrography: transformation of image during reconstruction a posteriori. G. W. Ellis. bibliog il Science 154:1195-7 D 2 '66
In holograms, lasers give pictures a third dimension; with report by M. Steinmann. il Life 61:116-17+ D 23 '66
Photography in 3-D; laser-holography. il Newsweek 68:88 Jl 18 '66
Picture that hangs in midair. J. Reinert. il Sci Digest 60:30-4 S '66
Pictures by laser light; holography. P. Farber. il U S Camera 29:52-3+ S '66
Pure light for practical pictures; holography. il Time 87:60 Mr 18 '66
Those incredible holograms; amazing frozen light waves give first true 3D pictures. C. P. Gilmore. il Pop Sci 189:78-82+ Jl '66
Three-D home TV foreseen. A. Ewing. il Sci N 89:468-9+ Je 11 '66
3-D image made at home. il Sci N 90:185 S 10 '66
3-D magic of holography. il Bsns W p96 S 10 '66
HOLOMICROGRAPHY. See Holography
HOLOTHURIANS
Sea cucumber sibling species; polypeptide chain types and oxygen equilibrium of hemoglobin. C. Manwell. bibliog il Science 152:1393-6 Je 3 '66
HOLROYD, J. C.
Wild spectacle. il Field & S 71:31-3+ Ag '66
HOLSAPPLE, Resa
In my opinion. por Seventeen 25:448 Ag '66
HOLST, Gustav
On Everest, Gustav Holst; some rare and beautiful music. J. Diether. por Am Rec G 32:952-3 Je '66
HOLSTEIN, Henri
Holland, 1966. Cath World 203:98-9 My '66
HOLT, Barbara
Closeup: Barbara Holt, fisherman. J. Mazurki. il pors Motor B 117:48-9+ My '66
HOLT, Harold Edward
Australia today; address, July 5, 1966. Vital Speeches 32:613-17 Ag 1 '66
Australia's answer to the Vietnam critics; interview. por Read Digest 89:67-72 D '66
Australia's Holt: a backer of LBJ's war policy; excerpts from address, June 30, 1966. por U S News 61:22 Jl 11 '66
United States and Australia reaffirm common goals; exchange of greetings: exchange of toasts, June 29, 1966. Dept State Bul 55: 131-2, 134-7 Jl 25 '66
Why Australia backs U.S. in the Vietnam war; interview. por U S News 62:58-61 Ja 2 '67

about

End of a fiery campaign. M. Tatlow. Nat R 18:1208 N 29 '66
End of the Ming dynasty. il por Time 87:23 Ja 28 '66
Establishing an identity. il por Time 88:39 N 25 '66
Man on top Down Under. H. Gordon. il pors N Y Times Mag p38-9+ O 23 '66
New man in Canberra. D. Warner. il Reporter 34:33-6 Ap 21 '66
President and Australian Prime Minister conclude talks: text of joint communique, July 14, 1966. Dept State Bul 55:212-13 Ag 8 '66

HOLT, Harold Edward—About—*Continued*
  Vanquished Vietniks. Time 88:43 D 2 '66
  Vital election. M. Tatlow. Nat R 18:837+
    Ag 23 '66
HOLT, John
  Fourth R, the rat race. N Y Times Mag p46-
    7+ My 1 '66
  How young children learn. Parents Mag 41:
    60-3+ S '66
  On schools; are the children in the running?
    Harper 232:102-3 My '66
HOLT, Raymond M.
  Three patios in Pomona. Library J 91:5859-61
    D 1 '66
HOLT, Rinehart and Winston, incorporated
  CBS buys Murchisons' 11 per cent interest
    in Holt. Pub W 190:44 S 19 '66
  Holt, B&T ship jointly, sharply cut time to
    coast. il Pub W 189:82-3 Ap 25 '66
  Holt marks its 100 years. il Pub W 189:32-9
    My 9 '66
HOLTON, George
  Restless camera of George Holton. L. Barry.
    il Pop Phot 58:86-95+ Je '66
HOLTZMAN, Richard B. and Ilcewicz, F. H.
  Lead-210 and polonium-210 in tissues of
    cigarette smokers. bibliog Science 153:1259-
    60 S 9 '66
HOLY family. See Jesus Christ—Family
HOLY Ghost. See Holy Spirit
HOLY Grail. See Grail
HOLY Office. See Catholic church—Congre-
    gation of the Holy Office
HOLY rollers. See Church of God
HOLY Roman empire
    See also
  Charlemagne, king of the Franks
HOLY Sepulcher, Church of. See Jerusalem—
    Church of the Holy Sepulcher
HOLY Spirit
  Stress on the Spirit; God of the present.
    Time 88:69-70 Ag 5 '66
    See also
  Pentecost
  Trinity
HOLY week
  Letter from abroad; Seville, Spain. W. San-
    som. il McCalls 93:48+ My '66
HOLYOKE, Mass.
  Sludge-disposal solution: thicken, filter, dry
    and burn. E. J. Bayon. il Am City 81:
    95-7 Je '66
HOLZBAUER, Herbert
  Bibliographic organization in the federal gov-
    ernment. bibliog por Wison Lib Bul 40:719-
    20+ Ap '66
HOLZMAN, Jac
  Originality and success; Nonesuch and Elek-
    tra records. H. Kupferberg. il Atlan 217:
    150+ Mr '66
HOMANS, Abigail Adams
  My Adams uncles: Charles, Henry, Brooks.
    Yale R 55:321-46 Mr '66
    about
  Memoirs of a spry matriarch. il pors Life
    61:61-2+ O 28 '66
HOMBURGER, Freddy. See Bajusz, E. jt. auth.
HOME, Alexander Frederick Douglas-Home,
    14th earl of. See Douglas-Home, A. F.
HOME
  Opinion; on staying put. R. Eddy. Mlle 63:
    108+ My '66
    See also
  Fathers
HOME accidents. See Accidents
HOME and the school. See School and the
    home
HOME bars. See Bars for the home
HOME building. See Building
HOME building industry. See Building industry
HOME decoration. See House decoration
HOME economics
  Bon appétit! concerning Food and home
    notes, service of the Department of agricul-
    ture. Reporter 35:9 D 29 '66
  How to work with a kitchen planner. E. S.
    Oshin. House & Gard 130:240-1+ O '66
  Notes of a happy housekeeper. M. E. Falter.
  See issues of House & garden incorporating
    Living for young homemakers
    See also
  Domestic finance
  House cleaning
  Housewives
  Storage in the home

    Anecdotes, facetiae, satire, etc.
  Please re-pot the sauerkraut. C. Simmons.
    il Sat Eve Post 239:22 Ja 29 '66; Same abr,
    Read Digest 88:21-2+ Ap '66

        Study and teaching
    See also
  Consumer education
HOME equipment. See Household appliances
HOME freezers. See Freezers
HOME furnishings. See Household furnishings
HOME grounds
  How the Cederbloms hide their house trailer.
    il Sunset 136:96 F '66
  How to turn your lot into a landscape. il
    House & Gard 129:164-7 Mr '66
  It delights the kids! it handles the cars! il
    Bet Hom & Gard 44:38-9 Ag '66
  Too much lawn? il Flower Grower 53:34 S '66
    See also
  Back yards
        Care
  That trim look. il Flower Grower 53:32-3
    S '66
  This good-looking garden takes little upkeep.
    il Sunset 136:254-5 Ap '66
HOME improvements. See Houses—Mainten-
    ance and repair
HOME insurance. See Insurance—All risk
    policies
HOME libraries. See Libraries, Private
HOME life. See Family life
HOME loan bank board. See United States—
    Federal home loan bank board
HOME loans. See Loans, Personal
HOME management. See Home economics
HOME mechanics. See Mechanics, Household
HOME offices. See Offices
HOME ownership
  Buy a house, or wait awhile? il Changing T
    20:29-32 Ap '66
  Buying a house: the nine most common
    questions. il Changing T 20:13-15 F '66
  Do-it-yourself homes. il Parents Mag 41:74-
    5+ Je '66
  How to plan a home you'll always like; inter-
    view, ed. by R. Martens. B. Tarke and
    L. Tarke. il Farm J 90:82+ N 11 '66
  How to shop for an older house. il Bet Hom
    & Gard 44:144+ O '66
  New house now? Bet Hom & Gard 45:34 Ja
    '67
  Personal business; house-hunting. Bsns W
    p 113 F 5 '66
  Setback in home buying; how bad? il U S
    News 61:50-2 N 28 '66
  When you buy a house; how much for clos-
    ing costs? il Changing T 20:30 Jl '66
    See also
  Mortgages
  Savings and loan associations
HOME service industries. See Service indus-
    tries
HOME study
  Denver's home teaching program. C. Mul-
    ford. NEA J 56:14-16 Ja '67
  Help children with homework the right way.
    il Good H 162:158 F '66
  Homework in American school and commun-
    ity. H. H. Punke. Sch & Soc 94:327-30 O
    15 '66
  Homework: will parents ever learn? A. P.
    Eliasberg. il N Y Times Mag p 114+ O 30
    '66
  TV vs homework; teacher-opinion poll. il
    NEA J 55:26 F '66
HOME study courses. See Correspondence
    schools and courses
HOME work. See Home study
HOMECOMING; drama. See Pinter, H.
HOMEMAKERS. See Housewives
HOMEMAKERS extension. See United States
    —Federal extension service
HOMEMAKING. See Home economics
HOMER
  From the Greek. G. Davenport. Poetry 108:
    417-19 S '66
HOMER, Winslow
  Chanties in color. il por Time 88:54-5 Jl 15 '66
  Portrait of the artist as a person. G. H.
    Hamilton. il Sat R 49:89 Ap 9 '66
  Winslow Homer. N. Lopes Filho. il Américas
    18:9-13 O '66
HOMESTAKE mine. See Gold mines and min-
    ing—United States
HOMESTEADS
  Here's how to get that hideaway homesite.
    M. R. Cutler. il Pop Mech 125:122-5+ Ap
    '66
  Land! Oklahoma Territory. R. E. Cunning-
    ham. il Am Heritage 17:48-55+ F '66
HOMEWORK. See Home study

HOMICIDE
See also
Murder
HOMING instinct. See Orientation
HOMMA, Masaharu
Fall of Corregidor; excerpts from Battles lost and won; great campaigns of World war II. H. W. Baldwin. il Am Heritage 17:18-23+ Ag '66
HOMMANN, Mary
Symbolic bells in Dixwell. Arch Forum 125: 54-9 Jl '66
HOMO erectus. See Man, Prehistoric
HOMOCYSTINURIA. See Cystathionine
HOMOGENEOUS grouping. See Ability grouping in education
HOMOLKA, Larry J.
Richardson's North Easton. Arch Forum 124: 72-7 My '66
HOMOSEXUALITY
Boxed in; homosexuals' exclusion from military service. D. Sanford. New Repub 154: 8-9 My 21 '66
Case of the elusive euphemism; barring of homosexuals by 1952 Immigration act. il Time 88:45-6 Jl 22 '66
Dealing with deviates; new bill passed in Great Britain. Time 88:17 D 30 '66
Death of Ahmed el Osamy; changes in Yemen. Time 88:27 Ag 12 '66
Erotic minorities, by L. Ullerstam. Review Sat R 49:29-30 Jl 9 '66. R. J. Levin
Female homosexuals. F. R. Schreiber and M. Herman. Sci Digest 60:13-14 O '66
Homosexual acts; Britain. Newsweek 69:28+ Ja 2 '67
Homosexual law reform. America 114:278 F 26 '66
Homosexuality: society's attitude. America 114:316 Mr 5 '66
Ordinariness of sodomy. J. Leavitt. Nation 204:54-7 Ja 9 '67
Sad gay life. J. Star. il Look 31:30-3 Ja 10 '67
Sex spies; UCLA study of law-enforcement policies and practices. Nation 202:572-3 My 16 '66
Sin or crime? problem in Great Britain. Newsweek 67:54 F 21 '66
What you should know about homosexuality; with discussion group program, by M. S. Smart. I. Bieber. bibliog Parents Mag 41: 31-2, 62+ My '66
HONAN, William H.
Christmas (ka-pow!) again. New Repub 155: 7-8 D 17 '66
Good case of the poll sniffles. N Y Times Mag p34-5+ Ag 21 '66. 12+ S 18 '66
Meet the generals (yes, sir!) N Y Times Mag p42-3+ D 18 '66
HONDA, Soichiro
Honda's new wheels. il por Time 88:111-12 O 7 '66
World's no. 1 thunderer. G. Kent. il por Read Digest 89:13-14+ D '66
HONDA motor company, Japan. See Motorcycle industry and trade
HONDURAS
See also
Fishing—Honduras
Hunting—Honduras
Medical relief work—Honduras
HONESTY
See also
Business ethics
Cheating in schoolwork
Integrity
Sincerity
Truthfulness
HONEY bees. See Bees
HONEY West (literary character) See Characters in literature
HONEYMOON
Traveling with Mlle; what makes a good honeymoon, besides a good man? L. Gottlieb. il Mlle 62:117-18 Ja '66
HONEYMOON; story. See Pritchett, V. S.
HONEYWELL, incorporated
Honeywell bets on automation. il Bsns W p60-2+ F 5 '66
Honeywell links data operations; acquires Computer control co. Bsns W p 174 Je 11 '66
Technique ranks space objectives; Honeywell's planning assistance through technical evaluation of relevance numbers. W. S. Beller. il Miss & Roc 18:22-4 F 7 '66
HONEYWELL Pentax infrared cameras. See Cameras
HONFLEUR, France
La bonne vie à Honfleur. H. Sutton. Sat R 49:38-9 Jl 2 '66

HONG, Jerry S. and Bauer, R. S.
Have you a halfway house program? Parks & Rec 1:914-15 N '66
HONG KONG
Trouble in the toy store. il Newsweek 68:39 S 12 '66
See also
Communism—Hong Kong
Moving picture industry—Hong Kong
Restaurants—Hong Kong
Shopping and shoppers—Hong Kong
Water supply—Hong Kong

Commercial treaties and agreements
United States and Hong Kong sign cotton textiles agreement; Department announcement with texts of agreement and related documents. Dept State Bul 55:467-72 S 26 '66

Description
Let's travel; New Year's collectors' items. il Mlle 62:119-21 Ja '66
HONG KONG conference. See Asian faith and order conference
HONIG, Albert M.
Breakthrough in psychiatry; revolutionary treatment of the mentally ill. C. Brossard. il pors Look 30:30-4+ Ap 5 '66
HONIG, Edwin
All summer; a fairy tale; poem. Sat R 50:20 Ja 21 '67
Sometimes a soft voice is needed; poem. Sat R 49:63 Ap 16 '66
Three poets. P. Weiss. Poetry 108:62-4 Ap '66
HONIG, Joel
Richard Strauss. Opera N 30:32 My 7 '66
Transfigured knight. Opera N 30:26-7 Ap 2 '66
HONOLULU
There's barely time for a hula; biggest boom in its history. il Bsns W p84-6 D 3 '66

Airports
Stretched jets to tax Honolulu facilities. R. G. O'Lone. il Aviation W 85:47-8 N 28 '66

Churches
Christmas eve in Honolulu; Kawaiahao church. il Sunset 137:31 D '66

Music
Honolulu. W. Aguiar, jr. Opera N 30:30 Mr 19 '66

Newspapers
See also
Honolulu advertiser
HONOLULU advertiser
Century of stubbornness. il Time 88:82 S 23 '66
HONOLULU international airport. See Honolulu—Airports
HONOR
Honor bright! M. G. Baker. Seventeen 25: 124+ Je '66
See also
Sportsmanship
HONOR system. See Self government in education
HONORARY degrees. See Degrees, Honorary
HOOD pins. See Fastenings
HOOF-and-mouth disease. See Foot-and-mouth disease
HOOFT, Willem Adolf Visser 't. See Visser 't Hooft, W. A.
HOOK, Sidney
Liberal Catholic thought. Commentary 41: 94-100 Ap '66
Neither blind obedience nor uncivil disobedience. N Y Times Mag p52-3+ Je 5 '66
HOOKENA, Hawaii. See Abandoned towns
HOOKER, John Jay, jr
Straws in the wind. por Time 87:22 Ap 22 '66
HOOKER, Leland W.
Selection and use of chain saws for the non-professional user. Consumer Bul 49:14-16 O '66
HOOKY holiday; drama. See Miller, H. L.
HOOPER, Frank F. See Kent, F. jt. auth.
HOOPER, Henry J. C.
U.S. informs U.N. Security council of action on Rhodesian agent; letter to Security council, containing letter to H. J. C. Hooper, February 28, 1966. A. J. Goldberg. Dept State Bul 54:588-9 Ap 11 '66
HOOPER, Noreen Creelman
Let's call a stork a stork. Read Digest 89: 139-40 S '66

HOOPES, Roy
Advice to future Peace corps volunteers. Seventeen 25:24+ My '66
Upper Darby senior high builds a school in Africa. Seventeen 25:98-9+ Ap '66

HOORAY!! it's a glorious day... and all that; musical comedy. See Musical comedies, revues. etc.—Criticisms, plots. etc.

HOOSIER tale: opera. See Kaufmann, W.

HOOVER, Herbert Clark
My visit with Herbert Hoover. C. Clemens. Hobbies 71:106-7 Ap '66

HOOVER, Herbert William, 1918-
Keeping Islandia isolated. R. H. Boyle. il por Sports Illus 25:80+ O 17 '66

HOOVER, John Edgar
FBI's war on organized crime. por U S News 60:102-4 Ap 18 '66
How red China spies on U.S. por Nations Bsns 54:84-8 Je '66
Turbulence on the campus. PTA Mag 60:4-6 F '66
    about
Battle of the bugs. por Time 88:19 D 23 '66
Bugging. Nat R 18:1306-7 D 27 '66
Chair for Hoover. Nation 203:629 D 12 '66
Christian virtues. Nation 203:37 Jl 11 '66
Dirty business. Nation 203:690-1 D 26 '66
Hoover's successor. Nation 202:254-5 Mr 7 '66
Passing the bug. Newsweek 68:19-20 D 26 '66
Who knew about bugging: RFK's story, and the FBI's. il por U S News 61:32-5 D 26 '66
Wiretap war: Kennedy, Johnson and the FBI. R. M. Cipes. New Repub 155:16-22 D 24 '66

HOOVER, Mary Bidgood. See Mayer, G. jt. auth.

HOOVER, Richard E.
Vision: the most valuable sense; with bibliography. por Wilson Lib Bul 40:818-23 My '66

HOOVER wilderness area. See Wilderness areas—California

HOPE Namgyal, maharani of Sikkim
How is Queen Hope getting along? with report by J. Howard. il pors Life 60:51-4+ My 20 '66
Queen of Sikkim: an intimate portrait. A. Kandell. il pors Redbook 127:52-5+ Je '66

HOPE, A. D.
Coup de grace; poem. Sat R 49:10 Mr 26 '66

HOPE, Bob
Bob Hope on Viet Nam; interview. pors Nations Bsns 54:44-6+ F '66
Things aren't that simple. por Seventeen 25:130+ D '66
Well. that's what it says in my crystal ball. por Ladies Home J 84:14 Ja '67
    about
GI's best friend. T. Armbrister. il pors Sat Eve Post 239:93-7 Mr 12 '66

HOPE, Marjorie
Vietnam's wounded waifs. Christian Cent 83:1111-12 S 14 '66

HOPE
Hope. F. J. Sheen. Vogue 148:216-17 D '66
Love, faith, hope; three attitudes in contemporary theology. J. W. Woelfel. Christian Cent 83:1570-3 D 21 '66

HOPE (ship) See Hospital ships

HOPE, ISLE OF. See Isle of Hope

HOPE college, Holland, Mich.
Heave ho lock in and rock: sophomores doused the freshmen in annual tug-of-war. L. Simross. il Sports Illus 25:40-1 O 17 '66

HOPFIELD, J. J.
Mechanism of lunar polarization. bibliog Science 151:1380-1 Mr 18 '66

HOPI Indians
Two ways to grow up; study of the social growth of the Hopi child contrasted with other American children. D. McNickle. Nation 202:365-6 Mr 28 '66

HOPKINS, David M. and Einarsson, Thorleifur
Pleistocene glaciation on St George. Pribilof Islands. bibliog Science 152:343-5 Ap 15 '66

HOPKINS, John F.
New York in fiction. por Library J 91:3097-9 Je 15 '66

HOPKINS, Steve
Brain surgery by computer. Pop Mech 126:94-7 D '66

HOPPER, Hedda
Hedda. por Newsweek 67:91 F 14 '66
Obituary
Time pors 87:52 F 11 '66

HOPPER, Robert L.
Strength where it counts. Am Ed 2:20-1 Je '66

HOPPER, Stanley Romaine
Nails; poem. Christian Cent 83:422 Ap 6 '66

HOPPOUGH, Robert
Sculptured garden ornament. Pop Mech 125:136-7 Je '66
—See Youngquist, A. jt. auth.

HORAN, Ellen
Maritime museum for the Chesapeake. il Yachting 119:158-9 Mr '66

HORCH, Kenneth W. See Waterman, T. H. jt. auth.

HORCHLER, Richard
Time bomb in Catholic education. Look 30:23-5 Ap 5 '66

HORDERN, William
Challenge to ethics. Christian Cent 84:84 Ja 18 '67

HORI, Makoto. and others
Tryptophan deficiency in rabbit reticulocytes: polyribosomes during interrupted growth of hemoglobin chains. bibliog Science 155:83-4 Ja 6 '67

HORICON national wildlife refuge. See Wildlife sanctuaries

HORMONAL contraceptives. See Contraceptives

HORMONE fattening of cattle. See Cattle—Hormone fattening

HORMONE research
Synthesized hormone will reduce shortage. Sci N 90:66 Jl 30 '66

HORMONES
Code that controls growth. il Life 61:93-4+ O 14 '66
Growth-hormone deficiency in man: an isolated, recessively inherited defect. D. L. Rimoin and others. bibliog il Science 152:1635-7 Je 17 '66
Growth hormone mapped. Sci N 89:393 My 21 '66
Hormonal influences on brain organization in infant rats. S. Levine and R. F. Mullins, jr. bibliog il Science 152:1585-92 Je 17 '66
Hypophyseal control of genetic expression during chick feather and skin differentiation. M. B. Yatvin. bibliog il Science 153:184-5 Jl 8 '66
Insect hormones synthesized. Sci Am 214:52-3 My '66
Juvenile hormone: identification of an active compound from balsam fir. W. S. Bowers and others. bibliog il Science 154:1020-1 N 25 '66
Lethal effects of synthetic juvenile hormone on larvae of the yellow fever mosquito, aedes aegypti. A. Spielman and C. M. Williams. bibliog il Science 154:1043-4 N 25 '66
Mystery gland: pineal gland. S. F. Yolles. il Todays Health 44:76-9 Mr '66
Parathyroid hormone in plasma in adenomatous hyperparathyroidism, uremia, and bronchogenic carcinoma. S. A. Berson and R. S. Yalow. bibliog il Science 154:907-9 N 18 '66
Progress in study of adrenal hormones. Sci N L 89:153 Mr 5 '66
Retention of the biological potency of human pituitary growth hormone after reduction and carbamidomethylation. J. S. Dixon and C. H. Li. bibliog il Science 154:785-6 N 11 '66
Stimulation of the proliferation of cortical neurons by prenatal treatment with growth hormone. S. Zamenhof and others. bibliog il Science 152:1396-7 Je 3 '66
Stress causes rise in hormone output; experiment to study growth hormone secretion. Sci N 89:371 My 14 '66
Which hormone to take when. R. A. Wilson. il Vogue 147:92-5+ Je '66
    See also
Aldosterone
Thyroxine

HORMONES. Plant
Germination of witchweed striga lutea lour.: isolation and properties of a potent stimulant. C. E. Cook and others. bibliog il Science 154:1189-90 D 2 '66
Plant hormones and regulators. J. van Overbeek. bibliog il Science 152:721-31 My 6 '66; Reply. M. A. Venis. 153:1022 Ag 26 '66
    See also
Auxins
Gibberellic acid

HORMONES, Sex
Automation of steroid analysis. I. E. Bush. bibliog il Science 154:77-83 O 7 '66
Can a woman be feminine forever? N. Sommers and J. Ridgeway. New Repub 154:15-16 Mr 19 '66
Control of conception by hormonal steroids; address, 1965. G. Pincus. bibliog il Science 153:493-500 Jl 29 '66

HORSE racing—*Continued*
Galloping granddad of the Grand national; T. Durant; with report. il Life 60:80A-80B+ Ap 8 '66
Good word in the Arc at Paris was Bon Mot. W. Tower. Sports Illus 25:78-9 O 17 '66
Hail the magnificent chestnut. W. Tower. Sports Illus 24:82 Ap 25 '66
High rollers of Ruidoso; All American quarter horse futurity in N.Mex. P. Ryan. il Sports Illus 25:36-8+ S 26 '66
Hopes go up and some come down; confused result of the Florida Derby. W. Tower. il Sports Illus 24:24-7 Ap 11 '66
King closes in on a crown; Derby winner Kauai King wins at Preakness. W. Tower. il Sports Illus 24:26-7 My 30 '66
King from wire to wire; Kauai King wins Kentucky Derby. W. Tower. il Sports Illus 24:30-3+ My 16 '66
Last, triumphant ride of Johnny Longden. A. Stump. il Sat Eve Post 239:74-6+ Je 4 '66
Muddy horse of the year; Buckpasser wins Woodward stakes at Aqueduct. W. Tower. il Sports Illus 25:30-2+ O 10 '66
Old Johnny Longden, his hail and farewell; won a record 6,032 races. J. Tobin. il Sports Illus 24:88-9+ Mr 21 '66
Out-of-state favorite; Kentucky Derby; winner Kauai King. il Newsweek 67:96 My 16 '66
Pink Chicken and a bold Derby; Buckpasser wins the betless Flamingo at Hialeah. W. Tower. il Sports Illus 24:24-6+ Mr 14 '66
Pot of gold for a nervy Cajun. W. Tower. Sports Illus 25:112-13 S 19 '66
Race that scrambled the Derby; Graustark loses to Abe's Hope at Keeneland. W. Tower. il Sports Illus 24:22-7 My 9 '66
Race track. A. Minor. See issues of New Yorker
Speed to burn; Travers stakes. Newsweek 68:65 Ag 29 '66
Sporting scene; Royal Ascot meeting. R. Angell. New Yorker 42:76+ Jl 23 '66
Successor got the message; beats the favorite, Dr Fager in the Champagne stakes. P. Axthelm. il Sports Illus 25:28-9 O 24 '66
Supersore superhorse; Kentucky Derby. Newsweek 67:88 My 9 '66
They are not just along for the ride; with account by F. Graham, jr. il Sports Illus 24:40-6+ Ap 11 '66
They made the stakes too long; Kauai King and the Belmont stakes. Time 87:92 Je 10 '66
Tradin' platers is Mr Van's game. J. Mann. il Sports Illus 24:42-4+ Mr 21 '66
Trotter. P. C. Welsh. il Am Heritage 18:30-49 D '66
Two out of three came back; Kentucky Derby favorites. W. Tower. il Sports Illus 24:107-9 Ap 18 '66
Year of drought in the West; few California horses for Kentucky Derby. W. Tower il Sports Illus 24:18-19 F 7 '66
See also
Harness racing
Race tracks

HORSE shows
Amateurs took the honors. A. Higgins. Sports Illus 24:90 Ap 25 '66
Blue ribbon for looks, too; National horse show in Madison Square Garden. A. Higgins. Sports Illus 25:86+ N 14 '66
Days out of the Arabian nights; photographs by R. Meek; with account by A. Higgins. il Sports Illus 24:28-33 F 21 '66
Hiram at the horse show; National horse show at Madison Square Garden. New Yorker 42:54-6 N 5 '66
Maple leaf forever; Devon, Pa. horse show. A. Higgins. Sports Illus 24:54+ Je 20 '66
Mr Baker builds his blue-ribbon dream course; European-style Grand prix, Oak Brook near Hinsdale, Ill. A. Higgins. Sports Illus 25:52-3 Ag 8 '66
Show with a big-top flavor; Kansas City American Royal; photographs by R. Meek; with account by A. Higgins. Sports Illus 25:46-51 O 10 '66

HORSE TAIL FALLS
Worthwhile detour to Horse Tail Falls. il Sunset 137:38+ S '66

HORSE training
Boo made a boo-boo; Graustark, Kentucky Derby favorite reduced to cripple. P. Axthelm. il Sports Illus 24:26-9+ My 23 '66
Inexact but incorporated; E. Neloy. il Time 88:63 Ag 19 '66

Tame a wild horse in 30 minutes. G. Lorang. il Farm J 90:32-3+ Jl '66
Wild transistorized West. J. E. Boykin. il Pop Mech 125:118-19 F '66
Wizard of Longchamp; F. Mathet. W. Tower. il Sports Illus 24:51-4+ Je 6 '66
See also
Horse racing
Horses, Educated

HORSEMANSHIP
If you are new to trail riding, here are pointers. il Sunset 136:36+ My '66
See also
Polo

HORSES
Crazy over quarter horses. J. Stewart-Gordon. il Read Digest 89:124-7 Ag '66
Desert prince. A. Higgins. Sports Illus 24:33 F 21 '66
Florida sets itself up to rival the bluegrass; Hialeah auction of Florida-bred yearlings. il Bsns W p28-9 F 5 '66
How to buy your first horse. W. O. Kester. il Consumer Bul 49:35-6 F '66
Moriarty's trap; carriage advertising P. J. Moriarty's restaurant; interview. F. Smith. New Yorker 42:38-40 My 7 '66
See also
American quarter horse association
Polo ponies
Race horses

Training
See Horse training

HORSES, Educated
Diving horses, and a three-sheet on a downtown corner; interviews. L. Carver; B. Doll. New Yorker 42:19-21 Jl 2 '66

HORSES in art
See also
Design, Decorative—Animal forms

HORSESHOE pitching
Let's pitch horseshoes. il Pop Gard 17:75+ D '66

HORSESHOEING
Blacksmith for the horsey set. il Ebony 21:83-4+ S '66

HORST
House that Horst grew. V. Lawford. il Vogue 147:134-9+ Je '66

HORTICULTURAL societies
Members' news. See issues of Horticulture

HORTICULTURAL stamps. See Postage stamps

HORTICULTURAL therapy. See Garden therapy

HORTICULTURE
H&G's gardener's month. See issues of House & garden incorporating Living for young homemakers
See also
Gardening

Bibliography
Books and reviews. See issues of Horticulture

HORTICULTURE (periodical)
Garden club yearbook winners (cont) Horticulture 44:54 Ap '66
Yearbook contest rules. Horticulture 44:14-15+ My '66

HORTON, Douglas
Boswell in St Peter's; D. Horton's Vatican diary. C. Northcott. Christian Cent 83:359 Mr 23 '66

HORTON, Frank L.
Museum of early southern decorative arts. Antiques 91:72-101 Ja '67

HORWITZ, Elinor Lander
But you haven't changed a bit! McCalls 93:63+ Je '66
How to earn money writing for the European market; exchange of letters. Writer 79:25-7 Ag '66

HORWITZ, Julius
Lady fights back. Look 30:32+ O 4 '66
Nursing home industry tools up. N Y Times Mag p26-7+ My 1 '66

HORWITZ, Sylvia L.
Employment lab for teenagers in trouble. il Parents Mag 41:64-7+ D '66

HOSEGOOD, R. A.
Electronics makes a better water system. Am City 81:137+ N '66

HOSIERY
How high the thigh? new styles. il Newsweek 67:76 Mr 28 '66

HOSKINS, Fred
Obituary
Christian Cent 83:578 My 4 '66

HOSKINS, Halford L.
Africa'a, Arab fringe. Cur Hist 50:136-41 Mr '66
Aid and diplomacy in the Middle East. Cur Hist 51:14-19 Jl '66

HOSKINS, Katherine
  December; Da Ming; poems. Poetry 108:11-15 Ap '66
  Roethke in his prose. Poetry 107:400-1 Mr '66
HOSMANN, Elena
  Arequipa. Américas 18:24-9 N '66
  Ayacucho. Américas 18:32-8 O '66
  Cajamarca. Américas 18:31-8 S '66
HOSMER, Craig
  Why synthetics? Newsweek 67:35 F 28 '66
HOSOE, Eikoh
  Killed by roses. H. Keppler. Mod Phot 30: 56-61 F '66
HOSPITAL bills. See Billing
HOSPITAL care
  It's a miracle that we save any of them: re-modeling plans for Georgetown hospital, Washington, D.C. W. R. Young. il Life 61:102-4+ D 2 '66
  Jon goes to the hospital. M. D. Farnham. il Parents Mag 41:80-3+ N '66
  Journey through a city of care; following a patient through Kenosha memorial hospital, Wis. C. Carner. il Todays Health 44:32-9 Ag '66
  Miracles and mishaps. M. Clark. il Atlan 218:88-94 Jl '66
  Overcare? intensive care can be frightening. il Newsweek 68:83 O 24 '66
  Your complete guide to hospital care. Bet Hom & Gard 44:60-1+ Ag '66
HOSPITAL interns. See Interns (medicine)
HOSPITAL laundries. See Laundries, Hospital
HOSPITAL nursing. See Nurses and nursing
HOSPITAL patients. See Sick, The
HOSPITAL service, Cost of. See Medical service, Cost of
HOSPITAL service, State. See Medical service, State
HOSPITAL ships
  In repose; navy hospital ship in the South China Sea. il Newsweek 68:35-6 Ag 15 '66
  Yanqui, come back! the voyage of the S.S. Hope to Peru; condensation. W. B. Walsh. il Read Digest 89:236-40+ D '66
HOSPITAL visiting. See Hospitals—Visitors
HOSPITALIZATION insurance. See Insurance, Hospitalization
HOSPITALS
  See also
  Children—Hospitals
  Hospital ships
  Nursing homes

  Architecture
  Building types study (cont) il Arch Rec 140: 197-8 O '66
  Building types study; with introductory statement by W. B. Foxhall. il Arch Rec 139:159-78 Mr '66
  It's a miracle that we save any of them; re-modeling plans for Georgetown hospital, Washington, D.C. W. R. Young. il Life 61:102-4+ D 2 '66

  Automation
  From site plan to sutures: planning the computerized hospital; Nassau County, N.Y. public general hospital. il Arch Rec 140:199-203 O '66

  Desegregation
  Confusion compounded; HEW's desegregation guidelines. Reporter 35:16+ O 20 '66

  Emergency services
  Emergency ward. J. H. Knowles. il Atlan 218:116-21 Jl '66
  Heart cart may save your life. H. Fantel. il Pop Sci 189:54-7 Jl '66
  Mobile emergency unit speeds care of critically ill patients. il Todays Health 44:71 My '66
  They guard against heart attack. M. Ferrigan. il Todays Health 44:10-11 Je '66

  Equipment and supplies
  Miracles and mishaps. M. Clark. il Atlan 218:88-94 Jl '66

  Federal aid
  Carrot and the stick: L. B. Johnson's policy on hospital desegregation requirements and qualifications for medicare. Reporter 34: 7-8 Je 30 '66
  Federal support for construction of health-related facilities. T. H. Klausmeyer. Arch Rec 139:160-3 Mr '66
  Help on way for hospitals; proposal for a large-scale hospital modernization program. America 114:345 Mr 12 '66

Hospital integration: equality versus availability. E. Langer. Science 152:1727 Je 24 '66
No crisis; meeting integration requirements. Newsweek 68:84-5 Jl 18 '66
Raid on medicare; hospitals to operate programs on profit basis. Nation 203:36 Jl 11 '66
Withholding money from hospitals that segregate. E. B. Drew. New Repub 155:11-12 Jl 30 '66

  Finance
  Public pays the bill. G. Rosenthal. il Atlan 218:107-10 Jl '66; Discussion. 218:45 S '66

  Gifts, legacies, etc.
  How to raise money; Eye foundation hospital, Birmingham. il Time 88:36 D 30 '66

  Management and regulation
  British medicine; doctors carry on but show new militancy. J. Walsh. Science 154:365-8 O 21 '66
  Creative hospital administrator; Cleveland Metropolitan general hospital. il Ebony 22: 73-4+ D '66
  Hidden death threats in our hospitals; excerpts from The doctors. M. L. Gross. il Look 30:27-30 Mr 22 '66; Excerpts. U S News 60:19 Mr 21 '66
  Journey through a city of care; following a patient through Kenosha memorial hospital, Wis. C. Carner. il Todays Health 44:32-9 Ag '66
  Wasteful duplication in our hospitals. J. Randall. Reporter 35:35-8 D 15 '66

  Outpatient service
  Independent outpatient annex looks to the future; Mt Zion hospital and medical center, San Francisco. il Arch Rec 139: 172-3 Mr '66
  Pediatric outpatient department; report on conference on conceptual and methodological approaches to research in pediatric out-patient departments. R. W. Olmsted. Science 153:1026 Ag 26 '66

  Standards
  ℞ for sick hospitals. il Newsweek 68:57-61 Jl 11 '66

  Visitors
  ℞ for happy hospital visiting. il Todays Health 45:70-1 Ja '67

  Volunteer workers
  Adventure in creative volunteering; programs of the Highlights club. John J. Kane hospital, Allegheny County, Pa. H. Ryman. il Parks & Rec 1:36-8 Ja '66
  What money cannot buy. J. de Hartog. il Atlan 218:111-15 Jl '66

  Alaska
  Alaska gets hospital; U.S. public health service Alaska native hospital, Barrow. Sci N 89:290 Ap 23 '66

  Great Britain
  After years of state medicine: a hospital crisis. U S News 60:52 Je 6 '66

  Ireland
  When a U.S. traveler abroad became ill; care in Regional hospital, Dooradoyle, Limerick. il U S News 61:16 O 31 '66

  Ontario
  First-phase plan of Ontario hospital looks ahead to regional needs; Ajax & Pickering general hospital. il Arch Rec 140:212-13 O '66

  United States
  Crisis now near in medical care? il U S News 60:38-41 Mr 7 '66
  Disgraceful facts about infant deaths in the U.S; with list of 376 American hospitals where childbirth is safest. R. Brecher and E. Brecher. McCalls 93:82-3+ F '66
  Gradualism at HEW; concerning discrimination of hospitals approved to participate in medicare program. D. Sanford. New Repub 155:8-10 Ag 27 '66
  Hidden death threats in our hospitals; excerpts from The doctors. M. L. Gross. il Look 30:27-30 Mr 22 '66; Excerpts. U S News 60:19 Mr 21 '66
  Hill-Burton at twenty; hospital progress and challenge. L. Hill. Todays Health 44:76 Ag '66
  Hill-Burton health act marks second decade. Sci N 90:137 Ag 27 '66

HOSPITALS—United States—*Continued*
Hospitals are worried as medicare nears; with interview with E. Henderson. il U S News 60:50-4 Je 6 '66
Hospitals update maternity care; St Mary's, Evansville, Ind. and other programs. Farm J 90:85 My '66
Medicine thinks big on the prairie: Hopedale, Ill. medical complex. C. Smith. il Read Digest 88:149-52 Ap '66
Now under fire: guidelines for integration. il U S News 61:74-6 O 17 '66
R for sick hospitals. il Newsweek 68:57-61 Jl 11 '66
Shortages medicare will face. U S News 60: 35 My 30 '66
Trouble with hospitals; symposium. il Atlan 218:87-104+ Jl '66
Wasteful duplication in our hospitals. J. Randal. Reporter 35:35-8 D 15 '66
Why crisis in medical care keeps growing. il U S News 62:60-4 Ja 23 '67
Your complete guide to hospital care. Bet Hom & Gard 44:60-1+ Ag '66
See also
United States public health service hospital, Lexington, Ky.
also subhead Hospitals under names of cities, e.g. New York (city)—Hospitals
HOSPITALS, Animal
Pet news; Angell memorial animal hospital, Boston. B. McGuire. Ladies Home J 83:26 F '66
HOSPITALS, Naval and marine
See also
Hospital ships
HOSPITALS, Psychiatric
Psychiatrist's notebook: questions and answers. T. I. Rubin. McCalls 94:160 O '66
See also
Mentally ill—Care and treatment
HOSTAGES
Notes and comment; seizure of U.S. ambassador, R. McIlvaine, by Guinea. New Yorker 42:51 N 12 '66
HOSTAGES; story. See Israel, C. E.
HOSTAS. See Plantain lilies
HOSTELS. See Youth hostels
HOSTESSES, Air. See Airlines—Hostesses
HOSTETLER, Robert D. See Murphy, W. A. jt. auth.
HOSTICK, King V.
(ed) Autographs. See issues of Hobbies
HOSTILE witness; drama. See Roffey, J.
HOT cross buns. See Buns
HOT dogs. See Cookery—Meat
HOT rod (periodical)
Rich on wheels. il Time 87:98 Je 24 '66
HOT rod magazine championship drags. See Automobile racing
HOT rod racing. See Automobile racing
HOT springs
Niagaras of stone; thermal springs at Pamukkalé, near Izmir, western Turkey. il UNESCO Courier 19:14-15 D '66
HOT water supply
How to have instant hot water. L. F. Gray. il Pop Sci 188:142 Mr '66
HOT weather
Heat; temperatures in New York city. New Yorker 42:21-2 Jl 23 '66
Heat wave: what caused it, what's next. il U S News 61:8 Jl 25 '66
Hottest town: Quartzsite, Ariz. il Travel 126: 40-1 Ag '66
It's Sirius; first two weeks in July. Time 88:24 Jl 22 '66
Making the most of summer. J. W. Parks. Parents Mag 41:42-3+ Ag '66
No escape; causes; effects. Newsweek 68:20 Jl 25 '66
Tony Karp on 35mm; man against the elements. T. Karp. Mod Phot 30:22+ Ag '66
HOT weather and business. See Weather and business
HOTCHNER, A. E.
Papa Hemingway; excerpts. por Sat Eva Post 239:32-8+ Mr 12; 36-40+ Mr 26; 34-40+ Ap 9 '66
about
Hemingway si, papa no. W. Sheed. Commonweal 84:221-3 My 13 '66
Hemingway to his Boswell. G. Wickes. New Repub 154:24-7 Ap 23 '66
Mrs Hemingway denied injunction on memoirs. Pub W 189:52-3 Mr 7 '66
On dismembering Hemingway. P. Young. Atlan 218:45-9 Ag '66; Discussion. 218:47-9 N '66
Papa's troubled legacy. J. Tebbel. il por Sat R 49:30-1+ Ap 9 '66

Peripatetic reviewer. E. Weeks. Atlan 217: 122+ My '66
Pique at biography. il por Time 87:50 F 11 '66
Privacy cases versus freedom of expression. H. F. Pilpel. Pub W 189:42 Mr 28 '66
HOTEL architecture. See Hotels, taverns, etc.
HOTEL decoration
Princely suite; Prince Philip's suite in the Hotel Pierre. il McCalls 93:74-5 Jl '66
HOTEL entertainers. See Entertainers
HOTEL management

Study and teaching

FEAST attracts job-hungry students; Project FEAST program in California. C. Larsson. il NEA J 55:20-2 D '66
HOTEL Pierre. See New York (city)—Hotels, restaurants, etc.
HOTELS, taverns, etc.
Borscht belt. by J. Adams and H. Tobias. Review
Newsweek il 67:120+ Je 13 '66
Building types study. il Arch Rec 140:123-36 Ag '66
Hotel headliners. See issues of Travel
Hotels and motels reflect a changing world. H. Mullikin. Arch Rec 140:137 Ag '66
Library at the St Regis. R. Kirk. Nat R 18:730 Jl 26 '66
See also
Hilton hotels corporation

Designs and plans

Sand, sea and SOM; Manua Kea beach hotel. J. Bailey. il Arch Forum 124:80-6 My '66

Employees
Anecdotes, facetiae, satire, etc.

Room 306 doesn't tip! W. P. Fox, jr. il Holiday 40:78-81+ D '66

Furniture, equipment, etc.

Closing a hotel, at a profit; British commercial property administration sells furnishings of Sheraton East hotel. il Bsns W p64-6 Jl 23 '66

Bahama islands

Fresh landfalls in the Out Islands. F. Rohr. il Motor B 118:39-42 O '66

Europe, Western

Your castle awaits you, sire! castle hotels in Europe; with report by M. Leatherbee. il Life 61:34-42A S 2 '66

Germany (Federal Republic)

Germany's castle hotels. H. Johnson. il House & Gard 129:52-3+ My '66

Great Britain

Bailiffscourt; Birer's hotel. T. Prittie. Atlan 219:109-10 Ja '67

Hawaii

Let's travel. il Mlle 63:200-1 My '66
Mauna Kea, one on the isle. C. Stinnett. Holiday 39:26+ Mr '66
Sand sea and SOM. J. Bailey. il Arch Forum 124:80-6 My '66

India

India's grandest hotel; the Oberoi intercontinental, New Delhi and other Oberoi achievements and plans. H. Sutton. il Sat R 49:54+ Ap 16 '66

Japan

For the mildly adventurous traveler: field notes on three varieties of Japanese inns. J. Fischer. Harper 232:16+ Je '66
Overnight in a Japanese inn. il Sunset 136:27 Mr '66

Nepal

Yaks and yeti. V. Gilmore. il Sat R 49:38+ Ap 23; 51-2 Ap 30 '66

United States

Driftwood inn; Vero Beach, Fla. M. Candee. il Travel 125:63 My '66
My mother said I should give it a try; hunt for a husband in Catskills. W. Kloman. il Sat Eve Post 239:36-41 O 8 '66
Old gold country inns at Christmas; the California scene. il Sunset 137:20+ D '66
Urban building: hotels vs. offices. G. A. Christie. Arch Rec 140:44 Ag '66
Vacation guide. Ebony 21:38 Je '66
See also subhead Hotels, restaurants, etc. under names of cities, e.g. Chicago—Hotels, restaurants, etc.

HOTTELET, Richard C.
Vietnam in perspective. Reporter 35:20-7 N 3 '66
HOUCK, Carter
Machine embroidery, Mexican style. Parents Mag 41:120 O '66
Parents' magazine's sewing circle. See issues of Parents' magazine and better home-making
HOUGH, Joseph C. jr
Reapportionment controversy. Christian Cent 83:171-3 F 9 '66
HOUGH, Richard
Annals of the sea. New Yorker 42:41-4+ Ag 20 '66
HOUGHTON Mifflin company
Houghton & Penguin books terminate sales agreement. Pub W 189:31 Ap 4 '66
HOUK, Ralph
Big Yankee turnabout. L. Koppett. il por Sports Illus 24:22-4+ Je 20 '66
Cellar that Houk built. il por Time 88:72 S 16 '66
HOULTON, William
England's colorful Kent. Travel 125:60-2 My '66
HOUND of the Maskervilles; drama. See Miller, H. L.
HOUNDS
See also
Afghan hounds
Beagles (dogs)
Foxhounds
Irish wolf-hounds
HOUPHOUET-BOIGNY, Félix
Houphouet-Boigny wins a bet. C. Sterling. Reporter 34:27-9 Je 16 '66
Where Africans welcome the businessman. il por Bsns W p 132-3+ Je 11 '66
HOUR in September; story. See Enright, E.
HOURS, Books of
How Braziller reproduced The hours of Catherine of Cleves. il Pub W 191:88+ Ja 2 '67
HOURS of labor
Any old time; variable hours system, West Germany. Newsweek 68:86 Ag 22 '66
Earnings and hours; tables. See issues of Monthly labor review
Leisure and the long workweek. P. Henle. il Mo Labor R 89:721-7 Jl '66
Overtime hours and premium pay, May 1965. J. R. Wetzel. il Mo Labor R 89:973-7 S '66
See also
Part time employment
also subhead Wages and hours under names of industries, e.g. Automobile industry and trade—Wages and hours
HOUSE, Annette
My year in the five and ten. Seventeen 25:162-3+ S '66
HOUSE, Elizabeth
In my opinion. por Seventeen 25:184 Je '66
HOUSE administration committee. See United States—Congress—House of representatives—Administration committee
HOUSE boats
Build yourself a houseboat. F. M. Paulson. il Field & S 71:108-13 N '66
Floating down the river in a house. M. Hunn. il Pop Mech 125:129-31 My '66
For family vacation fun; rent a houseboat. P. Czura. il Todays Health 44:22-4+ Ap '66
Heyday for houseboats. J. Gribbins. il Motor B 118:86 Ag '66
House ahoy! B. Plumb. il N Y Times Mag p56-7 Ag 14 '66
Houseboat holiday. J. R. Gregg. il Motor B 117:34-5+ Je '66
Houseboats, 1966. il Motor B 117:164-6 Ja '66
New look of houseboats. il Yachting 120:48-9+ Jl '66
1967 houseboats. il Motor B 119:158-61 Ja '67
Now there's even a regatta for houseboats; International houseboat regatta, Ohio River, Louisville, Ky. P. Hadley. il Pop Sci 189:142-5 O '66
HOUSE building. See Building
HOUSE buying. See Home ownership
HOUSE cleaning
Housekeeping wasn't for Aunt Gertie. H. Chadwick. il Todays Health 45:60-1 Ja '67
HOUSE committee on un-American activities. See United States—Congress—House of representatives—Un-American activities committee
HOUSE committees. See United States—Congress—House of representatives—Committees
HOUSE decoration
Art of stenciling. il House & Gard 130:198-9+ S '66
Big effect for little money. M. Garrity. il Bet Hom & Gard 44:68-9 S '66

Bring summer inside. il McCalls 93:76-9 Je '66
Carpets & rugs are better than ever! il Good H 162:116-23 F '66
Challenge of a big room; with editorial comment. il House & Gard 129:155, 156-65 Ap '66
Chez Mlle. B. Plumb. il Mlle 62:64-5 Mr; 96-7 Ap '66
Comfort is a whole way of life. il House & Gard 131:80-7 Ja '67
Decorating wrongs made right. il Bet Hom & Gard 44:49-59 F; 20 My '66
Eighteenth century, a furniture style of many moods. il House & Gard 130:214-17 O '66
Every well-decorated room should have evidence of a family. P. Rumely. il Bet Hom & Gard 44:44-59 S '66
Finest of America's design heritage. il Good H 162:132-9 Ap '66
Fresh, swingy ideas from rooms of the young pros. il House & Gard 129:168-75 My '66
From a tumbledown barn, a spirited house. il House & Gard 130:80-5 Ag '66
Give us courage and gaiety. House & Gard 129:147 My '66
Give your home that personal touch. S. Kaiser. il Farm J 90:98-9 Ap '66
Good decorating starts with a theme. il Good H 162:128-36 Je '66
Happy ideas for a basement playroom. R. Charles. il Parents Mag 41:70-3+ Je '66
Happy rediscovery of Romanesque. il House & Gard 129:118-23 F '66
House that Horst grew. V. Lawford. il Vogue 147:134-9+ Je '66
House with a place for everything! Good housekeeping-Weyerhaeuser company house in Beacon, N.Y. il Good H 162:134-44 Mr '66
Improve your home. Pop Sci 188:131-70+ Ap '66
Lord and Lady Iliffe's triple entente: country, city, and sun. L. Blanch. il Vogue 148:102-9+ Jl '66
Man's castle; remodeled carriage house and stables. M. White. il Ladies Home J 83:102-7 N '66
New for home owners who do. R. M. Howe. il Pop Mech 125:116-19+ Ap '66
Personality decorating. P. Rumely and N. Cordts. il Bet Hom & Gard 44:44-53 Ap '66
Plan for farmers to conquer space; farm home's problems. J. LemMon. il Suc Farm 64:97+ Ap '66
Red, white and what? M. White. il Ladies Home J 83:90-1 Mr '66
Rooms full of roses. il McCalls 93:66-73 Ag '66
Small gem of a house where reason and poetry meet. il House & Gard 130:166-71 D '66
Spring spree: new fabrics, new looks. il Ladies Home J 83:92-7+ My '66
Take-it-easy rooms. il House & Gard 129:102-13 Je '66
Thirty-five ideas under $100. J. LemMon. il Suc Farm 64:59-65 N '66
Today's miracle fabrics, fibers, finishes and fashion. P. Rumely. il Bet Hom & Gard 44:46-59 My '66
Treillage indoors. il House & Gard 129:120-3 Je '66
Two designers' apartments: the constant adventure. il House & Gard 129:110-17 F '66
Two hideouts for paterfamilias; rule 1: wives, children stay out. il Esquire 66:120-3 O '66
Wallpaper whizz-ardry. M. White. il Ladies Home J 83:78-83 Ap '66
When you decorate for the first time. M. Kraft. Good H 162:138 Je '66
Why women never stop decorating. C. B. Luce. McCalls 93:64+ F '66
Wonderful, whimsical wicker. il House & Gard 129:148-55 My '66
See also
Antiques
Apartments
Bathrooms
Bedrooms
Ceilings
Color in house decoration
Decoration and ornament, Architectural
Display of antiques, art objects, etc.
Floor coverings
Furniture
Halls
Hardware
Houses, Model
Interior decorators
Kitchens
Laundries
Music rooms and equipment
Painting, Industrial and practical
Shutters
Table decoration

HOUSE decoration—Continued

Cost

Remodeling with a price tag. il House & Gard 130:106-11 Ag '66

History

Some thoughts on the environmental arts; Adams-Emery wing at the Cincinnati art museum. P. R. Adams. il Antiques 89:391-9 Mr '66

HOUSE decoration, English
See also
Furniture, English

HOUSE decoration, Exterior
Pattern of the street; Western Native Township; Johannesburg. J. Beinart. il Arch Forum 125:58-63 S '66
Pot screen: it's good looking. it tinkles. il Sunset 137:114 O '66
See also
House painting

HOUSE decoration, Hawaiian
Hawaiian inspiration. il House & Gard 130:112-19 Ag '66

HOUSE decoration, Italian
See also
Furniture, Italian

HOUSE decoration, Lebanese
House of many treasures; Beirut. il House & Gard 130:236-41 N '66
Translated from the Lebanese: piquant party touches, buoyant decoration. il House & Gard 130:184-5 D '66

HOUSE decoration, Turkish
Lee Radziwill; in her London Turquerie room. il Vogue 148:220-3 D '66

HOUSE dust allergy. See Allergy

HOUSE expansion. See Houses, Remodeled

HOUSE guests. See Guests

HOUSE lighting. See Electric lighting

HOUSE of commons. See Great Britain—Parliament—House of commons

HOUSE of David
Moribund kingdom of Ben. il Time 87:27-8 Je 17 '66

HOUSE of lords. See Great Britain—Parliament—House of lords

HOUSE of representatives. See United States—Congress—House of representatives

HOUSE of the famous poet; story. See Spark, M.

HOUSE paint. See Paint

HOUSE painting
Bloom in the slums; paint job sponsored by a business-labor organization in Cleveland's run-down areas. il Bsns W p 178+ O 15 '66
Give your home a fresh start. il Pop Gard 17:60-2 D '66
When it's time to paint a vine-covered house. il Sunset 137:88+ S '66
See also
House decoration, Exterior

HOUSE painting, Interior. See Painting. Industrial and practical

HOUSE pets. See Pets

HOUSE plans. See Architecture, Domestic—Designs and plans

HOUSE plants
Character pruning with small container plants. il Sunset 137:60-1 Ag '66
Control plant pests indoors. L. Pyenson. il Horticulture 45:22-3+ Ja '67
Cymbidiums fit into every home. R. W. Jones. il Horticulture 44:22-3 N '66
Ferns in your house. K. Berggrav. il Horticulture 44:18-21+ Je '66
Summer primer on house plants. il Pop Gard 17:18 Ag '66
These indoor plants are really living works of art. il Sunset 138:64-5+ Ja '67
Unusual indoor garden. E. D. Ballard. il Horticulture 45:24-5 Ja '67
See also
African violets
Bromeliads
Episcias
Flower boxes, planters, etc.
Gloxinias
Norfolk Island pine
Plants, Potted
Window gardening

HOUSE prices. See Housing—Costs

HOUSE rules committee. See United States—Congress—House of representatives—Rules committee

HOUSE selling. See Home ownership

HOUSE space committee. See United States—Congress—House of representatives—Committees

HOUSE sparrows. See Sparrows

HOUSE trailers. See Automobile trailers

HOUSE-tree-person-person test. See Personality tests

HOUSE visits. See Medical service

HOUSEBOAT regattas. See Regattas

HOUSEBOATS. See House boats

HOUSEHOLD accounts. See Domestic finance

HOUSEHOLD appliances
Bedroom amenities. il House & Gard 130:238-9+ O '66
Housing's gloom seeps into home equipment. Bsns W p36-7 D 17 '66
New for your home. M. Morey. See issues of Popular mechanics
Putting good taste in a can opener. il Bsns W p80-2 Jl 9 '66
What's new for living. See issues of House & garden incorporating Living for young homemakers
What's new in homemaking. See issues of Successful farming
See also
Kitchen utensils
also names of household appliances, e.g. Vacuum cleaners

HOUSEHOLD budget. See Budget, Household

HOUSEHOLD employees
Foreign maids. il Newsweek 68:104+ N 14 '66
How reliable is teen help? J. Fithian. il Farm J 90:96+ My '66
Servants I have worked for. A. Gingrich. Esquire 66:74-5+ Ag '66
Summer baby sitter. S. Peck. il N Y Times Mag p 118+ My 22 '66
Trouble finding household help? il Changing T 20:20 N '66

HOUSEHOLD furnishings
Basic best buys for your bedroom. il House & Gard 130:230-7 O '66
Bedroom amenities. il House & Gard 130:238-9+ O '66
Colorful accessories to make yourself. M. Garrity. il Bet Hom & Gard 44:68-9 S '66
Comfort for a triple life. il House & Gard 131:112-15 Ja '67
Connoisseur's corner. See issues of House & garden incorporating Living for young homemakers
Design winners. il House & Gard 130:62 N '66
Every well-decorated room should have evidence of a family. P. Rumely. il Bet Hom & Gard 44:44-59 S '66
Home is what you make it! eleven weekend projects. il Pop Mech 126:112-51+ S '66
Housing's gloom seeps into home equipment. Bsns W p36-7 D 17 '66
How to furnish your rooms for quiet. il House & Gard 131:132-5 Ja '67
Ideas in action. D. Jordan. il Bet Hom & Gard 44:54-71 O '66
Island bounty. il House & Gard 131:120-9 Ja '67
Lights! camera! model rooms! B. Plumb. il N Y Times Mag p 106-7 Mr 20 '66
1966 was a happening. B. Plumb. il N Y Times Mag p82-3+ Ja 8 '67
100 ideas under $100. il Bet Hom & Gard 44:22+ Jl '66
Spotlights in a studio; brightening your room. il Seventeen 25:186 Mr '66
That little dress goes over big; Helsinki-based business of Marimekko dresses and home furnishings. il Bsns W p88-90 D 10 '66
Things I must take back to school. il Seventeen 25:306 Ag '66
Up, up, up, up; household stackables. B. Plumb. il N Y Times Mag p58-9 F 20 '66
What's new for living. See issues of House & garden incorporating Living for young homemakers
See also
Color in house decoration

Exhibitions

Museum of early southern decorative arts; the rooms and their furnishings. F. L. Horton. il Antiques 91:72-95 Ja '67

HOUSEHOLD furnishings, Moving of. See Moving

HOUSEHOLD management. See Home economics

HOUSEHOLD mechanics. See Mechanics, Household

HOUSEHOLD pests
See also
Cockroaches
Insects, Injurious and beneficial

HOUSEKEEPING. See Home economics

HOUSELEEKS
Hen-and-chickens: dramatic in a well designed garden. il Sunset 137:161 Jl '66

HOUSEMAN, William
Going places, finding ghosts in Colorado's nostalgic mining towns. House & Gard 129:40-2+ Je '66
How to work with an architect. House & Gard 130:124-5+ Ag '66

HOUSEPIAN, Marjorie
Unremembered genocide. Commentary 42:55-61 S; 8+ D '66

HOUSES
Ideas in houses (cont) il Life 60:70-3+ Ja 28; 84-7+ F 11; 104-7+ Ap 1; 116-19+ My 6; 108-11+ Je 24; 61:74-7+ Ag 5; 90-3+ S 23; 140-4+ D 9 '66
See also
Architecture, Domestic
Doll houses
Farmhouses
Storage in the home

Air conditioning
See Air conditioning

Maintenance and repair
Give your home a fresh start. il Pop Gard 17:60-2 D '66
Homeowners' clinic; questions and answers. W. C. Lammey. See issues of Popular mechanics
Solved: the toughest problems any house can have! il Bet Hom & Gard 44:60-81 Mr '66

Prices
See Housing—Costs

HOUSES, Air conditioned. See Air conditioning

HOUSES, Model
House with a place for everything! Good housekeeping-Weyerhaeuser company house in Beacon, N.Y. il Good H 162:134-44 Mr '66
1,580-square-foot house by the editors of Better homes and gardens; Cape Cod. N. Seney and R. Kruse. il Bet Hom & Gard 44:60-7+ Ap '66
2,084-square-foot house, by the editors of Better homes and gardens; Downers Grove, Ill. N. Seney and R. Kruse. il Bet Hom & Gard 44:60-9+ My '66

HOUSES, Plastic
People in plastic houses; migratory farm-workers in California. il Fortune 73:170 Ap '66

HOUSES, Prefabricated
Good news for men! self-contained vacation houses. D. L. Gregg. il Bet Hom & Gard 44:16+ Mr '66
New ideas in prefab cabins. J. Rutherfoord. il Field & S 71:64-6+ Je '66
Prefabricated housing. C. M. Edwards. il Consumer Bul 49:13-18 Ag '66

HOUSES, Remodeled
Add-on bay takes load off garage. il Pop Mech 126:150-1+ S '66
And a corner for mother. B. Plumb. il N Y Times Mag p 116-17 O 16 '66
Bold new style of Spain; home of Paul and Karen Radkai. J. Peter. il Look 30:63-5 N 1 '66
Converting the garage or carport. il Sunset 136:120+ Ap '66
Dig he did; remodeled brownstone in New York. B. Plumb. il N Y Times Mag p80-2 Ag 28 '66
Doing over the home place. R. Martens. il Farm J 90:66-7 Je '66
Far from factory-built; house formerly a factory. B. Plumb. il N Y Times Mag p 104-5+ N 6 '66
Getting a lift from facelifting; remodeling money available. Bsns W p35 S 3 '66
Home is what you make it! eleven weekend projects. il Pop Mech 126:112-51+ S '66
New bedrooms above, playroom, laundry, and car below. il Sunset 137:116 N '66
New breakfast room solved a traffic problem. il Sunset 137:128 O '66
New family room looks out on a new terrace, new veranda overlooks the pool. il Sunset 136:114-15 My '66
Personal business; old houses. Bsns W p 133-4 Jl 23 '66
PM's guide to basic remodeling measurements. il Pop Mech 126:171-2 S '66
Remodeled houses solve many problems. il Arch Rec 139:155-8 Mr '66
Remodeling: hard work but worth it. R. Nelson. il Farm J 90:52-3 Ag '66

Remodeling on a grand scale. B. Plumb. il N Y Times Mag p 170-2 N 13 '66
Remodeling with a price tag. il House & Gard 130:106-11 Ag '66
Remodeling's rewards. il House & Gard 130:79-99 Ag '66
Rings update their farm home. J. LemMon. il Suc Farm 64:68-9 Ag '66
Seven smart ways to gain living space in the home. C. T. Sigman. il Pop Sci 189:142-8 S '66
Sometimes your front yard is simply opportunity. il Sunset 137:90 Jl '66
Spacemaking! six families' remodeling projects. il Bet Hom & Gard 44:16+ Ap '66
They bought an old box, and surrounded it. il Sunset 136:121-2 Je '66
They remodeled for space and for spaciousness. il Sunset 136:138+ Ap '66
Thin home in an old row; Cafritz house. Georgetown. il Life 61:88-91+ N 4 '66
Three old-timers off to a fresh start; American institute of architects-Sunset magazine Western home awards. il Sunset 136:78-85 Mr '66
To gain space they went up. il Sunset 137:164 O '66
What's your choice in remodel financing. Sunset 136:101-2 F '66
Would you believe a garage could look like this? il Bet Hom & Gard 44:44-5 Ag '66

HOUSES, Round. See Buildings, Round

HOUSES, Seashore. See Beach architecture

HOUSES, Toy. See Doll houses

HOUSEWARES. See Household appliances

HOUSEWIVES
Angry housewives win key skirmish; support from FTC against high food prices. il Bsns W p42 O 29 '66
Bored housewife. L. Tornabene. il Ladies Home J 83:97-9+ N '66
Boycotts; action protesting high food prices. Nation 203:498-9 N 14 '66
Boycotts and prices. M. Friedman. Newsweek 68:92 N 28 '66
Everywoman's village stirs up the housewives. E. Perry. il Life 60:46+ Mr 25 '66; Same abr. with title Housewives' school to beat the boredom. Read Digest 88:41-2+ Je '66
Grocers' answer on prices: if women really want a change it can be arranged; elimination of games, gimmicks and extra services. il U S News 61:110+ N 14 '66
Housewives' revolt. Sr Schol 89:18-19 N 11 '66
Housewives skewer high food prices; organized action against chain food stores. il Bsns W p42-3 O 22 '66
I've learned to put first things first. J. Fithian. Farm J 90:83 O '66
Mrs Parkinson's law; scientific solution for those days when everything seems to go wrong. C. N. Parkinson. il McCalls 93:104-5+ F '66
Small lesson in relative importance; a wife's devotion to polished floors. B. Boris. il Redbook 127:6+ Jl '66
See also
Home economics

HOUSING
See also
Building
Discrimination in housing
Home ownership
Savings and loan associations
Slums

Costs
It will cost more. il Time 87:80 Ja 28 '66
Where it costs less to build a home. il U S News 61:18 O 24 '66

Desegregation
Checkerboard communities, pattern for living. il Newsweek 67:86+ Ap 25 '66
Desegregated housing. F. F. Piven and R. A. Cloward. New Repub 155:17-22 D 17 '66; Discussion. 156:44 Ja 7; 44-5 Ja 14 '67
Formula for racial peace in Chicago? U S News 61:6 S 5 '66
Not even a boo; William J. Levitt's open-occupancy measure. Newsweek 67:74 My 30 '66
Stamford's attempt to integrate suburbia; scattered sites program. J. R. Wolf. il Reporter 35:20+ D 29 '66
Victory in the North; open-housing agreement; Chicago. il Newsweek 68:20-1 S 5 '66
When black and white live together: Rochdale village, Queens, N.Y. H. Swados. il N Y Times Mag p47+ N 13 '66

HOUSING—*Continued*

Federal aid
Follow that vote; rent-subsidy bill carried by House. Newsweek 67:44 My 23 '66
This month's feature: Congress & the rent supplement program. Cong Digest 45:1-32 Ja '66

Finance
See Housing finance

Slum clearance
See Slums

California
California apartments make skillful use of Hillside sites. il Arch Rec 139:133-40 Mr '66
Court vs. the voters on open housing; California Supreme court declares Proposition 14 unconstitutional. L. T. King. Commonweal 84:491-2 Ag 5 '66
Court votes no. Newsweek 67:47 My 23 '66
Upset: California law on homeowners' rights. U S News 60:13 My 23 '66

United States
City is the frontier, by C. Abrams. Review New Repub 154:42+ My 14 '66. W. Thabit
Desegregated housing. F. F. Piven and R. A. Cloward. New Repub 155:17-22 D 17 '66; Discussion. 156:44 Ja 7; 44-5 Ja 14 '67
Doing something about slums. H. J. Gans. Commonweal 83:688-93 Mr 18 '66
Rebuilding the slums. J. Ridgeway. New Repub 156:22-5 Ja 7 '67
See also
Building industry
Housing laws and legislation—United States
Negroes in the United States—Housing
United States—Housing and urban development, Department of
also subhead Housing under names of cities, e.g. Chicago—Housing

HOUSING, Company. See Company towns
HOUSING, Discrimination in. See Discrimination in housing
HOUSING and urban development, Department of. See United States—Housing and urban development, Department of
HOUSING construction. See Building industry
HOUSING finance
Financing a house. Consumer Rep 31:394-7 D '66
House of troubles. il Time 87:97-8 Je 10 '66
See also
Federal national mortgage association
Mortgages
United States—Federal housing administration

HOUSING for the aged. See Aged—Housing
HOUSING laws and legislation

United States
Back at the office: House furor and Title IV. Newsweek 68:21-2 Ag 15 '66
This month's feature: Congress & the rent supplement program. Cong Digest 45:1-32 Ja '66
See also
Housing—Federal aid

HOUSING projects
Senator contends church maligned. Christian Cent 83:454, 1137 Ap 13, S 21 '66
Where D(3) helped wipe out a slum; St Louis' 12-acre La Clede town. il Bsns W p 162-4+ D 17 '66
See also
Queens, N.Y.—Housing

Site planning
Cluster house divides itself into separate units for quiet living. N. Seney. il Bet Hom & Gard 45:68-9 Ja '67
Framework for new kind of living; Redwood Shores. il Arch Rec 139:159-66 Je '66
Rape of the land. B. H. Bagdikian. il Sat Eve Post 239:25-9 Je 18 '66
Riis plaza; design with keen understanding of human needs. il Arch Rec 140:134-5 D '66
When to sell to the developer; farm land grab. G. Logsdon. il Farm J 90:38-9+ Mr '66

HOUSING projects, Company. See Company towns
HOUSING projects, Government
Goldberg's variation on Chicago public housing. Raymond M. Hilliard center. J. M. Dixon. il Arch Forum 125:25-33 N '66
Seven winners named for urban design excellence. il Am City 81:89 N '66

HOUSING subsidies. See Housing—Federal aid
HOUSLEY, Mary Frances
Girl named Frankie. M. Kantor. por Read Digest 88:86-90 My '66
HOUSTON, L. B.
Endowment management for parks. por Parks & Rec 1:328-30+ Ap '66
HOUSTON, R. L.
It would be idiotic to deal with the Viet Cong; interview. por U S News 61:44-5 O 17 '66
HOUSTON, Walter Scott
Deep-sky wonders. See issues of Sky and telescope
HOUSTON, Tex.
Big deal that got away. S. H. Brown. Fortune 74:164-6+ O '66
Houston wins its big-city sp ırs. il Bsns W p 130-3+ N 19 '66
Multiple solutions through central microfilming. E. A. Newgren. Am City 81:146+ F '66
One city that cares, enough to make every mother's day care dream come true. J. Robbins and J. Robbins. Ladies Home J 83:71+ Jl '66

Airports
Texas expanding to meet air traffic growth. E. J. Bulban. il Aviation W 85:39+ D 19 '66
World's first supersonic jet airport; Houston intercontinental airport. il Pop Sci 188:90-1 F '66

Anti-poverty program
Will success spoil a poverty program? W. P. Pannill. New Repub 154:10 F 26 '66

Architecture
Challenge to Apollo; Jones hall. il Time 88:90 O 14 '66
Dealer who's remaking Houston; combination of financial acumen and architectural knowhow. il Bsns W p 170-2+ D 3 '66
Debut in Houston: Jesse H. Jones hall. il Newsweek 68:108-9 O 17 '66
Jesse H. Jones hall, a grand slam play. R. C. Marsh. il Hi Fi 16:MA20-1 D '66
Keeping up with the Cliburns (and the Joneses) Jesse H. Jones hall. P. Hume. il Sat R 49:72 O 29 '66

Hospitals
St Joseph's grows on a crowded urban site while services continue. il Arch Rec 140:206-7 O '66
What money cannot buy; City county hospital. J. de Hartog. il Atlan 218:111-15 Jl '66

Music
Houston's culture gets a new glow. Jesse H. Jones hall. il Bsns W p 150-2 O 8 '66
Keeping up with the Cliburns (and the Joneses) Jesse H. Jones hall; first concert. P. Hume. il Sat R 49:72 O 29 '66
See also
Houston grand opera association

Newspapers
See also
Houston chronicle
HOUSTON astrodome. See Stadiums
HOUSTON Astros (baseball) See Baseball clubs
HOUSTON chronicle
Deal done in. il Time 87:62 Je 17 '66
Houston's shackled press. B. H. Bagdikian. Atlan 218:87-8+ Ag '66; Discussion. 218:44+ O '66
If you want a paper. . . il Newsweek 67:62+ Je 20 '66
HOUSTON endowment, incorporated
Big deal that got away. S. H. Brown. Fortune 74:164-6+ O '66
HOUSTON grand opera association
Houston. A. Holmes. il Opera N 30:28 F 19; 31 Mr 12 '66
Houston; celebrating the opening of Jesse H. Jones hall for the performing arts. A. Holmes. Opera N 31:23-4 N 19 '66
Houston; production of Hansel and Gretel in Jesse H. Jones hall for the performing arts. A. Holmes. Opera N 31:28 D 31 '66
HOUSTON intercontinental airport. See Houston, Tex.—Airports
HOUSTON museum of fine arts
American decorative arts in Texas; the Bayou bend collection. D. B. Warren. il Antiques 90:796-815 D '66
HOUSTON symphony orchestra
Musical events; concert in Carnegie Hall. W. Sargeant. New Yorker 42:169-70 Ap 2 '66
HOUSTON tournament. See Golf—Tournaments

HOVDA, Robert W.
Priests as witnesses. Commonweal 83:532-4
F 4 '66

HOVERCRAFT. See Ground effect machines

HOVING, Lucas
Lucas Hoving, Nancy Lewis, Chase Robinson; 92nd street Y. M. Marks. Dance Mag
40:67 Jl '66

HOVING, Thomas Pearsall Field
Beauty and horror; remarks. New Yorker 42:
28-31 My 28 '66
Outdoorsman of the big city; interview, ed.
by S. Davis. pors Life 60:39-40+ Ap 29
'66
Think big about small parks. N Y Times
Mag p 12-13+ Ap 10 '66
Two commissioners; interview. New Yorker
42:35-7 Mr 5 '66

about

Happening at the Met. il por Time 88:46 D
23 '66
Happening called Hoving. B. Weinraub. il
pors N Y Times Mag p 10-11+ Jl 10 '66
Hoving is a happening in the parks. Life
61:4 S 9 '66
Metropolitan's man. por Newsweek 68:46 D
26 '66
Peopling the parks. il por Time 88:48 S 2 '66
S.R.O. at Mr Hoving's Met. R. Lynes. il
N Y Times Mag p8-11+ Ja 1 '67
Summer romance. il por Newsweek 68:26
Jl 18 '66

HOVING, Walter
Mutual antipathy. por Time 87:82 Ap 1 '66

HOW I spent my summer vacation; story. See
Loeser K.

HOW-to-do-it books. See Instruction manuals

HOW to succeed in business without really
trying; musical comedy. See Musical
comedies, revues, etc.—Criticisms, plots,
etc.

HOW to write New Yorker stories; story. See
Karp, E.

HOWAR, Barbara
Here comes, there goes Barbara; interview,
ed. by deRosset Morrissey. il pors Life 61:
48-50+ Jl 29 '66
Washington's swinging scene. il por Newsweek 67:34-8 Je 20 '66

HOWARD, Alan
With the guerrillas in Guatemala. N Y Times
Mag p8-9+ Je 26 '66

HOWARD, Anthony
Behind the bureaucratic curtain. N Y Times
Mag p34-5+ O 23 '66

HOWARD, Edward N.
Paperback wearability. por Library J 91:
4057-60 S 15 '66

HOWARD, Jane
Busiest copycat of them all. Life 61:69-70+
Jl 1 '66
Can a nice novelist finish first? Life 61:74-
74A+ N 4 '66
Happiness is being number 1. Life 61:68-70+
Ag 19 '66
Host with a genius for jarring juxtapositions.
Life 61:61+ D 9 '66
Leading lady of U.S. verse. Life 62:37-8+
Ja 13 '67
Man for all disasters. pors Life 61:57-8+
N 25 '66
Oracle of the electric age. Life 60:91-2+
F 25 '66
What's special is the mood here? Life 60:54+
My 20 '66

HOWARD, John
Individual in society; address, May 25, 1966.
Vital Speeches 32:593-6 Jl 15 '66

HOWARD, Lawrence C.
Teach them the arts of freedom. Sat R 49:66-
7+ Je 18 '66

HOWARD, Richard
Bonnard: a novel; poem. New Yorker 42:32-3
S 3 '66
British chronicle. Poetry 108:399-407 S '66
Canadian chronicle. Poetry 108:45-53 Ap '66
Hispanic chronicle. Poetry 107:338-42 F '66
Illusion wedded to simple need. Poetry 108:
329-35 Ag '66
Jewelry by Resia Schor. Craft Horiz 26:8-11+
Jl '66
Landscape garden; poem. New Yorker 42:62
N 5 '66
New York: the bed. Craft Horiz 26:8-15 S
'66
Panoptic shoehorns. Art N 65:44-5+ Ap '66
People figures. Craft Horiz 26:36-41 N '66
To a known place. Poetry 107:253-8 Ja '66

HOWARD, Steven J.
Keeping electric garden tools cutting. Pop
Mech 125:126-9+ Je '66

HOWARD, William
Judges v. jailers. por Time 88:69 S 16 '66

HOWARD Johnson company. See Johnson,
Howard, company

HOWARD Johnson restaurants. See Restaurants—United States

HOWARD W. Sams and company. See Sams,
Howard W. and company

HOWE, Florence
Victims and witnesses. Nation 202:432-3 Ap
11 '66

HOWE, Gordon
Sporting scene. H. W. Wind. il New Yorker
41:116+ F 12 '66

HOWE, Harold, 2d
Blueprint for education. Parents Mag 41:58-
61+ O '66
Federal money in public schools; interview.
por U S News 61:68-74 D 5 '66
In defense of the guidelines; statement, Sep-
tember 27, 1966. Library J 91:5002+ O 15
'66
Nation of amateurs in educaton; adaptation
of address, July 14, 1966. Sch & Soc 94:
448-51 D 10 '66
Time is now. Sat R 49:57-8 Jl 16 '66
Tolstoi and teachers. por NEA J 55:19 My '66
U.S. office of education. Sat R 49:68-70+
D 17 '66
View from afar. por Am Ed 2:inside cover
S '66
Washington report; excerpts from testimony,
ed. by J. Lloyd. por Sr Schol 89:sup9 O 28
'66
What are Americans receiving in return for
their heavy investment in education? ex-
cerpts of testimony. por Am Ed 2:24-6
N '66

about

Education: racial controversy dogs U.S. com-
missioner. L. J. Carter. por Science 154:
242-3+ O 14 '66
Failure of gradualism. Newsweek 68:80 Jl 4
'66
Here's Harold Howe new education chief. il
por Sr Schol 87:sup2 Ja 14 '66
Howe of integration. il por Newsweek 68:74
O 24 '66
Mr Howe and his racial views; center of
controversy. U S News 61:24 O 17 '66
New U.S. commissioner of education. Sch
& Soc 94:84 F 19 '66
Official under fire for racial views. por U S
News 61:16 Ag 29 '66
Washington report. J. Lloyd. Sr Schol 89:
sup7 D 2 '66

HOWE, Henry H. 1942?-
Conduct unbecoming. J. Rechy. il Nation
202:204-8 F 21 '66; Reply. J. L. Howe. 202:
346+ Mr 28 '66
Lieutenant at liberty. Nation 202:413 Ap 11
'66

HOWE, Irving
Other Singer. Commentary 41:78+ Mr '66

about

Freedom is a full-time job. M. R. Konvitz.
Sat R 50:47 Ja 21 '67

HOWE, Richard L.
Shopping for tools. See Issues of Popular
mechanics

HOWE, Russell Warren
Ghana without The Redeemer. New Repub
154:9-11 Mr 12; 36+ Ap 2 '66
Old hand's new look at seventeen countries.
New Repub 155:15-17 Ag 27 '66
Rock that does not roll to Franco's beat.
New Repub 156:16-17 Ja 21 '67
Wrangling over Rhodesia: Commonwealth's
venture into controversy. New Repub 155:
8-9 O 1 '66
Year of the mandarins. New Repub 155:13-14
D 10 '66

HOWELL, Douglass
Fine papermaking described by craftsman at
Brentano's. il por Pub W 190:120 Jl 4 '66
Hand-made paper still flourishes. il Pub W
190:104+ S 5 '66; Correction. 190:146 O 3
'66; Discussion. 190:20 N 7 '66

HOWELL, Ted
Hunter against odds. pors Outdoor Life 138:
39-41+ O '66

HOWELLS, William W.
Homo erectus: with biographical sketch. Sci
Am 215:28, 46-53 N '66

HOWER, Ralph M.
Opus Dei defended. Christian Cent 83:338-9
Mr 16 '66

HOWES, Barbara
Bay at West Falmouth; poem. New Yorker
42:44 My 14 '66

HOWES, Barbara—*Continued*
For Katherine Anne Porter May 15, 1965;
poem. Sat R 49:104 F 19 '66
Hourglass; poem. New Repub 154:23 My 21
'66
Leaning into light; poem. New Repub 154:23
My 7 '66
Letter from the Caribbean; poem. New Yorker
41:34 F 19 '66
Miss Moore herself. New Repub 155:31 D
17 '66

HOWEY, Joseph, and McKenney, Elizabeth
Point of increasing returns. pors Library J
91:6039-42 D 15 '66

HOWIE, Virginia
Lilies for all summer. il Horticulture 44:24-5+
F '66

HOWLIN' Wolf. See Wolf, H.

HOW'S the world treating you? drama. See
Milner, R.

HOYEM, Andrew
Diana; When we meet I will wear a rose;
Love seat; Zeal; poems. Poetry 109:86-8 N
'66

HOYER, Linda Grace
Burning bush; story. New Yorker 42:50-5 O
1 '66

HOYLE, Fred. See Burbidge, G. jt. auth.

HOYT, Norris D.
Boating. Sports Illus 25:48-9 Ag 8 '66
Famed sailor Norrie Hoyt comments on Passagemaker. Motor B 117:39+ My '66
Once over heavily. il Yachting 120:37-9+ Ag
'66
Once over lightly. Yachting 120:51-3+ S '66

HRABA, Tomas. See Merchant, B. jt. auth.

HROMÁDKA, Josef Luki
Doctor Hromadka and the will to peace;
reply. J. C. Heidbrink. America 114:367
Mr 19 '66

HSU, Jeng M. and others
Pancreatic carboxypeptidases: activities in
zinc-deficient rats. bibliog Science 153:882-3
Ag 19 '66

HSU, Oon-bee, and Carter, M. D.
Singapore national library. bibliog Wilson Lib
Bul 40:629-33 Mr '66

HSU, Tzu-tsai
Mystery of the locked legation: who killed
Mr Hsu? R. Chelminski. il por Life 61:30B
Ag 19 '66

HU, C. T.
How school keeps in China. Sat R 49:66-7+
Ag 20 '66

HUALAPAI DAM (proposed) See Dams

HUANG, Su-shu
Synchronization in close binaries. Sky & Tel
31:215-17 Ap '66

HUBBARD, Fred D.
Battle in the ghetto. Newsweek 67:44+ Je 13
'66

HUBBARD, Timothy William
Battle at Valcour Island: Benedict Arnold as
hero. Am Heritage 17:8-11+ O '66

HUBBELL, John G.
Brave men in frail planes. Read Digest 88:
76-80 Ap '66
Case of the missing H-bomb. Read Digest
89:239-44+ S '66
Confessions of a Little league coach. Read
Digest 88:157-60 My '66
Guardian mountain of our continent. Read
Digest 88:149-52+ Je '66

HUBERT, Adelyn C.
Love that luau! Motor B 118:43-4+ Jl '66

HUBERTSON, Amanda Labarca. See Labarca
Hubertson, A.

HUCH, William F. See Ney, E. P. jt. auth.

HUCK, Susan
El gallo colorao ha ganao, or, What happened in Santo Domingo. Nat R 18:617-18
Je 28 '66

HUDGINS, William R.
Relating to the community. il por Time 87:
80+ Ja 28 '66

HUDSON, Charles L.
Making school days healthy days. por Todays
Health 44:92 S '66

HUDSON, Helen
Constant caller; story. Reporter 36:50 Ja 12
'67
Send a patrol car to Spartanburg; story.
Mlle 63:118-19 Je '66

HUDSON, Lois Phillips
Battle in the wilderness: benevolent wreckers. Nation 202:393-6 Ap 4 '66

HUDSON, Peggy
Look and listen. See issues of Senior
scholastic
Looking and listening. See issues of Senior
scholastic
Previewing the '66-'67 season. Sr Schol 89:30,
sup 15 S 16 '66

HUDSON, William L.
Ice ahead! R. K. Andrist. il Am Heritage
17:92-103 Ag '66

HUDSON BAY company. See Hudson's Bay
company

HUDSON institute, Incorporated
Where they think about the unthinkable.
B. Riggan. il Horizon 8:40-4+ Sum '66

HUDSON RIVER
Congress and the Hudson. Natur Hist 75:70+
O '66
Hudson River. E. J. Kahn, jr. il Holiday 40:
40-55+ O '66
Hudson River clean-up: it can be clear, blue
and wonderful again. P. T. White. il N Y
Times Mag p8-9+ Jl 17 '66
Hudson's six geologies. C. J. Schuberth. il
Natur Hist 76:46-55 bibliog(p73) Ja '67
Storm King. Liv Wildn 29:42-3 Wint '65
Storm King. New Yorker 42:17-19 Ja 7 '67
Storm King gets a reprieve. il Am For 72:5
F '66
Storm on the Hudson. Natur Hist 75:6-7 Je
'66
Water proposals for New York. Science 154:
215-16 O 14 '66

HUDSON RIVER day line
Full ahead on the Hamilton. New Yorker 42:
29-31 Je 4 '66

HUDSON RIVER marathon. See Motor boat
racing

HUDSON RIVER school. See Painting, American

HUDSON RIVER VALLEY
Hudson River. E. J. Kahn, jr. il Holiday 40:
40-55+ O '66

HUDSON'S BAY company
Hudson's Bay mushes along the urban trail;
drive to expand department store business
throughout Canada. il Bsns W p64-8 S 3 '66

HUÉ, Vietnam
God-given mission. Newsweek 67:49 Je 13 '66

HUEFTLE, Keene
Get a good thing going. il por Outdoor Life
137:62-3+ My '66

HUET, Henri
On with the war and Operation Masher;
and Operation Double Eagle; photographs.
Life 60:20-24E F 11 '66

HUFF, Betty Tracy
Girl and the gold mine; drama. Plays 26:
29-39 O '66
Penelope, pride of the pickle factory; drama.
Plays 25:39-49 F '66

HUFF, Corrine
Growing troubles of Chairman Powell. il por
U S News 62:10 Ja 2 '67

HUFF, Darrell
Extend your living space with a deck. por
Pop Sci 188:137-41+ Ap '66
Rough stuff: the big news in wall paneling.
Pop Sci 188:132-6+ Ap '66
Which fireplace should you choose? Pop Sci
189:156-61 O '66
You can't beat slate underfoot. Pop Sci 189:
120-2 Ag '66

HUFF, Robert
Lamb, the clocks, the blue light. Poetry 109:
44-8 O '66
On the death of Theodore Roethke; To
Francey; For Philip Booth; poems. Poetry
107:360-2 Mr '66
Watching my son watch Botticelli; poem.
Mlle 62:158 Ap '66

HUFF, William H. See Brown, N. B. jt. auth.

HUFFINES, Robert Luther, 1905–
Moves. Time 88:72+ Jl 15 '66

HUFFMAN, John W.
Expectant mother. Redbook 127:28+ Ag '66

HUG, George, and others
Phosphorylase kinase of the liver: deficiency
in a girl with increased hepatic glycogen.
bibliog Science 153:1534-5 S 23 '66

HUG, Russell John
New baker adds yeast to Ward. il por Bsns W
p80-2+ Jl 16 '66

HUGGINS, Charles Brenton
Belated recognition. il por Time 88:77 O 21
'66
Cancer fighters. il por Newsweek 68:78+ O
24 '66
1966 Nobel laureates in medicine and physiology. P. Talalay and G. Williams-Ashman. por Science 154:362-4 O 21 '66
Two share Nobel prize. por Sci N 90:319 O 22
'66

HUGGINS, Edith
TV news hens. il pors Ebony 21:44-6+ O '66

HUGHES, Charles E. See Nadler, C. F. jt.
auth.

HUGHES, Elizabeth (Sullivan)
Ten for the road. por McCalls 94:54+ N '66

HUGHES, Emmet John
[Current events column] See issues of Newsweek

HUGHES, H. Stuart
Keeping an eye on tourists. D. Sanford. New Repub 154:9-10 Ap 9 '66
Snooping industry. Nation 202:412 Ap 11 '66

HUGHES, Howard Robard
Big grab-up of Howard Hughes's sell-off. il Life 60:45 My 13 '66
Eccentric. il por Time 87:89 Ap 15 '66
Goodman position clarified on Howard Hughes biography. Pub W 190:49 Jl 18 '66
Howard Hughes, by J. Keats. Review Newsweek por 67:95 My 30 '66
Reporter 35:57-8 Jl 14 '66. J. R. Phelan
Howard Hughes' lucrative beating. il por Newsweek 67:75-6 Ap 18 '66
Howard Hughes's biggest surprise. J. McDonald. il Fortune 74:119-20+ Jl 1 '66
Piracy or champerty? por Newsweek 68:54-5 Ag 8 '66
Putting on the Ritz. por Newsweek 68:32-3 N 28 '66
Random house asks court to void Hughes injunction. Pub W 190:39-40 Ag 8 '66
Random house enjoined on Hughes biography. Pub W 190:193-4 Jl 11 '66
Some precedents in the Howard Hughes verdict. R. H. Smith. Pub W 190:312 Ag 29 '66
Stuart, Random et al. vs. Hughes. Rosemont, etc. Pub W 189:47-8 My 16 '66
Stuart wins award in Goodman, Hughes case. Pub W 190:28 D 12 '66
U.S. court voids injunction on biography of Hughes. Pub W 190:308-9 Ag 29 '66
What's behind the big TWA sale. por Bsns W p 145-6+ Ap 16 '66

HUGHES, John
Indonesia for Indonesians. New Repub 154:11-12 Ap 30 '66

HUGHES, John F.
Title I ESEA: the way and the means. por Sr Schol 89:sup 11 N 4 '66

HUGHES, Judith Coolidge
North European export mirrors: the evidence and some suggestions. Antiques 89:856-61 Je '66

HUGHES, Langston
Crowns and garlands; poem. Nation 204:92 Ja 16 '67

HUGHES, Patrick J.
Entrepreneur in Ireland. J. Perham. por Duns R 87:65 F '66

HUGHES, R. D. See Bustard, H. R. jt. auth.

HUGHES, Richard
Orientalization of the West. Sat R 49:47-8+ O 8 '66

HUGHES, Richard Joseph
New Jersey obscenity bill vetoed by governor. Pub W 189:275 Ja 24 '66

HUGHES, Richard Joseph, family
Ten for the road; trip across the country. B. Hughes. il McCalls 94:54+ N '66

HUGHES, Sarah (Tilghman)
Woman who swore in President Johnson recalls what happened aboard Air force one, 2:38 p.m. Dallas, November 22, 1963; ed. by M. Drury. McCalls 94:66+ N '66

HUGHES, Spike
Balance regained. Opera N 30:24-5 Ja 29 '66
Eating with opera. Opera N 31:8-12 N 19 '66
Irrepressible spirit. Opera N 30:24-5 Mr 19 '66

HUGHES, Ted
Pause for breath; poem. New Yorker 42:90 Ag 27 '66

HUGHES, Thomas L.
Policy-making in a world turned upside down. For Affairs 45:202-14 Ja '67

HUGHES, Vernon W.
Muonium atom; with biographical sketch. Sci Am 214:20, 93-100 Ap '66

HUGHES tool company
Hughes designing civil, military hot-cycle aircraft. H. D. Watkins. il Aviation W 84:48-9+ F 28 '66
TWA to press claim against Hughes tool. Aviation W 84:33 Ap 18 '66

HUGO, Richard F.
Point no point; poem. Poetry 108:236 Jl '66

HUGO, Victor Marie, comte
Victor Hugo, decorator; Guernsey house. E. Schlumberger. il pors Vogue 147:224-31+ My '66

HUIZINGA, J. H.
Captain O'Neill and the anti-Papist. Reporter 35:43-4 O 20 '66

HUJER, Karel
Blaeuw's celestial globe and three new stars. K. Hujer. il Sky & Tel 32:278-9 N '66

HUKBALAHAPS
Hunt for the Huks. Time 88:27 Ag 5 '66
Lesson for Oscar. Time 88:29 D 23 '66
President Marcos and the Huk resurgence. D. Warner. il Reporter 35:28-31 N 3 '66
Red terror rising: Huks' comeback in Philippines. il U S News 61:68-9 S 19 '66

HULBURT, E. O. center for space research. See United States—Naval research laboratory

HULL, Bobby
Golden goal. il por Time 87:63-4 Mr 25 '66
Hockey's biggest moment: no. 51. M. Kane. il pors Sports Illus 24:26-9 Mr 21 '66
Hull of fame. H. L. Masin. por Sr Schol 88:22 Ap 22 '66
Sportsman of the year: J. Ryun; four others excelled. por Sports Illus 25:55 D 19 '66

HULL, Clinton R.
Build this white-water riverboat. Pop Mech 126:154-7+ D '66
Line of scrimmage. Outdoor Life 138:58-61+ O '66

HULL, Dale O.
How to buy a used tractor. Suc Farm 64:42-3 Je '66

HULL, Helen S.
Trillium triumph. il Flower Grower 53:38-9+ My '66

HULL, Raymond
Peter principle. Esquire 67:76-7 Ja '67

HULL, Robert W.
Protozoology. Science 151:596-7 F 4 '66

HULLOW, Warren
Welded metal sculpture. Sch Arts 65:24 F '66

HULLS (naval architecture)
Cool new three-keeler is stable and sassy; Starcraft's Daytona. J. Roe. il Pop Sci 189:120-2 N '66
New boats by Chrysler. M. Crook. il Yachting 120:49+ O '66
New look at planing hull design. J. Stoltz. il Motor B 118:98-101+ S; 48-51 O; 46-9+ N; 48-50+ D '66
Study of sailing yachts. H. C. Herreshoff and J. N. Newman. il Sci Am 215:60-8 bibliog(p 114) Ag '66
What hull shape is for you? J. Atkin. il Motor B 117:40-1+ My '66

HULTQUIST, Kay Bacon
Sounds of a river. Nat Parks Mag 40:9-12 Ag '66

HUMAN behavior. See Behavior (psychology)
HUMAN beings. See Man
HUMAN ecology
Allergies: ecological approach; report on first annual meeting of the Society for clinical ecology. M. Spetz. Science 153:903 Ag 19 '66
Plant pathology and human welfare. A. J. Riker. bibliog il Science 152:1027-32 My 20 '66

See also
Man—Influence of environment
Man—Influence on nature

HUMAN electricity. See Electrophysiology
HUMAN embryo. See Fetus
HUMAN engineering
How human engineering is making better tools for you. J. G. Busse. il Pop Sci 189:114-17+ O '66

HUMAN evolution. See Evolution
HUMAN fertility. See Fertility, Human
HUMAN figure in art
Against the cold; S. Drexler. il Newsweek 67:91 F 21 '66
Modigliani's subject of desire. J. Perreault. il Art N 65:42-3+ O '66
Paul Georges paints a nude. L. Campbell. il Art N 64:52-5+ Ja '66
People figures; exhibition at New York's Museum of contemporary crafts. R. Howard. il Craft Horiz 26:36-41 N '66

See also
Human figure in photography
Nude in art

HUMAN figure in photography
Cande in a curtain. P. Gowland. il Pop Phot 59:12+ Ag '66
Changes on a classic theme; the nude appears in new moods and guises. il Life 61:53-61 D 23 '66
Fashionable figure; photographs, excerpts from The photographer and his model. U S Camera 29:50-1 O '66
Follow the form. il U S Camera 30:60-1 Ja '67
Good nudes: Rawlings is back. H. Keppler. il Mod Phot 31:74-5 Ja '67
Hattersley class: nudes. il Pop Phot 58:51-4 Je '66

HUMAN figure in photography—*Continued*
No place for nudes. P. Gowland. il Pop Phot 58:20+ Je '66
Sexy sandwich. il U S Camera 29:62-5 O '66
Some of the parts can be as exciting as the whole girl. P. Gowland. il Pop Phot 59:120-1+ N '66

HUMAN genetics. See Genetics

HUMAN heredity. See Heredity

HUMAN nature
Man has no killer instinct. G. Gorer. N Y Times Mag p47+ N 27 '66

HUMAN race. See Man

HUMAN relations
Help fight heartache. G. Nash. America 114: 835-6 Je 11 '66
Ones who wait. N. Rosten. il Sat Eve Post 239:62-5 D 31 '66
See also
Brotherhood of man
Conversation
Friendship
Loneliness
Love
Marriage
Sex relations
Teachers—Adjustment

HUMAN rights. See Civil rights

HUMAN rights, Universal declaration of. See Universal declaration of human rights

HUMAN rights commission. See United Nations —Commission on human rights

HUMAN rights conference. See International conference on human rights (proposed)

HUMAN rights day and week
Human rights day 1966; texts of messages. A. R. Pazhwak; Thant. UN Mo Chron 3: i-iii D '66

HUMAN rights year. See International human rights year (proposed)

HUMAN voice. See Voice

HUMANE societies
Concentration camps for dogs; L. W. Brown's Maryland compound raided; with report by M. Silva. il Life 60:22-9 F 4 '66

HUMANE society of the United States
National humane center. Nat Parks Mag 40: 20 Ap '66

HUMANE treatment of animals. See Animals— Treatment

HUMANISM
New secular ecumenism. J. B. Sheerin. Cath World 203:261-4 Ag '66

HUMANISTIC education. See Liberal education

HUMANITIES
Arts, the humanities, and the school library; symposium. ed. by E. E. Ahlers. il ALA Bul 60:899-908+ O '66
Bibliographic organization in the humanities. C. H. Rawski. bibliog il Wilson Lib Bul 40:738-50 Ap '66; Correction. 41:26 S '66
Schism in American scholarship; address, November 6, 1965. J. Higham. bibliog f Am Hist R 72:1-21 O '66
See also
Liberal education
Science and the humanities

Study and teaching
High school and the cultural illiterate. G. Culligan. il Am Ed 2:1-5 N '66
Humanities move into social studies world. Sr Schol 89:sup3+ D 9 '66
Saving the humanities. E. Larrabee. bibliog f Commentary 42:53-60 D '66
Teach them the arts of freedom. L. C. Howard. il Sat R 49:66-7+ Je 18 '66

HUMANITY (mankind) See Man

HUMBLE oil and refining company
Playing the games; Esso's promotional game, Tigerino. New Repub 156:10 Ja 21 '67

HUME, Ivor Noël. See Noël Hume, I.

HUME, Paul
Keeping up with the Cliburns (and the Joneses) Sat R 49:56-7+ O 29 '66

HUMETRICS division. See Thiokol chemical corporation

HUMIDIFIERS
Humidifiers work wonders in winter. R. Hoefgen. Parents Mag 41:26 N '66
In winter you need both heat and humidity. il McCalls 93:32 F '66
Which humidifier? il Bet Hom & Gard 44:28-9 F '66

HUMIDITY
See also
Hygrometers

HUMMEL, Horace D.
Archaeological finds. Christian Cent 83:499-500 Ap 20 '66
Harvest of books in the biblical field. Christian Cent 83:431-3 Ap 6 '66
Israel before Christ. Christian Cent 83:868 Jl 6 '66

HUMMEL, Katharine P. and others
Diabetes, a new mutation in the mouse. Science 153:1127-8 S 2 '66

HUMMINGBIRDS
Albino adventure nets rare Anna's. P. W. Colburn. il Audubon Mag 68:476-8 N '66
Marvelous hummingbird rediscovered. C. H. Greenewalt. il Nat Geog Mag 130:98-101 Jl '66

HUMOR
Bill Cosby talks about life, laughter and the pursuit of wonderfulness; interview, ed. by J. Long. B. Cosby. il Seventeen 26:94-5+ Ja '67
Books to watch television by: novelty books on nonbooks. B. Rollin. Look 30:M10 Ap 19 '66
Label on the package: titles. R. Armour. Writer 79:25-6 N '66
Manner of speaking; wit and grace. J. Ciardi. Sat R 49:22 Jl 9 '66
Speaking out; only fools laugh at their woes. A. Wilson. Sat Eve Post 239:12+ My 21 '66
Tallest dwarf in the world; ed. by E. Miller. W. Allen. il Seventeen 25:158-9+ My '66
See also
Comedy
Television broadcasting—Humor

Bibliography
Curl up and read. H. Hierth. Seventeen 25:13 Jl '66

HUMOR, American
American humor: hardly a laughing matter; Time essay. Time 87:46-7 Mr 4 '66
American humor, 1966. W. K. Zinsser. il Horizon 8:116-20 Spr '66

HUMOR, English
Speaking out; only fools laugh at their woes. A. Wilson. Sat Eve Post 239:12+ My 21 '66

HUMOR, Negro. See Negro humor

HUMOR, Pictorial
What's so funny? P. Caulfield. il Mod Phot 30:68-75 My '66
See also
Caricatures and cartoons
Comics (books, strips, etc)

HUMOR, Russian
Russia cracks jokes about China. A. Parry. il N Y Times Mag p 14-15+ Je 26 '66

HUMORISTS
See also
Negro comedians

HUMPERDINCK, Engelbert
Sadler's Wells Hansel and Gretel; does Angel have the dark horse of the season's operatic recordings? J. Maclain. Am Rec G 32:546 F '66

HUMPHREY, Doris
Turtle and the bee. E. Stodelle. il Dance Mag 40:16-19 Mr '66

HUMPHREY, Hubert Horatio, 1882?-1949
My father. H. H. Humphrey. por Atlan 218:81-4+ N '66; Same abr. with title Legacy my father left me. Read Digest 90:75-9 Ja '67

HUMPHREY, Hubert Horatio. 1911-
Excerpt from address, August 27, 1965. Cong Digest 45:76+ Mr '66
GH and the VP; comments during visit to GH. pors Good H 162:56+ Ap '66
Humphrey: space program is here to stay; interview. pors Tech W 19:12-13 S 5 '66
Humphrey: the man with one arrow; interview. ed. by E. J. Hughes. por Newsweek 67:28-9 Ap 4 '66
Impact of technology on world trade and economic development; address, November 16, 1966. Dept State Bul 55:960-5 D 26 '66
My father. por Atlan 218:81-4+ N '66; Same abr. with title Legacy my father left me. Read Digest 90:75-9 Ja '67
New aspects of the Alliance for progress; address, November 10, 1966. Dept State Bul 55:878-82 D 12 '66
Perspective on Asia; address, June 8, 1966. Dept State Bul 55:2-6 Jl 4 '66; Same. Vital Speeches 32:532-5 Jl 15 '66
Remarks, February 8, 1966. Dept State Bul 54:309 F 28 '66
Responsibilities of world leadership; address, April 25, 1966. Dept State Bul 54:769-72 My 16 '66

HUMPHREY, Hubert Horatio, 1911- —*Cont.*
Science forecast by HHH; excerpts from address. Sci N 90:52 Jl 23 '66
Solving the Nation's travel arithmetic. Sat R 49:52 Mr 12 '66
United States tasks and responsibilities in Asia; address, March 11, 1966. Dept State Bul 54:523-8 Ap 4 '66
Vice President Humphrey reports to President on Asian trip; text of memorandum; March 6, 1966. Dept State Bul 54:489-91 Mr 28 '66
Vice President Humphrey returns from Far East mission; remarks, January 3, 1966. Dept State Bul 54:114-15 Ja 24 '66
Vietnam: why we stay; excerpt from address, April 25, 1966. Read Digest 89:47-9 Jl '66
We do not want a group to shoot its way into power; excerpts from interview. por U S News 60:71-2+ Mr 14 '66
We need your inventive skill! pors Pop Sci 188:102-5 Te '66
World food and population crisis: DAC's fifth annual high-level meeting; remarks, July 20, 1966. Dept State Bul 55:202-5 Ag 8 '66
Your government and your schools; summary of address. por PTA Mag 61:8-10 S '66
—and Kittikachorn, Thanom
Vice President reviews Asian problems with Thai premier; joint communique, February 15, 1966. Dept State Bul 54:396-7 Mr 14 '66

about

Back of the Humphrey mission. il por U S News 60:33 F 21 '66
Be it ever so humble. Newsweek 67:34 Mr 28 '66
Bright spirit. il pors Time 87:21-5 Ap 1 '66
Can Hubert Humphrey's dream come true? A. H. Sypher. il por Nations Bsns 54:27-8 Ag '66
Diligent student who is nothing but may be everything. H. Sidey. il por Life 61:50 S 16 '66
For now, at least, apartment for the veep. il U S News 61:22 O 10 '66
Front runners for '72. W. Weaver, jr. il pors N Y Times Mag p26-7+ My 22 '66
Globe-trotting with the veep. il pors Newsweek 67:39-40 F 28 '66
Have talking cell, will travel. il por Time 87:24 F 25 '66
HHH as I knew him. O. Doty. NEA J 55: 16-17 S '66
Humphrey and 1972. W. V. Shannon. Commonweal 83:629-30 Mr 4 '66
Humphrey mission: questions abroad, and in Congress. il pors U S News 60:16 F 28 '66
Humphrey on Kennedy, a remark, then a rollback. por U S News 61:22 O 10 '66
Humphrey's chickens. K. Crawford. Newsweek 67:38 Mr 14 '66
Humphrey's dilemma. Christian Cent 83: 325-6 Mr 16 '66
Humphrey's old pals. A. Kopkind. New Repub 154:19-22 My 7 '66; Discussion. 154: 37-8 My 21 '66
Humphrey's role: selling a consensus. il por U S News 60:20 Mr 7 '66
Kennedy vs. Humphrey: what it's all about. il por U S News 60:54-5 Mr 28 '66
Life of a salesman. il Newsweek 67:25-6 Mr 7 '66
Little White House for vice president? il por U S News 60:58-9 Mr 28 '66
Not so ancient history: annual meeting of ADA. Nation 202:538 My 9 '66
Old characters in new roles. C. Fritchey. Harper 233:30+ Jl '66
Old Hubert: cheerleader for the war in Vietnam. New Repub 154:7 Mr 12 '66
Restrained optimism. il Time 87:25-6 Mr 4 '66
Rugged road ahead for Hubert Humphrey. por U S News 61:21 S 12 '66
Second front. il Newsweek 67:35-6 F 21 '66
Still talking. por Time 87:27A-27B Mr 18 '66
Twelfth annual Mr Travel award. il pors Travel 126:38-40+ Jl '66
Washington: ten of its most powerful men. il por Vogue 148:150-1 N 15 '66
What party leaders think of Bobby Kennedy's future. il por U S News 61:54-6 S 26 '66
While LBJ was under surgery. por U S News 61:15 N 28 '66
Who is Hubert, what is he? J. Richardson. por Esquire 66:106-8+ N '66
Why Humphrey believes he'll be on the ticket in '68. il U S News 61:28 O 3 '66

HUMPHREY, Hubert Horatio, family
Hubert Humphrey takes time off. V. Glaser. il pors Look 30:47-8+ Ap 19 '66

HUMPHREY, Richard
VHF/FM marine radio service. Pop Electr 24: 67-70+ Je '66
VHF marine radio's new horizon. Electr World 75:50-2 Ja '66
V.H.F. radio conference at boat show. Electr World 75:29+ Ap '66
Weather when you want it. Motor B 119:107-8+ Ja '67
Who do you call when there's nobody there? Motor B 117:114+ Ap '66
HUMPHREYS, Richard F.
Engineering education for what? adaptation of address, April 1, 1965. Sch & Soc 94: 39-41 Ja 22 '66
HUMPHRIES, Lynn
Businessmen's expectations. Duns R 88:13 S '66
HUMPHRIES, Rolfe
(tr) See Garcia Lorca, F. Song of the little death
Virtue intense, most bright and active grace. B. Spacks. Poetry 108:337-9 Ag '66
HUMPHRY, James, 3d
Books in the field: art. bibliog por Wilson Lib Bul 41:296-300+ N '66
HUNGARIAN language
Notes from a European diary, 1963-64. E. Wilson. New Yorker 42:103-4+ Je 4 '66
HUNGARIAN national ballet. See Ballet—Hungary
HUNGARIANS
Budapest: ten years after the Hungarian revolution. L. Gross. il Look 30:106-10+ N 1 '66
Road back to Budapest. T. Foote. il N Y Times Mag p56-7+ N 20 '66
HUNGARY
See also
Arts and crafts—Hungary
Ballet—Hungary
Budapest
Catholic church in Hungary
Communism—Hungary
Sopron

Economic conditions

Atlantic report. Atlan 218:36+ O '66
Painful cure; profit-oriented system. Newsweek 67:33-4 F 7 '66

Foreign relations

Little boxes; Hungarian mines washed over to Austria. il Time 87:41 My 20 '66

History
Revolution, 1956

Hungary in revolt, November 1956; reprints from November 1956 issue. S. Parry and others. il Nat R 18:1105-10 N 1 '66
Hungary's ill-fated fight for freedom. il Sr Schol 89:4-6 O 21 '66
Road back to Budapest. T. Foote. il N Y Times Mag p56-7+ N 20 '66
HUNGER
Food processing, key to economic development. G. C. Lodge. Harvard Bsns R 44:6-8+ S '66
See also
Famines
HUNGER strikes
Hero or a fool? T. MacSwiney, rebel during Irish revolt. Sr Schol 89:3 O 28 '66
HUNGRY I, San Francisco. See Night clubs
HUNN, Max
Cruising Florida's cricks. Motor B 117:180+ Mr '66
Floating down the river in a house. Pop Mech 125:129-31 Mr '66
Look at Georgia's Lake Lanier. Motor B 118:36-7+ S '66
Small boats are tops for tarpon. Motor B 117:40-1+ Ap '66
This tree builds land. il Am For 72:13 My '66
HUNNICUTT, J. M.
Meet parking demands before they beat you. Am City 81:113+ D '66
HUNSICKER, H. N.
Farmers of the future. por Am Ed 2:20-2 F '66
HUNT, Elsie D.
Why I've changed my mind about our mortgage with a view. Farm J 90:75+ O '66
HUNT, Haroldson Lafayette
Just plain H. L. Hunt. T. Buckley. il por Esquire 67:64-9+ Ja '67
HUNT, James F.
Great rewards and great frustrations. Motor B 117:54-5+ F '66
HUNT, James R.
System in Hawaii; address, July 1966. pors ALA Bul 60:1142-6 D '66

HUNT, James Stone
Bored by retirement, he builds an empire. il pors Bsns W p 162-4+ F 26 '66
HUNT, Jane
Sarah, waiting; story. Seventeen 25:108-9 Je; 96-7 Jl '66
HUNT, Janet
Easy desserts children can make. Parents Mag 41:87 O '66
HUNT, John Clark
Forest that men made. Am For 71:18-21+ N; 32-5+ D '65; Correction. 72:3 Ja '66
HUNT, Joseph McVicker
Can we make human beings more intelligent? interview, ed. by J. K. Lagemann. Read Digest 88:77-81 My '66
HUNT, Mabel Leigh
On high ground. Horn Bk 42:398 Ag '66
HUNT, Morton M.
Help wanted: divorce counselor. N Y Times Mag p 14-17 Ja 1 '67
World of the formerly married; excerpts. McCalls 93:53-5+ Ag; 94-5+ S; 94:126-7+ O '66
HUNT, Naomi L.
Creative leisure in the Nation's capital. Parks & Rec 1:564-5+ Jl '66
HUNT, Pearson
Fallacy of the one big brain. Harvard Bsns R 44:84-90 Jl '66
HUNT, Wilson Price
Ordeal in Hell's Canyon. A. M. Josephy, jr. il por Am Heritage 18:72-9+ D '66
HUNT foods and industries, incorporated
Simon says it with a broad brush. il Bsns W p62-4+ My 14 '66
HUNTER, Evan
Paper dragon; condensation of novel. Ladies Home J 83:89-96 Je '66
HUNTER, John M.
Colombia: a tarnished showcase. bibliog f Cur Hist 51:276-83+ N '66
HUNTER, Madeline C.
Teachers in the nongraded school. NEA J 55:12-15 F '66
HUNTER-farmer relations. See Farmer-hunter relations
HUNTERS
Alaska's greatest hunter: Peter Koonuknoruck. C. E. Gillham. il Field & S 71:28-30+ Ag '66
   See also
Farmer-hunter relations
HUNTING
Gist of it: digest of the outdoor news, ed. by H. Moore. See issues of Outdoor life
Hit them exactly right. J. O'Connor. il Outdoor Life 138:68+ Ag '66
Sportsman's notebook. H. G. Tapply. See issues of Field & stream
Twenty ways to improve your hunting. S. Dolley. il Field & S 71:52-3+ D '66
Where to go fishing, vacationing, hunting. C. Fish. See issues of Outdoor life
   See also
Falconry
Poaching
Whaling
   also Deer hunting and similar headings
   Accidents and injuries
Blood sport. Time 88:45 D 30 '66
   Anecdotes, facetiae, satire, etc.
What is good shooting? J. O'Connor. il Outdoor Life 139:28+ Ja '67
   Equipment and supplies
   See Hunting outfits
   History
Study of hunters urged. il Sci N 89:315 Ap 30 '66
   Safety devices and measures
Color blindness. S. Lowell. Field & S 71:146+ My '66
   Alabama
Reformation of Bill. S. B. Holleman. il Outdoor Life 137:52-3+ Mr '66
Shooting on Mr Bud's place; L. B. Maytag's plantation in Union Springs. V. Kraft. il Sports Illus 25:50-4 N 21 '66
   Alaska
Big game hunting forecast. il Field & S 71:98-9 Ag '66
Haystack bear. J. Rearden. il Outdoor Life 137:44-6+ Je '66
Hunter against odds. T. Howell. il Outdoor Life 138:39-41+ O '66
Jan Koslosky of Alaska: new breed of frontiersman. H. Ehrlich. il Look 31:46-9 Ja 10 '67

Nemesis of the black brant. R. Cantwell. il Sports Illus 24:44-6+ My 16 '66
Roy Rogers goes north. W. E. A. Anderson. il Outdoor Life 137:52-5+ Ap '66
Trail to buck mountain. F. Dufresne. il Field & S 71:40-1+ O '66
Trophy you'll never get. R. W. Young. il Field & S 71:42-3+ Ag '66
Two-time loser. E. Stevens. il Outdoor Life 137:36-9+ My '66
Wolves ain't so smart. W. Page. il Field & S 70:65-7+ Mr '66

   Arctic Regions
Luck of the Yukon. B. O'Connor. il Outdoor Life 138:20-3+ Jl '66

   Arizona
Conning and killing cunning coyotes. R. Cantwell. il Sports Illus 25:61-4 N 7 '66

   British Guiana
Devil jaguar. S. E. Brock. il Outdoor Life 137:44-7+ F '66

   California
All-season big game; wild pigs. J. Ruch. il Field & S 71:48-9+ Ag '66
Bandtail flyby. J. Mears. il Outdoor Life 138:46-7+ S '66
Ducks are flying again. V. Kraft. il Sports Illus 25:50-2+ O 3 '66
Magic circle, shortcut to weekend sport. J. Freeman. il Outdoor Life 138:64-6+ O '66
More chukar hunters needed. C. Dickey. il Field & S 71:68-71+ S '66
Old Wino's last stand. F. J. Evans. il Outdoor Life 138:44-7+ Ag '66
Very easy birds to miss; valley quail. T. Trueblood. il Field & S 71:28-30+ N '66

   Canada
All American goose; Canada goose. F. Dufresne. il Field & S 71:62-3+ N '66
Bad luck *oogruk.* C. E. Gillham. il Field & S 70:46-8+ Mr '66
Big game hunting forecast. il Field & S 71:98-9 Ag '66
Fabulous Smoky River; Alberta. R. M. Hobbs. il Field & S 71:54-5+ O '66
Farewell, Eric Collier. E. Collier. il Outdoor Life 139:54-5+ Ja '67
Hunt for the records; trophies to qualify for Boone and Crockett listings. A. F. Benson. il Outdoor Life 138:20-3+ Ag '66
Invisible moose. E. Westgarde. il Outdoor Life 137:32-5+ Je '66
Last frontier; new hunting country. R. M. Hobbs. il Outdoor Life 137:44-7+ Mr '66
Long quest. L. T. Empey. il Outdoor Life 137:50-3+ Je '66
October holiday. C. Ford. il Field & S 71:42-5+ O '66
Ross and his ram. D. Peck. il Outdoor Life 138:34-5+ Ag '66
Rugged place for a picnic; desolate Northwest Territories. D. Barnes. il Sports Illus 24:78-80+ My 2 '66
Two for the book. W. Page. il Field & S 71:23-5+ Jl '66

   Colorado
Elk to whistle about. F. W. Davis. il Outdoor Life 137:62-4+ F '66
Harder they come; ed. by B. East. C. Atwood. il Outdoor Life 138:64-7+ O '66
Hunting's best-kept secret; postseason on deer. R. Tinsley. il Field & S 71:25-7+ Ag '66
Summer deer hunt. P. Barrett. il Outdoor Life 138:28-31+ Jl '66

   Connecticut
Snow hunt for stew. G. Heinold. il Outdoor Life 138:62-4+ S '66

   Delaware
Bobwhites teach me a lesson. T. Janes. il Outdoor Life 138:54-5+ D '66

   Europe, Eastern
Don't shoot unless you're loaded; hunting behind the iron curtain. C. Thayer. il Sports Illus 25:96-102+ D 5 '66

   Florida
New gamebird for the South? pheasant. G. X. Sand. il Outdoor Life 137:40-1+ Je '66

   France
Mixed bag in the chateau country. W. Page. il Field & S 71:60-1 O '66

HUNTING—*Continued*

Great Lakes Region

Compleat hunter; Plains states. M. Ellis. il Field & S 71:117-20 S '66

Georgia

No hunting and fishing; Pioneer Georgia project. G. H. Gillelan. il Outdoor Life 137:29-31+ Mr '66

Guyana

Cattle slayers of Shiwishi-win. S. E. Brock. il Outdoor Life 138:66-9+ N '66

Honduras

Big Red's jaguar. W. Page. il Field & S 71:44-5+ Ja '67

Idaho

Bighorn by the seat of my pants. G. Gresham. il Field & S 71:37-9+ O '66
Where hunters never fail. L. Miracle. il Outdoor Life 137:60-1+ Je '66

Illinois

Ghosts of the Shawnee; whitetail-deer hunting. B. Cary. il Outdoor Life 138:32-7 N '66

India

Bold, bad tiger of Ghatpiparia. J. O'Connor. il Outdoor Life 137:36-9+ Mr '66
Man-eaters of Naini Tal. F. Turner. il Outdoor Life 138:67-81 D '66

Iowa

Grandest hunting of all; cottontail. H. Bradshaw. il Field & S 71:66-7+ N '66
Hitting the hot line; hunting rabbits with a beagle. H. Bradshaw. il Outdoor Life 137:56-8+ F '66

Kansas

Kansas' first deer hunt; whitetails and mule deer. A. Weaver. il Outdoor Life 138:64-5+ N '66

Kentucky

I shot Big Red. C. W. Shelton. il Outdoor Life 139:44-5+ Ja '67
Kentucky's happiest hunting ground; Primitive weapons hunting area, Cumberland national forest. J. Hayes. il Field & S 71:58-61+ N '66

Louisiana

Bee thrashing in Louisiana. J. Blanchard. il Field & S 71:146-8+ S '66

Maine

Charley Varney's deer farm. N. Karas. il Field & S 71:58-9+ O '66
Comfort in cold covers. B. Elliot. il Outdoor Life 139:56-7+ Ja '67
Farm-fed whitetails. B. Geagan. il Field & S 71:68-9+ N '66
Go to sea for ducks. J. B. Robinson. il Outdoor Life 138:39-41+ N '66
Greatest hunting of all; black bear. B. Mason. il Outdoor Life 138:42-5+ N '66
Old hole-in-the-head. P. D. Smith. il Outdoor Life 138:32-3 D '66
Think like a deer. M. E. Barker. il Field & S 71:46-7+ O '66

Maryland

Deer you hunt like rabbit. C. Robinson. il Field & S 71:52-3+ O '66
High-tide tidbit. C. Robinson. il Field & S 71:53-5+ S '66

Massachusetts

Custom-made hunters; introducing waterfowl shooting; project by the Boston office of U.S. bureau of sport fisheries and wildlife. H. Titus. il Field & S 71:72-3+ N '66

Mexico

Bargain jaguar. O. A. Washburn. il Field & S 71:50-2+ Ag '66
Tigre is behind us! C. J. McElroy. il Outdoor Life 139:35-7+ Ja '67

Michigan

Death walked the duck marsh; ed. by B. East. E. La Fountain. il Outdoor Life 137:60-1+ Ap '66
Michigan elk, no longer sacred cows. J. Chiappetta. il Field & S 71:36-7+ Ag '66
Thanksgiving hunt. J. McPhee. il Outdoor Life 137:60-1+ My '66
Whitetails in the sands. J. O. Cartier. il Outdoor Life 138:46-9+ N '66

Middle western states

Compleat hunter; Plains states. M. Ellis. il Field & S 71:117-20 S '66

Missouri

Ozark quail with a twist. D. Duffey. pors Outdoor Life 139:68-9+ Ja '67
Talk about doves; interviews. J. Parks: H. Banks. il Field & S 71:56-7+ S '66

Mongolia

I hunt Mongolia's argali. G. H. Landreth. il Outdoor Life 138:32-5+ S '66

Montana

Giant of Mission creek; ed. by J. O. Cartier. L. L. Julie. il Outdoor Life 138:46-7+ D '66
Montana mixture. G. Gresham. il Field & S 71:44-7 Ag '66

Mozambique

Africa's meanest game. F. Bear. il Outdoor Life 137:32-5+ F '66
My greatest trophy. F. Bear. il Outdoor Life 137:36-9+ Ap '66

Nebraska

More deer than hunters. G. Hornbeck. il Field & S 71:49-51+ O '66

Nepal

Yaks and yeti. V. Gilmore. il Sat R 49:38+ Ap 23 '66

Nevada

Get a good thing going. K. Hueftle. il Outdoor Life 137:62-3+ My '66
New kind of trophy hunt. J. K. Cope. il Outdoor Life 139:66-7+ Ja '67

New Jersey

Pigeons vs. pints. E. Zern. il Field & S 71:64-5+ My '66
They don't yell yoicks! in New Jersey. B. Lefferts. il N Y Times Mag p52-3+ D 4 '66

New Mexico

Pronghorns in the pasture. D. Hamilton. il Outdoor Life 137:54-5+ F '66
Truth or consequences quail. P. Czura. il Field & S 71:47-9 S '66

New York (state)

Fire Island fox hunt. N. Karas. il Field & S 71:48-9 Ja '67
New place for rabbits. N. Karas. il Outdoor Life 138:70-1+ O '66

New Zealand

New Zealand at the crossroads. F. C. Hibben. il Field & S 71:12-13+ Ag '66

North Dakota

Found; new duck bonanza. J. O. Cartier. il Outdoor Life 138:52-5+ S '66

Northeastern states

Compleat hunter. H. Grey. il Field & S 71:153-6 S '66

Northwestern states

Pheasant is a clever bird. T. Trueblood. il Field & S 71:64-7+ S '66

Ohio

Longest coon hunt. M. Mudd. il Outdoor Life 137:44-7+ My '66
Luck of Irish ridge; ed. by M. C. Gilfillan. D. Allison. il Outdoor Life 138:56-7+ D '66
New look of duck hunting. E. A. Bauer. il Outdoor Life 138:42-5+ O '66
Shot in the dark; hunting with bow-and-arrow. H. Cox. il Outdoor Life 137:56-9+ Mr '66
Turkey are back. G. Laycock. il Field & S 71:70-1+ N '66

Oregon

Bird hunter's Shangri-la; chukars in Hell's Canyon. L. Miracle. il Outdoor Life 138:62-3+ N '66
Pleasure before work. L. Miracle. il Outdoor Life 137:42-3+ Ap '66
Very easy birds to miss; valley quail. T. Trueblood. il Field & S 71:28-30+ N '66

Pennsylvania

Born to tree coon. D. J. Anderson. il Field & S 71:52-3+ N '66
Cottontails or snowshoes? J. Chiappetta. il Field & S 71:50-2+ Ja '57
Giant of Newcomer Hollow; ed. by J. Hayes. R. E. Miller. il Outdoor Life 137:38-9+ F '66
Harsh-voice fever. D. Sweigard. il Outdoor Life 139:62-5+ Ja '67

HUNTING—Pennsylvania—Continued

Long Tom. D. J. Anderson. il Field & S 70: 38-40+ F '66

One thousand yard bucks. K. C. Hinman. il Field & S 71:56-7+ O '66

South Carolina

Hunting atomic energy reserve. C. Elliott. il Outdoor Life 138:42-3+ Ag '66

South Dakota

Come hither coyote. H. Bradshaw. il Field & S 71:44-5+ D '66

Southern states

Compleat hunter. G. Gresham. il Field & S 71:133-6 S '66

Yankee dog hunts in Dixie. C. Ford. il Field & S 70:138-40+ F '66

Southwestern states

What's tough about javelina. B. W. Dalrymple. il Outdoor Life 138:52-3+ N '66

Tanganyika

My heart-attack trophies; hunting Cape buffalo. E. A. Bauer. il Field & S 70:43-5+ Mr '66

Tanzania

Put a lion in your tank; tennis players on African safari. B. Collins. il Sports Illus 25:36-8+ Jl 25 '66

Tennessee

Alone with the squirrels. C. Vinson. il Outdoor Life 138:62-3+ O '66

Texas

Deep in the heart of darkest Texas. D. Barnes. il Sports Illus 24:57-8+ My 23 '66

Surefire deer country; west Texas' Big Bend country. B. W. Dalrymple. il Outdoor Life 138:38-41+ D '66

Uganda

We found the elephant place. E. A. Bauer. il Outdoor Life 138:28-31+ Ag '66

United States

All American goose; Canada goose. F. Dufresne. il Field & S 71:62-3+ N '66

Field & stream 1966 hunting forecast, small & big game. Field & S 71:119-26 O '66

Forty-five experts tell where to hunt deer; symposium. il Outdoor Life 138:54-7+ O '66

How to hunt prairie grouse. D. Harbour. il Field & S 71:62-3+ S '66

October holiday. C. Ford. il Field & S 71: 42-5+ O '66

Off and gunning. Sports Illus 25:10 O 31 '66

Utah

Lion hunters are nuts; cougar chasing in Zion National Park. W. Page. il Field & S 71:64-5 N '66

Too many bucks. G. H. Gillelan. il Outdoor Life 138:60-1+ S '66

Vermont

Fugitive of Black Mountain. D. Lawrence. il Outdoor Life 138:50-1+ O '66

Picking the pockets. H. G. Tapply. Field & S 71:137 My '66

Virginia

Chincoteague clappers. M. Rosko. il Outdoor Life 138:52-3+ O '66

New trophy for bowmen. G. H. Gillelan. il Outdoor Life 137:24+ My '66

Washington (state)

Feel free to hunt. C. Chatfield. il Outdoor Life 138:70-1+ N '66

McCormick's preposterous law. C. Chatfield. il Outdoor Life 139:42-3+ Ja '67

Our most neglected gamebird; the chukar. C. Chatfield. il Outdoor Life 137:52-3+ F '66

West Virginia

Black bear mountain; Monongahela national forest. D. Knight. il Field & S 71:34+ N '66

Mountain hospitality. E. A. Bauer. il Outdoor Life 137:14-7+ Ap '66

Western states

Compleat hunter. T. Trueblood. il Field & S 71:89-92 S '66

Wyoming

Late hunting is great hunting. B. Milek. il Field & S 71:49-51+ N '66

This is trophy hunting; mule deer. C. Elliott. il Outdoor Life 138:54-7+ N '66

Wow! what a wapiti! J. Cook. il Outdoor Life 138:56-7+ S '66

HUNTING, Primitive

Study of hunters urged. il Sci N 89:315 Ap 30 '66

HUNTING dogs

Born to tree coon. D. J. Anderson. il Field & S 71:52-3+ N '66

Dog hunters; coon hunting. G. Logsdon. il Farm J 90:68Q Mr '66

Dogs. D. M. Duffey. See issues of Outdoor life

Fox went out on a chilly night. L. Dietz. il Field & S 71:48-50+ My '66

Greatest hunting of all; black bear. B. Mason. il Outdoor Life 138:42-5+ N '66

Hunter, pet, or both? C. Dickey. il Field & S 71:106-9 Jl '66

Lost dogs; if your bird shoot turns into a dog hunt. R. Beck. il Field & S 71:116-18+ D '66

Yankee dog hunts in Dixie. C. Ford. il Field & S 70:138-40+ F '66

See also

Dachshunds

HUNTING knives. See Bowie knives

HUNTING laws. See Game laws

HUNTING on farm lands. See Farmer-hunter relations

HUNTING outfits

Motorized buck buggy. R. Chaplin. il Outdoor Life 138:74 N '66

One thousand yard bucks. K. C. Hinman. il Field & S 71:56-7+ O '66

HUNTING preserves. See Game preserves

HUNTING rifles. See Rifles

HUNTING season; story. See Greenberg, J.

HUNTING trophies. See Trophies, Sport

HUNTING with bow and arrow

Africa's meanest game. F. Bear. il Outdoor Life 137:32-5+ F '66

Archery. G. H. Gillelan. See issues of Outdoor life

Backyard record deer; ed. by H. Kenny. M. Johnson. il Field & S 71:50-1+ Jl '66

Bear that broke a jinx. F. Bear. il Outdoor Life 138:35-7+ D '66

Kansas' first deer hunt; whitetails and mule deer. A. Weaver. il Outdoor Life 138: 64-5+ N '66

My greatest trophy. F. Bear. il Outdoor Life 137:36-9+ Ap '66

Shot in the dark; hunting with bow-and-arrow. H. Cox. il Outdoor Life 137:56-9+ Mr '66

Too many bucks. G. H. Gillelan. il Outdoor Life 138:60-1+ S '66

Whitetails vs. mule deer. G. H. Gillelan. il Outdoor Life 138:26+ S '66

HUNTINGTON, James

On the edge of nowhere; condensation. ed. by L. Elliott. por Read Digest 89:189-93+ Ag '66

HUNTINGTON, Roger

ABCs of carburetion. Pop Mech 126:120-3+ D '66

Belt drives. Hot Rod 19:60-2 Mr '66

Important features of Detroit's 1967 models. Consumer Bul 49:18-23 N '66

HUNTINGTON, N.Y.

Deep water harbors, gratis! B. D. Barker. 3d. il Yachting 119:218+ Mr '66

Historic houses, etc.

Walt Whitman's home. il Travel 126:43-5 O '66

HUNTINGTON, N.Y. public library

Huntington pl tries Sunday library hours. Library J 91:2184+ Ap 15 '66

HUNTLEY, Chet

Anniversary talk with Huntley & Brinkley; interview. ed. by J. F. Fixx. por McCalls 94:56+ O '66

HUNTZINGER, Robert

Big Hoosier hurry; photographs. Sports Illus 24:30-5 My 30 '66

HUPÉ, Robert Strausz-. See Strausz-Hupé, R.

HUPP, Burr W.

Distribution's endless route. Duns R 87:pt2 134-6+ Mr '66

HURD, Clement

Clement Hurd; children's book illustrator as artist and exhibitor. il por Pub W 189:106-8 F 7 '66

HURD, E. S.

Better forests from blue ribbon trees. Am For 72:12-14+ Je '66

HURD, Peter
Another image problem. il por Newsweek 69:22 Ja 16 '67
Critic's choice. il por Time 89:12-13 Ja 13 '67
LBJ on canvas. il por Newsweek 67:19 F 7 '66

HURLBURT, Marjorie L. See Gott, H. T. jt. auth.

HURLER syndrome. See Lipochondrodystrophy

HURLEY, Mark J.
Vatican II and Catholic education; interview, ed. by W. K. Richards. por Sr Schol 88:sup5 My 13 '66

HURLEY, Neil P.
Satellite communications. America 115:204-6 Ag 27 '66

HURRICANE simulators. See Simulators

HURRICANES
At war with the weather. B. Tufty. il Sci N 90:26-7 Jl 9 '66
Hold back the sea; New Bedford, Mass. F. C. Gray, jr. il Yachting 120:54+ Jl '66
Hurricane barrier for New Bedford. W. F. Mackie. il Motor B 117:197-8 Ap '66
Hurricane protection; Fox Point Hurricane Dam project in Providence, R.I. il Am City 81:78 Jl '66
Lessons learned from hurricane Betsy. il Am City 81:93-6 Ap '66
Long lurid life of hurricane Betsy. A. E. Sik. il Motor B 118:38-40+ Ag '66
Storm tests launch mobility concept. il Aviation W 84:175 Je 20 '66
Time of the twister; Alma's path. Newsweek 67:34 Je 20 '66
What to do in a hurricane. E. Crimmin. il Sci Digest 60:80-2 Ag '66

HURSTON, Zora Neale
Zora Neale Hurston: author and folklorist. E. L. Blake. por Negro Hist Bul 29:149-50+ Ap '66

HURT, Henry
Boycott and ballot. Reporter 35:23+ Ag 11 '66

HURWITZ, Al
Creativity; questions and answers. pors Sch Arts 65:30-3 Ja '66
Project; a living community park. Sch Arts 65:17-19 Ap '66

HURWITZ, Howard L.
New books on American history. Sr Schol 88:sup 12+ Mr 4; sup9-10 Mr 11 '66
[New books on world history] Sr Schol 88: sup 10-11 Mr 11 '66
(ed) What's new in social studies; summaries of articles and reports. Sr Schol 88:sup21 F 11; sup20-1 Mr 25; 89:sup39 S 23 '66
What's your P.S.Q? Sr Schol 89:sup26 S 23 '66

HUSAIN, L. and Kuroda, P. K.
Magnesium-28 in rain: produced by cosmic rays. bibliog Science 154:180-1 D 2 '66

HUSBAND and wife. See Domestic relations; Husbands; Marriage; Marriage counseling; Wives

HUSBANDS
More secret thoughts of a happy husband. E. Joseph. McCalls 93:125 Ag '66
Pregnancy among husbands quite common. Todays Health 44:6 S '66
Stubborn husband; case of a hard of hearing husband. il Good H 162:12+ Mr '66
What kind of man will you marry? N. Goodman and D. Klein. il Seventeen 25: 156-7+ Ap '66
When can infidelity be justified or forgiven? results of McCall's questioning 1,112 men and women. S. Blum. il McCalls 93:73+ My '66
Why husbands don't say what they really think; summary of survey. A. Whitman. il McCalls 93:75+ S '66
Why men don't listen or talk to their wives. S. Blum. il McCalls 93:78-9+ F '66; Same abr. with title Why men don't talk to their wives. Read Digest 88:55-8 My '66
Why shouldn't husbands dry the dishes! J. Brothers. Good H 162:26 +Mr '66
See also
Domestic relations
Marriage
Widowers
Wives

HUSSEIN, king of Jordan
What the Russians are up to in the Middle East; interview, ed. by J. Law. por U S News 61:39-42 D 26 '66

about

Arab and Jew. il Newsweek 68:44 D 19 '66
Everybody loses. Newsweek 68:42+ D 5 '66
Flare-up in Mideast; another danger spot. J. Law. il por U S News 61:50 D 19 '66

Gamble on the Jordan. J. A. Morris, jr. il Nation 204:6-8 Ja 2 '67
In Jordan a spunky king again fights to hold on. G. DeCarvalho. il por Life 61:50B D 9 '66
King on the spot. il por Time 88:30+ Jl 8 '66
Ready for trouble. il por Time 88:44 D 9 '66
Second thoughts. il por Newsweek 68:56+ D 12 '66
Sequel to Samu. Time 88:38+ D 2 '66
Tension below the surface. Time 88:42 D 16 '66
Three kings in accord. por Time 87:37 F 4 '66

HUSTON, John
Maestro Huston. por Newsweek 67:89 Mr 7 '66

HUSTON, Perdita
Chick off the literary block. Life 60:59-60 My 13 '66

HUSTWITT, Arthur
CBA meets in Chicago; report of convention. Pub W 190:34-6 S 5 '66

HUTCHENS, James
Chopper chaplains. por Time 87:68 F 11 '66

HUTCHENS, John K.
One thing and another (cont) Sat R 49:35 Mr 5; 25+ My 21; 44-5 Je 11; 25-6 Ag 13; 97-9 O 8; 45-6 D 24 '66

HUTCHIN, Kenneth Charles
The change and what husbands should know about it; adaptation from How not to kill your wife. Todays Health 44:54-6+ S '66

HUTCHINGS, Hugh M.
You are invited to attend U.S. power squadrons free instruction classes in boat operation. por Motor B 118:74-6 Ag '66

HUTCHINSON, Ann
New approaches to new questions; report on the fifth National notation conference. Dance Mag 40:20-1 Ag '66

HUTCHINSON, Edward P.
(ed) New immigration. bibliog f Ann Am Acad 367:1-149 S '66
New immigration: an introductory comment. Ann Am Acad 367:1-3 S '66

HUTCHINSON, James
Painting among the Seminoles. Am Artist 30:52-7+ Ap '66

HUTCHISON, Bruce. See Reston, J. jt. auth.

HUTCHISON, Victor H. and others
Thermoregulation in a brooding female Indian python, python molurus bivittatus. bibliog Science 151:694-6 F 11 '66

HUTH, Hans
German japanned wares. Antiques 89:695-9 My '66

HUTTER, Donald
Valedictory; story. Esquire 65:110-11 My '66

HUTTO, Henry
Meditation on the Nicene creed; poem. Christian Cent 83:1177 S 28 '66
We yawned; poem. Christian Cent 83:334 Mr 16 '66

HUXLEY, Aldous
Aldous Huxley, ed. by J. Huxley. Review
New Repub 154:23-4 Mr 26 '66. F. Getlein
Aldous Huxley, cordial, witty, civilized man. J. Stafford. Vogue 147:57 F 15 '66
Man who tried everything. R. Bradbury. Life 60:12 F 11 '66

HUXLEY, Elspeth
African affairs (cont) por Nat R 18:163-4, 435, 877-8, 989 F 22, My 3, S 6, O 4 '66
Letter from Africa. por Nat R 18:268-70, 569 Mr 22, Je 14 '66
What a top authority says about Africa's future; interview, ed. by J. Fromm. por U S News 60:56-7 Mr 14 '66

HUXTABLE, Ada Louise (Landman)
Home. N Y Times Mag p64-5+ F 13 '66

HUYCK, Dorothy Boyle
Honeymoon year. Am For 72:22-5+ D '66
National forests come alive: new vistas through VIS. Am For 72:12-16 Ap '66

HWUI Shan
Was America the wonderful land of Fusang? R. Larson. il Am Heritage 17:42-5+ Ap '66

HYACINTHS
Here's help in buying hyacinths. il Sunset 137:256 O '66
New ways with hyacinths. W. Meachem. il Horticulture 44:18-19+ O '66

HYALINE membrane disease
Newborns' disease linked to high-risk mothers. Todays Health 45:17 Ja '67
Pulmonary arterial vasculature in neonatal hyaline membrane disease. J. M. Lauwer-yns. bibliog il Science 153:1275-7 S 9 '66

HYAMS, Joe
Haunted. pors Sat Eve Post 239:28-31 Jl 2 '66; Same abr. with title Our haunted house. Read Digest 89:74-8 N '66

HYBRID corn. See Corn—Hybrids

HYBRID lilies. See Lilies

HYBRIDIZATION
Glucuronidase gene expression in somatic hybrids. R. Ganschow. bibliog il Science 153:84-5 Jl 1 '66
See also
Heterosis (biology)
Tree breeding

HYDE, Bryden B.
Living with antiques. Antiques 89:233-7 F '66

HYDE, Donald Frizell
Obituary
Pub W 189:109-10 F 14 '66

HYDE, George A.
Hollow tree. America 115:833-4 D 24 '66

HYDE, Rosei Herschel
Reluctant regulator heads the FCC. por Bsns W p42 Je 25 '66

HYDE PARK Vanderbilt estate. See Vanderbilt national historic site

HYDLE, Lars
Our man in Saigon. por Am Ed 3:6-8 D '66

HYDRATES
Pressure-induced dehydration reactions and transitions in inorganic hydrates. R. R. Sood and R. A. Stager. bibliog il Science 154:388-90 O 21 '66

HYDRAULIC control
High rise in hydraulics. G. Berkwitt. il Duns R 88:43-5+ S '66
Taking a fluid approach. il Time 88:49 D 2 '66

HYDRAULIC engineering
High rise in hydraulics. G. Berkwitt. il Duns R 88:43-5+ S '66

HYDRAULIC equipment for airplanes. See Airplanes—Hydraulic equipment

HYDRAZIDES
See also
Isoniazid

HYDRAZINE
Editorially speaking; banning use of hydrazine by American hot rod association. R. Brock. Hot Rod 19:6 D '66

HYDROCARBONS
Alkanes in fungal spores. J. Oro and others. bibliog il Science 154:399-400 O 21 '66
High-temperature synthesis of aromatic hydrocarbons from methane. J. Oró and J. Han. bibliog il Science 153:1393-5 S 16 '66
Protective action of polycyclic hydrocarbons against induction of adrenal necrosis by dimethylbenzanthracene. P. H. Jellinck and B. Goudy. bibliog il Science 152:1375-6 Je 3 '66
Terpenoid precursors of hydrocarbons from the gasoline range of petroleum. B. J. Mair and others. bibliog il Science 154:1339-41 D 9 '66

HYDROCEPHALUS
Pump aids watery brain. Sci N 90:320 O 22 '66

HYDROCORTISONE
Glucagon, starvation, and the induction of liver enzymes by hydrocortisone. O. Greengard and G. T. Baker. bibliog il Science 154:1461-2 D 16 '66
Plasma kinins and cortisol: a possible explanation of the anti-inflammatory action of cortisol. M. J. Cline and K. L. Melmon. bibliog il Science 153:1135-8 S 2 '66
Tryptophan pyrrolase induced in human liver by hydrocortisone: effect on excretion of kynurenine. K. Altman and O. Greengard. bibliog il Science 151:332-3 Ja 21 '66

HYDROCYANIC acid
Primeval soup poisonous; life-like substances formed from hydrogen cyanide. Sci N 90: 69 Jl 30 '66

HYDRODYNAMICS
Chains of particles in shear flow. I. Y. Z. Zia and others. bibliog il Science 153:1405-6 S 16 '66

HYDROELECTRIC plants
Congress and the Hudson. Natur Hist 75: 70+ O '66
French harness tides for power; St Malo tidal dam. il Bsns W p 108-10 Ap 30 '66
Guns and butter plus; Dickey-Lincoln scheme. R. Moley. Newsweek 67:96 F 28 '66
Imperial power; Churchill Falls project. il Time 88:105 O 14 '66
Nam Ngum development fund. UN Mo Chron 3:34-5 Ap; 38 Je '66
Power from Labrador; Churchill Falls hydroelectric plant. Bsns W p52 O 15 '66
Storm King. Liv Wildn 29:42-3 Wint '65
Storm King gets a reprieve. il Am For 72:5 F '66
Storm King opinion: stunning conservation victory. R. E. Train. Am For 72:10-11 Mr '66

Storm King project; licensing order set aside by United States Court of appeals. Nat Parks Mag 40:20 F '66
Storm on the Hudson. Natur Hist 75:6-7 Je '66
World's biggest power station gets go-ahead; Churchill Falls, Labrador. Sci N 90:376 N 5 '66
See also
Electric transmission

HYDROELECTRIC power
Abundance of alternatives; Colorado River basin fund. A. W. Smith. Nat Parks Mag 40:2+ Jl '66
Canada's coming export; hydroelectric power. il U S News 60:74-6 F 7 '66
U.S. and Canada to negotiate for development of Saint John River; Department announcement; with texts of notes exchanged. Dept State Bul 54:67-8 Ja 10 '66
See also
Tennessee Valley authority
Tide power

HYDROFOIL models
Up-and-flying model sailboat; aerohydrofoil. R. L. Clough, jr. il Pop Mech 126:165-7 Ag '66

HYDROFOILS
New designs seen for patrol boats. il Miss & Roc 18:79-81 Mr 28 '66
UAC planing hull craft aimed at oilmen. R. W. Niblock. il Tech W 19:12-13 Ag 1 '66

HYDROGEN
Gas clouds speed to earth. Sci N 90:103 Ag 13 '66
High-latitude hydrogen clouds. il Sky & Tel 32:206 O '66
Hydrogen bonding specificity of nucleic acid purines and pyrimidines in solution. Y. Kyogoku and others. bibliog il Science 154:518-20 O 28 '66
Neutral hydrogen survey of Andromeda galaxy. W. D. Brundage and J. D. Kraus. bibliog il Science 153:411-14 Jl 22 '66

Isotopes

See also
Deuterium

HYDROGEN, Liquid
Fuel with fizz. Newsweek 68:88 Jl 18 '66
Taming liquid hydrogen. il Time 88:57 Jl 15 '66
Taming the tiger in Apollo's tank. il Bsns W p66+ Jl 16 '66
Uprated Saturn flight confirms, S-4B role. G. Alexander. il Aviation W 85:32-3 Jl 11 '66

HYDROGEN bombs
Bomb hunt; B-52 bomber collides over Spain. Nation 202:141-2 F 7 '66
Bomb is found. il Time 87:27 Mr 25 '66
¡La bomba recuperada! recovery of bomb lost off Spanish coast. il Time 87:27 Ap 15 '66
Case of the missing H-bomb. J. G. Hubbell. il Read Digest 89:239-44+ S '66
Case of the missing H-bomb; Palomares search. R. Oulahan. il Life 60:106A-106B F 25 '66
Deep mystery; U.S. hydrogen bomb lost off the southeast Spanish coast. Newsweek 67: 61 F 21 '66
Dunderball; H-bomb search off Spanish coast. il Time 87:33 F 4 '66
Enter the poodle; efforts to retrieve H-bomb. Newsweek 67:55 Ap 4 '66
Fabulous machines that recovered our lost H-bomb. G. Soule and A. P. Armagnac. il Pop Sci 188:86-90+ Je '66
Found; missing H-bomb. Sr Schol 88:22 Ap 1 '66
How they found the bomb; calculation by Sandia scientists of location of bomb missing off Spain. il Time 87:53 My 13 '66
How we found the missing H-bomb; rescue operation by Alvin and Aluminaut. W. O. Rainnie. il Pop Mech 126:72-8+ Ag '66
H-bomb is missing and the hunt goes on. il Newsweek 67:55-7 Mr 7 '66
H-bombs on the loose; what about the dangers? questions and answers. il U S News 60:66-8 Ap 4 '66
Is it or isn't it? finding and retrieving a missing bomb off Palomares, Spain. il Newsweek 67:47-8 Mr 28 '66
Is poison safe? Sat Eve Post 239:102 Ap 23 '66
Little sub's big score: the H-bomb is found; drama of the bomb lost off Palomares. il Life 60:34-5 Ap 1 '66
Lost H-bomb. il Sr Schol 88:6 F 25 '66
Missing bomb. Commonweal 83:549 F 11 '66

HYDROGEN bombs—*Continued*
Mystery of the missing H-bomb; bomber collision over the Spanish coast. il U S News 60:10 F 14 '66
Navy dives deep for a lost H-bomb; hunt for nuclear warhead sunk off Spanish coast. il Bsns W p32 F 5 '66
Navy presses deep-sea probes: search for H-bomb sunk off Spain. il Bsns W p72-4+ Mr 12 '66
Nuke fluke; U.S. misplaced H-bomb. Time 87:37 Mr 11 '66
Palomares learns to love the bomb. T. Szulc. il N Y Times Mag p22-3+ F 20 '66
Rescue and unveiling of an H-bomb. il U S News 60:11 Ap 18 '66
Rough sea for Charlie; attempts fail to raise bomb off Palomares. Time 87:33 Ap 1 '66
Sigh of relief; hydrogen bomb recovery off coast of Spain. il Newsweek 67:62-3 Ap 18 '66
Spanish bomb; US bomb missing in Spain. New Repub 154:8 Mr 19 '66
Still looking; H-bomb missing after the mid-air crash over Spain. Newsweek 67:33 F 7 '66
Tossing a Curv; H-bomb recovered by cable-controlled underwater research vehicle. il Bsns W p93-4 Ap 16 '66

Testing
See Atomic bombs—Testing

HYDROGEN bonding. See Hydrogen
HYDROGEN clocks. See Atomic clocks
HYDROGEN cyanide. See Hydrocyanic acid
HYDROGEN ion concentration
Mechanism for intercalation of kaolinite by alkali acetates. D. L. Smith and others. bibliog il Science 153:741-3 Ag 12 '66
HYDROLOGIC research
Meandering rivers take easiest route to the sea. il(p33) Sci N 90:38 Jl 16 '66
HYDROLOGICAL cycle. See Water
HYDROLOGY. See Water
HYDROMAGNETIC waves. See Magnetohydrodynamics
HYDROMECHANICS
Density-current plumes. D. T. Mason. bibliog il Science 152:354-6 Ap 15 '66
HYDRONIC waves. See Radio waves
HYDRONICS, incorporated
Sarasota mystery; plasmonics? hydronics? K. Warner. il Pop Electr 24:50-3 Mr '66
HYDRONICS receivers. See Radio receiving apparatus
HYDROPLANE accidents. See Boats and boating—Accidents
HYDROPLANE racing. See Motor boat racing
HYDROPLANES
New Miss B! R. Musson. il Pop Mech 125:106-8+ Mr '66
HYDROPSYCHOTHERAPY. See Psychotherapy
HYDROSKIMMERS. See Ground effect machines
HYDROSTATICS
See also
Specific gravity
HYDROXYBENZYLOXYAMINE. See Benzyloxyamine
HYDROXYL
Chemisorption of water at high temperatures on kaolinite: effect on dehydroxylation. G. W. Brindley and G. L. Millhollen. bibliog il Science 152:1385 Je 3 '66
Infrared study of the hydroxyl bands in clinoamphiboles. R. G. Burns and R. G. J. Strens. bibliog il Science 153:890-2 Ag 19 '66
HYDROXYLATION
6-Hydroxylation: effect on the psychotropic potency of tryptamines. R. G. Taborsky and others. bibliog il Science 153:1018-19 Ag 26 '66
HYDROXYPROLINE
Formation of hydroxyproline in collagen. S. Udenfriend. bibliog il Science 152:1335-40 Je 3 '66
Hydroxylation of proline and the intracellular accumulation of a polypeptide precursor of collagen. K. Juva and others. bibliog il Science 152:92-4 Ap 1 '66
HYGIENE
See also
Health
Study and teaching
What our kids don't know about health. T. Irwin. il Todays Health 44:18-21 My '66
HYGROMETERS
Isopiestic technique: measurement of accurate leaf water potentials. J. S. Boyer. bibliog il Science 154:1459-60 D 16 '66

HYLAND, Janet
For the single girl: a new way of life in California. G. Greene. il pors Ladies Home J 83:58-9+ Jl '66
HYMAN, Mervin
Football's week. See issues of Sports illustrated published during football season
HYMAN, Stanley Edgar
Well-tempered critic. J. W. Aldridge. Commentary 42:72-3 Jl '66
HYMNALS. See Hymns
HYMNS
Hymns: like salted peanuts; concerning Katharine Smith Diehl's Hymns and tunes —an index. Christian Cent 83:1523 D 7 '66
New songs for Methodists; brand-new hymnal. Time 88:66 Jl 22 '66
Sing to the Lord a new song. W. R. Miller. Christian Cent 83:771-6 Je 15 '66; Discussion. 83:1031-2, 1217 Ag 24, O 5 '66
HYMOFF, Edward
Deadly booby traps in a dirty war. Pop Mech 125:70-3+ Je '66
HYND, Alan
Other plot to kill Lincoln. Read Digest 88:92-7 F '66
HYNEK, Josef Allen
Are flying saucers real? por Sat Eve Post 239:17-21 D 17 '66
about
UFO's for real? Newsweek 68:70 O 10 '66
HYPERBARIC oxygenation
Hyperbaric oxygenation: the eye as a limiting factor. G. Margolis and I. W. Brown, jr. bibliog il Science 151:466-8 Ja 28 '66
HYPERCALCEMIA
Thyrocalcitonin: effect on idiopathic hypercalcemia. G. Milhaud and J. C. Job. bibliog il Science 154:794-6 N 11 '66
Too much vitamin D? Consumer Rep 31:52-4 F '66
HYPERPLASIA
Hypertrophy versus hyperplasia. R. J. Goss. bibliog il Science 153:1615-20 S 30 '66
HYPERSENSITIVITY. See Allergy
HYPERTENSION
Cadmium & blood pressure. il Time 88:61-2+ N 4 '66
Creeping up on hypertension; disease called aldosteronism. il Bsns W p 173-4 S 10 '66
I prescribe. . . . J. D. Wassersug. il Sci Digest 60:79-83 D '66
Increased cardiovascular reactivity to angiotensin caused by renin. G. M. C. Masson and others. bibliog il Science 153:1002-4 Ag 26 '66
Killer cadmium. il Newsweek 68:73 N 7 '66
Lysosomal nature of juxtaglomerular granules. E. R. Fisher. bibliog il Science 152:1752 Je 24 '66
HYPERTROPHY
Hypertrophy versus hyperplasia. R. J. Goss. bibliog il Science 153:1615-20 S 30 '66
HYPERVENTILATION. See Respiration
HYPNOANALYSIS. See Hypnotism
HYPNOTISM
How to hex, unhex. Sci Digest 60:21-2 S '66
Hypnosis therapy helps; sensory hypnoanalysis. Sci N 90:346 O 29 '66
Martyrs may not feel pain: contemplation practiced by people in eastern religions akin to auto-hypnosis. P. McBroom. il Sci N 89:505-6 Je 25 '66
Most entrancing man in Hawaii; A. DeMello. il Ebony 21:116-18+ O '66
Should police use hypnosis? F. R. Schreiber and M. Herman. il Sci Digest 59:17-21 My '66
HYPOCRISY
Art of apology. M. H. Freydberg. McCalls 93:87+ Mr '66
HYPOTENSIVE peptides. See Peptides
HYPOTHALAMUS
Control of sensory fields by stimulation of hypothalamus. M. F. MacDonnell and J. P. Flynn. il Science 152:1406-8 Je 3 '66
Copulation-reward site in the posterior hypothalamus. A. R. Caggiula and B. G. Hoebel. bibliog il Science 153:1284-5 S 9 '66
Electron-microscopic autoradiography of rat hypothalamus after intraventricular H[3]-norepinephrine. G. K. Aghajanian and F. E. Bloom. bibliog il Science 153:308-10 Jl 15 '66
Light-induced changes in pineal hydroxyindole-O-methyltransferase: abolition by lateral hypothalamic lesions J. Axelrod and others. bibliog il Science 154:898-9 N 18 '66
Lipolysis in homogenates of adipose tissue: an inhibitor found in fat from obese rats. H. A. Haessler and J. D. Crawford. bibliog il Science 154:909-10 N 18 '66

HYPOTHALAMUS—*Continued*
Reserpine: inhibition of olfactory blockage of pregnancy in mice. C. J. Dominic. bibliog Science 152:1764-5 Je 24 '66
Severe impairment of heat-induced saliva-spreading in rats recovered from lateral hypothalamic lesions. F. R. Hainsworth and A. N. Epstein. bibliog il Science 153:1255-7 S 9 '66

HYSLOP, Beatrice F.
(comp) Articles and other books received; France. See issues of American historical review

HYSTERIA
Both sexes are affected by hysteria, study finds. Todays Health 44:3 Je '66
Culture shapes mental ills. Sci N 90:417 N 19 '66

HYSTERIA (social psychology)
Culture shapes mental ills. Sci N 90:417 N 19 '66

I

IACC. See Inter-American cultural council
IACW. See Inter-American commission of women
IAEA. See International atomic energy agency
IA-ECOSOC. See Inter-American economic and social council
IAF. See Industrial areas foundation; International astronautical federation
IAM. See International association of machinists
IATA. See International air transport association
IATUL. See International federation of library associations—International association of technological university libraries
IBA. See Investment bankers association of America
IBEW. See International brotherhood of electrical workers
IBM. See International business machines corporation
ICAF. See United States—Industrial college of the armed forces
ICAO. See International civil aviation organization
ICBM (intercontinental ballistic missiles) See Guided missiles
ICC. See International control commission for Indochina; United States—Interstate commerce commission
ICO. See United States—Interagency committee on oceanography
ICS. See International correspondence schools
I can always stop; story. See Bongartz, R.
I can't imagine tomorrow; drama. See Williams, T.
ID cards. See Identification cards, certificates, etc.
IDA. See Institute for defense analyses
IDB. See Inter-American development bank
IDCSP (initial defense communications satellite program) See Communications satellites—Military applications
IDEA project. See Institution for the development of educational activities
I do! I do! musical comedy. See Musical comedies, revues, etc.—Criticisms, plots, etc.
IEEE. See Institute of electrical and electronics engineers
IESC. See International executive service corps
IFLA. See International federation of library associations
IFMA. See Interdenominational foreign mission association
IGY. See International geophysical year
IHAS (integrated helicopter avionics systems) See Aeronautic instruments
ILA. See International longshoremen's association
ILC. See United Nations—International law commission
ILGWU. See International ladies' garment workers union
ILO. See International labor organization
ILS (instrument landing system) See Airplanes, Light—Landing
ILWU. See International longshoremen's and warehousemen's union
IMCO. See Intergovernmental maritime consultative organization

IMF. See International monetary fund
IMP (interplanetary monitoring platform) See Artificial satellites—Use in research
INCO. See International nickel company
INSEA. See International society for education through art
IOS. See Investors overseas services, limited
IPA. See International publishers association
IQ. See Intelligence quotient
IQSY. See International years of the quiet sun
IRA. See International reading association; Irish republican army
IRRI. See International rice research institute
IRS. See United States—Internal revenue service
ISAD. See American library association—Information science and automation division
ISCM. See International society for contemporary music
I see you, Bianca; story. See Brennan, M.
IT and T. See International telephone and telegraph corporation
ITCA. See International typographic composition association
ITV (instructional television) center. See National center for school and college television
ITY. See International tourist year, 1967
IUCD (intra-uterine contraceptive device) See Contraceptives
IUD. See American federation of labor and Congress of industrial organizations—Industrial union department
IUE. See International union of electrical, radio and machine workers
IA DRANG VALLEY, Battle of. See Vietnamese war, 1957- —Campaigns and battles

IAKOVLEV, Aleksandr Sergeevich
Yakovlev urges more integration of Russian research, production; excerpts from Izvestia article. por Aviation W 84:83+ Ap 25 '66

IAKOVOS, abp
Ecumenism is no trivial thing. America 115:55 Jl 16 '66

IAN, Janis
42nd street psycho blues. por Seventeen 26:44+ Ja '67

IASHAPENKO, Iurii
Soviet spellbinder. Nat R 18:1206 N 29 '66

IATROGENIC diseases
Drug disease. Newsweek 67:64+ My 2 '66
Imaginary heart disease; cardiac neurotics, vexing medical problem. W. Kitay. Sci Digest 60:53-7 S '66

IBARRURI, Dolores
I become La pasionaria; excerpt from They shall not pass. Nation 203:94-8 Jl 25 '66

IBERIA airlines. See Airlines—Spain

IBN Khaldūn
Ibn Khaldūn: man of history; excerpts from radio program. B. Bray. il UNESCO Courier 19:4-10 Je '66

IBOGAINE
New African drug aids psychotherapy. Sci N 90:9 Jl 2 '66

IBSEN, Henrik
Wild duck; tr. by E. Le Gallienne. Criticism Time 89:70-1 Ja 20 '67

IBUKA, Masaru
Sony: how to grow big by thinking small. il por Newsweek 67:88-90 Je 13 '66

ICE, Anne Mare
Report on trip to Scandinavia. por Negro Hist Bul 29:94-6 Ja '66

ICE
History on the rocks; army scientists date Greenland ice cores. Time 88:115 S 30 '66
Ice. L. K. Runnels. il Sci Am 215:118-24+ bibliog(p 156) D '66
Ice nuclei from automobile exhaust and iodine vapor. V. J. Schaefer. bibliog Science 154:1555-7 D 23 '66
Nature note. il Sci N 90:411 N 12 '66

Polar Regions

Antarctic pack ice: boundaries established from Nimbus I pictures. M. C. Predoehl. il Science 153:861-3 Ag 19 '66
Ice cap age disputed. Sci N 90:348 O 29 '66
On a floating island; U.S. Arctic drifting stations. V. P. Hessler. il Science 151:1360-2 Mr 18 '66
See also
Glaciers

ICE age. See Glacial epochs
ICE buckets. See Buckets (pails)
ICE cream, ices, etc.
Frosty finales; bombes; with recipes. P. Cannon. il Ladies Home J 83:80-1+ Jl '66

ICE cream, ices, etc.—*Continued*
How the fine Italian hand shapes ice cream. il Sunset 137:100-1 O '66
Ice cream desserts. il Bet Hom & Gard 44:105-6 Je '66
Ice cream incognito; with recipes. il McCalls 93:96-7+ Ag '66
Ice cream stars; with recipe. il Sunset 137:136 D '66
Ice cream surprises. il Farm J 90:98 F '66
Ja, das ist ein Sealtest; Austria. il Newsweek 68:100-1 D 19 '66
Look what's happened to ice cream. D. Wharton. il Read Digest 88:101-3 Je '66
Summer coolers; with recipes. il Ebony 21:134+ Ag '66
Twelve-minute ice cream; with recipes. il Seventeen 25:182-3+ My '66
Two homemade mint ice creams; with recipes. Sunset 137:136 S '66
Vanilla ice cream dressed up for dessert. Good H 162:147 Mr '66

ICE cream industry. See Ice cream, ices, etc.

ICE cream sauces. See Sauces

ICE cream sodas. See Beverages

ICE crushers
Ice crushers; with electric-blender attachments. il Consumer Rep 31:276-9 Je '66

ICE cutting. See Ice industry

ICE fishing. See Fishing, Winter

ICE hazards in aviation. See Airplanes—Ice protection

ICE hockey. See Hockey

ICE industry
Natural ice; cutting and shipping. E. Sloane. il Am Heritage 17:82-3 Ag '66

ICE islands. See Ice—Polar Regions

ICE patrol. See United States—Coast guard

ICE removal. See Snow and ice removal

ICE skating. See Skating

ICE wagons. See Wagons

ICE water. See Water

ICED tea. See Tea

ICELAND
Iceland: a nation hurrying toward tomorrow. J. H. Winchester. il Read Digest 88:197-200+ Je '66

ICINGS
Successful recipes; frosting favorites. il Suc Farm 64:105-6 Ap '66

IDAHO
See also
Craters of the Moon National Monument
Fishing—Idaho
Hell's Canyon
Hunting—Idaho
Salmon River
Skis and skiing—Idaho
Wilderness areas—Idaho

Politics and government
Ironic defeat; R. E. Smylie. Time 88:12-13 Ag 12 '66
Price of the meal. il Time 88:28-9 O 28 '66

Religious institutions and affairs
Part-time priesthood. il Newsweek 68:72 Ag 15 '66

IDAHO FALLS, Idaho
One-trip hole patching. L. Lowe. il Am City 81:38 O '66

IDEA files. See Fiction—Technique

IDEA project. See Institution for the development of educational activities

IDEAL states. See Utopias

IDEALISM
Idealism without illusions; address, June 11, 1966. L. A. Townsend. Vital Speeches 32:626-9 Ag 1 '66

IDEALS
See also
Idealism

IDEAS in business
Management concepts: fads and fancies. J. W. McGuire. il Duns R 87:47-8+ Mr '66
Open your mind to fresh ideas. C. A. Cerami. il Nations Bsns 54:86+ S '66
See also
Imitation in business

IDENTIFICATION
Call me by my rightful number; computers cause anonymity. E. P. Paullin. il Sat R 49:76 F 19 '66
Chicago cop faces crime; illustrator catches suspects. il Ebony 21:48-50+ Ap '66
Living by the numbers. il Life 60:76A-78+ F 18 '66
See also
Voiceprints

IDENTIFICATION cards, certificates, etc.
ID cards for forty-three cents each; Rochester, N.Y. E. C. Traugott. il Am City 81:45 Jl '66
Polaroid trains lens on quickie ID cards. il Bsns W p 132-4 O 1 '66
Teen travel talk; International student identity card through United States national student association. il Seventeen 25:204 Mr '66

IDENTITY, Personal. See Personality

IDENTITY crisis; story. See Schoen, B.

IDEOLOGY
Nationalism and ideology. by B. Ward. Review
Sat R 49:27-8 Ag 20 '66. J. Real
Virtues of ideology. J. O'Gara. Commonweal 84:250 My 20 '66

IDIOCY
See also
Mongolism

IDIOPATHIC hypercalcemia. See Hypercalcemia

IDIOT savant. See Mentally handicapped

IDOMENEO; opera. See Mozart, J. C. W. A.

IDRIS I, king of Libya
Peanuts to prosperity. il por Time 87:40 F 25 '66

IDZERDA, Stanley J.
Good teacher is a good teacher. NEA J 55:14-16 N '66

IERARDI, Gordon S.
Obituary
Pub W por 189:73-4 F 28 '66

IF you need me, let me know; story. See Conaway, R.

IGER, Eve Marie
How to fly to Europe without buying a ticket. Esquire 67:70-5 Ja '67

IGLAUER, Edith
Beautiful day; story. New Yorker 42:53-6 Mr 19 '66
Reporter at large (cont) New Yorker 42:188-92+ S 24 '66

IGNACIO, Ricardo
Lesson for Oscar. Time 88:29 D 23 '66

IGNACIO RASCO, José
Integration or disintegration. Américas 18:29-34 Jl '66

IGNATIUS, Mary S.
Some classroom-tested ideas. NEA J 55:39 N '66

IGNATIUS, Paul Robert
Where the Vietnam pipeline begins. por Bsns W p 188+ Ap 16 '66

IGNATOW, David
American parable; poem. Nation 202:783 Je 27 '66
On the death of Winston Churchill; All quiet; poems. Poetry 108:16 Ap '66
Permanent hell. Nation 202:752-3 Je 20 '66
Rescue the dead; Hope; poems. Poetry 109:156-7 D '66
Sediment; poem. New Yorker 42:199 D 17 '66

IGNEOUS rocks. See Rocks, Igneous

IGNITION devices. See Automobile engines—Ignition; Marine engines—Ignition

IK (native race) See Uganda—Native races

IKEDA, Daisaku
Reporter at large. J. M. Flagler. New Yorker 42:152+ N 26 '66

IKEYA-Seki comet. See Comets

IKKAI, Takamitsu, and others
Actin: volume change on transformation of G-form to F-form. bibliog Science 152:1756-7 Je 24 '66

IKOMA, Tatsuo. See Kuroda, Y. jt. auth.

ILCEWICZ, Frank H. See Holtzman, R. B. jt. auth.

ILG, Frances L. and Ames, L. B.
Your child may be in the wrong grade at school. Read Digest 89:56-60 Ag '66

ILIFFE, Edward Langton Iliffe, 2d baron
Lord and Lady Iliffe's triple entente: country, city, and sun. L. Blanch. il por Vogue 148:102-9+ Jl '66

ILIFFE, Renée (Merandon du Plessis) Iliffe, baroness
Lord and Lady Iliffe's triple entente: country, city, and sun. L. Blanch. il pors Vogue 148:102-9+ Jl '66

ILLEGAL radio broadcasting stations. See Radio stations, Illegal

ILLEGITIMACY
Born between East and West; concerning Pearl S. Buck foundation. M. Macmillan. Sat R 49:51 Jl 23 '66

ILLEGITIMACY—*Continued*
Conversations parents never hear: unwed mother. il Look 30:71 S 20 '66
Illegitimacy in U.S; it's on the rise. il U S News 61:87 Jl 18 '66
See also
Mothers, Unmarried

ILLIA, Arturo Umberto
Argentina: still afraid of Peron. por Bsns W p92+ My 21 '66
Down on his luck. il por Time 88:45 S 16 '66
How much longer? il Time 87:35 F 11 '66
Last coup? il por Newsweek 68:52 Jl 11 '66
Why the military took over in Argentina. il por U S News 61:59-60 Jl 11 '66

ILLICH, Ivan
To be perfectly frank. America 116:88-91 Ja 21 '67

ILLINOIS
See also
Architecture, Domestic—Illinois
Booksellers and bookselling—Illinois
Hunting—Illinois
Libraries—Illinois
Unemployment—Illinois

Hospitals
See Hospitals—United States

Politics and government
Adlai Stevenson: a new vision; achievements as governor. E. Roper. Sat R 49:20 Jl 9 '66
Adlai III: another Stevenson stirs Illinois politics. J. Star. il Look 30:28-31 O 4 '66
Boy wonder grows up. P. M. Deuel. il Nation 203:374-6 O 17 '66
Douglas and the devil theory; election issues and candidates. Nation 202:315 Mr 21 '66
Hardest campaign of Paul Douglas' career. R. T. Cooper. New Repub 155:9-10 O 22 '66
Percy vs. Douglas; the blighted campaign. S. Alsop. il Sat Eve Post 239:26-9 N 5 '66
Second campaign; C. H. Percy. il Newsweek 68:42 O 24 '66
Whiz kid switches to politics. Bsns W p71-2 N 26 '66
Yorktown revisited; Senate race. il Time 88:33 N 4 '66

Race problems
See also
Chicago—Riots

ILLINOIS freedom to read committee
Illinois group formed to fight censorship. Pub W 190:37-8 O 17 '66

ILLINOIS institute of technology, Chicago
IIT, the house that Mies built. il Sci Digest 59:48-53 Mr '66

ILLINOIS. University
College or career for dancers? University of Illinois' answer. E. Stodelle. il Dance Mag 40:52-5 Ap '66
Multiversity, by N. von Hoffman. Review Sat R 49:65 Ag 20 '66. P. Woodring
Pressure cooker for four-year-old minds; Institute for research on exceptional children. M. Pines. il Harper 234:55-61 Ja '67

Chicago campus
New campus. O. Newman. il Arch Forum 124:50-1 My '66

ILLITERACY
India's literacy lady: W. H. Fisher. il Time 88:55 Ag 5 '66
International campaign against illiteracy; World congress of ministers of education on the eradicaton of illiteracy. E. Sochor. Sch & Soc 94:76+ F 5 '66
Library trustees and the literate society. C. T. Senft. ALA Bul 60:942-5 O '66
Literacy by decree in Indonesia. R. M. Thomas. bibliog f il Sch & Soc 94:279-83 Sum '66
Military credits freed for knowledge; historic decision by Iran. il UNESCO Courier 19:44-5 Jl '66
One day's expenditure on arms: gift from Iran: letter. Mohammed Reza Pahlevi. UNESCO Courier 19:33 Je '66
Preparing adults for rapid change. R. H. Coates. il NEA J 55:23-5 D '66
Progress in literacy: Mexico. A. Zambrano. Christian Cent 83:1061 Ag 31 '66
Rising illiteracy. Sci Am 215:66+ N '66
Swans into Larks; project of LARK (Literacy and related knowledge) foundation. H. Gilbert. il Library J 91:2780-2 Je 1 '66
Trade winds; D. N. Fader plan to arouse reading interest. J. Beatty, jr. il Sat R 49: 10 Je 25 '66
UNESCO and literacy: progress report; new literacy projects of the United Nations development program. R. L. Tobin. Sat R 49:24 Jl 30 '66

UNESCO experimental literacy projects. Sch & Soc 94:120 Mr 5 '66
UNESCO's world literacy programme enters operational phase. UNESCO Courier 19:33 Ap '66
We are courting disaster: Shah of Iran's donation to U.N. Newsweek 67:50 My 16 '66
What happened to Farmer? Center for community-action education. New Repub 154: 7-8 Ap 2 '66
See also
International literacy day

ILLUMINATED manuscripts. *See* Illumination of books and manuscripts

ILLUMINATION of books and manuscripts
Medieval splendors; manuscript illuminations. A. Werner. il Am Artist 30:38-42+ D '66

ILLUSIONS and hallucinations
Offerings at the psychedelicatessen. R. R. Lingeman. il N Y Times Mag p6-7+ Jl 10 '66; Discussion. p2 Jl 31 '66
Pleasure dome '66: psychedelic overload. R. Kotlowitz. il Harper 233:99-100 Jl '66
See also
Apparitions
Mushroom ceremony

ILLUSTRATED books
Big books: 1966. H. Yglesias. Nation 203:680-1 D 19 '66
Child of affluence. W. Miller. Nation 202:338-9 Mr 21 '66
Holiday hoard. il Time 88:117-18+ D 9 '66

ILLUSTRATION of books and periodicals
Alan E. Cober: artist of the year '65. H. C. Pitz. il Am Artist 30:36-41+ Je '66
Art of art for children's books, by D. Klemin. Review
  Pub W 190:88-90 N 7 '66. P. A. Bennett
Art of Eugene Karlin. J. H. Michel. il Am Artist 30:50-4+ Mr '66
Artist at work (cont) il Horn Bk 42:83-6, 553-5, 690-3 F. O-D '66
Books in review; the illustrator's art. E. E. Dee. Natur Hist 75:58+ O '66
Boris Artzybasheff. L. S. Bechtel. Horn Bk 42:176-80 Ap '66
Calico pictures of storybook tales. R. Grabner. il Sch Arts 66:35 D '66
Clement Hurd: children's book illustrator as artist and exhibitor. il Pub W 189:106-8 F 7 '66
Design: a free-for-all wrestling match. Pub W 190:100+ N 7 '66
Designer and photographer; designing of the book. This was Toscanini. S. Salter. il Pub W 190:111-13 S 5 '66
Designer-publisher relations. S. Salter. Pub W 189:166+ Je 13 '66
High technical level in illustrators '66; eighth annual exhibition; of the Society of illustrators il Pub W 189:110-12 Mr 7 '66
House that Jack built; R. Briggs' illustrations for Mother Goose treasury. J. Fritz. il Horn Bk 42:681-3 D '66
Illustration discussed by children's book council; summary of addresses. Pub W 189:83 Ap 18 '66
Interpretive portraits of Fred Steffan; with commentary by the editors. il Am Artist 31: 38-43+ Ja '67
Meteoric career of Ed Emberley. D. Waugh. il Am Artist 30:54-61 N '66
Milton Glaser of push pin studios. D. Waugh. il Am Artist 30:56-61+ Je '66
New techniques and images illustrate Abrams Inferno. il Pub W 189:106-7 Ap 4 '66
Nonny Hogrogian: decorator of books for children. D. Waugh. il Am Artist 30:52-7 O '66
Photogravure used for MOMA photography books. il Pub W 189:104 Ap 4 '66
Story sets the pace: an illustrator's view of design. N. Hogrogian. il Pub W 189:100-3 F 21 '66
Textbook artist. il Design 67:4-7 Ja; 16-25 Mr '66
3-D photos in Golden's fairy tale series and other books. il Pub W 190:104-6 N 7 '66
Two worlds of Naoko Matsubara. F. Eichenberg. il Am Artist 30:34-9+ N '66
See also
Picture books for children

ILLUSTRATORS
Artist at work (cont) il Horn Bk 42:83-6, 553-5, 690-3 F, O-D '66
See also
Beardsley, A. V.
Sendak, M.
Society of illustrators

ILLYA darling; musical comedy. *See* Musical comedies, revues, etc.—Criticisms, plots, etc.

IMMUNOGLOBULINS. See Serum globulins

IMPACT, Tex.
Liquorville; Impact, inc. il Newsweek 67:77 F 14 '66

IMPEACHMENTS
One hundred years ago; attempt in Congress to impeach President Johnson. R. L. Strout. New Repub 154:17-18 F 12 '66

IMPEDANCE (electricity)
T and H attenuator pad nomograms. M. H. Applebaum. il Electr World 75:31 Mr '66
Why 50-OHM coax? il Electr World 75:61 F '66

IMPERIAL chemical industries, limited
British company that found a way out. M. J. Gart. il Fortune 74:104-9+ Ag '66

IMPERIAL Russian bonds. See Bonds, Government—Russia

IMPERIAL smelting corporation. See Great Britain—Industries

IMPLEMENTS, utensils, etc.
See also
Indians of North America—Implements
Kitchen utensils

IMPORT quotas
Chemicals get their oil; petrochemical makers win import quotas. Bsns W p46 S 17 '66
Oil woes: fight over imports at home; petrochemical makers scrambling for special feedstock allotments. Bsns W p48 O 8 '66

IMPORT tax. See Tariff

IMPORTS. See United States—Commerce

IMPOSTORS and imposture
Preserving la différence; physical examination to prove sex; European track-and-field championships. il Time 88:70 S 16 '66
See also
Quacks and quackery

IMPRESARIOS
So you want to be an impresario? B. Jacobson. il Hi Fi 16:29-32 D 15 '66

IMPRESSIONISM (art)
Art galleries. R. M. Coates. il New Yorker 42:192-5 N 19 '66
Importance of Cézanne. G. Laderman. il Art N 65:39-41+ O '66
Unknown Sisley. J. Ashbery. il Art N 65:44-5+ N '66
See also
Painting, French

IMPRIMATUR. See Catholic church—Discipline

IMPROVISATION (acting)
Happenings are happening. il Time 87:76-7 Mr 4 '66
Improvisation bit; San Francisco and Chicago companies. J. Novick. Nation 203:613-15 D 5 '66

IMPROVISATION (dance)
Improvisation: the most creative approach to dance. B. Mettler. il Dance Mag 40:42-5+ Jl '66

IN-flight movies. See Airlines—Passenger service

IN-laws. See Relatives

IN-service librarian education. See Librarians—Education in service

IN service training of employees. See Employees—Training

IN the beginning; story. See Siegel, B.

IN the fun house; story. See Moulton, E.

IN the region of ice; story. See Oates, J. C.

IN trouble; story. See Roth, P.

INADMISSIBLE evidence; drama. See Osborne, J.

INBAU, Fred E.
Behind those police brutality charges. Read Digest 89:41-6 Jl '66

INBOARD motors. See Gas and oil engines, Inboard

INBOARD-outboard motors. See Marine engines

INBREEDING
Inbreeding of zoo animals. R. Bogart. bibliog il Parks & Rec 1:254-7 Mr '66

INCARNATION
Man revealed. C. Davis. America 114:445 Ap 2 '66
See also
Jesus Christ

INCAS
Cajamarca. E. Hosmann. il Américas 18:31-8 S '66
Royal commentaries of the Incas and general history of Peru, by G. de la Vega. Review
Sat R 50:33-4 Ja 7 '67. J. H. Parry
See also
Machu Picchu, Peru

INCENTIVE financing. See Corporations—Finance

INCENTIVE pay. See Incentives in industry

INCENTIVES in education
Golden grades; paying kids for grades. Newsweek 67:62 Ap 4 '66

INCENTIVES in industry
Attack on incentive system seen in rising debate on contracting; address. J. R. Russell. Aviation W 84:119+ My 23 '66
Major contracts keyed to performance. K. Johnsen. il Aviation W 84:101-2 F 21 '66
Manpower development and incentives to change. Mo Labor R 89:1123-5 O '66
NASA awards list shows incentives push. il Aviation W 84:55+ Je 27 '66
NASA tightening incentive fee system. il Aviation W 85:150+ Ag 15 '66
Senate battles over patents rights. F. Sartwell. Sci N 90:558 D 31 '66
$25.6-million Gemini incentive seen for near-perfect effort. Aviation W 86:32 Ja 16 '67

INCEST
Incest of Tieng and Aang who had a common ancestor fifteen generations ago; excerpt from Nous avons mangé la forêt de la Pierre-Génie Gôo, tr. by V. Bordaz. G. Condominas. il Natur Hist 75:13-19 Je '66
Incest taboo uncovered. Sci N 90:111 Ag 13 '66

INCIDENT before Troy; drama. See Nightingale, E. M.

INCIDENT on the tenth floor; story. See Brown, J.

INCIDENTS in connection with a crash landing; opera. See Blacher, B.

INCOME
Calculation and uses of spendable earnings series. il Mo Labor R 89:405-9 Ap '66
Effects of employment redistribution on earnings. C. Hodge. il Mo Labor R 89:744-8 Jl '66
Geographic study of employment and earnings from 1939 to 1964. C. Utter. il Mo Labor R 89:132-7 F '66
Getting more money now? here's what it's worth. il U S News 61:39-40+ Ag 1 '66
Guaranteed income; address, May 21, 1966. R. Theobald. Vital Speeches 32:573-6 Jl 1 '66
Guaranteed income and the Protestant ethic. Christian Cent 83:260-2 Mr 2 '66
How about a negative income tax for the poor? pro and con discussion. Sr Schol 88:14-15 Ap 22 '66
Job or subsidy for everybody? summary of report. U S News 60:102 F 14 '66
Lutherans support minimum income. America 115:52-3 Jl 16 '66
Measure of personal income (title varies) tables. See issues of Business week
Should they have to work at all? il Nations Bsns 54:34-5+ S '66
T.R.B. From Washington; guaranteed income. New Repub 155:4 D 17 '66
Take-home game; western Europe. il Time 88:75 Ag 26 '66
Washington should pay taxes to the poor; advantages of a negative income tax. M. D. Reagan. il N Y Times Mag p24-5+ F 20 '66; Discussion. p 19+ Mr 13 '66
See also
Gross national product
Purchasing power
Retirement income
Salaries

INCOME protection insurance. See Insurance—Policies

INCOME tax

Anecdotes, facetiae, satire, etc.
Collector's items; excerpts from Dear Internal revenue, comp. by B. Adler. Look 30:86 Ap 5 '66

Capital gains tax
Bill seeks capital gains tax status for copyrights. Pub W 189:47 My 16 '66
That locked-in feeling. Fortune 73:207 F '66

Collection
See Withholding tax

Deductions
Can you deduct auto expenses without detailed records? Bet Hom & Gard 44:6 F '66
Check these year-end tax savers. il Changing T 20:40 D '66
Depreciation for savers. H. C. Wallich. Newsweek 67:88 Ap 4 '66
Educational deductions: IRS wants to tighten up. E. Langer. Science 153:845-6 Ag 19 '66
Eight little-known ways to cut your tax bill. M. E. Holbrook. il Nations Bsns 54:36-7+ Mr '66

INCOME tax—Deductions—*Continued*

How to be a good tax manager. F. Bailey, jr. Suc Farm 64:36+ N '66

Just what qualifies as a casualty loss? Bet Hom & Gard 44:8 F '66

Keeping Christians honest; all Canadian income-tax-deductible contributions must so register. Christian Cent 83:517 Ap 27 '66

Last-minute tax tips. il Changing T 20:13-15 Ap '66

New millions in tax savings. U S News 61: 102 N 28 '66

New tax rules out. don't miss your 7 per cent. C. W. Gifford. Farm J 90:38L Je '66

Save on taxes? find your best bets here. il Changing T 20:25-9 F '66

Tax break for working mothers. America 115:108 Jl 30 '66

Tax deduction picture brighter; teacher-tax-payers. Sr Schol 89:sup2 O 28 '66

Tax deductions for educational expenses. W. W. Brickman. Sch & Soc 94:341 O 29 '66

Tax reminders: how to save by acting now. U S News 61:125-8 N 14 '66

Tax saving tips for electronics moonlighters. K. Kirkpatrick. il Pop Electr 24:67-9 Mr '66

Tax-saving trick: the arts dodge. U S News 61:113-14 S 19 '66

Tips on saving income tax dollars. D. D. Crumley. Suc Farm 64:41+ F '66

What every young father should know about taxes. J. D. Bierman. il Parents Mag 41: 54-5+ Mr '66

You can cut your next tax bill right now. il Changing T 20:29-30 Je '66

See also
Amortization deductions
Expense accounts (business)

Forms
See Tax forms

Returns
See Tax returns

Brazil
Antipatriotic triumph of Travancas the terrible. Time 87:41 Je 24 '66

United States
Another push for tax rise; summary of address. October 31. 1966. W. M. Martin, jr. U S News 61:128 N 14 '66

As city taxes rise, the latest favorite. il U S News 61:86 Ag 8 '66

Blessed are the work-makers; creation of jobs providing income-tax revenues of our government. D. Lawrence. U S News 61:92 S 5 '66

Budget that doesn't give; why there's growing pressure for a tax increase. il U S News 61:100-2 O 10 '66

Campaign fund; question of income tax financing presidential candidates. New Repub 155:6 N 5 '66

Chances now for a tax increase; with excerpt from address by A. F. Burns. il U S News 61:27-9 D 12 '66

How war spending is forcing a tax rise. il U S News 62:49-50 Ja 2 '67

If income taxes go up; the cost to you. il U S News 60:97-9 Mr 7 '66

Income tax answers you need. N. Harl. Suc Farm 64:25+ D '66

Income tax: how good? excerpts from Federal tax policy. J. A. Pechman. U S News 61:115-16 S 26 '66

Now: a tax plan that pays people; negative income tax. il U S News 60:63 F 14 '66

Now: politicians to get a tax check-off. U S News 61:39 N 28 '66

See how they run; survey concerned with tax disincentive effect on higher-income people. Newsweek 68:80 D 5 '66

So you get more money; are you better off? U S News 60:28 Ap 4 '66

Squeeze in LBJ's tax plan: how millions would be hurt. U S News 60:87-8 Ja 31 '66

Uncle Sam's pound of flesh; our loophole-ridden tax system. S. Alsop. il Sat Eve Post 239:18 My 7 '66

Unexpected receipts fill government's till: revenues higher than Treasury estimates. il Bsns W p66+ S 10 '66

Unmarried people are overtaxed; J. A. Pechman's views. Life 61:8 S 30 '66

See also
Tax returns

INCOME tax consultants. See Tax consultants

L'INCORONAZIONE di Poppea; opera. See Monteverdi, C.

INCREASE of population. See Population, Increase of

INCUBATION
Egg communication; eggs in nest tend to hatch at about the same time. il Time 87:76 My 27 '66

INCUBATORS, Baby. See Infants. Premature

INDEMNITY, Civilian. See Vietnamese war. 1957- —Compensation of non-combatants

INDEPENDENCE (airplane carrier) See Aircraft carriers

INDEPENDENCE day. See Fourth of July

INDEPENDENCE Hall, Philadelphia
Restoration in Independence Hall: a continuum of historic preservation. L. H. Nelson. il Antiques 90:64-8 Jl '66

INDEPENDENT moving picture producers. See Moving picture production and direction

INDEPENDENT regulatory commissions
Executive and independent agencies. Sr Schol 88:21 F 18 '66

INDEPENDENT schools education board. See Books and reading—Best books

INDEPENDENT study
Independent study and the campus crisis. L. C. Rhett. il Sat R 49:62-4 Jl 16 '66

Independent study in medical school. Sch & Soc 94:262+ Sum '66

Library college idea. L. Shores. bibliog il Library J 91:3871-5 S 1 '66

INDEX expurgatorius. See Index librorum prohibitorum

INDEX librorum prohibitorum
French authors and Roman indexers. H. M. Watson; reply with rejoinder. J. C. McDonald. America 114:212 F 12 '66

Index becomes an appendix. Christian Cent 83:608 My 11 '66

Index indexed; never to be updated or reprinted. Time 87:74 Ap 29 '66

Index R.I.P. Commonweal 84:193 My 6 '66

INDEX numbers
Economic indexes: keeping tabs on the economy. il Sr Schol 88:19 My 13 '66

Research and development price indexes. A. D. Searle. il Mo Labor R 89:57-61 Ja '66

INDEX of prohibited books. See Index librorum prohibitorum

INDEXING
Instant indexing; system for locating past photo magazine articles. N. S. Smith. il U S Camera 29:16-18+ F '66

INDIA
India in perspective; address. March 29, 1966. I. Gandhi. Vital Speeches 32:423-5 My 1 '66

India: too poor to be effective, too big to be ignored. E. Dunbar. il Look 30:19-32 Jl 12 '66

India's long hot summer. M. Fishwick. Sat R 49:19-21 Jl 16 '66

See also
Agriculture—India
Americans in India
Architecture—India
Benares
Christmas—India
Cows (in religion, folklore, etc.)
Dewata
Economic assistance in India
Famines—India
Fatehpur Sikri
Food relief—India
Hotels. taverns, etc.—India
Hunting—India
Jaipur
Kashmir
Kerala
Khajuraho
Land—India
Medicine—India
Money—India
Moving pictures—India
Negroes in India
New Delhi
Political parties—India
Punjab
Rajasthan Desert
Science—India
Sikhs
Taj Mahal
Technical assistance in India
Temples—India
Water supply—India
Women—India

Antiquities
See also
Harappa culture

Cabinet
Casualty list. il Time 88:48 N 18 '66

Show of independence. Time 88:40 N 25 '66

INDIA—*Continued*

Description and travel

Travel notes. R. Joseph. Esquire 65:24+ Mr '66

Traveler, consider my India; ed. by R. Joseph. C. Bowles. il Esquire 65:110-11+ Mr '66

Traveling with Mlle: travel, temples, and tolerance. S. Rama Rau. il Mlle 64:132-4 D '66

Wonders of India. J. P. Gabriel. il Travel 126:56-62 O '66

Economic conditions

Cities of the dreadful night. E. R. F. Sheehan. Nation 202:300-2 Mr 14 '66

India: a huge country on the verge of collapse. S. W. Sanders. il U S News 61:68-71 N 28 '66

India; address, January 17, 1966. S. Sherwood. il Vital Speeches 32:305-7 Mr 1 '66

Mrs Gandhi's legacy: the starving nation of India. V. J. Dunigan. Cath World 203:34-9 Ap '66

Mrs Gandhi's mission. A. Campbell. New Repub 154:13-17 Ap 2 '66

Report from India; ed. by D. Hanson. L. Webster. Suc Farm 64:6 Mr '66

We've never had it so bad. K. Singh. il N Y Times Mag p5+ Ja 23 '66
See also
Famines—India

Economic policy

Every dogma has its day. il Newsweek 68: 41 Jl 18 '66

Indira's India, a hopeful surprise. Life 61:4 S 2 '66

Toward a freer economy. Time 87:41 Je 24 '66

Foreign opinion
American

Myths that divide India and us. L. Markel. il N Y Times Mag p29+ Ja 15 '67

Foreign relations
Pakistan

Whiff of normalization. Time 87:33-4 Mr 11 '66

United States

India speaks to America, by B. N. Chakravarty. Review
Sat R 49:33-4 Ap '66. W. Hangen

President Johnson and Prime Minister Gandhi of India confer at Washington; exchange of greetings; exchange of toasts; with joint communique. March 29, 1966. L. B. Johnson; I. Gandhi. Dept State Bul 54:598-605 Ap 18 '66

Sari-clad visitor from India. il Sr Schol 88:21 Ap 15 '66

Hindu-Muslim relations

India for the Hindus, says the Jan Sangh; All-India people's party. J. A. Lukas. il N Y Times Mag p20-1+ Ag 14 '66

Violence in India; cow riots. il Sr Schol 89: 25-6 D 9 '66

Where cows eat and people starve. il U S News 61:111 N 21 '66

History
Afghan wars
See Afghan wars

Industries

Fertilizer to fight hunger. il Time 87:93 My 27 '66

Schoolboys come of age; Indian businessmen. il Time 87:74 Ap 22 '66
See also
Textile industry—India

Native races

By spear and gun; cooperation between Nagas and Mizos in wars of independence. il Newsweek 67:54 My 30 '66

Politics and government

Every dogma has its day. il Newsweek 68: 41 Jl 18 '66

Explosive quality. il Time 88:41-2 N 11 '66

First duty. il Newsweek 67:37-8 F 7 '66

India: a huge country on the verge of collapse. S. W. Sanders. il U S News 61:68-71 N 28 '66

Mrs Gandhi elected. Sr Schol 88:17 F 4 '66

Mrs Gandhi's mission. A. Campbell. New Repub 154:13-17 Ap 2 '66

Muddling through; wave of disenchantment with lady Prime Minister. Newsweek 68: 56+ N 28 '66

Nehru will. Newsweek 67:41-2 Ja 31 '66

Return of the rosebud. il Time 87:24-6+ Ja 28 '66; Same abr. Read Digest 88:83-7 Ap '66

Rupees and rice. G. Woodcock. Commonweal 84:414-17 Jl 1 '66

Shastri dies. Sr Schol 87:15 Ja 21 '66

She stands remarkably alone. J. A. Lukas. il N Y Times Mag p34-5+ Mr 27 '66
See also
India—Cabinet
India—Hindu-Muslim relations
Political parties—India

Population
See also
Birth control—India

Religious institutions and affairs

World around us. Christian Cent 83:344-6 Mr 16 '66
See also
Christians in India
Church of south India
Cows (in religion, folklore, etc.)
Hinduism
India—Hindu-Muslim relations
Protestant churches—India
Sadhus
Sikhs

Riots

After freedom; Sikh state plan causes riots. Newsweek 67:49-50 Mr 28 '66

Explosive quality. Time 88:41-2 N 11 '66

For mother cow; clash over slaughter of cow by Moslems il Newsweek 68:66 N 21 '66

Old order; Adivasi tribesmen rebel. Newsweek 67:53 Ap 11 '66

Riots in India; prelude to a visit to U.S. U S News 60:16 Mr 28 '66

Social conditions

Cities of the dreadful night. E. R. F. Sheehan. Nation 202:300-2 Mr 14 '66
See also
Caste

Social life and customs

It's a long, long way from old Camp Shawnee; volunteers being trained for service in India. S. Rama Rau. il N Y Times Mag p52-3+ N 13 '66
See also
Caste
Women—India

Social policy

Her father's daughter. il Time 87:28-9 Je 3 '66

INDIA and the United States
Myths that divide India and us. L. Markel. il N Y Times Mag p29+ Ja 15 '67

INDIA-Pakistan dispute. See Kashmir

INDIAN affairs, Bureau of. See United States —Indian affairs, Bureau of

INDIAN agencies. See Indians of North America —Reservations

INDIAN art (East Indian) See Art, Indian (East Indian)

INDIAN businessmen. See Businessmen

INDIAN butter tree. See Butter trees

INDIAN cookery (East Indian) See Cookery, Indian (East Indian)

INDIAN legends (East Indian) See Legends, Indian (East Indian)

INDIAN literature (East Indian)
From *sivas* to civil servants. R. L. Stilwell. Sat R 49:42-3 S 24 '66

INDIAN music (East Indian) See Music, Indian (East Indian)

INDIAN national congress
Political python of India. J. A. Lukas. il N Y Times Mag p26-7+ F 20 '66

INDIAN OCEAN
Ocean mysteries revealed. Sci N 90:85 Ag 6 '66

INDIAN pipes (plants)
Indian pipe's secret. R. L. Scheffel. il Audubon Mag 68:224-5 Jl '66

INDIAN relics. See Indians of North America— Antiquities

INDIAN reservations. See Indians of North America—Reservations

INDIAN rhinoceros. See Rhinoceros

INDIAN schools. See Indians of North America—Education

INDIAN students (East Indian)
Majoring in mayhem; student rioting. Time 88:37 O 28 '66

INDIAN weaving. See Weaving

INDIANA, Robert
Horizons of Robert Indiana. G. R. Swenson. il Art N 65:48-9+ My '66

INDIANA
See also
Festivals—Indiana
Libraries—Indiana

History
Hush-a-bye, Indiana; changing of historical facts by local pride and press agentry. W. E. Wilson. il Am Heritage 18:68-71 D '66

Hospitals
See Hospitals—United States

INDIANA DUNES NATIONAL LAKESHORE
Battle of the dunes; bill passed. Newsweek 68:44+ O 24 '66
Indiana dunes lakeshore. Nat Parks Mag 40:23 My '66
Park system expands. Nat Parks Mag 40:18 D '66
Saving the dunes. Time 88:80 O 21 '66
Sleeping Bear Dunes National Lakeshore. H. A. Raup. il Nat Parks Mag 40:10-14 F '66

INDIANA general corporation
Flying Dutchman. R. Levy. Duns R 88:60-1+ N '66

INDIANA university press
Indiana press organizes international department. Pub W 190:42 Jl 25 '66

INDIANAPOLIS
Crime
Addenda to De Sade; murder of S. M. Likens. il Time 87:25 My 6 '66
Avenging Sylvia; death by torture of S. M. Likens. Time 87:22-3 My 27 '66

INDIANAPOLIS automobile races. See Automobile racing

INDIANS
Art
See also
Indians of North America—Art
Totem poles
Education
See also
Indians of North America—Education
Weaving
See Weaving

INDIANS (Hindus) See Hindus
INDIANS (of India) See East Indians

INDIANS, Treatment of
Blasphemy. Nation 202:476 Ap 25 '66
Defender of the Indians; with editorial comment. R. Gallardo. il Américas 18:inside cover, 23:31 O '66

INDIANS in art
George Catlin revival. H. McCracken. il Am Artist 30:26-31+ Mr '66
Painting among the Seminoles. J. Hutchinson. il Am Artist 30:52-7+ Ap '66
Roundup time. il Time 88:56-8 Ag 12 '66
Sculpture of Eugenie Shonnard. E. Bell. il Am Artist 30:62-7+ Je '66

INDIANS of Alaska. See Indians of North America—Alaska

INDIANS of Central America
Antiquities
Gold of Coclé, Panama. R. A. Cowes. bibliog il Américas 18:18-25 F '66
See also
Mayas

INDIANS of Mexico
Lonely tribe of long-distance runners; Mexico's Tarahumare Indians. E. Shrake. il Sports Illus 26:56-62+ Ja 9 '67
See also
Aztecs
Antiquities
Digging up prehistoric America; discoveries of ancient cultivated corn solve prehistoric mystery. R. Claiborne. il Harper 232:69-74 Ap '66
Gallery for young people; dog; funeral offerings. C. B. Johnson. il Sch Arts 65:44 My '66
Rock carvings at Chalcacingo; bas-reliefs add to knowledge of ancient Olmec culture in Mexico. C. T. E. Gay. il Natur Hist 75:56-61 Ag '66
Science in action; choosing a site to dig. S. Gorenstein. Natur Hist 75:64-7 F '66
Suggested revision for west Mexican archeological sequences. S. V. Long and R. E. Taylor. bibliog il Science 154:1456-9 D 16 '66
See also
Mayas
Sculpture, Pre-Columbian

Dances
Dances of Anáhuac, by G. P. Kurath and S. Martí. Review
  Américas 18:46-7 Ap '66. M. C. Moyano
Music
Dances of Anáhuac, by G. P. Kurath and S. Martí. Review
  Américas 18:46-7 Ap '66. M. C. Moyano

INDIANS of North America
See also
Apache Indians
Arapaho Indians
Eskimos
Havasupai Indians
Hopi Indians
Navaho Indians
Nez Percé Indians
Paiute Indians
Pueblo Indians
Seminole Indians
Seneca Indians
Totem poles

Antiquities
Indian relics. C. Miles. il Hobbies 70:113-15 F '66
Paleo-Indian bison kill. J. B. Wheat. il Sci Am 216:44-52 Ja '67

Alaska
Alaska's vanishing art. K. Kuh. il Sat R 49:25-31 O 22 '66

Arizona
Willow figurines from Arizona. R. C. Euler. il Natur Hist 75:62-7 Mr '66

Nevada
Paiute trail; or, Collecting in Nevada. C. Miles. Hobbies 71:113-14 S '66

New Mexico
Oldest New World community; Rio Rancho, Albuquerque. Sci Am 214:51 Ap '66

North Dakota
Copper artifacts from prehistoric archeological sites in the Dakotas. W. E. Hill, jr. and R. W. Neuman. bibliog Science 154:1171-3 D 2 '66

South Dakota
Copper artifacts from prehistoric archeological sites in the Dakotas. bibliog Science 154:1171-3 D 2 '66

Art
Alaska's vanishing art. K. Kuh. il Sat R 49:25-31 O 22 '66
Flagstaff's permanent Indian show; Museum of northern Arizona. il Sunset 136:78 My '66

Culture
Enduring Indian. N. O. Lurie. Natur Hist 75:10+ N '66
Intermountain plateau area. C. Miles. il Hobbies 71:114-16 D '66
Northwest Coast culture area. C. Miles. il Hobbies 70:113 F '66
Plains Indian culture area. C. Miles. il Hobbies 71:112-14+ Ja '67
Sub-areas of the Northwest coast culture. C. Miles. il Hobbies 71:114-16 Mr; 114-15 Ap; 114-16 My; 114-15+ Je; 114-16 Jl; 114-15+ Ag '66
Tales of the Amerinds. J. K. Hutchens. il Sat R 49:25-6 Ag 13 '66

Dances
Summertime is powwow time; versions of Indian ritual dances across the country. G. P. Kurath. il Dance Mag 40:40-1+ My '66

Economic conditions
Indian tests the mainstream. D. McNickle. il Nation 203:275-9 S 26 '66
Indians and their benefactors; Office of economic opportunity's project at Rosebud Sioux reservation. New Repub 155:9 Jl 16 '66
Let's get the Indians into the economy. H. B. Meyers. Fortune 74:104 S '66
Private-plus plan to ease poverty; Anadarko, Okla. J. P. Eddy. Christian Cent 83:1064 Ag 31 '66
Red backlash in Minnesota. Christian Cent 83:1400-1 N 16 '66

Education
Panacea; teaching on Christian Island in Lake Huron. E. Beeson. il Sr Schol 88:sup 12-13 Mr 18 '66

INDIANS of North America—*Continued*

Fishing

Dick Gregory goes fishing: fish-in on the Nisqually River. R. C. Lee. Nation 202:487-9 Ap 25 '66

Udall and the Indians; National Indian youth council fight to preserve 1854 fishing treaty. New Repub 154:8 Ap 30 '66

Government relations

Enduring Indian. N. O. Lurie. Natur Hist 75:10+ N '66

Indian tests the mainstream. D. McNickle. il Nation 203:275-9 S 26 '66

See also

Indians of North America—Reservations

Indians of North America—Treaties

United States—Indian affairs, Bureau of

History

Disinherited by D. Van Every. Review Sat R 49:39 Ap 2 '66. J. Collier. sr

Tales of the Amerinds. J. K. Hutchens. il Sat R 49:25-6 Ag 13 '66

Implements

Storied rock becomes a bird oasis: Indian metate, or milling stone. H. Carleton. il Audubon Mag 68:273-4 Jl '66

Legal status, laws, etc.

See Indians of North America—Government relations

Missions

Mission; journeying through New Mexico. C. Walter. il U S Camera 29:16-17 Mr '66

Religion and mythology

Chicago's Indian priest; P. J. Powell of the St Augustine center for American Indians. il Newsweek 69:91 Ja 23 '67

See also

Totem poles

Reservations

Indians and their benefactors: Office of economic opportunity's project at Rosebud Sioux reservation. New Repub 155:9 Jl 16 '66

Long way from the buffalo road; excerpt from The Arapaho way, ed. by A. Bass. C. Sweezy. il Am Heritage 17:22-5+ O '66

Monument Valley: a Navajo tribal park. O. F. Oldendorph. il Nat Parks Mag 40:4-8 Ag '66

Udall's Indians: proposed legislation to manage own lands. New Repub 155:7-8 O 15 '66

Maps

New guide to your vacationlands. H. E. Paine. il Nat Geog Mag 130:94-7, sup(folded map) Jl '66

Social conditions

Under the Indian sign: Indians of Maine. L. Spiker. il Nation 202:483-6 Ap 25 '66

Where the real poverty is: plight of American Indians. il U S News 60:104-8 Ap 25 '66

Treaties

Dick Gregory goes fishing; Indian rights. R. C. Lee. Nation 202:487-9 Ap 25 '66

Treatment

See Indians, Treatment of

Wars

See also

Little Big Horn, Battle of the, 1876

Alaska

Tycoons of Tyonek. il Time 88:19 Jl 1 '66

Maine

Under the Indian sign. L. Spiker. il Nation 202:483-6 Ap 25 '66

INDIANS of North America in art. See Indians in art

INDIANS of South America

Antiquities

See also

Sculpture, Pre-Columbian

Colombia

Aboriginal sophisticates; ancient manmade ridges in Colombia. il Time 88:81 Ag 5 '66

Jungle gods of San Agustin. G. Reichel-Dolmatoff. il Natur Hist 75:42-9 D '66

Mystery of an engineering wonder. J. Reinert. il Sci Digest 60:8-9 O '66

Ecuador

Japanese in B.C. America? Jomon-like pottery unearthed at Valdivia, Ecuador. il Sci N L 89:53 Ja 22 '66

Peru

City wrested from the jungle; city of pre-Inca times found in the region of Pajaten. il UNESCO Courier 19:33 D '66

Gold of ancient Peru. D. T. Easby, jr. Américas 18:24-33 D '66

See also

Pottery, Peruvian

Social conditions

Blow-up in the Andes; new trouble for U.S. J. N. Wallace. il U S News 60:72-4 Ap 11 '66

Treatment

See Indians, Treatment of

Brazil

[Portfolio of photographs from the Mato Grosso] C. Andujar. Mod Phot 30:51-7 Je '66

Peru

See also

Incas

Venezuela

Jungle journal. J. Liedloff. Esquire 65:44+ My '66

Yanomamö, the fierce people. N. A. Chagnon. il Natur Hist 76:22-31 Ja '67

INDICATORS, Target. See Target locators

INDIGNATION. See Anger

INDIGO buntings

North sky guides birds. P. McBroom. Sci N 90:152 S 3 '66

INDIVIDUAL and society

I can't swim; citizen responsibility; address, May 24, 1966. R. G. Wingerter. Vital Speeches 32:631-8 Ag 1 '66

Individual in society; commitment to discipline and compassion; address, May 25, 1966. J. Howard. Vital Speeches 32:593-6 Jl 15 '66

Why young people are seeking new values. R. Schickel. il Redbook 127:73+ My '66

INDIVIDUAL and state

I can't swim; citizen responsibility; address, May 24, 1966. R. G. Wingerter. Vital Speeches 32:631-8 Ag 1 '66

INDIVIDUAL differences

See also

Sex differences

INDIVIDUAL instruction

Individualizing instruction; symposium. il NEA J 55:31-40 N '66

INDIVIDUAL liberty. See Liberty

INDIVIDUALISM

See also

Individual and state

Personalism

INDIVIDUALITY

Do you see your children as they really are? with quiz. W. Abraham. il PTA Mag 60:28-30 Je '66

Pretty, lascivious, undignified: individuality of women. J. Mitford. Vogue 147:92-3 Mr 15 '66

See also

Personality

INDIVIDUALIZED instruction. See Individual instruction

INDOCHINA, FRENCH

History

Civil war, 1946-1954

And still the little men of the Vietcong keep coming. B. B. Fall. il N Y Times Mag p20-1+ Mr 6 '66

Enclave warfare: France's experience; report. S. W. Sanders. il U S News 60:37 F 28 '66

General de Gaulle and Vietnam. J. Lacouture. New Repub 154:19-21 Mr 12 '66

1954 and 1966: is U.S. repeating French mistakes in Vietnam? interview. M. Taylor. il U S News 60:36-7 F 28 '66

Two sides to the Dienbienphu story; concerning assessments by Bernard Fall and VO Nguyen Giap. J. Mirsky. Nation 202:781-4 Je 27 '66

Civil war, 1946-1954—Peace and mediation

See also

Council of foreign ministers, Geneva, 1954

INDOLEACETIC acid

Reversible inactivation of aged solutions of indolyl-3-acetic acid. A. A. Bitancourt. bibliog il Science 154:1327-9 D 9 '66

INDONESIA
Five journeys from Jakarta, by M. Williams.
Review
   Newsweek il 67:92+ F 28 '66
  See also
Anti-Communist movements—Indonesia
Bali
Chinese in Indonesia
Education—Indonesia
Foreign visitors in Indonesia
Immigration and emigration—Indonesia
Investments, Foreign (in Indonesia)
Jogjakarta
Political parties—Indonesia
Trials—Indonesia
United Nations—Indonesia

Army
As Indonesia tries military rule. il U S News
  60:46 Mr 28 '66
Bloodbath with reds on receiving end. il
  U S News 60:34 Ja 31 '66
Indonesia: the plot that failed. L. M.
  Taubinger. Nat R 18:160 F 22 '66

Cabinet
Bung's bounce; new cabinet. il Time 87:40
  Mr 4 '66
Temper tantrum. Newsweek 68:34 Ag 8 '66

Economic conditions
Forward to chaos. Newsweek 67:35 F 7 '66
Hopes rise for Indonesia. il Bsns W p92-4+
  Jl 30 '66
Indonesia back to realism. America 115:126
  Ag 6 '66
Indonesia dusts off welcome mat: new foreign
  investment law. Bsns W p24 D 31 '66
Indonesia: generation of '66. R. Littell. il
  Newsweek 67:36+ My 16 '66
Indonesia: hope, where once there was none.
  R. P. Martin. il U S News 60:70-2 Je 6 '66
Indonesia's unfinished revolution. D. Warner.
  il Reporter 35:28-9+ Jl 14 '66
Land of *ngobjek*. il Fortune 74:69-70+ O '66
Peace breaks out. Newsweek 68:71 Ag 22 '66
Struggle for power in Indonesia. D. Kirk. il
  Reporter 34:38-40 F 24 '66

Foreign population
  See also
Chinese in Indonesia

Foreign relations
Friends again? relations with U.S. Sr Schol
  88:18 My 13 '66
Indonesia for Indonesians; what the latest
  upheaval may mean. J. Hughes. New Re-
  pub 154:11-12 Ap 30 '66
Indonesian foreign minister meets with
  Secretary Rusk; joint statement, September
  27, 1966. D. Rusk and A. Malik. Dept State
  Bul 55:652 O 24 '66
King of kings; new policy emerging. il News-
  week 67:59 My 2 '66
Maphilindo again. Newsweek 67:53-4 My 30 '66
Mission to Malaysia. il Time 87:27 Je 3 '66
Peace breaks out; agreement with Malaysia.
  Newsweek 68:70-1 Ag 22 '66
Peace talks; ending the three-year-old war
  with Malaysia. il Newsweek 67:52 Je 13 '66
Uproar of peace; end of Indonesia's *kon-
frontasi* with Malaysia. il Time 87:39-40
  Je 10 '66

Industries
  See also
Indonesia—Economic conditions

Politics and government
Anti-Communist crusade of Indonesia's Mos-
  lems. D. Kirk. il Reporter 34:41-2+ Ja 27
  '66
As Indonesia tries military rule. il U S News
  60:46 Mr 28 '66
Atlantic report. Atlan 219:12+ Ja '67
Convenient confession; Aidit's reputed con-
  fession. il Newsweek 67:41 F 21 '66
Counter-counterattack. il Newsweek 67:46
  Mr 7 '66
Coup a la Java. Sr Schol 88:7 Mr 25 '66
De-communization. Newsweek 67:40+ F 28
  '66
Dilemma in Djakarta. Newsweek 68:34-5 D
  26 '66
Eclipse. Newsweek 68:38+ Jl 18 '66
Emergency time. il Time 87:25 Mr 25 '66
End of the line for Sukarno; more power
  for his successor. il U S News 61:20 Jl
  18 '66
Five journeys from Jakarta, by M. Williams.
Review
  Nat R 18:375-7 Ap 19 '66. A. Lejeune
General at the palace. il Time 87:35 Ap 8 '66

Getting rid of Sukarno; Indonesia's leaders
  have a surplus of opponents. R. Butwell.
  New Repub 155:12-13 O 8 '66
Great purge Indonesia; slaughter of Indo-
  nesian Communist party. S. S. King. il
  N Y Times Mag p25+ My 8 '66
Haunted face of a red defeat; vengeance
  against Communists; with report by D.
  Moser. il Life 61:24-33 Jl 1 '66
Indonesia after gestapu. Nat R 18:161 F 22
  '66
Indonesia: change at the top. Newsweek 67:
  42 Mr 21 '66
Indonesia: complete overhaul. B. Krisher. il
  Newsweek 67:48+ Ap 4 '66
Indonesia for Indonesians; what the latest
  upheaval may mean. J. Hughes. New Re-
  pub 154:11-12 Ap 30 '66
Indonesia: generation of '66. R. Littell. il
  Newsweek 67:36+ My 16 '66
Indonesia: hope after massacre. A. Josey. il
  Nation 203:565-70 N 28 '66
Indonesia: hope, where once there was
  none. R. P. Martin. il U S News 60:70-2
  Je 6 '66
Indonesia: night of terror, dawn of hope;
  September 1965 coup. C. W. Hall. il Read
  Digest 89:275-8+ O '66
Indonesia's Chinese are people without a
  country. D. Kirk. il N Y Times Mag p32-3+
  O 23 '66; Reply. E. Tepper. p22+ N 6 '66
Indonesia's quasi-military regime. F. Bun-
  nell. bibliog f Cur Hist 52:22-8+ Ja '67
Indonesia's unfinished revolution. D. Warner.
  il Reporter 35:28-9+ Jl 14 '66
King of kings; new policy emerging. il News-
  week 67:59 My 2 '66
Man on trial; Subandrio. il Time 88:44 O 14
  '66
Now you see him . . . il Time 87:33 Mr 18 '66
President, the generals, and the angry young
  men; Sukarno's wife mediates. Time 87:30
  Ap 1 '66
Pride and fall. Nation 202:346 Mr 28 '66
Reducing the aura. Time 87:36 Ap 22 '66
Sentence of death, a sentence of advice. Time
  89:26+ Ja 6 '67
Situation normal; arrests and appointments.
  il Newsweek 67:48-9 Mr 28 '66
Small price to pay. il Newsweek 69:42+ Ja
  23 '67
Streamlined cabinet. Time 88:28 Ag 5 '66
Struggle for power in Indonesia. D. Kirk. il
  Reporter 34:38-40 F 24 '66
Suharto is the name, not Sukarno. D. Kirk.
  il N Y Times Mag p 18-19+ Jl 24 '66
Sukarno's holdouts in central Java; Nation-
  alist-Moslem conflict. D. Kirk. il Reporter
  35:39-41 S 8 '66
Talk with General Suharto; interview; ed.
  by B. Krisher. Suharto. Newsweek 68:43
  S 5 '66
Terrible toll; post coup death figures. News-
  week 67:50 Ja 31 '66
Thousand cuts; Peoples' consultative con-
  gress session. il Newsweek 68:42 Jl 4 '66
Tightening the noose. il Time 87:27 My 27
  '66
Triumvirate at the top. Bsns W p95 Jl 30 '66
Turmoil rules in Indonesia; Sukarno's battle
  with army leaders. Bsns W p44 Mr 19 '66
Ultimatum for Sukarno? Newsweek 69:31 Ja
  9 '67
Uncertain balance. il Time 87:35 My 13 '66
Unmaking of a president. il Time 88:29-30
  Jl 1 '66
Vengeance with a smile. il Time 88:22-6 Jl
  15 '66
View from Jakarta; public reaction to the
  Indonesian crisis. Nation 202:171 F 14 '66
Where the girls were; tales of corruption,
  embezzlement and sexual promiscuity in
  the days of President Sukarno. Newsweek
  68:40 S 12 '66
Who's on trial? former Cabinet members
  put on trial. Time 88:36 S 9 '66
Young wives' tale; charges of corruption
  against former ministers. il Newsweek 67:
  53 Ap 11 '66
  See also
Indonesia—Cabinet

Religious institutions and affairs
Anti-Communist crusade of Indonesia's Moslems. D. Kirk. il Reporter 34:41-2+ Ja 27
  '66

Riots
Bung's bounce; anti-red students storm
  Djakarta. il Time 87:40 Mr 4 '66
INDONESIAN students
Asian flu; riots after Sukarno's Independence
  day speech. il Newsweek 68:42+ S 5 '66
Impatient '66 generation driving hard for
  reforms. il Life 61:32-3 Jl 1 '66

INDONESIAN students—*Continued*
Students boot out the Communists. H. C. Atyeo. Nat R 18:458 My 17 '66
Suharto is the name, not Sukarno. D. Kirk. il N Y Times Mag p 18-19+ Jl 24 '66
INDOOR birdwatcher; story. See Rogin, G.
INDOOR gardening. See Window gardening
INDOOR gardens. See Gardens, Indoor
INDOOR plants. See House plants
INDOOR tennis. See Tennis
INDOOR tennis courts. See Tennis courts, Indoor
INDUCTANCE
Build the crowd stopper; demonstrating principle of mutual induction. W. B. Ford. il Pop Electr 24:48-51+ My '66
Power inductors. R. E. Coy. il Electr World 76:33-5+ N '66
Special section: chokes and coils: symposium. il Electr World 76:37-52 O '66
Straight-wire inductance graph. D. W. Moffat. il Electr World 75:27 F '66
Testing and measuring inductors. S. Zwass. il Electr World 76:30-2+ S '66
INDUCTION (electricity)
See also
Inductance
INDUCTION coils
Life testing of R.F. inductors. W. D. Hauser. il Electr World 76:60 S '66
Power inductors. R. E. Coy. il Electr World 76:33-5+ N '66
Special section: chokes and coils; symposium. il Electr World 76:37-52 O '66
INDUCTIVE reactance. See Inductance
INDUS VALLEY
Antiquities
See also
Mohenjo-daro
INDUSTRIAL agreements. See Trade agreements
INDUSTRIAL arbitration. See Arbitration, Industrial
INDUSTRIAL areas foundation
Making trouble is Alinsky's business. P. Anderson. il N Y Times Mag p28-31+ O 9 '66
INDUSTRIAL arts
Study and teaching
Learning the art of industry. M. L. Schmitt. il Am Ed 2:8-11 My '66
INDUSTRIAL bonds. See Bonds
INDUSTRIAL buildings
Building types study; with introd. by J. Barnett. il Arch Rec 139:173-88 Je '66
Dark steel pavilion designed for export; Cummins engine co. plant, Darlington, England. il Arch Forum 125:82-7 O '66
Four small industrial plants, simple in concept, and designed with a skilled restraint. il Arch Rec 140:151-5 N '66
Industrial construction: too much too soon? G. A. Christie. il Arch Rec 140:44 D '66
IBM thinks twice. J. M. Dixon. il Arch Forum 124:32-9 Mr '66
Leaving the columns outside; computer plant, Scientific data systems inc. il Arch Forum 125:70-7 N '66
Three buildings for industrial research; facilities at Climax molybdenum company of Michigan, Ann Arbor. il Arch Rec 140: 178-81 O '66
See also
Factories
Designs and plans
Secret of plant layout is rational analysis and evaluation. il Arch Rec 139:178-81 Je '66
Heating and ventilation
Swiss engineers explain incinerator income. il Am City 81:24 Je '66
INDUSTRIAL college of the armed forces. See United States—Industrial college of the armed forces
INDUSTRIAL control. See Industry and state
INDUSTRIAL cooperation
Big business can help you be your own boss. L. Velie. Read Digest 88:141-4 My '66
INDUSTRIAL corporation bonds. See Bonds
INDUSTRIAL development bonds. See Bonds, Industrial development
INDUSTRIAL districts
Research park thrives in academic neighborhood; North Carolina's Research triangle park. il Bsns W p 184-5+ D 10 '66
INDUSTRIAL diversification. See Diversification in industry

INDUSTRIAL education
Teaching Ivan a trade; training factory workers. il Bsns W p80+ Ap 30 '66
See also
Business education
Employees—Training
Engineering education
Industrial arts—Study and teaching
Technical education
Vocational education
INDUSTRIAL efficiency. See Efficiency, Industrial
INDUSTRIAL engineering
Systems approach to automation is explained to R&E council; annual conference. Pub W 189:154-6+ Je 13 '66
INDUSTRIAL equipment
Making do with the old; McGraw-Hill economics dept. survey. il Bsns W p 101-2 N 26 '66
INDUSTRIAL espionage. See Spies, Industrial
INDUSTRIAL exhibitions. See Exhibitions
INDUSTRIAL exhibitions, Traveling. See Exhibitions, Traveling
INDUSTRIAL expansion
Expansion runs into a logjam; construction headaches; lack of men and material. il Bsns W p 169-70+ Ap 16 '66
See also
Capital investments
INDUSTRIAL gaming. See Management games
INDUSTRIAL gases. See Gases—Industrial applications
INDUSTRIAL know-how. See Technical information
INDUSTRIAL location. See Location in business and industry
INDUSTRIAL management and organization
Affluent organization; excerpts from address, April 8, 1966. R. E. Miles. bibliog f Harvard Bsns R 44:106-14 My '66
Armco peps up service by overhauling itself. il Bsns W p96-8+ F 26 '66
How Thiokol weathered the storm; top-to-bottom reorganization. il Bsns W p98-100+ N 12 '66
Industry action to combat pollution. J. J. Hanks and H. D. Kube. bibliog f il Harvard Bsns R 44:49-62 S '66
Russia upgrades its managers; growing management movement; with editorial comment. Bsns W p76+. 196 Ap 16 '66
Why the ink is black at Harris-Intertype; planning, the watchword. il Bsns W p34-6 D 31 '66
See also
Assembly line methods
Business management and organization
Linear programming
Management rights
Railroads—Management

Study and teaching
Mentors for Britain's flagging management; London business school helping to instill professionalism in industry's managers. il Bsns W p 190-1+ O 15 '66
See also
Harvard university—Graduate school of business administration

Great Britain
What's the matter with the British businessman? S. White. Read Digest 88:207-8+ Ap '66
Russia
Economic reforms: big changes, big headaches, at Rostelmash; giant farm equipment manufacturing enterprise at Rostov. Bsns W p 140 Jl 23 '66
Labor aspects of the economic reform in the Soviet Union. E. Nash. Mo Labor R 89: 597-602 Je '66
Russia's brass tells how it's done; international management session at Rotterdam hears Soviet experts. il Bsns W p 171-2+ O 8 '66
INDUSTRIAL missions. See Missions—Industrial work
INDUSTRIAL mobilization
Business and Vietnam. J. Perham. il Duns R 87:40-2+ Ap '66
Getting guns, and butter. il Bsns W p94-8 Ap 30 '66
Industry acts to meet novel problems; company-by-company examination of efforts to satisfy unprecedented limited-war needs of military. W. E. Wilks. il Miss & Roc 18: 123+ Ap 4 '66
Lag in deliveries puts squeeze on Pentagon. il Bsns W p 18-19 D 24 '66

INDUSTRIAL morale. See Employee morale
INDUSTRIAL noise. See Noise
INDUSTRIAL organization. See Industrial management and organization
INDUSTRIAL packaging. See Packaging
INDUSTRIAL parks. See Industrial districts
INDUSTRIAL pensions. See Pensions, Industrial
INDUSTRIAL psychology. See Psychology, Industrial
INDUSTRIAL relations
Canada getting set for a rough year; labor to press hard for greater gains. il Bsns W p51-2+ Ja 7 '67
Close-up: talk with George W. Taylor; interview. ed. by J. Berry. il Duns R 88: 8-9+ O '66
Demand is: more, much more; business resistance stiffens, potential trouble looms. il Bsns W p 118+ Ag 6 '66
Developments in industrial relations. See Issues of Monthly labor review
Gathering storm in labor relations. Bsns W p 116 Jl 30 '66
Just ahead: seventeen months of strike threats. il Nations Bsns 54:36-7+ Ag '66
Labor in a year of expansion. P. Groom. bibliog f Mo Labor R 88:1414-22 D '65
Papers from the IRRA annual meeting; excerpts. Mo Labor R 89:125-31 F '66
Recommendation for maritime labor relations policies. Mo Labor R 89:19-21 Ja '66
Review of labor relations in 1966. K. E. Ondras. Mo Labor R 89:1356-61 D '66
Significant decisions in labor cases. See Issues of Monthly labor review
Unions close ranks for next year's bargaining; AFL-CIO helping to set up new coalitions for 1967. Bsns W p90+ N 12 '66
What to do when the union knocks. W. Wingo. il Nations Bsns 54:42-5+ N; 40-1+ D '66; 55:82-5+ Ja '67
    See also
Arbitration, Industrial
Collective bargaining
Communication in management
Strikes
Trade agreements
United States—Labor policy
United States—National labor relations board
INDUSTRIAL relations research association
Papers from the IRRA annual meeting; excerpts (cont) Mo Labor R 89:125-31 F '66
Papers from the IRRA spring meeting; excerpts. Mo Labor R 89:603-16 Je '66
INDUSTRIAL research
Basic research in the university and industrial laboratory; excerpts from address, 1966. R. E. Marshak. Science 154:1521-4 D 23 '66
High technology of 1965. il Fortune 74:216-23 Jl 15 '66
How to make R&D more productive; through a program appraisal staff. L. G. Cook. Harvard Bsns R 44:145-50+ Jl '66
Industry research plan. Sci N 89:279 Ap 16 '66
Pouring more billions into R&D; pursuit for new products. il Bsns W p 164-6+ My 7 '66
Research outlook; austerest research budget in memory. Bsns W p 109 My 21 '66
Road to glory? Sci N 90:551 D 24 '66
Soviets' new profit lure: overhaul of Russia's R&D establishment. Bsns W p 115 S 17 '66
What's needed to keep new products coming; symposium. il Nations Bsns 53:42-3+ D '65
    See also
Fire protection—Research
National research corporation
Operations research
Products, New
INDUSTRIAL revenue bonds. See Municipal bonds
INDUSTRIAL revolution
    See also
Social revolution
INDUSTRIAL schools. See Trade schools
INDUSTRIAL secrets. See Trade secrets
INDUSTRIAL security measures. See Industry —Security measures
INDUSTRIAL spies. See Spies, Industrial
INDUSTRIAL statistics
Business markets. il Duns R 88:pt2 70-6 Jl '66
    See also
Employment—Statistics
INDUSTRIAL tours
Plant tours. J. E. Frazer. il Travel 126:31-4 Jl '66; Same abr. Read Digest 89:19-20+ Jl '66

INDUSTRIAL towns. See Company towns
INDUSTRIAL trusts. See Trusts, Industrial
INDUSTRIAL union department. See American federation of labor and Congress of industrial organizations—Industrial union department
INDUSTRIAL waste. See Trade waste
INDUSTRIALIZATION
Industrial development. UN Mo Chron 3:71-8 Je '66
Spanish temper heats up; economy out of balance. il Bsns W p78-9+ Ag 6 '66
Technology in China. G. Uchida. il Sci Am 215:37-45 N '66
    See also
Economic development
Underdeveloped areas
INDUSTRIAS Romi. See Machine tool industry and trade
INDUSTRIES, Seasonal. See Seasonal industries
INDUSTRY
    See also
Business
        Charitable contributions
    See Corporations—Charitable contributions
        Location
    See Location in business and industry
        Security measures
Spying for industry; private police and detective firms. J. Ridgeway. New Repub 154:10-11 My 14 '66
INDUSTRY and art. See Art and industry
INDUSTRY and education. See Business and education
INDUSTRY and state
Accidents will happen; possible consequences of government interference in automotive industry. Reporter 34:9 My 5 '66
After the honeymoon; four leading business executives views. L. L. L. Golden. Sat R 49:121 O 8 '66
Aluminum: the classic rollback. G. Burck. il Fortune 73:106-11+ F '66
America's next ten years. Nations Bsns 54: 42 Ap '66
As new controls threaten, would you rather fight than switch? il Nations Bsns 54: 44-6+ O '66
At issue: should government plan for business? il Nations Bsns 54:35-7 F '66
Automobile smashup. R. A. Webber. America 114:851-3 Je 18 '66
Big business and the national interest. il Sr Schol 88:9-11+ My 20 '66
Bobby Kennedy and the businessmen. G. R. Rosen. il Duns R 88:32-3+ O '66
Bridging the gap; State department opens exchange program. Newsweek 68:64+ Ag 15 '66
Business and government, do they speak the same language? exclusive economic survey. D. M. Keezer; A. Balk. il Sat R 49: 23-9+ Mr 5 '66
Business and the G.O.P. J. Berry; reply. B. Goldwater. Duns R 87:16 Ja '66
Car safety; concerning auto safety legislation. New Repub 154:10 Ap 16 '66
Challenge to business: create its own Great society; condensation of address, March 24, 1966. G. Champion. Read Digest 89:107-10 Ag '66
Changes in store for AF non-profits; with editorial comment. M. Getler. Miss & Roc 18:14-15, 54 Ap 25 '66
Closeup: interview. T. C. Sorensen. il Duns R 88:8-9 Jl '66
Company's man in Washington. R. A. Smith. il Fortune 73:132-5+ Ap '66
Controls close in on business, and more are on the way. il U S News 61:74-5 Jl 4 '66
Conversion of defense resources. B. G. Lall. Bul Atomic Sci 22:46-8 Ja '66
DOD emphasis on concept stage to benefit industry. M. Getler. Miss & Roc 18:15-16 My 23 '66
Do stiffer controls lie ahead? defense pressures. Bsns W p61-2 O 15 '66
Eyes on industry; auto and drug industries. Commonweal 84:143 Ap 22 '66
Fighting influence with influence; John D. Harper's comment on Washington power. il Time 87:96 F 4 '66
FSO and business executive exchanged in pilot project. Dept State Bul 55:279 Ag 22 '66
Government and business; must they be enemies? address, January 12, 1967. H. Ford, 2d. il U S News 62:82-5 Ja 23 '67

INDUSTRY and state—*Continued*
Government tightens the red tape noose. il Nations Bsns 54:54-6+ Jl '66
House unit drops non-profit investigation. K. Johnsen. Aviation W 84:29-30 Ap 25 '66
How steel is winning luster in Washington. il Bsns W p 146+ N 26 '66
How to reduce business' credibility gap; government industry relations; address, March 24, 1966. B. C. Goss. Vital Speeches 32:396-8 Ap 15 '66
Keeping an eye on Washington; interview. W. M. Kiplinger. il Nations Bsns 54:68-72+ Ag '66
Let's give business a square deal. R. M. Nixon. Nations Bsns 54:46-7+ Ap '66
LBJ's mail; reaction to cooperation from business. Newsweek 67:68 Ap 25 '66
New partnership; big government and big business. R. J. Barber. New Repub 155:17-22 Ag 13 '66
News lines. See issues of U.S. news & World report
Ominous swipe at profits. Fortune 73:103-4 Je '66
People speak softly when government carries big stick. A. H. Sypher. il Nations Bsns 54:29-30 Ja '66
Politics of auto safety; background of bill's introduction. E. B. Drew. il Atlan 218:95-102 O '66
Private enterprise and public intelligence. G. J. Stigler. Duns R 88:17+ O '66
Push-button snooping; the threat to business. Nations Bsns 54:40-1+ N '66
Regulation, by business or government? J. G. Van Cise. bibliog f Harvard Bsns R 44:53-63 Mr '66
Safety strugle; possibility of an auto-safety law. il Time 87:90+ Ap 15 '66
Standing corporate watch on the Potomac; U.S. companies' full-time offices in Washington. il Newsweek 68:90-1 D 12 '66
Trouble with antitrust; excerpts from address. M. A. Wright. il Duns R 88:50-1+ N '66
Uncle Sam finds hot potato in beet field; Aroostook County, Me. il Nations Bsns 54:58-9 N '66
We can fight inflation without controls; interview. R. J. Saulnier. Nations Bsns 54:33-5+ Mr '66
We need a new capitalism in America. G. Romney. Nations Bsns 54:34-5+ Jl '66
What's needed to keep new products coming; symposium. Nations Bsns 53:42-3+ D '65
Why business dislikes the curbs LBJ proposes; excerpts from address, September 19, 1966. R. M. Blough. U S News 61:22 O 3 '66
Why politics needs business in '66; symposium. il Nations Bsns 54:42-5+ Je '66
See also
Economic planning
Free enterprise
Government aid to business
Industrial mobilization
Labor laws and legislation—United States
Price regulation by government
Public utilities—Regulation
Stock exchange—Regulation
Strikes—United States—Government intervention
Sweden—Labor policy
Trusts, Industrial
United States—Federal trade commission
United States—Interstate commerce commission
United States—Labor policy

Anecdotes, facetiae, satire, etc.
If Thomas Jefferson came back today. L. B. Mason. il Nations Bsns 54:70-1+ Ap '66
INDUSTRY and war. See War—Economic aspects
INEQUALITY. See Equality
INERTIAL guidance systems
Air force receives low-cost, accurate navigation system. R. G. Barnhart. il Miss & Roc 18-42 Ap 25 '66
C-5A platform tests reveal problems. Aviation W 85:31 Jl 11 '66
C-5A to use gimbal-less stable platform; integrated navigation system for military jet transports. B. Miller. il Aviation W 85:52-3+ D 5 '66
Faster carrier inertial alignment sought. B. Miller. il Aviation W 85:105-6+ N 21 '66
Inertial navaid business expands sharply. B. Miller. il Aviation W 85:136-7+ Ag 15 '66
Pan Am beginning Pacific navaid flights; using Sperry gyroscope SGN-10 inertial navigation system. K. J. Stein. Aviation W 85:43 S 19 '66

INERTIAL navigation. See Navigation, Aerial
INFALLIBILITY. See Catholic church—Infallibility
INFANCY of animals. See Animals, Infancy of
INFANT feeding. See Infants—Nutrition
INFANT mortality
Crib deaths: search for a mystery killer. S. M. Spencer. il Sat Eve Post 239:78-80+ N 19 '66
How disgraceful are the facts about infant deaths in the United States? J. R. Evrard and C. Evrard. Todays Health 44:72+ Jl '66
Nine deaths, no answers; crib deaths enigmas. il Newsweek 67:92 Mr 21 '66
See also
Obstetrics
INFANT psychology. See Child study
INFANTS
Shape perception in infants. Sci Am 214:56 My '66

Anecdotes, facetiae, satire, etc.
How to talk to a baby. J. Kerr. il Ladies Home J 83:56 F '66

Care and hygiene
America's unhealthy children; an emerging scandal. R. Tunley. Harper 232:41-6 My '66; Discussion. 233:4 Jl; 8 Ag '66
First days at home with the baby; excerpt from Your child and you. D. T. Hellyer. il Parents Mag 41:36-7+ Ap '66
Newborn baby; excerpt from The infant world. M. Liley and B. Day. il McCalls 93:26+ Ag '66; Same abr. with title Wondrous world of the newborn. Read Digest 89:193-4+ N '66
Play it cool with your baby. D. Siegel. il Parents Mag 41:28-9 Jl '66
See also
Children—Care and hygiene
Infants, Premature

Crying
Baby's cries a clue to intelligence; finding of Samuel Karelitz. Todays Health 45:69 Ja '67
Crying in infancy. B. Spock. il Redbook 127:26+ S '66
Nightly crybabies; search for a cause. il Time 88:79 S 23 '66
When a baby's cry means danger. P. M. Wright. Ladies Home J 83:68 Mr '66

Growth and development
Age differences in infants' attention to patterns of different complexities. W. M. Brennan and others. bibliog Science 151:354-6 Ja 21 '66
Beginning of character; how babies learn to meet the world. B. Spock. il Redbook 127:28+ O '66
How does a baby learn? M. A. Wessel. il Parents Mag 41:48-9+ Mr '66
Love is a baby's best teacher. D. S. Peet. il Parents Mag 41:58-9+ My '66
New born; dramatic story of the first days of life. J. Star. il Look 30:51-9 My 31 '66
Ontogenetic development of the human sleep-dream cycle. H. P. Roffwarg and others. bibliog il Science 152:604-19 Ap 29 '66

Language
See Children—Language

Management and training
See Children—Management and training

Names
See Names, Personal

Nutrition
Baby meats are versatile. il Parents Mag 41:104-5 Ap '66
Breast feeding; facts and fallacies. B. B. Smith. il Todays Health 44:36-7 F '66
Foods catered to baby's taste; Beech-Nut baby foods. M. B. Keiser. il Parents Mag 41:34+ My '66
Intestinal alkaline phosphatase; regulation by a strain-specific factor in mouse milk. P. R. V. Nayudu and F. Moog. bibliog il Science 152:656-7 Ap 29 '66
What's new in feeding babies. il Good H 162:175 My '66
See also
Gerber products company

Photographs
Young gourmet: Andrew Sirkis. N. Sirkis. il Look 30:M14-16 Ap 19 '66

INFANTS—*Continued*

Sight
See Sight

Sleep
See Sleep

INFANTS, Newborn
Attention in the newborn: effect on motility and skin potential. G. Stechler and others. bibliog il Science 151:1246-8 Mr 11 '66
Babies recognize early. Sci N 90:362 O 29 '66
New born: dramatic story of the first days of life. J. Star. il Look 30:51-9 My 31 '66
Optomotor response in human infants to apparent motion: evidence of innateness. E. S. Tauber and S. Koffler. bibliog Science 152: 382-3 Ap 15 '66
Slant perception and shape constancy in infants. T. G. R. Bower. bibliog il Science 151:832-4 F 18 '66
What you don't know about mothering. S. F. Yolles. Ladies Home J 83:50 Ag '66

INFANTS, Photography of. See Photography of children

INFANTS, Premature
Canopy protects premies. Sci N 90:368 N 5 '66
Heart standards set for premature babies. Sci N L 89:72 Ja 29 '66

INFECTION
Aerobiology: report on second International conference on aerobiology. R. Ehrlich. Science 154:293-4+ O 14 '66
Bye-bye, bacteria! T. Irwin. il Pop Mech 125:90-3+ Je '66
Chromosome changes induced by infections in tissues of rhynchosciara angelae. C. Pavan and R. Basile. bibliog il Science 151: 1556-8 Mr 25 '66
Goodbye to infection: laboratory-made antibodies: reprint. W. Sullivan. Sci Digest 59: 71-4 Mr '66

INFECTIOUS diseases. See Communicable diseases

INFECTIOUS mononucleosis. See Mononucleosis, Infectious

INFERIORITY complex. See Complexes (psychology)

INFERNO. See Dante Alighieri

INFINITE
Religious slum-dwellers. D. Callahan. Commonweal 84:530-3 Ag 19 '66; Discussion. 84:625+; 85:5+, 86-7 S 30-O 7, 21 '66

INFINITY. See Infinite

INFLAMMABLE materials
AF probes fires in 100 per cent oxygen. Miss & Roc 18:31-2 Mr 7 '66

INFLATABLE rafts. See Rafts

INFLATION (finance)
Anatomy of inflation: effect on companies. il Newsweek 67:66-8 Mr 28 '66
Attack on profits: concerning Gardner Ackley's Chamber of commerce speech. H. Hazlitt. Newsweek 67:90 My 23 '66
Avoiding overcure. il Time 87:93 My 13 '66
Bad means good; threat remains. Newsweek 67:78+ Ap 18 '66
Boom now getting out of hand? il U S News 60:25-6 My 9 '66
Brazil tries traveling the tight-money road. il Bsns W p76+ O 15 '66
Buck's being passed to you. il Nations Bsns 54:40-1 Je '66
Businessman's formula to head off inflation: excerpts from address, February 19, 1966. R. M. Blough. U S News 60:87-8 Mr 7 '66
Case for doing almost nothing. Fortune 74: 113-14 O '66
Check the boom? J. Tobin. New Repub 155: 9-14 S 3 '66
Councilor to Canute. Time 87:22 Ap 15 '66
Desert guideposts. H. C. Wallich. Newsweek 68:82 Ag 22 '66
Do the signs read inflation? with charts. il Bsns W p27-9 F 19 '66
Dose of taxes, but enough? tax bill to curb inflation. il Newsweek 67:66 Mr 28 '66
Doubts that won't go away: worries over inflation, prices, and Vietnam-boom pressures. il Bsns W p40-1 S 17 '66
Experts turn against tax boosts: survey of 100 top men finds 60 per cent opposed. il Bsns W p 154-5+ My 28 '66
From mist to rain. il Time 87:15-16 Mr 25 '66
Future of U.S. boom as Europe sees it. il U S News 60:62-4 My 2 '66
Get ready for more inflation. il Changing T 20:33-5 Je '66
Gone guideposts. Time 88:65 Ag 12 '66
Guidelines for the guidelines. L. B. Johnson. il Newsweek 68:79 Ag 22 '66

Home building: inflation casualty. il U S News 60:27-8 Je 27 '66
How inflation baffles investment markets: U.S, Europe, Japan. il U S News 60:62-3 Mr 21 '66
How much inflation ahead? what economists say. il U S News 60:42-5 Mr 14 '66
If inflation becomes a way of life in U.S: what to expect. il U S News 60:29-31 Je 27 '66
Inflation? Nat R 18:255-6 Mr 22 '66; Reply. D. Coxe. 18:338 Ap 19 '66
Inflation: bugbear and battle cry; with excerpts from L. B. Johnson's addresses. il Newsweek 67:27-8 Ap 11 '66
Inflation everywhere. Time 87:96 Mr 4 '66
Inflation: getting less for your money. il Sr Schol 88:18-19 F 11 '66
Inflation is Saigon's other enemy. il Bsns W p54+ Mr 5 '66
Inflation isn't easy to measure; BLS chief urges five-year study. il Bsns W p54+ Je 4 '66
Inflation: pro and con debate over LBJ's program. il Life 60:83-4+ Ap 15 '66
Inflation? recession? or both? il Nations Bsns 54:38-41+ O '66
Inflation requires action now. Life 60:4 Ap 1 '66
Inflation: the elusive pickpocket. il Sr Schol 89:11-13 N 4 '66
Investing in a time of inflation, advice of economists; symposium. il U S News 60: 58-65 Ap 4 '66
Investors tremble over indecision; Wall Street blames White House policymakers. il Bsns W p 158-9 Mr 19 '66
Is there inflation ahead? symposium. Duns R 87:38-40+ F '66
Johnson tries for a fresh formula; need for wage-price guidepost reinforcement. il Bsns W p25-6 Ag 13 '66
Johnson's new consensus; Business week survey of top executives; with editorial comment. il Bsns W p25-6, 172 Ap 9 '66
Little anti-inflation tonic; how foreign bankers size up health of the U.S. economy. U S News 61:74 O 10 '66
LBJ's anti-inflation plan: how business will be affected. il U S News 61:31-3 S 19 '66
LBJ's economic baling wire: anti-inflation moves. il Newsweek 68:79 O 3 '66
Moderate inflation? il Fortune 73:37-8 F '66
Must full employment mean inflation? G. Burck. il Fortune 74:120-3+ O '66
Now it's up to Congress: to slow inflation and ease strain on the money market. il Bsns W p35-8 S 17 '66
Only way to stop inflation. Bsns W p200 S 10 '66
Open door to inflation? A. H. Raskin. il Reporter 35:24-7 S 8 '66
Operation reassurance; President Johnson & advisers. il Time 88:18 Ag 19 '66
Other nations fight inflation: how they're making out; Europe, Japan, Canada. il U S News 61:86-7 S 26 '66
Politics of inflation. Fortune 74:101-2 S '66
Power of persuasion; R. P. Gerholz talks with President Johnson. Newsweek 67:67-8 Ja 31 '66
President's dilemma; inflationary problems; with editorial comment. il Bsns W p33-5, 200 Mr 19 '66
Prices going up. il Newsweek 68:13-14 Ag 29 '66
Prices, taxes, credit depress the consumer; findings of Survey research center, University of Michigan. il Bsns W p39 Je 18 '66
Problems of inflation; excerpts from statement before the Joint economic committee of Congress. E. Gray. Duns R 87:21-2+ Ap '66
Profits will feel the bite. il Bsns W p35-7 O 1 '66
Protecting the family budget; address, September 4, 1966. G. Meany. Vital Speeches 32:749-51 O 1 '66
Raise taxes now. H. C. Wallich. Newsweek 67:90 Mr 21 '66
Relax and enjoy. H. C. Wallich. Newsweek 67:84 F 21 '66
Retarding growth: government's role in creating inflation. H. Hazlitt. Newsweek 67:87 My 9 '66
Rising prices: how long, how high? with report by H. C. Wallich. il Newsweek 68: 69-75 S 5 '66
Rising risk of runaway inflation. W. L. White. Read Digest 89:128-32 Ag '66
Runaway boom? what business leaders think now. il Nations Bsns 54:40-1+ Ap '66

INFLATION (finance)—Continued

Senate sugars the tax bill. Bsns W p41-2 O 15 '66

Slash the spending. H. Hazlitt. Newsweek 67:76 Mr 28 '66; Same abr. Read Digest 88:129-30 Je '66

Spiral cloud. il Time 87:91 F 25 '66

Step in the right direction? five-point anti-inflation program. il Newsweek 68:82+ S 26 '66

Stronger dose to curb inflation? with editorial comment. il Bsns W p29-30, 140 Ap 2 '66

Sweden's decision: inflation is better than strikes. il U S News 60:92+ Ap 25 '66

Tax boost soon? adaptation of address. May 2, 1966. W. W. Heller. New Repub 154:9-11 My 21 '66

Tax boost: too late to help? il Newsweek 67:73 My 9 '66

Time to touch the brakes. Time 87:27-27A Mr 18 '66

Trouble in paradise. K. Crawford. Newsweek 67:41 Ap 11 '66

Virtues of penny pinching. il Time 87:23-4 Ap 8 '66

We can fight inflation without controls; interview. R. J. Saulnier. Nations Bsns 54:33-5+ Mr '66

What comes after the guideposts? Bsns W p 148 Ag 13 '66

What makes inflation go and stops it. il Bsns W p 196-8 My 14 '66

What more inflation would do to you. il Nations Bsns 54:44-5 Ap '66

What the President could do; former economic advisers statements at Washington symposium. il Time 87:91 Mr 4 '66

When prosperity hurts. il Time 87:91-2 Ap 29 '66

Where tight money is pinching; credit squeeze cuts into housing. il Newsweek 68:65-6+ Jl 4 '66

Why all this inflation? J. Daniel. Read Digest 89:70-3 Jl '66

Why inflation grows. H. Hazlitt. Newsweek 67:76 Ap 25 '66

Wilson's double trouble; both political left and right oppose anti-inflationary program. il Bsns W p24 Jl 30 '66

With baling wire; latest anti-inflation moves. il Time 88:103 S 30 '66

Worried advisers; CEA chiefs past and present. il Newsweek 67:71-2 Mr 7 '66

INFLUENCE (psychology)

How persuasive are you? with test questions and answers. J. H. Wolfe. Read Digest 89:37-8+ D '66

INFLUENCE of altitude. See Altitude, Influence of

INFLUENCE of literature. See Literature, Influence of

INFLUENZA

Drifting flu; California, hardest hit. Time 87:54+ Mr 4 '66

Du Pont writes a new Rx; drug to prevent Asian flu; amantadine hydrochloride called Symmetrel. Bsns W p44 O 29 '66

Epidemic influenza, 1966. L. W. Sauer. PTA Mag 60:35+ My '66

Influenza epidemic hits West coast. Sci N 89:169 Mr 12 '66

Latest official word on the flu. U S News 60:10 Mr 7 '66

Vaccines

Flu vaccine developed by Australians patented. Sci N 90:191 S 10 '66

INFLUENZA virus

Influenza virus purification with the zonal ultracentrifuge. C. B. Reimer and others. bibliog il Science 152:1379-81 Je 3 '66

INFORMATION. See Knowledge

INFORMATION, Freedom of

Falsification of history; discrepancies between published and unpublished accounts by State department of Franco-American relations. Nation 203:235 S 19 '66

See also

Freedom of the press
Government and the press

INFORMATION, Government. See Government information

INFORMATION, Technical. See Technical information

INFORMATION agency (United States) See United States—Information agency

INFORMATION exchange groups. See Communication in science

INFORMATION science and automation division. See American library association—Information science and automation division

INFORMATION services

Dial for satellite count; automatic phone-answering service by Smithsonian astrophysical observatory. Sci N L 89:52 Ja 22 '66

Electronic speechmaker; dial stock quotations from American stock exchange. il Electr World 75:68 Je '66

Information becomes a hot item. il Bsns W p 164-6 My 14 '66

Information please. P. Villiard. il Read Digest 88:62-5 Je '66

INFORMATION storage and retrieval systems

Biosciences information service of biological abstracts. P. V. Parkins. bibliog il Science 152:889-94 My 13 '66

Box finds a memory for film; Mosler's selectriever. il Bsns W p 188 My 28 '66

Closing the circuit: automation and data processing for libraries; address, June 24, 1965, with reply by C. F. J. Overhage. V. W. Clapp. bibliog il Library J 91:1165-71 Mr 1 '66

Computers and copyrights. C. G. Benjamin. Science 152:181-4 Ap 8 '66

Coping with the information explosion. P. H. Abelson. Science 154:75 O 7 '66

EDUCOM: Interuniversity communications council. J. G. Miller. bibliog Science 154:483-8 O 28 '66

Foundations of access to knowledge; report on summer symposium. D. Bergen. Science 151:711 F 11 '66

Future of printing in a data-hungry society; summary of address. L. C. Deighton. Pub W 189:55-60 Ja 31 '66

How to put two and a half tons of research into one handy little box; service by the Educational research information center. L. G. Burchinal and H. A. Haswell. il Am Ed 2:23-5 F '66

Information becomes a hot item. il Bsns W p 164-6 My 14 '66

Information revolution. il Duns R 88:pt2 130-1+ S '66

Information storage and retrieval. B. A. Lipetz. il Sci Am 215:224-8+ S '66

Information storage, retrieval and dissemination. il Duns R 88:pt2 145-6+ S '66

National document-handling systems in science and technology; federal government's responsibilities. L. F. Carter. bibliog Science 154:1299-304 D 9 '66

National information system planning featured at ARL meeting in New York. Library J 91:3888-9 S 1 '66

Plans for Project Intrex. C. F. J. Overhage. bibliog il Science 152:1032-7 My 20 '66

Push-button snooping: the threat to business. Nations Bsns 54:40-1+ N '66

Techniques tomorrow. B. Sherman. Mod Phot 30:22 Ap '66

U.S. service cuts British research time; computer-operated information-retrieval service of medical literature. Sci N 90:339 O 22 '66

Use of computer in libraries analyzed at joint meeting. Library J 91:2301-2 My 1 '66

See also

Computers
Electronic data processing
Libraries—Automation
Programming (computers)

INFORMATION systems, Management

Myth of real-time management information. J. Dearden. il Harvard Bsns R 44:123-32 My '66

INFORMATION tests

And not a drop to drink. J. Daugherty and M. Daugherty. il Sci Digest 61:94-6 Ja '67

Are there diamonds on the moon? quiz. J. Daugherty and M. Daugherty. il Sci Digest 59:85-7 Je '66

Are you smart enough to beat the draft, stay in college and read this issue of Esquire? Esquire 66:109 S '66

Bomb something! test to take on the Vietnamese war. il Esquire 66:59-61 Ag '66

Changing times quiz (cont) Changing T 20:44 Ap; 47 Ag; 43 D '66

Contemporary affairs test (cont) il Sr Schol 89:19-20 S 16 '66

Family quiz game. K. Buchanan and I. Buchanan. See issues of Parents' magazine and better homemaking

For dreamers only; quiz. J. Daugherty and M. Daugherty. il Sci Digest 59:87-9 My '66

How much do you really know about Viet Nam? il Sr Schol 89:8-9+ O 28 '66

How to spend the winter; quiz. J. Daugherty and M. Daugherty. il Sci Digest 59:93-5 F '66

It's a moldy world. J. Daugherty and M. Daugherty. il Sci Digest 60:88-90 N '66

INFORMATION tests—*Continued*
Killer wind; quiz. J. Daugherty and M. Daugherty. il Sci Digest 60:83-5 S '66
Making the earth flat; quiz. J. Daugherty and M. Daugherty. Sci Digest 60:90-3 D '66
National health test. PTA Mag 60:24-8 My; 24-7 Je '66
Painful subject; quiz. J. Daugherty and M. Daugherty. il Sci Digest 60:89-91 Jl '66
Quiz; glass that almost isn't. J. Daugherty and M. Daugherty. il Sci Digest 59:85-7 Mr '66
Races of mankind. J. Daugherty and M. Daugherty. il Sci Digest 60:85-7 O '66
Senior scholastic end-term review test (cont) il Sr Schol 87:17-18 Ja 21; 88:21-2 My 20 '66
Test your astronaut I.Q. il Pop Mech 126: 130-1+ N '66
Your body chemistry; quiz. J. Daugherty and M. Daugherty. il Sci Digest 59:89-91 Ap '66
Your literary I.Q; ed. by J. T. Winterich and D. M. Glixon. See issues of Saturday review
See also
Vocabulary tests
INFORMATION theory
Information theory after eighteen years. E. N. Gilbert. bibliog il Science 152:320-6 Ap 15 '66; Discussion. 152:1330; 153:688+ Je 3, Ag 12 '66
INFORMATIONAL media guaranty program. See United States—Information agency
INFORMERS (law)
Hoffa decision; government informer issue. Nation 204:5-6 Ja 2 '67
Revenuer and the red in the red; Albert Deschenes' witch-hunt on R. G. Lenske. New Repub 155:9 N 19 '66
INFRARED apparatus and appliances
Infra-red divining rod; underground fresh-water flows. il Time 88:88 N 11 '66
INFRARED cameras. See Cameras
INFRARED photography. See Photography, Infrared
INFRARED rays
Seeing the unseen with infrared. M. J. Walker. il Sci N 90:273-4 O 8 '66
INFRARED thermography. See Photography, Infrared
INGE, William
Where's daddy? Criticism
Commonweal 84:83 Ap 8 '66
New Repub 154:36 Mr 26 '66
New Yorker 42:110 Mr 12 '66
Newsweek 67:94 Mr 14 '66
Sat R 49:55 Mr 19 '66
Time por 87:52 Mr 11 '66
Vogue 147:64 Ap 15 '66
INGERSOLL, John H.
Build a care-free concrete patio. Pop Gard 17:46-7 Mr '66
Second kitchen goes outdoors. Pop Gard 17: 40-3 My '66
INGLIS, Brian
Heed the cries of appetite and stay thin. Vogue 148:146-7+ N 15 '66
Power to resist disease. Vogue 147:84-5+ F 15 '66
INGRAHAM, Hollis S.
Immunization facts and figures. Parents Mag 41:77-9 N '66
Public health and drug safety; address, October 14, 1965. Vital Speeches 32:231-4 F 1 '66
INGRAHAM, Leonard W.
8mm single-concept films. Sr Schol 87:sup28-9 Ja 14 '66
INGRES, Jean Auguste Dominique
Portrait of the artist as a music-lover. F. V. Grunfeld. il por Opera N 30:8-13 Ja 29 '66
INHERITANCE
Estate planning for farmers; avoid losing your estate in taxes. N. G. P. Krausz and B. Brantley. il Suc Farm 64:31+ My '66
Killing an inheritance; slayer made constructive trustee. Time 88:38 Jl 29 '66
Plus for probate; court locates illegitimate niece of man who left no will. il Time 88:73-4 N 4 '66
See also
Estate planning
Estates, Decedents
Probate law and practice
Property, Intellectual
Wills
INHERITANCE (biology) See Heredity
INHERITANCE of disease. See Heredity of disease
INHERITANCE tax
For your family's future: how to save taxes on an estate. il U S News 61:48-52 Ag 8 '66

Making sense of transfer taxes. il Bsns W p98+ Jl 9 '66
What would happen if you died tonight? questions and answers. C. W. Gifford. il Farm J 90:36-7+ Ap '66
See also
Gifts—Taxation
INHIBITING substances, Growth. See Growth inhibiting substances (plants)
INITIAL defense communications satellite program. See Communications satellites—Military applications
INITIALISMS. See Acronyms
INJECTIONS
See also
Inoculation
INJECTIONS, Intravenous
Intravenous therapy: routine but vital. il Todays Health 44:35 N '66
INJURIES from sports. See Sports—Accidents and injuries
INJUSTICE. See Justice
INK brushwork. See Brush drawing
INKSTANDS
English inkstands in silver and Sheffield plate. J. Stone. il Antiques 90:342-6 S '66
INLAND navigation
Personal business; inland waterway to Florida. Bsns W p 137-8 S 3 '66
See also
Congo River
River trips
INLAND SEA
Through the Inland Sea in daylight. il Sunset 137:40+ N '66
INLAND shipping. See Inland water transportation
INLAND steel company
Steel price increase hits where it hurts; Inland steel's lead in price rise. Bsns W p28 Ag 6 '66
INLAND water transportation
From romance to riches: the waterway boom; with report by P. Carter. il Newsweek 67:79-80 Je 6 '66
Lakers open 111th season; Great Lakes shipping. il Bsns W p36 Ap 9 '66
National transportation policy; address, February 8, 1966. J. Miller. Vital Speeches 32: 292-4 Mr 1 '66
INLAND waterways. See Waterways—United States
INNISFREE garden, Millbrook. See Gardens—New York (state)
INNOVATIONS (economics)
Innovative imitation. T. Levitt. il Harvard Bsns R 44:63-70 S '66
INNOVATIONS, Technological. See Technological innovations
INOCULATION
Warriors against disease; Brother's brother team in Nicaragua and Liberia. C. M. Davis. il Todays Health 44:30-4 N '66
See also
Immunity
Vaccination
INORGANIC hydrates. See Hydrates
INPUT-output analysis. See Linear programming
INPUT-output equipment. See Computers—Input-output equipment
INQUESTS, Coroners'. See Coroners
INQUISITION
Spanish inquisition, by H. Kamen. Review
America 114:673 My 7 '66. J. A. Brundage
Commonweal 84:587-8 S 16 '66. T. P. Anderson
Newsweek il 67:112A-112B+ Ap 18 '66
Victims of a pious cruelty. A. L. Sachar. il Sat R 49:36-7 Je 18 '66
INSANE
See also
Mentally ill

Legal status, laws, etc.
See Mental health laws
INSANE, Criminal and dangerous
Society and the sex criminal; excerpt from How many more victims? G. D. Shultz. Read Digest 89:139-46 N '66
Symptoms of mass murder. Time 88:18-19 Ag 12 '66
See also
Forensic psychiatry
INSANITY
You have to be insane not to pay taxes. Time 89:80 Ja 6 '67
See also
Hysteria
Schizophrenia

INSANITY—*Continued*

Jurisprudence

Doing in M'Naghten; Court of appeals for the second circuit's decision binding in federal cases in New York, Connecticut and Vermont. Time 87:57 Mr 11 '66

Mental illness is a myth. T. S. Szasz. il N Y Times Mag p30-1+ Je 12 '66; Discussion. p4+ Jl 3: 2 Jl 10 '66

Rebuttal to the Queen; overturning M'Naghten. il Newsweek 67:30 Mr 14 '66

See also
Forensic psychiatry

INSANITY, Delusional. See Paranoia

INSATIABLE dragon; drama. See Boiko, C.

INSCRIPTIONS
See also
Graffiti

INSECT baits and repellants
Cucurbitacins: specific insect attractants in cucurbitaceae. O. L. Chambliss and C. M. Jones. bibliog il Science 153:1392-3 S 16 '66

Insect repellents. Consumer Rep 31:305-7 D '66

INSECT bites and stings
Insect stings can kill. F. Marley. il Sci N 90:42-3 Jl 16 '66

Never swing at a honeybee. E. A. Bauer. il Field & S 70:73+ Mr '66

INSECT calls. See Insect sounds

INSECT control. See Insects, Injurious and beneficial—Control

INSECT flight. See Insects—Flight

INSECT intelligence. See Insects—Habits and behavior

INSECT mating behavior. See Courtship of insects

INSECT personnel detector. See Detectors

INSECT pests. See Insects, Injurious and beneficial

INSECT repellents. See Insect baits and repellents

INSECT secretions. See Secretions

INSECT sex attractants
Birth control for bugs. H. Fantel. il Pop Mech 126:116-19+ Ag '66

Sex attractant of the pink bollworm moth: isolation, identification, and synthesis. W. A. Jones and others. bibliog Science 152:1516-17 Je 10 '66

Sex attractants in frass produced by male ips confusus in ponderosa pine. R. M. Sliverstein and others. bibliog il Science 154:509-10 O 28 '66

INSECT sonar. See Sonar

INSECT song. See Insect sounds

INSECT sounds
Allure of the female mosquito. M. Roth and others. il Natur Hist 75:26-31 bibliog(p70) D '66

Evolution of cricket chirps. R. D. Alexander. il Natur Hist 75:26-31 bibliog(p82) N '66

INSECT tagging
Tagging the migratory monarch. E. Stobbe. il Audubon Mag 68:343-6 S '66

INSECT traps
Yellowjackets trapped. Sci N 90:214 S 17 '66

INSECTICIDES
Death in the afternoon; studies of circadian rhythms of insects and effectiveness of insecticides. Sci N 91:12 Ja 7 '67

Recommended time intervals between insecticide application and harvest. Suc Farm 64:85 Mr '66

Safe and accurate dilution of garden chemicals. il Sunset 136:240 Je '66

Soil insects cut corn yields. Suc Farm 64:87 Mr '66

Ten rules to follow. Pop Gard 17:69 Ag '66

What to spray at, and what to spray with. il Sunset 136:230-2+ Je '66

See also
Endrin

Injurious effects

Heritage in peril. M. L. Grossman. il Am Heritage 17:14-15+ Ag '66

Pure water is basic. C. K. Fox. Esquire 66:48+ O '66

Residues

Biodegradation of the gamma isomer of benzene hexachloride in submerged soils. K. Raghu and I. C. MacRae. bibliog il Science 154:263-4 O 14 '66

See also
Insecticides—Injurious effects

INSECTICIDES, Resistance to. See Insects, Injurious and beneficial—Resistance to control

INSECTIVOROUS plants
See also
Venus's flytraps

INSECTS
Crossroads of the insect world. J. W. MacSwain. il Nat Geog Mag 130:844-57 D '66

Insects, by R. E. Hutchins. Review
Time 87:111 Ap 15 '66

See also
Embryology—Insects
Orthoptera
also names of insects, e.g. Ants

Anatomy

Contribution toward encyclopedia of insect anatomy, by R. E. Snodgrass. Review
Hobbies 71:130 Jl '66

Collection and preservation

How to bag a bug. il Sci Digest 59:9 Je '66

Control

See Insects, Injurious and beneficial—Control

Development

Birth of a butterfly. D. G. Schleisner. il Flower Grower 53:34+ Jl '66

Electron microscopy of living insects. R. F. W. Pease and others. bibliog il Science 154:1185-6 D 2 '66

Hormonal termination of diapause in the alfalfa weevil. W. S. Bowers and C. C. Blickenstaff. bibliog il Science 154:1673-4 D 30 '66

Internal clocks and insect diapause. P. L. Adkisson. bibliog il Science 154:234-41 O 14 '66

Eggs

Tanning of grasshopper eggs by an exocrine secretion. T. Eisner and others. bibliog il Science 152:95-7 Ap 1 '66

Flight

Differential anemometer for measuring the turning tendency of insects in stationary flight. K. D. Roeder. il Science 153:1634-6 S 30 '66

Insect aerodynamics: vertical sustaining force in near-hovering flight. L. Bennett. bibliog il Science 152:1263-6 My 27 '66

Radar observations of insects in free flight. K. M. Glover and others. bibliog il Science 154:967-72 N 25 '66

Food

Gibberellic acid; effects of feeding in an artificial diet for honeybees. J. L. Nation and F. A. Robinson. bibliog Science 152:1765-6 Je 24 '66

Habits and behavior

Accessory burrows of digger wasps; excerpts from Comparative ethology and evolution of the sand wasps. H. E. Evans. bibliog il Science 152:465-71 Ap 22 '66

Ants, bees can learn but flies cannot. Sci N 89:370 My 14 '66

See also
Courtship of insects
Sex behavior

Anecdotes, facetiae, satire, etc.

Power of the press; effects of newspapers. C. M. Curtis. Atlan 218:141-2 N '66

Migration

See also
Insect tagging

Orientation

See Orientation

Physiology

Chromosome variability and geographic distribution in insects. B. John and K. R. Lewis. bibliog il Science 152:711-21 My 6 '66

Iphita limbata stal.: components of neurosecretory material. K. R. Seshan and P. I. Ittycheriah. bibliog il Science 153:427-8 Jl 22 '66

Ultrasonic sensitivity: a tympanal receptor in the green lace wing chrysopa carnea. L. A. Miller and E. G. MacLeod. bibliog il Science 154:891-3 N 18 '66

Protective equipment

See Defense mechanisms (biology)

Resistance to control

See Insects, Injurious and beneficial—Resistance to control

INSECTS, Effect of radiation on. See Insects, Injurious and beneficial—Control

INSECTS, Geographical distribution of. See Geographical distribution of animals and plants

INSECTS, Injurious and beneficial
Bugs' battle against man. D. Belveal. il Todays Health 44:48-51 F '66
What to spray at, and what to spray with. il Sunset 136:230-2+ Je '66
See also names of insects, e.g. Tent caterpillars

Control
Birth control for bugs. H. Fantel. il Pop Mech 126:116-19+ Ag '66
Common sense pest control. il Flower Grower 53:48-9 My '66
Control plant pests indoors. L. Pyenson. il Horticulture 45:22-3+ Ja '67
Gamma rays stop food-destroying insects. Sci N 90:247 O 1 '66
Good housekeeping guide to pest control. il Good H 162:178-9 Je '66
Pest control progresses; biological and environmental control. B. Tufty. Sci N L 89:119 F 19 '66
Pesticide program in Grand Teton National Park; control of bark beetle. A. Murie. il Nat Parks Mag 40:17-19 Je '66
Population flushing with sexually sterile insects. J. Monro. bibliog il Science 151:1536-8 Mr 25 '66
Second look at silent spring. il Pop Gard 17:64-9 Ag '66
Secret weapons. D. Belveal and D. Phillips. il Todays Health 44:38-41 Je '66
Seduction of bark beetles; biological control. Sci Am 215:64-5 D '66
Sound, light lure bugs. Sci N 91:10 Ja 7 '67
Spray away summer pests. il Flower Grower 53:9 Jl '66
Sterile flies used to combat dacus; enemy of olives subjected to radioisotope technique. D. Whitney. il Natur Hist 75:30-5 Mr '66
Twenty days in June, the cautious war; tussock moth. H. E. McLean. il Am For 72:28-31+ Mr '66
Weed and insect control guide. L. E. Zeman. il Suc Farm 64:69+ Mr '66
See also
Chemosterilants
Flies—Extermination
Insecticides
Mosquitoes—Extermination
Spraying and dusting

Resistance to control
Insects winning struggle. il Sci N 89:320 Ap 30 '66

INSECTS, Sound production by. See Insect sounds

INSECTS as carriers of infections
See also
Insects, Injurious and beneficial

INSELBERG, Rachel M. See Burke, L. jt. auth.

INSEMINATION, Artificial. See Artificial insemination

INSHA, Ibne
Reading habits and book publishing in Asia; adaptation of address, May 1966. UNESCO Courier 19:12-16 N '66

INSIDE a pyramid; story. See Golding, W.

INSIDER trading. See Stocks—Insider trading

INSIGNIA
See also
Schools—Insignia

INSOLVENCY. See Bankruptcy

INSOMNIA
Rx for insomniacs. J. Brothers. Good H 162:26+ My '66
See also
Sleep

INSPIRATION
Butter the size of a walnut; recipe for a story. I. Foster. Writer 79:23-5 D '66
Digging for ideas. J. Nelms. Writer 79:27-8 Mr '66
Fortunate failures. S. K. Boyd. Writer 79:13-15+ Ag '66
Off the cuff; literary and poetic results of insomnia. L. Conger. Writer 79:6-8 Mr '66

INSPIRATION of the Bible. See Bible—Inspiration

INSTALMENT plan
Are changes coming in those one-sided credit laws? il Consumer Rep 31:108-12 Mr '66
Buying credit wisely. H. Black. NEA J 55:23 My '66

Everything you should know to finance a new car. D. L. Gregg. il Bet Hom & Gard 44:42+ O '66
Financing and insurance, tips & traps. R. Gottlieb. Motor T 18:40-2 Je '66
Let the borrower beware! R. C. Jancauskas. il America 115:774-6 D 10 '66
Loan costs don't stop consumers. il Bsns W p32-3 Je 25 '66
On the way: rules for buy now, pay later; Federal trade commission code. U S News 62:11 Ja 9 '67
Pitfalls of credit buying. A. Poinsett. il Ebony 21:67-8+ Ap '66
Pitfalls of financing. R. J. Gottlieb. Motor T 18:84 N '66
Tight credit hits installment loans. U S News 60:109-10 Ap 18 '66
Wait and save. il Changing T 20:24 Je '66
See also
Credit
Land contracts

Laws and regulations
Is a purchase on credit an asset or a liability? Consumer Bul 49:28-9 S '66
Some victories for truth-in-lending. Consumer Rep 31:394-5 Ag '66

INSTAMATIC cameras. See Cameras

INSTANT coffee. See Coffee

INSTINCT
Books in review; instinct and aggression. T. C. Schneirla. Natur Hist 75:16+ D '66
Instincts and prophecies. G. H. T. Kimble. Reporter 35:40+ D 29 '66
Use that sixth sense, instinct. R. Dreyfack. il Nations Bsns 54:80-2+ D '66
See also
Animals—Habits and behavior
Fighting (psychology)

INSTITUTE for advanced study, Princeton, N.J.
Generalist takes the helm; C. Kaysen. il Bsns W p 152+ Ap 30 '66
Paradise in Princeton. il Newsweek 67:82 F 28 '66
Paradise in Princeton. il Time 88:70+ Jl 8 '66
Visit to an intellectual hotel. J. Corry. il N Y Times Mag p50-1+ My 15 '66

INSTITUTE for applied technology. See United States—Institute for applied technology

INSTITUTE for college and university administrators
Institute for college and university administrators. Sch & Soc 94:85 F 19 '66

INSTITUTE for defense analyses
IDA reform may revise non-profits role. G. C. Wilson. Aviation W 84:31 Je 27 '66

INSTITUTE for educational development
IED gets USOE grant for purchasing advice project; Educational products information exchange. Pub W 190:38 N 28 '66

INSTITUTE for freedom in the church
Rocky road of peacemakers. America 115:407 O 8 '66

INSTITUTE for the study of nonviolence
Just folks at a school for nonviolence. J. Didion. il N Y Times Mag p24-5+ F 27 '66

INSTITUTE of aerospace sciences. See American institute of aeronautics and astronautics

INSTITUTE of electrical and electronics engineers
IEEE focuses on IC radiation hardening. il Tech W 19:34-6 Ag 1 '66
IEEE told of its undersea challenges. Miss & Roc 18:14 Mr 28 '66
On-site processing needed for data boom; discussions at first IEEE ocean electronics symposium. R. Pay. il Tech W 19:26+ O 3 '66
Radio astronomy aired at IEEE. C. D. LaFond. il Miss & Roc 18:31-2+ Ap 4 '66
Scientific explanation for the UFOs? J. Lear. il Sat R 49:67-9 O 1 '66
Techniques tomorrow; future potentials. B. Sherman. il Mod Phot 30:44+ Jl '66
Ultrasonics; report on fifth annual symposium. W. P. Mason. Science 152:1286-7 My 27 '66

INSTITUTE of forest genetics
Better forests from blue ribbon trees; Rhinelander station, Wis. E. S. Hurd. il Am For 72:12-14+ Je '66

INSTITUTE of high fidelity, incorporated
New IHF standard on amplifiers. W. A. Stocklin. Electr World 75:6+ Ap '66

INSTITUTE of international education
Next decade of the IIE. Sch & Soc 94:185 Ap 2 '66

INSTITUTE of marine resources, La Jolla, Calif.
California pioneering new technology. W. E. Wilks. Tech W 19:29-30 Jl 4 '66
California study opens broad potential. W. E. Wilks. Tech W 19:23+ Jl 11 '66
INSTITUTE of oceanography. See United States—Commerce, Department of—Institute of oceanography
INSTITUTE of student opinion. See Scholastic research center
INSTITUTE of Verdi studies of Parma. See Parma. Italy
INSTITUTES, Library. See Library institutes and workshops
INSTITUTES, Teachers. See Teachers institutes
INSTITUTES for the achievement of human potential, Philadelphia
Run away, little girl; condensation. M. M. Segal. il Read Digest 89:259-62+ N '66
INSTITUTION for the development of educational activities
IDEA: prescription for change. T. Kaser. il Sat R 49:68-9 Je 18 '66
INSTITUTIONAL investors. See Stockholders
INSTITUTIONS, Non-profit
Congress: private universities say unemployment pay should not cover their faculty, students. J. Walsh. Science 152:185-7 Ap 8 '66
Government use of nonprofit companies. J. L. Trainor. Harvard Bsns R 44:38-40+ My '66
See also
Urban America, incorporated
INSTITUTO cultural peruano norteamericano. See United States—Cultural relations
INSTRUCTION. See Teaching
INSTRUCTION manuals
Anecdotes, facetiae, satire, etc.
Merry crisis! happy solenoid! not getting nervous-breakdown from Easy instruction booklets! L. Rosten. il Look 31:10 Ja 10 '67
INSTRUCTIONAL materials. See Teaching—Aids and devices
INSTRUCTIONAL materials centers
Audio-visuals at your fingertips. A. De Bernardis. il Sr Schol 87:sup26 Ja 14 '66
CUE: an experiment in the humanities; adaptation of address, July 1966. G. Lacy. il ALA Bul 60:918-22 O '66
Gadfly of the Education act, title III: supplementary educational centers and services; ed. by H. Phillips and others. il Library J 91:1020-4 F 15 '66
INSTRUMENT flying. See Aviation—Instrument flying
INSTRUMENT landing. See Airplanes—Landing
INSTRUMENTAL music
See also
Phonograph records—Instrumental music
INSTRUMENTS
See also
Aeronautic instruments
Optical instruments
Scientific apparatus and instruments
INSTRUMENTS, Testing. See Testing instruments
INSULATED jugs. See Thermos containers
INSULATION (electric)
Double-insulated portable saber saw; Rockwell Porter-cable model 60. il Consumer Rep 31:100-1 Mr '66
Double insulation, not just for drills. Consumer Rep 31:56-7 F '66
INSULIN
Automatic insulin. Sci Am 215:58+ D '66
Break for diabetics; research in U.S. and red China in synthesizing human insulin. Bsns W p94 O 1 '66
First for China: synthesis of insulin by Chinese researchers. Newsweek 68:70 S 26 '66
Inhibition of insulin release by norepinephrine in man. D. Porte, jr and R. H. Williams. bibliog il Science 152:1248-50 My 27 '66
Insulin discovery: production of artificial insulin in red China. Sr Schol 89:20-1 O 14 '66
Iodoinsulin used to determin specific activity of iodine-131. S. A. Berson and R. S. Yalow. bibliog il Science 152:205-7 Ap 8 '66
Protein synthesis by heart muscle ribosomes: an effect of insulin independent of substrate transport. W. S. Stirewalt and I. G. Wool. bibliog il Science 154:284 O 14 '66

Synthesis of insulin. P. G. Katsoyannis. bibliog il Science 154:1509-14 D 23 '66
Total synthesis of insulin in red China. V. K. McElheny. bibliog Science 153:281-3 Jl 15 '66
INSURANCE
Credit-card premiums; insurance. Time 87: 96+ My 13 '66
Insurance ethics: from the inside looking out. H. K. Duke. bibliog f Ann Am Acad 363: 102-7 Ja '66
Teacher insurance: who foots the bill? E. S. Crowley. NEA J 55:51+ S '66
Adjustment of claims
Way-out world of wacky insurance claims. C. B. Hicks. il Pop Mech 126:110-13+ Ag '66
All risk policies
Best insurance for your home & belongings; homeowners policy. il Changing T 20:17-20 Jl '66
Fraudulent promotion
Good for Dodd; Senator reveals fraudulent practices by insurance companies. Nation 202:142 F 7 '66
Policies
Who pays for child care when your wife is sick? Bet Hom & Gard 44:10+ Ap '66
Reinsurance
International reinsurance problems examined by UNCTAD expert group. UN Mo Chron 3:36 O '66
Taxation
Is what you get from insurance taxed? Changing T 20:14 O '66
INSURANCE, Agricultural
How to use crop insurance as a farm management tool. Suc Farm 64:36 Mr '66
INSURANCE, Automobile
A's to your Q's about auto insurance. T. Irwin. Pop Sci 189:72-4+ Jl '66
Buying auto insurance. il Consumer Rep 31: 398-402 D '66
Crash artists. Newsweek 68:80 Ag 22 '66
Does your auto insurance protect your passengers? Changing T 20:12 Mr '66
Easing the pain of auto accidents: basic protection plan. Time 87:40+ Mr 25 '66
Financing and insurance, tips & traps.. R. Gottlieb. Motor T 18:40-2 Je '66
Good for Dodd; Senator reveals fraudulent practices by insurance companies. Nation 202:142 F 7 '66
How much auto liability insurance do you really need? Bet Hom & Gard 44:10+ My '66
Insure, but insure wisely. G. P. Nicholas. Motor T 18:86 N '66
More on auto insurance. J. Ridgeway. New Repub 156:21-3 Ja 14 '67
Notes on car insurance. Sr Schol 88:40 Ap 22 '66
Riddle of the vanishing insurance companies; G. Head's operations against companies fraudulent manipulations. L. Velie. Read Digest 89:109-13 S '66
Underground war on auto insurance. J. Ridgeway. New Repub 155:19-21 D 3 '66
What control do you have over car repairs paid by the insurance company? Bet Hom & Gard 44:20+ F '66
Why auto insurance costs more and more; questions and answers. il U S News 61: 60-3 S 12 '66
See also
State farm mutual automobile insurance company
INSURANCE, Aviation
Great insurance mystery. A. Trammell. Flying 78:62-3 Ap; 58-61 My '66
747 looms as insurance test case. W. H. Gregory. il Aviation W 86:25-6 Ja 2 '67
United States and the Warsaw convention; statements. February 1, 14, 1966. A. F. Lowenfeld. il Dept State Bul 54:580-8 Ap 11 '66
U.S. expected to stand on liability accord. Aviation W 84:40 My 23 '66
INSURANCE, Business
Shield against stockholder suits. il Bsns W p56-7 Jl 2 '66
INSURANCE, Dental
When denticare comes: here's how it will work. il U S News 60:53-4 Je 13 '66
INSURANCE, Fire
How to update fire insurance. Suc Farm 64: 8 O '66
INSURANCE, Fraudulent. See Fraud

INSURANCE, Group
Group insurance is growing. J. H. Kleinmann. il NEA J 55:48-9 My '66
  See also
Insurance, Hospitalization

INSURANCE, Health
Buy the right health insurance. F. Bailey. jr. Suc Farm 64:90 S '66
Health insurance coverage for workers on layoff. W. W. Kolodrubetz. Mo Labor R 89:851-5 Ag '66
No crisis; reaction to medicare program. Newsweek 68:84-5 Jl 18 '66
UAW gets coverage on mental illness. Bsns W p 156+ S 10 '66
What every young father should know about health insurance. J. R. Williams. il Parents Mag 41:86+ N '66
  See also
Insurance, Dental
Insurance, Hospitalization
Insurance, Mental health

Canada
Medicare plan for Ontario. J. R. Mutchmor. Christian Cent 83:692-3 My 25 '66

Europe, Western
Europe's advice to U.S. on medical care. il U S News 62:64-6 Ja 23 '67

United States
Adapting group health insurance to medicare. E. H. Beier. Mo Labor R 89:491-5 My '66
A.M.A. & medicare. il Time 88:42 Jl 8 '66
Annals of legislation; medicare. R. Harris. New Yorker 42:29-38+ Jl 2 '66
Annals of legislation; medicare; all-out effort of AMA to defeat bill from 1961 through 1964. R. Harris. New Yorker 42:35-8+ Jl 16 '66
Annals of legislation; medicare, Forand bill, Kerr-Mills act. R. Harris. New Yorker 42:30-6+ Jl 9 '66
Annals of legislation; medicare; the passage of the bill. R. Harris. New Yorker 42:35-40+ Jl 23 '66
As medicare begins. America 115:6 Jl 2 '66
As medicare begins. Consumer Rep 31:288-93 Je '66
Buildup for a letdown? predicted increased demand for doctors' and hospitals' services. Reporter 34:6 Je 2 '66
Care for the not-so-poor. D. Sanford. New Repub 154:8 Je 4 '66
Carrot and the stick; L. B. Johnson's policy on hospital desegregation requirements and qualifications for medicare. Reporter 34:7-8 Je 30 '66
Changes in negotiated health and insurance plans, 1962-66. R. C. Joiner. Mo Labor R 89:1246-9 N '66
Countdown for medicare; search for eligibles; benefits. il Newsweek 67:78+ Mr 28 '66
Crisis now near in medical care? il U S News 60:38-41 Mr 7 '66
Deadline for medicare. Consumer Rep 31:134 Mr '66
Enrolling for medicare. H. H. Miller. New Repub 154:10-11 F 12 '66
Friendly man from medicare. F. J. Taylor. Read Digest 88:175-6+ Ap '66
Great salesmanship; signing up for medicare. il Time 87:27 Ap 8 '66
Guide to medicare; ABC's of starting plan. il U S News 61:34-5 Jl 4 '66
Guidelines for doctors on medicare fees. U S News 60:8 Je 13 '66
Hospitals are worried as medicare nears; with interview with E. Henderson. il U S News 60:50-4 Je 6 '66
How to use medicare. il Changing T 20:7-11 My '66
If you have questions about medicare; here are the answers; interview. A. Hess. il U S News 60:58-63 My 9 '66
Let's all get sick; medicare. Nat R 18:566 Je 14 '66
Medicaid; apples and oranges. B. J. Culliton. Sci N 90:569 D 31 '66
Medicare; a slow start, but big test still to come. il U S News 61:35-6 Jl 18 '66
Medicare and health insurance, too? il Changing T 20:17-20 Je '66
Medicare and medicaid. Sci Am 215:100-1 S '66
Medicare bonanza. S. Greenberg. il Nation 203:513-16 N 14 '66; Discussion. 204:34+ Ja 9 '67
Medicare bottleneck. New Repub 154:9-10 Ja 29 '66
Medicare for all: how near? il U S News 61:30+ Jl 4 '66

Medicare; progress report. J. L. Breeling. Todays Health 45:38 Ja '67
Medicare: promises and pitfalls. S. Greenberg. il Nation 202:617-20 My 23 '66
Medicare ready to roll. F. Marley. Sci N 90:4 Jl 2 '66
Medicare sign-up; dates and deadlines. U S News 60:8 Ap 11 '66
Medicare will provide home health services. Sci N L 89:121 F 19 '66
Medicare's effect on health insurance. il U S News 60:42-4 Ap 11 '66
Medicare's expensive companion; with editorial comment. il Bsns W p38-9, 190 Je 25 '66
Medicare's Mccarthyite clause. Christian Cent 83:228 F 23 '66
More federal billions for medical bills; medicaid, Title XIX in the medicare act. U S News 61:13 N 28 '66
More medicare information needed. Consumer Rep 32:4-5 Ja '67
New medicare rules; what farmers want to know. F. Bailey, jr. Suc Farm 64:94 F '66
New over-65 health insurance policies, to supplement medicare. Suc Farm 64:76 Jl '66
New worry for medicare: a little-noticed giveaway; health aid for medically needy of all ages. il U S News 60:54-5 Je 20 '66
Now: more help for old people; latest on medicare and its problems, nursing-home program. il U S News 62:60-2 Ja 9 '67
Nursing home industry tools up. J. Horwitz. il N Y Times Mag p26-7+ My 1 '66
Nursing homes, just how much will medicare pay? Bet Hom & Gard 44:122-3 N '66
Nursing homes offer an investment lure; medicare expected to spark a nursing home boom. il Bsns W p 113:14 Jl 23 '66
Nursing homes: one more problem for medicare. il U S News 60:50-2 Je 13 '66
On M day for medicare. il U S News 61:8 Jl 11 '66
On the way: a program broader than medicare. U S News 60:16 My 16 '66
Preventicare needed. Sci N 90:244 O 1 '66
Provisions for paid sick leave in metropolitan areas. K. J. Hoffmann. il Mo Labor R 89:164-9 F '66
Public pays the bill. G. Rosenthal. il Atlan 218:107-10 Jl '66; Discussion. 218:45 S '66
R for sick hospitals. il Newsweek 68:57-61 Jl 11 '66
Sacred trust, by R. Harris. Review New Repub 156:35-6 Ja 21 '67. R. Yoakum
Shortages medicare will face. U S News 60:35 My 30 '66
Substitute for state medicine: how it works; Kaiser foundation health plan (KFHP) il U S News 60:64-5 F 14 '66
Surprising facts about medicare. C. P. Anderson. Look 30:78+ My 17 '66
$36 a year for medicare: the service it buys; questions and answers. il U S News 60:56-7 Ja 31 '66
Watch out for Title 19; medicaid. Life 61:4 Jl 29 '66
What the doctor ordered; problems of medicare and medicaid. Time 88:13 Ag 26 '66
Will it work? il Time 87:33-4 Je 10 '66
Will medicare push up the doctor's bill? il Bsns W p 192+ Je 18 '66
Will they, won't they? question of overcrowding hospitals with medicare patients. New Repub 155:10 Jl 2 '66
Your health-insurance checkup. Todays Health 44:6+ Je '66

INSURANCE, Hospitalization
Changes in negotiated health and insurance plans, 1962-66. R. C. Joiner. Mo Labor R 89:1246-9 N '66
Who decides what is reasonable cost for hospital care? Washington, D.C. hospitals vs. Blue cross agency; Group hospitalization, inc. il U S News 60:44 Ap 11 '66
Why hospitals overcharge patients; with case history. R. H. Berg. il Look 30:29-33 Je 14 '66

INSURANCE, Liability
Shield against stockholder suits. il Bsns W p56-7 Jl 2 '66
What if you're sued for a million? il Changing T 20:24 Je '66
  See also
Insurance, Automobile
Insurance, Aviation

INSURANCE, Library
Pricing library materials for insurance purposes. J. M. O'Brien and others. il ALA Bul 60:729-30 Jl '66

INSURANCE, Life
Does it pay to convert your GI insurance? Bet Hom & Gard 44:6+ Jl '66

INSURANCE, Life—*Continued*
How much life insurance should you carry on your children? Bet Hom & Gard 44:12 F '66
Life insurance for single women. il Changing T 20:33-5 D '66
Nonsmokers given lower life insurance rates. Sci N L 89:150 Mr 5 '66
Why does your wife's life insurance cost less than yours? Bet Hom & Gard 44:8 My '66

Credit aspects
Another victim of tight money. U S News 61:80 D 26 '66
Dirty deal in small loans; relations of finance and insurance companies. J. Ridgeway. New Repub 155:11-12 O 8 '66

Policies
How to buy life insurance. Consumer Rep 32:14-25 Ja '67
How to use life insurance in your estate. B. Brantley. il Suc Farm 64:32-3+ N '66
Life insurance: par or nonpar? Bet Hom & Gard 44:8+ Ap '66
What every young father should know about life insurance. B. T. Newton, jr. Parents Mag 41:71+ O '66
Who should own your child's life insurance? P. Lindberg. Bet Hom & Gard 45:6 Ja '67

Policy loans
Easy-money market. Time 88:105-6 S 16 '66
Should you borrow on life insurance? il Good H 162:186 Mr '66

Rates
Cheap life insurance. J. Ridgeway and D. Wiggins. New Repub 155:11-12 N 12 '66

Taxation
See Insurance—Taxation

INSURANCE, Marine
Insurance. D. M. Mitchell. Yachting 119:75+ Ap '66

INSURANCE, Medical. See Insurance, Health

INSURANCE, Mental health
$5-a-session psychiatry; health insurance plans and other programs provide psychiatric care to employed and retired persons. F. R. Schreiber and M. Herman. il Sci Digest 60:14-17 D '66
Insurance plans help to foot the bills. Bsns W p 180 N 5 '66

INSURANCE, Property
Insurance, a special kind of comfort. House & Gard 131:30+ Ja '67
What every photographer should know about insurance. D. Linton. Pop Phot 58:63+ Ap '66

INSURANCE, Psychiatric. See Insurance, Mental health

INSURANCE, Social

United States
Free ride starts in social security. U S News 60:94-5 Mr 28 '66
Personal business: social security: it's a bargain, and tax-free, too. Bsns W p 137 Ap 23 '66
See also
Insurance, Health—United States
Insurance, Unemployment—United States
Old age pensions—United States

INSURANCE, Unemployment

Great Britain
Winston Churchill versus the Webbs: the origins of British unemployment insurance. B. B. Gilbert. bibliog f Am Hist R 71:846-62 Ap '66

Pennsylvania
Farewell to loafers' paradise; loopholes plugged. E. Selby. Read Digest 89:161-2+ S '66

United States
Broad extension of jobless pay? unemployment compensation. U S News 61:62-3 Jl 4 '66
Congress: private universities say unemployment pay should not cover their faculty, students. J. Walsh. Science 152:185-7 Ap 8 '66
Financial aspects of SUB plans. E. H. Beier. il Mo Labor R 89:385-9 Ap '66
Looming fight over jobless pay: showdown to federalize unemployment compensation system. Bsns W p76+ Ap 30 '66
New grab for federal power: unemployment benefits. E. Selby and A. Selby. Read Digest 88:56-9 F '66

Research in unemployment insurance. R. Munts. bibliog f Mo Labor R 89:1230-5 N '66
Will you pay more to support loafers? il Nations Bsns 53:38-41 D '65

INSURANCE agents
Good-humored salesmen; mobile office of John Hancock mutual life insurance company. il Time 88:72+ Jl 1 '66
River view home. il Ebony 21:123-6 Mr '66

INSURANCE companies
Cheap life insurance. J. Ridgeway and D. Wiggins. New Repub 155:11-12 N 12 '66
Insurance men expand their lines: holding companies being set up to broaden industry's financial services. Bsns W p70+ Mr 19 '66
Life insurance: the monolithic sect; concerning the book Pay now. die later. J. Gollin. il Nation 203:670-4 D 19 '66
Riddle of the vanishing insurance companies; G. Head's operations against companies fraudulent manipulations. L. Velie. Read Digest 89:109-13 S '66
See also
John Hancock mutual life insurance company
Sentry insurance companies
State farm mutual automobile insurance company

Anecdotes, facetiae, satire, etc.
Top of my head; O yez, O yez, O yez. G. Ace. Sat R 49:5 Jl 2 '66

Investments
New interest in incentive financing; study of twenty-nine life insurance companies. S. L. Hayes, 3d. il Harvard Bsns R 44:99-112 Jl '66

INSURANCE rates. See Insurance, Life—Rates
INSURANCE salesmen. See Insurance agents
INSURRECTIONS. See Revolutions
INTEGRATED circuits. See Electronic circuits
INTEGRATED helicopter avionics system. See Aeronautic instruments
INTEGRATION of libraries. See Libraries and Negroes
INTEGRATION of public schools. See Public schools—Desegregation
INTEGRITY
Foolproof formula for success. A. Gordon. Read Digest 89:88-90 D '66
INTELLECT
See also
Intelligence
Thought and thinking
INTELLECTUAL cooperation
See also
Exchanges, Literary and scientific
United Nations educational scientific and cultural organization
United States—Cultural relations
United States—State, Department of—International scientific and technological affairs, Office of
INTELLECTUAL liberty
Federal aid and the freedom to read. E. Geller. Library J 91:298 Ja 15 '66
International evening at the ABA convention; summary of address, June 6, 1966. A. J. Goldberg. il Pub W 189:36-7 Je 20 '66
See also
Academic freedom
American civil liberties union
INTELLECTUAL life
See also
Books and reading
INTELLECTUAL property. See Property, Intellectual
INTELLECTUAL snobs. See Snobs and snobbishness
INTELLECTUALS
American intellectual; address, June 1, 1966. R. C. Nairn. Vital Speeches 32:667-70 Ag 15 '66
Failure of a mission; relations between intellectuals and the President. Nation 203:236 S 19 '66
Ideas in action: relations between the academic community and elected representatives; address, December 4, 1965. S. Horn. Vital Speeches 32:283-8 F 15 '66
Johnson & the intellectuals. H. Fairlie; discussion. Commentary 41:4+ Ja; 6+ F '66
Let's all be eggheads. H. Downs. Sci Digest 59:90-3 My '66
LBJ at Princeton: some words about intellectuals and government. D. S. Greenberg. il Science 152:1223-5 My 27 '66
Making a mass élite. E. Hoffer. il Holiday 39:10+ Mr '66

INTELLECTUALS—*Continued*
Notes on cult; or, How to join the intellectual establishment. V. S. Navasky. il N Y Times Mag p28-9+ Mr 27 '66
Problems of the Negro woman intellectual. P. Pierce. il Ebony 21:144-9 Ag '66
Profiles; E. Hoffer. C. Tomkins. New Yorker 42:34-6+ Ja 7 '67
Truth and power: the intellectuals and the Johnson administration. H. J. Morgenthau. New Repub 155:8-14 N 26 '66; Discussion. 155:15-17 D 17; 35-6 D 24 '66; 156:42-3 Ja 7 '67
Unfortunate standoff: Johnson versus the intellectuals. H. Sidey. il Life 61:42D S 23 '66

See also
Scholars

INTELLIGENCE
Baby's cries a clue to intelligence; finding of Samuel Karelitz. Todays Health 45:69 Ja '67
Can we make human beings more intelligent? interview, ed. by J. K. Lagemann. J. M. Hunt. Read Digest 88:77-81 My '66
Savage mind, by C. Lévi-Strauss. Review New Repub 156:38-40 Ja 7 '67. P. Gallagher

INTELLIGENCE, Artificial. See Artificial intelligence

INTELLIGENCE, Military. See Military intelligence

INTELLIGENCE levels
Equality: a geneticist's view; reprint. T. Dobzhansky. il Cath World 204:104-12 N '66

Negroes
Lesson in bias; H. E. Garrett's pamphlet, How classroom desegregation will work. Newsweek 67:63 My 30 '66

INTELLIGENCE quotient
Frenzy over IQ tests; with study-discussion program, by E. Harris and D. Harris. G. R. Hawes. bibliog il PTA Mag 60:7-9, 35 Mr '66
I.Q. is an intelligent test. D. Wechsler. il N Y Times Mag p 12-13+ Je 26 '66; Reply with rejoinder. J. Laspro. p2+ Jl 17 '66

INTELLIGENCE service. See Secret service

INTELLIGENCE tests
Are intelligence tests unfair? P. Woodring. Sat R 49:79-80 Ap 16 '66
How good are our schools? armed forces qualification test provides a clue. R. De Neufville and C. Conner. il Am Ed 2:1-7 O '66
I.Q. is an intelligent test. D. Wechsler. il N Y Times Mag p 12-13+ Je 26 '66; Reply with rejoinder. J. Laspro. p2+ Jl 17 '66
Russians test failures. Sci N 90:3 Jl 2 '66
Stretch your mind! mental exercises. R. W. Samson. il Read Digest 88:37+ Mr '66
Teacher-opinion poll; group intelligence tests. NEA J 55:31 Ap '66
Testing results of preschoolers from some predominantly disadvantaged neighborhoods in St Petersburg, Fla; using Kuhlmann-Anderson test. W. E. Rouson. bibliog il Negro Hist Bul 29:111+ F '66
What are IQ tests good for? A. Loomer. Parents Mag 41:80+ S '66

See also
Intelligence quotient

INTELSAT. See International telecommunications satellite consortium

INTERAGENCY committee on oceanography. See United States federal council for science and technology

INTER-AGENCY group on international aviation (proposed)
Inter-agency group drafts U.S. position on aeronautical comsat. Aviation W 85:35 Ag 15 '66

INTERAMA. See Inter-American cultural and trade center, Miami

INTER-AMERICAN commission of women
Commission of women: fourth special assembly. Américas 18:48 Jl '66
IACW: fourth special assembly. M. O. De Macaya. il Américas 18:37-41 Ag '66
Women and progress. G. de Zéndegui. Américas 18:inside cover Je '66

INTER-AMERICAN committee on the Alliance for progress. See Alliance for progress

INTER-AMERICAN conferences
Charter amendments; preparation for the forthcoming third special Inter-American conference. G. Meek. Américas 18:43 Ag '66
Major Inter-American resolutions concerning folk and popular arts. il Américas 18: 26-7 Ja '66

Summit plans; eleventh meeting of consultation of ministers of foreign affairs. G. Meek. il Américas 18:40 D '66
Toward new dimensions for the OAS: second special inter-American conference; with excerpts from statements by delegates. G. Meek. il Américas 18:1-14 Ja '66

INTER-AMERICAN cooperation. See Inter-American relations

INTER-AMERICAN cultural and trade center, Miami
Interama interruption; CFA suspends loan. Reporter 34:18 Mr 10 '66

INTER-AMERICAN cultural council
Cultural cooperation; meeting. G. de Zéndegui. Américas 18:inside cover Ja '66
Culture in the limelight; with declaration on education, science and culture, and excerpts from address by J. Mora, G. de Zéndegui. il Américas 18:inside cover. 5-9 F '66
Toward deeper cultural relations in the hemisphere; address, January 18, 1966; with message of President Johnson. C. Frankel. Dept State Bul 54:202-7 F 7 '66

INTER-AMERICAN development bank
U.S.-Latin American relations; address, March 24, 1966. T. G. Upton. il Vital Speeches 32:400-4 Ap 15 '66

INTER-AMERICAN economic and social council
Alliance for progress: next steps for effective action; address, March 29, 1966. L. Gordon. Dept State Bul 54:738-46 My 9 '66
Committee on ports. G. Meek. Américas 18: 44-5 Ag '66
First five years; evaluation of Alliance for progress. F. Harmon. il Américas 18:1-7 Ag '66

Meetings, 1966
IA-ECOSOC meetings: fourth annual. Américas 18:40 Ap '66
Socioeconomic affairs: fourth special meeting. il Américas 18:46 Jl '66

INTER-AMERICAN education
Learning in two languages; Elbert Covell college; Inter-American studies program. A. J. Cullen. il Américas 18:12-18 My '66

INTER-AMERICAN relations
Hemisphere cooperation for economic and social progress; address, April 14, 1966. T. C. Mann. Dept State Bul 54:734-7 My 9 '66
Inter-American cooperation: the road ahead; address, December 1, 1966. L. Gordon. Dept State Bul 55:946-52 D 26 '66
President Johnson visits Mexico city; remarks upon his arrival, April 14, 1966; address at dedication of Abraham Lincoln statue, remarks to the staff of the U.S. embassy, with text of joint statement, April 15, 1966. L. B. Johnson. Dept State Bul 54:726-33 My 9 '66
See also
Alliance for progress
Inter-American commission of women
Latin America and the United States
Organization of American states
Pan American day and week

INTER-AMERICANISM. See Inter-American relations

INTERARMCO. See International armaments corporation

INTERCHANGE of persons. See Exchange of persons programs

INTERCHANGE of students. See Students. Interchange of

INTERCHANGE of teachers. See Teachers, Interchange of

INTERCITY transportation. See Transportation—United States

INTERCOLLEGIATE athletics. See College athletics

INTERCOLLEGIATE rowing association championships. See Rowing

INTERCOMMUNICATING systems
Build a hip squawk box; intercom doubles as a burglar and fire alarm. C. Vlahos and B. G. Wels. il Pop Electr 25:97-8+ O '66
Build this CB intercom and keep track of your kids. C. Stevens. il Pop Mech 126:166-8+ S '66
Super-simple intercom you can build. R. M. Benrey. il Pop Sci 189:102-3 Ag '66

INTERCOMMUNION. See Lords Supper

INTERCONNECTION of power systems. See Electric plants—Interconnection

INTERCONTINENTAL ballistic missiles. See Guided missiles

INTERCULTURAL education
See also
Colleges and universities—International cooperation

INTERDENOMINATIONAL cooperation. See Religious cooperation

INTERDENOMINATIONAL foreign mission association
Evangelical congress on worldwide mission; Wheaton, Ill. college campus April 9-16, 1966. M. Shelly. Christian Cent 83:695-7 My 25 '66

INTEREST
Bank depositor; government fixes maximum interest rate and sets minimum prices. M. Friedman. Newsweek 68:88 N 7 '66
Bank stocks and interest rates. il Duns R 87:98-9 F '66
Bankers report on the outlook for borrowers. U S News 61:90+ N 7 '66
Borrow with money in the bank? why? interest-saving passbook loans. il Changing T 20:20 S '66
Borrowing costs: headed higher. U S News 60:110 F 14 '66
Businessmen shrug off the prime rate boost. il Bsns W p23 Ag 27 '66
Clash of interest. il Time 88:77 Jl 8 '66
Creating new strains. il Time 87:79-80 Mr 25 '66
Et tu, Harry? concerning criticism from H. S. Truman. il Newsweek 68:23 S 12 '66
First faint signs of an easing in money. il U S News 61:90+ D 19 '66
Growing dilemma over money to lend. il U S News 60:97-9 Je 20 '66
Hidden clause; savings-and-loan associations use escalation clauses to boost rates. il Newsweek 68:80 O 17 '66
Interest rise hurts budget. U S News 60:114 F 28 '66
Investing in a time of inflation, advice of economists; symposium. il U S News 60:58-65 Ap 4 '66
Is money tight, or isn't it? never been tighter since the 1920s. il Bsns W p96-8 Ag 6 '66
Is the country running out of money? il U S News 61:85-7 Jl 11 '66
It's getting harder to borrow money; why. il U S News 60:66-8 Mr 28 '66
Latest on what your savings can earn. il U S News 60:60-1 Mr 21 '66
Let interest rates find their own levels. il Fortune 74:100 Ag '66
Little man grabs hard for that 5 per cent yield. il Bsns W p 151-2 +F 19 '66
Loan costs don't stop consumers. il Bsns W p32-3 Je 25 '66
LBJ clamps down a bit; more restrictive fiscal policy. il Bsns W p37-8 S 10 '66
Money at a price. il Fortune 73:40+ Ap '66
Money is heading to lusher pastures; S&L losing out to stiff bank competition. il Bsns W p 147-8+ My 28 '66
Money tighter, interest higher. U S News 61:90 Jl 18 '66
More bad news for borrowers, cost of money keeps rising. il U S News 61:89-90 Jl 25 '66
New age of five percent. il Fortune 73:209-10+ Mr '66
New hike in interest: money crisis ahead? U S News 60:13 Mr 21 '66
New look at interest rates. U S News 60:105-6 Je 13 '66
New rules on interest: meaning for savers, borrowers. il U S News 61:101-2 O 3 '66
Outlook now: tighter credit, higher interest rates. il U S News 60:113-14 Mr 14 '66
Pinch of tight money, meaning to the U.S. il U S News 61:36-8 Ag 1 '66
Prime rate starts up, again. Bsns W p22 Jl 2 '66
Race is on to borrow before the rate rises. il Bsns W p28-9 Ag 13 '66
Rates up, money vanishing, and new troubles for borrowers. U S News 61:85-7 Ag 22 '66
Some victories for truth-in-lending. Consumer Rep 31:394-5 Ag '66
Squeeze on money gets still tighter. Bsns W p30 Ag 20 '66
Squeeze: up goes the prime rate. il Newsweek 68:65 Jl 11 '66
Swatting at high rates. Bsns W p58 S 24 '66
Tighter, costlier cash may bring a slowdown. il Bsns W p36-7 Mr 19 '66
Trying to ease up on the money markets. il Bsns W p38-9 S 17 '66
Usury, what else? Nation 203:301 O 3 '66
Where to get the most for money. il Bsns W p 154+ O 8 '66
Will higher taxes mean lower interest rates? concerning State-of-the-Union message. U S News 62:99-100 Ja 23 '67

Will new issue flood push interest rates up? il Bsns W p46 Je 18 '66
See also
Instalment plan
Investments

INTEREST groups, Political. See Pressure groups

INTERFACES, Chemistry of. See Surface chemistry

INTERFAITH cooperation. See Religious cooperation

INTERFERENCE, Radio. See Radio interference

INTERFERING parents. See Parents

INTERFEROMETERS
Instrument proposed for measuring stars. Sci N 90:120 Ag 20 '66
Long-base-line interferometer at Jodrell Bank. A. D. Frost and H. P. Palmer. il Sky & Tel 32:21-4 Jl '66
Measurement of stellar diameters. R. H. Miller. bibliog il Science 153:581-7 Ag 5 '66

INTERFERON
Effect of interferon on early interferon production. H. B. Levy and others. bibliog il Science 152:1274-6 My 27 '66
Interferon: lack of detectable uptake by cells. C. E. Buckler and others. bibliog il Science 152:80-2 Ap 1 '66
Interferon protection against virus explained. Sci N 89:370 My 14 '66

INTERGOVERNMENTAL maritime consultative organization
U.S. welcomes IMCO action on passenger-ship safety. Dept State Bul 55:965 D 26 '66

INTERGOVERNMENTAL oceanographic commission
International oceanography; way scientific co-operation develops. K. N. Fedorov. il UN Mo Chron 3:28-37 Mr '66

INTERINDUSTRY analysis. See Linear programming

INTERIOR decoration
Report on residential interior design. G. O'Brien. il Arch Rec 139:29+ mid-My '66
Those Manhattan designers of good living. il Fortune 73:132-7 Mr '66
See also
Hotel decoration
House decoration
Mural painting and decoration
Office decoration

INTERIOR decorators
How to work with an interior decorator. C. O. Richardson. House & Gard 130:206-7+ S '66
Those Manhattan designers of good living. il Fortune 73:132-7 Mr '66

INTERLIBRARY loans
Proposed revision of the interlibrary loan form; Interlibrary loan committee of the Reference services division. il ALA Bul 61:9 Ja '67

INTERLINGUA
Interlingua expanding. Sci N 89:297 Ap 23 '66

INTERMARRIAGE of races
Belly-dancer who became a lady. C. Davis and M. J. Bellenger. il Ebony 21:78-80+ Jl '66
Colorless conjugality; Maryland bars Kovacs-Toalepai marriage. il Time 87:25 F 25 '66
Crime of being married; Lovings' fight against miscegenation. il Life 60:85-6+ Mr 18 '66
Happy end for Prince Seretse and Ruth. il Ebony 21:119-22+ My '66
Is my mixed marriage mixing up my kids? reprint. S. Davis. il Ebony 21:124-6+ O '66
Odds against a GI marrying a Vietnamese. U S News 61:10 Ag 22 '66
Science used in race case; Loving vs. Virginia. Sci N 90:465 D 3 '66

INTERMARRIAGES, Religious. See Marriages, Mixed

INTERNAL revenue service. See United States—Internal revenue service

INTERNAL structure of the earth. See Earth—Internal structure

INTERNATIONAL aeronautic federation
FAI explained; ed. by J. Gilbert. M. Obregon. il Flying 79:64-7 D '66

INTERNATIONAL agencies
International agencies for development. A. Rivkin. bibliog f Cur Hist 51:96-101+ Ag '66
President urges careful review of international agency budgets; statement, with texts of memorandums, March 15, 1966. L. B. Johnson. Dept State Bul 54:576-8 Ap 11 '66
See also
United States-South Africa leader exchange program, incorporated

INTERNATIONAL air transport association
Air of caution expected to mark annual IATA meeting; with editorial comment. Aviation W 85:21, 30-1 O 31 '66
Atlantic tour fare agreement seen. J. W. Carter. Aviation W 85:35-6 D 5 '66
Cautious mood stalls IATA talks. R. G. O'Lone. Aviation W 85:36-7 O 10 '66
CAB may boost pressure on IATA. R. G. O'Lone. Aviation W 85:41-2 O 24 '66
CAB views IATA; comments. C. S. Murphy. Aviation W 85:17 N 28 '66
IATA balks at basic fare cuts. R. G. O'Lone. Aviation W 85:34-7 O 17 '66
IATA chief sees major handling procedure changes for giant jets. Aviation W 84:44 My 30 '66
New chief will modify IATA's philosophy. L. L. Doty. Aviation W 84:50 Ap 4 '66
New jets peril small flag carriers. H. D. Watkins. Aviation W 85:36-7 N 7 '66
North Atlantic air traffic surging. J. W. Carter. Aviation W 85:26-7 D 26 '66
Pacific fare battle due at IATA meeting. J. W. Carter. Aviation W 85:39 Ag 8 '66
Rate proposals key IATA issue. L. L. Doty. Aviation W 85:25-6 D 19 '66
Tariff simplification challenging IATA. L. L. Doty. Aviation W 85:27-8 D 26 '66
Time for a diplomat. il Time 87:75 Ap 22 '66
INTERNATIONAL arbitration. See Arbitration, International
INTERNATIONAL armaments corporation
Planning a war? See Sam! A. Whitman. il Pop Mech 125:90-2+ My '66
INTERNATIONAL arts and crafts exhibition. See Arts and crafts—Exhibitions
INTERNATIONAL aspects of art. See Art—International aspects
INTERNATIONAL association for the exchange of students for technical experience
Student exchange. D. Wolfle. Science 152: 1461 Je 10 '66
INTERNATIONAL association of machinists
Airline labor groups to push for larger share of earnings. J. W. Carter. Aviation W 84: 40-1 Ja 24 '66
Airline strike signals new labor struggle. il Aviation W 85:34-6+ Jl 18 '66
Getting upstaged by the union wasn't in the scenario; L. B. Johnson intervention. H. Sidey. il Life 61:32 Ag 12 '66
Grounded; machinists strike against airlines. il Time 88:16-17 Jl 15 '66
Guideposts for pay raises discarded? Machinists union vs. five major airlines. U S News 60:94 Je 20 '66
IAM cool to proposed airline settlement; July 5 strike threat. J. W. Carter. Aviation W 84:45 Je 13 '66
Labor feels its oats; deadlock between airlines and machinists. il Bsns W p90-2+ My 14 '66
Labor-for-rent war; machinists and UAW attack aerospace practice of leasing extra craftsmen from agencies. il Bsns W p 160+ N 5 '66
Machinist negotiations continue under Labor dept. sponsorship. Aviation W 84:34 Je 27 '66
Not off the ground yet; airline machinists force Congress to take action. il Bsns W p30 Ag 13 '66
Qantas pilots threaten walkout; strike at Air Canada continues. Aviation W 85:41 N 28 '66
Strike economic, social impact deepens. il Aviation W 85:40-2 Ag 8 '66
Strike socks in the airlines; five carriers grounded. il Bsns W p28-9 Jl 16 '66
Taking the lid off wages? strike against airlines. il Newsweek 68:17-18 Ag 8 '66
Up in the air; no settlement. Newsweek 68: 64 Ag 1 '66
When a union struck five major airlines; Machinists union. il U S News 61:105-6 Jl 18 '66
Woodshed solution. il Time 88:17-18 Ag 5 '66
INTERNATIONAL astronautical congress. See International astronautical federation
INTERNATIONAL astronautical federation
New Soviet manned flights expected soon. Tech W 19:13-14 O 24 '66
Reporter at large; seventeenth annual congress. D. Lang. New Yorker 42:37-40+ D 24 '66
Russian data scanty at IAF gathering; with editorial comment. Tech W 19:16-17, 50 O 17 '66
Space club's roster goes international; Madrid meeting of international space scientists. il Bsns W p 112+ O 22 '66
USSR finds drugs vital in space. D. E. Fink. Aviation W 85:30-1 O 17 '66

INTERNATIONAL atomic energy agency
Assembly takes note of report. UN Mo Chron 3:63-4 D '66
INTERNATIONAL automobile show. See Automobiles—Exhibitions
INTERNATIONAL B. F. Goodrich company. See Goodrich, B. F. company
INTERNATIONAL balance of payments. See Balance of payments
INTERNATIONAL bank for reconstruction and development
As good as gold; annual meeting of the directors of the World bank and the IMF. Time 88:111 O 7 '66
International agencies for development. A. Rivkin. bibliog f Cur Hist 51:96-101+ Ag '66
Muddy road to monetary reform; meeting in Washington. il Bsns W p40-1 O 1 '66
Stride toward monetary reform; IMF-World bank meeting. il Newsweek 68:82-4 O 10 '66
Toward a more rational world economic order; statement, September 29, 1966. G. W. Ball. Dept State Bul 55:633-7 O 24 '66
World bank's 20th anniversary; summary of message of congratulations. Thant. UN Mo Chron 3:57 Jl '66
INTERNATIONAL BB-gun shooting championship. See Shooting—Competitions
INTERNATIONAL bibliography. See Bibliography, International
INTERNATIONAL brain research organization. See Brain
INTERNATIONAL brigades. See Spain—History—Civil war, 1936-1939—Volunteers
INTERNATIONAL brotherhood of electrical workers
Electrical brotherhood makes its power play; IBEW bid for prestige. il Bsns W p50+ N 5 '66
Where a strike hurts war effort. U S News 61:80 D 19 '66
INTERNATIONAL brotherhood of firemen and oilers
Dead issue comes to life; why firemen went on strike. U S News 60:79 Ap 11 '66
That railroad strike, & co; firemen's union. Nat R 18:346-8 Ap 19 '66
What's next in rail dispute. U S News 60: 88 Ap 18 '66
INTERNATIONAL brotherhood of teamsters, chauffeurs, warehousemen and helpers of America
As Hoffa's deadline nears; a strike deadline too. il U S News 62:85-7 Ja 16 '67
Bargaining and wages in local cartage. V. J. Sheifer. il Mo Labor R 89:1076-84 O '66
DRIVE; teamsters in politics; Democrat Republican independent voter education. T. E. Tornek. il Nation 203:663-5 D 19 '66
Elusive heel; Hoffa to ask convention to change the union's bylaws. Time 87:21 F 11 '66
Fighting Hoffa's blues. il Time 88:17-18 Jl 15 '66
Hell with everybody! convention in Miami Beach. il Newsweek 68:80 Jl 18 '66
Hoffa seeks stand-in, in case he's needed; hand-picked successor if sent to jail. Bsns W p 144 Je 4 '66
Hoffa still holds the reins, for now. il Bsns W p 128-30 Jl 9 '66
Hoffa's funeral. il Newsweek 68:20-1 D 26 '66
How a union can be run from prison. il U S News 61:76+ Jl 11 '66
If Jimmy Hoffa goes to jail. il U S News 61:65-6 D 26 '66
Jimmy's boy; Hoffa's caretaker succession plan. Newsweek 67:76 My 16 '66
Teamsters prepare for nationwide contracts. Mo Labor R 89:III-IV Jl '66
Teamsters take a dare and lose a vote. il Bsns W p 152-3+ Ap 16 '66
Will jailing Hoffa hurt the teamsters? Bsns W p44 D 17 '66
INTERNATIONAL business machines corporation
$5-billion world market for computers; special report. il Bsns W p 110-14+ F 19 '66
Foreign hands see employer's home base; cutrate U.S. tour for IBM overseas workers. il Bsns W p78-9 Ag 13 '66
IBM thinks twice; building policies. J. M. Dixon. il Arch Forum 124:32-9 Mr '66
I.B.M.'s $5,000,000,000 gamble; system/360 computer. T. A. Wise. il Fortune 74:118-23+ S; 139+ O '66
New IBM lab will attack variety of space problems. Tech W 20:41 Ja 16 '67
R&E council is briefed on new tools from IBM. il Pub W 189:82-5 My 2 '66

INTERNATIONAL business machines corpora-
tion—*Continued*
SR's businessman of the year: T. J. Watson,
jr. W. D. Patterson. Sat R 50:74+ Ja 14
'67
Taking & offering stock. il Time 87:92 My 6
'66
Taking the hard sell to eastern Europe: In-
comex 66 exhibit in Czechoslovakia. il Bsns
W p34-6 Je 4 '66
INTERNATIONAL cartels. See Trusts, Indus-
trial—International trusts
INTERNATIONAL childrens emergency fund.
See United Nations childrens fund
INTERNATIONAL civil aviation organization
Inter-agency group drafts U.S. position on
aeronautical comsat. Aviation W 85:35 Ag
15 '66
ICAO may resort to diplomatic conference to
save Warsaw pact. Aviation W 84:36 F 21
'66
ICAO unit opposes early airline comsat. Aviation W 85:50 O 31 '66
INTERNATIONAL coffee council
U.S. welcomes recent decisions by International coffee council; Department statement, September 7, 1966. Dept State Bul
55:463 S 26 '66
INTERNATIONAL competition of artistic ceramics. See Pottery—Competitions
INTERNATIONAL conference of Christians
and Jews
Christians and Jews in international conference. R. C. Dodds. Christian Cent 83:
1359-62 N 2 '66
INTERNATIONAL conference on education
International conference on education; text
of letter to Dr James Perkins, November
24, 1966. L. B. Johnson. Dept State Bul
56:15 Ja 2 '67
INTERNATIONAL conference on human rights
(proposed)
International conference on human rights.
UN Mo Chron 3:39-40 Jl '66
Meeting of preparatory committee. UN Mo
Chron 3:42-3 Je '66
INTERNATIONAL conference on public educa-
tion
28th International conference on public edu-
cation. R. Gampert. Sch & Soc 94:48-9 Ja
22 '66
INTERNATIONAL conference on water for
peace (proposed)
Water for peace conference to be held at
Washington; statement, November 8, 1966.
L. B. Johnson. Dept State Bul 55:868-9 D
5 '66
INTERNATIONAL conferences
Asian summit, what to expect. U S News
61:35 O 10 '66
Calendar of international conferences and
meetings. See occasional issues of De-
partment of state bulletin
How the balance has changed; secret sum-
mit in Moscow; nonaligned nations meet
in New Delhi. il Time 88:34 O 28 '66
Moscow meeting; Communist leaders from
nine nations. Sr Schol 89:18 N 4 '66
Vietnam: the U.S. tries harder; President
Johnson accepts invitation of President
Marcos to summit conference in Manila. il
Bsns W p38-9 O 1 '66
Waiting for the end; four-day meeting of
the nonaligned statesmen in New Delhi. il
Newsweek 68:62-3 N 7 '66
See also
Council of foreign ministers, Geneva, 1954
Inter-American conferences
Manila conference, 1966
Pugwash conferences on science and world
affairs
INTERNATIONAL Congregational council
Dying to live. C. Northcott. Christian Cent
83:955 Ag 3 '66
INTERNATIONAL congress for scientific man-
agement
Russia's brass tells how it's done; interna-
tional management session at Rotterdam
hears Soviet experts. il Bsns W p 171-2+
O 8 '66
INTERNATIONAL congress of mathematicians
Fields math medal awarded two in Moscow.
Sci N 90:137 Ag 27 '66
INTERNATIONAL congress on air technology.
See Aviation—International aspects
INTERNATIONAL congress on metallic cor-
rosion
For world science: a bear hug; third Interna-
tional congress on metallic corrosion in Mos-
cow's Sovetskaya hotel. il Bsns W p92+
Je 4 '66

INTERNATIONAL control commission for
Indochina
It would be idiotic to deal with the Viet
Cong; interview. R. L. Houston. U S News
61:44-5 O 17 '66
Policemen without power. il Newsweek 68:
30-1 S 5 '66
INTERNATIONAL convention of Christian
churches. See Disciples of Christ
INTERNATIONAL convention on the elimi-
nation of all forms of racial discrimination
International convention on the elimination
of all forms of racial discrimination; state-
ment, December 21, 1965; with text of
convention. Thant. UN Mo Chron 3:103-15
Ja '66
United Nations adopts convention on racial
discrimination; statements, December 14, 21,
1965. A. J. Goldberg; F. E. Willis. Dept
State Bul 54:212-16 F 7 '66
U.S. signs convention on racial discrimina-
tion; statement, September 28, 1966. A. J.
Goldberg. Dept State Bul 55:653 O 24 '66
INTERNATIONAL cookery. See Cookery, In-
ternational
INTERNATIONAL cooperation
Problems abroad; findings of educational re-
search and opportunities for teachers
abroad, at International conference on pub-
lic education, Geneva. Sch & Soc 94:447+
D 10 '66
See also
Colleges and universities—International co-
operation
Economic assistance
Inter-American economic and social council
Inter-American relations
International agencies
International education
Patents—International aspects
Science—International aspects
United Nations
United States book exchange, incorporated
White House conference on international co-
operation, 1965
INTERNATIONAL correspondence schools
Button, button, which has the answer? FM
radio educational broadcasting. il Bsns W
p 188+ Je 18 '66
INTERNATIONAL council of community
churches
Council of community churches. R. H. Tay-
lor. Christian Cent 83:1154 S 21 '66
INTERNATIONAL council of scientific unions
NAS, ICSU statements on international meet-
ings; October 1966. Science 154:369 O 21 '66
Smale aftermath: ICSU and academy urge
ban on politics at meetings. D. S. Greenberg. Science 154:368-70 O 21 '66

Committee on space research

Soviet spacecraft sterilization methods aired
at COSPAR. W. S. Beller. Miss & Roc 18:
17-18 My 16 '66
INTERNATIONAL court of justice. The Hague
Apartheid: catalyst in the U.N; World court's
unfavorable verdict in regard to South West
Africa. A. A. D'Amato. Christian Cent 83:
1303-6 O 26 '66
Election of members of International court
of justice. UN Mo Chron 3:93 D '66
ICJ South-West Africa judgment: U.S. ap-
praises legal situation; Department state-
ment. Dept State Bul 55:231 Ag 15 '66
South West Africa case: what happened? E.
A. Gross. For Affairs 45:36-48 O '66
South West Africa: World court's ticklish
case. il Nation 202:389-93 Ap 4 '66
Vote on apartheid. Time 88:22 Jl 29 '66

Decisions

Judgement in South West Africa cases. UN
Mo Chron 3:67-74 Ag '66
Shock from The Hague; Southwest Africa.
il Newsweek 68:42+ Ag 1 '66
South Africa's victory; analysis of South-
west Africa decision. Nation 203:107-8 Ag
8 '66
INTERNATIONAL dance festival. See Dance
festivals
INTERNATIONAL design conference
Art and life at Aspen Meadows; report of
conference. J. Barnett. Arch Rec 140:121-2
Ag '66
Aspen design conference stresses human
values. Pub W 190:113-14 Ag 1 '66
INTERNATIONAL economic affairs committee.
See National association of manufacturers
INTERNATIONAL education
Aid to African education. Sch & Soc 94:447
D 10 '66

INTERNATIONAL education—*Continued*
Aid to the understudied; Congress passes act.
Newsweek 68:96-7 O 31 '66
American education and the developing
areas; address; with questions and answers. K. W. Thompson. Ann Am Acad
366:17-32 Jl '66
Anniversary of the Fulbright act; Interna-
tional education act now in Congress. J.
Cass. Sat R 49:47-8 Ag 20 '66
As nations become neighbors; symposium.
il Sat R 49:50-2+ Ag 20 '66
Education as an instrument of American
foreign policy; address, April 16, 1966. W.
Benton. Ann Am Acad 366:33-40 Jl '66
Education for international communication
and understanding in the technological
age; summary of address, November 2,
1965. W. W. Brickman. Sch & Soc 94:31-2
Ja 22 '66
Education for world responsibility; address,
July 16, 1966. C. Frankel. Vital Speeches
32:621-5 Ag 1 '66
International education act of 1966; state-
ment, March 31, 1966. C. Frankel. Dept
State Bul 54:754-7 My 9 '66
Major provisions of the International educa-
tion act. Sat R 49:53 Ag 20 '66
National foreign policy conference for educators; Washington, D.C. June 16-17, 1966;
with introd. by R. I. Phillips; symposium.
Dept State Bul 55:71-109 Jl 18 '66
Neglected aspect of foreign affairs; Ameri-
can educational and cultural policy abroad,
by C. Frankel. Review
Sat R 49:42 Mr 5 '66. M. R. Konvitz
Opportunity; proposals of E. U. Condon. Na-
tion 203:533 N 21 '66
President asks global attack on ignorance;
statements. L. B. Johnson. Sr Schol 88:sup
1-2 F 25 '66
Toward deeper cultural relations in the hem-
isphere; address, January 18, 1966. C.
Frankel. Dept State Bul 54:202-7 F 7 '66
Two decades in the world of education. L.
Elvin. il UNESCO Courier 19:24-7 Jl '66
U.S. government and international education.
W. W. Brickman. Sch & Soc 94:254 Sum '66
Widening campus horizons; concerning Edu-
cation and world affairs; study of inter-
national activities at six U.S. universities.
G. A. Olds. Sat R 49:67-8 Ag 20 '66
See also
Colleges and universities—International co-
operation
Experiment in international living (organi-
zation)
Institute of international education
Inter-American education
International relations—Study and teaching
Travel study courses
United Nations educational, scientific and cul-
tural organization
INTERNATIONAL emergency childrens fund.
See United Nations childrens fund
INTERNATIONAL executive service corps
Globe-trotting troubleshooters of IESC. D. Ro-
binson. Read Digest 89:25-6+ N '66
Paunch corps in action. Newsweek 67:68+
F 28 '66
Work is a proper noun. H. Bowser. Sat R
49:32 O 22 '66
INTERNATIONAL exports, limited. See Night
clubs
INTERNATIONAL expositions. See Exhibitions
INTERNATIONAL federation. See International
organization
INTERNATIONAL federation of campers and
caravaners
Togetherness under canvas; annual rally in
Hungary. il Time 88:26 Ag 26 '66
INTERNATIONAL federation of library asso-
ciations
IFLA/FIAB report. R. Vosper; K. Molz. il
Wilson Lib Bul 41:276-83+ N '66
Shared cataloging; feature of LC's plan. E.
Hamer and A. McCormick. ALA Bul 60:
1127 D '66

International association of
technological university
libraries
IATUL: what it is and what it does. G. T.
Piez. ALA Bul 60:712-13 Jl '66
INTERNATIONAL federation of medical stu-
dent associations
Busmen's holiday for medical students. Sch
& Soc 94:343 O 29 '66

INTERNATIONAL festival of music and drama,
Edinburgh
Edinburgh. T. Urquhart. Opera N 31:27
N 5 '66
INTERNATIONAL film festival, Cannes. See
Cannes international film festival
INTERNATIONAL finance. See Finance, Inter-
national
INTERNATIONAL finance corporation
New verve for worldwide financing. il Bsns
W p 106+ Jl 9 '66
INTERNATIONAL flower show. See Flower
exhibits
INTERNATIONAL furniture fair, Cologne. See
Exhibitions
INTERNATIONAL geophysical year
Statement by eleven distinguished geophysi-
cists; letter. UNESCO Courier 19:30-1 O
'66
INTERNATIONAL government. See Interna-
tional organization
INTERNATIONAL harvester company
Firm seeks bigger beryllium market. J. F.
Judge. il Miss & Roc 18:22-3 Ap 11 '66
INTERNATIONAL house of pancakes. See Res-
taurants—United States
INTERNATIONAL houseboat regatta. See Re-
gattas
INTERNATIONAL human rights year (pro-
posed)
Recommendations for twentieth anniversary.
UN Mo Chron 3:22-4 Mr '66
INTERNATIONAL hydrological decade
Instant information on water needed; data
from satellites and computers. Sci N 89:
207 Mr 26 '66
INTERNATIONAL ice patrol
See also
United States—Coast guard
INTERNATIONAL inventors and new products
exhibition. See Inventions—Exhibitions
INTERNATIONAL investment computers. See
Intinco limited
INTERNATIONAL joint commission (United
States and Canada)
Congress receives IJC report on pollution of
lakes. Dept State Bul 54:293-4 F 21 '66
U.S. and Canada request IJC study on air pol-
lution; text of letter, September 23, 1966.
Dept State Bul 55:688-9 O 31 '66
INTERNATIONAL labor movement. See Trade
unions—International aspects
INTERNATIONAL labor organization
Adamant Mr Meany; AFL-CIO walkout. Na-
tion 202:764 Je 27 '66
AFL-CIO foreign policy; U.S. delegates walk-
out. New Repub 154:7 Je 25 '66
Conflicts shake labor's house. Bsns W p 110
Je 25 '66
International labor conference of 1966. H. M.
Douty. Mo Labor R 89:841-6 Ag '66
President Johnson urges Senate to ratify
ILO convention 122; statement, June 2,
1966. L. B. Johnson. Dept State Bul 54:
1026-7 Je 27 '66
Teaching the Kenyans to take a letter; sec-
retarial training sponsored by ILO. il Bsns
W p 126-7 My 7 '66
INTERNATIONAL ladies' garment workers'
union
D.D. New Repub 154:10 Ap 2 '66
D.D. of the ILG. Sr Schol 88:22-3 Ap 1 '66
Hail and farewell; president retires. News-
week 67:74+ Mr 28 '66
Hell raisers' adieux. il Time 87:20 Mr 25 '66
On the heels of a giant; L. Stulberg succeeds
D. Dubinsky as ILGWU president. il Bsns
W p54+ Jl 16 '66
INTERNATIONAL language. See Language,
Universal
INTERNATIONAL law
Assembly adopts two resolutions; principles
of international law concerning friendly re-
lations and co-operation among states. UN
Mo Chron 3:95-8 Ja '66
Principles of international law concerning
friendly relations and cooperation among
states; statement, December 8, 1965. W. P.
Rogers. Dept State Bul 54:168-75 Ja 31
'66
Revolution in peace education; Clark-Sohn
plan and the World law fund. R. A. Falk.
il Sat R 49:59-61+ My 21 '66
Special committee session concluded; with
texts adopted. UN Mo Chron 3:55-6 My
'66
United Nations programme of assistance and
exchange in the field of international law.
C. A. Stavropoulos. UN Mo Chron 3:41-7
Ap '66

INTERNATIONAL law—*Continued*
World peace through law; address, March 12, 1966. E. Warren. Vital Speeches 32:387-90 Ap 15 '66
See also
Aggression (international law)
Alien property
Conquest, Right of
Maritime law
Rule of law
Sanctions (international law)
Space law
United Nations—International law commission
United Nations—Legal committee
United Nations—Special committee on principles of international law concerning friendly relations and cooperation among states

INTERNATIONAL law commission. See United Nations—International law commission

INTERNATIONAL literacy day
International literacy day; proclamation, August 30, 1966. L. B. Johnson. Dept State Bul 55:464 S 26 '66

INTERNATIONAL longshoremen's and warehousemen's union
Decks cleared for new dock pact. il Bsns W p 108-10 Jl 30 '66
1966 West coast longshore negotiations. M. D. Kossoris. Mo Labor R 89:1067-75 O '66

INTERNATIONAL longshoremen's association
ILA tries its hand at unclogging Saigon; effort to move supplies delayed by antiquated docks and working habits. il Bsns W p53+ F 19 '66

INTERNATIONAL management congress. See International congress for scientific management

INTERNATIONAL monetary and financial policies, National advisory council on. See United States—National advisory council on international monetary and financial policies

INTERNATIONAL monetary fund
As good as gold; annual meeting of the directors of the World bank and the IMF. Time 88:111 O 7 '66
Edging near a new money; unexpected progress at IMF. Bsns W p 136 D 3 '66
It's an uphill fight for monetary reform; twenty member nations join in the talks. il Bsns W p73-4+ S 24 '66
Muddy road to monetary reform; meeting in Washington. il Bsns W p40-1 O 1 '66
Toward a more rational world economic order; texts of statements, September 29, 1966. H. H. Fowler. Dept State Bul 55:626-33 O 24 '66

INTERNATIONAL multihull boat race. See Yacht racing

INTERNATIONAL music festival, Daytona Beach. See Music festivals—Florida

INTERNATIONAL nickel company
Nickel comes up short. Bsns W p35 Ag 6 '66

INTERNATIONAL nickel company of Canada
Inco puts new dent in guideposts; Canadian nickel producer posts a 9.6 per cent boost. il Bsns W p 152 N 12 '66

INTERNATIONAL oceanographic congress, Moscow, 1966
Oceanographic congress. UN Mo Chron 3:58 Jl '66

INTERNATIONAL officials and employees
See also
United Nations—Secretariat

INTERNATIONAL Olympic committee. See Olympic games

INTERNATIONAL one-designs. See Sailboat racing

INTERNATIONAL opera production association
Interopera; clearing house for productions. Q. Eaton. il Opera N 30:32 F 12 '66

INTERNATIONAL organization
Revolution in peace education; Clark-Sohn plan and the World law fund. R. A. Falk. il Sat R 49:59-61+ My 21 '66
Thought for the New Year; proposal for world federalism. N. Cousins. Sat R 49:28 D 24 '66
See also
United world federalists

INTERNATIONAL organizations. See International agencies

INTERNATIONAL organizations, Regional
See also
Asian and Pacific council (proposed)
Organization of the American states

INTERNATIONAL PEN club. See PEN club

INTERNATIONAL petroleum exposition. See Petroleum industry and trade—Exhibitions

INTERNATIONAL photography fair. See Photography—Exhibitions

INTERNATIONAL police
See also
United Nations—Armed forces

INTERNATIONAL printing pressmen's and assistants' union of North America
Two printing unions holding merger talks. Pub W 189:132 Mr 7 '66

INTERNATIONAL publishers association
I.P.A. educational group meets during the fair. il Pub W 190:29-32 N 7 '66

INTERNATIONAL publishers representatives (firm)
New book company formed to sell books abroad. Pub W 190:47 N 21 '66

INTERNATIONAL publishing corporation, limited
British combine buys share of U.S. publisher. Pub W 189:69 F 28 '66
Forty million books a year from new IPC company. Pub W 189:45 Mr 28 '66
Paul Hamlyn discusses possible U.S. activities; interview. P. Hamlyn. Pub W 189:46-7 Je 20 '66
Trade-technical magazines forge international chain. Pub W 190:41 Jl 25 '66

INTERNATIONAL reading association
Meeting, 1966. il Sr Schol 89:sup3 S 16 '66

INTERNATIONAL relations
Address to the Consultative assembly of the Council of Europe at Strasbourg, France, May 3, 1966. Thant. il UN Mo Chron 3:51-60 Je '66
China and Nazi Germany. W. Pfaff. Commonweal 84:70-1 Ap 8 '66
China watchers; Soviet strategy. H. Brandon. Sat R 49:18+ F 5 '66
De Gaulle, the U.S. and Russia: a look at the trends; interview, ed. by F. C. Painton. A. Grosser. U S News 60:42-3 Je 20 '66
Fairly peaceful world, except in Vietnam. il U S News 62:20-1 Ja 2 '67
Fatal arrogance of power. J. W. Fulbright. il N Y Times Mag p28-9+ My 15 '66
General assembly adopts resolution; prohibition of the use of force; with text. UN Mo Chron 3:55-63 D '66
Hard work ahead for the United Nations; address, March 18, 1966. J. J. Sisco. Dept State Bul 54:571-6 Ap 11 '66
How do you make peace? D. Lawrence. U S News 60:124 F 28 '66
Impact and potential of American diplomacy; address; with questions and answers. P. Findley. Ann Am Acad 366:68-77 Jl '66
Inadequate defense against World war III. D. Lawrence. U S News 61:88 D 26 '66
Lonely role of the U.S. U S News 61:119 O 17 '66
Missing brotherhood. D. Lawrence. U S News 60:120 Mr 14 '66
New year's thoughts 1966. E. Rabinowitch. Bul Atomic Sci 22:3-7+ Ja '66
Orient: a problem of nonexistence; attitudes toward two Chinas. W. J. Thorbecke. Sat R 49:38-9 Mr 26 '66
Peace and war, by R. Aron. Review
Sat R 50:30-1 Ja 7 '67. H. J. Morgenthau
Policy-making in a world turned upside down. T. L. Hughes. For Affairs 45:202-14 Ja '67
Progress toward a decent world order; address, June 14, 1966. D. Rusk. Dept State Bul 55:44-9 Jl 11 '66
Revolutions: the big problem in the world today. D. Lawrence. U S News 60:112 Mr 7 '66
Scholars face the future: bringing about peaceful change. P. Van Slyck. Sat R 49:75-6 Je 11 '66
Science of crisis diplomacy. H. Pryor. il Sci Digest 59:33-6 Ap '66
Secretary Rusk's news conference of November 18, 1966. D. Rusk. Dept State Bul 55:844-51 D 5 '66
'67: what will it be like in the outside world? il U S News 62:28-30 Ja 9 '67
This month's feature: congressional review of foreign policy. Cong Digest 45:225-56 O '66
Trade aid and world peace. America 114:580 Ap 23 '66
Twenty-five years after Pearl Harbor: an attack that remade the world. il U S News 61:40-4+ D 12 '66
U.S. and world affairs annual; ed. by R. Hemming and others. il Sr Schol 89:pt2 1-31 S 23 '66
U.S. takes on still more of world's defense. il U S News 60:34-6 Mr 7 '66

INTERNATIONAL relations—*Continued*
U.S, the Communists, and wars of national liberation. il Sr Schol 89:12-13+ O 7 '66
Warning, danger, loaded words ahead! il Sr Schol 88:5-7 Mr 11 '66
World politics and tension areas, by F. Gross. Review
  Sat R 49:53 Je 11 '66. H. H. Ransom
  See also
Arbitration, International
Atlantic community
Balance of power
Diplomacy
Disarmament
Europe—Politics
International conferences
International organization
International security
Intervention
Peace
Sea power
United Nations
War
World politics
  also subhead Foreign relations under names of countries, e.g. France—Foreign relations

Bibliography
Recent books on international relations; comp. by H. L. Roberts. See issues of Foreign affairs
Source material; comp. by D. Wasson. See issues of Foreign affairs
World scene (cont) V. S. Kearney. America 114:659-61; 115:692-3+ My 7, N 26 '66

Study and teaching
What colleges can do. W. W. Marvel. il Sat R 49:56-7+ Ag 20 '66
INTERNATIONAL rice research institute
IRRI fills empty rice bowls. P. Deutschman. il Sat R 49:16-17+ Ag 6 '66
INTERNATIONAL science fair. See Science fairs
INTERNATIONAL science foundation (proposed)
Editor comments on space, basic research, and an International science foundation. E. Rabinowitch. Bul Atomic Sci 22:2-3 O '66
INTERNATIONAL scientific and technological affairs, Office of. See United States—State, Department of—International scientific and technological affairs, Office of
INTERNATIONAL security
McNamara's new design for world peace and security; address, May 18, 1966. R. S. McNamara. il U S News 60:90-5 My 30 '66; Same with title Security in the contemporary world. Dept State Bul 54:874-81 Je 6 '66
Mutual defense assistance control act. Cur Hist 51:45-6 Jl '66
Reflections on international security. H. M. Guéron. Bul Atomic Sci 22:32-3 S '66
Secretary McNamara discusses Asian affairs and nuclear arms control in interview for Japanese magazine. R. S. McNamara. Dept State Bul 55:303-11 Ag 29 '66
Updating the world's biggest military machine; Time essay. Time 87:34-5 Je 3 '66
  See also
Aggression (international law)
Atomic power—International control
Disarmament
Peace
INTERNATIONAL security affairs division. See United States—Defense, Department of—International security affairs division
INTERNATIONAL settlements, Bank for. See Bank for international settlements
INTERNATIONAL socialist congress
Socialist conventioneers; 10th socialist international congress in Stockholm. W. S. Allen. Commonweal 84:409-10 Jl 1 '66
INTERNATIONAL society for contemporary music
Talent and trash from I.S.C.M. P. Moor. Hi Fi 16:MA26 D '66
INTERNATIONAL society for education through art
American art education in Japan; congress of the International society for education through art. M. F. Andrews. il Sch Arts 65:32-6 Mr '66
INTERNATIONAL society for the preservation of black-and-white photography. See Camera clubs
INTERNATIONAL student service
Unofficial ambassadors; ISS programs. C. Sutliff. il Sat R 49:58-9 Ag 20 '66

INTERNATIONAL Tchaikovsky competition. See Music—Competitions
INTERNATIONAL telecommunications satellite consortium
AT&T plans vast comsat net with 83,000-circuit capacity. K. Johnsen. Aviation W 85:24 D 26 '66
Comsat question. W. J. Coughlin. Tech W 19:50 O 24 '66
FCC ownership decision speeds construction of new terminals. K. Johnsen. Aviation W 85:17-18 D 19 '66
Global Comsat expansion delayed two years. Aviation W 84:31 My 30 '66
NASA-Intelsat conclude contract for Apollo communications work. Aviation W 84:33 Ap 4 '66
Satellites will compete for major role in commercial communications traffic. K. Johnsen. il Aviation W 84:124-5+ Mr 7 '66
Second Intelsat-2 is orbiting earth. Aviation W 86:34 Ja 16 '67
U.S. spurring overseas Comsat terminals. K. Johnsen. Aviation W 84:31 My 23 '66
INTERNATIONAL telephone and telegraph. American broadcasting company merger. See Business consolidations and mergers
INTERNATIONAL telephone and telegraph corporation
Broadcast ownership; questions presented by the ITT-ABC merger. New Repub 155:6 O 15 '66
Hard-nosed ITT; public relations department. L. L. L. Golden. il Sat R 49:148 Mr 12 '66
How modern management doubled ITT's European sales. Bsns W p 102 My 7 '66
How one man can move a corporate mountain. S. H. Brown. il Fortune 74:80-3+ Jl 1 '66
ITT plans to acquire Howard W. Sams & co. Pub W 189:54-5 My 23 '66
Sams board approves its merger proposal. Pub W 190:198 Jl 11 '66
Sams stockholders agree on acquisition by ITT. Pub W 190:52 O 10 '66
INTERNATIONAL television. See Television broadcasting—International aspects
INTERNATIONAL tin council
Tin council and U.S. officials discuss tin sales program. Dept State Bul 55:756 N 14 '66
INTERNATIONAL tourist year, 1967
Agenda for travel. W. D. Patterson. Sat R 50:24+ Ja 7 '67
International tourist year 1967; symposium. il Sat R 50:43-8+ Ja 7 '67
INTERNATIONAL trade. See Commerce
INTERNATIONAL trade mart, New Orleans. See New Orleans—International trade mart
INTERNATIONAL travel. See Travel
INTERNATIONAL travel regulations. See Travel regulations
INTERNATIONAL trusteeships
  See also
Trust Territory of the Pacific Islands
INTERNATIONAL typographic composition association
ITCA convention draws record attendance. Pub W 190:119 N 7 '66
INTERNATIONAL typographical union
Printers rise again; shut down of Boston's five dailies. il Time 87:77 Mr 18 '66
INTERNATIONAL understanding. See International understanding
INTERNATIONAL underwater film festival. See Moving picture festivals
INTERNATIONAL union of electrical, radio and machine workers
Bargaining basement; strike threat by GE. Newsweek 68:80 O 17 '66
GE puts unity to test. il Bsns W p94+ Je 25 '66
It takes a bigger offer now to head off a strike. U S News 61:92-3 O 17 '66
Johnson draws bead on GE fight; wins two-week delay in nationwide strike. il Bsns W p 145-7 O 8 '66
Shared victory. Time 88:103-4 O 21 '66
Who won in the GE settlement. il Bsns W p 149-50+ O 22 '66
INTERNATIONAL union of mine, mill and smelter workers
Peace pact opens way to merger; steelworkers may take over Mine, mill members. il Bsns W p 132 S 3 '66
Smelted; mutual assistance pact. Time 88:96 S 9 '66
INTERNATIONAL union of operating engineers
Reducing seasonal unemployment; in construction industry. Mo Labor R 89:990-3 S '66

INTERNATIONAL university sports federation
Mickey Mouse Olympics; American skiers at World university winter games, Sestriere. B. Ottum. il Sports Illus 24:43-6 F 28 '66
INTERNATIONAL violin competition. See Music—Competitions
INTERNATIONAL voluntary workcamps
Travel with a purpose; programs in less developed areas. il Sat R 49:92+ F 19 '66
INTERNATIONAL volunteer service. See Volunteer service, International
INTERNATIONAL writers conference
Writers confer: good show at the Paramount. J. Yglesias. Nation 202:460-2 Ap 18 '66
Writers talk in Brooklyn. America 114: 473 Ap 9 '66
INTERNATIONAL years of the quiet sun
Statement by eleven distinguished geophysicists; letter. UNESCO Courier 19:30-1 O '66
Years of the quiet sun. N. Pushkov and B. Silkin. il UNESCO Courier 19:22-8 S '66
INTERNATIONAL youth library, Munich
International youth library. H. Fotheringham. il Library J 91:5704-5 N 15 '66
INTERNATIONALISM
Soviet teaching of history and international understanding. V. G. Trukhanovsky. Sch & Soc 94:152-5 Mr 19 '66
See also
International education
INTERNS (medicine)
Exit the old GP? residency to replace internship recommendation. Newsweek 68:92 O 3 '66
INTEROCEANIC canal commission. See United States—Interoceanic canal commission
INTEROPERA. See International opera production association
INTERPERSONAL relations. See Human relations
INTERPLANETARY communication
Messages to the stars; address, 1965. D. M. A. Mercer. il UNESCO Courier 19:4-7+ Ja '66
INTERPLANETARY dust. See Matter, Interstellar
INTERPLANETARY flight. See Space flight
INTERPLANETARY monitoring platform. See Artificial satellites—Use in research
INTERPLANETARY navigation. See Navigation (space flight)
INTERPRETERS and interpretation. See Translations and translating
INTERRACIAL adoption. See Adoption
INTERRACIAL attitudes. See Attitudes
INTERRACIAL cooperation
Checkerboard communities, pattern for living. il Newsweek 37:86+ Ap 25 '66
London's interracial parish; Notting Hill. C. Northcott. Christian Cent 83:1475 N 30 '66
INTERRACIAL marriages. See Intermarriage of races
INTERRACIAL relations. See Race relations
INTERSTATE commerce
See also
United States—Interstate commerce commission
INTERSTATE commerce commission. See United States—Interstate commerce commission
INTERSTATE compacts
Interstate library compact. M. R. Vale. il Library J 91:2419-22 My '66
INTERSTATE highway system. See Express highways; Roads—United States
INTERSTELLAR matter. See Matter, Interstellar
INTERSTELLAR space. See Space, Outer
INTERUNIVERSITY communications council
EDUCOM: Interuniversity communications council. J. G. Miller. bibliog Science 154: 483-8 O 28 '66
INTERURBAN railroads. See Electric railroads
INTERVENTION
Assembly adopts declaration: concerning domestic affairs of other states and the protection of their independence and sovereignty; with text of resolution. UN Mo Chron 3:23-30 Ja '66
Nonintervention vs. containment. B. G. Lall. Bul Atomic Sci 22:21-4 My '66
Question of intervention in the domestic affairs of states; statement, December 10, 1965, with text of resolution, December 21, 1965. A. J. Goldberg. Dept State Bul 54: 124-9 Ja 24 '66
INTERVIEWING
Hollywood interview: canonizing the superficial. J. N. Bell. il Sat R 49:115-16+ O 8 '66
How Andy McGhee got a better job. W. Shelton. il Fortune 75:116-17+ Ja '67

Memo from an angry business writer; how executives handle and mishandle press interviews. R. Phalon. Duns R 87:38-9+ Ja '66
Symposium on oral history. bibliog il Wilson Lib Bul 40:599-608+ Mr '66
Take a fashion lesson; job-hunting: that big first impression. il Seventeen 25:165 Je '66
See also
Applications for positions
Employment systems
INTESTINAL and parasitic worms. See Worms, Intestinal and parasitic
INTESTINES
Conversion of p,p'-DDT to p,p'-DDD by intestinal flora of the rat. J. L. Mendel and M. S. Walton. bibliog il Science 151:1527-8 Mr 25 '66
Transport of sugars and amino acids in the intestine: evidence for a common carrier. F. Alvarado. bibliog il Science 151:1010-13 F 25 '66
See also
Appendix (anatomy)
Hernia
Diseases
Cystinuria: genetic heterogeneity and allelism. L. E. Rosenberg. bibliog il Science 154: 1341-3 D 9 '66
Intestinal parasites: the enemy within. M. J. E. Senn. McCalls 93:46+ Je '66
INTINCO limited
Taping instant data for investors. il Bsns W p 147-8+ N 5 '66
INTOLERANCE. See Prejudice
INTOXICANTS. See Liquors
INTRACOASTAL WATERWAY
Southward ho! il Motor B 118:27+ O '66
INTRA-UTERINE contraceptive devices. See Contraceptives
INTRAVENOUS feeding. See Injections, Intravenous
INTREX (information transfer experiments) See Information storage and retrieval systems
INTROVERSION and extroversion
See also
Autism
INVASION of Russia. See World war, 1939-1945 —Campaigns and battles—Russia
INVENTIONS
Expert's blueprint for successful inventing; interview, ed. by C. P. Gilmore. R. R. Walton. il Pop Mech 126:102-5+ D '66
First of the month; use of bedbugs as insect personnel detector. C. Amory. Sat R 49:6 Ag 6 '66
Get inventions off the shelf; concerning patent rights of the said-to-invent inventor. C. E. Barnes. Harvard Bsns R 44:138-9 Ja '66
Inventions, patents, processes. See issues of Science digest
Inventors win an ally. Sci N 90:444 N 26 '66
New ideas from the inventors. See issues of Popular science monthly
7000 better mousetraps. M. J. Pedersen. il Pop Mech 126:70-7 S '66
We need your inventive skill! H. H. Humphrey. il Pop Sci 188:102-5 Je '66
See also
Creation (literary, artistic, etc)
Patents
United States—National inventors council
United States—Patent office
Exhibitions
7000 better mousetraps. M. J. Pedersen. Pop Mech 126:71 S '66
Where inventors turn ideas into hard cash; International inventors and new products exhibition at New York coliseum. il Bsns W p 116-18 S 17 '66
INVENTORIES
Inventories at the top. il Fortune 74:36+ N '66
Inventories at the turning point. il Fortune 74:24+ Ag '66
Inventory crosscurrents. il Fortune 73:38+ F '66
Keeping inventories geared to production. il Bsns W p34-5 F 26 '66
Stocked up. Fortune 73:32+ My '66
INVENTORS
Inventor of the month. S. V. Jones. See issues of Science digest
Inventor who still won't quit: E. E. Kleinschmidt. il Bsns W p 154-6+ S 3 '66
See also
Inventions

INVESTMENTS, Foreign (by Europe)
Bond flood rouses ire of Europe. il Bsns W
p 128+ Mr 5 '66
INVESTMENTS, Foreign (by Great Britain)
East of Suez up for grabs. J. Amery. il Re-
porter 35:16-21 D 1 '66
INVESTMENTS, Foreign (by Japan)
Japan discovers America in its scramble for
resources; Alaska and western Canada. il
U S News 61:127-9 S 26 '66
INVESTMENTS, Foreign (in Alaska)
Alaska: a treasure house for Japanese in-
dustry? il U S News 61:128-9 S 26 '66
INVESTMENTS, Foreign (in Asia)
Capital's last frontier; why U.S. invests. J.
Henry. il Nation 202:480-3 Ap 25 '66
INVESTMENTS, Foreign (in Belgium)
Antwerp's Texas touch brings in the big
ones. il Bsns W p48-9+ F 12 '66
Belgium lays out the welcome mat; inter-
view. A. de Winter. Nations Bsns 54:68
D '66
Where U.S. industry booms abroad. il Na-
tions Bsns 54:66-7+ D '66
INVESTMENTS, Foreign (in Brazil)
Back with backing from abroad. il Time 88:94
D 16 '66
Brazil: some success, much to do. il Bsns W
p61-2+ Ja 22 '66
INVESTMENTS, Foreign (in Canada)
Canada for Canadians again. il U S News
60:48 My 30 '66
Japan discovers America in its scramble for
resources. il U S News 61:127-8 S 26 '66
INVESTMENTS, Foreign (in Chile)
Chile's copper beckons once again; U.S.
producers $500-million expansion program
in partnership with Chilean government. il
Bsns W p76+ O 1 '66
INVESTMENTS, Foreign (in China)
China goes west for steel mill; West Ger-
many to build steel-finishing complex. il
Bsns W p 105-6 Mr 26 '66
China traders thrive again; Westerners
getting more of the business. il Bsns W
p80-4+ S 24 '66
INVESTMENTS, Foreign (in Congo [capital
Kinshasa])
Papa is dead. Newsweek 69:46+ Ja 16 '67
INVESTMENTS, Foreign (in Europe)
As U.S. businessmen in Europe look to the
future. il U S News 61:64-5 D 5 '66
Big, bigger, biggest; American business goes
global; effect on Atlantic alliance. R. J.
Barber. New Repub 154:14-18 Ap 30 '66
Bond flood rouses ire of Europe. il Bsns W
p 128+ Mr 5 '66
Changing course; U.S. companies. il Time 89:
88-9 Ja 6 '67
Toward a trillion; world's most promising
growth market. il Time 87:84 Mr 25 '66
U.S. aid to east Europe. V. E. Mares. bib-
liog f il Cur Hist 51:43-4 Jl '66
INVESTMENTS, Foreign (in France)
Hello, dollar! renewed welcome for U.S. in-
vestments. Time 87:85B-86 Ap 1 '66
If you can't lick 'em; French decisions, re-
garding management of U.S. firms. News-
week 67:88+ My 23 '66
Now de Gaulle likes those Yankee dollars.
il Bsns W p44+ My 14 '66
INVESTMENTS, Foreign (in Germany [Fed-
eral Republic])
Bonn sends up warning on U.S. investments;
curtailing Texaco-Deutsche Erdoel negotia-
tions. Bsns W p36 My 7 '66
INVESTMENTS, Foreign (in Greece)
Esso Pappas complex. il Fortune 73:69-70+
F '66
INVESTMENTS, Foreign (in Indonesia)
Indonesia dusts off welcome mat; new for-
eign investment law. Bsns W p24 D 31 '66
INVESTMENTS, Foreign (in Ivory Coast)
Where Africans welcome the businessman;
Ivory Coast angling for U.S. money. il
Bsns W p 132-3+ Je 11 '66
INVESTMENTS, Foreign (in Jamaica)
Industry's new island in the sun. il Bsns W
p66+ F 12 '66
INVESTMENTS, Foreign (in Japan)
Expanding the fabric of U.S.-Japanese eco-
nomic relations; address, July 8, 1966. J.
T. Connor. Dept State Bul 55:215-21 Ag 8
'66
INVESTMENTS, Foreign (in Latin America)
Close-up: interview. ed. by J. Berry. G. C.
Lodge. Duns R 88:8-9+ Ag '66
Personal business. Bsns W p 119-20 Ap 2 '66
Why Latin Americans say, go home, Yanqui.
R. West. il N Y Times Mag p8-9+ My 29
'66
INVESTMENTS, Foreign (in Mexico)
Mexico's money men learn to lure capital;
promise of fat dividends and growth. il
Bsns W p 116-18+ N 26 '66

INVESTMENTS, Foreign (in Russia)
Where now the Yankee trader? Nation 202:
636 My 30 '66
INVESTMENTS, Foreign (in South Africa)
African investments. Commonweal 84:327 Je
10 '66
Banks and South Africa. New Repub 155:6-7
D 17 '66
South Africa; profitable U.S. firms. New
Repub 155:7-8 Ag 13 '66
INVESTMENTS, Foreign (in Spain)
Spanish temper heats up; economy out of
balance. il Bsns W p78-9+ Ag 6 '66
INVESTMENTS, Foreign (in underdeveloped
areas)
There's plenty of promise in the underde-
veloped land. W. Wilhelm. Fortune 74:150-2
O '66
INVESTMENTS, Foreign (in United States)
All roads lead to Wall Street; effect on New
York exchange. Time 87:93-4 Mr 11 '66
Congress opens a door to overseas investors;
no tax on investment income under law
aimed at aiding U.S. payments balance. il
Bsns W p 102+ O 29 '66
How companies are wooing investors abroad;
via Early bird and underwater cable. il
Bsns W p 154-5+ My 14 '66
How U.S. funds lure overseas investors. il
Bsns W p66-8 D 31 '66
SEC tackles Swiss fund. Bsns W p 128+
F 12 '66
Treasury department to control blocked for-
eign assets in U.S. Dept State Bul 54:945
Je 13 '66
INVESTMENTS, Foreign (in Venezuela)
Venezuela: there's more to it than oil; ore,
power, and new industry lure U.S. com-
panies. il Bsns W p 178-80+ N 12 '66
INVESTMENTS, Foreign (in Vietnam [Repub-
lic])
Capital's last frontier; why U.S. invests. J.
Henry. il Nation 202:480-3 Ap 25 '66
How business fights the war by contract. il
Bsns W p58+ Mr 5 '66
Saigon: a boomtown for U.S. businessmen.
W. Tuohy. il Newsweek 67:70-2 Ja 31 '66
INVESTMENTS, Foreign (in Yugoslavia)
Yugoslavia: a red carpet for foreign capital?
Bsns W p 118 D 3 '66
INVESTORS. See Stockholders
INVESTORS diversified services, incorporated
New chiefs lead IDS back into the race.
il Bsns W p 152-4+ Je 25 '66
INVESTORS overseas services, limited
Cornfeld's empire. il Newsweek 69:68+ Ja
16 '67
SEC tackles Swiss fund. Bsns W p 128+
F 12 '66
INVITATION to the dance; story. See Gerber,
M. J.
INVITATIONS
Wedding invitations; lore and laws that gov-
ern them. House & Gard 129:42+ My '66
INYO national forest. See National forests
IOANES, Raymond Andrew
World food problem; address, April 27, 1966.
Vital Speeches 32:533-6 Je 15 '66
IODINE
Ice nuclei from automobile exhaust and
iodine vapor. V. J. Schaefer. bibliog Sci-
ence 154:1555-7 D 23 '66

Isotopes

Iodoinsulin used to determine specific activity
of iodine-131. S. A. Berson and R. S. Yalow.
bibliog il Science 152:205-7 Ap 8 '66
IODINE compounds
Crystal and molecular structure of acetyl-
selenocholine iodide. E. Shefter and O.
Kennard. bibliog il Science 153:1389-90 S
16 '66
IODOINSULIN. See Insulin
ION engines
Ion devices move toward useful space ap-
plications. R. Pay. il Miss & Roc 18:43-4
Mr 14 '66
ION exchange
Tactoid formation in montmorillonite; effect
on ion exchange kinetics. A. Banin. bib-
liog il Science 155:71-2 Ja 6 '67
ION-scattering analyzer. See Counters (elec-
trons, ions, etc)
IONA community, Scotland
Peerage for a Presbyterian. il Time 89:66
Ja 13 '67
IONESCO, Eugène
Eugène Ionesco. C. Cate. por Atlan 217:114-
20 Ap '66

IONESCO, Eugène—*Continued*
Ionesco: the absurd and beyond. J. Weightman. il pors N Y Times Mag p24-5+ My 1 '66
Letter from Paris; le Theatre de Poche-Montparnasse: summer program of one-act playlets. Genêt. New Yorker 42:145-6+ S 10 '66
Pedestrian in the air. Criticism
  Sat R 49:53 F 5 '66
La soif et la faim. Criticism
  New Yorker 42:101-2 Jl 16 '66
IONIAN ISLANDS
  See also
  Corfu (island)
IONIC crystals. See Crystallography
IONIZATION, Gaseous
Thermal conductivity effect of carrier gases on flame-ionization detector sensitivity. R. L. Hoffmann and C. D. Evans. il Science 153:172-3 Jl 8 '66
IONIZATION chambers
Radiological survey meters. J. G. Ello. il Electr World 75:44-6+ Ja '66
IONIZATION detectors. See Detectors
IONIZATION of gases
  See also
  Plasma (ionized gases)
IONOSPHERE. See Atmosphere, Upper
IONOSPHERIC radio wave propagation
Ionospheric topside sounding. W. Calvert. bibliog il Science 154:228-34 O 14 '66
IONOSPHERIC research. See Atmospheric research
IONS
Framework rearrangement in boranes and carboranes. W. N. Lipscomb. bibliog il Science 153:373-8 Jl 22 '66
Magnesium ions: activity in seawater. R. M. Pytkowicz and others. bibliog Science 152:640-2 Ap 29 '66
Stay young with ions; experiments with air ion inhalation. T. W. Hill. il Sci Digest 61:74-7 Ja '67
  See also
  Plasma (ionized gases)
IOWA
  See also
  Agriculture—Iowa
  Architecture, Domestic—Iowa
  Booksellers and bookselling—Iowa
  Courts—Iowa
  Education—Iowa
  Hunting—Iowa
  Law—Iowa

Description and travel
Lakes of Iowa. R. V. Cassill. Holiday 40:18+ Ag '66

History
Pennsylvania boyhood; memoir. J. N. Culbertson. il Am Heritage 18:54-8 D '66
IOWA beef packers, incorporated
Management's rule-breakers: the ways of the winners. J. Weiner. Duns R 87:85-7 Ja '66
IOWA state fair. See Agricultural exhibitions
IPCAR, Dahlov
Combining Dinobase and wash on paper. il Horn Bk 42:83-6 F '66
IPHITA limbata. See Hemiptera
IPPOLITO, Felice
Appeal judges cut Ippolito's sentence in half. V. K. McElheny. Science 152:54-5 Ap 1 '66
IPS confusus. See Beetles
IRAN
White revolution; progress of the Shah's program. il Time 87:80 F 11 '66
  See also
  Azerbaijan
  Colleges and universities—Iran
  Economic assistance in Iran

Antiquities
Masterpieces from a lost kingdom; Marlik. E. O. Negahban. il UNESCO Courier 19:16-21 Je '66
Research in the prehistory of central western Iran. T. C. Young, jr. and P. E. L. Smith. bibliog il Science 153:386-91 Jl 22 '66
  See also
  Persepolis

Description and travel
Sparking tomorrow's tourist explosion. il UNESCO Courier 19:34-40+ D '66

Foreign relations
Politics of anti-Americanism. M. Tehranian. il Nation 203:415-18 O 24 '66

Religious institutions and affairs
Seven commandments of Zoroaster. A. S. Mehdevi. il N Y Times Mag p32-3+ Mr 27 '66
IRANIAN oil fire. See Oil fires
IRAQ
  See also
  Baghdad
  Kurds
  Petroleum industry and trade—Iraq

Antiquities
Temple changes view; ancient Assyrian temple, Tell al-Rimah. il Sci N 90:296 O 15 '66

Politics and government
Brother act. Newsweek 67:54+ My 2 '66
Miss no. 2; Abdel Razzak's coup attempt. Newsweek 68:53 Jl 11 '66
Moderate choice. Time 87:40 Ap 29 '66
No time for prudence. Time 88:28 Ag 19 '66
Truce for two nationalisms. Time 88:33 Jl 8 '66
IRAQ petroleum company. See Petroleum industry and trade—Iraq
IRBY, Kenneth
Faults along which the tremor runs. Robert Duncan; Fragments for Bill Dodd; poems. Poetry 107:365-8 Mr '66
IRELAND
Thaw in the Irish cold war; antagonism between north and south. W. R. Rodgers. il N Y Times Mag p30-1+ F 27 '66
  See also
  Banks and banking—Ireland
  Cashel
  Fishing—Ireland
  Folklore—Ireland
  Hospitals—Ireland
  Land tenure—Ireland
  Strikes—Ireland

Description and travel
Ireland: fifty years after the troubles. J. Vachon. il Look 30:61-7 Ap 19 '66
Irish interlude. Raja Rao. il Sat R 49:32+ Je 25 '66
Wild roses and Irish salmon. C. T. Coiner. il Esquire 65:94-7+ F '66

History
Ireland rehearses the future. K. Sullivan. Nation 203:485-6 N 7 '66

Bibliography
Articles and other books received; comp. by L. H. Carlson. See issues of American historical review

Sinn Fein rebellion, 1916
Ireland: fifty years after the troubles. J. Vachon. il Look 30:61-7 Ap 19 '66
Men that God made mad; Irish uprising celebrated on record. R. L. Tobin. il Sat R 49:61 O 15 '66
Where the martyrs died. S. Cronin. Nation 203:486-8 N 7 '66

Industries
  See also
  Mining industry and finance—Ireland

Politics and government
Choosing the chief. Newsweek 68:44 N 14 '66
  See also
  Elections—Ireland
  Ireland—History—Sinn Fein rebellion, 1916
  Northern Ireland

Religious institutions and affairs
World around us (cont of) News of the Christian world. Christian Cent 83:282, 1017-18 Mr 2, Ag 17 '66
  See also
  Catholic church in Ireland
  Protestant churches—Ireland

Social history
Requiem for potheen. T. Prittie. il Atlan 217:116-17 My '66
IRELAND, NORTHERN. See Northern Ireland
IREYS, Alice R.
Junipers are useful. il Horticulture 44:18-21 N '66
IRION, Mary Jean
Dogwood in December; poem. Christian Cent 83:1569 D 21 '66
Great Uncle Ezra; poem. Christian Cent 83:585 My 4 '66

IRION, Mary Jean—*Continued*
  Merry Christmas to the ladies society; poem. Christian Cent 83:1565 D 21 '66
  When the half-gods go; poem. Christian Cent 83:106 Ja 26 '66

IRISES
  Bearded iris. il Flower Grower 53:35-6 Jl '66
  Grow some iris winners. Flower Grower 53:54 Je '66
  How to divide or move spuria iris. il Sunset 137:252+ O '66
  How to enjoy iris. il Flower Grower 53:28 Je '66
  In pursuit of the rainbow. M. Price. il Flower Grower 53:24-7 Je '66
  Iris the more the merrier. J. E. Dwyer. il Pop Gard 17:16-17 Ag '66
  Leading iris for 1965. Flower Grower 53:67 My '66
  Some choice miniature iris for your garden. M. M. Graff. il Horticulture 44:30-1+ F '66

IRISH
  Thaw in the Irish cold war. W. R. Rodgers. il N Y Times Mag p30-1+ F 27 '66

IRISH authors. See Authors, Irish

IRISH cookery. See Cookery, Irish

IRISH in literature
  Hogan's goat; interview. ed. by D. L. Flaherty. W. Alfred. il America 114:378-81 Mr 19 '66

IRISH in the United States
  Thanks to the Irish. P. Gleason. America 114:696-8 My 14 '66
  World I grew up in; Chicago's south side. J. T. Farrell. Commonweal 83:606-7+ F 25 '66

IRISH language

Study and teaching
  Basic Irish made easy. America 115:127 Ag 6 '66

IRISH literature
  See also
  Authors, Irish

IRISH moss. See Carrageen

IRISH republican army
  Fears to speak of Easter week. America 114:369 Mr 19 '66

IRISH revolt, 1916. See Ireland—History—Sinn Fein rebellion, 1916

IRISH setters. See Setters

IRISH sweepstakes. See Lotteries

IRISH tweed. See Tweed

IRISH unification question
  See also
  Irish republican army

IRISH wolf-hounds
  Biggest dog of all was Finn MacCool's aunt: Irish wolfhound. R. H. Boyle. il Sports Illus 24:42-4+ F 14 '66

IRIZARRY, Carmen
  Moiseyev's army conquers Spain. Dance Mag 41:28-31 Ja '67

IRON
  Synthetic detergents: their influence upon iron-binding complexes of natural waters. F. Kent and F. F. Hooper. bibliog il Science 153:526-7 Jl 29 '66
  Zinc and cobalt: effect on the iron metabolism of ustilago sphaerogena, H. Komai and J. B. Neilands. bibliog il Science 153:751-2 Ag 12 '66
  See also
  Blast furnaces

Metallography
  Retrograde melting in the system Mg-Fe-Si. O. D. H. Speidel and R. H. Nafziger. bibliog il Science 152:1367-8 Je 3 '66

IRON alloys
  Polymorphism of shock loaded Fe-Mn and Fe-Ni alloys. T. R. Loree and others. bibliog il Science 153:1277-8 S 9 '66

IRON bacteria
  Direct evidence for the cathodic depolarization theory of bacterial corrosion. W. P. Iverson. bibliog il Science 151:986-8 F 25 '66

IRON curtain. See Europe, Eastern

IRON in the body
  Inhibition of protein synthesis: a mechanism for the production of impaired iron absorption. N. J. Greenberger and R. D. Ruppert. bibliog il Science 153:315-16 Jl 15 '66

IRON metallurgy
  Steel from idle resources; taconite-scrap process. Sci Am 214:56+ Je '66

IRON meteorites. See Meteorites

IRON mines and mining

Australia
  Australia's iron boom comes down to earth. il Bsns W p98-100 Ag 13 '66

Liberia
  Men of the iron mountain; mines of the Grängesberg company. M. Mayer. il Reporter 35:41-4 Jl 14 '66

Sweden
  Men of the iron mountain; mines of the Grängesberg company. M. Mayer. il Reporter 35:41-4 Jl 14 '66

IRON ores
  Deep-sea iron deposit from the South Pacific. E. Bonatti and O. Joensuu. bibliog il Science 154:643-5 N 4 '66
  Quartz and magnetite: oxygen-18-oxygen-16 fractionation in metamorphosed Biwabik iron formation. E. C. Perry, jr. and R. B. Bonnichsen. bibliog il Science 153:528-9 Jl 29 '66

IRONING
  See also
  Pressing of garments

IRONSI, Johnson Thomas Umunankwe Aguiyi-. See Aguiyi-Ironsi, J. T. U.

IROQUOIS Indians
  Iroquois research; report on conference. E. J. Tooker. Science 151:712 F 11 '66

IRRADIATED food. See Food, Effect of radiation on

IRRIGATION
  See also
  Arid regions
  Reclamation of land
  Watering of gardens. lawns. etc.

IRRIGATION, Underground
  New way to irrigate. C. E. Ball. il Farm J 90:58L My '66

IRVIN, Bob
  Detroit listening post. Pop Mech 126:38+ O; 30+ N '66

IRVIN, Robert W.
  Fallacy of the electric car. Motor T 19:78-81 Ja '67
  New federal safety czar's tough views on cars! Motor T 18:42-4 D '66

IRVING, George W. 1910-
  Man who runs agricultural research. por Bsns W p66 F 26 '66

IRVING, Jules
  Bleak house. Time 89:55 Ja 20 '67

IRVING P. Krick associates
  Your weather. See issues of Farm journal

IRVING, R. See Harrison, J. M. jt. auth.

IRVING, Washington
  Rip Van Winkle; dramatization. See Thane, A.

IRWIN, John B.
  Training of an astronomer. Science 152:1597-9; 154:1275-6 Je 17, D 9 '66

IRWIN, Patrick H. and Langham, F. W. Jr
  Change seekers. Harvard Bsns R 44:81-92 Ja '66

IRWIN, Richard D. incorporated
  Merger cancelled by Richard Irwin, Dow Jones. Pub W 190:76-7 N 14 '66
  Richard Irwin, Dow Jones propose merger plan. Pub W 190:50-1 O 10 '66

IRWIN, Robert W.
  Detroit listening post. See issues of Popular mechanics August 1966-

IRWIN, Samuel, and Benuazizi, Ali
  Pentylenetetrazol enhances memory function. bibliog Science 152:100-2 Ap 1 '66

IRWIN, Theodore
  A's to your Q's about auto insurance. Pop Sci 189:72-4+ Jl '66
  Bye-bye, bacteria! Pop Mech 125:90-3+ Je '66
  Crackdown on bootleg drugs. Todays Health 45:18-19+ Ja '67
  Don't be a weekend athlete! Todays Health 44:46-9 Jl '66
  Electronic eyes are watching your tax returns. Pop Mech 125:94-8+ Mr '66
  Making ends meet, by moonlight. N Y Times Mag p73+ Ap 3 '66
  Saving a city from a cloud of death. Pop Sci 188:108-11+ Ap '66
  What our kids don't know about health. Todays Health 44:18-21 My '66

ISAAC, Erich
  Before the beginning. Commentary 41:85-8 Je '66
  Forbidden foods. Commentary 41:36-41 Ja: 42:16-17 Jl '66

ISAACS, Harold R.
  Reporter at large. New Yorker 42:37-40+ Ag 27; 73-4+ S 3 '66

ISAACS, John D. and others
Satellite elongation into a true Sky-Hook.
bibliog Science 151:682-3 F 11 '66
ISABELLA I, queen of Spain
Symbolic gift; unveiling of statue. G. de
Zéndegui. Américas 18:inside cover My '66
ISAKSEN, Lone
Brief biography. S. Goodman. pors Dance Mag
40:50-1 N '66
ISHAM family
Isham coat-of-arms. H. K. Eilers. il Hobbies
71:126 Jl '66
ISHERWOOD, Christopher
Where are they now? il pors Newsweek 68:
20 D 5 '66
ISHIKURA, H. and others
Oligoribonucleotides: improvement in chro-
matographic separation. bibliog Science
153:300-1 Jl 15 '66
ISLAM
Ibn Khaldūn: man of history; excerpts from
radio program. B. Bray. il UNESCO Cou-
rier 19:4-10 Je '66
Modernizing Mohammed's law. Time 88:49 O
28 '66
See also
Mosques
ISLAND; story. See Wallace, M.
ISLAND airlines. See Local service airlines
ISLAND flyers club. See Aviation clubs
ISLANDIA NATIONAL MONUMENT (pro-
posed) See National monuments
ISLANDS
Fishingest way south. Z. Taylor. il Motor B
118:30-1+ O '66
ISLANDS cherry
They are the do anything cherries. il Sunset
137:287-8 O '66
ISLANDS of the Pacific
Major airlines eye Pacific local service. H. D.
Watkins. Aviation W 85:38-9 D 12 '66
See also
Guam
Micronesia
Trust Territory of the Pacific Islands
ISLE OF HOPE
Isle of Hope: the terrapin's last stand. C.
Stinnett. il Holiday 40:24+ S '66
ISLE OF RHODES. See Rhodes (island)
ISLER, Charlotte
Bronx junior high school sex quiz. Sat R
49:64-5 F 5 '66
ISOANTIGENS. See Antigens and antibodies
ISODENSITOMETRY. See Densitometry
ISOLATION, Sensory. See Sensory deprivation
ISOLATION, Social. See Social isolation
ISOLATIONISM (Europe) See Europe—Politics
ISOLATIONISM (United States) See United
States—Foreign relations
ISONIAZID
Mammary tumor inhibition and lung ade-
noma induction by isonicotinic acid hydra-
zide. B. Toth and P. Shubik. bibliog il
Science 152:1376-7 Je 3 '66
Nicotinamide-adenine dinucleotide in tuber-
cle bacilli exposed to isoniazid. A. Bekier-
kunst. bibliog il Science 152:525-6 Ap 22 '66
ISONICOTINIC acid hydrazide. See Isoniazid
ISOPODA
Copper and the role of isopods in degrada-
tion of organic matter. W. Wieser. bibliog
il Science 153:67-9 Jl 1 '66
Glycogen content in the wood-boring isopod,
limnoria lignorum. R. Y. George. bibliog
il Science 153:1262-4 S 9 '66
ISOSTASY
Three offshoots of astronomy. E. D. Dale. il
Sky & Tel 31:277-9 My '66
ISOTOPES
Kinetic isotope effects and organic reaction
mechanisms. M. J. Goldstein. bibliog il
Science 154:1616-21 D 30 '66
See also
Radioisotopes
also subhead Isotopes under names of
chemical elements, e.g. Strontium—Isotopes
ISRAEL, Adrian C.
Learn to listen. por Time 87:82 Ap 1 '66
ISRAEL, Charles E.
Hostages: story. Redbook 127:129 Jl '66
ISRAEL, Lawrence J.
Next logical step: multi-level shopping cen-
ters. Arch Rec 139:166-7 Ap '66
ISRAEL, Lee
Notes on stoop. Esquire 66:90-1 Ag '66
ISRAEL
Israel: land of unlimited impossibilities. B.
Tuchman. il Sat Eve Post 240:30-4+ Ja 14
'67

Man of Sde Boker. G. Samuels. il N Y
Times Mag p42+ O 16 '66
See also
Christians in Israel
Collective settlements—Israel
Dead Sea
Education—Israel
Forests and forestry—Israel
Jerusalem
Jews in Israel
Libraries—Israel
Marriage law—Israel
Masada (fortress) Israel
Negev
Newspapers—Israel
Technical assistance in Israel
United Nations—Israel
Water supply—Israel

Antiquities
Art that history shaped. K. Kuh. il Sat R
49:17-24 Ja 29 '66
Masada and its scrolls; excerpt from Masada.
Y. Yadin. Commentary 42:41-7 O '66
Masada, by Y. Yadin. Review
Sat R il 49:39 N 26 '66. J. B. Pritchard

Boundaries
Dangerous border. R. Chesnoff. il Newsweek
68:40+ Ag 15 '66

Commercial treaties and agreements
U.S. and Israel amend cotton textiles agreement; Department announcement; with text
of U.S. note, June 20, 1966. Dept State Bul
55:189 Ag 1 '66

Defenses
Defining the limit; U.S. sale of A-4 Sky-
hawks. il Newsweek 67:48 My 30 '66

Description and travel
Israeli mosaics... H. Mitgang. il Atlan 218:
108-12 Ag '66
Travel. D. Messinesi. Vogue 147:52-3 Mr 15 '66

Economic conditions
Atlantic report. Atlan 217:24+ F '66

Economic relations
Israel's aid to Africa. G. Gersh. Commonweal
85:226-8 N 25 '66

Foreign relations
Flight into Egypt; A. Nathan's peace flight.
il Newsweek 67:50+ Mr 14 '66
Gunfire over Galilee. il Time 88:28 Ag 26 '66
Incident at Samu; Israel attack on Jordan
rather than Syria. il Time 88:36 N 25 '66
Israeli army retaliates; raid against Jordanian
village of Es Samu. il Sr Schol 89:24 D 9
'66
Jews; A. Eban visit to Poland. il Newsweek
67:54+ My 23 '66
Massive retaliation; Israeli army units in
Jordan. il Newsweek 68:42 N 28 '66
OAS-Israel cooperation. G. Meek. Américas
18:45 S '66
Second thoughts; fighting on Israel-Jordan
border. il Newsweek 68:56+ D 12 '66
That new boy in Israel's foreign office. J.
Feron. il N Y Times Mag p40-1+ Ap 17 '66
Thunder over Galilee; reprisal for activities
by Syrian infiltrators. il Newsweek 68:44
Jl 25 '66
U.S. and Israel reaffirm ties of friendship;
exchange of toasts, August 2, 1966. L. B.
Johnson; Z. Shazar. Dept State Bul 55:
346-7 S 5 '66

Intellectual life
Poetry in Israel. R. Alter; discussion. Commentary 41:19-20 Mr; 22+ Je '66

Politics and government
Don't panic. il Newsweek 69:45-6 Ja 16 '67

Religious institutions and affairs
Reporter at large; American Jews in Israel.
H. R. Isaacs. New Yorker 42:32+ S 3 '66
See also
Christians in Israel
ISRAEL and Germany
Reconciliation in Israel; Service of reconcilia-
tion. I. Halperin. Christian Cent 83:216-22
F 16 '66
Touchy visit; demonstrations against Aden-
auer. il Newsweek 67:49 My 16 '66
ISRAEL and the United States
Atlantic report; American presence. Atlan
217:30+ F '66
ISRAEL-Arab relations. See Jewish-Arab re-
lations

ISRAEL-Arab war, 1948-1949
  Arab refugees: a Zionist view. M. Syrkin;
   reply with rejoinder. R. S. Goldman. Com-
   mentary 41:6+ Je '66
ISRAEL museum, Jerusalem. See Jerusalem—
  Israel museum
ISRAEL philharmonic orchestra
  Waiting for Mr Right. il Time 87:65 Je 17 '66
ISRAELI art. See Art, Israeli
ISRAELI economic assistance. See Economic
  assistance, Israeli
ISRAELI fiction
  Confronting the holocaust: three Israeli
   novels. R. Alter. Commentary 41:67-73 Mr
   '66
ISRAELI-Franco-British aggression. See Egypt
  —History—Invasion. 1956
ISRAELI literature
    See also
  Israeli fiction
ISRAELI poetry
  Poetry in Israel. R. Alter; discussion. Com-
   mentary 41:19-20 Mr; 22+ Je '66
ISRAELIS
  Israel: land of unlimited impossibilities. B.
   Tuchman. il Sat Eve Post 240:30-4+ Ja
   14 '67
ISTANBUL
    See also
  Golden Horn
    Description
  Alla Turca. L. Blanch. il Vogue 148:182-4+ D
   '66
  Istanbul: city tinged with blood and gold;
   tr. by A. Foulke. A. Robbe-Grillet. Vogue
   147:58-9+ F 1 '66
ITALIAN architecture. See Architecture,
  Italian
ITALIAN armistice. See World war, 1939-1945
  —Armistices
ITALIAN art. See Art, Italian
ITALIAN automobiles. See Automobiles, For-
  eign
ITALIAN cookery. See Cookery, Italian
ITALIAN furniture. See Furniture, Italian
ITALIAN music. See Music, Italian
ITALIAN opera singers. See Opera singers
ITALIAN poetry
  Great poet, a continuing task. N. J. Perella.
   Poetry 107:333-7 F '66
    Translations into English
  Here's your letter, asking me; tr. by J. W.
   Freeman. G. Puccini. il Opera N 31:17 D 3
   '66
ITALIAN sculpture. See Sculpture, Italian
ITALIAN wines. See Wine
ITALIANS
  Italian men are lousy lovers; concerning
   G. Parca's book The sultans. J. Bonfante.
   il Life 60:81-2+ F 4 '66
  Those remarkable Italians; excerpt from The
   Italians. L. Barzini. il Read Digest 88:143-
   6 Ap '66
    See also
  Florentines
ITALY
    See also
  Aerospace industries—Italy
  Americans in Italy
  Architecture, Domestic—Italy
  Astronomical observatories—Italy
  Automobile industry and trade—Italy
  Banks and banking—Italy
  Booksellers and bookselling—Italy
  Chemical industries—Italy
  Colleges and universities—Italy
  Floods—Italy
  Florence
  Gardens—Italy
  Law—Italy
  Money—Italy
  Music—Italy
  Music festivals—Italy
  Opera—Italy
  Parma
  Phonograph record industry—Italy
  Political parties—Italy
  Restaurants—Italy
  Rome (city)
  Sardinia
  Science—Italy
  Trials—Italy
  Venice
  World war, 1939-1945—Italy
  Zagarolo
    Antiquities
    See also
  Herculaneum
  Pompeii
  Rome—Antiquities
  Sybaris

    Cabinet
Fine Italian hand; new coalition cabinet.
  Time 87:39-40 Mr 4 '66
    Description and travel
Highlighting Italy. M. M. Davis. il Travel
  125:28-33+ Je '66
Home to Italy. A. Waugh. Nat R 18:996+
  O 4 '66
    Economic conditions
New miracle? Newsweek 68:95 S 26 '66
Special report. il Bsns W p 130-2+ S 10 '66
    Economic policy
Quite a comeback. il Time 88:72 S 2 '66
    History
Garibaldi and his enemies, by C. Hibbert.
  Review
    Sat R 49:40-1 Mr 5 '66. C. F. Delzell
    Time 87:102+ Mr 11 '66
Glorious revolutionist. il Newsweek 67:108+
  Mr 21 '66
Stormy road to grandeur; with historical
  chart showing great events. E. Kern. il
  Life 60:40-6+ Mr 11 '66
    Bibliography
Articles and other books received; comp. by
  E. P. Noether. See issues of American his-
  torical review
    Industries
Addio red heads; effect of US bans on Italian
  wig industry. il Time 87:86 Mr 25 '66
Building like the Caesars; Italian construc-
  tion companies working throughout the
  world. il Time 87:92 Je 24 '66
How to insulate; Pirelli group. Time 87:100+
  Ap 8 '66
    See also
Electric apparatus industry
Food industry and trade
    Politics and government
All aboard. Newsweek 67:47 Mr 28 '66
All in the family; nursery bill defeats gov-
  ernment. Newsweek 67:44 Ja 31 '66
Cabinet reshuffle changes Italy's science
  minister. V. K. McElheny. Science 152:
  336-7 Ap 15 '66
Italy's feuding politicians. America 114:185
  F 5 '66
Mystic mayor, and Fanfani outfoxed. C.
  Sterling. il Reporter 34:34-6 Ja 27 '66
Non-crisis in Italy. E. A. Bayne. For Af-
  fairs 45:353-62 Ja '67
Patching it up. Newsweek 67:42 F 28 '66
Snipers of Rome; routed center-left coali-
  tion government of Premier Aldo Moro.
  Time 87:34 Ja 28 '66
    See also
Elections—Italy
Fascism—Italy
Italy—Cabinet
Political parties—Italy
    Religious institutions and affairs
World around us. Christian Cent 83:1356-7 N 2
  '66
    See also
Catholic church in Italy
    World war, 1939-1945
  See World war, 1939-1945—Italy
ITALY and the United States
    History
Flirtation with fascism: American pragmatic
  liberals and Mussolini's Italy. J. P. Dig-
  gins. bibliog f Am Hist R 71:487-505 Ja '66
IT'S a bird, it's a plane, it's Superman; musical
  comedy. See Musical comedies, revues, etc.
  —Criticisms, plots, etc.
IT'S magic time; story. See Whedon, J.
ITTA, John Paul
  Nonny Hogrogian. Horn Bk 42:421-5 Ag '66
ITTYCHERIAH, P. I. See Seshan, K. R. jt.
  auth.
ITZKOFF, Seymour W.
  Cultural pluralism in urban education. bib-
  liog f Sch & Soc 94:383-6 N 12 '66
IUSUPOV, Feliks Feliksovich, knîaz'
  I killed Rasputin; excerpt from Lost splendor.
  Read Digest 88:133-7 Mr '66
IVANOV; drama. See Chekhov, A.
IVERSON, Warren P.
  Direct evidence for the cathodic depolar-
  ization theory of bacterial corrosion. bibliog
  Science 151:986-8 F 26 '66

IVES, Burl
Ives sings a song of the sea; interview, ed. by. G. Sloane. il por Motor B 117:42-3 Mr '66

IVES, Charles Edward
From RCA Victor: after sixty-eight years, the first symphony of Chas. E. Ives. A. Cohn. il por Am Rec G 32:1032-3 Jl '66
New stereo discs for a further look at Ivesian questions and answers. E. Salzman. il Hi Fi 16:70-1 Je '66
Recordings. M. Mayer. Esquire 66:54+ O '66
Records:
Songs. Opera N 31:30 N 19 '66

IVES, Ronald L.
Power-line spike absorber. Electr World 75: 88 Mr '66

IVEST-Wellington management merger. See Business consolidations and mergers

IVEY, Robert
On the gypsy circuit. W. Como. por Dance Mag 40:20 N '66

IVORY, James
Music of Satyajit Ray. por Am Rec G 32:1109-11 Ag '66

IVORY COAST
Houphouet-Boigny wins a bet. C. Sterling. Reporter 34:27-9 Je 16 '66
Peace corpsman looks back. E. Sigel. il Reporter 35:12-16 D 29 '66
Le plan in Africa; flourishing country. il Time 88:114 S 16 '66
See also
Investments, Foreign (in Ivory Coast)

Economic conditions
Where Africans welcome the businessman: Ivory Coast angling for U.S. money. il Bsns W p 132-3+ Je 11 '66

IVY, Andrew Conway
Case of the cancer cure. il por Newsweek 67:65-6 F 14 '66
Krebiozen verdict. il por Time 87:49 F 11 '66
IVY-leaved geraniums. See Geraniums
IVY poisoning. See Poison ivy

IYEDA, Ryuji
From the Orient with guile. il por Time 87:82 Ap 22 '66

J

J. C. Penney company. See Penney, J. C. company
JCS. See United States—Joint chiefs of staff
J.D. degree. See Degrees, Academic
J. P. Morgan and company See Morgan guaranty trust company
J. W. Stacey, incorporated. See Stacey, J. W. incorporated
J. Walter Thompson company. See Thompson, J. Walter, company
JO (justitieombudsman) See Administrative remedies

JABLONSKI, Edward
Unlikely corners. See issues of American record guide to July 1966

JABRI, Marwan
France and the Common market. Cur Hist 50:228-31+ Ap '66

JABUSCH, Willard F.
New seminaries in Europe. Commonweal 85: 17-21 O 7 '66

JACCOUX, Claude
Our far-flung correspondents. J. Bernstein. il New Yorker 42:148+ Mr 26 '66

JACK, Homer A.
Toward a world disarmament conference. Bul Atomic Sci 22:47-8 Ap '66

JACK-ó-lanterns. See Halloween

JACKETS, Mens. See Clothing and dress—Men

JACKSON, Andrew
House divides. by P. I. Wellman. Review Sat R por 49:37 F 12 '66. H. Hansen

JACKSON, Barbara (Ward) lady. See Ward, B.

JACKSON, Bruce
Exiles from the American dream. Atlan 219: 44-51 Ja '67
White-collar pill party. Atlan 218:35-40 Ag '66

JACKSON, Carolyn
I don't mind; poem. Nation 203:520 N 14 '66

JACKSON, Charlotte
Books for children. Atlan 218:148+ D '66
Christmas stories. Atlan 218:156+ D '66

JACKSON, D. B. See Spoor, R. P. jt. auth.

JACKSON, D. I. and Coombe, B. G.
Gibberellin-like substances in the developing apricot fruit. bibliog Science 154:277-8 O 14 '66

JACKSON, Donald
Constitutional rights break down the squeal room door. Life 61:40-1 O 21 '66
Protesters, fugitives and a law shot full of holes. Life 61:42-3 D 9 '66

JACKSON, Gabriel
Heat in Spain. Commonweal 84:327-9 Je 10 '66
Siege and the commune. Nation 202:786 Je 27 '66

JACKSON, Harriet
American dancer, Negro. Dance Mag 40:35-42 O 8 '66

JACKSON, Henry Martin
Excerpt from address, September 1, 1966. Cong Digest 45:241+ O '66

JACKSON, J. B.
Abolish the highways! Nat R 18:1213-17 N 29 '66

JACKSON, James P.
Fishing ponds, unlimited. Am For 71:36-7+ O '65
Growing up with family camping. Am For 72:48-50+ My '66
Up on Yellowstone Lake. Am For 72:14-17+ N '66

JACKSON, Katherine Gauss
Books in brief. See issues of Harper's magazine

JACKSON, Kennell, Jr
Reducing kids to dust. Nation 203:521-2 N 14 '66

JACKSON, Luther P. Jr
Communicating research on the poor: the problem of telling it like it is: some ways of telling it: address. bibliog por Negro Hist Bul 29:151-2+ Ap '66

JACKSON, Miles M. Jr
Library development abroad. por Library J 91:1354-61 Mr 15 '66

JACKSON, Norman
So now it's optional; Widower; poems. Reporter 35:58 D 15 '66

JACKSON, Paul T.
Record, record, who's got the record? Am Rec G 32:676-8 Ap '66

JACKSON, Renwick
Educational enrichment. Christian Cent 83: 621 My 11 '66

JACKSON, Richard Montgomery
U.S. international aviation policy; address, January 20, 1966. Vital Speeches 32:398-400 Ap 15 '66

JACKSON, Roy, and Wieting, Roger
Two plants in one remove 97.5 percent BOD. Am City 81:158+ O '66

JACKSON, Shirley
Nightmare in reality. G. Hicks. Sat R 49: 31-2 S 17 '66
We have always lived in the castle; dramatization of novel. Criticism
Commonweal 85:167 N 11 '66

JACKSON, Violette N.
Great Gomberg. Am Rec G 32:771 My '66

JACKSON, Warren, Jr
Inventor of the month. S. V. Jones. por Sci Digest 60:25 S '66

JACKSON, Ga.
English is to enjoy. J. A. Settle. il Sr Schol 88:sup20 F 11 '66

JACKSON, Miss.
Historic reversal for the FCC; Court of appeals rules FCC erred in renewing license of WLBT. R. L. Shayon. Sat R 49:102 My 7 '66

Churches
Responding creatively to hatred and violence; contributions to help rebuild Negro churches. Christian Cent 83:103 Ja 26 '66

JACKSON COUNTY, Mo.
How to use landmarks in program. W. L. Landahl. il Parks & Rec 1:642-3 Ag '66

JACKSON HOLE VALLEY
Ladybird country. H. Sutton. il Sat R 49: 40+ O 1 '66
Ski time in Sun Valley and Jackson Hole. G. E. Maxwell. il Todays Health 44:42-7+ N '66

JACKSONVILLE, Fla.

Parks and playgrounds
Marina park. il Parks & Rec 1:406-8 My '66

Politics and government
Housecleaning. Newsweek 68:34+ S 26 '66

JACKSONVILLE, Fla. public library
Jacksonville accents color. H. Brinton. il Library J 91:5852-4 D 1 '66

JACKSONVILLE, Ill.

Churches

Gratuitous data. Christian Cent 83:795 Je 22 '66

JACOB, Dorothy
Folklore and nature; the immortal holly tree. Natur Hist 75:6+ D '66

JACOB, François
Genetics of the bacterial cell; address. December 11, 1965. bibliog Science 152:1470-8 Je 10 '66

JACOBEAN lilies
Quick flowering bulb. E. Javorsky. il Flower Grower 53:20+ D '66

JACOBS, Arthur P.
Rights and permissions. P. Nathan. Pub W 189:120 Je 13 '66

JACOBS, David
Habitat 67. Horizon 9:70-3 Wint '67
Saarinen's CBS skyscraper. Holiday 39:122+ Je '66

JACOBS, Flora Gill
Miniature shops. Hobbies 71:124-5+ Jl '66

JACOBS, George R.
Fourth annual review of the Long-term cotton textile arrangement; statement, September 27, 1966. Dept State Bul 55:903-5 D 12 '66
Third-year major review of the Long-term cotton textile arrangement; statement, December 7, 1965. Dept State Bul 54:134-9 Ja 24 '66

JACOBS, Harvey
Note on the universe-building business. Writer 79:17-18 Mr '66

JACOBS, Hayes B.
Behind the hair curtain. Sat R 49:6+ O 8 '66
Just for laughs. Look 30:15 O 4 '66
Unpacific genius. Reporter 35:46-8 Ag 11 '66
Work and worries of non-sleeping Beauty. Look 30:53 Jl 12 '66

JACOBS, Jay
Are they trying to tell us something? Reporter 34:38-9 Je 16 '66
Flawed diamond. Reporter 34:57-8 Ja 27 '66
Silver-tongued southpaw. Reporter 35:51-2+ Jl 14 '66
Within the madding crowd. Reporter 34:44+ My 5 '66

JACOBS, Jimmy
It was action day in Brooklyn. T. Brody. il por Sports Illus 25:20-1 S 5 '66
Really the greatest. R. H. Boyle. il pors Sports Illus 24:64-70+ Mr 7 '66

JACOBS, Lewis
Lewis Jacobs: film-maker, director, author, teacher; interview. ed. by J. Deschin. por Pop Phot 58:12+ F '66

JACOBS, Paul
Death of the recital. B. Boretz. Nation 203:125-7 Ag 8 '66

JACOBS, Paul, 1918-
Los Angeles police. Atlan 218:95-101 D '66

JACOBS, Walter Darnell
Essence and the tactics. Nat R 18:792 Ag 9 '66

JACOBS, Wilbur R.
Kind words for founding fathers. Sat R 49:38 Ap 2 '66
New nation in a New World. Sat R 46:35-6 N 26 '66

JACOB'S Pillow dance festival. See Dance festivals

JACOBSEN, E. H.
Microwave ultrasonics. bibliog Science 151:1179-87 Mr 11 '66
—See Ilukor, J. jt. auth.

JACOBSEN, Josephine
Greek wind; poem. Sat R 49:26 Mr 19 '66
Return from Delphi; poem. Poetry 108:301-2 Ag '66

JACOBSON, A. G.
Inductive processes in embryonic development. bibliog Science 152:25-34 Ap 1 '66

JACOBSON, Bernard
Authentic Messiah. Hi Fi 16:56-9 D '66
Busoni centenary. Hi Fi 16:135 My '66
By an unkown master. The baroque Beatles book. Hi Fi 16.67 F '66
Elgar's violin concerto, as played by Menuhin today and by Menuhin yesterday. Hi Fi 16:86-7 S '66
Four fine virtuosos of the honorable oboe. Hi Fi 16:87-8 My '66
In Bach's cello suites, playing both cerebral and passionate. Hi Fi 16:87 Ap '66
In composer. Hi Fi 16:40-2+ F '66
In the service of Heinrich Schütz, choral masterworks revealed. Hi Fi 16:73+ Mr '66
LSO comes to Florida. Hi Fi 16:MA14-15 O '66
So you want to be an impresario? Hi Fi 16:29-32 D 15 '66
Stravinsky, his heritage and his legacy. Hi Fi 16:MA9+ O '66
Stravinsky's new Requiem canticles. Hi Fi 16:MA11 D '66
Three Mahler symphonies. Hi Fi 16:131 F '66
(ed) See Darré, J. M. And we quote

JACOBSON, Dan
Beyond whose culture? Commentary 41:87-93 Mr '66
End to pornography? Commentary 42:76-8+ N '66
Literary vocation. Commentary 41:92+ My '66

JACOBSON, Eugene D.
Gastrointestinal circulation. Science 154:1366+ D 9 '66

JACOBSON, Robert
Donizetti's Campanello. Sat R 49:65 O 29 '66
Life music review. Life 62:18 Ja 20 '67
Los Angeles in Carthage. Sat R 49:63 D 17 '66

JACOBSON, Stanley
Study plus action. NEA J 55:41-2+ N '66

JACOBY, Ed
Follow the form. il U S Camera 30:60-1 Ja '67

JACOBY, Gale
Lipstick may fall in the bilge. B. Ottum. il por Sports Illus 24:64-6+ F 14 '66

JACOBY, Rene
Lipstick may fall in the bilge. B. Ottum. il por Sports Illus 24:64-6+ F 14 '66

JACQUELINE Grennan, Sister. See Grennan, J.

JACQUEMARTS. See Jaquemarts

JACQUES, Amédée Florent
Amadeo Jacques. A. A. Roig. il por Américas 18:7-13 Jl '66

JACQUES, Richard G.
Performance criteria; a system of communication. Arch Rec 139:191-5 My '66

JACQUETTE, Tommy
In burned-out Watts: it's now baby. J. Shepherd. il pors Look 30:94-6+ Je 28 '66

JADE carving. See Carving (art industries)

JADID, Salah
Doctors of Damascus. por Newsweek 68:34 D 26 '66

JAEGER, Joseph, Jr
National recreation areas. por Parks & Rec 1:629+ Ag '66

JAEGER, R. R. See Lipschutz, M. E. jt. auth.

JAFFE, Christopher
Musical shell game. il por Fortune 73:160 F '66

JAFFE, Dan
All-American muse. Sat R 49:29-30 O 15 '66

JAFFE, L. D. and Scott, R. F.
Lunar surface strength: implications of Luna 9 landing. bibliog Science 153:407-8 Jl 22 '66

JAFFE, Leonard
House doctor. il por Newsweek 67:75 Mr 7 '66

JAFFE, Rona
Rose white and rose red; story, excerpt from The cherry in the martini. por Sat Eve Post 239:66-8 S 10 '66

JAGAN, Cheddi
Atlantic report. Atlan 217:14+ Mr '66
Guyana is free, to go where? A. Verrier. il por N Y Times Mag p54-5+ My 22 '66
Guyana on the eve. P. Crane. America 114:297-8 F 26 '66

JAGDTERRIERS. See Terriers

JAGGERS, O. L.
Miss Velma descends. A. B. Haines. Christian Cent 83:992+ Ag 10 '66

JAGGERS, Velma Mary Lee
Miss Velma descends. A. B. Haines. Christian Cent 83:992+ Ag 10 '66
Swinging sermon. il por Newsweek 68:62+ N 14 '66

JAGUAR hunting
Bargain jaguar. O. A. Washburn. il Field & S 71:50-2+ Ag '66
Big Red's jaguar. W. Page. il Field & S 71:44-5+ Ja '67
Cattle slayers of Shiwishi-win. S. E. Brock. il Outdoor Life 138:66-9+ N '66
Devil jaguar. S. E. Brock. il Outdoor Life 137:44-7+ F '66
Tigre is behind us! C. J. McElroy. il Outdoor Life 139:35-7+ Ja '67

JAINA figurines. See Figurines

JAIPUR, India
India's city of pink. H. Sutton. Sat R 49:46+ My 14 '66

JAKOBOVITS, Immanuel
Chief rabbi from Fifth avenue. por Time 88:58-9 Ag 26 '66

JAKOBY, W. B. and others
Thyroglobulin: evidence for crystallization and association. bibliog Science 153:1671-2 S 30 '66

JAM. See Jelly, jam etc.

JAMA; story. See O'Hara, J.

JAMAICA
See also
Art—Jamaica
Investments, Foreign (in Jamaica)
Technical assistance in Jamaica

JAMAICAN cookery. See Cookery, Jamaican

JAMES, Edwin
Edwin James, pioneer naturalist. R. G. Beidleman. il Horticulture 44:32-4 D '66

JAMES, Ewing S.
Careful now, Dr James! Christian Cent 83: 768 Je 15 '66

JAMES, Henry
Lesson of the master: Henry James and James Baldwin. C. Newman. Yale R 56:45-59 O '66

JAMES, J. N.
Voyage of Mariner IV; with biographical sketch. Sci Am 214:20, 42-52 bibliog(p 143) Mr '66

JAMES, Kenneth W.
Book binderies and the information explosion; excerpts from address, April 13, 1966. Pub W 189:97-8+ My 2 '66

JAMES, L. Eldon
This is the week that will be. PTA Mag 61:11 N '66

JAMES, Pat
Horse in Ireland, or anywhere. U S Camera 29:46-7 My '66
Valley Forge. U S Camera 29:64-5 Mr '66

JAMES, Weldon
I resign. por Time 87:63-4 Ap 22 '66

JAMES, William, jr
John Singer Sargent in his studio. Atlan 217:91-2 Mr '66

JAMES Bond (literary character) See Spies in literature

JAMESON, Henry
When a county tried to cut relief bill. il U S News 60:44-7 Ja 31 '66

JAN Sangh (All-India people's party) See Political parties—India

JANÁČEK, Leoš
Edge of truth. J. W. Freeman. il por Opera N 31:6-7 N 19 '66
New York; performance of Jenufa. F. Merkling. Opera N 31:28 D 3 '66

JANCAUSKAS, Raymond C.
Let the borrower beware! America 115:774-6 D 10 '66

JANER, Albert Christ-. See Christ-Janer, A.

JANER, Arland Frederick Christ-. See Christ-Janer, A. F.

JANES, Ted
Bass with a bang. Outdoor Life 138:32-3+ Ag '66
Bobwhites teach me a lesson. Outdoor Life 138:54-5+ D '66
New muskie water. Outdoor Life 138:36-9+ Jl '66
Spring on the Miramichi. por Outdoor Life 137:48-9+ My '66
Strange doings on Otsego Lake. Outdoor Life 137:42-3+ Mr '66

JANEWAY, Elizabeth (Hall)
Nostalgic smells. House & Gard 129:106-7 F '66
Skeptical report on the experts who tell women how to be women. McCalls 93:94-5+ Ap '66
Toad beneath the harrow knows. por Library J 91:887-91 F 15 '66

JANEY, Sue Ellen
Million-dollar quiz show; drama. Plays 25: 92-5 Ap '66

JANKOWSKI, Horst
Lively arts; interview, ed. by R. Hemming. por Sr Schol 89:22 O 14 '66

JANKOWSKI, J. Moor-. See Moor-Jankowski, J.

JANSEN, Guenter
New Orleans librarian resigns after attacks. Library J 92:41-2 Ja 1 '67

JANSON, Donald
People of the blue-green waters. Audubon Mag 68:464-9 N '66

JANSSEN, Horst
Newest Gothic. il Time 89:63 Ja 20 '67

JANSSEN, Peter A.
College conundrum: how to choose. Am Ed 2:24-7 S '66
Next step: teacher integration. Reporter 35: 32-4 N 3 '66
St John's college of Annapolis. Am Ed 2:13 O '66

JANSSENS, Peter A. and Cohen, P. P.
Ornithine-urea cycle enzymes in the African lungfish, protopterus aethiopicus. bibliog Science 152:358-9 Ap 15 '66

JANUARY nuptials for Miss Fairweather; story. See Loeser, K.

JANUS, Judith
Songs that dance: Ethical culture auditorium. M Marks. Dance Mag 40:65 Jl '66

JAPAN
Japan is one of the biggest countries in the world. E. O. Reischauer. il N Y Times Mag p34-5+ O 16 '66
See also
Aeronautics, Military—Japan
Airlines—Japan
Airplane industry and trade—Japan
Automobile industry and trade—Japan
Birds—Japan
Colleges and universities—Japan
Crime and criminals—Japan
Education—Japan
Elections—Japan
Electronic apparatus industry and trade—Japan
Fishing—Japan
Foreign visitors in Japan
Gardens—Japan
Hiroshima
Hokkaido (island)
Hotels, taverns, etc.—Japan
Inland Sea
Investments, Foreign (by Japan)
Investments, Foreign (in Japan)
Japanese
Music festivals—Japan
Nagasaki
Political campaigns—Japan
Prices—Japan
Radioactive fallout—Japan
Railroads—Japan
Recreation—Japan
Shopping and shoppers—Japan
Space research—Japan
Tokyo
Women—Japan
World war, 1939-1945—Japan
Youth—Japan

Commerce

Japan plays the field; peace and trade with everyone. A. Campbell. New Repub 154: 19-22 Mr 5 '66
See also
Japan—Industries
Joint United States-Japan committee on trade and economic affairs

Commercial treaties and agreements

King crab fishery agreement with Japan extended: text of U.S. note, November 29, 1966. D. Rusk. Dept State Bul 55:984 D 26 '66
New co-prosperity sphere; raw materials agreements signed. Time 87:98 F 25 '66
U.S. and Japan sign agreement updating U.S. concessions; with list of concessions. Dept State Bul 55:466 S 26 '66

Cultural relations

U.S.-Japan cultural conference held at Tokyo. Dept State Bul 54:405 Mr 14 '66

Defenses

Japan's defense rests on U.S. technology. S. Nagashima. il Tech W 19:32-3 D 5 '66

Description and travel

Great fur caravan: Vogue's crew in northern Japan. M. Evans. il Vogue 148:89-90+ O 15 '66
Japan's winter bloom. D. Messinesi. Vogue 148:77-8 O 15 '66
350 must miles in Japan. L. Barry. il Pop Phot 58:86-9+ Ap '66

Economic conditions

Japan: a brisker pace in bar and board room. il Bsns W p 198 S 10 '66
Miracle of Japan: where is it headed now? interview; ed. by K. M. Chrysler. E. O. Reischauer. il U S News 61:58-62 Ag 8 '66
Thermometer; department-store sales. il Time 88:75 Ag 26 '66
Two island nations: a study in contrasts. il U S News 62:58-60 Ja 16 '67
See also
Japan—Industries

Economic relations

Japan's aid push; nine southeast Asian nations to postwar trade-and-aid conference. il Time 87:97 Ap 15 '66
See also
Joint United States-Japan committee on trade and economic affairs

JARMAN, Walton Maxey
Mutual antipathy. por Time 87:82 Ap 1 '66
JARRELL, Randall
On Randall Jarrell. R. W. Flint. Commentary 41:79-81 F '66
Prince of reviewers. A. Kazin. il Reporter 35:45-6+ S 8 '66
JARRELL, Temple R.
South. por Parks & Rec 1:635 Ag '66
JARRETT, James L.
Santa Cruz after one year. Sat R 50:67+ Ja 21 '67
JARS, Cookie. See Cookie jars
JARVIK, Murray E. See Slotnick, B. M. jt. auth.
JARVIS, Esther
Bright swingers stop collisions. Audubon Mag 68:373-4 S '66
JARVIS, P. G. and Slatyer, R. O.
Calibration of β gauges for determining of leaf water status. bibliog Science 153:78-9 Jl 1 '66
—See Slatyer, R. O. jt. auth.
JASINSKI, Andrzej, and others
Rate of movement and redistribution of stainable neurosecretory granules in hypothalamic neurons. bibliog Science 154:776-8 N 11 '66
JASMINE
Most jasmines are fragrant; all are easy to grow. il Sunset 137:150-1 Jl '66
JASPERS, Karl
Criminal state and German responsibility; tr. by W. J. Dannhauser. Commentary 41:33-9 F '66

about

Surprise for Karl Jaspers. W. S. Schlamm. Nat R 18:620 Je 28 '66
JASPERSON, Robert W.
Is the National park service obliged to complete the north shore road? letter to George Marshall, March 31, 1966. Liv Wildn 30:31-5 Spr '66
JASS, Rudolph F.
Pocket parks. Am City 81:86-7 D '66
JATLOW, J. L.
Microwave for data transmission. Duns R 88:pt2 150 S '66
JAVA
Sukarno's holdouts in central Java; Nationalist-Moslem conflict. D. Kirk. il Reporter 35:39-41 S 8 '66
See also
Botany—Java
JAVELINA hunting. See Peccary hunting
JAVITS, Jacob Koppel
Consensus government and the opposition role; address, March 21, 1966. Vital Speeches 32:391-3 Ap 15 '66
Excerpt from debate, September 24, 1965. Cong Digest 45:77+ Mr '66
Excerpts from addresses, September 1, 6, 1966. Cong Digest 45:245+ O '66
about
CPNY and Mr Javits. Nat R 18:1304-5 D 27 '66
Could this Jew be President? M. Viorst. il por Esquire 65:100-4+ Ap '66
Cry for progress il por Time 87:39 Ap 8 '66
Liebman on the burning deck. Nation 204:4-5 Ja 2 '67
Mormon-Jewish ticket? Time 87:31-2 My 13 '66
Romney-Javits ticket for Republicans? il por U S News 60:20 Je 6 '66
Senator Javits and the Committee of one million. Nat R 19:14+ Ja 10 '67
Trustee for tomorrow. il pors Time 87:25-9 Je 24 '66
JAVITS, Joan. See Wyse, L. jt. auth.
JAVITS, Marion Ann (Borris)
Will Marion Javits move the White House to New York? interview, ed. by B. Walters. Ladies Home J 83:40 Ag '66
JAVORSKY, Emil
Quick flowering bulb. il Flower Grower 53:20+ D '66
Subtropic flora thrives on 50th parallel. Natur Hist 75:18-23 F '66
JAWS
Intracranial mobility in the coelacanth; jaw mechanism of latimeria. K. S. Thomson. bibliog il Science 153:999-1000 Ag 26 '66

Surgery

See Oral surgery
JAYCEE awards. See United States junior chamber of commerce
JAYCEES. See United States junior chamber of commerce

JAYNE, John Franklin
Stowing the anchor rode. Motor B 117:152+ Mr '66
JAYNES, Mary
Segregation fence: a young mother gets involved. por Redbook 126:8+ Mr '66
JAYS
How to make up to a jay. il Sunset 136:144+ Je '66
JAZY, Michel
Al-lez! jaz-y! al-lez! jaz-yl A. Crichton. Sports Illus 25:25 Jl 4 '66
JAZZ bands. See Bands (music)
JAZZ festivals. See Music festivals—United States
JAZZ music
Cool cat against the reds' cherry bombs; interview, ed. by R. Hemming. P. Winter. il Sr Schol 87:2+ Ja 21 '66
Demurrer on jazzy Lord's suppers. L. Kinsolving. Christian Cent 83:803-4 Je 22 '66; Discussion. 83:1084 S 7 '66
Is new music new? N. Rorem. Am Rec G 32:776-9+ My '66
Jazz concerts. W. Balliett. New Yorker 42:78+ F 26; 210-14+ O 1 '66
Jazz goes to church. il Ebony 21:76-80 Ap '66
Liturgy and headlines; jazz masses. America 116:79 Ja 21 '67
New jazz. N. Hentoff. il Vogue 147:177+ F 1 '66
New jazz. il Newsweek 68:101-4+ D 12 '66
New jazz, black, angry, and hard to understand. N. Hentoff. il N Y Times Mag p 10-11+ D 25 '66
New Orleans jazz archive at Tulane. R. B. Allen. il Wilson Lib Bul 40:619-23 Mr '66
Our footloose correspondents; New Orleans. W. Balliett. il New Yorker 42:128+ Je 11 '66
Profiles: Red Allen. W. Balliett. il New Yorker 42:33-6+ Je 25 '66
Where's the melody? M. Williams. Am Rec G 32:774-5+ My '66
See also
Phonograph records—Jazz music
Rock 'n' roll music

Anecdotes, facetiae, satire, etc.

Temptation of Professor Tillich. G. Cali. Esquire 65:68-9 My '66
JAZZ musicians
New jazz. il Newsweek 68:101-4+ D 12 '66
Our footloose correspondents; New Orleans. W. Balliett. il New Yorker 42:128+ Je 11 '66
JEALOUSY
Bobby's new baby; brand-new little sister. il Good H 162:52+ My '66
Dialogue with mothers; jealousy in the younger sibling. B. Bettelheim. Ladies Home J 83:39-40 Jl '66
JEAN Marie Kann, Sister. See Kann, J. M.
JEANNE d'Arc, Saint. See Joan of Arc
JEANNERET-GRIS, Charles Édouard. See Le Corbusier
JEEPS. See Automobiles; Motor vehicles
JEEPSTERS. See Automobiles
JEFFERSON, Thomas
Mr Jefferson's Monticello. J. Judge. il por Nat Geog Mag 130:426-44 S '66
JEFFERSON COUNTY, Colo.
Local cooperation means strength; North Jeffco metropolitan recreation and park district, Arvada. Parks & Rec 1:897 N '66
JEFFERSON COUNTY, Ky.
We merged city and county purchasing. R. S. Greer. il Am City 81:114-15 O '66
JEFFERSON national expansion memorial. See St Louis—Monuments, statues, etc.
JEFFERYS, William H.
Rotation of the planet Mercury. bibliog Science 152:201 Ap 8 '66
JEFFRIES, Christie
Naval recruit; poem. Farm J 90:106 My '66
JEHOVAH'S Witnesses
Witnesses' Spartan trials; Greece. il Time 88:84+ S 9 '66
JELINEK, Arthur J.
Correlation of archeological and palynological data. bibliog Science 152:1507-9 Je 10 '66
JELLINCK, P. H. and Goudy, Barbara
Protective action of polycyclic hydrocarbons against induction of adrenal necrosis by dimethylbenzananthracene. bibliog Science 152:1375-6 Je 3 '66
JELLINEK, Hedy D.
Guide to European music festivals, 1966. Sat R 49:58-9 Mr 26 '66
Music festivals U.S.A.: summer 1966. Sat R 49:50-3 My 28 '66

JELLY, Jam. etc.
Berry jams that you freeze; with recipes.
Sunset 137:137 Jl '66
Citrus preserves. il Sunset 136:177-8 F '66
Jam. jelly. marmalade: the differences. il
Good H 162:183 Ap '66
Treasure trove of gifts to make; with recipes. il Ladies Home J 83:78-9+ D '66
JELLYFISH
Nettlesome; government matching grants to
states for jellyfish control. il Newsweek 68:
68+ N 14 '66
JELM, Lloyd
How I decided to go narrow row, even on a
rented farm; ed. by W. J. Fletcher. Suc
Farm 64:46-7+ Mr '66
JENCKS, Christopher
Accommodating whites. New Repub 154:19-
22 Ap 16 '66
Education: the racial gap. New Repub 155:
21-6 O 1 '66
Speaking out. por Sat Eve Post 239:14+
Ap 23 '66
JENKINS, Dan
College football (cont) Sports Illus 25:44-6 N 7
'66
Pro football (cont) Sports Illus 25:54-6 Jl
18 '66
Skiing. Sports Illus 24:88-9 Ap 4 '66
Sporting look. Sports Illus 24:86-7 Ap 25 '66
JENKINS, Joseph Alton
Labor board gags your freedom of speech.
por Nations Bsns 54:52-3+ Ap '66
JENKINS, Paul
Jenkins paints an opinion. Art N 65:54-5+
N '66
JENKINS, Ray
Mr & Mrs Wallace run for governor of
Alabama. N Y Times Mag p28-9+ Ap 24
'66
JENKINS, Roy Harris
Sex and the lords. B. Wenham. New Repub
154:9-10 F 12 '66
JENKINS, Speight, Jr
Kaleidoscope. Opera N 31:25-7 D 17 '66
JENKS, George F. and Brown, D. A.
Three-dimensional map construction. bibliog
Science 154:857-64 N 18 '66
JENNING, Michael Bryant
Kissing Jamie Cary; story. Seventeen 25:158-9
N '66
JENNINGS, Eugene E.
You can't succeed in business by merely
trying. Nations Bsns 54:110-12+ My '66
JENNINGS, Frank G.
Education of educators. Sat R 49:79-80 N 19
'66
Of books and engagement; excerpts from
address. July 1965. por Library J 91:2149-52
Ap 15 '66
JENNINGS, Gary
I still love a parade. Writer 79:15-17+ S '66
Speaking Scandinavian. Holiday 40:8+ N '66
JENNINGS, John Q.
Why all the confusion over profits? Nations
Bsns 54:106+ S '66
JENNINGS, Paul Francis
From an age of innocence, a sport with size.
Sports Illus 24:41 F 14 '66
JENNY, John H.
More and better substitutes. NEA J 55:15
O '66
JENSEN, David
Hagfish; with biographical sketch. Sci Am
214:17, 82-90 F: 8 My '66
JENSEN, E. J. and Ellis, H. S.
Pipelines; with biographical sketches. Sci Am
216:22, 62-70+ bibliog(p 146) Ja '67
JENSEN, Eileen
First love, the second time; story. Ladies
Home J 83:90-1 Ap '66
JENSEN, Michael C.
Gamesmanship with the guideposts. Harvard
Bsns R 44:168-70+ N '66
JENSEN, Oliver
Shape of things practically here; fable. Am
Heritage 17:44-9 Je '66
JEPSEN, Glenn L.
Early eocene bat from Wyoming. bibliog Science 154:1333-9 D 9 '66
JERNIGAN, William W.
Oral Roberts favors futuristic. Library J 91:
5889-91 D 1 '66
JEROME, Judson
At the dancing school of the sisters Schwarz:
poem. Sat R 49:18 Jl 2 '66
In the faculty lounge; poem. Atlan 218:105
Ag '66
Tipping; poem. Sat R 49:41 S 10 '66
JERSEY aero club. See Aviation clubs
JERSEY CITY, N.J.

Architecture
Requiem for a courthouse. D. G. Lowe. il Am
Heritage 17:26-9+ O '66

Galleries and museums
Manner of speaking; objection to Mia Le-
Comte's painting. J. Ciardi. Sat R 49:12
Ap 23 '66
JERUSALEM
Incident in Jerusalem. D. Wakefield. Commentary 41:49-55 F '66

Church of the Holy Sepulcher
Unholy row over the tomb of Christ. D.
Holden. il Sat Eve Post 239:80-5 Ap 9 '66

Israel museum
Art that history shaped. K. Kuh. il Sat R
49:17-24 Ja 29 '66
Shrine of the book. excerpt from address.
A. Eban. il Sch Arts 65:43-5 Ap '66
JERUSALEM Bible. See Bible—Versions
JERUSALEM'S biblical zoo. See Zoological
gardens
JESPERSON, Margaret
Me; poem. Horn Bk 42:234 Ap '66
JESSE H. Jones hall, Houston, Tex. See Concert halls
JESSEL, George
Loved one. por Time 88:52+ Ag 26 '66
JESSUP, John K.
New boy survives a hazing. Life 60:17 Ja
28 '66
Urgent new reach to be equal. Life 60:88-90+
Je 3 '66
JESUIT high schools. See Catholic church—
Education
JESUITS
Pope and Jesuits: invitation and response.
America 115:729-30 D 3 '66
Pope Paul's mournful November warning.
Christian Cent 83:1497-8 D 7 '66
Rebuke to the Jesuits; scolding by Pope. il
Newsweek 68:95 N 28 '66
Standpat in Rome. Time 88:98+ N 25 '66
Warning from the Pope: its meaning; summary of address, November 16, 1966. Paul
VI. il U S News 61:15 N 28 '66

Missions
Jesuits plan mission progress. America 114:
245 F 19 '66
JESUS, Carolina Maria de
Better to be poor. il pors Ebony 22:100-4 D
'66
JESUS, Society of. See Jesuits
JESUS CHRIST
Finding the historical Jesus. by J. F. Peter.
Review
Christian Cent 83:273-4 Mr 2 '66. N. Perrin
Heretic or prophet? il Time 88:56-8+ N 11
'66
Human Christ. V. P. McCorry. America 114:
757-8 My 21 '66
Jesus Christ, by Y. Congar. Review
America 114:748+ My 21 '66. H. Musurillo
Quest through the centuries: the search
for the historical Jesus, by H. K. McArthur. Review
Christian Cent 83:1114+ S 14 '66. H. C.
Kee
Reassembling the face of Christ R. W. Gilsdorf. America 115:131-5 Ag 6 '66
Shape of Christology, by J. McIntyre. Review
Christian Cent 83:1342-3 N 2 '66. D. A.
Fox
Suffering with Christ. C. Davis. America
115:157 Ag 13 '66
Sunday Christology. V. P. McCorry. America
115:398 O 1 '66
Who is this man? V. P. McCorry. il America 114:633-4 Ap 30 '66
See also
Salvation
Second advent

Art
Art: Barnett Newman show at Guggenheim
museum. M. Kozloff. Nation 202:598 My
16 '66
Last supper; Milan's deathless treasure. E.
O. Hauser. il Read Digest 88:166-8+ Ap
'66
Native expression; Nativity as a subject
during renaissance. il Time 88:46-51 D 23 '66
Unanswerable question; B. Newman's abstract Passion. il Newsweek 67:100 My 9
'66

Birth
See Jesus Christ—Nativity

Crucifixion
Crucifixion plot; theories of Hugh J. Schonfield and others. il Newsweek 68:51 Ag 8
'66

JESUS CHRIST—Crucifixion—_Continued_
Passover plot, by H. J. Schonfield. Review
America 115:258 S 10 '66. H. Musurillo
Road between Rome and Jerusalem. S. Sand-
mel. Sat R 49:42-3 D 3 '66
Suffocation of Christ. il Time 88:49 Jl 29 '66
Why did you let us kill him? excerpt from
The mind of Christ. H. A. Bosley. Christian
Cent 83:387 Mr 30 '66

Divinity

Easter 1966, a quest for the true Jesus. il
pors Newsweek 67:71-3 Ap 11 '66
Facts of the matter. V. P. McCorry. America
115:527 O 29 '66
Synoptic problem and the contemporary theological chaos. W. R. Farmer, jr. Christian
Cent 83:1204-6 O 5 '66; Discussion. 83:1345-
6 N 2 '66
We thank you, John. V. P. McCorry. America
114:606 Ap 23 '66

Family

Quiet, kind companion. V. P. McCorry.
America 116:28 Ja 7 '67

Forty days in the wilderness

See Jesus Christ—Temptation

Incarnation

See Incarnation

Nativity

Christmas sky. F. M. Branley. il Redbook
128:45+ D '66
Christmas story, from the Gospels of Matthew
and Luke; excerpts from the Metropolitan
museum of art's current book, ed. by M.
Northrup. il McCalls 94:59-65 D '66
Sign of the manger; St Luke's account of the
Nativity. C. H. Giblin. il America 115:826-8
D 24 '66
Way of it. V. P. McCorry. America 115:838-9
D 24 '66
See also
Christmas
Christmas cribs

Parables

See also
Good Samaritan (parable)

Passion

Crucifixion plot; theories of Hugh J. Schonfield and others. il Newsweek 68:51 Ag 8 '66

Poetry

Sonnets on the seven last words. R. Spargur.
Christian Cent 83:399 Mr 30 '66

Teaching

First and last word. V. P. McCorry. America
115:787 D 10 '66

Temptation

Clarity in mystery. V. P. McCorry. America
114:310 F 26 '66

Trial

Trial of Jesus. S. G. F. Brandon. il pors
Horizon 9:4-13 Wint '67
JET air travel. See Air travel
JET airplane engines
Cryogenic engine is latest DOD/NASA joint
project. Miss & Roc 18:31-2 My 30 '66
GE offering SST engine growth; new com-
bustor unveiled by P&W. Aviation W 84:41
My 2 '66
G.E.'s hard-driving jockey in the jet-engine
race. J. Mecklin. il Fortune 74:116-18+
Jl 1 '66
JT9D engine for 747 emphasizes thrust for
cruise. M. L. Yaffee. il Aviation W 84:42-3
Ap 18 '66
Marquardt developing composite engines.
M. L. Yaffee. il Aviation W 85:93+ D 12 '66
Mid-1968 engine deliveries slated for opera-
tional F-111B. il Tech W 19:15 S 5 '66
Plating reclaims worn jet engine parts. M.
L. Yaffee. il Aviation W 85:63+ O 17 '66
P&W increases airflow for SST engine. M.
L. Yaffee. il Aviation W 85:50+ Ag 29 '66
Rolls explores third-generation lift jets. H. J.
Coleman. il Aviation W 84:54-5+ Ap 18
'66
Rolls plans multiple versions of RB.178. H. J.
Coleman. il Aviation W 85:40-1 Jl 18 '66

Cooling

Rigimesh now heavily used in cooling; application in jet and rocket engines. R.
Barnhart. il Tech W 19:36+ D 19 '66

Design

Concorde engine goes up and so does the
cost; changes in supersonic engine design. Sci N 90:252 O 1 '66
GE boosts thrust in phase 3 SST engine. M.
L. Yaffee. il Aviation W 85:42-3+ S 26 '66

Fuel

Flame-resistant jet fuel and fireproofed
people. il Life 60:38-9 Ap 15 '66
Liquefied natural gas considered promising as
Mach 3 SST fuel. Aviation W 84:47 My 23
'66
Liquid methane may be suitable fuel for SST.
Sci N 89:515 Je 25 '66

Maintenance and repair

Maintainability becomes engine byword. M.
L. Yaffee. il Aviation W 85:106-7+ O 31
'66
JET business planes. See Airplanes, Business
JET engine noise. See Airplanes—Noise
JET pilots. See Air pilots
JET propelled airplanes. See Airplanes, Jet
propelled
JET propulsion
Ground labs hamper work in supersonic com-
bustion; application of supersonic combus-
tion to hypersonic ramjets. Tech W 19:
37+ O 17 '66
NASA/Lewis revives air-breather effort;
emphasis on supersonic transport propul-
sion. M. L. Yaffee. il Aviation W 84:71+
Je 13 '66
See also
Jet airplane engines
JET propulsion laboratory
JPL abandons Surveyor photo attempts. il
Aviation W 85:28 Jl 18 '66
JPL story. H. L. Nieburg. Bul Atomic Sci
22:35-8 O '66
Moon is brown; Surveyor's pictures. Time
87:70 Je 24 '66
Personality of the month; Bill Pickering,
master scientist. A. Hamilton. il Sci Digest
59:12-17 Mr '66
Voyager, planet probe technology in hand.
R. Pay. il Tech W 19:95-8+ N 28 '66
JET railcars. See Railroads—Trains
JET transition training. See Air pilots—Train-
ing
JETS (football club) See Football clubs
JETT, T. Sutton
Renaissance of the grand Mall. por Parks &
Rec 1:324-6 Ap '66
JEUNE Afrique. See Periodicals—Tunisia
JEUNESSES musicales. See Musical societies
JEWEL wasps. See Wasps
JEWELERS
Metalworkers of Europe. J. Skoogfors. il
Craft Horiz 26:36+ S '66
See also
Tiffany and company
JEWELRY
All the trimmings. il Seventeen 25:102-3+
D '66
Casting. F. Marlow. il Sch Arts 65:19-20 Ja
'66
Jewelry by Resia Schor. R. Howard. il Craft
Horiz 26:8-11+ Jl '66
Metals; a discussion. J. Prip; R. Pearson.
Craft Horiz 26:29-31 Je '66
Personal business: fine jewelry for Christ-
mas. Bsns W p 159-60 N 26 '66
Rudolf Dentler. D. Masuhr. il Craft Horiz
26:16-17 Mr '66
Schubert's shards; old Indian pottery frag-
ments in modern bracelet. A. Thorpe. il
Craft Horiz 26:18-19 Ja '66
Take a fashion lesson. il Seventeen 25:230
My '66
They bug me; K. J. Lane. il Newsweek 68:
110+ N 28 '66
See also
Goldsmithing
Precious stones
JEWELRY trade
In Brazil, it's breakfast at Stern's; H. Stern's
jewelry business. il Bsns W p 110-12+ My
14 '66
See also
Cartier, incorporated
Tiffany and company
JEWISH Americans in Israel. See Americans
in Israel
JEWISH-Arab relations
Arab and Jew. il Newsweek 68:44 D 19 '66
Arab refugees: a Zionist view. M. Syrkin;
reply with rejoinder. R. S. Goldman. Com-
mentary 41:6+ Je '66

JEWISH-Arab relations—*Continued*
Arabs bar Coke, Ford; boycott list of companies doing business in Israel. Bsns W p52 N 26 '66
Business in Mideast walks on shifting sands. il Bsns W p26+ Jl 2 '66
Diary of the Sinai campaign, by M. Dayan. Review
  Time 87:111+ Je 24 '66
For the Arabs Israel does not exist. A. Carthew il N Y Times Mag p30-1+ D 18 '66; Reply. M. Arnon. p37 Ja 8 '67
Gamble on the Jordan. J. A. Morris, jr. il Nation 204:6-8 Ja 2 '67
Highly volatile; state of the Middle East. il Newsweek 68:56 O 24 '66
  See also
United Nations—Israel
JEWISH art. See Art, Jewish
JEWISH authors. See Authors, Jewish
JEWISH baseball players. See Baseball players
JEWISH children
Children, by C. Blackstock. Review
  Sat R 49:42+ N 26 '66. I. Halperin
How to survive childhood. M. Polner. Nation 203:523 N 14 '66
JEWISH cookery. See Cookery, Jewish
JEWISH fiction
Books: the Jewish novel. L. Kahn. Cath World 204:242-4 Ja '67
JEWISH folk music society. See Musical societies
JEWISH heritage award
Elie Wiesel wins first Jewish heritage award. Pub W 189:37 Ap 4 '66
JEWISH holidays. See Holidays
JEWISH law
What's in a name? restrictions on *kohanim*. Time 87:61 My 27 '66
JEWISH literature (American)
Jew as modern writer. A. Kazin. Commentary 41:37-41 Ap '66
JEWISH newspapers
Germany's Jewish watchdog; Allgemeine unabhängige jüdische wochenzeitung (General independent Jewish weekly) of the West German republic. Time 88:41 D 30 '66
JEWISH periodicals
  See also
Commentary (periodical)
JEWISH sects
  See also
Hasidism
Zealots (Jewish party)
JEWISH students
Yarmulke in school; New York city's school board decision. Newsweek 67:86 Mr 28 '66
JEWISH theological seminary of America, New York
Library collections badly damaged in Jewish theological seminary fire. il Library J 91: 2450 My 15 '66
JEWISH theology
What God thinks of man; A. J. Heschel's philosophy. Newsweek 67:57 Ja 31 '66
JEWISH youth. See Youth, Jewish
JEWISON, Norman
New faces. A. Knight. por Sat R 49:25 D 24 '66
JEWS
Does the Jew exist? excerpt from The liberation of the Jew. A. Memmi. Commentary 42:73-4+ N '66
State of Jewish belief; symposium; with introd. by M. Himmelfarb. Commentary 42: 71-160 Ag '66
  See also
Anti-Semitism
Catholic church—Relations—Jews
Israel

Dietary laws
Forbidden foods; kashruth doctrine. E. Isaac; discussion. Commentary 42:12-13+ Jl '66
Trefa banquet: Cincinnati dinner, 1883; first steps toward reform. J. J. Appel. Commentary 41:75-8 F '66; Reply with rejoinder. A. Marks. 41:18+ My '66

History
At the dawn of civilization, ed. by E. A. Speiser. Review
  Commentary 41:85-8 Je '66. E. Isaac
European Jewry, past and present. S. D. Temkin. Christian Cent 83:1422+ N 16 '66
Jews in their land; ed. by D. Ben-Gurion. Review
  Sat R il 49:26 Ag 20 '66. A. L. Sachar
Myth of the Jewish world-conspiracy; excerpt from Warrant for genocide. N. Cohn. Commentary 41:35-42 Je '66; Discussion. 42: 10+ D '66
  See also
David, king of Israel

Law
  See Jewish law

Liturgy and ritual
Going to shul. M. Himmelfarb. Commentary 41:66-70 Ap '66

Persecutions
Myth of the Jewish world-conspiracy; excerpt from Warrant for genocide. N. Cohn. Commentary 41:35-42 Je '66; Discussion. 42:10+ D '66
Treblinka, by J. F. Steiner. Review
  Time 87:37-8 Ap 29 '66
Victims of a pious cruelty. A. L. Sachar. il Sat R 49:36-7 Je 18 '66
  See also
Blood accusation

Political and social conditions
Jews and Germans; excerpt from address at World Jewish congress, 1966; tr. by W. J. Dannhauser. G. Scholem. Commentary 42: 31-8 N '66
  See also
Protocols of the wise men of Zion

Religion
  See Judaism

Rites and ceremonies
Forbidden foods; kashruth doctrine. E. Isaac; discussion. Commentary 42:12-13+ Jl '66
JEWS, Negro
Black Jews. il Newsweek 68:44 D 26 '66
JEWS and Catholics. See Catholic church—Relations—Jews
JEWS and Christians, International conference of. See International conference of Christians and Jews
JEWS and Germans
German and Jew, difficult encounter. L. Kahn. Christian Cent 83:1207-10 O 5 '66
Germans and Jews. Newsweek 68:72+ Ag 15 '66
Jews and Germans; excerpt from address at World Jewish congress, 1966; tr. by W. J. Dannhauser. G. Scholem. Commentary 42: 31-8 N '66
JEWS and Negroes
Negro-Jewish confrontation. M. Geltman. Nat R 18:621-3 Je 28 '66
Negroes, Jews, and muzhiks. M. Himmelfarb. Commentary 42:83-6 O '66; Reply. America 115:641 N 19 '66
Study proves Negroes not strongly anti-Semitic. Christian Cent 83:1265 O 19 '66
JEWS and the World war. See World war, 1939-1945—Jews
JEWS in Canada
Un-American Jew. E. Berger. Commentary 42:82-5 S '66
JEWS in Denmark
Denmark's heroic week. il Sr Schol 89:3 O 7 '66
JEWS in eastern Europe. See Jews in Europe
JEWS in Ethiopia
  See also
Falashas
JEWS in Europe
European Jewry, past and present. S. D. Temkin. Christian Cent 83:1422+ N 16 '66
Jews; East European Jews. il Newsweek 67:54+ My 23 '66
Life they left behind; Jewish immigrants between 1880 and World war I; portfolio. Am Heritage 17:15-21 O '66
Negroes, Jews, and muzhiks. M. Himmelfarb. Commentary 42:83-6 O '66
JEWS in France
New life in France's Jewish community. S. D. Temkin. Christian Cent 83:1519-21 D 7 '66
JEWS in Germany
Jews and Germans; excerpt from address at World Jewish congress, 1966; tr. by W. J. Dannhauser. G. Scholem. Commentary 42: 31-8 N '66
JEWS in Great Britain
British Jewry: the curtain maintained. S. D. Temkin. Christian Cent 83:1606-8 D 28 '66
Chief rabbi from Fifth avenue; chief rabbi of the British Commonwealth. Time 88:58-9 Ag 26 '66
JEWS in Israel
Jews in their land; ed. by D. Ben-Gurion. Review
  Sat R il 49:26 Ag 20 '66. A. L. Sachar
JEWS in Palestine
  See also
Jewish-Arab relations

JEWS in Palestine—*Continued*

Resistance movement

See also

Haganah

JEWS in Russia

Jews of silence, by E. Wiesel. Review
  Sat R 49:42 N 26 '66. H. Schwartz

Jews of silence; tr. by N. Kozodoy; excerpt.
  E. Wiesel. il Sat Eve Post 239:38-40+ N 19
  '66

Of many things. T. N. Davis. America 114:
  607 Ap 30 '66

Time runs out for Russia's Jews; ed. by J.
  Star. A. Schneier. il Look 30:100+ N 29
  '66

Tisha B'av in Moscow; Judaism's national
  day of mourning. B. I. Rubin. Christian
  Cent 83:1186-7 S 28 '66

JEWS in the United States

Brothers but not identical twins; American
  Christians and Jews. Christian Cent 83:641
  My 18 '66

Christian beliefs and anti-Semitism, by C. Y.
  Glock and R. Stark. Review
  Commentary 42:96-9 D '66 S. Monas

In the land of promise; lower East side exhibition at the Jewish museum. A. Werner.
  il Reporter 35:50-2 O 6 '66

Jews in America, by R. Gay. Review
  Commentary 42:77-9 Jl '66. J. J. Appel

Jews in the mind of America, by C. H.
  Stember and others. Review
  Christian Cent 84:14-15 Ja 4 '67. M.
  Polner

Johnson and his Jewish critics; concerning
  criticism of Vietnamese policy. Nation 203:
  268-9 S 26 '66

Little milk, a little honey. D. Boroff. il Am
  Heritage 17:12-14+ O '66

Negroes, Jews, and muzhiks. M. Himmelfarb.
  Commentary 42:83-6 O '66

Several worlds of American Jews; activities
  of the secular organizations. M. K.
  Sanders. Harper 232:52-62 Ap '66; Discussion. 232:4+ Je '66

Trefa banquet; Cincinnati dinner, 1883; first
  steps toward reform. J. J. Appel. Commentary 41:75-8 F '66; Reply with rejoinder.
  A. Marks. 41:18+ My '66

When reform was young. L. S. Dawidowicz.
  Commentary 42:63-7 Jl '66

JHABVALA, R. Prawer

Man with a dog; story. New Yorker 42:52-
  60 N 19 '66

JHUNG, Finis

Brief biography. S. Goodman. pors Dance
  Mag 40:50-1 Ag '66

JIGERS (motor vehicles) See Motor vehicles

JIGS

Jig-of-all-work for your table saw. R. J. De
  Cristoforo. il Pop Sci 189:180-4 O '66

Three jigs for cutting wood discs. C. E.
  Banister. il Pop Mech 125:148-51+ Je '66

JIGSAW puzzles. See Puzzles

JIU-Jitsu

Honor's judo defense of honor. M. E. Smith.
  il Life 60:127-8 My 20 '66

JOAN of Arc, Saint

Joan of Arc, by R. Pernoud. Review
  Sat R 49:56 D 3 '66. O. Prescott

JOB, Jean Claude. See Milhaud, G. jt. auth.

JOB, Book of. See Bible—Old Testament—Job

JOB aptitude tests. See Aptitude tests

JOB corps. See United States—Job corps

JOB discrimination. See Discrimination in employment

JOB instruction training. See Employees—
  Training

JOB interviews. See Interviewing

JOB placement guidance. See Vocational
  guidance

JOB satisfaction

How Andy McGhee got a better job. W.
  Shelton. il Fortune 75:116-17+ Ja '67

How do you like your job? il Todays Health
  44:34-5+ F '66

See also

Employee morale

JOB security. See Employment systems—Guaranty of employment

JOB shops. See Employment agencies

JOB tenure. See Seniority, Employee

JOB training. See Employees—Training

JOBBERS, Book. See Book jobbers

JOBS. See Employment: Occupations

JOCKEY club of Paris. See Paris—Clubs

JOCKEYS

They are not just along for the ride; with
  account by F. Graham, jr. il Sports Illus 24:
  40-6+ Ap 11 '66

See also

Baeza, B.

Horse racing

Longden, J.

JODRELL Bank telescope. See Radio telescope

JOEL, Lydia

Dancer prepares; introduction. Dance Mag 40:
  49-51 Mr '66

JOENSUU, Oiva. See Bonatti, E. jt. auth.

JOFFREY, Robert

In Balanchine's footsteps? il por Newsweek
  68:96 O 3 '66

JOFFREY ballet. See City Center Joffrey ballet

JOGJAKARTA, Indonesia

In deepest Java. H. Sutton il Sat R 50:100+
  Ja 14 '67

JOHANN, Robert O.

Philosopher's notebook (cont) America 114:
  260, 591, 876; 115:207, 513; 116:95 F 19, Ap
  23, Je 25, Ag 27, O 29 '66, Ja 21 '67

JOHANNESBURG

Architecture

Pattern of the street; Western Native Township. J. Beinart. il Arch Forum 125:58-63
  S '66

JOHANSEN, John M.

John M. Johansen declares himself. Arch
  Forum 124:64-7 Ja '66

about

Rear end of the Xerox, or how I learned to
  love that library. M. Charney; S. Moholy-
  Nagy. il Arch Forum 124:60-1 My '66

JOHN, Saint, the Evangelist

Saint John the thunderer. E. O. Hauser. il
  Read Digest 88:162-4+ My '66

JOHN XXIII, pope

John XXIII and the city of man, by P. Riga.
  Review
  Cath World 203:315-16 Ag '66. E. C.
  Bianchi

JOHN, Bernard, and Lewis, K. R.

Chromosome variability and geographic distribution in insects. bibliog Science 152:
  711-21 My 6 '66

JOHN, Erwin Roy

American in Cuba. Nation 202:296-9, 327-
  9 Mr 14-21 '66

—See Ruchkin, D. S. jt. auth.

JOHN, Godfrey

Judas; poem. Christian Cent 83:366 Mr 23 '66

JOHN, Gospel of. See Bible—New Testament
  —John

JOHN Birch society

Bedeviled Birchers. Time 88:25 S 9 '66

Birch tree grows. J. Freedman. il Library
  J 91:624-8 F 1 '66; Reply. L. Newman. 91:
  1952 Ap 15 '66

Birchers' revolt; two top members resign.
  Newsweek 68:20 Ag 29 '66

Birchism at the grass roots; Birch watchers
  retaliatory group. A. Forster. il Nation 203:
  73-6 Jl 25 '66

Cranston on Birch. Nation 203:108-9 Ag 8 '66

Is Robert Welch's doctrine Christian? A.
  Croce. Nat R 18:762 Ag 9 '66; Discussion.
  18:910+ S 20 '66

What makes Catholics Birchers? America 114:
  686-7 My 14 '66

When good Birchers get together. T. Buckley.
  il N Y Times Mag p48-9+ Je 5 '66

Whose hand to shake? W. F. Buckley, jr.
  Nat R 18:352 Ap 19 '66

JOHN Carroll university, Cleveland

When your real job is son; seminars for
  executives of family-run companies. il
  Bsns W p98+ O 15 '66

JOHN Cotton Dana publicity awards

Seven libraries share top honors in John Cotton Dana awards. Library J 91:3376-7 Jl
  '66

JOHN F. Kennedy airport. See New York (city)
  —Airports

**JOHN F. Kennedy Center for the performing
  arts, Washington, D.C.**

Capital cultural crusader. H. Brandon. Sat R
  49:7 Ag 27 '66

JOHN F. Kennedy library, Cambridge

Jacqueline Kennedy goes public. L. Bergquist.
  il Look 30:46+ Mr 22 '66

JOHN F. Kennedy space center. See United
  States—National aeronautics and space administration—John F. Kennedy space center

JOHN Fitzgerald Kennedy school of government. See Harvard university—John Fitzgerald Kennedy school of government

JOHN Hancock mutual life insurance company
Good-humored salesmen; mobile office. il Time 88:72+ Jl 1 '66

JOHN LaFarge institute
New commitments of religions in civil rights. il America 114:292-3 F 26 '66
Of many things. America 115:inside cover Ag 27 '66

JOHN Muir trail. See Trails

JOHN Simon Guggenheim foundation
Viewpoint; grants in photography. J. Deschin. Pop Phot 59:26+ Ag '66

JOHN Stands in Timber (Cheyenne Indian)
Last ghastly moments at the Little Bighorn; ed. with introd. by M. Liberty. Am Heritage 17:14-21+ Ap '66

JOHNNY on the spot; drama. See Fisher, A. and Rabe, O.

JOHNS, Jasper
Brooms and prisms. J. Ashbery. il Art N 65:58-9+ Mr '66

JOHNS, Robert. See Coplen, L. jt. auth.

JOHN'S bargain stores corporation
Friendly undertaker. R. Levy. il Duns R 88:69-70 N '66

JOHNS Hopkins press
Authors & editors; The Eisenhower papers. W. Gellhorn. Pub W 191:25 Ja 9 '67

JOHNS Hopkins university
Johns Hopkins' humanities center. Sch & Soc 94:343-5 O 29 '66
Libraries, lasagna, and leaning towers; Bologna center. J. A. Hoffberg. il Wilson Lib Bul 40:948-52 Je '66

JOHNSON, A. M.
Why we add asbestos. Am City 81:98-9 Mr '66

JOHNSON, A. R. and others
Strontium incorporation into dental enamel. bibliog Science 153:1396-7 S 16 '66

JOHNSON, Alexis
Issue and goal in Viet-Nam; address March 14, 1966. Dept State Bul 54:529-36 Ap 4 '66

JOHNSON, Andrew
One hundred years ago. R. L. Strout. New Repub 154:17-18 F 12 '66

JOHNSON, Arthur G. See Han, S. S. jt. auth.

JOHNSON, Betsey
We orbit around; interview by Mademoiselle's guest editors. por Mlle 63:349 Ag '66

about
[Mademoiselle Merit award winner] il por Mlle 64:51 Ja '67

JOHNSON, Body. See Johnson, J. W.

JOHNSON, C. R.
Fresh water from a brackish source. Am City 81:122-3 Ap '66

JOHNSON, Carol
Art (before a painting of Pisanello, Verona) poem. Commonweal 85:399 Ja 13 '67
Toward a poem unwritten on a journey south. Commonweal 84:200 My 6 '66

about
Strategies of reason reasoning. W. A. McBrien. Commonweal 84:476-7 Jl 22 '66

JOHNSON, Charlotte Buel
Gallery for young people. See issues of School arts

JOHNSON, Chester
Tortuous shore. Nation 202:561-3 My 9 '66

JOHNSON, Clarence Leonard
Variable sweep vs. the fixed Delta. C. Welles. por Life 61:79+ O 28 '66

JOHNSON, Claudia Alta (Taylor)
Conservation's big one-two; excerpts from address, February 23, 1966. por Am For 72:6-7+ Ap '66
Jackie Kennedy and Lady Bird Johnson; what they say about love, marriage and faith; excerpts from Common sense wisdom of three first ladies, ed. by B. Adler. por Good H 162:92-4 Je '66
Let's work together for a more beautiful America; adaptation of addresses, with text of letter to readers of Parents' magazine. por Parents Mag 41:22+ Jl '66
Mrs LBJ country; ed. by M. Simons. pors Look 30:35-41 Jl 12 '66
My first trip. il McCalls 93:80 Ap '66

about
America the more beautiful. il por Time 88:53 S 30 '66
British editor's size-up of President Johnson; excerpts from LBJ. M. Davie. il por U S News 61:46 Ag 29 '66

Home on the range; beautifying and sightseeing trip in Texas. Time 87:26-7 Ap 8 '66
In Asia, a reassuringly real First lady. S. Alexander. Life 61:22B N 4 '66
Lady Bird, says L.B.J, will beautify us out of existence. H. Sidey. il por Life 61:30B Jl 22 '66
Lady Bird's boat ride. S. Alexander. Life 60:34 Ap 15 '66
Let's travel; with Mrs LBJ to Big Bend. F. Koltun. il por Mlle 63:26+ Jl '66
Mrs Johnson talks about her love for the White House. R. F. Pomeroy. il por Redbook 127:72-8+ Jl '66
Natural beauty, the follow through. J. B. Craig. il pors Am For 71:12-15+ O '65
Place where people really live. S. Lanahan. House & Gard 130:202+ O '66
Quickening tick of the conservation clock. J. B. Craig. il pors Am For 72:10-13+ N '66

JOHNSON, Daniel
Quebec changes governments. C. Ryan. For Affairs 45:148-61 O '66
Quebec; separatism in a new guise. D. O'Leary. il Nation 203:6-8 Jl 4 '66

JOHNSON, Dorothy M.
Ten-pound box of candy; story. McCalls 93:92-3 Ap '66

JOHNSON, Electa
Yankee sails again. il pors Motor B 117:36-9 Mr '66

JOHNSON, Eric W.
Be grateful for grammar. Parents Mag 41:67-8+ Mr '66
What to do for the child who has no friends. Parents Mag 41:56-8+ Ag '66

JOHNSON, Evelyn P.
Selling to juvenile publications. Writer 79:30-1 F '66

JOHNSON, F. M.
Drosophila melanogaster; inheritance of a deficiency of alkaline phosphatase in larvae. Science 152:361-2 Ap 15 '66

JOHNSON, Frank H.
Bioluminescence. Science 153:1141-2 S 2 '66

JOHNSON, Frederick
Archeology in an emergency. Science 152:1592-7 Je 17 '66

JOHNSON, Fridolf
Amado Gonzalez; San Francisco artist. por Am Artist 30:56-61+ F '66
European sketches of Frank di Gioia. Am Artist 30:46-51+ Ap '66

JOHNSON, Gerald W.
Baltimore might make it. New Repub 154:17-18 Ap 9 '66
But Mahoney stood outside. New Repub 155:8 O 22 '66
Democratic borah. New Repub 155:25-6 D 3 '66
Javits comes to the aid of his party. New Repub 155:20-2 S 3 '66
Making the Constitution. New Repub 155:28 N 26 '66
Marshall's ordeal. New Repub 156:32 Ja 14 '67
Mormons. New Repub 156:40 Ja 7 '67
Which GOP is it to be? New Repub 154:27-9 Je 25 '66

JOHNSON, Hamp, family
Incurable Negro disease strikes five in family. il Ebony 21:154-6+ My '66

JOHNSON, Harold L.
Infrared stars. bibliog Sky & Tel 32:73-7 Ag '66

JOHNSON, Harry J.
Advice to businessmen on health and retirement; interview. por U S News 60:62-7 Mr 7 '66
That tired feeling, its cause and cure. Read Digest 88:142-4 Mr '66

JOHNSON, Howard Brennan
Daddy's boy. il pors Newsweek 68:70 Ag 8 '66

JOHNSON, Howard Wesley
M.I.T; new president will pursue broadened goals. L. J. Carter. il por Science 151:1511-15 Mr 25 '66

JOHNSON, Howard, company
Daddy's boy. il Newsweek 68:70 Ag 8 '66
Tinting supermarkets with orange and blue. il Bsns W p42-3+ Jl 2 '66

JOHNSON, Hugh
Cognac, the soul of wine. House & Gard 129:138+ F '66
Comforting wines for cold weather. House & Gard 131:136+ Ja '67
Germany's castle hotels. House & Gard 129:52-3+ My '66
Going places, finding things in the wine towns of Europe. House & Gard 130:56-8+ S '66

JOHNSON, Hugh—*Continued*
Hot weather wines for cold meals. House & Gard 129:148+ Je '66
Tour of California wineries. House & Gard 130:248+ O '66
Wine for holiday feasts. House & Gard 130:188+ D '66

JOHNSON, Irving
Saga of a ship, the Yankee. L. Marden. il pors Nat Geog Mag 129:262-9 F '66
Yankee sails again. il pors Motor B 117:36-9 Mr '66

JOHNSON, J. Stewart
Egyptian revival in the decorative arts. Antiques 90:489-94 O '66

JOHNSON, James B.
Discovery. P. Caulfield. il Mod Phot 30:74-5+ Mr '66

JOHNSON, James Douglas
Arkansas: the rage of the rednecks. T. Dearmore. il Reporter 35:24-8 O 20 '66
Different kind of Johnson. il por Time 88:22 Ag 19 '66
Other Johnson: an LBJ critic. il por U S News 61:12 Ag 22 '66

JOHNSON, James W.
Fight that won't stay dead. Sports Illus 25:64-70+ Jl 4 '66

JOHNSON, Jed
Happy marriage of love and politics. M. Miller. il pors Ladies Home J 83:94-5+ Mr '66

JOHNSON, John L. and Chilton, W. S.
Galactosamine glycan of chondrococcus columnaris. bibliog Science 152:1247-8 My 27 '66

JOHNSON, Keith R.
Volunteer programs. Atlan 217:69 F '66
Who should serve? Atlan 217:63-8 F '66

JOHNSON, Kelly. See Johnson, C. L.

JOHNSON, Lady Bird. See Johnson, C. A. T.

JOHNSON, Lee
Sexy sandwich. il U S Camera 29:62-5 O '66

JOHNSON, Lester
Combining man & the monument; show at Martha Jackson gallery, N.Y. il por Time 87:74 F 18 '66
Image as counterforce. H. Rosenberg. il Art N 64:48-9+ F '66

JOHNSON, Lila R.
College at your doorstep. Parents Mag 41:70-1+ S '66

JOHNSON, Luci Baines
Luci Johnson: I've been forced to grow up! ed. by J. Baer. pors Seventeen 25:166-7+ My '66
No one can be sure it will be marvy; interview, ed. by C. Morrissey. pors Life 61:79-80 Jl 15 '66

about
Abandoning abandon. Time 87:26 My 6 '66
Approaching wedding of Pat and the President's daughter. il pors Life 61:76-8 Jl 15 '66
Behind the scenes at the big wedding. por U S News 61:12-13 Ag 22 '66
Business watches Luci. il Bsns W p34-5 Ag 6 '66
Great American wedding. J. Neubauer; B. Brown; F. Ward. il pors Pop Phot 59:85-9+ D '66
Great society all wound up in a wedding. H. Sidey. il por Life 61:34B Ag 5 '66
It's wedding week at the White House. il por U S News 61:36-7 Ag 8 '66
Life with Luci. il por Newsweek 68:20-1 Ag 1 '66
Luci Johnson and Pat Nugent talk about life without father. M. Means. por Ladies Home J 83:73+ Ag '66
Luci Johnson's engagement. C. Sadler. il pors McCalls 93:104-5+ Mr '66
Luci's White House wedding. M. Simons and M. Kaytor. il pors Look 30:34-9 Ag 9 '66
Pat Nugent's parents tell; how to be a White House in-law. F. R. Schreiber. il Ladies Home J 83:110-12 Ag '66
Secrets, showers & soufflés. il por Time 88:21 Jl 8 '66
Something blue: shopping for trousseau. il por Time 87:36 Je 10 '66
Splendor of Luci's wedding. il pors Life 61:20-7 Ag 19 '66
Three-ring wedding. il por Time 88:19-23 Ag 5 '66
Unusual ceremony; wedding. il pors Time 88:9-11 Ag 12 '66
Wedding in Washington. il pors Newsweek 68:17-21 Ag 15 '66
When a president's daughter marries. il por U S News 61:10 Ag 1 '66

Who are the 400? wedding invitations. il por Newsweek 68:22-3 Jl 18 '66
Wonderful, terrible life of the President's daughters. il pors Newsweek 67:36-8+ My 23 '66

JOHNSON, Lynda Bird
A look back at college. por McCalls 94:68-9+ Ja '67

about
Charley, my boy? il por Time 88:37 O 7 '66
Hollywood house party. il por Newsweek 67:36 Mr 28 '66
New girl in town; visit to Hollywood. por Time 87:21 Mr 25 '66
Señorita L.B.J; visit to Spain. il por Time 88:18-19 Jl 1 '66
Something blue: shopping for Luci's trousseau. il Time 87:36 Je 10 '66
Step by step: Lynda Bird Johnson's Hollywood beauty treatment. V. Scott. pors Ladies Home J 83:62+ Jl '66
That Hamilton man. il Newsweek 67:27 Ap 4 '66
Wonderful, terrible life of the President's daughters. il pors Newsweek 67:36-8+ My 23 '66

JOHNSON, Lyndon Baines
Additional documentation on President Johnson's trip to Asia; addresses and remarks at various points on itinerary; October 17-30, 1966. Dept State Bul 55:812-34 N 28 '66
Advancement of peace; remarks, January 20, 1966. Dept State Bul 54:186-9 F 7 '66
After the big freeze, defrosting? summary of address. Newsweek 68:42+ O 17 '66
Alliance for progress: a new kind of revolution; address, August 17, 1966. Dept State Bul 55:330-4 S 5 '66; Excerpts. Cur Hist 51:307 N '66
Budget message; January 24, 1966; excerpts. Dept State Bul 54:247-9 F 14 '66
Building a better society, the main test in Viet-Nam; excerpt from address, February 16, 1966. Dept State Bul 54:363-4 Mr 7 '66
Camranh Bay; address, October 26, 1966. Vital Speeches 33:66-7 N 15 '66
Challenge of the Americas; address, April 15, 1966. Vital Speeches 32:418-20 My 1 '66; Same with title Address at dedication of Abraham Lincoln statue. Dept State Bul 54:727-31 My 9 '66
Civic meeting, Anchorage; signing fish protein concentrate act, excerpts from remarks, November 2, 1966. Dept State Bul 55:809 N 28 '66
Columbus day, 1966; remarks, with text of proclamation, September 22, 1966. Dept State Bul 55:602-4 O 17 '66
Continuing the search for areas of common understanding with eastern Europe; remarks, June 15, 1966. Dept State Bul 55:56-8 Jl 11 '66
Counterattack; answer to critics; excerpts from addresses. Newsweek 67:31 Je 27 '66
Crowds. por Parks & Rec 1:821-2 O '66
Economic report to Congress, January 27, 1966; excerpts. Mo Labor R 89:278-82 Mr '66; por U S News 60:88-93 F 7 '66
Enemy we face in Viet-Nam; excerpt from address, July 23, 1966. Dept State Bul 55:226-8 Ag 15 '66
Exchange of greetings; exchange of toasts; Prime Minister Gandhi's visit. Dept State Bul 54:598-9+ Ap 18 '66
Exchange of toasts with Chancellor Erhard, December 20, 1965. Dept State Bul 54:46-8 Ja 10 '66
Fifth anniversary of the Peace corps; remarks, March 1, 1966. Dept State Bul 54:441-3 Mr 21 '66
Florence agreement to govern scientific instrument imports; statement, November 10, 1966. Dept State Bul 55:895 D 12 '66
Food for freedom; message to Congress; February 10, 1966. Dept State Bul 54:336-41 F 28 '66
Food for peace act of 1966 signed into law; statement, November 12, 1966. Dept State Bul 55:866-7 D 5 '66
Foreign aid; message to the Congress; February 1, 1966. Dept State Bul 54:320-7 F 28 '66
Foreign assistance act of 1966 signed by President Johnson; statement, September 19, 1966. Dept State Bul 55:602 O 17 '66
Foreign assistance program; address, February 1, 1966. Cur Hist 50:358-9 Je '66
Foreign service: constructive tasks ahead; remarks, June 9, 1966. Dept State Bul 55:25-7 Jl 4 '66
Four essentials for peace in Asia; address, July 12, 1966. Dept State Bul 55:158-62 Ag 1 '66; Same with title United States Asian policy. Vital Speeches 32:610-13 Ag 1 '66

JOHNSON, Lyndon Baines—Continued

Four fundamental facts of our foreign policy; excerpt of address, September 5, 1966. Dept State Bul 55:453-4 S 26 '66

Freedom is an indivisible word; U.S. aims; statement. Time 87:26 Mr 4 '66

Guidelines for the guidelines. por Newsweek 68:79 Ag 22 '66

How LBJ would clean up the water and air; summary of message, February 23, 1966. U S News 60:14 Mr 7 '66; Excerpts. Am For 72:6-7+ Ap '66

International economic policies for 1966; excerpts from Economic report of the President. Dept State Bul 54:290-3 F 21 '66

International education and health; message to the Congress, February 2, 1966. Dept State Bul 54:328-35 F 28 '66; Same abr. with title Proposed international education act of 1966; excerpts. Sch & Soc 94:186-9 Ap 2 '66

International negotiations for arms control and disarmament; letter, February 15, 1966. Dept State Bul 54:410-11 Mr 14 '66

Interview; reprint from America illustrated, September, 1966. Dept State Bul 55:574-8 O 17 '66

Job for a new department: safer cars, fewer traffic jams, faster planes, better ships; summary of message. March 2, 1966. U S News 60:39-40 Mr 14 '66

LBJ tells Hanoi: agree to peace talks, or face more bombing; excerpts from addresses, June 30, 1966. pors U S News 61:20 Jl 11 '66

LBJ's dream of a Great society; excerpts from statements. pors U S News 61:33 D 19 '66

Making Europe whole: an unfinished task; address, October 7, 1966. Dept State Bul 55:622-5 O 24 '66

Meeting with Vice President, Los Angeles, February 8, 1966; remarks. Dept State Bul 54:307-9 F 28 '66

Memorial day, 1966; address, May 30, 1966. Dept State Bul 54:962-4 Je 20 '66

Message to Congress on food aid to India; March 30, 1966. Dept State Bul 54:605-7 Ap 18 '66

Mr Johnson's ten questions: U.S. policy in the Vietnam war. with answers. Newsweek 67:24 Mr 7 '66

Most urgent work of our times; epilog for the book. This America. Dept State Bul 55:715-16 N 7 '66

NSC reviews Viet-Nam problems; remarks, May 10, 1966. Dept State Bul 54:834 My 30 '66

Need for scholars; address, May 11, 1966. Vital Speeches 32:482-4 Je 1 '66; Excerpts. Dept State Bul 54:835-6 My 30 '66

New law a first step to protect Great seal of the United States; statement, November 12, 1966. Dept State Bul 55:924-5 D 19 '66

NATO: an instrument of peace; statement, April 4, 1966. Dept State Bul 54:650-1 Ap 25 '66

Our objective in Viet-Nam; address, August 20, 1966. Dept State Bul 55:368-71 S 12 '66

Our view of NATO: address. March 23 1966. Dept State Bul 54:554-6 Ap 11 '66; Same with title Stronger NATO. Vital Speeches 32:386-7 Ap 15 '66

Pacification and development programs in Viet-Nam; statement. June 16, 1966. Dept State Bul 55:55 Jl 11 '66

Peace, our most compelling task; remarks made at the lighting of the national Christmas tree, December 17, 1965. Dept State Bul 54:51-2 Ja 10 '66

Peking's threats; address, August 30, 1966. Vital Speeches 32:706-8 S 15 '66; Same with title True meaning of patriotism. Dept State Bul 55:424-7 S 19 '66

Philippine veterans benefits signed into law; statements, September 30 and October 11, 1966. Dept State Bul 55:684-6 O 31 '66

President announces resumption of bombing against military targets in North Viet-Nam; statement. January 31, 1966. Dept State Bul 54:222-3 F 14 '66

President answers congressional letter on Viet-Nam situation; text of letter, January 22, 1966. Dept State Bul 54:253-4 F 14 '66

President asks global attack on ignorance; statements. Sr Schol 88:sup 1-2 F 25 '66

President comments on internal developments in Viet-Nam; statement. May 21, 1966. Dept State Bul 54:888 Je 6 '66

President hails congressional support of food aid to India; statement, April 19, 1966. Dept State Bul 54:747-8 My 9 '66

President hails fifth anniversary of the Alliance for progress; statement, March 14, 1966. Dept State Bul 54:537-8 Ap 4 '66

President hails OECD progress; text of message, September 28, 1966. Dept State Bul 55:675 O 31 '66

President Johnson and Chancellor Erhard hold talks at Washington; joint communique. Dept State Bul 54:46-51 Ja 10 '66

President Johnson and General Westmoreland discuss the situation in Viet-Nam; statement, August 14, 1966. Dept State Bul 55:335-6 S 5 '66

President Johnson and King Faisal of Saudi Arabia exchange views on matters of common interest; exchange of greetings, exchange of toasts, June 21, 1966. Dept State Bul 55:38-9, 40 Jl 11 '66

President Johnson and Prime Minister Gandhi of India confer at Washington; exchange of greetings; exchange of toasts; with joint communique, March 29, 1966. Dept State Bul 54:598-605 Ap 18 '66

President Johnson begins his tour of Asia; statement upon departure and texts of statements and remarks on various occasions during portion of trip in Hawaii, New Zealand and Australia; October 17-20, 1966. Dept State Bul 55:698-711 N 7 '66

President Johnson confers with British Prime Minister; exchange of toasts, July 29, 1966. Dept State Bul 55:265-6 Ag 22 '66

President Johnson confers with the Prime Minister of Laos; statement at news conference, October 13, 1966. Dept State Bul 55:667-9 O 31 '66

President Johnson discusses forthcoming Asian trip; excerpts from opening statements at news conferences, October 6 and 13, 1966. Dept State Bul 55:664-7 O 31 '66

President Johnson hails U.N. accord on treaty governing exploration of outer space; statement, December 8, 1966. Dept State Bul 55:952 D 26 '66

President Johnson lights the Nation's Christmas tree; remarks, December 15, 1966. Dept State Bul 56:14 Ja 2 '67

President Johnson pays tribute to Peace corps volunteers; remarks, September 13, 1966. Dept State Bul 55:496-9 O 3 '66

President Johnson returns to the United States after seventeen day trip to the Asian-Pacific area; remarks at Anchorage, November 1, 2 and at Dulles airport, November 2, 1966. Dept State Bul 55:806-12 N 28 '66

President Johnson urges Senate to ratify ILO convention 122; statement, June 2, 1966. Dept State Bul 54:1026-7 Je 27 '66

President Johnson visits Mexico city; remarks upon his arrival, April 14, 1966; address at dedication of Abraham Lincoln statue, remarks to the staff of the U.S. embassy, with text of joint statement with President G. Diaz Ordaz. April 15, 1966. Dept State Bul 54:726-33 My 9 '66

President Johnson visits Mexico to inspect Amistad Dam; statement, November 29; remarks, December 3; with text of joint statement, December 3, 1966. Dept State Bul 56:12-13 Ja 2 '67

President Johnson's appraisal of the election; excerpts from news conference, November 10, 1966. por U S News 61:57 N 21 '66

President Johnson's trip to Asia; visits to Thailand and Korea; texts of addresses, remarks, and statements made October 28-November 2, 1966. Dept State Bul 55:766-77 N 21 '66

President Marcos of the Philippines visits the United States; exchange of greeting and toast, September 14, 1966. Dept State Bul 55:526, 528-9 O 10 '66

President marks Poland's national millennium; calls for wider East-West contracts; remarks, with text of proclamation, May 3, 1966. Dept State Bul 54:794-7 My 23 '66

President presents Medal of science awards; remarks, February 10, 1966. Science 151:804 F 18 '66

President reaffirms support for foreign aid program; remarks, August 3, 1966. Dept State Bul 55:276-7 Ag 22 '66

President reports to Congress on Communications satellite act; text of letter, March 3, 1966. Dept State Bul 54:503 Mr 28 '66

President Schick of Nicaragua visits Washington; texts of greetings exchanged, June 9, 1966. Dept State Bul 55:14-15 Jl 4 '66

President sends convention on investment disputes to Senate; letter, February 16, 1966. Dept State Bul 54:419-20 Mr 14 '66

President Senghor of Senegal visits the United States; exchange of greetings; with exchange of toasts; September 28, 1966. Dept State Bul 55:649-52 O 24 '66

JOHNSON, Lyndon Baines—*Continued*
President signs LSCA 1966 amendments; announces National library commission. excerpts from address. July 19, 1966. Library J 91:3666 Ag '66
President signs supplemental military authorization bill; remarks, March 15, 1966. Dept State Bul 54:578-9 Ap 11 '66
President tells mayors: slow down spending; remarks, October 15. 1966. U S News 61:14 O 31 '66
President transmits fourth annual report of Peace corps to Congress; March 14, 1966. Dept State Bul 54:634-5 Ap 18 '66
President urges action on funds for southeast Asia operations; text of letter, January 19, 1966. Dept State Bul 54:254-5 F 14 '66
President urges participation in Asian development bank; message. January 18. 1966. Dept State Bul 54:255-7 F 14 '66
President's message; international education. Sat R 49:55 Ag 20 '66
President's reply to Senator Fulbright; excerpts from address, May 10, 1966. por U S News 60:121 My 23 '66
Prime Minister of Guyana visits the United States; exchange of greetings and exchange of toasts, July 21, 1966. Dept State Bul 55: 229-30 Ag 15 '66
Remarks at Cape Kennedy, Fla, September 27, 1966. Dept State Bul 55:581-3 O 17 '66
Roosevelt legacy: facing the realities of our time; remarks, August 21, 1966. Dept State Bul 55:371-2 S 12 '66
Search for agreements in the cause of peace; address, August 26, 1966. Dept State Bul 55:410-13 S 19 '66
Seven nations declare unity at Manila conference; texts of the three documents issued at the close of conference. Dept State Bul 55:730-9 N 14 '66
State of the Union; address, January 12, 1966. Vital Speeches 32:226-30 F 1 '66; Excerpts. Dept State Bul 54:150-5 Ja 31 '66
Steps toward an honorable peace in South Viet-Nam; statement, June 18, 1966. Dept State Bul 55:42-4 Jl 11 '66
Talking at a distance; summary of statement on Asian policy. Newsweek 68:39+ Jl 25 '66
Two threats to peace: hunger and aggression; address, June 30, 1966. Dept State Bul 55:114-19 Jl 25 '66; Same with title Vietnam war. Vital Speeches 32:578-82 Jl 15 '66
U.S. accepts Beirut agreement; implements Florence agreement; statement, October 14, 1966. Dept State Bul 55:894 D 12 '66
United States and Africa: a unity of purpose; address, May 26, 1966. Dept State Bul 54:914-18 Je 13 '66
United States and Australia reaffirm common goals; exchange of greetings; exchange of toasts, June 29, 1966. Dept State Bul 55: 130-1, 133 Jl 25 '66
U.S. and Burma reaffirm bonds of friendship and cooperation; exchange of greetings, toast, September 8; with text of joint communique, September 9, 1966. Dept State Bul 55:483-6 O 3 '66
United States and Germany reaffirm community of interest; exchange of toast, September 26; with text of joint communique, September 27, 1966. Dept State Bul 55: 578-9, 583-5 O 17 '66
U.S. and Israel reaffirm ties of friendship; toast at state dinner, August 2, 1966. Dept State Bul 55:346 S 5 '66
U.S. and Mexico to cooperate in screw-worm eradication plan; statement, July 27, 1966. Dept State Bul 55:232 Ag 15 '66
United States and Poland: strengthening traditional bonds; address, October 16, 1966. Dept State Bul 55:712-15 N 7 '66
U.S. and Venezuela inaugurate undersea telephone cable; remarks, August 3, 1966. Dept State Bul 55:275 Ag 22 '66
United States calls for treaty on exploration of the moon; statement, May 7, 1966. Dept State Bul 54:900 Je 6 '66
U.S.-Canadian friendship symbolized by new park; statement, September 9, 1966. Dept State Bul 55:499 O 3 '66
United States foreign policy begins at home; address, August 26, 1966. Dept State Bul 55:406-10 S 19 '66
U.S. marks anniversary of Arms control act; statement, September 24, 1966. Dept State Bul 55:687 O 31 '66
U.S. Mexico to join in solving Rio Grande salinity problem; statement, with text of telegram to President G. Diaz Ordaz, September 19, 1966. Dept State Bul 55:686-7 O 31 '66

U.S. participation in the U.N. during 1964; text of message. Dept State Bul 54:504-6 Mr 28 '66
U.S. support for Central American common market reaffirmed; statement, June 3, 1966. Dept State Bul 54:1004-5 Je 27 '66
U.S. to cooperate in economic and social development in Asia; remarks, March 16, 1966. Dept State Bul 54:521-2 Ap 4 '66
U.S. withdrawal from Viet-Nam depends on halt of aggression; excerpt from remarks, September 5, 1966. Dept State Bul 55:455 S 26 '66
Vietnam; address, February 23, 1966. Vital Speeches 32:322-5 Mr 15 '66; Same with title Vietnam: the struggle to be free. Dept State Bul 54:390-6 Mr 14 '66; Excerpt. Cong Digest 45:105-6 Ap '66
War, taxes, Great society, Johnson's blueprint for '67; State-of-the-Union message, January 10, 1967. por U S News 62:104-10 Ja 23 '67
Water for peace; excerpt from remarks, September 3, 1966. Dept State Bul 55:456-7 S 26 '66
Welcoming of Vietnamese leaders, Honolulu; remarks, February 6, 1966. Dept State Bul 54:302-3 F 28 '66
Why LBJ visited Vietnam; excerpt from address, October 26, 1966. U S News 61:19 N 7 '66
World food and population crisis; DAC's fifth annual high-level meeting; message, July 21, 1966. Dept State Bul 55:209-10 Ag 8 '66
World meteorological day; statement, March 23, 1966. Dept State Bul 54:618-19 Ap 18 '66
Year of harvest: the 1966 manpower report; excerpt. March 8, 1966. Mo Labor R 89:11+ Mr '66
—and Park, C. H.
Visits to Thailand and Korea; text of joint statement, November 2, 1966. Dept State Bul 55:777-80 N 21 '66
—See Diaz Ordaz, G. jt. auth.

about

Achilles heel. K. Crawford. Newsweek 67:37 Je 20 '66
Action at last; anti-inflation program. il por Time 88:29-30 S 16 '66
Address on the State of the Union. America 116:78 Ja 21 '67
Affection gap; popularity. il por Time 88:21-2 S 23 '66
Appointment in Manila. por Newsweek 68:36 O 10 '66
As Congress starts new term; LBJ's wishes, his chances. il por U S News 60:32-3 Ja 31 '66
As LBJ asks more and more laws. il por U S News 60:25-6 Ap 4 '66
As the book appears; a close look at the facts; concerning The death of a President by W. Manchester. il por U S News 62:50-2 Ja 23 '67
As world problems mount for LBJ. il U S News 61:6+ S 12 '66
Asian doctrine: what it's all about. il por U S News 61:30-2 Ag 8 '66
Atlantic report (cont) Atlan 217:6 Mr; 6+ Ap; 26+ My '66
Atlantic report: self-imposed isolationism. D. Kiker. Atlan 218:6+ S '66
Atlantic report: Washington. D. Kiker. Atlan 218:4+ D '66
Awesome twosome. T. Wicker. il pors N Y Times Mag p8-9+ Ja 30 '66
Back at the office. Newsweek 68:21-2 Ag 15 '66
Back of the uproar about LBJ managing the news. il pors U S News 60:42-3 Ja 31 '66
Balance-sheet Barnum: budget-making. il por Newsweek 68:25-7 D 12 '66
Basic research: the political tides are shifting. D. S. Greenberg. Science 152:1724-6 Je 24 '66
Bit of limbo: keeping mum about plans. Time 89:15 Ja 6 '67
Bone weariness brought on by a driving boss and the sleep gap. H. Sidey. il Life 60:48 Je 10 '66
Bonfire of discontent; cities' problems, three-day trip through Northeast. il por Time 88: 9-10 Ag 26 '66
Born hero-worshiper who serves his hero. P. Anderson. il pors N Y Times Mag p28-9+ F 20 '66
Brief silence of loquacious Lyndon. H. Sidey. il pors Life 61:48 D 2 '66
British editor's size-up of President Johnson; excerpts from LBJ. M. Davie. il pors U S News 61:40-6 Ag 29 '66

JOHNSON, Lyndon Baines—about—*Continued*

Can LBJ reverse the polls? por U S News 60:33 Je 20 '66

Captive of consensus; popular approval at low ebb. il por Time 87:23-4 Je 24 '66

Cautious, candid & conciliatory; State of Union address. il Time 89:13-14 Ja 20 '67

Changing mood of Congress; how outlook is shifting. il por U S News 60:28-30 My 2 '66

Close look at election trends. il por U S News 61:37-40 O 17 '66

Closer ties for LBJ and Fulbright? il por U S News 60:15 Je 27 '66

Comradely combat; J. B. Connally & President Johnson. il por Time 87:25 Ap 15 '66

Consensus politics: end of an experiment. D. S. Broder. il por Atlan 218:60-5 O '66

Consensus that isn't. Nation 202:282 Mr 14 '66

Counting blessings; campaign trail. Time 88:20-1 S 9 '66

Credibility gap. K. Crawford. Newsweek 69:32 Ja 16 '67

Crisis in the cities: LBJ's plan of action. il U S News 60:55-7 F 7 '66

Cross-purposes and crossed fingers; rating plunges to new low. il Newsweek 67:25-6 My 30 '66

Decision of mind and experience, not of heart and hope. H. Sidey. il Life 61:28B Jl 8 '66

Did LBJ make John Kennedy president? with interview with J. N. Garner. il pors U S News 62:42-6+ Ja 16 '67

Doctor Lyndon B. Fell. S. Alsop. pors Sat Eve Post 239:16 Jl 30 '66

End in sight for LBJ's honeymoon with business? what business leaders say; symposium. il por U S News 61:32-5 Ag 22 '66

Every man for himself. Newsweek 68:21 Jl 25 '66

Everything but peace. Nation 202:197 F 21 '66

Exit Goldman, enter Roche: can LBJ and intellectuals be friends? B. Nelson. Science 153:1505-7 S 23 '66

Ezra's way; hitting the campaign trail with a bang. il por Time 88:29 O 21 '66

Face of the President 1966. S. Alsop. por Sat Eve Post 239:23-5 S 24 '65

Fooling the people. New Repub 155:5-7 Ag 13 '66

Foreign aid under Lyndon Johnson. A. Roseman. Cur Hist 50:335-41+ Je '66

Foreigner looks at LBJ; excerpts from LBJ: a foreign observer's viewpoint. M. Davie. Newsweek 67:22-3 Ap 25 '66

Fresh slant on polls; President at lowest popularity level. il Newsweek 67:33 Je 20 '66

From Fulbright: a sweeping attack on LBJ's Asian doctrine. U S News 61:12 Ag 1 '66

Games Johnson plays: deeper and deeper into the credibility gap. J. Deakin. New Repub 156:10-11 Ja 14 '67

Getting upstaged by the union wasn't in the scenario. H. Sidey. il por Life 61:32 Ag 12 '66

Good-neighbor policy. il Newsweek 67:30+ Mr 21 '66

Great American presidents; address, February 3, 1966. J. A. Farley. Vital Speeches 32:393-6 Ap 15 '66

Greatest drama; press conference. il Time 87:19-20 Ap 1 '66

Growing drama in U.S. politics: new front runner? il por U S News 61:15 Ag 29 '66

Growing rift of LBJ and Kennedys; behind the furor over a book; concerning The death of a President, by W. Manchester. il pors U S News 62:22-7 Ja 2 '67

Grumblings at the ranch; gubernatorial critics. il por Time 88:10 D 30 '66

Guns plus butter; State of the Union message. Sr Schol 88:17 F 4 '66

Hawaii conference. il Time 87:19-20 F 11 '66

He is what he is. il pors Newsweek 68:17-18 Ag 1 '66

He makes a truce with a man he came almost to hate, L.B.J.; R. Kennedy-L. B. Johnson relationship. H. Sidey. il pors Life 61:38-9 N 18 '66

He was Mr Equal, not Mr Big. H. Sidey. il por Life 61:36 N 4 '66

Heresy at Omaha. W. Lippmann. Newsweek 68:17 Jl 18 '66

Hitting the trail; LBJ's upstate New York, New England tour. il por Newsweek 68:14-15 Ag 29 '66

Hopeful President joins the debate. il por Newsweek 67:23 Mr 7 '66

How much of the way with LBJ? il pors Newsweek 68:25-8+ S 26 '66

How things are changing for LBJ. il pors U S News 60:40-3 Je 6 '66

How to fight the war in Vietnam: growing differences between Pentagon and the President. il por U S News 60:37 Ap 11 '66

I, we and they, according to L.B.J. Life 61:4 N 25 '66

If you wonder where government spending is headed. por U S News 60:51-2 F 14 '66

In a spirit of prayer: decision on Vietnam. M. Ascoli. Reporter 34:14 F 10 '66

In Johnson land; some marks of the President across his part of Texas. R. Dudman. New Repub 155:11-12 D 17 '66

Inflation: bugbear and battle cry; report and excerpts from addresses. il Newsweek 67:27-8 Ap 11 '66

Intuition's reward; visit to Mexico. il por Time 87:19-20 Ap 22 '66

Is dissent traitorous? concerning President Johnson's Chicago address, May 17, 1966. Christian Cent 83:703 Je 1 '66

Is war in Vietnam to blame for the decline in LBJ's popularity? il U S News 60:22 Ap 11 '66

Issues that will tip the '66 elections. C. B. Seib. il Nations Bsns 54:38-9+ Mr '66

It was no monolith. R. Moley. Newsweek 69:104 Ja 23 '67

Johnson and his Jewish critics; concerning criticism of Vietnamese policy. Nation 203:268-9 S 26 '66

Johnson and Kennedy; the two thousand days. T. A. Bailey. il pors N Y Times Mag p30-1+ N 6 '66; Discussion, p22 D 4 '66

Johnson and Marcos. M. Meadows. New Repub 155:12 S 17 '66

Johnson and Moyers. New Repub 155:4 D 24 '66

Johnson & the intellectuals. H. Fairlie; discussion. Commentary 41:4+ Ja; 6+ F '66

Johnson and the press. F. Cormier. il por Sat R 49:70-2 S 10 '66

Johnson the genius. S. Alsop. il por Sat Eve Post 239:18 Ja 29 '66

Johnson touch. Nation 203:531-2 N 21 '66

Johnson trade policy; excerpts from address. W. M. Roth. bibliog f Dept State Bul 54:856-9 My 30 '66

Johnson's cure for government deficits. il U S News 61:78-80 D 26 '66

Kennedy hurricane. S. Alsop. Sat Eve Post 239:14 Ag 27 '66

Letter from Washington (cont) R. H. Rovere. New Yorker 42:197-203 O 8 '66

Letter from Washington; concerning State of the Union message. R. H. Rovere. New Yorker 41:88+ Ja 22 '66

Literary style of L.B.J. C. Ricks. Esquire 66:117+ N '66

A look at the inner workings of the White House; interview. B. D. Moyers. il pors U S News 60:78-85 Je 13 '66

Looking at Lyndon. R. I. Rubin. Christian Cent 83:1276-7 O 19 '66

Loss column; midterm upset election. K. Crawford. Newsweek 68:49 N 21 '66

Lying low; impending State of the Union address. por Time 89:12 Ja 13 '67

Lyndon B. Johnson. Constella. il por Sat Eve Post 239:27 Mr 26 '66

LBJ. N. Freeman. Nat R 18:1330-2 D 27 '66

LBJ and Congress; a new ball game. U S News 61:34 N 28 '66

LBJ and Congress: why the magic is gone. il pors U S News 60:53-5 Mr 21 '66

LBJ and the Democrats. M. Greenfield. il Reporter 34:8-13 Je 2 '66

LBJ and the elections: trouble ahead. L. H. Bean and R. Drummond. Look 30:89-90 O 4 '66

Lyndon B. Johnson and the world, by P. L. Geyelin. Review
New Repub 155:29-30 Jl 16 '66. M. W. Childs
Sat R 49:33-4 Je 18 '66. J. H. Plumb
Time 88:90+ Jl 22 '66

LBJ at Princeton: some words about intellectuals and government. D. S. Greenberg. il por Science 152:1223-5 My 27 '66

LBJ broods about his image. M. McGrory. America 115:410 O 8 '66

Lyndon B. Johnson, by R. Evans and R. Novak. Review
New Repub 155:35-7 N 12 '66. L. L. King
Newsweek il 68:110B+ O 17 '66. S. Maloff

LBJ: he's turned the other cheek. J. Neubauer. il Pop Phot 60:118-19+ Ja '67

LBJ: in a dilemma, and no consensus. por U S News 60:19 F 14 '66

LBJ in action: what those nonpolitical trips are like. il pors U S News 61:38-9 S 12 '66

LBJ in Hawaii: a look and a promise. il pors Newsweek 67:24-7 F 21 '66

L.B.J. isn't really the master politician everybody thinks he is. H. Sidey. il Life 61:30B Jl 15 '66

LBJ, near great. W. V. Shannon. Commonweal 85:361-2 Ja 6 '67

JOHNSON, Lyndon Baines—about—*Continued*
Unlike old soldiers, labels never fade away.
P. Lisagor. il Nations Bsns 54:21-2 S '66
Waiting for Lyndon. por Bsns W p29-30 Ja
7 '67
War in Washington: the temper of the
capital. M. Greenfield. il por Reporter 34:
29+ Mr 10 '66
What party leaders think of Bobby Kennedy's
future. il por U S News 61:54-6 S 26 '66
When friends fall out. P. Lisagor. Nations
Bsns 54:23-4 Je '66
When LBJ just can't say no. il por News-
week 67:19 My 2 '66
When LBJ went on tour out West. U S News
61:6 S 5 '66
Where U.S. is winning in the world. il por
U S News 61:48-51 Jl 11 '66
Who could ask for anything more? P. Lisagor.
il por Nations Bsns 54:23-4 N '66
Who'll be helped, hurt by LBJ plans: con-
cerning State-of-the-Union message. il por
U S News 62:27-30 Ja 23 '67
Who's nervous? Nation 202:666 Je 6 '66
Why Democrats are losing ground. il pors
U S News 61:37-9 Jl 18 '66
Why LBJ can't pull victory rabbit from
Viet Nam hat. P. Lisagor. il Nations Bsns
54:23-4 O '66
Wilson's mission: a test of U.S.-British part-
nership. il U S News 61:33-4 Ag 1 '66
Winding line of LBJ. Nat R 18:250-2 Mr 22
'66
Wiretap war: Kennedy, Johnson and the
FBI. R. M. Cipes. New Repub 155:16-22
D 24 '66
With a hep-ful exegesis; President John-
son's pronunciation. J. P. Degnan. Esquire
66:243+ D '66
Woman who swore in President Johnson re-
calls what happened aboard Air force one,
2:38 p.m. Dallas, November 22, 1963; ed. by
M. Drury. S. T. Hughes. il por McCalls 94:
66+ N '66
World and L.B.J: President's style in foreign
policy. D. M. Cregier. por Christian Cent
83:859-61 Jl 6 '66
Yet another debate. K. Crawford. Newsweek
67:32 F 28 '66
You gettin' that deer? Newsweek 67:97 Ap 18
'66

Anecdotes, facetiae, satire, etc.
Joy to the world and especially to Pickens,
S.C. C. Trillin. il por Esquire 66:242-3
D '66

Health
Different kind of cuttin'. il por Time 88:22-3
D 2 '66
LBJ: back with a surprise; preparation for
surgery. por Newsweek 68:27-8 N 14 '66
LBJ: new operation. Sr Schol 89:26 N 18 '66
Minor surgery, Johnson style. il pors News-
week 68:27-8 N 28 '66
New surgery for the President, facts about
LBJ's health; with statement by G. Burkley.
il pors U S News 61:48-9 N 14 '66
Operational withdrawal; cancellation of cam-
paign plans. il Time 88:27 N 11 '66
Patient on the move. Time 88:28 D 9 '66
Polyp, hernia like LBJ's not rare. Sci N
90:393 N 12 '66
President's surgery no small matter. F. Mar-
ley. Sci N 90:443 N 26 '66
President's surgery; summary of postopera-
tive statements by physicians. il por U S
News 61:28 N 28 '66
Recuperating in Texas, the LBJ way. il pors
U S News 61:14 D 5 '66
Rest for LBJ. after a schedule that left oth-
ers tottering. U S News 61:28 N 14 '66
Rupture & a polyp. il Time 88:66 N 11 '66
Surgery: a diagnosis. por Newsweek 68:28-9
N 14 '66
With a good cough; operations to remove a
polyp from throat and repair an abdominal
hernia. il pors Time 88:30-2 N 25 '66

Relations with Congress
See Presidents—United States—Relations
with Congress

Statues, portraits, etc.
Another image problem; Hurd portrait.
Newsweek 69:22 Ja 16 '67
Critic's choice; Hurd portrait. Time 89:12-13
Ja 13 '67
LBJ on canvas. il por Newsweek 67:19 F 7
'66
Story of a portrait which LBJ turned down.
U S News 62:12 Ja 16 '67
Ugliest thing L.B.J. ever saw; Peter Hurd
painting. Life 62:34-34A Ja 20 '67

Visit to the Far East, 1966
Additional documentation on President John-
son's trip to Asia; addresses and remarks
at various points on itinerary; October 17-
30, 1966; with chronological list of material
on trip as published in the Bulletin. L. B.
Johnson. Dept State Bul 55:812-35 N 28 '66
Big fellow is a part of their future. H. Sidey.
il por Life 61:54 N 11 '66
End of a journey. Nat R 18:1144 N 15 '66
End of the odyssey; last leg of journey. il
por Time 88:28-9 N 11 '66
Glad to be back. il pors Newsweek 68:26-30
O 31 '66
Grand finale deep in the heart of Asia. il
Life 61:44-5 N 11 '66
Great road show. Nation 203:466 N 7 '66
I'd know him anywhere. S. Alexander. Life
61:36 N 25 '66
In Asia, a reassuringly real First lady. S.
Alexander. Life 61:22B N 4 '66
Johnson visit. N. Brennan. Commonweal 85:
215-16 N 25 '66; Reply. R. A. De Gregorio.
85:391+ Ja 13 '67
LBJ comes home. il pors Sr Schol 89:24-5 N
18 '66
LBJ goes away. Commonweal 85:95 O 28 '66
LBJ hits the trail to the Pacific. il pors
Newsweek 68:27-9 O 24 '66
LBJ meets allies at Manila; with press com-
ments. il pors Sr Schol 89:16-18 N 11 '66
LBJ moves out for peace; Asian trip plans.
il por Bsns W p37-9 O 15 '66
LBJ to meet allies in Manila. il Sr Schol 89:
18 O 14 '66
LBJ's Far-East goal: a united Asia. il U S
News 61:6 O 17 '66
LBJ's travels; peace, politics. il por News-
week 68:27-8 O 17 '66
Manila summit. H. Sutton. Sat R 49:14+
N 12 '66
Measure of a mission. il pors Newsweek 68:
29-30 N 14 '66
Mission for humanity. D. Lawrence. U S
News 61:144 N 14 '66
On top Down Under. il pors Time 88:25-7 O
28 '66
Pacific mission. il Time 88:32-3 O 14 '66
President and the lures of lava-lava land. il
por Life 61:40B-40C O 28 '66
President Johnson begins his tour of Asia;
statement upon departure and texts of
statements and remarks on various oc-
casions during portion of trip in Hawaii,
New Zealand and Australia; October 17-20,
1966. L. B. Johnson. Dept State Bul 55:
698-711 N 7 '66
President Johnson discusses forthcoming
Asian trip; excerpts from opening state-
ments at news conferences, October 6 and
13, 1966. L. B. Johnson. Dept State Bul
55:664-7 O 31 '66
President Johnson returns to the United
States after seventeen day trip to the
Asian-Pacific area; remarks at Anchorage,
November 1, 2 and at Dulles airport,
November 2, 1966. L. B. Johnson. Dept
State Bul 55:806-12 N 28 '66
President Johnson's trip to Asia; remarks
at Cam Ranh Bay, October 26, and report
to the Nation, October 27, 1966. L. B. John-
son. Dept State Bul 55:735-9 N 14 '66
President Johnson's trip to Asia; visits to
Thailand and Korea; texts of addresses,
remarks, and statements made October 28-
November 2, 1966. L. B. Johnson. Dept State
Bul 55:766-77 N 21 '66
Protecting the flank. il pors Time 88:25-30 N
4 '66
Rest for LBJ. after a schedule that left oth-
ers tottering. U S News 61:28 N 14 '66
Togetherness in the Pacific. il pors News-
week 68:27-9 N 7 '66
United States and the new Asia; address,
November 16, 1966. W. W. Rostow. Dept
State Bul 55:910-14 D 19 '66
Visit of heart, a mission of purpose; with
accounts by S. Alexander, D. Moser and
R. B. Stolley. il pors Life 61:24-35 N 4 '66
Visit to Cam Ranh Bay. il pors Newsweek
68:24-7 N 7 '66
Westward ho! Nat R 18:1083+ N 1 '66
What LBJ is offering the Asians. il por U S
News 61:33-4 O 31 '66
What LBJ will find in Asia; Allies say; win
the war il por U S News 61:37-40 O 24 '66
What was decided in Manila; new plan for
peace. il pors U S News 61:33-4 N 7 '66
When paint spattered LBJ's car; Melbourne,
Australia. il U S News 61:10 O 31 '66
When President Johnson went to the war
front; with excerpt from address. il pors
U S News 61:19-20 N 7 '66

JOHNSON, Lyndon Baines, family
Family next door in the big White House. R. Sherrill. il N Y Times Mag p6-7+ Jl 31 '66
Growing: TV empire of the LBJ family. U S News 60:10 F 7 '66
Luci Johnson: I've been forced to grow up! ed. by J. Baer. L. B. Johnson. il Seventeen 25:166-7+ My '66
Lyndon's set. Nation 202:637 My 30 '66
Wonderful, terrible life of the President's daughters. il Newsweek 67:36-8+ My 23 '66
JOHNSON, Lyndon Baines, library (proposed)
See Texas. University, Austin—Libraries
JOHNSON, M. Glen
Aid success in west Europe. bibliog f Cur Hist 51:1-6+ Jl '66
JOHNSON, Mel
Backyard record deer; ed. by H. Kenny. Field & S 71:50-1+ Jl '66
JOHNSON, Napoleon Bonaparte
All the justice money can buy. B. Bailey. New Repub 154:8-9 Je 11 '66
JOHNSON, Nora
My life as a nearsighted fish. Sports Illus 26:42-6 Ja 9 '67
JOHNSON, P. L. See Likens, G. E. jt. auth.
JOHNSON, Pamela Hansford
In ghastly transcripts, a test of our times. Life 61:62+ Ag 12 '66
Letter from abroad. McCalls 94:28+ D '66
Speaking out. por Sat Eve Post 240:8+ Ja 14 '67
JOHNSON, Patty
Are we a nation of hoods? Read Digest 89: 127-9 D '66
JOHNSON, Paul Burney, 1916?-
Bourbon borealis. Time 87:24 F 11 '66
JOHNSON, Pearl Patterson
Morning fog; poem. Farm J 90:109 F '66
JOHNSON, Philip Cortelyou
Philip Johnson explains his remarkable underground museum. il por Vogue 147:200-1 My '66
We shall not be thanked by posterity. por Fortune 74:68 Jl 1 '66
JOHNSON, Pyke, Jr
Rosengren's, a San Antonio institution for more than thirty years. Pub W 189:78-81 My 30 '66
Western Americana, juveniles, stressed in Montana bookshop. Pub W 189:66-7 Mr 14 '66
JOHNSON, Quintin
High-pressure polymorphism in sodium chloride: a reinvestigation. bibliog Science 153: 419 Jl 22 '66
JOHNSON, Randy
Randy passes a test in his new home. D. Jenkins. il Sports Illus 25:54-6 Jl 18 '66
JOHNSON, Rebekah (Baines)
Reminder of Rebekah Baines; novel, Hannah Jackson. H. Sidey. il por Life 61:42 D 16 '66
JOHNSON, Rex
Memories of the woods; poem. Am For 72:35 O '66
JOHNSON, Richard Mentor
Undistinguished and unique. il Sr Schol 88:5 F 4 '66
JOHNSON, Robert I.
Want a planetarium? bibliog por Parks & Rec 1:831-3+ O '66
JOHNSON, Robert Livingston
Obituary
Pub W 189:76-7 Ja 31 '66
JOHNSON, Robert R.
Never too late! Motor B 118:34-5+ S '66
JOHNSON, Robert S.
Americans view the war: to get the truth, I just don't know. Nation 203:502-5 N 14 '66
JOHNSON, Robin
Audience; poem. Sat R 49:51 Mr 26 '66
Bus driver; poem. Reporter 35:56 D 1 '66
JOHNSON, Ronald
Letters to Walt Whitman; poem. Poetry 108: 152-61 Je '66
JOHNSON, Samuel
Boswell without Johnson? G. Wills. Nat R 18:790-1 Ag 9 '66
JOHNSON, Samuel Curtis
Businessmen in the news. il por Fortune 74: 51 N '66
JOHNSON, Sydney
Happy marriage of love and politics. M. Miller. il pors Ladies Home J 83:94-5+ Mr '66
JOHNSON, U. Alexis
Free Asia; address, October 4. 1966. Dept State Bul 55:638-43 O 24 '66; Excerpts. por U S News 61:98-100+ O 17 '66
Seminar on communication satellite earth-station technology; statement. May 16, 1966. Dept State Bul 54:949-52 Je 13 '66

about
Dialogue restored. il Time 88:23 Ag 5 '66
U.S. envoy to Tokyo: State department's old pro. por U S News 61:16 Ag 8 '66
JOHNSON, Virginia
Two sex researchers on the firing line; interview. ed. by W. Bradbury. pors Life 60: 43-4+ Je 24 '66
—See Masters, W. H. jt. auth.

about
Margaret Mead answers questions about: concerning study on the physiology of sex. M. Mead. Redbook 127:36+ O '66
Problems of sex. il por Time 87:51 Ap 29 '66
Sex under scrutiny. il Newsweek 67:80 Ap 25 '66
Should this sex research be allowed to go on? L. R. Chevalier. Ladies Home J 83: 26+ My '66
JOHNSON, Walter
President's public relations. Sat R 49:43 Ap 16 '66
JOHNSON-MARSHALL, Percy
Shapes of the new Southwest. Arch Forum 125:60-7 Jl '66
JOHNSON CITY, Tex.
Journey to Johnson City. S. Young. il Holiday 39:70-5 My '66
LBJ country: from poverty to riches. il U S News 60:52-5 My 2 '66
JOHNSTON, D. Gordon. See Ridgway, S. H. jt. auth.
JOHNSTON, Frances B.
Innocent eye; show at Museum of modern art. New York. H. Cohen. il Reporter 34:45-8 Mr 10 '66
JOHNSTON, J. Richard
University government and the teach-ins. Bul Atomic Sci 22:30-1 F '66
JOHNSTON, Marjorie
Library title; progress report. por Library J 91:1017-19 F 15 '66
JOHNSTON, Paul F.
Regional approaches to educational problems. NEA J 55:27-8+ Ap '66
JOHNSTON, W. T.
Useful reference books. Consumer Bul 49:2+ Je '66
JOHNSTONE, Kathleen Yerger
Collecting seashells. Holiday 40:99-104 Jl '66
JOHNSTONE, Margaret Blair
How to live with a woman; reprint. Read Digest 88:75-7 F '66
JOHNSTONE, Ronald L.
Parochial pedagogy. Christian Cent 84:48 Ja 11 '67
JOHNSTONE, William C.
U.S. policy in southeast Asia: what's ahead? Cur Hist 50:106-11+ F '66
JOHNSTOWN flood, 1889
Run for your lives! D. G. McCullough. il Am Heritage 17:4-11+ Je '66
JOINING up; story. See Beal, M. F.
JOINT adventures
Architect in practice; joint-venture practice. il Arch Rec 139:99+ My '66
FTC hits at joint ventures; Phillips-National distillers agree to dissolve joint efforts in petrochemicals. Bsns W p33 Ag 13 '66
Hercules, Thiokol unique in Poseidon team; rocket motor. J. F. Judge. il Tech W 19:23-4 S 5 '66
Joint-venture troubles; Japan. Fortune 73: 74+ F '66
JOINT chiefs of staff. See United States—Joint chiefs of staff
JOINT committee on internal revenue taxation. See United States—Congress—Joint committee on internal revenue taxation
JOINT economic committee. See United States —Congress—Joint economic committee
JOINT tenancy
Estate planning for farmers; whose name should be on the titles? N. E. Harl and B. Brantley. Suc Farm 64:33+ Je '66
JOINT undertakings. See Joint adventures
JOINT United States-Canadian committee on trade and economic affairs
U.S.-Canada economic committee concludes tenth meeting; text of communique. Dept State Bul 54:464-6 Mr 21 '66
JOINT United States-Japan committee on scientific cooperation
Cancer research: U.S.-Japan cooperative science program; report on symposium. Y. Nishizuka and others. Science 152:1524-6 Je 10 '66
United States-Japan committee on scientific cooperation: neurochemistry conference; report on conference on the function and metabolism of the nervous system. Y. Tsukada and A. Lajtha. Science 152:801-3 My 6 '66

JOINT United States-Japan committee on scientific cooperation—*Continued*
U.S.-Japan scientific committee holds sixth annual meeting; Department of state announcement, October 7; with messages from President Johnson and Prime Minister Sato, opening remarks by Secretary Rusk, and text of joint communique, October 13, 1966. Dept State Bul 55:681-4 O 31 '66
JOINT United States-Japan committee on trade and economic affairs
Secretary Rusk meets with Asian leaders; statement before U.S-Japan committee on trade and economic affairs, July 5; with text of Joint U.S.-Japan communique, July 7, 1966. D. Rusk. Dept State Bul 55:177-80 Ag 1 '66
U.S.-Japan trade committee to meet at Kyoto July 5-7. Dept State Bul 54:1027 Je 27 '66
JOINT ventures. See Joint adventures
JOINTS

Diseases
See also
Arthritis
JOINTS (engineering)
Bad ball-joints can bury you! M. J. Schultz. il Pop Mech 125:179-83+ F '66
JOINVILLE, François Ferdinand Philippe Louis Marie d'Orléans, prince de
Princely service; excerpts from Civil war album of paintings by the Prince de Joinville. A. Maurois. il por Am Heritage 17:52-63+ Ap '66
JOKES, Russian. See Humor, Russian
JOLLY, Alison
Lemur social behavior and primate intelligence. bibliog Science 153:501-6 Jl 29 '66
JOMON pottery. See Pottery, Japanese
JONAH; drama. See Goodman, P.
JONAS, Gerald
Discontinuity; poem. New Repub 155:21 O 8 '66
In the land of plenty; poem. New Repub 154:24 My 14 '66
Lines for a private celebration; poem. Atlan 218:66 N '66
Marching blues; poem. New Repub 155:19 O 1 '66
Portrait of the poet; poem. Sat R 49:55 D 10 '66
Prince; story. Commentary 42:55-68 O '66
Private truce; poem. New Yorker 42:63 Jl 30 '66
JONAS, Louis Paul
World of Louis Paul Jonas. Z. J. Merritt. il por Am Artist 31:54-60 Ja '67
JONATHAN, Will
Doer's model. Sat R 49:57 S 3 '66
JONES, Alan Pryce-. See Pryce-Jones, A.
JONES, Alexander
Curt, clear, complete. por Time 88:53-4 N 4 '66
JONES, Alfred Winslow
Funds that use short-sale tactics. por Bsns W p 108+ Ap 2 '66
Jones nobody keeps up with. C. J. Loomis. il por Fortune 73:237+ Ap '66
JONES, Antony Charles Robert Armstrong-, 1st earl of Snowdon. See Snowdon, A. C. R. A.-J.
JONES, Arthur Gwynne, baron Chalfont. See Chalfont, A. G. J.
JONES, Bobby
Golf (cont) C. Price. Esquire 66:44+ S '66
JONES, C. Garrett-. See Garrett-Jones, C.
JONES, Carter
Girl's the thing. il U S Camera 29:44-5 Je '66
Good skates. il U S Camera 29:42-3 Je '66
JONES, Charles F.
High tide for business; address, December 2, 1965. Vital Speeches 32:210-12 Ja 15 '66
JONES, Charles M. See Chambliss, O. L. jt. auth.
JONES, Clarence T.
Spot billiards for the cerebral palsied. por Parks & Rec 1:159 F '66
JONES, Clint
Spartan swifty. H. L. Masin. por Sr Schol 89:21 N 11 '66
JONES, Curtis H.
Applied math for the production manager. Harvard Bsns R 44:20-2+ bibliog(p 182) S '66
JONES, David Pryce-. See Pryce-Jones, D.
JONES, Ernest A.
Man with the split-level head; address, February 21, 1966. Vital Speeches 32:359-63 Ap 1 '66
JONES, Franklin
Paintings of Franklin Jones. F. Whitaker. il por Am Artist 30:24-9+ D '66

JONES, Gwyneth
Lady from Wales; interview, ed. by T. Urquhart. por Opera N 31:19 N 19 '66
about
Music to my ears. I. Kolodin. Sat R 49:30 D 24 '66
JONES, Harry
Dream as big as a mountain. Sat Eve Post 239:30-1 S 10 '66
JONES, Harry (football player)
Save the bones for Harry Jones! H. L. Masin. por Sr Schol 89:32 N 18 '66
JONES, Howard Mumford
Politics, Mr O'Connor, and the family novel. Atlan 218:117-18+ O '66
JONES, Jack E.
Letter to Commentary. Nat R 18:983-8, 1078+ O 4, N 1 '66
JONES, Jesse Holman
Houston's shackled press. B. H. Bagdikian. Atlan 218:87-8+ Ag '66
JONES, Jim
Dixie city in Brazil. il pors Ebony 22:89-90+ N '66
JONES, John Paul
I have not yet begun to fight. por Sr Schol 89:5 S 23 '66
JONES, John W.
Visually handicapped child; address, March 15, 1966. Wilson Lib Bul 40:824-8 My '66
JONES, Judith McKnight
Dixie city in Brazil. il pors Ebony 22:89-90+ N '66
JONES, Kirby
Peace corps volunteer in the field: community development. Ann Am Acad 365:63-71 My '66
JONES, Kit
Key. Criticism
Nation 203:718 D 26 '66
JONES, L. H. P. and others
Tabashir: an opal of plant origin. bibliog Science 151:464-6 Ja 28 '66
JONES, Landon Y.
Open letter to Princeton Charlie. Horizon 9:67 Wint '67
JONES, LeRoi
Blues for Mr Jones. J. Richardson. por Esquire 65:106-8+ Je '66
Jones boy. por Newsweek 67:105A+ My 2 '66
Opinion: on Negro aims. J. Meyer. Mlle 62:84+ Ap '66
JONES, Paul
This little car went to high school. PTA Mag 61:4-6 bibliog(p36) Ja '67
JONES, Phil B.
What's new. Suc Farm 64:58 Jl; 30 Ag '66
—See Maddex, R. L. jt. auth.
JONES, Richard T. and others
Hemoglobin Freiburg: abnormal hemoglobin due to deletion of a single amino acid residue. bibliog Science 154:1024-7 N 25 '66
Hemoglobin Sphakiá: a delta-chain variant of hemoglobin A₂ from Crete. bibliog Science 151:1406-8 Mr 18 '66
JONES, Robert R.
You need a will. Parents Mag 41:48-50+ Ap '66
JONES, Rodney W.
Cymbidiums fit into every home. il Horticulture 44:22-3 N '66
JONES, Rudolph
Are all men equal? address, November 30, 1965. Vital Speeches 32:271-2 F 15 '66
JONES, Stacy V.
Inventor of the month. See issues of Science digest
JONES, Virginia Lacy
Savannah state college award to Virginia L. Jones & Lj editor. Library J 91:2300 My 1 '66
JONES, William A. and others
Sex attractant of the pink bollworm moth: isolation, identification, and synthesis. bibliog Science 152:1516-17 Je 10 '66
JONES and Laughlin steel corporation
Small town prepares for a big change: Hennepin and five other villages of Putnam County, Ill. prepare a comprehensive plan. il Fortune 74:187+ N '66
JONSON, Ben
Alchemist. Criticism
America 115:668 N 19 '66
Nation 203:460 O 31 '66
New Repub 155:32-3 O 29 '66
New Yorker 42:83 O 22 '66
Newsweek 68:108 O 24 '66
Sat R 49:49 O 29 '66
Time il 85:85 O 21 '66
Vogue 148:161 D '66
Works of Ben Jonson. K. Rexroth. Sat R 49:25 D 17 '66

JONSON, Jim
Emotion in motion; paintings. Sports Illus 24:48-55 My 23 '66
JORDAN, Alexander T.
New for amputees: instant limbs. Todays Health 44:37-9+ D '66; Same abr. with title They walk again, at once. Read Digest 89:61-4 D '66
JORDAN, Barbara C.
Quiet change. il por Time 87:31-2 My 20 '66
JORDAN, Donald L.
American industry; address, February 24, 1966. Vital Speeches 32:381-4 Ap 1 '66
JORDAN, Eileen Herbert
Bed Elizabeth Taylor once slept in; story. Redbook 127:50-1 My '66
JORDAN, F. G. Jr
How to get the most out of a city's street system. por Am City 81:77-9+ N '66
JORDAN
See also
Airplanes, Military—Jordan
Bethlehem
Dead Sea
Jerusalem
Shopping and shoppers—Jordan
United Nations—Jordan

Antiquities
Ancient Hebron, the city of David. P. C. Hammond. il Natur Hist 75:42-9 My '66

Defenses
Jordan's purchase of F-104 adds to jumble of Arab arms buildup. L. L. Doty. Aviation W 84:34 Ap 11 '66

Foreign relations
Everybody loses. Newsweek 68:42+ D 5 '66
Sequel to Samu. Time 88:38+ D 2 '66

Politics and government
Flare-up in Mideast: another danger spot. J. Law. il U S News 61:50 D 19 '66
Gamble on the Jordan. J. A. Morris, jr. il Nation 204:6-8 Ja 2 '67
Israeli army retaliates; raid against Jordanian village of Es Samu. il Sr Schol 89:24 D 9 '66
King on the spot. il Time 88:30+ Jl 8 '66
Ready for trouble. il Time 88:44 D 9 '66
JORDAN VALLEY
Abraham, the friend of God. K. MacLeish. il Nat Geog Mag 130:739-89 D '66
JORGENSEN, Kathryn
New approach to teaching social studies. Sr Schol 89:sup9 N 4 '66
JOSEPH, Elliot
More secret thoughts of a happy husband. McCalls 93:125 Ag '66
JOSEPH, James
Can electronics pick your mate? Pop Electr 24:70-3+ Mr '66
Deadly loopholes in driver licensing. Motor T 19:48-50 Ja '67
How you can survive a high-speed blowout! Motor T 18:46-8+ D '66
JOSEPH, Lou
Now, they're saving dead teeth. Todays Health 44:14-16 O '66
JOSEPH, Richard
Europe for the 2-S set. Esquire 66:148-9 S '66
Montreal: super city. Esquire 65:140+ My '66
Ten enchanted evenings. Esquire 66:96-105 Ag '66
To live in Madrid. Esquire 66:90-1+ Jl '66
Travel notes. See issues of Esquire
(ed) See Collins, L. Traveler, consider my Florida
(ed) See Goldwater, B. M. Traveler, consider my Arizona
JOSEPH H. Hirshhorn collection. See Art—Private collections
JOSEPH Hirshhorn museum, Washington, D.C. See Washington, D.C.—Galleries and museums
JOSEPH P. Kennedy Jr. foundation
Food & the mind; awards. Time 87:52+ Ap 22 '66
JOSEPHSON effects. See Superconductivity
JOSEPHUS, Flavius
Account of Josephus; excerpts from The Jewish war. por Horizon 8:26-7 Wint '66
JOSEPHY, Alvin M. Jr
Ordeal in Hell's Canyon. Am Heritage 18:72-9+ D '66
JOSEY, Alex
Indonesia: hope after massacre. Nation 203:565-70 N 28 '66
Singapore: one-party democracy. Nation 203:661-3 D 19 '66

JOSEY, E. J.
Giving disadvantaged Negro children a reading start. por Negro Hist Bul 29:155-6 Ap '66
Librarian-trustee. Library J 91:2438-9 My 15 '66
JOSLIN, Holly
Pirate; poem. Horn Bk 42:474 Ag '66
JOURNALISM
Journalism: public enlightenment or private interest? J. Tebbel. Ann Am Acad 363:79-86 Ja '66
See also
Editorials
Libel and slander
News
Newspaper court reporting
Newspapers
Reporters and reporting

Anecdotes, facetiae, satire, etc.
Adversaria. Esquire 65:82-3 F; 116-17 Mr; 138-9 Ap '66

Study and teaching
Fleet Street fortune at work: two seminars in understanding; enterprises of the Thomson foundation. J. Tebbel. Sat R 49:101-2 N 12 '66
Journalism, open to all students; MacArthur high school, Saginaw, Mich. G. J. Egan. NEA J 55:53-4 My '66
Off-the-job training; scholarships for experienced journalists. il Time 87:74 Je 3 '66
Stanford's Niemans: Professional journalism fellowships program. Newsweek 67:72 F 7 '66
Toward a native press: Nairobi press institute. il Time 88:46 Jl 15 '66
Training for the journalist in Africa and Vietnam; International federation of journalists projects. J. Tebbel. Sat R 49:84-5+ D 10 '66
Urban renewal. Newsweek 67:93 My 16 '66
What are the journalism schools teaching? analysis of curricula. J. Tebbel. il Sat R 49:48-50 Ag 13 '66
Where are tomorrow's journalists? A. Balk; discussion. Sat R 49:57+ F 12 '66

Africa
Toward a native press: Nairobi press institute. il Time 88:46 Jl 15 '66
Training for the journalist in Africa and Vietnam; International federation of journalists projects. J. Tebbel. Sat R 49:84-5+ D 10 '66

Great Britain
See also
Newspapers—Great Britain

United States
English lesson; criticism by H. Fairlie. il Newsweek 67:60-2 Je 6 '66
Journalism's next assignment: to see life in its full dimensions; excerpts from address. H. R. Luce. Fortune 75:88 Ja '67
New journalism. J. F. Fixx. Sat R 49:65 F 12 '66
See also
Catholic press
Newspapers—United States
Periodicals—United States

Vietnam (Republic)
Training for the journalist in Africa and Vietnam; International federation of journalists projects. J. Tebbel. Sat R 49:84-5+ D 10 '66
JOURNALISTIC ethics
See also
Crime and the press
JOURNALISTIC photography. See Photography, Journalistic
JOURNALISTS
Where are tomorrow's journalists? A. Balk; discussion. Sat R 49:57+ F 12 '66
See also
Foreign correspondents
JOURNALS. See Periodicals
JOURNALS of opinion. See Periodicals
JOURNEY of the fifth horse; drama. See Ribman, R.
JOUSTING. See Tournaments
JOVANOVICH, William
Misuses of the past. Sat R 49:21-4 Ap 2 '66
JOY. See Happiness
JOY cometh in the morning; story. See Thomas, D.
JOYCE, Donald V.
Recreation with the marines in Vietnam. por Parks & Rec 1:842-4 O '66

JOYCE, James
Distinguished simplicity. il por Time 88:78
D 23 '66
His fame proceeds in giant steps. R. Hatch.
Harper 232:142-3+ Mr '66
James Joyce. S. Kauffmann. New Repub 156:
33+ Ja 7 '67
Letters of James Joyce. ed. by R. Ellmann.
Review
Newsweek por 68:110-110A+ D 5 '66. S.
Maloff
Sat R 50:38 Ja 21 '67. L. Edel
Re Joyce, by A. Burgess. Review
Commonweal 83:645-6 Mr 4 '66. T. F.
Staley
JOYCE, James Avery
NATO: the painted corpse. Christian Cent
83:265-7 Mr 2 '66
JOYFUL noise: musical comedy. See Musical
comedies, revues, etc.—Criticisms, plots,
etc.
JUAN Carlos, count of Barcelona
Pretender's cabinet. Time 87:40 Je 17 '66
JUDAISM
British Jewry: the curtain maintained. S. D.
Temkin. Christian Cent 83:1606-8 D 28 '66
European Jewry, past and present. S. D.
Temkin. Christian Cent 83:1422+ N 16 '66
Jewish affirmation. M. Geltman. il Nat R
18:977-83 O 4 '66; Discussion. 18:1020+ O 18
'66
On reading Matthew: question of a Judeo-
Christian tradition. M. Himmelfarb; dis-
cussion. Commentary 41:12+ Mr '66
Orthodox thinking: report of convention of
Union of Orthodox Jewish congregations of
America. Newsweek 68:96 D 12 '66
Pulling toward unity. Time 87:82 Je 24 '66
Rediscovering Judaism. A. A. Cohen. il Com-
monweal 83:634-5 Mr 4 '66
Rediscovering Judaism. ed. by A. J. Wolf.
Review
Commentary 41:88+ F '66. M. Fox; Reply
with rejoinder. E. L. Fackenheim. 41:
24+ Je '66
Seek Jewish unity: Rabbinical assembly in
Toronto. Christian Cent 83:705 Je 1 '66
State of Jewish belief: symposium; with in-
trod. by M. Himmelfarb. Commentary 42:
71-160 Ag '66; Reply. Christian Cent 83:1104
S 14 '66
Trefa banquet: Cincinnati dinner, 1883; first
steps toward reform. J. J. Appel. Commen-
tary 41:75-8 F '66; Reply with rejoinder.
A. Marks. 41:18+ My '66
Unfreezing the law. il Time 88:94+ O 14 '66
When reform was young. L. S. Dawidowicz.
Commentary 42:63-7 Jl '66
See also
Philosophy, Jewish
JUDAISM and Christianity. See Christianity
and other religions
JUDD, Donald
Questions to Stella and Judd: interview. ed.
by L. R. Lippard. il por Art N 65:55-61 S
'66
JUDD, Walter H.
United States policy toward China. Nat R
18:520-3 My 31 '66

about
Washington insight. C. Fritchey. Harper 232:
49 Ap '66
JUDGE, Joseph
Mr Jefferson's Monticello. Nat Geog Mag 130:
426-44 S '66
Operation Brownsville. Commonweal 84:193-
4 My 6 '66
JUDGES
High court's 20th century men: four younger
justices. il Bsns W p 190+ O 1 '66
Prisoners on principle: Kentucky counties
fiscal courts Time 88:74 N 18 '66
Report on judicial ethics. G. Thoron. bib-
liog f Ann Am Acad 363:36-43 Ja '66
Should the Supreme court's power be curbed?
pro and con discussion. Sr Schol 88:6-7 Mr
4 '66
Supreme court: summit of the U.S. judiciary.
il Sr Schol 87:11-13 Ja 7 '66
Supreme court: the silent arm of government.
il Sr Schol 88:12-13 F 18 '66
Who's who on Supreme court. il U S News
60:50-1 Je 20 '66
Winds of change in how we pick our judges.
il Sr Schol 87:20-1 Ja 7 '66
See also
Negro judges

**Appointment, qualifications,
tenure, etc.**
Answer to aging judges. Life 60:4 F 4 '66
How to remove them. Time 87:82 F 4 '66

Is that judge fit to sit? P. Friggens. Read
Digest 89:127-31 Jl '66
Let's make government work better! re-
form proposals. D. D. Eisenhower. Read
Digest 90:61-7 Ja '67; Reply. D. Lawrence.
U S News 62:88 Ja 9 '67
JUDGMENTS
Of alimony, embezzlers, lifers & immoral
pilots; current sampler of recent decisions.
il Time 88:74 N 18 '66
Of fright, nudists & spinsters; individual
human conflicts; current examples. il Time
89:82 Ja 6 '67
Of love, kisses & nudism; decisions. Time 88:
58-9 Jl 15 '66
Who can't have what; current examples.
Time 88:81-2 D 16 '66
JUDICIAL decisions. See Judgments
JUDICIAL procedure. See Procedure (law)
JUDICIARY. See Judges
JUDO. See Jiu-jitsu
JUDSON, Edward Zane Carroll
Faces from the past. R. M. Ketchum. por Am
Heritage 17:64-5 Ap '66
JUDSON, Horace
I had this sense of lurking magic. Life 61:
98+ N 25 '66
JUDSON dance theatre. See Dance companies
JUDSON memorial church. See New York
(city)—Churches
JUDSON poets' theatre. See New York (city)—
Theater
JUETTNER, W. R.
Fierce and foggy first for Thunderballs. il
Motor B 118:80-2 D '66
JUGOSLAVIA. See Yugoslavia
JUICE extractors. See Fruit juice extractors
JUILLIARD dance ensemble
Juilliard dance ensemble, Juilliard concert
hall. M. Marks. Dance Mag 40:83 Je '66
JUILLIARD opera theater
New York; production of La Bohème. J.
Honig. Opera N 30:28 Ap 16 '66
JUILLIARD school of music, New York
Music to my ears; H. Weisgall's Purgatory
and R. Sessions' The trial of Lucullus
performed. I. Kolodin. Sat R 49:38 Je 4 '66
Musical events; performance of two atonal
operas: Purgatory, by H. Weisgall, and
Trial of Lucullus, by R. Sessions. W.
Sargeant. New Yorker 42:85-6 My 28 '66
New York. R. D. Daniels. Opera N 31:28
S 10 '66
JULESZ, Bela
Binocular disappearance of monocular sym-
metry. Science 153:657-8 Ag 5 '66
JULIANA, queen of the Netherlands
Crowned with money. il por Time 88:100 S 9
'66
Inflation is a royal nuisance. Life 61:4 S 9
'66
JULIUS Caesar; opera. See Händel, G. F.
JULIUS Garfinckel and company
Mutual antipathy; antitrust suit filed to stop
Genesco takeover. il Time 87:82 Ap 1 '66
JULLIAN, Philippe
Montesquiou, professor of beauty. Vogue 148:
184-5+ N 1 '66
JULLIE, Louis L.
Giant of Mission creek; ed. by J. O. Cartier.
por Outdoor Life 138:46-7+ D '66
JULY fourth. See Independence day
JUMSAI NA AYUTYA, Sumet
Ayutya Venice of south Asia. UNESCO
Courier 19:4-11 O '66
JUNCOS
Long night of the snowbirds. J. George. il
Read Digest 89:161-2+ D '66
JUNE
Line a day. P. Cannon. il Ladies Home J
83:104 Je '66
JUNGLE
By car into Venezuela's high jungle. il Sun-
set 136:34+ Mr '66
New conquistadors in the Amazon jungle. E.
P. Hanson; reply with rejoinder. J. H.
Norton. Américas 18:48 F '66
See also
Rain forests
JUNGLE of love; story. See O'Faolain, S.
JUNGLE warfare
Students of survival; Australia's Jungle war-
fare center. P. Harvey. il Newsweek 68:30
Ag 29 '66
Vietnam: jungle conflict poses new R&D
problems. L. J. Carter. il Science 152:187-90
Ap 8 '66
JUNGLES
Just beyond the Caribbean, the tranquil
Surinam jungle. il Sunset 136:58+ Je '66

JUNIOR chambers of commerce. See United States junior chamber of commerce

JUNIOR college libraries. See College libraries

JUNIOR colleges
College at your doorstep; two-year community colleges. L. R. Johnson. il Parents Mag 41: 70-1+ S '66
Cooperation between two-year and four-year colleges. C. E. Blocker. bibliog f Sch & Soc 94:218-22 Ap 16 '66
How good are the junior colleges? R. Lynes. il Harper 233:53-60 N '66
Increase. Sch & Soc 94:380+ N 12 '66
Junior college and technical education. Sch & Soc 94:340 O 29 '66
Technical education and society: the community college; address, May 12, 1966. E. J. Gleazer, jr. Vital Speeches 32:540-3 Je 15 '66
What about the junior college? D. Klein. Seventeen 25:22+ Jl '66
See also
Berkshire community college, Pittsfield, Mass.

JUNIOR curators. See Museum workers

JUNIOR high school buildings. See School buildings

JUNIOR miss contests. See Beauty contests

JUNIOR year abroad. See Foreign study

JUNIPER
It's the conifer that grows every which way. il Sunset 137:238+ N '66
Junipers are useful. A. R. Ireys. il Horticulture 44:18-21 N '66

JUNIPERUS chinensis. See Juniper

JUNK dealers
Car junkyards try sophistication. il Bsns W p 108-10+ F 26 '66

JUNKER, Howard
Art of animation. Nation 202:249-50 F 28 '66
Common scolds. Nation 202:307-9 Mr 14 '66
New silver screen. Esquire 66:62+ O '66

JUNKYARDS
Car junkyards try sophistication. il Bsns W p 108-10+ F 26 '66

JUPITER (planet)
Unusual widespread colors on Jupiter. J. Olivarez. il Sky & Tel 31:306-7 My '66
See also
Space flight to Jupiter

Atmosphere
Hot shadows of Jupiter. R. L. Wildey; reply with rejoinder. W. T. Plummer. Science 153:1418-19 S 16 '66

Radiation
Decametric radio pulses from Jupiter; characteristics. C. N. Olsson and A. G. Smith. bibliog il Science 153:289-90 Jl 15 '66

Rotation
Radio rotation period of Jupiter. S. Gulkis and T. D. Carr. bibliog il Science 154:257-9 O 14 '66

Surface
Red spot explained. Sci N 89:335 My 7 '66

JURACK, Charles A.
La Mouette II. il Yachting 119:99+ Ja '66

JURIES, Art
Trial by jury. N. Kent. Am Artist 30:3+ D '66

JURY
Community conscience; results of study in the book, The American jury. Time 88:36 Ag 12 '66
How good are our juries? concerning American jury, by H. Kalven, jr. and H. Zeisel. F. Knebel. il Look 30:75-6+ Ag 23 '66; Same abr. Read Digest 89:239-41+ N '66
Inverted racism; all-white jury for trial of D. Gregory in Chicago. Christian Cent 83: 575-6 My 4 '66
Juries: cornerstone or millstone to justice? Sr Schol 87:18-19 Ja 7 '66
Kafka goes to court; concerning J. Marshall's book, Law and psychology in conflict. il Time 88:58 Jl 15 '66
LBJ's civil rights bill. A. M. Bickel. New Repub 154:12-14 My 21 '66
Morgan's crusade for Negro jurors. J. B. Cumming, jr. Reporter 34:39-40 F 10 '66

JUST among friends; story. See Lee, M.

JUSTICE, Donald
Missing person; poem. New Yorker 42:202 O 15 '66
To the hawks; Men at forty; Man closing up; poems. Poetry 108:79-84 My '66
To waken a small person; poem. New Yorker 42:66 N 5 '66

JUSTICE
Moral indignation. V. P. McCorry. America 115:496 O 22 '66

JUSTICE, Administration of
See also
Criminal law
Criminal procedure
Judges
Jury
Legal aid
Punishment

Alabama
Alabaman condemns Alabama justice; E. Thomas acquitted of V. Liuzzo murder. Christian Cent 83:1233 O 12 '66

California
Delayed injustice; San Francisco's 1964 sitins. Nation 203:109 Ag 8 '66
Jail or sterilization? sentence of Judge Kearney in Santa Barbara, Calif. il Time 87:46 Je 3 '66
Sterilize that woman! jail or sterilization, decree by Judge Kearney in Santa Barbara, Calif. W. F. Buckley, jr. Nat R 18:666 Jl 12 '66

Canada
Canadian justice: ordeal of Steven Truscott; case to be reviewed pending publication of I. LeBourdais book. E. Stafford. il Nation 202:614-17 My 23 '66

Germany (Federal Republic)
Out of the night; courts asked to reopen cases involving Reichstag fire and Remagen bridge. il Newsweek 69:32+ Ja 2 '67

Great Britain
Justice too late; posthumous pardon for Timothy John Evans. Christian Cent 83: 1328 N 2 '66
Too late to be happy; posthumous pardon for T. J. Evans. Newsweek 68:56 O 31 '66
Wrong man; Evans' case. Time 88:41 O 28 '66

Mississippi
Yankee lawyers in Mississippi courts. R. Hammer. Harper 233:79-84+ N '66

Oklahoma
All the justice money can buy. B. Bailey. New Repub 154:8-9 Je 11 '66

South Africa
Pimpernel's exit. Time 87:42 My 20 '66

Southern states
Breaching the white wall of southern justice; Time essay. Time 87:46-7 Ap 15 '66
Integrating the jury; case of Alabama's Lowndes County. Time 87:24 F 18 '66
Jury of their peers; defense attorneys in connection with 1964 murder of civil-rights workers seek to call off trial. Reporter 35: 24 O 6 '66

United States
Credit for time served; found guilty a second time. il Time 88:46 S 2 '66
Criminal justice; address, August 9, 1966. N. deB. Katzenbach. Vital Speeches 32:708-12 S 15 '66
Dangerous poor. S. Alsop. il Sat Eve Post 239:18 Jl 16 '66
End to copping; ruling of federal judge, E. Weinfeld. Time 87:54 Je 24 '66
Judge Raymond Pace Alexander speaks to Vietnamese law faculty; address, August 16, 1965. R. P. Alexander. Negro Hist Bul 29:109+ F '66
Judges go back to school; Sentencing institutes. G. Samuels. il N Y Times Mag p36-7+ N 6 '66
Justice in the courtroom, can the poor get it? public defender system. G. Samuels. Sat R 49:25+ Ja 29 '66
Justice, the law and the lawyer. M. Mayer. il Sat Eve Post 239:36-9+ F 26 '66
U.S. courts and the law explosion; symposium, ed. by D. Reische. il Sr Schol 87:6-21 Ja 7 '66
We're taking too many liberties with freedom. A. H. Sypher. il Nations Bsns 53: 29-30 D '65
See also
Courts—United States
Judgments
Trials

Virginia
Science used in race case; Loving vs. Virginia. Sci N 90:465 D 3 '66

JUSTICE, Department of. See United States—
Justice, Department of

JUSTICE, Miscarriage of
For a stolen life: $115,000; case of S. Dennison. il Time 87:43 Mr 25 '66
Justice too late; posthumous pardon for Timothy John Evans. Christian Cent 83:1328 N 2 '66
Too late to be happy; posthumous pardon for T. J. Evans in Britain. Newsweek 68:56 O 31 '66
Wrong man; Evans' case. Time 88:41 O 28 '66

JUSTICES. See Judges

JUSTITIEOMBUDSMAN. See Administrative remedies

JUVA, Kale, and others
Hydroxylation of proline and the intracellular accumulation of a polypeptide precursor of collagen. bibliog Science 152:92-4 Ap 1 '66

JUVENILE courts
Reformers in crisis. il Time 87:114 My 20 '66
See also
Juvenile delinquency

JUVENILE delinquency
Causes and cures of delinquency. R. Coles. New Repub 154:28-9+ Ja 29 '66
Godfather to delinquent boys. il Ebony 21:110-12+ My '66
Many delinquent boys follow dads' footsteps. Sci N L 89:121 F 19 '66
Passive delinquent may end in prison. Sci N 90:253 O 1 '66
Pills, glue and kids: an American tragedy. E. Selby and A. Selby. Read Digest 88:66-70 Je '66
Suburbs: made to order for crime. J. R. Moskin. il Look 30:20-7 My 31 '66
World of Rufus Henry; juvenile gangs of Los Angeles. F. Bonham. Horn Bk 42:34-6 F '66
Young adult offender; current practices and programmes in prevention and treatment; based on study by National council on crime and delinquency. UN Mo Chron 3:38-44 Mr '66
See also
Gangs
Juvenile courts
Problem children
Reformatories
Rehabilitation of juvenile delinquents

Prevention
Children and the badge; Atlanta board of education's school detective department. R. Hardwick. il Am Ed 2:1-4 D '65
Keeping kids out of trouble; program in New Castle, Pa. W. F. Burmester. il Parents Mag 41:50-1+ F '66
Night-time basketball fights juvenile delinquency; Leonia, N.J. il Am City 81:124 Ag '66
Noble experiment; opposition to School resource officer program. Reporter 35:14+ O 20 '66
On the classroom beat; School resource officers experiments. il Newsweek 68:76-7 Ag 8 '66
Tucson's dangerous alliance; school-police liaison. Christian Cent 83:879-80 Jl 13 '66
Youth, crime, and the Great society; major prevention projects. J. Symington. il Reporter 34:41-3 F 24 '66

Russia
USSR delinquents bored. Sci N 90:208 S 17 '66

JUVENILE hormones. See Hormones
JUVENILE literature. See Childrens literature
JUXTAGLOMERULAR granules. See Lysosomes

K

KFHP (Kaiser foundation health plan) See Insurance, Health—United States
KGB. See Secret service—Russia
KKK. See Ku Klux klan
KLM (airline) See Airlines—Netherlands
KAAT, Jim
Kaat's meow. Sports Illus 25:24+ O 17 '66
KABRISKY, Matthew
Doer's model. W. Jonathan. Sat R 49:57 S 3 '66
KACKLEY, George Landon
Greek was Greek to us! Sr Schol 88:sup 18 Ap 15 '66

KADAR, Jan
Director. New Yorker 41:23-5 F 12 '66
KADISON, Margaret
Junior journal (title varies) Ladies Home J 83:52 Je; 18 Jl; 20 Ag; 34 O '66; 84:4 Ja '67
KAEL, Pauline
At the movies. See issues of McCall's
Films. See issues of New republic, September 10, 1966-
Goddess upstages the girls. Life 60:118+ Ap 8 '66
Incredible shrinking Hollywood. Holiday 39:86-93+ Mr '66
Marlon Brando: an American hero. Atlan 217:72-5 Mr '66
about
Perils of Pauline. por Newsweek 67:80+ My 30 '66
KAELIN, Al
Wall of the winds. Sch Arts 66:18-19 N '66
KAEMPFERT, Bert
Do not disturb. Time 87:81 Je 24 '66
KAFKA, Barbara
Wood: two approaches to modern sculpture. por(p7) Craft Horiz 26:12+ Jl '66
KAFKA, Franz
It's a Kafkaesque world. M. Greenberg. il pors N Y Times Mag p 12-13+ My 29 '66
Kafka's Prague. S. Bullaty and A. Lomeo. il por Horizon 9:88-99 Wint '67
KAHAHAWAI, Joseph
Sailor confesses to old Hawaii killing; Albert Jones confession. il Life 61:49 O 7 '66
KAHALA Hilton hotel. See Hotels, taverns, etc.—Hawaii
KAHLENBERG, Richard S.
Negro radio. bibliog por Negro Hist Bul 29:127-8+ Mr '66
KAHN, David
Modern cryptology; with biographical sketch. Sci Am 215:15, 38-46 Jl '66
KAHN, Ely Jacques, 1916-
Heads you win? Reporter 35:39-42 O 20 '66
Hudson River. Holiday 40:40-55+ O '66
Letter from Cape Town. New Yorker 42:182+ N 5 '66
Reporter at large. New Yorker 42:42-6+ Je 11; 42-4+ Je 18; 56+ Je 25 '66
Small islands. Sat R 49:45-6 O 8 '66
KAHN, Herman
Vietnam: what should we do now? por Look 30:29+ Ag 9 '66
—and Pfaff, William
Our alternatives in Europe. For Affairs 44:587-600 Jl '66
about
Doctor Jekyll and Mr Kahn. J. C. Fleck. Christian Cent 83:680-3 My 25 '66; Reply with rejoinder. J. Fletcher. 83:935 Jl 27 '66
KAHN, Joan
Editing the mystery and suspense novel. Writer 79:18-21 Jl '66
KAHN, Joseph
Speaking out. por Sat Eve Post 239:8+ D 17 '66
KAHN, Journet
Freedom in the Catholic church. Christian Cent 83:461-3 Ap 13 '66
KAHN, Lothar
Books: the Jewish novel. Cath World 204:242-4 Ja '67
German and Jew, difficult encounter. Christian Cent 83:1207-10 O 5 '66
KAHN, Louis I.
Avant-garde anachronist. il por Time 87:70-1 Je 10 '66
Landmark for medical research. J. Peter. il por Look 31:52-3 Ja 10 '67
Louis Kahn in India: an old order at a new scale. J. Bailey. il Arch Forum 125:39-47 Jl '66
KAHN, Mark L.
Pilot's dilemma. Mo Labor R 89:264-7 Mr '66
KAHN, Roger
I'm not discouraged either, got it? Sat Eve Post 239:85-9 Ja 29 '66
They ain't getting no maiden. Sat Eve Post 239:97-101 Je 18 '66
KAHN, Tom
Problem of the new left. Commentary 42:30-8 Jl; 8+ N '66
KAHNEMAN, Daniel, and Beatty, Jackson
Pupil diameter and load on memory. bibliog Science 154:1583-5 D 23 '66
KAIETEUR FALLS
Potaro goes over the edge. il Sunset 136:50+ My '66

KAIN, Jay D.
Sand mold casting with styrofoam. Sch Arts
65:36-8 Je '66
KAISER, Edgar Fosburgh
Mr Kaiser named U.S. national chairman
for United Nations day. L. B. Johnson.
Dept State Bul 54:976 Je 20 '66
KAISER, Henry J, company
Kaiser plans appeal in BOF case. il Bsns W
p97 Jl 23 '66
KAISER foundation health plan. See Insurance,
Health—United States
KAISER industries corporation
Where Kaiser's cars lead the pack; produc-
tion abroad. il Bsns W p 114-16+ N 5 '66
KAISER jeep corporation
Holy toledo! new jeep line. il Time 89:89
Ja 6 '67
Jeepster reborn; Kaiser revives sporty car.
il Bsns W p62-4 Ja 7 '67
Taking the hard sell to eastern Europe; In-
comex 66 exhibit in Czechoslovakia. il Bsns
W p34-6 Je 4 '66
KAKIHANA, Ryoko, and others
Brain sensitivity to alcohol in inbred mouse
strains. bibliog Science 154:1574-5 D 23 '66
KALAMAZOO, Mich.

Sanitary affairs
City-industry treatment plant. Am City 81:26
F '66

Streets
No more dumping on the street; two new
sweepers. D. H. Swets. il Am City 81:92-3
Mr '66
KALANCHOES
Red-blooming succulent gift. il Sunset 137:
181 D '66
KALB, Marvin
Soviet Union's 50th: is Russia a tourist
country? Sat R 50:51-2+ Ja 7 '67
Vital interests of Mr Kennan. N Y Times
Mag p30-1+ Mr 27 '66
KALCHEIM, Lee
Match-play. Criticism
New Yorker 42:83+ O 22 '66
Party for divorce. Criticism
New Yorker 42:83+ O 22 '66
KALCKAR, Herman M.
Galactose metabolism and cell sociology. bib-
liog Science 150:305-13; 151:478 O 15 '65,
Ja 28 '66
KALER, Grace
Old metals. See issues of Hobbies
KALETTA, Jim
Flying photographer. il Flying 79:98 O '66
KALINGA prize
Rabinowitch awarded Kalinga prize. A. K.
Smith. Science 153:1627 S 30 '66
KALISH, G. H. and Di Luzio, N. R.
Peroxidation of liver lipids in the patho-
genesis of the ethanol-induced fatty liver.
bibliog Science 152:1390-2 Je 3 '66
KALLEN, Horace Meyer
How I bet my life. por Sat R 49:27-30+ O 1
'66
KALLET, Nathan
Olivier and the Moor. Holiday 39:143-4 Ap '66
KALMAN, Paul
Little boats for big fish. Field & S 70:57-9+
Mr '66
KALS, William S.
And a star to steer her by. Motor B 118:
36-7 Jl '66
Boat-wife handling. Motor B 117:90-1 Ja '66
Columbus sights the New World. Motor B
118:102+ O '66
Tidal currents. Motor B 117:32-3+ Ap '66
What do you know about coral? Yachting
120:49+ N '66
KALTENBORN, Howard Stanley
Anniversary remarks. Sci N 89:182 Mr 19 '66
KALTHUM, Om
Nightingale of the Nile. por Time 88:72 Ag 5
'66
KALTSOYA, Anastasia, and others
Hemoglobins of early human embryonic de-
velopment. bibliog Science 153:1417-18 S 16
'66
KALVEN, Harry, Jr
Community conscience. Time 88:36 Ag 12 '66
KAM, King. See Cameron, C. B.
KAMARAJ, Kumaraswami
Political python of India. J. A. Lukas. il
por N Y Times Mag p26-7+ F 20 '66
KAMIKAZE. See World war, 1939-1945—Japan
KAMINER, Benjamin, and Bell, A. L.
Synthetic myosin filaments. bibliog Science
151:323 Ja 21 '66
KAMISAR, Yale
Gifted gadfly. por Time 88:77+ N 11 '66

KAMMERER, Rafael
Golden art of Sergei Rachmaninoff. Am Rec
G 33:156-65 O '66
More keyboard giants of the past. Am Rec G
32:806-9 My '66
Three via London imports: by far the best
piano-roll transfers. Am Rec G 33:296-8
D '66
KAMP, Irene
Great indoors. Criticism
Commonweal 83:699-700 Mr 18 '66
Vogue 147:58 Mr 15 '66
KAMPEN, Irene
Pleasure of your company is requested. Mc-
Calls 93:49 Mr '66
KAMPINE, John P. and others
Diagnosis of Gaucher's disease and Niemann-
Pick disease with small samples of venous
blood. bibliog Science 155:86-8 Ja 6 '67
KAMRIN, Benjamin B.
Alpha globulin injections and decreased
gamma globulin production in chickens. bib-
liog Science 153:1261-2 S 9 '66
KANDEL, Lenore
Judge orders Love book to be returned for
sale. Pub W 191:58 Ja 16 '67
San Francisco police arrest booksellers. Pub
W 190:27-8 D 12 '66
KANDELL, Alice
Queen of Sikkim: an intimate portrait. Red-
book 127:52-5+ Je '66
KANDINSKY, Wassily
Abstract icons. Time 88:84-5 D 16 '66
Art galleries: exhibition at the Marlborough-
Gerson gallery. R. M. Coates. New Yorker
42:135-6+ Ap 23 '66
Kandinsky, no great master but a great in-
fluence. H. Kramer. il por N Y Times Mag
p28-9+ D 18 '66
KANE, James
Book of the month. Cath World 202:308 F '66
KANE, Martin
Boxing (cont) Sports Illus 25:72+ O 3 '66
Tennis. Sports Illus 24:84-6 Ap 4 '66
KANEHL, Rod
Can't anyone here use Kanehl? L. Shecter.
il pors Sports Illus 25:54-6+ Ag 8 '66
KANGAROO lottery; story. See Lamott, K.
KANGAROOS
Federal controls needed for kangaroo indus-
try; protecting kangaroos and wallabies
from indiscriminate slaughter. il Sci N 90:
251 O 1 '66
Nature note; wallaby. il Sci N 91:30 Ja 14
'67
KANICLIDES, Penny
Prettiest veep. il por Newsweek 67:69 F 7
'66
KANIN, Garson
(ed) See Maugham, W. S. Remembering Mr
Maugham
KANN, Sister Jean Marie
Everything that rises must converge. Cath
World 204:154-9 D '66
KANNY, Mark N.
Schmidt-Isserstedt's Ninth, the most satis-
fying in ten years. Am Rec G 33:208-9 N
'66
KANO, Nigeria
Massacre in Kano. il Time 88:44+ O 14 '66
KANOVITZ, Howard
Focus as physical reality. B. H. Friedman.
il Art N 65:47-9+ O '66
KANSAS
See also
Crime and criminals—Kansas
Geology—Kansas
Hunting—Kansas
Public health—Kansas
Public welfare—Kansas

Description and travel
Wagons ho! prairie schooner trips across
western Kansas. H. J. Samuels. il Travel
126:37-9+ Ag '66
KANSAS CITY, Kan, public library
Kansas City combo. W. K. Dennis. il Li-
brary J 91:5862-3 D 1 '66
KANSAS CITY, Mo.

Churches
Four for St Mark's. il Time 88:65 Jl 22 '66
Galleries and museums
See also
William Rockhill Nelson gallery of art
Music
Appetite-whetting thing. il Time 87:69 Je 10
'66
Celebration of Henry Purcell; orchestral-
ballet-opera triple bill. J. Haskins. il Hi Fi
16:MA9 Ag '66

KANSAS City, Mo.—Music—*Continued*
Doctor Moore's Carry Nation; commissioned by University of Kansas City. A. Rich. il Hi Fi 16:MA27 Jl '66
Kansas City; Performing arts foundation. F. Merkling. il Opera N 31:25 S 10 '66
Purcell in Missouri. J. Ardoin. il Sat R 49: 49+ Je 18 '66
See also
Kansas City lyric theater

Sanitary affairs
Kansas City's West side story. L. W. Weller. il Am City 81:108-11 F '66
KANSAS CITY American Royal (horse show) See Horse shows
KANSAS CITY Athletics (baseball) See Baseball clubs
KANSAS CITY Chiefs (football club) See Football clubs
KANSAS CITY lyric theater
Kansas City. J. Haskins. Opera N 31:24 N 5 '66
Kansas City stock; interview, ed. by F. Merkling. R. Patterson. Opera N 31:13 S 10 '66
KANSAS, University
Kansas centennial. il Time 87:49 Ap 22 '66
Student doctor learns to care. R. H. Berg. il Look 30:24-9 F 8 '66
KANTOR, MacKinlay
Girl named Frankie. Read Digest 88:86-90 My '66
My most unforgettable character. Read Digest 89:221-2+ D '66
KAOLINITE
Chemisorption of water at high temperatures on kaolinite: effect on dehydroxylation. G. W. Brindley and G. L. Millhollen. bibliog il Science 152:1385 Je 3 '66
Mechanism for intercalation of kaolinite by alkali acetates. D. L. Smith and others. bibliog il Science 153:741-3 Ag 12 '66
KAPELL, William
Brief candles. H. Goldsmith. por Hi Fi 16: 52-3 F '66
KAPINGAMARANGI
Reporter at large. E. J. Kahn, jr. New Yorker 42:52+ Je 18 '66
KAPITZA, Peter Leonidovich
Kapitsa to visit England. V. K. McElheny. Science 152:744 My 6 '66
Kapitsa's visit to England. V. K. McElheny. Science 153:725-7 Ag 12 '66
Return of the vanished. il por Time 87:40+ My 13 '66
Science in U.S. far ahead, says top Russian. il por Bsns W p74-5 D 24 '66
KAPLAN, Abraham
Profess with a passion. il por Time 87:85 My 6 '66
KAPLAN, Allan
Orange; poem. Nation 202:750 Je 20 '66
KAPLAN, Ethel
Be glad you're not beautiful. Todays Health 44:22-5+ Ag '66
KAPLAN, Flora
Artist & agent. M. Orovan. il U S Camera 29:54-7+ Ap '66
KAPLAN, George D.
Middleman on the production line. il por Bsns W p 171-2 Je 11 '66
KAPLAN, H. R.
Unluckiest island. Motor B 117:193-5 Mr '66
KAPLAN, I. R. and Nissenbaum, A.
Anomalous carbon-isotope ratios in nonvolatile organic material. bibliog Science 153: 744-5 Ag 12 '66
KAPLAN, Jack
Doctor Abrams, dean of machine quacks. Todays Health 44:20-1+ Ap '66
KAPLAN, Jacques
Furrier to the art world. G. Glueck. il por N Y Times Mag p38-9+ O 2 '66
KAPLAN, Martin
Social effects of animal diseases in developing countries. Bul Atomic Sci 22:15-21 N '66
KAPLAN, Ralph
PPA hears views on impact of new technology; excerpts from address, May 27, 1966. Pub W 189:73-4 Je 27 '66
KAPLAN, Robert. See Hinrichs, M. A. jt. auth.
KAPLAN, Stanley
Challenge of a plank of wood. por Am Artist 30:31-5+ My '66
KAPLEAU, Philip
All is one, one is none, none is all. pors N Y Times Mag p26-7+ Mr 6 '66
KAPLOW, Jeffry
Left tradition. Nation 202:784-6 Je 27 '66
Saint Charles. Nation 202:368-70 Mr 28 '66
KAPPEL, Frederick R.
Aspects of leadership; address, January 18, 1966. Vital Speeches 32:254-6 F 1 '66

KAPROW, Allan
Experimental art. Art N 65:60-3+ Mr '66
Happenings in and out of school; interview, ed. by D. W. Ecker. Sch Arts 65:23-8 Mr '66
about
Happening at the Hamptons. il Time 88:42+ Ag 19 '66
KARAJAN, Wolfgang von
Pipe line. Newsweek 67:90 F 14 '66
KARAMU house. See Cleveland, Ohio—Theater
KARANKAWAY country. See Texas
KARAS, Nicholas
Charley Varney's deer farm. Field & S 71: 58-9+ O '66
Crows in the pigpen. Field & S 71:56-7+ D '66
Dogs that decoy ducks. Field & S 71:80-2+ S '66
Fire Island fox hunt. Field & S 71:48-9 Ja '67
Hickory shad on the Susquehanna. Field & S 70:66-7+ Ap '66
New place for rabbits. por Outdoor Life 138: 70-1+ O '66
Pack-in ponds. por Field & S 71:34-5+ Jl '66
KARCH, Carroll Schauer
Patch the pony says. PTA Mag 60:23 My '66
Pony with a safety message. Todays Health 44:5+ My '66
KARCH, Krekel
Walls for wandering farms. A. Whitman. il pors Pop Mech 125:95-7+ Je '66
KARDORFF, Ursula von
Where dreams ended, terror began. R. Plant. Sat R 49:29 My 21 '66
KARIEL, Henry S.
Behind pluralism's facade. Nation 203:22-3 Jl 4 '66
Private acts & public goals: ideological vacuum. Nation 202:449-52 Ap 18 '66
KARL, Jean
Real and the unreal; address, October 13, 1965. por Wilson Lib Bul 41:162-7 O '66
KARLEN, Arno
Sweden. Holiday 40:44-51+ N '66
KARLIN, Eugene
Art of Eugene Karlin. J. H. Michel. il Am Artist 30:50-4+ Mr '66
KARLINSKY, Simon
Uses of Dostoevsky. Nation 203:164-5 Ag 22 '66
Yevtushenko and the underground poets. Nation 203:549-53 N 21 '66
KARNER, Erwin F.
Your fishing club; reprint. Parks & Rec 1: 563 Jl '66
KARNOW, Stanley
Asian name game. Sat R 49:84 My 7 '66
Bad news from the north. New Repub 155: 18-19 N 19 '66
Bewildering collision. Sat R 49:41-2+ O 8 '66
KAROLUS, August
German TV pioneer. H. F. Kutschbach. il por Pop Electr 25:72 Jl '66
KARP, David
TV shows are not supposed to be good. N Y Times Mag p6-7+ Ja 23 '66
KARP, Eleanor
How to write New Yorker stories; story. Harper 233:69-74 Jl '66
KARP, Irwin
Author's right to write. Sat R 50:28-9 Ja 21 '67
KARP, Tony
Tony Karp on 35mm. See issues of Modern photography
KARPATKIN, Marvin M.
How it was. Nation 202:134-6 Ja 31 '66
Puerto Rico. New Repub 154:12-15 My 7 '66
KARSH, Yousuf
Through native eyes. Library J 91:3079-80 Je 15 '66
KART enduro nationals. See Karting
KART racing. See Karting
KARTH, Joseph Edward
What next in space? excerpts from remarks. Aviation W 85:11 Ag 1 '66
about
Space science: congressmen want larger voice. L. J. Carter. por Science 153:615+ Ag 5 '66
KARTING
Kart enduro nationals. T Medley. il Hot Rod 19:94-5 O '66
KARWAKI, Thomas. See Lauver, J. L. jt. auth.
KASER, David
Korean micro-libraries and private reading rooms. por Library J 91:6035-8 D 15 '66

KASER, Tom
IDEA: prescription for change. Sat R 49:
68-9 Je 18 '66

KASHMIR
Exchange of messages on Tashkent declara-
tion. UN Mo Chron 3:8-9 F '66
Guns of September. Time 88:45 S 16 '66
Indian hara-kiri; Indian-Pakistani war; dis-
cussion. Christian Cent 82:1515-16; 83:148
D 8 '65, F 2 '66
Tashkent declaration registered with UN;
with text of declaration. UN Mo Chron 3:
37-9 Ap '66
Vale of Kashmir won't be undersold. R.
Girson. il Atlan 217:122-4 F '66
See also
United Nations—Kashmir

Description and travel
Going places, finding things in Kashmir.
N. Barry. il House & Gard 130:54-6+ O '66

KASLER, James H.
Hero lost. Time 88:27 Ag 19 '66
Wall of lead. por Newsweek 68:64 Ag 22 '66
Way to survive. il por Time 88:20-1 Ag 12
'66

KASS, Jerome
Monopoly. Criticism
Commonweal 84:57 Ap 1 '66
New Yorker 42:120+ Mr 26 '66

KASTENDIECK, Miles
Tenor of the House. Opera N 30:18-19 Je 4
'66

KASTLER, Alfred
Lauded at last. por Time 88:88 N 11 '66
1966 Nobel laureate in physics. F. M. Pipkin.
por Science 154:747-9 N 11 '66
Nobel prize winners. por Sci N 90:400 N 12 '66
Practical theorists. il por Newsweek 68:73
N 14 '66

KÄSTNER, Erich
Young man: five a.m; poem. tr. by J. Simon.
Mlle 62:112 F '66

KASTON, B. J.
Evolution of the web. il Natur Hist 75:26-33
Ap '66

KATALLAGETE (periodical)
Katallagete, what? new magazine under
auspices of the Committee of southern
churchmen. Christian Cent 83:1265 O 19 '66

KATANGA
Armed forces
Crushing the Kats. il Time 88:47 O 14 '66

KATCHALSKY, Aharon
Man's first robot with muscles. J. Lear. il
Sat R 49:83-6 D 3 '66

KATEB, George
Common-sense communism. Nation 203:254-5
S 19 '66
Kennedy as statesman. Commentary 41:54-60
Je '66

KATES, Stephen
Testing their medals. il por Time 88:39 Ag
26 '66

KATHLEEN Thérèse Connor, Sister. See Connor, K. T.

KATHY'S papa; story. See Cope, J.

KATMAI, MOUNT
See also
Katmai National Monument

KATMAI NATIONAL MONUMENT
Katmai National Monument. D. L. Coe. il
Nat Parks Mag 40:4-9 Je '66

KATO Zakro, Crete. See Crete—Antiquities

KATOSKI, Leonard T.
Injun country nature area. por Parks & Rec
1:251-3 Mr '66

KATS, Madeleine
Sweden. Dance Mag 40:25+ Ap '66

KATSOYANNIS, P. G.
Synthesis of insulin. bibliog Science 154:1509-
14 D 23 '66

KATSUKI, Y. and others
Tetraethylammonium and tetrodotoxin: effects
on cochlear potentials. bibliog Science 151:
1544-5 Mr 25 '66

KATZ, Arnold M. and Repke, D. I.
Control of myocardial contraction: the sensitivity of cardiac actomyosin to calcium
ion. bibliog Science 152:1242-3 My 27 '66

KATZ, Bill
Day at LJ. por Library J 91:3110-16 Je 15 '66
(ed) Magazines. Library J 92:91-2 Ja 1 '67

KATZ, Daniel
Attitude formation and public opinion. bibliog f Ann Am Acad 367:150-62 S '66

KATZ, Joseph J. and Crespi, H. L.
Deuterated organisms: cultivation and uses.
bibliog Science 151:1187-94 Mr 11 '66

KATZ, William
George Henry White: a militant Negro con-
gressman in the age of Booker T. Wash-
ington. bibliog por Negro Hist Bul 29:125-6+
Mr '66
Ignored by historians. Sat R 49:67-8 Jl 16 '66
Much yet to overcome. Sat R 49:26-7 Ag 13
'66

KATZBERG, Allan A. and Hendrickx, A. G.
Gonadotropin-induced anomalies of the zona
pellucida of the baboon ovum. bibliog Science 151:1225-6 Mr 11 '66

KATZENBACH, Nicholas deBelleville
Crime reporting; address, February 14, 1966.
Vital Speeches 32:351-2 Mr 15 '66
Criminal justice; address, August 9, 1966.
Vital Speeches 32:708-12 S 15 '66
Excerpt from testimony, February 15, 1966.
Cong Digest 45:141+ My '66
Excerpt from testimony, May 4, 1966. Cong
Digest 45:266+ N '66
Excerpt from testimony, May 19, 1965. Cong
Digest 45:296+ D '66
Growth of the foreign service; an index of
world responsibility; remarks. October 27,
1966. Dept State Bul 55:781-3 N 21 '66
Issues of East-West trade; address, Decem-
ber 9, 1966. Dept State Bul 56:2-5 Ja 2 '67

about
Duty to defy. Time 87:25 F 25 '66
LBJ makes some changes. il por U S News
61:39 O 3 '66
New U in the fudge factory. il por Time
88:29 N 11 '66
Poker-faced lawman on the spot; with report
by J. Neary. il pors Life 60:49-50+ My 6
'66
Shaking up the jelly. il por Newsweek 69:
22-3 Ja 16 '67
State's new team. por Time 88:24 S 30 '66

KAUAI (island)
Olulaau O Kauai (the forest of Kauai) R.
Wenkham. il Audubon Mag 68:430-5 N '66
Resort hotel on beach; Waiohai resort hotel.
il Arch Rec 140:134 Ag '66

KAUFFMAN, Henry J.
American copper teakettle. Antiques 89:570-
2 Ap '66

KAUFFMANN, Stanley
Almost-English. New Repub 155:26+ D 10 '66
Business of books. New Repub 155:24+ N
5 '66
But for whom? New Repub 155:17+ N 19 '66
Childe Harold. New Repub 155:22+ N 12 '66
Explosion explosion. New Repub 155:18+ O 1
'66
Frightened writer. New Repub 155:20+ O 8
'66
James Joyce. New Repub 156:33+ Ja 7 '67
Mayhem by Muggeridge. New Repub 155:23+
D 17 '66
Nothing new. New Repub 156:26+ Ja 14 '67
Onward with Updike. New Repub 155:15-17
S 24 '66
Politics as romance. New Repub 155:14+
O 15 '66
Really lost generation. New Repub 155:22+
D 3 '66
Teleprromptings. New Repub 156:24+ Ja 21
'67
Tenor on horseback. New Repub 155:23+
O 22 '66
Up from cleverness. New Repub 155:24+ D
24 '66
(ed) See Ford, H. Looks of books

about
Common scolds; preview and review. H.
Junker. Nation 202:307-9 Mr 14 '66
Merrick plan; concerning canceled preview.
Newsweek 67:86 F 28 '66
Smelling a rat; Kauffmann, Merrick and
previews. il por Time 87:64 F 25 '66
Supercritic: replacement by W. Kerr. News-
week 68:94-5 S 12 '66

KAUFMAN, Arnold S.
Compleat cold warrior. Nation 202:214-16 F
21 '66
Murder in Tuskegee. Nation 202:118-25 Ja
31 '66

KAUFMAN, Bel
Echoes of Sholom Aleichem. por Sat R 49:
61-2 O 1 '66
Editor interviews; ed. by M. S. Fenner. pors
NEA J 55:71-2 S '66
Plea for professional dignity; interview. ed.
by H. Ravis. por Sr Schol 89:sup5 O 14 '66

about
High school classic. il por Time 87:74 Mr 18
'66

KAUFMAN, Betty
Art. See occasional issues of Commonweal to June 24, 1966
KAUFMAN, Felix
Data systems that cross company boundaries. Harvard Bsns R 44:141-5+ Ja '66
KAUFMAN, George S.
Butter and egg man. Criticism
America 115:524 O 29 '66
Nation 203:493 N 7 '66
New Yorker 42:98-9 O 29 '66
By George S. Kaufman and . . . H. Teichmann. il pors N Y Times Mag p64-5+ N 13 '66
Happy encore for Kaufman's classics. T. Prideaux. il por Life 61:127-30 N 25 '66
—and Ferber, Edna
Dinner at eight. Criticism
America 115:524 O 29 '66
Commonweal 85:78 O 21 '66
Life 61:127-30 N 25 '66
Nation 203:397-8 O 17 '66
New Yorker 42:116 O 8 '66
Newsweek 68:104 O 10 '66
Sat R 49:63 O 15 '66
Time il 88:92 O 7 '66
KAUFMAN, Gordon D.
Theological historicism as an experiment in thought. Christian Cent 83:268-71 Mr 2 '66
KAUFMAN, Irving R.
Confession debate continues. N Y Times Mag p36-7+ O 2 '66
KAUFMAN, Murray
Pleasure dome '66: the world of Murray the K. R. Kotlowitz. il Harper 233:96-100 Jl '66
KAUFMAN, Ruth M. and Richstone, May
Teachers with the guidance point of view. NEA J 55:32-4 O '66
KAUFMAN, Shirley
Beetle on the shasta daylight; poem. New Yorker 42:48 Ap 2 '66
For a cold night; poem. Poetry 108:378 S '66
KAUFMAN, William I.
Hot dog cookbook; excerpts. Ladies Home J 83:100-1+ Je '66
KAUFMANN, Edgar, jr
Design sans peur et sans ressources. Arch Forum 125:68-70 S '66
KAUFMANN, Walter
Hoosier tale. Criticism
Opera N 31:28 S 10 '66
KAULONG. See New Britain (island)—Native races
KAUNDA, Kenneth David
Address to Assembly; summary, November 15, 1966. UN Mo Chron 3:64-6 D '66

about

Africa's good guy under pressure. L. Garrison. il pors N Y Times Mag p 14-15+ Ag 7 '66
Challenge in Africa. America 115:311 S 24 '66
KAVALER, Lucy
And not a drop to drink. Redbook 126:80-1+ Ap '66
Science in action; mold-made flavors; excerpts from Mushrooms, molds and miracles. Natur Hist 75:62+ Ap '66
There's something in the air. Redbook 127:52-3+ Ag '66
KAVANAUGH, James J.
Priest's income. America 114:585-7 Ap 23 '66
KAWAIAHAO church. See Honolulu—Churches
KAWAKAMI, Genichi
Yamaha's potpourri finds a market. il Bsns W p82-4+ O 1 '66
KAYAK racing
Co-ed in a cold-water kayak. C. S. Wren. il Look 30:52+ D 13 '66
KAYAKS
He stalks sharks by kayak. G. X. Sand. il Pop Mech 125:120-2 My '66
Kayak-camping Lake Powell. J. Clark. il Field & S 71:56-9 Je '66
Making your own glass kayak. il Sunset 137:144+ O '66
KAYE, Leo
Camping fun for diabetic youngsters. Todays Health 44:50-3 Je '66
KAYSEN, Carl
Allocating federal support for basic research. Bul Atomic Sci 22:16-22 Ja '66

about

Generalist takes the helm. il por Bsns W p 152+ Ap 30 '66
Paradise in Princeton. il por Newsweek 67:82 F 28 '66
Visit to an intellectual hotel. J. Corry. il por N Y Times Mag p50-1+ My 15 '66

KAZAKHSTAN
Eagles of Kazakhstan. E. S. Staples. Atlan 219:92-5 Ja '67
KAZAN-KOMAREK, Vladimir
Never forget! por Newsweek 68:52+ N 28 '66
KAZIN, Alfred
Hawthorne: the artist of New England. Atlan 218:109-13 D '66
Imagination and the age. Reporter 34:32-5 My 5 '66
Innocents of 1914. Reporter 35:43-5 N 3 '66
Jew as modern writer. Commentary 41:37-41 Ap '66
Prince of reviewers. Reporter 35:45-6+ S 8 '66
Theatre. Vogue 149:52 Ja 1 '67
KAZMAIER, Richard William
Winner. por Time 87:100 Je 10 '66
KEANE, Clif
Lots of fun with a poison pen. F. Deford. il por Sports Illus 25:56-8 O 3 '66
KEANE, Johnny
Big Yankee turnabout. L. Koppett. il por Sports Illus 24:22-4+ Je 20 '66
Dying team screams for help. W. Leggett. il pors Sports Illus 24:34-7 My 16 '66
Good man, a good manager. Sports Illus 26:8-9 Ja 16 '67
Jaundiced eye. il por Newsweek 67:96-7 My 23 '66
KEARFOTT systems division. See General precision, incorporated—Kearfott systems division
KEARNEY, Frank Patrick
Jail or sterilization. il Time 87:46 Je 3 '66
Sterilize that woman! W. F. Buckley, jr. Nat R 18:666 Jl 12 '66
KEARNEY, Hal
Theory of illustration. Design 67:4-7 Ja '66
KEARNEY, Paul W.
Kill that fire with the right extinguisher. Pop Mech 127:102-5+ Ja '67
Shut the windows! the fire suds are coming through the doors. Pop Mech 125:136-9+ F '66
KEARNEY, Vincent S.
Question of Burma. America 115:421 O 8 '66
World scene (cont) America 114:659-61; 115:692-3+ My 7. N 26 '66
KEATING, Bern
Cajunland, Louisiana's French-speaking coast. Nat Geog Mag 129:352-91 Mr '66
High life in Mexico city. Holiday 39:58-63+ Je '66
Problems of a two-part land. Nat Geog Mag 131:1-47 Ja '67
KEATING, Edward M.
New left; what does it mean? Sat R 49:25-7+ S 24 '66
KEATING, Stephen F.
Honeywell bets on automation. il por Bsns W p60-2+ F 5 '66
KEATON, Buster
Buster Keaton; excerpt from Agee on film. J. Agee. il pors Life 60:63-4 F 11 '66
Keaton, by R. Blesh. Review
Nat R por 18:786-7 Ag 9 '66. H. Kenner
Obituary
Nat R por 18:167+ F 22 '66. H. Kenner
Time pors 87:52+ F 11 '66
What a Buster! J. Morgenstern. il pors Newsweek 67:30+ F 14 '66
KEATS, Ezra Jack
Ezra Jack Keats on college as an illustrative medium. il Pub W 189:94-5 Ap 4 '66
KEATS, John, 1795-1821
John Keats, by D. Bush. Review
Nat R 18:371+ Ap 19 '66. J. Hart; Reply with rejoinder. M. J. Howell. 18:547 My 31 '66
KECK, George E.
Traffic and airports; excerpts from address. Aviation W 85:21 N 21 '66
KEE, Howard Clark
Tangled path. Christian Cent 83:1114+ S 14 '66
KEEBLER company
Third man's theme. R. Levy. il Duns R 88:43 Ag '66
KEEFE, Frederick L.
Interpreter. New Yorker 42:178+ D 10 '66
KEELING, Gerald F.
Total procurement package; excerpts from remarks. Aviation W 84:21 Ap 25 '66
KEEN, Sam
Jean-Paul Sartre: no Christian theist! Christian Cent 83:1578 D 21 '66
Oracular. Christian Cent 83:715 Je 1 '66
KEENEY, Barnaby C.
New blood for Brown. Time 87:43 Ja 28 '66
Salty spokesman for the humanities; with statements by Keeney. il pors Life 61:53-4+ S 16 '66

KEEP-America-green campaign. See Forest fire protection
KEEPSAKES
How to live with memories. D. Goldberg. Redbook 127:57+ O '66
Mothers keep all these things. M. Holmes. il Todays Health 44:34-6 D '66
KEESHAN, Bob
Backstage with Captain Kangaroo. pors Parents Mag 41:40-1+ Ag '66
KEETON, William T.
Evolution: basic to biology. Christian Cent 84:71-6 Ja 18 '67
KEEZER, Dexter M.
Business and government, do they speak the same language? Sat R 49:23-8+ Mr 5 '66
Commerce and comity. Sat R 49:37+ O 15 '66
KEGLEY, Charles W.
Time for evaluation. Christian Cent 83:833 Je 29 '66
KEHMEIER, Gale C.
Pilots and the 727. New Repub 154:10 Mr 19 '66
KEIFER, William
So you want to own a weekly. Sat R 49:69-70 My 14 '66
KEINO, Kipchoge
Everyone's keen on Keino. C. E. Brown. il pors Ebony 21:100-2+ My '66
Hats off. il por Newsweek 67:84 F 14 '66
Kama for the Angelenos. G. S. Brown. il por Sports Illus 24:18-19 Ja 31 '66
KEISER, Marjorie
Consumer service bureau report. See issues of Parents' magazine and better homemaking
KEITEL, Wilhelm
Memoirs of Field-Marshal Keitel, ed. by W. Görlitz. Review Sat R por 49:37+ Mr 5 '66. L. L. Snyder
KEITH, G. Stuart
Can I count that bird? Audubon Mag 68:24-6 Ja '66
KEITH, Joseph A.
Pawtucket's two-pronged attack. Am City 81:108-9 Ag '66
KEITHLY, George
Hill coast; poem. Commonweal 85:225 N 25 '66
KEKKONEN, Sylvi (Uino)
Reflections of a first lady; excerpts from Crystals, tr. by K. Collings. McCalls 93:56 Je '66
KELEMEN, Pál
Weaver's high art; reprint. Américas 18:1-10 D '66
KELIHER, Alice V.
What parents should teach. PTA Mag 60:14-16 bibliog(p34) Mr '66
KELL, G. S. See Falk, M. jt. auth.
KELLENBERGER, Edouard
Genetic control of the shape of a virus; with biographical sketch. Sci Am 215:16, 32-9 bibliog(p 154) D '66
KELLER, Anthony
Composers on campus. Hi Fi 16:104-7 O '66
KELLER, David N.
Buy your own hunk of the outdoors. Field & S 71:8-11+ Ja '67
KELLER, Kaufman Thuma
Obituary Newsweek 67:73-4 Ja 31 '66
KELLERTH, J. O. See Green, D. G. jt. auth.
KELLEY, Charles F.
Volts, amperes and headaches. Motor B 118:39+ Jl '66
Yacht safety bureau. Yachting 119:87-9+ Ap '66
KELLEY, Dean M.
Church and the poverty program. Christian Cent 83:741-4 Je 8 '66
—and Nelson, C. D.
Religious liberty: toward consensus. Christian Cent 83:651-3 My 18 '66
KELLEY, Reeve Spencer
Down at the health store; poem. Sat R 49:48 Jl 16 '66
Snore; poem. Sat R 49:56 O 22 '66
KELLEY, Robert
Cameras worked, the balloon failed. G. P. Hunt. Life 60:3 My 13 '66
KELLOGG, Jean D.
Serious comedy. Christian Cent 83:1575-6 D 21 '66
KELLS, Rosemary
Pick your picture. Seventeen 26:120 Ja '67
KELLY, Dave
What happened; poem. Atlan 218:93 S '66
KELLY, Donald N.
Minister in the marketplace. L. Pompian. il Read Digest 88:29-30+ Je '66
KELLY, Edward E.
Newman, Vatican I and II, and the church today. Cath World 202:291-7 F '66

KELLY, Grace. See Grace Patricia, consort of Rainier III, prince of Monaco
KELLY, John
Tomorrow's printing processes and the human element; excerpts from address. Pub W 189:98-9+ Mr 7 '66
KELLY, Joyce
Painting technique of John McCrady. Am Artist 30:50-5+ F '66
KELLY, Lawrence Vincent
Kelly of Dallas. F. Stevenson. por Opera N 31:18-19 N 5 '66
KELLY, Robert
Seven books by eight poets. A. R. Ammons. Poetry 108:191-3 Je '66
KELLY, Robert A.
Six trick billiard shots you can make. Pop Mech 125:144-7+ F '66
KELLY, Roz
Discovery. P. Caulfield. il por Mod Phot 30:70-1+ Ap '66
KELLY, Virginia
Loud the twang of the guitar. Read Digest 90:143-6 Ja '67
KELLY, Wallace
Ink resist technique, with variations. il por Am Artist 31:50-3+ Ja '67
KELLY, William Doane
What is a Catholic college? Commonweal 83:494-7 Ja 28 '66
KELLY girl service, incorporated. See Kelly services, incorporated
KELLY services, incorporated
Kelly boys; name change of Kelly girl service, inc. Newsweek 67:86 Ap 18 '66
KELMAN, Steven
Face to face with a successful political writer; ed. by C. Schwalberg. por Seventeen 25:169 D '66
Feud among the radicals. Harper 232:67-72+ Je '66
Freshman paper on Harvard freshmen. N Y Times Mag p50-3+ D 11 '66
Speaking out. por Sat Eve Post 239:12+ N 19 '66
KELP
Kelp forests of the Pacific. W. Marx. Atlan 218:107-10 S '66
Seaweed; report from International seaweed symposium. E. Conway and E. G. Young. Science 151:358-9 Ja 21 '66
KELSEY, Robert J.
Backpacking family style. Field & S 70:56-9 F '66
KELSEY, Seth L.
Uncommon evergreens. Horticulture 45:30-1+ Ja '67
KELUD, MOUNT. See Mud volcanoes
KEMP, Jack
Insiders scout the Super bowl. por Newsweek 69:83 Ja 16 '67
KEMPER, James S.
Setting the right example; interview. por Nations Bsns 54:42-4+ Ja '66
KEMPER, Robert Graham
Allegory of the American dream. Christian Cent 83:1214+ O 5 '66
Drama. Christian Cent 83:1447, 1540-1; 84:16-17, 86 N 23, D 14 '66, Ja 4 18 '67
That parochial syndrome: two views, one lay, one clerical. Christian Cent 83:205-6 F 16 '66
KEMPNER, Mary Jean
Père Bise and the swans. Harper 232:86-7 Je '66
KEMPTON, Murray
From the depths of the thirties. New Repub 155:25-8 N 5 '66

about
Bugging. Nat R 18:1306-7 D 27 '66
KENAWI, Ibrahim Zaki
Great dam thunders ahead. L. Griggs. il por Life 60:101-2+ Je 17 '66
KENDALL, Dave
Warm words for fall cruisingmen. Motor B 118:25-7+ S '66
KENDALL, Elaine
Ouch! I love it! Holiday 40:116+ Jl '66
Speaking out. por Sat Eve Post 239:10+ Jl 16 '66
KENDALL, Gordon
Baptist students select Catholic adviser. Christian Cent 84:5 Ja 4 '66
KENDALL, Parker H.
Let's bring back the old games. PTA Mag 60:27+ Mr '66
See Jim read the book. Reporter 34:37-8 Je 30 '66
KENDALL, William H.
Go west; but do it soon. Motor B 117-36-9+ Ap '66
KENDREW, John
What switches it on? excerpt from Thread of life. Sat R 49:76-7 O 1 '66

KENILWORTH ivy
Do you know the Kenilworth-ivy? V. Grieff.
il Flower Grower 53:12 Je '66
KENISTON, Kenneth
College students: most are earnest, a few
rebel; interview. por U S News 60:44-7 My
30 '66

about

New set of labels. il por Time 87:71+ Ap 29
'66
New student. Newsweek 67:92 My 2 '66
KENKO fish-eye attachment. See Lenses,
Photographic
KENMIR, Russell C. See Yaberg, F. L. jt.
auth.
KENNAN, George Frost
Excerpt from testimony, February 10, 1966,
before Senate committee on foreign rela-
tions. Cong Digest 45:108-10 Ap '66
From containment to isolation; excerpts
from address. por Time 87:20 F 18 '66
Kennan on Vietnam; statement; with ques-
tions and answers. New Repub 154:19-30
F 26 '66
Voices of dissent: Gavin and Kennan; testi-
mony before the Senate foreign relations
committee; excerpts. il Newsweek 67:28-9
F 21 '66

about

Heart of the matter in Vietnam. America
114:282-3 F 26 '66
Letter from Washington. R. H. Rovere. New
Yorker 41:146+ F 19 '66
Vital interests of Mr Kennan. M. Kalb.
il pors N Y Times Mag p30-1+ Mr 27 '66
KENNARD, C. H. L. See Sullenger, D. B. jt.
auth.
KENNARD, Olga. See Shefter, E. jt. auth.
KENNEDY, Caroline
My life with Caroline and John-John; ex-
cerpts (cont) M. Shaw. il por Ladies Home
J 83:68-9+ F '66
KENNEDY, Cora Wright
Tools & techniques. See issues of Popular
photography
KENNEDY, Donald, and others
Release of coordinated behavior in crayfish
by single central neurons. bibliog Science
154:917-19 N 18 '66
KENNEDY, Edward Moore
Fresh look at Vietnam. pors Look 30:21-3 F
8 '66
Immigration act of 1965. bibliog f Ann Am
Acad 367:137-49 S '66

about

Instant U. il por Newsweek 67:34-5 My 16
'66
Kennedy campaigning, by M. B. Levin. Re-
view
Sat R 49:100-1 O 8 '66. D. Young
Kennedys at home have a few problems. M.
F. Nolan. New Repub 154:10-11 Je 25 '66
Senior Senator Kennedy. M. Greenfield. il
por Reporter 35:19-24 D 15 '66
Teddy and Eddie revisited. M. F. Nolan. Re-
porter 35:33-5 S 8 '66
This one is about Teddy: Kennedy books.
J. N. Eller. America 115:316 S 24 '66
KENNEDY, Ethel (Skakel)
Ethel Kennedy: meddler or good samaritan?
il por U S News 62:16 Ja 23 '67
KENNEDY, George Clayton
Cooler at the core. Time 87:52 F 18 '66
KENNEDY, Gerta
Chesapeake; poem. New Yorker 42:54 N 26
'66
KENNEDY, Jacqueline Lee (Bouvier)
Jackie Kennedy and Lady Bird Johnson: what
they say about love, marriage and faith;
excerpts from Common sense wisdom of
three first ladies, ed. by B. Adler. por Good
H 162:92-4 Je '66
Sea; Dream; poems. por McCalls 93:80 Je '66

about

As the book appears: a close look at the
facts; concerning The death of a President
by W. Manchester. il por U S News 62:50-2
Ja 23 '67
Battle of the book: Manchester's The death
of a President. il pors Time 88:15-18 D 23
'66
Battle over a book; new role for Mrs JFK.
U S News 62:6 Ja 2 '67
Bishop plans Kennedy book despite family's
objection. Pub W 190:107 S 26 '66
Book that has backfired; concerning The
death of a President, by W. Manchester. il
por U S News 61:36 D 26 '66

Chapter II, or finis? il por Time 88:10-12 D 30
'66
Controversy that has only just begun. M.
McGrory. America 116:10 Ja 7 '67
Death of a husband. G. Ace. Sat R 50:31
Ja 14 '67
Fairest of the fair; vacation in Seville. il pors
Time 87:102-3 Ap 29 '66
Growing rift of LBJ and Kennedys: behind
the furor over a book; concerning The death
of a President, by W. Manchester. il pors
U S News 62:22-7 Ja 2 '67
History makers. Nation 204:4 Ja 2 '67
Holiday spirit; controversy over W. Man-
chester's book. K. Crawford. Newsweek 69:
25 Ja 9 '67
Jackie Kennedy, the radiant conquistadora;
visit to Spain; with report. il pors Life 60:
78A-80+ My 6 '66
Jacqueline B. Kennedy, plaintiff. il pors News-
week 68:39-43 D 26 '66
Jacqueline Kennedy. Z. S. Mason. il por Sat
Eve Post 239:25 Mr 26 '66
Jacqueline Kennedy goes public. L. Bergquist.
il pors Look 30:46+ Mr 22 '66
Jacqueline Kennedy's new life. V. T. Strat-
ford. por Ladies Home J 83:70+ F '66
Jacqueline Kennedy's victory; W. Manchester's book. il por Newsweek 69:16-19 Ja 2
'67
JFK book: accord reached as publisher's seek
compromise on revisions asked by Kennedys. Pub W 190:57-8 D 26 '66
JFK censored? il por Newsweek 68:65-6 O 3
'66
Kennedy book. Commonweal 85:360-1 Ja 6 '67
Kennedy-Manchester book controversy; symposium. il por Sat R 50:18-29 Ja 21 '67
Kennedys look at history. Nat R 19:12-13 Ja
10 '67
Manchester book. Reporter 35:8 D 29 '66
Mrs Kennedy and Harper & Row continue
negotiations on editorial content of Death
of a President. Pub W 191:33-4 Ja 2 '67
Perils of hasty history; tragedy of the Man-
chester story. H. Bowser. Sat R 49:14 D 31
'66
Spreading controversy; dispute over W. Man-
chester's book. il por Time 89:16 Ja 6 '67
Steam from the bubble bath; anecdotes from
P. Salinger's forthcoming book. Time 88:17
Jl 29 '66
Temporary cease-fire; war over W. Man-
chester's book. il por Newsweek 69:20 Ja 9
'67
Widow vs. author; concerning W. Man-
chester's The death of a President. por Sr
Schol 89:16 Ja 6 '67
KENNEDY, James Bullard
Needful rites. 1966; poem. New Repub 155:23
D 3 '66
KENNEDY, James F.
Square-wave testing. Electr World 75:94-5 Mr
'66
KENNEDY, John Fitzgerald, 1917-1963
Annals of legislation. R. Harris. New York-
er 42:35-6+ Jl 9; 35-8+ Jl 16 '66
Best Kennedy book? The death of a Pres-
ident. Newsweek 68:21-2 S 5 '66
Did LBJ make John Kennedy president?
with interview with J. N. Garner. il pors
U S News 62:42-6+ Ja 16 '67
Johnson and Kennedy; the two thousand
days. T. A. Bailey. il pors N Y Times Mag
p30-1+ N 6 '66; Discussion. p 159-60 N 27;
22 D 4 '66
Kennedy as statesman. G. Kateb. Commen-
tary 41:54-60 Je '66
Kennedy image, three years later. il Sr
Schol 89:10-13+ N 18 '66
Peace corps; JFK's bold legacy. il por Look
30:34-9 Je 14 '66
Pleasure of his company. by P. B. Fay, jr.
Review
Time Jl por 88:118 O 28 '66
Pleasure of his company; excerpts. P. B.
Fay, jr. il pors McCalls 93:62-5+ Jl; 74-5+
Ag '66
Salinger tells how Kennedy tried to hide
Vietnam build-up; excerpts from With
Kennedy. P. Salinger. il por U S News 61:
103 S 12 '66
Sunday painters; Churchill, Eisenhower and
Kennedy. C. B. Luce. McCalls 94:12+ Ja
'67
Tale of one city, and two men; foreign poli-
cies of Kennedy and Johnson. C. Fritchey.
Harper 233:108-10+ D '66
Was John F. Kennedy a great man? S.
Alsop. il pors Sat Eve Post 239:16 D 3 '66
When J.F.K. was rich, young, and happy. H.
Muheim. il Esquire 66:64-6+ Ag '66
With Kennedy, by P. Salinger Review
Atlan 218:133-4 S '66 O. Handlin
Nat R 18:1052-3 O 18 '66. F. Russell
New Repub 155:16-17 S 10 '66. M. W.
Childs
Sat R 49:25 S 3 '66. J. M. Burns

KENNEDY, John Fitzgerald, 1917-1963—*Cont.*

Assassination

Any number can play; question of whether the assassination was the work of one man. Newsweek 68:37-8 N 7 '66

As the book appears: a close look at the facts; concerning The death of a President by W. Manchester. il pors U S News 62:50-2 Ja 23 '67

Battle of the book; Manchesters's The death of a President. il Time 88:15-18 D 23 '66

Book that backfired; concerning The death of a President, by W. Manchester. il U S News 61:36 D 26 '66

Chapter I; Manchester book. Newsweek 69:29-30 Ja 16 '67

Death of a President; excerpts. W. Manchester. il por Look 31:36-42+ Ja 24 '67 (to be cont)

Enough is enough. W. V. Shannon. Commonweal 85:191-2 N 18 '66; Discussion. 85:331, 410-11 D 16 '66, Ja 13 '67

Eyewitness in Dallas. C. Roberts. il Newsweek 68:26-9 D 5 '66

Growing rift of LBJ and Kennedy; behind the furor over a book; concerning The death of a President, by W. Manchester. il U S News 62:22-7 Ja 2 '67

Inquest. by E. J. Epstein. Review
    Esquire 66:14+ O '66. M. Muggeridge

Into the archives; X rays and photographs of body of John Kennedy. Time 88:33 N 11 '66

Jacqueline Kennedy's victory; W. Manchester's book. il Newsweek 69:16-19 Ja 2 '67

JFK censored? il Newsweek 68:65-6 O 3 '66

JFK; the death and the doubts. il Newsweek 68:25-6 D 5 '66

Kennedy assassination; question of a second investigation. New Repub 155:8 N 12 '66

Manchester book. Reporter 35:8 D 29 '66

Matter of reasonable doubt. il Life 61:38-48B+ N 25 '66

Missing link; photos and X-rays of autopsy. il Newsweek 68:30-1 N 14 '66

Mythmakers; mysterious deaths of people involved in case. il Time 88:33-4 N 11 '66

New inquiry is needed; questions concerning the assassination. H. Mitgang. N Y Times Mag p 14 D 25 '66; Discussion. p 15 Ja 8 '67

Notes for a new investigation. S. Meagher. Esquire 66:211+ D '66

Phantasmagoria; who murdered Kennedy? il Time 88:34-5 N 25 '66

Plans for official book on Kennedy assassination; W. Manchester's book. Pub W 190:40-1 S 5 '66

Primer of assassination theories. il Esquire 66:205-10+ D '66

Tragic day in Texas. il Sr Schol 89:7 N 18 '66

Widow vs. author; concerning W. Manchester's The death of a President. Sr Schol 89:16 Ja 6 '67
    See also
United States—President's commission on the assassination of President Kennedy

Bibliography

Assassination: some serious exceptions to the Warren report. R. Butterfield. Harper 233:122+ O '66

JFK in Dallas. A. L. Fein. il pors Sat R 49:36-8+ O 22 '66

Memorials

Assassination in Boston; abstract mural in John F. Kennedy federal building. il Time 88:60 Ag 26 '66

How some of the world remembers Kennedy. il Sr Schol 89:8-9 N 18 '66

Israeli memorial to President Kennedy. il U S News 61:14 Jl 18 '66

Little D; roadside marker at location of assassination. Time 87:25 Ap 15 '66

Living with history; Dallas citizens oppose assassination site marker text. Newsweek 67:48+ Ap 18 '66

Musical events; performance of Sydeman's In memoriam John F. Kennedy. W. Sargeant. New Yorker 42:128-9 N 26 '66

Tribute to JFK at Runnymede. E. Kolowrat. il Sr Schol 89:13 N 18 '66
    See also
John F. Kennedy library. Cambridge

Poetry

Three presidents. R. Bly. Nation 202:108 Ja 24 '66

Tomb

As the Kennedy gravesite takes shape. il U S News 60:16 Ja 10 '66

As the Kennedy tomb takes its final form. il U S News 61:12 N 28 '66

KENNEDY, John Fitzgerald, 1960-
My life with Caroline and John-John; excerpts (cont) M. Shaw. il por Ladies Home J 83:68-9+ F '66

KENNEDY, John Fitzgerald, family
My life with Caroline and John-John; excerpts (cont) M. Shaw. il Ladies Home J 83:68-9+ F '66

Skiing threesome. il pors Look 30:42-5 Mr 22 '66

KENNEDY, John F, library. See John F. Kennedy library, Cambridge

KENNEDY, John Fitzgerald, school of government. See Harvard university—John Fitzgerald Kennedy school of government (proposed)

KENNEDY, Joseph Patrick
Kennedy nobody knows. G. Cameron. il Ladies Home J 83:70-1+ Je '66

KENNEDY, Joseph Patrick, family
U.S. government-in-exile: the Kennedys. E. J. Hughes. Newsweek 67:21 Mr 7 '66

KENNEDY, Lois J.
Junior sailing. il Yachting 120:40-1+ Ag '66

KENNEDY, Louise
Face to face with a Bangkok recording star. il pors Seventeen 25:179 S '66

KENNEDY, Mary
I am a thought of you. Vogue 147:66 Ap 1 '66
Presence; poem. Cath World 203:238 Jl '66

KENNEDY, Robert Francis
Alliance for progress: symbol and substance. Bul Atomic Sci 22:28-34 N '66

Excerpt from testimony, May 20, 1965. Cong Digest 45:304+ D '66

Senator Robert Kennedy explains his position; interview. por U S News 60:68-70 Mr 14 '66

Suppose God is black. pors Look 30:44-6+ Ag 23 '66

Vietnam: pro and con of Kennedy's peace plan; statement, February 19, 1966. por U S News 60:104-7 Mr 7 '66

about

Another Kennedy seeks the presidency. il pors U S News 60:56-61 Je 27 '66

Battle of the bugs. por Time 88:19 D 23 '66

Bill & Bobby show. por Time 87:29 Ap 8 '66

Bob Kennedy's future. W. V. Shannon. Commonweal 83:686-7 Mr 18 '66

Bobby and the political battle between the generations. H. Sidey. il por Life 61:34D Jl 1 '66

Bobby Kennedy and the businessmen. G. R. Rosen. pors Duns R 88:32-3+ O '66

Bobby Kennedy's shadow cabinet. S. V. Roberts. por Esquire 66:163-9+ S '66

Bobby Kennedy's tactics; a view from abroad; excerpts from report. P. Worsthorne. U S News 61:10 S 19 '66

Bobby on Vietnam. K. Crawford. Newsweek 67:33 Mr 7 '66

Bobby phenomenon. J. Newfield, por Nation 203:505-7 N 14 '66

Bobby phenomenon. il pors Newsweek 68:30+ O 24 '66

Bobby raises a ruckus. M. McGrory. America 114:348 Mr 12 '66

Book that has backfired; concerning The death of a President, by W. Manchester. il por U S News 61:36 D 26 '66

Compulsive candidate. A. J. Glass. il pors Sat Eve Post 239:36-8+ Ap 23 '66

Did LBJ make John Kennedy president? il por U S News 62:42-6+ Ja 16 '67

Dirty business. Nation 203:690-1 D 26 '66

Fight RFK started: should we negotiate with the Viet Cong? por U S News 60:20 Mr 7 '66

Fox in a chicken coop. Time 87:26-7 Mr 4 '66

Front runners for '72. W. Weaver, jr. il pors N Y Times Mag p26-7+ My 22 '66

Growing drama in U.S. politics: new front runner? il por U S News 61:15 Ag 29 '66

Growing rift of LBJ and Kennedy; behind the furor over a book; concerning The death of a President, by W. Manchester. il por U S News 62:22-7 Ja 2 '67

He's a happening. A. Kopkind. New Repub 154:18-22 Ap 2 '66

Humphrey on Kennedy, a remark, then a rollback. por U S News 61:22 O 10 '66

Instant U. il por Newsweek 67:34-5 My 16 '66

Kennedy act. New Repub 155:4 N 12 '66

Kennedy caper; RFK in van of a new, anti-LBJ bloc of Peace Democrats. Newsweek 67:24-5 Mr 7 '66

Kennedy chemistry. Newsweek 68:21 O 3 '66

Kennedy hurricane. S. Alsop. por Sat Eve Post 239:14 Ag 27 '66

Kennedy in New York. New Yorker 42:39-42 My 14 '66

Kennedy in '68? H. H. Miller. New Repub 155:11-13 O 15 '66

KENNEDY Robert Francis—about—*Continued*
Kennedy initiative. Nation 202:253 Mr 7 '66
Kennedy on Latin America. J. O'Gara. Commonweal 84:304 Je 3 '66
Kennedy vs. Humphrey; what it's all about. il por U S News 60:54-5 Mr 28 '66
Kennedys at home have a few problems. M. F. Nolan. New Repub 154:10-11 Je 25 '66
Kennedy's prescription for Latin America. New Repub 154:8-10 My 28 '66
Look of '72? por Time 88:31 O 21 '66
Loss column; midterm upset election. K. Crawford. Newsweek 68:49 N 21 '66
LBJ vs. RFK? C. Roberts. il por Newsweek 67:35 Je 13 '66
Making of president Robert Kennedy. W. V. Shannon. il pors Harper 233:62-8 O '66
Making of the president, 1972? Newsweek 68:17-18 S 5 '66
Making of the surrogate. por Time 88:19-20 Jl 8 '66
Man from D.E.L.P.H.I. il por Time 87:33 My 20 '66
Missile crisis, by E. Abel. Review Sat R 49:43 Mr 12 '66. D. Kurzman
Mr Nixon advises Mr Kennedy. Nat R 18:1146 N 15 '66
Next president. K. Crawford. Newsweek 68:24 S 5 '66
On the campaign trail with Robert Kennedy. il por U S News 61:40-1 N 7 '66
One of the boys. por Time 88:14-15 Ag 26 '66
Passing the buck. Newsweek 68:19-20 D 26 '66
RFK: how he's building his own party. H. M. Alexander. il por Nations Bsns 54:38-9+ Jl '66
Robert Kennedy and the what if game. D. Kiker. il Atlan 218:66-70 O '66
Robert Kennedy, as Mexico's reds see him; excerpts from United press international dispatch. U S News 61:18 O 10 '66
Robert Kennedy moves up. H. Brandon. Sat R 49:8 Je 25 '66
Robert Kennedy on tour. J. Witcover. New Repub 155:9-10 O 1 '66
Shadow & the substance. il pors Time 88:32-6 S 16 '66
They don't dig this security jazz. P. Lisagor. il Nations Bsns 54:19-20 Ag '66
Washington: ten of its most powerful men. il por Vogue 148:156-7 N 15 '66
Welcome aboard. Nation 203:339-40 O 10 '66
What is Robert Kennedy up to? with reports by H. Sidey and P. Kimball. il pors Life 61:34-43+ N 18 '66
What party leaders think of Bobby Kennedy's future. il por U S News 61:54-6 S 26 '66
Who knew about Kennedy; RFK's story, and the FBI's. il por U S News 61:32-5 D 26 '66
Winning non-candidate. il por Newsweek 68:25 Jl 11 '66
Wiretap war: Kennedy, Johnson and the FBI. R. M. Cipes. New Repub 155:16-22 D 24 '66
You Wild thing, you. Time 89:42 Ja 13 '67
Youth myth. K. Crawford. Newsweek 68:44 N 7 '66

Visit to Africa, 1966

Favorite American; assessment of African tour. A. Deming. il pors Newsweek 67:53 Je 27 '66
Kennedy on Africa. New Yorker 42:19-21 Jl 9 '66
Kennedy safari. Nation 203:2 Jl 4 '66
Under fire: Robert Kennedy's African trip. por U S News 60:22 Je 6 '66

Visit to South Africa, 1966

Breath of fresh air? il New Repub 89:16 S 16 '66
Kennedy reception. New Repub 154:13-14 Je 11 '66
Senator Kennedy crosses the color line. A. P. Goller. Commonweal 84:455-6 Jl 22 '66
Superannuated youth. Reporter 34:7 Je 30 '66
Sympathetic chord. il pors Newsweek 67:44A-44B Je 20 '66
With Bobby in darkest Africa. il Time 87:27 Je 17 '66
With Robert Kennedy in white Africa. A. J. Meyers. il por U S News 60:46 Je 20 '66

KENNEDY, Robert Francis. family
Wilderness trip with the Kennedys. D. Connelly. il pors McCalls 93:66+ My '66

KENNEDY, Ted. See Kennedy, E. M.

KENNEDY, Widge. See Kennedy, L.

KENNEDY, William V.
Problems of peacemaking. America 114:855-7 Je 18 '66

KENNEDY, X. J.
Choice and range. Poetry 109:184-5 D '66

KENNEDY, CAPE
Airport to the moon. il Electr World 75:6, 94 Ja '66

Buildup of Titan 3 shown at Kennedy complex; photographs. Aviation W 84:86-9 Je 13 '66
Kennedy space center; springboard to the moon; with editorial comment. il Aviation W 84:21, 71-80+ Je 20 '66

KENNEDY half dollar. See Money—United States

KENNEDY international airport. See New York (city)—Airports

KENNEDY library. See John F. Kennedy library, Cambridge

KENNEDY space center. See United States—National aeronautics and space administration—John F. Kennedy space center

KENNEDY stamps. See Postage stamps

KENNELLY, Norman
Undercover man. Criticism
    Commonweal 84:418 Jl 1 '66

KENNELS
How to plan a dog run. il Sunset 136:134+ Je '66
Puppy pen, catwalk. dog deck, high feeder, A-frame dog house. il Sunset 138:62-3 Ja '67
Sanitize your dog kennel. N. Nider. il Field & S 71:114-15+ Ja '67

KENNER, Hugh
Buster agonistes. Nat R 18:786-7 Ag 9 '66
Evelyn Waugh: in memoriam. por Nat R 18:418+ My 3 '66
Movies. Nat R 18:281-3 Mr 22 '66
Torch in the labyrinth. Nat R 18:938-9+ S 20 '66
Understanding McLuhan. Nat R 18:1224-5 N 29 '66
Wisdom on the cello. Nat R 18:420-1 My 3 '66

KENNERLY, Adele, and Kennerly, Mitchell, Jr
Taxing problem solved. Sat R 49:6 Mr 19 '66

KENNERLY, Mitchell, Jr. See Kennerly, A. jt. auth.

KENNETT, James P.
Foraminiferal evidence of a shallow calcium carbonate solution boundary, Ross Sea, Antarctica. bibliog Science 153:191-3 Jl 8 '66

KENNEY, Ann D.
(ed) Family movie guide. See issues of Parents' magazine and better homemaking

KENNEY, John P. See Beattie, R. H. jt. auth.

KENNINGTON, Garth S. and Ching, C. F. T.
Activation analysis of ungulate hair. bibliog Science 151:1085-6 Mr 4 '66

KENNISON, James L.
Publicize, publicize. Parks & Rec 1:699+ S '66

KENNY, Howard
(ed) See Johnson, M. Backyard record deer

KENOSHA, Wis.
Snorkel that goes on loan. E. Spitzer. il Am City 81:117 Ap '66

Hospitals

Journey through a city of care; following a patient through Kenosha memorial hospital. C. Carner. il Todays Health 44:32-9 Ag '66

Streets

Slurry seal cures spalled-concrete ills. D. K. Holland. il Am City 81:103 F '66

KENOSHA memorial hospital. See Kenosha, Wis.—Hospitals

KENSETH, Arnold
Christmas pageant; poem. Christian Cent 83:1565 D 21 '66
Sonnet for Christmas. Christian Cent 83:1569 D 21 '66

KENSETT, John Frederick
John Frederick Kensett; a tribute to man and artist. F. Lewison. il por Am Artist 30:32-7+ O '66

KENSHALO, Dan R. and Scott, H. A. Jr
Temporal course of thermal adaptation. bibliog Science 151:1095-6 Mr 4 '66

KENT, Charles Deane
(ed) Canadian libraries. bibliog por Library J 91:5521-64+ N 15 '66

KENT, Fred, and Hooper, F. F.
Synthetic detergents: their influence upon iron-binding complexes of natural waters. bibliog Science 153:526-7 Jl 29 '66

KENT, George
Hottest job on earth. Read Digest 90:184-6+ Ja '67
Shock of happiness. Read Digest 88:97-100 Mr '66
World's no. 1 thunderer. Read Digest 89:13-14+ D '66

KENT, Leticia
Aerial garbage. New Repub 154:8 F 12 '66

KENT, Louise Andrews
Vermont year round cookbook; excerpts. Ladies Home J 83:106-7+ Ap '66

KENT, Rockwell
Art news from nowhere. il por Esquire 67:
127 Ja '67
KENT, England
England's colorful Kent. W. Houlton. il
Travel 125:60-2 My '66
KENTFIELD, Calvin
Frenchman in the kitchen. Holiday 40:66-8
Ag '66
Norway. Holiday 40:52-61+ N '66
KENTUCKY
See also
Cumberland Gap
Cumberland Plateau
Hunting—Kentucky

Description and travel
Sun shines bright. M. Cohen. il Redbook
127:60-1+ My '66
Travel report: Kentucky. L. Barry. il Pop
Phot 59:76-7+ Jl '66

Historic houses, etc.
Living with antiques; Stony Lonesome in
Kentucky. E. O. O'Rear. il Antiques 89:
851-5 Je '66

Parks and reserves
Hunting banned in Kentucky state parks. Nat
Parks Mag 40:21 O '66
KENTUCKY caves. See Mammoth Cave Na-
tional Park
KENTUCKY Derby. See Horse racing
KENTUCKY opera association
Blue grass winner. R. D. Daniels. il Opera N
30:14-16 Ap 9 '66
Louisville. W. Mootz. Opera N 30:31 F 5;
27 Je 4 '66
Louisville; production of The marriage of
Figaro. W. Mootz. Opera N 31:31 D 24 '66
KENTUCKY. University, Lexington
Educare for elders. il Time 88:44 Ag 12 '66
KENYA
See also
Education—Kenya
Natural resources—Kenya
Sports—Kenya

Boundaries
War in the desert. Newsweek 68:46 Jl 25 '66

Economic conditions
Whites in Kenya: what's their fate? A. J.
Meyers. il U S News 60:82-3 F 14 '66

Industries
Kenya. D. N. McMaster. bibliog il Focus
16:1-6 F '66

Politics and government
Another sweep for Jomo. il Time 88:33 Jl 8
'66
Clipped wings; Kenyatta's crackdown on
Odinga's breakaway movement. il News-
week 67:48+ My 9 '66
Exit double O; Odinga's resignation. News-
week 67:46 Ap 25 '66
Kenyatta of Kenya; with report by H. Moffet.
il pors Life 61:36-49+ Ag 5 '66
Kenyatta's country, by R. Cox. Review
Sat R il 49:37-8+ Jl 9 '66. C. Miller
Rolls, gold and ivory; storm over Nairobi's
mayor's transportation. il Newsweek 67:56
F 21 '66
Sharper panga. Time 87:36 My 13 '66
Transformation of Jomo Kenyatta. C. Sanger.
Reporter 34:37-9 Mr 10 '66
Trouble for Kenyatta. Time 87:40 Ap 29 '66
Trouble with Odinga. il Time 87:28 Mr 25 '66

Race problems
Whites in Kenya: what's their fate? A. J.
Meyers. il U S News 60:82-3 F 14 '66
KENYATTA, Jomo
Another sweep for Jomo. il por Time 88:33
Jl 8 '66
Kenyatta of Kenya; with report by H. Moffet.
il pors Life 61:36-49+ Ag 5 '66
Metamorphosis of Jomo Kenyatta. C. T.
Rowan. Read Digest 88:119-23 Mr '66
Our Eisie and Kenya's Kenyatta. G. P.
Hunt. pors Life 61:3 Ag 5 '66
Sharper panga. por Time 87:36 My 13 '66
Transformation of Jomo Kenyatta. C. Sanger.
por Reporter 34:37-9 Mr 10 '66
KEOHANE, Robert Owen
Political influence in the General assembly.
bibliog f por(back cover) Int Council 557:
5-64 Mr '66
KEPES, Gyorgy
Where is science taking us? excerpts from
addresses. por Sat R 49:66-7 Mr 5 '66

KEPPEL, Francis
Interview with Francis Keppel. pors Am Ed
2:11-13 Jl '66
National educational assessment. NEA J 55:
24+ F '66

about
Education: Keppel to leave HEW. L. J. Car-
ter. Science 152:328 Ap 15 '66
Keppel to head new G.E.-Time education
firm. Pub W 189:57-8 My 30 '66
Quitting time. Newsweek 67:37 Ap 18 '66
KEPPLER, Herbert
Keppler on the SLR. See issues of Modern
photography
KERALA, India
Breakaway from the C.S.I; new Independent
Anglican church of Kerala. V. Koilpillai.
Christian Cent 83:872 Jl 6 '66
Namboodiri Brahmans of Kerala. J. Mencher.
il Natur Hist 75:14-21 bibliog(p64) My '66
Rice prejudice. il Newsweek 67:42 F 14 '66
Sounds of hunger. Time 87:37 F 4 '66
KERATOSULFATES. See Sulfates
KERFOOT, Oliver. See Wright, I. M. jt. auth.
KERGUELEN ISLANDS
Father Perry's expedition to Kerguelen
Island. J. Ashbrook. il Sky & Tel 31:340-1
Je '66
KERMAN, Joseph
Majesty restored. Opera N 31:8+ N 5 '66
Night music. Opera N 31:24-5 Ja 14 '67
KERN, Edward
Crucible of Christendom. Life 60:77-8+ Je 17
'66
Stormy road to grandeur. Life 60:40-6+ Mr
11 '66
Swinging hub of the world. Life 60:66-79 Je
10 '66
KERN, Florence
Marine phone. Yachting 120:46-7+ S '66
KERNAN, Henry
Forest riddle of New York. Am For 72:21
S '66
KERNAN, John Devereux
China trade silver. Antiques 90:195-9 Ag '66
Gold funeral rings. Antiques 89:568-9 Ap '66
KERNELL, Daniel
Input resistance, electrical excitability, and
size of ventral horn cells in cat spinal cord.
bibliog Science 152:1637-40 Je 17 '66
KERNER, Ben
Boob bows out. Sports Illus 26:8 Ja 16 '67
KERNITE
Crystal structure of kernite, $Na_2B_4O_6$
$(OH)_2 \cdot 3H_2O$. R. F. Giese. bibliog il Science
154:1453-4 D 16 '66
KERNS, Mary Elenor
Ink & tempera prints. Sch Arts 65:17-20 F
'66
KEROSENE lanterns. See Lanterns
KERR, Alix. See Bailey, R. jt. auth.
KERR, Belle
Pressures on students. NEA J 55:30-1 S '66
KERR, George R. and Waisman, H. A.
Phenylalanine: transplacental concentrations
in rhesus monkeys. bibliog Science 151:824-
5 F 18 '66
KERR, Jean
How to talk to a baby. Ladies Home J 83:56
F '66
I just stepped out of Vogue. Ladies Home J
83:109+ My '66
Life's ambition; poem. McCalls 93:81 Je '66
KERR, Myrtle
Blotter press. Sch Arts 66:14-17 N '66
KERR, Walter
How playwrights lose. Harper 233:75-80 S '66

about
Dear Kerr: you, sir! por Time 88:68 S 9 '66
Supercritic. por Newsweek 68:94-5 S 12 '66
KERR, Walter B.
Herald tribune vs. Times: war of the Paris
editions. Sat R 49:104-5 N 12 '66
I discover America. Sat R 49:95+ Mr 12 '66
KERR-Mills act. See Insurance, Health—
United States
KERRIGAN, Anthony
(tr) See Borges, J. L. Three stories
KERTESZ, Istvan
Musical events: concert performed by Lon-
don symphony orchestra in Carnegie Hall.
W. Sargeant. New Yorker 42:125-6 Ap 16
16 '66
KESSEL, David, and others
Nucleotide formation as a determinant of 5-
fluorouracil response in mouse leukemias.
bibliog Science 154:911-13 N 18 '66
KESSLE, Gun
Child of affluence. W. Miller. Nation 202:338-9
Mr 21 '66

KESSLER, Edward
Alfred jewel; poem Sat R 49:27 S 17 '66
Cowbird; poem. Sat R 49:53 F 12 '66
KESSLER, Edwin
Storm's incalculable energy. Natur Hist 75:
12-17 Ap '66
KESSLER, Jascha
Three poems. Sat R 49:99 Ap 16 '66
KESSLER, Stephen Henry
Dangers of LSD. il por Time 87:52 Ap 22 '66
Murder by LSD? Newsweek 67:29 Ap 25 '66
KESTER, Wayne O.
How to buy your first horse. Consumer Bul
49:35-6 F '66
KESTNER, Jack
(ed) See Mandeville, R. C. What U.S. bombs
in North Vietnam; a navy pilot's account
Is U.S. stripping Atlantic defenses? il U S
News 62:10 Ja 9 '67
KETCHAM, Charles B.
Search for the new morality. Christian Cent
83:1236-9 O 12 '66
KETCHUM, Richard M.
Faces from the past (cont) Am Heritage 17:
24-5 F; 64-5 Ap '66
KETONES
Ants use chemical alarm. Sci N 90:270 O 8
'66
KETOSIS. See Cattle—Diseases and pests
KETTLES
American copper teakettle. H. J. Kauffman.
il Antiques 89:570-2 Ap '66
Ceramic kettles with stands. H. Newman. il
Antiques 89:240-4 F '66
KEVANE, Raymond A.
Different cultures but a common ideal.
America 114:326-8 Mr 5 '66
KEW botanical gardens. See Royal botanic
gardens, Kew
KEY; drama. See Jones, K.
KEY deer. See Deer
KEY WEST, Fla.
Key West gets largest desalting plant. Am
City 81:22 Jl '66
KEY WEST bridge. See Bridges
KEYES, Charlotte E.
Suppose they gave a war and no one came.
McCalls 94:26+ O '66
KEYES, Frances Parkinson
Fiesta San Antonio. Travel 125:29-31+ Mr '66
See also
KEYES, Gene
Suppose they gave a war and no one came.
C. E. Keyes. por McCalls 94:26+ O '66
KEYFITZ, Nathan
Privilege and poverty: two worlds on one
planet. Bul Atomic Sci 22:9-14 Mr '66
KEYNES, John Maynard Keynes, 1st baron
Age of Keynes, by R. Lekachman. Review
Commentary 42:91-2+ N '66. A. Shon-
field
Duns R 88:139 O '66. J. Berry
New Repub 155:26+ S 17 '66. A. Camp-
bell
Newsweek por 68:117A+ S 19 '66
Sat R 49:32+ O 15 '66. A. E. Burns
Economics and freedom. E. T. Chase. Com-
monweal 85:254-6 D 2 '66
Rise of the new economics. il Sr Schol 87:
12-16 Ja 14 '66
KEYS, Leonard F.
Sitting ducks of aerial war. il pors Ebony
22:58-60+ N '66
KEYS, FLORIDA. See Florida Keys
KEYS. See Locks and keys
KEYSERLING, Leon H.
Economic growth; letter. New Repub 155:
44-5 N 26 '66
Soliloquy for the guideposts; interview. por
Duns R 88:32 S '66
T.R.B. from Washington. New Repub 154:
4 Mr 5 '66
KHADEJHA (costume designer)
Khadejha: the girl who started it. I. Neves.
il pors Life 61:147-8 S 16 '66
KHAJURAHO, India
Day in Khajuraho. H. Sutton. il Sat R 49:
79-80+ My 7 '66
KHALDūN, Ibn. See Iban Khaldūn
KHAMA, Ruth (Williams)
Happy end for Prince Seretse and Ruth. il
pors Ebony 21:119-22+ My '66
KHAMA, Seretse
Botswana's cheerless freedom. T. Land. Re-
porter 34:41-2 F 10 '66
Happy end for Prince Seretse and Ruth. il
pors Ebony 21:119-22+ My '66
Two new nations. il por Time 88:46 O 7 '66
Whimsy can change the world. C. D. Downes.
America 115:386 O 1 '66
KHAN, Ali Akbar
Sarodist; interview. New Yorker 42:23-4 Ag
27 '66

KHAN, Mohammad Ayub. See Ayub Khan, M.
KHEEL, Theodore Woodrow
How the big strikes are settled. L. Velie.
Read Digest 88:135-9 Je '66
KHIDER, Mohammed
Death in exile. Newsweek 69:44-5 Ja 16 '67
KHRUSHCHEV, Nikita Sergeevich
Footnote to history. Newsweek 67:41 F 14
'66
Khrushchev, by E. Crankshaw. Review
America 115:99 Jl 23 '66. G. J. Prpic
Commentary 42:135-7 O '66. M. Rush
Newsweek il pors 67:106 Je 20 '66
Sat R 49:23-4 Je 25 '66. M. MacDuffie
Vote in peace; first public outing in a year.
Time 87:36 Je 24 '66
KIBBUTZIM. See Collective settlements—Is-
rael
KIDD, Susan
Face to face: with a girl who likes walking,
waltzes and witchcraft. por Seventeen 25:
78 My '66
KIDD, William Winston
Year of Billy the Kidd. D. Jenkins. il pors
Sports Illus 24:10-13 Ja 24 '66
KIDDE, Walter, and company
501st-largest industrial. Fortune 74:280 Jl 15
'66
Professional. il Newsweek 68:74 Jl 4 '66
KIDNAPPING
Battle of Gobbler's Knob; kidnapping of P.
Bradnick. il Time 87:23 My 27 '66
Ben Barka affair. C. Sterling. il Reporter
34:22-8 Mr 10 '66
Diminished fifth; l'affaire Ben Barka erupts
into scandal. il Newsweek 67:44+ Ja 31 '66
Fine French scandal over a missing Moroc-
can. il Life 60:30-32B F 4 '66
Kidnapped! interview, ed. by J. Bird.
P. A. Bradnick. il Sat Eve Post 239:25-9+
Jl 16 '66
Silent witnesses; Ben Barka affair. Time
87:32 F 4 '66
Stalking the terror of Shade Gap; Peggy
Ann Bradnick case. M. Mok. il Life 60:32B-
32E My 27 '66
Terror in the Tuscaroras; Peggy Ann Brad-
nick case. il Newsweek 67:29-30 My 30 '66
Watch for a kidnaped son; D. Goldman
mystery. L. Wainwright. Life 60:25 Je 3
'66
See also
Brigands and robbers
KIDNEYS
Acceleration of ureteral peristalsis by adrenal
compression. S. Boyarsky and others. il
Science 154:669 N 4 '66
DNA synthesis and differentiation in em-
bryonic kidney mesenchyme in vitro. J.
S. Sobel. bibliog il Science 153:1387-9 S 16
'66
Lysosomal nature of juxtaglomerular gran-
ules. E. R. Fisher. bibliog il Science 152:
1752 Je 24 '66
See also
Diuretics and diuresis
Glomerulus

Diseases
Kidney patients have higher hopes now; new
surgery, machinery, and research are com-
bating the scourge of kidney failure. il
Bsns W p 124+ O 15 '66
See also
Nephritis
KIDNEYS, Artificial
Artificial kidney saves accident victim. To-
days Health 44:72 My '66
Cheap kidney developed. Sci N 90:286 O 8 '66
Do-it-yourself kidney. il Time 87:51 Je 10 '66
Machine of life; dialysis centers. Newsweek
68:62 Jl 25 '66
New kidney to be smaller. Sci N 90:99 Ag
13 '66
KIDNEYS, Transplantation of. See Trans-
plantation of organs, tissues, etc.
KIEFER, John E. See Walker, T. R. jt. auth.
KIEFFER, Burt
(ed) See Thomas, G. Great antiques; the
Curtiss Fledgling
KIELMAN, Chester V.
Texas oil industry project. por Wilson Lib
Bul 40:616-18 Mr '66
KIELMANSEGG, Johann Adolf, graf von
Germany's Kielmansegg commander for
300,000 GI's? por U S News 61:22 Jl 11 '66
KIENHOLZ, Edward
Savonarola in the City of Angels. il por Time
87:78 Ap 8 '66
KIEPENHEUER, K. O.
Domeless solar refractor of Capri observatory.
Sky & Tel 31:256-9 My '66
KIEPURA, Jan
Obituary
Opera N por 31:34 O 15 '66

KIERKEGAARD, Søren Aabye
Lowest depths; excerpts from Last years. por Time 87:43 My 6 '66

about

Books. J. Updike. New Yorker 42:115-18+ F 26 '66

KIES, Marian W. and others
Encephalitogenic activity of bovine basic proteins. bibliog Science 151:821-2 F 18 '66

KIESINGER, Kurt Georg
Bonn tries consensus. il por Bsns W p41 D 3 '66
Germany: government by compromise. il por Newsweek 68:50+ D 12 '66
Germany: the arithmetic of politics. il por Newsweek 68:60+ N 21 '66
Grand coalition. Sr Schol 89:14-15 Ja 13 '67
In search of coalition. il por Time 88:40 N 18 '66
Order of the day; German equivalent of a state-of-the-union message. por Newsweek 68:32 D 26 '66
Quiet is shattered on Bonn front. il por Bsns W p44-5 N 19 '566
Renewal on the Rhine. il pors Time 88:34-8 D 9 '66
Resurgence of the spirit; in Paris. por Time 89:26+ Ja 20 '67
Romanized Teuton. il por Newsweek 68:50+ D 19 '66
Stalking the elusive coalition. il por Newsweek 68:41 N 28 '66

KIESLER, Frederick John
Grotto for meditation. Craft Horiz 26:22-7 Jl '66
Obituary
Art N 64:6 F '66

KIEV, Russia
Dina Mironovna Pronichev remembers Babi Yar; excerpt from novel, Babi Yar. A. Kuznetsov. N Y Times Mag p45+ D 11 '66
KIEV massacre. See World war, 1939-1945—Atrocities

KIEWIT, Peter
Biggest invisible builder in the world. H. B. Meyers. il pors Fortune 73:146-51+ Ap '66

KIGHT, Murley Kay
Mosaic. Sch Arts 66:31 N '66

KIKER, Douglas
Atlantic report: Washington. See issues of Atlantic, September 1966
Robert Kennedy and the what if game. Atlan 218:66-70 O '66
Russell of Georgia: old guard at its shrewdest. Harper 233:101-4+ S '66

KILAUEA (crater)
Nature note; Pele's hair. il Sci N 90:486 D 10 '66

KILIMANJARO
Up Kilimanjaro. G. M. Orenstein. il Atlan 218:128-31 Jl '66

KILLENS, John Oliver
Speaking out. por Sat Eve Post 239:10+ Jl 2 '66

KILLER whales. See Whales
KILLING, Mercy. See Euthanasia
KILLING of animals. See Hunting
KILLING of Sister George; drama. See Marcus, F.

KILLINGER, Madeline (Wyer)
Malcolm Glenn Wyer. ALA Bul 69:383-4 Ap '66

KILLINGSWORTH, Edward A, family
Family terrace: teen-age theatre. il House & Gard 130:104-5+ Jl '66

KILLINGSWORTH, Jeannette
You can't send a girl there! il pors Mlle 63: 33-40 Jl '66

KILLY, Jean Claude
Skiing's darling of derring-do. D. Jenkins. il pors Sports Illus 24:20-2+ F 21 '66
Sportsman of the year: J. Ryun; four others excelled. por Sports Illus 25:50 D 19 '66

KILPATRICK, James Jackson
New right: what does it seek? Sat R 49:29-31+ O 8 '66
Special report. Nat R 18:258+ Mr 22 '66

KILPATRICK, Walter S.
Ecumenical gap. Christian Cent 83:296-300 Mr 9 '66

KILSTON comet. See Comets

KILTS
Kilts for kids; sewing instructions. C. Houck. il Parents Mag 41:134 S '66

KILVERT, B. Cory, Jr
Home garden notebook. Flower Grower 53:61-2 My '66
Peat moss fact & fiction. il Flower Grower 53:63-4 My '66
Plot to produce more. Flower Grower 53:42-3 Mr '66
When the chips are down. Flower Grower 53: 43 N '66

KIM, Chong Pil
Dawn over Asia; address, October 6, 1966. Vital Speeches 33:42-6 N 1 '66

KIM, Richard E.
O my Korea! por Atlan 217:106-17 F '66

KIMBALL, John T.
Age of the intuitive manager. Duns R 87: 42-3+ Ja '66

KIMBALL, Penn
He builds his own Kennedy identity and the power flows freely to him. Life 61:42-3+ N 18 '66

KIMBALL, Ruth F.
Theatrical exhibitions at Lincoln Center. Wilson Lib Bul 40:513-16+ F '66

KIMBELL museum. See Fort Worth, Tex.—Galleries and museums

KIMBERLY-CLARK corporation
Femininely yours. M. B. Keiser. il Parents Mag 41:16+ F '66
Super trees. il Am For 72:10-11 O '66

KIMBLE, Daniel P.
Learning, remembering, and forgetting. Science 151:712-13 F 11 '66

KIMBLE, George H. T.
Instincts and prophecies. Reporter 35:40+ D 29 '66
Nor any drop to drink. Reporter 35:55-6 S 8 '66

KIMBROUGH, Emily
Muzzy's heart was young and gay. Life 16: 17 Jl 1 '66

KIMBROUGH, Robert A.
Expectant mother. Redbook 126:42+ Mr '66

KIMMEL, Husband E.
Admiral Kimmel: why was he not warned? excerpts from statement, 1966. por U S News 61:20 D 19 '66

KIMPTON, Lawrence A.
Unrest on the campus; address, November 9, 1965. Vital Speeches 32:302-5 Mr 1 '66

KIMSEY, Ada R.
Women who do things. Parks & Rec 1:836-8+ O '66

KIND, Joshua
Art news from Chicago (cont) Art N 64:46+ F; 65:56 Sum '66

KINDERGARTEN
End of the beginning. E. Maloney. il Ladies Home J 83:57 Ag '66
Miss Marsh, I love you. E. Maloney. Ladies Home J 83:80+ O '66
Planning preschool facilities. M. P. Berson and W. W. Chase. il Am Ed 2:7-11 D '65
Water the hibernating toads! experiences with a variety of small animals. R. J. Moscrip. il NEA J 55:30-2 F '66

KINETIC art. See Art in motion

KINETIN
Auxin effects on the mobility of kinetin in the plant. A. K. Seth and others. bibliog il Science 151:587-8 F 4 '66

KING, Alan
Chopped liver à la King. il por Time 87:48 My 13 '66

KING, Arthur R. Jr, and Brownell, J. A.
Monolithic theories of the curriculum; excerpt from Curriculum and the disciplines of knowledge. bibliog Sch & Soc 94:190-8 Ap 2 '66

KING, Billie Jean
Duel on grass at 26 paces. B. Collins. Sports Illus 25:54-5 S 5 '66
Manolo is king, and a king is queen. J. Lovesey. il por Sports Illus 25:50+ Jl 11 '66

KING, Cecil Harmsworth
Trade winds. H. R. Mayes. Sat R 49:12 O 29 '66

KING, Donald West. See Saunders, G. C. jt. auth.

KING, Edward Lee
Voice from Watts. il Newsweek 67:68 Je 20 '66

KING, Larry L.
Bob Jones university: the buckle on the Bible belt. Harper 232:51-8 Je '66
Joe Pool of HUAC. Harper 233:61-5 N '66
Lyndon Johnson as literary critic. New Repub 155:35-7 N 12 '66
My hero LBJ. Harper 233:51-61 O '66
Poeme d'extase. New Repub 155:34-5 N 26 '66
They couldn't cut old Ollie, could they? Sat Eve Post 239:107-11 O 22 '66

KING, Lawrence T.
Court vs. the voters on open housing. Commonweal 84:491-2 Ag 5 '66

KING, M. G. See Mangan, G. L. jt. auth.

KING, Martin Luther, 1929-
Freedom's crisis: last steep ascent. Nation 202:288-92 Mr 14 '66
Gift of love. McCalls 94:146-7 D '66
Nonviolence: the only road to freedom. por Ebony 21:27-30+ O '66

KING, Martin Luther, 1929- —*Continued*

about

As Negro unrest continues to spread—. il
    U S News 61:30 Jl 25 '66
Chicago summer: bossism, racism and Dr
    King. P. Good. il Nation 203:237-42 S 19 '66
Dilemma for Dr King. C. E. Fager. Christian
    Cent 83:331-2 Mr 16 '66
Doctor King carries fight to northern slums.
    il pors Ebony 21:94-6+ Ap '66
Doctor King's case for nonviolence. America
    115:578 N 12 '66
Gamble in the ghetto. Newsweek 67:24-5
    Ja 31 '66
Graham and King as ghetto-mates. Chris-
    tian Cent 83:976 Ag 10 '66
King in Chicago. B. Cook. Commonweal 84:
    175-7 Ap 29 '66
New white backlash? por Sat Eve Post 239:88
    S 10 '66
One last chance. Christian Cent 83:792-3 Je 22
    '66
Racial scene. Christian Cent 83:930 Jl 27 '66
Render unto King. il por Time 87:18-19 Mr 25
    '66
Requiem or revival? T. B. Morgan. il pors
    Look 30:70-3+ Je 14 '66
Still King. Christian Cent 83:1071 S 7 '66
Too many cooks, too much spice. Christian
    Cent 83:880 Jl 13 '66
Touchiest target. il por Newsweek 68:29 Ag
    15 '66

KING, Maureen
Princess Grace: how she lovingly raises her
    children; ed. by S. Fliegers. por Good H
    162:74-7+ F '66
KING, Robert H.
Preseminary theology? Christian Cent 83:558-
    61 Ap 27 '66
KING, Seth S.
Great purge in Indonesia. N Y Times Mag
    p25+ My 8 '66
KING, Terry Johnson
Strangest yachting crowd. Yachting 119:224-5
    Mr '66
KING, William Dickey
Gathering of Kings; photographs. Horizon
    8:38-9 Wint '66
KING, William H.
You've never had it so good. Sr Schol 87sup 19
    Ja 14 '66
KING Kam. See Cameron, C. B.
KING Alfred and the cakes; drama. See Thane,
    A.
KING brothers
Monkey business grows in Maryland. il pors
    Ebony 21:97-100 Mr '66
KING crabs
Intracellular absorption difference spectrum
    of limulus extra-ocular photolabile pigment.
    G. C. Murray. bibliog il Science 154:1182-3
    D 2 '66
Simple photoreceptors in limulus polyphemus.
    R. Millecchia and others. bibliog il Science
    154:1199-201 D 2 '66
KING ISLAND, Alaska
Our far-flung correspondents; summer's first
    boat. B. Roueché. New Yorker 42:98+ O
    22 '66
KING salmon fishing. See Salmon fishing
KING snakes. See Snakes
KING VALLEY recreation area, Calif. See
    Recreation areas
KINGEN, W. R.
Phone tattles on burglars. Pop Mech 126:
    174-7+ D '66
KINGFISH fishing
Sweet king. G. Heinold. il Outdoor Life
    138:30+ D '66
KINGFISHERS
Freshest thing in feathers. G. Heinold. il
    Read Digest 89:211-12+ S '66
KINGS and rulers
Crowned with money; base pay. il Time 88:
    100 S 9 '66
Mistresses, by B. Kelen. Review
    Sat R 49:28 Jl 9 '66. P. MacManus
    See also
Africa—Kings and rulers
Monarchy
Pretenders, Royal
KINGS CANYON NATIONAL PARK
Yosemites of the Kings River. R. H. Rose.
    il Nat Parks Mag 40:4-9 O '66
KINGSPORT press, incorporated
Allied Kingsport unions refile unfair labor
    charges. Pub W 190:194-5 Jl 11 '66
Education board asks delay on Kingsport
    injunction. Pub W 189:29-30 Ap 4 '66
Judge enjoins school board in Kingsport
    strike case. Pub W 189:46-7 Mr 28 '66

Kingsport press upheld against union charges.
    Pub W 190:45 S 19 '66
N.Y. Board of education to vote on union
    plea; proposal to discontinue buying books.
    Pub W 189:50 Mr 21 '66
N.Y.C. schools enjoined from Kingsport boy-
    cott. Pub W 190:27 O 24 '66
New York schools asked to boycott Kings-
    port press. Pub W 189:152 F 21 '66
Unions drop NLRB charges against Kings-
    port press. Pub W 189:45-6 Je 20 '66
KINGTON, Brent
Brent Kington's wheeling world. il Craft
    Horiz 26:43-5 N '66
KININS. See Peptides
KINKEL, Jack
When the tail wags the dog. Sat R 49:140+
    Mr 12 '66
KINNE, Russ
Flying photographer. Flying 78:94-5 F '66
KINNELL, Galway
La Bagarède: poem. New Yorker 42:58 S
    24 '66
Last songs. Nation 202:528 My 2 '66
Night in the forest; poem. Nation 203:398 O
    17 '66
Poem of Negro boys I swam with in the
    Mississippi seven years ago. Nation 203:
    126 Ag 8 '66
Poem: On this hill crossed; Correspondence-
    school instructor says goodbye to his poetry
    students; Poetry shelf; poems. Poetry 108:
    217-24 Jl '66
KINNEY service corporation
Kinney spreads umbrella wider; expanding
    service, from autos to funerals. il Bsns W
    p 101-2+ Ap 16 '66
KINROSS, John Patrick Douglas Balfour, 3d
    baron
Nile. Horizon 8:80-99 Sum '66
KINSEY, Bill Haywood
Grudging acquittal. Time 88:62 S 30 '66
In another country. Newsweek 68:40+ O 3
    '66
Peace corps murder case. il pors Time 88:64+
    S 16 '66
KINSOLVING, Lester
Demurrer on Jazzy Lord's suppers. Chris-
    tian Cent 83:803-4 Je 22 '66
Entertainment; Fr Boyd at the hungry i.
    Christian Cent 83:1244 O 12 '66
KINTNER, Robert Edmonds
Playing all the bases. por Time 87:25 Ap 8
    '66
Utility men. Newsweek 67:28 Ap 11 '66
White House staff. New Repub 154:8-9 Ap
    16 '66
KINZER, H. M.
Shoot now, think later? Pop Phot 58:65+ My
    '66
KIPLING, Rudyard
Rudyard Kipling, by J. I. M. Stewart. Re-
    view
    Sat R por 49:58 O 22 '66. O. Prescott
Unexplored territory. J. Hart. Nat R 18:
    1233-4 N 29 '66
KIPLINGER, Willard Monroe
Chat with W. M. Kiplinger. por Changing T
    21:inside cover Ja '67
Keeping an eye on Washington; interview.
    por Nations Bsns 54:68-72+ Ag '66
KIRA, Alexander
Futuristic features, a fountain sink, low toilet,
    lounge-like tub. M. Mok. il por Life 60:
    84-6 My 20 '66
Getting set for tomorrow's bath. il Bsns W
    p 103-4+ My 21 '66
Guess what! L. Benjamin. Ladies Home J
    83:8 S '66
KIRBY, Thomas F.
Infringers beware! Pop Electr 25:75-6 Jl '66
KIRBY, William D.
Job-matched units spur snow-fighting. Am
    City 81:98-9 F '66
KIRCHNER-DEAN, Otto
Book selection and the democratic dialogue.
    por Library J 91:2765-7 Je 1 '66
KIRK, Ben T. and Sinclair, J. B.
Plasmodesmata between hyphal cells of geo-
    trichum candidum. bibliog Science 153:1646
    S 30 '66
KIRK, Claude
Wave either way. Time 88:29-30 O 28 '66
KIRK, Donald
Anti-Communist crusade of Indonesia's Mos-
    lems. Reporter 34:41-2+ Ja 27 '66
Bali exorcises an evil spirit. Reporter 35:42-3
    D 15 '66
Election to test Laotian stability. Reporter
    35:26-9 D 29 '66
Indonesia's Chinese are people without a
    country. N Y Times Mag p32-3+ O 23 '66
Struggle for power in Indonesia. Reporter
    34:38-40 F 24 '66
Suharto is the name, not Sukarno. N Y Times
    Mag p 18-19+ Jl 24 '66

KIRK, Donald—*Continued*
Sukarno's holdouts in central Java. Reporter 35:39-41 S 8 '66
KIRK, Grayson
University in contemporary society; adaptation of address. June 1, 1965. Sch & Soc 94:63-5 F 5 '66
Youth on the college campus; address. November 3, 1965. Vital Speeches 32:248-52 F 1 '66
KIRK, Lucile D.
Good looks. See issues of Parents' magazine and better homemaking
KIRK, Roland
Roland Kirk: modern one-man band. il pors Ebony 21:181-4+ My '66
KIRK, Russell
Dogma of the South. por Nat R 19:38 Ja 10 '67
From the academy. See issues of National review
New direction in the U.S. right? N Y Times Mag p20-1+ Ag 7 '66
Scholar is not a lion or a fox. N Y Times Mag p28-9+ My 1 '66
KIRK, Ruth
Rain forest; excerpt from Olympic rain forest. il Audubon Mag 68:314-27 S '66
Vacation U.S.A. a Redbook guide to the national parks. Redbook 126:43-50 Ap '66
KIRKENDALL, Lester A.
Away with stereotypes. PTA Mag 61:6-7 S '66
KIRKPATRICK, Curry
Basketball. Sports Illus 25:60+ Jl 4 '66
Basketball's week. Sports Illus 26:68-9 Ja 9 '67
Celtics stretch an era. Sports Illus 24:30-1 Ap 11 '66
College basketball. Sports Illus 26:42-3 Ja 2 '67
Pro basketball. Sports Illus 24:88-9 Ap 25 '66
KIRKPATRICK, Ken
Tax saving tips for electronics moonlighters. Pop Electr 24:67-9 Mr '66
KIRKUP, James
Earth tremor in Lugano; poem. New Yorker 42:62 S 24 '66
KIRLOSKAR, Shantanu Laxman
M.I.T. man in Poona. por Fortune 73:75 Mr '66
KIROV ballet
Kirov ballet's Sleeping beauty film. C. Barnes. il Dance Mag 40:44-5 Ap '66
KIRSHNER, Donald
Man with the golden ear. il por Time 87:44 Ap 22 '66
KIRSHNER, Norman, and others
Release of catecholamines and specific protein from adrenal glands. bibliog Science 154:529-31 O 28 '66
KIRTLAND, Robert
Changing the church's attitude toward change. America 115:274-6 S 17 '66
KIRTLAND warblers. See Warblers
KIRWAN, John D.
Movies. Nat R 18:1178-9 N 15 '66
Plea for sanity. Nat R 18:1275 D 13 '66
KISS; story. See Taube, M.
KISSING disease. See Mononucleosis, Infectious
KISSING Jamie Cary; story. See Jenning, M.
KISSINGER, Henry A.
For a new Atlantic alliance; address, June 1966. Reporter 35:18-27 Jl 14 '66
Vietnam: what should we do now? por Look 30:26 Ag 9 '66
KISTER, Kenneth F.
Of luvs and lights. por Wilson Lib Bul 41:510-13+ Ja '67
Why not work in England next year? por ALA Bul 61:72-6 Ja '67
KISTIAKOWSKY, G. B.
Allocating support for basic research, and the importance of practical applications. Bul Atomic Sci 22:12-18 F '66
KIT building
Gift idea: the serious kit. il Sunset 137:95-6+ D '66
KITAGAWA Utamaro. See Utamaro
KITAY, William
Imaginary heart disease. Sci Digest 60:53-7 S '66
Let's retain the dignity of dying. Todays Health 44:62-4+ My '66
KITCHEN; drama. See Wesker, A.
KITCHEN cabinets
Parts of this kitchen roll around. il Sunset 138:75 Ja '67
Swing-down cupboards. B. Baker. il Pop Mech 126:126-7 S '66
Tall storage ideas. il Bet Hom & Gard 44:110+ N '66

KITCHEN furniture
Galley spices up patio fun. S. Ellingson. il Pop Mech 125:148-50 My '66
Good food happens here! il Bet Hom & Gard 44:54-69 N '66
Kitchen of ideas. il Sunset 137:82-9 N '66
More about our mix-bake-center kitchen. il Bet Hom & Gard 44:104 N '66
Place for the cook in the garden. il Sunset 136:88-93 Je '66
Small, but still a place to sit down. il Bet Hom & Gard 44:142 Je '66
What's right for counter height? il Bet Hom & Gard 44:86 Ap '66
Wheel-about kitchen. il House & Gard 129:100-5 F '66
You are seeing it now without one wall. il Sunset 136:70-1 F '66
See also
Kitchen cabinets
Snack bars
KITCHEN gadgets. See Gadgets
KITCHEN madonna; story. See Godden, R.
KITCHEN physics. See Physics—Experiments
KITCHEN planning. See Home economics
KITCHEN ranges. See Stoves
KITCHEN sinks. See Sinks
KITCHEN storage. See Storage in the home
KITCHEN utensils
Dictionary of pots and pans. il McCalls 94:42+ N '66
Gift list for cooks. M. Davidson. il Ladies Home J 83:64+ D '66
Good food happens here! il Bet Hom & Gard 44:54-69 N '66
Household gadgets: inexpensive, ingenious, invaluable. il Good H 162:188+ Je '66
Kitchen of ideas. il Sunset 137:82-9 N '66
Lowdown on nonstick kitchen stuff. il Changing T 20:23-4 O '66
More about our mix-bake-center kitchen. il Bet Hom & Gard 44:104 N '66
More good news about non-stick cookware. il House & Gard 129:30 Mr '66
Ten ways to make a little kitchen seem bigger. M. Davidson. il Ladies Home J 83:56+ My '66
Tougher Teflon coatings for cookware. il Consumer Bul 49:2+ My '66
Western kitchen. See issues of Sunset
What's cooking here? guessing game for gourmets. il House & Gard 129:182-3+ My '66

Anecdotes, facetiae, satire, etc.
As the pot boils. M. Davidson. il Ladies Home J 83:58+ Ap '66

Care
Dictionary of pots and pans; hints on care. McCalls 94:161 N '66
KITCHEN ware. See Kitchen utensils
KITCHENS, J. H. Jr. See Mixon, J. E. jt. auth.
KITCHENS
Beautiful kitchens come in all sizes. il McCalls 93:116-21+ Ap '66
Bold, bright kitchens. il House & Gard 129:186-9 My '66
Breakfast beside a cheerful new kitchen. il Sunset 136:126-7 Je '66
Build easy living into your kitchen. J. LemMon. il Suc Farm 64:134-5 Mr '66
Can you reduce the noise in your kitchen? D. Hasleiet. Bet Hom & Gard 44:104+ My '66
Combine modern utility with old-fashioned charm. J. LemMon. il Suc Farm 64:72-3 My '66
Compact kitchen has everything right. H. A. Dawson and G. V. Young. il Bet Hom & Gard 44:68-9 Ap '66
Cook can talk to her guests, and they don't get in her way. il Sunset 136:164-5 My '66
Creative kitchen decor. S. Kaiser. il Farm J 90:114 F '66
Diary of a remodeled kitchen. il House & Gard 130:128-30 Ag '66
European cooks' tour. B. Plumb. il N Y Times Mag p82-3+ My 22 '66
Everything hangs out in plain sight. il Sunset 137:112 O '66
Here's a kitchen with plenty of everything. J. LemMon. il Suc Farm 64:66-7 Je '66
How to detour kitchen traffic. J. Gillies. il Farm J 90:114-15 Ap '66
How to make a kitchen bigger without adding space. il Bet Hom & Gard 44:134 S '66
How to work with a kitchen planner. E. S. Oshin. House & Gard 130:240-1+ O '66
In this new kitchen-family room, there's music, a warm fire, and bright carpet on the floor. il Sunset 136:124-5 My '66

KITCHENS—*Continued*
  Kitchen cooks as easily for twenty-four as
    for two. il House & Gard 131:118-19 Ja '67
  Kitchens à la carte. N. S. Hazelton. Nat R
    18:317-18 Ap 5 '66
  Look-see kitchens give up storage for view.
    il Sunset 136:119-20 Mr '66
  Louvered kitchen wall. il Sunset 137:118 O '66
  Make the most of kitchen storage. J. Lem-
    Mon. il Suc Farm 64:79-83+ O '66
  More about our mix-bake-center kitchen. il
    Bet Hom & Gard 44:104 N '66
  More kitchens with positive points of view.
    il Good H 162:124-9 F '66
  Now here's a kitchen addition that goes
    all out! il Bet Hom & Gard 44:40-1 Ag '66
  One catalog kitchen, two different ways.
    J. LemMon. il Suc Farm 64:66-7 Jl '66
  One-wall kitchen with a room full of ideas!
    il Bet Hom & Gard 44:90 Je '66
  This kitchen fits the space you have! il Bet
    Hom & Gard 44:80 My '66
  Very versatile kitchen dividers. il Bet Hom
    & Gard 44:98 My '66
  Well-designed laundry can complement even
    the most distinguished kitchen. il Bet Hom
    & Gard 44:74-5 F '66
  What makes a kitchen really work? il Bet
    Hom & Gard 44:110+ O '66
  What's wrong with this kitchen? il Redbook
    127:78-9+ Je '66
  Wheel-about kitchen. il House & Gard 129:
    100-5 F '66
  Where the pros cook: workshops of profes-
    sional home economists. M. Davidson. il
    Ladies Home J 84:74-7 Ja '67
  You are seeing it now without one wall. il
    Sunset 136:70-1 F '66
  Young family, old house, new kitchen. M.
    Davidson. il Ladies Home J 83:88-90 S '66

  Lighting
  See Electric lighting
KITCHENS, Institutional

  Equipment
  Changes in food service technology and how
    they affect design. E. G. Daniels. il Arch
    Rec 140:145-8 Ag '66
KITCHENS, Outdoor
  Second kitchen goes outdoors. J. H. Inger-
    soll. il Pop Gard 17:40-3 My '66
KITE fishing. See Fishing
KITES
  Go fly a kite! N. Mallison. il Parks & Rec
    1:236-7 Mr '66
  How to build and fly Chinese kites. W. H.
    Paxton. il Pop Sci 188:144-7 My '66
  Kites restored: weekends in Sheep Meadow,
    Central park. New Yorker 42:24-5 Ag 27 '66
KITMAN, Marvin
  My slice of the real-estate pie. Sat Eve Post
    240:16 Ja 14 '67
  My son the outfielder, and my major-leaguer,
    Dick Stuart. Sat Eve Post 239:20 S 10 '66

  about
  Man from Monocle. Newsweek 67:101-2 Je
    13 '66
  Soon to be a major motion picture. C. D. B.
    Bryan. New Repub 154:23-5 Je 11 '66
  Trade winds. J. Beatty, jr. Sat R 49:10 Je
    4 '66
KITT PEAK national observatory. See Astro-
    nomical observatories
KITTAY, Sol
  How BVD bought its new outfit. il por Bsns
    W p98-100 Je 4 '66
  Renaissance man in B.V.D.s. R. Levy. por
    Duns R 88:41-2 Jl '66
KITTERY POINT, Me.
  Living with antiques; Pepperrell mansion.
    J. W. P. Frost. il Antiques 89:368-73
    Mr '66
KITTIKACHORN, Thanom. See Humphrey, H.
    H. jt. auth.
KITTO, G. B. and Wilson, A. C.
  Evolution of malate dehydrogenase in birds.
    bibliog Science 153:1408-10 S 16 '66
KITTY Hawk (aircraft carrier) See Aircraft
    carriers
KIVITT, Ted
  Brief biography. S. Goodman. pors Dance
    Mag 40:50-1 O '66
KIWANIS clubs
  Top ten; men of the year. il Am City 81:
    169 Je '66
KIWANUKA, Joseph, abp
  Death of an archbishop. America 114:371 Mr
    19 '66
KIZER, Carolyn
  What we are, and are not. B. Cutler. Poetry
    108:269 Jl '66
KLABER, Eugene Henry
  Who needs new cities? Arch Forum 124:68-9
    Ap '66

KLASCHIK, Lothar H.
  Design technique of visual persuasion. De-
    sign 67:8-11 Ja '66
KLASS, Philip J.
  Scientific explanation for the UFOs? il J.
    Lear. il Sat R 49:67-9 O 1 '66
KLASSEN, E. T.
  Test of the total product. Duns R 88:139-40
    N '66
KLAUS, Joseph
  Address in General assembly, December 1,
    1965; summary. por UN Mo Chron 3:70-1 Ja
    '66
KLAUSMEYER, Thomas H.
  Federal support for construction of health-
    related facilities. Arch Rec 139:160-3 Mr '66
KLAW, Spencer
  Man with the golden touch. Sat Eve Post
    239:83-5+ Mr 12 '66
  Perils of running a nonprofit. Fortune 74:158-
    61+ N '66
KLEBER, Norbert
  Gallery that's on the go. M. Orovan. il por
    U S Camera 30:38+ Ja '67
KLEIHAUER, Aylsworth
  On the beach, with sculpture. il Sch Arts 65:
    9-13 F '66
KLEIN, Arthur. See Belvin, W. jt. auth.
KLEIN, Carole
  Parent and child. N Y Times Mag p 102+
    O 16 '66
KLEIN, Daniel Martin
  Wolves in the attic; story. Sat Eve Post
    239:78-9 Je 18 '66
KLEIN, David
  College & careers. See issues of Seventeen
  Families on the move. Parents Mag 41:48-9+
    F '66
  Team or tug of war? Seventeen 25:146-7+
    F '66
  —See Goodman, N. jt. auth.
KLEIN, Herbert E.
  High-powered drive in material handling.
    Duns R 87:pt2 128-9+ Mr '66
  Transformation in the office. Duns R 87:pt2
    124-5+ Mr '66
KLEIN, Howard
  Aglow with life. Opera N 30:24-5 Mr 5 '66
  Birth of an opera. N Y Times Mag p32-3+
    Ag 28 '66
  Cesare means emperor of bassos. N Y Times
    Mag p44+ Mr 20 '66
  Instinct for drama. Opera N 31:46-7 S 17 '66
KLEIN, Julius
  Dodd's case: what's ethical? il por Newsweek
    68:22+ Ag 1 '66
  Dodd's trip: how helpful to Klein? por U S
    News 61:8 Ag 1 '66
  Focus on Washington. Cato. Nat R 18:663
    Jl 12 '66
  From Senator Dodd: a denial of misconduct;
    summary of testimony, June 27, 1966.
    T. J. Dodd. U S News 61:14-15 Jl 11 '66
  Private lives. il Time 88:15 Jl 1 '66
  Senate looks at a member's conduct. il por
    U S News 61:6 Jl 4 '66
  Senator & the lobbyist. il Time 88:19 Jl 8 '66
KLEIN, Marcus
  Gods and goats. Reporter 35:60-2 S 22 '66
  Key is loneliness. Reporter 34:43-4 Je 30 '66
KLEIN, Norma
  Garnet necklace; story. Mlle 62:184-5 Ap '66
KLEIN, Tobias
  Teen-age culture. America 115:10 Jl 2 '66
KLEINE-AHLBRANDT, Laird
  Real poet. Opera N 30:22-3 F 5 '66
KLEINMANN, Jack H.
  Group insurance is growing. NEA J 55:48-9
    My '66
  What makes a good school system? NEA J
    55:45 N '66
KLEINSCHMIDT, Edward Ernst
  Inventor who still won't quit. il pors Bsns W
    p 154-6+ S 3 '66
KLEINSMITH, Lewis J. and others
  Phosphorylation of nuclear protein early in
    the course of gene activation in lympho-
    cytes. bibliog il Science 154:780-1 N 11 '66
KLEKOWSKI, Edward J. Jr, and Baker, H. G.
  Evolutionary significance of polyploidy in the
    pteridophyta. bibliog Science 153:305-5 Jl 15
    '66
KLEMENT, William, Jr, and Cohen, L. H.
  Melting of tin telluride at high pressures.
    bibliog Science 154:1176-7 D 2 '66
KLEMM, Eugene
  Parents and report cards. PTA Mag 61:24-6
    bibliog(p36) O '66
KLEPPA, O. J.
  Calorimetry. Science 154:431 O 21 '66
KLIGMAN, Albert M.
  Investigating the investigator. Time 88:65 Ag
    5 '66
KLINCK, Richard E.
  Conservation is unselfishness. Sr Schol 88:sup
    17-18 Ap 29 '66

KLINGENBERG, John.   See Olson, O. O. jt.
    auth.
KLOMAN, William
    My mother said I should give it a try. Sat
    Eve Post 239:36-41 O 8 '66
KLOPSTEG, Paul E.
    Environmental sciences. Science 152:595, 1693
    Ap 29, Je 24 '66
KLOR, Robert A.
    Ginzburg as precedent. Time 88:46 Jl 22 '66
KLUCIS, E. S. and Gould, H. J.
    Zonal ultracentrifuge for the separation of
    ribosomal subunits. bibliog Science 152:373
    Ap 15 '66
KLUGE, Alexander
    Experiment in love; story. Esquire 66:111 O
    '66
KLUGER, Richard
    What I did to books and vice versa. Harper
    233:69-74 D '66
KLUTTZ, Jerry
    What new federal ethics code means to busi-
    ness. Nations Bsns 54:108+ O '66
KLÜVER, Johan Wilhelm
    Good janitor becomes as important as a
    curator. D. Bourdon. il por Life 61:46-7+
    Ag 12 '66
KNAKE, Ellery
    Postemergence weed killers for corn and soy-
    beans. Suc Farm 64:80+ Mr '66
KNAPP, Arthur, 1907-
    Founding the Frostbite fleet. il Newsweek
    69:8 Ja 9 '67
KNAPP, Sherman Richmond
    Knapp of Northeast utilities. por Fortune 74:
    31 Ag '66
KNAPP school libraries project
    Knapp high schools and the ALA standards.
    P. Sullivan. il Library J 91:2609-11 My 15
    '66; Correction. 91:4243 S 15 '66
    Knapp school libraries project, phase III:
    three high schools; symposium. il Sr School
    88:sup9-10 My 13 '66
KNAPSACKS
    We got this idea in Crete. il Sunset 136:130+
    F '66
KNEBEL, Fletcher
    How good are our juries? Look 30:75-6+ Ag
    23 '66; Same abr. Read Digest 89:239-41+
    N '66
    Las Vegas: it wins, it worries, it weeps.
    Look 30:75-8+ D 27 '66
    New wave of doubt. Look 30:66-72 Jl 12 '66
KNEELAND, Jo Anna
    Dancer prepares. por Dance Mag 40:51-3+
    Mr; 57-9 Ap; 65-7 My; 67-9 Je; 28+ S '66
    Dancer prepares; address. por Dance Mag
    40:51+ Mr '66

                    about
    Dancer prepares. L. Joel. il Dance Mag 40:
    49-53+ Mr '66
KNERER, G. and Atwood, C. E.
    Polymorphism in some nearctic halictine bees.
    bibliog Science 152:1262-3 My 27 '66
KNICKERBOCKER ice company
    Ice wagon cometh. il Am Heritage 17:54
    5 Je '66
KNIFE rests. See Tableware
KNIGHT, Arthur
    Behind the screen scenes. Sat R 49:39 S
    24 '66
    SR goes to the movies. See issues of Satur-
    day review
    Where is the new talent? Sat R 49:20-2 D 24
    '66
    Why we need a film institute. Sat R 49:50+
    Ag 13 '66
KNIGHT, Damon
    Science fiction basics. por Library J 91:2777-9
    Je 1 '66
KNIGHT, Doug
    Black bear mountain. Field & S 71:34+
    N '66
KNIGHT, Douglas
    Three poems: Memorandum: from another
    country; In the brute air; At the church
    door. Yale R 56:109-10 O '66
KNIGHT, Frances G.
    Frances Knight, ogress of the passport office;
    interview, ed. by S. McBee. pors Life 61:
    31-3 Jl 8 '66
    Inside look at a struggle over policy; ex-
    cerpts from interview, ed. by V. Glaser.
    por U S News 60:16 Ap 4 '66

                    about
    All together now, Frances Knight is a bad
    woman. Nat R 18:351 Ap 19 '66
    Frances and the creeps. Newsweek 67:30 Ap
    4 '66
    Keeping an eye on tourists. D. Sanford.
    New Repub 154:9-10 Ap 9 '66
    Truth about the Abba Schwartz case. C.
    Fritchey. Harper 232:33-4+ Je '66

KNIGHTS of Columbus
    Knights & Masons together. Time 88:74-**5**
    Ag 19 '66
KNIGHTS of the golden horseshoe. See Explor-
    ers, American
KNIPHOFIA. See Torch lilies
KNIVES
    Christmas list; holiday greeting; Randall
    knives. J. Fischer. Harper 233:23-4+ D '66
    Electric carving knife in action. il House &
    Gard 130:312-13 N '66
    How to use and care for an electric carving
    knife. il House & Gard 130:310-11 N '66
    Knives for astronauts and everyone. G. X.
    Sand. il Pop Mech 127:144-7+ Ja '67
KNOEPFLE, John
    Three firsts. G. Malanga. Poetry 108:130-1
    My '66
KNOLL, Erwin
    Our Model T copyright law. Reporter 34:
    39-41 Mr 10 '66
KNOPF, Blanche (Wolf)
    Blanche W. Knopf wins WNBA's Skinner
    award. Pub W 189:62 My 30 '66
    Obituary
    Pub W por 189:103-4 Je 13 '66
    WNBA dinner to honor Mrs Knopf in me-
    moriam. Pub W 190:109 S 26 '66
    WNBA's Skinner award honors memory of
    Blanche W. Knopf. il Pub W 190:25 O 24 '66
KNOPF, Hans
    Round one at Forest Hills; photographs.
    Sports Illus 25:40-5 Ag 29 '66
KNORR, Klaus
    On the cost-effectiveness approach to military
    research and development. Bul Atomic Sci
    22:11-14 N '66
KNOSSOS, Crete. See Crete—Antiquities
KNOTS and splices
    Stoppers! G. S. Smith. il Motor B 118:41
    Ag '66
KNOTT, Frederick
    Wait until dark. Criticism
        Look il 30:112-13+ My 17 '66
        Newsweek 67:88 F 14 '66
        Sat R 49:52-3 F 19 '66
        Time 87:66 F 11 '66
KNOWLAND park zoo, Oakland, Calif. See
    Zoological gardens
KNOWLEDGE
    Communications; address, June 5, 1966. R. W.
    Sarnoff. Vital Speeches 32:670-2 Ag 15 '66
    Diversity; excerpts from address. J. R. Platt.
    Science 154:1132-9 D 2 '66
    Policy problems of a data-rich civilization;
    address, October 1965. H. D. Lasswell. bib-
    liog il Wilson Lib Bul 41:58-65 S '66
        See also
    Research
KNOWLEDGE, Theory of
    Knower and the known, by M. Grene. Review
    Commentary 42:100-2 N '66. M. Natanson
        See also
    Education—Philosophy
    Reality
KNOWLES, James Wiley
    Congress' own economic adviser. il por Bsns
    W p 102+ Je 11 '66
KNOWLES, John
    All split up, por Seventeen 25:184+ My '66
KNOWLES, John H.
    Emergency ward. Atlan 218:116-21 Jl '66
KNOWLES, Ruth Sheldon
    Pouring oil on troubled sands. Read Digest
    89:171-2+ Ag '66
    Three-R war in Vietnam. Read Digest 90:
    171-4 Ja '67
KNOWLTON, Perry
    He likes to cook. por Bet Hom & Gard 44:82
    My '66
KNOWLTON, Robert A.
    Couple across the street; story. Good H 162:
    98-9 My '66
    Lucky bridegroom; story. Good H 162:80-2
    Je '66
KNOX, Cameron
    Holographic microscopy as a technique for
    recording dynamic microscopic subjects.
    bibliog Science 153:989-90 Ag 26 '66
KNOX, Franklin
    Mystery of Pearl Harbor. H. E. Barnes;
    F. E. Beatty; P. Greaves. il Nat R 18:1260-
    72 D 13 '66
KNOX, Henry
    Lady Knox. D. Forbes-Robertson. il por
    Am Heritage 17:46-7+ Ap '66
KNOX, Lucy (Flucker)
    Lady Knox. D. Forbes-Robertson. il Am
    Heritage 17:46-7+ Ap '66
KNUDSON, Rozanne
    My mother, the censor; reprint. por ALA Bul
    60:613-16 Je '66
KNUTSON, Robert C.
    Old sexton; poem. Christian Cent 83:1009
    Ag 17 '66

KOBELL, Stina
Stuttgart: International crafts exhibition.
Craft Horiz 26:22-7 S '66
KOBLER, John
Britain's Rx for our drug addicts. Sat Eve
Post 239:74-8 Ag 13 '66
Here's child care for every working mother.
Ladies Home J 83:34+ Ag '66
Out for a night at the local caldron. Sat Eve
Post 239:76-8 N 5 '66
Pet news. Ladies Home J 83:44 N '66
Sex criminal: I don't know why I did it. Sat
Eve Post 240:23-9+ Ja 28 '67
Who is Bourbaki? Sat Eve Post 239:34-5 F 26
'66
KOC, Vehbi
Turkish tycoon rolls his own. il pors Bsns W
p66-8+ Ja 7 '67
KOCH, Christopher
Giving them what they want. Nation 202:
337-8 Mr 21 '66
KOCH, John
Realism of John Koch; with commentaries.
il Am Artist 30:30-5+ S '66
KOCH, Kenneth
Test in art. Art N 65:54-7 O '66
KOCH, Stephen
Games of the poet. Nation 203:649-50 D 12 '66
Images of loathing. Nation 203:25-6 Jl 4 '66
KOCHER, Robert L.
Coil construction and packaging. Electr World
76:45-7 O '66
KOCHTIZSKY, Robert B.
LAOS: laymen in mission. J. C. Cosby, jr.
Christian Cent 83:931-3 Jl 27 '66
KOCZY, Friedrich Frans
Tropical oceanography. Science 153:557-9 Jl
29 '66
KODACHROME II films. See Moving picture
films
KODACOLOR films. See Photography—Films
KODÁLY, Zoltán
Kodály education in action. E. Helm. Hi Fi
16:MA30-1 Jl '66
Salty saint of Budapest. il por Time 88:39-40
Ag 26 '66
KODAMA, H. See Schnitzer, M. jt. auth.
KOECHLIN, Charles
Music of the birds and beasts. O. Daniel.
Sat R 49:68-9 Mr 26 '66
Postscript: that day I visited Charles Koech-
lin. A. Cohn. Am Rec G 32:782-3+ My '66
KOEFOED, Jean
Selling how-to art, craft books to hobbyists
and gift shoppers. il Pub W 190:49-53 Ag
22 '66
KOEGLER, Horst
Reports from abroad; Prague. Dance Mag
40:18+ Ap '66
KOEHLER, Charles R.
Cape Code seashore's white cedar swamp. il
Nat Parks Mag 40:11 D '66
—and Koehler, Margaret
Cape Cod's fresh water lakes. Travel 126:45-8
S '66
Circling the Gaspe Peninsula. Travel 125:56-62
Je '66
KOEHLER, Margaret. See Koehler, C. jt. auth.
KOENIG, H. P.
Monte Carlo. Travel 125:45-7 My '66
KOENIG, Richard E.
Two consider revelation. Christian Cent 83:
808-10 Je 22 '66
KOERNER, James D.
Paradise for planners. Sat R 49:59-61+ Jl 16
'66
Reform and revolution in English education.
il Sat R 50:61-3+ Ja 21 '67
KOFFLER, Sandra. See Tauber, E. S. jt.
auth.
KOH, Soon-duk, and Koh, T. H.
Scaling of musical preferences by the men-
tally retarded. bibliog Science 153:432-4 Jl
22 '66
KOH, Tong-he. See Koh, S. D. jt. auth.
KOHALA PENINSULA, Hawaii
Kohala. il Sunset 137:64-71 N '66
KOHLBERG, Edith Rose
Battleground of the spirit. Mlle 63:162-3+
My '66
KOHLER, Carl
Connubially-oriented computer of Otto Tronix.
il Pop Electr 25:53-5+ Jl '66
Di-di-di-di-di-di-di-di-dit. Pop Electr 25:79-
81+ N '66
Unpopular electroniks. Pop Electr 25:80-1 O
'66
KOHLER, Foy David
East-West relations: shaping a stable world;
address, December 11 1966. Dept State Bul
56:6-11 Ja 2 '67; Excerpts. por U S News
61:52-3 D 26 '66
about
LBJ makes some changes. il por U S News
61:39 O 3 '66
State's new team. Time 88:24 S 30 '66

KOHN, Hans
Russians against revolution. Sat R 49:38 S
17 '66
West Germany and the United States. Cur
Hist 50:277-80+ My '66
KOHN, Linda
In my opinion. Seventeen 25:272 Ap '66
KOKANEE fishing. See Salmon fishing
KOKOSCHKA, Oskar
Still O.K. il por Time 88:76 O 28 '66
Wild one. il por Newsweek 68:90 N 7 '66
KOLASA, Elaine
Black cat and the grinning pumpkin. Sch
Arts 66:9 O '66
KOLB, Ken
Been here and gone again; story. Ladies
Home J 83:100-1 N '66
KOLFF, Willem H. Van Breda. See Van Breda
Kolff, W. H.
KOLIPINSKI, Milton C. and Higer, A. L.
Ecological research in Everglades National
Park. Nat Parks Mag 40:14-17 O '66
KOLLER, James
Eyes and I. R. Duerden. Poetry 108:126-30
My '66
KOLMAS, Josef
Minority nationalities. Bul Atomic Sci 22:71-4
Je '66
KOLODIN, Irving
Big world of Don Pablo. Sat R 49:43-5+ D 31
'66
Great artists of our time. Sat R 49:47-9+
F 26 '66
Music to my ears. See issues of Saturday
review
New world of tape. Sat R 49:63-4 N 26 '66
Recordings in review. See issues of Saturday
review
Recordings reports: miscellaneous LPs. See
issues of Saturday review
Recordings reports: orchestral LPs. See is-
sues of Saturday review
KOLODZIEJ, Edward A.
Congress & foreign policy: timid political
will. Nation 202:292-4 Mr 14 '66
KOLTIN, Y. and Raper, J. R.
Schizophyllum commune: new mutations in
the B incompatibility factor. bibliog Sci-
ence 154:510-11 O 28 '66
KOMAI, H. and Neilands, J. B.
Zinc and cobalt: effect on the iron metabolism
of ustilage sphaerogena. bibliog Science 153:
751-2 Ag 12 '66
KOMAIKO, Jean R.
Wonderful world of play. Parents Mag 41:
50-3+ D '66
KOMAREK, Edwin Vaclav
Lightning as a sculptor of life. J. Lear. il por
Sat R 49:57-62 Je 4 '66
KOMAREK, Vladimir Kazan-. See Kazan-
Komarek, V.
KOMER, Robert
Mr Komer reports on progress in the other
war in Viet-Nam; statement, November 7,
1966. Dept State Bul 55:892-4 D 12 '66
Mr Komer reports to President on civil
programs in Viet-Nam; excerpts from re-
port. Dept State Bul 55:128-9 Jl 25 '66
Other war in Vietnam; progress report; with
text of letter of transmittal, September 13,
1966. Dept State Bul 55:549-67, 591-601 O
10-17 '66
about
Moving forward. il Time 88:23-4 S 23 '66
NSC reviews Viet-Nam problems; remarks,
May 10, 1966. L. B. Johnson. Dept State
Bul 54:834 My 30 '66
KOMISCHE oper, Berlin. See Opera houses
KOMORNY, Annie
Vacation; poem. McCalls 94:172 O '66
Wonderer; poem. McCalls 94:113 Ja '67
KOMOROWSKI, Tadeusz
Obituary
Nat R 18:921 S 20 '66. P. P. Witonski
KOMOSKI, P. Kenneth
Programed instruction: an evaluation. Sr
Schol 88:sup 13 F 11 '66
KONECCI, Eugene
Second-generation spacecraft; excerpts from
remarks. Aviation W 85:21 Ag 8 '66
KONINGSBERGER, Hans
Reporter at large. New Yorker 42:57-8+
Ap 23; 87-8+ Ap 30 '66
KONVITZ, Milton R.
Freedom is a full-time job. Sat R 50:47 Ja 21
'67
Learning for export. Sat R 49:42 Mr 5 '66
KÓNYA, Sándor
Master of style. A. Wagner. por Opera N
30:26-7 F 19 '66
KOOKABURRAS
Extinction threatens; conservationists fight-
ing to protect Australian wildlife. il Sci N
90:483 D 3 '66

KOOLISH, Abraham L.
Million-dollar trinket. R. L. Smith. il Nation 203:354-5 O 10 '66
KOOTENAI RIVER
See also
Libby Dam project (proposed)
KOOYMAN, Gerald L.
Maximum diving capacities of the Weddell seal, leptonychotes weddelli. bibliog Science 151:1553-4 Mr 25 '66
KOPIN, Irwin J. See Baldessarini, R. J. jt. auth.
KOPIT, Arthur
Thank you, Annette Funicello. por Sat Eve Post 239:74-7 Jl 16 '66
KOPKIND, Andrew D.
Adventures of Arthur Goldberg. New Repub 155:15-18 O 8 '66
Anti-Vietnam politics. New Repub 154:15-18 Je 4 '66
Down the down staircase. New Repub 155:11-14 O 22 '66
Future of black power. New Repub 156:16-18 Ja 7 '67
Goodbye to all that. New Repub 155:7-8 N 19 '66
Grape pickers' strike. New Repub 154:12-15 Ja 29 '66
How do you fight it? New Repub 155:6-7 S 3 '66
Humphrey's old pals. New Repub 154:19-22 My 7 '66
Lair of the Black Panther. New Repub 155:10-13 Ag 13 '66
No fire this time. New Repub 154:15-16 Je 18 '66
Poor politics. New Repub 154:15-17 Je 25 '66
Powell and black bravado. New Repub 156:13-15 Ja 21 '67
Taking radicals seriously. New Repub 155:28-30 D 10 '66
Ten days that shook the capital. New Repub 155:9-11 N 5 '66
Watts, waiting for D-day. New Repub 154:15-17 Je 11 '66
—and Ridgeway, J. F.
Washington: life in the lost colony. New Repub 154:19-22 Ap 30 '66
Washington: the lost colony. New Repub 154:13-17 Ap 23 '66
about
Art of finding out. il por Newsweek 67:80 My 30 '66
KOPP, Rudolf, and others
Long temporal gradient of retrograde amnesia for a well-discriminated stimulus. bibliog Science 153:1547-9 S 23 '66
KOPPETT, Leonard
Big Yankee turnabout. Sports Illus 24:22-4+ Je 20 '66
Yankee dynasty can never come back. N Y Times Mag p44-5+ O 2 '66
KORALL, Burt
Art Farmer, a natural evolution. Sat R 49:68-9 Ap 16 '66
Measure of Sinatra. Sat R 49:58-9 O 15 '66
KORB, George M.
Church support. America 114:440-2 Ap 2 '66
KORBOBO, Raymond P.
Summer-blooming shrubs? Horticulture 44:16-17+ Ag '66
KORDA, Michael V.
Camera that thinks it's a duck. il Pop Phot 58:62-5+ Mr '66
Subminiatures, the giant-killers? Pop Phot 58:88-90+ My '66
about
Child has 10,000 faces. K. Poll. il Pop Phot 58:78-9 Je '66
KOREA
See also
United Nations—Korea
KOREA (People's Democratic Republic)
See also
Communist party (Korea)
Panmunjom
Army
Death of a patrol. il Newsweek 68:50+ N 14 '66
KOREA (Republic)
Korea. Progress and prospects; address, May 7, 1966. S. D. Berger. Dept State Bul 54:860-5 My 30 '66
See also
Libraries—Korea (Republic)
Commerce
See also
Korea (Republic)—Industries

Commercial treaties and agreements
United States and Korea amend cotton textile agreement; Department announcement; with texts of U.S. note and letter, November 22, 1966. Dept State Bul 55:982-3 D 26 '66

Economic conditions
Ready for take-off. il Newsweek 67:36-7 F 7 '66
South Korea takes off; an Asian success story. il U S News 61:42-3 O 31 '66
See also
Korea (Republic)—Industries

Foreign relations
South Korea takes off; an Asian success story. il U S News 61:42-3 O 31 '66
Visits to Thailand and Korea; text of joint statement, November 2, 1966. L. B. Johnson and C. H. Park. Dept State Bul 55:777-80 N 21 '66

Industries
Koreans build a peacetime economy; bid for export markets. il Bsns W p 170-2+ My 7 '66

Politics and government
O, my Korea! R. E. Kim. Atlan 217:106-17 F '66
Point of disorder; saccharine-smuggling scandal; National assembly incident. il Newsweek 68:51 O 3 '66
Saccharin; resignations of cabinet. Time 88:46 S 30 '66

Religious institutions and affairs
World around us (cont of) News of the Christian world. Christian Cent 83:505-6, 1489-90 Ap 20, N 30 '66

Social conditions
O my Korea! R. E. Kim. Atlan 217:106-17 F '66
KOREA, NORTHERN. See Korea (People's Democratic Republic)
KOREAN armistice. See Korean war, 1950-1953 —Peace and mediation
KOREAN businessmen. See Businessmen
KOREAN war, 1950-1953
American participation
Pull-out, all-out, or stand fast in Vietnam? M. B. Ridgway. Look 30:81-2+ Ap 5 '66
Economic aspects
When wartime controls were last used in U.S. U S News 61:37 S 12 '66
Peace and mediation
Ambush in Korea. Sr Schol 89:25 N 18 '66
Pantomime at Panmunjom; role of the Military armistice commission. B. Atkinson. il Sat R 49:61+ O 8 '66
Suddenly, a crisis on the Korean front. il U S News 61:13 N 14 '66
What it's like to negotiate with the Chinese; negotiations at Panmunjon to settle Korea's future. A. H. Dean. il N Y Times Mag p44-5+ O 30 '66
Strategy
Pull-out, all-out, or stand fast in Vietnam? M. B. Ridgway. Look 30:81-2+ Ap 5 '66
KORKUNOV, Nikolai Mikhailovich
Bureaucracy and freedom; N. M. Korkunov's theory of the state. G. L. Yaney. bibliog f Am Hist R 71:468-86 Ja '66
KORMEIER, Lucy C. See Mandy. W. J. jt. auth.
KORMENDI, Ferenc
Emperor s war games. Reporter 35:50-4+ N 17 '66
KORN, Edward D.
Structure of biological membranes. bibliog Science 153:1491-8 S 23 '66
KORN, Peter Jona
Max Reger festival. Hi Fi 16:MA20-1 Ag '66
KORNBERG, Warren
Policy shifts mark science's year. por Sci N 90:545 D 24 '66
about
Science service gets new managing editor. por Sci N 90:447 N 26 '66
KOROLEV, Sergei Pavlovich
Soviet space designer Korolev dies; built Sputniks, Voskhods. por Aviation W 84:37 Ja 24 '66
KORSAKOV, Nikolai Andreevich Rimskii-. See Rimskii-Korsakov, N. A.

KORSON, George Gershon
George Korson: a folk-music classic revisited. H. Yurchenco. Am Rec G 32:475-7 Ja '66

KORVETTE, E. J, incorporated
How confusion caught up with Korvette. L. A. Mayer. il Fortune 73:153-4+ F '66
Korvette gets a new driver; company to be run by Spartans. Bsns W p50 S 17 '66
Romance at Korvette. Time 87:90 Je 3 '66

KOŠ, Erih
Writer as craftsman. por Sat R 49:11-14 Ag 13 '66

KOSAMBI, D. D.
Scientific numismatics; with biographical sketch. Sci Am 214:17, 102-8+ bibliog(p 139) F '66

KOSLOSKY, Jan
Jan Koslosky of Alaska: new breed of frontiersman. H. Ehrlich. il pors Look 31: 46-9 Ja 10 '67

KOSTELANETZ, Richard
Artist as playwright and engineer. N Y Times Mag p32-3+ O 9 '66
In darkest Fulbright. Nation 202:725-6 Je 13 '66
Marshall McLuhan. Commonweal 85:420-6 Ja 20 '67
Our greatest living man of letters. Reporter 34:53-4 Ja 27 '66
Prevalence of Paul Goodman. N Y Times Mag p70-1+ Ap 3 '66
Two extremes of avant-garde music. N Y Times Mag p34-5+ Ja 15 '67

KOSTROWISKY, Guillaume Apollinaire de. See Apollinaire, G. pseud.

KOSTRUBALA, Ingrid
Cold weather, warm hearts. C. L. Sanders. il pors Ebony 21:27-30+ Ap '66

KOSYGIN, Aleksei Nikolaevich
Alexei goes to Paris. America 115:789-90 D 17 '66
Brezhnev and Kosygin: the cult of impersonality. P. Grose. il pors N Y Times Mag p34-7+ O 9 '66
Defining the limit. il por Newsweek 67:48 My 30 '66
Kosygin in Paris: differences within amity. A. Werth. Nation 203:693-6 D 26 '66
Kremlin travelers: what they're up to. il por U S News 61:16 D 12 '66
Lively robot. il por Time 88:38+ D 16 '66
Marxist mellowed: visit to France. il por Newsweek 68:50 D 19 '66
Mrs Gandhi: peaceful, Kosygin: hostile. il U S News 61:20 Jl 25 '66
No changes. il por Time 88:25 Ag 12 '66
On the road again. Nat R 18:506-7 My 31 '66
Russia at the crossroads. R. Sherrod. il por Sat Eve Post 239:28-33 Mr 26 '66
Russian dilemma. il Newsweek 67:40+ Je 20 '66
Small hello. il Newsweek 67:47 Je 27 '66
Traveling abroad with B and K. il Newsweek 67:51 My 23 '66

KOTEN, Bernard L.
(tr) See Evtushenko. E. A. Delicate tinkle of icicles

KOTHE, D. W.
Put all reproduction equipment in one place and save. Am City 81:106-7 Ap '66

KOTKER, Norman
Turkish delights. Horizon 8:78-89 Aut '66

KOTLOWITZ, Robert
Ballerinas famous and flawed. Harper 233: 98-100 Ag '66
Performing arts. See issues of Harper's magazine, April 1966-

KOTO, K. See Morimoto, N. jt. auth.

KOTOK, Edward I.
Obituary
Am For 72:54 N '66

KOUFAX, Sandy
Sandy Koufax story: my battle with arthritis; excerpts from Koufax, ed. by E. Linn. pors Look 30:80-6 Jl 12 '66
Sandy Koufax story: my salary fights; excerpts from Koufax, ed. by E. Linn. pors Look 30:90-2+ Je 14 '66
Sandy Koufax story: what baseball means to me; excerpts from Koufax, ed. by E. Linn. pors Look 30:33-4+ Jl 26 '66

about

Arm and the man. Newsweek 68:74-5 Ag 8 '66
Best. Sports Illus 25:13 N 28 '66
Double play. il por Time 87:63 Mr 25 '66
Koufax the incomparable. M. Richler. Commentary 42:87-9 N '66
New union's million-dollar pitch. il por Life 60:77-8 Ap 1 '66
$1,000,000 holdout. J. Mann. il por Sports Illus 24:26-9 Ap 4 '66
Sandy Koufax draws thousands to Elson's in Atlanta shopping center. il por Pub W 190:58-9 S 5 '66

Sandy's agony. por Time 88:50 S 9 '66
Sandy's painful choice. il por Newsweek 68: 64-5 N 28 '66
Sic transit tradition. Time 87:75 Ap 8 '66
Super-holdouts. il por Newsweek 67:84 Mr 28 '66
Too many shots, too many pills. il por Time 88:64 N 25 '66
Two stores rack up large sales of Koufax. il por Pub W 190:73-5 O 3 '66

KOUNKEL, Gary L.
Precision wirewound adjustment potentiometers. Electr World 15:58-60 Ap '66

KOVACH, Bill, and Caldwell, Nat
Plight of the rural poor. Reporter 34:27+ Ap 21 '66

KOVACS, Imre
Journey in darkness. Reporter 35:46-9 O 20 '66

KOVNER, Amy
Plea from the ghetto. Am Ed 3:12 D '66

KOWALD, Kenneth
Air pollution control news. See issues of American city

KOYAMA, Seitaro. See Sotobayashi, T. jt. auth.

KOZLICK, Joseph C.
See how de mainsail sets. Motor B 118:43+ O '66
Thorny path. por Motor B 119:81-5+ Ja '67

KOZLOFF, Max
Art See issues of Nation

KOZODOY, Neal
(tr) See Agnon, S. J. First kiss
(tr) See Wiesel, E. Jews of silence

KRAFT, Christopher Columbus, 1924-
Double troubles. il Newsweek 67:58 My 30 '66

KRAFT, Ivor
Head Start to what? Nation 203:179-82 S 5 '66
Pedagogical futility in fun and games? NEA J 56:71-2 Ja '67

KRAFT, John A. Jr
How to get a science job at home. Sci Digest 59:77-9 F '66
Restring a tennis racket like a pro. Pop Sci 188:140-3 Je '66

KRAFT, Joseph
Patrician. Commentary 41:92+ F '66

about

Kraftsmanship. por Newsweek 68:54 Jl 4 '66

KRAFT, Ken, and Kraft, Pat
Case of the plodding highwayman or the Po8 of crime. Am Heritage 18:50-3+ D '66

KRAFT, Leonard E.
Teachers must leave retirement benefits behind. NEA J 55:50+ F '66

KRAFT, Pat. See Kraft, K. jt. auth.

KRAG, Jens Otto
New twist, the LBJ; U.S. visit; White House dance. il por Newsweek 67:27-8 My 9 '66

KRAININ, Ewing
World is his beat. T. Maloney. il U S Camera 29:44-5 My '66

KRAKATOA (island)
Air-sea waves from the explosion of Krakatoa. F. Press and D. Harkrider. bibliog il Science 154:1325-7 D 9 '66

KRALOVA, Eva
Face to face with a circus web girl. por Seventeen 25:101 Jl '66

KRAM, Mark
Boxing. Sports Illus 24:70-2 My 9 '66
When Emile got his Irish up. Sports Illus 25:14-15 Jl 25 '66
Wink at a homely girl Sports Illus 25:86-8+ O 10 '66

KRAMER, A. Ray
Documentation. Motor B 117:27+ Ap '66

KRAMER, Hilton
Kandinsky, no great master but a great influence. N Y Times Mag p28-9+ D 18 '66
True father of modern painting. N Y Times Mag p30+ Mr 20 '66

KRAMER, Jack
Choose bromeliads for outdoor decorating. il Flower Grower 53:8-10 Ag '66
Orchid for a winter window. Flower Grower 53:38 S '66

KRAMER, Jane
Profiles; R. C. Scull. New Yorker 42:64-6+ N 26 '66
Reporter at large. New Yorker 42:138+ Ap 2 '66

KRAMER, Larry
Transatlantic view (cont) por Pub W 189: 61-4 Ja 31; 61-3 F 28 '66

KRAMER, Paul J. and others
Terminology of cell-water relations. bibliog Science 153:889-90 Ag 19 '66

KRAMER, Rita
Parent and child (cont) N Y Times Mag p72+ F 13; 104+ Ap 24 '66

KROWN, Leo
Israel's new prophet. il por Time 88:77 D 16 '66
KRUEGER, Karl K.
Some facts for writers about The Rotarian magazine. Writer 79:25 Ap '66
KRUGER, Kai
(ed) See North, L. Lowell North on sails
KRUGER NATIONAL PARK
Bringing us back alive. P. L. Buckley. Nat R 18:625-6 Je 28 '66
KRUIJFF, Jan de
Notes from our correspondents (cont) Hi Fi 16:20 Ap; 18+ Ag '66
KRUMMEL, Donald W.
Books in the field: music. bibliog por Wilson Lib Bul 41:284-95 N '66
Merrill at 100. Library J 91:205 Ja 15 '66
KRUPP, George
Sex in laboratory. Sat R 49:38-9 N 19 '66
KRUSE, Arthur S.
Plus for probate. il por Time 88:73-4 N 4 '66
KRUTCH, Joseph Wood
Dam the Grand Canyon? no! cries an Arizonan. Audubon Mag 68:308-11 S '66
Danger: utopia ahead. Sat R 49:17-18+ Ag 20 '66
Man is more than a statistic. Sat R 49:14-16 My 21 '66
KRUUK, Hans
Defense against killers. il Natur Hist 75: 48-55 Ap '66
KRYTER, Karl D.
Psychological reactions to aircraft noise. bibliog Science 151:1346-55 Mr 18 '66
KU, Lily, and Romani, R. J.
Ribosomes from pear fruit. bibliog Science 154:408-10 O 21 '66
KU, Teh-lung, and Broecker, W. S.
Atlantic deep-sea stratigraphy: extension of absolute chronology to 320,000 years. bibliog Science 151:448-50 Ja 28 '66
KU KLUX klan
End of hearings on the Klan. America 114: 343 Mr 12 '66
Loaded pistol; G. Mars, Grand Klaliff of the KKK. S. Alsop. il Sat Eve Post 239:22 '66
Malice toward some; S. H. Bowers and the Dahmer murder. il Newsweek 67:39-40 Ap 11 '66
Mississippi mayor fights the Klan. A. Schardt. Reporter 34:39-40 Ja 27 '66
Portrait of a Klansman; R. Cranford. S. Alsop. il Sat Eve Post 239:23-7 Ap 9 '66
Southern plain talk about the Ku Klux klan. R. Flowers. il Look 30:36+ My 3 '66
See also
Government investigations—Ku Klux klan
KUBE, Harold D. See Hanks, J. J. jt. auth.
KUBIC, Milan J.
Top brass in Brazil. New Repub 155:11-13 S 10 '66
KUBISTOVA, J. and Seth, D.
1,2-propanediol-2-phosphate in ascaris lumbricoides. bibliog Science 154:1461 D 16 '66
KUBITSCHEK, Juscelino
Roads start to tame Brazil's green hell. il Bsns W p 192-4+ S 10 '66
KUBLY, Herbert
Holy mountain. Holiday 40:68-77+ D '66
Value of writers' workshops. Writer 79:22-4 O '66
KUBRICK, Stanley
Kubrick, farther out. il por Newsweek 68: 106+ S 12 '66
Profiles. J. Bernstein. por New Yorker 42: 70-2+ N 12 '66
To prepare man for the extraordinary. il por Esquire 65:117 My '66
KUCZO, Joe
If it can move, then tape it. B. Gilbert. il por Sports Illus 25:38-40+ N 28 '66
KUEHNELT-LEDDIHN, Erik Maria, ritter von
How Catholic are American Catholics? Cath World 203:42-7 Ap '66
Letter from Down Under. por Nat R 18:310 Ap 5 '66
Letter from southeast Asia. Nat R 18:359 Ap 19 '66
Letter from the Continent. See occasional issues of National review
KUEHNL, Neil
What your family should know about emphysema. Bet Hom & Gard 44:28 My '66
—and Bush, George
Family money management. See issues of Better homes and gardens
KUEPPERS, Friedrich, and Bearn, A. G.
Inherited variations of human serum α-antitrypsin. bibliog Science 154:407-8 O 21 '66
KUGELBLITZ. See Lightning
KUH, Frederick
Is peace naive? Nation 203:69 Jl 25 '66

KUH, Joyce
Would this day-care plan work for you? Ladies Home J 83:78 O '66
KUH, Katharine
Alaska's vanishing art. Sat R 49:25-31 O 22 '66
Art that history shaped. Sat R 49:17-24 Ja 29 '66
Fine arts. See occasional issues of Saturday review
Golden loans for a silver anniversary. Sat R 49:45-51 Mr 19 '66
KUHLMAN, Raymond L.
Approach with care. Flying 78:88-90 Ap '66
KUHLMANN-Anderson tests. See Intelligence tests
KUHN, Irene Corbally
Surprising Surinam. Travel 126:30-4 N '66
KUHN, Philip
From Japan. Bul Atomic Sci 22:26-7 Mr '66
KUIPER, Gerard P. and others
Russian Luna IX pictures: provisional analysis. Science 151:1561-3 Mr 25 '66
KULIANG, K. K. L.
View toward change. Sat R 49:34 Je 18 '66
KULJIAN corporation
Giving American ways to foreign engineers. il Bsns W p 170+ O 1 '66
KULKA, Marshall. See Von Schmeling, B. jt. auth.
KULLGREN, Birgitta. See Hard, R. C. jr, jt. auth.
KULLMAN, V. S. See Lindsay, H. A. jt. auth.
KUMIN, Maxine W.
Country house; poem. Harper 233:89 N '66
about
Down from the forked hill unsullied. R. Wallace. Poetry 108:121-2 My '66
KUNASZ, Paul
All the little swingers; story. Redbook 127: 60-1 S '66
KUNHARDT, Philip
Big idea. Life 62:23 Ja 20 '67
KUNITZ, Stanley
Auden on poverty; a conversation. Atlan 218:94-102 Ag '66
Hartford walker. New Repub 155:23-6 N 12 '66
(tr) See Voznesenskiĭ, A. First frost; I am Goya
(tr) See Voznesenskiĭ, A. My Achilles heart; Striptease; Ballad of the full stop
(tr) See Voznesenskiĭ, A. Two poems
KUNKEL, H. G. and others
Genetically determined antigen of the Ne subgroup of gamma-globulin: detection by precipitin analysis. bibliog Science 154: 1041-3 N 25 '66
KUNKEL, John Crain
Excerpt from January 27, 1966, newsletter to his constituents. Cong Digest 45:152+ My '66
KUNKEL, Marguerite
Cimicifugas. Horticulture 44:41+ Je '66
KUNNEMAN, Horst H.
Twenty years later. por Library J 91:5699-703 N 15 '66
KUNSTADTER, Peter
Living with Thailand's gentle Lua. il por Nat Geog Mag 130:122-52 Jl '66
KUNSTLER, William M.
Deep in my heart, by W. M. Kunstler. Review
Sat R 49:40-1 Mr 12 '66. J. R. Waltz
KUNTNER, Rudolph
New house. F. Stevenson. il Opera N 31:28-9 D 24 '66
KUNTZE, Archie Carlyn
Captain's paradise. il por Newsweek 68:36 Ag 15 '66
Closed case. Newsweek 68:36 N 28 '66
Mayor. il por Time 88:21 Ag 12 '66
Paying for prowess. il por Time 88:36 N 25 '66
Time of trial. por Newsweek 68:55 N 14 '66
KUNZ, Alma
Where the trout sleep late in the morning. J. Olsen. il por Sports Illus 24:86-90+ My 16 '66
KUPERSTOCK, Kit
My kids love the school lunch. Parents Mag 41:86-7+ S '66
KUPFERBERG, Herbert
Going full blast. Opera N 31:9-11 S 10 '66
Record reviews. See issues of Atlantic
Records at half price. Atlan 218:128-30 D '66
They shall have music. See issues of Atlantic
Le véritable Maurice. Atlan 219:111-13 Ja '67
KUPFERMAN, Theodore Roosevelt
Bill seeks capital gains tax status for copyrights. Pub W 189:47 My 16 '66
Campaign by consensus. il por Time 87:28-9 F 4 '66
Gracious race. il por Newsweek 67:31A F 21 '66
Man like Lindsay. il por Time 87:24 F 18 '66

KURATH, Gertrude Prokosch
Summertime is powwow time. Dance Mag 40:40-1+ My '66
KURDS
Whose bodies? Iraq's Kurdish terrorists. il Time 87:28 Je 3 '66
KURITA, Takeo
Battle off Samar. W. P. Deac. il Am Heritage 18:22-3+ D '66
KURKA, Robert
Good soldier Schweik. Criticism
Opera N il 30:35 Ap 2 '66
Opera N il 31:24 N 19 '66
KURLAND, Norman D.
More Negroes in college: a program for action now; remarks, February 24, 1965. Sch & Soc 94:41-3 Ja 22 '66
KURODA, P. K. See Husain, L. jt. auth.
KURODA, Yoshio, and Ikoma, Tatsuo
N-acetylhistidine isolated from frog heart. bibliog Science 152:1241-2 My 27 '66
KURTZ, E.
Public understanding of science. Science 154: 800-1 N 11 '66
KURUMADA, Takao, and Labbe, R. F.
Fumarate reductase in the control of heme biosynthesis. bibliog Science 151:1228-9 Mr 11 '66
KURZMAN, Dan
Confusion brought cataclysm. Sat R 49:24-5 Je 25 '66
Democracy vs. dictator's ghost. Sat R 49:48-9 D 24 '66
Lovestone's cold war. New Repub 154:17-22 Je 25 '66
World in the balance. Sat R 40:43 Mr 12 '66
KUSCHEL, C. E.
Once too often. Outdoor Life 138:42-5+ Jl '66
KUSCHMAN, William E.
Education and society in disadvantaged suburbia. Sch & Soc 94:386-7 N 12 '66
KUSNER, Kathy
Blue ribbon for looks. too. A. Higgins. por Sports Illus 25:86+ N 14 '66
KUSS, Henry J. 1922?-
Kuss of death. Nation 202:85-6 Ja 24 '66
KUWAIT
Country that oil built: quick rise to riches. J. Law. il U S News 60:70-2 Je 13 '66
KUWAITI cookery. See Cookery, Kuwaiti
KUZNETSOV, Anatolii
Dina Mironovna Pronichev remembers Babi Yar; excerpt from novel, Babi Yar. N Y Times Mag p45+ D 11 '66
KVAKA, Margaret
Weekend fling. Flying 79:62-4 S '66
KY, Nguyen-cao-. See Nguyen-cao-Ky
KY, Nguyen-cao-, Mme. See Nguyen-cao-Ky, Mme
KYANITE
Kyanite-andalusite equilibrium from 700° to 800°C. R. C. Newton. bibliog il Science 153: 170-2 Jl 8 '66
Kyanite-sillimanite equilibrium at 750°C. R. C. Newton. bibliog il Science 151:1222-5 Mr 11 '66
KYGER, Joanne
Pigs for Circe in May; poem. Poetry 108: 175-7 Je '66
KYLE, Jim
Supersensitive communications systems. Electr World 75:41-4 F; 76:6+ Jl '66
KYLE, Keith
Beating de Gaulle's veto. New Repub 155: 17-20 D 10 '66
Behind the Aspida trial. New Repub 156: 17-18 Ja 21 '67
Rhodesia through the looking glass. New Repub 155:10-12 D 24 '66
KYNURENINE
Tryptophan pyrroclase induced in human liver by hydrocortisone: effect on excretion of kynurenine. K. Altman and O. Greengard. bibliog il Science 151:332-3 Ja 21 '66
KYOGOKU, Yoshimasa, and others
Hydrogen bonding specificity of nucleic acid purines and pyrimidines in solution. bibliog Science 154:518-20 O 28 '66

L

LAD. See American library association—Library administration division
LAOS. See Laymen's overseas service (organization)
LAPL. See Los Angeles public library

LAS (large astronomical satellite) See Artificial satellites—Astronomical applications
LCFO. See Lowndes County freedom organization
LDH (lactic dehydrogenase) See Dehydrogenases
LEED (laser-energized explosive device) See Explosives—Ignition
LEM (lunar excursion module) See Space vehicles—Landing systems—Moon
LHA amphibious assault ship. See Warships—United States
LINC (laboratory instrument computer) See Computers—Medical applications
LL.B. degree. See Degrees, Academic
LLRV (lunar landing research vehicle) See Space vehicles—Landing systems—Moon
LNG (liquefied natural gas) See Gas, Natural—Liquefaction
LP gas. See Liquefied petroleum gas
LRS. See United States—Library of Congress—Legislative reference service
LSCA (Library services and construction act) See Library laws and legislation
LSD. See Lysergic acid diethylamide
LSE. See London school of economics and political science
LSSM (Local scientific survey module) See Lunar vehicles
LABANOTATION. See Dance notation
LABARCA HUBERTSON, Amanda
Word with Amanda Labarca; with excerpts from an interview. J. Villaverde. il pors Américas 18:32-5 Mr '66
LABAT, Edgar
In the shadow of the chair. il por Time 88:78 Ag 26 '66
LABBE, Robert F. See Kurumada, T. jt. auth.
LABELS
Balloting by bumper; cars by millions plug candidates. il Bsns W p44 O 15 '66
Bit of good news on cents-off; labels ruled fictitious pricing. Consumer Rep 31:52 F '66
Soft drink labels now speak softly. Consumer Rep 31:218-19 My '66
Some gains, and a loss, in safety; Federal hazardous substances act. Consumer Rep 32:4 Ja '67
Stricter labels for some common drugs. Consumer Rep 31:426-7 S '66
Trade winds; readership of labels on bottles, cereal boxes, cans, and jars. J. G. Fuller. Sat R 49:14+ S 10 '66
See also
Plant labels

Law
See Packaging—Laws and regulations

Manufacture
Stick 'em up; Avery products corp. il Newsweek 68:66-7 D 26 '66
LABER, Jeri L.
Trial ends. New Repub 154:26-9 Mr 19 '66
LABINO, Dominick
Dominick Labino: the color of glass dictates form. R. Florian. il por Craft Horiz 26: 28-31 Jl '66
LABOR, Department of. See United States—Labor, Department of
LABOR, Farm. See Farm labor
LABOR, Migrant. See Migrant labor
LABOR, Skilled. See Skilled labor
LABOR agreements. See Trade agreements
LABOR and laboring classes
Foreign labor briefs. Mo Labor R 89:410-14, 528-31, 659-61, 774-5, 890-1, 1000-1, 1126-7, 1267-8, 1389-90 Ap-D '66
Labor front. T. R. Brooks. See issues of Dun's review and modern industry
Manpower development and incentives to change. Mo Labor R 89:1123-5 O '66
See also
Employment
Farm labor
Poor—United States
Skilled labor
Trade unions

Bibliography
Book reviews and notes. See issues of Monthly labor review

Education
Educational attainment of workers in March 1965. D. F. Johnston and H. R. Hamel. il Mo Labor R 89:250-17 Mr '66
Steelworkers on campus. H. J. Golatz. America 114:652-4 My 7 '66
See also
Trade unions—Educational work

LABOR and laboring classes—*Continued*

International aspects
See Trade unions—International aspects

Non-wage payments
See Non-wage payments

Political activities
See Trade unions—Political activities

Statistics
Current labor statistics. See issues of Monthly labor review
See also
Strikes—Statistics

Wages
See Wages

Brazil
See also
Trade unions—Brazil

Canada
Canadian automation code; excerpt from address, September 1965. A. Balloch. Mo Labor R 89:520-2 My '66
Country that really has labor troubles. il U S News 61:100+ S 26 '66
See also
Labor supply—Canada
Strikes—Canada
Wages—Canada

China (People's Republic)
Cities say no; Red guards opposed by urban workers. Time 89:24-6 Ja 20 '67

Cuba
Premier Castro's speech on Cuba; excerpts from address, August 30, 1966. F. Castro. Cur Hist 51:363+ D '66

France
See also
Strikes—France

Germany (Federal Republic)
Any old time; variable hours system. Newsweek 68:86 Ag 22 '66

Great Britain
How the tea break could ruin England; Time essay. Time 88:20-1 S 2 '66
See also
Labor party (Great Britain)
Strikes—Great Britain
Trades union congress
Wages—Great Britain

Latin America
Latin America: labor between bread and revolution. S. Lens. il Nation 203:248-51 S 19 '66

Netherlands
See also
Wages—Netherlands

North Carolina
New place in life for the unskilled; Pilot project in North Carolina, relocating and training of unemployed agricultural workers. il Bsns W p 110-12 Mr 26 '66

Pennsylvania
See also
Unemployment—Pennsylvania

Poland
Two days that shook the Communist world. F. Lewis. il N Y Times Mag p25+ Je 12 '66

Russia
See also
Labor supply—Russia

Spain
See also
Labor laws and legislation—Spain
Strikes—Spain

Sweden
Model strikeless state: Sweden now has labor trouble. U S News 60:82-5 Mr 28 '66
See also
Wages—Sweden

United States
Building the Great society; new opportunities and responsibilities for labor and management; address, January 17, 1966. W. P. Reuther. Vital Speeches 32:432-5 My 1 '66
Chronology of recent labor events. See issues of Monthly labor review
Few drones in the hive. America 115:310-11 S 24 '66
Labor and the economy; the big push. il Sr Schol 89:14-15 D 9 '66

Labor month in review. See issues of Monthly labor review
Labor: toward full employment. il Sr Schol 88:9-11 Ap 1 '66
Protestantism and the American labor movement: the Christian spirit in the gilded age; excerpts from address, April 1965. H. G. Gutman. bibliog f Am Hist R 72: 74-101 O '66
Special labor force report. See issues of Monthly labor review
Strike curbs are labor's no. 1 issue. il Bsns W p 104+ O 1 '66
Tool men fret amid rising tide of orders; skilled labor shortage. il Bsns W p29-30 F 19 '66
Unemployment takes back seat; it's a worker's market. il Bsns W p42-4 N 5 '66
See also
American federation of labor and Congress of industrial organizations
Arbitration, Industrial—United States
Contracts, Government—Labor problems
Labor day
Labor laws and legislation—United States
Labor supply—United States
Negroes in the United States—Employment
Strikes—United States
Trade unions—United States
Unemployment—United States
United States—Labor, Department of
Wages—United States

History
Rebel in a wing collar; march on Washington: J. Coxey and his Commonweal army, 1894. G. A. Gipe. il Am Heritage 18:24-9+ D '66

Political activities
See Trade unions—Political activities

Vietnam (Republic)
Toward negotiation; labor problems of U.S. construction combine in Vietnam. Time 87: 90 Je 17 '66

Yugoslavia
Mijo. Sava. Vojislav and Mila. F. Y. Blumenfeld. il Newsweek 68:50-1 O 17 '66

LABOR board. See United States—National labor relations board

LABOR camps
See also
International voluntary workcamps

LABOR conferences
See also
International labor organization

LABOR contracts
See also
Trade agreements

LABOR cost
As raises push up labor costs; U.S. to follow Europe's path? il U S News 61:68+ N 7 '66
New look at labor costs. U S News 61:80 D 5 '66

LABOR day
Labor: the issues that remain. Christian Cent 83:1047-8 Ag 31 '66
Statement for Labor day, 1966; plea for social awareness by Social action department. NCWC. America 115:220 S 3 '66

LABOR displacement. See Unemployment, Technological

LABOR disputes
How union shop breeds corruption. il Nations Bsns 54:42-3+ F '66
Violence in American labor disputes. P. Taft. bibliog f Ann Am Acad 364:127-40 Mr '66
See also
Grievance procedures
Strikes
United States—National labor relations board

LABOR in politics. See Trade unions—Political activities

LABOR laws and legislation

New York (state)
Lindsay, Quill & the transit strike. T. R. Brooks. Commentary 41:50-7 Mr '66
Sic transit; improvement needed in machinery for negotiating with government workers. Reporter 34:14+ Ja 27 '66
Striking down the strike; Condon-Wadlin act violation; G. Weinstein's suit. il Time 87:50 F 18 '66

Spain
Labor and the Spanish syndical system; excerpt from Labor policy and practices in Spain. F. Witney. Mo Labor R 89:867-70 Ag '66

LABOR laws an legislation—*Continued*

United States

Bad news for union bosses; fight over the right to work. il Nations Bsns 53:36-7+ D '65

Chance on the outside; MDTA project at Lorton youth center. T. R. Sard. il Am Ed 2:29-32 Ap '66

Emergency strikes; weaknesses of present antistrike legislation. America 114:165-6 Ja 29 '66

Ethical aspects of union policy and conduct; Labor-management reporting and disclosure act. E. Stein. bibliog f Ann Am Acad 363: 117-25 Ja '66

How union shop breeds corruption. il Nations Bsns 54:42-3+ F '66

In Court; low score for unions. U S News 61:105-6 N 21 '66

Irresponsible unionism, right to strike; excerpts from a New York times editorial. U S News 60:112 Je 6 '66

Job for Jim; training under Manpower development and training act. J. N. Miller. il Read Digest 88:78-82 F '66

Johnson readies bill to ban strikes. il Bsns W p 117-18 Mr 12 '66

Labor bills may get a break: three controversial bills. Bsns W p 115 Mr 26 '66

Landmarks in labor. Nat R 18:144-5 F 22 '66

Limiting the right to strike. D. Lawrence. U S News 60:100 F 7 '66

On the trail of runaway plants; tax-exempt bonds lure industry. il Bsns W p 114-16 Ag 6 '66

Right to work controversy. G. J. Skibbins and C. S. Weymar. bibliog f il Harvard Bsns R 44:6-8+ Jl '66

Significant decisions in labor cases. See issues of Monthly labor review

Six characters in search of a posture. il Bsns W p 152+ Mr 5 '66

Spotlight on business; strikebreaking law; Senate labor committee debate; excerpts. Newsweek 68:62+ Ag 15 '66

State labor legislation in 1966. D. T. Bond. Mo Labor R 89:1378-84 D '66

State labor legislation passed in 1965. D. T. Bond. Mo Labor R 88:1445-50 D '65

Strike prevention. K. Crawford. Newsweek 68:20 Ag 29 '66

Strikes and people: a proposal. L. Hazard. Atlan 218:116-18 D '66; Discussion. 219:30+ Ja '67

What a new antistrike law will be like. il U S News 61:30-1 N 28 '66

What kind of law to limit strikes? U S News 60:71 F 7 '66

Where will labor turn? legislative setbacks on Capitol hill. Bsns W p29-31 Je 4 '66

Why tolerate the excesses of unions. Life 61:4 Ag 26 '66

See also
Arbitration, Industrial—United States
Insurance, Unemployment—United States
Minimum wage—United States
Trade unions—United States

Taft-Hartley law

Cattlemen oppose repeal of right-to-work law. Suc Farm 64:126 Mr '66

Filibustering 14(B) Newsweek 67:19 F 7 '66

Friendly Congress turns sour; 14(b) hopes dying, threat of tough anti-strike laws. il Bsns W p47-8 F 5 '66

How LBJ fights defense strikes. U S News 62:46 Ja 2 '67

Jim Crow and 14-B. H. Golden. New Repub 155:16-18 N 12 '66

Perils of HR 10027; secondary boycotts. Nat R 18:255 Mr 22 '66

R.I.P; repeal of 14(b) dead for session. Time 87:22 F 18 '66

Speaking out; right-to-work fight misses the point; with editorial comment. R. P. Griffin. Sat Eve Post 239:12+, 96 F 26 '66

Unmutual friends; Everett M. Dirksen's filibuster against repeal of section 14 (b) Reporter 34:14+ F 10 '66

Why 14(b) wasn't repealed. M. S. Evans. Nat R 18:214-15 Mr 8 '66

LABOR leaders. See Trade unions—Officials

LABOR-management advisory committee. See United States—President's advisory committee on labor-management policy

LABOR-management relations. See Industrial relations

LABOR-management reporting and disclosure act of 1959. See Labor laws and legislation —United States

LABOR market. See Labor supply

LABOR officials. See Trade unions—Officials

LABOR output. See Labor productivity

LABOR party (Great Britain)

Britain's Labor. Commonweal 84:96 Ap 15 '66

Chips are down for Harold Wilson. G. Bailey. il Reporter 34:31-4 Je 2 '66

For Wilson and labor, 150-seat gain? or fifty? U S News 60:24 Mr 14 '66

From Britain; a long Parliament. J. M. Cameron. Commonweal 84:144-5 Ap 22 '66

On from Highgate; Brighton conference. il Newsweek 68:44 O 17 '66

LABOR productivity

As raises push up labor costs; U.S. to follow Europe's path? il U S News 61:68+ N 7 '66

Business can live with the labor shortage. C. E. Silberman. Fortune 73:112-15+ My '66

Output per man-hour in the footwear industry. F. T. Moss. il Mo Labor R 89: 401-4 Ap '66

Productivity management. D. Sirota. Harvard Bsns R 44:111-16 S '66

Projecting industry productivity. B. P. Klotz. il Mo Labor 89:514-17 My '66

Understanding economic growth. R. S. Schultz. Harvard Bsns R 44:32-4+ N '66

See also
Work measurement

LABOR relations board, National. See United States—National labor relations board

LABOR requirements (for production)

Labor and material requirements for sewer works construction. R. V. Murray. il Mo Labor R 89:288-90 Mr '66

LABOR saving devices

Problem; his hired man left. J. Harvey. il Suc Farm 64:44-5 Ag '66

Anecdotes, facetiae, satire, etc.

Ingenious new laborsaving devices; excerpt from My war wilth the 20th century. P. Berton. il Read Digest 88:147-8 Ap '66

LABOR shortage. See Labor supply

LABOR supply

Brain drain: a U.S. dilemma. H. G. Grubel. bibliog Science 154:1420-4 D 16 '66

Help! il Time 87:79 Mr 25 '66

See also
Manpower

Canada

Canada riled by imported labor: recruitment of Britons by Douglas aircraft co. of Canada. Bsns W p97 O 29 '66

Where imports beat the skills shortage; Douglas aircraft of Canada imports workers from England. il Bsns W p58-60 Ag 20 '66

Europe, Western

Western Europe's business worry: a shortage of workers. U S News 61:122 N 14 '66

Germany (Federal Republic)

German solution for labor pinch. U S News 61:103-4 S 26 '66

Russia

Soviet manpower report. M. Feshbach. Mo Labor R 89:III-IV N '66

Sweden

Sweden's manpower programs. S. Swerdloff. Mo Labor R 89:1-6 Ja '66

United States

Adaptation of labor resources to changing needs; excerpt from Manpower planning in a free society. R. A. Lester. Mo Labor R 89:245-9 Mr '66

Business can live with the labor shortage. C. E. Silberman. Fortune 73:112-15+ My '66

Estimated need for skilled workers, 1965-75. A. F. Salt. il Mo Labor R 89:365-71 Ap '66

Help wanted and very badly; tight market for labor. il Bsns W p 101-3 Ap 2 '66

How Wirtz sees labor shortages. U S News 60:72 F 7 '66

Immigration and the Department of labor. F. H. Cassell. bibliog f Ann Am Acad 367: 105-14 S '66

Immigrant worker. F. L. Mott. il Ann Am Acad 367:23-32 S '66

Job agencies sprout satellites; tight labor market. il Bsns W p52-4 Ap 9 '66

Labor force projections, by color, 1970-80. S. Cooper and D. F. Johnston. il Mo Labor R 89:965-72 S '66

Labor force projections by state, 1970 and 1980. D. F. Johnston and G. R. Methee. il Mo Labor R 89:1098-104 O '66

Machines won't take over after all: highlights of Labor department study. America's Industrial and occupational manpower requirements 1964-75. il Bsns W p93-4+ O 8 '66

LABOR supply—United States—*Continued*
Manpower hunt puts recruiters to the test.
il Bsns W p41-2 Jl 9 '66
Watching for manpower shortages. Mo Labor
R 89:III-IV Je '66
West and South: where number of workers
is growing fastest. il U S News 61:78 O 31
'66
When the worker is king, industry's big hunt
for talent. il U S News 60:98+ F 14 '66
Where shortages are beginning to pinch. il
U S News 60:49-50 Mr 14 '66
Why the draft won't hurt your labor supply.
il Nations Bsns 54:35-7+ N '66
Year of harvest; the 1966 manpower report;
excerpt . March 8, 1966. L. B. Johnson. Mo
Labor R 89:II+ Mr '66

LABOR turnover
Labor turnover; tables. See issues of Monthly
labor review

LABOR unions. See Trade unions

LABOR vote. See Trade unions—Political activities

LABORATORIES
Research labs swarm to capital. il Bsns W
p 144-6+ Ap 23 '66
See also
Atomic research laboratories
Criminological laboratories
School laboratories
Testing laboratories
Underwater laboratories

Architecture
Building as a system; new laboratory buildings at Birmingham university, England.
T. Alexander. il Arch Forum 125:90-7 Jl '66
Engineering laboratory. il Arch Rec 139:
184-5 Ap '66
Laboratory as a machine; Standard oil. il
Arch Forum 124:40-7 Ap '66
Research raised on high; Laboratory of clinical investigation, Yale-New Haven hospital
buildings, and Henry Moses research institute, Montefiore hospital, Bronx, N.Y. il
Arch Forum 125:72-7 O '66

Equipment
Multicapillary mixer of solutions. G. W.
Moskowitz and R. L. Bowman. il Science
153:428-9 Jl 22 '66
See also
School laboratories—Equipment

LABORATORIES, Government
Federal laboratories: are they adjusting to
changing needs? L. J. Carter. Science 154:
1529-30 D 23 '66

LABORATORIES, Testing. See Testing laboratories

LABORATORY animals
Ages of experimental animals. N. O. Calloway; discussion. Science 152:15-16; 153:121-2
Ap 1, Jl 8 '66
Animal care: the humane movement is pulling ahead. E. Langer. il Science 151:1515-18
Mr 25 '66
Diseases of laboratory animals; report on
fourth annual meeting of the Gesellschaft
für versuchstierkunde. R. J. Flynn. Science 153:906 Ag 19 '66
Laboratory animal law. Sci Am 215:65 N '66
Lost pets that stray to the labs; unscrupulous
dognappers. C. Phinizy. Read Digest 88:
131-4 Ap '66
Pedigreed frogs anyone? Sci N 90:267 O 8
'66
Pet news; report of congressional hearings on
pet stealing. J. Dattel. il Ladies Home J
83:20+ Je '66
Pigs in the laboratory. L. K. Bustad. il Sci
Am 214:94-100 bibliog(p 144) Je '66
Researchers fear animal restrictions. Sci N
89:317 Ap 30 '66
Researchers menace British frogs. Sci N 90:
207 S 17 '66
Scientists vs. animal lovers. L. Eisenberg. il
Harper 233:101-2+ N '66; Discussion. 234:
4+ Ja '67
See also
Animals—Treatment
Chimpanzees
Gerbils
Rats

Feeding
Weaning of young rats: effect of time on
behavior. V. Nováková. bibliog il Science
151:475-6 Ja 28 '66

LABORATORY architecture. See Laboratories—Architecture

LABORATORY instrument computer. See Computers—Medical applications

LABORATORY technicians
See also
Medical workers

LABORATORY work. See Science—Study and
teaching

LABORDE, Ellis P.
Licking the coontail problem. Parks & Rec
1:174 F '66

LABOUISSE, Henry R.
Nobel peace prize: acceptance speech,
December 10, 1965. por UN Mo Chron 3:99-
102 Ja '66

LABRADOR dogs
Cotton fires up Little Smoky; National at
Bombay Hook national wildlife refuge. D.
Barnes. il Sports Illus 24:28-33 Ja 31 '66

LABRADOR retrievers. See Labrador dogs

LABYRINTH (ear)
See also
Ménière's disease

LAC des cygnes; ballet. See Ballets—Criticisms

LACE and lace making
Three centuries of bobbin lace. C. C. Mayer.
il Antiques 90:186-91 Ag '66

LACEWINGS
Ultrasonic sensitivity: a tympanal receptor in
the green lace wing chrysopa carnea. L. A.
Miller and E. G. MacLeod. bibliog il Science
154:891-3 N 18 '66

LACEY, Paul A.
Two similes for Advent; poem. Christian
Cent 83:1564 D 21 '66

LACHANCE, Leo E. See Palmquist, J. jt. auth.

LACHAPELLE, Edward R.
Control of snow avalanches; with biographical sketch. Sci Am 214:17, 92-9+ F '66

LACHS, John
Dogmatist in disguise. Christian Cent 83:1402-
5 N 16 '66

LACOUTURE, Jean
General de Gaulle and Vietnam. New Repub
154:19-21 Mr 12 '66

LACQUER and lacquering
See also
Japanning

LACRIMAL organs
Lactoperoxidase: identification and isolation
from harderian and lacrimal glands. M.
Morrison and P. Z. Allen. bibliog il Science 152:1626-8 Je 17 '66

LACROSSE
Game of the brave. il Newsweek 67:97-8
My 23 '66
Lacrosse gets off to a faster start. il Bsns
W p44-5 Jl 9 '66
Lacrosse watching this spring. il Sunset
136:54+ Mr '66
Navy's star with a stick; J. Lewis. F. Deford.
il Sports Illus 24:44-6+ My 30 '66
Ugliest day for army; navy won its seventh
straight national lacrosse championship. F.
Deford. Sports Illus 24:88+ Je 13 '66

LACTIC dehydrogenases. See Dehydrogenases

LACTOPEROXIDASE. See Enzymes

LACTOSE
Milk, enzymes & ulcers. il Time 87:60 Mr
25 '66

LACY, Dan
Impact of universal education; remarks, June
1965. por Library J 91:3866-70 S 1 '66
Net prices, library editions: Senate hearings
reviewed; summary of testimony. Pub W
190:26-9 Jl 25 '66
New responsibilities for publishing; summary
of address, June 13, 1966. por Pub W 190:
39-40 Jl 4 '66

LACY, Grace Nelson
CUE: an experiment in the humanities; adaptation of address. July 1966. por ALA Bul
60:918-22 O '66
CUE system. por Sr Schol 88:sup8 Ap 29 '66

LA DANY, L.
New look at red China, an authoritative
size-up; interview, ed. by K. M. Chrysler.
por U S News 60:56-8 F 28 '66

LADD, Ernie
Big rookie bonuses start a battle. E. Shrake.
Sports Illus 24:44 Ja 24 '66

LADD, H. S. See Hess, H. H. jt. auth.

LADDERS
Build your own rope ladder. G. P. Manning.
il Motor B 118:29 D '66

LADEN, Norman
Treatment for snakebite. Field & S 71:162-
3+ S '66

LADER, Lawrence
Let's speak out on abortion; excerpt from
Abortion. Read Digest 88:82-5+ My '66
Three men who made a revolution. N Y
Times Mag p8-9+ Ap 10 '66

LADERMAN, Ezra
Avant-garde makes a noise. N Y Times Mag
pt2 p 17-8 S 11 '66

LADERMAN, Gabriel
Importance of Cézanne. Art N 65:39-41+ O '66
LADIES world series of golf. See Golf—Tournaments
LADY and the peddler; story. See Agnon, S. J.
LADY slippers. See Ladys slippers
LADYBIRDS
It's a happy sight to see ladybugs lunching away on aphids. il Sunset 136:108-9 Mr '66
LADYBUGS. See Ladybirds
LADYS slippers
Challenging lady-slipper. C. C. Trubey. il Flower Grower 53:61 Je '66
Orchids in your house. J. Lonski. il Horticulture 44:28-9+ F '66
LAESTAR, Carl H. and Laestar, M. E.
How to pack for mail order shipping; excerpt from Successful selling of antiques by mail. Hobbies 71:84 Ag '66
Methods and rules of shipping; excerpt from Successful selling of antiques by mail. Hobbies 71:76+ S '66
LAESTAR, Martha E. See Laestar, C. H. jt. auth
LA FARGE, Henry A.
Come to Christie's. Art N 65:42-3+ D '66
John La Farge: a reappraisal. Art N 65:29-31+ My '66
Music of flowers. Art N 65:40-1+ N '66
LA FARGE, John
John La Farge: a reappraisal. H. A. La Farge. il por Art N 65:29-31+ My '66
Meticulous mandarin. il Time 87:64 Je 3 '66
LAFARGE, John, institute. See John LaFarge institute
LA FAVE, Lawrence
Need for a third party. Bul Atomic Sci 22:39 O '66
LA FAY, Howard
Gibraltar, rock of contention. Nat Geog Mag 130:102-21 Jl '66
LAFAYETTE college, Easton, Pa.
Student attitudes at Lafayette, 1964-65. K. R. Bergethon. Sch & Soc 94:74-6 F 5 '66
LAFLEUR, Lydia
Worth fighting for. bibliog por Library J 91: 1582-6 Mr 15 '66
LA FONTAINE, Barbara
Babes in the woods. Sports Illus 25:60-2+ Jl 11; 44-6+ Jl 18 '66
LA FOUNTAIN, Edward
Death walked the duck marsh; ed. by B. East. por Outdoor Life 137:60-1+ Ap '66
LAGARDE, Jocelyn
Big bundle of royalty; with report by D. Zeitlin. il pors Life 61:69-70+ O 14 '66
LAGEMANN, John Kord
Bring to it the rainbow. Read Digest 89:87-9 N '66
Conversation can nourish your life. Read Digest 88:131-4 Je '66
Rewards of risking it. Read Digest 90:191+ Ja '67
(ed) See Hunt, J. M. Can we make human beings more intelligent?
LAGERKVIST, Pär
Quest of Pär Lagerkvist. K. Lamott. il por Holiday 40:151+ N '66
LAGUARDIA airport. See New York (city)—Airports
LAGUNA BEACH, Calif.

Music

Laguna Beach, Cal. W. Aguiar, jr. Opera N 31:23 O 15 '66
LAHR, Bert
Manner of speaking; on purifying the antiquities in Ypsilanti. J. Ciardi. Sat R 49: 22 Ag 13 '66
LAHR, Georgiana Lieder
Enchanted broom; drama. Plays 26:72-4 O '66
LAICH, Katherine
ALA headquarters space problem grows. ALA Bul 60:501-2 My '66
Keep the lines open. ALA Bul 60:1161-2 D '66
LAING, Alexander
Good treason; poem. Sat R 49:38 Jl 9 '66
LAING, Dilys
Carol to be sung to lutes or banjos; with respects to Piero Della Francesca. Commonweal 85:344 D 23 '66
LAING, Gerald
Hybrid. New Yorker 42:35-6 Ap 30 '66
Pollsters began with kits, questionaires, no know-how. il por Life 60:72 My 20 '66
LAING, Mack
Ungathered harvests in the ocean. UNESCO Courier 19:11-15+ S '66
LAIRD, Melvin R.
Excerpt from February 2, 1966, statement to the press. Cong Digest 45:144 My '66
If a coalition is acceptable, the fighting makes no sense; statement, March 1, 1966. por U S News 60:76+ Mr 14 '66
Tax-sharing with the states; address, November 17, 1966. Vital Speeches 33:184-9 Ja 1 '67
LAIRD, Roland
Birth control; letter. Commonweal 84:3+ Mr 25 '66
LAISE, Caroline Clendening
Entente cordiale. por Newsweek 69:23 Ja 16 '67
LAITY
Asia, a challenge to the individual apostolate; opportunities for the Catholic lay worker. G. Caulfield. Cath World 202:283-7 F '66
Catholic layman confronts his changing church. D. Norton-Taylor. il Fortune 74: 172-5+ D '66
Different cultures but a common ideal; lay volunteers forming international bond of charity. R. A. Kevane. America 114:326-8 Mr 5 '66
Laity lose their chains. J. B. Sheerin. Cath World 202:262-6 F '66
Lay people in the church; a study for a theology of laity, by Y. M. J. Congar. Review
Cath World 202:308 F '66. J. Kane
Lay trusteeism: yesterday and today. G. P. Fogarty. America 115:656-9 N 19 '66
Laymen in the parish. J. O'Gara. Commonweal 84:4 Mr 25 '66
Man in the pew. C. S. Calian. Cath World 204:170-3 D '66
Of many things. T. N. Davis. America 115: 759 D 10 '66
Part-time priesthood; Episcopal laymen with full-time jobs trained to be part-time priests. il Newsweek 68:72 Ag 15 '66
Prophets to the world: priests and laymen. America 114:218 F 12 '66
Psychologist views the new liturgy. A. J. Summo. Cath World 202:272-7 F '66
Today's layman: an uncertain Catholic. D. J. Thorman. America 116:39-41 Ja 14 '67
What makes a Catholic conservative conservative? E. F. Tyhanic. Cath World 203: 11-16 Ap '66; Discussion. 203:258 Ag '66
Who can afford to work for the church? J. J. Gallagher. America 114:192-4 F 5 '66
Will the bishops speed up renewal? J. B. Sheerin. Cath World 204:132-3 D '66
See also
World congress for the lay apostolate
LAJTHA, Abel, and others
Brain research. Science 152:550+ Ap 22 '66
—See Tsukada, Y. jt. auth.
LAKE, Alice
Drugs; a student report. Seventeen 25:170-1+ S '66
How doctors heal the unborn. Sat Eve Post 239:39-42 F 12 '66
Mother who learned to fight. Redbook 128:62-3+ N '66
Tell me doctor. Ladies Home J 83:42+ F '66
LAKE COUNTY, Ind.
Abandoned county. il Time 87:31 Ap 29 '66
LAKE COUNTY, Ind. public library system
Seven for Lake County. R. P. Bartolini. il Library J 91:5874-7 D 1 '66
LAKE CREEK Water Yield Improvement project, Colo. See Water storage
LAKE cruises. See Cruising
LAKE ERIE. See Erie, Lake
LAKE ERIE opera theater
Cleveland. R. Finn. il Opera N 31:25 N 5 '66
LAKE FORK recreation area, Colo. See Recreation areas
LAKE GEORGE opera festival. See Music festivals—New York (state)
LAKE HAVASU. See Havasu Lake
LAKE HAVASU CITY, Ariz.
Have fun, Havasu! il Travel 125:6-7 Ap '66
LAKE MICHIGAN. See Michigan, Lake
LAKE OF THE OZARKS
Lake of the Ozarks. W. E. Swegle. il Motor B 118:22-5 Ag '66
LAKE pollution. See Water pollution
LAKE POWELL. See Lakes, Artificial
LAKE TAHOE. See Tahoe, Lake
LAKE TAHOE state park. See Nevada—Parks and reserves
LAKER, Dorothy
Footpath in the wilderness. Travel 126:61-3 Ag '66
LAKES
Chemically stratified lake in Alaska; Pingo Lake. G. E. Likens and P. L. Johnson. bibliog il Science 153:875-7 Ag 19 '66
Drought shrinks lakes on Long Island. Sci N 90:329 O 22 '66
Lakes of Iowa. R. V. Cassill. Holiday 40:18+ Ag '66
Unmapped Adirondack Lake; glacial lake. P. Schaefer. il Liv Wildn 30:10 Sum '66
See also
Great Lakes
Water pollution

LAKES—*Continued*

Clearing

Licking the coontail problem; how New Orleans rid its lagoons of obnoxious aquatic plant life. E. F. Laborde. il Parks & Rec 1:174 F '66

LAKES, Artificial
Lake Powell. W. Stegner. il Holiday 39:64-9+ My '66
Lakemaker; T. J. Perine. il Time 88:67 S 23 '66
Look at Georgia's Lake Lanier. M. Hunn. il Motor B 118:36-7+ S '66
Offbeat travel opportunity; cruising up Lake Powell. A. H. Hepburn. il Sr Schol 88: sup21 F 25 '66
Six new Arizona fishing lakes. il Sunset 136: 44+ Ap '66

LAKEWOOD, N.J.
Our neighbors helped us rebuild out of the ashes; Negro family's house burned; ed. by L. Shecter. B. DeCausey. il Good H 162: 98-9+ Je '66

LAKING, Leslie
Royal botanical gardens. Horticulture 45:34-5+ Ja '67

LAKOFF, Sanford A.
Tizard record. Bul Atomic Sci 22:39-41 Ja '66

LAL, D. and Venkatavaradan, V. S.
Low-energy protons; average flux in interplanetary space during the last 100,000 years. bibliog Science 151:1381-4 Mr 18 '66

LALL, Betty Goetz
Arms control in Congress, 1966. Bul Atomic Sci 22:35-7 D '66
Arms reduction impact. Bul Atomic Sci 22: 41-4 S '66
Conversion of defense resources. Bul Atomic Sci 22:46-8 Ja '66
Cooperation and arms control in outer space. Bul Atomic Sci 22:34-7 N '66
International cooperation at the White House. Bul Atomic Sci 22:41-3 F '66
New frontiers of urban excellence? Bul Atomic Sci 22:37-40 Mr '66
Next: a proliferation ban. Bul Atomic Sci 22:42-5 Ja '66
Nonintervention vs. containment. Bul Atomic Sci 22:21-4 My '66
Peacekeeping at the U.N. Bul Atomic Sci 22:43-5 O '66
U.S. China policy is changing: travel comes first. Bul Atomic Sci 22:93-6 Je '66

LALONDE, L. E.
Good water-meter management. Am City 81: 167-8 My '66

LAMARR, Hedy
Court denies injunction against Hedy Lamarr book. Pub W 190:52 O 10 '66
Poeme d'extase. L. L. King. New Repub 155: 34-5 N 26 '66

LAMB (meat)
Which lamb chop is which? il Sunset 137: 134-5 S '66
See also
Cookery—Meat

LAMB stew. See Stew

LAMBERT, Darwin
Over the years with Great Basin Park. bibliog f il Nat Parks Mag 40:12-16 Je '66

LAMBERT, Frank I.
In marine communications here's how VHF fits in. Motor B 119:109-11+ Ja '67

LAMBERT, Gavin
Gavin Lambert wins first Thomas R. Coward award. Pub W 189:58 Mr 7 '66

LAMBERT, John M.
Inventor of the month. S. V. Jones. il por Sci Digest 60:44 D '66

LAMBERT, Peter B. and Frank, H. A.
Local recognition of histocompatibility differences in skin grafts. bibliog Science 155:99-101 Ja 6 '67

LAMBERT, Richard D.
(ed) Americans abroad. Ann Am Acad 368: 1-170 N '66
Some minor pathologies in the American presence in India. bibliog f Ann Am Acad 368:157-70 N '66

LAMBERT, Sam M.
Signs of a maturing profession. NEA J 55: 52-5 D '66

LAMBERT, William. See Wheeler, K. jt. auth.

LAMBERT pharmacal company. See Warner-Lambert pharmaceutical company

LAMBS
Extra lamb crops closer to reality. il Farm J 90:50J S '66

LAME White Man (Cheyenne Indian)
Last ghastly moments at the Little Bighorn; ed. with introd. by M. Liberty. John Stands in Timber. il Am Heritage 17:18-21+ Ap '66

LAMESA, Tex.
Old city hall gets a new face. C. A. Taylor. il Am City 81:91 Mr '66

LAMHUT, Phyllis
Brief biography. S. Goodman. pors Dance Mag 40:46-7 Ap '66
Phyllis Lamhut, Henry street playhouse. M. Marks. Dance Mag 40:30-1 Mr '66

LAMINATED construction. See Sandwich construction

LAMM, Michael
How warranties work. Motor T 18:124 N '66
Opting for options. Motor T 18:120-1 N '66

LAMMEY, W. Clyde
Homeowners' clinic; questions and answers. See issues of Popular mechanics
How to get started in metal turning. Pop Mech 127:186-9+ Ja '67 (to be cont)
Twelve ways to attach legs. Pop Mech 126: 122-3 Jl '66

LAMOLA, Angelo A. and Mittal, J. P.
Solution photochemistry of thymine and uracil. bibliog Science 154:1560-1 D 23 '66

LAMON, James D.
Rough water bass. Outdoor Life 138:36-9+ Ag '66

LAMONT, Lansing
Crucial struggle for forty-five congressional seats. Fortune 74:124-7+ S '66

LAMOTT, Kenneth
Career of Richard Sorge. Nation 202:687-8 Je 6 '66
Cells as second homes. Holiday 39:12+ F '66
Gatsby and the sea gull; story. Harper 233: 113-17 O '66
Kangaroo lottery; story. Sat Eve Post 239: 84-93 Mr 26 '66
La Jolla's new university: Olympus on a mesa. Harper 233:82-4+ Ag '66
Quest of Pär Lagerkvist. Holiday 40:151+ N '66
Report from a racing sailor. Holiday 40:8+ Jl '66

LAMP bulbs. See Electric lamps

LAMP tables. See Tables

LAMPEDUSA, Giuseppe di
Notes from a European diary: 1963-64. E. Wilson. New Yorker 42:42-6+ My 28 '66

LAMPORT, Felicia
Ecumenical economy; poem. Atlan 218:130 O '66
Hypocritics. Atlan 218:104-6 Ag '66
Plaintive geometry; poem. Harper 232:58 Je '66

LAMPORT, Sol
Sail means only a sale to Sol. H. Whall. il pors Sports Illus 24:26-9 Ja 24 '66

LAMPS
Easiest lamp you'll ever make! il Bet Hom & Gard 44:134 My '66
See also
Electric lamps
Lighting fixtures

LAMPS, Reflector. See Reflectors

LAMPS, Three-way. See Electric lamps

LAMSON, Peggy
White northerner's choice. Atlan 217:58-62 Je '66

LANAHAN, Scottie
Place where people really live. House & Gard 130:202+ O '66

LANCASTER, Donald E.
Amplification using switching techniques. Electr World 75:30-2+ F '66
Electronic metal locators. Electr World 76: 39-42+ D '66
Hi-fi à go-go lamps. Pop Electr 24:64-6+ Ja '66
IC-67 metal locator. Pop Electr 26:41-8+ Ja '67
Insulated gate transistor. Electr World 76: 34-6+ Jl '66
Integrated circuit amplifier you can build for under $6! Pop Electr 25:57-9+ O '66
Integrated circuits. Pop Electr 25:52-6+ O '66
Linear integrated circuits: what's available? Electr World 76:38-42+ N '66
Musette color organ. Pop Electr 25:56-62+ Jl '66
Nanosecond pulses: techniques & applications. Electr World 75:37-9+ F '66
Parts profiles. See issues of Popular electronics to May 1966
Pulse generator. Pop Electr 24:60-2 Ap '66
Semiconductor interval timer. Electr World 75:82-4 My '66
Square deal audio generator. Pop Electr 25: 59-63 N '66
Switching-mode power conversion. Electr World 76:87-90 S '66
Using new low-cost integrated circuits. Electr World 75:50-2+ Mr '66
Varactor diode applications. Electr World 75: 43-6+ Je '66

LANCEY, Roderic C. See Smalter, D. J. jt. auth.

LANCHESTER, Elsa
Isadora Duncan had nothing to pass on to the future; interview. ed. by V. H. Swisher. pors Dance Mag 40:52-3 S '66

LAND, Edwin Herbert
Instant photography; the impossible that happened. il pors Pop Sci 189:130-1 O '66
Michelson winner named. por Sci N 90:327 O 22 '66

LAND, Irene Ellen (Stokvis) See Stokvis, I. E.

LAND, Thomas
Abram Fischer: Afrikaner fights apartheid. Nation 202:650-1 My 30 '66
Botswana's cheerless freedom. Reporter 34: 41-2 F 10 '66

LAND
See also
Real property
Reclamation of land

Anecdotes, facetiae, satire, etc.
Why I've changed my mind about our mortgage with a view. E. D. Hunt. il Farm J 90:75+ O '66

Prices
See Land values

Subdivision
Headache-free subdivision review; Fort Worth, Tex. il Am City 81:109 S '66
See also
Taxation
Property tax

India
Asia needs cropland areas immediately. Sci N 90:405 N 12 '66

Tennessee
Man who wouldn't law with Uncle Sam; case of W. Metcalf and government suit. W. Ogden. Read Digest 88:39+ F '66
See also
United States
Public lands—United States

LAND contracts
Will selling land on contract save you tax dollars? N. G. P. Krausz. il Suc Farm 64: 33+ O '66

LAND fills. See Municipal dumps

LAND grant colleges
Bad news for farmers. D. Hanson. Suc Farm 64:8+ My '66
Proposed federal cuts in land-grant college funds; statement, February 4, 1966. Sch & Soc 94:189-90 Ap 2 '66

LAND management, Bureau of. See United States—Land management, Bureau of

LAND mines. See Mines, Military

LAND reclamation. See Reclamation of land

LAND reform. See Land tenure

LAND reform conference. See World land reform conference

LAND retirement program. See Agricultural administration—United States

LAND sinking
City sinking in a sea of mud. R. S. Strother. il Read Digest 89:99-103 Ag '66

LAND slides. See Landslides

LAND speculation
Good earth; investments in land. Fortune 74:241-2 N '66

LAND tenure
Land reform and the world food crisis; summary of conference. UN Mo Chron 3:45-8 Jl '66
See also
Real property
World land reform conference

Alaska
See also
Homesteads

Bolivia
See also
Agricultural colonization—Bolivia

China (People's Republic)
Development of agriculture. J. Robinson; J. Gray. il Bul Atomic Sci 22:27-39 Je '66

Colombia
Journey in darkness; preparations for first land-redistribution project in Cunday. I. Kovacs. il Reporter 35:46-9 O 20 '66

Ireland
Struggle for the land. R. Moley. Newsweek 92 Jl 4 '66

Latin America
Land reform in Latin America. R. J. Bocklet. America 115:458-60 O 15 '66; Discussion. 115:566-8 N 12 '66
Latin American land reform; enemies of promise. W. C. Thiesenhusen. il Nation 202:90-4 Ja 24 '66

Peru
Peruvian politics stalls Belaúnde's reforms. S. Rodman. il Reporter 35:37-40 Jl 14 '66

Russia
See also
Agricultural colonialization—Russia

United States
Finders keepers; attempt by group of Spanish Americans to seize land in New Mexico. Newsweek 68:40 N 7 '66
Keeping suburbia green; the land trust. Newsweek 68:113 N 28 '66
See also
Homesteads

Vietnam (Republic)
Why we fail as revolutionaries. I. F. Stone. New Repub 155:23-5 Jl 30 '66

LAND utilization
Geology and the new conservation movement; address, December 6, 1965. P. T. Flawn. bibliog Science 151:409-12 Ja 28 '66; Discussion. 152:152+. 1568-9 Ap 8. Je 17 '66
Greenspan program. O. L. Freeman. il Parks & Rec 1:829-30 O '66
See also
City planning

LAND valuation. See Real property—Valuation

LAND values
Fat of the land; farm land. Time 87:96 Ap 29 '66
What tight money is doing to land prices. il U S News 61:32-3 D 5 '66
When to sell to the developer; farm land grab. G. Logsdon. il Farm J 90:38-9+ Mr '66

LANDAHL, William L.
How to use landmarks in program. por Parks & Rec 1:642-3 Ag '66

LANDAU, Jacob
Yes—no, art—technology; address, July 1965. por Wilson Lib Bul 41:42-57 S '66

LANDAU, Joseph V.
Protein and nucleic acid synthesis in escherichia coli; pressure and temperature effects. bibliog Science 153:1273-4 S 9 '66

LANDAU, Nina Serrano
Agit-prop pop opera. J. O'Connor. Nation 203:716-17 D 26 '66

LANDERS, Ann, pseud.
Behind the advice column. Sat R 49:108-10 N 12 '66
Sickness of our times. PTA Mag 61:4-5 S '66

about
Second decade for the Ann Landers style. J. M. Flagler. il pors Look 30:66+ O 18 '66

LANDFILLS. See Municipal dumps

LANDI, Gino
Hellzapoppin, Roman style. il Time 88:80 O 7 '66

LANDING gear, Airplane. See Airplanes—Landing gear

LANDING mats. See Aviation landing stations —Landing mats

LANDING of airplanes. See Airplanes—Landing

LANDING strips, Airplane. See Aviation landing stations

LANDING systems for space vehicles. See Space vehicles—Landing systems

LANDINO, A.
City survey that saves. Am City 81:94-5+ D '66

LANDLORD and tenant
Speaking out; we need more slumlords. J. Kahn. Sat Eve Post 239:8+ D 17 '66
White slumlord confesses. B. Dahl. il Esquire 66:92-4+ Jl '66
See also
Rent

LANDMARKS, Historic. See Historic houses, etc.; United States—Historic houses, etc.

LANDMARKS, Literary. See Literary landmarks

LANDON, Kenneth P.
1954 Geneva agreements. bibliog f Cur Hist 50:79-84+ F '66

about
Where are they now? pors Newsweek 68:16 D 19 '66

LANDOR, Ronald A.
Fallacy of balance in public library book selection; excerpts from address, October 1965. por Library J 91:629-32 F 1 '66

LANDRETH, George H.
I hunt Mongolia's argali. pors Outdoor Life 138:32-5+ S '66

LANDRY, Tom
Thinking man's Cowboy. E. Linn. il por Sat Eve Post 239:76-8+ D 17 '66

LANDSCAPE
Blight or a noble city? I. McHarg. il Audubon Mag 68:47-52 Ja '66
Offense against America; a mountain is ravaged, a valley shattered; Big Black Mountain. H. M. Caudill. il Audubon Mag 68:356-9 S '66

LANDSCAPE gardening
Campus landscape. J. Du Von. il Am Ed 2: 18-24 My '66
Front garden done over with screens, trellises. il Sunset 138:128-9 Ja '67
Holly in the landscape. C. E. Lewis. il Horticulture 44:24-5+ D '66
How to turn your lot into a landscape. il House & Gard 129:164-7 Mr '66
How to unflatten your lot! il Bet Hom & Gard 44:66-7 S '66
How to work with a landscape architect. R. Bailey. House & Gard 130:266-7+ N '66
Impact from one kind of plant. il Flower Grower 53:52-3 My '66
Junipers are useful. A. R. Ireys. il Horticulture 44:18-21 N '66
Landscape idea collecting; Foothill college campus. il Sunset 137:78-81 S '66
More summer color for problem spots! H. Mason and L. Grove. il Bet Hom & Gard 44:54-9 Je '66
New look in near-the-house planting. J. R. Rebhan. il Flower Grower 53:34-6+ Mr '66
Plant for privacy. il Flower Grower 53:34-6 Je '66
Quick summer color for problem spots. H. Mason. il Bet Hom & Gard 44:70-3 My '66
Raised plant bed. il House & Gard 131:130-1+ Ja '67
Roses that do a real landscaping job. il Bet Hom & Gard 44:66-71 F '66
Showmanship helps to make good landscaping. il House & Gard 129:198-200 Mr '66
Sort out your garden now. B. Black. il Pop Gard 17:42-5 Mr '66
They landscaped for the children as well as for the adults. il Sunset 138:124-5 Ja '67
What is the cost of good landscaping? il House & Gard 129:132-5+ F '66
See also
Garden design
Gardens, Japanese
Hedges
Waterfalls in gardens

LANDSCAPE improvement
Abolish the highways! J. B. Jackson. Nat R 18:1213-17 N 29 '66
America the more beautiful. il Time 88:53 S 30 '66
Billboards, glass houses, and the law; excerpt from address. R. F. Babcock. Harper 232: 20+ Ap '66
Business and beauty: address, December 2, 1965. L. S. Rockefeller. Vital Speeches 32: 219-21 Ja 15 '66; Same. il Audubon Mag 68: 112-15 Mr '66
How to wage war on ugliness. E. K. Faltermayer. il Fortune 73:130-4+ My '66
Lady Bird, says L.B.J., will beautify us out of existence. H. Sidey. il Life 61:30B Jl 22 '66
Let's work together for a more beautiful America; adaptation of addresses, with text of letter to readers of Parents' magazine. C. A. T. Johnson. Parents Mag 41: 22+ Jl '66
Neighborhood well; site beautified. il Newsweek 68:89-90+ O 10 '66
1966 legislative roundup; legislation of significance to the park and recreation field; comp. by K. J. Smithee. Parks & Rec 1:960-1+ D '66
Politics of beauty. W. F. Buckley, jr. il Esquire 66:50-3+ Jl '66

LANDSCAPE in poetry. See Nature in poetry

LANDSCAPE painting
John Frederick Kensett; a tribute to man and artist. F. Lewison. il Am Artist 30: 32-7+ O '66
Landscape paintings of William Palmer. L. Schmeckebier. il Am Artist 30:50-5+ Je '66
St Augustine: city of artists, 1883-1895. F. A. Sharf. il Antiques 90:220-3 Ag '66

LANDSCAPE protection
Crowds. L. B. Johnson. Parks & Rec 1:821-2 O '66

Keynote address: America the beautiful; with editorial comment. R. E. Train. il Am For 71:11, 16-19+ O '65
Natural beauty, the follow through. J. B. Craig. il Am For 71:12-15+ O '65
Offense against America; a mountain is ravaged, a valley shattered; Big Black Mountain. H. M. Caudill. il Audubon Mag 68:356-9 S '66
Politics of beauty; excerpts from addresses. H. L. Diamond. il Parks & Rec 1:138-41+ F '66
Rape of the land. B. H. Bagdikian. il Sat Eve Post 239:25-9+ Je 18 '66
Strip-mine morality: landscaping of hell; regulations proposed by the Strip mining and reclamation division of the Kentucky department of natural resources. W. Berry. il Nation 202:96-100 Ja 24 '66
To save the Grand Canyon; Colorado River basin bill proposals. W. Stegner. Sat R 49:20 Ag 20 '66
See also
Shore protection

LANDSLIDES
Action at Agrigento; Sicily. Newsweek 68: 42 Ag 1 '66
Highground haven; Lake Fork recreation area, Colo. N. W. Noble. il Am For 72:30-1+ Je '66
Sherman landslide, Alaska. R. L. Shreve. bibliog il Science 154:1639-43 D 30 '66
What to do in a landslide. E. Crimmin. il Sci Digest 60:75-7 Jl '66

LANDYMORE, William Moss
Admirals' revolt. il por Newsweek 68:41-2 Ag 1 '66

LANE, Ann J.
Longest journey. Nation 202:530-1 My 2 '66

LANE, Frederic C.
At the roots of Republicanism. bibliog f Am Hist R 71:403-20 Ja '66

LANE, Kenneth J.
They bug me. il por Newsweek 68:110+ N 28 '66

LANE, Mark
Again, the assassination; analysis of criticisms of Warren commission report. il Por Newsweek 68:30-3 Ag 15 '66
Lane says JFK death is still unsolved murder. Pub W 190:58 Ag 22 '66
Warren commission: the critics and the law; theories of E. J. Epstein and M. Lane. K. Goodall; A. L. Goodhart. Reporter 35:44-8+ D 15 '66

LANE, Will
Vagabond camera. See issues of Travel

LANES, Jerrold
Surrealism in the round. New Repub 155:28+ D 17 '66

LANG, Barbara
Magic sentence. Writer 79:20-1+ O '66

LANG, Daniel
Letter from Geneva. New Yorker 42:108-10+ Je 25 '66
Reporter at large. New Yorker 42:37-40+ D 24 '66

LANG, David J. See Mella, B. jt. auth.

LANG, Paul Henry
Art of the second guess. Sat R 49:50+ F 26 '66
Baroque flourishes. Opera N 31:16-17 N 19 '66
Baroque on the Time-Life plan. Sat R 49: 62-3 Ap 30; 62-3 Jl 30 '66

LANG, Thomas G. and Norris, K. S.
Swimming speed of a Pacific bottlenose porpoise. bibliog il Science 151:588-90 F 4 '66
—and Pryor, Karen
Hydrodynamic performance of porpoises, stenella attenuata. bibliog Science 152: 531-3 Ap 22 '66
—and Smith, H. A. P.
Communication between dolphins in separate tanks by way of an electronic acoustic link (cont) Science 152:387 Ap 15 '66

LANG, Wilfred
Wilfred Lang: artist, critic of today's church. D. Devereux. Christian Cent 83:1515-19 D 7 '66

LANGBEIN, W. B. See Leopold, L. B. jt. auth.

LANGBORNE, Leon
Book review. Negro Hist Bul 29:117 F '66

LANGE, Dorothea
This is the way it is, look at it! look at it! interview; ed. by J. Deschin. Pop Phot 58:58+ My '66
about
Camera as a sociological weapon. P. Stackpole. U S Camera 29:16+ My '66
Dorothea Lange and her printer. J. Deschin. il Pop Phot 59:28+ Jl '66
Dorothea Lange; friend of vision. C. Morrison. il Look 30:34-8 Mr 22 '66

LANGE, Dorothea—about—*Continued*
One whom I admire, Dorothea Lange (1895–1965) W. E. Smith. il por Pop Phot 58:86-8 F '66
Paintings and photographs. F. Getlein. New Repub 154:33-5 Mr 19 '66
Recording life-in-process. M. R. Weiss. il por Sat R 49:50-1 Mr 5 '66
LANGE, Victor
Polyphony in letters. New Repub 154:33-5 My 14 '66
LANGENBERG, Donald N. and others
Josephson effects; with biographical sketches. Sci Am 214:16, 30-9 bibliog(p 146) My '66
LANGEWIESCHE, Wolfgang
Kinderdorf kids and their professional mothers. Read Digest 89:123-6 D '66
LANGGUTH, Jack
Doctor Berne plays the celebrity game. N Y Times Mag p 10-11+ Jl 17 '66
Political fun and games in California. N Y Times Mag p27-9+ O 16 '66
LANGHAM, Frank W. Jr. See Irwin. P. H. jt. auth.
LANGKAMMER, David M.
Great Lakes. por Parks & Rec 1:644 Ag '66
LANGLAIS, Bernard
Bernard Langlais. E. Dugmore. il Craft Horiz 26:22-5 Mr '66
LANGLEY, Samuel P.
Profiles; Smithsonian institution. G. T. Hellman. New Yorker 42:87-8+ D 10 '66
LANGLEY research center. See United States—National aeronautics and space administration—Langley research center
LANGLIE, Arthur B.
Report from Montesano. por Am For 72:6 Jl '66
LANGLOIS, Pierre
Pierre Langlois, *ébéniste* extraordinary. J. Stuart. il Antiques 89:652+ My '66
LANGONE, John
Head keeper of the new cathedral. Sat R 49:53-4 Ap 2 '66
LANGSNER, Jules
Art from Los Angeles (title varies) Art N 65:58 D '66
LANGUAGE, Universal
One world, but which language? Redbook 126:34+ Ap '66
LANGUAGE and languages
See also
Communication (speech, writing, etc)
Figures of speech
Semantics
Translations and translating

Study and teaching
Quick lesson in every language. E. Siegelman. Travel 125:65-7 F '66
See also
Languages, Modern—Study and teaching
Summer institute of linguistics
LANGUAGE and thought. See Thought and language
LANGUAGE of animals. See Animal communication
LANGUAGE teaching records. See Phonograph records—Language teaching records
LANGUAGES, Artificial
See also
Interlingua
LANGUAGES, Modern
See also
Modern language association of America

Anecdotes, facetiae, satire, etc.
Wallop yon horse with a parachute; results of mistakes when using basic foreign phrases. L. Rosten. il Look 30:16 Mr 8 '66; Same abr. with title Please pardon my French, German, Italian, etc. Read Digest 89:143-6 Ag '66

Study and teaching
Foreign language in high school. M. E. Barker; N. S. MacKeigan; G. D. Matlock. NEA J 55:47-9 O '66
Language requirements for the Ph.D; letter. S. Ross and C. W. Shilling. Science 153:1595 S 30 '66; Discussion. 154:1603 D 30 '66
Scholar gap; U.S. agencies increase Vietnamese language enrollment. il Newsweek 67:58-9 Ja 31 '66
To and from babel. S. Zoll. Nation 202:398-9+ Ap 4 '66
See also
Phonograph records—Language teaching records
LANIER, G. N. and Oliver, J. H. Jr
Sex-ratio condition: unusual mechanisms in bark beetles. bibliog Science 153:208-9 Jl 8 '66

LANIER, R. S.
Buildings and the sonic boom. Arch Forum 125:54-5+ D '66
LANIER, LAKE. See Lakes, Artificial
LANNI, Yvonne Théry, and others
Bacteriophage T5 chromosome fractionation: genetic specificity of a DNA fragment. bibliog Science 152:208-10 Ap 8 '66
LANPHIER, Thomas G. Jr
I shot down Yamamoto. Read Digest 89:82-7 D '66
LANSBURGH, Therese
One woman can make the difference: a blueprint for day care action. G. Gibson. il Ladies Home J 83:62+ S '66
LANSBURY, Angela
Dame in Mame. il pors Time 87:59-60 Je 17 '66
No shame for Mame. por Newsweek 67:89 Je 6 '66
Smashing new dame to play Mame; with report by J. Hallowell. il pors Life 60:88-92+ Je 17 '66
LANSDOWNE, James Fenwick
Portfolio; paintings, with biographical sketch. por Audubon Mag 68:454-61 N '66
LANSDOWNE, Stuart
Washington front. America 115:27, 246 Jl 9, S 10 '66
LANSKY, Meyer
Island in the sun. il por Newsweek 69:22-4 Ja 9 '67
LANTERNS
Battery camp light. C. Conley. il Field & S 71:123 Je '66
Camp lanterns. Consumer Rep 31:298-301 D '66
Lanterns that give more light. W. Radcliffe. il Pop Gard 17:68-9 Mr '66
Treasure hunt: kerosene lanterns. J. Mebane. il Bet Hom & Gard 44:122 My '66
LANTOS, Thomas P.
Should teachers form their own political action groups? yes. NEA J 55:58-9 D '66
LANTZ, Ragni
Bachelor girl. Ebony 21:102-4+ Ag '66
LANTZ, Thomas
Making the budget work; reprint. por Parks & Rec 1:744-5 S '66
LANYI, George A. See McWilliams, W. C. jt. auth.
LAOS
See also
Elections—Laos
United States—Armed forces—Forces in Laos

Armed forces
Air strike. Newsweek 67:56 Je 27 '66
Situation normal; chiefs of staff dispute. Newsweek 68:56 O 31 '66

Foreign relations
President Johnson confers with the Prime Minister of Laos; statements at news conference, October 13, 1966. L. B. Johnson; Sowanna Phouma. Dept State Bul 55:667-9 O 31 '66

Native races
Laos report: gains in a forgotten war; team of Americans and Meo tribesmen. S. W. Sanders. il U S News 61:24-5 Jl 4 '66

Politics and government
Election to test Laotian stability. D. Kirk. il Reporter 35:26-9 D 29 '66
Gathering the pieces; anti-Communist forces in chaos. Time 88:37 N 4 '66
Just a little rebellion; revolt failed. Time 88:36 O 28 '66
Kong Le & the dragon. il Time 88:48 O 21 '66
Laosing it up. Newsweek 68:59-60 O 3 '66
See also
Elections—Laos
LAP trays. See Trays
LA PAZ, Bolivia
Letter from La Paz. C. Rand. il New Yorker 42:35-40+ D 31 '66
LAPHAM, Lewis
Miami Beach: swinging in the city of illusion. Sat Eve Post 239:25-33 F 26 '66
Trials of Candy and Mel. Sat Eve Post 239:28-32+ Ag 27; 32-6+ S 10 '66
LAPIDARY work
Lapidary equipment. H. D. Brown. il Hobbies 71:117 Je '66
LAPIDE, Pinchas E.
Jerusalem's biblical zoo. Christian Cent 84:17-18 Ja 4 '67

LAPIERE, Cheryl
Sonny & Chér: they're what's happening, baby. P. Bogdanovich. il pors Sat Eve Post 239:46-50+ Ap 23 '66
Sonny talks about Chér; interview. ed. by P. Bogdanovich. S. Bono. pors Vogue 148: 137-8 N 15 '66

LAPIN, Al, Jr
Fortune in flapjacks. R. Levy. il por Duns R 87:53-4 Je '66

LAPINSKI, Susan
In my opinion. por Seventeen 25:26 Mr '66

LA PIRA, Giorgio
Mystic mayor, and Fanfani outfoxed. C. Sterling. il Reporter 34:34-6 Ja 27 '66

LAPLAND
See also
Botany—Lapland

LAPP, Ralph E.
But what comes after the moon? excerpt from address, November 11, 1966. New Repub 155:10-12 N 19 '66
Where the brains are. Fortune 73:154-6+ Mr '66

LAQUER, Walter Z.
Lenin's Russia. Commentary 41:100-4 Mr '66

LARCENY. See Stealing

LARDNER, George
Campaign spending. New Repub 155:9-10 O 8 '66

LARDNER, Rex
Can basketball survive Lew Alcindor? Sat Eve Post 240:70-3 Ja 14 '67
Handbook of dishonorable tennis. N Y Times Mag p36-7+ Ap 24 '66

LARDNER, Ring
Unforgettable Ring Lardner. J. Wheeler. por Read Digest 89:113-17 O '66

LARDNER, Susan
Current cinema (cont) New Yorker 42:78+ Jl 9; 92 Jl 16; 75 Jl 23; 64+ Jl 30 '66
Older man; story. Seventeen 25:176-7 S '66

LAREDO, Tex.

Anti-poverty program
Laredo learns about the war on poverty. K. O. Gilmore. Read Digest 90:44-9 Ja '67

LARGE families. See Family, Size of

LARGE print books. See Printing—Legibility

LARGENT, Robert E.
Dry mounting with a dryer. U S Camera 29:72-3+ My '66

LARGILLIÈRE, Nicolas de
Largilliere's portrait of Elizabeth Throckmorton. B. Teyssèdre. il por Art N 64:44-7+ Ja '66

LARIMER Childrens center, Fort Collins, Colo.
See Child guidance clinics

LARK, K. G. and others
Segregation of sister chromatids in mammalian cells. bibliog il Science 154:1202-5 D 2 '66

LARKIN, Margaret
As many as God sends? family planning in Mexico. Nation 203:508-11 N 14 '66

LARMOUR, Peter J.
De Gaulle and the new France. Yale R 55:500-20 Je '66

LARNER, Jeremy
Basketball: the graceful game. Holiday 39: 30+ F '66

LA ROCHEFOUCAULD, François, duc de
Some maxims of La Rochefoucauld; excerpts from Maxims, tr. by L. W. Tancock. Horizon 8:65 Wint '66

about
Making of a cynic. M. Bishop. il por Horizon 8:56-64 Wint '66

LARRABEE, Eric
Jazz notes. See issues of Harper's magazine to July 1966
Saving the humanities. bibliog f Commentary 42:53-60 D '66
Science and the common reader. Commentary 41:43-8 Je '66
Written in cold fury. Harper 232:117-19 Ap '66

LARRICK, Nancy
Are national tests fair? Parents Mag 41:54-6+ D '66

LARROCHA, Alicia de
Mephisto's musings. por Hi Fi 16:136+ Ap '66
Musical events; performance of Albéniz' Iberia suite. W. Sargeant. New Yorker 42: 53 D 24 '66

LARSEN, Bruno M.
Don't panic, push the button! Pop Electr 24: 45-7 Ja '66

LARSEN, Emil
More about the glass of Emil Larsen. L. F. Reals. il Hobbies 71:98 S '66

LARSEN, Finn Jacob
Soviet ICBM report awesome; summary of address, June 2, 1966. Tech W 18:10 Je 6; 11 Je 13 '66

about
Soviet ICBM strength: letter. A. Sylvester. Tech W 18:8 Je 13 '66

LARSEN, Joseph R. and others
d-Tubocurarine chloride: effect on insects. bibliog Science 152:225-6 Ap 8 '66

LARSEN, Otto N.
Controversies about the mass communication of violence. bibliog f Ann Am Acad 364:37-49 Mr '66

LARSON, Carl H.
Pencil thinks big. Design 68:13-15 N '66

LARSON, Charles R.
Seal of approval. Nation 203:425-6 O 24 '66

LARSON, Geraldine B.
Whitaker's forest. Am For 72:22-5+ S '66

LARSON, Karen, and Swan, Jeanne
Spelling the words they need today. NEA J 55:51-2 F '66

LARSON, Robert
Was America the wonderful land of Fusang? Am Heritage 17:42-5+ Ap '66

LARSON, Stephen M.
Lunar photography with a 5-inch refractor. il Sky & Tel 32:164-8 S '66

LARSSON, Carl
FEAST attracts job-hungry students. NEA J 55:20-2 D '66

LARTIGUE, Jacques Henri
And what were you doing at seven? H. Keppler. il Mod Phot 30:66-9 O '66

LARVAE
Drosophila melanogaster: inheritance of a deficiency of alkaline phosphatase in larvae. F. M. Johnson. il Science 152:361-2 Ap 15 '66
Kill grubs to control moles. il Suc Farm 64:110 Ap '66

LARYNX

Surgery
Finding his voice again; Walter Lopata operation. il Newsweek 69:86 Ja 23 '67

LARYNX, Artificial
Finding his voice again; Walter Lopata operation il Newsweek 69:86 Ja 23 '67

LASAGNA, Louis
Clinical pharmacology: present status and future development. Science 152:388-91 Ap 15 '66

LA SCALA opera house. See Opera houses

LASCELLES, George Henry Hubert, 7th earl of Harewood. See Harewood. G. H. H. L.

LASCH, Christopher
Divorce and the family in America. Atlan 218:57-61 N '66
Feminist ideology. Commentary 41:100-2+ Ap '66
Profusion of information. Nation 202:397-8 Ap 4 '66
What shall a moral man do? Nation 203: 581-6 N 28 '66

LA SELVA, Vincent
Sense of theater; interview. ed. by F. Stevenson. por Opera N 30:16 Ap 16 '66

LASER communication systems. See Light communication systems

LASER gyro. See Gyroscope

LASER-holography. See Holography

LASER sensors. See Aeronautic instruments

LASER surgery. See Lasers—Medical applications

LASERS
BTL units impress signals on laser beams. il Tech W 20:40 Ja 2 '67
Chemical lasers. G. C. Pimentel. il Sci Am 214:32-9 bibliog(p 140) Ap '66
Color laser stores data. J. Eberhart. il Sci N 90:51 Jl 23 '66
Generation of light from free electrons. W. W. Salisbury. il Science 154:386-8 O 21 '66
Helium-neon laser: thermal high-resolution recording. C. O. Carlson and others. il Science 154:1550-1 D 23 '66
High-energy liquid laser. Sci Am 215:48 O '66
How to predict an earthquake; dual laser beam technique. il Sci Digest 60:26 S '66
Laser beams may predict earthquakes; geodetic laser survey system. Sci N 89:349 My 7 '66
Laser replaces TV tube. Bsns W p 123 O 8 '66
Laser watches space. il Sci N 90:349 O 29 '66
Lasers are now big business. Electr World 75:69 Je '66
Lasers break gas atoms. Sci N 90:222 S 24 '66
Laser's bright magic. T. Meloy. il Nat Geog Mag 130:858-81 D '66

LASERS—*Continued*
Lasers, fiber bundles yield rfi-immune explosive initiator; laser-energized explosive device system. R. Pay. il Tech W 19:33+ N 14 '66
Lasers move into the marketplace; revolutionize everything from surgery to military tactics. il Bsns W p90-1+ S 10 '66
Measuring length with a laser. il Electr World 75:85 Mr '66
New laser can find lost targets. il Sci N 89:510 Je 25 '66
New liquid laser works without cooling. Sci N 90:143 Ag 27 '66
Standards for laser safety advocated. C. D. LaFond. Tech W 18:46-7 Je 6 '66
Sun laser passes tests. il Sci N 90:103 Ag 13 '66
Two new laser uses. il Sci Digest 60:18-19 O '66
When the subject is lasers. T. Sturgeon. Nat R 18:681-3 Jl 12 '66
Wideband video in digital form transmitted over laser system. B. Miller. il Aviation W 85:61+ Ag 22 '66

Medical applications
Lasers kill cancers in living bodies. Sci N 89:201 Mr 26 '66
Red flag on laser use. Sci N 91:47 Ja 14 '67
Scanner to examine chromosome changes. R. D. Hibben. il Aviation W 85:95+ D 5 '66

Military applications
Army developing fog-piercing millimeter-wave imaging unit. R. Pay. il Miss & Roc 18:34+ Ap 25 '66
Laser technique may aid A-ICBM systems. R. Pay. Tech W 19:33-4 N 7 '66
Vietnam war needs spur laser research. B. Miller. il Aviation W 84:236-7+ Mr 7 '66

Photographic applications
Laser as light source for optical diffractometers: Fourier analysis of electron micrographs. J. E. Berger and others. bibliog il Science 153:168-70 Jl 8 '66
Laser TV system sees in the dark. il Pop Sci 188:119 F '66
See also
Holography
LASKER, Florence award. See Florence Lasker civil liberties award
LASKER, Mary (Woodard)
Elegant frame for masterpieces. il House & Gard 130:78-83 Jl '66
LASKER awards. See Albert Lasker awards
LASKI, Marghanita
Nature and the higher things. Sat R 49:33-4 F 26 '66
LASLETT, L. Jackson, and Sessler, A. M.
Rotation of mercury: theoretical analysis of the dynamics of a rigid ellipsoidal planet. bibliog Science 151:1384-5 Mr 18 '66
LASS, Abraham H.
Joy has gone out of learning. por Sat R 49:65 Je 18 '66
LASSEN VOLCANIC NATIONAL PARK
It's 1.3 miles to Bumpass Hell. il Sunset 137:10 O '66
Wilderness plan for Lassen Volcanic National Park and the surrounding region. A. W. Smith and W. J. Hart. il Nat Parks Mag 40:12-17 D '66
LASSITER, Luther
Wimpy was a sleeping beauty. B. Ottum. il por Sports Illus 26:18-19 Ja 9 '67
LASSON, Robert
Just for laughs. Look 30:M8 N 29 '66
LASSUDRIE-DUCHÊNE, B.
Socialist crisis of faith. America 114:319 Mr 5 '66
LASSWELL, Harold D.
Policy problems of a data-rich civilization; address, October 1965. bibliog por Wilson Lib Bul 41:58-65 S '66
LAST gentleman; novel. See Percy, W.
LAST of the suffragettes; story. See Sherris, R.
LAST stop before the carbarn; story. See Maloney, R.
LAST time home; story. See Robinson, B.
LASTRA, Luis
Old masters in Puerto Rico. Américas 18:11-16 N '66
Summer without smoke. Américas 18:40-1 O '66
LAS VEGAS, Nev.

Description
Alice in Vegas. S. Hochman. Holiday 39:30+ My '66
Family Las Vegas: vacation jackpot. F. Swartz. il Todays Health 44:44-9 O '66

Las Vegas: it wins, it worries, it weeps. F. Knebel. il Look 30:75-8+ D 27 '66

Hotels, restaurants, etc.
Notes and comment; Caesars palace. New Yorker 42:25-6 Ag 20 '66
See also
Night clubs

Theater
On the gypsy circuit. W. Como. il Dance Mag 40:24-6 Je '66
LASZLO, John, and others
Actinomycin D: inhibition of respiration and glycolysis. bibliog Science 151:1007-10 F 25 '66
LATCH, Edward Gardiner
Erastianism on the Potomac. Christian Cent 83:484 Ap 20 '66
LATEINER, Jacob
Later vintage. il por Time 88:50 Ag 19 '66
Treat worth the travail. il por Time 89:44 Ja 13 '67
LATEX paint. See Paint
LATHAM, Marte
Capturing strange creatures in Colombia. Nat Geog Mag 129:682-93 My '66
LATHES
Circular bits for your lathe. W. E. Burton. il Pop Mech 126:160-2+ Jl '66
East meets West to develop a lathe; Krupp-Hungarian machine, tape controlled lathe, called CER 200. il Bsns W p64+ Ap 30 '66
Give your lathe a brake. W. E. Burton. il Pop Mech 126:188-91 O '66
LATHROP, Peter
Criticism sans action. Nation 203:23-5 Jl 4 '66
LATHYRISM
Lathyrism; report on series of informal talks and discussions. H. B. Bensusan. Science 153:322-3 Jl 15 '66
LATICIFERS. See Plant cells and tissues
LATIMERIA. See Coelacanths
LATIN AMERICA
Bitter Latins. J. Bishop. il Commonweal 84:331-3 Je 10 '66
Latin America; the shadow of coming events. T. Aitken, jr. Harper 232:100-1 Je '66
Profile of Latin America: new optimism plus nagging doubts. il Sr Schol 89:pt2 10-11 S 23 '66
See also
Agriculture—Latin America
Anti-Communist movements—Latin America
Architecture—Latin America
Art—Latin America
Arts and crafts—Latin America
Canals—Latin America
Catholic church in Latin America
Central America
Church and state in Latin America
Colleges and universities—Latin America
Communism—Latin America
Cooperation—Latin America
Economic assistance in Latin America
Education—Latin America
Ethnology—Latin America
Food relief—Latin America
Guerrillas—Latin America
Labor and laboring classes—Latin America
Land tenure—Latin America
Library schools and education—Latin America
Natural resources—Latin America
Political parties—Latin America
Strikes—Latin America
Taxation—Latin America
Trade unions—Latin America

Armed forces
Internal security and military power; counterinsurgency and civic action in Latin America, by W. F. Barber and C. N. Ronning. Review
New Repub 155:31+ N 5 '66. J. A. Page

Bibliography
Recent books on Latin America; comp. by M. N. Gerassi. Nation 204:26 Ja 2 '67

Commerce
Europeans gain edge in South America; market for aircraft appears lost to U.S. C. Brownlow. Aviation W 85:26-7 S 19 '66

Defenses
Arms race in Latin America; what is the U.S. doing? D. D. Ranstead. Commonweal 85:313-14 D 16 '66
Great arms race. Time 88:43 N 11 '66

LATIN AMERICA—*Defenses*—*Continued*

Inter-American cooperation: the road ahead; address, December 1, 1966. L. Gordon. Dept State Bul 55:950-2 D 26 '66

Soldiers all; race for big arms. Newsweek 68:56 N 14 '66

Description and travel

Month of adventure in South America. J. Riggs. il Bet Hom & Gard 44:133-8 N '66

Discovery and exploration

Defender of the Indians; with editorial comment. R. Gallardo. il Américas 18:inside cover, 23-31 O '66

Dog and the conquistador. J. J. de Madariaga. il Américas 18:16-25 Je '66

Remarkable voyage of the Water Witch; Paraná River expedition of 1853-56. R. Wood. il Américas 18:4-9 Ap '66

Economic conditions

Hemisphere cooperation for economic and social progress; address, April 14, 1966. T. C. Mann. Dept State Bul 54:734-7 My 9 '66

New conquistadors in the Amazon jungle. E. P. Hanson; reply with rejoinder. J. H. Norton. Américas 18:48 F '66

Private enterprise, economic integration, and the Alliance for progress; address, June 1, 1966. L. Gordon. Dept State Bul 55:18-23 Jl 4 '66

U.S.-Latin American relations; address, March 24, 1966. T. G. Upton. il Vital Speeches 32:400-4 Ap 15 '66

Whose backyard? doubting a doctrine. R. Christopher. Newsweek 67:50-1 Je 20 '66
See also
Inter-American economic and social council

Economic integration

Alliance for progress essay. Américas 18:45 O '66

Inter-American cooperation: the road ahead; address, December 1, 1966. L. Gordon. Dept State Bul 55:946-52 D 26 '66

Junior summit. il Newsweek 68:36 Ag 29 '66

Latin America: economic integration for progress. F. G. Gil. Nation 203:280-3 S 26 '66

Economic policy

Close-up: interview, ed. by J. Berry. G. C. Lodge. Duns R 88:8-9+ Ag '66

Real revolution in Latin America: Chile, Peru and Venezuela. il U S News 60:90-2 Je 13 '66

What private enterprise means to Latin America. D. Rockefeller. For Affairs 44:403-16 Ap '66

Foreign relations
Israel

OAS-Israel cooperation. G. Meek. Américas 18:45 S '66

Secretary General's visit to Israel. il Américas 18:42 D '66

United States

Latin America 1966. C. A. Floria. Cath World 204:42-5 O '66

Tensions in U.S.-Latin American relations. W. J. Hinson. Christian Cent 83:1004-7 Ag 17 '66

History

Fortresses of the past. E. C. Uriburu. il Américas 18:33-6 My '66

Bibliography

Articles and other books received; comp. by D. E. Worcester. See issues of American historical review

Wars of independence, 1806-1830

Integration or disintegration: Latin American dilemma. J. Ianacio Rasco. il Américas 18:29-34 Jl '66

Sweeping the Spanish from Spanish America. il Sr Schol 88:2 F 25 '66

Maps

Map of Latin America (cont) Sr Schol 89: pt2 13 S 23 '66

Nationalism

South America's place in the sun. J. N. Goodsell. il Sat R 49:35 Jl 9 '66

Politics

Integration or disintegration: Latin American dilemma. J. Ianacio Rasco. il Américas 18:29-34 Jl '66

Latin America: a new exploration; address, April 22, 1966. A. Morales-Carrión. Vital Speeches 32:524-6 Je 15 '66

Latin America 1966. C. A. Floria. Cath World 204:42-5 O '66

Latin America: revolution without revolutionaries. N. Gall. il Nation 203:145-9 Ag 22 '66

Latin America: search for a politics. E. A. Triveri. il Nation 203:182-5 S 5 '66

Latin left; rise of the social Christians. S. Lens. Commonweal 85:52-5 O 14 '66; Reply. P. E. Sigmund. 85:182-3 N 11 '66

Rocky road for the alliance. il Bsns W p 126+ Je 11 '66

South America, 1966; symposium. bibliog f Cur Hist 51:257-307+ N '66

Whose backyard? doubting a doctrine. R. Christopher. Newsweek 67:50-1 Je 20 '66
See also
Elections—Latin America
Tricontinental conference, Havana, 1966

Religious institutions and affairs
See also
Catholic church in Latin America
Methodist church in Latin America

Social conditions

Kennedy on Latin America. J. O'Gara. Commonweal 84:304 Je 3 '66

Latin America: a new exploration; address, April 22, 1966. A. Morales-Carrión. Vital Speeches 32:524-6 Je 15 '66

Latin America: revolution without revolutionaries. N. Gall. il Nation 203:145-9 Ag 22 '66

Social policy

Real revolution in Latin America: Chile, Peru and Venezuela. il U S News 60:90-2 Je 13 '66

LATIN AMERICA and the United States

Compulsive candidate: R. Kennedy. A. J. Glass. il Sat Eve Post 239:36-8+ Ap 23 '66

End to Yankee, no! America 115:202 Ag 27 '66

Kennedy's prescription for Latin America. New Repub 154:8-10 My 28 '66

What private enterprise means to Latin America. D. Rockefeller. For Affairs 44:403-16 Ap '66

Whose backyard? doubting a doctrine. R. Christopher. Newsweek 67:50-1 Je 20 '66

Why Latin Americans say, go home, Yanqui. R. West. il N Y Times Mag p8-9+ My 29 '66
See also
Inter-American education
Inter-American relations
Pan American day and week

LATIN AMERICAN artists. See Artists, Latin American

LATIN AMERICAN book programs, incorporated

New book program. Américas 18:43 Ja '66

LATIN AMERICAN cookery. See Cookery, Latin American

LATIN AMERICAN folk art. See Folk art

LATIN AMERICAN music festival of Caracas. See Music festivals—Venezuela

LATIN AMERICAN musicians. See Musicians, Latin American

LATIN AMERICAN painting. See Painting, Latin American

LATIN AMERICAN philosophy. See Philosophy, Latin American

LATIN AMERICAN poetry

Hispanic chronicle. R. Howard. Poetry 107: 338-42 F '66

LATIN AMERICAN scientists. See Scientists, Latin American

LATIN AMERICAN studies. See Inter-American education

LATIN AMERICANS
See also
Brazilians

LATIN AMERICANS in the United States

Finders keepers; attempt by group of Spanish Americans to seize land in New Mexico. Newsweek 68:40 N 7 '66

Three cultures of New Mexico. W. T. Le Viness. il Américas 18:8-15 Je '66

U.S. Latins on the march; political activity. il Newsweek 67:32-6 My 23 '66

LATIN language

Study and teaching

Latina vivat; work of W. E. Sweet. il Newsweek 68:64 D 5 '66

What's happened to Latin? J. Parker. il Look 30:79-80+ O 18 '66

LATIN literature

Julius Caesar. K. Rexroth. Sat R 49:23 Jl 30 '66

Translations into English

Roman culture, ed. with introds. by G. Wills. Review

Nat R 18:938-9+ S 20 '66. H. Kenner

LATIN poetry

Translations into English

Four modes of translation. G. Davenport. Poetry 107:264-6 Ja '66

LATNER, A. L. and others

Pyruvate inhibition of lactate dehydrogenase activity in human tissue extracts. bibliog Science 154:527-9 O 28 '66

LATORTUE, Gerard R.

Haiti: chaotic and corrupt. Nation 203:539-41 N 21 '66

Tyranny in Haiti. bibliog f Cur Hist 51:349-53+ D '66

LATOUR, Henri Fantin-. See Fantin-Latour, H.

LATOURETTE, Kenneth Scott

Missionaries abroad. Ann Am Acad 368:21-30 N '66

LATTER-day saints. See Mormons and Mormonism

LATTERELL, R. L.

Nitrogen- and helium-induced anoxia: different lethal effects on rye seeds. bibliog Science 153:69-70 Jl 1 '66

LATTICES. See Trellises

LATTIMORE, Owen

Point beyond decency. Nation 202:212-13 F 21 '66

about

Blue chip foreign policy opinion. W. F. Buckley, jr. Nat R 18:719 Jl 26 '66

LATTIMORE, Richmond

(tr) See Aeschylus. Oresteia

LAUER, Rosemary

Naturalization process. Christian Cent 83:685-6 My 25 '66

Women clergy for Rome? Christian Cent 83:1107-10 S 14 '66

LAUNCHING pads for space vehicles. See Space vehicles—Launching pads

LAUNCHING sites for space vehicles. See Space vehicles—Launching sites

LAUNDRIES

Big little laundries. il Bet Hom & Gard 44:134 Je '66

Clothes care center in space you didn't know you had. H. A. Dawson. il Bet Hom & Gard 44:72-3 F '66

Compact but convenient. il Bet Hom & Gard 44:118 Ap '66

Drip-dries drip-dry here. il Sunset 137:152 O '66

Give your wife a break; step-saving work center. H. Clark. il Pop Mech 126:120 3 S '66

It's her sewing and laundry room. il Sunset 137:126+ S '66

Look where the laundry is now. M Davidson. il Ladies Home J 83:50+ N '66

New locales for laundry. il McCalls 94:46+ O '66

Revolutionize your laundry with this unit. D. Jordan. il Bet Hom & Gard 44:66 O '66

Successful farming designs two top efficiency laundries. J. LemMon. il Suc Farm 64:74-5 My '66

They put their laundry on the upstairs landing. il Sunset 137:76 Jl '66

Well-designed laundry can complement even the most distinguished kitchen. il Bet Hom & Gard 44:74-5 F '66

LAUNDRIES, Hospital

New concepts in hospital laundry design; excerpts from The hospital laundry. il Arch Rec 140:219-24 O '66

LAUNDRY

Laundering tips to try. Good H 162:230 Mr '66

Laundry detergents, should you launder in cold water? il Consumer Bul 49:2+ Mr '66

Men's shirts don't have to be a problem. E. Taylor. il Good H 162:167 Mr '66

Miracle fabrics and new equipment add up to easier laundering. R. Charles. il Parents Mag 41:89-92+ O '66

LAUNOIS, John

No place is not for color. il Pop Phot 58:64-7+ F '66

LAUREL International. See Horse racing

LAURENTS, Arthur

Look, girls, there's the man with our tap shoes! N Y Times Mag pt2 p42-3+ S 11 '66

LAURINCHUKAS, Albertas

Why the Statue of Liberty looks to the east, etc; excerpts from The third side of the dollar. N Y Times Mag p8-9+ D 25 '66

LAURY, Jean Ray

Be creative with appliqué. Farm J 90:88-9 My '66

LAURY, John

Step by step to a perfect mess! Bet Hom & Gard 44:92 Mr '66

LAUSCHE, Frank J.

Excerpt from debate, July 27, 1966. Cong Digest 45:211+ Ag '66

LAUTREC MONFA, Henri Marie Raymond de Toulouse-. See Toulouse-Lautrec Monfa, H. M. R. de

LAUVER, James L. and Karwaki, Thomas

Asian cultural meaning for western art. Sch Arts 65:9-11 Ja '66

LAUVRAY, Abel

Letter from Paris; discovery of his Impressionist paintings. Genêt. New Yorker 42:225-6 N 19 '66

LAUWERYNS, J. M.

Pulmonary arterial vasculature in neonatal hyaline membrane disease. bibliog Science 153:1275-7 S 9 '66

LAUX, P. J.

Fly now, pay later. America 115:340-1 S 24 '66

LAVA

Nature note; Pele's hair. il Sci N 90:486 D 10 '66

See also

Volcanoes

LAVA foam. See Rocks, Igneous

LAVALLEE, David

Coldest swim in the world. Pop Mech 126:70-4 Jl '66

LAVANOUX, Maurice

Anniversary and a wedding. C. J. McNaspy. America 115:234 S 3 '66

LAVATORIES

See also

Washbasins

Water closets

LAVENDER

Favorite subshrub: English lavender. il Sunset 137:152-3 Jl '66

LAVIN, Irving

Great discovery: Bernini's work at the age of thirteen. il por Life 62:66-72+ Ja 20 '67

Prodigy Bernini. Newsweek 69:85 Ja 23 '67

LAVINE, Harold

Dominican despot. Sat R 49:28-9 Ag 13 '66

Lethal license. Sat R 49:23-4 Ag 27 '66

Poet and patriot. Sat R 49:28 Ag 6 '66

LAVKER, Judith, and Rosett, Nancy

Teenagers provide recreation for the mentally retarded. Parks & Rec 1:487 Je '66

LAW, Warren Aubrey

How to carve your niche in the economy. il por Nations Bsns 54:96-8+ My '66

LAW

See also

Confession (law)

Copyright

Criminal law

Game laws

Inheritance

International law

Juvenile courts

Legal ethics

Libel and slander

Probate law and practice

Rule of law

Trespass

Trials

Wills

also special branches of law, e.g. Maritime law; *also* law on special subjects, e.g. Boats and boating—Laws and regulations

Curiosa and miscellany

Recent rulings; comp. by H. Helfer (cont) il N Y Times Mag p 19 Je 12 '66

When the law is a ass, a idiot. Life 60:4 Mr 4 '66

Language

Glossary of legal terms. Sr Schol 87:21 Ja 7 '66

Study and teaching

Learning by trying; trial training. il Time 87:67 Ap 8 '66

Peek at the pros; Michigan's annual advocacy institute. il Time 87:43-4 Mr 25 '66

See also

Law schools

Terminology

See Law—Language

Alabama

Crime to publish an editorial on Election day; Supreme court decision: Mills v. Alabama. Pub W 189:71 Je 27 '66

California

Capital punishment; Ronald Reagan's position. Reporter 36:14+ Ja 12 '67

Mental health trap; R. Simpson case. T. E. Schulz. Nat R 18:510-12+ My 31 '66

LAW—*Continued*

Great Britain

Sex and the lords; liberalizing the laws on homosexuality and abortion. B. Wenham. New Repub 154:9-10 F 12 '66

See also
Divorce—Great Britain

Iowa

Fathers and small sons; M. Painter custody case. S. Alexander. Life 60:20 Mr 11 '66
Iowa farm life vs. Walnut Creek; custody battle of five-year-old Mark Painter. A. B. Haines. Christian Cent 83:378-80 Mr 23 '66

Italy

Amnesty time in Italy. Time 87:114 My 20 '66

Kentucky

Controlling the strippers. Time 87:96 F 4 '66
For the long tomorrow; Kentucky's governor signs state civil rights bill. il Time 87:27 F 4 '66

Mississippi

Yankee lawyers in Mississippi courts. R. Hammer. Harper 233:79-84+ N '66

Nevada

Lawless lawmen; violations of eavesdropping prohibitions by FBI. A. Barth. New Repub 155:19-22 Jl 30 '66

North Carolina

Speaker-ban law still news in North Carolina. W. M. Wells, jr. Christian Cent 83:783 Je 15 '66

Russia

Socialist legality on trial; A. Sinyavsky-Y. Daniel trial. A. Brumberg. il Reporter 34:34-6 Mr 10 '66

Sudan

Reporter at large; MIT Fellows in Africa program. J. McPhee. New Yorker 42:101-2+ Mr 5 '66

Texas

Bolstering the barriers in Connally's corral; Texas voter registration law. J. C. Evans. Christian Cent 83:487 Ap 20 '66

United States

U.S. courts and the law explosion; symposium, ed. by D. Reische. il Sr Schol 87:6-21 Ja 7 '66
See also
Justice, Administration of—United States
Law enforcement
Legislation—United States
United States—Constitution

Virginia

See also
Justice, Administration of—Virginia

LAW, Jewish. See Jewish law

LAW and mental illness. See Mental health laws

LAW enforcement
Crime wave, what can be done about it? il U S News 61:46-51 Ag 1 '66
Former justice warns: return to law, or face anarchy; address, April 12, 1966. C. E. Whittaker. U S News 60:58-60+ Ap 25 '66
See also
Police

LAW libraries
See also
American association of law libraries

LAW makers. See Legislators
LAW making. See Legislation
LAW of relativity. See Relativity (physics)
LAW schools
Matter of degree; law school degrees. Time 88:34 D 30 '66
See also
Law—Study and teaching
Mississippi. University—School of law
Yale university—School of law

LAW students
Yales vs. the Harvards (legal division) V. S. Navasky. il N Y Times Mag p47-9+ S 11 '66

LAWFORD, Patricia (Kennedy)
Catholic church opposes divorce reform. Christian Cent 83:197 F 16 '66

LAWFORD, Valentine
America's head gardener. Henry Francis Dupont. Vogue 147:150-3 Mr 1 '66
Doris Duke's shangri-la. Vogue 148:224-9+ N 1 '66
House that Horst grew. Vogue 147:134-9+ Je '66

Queen Helen's garden. Vogue 147:154-7+ Mr 1 '66
Roman classic surprise. Vogue 148:182-7+ N 15 '66
Taylor Pryors' ocean adventure. Vogue 148:208-11+ N 1 '66
Upswing young. Vogue 148:140-7+ Ag 1 '66
Wizardry of Oise. Vogue 148:256-9+ O 1 '66

LAWICK, Jane (Goodall) van, baroness. See Van Lawick, J. G.

LAWLER, Justus George
Elbowroom for the mind. America 116:41-3 Ja 14 '67

LAWLESSNESS. See Moral attitudes

LAWLOR, John
Customizer and the car maker. Motor T 18:28-9 Ap '66
Fastback becomes a fastbagon. Motor T 18:20-1 S '66
Ghia: third in a connoisseur's series. Motor T 18:30-1 Ap '66
Poor man's classics. Motor T 18:78-80+ Je '66

LAWN fertilizers. See Fertilizers and manures
LAWN mowers
Build this creeping sulky to ease grass-cutting chores. G. W. Bahrt. il Pop Mech 126:140-4 Jl '66
Handyman how-to: tips to help make outdoor work easier. il Bet Hom & Gard 44:121 Ap '66
How safe is your power mower? il Flower Grower 53:30 Jl '66
New mower engine: cheaper than an overhaul? il Pop Sci 188:132-3 My '66
Playing safe with a rotary mower. Sunset 137:110 S '66
Power equipment is safe. il Pop Gard 17:64-7 Mr '66
Power mowers. Consumer Rep 31:176-84 D '66
Power mowers: danger in the yard. il Changing T 20:31-2 My '66
Riding rotary lawn mower. il Consumer Bul 49:13-18 Jl '66
Safe mowing. W. V. White. il Horticulture 44:32-3 Ag '66
Safe power mowing. il Todays Health 44:5 Jl '66
Self-propelled lawn mowers. il Consumer Rep 31:281-6 Je '66
Still a tiger in your toolshed. R. P. Crossley. il Pop Mech 125:100-3+ Je '66
They've thrown away the carb on new Sears mower. H. Walton. il Pop Sci 188:154-6 Je '66
Why the new power mowers are safer. J. Hand. il Pop Sci 188:158-62+ Mr '66
Why you should want a yard-care rider. J. M. Liston. il Pop Sci 188:122-7 My '66
Your new mower, safest one yet. H. Shuldiner. il Pop Sci 189:130-2 Jl '66

Care

Tips on care of a hand mower. il Flower Grower 53:45 F '66

LAWN mule. See Tractors
LAWN sprinklers. See Sprinklers
LAWN sweepers
Lawn sweepers. Consumer Rep 31:184-6 D '66

LAWN tennis. See Tennis
LAWNS
Common sense lawn care. R. W. Schery. Flower Grower 53:30-1+ Ap '66
Five basic steps in lawn maintenance. R. H. Brewster. il Pop Gard 17:76-9 Mr '66
For an instant lawn, roll your own. il Flower Grower 53:55 Je '66
Formula for lawn success. N. L. Carleton; C. J. Hudson, jr; R. D. Westcott. il Pop Gard 17:60-3+ My '66
Green elephant; grass to the homeowner. B. La Fontaine. il Sports Illus 24:68-70+ Ap 4 '66
Lawns. R. W. Schery. il Horticulture 44:34-6 S '66
Solving your summer lawn problem. R. M. Carleton. Flower Grower 53:29 Jl '66
Steps to assure a good lawn. R. W. Schery. House & Gard 130:146-7+ Ag '66
Turf maintenance costs; excerpt from report. il Parks & Rec 1:239-41+ Mr '66

LAWNS, Watering of. See Watering of gardens, lawns, etc.

LAWRENCE, Chester H.
Twenty ways to get more out of your tape recorder. Pop Mech 126:197-9+ N '66

LAWRENCE, David
Era of anarchy. U S News 61:96 Ag 29 '66; Same abr. Read Digest 89:127-8 N '66
Who is to blame? U S News 61:84 Ag 1 '66

LAWRENCE, David C.
Fugitive of Black Mountain. Outdoor Life 138:50-1+ O '66

LAWRENCE, David Herbert
Last glowing isolation: countryside that inspired. D. Pryce-Jones. Reporter 34:49-50 F 10 '66
Lawrence as playwright. D. J. Gordon. Nation 202:686 Je 6 '66
Out of the closet. Time 87:104 Ap 1 '66
Two anti-puritan Puritans; Bernard Shaw and D. H. Lawrence. D. J. Gordon. Yale R 56:76-90 O '66

LAWRENCE, David Leo
Old class. il por Time 88:28-9 D 2 '66

LAWRENCE, Ernest Orlando memorial awards. See Ernest Orlando Lawrence memorial awards

LAWRENCE, Howard C.
Tip top electronics. Motor B 117:24-7+ Mr '66

LAWRENCE, Robert
Berlioz or Crespin? Sat R 49:52+ Ja 29 '66
Child of the baroque. Sat R 49:53 Je 25 '66
Let there be light (operas) Sat R 49:55 Jl 30 '66
Majesty restored. Opera N 31:9+ N 5 '66
Ring completed Sat R 49:70-1+ O 29 '66
Sitting pretty. Opera N 30:24-5 Ap 9 '66
Unfinished symphony. Opera N 31:24-5 D 3 '66
Verrett-Fasano Orfeo. Sat R 49:69 Ap 30 '66

LAWRENSON, Helen
Caine file. Esquire 66:260-2+ D '66
Fu Manchu strikes again. Holiday 39:128+ F '66
Life and suspiciously hard times of Anthony Quinn. Esquire 66:93-5+ O '66
Thirteenth Duke of Bedford sells shoes. Esquire 66:86-8+ Ag '66

LAWSON, Ann
They couldn't have a baby, and then quintuplets! B. Day. il por McCalls 93:82-3+ Je '66

LAWSON quintuplets. See Quintuplets

LAWSUITS. See Actions and defenses

LAWTON, Edith
Should teachers see student records? NEA J 55:36-7 O '66

LAWTON, Fred E.
All-weather, long range electronic pelorus: RDF. Motor B 117:78-81+ Ja '66

LAWYERS
Boston prodigy; F. L. Bailey. il Time 88:52+ D 9 '66
Brothers in a law fraternity and how they have bloomed. il Life 60:48-48A My 20 '66
Corpus Christi's squad car lawyer. J. Biery. il Reporter 36:43-5 Ja 12 '67
Experiments on humans: where are the lawyers? A. S. Miller. Sat R 49:48-50 Jl 2 '66
How to deal with a lawyer. C. W. Gifford. il Farm J 90:B6+ Jl '66
Justice, the law and the lawyer. M. Mayer. il Sat Eve Post 239:36-9+ F 26 '66
Lawyer despite himself; T. Hallinan. il Time 89:39 Ja 13 '67
Personal business; family lawyer. Bsns W p 129-30 Ag 13 '66
They build a bridge to Washington; top lawyers of capital. il pors Bsns W p86-7+ Ap 23 '66
What can be done about pettifoggery and legal delays? G. R. Winters. bibliog f Ann Am Acad 363:52-9 Ja '66
Yankee lawyers in Mississippi courts. R. Hammer. Harper 233:79-84+ N '66
See also
American bar association
Attorney and client
District attorneys
Judges
Legal aid
Right to counsel

Salaries, fees, etc.
See Cost (law)

Training
See Law—Study and training

LAXALT, Robert
Basque sheepherders, lonely sentinels of the American West. por Nat Geog Mag 129:879-88 Je '66

LAY missionaries. See Missionaries

LAYCOCK, George
Exploring the Kuujjua. Field & S 71:45-7 My '66
He's always ready to go fishing. Pop Mech 126:102-5 S '66
How wild the Wolf? por Outdoor Life 137:48-51+ F '66
Jigging for lake trout. Field & S 70:58-60+ Ap '66
New nurseries for pike. Field & S 70:10-12+ Mr '66

Trail of the ten-pound bass. pors Outdoor Life 137:48-9+ Ap '66
Turkey are back. Field & S 71:70-1+ N '66

LAYING up of boats. See Boats—Storage

LAYMEN. See Laity

LAYMEN'S overseas service (organization)
LAOS: laymen in mission. J. C. Cosby, jr. Christian Cent 83:931-3 Jl 27 '66

LAYS, Nancy Jane
Whaleboat to pleasure boat. Motor B 117:44+ Mr '66

LAYSAN albatrosses. See Albatrosses

LAZAR, Anita
Sherry stopover. Travel 126:49 S '66

LAZAR, Irving Paul
Big sell. por Newsweek 67:99-100 Mr 7 '66

LAZARO, Hipolito
Collectors' records. A. Favia-Artsay. por Hobbies 71:36+ S '66

LAZARUS, A. L.
Some people; poem. Christian Cent 83:1028 Ag 24 '66

LAZARUS, Arnold
House named Sylvia; poem. Sat R 49:25 Ap 30 '66

LAZARUS, Emma
Americans not everybody knows. A. A. Goldstein. por PTA Mag 60:10-12 Ap '66
I lift my lamp beside the golden door. E. M. Halliday. por Am Heritage 17:97 F '66

LAZARUS, Fred R. Jr
Expanding with confidence: interview. por Nations Bsns 54:40-1+ Jl '66

LE, Nguyen-quang-. See Nguyen-quang-Le

LE Duan
Tough boss. por Newsweek 67:34 Ja 31 '66

LEACH, Charles M. See McWhorter, F. P. jt. auth.

LEACOCK, Stephen
He left us laughing. E. Logan. Sr Schol 88:sup6 Mr 18 '66

LEACOCK memorial home. See Orillia, Ontario—Historic houses, etc.

LEAD
Source of lead-210 and polonium-210 in tobacco. T. C. Tso and others. bibliog il Science 153:880-2 Ag 19 '66

Isotopes
Lead-210 and polonium-210 in biological samples from Alaska. T. M. Beasley and H. E. Palmer. bibliog il Science 152:1062-4 My 20 '66
Uranium and lead isotopic stability in a metamict zircon under experimental hydrothermal conditions. R. T. Pidgeon and others. bibliog il Science 154:1538-40 D 23 '66

LEAD poisoning
Chronic lead poisoning no threat to U.S. Sci N 90:225 S 24 '66
Lead among the Romans. il Time 88:79 S 23 '66
Moonshiners get gout from lead poisoning. Sci N 90:9 Jl 2 '66

LEADER, Robert W.
Kinship of animal and human diseases; with biographical sketch. Sci Am 216:22, 110-16 bibliog(p 148) Ja '67

LEADERSHIP
Education for the modern age; address, February 25, 1966. S. D. Cornell. Vital Speeches 32:372-6 Ap 1 '66
Leaders where the action is; youth disinterest. Life 60:4 Mr 4 '66
Leadership; address, May 20, 1966. H. C. Krannert. Vital Speeches 32:663-7 Ag 15 '66
Leadership and scholarship; concerning report of the Carnegie corporation of New York. W. W. Brickman. Sch & Soc 94:116 Mr 5 '66
Lessons of leadership; symposium (cont) il Nations Bsns 53:44-6+ D '65; 54:42-4+ Ja; 66-70+ F; 42-4+ Mr '66
Need for leaders, excerpts from Antileadership vaccine. J. W. Gardner. Science 151:283 Ja 21 '66
Responsibilities of world leadership; address, April 25, 1966. H. H. Humphrey. Dept State Bul 54:769-72 My 16 '66

LEADING men (moving pictures) See Characters in moving pictures

LEAF-cutting ants. See Ants

LEAF proteins. See Plant proteins

LEAFLETS. See Pamphlets

LEAGUE for spiritual discovery
Celebration #1. New Yorker 42:42-3 O 1 '66
Chemical salvation. America 115:403 O 8 '66
Doctor Leary and Dr Pusey. America 115:440 O 15 '66
Impresario religioso; Leary's new show. il Time 88:56 S 30 '66

LEAGUE for spiritual discovery—*Continued*
Is this trip really necessary? Dr Leary's LSD road show. R. Vaughan. Life 61:24 N 11 '66
Two for the show; T. Leary's LSDism. il Newsweek 68:68 O 3 '66
LEAGUE of federal recreation associations 120,000 strong. K. Edler. Parks & Rec 1:233-4 Mr '66
LEAGUE of women voters of the United States
League of women voters. il Ebony 21:107-8+ O '66
LEAKAGE
Repairing basement leaks. H. R. Pfister. il Pop Sci 189:121 Jl '66
LEAKE, Chauncey D.
Dimethyl sulfoxide. Science 152:1646-9 Je 17 '66
LEAKS in pipes. See Gas pipes—Leakage
LEANDER McCormick observatory, Charlottesville, Va. See Astronomical observatories
LEANING tower of Pisa. See Pisa—Campanile (leaning tower)
LEAR, John
Research in America. See issues of Saturday review
Whither personal privacy? Sat R 49:36+ Jl 23 '66
LEAR, Martha Weinman
Greenhouse for wilted women. N Y Times Mag p 16-17+ Je 19 '66
Not whodunit, but whatdidit? N Y Times Mag p48-9+ D 4 '66
LEAR Jet corporation
Customers' reaction enlarges Lear liner. E. J. Bulban. il Aviation W 84:60+ My 30 '66
Lear jet expands varied avionics effort. P. J. Klass. il Aviation W 84:57+ F 28 '66
LEAR Siegler, incorporated
Lear Siegler's fast mover. J. F. Olesky. Duns R 87:63-4 F '66
LEARNED, Edmund P.
Problems of a new executive; reprint from May 1949 issue. por Harvard Bsns R 44:20-4+ Jl '66
LEARNED journals. See Periodicals
LEARNING, Maze. See Maze tests
LEARNING, Psychology of
Anxiety slows response; learning deficit. Sci N 90:154 S 3 '66
Chimps that may learn to talk. il Sci Digest 59:9-11 My '66
Class socialization patterns and their relationship to learning. G. L. Cary. bibliog f Sch & Soc 94:349-52 O 29 '66
Common blocks of learning; with study-discussion program by E. Harris and D. Harris. R. L. Spaulding. bibliog il PTA Mag 61:28-30, 35 S '66
Discrimination learning and inhibition. H. S. Terrace. bibliog il Science 154:1677-80 D 30 '66
Education as social invention; excerpt from Toward a theory of instruction. J. S. Bruner. il Sat R 49:70-2+ F 19 '66
How young children learn. J. Holt. il Parents Mag 41:60-3+ S '66
Invertebrate learning. M. J. Wells. il Natur Hist 75:34-41 bibliog(p68) F '66
Moment of learning: Fifteenth street school, New York. G. B. Leonard. il Look 30:24-30 D 27 '66
Secrets of how we think and how we learn; reprint. Sci Digest 59:41-7 Mr '66
Special journal feature on learning; symposium. NEA J 55:10-24 Mr '66
Toward a theory of instruction, by J. S. Bruner. Review
    Sr Schol il 89:sup50 S 23 '66. D. L. Burleson
Will to learn: excerpt from Toward a theory of instruction. J. S. Bruner. bibliog f Commentary 41:41-6 F '66
    See also
Conditioned response
Maze tests
Memorizing
Memory
Problem solving
Transfer of training
LEARNING ability. See Ability
LEARNING and scholarship
    See also
College professors and instructors
Humanities

LEARNING materials. See Teaching—Aids and devices
LEARY, Daniel J.
New books. Cath World 203:373-4 S '66
Voices of convergence: Teilhard, McLuhan and Brown. por Cath World 204:206-11 Ja '67
LEARY, Howard
Finest could be finer. T. R. Brooks. il N Y Times Mag p28-9+ Ap 3 '66
Not exactly a Jimmy Cagney cop. B. Weinraub. il pors N Y Times Mag p28-9+ O 30 '66
LEARY, John P.
Bias for the new. Commonweal 83:677-9 Mr 11 '66
Wisdom of being apart. America 115:224-7 S 3 '66
LEARY, Ray D.
No storm-water bypass. Am City 81:93-5 Ag '66
LEARY, Susan
Young people and LSD: a talk with Susan Leary; ed. by M. Mannes. McCalls 93:14+ Jl '66
    about
Silver snuffbox. por Time 87:85 Mr 18 '66
LEARY, Timothy
Are the country's youth in the midst of a passing fad, satanic possession, or genuine exploration? M. Lerner. Mlle 64:52+ Ja '67
Celebration #1. New Yorker 42:42-3 O 1 '66
Chemical salvation. America 115:403 O 8 '66
Doctor Leary and Dr Pusey. America 115:440 O 15 '66
Doctor Leary's conviction. Commonweal 84:95 Ap 15 '66
Growth of a mystique; ed. by J. Mitchell. il por Newsweek 67:60-1 My 9 '66
Impresario religioso. il por Time 88:56 S 30 '66
On and off. il por Newsweek 67:21-2 My 2 '66
Psychedelic game; excerpt from Psychedelic reader. R. Hoffmann. Mlle 62:179+ Mr '66
Psychedelic sentence. Newsweek 67:35 Mr 21 '66
Raid on Castalia. M. Mannes. Reporter 34:27-8+ My 19 '66
Scientists, theologians, mystics swept up in a psychic revolution. B. Farrell. il Life 60:30D-33 Mr 25 '66
Silver snuffbox. por Time 87:85 Mr 18 '66
Time to mutate. il por Time 87:30-1 Ap 29 '66
Two for the show. il Newsweek 68:68 O 3 '66
LEASES
What to look for in an apartment lease. il Good H 162:183 Mr '66
LEASING of airplanes. See Airplanes—Leasing
LEASOR, James
Dr Love, hero, and heroin; story. Vogue 147:144 F 15 '66
LEASURE, Bob
Wilderness dog walking. il Todays Health 44:28-9 O '66
LEASURE, J. Keith. See Holmsen, T. W. jt. auth.
LEATHERBEE, Mary
One toot to stay up and three to come down. por Life 61:72+ N 18 '66
Over a drawbridge to the past. Life 61:42-42A S 2 '66
Wily old man of the sea and Othello on the rocks. Life 60:62-3 My 27 '66
LEATHERMAN, Leroy
Martha Graham: portrait of the lady as an artist; excerpt. Dance Mag 40:60-5 N '66
LEAVE of absence
Steel men thrive on sabbaticals; thirteen weeks of paid vacation every five years. il Bsns W p 166-8 N 26 '66
    See also
Teachers—Leaves of absence
LEAVENWORTH, J. Lynn
Toward seminary merger. Christian Cent 83:527-8+ Ap 27 '66
LEAVES
Gaseous-diffusion porometer for continuous measurement of diffusive resistance of leaves. R. O. Slatyer and P. G. Jarvis. bibliog il Science 151:574-6 F 4 '66
Leaves provide protein. Sci N 90:43 Jl 16 '66
Mulch or compost. P. F. Frese. il Pop Gard 17:87+ D '66
LEAVES, Fragrant. See Gardens, Fragrant
LEAVES, Pressed. See Flowers, Dried
LEAVES of absence. See Leave of absence; Teachers—Leaves of absence
LEAVITT, Jack
Ordinariness of sodomy. Nation 204:54-7 Ja 9 '67

LEAVITT, Scot
Today's subtle art of China watching. Life 61:90B+ O 7 '66
LEBANESE house decoration. See House decoration, Lebanese
LEBANON
See also
Airlines—Lebanon
Architecture—Lebanon
Baalbek
Banks and banking—Lebanon
Music festivals—Lebanon
Antiquities
See also
Baalbek
Description and travel
Travel notes. R. Joseph. Esquire 65:34+ Mr '66
Economic conditions
Beirut is where the action is. il Bsns W p68-71 Ap 30 '66
Politics and government
Tiger at the helm. Time 87:30 F 11 '66
LEBEUF, LeRoy L.
Those critical five days. Suc Farm 64:54-5 O '66
LEBLANC, Richard
Thief-proofing our art museums. Am Artist 30:16-17+ F '66
Unesco and education. NEA J 55:42-3 Ap '66
LEBOURDAIS, Isabel
Canadian justice: ordeal of Steven Truscott. E. Stafford. il Nation 202:614-17 My 23 '66
LEBOWITZ, Martin
Making the violent scene. Nation 204:57-9 Ja 9 '67
LECANUET, Jean
Two faces of JFK. il por Newsweek 68:63-4 N 21 '66
LE CARRÉ, John, pseud. See Cornwell, D. J. M.
LECHNER, Harry
Custom channelization tames an intersection. Am City 81:120+ F '66
LECHNER, R. J. See Weertman, W. L. jt. auth.
LE CLEDE town, St Louis. See Housing projects
LECLER, René
Born to be king. Seventeen 25:156-7+ N '66
England's teen-age princess. Seventeen 25:154-5+ S '66
Queen Elizabeth turns forty. McCalls 93:76-9+ My '66
LE CORBUSIER
Books. P. Goodman. il Arch Forum 124:78-9 My '66
Farewell to Corbu. G. Barford. il por Sch Arts 65:25-9 Ap '66
Last works of Le Corbusier. J. Barnett. il Arch Rec 139:187-94 Ap '66
LECTURE; story. See Mountzoures, H. L.
LECTURE method in teaching
Do lectures teach? Sci Digest 60:26 O '66
LEDBETTER, Alvin L.
Advantages of the Anco plan of inventory control. Pub W 190:56-7 D 5 '66
LEDDIHN, Erik Maria, ritter von Kuehnelt-. See Kuehnelt-Leddihn, E. M. von
LEDDY, John Marshall
Department presents views on Senate resolutions on closer relations among Atlantic nations; statement, March 24, 1966. Dept State Bul 54:672-4 Ap 25 '66
LEDEBUHR, Albert F.
Military chaplaincy: an apologia. Christian Cent 83:1332-5 N 2 '66
LEDERBERG, Joshua
Experimental genetics and human evolution. Bul Atomic Sci 22:4-11 O '66
New proposal for European security. Bul Atomic Sci 22:28-9 D '66
LEDERER, Esther Pauline (Friedman) See Landers, A. pseud.
LEDERER, Muriel
Let's teach our teens to drive at night. Todays Health 44:68-71 S '66
LEDERER, William J.
Story of pink jade; story; excerpt. McCalls 94:100-1 D '66
LEDLEY, Robert S. and Ruddle, F. H.
Chromosome analysis by computer; with biographical sketches. Sci Am 214:20, 40-6 Ap '66
LEDLIE, Mary Elizabeth. See Bergmann, W. L. jt. auth.
LEDOGAR, Robert J.
Poverty or pretense. C. J. McNaspy. America 114:632-3 Ap 30 '66
LEDUC, Violette
Steal-scening with Hepburn & O'Toole. Vogue 147:172-3+ Ap 1 '66

LEE, Brenda
Secretary on the edge of war. il pors Ebony 21:27-30+ Je '66
LEE, Charlotte Ann
International vacation study course in Scandinavia; report. Negro Hist Bul 29:108 F '66
LEE, Clyde
That Vandy dandy. H. L. Masin. por Sr Schol 87:22 Ja 21 '66
LEE, David B.
Dave Lee takes a poke at pollution. pors Am City 81:101-4 S '66
LEE, Gypsy Rose
Gypsy Rose Lee: dowager stripper. J. Hamilton. il pors Look 30:58-9+ F 22 '66
LEE, James A.
Cultural analysis in overseas operations. Harvard Bsns R 44:106-14 Mr '66
LEE, Kuan-yew
Resort to candor; summary of address. il por Newsweek 68:30+ Jl 4 '66
about
Letter from Singapore. R. Shaplen. il New Yorker 42:57-8+ Ja 14 '67
Rupture in Malaysia. C. P. Bradley. bibliog f Cur Hist 50:98-105 F '66
LEE, Laurie
What love must be. Read Digest 88:124-6 Mr '66
LEE, Marjorie
Alone at last; story. Redbook 127:62-3 Jl '66
Just among friends; story. Redbook 127:82-3 Je '66
LEE, Maryat
Tightrope walker. Criticism
Nation 203:718 D 26 '66
LEE, Rex
Coming of the jet age in Samoa. H. Sutton. Sat R 49:56+ F 5 '66
LEE, Richard Charles
New Haven and its mayor. G. Nelson. Holiday 39:62-3+ My '66
LEE, Robert C.
Dick Gregory goes fishing. Nation 202:487-9 Ap 25 '66
LEE, Robert Edward
Lee raised his hat. J. Ritter. Negro Hist Bul 29:59-60 D '65
Son's tribute; with paintings. D. G. Lowe. Am Heritage 17:18-19+ F '66
LEE, Sherman Emery
Aristocrat. il por Time 88:88 S 16 '66
LEE, Vin-Jang
Heterogeneous catalysis: effect of an alternating electric field. Science 152:514 Ap 22 '66
LEE, Vivian
Babies spend half their time REM-ing. Life 60:116 My 20 '66
LEE Higginson corporation
Good night, Lee Hig. Time 88:68+ Ag 26 '66
LEECH, Michael T.
Punch and Judy; drama. Plays 26:91-8 N '66
LEED, Jacob
Two poems: This morning; Often I've thought. Poetry 108:309-10 Ag '66
LEEK, Sybil
Horoscope. Ladies Home J 84:16+ Ja '67
Horoscope for gift-giving. Ladies Home J 83:61-2 D '66
Weight-watchers' horoscope. Ladies Home J 83:78+ N '66
LEEN, Nina
From fighting turtles to flying kittens. G. P. Hunt. por Life 61:3 Jl 29 '66
LEENHARDT, Olivier. See Edgerton, H. E. jt. auth.
LEER, Oscar van
Three lives of Oscar van Leer. il por Fortune 73:76 F '66
LEES, Gene
Pot luck. Holiday 40:129-30 O '66
LEES, Hannah
Negro response to birth control. Reporter 34:46-8 My 19 '66
LEESON, Jim
Desegregation in the South. Sat R 49:74+ D 17 '66
LEEWARD ISLANDS
Fresh breeze stirs the Leewards. C. Mitchell. il Nat Geog Mag 130:488-537 O '66
LEFAIVRE, Wesley
Ivy; Progress; poems. Am For 72:46 Jl '66
Poems: A solitary lily; To a dead sparrow. Am For 72:46 Je '66
LEFF, Mike, and others
Partnerships in purchasing. Am City 81:145-6 Je '66
LEFFERTS, Barney
They don't yell yoicks! in New Jersey. N Y Times Mag p52-3+ D 4 '66

LEFKOWITZ, Louis J.
First steps in legislation for the arts. Art N 65:29 S '66
LEFRAK City. See Queens, N.Y.—Housing
LEFT and right (political science) See Right and left (political science)
LEFT wing (politics) See Right and left (political science)
LEFTOVERS. See Cookery—Leftovers
LEFTWICH, E. H.
Technician band antenna coupler. Pop Electr 25:87-8 Ag '66
LEG
Have you read any good legs lately? R. Warfield. Vogue 148:98+ Jl '66
Lovely leggy look. il Seventeen 25:168-9 S '66
See also
Femur
LEG braces. See Orthopedic apparatus
LEG exercisers. See Exercising equipment
LEG exercises. See Exercise
LEG grafting. See Transplantation of organs, tissues, etc.
LEG make-up. See Cosmetics; Make-up
LEGACIES
See also
Wills
LEGACIES, Unclaimed
Mallet's millions. Time 87:33-4 Ja 28 '66
LEGACY; story. See Gordon, E. E.
LEGAL aid
And now, judicare. Time 87:24 My 6 '66
For the poor; independent appraisal from a dispassionate Philadelphia judge. il Time 88:41-2 Ag 5 '66
Poor find a friend in court: ABA pushing program to supply legal aid with federal anti-poverty funds. il Bsns W p92-4+ D 10 '66
Storefront law: anatomy of a grant; Ford backed legal aid project in New Haven, Conn. il Newsweek 67:90-1 Mr 14 '66
LEGAL confession. See Confession (law)
LEGAL education. See Law schools
LEGAL ethics
Lies & lawyers; critic M. Freedman. Time 87:81 My 13 '66
What can be done about pettifoggery and legal delays? G. R. Winters. bibliog f Ann Am Acad 363:52-9 Ja '66
See also
Attorney and client
LEGAL fees. See Cost (law)
LEGAL insanity. See Insanity
LEGAL language. See Law—Language
LEGAL medicine. See Medical jurisprudence
LEGAL procedure. See Procedure (law)
LEGAL profession. See Lawyers
LE GALLIENNE, Eva
(tr) See Ibsen, H. Wild duck
LEGENDS
See also
Christmas legends
Grail
Saints
LEGENDS, American
Hush-a-bye, Indiana; changing of historical facts by local pride and press agentry. W. E. Wilson. il Am Heritage 18:68-71 D '66
LEGENDS, Chinese
Chinese legend & lore. G. Kaler. il Hobbies 71:50 S; 50-1 O '66
Story of pink jade; excerpt. W. J. Lederer. il McCalls 94:100-1 D '66
LEGENDS, Indian (East Indian)
Nagas, their lore and legend. G. Kaler. il Hobbies 71:50 D '66
LEGENDS, Japanese
Chronicle of Yoshitsune; tr. by H. Craig. Review
Sat R 49:58 Je 11 '66. E. Miner
LEGER, Paul Emile, cardinal
Ecumenism is no trivial thing. America 115:55 Jl 16 '66
LEGG, Ken
Look under the bark. Audubon Mag 68:193-4 My '66
LEGGE, Walter
At La Scala: new Faust, revived Bohème. Hi Fi 16:158-9 My '66
Mines of sulphur: recital in Geneva. Hi Fi 16:128-9 Je '66
Opera on three fronts. Hi Fi 16:136-9 Mr '66
LEGGETT, Jim
How you can survive a high-speed blowout! J. Joseph. il Motor T 18:46-8+ D '66
LEGGETT, John
You take the easy road to success in writing; story. Harper 232:49-52 F '66

LEGGETT, Robert Louis
Excerpt from debate, July 28, 1966. Cong Digest 45:284+ N '66
LEGGETT, William
Baseball. Sports Illus 25:53-5 Jl 4; 50-1 Ag 15; 60-1 Ag 29 '66
LEGIBILITY of printing. See Printing—Legibility
LEGIONS, Roman. See Rome—Army
LEGISLATION
Terminology
See Law—Language
United States
As Congress heads home: decisions that affect everybody. il U S News 61:47-8 O 24 '66
B+ Congress: key votes in the 89th. il New Repub 155:15-22 O 22 '66
Congressional box score. Newsweek 68:36 O 31 '66
Lady blocks the pork barrel; exemptions dropped from Housing and urban development bill. Life 61:6 S 23 '66
Low-gear year. Newsweek 67:38+ Je 13 '66
LBJ's domestic plans face a cool Congress. il Bsns W p28-30 Ja 22 '66
There ought to be a law. il Changing T 20:39-41 Ag '66
See also
Labor laws and legislation—United States
Library laws and legislation
Social legislation—United States
United States—Congress
United States—Supreme court
LEGISLATIVE bodies
United States
See also
State legislatures
United States—Congress
LEGISLATIVE reference service, Library of Congress. See United States—Library of Congress—Legislative reference service
LEGISLATORS
Octopus in the state house; report. T. Armbrister. il Sat Eve Post 239:25-9+ F 12 '66
See also
Negro legislators
LEGISLATURES, State. See State legislatures
LEGLER, Philip
Hunter; poem. Commonweal 84:153 Ap 22 '66
Seasonal; poem. Commonweal 85:344 D 23 '66
LEGS. See Leg
LEGS, Artificial. See Artificial limbs
LEGUMES
See also
Harvesting
Lentils
LEHMAN, Eileen F. and Hall, R. E.
Who is this child? pors Am Ed 2:10-12 Ap '66
LEHMAN, Orin
Campaign by consensus. il por Time 87:28-9 F 4 '66
LEHMAN, Robert
Department store of investment. il por Time 87:96 F 25 '66
LEHMAN brothers (brokers)
Department store of investment. il Time 87:96 F 25 '66
LEHMANN, Gerhard, and Moore, W. J.
Color center in amethyst quartz. bibliog Science 152:1061-2 My 20 '66
LEHMANN, Otto
New richness. Opera N 30:24-5 F 26 '66
LEHMANN-Peterson, Incorporated
Str-r-r-etch to a luxury limousine. A. Whitman. il Pop Mech 125:116-19+ Je '66
LEHN and Fink products corporation
Sales & marketing; familiar face gets lifted. J. F. Olesky. Duns R 87:55-7 Ja '66
LEHRMAN, Hal
Underground to independence. Sat R 40:32-3 Mr 26 '66
LEIBER, Fritz
Books must balance. Nat R 18:1003-5 O 4 '66
LEIBER, Robert
(ed) See Friedländer, S. Pius XII and the Third Reich
LEIBNIZ, Gottfried Wilhelm, freiherr von
Leibniz commemoration; report on symposium to commemorate the 250th anniversary of death. F. Kreiling. Science 152:1411-12 Je 3 '66
LEIBOWITZ, Sarah Fryer. See Deutsch, J. A. jt. auth.
LEIDER, Frida
Collectors' records. A. Favia-Artsay. Hobbies 71:36 S '66

LEIFER, Neil
They are not just along for the ride; photographs. Sports Illus 24:40-4 Ap 11 '66
LEIGH, Gertrude
Expectant mother; or, Cleaner demeanor; poem. McCalls 94:169 O '66
LEIGH, Mitchell
Gold pan alley. por Newsweek 68:64 Ag 15 '66
LEIGHTON, Ann
Look down at the plants. Antiques 90:200-3 Ag '66
Take a handful of bugloffe; excerpt from For meate and medicine. Am Heritage 17: 66-71 O '66
LEIGHTON, Claire
Ideal mate; poem. McCalls 93:136 Jl '66
In defense of forty; poem. McCalls 94:110 Ja '67
LEIGHTON, Robert B.
Photographs from Mariner IV; with biographphical sketch. Sci Am 214:20, 54-68 bibliog(p 140) Ap '66
—and Murray, B. C.
Behavior of carbon dioxide and other volatiles on Mars. bibliog Science 153:136-44 Jl 8 '66
LEIMBACH, Patricia P.
Harvest reflections. por Farm J 90:67 S '66
LEININGER, R. I. and others
Nonthrombogenic plastic surfaces. bibliog Science 152:1625-6 Je 17 '66
LEINSDORF, Erich
Sound versus fury. Atlan 217:82-4+ Ap '66
What makes opera run. Atlan 217:53-8 Mr '66
LEIPZIG, Arthur
Almost calculated disorder. J. Deschin. il Pop Phot 60:120-1 Ja '67
LEIS
Flowers that say aloha. D. Clark. il Nat Geog Mag 131:120-31 Ja '67
LEISTER, Mary McFarland
Epimediums, plants that dance with the wind. Flower Grower 53:24+ Ap '66
Gardens & vacations. Flower Grower 53:37-8 Jl '66
LEISURE, George S.
Landmark in conservation writing: a Wilderness bill of rights. por Nat Parks Mag 40: 18-19 Mr '66
LEISURE
How do you spend your time? findings of poll by Opinion research corporation of Princeton, N.J. Sr Schol 88:32 Ap 15 '66
Leisure and the split man. H. Rosenberg. Vogue 147:142-3+ F 1 '66
Looms weave by themselves; challenge of leisure time; excerpts from address. G. B. Hartzog, jr. il Parks & Rec 1:20-2 Ja '66
Voice of the recreator. S. Lutzin. Parks & Rec 1:895 N '66
You only go around once. M. A. Guitar. Mlle 63:132+ Je '66
LEISURE World, Walnut Creek, Calif. See Aged—Housing
LEJEUNE, Anthony
Bending to the wind. Nat R 18:1231-2 N 29 '66
Indonesian backdrop. Nat R 18:375-7 Ap 19 '66
Legacy of Richard Weaver. Nat R 18:473-4 My 17 '66
Letter from London (cont) Nat R 18:354-5, 879+ Ap 19, S 6 '66
Letters on Rhodesia. Nat R 18:1309-10 D 27 '66
Man behind the golden myth. Nat R 19:41+ Ja 10 '67
More triumph than tragedy. Nat R 18:581-2 Je 14 '66
LEKACHMAN, Robert
Automation report. Commentary 41:65-71 My '66
What's up with taxes. Atlan 218:65-6+ Ag '66
LEKSELL, Lars
Brain surgery by computer. S. Hopkins. il por Pop Mech 126:94-7 D '66
LELAND, Dorothy E.
Books for boys & girls. See issues of Parents' magazine and better homemaking
LELLO, Elizabeth
Mystery at Tumble inn; drama. Plays 25:15-25 My '66
LELYVELD, Joseph
Afrikaner feels lonely in the world. N Y Times Mag p9+ F 6 '66
Dadaists in politics. N Y Times Mag p32-5+ O 2 '66
Minority of one in South Africa's Parliament. N Y Times Mag p34-5+ Mr 20 '66
When God threw the dice they fell wrong for us. N Y Times Mag p24-5+ My 15 '66
Where 78 per cent of the people are the others. N Y Times Mag p 10-11+ Je 19 '66

LEMA, Tony
Obituary
Sports Illus 25:10 Ag 1 '66
Pro with laughing eyes and bitter moods. J. R. McDermott. il pors Life 61:56-8 Ag 5 '66
LEMAN, Eugene
Video tape recorder for home use. Electr World 75:49-52+ F '66
LE MANS Grand prix. See Automobile racing
LEMASS, Seán Francis
New taoiseach. Time 88:47 N 18 '66
LEMAY, Curtis E.
General LeMay tells how to win the war in Vietnam. por U S News 61:36-8+ O 10 '66
about
Brutal logic of power. W. Millis. Sat R 49:36 Ja 29 '66
LEMERCIER, Grégoire
Monks in psychoanalysis. por Time 88:80 D 2 '66
LEMIRE, Clement
Debut of a children's theater. por Parks & Rec 1:142-4 F '66
LEMOINE, George
Pleasure, pain, & the performers. il Pop Phot 59:86-9+ S '66
LEMON, Richard
Daddy is a hippy. Sat Eve Post 239:22 Jl 2 '66
Message in Billy Wilder's Fortune cookie: well, nobody's perfect. Sat Eve Post 239:30-4+ D 17 '66
Ollie who? Sat Eve Post 239:26 Ap 23 '66
LEMON Hill mansion. See Philadelphia—Historic houses, etc.
LEMONE, Evelyn
Records for teachers. See issues of Dance magazine
LEMONS
See also
Cookery—Fruit
LEMURS
Lemur social behavior and primate intelligence. A. Jolly. bibliog il Science 153: 501-6 Jl 29 '66
LENARD, John F. See McPhee, W. T. jt. auth.
LENDING of prints. See Prints—Circulation, loans, etc.
LENG, Russell J.
Vietnam: what role for the UN? Nation 202: 227-9 F 28 '66
L'ENGLE, Madeleine
Before Babel. Horn Bk 42:661-70 D '66
LENGTH measurement
Measuring length with a laser. il Electr World 75:85 Mr '66
LENGTH of service. See Seniority, Employee
LENGYEL, Peter. See Eisenstadt, J. jt. auth.
LENHOFF, Howard M. See Blanquet, R. jt. auth.
LENIN, Vladimir Il'ich
Lenin's Russia. W. Laqueur. Commentary 41: 100-4 Mr '66
LENINGRAD
Description
Notes on Leningrad. P. de Rothschild. Vogue 148:142-3+ O 15 '66
Music
Listening in Leningrad. A. Darack. Sat R 49:90-1 N 26 '66
LENK, John D.
Small boat electronics: what should you install yourself? Motor B 118:33-5 N '66
Time domain reflectometry. Electr World 76: 48-50+ S '66
What the surveyor looks for. Motor B 118: 52+ S '66
LENNON, John
According to John. il Time 88:38 Ag 12 '66
Bards of pop. il Newsweek 67:102 Mr 21 '66
Blues for the Beatles. il por Newsweek 68: 94 Ag 22 '66
John Lennon: Beatle on his own. L. Gross. il pors Look 30:58-60+ D 13 '66
Of many things; Beatle John Lennon's statement. T. N. Davis. America 115:164 Ag 20 '66
Old Beatles, a study in paradox. M. Cleave. il pors N Y Times Mag p 10-11+ Jl 3 '66
LE NÔTRE, André
Gardener and the king. J. Barry. il Read Digest 89:158-63 O '66
LENS, Sidney
Labor and politics. Commonweal 84:278-80 My 27 '66
Latin America: labor between bread and revolution. Nation 203:248-51 S 19 '66
Latin left; rise of the social Christians. Commonweal 85:52-5 O 14 '66

LENS, Sidney—*Continued*
Santo Domingo: unfinished revolution. Nation 202:520-3 My 2 '66
Shriver's limited war. Commonweal 84:412-14 Jl 1 '66
What Bundy demanded. Nation 203:658 D 19 '66
LENS extenders. See Photography—Apparatus and supplies
LENSE adapters. See Photography—Apparatus and supplies
LENSES
Nature's amazing lenses. il Life 61:22-9 D 23 '66
LENSES, Photographic
Auxiliary lenses. Pop Phot 59:185-6 N '66
Broad range of Macro lenses. il U S Camera 29:52-3+ Ap '66
Can lens X fit camera Y? sometimes yes, sometimes no! D. L. Miller. il Mod Phot 30:80-1+ O '66
Can you control a lens's definition? reprint from Here's how. J. W. McFarlane. il Mod Phot 30:74-7+ Je '66
Everyman's fish-eye. H. Keppler. il Mod Phot 30:72-3+ N '66
Great through-the-lens meter explosion; with foreword by H. Keppler. il Mod Phot 30:52-73 S '66
Handhold a 300mm lens. il U S Camera 29:60-1 Je '66
How to get the most out of lens extenders. C. W. Kennedy. il Pop Phot 58:68-9+ Ap '66
It's long but is it good? E. Meyers. il Mod Phot 30:54-5 My '66
Keppler on the SLR; tele lenses. H. Keppler. il Mod Phot 30:34+ Ag '66
Keppler on the SLR; wide-angle dilemma. H. Keppler. il Mod Phot 30:32+ S '66
Lens explosion; Photokina. P. Leonian. il U S Camera 30:58-9+ Ja '67
Lens guide. Pop Phot 59:171-84 N '66
Lenses for 35mm and other jollies. Mod Phot 30:69+ Je '66
Long lenses on short budgets. M. Morrison. il U S Camera 29:48-9+ Ap '66
Love for lenses. il U S Camera 29:48-9 Jl '66
Make the most of your slow lens. M. Edelson. il U S Camera 29:58-9+ F '66
Matzkin on movies; difficulties with super 8 M. A. Matzkin. Mod Phot 30:32+ Ap '66
Matzkin on movies; twin-lens reflex. M. A. Matzkin. Mod Phot 30:28 Mr '66
Meyers on technique; secrets of a careful camera and lens buyer. E. Meyers. Mod Phot 30:18+ D '66
New Fisheye lens. I. Shirley and P. Schleifer. il U S Camera 29:16+ D '66
New front lenses: two easy ways to close-ups. N. Rothschild. il Pop Phot 59:78-9+ Ag '66
New two-stage Macro lenses. N. Rothschild. il Pop Phot 59:112-13+ N '66
1966/67 interchangeable lens list; comp. by D. L. Miller. Mod Phot 30:70-9 O '66
Not so close close-ups. il Mod Phot 30:55+ F '66
Ruddy satellite: cavernous vessel. il Life 61:114 D 23 '66
Simon says; camera features fifty-seven lenses. N. Simon. Mod Phot 31:110+ Ja '67
Swinging lens gives 35mm SLR the right view. D. L. Miller. il Mod Phot 30:26+ S '66
Techniques tomorrow. B. Sherman. Mod Phot 30:26+ Je; 42+ S '66
Techniques tomorrow; optical tolerances in lens making. B. Sherman. Mod Phot 30:34+ My '66
Techniques tomorrow; tele lens assist from electronics. B. Sherman. Mod Phot 30:96+ Ag '66
To hell with instructions. H. Keppler. il Mod Phot 30:64+ D '66
Try these vision-stretchers. M. D. Grennan. il Pop Phot 59:98-101+ S '66
Vagabond camera; wide-angle lenses. W. Lane. il Travel 126:68 Ag '66
What's new in tele lenses. B. Sherman. il Mod Phot 30:68-9 Ag '66
What's new that's good? C. W. Kennedy. il Pop Phot 58:108-10 Je '66
Wide-angle. C. Reynolds. il Pop Phot 59:82-9+ O '66
Wide: from not so to very. H. Keppler. il Mod Phot 30:50-9 Ap '66
Wide lenses: how they grew, where they're going. B. Sherman. il Mod Phot 30:60-1+ Ap '66
See also
Zoom lenses
Testing
How to test your lenses. il Mod Phot 30:127-8 D '66
How wide's wide? H. Keppler. il Mod Phot 30:66-7 Ap '66

Is it true? H. N. Todd and R. D. Zakia. Pop Phot 58:62 My '66
Keppler on the SLR. H. Keppler. il Mod Phot 30:16+ Ap '66
Why you should forget lens testing! W. Hanson. il Pop Phot 58:72-3+ Mr '66
LENSKE, Reuben G.
Revenuer and the red in the red. New Repub 155:9 N 19 '66
LENSLESS photography. See Holography
LENT
Breaking the fast; limited Lenten regulations on fasting and abstinence. Newsweek 67:61 F 28 '66
Easier law: more commitment. America 114:372 Mr 19 '66
Lenten fast. Commonweal 83:628 Mr 4 '66
LENTE, Elinor
Vietnam hero salutes his teacher. D. Chapman. il pors Look 30:68+ F 22 '66
LENTEN menus
Fine fish dishes. B. M. Stover. il Parents Mag 41:71-4+ Mr '66
Milk, eggs, and cheese, your big Lenten helpers. G. Maddox. il Todays Health 44:70-5 Mr '66
World's best dishes made easy for Lent; with recipes. il Ladies Home J 83:121-40 Mr '66
LENTILS
Grow lentils on your windowsill. G. Taloumis. il Flower Grower 53:47 D '66
LENTRICCHIA, Frank, Jr
Some coordinates of modern literature. Poetry 108:65-7 Ap '66
Wallace Stevens: emergence of the poet. Poetry 109:201-3 D '66
LENTZ, John J.
Malady of Mary Mallon. Todays Health 44:34-6 Ap '66
LENYA, Lotte
Lady known as Lenya. R. Reed. il pors N Y Times Mag p 128+ N 20 '66
LEO XIII, pope
Rerum novarum. Commonweal 84:326 Je 10 '66
LEO, John
Cody in Chicago. Commonweal 84:334-6 Je 10 '66
Consensus on birth control. New Repub 155:10 N 12 '66
Outside Catholicism. Reporter 35:48-50 D 1 '66
LEO, Richard F. and Parker, P. L.
Branched-chain fatty acids in sediments. bibliog Science 152:649-50 Ap 29 '66
LEON, Dennis
Art galleries; exhibition at the Kraushaar. R. M. Coates. New Yorker 41:142 F 19 '66
LEONARD, C. Gomez, and others
Transformation of auxotrophic mutants of group H. streptococci. bibliog Science 152:1255-6 My 27 '66
LEONARD, Justin W. See Leopold, A. S. jt. auth.
LEONARD, Virginia
Book selection in Grosse Pointe: where school librarians advise the public library. ALA Bul 60:627-9 Je '66
LEONARD; story. See O'Hara, J.
LEONARDO da Vinci
Last supper; Milan's deathless treasure. E. O. Hauser. il Read Digest 88:166-8+ Ap '66
LEONCAVALLO, Ruggiero
Cav 'n' Pag from La Scala; with editorial comment. P. L. Miller. Am Rec G 33:336-7 D '66
Records:
Pagliacci. Opera N 31:34 D 17 '66
LEONHARD, Wolfgang
Moscow, the new party line. New Repub 154:12-14 Ap 30 '66
LEONI, Raúl
U.S. and Venezuela inaugurate undersea telephone cable; remarks, August 3, 1966. Dept State Bul 55:274-5 Ag 22 '66
about
Castro terrorists on the move again. il por U S News 61:8 D 26 '66
Rooting out the rebels. il Newsweek 68:36 D 26 '66
War on subversion. il por Time 88:29 D 23 '66
LEONIA, N.J.
Night-time basketball fights juvenile delinquency. il Am City 81:124 Ag '66
LEONIAN, Philip
Lens explosion. U S Camera 30:58-9+ Ja '67
LEONIDS. See Meteors
LEOPARDI, Giacomo, conte
Great poet, a continuing task. N. J. Perella. Poetry 107:333-7 F '66

LEOPARDS
Forsaken pair of rare specimens; zooborn snow leopards; foster-mothered by curator. il Life 61:121+ O 7 '66
Great cats of Africa. J. Dominis. il Life 62:36-52 Ja 6 '67

Photographs
See Animals—Photographs
LEOPOLD, A. Starker, and Leonard, J. W.
Alaska Dam would be resources disaster. Audubon Mag 68:176-8 My '66
LEOPOLD, Luna B. and Langbein, W. B.
River meanders; with biographical sketches. Sci Am 214:16, 60-70 Je '66
LEOS, Ed
Reporting an intense awareness of things as they are. Sch Arts 66:14-18 S '66
LEOVY, C.
Mars ice caps. bibliog Science 154:1178-9 D 2 '66
LE PARC, Julio
Argentine in Venice. O. Masotta. il Américas 18:19-22 Ag '66
LEPERS. See Leprosy and lepers
LEPP, Ignace
Second thoughts on second marriages. Time 88:65 Jl 22 '66
LEPRECHAUN shoemakers; drama. See Watts, F. B.
LEPROSY and lepers
All we had to give was ourselves; two Peace corps volunteers in leper colony; Bolivia. L. Elliott. il Redbook 127:58-9+ My '66
Coming, leprosy's end; reprint. E. Ubell. il Sci Digest 59:87-9 F '66
Shun them no more! Christian Cent 83:1295-6 O 26 '66; Reply. M. L. Brubaker. 84:55 Ja 11 '67
Two-drug cure for leprosy. Sci N 90:78 Jl 30 '66
LEPROSY research
Coming, leprosy's end; reprint. E. Ubell. il Sci Digest 59:87-9 F '66
Sahib doctor: the healing surgeon of Vellore; condensation of Ten fingers for God. D. C. Wilson. il Read Digest 88:207-10+ Je '66
LEPTOSPIRA
Danger in swimming hole. Sci N 89:362 My 14 '66
LERCHE, Charles Olsen, 1918-
After the cold war. Nation 202:673-6 Je 6 '66
LERMAN, Leo
Catch up with. See issues of Mademoiselle
Expo 67: man and his world. Mlle 64:116-19 Ja '67
Imports. Mlle 62:156-9 F '66
Something to talk about. Mlle 63:134-5 O '66
Third stream: off Broadway. Mlle 62:146-7 Mr '66
Will the real work of art please stand up? Mlle 62:114-16 Ja '66
LERNER, Alan Jay
Interview; ed. by R. Heffner. por McCalls 94:104-5+ N '66
LERNER, Max
Are the country's youth in the midst of a passing fad, satanic possession, or genuine exploration? Mlle 64:52+ Ja '67
Talks to teens. por Seventeen 25:162+ Mr '66
What sex means to college girls today. Redbook 127:51+ Je '66
LESAGE, Jean
Quebec changes governments. C. Ryan. For Affairs 45:148-61 O '66
LESAGE, Laurent
Rose petals among the postscripts. Sat R 49:34-5 Ap 2 '66
LESHAN, Eda J.
Answer to young mothers who feel lost. Redbook 127:43+ Ag '66
Anxious child can learn, but what? PTA Mag 61:8-10 bibliog(p35) Ap '66
Parent and child (cont) N Y Times Mag p83-4 Ap 3; 112+ My 15; 76+ Ag 28 '66
Parents with too much knowledge. Redbook 126:49+ F '66
Teen-ager and the telephone. McCalls 93:84+ Mr '66
LESLIE, Sir Shane
His own biographer. Nat R 18:1114-15 N 1 '66
Holy-Fox. Nat R 18:844+ Ag 23 '66
Long shots and the long run. Nat R 18:537-8 My 31 '66
LESLIE; drama. See Phelps, H.
LES MARECOTTES, Switzerland
Traveler's choice. E. D. Clason. Travel 125:11 Je '66
LESNEY products and company. See Great Britain—Industries
LESOTHO
Decline of kings. il Time 89:31 Ja 6 '67
Drama in two acts. il Newsweek 68:54+ O 17 '66

Two new nations. il Sr Schol 89:18-19 O 7 '66
Two new nations. il Time 88:46 O 7 '66
See also
United Nations—Lesotho
LESOURNE, Jacques
Linking computers to French logic. il por Bsns W p96-8 D 24 '66
LESSER ANTILLES. See West Indies
LESSING, Doris May
All about a modern Eve. G. Hicks. Sat R 49:31-2 Ap 2 '66
Commonplace book of Doris Lessing. L. Graver. New Repub 154:27-9 Ap 2 '66
LESSING, Lawrence
At the controls of the living cell. Fortune 73:154-8+ My '66
Bringing the fuel cell down to earth. Fortune 74:128-31+ S '66
Inside the molecules of the mind. Fortune 74:100-5+ Jl 1 '66
Into the core of life itself. Fortune 73:146-51+ Mr '66
Where the industries of the seventies will come from. Fortune 75:96-9+ Ja '67
LESSING, Pieter
Peking's stake in Africa. Nat R 18:262-4 Mr 22 '66
LESTER, Elenore
Happenings and happiness. Commonweal 84:466+ Jl 22 '66
LESTER, Richard
New faces. H. Alpert. il por Sat R 49:21 D 24 '66
LESTER, Richard A.
Adaptation of labor resources to changing needs; excerpt from Manpower planning in a free society. Mo Labor R 89:245-9 Mr '66
LESURE, James S.
And gladly strike? por Sat R 49:79 F 19 '66
LESURE, Thomas B.
Arizona's Colorado. Travel 126:59-63 D '66
Best U.S. golf resorts. Travel 125:24-8+ Mr '66
Wyoming's Snake River float trip. Travel 125:36-8 My '66
LET George do it; drama. See Hark, M. and McQueen, N.
LETCHER, John S. Jr
Singlehanded to Alaska. Yachting 119:66-8+ Je '66
LETHAL genes. See Genes
LETICIA, Colombia
Mike's revolution. S. Seegers and K. Seegers. il Américas 18:30-5 Ap '66; Same abr. with title One-man revolution on the Amazon. Read Digest 88:185-8+ My '66
LE TOURNEAU, Robert Gilmour
Man who can move mountains. S. James. il por Pop Mech 16:96-100+ Jl '66
LET'S be friends; story. See White, V. R.
LET'S sing Yiddish; musical comedy. See Musical comedies, revues, etc.—Criticisms, plots, etc.
LETTER paper. See Stationery
LETTER writing
I am, yours &c; the art of writing letters. L. Kronenberger. Atlan 217:97-100 Mr '66
Write-in campaign. il Seventeen 25:152-3 Je '66
LETTERING
Freeman Craw, graphic designer. E. M. Ettenberg. il Am Artist 30:32-7+ Mr '66
Stick lettering. S. Hanson. il Sch Arts 65:12-15 Ja '66
LETTERPRESS printing. See Printing
LETTERS
Letters of Petrarch; selection, tr. by M. Bishop. F. Petrarca. Horizon 9:42-5 Wint '67
Mimeographiti; the Christmas letter. J. A. Murdock. Christian Cent 83:1573-4 D 21 '66
See also
Letter writing
LETTERS by children
Children's letters to God; comp. by E. Marshall and S. Hample. il Sat Eve Post 239:30-1 N 19 '66
LETTERS of complaint. See Complaints
LETTERS of reference. See Recommendations for positions
LETTERS to congressmen. See Lobbying
LEUCHTENBERG, William E.
Genesis of the Great society. Reporter 34:36-9 Ap 21 '66
LEUCINE
Leucine incorporation into the membranellar bands of regenerating and non-regenerating stentor. N. De Terra. bibliog il Science 153:543-5 Jl 29 '66

LEUCOCYTES
Evidence from cultured leucocytes of blood cell chimerism in ex-parabiotic frogs. E. P. Volpe and B. M. Gebhardt. bibliog il Science 154:1197-9 D 2 '66
Leukocyte mitosis: suppression in vitro associated with acute infectious hepatitis. B. Mella and D. J. Lang. bibliog il Science 155:30-1 Ja 6 '67
Leukocytes test tissues. Sci N 90:261 O 1 66
One-way stimulation in mixed leukocyte cultures. F. H. Bach and N. K. Voynow. bibliog il Science 153:545-7 Jl 29 '66
Vesicular stomatitis virus replication in human leukocyte cultures: enhancement by phytohemagglutinin. R. Edelman and E. F. Wheelock. bibliog il Science 154:1053-5 N 25 '66

LEUKEMIA
All-out assault on leukemia; with reports by W. Bradbury and A. Rosenfeld. il Life 61:88-108+ N 18 '66
Cancer, other ills linked; congenital defects increase risk of leukemia. Sci N 90:395 N 12 '66
Cancer tied to bombing; cases of leukemia in Hiroshima and Nagasaki. F. Marley. Sci N 89:437 Je 4 '66
Enzyme found in tears is in excess in leukemia; lysozyme. Sci N 89:377 My 14 '66
Leukemia cure hinges on way virus behaves. Sci N 90:101 Ag 13 '66
More whites get leukemia. Sci N 90:82 Ag 6 '66
Nucleotide formation as a determinant of 5-fluorouracil response in mouse leukemias. D. Kessel and others. bibliog il Science 154:911-13 N 18 '66
Rare Chinese tree may help fight leukemia; Camptotheca tree. il Sci N 90:115 Ag 20 '66
World without cancer? work of S. Farber. il Newsweek 68:74 N 28 '66

Therapy
Drugs help leukemics. Sci N 89:456 Je 11 '66
Leukemia remissions; following drug or X-ray treatment. Sci N 89:460 Je 11 '66

LEUKEMIA viruses
All-out assault on leukemia; with reports by W. Bradbury and A. Rosenfeld. il Life 61:88-108+ N 18 '66
Murine leukemia viruses: antigenic studies by quantitative complement fixation. P. Gerber and others. bibliog il Science 152:1074-5 My 20 '66
Virus-induced murine leukemia: its inhibition and suppression by serum containing erythropoietin. P. G. Stansly and P. E. Schiop. bibliog il Science 152:1082-3 My 20 '66

LEUKOCYTES. See Leucocytes

LEUKOENCEPHALITIS. See Encephalitis

LEUSER, Eleanore
Wise people of Gotham; drama. Plays 25:79-84 F '66

LEVEAU, Carl Walter
Aluminum maintenance. Yachting 119:80+ Ap '66

LEVEL control, Liquid. See Liquid level control

LEVENSON, Sam
Sam Levenson recalls; when it was a privilege; excerpt from Everything but money. por Nations Bsns 54:40-1 S '66

about

Matzo-barrel philosopher. por Time 88:108+ S 9 '66

LEVER brothers and Unilever, limited
Big daddy stays & grows; African enterprise. il Time 87:90+ Je 24 '66
Two-headed giant comes back fighting; Anglo-Dutch Unilever. il Bsns W p 120-2+ Ap 9 '66

LEVER brothers company
Detergent bar for skin care; Dove beauty bar. M. B. Keiser. il Parents Mag 41:20+ Ag '66

LEVERTOV, Denise
Life at war; poem. Poetry 108:149-51 Je '66
What were they like? poem. Nation 202:781 Je 27 '66

LEVETEAU, J. and MacLeod, P.
Olfactory discrimination in the rabbit olfactory glomerulus. bibliog Science 153:175-6 Jl 8 '66

LEVI, Shelley
Achilles' heel; drama. Plays 25:69-72 My '66

LEVI, Werner
China's Asian policy. Cur Hist 51:153-8 S '66

LÉVI-STRAUSS, Claude
Lévi-Strauss mind. il por Newsweek 69:90 Ja 23 '67

Sartre vs. Lévi-Strauss; who are the radicals today? L. Abel. Commonweal 84:364-8 Je 17 '66

LEVIANT, Curt
Blood in the recipe. Nation 203:394-5 O 17 '66
Nobel laureate of Hebrew literature. Nation 203:645-7 D 12 '66

LEVIN, Harry
Unbanning of the books. por Atlan 217:77-81 F '66

LEVIN, Martin
(ed) Phoenix nest. See issues of Saturday review

LEVIN, Meyer
$500 misunderstanding. Sat R 49:58+ S 24 '66
Poster passion. Travel 125:39-41 F '66
Screening the festivals. Travel 125:44-6 Ap '66

LEVIN, Phyllis Lee
Short, short, short skirt story. N Y Times Mag p36-7+ Mr 20 '66; Same abr. with title Short short story of the skirt. Read Digest 88:112-14 Je '66

LEVIN, Robert J.
From I-thou to I-it. Sat R 49:29-30 Ag 20 '66
In defense of modern romance. Sat R 49:36-7 N 26 '66
Sex, morality, and society. Sat R 49:29-30 Jl 9 '66
When listening means life. Sat R 49:65 O 1 '66
(ed) See Perry, R. E. Where the innocent die
—See May, R. jt. auth.

LEVINE, Carol. See Balaban, V. jt. auth.

LEVINE, Daniel U.
Crisis in the administration of inner city schools. Sch & Soc 94:322-4 O 15 '66

LEVINE, David
Peaceable kingdom; caricature. Newsweek 68:14-15 D 26 '66

LEVINE, Faye
Life, love, and the movies in India. Atlan 218:90-3 N '66

LEVINE, Joseph E.
Last of the movie barons. il pors Newsweek 67:102+ My 2 '66

LEVINE, Lawrence, and others
Antibodies to photoproducts of deoxyribonucleic acids irradiated with ultraviolet light. bibliog Science 153:1666-7 S 30 '66

LEVINE, Leo
Ol' Jack was nimble, ol' Jack was quick, with his Brabham machine he turned the trick. Motor T 19:56-9+ Ja '67
Porsche 911-S. Motor T 19:22-3 Ja '67

LEVINE, Philip
Cemetery at academy, California; poem. New Yorker 42:116 Ag 20 '66
They got our leader; Looking for Levine; poems. Poetry 109:94-6 N '66

LEVINE, Philip T. and others
Noncollagenous nature of the proteins of shark enamel. bibliog Science 154:1192-4 D 2 '66

LEVINE, Robert J.
Histamine synthesis in man: inhibition by 4-bromo-3-hydroxybenzyloxyamine. bibliog Science 154:1017-19 N 25 '66

LEVINE, Seymour
Sex differences in the brain; with biographical sketch. Sci Am 214:20, 84-90 Ap '66
—and Mullins, R. F. Jr
Hormonal influences on brain organization in infant rats. bibliog Science 152:1585-9 Je 17 '66

LEVINE, Sumner N.
Enzyme amplifier kinetics. Science 152:651-3 Ap 29 '66

LE VINESS, W. Thetford
Three cultures of New Mexico. Américas 18:8-15 Je '66

LEVINSON, Deirdre
Crouch; story. Commentary 41:60-4 My '66

LEVINSON, Norma
Paradise on Tuesday; story. Redbook 127:64-5 Ag '66

LEVINSON, Robert E.
How to get through to people. Nations Bsns 54:92+ N '66

LEVINTHAL, Cyrus
Molecular model-building by computer; with biographical sketch. Sci Am 214:16, 42-52 bibliog(p 144) Je '66

LEVIT, Stephen
Technical representative. G. Smith. il pors Electr World 76:40-1+ Ag '66

LEVITAN, Sar A. and Mangum, G. L.
Coming to grips with unemployment. Reporter 35:44-6 N 17 '66

LEVITAS, Mitchel
One man is an island. N Y Times Mag p46-7+ Je 5 '66
Rise, fall and... of F.D.R. jr. N Y Times Mag p27+ O 23 '66
2-S, too smart to fight? N Y Times Mag p27+ Ap 24 '66

LEWY, Guenter
Was silence the only solution? Sat R 49:26-7 My 21 '66

LEXINGTON, Mass.
See also
Cary memorial library

LE-xuan-Chuyen
Encouraging returns. Time 88:43 D 9 '66

LEY, Willy
Cold war in space. Pop Sci 189:41-5+ Ag '66

LEYMARIE, Jean
Force of nature. il Newsweek 68:102 N 28 '66

LEYTON, Lawrence
Excerpt from testimony, June 16, 1965. Cong Digest 45:55+ F '66

L'HEUREUX, John
Cain; poem. Cath World 204:91 N '66
Compliance; poem. Atlan 217:142 Mr '66
Fabrication; poem. Harper 233:55 D '66
Gift; poem. Atlan 217:92 My '66

LI, Ching
Hong Kong's China doll. J. R. Moskin. il pors Look 30:M12-15 My 3 '66

LI, Choh Hao. See Dixon, J. S. jt. auth.

LIABILITY (law)
Case of the injured wife; suing under New Hampshire law for accident in Vermont. Time 88:56 O 21 '66
Conundrums of causation. il Time 88:39 Jl 29 '66
Decline & fall of privity. il Time 88:78 Ag 26 '66
Duffer's dilemma; golfing accident. Time 87:74 My 6 '66
Fasten your seat belt; failure to use a seat belt may bar recovery in a personal-injury suit. Time 88:46 Jl 22 '66
More protection for drunks; question of tavernkeepers' liability. Time 87:80 Ap 15 '66
Of love, kisses & nudism; decisions. Time 88:58-9 Jl 15 '66
Practical pressures pushing the profession; excerpts from address, with reply by E. Goble. R. F. Hastings. Arch Rec 140:9 O '66

LIABILITY insurance. See Insurance, Liability

LIAO, Shu-huei, and Hamilton, R. H.
Intracellular localization of growth hormones in plants. bibliog Science 151:822-4 F 18 '66

LIBBY, Paul R. and Dao, T. L.
Rat mammary gland RNA; incorporation of C14-formate and effect of hormones and 7,12-dimethylbenzanthracene. bibliog Science 153:303-5 Jl 15 '66

LIBBY DAM project (proposed)
U.S. exercises its option to build Libby Dam. Dept State Bul 54:297-8 F 21 '66

LIBEL and slander
Another clash between fundamental principles; Gilligan case. H. F. Pilpel. Pub W 189:64-5 F 28 '66
Libel based on letter dictated to a secretary. H. F. Pilpel Pub W 189:66 Ja 31 '66
Libel pendulum continues to swing. H. F. Pilpel. Pub W 189:40-1 Mr 28 '66
Linus Pauling takes the stand; excerpts from proceedings. Nat R 18:459-66 My 17 '66
Linus Pauling: TKO; lawsuit against National review. Nat R 18:403 My 3 '66
Meanwhile in another libel case; New Hampshire. H. F. Pilpel. Pub W 189:45 My 9 '66
National review vindicated; Linus Pauling case thrown out; Court's opinion, and Obiter dicta, by National review. Nat R 18:404-7 My 3 '66
New clarity, new hazards in the law of libel; New York Court of appeals decision. H. F. Pilpel. Pub W 190:39-40 Jl 25 '66
Pauling and libel; case against National review dismissed. Commonweal 84:192 My 6 '66
Privacy and libel again; case concerning Massachusetts physician's objection to his name being used in connection with national advertising campaign. H. F. Pilpel. Pub W 189:55-6 My 30 '66
Recent libel decision expands Times case doctrine. H. F. Pilpel. Pub W 189:43-5 My 9 '66
Right of public to criticize. H. F. Pilpel. Pub W 189:65 Ja 31 '66
Stevens asks court to enjoin Frick suit. Pub W 190:49-50 O 10 '66
Stevens presents case to U.S. Court of appeals Pub W 190:58-60 D 26 '66
Times' contention it was not present in Alabama upheld. H. F. Pilpel. Pub W 190:31-2 N 28 '66
Who decides a question of law? recent New York prosecution. H. F. Pilpel. Pub W 190:51-2 O 3 '66
See also
Trials (libel)

LIBEN, Meyer
CCNY; a memoir. Commentary 40:64-70 S 65; 41:16+ Ap '66

LIBERAL arts colleges. See Colleges and universities; Liberal education

LIBERAL colleges. See Liberal education

LIBERAL education
Conserving liberal education. J. G. Dwyer. Cath World 204:82-6 N '66
Cooperative relations involving the liberal arts colleges. W. E. Cadbury, jr. Sch & Soc 94:213-17 Ap 16 '66
Editor's bookshelf; concerning Earl J. McGrath's observations on sacrificing undergraduate liberal education to research in state institutions. P. Woodring. Sat R 49:85 D 17 '66
Education for the modern age; address, February 25, 1966. S. D. Cornell. Vital Speeches 32:372-6 Ap 1 '66
Liberal education for adults in a changing society; adaptation of address, May 7, 1966. J. E. Allen, jr. Sch & Soc 94:454-8 D 10 '66
Plight of the small college. W. A. Wallis; discussion. Atlan 217:38 Ja; 44 F '66
Reforming of general education, by D. Bell. Review
Sat R 49:98 Ap 16 '66. P. Woodring
Small college: another view; with reply by A. Wallis. H. Lowry. Atlan 217:50, 76-8 Mr '66
See also
Humanities

LIBERAL party (Great Britain)
Diminishing third. Newsweek 67:47 Mr 21 '66

LIBERAL party (United States)
CPNY and Mr Javits. Nat R 18:1304-5 D 27 '66

LIBERALISM
Agenda for American liberals; excerpt from address, April 1966. J. K. Galbraith. Commentary 41:29-34 Je '66; Discussion. 42:6+ S '66
Bankruptcy of the liberals; address, November 27, 1965. C. Oglesby; discussion. Commonweal 83:400-1, 547+ Ja 7, F 11 '66
Great liberal death-wish. M. Muggeridge. Nat R 18:573-4 Je 14 '66
Humphrey's dilemma. Christian Cent 83:325-6 Mr 16 '66
Letter to a new leftist, from a tired liberal. J. Fischer. Harper 232:16+ Mr '66; Same abr. with title Letter to a young leftist. Read Digest 88:137-40 My '66; Discussion. Harper 232:6 My '66
Liberalism: opportunity from impasse. F. A. Warren, 3d. Nation 202:238-41 F 28 '66
Liberals' new fundamentalism. Pyrrho. Nat R 18:219 Mr 8 '66
Shortage of liberals. W. V. Shannon. Commonweal 84:46-7 Ap 1 '66
Sound liberalism is still the answer; reprint. D. Lawrence. U S News 61:120+ Jl 18 '66
See also
Conservatism
Right and left (political science)

LIBERIA
See also
Medical relief work—Liberia

Industries
See also
Iron mines and mining—Liberia

LIBERTY, Margot
(ed) See John Stands in Timber. Last ghastly moments at the Little Bighorn

LIBERTY
Academic freedom and political liberty. A. Lepawsky; discussion. Science 151:1034; 152:1567 Mr 4, Je 17 '66
Bureaucracy and freedom: N. M. Korkunov's theory of the state. G. L. Yaney. bibliog f Am Hist R 71:468-86 Ja '66
Expanding liberties, by M. R. Konvitz. Review
Nation 203:289-90 S 26 '66. F. J. Donner
Freedom in the modern world, by H. J. Muller. Review
Sat R 49:39 F 5 '66. G. Bruun
Freedom is a two-edged sword. A. Gordon. Read Digest 89:37-9 Jl '66
Great free society; address, May 9, 1966. A. H. Motley. Vital Speeches 32:684-7 S 1 '66
Right to work controversy. G. J. Skibbins and C. S. Weymar. bibliog f il Harvard Bsns R 44:6-8+ Jl '66
Seven steps to greater personal freedom. V. Packard. Read Digest 88:123-7 Ap '66
Theology of nonresistance. V. Eller. Christion Cent 83:1534-7 D 14 '66
Thoughts for young Americans. D. D. Eisenhower. Read Digest 88:88-92 Ap '66

LIBERTY—*Continued*
Vietnam; cause of human freedom; address, February 23, 1966. L. B. Johnson. Vital Speeches 32:322-5 Mr 15 '66; Same with title Vietnam; the struggle to be free. Dept State Bul 54:390-6 Mr 14 '66; Excerpt. Cong Digest 45:105-6 Ap '66

See also
American civil liberties union
Assembly, Right of
Civil rights
Democracy
Equality
Liberalism

LIBERTY, Religious. See Religious liberty
LIBERTY, Statue of. See Statue of Liberty
LIBERTY of conscience
Helping prisoners of conscience; Amnesty international. Time 87:79 Ap 15 '66
See also
Religious liberty

LIBERTY of speech. See Free speech
LIBERTY of the press. See Freedom of the press
LIBERTY STATE PARK (proposed) See New Jersey—Parks and reserves

LIBRARIANS
As attractive as Buddhism? Conference on the present status and future prospects of reference information service, Columbia university. il Library J 91:2423-30 My 15 '66
Conference on the present status and future prospects of reference/information service, Columbia university. Wilson Lib Bul 40:909 Je '66
Escalation and librarians; question of material on all sides of the Vietnam issue. J. Berry. Library J 91:211 Ja 15 '66
First lady; libraries, readers and librarians in Great Britain, ed. by G. R. Davies. L. Paulin. Library J 91:4052-3 S 15 '66
Foreign librarians on U.S. tour. Wilson Lib Bul 40:803 My '66
Invisible librarian; report on The university in America, a convocation held in Beverly Hills, Calif. F. Blake. il Library J 91:3360-2 Jl '66
Librarian-trustee. E. J. Josey. Library J 91:2438-9 My 15 '66
Librarians and the everlasting now; excerpts from address, October 17, 1965. L. Q. Mumford. il Library J 91:901-6 F 15 '66
Long side of the rectangle; misuse of qualified professional staff. J. Berry. Library J 91:3884 S 1 '66
Masters of the raging book? address, July 15, 1966. M. V. Gaver. bibliog f il ALA Bul 60:794-9+ S '66
Medusa revisited. K. Nyren. Library J 91:5344 N 1 '66
New librarian. il Newsweek 68:85 Jl 25 '66
Old order and the new breed, or, Will automation spoil Mel Dewey? P. Papazian. ALA Bul 60:644-6 Je '66
Pool of paragons: faculty wives as helpers for college librarians. J. Weatherford. Library J 91:1790 Ap 1 '66
Pornographic convention: role as arbiters of taste; reprint. J. R. Coyne. bibliog Library J 91:2768-73 Je 1 '66; Discussion. 91:3290+ Jl '66
Price of obsolescence. J. Weatherford. Library J 91:1182 Mr 1 '66
Pushing the book; sharing love of reading with young people. M. A. Edwards. Library J 91:6166-8 D 15 '66
Reference librarian in an urban public library; excerpts from address, July 1965. E. J. Gaines. il Library J 91:2003-7 Ap 15 '66
Russian library delegation on U.S. study tour. Pub W 189:74 Ja 31 '66
See also
Catalogers
Childrens librarians
Library staffs
School librarians

Education
See Library schools and education

Education in service
Staffing of technical processes; programmed instruction for nonprofessionals. J. M. Elrod. Library J 91:2275-7 My 1 '66

Placement
See Librarians—Selection and appointment

Political activities
Join the picket line! concerning letter from union to librarians to boycott annual congress at St John's. J. N. Berry, 3d. il Library J 91:1782-7 Ap 1 '66

Qualifications
Civil service reform; letter to the editor. J. A. Ruef. Library J 92:30 Ja 1 '67

Recruiting
Land of Lincoln recruits librarians. D. J. Anderson. ALA Bul 60:1174-6 D '66
Namath system; bonus for beginning professional. E. Moon; reply. B. Schein. Library J 91:1092+ Mr 1 '66
Pioneer library system's cadet program. Mrs D. Connors. ALA Bul 61:86-9 Ja '67
Priority in Indiana. R. R. McClarren. ALA Bul 60:951+ O '66

Recruiting
Recruitment (cont) M. Ricking. ALA Bul 60:665-9, 731 Je-Jl '66

Salaries
Librarians pass teachers' salaries, six-year Canadian survey reveals. Library J 91:2788+ Je 1 '66
Persecuted minority; low salaries in the face of great demand for professionals. S. Sass. Library J 91:3126-7 Je 15 '66
Placement situation 1965 (with a preview of 1966) D. E. Strout and R. B. Strout. Library J 91:3117-26 Je 15 '66

Selection and appointment
Placement situation 1965 (with a preview of 1966) D. E. Strout and R. B. Strout. Library J 91:3117-26 Je 15 '66

Supply and demand
Current topics: a new year's roundup of some of librarianship's problems; symposium. il Library J 92:72-5 Ja 1 '67
Golden egg of federal support; not enough available librarians nor enough library school teachers. J. Shera. Wilson Lib Bul 41:327+ N '66
Persecuted minority; low salaries in the face of great demand for professionals. S. Sass. Library J 91:3126-7 Je 15 '66
Profile of an alumni body: graduates of Columbia university's school of library service. C. J. Frarey. il Library J 91:1776-81 Ap 1 '66
Search for status: Canadian libraries; the profession. J. Marshall. bibliog il Library J 91:5556-63 N 15 '66
Washington report. J. Lloyd. Sr Schol 88:sup8 Ap 15 '66

Tenure
Tenure for librarians. G. Coen. Library J 91:212-13 Ja 15 '66; Reply with rejoinder. E. W. Allen, jr. 91:1744 Ap 1 '66

Trade unions
See Librarians unions

LIBRARIANS, Professional ethics for
Code of ethics for librarians; reprint. Library J 91:5336-7 N 1 '66
Ethics: the creaking code; LAD's Code revision committee. J. F. Anderson. Library J 91:5333-5 N 1 '66; Reply. R. S. Gregory. 92:29 Ja 1 '67
Gored from within; concerning D. Gore's article in March 1966 issue of AAUP bulletin, letter to the editor. M. C. M. Souza. Library J 91:3014+ Je 15 '66

LIBRARIANS as authors
Cherchez l'homme; seven best librarian-authors all women! J. Shera. Wilson Lib Bul 41:423+ D '66

LIBRARIANS unions
Brooklyn gambit; decision by professional librarians to join AFL-CIO American federation of state, county, and municipal employees. K. Nyren. Library J 91:5905 D 1 '66
Brooklyn library union to seek better service. Library J 92:38+ Ja 1 '67

LIBRARIANSHIP
Brazil's library law; victory in the struggle for professional status. M. A. Gelfand. bibliog Library J 91:1362-4 Mr 15 '66
Careers in librarianship. R. Warncke. ALA Bul 60:805-9 S '66
Changing patterns in librarianship; implications for library education; adaptation of address, September 1966. L. Carnovsky. il Wilson Lib Bul 41:484-91 Ja '67

LIBRARIANSHIP—*Continued*
Current topics: a new year's roundup of some librarianship's problems; symposium. il Library J 92:72-8 Ja 1 '67
Headsets. Gore. & professors. J. Weatherford. Library J 91:5906 D 1 '66
Institute of library research; University of California. R. M. Hayes. il Library J 91: 4579-85 O 1 '66
Last one in bed's a librarian! concerning article: The mismanagement of college libraries by D. Gore. B. E. Richardson. il Library J 91:4904-7 O 15 '66; Discussion. 91:5792+ D 1 '66
Librarians and the everlasting now; excerpts from address, October 17, 1965. L. Q. Mumford. il Library J 91:901-6 F 15 '66
Masters of the raging book? address, July 15, 1966. M. V. Gaver. bibliog f il ALA Bul 60:794-9+ S '66
More than deliberate speed; better utilization of both clerical and professional personnel. M. T. Boaz. ALA Bul 60:286-8 Mr '66
New era for the public library; address, April 1966. S. B. Gould. ALA Bul 60:585-90 Je '66
New patterns for library service; excerpts from address, October 1964. M. Monroe. il Library J 91:1366-70 Mr 15 '66
Scrimp or splurge? J. E. Daily. Library J 91:2431-4 My 15 '66
Technology in the library. L. H. Freiser. il Wilson Lib Bul 41:69-71 S '66
What is past is prologue: beyond 1984. J. H. Shera. bibliog f il ALA Bul 61:35-47 Ja '67
What the historian has been missing. J. Shera. Wilson Lib Bul 40:639+ Mr '66
See also
Library science as a profession

International aspects
Library development abroad. M. M. Jackson, jr. il Library J 91:1354-61 Mr 15 '66
Why comparative librarianship? L. Shores. bibliog il Wilson Lib Bul 41:200-6 O '66

LIBRARIES
Library development abroad. M. M. Jackson, jr. il Library J 91:1354-61 Mr 15 '66
Useful services that can improve any public library. Good H 162:184-5 Ap '66
See also
American libraries abroad
Books and reading
College libraries
High school libraries
Prison libraries
School libraries
United Nations—Library

Acquisitions
Acquisitions: missing link in the library school curriculum? excerpts from address, 1965. W. R. Butler. il Library J 91:2271-4 My 1 '66
ALA & National league of cities to study book binding practices. Library J 91:5566-7 N 15 '66
How many copies are enough? Toledo. Ohio, public library; reprint. R. D. Franklin. il Library J 91:4573-5 O 1 '66
Publishers, computers, & consumers; excerpts from reports of University of California libraries. Los Angeles and Davis. Library J 91:1365 Mr 15 '66
Study to correct abuses in book purchasing; ALA and the National league of cities. Wilson Lib Bul 41:368+ D '66
Suppose butter; problems in spending federal money. J. Weatherford. Library J 91:3366 Jl '66

Administration
See Library administration

Advertising
See Library publicity

Architecture
See Library architecture

Audio-visual materials
See Libraries and audio-visual materials

Automation
Closing the circuit: automation and data processing for libraries; address, June 24, 1965. with reply by C. F. J. Overhage. V. W. Clapp. bibliog il Library J 91:1165-71 Mr 1 '66
Computer cycle: enthusiasm and despair; excerpts from annual report of library, School of medicine, Washington university. Library J 91:4907 O 15 '66

Computer produced book catalog. T. W. McConkey. il Library J 91:1864-5 Ap 1 '66
Computers challenge cards in library cataloging study; New York public library. Pub W 189:71 F 28 '66
Data processing in the library; symposium. bibliog il Wilson Lib Bul 41:382-417+ D '66
Fully automated registration system instituted at Los Angeles library. Library J 91:3134+ Je 15 '66
Information explosion hits our libraries. il Read Digest 88:153-5 Ap '66
Lack of machine-readable book data stymies automation advance, says CLR; excerpts from introduction to report. V. W. Clapp. Library J 91:220 Ja 15 '66
Library study reckons catalog conversion cheap; National union catalog at the Library of Congress. Pub W 189:71 F 28 '66
New librarian. il Newsweek 68:85 Jl 25 '66
Old order and the new breed, or, Will automation spoil Mel Dewey? P. Papazian. ALA Bul 60:644-6 Je '66
R&E council is briefed on new tools from IBM; members attend library session. Pub W 189:85 My 2 '66
Technology in the library. L. H. Freiser. il Wilson Lib Bul 41:69-71 S '66
What is past is prologue: beyond 1984. J. H. Shera. bibliog f il ALA Bul 61:35-47 Ja '67
See also
Information storage and retrieval systems
United States—Library of Congress—Automation

Anecdotes, facetiae, satire, etc.
Open letter: to Melvil Dewey on a symposium. C. A. McIsaac. il Library J 91:6047-8 D 15 '66
Time tunnel; possible quotations from future librarians. J. Weatherford. Library J 91: 5346 N 1 '66

Book discarding
Disposal delusions: items later needed by historians and librarians; letter to the editor. R. Higham. Library J 91:1094+ Mr 1 '66

Book losses
See also
Book thefts

Book sales
See Book sales

Book selection
See Book selection

Censorship
Birch tree grows. J. Freedman. il Library J 91:624-8 F 1 '66; Reply. L. Newman. 91: 1952 Ap 15 '66
Censorship obsession; letter to the editor. M. R. Boring. Library J 91:2248 My 1 '66
Controversial books; excerpt from policy statement, by trustees of Cary memorial library, Lexington, Mass. Library J 91:4572 O 1 '66
Drapery for Diego. J. Weatherford. Library J 91:646 F 1 '66
Intellectual freedom. ALA Bul 60:691+ Jl '66
Intellectual freedom. E. J. Gaines. See issues of ALA bulletin to June 1966
My mother, the censor; reprint. R. Knudson. ALA Bul 60:613-16 Je '66
Route '66: of obscenity and such. E. Moon. il Library J 92:53-5 Ja 1 '67
See also
School libraries—Censorship

Charging systems
Your charging system: is it thiefproof? R. F. Clarke and H. G. Clarke. Library J 91:642-3 F 1 '66; Discussion. 91:1332+ Mr 15 '66

Childrens rooms
See Libraries, Childrens

Circulation, loans, etc.
Dilemmas, problems, troubles. D. Dempsey. Sat R 49:39-40 N 12 '66
What is happening to public library circulation? E. Moon. il Library J 91:3851-63 S 1 '66; Reply. M. J. Bailey. 91:5504+ N 15 '66
See also
School libraries—Circulation, loans, etc.

Classification
See Classification

Cooperative service
See Library cooperation

LIBRARIES—*Continued*

Equipment and supplies
See Library furniture and equipment

Extension work
See Library extension

Federal aid
See Libraries and state

Finance
Everything in a low key; Canadian libraries: public; legislation and finance. R. L. Davison. il Library J 91:5533-6 N 15 '66
Intellectual freedom also requires money. E. J. Gaines. ALA Bul 60:119-21 F '66
Lift the ceiling. G. K. Schenk. Wilson Lib Bul 41:233+ O '66
See also
Libraries—Statistics
Libraries and state

Bibliography
Performance and program budgeting; comp. by H. Young. ALA Bul 61:63-7 Ja '67

Fires and fire protection
Library collections badly damaged in Jewish theological seminary fire. il Library J 91:2450 My 15 '66

Foreign language collections
PL-480 budget increased by $303,400; new programs and participants added. Library J 91:911 F 15 '66

Furniture
See Library furniture and equipment

Gifts, legacies, etc.
Equus donatus and the IRS: deductions for gifts to publicly supported nonprofit organizations. J. Shera. Wilson Lib Bul 40:545+ F '66
Notable acquisitions. Wilson Lib Bul 40:662+ Ap '66
Welcome gift; Journal of Negro history presented to Yesler branch's Negro life and history collection, Seattle public library. J. A. Welsh. il Negro Hist Bul 29:156+ Ap '66

Hours of opening
See also
School libraries—Hours of opening

Information service
See Libraries—Reference work

Instruction in use
A-V showtime; preconference institute: Library orientation programs. E. Moon. il Library J 91:3640-2 Ag '66
Catalog-first theory; San Diego Mesa college library, San Diego, Calif; letter to the editor. K. P. Anderson. Library J 91:5506+ N 15 '66
Drab skits and fine print: college library orientation. J. Weatherford. Library J 91:3886 S 1 '66
Introducing the library through film; list of films and filmstrips. H. Wheeler. Wilson Lib Bul 41:197-9 O '66
Library workshop for adults; Dayton and Montgomery County public library. M. T. Stibitz. il ALA Bul 60:937-41 O '66

International aspects
Bridge of children's books; symposium, ed. with introd. by E. Geller. bibliog il Library J 91:5683-92 N 15 '66
International exchange (cont) il Wilson Lib Bul 40:629-33, 759-63, 948-52; 41:418-20 Mr-Ap, Je, D '66
Why comparative librarianship? L. Shores. bibliog il Wilson Lib Bul 41:200-6 O '66
See also
United States—Library of Congress—National program for acquisitions and cataloging

Legislation
See Library laws and legislation

Management
See Library administration

Microfilm collections
Preservation of deteriorating books; excerpts from report (cont) G. R. Williams. Library J 91:189-94 Ja 15 '66; Reply to Ja 1 issue. G. B. Van Schaack. 91:870+ F 15 '66
Reproduction vs. preservation; excerpt from Care and preservation of books. J. Alden. Library J 91:5319-22 N 1 '66

Moving picture collections
8mm revolution. J. L. Limbacher. il Library J 91:6162-3 D 15 '66

Music collections
New Orleans jazz archive at Tulane. R. B. Allen. il Wilson Lib Bul 40:619-23 Mr '66

Oral history collections
Symposium on oral history. bibliog il Wilson Lib Bul 40:599-608+ Mr '66

Organization
See Library administration

Paperback books
ALA to report on use of paperbacks in libraries. Pub W 190:39 O 17 '66
Book by any other name. E. Moon. Library J 91:4061 S 15 '66; Discussion. 91:5278+ N 1 '66
Invisible chains; medieval philosophy of hardbacks. D. P. Weill. il Library J 91:4054-6 S 15 '66
Paperback wearability; evaluation at Monroe County public library, Bloomington, Ind. E. N. Howard. il Library J 91:4057-60 S 15 '66
Role of paperbacks in libraries; summary of ALA's paperback sessions: The literate unreached. Pub W 190:32-6 Ag 8 '66

Periodical collections
Foreign press in US libraries. C. Wall. il Library J 91:638-41 F 1 '66

Phonograph and phonograph records
Using your public library's record collection; Chicago public library. M. R. Adkins. Sr Schol 88:sup9 Ap 1 '66

Public relations
Focus on public relations; symposium. il Wilson Lib Bul 40:508-31 F '66
See also
Adult education—Library participation

Readers advisory service
Education, the common reader, and the future; address, June 1965. R. D. Altick. ALA Bul 60:275-82 Mr '66

Reference work
Adventures in the reference room; address, July 13, 1966. R. B. Morris. il Wilson Lib Bul 41:492-501 Ja '67
As attractive as Buddhism? Conference on the present status and future prospects of reference information service, Columbia university. il Library J 91:2423-30 My 15 '66
Conference on the present status and future prospects of reference/information service, Columbia university. Wilson Lib Bul 40:909 Je '66
Library cooperation for reference and research; symposium, with introd. by R. G. Vosper. il ALA Bul 60:1133-46+ D '66
Reference librarian in an urban public library; excerpts from address, July 1965. E. J. Gaines. il Library J 91:2003-7 Ap 15 '66
Will the real reference problem please stand up? T. Freides. bibliog il Library J 91:2008-12 Ap 15 '66; Discussion. 91:2736+, 3018 Je 1, 15 '66

Registration
Appendectomy: nonresident fee. W. Brahm; discussion. Library J 91:2+, 1334+ Ja 1, Mr 15 '66
LAPL and the data service bureau. D. W. Bass. il Wilson Lib Bul 41:404-8 D '66

Reports
See Library reports

Special collections
Look to the East; preconference of ACRL's college libraries section: Library collections for non-western studies, at Douglass college. S. Stowe. Library J 91:3645 Ag '66
See also
Libraries—Foreign language collections
Libraries—Moving picture collections

Standards
Layman's dilemma: better standards for small libraries by joining together to establish library systems. G. K. Schenk. Wilson Lib Bul 40:555 F '66
Public library standards went that-a-way; meanwhile, back at the convention. D. Curley. Library J 91:3864-5+ S 1 '66; Reply. W. L. Emerson. 91:4866+ O 15 '66

LIBRARIES—Standards—*Continued*
Standards no longer exist; letter to the editor. A. H. Rinee, jr. Library J 91:4010 S 15 '66
Why revise public library standards now? E. A. Ferguson. ALA Bul 60:590-4 Je '66

Statistics
Indexes of American public library statistics. ALA Bul 60:347 Ap '66
Library statistics and the measurement of library services. J. Krikelas. bibliog f ALA Bul 60:494-9 My '66
National conference on library statistics. F. L. Schick and A. F. Trezza. ALA Bul 60:499-500 My '66
National conference on library statistics. R. J. Shaw. il ALA Bul 60:727-8 Jl '66
Statistical ammunition; report on a National conference on library statistics. M. Chicorel. Library J 91:3363-4+ Jl '66
Statistical chaos: technical services in public libraries. C. J. Adams. Library J 91:2278-80 My 1 '66
What is happening to public library circulation? E. Moon. il Library J 91:3851-63 S 1 '66; Reply. M. J. Bailey. 91:5504+ N 15 '66

Student assistants
See Library assistants

Technical processes
Technical services; symposium. il Library J 91:2267-80 My 1 '66
See also
School libraries—Technical processes

Technology departments
Information technology: problems and promises; excerpts from address, May 27, 1965. M. Taube. Library J 91:1155-8 Mr 1 '66

Trustees, boards, committees, etc.
Across the board; ed. by D. Corrigan. Library J 91:212-13, 908, 1372+ Ja 15, F 15, Mr 15 '66
Choosing the board. V. G. Young. Library J 91:3130 Je 15 '66
Librarian-trustee. E. J. Josey. Library J 91:2438-9 My 15 '66
Library trustees and the literate society. C. T. Senft. ALA Bul 60:942-5 O '66
Rise and fall of a library; headquarters of Daniel Boone regional library; Columbia, Mo. public library. A. T. Hamlin. il ALA Bul 60:339-47 Ap '66
Why boards and trustees? Mrs W. Lynch. Library J 91:2018 Ap 15 '66
See also
American library trustee association

Work with blind
Extension of library services to physically handicapped proposed; persons who cannot read conventional printed matter. Library J 91:2294-5 My 1 '66
Libraries and the visually handicapped. C. Avery and H. H. Lyman. Wilson Lib Bul 40:854-7 My '66
Talking book: a prelude to action. V. R. Boyles. il Library J 91:201-4 Ja 15 '66

Work with children
See Libraries, Childrens

Work with foreign born
Los amigos: for the Spanish-speaking mother; New Haven library neighborhood center. J. Coyne. il Library J 91:329-31 Ja 15 '66

Work with schools
See Libraries and schools

Work with the handicapped
Service for everyone; symposium, ed. by R. S. Bray and L. K. Volin. bibliog il Wilson Lib Bul 40:816-57 My '66

Work with young people
Out of the ivory tower into the grease pit; National library week at Ossining, N.Y. public library; with bibliography. E. Sclar. il Library J 91:2162-4+ Ap 15 '66
Worth fighting for. L. LaFleur. bibliog il Library J 91:1582-6 Mr 15 '66
See also
Libraries and students

Brazil
Brazil's library law; victory in the struggle for professional status. M. A. Gelfand. bibliog Library J 91:1362-4 Mr 15 '66

California
See also
Los Angeles public library
Pomona, Calif, public library

Canada
Canadian libraries; symposium, ed. with introd. by C. D. Kent, and with editorial comment. bibliog il Library J 91:5521-64+ N 15 '66
See also
Canadian library association
Libraries—Ontario

China (People's Republic)
Libraries and publishing in mainland China; excerpts from Publishing in mainland China. G. R. Nunn. bibliog f il Library J 91:3327-32 Jl '66

Colombia
Culture in the bank; achievements sponsored by Bank of the Republic through Luis Angel Arango library, Bogotá. F. De Castro. il Américas 18:14-16 Jl '66

Connecticut
See also
Greenwich, Conn. library
New Haven, Conn, free public library

England
See also
British museum
Libraries—Great Britain
Luton, England, public libraries
Nottingham, England, public library

Florida
See also
Jacksonville, Fla. public library

France
See also
Paris—Libraries

Germany (Federal Republic)
Germany. H. H. Kunneman; H. Fotheringham. bibliog il Library J 91:5699-705 N 15 '66

Great Britain
London letter. G. R. Davies. Library J 91:2435-6, 4052-3 My 15, S 15 '66

Hawaii
System in Hawaii; address, July 1966. J. R. Hunt. il ALA Bul 60:1142-6 D '66

Illinois
Land of Lincoln recruits librarians. D. J. Anderson. ALA Bul 60:1174-6 D '66
See also
Chicago public library
Decatur, Ill. public library

Indiana
Priority in Indiana. R. R. McClarren. ALA Bul 60:951+ O '66
See also
Bloomington public and Monroe County library, Ind.
Lake County, Ind, public library system

Israel
Books of a pioneer culture. U. Ofek. il Library J 91:5706-8 N 15 '66

Italy
See also
Florence—Libraries

Kansas
See also
Kansas City, Kan, public library

Korea (Republic)
Korean micro-libraries and private reading rooms. D. Kaser. il Library J 91:6035-8 D 15 '66

Latin America
Report on Latin American libraries; Round table on international cooperation for library and information services in Latin America. M. D. Shepard. il Wilson Lib Bul 40:538-42 F '66

Louisiana
See also
New Orleans public library

Maryland
New concepts of library service proposed for unborn Maryland city: Columbia. Library J 91:648 F 1 '66
See also
Enoch Pratt free library, Baltimore
Prince Georges County memorial library, Hyattsville

LIBRARIES—*Continued*

Massachusetts
Eastern regional public library system born in Mass. after six years labor. Library J 91: 5913-14 D 1 '66
Money and standards, not advice; results of state aid, letter to the editor. Library J 91:3022+ Je 15 '66
Regional cooperation in Massachusetts realized. Wilson Lib Bul 41:368 D '66
See also
Cary memorial library, Lexington
Fitchburg, Mass. public library

Michigan
See also
Grosse Pointe, Mich. public library

Minnesota
See also
Minneapolis public library

Missouri
See also
Columbia, Mo. public library
Missouri state library, Jefferson City

Netherlands
See also
Amsterdam, Netherlands—Libraries

New Jersey
New Jersey plan; address, July 1966. M. V. Gaver. il ALA Bul 60:1138-42 D '66

New Mexico
See also
New Mexico state library, Santa Fe

New York (state)
Nelson associates survey recommends one catalog center for state of N.Y. Library J 91:3132 Je 15 '66
Pioneer library system's cadet program. Mrs D. Connors. ALA Bul 61:86-9 Ja '67
Three R's in New York: library reference and research resources; address, July 1966. E. B. Nyquist. il ALA Bul 60:1134-8 D '66
See also
Nassau library system
New York library association
New York public library
Ossining, N.Y. public library

North Carolina
See also
Charlotte and Mecklenburg County, N.C. public library

Ohio
Blasingame appointed consultant to Ohio public library survey. Library J 91:5567+ N 15 '66
See also
Cleveland public library
Columbus, Ohio, public library
Dayton and Montgomery County public library
Toledo public library

Ontario
Ontario libraries lag, St John says; education minister promises new laws. Library J 91:1856 Ap 1 '66
Report on the St John report. L. H. Freiser. Library J 91:5693-5 N 15 '66

Puerto Rico
See also
San Juan, Puerto Rico—Libraries

Quebec (province)
Breaking the vicious circle. G. Martin. il Library J 91:5550-5 N 15 '66

Russia
USSR libraries: a status report; excerpts from editorial from Biblioteki SSSR. V. Orlov. ALA Bul 60:648-50 Je '66
See also
Moscow—Libraries

Singapore
Singapore national library. O. B. Hsu and M. D. Carter. bibliog il Wilson Lib Bul 40:629-33 Mr '66; Correction. 41:26 S '66

United States
Commission on libraries set up by President. Pub W 190:44 S 19 '66
Escalation and librarians; question of material on all sides of the Vietnam issue. J. Berry. Library J 91:211 Ja 15 '66
Information explosion hits our libraries. il Read Digest 88:153-5 Ap '66

Library support; address, March 23, 1966. R. Vosper. Vital Speeches 32:504-6 Je 1 '66
Metropolitan public library; symposium. il Wilson Lib Bul 40:916-29 Je '66
New era for the public library; address, April 1966. S. B. Gould. ALA Bul 60:585-90 Je '66
Resources for research in urban areas; address, July 12, 1966. E. G. Holley. bibliog il Wilson Lib Bul 41:502-9 Ja '67
Route '66: a selective review and commentary on the (mostly American) library scene and its events of the past year. E. Moon. il Library J 92:51-63 Ja 1 '67
See also
Council on library resources, incorporated
Libraries—Statistics
Library surveys
National library week
United States—Library of Congress

Washington (state)
See also
Renton, Wash. public library
Seattle public library

Wisconsin
Along the migrant stream. E. Burr. Library J 91:335-6 Ja 15 '66

LIBRARIES (rooms)
Two hideouts for paterfamilias; rule 1: wives, children stay out. il Esquire 66:120-3 O '66

LIBRARIES, Childrens
Boy, this place sure has changed! North Manhattan library center project. New York public library. M. Robbins. il Wilson Lib Bul 41:186-9 O '66
Bridge of children's books; symposium, ed. with introd. by E. Geller. bibliog il Library J 91:5683-92 N 15 '66
Children's library in Mississippi does double duty. E. B. Zeigler. Horn Bk 42:292-7 Je '66
For children only: new library at Clamart, near Paris. il UNESCO Courier 19:16-19 Mr '66
No roses for Harry. M. Robbins. bibliog il Library J 91:1587-90 Mr 15 '66
See also
Book week

Book selection
See Book selection

Projects
Cooperative ventures in children's reading: Children's book council vacation reading program. B. Beilenson. il Library J 91:2170-1 Ap 15 '66

LIBRARIES, College. See College libraries

LIBRARIES, Employee
Bookstore promotes employee libraries for industries. Pub W 190:53 N 28 '66

LIBRARIES, Instruction in use of. See Libraries—Instruction in use

LIBRARIES, Medical. See Medical libraries

LIBRARIES, Moving of. See Moving of libraries

LIBRARIES, Prison. See Prison libraries

LIBRARIES, Private
And the books came tumblin' in; Tumblin' Creek cabin library, Tennessee mountains. S. C. Gross. il Sr Schol 88:sup9-10 My 6 '66
What unrequired books do students buy? Moderator survey. il Pub W 190:65-7 S 19 '66

LIBRARIES, Regional
Provincial diversity: Canadian libraries. H. Harbord. bibliog il Library J 91:5537-43 N 15 '66

LIBRARIES, School. See School libraries

LIBRARIES, Scientific. See Scientific libraries

LIBRARIES, Ship
Books under water: library life aboard a Polaris submarine. G. P. Steele. il Library J 91:2281-5 My 1 '66

LIBRARIES, Special
Federal assistance to special libraries. R. J. Havlik. ALA Bul 60:166-8 F '66
Resources for research in urban areas; address, July 12, 1966. E. G. Holley. bibliog il Wilson Lib Bul 41:502-9 Ja '67
See also
Medical libraries
Research libraries
Scientific libraries

LIBRARIES, State
State of the states. E. Moon. Library J 91: 1181 Mr 1 '66; Discussion. 91:2246+ My 1 '66

LIBRARIES, Thefts from. See Book thefts

LIBRARIES, Traveling
See also
Bookmobiles

LIBRARIES, University. See College libraries

LIBRARIES and adult education. See Adult education—Library participation

LIBRARIES and art
Arts, the humanities, and the school library; symposium; ed. by E. E. Ahlers. il ALA Bul 60:899-908+ O '66
Chicago pl censors art exhibit; says pictures were suggestive. Library J 91:214 Ja 15 '66
Indoor and outdoor sculpture; Brentano collection. T. W. McConkey. il Library J 91: 5930 D 1 '66

LIBRARIES and audio-visual materials
A-V showtime; preconference institute: Library orientation programs. E. Moon. Library J 91:3640-2 Ag '66
Obligated funds, fiscal 1966 and 1967, for instructural and A-V materials under recent federal legislation; chart. Pub W 190:44-5 Jl 25 '66

LIBRARIES and authors
Toad beneath the harrow knows; Copyright revision bill and photocopying. E. Janeway. il Library J 91:887-91 F 15 '66; Correction. 91:2740 Je 1 '66

LIBRARIES and booksellers
ALA & National league of cities to study book binding practices. Library J 91:5566-7 N 15 '66
Study to correct abuses in book purchasing: ALA and the National league of cities. Wilson Lib Bul 41:368+ D '66

LIBRARIES and civil defense. See Libraries and war

LIBRARIES and communication. See Communication

LIBRARIES and moving pictures
See also
Libraries—Moving picture collections

LIBRARIES and Negroes
Institutional membership in ALA; report of a Council committee on a membership proposal that institutional membership in ALA be restricted. ALA Bul 60:362-74 Ap '66
Negro library protests upheld by Supreme court; Clinton, Louisiana, public library. Library J 91:1374 Mr 15 '66
Saturday's children: Countee Cullen story; North Manhattan project. L. LaFleur; M. Robbins. bibliog il Library J 91:1581-90 Mr 15 '66
Word to the wise; Supreme court conviction reversed in Clinton, La. library demonstration. Time 87:61 Mr 4 '66

LIBRARIES and publishers
Book bind tight as ESEA nears deadline; difficulties of manufacturers, publishers, and wholesalers in filling school orders. Library J 91:2612-13 My 15 '66
Melodramatic world of librarians and copyright; report of ALA copyright workshop. R. H. Smith. Pub W 190:40 Ag 1 '66; Discussion. 190:22-3 Ag 15 '66
Publishers, computers, & consumers; excerpts from reports of University of California libraries, Los Angeles and Davis. Library J 91:1365 Mr 15 '66
Publishers study impact of U.S. school-aid funds; ABPC meeting on Changing nature and scope of the school and library market; summary of conference. il Pub W 189:28-50 My 23 '66; Correction. 189:49 Je 20 '66
Schools and scholarly books; summary of address, June 14, 1966. M. V. Gaver. il Pub W 190:44-6 Jl 4 '66
Truce with the publishers; discussion of net pricing between a publisher, wholesaler, and a librarian. Library J 91:2579-83 My 15 '66

LIBRARIES and readers
Access and the Supreme court: discrimination against students and nonresidents. E. Moon. Library J 91:1788 Ap 1 '66; Reply. E. M. Oboler. 91:2738+ Je 1 '66
Caught in the draft; providing materials for both conscientious objectors and service men. J. Berry. Library J 91:907+ F 15 '66
First lady; libraries, readers and librarians in Great Britain, ed. by G. R. Davies. L. Paulin. Library J 91:4052-3 S 15 '66
Metropolitan public library; symposium. il Wilson Lib Bul 40:916-29 Je '66
My mother, the censor; reprint. R. Knudson. ALA Bul 60:613-16 Je '66

LIBRARIES and research
Compleat collector; building and maintenance of source material collections for history; three-day colloquium at Harvard university. K. Nyren. il Library J 91:6029-34 D 15 '66
Forgotten key; independent research a myth? school libraries. M. Rossoff. Library J 91: 5126-8+ O 15 '66
Institute of library research; University of California. R. M. Hayes. il Library J 91: 4579-85 O 1 '66

Library college idea: inevitable culmination of the independent study movement. L. Shores. bibliog il Library J 91:3871-5 S 1 '66
Library cooperation for reference and research; symposium, with introd. by R. G. Vosper. il ALA Bul 60:1133-46+ D '66
Mind-saving stations. Library J 91:2002 Ap 15 '66
Resources for research in urban areas; address, July 12, 1966. E. G. Holley. bibliog il Wilson Lib Bul 41:502-9 Ja '67
Self-sufficiency paradox; letter to the editor. H. G. Brown. Library J 91:870 F 15 '66
Seven league boots for the scholar? problems and prospects of library telefacsimile. D. W. Heron and J. R. Blanchard. il Library J 91: 3601+ Ag '66
Trickster in library research. J. Shera. Wilson Lib Bul 41:521+ Ja '67

LIBRARIES and schools
Book selection in Grosse Pointe: where school librarians advise the public library. V. Leonard. ALA Bul 60:627-9 Je '66
Communication is the key. G. Raftery. il Sr Schol 89:sup21 O 28 '66
Impact of universal education; remarks, June 1965. D. Lacy. il Library J 91:3866-70 S 1 '66
Sample projects, title III, ESEA; Nassau school-public library project. D. S. Lindauer. il Library J 91:1024-8 F 15 '66

LIBRARIES and social and economic problems
Books for adults beginning to read. Wilson Lib Bul 41:83-7 S '66
Boy, this place sure has changed! North Manhattan library center project, New York public library. M. Robbins. il Wilson Lib Bul 41:186-9 O '66
Education act; off the ground, new developments for school libraries; symposium. il Library J 91:1009-32+ F 15 '66
Federal legislation relevant to library antipoverty efforts: 1966; comp. by P. Winnick. Library J 91:347-53 Ja 15 '66
Getting into the ghetto; preconference Workshop on books for adults beginning to read. J. N. Berry, 3d. il Library J 91:3642-4 Ag '66
Library and the functionally illiterate in Cleveland; excerpts from letter, ed. by W. Woulfe. F. Long. ALA Bul 60:637-8 Je '66
Library service in the inner city; Community action program and Enoch Pratt free library, Baltimore. E. Levy. il Wilson Lib Bul 41:470-7 Ja '67
Metropolitan public library; symposium. il Wilson Lib Bul 40:916-29 Je '66
Minority groups in texts and library books; hearings before the House ad hoc subcommittee on de facto school segregation. G. Krettek and E. D. Cooke. Wilson Lib Bul 41:235 O '66
Powell committee considers treatment of minority groups in school books. Library J 91:5720 N 15 '66
Return to Durango street; address, July 1966. F. Bonham. il Library J 91:4188-91 S 15 '66
Saturday's children: Countee Cullen story; North Manhattan project. L. LaFleur; M. Robbins. bibliog il Library J 91:1581-90 Mr 15 '66
Time for self-renewal; a special issue on the antipoverty programs; symposium, ed. by P. Winnick. Library J 91:317-53+ Ja 15 '66
Two blocks apart:YASD preconference on the disadvantaged. E. Geller. il Library J 91:4222-9 S 15 '66
Unparalleled opportunity; antipoverty work. G. K. Schenk. Wilson Lib Bul 40:777 Ap '66
Widening the horizons of the culturally deprived; excerpts from address, July 1965. G. H. Esser, jr. ALA Bul 60:175-8 F '66

LIBRARIES and state
Academic library construction: federal support. ALA Bul 60:775-6 S '66
Authorizations and funds set for library programs in '67; Appropriations uncertain till final hours. G. Krettek and E. D. Cooke. il ALA Bul 60:1123-5 D '66
Bugbear of school library education; results of ESEA. J. Rowell. Library J 91:5123-5 O 15 '66
Defense never rests; testifying for the extension and expansion of the Library services and construction act. L. G. Currier. ALA Bul 60:705-10 Jl '66
Education act enters second year with larger funding probable. Library J 91:4230+ S 15 '66
Education act: off the ground, new developments for school libraries; symposium. il Library J 91:1009-32+ F 15 '66

LIBRARIES and state—*Continued*

Education pentagon; story of an Lj visit. J. N. Berry, 3d. il Library J 91:195-200 Ja 15 '66; Reply. W. L. Morin. 91:1092 Mr 1 '66

89th Congress adjourned; eleventh-hour vote on appropriations; G. Krettek and E. D. Cooke. Wilson Lib Bul 41:433+ D '66

ESEA amendments of 1966. G. Krettek and E. D. Cooke. ALA Bul 60:417-18 My '66

Evaluations under way for Title I, Head Start. Library J 91:6173+ D 15 '66

Federal aid and the freedom to read. E. Geller. Library J 91:298 Ja 15 '66

Federal commitment to education; aid to schools and libraries. C. B. Grannis. Pub W 190:69 Ag 1 '66

Federal library legislation, programs, and services; symposium, ed. by H. Drennan; with editorial comment. ALA Bul 60:107, 139-68 F '66

Golden egg of federal support; not enough available librarians nor enough library school teachers. J. Shera. Wilson Lib Bul 41:327+ N '66

Grants and loans for seventeen libraries awarded under HEFA in February. Library J 91:1186 Mr 1 '66

Hasty action imperative for '66 HEA funds. Pub W 189:57 My 30 '66

How a library won an election; Minneapolis public library. K. C. Busch and E. J. Gaines. il Library J 91:5338-43 N 1 '66

Involvement in federal programs; Enoch Pratt free library; address, 1966. E. Castagna. il Wilson Lib Bul 41:478-83 Ja '67

Libraries must be mandated. C. E. Reid. Library J 91:1372+ Mr 15 '66

Library support; address, March 23, 1966. R. Vosper. Vital Speeches 32:504-6 Je 1 '66

LBJ signs bills in Thailand for 1967 library aid funds. L. B. Johnson. Library J 91:5908 D 1 '66

Money and standards, not advice; results of state aid in Massachusetts, letter to the editor. Library J 91:3022+ Je 15 '66

National dimension: a report on the impact of federal aid to libraries. K. Nyren. il Library J 92:64-71 Ja 1 '67

President Johnson recommends ESEA extension and expansion. Library J 91:2178 Ap 15 '66

Route '66: a selective review and commentary on the (mostly American) library scene and its events of the past year. E. Moon. il Library J 92:51-63 Ja 1 '67

School aid bill passed by Congress; Education act for 1966-67. Library J 91:5720 N 15 '66

Service to schools: Elementary and secondary education act. G. K. Schenk. Wilson Lib Bul 40:968 Je '66

Singin' those federal blues: unprecedented mobilization of school library profession on pain of losing federal benefits. E. Geller. Library J 91:992 F 15 '66

Strong book and library components cited in ESEA Title I by USOE spokesman; excerpts from address, March 1966. M. Black. Library J 91:2180-1 Ap 15 '66

Struggling with Education act; ALA midwinter report. E. Geller. Library J 91:1615-17 Mr 15 '66

Tied with a red tape ribbon: knots in the NDEA program. T. P. Lewis. il Library J 91:2157-61 Ap 15 '66

Title II plans show clear predominance of library over textbooks and audiovisuals; school library resources. Library J 91:1038 F 15 '66

USOE worried about Title I laggards. Library J 91:1630-1 Mr 15 '66

Whither cooperation? ESEA Titles II and III at same time as new LSCA amendment, Title III school libraries. E. Geller. Library J 91:5664 N 15 '66

LIBRARIES and students

Impact of universal education; remarks, June 1965. D. Lacy. il Library J 91:3866-70 S 1 '66

Many-splintered thing. E. Moon. Library J 91:3663+ Ag '66

LIBRARIES and war

Libraries and civil defense; with bibliography. J. F. Hanna. ALA Bul 60:655-6 Je '66; Reply. E. M. Oboler. 60:755-6 S '66

LIBRARIES as social centers. See Library buildings as social centers

LIBRARIES for the handicapped. See Handicapped, Libraries for the

LIBRARY administration

Bugbear of school library education; results of ESEA. J. Rowell. Library J 91:5123-5 O 15 '66

Current issues facing leadership in the school library field; adaptation of address, July 1966. H. G. Shane. ALA Bul 60:923-6 O '66

Focus on the supervisor. G. K. Schenk. Wilson Lib Bul 41:435 D '66

Last one in bed's a librarian! concerning article: The mismanagement of college libraries by D. Gore. B. E. Richardson. il Library J 91:4904-7 O 15 '66; Discussion. 91:5792+ D 1 '66

Library education and the talent shortage: poll of library administrators; symposium. il Library J 91:1761-73 Ap 1 '66; Discussion. 91:2390+, 4866, 6020 My 15, O 15, D 15 '66

Management training advocated; letter to the editor. J. J. Oliva. Library J 91:5284 N 1 '66; Same. ALA Bul 60:1115 D '66

Some of my best friends; librarians and trustees. G. Gordon. Library J 91:908 F 15 '66

See also

Libraries—Trustees, boards, committees, etc.

LIBRARY administration division of ALA. See American library association—Library administration division

LIBRARY advertising. See Library publicity

LIBRARY and museum of the performing arts. See Lincoln Center for the performing arts, New York—Library and museum of the performing arts

LIBRARY architecture

Anti-academic library; new Robert Hutchings Goddard library at Clark university, Worcester, Mass. il Library J 91:2286-7 My 1 '66

Architectural issue (cont) Library J 91:5827-904 D 1 '66

Bricks and mortar. Library J 92:47 Ja 1 '67

Building briefs (cont) Library J 91:1389-90, 2303, 3900, 4070-1 Mr 15, My 1, S 1-15 '66

Coast range gem: the Los Gatos high school library. E. Mason. il ALA Bul 60:270-4 Mr '66; Reply with rejoinder. E. T. Schofield. 60:529-31 Je '66

Design awards. P. P. Price and H. A. Carl. ALA Bul 61:29-30 Ja '67

Design for the campus; building types study. il Arch Rec 140:204-18 S '66

John M. Johansen declares himself; library for Clark university. J. M. Johansen. il Arch Forum 124:64-7 Ja '66

Library building program. A. B. Martin. il Wilson Lib Bul 41:514-16 Ja '67

Library buildings awards announced; one first honor, ten awards of merit. il Library J 91:2445 My 15 '66

Making libraries useable; provisions for those with handicaps. E. H. Noakes. il Wilson Lib Bul 40:851-3 My '66

New buildings. Library J 91:223, 663-4 Ja 15-F 1 '66

No perfect diamonds; Canadian libraries. A. W. Bowron. il Library J 91:5544-9 N 15 '66

Pittsburgh library; class amid the clutter. il Arch Forum 124:58-61 Mr '66

Rear end of the Xerox, or how I learned to love that library. M. Charney; S. Moholy-Nagy. il Arch Forum 124:60-1 My '66

Third Library buildings awards. il ALA Bul 60:576-83 Je '66

Toplighted, protected spaces for reading. il Arch Rec 140:103-5 Ag '66

Two of New York's newest: Queens borough public library; the Library and museum of the performing arts in Lincoln Center. il Library J 91:3108-9 Je 15 '6

Where should the library be? University of Massachusetts. il Arch Rec 139:178-9 My '66

LIBRARY assistants

Academic librarians discuss nonprofessionals: Eastern college librarians at 52nd annual conference. Library J 92:40-1 Ja 1 '67

See also

Catalogers

LIBRARY associations

Counselors revisited: five largest national library associations working with APGA. M. Ricking. ALA Bul 60:665-7 Je '66

How shall librarians organize? problem of professional organizations based on political, religious, or racial interests. R. Burgess. Library J 91:6043-4 D 15 '66

LIBRARY boards. See Libraries—Trustees, boards, committees, etc.

LIBRARY bookbinding. See Bookbinding

LIBRARY budgets. See Libraries—Finance

LIBRARY building consultants. See Library consultants

LIBRARY buildings. See Library architecture

LIBRARY buildings as social centers

From supermarket to superlibrary. W. Cahn and R. Cahn. il Parents Mag 41:47-9+ Je '66

Little miracle on Chapel street. H. T. Drennan. il Am Ed 2:1-5 Jl '66

LIBRARY carpets. See Rugs and carpets
LIBRARY catalogs. See Catalogs, Library
LIBRARY censorship. See Libraries—Censorship
LIBRARY classification. See Classification
LIBRARY compacts, Interstate. See Interstate compacts

LIBRARY conferences
As attractive as Buddhism? Conference on the present status and future prospects of reference information service. Columbia university. il Library J 91:2423-30 My 15 '66
Calendar. See second issue of each month of Library journal
Compleat collector: building and maintenance of source material collections for history; three-day colloquium at Harvard university. K. Nyren. il Library J 91:6029-34 D 15 '66
Conference on the present status and future prospects of reference/information service, Columbia university. Wilson Lib Bul 40:909 Je '66
Conference papers logjam; use of University microfilms; letter to the editor. Library J 91:3578 Ag '66
Library education in Asia: topic of Hawaii conference. Library J 91:2790 Je 1 '66
Maryland classification symposium has international all-star cast. Library J 91:2795 Je 1 '66
Meetings, courses, associations, etc. See issues of Wilson library bulletin
National conference on library statistics. F. L. Schick and A. F. Trezza. ALA Bul 60:499-500 My '66
National conference on library statistics. R. J. Shaw. il ALA Bul 60:727-8 Jl '66
See also
Conference of eastern college librarians

Anecdotes, facetiae, satire, etc.
Open letter: to Melvil Dewey on a symposium. C. A. McIsaac. il Library J 91:6047-8 D 15 '66

LIBRARY consultants
Action vs. advice: conflict in consulting: excerpts from report on state library consultants. M. A. Long. ALA Bul 60:357-61 Ap '66; Discussion. 60:711-12, 882-3 Jl, O '66
Library building program. A. B. Martin. il Wilson Lib Bul 41:514-16 Ja '67
Super-librarian and sub-architect; role of the building consultant. N. R. McAdams. Library J 91:5827-31 D 1 '66

LIBRARY cooperation
Interstate library compact. M. R. Vale. il Library J 91:2419-22 My '66
Science library cooperation in three colleges: Bryn Mawr, Haverford, and Swarthmore, Pa. S. Newhall. ALA Bul 60:380-1 Ap '66
Whither cooperation? ESEA Titles II and III at same time as new LSCA amendment, Title III school libraries. E. Geller. Library J 91:5664 N 15 '66
Widening the horizons of the culturally deprived; excerpts from address, July 1965. G. H. Esser, jr. ALA Bul 60:175-8 F '66
See also
United States—Library of Congress—National program for acquisitions and cataloging

LIBRARY discipline. See Library administration
LIBRARY education. See Library schools and education
LIBRARY equipment. See Library furniture and equipment

LIBRARY exhibits
Greenwich reading time. J. W. Bryant. il Wilson Lib Bul 40:530-1 F '66
Ideas for summer displays. il Wilson Lib Bul 40:966-7 Je '66
Theatrical exhibitions at Lincoln Center. R. F. Kimball. il Wilson Lib Bul 40:513-16+ F '66

LIBRARY extension
Extending library service: ed. by G. K. Schenk. See issues of Wilson library bulletin
See also
College library extension
Libraries, Regional
School library extension

LIBRARY finance. See Libraries—Finance
LIBRARY for the blind, Philadelphia. See Philadelphia—Free library—Library for the blind

LIBRARY furniture and equipment
Buyers' guide (cont of) Products and equipment; ed. by T. W. McConkey. See first issue of each month of Library journal

Furniture specifications and bidding documents. M. Van Buren. il Library J 91:5845-50 D 1 '66
Goods and gadgets. See issues of ALA bulletin
Library technology. G. T. Piez. See issues of ALA bulletin
On being specific; pre-conference institute on library equipment. S. Havens. il Library J 91:3646-8 Ag '66
Products & equipment; ed. by T. W. McConkey. See first issue of each month of Library journal

LIBRARY gifts. See Libraries—Gifts, legacies, etc.

LIBRARY institutes and workshops
As good as librarians make them; NDEA institutes for school librarianship. F. Henne. Library J 91:2565-9 My 15 '66
Meetings, courses, associations, etc. See issues of Wilson library bulletin
Missouri librarians go literary at state library winter institute. Library J 91:2788 Je 1 '66

LIBRARY instruction. See Libraries—Instruction in use
LIBRARY insurance. See Insurance, Library

LIBRARY journal
Day at Lj; with editorial comment. B. Katz. il Library J 91:3110-16 Je 15 '66
Dewey proportions: comparison of Toledo public library adult circulating book stock at main library and at typical Toledo branch library with Lj adult book review coverage. E. Moon. Library J 91:2783 Je 1 '66
Lj and LC win Edpress awards for excellence in educational journalism. il Library J 91:3370 Jl '66
Living end: new format. E. Moon. Library J 91:6049 D 15 '66
Major changes announced in Lj editorial staff. il Library J 91:4590+ O 1 '66

LIBRARY laws and legislation
ALA Washington notes. G. Krettek and E. D. Cooke. See issues of Wilson library bulletin
Bills introduced in January to extend and expand LSCA. Library J 91:1184 Mr 1 '66
Brazil's library law; victory in the struggle for professional status. M. A. Gelfand. bibliog Library J 91:1362-4 Mr 15 '66
Compromise bills to extend LSCA introduced in House and Senate. Library J 91:2294 My 1 '66
Defense never rests; testifying for the extension and expansion of the Library services and construction act. L. G. Currier. ALA Bul 60:705-10 Jl '66
Everything in a low key; Canadian libraries: public; legislation and finance. R. L. Davison. il Library J 91:5533-6 N 15 '66
Federal library legislation, programs, and services; symposium, ed. by H. Drennan, with editorial comment. ALA Bul 60:107, 139-68 F '66
LSCA amendments voted by Congress: House, 336 to 2; Senate, unanimous. Library J 91:3368 Jl '66
LSCA program developments. P. P. Price and H. A. Carl. ALA Bul 60:127-9 F '66
Ontario libraries lag, St John says; education minister promises new laws. Library J 91:1856 Ap 1 '66
President signs LSCA 1966 amendments; announces National library commission, excerpts from address, July 19, 1966. L. B. Johnson. Library J 91:3666 Ag '66
Presidential signature: Library services and construction act amendments of 1966. P. P. Price and H. A. Carl. ALA Bul 60:773-4 S '66
Report on the St John report; chaotic situation in Ontario. L. H. Freiser. Library J 91:5693-5 N 15 '66
Washington report: from the ALA Washington office. G. Krettek and E. D. Cooke. See issues of ALA bulletin
Whither cooperation? ESEA Titles II and III at same time as new LSCA amendment, Title III school libraries. E. Geller. Library J 91:5664 N 15 '66

LIBRARY loans. See Libraries—Circulation, loans, etc.
LIBRARY management. See Library administration
LIBRARY of Congress. See United States—Library of Congress
LIBRARY of Congress catalog cards. See Catalog cards
LIBRARY orientation. See Libraries—Instruction in use
LIBRARY patrons. See Libraries and readers
LIBRARY personnel. See Library assistants; Library staffs

LIBRARY publicity
Focus on public relations; symposium. il Wilson Lib Bul 40:508-31 F '66
How a library won an election; Minneapolis public library. K. C. Busch and E. J. Gaines. il Library J 91:5338-43 N 1 '66
See also
National library week

LIBRARY purchasing
Suppose butter; problems in spending federal money. J. Weatherford. Library J 91:3366 Jl '66

LIBRARY reports
Microscope vs. telescope: large part of annual report devoted to single day; Luton public libraries, England. E. Moon. Library J 91:644 F 1 '66

LIBRARY schools and education
Accredited library schools. ALA Bul 60: 1071-2 N '66
Acquisitions: missing link in the library school curriculum? excerpts from address, 1965. W. R. Butler. il Library 91:2271-4 My 1 '66
Bugbear of school library education: results of ESEA. J. Rowell. Library J 91:5123-5 O 15 '66
Changing patterns in librarianship: implications for library education; adaptation of address, September 1966. L. Carnovsky. il Wilson Lib Bul 41:484-91 Ja '67
Current topics: a new year's roundup of some of librarianship's problems; symposium. il Library J 92:72-5 Ja 1 '67
Federal government and professional library education. S. R. Reed. ALA Bul 60:163-6 F '66
Golden egg of federal support: not enough available librarians not enough library school teachers. J. Shera. Wilson Lib Bul 41:327+ N '66
Je crois qu'elle ose regarder mon nez; chasm of misunderstanding between the practitioner and the educator. J. Shera. Wilson Lib Bul 41:215+ O '66
Library education and the shortage of both manpower and talent, symposium; ed. by D. Bendix with editorial comment. il Library J 91:4881-98, 4908 O 15 '66; Discussion. 91: 6020+; 92:32 D 15 '66, Ja 1 '67
Library education and the talent shortage: poll of library administrators; symposium. il Library J 91:1761-73 Ap 1 '66; Discussion. 91:2390+, 4866, 6020 My 15, O 15, D 15 '66
Library education; Title XI of the National defense education act. P. P. Price and H. A. Carl. ALA Bul 61:27-8 Ja '67
Management training advocated: letter to the editor. J. J. Oliva. Library J 91:5284 N 1 '66; Same. ALA Bul 60:1115 D '66
Meetings, courses, associations, etc. See issues of Wilson library bulletin
More than deliberate speed; better utilization of both clerical and professional personnel. M. T. Boaz. ALA Bul 60:286-8 Mr '66
To kill a whooping crane; fresh approach to the problem of educating librarians. P. Sexton. il Library J 91:5327-32 N 1 '66
What's wrong with our library schools? discussion by six 1965 library school graduates; reprint. U. Cameron and others. il Library J 91:1773-5 Ap 1 '66; Discussion. 91:2394+ My 15 '66
Will the real reference problem please stand up? T. Freides. bibliog il Library J 91:2008-12 Ap 15 '66; Discussion. 91:2736+, 3018 Je 1, 15 '66
See also
American library association—Office for library education

Asia, Southeastern
Library education in Asia; topic of Hawaii conference. Library J 91:2790+ Je 1 '66

Canada
Search for status. J. Marshall. bibliog il Library J 91:5556-63 N 15 '66
Three levels of library education. D. D. Sudar. bibliog Library J 91:4899-903 O 15 '66

Latin America
Report on Latin American libraries; Round table on international cooperation for library and information services in Latin America. M. D. Shepard. il Wilson Lib Bul 40:538-42 F '66

LIBRARY science
See also
Bibliography
Librarianship
Bibliography
Professional reading. See issues of Library journal

Periodicals
See also
Library journal
Wilson library bulletin

Study and teaching
See Library schools and education

LIBRARY science as a profession
Cause, or effect? our image. J. Weatherford. Library J 91:4588 O 1 '66
Long side of the rectangle; misuse of qualified professional staff. J. Berry. Library J 91:3884 S 1 '66
Search for status; Canadian libraries: the profession. J. Marshall. bibliog il Library J 91:5556-63 N 15 '66

LIBRARY services and construction act. See Library laws and legislation

LIBRARY staffs
Plans for a project to set up a nationwide investigation of manpower problems; University of Maryland school of library and information services. Wilson Lib Bul 40: 687 Ap '66
Staffing of technical processes. J. M. Elrod. Library J 91:2275-7 My 1 '66
See also
Librarians unions

LIBRARY standards. See Libraries—Standards; School libraries—Standards

LIBRARY statistics. See Libraries—Statistics

LIBRARY surveys
Action vs. advice: conflict in consulting; state libraries; excerpts from report. M. A. Long. ALA Bul 60:357-61 Ap '66; Discussion. 60: 711-12, 882-3 Jl, O '66
In, out, or neglected? books chosen in response to an Lj book selection survey. E. Moon. il Library J 91:633-7 F 1 '66
Ontario libraries lag, St John says; education minister promises new laws. Library J 91:1856 Ap 1 '66
Placement situation 1965 (with a preview of 1966) D. E. Strout and R. B. Strout. Library J 91:3117-26 Je 15 '66
Profile of an alumni body: graduates of Columbia university's School of library service. C. J. Frarey. il Library J 91:1776-81 Ap 1 '66
Statistical chaos: technical services in public libraries. C. J. Adams. Library J 91:2278-80 My 1 '66
Survey milestones; Canadian libraries: national. J. E. Brown. bibliog il Library J 91:5525-8 N 15 '66
Tied with a red tape ribbon: knots in the NDEA program. T. P. Lewis. il Library J 91:2157-61 Ap 15 '66
What is happening to public library circulation? E. Moon. il Library J 91:3851-63 S 1 '66
What should PLA be doing? report on an informal survey conducted by Activities committee, with comment by E. A. Ferguson. K. Molz. ALA Bul 60:595-9+ Je '66

LIBRARY trustees. See Libraries—Trustees, boards, committees, etc.

LIBRARY week. See National library week

LIBRARY workshops. See Library institutes and workshops

LIBRATION of the moon. See Moon—Libration

LIBRETTISTS
See also
Metastasio, P. A. D. B.

LIBRETTO
In the grand tradition; libretto and music for Shakespeare's Antony and Cleopatra. J. W. Freeman. il Opera N 31:40-1 S 17 '66
Unanswered question; music or words first. R. Berges. il Opera N 30:6-7 Mr 26 '66

LIBYA
Children of Allah, by A. N. Keith. Review Atlan 217:160-2 Mr '66. O. Handlin Sat R 49:41-2 Mr 5 '66. C. Miller
See also
Reclamation of land—Libya

Economic conditions
Peanuts to prosperity. il Time 87:40 F 25 '66

History
Libya. R. S. Harrison. bibliog il Focus 17:1-6 N '66

Industries
See also
Petroleum—Libya

LICENSE plates, Automobile. See Automobiles—License plates

LICENSES
See also
Air pilots—Licenses
Automobile drivers—Licenses

LICENSES, Radio operator. See Radio operators—Licenses

LIFE saving equipment
Lifesaving gear. J. A. Emmett. il Outdoor Life 137:126-9 My '66
Your spare tire can prevent a drowning. S. M. Gerard. il Read Digest 88:109-11 Je '66

See also
Parachutes
Rafts

LIFE support systems (space environment)
AF, AEC buying more study of long-mission isotope use. Tech W 19:24-5 Ag 8 '66
Air force funding GE tests of possible space lifeboat. H. M.. David. Miss & Roc 18:28 My 2 '66
Apollo lunar flight package readied. H. M. David. il Miss & Roc 18:24-6 My 23 '66
Convair examines closed-loop prospects. il Tech W 19:39 Ag 15 '66
Cryogenic fuels keyed to water cycle; concerning lunar water supply. W. S. Beller. il Tech W 19:28-9 Ag 29 '66
Electrolytic reduction of CO_2 promising; changing carbon dioxide into breathable oxygen and carbon powder. Tech W 19:45 D 5 '66
ECS elements for LEM nearing delivery. R. D. Hibben. il Aviation W 84:76-7+ My 30 '66
Gemini 9A brings scrutiny for personal equipment, workloads; program of testing extravehicular activity flight equipment. E. J. Bulban. Aviation W 84:37 Je 13 '66
GE facility to study zero-G performance. K. Voss. il Tech W 20:17 Ja 2 '67
Hybrid maneuvering unit design progresses; dual maneuvering unit. H. M. David. il Tech W 19:36-7 O 17 '66
NASA gets full-size moon-balloon shelter; stay time extension module. il(p 193) Sci N 89:194 Mr 26 '66
NASA seeks breakthrough in oxygen recovery systems. H. M. David. Miss & Roc 18:29 Ap 4 '66
Soviets predict spaceflight maturation. H. M. David. Miss & Roc 18:39+ Ap 25 '66
Special report on space bio-science; with editorial comment. D. E. Fink. il Aviation W 85:21, 54-65+ Ag 15 '66
Stabilize men in space; astronaut maneuvering unit. Sci N L 89:52 Ja 22 '66
USSR may aim to settle and farm moon. H. M. David. Tech W 20:18-19 Ja 2 '67
Waste treatment plant to improve system. H. M. David. il Tech W 20:28 Ja 9 '67
See also
Space vehicles—Cabin atmospheres

LIFEBOATS, Motor
Unsinkable, high-powered rescue; coast guard's latest 44-foot motor lifeboat. il Pop Mech 125:146-7 Mr '66

LIFEGUARDS
Awesome Aussie plunge! Burleigh heads lifesaving club initiation. il Travel 126:59-63 N '66
Through the green lenses. J. Carlisle. il Seventeen 25:106-7+ Je '66

LIFETIME sports foundation
Lifetime sports grant to NRPA. il Parks & Rec 1:493 Je; 627-8 Ag '66
Lifetime sports project kickoffs. il Parks & Rec 1:627-8 Ag '66
100-plus comes of age; nonprofit children's bowling program. il Parks & Rec 1:557 Jl '66
Quality of fitness; excerpt from address. C. B. Wilkinson. Parks & Rec 1:149-50 F '66

LIFT-fan engines. See Gas turbines, Aircraft
LIFT locks. See Locks (hydraulic engineering)
LIFTING. See Weight lifting
LIFTING systems. See Materials handling
LIGAND-exchange chromatography. See Chromatographic analysis
LIGHT, Goddard
Truth about bookselling; review. Pub W 189: 68-9 Je 27 '66

LIGHT
See also
Photography—Light
Polarization (light)

Physiological effects
Activity rhythms and adiurnal light-dark control. M. L. R. Goff and F. W. Finger. bibliog il Science 154:1346-9 D 9 '66
Light-induced changes in pineal hydroxyindole-O-methyltransferase: abolition by lateral hypothalamic lesions. J. Axelrod and others. bibliog il Science 154:898-9 N 18 '66
Light-stimulated electrical responses from skin. H. E. Becker and R. A. Cone. bibliog il Science 154:1051-3 N 25 '66

Open-field behavior in mice: evidence for a major gene effect mediated by the visual system. J. C. DeFries and others. bibliog il Science 154:1577-9 D 23 '66
Reproduction in lizards: influence of temperature on photoperiodism in testicular recrudescence. P. Licht. bibliog il Science 154: 1668-70 D 30 '66
See also
Plants, Effect of light on

Velocity
Is the speed of light ultimate? I. Asimov. il Sci Digest 60:87-8 D '66

LIGHT airplanes. See Airplanes, Light
LIGHT amplification by stimulated emission of radiation. See Lasers
LIGHT amplifiers. See Lasers
LIGHT bulbs. See Electric lamps
LIGHT communication systems
Laser potential in deep-space link grows. B. Miller. il Aviation W 84:71+ Ja 31 '66
LIGHT filters
Color exposure guaranteed! D. B. Eisendrath, jr. Pop Phot 59:122-3+ N '66
Filters: how to get the most out of the basic ten. N. Rothschild. il Pop Phot 59: 76-9+ S '66
Keppler on the SLR. H. Keppler. Mod Phot 30:18 My '66
New crazy-color reconnaissance system spies out the secrets of a beachfront. il Life 61: 110-11 D 23 '66
Two heads are better than one, when one is the Omega variable-contrast head. B. Hoffman. il Pop Phot 59:112-13 D '66
LIGHT meters. See Exposure meters; Photometers
LIGHT projection
Community effort lights and athletic field: Del Oro high school athletic field at Loomis, Calif. il Am City 81:132 F '66
Test planned for battlefield illuminator; airborne device to light area of two square miles. M. L. Yaffee. il Aviation W 85:65+ N 7 '66
LIGHT sensitization
Photosensitizing compounds in extracts of drinking water. S. S. Epstein and F. B. Taylor. bibliog il Science 154:261-3 O 14 '66

LIGHTERS, Cigarette. See Cigarette lighters
LIGHTFOOT, Robert M. jr
Bradley builds an addition. Library J 91:5895-6 D 1 '66
LIGHTHILL, Michael James
Science center in Siberia. V. K. McElheny. Science 152:1047 My 20 '66
LIGHTHOUSES
Lighthouse knee deep in sea. il Sci N 90: 278+ O 8 '66
Lighthouses. B. Finnegan. il Hobbies 71:118-19 Ja '67
LIGHTING
Johnson residence, Old Lyme, Connecticut. il Arch Rec 139:106-9 mid-My '66
Man of many lights; E. Price. il Fortune 73:170+ Ap '66
See also
Candles
Electric lighting
Opera—Stage lighting
LIGHTING, Christmas. See Christmas decorations, Outdoor
LIGHTING, Outdoor
New form of night lighting for a party in the dark. il House & Gard 130:120-3 Ag '66
New lights refresh their entry. il Sunset 136:147-8 Ap '66
Outdoor lighting. See issues of American city
Sports under lights; address, March 1965. R. E. Faucett. il Parks & Rec 1:726-7+ S '66
See also
Campus lighting
Electricity on the farm
Light projection
also subhead Lighting under various subjects, e.g. Golf courses—Lighting
LIGHTING, Underwater
Leakproofing a pool light. il Sunset 137:124+ O '66
LIGHTING fixtures
Approach to residential lighting. D. A. Mintz. il Arch Rec 139:7+ mid-My '66
Easy living means easy seeing. il House & Gard 131:110-11 Ja '67
Garden lighting that's simple and safe. il Sunset 137:54-7 Jl '66
Hanging lamps. J. Mebane. il Bet Hom & Gard 44:36-7 Je '66

LIGHTING fixtures—*Continued*
Lights from pots. il Bet Hom & Gard 44:139
My '66
Newly designed electrical fixtures have neat,
compact appearance. il Arch Rec 139:207 My
'66
Twenty-five marvelous ideas for Sunday art-
ists, over half our panel, and collectors al-
most everyone. il House & Gard 130:98-101
Jl '66
Twenty-three ways to improve your home
lighting. C. P. Gilmore. il Pop Sci 189:
172-7 S '66
See also
Chandeliers
Spotlights
LIGHTING laboratories. See Testing labora-
tories
LIGHTING panels. See Paneling
LIGHTNING
High-speed, time-resolved spectrum of a
lightning stroke. R. E. Orville. bibliog il
Science 151:451 Ja 28 '66
Lightning as a sculptor of life; E. V. Koma-
rek's and other theories on value of con-
trolled fires. J. Lear. il Sat R 49:57-62 Je 4
'66
Lightning greater hazard than believed. il
(p341) Sci N 90:351 O 29 '66
Lightning seen cause of puzzling chondrules.
Sci N 90:39 Jl 16 '66
Lightning stroke measured. Sci N 90:272 O 8
'66
Many UFOs are identified as plasmas. P. J.
Klass. il Aviation W 85:54-5+ O 3 '66
Nature note. Sci N 90:27 Jl 9 '66
Plasma theory may explain many UFOs;
special form of ball lightning. P. J. Klass.
il Aviation W 85:48-50+ Ag 22 '66; Dis-
cussion. 85:130 O 10 '66
Scientific explanation for the UFOs? J. Lear.
il Sat R 49:67-9 O 1 '66
Truly remarkable fly; ball lightning; letter.
F. B. Mohr. Science 151:634+ F 11 '66
U.F.O.'s or kugelblitz? il Pop Electr 25:84
S '66
What to do when lightning strikes. G. R.
Von Kronenberger. Read Digest 89:169-70+
S '66
LIGHTNING bugs. See Fireflies
LIGHTNING conductors
Plan now for adequate lightning protection.
il Suc Farm 64:27 Ap '66
LIGHTNING protection
What to do when lightning strikes. G. R. Von
Kronenberger. Read Digest 89:169-70+ S '66
LIGHTNING rods. See Lightning conductors
LIGHTS, Traffic. See Traffic signals
LIGHTSHIPS
Lighthouse knee deep in sea. il Sci N 90:278+
O 8 '66
LIKENS, G. E. and Johnson, P. L.
Chemically stratified lake in Alaska. bib-
liog Science 153:875-7 Ag 19 '66
LIKENS, Sylvia Marie
Addenda to De Sade. il por Time 87:25 My 6
'66
Avenging Sylvia. Time 87:22-3 My 27 '66
LILES, Margaret
Pony with a safety message. C. S. Karch.
il Todays Health 44:5+ My '66
LILEY, Margaret, and Day, Beth
Fascinating story of life before birth. Par-
ents Mag 41:62-3+ O '66
Newborn baby; excerpt from The infant
world. McCalls 93:26+ Ag '66; Same abr.
with title Wondrous world of the newborn.
Read Digest 89:193-4+ N '66
LILIENFIELD, Lawrence S.
Medical bootstrap in Saigon. Sci N 90:451
N 26 '66
LILIENTHAL, David Eli
From Capitol hill to capital gains. R. D.
Heffner. Sat R 50:84+ Ja 14 '67
Venturesome years. S. Maloff. por Newsweek
68:120+ O 24 '66
LILIES
Easy to grow lilies. H. V. Wilson. il Flower
Grower 53:26-7 Ag '66
Lilies for all summer. V. Howie. il Horti-
culture 44:24-5+ F '66
See also
Day-lilies
LILJE, Hanns, bp
Bishop Hanns Lilje in Denver. R. Spargur.
Christian Cent 83:1129-30 S 14 '66
LILLARD, Richard G.
Deserts in the sea. Nation 202:268-70 Mr 7 '66
LILLE, France
Return of the native. il Time 87:30 My 6 '66
LILLYWHITE, Ray L. and Ware, M. L.
Retirement benefits and teacher mobility.
NEA J 55:15-16 Ap '66
LIMA, Luis Augusto Turcios. See Turcios
Lima, L. A.

LIMA, Ohio
Street traffic
Meters came back. il Am City 81:120 Jl '66
LIMA, Peru
City planning
Streetcar named desire; demolition of prosti-
tutes shacks. Newsweek 67:60 My 2 '66
Description
Leap to Lima. M. M. Davis. il Travel 125:48-9
F '66
LIMBACHER, James L.
8mm revolution. Library J 91:6162-3 D 15 '66
On the record; Words (cont of) Recorded
word. See issues of Library journal
Recorded word. See second issue of each
month of Library journal
(ed) Records for young people (cont) Li-
brary J 91:1596-8 Mr 15 '66
(ed) Recordings for young people (cont)
Library J 91:5139-41 O 15 '66
LIMITATION of actions
Criminal state and German responsibility: a
dialogue; tr. by W. J. Dannhauser. K.
Jaspers; R. Augstein. Commentary 41:33-9
F '66
LIMITED war. See War
LIMNOLOGY
Chemically stratified lake in Alaska; Pingo
Lake. C. E. Likens and P. L. Johnson.
bibliog il Science 153:875-7 Ag 19 '66
LIMNORIA. See Isopoda
LIMULUS polyphemus. See King crabs
LIN, E. C. C. See Zwaig, N. jt. auth.
LIN, Piao
Lin Piao on the people's war; excerpts from
article. Cur Hist 51:172-4+ S '66
Red China's plan to conquer the world;
excerpts from document. Nations Bsns 54:
40-1 Ja '66
about
Back to the cave! il por Time 88:28-32 S 9
'66; Same abr. with title Red guard:
nightmare in the streets. Read Digest 89:
196+ D '66
Dear comrade. il por Time 88:16 Ag 26 '66
From a single spark. por Newsweek 67:46 Je
27 '66
How to succeed in China by really trying.
por Newsweek 68:33 S 5 '66
Lin Piao on deck. Nat R 18:868-9 S 6 '66
Long live Chairman Mao! long live Lin Piao!
S. Topping. il pors N Y Times Mag p 18-
19+ Jl 17 '66
Man alongside Mao. E. Snow. New Repub
155:15-18 D 3 '66
Mao's closest comrade: Lin. il por News-
week 68:26+ Ag 29 '66
Mystery of red China: a real blowup coming?
il por U S News 62:46-8 Ja 23 '67
Red army boss Lin Piao: is he Mao's real
heir? il por U S News 61:16 Ag 29 '66
LIN, Teh-ping
Microinjection of mouse eggs. bibliog Science
151:333-7 Ja 21 '66
LINARIA cymbalaria. See Kenilworth ivy
LINCEAN academy. See Scientific societies—
History
LINCIR, Rosalie
Dancer's character. Dance Mag 40:88-9 O '66
LINCOLN, Abraham
House divides, by P. I. Wellman. Review
Sat R por 49:37 F 12 '66. H. Hansen
Lincoln papers in the Stern bequest; reprint.
J. M. Edelstein. Hobbies 70:110-12 F; 71:
106-7+ Mr '66
One hundred years ago. R. L. Strout. New
Repub 154:17-18 F 12 '66
There I grew up. W. E. Wilson. il Am
Heritage 17:30-1+ O '66
Two about Lincoln. P. Simon. Christian Cent
83:176 F 9 '66
Assassination
End of a manhunt; excerpt from lecture, ed.
by B. Fleet. R. B. Garrett. il Am Heritage
17:40-3+ Je '66
Other plot to kill Lincoln. A. Hynd. il por
Read Digest 88:92-7 F '66
Bibliography
Lincolniana in 1965; the Civil war centen-
nial. B. E. Wheeler. il Hobbies 70:28-9+
F '66
Drama
Link with Lincoln. H. L. Miller. Plays 25:
1-14 F '66
Time for purpose. M. Rawe. Plays 25:27-38
F '66

LINDSAY, F. K.
How soft is soft water? Am City 81:148+ Je '66

LINDSAY, H. A. and Kullman, V. S.
Pentobarbital sodium: variation in toxicity. bibliog Science 151:576-7 F 4 '66

LINDSAY, John Vliet
Beginning. F. R. Weissberg. New Yorker 42:22-3 Ag 13 '66
Deeper troubles for a top Republican. il por U S News 60:20 Je 20 '66
Dinner for none, please John; or How you could have treated King Faisal. G. Ace. Sat R 49:10 Jl 16 '66
Election night. New Yorker 42:50-1 N 19 '66
Fun city: life with Lindsay. il pors Newsweek 68:33-4 D 12 '66
Get the image? Nat R 18:104 F 8 '66
Gladiator of the East. T. Wicker. Atlan 217:77-8 Ap '66
Governing the ungovernable. il por Time 88:30-1 D 16 '66
Great mayor, that bum? R. Reeves. il pors N Y Times Mag p6-7+ Ja 1 '67
Hearing. New Yorker 42:40-1 My 7 '66
Innocent bystander. R. Moley. Newsweek 67:104 Ap 4 '66
Is New York's new mayor solving the city's problems? il por U S News 61:66-8 Ag 15 '66
Lindsay, Quill & the transit strike. T. R. Brooks. Commentary 41:50-7 Mr '66
Lindsay, the first six months. W. V. Shannon. New Repub 155:16-19 Jl 16 '66
Look of '72? por Time 88:31 O 21 '66
Mayor for the times. E. J. Hughes. por Newsweek 68:32-3 O 3 '66
Mayor on Vietnam. Nat R 18:1254+ D 13 '66
New boy survives a hazing. J. K. Jessup. Life 60:17 Ja 28 '66
No honeymoon. il por Time 87:29B Mr 18 '66
Notes and comment; prevention of possible riot July 23 in East New York. New Yorker 42:17-18 Ag 6 '66
Painful step toward solvency. il por Time 87:29 Je 24 '66
Politics and police. R. Moley. Newsweek 67:104 Mr 7 '66
Pow! zonk! blam! il pors Newsweek 67:23 Ja 31 '66
Sixteen-hour day with his honor. T. Meehan. il pors N Y Times Mag p6-7+ Jl 3 '66
That tired feeling. por Newsweek 67:29 Mr 14 '66
This Lindsay takes on that city. R. J. Whalen. il pors Fortune 73:126-9+ Je '66
Underdeveloped Manhattan. Nat R 18:970-1 O 4 '66
Unmaking of a mayor, by W. F. Buckley, jr. Review
Nat R 18:1171-4 N 15 '66. C. B. Luce

LINDSAY, LeRoy R.
Letter from the fringe, the nonpastoral ministry. Christian Cent 83:1075-7 S 7 '66

LINDSAY, Mary (Harrison)
Mayor's mansion; interview. New Yorker 42:47-8 O 15 '66

LINDSAY, Robert, and Nixon, R. B.
Two decades in the world of the mass media. UNESCO Courier 19:36-9 Jl '66

LINDSAY, Vachel
Vachel Lindsay's lost weekend in Urbana. M. M. Marberry. por Horizon 9:112-15 Wint '67

LINDSEY, David A.
Sediment transport in a Precambrian ice age: the Huronian Gowganda formation. bibliog Science 154:1142-3 D 16 '66

LINDSEY, Dorothea M.
MUST: project for urban service. Christian Cent 83:1041-2 Ag 24 '66

LINDSEY, Robert
Aircraft video system allows radar intercept ground replay. Tech W 19:45+ S 19 '66
LMSC foresees steady Agena demand. Tech W 19:29 S 5 '66
LMSC plans to use Gemini spray process in architecture. Tech W 19:30+ S 12 '66
Materials refinement assists Poseidon launcher designers. Tech W 18:32-3 Je 13 '66
New TVC development uses free air. Miss & Roc 18:35-6 Mr 14 '66
No static firing scheduled for Gemini 8 Agena target. Miss & Roc 18:31-2 Ja 24 '66
Similarity to space beckons scientists. Tech W 19:34+ D 5 '66
Tactical Polaris proposed for Vietnam. Tech W 19:31-2 Jl 4 '66

LINDSLEY, E. F.
How to buy a paint sprayer and make it pay. Pop Sci 189:160-3 S '66

LINDSTROM, Thais S.
Time passing, man enduring. Sat R 49:49-50 F 19 '66

LINDY, Seppo, and Rajasalmi, Matti
Lactate dehydrogenase isozymes of chick embryo: response to variations of ambient oxygen tension. bibliog Science 153:1401-3 S 16 '66

LINE, Les
First lady of agriculture visits an Audubon center; picture story. Audubon Mag 68:347-50 S '66
Fruits of autumn. il Audubon Mag 68:328-9 S '66

LINEAR accelerators. See Accelerators (electrons, etc)

LINEAR programming
Applied math for the production manager. C. H. Jones. Harvard Bsns R 44:20-2+ bibliog(p 182) S '66
Lifting the haze from the future; Clopper Almon's input-output models. il Bsns W p 100-2 D 17 '66
Marketers meet input-output; Pittsburgh executives hear Commerce dept.'s exposition of business applications of input-output technique. il Bsns W p 146-8 O 29 '66

LINEAWEAVER, Marion
Things that were still alive; poem. Atlan 218:60 Ag '66
Two ways of dying; poem. Harper 232:79 Je '66

LINEAWEAVER, Thomas H. 3d
Huzza porpoise. Holiday 40:20+ Jl '66

LINERS. See Ocean liners

LINFORD, Ernest
BLM gets third director in five years; editorial. por Am For 72:13 S '66

LING, James Joseph
Jimmy Ling's wonderful growth machine. S. H. Brown. il por Fortune 75:136-8+ Ja '67
Swinging Ling. por Newsweek 69:78-80 Ja 23 '67

LING-Temco-Vought, Incorporated
Jimmy Ling's wonderful growth machine. S. H. Brown. il Fortune 75:136-8+ Ja '67
Swinging Ling; acquisition of Wilson & co. Newsweek 69:78-80 Ja 23 '67

LINGEMAN, Richard R.
Big, happy, beating heart of the Detroit sound. N Y Times Mag p48-9+ N 27 '66
Offerings at the psychedelicatessen. N Y Times Mag p6-7+ Jl 10 '66
Visit with Mary Poppins and P. L. Travers. N Y Times Mag p 12-13+ D 25 '66

LINGERIE. See Underwear

LINGG, Ann M.
New York's brand-new opera house. Read Digest 89:19-20+ S '66
Port of call. Opera N 30:26-7 Ap 16 '66
Singer vs. public. Opera N 31:6-7 Ja 14 '67
Strauss vs. Wagner. Opera N 31:6 D 10 '66

LINK with Lincoln: drama. See Miller, H. L.

LINKE, Richard O.
Jes' rich folks. il por Newsweek 68:94 O 17 '66

LINKLETTER, Art
He likes to cook! with recipes. il Bet Hom & Gard 44:70-1+ Ap '66

LINN, Edward
F. Lee Bailey: renegade in the courtroom. Sat Eve Post 239:80-2+ N 5 '66
Thinking man's Cowboy. Sat Eve Post 239:76-8+ D 17 '66
World's finest miler? Sat Eve Post 239:90+ Ap 23 '66
(ed) See Koufax, S. Sandy Koufax story: my battle with arthritis
(ed) See Koufax, S. Sandy Koufax story: my salary fights
(ed) See Koufax, S. Sandy Koufax story: what baseball means to me

LINN, Karl
Environmental art. Sch Arts 66:26-8 D '66

LINOLEUM block prints
Linoleum blocks. J. L. Dorsey. Design 68:4-6+ S '66

LINOWITZ, Sol Myron
Public affairs; address, April 21, 1966. Vital Speeches 32:477-80 My 15 '66

about

Ambassador Linowitz. por Américas 18:41 D '66
Anti-intellectualism in the government. W. W. Brickman. Sch & Soc 94:437 D 10 '66
Busiest copycat of them all. J. Howard. il pors Life 61:69-70+ Jl 1 '66
Man from Xerox multiplies his roles. M. Mayer. il pors N Y Times Mag p44-5+ Ap 24 '66
New boy at State. il por Newsweek 69:53-4 Ja 16 '67
Old pros. por Time 88:34 O 14 '66

LINTON, David
  Grazing mollusks in the weeds. Natur Hist 75:58-61 Mr '66
  Nature and the camera. Natur Hist 75:66-7 Je '66
  What every photographer should know about insurance. Pop Phot 58:63+ Ap '66

LION; story. See Zamyatin, Y.

LION cubs. See Lions

LION hunting
  My greatest trophy. F. Bear. il Outdoor Life 137:36-9+ Ap '66
    See also
  Puma hunting

LION in winter; drama. See Goldman, J.

LION press
  Lion press: new children's book firm. Pub W 190:198-9 Jl 11 '66

LION rock, Ceylon. See Sigiriya, Ceylon

LIONEL, Daniel L.
  Are prospects people? Sat R 49:64+ My 14 '66

LIONNI, Leo
  Mrs Sanborn, I love you. Pub W 189:134-5 Jl 11 '66

LIONS
  All in a dog's life; dachshund and motherless lion cub. il Look 31:M8 Ja 24 '67
  The lion; with report by G. B. Schaller. il Life 62:44-58+ Ja 20 '67
  Lions loose on a lonely road; fate of lions after highway accident in France. il Life 61:99-100 O 28 '66

    Photographs
    See Animals—Photographs

LIONS in moving pictures. See Animals in moving pictures

LIP make-up. See Make-up

LIPATTI, Dinu
  Brief candles. H. Goldsmith. por Hi Fi 16:53-4 F '66

LIPCHITZ, Jacques
  Man always wins; statue of Pegasus and Bellerophon to top New York's Columbia university school of law. il por Newsweek 68:82-3 S 5 '66

LIPE, William N. and Crane, J. C.
  Dormancy regulation in peach seeds. bibliog Science 153:541-2 Jl 29 '66

LIPETZ, Ben-Ami
  Information storage and retrieval; with biographical sketch. Sci Am 215:51, 224-8+ S '66

LIPID film transducers. See Transducers

LIPIDES
  Action of anionic and cationic nerve-blocking agents: experiment and interpretation. M. P. Blaustein and D. E. Goldman. bibliog il Science 153:429-32 Jl 22 '66
  Composition of combustible concretions of the alewife, alosa pseudoharengus. E. Sondheimer and others. bibliog il Science 152:221-3 Ap 8 '66
  Drugs affecting lipid metabolism; report on second international symposium. D. Kritchevsky. Science 151:1016-17 F 25 '66
  Ethylene formation in rat liver microsomes. M. Lieberman and P. Hochstein. bibliog il Science 152:213-14 Ap 8 '66
  Lipids of the living coelacanth, latimeria chalumnae. J. C. Nevenzel and others. bibliog il Science 152:1753-5 Je 24 '66
  Phospholipids of bacteria with extensive intracytoplasmic membranes. P. O. Hagen and others. bibliog il Science 151:1543-4 Mr 25 '66
  Seed lipids. I. A. Wolff. bibliog il Science 154:1140-9 D 2 '66

LIPOCHONDRODYSTROPHY
  Vitamin C-induced increase of dermatan sulfate in cultured Hurler's fibroblasts. I. A. Schafer and others. bibliog il Science 153:1008-10 Ag 26 '66

LIPOPROTEINS
  Lipoprotein patterns in acrylamide gel electrophoresis. S. Raymond and others. bibliog il Science 151:346-7 Ja 21 '66
  Serum high-density lipoprotein: effect of change in structure on activity of chicken adipose tissue lipase. A. Scanu. bibliog il Science 153:640-1 Ag 5 '66

LIPP, Solomon
  Books. Américas 18:40-2 N '66

LIPPARD, Lucy R.
  (ed) Questions to Stella and Judd; interview. Art N 65:55-61 S '66

LIPPINCOTT and Margulies, incorporated
  Fine art of namesmanship. R. Levy. il Duns R 87:51-2 Ap '66

LIPPMANN, Walter
  [Current events column] See issues of Newsweek
  University; excerpt from address, May 1966. New Repub 154:17-20 My 28 '66
    about
  Farewell to Washington. Time 89:36 Ja 6 '67
  Isolationism confirmed. Time 88:95 N 25 '66

LIPSCHUTZ, M. E. and Jaeger, R. R.
  X-ray diffraction study of minerals from shocked iron meteorites. bibliog Science 152:1055-7 My 20 '66

LIPSCOMB, Charles T. Jr
  Advertising; address, November 4, 1966. Vital Speeches 33:145-8 D 15 '66

LIPSCOMB, William N.
  Framework rearrangement in boranes and carboranes. bibliog Science 153:373-8 Jl 22 '66

LIPSKY, Yuri N.
  What Luna 9 told us about the moon; tr. by A. Boyko. Sky & Tel 32:257-60 N '66

LIPTON, Leonard
  Movie report. Pop Phot 58:127 Mr '66
  My son, the film maker. Pop Phot 58:128-9 Ap '66

LIPTON, Sir Thomas Johnstone, bart
  Wanted: wholesome boats for the America's cup; reprint. por Yachting 120:43+ D '66

LIQUEFIED natural gas. See Gas, Natural—Liquefaction

LIQUEFIED petroleum gas
  Use LP gas and save; Orlando, Fla. J. E. Pipkin. il Am City 81:88-9 Je '66
    See also
  Gas, Natural—Liquefaction

LIQUEURS
  Spirits to eat with a spoon; recipes. il Vogue 148:146 D '66
  Wine, women & so on. P. Cannon. Ladies Home J 83:122 Ap '66
    See also
  Cookery—Liquors

LIQUID chlorine. See Chlorine, Liquid

LIQUID fuel
    See also
  Coal liquefaction

LIQUID hydrogen. See Hydrogen, Liquid

LIQUID level control
  Cryogenic liquid level controls. W. W. Schopp. il Electr World 76:36-8+ D '66

LIQUID methane. See Methane

LIQUID neoprene. See Rubber, Artificial

LIQUID nitrogen. See Nitrogen, Liquid

LIQUID propellant rockets
  Aerospike liquid rocket nozzle detailed. J. F. Judge. il Tech W 19:26+ D 5 '66
  Flight of Saturn IB will test J-2 engine. I. Stone. il Aviation W 84:53+ F 14 '66
  M-1 engine demonstrated; liquid hydrogen-liquid oxygen engine. il Aviation W 85:79+ O 10 '66
  Rocketdyne unveils new rocket engine; versatile and compact Aerospike. M. L. Yaffee. Aviation W 85:24-5 D 5 '66

    Testing
  Aerojet ending final tests of M-1 engine components. il Tech W 19:28 S 5 '66

LIQUIDITY (economics)
  Crus of the matter; plan to establish collective reserve unit. il Time 87:101 F 4 '66

LIQUOR habit. See Alcoholism

LIQUOR industry
  Liquorville; Impact, inc; Impact, Tex. il Newsweek 67:77 F 14 '66
  Making much of a mess; Ricard inc, France. il Time 87:98 F 25 '66
  Young market boosts light-spirited drinks. il Bsns W p84-5 F 19 '66
    See also
  Seagram, Joseph E, and sons

    Advertising
  Big pitch in Life. Christian Cent 84:5 Ja 4 '67

LIQUOR laws and regulations

    Australia
  10 o'clock swill; curfew extended in Melbourne. Time 87:30 F 11 '66

    Southern states
  Dry to the last drop. Time 88:40 Jl 1 '66
  Wets on the rocks. Newsweek 67:26+ Ap 25 '66

LIQUOR problem
  Teen-age drinking and drug addiction. J. H. Pollack. il NEA J 55:8-12 My '66
    See also
  Alcoholism

LIQUOR problem—*Continued*

Finland

Case for genetic drinking. P. McBroom. Sci N 90:543 D 24 '66

Russia

Russian view of drinking changes. Sci N 89:275 Ap 16 '66

United States

Drinking approved at Stanford. Sch & Soc 94:340-2 29 '66

Teenagers and alcohol; too explosive a mixture? Sr Schol 89:13-14 S 16 '66; Discussion. 89:14-16+ N 4 '66

LIQUOR traffic

United States

Tight little island; demise of prohibition in Mississippi. Newsweek 68:33-4 S 19 '66

See also

Moonshining

Prohibition—United States

LIQUORS

Aspirin, liquor and LSD. H. Downs. Sci Digest 61:91-3 Ja '67

Drinks on a grand scale; dispensers and coolers for drinks. il House & Gard 129:218-19 Ap '66

Manner of speaking; calories in liquors. J. Ciardi. Sat R 49:24 S 10; 18+ O 1; 19 O 22 '66

Mead. M. Sharp. il Atlan 218:116 S '66

Percipient aperitifs; kinetic cordials. il Esquire 65:80-1 Mr '66

Traveler's guide to native drinks in Germany and Switzerland. N. S. Hazelton. il House & Gard 129:174+ Mr '66

What's in. Time 88:87 O 14 '66

See also

Liqueurs

Whiskey

Analysis

It's the poison; effects of congeners in liquor. D. Valentry. Sci Digest 60:66-8 D '66

LIRA. See Money—Italy

LISAGOR, Peter

Trends: Washington mood. See issues of Nation's business

LISBON, Portugal

Galleries and museums

New museum of tiles in Lisbon; Museu do azulejo. R. C. Smith. il Antiques 89:828-33 Je '66

Music

Great opera houses: Lisbon; Teatro nacional de São Carlos. F. Teixeira Direito. il Opera N 31:26-9 Ja 14 '67

Lisbon. F. Teixeira Direito. il Opera N 30:31 Mr 5; 32 Mr 26; 32 Ap 16 '66

LISCANO, Juan

Diary of Venezuelan literature. Américas 18:6-11 My '66

LISE LOTTE

America cottons to Lise Lotte. il pors Life 60:53-4 Ap 1 '66

LISK, Donald J.

Detection and measurement of pesticide residues. bibliog Science 154:93-8 O 7 '66

LISK, Robert D.

Inhibitory centers in sexual behavior in the male rat. bibliog Science 152:669-70; 153:770 Ap 29, Ag 12 '66

LISTENING. See Attention

LISTENING devices, Electronic. See Electronics in criminal investigation, espionage, etc.

LISTER, Richard Percival

Prestige. Atlan 218:125-6 Jl '66

LISTERINE. See Mouthwashes

LISTON, James M.

Little tractor that can. Pop Gard 17:50-3+ D '66

Why you should want a yard-care rider. Pop Sci 188:122-7 My '66

LISZT, Franz

At last, The years of pilgrimage on Odeon. R. Kammerer. Am Rec G 32:1138 Ag '66

Records. Opera N 31:30 N 19 '66

LIT, Theodore

(ed) Four against the red China lobby. Nat R 18:513-28 My 31 '66

LITCHFIELD, Edward Harold

Pittsburgh: the rocky road to academic excellence. D. S. Greenberg. il pors Science 151:549-52, 658-62, 799-801 F 4-18 '66

LITCHFIELD COUNTY choral union. See Music festivals—Connecticut

LITCHIS

See also

Cookery—Fruit

LITERACY. See Illiteracy

LITERARY ability. See Creation (literary, artistic, etc)

LITERARY agents

Literary agent: his function, life, and power. P. R. Reynolds. il Sat R 49:113-14 O 8 '66

New role for French literary agents? H. R. Lottman. Pub W 190:27-9 Ag 1 '66

LITERARY and scientific exchanges. See Exchanges, Literary and scientific

LITERARY blunders. See Blunders

LITERARY censorship. See Censorship

LITERARY characters. See Characters in literature

LITERARY clubs

See also

PEN club

LITERARY contests. See Literature—Competitions

LITERARY correspondence. See Letters

LITERARY criticism

Bit between my teeth, by E. Wilson. Review New Repub 155:23-8 Jl 2 '66. R. Gilman; Reply. H. A. Perluck. 155:35-7 Ag 13 '66

Dying breed: Arthur Sturbridge speaks out, by S. Quarles. Review Atlan 217:141-2 Mr '66. P. Davison

Modern movement, by C. Connolly. Review Atlan 218:76-9 Jl '66. L. Kronenberger

Standards, by S. E. Hyman. Review Commentary 42:72-3 Jl '66. J. W. Aldridge

To criticize the critic and other writings, by T. S. Eliot. Review Commentary 42:87-91 S '66. J. Frank Nation 203:324-5 O 3 '66. F. J. Hoffman

See also

Book reviews

Critics

Literature—Appreciation and interpretation

LITERARY critics. See Critics

LITERARY fads. See Fads

LITERARY fantasies. See Fantasies, Literary

LITERARY forgeries and mystifications

North Koreans accused of forging Bibles; counterfeit issues of some 1000 publications. Pub W 189:103 F 14 '66

LITERARY form. See Style, Literary

LITERARY inspiration. See Inspiration

LITERARY landmarks

Victor Hugo, decorator; Guernsey house. E. Schlumberger. il Vogue 147:224-31+ My '66

Walt Whitman's home; West Hills, Huntington, L.I. il Travel 126:43-5 O '66

LITERARY periodicals. See Literature—Periodicals

LITERARY piracy. See Copyright—Unauthorized reprints

LITERARY prizes. See Rewards, prizes, etc.

LITERARY property. See Copyright; Property, Intellectual

LITERARY research

How to research articles by mail; facts to build magazine articles. M. Gunther. Writer 79:13-16 Ap '66

Study and teaching

Practical program in literary research. P. T. Nolan. Sr Schol 89:sup 16 O 14 '66

LITERARY style. See Style, Literary

LITERARY titles. See Titles of books, stories, etc.

LITERARY topics. See Literature—Themes

LITERATURE

Avant-garde and contemporary literature; excerpts from address, October 28, 1965. S. Sontag. il Wilson Lib Bul 40:930-2+ Je '66

Enemy is academe; summary of address. S. Bellow. il Pub W 190:34 Jl 18 '66

Your literary I.Q; ed. by J. T. Winterich and D. M. Glixon. See issues of Saturday review

See also

Authorship

Best sellers

Biography

Books and reading

Censorship

Fiction

Immoral literature and pictures

Letters

Modernism (literature)

Style, Literary

Translations and translating

War and literature

also literature of special subjects, e.g. Travel literature

LITERATURE—*Continued*

Appreciation and interpretation

Beyond culture, by L. Trilling. Review
    Commentary 41:87-93 Mr '66. D. Jacobson
Criterions for criticism. G. W. Allen. Sat R
    49:64+ Je 11 '66
Opinion: on reading fiction. O. Prescott. Mlle
    63:68+ S '66
Toppling the ivory tower. H. Gold. Holiday
    30:10+ My '66
    See also
Poetry—Appreciation

Collections

    See also
Anthologies

Competitions

English madness; Weekend literary compe-
    titions. P. Rowlett. Commonweal 84:475-6
    Jl 22 '66
First prizewinner in the Teachers' writing
    competition. il NEA J 55:12-14 O '66
Using students to evaluate manuscripts;
    Rosary H.S. Detroit. Sister Marie Virginia.
    Sr Schol 89:sup 18-19 O 14 '66

History

European literary scene; Gorki institute of
    world literature, Moscow embarks on a
    history of world literature. R. J. Clements.
    Sat R 49:31 F 26 '66
Great men, great events. UNESCO Courier
    19:30-1 Mr '66
Studies in medieval and renaissance litera-
    ture, by C. S. Lewis. Review
    Nat R 18:1332-3 D 27 '66. J. Lobdell

Moral and religious aspects

See Literature and morals

Periodicals

Literary newspapers and book reporting
    media in France. H. R. Lottman. Pub W
    189:51-3 My 23 '66

Philosophy

Nil, by R. M. Adams. Review
    Nation 204:26-7 Ja 2 '67. H. R. Wolf

Study and teaching

New records. M. Muri. Sr Schol 89:sup 17
    S 30 '66
Social studies and English combine in hu-
    manities approach; Gunn high school. Palo
    Alto, Calif. R. Goben. Sr Schol 88:sup8
    Ap 22 '66

Technique

    See also
Characterization
Fiction—Technique

Themes

Edwin Muir: the story and the fable. D.
    Hoffman. Yale R 55:403-26 Mr '66
I still love a parade. G. Jennings. Writer 79:
    15-17+ S '66
Lonesome boy theme; address, May 5, 1966.
    A. Bontemps. il Horn Bk 42:672-80 D '66
Malamud's 'heroes; fate of fixers. J. Baum-
    bach. Commonweal 85:97-9 O 28 '66
Pre-empted domain. R. Macauley. Sat R 49:
    20-1 Je 4 '66
Prejudice and hope. V. Peterson. Reporter
    35:34-6 Ag 11 '66
Prisoner of time; theme of The pawn-
    broker. R. A. Schroth. America 115:98 Jl
    23 '66
Search for the ideal absurdity. G. Hicks.
    Sat R 49:21-2 S 3 '66
Set in Africa. J. Arundel. il Horn Bk 42:
    548-52 O '66
Two anti-puritan Puritans: Bernard Shaw
    and D. H. Lawrence. D. J. Gordon. Yale
    R 56:76-90 O '66
Violence: a neglected mode of behavior. B.
    Bettelheim. bibliog f Ann Am Acad 364:
    50-9 Mr '66
Violence in American literature. D. B.
    Davis. Ann Am Acad 364:28-36 Mr '66
What's happening to fiction? O. Prescott.
    Sat R 49:21-2 N 26 '66
    See also
Christmas in literature
Haiti in literature
Love in literature
Negroes in literature
New York city in literature
Religion in literature
Sex in literature
Social problems in literature
War and literature

LITERATURE, Childrens. See Childrens lit-
    erature

LITERATURE, Comparative
Dostoevsky and romantic realism, by D.
    Fanger. Review
    Nation 203:164-5 Ag 22 '66. S. Karlinsky
There was something about the twenties.
    A. MacLeish. Sat R 49:10-13 D 31 '66
LITERATURE, Educational. See Educational
    literature
LITERATURE, Immoral. See Immoral litera-
    ture and pictures
LITERATURE, Influence of
Mood of the writer. J. Myrdal. Sat R 49:15-
    16+ Ag 13 '66
Storm over A cat called Jesus; one act play
    by G. T. Davis. A. B. Haines. Christian
    Cent 83:250-2 F 23 '66
Then he wrote a book; effect of Upton Sin-
    clair's The jungle. L. L. L. Golden. Sat
    R 49:103 N 12 '66
Who's to blame when a murderer strikes?
    with report by P. H. Johnson. il Life 61:
    60-2+ Ag 12 '66
    See also
Childrens literature, Influence of
LITERATURE, Theatrical. See Theatrical liter-
    ature
LITERATURE and art. See Art and literature
LITERATURE and communism. See Com-
    munism and literature
LITERATURE and morals
Pilgrim's progress. K. Rexroth. Sat R 49:20
    Ag 13 '66
LITERATURE and science
Science and literature; adaptation of address.
    E. Sewell. Commonweal 84:218-21 My 13
    '66; Discussion 84:448-9 Jl 8 '66
Science is where the action is. A. Rosenfeld.
    Life 61:16 Jl 29 '66
    See also
Science fiction
LITERATURE and social problems. See Social
    problems in literature
LITERATURE and society
Writer as independent spirit; questions to be
    explored at New York congress; symposium.
    il Sat R 49:16-30+ Je 4 '66
Writer as world citizen. N. Cousins. Sat R
    49:14+ Ag 13 '66
LITERATURE and war. See War and litera-
    ture
LITERATURE classification, Decimal. See
    Classification, Decimal
LITHIUM
Lithium's failure to replace sodium in mam-
    malian sympathetic ganglia. A. J. Pappano
    and R. L. Volle. bibliog il Science 152:85-7
    Ap 1 '66
LITHOGRAPHERS and photoengravers inter-
    national union
Several printing unions plan merger in 1967.
    Pub W 190:126 D 5 '66
Two printing unions holding merger talks.
    Pub W 189:132 Mr 7 '66
LITHOGRAPHIC technical foundation, incor-
    porated. See Graphic arts technical founda-
    tion
LITHOGRAPHS
Escher's eerie games. il Horizon 8:110-15
    Aut '66
Resurgence of Robert Riggs. H. C. Pitz. il
    Am Artist 30:50-5+ My '66
LITHOGRAPHY
Color lithographs of Richard Florsheim; with
    technical commentary by the artist. il Am
    Artist 30:25-30+ My '66
Litho platemakers meet, adopt trade customs.
    Pub W 190:123-4 D 5 '66
LITHOPS. See Flowering stones
LITTELL, Franklin H.
State of Iowa vs. the Amish. Christian Cent
    83:234-5 F 23 '66
LITTER. See Refuse and refuse disposal
LITTER baskets. See Refuse receptacles
LITTERBAGS. See Refuse receptacles
LITTLE, Floyd
Floyd Little: portrait of an All America.
    G. Astor. il pors Look 30:90-2+ N 1 '66
Half a glass of fresh blood on Saturday
    morning. M. Cope. il pors Sat Eve Post 239:
    84-6+ N 19 '66
LITTLE, Jean
People in books. Horn Bk 42:159-62 Ap '66
LITTLE, Malcolm. See Malcolm X
LITTLE affair in Paris; story. See Durrell, L.
LITTLE ark; story. See Vivante, A.
LITTLE BIG HORN, Battle of the, 1876
Bad day ahead for the army's greatest loser;
    Hardin, Mont, re-enactment of the battle.
    A. Chamberlin. il Sat Eve Post 239:70-3
    Ag 27 '66
Battle of the Little Big Horn, by M. Sandoz.
    Review
    America 115:73-4 Jl 16 '66. W. H. Russell
    Sat R 49:25+ My 21 '66. J. K. Hutchens

LITTLE BIG HORN, Battle of the 1876—*Cont.*
Grisly epilogue. M. Sandoz. Am Heritage 17:
73 Ap '66
Guns of the 7th cavalry. C. G. Worman. il
Hobbies 71:126-7 N '66
Last ghastly moments at the Little Bighorn;
ed. with introd. by M. Liberty. John Stands
in Timber. il Am Heritage 17:14-21+ Ap '66
LITTLE Christmas; story. See Fritz, J.
LITTLE dance group. See Dance companies
LITTLE leagues
Confessions of a Little league coach. J. G.
Hubbell. il Read Digest 88:157-60 My '66
LITTLE magazines. See Periodicals
LITTLE orchestra society, New York
Music and dance; Philharmonic Hall. M.
Marks. Dance Mag 41:62 Ja '67
Musical events; concert performance of
Janáček's Jenufa. W. Sargeant. New Yorker
42:131 N 12 '66
New York; performance of Janáček's Jenufa.
F. Merkling. Opera N 31:28 D 3 '66
LITTLE ROCK, Ark.

Lighting

Fewer lights, more illumination; War memorial field. J. Breckling. il Am City 81:121
D '66

Street traffic

Some remedies for traffic chaos. H. M.
de Noble. il Am City 81:106-8 D '66
LITTLE TENNESSEE RIVER
Sounds of a river. K. B. Hultquist. il Nat
Parks Mag 40:9-12 Ag '66
LITTLEJOHN, David
Immortal snob. Reporter 35:47-8 N 3 '66
LITTLER, Gene
Sorry about that. il por Time 88:80-1 S 23
'66
LITTLEWOOD, Tom
Trials of statehouse journalism. Sat R 49:82-3
D 10 '66
LITTON industries, Incorporated
Anatomy of an acquisition. J. B. Weiner.
Duns R 87:34+ My '66
How Litton keeps it up, the view from in-
side; interviews. ed. by D. Seligman and
T. A. Wise. H. Gray; R. Ash. il Fortune
74:152-4+ S '66
Litton, American book revise merger terms.
Pub W 190:45 N 21 '66
Litton to acquire American book company.
Pub W 190:37 Ag 8 '66
Management of Litton industries. J. B.
Weiner. il Duns R 87:32-3+ My '66
Opportunity list. Time 87:96 Ap 29 '66
Stock for all reasons. Newsweek 67:77 F 14
'66
Switching job refined at ETR by Westrex.
K. Voss. Tech W 19:33-4 O 10 '66
What puts the whiz in Litton's fast growth;
unique blend of finance and management. il
Bsns W p 174-6+ Ap 16 '66
LITURGICAL arts quarterly
Anniversary and a wedding. C. J. McNaspy.
America 115:234 S 3 '66
LITURGICAL arts society
See also
Liturgical arts quarterly
LITURGICAL drama. See Religious drama
LITURGICAL language
Call for a new translation. America 114:249
F 19 '66; Reply. M. M. Bourke. 114:399-
400 Mr 26 '66
Latin liturgy for seminaries? America 114:
470 Ap 9 '66
Living language for the liturgy; use of Eng-
lish in Catholic church. Christian Cent 83:
517 Ap 27 '66
Modern English in the mass. G. Edwards.
America 115:483-6 O 22 '66; Discussion. 115:
742-6 D 3 '66
LITURGICAL movement

Catholic church

Dull new day; reform is being limited to
externals. J. B. Mannion. Commonweal 84:
519-21 Ag 19 '66
Worship in the city of God. C. J. McNaspy.
America 115:176-7 Ag 20 '66

Protestant churches

Protestants and liturgy. M. E. Marty. Com-
monweal 84:522-4 Ag 19 '66
LITURGICAL music. See Church music
LITURGICAL week
Worship in the city of God. C. J. McNaspy.
America 115:176-7 Ag 20 '66

LITURGIES
Gospel is in the verb. P. Sanders. Christian
Cent 83:400 Mr 30 '66
See also
Catholic church—Liturgy and ritual
LITURGY, Catholic. See Catholic church—
Liturgy and ritual
LITVINOFF, Ivy
Sowing asphodel; story. New Yorker 42:50-6
Ap 23 '66
LITZ, A. Walton
Wallace Stevens: business and a sonnet.
Nation 204:85-7 Ja 16 '67
LITZ, Katherine
Katherine Litz; interview, ed. by O. May-
nard. pors Dance Mag 41:52-9 Ja '67 (to
be cont)
LIU, Jane Hu. See Nastuk, W. L. jt. auth.
LIU, Shao-chi
Dance of the scorpion. il por Time 89:20-3
Ja 13 '67
Numbers game, Chinese style. por Newsweek
69:28 Ja 9 '67
LIU, Tsing-keu
Shanghai's repentant capitalists. R. Guillain.
il Reporter 34:39-40 Ap 7 '66
LIUNI, Michael
Who is fair to Beth? il por Newsweek 68:
33-4 N 28 '66
LIUNI, Michael, family
Bringing up Beth. Newsweek 69:30 Ja 16 '67
LIVANT, Rose A.
Magic garden. Opera N 30:6-7 Ap 2 '66
LIVE-pigeon shooting. See Shooting
LIVER
Feedback inhibition of key glycolytic enzymes
in liver; action of free fatty acids. G.
Weber and others. bibliog il Science 154:
1357-60 D 9 '66
Hepatic synthesis of alpha$_2$ acute phase-
globulin of rat plasma. E. J. Sarcione and
A. E. Bogden. bibliog il Science 153:547-8
Jl 29 '66
Hexose-6-phosphate dehydrogenase found in
human liver. S. Ohno and others. bibliog
il Science 153:1015-16 Ag 26 '66
Nuclei from rat liver; isolation method that
combines purity with high yield. G. Blobel
and V. R. Potter. bibliog il Science 154:
1662-5 D 30 '66

Diseases

Color blindness genes not basis for cirrhosis.
Sci N 90:223 S 24 '66
Liquor vs. the liver. il Newsweek 69:48 Ja 9
'67
Peroxidation of liver lipids in the patho-
genesis of the ethanol-induced fatty liver.
G. H. Kalish and N. R. Di Luzio. bibliog
il Science 152:1390-2 Je 3 '66
Phosphorylase kinase of the liver; deficiency
in a girl with increased hepatic glycogen.
G. Hug and others. bibliog il Science 153:
1534-5 S 23 '66
See also
Hepatitis
LIVER as food
See also
Cookery—Meat
LIVER cancer. See Cancer
LIVER cells. See Cells
LIVER enzymes. See Enzymes
LIVESTOCK
News. See issues of Farm journal

Branding

Freeze-branding, slick way to mark livestock. G. Lorang. il Farm J 90:40H+ Ag
'66

Diseases and pests

Animal health guide; symposium. il Suc
Farm 64:51+ O '66
We must eradicate animal disease. O. L.
Freeman. Suc Farm 64:6+ O '66
See also
Cattle—Diseases and pests
Screwworms

Marketing

Livestock marketing. J. Harvey and D.
Malena. il Suc Farm 64:37-9 Jl '66

Prices

See also
Swine—Prices
LIVESTOCK, Cooling of
How to cool hogs indoors or outdoors. D.
Wolf. il Farm J 90:A4-5 Ag '66
See also
Swine, Effect of temperature on
LIVESTOCK, Weight and measurements of
See also
Cattle, Weight and measurements of

LIVING. See Conduct of life; Life

LIVING on the box; story. See Gilliatt, P.

LIVING rooms
In this new kitchen-family room, there's music, a warm fire, and bright carpet on the floor. il Sunset 136:124-5 My '66
It's the family studio. il Sunset 136:100-1 Ap '66
They remodeled for space and for spaciousness. il Sunset 136:138+ Ap '66
This garden room is the living end! il Bet Hom & Gard 44:58-9 Ag '66

LIVING rooms, Outdoor. See Outdoor rooms

LIVINGS, Henry
Eh? Criticism
Commonweal 85:229 N 25 '66
Life 61:17 Ag 12 '66
Nation 203:262 S 19 '66
Nation 203:494 N 7 '66
New Yorker 42:96+ O 29 '66
Newsweek 68:98 O 31 '66
Reporter 36:55 Ja 12 '67
Sat R 49:39 Ag 13 '66
Time 88:90 O 28 '66

LIVINGSTON, Dinah
Grow old along with me; story. Mlle 63:292-3 Ag '66

LIVINGSTON, Howard
My brother in Jerusalem; poem. Negro Hist Bul 29:31 Ja '66

LIVINGSTON, Norman S.
Inventor of the month. S. V. Jones. il por Sci Digest 60:11 Ag '66

LIVINGSTON, Samuel
What the teacher can do for the student with epilepsy. NEA J 55:24-6 N '66

LIVINGSTON, William C.
Magnetic fields on the quiet sun; with biographical sketch. Sci Am 215:28, 54-62 bibliog(p 160) N '66

LIZARDS
Gekkonid lizards: average ages derived from tail-loss data. H. R. Bustard and R. D. Hughes. bibliog il Science 153:1670-1 S 30 '66
Reproduction in lizards: influence of temperature on photoperiodism in testicular recrudescence. P. Licht. bibliog il Science 154:1668-70 D 30 '66
Sceloporus occidentalis: preferred body temperature of the western fence lizard. S. M. McGinnis. bibliog il Science 152:1090-1 My 20 '66
See also
Chameleons
Horned toads

Eggs
Geographic variation in ovarian cycles and clutch size in cnemidophorus tigris (teiidae) C. J. McCoy and G. A. Hoddenbach. bibliog il Science 154:1671 D 30 '66

LLERAS RESTREPO, Carlos
Landslide for Lleras. Time 87:36+ My 13 '66
Liberals' choice. Newsweek 67:60 My 16 '66

LLEWELLYN, Richard
O, feast of Happy Marl; story. McCalls 94:70-1 D '66

LLOYD, Audrey Walls
Cruising the Karankaway country. Motor B 118:22-5+ N '66

LLOYD, Harvey
Shades of Lammermoor; photographs. Opera N 30:14-16 F 19 '66

LLOYD, John
Federal aid: teachers lead the way. Sr Schol 89:sup4 O 21 '66
Washington report. See issues of Senior scholastic

LLOYD, Kate
Peru: notes on the wing. Vogue 148:116 Jl '66
Trance music of La Monte Young. Vogue 147:198+ My '66
Travel. Vogue 148:102-4 N 15 '66

LOADING and unloading
Loading chute ideas that work. il Suc Farm 64:46 Je '66
Tractor loaders, selection and use. P. B. Jones. il Suc Farm 64:34-5 D '66
See also
Materials handling

LOADING chutes. See Swine farms—Equipment

LOAN, Nguyen-ngoc-. See Nguyen-ngoc-Loan

LOAN associations. See Credit unions; Savings and loan associations

LOANS
Should you ever lend money to a relative? Bet Hom & Gard 44:6+ Ap '66
See also
Credit
Government lending
Insurance, Life—Policy loans
Interest
Mortgages
Pawnbroking
Student loans

LOANS, Bank
Borrow with money in the bank? why? interest-saving passbook loans. il Changing T 20:20 S '66
Business borrowing surges ahead. il Bsns W p 100-2 Ja 22 '66
Discount hike starts to pinch bank loans. Bsns W p26-7 F 5 '66
Forecast for loans: tight, dear; ABA bankers see demand outrunning supply. il Bsns W p 171-2 N 5 '66
Money should be tight but not out of reach; outlook for '67. il Bsns W p42-4 D 31 '66
What makes you a good credit risk? il Changing T 20:39-40 F '66; Same abr. with title Are you a good credit risk? Read Digest 88:85-7 Je '66

LOANS, Foreign
See also
Economic assistance

LOANS, Government. See Government lending

LOANS, Mortgage. See Mortgages

LOANS, Personal
Borrowers turn to odd spots; offbeat sources. Bsns W p65-6 O 8 '66
Dirty deal in small loans: relations of finance and insurance companies. J. Ridgeway. New Repub 155:11-12 O 8 '66
Getting money for a home: why it's tough, the outlook; interview. J. E. Horne. il U S News 61:82-5 Ag 8 '66

LOANS, Student. See Student loans

LOBATE bowls. See Bowls

LOBBYING
Bad news for union bosses: fight over the right to work. il Nations Bsns 53:36-7+ D '65
City lobbyists head for Washington. il Bsns W p88-9+ Jl 9 '66
Handbook for arm twisters; letters to legislators. R. Starnes. Field & S 70:20+ Mr '66
Letters to congressmen. D. Wolfle. Science 151:639 F 11 '66
Lobbyists, by J. Deakin. Review
New Repub 155:32-4 D 10 '66. H. Fuller
Sugar: a sticky mess in Congress. P. Findley. Read Digest 88:88-92 Je '66
University lobbyists. M. Levy. Reporter 34:31-3 Je 30 '66
What can I do? letters to congressmen. D. Lawrence. U S News 61:116 S 12 '66

LOBBYISTS
Lobbyists, by J. Deakin. Review
New Repub 155:32-4 D 10 '66. H. Fuller
Reaching for the pie; university lobbyists. Time 88:48 Jl 15 '66
University lobbyists. M. Levy. Reporter 34:31-3 Je 30 '66; Discussion. 35:6 Ag 11 '66

LOBDELL, Helen
Dark splinters; story. NEA J 55:12-13 N '66
Why not a domestic teacher exchange program? NEA J 55:15 F '66

LOBDELL, Jared
C. S. Lewis' renaissance. Nat R 18:1332-3 D 27 '66
What the farmers believed. Nat R 18:539-40 My 31 '66

LO BELLO, Nino
Coming soon: world's first artificial baby. Sci Digest 59:40-4 F '66
These creatures are 5 hundred million years old. Sci Digest 61:70-3 Ja '67

LOBSENZ, Norman M.
What good is Sunday school? Redbook 127:60-1+ O '66

LOBSTERS
Fewer lobsters reach their destination. il Bsns W p32 Ag 13 '66
Lobster: oddball of the ocean. D. MacDonald. il Read Digest 89:203-4+ D '66
See also
Cookery—Fish

LOCAL defense. See Civil defense

LOCAL finance
Consolidation issue. Am City 81:7 N '66

LOCAL government
Revolution in local government recommended by CED report. Library J 91:3669 Ag '66
See also
Townships

United States
Consolidation issue. Am City 81:7 N '66
Now the super county; CED study urges larger and stronger county units. Bsns W p 101 Jl 23 '66
See also
Town meeting

LOCAL history pageants. See Pageants

LOCAL scientific survey module. See Lunar vehicles

LOCAL service airlines

Canada to strengthen regional carriers. R. G. O'Lone. Aviation W 85:38-9 N 14 '66

Commuter airlines. D. A. Brown. il Aviation W 85:125+ N 14; 121+ N 21; 99+ N 28 '66

Commuterlines urged to seek firm rules. R. G. O'Lone. Aviation W 85:116-18 D 12 '66

Commuters; Commuter airlines. il Time 88:66 D 23 '66

Flying high in vintage Fords; Lake Erie route of Island airlines. il Bsns W p 132-4 Ja 7 '67

Local carriers move to increase cargo business as demand rises. R. G. O'Lone. Aviation W 85:38 O 3 '66

Local hearings may speed route cases. Aviation W 84:51-2 Mr 21 '66

Local revenues rise as strike continues. Aviation W 85:40-1+ Ag 15 '66

Local service revenue to double by 1970. W. Wright. Aviation W 84:185-7 Mr 7 '66

Locals ask densest short-haul markets. W. Wright. Aviation W 84:35 F 7 '66

Major airlines eye Pacific local service. H. D. Watkins. Aviation W 85:38-9 D 12 '66

Record profit forecast for local airlines. W. Wright. Aviation W 84:41 My 16 '66

Small jets get into a dogfight; American-Mohawk squabble over Syracuse air travelers. il Bsns W p 163 My 7 '66

Third Florida route backed. Aviation W 85:52 N 14 '66

Trunks set revenue record in first half. H. D. Watkins. Aviation W 85:43 Ag 8 '66

U.S.-industry urban VTOL drive urged. il Aviation W 84:39-40 My 9 '66

VTOLs proposed for Northeast corridor. J. R. Ashlock. il Aviation W 84:34-6 Ap 4 '66

See also
Air America, incorporated
Frontier airlines, incorporated
Pacific Southwest airlines

LOCAL taxation

As city taxes rise, the latest favorite: personal income taxes. il U S News 61:86 Ag 8 '66

State, local tax rise steepens. U S News 61:87-8 Jl 11 '66

Taxes: are you getting your money's worth? M. Mayer. Bet Hom & Gard 44:14 D '66

LOCALISM. See Provincialism

LOCATION in business and industry

Business markets. il Duns R 88:pt2 70-6+ Jl '66

Desirable location: factories wanted. R. J. Whiteside. America 114:261 F 19 '66

Management's critical choice: to build or modernize. il Duns R 87:pt2 104-7+ Mr '66

Manchester concept and how it paid off; Maple press. Pub W 190:86-91 Ag 1 '66

On the trail of runaway plants; tax-exempt bonds lure industry. il Bsns W p 114-16 Ag 6 '66

Plant moves house. D. Balaban. il Duns R 87:pt2 114-16+ Mr '66

Real estate decisions are different. A. M. Weimer. il Harvard Bsns R 44:105-12 N '66

Site selection: industrial gamesmanship. D. Balaban. il Duns R 87:pt2 110-13+ Mr '66

Site selection: simple factors add up to a complex decision; with checklist guide by Oswald Stewart. Arch Rec 139:174-7 Je '66

Small town prepares for a big change; Hennepin and five other villages of Putnam County, Ill. prepare a comprehensive plan. il Fortune 74:187+ N '66

Welcome mat out for aerospace industry. M. L. Yaffee. il Aviation W 84:65-6+ F 14 '66

Wooing the plants; competitive struggle among states and cities. il Time 88:110 N 25 '66

LOCATION of metals. See Metal detectors

LOCATIONS, Moving picture. See Moving pictures—Setting and scenery

LOCATORS, Metal. See Metal detectors

LOCATORS, Target. See Target locators

LOCH NESS, Scotland. See Ness, Loch, Scotland

LOCH NESS monster

Looking for the monster. D. Cohen. il Sci Digest 61:20-2 Ja '67

New evidence spurs hunt for Loch Ness monster. D. Scott. il Pop Sci 189:112-15+ N '66

LOCHER, Barbara

Occupational therapy. por Wilson Lib Bul 40:849-50+ My '66

LOCHER, David

Corner of December; poem. America 115:824 D 24 '66

LOCICERO, T. V.

Murder of Rabbi Adler. Commentary 41:49-53 Je; 42:26+ O '66

LOCKABEY, Almon

Mexican scalp for Ondine. Yachting 119:102-3+ Ap '66

LOCKERS

Lockers instead of baskets; municipal swimming pools. il Am City 81:57 O '66

LOCKHEED aircraft corporation

C-5A subcontract team being formed. Aviation W 84:34 Ap 18 '66

$50 billion battle to build the giant SST; with report by C. Welles. il Life 61:68-77+ O 28 '66

Golden goose; Lockheed mockup at Burbank, Calif. il Time 88:71 Jl 1 '66

Lockheed aims at the airlines; Defense dept.'s leading contractor. il Bsns W p46-9+ D 24 '66

Lockheed bets big on new controls; air force contract to design and build giant C-5As. il Bsns W p 116+ Je 4 '66

Lockheed names first AAFSS subcontractors; advanced aerial fire support system. Aviation W 85:87 O 3 '66

Lockheed pushes CL-1011 airbus study. C. M. Plattner. Aviation W 85:31 D 26 '66

Lockheed studies civil C-5A with 330,000 lb. payload. Aviation W 85:41 N 14 '66

Lockheed tops RDT&E list. Tech W 20:19 Ja 9 '67

No end in sight; history, projects administrators and competitors. il Time 87:72-6+ F 11 '66

SST race, biggest of all. il Newsweek 68:48-52+ Ag 29 '66

SST's decisive moment; will contract go to Boeing, Lockheed, both, or neither? il Bsns W p35-7 D 24 '66

Why do they fall? Luftwaffe's 51st Starfighter crash since 1961. il Bsns W p54+ Ap 2 '66

Lockheed missile and space division

LMSC foresees steady Agena demand. R. Lindsey. il Tech W 19:29 S 5 '66

LMSC plans to use Gemini spray process in architecture; gold coating. R. Lindsey. Tech W 19:30+ S 12 '66

LOCKHEED-California company. See Lockheed aircraft corporation

LOCKHEED-Georgia company. See Lockheed aircraft corporation

LOCKHEED missile and space division. See Lockheed aircraft corporation—Lockheed missile and space division

LOCKS (hydraulic engineering)

Locksmanship; how to cope with the ups and downs of canal linking Lake Champlain with the Hudson River. J. Hart. il Yachting 119:72-3 My '66

LOCKS and keys

Build the electrolock; electronic combination lock. M. E. Coultes. il Pop Electr 24:60-1 Ja '66

How to lock burglars out. J. A. Morris. il Read Digest 89:137-40 D '66

Keying system improves security. il Arch Rec 139:189-90 Ja '66

Sequence-operated lock. G. L. Anderson. il Pop Electr 26:73-4+ Ja '67

You've never seen a key like this! Sargent maximum security system. il Pop Mech 125:165 F '66

LOCKSHIN, Richard A.

Insect embryogenesis; macromolecular syntheses during early development. bibliog Science 154:775-6 N 11 '66

LOCKSPEISER, Edward

Bout with Boulez. Hi Fi 16:65-8+ My '66

LOCOMOTION

See also
Animal locomotion

LOCOMOTIVE models. See Railroad models

LOCOMOTIVES

Drive your own locomotive. H. Fast. Esquire 65:36+ My '66

See also
Steam engines

LOCOMOTIVES, Gas turbine

Budd-AiResearch turbine railcar to begin trial runs this summer. R. D. Hibben. il Aviation W 84:65+ Ap 18 '66

Turbine-driven railcar is undergoing tests. il Am City 81:14 D '66

LODGE, David

Graham Greene's comedians. Commonweal 83:604-6 F 25 '66

LODGE, George C.

Close-up; interview, ed. by J. Berry. pors Duns R 88:8-9+ Ag '66

Food processing, key to economic development. Harvard Bsns R 44:6-8+ S '66

LODGE, Henry Cabot, 1902–
Outlook now for the war in Vietnam; interview. por U S News 61:66-8 N 21 '66

about

NSC reviews Viet-Nam problems; remarks, May 10, 1966. L. B. Johnson. Dept State Bul 54:834 My 30 '66
Surprise? Nation 202:634 My 30 '66

LODGE, James P. Jr, and Pate, J. B.
Atmospheric gases and particulates in Panama. bibliog Sciene 153:408-10 Jl 22 '66

LODISH, Harvey F. and Zinder, N. D.
Replication of the RNA of bacteriophage f2. bibliog Science 152:372-8 Ap 15 '66

LOEFFLER, Theodore B.
Bigots' book shelf; campus scare campaign. Nation 203:206-9 S 12 '66

LOESCHER, Frank S.
New bridge of understanding and cooperation. Sch & Soc 94:126-8 Mr 5 '66

LOESER, Katinka
How I spent my summer vacation; story. Redbook 127:64-5 S '66
January nuptials for Miss Fairweather; story. New Yorker 41:27-31 Ja 29 '66
Life and death of little children; story. New Yorker 42:26-7 Ag 27 '66
Marmee; story. New Yorker 42:28-32 Je 25 '66
To all a good night; story. Redbook 128:58-9 D '66
Where early falls the dew; story. McCalls 93:98-9 Mr '66

LOESER brothers
Three California brothers; School of American ballet reports on its 1964-65 Ford foundation national scholarship program. M. Moseley. il Dance Mag 40:32-3 Mr '66

LOESSER, Frank
Loesser the wit, the greater the hit. T. Prideaux. il Life 60:18 Je 17 '66
One-man gang. por Newsweek 67:98-9 My 16 '66

LOEWENSTEIN, Karl
Berlin revisited; thoughts on unification. bibliog f Cur Hist 50:263-8+ My '66

LOEWINSOHN, Ron
Flowers, because they've come to be; From The step; poems. Poetry 108:178-84 Je '66
Some uses of landscape. Poetry 109:123-6 N '66

about

California hybrid. J. Harrison. Poetry 108:198-201 Je '66

LOFTING, Christopher
Trouble in Puddleby-on-the-Marsh. por Life 61:7 S 30 '66

LOFTING, Colin
Mortifying visit from a dude dad. por Life 61:128+ S 30 '66

LOFTING, Hugh
Mortifying visit from a dude dad. C. Lofting. il pors Life 61:128+ S 30 '66

LOG cabins
Log houses in Wisconsin. R. W. E. Perrin. il Antiques 89:867-71 Je '66

LOGAN, Ben
He stalks sharks by kayak. G. X. Sand. il pors Pop Mech 125:120-2 My '66

LOGAN, Edgar
Federal aid; bonanza for the disadvantaged. Sr Schol 89:sup8+ O 21 '66
He left us laughing. Sr Schol 88:sup6 Mr 18 '66
Where the streets are paved with gold. Sr Schol 88:sup22 Ap 15 '66

LOGAN, John
On the death of Keats; poem. Poetry 109:1-3 O '66
Rescue; poem. New Yorker 42:54 S 17 '66
White Pass ski patrol; poem. Nation 203:358 O 10 '66

LOGAN, Rayford W.
Assessment of current American influence in Africa. Ann Am Acad 366:99-107 Jl '66

LOGBOOKS
Right log for your boat. E. S. Maloney. il Motor B 117:26+ Ap '66

LOGGERS. See Lumberjacks

LOGGING. See Lumbering

LOGIC
Anecdotes, facetiae, satire, etc.
Infuriating man. L. Rosten. Look 30:14 N 15 '66

LOGISTICS
See also
Aeronautics, Military

LOGS, Ships. See Logbooks

LOGSDON, Gene
Dog hunters. Farm J 90:68Q Mr '66
Fight for farm labor. Farm J 90:89 Mr '66

Our cows never talk back. Farm J 90:22 Mr '66
When to sell to the developer. Farm J 90:38-9+ Mr '66
Will a minimum wage law hurt you? Farm J 90:25 Jl '66

LOGUE, Edward J.
Boston's bristly Mr Logue. A. R. Talbot. Harper 233:18+ N '66
Boston's powerful model for rebuilders. il por Bsns W p 152-4 N 26 '66

LOHENGRIN (operatic character) See Characters in opera

LOHENGRIN; opera. See Wagner, R.

LOHR, Helga
Letter from Berlin. Nation 202:51-4 Ja 10; inside cover F 28 '66

LOIRE RIVER
River of counts and kings: the Loire. K. MacLeish. il Nat Geog Mag 129:822-69 Je '66

LOIRE VALLEY
River of counts and kings: the Loire. K. MacLeish. il Nat Geog Mag 129:822-69 Je '66

LÖKEN, Olav H.
Baffin Island refugia older than 54,000 years. bibliog Science 153:1378-80 S 16 '66

LOMBARD, Alain
Music to my ears. Sat R 49:34 F 5 '66

LOMBARDI, John
Standards at the grass roots; excerpts from address, July 14, 1965. bibliog f ALA Bul 60:377-80 Ap '66

LOMBARDI, Vince
Great man. Sports Illus 26:5-6 Ja 2 '67
Pro pecunia sunt. il por Time 88:44 D 30 '66
Stop those Chiefs! T. Maule. il por Sports Illus 26:10-13 Ja 16 '67

LOMBARDO, Kathleen
We sat on the mountain's back; poem. Sat R 49:23 Ap 16 '66

LOMEO, Angelo. See Bullaty, S. jt. auth.

LONDON, Brian
If Cassius can't punch, then London isn't down. J. Lovesey. il Sports Illus 25:16-19 Ag 15 '66

LONDON, Jack
To keep the pot boiling. F. Walker. Nation 202:105-7 Ja 24 '66

LONDON, Kurt L.
Sino-Soviet conflict. bibliog f Cur Hist 51:206-12+ O '66

LONDON, Perry
Psychoanalysis and morality. L. H. Farber; discussion. Commentary 41:23+ Mr; 6+ Ap '66

LONDON
Letter from London. M. Panter-Downes. See issues of New Yorker
Letter home; new wave of nostalgia. J. Crosby. Esquire 65:60+ Je '66
London, center of tactility. il Esquire 66:172-3 D '66
Sight and sound from London. L. Hershey. il McCalls 93:10+ S '66

Airports

BOAC, BEA planning joint cargo terminal; Heathrow international airport. H. J. Coleman. il Aviation W 85:49-50 N 21 '66
London focuses on rail links for airports; Heathrow international airport. H. J. Coleman. il Aviation W 86:39-41 Ja 2 '67

Architecture

Ceremonial modern for the establishment; Royal college of physicians. il Arch Rec 140:179-84 S '66

Art

Art news from London. J. Russell. See issues of Art news

Banks

Daring & the elite; Hill, Samuel & co, ltd. Time 88:73 Ag 19 '66
Profiles; merchant bank, Hambros bank, ltd. J. Wechsberg. New Yorker 41:42-6+ F 5 '66
Profiles; Siegmund G. Warburg. J. Wechsberg. New Yorker 42:45-8+ Ap 9 '66

British museum

See British museum

Clubs

London's clubland. A. Waugh. il Nat R 18:1111+ N 1 '66

Covent Garden

London; Tchaikovsky. F. Aprahamian. Opera N 31:26 N 19 '66

LONDON—*Continued*

Crime

Bullets on Braybrook street; fatal shooting of three policemen. Time 88:33 Ag 19 '66
Slip in the system; three policemen murdered; arrests. il Newsweek 68:30-1 Ag 29 '66

Description

Gin fizz. C. Brogan. Nat R 18:722-3+ Jl 26 '66
One man's London. A. C. Fisher, jr. il Nat Geog Mag 129:743-91 Je '66
Soho. A. Waugh. il Nat R 18:1223+ N 29 '66
We four teens in London town; report on the making of A man for all seasons; ed. by E. Miller. C. Crawford. il Seventeen 26:80-1+ Ja '67
You can walk across it on the grass. il Time 87:30-4 Ap 15 '66

Fire, 1666

300 years ago, fire! C. V. Wedgwood. il N Y Times Mag p6+ Ag 28 '66

Galleries and museums

See also
British museum

Hotels, restaurants, etc.

And at long last they are doing something about the food. J. Crosby. il Esquire 66: 66-7+ Jl '66
Soho. A. Waugh. il Nat R 18:1223+ N 29 '66

Libraries

See also
British museum

Maps

London colossus astride the Thames. Nat Geog Mag 129:750-2 Je '66

Music

Bennett's premiere, Hungarians' Beethoven; London report. E. Greenfield. Hi Fi 16: 156-7 My '66
Bernstein eruption, new Rosenkavalier. E. Greenfield. il Hi Fi 16:MA28-9 Jl '66
Birthday party. il Newsweek 68:57 Ag 15 '66
Britain's swinging festival; Henry Wood promenade concerts. E. Greenfield. Hi Fi 16:MA31 D '66
Letter from London; third City of London festival; B. Britten's work, the Burning fiery furnace. M. Panter-Downes. New Yorker 42:70+ Jl 23 '66
London. F. Aprahamian. il Opera N 30:32 Mr 5; 32 Mr 26 '66
New hall for London; home for London symphony orchestra. T. Heinitz. Sat R 49:71 Ap 16 '66
Notes from our correspondents. E. Greenfield. See issues of High fidelity incorporating Musical America
Other side: music and opera productions. T. Heinitz. Sat R 49:57 Ag 27 '66
Tippett premiere, Britten revivals. E. Greenfield. Hi Fi 16:160-1 Ap '66
Wallenstein's Beethoven. T. Heinitz. Sat R 50:107 Ja 14 '67

Newspapers

Letter from London; unhappy New Year all around. M. Panter-Downes. New Yorker 42:102-3 Ja 14 '67
See also
Morning star (newspaper)
Times, London

Police

Bullets on Braybrook street; fatal shooting of three policemen. Time 88:33 Ag 19 '66
Slip in the system; three policemen murdered; arrests. il Newsweek 68:30-1 Ag 29 '66

Religious institutions and affairs

London's interracial parish; Notting Hill. C. Northcott. Christian Cent 83:1475 N 30 '66

Social life and customs

London: the cutting edge. G. Zimmermann. il Look 30:82-4 S 20 '66
You can walk across it on the grass. il Time 87:30-4 Ap 15 '66

Stores

New York, London, Paris collect. L. Lerman. Mlle 63:105 Je '66

Subways

Automate mass-transit fare sales; computer-controlled ticketing in London underground. R. S. Silver. il Am City 81:83-5 F '66

Theater

New Elizabethans. il Time 87:62-9 F 4 '66
Surveying London's season. H. Hewes. Sat R 49:101 My 7 '66

Westminster abbey

House of kings; ed. by E. Carpenter. Review
Sat R 49:34 Jl 30 '66. R. Branner

LONDON, Great fire of. See London—Fire, 1666
LONDON business school. See Business education
LONDON festival. See Music festivals—England
LONDON school of economics and political science
Berkeley-on-Thames. il Newsweek 68:64-5 D 5 '66
Something new in Britain; concerning the appointment of Dr W. Adams. R. Rosenblatt. New Repub 155:9-10 D 17 '66
LONDON symphony orchestra
LSO comes to Florida; Daytona Beach report. B. Jacobson. il Hi Fi 16:MA14-15 O '66
Musical events; concerts in Carnegie Hall, conducted by I. Kertesz. W. Sargeant. New Yorker 42:125-6 Ap 16 '66
Not just naked girls; Florida international music festival. il Time 88:48 Ag 12 '66
LONDON Times. See Times, London
LONELINESS
See also
Social isolation
LONERGAN, Lawrence Anthony
Paintings of Claude Ponsot. Cath World 203: 191-2 Je '66
LONEY, Glenn
Mystery plays and Monteverdi. Hi Fi 16: MA28-9 O '66
LONG, Barbara
In cold comfort. Esquire 65:124+ Je '66
Winner who lost. Vogue 148:70+ N 15 '66
LONG, Durward
Faculty responsibility and the executive conquest of academe. Sch & Soc 94:89-92 F 19 '66
LONG, E. John
Island. Am For 72:22-4+ F '66
LONG, Earl Kemp
Long, Long trail; excerpts from America's political dynasties: from Adams to Kennedy. S. Hess. il por Am Heritage 17:40-2+ Ag '66
LONG, Edward M.
Build a handful of power. Pop Electr 25:53 S '66
LONG, Edward Vaughan
Burgeoning Big brotherism. Christian Cent 83:645-7 My 18 '66
You ought to be left alone. Esquire 65:102-3 My '66
LONG, Fern
Library and the functionally illiterate in Cleveland; excerpts from letter, ed. by W. Woulfe. ALA Bul 60:637-8 Je '66
LONG, George
Parade. U S Camera 30:74 Ja '67
LONG, Harold M.
Improving the teaching of world affairs. Sr Schol 89:sup 16 D 2 '66
New books for teaching world history. Sr Schol 89:sup20-2 N 18 '66
LONG, Huey Pierce
Long, Long trail; excerpts from America's political dynasties: from Adams to Kennedy. S. Hess. il por Am Heritage 17:40-2+ Ag '66
LONG, Inez
Brethren take to the hills and the alleys. Christian Cent 83:916-17 Jl 20 '66
LONG, Irl R. See Ross, M. H. jt. auth.
LONG, Janet
(ed) See Cosby, B. Bill Cosby talks about life, laughter and the pursuit of wonderfulness
LONG, Marie Ann
Action vs. advice: conflict in consulting; excerpts from report on state library consultants. por ALA Bul 60:357-61 Ap '66
LONG, Paul F.
Sound of wings; poem. Nat Parks Mag 40:18 F '66
LONG, Russell Billiu
Excerpt from addresses, January 27, 29 and February 16, August 31, 1966. Cong Digest 45:121-3, 238+ Ap, O '66

LONG, Russell Billiu—*Continued*

about

How Long will play his new Senate role. por Bsns W p36+ F 19 '66

Long, Long trail; excerpts from America's political dynasties: from Adams to Kennedy. S. Hess. il por Am Heritage 17:40-2+ Ag '66

Long view. K. Crawford. Newsweek 67:36 Mr 21 '66

Medicine men and public health. R. Yoakum. New Repub 156:35-6 Ja 21 '67

Powwows and sinners. Newsweek 67:74 F 21 '66

Tax credit is the target. il Bsns W p29 S 3 '66

Washington: ten of its most powerful men. il por Vogue 148:153 N 15 '66

LONG, S. V. and Taylor, R. E.
Suggested revision for west Mexican archeological sequences. bibliog Science 154:1456-9 D 16 '66

LONG, Sumner Adam
Will the real Huey Long please stand up. S. M. Fertitta. il Motor B 118:88+ Ag '66

LONG ago in Bethlehem; drama. See Newman, D.

LONG BEACH, N.Y.
New lights make a city garbage-pail conscious. F. E. Vogel. il Am City 81:111 Jl '66

LONG BEACH-San Francisco ocean powerboat race. See Motor boat racing

LONG BEACH state college, Long Beach, Calif.
Sculptors in the factory. il Fortune 73:140-5 Ap '66

LONG Christmas dinner; drama. See Wilder, T.

LONG flight of stairs; story. See Brown, M. F.

LONG ISLAND, N.Y.
Goof-ball set: addiction in the suburbs. M. Schram. il Nation 203:242-5 S 19 '66
Island: any future for the good life? il Newsweek 68:48-50 Ag 8 '66

See also
Architecture, Domestic—Long Island
Gardens—Long Island

Industries

Growing its own economy; expanding and diversifying its industry. il Bsns W p 184-6+ Mr 26 '66

New plants sprout on Long Island. Hi Fi 16:43+ My '66

LONG ISLAND center, Stony Brook. See New York state university—Long Island center, Stony Brook

LONG ISLAND railroad strike. See Strikes—United States—Railroads

LONG ISLAND SOUND
Circumnavigation of Long Island. B. Robinson. il Yachting 119:82-4+ Ja '66
L.I. lake proposed; turning Sound into a freshwater reservoir. B. Tufty. il Sci N 90:149 S 3 '66
Potential freshwater reservoir in the New York area. R. D. Gerard. bibliog il Science 153:870-1 Ag 19 '66; Discussion. 154:215-16 O 14 '66

LONG letter; story. See Henderson, R.

LONG playing records. See Phonograph records

LONG range navigation. See Loran

LONG way home; story. See Ernst, P.

LONGANS
See also
Cookery—Fruit

LONGDEN, Johnny
Last, triumphant ride of Johnny Longden. A. Stump. il pors Sat Eve Post 239:74-6+ Je 4 '66
Old Johnny Longden, his hail and farewell. J. Tobin. il por Sports Illus 24:88-9+ Mr 21 '66
Pumper's last purse. il por Time 87:72 Mr 18 '66

LONGEST time; story. See Glaze, E.

LONGEVITY
See also
Aging

LONGLEY, William. See Cohen, C. jt. auth.

LONGSHOREMEN
See also
International longshoremen's and warehousemen's union

Wages and hours
Decks cleared for new dock pact. il Bsns W p 108-10 Jl 30 '66

Where automation pays workers; dock workers on the West coast. U S News 62:88 Ja 16 '67

Where pay rise tops 5 per cent. U S News 61:79 Ag 1 '66

LONGWELL, Maude. See Sharkey, M. B. jt. auth.

LONGWOOD gardens. See Gardens—Pennsylvania

LONGWORTH, Alice Roosevelt
Washington's other monument. J. Alsop. por Vogue 147:178-9+ F 1 '66

LONSDALE, Gordon Arnold
My spy can lick your spy. M. Frankel. il Atlan 217:103-4+ Ap '66

LONSDALE, Kathleen, and Mason, Phoebe
Uric acid, uric acid dihydrate, and urates in urinary calculi, ancient and modern. bibliog Science 152:1511-12 Je 10 '66
—and Sutor, D. J.
Newberyite in ancient and modern urinary calculi: identification and space group. bibliog Science 154:1353-4 D 9 '66

LONSKI, Joseph
Orchids in your house. Horticulture 44:28-9+ F '66

LOOK (periodical)
Chapter II, or finis? Manchester book. il Time 88:10-12 D 30 '66
Jacqueline Kennedy's victory; W. Manchester's book. il Newsweek 69:16-19 Ja 2 '67
Look-alike; Savings and loan foundation ad in Look. Newsweek 67:86 Je 27 '66
Look 1966 All America. G. Astor. il Look 30: 89-91 D 13 '66
Look to the future; end of thirtieth year, beginning of 31st year of publication. G. Cowles. Look 31:13 Ja 10 '67
Look youth survey: are you a teen-ager? yeah, I'm afraid so. J. Shepherd. Look 30:44+ S 20 '66
Memorandum to Look's readers. W. Attwood. Look 30:6 Ag 9 '66
Mrs Kennedy and Harper & Row continue negotiations on editorial content of Death of a President. Pub W 191:33-4 Ja 2 '67
Random house asks court to void Hughes injunction. Pub W 190:38-9 Ag 8 '66
Teacher of the year; Mona Dayton's magical classroom. D. Chapman. il Look 30: 85-6+ Ap 19 '66
Truth as personal property. A. Gingrich. Sat R 50:22-3 Ja 21 '67
Washington report: National teacher of the year award. J Lloyd. Sr Schol 88:sup7 Ap 29 '66
What the fuss was about; first installment of The death of a President. Time 89:47-8 Ja 20 '67
See also
All-America cities
Collier trophy

LOOMER, Alice
Every child needs to be loved for himself. Parents Mag 41:66-7+ O '66
What are IQ tests good for? Parents Mag 41:80+ S '66

LOOMIS, Carol J.
The 500: a decade of growth. Fortune 74: 212-15+ Jl 15 '66
Pension funds still want stocks. Fortune 73:130-1+ Je '66
SEC has a little list. Fortune 75:110-15+ Ja '67
Where Manny Cohen is leading the SEC. Fortune 74:163-5+ D '66 (to be cont)

LOOMIS, Roger Sherman
Obituary
Pub W 190:29 O 24 '66

LOOMIS, Calif.
Community effort lights an athletic field. il Am City 81:132 F '66

LOOMS
Here's a loom to start on. il Sunset 136:124+ F '66

LOOS, Adolf
Adolf Loos: pioneer of modern architecture, by L. Munz and G. Kunstler. Review
Arch Forum il 125:88-9+ Jl '66. R. Neutra

LOOS, Anita
Behind the screen scenes. A. Knight. por Sat R 49:39 S 24 '66
Why gentlemen preferred Anita. E. Weeks. Atlan 218:138 O '66

LOPERT, Tanya
La dolce Venezia. il por Time 88:85 S 16 '66

LOPES, J. Leite
Science for development, a view from Latin America. Bul Atomic Sci 22:7-11 S '66

LOPES FILHO, Napoleao
Winslow Homer. Américas 18:9-13 O '66

LOPEZ, Antoine
Ben Barka affair. C. Sterling. il Reporter 34:22-8 Mr 10 '66

LOPEZ, Enrique Hank
Back to Bachimba. Horizon 9:80-3 Wint '67

LÓPEZ-FRESQUET, Ruto
Bridge to disenchantment. K. Wagenheim. Nation 204:25-6 Ja 2 '67

LOPEZ TIJERINA, Reies. See Tijerina. R. L.

LOPOKOV, Feodor V.
Lopukhov and his Tanzsymphonia; excerpt from Era of the Russian ballet. N. Roslavleva. Dance Mag 41:72-4 Ja '67

LOPOKOV, Feodor V. family
Lopukhov dynasty. L. Yoffe. il Dance Mag 41:35-9+ Ja '67

LORAN
Army seeks to improve ground positioning; man-pack receiver version of Loran tactical radio navigation system. M. Getler. il Tech W 19:14-15 O 17 '66
Small radio navigation pinpoints position; Manpack Loran. Sci N 90:328 O 22 '66
USAF evaluates Loran-inertial system. B. Miller. il Aviation W 84:83+ My 9 '66

LORANG, Glenn, and Snyder, John
Barbered trees. Farm J 90:68T Mr '66

LORCA, Federico García. See García Lorca, F.

LORD, Albert B.
Father of Serbian literature. Sat R 49:29-30 Ap 30 '66

LORD, Deane W.
(ed) See Root, H. F. Brighter future for children with diabetes

LORD, John
Whirl of kilts, the skirl of pipes. Life 61:12 O 21 '66

LORD, Ruth K.
Oh Lord, remember me; story. Ladies Home J 83:88-9 Ap '66

LORDS prayer
Interpretation of prayer in the early church, by R. L. Simpson. Review
Christian Cent 83:272 Mr 2 '66. G. T. Armstrong
Lord's prayer updated; Australian reactions. Newsweek 68:104+ O 10 '66

LORDS Supper
Ecumenism and the eucharist. America 115: 441 O 15 '66
Exploring intercommunion. America 114:281 F 26 '66
See also
Catholic church—Eucharist

LOREE, T. R. and others
Polymorphism of shock loaded Fe-Mn and Fe-Ni alloys. bibliog Science 153:1277-8 S 9 '66

LOREN, Sophia
Men in my life. pors Ladies Home J 83:84-7+ Ap '66
Sophia Loren writes about Sophia Loren. pors Ladies Home J 83:73-9 Mr '66
about
Real treasure. il pors Newsweek 67:92 Je 6 '66
Sophia Loren: on women who are bored and boring. A. Menen. por McCalls 94:54-5+ Ja '67
Sophia plays a museum; photographs at the Museum of modern art. N Y Times Mag p38+ My 15 '66

LORENGAR, Pilar
Music to my ears; Metropolitan's newest Elvira. I. Kolodin. Sat R 49:41 F 26 '66

LORING, Eugene
Eugene Loring talks; ed. by O. Maynard. pors Dance Mag 40:35-9 Jl; 52-4+ Ag '66

LORING, Paule
Geriatric a-go-go. Yachting 120:60-1+ Jl '66

LORR, John S.
How to make a sun-dial fire pit. Pop Sci 188:132-5 Je '66

LORRINSON, Leverret
Washington front. America 114:769 My 28 '66

LORTON reformatory. See Reformatories

LOS ANGELES
Los Angeles, center of vulgarity. il Esquire 66:178-9 D '66
Magnet in the West. il Time 88:14-19 S 2 '66
Meanwhile back at the pueblo: Los Angeles dance. V. H. Swisher. il Dance Mag 40:41-4 D '66

Airports
Los Angeles working to ease road jams. H. D. Watkins. il Aviation W 85:55+ N 14 '66

Anti-poverty program
Reprise of a nightmare; more rioting in Watts. il Time 87:19 Mr 25 '66

Architecture
Century plaza: a resort in mid-city. il Arch Rec 140:124-7 Ag '66

Community action in the West: Chatsworth moves its church. il Sunset 136:154 Ap '66
Motel and restaurant on busy city corner; Park Plaza lodge. il Arch Rec 140:130-1 Ag '66

Art
Art news from Los Angeles (title varies) il Art N 65:20+ Mr; 57 Sum; 58 D '66
Los Angeles: object lesson. J. Coplans. il Art N 64:40+ Ja '66

Cemeteries
Dead right; trouble over Court of liberty inscriptions. il Newsweek 67:44 Ap 18 '66
First step up to heaven; Forest Lawn memorial park in Glendale, Calif. il Time 88: 54 S 30 '66
Living end. il Newsweek 68:95 O 3 '66

City planning
Century city, Los Angeles' new ultra-uptown; Alcoa, building on 20th Century-Fox's old movie lot. il Bsns W p98-101 Jl 23 '66
Why megalopolis grows; a report from Los Angeles. il U S News 60:81 Mr 21 '66

Courts
Justice in the courtroom, can the poor get it? public defender system. G. Samuels. Sat R 49:25+ Ja 29 '66

Description
Profiles. C. Rand. New Yorker 42:56-60+ O 1; 64-6+ O 8 '66
250 things to see and do in and around Los Angeles. il Sunset 137:61-8 Jl '66

Education
8 across, 3 down; crossword puzzles to build vocabulary and improve spelling; Alexander Hamilton H. S. S. Cochell. Sr Schol 89: sup 13 D 2 '66

Fire department
Scuba-diving fire-eaters. R. Grant. il Pop Mech 126:102-4 Ag '66

Foreign population
Profiles. C. Rand. New Yorker 42:64-6+ O 15 '66

Galleries and museums
See also
Los Angeles County museum of art
Los Angeles County museum of history, science and art

Gardens
Japanese garden in Los Angeles. il Sunset 136:104-7 Mr '66

Historic houses, etc.
Will salvation spoil the Dodge house? D. S. Brown. il Arch Forum 125:68-71 O '66

Hospitals
Unforgettable Sister Winifred. L. Young. il Read Digest 88:173-4+ Mr '66

Hotels, restaurants, etc.
Prestige acropolis; Century Plaza hotel. il Time 87:62 Je 10 '66

Immigrants
See Los Angeles—Foreign population

Libraries
See also
Los Angeles public library

Moral conditions
Mad new scene on Sunset Strip; with report by R. Vaughan. il Life 61:75-6+ Ag 26 '66
Special island; Palisades high school students and narcotics. Newsweek 67:40 Ap 11 '66

Music
Los Angeles. A. Goldberg. Opera N 30:29 F 19 '66
New audiences in new buildings. W. Malloch. Hi Fi 16:156-7 Ap '66
Notes from our correspondents. W. Malloch. il Hi Fi 16:12+ Ag '66
Second city, lack of home-based opera. N. Melnick. il Opera N 31:8-12 D 3 '66

Negroes
Another civil-rights headache: plight of Mexican-Americans. il U S News 60:46-8 Je 6 '66
Burn, baby, burn! excerpts. J. Cohen and W. S. Murphy. il Life 61:36-8+ Jl 15 '66

LOS ANGELES—Negroes—_Continued_

How it is: my home is Watts. J. Scott. Harper 233:47-8 O '66; Correction. 234:92 Ja '67

In burned-out Watts: it's now baby. J. Shepherd. il Look 30:94-6+ Je 28 '66

Journey into the mind of Watts. T. Pynchon. il N Y Times Mag p34-5+ Je 12 '66

Minority groups in California. il Mo Labor R 89:978-83 S '66

Return to Durango street; address, July 1966. F. Bonham. il Library J 91:4188-91 S 15 '66

Ugly mood of Watts. J. G. Dunne. il Sat Eve Post 239:83-7 Jl 16 '66

Uneasy calm. il Newsweek 67:43 Je 13 '66

Watts manifesto & the McCone report. B. Rustin. Commentary 41:29-35 Mr '66; Reply with rejoinder. K. A. Martyn. 42:6+ Ag '66

Watts today. il Life 61:54-65 Jl 15 '66

Watts, waiting for D-day. A. Kopkind. New Repub 154:15-17 Je 11 '66

Police

Burn, baby, burn! excerpts. J. Cohen and W. S. Murphy. il Life 61:36-8+ Jl 15 '66

Civic lesson on homicide; coroner's inquest to determine cause of Leonard Deadwyler's death. S. Alexander. Life 60:29 Je 10 '66

Deadwyler verdict; shooting of Leonard Deadwyler accidental. Time 87:38 Je 10 '66

Flashpoint in Watts? repercussions of L. Deadwyler killing by police. il Newsweek 67:30+ My 30 '66

Watts again; testimonies of police officer Jerold Bova and Mrs Barbara Deadwyler. il Time 87:19-20 Je 3 '66

Watts today. il Life 61:54-65 Jl 15 '66

Police department

Los Angeles police. P. Jacobs. il Atlan 218:95-101 D '66

Public buildings

Beauty plus utility; municipal water and power office complex provides landmark attractiveness. il Am City 81:114+ Mr '66

Public library

See Los Angeles public library

Recreation and parks, Department of

Public seashores: their administration. W. Frederickson, jr. il Parks & Rec 1:638-40 Ag '66

Religious institutions and affairs

Miss Velma descends. A. B. Haines. Christian Cent 83:992+ Ag 10 '66

Riots

Burn, baby, burn! excerpts. J. Cohen and W. S. Murphy. il Life 61:36-8+ Jl 15 '66

Flashpoint in Watts? repercussions of L. Deadwyler killing by police. il Newsweek 67:30+ My 30 '66

In burned-out Watts: it's now baby. J. Shepherd. il Look 30:94-6+ Je 28 '66

Journey into the mind of Watts. T. Pynchon. il N Y Times Mag p34-5+ Je 12 '66

Lesson from Watts: it can happen here. C. C. Trillingham. il PTA Mag 61:12-14 O '66

New outburst in Watts. M. McGrory. America 114:437 Ap 2 '66

Night Watts blew up again. il Newsweek 67:33-4 Mr 28 '66

Once again hatred flashes in Watts. il Life 60:80-1 Mr 25 '66

Race riots: erupting now, and threats of more to come; Watts. il U S News 60:8-9 Mr 28 '66

Racial hot spot erupts once more. il U S News 60:8 My 30 '66

Reprise of a nightmare; more rioting in Watts. il Time 87:19 Mr 25 '66

Ugly mood of Watts. J. G. Dunne. il Sat Eve Post 239:83-7 Jl 16 '66

Voice from Watts; E. L. King to be arraigned on four counts of arson. il Newsweek 67:68 Je 20 '66

Watts manifesto & the McCone report. B. Rustin. Commentary 41:29-35 Mr '66; Reply with rejoinder. K. A. Martyn. 42:6+ Ag '66

Watts riots: new violence. Sr Schol 88:24 Ap 1 '66

Watts, waiting for D-day. A. Kopkind. New Repub 154:15-17 Je 11 '66

Watts: where welfare bred violence. E. Selby and A. Selby. Read Digest 88:67-71 My '66

Sanitary affairs

Double-barreled clay-pipe sewer. L. A. Pardee. il Am City 81:82-3 D '66

Social conditions

How it is: my home is Watts. J. Scott. Harper 233:47-8 O '66; Correction. 234:92 Ja '67

Profiles. C. Rand. New Yorker 42:64-6+ O 15 '66

Social life and customs

For the single girl: a new way of life in California; South Bay club, in a Los Angeles suburb. G. Greene. il Ladies Home J 83:58-9+ Jl '66

Streets

Mad new scene on Sunset Strip; with report by R. Vaughan. il Life 61:75-6+ Ag 26 '66

Sunset along the Strip. il Time 88:69 D 2 '66

Sunset for the Strip? il Newsweek 68:22+ Jl 4 '66

Theater

Mock murder to cool Watts: street pantomimes given, to promote better understanding between races. il Life 61:85-6 Ag 19 '66

LOS ANGELES ballet. See Ballet companies

LOS ANGELES COUNTY, Calif.

Dog control by county contract. M. J. Golden. il Am City 81:197 S '66

Courts

Computerized docket; speedup record of the Los Angeles County Superior court. il Time 88:38 Jl 29 '66

LOS ANGELES COUNTY museum of art

Great Assyrian affair; feud over Nimrud reliefs with Kimbell museum. il Time 87:66 Mr 25 '66

New audiences in new buildings. W. Malloch. Hi Fi 16:156-7 Ap '66

Wars of the instant Medicis. R. Wernick. il Life 61:102-3+ O 28 '66

LOS ANGELES COUNTY museum of history, science and art

Los Angeles: complex creates a civic space. il Arch Rec 139:200-3 Ap '66

LOS ANGELES Dodgers (baseball) See Baseball clubs

LOS ANGELES international airport. See Los Angeles—Airports

LOS ANGELES public library

Fully automated registration system instituted at Los Angeles library. Library J 91:3134 Je 15 '66

LAPL and the data service bureau. D. W. Bass. il Wilson Lib Bul 41:404-18 D '66

Branches

Experiment in Watts: Vernon branch. E. P. Bishop. il Library J 91:338-9 Ja 15 '66

LOS ANGELES Rams (football club) See Football clubs

LOS ANGELES suicide prevention center. See Suicide prevention center, Los Angeles

LOS ANGELES times. See Times, Los Angeles

LOS ANGELES times Grand prix. See Automobile racing

LOS GATOS, Calif.

Coast range gem: the Los Gatos high school library. E. Mason. il ALA Bul 60:270-4 Mr '66; Reply with rejoinder. E. T. Schofield. 60:529-31 Je '66

LOSS of memory. See Amnesia

LOSSING, Benson John

Son's tribute; with paintings. D. G. Lowe. Am Heritage 17:18-19+ F '67

LOST city of the Incas. See Machu Picchu, Peru

LOST continent. See Atlantis

LOST: one kaleidoscope; story. See Magilligan, S.

LOST persons. See Missing persons

LOTOS club. See New York (city)—Clubs

LOTTERIES

Animal game: flourishing numbers game in Brazil. Time 87:31-2 Mr 25 '66

Draft: a slowdown in calls, and new talk of a lottery. il U S News 61:18 N 21 '66

Draft by lottery? pro and con discussion. Sr Schol 89:12-13 S 23 '66

Good thing in the Irish sweepstakes, for the owners; Hospitals' trust. T. O'Hanlon. il Fortune 74:170-3 N '66

New Hampshire backs slow nag. Bsns W p38 S 3 '66

LOTTERIES—*Continued*
Run for the money; New Hampshire's statistics. Newsweek 68:24+ O 3 '66
Search for Santa Claus; state lottery in New York. Nation 203:436-7 O 31 '66
State lotteries: safe bet or bad risk? pro and con discussion. Sr Schol 88:14-15 Mr 11 '66
Way a draft lottery would work. il U S News 61:29 Jl 4 '66
Why take a chance? by P. W. Rishell. Review
    Christian Cent 83:1157-8 S 21 '66. T. L. Conklin
Winning ticket; New Hampshire sweepstakes; other states interested. il Time 87: 80 Ap 1 '66

LOTTMAN, Herbert R.
Baedeker of Beatnik territory. N Y Times Mag p40-1+ Ag 7 '66
Best sellers in France. Pub W 190:43-5 O 10 '66
Crime, violence, espionage: 1000 volumes of *Série noire.* Pub W 189:44-8 Mr 7 '66
La dolce vita; Italian publishers discover Rome. Pub W 191:31-2 Ja 2 '67
French bookselling may enter the 20th century. Pub W 190:34-6 Ag 15 '66
French literary prizes confound, somewhat, their critics. Pub W 190:43-7 D 26 '66
French publishers cope with state censorship. Pub W 189:51-4 F 7 '66
Interdit: censorship in France. Wilson Lib Bul 40:759-63 Ap '66
Lire: the French try institutional promotion. Pub W 190:41-3 S 19 '66
Literary newspapers and book reporting media in France. Pub W 189:51-3 My 23 '66
Mergers and changes in French publishing. Pub W 189:38-42 Mr 21 '66
New imprint in Paris. Pub W 190:34-6 N 21 '66
New role for French literary agents? Pub W 190:27-9 Ag 1 '66
Newspaper de Gaulle has to read. Harper 234:62-6 Ja '67
No time for childhood. Library J 91:5709-12 N 15 '66
Paperback revolution hits France. Pub W 190:41-4 Jl 18 '66
Plantin-Moretus museum in Antwerp. Pub W 190:78-9+ S 5 '66
Pléiade library. Pub W 191:49+ Ja 16 '67
Printing monks of Venice. Pub W 190:110-11 D 5 '66
Skeptical guide to Michelin. Harper 232:82-5 Je '66

LOTZ, Norm
I've got the band and that's all I need. por Seventeen 26:82-3+ Ja '67

LOUCHHEIM, Katie (Scofield)
Eligible man; poem. Ladies Home J 83:185 O '66
Human comedy; poem. Commonweal 84:177 Ap 29 '66
Unripe day; poem. Mlle 63:108 O '66

about
Kiss of the muse: State appointment: poems published. por Newsweek 68:32 O 17 '66
With pen & dream. por Time 88:38 O 14 '66

LOUCKS, Orie L. See Anderson, R. C. jt. auth.

LOUD speaking apparatus
Build a fantastic coneless loudspeaker! il Pop Mech 125:168-70 Je '66
Cheapest solid-state receiver kit yet. R. Benrey. il Pop Sci 189:95 Ag '66
Compact speakers. H. Fantel. Opera N 30:37 Ap 2 '66
Loudspeaker systems. il Consumer Rep 31: 222-9 D '66
Loudspeakers: their choice and installation. N. Eisenberg. il Hi Fi 16:51-8 Je '66
Low-cost loudspeakers. il Consumer Rep 31:242-5 My '66
Microphones for public address. P. K. Franklin. il Electr World 75:50-2+ Je '66
Music, of sorts, to read by: loudspeaker disguised as table lamp. il Consumer Rep 31: 264 Je '66
New equipment: a styling bonanza for stereo sound. Hi Fi 16:98 O '66
P.A. loudspeaker principles and practice. A. B. Cohen. il Electr World 75:23-6+ Je '66
Selecting a P.A. amplifier. M. S. Sumberg. il Electr World 75:39-42+ Je '66
Speaker trends. H. Fantel. Opera N 31:33 D 10 '66
Why are they still inventing speakers? H. Fantel. il Pop Electr 25:49-52+ N '66

Cabinets
Build a long-tailed phase inverter. D. B. Weems. il Pop Electr 25:69-72+ S '66

Cabinets, the new look in stereo housing; with editorial comment. N. Eisenberg. il Hi Fi 16:55, 56-9 S '66
Designing a ducted-port bass-reflex enclosure. J. F. Novak. il Electr World 75:25-8+ Ja '66
Enclosures for high-compliance loudspeakers. R. H. Russell. il Electr World 76:25-8+ Ag '66
Four on the floor. D. B. Weems. il Pop Electr 25:74-6 N '66
Put an air brake on your woofer. D. B. Weems. il Pop Electr 24:60-3 Mr '66
Stereo on wheels. il Hi Fi 16:103 O '66
Totem poles for stereo; Sweet sixteen concept. D. B. Weems. il Pop Electr 24:48-52+ Ja '66

Terminology
Speaking of speakers. Hi Fi 16:57 Je '66

LOUD speaking apparatus, Used
See also
Stereophonic sound systems, Used

LOUDNESS
Direct test of the power function for loudness. L. F. Marks and A. W. Slawson. bibliog il Science 154:1036-7 N 25 '66

LOUGHRAN, Bernice
Should design principles be taught? Sch Arts 66:20-4 O '66

LOUIS II, king of Bavaria
Ludwig's world. H. Bailey. il Opera N 30:26-9 Mr 26 '66

LOUIS XIV, king of France
Setting of the Sun King. L. Kronenberger. il Atlan 219:58-61 Ja '67
Sun King, by N. Mitford. Review
    Sat R 49:34 N 5 '66. L. Gershoy
    Time 88:130+ O 14 '66

LOUIS, Father M. See Merton, T.

LOUIS, Jean Claire-. See Claire-Louis, J.

LOUIS, Murray
Murray Louis & company, Henry street settlement playhouse. M. Marks. Dance Mag 40:70-1 Ap '66
Murray Louis dance company, Hunter college playhouse. J. Maskey. Dance Mag 40:76 D '66

LOUIS, William Roger
Great Britain and the African peace settlement of 1919. bibliog f Am Hist R 71:875-92 Ap '66

LOUISIANA
See also
Booksellers and bookselling—Louisiana
Fishing—Louisiana
Roads—Louisiana

Description and travel
Cajunland, Louisiana's French-speaking coast. B. Keating. il Nat Geog Mag 129: 352-91 Mr '66

History
Louisiana: black governors, white sugar and blood. L. Bennett, jr. il Ebony 21:121-4+ Ap '66

Politics and government
Constitutional disenfranchisement of the Negro in Louisiana. 1898. G. E. Cunningham. bibliog Negro Hist Bul 29:147-8+ Ap '66
Long, Long trail; excerpts from America's political dynasties: from Adams to Kennedy. S. Hess. il Am Heritage 17:40-2+ Ag '66

Race problems
Constitutional disenfranchisement of the Negro in Louisiana. 1898. G. E. Cunningham. bibliog Negro Hist Bul 29:147-8+ Ap '66
Louisiana: black governors, white sugar and blood. L. Bennett, jr. il Ebony 21:121-4+ Ap '66

LOUISVILLE
City planning
Fresh pattern for inner-city renewal. il Am City 81:97+ F '66

Finance
We merged city and county purchasing. R. S. Greer. il Am City 81:114-15 O '66

Music
See also
Kentucky opera association

Newspapers
See also
Courier-journal

LOUISVILLE philharmonic orchestra
Orchestra of record. Newsweek 67:102+ Mr 21 '66

LOUISVILLE. University

Medical center

Medical complex. il Arch Rec 140:184-5 O '66

LOUTH, John D.

Changing face of marketing. Duns R 87: 46-7+ Ap '66

LOUTTIT, Henry Irving, bp

Bishop on trial. por Time 88:69 O 21 '66

LOUVAIN university. See Colleges and universities—Belgium

LOVAAS, O. Ivar, and others

Acquisition of imitative speech by schizophrenic children. bibliog Science 151:705-7 F 11 '66

LOVANO, Jessie J. and McFee, J. K.

Art judgment & social responsibility. bibliog Sch Arts 65:23-4 Ap '66

LOVE, Edmund G.

Biggest day in Flushing; excerpt from Situation in Flushing. Read Digest 88:69-74 F '66

LOVE, George H.

Uniting for strength; interview. por Nations Bsns 55:44-5+ Ja '67

LOVE, Joseph

Hans Hoffman, 1880-1966. America 114:396 Mr 19 '66

about

In many voices; one-man show of ink paintings at Alonzo gallery. T. F. Mathews. America 116:62 Ja 14 '67

LOVE, Nancy

Northwest Florida. Travel 126:26-30 Jl '66

LOVE

Could you have loved as much? Edith Taylor's story. B. Considine. Read Digest 88: 73-5 Ap '66

Dogmatist in disguise; concerning J. Fletcher's Situation ethics. J. Lachs. Christian Cent 83:1402-5 N 16 '66

Gift of love; seven vignettes. McCalls 94: 72-5+ D '66

Henry Miller's real woman; conversation, ed. by D. Dury. H. Miller. Mlle 64:90-1+ D '66

In my opinion; Americans should stop being afraid to show affection. J. Wales. Seventeen 25:154 Jl '66

Love in America; with editorial comment. il Sat Eve Post 239:8+, 78 D 31 '66

Love, love, love; questions and answers. A. Wood. Seventeen 25:404-5 Ag '66

Man talk; you can't hurry love. D. Newman and R. Benton. Mlle 64:30 Ja '67

My dear children of God. R. J. Cushing. McCalls 94:98-9 D '66

Open letter to the girl my son didn't marry. Good H 162:61-2+ My '66

Personal fulfillment in man and woman; excerpt from Man and woman. M. O'Keefe and J. J. Evoy. America 115:582-6 N 12 '66

What love must be. L. Lee. il Read Digest 88:124-6 Mr '66

See also

Marriage

Anecdotes, facetiae, satire, etc.

Variations on a four-letter word; drawings. M. Ramus. Horizon 8:98-103 Spr '66

Caricatures and cartoons

American way of love. R. Osborn. Sat Eve Post 239:28-9 D 31 '66

LOVE (charity) See Charity

LOVE (theology)

Evil and the God of love, by J. Hick. Review

Sat R 49:35 Ag 13 '66. R. C. Muska

God, man and Christian man. V. P. McCorry. America 114:841-2 Je 11 '66

How does love reign? J. M. Gustafson. Christian Cent 83:654-5 My 18 '66

Love, faith, hope: three attitudes in contemporary theology. J. W. Woelfel. Christian Cent 83:1570-3 D 21 '66

Thou shalt love. V. P. McCorry. America 115:363-4 S 24 '66

LOVE, Maternal

Every child needs to be loved for himself. A. Loomer. il Parents Mag 41:66-7+ O '66

See also

Maternal deprivation

Mothers

LOVE and hate and Dr Tisch; story. See Sterba, M.

LOVE experts; story. See Dworkin, S.

LOVE feast motive. See Music—Themes, motives, etc.

LOVE field airport. See Dallas—Airports

LOVE in literature

Elderly lover; tr. by J. W. Freeman. A. Maurois. il Opera N 30:8-12 Mr 19 '66

See also

Love poetry

LOVE on trial; opera. See Rossini, G.

LOVE poetry

Robert Graves's secret vice pays off; love poetry. A. S. Mehdevi. il N Y Times Mag p36-7+ O 30 '66

To the love song, with love. R. Rodgers. il Sat Eve Post 240:36-7 Ja 28 '67

Voices of love. il Sat Eve Post 239:42-3 D 31 '66

LOVE stories. See Short stories

LOVE story magazines. See Periodicals

LOVELL, Sir Bernard

Sir Bernard Lovell's exclusive cabled report on the Luna 9 pictures received at Jodrell bank. por Sat R 49:60-1 Mr 5 '66

about

Bringing credit to Jodrell bank. por Time 87: 52 Ap 15 '66

Handicapping the moon. Reporter 34:16 F 24 '66

Robot on the moon. J. Lear. il por Sat R 49:57-65 Mr 5 '66

LOVELL, Enid Baird

Overseas pilot without a chart. Bsns W p 185-6+ S 24 '66

LOVELL, James A. Jr

See also

Space flight—Manned flights—Lovell-Aldrin flight, 1966

LOVELORN columns. See Newspapers—Advice columns

LOVEMAN, Amy, national award. See Loveman award

LOVEMAN award

1966 Amy Loveman awards. J. F. Fixx. Sat R 49:20 Jl 2 '66

LOVER, is that you? story. See Morris, W.

LOVERS; story. See Blyth, M.

LOVES of Cass McGuire; drama. See Friel, B.

LOVESEY, John

College basketball. Sports Illus 24:66-7 Mr 14 '66

Tennis. Sports Illus 25:50+ Jl 11 '66

LOVESTONE, Jay

Adamant Mr Meany. Nation 202:764 Je 27 '66

CIA-AFL-CIO. Nation 202:700 Je 13 '66

Lovestone's cold war. D. Kurzman. New Repub 154:17-22 Je 25 '66

LOVIN' Spoonful (singers) See Singers

LOVING, Richard

Crime of being married. il pors Life 60:85-6+ Mr 18 '66

LOVOOS, Janice

Metal sculpture of Russ Shears. Am Artist 30:38-42+ Mr '66

Powerful art of Franz Rederer. Am Artist 30:42-7+ N '66

Three California ceramists. Am Artist 30: 50-5+ D '66

LOW, Barbara W. and Chen, C. C. H.

Deamino-oxytocin and 1-γ-mercaptobutyric acid-oxytocin; X-ray crystallographic data. bibliog Science 151:1552-3 Mr 25 '66

LOW Archipelago. See Tuamotu Islands

LOW fat diet. See Diet in disease

LOW-sodium diet. See Diet in disease

LOW temperature cameras. See Cameras

LOW temperature research

Effect of temperature on the life of soap bubbles, and their solidification at low temperature. A. V. Grosse. bibliog il Science 153:894-5 Ag 19 '66

LOW temperatures

Conditions for purine synthesis: did prebiotic synthesis occur at low temperatures? R. Sanchez and others. bibliog il Science 153: 72-3 Jl 1 '66

Cryogenic fuels keyed to water cycle; concerning lunar water supply. W. S. Beller. il Tech W 19:28-9 Ag 29 '66

Cryogenic liquid level controls. W. W. Schopp. il Electr World 76:36-8+ D '66

Frozen Christian: cryogenic interment. R. C. W. Ettinger; discussion. Christian Cent 82:1550+; 83:183-4 D 15 '65, F 9 '66

Stimulated Brillouin and Raman scattering in quartz at 2.1° to 293° Kelvin. P. E. Tannenwald and J. B. Thaxter. bibliog il Science 154:1319-20 D 9 '66

LOWE, Ann

Dean of American designers. G. Major. il pors Ebony 22:136-8+ D '66

LOWE, Charles F.

Tripped on the riggings. il por Time 88:60+ Jl 15 '66

LOWE, Charles U. and others
Mucopolysaccharide from patients with cystic fibrosis of the pancreas. bibliog Science 153:1124-5 S 2 '66
LOWE, David G.
Requiem for a courthouse. Am Heritage 17: 26-9+ O '66
Son's tribute. Am Heritage 17:16-21+ F '66
LOWE, George E.
Camelot affair. Bul Atomic Sci 22:44-8 My '66
LOWE, John
Ever go to a rooster crow? Farm J 90: 64X F '66
LOWELL, James
Cleveland bookman arrested; police fascism charged. Pub W 191:57-8 Ja 16 '67
LOWELL, James Russell
James Russell Lowell, by M. Duberman. Review
Newsweek por 69:61-2 Ja 2 '67. S. Maloff
Person first, a poet second. L. Untermeyer. Sat R 49:54+ D 3 '66
LOWELL, Robert
Fourth of July in Maine: poem. Atlan 217:66-7 Mr '66
1958: poem; excerpt from Near the ocean. Harper 233:63 S '66

about
Master as servant. S. Moon. Poetry 108:189-90 Je '66
LOWENFELD, Andreas F.
United States and the Warsaw convention; statements, February 1, 14, 1966. Dept State Bul 54:580-8 Ap 11 '66
LOWENSTEIN, Allard K.
Candidate; interview. New Yorker 42:41-4 Mr 12 '66
LOWENSTEIN, Amy
Ballade des professeurs du temps fadis; poem. Atlan 217:121 F '66
LOWENTHAL, Richard
Germans feel like Germans again. N Y Times Mag p36-7+ Mr 6 '66
LOWER CALIFORNIA. See California, Lower
LOWER East side. See New York (city)—Description
LOWMAN, Paul D. Jr
Earth from orbit. por Nat Geog Mag 130:644-71 N '66
LOWNDES COUNTY, Ala.
Making up for the past; school-aid measure. New Repub 154:10-11 Mr 19 '66
Test for black power. il Newsweek 68:37 N 7 '66
LOWNDES COUNTY freedom organization
Black power. F. Millspaugh. Commonweal 84:500-3 Ag 5 '66
Lair of the Black Panther. A. Kopkind. New Repub 155:10-13 Ag 13 '66
LOWRY, Howard
Small college: another view. Atlan 217:76-8 Mr '66
LOWRY, Laurence Stephen
Letter from London; exhibition at the Tate. M. Panter-Downes. New Yorker 42:56+ D 24 '66
Rogue at seventy-nine. il por Newsweek 69: 67 Ja 2 '67
LOWRY, Malcolm
Lowry's subjective equipment. J. Wain. New Repub 154:23-4 Ja 15 '66; Correction. 154: 37 F 5 '66
Malcolm Lowry: a reminiscence. D. Markson. Nation 202:164-7 F 7 '66
LOYALTY
See also
Patriotism
LOYALTY, Oaths of
Teach-in in Tucson; Supreme court upholds Elfbrandts' stand. il Newsweek 67:21 My 2 '66
LOYOLA university of Los Angeles
Loyola protest; letter. Commonweal 84:325+ Je 10 '66; Reply. K. Carreiro. 84:452 Jl 22 '66
LUA (native race) See Thailand—Native races
LUBELL, Samuel
Mood of caution; excerpts from address, October 27, 1966. U S News 61:46-7 N 14 '66
LUBOLD, Joyce Kissock
Where have all the children gone? Read Digest 88:135-7 Ap '66
Wouldn't it be easier if I just wore a sign on my back? Pub W 189:43-6 Mr 21 '66
LUBOVE, Roy
Welfare industry: social work & the life of the poor. Nation 202:609-11 My 23 '66

LUBRICATION and lubricants
Notes on motor oil. il Sr Schol 88:34-5+ Ap 22 '66
Useful facts on motor oil. il Consumer Bul 49:27-30 O '66
See also
Automobiles—Lubrication
LUBY, James P.
Annals of medicine; two cases of Vivax malaria, report. B. Rouché. New Yorker 42:219-22+ N 12 '66
LUC Gabrielle, Sister
Solid sister. Newsweek 67:100 Mr 28 '66
LUCAL, John
On misunderstanding Africa. Cath World 203:220-3+ Jl '66
LUCAS COUNTY, Ohio
New county recreation center in action. A. G. Morse. il Parks & Rec 1:720-1+ S '66
LUCE, Clare (Boothe)
Victor belongs to the spoils. Nat R 18:1171-4 N 15 '66
Without portfolio. See issues of McCall's
LUCE, Gay Gaer, and Segal, Julius
Sleep, from alpha to delta. N Y Times Mag p28-9+ Ap 17 '66; Same abr. with title What happens when you sleep. Read Digest 89:84-8 Ag '66
What time is it? the body's clock knows. N Y Times Mag p28-9+ Ap 3 '66
When children sleep. Redbook 128:50-1+ Ja '67
LUCE, Henry Robinson
Journalism's next assignment; excerpts from address. Fortune 75:88 Ja '67
LUCET, Charles
France today: address, September 16, 1966. Vital Speeches 32:746-9 O 1 '66
LUCEY, Patrick J.
Straws in the wind. Time 87:22 Ap 22 '66
LUCEY, William L.
Home scene (cont) America 114:661-2; 115: 696+ My 7, N 26 '66
LUCIA di Lammermoor: opera. See Donizetti, G.
LUCIENTES, Francisco José de Goya y. See Goya y Lucientes F. J. de
LUCK
See also
Superstition
LUCKETT, Hubert
New rectangular 25-inch color TV you build from a kit. Pop Sci 188:102-3 My '66
LUCKNER, Felix, graf von
Obituary
Nat R 18:402 My 3 '66. L. Thomas
Sea devil. il por Newsweek 67:42+ Ap 25 '66
LUCKY bridegroom; story. See Knowlton, R. A.
LUDENDORFF, Erich
Ludendorff, by D. J. Goodspeed. Review
Sat R 49:59 O 22 '66
LUDINGTON, Ivan
Is reading for everyone? the Ludington plan to make a slogan a reality. il por Pub W 190:30-4 N 21 '66
LUDLOW fair; drama. See Wilson, L.
LUDLUM, David B. See Wilhelm, R. C. jt. auth.
LUDWIG II, king of Bavaria. See Louis II, king of Bavaria
LUDWIG, Christa
Man and wife; interview. ed. by R. Eyer. por Opera N 31:14-15 D 17 '66
LUDWIG, Donald
Testing diodes. Electr World 75:95 Ja '66
LUECKE, Richard
Autocratic statement. Christian Cent 83:368-9 Mr 23 '66
LUFTHANSA. See Airlines—Germany (Federal Republic)
LUGGAGE
Countdown to travel! il Seventeen 25:148-9 My '66
Globe-trotting notes on knits and totes. il Seventeen 25:252-3 Ag '66
Individual luggage. il House & Gard 130: 282-3 O '66
Molded luggage. il Consumer Rep 31:324-9 Jl '66
More globe-trotting totes. il Seventeen 25: 334 Ag '66
Visit from Santa. il Seventeen 25:179 D '66
What to look for in luggage. il Good H 162:156 Je '66
What's new in luggage? Bet Hom & Gard 44:29 D '66
See also
Packing of luggage
LUGRIS, Beatriz
Books. Américas 18:41 Jl '66
LUIS Angel Arango library. See Banks and banking—Colombia

LUKAS, J. Anthony
India for the Hindus, says the Jan Sangh.
N Y Times Mag p20-1+ Ag 14 '66
Political python of India. N Y Times Mag
p26-7+ F 20 '66
She stands remarkably alone. N Y Times
Mag p34-5+ Mr 27 '66
Village of hunger and lethargy. N Y Times
Mag p30-1+ O 2 '66
LUKE, Gospel of. See Bible—New Testament—
Luke
LUKIN, Sven
And now: Top. il por Time 87:58-9 F 11 '66
Solid anti-geometry. E. C. Baker. il Art N
65:56-7+ Mr '66
LULVES, John F. Jr
Is there a student conservatism? Nat R 18:
530-1 My 31 '66
LUMBAGO. See Backache
LUMBER industry and trade
New wonders of wood. il Duns R 87:42-4+ Mr
'66
See also
Wood waste
LUMBERING
Liquid logging; log flume. B. Goldrath. il Am
For 72:34-6 F '66
What's wrong with logging? R. G. Reid.
Am For 72:3+ Jl '66
See also
Lumberjacks
LUMBERJACKS
Darts, Paul Bunyan size; ax throwing loggers
vie for world title. J. E. Boykin. il Pop
Mech 125:118-19 Mr '66

Training
School for loggers; Community college, Coos
Bay, Ore. W. B. Morse. il Am For 72:26-
7+ O '66
LUMEMIN. See Musical instruments. Elec-
tronic
LUMET, Sidney
Group embalmed. P. Benchley. Holiday 39:
155-6+ My '66
LUMINESCENCE
Ozone-induced chemiluminescence of organic
compounds. R. L. Bowman and N. Alexan-
der. bibliog il Science 154:1454-6 D 16 '66
LUMINESCENCE, Biological
Bioluminescence; report on Luminescence
conference. F. H. Johnson. Science 153:1141-
2 S 2 '66
Subcellular sources of luminescence in
noctiluca. R. Eckert. bibliog il Science 151:
349-52 Ja 21 '66
LUMINOUS ceilings. See Ceilings
LUMUMBA, Patrice Emergy
Revenant Lumumba. Nat R 18:306-7 Ap 5
'66
LUNA, Donyale
Luna year. il pors Time 87:47 Ap 1 '66
LUNA flights. See Space flights to the moon—
Luna flights
LUNAR bases
Astronomical, lunar surface stations eyed.
M. Getler. il Tech W 19:48-52 N 28 '66
Emplaced data station may extend ALSEP.
C. D. LaFond. il Tech W 20:30+ Ja 9 '67
USSR may aim to settle and farm moon.
H. M. David. Tech W 20:18-19 Ja 2 '67
We'll build a city on the moon. D. Q. Posin.
il Todays Health 44:30-5 My '66
What earthly use is the moon? W. Sullivan.
il N Y Times Mag p39+ Ag 28 '66
LUNAR construction engineering. See Lunar
bases
LUNAR drilling apparatus. See Drilling and
boring machinery
LUNAR environment chamber. See Simulators
LUNAR landing research vehicle. See Space
vehicles—Landing systems—Moon
LUNAR landing systems. See Space vehicles—
Landing systems—Moon
LUNAR magnetic fields. See Magnetic fields
(cosmic physics)
LUNAR models. See Astronomical models
LUNAR modules. See Space vehicles— Land-
ing systems—Moon
LUNAR names. See Names, Lunar
LUNAR Orbiter. See Artificial satellites
LUNAR photography. See Astronomical photog-
raphy; Space photography
LUNAR polarization. See Polarization (light)
LUNAR radiation
Radioactivity of the lunar surface. H. W.
Kraner and others. bibliog Science 152:1235-
6 My 27 '66
LUNAR research. See Moon
LUNAR roving vehicle. See Lunar vehicles

LUNAR simulators. See Simulators
LUNAR stations. See Lunar bases
LUNAR tides. See Tides
LUNAR vehicles
Lunar international laboratory. B. Friedman.
il UNESCO Courier 19:31-2+ My '66
Lunar metal production plant seen feasible;
mobile plant may use electrolysis to melt
lunar surface material. J. F. Judge. il
Tech W 19:28-9 O 17 '66
MTA augurs man's travel on moon surface;
mobility test article and local scientific
survey module. il Sci N 90:3 Jl 2 '66
NASA given lunar surface experiment
demonstration; Apollo lunar surface experiments package. W. J. Normyle. il Aviation W 85:94-5+ Jl 25 '66

Testing
Bendix lunar rover tested at Marshall. il
Tech W 18:42-3 Je 13 '66
Lunar survey module design under test;
Molab and LSSM. W. J. Normyle. il Avia-
tion W 85:97-8+ Jl 18 '66
Moonobile; mobility test article. il Sci Di-
gest 60:inside cover Ag '66
LUNCHEONS
Effortless summer lunch; with recipes.
M. Kaytor. il Look 30:76-7 Jl 26 '66
Open season for entertaining; luncheon on
the terrace; with recipes. il McCalls 93:
112+ My '66
What do you serve when the ladies come to
lunch? with recipes. il Redbook 126:80-4+
F '66
LUNCHES
Good lunches to go! il Bet Hom & Gard 44:
98+ S '66
Lunches kids like. B. B. Smith. il Parents
Mag 41:104 F; 122 Mr; 102 Ap; 108 My;
90 Je; 82 Jl '66
My kids love the school lunch; with recipes.
K. Kuperstock. il Parents Mag 41:86-7+
S '66
New treats for lunch boxes; with recipes.
il Redbook 127:92-3 O '66
Pointers on packing a lunch box. Good H
162:229 Mr '66
Sunday summer lunch at Horst's. Vogue
147:155 Je '66
LUNCHES, School. See School lunches
LUNCHROOMS
See also
Cafeterias

Equipment
Robot dons chef's hat to speed up burgers;
new automatic system, called AMFARE.
il Bsns W p42 Ap 23 '66
LUND, Mary Graham
Adolescent; poem. Christian Cent 83:1106 S
14 '66
LUND, R. D. and Westrum, L. E.
Neurofibrils and the Nauta method. bibliog
Science 151:1397-9 Mr 18 '66
LUND, Richard
Intermuscular bones in pholidophorus bechei
from the lower lias of England. bibliog
Science 152:348-9 Ap 15 '66
LUNDKVIST, Ulf, and Perlmann, Peter
Immunochemical studies of submicrosomal
membranes from liver of normal and
phenobarbital-treated rats. bibliog Science
152:780-2 My 6 '66
LÜNEBURGER HEIDE, Germany
Mike Frome. M. Frome. Am For 72:6+ Mr
'66
LUNG adenomas. See Tumors
LUNG cancer. See Cancer
LUNGFISHES
Nature note. il Sci N 90:560 D 31 '66
Ornithine-urea cyle enzymes in the African
lungfish, protopterus aethiopicus. P. A.
Janssens and P. P. Cohen. bibliog il Science 152:358-9 Ap 15 '66
Urea synthesis in the lungfish: relative importance of purine and ornithine cycle pathways. R. P. Forster and L. Goldstein.
bibliog il Science 153:1650-2 S 30 '66
Uricolytic enzymes in liver of the dipnoan
protopterus aethiopicus. G. W. Brown, jr.
and others. bibliog il Science 153:1653-4 S
30 '66
LUNGS
Lung. J. H. Comroe, jr. il Sci Am 214:56-
66+ F '66
Metabolism of alveolar calls: histochemical
evidence and relation to pulmonary surfactant. S. I. Said and others. bibliog il
Science 152:657-9 Ap 29 '66

LUNGS—*Continued*

Diseases

Should include lung diseases in program; emphysema and chronic bronchitis. Sci N 90:353 O 29 '66

See also
Chest—Diseases
Cystic fibrosis
Emphysema
Pneumothorax

LUNIK probes. See Lunar probes, Russian

LUPU, Radu
Keeping up with Cliburns (and the Joneses) P. Hume. il por Sat R 49:56-7+ O 29 '66
Success by short cut. il por Time 88:96 O 21 '66

LURIE, Diana
They all come thinking I can't be that great. Life 60:96-96B+ Mr 18 '66

LURIE, Nancy Oestreich
Enduring Indian. Natur Hist 75:10+ N '66

LUTEN, C. J.
Bluebeard's castle; London edition. Am Rec G 33:100-1 O '66
Complete, on Vox, Chabrier's piano works: the very heart of his art. Am Rec G 32: 949+ Je '66
In Telefunken's historical series mementoes of the Berlin opera in its golden age. Am Rec G 32:592-4 Mr '66
Tristan und Isolde. Am Rec G 33:284-8 D '66

LUTEN, Carol Ann
Back to school, and all like that. Am Rec G 33:26-7 S '66

LUTEOMAS. See Tumors

LUTHERAN church in America. See Lutheran church in the United States

LUTHERAN church in Norway
Suffer religious oppression in Norway. Christian Cent 83:1024 Ag 24 '66

LUTHERAN church in Sweden
Second spring in Sweden. V. P. McCorry. America 114:551 Ap 16 '66
Sex, sin and salvation in Sweden. D. W. Ferm. Christian Cent 83:1142-6 S 21 '66; Discussion. 83:1343-5 N 2 '66

LUTHERAN church in the United States
Biennial American Lutheran convention. W. L. Thorkelson. Christian Cent 83:1452 N 23 '66
L.C.A. gives final push to L.C.U.S.A.; Lutheran council in the U.S.A.; proposed. W. L. Thorkelson. Christian Cent 83:917+ Jl 20 '66
Reformed-Lutheran conversations. T. G. Tappert. Christian Cent 83:412-14 Mr 30 '66

LUTHERANS in the United States
School v. family; survey of religious attitudes and beliefs among parochial-school children. Time 88:56 S 16 '66

LUTHERMAN, Marjorie
Curl up and read. Seventeen 25:191 D '66

LUTON, England, public libraries
Microscope vs. telescope: large part of annual report devoted to single day. E. Moon. Library J 91:644 F 1 '66

LUTOSŁAWSKI, Witołd
New music of Poland. O. Daniel. por Sat R 49:51-2 Jl 30 '66

LUTTGES, Marvin, and others
Examination of transfer of learning by nucleic acid. bibliog Science 151:834-7 F 18 '66

LUTZ, Paul V.
Greetings, or, Do I feel a draught? Am Heritage 17:112 Ag '66

LUTZIN, Sid
Voice of the recreator. por Parks & Rec 1:895-6 N '66

LUXOR
Alive for 3,400 years? azotobacter bacterial culture from wall of the Great temple of Amun. il Sci Digest 59:48 Ap '66

LUXURY
Luxury: the personal view; opinions of famous women. il Vogue 148:158-9+ N 1 '66

LUZ, Oskar
Proud primitives, the Nuba people. Nat Geog Mag 130:672-99 N '66

LUZBETAK, Louis Joseph
Of many things. T. N. Davis. America 115: inside cover Jl 23 '66

LWOFF, André
Interaction among virus, cell, and organism; address, December 11, 1965. Science 152: 1216-20 My 27 '66

LYE, Len
Gallery for young people. C. B. Johnson. il Sch Arts 65:48 Ja '66

LYING
Why youngsters lie. V. Balaban and C. Levine. il Parents Mag 41:41-3+ My '66
See also
Lie detectors
Truthfulness

LYKES, Richard W.
Teachers from abroad take a look at America. Am Ed 2:14-19 S '66

LYLE, David
Logistics of junk. Esquire 65:59-67+ Mr '66
Plague and war, 1966. Esquire 66:158-63+ S '66

LYMAN, Helen H. See Avery, C. jt. auth.

LYMON, Frankie
Comeback of a child star. A. Peters. il pors Ebony 22:42-4+ Ja '67

LYMPH nodes. See Lymphatic glands

LYMPHATIC glands
Transmigration of lymph nodes by tumor cells. B. Fisher and E. R. Fisher. bibliog Science 152:1397-8 Je 3 '66

LYMPHOCYSTIS. See Fishes—Diseases and pests

LYMPHOCYSTIS viruses. See Viruses

LYMPHOCYTES
Antiserum to lymphocytes: prolonged survival of canine renal allografts. A. F. Monaco and others. bibliog il Science 153: 1264-7 S 9 '66
Lymphocytes from thymectomized rates: immunologic, proliferative, and metabolic properties. W. O. Rieke. bibliog il Science 152:535-8 Ap 22 '66
Mitosis: induction by cultures of human peripheral lymphocytes. N. Hashem; discussion. Science 152:231; 153:659 Ap 8, Ag 5 '66
Phosphorylation of nuclear protein early in the course of gene activation in lymphocytes. L. J. Kleinsmith and others. bibliog il Science 154:780-1 N 11 '66
Radioautographic and electron-microscopic evidence of rapid uptake of antigen by lymphocytes. S. S. Han and A. G. Johnson. bibliog il Science 153:176-8 Jl 8 '66
Synthesis of nonribosomal RNA by lymphocytes: a response to phytohemagglutinin treatment. H. L. Cooper and A. D. Rubin. bibliog il Science 152:516-18 Ap 22 '66

LYMPHOID cells
Immunoglobulin synthesis in vitro by established human cell lines. J. L. Fahey and others. bibliog il Science 152:1259-61 My 27 '66; Reply. G. E. Moore and others. 153: 212-13 Jl 8 '66
Lymphoid cells producing antibody against simple haptens: detection and enumeration. B. Merchant and T. Hraba. bibliog il Science 152:1378-9 Je 3 '66

LYMPHOMAS. See Tumors

LYNCH, Connie
Lynch mob. il Newsweek 68:22+ Ag 8 '66

LYNCH, John
Choosing the chief. Newsweek 68:44 N 14 '66
New taoiseach. por Time 88:47 N 18 '66

LYNCH, Russell G.
Do they dig you, daddio? adaptation of address; reprint. Am For 72:30-1+ F '66

LYNCH, Mrs Weldon
Why boards and trustees? Library J 91: 2018 Ap 15 '66

LYNCH, William F.
Can ministers and psychiatrists work together? Redbook 128:52-3+ D '66

LYND, Staughton
Blistering by Brewster. por Time 87:43 Ja 28 '66
Citizen diplomacy. Nation 202:87 Ja 24 '66
Mission of Staughton Lynd. W. F. Buckley, jr. Nat R 18:105 F 8 '66
One last fling; denounces U.S. involvement in Viet Nam on BBC TV. Time 87:21 F 11 '66
Spokesman for the new left. J. Corry. il pors N Y Times Mag p 12-13+ Ja 23 '66

LYNDHURST (manor house) See New York (state)—Historic houses, etc.

LYNDON, Donlyn
Big happening in Berkeley. Arch Forum 124: 56-63 Ja '66
Concrete cascade, in Portland. Arch Forum 125:74-9 Jl '66
Student dorms: a university tries variety. Arch Forum 124:62-7 Mr '66

LYNDON Baines Johnson library (proposed) See Texas. University, Austin—Libraries

LYNDS, Ronald C. and Quimby, David
Testing and measuring capacitors. Electr World 76:39-41+ S '66

LYNES, Russell
After hours. See issues of Harper's magazine
How good are the junior colleges? Harper 233:53-60 N '66
San Francisco's cultural donnybrook. Harper 232:31-2+ Mr '66
S.R.O. at Mr Hoving's Met. N Y Times Mag p8-11+ Ja 1 '67

LYNN, Kenneth S.
Dos Passos' Chosen country. New Repub 155: 15-18+ O 15 '66

LYON, Peter
Long live the railroads. Holiday 39:50-61+ My '66

LYONS, Augusta Wallace
First flower; story. Parents Mag 41:64-6 Mr '66

LYONS, Daniel
Bomb here, bomb there. America 114:718 My 21 '66

LYONS, Eugene
Licensed to kill in real life. Nat R 18:259-61 Mr 22 '66
Moscow-brewed LSD. Nat R 18:475+ My 17 '66

LYONS, France
Music
Lyons. D. A. Mackinnon. Opera N 30:33 Mr 26 '66

LYRIC opera of Chicago
Chicago. J. Stedman. il Opera N 31:29 D 10 '66
Chicago; Bizet's Pêcheurs de perles. J. W. Stedman and G. McElroy. Opera N 31:27 D 31 '66
Chicago; Boris Godunov and Otello. G. McElroy. il Opera N 31:23 N 19 '66
Chicago; Monteverdi's Coronation of Poppaea. F. M. Merkling. il Opera N 31:29 D 17 '66
Chicago; Prokofiev's Angel of fire and Verdi's La Traviata. J. W. Stedman and G. McElroy. il Opera N 31:30 Ja 21 '67
Majesty restored. J. Kerman. Opera N 31: 8+ N 5 '66
Opera after the schism; Dallas-Chicago report. R. C. Marsh. il Hi Fi 16:142-3 F '66

LYRICS (songs) See Songs
LYSENKO, Trofim Denisovich
Soviet biologists push revolt against old boss. por Bsns W p72 F 26 '66
LYSERGIC acid diethylamide
Aspirin, liquor and LSD. H. Downs. Sci Digest 61:91-3 Ja '67
Congress: a new option for addicts; a look at LSD. J. Walsh. Science 152:1728-9 Je 24 '66
Dangerous LSD? Sci Am 214:54 F '66
Dangers of LSD; Kessler case. il Time 87:52 Ap 22 '66
Dangers of the drug called LSD. L. W. Sauer. PTA Mag 61:31-2 S '66
Donna and the sugar cube. il Newsweek 67: 100 Ap 18 '66
Epidemic of acid heads; post-LSD symptoms after non-medical use. il Time 87: 44+ Mr 11 '66
Four ways to go: the end of the trip. J. Brackman. Esquire 66:126+ S '66
Growing peril: teenage use of drugs for kicks. Good H 162:168 My '66
Growth of a mystique; ed. by J. Mitchell. il Newsweek 67:60-1 My 9 '66
I tried LSD. I. Michele. Ladies Home J 83: 52+ Ag '66
If you want to know about LSD... il U S News 61:82 Jl 18 '66
Illicit LSD traffic hurts research efforts. Sci N 89:327 Ap 30 '66
Is the trip over for LSD? journey into the human subconscious with unknown consequences. Bsns W p 141-2 Ap 23 '66
Is this trip really necessary? Dr Leary's LSD road show. R. Vaughan. Life 61:24 N 11 '66
Kick; government agencies efforts to stamp out drugs. New Repub 154:10 Ap 16 '66; Discussion. 154:33-6 Ap 30; 34-6 My 7 '66
Law & LSD. Time 87:34 Je 10 '66
LSD and the drugs of the mind; uses, abuses, promise and perils; ed. by M. Clark. il Newsweek 67:59-60+ My 9 '66
LSD and the third eye; theories on the role of the pineal organ and its chemicals. J. N. Bleibtreu. Atlan 218:64-9 S '66
LSD, by R. Alpert and S. Cohen. Review Esquire 66:48+ N '66. M. Muggeridge
LSD: control, not prohibition. Life 60:4 Ap 29 '66
LSD helps alcoholics. Sci N 90:22 Jl 9 '66
LSD helps severely disturbed children. Sci N 89:378 My 14 '66

LSD is not a tonic. P. McBroom. Sci N 89:433 Je 4 '66
LSD may become legal if it gets religion. Sci N 90:22 Jl 9 '66
LSD pother. America 115:377 O 1 '66
LSD: research & joy ride. J. T. Ungerleider and D. D. Fisher. il Nation 202:574-6 My 16 '66
LSD spelled out. M. Lerner; H. A. Abramson. Mlle 64:52-3+ Ja '67
LSD: tamed for research; letter. C. C. Dahlberg. Science 153:1595 S 30 '66
LSD; Time essay. Time 87:30-1 Je 17 '66
LSD trigger; crystal palaces and absolute horror. T. Buckley. New Repub 154:15-21 My 14 '66
More light, less heat over LSD. il Bsns W p78+ Je 25 '66
Murder by LSD? Kessler case. Newsweek 67:29 Ap 25 '66
On and off; T. Leary and guests arrested. il Newsweek 67:21-2 My 2 '66
Other side of LSD: the promise & the peril. J. A. Osmundsen. il Look 30:78 Jl 26 '66
Psychedelic art. il Life 61:60-6+ S 9 '66
Psychedelic game; excerpt from Psychedelic reader. R. Hoffmann. Mlle 62:179+ Mr '66
Psychedelic state fluid. Sci N 90:238 S 24 '66
Raid on Castalia. M. Mannes. Reporter 34: 27-8+ My 19 '66
Shrouds around LSD; letter. J. C. Pollard. Science 154:844 N 18 '66
Spread and perils of LSD; with reports by A. Rosenfeld and B. Farrell. il Life 60:28-33 Mr 25 '66
Three motives for good behavior; youthful experimentation with LSD. America 114:579 Ap 23 '66
Time to mutate: T. Leary. il Time 87:30-1 Ap 29 '66
Truth about LSD. W. R. Young. Read Digest 89:56-9 S '66
Turned-on and super-sincere in California. R. Todd. il Harper 234:42-7 Ja '67
Turned on, turned off; researchers meeting, San Francisco. il Newsweek 67:63 Je 27 '66
Turned-on way of life. il Newsweek 68:72+ N 28 '66
Turning it on with LSD; doses to mental patients. Time 88:58 N 25 '66
UCLA treats large number of LSD cases. Sci N 90:117 Ag 20 '66
What is the clinical evidence? L. Ochota. New Repub 154:21-2 My 14 '66
Young people and LSD: a talk with Susan Leary; ed. by M. Mannes. S. Leary. McCalls 93:14+ Jl '66

LYSOSOMES
Lysosomal nature of juxtaglomerular granules. E. R. Fisher. bibliog il Science 152: 1725 Je 24 '66

LYSOZYME
Three-dimensional structure of an enzyme molecule. D. C. Phillips. il Sci Am 215:78-90 bibliog(p 160) N '66

LYTTON, Bart
Will salvation spoil the Dodge house? D. S. Brown. il Arch Forum 125:68-71 O '66

M

MAC. See United States—Military airlift command
M&M. See Manufacturing and machining services corporation
MCA. See Music corporation of America
M. H. de Young memorial museum, San Francisco
Coming June 11, the Brundage opening. il Sunset 136:36+ Je '66
Gateway's Oriental treasure; Brundage collection. il Time 87:92 Je 17 '66
Lotus-eater; Brundage wing dedicated. il Newsweek 67:66-7 Je 20 '66
MHMA. See Mobile homes manufacturers association
MILA (Merritt Island launch area) See Proving grounds
MINEAC (miniature electronic autocollimator) See Collimators
MIT. See Massachusetts institute of technology, Cambridge
M.I.T. press
M.I.T. press demonstrates its computer system. il Pub W 190:73-5 N 14 '66
MLF (multilateral force) See North Atlantic treaty organization—Multilateral force (proposed)

MOL (manned orbiting laboratory) See Space stations
MPAA. See Motion picture association of America
MRCA. See Market research corporation of America
MSU. See Michigan state university of agriculture and applied science, East Lansing
MTA (mobility test article) See Lunar vehicles
MUST (metropolitan urban service training) See Religious cooperation
MA, Thao
Situation normal. Newsweek 68:56 O 31 '66
MAAS, Peter
Government asks ban against Valachi memoirs. Pub W 189:56-7 My 23 '66
Whose thing? Newsweek 67:93 My 23 '66
MAAZEL, Lorin
Maazel, classicist. E. Salzman. Sat R 49: 51 D 31 '66
Music to my ears. I. Kolodin. Sat R 49:76 N 19; 58+ N 26 '66
Musical events; performance of Beethoven's Ninth symphony by New York philharmonic. W. Sargeant. New Yorker 42:229-30 N 19 '66
Presto! Newsweek 67:89 My 30 '66
MACACA nemestrina. See Monkeys
MCADAMS, Nancy R.
Super-librarian and sub-architect. por Library J 91:5827-31 D 1 '66
MACALESTER college, St Paul, Minn.
World press institute. A. Rodríguez Villar. il Américas 18:2-7 Je '66
MACALISTER, Paul Ritter
Imaginative ideas for display. il House & Gard 130:70-7 Jl '66
MACANDREW, Andrew R.
Hazardous art of mistranslation. Harper 232: 94-6+ Ap '66
MACAO
Breath of trouble. il Time 88:37-8 D 16 '66
Eastward Ho; Peking's influence. il Newsweek 68:56 O 17 '66
Macao: the vanishing sin. C. Stinnett. il Holiday 40:16+ O '66
Object lesson. Newsweek 68:44+ D 19 '66
MACAQUES. See Monkeys
MACARONI
Adventures in pasta. J. D. Scott. il Holiday 40:74-6 O '66
Gastronomy. J. Wechsberg. il Esquire 65: 66-7 My '66
Gnocchi is simply Italian for lumps. il Sunset 136:196+ My '66
Macaroni with cheese, the ways are almost unlimited. il Sunset 136:164 Je '66
World of fine cooking; pasta. M. Field. il McCalls 93:59-60+ Je '66
MACARTHUR, Douglas, 1880-1964
Fall of Corregidor; excerpts from Battles lost and won; great campaigns of World war II. H. W. Baldwin. il Am Heritage 17:16-23+ Ag '66
Late General MacArthur, warts and all. F. Bowers. por Esquire 67:90-1+ Ja '67
MACARTHUR, Douglas, 1909-
Free world's stake in Viet-Nam; address, October 19, 1966. Dept State Bul 55:745-50 N 14 '66
Your stake in the balance-of-payments problem; address, April 26, 1966. Dept State Bul 54:812-17 My 23 '66
MACARTHUR, Robert Helmer
Correction to one of MacArthur's species-abundance formulas. E. C. Pielou and A. N. Arnason. bibliog il Science 151:592 F 4 '66
MACAULAY, Pauline
Astrakhan coat. Criticism
Time 89:71 Ja 20 '67
MCAULEY, Karen
To my sister, Susan; poem. Mlle 63:322 Ag '66
MACAULEY, Robie
Pre-empted domain. Sat R 49:20-1 Je 4 '66
MCAVOY, Thomas D.
In memory of Tom McAvoy. G. P. Hunt. por Life 60:3 F 25 '66
Talent for candids. P. Stackpole. U S Camera 29:26+ Je '66
MACBAIN, Alastair
Crazy quail. Field & S 71:43+ Jl '66
MCBEE, Susanna
He saw dad and uncles first, then switched. Life 60:46+ Ap 1 '66
Long void is filled at last. Life 62:32-32B Ja 13 '67
(ed) See Whalen, W. H. Bizzarre account of what Whalen says he did

about

Interviewing an accused spy. G. P. Hunt. por Life 61:3 Jl 22 '66

MACBETH, George
Bats; poem. New Yorker 42:159 S 17 '66
Star; poem. New Yorker 42:56 O 15 '66
Ward; poem. New Yorker 42:42 Ap 30 '66
MACBETH; drama. See Shakespeare, W.—Plays
MCBRIDE, C. H.
Ground floor. Esquire 65:94-5 Mr '66
MCBRIDE, Joe
Make a vacuum cleaner for your car. Pop Sci 188:143 Mr '66
MCBRIDE, R. A. and Schierman, L. W.
Antibody-forming cells: population patterns after simultaneous immunization with different isoantigens. bibliog Science 154:655-7 N 4 '66
MCBRIEN, Richard P.
Radical theology. Commonweal 84:605-8 S 23 '66
MCBRIEN, William A.
Strategies of reason reasoning. Commonweal 84:476-7 Jl 22 '66
MCCABE, Bernard
Books. Commonweal 83:561-2; 84:443-4 F 11, Jl 8 '66
MCCABE, Ralph. See Pyrrho, pseud.
MCCABE, Robert Karr
When China spits, we swim. N Y Times Mag p26-7+ F 27 '66
MCCAFFERTY, Phil
For thrifty shooting, try a BB trap range. Pop Sci 189:142-3 Ag '66
How to buy a fishing rod. Pop Sci 189: 148-50+ Jl '66
Repairing window shades. Pop Sci 188:180-1 Mr '66
Which type of camper should you buy? Pop Sci 188:148-53+ My '66
—and Van Alstyne, T. C.
Color those metal projects chemically. Pop Sci 188:124-8 F '66
MCCAIN, Dennis, family
How America lives; their home is wherever they like it. G. Greene. il Ladies Home J 83:74-5+ Je '66
MCCAIN, John S. jr
Total wet war; address, May 2, 1966. Vital Speeches 32:514-18 Je 15 '66
MACCALL, George
Reasons why the roof fell in. W. Bingham. Sports Illus 25:73-4+ N 21 '66
MCCALL'S (periodical)
When McCall's looks for stories. B. Blakemore. Writer 79:25 F '66
MCCALLUM, Daniel Craig
Big business takes the management track. por Bsns W p 104+ Ap 30 '66
MCCALLUM, David
Illya goes home to the heather. il pors Life 60:45-6 Ap 29 '66
Illya woodwind blows good. K. Gouldthorpe. Life 60:12 Ap 29 '66
MCCALMON, George, and Moe, Christian
Why communities dramatize history; excerpts from reprint. Parks & Rec 1:778+ S '66
MCCANDLESS, Boyd
Children's research can go wrong. PTA Mag 61:23-5 bibliog(p36) D '66
MCCANN, Frances V.
Curare as a neuromuscular blocking agent in insects. bibliog Science 154:1023-4 N 25 '66
MCCANN, Hugh Wray-. See Wray-McCann, H.
MCCARTEN, John
Theatre. See issues of New Yorker
MCCARTHY, Charles R.
Personal freedom and community responsibility. Cath World 203:165-8 Je '66
MCCARTHY, Colman
After the noise: the hope of Vatican II. Christian Cent 83:167-70 F 9 '66
MCCARTHY, Eugene J.
My hopes for the Democrats. por Sat R 49: 21-3+ N 5 '66
U.S: supplier of weapons to the world. Sat R 49:13-15 Jl 9 '66
MCCARTHY, Ginny
What it takes to feed your family well. Parents Mag 41:94-5+ N '66
MCCARTHY, Joe
Honeymoon that reran for ten years. Life 60: 12 Mr 25 '66
MCCARTHY, John
Information; with biographical sketch. Sci Am 215:45, 64-73 S '66
MCCARTHY, Mary
Letter from abroad; M. McCarthy versus Paris. J. Barry. il McCalls 93:40+ Je '66
MCCARTHY, Tom
Color odds are ten to one against Tom McCarthy. il por Pop Phot 59:88-97+ Jl '66

MCCARTNEY, Paul
Bards of pop. il por Newsweek 67:102 Mr 21 '66
Old Beatles, a study in paradox. M. Cleave. il pors N Y Times Mag p 10-11+ Jl 3 '66

MCCARTY, John T.
Role of the professional manager; address, August 22, 1966. Vital Speeches 32:751-4 O 1 '66

MCCASKILL, Henry
Night, what of the watchman? Nation 202: 766 Je 27 '66

MCCAULEY, John F.
His Honor is a teacher. M. W. Krey. por NEA J 55:47+ Mr '66

MCCAULEY, Patt Kirby
What good are report cards? Parents Mag 41:42-3+ Je '66

MCCHAN, George
McChan's luck. por Time 88:35 D 30 '66

MACCHI, Angelo
Italy, 1966. Cath World 202:288-90 F '66

MCCHRISTIAN, Joseph A.
Men who run the war. por Newsweek 68:54 D 5 '66

MCCLAIN, Edward F.
High-precision 85-foot radio telescope. Sky & Tel 32:4-6 Jl '66

MCCLANE, A. J.
(ed) Fishing. See issues of Field & stream
Fly fishing for bones. Field & S 71:54-7 N '66
Perfect boats for fishermen. Field & S 71: 28-9+ Ja '67
                    about
Fishing with Al McClane. T. Trueblood. Field & S 70:24+ Ap '66

MCCLARREN, Robert R.
Priority in Indiana. ALA Bul 60:951+ O '66
—and Thompson, D. E.
Architectural checklist. bibliog pors Library J 91:5832-7 D 1 '66

MCCLELLAN, Daniel
Father Dan the money man. il por Time 87:75+ Ap 22 '66

MCCLELLAN, Edwin
From the eighth century. Poetry 107:404-6 Mr '66

MCCLELLAN, R. O. See Bustad, L. K. jt. auth.

MCCLELLAND, Howard D.
Executive investment: citrus groves. T. J. Murray. il Duns R 88:33 Ag '66

MCCLORY, Kevin
Life of Ian Fleming. Pub W 191:36-7 Ja 9 '67

MCCLOSKEY, Mark
Five poets. Poetry 108:272-6 Jl '66
Minor change; poem. New Yorker 42:96 Mr 5 '66
Of war; poem. Commonweal 85:171 N 11 '66
Out of touch; poem. Poetry 108:235 Jl '66
                    about
Three English poets. Poetry 109:126-9 N '66

MCCLOSKEY, Robert James
Mr Harriman to supervise U.S. actions on POW's in Viet-Nam; statement, May 18 1966. Dept State Bul 54:888 Je 6 '66
Senior scholastic interview. il por Sr Schol 89:21 N 4 '66

MCCLOY, John J.
Secretary Rusk, Secretary McNamara, Mr McCloy meet with President Johnson; excerpts from press briefing, November 23, 1966. Dept State Bul 55:923-4 D 19 '66

MCCLUER, Robert H. See Meisler, M. H. jt. auth.

MCCLURE, Claude
Charges dismissed. Newsweek 67:24 Ap 25 '66
Out of action. Commonweal 84:45-6 Ap 1 '66
Two GI's in limbo. H. W. Ernst. il Nation 202:294-5 Mr 14 '66

MCCLURE, Eleanor
Concentrate, don't scatter flowers. Pop Gard 17:40-1 Ag '66

MCCLURE, John T.
More Stravinsky by Stravinsky, and Ivesian explorations. W. Malloch. il por Hi Fi 16: 12+ Ag '66

MCCLURG, A. C, and company
Chicago finance company plans to acquire McClurg. Pub W 190:55-6 O 31 '66
Finance firm completes acquisition of A. C. McClurg. il Pub W 191:59 Ja 16 '67

MCCLUSKEY, Sally
Private papers of a very new mother. Good H 162:58+ Mr '66

MCCOLGAN, Robert
People won't drink cedar water. Am City 81: 103-5+ D '66

MCCOMBS, Philip A.
Who is behind the race riots? Nat R 18:934-5 S 20 '66

MCCONKEY, Thomas W.
(ed) Buyers' guide (cont of) Products and equipment. See first issue of each month of Library journal
(ed) Library buying guide 1966. Library J 91:1792+ Ap 1 '66
(ed) Products & equipment. See first issue of each month of Library journal

MCCONNAUGHY, Mary Jean, and Fox, Bernie
Alice in Wonderland. Sch Arts 65:29-30 My '66

MCCONNELL, Bonnie
Entreaty; poem. Farm J 90:89 S '66

MCCONNELL, Charles
There is a difference. por Seventeen 26:98 Ja '67

MCCONNELL, John Paul
Air power: what it is doing in Vietnam war; interview. por U S News 60:28-9 My 9 '66
Fallacy of the nuclear stalemate; address, March 24, 1966. Vital Speeches 32:456-9 My 15 '66

MCCORD, Andrew King
Pulling the big switch. il por Bsns W p 182-4+ F 19 '66

MCCORKLE, Grady
Stacey speeds delivery with new billing system. Pub W 189:46-9 Ap 18 '66

MCCORKLE, S. A.
Who really fathered the city-manager plan? bibliog Am City 81:106-7 Mr '66

MCCORMAC, Billy M. and Ash, J. E.
Great Lakes research. Science 152:1773-4+ Je 24 '66

MCCORMACK, Clyde R.
Heresy by translation. Christian Cent 83: 437-8 Ap 6 '66

MCCORMACK, Edward Joseph
Teddy and Eddie revisited. M. F. Nolan. Reporter 35:33-5 S 8 '66

MCCORMACK, James
Amazing story of earth satellites; interview. por U S News 61:58-62 D 26 '66
                    about
Speeding Comsat into a fast orbit. por Bsns W p 128+ Mr 26 '66

MCCORMACK, John J.
New general for Maryknoll. America 115: 269 S 17 '66

MCCORMICK, Adoreen, and Carl, H. A.
Library of Congress assistance to the Nation's libraries. ALA Bul 60:159-63 F '66
—See Hamer, E. E. jt. auth.

MCCORMICK, Cyrus Hall
Famous firsts: U.S. seedbed of the manager's art. por Bsns W p53-4 Ag 27 '66

MCCORMICK, Richard A.
Book review. America 114:859-60 Je 18 '66
Modern morals in a muddle. America 115:116 Jl 30 '66

MCCORMICK, Robert Rutherford
McCormick of Chicago, by F. C. Waldrop. Review
    Christian Cent 83:236 F 23 '66. E. Gertz
    New Repub 154:39-40 F 26 '66. E. Norlander
    Newsweek il pors 67:60+ Mr 7 '66

MCCORMICK, Robert V.
Curse of the North. Field & S 71:47+ Je '66

MCCORMICK, Leander observatory. See Astronomical observatories

MCCORRY, Vincent P.
Our oldest mission; symbol of peace. America 114:625 Ap 30 '66
Word. See issues of America

MCCOY, C. J. and Hoddenbach, G. A.
Geographic variation in ovarian cycles and clutch size in cnemidophorus tigris (teiidae) bibliog Science 154:1671 D 30 '66

MCCOY, Penny
Found: a pretty Penny. B. Ottum. il por Sports Illus 25:12-15 Ag 15 '66

MCCRACKEN, Harold
George Catlin revival. Am Artist 30:26-31+ Mr '66

MCCRACKEN, James
Tenor who busted loose. por Hi Fi 16:111+ Je '66

MCCRACKEN, K. G.
Energy spectra of a number of celestial X-ray sources in the energy range from 2 to 60 kiloelectron volts. bibliog Science 154:1000-2 N 25 '66

MCCRADY, John
Painting technique of John McCrady. J. Kelly. il pors Am Artist 30:50-5+ F '66

MCCRAW, Harry Wells
Floyd's Markheim caps the season. Hi Fi 16:124-5 Je '66

MCCRAY, Richard
Possibility of maser action in cosmic radio sources. bibliog Science 154:1320-3 D 9 '66

MCCROSSIN, G. Michael
Pentecost in our lives. America 114:770-2 My 28 '66

MCCULLERS, Carson (Smith)
Key is loneliness. M. Klein. Reporter 34: 43-4 Je 30 '66

MCCULLOCH, Frank
Saigon's Buddhists get the Premier's message. Life 60:28-9 Je 3 '66
Young generals who run the country. Life 60:52B+ F 25 '66

MCCULLOCH, William F. and Diesch, S. L.
You can catch animal diseases. Suc Farm 64:70 O '66

MCCULLOCH, William M.
Excerpt from debate, July 26, 1966. Cong Digest 45:272+ N '66

MCCULLOUGH, David G.
Hail Liberty! Am Heritage 17:22-3+ F '66
Run for your lives! Am Heritage 17:4-11+ Je '66

MCDANIEL, Robert G. and Sarkissian, I. V.
Heterosis: complementation by mitochondria. bibliog Science 152:1640-2 Je 17 '66

MCDERMOTT, John
Portent for the future: welfare imperialism in Vietnam. Nation 203:76-88 Jl 25 '66

MCDERMOTT, John A.
Chicago Catholic asks: where does my church stand on racial justice? por Look 30:82+ N 1 '66

MCDERMOTT, John R.
Cries of pig, stupid, as the red light flashes. Life 60:36+ Mr 4 '66
Pro with laughing eyes and bitter moods. Life 61:56-8 Ag 5 '66
Toughest bird in Baltimore. Life 61:48A-48B Jl 8 '66

MACDONALD, Brian
Rose Latulippe; notes from diary. por Dance Mag 40:58-62 D '66

MACDONALD, David
Lobster: oddball of the ocean. Read Digest 89:203-4+ D '66
Mayhem on ice. Read Digest 88:17-18+ Mr '66
They couldn't beat Bluenose. Read Digest 89:118-22 O '66

MACDONALD, Don
Way we see it. por Motor T 18:18 S; 8 O; 8 N; 8 D '66; 19:6 Ja '67

MACDONALD, Dwight
Films. See issues of Esquire to November 1966
Politics. Esquire 67:26+ Ja '67
Valedictory. Esquire 66:70+ N '66

about

Big bad Wolfe? por Newsweek 67:60 Ja 31 '66
Look out, politics, here comes MacDonald. A. Gingrich. il Esquire 67:6 Ja '67

MACDONALD, Flora
Flora, by E. G. Vining. Review
Sat R 49:88 Ap 9 '66. A. Pippett

MCDONALD, John
Howard Hughes's biggest surprise. Fortune 74:119-20+ Jl 1 '66
Now the bankers come to Disney. Fortune 73:138-41+ My '66
Steel is rebuilding for a new era. Fortune 74:130-7+ O '66
There wasn't any panic at 23 Wall. Fortune 74:152-5+ D '66

MACDONALD, John D.
Funny man; story. Sat Eve Post 239:64-6 My 21 '66

about

Authors & editors. Pub W 191:21 Ja 2 '67

MCDONALD, Katherine (Griffith)
Fatal meeting. Opera N 30:24-5 F 19 '66

MCDONALD, Michelle
November; poem. Horn Bk 42:751 D '66

MCDONALD corporation
Hamburger university. N. Fraser. il Life 61:100 O 21 '66

MCDONNELL, James Smith
Mr Mac & Messrs Douglas. il por Time 89: 73-4 Ja 20 '67

MACDONNELL, Malcolm F. and Flynn, J. P.
Control of sensory fields by stimulation of hypothalamus. Science 152:1406-8 Je 3 '66

MCDONNELL aircraft corporation
Mr Mac tries again; concerning takeover of Douglas aircraft co. il Time 88:90 D 16 '66
$25.6-million Gemini incentive seen for near-perfect effort. Aviation W 86:32 Ja 16 '67
We did our homework. il Newsweek 68:68 N 14 '66

MCDONNELL company-Douglas aircraft company merger. See Airplane industry and trade—Consolidations and mergers

MACDOUGALL, Allister
White alder berries. Horticulture 44:52 O '66

MACDOUGALL, Michael
Spy and the coin collector. Nat R 18:355 Ap 19 '66

MCDOWALL, Roddy
(comp) Double exposure; excerpts. por Mc-Calls 94:97-107 O '66

MCDOWELL, Edwin
Helping them bury us. Nat R 18:540-2 My 31 '66

MCDOWELL, Samuel Edward
Sam, you make the ball too small. J. Mann. il pors Sports Illus 24:40-2+ My 23 '66
Sudden Sam, the shutout man. il por Time 87:54-5 My 13 '66
Sudden Sam, the strike-out man. H. L. Masin. por Sr Schol 88:26 Ap 15 '66

MACDUFFIE, Malcolm
Think small (boat that is) Yachting 120:62-4 N '66

MACDUFFIE, Marshall
From the Ukraine to the Kremlin. Sat R 49: 23-4 Je 25 '66
Indictment of ideas. Sat R 49:25 Ag 6 '66

MACE, Myles L.
President and international operations. bibliog Harvard Bsns R 44:72-84 N '66

MACEDONIA
See also
Pella, Greece (ancient city)

MCELROY, C. J.
Tigre is behind us! pors Outdoor Life 139: 35-7+ Ja '67

MCELROY, George
(ed) See Suliotis, E. Gift of the Greeks
—See Stedman, J. W. jt. auth.

MCELROY, Michael B. See Chamberlain, J. W. jt. auth.

MCELWAIN, Franklin R.
Overhead transparencies: a new service for teaching. Sr Schol 89:sup7 S 16 '66

MCENROE, W. D. and Dronka, Kazimierz
Color vision in the adult female two-spotted spider mite. bibliog Science 154:782-4 N 11 '66

MCENTEE, Howard G.
Magic box that calls you to the telephone. Pop Sci 188:116-19 Je '66

MACEOIN, Gary
American Catholicism: wind from Rome. Nation 204:42-6 Ja 9 '67
Hollow tree. America 115:591 N 12 '66

MCEWEN, Alexander, family
Alexander McEwen young. il pors Vogue 148: 250-1 D '66

MACEWEN, Gwendolyn
Canadian chronicle. R. Skelton. Poetry 109: 55 O '66

MCEWEN, Roderick, family
Rory McEwen girls. il pors Vogue 148:248-9 D '66

MCFADDEN, J. P.
Who will protect the police? Nat R 18:311-13+ Ap 5 '66

MCFADDEN, James J.
Reporter at large. F. C. Shapiro. New Yorker 42:181-98 O 22 '66

MCFADDEN, William C.
It's what's bugging them. America 114:502-3 Ap 9 '66

MACFADDEN-Bartell corporation
Macfadden-Bartell titles used for sales promotion. Pub W 189:274-5 Ja 24 '66

MCFALL, Wilfred M.
Yen for Zen; poem. Christian Cent 83:1055 Ag 31 '66

MCFARLAN, Ethel
Tiger catcher; dramatization of a Chinese folk tale. Plays 26:65-8 Ja '67

MCFARLAND, Gary
Jazz concerts. W. Balliett. New Yorker 42: 80+ F 26 '66

MCFARLAND, Jim
Shop talk. See issues of Hot rod

MCFARLANE, John W.
Can you control a len's definition? reprint from Here's how. Mod Phot 30:74-7+ Je '66

MACFARLANE, Norman
Navy chaplaincy: muzzled ministry. Christian Cent 83:1338-9 N 2 '66

MCFARLANE, Samuel B.
Inventor of the month. S. V. Jones. por Sci Digest 59:27 F '66

MCFARLIN, Peter F. See Pratt, R. M. jt. auth.

MACFARQUHAR, Roderick
Mao's last revolution. bibliog f For Affairs 45:112-24 O '66

MCFEE, June King. See Lovano, J. J. jt. auth.

MCFEGGAN, James
Don't trade that police car. Am City 81: 100-2 F '66

MCGARRAH, Robert E.
Logistics for the international manufacturer. Harvard Bsns R 44:154+ Mr '66

MCGARRIGLE, Francis J.
To God, thanks. America 115:690 N 26 '66
MCGAUGH, James L.
Time-dependent processes in memory storage. bibliog Science 153:1351-8 S 16 '66
—and Alpern, H. P.
Effects of electroshock on memory; amnesia without convulsions. bibliog Science 152:665-6 Ap 29 '66
MCGAW, Bill
Showdown in the Southwest. il por Time 87:44 F 11 '66
MCGEE, Gale W.
Arrogance of dissent; irresponsible quality of much political dissent; remarks at Oregon state university forum. Life 61:4 Jl 15 '66
Excerpt from address, February 10, 1966. Cong Digest 45:147+ My '66
Excerpt from debate, July 27, 1966. Cong Digest 45:213+ Ag '66

about
Arrogance of dissent. K. Crawford. Newsweek 68:27 Jl 18 '66
MCGEE, Henry W.
Super postmen. il pors Ebony 22:48-50+ D '66
MCGEE, James
How I lost 180 pounds; interview, ed. by L. Robinson. pors Ebony 21:36-8+ Jl '66
MCGEE, Reece
Welfare in affluence: the mirage of rationalism. Nation 202:174-80 F 14 '66
MCGEER, Edith G. and McGeer, P. L.
Circadian rhythm in pineal tyrosine hydroxylase. bibliog Science 153:73-4 Jl 1 '66
MCGEER, Patrick L. See McGeer, E. G. jt. auth.
MCGHEE, Andrew White
How Andy McGhee got a better job. W. Shelton. il por Fortune 75:116-17+ Ja '67
MCGHEE, George C.
East-West trade: a realistic appraisal; address, March 31, 1966. Dept State Bul 54:1019-26 Je 27 '66
International scientific cooperation: an American view; reprint. Dept State Bul 54:369-78 Mr 7 '66
Roots of American foreign policy; address, November 9, 1965. Dept State Bul 54:53-8 Ja 10 '66
Space exploration, a new dimension in U.S.-European cooperation; excerpts from address, January 14, 1966. Dept State Bul 54:460-3 Mr 21 '66
United States and Germany: our mutual responsibilities and our mutual dependence; address, February 18, 1966. Dept State Bul 54:657-63 Ap 25 '66
U.S. responsibilities toward Europe and Germany; address, July 14, 1966. Dept State Bul 55:269-73 Ag 22 '66
MCGINLEY, Phyllis
Threnody; poem; reprint. Horizon 8:49 Wint '66
Wonderful time; poems; excerpts. McCalls 93:60-1 Jl '66
Wreath of Christmas legends; poems. Ladies Home J 83:73-7 D '66
MCGINNIS, Bret
Department accreditation plan. por Parks & Rec 1:217 Mr '66
Hoosier senior citizens camp. por Parks & Rec 1:419+ My '66
MCGINNIS, Samuel M.
Sceloporus occidentalis: preferred body temperature of the western fence lizard. bibliog Science 152:1090-1 My 20 '66
MCGLANNAN school for dyslexics, Miami, Fla. See Special classes and special schools
MCGOLDRICK, Redmond
Vacancies; poem. America 114:808 Je 4 '66
MCGOVERN, Donald H.
Men who run the war. por Newsweek 68:55 D 5 '66
MCGOVERN, George S.
Foreign policy and the crisis mentality. Atlan 219:55-7 Ja '67
Opinion: on Vietnam. Mlle 62:66+ Mr '66
MCGOVERN, John P.
How to control allergies. Parents Mag 41:68-9+ N '66
MCGOWEN, Jackson Ramsey
Why Douglas is in a downdraft. il por Bsns W p 175-8+ O 22 '66
MCGRADY, Hope H.
Books for beginners. Library J 91:1033-5 F 15 '66
MCGRAW-HILL, Incorporated
Fall regional distribution is a hit at McGraw-Hill. il Pub W 191:22-7 Ja 2 '67
Justice dept. ok's merger of McGraw-Hill and S&P. Pub W 189:53 Mr 7 '66
McGraw-Hill completes Midwest distribution center. Pub W 189:198 Je 6 '66

McGraw-Hill to buy medical publisher. Pub W 190:41 Jl 25 '66
Major new series on Communist China and U.S.A. Pub W 189:64 F 7 '66
MCGRAW-Hill book company. See McGraw-Hill, incorporated
MACGREGOR, Felipe E.
America personality. por America 114:back cover Ap 16 '66
MCGREW, Jay L. and others
Marangoni flow: an additional mechanism in boiling heat transfer. bibliog Science 153:1106-7 S 2 '66
MCGRORY, Mary
Washington front. See issues of America
MCGUIGAN, Dorothy
Mother to the fatherland. Horizon 8:16-23 Sum '66
MCGUIRE, Frank G.
Government expresses interest in small-arms rocket family. Tech W 18:34+ Je 13 '66
MCGUIRE, Garth R.
Practice waterskiing indoors. Parks & Rec 1:754-5 S '66
MCGUIRE, James
Your bank is defunct. por Newsweek 68:87-8 O 24 '66
MCGUIRE, Joseph W.
Management concepts? fads and fancies. Duns R 87:47-8+ Mr '66
MCGUIRE, Tom
New England tombstone rubbings. Sch Arts 65:21-3 Je '66
MACHADO, Antonio
Elegy for Don Francisco Giner de los Ríos; tr. by R. Bly. Nation 202:464 Ap 18 '66

about
Heat in Spain. G. Jackson. Commonweal 84:327-9 Je 10 '66
Spain: no homage allowed! Nation 202:462-4 Ap 18 '66
MCHARG, Ian L.
Blight or a noble city? por Audubon Mag 68:47-52 Ja '66
MACHIAVELLI, Niccolò
Old Nick. S. K. Oberbeck. por Newsweek 69:97 Ja 23 '67
MACHINE age
See also
Technocracy
Technology and civilization
MACHINE billing. See Billing
MACHINE embroidery. See Embroidery
MACHINE shop workers. See Machine shops—Employees
MACHINE shops
Employees
Tool and die makers. C. Peet. Pop Mech 127:20+ Ja '67
MACHINE tool industry and trade
Machine tool maker with taste for expansion; Giddings & Lewis. il Bsns W p 156+ D 3 '66
Revolution from Brazil, in machine tool making; Industrias Romi. il Bsns W p92-4+ Ag 20 '66
Tool makers in Russia gear up for business; aim for export markets. il Bsns W p 175-6 N 26 '66
Tool men fret amid rising tide of orders; skilled labor shortage. il Bsns W p29-30 F 19 '66
When business is almost too good. il Bsns W p 198+ S 24 '66
See also
Ex-cell-o corporation
MACHINE tools
Roundup of new tools for the hardware show. il Pop Sci 189:198+ N '66
Shop talk. R. P. Stevenson. See issues of Popular science monthly
See also
Drilling and boring machinery
Jigs
Machine tool industry and trade
Milling tools
Control
East meets West to develop a lathe; Krupp-Hungarian machine. tape controlled lathe, called CER 200. il Bsns W p64+ Ap 30 '66
Exhibitions
Tool makers in Russia gear up for business; aim for export markets. il Bsns W p 175-6 N 26 '66
MACHINE translators. See Translating machines
MACHINE works
Employees
See also
Machinery industry—Wages and hours

MACHINERY
See also
Labor saving devices

Design
See also
Human engineering

Stands
Rolling saw stand features handy bins. R. Treves. il Pop Mech 126:149 Ag '66

Taxation
Tax credit that business may lose. U S News 60:102+ My 9 '66

MACHINERY, Automatic
High-powered drive in material handling. H. E. Klein. il Duns R 87:pt2 128-9+ Mr '66

MACHINERY in industry
See also
Automation

MACHINERY industry
See also
Agricultural machinery industry and trade

Wages and hours
Earnings in the machinery industries, April-June 1965. F. W. Mohr. il Mo Labor R 89: 36-9 Ja '66

MACHINISTS
See also
Machine shops—Employees

MACHINISTS union. See International association of machinists

MACHU PICCHU, Peru
Machu Picchu; an anthology; excerpts, comp. by H. Buse. il Américas 18:15-21 Ja '66
Something lost behind the ranges. G. F. Hobart. Nat R 18:166 F 22 '66
Tombs of Machu Picchu; with bibliography. C. W. Goff. il Américas 18:8-18 Ag '66

MCHUGH, Keith Stratton
New York's novel export plan; interview. por Duns R 87:55-6+ F '66

MCILVAINE, Robinson
Notes and comment; seizure. New Yorker 42:51 N 12 '66

MCINERNY, Ralph
Pain of possession; story. Redbook 128:46-7 D '66

MACINNES, Colin
Mauritius: world strains in microcosm. Nation 203:447-9 O 31 '66
Mothers & daughters. Mlle 62:186-7+ Mr '66

MACINNES, Helen
Queen of the spies. il Time 87:114 Mr 18 '66

MACINNES, James W. and Uretz, R. B.
Organization of DNA in dipteran polytene chromosomes as indicated by polarized fluorescence microscopy. bibliog Science 151:689-91 F 11 '66

MCINNIS, Frank G.
Reaching our goals. por Parks & Rec 1:401 My '66

MACINNIS, Joseph B.
Living under the sea; with biographical sketch. Sci Am 214:20, 24-33 bibliog(p 143) Mr '66

MCINTIRE, Carl
McIntire followers rally to his cause. R. J. Wagner. Christian Cent 83:317-18 Mr 9 '66
Radio station calls McIntire's bluff. C. W. Zunkel. Christian Cent 83:1551-2 D 14 '66

MCINTOSH, Alan
I am a tired American; reprint. U S News 60:120 F 14 '66

MCINTYRE, Edward F.
Stereo cartridges in '66. Hi Fi 16:45-9+ F '66

MCINTYRE, Loren
Flamboyant is the word for Bolivia. il Nat Geog Mag 129:153-95 F '66

MCINTYRE, Thomas J.
Excerpt from address, June 1, 1966. Cong Digest 45:248+ O '66

MCISAAC, Charles A.
Open letter. Library J 91:6047-8 D 15 '66

MACIVER, Loren
Art galleries; exhibition at the Pierre Matisse. R. M. Coates. New Yorker 42:158 Ap 9 '66

MACK trucks, incorporated
Bulldog tenacity puts truck maker on the high road. il Bsns W p 182-4+ O 15 '66

MCKAY, Vernon
Africa and the American right. New Repub 154:13-16 Mr 26 '66
Cooperation for order in Africa. Cur Hist 50: 129-34+ Mr '66

MACKAYE, Benton
Notes from a diarist. Liv Wildn 29:27-8 Wint '65

MCKEAN, Brad
He makes a splash with a ripple. C. Phinizy. il pors Sports Illus 24:60-2+ My 16 '66

MCKEE, William F.
When $4-billion is up in the air. il por Bsns W p 190-2+ O 8 '66

MACKEIGAN, Niels S.
Foreign language in high school. NEA J 55: 48 O '66

MCKENNEY, Elizabeth. See Howey, J. jt. auth.

MCKENNEY, J. Wilson
Teaching the Bill of rights in California. Sat R 49:68-9+ Mr 19 '66

MCKENNY, Betsy
Curl up and read. Seventeen 25:196 Ap '66

MCKENZIE, Donald
Burn up those lift-station odors. Am City 81:80-2 N '66

MCKENZIE, John Lawrence
Priest incubators. Christian Cent 83:1602-3 D 28 '66
Reflections on the church's teaching authority; excerpt from Authority in the church. por Cath World 203:86-90 My '66

about
In his own society. por Time 87:86+ My 13 '66

MCKETA, Robert F.
Youth activities in Okinawa. por Parks & Rec 1:156-8 F '66

MACKEY, Ernan
Oh, my darling daughter; story. Redbook 127:66-7 O '66

MACKIE, Walter F.
Hurricane barrier for New Bedford. Motor B 117:197-8 Ap '66

MCKIERNAN, Eoin
Ecumenical backlash. America 115:31-3 Jl 9 '66

MCKINLEY, Donald
Twenty-fourth Ceramic national. Craft Horiz 26:10-15+ N '66
Wood; a discussion. por Craft Horiz 26:16-19 Je '66

MCKINLEY, Fred
Perfect camper. Outdoor Life 137:48-51+ Mr '66

MCKINNEY, C. S.
Construct the critical units first. Am City 81:112-13 My '66

MCKINNEY, Jack
Trade winds; telephone talk-jockey show. J. C. Fuller. il Sat R 49:12-13 Mr 5 '66

MACKINTOSH, Helen K.
Washington report. J. Lloyd. Sr Schol 87: sup4 Ja 14 '66

MCKISSICK, Floyd B.
Is integration necessary? letter. New Repub 155:33-6 D 3 '66
Negro leader warns of violence, and gives reasons; interview. por U S News 60:40-2 My 23 '66

about
Chilling shift. il por Time 87:35-6 Je 10 '66

MCKITTERICK, Nathaniel
Government and big money. New Repub 154: 32-3 F 5 '66
Some hard facts about foreign aid. New Repub 154:27-28+ My 21 '66

MCLAFFERTY, F. W.
High-resolution mass spectrometry. bibliog Science 151:641-9 F 11 '66

MACLAIN, Jon
In retrospect, Richard Crooks. Am Rec G 32:819+ My '66

MCLAIN, Pete
Light-tackle stripers. Field & S 71:92-5+ Jl '66

MACLAINE, Shirley
Redbook dialogue. pors Redbook 127:52-3+ My '66

MACLANE, Gretchen
Choreography by Gretchen MacLane, Constance Sullivan, James Waring, Deborah Lee; Judson memorial church. J. Anderson. Dance Mag 40:65-6 Jl '66

MCLAREN, A. D. See Schurr, J. M. jt. auth.

MCLAREN, I. A. and others
Polyteny: a source of cryptic speciation among copepods. bibliog Science 153:1641-2 S 30 '66

MCLAREN, Robert Bruce
Science and contemporary theology. Bul Atomic Sci 22:25-6 Mr '66

MCLAUGHLIN, Dean B.
Michigan stellar spectroscopist. K. O. Wright. por Sky & Tel 31:91 F '66

MCLAUGHLIN, Lorrie
Editor over my shoulder. Writer 79:29-30+ My '66
Ten article ideas that pay off. Writer 79: 18-20 Je '66

MCLAUGHLIN, Mignon
Neurotic's notebook (cont) Atlan 217:121 F; 218:127 Jl; 106 Ag '66

MCLAUGHLIN, W. Earle
Balance of payment; address, April 27, 1966. Vital Speeches 32:521-4 Je 15 '66

MCLEAN, Herbert E.
Alaska by jet, new boating fun! Motor B 118:30-3+ Jl '66
Here comes the Fire bike brigade! il Am For 72:4-5 O '66
Twenty days in June, the cautious war. Am For 72:28-31+ Mr '66
What's all this about Admiralty? Am For 72:38-41+ My '66

MACLEAN, John A. Jr
U.S. should adopt a whole new system of measurement. por Nations Bsns 54:87-9 Ja '66

MCLEAN, Robert
Marred victory. il Time 87:65 Ap 1 '66

MCLEAN, William B.
Navy's top handyman; interview, ed. by J. Riley. pors Life 62:31-2+ Ja 6 '67

MCLEAN, Wilmer
Tale of a table. M. A. Benjamin; reply. Am Heritage 17:100 Je '66

MACLEISH, Archibald
There was something about the twenties. Sat R 49:10-13 D 31 '66

MACLEISH, Kenneth
Abraham, the friend of God. Nat Geog Mag 130:739-89 D '66
River of counts and kings: the Loire. Nat Geog Mag 129:822-69 Je '66
Singapore, reluctant nation. Nat Geog Mag 130:268-300 Ag '66

MCLENDON, Gordon Barton
Stadium inside a studio; excerpt from Backstage at the Mets. L. Nelson and A. Hirshberg. il por Sports Illus 24:38-40+ Mr 28 '66

MACLEOD, Ellis G. See Miller, L. A. jt. auth.

MACLEOD, George Fielden, baron
Peerage for a Presbyterian. il por Time 89:66 Ja 13 '67

MACLEOD, Iain
Reports of Britain's death. For Affairs 45:88-97 O '66

MCLEOD, N. Bruce
Dissent on China. C. P. Tung. Christian Cent 83:1183 S 28 '66

MACLEOD, P. See Leveteau, J. jt. auth.

MCLOUTH steel corporation
Kaiser plans appeal in BOF case. il Bsns W p97 Jl 23 '66

MCLUHAN, Herbert Marshall
Great change-overs for you. Vogue 148:62-3+ Jl '66
Understanding Canada and sundry other matters; interview. por Mlle 64:114-15+ Ja '67

about

Against McLuhan. B. DeMott. Esquire 66:71-3 Ag '66
Artist and/in the electronic environment. D. Smith. Craft Horiz 26:42+ N '66
Is technology taking over? C. E. Silberman. il por Fortune 73:112-15+ F '66
McLuhan appointed to Fordham's Schweitzer chair. Pub W 191:59 Ja 16 '67
McLuhanisms. M. Walsh. America 114:784-5 My 28 '66
Marshall McLuhan. R. Kostelanetz. Commonweal 85:420-6 Ja 20 '67
Old wine in new bottles. T. Schwartz. il Pop Phot 59:50 N '66
Oracle of the electric age. J. Howard. il pors Life 60:91-2+ F 25 '66
People are talking about... por Vogue 148:60-1 Jl '66
Understanding McLuhan. H. Kenner. il Nat R 18:1224-5 N 29 '66
Understanding McLuhan. pors Newsweek 67:56-7 F 28 '66
Voices of convergence: Teilhard, McLuhan and Brown. D. J. Leary. Cath World 204:206-11 Ja '67
What nature abhors; current tour. Nation 203:596 D 5 '66

MCLUHAN, Marshall. See McLuhan, H. M.

MCMAHAN, H. D.
Small cities can have pension plans. Am City 81:200+ S '66

MCMAHAN, Ida, and Whitehorn, Ethel
Motion picture previews. See issues of PTA magazine

MCMAHON, Bernice
Finding the Mason Dixon line. Travel 126:45-7 D '66

MCMAHON, Michael
Hanging gardens; poem. Atlan 218:147 N '66

MACMANUS, Patricia
Some affairs of state. Sat R 49:28 Jl 9 '66
Women out of this world. Sat R 50:87-8 Ja 14 '67

MCMASTER, Beth
Enjoying nature; on an Algonquin howl-along. Audubon Mag 68:472-5 N '66

MCMASTER, D. N.
Kenya. bibliog Focus 16:1-6 F '67

MCMICHAEL, Robert
Generous example. Am Artist 30:4+ F '66

MACMILLAN, Donald Baxter
Most unforgettable character I've met. R. Platt. il por Read Digest 88:49-55 F '66

MCMILLAN, Edwin M.
Current problems in particle physics; address, December 27, 1965. Science 152:1210-15 My 27 '66

MCMILLAN, George
I've served my time in hell. Am Heritage 17:10-15 F '66

MACMILLAN, Harold
Christmas at Chatsworth. Horizon 9:84-7 Wint '67

about

Bending to the wind. A. Lejeune. Nat R 18:1231-2 N 29 '66
Gentleman's code. por Newsweek 68:109-10 O 3 '66
In the best Tory tradition. E. M. Yoder, jr. Sat R 49:99-100 O 8 '66
Supermac looks back. por Time 88:124+ S 30 '66
Unflappable supermac. A. Campbell. New Repub 155:30-1 O 1 '66

MCMILLAN, John Lanneau
Washington: the lost colony. A. Kopkind and J. Ridgeway. New Repub 154:14-17 Ap 23 '66

MACMILLAN, Mary
Born between East and West. Sat R 49:51 Jl 23 '66

MCMILLAN, Tom
Stoneware: an ancient art makes an exciting comeback. W. Radcliffe. il por Pop Gard 17:58-61 Ag '66

MACMILLAN company
Macmillan to abandon library bindings. Pub W 191:56 Ja 16 '67
Macmillan's author files, 1892-1960; gift to the NYPL. il Pub 190:21-4 O 24 '66
Noted acquisitions; author files to NYPL. Wilson Lib Bul 41:363 D '66

MCMILLEN, Charlotte
Architecture for junior high. Design 67:36-7 Mr '66

MACMINN, Strother
How to become a stylist. Motor T 18:39+ Ap '66

MCMULLEN, Roy
Americans abroad. Hi Fi 16:MA25+ O '66
Art news from Paris. See issues of Art news to June 1966
Courage of Aimé Maeght. Hi Fi 16:MA26 N '66
Music and dance. Hi Fi 16:144-5 F '66
Music in the Marais. Hi Fi 16:69-72 My '66
Notes from our correspondents. See issues of High fidelity incorporating Musical America
Opera on the Mediterranean; Riviera report. Hi Fi 16:154-6 My '66
(comp) Phantom of the Festspielhaus. Hi Fi 16:60-4 N '66
Virgil Thomson's self-portrait. Hi Fi 16:MA21+ N '66

MCMURRIN, Sterling M.
What tasks for the schools? Sat R 50:40-3 Ja 14 '67

MCMURRY, Robert N.
Sell more with fewer salesmen. Nations Bsns 54:96-8+ Je '66

M'NAGHTEN rules. See Insanity—Jurisprudence

MCNALLY, Robert E.
Books. Commonweal 84:506-7; 85:376 Ag 5 '66, Ja 6 '67
Catholic professors on the secular campus. por America 115:321 S 24 '66
Disappearing priesthood. America 114:877-8 Je 25 '66

MCNALLY, Tom
Dolphin on the fly. pors Field & S 70:148-9+ Ap '66

MCNAMARA, Louise
Center for ITV. E. Cohen. il Am Ed 2:22-4 Je '66

MCNAMARA, Patrick H.
Mexican-Americans in the Southwest. America 114:352-4 Mr 12 '66

MCNAMARA, Robert Strange
Excerpt from testimony, April 20, 1966. Cong Digest 45:207+ Ag '66
Excerpt from testimony, June 21, 1966. Cong Digest 45:237+ O '66
In a nuclear attack on America; summary of testimony, March 8, 1966. U S News 60:14 Mr 21 '66

MCNAMARA, Robert Strange—Continued
Is bombing the answer? excerpts from statement, January 21, 1966. por U S News 60:47-8 F 28 '66
McNamara outlines MOL schedule; summary of statement; ed. by M. Getler. Miss & Roc 18:14-16 F 28 '66
McNamara's new design for world peace and security; address, May 18, 1966. U S News 60:90-5 My 30 '66; Same with title Security in the contemporary world. Dept State Bul 54:874-81 Je 6 '66
McNamara's plan for rejectees; excerpts from address, August 23, 1966. por U S News 61:27 S 5 '66
O positive; summary of address to American society of newspaper editors. il por Time 87:18 My 27 '66
Red China in the nuclear race; excerpts from testimony, January 25, 1966. por U S News 60:8 F 7 '66
Revelation in the Defense department; summary of address to the American society of newspaper editors in Montreal, May 18, 1966. America 114:794 Je 4 '66
Review of United States foreign and military policy; transcript of press conference, August 25, 1966. Dept State Bul 55:417-19, 423-4 S 19 '66
Secretary McNamara discusses Asian affairs and nuclear arms control in interview for Japanese magazine. Dept State Bul 55:303-11 Ag 29 '66
Secretary McNamara's views on ammunition shortages; excerpts from testimony. U S News 60:41 Ap 25 '66
Secretary Rusk, Secretary McNamara, Mr McCloy meet with President Johnson; excerpts from press briefing, November 23, 1966. Dept State Bul 55:921-3 D 19 '66
Stennis vs. McNamara; how ready for combat are U.S. forces? excerpts from statements. por U S News 60:21 Ap 11 '66
Vietnam bombing debate. Aviation W 84:17 F 21 '66
Vietnam war; as McNamara sees it; excerpts from statements. por U S News 60:21 Mr 14 '66
Voluntary service for all youth; address, May 19, 1966. Vital Speeches 32:484-8 Je 1 '66
Why U.S. decided to step up the air war; excerpts from news conference, June 29, 1966. U S News 61:32-3 Jl 11 '66
Yes and no; summary of address to American newspaper editors. por Newsweek 67:26 My 30 '66

about

Aberrations at Harvard. il por Time 88:95 N 18 '66
Anything goes; concerning his Montreal address. F. S. Meyer. Nat R 18:629 Je 28 '66
Awesome twosome. T. Wicker. il pors N Y Times Mag p8-9+ Ja 30 '66
Battle for a nuclear navy; will McNamara or Congress win? il por U S News 60:44-6 Je 27 '66
Bombs, bottlenecks & baloney. il Time 87:26 Ap 29 '66
Caesar's wars; bombardment from Capitol hill. il por Time 87:22 My 6 '66
Credibility gap widens; testimony before Senate foreign relations committee. R. Hotz. Aviation W 84:17 My 2 '66
For McNamara, a rougher round. il por Bsns W p 162-4+ F 19 '66
Gnawing debate. il por Newsweek 67:25-6 Mr 14 '66
His business is war. S. Alsop. il pors Sat Eve Post 239:29-33+ My 21 '66
Imaginary weaknesses. por Time 87:24-5 Mr 11 '66
Joint chiefs fear Soviet technical coup; with editorial comment. G. C. Wilson. Aviation W 84:11, 16-17 F 28 '66
Joint chiefs wear a different hat. il por Bsns W p68-72 Jl 30 '66
McNamara answers bomber critics. Miss & Roc 18:13 My 2 '66
McNamara says Soviets err on ABM. M. Getler. por Miss & Roc 18:12-14 My 2 '66
McNamara scales down his buying. por Bsns W p34 Jl 16 '66
McNamara story continues. J. J. Stone. Bul Atomic Sci 22:39-42 Ap '66
McNamara under fire; now it's bomber issue. U S News 60:10 My 2 '66
McNamara's balloon; concerning speech before American society of newspaper editors. Nation 202:667 Je 6 '66
McNamara's call for a new policy; its meaning and impact. por U S News 60:14 My 30 '66
McNamara's other war. il por Newsweek 67:23 My 9 '66
McNamara's salvation army. D. Sanford. New Repub 155:13-14 S 10 '66

McNamara's war; what the record shows. U S News 61:36-7 Jl 25 '66
Military starts to speak out; excerpts from Neither liberty nor safety. N. F. Twining. il por U S News 61:92-4 O 3 '66
More and more criticism of McNamara. il por U S News 60:14-15 My 9 '66
Now it's official; missile gap narrows. il por U S News 61:8 D 19 '66
Now it's Rivers vs. McNamara. U S News 60:15 Je 27 '66
Profits of war; putsch against McNamara. H. L. Nieburg. por Nation 203:696-701 D 26 '66
Real McNamara. por New Repub 154:5-7 Je 4 '66
Signs of backlash against student mobs. il U S News 61:14 N 21 '66
State of affairs. H. Brandon. Sat R 50:16+ Ja 14 '67
Steaming into Paris. por Newsweek 68:32+ Ag 8 '66
Stimulating talk from a new McNamara; concerning Montreal address. Life 60:4 Je 3 '66
Story of Robert McNamara. il pors U S News 61:32-8+ Jl 25 '66
10-billion gamble on a plane; how it's paying off. il por U S News 61:42-5 Ag 15 '66
Time for contemplation. W. J. Coughlin. Tech W 19:46 Jl 11; 50 Jl 18 '66
Vietnam; how wrong was McNamara? S. Alsop. il por Sat Eve Post 239:14 Mr 12 '66
Visitor. il por Newsweek 68:51 O 24 '66
War outlook; as McNamara sees it now. por U S News 61:26 O 24 '66
Washington; ten of its most powerful men. por Vogue 148:152-3 N 15 '66
What McNamara learned in Vietnam. il por U S News 61:41-2 O 24 '66
What the draft might blow up. C. Fritchey. por Harper 233:26-30 Ag '66
Who is man? M. Ascoli. Reporter 34:14 Je 16 '66
Why do they hate Robert Strange McNamara? J. Burnham. il pors Nat R 18:1152-62 N 15 '66

MCNASPY, Clement J.
Book reviews. America 114:418 Mr 26 '66
Fine arts. See occasional issues of America
Mississippi; a changing state. America 115:387-8 O 1 '66
Senghor of Senegal; philosopher president. America 115:516-17 O 29 '66
This restless generation. America 114:726-30 My 21 '66
Worship in the city of God. America 115:176-7 Ag 20 '66

MACNEIL, Cornell
Singer vs. public. A. M. Lingg. il Opera N 31:6-7 Ja 14 '67

MCNEIL, Elton B.
Violence and human development. Ann Am Acad 364:149-57 Mr '66

MCNEILL, David
Speaking of space. bibliog Science 152:875-80 My 13 '66

MCNETT, Thelma A.
Our wintering, tailless towhee. Audubon Mag 68:195 My '66

MCNICHOL, John F.
Name it, our computer can do it. por Am City 81:88-9 D '66

MCNICKLE, D'Arcy
In search of the white man's guidance. Nation 202:493-4 Ap 25 '66
Indian tests the mainstream. Nation 203:275-9 S 26 '66
Two ways to grow up. Nation 202:365-6 Mr 28 '66

MCNULTY, Faith
Reporter at large. New Yorker 42:31-6+ Ag 6 '66

MACOMBER, Peter B. and others
Chloroquine; physiological basis of drug resistance in plasmodium berkhei. bibliog Science 152:1374-5 Je 3 '66

MACON, Ga.
Indecisive decision; controversy over park willed for white people. il Time 87:40 Ja 28 '66

Religious institutions and affairs
Don't come unto me; Negro admissions cause clergy sackings. New Repub 155:9-10 N 12 '66

MCPHEE, Jack
Thanksgiving hunt. por Outdoor Life 137:60-1+ My '66

MCPHEE, John
Profiles. New Yorker 42:57-8+ Mr 19 '66
Reporter at large. New Yorker 42:101-2+ Mr 5; 142+ My 7; 144+ My 14 '66

MCPHEE, Walter T. and Lenard, J. F.
Design, build, operate and train. pors Am City 81:100-3 O '66
MCPHERSON, William
More Musil. New Repub 154:35-6 My 14 '66
MCQUADE, Kate. See Cooley, M. jt. ed.
MCQUADE, Lawrence C.
New tycoon. Am Ed 2:26-7 O '66
MCQUADE, Walter
[Monthly column] See issues of Architectural forum
—and Herrera, Philip
(eds) Structure & design. See issues of Fortune
MCQUEEN, Noel. See Hark, M. jt. auth.
MCQUEEN, Steve
I still get goose pimples; ed. by K. Rudeen. Sports Illus 25:39-42 Ag 8 '66
Loser makes it big. T. Armbrister. il pors Sat Eve Post 240:26-9 Ja 14 '67
Motorcycles: what I like in a bike, and why. pors Pop Sci 189:76-81 N '66
MCQUILKIN, R.
Purification; poem. Christian Cent 83:1077 S 7 '66
MACRAE, Duncan, Jr
Careers, science, and politics. Bul Atomic Sci 22:26-8 F '66
MACRAE, I. C. See Raghu, K. jt. auth.
MCREYNOLDS, David
Chinese communism, U.S.A. Commonweal 83: 528-31 F 4 '66
MACROMOLECULES. See Molecules
MACSHANE, Frank
Dahlberg: aphorisms & poetry. Nation 203: 225-6 S 12 '66
Revival of an old Ford. Holiday 39:160+ My '66
MACSWAIN, J. W.
Crossroads of the insect world. Nat Geog Mag 130:844-57 D '66
MACSWINEY, Terence
Hero or a fool? por Sr Schol 89:3 O 28 '66
MCTIGHE, Thomas P.
Books. Commonweal 85:144+ N 4 '66
MACURA, Miloš
Pop. 6,000,000,000; interview. New Yorker 42:47-9 S 10 '66
MCVAY, Scott
Last of the great whales; with biographical sketch. Sci Am 215:10, 13-21 bibliog(p 114) Ag '66
MCVEIGH, Linda
Crimson girl. por Newsweek 67:73 F 7 '66
Harvard's Mother Cobra; Crimson's managing editor; with report by C. Aitman. il pors Life 60:43-4+ Mr 4 '66
MCVICAR, Leonard
Pre-teenagers help improve their city. por Parks & Rec 1:32-3 Ja '66
MCVITTY, Marion H.
Should U.S. aid be channeled through the U.N? Cur Hist 51:102-7+ Ag '66
MCWHINNEY, Edgar
Clubs feed cattle, and the kitty. il pors Bsns W p 132-3+ Je 25 '66
MCWHORTER, Frank P. and Leach, C. M.
Contact photomicrography in the ultraviolet on high-resolution plates. Science 152:757-8 My 6 '66
MCWILLIAMS, Carey
Ethics in an affluent society. Christian Cent 83:797-802 Je 22 '66
Reagan vs. Brown: how to succeed with the backlash. Nation 203:438-42 O 31 '66
MCWILLIAMS, Stanley W.
Sitting ducks of aerial war. il pors Ebony 22:58-60+ N '66
MCWILLIAMS, Wilson Carey
Ending the cold war. Commonweal 85:363-5 Ja 6 '67
National interest and international ideology. Commonweal 84:442 Jl 8 '66
On time and history. Yale R 56:91-103 O '66
Poverty: public enemy number one. Sat R 49:48-9+ D 10 '66
Search for a unified portrait. Commonweal 83:643-5 Mr 4 '66
—and Hale, Dennis
Spain and Vietnam. Commonweal 84:575-7 S 16 '66
—and Lanyi, G. A.
Burghers in the Kremlin. Commonweal 84: 195-7 My 6 '66
MACY, John Williams, 1917-
Automated government. Sat R 49:23-5+ Jl 23 '66
Unless we begin now; address, July 25, 1966. Vital Speeches 32:678-82 S 1 '66
MAD show; revue. See Musical comedies, revues, etc.—Criticisms, plots, etc.
MADAM Tussaud's gallery of wax figures. See Wax figures

MADAR, Olga M.
Little room at top for labor's women. Bsns W p62+ My 28 '66
MADARIAGA, Juan José de
Dog and the conquistador. Américas 18:16-25 Je '66
MADDEN, Murdaugh Stuart, and Cohn, S. L.
Legal status and problems of the American abroad. bibliog f Ann Am Acad 368:119-31 N '66
MADDEN, Robert J.
High explosives on the highways; interview, ed. by T. Stimson. Pop Mech 126:88-92+ D '66
MADDEX, Robert L. and Jones, P. B.
Shelled corn, how to handle it this fall. Suc Farm 64:46-7 Ag '66
MADDOW, Ben
Wind machine; story. Harper 233:55-60 Ag '66
MADDOX, Gaynor
February's fine for fancy recipes. Todays Health 44:52-7 F '66
Frozen foods streamline your favorite recipes. Todays Health 44:52-7 Ap '66
Here is hearty variety for hungry beefeaters. Todays Health 44:50-5 My '66
Milk, eggs, and cheese, your big Lenten helpers. Todays Health 44:70-5 Mr '66
[Monthly column on cookery] See issues of Today's health
Summertime splendors: fresh fruit and berry treats. Todays Health 44:56-7+ Je '66
'Tis the season for chocolate and mistletoe. Todays Health 44:54-9 D '66
Togetherness meals for your family. Todays Health 44:48-53 S '66
MADDOX, John
John Maddox: crusading science editor. J. Lear. por Sat R 49:67-9 N 5 '66
MADDOX, Lester
Georgia: Lester Maddox and the mad Democrats. A. Schardt. Reporter 35:29-30 O 20 '66
Georgian quits in protest. por Sr Schol 89:18 O 21 '66
Great payoff. Newsweek 68:34-5 D 12 '66
Lester leaps in. il por Newsweek 69:29-30 Ja 23 '67
Mr White Backlash. R. Cleghorn. il pors N Y Times Mag p27-9+ N 6 '66
Peach state snarl. Sr Schol 89:18 D 2 '66
Picking Maddox. por Newsweek 68:20 D 26 '66
Politics: the white backlash, 1966. il Newsweek 68:27-8 O 10 '66
Refusal to go along with hate; with report by R. B. Stolley. il pors Life 61:109-10 O 14 '66
Seated & subdued. por Time 89:22 Ja 20 '67
Surprise from Maddox: he sounds a changed note. por US News 62:14 Ja 23 '67
Up to the legislature. Time 88:20-1 D 23 '66
MADDY, A. H. and Malcolm, B. R.
Protein conformations in the plasma membrane. bibliog Science 150:1616-18; 153:213 D 17 '65, Jl 8 '66
MADEIRA (island)
See also
Tourist trade—Madeira (island)
MADEMOISELLE (periodical)
Enter Mademoiselle's college board competition '66-'67. Mlle 63:211 O '66
Mademoiselle Merit awards, 1966. il Mlle 64: 47-51 Ja '67
Mademoiselle's annual Merit awards, 1965. il Mlle 62:45-9 Ja '66
Mlle's guest editors: '66. J. M. Savanyu. il Mlle 63:246-7 Ag '66
MADISON, Charles A.
Covici: Steinbeck's editor, collaborator, and conscience. Sat R 49:15-16 Je 25 '66
MADISON, Dolly (Payne) Todd
Faces from the past. R. M. Ketchum. por Am Heritage 17:24-5 F '66
MADISON, J. T. and others
Nucleotide sequence of a yeast tyrosine transfer RNA. bibliog Science 153:531-4 Jl 29 '66
MADISON, Wis.
D.E.D. goes underground. R. L. Carroll. il Am City 81:96-7 Jl '66
MADISON-Felicia, Camp. See Camps
MADISON Square Garden. See New York (city)—Madison Square Garden
MÄDLER, Johann Heinrich von
Pulkovo double stars and J. H. Madler. J. Ashbrook. Sky & Tel 31:79 F '66
MADNESS of Lady Bright; drama. See Wilson, L.
MADOCS, Rita
Chagall bride; story. Ladies Home J 83:58-9 Ag '66
Saturday people; story. McCalls 94:116-19 O '66
Stargazer; story. McCalls 94:46-7 Ja '67

MADRID

Music

In Spain, new music on the rise. E. Haines.
il Hi Fi 16:MA18-19 Ag '66

Newspapers

Monarchy si, liberal no; new liberalized press
law against Spanish newspaper, A.B.C.
Time 88:24 Jl 29 '66

Social life and customs

To live in Madrid. R. Joseph. il Esquire 66:
90-1+ Jl '66

MADRIGALS

See also

Phonograph records—Madrigals

MADSON, John

Ringnecks, humbler of hunters. Farm J 90:
50B-50C+ N '66

MADURODAM, The Hague. See Models of cities, towns, etc.

MAERKI, Vic

Power politics in New England. New Repub
154:10 Ja 29 '66

MAFIA

Big tab; thirteen Cosa nostra bosses collared
at a Queens restaurant. Newsweek 68:23
O 3 '66

Justice for Franca; challenging Mafia traditions by prosecuting her abductor in Sicily.
il Newsweek 69:37 Ja 2 '67

Larry Gallo, Crazy Joe and Kid Blast; Robin
Hoods or real tough boys? F. J. Cook. il
N Y Times Mag p36-7+ O 23 '66

Mafia and politics, by M. Pantaleone. Review
Nation 203:360-1 O 10 '66. G. Gersh
Sat R 49:29 Ag 13 '66. C. F. Delzell
Time 88:92+ Ag 5 '66

Panic in Chicago's Mafia. B. Davidson and
S. Smith. il Sat Eve Post 239:102-5 My
21 '66

Secret rulers, by F. J. Cook. Review
Sat R 50:92 Ja 14 '67. J. Haas

MAGAZINE advertising. See Advertising me- diums—Periodicals

MAGAZINE articles. See Periodical literature

MAGAZINE editors. See Editors and editing

MAGAZINE fiction. See Fiction in periodicals and newspapers

MAGAZINE publishing. See Periodicals, Pub- lishing of

MAGAZINE stands, racks, etc.

Johnny magazine rack. il Pop Mech 125:42-3
F '66

MAGAZINES, Childrens. See Childrens period- icals

MAGGIO musicale fiorentino. See Music fes- tivals—Italy

MAGIC flute; opera. See Mozart, J. C. W. A.

MAGIC touch; story. See Heinemann, A.

MAGICIANS

Master magicians, by W. Gibson. Review
Life 61:20 S 30 '66. T. Prideaux

MAGID, Marion

Last word: the public fantasy versus the
private act. Esquire 65:128-9 My '66

MAGILLIGAN, Sue

Lost: one kaleidoscope; story. Seventeen 26:
78-9 Ja '67

MAGISTRATES. See Judges

MAGMA. See Rocks, Igneous

MAGNAVOX company

Only the best. Time 89:76+ Ja 20 '67

MAGNESIUM

Magnesium in sea water: an electrode measurement. M. E. Thompson. bibliog il Science 153:866-7 Ag 19 '66

Magnesium ions: activity in seawater. R. M.
Pytkowicz and others. bibliog Science 152:
640-2 Ap 29 '66

Magnesium-28 in rain: produced by cosmic
rays. L. Husain and P. K. Kuroda. bibliog
il Science 154:1180-1 D 2 '66

MAGNESIUM compounds

Diagenesis of carbonate sediments: interaction of magnesium in sea water with mineral grains. R. A. Berner. bibliog il Science
153:188-91 Jl 8 '66

See also

Magnesium pemoline

MAGNESIUM pemoline

Can this drug make you smarter? testing
Cylert. W. S. Bacon. il Pop Sci 189:82-5
N '66

Magnesium pemoline: enhancement of brain
RNA polymerases. A. J. Glasky and L. N.
Simon. bibliog il Science 151:702-3 F 11 '66

Magnesium pemoline: enhancement of learning and memory of a conditioned avoidance
response. N. Plotnikoff. bibliog il Science
151:703-4 F 11 '66; Reply with rejoinder.
R. Bowman. 153:902 Ag 19 '66

Memory and aging biological cousins; use of
Cylert to improve performance in the
elderly. P. McBroom. Sci N 90:399 N 12 '66

Memory pills; experimenting with Cylert. il
Time 87:56 Je 24 '66

Memory pills work; clinical reports on Cylert.
Sci Digest 60:22 S '66

Pill that helps you remember; Cylert. S. M.
Spencer. il Sat Eve Post 239:64-6+ S 24
'66

Pills to help us remember? Cylert. I. Asimov.
il N Y Times Mag p 148-51 O 9 '66

MAGNETIC fields

Flipping the magnetic field. Time 87:48 Je 17
'66

Shifts change life. il Sci N 89:495 Je 18 '66

Zero magnetic field achieved in lab. W S.
Beller. il Miss & Roc 18:16-17 Ap 11 '66

MAGNETIC fields (cosmic physics)

Chronic exposure to low lunar magnetism
considered harmful. Tech W 18:38 Je 27 '66

Magnetic fields on the quiet sun. W. C. Livingston. il Sci Am 215:54-62 bibliog(p 160) N
'66

Magnetic measurements in space. J. H.
Wujek, jr. il Electr World 75:36-7+ Ja '66

Solar and interplanetary magnetic fields.
J. M. Wilcox. bibliog il Science 152:161-6
Ap 8 '66

Terrestrial tail; earth's magnetic field. il
Time 87:58 Ap 22 '66

MAGNETIC measurements

See also

Magnetometers

MAGNETIC memory (computers)

Computer logic and memory. D. C. Evans.
il Sci Am 215:74-85 bibliog(p312) S '66

Giannini makes non-destruct memory unit. il
Tech W 19:34 O 31 '66

Tape memory unit awaits GT-9 test. C. D.
LaFond. il Miss & Roc 18:16-17 My 16 '66

MAGNETIC pole. See Magnetism, Terrestrial

MAGNETIC recorders and recording

Battery tape recorders. il Consumer Rep 31:
547-51 N '66

Buying guide to tape recorders. il Good H
162:185 Ap '66

Buypoints: tape recorders. M. D. Grennan. il
Pop Phot 59:179-93 O '66

Cartridge tape players; installation in automobiles. il Consumer Bul 49:20-2 D '66

High fidelity newsfronts. N. Eisenberg. il
Hi Fi 16:32+ Ap '66

How to buy a tape recorder. F. Bowers.
House & Gard 129:4-5+ F '66

Knight KG-415 tape recorder kit. L. Zide. il
Am Rec G 32:739-41 Ap '66

Look at new tape recorders and record players. R. H. Burgert. Sr Schol 89:sup8 N 11
'66

Music a la Bolognese by DGG in France. R.
McMullen. Hi Fi 16:16+ O '66

New equipment: making news in sight and
sound. Hi Fi 16:96-8 O '66

New sounds made by electronic musician. Sci
N 90:40 Jl 16 '66

Notes from our correspondents; Paris taping
of Wozzeck. R. McMullen. il Hi Fi 16:12+
My '66

Other side; launching in Britain of miniature
cartridge tapes and pocket-sized recorders.
T. Heinitz. Sat R 49:88-9 N 26 '66

Prospects of recording; electronic media, a
threat to the public concert? G. Gould.
Hi Fi 16:46-63 Ap '66

PS buyer's guide to personal tape recorders.
C. P. Gilmore. il Pop Sci 189:124-9+ N '66

Sound on your shoulder. C. Conley. il Field
& S 71:101 D '66

Sound photo tour. L. Barry. Pop Phot 58:38+
Mr '66

Sound; tape recorders can be the nucleus
of a high fidelity system. J. Wesson. U S
Camera 29:30-1 N '66

Stereo tape deck you build from a kit. R. M.
Benray. il Pop Sci 188:136-7 Mr '66

Tape cartridge comes of age. L. Coplen and
R. Johns. il Electr World 76:30-2+ N '66

Tape guide recorder. il Mod Phot 30:99+ N
'66

Tape it. J. R. Roberson. il Holiday 40:111-16
O '66; Same abr. with title Why not tape
it? Read Digest 89:231-2+ D '66

Tape recorder echo chamber. S. E. Auyer. il
Pop Electr 25:81-2 Ag '66

Tape recorder guide. il Hi Fi 16:125-44 N '66

Tape recorders insure accuracy at public
meetings; Westbury, L.I. N.Y. J. Sharkey.
il Am City 81:86 Jl '66

Tape recorders today, a guide to features
and performance. I. L. Grozny. il Hi Fi 16:
49-52 Ag '66

MAGNETIC recorders and recording—*Cont.*
Taping true, for less; Magnecord, Revox, Dynaco Beocord 2000. I. Berger. Sat R 49: 59+ Ag 27 '66
Ten years of the tape deck. R. D. Darrell. Hi Fi 16:73-4+ My '66
This recorder is your private secretary. R Benrey. il Pop Sci 189:153 O '66
To take and to tape; some random and differing thoughts by the editors on recording your trip with camera and recorder. M. S. Fenner; W. A. Graves; M. B. Tucker. il NEA J 56:62-4 Ja '67
You can build a tape player for your car. R. M. Benrey. il Pop Sci 188:186-90 Ap '66
    See also
Tape recordings
Video tape recorders and recording

Aeronautic applications
Concorde flight test recorder readied for June delivery. C. D. LaFond. il Tech W 19:34-6+ O 3 '66

Business applications
Spreading the message with tape. il Bsns W p87 Jl 9 '66

Educational applications
Happiness is your own carrel; first wholly electronic learning center. il Time 87:60 F 18 '66

Equipment
Directory of tape cartridge equipment. Sat R 49:67 N 26 '66
Tape-slide synchronizers. il Pop Phot 59:193 O '66

Space flight applications
Tape for space. J. Eberhart. il Sci N 89:240-1 Ap 9 '66

Stereophonic recorders
Car stereo boom! D. MacDonald. il Motor T 18:58-9 Ap '66
How to install automobile stereo tape players. H. L. Davidson. il Pop Electr 25:66-7+ N '66
Knight-kit KG-415 stereo tape deck B. Hartford. il Pop Mech 127:196-7 Ja '67
Stereo in your car; with editorial report. L. Marcus. il Hi Fi 16:57-64 My '66
Stereo tape players for autos. il Consumer Rep 31:220-1 My '66

Unauthorized recording
Piracy on the high C's; recording at concerts and operas. R. Freed. il Sat R 49: 55-6+ Mr 26 '66
Tape underground; privately pressed recordings. C. L. Osborne. il Hi Fi 16:44-8 Ag '66

Visual recordings
    See Video tape recorders and recording
MAGNETIC recorders and recording, Portable
Battery operated portables. il Mod Phot 30:115-16 N '66
Battery-powered tape recorders. Electr World 76:34-7 Ag '66
Portable tape recorders. H. Fantel. Opera N 30:33 Ap 16 '66
Tape as you travel. M. A. Matzkin. il Hi Fi 16:48-52 Jl '66
Tape talk; portable tape recorders. il Seventeen 25:232-3 My '66
MAGNETIC stars. See Magnetism, Stellar
MAGNETIC tape
Sound advice; cartridge loaded tape. L. Zide. Mod Phot 30:32+ Ag '66
Sound for shows, a buyer's guide to tape. J. Arthur. il Pop Phot 58:94+ Mr '66
Sound; Magnetic media corporation. J. Wesson. U S Camera 29:22-3 Mr '66
Tape cartridge comes of age. L. Coplen and R. Johns. il Electr World 76:30-2+ N '66
Tape makers prosper as computer sales soar. il Bsns W p 181-2 S 17 '66
Tape on the turnpike; cartridge systems for auto and home use. I. Berger. il Sat R 49:64+ N 26 '66
Tape recorders today, a guide to features and performance. I. L. Grozny. il Hi Fi 16:49-52 Ag '66
    See also
Tape recordings
MAGNETISM
Magnetic personality of matter; reprint. B. Shore. il Sci Digest 60:62-6 N '66
    See also
Magnetic field
Magnets
MAGNETISM, Lunar
    See also
Magnetic fields (cosmic physics)

MAGNETISM, Stellar
Peculiar A stars. L. C. Green. il Sky & Tel 31:84-8 F '66
MAGNETISM, Terrestrial
Earth's air shakes like jelly. A. Ewing. Sci N L 89:117 F 19 '66
Earth's magnetic field; a new look; address, December 26, 1965. N. F. Ness bibliog il Science 151:1041-52 Mr 4 '66
Galactic depolarization of the 21-centimeter-wavelength radiation of extragalactic sources J. M. Bologna and others. bibliog il Science 154:1656-8 D 30 '66
Geomagnetic polarity epochs: a new polarity event and the age of the Brunhes-Matuyama boundary. R. R. Doell and G. B. Dalrymple. bibliog il Science 152:1060-1 My 20 '66
Magnetic anomalies over the Pacific-Antarctic ridge. W. C. Pitman, 3d. and J. R. Heirtzler. bibliog il Science 154:1164-6+ D 2 '66
Magnetic poles were once reversed. il Sci N 89:263 Ap 16 '66
Paleomagnetic study of Antarctic deep-sea cores. N. D. Opdyke and others. bibliog il Science 154:349-57 O 21 '66
Spreading of the ocean floor: new evidence. F. J. Vine. bibliog il Science 154:1405-15 D 16 '66
    See also
Magnetic field
MAGNETOHYDRODYNAMICS
Space waves give new information about sun. Sci N 89:388 My 21 '66
MAGNETOMETERS
Magnetic measurements in space. J. H. Wujek, jr. il Electr World 75:36-7+ Ja '66
MAGNETS
Look what they're doing with magnets. H. Manchester. il Pop Mech 126:116-19+ D '66
Superconducting magnet able to operate in space. il Sci N 90:5 Jl 2 '66
Superconducting magnet in full-scale test. Sci N 89:263 Ap 16 '66
MAGNIER, Claude
Three bags full; adaptation. See Chodorov, J.
MAGNIN, I. and company. See Bullock's-Magnin company
MAGNITUDE. See Size
MAGNOLIAS
Choosing, planting, and growing your magnolia. Sunset 136:210+ F '66
Elegant Oriental magnolias. il Sunset 136: 72-5 F '66
Tree for spring. D. P. Wyman. il Flower Grower 53:27 F '66
MAGNUSON, Warren Grant
Magnuson answers Senate SST queries. por Aviation W 85:89+ S 12 '66
    about
Underwater harvest. Atlan 217:8 Mr '66
MAGRITTE, René
Enigmatic visions of René Magritte; exhibition to tour U.S. il pors Life 60:113-14+ Ap 22 '66
    about
Art of the possibility; show at Museum of modern art. H. Cohen. Reporter 34:51 F 10 '66
Paintings and photographs. F. Getlein. New Repub 154:33-5 Mr 19 '66
This is not Magritte. il pors Esquire 65: 100-3 F '66
MAGUIRE, Richard
Mystery in the countinghouse. W. Pincus. il Atlan 218:73-5 O '66
MAHAR, Mary Helen
Federal legislation and programs to assist school libraries. ALA Bul 60:153-6 F '66
el MAHDI, Sayed Sadik
Atlantic report. Atlan 219:20+ Ja '67
MAHER, Charles
(ed) See Breedlove, C. 600 mph, what it's really like!
MAHER, James T.
Music-making at home. Holiday 39:121-6 Ap '66
View of the water; American palaces by the sea. Holiday 40:48-53+ Jl '66
MAHEU, René
To all young people twenty years old. UNESCO Courier 19:30 F '66
UNESCO at twenty; Unesco: personal testimony toward an over-all appraisal; adaptation of address, July 7, 1966. Sch & Soc 94:404-11 N 26 '66
UNESCO'S twenty years; excerpts from address, July 7, 1966. UNESCO Courier 19:4-5 Jl '66
MAHLBERG, Paul, and Sabharwal, Pritam
Mitotic waves in laticifers of euphorbia marginata. bibliog Scence 152:518-19 Ap 22 '66

MAHLER, Gustav
Again. Mahler symphonies by Leinsdorf and Bernstein; the Sixth and Seventh. D. Newlin. Am Rec G 33:114-16+ O '66
By Bernstein, Mahler's Ten, minus one; with the New York philharmonic. P. G. Davis. Hi Fi 16:22 D '66
Gustav Mahler: the Ninth was not impassable. J. Bruck. il por Am Rec G 32:412-16 Ja '66
Gustav Mahler, the unfinished Tenth quickened to vibrant life. W. Malloch. Hi Fi 16:65-6 F '66
Mahler (and Cooke's) No. 10. I. Kolodin. Sat R 49:55 Ja 29 '66
Must for all Mahler lovers: Angel's Des knaben wunderhorn. J. Diether. Am Rec G 33:212-15 N '66
Three Mahler symphonies; New York concerts. B. Jacobson. Hi Fi 16:131 F '66
Vanguard offers a stereo première of the Mahler Seventh from Salt Lake City. D. Newlin. Am Rec G 32:950-1 Je '66

MAHON, George Herman
Is government spending getting out of hand? excerpt from address, October 25, 1966. por U S News 61:79-80 N 7 '66

about

Top congressman's warning to Hanoi. por U S News 61:11 Ag 1 '66

MAHONEY, Billie
Labanotation and me. por Dance Mag 40:56+ Ap '66

MAHONEY, Dan
Do the big-city police have popular support? interview; ed. by F. Clinton. pors Nat R 18:880-2 S 6 '66

MAHONEY, David Joseph, 1923-
Shuffle & cut. por Time 88:88+ D 2 '66

MAHONEY, George Perry
Loser's victory. il por Time 88:25 S 23 '66
Mahoney: a legend in his own time. J. Ridgeway. New Repub 155:13-15 O 29 '66

MAHONEY, Sally M. and Stokes, L. Z.
School library program for the blind. Wilson Lib Bul 40:829+ My '66

MAHONEY, Stephen
Master of foolishness. Life 61:89 Jl 1 '66
Milkman with plastic bombs in his icebox. Life 61:52 N 11 '66

MAIAKOVSKII, Vladimir Vladimirovich
Mayakovsky, ed. by H. Marshall. Review Nation 202:271-2 Mr 7 '66. M. Dalton

MAIDENHAIR tree. See Ginkgo

MAIDS (servants) See Household employees

MAI-hong-Nhi
Is North Vietnam weakening? interview; ed. by G. C. Troelstrup. por U S News 61:52-3 D 12 '66

MAIL advertising. See Advertising, Direct mail

MAIL handling
Automated post office zips along, but slowly. il Bsns W p38 Ja 29 '66
Crisis in the post office; reform aims. J. N. Miller. il Read Digest 88:127-32 Mr '66
Day the mails stopped; Chicago's problems. C. Remsberg. Sat R 49:21-4 D 17 '66
Great mail crisis of Norfolk, Illinois. J. Crittenden. Atlan 219:106+ Ja '67

MAIL order business
Back from the ashes in only three weeks. il Bsns W p92+ F 26 '66
Giants put on more muscle. il Bsns W p72-4+ Jl 23 '66
Keppler on the SLR; how to buy by mail. H. Keppler. il Mod Phot 30:34+ D '66
Mail-order dogs. H. Modavis. il Field & S 71:144-5+ Je '66
Success of Neckermann's pig: Germany. il Time 88:106+ O 21 '66
When a book hits the jackpot. J. Tebbel. Sat R 49:62-4 F 12 '66

MAIL order catalogs. See Catalogs, Mail order

MAIL service. See Postal service

MAIL service, Air. See Air mail service

MAILER, Norman
Modes and mutations: comment on the modern American novel. Commentary 41:37-40 Mr '66

about

Books. M. Muggeridge. il Esquire 66:104+ D '66
Imagination and the age. A. Kazin. Reporter 34:32-5 My 5 '66
Mailer's America. J. Wain. New Repub 155:19-20 O 1 '66

Man against his times. A. Darack. por Sat R 49:35 S 3 '66
Pasta fazool. por Newsweek 68:73+ Ag 29 '66
Victim & analyst. J. W. Aldridge. Commentary 42:131-3 O '66

MAILING lists
Onward and upward with the arts. C. Trillin. New Yorker 42:126+ S 24 '66

MAIMONIDES hospital. See Brooklyn—Hospitals

MAIN, A. R. and Hastings, F. L.
Carbamylation and binding constants for the inhibition of acetylcholin-esterase by physostigmine, eserine. bibliog Science 154:400-2 O 21 '66

MAIN, James H. P.
Retention of potential to differentiate in long-term cultures of tooth germs. bibliog Science 152:778-80 My 6 '66

MAINE
See also
Fishing—Maine
Hunting—Maine
Penobscot Bay
Saint John River
Wilderness areas—Maine

Climate
Classic coastal day; good days that boating people count on; excerpt from Between wind and water. G. W. Brace. il Yachting 120:55+ Jl '66

Description and travel
From Boston to Boothbay and beyond. H. Winters. il Motor B 117:28-31+ Ag '66
Maine's high country. L. Dietz. il Field & S 71:108-11+ D '66
Sunrise serenade: Maine. I. Robinson and J. Robinson. il Travel 126:39+ S '66

MAINE Chance, Ariz. See Health resorts, watering places, etc.

MAINHARDT, Robert
Deadly zip gun for the missile age. il pors Life 60:45-8 My 27 '66

MAINTENANCE men
Specifications for a maintenance specialist; creation maintenance man in Mount Vernon recreation department. J. M. Branca. Parks & Rec 1:39+ Ja '66; Reply with rejoinder. R. J. Lindl. 1:390+ My '66

MAINWARING, Marion
Away from Moby Dick and Jane. Sr Schol 89:sup 13-15 O 14 '66

MAIR, Beveridge J. and others
Terpenoid precursors of hydrocarbons from the gasoline range of petroleum. bibliog Science 154:1339-41 D 9 '66

MAISEL, Albert Q.
Facts you should know about funerals. Read Digest 89:81-6 S '66
Ten ways to cut your medical bills. Read Digest 89:80-4 O '66
Useless gland that guards our health. Read Digest 89:229-30+ N '66

MAIZE. See Corn

MAIZE dwarf mosaic. See Corn dwarf mosaic

MAIZEL, Jacob V. Jr
Acrylamide-gel electrophorograms by mechanical fractionation: radioactive adenovirus proteins. bibliog Science 151:988-90 F 25 '66

MAJOLI, Mario
Ad Hoc committee of experts; summary of statement; March 25, 1966. UN Mo Chron 3:36-7 Ap '66

MAJOR, Gerri
New image of the socialite. Ebony 21:63-4+ Ag '66

MAJOR, Reginald W.
Schools and race: integration for excellence. Nation 203:213-15 S 12 '66

MAJORITIES
Wanted: a responsible majority; congressional elections. D. Lawrence. U S News 61:112 O 31 '66

MAKARENKO, A. S.
Life, the inexorable teacher; excerpt from The collective family. Sat R 50:117 Ja 7 '67

MAKARIOS III, abp
Behind the Aspida trial. K. Kyle. New Repub 156:17-18 Ja 21 '67
Toward a boiling point. il por Time 87:39 Ap 1 '66

MAKARONAS, Ch. J.
Pella: capital of ancient Macedonia; with biographical sketch. Sci Am 215:16, 98-105 D '66

MAKE-up
Beauty bulletin: sound of makeup; with quotes from tape-recorded talk with A. Grey. il Vogue 147:172-5 F 1 '66
Beauty life: three smart girls and what they've learned about makeup. il Mlle 64:98-101+ Ja '67
Case for fakery in beauty; the case for reality in beauty. il Vogue 143:192-5+ N 1 '66
Change of face. il Mlle 63:140-1 Je '66
Color them kicky; painting knees, legs and toes. il Seventeen 25:134 Jl '66
Glitter, glow and glisten; the new make-up. il Redbook 127:62-3+ My '66
Hello, bright eyes! il Mlle 62:194-5 Ap '66
Kneedless art? new leg makeup and knee accessories. il Newsweek 678:110 Je 13 '66
Makeups that do more. il Mlle 63:126-7 My '66
Mlle makes more of four G.E.s C. Rush. Mlle 63:274-9 Ag '66
Real you. il McCalls 93:84-5+ S '66
Seeing double? S. Harney. il Ladies Home J 83:84 N '66
Shapely face; schemes and application techniques. il McCalls 93:124-5+ Ap '66
Soft-shadowed eyes; light-catching lips; makeup instructions. il McCalls 94:58-9+ Ja '67
Soft spring makeup in nine quick steps. il Good H 162:130-1 My '66
Touch of sable; makeup man, Pablo of Elizabeth Arden. il Time 87:67 Je 10 '66
Water-baby look; moon maid look. il Seventeen 25:82-3 Je '66
Why women make up. il Sci Digest 59:18 F '66
The you look in make-up. il Seventeen 25:150-1 Ap '66

MAKE-up, Leg. See Cosmetics

MAKE-up, Theatrical
Mark Twain tonight! Hal Holbrook this morning. New Yorker 42:44-5 Ap 23 '66

MAKINS, Roger Mellor, 1st baron Sherfield. See Sherfield, R. M. M.

MAKO shark fishing. See Shark fishing

MALAHOFF, Alexander, and others
Molokai fracture zone: continuation west of the Hawaiian ridge. bibliog Science 153:521-2 Jl 29 '66

MALAMUD, Bernard
Bernard Malamud. H. Frankel. por Sat R 49:39-40 S 10 '66
Between the lines. R. A. Schroth. America 115:284 S 17 '66
Malamud as Jewish writer. R. Alter. Commentary 42:71-6 S '66
Malamud's heroes. J. Baumbach. Commonweal 85:97-9 O 28 '66
Schlemiel triumphant. por Newsweek 68:108B-110 S 12 '66

MALANGA, Gerard
New stars develop in Orion; Third person; October in New York; poems. Poetry 107:373-4 Mr '66
Three firsts. Poetry 108:130-3 My '66

MALARIA
African malaria may not be rare in U.S. Sci N 89:467 Je 11 '66
Annals of medicine; two cases of Vivax malaris, with report by J. S. Luby. B. Roueché. New Yorker 42:198+ N 12 '66
Falciparum malaria: transmission to the gibbon by anopheles balabacensis. D. J. Gould and others. bibliog Science 153:1384 S 16 '66
Malaria eludes drugs; effects of sulfones on patients suffering from plasmodium falciparum malaria. B. Culliton. Sci N 90:417 N 19 '66
Malaria infection (plasmodium iophurae); changes in free amino acids. I. W. Sherman and J. B. Mudd. bibliog il Science 154:287-9 O 14 '66
No threat from malaria. il Sci N 90:468 D 3 '66
Plasmodium vivax transmitted from man to monkey to man. M. D. Young and others. il Science 153:1006 Ag 26 '66
Porotic hyperostosis, anemias, malarias, and marshes in the prehistoric eastern Mediterranean. J. L. Angel. bibliog il Science 153:760-3 Ag 12 '66
Scientists volunteer for 186 mosquito bites. Sci N 90:180 S 10 '66
Shooting malaria down; research effort to find and test drugs to fight it. il Bsns W p92-3 Ap 16 '66
See also
Antimalarials
Chloroquine

Prevention and control
Frontier malaria fighter. H. E. Dark. il Todays Health 44:28-9+ My '66
Malaria wins round two. C. P. Gilmore. il N Y Times Mag p44-5+ S 25 '66

MALARIAL parasites. See Plasmodium (parasite)

MALATHION
Malathion degradation by trichoderma viride and a pseudomonas species. F. Matsumura and G. M. Boush. bibliog il Science 153:1278-80 S 9 '66

MALAWI
Politics and government
One-man Banda. Newsweek 68:38 Jl 18 '66
What the doctor orders. il Time 88:34 Jl 15 '66

MALAY PENINSULA
See also
English in Malay Peninsula

MALAYA
See also
Malaysia
Zoology—Malaya

MALAYSIA
Changing world of Malaysia. R. Peritz. bibliog f Cur Hist 52:29-35+ Ja '67
Letter from Singapore. R. Shaplen. il New Yorker 42:57-8+ Ja 14 '67
Looking for an angel; sudden reduction in Britain's role as financial angel and protector. Time 88:36 N 4 '66
Peace breaks out; Indonesian agreement. Newsweek 68:70-1 Ag 22 '66
Peace talks; negotiations with Indonesia. il Newsweek 67:52 Je 13 '66
Rupture in Malaysia. C. P. Bradley. bibliog f Cur Hist 50:98-105 F '66
Singapore and Malaysia: a divorce of inconvenience. D. Warner. il Reporter 34:44-6 Ap 7 '66
Uproar of peace: end of Indonesia's konfrontasi with Malaysia. il Time 87:39-40 Je 10 '66

MALCOLM X
Malcolm X: mission and meaning. R. P. Warren. Yale R 56:161-71 D '66
Odyssey of a black man. N. Hentoff. Commonweal 83:511-12 Ja 28 '66
Who issued the orders? Newsweek 67:36 Mr 21 '66

MALCOLM, Janet
Books. New Yorker 42:210+ D 17 '66

MALCOLM; drama. See Albee, E.

MALE coiffure. See Hairdressing

MALE cosmetics. See Cosmetics for men

MALE dancers. See Dancers

MALE nurses. See Nurses and nursing

MALIC dehydrogenases. See Dehydrogenases

MALICK, Donald L.
Hawks of western North America: with biographical sketch. il por Audubon Mag 68:443-8 N '66

MALIGNANT tumors. See Cancer

MALIK, Adam. See Rusk, D. jt. auth.

MALIK, Charles Habib
Reflections on the Great society. por Sat R 49:12-15 Ag 6 '66

MALINA, J. F. jr
Don't waste, renovate and reuse. Am City 81:160+ Mr '66

MALKIN, Lawrence
Britain's aristocrats of crime. Reporter 35:46-8 S 22 '66

MALKIN, Martin F. and Zahalsky, A. C.
Interatcion of the water-soluble carcinogen 4-nitroquinoline N-oxide with DNA. bibliog Science 154:1665-7 D 30 '66

MALLAN, Lloyd
John Campbell syndrome. Nat R 18:415-16+ My 3 '66
about
Russians faked it. D. Cohen. il Nation 203:445-7+ O 31 '66

MALLAN, Rose
City-side sanctuary. Travel 125:12 Je '66

MALLARY, Robert
Ideologue in Lotosland. H. Rosenstein. il por Art N 65:36-8+ O '66

MALLERY, David
Something more. Sat R 49:70-1 Je 18 '66

MALLET, Jean Pierre
Mallet's millions. Time 87:33-4 Ja 28 '66

MALLETTE, Daniel J.
In the inner city. Commonweal 84:17-20 Mr 25 '66

MALLIK, Anne-Marie
Alice in wonderland. J. Miller. il pors Vogue 148:240-7+ D '66

MALLISON, Nathan
Go fly a kite! por Parks & Rec 1:236-7 Mr
'66
MALLOCH, William
Gustav Mahler, the unfinished Tenth quick-
ened to vibrant life. Hi Fi 16:65-6 F '66
New Audiences in new buildings. Hi Fi 16:
156-7 Ap '66
Notes from our correspondents. Hi Fi 16:12+
Ag '66
MALLON, Mary
Malady of Mary Mallon. J. Lentz. il Todays
Health 44:34-6 Ap '66
MALLOWAN, Max E. L.
Mallowans; interview. New Yorker 42:51-2
O 29 '66
MALLS, Shopping. See Business districts
MALMGREEN, Henry P.
Stories for Modern romances. Writer 79:
26-9 D '66
MALNUTRITION. See Children—Nutrition
MALOFF, Saul
Masquerade; story. Sat Eve Post 239:44-7
F 12 '66
MALONE, Thomas F.
World weather watch. Science 154:678-9 N 4
'66
MALONEY, Eileen
End of the beginning. Ladies Home J 83:57
Ag '66
Miss Marsh, I love you. Ladies Home J 83:
80+ O '66
MALONEY, Elbert S.
New charts. See issues of Motor boating
Right log for your boat. Motor B 117:26+ Ap
'66
MALONEY, J. J.
If I am elected; poem. Christian Cent 83:1371
N 9 '66
MALONEY, Ralph
Best man; story. Atlan 217:51-6 My '66
Last stop before the carbarn; story. Atlan
218:63-8 Jl '66
MALONEY, Tom
World is his beat. U S Camera 29:44-5 My '66
MALOOF, Sam
Wood; a discussion. por Craft Horiz 26:16-19
Je '66
MALOPROPISMS. See Blunders
MALPRACTICE
See also
Quacks and quackery
MALRAUX, André
Behind the mask of Africa. N Y Times Mag
p30-1+ My 15 '66
about
Far out to jail. il por Time 88:54 Jl 15 '66
Goodbye to all that. il Time 87:62 Je 24 '66
Letter from Paris. Genêt. New Yorker 42:
223-5 N 19 '66
MALTA
Elections in Malta. C. Cardona. America
114:412-14 Mr 26 '66
MALTHUS, Thomas Robert
Early warning of an explosion. il Sr Schol
88:5 F 11 '66
MALTHUSIANISM
Early warning of an explosion. il Sr Schol
88:5 F 11 '66
See also
Population, Increase of
MALVERNE, N.Y.
Malverne: integration is not enough. B. J.
De Noie. Nat R 18:679-81 Jl 12 '66
MALY, Eugene H.
New relationship of church to world; adapta-
tion of address, August 1965. Cath World
203:104-8 My '66
MAMAS and the Papas (singers) See Singers
MAME; musical comedy. See Musical comedies,
revues, etc.— Criticisms, plots, etc.
MAMMALS
Visual and nonvisual auditory systems in
mammals. J. M. Harrison and R. Irving.
bibliog il Science 154:738-43 N 11 '66
See also
Embryology—Mammals
Sloths
Whales
MAMMARY cancer. See Cancer
MAMMARY glands
Mammary glands of pregnant rats: develop-
ment stimulated by licking. L. L. Roth and
J. S. Rosenblatt. bibliog il Science 151:
1403-4 Mr 18 '66
Rat mammary gland RNA: incorporation of
C14-formate and effect of hormones and
7,12-dimethylbenzanthracene. P. R. Libby
and T. L. Dao. bibliog il Science 153:303-5
Jl 15 '66

MAMMOTH CAVE NATIONAL PARK
Unseen world of Kentucky's Mammoth cave.
J. Speiser. il Nat Parks Mag 40:4-9 F '66
MAMMOTHS
Elephant-hunting in North America. C. V.
Haynes, jr. il Sci Am 214:104-12 bibliog(p
144) Je '66
Elephant teeth found at sea. B. Tufty. il
Sci N 90:481 D 3 '66
Undersea elephants. Sci Am 216:58+ Ja '67
MAN
History of mankind; publication of Unesco.
il UNESCO Courier 19:32-3 Jl '66
Impact of the concept of culture on the con-
cept of man. C. Geertz. il Bul Atomic Sci
22:2-8 Ap '66
Man is really an animal and thus does he
respond. E. Goble. Arch Rec 140:9 D '66
Man's task: a union of contrasts. L. L.
Whyte. Sat R 49:32 N 12 '66
Personalising process; address, January 26,
1966. M. E. Parr. Vital Speeches 32:341-4
Mr 15 '66
Science on race. P. McBroom. Sci N 91:44
Ja 14 '67
See also
Civilization
Color of man
Common man
Ethnology
Human nature
Humanism
Man, Primitive
Men
Influence of environment
Evolution by mistake; changes in man's re-
lationship to his environment. Sci N 90:
221 S 24 '66
Man in the technological society; symposium.
bibliog il Wilson Lib Bul 41:40-75+ S '66
Science and symbol in the Turner frontier
hypothesis. W. Coleman. bibliog f Am
Hist R 72:22-49 O '66
See also
Human ecology
Influence on nature
Man and his bruised planet. il Sci N 91:5-6
Ja 7 '67
One man's trash; control of pollution. Sci
Am 214:52 My '66
Origin and antiquity
Adam, Eve and the Pope; contemporary
concepts of original sin; Catholic scholars
report. il Newsweek 68:93 Ag 22 '66
Correlation of archeological and palynological
data. A. J. Jelinek. bibliog il Science 152:
1507-9 Je 10 '66
One Adam or many? monogenism-polygenism
controversy. Christian Cent 83:951 Ag 3 '66
Origins of native Americans. C. Miles. il
Hobbies 71:113-16 O '66
Roots of human nature; evidence that apes
are contemporaries, not ancestors. N. J.
Berrill. il Atlan 217:92-6 Je '66
See also
Evolution
Man, Prehistoric
Stone age
Periodicity
See Periodicity
Survival
Delegation of the survival instinct. N.
Cousins. Sat R 49:24 Ap 9 '66
On survival. D. Shively. Bul Atomic Sci 22:
34 S '66
We could stockpile birds. S. Alsop. il Sat Eve
Post 239:16 F 12 '66
MAN, Effect of altitude on. See Altitude, In-
fluence of
MAN, Prehistoric
Homo erectus. W. W. Howells. il Sci Am
215:46-53 N '66
Man Dr Leakey dug up; Paranthropus from
Olduvai gorge. Africa. J. Reinert. il Sci
Digest 60:72-80 N '66
Man through time's mists; findings in Oldu-
vai gorge. J. Pfeiffer. il Sat Eve Post 239:
40-4 D 3 '66
Oldest Australian. il Sci Digest 59:26-7 Ap
'66
Preserving the treasures of Olduvai gorge.
M. M. Payne. il Nat Geog Mag 130:700-9
N '66
Research in the prehistory of central western
Iran. T. C. Young, jr. and P. E. L. Smith.
bibliog il Science 153:386-91 Jl 22 '66
When homo erectus tamed fire, he tamed
himself. J. Pfeiffer. il N Y Times Mag
p58-9+ D 11 '66; Discussion. p 18+ Ja 8
'67

MAN, Primitive
Lévi-Strauss mind. il Newsweek 69:90 Ja 23
'67
Savage mind, by C. Lévi-Strauss. Review
New Repub 156:38-40 Ja 7 '67. P. Gallagher
MAN amplifiers
GE developing man-amplifying equipment for
ARPA, army; walking truck and Hardiman. il Tech W 19:30 S 5 '66
MAN in the bicycle cap; story. See Corcoran, B.
MAN in the red suit; drama. See Messenger,
B.
MAN of La Mancha; musical comedy. See
Musical comedies, revues, etc.—Criticisms,
plots, etc.
MAN of war birds. See Frigate birds
MAN who made his home in the Los Angeles
international airport; story. See Crittenden, J.
MAN who saw through heaven; story. See
Weingarten, V.
MAN with a dog; story. See Jhabvala, R. P.
MAN with a load of mischief; musical comedy. See Musical comedies, revues, etc.—
Criticisms, plots, etc.
MANAGEMENT, Business. See Business management and organization
MANAGEMENT, Industrial. See Industrial
management and organization
MANAGEMENT education. See Industrial management and organization—Study and teaching
MANAGEMENT games
Games businessmen play. il Time 88:111 S
16 '66
It's just a game; GREMEX, Goddard research engineering management exercise.
J. Eberhart. Sci N 90:256 O 1 '66
MANAGEMENT information system. See Information systems, Management
MANAGEMENT of children. See Children—
Management and training
MANAGEMENT rights
Management rights provisions in major agreements. R. F. Groner and L. E. Lunden.
il Mo Labor R 89:170-4 F '66
MANAGERS. See Executives
MANAGERS, Baseball. See Baseball managers
MANAGERS, Concert. See Concert managers
MANCHESTER, Harland
Electric heat for your home? Read Digest 90:
157-8+ Ja '67
Look what they're doing with magnets. Pop
Mech 126:116-19+ D '66
Saga of Patsy and Oscar; story. Read Digest 89:41-2 O '66
You name it, we rent it. Read Digest 89:114-
16 Jl '66
MANCHESTER, William
Death of a President; excerpts. Look 31:36-
42+ Ja 24 '67 (to be cont)

about

As the book appears: a close look at the facts;
concerning his The death of a President.
il U S News 62:50-2 Ja 23 '67
Battle of the book. il Time 88:15-18 D 23 '66
Best Kennedy book? Newsweek 68:21-2 S 5
'66
Book that has backfired; concerning his The
death of a President. il U S News 61:36
D 26 '66
Chapter I. Newsweek 69:29-30 Ja 16 '66
Chapter II, or finis? il Time 88:10-12 D 30 '66
Controversy that has only just begun. M.
McGrory. America 116:10 Ja 7 '67
Growing rift of LBJ and Kennedys: behind
the furor over a book; concerning his The
death of a President. il U S News 62:22-7
Ja 2 '67
Harper & Row, Manchester file official answers. Pub W 191:57 Ja 16 '67
History makers. Nation 204:4 Ja 2 '67
Holiday spirit. K. Crawford. Newsweek 69:
25 Ja 9 '67
Jacqueline B. Kennedy, plaintiff. il por
Newsweek 68:39-43 D 26 '66
Jacqueline Kennedy's victory. il Newsweek
69:16-19 Ja 2 '67
JFK book: accord reached as publishers
seek compromise on revisions asked by
Kennedys. Pub W 190:57-8 D 26 '66
Kennedy book. Commonweal 85:360-1 Ja 6
'67
Kennedy-Manchester book controversy; symposium. il por Sat R 50:18-29 Ja 21 '67
Kennedys look at history. Nat R 19:12-13 Ja
10 '67
Manchester book. Reporter 35:8 D 29 '66
Mrs Kennedy and Harper & Row continue
negotiations on editorial content of Death
of a President. Pub W 191:33-4 Ja 2 '67

Perils of hasty history. H. Bowser. Sat R
49:14 D 31 '66
Plans for official book on Kennedy assassination. Pub W 190:40-1 S 5 '66
Spreading controversy. il Time 89:16 Ja 6 '67
Start the presses; The death of a President;
Harper & Row clearance. il Time 89:47 Ja
20 '67
Temporary cease-fire; war over book. il
Newsweek 69:20 Ja 9 '67
What the fuss was about; first installment
of The death of a President. Time 89:47-8
Ja 20 '67
Widow vs. author; concerning his The death
of a President. por Sr Schol 89:16 Ja 6 '67
MANCHESTER guardian. See Guardian (newspaper)
MANCINI, Marie
Uncompromising heart, by F. Mallet-Joris.
Review
Sat R 49:31-2 Ap 30 '66. J. H. Plumb
MANDAEANS
Text from the early church: beliefs of Nazarenes in medieval Arab manuscript. il
Time 88:64 Jl 15 '66
MANDARIN pancakes. See Griddle cakes
MANDEL, Emanuel
Do we need new rules for experiments on
people? J. Lear. il Sat R 49:64-70 F 5 '66
Research and responsibility. Nation 202:284-5
Mr 14 '66
MANDEL, Loring
Project immortality. Criticism
Sat R 49:53 F 5 '66
MANDELBAUM, Seymour J.
More and more alike. Nation 203:713-14 D 26
'66
MANDELL, A. J. and others
Dreaming sleep in man: changes in urine
volume and osmolality. bibliog Science 151:
1558-60 Mr 25 '66
MANDELL, N. and Roberts, C. F.
Piston extractor for the Hughes press. bibliog Science 152:799-800 My 6 '66
MANDEL'SHTAM, Osip Emil'evich
Messages from the lost. G. Davenport. Nat R
18:119 F 8 '66
MANDEVILLE, Robert C.
What U.S. bombs in North Vietnam; a navy
pilot's account; excerpt from statement,
December 28, 1966, ed. by J. Kestner. por
U S News 62:13 Ja 9 '67
MANDY. William J. and Kormeier, L. C.
Homoreactant: a naturally occurring autoantibody in rabbits. bibliog Science 154:651-
2 N 4 '66
MANET, Édouard
Art. M. Kozloff. Nation 203:588-90, 621-2 N
28-D 5 '66
Brilliance of light; exhibition at Philadelphia museum of art. A. Werner. Reporter
35:50+ N 3 '66
Fundamentalist. il por Time 88:80-3 N 11 '66
Manet's mental museum. H. G. Gardiner. il
Art N 65:48-50+ N '66
Poetry of the present. il por Newsweek 68:
104-6 N 28 '66
MANEUVERABILITY of boats. See Boats—
Maneuverability
MANGAN, G. L. and King, M. G.
Initial and resultant population densities in
chickens between brooding and sexual maturity. bibliog Science 154:1568-9 D 23 '66
MANGANESE
Crystal and molecular structure of a double
complex of manganese with phthalocyanato and pyridine ligands. L. H. Vogt,
jr. and others. bibliog il Science 151:569-70
F 4 '66
Manganese nodules: their evolution. M.
Bender and others. bibliog il Science 151:
325-8 Ja 21 '66
Manganese pavements on the Blake plateau.
R. F. Pratt and P. F. McFarlin. il Science
151·1080-2 Mr 4 '66
Neurological defect: manganese in phenocopy
and prevention of a genetic abnormality of
inner ear. L. Erway and others. bibliog
il Science 152:1766-8 Je 24 '66
Tetrodotoxin and manganese ions: effects
on electrical activity and tension in taenia
coli of guinea pig. Y. Nonomura and others.
bibliog il Science 152:97-9 Ap 1 '66
MANGER groups. See Christmas cribs
MANGIAROTTI, Giorgio, and others
Selection of sucrose-dependent escherichia coli
to obtain envelope mutants and fragile
cultures. bibliog Science 153:892-4 Ag 19 '66
MANGIERI, A. A.
Diode meter protectors. Electr World 76:56-
7+ N '66
MANGLAPUS, Raul S.
Asian revolution and American ideology. bibliog f For Affairs 45:344-52 Ja '67

MANGONE, Gerard J.
What does the U.S. want from the U.N?
Bul Atomic Sci 22:8-12 Ja '66

MANGROVE
Mangrove world. J. D. Multer and H. G.
Multer. il Am For 72:34-7 Ag '66
This tree builds land. M. Hunn. il Am For
72:13 My '66

MANGUM, Garth L. See Levitan, S. A. jt.
auth.

MANHATTAN. See New York (city)

MANHATTAN community college. See Borough
of Manhattan community college, New York

MANHATTAN festival ballet. See Ballet companies

MANHATTAN opera company
Oscar Hammerstein's Manhattan opera com-
pany, by J. F. Cone. Review
Sat R il 49:74-5 N 26 '66. H. Weinstock

MANHATTAN project. See Atomic bombs—
Manufacture

MANHATTAN school of music
New York; Nicolas Flagello's Judgment of
St Francis and Martin Kalmanoff's Empty
bottle. J. Honig. Opera N 30:22-3 My 7 '66
New York; performance of Chabrier's Educa-
tion manquée and Mascagni's Cavaleria
rusticana. R. D. Daniels. il Opera N 30:31
Ja 29 '66

MANHATTANVILLE college of the Sacred
heart, New York
Pius X at fifty; School of liturgical music.
America 115:52 Jl 16 '66

MANICURING
Electric manicure sets. il Consumer Bul 49:
25-7 D '66

MANIFOLD
Airing out the manifold. J. McFarland. il
Hot Rod 19:76-8 Je '66

MANIHI. See Tuamotu Islands

MANILA
Hotels, restaurants, etc.
Return to the Rock. H. Sutton. Sat R 49:
70-2 D 3 '66
Police
Sickly sleuths. Newsweek 68:49 D 19 '66

MANILA conference, 1966
Great road show. Nation 203:466 N 7 '66
He was Mr Equal, not Mr Big. H. Sidey. il
Life 61:36 N 4 '66
LBJ meets allies at Manila; with press com-
ments. il Sr Schol 89:16-18 N 11 '66
Manila and the President. M. Ascoli. Reporter
35:14+ N 17 '66
Manila conference communique; excerpts from
the closing comunique. Cur Hist 52:48-9 Ja
'67
Manila: is it only a gesture? E. Weintal.
Newsweek 68:28-9 O 24 '66
Manila makes it clear. il Bsns W p36-7 O 29
'66
Manila manifesto. New Repub 155:8 N 5 '66
Manila summit. H. Sutton. Sat R 49:14+ N 12
'66
New building blocs for Asia. C. J. V.
Murphy. Fortune 74:134+ D '66
President Johnson discusses forthcoming
Asian trip; excerpts from opening state-
ments at news conferences, October 6 and
13, 1966. L. B. Johnson. Dept State Bul
55:664-7 O 31 '66
President Johnson's trip to Asia; remarks at
Cam Ranh Bay, October 26, and report to
the Nation, October 27, 1966. L .B. Johnson.
Dept State Bul 55:735-9 N 14 '66
President Marcos and the Huk resurgence.
D. Warner. il Reporter 35:28-9 N 3 '66
Protecting the flank. il Time 88:25-30 N 4
'66
Seven nations declare unity at Manila con-
ference; texts of the three documents is-
sued at the close of conference. Dept State
Bul 55:730-5 N 14 '66
Solemn event in a fiesta city, no miracle, but
solid results. D. Moser; R. B. Stolley. il
Life 61:30-1 N 4 '66
Some hopeful signs in the Pacific. Bsns W
p 186 O 29 '66
Togetherness in the Pacific. il Newsweek
68:27 N 7 '66
United States and the new Asia; address,
November 16, 1966. W. W. Rostow. Dept
State Bul 55:910-14 D 19 '66
What LBJ is offering the Asians. il U S
News 61:33-4 O 31 '66
What LBJ will find in Asia; Allies say: win
the war. il U S News 61:37-40 O 24 '66
What was decided in Manila; new plan for
peace. il U S News 61:33-4 N 7 '66

MANIPULATORS
See also
Man amplifiers

MANITAS de Plata
Gypsy camp in a concert hall: 'Manitas'
flamenco tour. M. Acoca. Life 61:16 N 18
'66

MANITZAS, Frank N.
Crackdown on colleges, Argentina. New Repub
155:12-15 N 19 '66

MANKER, Don
To kiss a fool; poem. Ladies Home J 83:103
Jl '66

MANKS, Dorothy S.
Ephraim Bull and his Concord grape. Horti-
culture 44:30-1+ O '66
People and plant names. Horticulture 44:18-21
Ag '66

MANLEY, Fletcher, Jr
Renee Manley: medical technologist. il Todays Health 45:28-32 Ja '67

MANLEY, R. St John. See Blais, P. jt. auth.

MANN, Jack
Baseball (cont) Sports Illus 24:58-60 Je 27;
25:75-7 O 10 '66

MANN, Pete
I guess we're just impatient. por Am Ed
2:5-7 Mr '66

MANN, Stanley
Rooms. Criticism
Commonweal 83:613-14 F 25 '66
New Yorker 41:84+ F 5 '66

MANN, Thomas
Essays on Thomas Mann, by G. Lukacs.
Review
Nation 202:590-3 My 16 '66. I. Deutscher

MANN, Thomas Clifton
Coordination of policy on population matters;
statement, April 11, 1966. Dept State Bul
54:784-7 My 16 '66
Hemisphere cooperation for economic and
social progress; address, April 14, 1966.
Dept State Bul 54:734-7 My 9 '66
U.S. informs Security council of action on
Rhodesian agent; letter to H. J. C. Hooper.
Dept State Bul 54:589 Ap 11 '66
U.S. Shipowners formally notified of ban on
Rhodesian oil shipments; letter, May 4,
1966. Dept State Bul 54:859 My 30 '66

about
Shrinking inner circle. por Time 87:21-2 My 6
'66

MANNE, Henry G.
In defense of insider trading; excerpts from
Insider trading and the stock market. bib-
liog f Harvard Bsns R 44:113-22 N '66

about
On the side of the insiders. por Bsns W
p 160+ N 12 '66

MANNED orbiting laboratory. See Space stations

MANNED space flights. See Space flight—
Manned flights

MANNED spacecraft center. See United States
—National aeronautics and space administration—Manned spacecraft center

MANNEQUINS. See Models (persons)

MANNERS. See Etiquette

MANNERS and customs
Boston tea party. il Ladies Home J 83:110-
12+ O '66
Polite Americans, by G. Carson. Review
Time il 87:111+ Ap 8 '66
See also
Clothing and dress
Culture
Dating
Funeral rites and ceremonies
Hairdressing
Taboo

MANNES, Marya
America in Salzburg. Harper 232:91-5 F '66
Assignment; poem. New Repub 154:31 F 26
'66
Let's face it. See issues of McCall's
Movies. Vogue 147:111 Ap 1; 147 My; 148:50
Ag 15; 79 O 15; 100 N 15 '66
Raid on Castalia. Reporter 34:27-8+ My 19 '66
What every girl should know. Mlle 62:83+
Ja '66

MANNHEIM, Andrew
2¼ Rollei SLR! Mod Phot 30:84-5+ N '66

MANNING, Gordon P.
Build your own rope ladder. Motor B 118:29
D '66
Repowering? Motor B 117:30-1+ F '66
Secret of a successful cruise. il Motor B 117:
22-5+ Ap '66

MANNING, Robert
New man at the Atlantic. il por Newsweek
67:61 Ja 31 '66

MANNING, S. C.
How to keep school segregation. J. Osborne. New Repub 154:16-18 Mr 12 '67

MANNION, John B.
Dull new day. Commonweal 84:519-21 Ag 19 '66
Pope and Mr Dooley on jazz masses. Commonweal 85:416-17 Ja 20 '67

MANNIX, Daniel P.
Wizard who created Oz. Read Digest 88:104-8 Je '66

MANNOR, Frank
Fatuus season. il Time 87:25B Ap 1 '66
It wasn't no hullabillusion, said the farmer, and fifty-two agreed. P. O'Neil. il por Life 60:28-9 Ap 1 '66

MANON Lescaut; opera. See Puccini, G.

MANOS, Constantine
Sailors of the shadowed skies; photographs. Sports Illus 25:28-34 Ag 1 '66

MANPACK Loran. See Loran

MANPOWER
Coordination of manpower programs; excerpt. H. C. Taylor. Mo Labor R 89:959-64 S '66
Program proposals for manpower policy A. R. Weber. Mo Labor R 89:130-1 F '66
See also
Labor supply—United States
United States—Armed forces

MANPOWER development and training act. See Labor laws and legislation—United States

MANRY, Robert Neal
Crossing the Atlantic in a 13-foot sailboat; excerpts from Tinkerbelle. il por Harper 232:41-50 Je '66
Tinkerbelle; excerpt. Read Digest 89:195-8+ Jl '66

MANS, Lawrence, family
Man can't afford to get soft! P. Friggens. il pors Farm J 90:26-7+ D '66; Same abr. Read Digest 90:127-31 Ja '67

MANSFIELD, John Kenneth
Policeman of foreign aid. por Time 87:33 Je 10 '66

MANSFIELD, Michael Joseph
Excerpt from address, August 31. 1966. Cong Digest 45:244+ O '66
Mansfield appeal, new road to Vietnam peace? summary of statement. por U S News 60:19 My 2 '66

about
Freedom to end freedom. M. Ascoli. Reporter 34:10 My 5 '66
R.I.P: repeal of 14(b) dead for session. Time 87:22 F 18 '66
Washington: ten of its most powerful men. il por Vogue 148:154-5 N 15 '66

MANSFIELD, Portia
Help them move young. por Dance Mag 40:16-17 Ag; 82 S; 76-7 O; 78 N; 67 D '66 (to be cont)

MANSFIELD, Tex.
Fresh water from a brackish source. C. R. Johnson. il Am City 81:122-3 Ap '66

MANSON, Frank
Mystery beneath the waves. por Sr Schol 89:34 N 18 '66

MANSOURI, Lotfi
Man from Iran; interview. ed. by F. Stevenson. por Opera N 30:11 F 19 '66

MANTHORNE, Jane
Sex education: the common denominator; with bibliography. Library J 91:319-22 Ja 15 '66

MANTLE, Mickey
Ghost arises. Time 88:45 Jl 15 '66
Troubled time for a wounded hero. B. Gilbert. il pors Sat Eve Post 239:76-80 S 10 '66

MANTUA, Ohio
Wrong is what you think up by yourself; school children answer questions of right and wrong. W. Stanton. il Redbook 128:56-7+ D '66

MANUALS, Instruction. See Instruction manuals

MANUEL, Michael
Opera in motion. F. Stevenson. il Dance Mag 40:28-9+ F '66

MANUFACTURERS, National association. See National association of manufacturers

MANUFACTURES
Hewing to the old line; buggy whips, hand-cranked ice-cream freezers, player pianos, etc. il Newsweek 68:90-1+ S 19 '66
Labor turnover; tables. See issues of Monthly labor review
See also
Products, New

Statistics
Business markets. il Duns R 88:pt2 70-6+ Jl '66

Ratios of manufacturing; with table (cont)
Duns R 88:72-4+ N '66

Wages and hours
Wage developments in manufacturing, 1965. G. Ruben. il Mo Labor R 89:871-6 Ag '66

MANUFACTURING and machining services corporation
Middleman on the production line; contract manufacturing. il Bsns W p 171-2 Je 11 '66

MANUFACTURING districts. See Industrial districts

MANUFACTURING expense. See Cost accounting

MANURE odors. See Odors

MANUS tribe. See New Guinea—Native races

MANUSCRIPT division. See United States—Library of Congress—Manuscript division

MANUSCRIPTS
See also
Dead Sea scrolls

Prices
Book values. il Fortune 74:242 O '66

MANUSCRIPTS, Authors. See Authorship

MANUSCRIPTS, Illuminated. See Illumination of books and manuscripts

MANUSCRIPTS, Illumination of. See Illumination of books and manuscripts

MANUSCRIPTS, Medieval
Age of Charlemagne. R. Pernoud. bibliog il Horiz 8:16-22+ Spr '66

MANUSCRIPTS, Rejected. See Editors and editing

MANWELL, Clyde
Sea cucumber sibling species: polypeptide chain types and oxygen equilibrium of hemoglobin. bibliog Science 152:1393-6 Je 3 '66

MANZONI, Pablo Zappi-. See Zappi-Manzoni, P.

MANZÙ, Giacomo
Art galleries; exhibition at the Rosenberg. R. M. Coates. New Yorker 41:102-4 Ja 29 '66

MAO, Tse-tung
Another leap? Time 88:22+ Ag 12 '66
Can Mao keep the upper hand in China? por U S News 62:13 Ja 9 '67
China after Mao; excerpts. A. D. Barnett. il por Look 30:31-5 N 15 '66
China convulsed. M. Gayn. For Affairs 45:246-59 Ja '67
China leaps: where? R. S. Elegant. il Reporter 35:35-9 S 22 '66
China's crisis of foreign policy. D. S. Zagoria. il por N Y Times Mag p22-3+ My 1 '66
Communist China . . . after Mao what? il por Sr Schol 88:12-14 F 4 '66
Culture riots: Mao at bay. I. Deutscher. Nation 203:442-5 O 31 '66
Dance of the scorpion. il por Time 89:20-3 Ja 13 '67
Drums in the night; blast at opponents. Newsweek 68:37 D 26 '66
Great proletarian cultural revolution. il Newsweek 69:29 Ja 9 '67
Great splash forward; Mao enjoys swim. il por Time 88:27 Ag 5 '66
Hidden battle for power in red China. V. Zorza. por Look 30:25-8 Ag 23 '66
How to be mad for Mao. il pors Sr Schol 89:17-18 S 23 '66
Is Mao really back in the swim? il pors Life 61:32-3 Ag 5 '66
Mao's last revolution. R. MacFarquhar. bibliog f For Affairs 45:112-24 O '66
Mystery of red China: a real blowup coming? il por U S News 62:46-8 Ja 23 '67
No ordinary swim. il pors Newsweek 68:36-40 Ag 8 '66
Nuclear muscle. il por Newsweek 67:53 My 23 '66
Numbers game, Chinese style; attacks on Liu. por Newsweek 69:28 Ja 9 '67
Peking has a Yenan complex. M. Gayn. il pors N Y Times Mag p 10-11+ Ja 30 '66
Red China's god: Communists try to deify Mao. il por U S News 60:14 My 23 '66
Red China's sinking revolution. C. J. V. Murphy. il por Fortune 74:134-9+ N '66
Stalemate in Peking; not strong enough to eliminate the opposition. por Newsweek 68:49 D 19 '66
Weeds & the flowers; Mao's physical condition. il por Time 87:34 My 13 '66
Where's Mao? il por Newsweek 67:41 My 16 '66

MAO, Tse-tung, Mme
Star is born. il por Newsweek 68:54 S 26 '66

MAORIS. See New Zealand—Native races

MAP making. See Cartography

MAP reading
Map reading for fun. B. Riviere. il Field & S 71:76 S '66
MAPLE
Sweet maples may be improved by breeding. il Sci N 89:361 My 14 '66
Trouble with maple. D. Wolfe. il Am For 72:18-21+ Je '66
MAPLE press company
Manchester concept and how it paid off. il Pub W 190:86-91 Ag 1 '66
MAPLE syrup
Trouble with maple. D. Wolfe. il Am For 72:18-21+ Je '66
MAPP, Frances
Wonderful Wizard of Oz; dramatization of story by L. F. Baum. Plays 25:49-58. 80 Mr '66
MAPP gas. See Methylacetylene propadienc
MAPPING, Aerial
See also
Artificial satellites—Mapping applications
Photogrammetry
MAPS
Making the earth flat; quiz. J. Daugherty and M. Daugherty. Sci Digest 60:90-3 D '66
See also
Cartography
Map reading
also subhead Maps under various subjects, e.g. National parks and reserves—Maps
MAPS, Early
Early mapping of the land and sea. G. A. Rothrock. il Natur Hist 75:24-9 bibliog (p68) F '66
MAPS, Pictorial
Getting to know your state's literary map. B. W. Fuson. il Sr Schol 89:sup44-5 S 23 '66
Love was where they found it; from 1620 through 1966. il Sat Eve Post 239:40-1 D 31 '66
MARAT/Sade: drama. See Weiss, P.
MARATHON oil company
Marathon oil's fleet fills transport gap. D. A. Brown. il Aviation W 84:106-10+ Ap 25 '66
MARATHON running. See Running
MARBERRY, M. M.
Vachel Lindsay's lost weekend in Urbana. Horizon 9:112-15 Wint '67
MARBLE
How to care for marble. Bet Hom & Gard 44:111 F '66
MARBLE CANYON DAM (proposed) See Dams
MARCEL, Gabriel
Ascent to being: Gabriel Marcel's philosophy of communion, by V. P. Miceli. Review Nat R 19:45-7 Ja 10 '67. F. D. Wilhelmsen
MARCH
March is a promise. H. Borland. Read Digest 88:172F+ Mr '66
MARCHALONIS, J. and Edelman, G. M.
Polypeptide chains of immunoglobulins from the smooth dogfish (mustelus canis) bibliog Science 154:1567-8 D 23 '66
MARCHAND, Leslie A.
Byron & Rossini. Opera N 30:6-7 Mr 19 '66
MARCHANT, William
New ambassadors. Horizon 8:50-5 Wint '66
On learning from children. Holiday 40:8+ Ag '66
MARCHESE, Dolores
Some projects for children's art classes. Sch Arts 66:21-8 S '66
MARCHESSAULT, R. H. See Sarko, A. jt. auth.
MARCHING through Boston; story. See Updike. J.
MARCOS, Ferdinand
Asian leader explains America's role to Americans; address, September 15, 1966. por U S News 61:114-16+ O 3 '66; Same. Dept State Bul 55:534-17 O 10 '66; Same with title Philippines and the United States. Vital Speeches 33:2-10 O 15 '66
President Marcos of the Philippines visits the United States; exchange of greeting and toast, September 14, 1966. Dept State Bul 55:527-31 O 10 '66
What an ally sees ahead for U.S. in Asia; interview. ed. by K. M. Chrysler. por U S News 61:66-9 S 19 '66

about

Formula from the Philippines. il por Time 88:22-3 S 23 '66
Johnson and Marcos. M. Meadows. New Repub 155:12 S 17 '66
LBJ hosts Asians. il por Sr Schol 89:19 S 30 '66

Marcos proposal. il por Newsweek 68:20 O 3 '66
Mutual admiration alliance. il Life 61:133-4 S 30 '66
New voice in Asia. il por Time 88:38-42+ O 21 '66; Same abr. with title Marcos of Manila, new voice in Asia. Read Digest 90: 101-6 Ja '67
Outspoken U.S. ally; contain China, Marcos urges. il por U S News 61:24+ S 26 '66
Philippines. A. Campbell. New Repub 154:21-4 Mr 12 '66
Philippines and its president. E. J. Hughes. il por Newsweek 67:51-3 Ag 25 '66
Presence of Marcos. Nat R 18:969-70 O 4 '66
President Marcos and the Huk resurgence. D. Warner. Reporter 35:28-31 N 3 '66
Time for toughness. il por Newsweek 67:42+ F 14 '66
U.S. and Philippines: drawing closer? il por U S News 60:84-5 Ap 4 '66
Vietnam: the U.S. tries harder. il por Bsns W p38-9 O 1 '66
MARCOS, Imelda Romualdez
First lady's lilting diplomacy. il pors Life 61: 134 S 30 '66
MARCUS, Arthur
How to pick a dealer. Motor T 18:64 N '66
MARCUS, Frank
Killing of Sister George; text. Esquire 66: 118-29+ N '66

about

Killing of Sister George. Criticism
Christian Cent 84:16-17 Ja 4 '67
Commonweal 85:106 O 28 '66
Esquire 66:8+ N '66
Life 61:6 D 2 '66
Nation 203:459-60 O 31 '66
Newsweek il 68:98+ O 17 '66
Reporter 35:62-3 N 17 '66
Sat R 49:72-3 O 22 '66
Time il 88:93 O 14 '66
Vogue 148:99 N 15 '66
MARCUS, Leonard
Prospects in audio. Hi Fi 16:64-7+ Ap '66
Second-hand stereo. Hi Fi 16:68-70 S '66
Stereo in your car. Hi Fi 16:58-64 My '66
MARCUS, Ruth
Small wonders. See issues of Good housekeeping
MARCY, MOUNT
Bob Marshall, Mount Marcy, and, the wilderness. P. Schaefer. il Liv Wildn 30:6-9 Sum '66
MAR DEL PLATA festival. See Moving picture festivals
MARDEN, Luis
Saga of a ship, the Yankee. Nat Geog Mag 129:262-9 F '66
MARDEN, Orison
Let's X out the coroner system. por Todays Health 44:88+ N '66
MARDI gras. See Carnival
MARDI gras; musical comedy. See Musical comedies, revues, etc.—Criticisms, plots, etc.
MARDOR, Munya M.
Underground to independence. H. Lehrman. Sat R 49:32-3 Mr 26 '66
MARECHAL, Leopoldo
Books. A. A. Piñeiro. por Américas 18:40-2 My '66
MAREE, A. Morgan, Jr, and associates
Keeping the stars in fiscal shape. il Bsns W p 160-2+ Je 4 '66
MAREK, George R.
Toscanini and the others. Harper 233:40+ N '66
MAREK, Lois
Cook's treasure. Parents Mag 41:121 O '66
MAREMONT, Arnold H.
Business, management, and creative thinking. Duns R 87:45-6+ My '66
Plea for the abrasive personality. Duns R 88:48-9+ N '66
MARES, Vaclav E.
French planning experiment. bibliog f Cur Hist 50:221-7+ Ap '66
U.S. aid to east Europe. bibliog f Cur Hist 51:36-44 Jl '66
MARETZEK, Max
Impressario tells all. R. Ellsworth. Am Rec G 32:898+ My '66
MARGARET of Austria, regent of the Netherlands
Chanson albums of Marguerite of Austria, by M. Picker. Review Am Rec G por 32:892+ My '66. J. W. Barker
MARGARET, princess of Great Britain
White tie and tails; party at the Waldorf. R. Lynes. Harper 232:28+ F '66

MARGARINE
Oleomargarine territory: letter. B. Glass. Science 153:1595-6 S 30 '66
MARGARITA ISLAND
Margarita Island: on a clear day you can flee forever. C. Stinnett. Holiday 40:24+ Ag '66
MARGIN requirements, Stock. See Stock exchange—Regulation
MARGIOTTA, Mike
Crop the square anywhere. M. Edelson. il U S Camera 29:58-9 Mr '66
MARGOLIS, Ellen
Grandparents for the asking. Parents Mag 41:60-1+ D '66
MARGOLIS, Frank L. and others
Norepinephrine methylation in a fetal rat adrenals. bibliog Science 154:275-6 O 14 '66
MARGOLIS, George, and Brown, I. W. Jr
Hyperbaric oxygenation: the eye as a limiting factor. bibliog Science 151:466-8 Ja 28 '66
MARGOLIS, Howard
Civil defense: notes on Project Harbor. Bul Atomic Sci 22:19-21 F '66
From New York and Washington: talking about disarmament. Bul Atomic Sci 22:38-40 F '66
MARGOLIUS, Sidney
Why young couples spend more than they earn. Redbook 126:56-7+ F '66
MARGRAVE, John L. See Paul, M. A. jt. auth.
MARIA Cordis, Sister. See Cordis, M.
MARIA Theresa, empress of Austria
Empress Maria Theresa, by R. Pick. Review Sat R 49:29 Jl 16 '66. G. Brunn
Mother to the fatherland. D. McGuigan. il Horizon 8:16-23 Sum '66
MARIAN Frances, Sister
Dark Pietà; poem. Christian Cent 83:1110 S 14 '66
Establishing teacher-student rapport. NEA J 55:19-20 O '66
Spring inventory; poem. Christian Cent 83:752 Je 8 '66
MARIAN movement. See Mary, Virgin—Theology
MARIANO, Nicky
Life with the Berensons. F. Biddle. New Repub 155:29-32 D 24 '66
MARICHAL, Juan
Dandy Dominican. il pors Time 87:88-92 Je 10 '66
30-game winner? il Newsweek 67:98 Je 13 '66
MARIE Michael, Sister
Importance of Freud. por Cath World 204:212-18 Ja '67
MARIE Virginia, Sister
Using students to evaluate manuscripts. Sr Schol 89:sup 18-19 O 14 '66
MARIGOLDS
Bright new marigold. il Flower Grower 53:33 Je '66
MARIHUANA
Great marijuana hoax; excerpt from Marihuana papers. A. Ginsberg. bibliog f Atlan 218:104+ N '66; Discussion. 219:28+ Ja '67
Pot penalties too severe. P. McBroom. Sci N 90:270 O 8 '66
MARIJUANA. See Marihuana
MARILLEY, Jane
Capital care for the businessman. il por Bsns W p24-5 Jl 2 '66
MARIN CITY, Calif.
Watts with view. Time 87:24 Ap 22 '66
MARINA park. See Jacksonville, Fla.—Parks and playgrounds
MARINAS
Convenient boating from marina motel; Travelodge motel. il Arch Rec 140:132-3 Ag '66
Dry-slip marinas: kinder to your boat. J. Martenhoff. il Pop Sci 188:150-1 F '66
From the marina-man's point of view. E. Crimmin. il Motor B 119:112-13+ Ja '67
Fully found marina. A. P. Winters. il Motor B 118:26+ O '66
Marina life in St Thomas V.I. G. Sloane. il Motor B 118:46-7+ D '66
Marinas grow apace with boating. il Motor B 117:266-7 Ja '66

Electric power
Volts, amperes and headaches. C. F. Kelley. il Motor B 118:39+ Jl '66
MARINE algae. See Algae
MARINE bands. See Bands (music)
MARINE biology
Kelp forests of the Pacific. W. Marx. Atlan 218:107-10 S '66
Marine biology; report on fourth meeting. C. H. Oppenheimer. Science 152:108 Ap 1 '66

Prying medical secrets from creatures of the sea. J. C. Devlin. il Todays Health 44:29-33+ Ap '66
See also
Algae
Marine resources
MARINE cookery. See Cookery, Marine
MARINE corps. See United States—Marine corps
MARINE diesel engines. See Diesel engines, Marine
MARINE ecology
Diatoms and the ecological conditions of their growth in sea ice in the Arctic Ocean. H. Meguro and others. bibliog Science 152:1089-90 My 20 '66
MARINE electronics. See Boats—Electronic equipment
MARINE engineering

Study and teaching
What a union does to fill a shortage; helping sailors become marine engineers. il Bsns W p 105-6 Ap 2 '66
MARINE engines
Boats and motors for 1967. J. A. Emmett. il Outdoor Life 139:70-2+ Ja '67
Free piston engine seen; may be used in heavy trucks and boats. Sci N 90:375 N 5 '66
Marriage of inboard and outboard. L. Heiner. il Motor B 118:92-4+ N '66
1967 motor facts and figures. Outdoor Life 139:73 Ja '67
Outdrives: the in way to propel a boat. J. Roe. il Pop Sci 189:106-8 N '66
Repowering? G. P. Manning. il Motor B 117:30-1+ F '66
Spray makers; hot boaters with ski boats. E. Rickman. il Hot Rod 19:32-8+ S '66
Stern drives. il Motor B 119:144-7 Ja '67
Still under wraps, but soon to be seen. il Motor B 118:42-4 D '66
Switchables. J. McFarland. il Hot Rod 19:92-4+ S '66
Wankel engine goes to sea. D. Borden. il Pop Sci 188:148-9 F '66
Wankel, new auxiliary power. M. Crook. il Yachting 120:50-1+ D '66
Yachting's boat show. il Yachting 119:127-30+ Ja '66
See also
Electric engines, Outboard
Gas and oil engines, Inboard
Gas and oil engines, Outboard
Gas turbines, Marine

Care
Before you button-up the engine. J. Seville. il Motor B 118:38-9 N '66
Water in the gas. B. Wells. Motor B 117:66+ Mr '66

Ignition
Electronic ignition takes to the water. M. Gellman. il Pop Mech 125:200-3 Mr '66
Innovations in ignition systems. L. Heiner. il Yachting 120:53-5+ O '66
MARINE fauna
Deep scattering layer migration and composition: observations from a diving saucer. E. G. Barham. bibliog il Science 151:1399-403 Mr 18 '66
Long-term activity recording in small aquatic animals. A. A. Heusner and J. T. Enright. bibliog il Science 154:532-3 O 28 '66
Marine bioacoustics; report on symposium. W. N. Tavolga. Science 153:771+ Ag 12 '66
Marvels of a coral realm. W. A. Starck, 2d. il Nat Geog Mag 130:710-38 N '66
Pacific pleistocene cores: faunal analyses and geochronology. A. Blackman and B. L. K. Somayajulu. bibliog il Science 154:886-9 N 18 '66
See also
Fishes
Starfishes
Whales
MARINE finishes. See Finishing materials
MARINE flora
Tiny ocean plant foods checked by their light. Sci N 89:162 Mr 12 '66
See also
Algae
MARINE gas turbines. See Gas turbines, Marine
MARINE gasoline. See Gasoline
MARINE geology. See Submarine geology
MARINE insurance. See Insurance, Marine
MARINE marshes. See Salt marshes
MARINE microorganisms. See Microorganisms

MARINE painting
Figures and figureheads: the maritime collection at the State Street bank and trust company, Boston. W. D. Garrett. il Antiques 90:816-18 D '66
Frederick Waugh, America's most popular marine painter. G. R. Havens. il Am Artist 31:30-7+ Ja '67
Maintenance with new products. W. Andrews. il Yachting 119:73+ Ap '66
Thomas Birch: America's first marine artist. W. H. Gerdts. il Antiques 89:528-34 Ap '66

MARINE plants. See Marine flora

MARINE radiophone. See Radio telephone on ships, boats, etc.

MARINE resources
Big business takes a dive in the ocean. H. Fantel. il Pop Mech 125:80-3+ Je '66
High tide for business; below the oceans; address, December 2, 1965. C. F. Jones. Vital Speeches 32:210-12 Ja 15 '66
Investment risks cloud market outlook. il Tech W 19:19+ S 26 '66
Minerals for humanity in ocean storehouses. Sci N 90:44 Jl 16 '66
Ocean engineering takes the plunge. T. Alexander. il Fortune 73:144-7+ Je '66
Oceanography: Interior department bids for a major role. L. J. Carter. Science 154:749-51 N 11 '66
Oceanography nears high tide; biggest government-sponsored research program. il Bsns W p51-2 Ag 6 '66
Oceanography; report of International congress in Moscow. R. H. Charlier. Science 153:1421-3 S 16 '66
Our newest frontier is underwater! R. F. Crossley. il Pop Mech 125:94-8+ My '66
Profits under the sea. G. Berkwitt. il Duns R 87:32-3+ Je '66
Sea food exhaustible. Sci N 90:84 Ag 6 '66
Undersea farms could use fish as sheep dogs. Sci N 90:73 Jl 30 '66
Ungathered harvests in the ocean; man's vast potential food reserve. M. Laing. il UNESCO Courier 19:11-15+ S '66
See also
Institute of marine resources, La Jolla, Calif.
Salt
United States—National council for marine sciences

International aspects
Sharing the seas' riches. C. M. Eichelberger. Sat R 49:18 Ag 13 '66
Who owns which ocean? Sci N 90:23 Jl 9 '66

MARINE resources and engineering development act, 1966. See United States—National council for marine sciences

MARINE sedimentary rocks. See Rocks, Sedimentary

MARINE sediments. See Sedimentation and deposition

MARINE spark plugs. See Spark plugs

MARINE structures
Hardware of a New World. W. Chalk. il Arch Forum 125:46-51 O '66

MARINE transport lines, incorporated
At the eye of the shipping storm; building ships abroad. Bsns W p 132+ Je 18 '66

MARINER (space vehicle) See Space vehicles

MARINER probes. See Space probes

MARINERS museum, Newport News, Va.
Mariner's museum. il Parks & Rec 1:901 N '66

MARINI, Marino
Centaurian. il por Time 87:72-5 My 27 '66

MARITAL counseling. See Marriage counseling

MARITIME consultative organization, Intergovernmental. See Intergovernmental maritime consultative organization

MARITIME day, National. See National maritime day

MARITIME law
Who owns which ocean? Sci N 90:23 Jl 9 '66
See also
Mutiny

MARITIME museums. See Naval museums

MARITIME pine. See Pine

MARITIME subsidies. See Ship subsidies

MARITIME workers
See also
Longshoremen
Seamen

MARK, R. F. and Davidson, T. M.
Unit responses from commissural fibers of optic lobes of fish. bibliog Science 152:797-9 My 6 '66

MARK and the rest of the world; story. See Ellington, M.

MARK Smith planetarium, Macon, Ga. See Planetariums

MARK Twain, pseud. See Clemens, S. L.

MARKEL, Helen
Children Santa didn't forget after all. Ladies Home J 83:24 My '66

MARKEL, Lester
Europe in search of a future. N Y Times Mag p4-5+ Jl 17 '66
Myths that divide India and us. N Y Times Mag p29+ Ja 15 '67

MARKER, Leonard
Alban Berg. Opera N 30:32 My 7 '66

MARKERS
See also
Plant labels

MARKET hunting. See Poaching

MARKET plazas. See Business districts

MARKET research
Better jet marketing procedures urged; reprint. G. M. Munsinger and A. L. O'Connor. il Aviation W 85:71 D 26 '66
Book market research: Europe; report of international meeting in Berlin. G. R. Davies. Pub W 191:53-5 Ja 16 '67
Researchers snap up supermarket secrets; chains sell records of merchandise movement to market researchers. Bsns W p83 Mr 5 '66

MARKET research corporation of America
MRCA gets rich supermarket data. Bsns W p 134 Ap 30 '66

MARKET surveys
See also
Consumer surveys

MARKETING
Are prospects people? D. L. Lionel. Sat R 49:64+ My 14 '66
Case of the product priority; excerpts from Cases in marketing management. E. C. Bursk. il Harvard Bsns R 44:6-8+ Mr '66
Changing face of marketing. J. D. Louth. il Duns R 87:46-7+ Ap '66
Distribution's endless route. B. W. Hupp. il Duns R 87:pt2 134-6+ Mr '66
Product line pricing; effect various products have on one another and on the total line. A. R. Oxenfeldt. il Harvard Bsns R 44:137-44 Jl '66
Social values of marketing; address, October 27, 1966. C. W. Cook. Vital Speeches 33:86-91 N 15 '66
Test of the total product. E. T. Klassen. il Duns R 88:139-40 N '66
Tinting supermarkets with orange and blue; Howard Johnson co. il Bsns W p42-3+ Jl 2 '66
See also
Advertising
Exclusive agencies
Market research
Retail trade
Sales promotion
Salesmen and salesmanship
Supermarkets
also subhead Marketing under various subjects, e.g. Farm produce—Marketing

MARKETING, Cooperative
Symbiotic marketing. L. Adler. Harvard Bsns R 44:59-71 N '66

MARKETING research. See Market research

MARKETS, Black. See Black markets

MARKFIELD, Wallace
Burlesque returns, but the competition is fierce. N Y Times Mag p 10-11+ Je 26 '66
Dark geography of W. C. Fields. N Y Times Mag p32-3+ Ap 24 '66

MARKHEIM; opera. See Floyd, C.

MARKING-writing pens. See Pens

MARKOVICH, Alexander
Bring glamor to your yard with marble chips. Pop Sci 189:130-1 Ag '66
Ceramic tire studs, they really grab you! Pop Mech 126:148-51 N '66
In the driver's seat: the Toyota Corona. Pop Mech 127:38+ Ja '67
Microelectronics magnified. Pop Mech 126:194-6+ N '66
Owners report on Volkswagen's new fastback and squareback. Pop Mech 126:82-4+ Ag '66
Spotlight on the Alfa Romeo Giulia TI. Pop Mech 125:48+ My '66
Spotlight on the MGB-GT. Pop Mech 125:36-7 Je '66

MARKS, Bertram R.
City in a hurry. Hi Fi 16:MA17+ Ag '66

MARKS, Edward B.
Saigon; the impact of the refugees. Reporter 36:33-6 Ja 12 '67

MARKS, George A. Jr
  Cold heart; story. Redbook 128:56-7 Ja '67
  Good-by, kitten; story. Redbook 126:50-1 F
    '66
MARKS, Lawrence E. and Slawson, A. W.
  Direct test of the power function for loud-
    ness. bibliog Science 154:1036-7 N 25 '66
MARKS and Spencer, limited
  English unorthodoxy of Marks & Spencer. J.
    Ross-Skinner. il Duns R 88:45-7+ O '66
MARKSMANSHIP. See Shooting
MARKSON, David
  Malcolm Lowry: a reminiscence. Nation 202:
    164-7 F 7 '66
MARKSTEIN, David L.
  How to make money in science stocks. Sci
    Digest 59:82-5 Ap '66
MARLBORO festival of music. See Music fes-
    tivals—Vermont
MARLEY, C. F.
  Planter hitches that save trips. Farm J 90:
    66B Ap '66
MARLIK antiquities. See Iran—Antiquities
MARLOWE, Dan J.
  Is your story different enough? Writer 79:
    17-19 D '66
MARLOWE, Derek
  Assassin; story; excerpts from A dandy in
    aspic. Sat Eve Post 239:50-2 S 10; 44-54
    S 24; 60-2 O 8 '66
MARLOWE, Foster
  Casting. Sch Arts 65:19-20 Ja '66
MARLOWE, Sylvia
  Recordings. M. Mayer. Esquire 66:52+ O '66
MARMALADE. See Jelly, jam, etc.
MARMEE; story. See Loeser, K.
MARMOTTAN musée. See Paris—Galleries and
    museums
MARNE RIVER
  Meander down the Marne. P. R. Smyth. il
    Travel 126:31-6 Ag '66
MAROON, Fred J.
  He builds in color. por Pop Phot 58:78-83 My
    '66
MAROPIS, Petro S.
  Saturday night; story. Esquire 66:132 N '66
MARQUESAS ISLANDS
  Island-hopping the Marquesas. M. Petersen.
    il Motor B 118:92-3+ S '66
MARRIAGE
  About marriage; CBS telecast. Feedback:
    marriage, a game for kids? America 116:34-5
    Ja 14 '67
  Can this marriage be saved? case histories;
    ed. by D. C. Disney. See issues of Ladies'
    home journal
  Divorce and the family in America. C. Lasch.
    il Atlan 218:57-61 N '66
  For better, but not for worse. A. A. Messer.
    il Todays Health 44:62-6+ Ap '66
  How to live with a woman; reprint. M. B.
    Johnstone. Read Digest 88:75-7 F '66
  Luci Johnson and Pat Nugent talk about life
    without father. M. Means. il Ladies Home J
    83:73+ Ag '66
  Lutheran clergyman looks at marriage. Cath
    World 204:174-6 D '66
  Making a weak marriage work; excerpt from
    Advice from a failure. J. Coudert. Ladies
    Home J 83:106-8 My '66
  Man talk; first hundred days. D. Newman
    and R. Benton. il Mlle 62:34 Ja '66
  Marriage as a wretched institution. M. Cad-
    wallader. il Atlan 218:62-6 N '66
  Marriage, divorce and remarriage. F. R.
    Schreiber and M. Herman. il Sci Digest
    60:24-7 N '66
  Marriage in two steps. M. Mead. Redbook
    127:48-9+ Jl '66
  May I ask you a few questions about love?
    Elmo Roper's opinion poll. S. Brown. il Sat
    Eve Post 239:24-7 D 31 '66
  On being the man of the house. P. S. Beagle.
    Sat Eve Post 239:70+ D 31 '66
  Pregnant bride. A. Silberman. il Redbook 128:
    58-9+ N '66
  Private morality and public policy. America
    114:722 My 21 '66
  Teen-age marriage. Time 87:102 Ap 29 '66
  Three provactive views of modern marriage.
    R. F. Capon; J. Bell; D. Horowitz. Mlle 64:
    87-9+ Ja '67
  Total gift. J. T. Culliton. America 115:770-3
    D 10 '66
  Unsolved mystery of marriage. il Changing T
    20:19-22 O '66
  What would you tell the newlywed couple?
    ed. by M. Longwell. Farm J 90:50-1 Je '66
  When a man marries. J. L. Collier. Read
    Digest 89:76-9 O '66
  Young wife's world. H. Valentine. See issues
    of Good housekeeping

Young wives' tales; symposium. Mlle 62:58-
    62+ Ja '66
    See also
  Catholic church—Canon on marriage and
    divorce
  Divorce
  Domestic relations
  High school students, Married
  Husbands
  Intermarriage of races
  Love
  Polyandry
  Priests
  Weddings
  Wives
          Anecdotes, facetiae, satire, etc.
  Fly now, pay later. P. J. Laux. America 115:
    340-1 S 24 '66
  How fragile is your marriage? A. Buchwald.
    Ladies Home J 83:68 S '66
  Love in a nutshell; excerpt from I've only
    got two hands and I'm busy wringing
    them. J. Goodsell. il Read Digest 89:65-6
    D '66
  Unfaithful executive. A. Buchwald. Look 31:
    34 Ja 10 '67
          Annulment
  New thinking on divorce; Catholic church.
    il Time 87:103-4 Mr 18 '66
          Quotations, maxims, etc.
  Look before you—; comp. by E. F. Murphy.
    N Y Times Mag p44+ My 15 '66

          Japan
  Marriage, Japanese style. M. Evans. McCalls
    94:84+ N '66
          United States
    See Marriage
MARRIAGE counseling
  Can this marriage be saved? case histories;
    ed. by D. C. Disney. See issues of Ladies'
    home journal
  For better, but not for worse. A. A. Messer.
    il Todays Health 44:62-6+ Ap '66
  Group therapy valuable aid to married
    couples. Sci N L 89:153 Mr 5 '66
  Help for troubled marriages. V. W. Grant.
    il Parents Mag 41:25-7+ Jl '66
  Help wanted: divorce counselor. M. M. Hunt.
    il N Y Times Mag p 14-17 Ja 1 '67
  Playback: new aid in the ordeal of self-dis-
    covery; tool of Drs Peter Hogan and Ian
    Alger. D. Monaco. il Look 31:26-9 Ja 24
    '67
MARRIAGE customs and rites
    See also
  Weddings
MARRIAGE law
          Israel
  Black Jews; Falasha and Jew marry. il
    Newsweek 67:50 My 9 '66

          United States
  Colorless conjugality; Maryland bars Kovacs-
    Toalepai marriage. il Time 87:25 F 25 '66
  Crime of being married; Lovings' fight
    against miscegenation. il Life 60:85-6+
    Mr 18 '66
  Private morality and public policy. America
    114:722 My 21 '66
MARRIAGES, Interracial. See Intermarriage of
    races
MARRIAGES, Mixed
  Ecumenical curtsy; modification of Catholic
    church laws on mixed marriage. Christian
    Cent 83:419-20 Ap 6 '66; Reply. D. McCabe.
    83:807 Je 22 '66
  Ecumenism and marriage. America 115:312
    S 24 '66
  Gracious gesture or insult? Vatican instruc-
    tions on mixed marriages. Christian Cent
    83:769 Je 15 '66
  Marriage, mixed and invalid. America 114:
    213 F 12 '66
  Mixed decision; new Vatican ruling. News-
    week 67:86 Mr 28 '66
  Mixed marriage laws. Commonweal 84:44 Ap
    1 '66
  Mixed marriages made easier; Roman Cath-
    olics. Time 87:76 Mr 25 '66
  Mixed marriages. Protestant reaction; sym-
    posium. Cath World 203:181-3 Je '66
  On mixed marriages. Christian Cent 83:1278
    O 19 '66
MARRIED women
    See also
  Wives
          Employment
  How to be a working mother without really
    crying; excerpt from So you want to be
    a working mother. L. Benjamin. Ladies
    Home J 83:101-3 My '66

MARRIED women—Employment—*Continued*
Legal rights of working wives. il Good H 162:180 Mr '66
Marital and family characteristics of workers in March 1965. V. C. Perrella and E. Waldman. il Mo Labor R 89:258-63 Mr '66
More moms on payroll; highlights of NICB study. Bsns W p59 D 31 '66
One job too many. P. B. Card. il Redbook 126:8+ F '66
Tax break for working mothers. America 115:108 Jl 30 '66
When a mother works. L. Burke and R. M. inselberg. Todays Health 44:3-5 N '66
Why mothers work. America 114:166 Ja 29 '66; Reply. C. S. McCauley. 114:312 Mr 5 '66
Why working mothers feel guilty; discussion by young mothers and jobholders; ed. by B. Bettelheim. Redbook 126:55+ Mr '66
Young woman in a white world; beauty helps husband earn degree. il Ebony 21:69-70+ Ag '66
See also
Part time employment

Law
See Woman—Legal status, laws, etc.
MARRINER, E. H.
BC-454 goes maritime. Pop Electr 25:92 Jl '66
MARRYING kind; story. See Alexander, R. W.
MARS, Grady
Loaded pistol. S. Alsop. il por Sat Eve Post 239:22 Ap 23 '66
MARS (planet)
Ames researchers find Mars produces life forms. Miss & Roc 18:23 F 14 '66
Martian wave of darkening: a frost phenomenon? J. Otterman and F. E. Bronner. bibliog il Science 153:56-60 Jl 1 '66
Search for extraterrestrial life: adaptation of address, October 13, 1965. N. H. Horowitz. bibliog Science 151:789-92 F 18 '66
See also
Space flight to Mars
Space vehicles—Landing systems—Mars

Atmosphere
Atmosphere of Mars: Mariner IV models compared. G. Fjeldbo and others. bibliog il Science 153:1518-23 S 23 '66
Atmospheric probe stressed for Mars. W. S. Beller. il Miss & Roc 18:16-17 Ap 4 '66
Mars: upper atmosphere. S. H. Gross and others. bibliog il Science 151:1216+ Mr 11 '66
Marsh gas on Mars. Time 88:56 N 4 '66
Martian atmosphere: the Mariner occulation experiment. J. W. Chamberlain and M. B. McElroy. bibliog il Science 152:21-5 Ap 1 '66
Upper atmosphere and ionosphere of Mars. T. M. Donahue. bibliog il Science 152:763-4 My 6 '66
What's stirring on Mars? Franco-U.S. findings. Newsweek 68:66 O 31 '66

Photographs, maps, etc.
Mariner IV: analysis of preliminary photographs. A. B. Binder. bibliog il Science 152: 1053-5 My 20 '66
Photographs from Mariner IV. R. B. Leighton. Sci Am 214:54-68 bibliog(p 140) Ap '66
See also
Space photography

Spectra
Mars: new absorption bands in the spectrum. J. Connes and others. Science 153:739-40 Ag 12 '66

Surface
Behavior of carbon dioxide and other volatiles on Mars. R. B. Leighton and B. C. Murray. bibliog il Science 153:136-44 Jl 8 '66
Canals, oases on Mars may be cracks, craters. Sci N 90:72 Jl 30 '66
Controversy rages over Martian polar caps. Sci N 90:54 Jl 23 '66
Elevation differences on Mars. il Sky & Tel 32:261 N '66
How old is Mars' surface? G. S. Mumford. Sky & Tel 31:89 F '66
Mariner IV: analysis of preliminary photographs. A. B. Binder. bibliog il Science 152: 1053-5 My 20 '66
Mars ice caps. C. Leovy. bibliog il Science 154:1178-9 D 2 '66
Martian surface. E. J. Öpik. bibliog il Science 153:255-65 Jl 15 '66
Miniature laboratory will probe life on Mars; Automated biological laboratory. il Sci N 90:367 N 5 '66

Photographs from Mariner IV. R. B. Leighton. il Sci Am 214:54-68 bibliog(p 140) Ap '66
Variations in Mars' surface height found. Sci N 89:418 My 28 '66
Yes, there are canals. H. Pryor. il Sci Digest 59:32-4 Mr '66

Temperature
Mars ice caps. C. Leovy. bibliog il Science 154:1178-9 D 2 '66
MARS landing systems. See Space vehicles—Landing systems—Mars
MARS probe. See Space probes
MARSH, Ernest S.
Speakers or spectators; address, February 9, 1966. Vital Speeches 32:439-42 My 1 '66
MARSH, Jane
Agony of the Tchaikovsky. il por Time 88:60 Jl 8 '66
Broncobuster in Moscow. il por Newsweek 68:84 Jl 11 '66
[Mademoiselle Merit award winner] por Mlle 64:48 Ja '67
Sporting chance; interview, ed. by F. Merkling. por Opera N 31:12 S 10 '66
about
New diva who busts broncos. il pors life 61:86+ S 23 '66
MARSH, Robert C.
Basic tape library. Hi Fi 16:59-62+ Ag '66
Jesse H. Jones hall, a grand slam play. Hi Fi 16:MA20-1 D '66
Martinon, an evaluation: Chicago report. Hi Fi 16:151 My '66
Notes from our correspondents. Hi Fi 16: 16+ Jl '66
Opera after the schism. Hi Fi 16:142-3 F '66
Opera in the Lone Star state. Hi Fi 16:121-2 Je '66
Ravinia and Grant Park concerts. Hi Fi 16: MA22-3 N '66
MARSH, Tracy H.
Mill, my lady's bower, or a church? Hobbies 70:84-5 F '66
MARSH marigolds
Nature note; marsh marigold. Sci N 89:377 My 14 '66
MARSHAK, R. E.
Basic research in the university and industrial laboratory; excerpts from address, 1966. Science 154:1521-4 D 23 '66
MARSHAK, Samuil Îakovlevich
Great literature for little folk. M. Morton. Horn Bk 42:336-44 Je '66
MARSHALL, A. P.
Undeveloped potential of ALA. por ALA Bul 60:1157-9 D '66
MARSHALL, Albert
Railways to pathways. Parks & Rec 1:978+ D '66
MARSHALL, Bob
Bob Marshall, Mount Marcy, and the wilderness. P. Schaefer. il Liv Wildn 30:6-9 Sum '66
MARSHALL, Charles Burton
South Africa: an unhysterical report. Nat R 18:724-9 Jl 26 '66
MARSHALL, Eleanor
High cost of passing through. Motor T 18:67 O '66
MARSHALL, Eric, and Hample, Stuart
(comps) Children's letters to God. Sat Eve Post 239:30-1 N 19 '66
MARSHALL, George Catlett
George C. Marshall, by F. C. Pogue. Review
   New Repub 156:32 Ja 14 '67. G. W. Johnson
   Newsweek por 68:73-4 D 26 '66. S. K. Oberbeck
   Time por 88:78-9 D 23 '66
George C. Marshall oral history project. F. C. Pogue. il Wilson Lib Bul 40:606-8+ Mr '66
MARSHALL, James
Kafka goes to court. il Time 88:58 Jl 15 '66
MARSHALL, John
Search for status: the library profession. bibliog por Library J 91:5556-63 N 15 '66
MARSHALL, Lauriston C. See Berkner, L. V. jt. auth.
MARSHALL, Louise H.
Behavioral sciences: vocabulary. Science 153:323-4 Jl 15 '66
MARSHALL, Percy Johnson-. See Johnson-Marshall, P.
MARSHALL, Richard
Our cultural exchanges. Commonweal 84:150-3 Ap 22 '66
MARSHALL, S. L. A.
Fight at Monkey; excerpt from Battles in the monsoon. Harper 233:111-14+ N '66
He's winning our war in Vietnam. Look 31:57-9 Ja 10 '67

MARSHALL, S. L. A.—*Continued*
Men facing death: destruction of an American platoon; excerpt from Battles in the monsoon. Harper 233:47-55 S; 16+ D '66
Truth about the most publicized battle of Vietnam; excerpt from Battles in the monsoon. Harper 234:67-70+ Ja '67

about
Basic flaw in Viet Nam. il por Time 88:86 O 21 '66
MARSHALL, Sarah P.
To a magician: Beatrix Potter, 1866 to 1966; poem. Horn Bk 42:425 Ag '66
MARSHALL, Thurgood
Colored judges. J. H. Roy. por Negro Hist Bul 29:85-6 Ja '66
MARSHALL ISLANDS
See also
Eniwetok
MARSHALL space flight center. See United States—National aeronautics and space administration—Marshall space flight center
MARSHES
Death walked the duck marsh; ed. by B. East. E. La Fountain. il Outdoor Life 137: 60-1+ Ap '66
Humans, plants and animals in Florida's Fahkahatchee Strand. M. A. Finn. il Nat Parks Mag 40:10-13 Jl '66
Wetlands: stepchild of land use. F. G. Ashbrook. il Nat Parks Mag 40:17-19 Ag '66
Wetlands, wildlife and the army engineers; adaptation of address, October 2, 1965. J. S. Gottschalk. il Audubon Mag 68:116-18 Mr '66
See also
Everglades
MARSHES, Salt. See Salt marshes
MARSTON, Charles
Stars and stripes. Hobbies 71:36 Jl '66
MARTEL, C. W.
New digital readout system. Electr World 76: 85 Jl '66
MARTELL, Charles
Ouija message from JFK; poem. Nation 203: 460 O 31 '66
MARTELLI, George
Portugal's African provinces. Reporter 35: 17-19 D 29 '66
MARTENHOFF, Jim
Dry-slip marinas: kinder to your boat. Pop Sci 188:150-1 F '66
How an expert rigs an outboard for rough water. Pop Sci 188:124-8+ Mr '66
How to stretch your boat. Pop Sci 188:110-11 Je '66
Ruckus over the turbine. Motor B 117:181-5 My '66
Sextant in the sky. Motor B 117:85+ Ja '66
Southward ho! See issues of Motor boating to April 1966
Voices in the night. Motor B 117:40-1+ F '66
MARTENS, Anne Coulter
Visions of sugar plums; drama. Plays 26:33-43 D '66
MARTHA'S VINEYARD
There's no place else quite like the Vineyard. M. Wiley. il Yachting 120:58-9+ Jl '66
MARTI, Jorge L.
French thought in Latin America. Américas 18:8-15 S '66
MARTÍ, José
Poet and patriot. H. Lavine. por Sat R 49:28 Ag 6 '66
MARTIAL law
See also
Courts martial
MARTIN, Agnes
Art; show at the Robert Elkon gallery. M. Kozloff. Nation 203:524-5 N 14 '66
MARTIN, Allie Beth
Library building program. por Wilson Lib Bul 41:514-16 Ja '67
MARTIN, Baker
Five with enterprise. P. Rifield. il por Mlle 63:144 S '66
MARTIN, David
Life TV review (cont) Life 61:7 S 2 '66
Play that song you made up. Life 60:96+ Mr 4 '66
MARTIN, Dean
Dean Martin cools it, and makes it. B. Rollin. il pors Look 30:54-6+ My 17 '66
Old moderately. por Time 87:60 Mr 11 '66
MARTIN, Dennis
Formagrams. E. Meyers. il Mod Phot 30:70-1 Ag '66
MARTIN, Dick
Favorites from the funnies. Hobbies 70:118-19 F '66
MARTIN, Fran
Our boys took to embassy life. Parents Mag 41:68-9+ D '66

MARTIN, Frank R.
Dream trip for fall trout. Outdoor Life 138: 24-7+ Ag '66
MARTIN, George W.
Call of the open trail. por Parks & Rec 1: 630-2 Ag '66
MARTIN, Gerard
Breaking the vicious circle: libraries in Quebec. por Library J 91:5550-5 N 15 '66
MARTIN, Harold H.
My son in Vietnam. pors Sat Eve Post 239: 34-8+ Jl 16 '66
Race of the thousand clowns. Sat Eve Post 239:25-9 My 7 '66
MARTIN, Harrison P.
Designing a flag. Motor B 118:112A O '66
MARTIN, John
My son in Vietnam. H. H. Martin. il pors Sat Eve Post 239:34-8+ Jl 16 '66
MARTIN, John Bartlow
After Trujillo. S. Halper. New Repub 155:25-8 D 24 '66
Books. R. H. Rovere. New Yorker 42:224+ N 26 '66
Dominican rewrite. Commonweal 85:280 D 9 '66
Verdict on Santo Domingo. por Time 88:30 N 11 '66
MARTIN, Joy Logee
Dwarf bananas. Horticulture 44:28-9 My '66
MARTIN, Linda Grant
When crisis is a way of life. Mlle 64:172-3+ N '66
MARTIN, Paul
Canada's role in East-West relations; address, March 11, 1966. Vital Speeches 32: 409-14 Ap 15 '66
Independent foreign policy: address, January 31, 1966. Vital Speeches 32:311-14 Mr 1 '66
MARTIN, Paulette
Theater of mystery. Commonweal 84:582-5 S 16 '66
MARTIN, R. D.
Tree shrews: unique reproductive mechanism of systematic importance. bibliog Science 152:1402-4 Je 3 '66
MARTIN, Robert W. jr
Message from the publisher. Aviation W 84: 17 F 7; 85:15 mid-D '66
MARTIN, Warren Bryan
Freedom and restraint in the Christian college. Christian Cent 83:1372-4 N 9 '66
Will to be different. Sat R 50:68-9 Ja 21 '67
MARTIN, Will
In a bind. Flying 78:93 Je '66
MARTIN, William McChesney, 1906-
Another push for tax rise; summary of address, October 31, 1966. U S News 61:128 N 14 '66

about
Control the Fed? Atlan 217:10 F '66
Year of the Fed. Fortune 75:85-6 Ja '67
MARTIN company
Firm seeks greater knowledge of carbides. J. F. Judge. il Tech W 20:23-5 Ja 16 '67
Launching pad of zero defects. Duns R 88: 26 Ag '66
MARTIN houses. See Bird houses
MARTIN-Marietta corporation
Martin missile guidance development center opening. C. D. LaFond. il Miss & Roc 18:32-3 My 2 '66

Aerospace division
Martin builds guidance research facility. il Aviation W 84:191+ Je 20 '66
MARTIN Orlando aerospace division. See Martin-Marietta corporation—Aerospace division
MARTÍNEZ MONTERO, Homero
Of law and the river. Américas 18:1-4 F '66
Toward a South American canal. Américas 18:23-7 S '66
MARTINI, Hans Joachim
Economy through air power. il Time 87:70 F 4 '66
MARTINON, Jean
Martinon, an evaluation: Chicago report. R. C. Marsh. il por Hi Fi 16:151 My '66
Musical events; concert in Carnegie Hall, performed by Chicago symphony orchestra. W. Sargeant. New Yorker 42:197-8 Mr 19 '66
MARTINŮ, Bohuslav
Another first from Louisville. C. J. Luten. por Am Rec G 33:221 N '66
MARTS, Arnaud Cartwright
Meandering streams of plenty. R. C. Cornuelle. Nat R 18:1232 N 29 '66
MARTY, Martin E.
Protestant view. Commonweal 84:8-10 Mr 25 '66
Protestants and liturgy. Commonweal 84:522-4 Ag 19 '66

MARTYRS
Foxe's book of martyrs, ed. by G. A. Williamson. Review
Commonweal 85:82-4 O 21 '66. J. Ratte
MARVEL, David Thomas
Surinam. il U S Camera 29:70-1 Je '66
MARVEL, William W.
What colleges can do. Sat R 49:56-7+ Ag 20 '66
MARVELL, Andrew
Coy mistress caper. il por Life 61:99-102 N 11 '66
MARVER, Diana, and others
Correlation between location and time of expression for genes in a single operon. bibliog Science 153:1655-6 S 30 '66
MARVER, Harvey S. and others
Coordinate synthesis of heme and apoenzyme in the formation of tryptophan pyrrolase. bibliog Science 154:501-3 O 28 '66
MARX, Karl
Communism: world's greatest failure. il por U S News 61:59-63 D 5 '66
Rise and fall of scientific socialism. A. P. Mendel. bibliog f For Affairs 46:98-111 O '66
Works of Marx. K. Rexroth. Sat R 49:62+ S 17 '66
MARX, Wesley
Eviction of whales. Atlan 217:91-5 Ap '66
Kelp forests of the Pacific. Atlan 218:107-10 S '66
MARXHAUSEN, Benjamin W.
Case of the bottles. Sch Arts 65:18 Ja '66
MARXISM. See Communism; Socialism
MARY, Virgin

Apparitions and miracles (modern)
Fátima's 50th: the day the sun danced. F. J. Spellman. il Sat R 50:70+ Ja 7 '67

Art
Correggio's Virgin and Child with the infant St John. J. Maxon. il Art N 65:30-3+ Ap '66
Fra Angelico's Virgin and child. P. R. Adams. il Art N 65:34-5+ D '66
Madonna with child writing. D. Miner. il Art N 64:40-3+ F '66
Manner of speaking; Karoli Crivelli's Madonna and Child. J. Ciardi. Sat R 49:12 Jl 23 '66

Theology
Disappointing Marian development; Christi Matri Rosarii (Rosaries to the Mother of Christ) Paul VI's fourth encyclical. S. Benko. Christian Cent 84:79-80 Ja 18 '67
Mary and the Christian. M. W. Hess. Cath World 203:100-3 My '66
Pruned, healthy tree. V. P. McCorry. America 116:63-4 Ja 14 '67
MARY, Virgin, in art. See Mary, Virgin—Art
MARY Alice, Sister
Sculpture in homemade clay. Design 68:32-4 N '66
M. Bernarda Sharkey, Sister. See Sharkey, M. B.
MARY Claude, Sister
Dixie cup; poem. Christian Cent 83:804 Je 22 '66
M. Davida, Sister
Moon torsion; poem. America 115:70 Jl 16 '66
MARY Dorothy Ann, Sister
This younger generation; excerpts from address, August 1965. Cath World 203:175-80 Je '66
MARY Eusebio, Sister
Pine cone creations. Design 67:26-8 My '66
MARY Faith, Sister
To a convent; poem. Cath World 202:285 F '66
M. Ferdinand, Sister
How to help your doctor help you. Todays Health 44:74-6 Ap '66
M. Josepha Clark, Sister. See Clark, M. J.
MARY Maynard, Sister. See Maynard, M.
M. Michael, Sister
Nun enters the Newman apostolate. Cath World 203:293-6 Ag '66
MARY Poppins (literary character) See Characters in literature
M. Simplicia, Sister
Dandelions; poem. Commonweal 84:638 S 30 '66
MARY Thérèse, Sister
Concert; poem. America 115:70 Jl 16 '66
Potomac watergate; poem. America 115:691 N 26 '66
Space flight; poem. Commonweal 84:356 Je 17 '66
Spirit of place; poem. Cath World 203:33 Ap '66
Warming our tents like a lantern; poem. America 115:824 D 24 '66

MARY Winifred, Sister
Unforgettable Sister Winifred. L. Young. il Read Digest 88:173-4+ Mr '66
MARYKNOLL fathers. See Catholic church—Missions
MARYLAND
See also
Architecture, Domestic—Maryland
Crime and criminals—Maryland
Festivals—Maryland
Fishing—Maryland
Hunting—Maryland
Libraries—Maryland
Montgomery County
Plummers Island

Boundaries
See also
Mason and Dixon's line

Maps
Go exploring with a map. G. Cross. Read Digest 89:115-18 Ag '66

Marriage law
See Marriage law—United States

Politics and government
Loser's victory; Mahoney's win. il Time 88:25 S 23 '66
Lucky seventh? gubernatorial race. Time 88: 32-3 N 4 '66
Mahoney: a legend in his own time. J. Ridgeway. New Repub 155:13-15 O 29 '66
MARYLAND academy of sciences, Baltimore
Events of 1967 in the graphic time table. il Sky & Tel 33:33-5 Ja '67
MARYLAND-National capital park and planning commission
Unique answer to urban sprawl problem. J. P. Hewitt. il Parks & Rec 1:491-2 Je '66
MARYLAND poets. See Poets, American
MARYLAND. University, College Park

School of library and information services
Plans for a project to set up a nationwide investigation of manpower problems. Wilson Lib Bul 40:687 Ap '66
MASADA (fortress) Israel
Letter from London; exhibition at Festival Hall of finds of archeological dig. M. Panter-Downes. New Yorker 42:55-6 D 24 '66
Masada and its scrolls; excerpt from Masada. Y. Yadin. Commentary 42:41-7 O '66
Masada, by Y. Yadin. Review
Sat R il 49:39 N 26 '66. J. B. Pritchard
Masada; with introd. by N. Kotker. Y. Yadin. il Horizon 8:18-25+ Wint '66
MASCAGNI, Pietro
Cav 'n' Pag from La Scala; with editorial comment. P. L. Miller. Am Rec G 33:336-7 D '66
Cav & Pag, Karajan/La Scala style. C. L. Osborne. il Hi Fi 16:124-5 O '66
Records:
Cavalleria rusticana. Opera N 31:34 D 17 '66
MASERS
Possibility of maser action in cosmic radio sources. R. McCray. bibliog il Science 154: 1320-3 D 9 '66
See also
Lasers
MASIN, Herman L.
Sports. See issues of Senior scholastic
MASKED ball; opera. See Verdi, G.
MASKED balls. See Balls (parties)
MASKELL, Thomas W.
Amateur scientist. Sci Am 215:114-18 Jl '66
MASKEY, Jacqueline
Broadway: spring. Dance Mag 40:22 Je '66
Potluck-in-the-park. Dance Mag 40:80-1 S '66
Two film reviews. Dance Mag 40:22-5 O '66
MASKING creams. See Cosmetics
MASKS (for the face)
Anaktuvuk mask and cultural innovation; adaptation of address. September 1964. S. Atamian. bibliog il Science 151:1337-45 Mr 18 '66; Reply. W. S. Neff. 152:1283 My 27 '66
MASLAND, Richard L.
Tracking down the causes of birth defects. Todays Health 44:60-2+ Ag '66
MASLOW, Sophie
Sophie Maslow dance company, Brooklyn college. M. Marks. Dance Mag 40:81-2 Je '66
MASON, Alpheus Thomas
Warren court and the Bill of rights. Yale R 56:197-211 D '66

MASON, Bill
Greatest hunting of all. Outdoor Life 138:42-5+ N '66
MASON, Birny, 1909-
Man from UNCARB. R. Levy. por Duns R 87:46-8 Je '66
MASON, David T.
Density-current plumes. bibliog Science 152:354-6 Ap 15 '66
MASON, Edward S.
Formulation of aid policies. Cur Hist 50:328-34+ Je '66
MASON, Edwin A.
Distant end; excerpts from Trail blazers. Am For 72:25+ Jl '66
MASON, Ellsworth
Coast range gem: the Los Gatos high school library. ALA Bul 60:270-4, 530-1 Mr, Je '66
Writing a building program; adaptation of address. May 16, 1966. por Library J 91:5838-44 D 1 '66
MASON, Hamilton, and Grove, Larry
More summer color for problem spots! Bet Hom & Gard 44:54-9 Je '66
MASON, John
Birdbath from a can cover. Audubon Mag 68:196 My '66
MASON, Joseph G.
How to keep key executives. Nations Bsns 54:75 Ag '66
Innovation in management; excerpts from How to build your management skills. por Parks & Rec 1:170-1 F '66
No, not another committee. Nations Bsns 53:80-1+ D '65
MASON, Lowell B.
If Thomas Jefferson came back today. Nations Bsns 54:70-1+ Ap '66
MASON, Phoebe. See Lonsdale, K. jt. auth.
MASON, Sarah
War; poem. Nation 203:522 N 14 '66
MASON, Warren P.
Ultrasonics. Science 152:1286-7 My 27 '66
MASON, Zoltan S.
Jacqueline Kennedy. Sat Eve Post 239:25 Mr 26 '66
MASON and Dixon's line
Finding the Mason Dixon line. B. McMahon. il Travel 126:45-7 D '66
MASONS, Free. See Freemasons
MASOTTA, Oscar
Argentine in Venice. Américas 18:19-22 Ag '66
MASQUERADE; story. See Maloff, S.
MASS
Liturgy and headlines; jazz masses. America 116:79 Ja 21 '67
Pope and Mr Dooley on jazz masses (with sincere apologies to Finley Peter Dunne) J. B. Mannion. Commonweal 85:416-17 Ja 20 '67
See also
Liturgical language
MASS (music)
Aggiornamento: musical requirements of liturgical renewal. Cath World 203:196-7 Jl '66
Mass and the opera: Milan cathedral and Teatro alla Scala. V. Sheean. il Opera N 30:8-13 Ap 2 '66
See also
Phonograph records—Mass
MASS culture. See Popular culture
MASS hysteria. See Hysteria (social psychology)
MASS media
Art, technology and education; excerpt from address. February 1966. A. I. Cox. jr. Christian Cent 83:862-4 Jl 6 '66
Controversies about the mass communication of violence. O. N. Larsen. bibliog f Ann Am Acad 364:37-49 Mr '66
Howdy, neighbor; media are history. J. Burnham. Nat R 18:976 O 4 '66
McLuhanisms. M. Walsh. America 114:784-5 My 28 '66
Man is more than a statistic. J. W. Krutch. Sat R 49:14-16 My 21 '66
Masscomm: W. H. Ferry charges. Newsweek 67:98+ My 2 '66
New computerized age: McLuhanism reconsidered. E. Barnouw. il Sat R 49:19-21+ Jl 23 '66
News is where you find it. R. L. Tobin. Sat R 49:135-6 Mr 12 '66; Discussion. 49:60 Ap 9 '66
Two decades in the world of the mass media. R. Lindsay and R. B. Nixon. il UNESCO Courier 19:36-9 Jl '66
Understanding McLuhan. M. McLuhan. il Newsweek 67:56-7 F 28 '66
Where are today's muckrakers? A. Weinberg and L. Weinberg. Sat R 49:54-5 Jl 9 '66

MASS murder. See Murder
MASS scales. See Measuring instruments
MASS spectrometry
High-resolution mass spectrometry. F. W. McLafferty. bibliog il Science 151:641-9 F 11 '66
MASS stipends
Mass stipends. Commonweal 85:214 N 25 '66
Mass stipends: on the way out? America 115:727 D 3 '66
MASSACHUSETTS
See also
Architecture, Domestic—Massachusetts
Birds—Massachusetts
Booksellers and bookselling—Massachusetts
Crime and criminals—Massachusetts
Greylock. Mount
Hunting—Massachusetts
Libraries—Massachusetts
Nantucket Island

Description and travel
Massachusetts builds for tomorrow. R. De Roos. il Nat Geog Mag 130:790-843 D '66

Historic houses, etc.
See also
Newbury, Mass.—Historic houses, etc.

History
See also
Shays' rebellion, 1786-1787

History, Naval
Figures and figureheads: the maritime collection at the State Street bank and trust company. Boston. W. D. Garrett. il Antiques 90:816-23 D '66

Politics and government
Backlash in the Bay state. Nation 203:268 S 26 '66
Black man leading a G.O.P. march on Washington; E. Brooke J. Skow. il Sat Eve Post 239:82-7 S 10 '66
Crowded platform; Senate and gubernatorial race. il Time 88:32 N 4 '66
G.O.P. on top; odds-on favorites in November elections. Time 88:24 S 23 '66
JFK legatees. Newsweek 67:31A-31B F 21 '66
Kenny comes home. il Time 87:20 Ja 28 '66
Massachusetts mix-up; Brooke-Peabody campaign. il Newsweek 68:30-1 O 17 '66
Negro in the Senate. il Newsweek 68:37-8 N 21 '66
Teddy and Eddie revisited. M. F. Nolan. Reporter 35:33-5 S 8 '66
MASSACHUSETTS general hospital, Boston. See Boston—Hospitals
MASSACHUSETTS helicopter airlines, incorporated. See Air general, incorporated
MASSACHUSETTS horticultural society
How flower shows have changed! A. H. Nehrling. il Horticulture 44:22-5+ Mr '66
MASSACHUSETTS institute of technology, Cambridge
Beast of change at M.I.T. il Fortune 75:141-4 Ja '67
Caltech & M.I.T: rivalry between the best. il Time 88:82-3 N 4 '66
M.I.T: new president will pursue broadened goals. L. J. Carter. il Science 151:1511-15 Mr 25 '66; Reply. E. Hodgins. 152:1458 Je 10 '66
M.I.T.'s student center: Eduardo Catalano starts with systems and creates architecture. il Arch Rec 139:125-32 Mr '66
Plans for Project Intrex. C. F. J. Overhage. bibliog il Science 152:1032-7 My 20 '66
Reporter at large; MIT Fellows in Africa program. J. McPhee. New Yorker 42:101-2+ Mr 5 '66
See also
M.I.T. press

School of architecture and planning
Blend of many disciplines. il Fortune 75:144 Je '67
MASSACHUSETTS library association
Montgomery demotion case under Mass. L.A. scrutiny. Library J 92:42 Ja 1 '67
MASSACHUSETTS. University, Amherst
Distinguished architecture for a state university. il Arch Rec 139:165-7 My '66
Librarian fights demotion move in Univ. of Massachusetts shakeup. Library J 91:5914-16 D 1 '66
Montgomery demotion case under Mass. L.A. scrutiny. Library J 92:42 Ja 1 '67
Simplicity produces a neat, inexpensive stadium. il Arch Rec 139:185-6 F '66
MASSACRES (World war, 1939-1945) See World war, 1939-1945—Atrocities

MASSAQUOI, Hans J.
Journey into the past. pors Ebony 21:91-4+
F: 102-4+ Mr '66
MASSE, Benjamin Louis
Full employment or stable prices? America
115:646 N 19 '66
Guidepost crisis. America 115:222 S 3 '66
How goes the poverty war? America 115:281-3
S 17 '66
Mr Reuther to Mr Meany. America 116:53 Ja
14 '67
Pulpit and market place. America 115:182+
Ag 20 '66
Vatican II on social progress. America 114:
776-8 My 28 '66
MASSEE, May
Obituary
Pub W 191:38 Ja 2 '67
MASSEE, William
Waters one through four. Esquire 66:34 Ag
'66
MASSENGALE, Don
Stranger stars in a Crosby cliffhanger. A.
Wright. il por Sports Illus 24:40-1 Ja 31 '66
MASSES (periodical)
Something wonderful happened. G. Hicks.
Sat R 49:41-2 D 10 '66
MASSIE, Robert K.
Not the Dr Spock! Sat Eve Post 239:80-2+
My 7 '66
MASSILLON, Ohio
Town's troubled mood as a war comes home;
Massillon, Ohio questions administration's
position. il Life 61:50-7 Ag 12 '66
MASSON, Georges M. C. and others
Increased cardiovascular reactivity to angio-
tensin caused by renin. bibliog Science
153:1002-4 Ag 26 '66
MAST cells
Mast cells and necrosis. H. Selye. il Science
152:1371-2 Je 3 '66
MASTER mariners' regatta. See Regattas
MASTER of the hounds; story. See Budrys, A.
MASTERS, George
Man for all disasters. J. Howard. il pors
Life 61:57-8+ N 25 '66
Step by step: Lynda Bird Johnson's Holly-
wood beauty treatment. V. Scott. il Ladies
Home J 83:62+ Jl '66
MASTERS, John
Upon the mountain. Holiday 40:6+ S '66
MASTERS, Marcia Lee
Four poets. L. Mueller. Poetry 109:51 O '66
MASTERS, Roger
French perspective on strategy. Bul Atomic
Sci 22:38-40 S '66
Goals for American power. Yale R 55:365-88
Mr '66
Modern man's ancient instincts. Sat R 49:
34-5 S 17 '66
Rusk's Francophobia: de Gaulle and NATO.
Commonweal 84:431-3 Jl 8 '66
MASTERS, William Howell
B to keep men vital; interview, ed. by R.
West. por Look 31:76+ Ja 10 '67
Two sex researchers on the firing line; in-
terview. ed. by W. Bradbury. pors Life
60:43-4+ Je 24 '66
—and Johnson, Virginia
Defense of love and morality. McCalls 94:102-
3+ N '66
about
Margaret Mead answers questions about:
concerning study on the physiology of sex.
M. Mead. Redbook 127:36+ O '66
Problems of sex. il por Time 87:51 Ap 29 '66
Sex study raises ruckus. il Sci Digest 60:29-
30 Jl '66
Sex under scrutiny. il Newsweek 67:80 Ap 25 '66
Should this sex research be allowed to go
on? L. R. Chevalier. Ladies Home J 83:
26+ My '66
MASTERS golf tournament. See Golf—Tourna-
ments
MASTITIS
Mastitis cleanup pushes ahead. Farm J 90:
50 Mr '66
Now you can see mastitis. C. E. Ball. il
Farm J 90:34+ N '66
Why play mastitis poker? il Farm J 90:A4+
O '66
MASTODON
Elephant teeth found at sea. B. Tufty. il
Sci N 90:481 D 3 '66
MASTROIANNI, Marcello
Great undashing lover of our time. A. Cham-
berlin. il pors Sat Eve Post 239:81-5 Ag 13
'66
MASTS and rigging
Happy drop out. F. Adams. il Yachting 120:
41-3+ O '66
MASUHR, Dieter
Rudolf Dentler. Craft Horiz 26:16-17 Mr '66

MATANZIMA, Kaiser
Tiger snarls. P. Webb. il por Newsweek
67:44 Ap 25 '66
MATAQUESCUINTLA, Guatemala
School-to-school: a partnership in under-
standing. J. Vaughn. Parents Mag 41:30+
Je '66
MATCH Box project. See Boston children's
museum
MATCH making by computers. See Compu-
ters—Social applications
MATCH-play; drama. See Kalcheim, L.
MATELL, Anne, and Matell, Robin
Taking baby abroad. Travel 126:56-8+ N '66
MATELL, Robin. See Matell, A. jt. auth.
MATER et magistra. See Encyclicals
MATERIAL handling. See Materials handling
MATERIALS
SAMPE blankets reinforced composites. J.
F. Judge. il Tech W 19:24-5+ N 21 '66
What makes a well-decorated room: natural
materials. P. Rumely. il Bet Hom & Gard
44:58-9 S '66
See also
Building materials

Handling
See Materials handling

Testing
See Testing
MATERIALS, Strength of. See Strength of
materials
MATERIALS centers. See Instructional mate-
rials centers
MATERIALS handling
Construction technology: can new lifting sys-
tems cut construction costs? il Arch Rec
139:203-4 Je '66
Harnessing air to do warehousing chores;
Clark equipment's load glide. il Bsns W
p 172+ Je 18 '66
High-powered drive in material handling. H.
E. Klein. il Duns R 87:pt2 128-9+ Mr '66
Look out! that forklift is after you. J. N.
Miller. Read Digest 89:142-5 O '66
MATERIALS of instruction. See Teaching—
Aids and devices
MATERIALS research
Federal report pinpoints problems. J. F.
Judge. Miss & Roc 18:30+ F 28 '66
SAMPE blankets reinforced composites. J. F.
Judge. il Tech W 19:24-5+ N 21 '66
MATERNAL deprivation
Motherless monkeys; with photographs. Sci
Digest 60:48-51 D '66
MATERNAL effect. See Prenatal influences
MATERNAL love. See Love, Maternal
MATH, Irwin
Identifying surplus crystals. Electr World 76:
57 Ag '66
Receiver noise measurements. Electr World
76:24+ Ag '66
MATHAI, Ciaramma K. and Beutler, Ernest
Electrophoretic variation of galactose-1-phos-
phate uridyltransferase. bibliog Science
154:1179-80 D 2 '66
MATHEMATICAL literature
Quantitative growth of the mathematical
literature. K. O. May. bibliog il Science
154:1672-3 D 30 '66
MATHEMATICAL programming. See Linear
programming
MATHEMATICAL recreations
Mathematical games. M. Gardner. See issues
of Scientific American
MATHEMATICAL societies
See also
International congress of mathematicians
MATHEMATICIANS
What are mathematicians doing? address. De-
cember 27, 1965. B. Friedman. bibliog il Sci-
ence 154:357-62 O 21 '66
Who is Bourbaki? pen name of six French
mathematicians. J. Kobler. il Sat Eve Post
239:34-5 F 26 '66
See also
International congress of mathematicians
MATHEMATICS
Early pragmatists; letter. E. E. Sellers.
Science 154:1604 D 30 '66
What are mathematicians doing? address,
December 27, 1965. B. Friedman. bibliog il
Science 154:357-62 O 21 '66
Who is Bourbaki? pen name of six French
mathematicians. J. Kobler. il Sat Eve Post
239:34-5 F 26 '66
See also
Harmonic analysis
Topology

MATHEMATICS—*Continued*

Courses of study

Mathematics curriculum: new study; letter. E. G. Begle. Science 151:632 F 11 '66

Formulae

Dynamic programming. R. Bellman. il Science 153:34-7 Jl 1 '66

Study and teaching

Lively third R; with editorial comment. K. E. Brown and others. il Am Ed 2:inside cover, 9-13 Je '66

Mom and dad study the new math; course sponsored by PTA of Beaumont, Tex. J. L. Creswell. il Parents Mag 41:68-9+ S '66

Why 1101=13; new approaches to mathematics teaching. N. Picard. il UNESCO Courier 19:22-9 Je '66

Why parents can't add; new math; excerpt from Son of the Great society. A. Buchwald. il Read Digest 89:151-2 O '66

See also

Arithmetic—Study and teaching

MATHER, John Aked
Photographer to oildom. E. C. Miller and T. K. Stratton. Am Heritage 17:103 O '66

MATHER, P. Boyd
That Amish thing. Christian Cent 83:245-7 F 23 '66

MATHET, François
Wizard of Longchamp. W. Tower. il por Sports Illus 24:51-4+ Je 6 '66

MATHEWS, Richard
Society's just got to go; we all know that. Sat R 49:74-6+ S 17 '66

MATHEWS, Thomas
Three Guianas. Cur Hist 51:333-7+ D '66

MATHEWS, Thomas F.
In many voices. America 116:62 Ja 14 '67

MATHEWSON, Franklin T.
Films for the PTA. PTA Mag 60:33-4 My: 33-4 Je '66

MATHEWSON, Joseph
Aunt Ulrica answers your questions. Opera N 30:6 F 26 '66
Hobbit habit. Esquire 66:130-1+ S '66

MATHIAS, Charles McCurdy
Excerpt from debate, July 27, 1966. Cong Digest 45:280+ N '66
Excerpt from February 4, 1966, newsletter to his constituents. Cong Digest 45:148+ My '66

MATHIESEN, Egon
Artist and the picture book; excerpts from address. Horn Bk 42:93-7 F '66

MATHIEU, Mireille
New sparrow stirs France. il por Life 60:115-16 Je 10 '66
Rising sparrow. por Time 88:68-9 N 4 '66

MATHIS, Buster
Cus is back aboard a big new Bus. R. H. Boyle. il por Sports Illus 26:18-22 Ja 16 '67

MATHIS der maler; opera. See Hindemith, P.

MATILLA, Alfredo
Festival and congress in Caracas. Américas 18:38-9 N '66

MATING behavior. See Sex behavior

MATING behavior (insects) See Courtship of insects

MATISSE, Henri
Art. M. Kozloff. Nation 202:498-500 Ap 25 '66
Distiller of sunshine: exhibition traveling across U.S. il Time 87:78-83 F 25 '66
Matisse: fabric vs. flesh. F. S. Wight. il Art N 64:26-9+ Ja '66

MATLOCK, Gene D.
Foreign language in high school. NEA J 55:49 O '66

MATRANGA, Frances
Tips for artists. Design 68:38 N '66

MATRIARCH; story. See Frater, A.

MATRIMONY. See Marriage

MATSCHINSKY, Martin
Welding their way up. il por Time 88:88 O 7 '66

MATSON, Ollie
They couldn't cut old Ollie, could they? L. L. King. il por Sat Eve Post 239:107-11 O 22 '66

MATSON navigation company
Containers race across Atlantic; international, door-to-door foreign service. Bsns W p76+ F 19 '66

MATSUBARA, Naoko
This month's cover artist. il (cover) por Willson Lib Bul 40:807 My '66
Two worlds of Naoko Matsubara. F. Eichenberg. il por Am Artist 30:34-9+ N '66

MATSUDA, Morihiro
Fishing for peace. il por Newsweek 67:46 Je 6 '66

Splendid blow to save our world. P. O'Neil. il por Life 60:85-6 Je 3 '66

MATSUI, Akira
Letter from president of Security council. UN Mo Chron 3:10 Mr '66
U.S. welcomes Security council views on Viet-Nam situation; letter, February 26, 1966. Dept State Bul 54:548 Ap 4 '66

about

Communications; concerning replies to letter to members of Security council. UN Mo Chron 3:9-10 Ap '66

MATSUI, Maremichi
What to do about group action... P. Caulfield. Mod Phot 30:74-5 S '66

MATSUMOTO, Fujiko
Thrushes two. il Audubon Mag 68:355 S '66

MATSUMURA, F. and Boush, G. M.
Malathion degradation by trichoderma viride and a pseudomonas species. bibliog Science 153:1278-80 S 9 '66

—and Hayashi, Masaki
Dieldrin; interaction with nerve components of cockroaches. bibliog Science 153:757-9 Ag 12 '66

MATSUNAGA, Spark Masayuki
Excerpt from testimony, August 18, 1965. Cong Digest 45:155+ My '66

MATT, Richard
On the water. il U S Camera 29:66-7+ O '66

MATTEL pre-school toys. See Toys

MATTER, Mercedes
I trembled with a terror I had never felt in my life before. Life 60:59-60 Ja 28 '66

MATTER
Bias for the positive; antimatter. Sci Am 215: 40-2 Ag '66
Opposite of you is uoy; antimatter. F. Warshofsky. il Esquire 66:82-3+ Ag '66

MATTER, Interstellar
Antimatter may matter. G. S. Mumford. Sky & Tel 31:264 My '66
Atmospheric noble gases from extraterrestrial dust. D. Tilles. bibliog Science 151:1015 F 25 '66
Implantation in interplanetary dust of rare-gas ions from solar flares. D. Tilles. bibliog il Science 153:981-4 Ag 26 '66
Low-energy protons; average flux in interplanetary space during the last 100,000 years. D. Lal and V. S. Venkatavaradan. bibliog il Science 151:1381-4 Mr 18 '66
Rubble orbits earth. Sci N 90:234 S 24 '66
See also
Plasma (ionized gases)

MATTER of time; story. See West, J.

MATTHEW, Eileen Holm
Amputees on skis. il Todays Health 45:12-13 Ja '67
Every child needs a doctor. Parents Mag 41: 52+ N '66
Flying rescuers of the Northwest. Todays Health 44:56-60 My '66
Samaritans of the ski slopes. Am For 72:34-7 Ja '66

MATTHEW, Gospel of. See Bible—New Testament—Matthew

MATTHEWS, Adelia Howland
Historic garden week in Virginia. Horticulture 44:46-7+ Mr '66

MATTHEWS, C. M.
History in the telephone book. Horizon 9:105-11 Wint '67

MATTHEWS, Herbert Lionel
Penance of Matthews. Nation 203:437-8 O 31 '66

MATTHEWS, Jessie
Jessie Matthews. R. C. Roman. il pors Dance Mag 40:66-71 S '66

MATTHEWS, Joseph Brown
Obituary
Nat R 18:763-4 Ag 9 '66

MATTHEWS, Luther F.
In the heart of it. il por Time 87:90 My 27 '66

MATTHEWS, Ronald
Forecast for Africa: more plots, more coups. N Y Times Mag p 10-11+ Ap 10 '66

MATTHEWS, Roy A.
Canada considers closer U.S. ties; excerpts from article. bibliog f Harvard Bsns R 44: 57-64 My '66

MATTHEWS, T. S.
James Agee, strange and wonderful. Sat R 49:22-3 Ap 16 '66
Portrait, with scratches: Adlai Stevenson. Vogue 147:192-3+ My '66

MATTHEWS, Walter Robert
Cleaner of St Paul's. C. Northcott. Christian Cent 83:238 F 23 '66

MATTHIAS, B. T. and others
Superconductivity of beta-uranium. bibliog Science 151:985-6 F 25 '66

MATTHIESSEN, Peter
Reporter at large (cont) New Yorker 41:94+ F 5 '66
MATTIOLI, Raffaele
Profiles. J. Wechsberg. por New Yorker 42: 52-4+ Ap 30 '66
MATTIS, Paul A. See Rubin. L. F. jt. auth.
MATTRESSES
Floating sores away; new hospital mattress. il Time 88:75 S 9 '66
MATTY, Carol
Bargain-priced Bolivia. Travel 125:45-8 Mr '66
MATURITY
Age of discretion. R. G. Gettell. Seventeen 25:162+ F '66
Don't brush off all the old rules. R. Goldberg. Seventeen 25:194+ S '66
Dreams tell of maturity. P. McBroom. Sci N 90:243 O 1 '66
Five roads to emotional maturity; excerpt from Hope for man. J. L. Liebman. Ladies Home J 83:104-5 My '66
How can I be me? G. Zimmermann. il Look 30:52-7 S 20 '66
How much freedom is too much freedom? panel discussion. il Seventeen 25:164-5+ Ap '66
How to begin the treasure hunt for your real self. R. E. Nixon and M. S. Welch. il Seventeen 25:140-1+ O '66
How to lose gracefully without really dying; questions and answers. A. Wood. il Seventeen 25:162-3+ My '66
I was a teen-age beatle; turns on the road to success. J. Peerce. Seventeen 25:170+ Ap '66
Luci Johnson: I've been forced to grow up! ed. by J. Baer. L. B. Johnson. il Seventeen 25:166-7+ My '66
Our creeping idiot savantism; maturity can be magnificent; address, June 12, 1966. J. Foxworth. Vital Speeches 32:596-9 Jl 15 '66
Talks to teens. F. Astaire. Seventeen 25:154+ O '66
Things aren't that simple. B. Hope. Seventeen 25:130+ D '66
What it means to be a girl now! D. A. Sugarman and R. Hochstein. Seventeen 25:172-3+ My '66
Whose life is it, anyway? questions and answers. A. Wood. il Seventeen 25:166-7+ S '66
Your Christmas moods. R. Nixon and M. S. Welch. il Seventeen 25:126-7+ D '66
MATZ, Judith Ann
Teaching young teenagers about sex. Parents Mag 41:60-1+ Mr '66
MATZ, Mary Jane
Decline of the diva. Opera N 30:12-16 Mr 12 '66
Forum for Verdi. Opera N 31:6-7 S 10 '66
Verdi's real roots. Opera N 30:24-5 F 12 '66
MATZKIN, Myron A.
Matzkin on movies. See issues of Modern photography
Tape as you travel. Hi Fi 16:48-52 Jl '66
MAUD, Ralph
(ed) See Thomas, D. Poems
MAUGHAM, Robin
My Uncle Willie. Sat Eve Post 239:78-81 Ja 29 '66
MAUGHAM, Syrie
Twisted marriage of Somerset Maugham; excerpts from A case of human bondage. B. Nichols. il pors Look 30:32-7 O 18 '66
MAUGHAM, William Somerset
Remembering Mr Maugham; ed. by G. Kanin; excerpts. Vogue 148:86-7+ Ag 15 '66

about

Maugham's bondage. F. Clinton. Nat R 18: 174-6 F 22 '66
My Uncle Willie. R. Maugham. il pors Sat Eve Post 239:78-81 Ja 29 '66
Remembering Mr Maugham, by G. Kanin. Review
    Reporter 36:60+ Ja 12 '67. S. Eimerl
    Sat R por 49:33-4 N 5 '66. B. Atkinson
Somerset and all the Maughams, by R. Maugham. Review
    Newsweek il por 67:102+ My 9 '66
    Sat R 49:28-9 Jl 9 '66. S. Weintraub
    Time 87:126 My 20 '66
Twisted marriage of Somerset Maugham; excerpts from A case of human bondage. B. Nichols. il pors Look 30:32-7 O 18 '66
MAUGHAN, Walter L.
Worth of a tree. Américas 18:34-6 D '66
MAULDIN, Bill
How to win over your children; excerpt. il Good H 162:100-1 Ap '66
1966: Mauldin on Vietnam. il New Repub 156:19-21 Ja 7 '67
MAULDIN, William Henry. See Mauldin, B.

MAUNA KEA
Deep layer of sediments in Alpine Lake in the tropical mid-Pacific. A. H. Woodcock and others. bibliog il Science 154:647-8 N 4 '66
MAUNA KEA Beach hotel. See Hotels, taverns, etc.—Hawaii
MAUNDER, Elwood R.
(ed) See Dana, S. T. Dana years
MAUNSBACH, Arvid B. See Miller, A. jt. auth.
MAURA, Christine Kropp, Sister. See Kropp, M. C.
MAUREEN O'Keefe, Sister. See O'Keefe, M.
MAURER, D. W.
Gumming up the syntax. Nation 203:456-7 O 31 '66
MAURER, Gilbert C.
Hazards of Roseville road. Pop Phot 58:60-2 Je '66
MAURER, W. E.
When to buy and sell cattle; ed. by O. Bay. por Farm J 90:62-3 My '66
MAURIAC, François
Saint Charles. J. J. Kaplow. Nation 202:368-70 Mr 28 '66
MAURICE, E. Ingersoll
E. Ingersoll Maurice prefers the wet method. il por Am Artist 30:36-7+ My '66
MAURIEL, John J. and Anthony, R. N.
Misevaluation of investment center performance. bibliog f Harvard Bsns R 44:98-105 Mr '66
MAURITIUS
Mauritius: world strains in microcosm. C. Macinnes. Nation 203:447-9 O 31 '66
MAUROIS, André
Elderly lover; tr. by J. W. Freeman. Opera N 30:8-12 Mr 19 '66
Princely service; excerpts from Civil war album of paintings by the Prince de Joinville. Am Heritage 17:52-63+ Ap '66
MAVERICK, Maury, Jr
Marching for a ghastly recompense in Texas. New Repub 155:11 S 24 '66
MAWHINNEY, Paul E.
Shoes; story. NEA J 55:12-14 O '66
MAX Reger festival. See Music festivals—Germany (Federal Republic)
MAXEY, Sylvia
Adventure in appreciation. Design 67:8-9 Mr '66
MAXIMS
Some maxims of La Rochefoucauld; excerpts from Maxims, tr. by L. W. Tancock. F. de La Rochefoucauld. Horizon 8:65 Wint '66
    See also
Aphorisms and apothegms
MAXIM'S de Tokyo. See Tokyo—Hotels, restaurants, etc.
MAXON, John
Correggio's Virgin and Child with the infant St John. Art N 65:30-3+ Ap '66
MAXWELL, G. Edward
(ed) Frank talk on how to choose, use, abuse your doctor. Todays Health 44:50-5+ O '66
Ski time in Sun Valley and Jackson Hole. Todays Health 44:42-7+ N '66
These housewives polish up their homemaking skills. Todays Health 44:8+ Mr '66
—See Hilligan, E. jt. auth.
MAXWELL, James A.
Heaven and earth in two dimensions. Reporter 35:56 N 3 '66
Not so funny. Reporter 35:39 D 29 '66
Ohio: can Bob Taft make a comeback? Reporter 35:31-2 O 20 '66
MAXWELL, James Clerk
Physics just before Einstein; adaptation of address, December 29, 1964. A. M. Bork. bibliog il Science 152:597-9 Ap 29 '66
MAXWELL, Jewell C.
Supersonic transport and you. V. Block. il por Sci Digest 60:60-7 Jl '66
MAXWELL, Michael
Dream of Gerontius. Am Rec G 32:796-7+ My '66
MAXWELL, Robert
To halt the retreat. il por Time 88:112+ N 18 '66
MAY, Allan
Ski school. NEA J 55:43 F '66
MAY, Catherine Dean
Congresswoman charges: Washington consumer aid is deceptive packaging; interview. pors Nations Bsns 54:54-6+ My '66
Excerpt from address, February 20, 1966. Cong Digest 45:173+ Je '66
MAY, Jürgen
Muddy day in East Berlin. J. Olsen. il pors Sports Illus 25:68-70+ Jl 18 '66
MAY, Kenneth O.
Quantitative growth of the mathematical literature. bibliog Science 154:1672-3 D 30 '66

MAY, Rollo
Antidotes for the new puritanism. Sat R 49:
19-21+ Mr 26 '66
—and Levin, R. J.
Sleeping beauty. Redbook 127:62-3+ S '66
MAY, William Frederic
New package at American can. il por Bsns W
p94-5+ S 17 '66
MAYA blue. See Pigments
MAYA figurines. See Figurines
MAYAKOVSKY, Vladimir Vladimirovich. See
Maiakovskii, V. V.
MAYAS
Clay sculpture from Jaina. L. Aveleyra
Arroyo de Anda and G. F. Ekholm. il
Natur Hist 75:40-7 Ap '66
In the land of the Maya. D. Puleston. il
Audubon Mag 68:146-50 My '66
Jade jaguar in ancient Maya tomb; Tikal,
Guatemala. il Sci N 89:482 Je 18 '66
Maya blue: a clay-organic pigment? H. Van
Olphen. Science 154:645-6 N 4 '66
MAYCOCK, J. N. and Grabenstein, D. E.
Piezoelectricity in secondary explosives. Sci-
ence 152:508-9 Ap 22 '66
MAYDAY (signal) See Signals and signaling
MAYER, Albert I.
Urban geography: city planning in the class-
room. Sr Schol 88:sup 12 Ap 22 '66
MAYER, Christa C.
Three centuries of bobbin lace. Antiques 90:
186-91 Ag '66
MAYER, Christian
Gruppe 47 at Princeton. Nation 202:588-90 My
16 '66
Letter from Germany: sword too heavy? Na-
tion 203:346-7 O 10 '66
No fun in Bavaria. Nation 203:637-9 D 12 '66
Whither West Germany? Nation 203:88-90
Jl 25 '66
MAYER, Frank C.
Teacher from Appalachia. Sch & Soc 94:324-
5 O 15 '66
MAYER, Frederick
Sober look at the new Germany. Christian
Cent 83:710-12 Je 1 '66
MAYER, George Louis
Awesome, superlative: Klemperer's Missa
solemnis. Am Rec G 33:8-9 S '66
Die entführung aus dem serail; satisfactory
recording. Am Rec G 33:104-6 O '66
Fond farewell to a great old lady, that be-
loved house, the Metropolitan opera. Am
Rec G 32:764-5+ My '66
Katerina Ismailova. Am Rec G 32:1116-19
Ag '66
Mann's superb study of the Strauss operas.
Am Rec G 32:890-1 My '66
Souvenir of a golden era. Am Rec G 32:690-1
Ap '66
MAYER, Greta, and Hoover, M. B.
Alone and not afraid. Redbook 127:58-9+
Je '66
MAYER, Jean
What should be done about teen-age over-
weight, and what shouldn't. por(p34) Ladies
Home J 84:36+ Ja '67
—and Sidel, V. W.
Crop destruction in South Vietnam. Chris-
tian Cent 83:829-32 Je 29 '66
—See Baile. C. A. jt. auth.
MAYER, Joseph E.
Solvay conference. Science 152:393 Ap 15 '66
MAYER, Lawrence A.
How confusion caught up with Korvette.
Fortune 73:153-4+ F '66
MAYER, Martha Hazzard
In Skansen park; poem. Christian Cent 83:
1139 S 21 '66
MAYER, Martin
Baedecker for volunteers. Sat R 49:82+ Mr
19 '66
Diminished responsibility. Commentary 41:
83-5+ F '66
Elaborately practical theater. Opera N 31:
14-25 S 17 '66
Goldberg represents Lyndon Johnson. N Y
Times Mag p 16-17+ F 6 '66
Golden age is now. N Y Times Mag pt2 p 16+
S 11 '66
Justice, the law and the lawyer. Sat Eve
Post 239:36-9+ F 26 '66
Man from Xerox multiplies his roles. N Y
Times Mag p44-5+ Ap 24 '66
Men of the iron mountain. Reporter 35:41-4
Jl 14 '66
Of the people. Opera N 30:8-13 F 26 '66
Price's Ballo, Grist and Lorengar debuts. Hi
Fi 16:134+ My '66
Recordings. See issues of Esquire
Routine murder in New York. Esquire 66:88+
S '66
Stop waiting for miracles; excerpt from ad-
dress. PTA Mag 61:19+ N '66

Understanding and using economics. Bet
Hom & Gard 44:112 S; 6 O; 7 N; 14 D '66;
45:44 Ja '67
Visitors; decade of cultural exchange. Sat R
49:53-5+ O 29 '66
Washington's grant to the Ford foundation.
N Y Times Mag p58-9+ N 13 '66
MAYER, Oscar Gottfried
Starry-eyed. Newsweek 68:78 Jl 11 '66
MAYER, Paul Avila
Three hand reel; adaptation of stories by
F. O'Connor. Criticism
New Yorker 42:178 N 19 '66
MAYER, Ralph
Ralph Mayer's technical question & answer
page. See issues of American artist
MAYER, Tom
Green-broke stud; story. Atlan 218:76-8 O
'66
My father and the fighter; story. Sat Eve
Post 239:78-80 O 22 '66
MAYERS, Thomas C.
Stamford's attempt to integrate suburbia.
J. R. Wolf. il Reporter 35:20+ D 29 '66
MAYERSON, Hymen S.
Physiological sciences. Science 152:1770+ Je
24 '66
MAYES, Herbert R.
Trade winds. See issues of Saturday review.
August 6, 1966-
MAYES, Paul E.
Designing an all-channel TV antenna. Electr
World 75:45-8+ F '66
MAYNARD, Fred
Build a swimming pool splash alarm. Pop
Electr 25:48-9+ Jl '66
MAYNARD, Sister Mary
Argonne national laboratory: educational
workshops. Science 154:1478-80 D 16 '66
MAYNARD, Olga
Backstage at television's Hollywood palace.
Dance Mag 40:36-8 F '66
College controversy. Dance Mag 40:62-5 S '66
(ed) See Litz, K. Katherine Litz
(ed) See Loring, E. Eugene Loring talks
(ed) See Paul, M. Why is a ballerina?
(ed) See Villella, E. Edward Villella talks
MAYNE, Richard
George Orwell and his critics. Reporter 35:
54+ O 6 '66
Giant slowly dying. Reporter 34:42+ Je 16
'66
Peace or nationalism for Europe? Reporter
34:53-4 Ap 7 '66
MAYNOR, Dorothy
Fine arts school. il por Ebony 21:80-2+ My '66
Making friends with music. O. Evans. il por
Opera N 31:15-17 N 5 '66
MAYO, Charles W.
I earnestly recommend... Ladies Home J
83:44 Ag '66
MAYOL, Jacques
How far down can he go? il pors Life 61:41-
2+ Jl 22 '66
MAYONNAISE
Mayonnaise; with recipes. S. M. Fertitta. il
Look 30:56-7 F 8 '66
Things to do with mayonnaise; with recipes.
il Ladies Home J 83:114 Ap '66
MAYORS
Cry of the cities. Nation 203:3-4 Jl 4 '66
Money riddle; U.S. conference of mayors. il
Newsweek 67:32 Je 27 '66
Urban pleas to Washington. America 115:
243-4 S 10 '66
See also subhead Mayors under names of
cities, e.g. Saigon—Mayors
MAYORS, Negro. See Negro municipal officers
MAYS, Benjamin E.
Achievements of the Negro colleges. por
Atlan 217:90-2 F '66
MAYS, Willie
Willie Mays: my story; excerpts from Willie
Mays: my life in and out of baseball, ed.
by C. Einstein. pors Look 30:62-3+ Mr 8;
116-17+ Mr 22; 72-4+ Ap 5 '66
about
Hand for Willie. il por Newsweek 68:65 Ag
29 '66
In pursuit of Ruth. il por Newsweek 67:88
My 9 '66
It's a long way to 714. J. G. Dunne. il pors
Sat Eve Post 239:78-81 Jl 30 '66
There's hope for Willie. il pors Ebony 21:96+
O '66
Which honor to choose? il por Time 88:44
Ag 26 '66
MAYTAG, L. B.
Shooting on Mr Bud's place. V. Kraft. il
Sports Illus 25:50-4 N 21 '66
MAZE tests
Stay young with ions. T. W. Hill. il Sci Di-
gest 61:74-7 Ja '67

MAZESS, Richard B. and Zimmerman, D. W.
Pottery dating from thermoluminescence. bibliog Science 152:347-8 Ap 15 '66
MAZOR, Julian
Rock creek; story. New Yorker 42:53-7 D 17 '66
MAZURKI, Jeannette
Closeup: Barbara Holt, fisherman. Motor B 117:48-9+ My '66
MAZUY, Kay K. See Treynor, J. L. jt. auth.
MAZZO, Kay
Brief biography. S Goodman. pors Dance Mag 40:46-7 Jl '66
MAZZULLA, Fred M.
Great collector, Fred Mazzulla. N. C. Lipton. il por Pop Phot 58:84-5+ Je '66
MBATA, Jeremiah
Another race official banned. J. Squire. Christian Cent 83:783-4 Je 15 '66
MBUTI. See Pygmies
MEACHAM, C. Parker
Birth and death of a pond. Nat Parks Mag 40:14-18 Jl '66
MEACHEM, William L.
New ways with hyacinths. Horticulture 44:18-19+ O '66
Which garden sprayer should you choose? Pop Sci 189:84-6 Jl '66
MEAD, Margaret
Anthropologists in the field. Holiday 40:113-15 Jl '66
Case for drafting all boys and girls. por Redbook 127:40+ S '66
Cruise into the past and a glimpse of the future. por Redbook 126:30+ F '66
Different lands, different friendships. por Redbook 127:38+ Ag '66
Gift of personal independence. por Redbook 128:26+ D '66
Letter from the field. por Redbook 127:30+ My '66
Margaret Mead answers questions. por Redbook 128:32+ Ja '67
Margaret Mead reviews. por Redbook 128:34+ N '66
Marriage in two steps. Redbook 127:48-9+ Jl '66
One world, but which language? por Redbook 126:34+ Ap '66
Rights of primitive peoples. For Affairs 45:304-18 Ja '67
MEAD, Matthew
(tr) See Bobrowski, J. Kaunas 1941
MEAD, Mrs Robert
Books the boys like: reported by their mother. por Pub W 189:107-10 F 21 '66
MEAD, Ruth
(tr) See Bobrowski, J. Kaunas 1941
MEAD. See Liquors
MEADOWS, George
Children and the badge. R. Hardwick. il por Am Ed 2:1-4 D '65
MEADOWS, Martin
Johnson and Marcos. New Repub 155:12 S 17 '66
MEADOWS
Thoughts afield. J. Stuart. il Am For 72:22-5+ Ja '66
MEAGHER, Sylvia
Notes for a new investigation. Esquire 66:211+ D '66
MEALS
Big meals for small budgets; with menus. il Redbook 127:84-5+ My '66
Dining, high style, in Manhattan; with recipes. il McCalls 93:102-3+ Je '66
Six February happenings; more fun than a party! with recipes. il Seventeen 25:156-61+ F '66
What makes a meal? a touch of love; with recipes. il Good H 162:112-29 My '66
  See also
Breakfasts
Cookery
Diet
Dinners and dining
Luncheons
Lunches
Menus
Snacks
Suppers
Thanksgiving dinners
MEANING of life. See Life
MEANING of words. See Semantics
MEANS, Marianne
Luci Johnson and Pat Nugent talk about life without father. Ladies Home J 83:73+ Ag '66
MEANY, George
Protecting the family budget; address, September 4, 1966. Vital Speeches 32:749-51 O 1 '66

about
Adamant Mr Meany. Nation 202:764 Je 27 '66
Breaking ranks at the top. por Bsns W p 149 Je 18 '66
Conflicts shake labor's house. Bsns W p 110 Je 25 '66
Different worlds. Newsweek 67:69-70 Je 27 '66
Labor and politics. S. Lens. il Commonweal 84:278-80 My 27 '66
Labor's love lost. Time 87:25 Ap 1 '66
Labor's political frustrations. A. H. Raskin. il por Reporter 34:26-8+ Ap 7 '66
Meany vs. Reuther: split widens in the AFL-CIO. U S News 61:82-3 N 28 '66
Two key figures in the LBJ-labor split. por U S News 60:24 Mr 14 '66
When Reuther crosses Meany. U S News 60:94 Je 27 '66
MEANY, John
Use of authority. America 114:409-11 Mr 26 '66
MEARS, Joe
Bandtail flyby. Outdoor Life 138:46-7+ S '66
Creek the crowds forgot. Field & S 71:154-7+ My '66
MEARS, Robert
Male animus. PTA Mag 61:7 S '66
MEASLES
End measles now; vaccination campaigns. il Time 87:51 F 4 '66
  Vaccines
End measles now; vaccination campaigns. il Time 87:51 F 4 '66
MEASLES, German. See Rubella
MEASLES virus
Encephalitis from virus. Sci N L 89:87 F 5 '66
MEASURE for measure; drama. See Shakespeare. W.—Plays
MEASUREGRAPHY company
Brass gets a quick polish; executive charm school. il Bsns W p 182+ Je 18 '66
MEASUREMENT
  See also
Frequency measurement
Geodesy
Length measurement
Tape measures
MEASUREMENT, Psychological. See Psychometrics
MEASUREMENTS, Astronomical. See Astronomical measurements
MEASURING instruments
New method to measure mass in space devised; linear spring/mass pendulum or mass scale. Sci N 90:256 O 1 '66
Yardstick that need not stand in a corner. Consumer Bul 49:33 O '66
MEASURING tapes. See Tape measures
MEAT
Cold cut pie; with recipes. il Seventeen 25:302-3+ Ag '66
Luncheon meats, sausage, frankfurters, hamburger; sources of high fat intake. il Consumer Bul 49:22-7 Je '66
Why meat today is better than ever. Good H 162:183 Ap '66
  See also
Beef
Carving (meat, etc)
Cookery—Meat
Lamb (meat)
  Grading and standardization
What's the difference between prime and choice meat? Good H 162:183 Je '66
  Marketing
He sells his own steaks. J. Albino. il Suc Farm 64:30H Ap '66
  Prepackaging
See-through meat trays. il Consumer Rep 31:330-1 Jl '66
  Prices
Meat's going to cost you more. il Changing T 20:44 F '66
Packers, cattlemen, bid up she stock. Farm J 90:38I Jl '66
Shopping tips from a butcher. S. E. Davis. il Consumer Bul 49:17-18 Mr '66
  Standards
See Meat—Grading and standardization
MEAT, Canned
Canned meats, mother's big helpers. B. M. Stover. il Parents Mag 41:61-4 Ap '66
Things to do with canned meats. il Ladies Home J 83:88 Ag '66

MEAT industry and trade
Should feeders invest in packing plants? O.
Bay. il Farm J 90:112-13 My '66
  See also
Iowa beef packers, incorporated
Meat—Prepackaging
Needham packaging company
Underwood, William, company
    Securities
Should feeders invest in packing plants? O.
Bay. il Farm J 90:38P+ Je '66
MEAT loaf, pies, etc. See Cookery—meat
MEAT packing industry. See Meat industry and
trade
MEAT thermometers. See Thermometers,
Cooking
MEATBALLS. See Cookery—Meat
MEBANE, John
Hanging lamps. Bet Hom & Gard 44:36-7 Je
'66
Treasure hunt (cont) Bet Hom & Gard 44:
30+ Mr; 116 Ap; 122 My; 29+ O '66
MECHANIC, Sylvia
(comp) Business books of 1965. por Library J
91:1159-64 Mr 1 '66
MECHANICAL aids in education. See Teach-
ing—Aids and devices
MECHANICAL devices
  See also
Automatons
Man amplifiers
MECHANICAL exercises. See Exercising equip-
ment
MECHANICAL handling. See Materials han-
dling
MECHANICAL heart. See Heart, Artificial
MECHANICAL toys. See Toys
MECHANICAL translating. See Translating ma-
chines
MECHANICS
  See also
Torque
Vibration
MECHANICS (persons)
  See also
Automobile mechanics (persons)
MECHANICS, Household
Home is what you make it! eleven weekend
projects. il Pop Mech 126:112-51+ S '66
MECHANISM (philosophy)
  See also
Cybernetics
MECHANIZATION, Military
Liddell Hart memoirs: the later years, by
B. H. Liddell Hart. Review
Nat R 18:937-8 S 20 '66. G. F. Eliot
Reporter il 34:52+ F 24 '66. B. W. Tuch-
man
MECHANIZED warfare. See Mechanization,
Military
MECKLIN, John
Building by the billion in Vietnam. Fortune
74:112-17+ S '66
Douglas aircraft's stormy flight path. For-
tune 74:166-71+ D '66
G.E.'s hard-driving jockey in the jet-engine
race. Fortune 74:116-18+ Jl 1 '66
Inside Vietnam. Reporter 35:57-8 O 6 '66
Sky's the limit with the C-5. Read Digest
88:83-6 F '66
U.S. airlines: into the wild blue what? For-
tune 73:146-8+ My '66
MECOM, John Whitfield
Big deal that got away. S. H. Brown. Fortune
74:164-6+ O '66
Deal done in. il por Time 87:62 Je 17 '66
Houston's shackled press. B. H. Bagdikian.
Atlan 218:87-8+ Ag '66
MEDAL of honor (United States)
Gallantry on the line; award to R. E. O'Mal-
ley. Newsweek 68:23 D 19 '66
Hero's courage on a nameless trail. L. Wain-
wright. Life 60:32 My 6 '66
Highest decision; L. B. Johnson presents
posthumous award to M. L. Olive. il News-
week 67:18 My 2 '66
Patriot's gift; award given to First Lieut.
C. Williams. il Time 88:14 Jl 1 '66
MEDALS
Some early American medals; commemora-
ting the opening of the Erie Canal. C.
French. Hobbies 71:102 N '66
  See also names of medals, e.g. Caldecott
medal
MEDCALFE, Maurice Lloyd
Maurice Medcalfe's bathing pillar. il Vogue
148:168-71 S 15 '66
MEDEA: drama. See Anouilh, J.
MEDEIROS, Margaret
In my opinion. por Seventeen 25:250 F '66
MEDELMAN, John
Loneliness of the long-distance runner over
forty. Esquire 65:120-3 Je '66

MEDIATION, International. See Arbitration,
International
MEDICAID. See Insurance, Health—United
States
MEDICAL art. See Medicine in art
MEDICAL assistants. See Medical workers
MEDICAL botany. See Botany, Medical
MEDICAL care. See Medical service
MEDICAL centers
Baltimore's inventive split-level medical cen-
ter. il Arch Rec 139:168-70 Mr '66
  See also
Health centers
Louisville. University—Medical center
MEDICAL colleges
Broad approach to planning for medical edu-
cation. I. Rosenfield and Z. Rosenfield. il
Arch Rec 139:164-7 Mr '66
Federal support for construction of health-
related facilities. T. H. Klausmeyer. Arch
Rec 139:160-3 Mr '66
New medical schools: building up for tomor-
row's patients. L. Prato. il Todays Health
44:36-41 N '66
Our backward medical schools. S. M. Creel.
Atlan 217:46-50 My '66; Discussion. 218:30+
Jl '66
Training for tomorrow's needs; arguments for
curriculum reform. Time 87:61 F 25 '66
MEDICAL delusions
What our kids don't know about health.
T. Irwin. il Todays Health 44:18-21 My '66
MEDICAL economics, incorporated
Stockholders OK merger of Reinhold. Medical
economics. Pub W 189:276 Ja 24 '66
MEDICAL education
Defining the new physician; excerpt from
report of the Citizens commission on grad-
uate medical education; with recommenda-
tions; ed. by J. Lear. Sat R 50:122-5 Ja 7
'67
Medical bootstrap in Saigon. Sci N 90:451
N 26 '66
New family physician; recommendations for
structural changes. J. L. Breeling. il Todays
Health 45:38-9 Ja '67
New profession within medicine? proposing
a graduate degree of medical practice. J.
Stokes, 3d. Sat R 49:90-2 D 3 '66; Discus-
sion. 50:120-2 Ja 7 '67
Prescription; excerpt from address, March 2,
1966. R. H. Ebert. Atlan 217:49 My '66
Quality versus quantity in American medi-
cal education. G. Williams. bibliog il Sci-
ence 153:956-61 Ag 26 '66; Discussion. 154:
723+ N 11 '66
Student doctor learns to care; University of
Kansas medical school. R. H. Berg. il Look
30:24-9 F 8 '66
  See also
Interns (medicine)
Medical colleges
    Federal aid
AAMC: a broader leadership role in health
education prescribed for Association of
medical colleges. J. Walsh; discussion. Sci-
ence 150:554, 1666; 151:1170+ O 29, D 24
'65, Mr 11 '66
Federal support for construction of health-
related facilities. T. H. Klausmeyer. Arch
Rec 139:160-3 Mr '66
MEDICAL electronics
Doctor's black bag is full of electronics. B.
Hartford. il Pop Mech 126:178-9 D '66
Electronic dental spies are bugging teeth.
Sci N 89:514 Je 25 '66
Mind control is good, bad. A. J. Budrys.
il Esquire 65:106-9 My '66
Persistent pain relief seen in new research;
miniature implantable electronic device.
Sci N 89:316 Ap 30 '66
  See also
Telemeter (physiological apparatus)
MEDICAL ethics
Are human tests ethical? F. Marley. Sci
N 90:115 Ag 20 '66
Breach of confidence? question of how the
Texas revelations on Whitman case will
affect student-doctor relations. il News-
week 68:89 Ag 22 '66
Coup de grâce. M. M. Shideler. Christian
Cent 83:1499-502 D 7 '66; Discussion. 84:20,
82-3 Ja 4, 18 '67
Doctors who profit from prescriptions;
doctor-merchants probed by Senate anti-
trust and monopoly subcommittee. Con-
sumer Rep 31:234-8 My '66
Ethical issues in research with human sub-
jects. W. Wolfensberger. bibliog Science
155:47-51 Ja 6 '67
Ethics for an international health profession.
C. E. Taylor. bibliog Science 153:716-20 Ag
12 '66

MEDICAL ethics—*Continued*
Experiments on people, the growing debate; symposium Sat R 49:41-50 Jl 2 '66; Discussion. 49:52 Ag 6; 51-2 S 3 '66
Human experimentation: New York verdict affirms patient's rights. E. Langer. Science 151:663-6 F 11 '66; Discussion. 152:448+, 865 Ap 22, My 13 '66
Medical ethics. I. H. Page. Science 153:371 Jl 22 '66
Morals of medicine. O. Garceau. bibliog f Ann Am Acad 363:60-9 Ja '66
Thanatopsis. C. W. Blaker. Christian Cent 83:1503-6 D 7 '66
Uneasy balance, ethics vs profits; physicians who profit from prescribed medications. K. Wheeler and W. Lambert. il Life 60: 86-8+ Je 24 '66
MEDICAL examinations. See Physical examinations
MEDICAL examiners (law)
Not whodunit, but whatdidit? M. W. Lear. il N Y Times Mag p48-9+ D 4 '66
See also
New York (city)—Chief medical examiner
MEDICAL fakers. See Quacks and quackery
MEDICAL fees. See Medical service, Cost of
MEDICAL fog. See Fog, Artificial
MEDICAL genetics. See Heredity of disease
MEDICAL hypnosis. See Hypnotism
MEDICAL instruments and apparatus
Chair that takes your pulse. il Sci Digest 60:27 Ag '66
Complexity, trouble & triumph. il Time 88: 65 Ag 5 '66
Device mass-screens for heart defects; PhonoCardioScan. J. F. Judge. il Tech W 19:20+ Ag 8 '66
Early tests can prevent chronic ills; Autoanalyzer. F. Marley. il Sci N 90:245 O 1 '66
Instrumented chair records vital functions. Sci N 89:450 Je 4 '66
Life detector; Doptone fetal pulse detector. il Sci Digest 60:53 N '66
Machines of progress. il Time 88:72-7 O 7 '66
New instrument aids spotting brain tumor. Sci N 90:166 S 3 '66
Pen-line diagnosis; autoanalyzer. il Time 88: 68 O 28 '66
Pump aids watery brain. Sci N 90:320 O 22 '66
Ten year pacemaker. Sci Digest 60:23-4 S '66
See also
Surgical instruments and apparatus
MEDICAL insurance. See Insurance, Health
MEDICAL interns. See Interns (medicine)
MEDICAL jurisprudence
Not whodunit, but whatdidit? M. W. Lear. il N Y Times Mag p48-9+ D 4 '66
Routine murder in New York; chief medical examiner of the City of New York. M. Mayer. Esquire 66:88+ S '66
MEDICAL laboratories
Research raised on high; Laboratory of clinical investigation, Yale-New Haven hospital buildings, and Henry Moses research institute, Montefiore hospital, Bronx, N.Y. il Arch Forum 125:72-7 O '66
MEDICAL libraries
Broad spectrum; training for various grades of medical library work. R. T. Lentz. Library J 91:4896-7 O 15 '66
MEDICAL library association
Medical powder keg; report on annual conference. E. Meyerhoff. il Library J 91:3355-9 Jl '66
Prizes, scholarships, membership available from the Medical LA. Library J 91:6056 D 15 '66
MEDICAL literature
Bibliographic organization in the biomedical sciences. S. Adams. bibliog il Wilson Lib Bul 40:714-18 Ap '66
See also
Booksellers and bookselling—Medical literature
MEDICAL microscopy. See Microscopy, Medical
MEDICAL practice. See Medicine—Practice
MEDICAL profession. See Medicine—Practice; Physicians
MEDICAL radiology. See Radiology, Medical
MEDICAL relief work

Haiti
And in Haiti, Focus; Foreign ophthalmological care. il Todays Health 44:25 Jl '66

Honduras
Volunteer foreign aid: M.Ds' mission to Honduras; Florida medical association. J. L. Breeling. il Todays Health 44:20-4 Jl '66

Liberia
Warriors against disease; Brother's brother team in Nicaragua and Liberia. C. M. Davis. il Todays Health 44:30-4 N '66

Nicaragua
Warriors against disease; Brother's brother team in Nicaragua and Liberia. C. M. Davis. il Todays Health 44:30-4 N '66

Underdeveloped areas
Appeal abroad of American medicine and public health; address; with questions and answers. L. L. Terry. Ann Am Acad 366: 78-88 Jl '66

Vietnam (Republic)
Brief report on the Cam Ne fund; projects. Sat R 49:26 D 3 '66
Cam Ne fund; visit of Mrs Janet Stark. N. Cousins. Sat R 49:25 My 14 '66
Enemy lies backfire, help promote immunization of South Viet children. il Todays Health 44:10 Jl '66
Healing the Montagnards. il Time 89:52 Ja 13 '67
It almost makes one cry: what a doctor sees in Vietnam; excerpts from diary. M. T. Hoekenga. il U S News 61:74-6+ S 19 '66
Medical help for Viet Nam. F. Marley. il Sci N 90:160-1 S 3 '66
Space time in Viet Nam; U.S. military doctors and corpsmen aid medical problems of civilians. Time 88:59-60 Ag 19 '66
Viet Nam: U.S. doctors are there. J. H. Winchester. il Todays Health 44:18-24+ Mr '66
Volunteers for Viet Nam: U.S. doctors. il Time 87:50 My 20 '66
Where the innocent die; ed. by R. J. Levin. R. E. Perry. il Redbook 128:46-7+ Ja '67
MEDICAL remedies. See Therapeutics
MEDICAL research
Air pollution medical research; report on eight in a series of air pollution medical research conferences. J. R. Goldsmith. Science 154:1588-91 D 23 '66
Blessed is the mother of twins; National organization of mothers of twins clubs. C. B. Hicks. il Todays Health 44:24-7 My '66
Brain research; report on third visiting seminar of the International brain research organization. A. Lajtha and others. Science 152:550+ Ap 22 '66
Do traces of metal decide our fate? J. D. Ratcliff. il Todays Health 44:34-6+ Mr '66; Same abr. with title Metals within us. Read Digest 88:109-13 Mr '66
Expedition to an idyll: Easter Island. C. Mydans. il Life 60:56+ F 4 '66
Mental retardation; report on conference on the Prevention of mental retardation through the control of infectious diseases. H. Eichenwald. Science 153:1290-3+ S 9 '66
Progress in medical research. F. Marley. Sci N 90:554 D 24 '66
Progress report on cures for the killer diseases. il U S News 60:60-1 My 2 '66
Prying medical secrets from creatures of the sea. J. C. Devlin. il Todays Health 44: 29-33+ Ap '66
Reflections on research and the future of medicine; report on two-day program at dedication of new research building for the Merck Sharp & Dohme research laboratories. T. L. Campbell. il Science 153:442-6+ Jl 22 '66
Sea treasure: New York aquarium, Coney Island. R. F. Nigrelli. New Yorker 42:22-3 Ag 27 '66
Swine in biomedical research; report on international symposium. L. K. Bustad and R. O. McClellan. Science 152:1526-8+ Je 10 '66
See also
Animal experimentation
Autopsy
Cancer research
Computers—Medical applications
Diabetes research
Drugs, Experimental
Heart research
Laboratory animals
Ophthalmology
Pasteur institute. Paris
Physiological research
Psychiatric research

MEDICAL research—*Continued*

Experimentation on man

Are human tests ethical? F. Marley. Sci N 90: 115 Ag 20 '66

Army fights bio-warfare; Ft Detrick's medical unit using volunteers as human guinea pigs. J. Eberhart. Sci N 90:268 O 8 '66

Consent required for drug experiments. Sci N 90:172 S 10 '66

Do we need new rules for experiments on people? J. Lear. il Sat R 49:61-70 F 5 '66; Discussion 49:58-9 Ap 2 '66

Ethical issues in research with human subjects. W. Wolfensberger. bibliog Science 155:47-51 Ja 6 '67

Ethics of human experiments; concerning Dr H. K. Beecher's study. Time 88:42+ Jl 8 '66

Experiments on man. Sci Am 215:44 Ag '66

Experiments on people, the growing debate; symposium. Sat R 49:41-50 Jl 2 '66; Discussion. 49:52 Ag 6; 51-2 S 3 '66

Human experimentation: New York verdict affirms patient's rights. E. Langer. Science 151:663-6 F 11 '66; Discussion 152: 448+, 865; 153:692 Ap 22, My 13, Ag 12 '66

Malaria wins round two. C. P. Gilmore. il N Y Times Mag p44-5+ S 25 '66

Medical experiments on humans; new guidelines. M. Alderman. New Repub 155:10-12 D 3 '66

Protecting human guinea pigs; PHS tightens rules. Bsns W p71 Jl 23 '66

Research and responsibility; concerning cancer cell injections case. Nation 202:284-5 Mr 14 '66

Research in America; three physicians dismissed from Jewish chronic disease hospital, Brooklyn. J. Lear. Sat R 49:65 Mr 5 '66

Volunteer prisoners aid flu vaccine study; tests at National institutes of health. Sci N 89:244 Ap 9 '66

Federal aid

Experiments on humans, the growing debate: invitation to open dialogue. W. H. Stewart. Sat R 49:43-4 Jl 2 '66

Government, the universities, and biomedical research; address, August 23, 1966. J. W. Gardner. Science 153:1601-3 S 30 '66

NIH: demand increases for applications of research. J. Walsh. Science 153:149-52 Jl 8 '66

MEDICAL schools. See Medical colleges

MEDICAL service

American health scandal, by R. Tunley. Review

New Repub 154:30+ Mr 5 '66. M. Alderman

Crisis now near in medical care? il U S News 60:38-41 Mr 7 '66

Health of the American people. F. E. Linder. il Sci Am 214:21-9 bibliog(p 144) Je '66

House calls aren't passe. Todays Health 44:74 My '66

Rx for sick hospitals. il Newsweek 66:57-61 Jl 11 '66

Trouble with hospitals; symposium. il Atlan 218:87-104+ Jl '66

Wasteful duplication in our hospitals. J. Randal. Reporter 35:35-8 D 15 '66

Where doctors don't reach; University of Colorado school of medicine program to lighten the work loads of physicians. il Time 88:71-2 Jl 22 '66

Why crisis in medical care keeps growing. il U S News 62:60-4 Ja 23 '67

See also
Airplanes in medical service
Hospitals
Physicians

China (People's Republic)

Observations on medical practices. G. L. Willox. Bul Atomic Sci 22:51-6 Je '66

France

Paris patrol; SOS service. Time 88:53 Jl 15 '66

Great Britain

British medicine. J. Walsh. Science 154:365-8 O 21 '66

New York (state)

Medicare's expensive companion; with editorial comment. il Bsns W p38-9, 190 Je 25 '66

Watch out for Title 19; medicaid. Life 61:4 Jl 29 '66

Russia

I had my baby in Moscow. B. Rosenfeld. il Redbook 127:52-3+ Jl '66

Underdeveloped areas

Medical problems of the developing countries. R. E. Brown. bibliog il Science 153:271-5 Jl 15 '66

MEDICAL service, Cost of

Are there ways around high health costs? medical-expense planning. Bet Hom & Gard 45:80+ Ja '67

As medicare begins. America 115:6 Jl 2 '66

$50 a day, and going up. E. L. Crosby. il Atlan 218:102-4+ Jl '66

Luxury of sickness. America 116:76 Ja 21 '67

Medical services: why costs are up. U S News 61:9 S 5 '66

Medicare bonanza. S. Greenberg. il Nation 203:513-16 N 14 '66; Discussion. 204:34+ Ja 9 '67

Medicare: promises and pitfalls. S. Greenberg. il Nation 202:617-20 My 23 '66

Public pays the bill. G. Rosenthal. il Atlan 218:107-10 Jl '66; Discussion. 218:45 S '66

Raid on medicare; hospitals to operate programs on profit basis. Nation 203:36 Jl 11 '66

Ten ways to cut your medical bills. A. Q. Maisel. Read Digest 89:80-4 O '66

Will medicare push up the doctor's bill? il Bsns W p 192+ Je 18 '66

MEDICAL service, Rural

Medicine thinks big on the prairie; Hopedale, Ill. medical complex. C. Smith. il Read Digest 88:149-52 Ap '66

They're country doctors no longer; Kansas rural health plan. H. Earl. il Todays Health 44:24-9 Je '66

MEDICAL service, State

America's unhealthy children: an emerging scandal. R. Tunley. Harper 232:41-6 My '66; Discussion. 233:4 Jl; 8 Ag '66

Annals of legislation; medicare. Wagner-Murray-Dingell bill. R. Harris. New Yorker 42:29-38+ Jl 2 '66

Europe's advice to U.S. on medical care. il U S News 62:64-6 Ja 23 '67

Medical care in New York. New Repub 154: 8-9 Je 18 '66

Medicare and medicaid. Sci Am 215:100-1 S '66

Medicare: awaiting the avalanche. E. Langer. Science 151:1366-8 Mr 18 '66

Medicare bottleneck. New Repub 154:9-10 Ja 29 '66

Medicare's expensive companion; with editorial comment. il Bsns W p38-9, 190 Je 25 '66

Trimming medicaid. Bsns W p42 Jl 9 '66

Watch out for Title 19; medicaid. Life 61:4 Jl 29 '66

What the doctor ordered; problems of medicare and medicaid. Time 88:13 Ag 26 '66

See also
Great Britain—National health service

MEDICAL societies

See also names of medical societies, e.g. American college of surgeons

MEDICAL students

Maybe he can become a doctor. C. Carner. il Todays Health 44:22-3+ My '66

MEDICAL supplies

Medical supplies. Consumer Rep 31:335-7 D '66

MEDICAL technicians. See Medical workers

MEDICAL technologists. See Medical workers

MEDICAL ultrasonics. See Ultrasonic waves—Medical applications

MEDICAL women's international association

Big man & the little lady; Elizabeth Blackwell award. il Time 88:71 Jl 22 '66

MEDICAL workers

Girls in white; AMA and ADA move to set up criteria for training and certifying assistants. J. Ridgeway. New Repub 154:10-12 F 19 '66

Good jobs in the health fields. il Changing T 20:33-5 S '66

More than a nurse, less than a doctor: ex-medical corpsmen as physicians' assistants at Duke university school of medicine. R. H. Berg. il Look 30:58-61 S 6 '66

Renee Manley: medical technologist. F. Manley, jr. il Todays Health 45:28-32 Ja '67

Wanted: 750,000 humanitarians. D. L. Wilbur. Todays Health 45:88+ Ja '67

Training

Health careers: challenge, change, opportunity; with list of training periods. il Todays Health 45:33-5 Ja '67

MEDICARE. See Insurance, Health—United States

MEDICINAL plants. See Botany, Medical

MEDICINE
Medical news of the month. M. Fishbein. See issues of McCall's
Medical sciences notes. Sci N 90:476, 500, 516, 536, 567; 91:42 D 3-31 '66, Ja 14 '67
Medicine today; ed. by V. Cohn. P. Wright. See issues of Ladies' home journal
News from the world of medicine. Read Digest 89:43-4 S; 51-2 O; 55-6 N; 23-4 D '66; 90:33-4 Ja '67
Progress of medicine. A. J. Snider. See issues of Science digest
See also
Acupuncture
Biomedical engineering
Drugs
Health
Medical research
Pharmacology
Poisons
Prescriptions
Therapeutics

Anecdotes, facetiae, satire, etc.
Silver lining. R. G. G. Price. il Atlan 218: 126-7 O '66

Bibliography
Curl up and read. J. Stone. il Seventeen 25:38 Mr '66
Medical books for the public library; comp. by V. S. Flandorf. Library J 90:4718-23 N 1 '65; Correction. 91:464 F 1 '66
Scientific, technical, and medical books to come; ed. by J. Putnam. Library J 91:5441-90 N 1 '66
Scientific, technical, and medical books to come; ed. by J. Putnam and J Lindheim (cont) Library J 91:1264-313 Mr 1 '66
Scientific, technical, and medical books to come; ed. by J. Putnam and K. Ahrens. Library J 91:3481-524+ Jl '66

Exhibitions
Walk through medicine's past; displayed in Smithsonian's hall of medical sciences. P. D. Rush. il Todays Health 45:46-51 Ja '67

History
Frontier malaria fighter. H. E. Dark. il Todays Health 44:28-9+ My '66
William Halsted: tragic figure, great surgeon; excerpt from The great doctors. R. Silverberg. il Todays Health 45:62-7 Ja '67
See also
Medicine—United States—History

Practice
Defining the new physician; excerpt from report of the Citizens commission on graduate medical education; with recommendations; ed. by J. Lear. Sat R 50:122-5 Ja 7 '67
Doctor's image is sickly. W. Goodman. il N Y Times Mag p38-9+ O 16 '66; Discussion. p 12+ O 30; 12+ N 6; 42+ N 13 '66
New profession within medicine? proposing a graduate degree of medical practice. J. Stokes, 3d. Sat R 49:90-2 D 3 '66; Discussion. 50:120-2 Ja 7 '67
Saying ah. J. Miller. Vogue 149:40+ Ja 1 '67
Sodbuster surgeons who helped win the West; excerpts from Doctors of the American frontier. R. Dunlop. il Todays Health 44:32-3+ Je '66
See also
Interns (medicine)
Medical ethics
Medical service
Physicians
Physicians and patients
Quacks and quackery
Therapeutics

Scholarships and fellowships
Aiding developing nations; Smith Kline & French foreign fellowships. L. L. L. Golden. Sat R 49:71 My 14 '66

Study and teaching
They're country doctors no longer; Kansas rural health plan. H. Earl. il Todays Health 44:24-9 Je '66
See also
Medical colleges
Medical education

China (People's Republic)
Insulin discovery. Sr Schol 89:20-1 O 14 '66
Total synthesis of insulin in red China. V. K. McElheny. bibliog Science 153:281-3 Jl 15 '66

Denmark
Unfit: Denmark's solution. il U S News 60: 74 Mr 7 '66

Europe, Western
A look at the nursing homes of Europe. il U S News 60:52 Je 13 '66

India
Sahib doctor: the healing surgeon of Vellore; condensation of Ten fingers for God. D. C. Wilson. il Read Digest 88:207-10+ Je '66

Russia
Appalling state of Russian hospitals; R. M. Hall's visit. il Time 88:85 S 30 '66
Diary of a Russian surgeon. N. M. Amosov. il Harper 233:79-86 D '66

United States
Health: latest in cures and research; meetings of American medical association and American therapeutic society. U S News 61:16 Jl 11 '66
Medicine '66; achievements, changes, new directions. J. L. Breeling. il Todays Health 45:36-40 Ja '67
New treatments for some old ailments; annual convention of American medical association. U S News 61:12-13 D 12 '66
What doctors see as top medical advances; comp. by the American medical association. U S News 61:14 D 19 '66

History
Blunderbuss doctors of early America. J. H. Winchester. il Todays Health 44:26-9+ N '66
Doctors of the new United States. J. H. Winchester. il Todays Health 44:40-3 D '66

Vietnam (Republic)
See also
Medical relief work—Vietnam (Republic)

MEDICINE, Aviation. See Aviation—Medical aspects
MEDICINE, Experimental. See Medical research

MEDICINE, Military
Dust-off! Dust-off! lifeline home from Vietnam. J. H. Winchester. il Read Digest 88: 60-6 My '66
See also
Vietnamese war, 1957- —Medical and sanitary affairs

MEDICINE, Preventive
Here's a lifesaving plan for your business. E. H. Bellows and M. R. Gasque. il Nations Bsns 54:94+ Ap '66
Preventicare needed. Sci N 90:244 O 1 '66

MEDICINE, Psychosomatic
Colitis tied to family type; psychosomatic illness. Sci N 90:399 N 12 '66
How we get psychosomatic disorders. F. R. Schreiber and M. Herman. il Sci Digest 59: 35-9 Mr '66
Man may learn to be ill. P. McBroom. Sci N 89:331 My 7 '66
See also
Iatrogenic diseases
Mind and body

MEDICINE, State. See Medical service, State
MEDICINE, Veterinary. See Veterinary medicine

MEDICINE and religion
Pastor's guidelines on some tough issues; excerpt from sermon, November 20, 1966. M. Hamilton. U S News 61:11 D 5 '66

MEDICINE in art
Doctor on buttons. D. F. Brown. il Hobbies 71:52-3+ O '66
Relics show their merits; Dr Weisman's collection of medical figures of the pre-Columbian era. F. Marley. il Sci N 90:396-7 N 12 '66

MEDICINE LAKE
Summer fishing at Medicine Lake. il Sunset 137:31-2 Jl '66

MEDICINE men in art. See Medicine in art
MEDICINES. See Drugs
MEDICINES, Patent, proprietary, etc.
Fast relief; examination of cold remedies; claims; NET. Newsweek 67:94+ Ap 4 '66
MEDIEVAL art. See Art, Medieval
MEDIEVAL drama. See Drama, Medieval
MEDIEVAL manuscripts. See Manuscripts, Medieval
MEDILL school of journalism. See Northwestern university, Evanston, Ill.—Medill school of journalism
MEDINA, Fernando Díez de. See Díez de Medina, F.

MEDITATION
Martyrs may not feel pain; contemplation practiced by people in eastern religions akin to auto-hypnosis. P. McBroom. il Sci N 89:505-6 Je 25 '66

MELANCHTHON
Quiet reformer. R. R. Caemmerer. Christian
Cent 83:141 F 2 '66
MELANIN
Terminology of vertebrate melanin-containing
cells: 1965. T. B. Fitzpatrick and others.
bibliog Science 152:88-9 Ap 1 '66
MELARO, Constance L.
Comments on teacher certification. NEA J
55:18 S '66
MELARTIN, Liisa, and Blumberg, B. S.
Albumin naskapi: a new variant of serum
albumin. bibliog Science 153:1664-6 S 30 '66
MELATONIN
Light-induced changes in pineal hydroxy-
indole-O-methyltransferase: abolition by
lateral hypothalamic lesions. J. Axelrod
and others. bibliog il Science 154:898-9 N 18
'66
MELBOURNE, Fla.

Water supply
People won't drink cedar water. R. McCol-
gan. il Am City 81:103-5+ D '66
MELCHER, Daniel
Are books overpriced? Library J 91:2542+ My
15 '66
British books to be numbered beginning this
month. Pub W 191:28-30 Ja 2 '67
Comments on the survey of bookstore operat-
ing ratios. Pub W 190:32-5 D 26 '66
Fred Melcher: as I knew him; address, July
1966. por ALA Bul 61:56-62 Ja '67
Narrow view of the book revolution. Pub W
190:24-6 D 12 '66
MELCHER, Frederic Gershom
Fred Melcher: as I knew him; address, July
1966. D. Melcher. ALA Bul 61:56-62 Ja '67
MELCHIOR, Lauritz
Mephisto's musings. por Hi Fi 16:119+ Mr
'66
MELFI, Leonard
Birdbath. Criticism
Nation 202:404 Ap 4 '66
New Yorker 42:126 Ap 23 '66
MELILLO, Louis. See Wunderlich, B. jt. auth.
MELIOIDOSIS
Delayed symptoms occur in rare swamp dis-
ease. Sci N L 89:131 F 26 '66
MELL, Jack G.
How to catch bass at midday. Field & S 71:
80+ My '66
MELLA, Barbara, and Lang, D. J.
Leukocyte mitosis: suppression in vitro asso-
ciated with acute infectious hepatitis. bbliog
Science 155:80-1 Ja 6 '67
MELLINGER, Marie B.
Path through the mist forest. Nat Parks
Mag 40:21-2 My '66
MELLON, Ailsa. See Bruce, A. M.
MELLON, Andrew William
Four miracles, and a masterpiece. J. A.
Michener. il Read Digest 89:160-5 N '66
MELLON, Andrew William, collection. See Na-
tional gallery of art, Washington, D.C.
MELLON, Bruce, collection. See Art—Private
collections
MELLON, Paul
Celebration of masterpieces. J. Walker. il
Vogue 147:94-5+ Mr 15 '66
Family reunion. il por Newsweek 67:99-100
Mr 21 '66
National gallery: preview of an anniversary
exhibition. A. Saarinen. il McCalls 93:96-
103+ Ap '66
Old England for new; Mellon's English paint-
ing collection to Yale. Time 88:84 D 16 '66
Throwing a party. H. Brandon. Sat R 49:20
Mr 19 '66
Treasure for Yale. il por Newsweek 68:104
D 19 '66
MELLON, Paul, collection. See Art—Private
collections
MELLON institute
New U. at Carnegie tech. Time 88:43+ S 23
'66
MELLORS, G. W. See Senderoff, S. jt. auth.
MELLOW, James R.
Books (cont) Commonweal 85:57-9 O 14 '66
MELMAN, Seymour
Great society priorities. Commonweal 84:494-7
Ag 5 '66
MELMON, Kenneth L.   See Cline. M. J. jt.
auth.
MELNICK, Joseph L. See Rapp, F. jt. auth.
MELNICK, Norman
Second city. Opera N 31:8-12 D 3 '66
MELNYKOVYCH, George
Glucocorticoid-induced resistance to deoxy-
cholate lysis in HeLa cells. bibliog Science
152:1086-7 My 20 '66

MELONS
How to pick a melon. il Bet Hom & Gard
44:69 Ag '66
M is for melons. il Ladies Home J 83:97 Je
'66
Melon full of cool and colorful ideas for
summer eating! il Bet Hom & Gard 44:64-
5+ Ag '66
MELOY, Thomas
Laser's bright magic. Nat Geog Mag 130:
858-81 D '66
MELTING points
See also
Eutectics
MELVIN, A. Gordon
Carrier shells. Hobbies 70:130 F '66
Natural history. See issues of Hobbies
MELVIN, Glen E.
540 or 1,000-rpm PTO: how to use both. Suc
Farm 64:52-3+ F '66
Tractor air cleaner, service it right. Suc
Farm 64:48 Jl '66
MEMBRACIDAE. See Tree hoppers
MEMBRANES (biology)
Immunochemical studies of submicrosomal
membranes from liver of normal and phe-
nobarbital-treated rats. U. Lundkvist and
P. Perlmann. bibliog il Science 152:780-2
My 6 '66
Membranes of cells only one molecule thick.
Sci N 90:78 Jl 30 '66
Muscle postjunctional membrane: changes in
chemosensitivity produced by calcium. W.
L. Nastuk and J. H. Liu. bibliog il Science
154:266-7 O 14 '66
Structure of biological membranes. E. D.
Korn. bibliog il Science 153:1491-8 S 23 '66
Structure of cell membranes at the molecular
level; report on conference. D. T. Warner.
Science 153:324-6 Jl 15 '66
See also
Epithelium
Plasma membranes
MEMBRANES (technology)
Gills for humans, they're here. il Sci Digest
59:36-8 My '66
MEMENTO, memento; story. See Amft, M. J.
MEMENTOS. See Keepsakes
MEMMEL, Bernard G.
Fees and charges; a legitimate source of
revenue; address. por Parks & Rec 1:152-
3 F '66
MEMMI, Albert
Does the Jew exist? excerpt from The lib-
eration of the Jew. Commentary 42:73-4+
N '66
MEMORANDUMS
In praise of memos. S. B. Vitt. Nations
Bsns 54:70 N '66
MEMORIAL gardens. See War memorials
MEMORIALS
Memorial to Joe Fortes; Vancouver, B.C.
J. Bellinger. il Negro Hist Bul 29:168 Ap
'66
See also
Kennedy, John Fitzgerald, 1917-1963—Memor-
ials
War memorials
MEMORIZING
Memorizing poetry: it can be fun. H. Al-
dridge. il Sr Schol 89:sup 16 S 23 '66
MEMORIZING, Music. See Music—Memorizing
MEMORY
Chemicals may color memories with emo-
tion. Sci N 89:466 Je 11 '66
Chemistry of memory. Sci Am 215:42 Ag '66
Components of skilled performance. M. I.
Posner. bibliog il Science 152:1712-18 Je 24
'66
Gabbernot has got me. S. Alexander. Life
61:38 S 16 '66
Inside the molecules of the mind. L. Lessing.
il Fortune 74:100-5+ Jl 1 '66
Learning, remembering, and forgetting; re-
port on conference. D. P. Kimble. Science
151:712-13 F 11 '66
Memory and aging biological cousins. P.
McBroom. Sci N 90:399 N 12 '66
Memory improvement. Sci N 89:248 Ap 9 '66
Memory still elusive. Sci N 91:9 Ja 7 '67
Memory three processes. Sci N 90:248 O 1 '66
Memory transfer unlikely. P. McBroom. Sci
N L 89:151 Mr 5 '66
Pupil diameter and load on memory. D. Kahn-
eman and J. Beatty. bibliog il Science 154:
1583-5 D 23 '66
Recovery of memory after amnesia induced
by electroconvulsive shock. S. Zinkin and
A. J. Miller. bibliog il Science 155:102-4
Ja 6 '67
Short-term memory. L. R. Peterson. il Sci
Am 215:90-5 bibliog(p 131) Jl '66

MEMORY—*Continued*
Time-dependent processes in memory storage.
   J. L. McGaugh. bibliog il Science 153:1351-8
   S 16 '66
Understanding memory. P. McBroom. il Sci
   N 89:186-7 Mr 19 '66
Watching Johnny's memory grow. F. R. Sch-
   reiber. il Todays Health 44:22-4+ O '66
   See also
Maze tests
Music—Memorizing
Reminiscence
Retention (psychology)
MEMORY, Loss of. See Amnesia
MEMORY devices (computers)
Box finds a memory for film; Mosler's se-
   lectriever. il Bsns W p 188 My 28 '66
Color laser stores data; IBM invention.
   J. Eberhart. il Sci N 90:51 Jl 23 '66
Computer logic and memory. D. C. Evans.
   il Sci Am 215:74-85 bibliog(p312) S '66
This magic box plays a game, can you beat
   it? building electronic brain. R. M. Benrey.
   il Pop Sci 189:100-1+ Ag '66
   See also
Magnetic memory (computers)
MEMORY pills. See Magnesium pemoline
MEMOS. See Memorandums
MEMPHIS Slim
Memphis Slim: la vie est bonne. il pors
   Ebony 21:56-8+ Je '66
MEMPHIS, Tenn.
Theater
[Theatre across America] J. Novick. Nation
   202:692-3 Je 6 '66

Water supply
Maintain your water meters. J. Baker. il
   Am City 81:99-101+ N '66
MEN
American male; by M. Brenton. Review
   Sat R 49:29-31 Jl 30 '66. R. Taplinger
American man; symposium, ed. by P. Coffin.
   il Look 31:14-34+ Ja 10 '67
American pastime of ridiculing American
   men. M. Mannes. McCalls 93:52+ F '66
Male attitude, by C. W. Ferguson. Review
   Sat R 49:41 N 19 '66. F. Brennan
Trade winds; masculinity crisis. J. G. Fuller.
   Sat R 49:16-17 Jl 30 '66
   See also
Cookery by men
Great men
Husbands
Sex differences
Widowers
Women and men
Young men

Anecdotes, facetiae, satire, etc.
Pride and prejudice. D. Newman and R.
   Benton. Mlle 62:44+ F '66

Clothing
See Clothing and dress—Men

Health and hygiene
Advice to businessmen on health and retire-
   ment; interview. H. J. Johnson. il U S
   News 60:62-7 Mr 7 '66
Congress' doctor prescribes: how to stay
   healthy under pressure; interview. G. W.
   Calver. il Nations Bsns 54:92+ O '66
Funny thing happened on my way to the
   sybaritic bath. L. Botto. il Look 31:84-6
   Ja 10 '67
How the American male can be fit. S. Musial.
   Parks & Rec 1:695+ S '66
How to keep an executive healthy. A. J.
   Snider. il Sci Digest 61:28-9 Ja '67
Over the hill at forty? nonsense! say these
   experts; findings of UCLA specialists. To-
   days Health 45:3-4 Ja '67
R for executive health: garden therapy. il
   Pop Gard 17:14-19+ D '66

Psychology
Man talk: endgame, or it's all over now,
   baby blue. D. Newman and R. Benton. Mlle
   63:40+ O '66
MENAKER, Michael, and Eskin, Arnold
Entrainment of circadian rhythms by sound
   in passer domesticus. bibliog Science 154:
   1579-81 D 23 '66
MENARD, Edith
Book review. Negro Hist Bul 29:41 N '65
Star; Of color; It; Opportunity; poems. por
   Negro Hist Bul 29:67 D '65
MENARD, H. W.
Extension of northeastern-Pacific fracture
   zones. bibliog Science 155:72-4 Ja 6 '67

MENCHER, Joan
Namboodiri Brahmans of Kerala. Natur Hist
   75:14-21 bibliog(p64) My '66
MENCKEN, Henry Louis
Wink at a homely girl. M. Kram. il Sports
   Illus 25:86-8+ O 10 '66
MENDEL, Arthur P.
Current Soviet theory of history: new trends
   or old? bibliog f Am Hist R 72:50-73 O '66
Rise and fall of scientific socialism. bibliog f
   For Affairs 45:98-111 O '66
MENDEL, Julius L. and Walton, M. S.
Conversion of p,p'-DDT to p,p'-DDD by in-
   testinal flora of the rat. bibliog Science
   151:1527-8 Mr 25 '66
MENDELISM
   See also
Genetics
MENDELS, Joe
Do you resent your children? Parents Mag
   41:33-5+ Ag '66
MENDELSOHN, Harold
TV and youth: new style for politics. Na-
   tion 202:669-73 Je 6 '66
MENDELSOHN, Jack
Dominican election and the role of the ob-
   servers. Christian Cent 83:894-8 Jl 13 '66
MENDELSSOHN, Felix
Belated birthday greetings to Sir Malcolm.
   M. Maxwell. Am Rec G 33:43+ S '66
Mendelssohn and Mozart marvels at Marlboro.
   A. Cohn. Am Rec G 32:986 Je '66
MENDEZ, Ann
Query from a practical Bostonian; poem.
   Christian Cent 83:422 Ap 6 '66
Valentine for Mr Hefner; poem. Christian
   Cent 83:166 F 9 '66
MÉNDEZ MONTENEGRO, Julio César
Against the odds. Time 88:27 Jl 8 '66
Two for the seesaw. Time 87:52 Mr 18 '66
MENDING
Stitch in time. Consumer Bul 49:26 O '66
MENDIOLA, Leticia R. and others
Isolation of nuclei from a marine dinoflagel-
   late. bibliog Science 153:1661-3 S 30 '66
MENDL, Elsie (De Wolfe) lady
Miss De Wolfe who decorated. il por Arch
   Forum 124:88 Mr '66
MENDOZA, Gunnar
Imperial city of Potosí. Américas 18:1-6 Jl
   '66
MENEN, Aubrey
How Mr Menen taught the Dangs primitive
   art. N Y Times Mag p20-2+ Jl 24 '66
How to live in a palazzo. House & Gard
   129:132-3+ Je '66
Letter from abroad. McCalls 93:76 +Ap '66
New Europe. Holiday 41:46-57+ Ja '67
Roman roulette. N Y Times Mag p24-5+ Ja
   30 '66
Sophia Loren: on women who are bored and
   boring. McCalls 94:54-5+ Ja '67
MENGIN, Robert
Books. N. Bliven. New Yorker 42:242-7 O 22
   '66
MÉNIÈRE'S disease
Pill for Ménière's. Time 88:55 D 16 '66
MENINGITIS
Cold that kills; outbreaks at military bases.
   Newsweek 67:58 F 28 '66
Trying too hard for the fast knockout. Time
   89:44 Ja 6 '67
MENK, Louis Wilson
Casey Jones is dead. il por Time 87:98 Je
   10 '66
No. 1 wheel. por Newsweek 68:84 O 10 '66
MENNINGER, Edwin A.
Trees that twist; excerpt from Fantastic
   tree. Am For 72:30-3+ Jl '66
MENNINGER, William Claire
Obituary
   Christian Cent 83:1139 S 21 '66
MENNONITES
Amish controversy: temporarily settled; Gov.
   Hughes acts. P. B. Mather. Christian Cent
   83:474-6 Ap 13 '66
Amish in Iowa; letter. L. E. Smartt. Com-
   monweal 83:707 Mr 18 '66
No worldly schools; Iowa. Sr Schol 88:17-18
   Mr 11 '66
Plain people vs. the common schools; efforts
   to improve Amish education D. A. Erick-
   son. il Sat R 49:85-7+ N 19 '66
State of Iowa vs. the Amish; school dispute.
   F. H. Littell. Christian Cent 83:234-5 F 23
   '66; Discussion. 83:468-72 Ap 13 '66
That Amish thing; education dispute in
   Iowa. P. B. Mather. Christian Cent 83:245-
   7 F 23 '66; Discussion. 83:468-72 Ap 13 '66
MENOCAL, Mario G.
Shooting. Sports Illus 24:76-8+ Mr 21 '66
MENON, Vengalil Krishnan Krishna. See
   Krishna Menon, V. K.

MENUHIN, Yehudi
Chip off the old prodigy. il pors Life 60: 63-4+ My 20 '66
Golden age. il por Newsweek 67:90-1 My 9 '66
Menuhin at fifty; disc issued by HMV. T. Heinitz. Sat R 49:72 Ap 30 '66
Repeat performance at fifty. E. Greenfield. il pors Hi Fi 16:24+ Ap '66
Yehudi Menuhin: musician of the year. G. Gould. il por Hi Fi 16:7-9 D 15 '66
MENUS
Classic menu mates; with recipes. il Redbook 127:94-8+ O '66
Epicure reminisces. A. L. Simon. il Holiday 40:34+ D '66
Fabulous dinner you don't slave over. il Bet Hom & Gard 44:84-5+ O '66
Go-go parties; with recipes. il Seventeen 25: 166-9+ Ap '66
Guide to dining out in another language. Bet Hom & Gard 44:78+ Ap '66
Happy marriage: spring menu. il McCalls 93:54 Ap '66
[Month] menus; with recipes. See issues of Sunset
Waiter, what does that mean? il Changing T 20:43-4 O '66
See also
Breakfasts
Buffet meals
Dinners and dining
Luncheons
Lunches
Meals
Thanksgiving dinners
MENZEL, Donald H.
Eclipse over the Andes. il pors Sky & Tel 33:11-15 Ja '67
MENZIES, Sir Robert Gordon
End of the Ming dynasty. il por Time 87: 23 Ja 28 '66
MEOS (native race) See Laos—Native races
MEPROBAMATES
Miltown's effect on brain a mystery. Sci N 90:24 Jl 9 '66
MERAS, Phyllis L.
Author; L. A. Fiedler. Sat R 49:32 Jl 30 '66
Princes' Islands. Travel 125:48-9 Je '66
MERCANTILE bank of Canada. See Banks and banking—Canada
MERCANTILE financial corporation
Finance firm completes acquisition of A. C. McClurg. il Pub W 191:59 Ja 16 '67
MERCENARIES (soldiers) See Mercenary troops
MERCENARY troops
Guns for hire; training camp exposure in France and ownership dispute. Newsweek 68:46+ O 3 '66
MERCER, D. M. A.
Messages to the stars; address. 1965. UNESCO Courier 19:4-7+ Ja '66
MERCER, Jinx
Apollo land recovery tests continue. Miss & Roc 18:24-5 F 28 '66
First Saturn IB launch will test Apollo heat shield design. Miss & Roc 18:16 F 7 '66
Gemini crew to photograph solar eclipse. Tech W 19:18-19 O 17 '66
Manned-Apollo flight to test optics. Miss & Roc 18:18 Ja 24 '66
NASA official details current plans for prelunar Apollos. Tech W 19:17 O 31 '66
No problems for next Saturn-Apollo. Miss & Roc 18:22 Mr 14 '66
S-IVB stage may become space station. Miss & Roc 18:17 Ap 25 '66
Successful Gemini 11 flight leaves EVA stress unsolved. Tech W 19:10+ S 26 '66
—and others
Beyond Gemini, Apollo problems loom. Tech W 19:13-17 N 21 '66
MERCER, Lucy Page. See Rutherfurd, L. P. M.
MERCER ISLAND, Wash.
Community action: a children's dragon comes to life. il Sunset 137:72-3 S '66
MERCHANDISE, Quality of. See Quality of products
MERCHANDISING
Batboom; Batman moving into retail trade. Time 87:88+ Mr 11 '66
Door belles; overabundance of greeting services. il Newsweek 68:106 O 17 '66
Selling the green berets. il Newsweek 67: 100+ My 2 '66
Sharp practice in merchandising and advertising. E. T. Grether. bibliog f Ann Am Acad 363:108-16 Ja '66
See also
Samples (merchandising)
MERCHANT, Bruce, and Hraba, Tomas
Lymphoid cells producing antibody against simple haptens: detection and enumeration. bibliog Science 152:1378-9 Je 3 '66

MERCHANT, Jane
Array of terms; poem. Horn Bk 42:349 Je '66
Gentle one; poem. Suc Farm 64:82 F '66
Of light and shade; poem. Farm J 90:89 S '66
MERCHANT bankers. See Bankers
MERCHANT banks, London. See London— Banks
MERCHANT marine
See also
Seamen

Germany (Democratic Republic)
On the ways. il Time 89:65 Ja 13 '67

Great Britain
Rule Britannia, without a ship at sea? economic effects. il Newsweek 67:38+ Je 6 '66

Norway
Surge to the sea; Bergesen's fleet. il Time 88:102-3 N 11 '66

Russia
Cold wet war. R. Moley. Newsweek 68:104 Ag 22 '66
Russia bids for ocean supremacy. N. Mostert. il Reporter 34:24-8 F 10 '66
U.S. views on developments in Viet-Nam given to U.S.S.R: Russian charges of US threat to Soviet merchant vessels; texts of U.S. note, July 23 and Soviet note, July 9, 1966. Dept State Bul 55:213-14 Ag 8 '66

United States
At sea with Johnson. J. Ridgeway. New Repub 154:10 Mr 5 '66
Cargo rates run into heavy seas; competitive bidding for military cargoes. Bsns W p82 Jl 30 '66
Our merchant marine in trouble. J. D. Hayes; discussion. Reporter 34:8+ F 10; 6+ F 24 '66
Recommendation for maritime labor relations policies. Mo Labor R 89:19-21 Ja '66
Shipping: storm signals lowering? il Duns R 87:pt2 125-7+ My '66
U.S. shipbuilding: mighty no more. il U S News 60:47 Je 27 '66
Vanishing merchant fleet. il U S News 60:80-1 My 2 '66
See also
Freight vessels
Merchant ships
National maritime day
Shipping—United States
MERCHANT ships
Our leaky pipeline to Vietnam. L. Velie. il Read Digest 89:113-18 D '66
MERCIER, Vivian
My life in the new novel. Nation 202:434-6 Ap 11 '66
MERCK and company
Reflections on research and the future of medicine; report on two-day program at dedication of new research building for the Merck Sharp & Dohme research laboratories. T. L. Campbell. il Science 153: 442-6+ Jl 22 '66
MERCOURI, Melina
Melina Mercouri. por Vogue 148:114-15 N 15 '66
about
Melina Mercouri rehearses Never on Sunday for Broadway. J. Hamilton. il pors Look 31:66-71 Ja 24 '67
People are talking about... M. Duras. por Vogue 147:108-9+ Ap 15 '66
Taming Melina to be a hoofer; with report by J. Hallowell. il pors Life 61:52-2+ D 2 '66
MERCURY
Singular metal from cinnabar. P. M. Tilden. il Natur Hist 75:26-31 Je '66
MERCURY (planet)
Luminescent effects seen possible on Mercury. Sci N L 89:130 F 26 '66
Mercury: anomalous absence from the 3.4-millimeter radio emission of variation with phase. E. E. Epstein. bibliog il Science 151: 445-7 Ja 28 '66
Rotation of Mercury. G. S. Mumford. Sky & Tel 31:213 Ap '66
Rotation of the planet Mercury. W. H. Jefferys. bibliog Science 152:201 Ap 8 '66
Temperature anomaly of Mercury. Sky & Tel 31:143 Mr '66
Rotation
Mercury: infrared evidence for non-synchronous rotation. S. L. Soter. bibliog il Science 153:1112-13 S 2 '66
Rotation of mercury: theoretical analysis of the dynamics of a rigid ellipsoidal planet. L. J. Laslett and A. M. Sessler. bibliog Science 151:1384-5 Mr 18 '66

MERCY killing. See Euthanasia

MEREDITH, Don
Insiders scout the Super bowl. por Newsweek 69:83 Ja 16 '67

about

Hard times for heroes. G. Astor. il pors Look 31:82-3 Ja 10 '67
When the booing stopped. T. Maule. il Sports Illus 25:32-5 S 26 '66

MEREDITH, James Howard
Big changes are coming. pors Sat Eve Post 239:23-7 Ag 13 '66

about

Blind bigotry on U.S. 51. Christian Cent 83: 793 Je 22 '66
He shot me like a goddam rabbit. K. Fleming. Newsweek 67:30 Je 20 '66
Heat on Highway 51. il por Time 87:26-7 Je 17 '66
Historic return to college. B. D. Diamonstein. Sat R 49:31-2 My 28 '66
How guilty is the South? W. F. Buckley, jr. Nat R 18:611 Je 28 '66
Is Meredith right? Nation 202:765 Je 27 '66
March Meredith began. il pors Newsweek 67: 27-31 Je 20 '66
Meredith ambush. Nation 202:731 Je 20 '66
Only believe. Nat R 18:1258 D 13 '66
Proud man. il por Newsweek 67:112+ Ap 18 '66
Race issue inflamed again: aftermath of a shooting; with editorial comment. il pors U S News 60:36-8, 112 Je 20 '66
Surprise package; A. J. Norvell sentenced. Newsweek 68:32 D 5 '66
Walk in the South to conquer old fears. il pors Life 60:30-5 Je 17 '66

MEREDITH, William
About opera; poem. Opera N 30:15 Je 4 '66
Dove; poem. Opera N 30:2 Mr 5 '66
Poem about morning. New Yorker 42:213 D 3 '66
Weather; poem. New Yorker 41:115 F 12 '66

MEREDITH college, Raleigh, N. C.
Baptist students select Catholic adviser. Christian Cent 84:5 Ja 4 '67

MEREDITH march through Mississippi. See Civil rights demonstrations

MERGERS. See Business consolidations and mergers

MERGERS, Railroad. See Railroads—Consolidations and mergers

MERINGUE
How to make perfect meringue shells. il Bet Hom & Gard 44:96 Ap '66
To cook a cloud; with recipes. il Ladies Home J 83:110-11+ Mr '66

MERIONES. See Gerbils

MERIT for leadership awards. See American city (periodical)

MERKLING, Frank, and others
They played the Metropolitan. Opera N 30: 8-13 F 5 '66

MERLIS, George
Why are we striking? Nat R 18:532-4 My 31 '66

MERMAN, Ethel
At 78, Berlin gives Annie a new showstopper, and is pleased with himself. T. Prideaux. por Life 60:47 Je 10 '66

MEROM, Peter
Reclamation of Israel's desert; photographs. Natur Hist 75:30-3 F '66

MEROMICTIC lakes. See Lakes

MERRIAM, Robert
Pigments for your imagination. Hot Rod 19: 68-71 F '66

MERRICK, David
Clean breast and the fell swoop. S. Alexander. Life 62:12 Ja 6 '67
He's Broadway today. il por Newsweek 67: 96-7 Mr 21 '66
Holly go quickly. M. Gussow. il por Newsweek 68:45 D 26 '66
Merrick plan; concerning canceled preview. Newsweek 67:86 F 28 '66
Presentation and examination of the be(a)st of Broadway as published by the writers and editors of Time. il pors Time 87:52-4+ Mr 25 '66
Smelling a rat; Kauffmann, Merrick and previews. il Time 87:64 F 25 '66
Who's afraid of David Golightly? il por Time 88:102-3 N 25 '66

MERRILL, James
Illusion wedded to simple need. R. Howard. Poetry 108:329-35 Ag '66
Words for Maria; poem. New Yorker 42:28 Jl 9 '66

MERRILL, Robert
Robert Merrill. A. M. Lingg. Opera N 30:35 Ap 16 '66
Staying power. A. Hughes. por Opera N 30: 26-7 F 26 '66

MERRILL, William Stetson
Merrill at 100. D. W. Krummel. il Library J 91:205 Ja 15 '66

MERRILL Lynch, Pierce, Fenner and Smith, incorporated
Heads you win? activities of the Center for research in security prices. E. J. Kahn, jr. il Reporter 35:39-42 O 20 '66
Long look upward. il Time 88:66-70 Ag 19 '66

MERRITT, Zella Jonas
World of Louis Paul Jonas. Am Artist 31:54-60 Ja '67

MERRITT ISLAND launch area. See Proving grounds

MERRY Christmas; drama. See Hackett, W.

MERSAND, Joseph
Books for English teachers. Sr Schol 89:sup62 S 23 '66
Potpourri of new books. Sr Schol 89:sup 18-19 D 2 '66

MERSON, Ben
New miracles to fight tooth decay. Good H 162:80-1+ F '66

MERTON, Thomas
Conjectures of a guilty bystander; excerpts. pors Life 61:60-2+ Ag 5 '66
Elegy for a Trappist. Commonweal 85:294 D 9 '66
How it is: apologies to an unbeliever. Harper 233:36+ N '66
Is the world a problem? Commonweal 84: 305-9 Je 3 '66

MERWIN, W. S.
Asians dying; poem. New Yorker 42:28 Ag 13 '66
Child; poem. New Yorker 42:50 D 17 '66
Dusk in winter; poem. Atlan 217:86 Mr '66
Evening; poem. Atlan 217:102 Ap '66
Finding of reasons; poem. Atlan 217:50 My '66
Gods; Looking east at night; April; Whenever I go there; poems. Poetry 107:299-302 F '66
When you go away; poem. Sat Eve Post 239: 42 D 31 '66
Widow; poem. New Yorker 42:174 My 21 '66

MERYMAN, Richard
Behind the myth the face of Norma Jean. Life 61:49-54 N 4 '66
Interview with Louis Armstrong. Life 60:94-102+ Ap 15 '66

MESA, Ariz.
Crime
Quiet one; murder of five. il Newsweek 68: 32 N 28 '66
Slaughter in the college of beauty; multiple murder. Time 88:33 N 18 '66

MESONS
Siding with symmetry. Time 88:78 S 16 '66
Step away from symmetry. il Time 88:54 Jl 8 '66
See also
Muonium

MESOPOTAMIA
See also
Iraq
Antiquities
Investigating the origins of Mesopotamian civilization. F. Hole. bibliog il Science 153: 605-11 Ag 5 '66
See also
Nimrud
Ur

MESOSCAPH. See Submarine boats

MESSENGER, Bill
Man in the red suit; drama. Plays 26:81-7 D '66

MESSENGER, what tidings? story. See Durant, M.

MESSER, Alfred A.
For better, but not for worse. Todays Health 44:62-6+ Ap '66
Malady of our times: alienation. Todays Health 44:40-3+ S '66

MESSERLY, Wayne
Should you hire help or get more machinery? Suc Farm 64:40 Mr '66

MESSIAEN, Olivier
Music of the birds and beasts. O. Daniel. Sat R 49:68-9 Mr 26 '66
Music today via Angel, a superlative HMV project. A. Cohn. por Am Rec G 32:780-1 My '66

MESSIER catalog. See Stars—Catalogs

MESSINESI, Despina
Their majesties King Constantine II and Queen Anne Marie of the Hellenes with H.R.H. Crown Princess Alexia. Vogue 148:116-19+ S 15 '66
Travel. See occasional issues of Vogue
Travel comforts collected by a cagey traveller. Vogue 147:56-7 F 1 '66
Tunisia; extravagant space and serenity. Vogue 147:21+ F 15 '66
MESSRASTER projection screen. See Projection apparatus
MESTHENE, Emmanuel G.
What modern science offers the church. Sat R 49:29-31+ N 19 '66
METABOLISM
Bliss, metabolism linked. Sci N 89:432 Je 4 '66
Drugs affecting lipid metabolism; report on second international symposium. D. Kritchevsky. Science 151:1016-17 F 25 '66
Metabolism of alveolar cells: histochemical evidence and relation to pulmonary surfactant. S. I. Said and others. bibliog il Science 152:657-9 Ap 29 '66
N-cyclohexyl linoleamide: metabolism and cholesterol-lowering effect in rats. H. Nakatani and others. bibliog il Science 153:1267-9 S 9 '66
See also
Galactose metabolism
Lipochondrodystrophy
Plants—Metabolism
METACHROMATIC leucodystrophy. See Nervous system—Diseases
METACONTRAST. See Sight
METAL carbonyls. See Carbonyls
METAL coating
Coherent coatings of refractory metals. S. Senderoff and G. W. Mellors. bibliog il Science 153:1475-81 S 23 '66
LMSC plans to use Gemini spray process in architecture; gold coating. R. Lindsey. Tech W 19:30+ S 12 '66
Plating reclaims worn jet engine parts; Linde's flame plating operation. M. L. Yaffee. il Aviation W 85:63+ O 17 '66
METAL coloring
Color those metal projects chemically. P. McCafferty and T. C. Van Alstyne. il Pop Sci 188:124-8 F '66
METAL containers. See Containers
METAL crystals
Eutectics provide possible one-step whisker composites. J. F. Judge. il Tech W 19:32-4 D 19 '66
Whisker-carrying filaments may solve alignment problem. il Tech W 19:34 D 19 '66
Whisker for transistor; resonant-gate transistor. Sci N 90:143 Ag 27 '66
METAL detection. See Metal detectors
METAL detectors
Electronic metal locators. D. E. Lancaster. il Electr World 76:39-42+ D '66
IC-47 metal locator. D. Lancaster. il Pop Electr 26:41-8+ Ja '67
Treasure finder you can build. R. M. Benrey. il Pop Sci 189:110-14 Jl '66
METAL finishing
See also
Japanning
METAL locators. See Metal detectors
METAL plating. See Metal coating
METAL powders
See also
Titanium, Powdered
METAL protection
See also
Chromium plating
METAL sculpture
Engineer of movement; kinetics of George Rickey. il Time 88:76-7 N 4 '66
Idealogue in Lotosland. H. Rosenstein. il Art N 65:36-8+ O '66
Metal sculpture of Russ Shears. J. Lovoos. il Am Artist 30:38-42+ Mr '66
News of art. il Horizon 9:76-7 Wint '67
Welded metal sculpture. W. Hullow; I. Parks. il Sch Arts 65:21-4 F '66
See also
Bronzes
METAL shapers. See Shapers
METAL spraying. See Metal coating
METAL trade
See also
Allegheny Ludlum steel corporation
METAL turning. See Turning
METAL whiskers. See Metal crystals
METAL work
See also
Art metal work
Sheet metal work

METALAW. See Space law
METALLOGRAPHY
Cubic carbides. W. S. Williams. bibliog il Science 152:34-42 Ap 1 '66
See also
Metal crystals
METALLURGY

History

Evidence of early pyrometallurgy in the Kerman Range in Iran. bibliog il Science 153:984-5 Ag 26 '66
METALLURGY, Dental. See Dental metallurgy
METALS
Microbes sort metals. Sci N 90:135 Ag 27 '66
Reversible combination of carbon monoxide with a synthetic oxygen carrier complex. L. Vaska. bibliog il Science 152:769-71 My 6 '66
See also
Alloys
Metallography
also names of metals, e.g. Copper

Cold working

Make yourself a shrink plate. W. E. Burton. il Pop Mech 125:192-3 Mr '66

Coloring

See Metal coloring

Detection

See Metal detectors

Prices

Gamesmanship with the guideposts. M. C. Jensen. Harvard Bsns R 44:168-70+ N '66
Inco puts new dent in guideposts; Canadian nickel producer posts a 9.6 per cent boost. il Bsns W p 152 N 12 '66
Metal shortages forcing delivery delays. M. L. Yaffee. Aviation W 85:31-2 S 19 '66
See also
Copper—Prices
METALS, Effect of temperature on
Oxygen isotope fractionation in the system dolomite-calcite-carbon dioxide. J. R. O'Neil and S. Epstein. bibliog il Science 152:198-201 Ap 8 '66
Superconductivity of alpha-uranium and the role of 5f electrons. T. H. Geballe and others. bibliog il Science 152:755-7 My 6 '66
Weakening of dunite by serpentine dehydration. R. E. Riecker and T. P. Rooney. bibliog il Science 152:196-8 Ap 8 '66; Reply with rejoinder. C. B. Sclar and L. C. Carrison. 153:1285-7 S 9 '66
METALS, Nonferrous
Ease the shortage. Time 87:90+ Mr 18 '66
METALS, Rare. See Earths, Rare
METALS, Transmutation of. See Transmutation (chemistry)
METALS in the body. See Minerals in the body
METAMORPHIC rocks. See Rocks
METAMORPHISM
Shock metamorphism of natural materials. B. M. French. Science 153:903-6 Ag 19 '66
METAMORPHOSIS
See also
Amphibia—Development
METAMORPHOSIS (insects) See Insects—Development
METAPHYSICS
Christian metaphysics, by C. Tresmontant. Review
Christian Cent 83:368-9 Mr 23 '66. R. Luecke
Commonweal 84:122-4 Ap 15 '66. E. Fontinell
Where has all philosophy gone? T. J. Cunningham. America 114:496-9 Ap 9 '66
See also
Ontology
METASTASIO, Pietro Antonio Domenico Buonaventura
Metastasio: librettist to a century. W. Weaver. por Hi Fi 16:53-5 Jl '66
METATE stones. See Indians of North America —Implements
METCALF, George R.
Metro North moves mountains. Reporter 35:24-9 N 17 '66
METCALF, Gordon M.
Company man. por Newsweek 68:88 N 14 '66
Metcalf of Sears, Roebuck. por Fortune 74:55 S '66
Pick of the rack. il por Time 88:101 N 11 '66
METCALF, Katherine
Art news from San Francisco. Art N 64:46-7 F; 65:66 Sum '66
METCALFE, Vern
North Tongass timber sale. Am Forest 72:10 Ja '66

METEORITE craters
Meteorite yields diamond; Arizona meteorite crater. Sci N 89:267 Ap 16 '66
Nickel-iron spherules from Aouelloul glass. E. C. T. Chao and others. Science 154:759-60+ N 11 '66

METEORITES
Artifacts in polarimetry and optical activity in meteorites. R. Hayatsu. bibliog il Science 153:859-61 Ag 19 '66
Barwell meteorite. P. L. Brown. il Sky & Tel 32:7-11 Jl '66
Butler, Missouri: an iron meteorite with extremely high germanium content. J. T. Wasson. bibliog Science 153:976-8 Ag 26 '66
Butler, Missouri: an unusual iron meteorite. J. I. Goldstein. bibliog il Science 153:975-6 Ag 26 '66
Chainpur-like chondrites: primitive precursors of ordinary chondrites? R. A. Schmitt and others. bibliog Science 153:644-7 Ag 5 '66
Cohenite in meteorites: a proposed origin. R. Brett. bibliog il Science 153:60-2 Jl 1 '66
Dislocations in a Campo del Cielo meteorite. K. H. G. Ashbee and L. F. Vassamillet. il Science 151:1526-7 Mr 25 '66
Distribution of uranium in some natural minerals. E. I. Hamilton. bibliog il Science 151:570-2 F 4 '66
Djerfisherite, alkali copper-iron sulfide: a new mineral from enstatite chondrites. L. H. Fuchs. bibliog il Science 153:166-7 Jl 8 '66
Electrolytic dissolution of iron meteorites. S. L. Tackett and others. bibliog il Science 153:877-80 Ag 19 '66
Fallen Christmas star; Barwell meteorite. Sci Am 215:109 S '66
Iron meteorites with low cosmic ray exposure ages. J. C. Cobb. bibliog il Science 151:1524 Mr 25 '66
Meteorite found in western Australia; octahedrite meteorite of nickel-iron alloy. Sci N 90:513 D 17 '66
Meteorites: optical activity in organic matter. W. G. Meinschein and others. bibliog il Science 154:377-80 O 21 '66
Organic compounds in carbonaceous chondrites. M. H. Studier and others; discussion. Science 152:102-7 Ap 1 '66
Shock-lithification of unconsolidated rock materials. N. M. Short. bibliog il Science 154:382-4 O 21 '66
Shock metamorphism of natural materials. B. M. French. Science 153:903-6 Ag 19 '66
Tracks of charged particles in meteorites. G. S. Mumford. il Sky & Tel 31:144 Mr '66
Weighing micrometeorites. il Sky & Tel 32:207 O '66
X-ray diffraction study of minerals from shocked iron meteorites. M. E. Lipschutz and R. R. Jaeger. bibliog il Science 152:1055-7 My 20 '66
Young iron meteorites found by radioactivity. Sci N 89:245 Ap 9 '66
See also
Chondrules
Meteors

METEORITIC diamonds. See Diamonds
METEOROIDS. See Meteors
METEOROLOGICAL buoys. See Oceanographic buoys
METEOROLOGICAL optics
See also
Airglow
METEOROLOGICAL research
Dust devils produced. il Sci N 90:234 S 24 '66
Peaceful uses of the earth's atmosphere. W. O. Roberts. Science 152:159 Ap 8 '66; Correction. 153:575-6 Ag 5 '66
Weather on a lab bench. A. Ewing. il Sci N 90:535 D 24 '66
See also
Artificial satellites—Meteorological applications
Rain making
Weather control
Weather research
World meteorological organization
METEOROLOGICAL stations
Nimbus B package is designed to talk to weather stations. il Tech W 19:42+ Ag 15 '66
METEOROLOGY
See also
Balloons, Meteorological
Climate
Computers—Meteorological applications
Lightning
Radar meteorology
Rain and rainfall
Sun and meteorology
Tornadoes

Trade winds
Weather
Weather forecasts
Winds
World meteorological organization

International cooperation
Joint global research project described; global atmospheric research program or global meteorological experiment. W. S. Beller. Tech W 20:16 Ja 2 '67

METEOROLOGY, Aeronautic
Fine art of forecasting. F. C. Bates. Flying 79:50-1 Ag '66
More flying weather signposts. H. T. Harrison. il Flying 78:73-5 Mr; 78:79-81 Ap '66
Solid-state air-data computer developed. B. Miller. il Aviation W 85:96-7+ N 14 '66
Temperature can clip SST range. Aviation W 84:41+ My 2 '66
Things upstairs. F. C. Bates. il Flying 79:52-4 Jl '66
Weather check. R. B. Parke. il Flying 79:32 Jl '66
See also
Radar meteorology
METEOROLOGY, Agricultural
Food crisis heals slowly; technical improvements suggested at symposium on agroclimatology. Sci N 90:250 O 1 '66
METEORS
Do comets really break down to produce meteor showers? T. D. Nicholson. il Natur Hist 75:50-2 D '66
First major Leonid shower since 1932 may occur this month. T. D. Nicholson. il Natur Hist 75:42-5 N '66
Good Leonid year? Sky & Tel 32:251 N '66
Great Lakes fireball. il Sky & Tel 31:78-9+ F '66
Great Leonid meteor shower of 1966. il Sky & Tel 33:4-10 Ja '67
Intruder from the Cosmos: Maine to North Carolina, trail. il Newsweek 67:90 My 9 '66
Leonids fulfill promise. il Sci N 90:453 N 26 '66
Lost comet showers sky; Leonid meteor shower. Sci N 89:459 Je 11 '66
Many observers watch summer meteors. il Sky & Tel 32:233-6 O '66
Meteor in full view; northeastern U.S. sighting. il Life 60:42-3 My 6 '66
November showers; Leonid showers. il Time 88:118+ N 18 '66
Observations of three meteor showers. L. J. Robinson. il Sky & Tel 31:112-15 F '66
Splendid April 25th fireball. il Sky & Tel 31:324-6 Je '66
Stars fell on Arizona; Leonid meteor shower. il Time 88:71 N 25 '66
These spacecraft say ouch! W. von Braun. il Pop Sci 189:76-7+ Jl '66
To catch a falling star; Leonid shower. il Sci N 90:495 D 10 '66
Venus flytrap rocket to collect space dust; air force to study Leonid meteor shower. Sci N 90:401 N 12 '66
METERS
See also
Electric meters
Exposure meters
Radiometers
METHADONE
No way out? drugs and therapeutic community programs. il Newsweek 68:77-8 O 10 '66
Stoned on methadone; disagreement over Dole-Nyswander treatment; with excerpts from interview with Synanon staff. L. Yablonsky. New Repub 155:14-16 Ag 13 '66; Discussion. 155:28-9 S 3; 37-8 S 17 '66
METHANE
High-temperature synthesis of aromatic hydrocarbons from methane. J. Oró and J. Han. bibliog il Science 153:1393-5 S 16 '66
Liquid methane may be suitable fuel for SST. Sci N 89:515 Je 25 '66
METHANOL
Dogs produce methanol. Sci N 89:286 Ap 23 '66
METHIONINE
Formylmethionine codon AUG as an initiator of polypeptide synthesis. R. E. Thach and others. bibliog il Science 153:416-18 Jl 22 '66
METHISAZONE. See Methyl isatin
METHODIST church
COSMOS in conference. J. R. Nelson. Christian Cent 83:1433-5 N 23 '66
Methodist women in quadrennial assembly. B. Thompson. Christian Cent 83:784-6 Je 15 '66

METHODIST church—*Continued*
  S.D.S. camps on the old campground; North
    Iowa Methodist annual conference. P. B.
    Mather. Christian Cent 83:1251-2 O 12 '66
  United Methodist church: critique and pro-
    posal. P. M. Minus, jr. and A. C. Core.
    Christian Cent 83:174-5+ F 9 '66

Board of missions
  What would John Wesley do about it? Union
    theological students vs. Methodist church's
    board of missions. Christian Cent 83:1264
    O 19 '66; Reply. D. W. Hornbeck and
    others. 83:1506-7 D 7 '66

Missions
  Definition attempted. B. Thompson. Christian
    Cent 83:214-16 F 16 '66
METHODIST church discipline. See Church dis-
  cipline
METHODIST church in Latin America
  Methodists and evangelism in Latin Amer-
    ica; report of consultation in Cochabamba,
    Bolivia. J. Bishop. Christian Cent 83:1059-
    61 Ag 31 '66
METHODIST church in Mexico
  Mexico's Methodists. A. Zambrano. Chris-
    tian Cent 83:1488 N 30 '66
METHODIST church in the United States
  E.U.B.-Methodist merger. M. Frakes. Chris-
    tian Cent 83:1432-3 N 23 '66
  Forever beginning; anniversary gathering.
    Time 87:76 My 6 '66
  Merging Methodists. Time 88:82 N 18 '66
  Methodists and the urban scene; fourth
    quadrennial convocation on urban life.
    A. P. Klausler. Christian Cent 83:348-50
    Mr 16 '66
  Motive for Methodists; monthly journal pub-
    lished for college students. il Newsweek
    67:60+ F 14 '66
METHODIST world conference
  Whither world Methodism? A. R. George.
    Christian Cent 83:1154+ S 21 '66
METHOTREXATE
  Autoradiography with tritiated methotrexate
    and the cellular distribution of folate
    reductase. Z. Darzynkiewicz and others.
    bibliog il Science 151:1528-30 Mr 25 '66
METHVIN, Eugene H.
  Extremism: danger to our schools; address,
    June 30, 1966. Vital Speeches 32:694-700 S 1
    '66
  Labor's new weapon for democracy. Read
    Digest 89:21-2+ O '66
  Let's have justice for non-criminals, too!
    Read Digest 89:53-60 D '66
METHYL iodide
  Electron paramagnetic resonance of methyl
    radicals on porous glass surface. M. Fuji-
    moto and others. bibliog il Science 154:381-2
    O 21 '66
METHYL isatin
  Adenovirus multiplication: inhibition by
    methisazone. D. J. Bauer and K. Apostolov.
    bibliog il Science 154:796-7 N 11 '66
METHYL radicals. See Radicals (chemistry)
METHYL sulfoxide
  Bringing back DMSO. Newsweek 69:48 Ja 9
    '67
  Dimethyl sulfoxide: lens changes in dogs
    during oral administration. L. F. Rubin
    and P. A. Mattis. il Science 153:83-5 Jl 1
    '66; Reply. L. J. Sacks. 154:543 O 28 '66
  Dimethyl sulfoxide; report on international
    conference. C. D. Leake. Science 152:1646-9
    Je 17 '66; Discussion. Science 153:576 Ag
    5 '66
  Razz-ma-tazz in the drug industry; lessons
    of the DMSO case. R. G. Sherrill. il Nation
    202:425-7 Ap 11 '66; Reply with rejoinder.
    J. H. Brown. 202:666+ Je 6 '66
METHYLACETYLENE propadiene
  Dow puts the heat on fuel gas; new product
    called MAPP. il Bsns W p92+ N 5 '66
METHYLAZOXYMETHANOL. See Cycasin
METHYLENE compounds
  Methylene-C[14]-dioxyphenyl compounds: metab-
    olism in relation to their synergistic action.
    J. E. Casida and others. bibliog il Science
    153:1130-3 S 2 '66
METHYLENEDIOXYPHENYL compounds. See
  Methylene compounds
METHYLGUANINE. See Guanine
METHYSERGIDE
  Headache drug harmful; possible relation-
    ship of Sansert to fibrosis. Sci N L 89:147
    Mr 5 '66
METRA International (firm) See Business con-
  sultants
METREVELI, Alexander
  Russian serves a warning. R. Ress. por
    Sports Illus 24:30+ Je 13 '66

METRIC system
  Big change to metric. il Sci N L 89:74-5 Ja
    29 '66
  House rules committee kills metric system
    study. Sci N 90:180 S 10 '66
  Why inches and ounces now are fighting
    words; pro and con discussion. D. V. Frost;
    J. A. MacLean, jr. il Nations Bsns 54:
    86-90 Ja '66
METRO air service
  American adds to New York taxi links.
    W. Wright. il Aviation W 84:50-1+ Mr 28
    '66
METRO Goldwyn Mayer pictures
  O'Brien of MGM: view from the 28th floor.
    H. Alpert. il Sat R 49:17-19+ D 24 '66
METROPOLITAN areas
  Blight or a noble city? I. McHarg. il Audu-
    bon Mag 68:47-52 Ja '66
  Earnings and hours in southern metropoli-
    tan areas, June 1965. A. Bauman. il Mo
    Labor R 89:984-9 S '66
  Great Lakes megalopolis. Sci Am 215:46+ O
    '66
  New designs for megalopolis. W. Buehr. il
    Horizon 8:56-65 Aut '66
  Poverty areas of our major cities. J. R.
    Wetzel and S. S. Holland. il Mo Labor R
    89:1105-10 O '66
  Problem of metropolis. D. J. Curran; reply.
    W. C. Kessel. America 114:183-4 F 5 '66
    See also
  Urban renewal

Anecdotes, facetiae, satire, etc.
  Grateful society: an urban fable. W. Owen.
    Arch Forum 125:92 O '66
METROPOLITAN club. See Washington, D.C.—
  Clubs
METROPOLITAN museum of art, New York
  Happening at the Met; possibility of T.
    Hoving as new director. il Time 88:46 D 23
    '66
  Metropolitan's man: T. Hoving. il Newsweek
    68:46 D 26 '66
  Rare bronze; purchase in London. Hobbies
    71:96+ S '66
  S.R.O. at Mr Hoving's Met. R. Lynes. il
    N Y Times Mag p8-11+ Ja 1 '67
  Treasury of ancient China; new gallery. il
    Time 87:79 F 4 '66
  Two hundred years of water color painting
    in America; preview of an exhibition. S. P.
    Feld. il Antiques 90:840-5 D '66
  What home for the temple? question of
    moving the Temple of Dendur to the Unit-
    ed States. K. Kuh. il Sat R 49:56-7 N 26
    '66

Junior museum
  Movers and Shakers. R. Lynes. il Harper
    233:33-4+ D '66
METROPOLITAN national company. See Me-
  tropolitan opera national company
METROPOLITAN opera association
  Front and center; relocating subscribers in
    Lincoln Center. Q. Eaton. Opera N 30:
    6-7 Je 4 '66
  Music to my ears; concerts in Lewisohn
    stadium. I. Kolodin. Sat R 49:48 Jl 16 '66
    See also
  Central opera service

Finance
  Open letter to guild members. A. A. Bliss.
    Opera N 31:7 D 10 '66
METROPOLITAN opera auditions. See Singing
  —Competitions
METROPOLITAN opera ballet
  Ballet's night. F. Stevenson. il Opera N 30:
    14-15 Mr 26 '66
  Evening of Tudor at the Met. I. Kolodin.
    Sat R 49:28 Ap 9 '66
  I have a turntable; first three new produc-
    tions. D. Hering. il Dance Mag 40:29-31 D
    '66
  Metropolitan opera ballet evening. Metro-
    politan opera house. M. Marks. Dance Mag
    40:35+ My '66
  Metropolitan opera ballet. Lewisohn stadium.
    D. Hering. Dance Mag 40:78+ S '66
  Musical events; performance in the Metropol-
    itan opera house. W. Sargeant. New Yorker
    42:161 Ap 9 '66
METROPOLITAN opera club
  Penguins. il Time 89:67 Ja 6 '67
METROPOLITAN opera company
  At the Met. Mehta, Tucci, Tebaldi, Caballe.
    C. L. Osborne. il Hi Fi 16:122-3+ Mr '66
  Atlanta's operatic mores; Opera guild lunch-
    eon boycott. Nation 202:701-2 Je 13 '66
  Exploring planet Met. il Time 88:92 S 16 '66
  Great opera houses: the Metropolitan. F.
    Merkling. il Opera N 30:8-13 Ap 16 '66

METROPOLITAN opera company—*Continued*
Is there a soprano in the house? or, Who's on Jordan tonight? H. Butler. il Harper 233:77-81 Ag '66
Lively arts. Sr Schol 89:26-7 S 16 '66
Lord of the manor. il Time 88:46-54+ S 23 '66; Same abr. with title Mr Bing calls the tune. Read Digest 89:130-4 D '66
Met: Giovanni, Chénier return. C. L. Osborne. il Hi Fi 16:142-3+ Ap '66
Met sets the stage for opening night. il Bsns W p 142-4+ Ag 20 '66
Met worth waiting for. G. Movshon. il Hi Fi 16:126-7 F '66
Metropolitan calendar. See issues of Opera news published during opera season
Metropolitan opera, 1883-1966, by I. Kolodin. Review
Sat R 49:31 D 17 '66. M. Davenport
Metropolitan opera 1966-67: repertory and roster. Opera N 31:42+ S 17 '66
Metropolitan opera spring tour casts. Opera N 30:inside back cover Mr 26 '66
Musical events; comparison with New York city opera. New Yorker 42:236-7 O 22 '66
Musical events; R. Bing in his sixteenth year as general manager. W. Sargeant. New Yorker 42:76+ Je 4 '66
New house. F. Stevenson. il Opera N 31:20-1 N 5 '66
New Met. L. Lerman. il Mlle 63:178-80+ My '66
New Met and its old master. il Newsweek 68:70-9 S 19 '66
New voices old house. R. Kotlowitz. Harper 232:126-7 Ap '66
Night the old Met died; program. I. Kolodin. Sat R 49:48+ Ap 30 '66
On the midway at Lincoln Center. R. Kolowitz. il Harper 233:136-7 D '66
Paris blues; Paris visit. il Newsweek 67:104 Je 13 '66
Peep show; performance of Barber of Seville at the Odéon theater, Paris. Time 87:69 Je 10 '66
Price's Ballo, Grist and Lorengar debuts. M. Mayer. il Hi Fi 16:134+ My '66
Profiles; R. Bing. J. Wechsberg. New Yorker 42:65-6+ S 17 '66
Sold-out castle; miscalculation in budgeting. Time 88:63 N 18 '66
Tannhäuser, Parsifal, and a cloud of promises. G. Movshon. il Hi Fi 16:113+ Je '66
With honor and insolence: Gounod's Faust; tr. by J. Gutman. J. L. Barrault. Opera N 30:17 Ap 9 '66
See also
Radio broadcasting—Music
METROPOLITAN opera guild
Gift of enthusiam; Eleanor Robson Belmont fund for student performances. R. A. Tuggle. il Opera N 30:12-13 Mr 5 '66
Preview; working rehearsal for supporting members. N. Ross. il Opera N 30:26-8 Mr 12 '66
METROPOLITAN opera house, New York
After eighty-three years the queen is dead, long live the queen; with report by T. Prideaux. il Life 60:24-33 Ap 29 '66
Finale; gala farewell benefit. il Newsweek 67:84-5 Ap 25 '66
Fond farewell to a great old lady, that beloved house, the Metropolitan opera. G. L. Mayer. il Am Rec G 32:764-5+ My '66
Gala farewell; April 16, 1966. il Opera N 30:16-21 My 7 '66
Glad good-bye to the old Met. H. Butler. il Look 30:41-2+ Ap 19 '66
Great opera houses: the Metropolitan. F. Merkling il Opera N 30:8-13 Ap 16 '66
Her tattered emblem. Nat R 18:399-400 My 3 '66
Is the old Met expendable? reprint from the Nation, January 13, 1964. il Arch Forum 125:82 N '66
Last days of the old lady; souvenir hunters. Time 87:76 Ap 1 '66
Last night at the old Met. il Sat R 49:54-5 My 14 '66
Metropolitan mementos. F. Stevenson. Opera N 30:13 Ap 9 '66
Night the old Met died. I. Kolodin. Sat R 49:48+ Ap 30 '66
Old Met, striking the tent; farewell gala performance. E. Gelatt. il Hi Fi 16:MA10+ Jl '66
They played the Metropolitan; opera house served as concert hall. F. Merkling and others. il Opera N 30:8-13 F 5 '66
See also
Lincoln Center for the performing arts, New York—Opera house
METROPOLITAN opera national company
Its own laurels; progress report. F. Merkling. il Opera N 31:18-19 S 10 '66
Mademoiselle's annual Merit awards, 1965. il Mlle 62:45-9 Ja '66

Metropolitan opera national company tour. Opera N 30:24-5 Ap 16 '66
Music to my ears; Mexico city visit. I. Kolodin. Sat R 49:35-6 Jl 2 '66
Musical events; performance of Britten's Rape of Lucretia. W. Sargeant. New Yorker 42:107 Ja 14 '67
National company takes its stand. C. L. Osborne. il Hi Fi 16:122-5 F '66
Opera hits the road. D. J. Henahan. il Holiday 39:111-14+ My '66
Opera in motion. F. Stevenson. il Dance Mag 40:28-9+ F '66
Reviews; dancing in Cinderella, Carmen, Susannah. J. Maskey; M. Marks. Dance Mag 40:18-20 F '66
METROPOLITAN opera national council
Council champagne; meeting of members. il Opera N 31:13 D 31 '66
METROPOLITAN opera standees. See Audiences
METROPOLITAN reference and research library, incorporated
Metro names officers appoints new director. Pub W 190:309 Ag 29 '66
METROPOLITAN urban service training. See Religious cooperation
METS (baseball) See Baseball clubs
METTLER, Barbara
Improvisation; the most creative approach to dance. por Dance Mag 40:42-5+ Jl '66
METZNER, Ralph
Psychedelic game; excerpt from Psychedelic reader. R. Hoffmann. Mlle 62:179+ Mr '66
MEXCALTITÁN, Mexico
Mexcaltitán, ancient island town. il Sunset 138:34 Ja '67
MEXICAN AMERICANS
Another civil-rights headache; plight of Mexican-Americans; Los Angeles. il U S News 60:46-8 Je 6 '66
Back to Bachimba. E. H. Lopez. il Horizon 9:80-3 Wint '67
Few Spanish-speaking children in high school in Southwest. Sch & Soc 94:376+ N 12 '66
Invisible minority; attitude of schools toward Spanish-speaking pupils. Newsweek 68:46 Ag 29 '66
Mexican-Americans in the Southwest; Mexican-American study project. P. H. McNamara. America 114:352-4 Mr 12 '66
Mexican-Americans: new wind from the Southwest. J. W. Moore and R. Guzman. il Nation 202:645-8 My 30 '66
Minority groups in California. il Mo Labor R 89:978-83 S '66
School bias toward Mexican Americans. Sch & Soc 94:378+ N 12 '66
MEXICAN cookery. See Cookery, Mexican
MEXICAN dancing. See Dancing, Mexican
MEXICAN embroidery. See Embroidery
MEXICAN war, 1845-1848. See United States—History—War with Mexico, 1845-1848
MEXICANS
Unsentimental report from Mexico. A. Auldecambe. Harper 232:80-4 Mr '66
MEXICANS in the United States
See also
Mexican Americans
MEXICO. D. D. Brand. bibliog il Focus 16:1-6 Je '66
Unsentimental report from Mexico. A. Auldecambe. Harper 232:80-4 Mr '66
See also
Agriculture—Mexico
Architecture—Mexico
Architecture, Domestic—Mexico
Birth rate—Mexico
California, Lower
Chihuahuan Desert
Colleges and universities—Mexico
Communism—Mexico
Cupatitzio River
Food supply—Mexico
Guadalajara
Horse Tail Falls
Hunting—Mexico
Mexcaltitán
Opium trade—Mexico
Railroads—Mexico
San Quintin, Mexico
Sports—Mexico
Trials—Mexico
Zihuatanejo

Antiquities
See Indians of Mexico—Antiquities

Commerce
Mexico taps a fat U.S. food market. il Bsns W p 104-6+ Mr 19 '66

MEXICO—*Continued*

Description and travel

Better homes and gardens tour: Mexico. il Bet Hom & Gard 45:29 Ja '67

Gone flying to Mexico. R. Mock. il Flying 78:46-51 Ap '66

Let's travel: briefing. il Mlle 62:233-43 Ap '66

Mexico's railroad in the sky; Ferrocarril Chihuahua al Pacifico. G. S. Wells. il McCalls 93:29-30+ F '66

Of lost days on a river; Mexico's Usumacinta River. C. Phinizy. il Sports Illus 24:62-4+ Mr 28 '66

Travel notes; Cantinflas' recommendations. R. Joseph. Esquire 66:18+ N '66

Traveler, consider my Mexico; ed. by R. Joseph. Cantinflas. il Esquire 66:144-5+ N '66

Travel's picture portfolio. Travel 125:50-5 Je '66

West coast of Mexico. B. Schulberg. il Holiday 39:46-59+ Ap '66

Discovery and exploration

Was America the wonderful land of Fusang? R. Larson. il Am Heritage 17:42-5+ Ap '66

Economic conditions

Mexico's economy: a new stage. D. S. Brothers. Cur Hist 51:344-8+ D '66

Our debts to Mexico. H. E. Fey. Christian Cent 83:1594-5 D 28 '66

Economic policy

See also
American property in Mexico

Expropriation policy

What Mexicanization means; expropriation of U.S. companies. Bsns W p 118 N 26 '66

Foreign relations

United States

Chain of common interest uniting the United States and Mexico; remarks, February 10 1966. D. Rusk. Dept State Bul 54:365-7 Mr 7 '66

History

Conquest, 1519-1540

Hernán Cortez and the Mexican Iliad. E. Ardura. il Américas 18:23-31 Ag '66

Spanish colony, 1540-1810

Century after Cortes, by F. Benitez. Review
Nation 203:287-8 S 26 '66. G. K. Lewis

Industries

See also
Food industry and trade

Religious institutions and affairs

World around us (cont of) News of the Christian world. Christian Cent 83:1190 S 28 '66

See also
Catholic church in Mexico
Methodist church in Mexico

Social conditions

Under the lid in Mexico: makings of an explosion. il U S News 60:50-1 My 2 '66

MEXICO (city)

City sinking in a sea of mud. R. S. Strother. il Read Digest 89:99-103 Ag '66

Description

Travel notes; Cantinflas' recommendations. R. Joseph. Esquire 66:18+ N '66

Traveler, consider my Mexico; ed. by R. Joseph. Cantinflas. il Esquire 66:145-6+ N '66

Description and travel

High life in Mexico city. B. Keating. il Holiday 39:58-63+ Je '66

Galleries and museums

Diego Rivera's gift to Mexico: Diego Rivera museum. Sunset 137:40 D '66

Mexico museum with sea-shells; Museum of anthropology. A. G. Melvin. il Hobbies 71:130+ Ja '67

Music

Mexico. L. Frick. Opera N 31:27 N 5 '66

Mexico city. L. Frick. Opera N 30:27 My 7; 31:27 N 19 '66

Theater

Mexico's strolling players; teatro Trashumante [Nomadic theater] J. Linde. il Américas 18:34-7 N '66

MEXICO, GULF OF

To Florida via the Gulf. J. L. Naumann. il Yachting 120:52-4+ D '66

See also
Fishing—Mexico, Gulf of

MEXICO and the United States

Challenge of the Americas; address, April 15, 1966. L. B. Johnson. Vital Speeches 32:418-20 My 1 '66; Same with title Address at dedication of Abraham Lincoln statue. Dept State Bul 54:727-31 My 9 '66

Chamizal highway to symbolize U.S.-Mexican friendship; statement, November 8, 1966. L. B. Johnson. Dept State Bul 55:882 D 12 '66

President Johnson visits Mexico to inspect Amistad Dam; statement, November 29; remarks, December 3; with text of joint statement, December 3, 1966. L. B. Johnson. Dept State Bul 56:12-13 Ja 2 '67

U.S., Mexico to join in solving Rio Grande salinity problem; statement, with text of telegram to President G. Diaz Ordaz, September 19, 1966. L. B. Johnson. Dept State Bul 55:686-7 O 31 '66

MEXICO city's stock exchange. See Stock exchange—Mexico (city)

MEYER, Alfred
Basil Ede's birds in a New York gallery. Natur Hist 75:32-41 D '66

MEYER, Carolyn
Villa vacations. House & Gard 129:72+ My '66

MEYER, Charles R.
How to install a fuel tank in your boat. Pop Sci 188:180-2 Ap '66

MEYER, Daniel
Build the ultrasonic omni-alarm. Pop Electr 24:41-5+ Ap '66

Reverb for your car. Pop Electr 24:50-3+ F '66

MEYER, Frank S.
Principles and heresies. See issues of National review

MEYER, Herbert M.
Beginning of the commonsense. Bul Atomic Sci 22:23-5 F '66

MEYER, Jane
Russell gallery at Great Falls. Am Artist 30:26-9+ N '66

MEYER, June
Opinion: on Negro aims. por Mlle 62:84+ Ap '66

Sons & mothers: the Harlem six. Nation 202:496-8 Ap 25 '66

MEYER, Karl. See Bhavanandan, V. P. jt. auth.

MEYER, Karl E.
English press: nasty, obsolete, the best in the world. Esquire 66:56-7+ Jl '66

MEYER, Sylvan
Georgia happening. Nation 203:640-4 D 12 '66

MEYER zoysia. See Grasses

MEYERHOFF, Erich
Medical powder keg. Library J 91:3355-9 Jl '66

MEYERKORD, Harold Dale
Water war in Viet Nam. G. L. Chapelle. il Nat Geog Mag 129:272-96 F '66

MEYERS, Edward
Meyers on technique. por Mod Phot 30:40 S; 50 O; 34 N; 18+ D '66

MEYERS, Frederic
Seniority as security: a rationale. Mo Labor R 89:127-8 F '66

MEYERS, Harold B.
FCC's expanding, demanding universe. Fortune 73:150-3 Je '66

It's time to turn the farmers loose. Fortune 74:140-5+ D '66

Paradoxical predicament of John Connor. Fortune 73:150-2+ F '66

MEYERS, Judith P.
What is a book? Sch Arts 65:34-7 Ja '66

MEYERS, Marina P.
STS alumni speak. Sci N 89:180+ Mr 19 '66

MEYERS, William
Doorbells: politics of activism. Nation 202:581-3 My 16 '66

MEYNELL, Sir Francis
Sir Francis Meynell lectures in New York; summaries of addresses; ed. by P. A. Bennett. por Pub W 189:86-9+ Ap 4 '66

MEZEY, Robert
Five poets. A. Freeman. Poetry 109:193 D '66

MIAMI, Fla.
Cubans in Miami. B. O. Walsh. America 114:286-9 F 26 '66

Airports

Miami congestion problem spurs dispute. G. Alexander. il Aviation W 85:54-5+ D 12 '66

Labor and laboring classes

Quick check; Miami employees and police checks. Nation 202:413 Ap 11 '66

MIAMI, Fla.—*Continued*

Music

Miami; Miami opera guild's 1966-67 family operas. D. Reno. Opera N 31:28 D 31 '66
Miami; production of Aida. G. Fitzgerald. il Opera N 30:30 Mr 19 '66
Miami; production of La Bohème. D. Reno. Opera N 30:31 Mr 12 '66

Newspapers

Biting the handout they feed you; Florida business leader treats handouts as ad-insertion orders. Time 88:41 Ag 19 '66
Pooling in Miami. Newsweek 68:54 Ag 8 '66
See also
Miami news
Newspapers—Consolidations and mergers

Parks and playgrounds

Project; a living community park. A. Hurwitz. il Sch Arts 65:17-19 Ap '66
MIAMI-Bahamas race. See Motor boat racing
MIAMI BEACH, Fla.

Description

Horsing around Miami. D. Messinesi. Vogue 149:154 Ja 1 '67
Miami Beach: swinging in the city of illusion. L. H. Lapham. il Sat Eve Post 239:25-33 F 26 '66

Hotels, restaurants, etc.

Miami Beach: swinging in the city of illusion. L. H. Lapham. il Sat Eve Post 239:25-33 F 26 '66
MIAMI COUNTY, Ohio
No painting required. il Am City 81:47 F '66
MIAMI Dolphins (football club) See Football clubs
MIAMI international airport. See Miami, Fla.—Airports
MIAMI-Nassau race. See Motor boat racing
MIAMI news
Miami news photogs shoot it long & wide... il U S Camera 29:64-7 S '66
MIAMI to Key West race. See Motor boat racing
MIAO, Chen-pai
First-hand report on red China today; interview. por U S News 61:58-61 N 7 '66
MICA
Polarized beauty. W. Patnode. il Natur H'st 75:24-5 Ap '66
MICE
Mice thrive in high gravity. il Sci N 89:237 Ap 9 '66
Of mice and men; study of diabetic mice. Newsweek 68:93 S 12 '66
See also
Pocket mice
MICE, White footed
Search for the golden mouse. J. K. Terres. il Audubon Mag 68:96-101 Mr '66
MICHAEL, Bernard, and Weinstein, Emanuel
Working one's way through tomorrow. pors Am Ed 2:29-32 D '65
MICHAEL, Charles R.
Receptive fields of directionally selective units in the optic nerve of the ground squirrel. bibliog Science 152:1092-5 My 20 '66
Receptive fields of opponent color units in the optic nerve of the ground squirrel. bibliog Science 152:1095-7 My 20 '66
MICHAEL, Franz
Communist China, Vietnam and United States policy. Nat R 18:523-6 My 31 '66
MICHAEL, Harold L.
Safety myths that mess up your driving. J. F. Pearson. il Pop Mech 126:93-7 N '66
MICHAEL, Lloyd
Catholic education examined. Sr Schol 89:sup20-1 D 9 '66
MICHAEL, Sister Marie. See Marie Michael, Sister
MICHAEL, Sister M. See M. Michael, Sister
MICHAEL, William H. Jr, and others
Lunar Orbiter: tracking data indicate properties of moon's gravitational field. Science 153:1102 S 2 '66
MICHAELIAN, Al
Autorandom. See issues of Motor trend
MICHAELIS, Arnold
(ed) See Gandhi, I. N. Interview with Indira Gandhi
(ed) See Stevenson, A. E. Adlai Stevenson: letters from his mother; his reactions
MICHALIK, A. S.
Balance plows and routes. Am City 81:110-11 S '66
MICHAUX, Lewis
Professor; interview. New Yorker 42:28-9 S 3 '66

MICHEL, Joan Hess
Art of Eugene Karlin. Am Artist 30:50-4+ Mr '66
Leonard Everett Fisher: illustrator & painter. Am Artist 30:42-7+ S '66
MICHELANGELI, Arturo Benedetti
Music to my ears; recital in Carnegie Hall. I. Kolodin. Sat R 49:34 F 5 '66
MICHELANGELO Buonarroti
Michelangelo tondo; treasure of Royal academy of arts. J. Stuart. il Antiques 90:36 Jl '66
MICHELE, Iris
I tried LSD. Ladies Home J 83:52+ Ag '66
MICHELIN guide. See Guidebooks
MICHELSON, Peter
Apology for pornography. New Repub 155:21-4 D 10 '66
MICHELSON stellar interferometers. See Interferometers
MICHENER, James Albert
Don't knock the rock. Read Digest 88:157-60+ F '66
Four miracles, and a masterpiece. Read Digest 89:158-65 N '66

about

Hawaii. J. Poppy. il Look 30:48-55 S 6 '66
People are talking about... por Vogue 148:180-1 N 1 '66
MICHENER, Martin C. and Walcott, Charles
Navigation of single homing pigeons: airplane observations by radio tracking. bibliog Science 154:410-13 O 21 '66
MICHIE company
Magnetic tape unit helps law publisher meet growth problem. W. O. Lewis and A. G. Colley, jr. il Pub W 189:24-5 Ap 4 '66
MICHIGAN
See also
Art—Michigan
Booksellers and bookselling—Michigan
Education—Michigan
Festivals—Michigan
Fishing—Michigan
Hunting—Michigan

Politics and government

Ballad of the green bow tie; Williams-Cavanagh contest. J. Ter Horst. il Reporter 35:36-8 S 8 '66
Faceless favorite; R. Griffin. il Time 88:25 S 30 '66
New generation. Time 87:20 Mr 25 '66
Ph.D. faces Ph.D. in classic congressional fight; Representative Weston Vivian vs GOP challenger Marvin Esch. il Bsns W p46 O 8 '66
Return of the boy wonder. il Time 88:12 Ag 12 '66
Teaching the mayor; Democratic senatorial primary result. New Repub 155:8 Ag 13 '66
What is a Romney? gubernatorial race. Time 88:33 N 4 '66

Religious institutions and affairs

Church relevant in Michigan. America 115:23-4 Jl 9 '66
MICHIGAN, LAKE
Perfect vacation blend: one Great Lake, four states. S. A. Mix. il Todays Health 44:42-9 Je '66
MICHIGAN national bank of Lansing. See Banks and banking—United States
MICHIGAN Small race. See Airplane racing
MICHIGAN state university of agriculture and applied science, East Lansing
In the Big ten. State wins the numbers game; Michigan state gets into the Western conference. J. Underwood. il Sports Illus 25:67-70 O 17 '66
Michigan state and the CIA: a dilemma for social science. I. L. Horowitz. Bul Atomic Sci 22:26-9 S '66
Rampartisanship; technical assistance program in Saigon indicted by Ramparts magazine. il Newsweek 67:78 Ap 25 '66
Spies beside the red cedar; Ramparts' indictment of MSU expedition to Saigon. R. Kirk. Nat R 18:630 Je 28 '66
With cap & cloak in Saigon. il Time 87:20 Ap 22 '66
MICHIGAN. University, Ann Arbor
Autumn on the campus. H. Sutton. il Sat R 49:48-9 N 5; 77-8+ N 12 '66
Law, speech and disobedience; sit-in case and trespass law. C. Cohen. il Nation 202:357-62 Mr 28 '66
2-S, too smart to fight? M. Levitas. il N Y Times Mag p27+ Ap 24 '66

MICHIGAN, University, Ann Arbor—*Continued*
Wave of the future; activities of the Short course in the administration of national parks, by University of Michigan and the National park service. G. W. Sharpe and others. il Am For 72:20-1+ F '66
Weak arm of the law; case of E. B. Power. Nation 202:350 Mr 28 '66

Libraries
Growth forces library reorganization; Univ. of Michigan reports on changes. Library J 91:1859 Ap 1 '66
Power resigns from U. of Michigan, cites conflict of interest opinion. Library J 91:2020-1 Ap 15 '66
Wagman blasts Michigan student paper, defends Power against conflict charge; excerpts from letter. F. H. Wagman. Library J 91:2296-7 My 1 '66

Medical center
Death watch in Washtenaw. A. Rothenberg. il Look 30:38-9 Ap 19 '66

School of music
Michigan's harvest. D. A. Sutherland. il Opera N 30:13-15 Mr 19 '66
MICHIKO, crown princess of Japan
Silk tree lullaby. McCalls 93:81 Je '66
MICHNICK, Irwin. See Leigh, M.
MICHOACÁN, Mexico
See also
Paricutín
MICROBES. See Microorganisms
MICROBIOLOGY
New IBM lab will attack variety of space problems. Tech W 20:41 Ja 16 '67
Recording microfluorospectrophotometer. W. J. Runge. bibliog il Science 151:1499-506 Mr 25 '66
See also
Microorganisms
MICROCARDS
How to put two and a half tons of research into one handy little box; service by the Educational research information center. L. G. Burchinal and H. A. Haswell. il Am Ed 2:23-5 F '66
Peril of the librain. H. Downs. il Sci Digest 60:94-6 N '66
MICROCIRCUITS. See Electronic circuits
MICRO-complement fixation. See Complement fixation
MICROCRUSTACEA. See Cladocera
MICROELECTRODES. See Electrodes
MICROELECTRONICS. See Miniature electronic equipment
MICROENCAPSULATION. See Capsules
MICROFILMS
Future of printing in a data-hungry society; summary of address. L. C. Deighton. Pub W 189:55-60 Ja 31 '66
Patents on microfilm seen speeding orders. Sci N 90:57 Jl 23 '66
U.S. patents issued since 1790 to be microfilmed. Pub W 190:78 N 14 '66
See also
Libraries—Microfilm collections
University microfilms, Ann Arbor, Mich.
MICROFLUOROSPECTROPHOTOMETERS. See Spectrophotometers
MICROMETEORITES. See Meteorites
MICROMETEOROIDS. See Meteors
MICROMINIATURIZATION. See Miniature electronic equipment
MICRONESIA
America's paradise lost, by W. Price. Review Nation 202:753-4 Je 20 '66. S. Zoll
See also
Trust Territory of the Pacific Islands
MICRONESIANS
Reporter at large. E. J. Kahn, jr. il New Yorker 42:42-6+ Je 11; 42-4+ Je 18; 56+ Je 25 '66
MICRONYL water filter. See Photography—Apparatus and supplies
MICROORGANISMS
Chlorinated hydrocarbon pesticides: degradation by microbes. C. I. Chacko and others. bibliog il Science 154:893-5 N 18 '66
Life in a drop of water. B. Tufty. il(p 129) Sci N L 89:134+ F 26 '66
Microbes sort metals. Sci N 90:135 Ag 27 '66
One cell protein from oil. Sci N 91:40 Ja 14 '67
Protect the friendly microbes. L. C. Cole. il Sat R 49:46-7 My 7 '66
Some earthly organisms survive heat of space. Sci N 90:89 Ag 6 '66

These creatures are 5 hundred million years old; bacteria revived from Precambrian era. N. Lo Bello. il Sci Digest 61:70-3 Ja '67
See also
American type culture collection
Staphylococci

Culture media
Bacterial growth rate in the sea: direct analysis by thymidine autoradiography; using leucothrix mucor growing epiphytically on pure cultures of marine algae. T. D. Brock. bibliog il Science 155:81-3 Ja 6 '67
MICROORGANISMS, Pathogenic
Antimicrobial specificity of leukocyte lysosomal cationic proteins. H. I. Zeya and J. K. Spitznagel. bibliog il Science 154:1049-51 N 25 '66
Are germs winning the war against people? J. A. Osmundsen. il Look 30:140-1 O 18 '66
Germs leave prints. Sci N 90:34 Jl 16 '66
Life in a drop of water. B. Tufty. il(p 129) Sci N L 89:134+ F 26 '66
New venereal disease; vibrio fetus infections. Time 87:62 F 25 '66
Sialic acid binding sites: role in hemagglutination by mycoplasma gallisepticum. B. Gesner and L. Thomas. bibliog il Science 151:590-1 F 4 '66
Tiny disease forms shaped like teardrops; mycoplasma. Sci N 89:394 My 21 '66
See also
Bacteria, Pathogenic
Leptospira
MICROPALEONTOLOGY
Life forms three billion years old discovered. Sci N 89:395 My 21 '66
Microorganisms three billion years old from the Precambrian of South Africa. E. S. Barghoorn and J. W. Schopf. bibliog il Science 152:758-63 My 6 '66
These creatures are 5 hundred million years old; bacteria revived from Precambrian era. N. Lo Bello. il Sci Digest 61:70-3 Ja '67
MICROPHONES
Get the microphone that's right for you. A. Zuckerman. il Pop Mech 125:196-200+ F '66
Microphones for public address. P. K. Franklin. il Electr World 75:50-2+ Je '66
Put a $9 wireless FM mike in your cigaret case. il Pop Mech 126:164-6 Jl '66
Sound advice. W. J. Weaver. Mod Phot 30:30 Jl '66
Sound advice; variable long distance mike to add sound to slides or movies. R. Flanzraich. il Mod Phot 30:44+ D '66
Wireless microphones. il Electr World 75:38 Je '66
MICROPHONES in criminal investigation, espionage, etc. See Electronics in criminal investigation, espionage, etc.
MICROPHOTOGRAPHY
Sears catalogue in postcard size? National cash register company's micro reproduction technique. Bsns W p48 D 3 '66
See also
Microfilms
MICROPRINTING of books. See Books—Photographic reproduction and projection
MICROPUBLICATIONS international (firm)
Gordon and Breach forms new publishing subsidiary; entry into microfiche field. Pub W 191:37 Ja 9 '67
MICROSCOPE and microscopy
Holomicrography: transformation of image during reconstruction a posteriori. G. W. Ellis. bibliog il Science 154:1195-7 D 2 '66
Low-cost microscopes. il Consumer Rep 31:317-19 D '66
Low-priced microscopes. il Consumer Rep 31:552-5 N '66
Nature and the microscope (cont) J. D. Corrington. il Natur Hist 75:59-63 My '66
New miscroscope based on astronomers' method. Sci N 90:72 Jl 30 '66
See also
Electron microscope and microscopy
Microscopy, Medical
Photomicrography
MICROSCOPIC slides
Nature and the microscope; mounting diatom slides. J. D. Corrington. il Natur Hist 75:59-63 My '66
MICROSCOPY, Medical
Microscope reduces risks in neurosurgery. Sci N 90:166 S 3 '66
MICROSOMES
Ethylene formation in rat liver microsomes. M. Lieberman and P. Hochstein. bibliog il Science 152:213-14 Ap 8 '66
MICROTUBULES. See Cells; Plant cells and tissues
MICROVISION. See Radio in aviation

MICROWAVE radiometers. See Radiometers
MICROWAVES
Microwave for data transmission. J. L. Jatlow. Duns R 88:pt2 150 S '66
Microwave ultrasonics. E. H. Jacobsen. bibliog il Science 151:1179–87 Mr 11 '66; Reply. T. A. Anderson. 152:1011 My 20 '66
Radiometry programs examine new uses. B. Miller. il Aviation W 85:71–2+ Jl 11 '66
Solid-state source of microwaves. R. Bowers. il Sci Am 215:22–31 Ag '66
MICTURITION reflex. See Reflexes
MID-AIR refueling of helicopters. See Helicopters—Refueling
MID-ATLANTIC ridge. See Ocean bottom
MIDDENS (archeology) See Excavations (archeology)
MIDDLE age
Command generation. il Time 88:50–4 Jl 29 '66; Same abr. with title Middle age: the command generation. Read Digest 89:201–4 O '66
Over the hill at forty? nonsense! say these experts; findings of UCLA specialists. Todays Health 45:3–4 Ja '67
MIDDLE ages
See also
Art, Medieval
Manuscripts, Medieval

History
Military origins of medieval representation. T. N. Bisson. bibliog f Am Hist R 71:1199–218 Jl '66

Bibliography
Articles and other books received; comp. by B. J. Holm. See issues of American historical review
MIDDLE AMERICA. See Central America
MIDDLE classes
Middle class in western Europe, 1815–1848. L. O'Boyle. bibliog f Am Hist R 71:826–45 Ap '66
Middlingness, by V. E. Starzinger. Review
Nat R 18:369 Ap 19 '66. R. Kirk
Mr White and Mr Blue; notes on the new middle class; excerpts from The great leap: from the old world of 1939 to the new era. J. Brooks. il Harper 232:88–91+ Je '66; Reply. A. B. Bridges. 233:6 Ag '66
Negro middle class is right in the middle. D. Cordtz. il Fortune 74:174–80+ N '66
MIDDLE ear. See Ear
MIDDLE EAST
See also
Architecture—Middle East
Armenia
Economic assistance in the Middle East
Petroleum—Middle East
Petroleum industry and trade—Middle East
Saudi Arabia

Defenses
Arab handicrafts; new arms race. New Repub 154:7 F 12 '66
Arming the Middle East. P. Seale; I. Beeson; P. Ben. New Repub 154:12–14 Je 4 '66
Atlantic report: Middle East arms race. Atlan 218:38+ S '66
Balance of weaponry; U.S. and Soviet arms sales of Israelis and Arabs. Time 87:39 F 25 '66
Pandora's ammunition box; U.S. policies. J. A. Morris, jr. il Nation 203:109–12 Ag 8 '66
Plutonium keg; danger of war in the Middle East steadily increasing. Nation 202:170 F 14 '66

Description and travel
Abraham, the friend of God. K. MacLeish. il Nat Geog Mag 130:739–89 D '66

Economic policy
Development and diplomacy in the Middle East; adaptation of address. J. S. Badeau. Bul Atomic Sci 22:5–10 My '66

History
Israel before Christ. H. D. Hummel. Christian Cent 83:868 Jl 6 '66

Bibliography
Articles and other books received; comp. by S. Glazer. See issues of American historical review

Maps
Map of the Middle East (cont) Sr Schol 89:pt2 15 S 23 '66

Politics
Arab and Jew. il Newsweek 68:44 D 19 '66
Arab boycott. Newsweek 68:88+ D 5 '66

Arming the Middle East. P. Seale; I. Beeson; P. Ben. New Repub 154:12–14 Je 4 '66
As tensions mount in the Middle East. il U S News 61:6 D 12 '66
Boomerang boycott; Arab world's boycott of Israel and foreign companies that do more than just sell finished goods to Israel. il Time 88:93–4 D 2 '66
Call to Mecca; Feisal's projected Islamic summit meeting. il Time 88:45 S 30 '66
Everybody loses. Newsweek 68:42+ D 5 '66
Flare-up in Mideast: another danger spot. J. Law. il U S News 61:50 D 19 '66
For the Arabs Israel does not exist. A. Carthew. il N Y Times Mag p30–1+ D 18 '66; Reply. M. Arnon. p37 Ja 8 '67
Gamble on the Jordan. J. A. Morris, jr. il Nation 204:6–8 Ja 2 '67
Highly volatile; state of the Middle East. il Newsweek 68:56 O 24 '66
In Jordan a spunky king again fights to hold on. G. DeCarvalho. il Life 61:50B D 9 '66
Incident at Samu; Israel attack on Jordan rather than Syria. il Time 88:36 N 25 '66
Intramural mayhem. Time 89:31 Ja 13 '67
Israeli army retaliates; raid against Jordanian village of Es Samu. il Sr Schol 89:24 D 9 '66
Massive retaliation; Israeli army units in Jordan. il Newsweek 68:42 N 28 '66
Middle East at the edge. America 115:766–7 D 10 '66
Ready for trouble. Time 88:44 D 9 '66
Rival Arabs. P. Seale and I. Beeson. New Repub 155:11 Ag 27 '66
Rough week. Newsweek 67:46 Ap 25 '66
Second thoughts; fighting on Israel-Jordan border. il Newsweek 68:56+ D 12 '66
Sequel to Samu. Time 88:38+ D 2 '66
Split over summitry. Time 88:26–7 Ag 12 '66
Tension below the surface. Time 88:42 D 16 '66
Thin edge of disaster. Nat R 18:1256–7 D 13 '66
Three kings in accord; Jordan-Saudi Arabia-Iran. Time 87:37 F 4 '66
U Thant's decision. New Repub 155:7–8 D 10 '66
What the Russians are up to in the Middle East; interview, ed. by J. Law. Hussein. il U S News 61:39–42 D 26 '66
Why Israel hit back. L. Muray. New Repub 155:7–8 N 26 '66

Religious institutions and affairs
World around us. Christian Cent 83:1088+ S 7 '66
See also
Orthodox Eastern church in the Near East
MIDDLE EAST airlines. See Airlines—Lebanon
MIDDLE EAST treaty organization
See also
Central treaty organization
MIDDLE EASTERN literature
Iran: goodby to the nightingale. F. M. Esfandiary. Nation 202:468–70 Ap 18 '66
MIDDLE WEST
See also
Agriculture—Middle western states
Colleges and universities—Middle western states
Fishing—Middle western states
Hunting—Middle western states

Politics
Heartland recaptured; election results. il Time 88:30–2 N 18 '66
Outlook in twenty-four states: little change. U S News 61:38–40 O 17 '66

Tornadoes
See Tornadoes
MIDDLETON, Christopher
Three English poets. M. McCloskey. Poetry 109:126–9 N '66
MIDDLETON, Mary
Pair of lubbers takes to the sea. il pors Ebony 21:112–14+ Ap '66
MIDDLETON, Olive
Born to sing; interview, ed. by F. Stevenson. por Opera N 30:29 Mr 5 '66
MIDDLETON, William D.
Goodbye to the interurban. Am Heritage 17:30–41+ Ap '66
MIDDLETOWN, N.J.
All the alarms in one console. il Am City 81:50 S '66
MIDDLETOWN, Ohio
Joint efforts build a shoppers' lot. il Am City 81:140 Ap '66
Put all reproduction equipment in one place and save. D. W. Kothe. il Am City 81:106–7 Ap '66

MIDGES
See also
Chironomus
MIDGET buses. See Station wagons
MIDGET motors corporation
One cylinder success car; King Midget. A. Rothenberg. il Look 30:M22+ N 15 '66
MIDLAND, Tex.

Sanitary affairs
When streets and buildings settle. G. H. Medley. il Am City 81:32 Mr '66
MIDSUMMER. See Special days, weeks and months
MIDSUMMER nights dream; ballet. See Ballets—Criticisms
MIDSUMMER night's dream; drama. See Shakespeare, W.—Plays
MIDWAY (island)
Midway's deadly antennas. H. I. Fisher. il Audubon Mag 68:220-3 Jl '66
MIDWEST. See Middle West
MIDWEST fall book festival. See Book fairs
MIDWOOD, Barton
Under the mount of Saturn; story. Esquire 66:124 Ag '66
MIELZINER, Jo
Mielziner; interview. New Yorker 42:44-5 Mr 19 '66
MIES VAN DER ROHE, Ludwig
Affirming the absolutes; drawings on view at Museum of modern art. il por Time 87: 58+ F 11 '66
IIT, the house that Mies built. il por Sci Digest 59:48-53 Mr '66
MIGDOLL, Herbert
It began with photograms. J. Deschin. il Pop Phot 60:38+ Ja '67
MIGRAINE. See Headache
MIGRANT labor
Along the migrant stream; library projects in Wisconsin. E. Burr. Library J 91:335-6 Ja 15 '66
Farm crisis, city crisis; Fay Bennett's report to National sharecroppers fund. Christian Cent 83:793 Je 22 '66
Migrants in the promised land; farm workers in Utah. J. F. Conway. America 115: 253-5 S 10 '66
Now they walk with us; Texas pickers. il Newsweek 68:54 S 12 '66
People in plastic houses. il Fortune 73:170 Ap '66
Plight of migrant America. A. Ogle. America 115:33-4 Jl 9 '66
Report on our migrant workers. America 114:346 Mr 12 '66
Stooping to conquer; Wirtz report. Newsweek 67:61-2 F 7 '66
See also
National farm workers' association
MIGRATION, Internal
See also
Negroes in the United States—Migration
MIGRATION of animals. See Animals—Migration
MIGRATION of Negroes. See Negroes in the United States—Migration
MIGRATORY workers. See Migrant labor
MIHAJLOV, Mihajlo
Unperson sings to the Russians. N Y Times Mag p26-7+ My 15 '66

about
Limits of freedom. Time 88:28-9 Ag 19 '66
Limits to liberalization. por Time 88:46 S 30 '66
One step backward. il Newsweek 68:48 O 3 '66
Publish and perish. Newsweek 68:71 Ag 22 '66
Strong constitution. il por Newsweek 68:42+ Ag 15 '66
MIJAS, Spain
How Generalissimo Franco got his consensus. D. Searl. New Repub 156:12-13 Ja 14 '67
MIKE Douglas show. See Television broadcasting—Programs
MIKESELL, Art
Bush buggy. Pop Mech 125:138-42+ My '66
MIKITA, Stan
Black Hawks' no. 2 tries harder. W. Leggett. il pors Sports Illus 24:34-6+ Ja 31 '66
MIKKELSEN, Robert S.
Party boat bonanza. pors Outdoor Life 137: 62-4+ Je '66
MILAN, Italy

Art
Last supper; Milan's deathless treasure. E. O. Hauser. il Read Digest 88:166-8+ Ap '66

Description
Mass and the opera; Milan cathedral and Teatro alla Scala. V. Sheean. il Opera N 30: 8-13 Ap 2 '66

Music
At La Scala: new Faust, revived Bohème. W. Legge. il Hi Fi 16:158-9 My '66
Milan. W. Weaver. il Opera N 30:31 Mr 5 '66
Milan; Elena Suliotis, Milan debut in La Scala's Nabucco. W. Weaver. il Opera N 31:32 Ja 21 '67
Milan; performance of La forza del destino. W. Weaver. il Opera N 30:32 Ja 29 '66
Mines of sulphur; recital in Geneva. W. Legge. il Hi Fi 16:128-9 Je '66
Opera on three fronts; Geneva-Munich-Milan. W. Legge. Hi Fi 16:136-9 Mr '66
La Scala's vogue; melds music and society. il Opera N 31:28-9 Ja 21 '67
MILDENBERGER, Karl
Hands of Clay. il Newsweek 68:68 S 19 '66
How about that whozis? Clay-Mildenberger fight. Time 88:70+ S 16 '66
Muslim ministers to a southpaw. M. Kane. il por Sports Illus 25:34-5+ S 19 '66
MILDEW
See also
Powdery mildew
MILEK, Bob
Late hunting is great hunting. Field & S 71:49-51+ N '66
Sheep fences or antelope? Field & S 71:10-12+ S '66
MILES, Charles
Indian relics. See issues of Hobbies
MILES, Dick
Bat about ping-pong. Sports Illus 25:90-2+ O 17 '66
MILES, Elizabeth B.
English silver pocket nutmeg grater. Antiques 90:828-31 D '66
MILES, Evelyn Adriance
Tenting across Europe. Travel 125:48-9+ My '66
MILES, Josephine
King; Civilian; Edge; Freedoms; Sundays; Countryside; poems. Poetry 108:324-8 Ag '66
MILES, Kenneth Henry
Miles: fast enough to win, slow enough to finish. B. La Fontaine. il por Sports Illus 24:16-17 F 14 '66
Obituary
Sports Illus 25:13 Ag 29 '66
Sports; fatal crash. Newsweek 68:65 Ag 29 '66
MILES, Raymond E.
Affluent organization; excerpts from address, April 8, 1966. bibliog f Harvard Bsns R 44: 106-14 My '66
MILES college, Birmingham, Ala.
Letter from the publisher. B. M. Auer. il Time 88:17 S 9 '66
MILFORD, Conn.
We put guts in our purchasing program. C. M. Oneto. il Am City 81:124-5 My '66
MILHAUD, Darius
Composer's life. por Opera N 30:8-11 Je 4 '66
MILHAUD, Gérard, and Job, J. C.
Thyrocalcitonin: effect on idiopathic hypercalcemia. bibliog Science 154:794-6 N 11 '66
MILHAVEN, John G.
Loyal opposition in the church. America 114: 622-4, 846 Ap 30, Je 18 '66

about
Ethics and evidence. D. Callahan. Commonweal 85:76-8 O 21 '66
MILHOLLEN, G. L. See Brindley, G. W. jt. auth.
MILI, Gjon
Romans; photographs. Life 60:56-74+ Mr 4 '66
Serenade to ninety years of greatness; photographs. Life 61:34-43 N 11 '66

about
Most un-alone alone man I ever knew. G. P. Hunt. il Life 61:3 N 11 '66
MILITARISM
Indonesia's quasi-military regime. F. Bunnell. bibliog f Cur Hist 52:22-8+ Ja '67
Military origins of medieval representation. T. N. Bisson. bibliog f Am Hist R 71:1199-218 Jl '66
Military rule in Burma. J. Silverstein. Cur Hist 52:41-7 Ja '67
Shifting authority in West Africa. C. E. Welch. bibliog f Cur Hist 50:153-8+ Mr '66

MILITARY administration
As generals take over, a look at military rule; with interview with E. Huxley. il U S News 60:54-7 Mr 14 '66

MILITARY air traffic control. See Air traffic control, Military

MILITARY airlift command. See United States —Military airlift command

MILITARY airplanes. See Airplanes, Military

MILITARY art and science
NASA presses research on limited war. Aviation W 85:75 Jl 4 '66
Soviet critique of China's total strategy. R. L. Garthoff. Reporter 34:48-9 My 19 '66
What we are learning in Viet Nam. il Nations Bsns 54:35-7+ Je '66
    See also
Camouflage
Chemical warfare
Guerrilla warfare
Jungle warfare
Mechanization, Military
Military research
Spies
Tactics
War
         History
Craftsmen in the art of war; Roman legions. il Life 60:54-9 Mr 18 '66
Herodotus and the strategy and tactics of the invasion of Xerxes. A. Ferrill. bibliog f Am Hist R 72:102-15 O '66

MILITARY assistance
Balance of weaponry; U.S. and Soviet arms sales to Israelis and Arabs. Time 87:39 F 25 '66

MILITARY assistance, American
AID report for fiscal 1965 transmitted to Congress; White House announcement; with President's letter of transmittal. L. B. Johnson. Dept State Bul 54:208-9 F 7 '66
Allies at cut rates: are they worth it? U S News 60:8 My 2 '66
Arms race in Latin America; what is the U.S. doing? D. D. Ranstead. Commonweal 85:313-14 D 16 '66
Competition for new weapons; arms race in the Middle East. P. Ben. New Repub 154: 13-14 Je 4 '66
Declaration of Honolulu; text, February 7, 1966. Nguyen-van-Thieu and others. Cur Hist 50:238-9+ Ap '66
Deep conviction; how the aid is earmarked. New Repub 154:5-6 My 7 '66
Foreign assistance program; address, February 1, 1966. L. B. Johnson. Cur Hist 50: 358-9 Je '66
Kuss of death; America's chief arms salesman. Nation 202:85-6 Ja 24 '66
New look in foreign aid, it will be harder to get. U S News 61:58 Jl 25 '66
New script. Time 87:20 F 11 '66
U.S. foreign aid: an overview; symposium. bibliog f il Cur Hist 50:321-57+ Je '66
U.S. foreign aid: case studies; symposium. bibliog f il Cur Hist 51:1-44+ Jl '66
U.S. foreign aid program: limit it to non-military aid? pro and con discussion. il Sr Schol 89:8-10 N 4 '66
U.S.: supplier of weapons to the world; with list of 1962-1965 sales. E. J. McCarthy. il Sat R 49:13-15 Jl 9 '66
U.S. takes on still more of world's defense. il U S News 60:34-6 Mr 7 '66
U.S. taking a second look at its world role. il U S News 60:40-2 My 16 '66
Updating the world's biggest military machine; Time essay. Time 87:34-5 Je 3 '66
Voluntary service for all youth; address, May 19, 1966. R. S. McNamara. Vital Speeches 32:484-8 Je 1 '66
William the terrible; Senate cuts administration's requests. il Newsweek 68:18 Ag 8 '66
    See also
United States—Armed forces—Forces in Vietnam (Republic)
         Bibliography
Readings on foreign aid. K. P. Dobkin. Cur Hist 51:50-1 Jl '66
         History
Evolution of U.S. foreign aid; excerpts from Foreign aid in international politics. J. D. Montgomery. Cur Hist 50:321-7+ Je '66
Roosevelt as friend of France. J. M. Haight, jr. bibliog f For Affairs 44:518-26 Ap '66

MILITARY assistance, Russian
Competition for new weapons; arms race in the Middle East. P. Ben. New Repub 154: 13-14 Je 4 '66

Our pilots call Hanoi Dodge City; Russian-made SA-2 anti-aircraft system. S. Butz. il N Y Times Mag p30-1+ O 16 '66
Soviet aid to Vietnam. A. Parry. il Reporter 36:28-33 Ja 12 '67

MILITARY aviators. See Air pilots

MILITARY bases
Britain dons shield of auxiliary police. Bsns W p36-7 F 26 '66
Cutback on bases. Sr Schol 87:18 Ja 14 '66
Ho Chi Minh trail and our Thai buildup. D. Warner. il Reporter 34:26-8 Ja 27 '66
Indian Ocean deal? center of Anglo-American military planning for the Far East. New Repub 154:7 F 5 '66
Ring around Asia: putting Peking on notice. il Newsweek 67:40 Ja 31 '66
U.S. and Philippines amend military bases agreement; joint announcement; exchange of notes; September 16, 1966. Dept State Bul 55:547-8 O 10 '66
    See also
Air bases

MILITARY bases, British
Auld song's end; new defense program. il Newsweek 67:48+ Mr 7 '66
East of Suez up for grabs. J. Amery. il Reporter 35:16-21 D 1 '66
Indian Ocean deal? center of Anglo-American military planning for the Far East. New Repub 154:7 F 5 '66

MILITARY budget. See United States—Armed forces—Appropriations and expenditures

MILITARY cemeteries. See National cemeteries—United States

MILITARY chaplains. See Chaplains, Military

MILITARY contracts. See Contracts, Government

MILITARY cooperation (United States) See Military assistance, American

MILITARY desertion. See Desertion, Military

MILITARY education
    See also
United States military academy, West Point

MILITARY engineering
    See also
United States—Army—Corps of engineers
Vietnamese war, 1957- —Engineering and construction

MILITARY equipment, supplies, etc. See Military supplies

MILITARY expenditures. See United States—Armed forces—Appropriations and expenditures

MILITARY government. See Military administration

MILITARY installations. See Military bases

MILITARY intelligence
Coastwatcher's diary: Guadalcanal; with introd. by S. W. Sears. M. Clemens. Am Heritage 17:104-10 F '66
    See also
Spies

MILITARY landing strips. See Aviation landing stations

MILITARY law
No one to sue; case of Shirley Shapiro. Time 88:98 O 7 '66
    See also
Courts martial
Military administration

MILITARY manpower. See United States—Armed forces

MILITARY mechanization. See Mechanization, Military

MILITARY mines. See Mines, Military

MILITARY mobilization. See United States—Armed forces—Mobilization

MILITARY officers, Retired. See Retired military officers

MILITARY parades. See Parades

MILITARY pilot training. See Air pilots—Training

MILITARY policy
    See also
United States—Military policy

MILITARY preparedness. See Preparedness, Military

MILITARY purchasing. See Purchasing, Military

MILITARY radio communication. See Radio communication, Military

MILITARY reconnaissance
Army seeks to improve ground positioning; man-pack receiver version of Loran tactical radio navigation system. M. Getler. il Tech W 19:14-15 O 17 '66
    See also
Aerial reconnaissance
Artificial satellites—Military applications

MILITARY research
ARPA team aids Thailand in developing R&D capability. M. Getler. Tech W 19:17-18 D 19 '66
TOD's guide to successful proposals; technical objective document release program. Miss & Roc 18:80 My 30 '66
Technological war. W. J. Coughlin. Tech W 19:54 N 14 '66
Vietnam needs cloud advanced projects; with table. C. Brownlow. Aviation W 84:16-21 Ja 31 '66
Vietnam research efforts accelerated; priority research objectives for Vietnam. il Aviation W 85:22-3 mid-D '66
What role for the think tanks? Defense dept. launches study of nonprofit research labs doing military work. il Bsns W p71-2+ My 14 '66
See also
Hudson institute, incorporated
Ordnance research
Rand corporation

Economic aspects
On the cost-effectiveness approach to military research and development. K. Knorr. Bul Atomic Sci 22:11-14 N '66
MILITARY science. See Military art and science
MILITARY secrets. See Defense information, Classified
MILITARY service
See also
Conscientious objectors

Physical and mental fitness
Four ways to go: the route of the draft reject. il Esquire 66:125 S '66
McNamara's plan for rejectees; excerpts from address, August 23, 1966. R. S. McNamara. U S News 61:27 S 5 '66
McNamara's salvation army; problem of the military reject. D. Sanford. New Repub 155:13-14 S 10 '66
Mental tests for 10 million Americans; what they show. il U S News 61:78-9 O 17 '66
Now that draft calls are so high; call-up of youths with lower mental and physical qualifications. il U S News 61:6 S 19 '66
Salvage operation; proposal to lower standards. Newsweek 68:20 S 5 '66
MILITARY service, Compulsory

Deferments and exemptions
Are you smart enough to beat the draft, stay in college and read this issue of Esquire? Esquire 66:109 S '66
As draft tests begin for students. il U S News 60:8 My 23 '66
Boxed in. D. Sanford. New Repub 154:8-9 My 21 '66
Draft by lottery? M. F. Nolan. New Repub 155:9-10 Jl 30 '66
Draft on the campus; Hershey's screening system. il Newsweek 67:58 Ja 31 '66
Draft standards for students: how they work; with sample questions. U S News 60:70 Ap 4 '66
Draft tests for college students. il U S News 60:10 Ja 31 '66
Ducking the draft and dodging the cameras: fathers and sons face charges. il Life 60:47 Ap 15 '66
Evading the draft: who, how and why; with report by D. Jackson and views of H. Drummonds and W. F. Wild. il Life 61:40-9 D 9 '66
How fair is the draft. J. Star. il Look 30:25-7 Ap 19 '66
Matching wits with a draft board; continued deferment; test questions and answers. Newsweek 67:35 Mr 28 '66
More unfair draft; qualifying tests. Life 60:4 Ap 29 '66
Multiple choice; students reactions to tests. New Repub 154:5-6 My 28 '66
Now hear this. General Hershey. J. Ciardi. Sat R 49:26 Jl 30 '66
Quaint notion of service. L. Wainwright. Life 60:28 Je 17 '66
Questioning the draft; students and the Selective service deferment test. il Newsweek 67:66-7 My 16 '66
Russian roulette in the classroom; grades and the draft. N. Cousins. Sat R 49:22 Ap 23 '66
Selective death sentence. Nation 202:604-5 My 23 '66
Selective service and student deferment. Sch & Soc 94:372-4 N 12 '66
Students and their deferment. Sat R 49:92 N 19 '66

2-S, too smart to fight? report from University of Michigan. M. Levitas. il N Y Times Mag p27+ Ap 24 '66
War comes to the campus; students take selective service tests. il Newsweek 67:29-30 My 23 '66

Australia
Sinister word; reactions to conscription for Vietnam. il Newsweek 67:44+ My 16 '66

Greece, Modern
Pay up or join up; government letters to Greeks in Australia. Newsweek 67:53 My 30 '66

United States
Abolish the draft? il Newsweek 68:23 D 19 '66
Are changes coming in the draft? il U S News 60:46-7 Je 13 '66
As odds shift on a military call-up—. il U S News 61:14 O 24 '66
As the draft reaches deeper and deeper. il U S News 60:4 F 28 '66
Better than the way George did it; Hershey's arguments. Time 88:72 D 23 '66
Big changes now coming in draft? il U S News 61:21-3 D 26 '66
Business worries about the draft. Bsns W p44 F 26 '66
By lot or not? idea of a conscription lottery. il Time 87:32 Je 10 '66
Canada: escape hatch for U.S. draft dodgers. il U S News 61:61-2 S 26 '66
Card is not for burning; concerning case of D. R. Miller. il Time 88:56 O 21 '66
Case for drafting all boys and girls. M. Mead. Redbook 127:40+ S '66
Changes in draft outlook; pressure on students is easing. il U S News 60:30-1 My 9 '66
Crisis of confidence: Vietnam; discussion between two senators and two student representatives. il Mlle 63:272-3 Ag '66
Deferring which college students? New Repub 154:7-8 Mr 5 '66
Double discrimination; civil rights activists and the draft. Nation 203:564 N 28 '66
Draft. F. S. Meyer. Nat R 18:785 Ag 9 '66
Draft: a question of pride or prejudice? il Sr Schol 89:6-11+ S 23 '66
Draft: a slowdown in calls, and new talk of a lottery. il U S News 61:18 N 21 '66
Draft: an old problem; Congress takes another look; summary of testimony, June 22, 1966. L. B. Hershey. U S News 61:28-9 Jl 4 '66
Draft by lot. New Repub 155:5-6 N 26 '66
Draft by lottery? M. F. Nolan. New Repub 155:9-10 Jl 30 '66
Draft by lottery? pro and con discussion. Sr Schol 89:12-13 S 23 '66
Draft debate. il Time 88:12 Ag 26 '66 ..
Draft gets its own reviewers. Bsns W p40-1 Jl 9 '66
Draft; inequalities and alternatives. D. Graham; J. Goodman; K. R. Johnson. Atlan 217:59-69 F '66
Draft is here to stay, but it should be changed. H. W. Baldwin. il N Y Times Mag p48-9+ N 20 '66; Discussion. p41 D 11 '66
Draft is unfair. J. Raymond; discussion. N Y Times Mag p6 F 6 '66
Draft run-around; needed attack on problems. Nation 203:660 D 19 '66
Draft tests set. Sr Schol 88:17 Mr 18 '66
Draft: the unjust vs. the unwilling; ed. by J. Sanders. il Newsweek 67:30-2+ Ap 11 '66
Drafting of protestors challenged. Sr Schol 87:16 Ja 21 '66
Drill sergeant; ordering up recruits. il Newsweek 67:21 F 28 '66
Equality does not exist; excerpts from testimony before the House armed services committee. L. B. Hershey. Time 88:13-14 Jl 1 '66
Evading the draft: who, how and why; with report by D. Jackson and views of H. Drummonds and W. F. Wild. il Life 61:40-9 D 9 '66
Future of the draft. J. C. Esty, jr. Nation 203:209-13 S 12 '66
Greeting. il Time 87:21-4 Je 3 '66
Greetings, or, Do I feel a draught? 1778. P. V. Lutz. il Am Heritage 17:112 Ag '66
Growing concern: is the draft unfair? U S News 61:10 Jl 11 '66
Here's the way the Pentagon would like to change the draft. il U S News 61:57-8 Jl 11 '66
How fair is the draft? J. Star. il Look 30:25-7 Ap 19 '66
How fair is the draft? a growing debate. U S News 60:8+ Je 6 '66

MILITARY service, Compulsory—United States
—*Continued*
How to fix it? Selective service system;
House armed services committee hearings.
Newsweek 68:19 Jl 4 '66
In my opinion; girls should be drafted just
as boys are. J. Stone. Seventeen 25:284
My '66
Incentives & inequities. Time 88:18 Jl 8 '66
Inglory boys: D. J. Miller and D. Mitchell.
Time 87:21 Mr 25 '66
Is Vietnam really a poor boys' war? il
U S News 61:58-9 N 14 '66
Jail's too good for them; reclassified Univer-
sity of Michigan students. New Repub 155:
8 O 8 '66
Just war and the selective objector. A.
Geyer. il Christian Cent 83:199-201 F 16 '66;
Reply. J. C. Fleck. 83:404 Mr 30 '66
Let every young man serve. Farm J 90:110
O '66
Letter from Washington; changes in the
draft. R. H. Rovere. New Yorker 42:200+
D 17 '66
Life & death grades; Selective service's
classification for draft deferment for stu-
dents. Time 87:70 Mr 25 '66
Lost report; campaign year delays the draft
study report. Nation 202:142-3 F 7 '66
McNamara's balloon; prescription for a less
inequitable selective service system. Na-
tion 202:667 Je 6 '66
Multiple choice. New Repub 154:5-6 My 28 '66
National service to replace the draft? pro
and con discussion. Sr Schol 89:16-17+ O
14 '66
New draft rules; who will be called now.
il U S News 61:26-7 S 5 '66
New proposals for changing the draft. U S
News 62:12 Ja 9 '67
Next: draft reservists? what it would mean.
il U S News 61:36 Ag 29 '66
Opinion: why the draft? A. Beichman. Mlle
62:6+ Ja '66
Pentagon report; civilian advisory board to
conduct study. Newsweek 68:33 Jl 11 '66
President who wouldn't get mad; draft pro-
testers at University of Chicago. il Time
87:72 My 20 '66
Quaint notion of service. L. Wainwright.
Life 60:28 Je 17 '66
Quick guide to the draft classifications. il
Changing T 20:39-40 N '66
Refilling the pool. il Time 88:32 N 11 '66
Republican Turks; draft under fire; with
editorial note. R. G. Sherrill. Nation 202:
284-8 Mr 14 '66
Salvage operation; proposal to lower stand-
ards. Newsweek 68:20 S 5 '66
Second chance; plans to draft men who failed
to meet requirements. il Time 88:13 S 2 '66
Secretary Rusk, Secretary McNamara, Mr
McCloy meet with President Johnson;
excerpts from press briefing, November 23,
1966. R. S. McNamara. Dept State Bul 55:
921-3 D 19 '66
Selective service and national needs; analysis
of reform proposals. B. K. Chapman. Re-
porter 34:15-18 Je 16 '66
Selective service and student deferment.
Sch & Soc 94:372-4 N 12 '66
Serious to-do about a silly law; trial of
D. J. Miller. L. Wainwright. Life 60:17
Mr 4 '66
Should farm boys wait for the draft? ed. by
J. D. Boyd. il Farm J 90:28-9+ Je '66
Speaking out; let's draft women too! C. Bird.
il Sat Eve Post 239:10+ Je 18 '66
Their students' military obligation. NEA J
55:45-6 O '66
These are the choices in military service.
il Changing T 20:37-41 Je '66
Time essay; new demands of the draft. Time
87:38-9 F 4 '66
Vietnam dodgers; refuge in Canada. News-
week 68:48+ O 3 '66
Vietnam: growing war and campus protests
threaten student deferments. E. Langer;
reply. B. M. Vetter. Science 151:517-18 F
4 '66
Volunteer army. M. Friedman. Newsweek
68:100 D 19 '66
War comes to the campus; students take
selective service tests. il Newsweek 67:29-
30 My 23 '66
What the draft might blow up. C. Fritchey.
Harper 233:26-9 Ag '66
What's happening in education? is draft system fair? W. D. Boutwell. PTA Mag 60:31-2
Je '66
Who gets in the army? D. P. Moynihan. New
Repub 155:19-22 N 5 '66; Reply with rejoinder. R. A. Freeman. 156:43-4 Ja 7 '67
Who should be drafted? student conference
at Antioch. L. Grauman, jr. New Repub
155:11-12 D 10 '66

Will the draft reach out for men over
twenty-five? U S News 61:12 O 17 '66
See also
Conscientious objectors
MILITARY service, Voluntary
Volunteer programs. K. R. Johnson. Atlan
217:69 F '66
MILITARY supplies
See also
United States—Army—Equipment and sup-
plies
Vietnamese war, 1957-   —Equipment and
supplies
Maintenance and repair
DOD stressing life cycle costing plan. P. J.
Klass. Aviation W 86:32-4 Ja 16 '67
MILITARY surplus. See Surplus products
MILITARY tactics. See Tactics
MILITARY terms. See War—Terminology
MILITARY topography
See also
Military reconnaissance
MILITARY training
Fort Dix: the new army game. M. Herr.
Holiday 39:68-9+ Ap '66
From BB to V.C; training in instinct shoot-
ing at Fort Polk, La. G. Gresham. il
Field & S 71:32+ S '66
Lessons of Vinh Hoa; training program for
Viet Nam-bound troops. il Time 87:30 F 4
'66
Little boy who plays Vietcong; with report
by D. Sider. il Life 61:50B-52+ Ag 5 '66
M; account of one company of American
soldiers. J. Sack. Esquire 66:79-86+ O '66
Making of a soldier USA; World war II. L.
Simpson. il Harper 232:76-80 F '66
Meet me in the middle of the air. J. Morris.
il Esquire 65:110-13+ Ap '66
Rebirth of the 5th marines; training at Camp
Pendleton; with report by L. Norman. il
Newsweek 68:33-4 Jl 11 '66
This country needs universal military train-
ing. D. D. Eisenhower. Read Digest 89:49-
55 S '66
Who should serve? K. R. Johnson. Atlan
217:63-8 F '66
MILITARY training camps
Essayons! Corps of engineers training regi-
ment at Fort Belvoir, Va. il Time 87:25
F 11 '66
Fort Dix: the new army game. M. Herr.
Holiday 39:68-9+ Ap '66
Getting GI's ready for war in jungle; Fort
Polk, La. il U S News 60:53-5 My 30 '66
Rebirth of the 5th marines; training at Camp
Pendleton; with report by L. Norman. il
Newsweek 68:33-4 Jl 11 '66
You'll need to know this if you're in Viet-
nam; training at Fort Leonard Wood, Mo.
il Newsweek 67:33 Ap 11 '66
MILK
Milk intolerance found among many Negroes.
Sci N 90:263 O 1 '66
See also
Dairying
Analysis
IRMA to analyze milk protein in one minute;
Infrared milk analyzer. Sci N 90:377 N 5
'66
Marketing
Can co-ops control all the milk? il Farm J
90:29+ S '66
Great milk pricing mystery. G. Logsdon. il
Farm J 90:65 F '66
Will the new base plan help you? N. Reeder.
Farm J 90:57+ F '66
Prices
Blocks price hike for New Jersey milk.
Farm J 90:50 Mr '66
Government moves to raise milk prices. Farm
J 90:48 Ap '66
Great milk pricing mystery. G. Logsdon. il
Farm J 90:65 F '66
Imitation milk gets a foothold. R. G. Fowler.
Farm J 90:64 O '66
Milk wars threaten Midwest dairymen. Farm
J 90:34 Je '66
Will the new base plan help you? N. Reeder.
Farm J 90:57+ F '66
Production
How I feed for high production. J. R. Bor-
cherding. il Suc Farm 64:44+ Je '66
Ideas for extra milk production. C. Peter-
son, jr. il Suc Farm 64:100B Mr '66
Milk production of cows on protein-free feed.
A. I. Virtanen. bibliog il Science 153:1603-14
S 30 '66

MILLER, James Nathan—*Continued*
Robert finds a friend. PTA Mag 60:4-7 Je
'66; Same abr. Read Digest 89:89-93 Jl '66
Wanted: new safety for older roads. Read
Digest 89:215-16+ D '66
We must stop choking our cities. Read
Digest 89:37-41 Ag '66
MILLER, John B.
Selecting a tent. Consumer Bul 49:16-18 Je
'66
Tents for automobile camping. Consumer Bul
49:32-6 Jl '66
MILLER, Jonathan
Alice in wonderland. Vogue 148:240-7+ D '66
Saying ah. Vogue 149:40+ Ja 1 '67

about

At last, an Alice unspoiled; with account
by H. Judson. il por Life 61:96A-98 N 25 '66
Child's-eye Alice. il por Newsweek 68:66-7
Ag 29 '66
MILLER, Joshua
Immunological competence: alteration by
whole body X-irradiation and shielding of
selected lymphoid tissues. bibliog Science
151:1395-7 Mr 18 '66
MILLER, Julius Sumner
His bag of tricks makes physics fun. W. S.
Griswold. il pors Pop Sci 188:95-9 My '66
MILLER, Larry
Two for the money. H. L. Masin. il por Sr
Schol 89:21 Ja 6 '67
MILLER, Lee A. and MacLeod, E. G.
Ultrasonic sensitivity: a tympanal receptor in
the green lace wing chrysopa carnea. bib-
liog Science 154:891-3 N 18 '66
MILLER, Lee D. and Miller, S. M.
Chromosomes from testicular preparations of
lepidoptera. bibliog Science 152:529-30 Ap
22 '66
MILLER, Lewis
Americans not everybody knows. C. W.
Ferguson. por PTA Mag 61:12-14 N '66
MILLER, Lois Mattox, and Monahan, James
To the cigarette makers: just the facts, please.
Read Digest 89:61-7 N '66
MILLER, Loren
How Supreme court overcame its racism;
excerpts from The petitioners. por Ebony
21:57-62+ Mr '66
MILLER, Lucille Marie (Maxwell)
How can I tell them there's nothing left?
J. Didion. il pors Sat Eve Post 239:38-42+
My 7 '66
MILLER, Merle
Carnival in Rio. Holiday 39:40-53+ F '66
Happy marriage of love and politics. Ladies
Home J 83:94-5+ Mr '66
MILLER, Philip L.
Anthology of American art song. Am Rec G
32:784-5 My '66
Columbia's Falstaff. Am Rec G 33:202-3 N '66
Donizetti's Lucrezia Borgia. Am Rec G 33:
292-3 D '66
First complete recording of a Wagner opera
ever made in the U.S.A; Lohengrin. Am
Rec G 32:1104-6 Ag '66
London's Don Carlo. Am Rec G 32:680-2 Ap
'66
On the record: Music (cont of) Recorded
music. See issues of Library journal
Opening nights at the Met. Am Rec G 33:
122-3 O '66
Pro musica in retrospect. Sat R 49:48-9 Je
25 '66
RCA Victor's Orfeo ed Euridice. Am Rec G
32:792-4 My '66
(ed) Recorded music. See issues of Library
journal
Two voices from the past: Thill and Teyte.
Am Rec G 32:422-4 Ja '66
Via Philips, the first recording of Rossini's
Mosè. Am Rec G 32:504-6 F '66
MILLER, R. H.
Measurement of stellar diameters. bibliog
Science 153:581-7 Ag 5 '66
MILLER, R. W. and Nishimura, H.
Congenital malformations and cancer: United
States-Japan cooperative science program.
Science 151:357-8 Ja 21 '66
MILLER, Ralph
Ralph Miller of Iowa: prophet of pressure.
F. Deford. il por Sports Illus 24:14-17 Ja 24
'66
MILLER, Raymond E.
Giant of Newcomer Hollow; ed. by J. Hayes.
por Outdoor Life 137:38-9+ F '66
MILLER, Russ
Made for the shade. Field & S 71:133-4 My
'66
MILLER, Ruth
Fitted baskets make unusual gifts. Farm J
90:119 Mr '66
MILLER, Susan M. See Miller, L. D. jt. auth.

MILLER, Sylvia
Shape of schools: today and tomorrow. To-
days Health 44:58-63 S '66
MILLER, Theresa M.
Is it always the child? Sat R 49:76-7+ O 15 '66
MILLER, Vernon F.
Town meeting reborn. Sat R 49:34-5 Jl 23 '66
MILLER, Walter B.
Violent crimes in city gangs. bibliog f Ann
Am Acad 364:96-112 Mr '66
MILLER, Warren
Child of affluence. Nation 202:338-9 Mr 21
'66
Spanish suit; story. Sat Eve Post 239:64-8
N 19 '66

about

Obituary
Commonweal 84:229 My 13 '66. W. Sheed
Newsweek 67:106-7 My 9 '66
MILLER, Wayne
Seven ages of love; photographs. Sat Eve
Post 239:19-23 D 31 '66
MILLER, William Robert
Chaplaincy vs. mission in a secular age.
Christian Cent 83:1335-7 N 2 '66
Christianity's new morality. New Repub 155:
22-4 S 3 '66
God and his men. New Repub 155:29-32 N 26
'66
Sing to the Lord a new song. Christian Cent
83:771-6 Je 15 '66
MILLER brewing company
Deal between grandchildren; W. R. Grace &
co. buys. il Time 88:108 S 30 '66
MILLIKAN, Clark H.
Cerebrovascular disease. Science 152:803-5+
My 6 '66
MILLIMAN, John D.
Submarine lithification of carbonate sedi-
ments. bibliog Science 153:994-7 Ag 26 '66
MILLING tools
Chip shields for milling machine W. E.
Burton. il Pop Mech 125:170-1 My '66
MILLION-dollar quiz show; drama. See Janey,
S. E.
MILLIONAIRES
Big spenders, by L. Beebe. Review
Sat R 49:41-2 Ap 16 '66. N. Samstag
How to be a millionaire at forty. Read Digest
88:114-18 Mr '66
Yes, you can make a million: here's the way
it's done today. U S News 60:111-12 My 16
'66
MILLIPEDES
1,2-dialkyl-4-(3H)-quinazolinones n the de-
fensive secretion of a millipede (glomeris
marginata) Y. C. Meinwald and others. bib-
liog il Science 154:390-1 O 21 '66
MILLIS, Walter
Brutal logic of power. Sat R 49:36 Ja 29 '66
MILLMAN, Peter M.
Big gun on Barbados. Sky & Tel 32:64-7 Ag
'66
MILLS, Ernest
Beware of the bunnies. Sch Arts 66:33 O '66
MILLS, James
Detective. Read Digest 88:219-23+ F '66
MILLS, John
El Morocco. F. Morton. il Holiday 39:78-80+
F '66
MILLS, Martha
Martha Mills' Little people of Drury lane.
C. H. Fawcett. il Hobbies 71:40+ S '66
MILLS, Ralph J. Jr
Three younger poets. Poetry 109:114-18 N '66
Two British chronicles. Poetry 107:406-10
Mr '66
MILLS, Richard C.
Not just for hurricanes. Am City 81:100-1
Ap '66
MILLS, Thomas J.
Scientific personnel and the professions. bib-
liog f Ann Am Acad 367:33-42 S '66
MILLS, Wilbur Daigh
Good news for taxpayers. pors Nations Bsns
53:50-2+ D '65

about

Nyet to Nicolae. por Time 87:29 My 20 '66
MILLS
See also
Windmills
MILLSPAUGH, Frank
Black power. Commonweal 84:500-3 Ag 5 '66
MILLSTONES, Indian. See Indians of North
America—Implements
MILMAN, Gregory, and others
Pentagonal aggregation of virus particles.
bibliog Science 152:1381-3 Je 3 '66
MILNER, Roger
How's the world treating you? Criticism
America 115:668 N 19 '66
New Yorker 42:128 N 5 '66
Sat R 49:34 N 12 '66
Time 88:85 N 4 '66

MILNES, L. W.
New downtown. Am City 81:86-7+ Je '66
MILNES, Sherrill
Made to measure; interview, ed. by A. M.
Lingg. Opera N 31:16 Ja 21 '67
MILO
164 bushels of milo/acre. E. Stout. il Suc
Farm 64:36-7+ My '66
Step up milo yields more than 50 per cent.
L. E. Zeman. il Suc Farm 64:30-1 N '66
MILT, Harry
Help for troubled families. Parents Mag 41:
84-5+ N '66
Parents aren't enough. Parents Mag 41:74-
5+ O '66
MILTON, Daniel
Drifting organisms in the Precambrian sea.
bibliog Science 153:293-4 Jl 15 '66
MILTON, John, 1608-1674
On Milton's poetry. R. Fraser. Yale R 56:
172-96 D '66
MILTOWN. See Meprobamates
MILWAUKEE
Home are the Braves; in Atlanta; divorce
from Milwaukee. G. Astor. il Look 30:60-
2+ My 3 '66

Hotels, restaurants, etc.
See also
Night clubs

Labor and laboring classes
Youthpower! summer jobs for teens. A. Gonzalez and G. Gonzalez. il Seventeen 25:156-
7+ Mr '66

Negroes
Pulpit v. the bench. il Time 88:23 S 9 '66
Still hot. il Newsweek 68:26-7 S 12 '66

Sanitary affairs
No storm-water bypass. R. D. Leary. il Am
City 81:93-5 Ag '66
MILWAUKEE art center
Corporate appreciation; Courbet masterpiece
and shareholders. il Time 87:73 My 6 '66
Milwaukee art center. T. Atkinson. il Antiques
90:663-7 N '66
MILWAUKEE Braves (baseball) See Baseball
clubs
MILWAUKEE Journal
They must be doing something right in
Milwaukee. G. A. Young. il Pop Phot 59:
98-101+ Jl '66
MILWAUKEE sentinel
They must be doing something right in Mil-
waukee. G. A. Young. il Pop Phot 59:98-
101+ Jl '66
MIM, pseud.
Sure sources of that sensation of warmth
and security. McCalls 93:105 Jl '66
MIME
See also
Pantomime
MIMEOGRAPH
Mimeographiti: the Christmas letter. J. A.
Murdock. Christian Cent 83:1573-4 D 21 '66
MINAMOTO Yoshitsune. See Yoshitsune
MIND and body
Beyond Darwinism. A. Portmann; M. Grene;
discussion. Commentary 41:6+ Mr '66
Psychiatrists study emotional intestine. Sci N
89:442 Je 4 '66
See also
Medicine, Psychosomatic
Psychology, Physiological
MINDANAO state university. See Colleges and
universities—Philippines
MINE, mill and smelter workers union. See
International union of mine, mill and
smelter workers
MINE accidents and explosions
See also
Coal mines and mining—Safety devices and
measures
MINE rescue work
Inquest on a premature burial; caved-in mine
near Sheppton, Pa. T. Buckley. il Esquire
65:75-81+ Je '66
MINER, Dorothy
Madonna with child writing. Art N 64:40-3+
F '66
MINER, Dwight Carroll
Profess with a passion. il por Time 87:82 My
6 '66
MINER, Earl
Lucky in love but not in life. Sat R 49:58 Je
11 '66
MINER, John W.
Costs of quackery. Todays Health 44:53 D '66
MINER, Robert G.
What a grind! il Flower Grower 53:39 Ag '66

MINER, S. S.
New revolver-like steam engine produces
4.25 hp. per cubic inch! Pop Sci 188:84-8
F '66
MINERAL resources. See Mines and mineral
resources
MINERAL resources in submerged lands
Mining future bright; payoff may come sur-
prisingly soon. Tech W 19:23 S 26 '66
Promise of the seas' bounty; why oceans'
riches should be placed under U.N. ad-
ministration. C. M. Eichelberger. il Sat R
49:21-3 Je 18 '66
See also
Gold in submerged lands
MINERAL waters
Corkscrew: mineral waters and mixers. P. S.
Brown. House & Gard 130:210+ S '66
Straight from the spa; French firm, Source
Perrier. il Time 88:114 S 16 '66
MINERALOGY
See also
Meteorites
Montmorillonite
MINERALS. See Mines and mineral resources
MINERALS in the body
Do traces of metal decide our fate? J. D.
Ratcliff. il Todays Health 44:34-6+ Mr '66;
Same abr. with title Metals within us.
Read Digest 88:109-13 Mr '66
See also
Chelation therapy
MINERS
See also
Coal miners
MINES, Military
Little boxes; Hungarian mines washed over
to Austria. il Time 87:41 My 20 '66
Thread of death; Viet Cong booby traps. il
Time 88:36 O 28 '66
MINES, Submarine
Close Haiphong? what mines could do. il
U S News 60:37 Mr 28 '66
MINES and mineral resources
Some commercial mineral oddities. H. D.
Brown. il Hobbies 71:117+ Ag '66
See also
Copper
Mica
Mineral resources in submerged lands
Prospecting

Arizona
Mineral rich Arizona. H. D. Brown. il
Hobbies 71:117 Ja '67

Australia
Bonanza Down Under. il Time 87:102 Je 10
'66

Belgium
See also
Coal mines and mining—Belgium

Bolivia
Mines in the sky. F. D. de Medina. il Amér-
icas 18:24-9 Ap '66
See also
Tin mines and mining—Bolivia

Canada
Timmins bonanza reaches the surface; de-
posits of copper, zinc, silver, and lead. il
Bsns W p92-4 N 26 '66

Greece, Modern
Aluminum under Parnassus. il Time 87:94+
Mr 11 '66

South Africa
See also
Gold mines and mining—South Africa

United States
See also
Oil shales

Utah
Reaping the minerals in Great Salt Lake. il
Bsns W p94-6 O 15 '66

Western states
Bonanza in Colorado: who gets it? J. Duscha.
il Atlan 217:82-6 Mr '66

Zambia
See also
Copper industry and trade—Zambia
MINES of sulfur; opera. See Bennett, R. R.
MINESTRONE. See Soups
MINH, Ho-chi-. See Ho-chi-Minh
MINIATURE cameras. See Cameras

MINIATURE electronic equipment
In electronics, the big stakes ride on tiny chips. P. Siekman. il Fortune 73:120-5+ Je '66
Microelectronics magnified; mystery of micro-electronics manufacturing. A. Markovich. il Pop Mech 126:194-6+ N '66
New surge for microelectronics. il Duns R 87:40-2+ Je '66
Saturn computer size may be cut by 2/3. K Voss. il Tech W 19:30+ O 17 '66

MINIATURE irises. See Irises

MINIATURE lamps. See Electric lamps

MINIATURE objects
Horse-drawn history. Hobbies 71:89+ N '66
Miniaturia at the spring show. J. H. Gray. Hobbies 71:123 Ag '66
Neck deep in miniaturitis. E. A. Fisher. il Hobbies 71:122-3 My '66
See also
Doll houses
Models of cities, towns, etc.

Collectors and collecting
John Blauer acquires the Jack Norworth miniature museum. S. A. Parvin. il Hobbies 71:122-3+ O '66

MINIATURE painting (portraits)
Miniatures by John Smart; Starr collection in the Nelson gallery-Atkins museum. D. Foskett. il Antiques 90:354-7 S '66

MINIATURE pig breeding. See Swine breeding

MINIATURE shops. See Shops, Miniature

MINIATURE weapons. See Weapons

MINIATURIZATION (electronics) See Miniature electronic equipment

MINIMUM wage
United States
AFL-CIO, LBJ, COPE, 14(b), $1.75 & co. Nat R 18:199 Mr 8 '66
Back minimum income proposal. Christian Cent 83:1202 O 5 '66
Billions more in wages: who will get the raises. U S News 61:77-8 S 12 '66
Broadest stride yet for minimum wage law. il Bsns W p44 S 10 '66
Hard decision on minimum wages. B. L. Masse. America 114:417-18 Mr 26 '66
High cost of the minimum wage. W. F. Buckley, jr. Nat R 18:922 S 20 '66
Labor's protectionism. H. C. Wallich. Newsweek 67:89 Ap 18 '66
Minimum-wage rates. M. Friedman. Newsweek 68:96 S 26 '66
Minimum wage vs. jobs; views of A. Burns. H. Hazlitt. Newsweek 67:90 Ap 11 '66
Minimum wages: the outlook now. U S News 60:88 Mr 21 '66
Raises for millions: here's the latest wage plan. U S News 60:101-2 Je 6 '66
Right time for a slowdown. Bsns W p204 Mr 12 '66
This month's feature: proposals to change minimum wage law. Cong Digest 45:37-64 F '66
What happens after minimum wage goes up. U S News 60:73-4 Ap 4 '66
Why minimum-wage bill is stalled. U S News 60:89 F 28 '66
Will a minimum wage law hurt you? G. Logsdon. il Farm J 90:25 Jl '66
Will Congress kill Main Street? il Nations Bsns 54:35-6+ My '66

MINING industry and finance
Brazil
Brazil's chief miner; Augusto Antunes. Fortune 73:76 Ap '66
Ireland
Entrepreneur in Ireland. J. Perham. Duns R 87:65 F '66

MINI-organ. See Organ

MINIPAN cameras. See Cameras

MINISTERIAL associations. See Religious co-operation

MINISTERS of the gospel. See Clergy; Theological students

MINISTRY of women. See Women as ministers

MINK coats, etc. See Fur coats, wraps, etc.

MINNEAPOLIS
New twin cities; cultural appetite. B. Hersh. il Holiday 39:50-5+ Je '66
Twins that dominate the northern plains. il Bsns W p74-6+ My 21 '66

Art
Lower edge: gallery exhibition of painting called The lovers, with judge's permission. E. J. Gaines. ALA Bul 60:411 My '66

City planning
Merchants' high hopes in Minneapolis. il Fortune 73:161-2 Je '66

Hotels, restaurants, etc.
Dining in/out with Esquire; Jay's Brookdale drive-in, Brooklyn center. Esquire 66:215-16 S '66

Libraries
See also
Minneapolis public library

Sanitary affairs
Burn up those lift-station odors. D. McKenzie. il Am City 81:80-2 N '66
Sewer within a sewer. W. G. Ridge. il Am City 81:112-13 O '66

Stores
Swinging store; Dayton's. il Newsweek 68:86 Ag 22 '66

Theater
As who likes it? season's productions of Tyrone Guthrie theatre. G. Weales. Reporter 35:40+ Ag 11 '66
Grandeur in Ypsilanti, gaiety in Minneapolis; Minnesota theater company. R. Kotlowitz. il Harper 233:118-19 S '66
Theatre; report on the Guthrie. J. Novick. Nation 203:427-8 O 24 '66

Water supply
Good water-meter management. L. E. LaLonde. il Am City 81:167-8 My '66

MINNEAPOLIS public library
How a library won an election. K. C. Busch and E. J. Gaines. il Library J 91:5338-43 N 1 '66

MINNEAPOLIS star and tribune company
Cowles knows how. L. L. L. Golden. Sat R 49:100 Je 11 '66

MINNELLI, Liza
Return to Oz. por Newsweek 67:88 F 28 '66

MINNESOTA
See also
Architecture, Modern—Minnesota
Booksellers and bookselling—Minnesota
Camping—Minnesota
Geology—Minnesota

Industries
See also
Minnesota mining and manufacturing company

Politics and government
Down with youth; Rolvaag wins. Time 88:25 S 23 '66
Minnesota's Democrats try to dump their governor. R. Steele. il Reporter 34:29-31 Je 2 '66
Poll vault; gubernatorial primary contenders. Reporter 35:10 Ag 11 '66
Smiling through. Newsweek 67:30+ Mr 14 '66
Statehouse to woodshed; A. M. Keith wrests gubernatorial nomination from K. F. Rolvaag. il Newsweek 68:20 Jl 4 '66
To the woodshed. Time 88:15-16 Jl 1 '66

MINNESOTA historical society
Annals of law; Lewis and Clark case; United States government's claim to field notes. C. Tomkins. New Yorker 42:106+ O 29 '66

MINNESOTA mining and manufacturing company
3M's self-help plan; setting up physically handicapped in copying-service businesses. il Bsns W p62 D 3 '66

MINNESOTA multiphasic personality inventory. See Personality tests

MINNESOTA theater company. See Minneapolis—Theater

MINNESOTA. University, Minneapolis
Minnesota puts own stamp on economics. il Bsns W p68-70+ O 1 '66

MINOAN civilization. See Civilization, Minoan

MINOR, Audax, pseud
Race track. See issues of New Yorker

MINOR, Spinoza
Is time dead? Nat R 18:456+ My 17 '66

MINOR league baseball. See Baseball

MINORITIES
Colored minorities and present British policies. E. M. Bussey. Mo Labor R 89:1111-15 O '66
Global apartheid? question of recognizing or doing business with a minority government. J. Burnham. Nat R 18:1036 O 18 '66
Minority nationalities; China. J. Kolmas. Bul Atomic Sci 22:71-4 Je '66
New melting pot; Time essay. Time 88:30-1 D 2 '66
See also
Race discrimination

MINOT, N.D.
Firm price for six years of service. V. Fahy. il Am City 81:106-7 My '66
MINSHEW, Velon H.
Stratigraphy of the Wisconsin Range, Horlick Mountains, Antarctica. bibliog Science 152:637-8 Ap 29 '66
MINSK, Russia
Minsk's 900th. B. Moore. Sat R 50:98 Ja 7 '67
MINSKY, Marvin L.
Artificial intelligence; with biographical sketch. Sci Am 215:51, 246-52+ S '66
MINSTREL show, or Civil rights in a cracker barrel; musical comedy. See Musical comedies, revues, etc.—Criticisms, plots, etc.
MINTO, Wallace L.
Is plasmonics for the birds? J. D. Drummond. Pop Electr 25:63-5 Jl '66
Sarasota mystery. K. Warner. il por Pop Electr 24:50-3 Mr; 48 Ap '66
MINTON, Robert M.
Tunnel diodes. por Electr World 76:41-4 Jl '66
MINTZ, David A.
Approach to residential lighting. Arch Rec 139:7+ mid-My '66
MINUJIN, Marta
Latin labyrinth. il Newsweek 67:90 F 21 '66
MINUS, Paul M. jr, and Core, A. C.
United Methodist church: critique and proposal. Christian Cent 83:174-5+ F 9 '66
MINUTEMEN (organization)
Arrest Minutemen. Sr Schol 89:20-1 D 2 '66
California: the Minuteman. J. Poppy. il Look 30:103-4 Je 28 '66
Patriots; raids in New York. il Newsweek 68:31 N 14 '66
Sunday patriots; raids. Time 88:32 N 11 '66
Zero hour for the Minutemen; with report by S. Mahoney. il Life 61:51-2 N 11 '66
MION, Renee
With regards & love to the editors of Esq. Esquire 66:20+ D '66
MIR, Marjorie
Haiku; poem. Horn Bk 42:698 D '66
MIRABILIS Jalapa. See Four o'clocks
MIRACLE, Leonard
Bird hunter's Shangri-la. Outdoor Life 138: 62-3+ N '66
Pleasure before work. pors Outdoor Life 137:42-3+ Ap '66
Silver from the sea. Outdoor Life 138:50-2+ Jl '66
Where hunters never fail. pors Outdoor Life 173:60-1+ Je '66
MIRACLE fruit. See Berries
MIRACLE, morality and mystery plays
Theater of mystery; from the absurd to the religious. P. Martin. Commonweal 84:582-5 S 16 '66
MIRACLES
See also
Faith cure
MIRÓ, Joan
Second fame: good food. N. Lyon. il por Vogue 147:188-90 Mr 1 '66
Visit to Joan Miró. E. Wolfe. Sr Schol 88: sup26 Ap 15 '66
MIRÓ, Pilar
Second fame: good food. N. Lyon. il por Vogue 147:188-90 Mr 1 '66
MIRRORS
More from mirrors. il Bet Hom & Gard 44:154-5 O '66
North European export mirrors; the evidence and some suggestions. J. C. Hughes. il Antiques 89:856-61 Je '66; Reply. B. G. Teller. 90:693 N '66
MIRRORS for telescopes
Bigger, better mirrors for gazing into space; reflectors for telescopes. il Bsns W p 184-6 My 28 '66
Optical telescope built; glass mirror with reflecting coat of aluminum. il Sci N 89: 297 Ap 23 '66
MIRSKY, Jonathan
Asia trap: what do we do now? Nation 202: 524-6 My 2 '66
Ho chi Minh: poet in leg irons. Nation 202: 302-3 Mr 14 '66
Two sides to the Dienbienphu story. Nation 202:781-4 Je 27 '66
MISANTHROPE; drama. See Moliere, J. B. P.
MISCARRIAGE of justice. See Justice, Miscarriage of
MISCEGENATION. See Intermarriage of races
MISCONDUCT in office
Correctives for dishonest and unfair public administrators. B. Bolles. Ann Am Acad 363:23-7 Ja '66
MISHELL, Robert I. and Dutton, R. W.
Immunization of normal mouse spleen cell suspensions in vitro. bibliog Science 153: 1004-6 Ag 26 '66

MISHIMA, Yukio, pseud.
Patriotism; story. Esquire 65:106-7 Ap '66
about
Japanese modern. J. Wain. New Repub 155: 25-8 Jl 30 '66
Japan's dynamo of letters; with report by J. Nathan. il pors Life 61:25-31 S 2 '66
MISHKIN, Edward
Bad news for smut peddlers. il Time 87:56+ Ap 1 '66
Court declines to review two censorship convictions. Pub W 189:49 My 9 '66
Obscenity test; legal poser. il Newsweek 67: 19+ Ap 4 '66
Police nail Mishkin in raid on Times square bookstore. Pub W 189:79 Ap 18 '66
MISS America contests. See Beauty contests
MISS Idella, the travelling hoe lady; story. See Morgan, B.
MISS Teen-age America contests. See Beauty contests
MISSILE sleds. See Rocket sleds
MISSILES, Guided. See Guided missiles
MISSILES and rockets (periodical)
Memo from the publisher (cont) J. W. Claar. Miss & Roc 18:7 F 21; 6 Mr 28; 5 Ap 4 '66
Note:
For material after June 6, 1966, see Technology week (periodical)
MISSION church buildings. See Church architecture
MISSION RANGE
1925-trip into the Missions. K. D. Swan. il Liv Wildn 29:3-8 Wint '65
Summer of riches; Montana's Mission Valley. H. Cruickshank. il Audubon Mag 68:86-91 Mr '66
MISSIONARIES
Crisis in mission. R. H. Bolton. Christian Cent 83:647-50 My 18 '66
Domestic missionaries. G. A. Hyde. il America 115:833-4 D 24 '66
Exit Burma's missionaries. America 114:763 My 28 '66
Killing them definitively; Protestant missionaries in Stanleyville area during massacre. P. F. Semonin. Nation 202:129-32 Ja 31 '66
Missionaries abroad. K. S. Latourette. Ann Am Acad 368:21-30 N '66
Persistent error: missionaries being identified with European or American colonizing powers. A. Sandilands. Christian Cent 84:54 Ja 11 '67
MISSIONS
Evangelical congress on worldwide mission; Wheaton, Ill. college campus April 9-16, 1966. M. Shelly. Christian Cent 83:695-7 My 25 '66
See also
Airplanes in church work
Evangelistic work
Laymen's overseas service (organization)
Methodist church—Missions
Missionaries

Indians of North America
See Indians of North America—Missions

Industrial work
Morality for managers: new form of experimental ministry in the U.S: the industrial missions. il Time 87:82 Je 24 '66

Africa
Persistent error: missionaries being identified with European or American colonizing powers. A. Sandilands. Christian Cent 84:54 Ja 11 '67
See also
Christians in Africa

Burma
Era ends; American missonaries expelled by Burmese government. Christian Cent 83:485 Ap 20 '66

California
See California—Missions

China
See also
Catholic church in China

Congo (capital Kinshasa)
Needed: new mission stance in the Congo. C. T. Underwood. Christian Cent 83:1091+ S 7 '66

Florida
See Florida—Missions

New Guinea
Mission to the stone age: Nancy and Dennis Cochrane among the Dunas. E. Nadel. il Look 31:30-4 Ja 24 '67

MISSIONS—*Continued*

United States

See also
Indians of North America—Missions

MISSISSIPPI
See also
Courts—Mississippi
Festivals—Mississippi
Jackson
Law—Mississippi
Prohibition—Mississippi

Anti-poverty program

CDGM muddle. New Repub 155:9 N 12 '66
Children and politics. Nation 203:501 N 14 '66
Mississippi: new plantations. M. Hoffman and J. Mudd. il Nation 203:411-15 O 24 '66
Shriver comes across; Child development group of Mississippi wins fight for funds from OEO. New Repub 156:10-11 Ja 7 '67
Small start in Mississippi. R. L. Shayon. Sat R 50:99 Ja 14 '67

Economic conditions

Delta: rich land and poor people. F. Davis. Reporter 34:41-3 Mr 24 '66
Thorntons of Mississippi; peonage on the plantation. P. Good. il Atlan 218:95-100 S '66

History

Democracy comes to Mississippi, 1870-1875. L. Bennett, jr. il Ebony 21:127-30+ F '66

Politics and government

Boycott and ballot; C. Evers aims. H. Hurt. Reporter 35:23+ Ag 11 '66
Mississippi: a changing state. C. J. Mc-Naspy. America 115:387-8 O 1 '66
Problems facing Mississippi; address, April 6, 1966. T. Webb. Vital Speeches 32:459-61 My 15 '66

Race problems

Accommodating whites. C. Jencks. New Repub 154:19-22 Ap 16 '66
Beware state policy bearing protection; task of the James Meredith march. J. Witcover. New Repub 154:11-12 Je 25 '66
Blind bigotry on U.S. 51; ambushing of J. H. Meredith. Christian Cent 83:793 Je 22 '66
Boycott and ballot; C. Evers aims. H. Hurt. Reporter 35:23+ Ag 11 '66
Br'er Fox; continuation of protest march begun by James Meredith. il Time 87:31 Je 24 '66
Curbing the Delta ministry. Time 87:84 Je 10 '66
Delta: rich land and poor people. F. Davis. Reporter 34:41-3 Mr 24 '66
Double discrimination; civil rights activists and the draft. Nation 203:564 N 28 '66
Grenada revisited. Newsweek 68:29-30 Jl 25 '66
Heat on Highway 51. il Time 87:26-7 Je 17 '66
March, in step and out; Meredith march. il Newsweek 68:14-16 Jl 4 '66
March Meredith began. il Newsweek 67:27-31 Je 20 '66
Marching where? Meredith march achievements. Reporter 35:12+ Jl 14 '66
Meredith ambush. Nation 202:731 Je 20 '66
Mission of Marian Wright. P. Pierce. il Ebony 21:94-7+ Je '66
Mississippi: a changing state. C. J. Mc-Naspy. America 115:387-8 O 1 '66
Mississippi mayor fights the Klan. A. Schardt. Reporter 34:39-40 Ja 27 '66
Problems facing Mississippi; address, April 6, 1966. T. Webb. Vital Speeches 32:459-61 My 15 '66
Race issue inflamed again; aftermath of a shooting; J. Meredith, with editorial comment. il U S News 60:36-8, 112 Je 20 '66
Strange march through Mississippi. il U S News 60:48 Je 27 '66
Uneasy silence; lack of historical literature after 1964 Mississippi summer project. P. Cowan. Nation 202:136-9 Ja 31 '66
Walk in the South to conquer old fears; J. Meredith's return to Mississippi. il Life 60:30-5 Je 17 '66
White look at black power. P. Good. il Nation 203:112-17 Ag 8 '66
Winter in the Delta; evicted Mississippi Negroes living in tent city. Commonweal 83:573 F 18 '66

Religious institutions and affairs

Showdown in the Delta; National council of churches report on Ministry. il Newsweek 67:67 Je 6 '66

Social conditions

Secret crisis in the Delta; Negro farm laborers. il Newsweek 67:28-9 Mr 7 '66
Strike that failed. D. R. Maxey. il Look 30:26-9 Mr 8 '66

MISSISSIPPI delta region. See Louisiana

MISSISSIPPI RIVER
Down the Mississippi; passage from Lake Michigan to New Orleans. J. L. Naumann. il Yachting 120:54-6+ N '66

Discovery and exploration

Mighty Mississippi: a full-length portrait. H. Sutton. McCalls 93:40+ Jl '66

Regulation

Plywood wall holds back the Mississippi. il Am City 81:171 My '66

MISSISSIPPI state university, State College
Fine, but not dandy; violators of M.S.U. parking rules to be prosecuted in local courts Time 88:40 Jl 29 '66

MISSISSIPPI test facility. See Proving grounds

MISSISSIPPI. University
If they wouldn't play Dixie so much; Ole Miss's Negro students. M. Frady. il Mlle 63:333+ Ag '66
Integration at Ole Miss. il Ebony 21:29-32+ My '66
Three years in Mississippi, by J. Meredith. Review
Sat R 49:31-2 My 28 '66. B. D. Diamonstein

School of law

New mood at Ole Miss. Time 88:76 S 23 '66

MISSOURI
See also
Booksellers and bookselling—Missouri
Fishing—Missouri
Hunting—Missouri

MISSOURI state library, Jefferson City, Mo.
Missouri librarians go literary at state library winter institute. Library J 91:2788 Je 1 '66

MISSOURI. University
Missouri's upward reach. il Time 87:72 F 4 '66

MISSOURI. University, Columbia
Photographers of the year: two for the title. M. R. Weiss. il Sat R 49:72-3 My 14 '66

MISTAKES. See Blunders

Mr Lazy man's family; drama. See Ward, M.

MR TRAVEL award
Twelfth annual Mr Travel award; Hubert H. Humphrey elected. il Travel 126:38-40+ Jl '66

MISTLETOE
Nature note. il Sci N 90:526 D 24 '66

MRS Barker; story. See West, A.

MRS Carroway, my name is Peabody, and I represent. . ; story. See Robinson, B.

MISUNDERSTANDINGS, International. See International relations

MITCHELL, Carleton
Fresh breeze stirs the Leewards. Nat Geog Mag 130:488-537 O '66
Great American sailboats; Finisterre; ed. by R. Stephens. Motor B 117:24-5+ Je '66

MITCHELL, Clarence
Excerpt from statement, June 29, 1965. Cong Digest 45:54+ F '66

MITCHELL, Cynthia
August white sales. Suc Farm 64:65+ Ag '66
What's behind your headaches. Suc Farm 64:131+ Mr '66

MITCHELL, D. Michael
Insurance. Yachting 119:75+ Ap '66

MITCHELL, David
Voices of spring; story. Redbook 127:68-9 S '66

MITCHELL, David H. 3d
Inglory boys. Time 87:21 Mr 25 '66

MITCHELL, George
Good living in Houston: at home beside the bayou. W. McQuade. il Fortune 74:110-15 Jl 1 '66

MITCHELL, Henry H.
Negro worship and universal need. Christian Cent 83:396-8 Mr 30 '66

MITCHELL, J. McD.
Renovate or rebuild? Am City 81:147-8+ O '66

MITCHELL, Mabel M.
Universal education for four-year-olds? NEA J 55:10-11 N '66

MITCHELL, Marion (Strobel) See Strobel, M

MITCHELL, Roger
Reading a book of poems; poem. Nation 202:565 My 9 '66

MITCHELL, Ronald
Gentleman Johnny. Opera N 30:6-7 Mr 5 '66

MITCHELL, William R.
Hear us singing; poem. Christian Cent 84:9 Ja 4 '67
MITCHELTREE, Wallace A.
Drought. Horticulture 44:36-7 Je '66
MITCHISON, Naomi
Dry days in Botswana. Sat R 49:65-6+ O 22 '66
Scottish mother for an African tribe. Harper 233:86-8+ S '66
MITES
Mites on a substrate. S. Radinovsky. il Natur Hist 75:38-43 Je '66
Nature note; red water mite. Sci N 89:187 Mr 19 '66
MITFORD, Jessica
American way of aging. McCalls 93:90-1+ Mr '66
Hello, there! you're on the air. Harper 232: 47-53 My '66
Pretty, lascivious, undignified. Vogue 147: 92-3 Mr 15 '66
Question of custody. McCalls 93:96-7+ My '66
MITGANG, Herbert
Israeli mosaics... Atlan 218:108-12 Ag '66
Looking for a war. N Y Times Mag p28-9+ My 22 '66
New inquiry is needed. N Y Times Mag p 14 D 25 '66
MITICH, Larry W.
Weeds in small grains, how to control them. Suc Farm 64:97+ Mr '66
MITOCHONDRIA
Biosynthesis of DNA by isolated mito-chondria: incorporation of thymidine triphosphate-2-C^{14}. P. Parsons and M. V. Simpson. bibliog il Science 155:91-3 Ja 6 '67
Heterosis: complementation by mitochondria. R. G. McDaniel and I. V. Sarkissian. bibliog il Science 152:1640-2 Je 17 '66
Mitochondrial DNA in yeast and some mammalian species. G. Corneo and others. bibliog il Science 151:687-9 F 11 '66
Nonphosphorylating respiration of mito-chondria from brown adipose tissue of rats. R. E. Smith and others. bibliog il Science 154:653-4 N 4 '66
Pyruvate oxidation and the permeability of mitochondria from blowfly flight muscle. C. C. Childress and B. Sacktor. bibliog il Science 154:268-70 O 14 '66
Respiratory control: loss in mitochondria from diseased plants. H. Wheeler and P. J. Hanchey. bibliog il Science 154:1569-71 D 23 '66
Salt transport organelle in artemia salenis (brine shrimp) E. Copeland. bibliog il Science 151:470-1 Ja 28 '66
MITOSIS. See Cell division (biology)
MITSUI trading company. See Japan—Industries
MITTAL, Jai P. See Lamola, A. A. jt. auth.
MITTERRAND, François
France is no longer a democracy. por N Y Times Mag p 14-15+ My 29 '66
MIX, Sheldon A.
Perfect vacation blend: one Great Lake, four states. Todays Health 44:42-9 Je '66
Solid wastes: every day, another 800 million pounds. Todays Health 44:46-9 Mr '66
That unforgettable month: December 1941. Todays Health 44:12-15 D '66
MIXED marriages. See Marriages, Mixed
MIXED-up feed and the silly bridegroom; story. See Singer, I. B.
MIXES, Food. See Food mixes
MIXING utensils
See also
Electric apparatus and appliances, Domestic
MIXON, James E. and Kitchens, J. H. Jr
When the South marched! pors Am For 72: 36-41 Mr '66
MIZER, Jean E.
Roots of failure; secondary school comment. NEA J 55:36 Ap '66
MIZOS. See India—Native races
MOB violence
Day I learned about prejudice: mob murder. E. A. Morrison. Mlle 63:122+ S '66
If mob rule takes hold in U.S: a warning from Richard Nixon. R. M. Nixon. U S News 61: 64-5 Ag 15 '66
MOBERG, Carl Axel
Spread of agriculture in the North European periphery. bibliog Science 152:315-19 Ap 15 '66
MOBIL oil company
New approach in automobile repair. C. Stevenson and K. W. Purdy. il Read Digest 90:123-6 Ja '67
Quiet aggression of Mobil oil. T. J. Murray. il Duns R 88:34-7+ S '66

MOBILE, Ala.
Newspapers
Sam hits 21; Newhouse empire. Time 88:47 Jl 15 '66
MOBILE homes. See Automobile trailers; Campers and coaches, Truck
MOBILE homes manufacturers association
Where housing market has lots of life; mobile homes gaining new respectability. il Bsns W p 150+ S 3 '66
MOBILE libraries. See Bookmobiles
MOBILE lunar laboratory. See Lunar vehicles
MOBILE service shops. See Automobile service stations
MOBILES
Decorate your yard and home with Walt Disney's Christmas mobile. W. C. Leckey. il Pop Mech 126:69-73+ D '66
MOBILITY test article. See Lunar vehicles
MOBILIZATION, Industrial. See Industrial mobilization
MOBILIZATION, Military. See United States—Armed forces—Mobilization
MOBILIZATION for youth, incorporated
Learning by doing; homework helpers. il Time 88:98+ O 21 '66
Teacher is a teen-ager. il Newsweek 68:89-90 Ag 22 '66
MOBS
See also
Mob violence
MOBUTU, Joseph Désiré
Black hoods in the square. il por Time 87:46 Je 10 '66
Crisis over copper. il por Time 89:31 Ja 13 '67
Crushing the Kats. il Time 88:47 O 14 '66
Death in the sun. il Newsweek 67:66 Je 13 '66
Last chance for Parliament. por Time 87:39 Ap 1 '66
New order. il Time 88:33+ Jl 22 '66
Papa is dead. Newsweek 69:46+ Ja 16 '67
MOCK, Russell C.
Gone flying to Mexico. Flying 78:46-51 Ap '66
MOCK oranges
Fragrant mock-orange. E. S. Henderson. il Flower Grower 53:56+ Mr '66
MOCKLER, Tony
Santo Domingo; labyrinth of policy. Nation 202:154-7 F 7 '66
MODAVIS, Howard
Mail-order dogs. Field & S 91:144-5+ Je '66
MODEL car racing. See Automobile models—Racing
MODEL houses. See Houses, Model
MODELS
See also
Molecules—Models
also specific types of models, e.g. Space vehicles models
MODELS (display figures)
New dress form helps home economics students. il Sci N L 89:54 Ja 22 '66
MODELS (persons)
Beauty gap; West Germany's need for foreign models to replace departed German girls. il Newsweek 67:74 My 30 '66
Handhold a 300mm lens. il U S Camera 29: 60-1 Je '66
Hold it, that's the pose! P. Gowland. il Pop Phot 58:76-7 My '66
Luna year. il Time 87:47 Ap 1 '66
Mad mad models of David Thorpe. il U S Camera 29:50-1 Ap '66
Model's day. R. Busch. il Pop Phot 59:82-3+ Jl '66
See also
Twiggy (model)
Veruschka
MODELS of cities, towns, etc.
1880 Tinytown, Dakota territory. A. Peterson. Hobbies 71:123+ N '66
Great American West in miniatures. R. J. Ward. il Hobbies 71:122-3 S '66
He built a prize-winning town; Wakarusa, Ind. S. A. Parvin. il Hobbies 70:120-2 F '66
Holland has a town in miniature; Maduro-dam, The Hague. il Sunset 138:36+ Ja '67
Miniature house started a town. W. Briner. il Hobbies 71:110 Ja '67
MODERN art museum, New York. See Museum of modern art, New York
MODERN civilization. See Civilization
MODERN dance. See Dancing
MODERN fiction. See Fiction
MODERN furniture. See Furniture

MODERN language association of America
English aided by Ford grant: Center for applied linguistics. Sr Schol 87:sup3 Ja 7 '66
First humanities grant: MLA receives $300,000; fund allocated to Center for editions of American authors. Pub W 190:39-40 Ag 8 '66

MODERN literature. See Literature

MODERN music. See Music

MODERN opera. See Opera—United States

MODERN photography (periodical)
Modern tests; how? T. Karp. il Mod Phot 30:58-61+ Je '66

MODERN sculpture. See Sculpture

MODERNISM (art)
And now: Top; pioneers of topographical art. il Time 87:58-9 F 11 '66
Art & information. D. Antin. il Art N 65:22-4+ Ap '66 (to be cont)
Art in orbit; kinetic art. il Newsweek 67:92-4 Ap 4 '66
Artist as playwright and engineer. R. Kostelanetz. il N Y Times Mag p32-3+ O 9 '66
Beautiful, Jean-Jacques; week-long Destruction in art symposium, London. il Time 88:37 S 23 '66
Big-city boy; show at New York's Janis gallery by C. Oldenburg. il Newsweek 67:100 Mr 21 '66
Calico dames in a frolic of art. il Life 60:58-60+ Ap 1 '66
Climbing Mt Oldenburg; pop art. H. Rosenstein. il Art N 64:21-5+ F '66
Everybody's object; consensus objet d'art of 1965. il Time 87:85 Ap 29 '66
Experimental art. A. Kaprow. il Art N 65:60-3+ Mr '66
Fourteen stations of the cross, 1958-1966. B. Newman. il Art N 65:26-8+ My '66
From Pollock to pop; twenty years of painting and sculpture. H. Rosenberg. il Holiday 39:96-105+ Mr '66
Guide for the unperplexed; anxiety of modern art. H. Rosenberg. Art N 65:46-7+ S '66
In my opinion; teens should open their eyes to pop, op, top and hop. L. Kohn. Seventeen 25:272 Ap '66
It; exhibition of her modular paintings at the East Hampton gallery; interview. C. Dantzic. New Yorker 42:27-8 My 28 '66
Latin labyrinth; M. Minujin. il Newsweek 67:90 F 21 '66
Mathematical games; eerie mathematical art of Maurits C. Escher. M. Gardner. il Sci Am 214:110-11+ Ap '66
Movement movement; kinetic artists. il Time 87:64-9 Ja 28 '66
Must everything be ugly? mother looks at contemporary arts. C. Seton. il Redbook 127:59+ S '66
News of art. il Horizon 9:78-9 Wint '67
News of art; cocktails, commotion, and creepies. il Horizon 8:92-3 Aut '66
One for the road; Segal's plaster driver in the truck. il Time 88:60 Ag 26 '66
Profiles; R. C. Scull, collector of pop art. J. Kramer. New Yorker 42:64-6+ N 26 '66
Progressive seebang; Seven decades of modernism in Manhattan. il Time 87:70-3 My 6 '66
Recent art in a climate of change. J. W. Moody. Christian Cent 83:401-3 Mr 30 '66
Savonarola in the City of Angels; assemblages of E. Kienholz. il Time 87:78 Ap 8 '66
Sort of the Svengali of pop; L. Castelli. J. Greenfeld. il N Y Times Mag p34-5+ My 8 '66
Story of pop. P. Benchley. il Newsweek 67:56-8+ Ap 25 '66
Times square of the mind; neon lighting. il Time 87:100-1 Mr 18 '66
True father of modern painting. H. Kramer. il N Y Times Mag p30-1+ Mr 20 '66
Valentine it is not. N. Kent. Am Artist 30:3+ F '66
Virtuosos of boredom. H. Rosenberg. Vogue 148:296-7+ S 1 '66
What is art coming to? R. Wraight. il Horizon 8:4-11 Spr '66
What modern art says about America. M. Fishwick. Sat R 49:19-20+ Ap 9 '66
See also
Dadaism
Happenings (art)
Impressionism (art)

MODERNISM (literature)
Modern movement, by C. Connolly. Review
Time 87:92 Mr 25 '66

MODERNISM in music. See Music

MODERNIZATION. See Social change

MODERNIZATION of houses. See Houses, Remodeled

MODESTO, Calif.
Electronics makes a better water system. R. A. Hosegood. il Am City 81:137+ N '66

MODIGLIANI, Amedeo
Modigliani's subject of desire. J. Perreault. il Art N 65:42-3+ O '66

MODULAR coordination (architecture)
Habitat 67; Fuller's Dymaxion house, and Safdie's Habitat 67. D. Jacobs. il Horizon 9:70-3 Wint '67
Steps down to the sea; private school in Spain. il Arch Forum 125:44-7 D '66

MODULAR design. See Modular coordination (architecture)

MOE, Christian. See McCalmon, G. jt. auth.

MOEDLAREUTH wall. See Germany (Democratic Republic)—Boundaries

MOELLER, Hans-Bernhard
Reshuffle in Bonn. Commonweal 85:281-2 D 9 '66

MOERDLER, Charles G.
Blue Moerdler. Newsweek 67:36+ Mr 28 '66

MOERS, Ellen
Victorian pornography and other fallibilities. Harper 233:119-20+ O '66

MOFFAT, Alex W.
Through a glass darkly. Yachting 119:194 F '66

MOFFAT, Donald W.
Straight-wire inductance graph. Electr World 75:27 F '66

MOFFAT, George
Long ride home. H. Peterson. il por Sports Illus 25:35-7 Ag 1 '66

MOFFETT, A. and Ettlinger, G.
Opposite responding in two sense modalities. bibliog Science 153:205-6; 154:799 Jl 8, N 11 '66

MOFFETT, Hugh
Anywhere, everywhere for the story, for the news, the meaning, the drama. Life 61:120B-120C+ D 23 '66
Cars fit drivers like gloves, and there's no belt. por Life 61:126A-126B O 28 '66
Don't call me Madame Prime Minister. Life 60:78B-78D Mr 25 '66
Hot spy writer on the lam. Life 60:84-6+ Mr 25 '66
Unflagging, septuagenarian Mzee and his statuesque Mama Ngina. Life 61:44-9+ Ag 5 '66
Unholy war of preacher Paisley. Life 61:35-6+ Ag 19 '66
Vacationist's verdict by our own gentil membre. Life 60:86 F 25 '66

MOFFIT, J. C. See Fulton, W. R. jt. auth.

MOFFITT, John
Among the waves; poem. America 114:262 F 19 '66

MOFFO, Anna
Do the things you love. por Seventeen 25:172+ N '66
about
Instinct for drama. H. Klein. por Opera N 31:46-7 S 17 '66

MOHAMMED Reza Pahlevi, shah of Iran
One day's expenditure on arms; letter. UNESCO Courier 19:33 Je '66

MOHAMMEDANISM. See Islam

MOHAN, Robert Paul
Seminarians and service. America 114:384-5 Mr 19 '66

MOHAWK airlines, incorporated
Small jets get into a dogfight; American-Mohawk squabble over Syracuse air travelers. il Bsns W p 163 My 7 '66

MOHENJO-DARO
Decline of the Harappans. G. F. Dales. il Sci Am 214:92-8+ bibliog(p 147) My '66

MOHOLE project
Drowning Mohole; Congress cuts off funds. Bsns W p62 S 3 '66
Haskins speaks out; summary of report. C. P. Haskins. Sci N 90:528 D 24 '66
Mohole: aground on Capitol hill. D. S. Greenberg. Science 153:963 Ag 26 '66
Mohole; preliminary drilling. H. H. Hess and H. S. Ladd. bibliog il Science 152:544-5 Ap 22 '66
Mohole; Senate is asked to restore funds. D. S. Greenberg. Science 153:38-9 Jl 1 '66
NSF appropriation; mutiny on the Mohole. D. S. Greenberg. Science 152:895-6 My 13 '66
No Mohole? Sci Am 215:48 Jl '66
Penny wise, pound foolish. P. H. Abelson. Science 152:1333 Je 3 '66
Point of the deal. Nation 203:172 S 5 '66
Politics and poker. W. J. Coughlin. Tech W 19:50 Ag 29 '66
Project nohole? House kills appropriation. Newsweek 68:60+ Ag 29 '66

MOHOLY-NAGY, Sibyl
Rear end of the Xerox, or how I learned to love that library. Arch Forum 124:61 My '66

MOHRHARDT, Foster E.
Invitation and a plea. ALA Bul 60:763 S '66
New ALA officer. V. W. Clapp. por ALA Bul 60:714+ Jl '66

MOHWA. See Butter trees

MOIRÉ patterns. See Design, Decorative

MOISEYEV dance company
Moiseyev's army conquers Spain. C. Irizarry. il Dance Mag 41:28-31 Ja '67

MOISTURE
Convection plumes from ulmus americana. L. E. B. Peterson and A. W. H. Damman; discussion. Science 149:764; 150:783, 1629; 152:387 Ag 13, N 5, D 17 '65, Ap 15 '66

MOK, Michael
Futuristic features, a fountain sink, low toilet, lounge-like tub. Life 60:84-6 My 20 '66
Stalking the terror of Shade Gap. Life 60: 32B-32E My 27 '66

MOLAB (mobile lunar laboratory) See Lunar vehicles

MOLARS. See Teeth

MOLDENHAUER, Hans
In quest of Webern. por Sat R 49:47-9+ Ag 27 '66

MOLDING plastics. See Plastics—Molding

MOLDINGS (architecture)
Custom look with wood moldings. il Bet Hom & Gard 44:70-1 S '66

MOLDS (botany)
Science in action; mold-made flavors; excerpts from Mushrooms, molds and miracles. L. Kavaler. Natur Hist 75:62+ Ap '66
Trehalase from dictyostelium discoideum: purification and properties. C. Ceccarini. bibliog il Science 151:454-6 Ja 28 '66
See also
Fungi
Phycomyces

MOLDS (for casting)
Sand mold casting with styrofoam. J. D. Kain. il Sch Arts 65:36-8 Je '66
Silicone molds for art; reproducing Aztec calendar stone and Altamira cave paintings. il Sci N 89:314 Ap 30 '66

MOLECULAR anatomy. See Molecules

MOLECULAR beams
Laboratory-made beam simulates outer space. Sci N 90:352 O 29 '66

MOLECULAR dynamics
See also
Molecular beams

MOLECULES
Antibody active sites and immunoglobulin molecules. S. J. Singer and R. F. Doolittle. bibliog il Science 153:13-25 Jl 1 '66
Circular dichroism of biological macromolecules. S. Beychok. bibliog il Science 154:1288-99 D 9 '66
Crystal and molecular structure of acetylselenocholine iodide. E. Shefter and O. Kennard. bibliog il Science 153:1389-90 S 16 '66
Framework rearrangement in boranes and carboranes. W. N. Lipscomb. bibliog il Science 153:373-8 Jl 22 '66
Genetic code. F. H. C. Crick. il Sci Am 215: 55-60+ bibliog(p 150) O '66
High-resolution mass spectrometry. F. W. McLafferty. bibliog il Science 151:641-9 F 11 '66
Interpretation of some organic photochemistry. H. E. Zimmerman. bibliog il Science 153:837-44 Ag 19 '66
Kinetic isotope effects and organic reaction mechanisms. M. J. Goldstein. bibliog il Science 154:1616-21 D 30 '66
Molecular basis of differentiation; report on workshop. G. L. Cantoni and A. Monroy. Science 151:597-8 F 4 '66
Molecular orbital densities: pictorial studies. A. C. Wahl. bibliog il Science 151:961-7 F 25 '66
New particle detected; excitonic molecule. Sci N 90:349 O 29 '66
New process discovered in molecules' dance. Sci N 89:331 My 7 '66
Spin label studies in chlamydomonas. E. C. Weaver and H. P. Chon. bibliog il Science 153:301-3 Jl 15 '66
Structure of cell membranes at the molecular level; report on conference. D. T. Warner. Science 153:324-6 Jl 15 '66
Three-dimensional structure of an enzyme molecule. D. C. Phillips. il Sci Am 215: 78-90 bibliog(p 160) N '66
Ultracentrifuge schlieren photographs: automatic analysis. R. Moore and others. il Science 152:1509-11 Je 10 '66

Very fast reactions in solution. G. G. Hammes. bibliog il Science 151:1507-11 Mr 25 '66
Zonal centrifuges and other separation systems. N. G. Anderson. bibliog il Science 154: 103-12 O 7 '66

Models
Molecular model-building by computer. C. Levinthal. il Sci Am 214:42-52 bibliog(p 144) Je '66

MOLES (animals)
Kill grubs to control moles. il Suc Farm 64: 110 Ap '66

MOLEY, Raymond
Perspective. See issues of Newsweek
Reminiscence of a braintruster. D. Young. Sat R 49:49-51+ D 24 '66

MOLIÈRE, Jean Baptiste Poquelin
Misanthrope; tr. by R. Wilbur. Criticism
Sat R 49:54 Mr 5 '66

MOLINA, Rafael Leonidas Trujillo. See Trujillo Molina, R. L.

MOLINARI-PRADELLI, Francesco
Fine Italian hand; interview, ed. by P. Elvins. por Opera N 30:13 F 12 '66
Music to my ears; Metropolitan's newest conductor. I. Kolodin. Sat R 49:41 F 26 '66

MOLLENHOFF, Clark
Mollenhoff cocktail. il por Time 88:35 Ag 12 '66

MOLLOY, Edward A.
Consider the lilies. Criticism
America 114:271-2 F 19 '66

MOLLUSKS
Bivalve mollusks: fluid dynamics of burrowing. E. R. Trueman. bibliog il Science 152: 523-5 Ap 22 '66
Improbable mollusk; glaucus atlanticus. W. M. Stephens. il Natur Hist 75:44-5 Ag '66
Species specific effect of acetylcholine on bivalve rectums. M. J. Greenberg. bibliog il Science 154:1015-17 N 25 '66
See also
Nautilus
Oysters
Parasites—Mollusks
Pearls
Sea hares

MOLLUSKS, Fossil
Pleistocene age determinations from California and Oregon. H. G. Richards and D. L. Thurber. bibliog il Science 152:1091-2 My 20 '66
Precambrian mollusc-like fossils from Inyo County, California. M. E. Taylor. bibliog il Science 153:198-201 Jl 8 '66

MOLNAR, Thomas
Imperial America. Nat R 18:409-11, 559+ My 3, Je 14 '66
No new road. Nat R 18:122+. 383 F 8, Ap 19 '66

MOLODY, Kenon Trofimovich. See Lonsdale, G. A.

MOLOKAI fracture zone. See Faults (geology)

MOLONEY, Jim
Whar ya headin' sailor, that ain't your bow! Motor B 117:108+ F '66

MOLTON, Warren Lane
Any Holy week; poem. Christian Cent 83: 423 Ap 6 '66
Good shepherd of goats; poem. Christian Cent 83:1565 D 21 '66
Key to kingdoms; poem. Christian Cent 83: 887 Jl 13 '66
Sacrum scrabbulium; poem. Christian Cent 83:1210 O 5 '66

MOLYBDENUM
Molybdenum diselenide: rhombohedral high pressure-high temperature polymorph. L. C. Towle and others. bibliog il Science 154:895-6 N 18 '66
Prices have work to do; price increase cancelled. H. Hazlitt. Newsweek 68:73 Ag 1 '66
RCA tests thermal energy pipe. J. F. Judge. il Miss & Roc 18:36-8 F 21 '66

MOLZ, Kathleen
Implications of the Ginzburg affair; address, April 20, 1966. Wilson Lib Bul 40:941-7 Je '66
What should PLA be doing? with comment by E. A. Ferguson. por ALA Bul 60:595-9+ Je '66

MOMMSEN, Theodor
Theodor Mommsen: neglected master of Roman history. W. H. Chamberlain. por Sat R 49:18-19+ My 21 '66

MONACCHIO, E. N. and Plevy, A. L.
Saw-tooth testing of audio-amp'ifiers. Electr World 76:74-6 Jl '66

MONACO, Anthony P. and others
Antiserum to lymphocytes: prolonged survival of canine renal allografts. bibliog Science 153:1264-7 S 9 '66

MONACO
  See also
  Monte Carlo
  Tourist trade—Monaco

Economic conditions
Putting Monaco back on the tourist's map;
  Prince Rainier vs Aristotle Onassis, the
  Greek shipping magnate. il Bsns W p28-9
  Jl 30 '66

Economic policy
Duel in the sun; economic dictatorship over
  Monte Carlo by A. S. Onassis. il Newsweek
  68:42 Jl 18 '66

MONAHAN, James. See Miller, L. M. jt. auth.

MONARCH butterflies. See Butterflies

MONARCHY
  Continuing magic of monarchy; Time essay.
  Time 88:32-3 D 9 '66

MONAS, Sidney
  Reasonable bigotry. Commentary 42:96-9 D '66

MONASTERIES
  All is one, one is none, none is all. P.
  Kapleau. il N Y Times Mag p26-7+ Mr 6
  '66
  Monks, nuns and monasteries, by S. Sitwell.
  Review
    Commonweal 84:159-60 Ap 22 '66. A.
    Fremantle
  Off the old Roman road to Jericho; Monastery
  of St George. il Sunset 137:60+ O '66
  See also
  Athos, Mount
  Convents and nunneries
  Escorial

MONASTICISM
  Monks in psychoanalysis. Time 88:80 D 2 '66
  Printing monks of Venice; Armenian Catholic
  monks of the Mechitarian order, printers
  of Books in Armenian. H. R. Lottman.
  Pub W 190:110-11 D 5 '66

Le MONDE. See Paris—Newspapers

MONDEL, Carl
  Chocolates. New Yorker 41:29-31 F 19 '66

MONDRIAAN, Pieter Cornelis
  Mondrian and romanticism; excerpt from
  catalogue of Toronto show. R. Rosenblum.
  il pors Art N 64:33-7+ F '66

MONET, Claude
  Diary of a Paris art dealer; excerpts from
  Diary of an art dealer. R. Gimpel. Vogue
  148:280-1+ O 1 '66
  Double windfall. por Newsweek 67:94+ Mr 28
  '66
  Lasting impression; Monet collection left to
  the Académie des beaux-arts. il Time 87:
  100 Mr 18 '66

MONET, Michel
  Monet's revenge. P. Schneider. il pors Horizon
  8:28-33 Aut '66

MONETARY and economic conference, London,
  1933
  1933, by H. Feis. Review
    Sat R 49:37 Ap 2 '66. L. J. Walinsky

MONETARY fund. See International monetary
  fund

MONETARY management. See Monetary policy

MONETARY policy
  Cheers for Fed strategy; survey of leading
  financial economists. il Bsns W p83-4+ O 8
  '66
  Current monetary policy; Fed policy regard-
  ing quantity of money. M. Friedman. il
  Newsweek 69:59 Ja 9 '67
  Financing freedom's future; address, April
  25, 1966. J. Exter. Vital Speeches 32:649-56
  Ag 15 '66
  Fiscal and monetary policy; address, Septem-
  ber 12, 1966. L. H. Olsen. Vital Speeches
  33:24-8 O 15 '66
  Is money tight, or isn't it? never been tighter since the 1920s. il Bsns W p96-8 Ag 6 '66
  LBJ clamps down a bit; more restrictive
  fiscal policy. il Bsns W p37-8 S 10 '66
  Trying to ease up on the money markets. il
  Bsns W p38-9 S 17 '66
  When should the Fed ease up? to continue
  the monetary freeze or allow bank reserves
  to grow again. Bsns W p200 O 8 '66
  Wright Patman: a lonely populist; head of
  the House banking and currency committee.
  il Bsns W p51-2+ Jl 23 '66

MONEX W rocket fuel. See Rockets—Fuel

MONEY
  Three more countries switching to the dollar.
  il U S News 60:17 F 21 '66
  See also
  Coins
  Currency convertibility
  Depreciation

Foreign exchange
Gold as money
Inflation (finance)
Interest
Investments

International aspects
Cold-blooded guardians of the world's moneys.
  R. Ball. il Fortune 74:124-9+ O '66
Contingency planning. H. C. Wallich. News-
  week 68:100 O 24 '66
Grim new grab for gold threatens your dollars.
  T. G. Harris. il Look 30:25-7 N 1 '66
Is gold at the end of its reign? il Bsns W
  p 129-30+ F 26 '66
Is the strongest economy in the world going
  bankrupt? interview. J. Rueff. il U S News
  61:60-3 O 17 '66
It's an uphill fight for monetary reform;
  twenty member nations join in the talks.
  il Bsns W p73-4+ S 24 '66
Mischief-maker; plan to create a new kind
  of international monetary reserve. Time 87:
  98 Mr 18 '66
Muddy road to monetary reform; meeting in
  Washington. il Bsns W p40-1 O 1 '66
Other side of the gold and dollar story; in-
  terview. W. S. Salant. il U S News 61:76-8
  O 24 '66
Playing for big chips in Eurodollars. il Bsns
  W p61-2+ D 10 '66
Stride toward monetary reform; IMF-World
  bank meeting. il Newsweek 68:82-4 O 10 '66
  See also
  Finance, International

Australia
Good-by pound, hello dollar. il Newsweek
  67:40 F 28 '66
Shedding shillings; Australia takes plunge
  into decimals. Time 87:39-40 F 25 '66

Brazil
  See also
  Finance—Brazil

France
Test of sobriety; the franc looking a trifle
  weak. Time 88:107 O 14 '66

Germany (Federal Republic)
Too short, too dear & too few; money shortage. il Time 88:70 Ag 12 '66

Great Britain
Britain gets a $1-billion breather; seamen's
  strike threatens ballance-of-payments. il
  Bsns W p44-5 Je 18 '66
Britain gets the point; decimalizing Britain's
  1,200-year-old coinage system. il Bsns W
  p37-8 D 17 '66
British economic situation; address, July 20,
  1966. H. Wilson. Vital Speeches 32:642-6 Ag
  15 '66
Coming: decimal system for Britain's coin-
  age. U S News 60:16 Mr 14 '66
Damn dots at last; decimalize the pound. il
  Time 88:69 D 23 '66
Future of sterling. H. C. Wallich. Newsweek
  68:73 Ag 8 '66
Helping the pound. il Time 88:94 S 23 '66
In for a pound; Bank for international settle-
  ments extends credit. Newsweek 67:78-9
  Je 27 '66
Radical cures, and radical dangers. il News-
  week 68:39-40 Ag 1 '66
Time for miracles; how to reduce the sterling
  drain. il Time 88:78 Jl 15 '66
Wilson clamps down on British economy;
  freeze on wages, prices and dividends. il
  Bsns W p31 Jl 23 '66

Anecdotes, facetiae, satire, etc.
Just for laughs. H. B. Jacobs. il Look 30:15
  O 4 '66

India
India's continuing crisis; rupee devaluated.
  P. Altbach. Christian Cent 83:1158-60 S 21
  '66

Italy
Money, Italian style. Newsweek 68:71-2 Jl
  4 '66
Shortchanged; coin shortage. Time 88:73 S
  2 '66

Russia
Communist cut-rates; campaign to acquire
  foreign money. il Newsweek 68:76 S 5 '66
In Russia: a big scramble for hard money.
  J. Fromm. il U S News 60:96-8 Ap 4 '66

United States
Business and finance; tight supply. il Newsweek 67:84 Mr 21 '66
Creating new strains. il Time 87:79-80 Mr
  25 '66

MONEY—United States—*Continued*
From dollars to doughnuts; the value of money. Sr Schol 89:10 D 9 '66
Grim new grab for gold threatens your dollars. T. G. Harris. il Look 30:25-7 N 1 '66
Half dollars on the way. Newsweek 67:79 Mr 14 '66
Is a money crisis near? il U S News 61:29-31 S 19 '66
Money: its care and nourishment. il Sr Schol 88:4 Ap 1 '66
Their world and our money. A. Campbell. New Repub 155:24-5 S 3 '66
U.S. running out of cash? pinch gets worse and worse. il U S News 61:72-3 O 31 '66
Wall Street: tight money. Newsweek 67:70-1 Mr 7 '66
When money is tightened; what the record shows. U S News 60:90-1 Ap 18 '66
Who's hiding all the half-dollars? il Changing T 21:33-4 Ja '67
See also
Paper money—United States
Silver as money
MONEY, Counterfeit. See Counterfeits and counterfeiting
MONEY management. See Budget, Household
MONEY market
Capital markets show the strain in Europe. il Bsns W p 118+ Je 18 '66
International flow of capital; concerning report of study. UN Mo Chron 3:37-8 Je '66
Where to get the most for money. il Bsns W p 154+ O 8 '66
MONEY raising campaigns. See Fund raising
MONEY rates. See Interest
MONFA, Henri Marie Raymond de Toulouse-Lautrec. See Toulouse-Lautrec Monfa, H. M. R. de
MONGOLIA
Forgotten part of world comes into the news. il U S News 60:80-1 Ap 18 '66
Galloping ahead; twenty-year friendship pact with Russia. il Newsweek 67:42-3 Ja 31 '66
Mongolia: odd prize in the red tug-of-war? C. W. Thayer. il Look 31:60+ Ja 24 '67
Outer Mongolia. L. F. Morris. il Travel 126: 56-8 D '66
See also
Gobi Desert
Hunting—Mongolia
Paleontology—Mongolia

Religious institutions and affairs
Mongolia. J. M. Flagler and J. A. Zill. il Look 31:52-9 Ja 24 '67
MONGOLISM
Lesson from David; concerning son of Bruce Roberts. C. Morrison. il Look 30:32-5 My 3 '66
MONGOLOIDS. See Mongolism
MONITOR, Radio. See Radio instruments
MONK, Edwin
Offshore cruiser. Yachting 119:74-6+ Mr '66
MONK, Meredith
Meredith Monk and Phoebe Neville; Judson memorial church. J. Maskey. Dance Mag 41:69 Ja '67
MONK, Thelonious Sphere
Yesterday's Monk again; new record release. M. Williams. por Sat R 49:60-1 Ja 29 '66
MONKEES. See Singers
MONKEY trial. See Tennessee evolution controversy
MONKEYS
Comparison of the effects of striate cortex and retinal lesions on visual acuity in the monkey. L. Weiskrantz and A. Cowey. bibliog il Science 155:104-6 Ja 6 '67
Free-ranging rhesus monkeys: age and sex differences in individual activity patterns. W. A. Draper. bibliog il Science 151:476-8 Ja 28 '66
Hemoglobin polymorphism in macaca nemestrian. M. H. Crawford. bibliog il Science 154:398-9 O 21 '66
Rhesus monkey bands; social patterns are studied in Puerto Rico. J. G. Vandenbergh. il Natur Hist 75:22-7 My '66
Roots of human nature; evidence that apes are contemporaries, not ancestors. N. J. Berrill. il Atlan 217:92-6 Je '66
Visual acuity in a stumptail macaque. M. Yarczower and others. bibliog il Science 152:1392-3 Je 3 '66
See also
Chimpanzees
Gibbons
Gorillas

Hybrids
Naturally occurring primate hybrid. I. S. Bernstein. il Science 154:1559 D 23 '66
MONKS. See Monasticism
MONOAMINE oxidase
Monoamine oxidase activity in various parts of the rat brain during the estrous cycle. A. J. Zolovick and others. bibliog il Science 154:649 N 4 '66
MONOCARBIDES. See Carbides
MONOCLE (periodical)
Man from Monocle. Newsweek 67:101-2 Je 13 '66
MONOCULARS. See Field glasses
MONOD, Jacques
From enzymatic adaptation to allosteric transitions; address, December 11, 1965. bibliog Science 154:475-83 O 28 '66
MONOGAMY. See Marriage
MONOGENISM. See Man—Origin and antiquity
MONONGAHELA national forest, W.Va. See National forests
MONONGAHELA RIVER VALLEY
Old steel valley starts to shake off its grime; mill towns along Monongahela. il Bsns W p72-3+ Ja 22 '66
Steel's jobless press for relief; steelworkers from McKeesport, Pa, descent on Washington. il Bsns W p90-2 Ja 22 '66
MONONUCLEOSIS, Infectious
College stress and illness. R. M. Osborn. Sci Digest 60:22-4 D '66
Kissing disease; new test developed by G. Hoff. il Life 60:81-2 Mr 18 '66
Mononucleosis not a serious disease. Sci N 90:352 O 29 '66
MONOPOLIES
New partnership; big government and big business. R. J. Barber. New Repub 155:17-22 Ag 13 '66
See also
Restraint of trade
MONOPOLY (game) See Games
MONOPOLY; drama. See Kass, J.
MONORAIL railroads. See Railroads, Single rail
MONOTROPA uniflora. See Indian pipes (plants)
MONRO, J.
Population flushing with sexually sterile insects. bibliog Science 151:1536-8 Mr 25 '66
MONROE, H. Chandler
Factors affecting academic standards; address, March 1, 1966. Vital Speeches 32:562-5 Jl 1 '66
MONROE, Keith
Johnny Weissmuller was a slow swimmer. N Y Times Mag p32-3+ D 18 '66
MONROE, Margaret
New patterns for library service; excerpts from address, October 1964. por Library J 91:1366-70 Mr 15 '66
MONROE, Marilyn
Behind the myth the face of Norma Jean. R. Meryman. il pors Life 61:49-54 N 4 '66
MONROY, A. See Cantoni, G. L. jt. auth.
MONSOONS
Monsoons fail to stop Viet air support. Aviation W 84:80-1 Mr 14 '66
MONSTERS
See also
Loch Ness monster
MONSTERS, Double. See Siamese twins
MONT BLANC
Harrowing freeze-up on the Needle. il Life 61:22B-22C S 2 '66
High performance; derring-do and tragedy on Dru Needle. il Newsweek 68:40+ S 5 '66
Our far-flung correspondents; complete circuit. J. Bernstein. il New Yorker 42:148+ Mr 26 '66
MONT BLANC tunnel. See Tunnels and tunneling
MONT SAINT MICHEL, France
Mont-Saint-Michel millennium. America 115: 574 N 12 '66
Our highwayman in France. H. Sutton. il Sat R 49:37-8 Ag 6 '66
MONTAGE
Montage as visual synthesis. D. Cyr. il Design 67:16-19 My '66
Photo posters in junior high school. J. Lidstone. il Sch Arts 66:27-30 N '66
Visual language. D. Cyr. bibliog il Sch Arts 66:32-5 N '66
See also
Photomontage

MONTAGNARDS
Black Tiger of Mang Buk; concerning special forces lieutenant. S. Booker. il Ebony 21: 68-70+ S '66
Fight at Monkey; excerpt from Battles in the monsoon. S. L. A. Marshall. il Harper 233:111-14+ N '66
Primitive life of Vietnam's mountain people. G. Condominas. il Natur Hist 75:8-13 Je '66
Rights for the mountain men. il Time 88:35-6 O 28 '66

MONTAGU, Lady Mary (Pierrepont) Wortley
Lady in pursuit of enlightenment. G. W. Stone, jr. il Sat R 49:30-1 F 12 '66
Lady Mary, quite contrary. por Time 87:105+ Mr 11 '66
Woman of mixed emotions. B. Boyce. por Sat R 49:58 D 3 '66

MONTAIGNE, Michel Eyquem de
Montaigne's essays. K. Rexroth. Sat R 49:25 F 26 '66

MONTALE, Eugenio
Name of the void. por Time 87:94 Je 3 '66

MONTANA
See also
Booksellers and bookselling—Montana
Fishing—Montana
Hunting—Montana
Mission Range
Wilderness areas—Montana
Zoology—Montana

History
See also
Little Big Horn, Battle of the, 1876

Legislature
One cow, one vote. M. Scherf. Harper 232: 103-9 Ap '66

Politics and government
Montana leans toward the liberal Democrat. New Repub 155:10-11 O 1 '66
One cow, one vote. M. Scherf. Harper 232: 103-9 Ap '66
Price of the meal. il Time 88:28-9 O 28 '66

MONTCLAIR, Calif.
Two toadstools and a wall of water. S. E. Scholl. il Am City 81:94-5 Mr '66

MONTE CARLO
Monte Carlo. H. P. Koenig. il Travel 125: 45-7 My '66

MONTE CARLO national orchestra. See Orchestras

MONTE CARLO opera orchestra
Opera on the Mediterranean; Riviera report. R. McMullen. il Hi Fi 16:154-6 My '66

MONTE CARLO race. See Automobile racing

MONTENEGRO, Julio César Méndez. See Méndez Montenegro, J. C.

MONTEREY BAY, Calif.
Meander in valley crossing a deep-ocean fan. F. P. Shepard. bibliog il Science 154:385-6 O 21 '66

MONTEREY COUNTY, Calif.
Just folks at a school for nonviolence. J. Didion. il N Y Times Mag p24-5+ F 27 '66

MONTEREY house. See Architecture, Domestic —California

MONTEREY jazz festival. See Music festivals —California

MONTERO, Homero Martínez. See Martínez Montero, H.

MONTES, Lola
Lola Montes; ed. by V. H. Swisher. pors Dance Mag 41:22-4 Ja '67

MONTESQUIOU-FEZENSAC, Robert, comte de
Montesquiou, professor of beauty. P. Jullian. il pors Vogue 148:184-5+ N 1 '66

MONTEVECCHI, Liliane
Las Vegas scene. W. Como. il pors Dance Mag 40:20-1 My '66

MONTEVERDI, Claudio
Coronation of Poppaea (L'incoronazione di Poppea) Criticism
Opera N 31:8+ N 5 '66
On records; Il ritorno d'Ulisse. Opera N 30: 34 F 5 '66

MONTEZUMA II, emperor of Mexico
Hernán Cortez and the Mexican Iliad. E. Ardura. il Américas 18:26-31 Ag '66

MONTGOMERY, Bernard Law, 1st viscount Montgomery of Alamein. See Montgomery of Alamein, B. L. M.

MONTGOMERY, Charles F.
American furniture of the Federal period, 1788-1825. Antiques 90:326-33 S '66

MONTGOMERY, Charlotte
Speaker for the house. See issues of Good housekeeping

MONTGOMERY, Hugh
Librarian fights demotion move in Univ. of Massachusetts shakeup. Library J 91:5914-16 D 1 '66
about
Montgomery demotion case under Mass. L.A. scrutiny. Library J 92:42 Ja 1 '67

MONTGOMERY, Jack
His greatest ride. D. S. Cary. il Read Digest 89:166-8+ N '66

MONTGOMERY, John D.
Evolution of U.S. foreign aid; excerpts from Foreign aid in international politics. Cur Hist 50:321-7+ Je '66

MONTGOMERY, Margaret
$25,000 bundle for a fat cat. il Ebony 22:106-8+ N '66

MONTGOMERY, Ruth
My psychic friends; excerpts from A search for the truth. Ladies Home J 84:101-6 Ja '67

MONTGOMERY of Alamein, Bernard Law Montgomery, 1st viscount
1066: Montgomery at Senlac Hill. Sat R 49: 44:6 Jl 9 '66

MONTGOMERY COUNTY, Md.
Is central processing for you? services for school libraries. R. L. Darling. Library J 91:6153-6 D 15 '66
Meet parking demands before they beat you. J. M. Hunnicutt. il Am City 81:113+ D '66
This farming business; Business of farming program. A. W. Tenney. il Am Ed 2:28-32 Jl '66
See also
Maryland-National capital park and planning commission

Negroes
Town that refused to go away. J. Bailey. il Arch Forum 125:78-81 O '66

MONTGOMERY Ward and company
Which guarantee do you use? Consumer Rep 31:472 O '66

MONTHERLANT, Henry de
Man absent from himself. J. O'Brien. Reporter 34:50 Mr 10 '66

MONTI, Eugenio
Just short of disaster. il Time 87:62 F 11 '66

MONTICELLO (historic house)
Mr Jefferson's Monticello. J. Judge. il Nat Geog Mag 130:426-44 S '66

MONTMORILLONITE
Montmorillonite: effect of pH on its adsorption of a soil humic compound. M. Schnitzer and H. Kodama. bibliog il Science 153:70-1 Jl 1 '66
Tactoid formation in montmorillonite: effect on ion exchange kinetics. A. Banin. bibliog il Science 155:71-2 Ja 6 '67

MONTREAL
Architecture
Affleck, Desbarats, Dimakopoulos, Lebensold & Sise. il Arch Rec 139:137-52 F '66
Downtown in 3-D. P. Blake. il Arch Forum 125:31-49 S '66
Moretti and Nervi's Place Victoria. il Arch Rec 139:141-6 Mr '66

City planning
Canadian cities rebuild on a three-layer plan. il Bsns W p42-3 Mr 12 '66
Downtown in 3-D. P. Blake. il Arch Forum 125:31-49 S '66
Photo report: when a city really sets out to rebuild. il U S News 61:62-5 Ag 22 '66

Description
Let's travel. M. Hodgson. il Mlle 64:121-3 Ja '67
Montreal: super city. R. Joseph. il Esquire 65:140+ My '66
Travel notes. R. Joseph. il Esquire 65:16+ My '66

Hotels, restaurants, etc.
Travel notes. R. Joseph. il Esquire 65:16+ My '66

Music
Mehta's Tosca in the Place des arts; Montreal report. C. L. Osborne. Hi Fi 16:154-5 Ap '66
Montreal; La Scala singers to perform in Canada. F. Campbell. Opera N 31:31 S 10 '66
Montreal; production of Tosca. R. Ubriaco. Opera N 30:32 Mr 19 '66
We, who are about to be disqualified, salute you! G. Gould. Hi Fi 16:MA23-4+ D '66

Subways
Subway with a French accent. il Bsns W p 118-19+ O 15 '66

MONTREAL—*Continued*

Worlds fair, 1967

Better homes and gardens tour: shipboard cruise to Canada for Expo '67. il Bet Hom & Gard 45:20 Ja '67

Bucky's biggest bubble; Crystal palace, U.S. pavilion at Canada's Expo 67. il Arch Forum 124:74-9 Je '66

Canada's 100th: the birthday party upstairs. Thomson of Fleet. il Sat R 50:60+ Ja 7 '67

Expo '67; man and his world; information. L. Lerman. il Mlle 64:116-19 Ja '67

Expo 67 marks Canada's birth. Sr Schol 88: sup2 Mr 18 '66

Fair winds in Montreal. il Newsweek 68:104+ D 5 '66

Forum for tomorrow; Expo 67. W. J. Coughlin. Tech W 19:50 O 31 '66

Great fair coming up. il Time 88:44-5 D 2 '66

Photo report: when a city really sets out to rebuild. il U S News 61:62-5 Ag 22 '66

Trnkaland. il Newsweek 67:99 Mr 28 '66

Trying to make a hit out of a world's fair; seventy nations sign for Montreal's Expo 67. il Bsns W p86-7+ Ag 20 '66

Architecture

Expo 67; an experiment in the development of urban space. il Arch Rec 140:169-76 O '66

Habitat H. D. Jacobs. il Horizon 9:70-3 Wint '67

Montreal's Expo 67. il Fortune 74:169+ O '66

Religious exhibits

Churches at Montreal's EXPO 67. C. De Mestral. il Christian Cent 83:1392-3 N 9 '66

MONTREAL Canadiens (hockey team)   See Hockey teams

MONTREAL planetarium. See Planetariums

MONTREAL symphony orchestra. See Orchestras

MONTREAL. University
University of Montreal: where the two Canadas meet. L. J. Carter. il Science 154: 868-72 N 18 '66

MONUMENT VALLEY, Utah and Arizona
Monument Valley: a Navajo tribal park. O. F. Oldendorph. il Nat Parks Mag 40: 4-8 Ag '66

MONUMENTS
Plastic surgery for concrete lions; Taft bridge, Washington, D.C. il Parks & Rec 1:593 Jl '66
See also
Statue of Liberty
Statues
also subhead Monuments, statues, etc. under names of cities, e.g. Washington, D.C.—Monuments, statues, etc.

MONUMENTS, National. See National monuments

MOOD music
Trivia market; canned classics. A. Rich. il Opera N 31:8-11 D 24 '66

MOODY, John Wallace
Recent art in a climate of change. Christian Cent 83:401-3 Mr 30 '66

MOODY, Mark
Painting poetry. Design 67:31 Ja '66

MOOG, Florence. See Etzler, M. E.; Nayudu, P. R. V. jt. auths.

MOON, Eric
COMSA and DISCUS. Sat R 49:50-1 F 5 '66
about
Savannah state college award to Virginia L. Jones & Lj editor. Library J 91:2300 My 1 '66

MOON, J. J.
Is J.J. really king of the surf? J. Bonfante. il por Life 60:81-2 Je 10 '66

MOON, Samuel
At the divide; This twisting; Late conversation; My wife, I will try; poems. Poetry 109:24-9 O '66
Creeley as narrator. Poetry 108:341-2 Ag '66
Master as servant. Poetry 108:189-90 Je '66

MOON
Birth of the moon; Luna 10; preliminary findings and U.S. theories. il Newsweek 67:71 My 2 '66
Circumlunation; significant findings by Luna 10. Sci Am 214:54-5 Je '66
Disarmament on the moon: the prospects look good. E. Langer. Science 153:153-4 Jl 8 '66
Lunar international laboratory. B. Friedman. il UNESCO Courier 19:31-2+ My '66
Moon is not only natural satellite. Sci N 89:201 Mr 26 '66
Moon's image blackened. Sci N 91:7 Ja 7 '67
Plastic quarantine envelope proposed; precautionary measures against contamination from moon-type organisms. H. M. David. Tech W 19:28-30 Ag 1 '66

Review of a yet-unwritten moon book. J. Ashbrook. Sky & Tel 32:334 D '66

Sun, moon, and planets this month. See issues of Sky and telescope

What earthly use is the moon? W. Sullivan. il N Y Times Mag p39+ Ag 28 '66

Why does the moon show only one face? I. Asimov. il Sci Digest 60:92-3 Jl '66

Year of the moon; 1966, period of fantastic achievements. il Newsweek 69:72-3 Ja 16 '67

See also
Lunar radiation
Moonlight
Occultations
Space flight to the moon
Space vehicles—Landing systems—Moon
Tides

Atmosphere

Lunar Orbiter reports safe atmosphere. R. Pay. il Tech W 19:20+ Ag 29 '66

Libration

Libration point useful: may be used as stopping point in space. Sci N 90:351 O 29 '66

Measurements

See Astronomical measurements

Names

See Names, Lunar

Orbit

Ring around the moon; Luna 10's path. Newsweek 67:90-1 Ap 18 '66

Photographs, maps, etc.

Clear and rugged 180 miles of moon; photographs taken by Lunar Orbiter II. Life 61: 50-50A D 9 '66

Close-up of Copernicus. Sci Am 216:55-6+ Ja '67

Dual cameras map lunar landing sites. I. Stone. il Aviation W 85:34-6 N 28 '66

East and West on the moon. J. Ashbrook. Sky & Tel 32:208 O '66

Eye on the moon; Soviet Union's Luna 9. Newsweek 67:54-6 F 14 '66

From Surveyor: the stark and airless beauty of the moon. Life 61:62-7 Jl 1 '66

In focus (cont) Sky & Tel 31:137, 276+ Mr, My '66

Luna IX pictures: a question of ethics; letter. D. C. Krause; with reply by B. Lovell. Science 151:1477 Mr 25 '66

Luna 9 pictures: implications. T. Gold and B. W. Hapke. bibliog il Science 153:290-3 Jl 15 '66

Lunar basins, lunar lineaments, and the moon's far side. W. K. Hartmann. bibliog il Sky & Tel 32:128-31 S '66

Lunar landscape; Soviets land softly. Time 87:42 F 11 '66

Lunar Orbiter delivers after brief scare. Tech W 19:13-14 N 28 '66

Lunar Orbiter photographs earth and moon. Sky & Tel 32:346-7 D '66

Lunar Orbiter reports safe atmosphere. R. Pay. Tech W 19:20+ Ag 29 '66

Lunar Orbiter-2 reveals crater details. Aviation W 85:26-7 D 5 '66

Manned landing plans boosted by Luna 13 photos, data. Aviation W 86:22-4 Ja 2 '67

Mapping the moon; Lunar Orbiter pictures. Newsweek 68:60 Ag 29 '66

Measure of achievement; Luna 9. Newsweek 67:60-1 F 21 '66

Moon is brown; Surveyor's pictures. Time 87:70 Je 24 '66

Moon photos enhanced. Aviation W 85:28-9 Ag 15 '66

NASA releases new Lunar Orbiter photos. Tech W 20:19 Ja 16 '67

New look at Copernicus; photographs by Lunar Orbiter 2. Time 88:50-1 D 9 '66

Photographing the moon; Lunar Orbiter I. Time 88:36 Ag 26 '66

Portrait in earthshine. Newsweek 67:65 Je 27 '66

Results from Lunar Orbiter 2. R. N. Watts, jr. and J. Ashbrook. Sky & Tel 33:22-6 Ja '67

Right down on the moon; Russia's Luna 9; with British and Soviet photographs. Life 60:26-30 F 11 '66

Robot on the moon; Luna 9 and how B. Lovell took pictures. J. Lear. Sat R 49:57-65 Mr 5 '66

Russian Luna IX pictures: provisional analysis. G. P. Kuiper and others. il Science 151:1561-3 Mr 25 '66

75 per cent achievement of Orbiter goals seen. I. Stone. Aviation W 85:16-19 Ag 29 '66

MOON—Photographs, maps, etc.—*Continued*

Shooting the moon: man's way-out view; photographs by Lunar Orbiter II. Newsweek 68:24-5 D 12 '66

Sir Bernard Lovell's exclusive cabled report on the Luna 9 pictures received at Jodrell bank. B. Lovell. Sat R 49:60-1 Mr 5 '66

Surveyor: candid camera on the moon. H. E. Newell. Nat Geog Mag 130:578-92 O '66

Surveyor 1: preliminary results; report by the Surveyor scientific evaluation and analysis team. bibliog Science 152:1737-50 Je 24 '66; Reply. E. A. Whitaker. 153:1550-1 S 23 '66

Surveyor sits softly on the moon. il Life 60:38-9 Je 10 '66

Unearthly vista. il Sci N 90:494-5 D 10 '66

See also
Space photography

Quotations, maxims, etc.

Moon talk; comp. by E. F. Murphy. N Y Times Mag p32 F 20 '66

Relay system

See Radio relay systems

Surface

Are there diamonds on the moon? quiz. J. Daugherty and M. Daugherty. il Sci Digest 59:85-7 Je '66

Bendix shows ALSEP system deployment; Apollo lunar surface experiment package. il Tech W 19:26-7 Ag 8 '66

Blocks or spines? il Sci N 90:465 D 3 '66

Child's toy may catch samples of moon. Sci N 90:73 Jl 30 '66

Clear and rugged 180 miles of moon; photographs taken by Lunar Orbiter II. Life 61:50-50A D 9 '66

Color events on the moon. P. Moore. il Sky & Tel 33:27 Ja '67

Control achievements stressed on Luna 9; with editorial comment. D. Winston. il Aviation W 84:21, 29-33 F 14 '66

Convex floor of the crater Mersenius. K. J. Delano. il Sky & Tel 31:309 My '66

Dust on the moon. H. C. Urey. bibliog Science 153:1419-20 S 16 '66

Emplaced data station may extend ALSEP. C. D. LaFond. il Tech W 20:30+ Ja 9 '67

Equipment devised for future flights; ALSEP (Apollo lunar surface experiment package) il Aviation W 85:74-7+ Ag 15 '66

Eye on the moon; Soviet Union's Luna 9. il Newsweek 67:54-6 F 14 '66

Flying photo lab lights astronauts' way to the moon; Orbiter II's mission yields 422 pictures of lunar surface. il Bsns W p 100-2 D 3 '66

Geological survey aiding NASA in landing site determination. R. Lindsey. il Tech W 20:40 Ja 9 '67

High central peaks. G. S. Mumford. Sky & Tel 32:275 N '66

High noon on the moon; Surveyor I's findings. Newsweek 67:76 Je 20 '66

Hot spots on the moon. J. M. Saari and R. W. Shorthill. il Sky & Tel 31:327-31 Je '66

How the first soft landing on the moon was achieved. L. A. DuBridge. il Read Digest 89:100-5 D '66

Inhospitable moon; Moscow discloses Luna 9's findings. il Time 87:52 F 18 '66

Luna firma. il Sci Am 214:56-7 Mr '66

Luna 9 photographs: evidence for a fragmental surface layer. D. E. Gault and others. bibliog il Science 153:985-8 Ag 26 '66

Luna 9 photos indicate surface erosion. W. C. Wetmore. Aviation W 84:34+ My 23 '66

Luna 9 pictures: implications. T. Gold and B. W. Hapke. bibliog il Science 153:290-3 Jl 15 '66

Luna photos encouraging for Surveyor; with editorial comment. R. Pay. il Miss & Roc 18:12-14, 46 F 14 '66

Lunar basins, lunar lineaments, and the moon's far side. W. K. Hartmann. bibliog il Sky & Tel 32:128-31 S '66

Lunar facts still scant. Sci N 90:441+ N 26 '66

Lunar landscape; Soviets land softly. il Time 87:42 F 11 '66

Lunar metal production plant seen feasible. J. F. Judge. il Tech W 19:28-9 O 17 '66

Lunar Orbiter photos reveal moonquakes. il Tech W 19:14-15 O 10 '66

Lunar Orbiter reports safe atmosphere. R. Pay. il Tech W 19:20+ Ag 29 '66

Lunar photography with a 5-inch refractor. S. M. Larson. il Sky & Tel 32:164-8 S '66

Lunar ring dikes from Lunar Orbiter I. J. A. O'Keefe and others. bibliog il Science 155:77-9 Ja 6 '67

Lunar rocks loom as hazard to Apollo. H. D. Watkins. il Aviation W 84:26-30 Je 13 '66

Lunar surface can support Apollo LEM. il Tech W 18:17 Je 20 '66

Lunar surface strength: implications of Luna 9 landing. L. D. Jaffe and R. F. Scott. bibliog il Science 153:407-8 Jl 22 '66

Man in the moon has two faces. il Sci N 90:531 D 24 '66

Man-made moonquakes. Sci N 91:45 Ja 14 '67

Measure of achievement; Luna 9. il Newsweek 67:60-1 F 21 '66

Moon photos enhanced. il Aviation W 85:28-9 Ag 15 '66

Moon-scraper may sample lunar surface. Sci N 90:39 Jl 16 '66

Moon: still a puzzle. J. Eberhart. il Sci N 90:420-2 N 19 '66

NASA given lunar surface experiment demonstration. W. J. Normyle. il Aviation W 85:94-5+ Jl 25 '66

New look at Copernicus; photographs by Lunar Orbiter 2. Time 88:50-1 D 9 '66

New Lunar Orbiter assigned thirteen prime photo target areas. Tech W 19:17 N 7 '66

New moon photos: spectacular; but mysteries remain unsolved; Copernicus by Lunar Orbiter II. il U S News 61:8 D 12 '66

Observing the moon, Bessarion B. A. K. Herring. il Sky & Tel 31:245 Ap '66

Observing the moon, Encke. A. K. Herring. il Sky & Tel 32:239 O '66

Observing the moon, Jansen B. A. K. Herring. il Sky & Tel 32:49 Jl '66

Observing the moon; Pico. A. K. Herring. il Sky & Tel 33:60 Ja '67

Orbiter increases landing site rejections. W. J. Normyle. il Aviation W 85:62-4 O 24 '66

Orbiter photo quality heightened by gridding technique. il Aviation W 85:28-31 O 10 '66

Origin of secondary lunar craters. G. S. Mumford. Sky & Tel 32:26 Jl '66

Pictures from the moon. R. N. Watts, jr. il Sky & Tel 32:16-19 Jl '66

Radioactivity of the lunar surface. H. W. Kraner and others. bibliog Science 152:1235-6 My 27 '66

Results from Lunar Orbiter 2. R. N. Watts, jr. and J. Ashbrook. il Sky & Tel 33:22-6 Ja '67

Right down on the moon; Russia's Luna 9; with British and Soviet photographs. Life 60:26-30 F 11 '66

Robot on the moon; Luna 9 and how B. Lovell took pictures. J. Lear. il Sat R 49:57-65 Mr 5 '66

Rotary-percussive system favored for moon drilling. M. Burns and L. A. Gardner. Tech W 18:33+ Je 20 '66

Russian moon lander yields data on lunar soil firmness, density. H. Rausch. Aviation W 86:81+ Ja 16 '67

Self-portrait; Lunar Orbiter's findings. il Newsweek 68:78 S 5 '66

75 per cent achievement of Orbiter goals seen. I. Stone. il Aviation W 85:16-19 Ag 29 '66

Shadow of a doubt; rock piles. il Newsweek 68:66 D 5 '66

Shock-lithification of unconsolidated rock materials. N. M. Short. bibliog il Science 154:382-4 O 21 '66

Shooting the moon: man's way-out view; photographs by Lunar Orbiter II. Newsweek 68:24-5 D 12 '66

Some Surveyor findings. Sky & Tel 32:63+ Ag '66

Soviet TV lands on moon. il Sci N L 89:114-15 F 19 '66

Soviet view of lunar surface reported. W. S. Beller. Miss & Roc 18:14-15 My 23 '66

Spiral lunar craters. il Sky & Tel 31:377 Je '66

Surveyor may survive lunar night; next launch scheduled; with editorial comment. R. Pay. il Tech W 18:16-17, 54 Je 13 '66

Surveyor I: preliminary results; report by the Surveyor scientific evaluation and analysis team. bibliog il Science 152:1737-50 Je 24 '66; Reply. E. A. Whitaker. 153:1550-1 S 23 '66

Surveyor I prompts confidence, caution. H. D. Watkins. il Aviation W 84:60-1+ Je 27 '66

Surveyor sits softly on the moon. il Life 60:38-9 Je 10 '66

Surveyor's pictures bolster LEM plans. il Aviation W 84:26-9 Je 6 '66

Vacuum welding of olivine. P. R. Bell. bibliog il Science 153:410-11 Jl 22 '66

Volcanic-like material seen in new views; with photographs. Tech W 19:20 O 17 '66

What Luna 9 told us about the moon; tr. by A. Boyko. Y. N. Lipsky. il Sky & Tel 32:257-60 N '66

MOON—Surface—*Continued*
What Lunar 9 proves, and doesn't. D. Cohen. il Sci Digest 59:10-12 Ap '66
What Russia found on the moon. il U S News 60:9 F 14 '66
What U.S. learns from moon landing. il Bsns W p 134-5 F 12 '66
What we'll do on the moon. W. Von Braun. il Pop Sci 189:90-2+ N '66

MOON, Flight to the. See Space flight to the moon

MOON, Photography of. See Astronomical photography

MOON and meteorology
Middle Devonian lunar month. A. F. Aveni. bibliog Science 151:1221-2 Mr 11 '66; Reply. S. K. Runcorn. 154:292 O 14 '66

MOON bases. See Lunar bases

MOON landing systems. See Space vehicles—Landing systems—Moon

MOON models. See Astronomical models

MOON probes. See Lunar probes

MOON settlements. See Lunar bases

MOON shelters. See Life support systems (space environment)

MOON vehicles. See Lunar vehicles

MOONEY, Christopher F.
Fresh look at man; excerpt from Teilhard de Chardin and the mystery of Christ. Sat R 49:20-4 F 26 '66

MOONEY, Mary Jane
Bullet through the window. J. L. Block. il por Good H 162:72+ Mr '66

MOONEY, Richard
France and the five. New Repub 154:11-12 F 26 '66

MOONEY aircraft, incorporated
Mooney sees 50 per cent increase in net billings in fiscal 1967. E. J. Bulban. il Aviation W 85:108-9+ S 19 '66

MOONEY positive control. See Automatic pilot (airplanes)

MOONEYE fishing
Ever try mooneyes? W. Davis. il Outdoor Life 139:94-6 Ja '67

MOONLIGHT
Doctor Sun & the moon. il Time 88:82 O 28 '66

MOONLIGHT polarization. See Polarization (light)

MOONLIGHTING. See Supplementary employment

MOONSHINING
Lost art of moonshine; illegal production of corn whiskey. W. P. Fox. il Sat Eve Post 239:34-5 Mr 26 '66
Requiem for potheen. T. Prittie. il Atlan 217:116-17 My '66

MOOR, Paul
Ginger in the opera house. Hi Fi 16:147 F '66
Gunther Schuller's The visitation. Hi Fi 16:MA28-9 D '66
New ideas for Wagner. Hi Fi 16:142-3 Mr '66
Speaking out. por Sat Eve Post 239:12+ S 10 '66
Talent and trash from I.S.C.M. Hi Fi 16:MA26 D '66

MOOR-JANKOWSKI, J. and others
Seroprimatology of chimpanzees; blood-group distribution as a racial characteristic. bibliog Science 152:219-20 Ap 8 '66

MOORE, Anne Carroll
Anne Carroll Moore urged withdrawal of Stuart Little. E. B. White reports; excerpts from article. E. B. White. Library J 91:2187 Ap 15 '66

MOORE, Barrington, jr
American nightmare: why we fear peasants in revolt. Nation 203:271-4 S 26 '66

MOORE, Betty
Baghdad's 1,000th: forthcoming celebrations. Sat R 50:74 Ja 7 '67
Mexico's 450th: commemorating the conquest of the Aztecs. Sat R 50:59 Ja 7 '67
Minsk's 900th. Sat R 50:98 Ja 7 '67

MOORE, Charles W. and Canty, Donald
Lincoln Center. Arch Forum 125:71-9 S '66

MOORE, Douglas Stuart
Ballad of Baby Doe. Criticism
Opera N il 30:30 Ja 29 '66
Carry Nation. Criticism
Hi Fi il 16:MA27 Jl '66
Newsweek il 67:115 My 16 '66
Opera N il 30:24 Je 4 '66

MOORE, Everett T.
CLEAN down the drain. por Library J 92:83-5 Ja 1 '67

MOORE, Gerald
Out of the cold, away from the roaches. Life 61:80+ S 30 '66

MOORE, Harold G.
Men who run the war. por Newsweek 68:54 D 5 '66

MOORE, Harry T.
People in a world full of things. Sat R 49:32 Mr 12 '66

MOORE, Henry
(ed) Gist of it. See issues of Outdoor life

MOORE, Irene
Accent on youth. Am For 72:22-5 Ag '66
Last of the Shenandoah settlers. Am For 72:10-11+ F '66
Teaching conservation in the city. Am For 72:22-5 O '66

MOORE, J. Edwin
Trees to sell? see a forester. Am For 72:20-7 Mr '66

MOORE, J. Hartwell. See Spector, S. jt. auth.

MOORE, Jack B.
Don't die, Jeff Chandler; story. Esquire 65:134-7 Ap '66

MOORE, James G. and others
1965 eruption of Taal volcano. Science 151:955-60 F 25 '66

MOORE, Joan W. and Guzman, Ralph
Mexican-Americans: new wind from the Southwest. Nation 202:645-8 My 30 '66

MOORE, John
Among the quiet folks; story. Sat Eve Post 240:52-4 Ja 14 '67

MOORE, John C.
Unexamined life of the professor. por Sat R 49:79 D 17 '66

MOORE, L. Daneo, and others
Cell-free protein synthesis: effects of age and state of ribosomal aggregation. bibliog Science 154:1350-3 D 9 '66

MOORE, L. W.
Some important business for business; address, September 12, 1966. Vital Speeches 33:28-32 O 15 '66

MOORE, Marianne
Four poems that show her mind's wide range: Sun; I may, I might, I must; O to be a dragon; The fox and the grapes. Life 62:44 Ja 13 '67
Granite and steel; poem. New Yorker 42:32 Jl 9 '66
Love in America? poem. Sat Eve Post 239:78 D 31 '66

about
Crystal for the metaphysical. M. Rukeyser. Sat R 49:52-3+ O 1 '66
Leading lady of U.S. verse. J. Howard. il pors Life 62:37-8+ Ja 13 '67
Miss Moore herself. B. Howes. New Repub 155:31 D 17 '66
Miss Moore in Manhattan. New Yorker 41:25-6 Ja 29 '66

MOORE, Mary Louise
Dichotomy; poem. Negro Hist Bul 29:70 D '65

MOORE, Mary Tyler
From TV to Tiffany's in one wild leap. J. Bowers. il pors Sat Eve Post 239:97-101 N 19 '66
Holly go quickly. M. Gussow. il por Newsweek 68:45 D 26 '66
Personality girl. il por Newsweek 68:78 Ag 1 '66

MOORE, Norman E.
Ceiling and visibility unlimited. Yachting 119:226+ Mr '66

MOORE, Patrick
Color events on the moon. il Sky & Tel 33:27 Ja '67

MOORE, R. and others
Ultracentrifuge schlieren photographs: automatic analysis. Science 152:1509-11 Je 10 '66

MOORE, Richard
Of a young mother; poem. Mlle 63:107 My '66
Sunlight at work; poem. Reporter 34:54 F 10 '66
Watch; poem. Reporter 35:48 N 3 '66

MOORE, Richard D.
Gene activation. Science 152:548-9 Ap 22 '66

MOORE, Robert H. See Carlton, L. jt. auth.

MOORE, Sam
1966 dream world series. Life 61:27 O 7 '66
Whatever happened to 40-love? Life 61:10 Jl 8 '66

MOORE, Samuel A. 2d, and Woodard, S. L.
School desegregation: localism or metropolitanism? bibliog f Sch & Soc 94:269-70 Sum '66

MOORE, Thomas F.
Long reign as king of the apes. Sports Illus 26:48-54 Ja 2 '67

MOORE, Trevor Wyatt
Passing of J. Corbel Flèche. Christian Cent 83:494-6 Ap 20 '66

MOORE, Virginia Bennett
Through a snorkeler's mask. Read Digest 89:133-8 Ag '66

MOORE, Walter J. See Lehmann, G. jt. auth.
MOORE, William
Scholar who went to the people. il pors Ebony 21:114-20 Mr '66
MOOREHEAD, Alan
Affinity with Australia. Sat R 49:43-4 O 8 '66
Opening of the South Seas; excerpts from Fatal impact. Harper 232:39-48 F; 121-2+ Mr '66
Our far-flung correspondents. New Yorker 42: 186-91 N 19 '66
Reporter at large. New Yorker 42:154+ O 29 '66
MOORHEAD, Jennelle
President's message. See issues of PTA magazine
MOORING of boats. See Boats—Mooring
MOOSE
Moose on the loose; incident in Northfield, Mass. il Newsweek 68:32+ O 17 '66
MOOSE hunting
Giant of Mission creek; ed. by J. O. Cartier. L. L. Jullie. il Outdoor Life 138:46-7+ D '66
Invisible moose. E. Westgarde. il Outdoor Life 137:32-5+ Je '66
MOPS and mopsticks
Shopping center for mops. il Good H 162:208 Je '66
MORA, José A.
Role of culture; excerpts from address, January 1966. Américas 18:inside cover F '66
about
Secretary General's visit to Israel. il por Américas 18:42 D '66
MORAL attitudes
Moral question; protest preferred to indifference. Nation 203:594 D 5 '66
Opinion: should God die? G. B. Blaine, jr. Mlle 63:138+ Ag '66
Planned lawlessness threatens to get out of hand; reprint. C. E. Whittaker. il U S News 61:37-8+ S 19 '66
Policeman looks at crime; interview. O. W. Wilson. U S News 61:51-2 Ag 1 '66
Romantic generation. P. F. Drucker. Harper 232:12+ My '66
We are not interested. America 115:129 Ag 6 '66
Who is to blame? D. Lawrence. U S News 61:84 Ag 1 '66
MORAL codes. See Ethics
MORAL conditions
See also
Moving pictures—Moral aspects
Television broadcasting—Moral aspects
also subhead Moral conditions under names of countries, cities, etc. e.g. United States—Moral conditions
MORAL education
Classroom incident; students' intolerance. NEA J 55:43-4 N '66
Educational values and goals: can morals be taught? address, January 21, 1966. J. Newsom. Vital Speeches 32:244-8 F 1 '66
Now a word about good kids. E. W. Buzbee. il N Y Times Mag p 132+ N 27 '66
Working with values in the classroom. M. Harmin and S. B. Simon. il Sr Schol 89: sup 16-17+ Ja 6 '67
MORAL philosophy. See Ethics
MORAL rearmament
Colossal escapism. Christian Cent 84:37 Ja 11 '67
MORAL sense. See Ethics
MORAL theology. See Christian ethics
MORALE
Teacher-opinion poll; teacher morale. il NEA J 55:55 D '66
MORALE, National
France
New mood in France. N. Cousins. Sat R 49:28+ S 24 '66
United States
Boom times, unhappy people, why? results of a nationwide survey. il U S News 60: 64-8+ Mr 21 '66
Election near: mood of voters. il U S News 61:50-2+ O 24 '66
Mood of Americans at this time; interview. G. Gallup. il U S News 61:50-4 S 19 '66
Speaking out; McCarthyism is threatening us again. A. Schlesinger, jr. Sat Eve Post 239:10+ Ag 13 '66
Trouble beyond Veitnam. N. Cousins. Sat R 49:20 My 21 '66
What's bothering Americans, as told to Congress. il U S News 61:56-9 Ag 15 '66

MORALES-CARRIÓN, Arturo
Latin America: a new exploration; address, April 22, 1966. Vital Speeches 32:524-6 Je 15 '66
MORALITY. See Ethics
MORALS. See Ethics
MORALS and literature. See Literature and morals
MORALS and war. See War—Moral aspects
MORAN, Charles McMoran Wilson, 1st baron
Winston Churchill: the struggle for survival 1940/65; excerpts. Life 60:92-3+ Ap 22; 74-6+ Ap 29 '66
about
Doctor who became a Boswell. G. P. Hunt. por Life 60:3 Ap 29 '66
Great patient; British and family reactions to biography of Churchill. il por Newsweek 67:45-6 My 9 '66
Inside Winston Churchill. il por Time 87:31 My 6 '66
More triumph than tragedy. A. Lejeune. Nat R 18:581-2 Je 14 '66
MORAN, Gabriel
Catechetics for the real world. America 115: 57-9 Jl 16 '66
Christianity: a religion for adults. Cath World 204:135-42 D '66
MORAN, W. R.
Heavy-duty phonograph turntables. Hobbies 70:35 F '66
MORATH, Kathy
Bruns stood guard to protect Kathy. D. Moser. il por Life 60:88+ Mr 4 '66
MORAVCSIK, Michael J.
Scientists in politics and out. Bul Atomic Sci 22:32-4 Ja '66
MORAVEC, Ivan
Connoisseur society edition of Chopin's Nocturnes by Ivan Moravec. S. Sell. por Am Rec G 32:954-5 Je '66
For Chopin, the voices of poets. H. Goldsmith. por Hi Fi 16:85 S '66
MORAVIA, Alberto
Ailments of the spirit. E. Capouya. por Sat R 49:30-1+ Ag 13 '66
Books. N. Bliven. New Yorker 42:165-8 Ap 9 '66
MORAVIAN music foundation
Music-making Moravians. S. Fleming. Hi Fi 16:MA16-17 S '66
MORAWETZ, Herbert
Reactivity of organic crystals. bibliog Science 152:705-11 My 6 '66
MORAY eels. See Eels
MORE, Sir Thomas, Saint
Sir Thomas More. por Sr Schol 89:4 Ja 13 '67
Works of Sir Thomas More. K. Rexroth. Sat R 49:22 My 21 '66
MORE, Wendell
Washington front. America 115:110, 172, 379, 479, 580, 797; 116:80 Jl 30, Ag 20, O 1, 22, N 12, D 17 '66, Ja 21 '67
MOREARTY, John E.
Books. Commonweal 84:445-6 Jl 8 '66
MOREAU, Jeanne
Moreau, she lives to love; interview, ed. by N. Liber. pors Life 62:39-40+ Ja 20 '67
MOREELL, Ben
Business, social progress and religion; address, October 27, 1966. Vital Speeches 33: 119-25 D 1 '66
MOREHEAD, Albert Hodges
When Culbertson's man outsmarted himself. C. Goren. il Sports Illus 25:66 N 7 '66
MORENO, Mario. See Cantinflas
MORETUS museum. See Plantin-Moretus museum, Antwerp
MOREY, Marion
New for your home. See issues of Popular mechanics
MORGAN, Berry
Andrew; story. New Yorker 42:25-8 Jl 2 '66
Miss Idella, the travelling hoe lady; story. New Yorker 42:53-5 D 10 '66
Organ piece; story. New Yorker 42:24-6 Ag 13 '66
Seven whiteface; story. New Yorker 42:32-3 Jl 23 '66
MORGAN, Buford
Moss man from Missouri. S. Althoff and D. Weddle. il pors Pop Mech 125:112-15 Je '66
MORGAN, Charles, Jr
Morgan's crusade for Negro jurors. J. B. Cumming, jr. Reporter 34:39-40 F 10 '66
MORGAN, Edward P.
Last big voice. por Newsweek 68:98 S 19 '66

MORGAN, Gaylin
  Hybrid wheat; here's a last-minute report. Suc Farm 64:36-7 O '66
  What's holding up hybrid alfalfa? Suc Farm 64:34-5 Je '66
MORGAN, J. P. family
  Fine art of making money. E. Streeter. Sat R 49:51-2 D 24 '66
MORGAN, Kenneth W.
  Buddhists in Saigon. Christian Cent 83:107-10 Ja 26 '66
MORGAN, Lael
  Stout hearts and strong stomachs. Motor B 117:96+ Ja '66
MORGAN, Neil
  Gilded South. Sat R 49:52+ O 8 '66
MORGAN, Richard S. and Uzman, B. G.
  Nature of the packing of ribosomes within chromatoid bodies. bibliog Science 152:214-16 Ap 8 '66
MORGAN, Thomas B.
  Requiem or revival? Look 30:70-3+ Je 14 '66
  Superbarbra. Look 30:54-61+ Ap 5 '66
MORGAN, Thomas Ellsworth
  Excerpt from debate, July 12, 1966. Cong Digest 45:217+ Ag '66
MORGAN (moving picture character)   See Characters in moving pictures
MORGAN guaranty trust company
  Fine art of making money. E. Streeter. Sat R 49:51-2 D 24 '66
  There wasn't any panic at 23 Wall. J. McDonald. il Fortune 74:152-5+ D '66
MORGELLO, Clem
  Wall Street. See issues of Newsweek
MORGENTHAU, Hans J.
  China (is; is not) an aggressive power; debate. por N Y Times Mag p28-9+ Mr 13 '66
  Domain of the contingent. Sat R 50:30-1 Ja 7 '67
  Johnson's dilemma. New Repub 154:12-16 My 28 '66
  Search for order without force. Sat R 49:37 S 17 '66
  Truth and power. New Repub 155:8-14 N 26 '66; 156:42-3 Ja 7 '67
  Vietnam: what should we do now? por Look 30:24-5 Ag 9 '66
MORHOUSE, L. Judson
  Influence peddler. Newsweek 67:28 My 30 '66
MORI, Michie
  Brown baby Olympic hopeful from Japan. il pors Ebony 21:58-60 O '66
MORIMOTO, N. and Koto, K.
  Crystal structure of umangite, Cu_3Se_2. Science 152:345 Ap 15 '66
MORISON, Elting E.
  It's two-thirds of a century; we've made it, so far. N Y Times Mag p34-5+ Ap 24 '66
MORISOT, Berthe
  Gallery for young people. C. B. Johnson. il Sch Arts 56:54 F '66
MORITA, Akio
  Sony: how to grow big by thinking small. il por Newsweek 67:88-90 Je 13 '66
MORLAND, Harold
  (tr) See Borges, J. L. Other tiger
MORLEY, Charles
  (comp) Articles and other books received: eastern Europe. See issues of American historical review
MORLEY, Felix
  Trends: the state of the Nation. See issues of Nation's business
MORMONS and Mormonism
  Church in the news: story of Morman success: hard work and sharing. il U S News 61:90-2+ S 26 '66
  For ruffled believers; quarterly publication, Dialogue. il Time 88:59 Ag 26 '66
  Is Mormonism reformable on race? Mormon view of Negro. Christian Cent 83:576 My 4 '66
  Mormon establishment. by W. Turner. Review
    Christian Cent 83:1473 N 30 '66. R. P. Nelson
    New Repub 156:40 Ja 7 '67. G. W. Johnson
  Story of Mormon gold. C. French. Hobbies 71:102 Ja '67
    See also
  Reorganized church of Jesus Christ of Latter day saints
MORNING star (newspaper)
  Swinging worker. Time 87:43 My 6 '66
MORO, Aldo
  All in the family. Newsweek 67:44 Ja 31 '66
  Fine Italian hand. Time 87:39-40 Mr 4 '66
MOROCCO
    See also
  Casablanca

Description and travel
  By rented car through Morocco. il Sunset 136: 62+ Ap '66
Foreign relations
  Ben Barka affair; CIA and the kidnapping. C. Sterling. il Reporter 34:27-8 Mr 10 '66
Politics and government
  Meanwhile, down in Morocco; Ben Barka affair; Morocco's silence. Reporter 34:26 Mr 10 '66
MORONEY, Clare
  Front and center. Q. Eaton. Opera N 30:6-7 Je 4 '66
MORPHINE
  Morphinist; incident at Hospital of the city of Vienna, 1928. R. Berczeller. New Yorker 42:141-2+ Ap 16 '66
    See also
  Opium
MORPHOGENESIS. See Morphology
MORPHOLOGY
  Genetic control of the shape of a virus. E. Kellenberger. il Sci Am 215:32-9 bibliog(p 154) D '66
  Lens differentiation; report on second conference. R. W. Reyer and others. Science 154:1682-4+ D 30 '66
  Morphogenesis in trichoderma: suppression of photoinduction by 5-fluorouracil. E. Galun and J. Gressel. bibliog il Science 151:696-8 F 11 '66
  Morphogenetic substance in legume nodule formation. A. G. Schaffer and M. Alexander. bibliog il Science 152:82-3 Ap 1 '66
  Morphology of nascent Ziegler-Natta polymers. P. Blais and R. S. Manley. bibliog il Science 153:539-41 Jl 29 '66
  Polysome morphology; evidence for endocrine control during chick embryogenesis. M. B. Yatvin. bibliog il Science 151:1001-3 F 25 '66
  Speciation in flowering plants. H. Lewis. bibliog Science 152:167-72 Ap 8 '66
MORRILL, Justin Smith
  Americans not everybody knows. C. W. Ferguson. por PTA Mag 61:20-2 D '66
MORRILL, Vaughn
  We're not taking the love out of love, we're making it more efficient. G. Shalit. il Look 20:34-5 F 22 '66
MORRILL land-grant college act of 1862. See School laws and legislation—United States
MORRILTON, Ark.
  Trials of an editor. il Newsweek 67:91-2 F 14 '66
MORRIS, Charles C.
  Proven transistor ignition system. Electr World 75:47-9 Ja '66
MORRIS, Edward A.
  Build a zener regulated power supply. Pop Mech 127:192-5+ Ja '67
MORRIS, Everett
  What is a cruising boat? Yachting 119:109-10 F '66
MORRIS, Ivan
  Movies. Vogue 148:207 S 1 '66
MORRIS, James, 1926-
  Alexandria reborn. Holiday 39:68-77 F '66
  Monarchs of the Beatle empire. Sat Eve Post 239:22-7 Ag 27 '66
  Rhodesia's enduring rebellion. Sat Eve Post 239:74-7 Jl 30 '66
  Speaking out. por Sat Eve Post 239:12+ O 22 '66
MORRIS, James, 1938?-
  Meet me in the middle of the air. Esquire 65: 110-13+ Ap '66
  Speaking out. por Sat Eve Post 239:10+ Mr 26 '66
MORRIS, Jill
  Four photographers. U S Camera 29:60-3+ F '66
  What's your sign? U S Camera 29:24+ D '66
MORRIS, Joe Alex
  At last: woolens you can wash by machine. Read Digest 89:233-7 O '66
  How to lock burglars out. Read Digest 89: 137-40 D '66
  Meet the Monster that checks your taxes. Read Digest 90:177-8+ Ja '67
MORRIS, Joe Alex, jr
  Gamble on the Jordan. Nation 204:6-8 Ja 2 '67
  Pandora's ammunition box. Nation 203:109-12 Ag 8 '66
MORRIS, John
  Poorest diocese in the U.S.A. America 114: 549-50 Ap 16 '66
MORRIS, John G.
  Cliff Edom: the man in Missouri. Pop Phot 59:96-7+ S '66
  Where is the money in photography? Pop Phot 59:75-9+ O '66

MORRIS, John N.
Hospital; poem. Nation 204:86 Ja 16 '67
MORRIS, Leavitt
Bulgaria's golden sands. Travel 126:56-7 S
'66
Outer Mongolia. Travel 126:56-8 D '66
MORRIS, Newbold
Obituary
Nat R 18:351 Ap 19 '66
MORRIS, Richard B.
Adventures in the reference room; address,
July 13, 1966. por Wilson Lib Bul 41:492-501
Ja '67
Career of a clever dissembler. Sat R 49:45 F
5 '66
MORRIS, Robert
Grey paint, Robert Morris. D. Antin. il Art N
65:22-4+ Ap '66
MORRIS, Robert Moore
Four hours from anywhere. il Time 87:86+
Je 24 '66
MORRIS, William J.
Fossil mammals from Baja California: new
evidence on early tertiary migrations. bib-
liog Science 153:1376-8 S 16 '66
MORRIS, Willie
Texas education. Commentary 42:23-32 Ag '66
MORRIS, Wright
Lover, is that you? story. Esquire 65:70 Mr '66
MORRISETT, Lloyd N.
Preschool education. Science 153:1197 S 9 '66
MORRISON, Allan
Women in the arts. Ebony 21:90-4 Ag '66
MORRISON, Alva
Socialism in Saskatchewan. Yale R 56:256-70
D '66
MORRISON, Charles Clayton
Apostle in print. por(p321) Christian Cent
83:323-5 Mr 16 '66; Discussion. 83:592 My
4 '66
Personal memoir. H. E. Fey. Christian Cent
83:326-7 Mr 16 '66
MORRISON, E. A.
Day I learned about prejudice. Mlle 63:122+
S '66
MORRISON, Howard A.
Precision non-wirewound potentiometers.
Electr World 75:40-1 Ap '66
MORRISON, Jack S.
Challenge of college dance education. por
Dance Mag 40:34+ Mr '66
MORRISON, Jane
Child reading; poem. Horn Bk 42:329 Je '66
MORRISON, Karl R.
Snare some space. por Design 68:21-2 S '66
MORRISON, Kenneth D.
Requiem for a woodland. Audubon Mag 68:185
My '66
MORRISON, Martin, and Allen, P. Z.
Lactoperoxidase: identification and isolation
from harderian and lacrimal glands. bib-
liog Science 152:1626-8 Je 17 '66
—See Ohno, S. jt. auth.
MORRISON, Morton
Analyzing color prints. U S Camera 29:46-7+
Mr '66
Long lenses on short budgets. U S Camera
29:48-9+ Ap '66
Reflections in my hubcaps. il U S Camera
30:6 Ja '67
MORRISON, Perry D.
Lost book campaign at Sacramento. Wilson
Lib Bul 40:526-9 F '66
MORRISON, Philip, and Morrison, Phylis
Books. Sci Am 215:141-6+ D '66
**MORRISON, Phylis. See Morrison, Philip, jt.
auth.**
MORRISON, Sandy
Bomb in the cellar. Nation 203:318-20 O 3
'66
MORRISROE, Richard F.
Let no drum be muffled; John F. Kennedy
award dinner; address, February 22, 1966.
T. C. Sorensen. Christian Cent 83:328-31
Mr 16 '66
MORRISSEY, James
Touch and sound of sight. por Am Ed 2:25-7
My '66
MORRISTOWN, N.J.
Highwaymen come to Morristown; Inter-
state highway system. J. Skow. il Sat Eve
Post 239:68-75 Ap 9 '66
MORROW, Anne L.
For sale, a new Jesus; poem. Christian Cent
83:493 Ap 20 '66
MORROW, William, and company
Scott, Foresman to buy William Morrow & co.
Pub W 190:26 O 24 '66
MORSE, Arthur G.
New county recreation center in action.
Parks & Rec 1:720-1+ S '66
MORSE, Hugh Bion
Sex criminal; I don't know why I did it. J.
Kobler. il Sat Eve Post 240:23-9+ Ja 28 '67

MORSE, Ralph
Get a good grip on anything. il Pop Phot
58:68-9+ F '66
Perfectly paired Gemini team falls to earth.
Life 60:34 Mr 11 '66
MORSE, Wayne
Excerpt from address, August 31, 1966.
Cong Digest 45:234+ O '66
Excerpt from address, February 25, 1966. Cong
Digest 45:123-5 Ap '66
Excerpt from debate. July 18, 1966. Cong
Digest 45:208+ Ag '66
Senator Morse's advice and dissent. A. R.
Smith. il pors N Y Times Mag p24-5+ Ap
17 '66
MORSE, William B.
Heterodyne vegetation meter. Pop Electr 26:
72+ Ja '67
Quiet revolution. Am For 72:6-9+ Jl '66
School for loggers. il Am For 72:26-7+ O '66
Their hearts are as big as their country.
il Am For 72:30-1+ Ag '66
Wilderness research. Am For 72:32-3+ Je '66
MORSE code. See Cipher and telegraph codes
MORTALITY
See also
Infant mortality
MORTENSEN, William
In memoriam. Pop Phot 58:4+ F '66
MORTGAGES
As mortgage costs climb to new high. il U S
News 61:23 N 14 '66
Builders squeezed by money troubles. il Bsns
W p34-5 My 28 '66
Financial engineering. H. C. Wallich. News-
week 68:92 D 5 '66
For home buyers and builders: help that's
in the works. il U S News 61:93-6 Ag 15 '66
Hidden clause; savings-and-loan associations
use escalaton clauses to boost rates. il
Newsweek 68:80 O 17 '66
Homebuilding sinks to a postwar low; tight
money situation. il Bsns W p46 N 26 '66
Homebuilding teeters. il Bsns W p34-5 S 3 '66
Mortgage crunch. il Fortune 74:32+ O '66
Mortgage loans are hard to get. il Changing
T 20:37-40 S '66
Mortgages shape up as costly and tighter.
Bsns W p34-5 Mr 5 '66
New money for home loans: will it ease
pinch? il U S News 61:82 S 5 '66
Scraping bottom; credit-starved housing in-
dustry. il Time 88:89 D 16 '66
Second mortgages: how & when to use 'em.
il Changing T 21:15-17 Ja '67
Usury, what else? Nation 203:301 O 3 '66
What they're charging for mortgage loans.
il Changing T 20:6 D '66
See also
Land contracts
United States—Federal housing administra-
tion
United States—Federal national mortgage
association
MORTIMER, Penelope
(ed) See Christie, J. Julie Christie talks
about mates and morals
MORTON, Charles W.
Accent on living. See issues of Atlantic
World of Erle Stanley Gardner. Atlan 219:
79-86+ Ja '67
MORTON, Frances
Rock gardens of the wilderness. Nat Parks
Mag 40:17 My '66
MORTON, Francis
Bonus vacation. Field & S 71:41+ Je '66
MORTON, Frederic
El Morocco. Holiday 39:78-80+ F '66
MORTON, Miriam
Great literature for little folk. Horn Bk 42:
335-44 Je '66
MORTON, Thruston B.
Excerpt from address, April 2, 1966. Cong
Digest 45:247+ O '66
MOSAICS
Engaging souvenirs of the Grand tour. J. T.
Butler. il Antiques 90:96-9 Jl '66
Mosaic; high school group project. M. K.
Kight. il Sch Arts 66:31 N '66
MOSCONI, Willie
Willie Mosconi comes out shooting. J. Tobin.
Sports Illus 24:74+ My 2 '66
MOSCOSO, Teodoro
Caracas's 400th; Bolivar and bulldozers. Sat R
50:94+ Ja 7 '67
MOSCOVITCH, Edward
Finding jobs for the poor. New Repub 155:
16-19 N 5 '66
MOSCOW
Airports
Happier landings ahead for Soviet air travel-
ers; Aeroflot modernizes airports in Mos-
cow. il Bsns W p 130-2 Ap 2 '66

MOSCOW—*Continued*

Description

American in Moscow. T. T. Hammond. il Nat Geog Mag 129:297-351 Mr '66

Moscow. R. J. Fuchs. il Focus 16:1-6 Ja '66

Hotels, restaurants, etc.

For world science: a bear hug; third International congress on metallic corrosion in Moscow's Sovetskaya hotel. il Bsns W p92+ Je 4 '66

See also

Night clubs

Libraries

House at 43 Gorky street; Moscow house of children's literature. I. Dyomin. il Library J 91:5696-8 N 15 '66

Stores

Moscow's stores that keep Ivan out; dollar shops. il Bsns W p96-8 N 5 '66

Theater

Illustrated letter from Moscow. K. Ambrose. il Dance Mag 40:36-7 Ap '66

MOSCOW American club. See Night clubs

MOSCRIP, Ruth J.

Water the hibernating toads! NEA J 55:30-2 F '66

MOSELEY, Monica

Dancer's bookshelf. Dance Mag 40:18 O '66

Mozart, Moliere, and Cupid. Dance Mag 40: 56-61 S '66

MOSER, Don

Far-out opera uproar Down Under. Life 62: 62-4+ Ja 6 '67

Fire in Alpha 107 Mike! Life 61:108+ N 25 '66

He cruised in a golden car, looking for the action. Life 60:23-24A+ Mr 4 '66

Host of candidates unperturbed by terrorist threats. Life 61:36-41 S 23 '66

Solemn event in a fiesta city, no miracle, but solid results. Life 61:30 N 4 '66

Vietnam: the week of wild uncertainty. Life 60:44-44C Ap 15 '66

Westmoreland: the four-star eagle scout. Life 61:68-70+ N 11 '66

Where the rivers ran crimson from butchery. Life 61:26-8 Jl 1 '66

MOSER, John C.

Trails of the leafcutters; with biographical sketch. Natur Hist 76:7, 32-5 bibliog(p73) Ja '67

MOSER, Lida

It's done in the darkroom. il U S Camera 29:54-5 Jl '66

MOSES, Robert, 1888-

Confessions of a reformed reformer; with biographical sketch. por Sat R 50:18-21+ Ja 7 '67

FDR in perspective. por Newsweek 68:109+ D 12 '66

MOSES, William Robert

Poetry chronicle. L. Mueller. Poetry 107:260 Ja '66

MOSES and Aron; opera. See Schönberg, A.

MOSKIN, J. Robert

(ed) See Wills, M. R. American defector comes home; why I quit China

about

Behind the scenes. il por Look 30:M2 F 8 '66

MOSKOW, Michael H.

Representation among teachers. Mo Labor R 89:728-32 Jl '66

MOSKOWITZ, Gerard W. and Bowman, R. L.

Multicapillary mixer of solutions. Science 153:428-9 Jl 22 '66

MOSKOWITZ, Morris

Menace of Moe's books. R. H. Smith. Pub W 190:41 N 7 '66

MOSKOWITZ, Ronald

Updating American education. New Repub 154:22-3 Je 11 '66

MOSQUES

Timeless Turkey. J. Lieber. il Travel 126: 30-6 O '66

MOSQUITOES

Allure of the female mosquito. M. Roth and others. il Natur Hist 75:26-31 bibliog(p70) D '66

Do mosquitoes love you? C. B. Hicks. il Todays Health 44:32-4 Jl '66

Falciparum malaria: transmission to the gibbon by anopheles balabacensis. D. J. Gould and others. bibliog Science 153:1384 S 16 '66

Extermination

How Florida licks mosquitoes. il Am City 81:159-60+ Ap '66

Instant mosquito control; aid of South American fish. il Time 88:66 O 14 '66

Lethal effects of synthetic juvenile hormone on larvae of the yellow fever mosquito, aedes aegypti. A. Spielman and C. M. Williams. bibliog il Science 154:1043-4 N 25 '66

MOSQUITOES as carriers of infection

Environmental control of ovarian development in mosquitoes of the culex pipiens complex. B. F. Eldridge. bibliog il Science 151:826-8 F 18 '66

MOSS, Bertram B.

Autopsy: an important medical aid; excerpts from Matter of caring. Todays Health 44: 65 My '66

MOSS, Frank Edward

Why I'm for a department of natural resources; address, February 7, 1966. por Am For 72:16-17+ Mr '66

MOSS, Howard

Front street; poem. New Yorker 42:26 Jl 2 '66

Meeting; poem. New Yorker 42:36 Ag 20 '66

Persistence of song. New Yorker 42:56 N 19 '66

Still pond, no more moving; poem. New Yorker 42:26 Ag 6 '66

Vase; poem. New Yorker 42:63 D 10 '66

about

By what is not the world. R. Roseliep. Poetry 107:394-6 Mr '66

MOSS, John Emerson, 1913-

Bureaucracy unbound. Time 88:14 Jl 1 '66

MOSS, Marvin J.

Square-wave generator. Electr World 75:75-7 F '66

MOSS, Stanley

Country boy. New Repub 155:23-4 N 19 '66

(tr) See Voznesensky, A. Laziness

about

Five poets. A. Freeman. Poetry 109:191-2 D '66

MOSS, Stirling

Stirling Moss on racing. See issues of Motor trend

MOSS, Valerie Jane

Thunder; poem. Horn Bk 42:234 Ap '66

MOSS, Peat. See Peat moss

MOSSES

See also

Carrageen

MOSSLER, Candace

Armored lady. il por Time 87:43 F 4 '66

Aunt Candy. il por Newsweek 67:26 Ja 31 '66

Candy trial. il por Newsweek 67:35 Mr 14 '66

Mesmerism in Miami. por Time 87:66 Mr 18 '66

Stale Candy. il Newsweek 67:64 Mr 14 '66

Trials of Candy and Mel. L. H. Lapham. il pors Sat Eve Post 239:28-32+ Ag 27; 32-6+ S 10 '66

MOSSMAN, Archie S.

Wildlife and the tsetse fly in Rhodesia. il Nat Parks Mag 40:10-15 S '66

MOSSMAN, James

Comic twist to an old familiar fez. W. Goodman. Life 61:10 Jl 15 '66

MOST elegant drawing room in Europe; story. See Hale, N.

MOST happy fella; musical comedy. See Musical comedies, revues, etc.—Criticisms, plots, etc.

MOSTAR, Roman

Seattle: sensitive and unaggressive. Library J 91:5878-9 D 1 '66

MOSTERT, Noel

Russia bids for ocean supremacy. Reporter 34:24-8 F 10 '66

World's most spectacular Rock. Read Digest 88:39-40+ Ap '66

Writing on the Rock. Reporter 34:28-31 Je 30 '66

MOTELS

Bedding down the budget-minded owner-operated Motel 6. il Bsns W p56-8+ Ag 27 '66

Building types study. il Arch Rec 140:123-36 Ag '66

Hotels and motels reflect a changing world. S. W. Brener. Arch Rec 140:137-8 Ag '66

In the heart of it: Downtowner corp. il Time 87:90 My 27 '66

MOTETS

See also

Phonograph records—Motets

MOTHER-child relationship. See Parent-child relationship

MOTHER goes modern; drama. See Arthur, K.

MOTHER Goose
House that Jack built; R. Briggs' illustrations for Mother Goose treasury. J. Fritz. il Horn Bk 42:681-3 D '66

MOTHER love. See Love, Maternal

MOTHER makes a choice; drama. See Whittaker, H.

MOTHER, mother! story. See Seager, L.

MOTHERS
Day I nearly turned in my apron; zany, true story with a warm valentine accent. C. T. Smith. il Farm J 90:87+ F '66
Happiness is bugs in the grass. M. Wentworth. il Redbook 127:10+ O '66
How doctors treat postpartum blues. il Good H 162:185 Mr '66
How to be a good mother without neglecting your husband. E. Desmond. il Parents Mag 41:32-3+ Jl '66
My mother, the censor; reprint. R. Knudson. ALA Bul 60:613-16 Je '66
Question and answer; stage mothers. Y. Yourlo and E. Yourlo. Dance Mag 40:24 D '66
Young mother's story. See issues of Redbook
    See also
Maternal deprivation
Stepparents

Anecdotes, facetiae, satire, etc.
Beat poems of a beat mother. W. Devlin. il Good H 162:54 Ap '66
Every day is mother's day. M. Brophy. See issues of Good housekeeping
Private papers of a very new mother. S. McCluskey. il Good H 162:58+ Mr '66

Caricatures and cartoons
How to win over your children; excerpt. M. Bolte; B. Mauldin. Good H 162:100-1 Ap '66

Employment
    See Married women—Employment

MOTHERS, Unmarried
Despised minority. A. Poinsett. il Ebony 21:48-50+ Ag '66
    See also
Illegitimacy

MOTHERS and daughters. See Parent-child relationship

MOTHERS and sons. See Parent-child relationship

MOTHERS day
Holiday treat for mother. il Ebony 21:158+ Ap '66

Drama
Mother makes a choice. H. Whittaker. Plays 25:73-8 My '66

MOTHER'S helpers. See Household employees

MOTHERS-in-law
Juanita was an oversolicitous mother. D. C. Disney. Ladies Home J 83:30+ Je '66
Three generations under one roof: a painful decision. Redbook 126:8+ Ap '66

MOTHERWELL, Helen Frankenthaler. See Frankenthaler, H.

MOTHERWELL, Robert
Assassination in Boston. il Time 88:60 Ag 26 '66
Second fame: good food. N. Lyon. il por Vogue 147:194-6 Ap 1 '66

MOTHS
Background selections of geometrid and noctuid moths. T. D. Sargent. il Science 154:1674-5 D 30 '66
Evolution by pollution; soot-colored forms multiplying. il Sci Digest 60:74-5 S '66
Hideaway for moths; symbiotic relationship with two- and three-toed sloths. R. S. Casebeer and C. L. Hogue. il Natur Hist 75:40-1 My '66
Twenty days in June, the cautious war; tussock moth. H. E. McLean. il Am For 72:28-31+ Mr '66

Ear
    See Ear (insects)

MOTION
    See also
Movement, Psychology of
Vibration

MOTION in art. See Action in art

MOTION picture association of America
New movie code. Sr Schol 89:17 O 7 '66

MOTION picture production code. See Moving picture censorship

MOTION pictures. See Moving pictures

MOTION study
    See also
Movement, Psychology of

MOTIONS of stars. See Stars—Motion

MOTIVATION (education)
Class socialization patterns and their relationship to learning. G. L. Cary. bibliog f Sch & Soc 94:349-52 O 29 '66
On motivating the disadvantaged child; address, August 8, 1966. E. Nightingale. Vital Speeches 33:18-24 O 15 '66
Prevention of failure. W. B. Waetjen; K. W. Clarke. il NEA J 55:37-40 Ap '66

MOTIVATION (psychology)
Are you a self-starter? O. Schisgall. Read Digest 89:99-102 Jl '66
Curiosity and exploration. D. E. Berlyne. bibliog il Science 153:25-33 Jl 1 '66; Reply. J. M. Burgers. 154:1680-1 D 30 '66
Implications of laboratory studies of aggression for the control and regulation of violence. R. H. Walters. bibliog f Ann Am Acad 364:60-72 Mr '66
Washroom wit; analytic study by H. Lomas and G. Weltman. il Newsweek 68:110+ O 10 '66
    See also
Conflict (psychology)

MOTIVE (periodical)
Jester for Wesleyans. il Time 88:69-70 O 21 '66
Motive for Methodists; monthly journal published for college students. il Newsweek 67:60+ F 14 '66

MOTLEY, Arthur H.
Great free society; address, May 9, 1966. Vital Speeches 32:684-7 S 1 '66

MOTLEY, Constance (Baker)
Unlimited visibility; interview. New Yorker 42:48-50 S 17 '66
    about
People of the week. por U S News 61:22 S 12 '66

MOTOR boat racing
Action-packed '66 program promises unlimited thrills. J. Schmale. il Motor B 117:150-2 Je '66
All-American racing team. M. Crook. il Yachting 119:93-5 Ja '66
Always in the shadow; D. Campbell. il Time 89:50 Ja 13 '67
At long last. J. Crouse. il Yachting 119:75+ Je '66
Bluebird's last run. il Life 62:87-8 Ja 13 '67
Boatman's year, '65. il Motor B 117:62-77 Ja '66
Crushing race on a cruel sea; Sam Griffith memorial race. F. Rohr. il Motor B 117:132-6 Ap '66
Donzi did and Donzi didn't; race from New York's Flushing Bay into the East River. H. Whall. il Sports Illus 25:16-17 Jl 25 '66
Donzi's 1-2-3 the Long Island marathon. M. Penzer. il Motor B 118:94-5+ S '66
Fierce and foggy first for Thunderballs. W. R. Juettner. il Motor B 118:80-2 D '66
Fire is put out; tragic death of D. Campbell. Sports Illus 26:7 Ja 16 '67
Fragile sport; President's cup regatta. il Time 88:58-9 Jl 1 '66
Glory and tragedy, lot of the unlimiteds; on-the-scene reports of the Suncoast, President's and Gold cup races. E. Crimmin; M. Penzer. il Motor B 118:84-5+ Ag '66
How an expert rigs an outboard for rough water. J. Martenhoff. il Pop Sci 188:124-8+ Mr '66
Lipstick may fall in the bilge; R. Jacoby and G. Jacoby challenge the men. B. Ottum. il Sports Illus 24:64-6+ F 14 '66
Madness off Miami; Miami to Bimini race. il Time 87:48 Mr 4 '66
Miami-Nassau: Wynne and wind. M. Penzer. il Motor B 117:154-5+ Je '66
Miami-to-Key West; Wynne wins all. M. Penzer. il Motor B 119:354-7 Ja '67
Mist+flip=a hectic Hudson. M. Penzer. il Motor B 118:81+ Ag '66
Month in yachting. See issues of Yachting
More power to you. M. Crook. See issues of Yachting
Motorboat racing records. Motor B 119:350-1 Ja '67
Offshore powerboat racing. M. Crook. il Yachting 119:70-2+ Ja '66
Powerboat racers; why do they do it? N. Counsell. il Motor B 117:156-8 Je '66
Powerboats in competition. M. L. Hersey. il Yachting 119:67-9+ F '66
Rooster tales. E. Rickman. See issues of Hot rod
Salton 500 sweet to old pro Ramos. il Motor B 117:338+ Ja '66

MOTOR boat racing—*Continued*
Salton's flagged ships. J. McFarland. il Hot Rod 19:94-5 Mr '66
Salton's savage 500. T. E. Stimson, jr. il Pop Mech 126:138-41+ N '66
Three was just one too many; Harold Els loses World outboard championship at Lake Havasu. H. Whall. il Sports Illus 25:62-4 D 12 '66
To Slovak/Tahoe Miss, the Governor's cup. C. D. Strang. il Motor B 118:41+ N '66
To Wynne/Ghost Rider, another offshore feather. E. F. Haylock. il Motor B 118:40+ N '66
Toughest chicken afloat; hydroplane driver M. Slovak. H. Whall. il Sports Illus 25:110-11 S 19 '66
Wet run to Painsville; 440-mile Long Beach-to-San Francisco ocean race. H. Whall. il Sports Illus 25:20-5 N 7 '66
Winning way to Nassau is Wynne's way; Miami-Nassau powerboat race. il Sports Illus 24:66-7 My 9 '66
Wynne conquers in a howling classic. il Motor B 118:83-4 D '66

MOTOR boat speed records
Motorboat racing records. Motor B 117:118+ Ja '66

MOTOR boats
Fastest, smoothest boat yet; Taylor boat. J. Gould. Esquire 65:108-9+ F '66
Highlights for '66; symposium. il Pop Sci 188:132-51 F '66
Inboards, 1966. il Motor B 117:120-35+ Ja '66
Moonshine; photographs. Hot Rod 19:72-3 F '66
1967 inboards. il Motor B 119:122-39+ Ja '67
Revamping the older powerboat. C. West. il Yachting 119:92-4+ Ap '66
Rooster tales. E. Rickman. See issues of Hot rod
'66 boats: it's a catch-up year. A. Mikesell. il Pop Mech 125:126-8 Mr '66
Spray makers; hot boaters with ski boats. E. Rickman. il Hot Rod 19:32-8+ S '66
Starcraft's Caravel-V with new MerCruiser 80 stern drive. A. Mikesell. il Pop Mech 127:126-8 Ja '67
See also
Hydrofoils
Hydroplanes
Lifeboats, Motor

Accidents
See Boats and boating—Accidents

Camping equipment
Try camping afloat. P. Perrett. il Pop Mech 125:124-6+ My '66

Design
Amazing Janie D. J. Stoltz. il Motor B 117:35 F '66
Designs. W. H. DeFontaine. il Yachting 119:120-6+ Ja '66
Down to the sea in stereo! J. Roe. il Pop Sci 188:114-16 My '66
Famed sailor Norrie Hoyt comments on Passagemaker. N. Hoyt. Motor B 117:39+ My '66
Plans for the perfect powerboat. il Esquire 65:106-7 F '66
Two ladies from the West coast. il Yachting 120:60-1 N '66
You can cross oceans in a motorboat. R. Beebe. il Motor B 117:36-8+ My '66

Electric equipment
See also
Motor boats—Starting

Electronic equipment
Electronics, 1966. il Motor B 117:168-73+ Ja '66
So you have bought a new cruiser. J. Roe. il Yachting 119:80-2+ Je '66

Equipment
Case of the capsule cruiser. I. Anthony. il Yachting 119:83+ My '66
Cypress Gardens driver tells: how to rig your ski boat. E. Rehling. il Pop Mech 125:138-40 Mr '66
New for outboards. il Yachting 119:86-7+ Mr '66
So you have bought a new cruiser. J. Roe. il Yachting 119:80-2+ Je '66
Swing-up stern ladder. H. Clark. il Pop Mech 126:148 Ag '66
Yachting's boat show. il Yachting 119:127-30+ Ja '66
You can cross oceans in a motorboat. R. Beebe. il Motor B 117:36-8+ My '66

Exhibitions
See Boats—Exhibitions

Fuel tanks
How to install a fuel tank in your boat. C. R. Meyer. il Pop Sci 188:180-2 Ap '66

History
Vintage power boats. M. Crook. il Yachting 120:45+ D '66

Speed
Fastest, smoothest boat yet; Taylor boat. J. Gould. Esquire 65:108-9+ F '66

Starting
In's and out's of electric starting. H. B. Notrom. il Pop Mech 125:170-3 Ap '66

Testing
First test-drive report on no-piston power for boats. J. Roe. il Pop Sci 189:88-91 Ag '66
Johnson's new Reveler. A. Mikesell. il Pop Mech 126:118-20 N '66
New Johnson surfer is fast, roomy, and stable. J. Roe. il Pop Sci 188:176-8+ Ap '66

MOTOR boats, Jet propelled
Ride your own jet stream for more fun and safety. J. Roe. il Pop Sci 189:102-4 Jl '66

MOTOR boats, Outboard
Antique outboards too frisky to retire. K. Warner. il Pop Mech 125:142-4+ Mr '66
Cool new three-keeler is stable and sassy; Starcraft's Daytona. J. Roe. il Pop Sci 189:120-2 N '66
How an expert rigs an outboard for rough water. J. Martenhoff. il Pop Sci 188:124-8+ Mr '66
1967 outboards. il Motor B 119:162-9 Ja '67
Outboards in shallow water. B. Whittier. il Yachting 119:118-19+ Ja '66
Outboards, 1966. il Motor B 117:144-9+ Ja '66
Rough and ready or smooth and sweet; Boston Whaler. J. Roe. il Pop Sci 189:132-4 S '66
See also
Electric engines, Outboard

Equipment
Perfect boat for campers. F. M. Paulson. il Field & S 71:32-3+ Ja '67

MOTOR bus accidents. See Traffic accidents

MOTOR buses
Germans mate bus and hotel; triple-decker rolling hotel. il Bsns W p 172-3 My 21 '66

Fares
Minibus + 5-cent fare=transit success story; Washington, D.C. il Am City 81:53 Mr '66

MOTOR caravans
Jeep patrol tour; trip sponsored by the Salida chamber of commerce. E. Orazem. il Travel 125:43-5 N '66

MOTOR fuels. See Motor truck engines—Fuel

MOTOR lodges. See Motels

MOTOR oils. See Lubrication and lubricants

MOTOR raceways. See Speedways

MOTOR sailers. See Motor boats

MOTOR scooters
For the fastest ride out of this world. take a motorbike. J. Contini. il Seventeen 25:152-3+ N '66
Take 'em aboard to ride 'em ashore. N. Phillips. il Motor B 117:82-4 Ja '66
Trail bikes for sportsmen. R. C. Renstrom. il Field & S 71:48-51+ D '66

MOTOR scooters, Police
Breakthrough in crime prevention? il U S News 60:14 F 14 '66
Fuzz with a buzz; motor scooter. il Time 89:39 Ja 13 '67
Scooter patrol puts zip in police work. Am City 81:45 Je '66
T.S.U: Tactical scooter units; N.Y. police department. New Yorker 41:31-2 F 5 '66

MOTOR sleds
Wild ride in the Rockies; snowmobile drive from Vail to Aspen. R. Cantwell. il Sports Illus 24:18-20+ Ja 24 '66

MOTOR trend award
Candidates! Car of the year award. D. Mac-Donald. il Motor T 19:64-5 Ja '67
Motor trend magazine's Car of the year award; eleven-year record. D. MacDonald. il Motor T 18:62-3 D '66

MOTOR trend-Riverside 500. See Automobile racing

MOTOR truck drivers
How to live with trucks. D. MacDonald. il Motor T 18:134 N '66
  See also
International brotherhood of teamsters, chauffeurs, warehousemen and helpers of America
Strikes—United States—Truck drivers

MOTOR truck engines
Free piston engine seen; may be used in heavy trucks and boats. Sci N 90:375 N 5 '66

        Fuel
Know your diesel. C. N. Hinkle and W. J. Fletcher. il Suc Farm 64:48 Ag '66

MOTOR truck industry and trade
Bulldog tenacity puts truck maker on the high road; Mack trucks. il Bsns W p 182-4+ O 15 '66
Trucks still pull the biggest load; in Japan truck making outranks cars. Bsns W p 114 D 3 '66

MOTOR truck lines
  See also
DC international

     Employees
Bargaining and wages in local cartage. V. J. Sheifer. il Mo Labor R 89:1076-84 O '66
Teamsters take a dare and lose a vote. il Bsns W p 152-3+ Ap 16 '66
  See also
Motor truck drivers

MOTOR truck tires. See Tires, Motor truck
MOTOR trucking. See Trucking
MOTOR trucks
More and heavier trucks in residential areas. il Am City 81:39 Jl '66
New trucks for 1967. il Farm J 90:58-9 N '66
What's new. il Suc Farm 64:58 Jl; 30 Ag; 36 S; 30 O; 38 N; 42 D '66
  See also
Mack trucks, incorporated

       Care
Rustproofing that pays for itself; Detroit. J. B. Garvie. il Am City 81:104-5 Mr '66

    Equipment
Four good ideas from one truck. il Suc Farm 64:64 Ap '66

     Testing
One for the road; Chevelle El Camino pick-up. E. Dahlquist. il Hot Rod 19:32-5 My '66
Town & country hauler; Ranchero. E. Dahlquist. il Hot Rod 19:30-3+ Ap '66

     Wheels
Now they've put motors inside every wheel. W. S. Bacon. il Pop Sci 189:86-7+ Ag '66

MOTOR trucks, Electric
Battery firm, affiliate aim for modest electric auto. L. J. Curran. il Tech W 19:36-7 N 7 '66

MOTOR trucks, Municipal
Rustproofing that pays for itself; Detroit. J. B. Garvie. il Am City 81:104-5 Mr '66

MOTOR trucks, Refrigerated
Produce sleeps and stays fresh. il Bsns W p49-50 Ja 29 '66

MOTOR vehicle accidents. See Traffic accidents

MOTOR vehicle laws and regulations
New federal rules for safety on the highways. U S News 61:12 D 19 '66

MOTOR vehicle racing
Creepers jeepers; second annual Four wheel drive Gran prix. E. Rickman. il Hot Rod 19:42-4 Je '66
Four-wheel frivolity. E. Rickman. il Hot Rod 19:77-80 F '66
Four wheels up and over. S. Kelly. il Motor T 18:26 Je '66
World's dirtiest drag race; swamp buggies race, Naples, Fla. K. Warner. il Pop Mech 126:128-31+ O '66

MOTOR vehicles
Buckin' Bronco V-8. D. MacDonald. il Motor T 18:48+ S '66
Personal car for roads and rail; StaRRcar combines mobility of automobiles and efficiency of rapid-transit systems. M. J. Pedersen. il Pop Mech 126:61A Ag '66
Terra firma funny cars. B. Greene. il Hot Rod 19:32-8+ Ag '66
That go-anywhere car again with new power! il Pop Sci 188:164-5 My '66
  See also
Automobiles
Motor buses
Motor scooters
Snowmobiles

     Accidents
See Traffic accidents

     Renting
Leasing: all systems go. il Duns R 87:pt2 136-9+ My '66

     Testing
MT road test:
Jeep with V-6 muscle. D. MacDonald. il Motor T 18:66-7 My '66
Utility with a flair; new Scout sportop. D. MacDonald. il Motor T 18:68-9 My '66

    Transmission
Amazing new cone drive is clutch, transmission, differential. H. Walton. il Pop Sci 188:59-62+ Je '66

     Wheels
Automotive engineers standardize wheel-loader rating. il Am City 81:219 S '66

MOTOR vehicles, Amphibious
Bush buggy. A. Mikesell. il Pop Mech 125:138-42+ My '66

MOTOR vehicles, Military
Mobility problems still vex army. W. S. Beller. il Miss & Roc 18:74-6 Mr 28 '66
Radio-packed jeeps for front-line talk. Sci N 90:103 Ag 13 '66

MOTOR vehicles, Police
  See also
Motor scooters, Police

MOTORAMA. See Automobiles—Exhibitions
MOTORBOATS. See Motor boats
MOTORCYCLE accidents. See Traffic accidents
MOTORCYCLE clubs
Rebels on wheels; Negro, white and integrated clubs. il Ebony 22:64-6+ D '66

MOTORCYCLE engines
Honda Grand prix four: summit of four-stroke technology. R. Renstrom. il Hot Rod 19:84-6 S '66

MOTORCYCLE industry and trade
Honda's hang-up; U.S. sales drop. Newsweek 68:66 Jl 11 '66
Mild ones roar off with a market. il Bsns W p 138-40 N 12 '66
World's no. 1 thunderer; Honda company. G. Kent. il Read Digest 89:13-14+ D '66

MOTORCYCLE racing
Daytona AMA style. B. Greene. il Hot Rod 19:70-3+ Je '66
Heir to the throne. E. Rickman. il Hot Rod 19:74-5 Mr '66
Rally on the rocks; Greenhorn enduro. il Hot Rod 19:82-3 Ag '66

MOTORCYCLE riding. See Motorcycling
MOTORCYCLES
BSA Victor 441. B. Greene. il Hot Rod 19:88-91+ Mr '66
Boss! Harley-Davidson Sportster. B. Greene. il Hot Rod 19:98-100+ N '66
Happiness is a hot Yamaha. B. Greene. il Hot Rod 19:82-5 F '66
Honda Grand prix four summit of four-stroke technology. R. Renstrom. il Hot Rod 19:84-6 S '66
Honda's technical masterpiece. B. Greene. il Hot Rod 19:81-5+ Ap '66
In wheels. J. H. Porter. il Mlle 62:160-1+ F '66
Outdoors. T. Williams. Esquire 65:18+ Ap '66
Take-along trail bikes add vacation fun. E. H. Arctander. il Pop Sci 188:166-9+ My '66
Trail bike basics. B. Behme. il Field & S 70:69-71+ F '66
Up on two wheels. B. Greene. See issues of Hot rod
  See also
Motor scooters
Motorcycling

   Maintenance and repair
Winter tune-up for your cycle (cont) M. J. Schultz. il Pop Mech 125:170-3+ F '66

  Safety devices and measures
Death by motorcycle. E. Maxwell. Todays Health 44:85 O '66

     Testing
Hustler. D. Evans. il Hot Rod 19:82-4+ My '66
Motorcycles: what I like in a bike, and why. S. McQueen. il Pop Sci 189:76-81 N '66
Three for the trail. S. James. il Pop Mech 127:140-3+ Ja '67

MOTORCYCLES, Police
See also
Motor scooters, Police

MOTORCYCLING
For the fastest ride out of this world, take a motorbike. J. Contini. il Seventeen 25:152-3+ N '66
News on wheels. Sr Schol 88:32 My 13 '66
Smothers brothers, crazy for wheels. W. S. Griswold. il Pop Sci 188:104-6 F '66
See also
Motorcycle clubs

MOTORISTS. See Automobile drivers

MOTOROLA, incorporated
There a new tune at Motorola; R. W. Galvin presses decentralization. il Bsns W p 110-12+ Ap 23 '66

MOTORS. See Electric motors; Engines

MOTOWN record corporation
Big, happy, beating heart of the Detroit sound; Motown's records. R. R. Lingeman. il N Y Times Mag p48-9+ N 27 '66
Triumph of a stay-at-home. il Ebony 21:32-4+ F '66

MOTRY, Barbara
I enjoyed having my baby. Parents Mag 41:36-7+ Ag '66

MOTT, Frank L.
Immigrant worker. Ann Am Acad 367:23-32 S '66

MOTT, Newcomb
Death on a train. por Sr Schol 88:6 F 25 '66
Deepening mystery. Newsweek 67:34-5 F 7 '66
Journey's end. il por Newsweek 67:44 Ja 31 '66
Obituary
Pub W 189:77 Ja 31 '66
Russian mystery: an American's death. il por U S News 60:12 F 7 '66

MOTTA (firm) See Food industry and trade

MOTTURA, Robert
Lo! le pauvre indien. il Newsweek 68:57-8 Ag 29 '66

MOUDY, James M.
Education without magic; address. November 19, 1965. Vital Speeches 32:275-8 F 15 '66

MOULTON, Elizabeth
Fall came in; poem. Mlle 63:108 O '66
In the fun house; story. Redbook 126:64-5 F '66

MOULTON, Priscilla Landis
Experiment in cooperative reviewing by scientists and librarians. Horn Bk 42:345-9 Je '66

MOUNT, Donald I. and others
Endrin: use of concentration in blood to diagnose acute toxicity to fish. bibliog Science 152:1388-90 Je 3 '66

MOUNT, Rick
Basketball's bright star in Indiana. F. Deford. il pors Sports Illus 24:28-30+ F 14 '66

MOUNT ATHOS. See Athos, Mount

MOUNT CLEMENS, Mich.
Ding dong, the bells are gone; Chippewa Valley high school. E. Stephens. Seventeen 25:410-11 Ag '66

MOUNT COOK NATIONAL PARK. See National parks and reserves—New Zealand

MOUNT JEFFERSON wilderness area (proposed) See Wilderness areas—Oregon

MOUNT KELUD. See Mud volcanoes

MOUNT MARCY. See Marcy, Mount

MOUNT OLYMPUS NATIONAL PARK. See Olympic National Park

MOUNT PALOMAR observatory. See Astronomical observatories

MOUNT RAINIER NATIONAL PARK
Little Tahoma's big slide. il Sunset 137:8 Jl '66

MOUNT SHASTA. See Shasta, Mount

MOUNT VERNON, N.Y.
Recreation
Specifications for a maintenance specialist; recreation maintenance man in Mount Vernon recreation department. J. M. Branca. Parks & Rec 1:39+ Ja '66

MOUNTAIN climbing. See Mountaineering

MOUNTAIN flying. See Aviation—Mountain flying

MOUNTAIN LAKES wild area. See Wilderness areas—Oregon

MOUNTAIN lion hunting. See Puma hunting

MOUNTAIN lions. See Pumas

MOUNTAIN sculpture
Dream as big as a mountain; 563 feet high memorial to Crazy Horse in Black Hills of S.D. H. Jones. il Sat Eve Post 239:30-1 S 10 '66
Largest; figure of Crazy Horse. Am Artist 30:6 S '66
See also
Stone Mountain memorial

MOUNTAIN sheep
Wild spectacle; bighorn rams in rutting season. J. Holroyd. il Field & S 71:31-3+ Ag '66

MOUNTAIN sheep hunting
Bighorn by the seat of my pants. G. Gresham. il Field & S 71:37-9+ O '66
Long quest. L. T. Empey. il Outdoor Life 137:50-3+ Je '66
New kind of trophy hunt. J. K. Cope. il Outdoor Life 139:66-7+ Ja '67
Ross and his ham. D. Peck. il Outdoor Life 138:34-5+ Ag '66
Two for the book. W. Page. il Field & S 71:23-5+ Jl '66
See also
Argali hunting

MOUNTAINEERING
California: climb beyond the possible; ascent of sheer rock in Yosemite Valley. C. S. Wren. il Look 30:70-2 Je 28 '66
Death on the Eiger; American climber. J. Harlin. Sports Illus 24:21+ Ap 4 '66
Harrowing freeze-up on the Needle; Mont Blanc. il Life 61:22B-22C S 2 '66
High performance; derring-do and tragedy on Dru Needle. il Newsweek 68:40+ S 5 '66
Metropolis mountain; Tokyo rock; photographs. Travel 125:49-51 Mr '66
Our far-flung correspondents; complete circuit of Mont Blanc by surrounding glacial passes and valleys before opening of tunnel. J. Bernstein. il New Yorker 42:148+ Mr 26 '66
Thousand feet of nothing down below; infamous north wall of the Eiger. J. Harlin. Sports Illus 24:69-70+ Ap 11 '66
Upon the mountain. J. Masters. il Holiday 40:6+ S '66
See also
Eiger (mountain), Switzerland
Trail riders of the wilderness

MOUNTAINEERING clubs
See also
Sierra club

MOUNTAINEERS (southern states)
And the books came tumblin' in; Tumblin' Creek cabin library, Tennessee mountains. S. C. Gross. il Sr Schol 88:sup9-10 My 6 '66
Crafts of the Southern highlands; portraits of craftsmen. Craft Horiz 26:35-56 Je '66

MOUNTAINS, Undersea. See Ocean bottom

MOUNTED animals. See Trophies, Sport

MOUNTING (taxidermy) See Taxidermy

MOUNTING of automobile engines. See Automobile engines—Mounting

MOUNTS, Gun. See Gun carriages

MOUNTZOURES, H. L.
Beating; story. New Yorker 42:30-2 Ag 20 '66
Epithalamion; story. New Yorker 42:46 Mr 26 '66
Lecture; story. New Yorker 42:170 Ap 23 '66
Pigeon; story. New Yorker 42:32-4 Jl 16 '66

MOURNING dove shooting
Talk about doves; interviews. J. Parks; H. Banks. il Field & S 71:56-7+ S '66

MOUSOLITE, Peter S.
Program for the talented college student. Sch & Soc 94:125-6 Mr 5 '66

MOUSSE. See Desserts

MOUSSIE, Curtis E.
Secrets of a society photographer. il U S Camera 29:44-5+ Ap '66

MOUSSORGSKY, Modest Petrovich. See Musorgskii, M. P.

MOUTH
See also
Jaws
Surgery
See Oral surgery

MOUTH hygiene
See also
Halitosis
Mouthwashes

MOUTHWASHES
Breathes there a mouth; TV advertising. il Time 88:74 D 9 '66
Contract that left the lawyers breathless; 1881 royalty agreement on Listerine mouthwash. il Bsns W p 122+ Ag 20 '66
Riches from royalties; royalty arrangement. il Time 88:92 D 16 '66

MOVEMENT, Notation. See Dance notation

MOVEMENT, Psychology of
Body dances to speech. P. McBroom. Sci N
89:483 Je 18 '66

MOVIE censorship. See Moving picture censorship

MOVING
Executives on the go. il Newsweek 68:102-4
N 21 '66
Families on the move. D. Klein. il Parents
Mag 41:48-9+ F '66
Family on the move. E. F. Liese. il Parents
Mag 41:64-5+ O '66
If you're thinking of moving. B. Surface. il
Read Digest 89:134-8 N '66
Moving day count-down. il House & Gard
129:62+ Ap '66
New rules for household movers; mildly consumer-oriented. Consumer Rep 31:450-1 S
'66
Pied Piper of personnel. R. Levy. Duns R 88:
49-50 S '66
Some pointers on moving. il Changing T
20:36 S '66

MOVING and storage companies
Moving the mobile American. il Duns R 87:
pt2 142-4 My '66

MOVING of libraries
Moving the library at Dutchess community
college. B. L. Feret. il ALA Bul 61:68-
71 Ja '67

MOVING of structures, etc.
Community action in the West: Chatsworth
moves its church. il Sunset 136:154 Ap '66

MOVING picture actors and actresses
Bing Crosby and his new movie: Stagecoach.
M. Davidson and J. Rale. il Sat Eve Post
239:30-3+ Ap 9 '66
Common market's glamor stock; beauties of
Europe. il Life 60:40-51 Ja 28 '66
Dorothy Dandridge: Hollywood's tragic enigma. L. Robinson. il Ebony 21:70-2+ Mr '66
Eight-sided gambol by The group; study of
the girls and their roles; with report by
P. Kael. il Life 60:116-18+ Ap 8 '66
France is mad for... Jerry Lewis? H. Alpert.
il N Y Times Mag p28-9+ F 27 '66
Great undashing lover of our time; M.
Mastroianni. A. Chamberlin. il Sat Eve
Post 239:81-5 Ag 13 '66
Hollywood sunset. G. Swanson. il Esquire
66:76-81 Ag '66
If you flunked the 2-S test, nice going; pinups from World war II and for Vietnamese
war. il Esquire 66:110-13 S '66
Incredible shrinking Hollywood; plus selected
short subjects. P. Kael. il Holiday 39:86-
93+ Mr '66
Keeping the stars in fiscal shape. il Bsns W
p 160-2+ Je 4 '66
Long reign as king of the apes; movie Tarzans. T. F. Moore. il Sports Illus 26:48-54
Ja 2 '67
Loser makes it big; S. McQueen. T. Armbrister. il Sat Eve Post 240:26-9 Ja 14 '67
Maurice Joseph Micklewhite, what's 'e got?
G. Steinem. il N Y Times Mag p66-7+ D 4
'66
Some day it will all be just wonderful. G.
Smith. il Sat Eve Post 239:34-7 Ja 29 '66
Spotlight! E. Miller. See issues of Seventeen
Very phony profession. T. Armbrister. il Sat
Eve Post 239:100-2+ O 8 '66
Where is the new talent? A. Knight. Sat R
49:20-2 D 24 '66
See also names of moving picture actors
and actresses. e.g. P. Newman

MOVING picture animal actors. See Animals
in moving pictures

MOVING picture authorship
Hollywood screen writers: who are they and
how do they work? P. R. Reynolds. il Sat
R 49:52-3+ Jl 9 '66
Tallest dwarf in the world; dir. by E. Miller. W. Allen. Seventeen 25:210+ My '66
To prepare man for the extraordinary. il
Esquire 65:117 My '66

MOVING picture awards
Who's to classify? church groups choices.
A. Knight. Sat R 49:42+ F 26 '66

MOVING picture cameras
Buypoints: movie cameras. M. D. Grennan.
il Pop Phot 59:132-45 O '66
Growing sophistication of Single 8. il U S
Camera 29:70 N '66
Here it is! the first double super 8 camera.
R. Benson. il Pop Phot 58:118+ My '66
Matzkin on movies: Bolex 150 super 8 movie
camera. M. A. Matzkin. il Mod Phot 30:68
D '66
Matzkin on movies; super 8's. M. A. Matzkin.
Mod Phot 30:28+ S '66

Motion-picture camera mount eliminates
helicopter's shakes. R. Barnhart. il Tech W
19:42-4 D 5 '66
Movie battle of the century? Fuji single 8
vs Kodapak super 8. il Pop Phot 58:124:7+
Ap '66
Movie test reports. See issues of Popular
photography
New French movie camera simplifies filming
of travelogues. W. Lane. il Travel 125:66-7
Ap '66
Single 8 grows up. M. Dultz. il Pop Phot
59:172+ D '66
Stampede of super 8. G. Gilbert. il U S
Camera 29:50-3 Je '66
Super 8 movie cameras. il Consumer Rep 31:
269-75 Je '66
Super 8 movie cameras. il Consumer Rep 31:
248-60 D '66
Super super 8 camera. L. Lipton. il Pop
Phot 58:116-17+ My '66
What's new that's good? H. Fondiller. il Pop
Phot 58:104+ Je '66

Sound equipment
And here, 007, is your camera. K. Poli. il
Pop Phot 60:128-31 Ja '67

MOVING picture censorship
Community standard should be a national
standard; Genet's Un chant d'amour. H. F.
Pilpel. Pub W 190:55-6 D 26 '66
Guilt despite association; J. Genet's Un chant
d'amour, film, Time 88:82 D 16 '66
Is nothing obscene? Swedish film 491. Time
88:70+ N 4 '66
Motion picture code and the new American
culture. J. Valenti. il PTA Mag 61:16-19
D '66
Movies, censorship and the law, by I. H.
Carmen. Review
Christian Cent 83:1416 N 16 '66. J. M.
Wall; Reply. W. Janssen, 83:1605 D 28
'66
New movie code; Motion picture association
of America. Sr Schol 89:17 O 7 '66
Three-and-a-half square; new code. Newsweek 68:22 O 3 '66
Washington report; statement, ed. by J.
Lloyd. S. Temple. Sr Schol 89:sup6 N 18 '66
When bare breasts are decent; new production code. il Time 88:56+ S 30 '66
Who's to classify? A. Knight. Sat R 49:42+
F 26 '66
See also
Moving pictures—Moral aspects

MOVING picture criticism. See Moving picture plays—Criticisms, plots, etc.

MOVING picture directors
Double-neos; Italy. il Newsweek 67:98 F 21
'66
Spotlight on Prague. il Newsweek 68:93-4
Jl 18 '66
Where is the new talent? A. Knight. Sat R
49:20-2 D 24 '66
See also
Brown, B.
Canutt, Y.
Forman, M.
Kubrick, S.
Truffaut, F.
Varda, A.
Watt, R.

MOVING picture editing. See Moving pictures
—Editing

MOVING picture festivals
Are these films offensive? Al Capp vs. the
modern young ladies of Wellesley. A. Capp;
R. Reisig. il Pop Phot 59:168-71 D '66
Art of animation; festival sponsored by the
Museum of modern art. H. Junker. Nation
202:249-50 F 28 '66
La dolce Venezia; Venice film festival. il
Time 88:85 S 16 '66
Eyes have it; New York film festival. il
Time 88:74-5 S 23 '66
Festival: fourth New York film festival. New
Yorker 42:54-5 S 24 '66
Film festival; New York film festival. P. T.
Hartung. Commonweal 85:56-7 O 14 '66
Film festivals, 1966; Berlin, San Sebastian;
and Cannes. H. Alpert; E. Archer; A. Sarris. Sat R 49:61-3 Jl 23 '66
Film festivals, 1966; New York, Venice,
Vancouver. H. Alpert; R. F. Hawkins; A.
Knight. il Sat R 49:91-2+ O 8 '66
Films at the Philharmonic; New York fourth
annual film festival. R. Steel. Christian Cent
83:1340-1 N 2 '66
Iron curtain festival; Carlsbad. A. Knight.
Sat R 49:36 Ag 6 '66
Lively arts; New York film festival. W.
Johnson and R. Hemming. il Sr Schol 89:
25 O 28 '66

MOVING picture festivals—*Continued*

Masters and mavericks; New York; best entries. il Newsweek 68:105-7 O 3 '66

New York is a foreign festival; entries in New York film festival. il Times 88:52 Ag 26 '66

Notes and comment; fourth annual New York film festival. New Yorker 42:48 S 17 '66

Plea for the *vieille vague*; San Francisco festival. S. Eimerl. Reporter 35:51-6 D 15 '66

San Francisco, festival rising. H. Alpert. Sat R 49:72 N 12 '66

SR goes to the movies; Mar del Plata entries. A. Knight. Sat R 49:30 Ap 2 '66

Sh-sh-sh-shark and other underwater festival goodies; International underwater film festival. P. Gowland. il Pop Phot 59:128-9 Ag '66

See also

Cannes international film festival

MOVING picture film collections

See also

Libraries—Moving picture collections

MOVING picture films

Fujichrome vs Kodachrome II, how do they compare? H. Keppler. il Mod Phot 30:88-9 Jl '66

Is super 8 good enough for professionals? questions and answers. E. A. Edwards. il Mod Phot 30:84+ S '66

Leonard Lipton's movie report; new Ektachrome II 8-mm emulsion. L. Lipton. Pop Phot 58:119 My '66

Matzkin on movies; difficulties with super 8. M. A. Matzkin. Mod Phot 30:32+ Ap '66

Movie films. Pop Phot 59:16C-18C D '66

Now! E.I. 1280 color movie film! W. Hanson; B. Pierce; N. Rothschild. il Pop Phot 58:35-6+ F '66

MOVING picture industry

See also

Moving picture production and direction

Finance

Supercolossalitis. P. Bart. il Sat R 49:14-16 D 24 '66

Where does the money go? H. Alpert. Sat R 49:16 D 24 '66

History

Movies: the history of an art and an institution, by R. Schickel. Review

Esquire 65:62+ Ap '66

Argentina

Geography lesson. A. Knight. Sat R 49:30 Ap 2 '66

Czechoslovakia

Spotlight on Prague; new films. il Newsweek 68:93-4 Jl 18 '66

Watch out for the hook, my friend. A. Levy. il Life 62:77-8+ Ja 20 '67

Great Britain

Moviemaking; slow, damp, and better now than Hollywood. il Esquire 66:60-1 Jl '66

Hong Kong

Imperial dynasty; empire of the Shaw brothers. il Newsweek 67:109-109A Ap 11 '66

Italy

Forty-cent stars; Franchi and Ingrassia films. il Newsweek 67:105A+ Mr 21 '66

Sweden

Scandinavian screen. R. Schickel. Holiday 40:156+ N '66

United States

American motion picture; 1966; SR's annual film survey; symposium. Sat R 49:11-25 D 24 '66

Creating with enthusiasm; interview. S. Goldwyn. Nations Bsns 54:46-8+ N '66

For movies; a boom, but new worries in Hollywood. il U S News 61:120-2 O 17 '66

Hollywood rides again. S. H. Brown. il Fortune 74:181-2+ N '66

Incredible shrinking Hollywood; plus selected short subjects. P. Kael. il Holiday 39:86-93+ Mr '66

Media-mex. R. Hatch. Nation 202:139 Ja 31 '66

New gold in the Hollywood hills; films for TV. il Time 88:108+ N 25 '66

New York is a foreign festival; entries in New York film festival. il Time 88:52 Ag 26 '66

TV and Hollywood sing a new duet; movies made for TV. Bsns W p 106-8 Ap 16 '66

See also

American international pictures (firm)

Metro Goldwyn Mayer pictures

Motion picture association of America

Twentieth century-Fox film corporation

MOVING picture locations. See Moving pictures—Setting and scenery

MOVING picture photography

Analysis of complex vascular systems in plants: optical shuttle method. M. H. Zimmermann and P. B. Tomlinson. bibliog il Science 152:72-3 Ap 1 '66

Focus on Bob Yung. H. V. Fondiller. il Pop Phot 58:100-3+ F '66

Images only your lens can see. N. Rothschild. il Pop Phot 59:122-5 Ag '66

Lewis Jacobs: film-maker, director, author, teacher; interview, ed. by J. Deschin. L. Jacobs. Pop Phot 58:12+ F '66

Matzkin on movies. M. A. Matzkin. See issues of Modern photography

Movie Q's and A's. J. R. Gregory. See issues of U.S. camera & travel, June 1966-

Novel movie effects. J. R. Oswald. il U S Camera 29:74-5 S '66

Watch the direction when cutting. M. A. Matzkin. il Mod Phot 30:84 Jl '66

Apparatus and supplies

Improved Tri-X, G.E.'s arc lamp, & super 8. L. Lipton. Pop Phot 58:108 F '66

Movie Q's and A's. J. R. Gregory. See issues of U.S. camera & travel, June 1966-

Movie report; good tools pay for themselves. L. Lipton. Pop Phot 58:127 Mr '66

Movie test reports. See issues of Popular photography

Competitions

Matzkin on movies; Eastman Kodak teenage movie contest. M. A. Matzkin. Mod Phot 30:98 My '66

Landscapes

New look for movie scenics. M. A. Matzkin. il Mod Phot 30:79 My '66

Lighting

Matzkin on movies. M. A. Matzkin. Mod Phot 26 Jl '66

Matzkin on movies; available light movies. M. A. Matzkin. Mod Phot 30:14+ Je '66

Portraits

Gowland à go-go. P. Gowland. il Pop Phot 59:136-9+ Jl '66

Study and teaching

Art of movie making. C. F. Trevelyan. il U S Camera 29:56-9 Je '66

Should you go to the Flaherty film seminar? L. Lipton. il Pop Phot 59:140+ Jl '66

MOVING picture photography, Submarine

Adventures of an underwater cameraman. W. Hartley and E. Hartley. il Pop Mech 126:92-5 S '66

Shark! P. R. Gimbel. il Sports Illus 25:68-76 Ag 29 '66

MOVING picture plays

Criticisms, plots, etc.

Are these films offensive? Al Capp vs. the modern young ladies of Wellesley. A. Capp; R. Reisig. il Pop Phot 59:168-71 D '66

At the movies. P. Kael. See issues of McCall's

Best of the year. M. Walsh. America 116:27 Ja 7 '67

Current cinema. B. Gill. See issues of New Yorker

Family movie guide; ed. by A. D. Kenney. See issues of Parents' magazine and better homemaking

Fear, games and Virginia Woolf; criteria for judging films. G. Wead. America 115:325-9 S 24 '66

Films. D. Macdonald. See issues of Esquire to November 1966

Films. M. Walsh. See issues of America

Films. P. Kael. See issues of New republic, September 10, 1966-

Films. R. Hatch. See occasional issues of Nation

Following the films. M. Ronan. See issues of Senior scholastic

Goings on about town. See issues of New Yorker

In my opinion; some movies are worse than ever: beach-ski-surf-rock soap operas. S. Lapinski. Seventeen 25:26 Mr '66

Incredible shrinking Hollywood; plus selected short subjects. P. Kael. il Holiday 39:86-93+ Mr '66

Life movie review. R. Schickel. See issues of Life

Lively arts. M. Ronan. il Sr Schol 89:28 D 9 '66

Motion picture previews. I. McMahan and E. Whitehorn. See issues of PTA magazine

MOVING picture plays—Criticisms, plots, etc.
—*Continued*

Movie report. C. Garibaldi. See issues of Good housekeeping

Movies. See issues of Consumer reports

Movies. See issues of National review

Movies in brief (cont) R. M. Hodgens. Nat R 18:229-30, 377-9, 850 Mr 8, Ap 19, Ag 23 '66

New films in review. D. Bates. See issues of Yale review

New movies. F. Somers. See issues of Redbook

Observations. W. Coffey. See issues of Commentary to August 1966

Odd-ball films. M. Walsh. America 114:838-9 Je 11 '66

Ratings of current motion pictures. See issues of Consumer bulletin

SR goes to the movies. H. Alpert. See issues of Saturday review

SR goes to the movies; ten best list. A. Knight. Sat R 50:97 Ja 14 '67

ST at the movies. M. Ronan. Sr Schol 88:sup 16+ Mr 4 '66

Screen. P. T. Hartung. See issues of Commonweal

Sense of disproportion. P. Kael. New Repub 156:39-42+ Ja 14 '67

Spotlight! E. Miller. See issues of Seventeen

Ten at the top; Newsweek's choicest. J. Morgenstern. il Newsweek 69:63+ Ja 9 '67

Ten best. P. T. Hartung. Commonweal 85:373 Ja 6 '67

Time listings. See issues of Time

Single works

A tout prendre
New Yorker 42:182 My 7 '66
Newsweek 67:106 My 16 '66

After the fox
New Yorker 42:89 Ja 7 '67
Newsweek 69:64 Ja 2 '67
Sat R 49:36 D 31 '66

Alfie
America 115:232-3 S 3 '66
Commonweal 84:585 S 16 '66
Life 61:6 S 2 '66
Nation 203:229 S 12 '66
New Yorker 42:90 Ag 27 '66
Newsweek 68:68 Ag 29 '66
Sat R 49:40 Ag 27 '66
Time il 88:66 S 2 '66
Vogue 148:207 S 1 '66

Alphabet murders
Newsweek il 68:89 Jl 25 '66
Sr Schol 88:20 Ap 29 '66
Time il 88:62 Jl 22 '66

Alvarez Kelly
Commonweal 85:294 D 9 '66
Newsweek 68:109-109A D 5 '66
Time 88:117 O 14 '66

American dream
New Yorker 42:103 S 10 '66
Newsweek il 68:88 S 5 '66
Sat R 49:30 S 17 '66

And now Miguel
Life 61:12 Jl 29 '66
Newsweek 67:94+ Je 27 '66
Sat R 49:50 My 14 '66
Time 87:115 Je 10 '66

Any Wednesday
America 115:560 N 5 '66
Commonweal 85:104 O 28 '66
New Repub 155:34 O 22 '66
New Yorker 42:164 O 22 '66

Appaloosa
Commonweal 84:638 S 30 '66
New Yorker 42:111 S 24 '66
Newsweek il 68:113+ S 26 '66
Sat R 49:30 S 17 '66
Sr Schol 89:29 O 21 '66
Time il 88:123 S 30 '66
Vogue 148:151 N 1 '66

Arabesque
America 114:754-5 My 21 '66
Christian Cent 83:810 Je 22 '66
Commonweal 84:257 My 20 '66
Life 60:12 My 13 '66
New Yorker 42:120 My 14 '66
Newsweek il 67:106 My 16 '66
Sat R 49:48 My 21 '66
Sr Schol 88:27-8 My 13 '66

Arrivederci, baby!
Newsweek il 69:88 Ja 16 '67
Time 89:83 Ja 20 '67

Assault on a Queen
Time 88:59 Ag 12 '66

Ballad of love
Commonweal 84:81 Ap 8 '66

Band of outsiders
Nation 202:406 Ap 4 '66
New Repub 155:27-9 S 10 '66
Newsweek 67:101 Mr 28 '66

Bang, bang, you're dead!
Newsweek il 68:88A S 5 '66

Battle of the bulge
Commonweal 83:507 Ja 28 '66
Sat R 49:43 Ja 29 '66
Sr Schol 88:18 F 25 '66

Beau Geste
America 115:298 S 17 '66
Sr Schol 89:26 O 7 '66

Bible
America 115:433-5 O 8 '66
Cath World 204:64 O '66
Christian Cent 83:1083 S 7 '66; Reply. R. Moore. 83:1410 N 16 '66
Commonweal 85:79 O 21 '66
Harper il 233:132-4 O '66
Life 61:22 O 7 '66
Look il 30:104+ O 18 '66
New Repub 155:30-2 O 22 '66
New Yorker 42:184-5 O 1 '66
Newsweek il 68:105 O 3 '66
Reporter 35:56 N 3 '66
Sat R 49:34 O 1 '66
Sr Schol 89:26 N 11 '66
Time il 88:119+ O 7 '66
Vogue 148:162 O 1 '66

Big hand for the little lady
Life 60:16 Je 24 '66
New Repub 155:33 O 22 '66
New Yorker 42:110 Je 18 '66
Newsweek il 67:104+ Je 20 '66
Sr Schol 88:37-8 My 6 '66
Time il 87:103 Je 24 '66

Big spenders
Mlle 63:92 Ag '66

Blindfold
Newsweek 67:104 Je 20 '66
Time il 87:112+ Je 10 '66

Blow-up
America 116:60-1 Ja 14 '67
Commonweal 85:403 Ja 13 '67
Life 62:8 Ja 20 '67
Nation 204:61-2 Ja 9 '67
New Yorker 42:60+ D 31 '66
Newsweek il 69:62 Ja 2 '67
Sat R 50:110 Ja 7 '67
Time il 88:37 D 30 '66

Blue Max
America 115:41-2 Jl 9 '66
Life 61:8 Jl 8 '66
Newsweek il 67:94 Je 27 '66
Sat R 49:43 Jl 16 '66
Time il 88:84 Jl 8 '66

Le bonheur
Commonweal 84:369 Je 17 '66
Life 60:22 My 20 '66
New Yorker 42:113-14 My 28 '66
Newsweek il 67:114-14A Je 13 '66
Sat R 49:45 My 28 '66
Time il 87:97-8+ My 27 '66
Vogue 147:147 My '66

Les bonnes femmes
Commonweal 84:285 My 27 '66
Newsweek 67:106 My 16 '66
Time il 87:117+ My 20 '66

Born free
America 115:42 Jl 9 '66
Commonweal 84:201 My 6 '66
Life 60:16 Ap 8 '66
Look il 30:106+ Ap 19 '66
Mlle 63:52 Je '66
New Yorker 42:78 Jl 9 '66
Newsweek 67:110 Ap 11 '66
Sr Schol 88:35 Ap 15 '66
Time il 87:105+ Ap 8 '66

Boy, did I get a wrong number!
Newsweek 67:102+ Je 20 '66
Time 87:104 Je 24 '66

Brig
New Yorker 42:131-2 Ap 23 '66
Newsweek il 67:90C+ Ap 25 '66

Casino royale
Look 30:50-4+ N 15 '66

Cast a giant shadow
America 114:631 Ap 30 '66
Newsweek il 67:110+ Ap 18 '66
Sat R 49:54 Ap 9 '66
Sr Schol 88:35 My 20 '66
Time il 87:103 Ap 15 '66

Chamber of horrors
Newsweek il 68:106D S 12 '66

Chase
America 114:337 Mr 5 '66
Commonweal 84:55 Ap 1 '66
Life 60:12 Mr 4 '66
McCalls 93:192-3 Ap '66
Nation 202:280 Mr 7 '66
Newsweek 67:91 F 28 '66
Sat R 49:64 F 19 '66
Sr Schol 88:32 Mr 18 '66
Time 87:105 F 25 '66

Chelsea girls
Newsweek il 68:109+ N 14 '66
Time 88:37 D 30 '66

Chushingura
Esquire 65:32+ F '66
Nation 203:526 N 14 '66

MOVING picture plays—Criticisms, plots, etc.
Single works—*Continued*
Group
    America 114:424 Mr 26 '66
    Commonweal 83:698-9 Mr 18 '66
    Holiday 39:155-6+ My '66
    Life il 60:116-17 Ap 8 '66
    McCalls 93:46 My '66
    Nat R 18:480-1 My 17 '66
    New Repub 154:25 Ap 9 '66
    New Yorker 42:173-4 Mr 19 '66
    Newsweek il 67:105A Mr 21 '66
    Reporter 34:55-6 My 19 '66
    Sat R 49:46 Mr 26 '66
    Time il 87:99+ Mr 11 '66
    Vogue 147:66 Ap 15 '66
Gypsy girl
    Life 61:17 S 30 '66
    Newsweek 68:105A O 17 '66
Hamlet
    Commonweal 83:615 F 25 '66
    New Yorker 42:125 Mr 26 '66
    Newsweek 67:99+ Mr 14 '66
    Sat R 49:49 My 21 '66
Harlot
    Esquire 66:22-3 Ag '66
Harper
    America 114:753-4 My 21 '66
    Commonweal 84:179 Ap 29 '66
    Life 60:16 Ap 1 '66
    McCalls 93:192 Ap '66
    New Yorker 42:162 Ap 2 '66
    Newsweek il 67:99 Ap 4 '66
    Sat R 49:46 Mr 12 '66
    Time il 87:99 Ap 1 '66
Harum scarum
    Sr Schol 87:24 Ja 14 '66
Hawaii
    America 115:560 N 5 '66
    Commonweal 85:104 O 28 '66
    Life 61:10 O 21 '66
    Life il 61:69-70+ O 14 '66
    Look il 30:48-57 S 6 '66
    New Repub 155:32-3 O 22 '66
    New Yorker 42:152 O 29 '66
    Newsweek il 68:117+ O 24 '66
    Sat R 49:26 O 15 '66
    Sr Schol 89:26 N 11 '66
    Time il 88:118+ O 21 '66
Hawks and the sparrows
    Time 88:75 S 23 '66
Help!
    Esquire 65:52+ Je '66
Heroes of Telemark
    Commonweal 84:56 Ap 1 '66
    Newsweek 67:94-5 F 14 '66
    Sr Schol 88:20 Mr 4 '66
    Time 87:101 F 18 '66
Hotel paradiso
    America 115:526 O 29 '66
    Time 88:112 O 28 '66
    Vogue 148:166 D '66
How I won the war
    Look il 30:58-60+ D 13 '66
How the West was won
    New Repub 154:34-6 Je 25 '66
How to steal a million
    America 115:193 Ag 20 '66
    Commonweal 84:534 Ag 19 '66
    Life 61:18 Ag 5 '66
    New Yorker 42:92 Jl 16 '66
    Newsweek il 68:89-90 Jl 25 '66
    Time il 88:62 Jl 22 '66
Hubbub
    Nation 202:139 Ja 31 '66
Hunger
    Time il 88:74-5 S 23 '66
Hunt
    Time 88:74 S 23 '66
Idol
    America 115:234 S 3 '66
    Commonweal 84:557 S 2 '66
    Life 61:20 S 16 '66
    Time il 88:78 Ag 19 '66
Impossible on Saturday
    America 114:631-2 Ap 30 '66
    Sat R 49:55 Ap 9 '66
Inside Daisy Clover
    America 114:397 Mr 19 '66
    Commonweal 83:667 Mr 11 '66
    Life 60:17 Mr 25 '66
    McCalls 93:38+ Ap '66
    New Yorker 42:109 F 26 '66
    Newsweek 67:91-2 F 28 '66
    Sat R 49:43 Ja 29 '66
    Time il 87:105-6 F 25 '66
    Vogue 147:58 F 15 '66
Intimate lighting
    Time 88:74 S 23 '66
Is Paris burning?
    America 115:715-16 N 26 '66
    Commonweal 85:262 D 2 '66
    Nat R 19:47+ Ja 10 '67
    New Yorker 42:167-8 N 5 '66
    New Yorker 42:183 N 19 '66
    Newsweek il 68:126-126A N 21 '66
    Reporter 36:56+ Ja 12 '67
    Sat R 49:59 N 26 '66
    Time il 88:122+ N 25 '66

It happened here
    America 115:260-1 S 10 '66
    New Yorker 42:98 Ag 13 '66
    Newsweek il 68:98 Ag 22 '66
    Sr Schol 89:26 O 28 '66
    Time il 88:80 Ag 26 '66
Italiano brava gente
    Commonweal 83:507-8 Ja 28 '66
    Life 60:15 F 11 '66
    Nation 202:221-2 F 21 '66
    New Yorker 41:140-2 F 12 '66
    Vogue 147:59 Mr 15 '66
It's what's happening
    Look il 30:108+ D 13 '66
Johnny tiger
    Sat R 49:50 My 14 '66
Joseph Kilian
    Nation 203:133-4 Ag 8 '66
    New Yorker 42:75 Jl 23 '66
Judex
    Newsweek 67:98B+ My 9 '66
    Sat R 49:100 My 7 '66
    Time il 87:103+ My 13 '66
Judith
    Newsweek 67:86 Ja 31 '66
    Time 87:88 Ja 28 '66
Juliet of the spirits
    Christian Cent 83:178 F 9 '66
    Esquire 65:18+ Mr '66
Kaleidoscope
    America 115:397 O 1 '66
    Life 61:18 O 14 '66
    New Yorker 42:185-6 O 1 '66
    Newsweek 68:116+ O 10 '66
    Time il 88:123 S 30 '66
Kanchenjungha
    Commonweal 84:503-4 Ag 5 '66
    Life 61:14 Ag 12 '66
    Newsweek il 68:79-80 Ag 8 '66
Khartoum
    America 115:78 Jl 16 '66
    Life il 60:93-5 My 27 '66
    New Yorker 42:75 Jl 23 '66
    Newsweek il 68:90 Jl 11 '66
    Sat R 49:43 Jl 16 '66
    Sr Schol 89:33-4 S 30 '66
    Time 88:56 Ag 5 '66
King and country
    America 114:271 F 19 '66
    Nation 202:221 F 21 '66
    New Yorker 41:124 F 5 '66
    Newsweek 67:85 Ja 31 '66
Lady L
    America 114:861 Je 18 '66
    Commonweal 84:337-8 Je 10 '66
    New Yorker 42:98+ My 21 '66
    Newsweek il 67:114B+ Je 13 '66
    Sat R 49:48 My 21 '66
    Vogue 148:30 Jl '66
Let's kill Uncle
    Time il 88:111 D 9 '66
Liquidator
    Commonweal 85:201 N 18 '66
    Time 88:121 O 21 '66
Lord love a duck
    America 114:424-5 Mr 26 '66
    Commonweal 83:667 Mr 11 '66
    McCalls 93:192 Ap '66
    New Yorker 42:106+ F 26 '66
    Newsweek il 67:100+ Mr 7 '66
    Sat R 49:45 F 12 '66
    Sr Schol 88:27 My 13 '66
Lost command
    America 115:78-9 Jl 16 '66
    Life 60:12 Je 3 '66
    New Yorker 42:111 S 24 '66
    Newsweek il 68:114 S 26 '66
    Sat R 49:50 Je 18 '66
Love and marriage
    Time il 88:80 Ag 26 '66
Loved one
    Christian Cent 83:178 F 9 '66
    Esquire 65:32 F '66
    Nat R 18:124-6 F 8 '66
Loves of a blonde
    America 115:812-13 D 17 '66
    Commonweal 85:166 N 11 '66
    Harper 233:137-8 D '66
    Nation 203:526 N 14 '66
    New Yorker 42:197 N 5 '66
    Newsweek il 68:110D+ S 19 '66
    Sat R 49:48 O 22 '66
    Time il 88:74 S 23 '66
Loving couples
    Commonweal 84:638 S 30 '66
    New Yorker 42:186 O 1 '66
    Time 87:110+ Mr 18 '66
    Vogue 147:111 Ap 1 '66
Lt. Robin Crusoe, U.S.N.
    Sat R 49:37 Jl 2 '66
Madame X
    America 114:706 My 14 '66
    McCalls 93:193 Ap '66
    Sat R 49:48 My 21 '66

MOVING picture plays—Criticisms, plots, etc.
Single works—*Continued*
Mademoiselle
  Life 61:20 S 16 '66
  New Yorker 42:84+ Ag 6 '66
  Newsweek 68:84A Ag 15 '66
  Sat R 49:40 Ag 27 '66
  Time il 88:78 Ag 19 '66
Male companion
  New Repub 154:24-5 Ap 9 '66
  New Yorker 41:145 F 19 '66
  Newsweek 67:85 Ja 31 '66
Man and a woman
  America 115:260 S 10 '66
  Life 61:12 S 9 '66
  New Repub 155:34 D 24 '66
  New Yorker 42:75 Jl 23 '66
  Newsweek 68:84 Ag 1 '66
  Sat R 49:38 Ag 13 '66
  Time il 88:60 Ag 12 '66
Man called Adam
  Newsweek 68:80 Ag 8 '66
  Time il 88:78 Ag 19 '66
Man could get killed
  America 114:754-5 My 21 '66
  Seventeen 25:158-9+ Mr '66
  Sr Schol 88:20 Ap 22 '66
  Time il 87:97 My 27 '66
Man for all seasons
  America 115:837-8 D 24 '66
  Commonweal 85:349-50 D 23 '66
  Life il 62:72-4 Ja 6 '67
  New Yorker 42:124 D 17 '66
  Newsweek il 68:113 D 19 '66
  Sat R 49:58 D 17 '66
  Sr Schol 89:18 Ja 13 '67
  Time il 88:119+ D 16 '66
Mandragola
  Commonweal 84:368 Je 17 '66
  New Yorker 42:112 Je 11 '66
  Time il 87:93 Je 3 '66
Marco the magnificent
  Sat R 49:30 S 17 '66
  Time il 88:123 S 30 '66
Masculine feminine
  Commonweal 85:22 O 7 '66
  Nation 203:366 O 10 '66
  New Repub 155:24+ N 19 '66
Meet me in Moscow
  Commonweal 83:585 F 18 '66
  New Yorker 42:120+ My 14 '66
  Newsweek il 67:94 F 14 '66
Merry wives of Windsor
  Opera N il 30:37 Ap 2 '66
Mirage
  Nation 202:222 F 21 '66
Mr Buddwing
  America 115:468 O 15 '66
  New Repub 155:34 O 22 '66
  Sat R 49:45 O 29 '66
Modesty Blaise
  Commonweal 84:557 S 2 '66
  Mlle 63:92 Ag '66
  New Yorker 42:96+ Ag 13 '66
  Newsweek il 68:98 Ag 22 '66
  Time il 88:81-2 Jl 15 '66
Moment to moment
  Time il 87:113 Mr 18 '66
  Vogue 147:101 F 1 '66
Money trap
  Newsweek 67:95 F 14 '66
  Time il 87:85 F 11 '66
Morgan!
  America 114:861 Je 18 '66
  Christian Cent 83:1604 D 28 '66
  Commonweal 84:225 My 13 '66
  Esquire 66:40+ O '66
  Life 60:16 My 6 '66
  Mlle 63:52+ Je '66
  Nation 202:502 Ap 25 '66
  New Repub 154:30+ Ap 30 '66
  New Yorker 42:86+ Ap 9 '66
  Sat R 49:65 Ap 16 '66
  Time il 87:99 Ap 1 '66
  Time il 87:80 Je 24 '66
Mule for the marquesa
  Commonweal 85:201 N 18 '66
Munster, go home!
  Sat R 49:37 Jl 2 '66
Murderers' row
  Newsweek 69:87 Ja 16 '67
  Time il 88:75 D 23 '66
My cousin
  Hobbies 71:36+ N '66
  Hobbies il 71:36 D '66
Naked prey
  Time il 87:101+ Je 17 '66
Namu, the killer whale
  Sr Schol 89:40 N 18 '66
Nevada Smith
  America 114:881 Je 25 '66
  Commonweal 84:419 Jl 1 '66
  Newsweek 68:90+ Jl 11 '66
  Sat R 49:50 Je 18 '66
  Time 88:81 Jl 15 '66

Night games
  Nation 204:94 Ja 16 '67
  Newsweek 69:64 Ja 2 '67
90 degrees in the shade
  Newsweek 68:72 D 26 '66
  Time 88:99 D 2 '66
Not with my wife, you don't!
  Time il 88:107+ N 11 '66
Ohayo
  Commonweal 83:586 F 18 '66
  Newsweek 67:83 F 7 '66
  Time il 87:88 Ja 28 '66
Oscar
  America 114:396-7 Mr 19 '66
  Commonweal 83:667 Mr 11 '66
  Life 60:17 Mr 25 '66
  Newsweek 67:99 Mr 14 '66
  Sat R 49:46 Mr 12 '66
  Time il 87:100-1 Mr 11 '66
  Vogue 147:111 Ap 1 '66
Othello
  Commentary 41:79-81 Ap '66
  Commonweal 83:614-15 F 25 '66
  Nat R 18:281-3 Mr 22 '66
  New Yorker 41:145 F 19 '66
  Sat R 49:60 F 5 '66
  Sr Schol il 88:23 F 11 '66
  Time il 87:103-4 F 4 '66
  Vogue 147:95 Mr 1 '66
Our man Flint
  America 114:209 F 5 '66
  Christian Cent 83:466+ Ap 13 '66
  Newsweek 67:84 F 7 '66
  Sat R 49:45 F 12 '66
  Time 87:104 F 4 '66
Pad (and how to use it)
  Commonweal 84:614 S 23 '66
  New Yorker 42:88+ Ag 27 '66
  Newsweek 68:88 S 5 '66
  Sr Schol 89:34 S 30 '66
  Time il 88:66 S 2 '66
  Vogue 148:79 O 15 '66
Paradise, Hawaiian style
  Newsweek 68:92A Jl 11 '66
Pawnbroker
  Esquire 65:48+ Je '66
Pearls on the ground
  Harper 233:138-9 D '66
Penelope
  Commonweal 85:230 N 25 '66
  Life 61:19 D 9 '66
  New Yorker 42:183-4 N 19 '66
  Newsweek 68:109 D 5 '66
Pitfall
  Holiday 40:34+ O '66
Plainsman
  Time 88:114 D 9 '66
Planet of vampires
  Sr Schol 87:24 Ja 14 '66
Professionals
  Commonweal 85:201 N 18 '66
  Life 61:18 N 4 '66
  New Repub 155:34 D 10 '66
  New Yorker 42:199 N 5 '66
  Newsweek 68:110 N 7 '66
  Sat R 49:74 D 3 '66
Promise her anything
  Newsweek 67:99 Mr 14 '66
  Time 87:105 F 25 '66
Quiller memorandum
  New Repub 156:42 Ja 14 '67
  Newsweek il 68:72 D 26 '66
  Time il 88:75 D 23 '66
Rare breed
  Sr Schol 88:28 Mr 11 '66
  Time il 87:109+ Ap 29 '66
Repulsion
  Esquire 65:60+ Ap '66
Russians are coming, the Russians are coming
  America 115:214 Ag 27 '66
  Commonweal 84:337 Je 10 '66
  Life 60:12 My 27 '66
  New Yorker 42:87 Je 4 '66
  Newsweek il 67:102 Je 20 '66
  Sat R 49:77 Je 11 '66
  Sr Schol 89:29 S 16 '66
  Time il 87:111-12 Je 10 '66
  Vogue 148:30 Jl '66
Salto
  Christian Cent 83:1416-17 N 16 '66
  Nation 203:429 O 24 '66
  Newsweek 68:88A S 5 '66
Sand pebbles
  America 116:27 Ja 7 '67
  Commonweal 85:428 Ja 20 '67
  Life 62:11 Ja 6 '67
  New Repub 156:40-1 Ja 14 '67
  Newsweek il 69:64 Ja 2 '67
  Sat R 49:62 D 24 '66
  Time il 89:96 Ja 6 '67
Sandra
  Commonweal 83:535 F 4 '66
  Esquire 65:37 F '66
  New Yorker 41:96+ Ja 22 '66
  Newsweek 67:85 Ja 31 '66
  Time 87:86 F 11 '66

MOVING picture plays—Criticisms, plots, etc.
—Single works—*Continued*
Who's afraid of Virginia Woolf?
America 115:121 Jl 30 '66
America 115:141-3 Ag 6 '66
Christian Cent 83:937-8 Jl 27 '66
Christian Cent 83:937-8 Jl 27 '66; Reply.
  R. G. Kemper. 83:1215+ O 5 '66
Commonweal 84:474 Jl 22 '66
Ladies Home J 83:59+ F '66
Life 61:8 Jl 22 '66
Life il 60:87-91 Je 10 '66
Look il 30:42-8 F 8 '66
Mlle 63:100 S '66
Nat R 18:943-6 S 20 '66
New Yorker 42:64-5 Jl 2 '66
Newsweek il 68:84 Jl 4 '66
Sat R 49:40 Jl 9 '66
Time il 88:78 Jl 1 '66
Vogue 148:59 Ag 1 '66
Wild angels
Sat R 49:40 Ag 27 '66
Sat R 49:53 S 10 '66
Wrong box
America 115:261 S 10 '66
Christian Cent 83:1243-4 O 12 '66
Nation 203:134 Ag 8 '66
New Yorker 42:64 Jl 30 '66
Newsweek il 68:83 Ag 1 '66
Sat R 49:38 Ag 13 '66
Sr Schol il 89:25 S 23 '66
Time il 88:59 Ag 12 '66
Vogue 148:207 S 1 '66
Young Aphrodites
New Yorker 42:90 Ja 7 '67
Newsweek 69:87-8 Ja 16 '67
Young world
Commonweal 84:314-15 Je 3 '66
Life 60:12 Je 10 '66
New Yorker 42:87 Je 4 '66
Newsweek 67:114A Je 13 '66
Sat R 49:45 My 28 '66
MOVING picture production and direction
Bawd of Avon; filming The taming of the
  shrew. il Time 87:58 Je 3 '66
Behind the scenes of a shocking movie;
  Who's afraid of Virginia Woolf? R. New-
  quist. il McCalls 93:86-9+ Je '66
Big bundle of royalty; making Hawaii; with
  report by D. Zeitlin. il Life 61:69-70+ O
  14 '66
Bing Crosby and his new movie; Stagecoach.
  M. Davidson and J. Raie. il Sat Eve Post
  239:30-3+ Ap 9 '66
Biography of a 120-second thriller. H. V.
  Fondiller. il Pop Phot 58:112-15+ My '66
Birth of an art. W. Johnson. il Sr Schol
  88:4-5+ Mr 4 '66
Charlie and his countess; filming of Countess
  from Hong Kong. J. Hamilton. il Look 30:
  96-100+ Ap 19 '66
Eight-sided gambol by The group; study of
  the girls and their roles; with report by P.
  Kael. il Life 60:116-18+ Ap 8 '66
Elizabeth Taylor and Richard Burton: the
  night of the brawl; filming of Who's afraid
  of Virginia Woolf? J. Roddy. il Look 30:
  42-8 F 8 '66
Entertainment film. C. F. Trevelyan. il U S
  Camera 29:70-3 O '66
Face to face with a boy whose life was
  changed by a movie; Up the down stair-
  case. L. Wallach. il Seventeen 25:143 O
  '66
Faye Dunaway; the farmer's grand-daughter;
  filming of It's what's happening! J. Hamil-
  ton. il Look 30:108+ D 13 '66
Filming Marat/Sade. A. Knight. Sat R 49:
  43 Jl 30 '66
Genius of Chaplin; Countess from Hong
  Kong. P. Gilliatt. il Vogue 148:94-7+ Jl '66
Gospel according to St Matthew. M. Walsh.
  America 114:307-8 F 26 '66
Great general slays 'em again; Y. Canutt;
  with report by D. Zeitlin. il Life 60:93-5+
  My 27 '66
Hawaii. J. Poppy. il Look 30:48-57 S 6 '66
Hip trip; Fantastic voyage; ed. by E. Miller.
  il Seventeen 25:116-17 O '66
Horror comedy; filming of Ken Burrows'
  Murder à la mod. New Yorker 42:23-5 Jl 23
  '66
James Garner really races in Grand prix.
  D. Scott. il Pop Sci 189:78-81+ Ag '66
John Lennon: Beatle on his own; filming of
  How I won the war. L. Gross. il Look
  30:58-60+ D 13 '66
Joycensors beware; making a movie out of
  James Joyce's Ulysses. il Newsweek 68:
  110+ S 19 '66
Kubrick, farther out; filming of 2001: a
  space odyssey. il Newsweek 68:106+ S 12
  '66

Letter from the set; role of magazine pho-
  tographer in The swinger. P. Gowland. il
  Pop Phot 58:42+ My '66
Little Cleopatra; shooting of Ian Fleming's
  Casino Royale. il Time 87:86 My 6 '66
Making of a movie: The chase. J. Brown.
  il Holiday 39:87-8+ F '66
Making the scene in Hollywood. M. Ronan.
  Sr Schol 88:28-9 My 6 '66
Message in Billy Wilder's Fortune cookie:
  well, nobody's perfect. R. Lemon. il Sat
  Eve Post 239:30-4+ D 17 '66
Monica Vitti: she's not that way at all;
  filming of Modesty Blaise. il Look 30:83-5
  Je 14 '66
Movie brutalists; style of young American
  film-makers. P. Kael. New Repub 155:23-
  4+ S 24 '66
New life for the new wave: MCA's European
  venture. A. Knight. Sat R 49:38 Ag 20 '66
Norman Rockwell; silent film star; new ver-
  sion of Stagecoach. C. Morrison. il Look
  30:40+ Mr 8 '66
O.K. everybody out of the pool; filming The
  swimmer. il Time 88:64 Ag 19 '66
Passionate clown comes back; C. Chaplin
  directs A countess from Hong Kong; with
  report by D. J. Hamblin. il Life 60:80-6
  Ap 1 '66
Paul Newman makes a western. R. W. Lewis.
  il N Y Times Mag p38-9+ N 6 '66
Peter Pan is out! filming of Man could get
  killed; ed. by E. Miller. S. Dee. il Seven-
  teen 25:158-9+ Mr '66
Profiles; S. Kubrick. J. Bernstein. New
  Yorker 42:70-2+ N 12 '66
Reel rods for show biz; automobiles of the
  entertainment world. J. McFarland. il Hot
  Rod 19:32-7 Je '66
Richard Burton to Liz: I love thee not... in
  Shakespeare's Taming of the shrew. R.
  Braddon. il Sat Eve Post 239:88-91 D 3
  '66
Shooting movies with a Nikon; marriage
  between still and motion picture photography. B. I. Gordon. il U S Camera 30:
  68-9+ Ja '67
Staking out a new world of film; new movie-
  makers. J. A. Rubin il Mlle 62:170-1+ Mr
  '66
Steal-scening with Hepburn & O'Toole; filming of How to steal a million. V. Leduc.
  il Vogue 147:172-3+ Ap 1 '66
Student and film; study of motion-picture
  production. J. A. Rubin. il Mlle 62:172 Mr
  '66
This time they're Taming the shrew. il Look
  30:58-63 O 4 '66
Typhoons and taxes; Sand pebbles; Taiwan
  location troubles. il Newsweek 67:98+ My
  9 '66
We four teens in London town; report on
  the making of A man for all seasons; ed.
  by E. Miller. C. Crawford. il Seventeen
  26:80-1+ Ja '67
Who's afraid of Dr Faustus? T. Sage. il
  Nat R 18:1319-20 D 27 '66
  See also
Moving picture directors
MOVING picture projection
Buypoints: movie projectors. M. D. Gren-
  nan. il Pop Phot 59:154-61 O '66
Filmotheques. R. Christgau. il Pop Phot 60:
  80+ Ja '67
Movies without a projector. G. Gilbert. il
  U S Camera 29:70-1+ Mr '66
One projector for two film sizes. G. Gilbert.
  il U S Camera 29:66-7 N '66
What's new that's good? H. Fondiller. il
  Pop Phot 58:105 Je '66
MOVING picture projectors. See Projection
apparatus
MOVING picture screens
New silver screen. H. Junker. Esquire 66:
  62+ O '66
MOVING picture sets. See Moving pictures—
Setting and scenery
MOVING picture sound recording
  See also
Moving pictures, Amateur—Sound recording
MOVING picture studios
Super 8 on the back lot; Universal City. L.
  Barry. il Pop Phot 59:36+ Ag '66
MOVING picture theaters
  See also
New York (city)—Radio City music hall
MOVING pictures
Current cinema; underground movies. B. Gill.
  New Yorker 42:130-2 Ap 23 '66
Down with bigness! J. Crist. Ladies Home J
  84:55 Ja '67
Film notes. H. V. Fondiller. Pop Phot 59:
  141 Jl; 132 Ag; 129 S '66; 60:84+ Ja '67
Films; bad good movies. D. Macdonald.
  Esquire 65:44+ Je '66

MOVING pictures—*Continued*
So off-beat we lose the beat. P. Kael. New Repub 155:42-5 N 5 '66
Up from underground. il Newsweek 67:90+ Ap 25 '66
See also
Animals in moving pictures
Moving picture production and direction
Television broadcasting—Moving pictures

Animal films
Woodlands are full of actors. H. V. Fondiller. il Pop Phot 59:126-7 S '66

Animated cartoons
Art of animation; festival sponsored by the Museum of modern art. H. Junker. Nation 202:249-50 F 28 '66
Computer-produced movies. K. C. Knowlton; reply. G. A. McCue and J. D. O'Keefe. il Science 151:839-40 F 18 '66
My son, the film maker. L. Lipton. il Pop Phot 58:128-9 Ap '66
See also
Disney, Walt, productions

Criticisms, plots, etc.
Winnie-the-pooh and the honey tree Reporter 34:46-7 Ap 21 '66

Biblical films
See Moving pictures—Religious films

Censorship
See Moving picture censorship

Comedy
Dark geography of W. C. Fields. W. Markfield. il N Y Times Mag p32-3+ Ap 24 '66
Forty-cent stars; Italian comics. il Newsweek 67:105A+ Mr 21 '66
Slapstick to satire. C. F. Trevelyan. il U S Camera 29:70-3 S '66

Dance films
George Balanchine at work on a permanent record; Midsummer night's dream. L. Joel. il Dance Mag 40:24-7 Ag '66
Monsters of the marriage. Time 88:103+ N 4 '66
Two film reviews: Royal ballet's Romeo and Juliet, Bolshoi ballet 67. J. Maskey. il Dance Mag 40:22-5 O '66

Dancing
Movies in the making: Les Demoiselles du Rochefort. L. Joel. il Dance Mag 40:20-1+ O '66
Toumanova in Hollywood. V. H. Swisher. il Dance Mag 40:26-7 Mr '66

Detective and mystery films
Fu Manchu strikes again. H. Lawrenson. Holiday 39:128+ F '66
Pins & needles. C. E. Trevelyan. il U S Camera 29:68-71+ D '66

Documentary films
Art of movie making. C. F. Trevelyan. il U S Camera 29:68-71 Ag '66
Charity plays the lead in reel buffs' movies; Reel fellows of Los Angeles. il Bsns W p34-5 Ja 22 '66
Films; Bell system movies; reprint. il U S Camera 29:54-5 Je '66
Films from Uncle Sam. il Newsweek 67:109-10+ Ap 18 '66
In search of realism; symposium. il Pop Phot 60:76-8 Ja '67
Juiced for you; foreign film program of U.S. department of agriculture. New Repub 155:7 S 10 '66
New films (cont) Am For 71:39 O '65
New films and filmstrips. V. M. Falconer. See occasional issues of Senior scholastic
New films for teaching. V. M. Falconer. il Sr Schol 89:sup 18 S 30 '66

Criticisms, plots, etc.
Anarchy, U.S.A.
   Christian Cent 83:1553 D 14 '66
Bolshoi ballet 67
   Dance Mag 40:24-5 O '66
   Sr Schol 89:26-7 O 14 '66
   Time 88:103+ N 4 '66
Cinderella
   Time 88:103 N 4 '66
Cinerama's Russian adventure
   New Yorker 42:121 Ap 16 '66
   Newsweek il 67:90 Ap 25 '66
   Vogue 147:56 Je '66
Eleanor Roosevelt story
   Christian Cent 83:178 F 9 '66
   Sr Schol 87:24 Ja 14 '66

Endless summer
   Commonweal 84:441 Jl 8 '66
   Life 61:19 N 25 '66. R. Vaughan
   New Yorker 42:78 Jl 9 '66
   Newsweek 68:84 Ag 1 '66
   Sat R 49:65 D 10 '66
   Sr Schol 89:33 S 30 '66
   Time 88:84 Jl 8 '66
Eyewitness. . . North Vietnam
   Sat R 49:65 D 10 '66
Flame and the fire
   Time il 87:104 Ap 15 '66
Goal!
   Sat R 49:65 D 10 '66
   Time il 88:120+ D 16 '66
John F. Kennedy: years of lightning, day of drums
   America 114:602-3 Ap 23 '66
   Christian Cent 83:655-6 My 18 '66
   Commonweal 84:154 Ap 22 '66
   Life 60:14 Ap 15 '66
   Nat R 18:694-6 Jl 12 '66
   New Yorker 42:121 Ap 16 '66
   Newsweek il 67:109-10 Ap 18 '66
   Sr Schol 88:37 My 6 '66
   Vogue 147:59 Mr 15 '66
Romeo and Juliet
   Dance Mag 40:22-4 O '66
   Sr Schol 89:28 N 4 '66
Sleeping beauty
   Commonweal 84:258 My 20 '66
   Dance Mag il 40:44-5 Ap '66
Time for burning
   Christian Cent 83:1604 D 28 '66
   Sat R 49:65 N 19 '66
To die in Madrid
   Christian Cent 83:178 F 9 '66
   Commentary 41:73 My '66
   Nat R 18:793-6 Ag 9 '66
Tokyo Olympiad
   Commonweal 84:441 Jl 8 '66
   Sat R 49:65 D 10 '66
Why Vietnam?
   New Repub 155:6 N 19 '66

Editing
Profiles; case of O. Preminger vs CBS over TV showing of Anatomy of a murder. L. Ross. New Yorker 41:42-6+ F 19 '66

Educational films
See Moving pictures in education

Foreign language films
Imperial dynasty; Chinese films made by the Shaw brothers of Hong Kong. il Newsweek 67:109-109A Ap 11 '66

History
Birth of an art. W. Johnson. il Sr Schol 88:4-5+ Mr 4 '66
You can't release Dante's Inferno in the summertime. S. N. Behrman. il N Y Times Mag p6-7+ Jl 17 '66

Medical films
See Moving pictures in medicine

Moral aspects
Film classification: a viewpoint. J. E. Fitzgerald. il Cath World 204:32-6 O '66
Guilt despite association; J. Genet's Un chant d'amour. film. Time 88:82 D 16 '66
Motion picture code and the new American culture. J. Valenti. il PTA Mag 61:16-19 D '66
Pornography and the new expression. R. Schechner. Atlan 219:74-8 Ja '67
Sex at the box office. S. T. Black. il McCalls 94:45+ Ja '67
Surprising Liz in a film shocker; Who's afraid of Virginia Woolf? with report by T. Thompson. il Life 60:87-92+ Je 10 '66
Teaching the screen arts. Brother DePaul. Cath World 203:109-12 My '66
See also
Moving picture censorship
National Catholic office for motion pictures

Music
See also
Phonograph records—Moving picture music

Natural history films
Films in review; some shorts of interest. L. S. Gordon. Natur Hist 75:11-13 My '66

Propaganda films
Films from the Vietcong. P. Gessner. Nation 202:110-11 Ja 24 '66
Image; films of the government services. New Repub 155:6 N 19 '66
New film smears civil rights cause. M. H. Bickham. Christian Cent 83:1553 D 14 '66

MOVING pictures—*Continued*

Psychological aspects
Mad about the boy; role of Morgan. il Time 87:80 Je 24 '66

Puppet films
Trnkaland. il Newsweek 67:99 Mr 28 '66

Religious films
King John version. A. Knight. Sat R 49:34 O 1 '66
Pasolini's passion. S. Kauffmann. New Republic 154:33-4 Mr 26 '66

Science fiction
Rape of the future. il Esquire 65:112-16 My '66
When a camera gets under the skin. A. Grant. il Pop Phot 59:118-19 O '66

Setting and scenery
Beginning: simpler procedure for permits to shoot on location in New York; interview. F. R. Weissberg. New Yorker 42:22-3 Ag 13 '66
Manhattan's towers become a set again; Mayor Lindsay welcomes film producers. il Bsns W p 178-80 S 10 '66
Muddle in Puddleby; protests by villagers in Castle Combe, England. il Newsweek 68: 40+ Jl 11 '66
19th Century Fox; filming of Story of Doctor Dolittle. il Time 88:28 Jl 8 '66
Trouble in Puddleby-on-the-Marsh; Castle Combe, England. P. Lofting. Life 61:7 S 30 '66

Social aspects
Notes and comment; world première of Troublemakers, movie about Newark community union project. New Yorker 42:47-8 D 10 '66

Sports films
Tokyo Olympiad. H. V. Fondiller. il Pop Phot 59:82-3 N '66

Spy films
Who is the real James Bond anyhow? J. Hamilton. il Look 30:50-4+ N 15 '66

Study and teaching
I was a teen-age movie teacher. J. M. Culkin. il Sat R 49:51-3+ Jl 16 '66; Discussion. 49: 48 Ag 20 '66
They found it at the movies; one-day seminar: School and motion pictures. W. Johnson. Sr Schol 88:sup6 My 6 '66

Suspense films
See Moving pictures—Detective and mystery films

Themes
Biggest money-making movie of all time, how come? The sound of music. J. Barthel. il N Y Times Mag p45-7+ N 20 '66
Creative business. P. Kael. New Repub 155: 32-5 O 8 '66
Fallen angels; American international pictures revises formula. il Newsweek 68:84 Ag 15 '66
Hollywood-haters: illusions and independents. A. Sarris. il Sat R 49:23-5 D 24 '66
Lexicon of youth. P. T. Hartung. Commonweal 84:314-15 Je 3 '66
Message in Billy Wilder's Fortune cookie: well, nobody's perfect. R. Lemon. il Sat Eve Post 239:30-4+ D 17 '66
Plea for the *vieille vague.* S. Elmerl. Reporter 35:51-6 D 15 '66
Spies who came into the fold; espionage craze. il Time 87:105-6 Mr 4 '66
Types & anti-types. W. Coffey. Commentary 42:54-9 Ag '66

Titles
Anecdotes, facetiae, satire, etc.
Smasheroo, she said softly. B. Conklin. il Sat Eve Post 239:16 Ag 13 '66

Travel films
Art of movie making. C. F. Trevelyan. il U S Camera 29:56-9 Je '66

War films
Following the films; It happened here and War game. W. Johnson. Sr Schol 89:26 O 28 '66

Czechoslovakia
Andula's dream. il Newsweek 68:110D+ S 19 '66

Director; New York première of Shop on Main Street. New Yorker 41:23-5 F 12 '66
Sweet light from a dark casino. il Time 88: 44 Jl 29 '66
Watch out for the hook, my friend. A. Levy. il Life 62:77-8+ Ja 20 '67
See also
Moving picture industry—Czechoslovakia

Europe, Western
New life for the new wave; MCA's European venture. A. Knight. Sat R 49:38 Ag 20 '66

France
Movie in the making; Les Demoiselles du Rochefort. L. Joel. il Dance Mag 40:20-1+ O '66
New life for the new wave; MCA's European venture. A. Knight. Sat R 49:38 Ag 20 '66
What's going on in Paris? R. Kotlowitz. Harper 234:101-3 Ja '67

India
Life, love, and the movies in India. F. Levine. Atlan 218:90-3 N '66
Screen; Satyajit Ray's Kanchenjungha. P. T. Hartung. Commonweal 84:503-4 Ag 5 '66

Italy
Double-neos. il Newsweek 67:98+ F 21 '66

Russia
Letter from Paris; first episode of War and peace called Prince Andrei and the battle of Austerlitz. Genêt. New Yorker 42:72 Jl 30 '66
Shakespeare à la Russe. A. Knight. Sat R 49:49 My 21 '66

United States
First 100 days; J. Valenti. il Time 88:38 S 2 '66
Hollywood-haters; illusions and independents. A. Sarris. il Sat R 49:23-5 D 24 '66
In my opinion; some movies are worse than ever: beach-ski-surf-rock soap operas. S. Lapinski. Seventeen 25:26 Mr '66
Movie brutalists; style of young American film-makers. P. Kael. New Repub 155:23-4+ S 24 '66
Where the action is? il Sr Schol 88:16-18 Ap 15 '66
See also
American film institute (proposed)
Moving picture industry—United States

Vietnam (Democratic Republic)
Films from the Vietcong. P. Gessner. Nation 202:110-11 Ja 24 '66

Vietnam (Republic)
Films from the Vietcong. P. Gessner. Nation 202:110-11 Ja 24 '66

MOVING pictures, Amateur
Charity plays the lead in reel buffs' movies; Reel fellows of Los Angeles. il Bsns W p34-5 Ja 22 '66
Consider the audience. E. Wildi. U S Camera 29:68-9+ Jl '66
Go way out for movie close-ups. M. A. Matzkin. il Mod Phot 30:84-5 F '66
Make your family movies more fun. il Changing T 20:31-2 F '66
Matzkin on movies; forget the conventions. M. A. Matzkin. Mod Phot 31:30 Ja '67
Slapstick to satire. C. F. Trevelyan. il U S Camera 29:70-3 S '66

Editing
Buypoints; movie editors. M. D. Grennan. il Pop Phot 59:148-53 O '66
Guide to the new super 8 editors. H. V. Fondiller. il Pop Phot 58:128-30 Mr '66
Ten ways to better cuts. E. Willdi. il Mod Phot 31:78-80+ Ja '67
Vagabond camera; running gag sequence can dramatize your travel films. W. Lane. il Travel 125:69 Je '66

Sound effects
Matzkin on movies. M. A. Matzkin. Mod Phot 30:48 F '66
Sound. J. Wesson. See issues of U.S. camera & travel
Voice in films. E. Wildi. U S Camera 29: 74-5+ O '66

Sound recording
Sound advice. R. Flanzraich. Mod Phot 31:48 Ja '67
Sound for silent films. J. I. Newmark. il U S Camera 29:72-3+ Ag '66

MOVING pictures, Amateur—*Continued*

Themes

Art of movie making. C. F. Trevelyan. il U S Camera 29:56-9 Je '66

Art of movie making; the documentary. C. F. Trevelyan. il U S Camera 29:68-71 Ag '66

Entertainment film. C. F. Trevelyan. il U S Camera 29:70-3 O '66

Make your house move. E. Wildi. il Mod Phot 30:72-3+ Ag '66

Titles

Matzkin on movies. M. A. Matzkin. il Mod Phot 30:18+ Ag '66

Movie titlers. il Pop Phot 59:146-7 O '66

Try rear-illuminated titles! J. R. Oswald. il U S Camera 30:70-1 Ja '67

MOVING pictures and children

See also

Moving pictures for children

MOVING pictures and reading

Confessions of a purist; on authenticity in films. D. M. Broderick. il Library J 91:1599-600 Mr 15 '66; Reply. M. R. Smith. 91:4156+ S 15 '66

MOVING pictures for children

Family movie guide; ed. by A. D. Kenney. See issues of Parents' magazine and better homemaking

Movies for young children. P. Kael. McCalls 93:36+ Je '66

To be secret; previewing of film The pleasure is mutual. R. H. Viguers. Horn Bk 42:521 O '66

MOVING pictures in education

8mm single-concept films. L. W. Ingraham. il Sr Schol 87:sup28-9 Ja 14 '66

Films for the PTA; starters for discussion of critical issues in our democracy. F. T. Mathewson. PTA Mag 60:33-4 My; 33-4 Je '66

New films for teaching world history. V. M. Falconer. il Sr Schol 89:sup 16-17 N 18 '66

Potent pictures; E.B.F. and Bell & Howell's Project Discovery. il Time 87:94+ Ap 1 '66

See also

Moving pictures—Documentary films

Moving pictures—Natural history films

Moving pictures—Study and teaching

Moving pictures in health education

MOVING pictures in health education

Films of interest. Todays Health 44:76 N '66

MOVING pictures in medicine

Films of interest. Todays Health 44:76 N '66

MOVING pictures in public relations

Hazards of Roseville road. G. C. Maurer. il Pop Phot 58:60-2 Je '66

MOVING pictures on airplanes. See Airlines—Passenger service

MOVSHON, George

Concert opera, Donizetti and Britten. Hi Fi 16:127+ Mr '66

Met worth waiting for. Hi Fi 16:126-7 F '66

New York opera; Met production of La Traviata. il Hi Fi 16:MA14-15 D '66

Tannhäuser, Parsifal, and a cloud of promises. Hi Fi 16:113+ Je '66

Wagner, legends and legacy. Hi Fi 16:MA22-3+ O '66

MOW, Joseph B.

Jean-Paul Sartre: Christian theist? Christian Cent 83:1437-9 N 23 '66

MOWAT, Farley

Men before Columbus; excerpt from Westviking, the ancient Norse in Greeland and North America. Read Digest 89:200-2+ N '66

MOWER, Jan

If one can do it. Yachting 119:186 F '66

MOWING machines

See also

Lawn mowers

MOWRER, Edgar Ansel

Analysis of appeasement. Nat R 19:40-1 Ja 10 '67

MOWRER, Orval Hobart

Sin, illness and guilt. R. J. Becker. Christian Cent 83:1007-9 Ag 17 '66

MOWSHOWITZ, Israel

Churchly particularism and the Jews. Christian Cent 83:988+ Ag 10 '66

MOYANO, Maria Clara

Books. Américas 18:46-7 Ap '66

MOYERS, Bill D.

A look at the inner workings of the White House; interview. U S News 60:78-85 Je 13 '66

White House rebuttal to Vietnam critics; interview. ed. by R. Pierpoint. Cath World 204:52-4 O '66

about

After Moyers leaves; the key men at the White House. il por U S News 61:12 D 26 '66

Bridge out. por Newsweek 68:18-19 D 26 '66

Johnson and Moyers. New Repub 155:4 D 24 '66

Moyers. J. Deakin. New Repub 154:13-14 Je 25 '66

No. 2 Texan in the White House. P. Anderson. il por N Y Times Mag p23+ Ap 3 '66

President's right-hand man. il por U S News 60:16 My 30 '66

Report on Washington. Atlan 217:10+ Mr '66

State of affairs. H. Brandon. Sat R 50:16+ Ja 14 '67

White House farewell. por Time 88:19-20 D 23 '66

MOYERS, Clyde, and Pinson, Gerald

Collective negotiations in colleges and universities. bibliog f Sch & Soc 94:389-90 N 12 '66

MOYERS, Ruby Jewel (Johnson)

Bill Moyers' mother. B. Weinraub. pors Esquire 66:96+ N '66

MOYLES, Lois

Report from California; poem. New Yorker 42:30 Ja 14 '67

MOYNIHAN, Antony Patrick Andrew Cairnes Berkeley Moynihan, 3d baron

Belly-dancer who became a lady. C. Davis and M. J. Bellenger. il pors Ebony 21:78-80+ Jl '66

MOYNIHAN, Daniel Patrick

Books. Commonweal 84:58-9 Ap 1 '66

Discarded third. por Look 30:27-9 My 17 '66

What kind of faith built the National shrine? adaptation of address. Commonweal 84:407-9 Jl 1 '66

Who gets in the army? New Repub 155:19-22 N 5 '66; 156:43-4 Ja 7 '67

about

A mother can't do a man's job. il por Newsweek 68:41+ Ag 22 '66

Moynihan of the Moynihan report. T. Meehan. il por N Y Times Mag p5+ Jl 31 '66; Discussion. p4 Ag 14 '66

Moynihan report; reply. H. L. Harrod. Christian Cent 83:180-2 F 9 '66

MOYNIHAN, Rodrigo

Abstract background; self-interview. il pors Art N 65:41+ My '66

Introducing Rodrigo Moynihan. J. Ashbery. il Art N 65:40+ My '66

MOYNIHAN, Shirin Roshan (Berry) Moynihan, baroness

Belly-dancer who became a lady. C. Davis and M. J. Bellenger. il pors Ebony 21:78-80+ Jl '66

MOZAMBIQUE

See also

Hunting—Mozambique

MOZART, Johann Chrysostom Wolfgang Amadeus

Abduction from the seraglio. Criticism

Opera N 30:30 Mr 5 '66

Sat R 49:70-1 O 22 '66

Don Giovanni. Criticism

New Yorker 41:114 F 12 '66

New Yorker 42:106 Ja 14 '67

Opera N 30:24-5 Ja 29 '66

Opera N il 30:18-20 Ja 29 '66

Sat R 49:26+ F 12 '66

Sat R 49:71 O 22 '66

Sat R 50:34 Ja 21 '67

Die entführung aus dem serail; satisfactory recording. G. L. Mayer. il Am Rec G 33:104-6 O '66

Great Mozart concerto marathon; on Epic, all the way with Lili Kraus. S. Sell. il Am Rec G 32:598-9 Mr '66

Idomeneo. Criticism

Opera N 30:30 Ap 9 '66

Magic flute. Criticism

New Yorker 42:238 O 22 '66

Opera N 30:31 Mr 26 '66

Sat R 49:50-1 O 29 '66

Magical month of Mozart. H. Goldsmith. Hi Fi 16:MA7+ N '66

Masterpieces galore. R. Gelatt. Reporter 34:40+ My 5 '66

Mendelssohn and Mozart marvels at Marlboro. A. Cohn. Am Rec G 32:986 Je '66

Mozart and opera seria. H. Weinstock. Sat R 49:67-8 Mr 26 '66

Mozart by Rudolf, et al. H. Glass. Am Rec G 33:47-8 S '66

Mozart with (and for) a song. I. Kolodin. Sat R 49:72-3 D 10 '66

Records:

Die entführung aus dem serail and Bastien und Bastiene. Opera N 31:34 D 3 '66

Requiem. Opera N 31:30 N 19 '66

MRKVA, Frank John
Carrot & careless George. por Time 88:23 Jl 22 '66
In the cold war, new charges of spying. il por U S News 61:12 Jl 25 '66
Red hot week for the spy business. il pors Life 61:20-3 Jl 22 '66
Way up. por Newsweek 68:23 Jl 25 '66

MROSE, Mary E. See Evans, H. T. jr. jt. auth.

MTSHALI, Benedict Vulindlela
New books. Cath World 203:52-3 Ap '66

MUCKRAKING
Then he wrote a book; effect of Upton Sinclair's The jungle. L. L. L. Golden. Sat R 49:103 N 12 '66
Where are today's muckrakers? A. Weinberg and L. Weinberg. Sat R 49:54-5 Jl 9 '66

MUCOPOLYSACCHARIDES. See Polysaccharides

MUCOVISCIDOSIS. See Cystic fibrosis

MUD
Death walked the duck marsh; ed. by B. East. E. La Fountain. il Outdoor Life 137:60-1+ Ap '66

MUD slides. See Landslides

MUD volcanoes
Boiling mud flows from volcano's lake; Mt Kelud, Java. Sci N 89:374 My 14 '66
Hot flowing mud is terror of volcano; Mt Kelud. Sci N 89:398 My 21 '66

MUDD, J. Brian. See Sherman, I. W. jt. auth.

MUDD, John. See Hoffman, M. jt. auth.

MUDD, Mike
Longest coon hunt. pors Outdoor Life 137:44-7+ My '66

MUDFISHES. See Gobies

MUDSLIDES. See Landslides

MUELLER, Lisel
Four poets. Poetry 109:48-52 O '66
Poetry chronicle. Poetry 107:258-63 Ja '66
Sun the other way around. Poetry 108:335-7 Ag '66

MUELLER, Walter J.
Department of state senior fellow program. Dept State Bul 55:436-40 S 19 '66

MUFFLERS. See Automobile engines—Mufflers

MUGGERIDGE, Malcolm
Book review of a very limited edition. Esquire 65:94+ My '66
Books. See issues of Esquire
Great liberal death-wish. Nat R 18:573-4 Je 14 '66
What's wrong in Britain; a noted editor looks at his country; interview, ed. by J. Fromm. por U S News 61:67-9 Jl 25 '66

about

Dance of the iconoclast. il por Time 89:36 Ja 6 '67
Enfant terrible. J. Epstein. Commentary 42:94-6 D '66
Mayhem by Muggeridge. S. Kauffmann. New Repub 155:23+ D 17 '66
Stop the milieu, I've got to get off. J. Hart. Nat R 18:999+ O 4 '66

MUGNAINI, Joseph
On drawing; excerpts from Drawing: a search for form. Am Artist 30:13+ Ap '66

MUHAMMAD Ali. See Clay, C.

MUHEIM, Harry
When J.F.K. was rich, young, and happy. Esquire 66:64-6+ Ag '66

MUHLFELD, Edward D.
Gone flying south to the Bahamas. Flying 78:127-33 Je '66
Publisher's memo. See issues of Flying

MUIR, Edwin
British chronicle. R. Howard. Poetry 108:399-400 S '66
Edwin Muir: the story and the fable. D. Hoffman. Yale R 55:403-26 Mr '66

MUIR, John
Yosemites of the Kings River. R. H. Rose. il Nat Parks Mag 40:4-9 O '66

MULCHERS. See Garden tools, equipment and supplies

MULCHING
How black plastic mulch made our garden really grow. M. V. Erickson. Flower Grower 53:60 Je '66
Pouring oil on troubled sands; asphalt and petroleum mulches. R. S. Knowles. Read Digest 89:171-2+ Ag '66
Try a pebble mulch; for low maintenance. il Pop Gard 17:30-1 D '66
What a grind! R. G. Miner. il Flower Grower 53:39 Ag '66
When the chips are down. B. C. Kilvert, jr. Flower Grower 53:48 N '66

MULDER, Karel Fredrik
Aftermath. Esquire 65:70-2 My '66

MULDOON, Joseph F. X.
How to rescue America from plumbers, carpenters, and people like that. J. Fischer. Harper 234:14+ Ja '67

MULE deer. See Deer

MULE deer hunting. See Deer hunting

MULFORD, Ann
What makes teachers burn? NEA J 55:13-15 My '66

MULHOLLAND, J. Derral, and Sjogren, W. L.
Lunar Orbiter ranging data: initial results. bibliog Science 155:74-6 Ja 6 '67

MULHOLLAND, Thomas, and Davis, Edward
Electroencephalographic activation: nonspecific habituation by verbal stimuli. bibliog Science 152:1104-6 My 20 '66

MULLANEY, Thomas E.
Blocking off the press. L. L. L. Golden. Sat R 49:78 S 10 '66

MULLEN, James
Subject matter? Sch Arts 65:8-11 Je '66

MÜLLER-BECK, Hansjürgen
Paleohunters in America: origins and diffusion. bibliog Science 152:1191-210 My 27 '66

MULLET fishing
Swinging fisherman. K. Warner. il Pop Mech 125:110-11 Ap '66

MULLEY, Frederick William
Mulley airs U.S. role in Saudi jet order. H. J. Coleman. Aviation W 84:32-3 My 23 '66

MULLICA RIVER
Mullica River. T. Paugh. il Motor B 118:28-9+ O '66

MULLIGAN, Hugh
Stand by to launch aircraft; excerpt from Vietnam: the confusing war. Read Digest 90:84-8 Ja '67
What it's like for the fighting man; excerpt from Vietnam: the confusing war. Read Digest 89:68-73 N '66

MULLIGAN, Joseph F.
Catholic campus today. Commonweal 83:497-9 Ja 28 '66
University in America. America 114:832-3 Je 11 '66

MULLIGAN, Timothy H.
Strong beginning. Opera N 30:24-5 Mr 26 '66

MULLIKEN, Robert Sanderson
Lauded at last. por Time 88:88 N 11 '66
1966 Nobel laureate in chemistry. J. R. Platt. por Science 154:745-7 N 11 '66
Nobel prize winners. por Sci N 90:400 N 12 '66
Practical theorists. il por Newsweek 68:73 N 14 '66

MULLIKIN, Harry
Hotels and motels reflect a changing world. Arch Rec 140:137 Ag '66

MULLINEX, C. D.
Parking under an island. Am City 81:164+ S '66

MULLINS, Richard F. Jr. See Levine, S. jt. auth.

MULTER, Abraham J.
Excerpt from statement, March 16, 1966. Cong Digest 45:151+ My '66

MULTER, H. Gray. See Multer, J. D. jt. auth.

MULTER, Julie D. and Multer, H. G.
Mangrove world. Am For 72:34-7 Ag '66

MULTICAPILLARY mixer. See Laboratories—Equipment

MULTI-EXPOSURE plates. See Photography—Plates

MULTILATERAL force. See North Atlantic treaty organization—Multilateral force (proposed)

MULTI-LAYER interconnection boards. See Electronic circuits

MULTIPHASIC screening. See Physical examinations

MULTIPLE access computer. See Computers—Cooperative use

MULTIPLE choice tests. See Educational tests and measurements

MULTIPLE guilt; story. See Sáiz, V.

MULTIPLE jobholding. See Supplementary employment

MULTIPLE myeloma
Low-molecular-weight proteins related to Bence Jones proteins in multiple myeloma. A. Solomon and others. bibliog il Science 151:1237-9 Mr 11 '66

MULTIPLE sclerosis. See Sclerosis, Multiple

MULTIPLEX radio broadcasting. See Radio broadcasting—Multiplex system

MULTIPLEX recording photography. See Photography

MULTIPLICATION
Properties of multiplication. il NEA J 55:23-5 Ap '66

MULTIPRONG connectors. See Connectors
MULTIPURPOSE furniture. See Furniture,
   Childrens
MULTIVIBRATORS
   Improving the low-frequency multivibrator.
      il Electr World 75:83 F '66
   Multi-master; solid-state multivibrator mod-
      ule. G. Boross. il Pop Electr 26:75-6 Ja '67
MULVANEY, D. J.
   Prehistory of the Australian aborigine; with
      biographical sketch. Sci Am 214:20+, 84-
      91+ bibliog(p 143) Mr '66
MULVEHILL, Larry
   B&W slides from B&W negatives. U S
      Camera 29:26 S '66
   Pretty Puerto Rico. U S Camera 29:62-3+ Ag
      '66
   Recreating old photos. U S Camera 29:20 Jl
      '66
            about
   Mulvehill, the great experimenter. H. M.
      Kinzer. il Pop Phot 58:96-101 Je '66
MULVOY, Mark
   Baseball (cont) Sports Illus 24:63-5 Mr 14; 25:
      58+ Jl 18 '66
   Baseball's week. See issues of Sports il-
      lustrated published during baseball season
   Golf. Sports Illus 25:62-4 S 26 '66
   Hockey. Sports Illus 26:44-6 Ja 2 '67
MUMFORD, George S. 3d
   News notes. See issues of Sky and telescope
MUMFORD, L. Quincy
   Annual report of the Librarian of Congress
      for the fiscal year ending June 30, 1965;
      summary. Wilson Lib Bul 40:893 Je '66;
      Same. Library J 91:2786 Je 1 '66
   International breakthrough. por Library J
      92:79-82 Ja 1 '67
   Librarians and the everlasting now; excerpts
      from address, October 17, 1965. por Library
      J 91:901-6 F 15 '66
   Pilot service for machine cataloging an-
      nounced by Mumford at ARL meeting;
      summary of report. Library J 91:1376 Mr
      15 '66
MUMMA, Ralph O. and others
   Dieldrin: extraction of accumulations by root
      uptake. bibliog Science 152:530-1 Ap 22 '66
MUMMERS theater, Oklahoma. See Oklahoma
   City—Theater
MUMPS
            Vaccines
   Live mumps vaccine shows promise in tests.
      il Sci N 90:21 Jl 9 '66
   Vaccine against mumps. il Time 88:46+ Jl
      1 '66
   Vaccine against mumps; Hilleman vaccine. il
      Newsweek 68:60-1 Jl 4 '66
MUNCH, Edvard
   Munch in America. W. Stevens. il Art N
      64:41-3+ Ja '66
MUNDLE, Winfred
   Vice mayor of Richmond. il pors Ebony
      22:176-8+ N '66
MUNDO, Fe del
   Big man & the little lady. il por Time 88:71
      Jl 22 '66
MUNDUS, Frank
   Deadly game. por Newsweek 68:88 Jl 11 '66
MUNGENAST, J. E.
   SCR revolution. Electr World 75:23-6 F '66
MUNICH
            Description
   Munich brews its own boom in new industry;
      West Germany's fastest-growing city. il
      Bsns W p 136-8+ Jl 16 '66

            Economic conditions
   Munich brews its own boom in new indus-
      try; West Germany's fastest-growing city.
      il Bsns W p 136-8+ Jl 16 '66
            See also
   International youth library

            Music
   Munich. E. D. Echols. il Opera N 30:32 Ja
      29; 31:26 N 5 '66
   Munich; Verdi's Rigoletto in original lan-
      guage at Bavarian state opera. E. D.
      Echols. Opera N 30:24 My 7 '66
   Opera on three fronts; Geneva - Munich -
      Milan. W. Legge. Hi Fi 16:136-9 Mr '66
MUNICIPAL accounting
   Computers occupy the royal suite; Chat-
      tanooga, Tenn. W. Zachry. il Am City 81:
      107 O '66

Up-to-the-minute management information
   reports; Wichita Falls, Tex. R. J. Neigh-
   bors. il Am City 81:102-4 Ag '66
         See also
Accounting—Mechanical aids
MUNICIPAL advertising
   City tells its story; ed. by P. D. Eimon.
      See issues of American city
   Get the public on the side of the repair crew;
      publicity methods used in Richmond, Va. il
      Am City 81:116-17 S '66
MUNICIPAL and federal relations. See Federal
   and municipal relations
MUNICIPAL bonds
   Biggest bonddoggle; Jerome, Ark, postpones
      issue. Newsweek 68:80+ O 31 '66
   Dog days in the municipals market; tight
      money causes trouble. il Bsns W p 122+
      O 1 '66
   How they'll rate your bonds. J. Pfeiffer. Am
      City 81:174+ O '66
   PR behind the yes; bond referendum. il Am
      City 81:136+ Mr '66
   Second look at municipal bonds. J. Perham.
      il Duns R 87:45-6+ Mr '66
   Tax-exempt bonds and the small investor. il
      Changing T 20:21-3 My '66
         See also
   Bonds, Revenue
MUNICIPAL buildings
   Let all the audience see what's showing;
      council chamber, Phoenix, Ariz. R. H.
      Sullivan. il Am City 81:90-1 N '66
         See also
   Municipal centers
MUNICIPAL centers
   Big steel; Chicago's civic center complete.
      il Arch Forum 125:33-7 O '66
   Charles center's latest; downtown Baltimore.
      il Arch Rec 140:173-8 S '66
   One good civic center doesn't make a city;
      Norfolk's municipal buildings. il Arch Rec
      139:157-62 F '66
   Tulsa civic center moves toward completion.
      il Am City 81:211 S '66
MUNICIPAL corporations
   Legal notes and decisions; prepared by Na-
      tional institute of municipal law officers.
      See issues of American city
MUNICIPAL debts. See Municipal finance
MUNICIPAL dumps
   How to make a landfill attractive; Chicago.
      J. Sexton. il Am City 81:92-3 N '66
   When streets and buildings settle; Midland,
      Tex. G. H. Medley. il Am City 81:32 Mr
      '66
MUNICIPAL elections
      See also subhead Elections under names
   of cities, New York (city)—Elections
MUNICIPAL employees
      See also
   Collective bargaining—Municipal employees
   Strikes—United States—Municipal employees
      also subhead Employees under names
   of cities, e.g. New York (city)—Employees
MUNICIPAL equipment
   Equipment-replacement plan; Reading, Mass.
      P. Welch. il Am City 81:84-5 D '66
   Firm price for six years of service; Minot,
      N.D. V. Fahy. il Am City 81:106-7 My '66
   More maintenance per man-hour; Highland
      Park, Ill. D. H. Fritz. il Am City 81:
      96-8 N '66
   Park adds an airport, subtracts maintenance
      costs; Decatur, Ill. L. Chandler. il Am City
      81:118-19 S '66
   Park plans can simplify maintenance; Santa
      Clara, Calif. E. R. Carmichael. il Am City
      81:104-6 O '66
   Snow melting for 64 cents per ton; Toronto.
      Am City 81:34 N '66

            Repairing
   Guaranteed maintenance puts strength in
      equipment purchases; Amarillo, Tex. E.
      Hill. il Am City 81:148+ Ap '66
   Some facts you should know about guaran-
      teed maintenance. A. C. Shepherd. Am
      City 81:92-3 D '66
MUNICIPAL expenditures. See Municipal
   finance
MUNICIPAL finance
   Cry of the cities; Conference of mayors calls
      for Vietnam cutback to aid cities problems.
      Nation 203:3-4 Jl 4 '66
   Firm price for six years of service; Minot,
      N.D. V. Fahy. il Am City 81:106-7 My '66
   Government by gambling; city and town debts;
      Italy. Newsweek 68:87 N 7 '66
   Mayor tells how to modernize America's
      cities. H. W. Goldner. Nations Bsns 54:
      108-10+ Ap '66

MUNICIPAL finance—*Continued*
Mendicant cities; who will finance renewal plans? R. Moley. Newsweek 67:116 Ap 11 '66
President tells mayors: slow down spending; remarks, October 15, 1966. L. B. Johnson. U S News 61:14 O 31 '66
State self-support. R. Moley. Newsweek 68: 116 D 12 '66
Surplus for local governments? U S News 61: 87 D 12 '66
Those lavish local spenders: state and local government spending. il Time 88:90 N 4 '66
Why big-city financing is in a mess; spread between expenditures and revenues growing. il Bsns W p36-8 Ap 23 '66
See also
Local taxation
New York (city)—Finance

MUNICIPAL garages. See Garages, Municipal
MUNICIPAL government
Alaska metro government. L. L. Woodman. Am City 81:212+ S '66
City tells its story; ed. by P. D. Eimon. See issues of American city
Our municipal notebook. See issues of American city
See also
Chicago—Politics and government
Complaints
Police
Townships

Germany (Federal Republic)
German council-manager form was anti-dictator measure. R. S. Childs. Am City 81:156+ My '66

MUNICIPAL improvement
America the more beautiful. il Time 88:53 S 30 '66
Billboards, glass houses, and the law; excerpt from address. R. F. Babcock. Harper 232:20+ Ap '66
Business and beauty: address, December 2, 1965. L. S. Rockefeller. Vital Speeches 32: 219-21 Ja 15 '66; Same. il Audubon Mag 68: 112-15 Mr '66
Can business be lured into urban rebirth? il Bsns W p 155-6+ D 17 '66
City lobbyists head for Washington. il Bsns W p88-9+ Jl 9 '66
Lady Bird, says L.B.J. will beautify us out of existence. H. Sidey. il Life 61:30B Jl 22 '66
Let's work together for a more beautiful America; adaptation of addresses, with text of letter to readers of Parents' magazine C. A. T. Johnson. Parents Mag 41:22+ Jl '66
Stop dissecting the urban community. Am City 81:106+ N '66
U.S. cities improving. Sci N 90:170 S 10 '66
Urban development part of HUD; interview. R. C. Weaver. il Am City 81:87-9+ Jl '66
Ventilating the crowded city. R. C. Weaver. Parks & Rec 1:893 N '66
We shall not be thanked by posterity. P. Johnson. Fortune 74:68 Jl 1 '66
See also
City planning
Urban renewal

MUNICIPAL industrial bonds. See Municipal bonds
MUNICIPAL motor trucks. See Motor trucks, Municipal
MUNICIPAL officers
See also subhead Public officers under names of cities, e.g. Richmond, Va.—Public officers
MUNICIPAL ordinances
Legal notes and decisions; prepared by National institute of municipal law officers. See issues of American city
MUNICIPAL parks. See Parks
MUNICIPAL publications

Bibliography
Municipal and civic publications. See issues of American city

MUNICIPAL purchasing. See Purchasing, Municipal
MUNICIPAL real estate. See Real property
MUNICIPAL records
Metal tax plates survive town-hall fire; Willingboro, N.J. J. T. McHugh. il Am City 81:90 Mr '66
Tape recorders insure accuracy at public meetings; Westbury, L.I. N.Y. J. Sharkey. il Am City 81:86 Jl '66
MUNICIPAL records on microfilm
Microfilm gives us 90 per cent more space; Dakota County, Minn. P. R. Welshons. il Am City 81:117 My '66

Multiple solutions through central microfilming; Houston, Tex. E. A. Newgren. Am City 81:146+ F '66
MUNICIPAL reports
Citizens dated up; city report-calendars il Am City 81:140+ Ag '66
MUNICIPAL revenue. See Municipal finance
MUNICIPAL swimming pools. See Swimming pools, Municipal
MUNICIPAL taxation. See Local taxation
MUNICIPAL universities. See Colleges and universities, Municipal
MUNICIPAL waterworks. See Waterworks
MUNITIONS
Increasing weaponry sales struggle seen. Aviation W 85:93-4 O 24 '66
Kuss of death; America's chief arms salesman. Nation 202:85-6 Ja 24 '66
Report from Vietnam. W. J. Coughlin and M. Getler. il Miss & Roc 18:44-8+ Mr 28 '66
See also
Atomic weapons
Weapons systems

MUNITIONS industries
When arms calls lag; defense companies to diversify into civilian work. Bsns W p 178 Mr 19 '66

Belgium
Belgian defense firm diversifying; S. A. Les Forges De Zeebrugge. J. F. Judge. il Miss & Roc 18:25-6+ F 7 '66

China (People's Republic)
Aerospace firms getting call to evaluate Chinese threat. R. Pay. Miss & Roc 18:23+ Ap 18 '66

United States
Aiming at the arms market overseas; U.S. ahead in weapon sales. il Bsns W p66-7+ D 3 '66
Boom boom; Norris-Thermador corp. il Newsweek 67:79 Mr 14 '66
Conversion of defense resources. B. G. Lall. Bul Atomic Sci 22:46-8 Ja '66
Defense predicts $15 billion in exports for next ten years. C. Brownlow. il Aviation W 83:18-20 mid-D '65

MUNITIONS list. See Defense information, Classified
MUNITIONS purchasing. See Purchasing, Military
MUNOZ, James. See Eugster, H. P. jt. auth.
MUNSINGER, Gary M. and O'Connor A. L. Better jet marketing procedures urged; reprint. Aviation W 85:71+ D 26 '66
MUNSINGER, Gerda
Canada's scandal: both sides losers? il por U S News 60:12-13 Mr 28 '66
Finding Gerda's goat. por Newsweek 67:50 Mr 21 '66
Gerda cooks up a Canadian stew. il pors Life 60:105-6 Mr 25 '66
Lunch at the Chateau Laurier. por Time 87: 28 Mr 25 '66
Man on the spot. il por Time 87:44 My 20 '66
Mounties get their men. Time 87:32 My 6 '66
Munsinger affair. il por Time 87:54 Mr 18 '66
Not very romantic. il por Newsweek 67:71 My 23 '66
Suspended degradation. Newsweek 67:58 Mr 28 '66
MUNSON, Gorham
Workshops for writers. Sat R 49:42-5+ Ap 30 '66
MÜNSTERBERG, Hugo
Famous firsts: measuring minds for the job. il por Bsns W p60+ Ja 29 '66
MUNTEANU, Robert L.
Global assault on the weather. bibliog UNESCO Courier 19:16-23 N '66
MÜNTER, Gabriele
Art galleries. R. M. Coates. New Yorker 42: 62+ D 24 '66
MUONIUM
Muonium atom. V. W. Hughes. il Sci Am 214:93-100 Ap '66
MUONS. See Muonium
MURACCIOLI, Pierre Antoine. See Antoine
MURAL painting and decoration
Alice in Wonderland; fourth grade project, Fairport school, Dayton. il Sch Arts 65:29-30 My '66
Christmas eve on our street. C. J. Alkema. il Sch Arts 66:12-13 D '66
Co-operative creativity; Pauline avenue public school, Toronto. M. V. Boyd. il Sch Arts 65:14-15 My '66

MURAL painting and decoration—*Continued*
Creative art in the classroom curriculum. M. L. Wooten. il Sch Arts 66:4-8 D '66
Hélène Aylon's Ruach palimpsest. L. Campbell. il Art N 65:47-9 D '66
Man needs space; Siqueiros' History of humanity. il Newsweek 68:69 Ag 29 '66
Mural painting can be fun. il Pop Mech 125:159 Ap '66
Painting the small mural. R. Barrio. il Design 68:8-12 N '66
Signs and symbols. N. Roukes. il Sch Arts 66:15-19 O '66
    See also
Photographic murals

MURALS, Photographic. See Photographic murals

MURAY, Leo
Why Israel hit back. New Repub 155:7-8 N 26 '66

MURAYAMA, Makio
Molecular mechanism of red cell sickling. bibliog Science 153:145-9 Jl 8 '66

MURCH, Walter
Short-range astronomy. R. Browne. il por Art N 64:37-9+ Ja '66

MURCHISON, Clint, Jr
Smiles of Texas are upon Clint's Cowboys. J. R. McDermott. il por Life 61:79-80+ D 16 '66

MURCHLAND, Bernard G.
Prophetic principle. Commonweal 84:171-5, 401 Ap 29, Je 24 '66

MURDER
Alien horror; killing of Miltiades Vlachos by son in Germany to avenge family honor. Time 87:32 Ja 28 '66
All-American boy; C. J. Whitman killings. il Newsweek 68:24-6+ Ag 15 '66
American amok; is the gun-ridden USA a violent nation? R. Coles. New Repub 155:12-15 Ag 27 '66
American nightmare; V. Percy murder. il Newsweek 68:22-3 O 3 '66
Besieged in suburbia; Cincinnati cases. Time 88:35 O 21 '66
Beyond grief; murder of V. Percy. il Time 88:22-4 S 30 '66
Blue Cadillac; E. W. Long confesses to killing Penny Van Orden. il Newsweek 67:41 Ap 11 '66
Boston strangler, by G. Frank. Review
    Newsweek 68:118+ O 31 '66. S. Schmidt
    Sat R 49:29-30 O 29 '66. R. Stout
Boston strangler; condensation. G. Frank. il Ladies Home J 83:65-72+ Ag; 91-8+ S '66
Can killers be predicted? concerning a psychiatrist's responsibility in cases like that of C. Whitman. P. McBroom. Sci N 90:117 Ag 20 '66
Crime of the country; killing by son in Germany to restore family honor. il Newsweek 67:33 F 7 '66
Day I learned about prejudice; mob murder. E. A. Morrison. Mlle 63:122+ S '66
Death of a wild man; Wilson-Green murders in San Francisco. il Newsweek 67:87 My 23 '66
Doctor is charged with two perfect murders. il Life 61:34 Ag 5 '66
Further reflections on mass murder. America 115:443 O 15 '66
In cold blood, by T. Capote. Review
    Commonweal 83:561-2 F 11 '66. B. McCabe
    Harper 232:108+ F '66. R. West; Reply with rejoinder. T. Caldwell. 232:4 My '66
    Nat R 18:226-9 Mr 8 '66. J. G. Dunne
    Nation 202:158-60 F 7 '66. S. Yurick
    Reporter 34:58 Mr 10 '66. J. K. Galbraith
Killing for kicks; murder of three Tucson teenagers. il Newsweek 67:35+ Mr 14 '66
McChan's luck; released convict held on suspicion of murder, Maryland. Time 88:35 D 30 '66
Madman in the tower; murders at University of Texas. il Time 88:14-19 Ag 12 '66
Malice toward some; S. H. Bowers and the Dahmer murder. il Newsweek 67:39-40 Ap 11 '66
Mass murder on a campus; Charles J. Whitman case. il U S News 61:6 Ag 15 '66
Mass murder that horrified the Nation; killing of student nurses in Chicago. U S News 61:8 Jl 25 '66
Mass murders in U.S. why? interview. H. A. Davidson. U S News 61:34-5 Ag 15 '66
Murder by LSD? Kessler case. Newsweek 67:29 Ap 25 '66
Murder in Tuskegee; day of wrath in the model town. A. S. Kaufman. il Nation 202:118-25 Ja 31 '66
Neighbors in Fox Run; indictment accusing Coppolino of murder. il Time 88:24 Ag 5 '66

One by one; murder of eight student nurses in Chicago. il Time 88:19-21 Jl 22 '66
Painters in blood; murder of D. Wilson. Time 87:30-1 My 20 '66
Pied Piper of Tucson; C. Schmid multiple murderer; with report by D. Moser. il Life 60:18-24A+ Mr 4 '66
Quiet life; C. A. Coppolino indicted for two murders. il Newsweek 68:28 Ag 8 '66
Quiet one; murder of five in Arizona. il Newsweek 68:32 N 28 '66
Routine murder in New York; chief medical examiner of the City of New York. M. Mayer. Esquire 66:88+ S '66
Slaughter in the college of beauty; multiple murder in Mesa, Ariz. Time 88:33 N 18 '66
Solid prospect; Supreme court ruling. Newsweek 67:34+ Ap 11 '66
Strangler; Cincinnati killings. Newsweek 68:46 O 31 '66
Symptoms of mass murder. Time 88:18-19 Ag 12 '66
Terror in the hills; triple murder; Sardinia. Newsweek 69:46 Ja 16 '67
They are all dead! murder of eight student nurses in Chicago. il Newsweek 68:18-20 Jl 25 '66
Torture of mothers, by T. Nelson. Review
    Nation 202:496-8 Ap 25 '66. J. Meyer
Toward outlawing murder; way opened for further Justice department prosecutions. Time 87:28-9 Ap 8 '66
Two celebrated mysteries are solved in new books; Boston stranglings and 1932 Hawaiian murder. il Life 61:48-9 O 7 '66
Under the clock, a sniper with 31 minutes to live; C. Whitman killings, Austin, Tex; with report by D. Nevin. il Life 61:24-31 Ag 12 '66
Until proven innocent; American serving death sentence in Mexico. il Time 88:87-8 O 28 '66
Who could kill Valerie Percy? il Life 61:47 S 30 '66
Who the gentle victims were. L. Wainwright. il Life 61:18-27 Jl 29 '66
Who's to blame when a murderer strikes? with report by P. H. Johnson. il Life 61:60-2+ Ag 12 '66
    See also
Assassination
Capital punishment
Trials (murder)

MURDER, Ritual. See Blood accusation

MURDER in the cathedral; drama. See Eliot, T. S.

MURDERERS. See Murder

MURDICK, Olin J.
Ecumenical high school. America 115:780-1 D 10 '66

MURDOCH, Iris
Choreography of despair. S. Eimerl. Reporter 35:45-6 N 3 '66
Odd fish in Iris Murdoch's kettle. M. Tucker. New Repub 154:26-8 F 5 '66

MURDOCH, Keith A.
City management speaks out; excerpts from address. Parks & Rec 1:413+ My '66

MURDOCK, John A.
Mimeographiti. Christian Cent 83:1573-4 D 21 '66

MURFITT, Rex
Choice small bulbs. Horticulture 44:16-17+ S '66
Lewisias. Horticulture 44:30-1 Jl '66

MURI, John
New records. Sr Schol 87:sup27 Ja 14; 88:sup 12-13 Ap 1; sup24-5 Ap 29; sup 12 My 13; 89:sup 17 S 30 '66

MURIE, Adolph
Pesticide program in Grand Teton National Park. Nat Parks Mag 40:17-19 Je '66

MURILLO, Luis
Fear on the high wire. B. Ballantine. il por Pop Sci 189:88-91 Jl '66

MURINE leukemia viruses. See Leukemia viruses

MURPHY, Abbie M.
How to prune old roses. Flower Grower 53:66 Mr '66
Trio of old roses. Flower Grower 53:46-7 F '66

MURPHY, Anselm
Book review. America 115:288 S 17 '66

MURPHY, Austin S.
War against personal thrift; address. November 21, 1966. Vital Speeches 33:169-73 Ja 1 '67

MURPHY, Charles J. V.
De Gaulle sets forth to change the face of Europe. Life 61:18-25+ Jl 8 '66; Same abr. with title What is de Gaulle up to? Read Digest 89:134-8 S '66

MURPHY, Charles J. V.—*Continued*
New multi-purpose U.S. army. Fortune 73:
122-4+ My '66
Red China's sinking revolution. Fortune 74:
134-9+ N '66
MURPHY, Charles S.
CAB views IATA; comments. Aviation W
85:17 N 28 '66
MURPHY, Cicero
Pool shark from Brooklyn. il pors Ebony 21:
44-6+ S '66
MURPHY, Edward F.
(comp) Accent on youth. N Y Times Mag
p 132 Ap 3 '66
(comp) Daddy, O! N Y Times Mag p 12+ Je
12 '66
(comp) For what it's worth. N Y Times Mag
p80 Mr 13 '66
(comp) Gift of giving. N Y Times Mag p74+
D 11 '66
(comp) Look before you—. N Y Times Mag
p44+ My 15 '66
(comp) Men in blue. N Y Times Mag p52
Mr 6 '66
(comp) Moon talk. N Y Times Mag p32 F
20 '66
MURPHY, Eugene F. See Freiberger, H. jt.
auth.
MURPHY, F. X.
To be perfectly frank. America 116:44-5 Ja
14 '67
MURPHY, Francis
Going it alone; estrangement in American
poetry. Yale R 56:17-24 O '66
MURPHY, Franklin David
Man from U.C.L.A. il por Time 88:98 O 21
'66
They're country doctors no longer. H. Earl.
il Todays Health 44:24-9 Je '66
MURPHY, G. A.
Break that habit. Flying 79:97 N '66
MURPHY, George Wesley
Tender invitation. por Time 87:92+ F 18 '66
MURPHY, John I.
What I have learned from diabetes. Read
Digest 88:197-200 My '66
MURPHY, Judith, and Gross, Ronald
Unfulfilled promise of ITV. Sat R 49:88-9+
N 19 '66
—See Gross, R. jt. auth.
MURPHY, Robert Cushman
Books in review (cont) Natur Hist 75:6+
Ag '66
MURPHY, Roland E.
Books. Commonweal 84:35-6 Mr 25 '66
Catholic professors on the secular campus.
por America 115:318 S 24 '66
MURPHY, Ruth Z. and Blumenthal, S. G.
American community and the immigrant. bib-
liog f Ann Am Acad 367:115-26 S '66
MURPHY, Sara
Men out of monkeys, or monkeys out of men?
New Repub 154:9-10 My 7 '66
MURPHY, Thomas J.
Why are we striking? G. Merlis. Nat R 18:
532-4 My 31 '66
MURPHY, William A. and Hostetler, R. D.
General-purpose composition potentiometers.
Electr World 75:50-1+ Ap '66
MURPHY, William Beverly
Campbell's; recipe for growth. J. B. Weiner.
il por Duns R 88:27-30+ Ag '66
MURPHY, William S. See Cohen, J. jt. auth.
MURRAY, Bain
Bright new light in Ohio. Hi Fi 16:134-5
Mr '66
MURRAY, Bruce C. and Davies, M. E.
Comparison of U.S. and Soviet efforts to
explore Mars. bibliog Science 151:945-54
F 25 '66
—See Leighton, R. B. jt. auth.
MURRAY, Catherine
Short poem: It's February. Poetry 109:21 O
'66
MURRAY, Don
Our fastest-growing health menace. Read
Digest 90:111-14 Ja '67
Secret of keeping your teeth. Read Digest
88:63-5 Mr '66
MURRAY, George C.
Intracellular absorption difference spectrum
of limulus extra-ocular photolabile pigment.
bibliog Science 154:1182-3 D 2 '66
MURRAY, James Richard
Hudson's Bay mushes along the urban trail.
il pors Bsns W p64-8 S 3 '66
MURRAY, Jim
Ronald Reagan to the rescue! Esquire 65:
76-8+ F '66
MURRAY, Joan
TV news hens. il pors Ebony 21:44-6+ O '66
MURRAY, John
Look, ma! no reflectors! il Pop Phot 58:64-
7+ Ap '66

MURRAY, John Courtney
Declaration on religious freedom: its deeper
significance; address. America 114:592-3 Ap
23 '66
Freedom, authority, community. America
115:734-7+ D 3 '66
MURRAY, Madalyn E.
Dialogue with Mrs O'Hair; interview, ed. by
N. C. Nielsen, jr. Christian Cent 83:615-18
My 11 '66
MURRAY, Stanley A.
Appalachian trail. Nat Parks Mag 40:4-7 D
'66
MURRAY, William
Culture boom. Holiday 39:70-5+ Mr '66
Europe by night. Holiday 41:58-71+ Ja '67
MURRAY the K. See Kaufman, M.
MURROW, Edward R.
Murrow in London, you can hear him now.
R. Gelatt. il por Hi Fi 16:123 O '66
Murrow remembers. R. L. Tobin. Sat R 49:
87 N 26 '66
MURTHY, V. Rama. See Stueber, A. M. jt.
auth.
MURVILLE, Maurice Couve de. See Couve de
Murville, M.
MUSA, Mark
Poet's epistles to posterity. Sat R 50:39 Ja
21 '67
MUSA cavendishi. See Bananas, Dwarf
MUSCLE
Muscle postjunctional membrane: changes in
chemosensitivity produced by calcium. W.
L. Nastuk and J. H. Liu. bibliog il Science
154:266-7 O 14 '66
Muscle relaxation: evidence for an intra-
fibrillar restoring force in vertebrate
striated muscle. C. Parsons and K. R.
Porter. bibliog il Science 153:426-7 Jl 22 '66
Postsynaptic versus presynaptic inhibition in
antagonistic stretch reflexes. D. G. Green
and J. O. Kellerth. bibliog il Science 152:
1097-9 My 20 '66
Synaptic activity in motoneurons during natural stimulation of muscle spindles. R. E.
Burke and P. G. Nelson. bibliog il Science
151:1088-91 Mr 4 '66
Tetrodotoxin and manganese ions: effects
on electrical activity and tension in taenia
coli of guinea pig. Y. Nonomura and others.
bibliog il Science 152:97-9 Ap 1 '66
Tropomyosin paracrystals formed by divalent
cations. C. Cohen and W. Longley. bibliog
il Science 152:794-6 My 6 '66
See also
Heart—Muscle

Proteins
Actin-myosin interaction: inhibition of the
myosin adenosine triphosphatase by actin.
S. Barron and others. bibliog il Science 151:
1541-2 Mr 25 '66
Actin: volume change on transformation of
G-form to F-form. T. Ikkai and others.
bibliog il Science 152:1756-7 Je 24 '66
MUSCLES
Parrots' muscles active. Sci N 90:338 O 22
'66
Your muscles: how they work, why they
hurt. il Changing T 20:21-3 N '66
See also
Myosin

Diseases
Myopathies: report on symposium. E. Ba-
jusz and F. Homburger. Science 152:1112-13
My 20 '66
See also
Dystrophy, Muscular
Myotonia

Fibrillation
Heart flutter explained; action of heart
fibrillation or irregular heart beats. Sci N
90:134 Ag 27 '66
MUSCULAR dystrophy. See Dystrophy, Muscu-
lar
MUSCULAR fatigue. See Fatigue
MUSCULAR sense
See also
Movement, Psychology of
MUSEO de arte de Ponce. See Ponce, Puerto
Rico—Galleries and museums
MUSEOLOGY. See Museum techniques
MUSEU do azulejo. See Lisbon, Portugal—
Galleries and museums
MUSEUM of early southern decorative arts,
Winston-Salem, N.C. See Winston-Salem,
N.C.—Galleries and museums
MUSEUM of fine arts, Houston. See Houston
museum of fine arts
MUSEUM of illustration art, New York
Museum of illustration art granted New
York charter. il Pub W 190:116-17 N 7 '66

MUSEUM of modern art, New York
Art of animation; festival sponsored by the
Museum of modern art. H. Junker. Nation
202:249-50 F 28 '66
Museum of modern art. M. Herr. il Holiday
40:115-18+ D '66
Paintings and photographs; retrospectives of
D. Lange and R. Magritte. F. Getlein. New
Repub 154:33-5 Mr 19 '66
True father of modern painting. H. Kramer.
il N Y Times Mag p30-1+ Mr 20 '66
MUSEUM of natural history. See American
museum of natural history, New York
MUSEUM of primitive art, New York
How Mr Menen taught the Dangs primitive
art. A. Menen. il N Y Times Mag p20-2+
Jl 24 '66
Rocky road to art; World of primitive art
show. il Newsweek 68:90 Jl 18 '66
MUSEUM of Spanish abstract art. See Cuenca,
Spain—Galleries and museums
MUSEUM techniques
Museum school; training the museologist. T.
D. Bernard. il Américas 18:30-2 My '66
MUSEUM workers
Turn left at the mummy, right at Van Gogh;
jobs for girls with museomania. K. Grove.
il Mlle 62:202-3+ Ap '66
MUSEUMS
From out of the past; wireless museums
preserve the early days. T. M. Hannah. il
Pop Electr 25:68-9 O '66
Many museums now welcome camera-toting
galleryites. W. Lane. il Travel 126:67 Jl '66
Museum world. J. L. Stoutenburgh. See is-
sues of Hobbies
Museums-a-go-go. S. Frieswyk. il Parks &
Rec 1:414-15+ My '66
    See also
Aeronautic museums
Art—Galleries and museums
Astronomical museums
Naval museums
    also subhead Galleries and museums un-
der names of cities, e.g. Chicago—Galleries
and museums

Architecture
Three museums. il Arch Rec 139:195-206 Ap
'66
Ziggurat for Whitney's art. il Life 61:95-6+
O 7 '66

Work with children
    See also
Metropolitan museum of art, New York—
Junior museum

Argentina
Museum school; training the museologist. T.
D. Bernard. il Américas 18:30-2 My '66
MUSEUMS, Traveling. See Artmobiles
MUSEUMS, Wax. See Wax figures
MUSGRAVE, Clifford
Royal pavilion, Brighton. Antiques 90:74-9,
320-5 Jl, S '66
MUSGRAVE, R. A.
Sharing the revenue; national taxes and local
needs. Nation 204:78-80 Ja 16 '67
MUSHROOM ceremony
Faith, mushrooms linked; soma, plant with
hallucinogenic properties worshiped by an-
cient Hindus. P. McBroom. Sci N 90:398
N 12 '66
MUSHROOMS
Cook's tour; what goes on at a mushroom
farm. il Sunset 137:224+ O '66
Dried mushroom powder is new U.S. product.
Sci N 90:159 S 3 '66
Magic of mushrooms. H. S. Witty. il Flower
Grower 53:39 F '66
Mushrooms; look before you eat. R. W. Buck.
il Horticulture 44:22-5 S '66
Nature note. Sci N 90:45 Jl 16 '66
What to know when buying mushrooms.
Good H 162:170 My '66
    See also
Cookery—Mushrooms
MUSIAL, Stan
Dramatic gains in youth fitness. por Parents
Mag 41:30 Ag '66
How the American male can be fit. por Parks
& Rec 1:695+ S '66
Out of the cellar but not in the first division;
America needs more than spring training.
Am Ed 2:28-30 S '66
MUSIC
Artist life. D. J. Soria. See issues of High
fidelity incorporating Musical America
Contemporary scene; excerpt from address,
May 1966. A. Copland. il Sat R 49:49 Je 25
'66

Distaste for music; excerpt from Virgil
Thomson. V. Thomson. il Vogue 148:292-5+
S 1 '66
Does anybody need the avant-garde? Discus.
il Harper 232:108-10 Je '66
From Bach to rock; accent's on youth. il
Sr Schol 88:20 My 6 '66
Here & there. See issues of High fidelity
incorporating Musical America
Is new music new? N. Rorem. Am Rec G 32:
776-9+ My '66
Life music review (cont) il Life 60:13 Ja 7;
16 F 25; 10 Mr 11; 12 Ap 29; 18 My 20; 61:18
Jl 1; 12 Ag 19 '66; 62:18 Ja 20 '67
Mephisto's musings. See issues of High
fidelity incorporating Musical America
Music and the statistical age; interview. I. F.
Stravinsky. Commentary 42:49-52 S '66
Music: how it's built. P. Glanville-Hicks.
Vogue 147:200-1 Mr 1 '66
Musical events; tonality dead? W. Sargeant.
New Yorker 42:200-2 My 14 '66
Musical rewards for the traveler. F. Bowers.
House & Gard 129:30+ Ap '66
New music. J. Peyser. il Vogue 147:176+
F 1 '66
1965-66 music season. S. Schultz. il Hi Fi
16:65-9 D 15 '66
Tomorrow's music today; classical music.
H. Evans. Seventeen 26:38 Ja '67
Two extremes of avant-garde music; J. Cage
and M. Babbitt. R. Kostelanetz. il N Y
Times Mag p34-5+ Ja 15 '67
What's what in modern music. R. Evett.
New Repub 156:36+ Ja 14 '67
    See also
Bands (music)
Birds in music
Copyright—Music
Jazz music
Mood music
Parody (music)
Rhythm
Television broadcasting—Music

Analysis, Interpretation, etc.
From a composer's journal; excerpts from
Music from inside out. N. Rorem. Com-
mentary 42:82-7 N '66

Appreciation
Circle of light. P. Wood. Opera N 30:8-10
F 19 '66
How to become an opera buff. F. Bowers.
House & Gard 130:92+ O '66
Scaling of musical preferences by the
mentally retarded. S. D. Koh and T. H.
Koh. bibliog il Science 153:432-4 Jl 22 '66
What makes a good pianist? F. Bowers. il
House & Gard 130:35+ N '66

Bibliography
Book reviews. See issues of American record
guide
From the editor; concerning book reviews.
J. Lyons. Am Rec G 32:888 My '66
    See also
Music literature

Competitions
Agony of the Tchaikovsky; Moscow's third
international Tchaikovsky competition. il
Time 88:60 Jl 8 '66
Competitions here and abroad. H. Kupfer-
berg. il Atlan 218:132+ O '66
Contests, foundations, awards, domestic and
foreign. Hi Fi 16:248-51 D 15 '66
Don't knock the rock. J. A. Michener. il
Read Digest 88:157-60+ F '66
Four for the future; Dimitri Mitropoulos in-
ternational music competition. il Time 87:
49 Ja 28 '66
Keeping up with the Cliburns (and the
Joneses) Cliburn international quadrennial
piano competition. P. Hume. il Sat R 49:
56-7+ O 29 '66
Success by short cut; Fort Worth's Van Cli-
burn international quadrennial piano com-
petition. il Time 88:96 O 21 '66
Testing their medals; Moscow winners. il
Time 88:39 Ag 26 '66
Van Cliburn contest for young pianists.
Américas 18:36 D '66
We, who are about to be disqualified, salute
you! Montreal report. G. Gould. Hi Fi
16:MA23-4+ D '66
    See also
Singing—Competitions

MUSIC—*Continued*

History and criticism
Avant-garde makes a noise. E. Laderman. il N Y Times Mag pt2 p 17+ S 11 '66
Unfinished symphony; Puccini's Turandot completed by F. Alfano. R. Lawrence. il Opera N 31:24-5 D 3 '66
See also
Jazz music
Opera—History and criticism

Instruction and study
Don't let summer stop the music! child's instruction. Bet Hom & Gard 44:34 Ap '66
How to select a musical instrument for a child. il Good H 162:181 Ap '66
Teaching music in the self-contained classroom. E. M. Badger; E. M. Covell. il NEA J 55:16-18 My '66
See also
Musical education

Memorizing
Recordings. M. Mayer. Esquire 66:52+ O '66

Periodicals
Magazines: foreign. Hi Fi 16:278-81 D 15 '66
Magazines: U.S. Hi Fi 16:231-2 D 15 '66

Themes, motives, etc.
Transfigured knight: Parsifal. J. Honig. il Opera N 30:26-7 Ap 2 '66

Theory
Music: how it's built. P. Glanville-Hicks. Vogue 147:200-1+ Mr 1 '66

Argentina
See also
Buenos Aires—Music

Austria
See also
Salzburg festival
Vienna—Music

Belgium
See also
Brussels—Music

Brazil
See also
Musicians, Brazilian
São Paulo (city), Brazil—Music

Canada
See also
Montreal—Music
Opera—Canada

Czechoslovakia
See also
Opera, Czech
Prague—Music

France
Goodbye to all that. il Time 87:62 Je 24 '66
See also
Paris—Music

Germany (Democratic Republic)
See also
Berlin (East Berlin)—Music
Dresden—Music

Germany (Federal Republic)
Presto! L. Maazel's Düsseldorf concert to be investigated. Newsweek 67:89 My 30 '66
See also
Berlin—Music
Cologne, Germany—Music
Munich—Music
Opera—Germany (Federal Republic)
Stuttgart, Germany—Music

Great Britain
See also
London—Music

India
See also
Music, Indian (East Indian)

Ireland
See also
Dublin—Music

Israel
See also
Israel philharmonic orchestra
Tel Aviv, Israel—Music

Italy
Before the opera, Italy's busy fall. W. Weaver. il Hi Fi 16:MA25+ D '66
See also
Florence—Music
Milan, Italy—Music
Music, Italian
Naples—Music
Rome (city)—Music

Mexico
See also
Mexico (city)—Music

Netherlands
See also
Amsterdam, Netherlands—Music

Portugal
See also
Lisbon, Portugal—Music

Russia
See also
Leningrad—Music

Spain
See also
Madrid—Music

Sweden
See also
Göteborg—Music
Music festivals—Sweden
Stockholm—Music

Switzerland
Switzerland, a musical tour through the cantons. P. G. Davis. Hi Fi 16:34+ S '66
See also
Geneva, Switzerland—Music
Zurich, Switzerland—Music

United States
Elite eleven: outstanding symphony orchestras. il Time 87:62+ Ap 8 '66
Lively arts. R. Hemming. Sr Schol 89:29 D 9 '66
Orchestras U.S.A, the season's forecast. Hi Fi 16:MA7-10 S '66
Retrospectives, healthy and other. C. J. McNaspy. America 115:161-2 Ag 13 '66
Serious music: in serious trouble. D. J. Henahan. il Holiday 39:106-9+ Mr '66
Sound progress, yeah, yeah, yeah! il Sr Schol 88:19 Ap 15 '66
Survey: North American cities: 1966-1967. Hi Fi 16:285-316 D 15 '66
Those were the days; fifty years ago. Hi Fi 16:75-6 D 15 '66
See also
Jazz music
Music, American
National music league
also subhead Music under names of cities, e.g. New Haven, Conn.—Music

MUSIC, American
Music in a new found land, by W. Mellers. Review
New Yorker 42:186+ Ap 23 '66. W. Sargeant
Music; newer American repertory. B. Boretz. Nation 202:437-8 Ap 11 '66
Musical events: concert of contemporary American compositions performed by Philharmonic, conducted by L. Bernstein. W. Sargeant. New Yorker 41:134 F 19 '66
See also
Composers, American
Jazz music
Music—United States
Opera, American
Phonograph records—American music

MUSIC, Austrian
Webern in perspective; excerpts from Anton von Webern, by E. Krenek; E. Wellesz; C. Bresgen. Sat R 49:47-9+ My 28 '66

MUSIC, Baroque
Baroque flourishes. P. H. Lang. Opera N 31:16-17 N 19 '66

MUSIC, Chamber. See Chamber music

MUSIC, Chinese
See also
Phonograph records—Chinese music

MUSIC, Church. See Church music

MUSIC, Czech
See also
Opera, Czech

MUSIC, Electronic
Does anybody need the avant-garde? Discus. il Harper 232:108-10 Je '66
Is new music new? N. Rorem. Am Rec G 32:776-9+ My '66
Musical events; demonstration of V. Vssachevsky's music at Bernard M. Baruch school of business and public administration. W. Sargeant. New Yorker 42:86+ My 28 '66
New music. J. Peyser. il Vogue 147:176+ F 1 '66
Prospects of recording: electronic media, a threat to the public concert? G. Gould. Hi Fi 16:46-63 Ap '66
Swurpledeewurpledeezeech! signature music. il Time 88:68 N 4 '66
See also
Phonograph records—Electronic music

MUSIC, English
Massive documentation of Byrd's technique. M. Serbin. Am Rec G 33:60-1 S '66
See also
Phonograph records—English music

MUSIC, French
Scoring the D train; E. Varese. F. V. Grunfeld. il Reporter 34:47-8+ Ap 7 '66
See also
Composers, French
Phonograph records—French music

MUSIC, Hebrew
See also
Phonograph records—Hebrew music

MUSIC, Hindu
See also
Phonograph records—Hindu music
Shankar, R.

MUSIC, Indian (East Indian)
Sarodist; interview. A. A. Khan. New Yorker 42:23-4 Ag 27 '66
See also
Phonograph records—Hindu music

MUSIC, Irish
See also
Phonograph records—Irish music

MUSIC, Italian
Mass and the opera; Milan cathedral and Teatro alla Scala. V. Sheean. il Opera N 30:8-13 Ap 2 '66

MUSIC, Japanese
See also
Phonograph records—Japanese music

MUSIC, Korean
See also
Phonograph records—Korean music

MUSIC, Latin American
Music. See issues of Américas

MUSIC, Mexican
See also
Phonograph records—Mexican music

MUSIC, Modern. See Music

MUSIC, Polish
See also
Phonograph records—Polish music

MUSIC, Popular (songs, etc)
Daddy is a hippy. R. Lemon. il Sat Eve Post 239:22 Jl 2 '66
Doodles and tenderness; rebirth of the gramophone sound. il Newsweek 69:66 Ja 2 '67
Encyclopedia of popular music, by I. Stambler. Review
Am Rec G 32:1002-4 Je '66. M. Kreuger
Evolution of Bob Dylan. A. E. Gollan. Nat R 18:638-40 Je 28 '66
Face to face with a Bangkok recording star. L. Kennedy. il Seventeen 25:179 S '66
Folk rock's tambourine man. S. Castan. il Look 30:76+ Mr 8 '66
42nd street psycho blues. J. Ian. Seventeen 26:44+ Ja '67
Girls from Motown; the Supremes. il Time 87:83-4 Mr 4 '66
Going to pot; new songs dealing with all kinds of taboo topics. Time 88:56-7 Jl 1 '66
Horns of plenty; the Alpert sound. il Newsweek 67:85 Ap 25 '66
Hot hundred: a surprise; patriotic songs. M. Geltman. Nat R 18:894-6 S 6 '66
In my opinion; with a few marvelous exceptions, folk rock is terrible. M. Medeiros. Seventeen 25:250 F '66
I've got the band that's all I need; teen-age band; Corporate image. N. Lotz. il Seventeen 26:82-3+ Ja '67
Lively arts; interview, ed. by R. Hemming. H. Jankowski. Sr Schol 89:22 O 14 '66
Newstalgia. il Time 88:64 D 2 '66
Off the record with the Supremes; ed. by E. Miller. D. Ross; M. Wilson; F. Ballard. il Seventeen 25:280-1+ Ag '66
Pop music on camera. N. Compton. Commentary 42:60-3 Jl '66
Popular records (cont) D. Watt. New Yorker 42:200-2+ Mr 19; 197-9 D 17 '66
Pot luck; discussion of dope in popular music. G. Lees. il Holiday 40:129-30 O '66
Le roi de pop; E. Barclay, king of French popular music. il Newsweek 69:56-8 Ja 9 '67
Teen-age money music; combo groups. il Life 60:102-4+ Je 3 '66
Well, what have we here? B. Dylan, king of rock 'n' roll. J. Siegel. il Sat Eve Post 239:32-6+ Jl 30 '66
Whatever happened to love songs? with report by T. Prideaux. il Life 61:61-2+ S 16 '66
See also
Phonograph records—Songs

MUSIC, South African
Songsters from a southern latitude; interview. A. Tracey and P. Tracey. New Yorker 42:27-9 Je 4 '66

MUSIC, Vietnamese
See also
Phonograph records—Vietnamese music

MUSIC and children
Shakespeare speaks to kids; how to encourage natural interest. H. Taubman. il Parents Mag 41:72-3+ O '66
They shall have music; project at Horace Mann elementary school, Bellflower, Calif. C. L. Herbert. il Am Ed 2:22 O '66

MUSIC as recreation
Music-making at home. J. T. Maher. il Holiday 39:121-6 Ap '66

MUSIC boxes
Philosopher's clock. New Yorker 42:39-41 My 21 '66

MUSIC collections in libraries. See Libraries—Music collections

MUSIC conductors. See Conductors (music)

MUSIC contests. See Music—Competitions

MUSIC copyright. See Copyright—Music

MUSIC corporation of America
New life for the new wave; European venture. A. Knight. Sat R 49:38 Ag 20 '66

MUSIC criticism. See Music—History and criticism

MUSIC critics. See Critics

MUSIC education. See Musical education

MUSIC festivals
Music festivals: foreign. Hi Fi 16:274-8 D 15 '66

Austria
Vienna; Vienna festival weeks. M. E. Peltz. il Opera N 31:30 S 10 '66
See also
Salzburg festival

Belgium
Ghent; Festival of Flanders. P. Affelder. il Opera N 31:29 O 15 '66

California
Aptos, Cal; Cabrillo music festival. C. Remolif. Opera N 31:24 O 15 '66
Festival small but powerful; Ojai report. P. Yates. Hi Fi 16:MA15 Ag '66
Jazz concerts: Monterey jazz festival. W. Balliett. New Yorker 42:210-14+ O 1 '66
New Mozart & twelve-tone captive maidens; Cabrillo festival. K. D. Wallace. Hi Fi 16:MA24-5 N '66
20th-century innovations, more or less; Stanford report. K. D. Wallace. Hi Fi 16:MA18-19+ O '66

Colorado
Central City, Aspen; Central City opera festival. A. Young. Opera N 31:27 S 10 '66
Mozart and Elliott Carter in Colorado; Aspen report. A. Young. il Hi Fi 16:MA20-1 O '66
University of Colorado: the musical panorama. A. Young. il Hi Fi 16:123+ Je '66

Connecticut
Shed at Norfolk: New England's oldest summer festival. H. Goldsmith. il Hi Fi 16:40-3 Je '66

England
Aldeburgh. A. Conner. il Opera N 31:29 S 10 '66
England; Glyndebourne festival. F. Aprahamian. il Opera N 31:27 O 15 '66
Festival in the ancient city; London report. E. Greenfield. Hi Fi 16:MA26-7 O '66
Festivals in England; Aldeburgh/Glyndebourne. E. Greenfield. Hi Fi 16:MA20-1 S '66
Mystery plays and Monteverdi; York festival. G. Loney. il Hi Fi 16:MA28-9 O '66

Europe, Western
Guide to European music festivals, 1966. H. D. Jellinek. Sat R 49:58-9 Mr 26 '66
Summer evenings (cont) Opera N 30:[37-8] Ap 9 '66

Florida
LSO comes to Florida; Daytona Beach report. B. Jacobson. il Hi Fi 16:MA14-15 O '66
Not just naked girls; Florida international music festival. il Time 88:48 Ag 12 '66

France
Aix-en-Provence. M. E. Davies. Opera N 31:27 O 15 '66
Americans abroad; Aix report. R. McMullen. Hi Fi 16:MA25+ O '66
Courage of Aimé Maeght; annual music and dance festival. R. McMullen. Hi Fi 16:MA26 N '66

MUSIC festivals—France—*Continued*
Estival festival foolishness. A. C. Schmidt.
il Reporter 35:50-1 O 20 '66
Gift of privilege; P. Casals. il Time 88:48+
Ag 12 '66
Music in the Marais. R. McMullen. il Hi Fi
16:69-72 My '66

Germany (Federal Republic)

Gunther Schuller's The visitation; Hamburg
report. P. Moor. il Hi Fi 16:MA28-9 D '66
Max Reger festival; Munich report. P. J.
Korn. Hi Fi 16:MA20-1 Ag '66
See also
Bayreuth festival

Greece, Modern

Athens, Opatija. F. Stevenson. Opera N 31:28
O 15 '66
Don Carlo and the Kirov in Greece; Athens
report. F. Stevenson. Hi Fi 16:MA24 O '66

Ireland

Wexford, M. E. Davies. Opera N 31:31 D 10
'66

Italy

New management for the Maggio; Florence
report. W. Weaver. il Hi Fi 16:MA22+
Ag '66

Japan

In Japan the arts of East and West; Osaka
report. E. Cunningham. il Hi Fi 16:MA16+
Ag '66

Lebanon

Gods were good to Baalbeck. J. Anderson. il
Dance Mag 40:26-8 My '66
Let's travel: Baalbek international festival.
G. Buckman. il Mlle 64:136-9 D '66

Massachusetts

See also
Berkshire symphonic festival

Mexico

To Puebla and return; first festival. I.
Kolodin. Sat R 49:20+ Je 25 '66

Netherlands

Amsterdam; Holland festival's Don Carlo.
J. Mindszenthy. il Opera N 31:25 O 15 '66
New concert hall in Rotterdam; Holland festi-
val. M. Seif. il Sat R 49:74 Jl 16 '66
Schat's Labyrinth; Rotterdam's new hall;
Holland festival. E. Helm. Hi Fi 16:MA22
S '66

New York (state)

At Caramoor: Curlew river, Escorial; Katonah
report. C. L. Osborne. Hi Fi 16:MA14-15
S '66
Katonah, N.Y. Caramoor festival. F. Merk-
ling. il Opera N 31:26 S 10 '66
New York; production of Handel's Giulio
Cesare, Puccini's La Bohème, and Kurt
Schwitters' Class struggle opera. F.
Merkling; R. D. Daniels; G. Fitzgerald.
il Opera N 31:22-3 N 5 '66
Saratoga, Lake George. F. Merkling. il Opera
N 31:23 O 15 '66
Small gem; Caramoor festival in Katonah. il
Time 88:61 Jl 8 '66
Summer opera, new and nervy; Saratoga
& Lake George. C. L. Osborne. Hi Fi 16:
MA16-17+ N '66

Portugal

Portugal's Gulbenkian festival; Lisbon report. N. Hirsch. Hi Fi 16:MA23 Ag '66

Rhode Island

Musical events: Newport jazz festival.
W. Balliett. New Yorker 42:95-7 Jl 16 '66

Sweden

Stockholm; Stockholm festival. K. Atterberg.
il Opera N 31:26 N 5 '66
Talent and trash from I.S.C.M. P. Moor.
Hi Fi 16:MA26 D '66

Switzerland

Yehudi Menuhin's festival; in Reformed
Lutheran church of Saanen-Gstaad. E.
Helm. il Hi Fi 16:MA27+ N '66

Texas

San Antonio. J. Rosenfield. il Opera N 30:28
Ap 16 '66

United States

George Wein: jazz by the sea. M. J. Arlen.
il Holiday 40:91-2+ Jl '66
Lively arts. R. Hemming. il Sr Schol 89:26-7
S 23 '66

Music festivals U.S.A: summer 1966. H. D.
Jellinek. il Sat R 49:50-3 My 28 '66
Place, a show, a win; concert country of the
Northeast. il Time 88:56-9 Jl 22 '66
Summer evenings (cont) Opera N 30:[37-8]
Ap 9 '66
This summer: festivals. U.S.A. Hi Fi 16:140-3
My '66

Venezuela

Festival and congress in Caracas. A. Matilla.
il Américas 18:38-9 N '66

Vermont

Musical events: chamber music concert:
Music from Marlboro; performed by artists
from Marlboro music festival. W. Sargeant.
New Yorker 42:74+ F 26 '66
Musicians at play; Marlboro report. S. Flem-
ing. il Hi Fi 16:MA12-13 O '66
Vermont magic; musicians rehearsals at
Marlboro college. H. Brandon. Sat R 49:8
Ag 13 '66

Yugoslavia

Music on the Adriatic; Dubrovnik summer
festival. P. Affelder. il Hi Fi 16:MA28-9
N '66

MUSIC for children
See also
Phonograph records—Childrens records
MUSIC foundations. See Foundations, Charit-
able and educational
MUSIC halls (variety theaters, cabarets, etc)
It's always warm here; Bobino music hall,
Paris. il Newsweek 69:69 Ja 9 '67
See also
New York (city)—Radio City music hall
MUSIC history. See Music—History and criti-
cism
MUSIC libraries
See also
Libraries—Phonograph and phonograph re-
cords
MUSIC literature
Books in the field: music. D. W. Krummel.
bibliog il Wilson Lib Bul 41:284-95 N '66
MUSIC patronage
Ludwig's world: R. Wagner's music. H.
Bailey. il Opera N 30:26-9 Mr 26 '66
Singers' friend; interview, ed. by A. M.
Lingg. J. W. Fisher. il Opera N 30:18 Ap 2
'66
MUSIC publishing
Bread & hyacinths; birthday salute to Boosey
and Hawkes. Q. Eaton. Opera N 30:12-13
F 19 '66
Man with the golden ear; D. Kirshner. il
Time 87:44 Ap 22 '66
Music publishers: U.S. Hi Fi 16:217-21 D 15
'66
MUSIC rooms and equipment
Cabinets, the new look in stereo housing;
with editorial comment. N. Eisenberg. il
Hi Fi 16:55, 56-9 S '66
Planned for music. il House & Gard 130:108-
12 Jl '66
Portfolio of stereo decor, 1966. il Hi Fi 16:
46-53 Mr '66
MUSIC schools
Fine arts school; cultural center in Harlem.
il Ebony 21:80-2+ My '66
Schools: the Americas. Hi Fi 16:233-47 D 15
'66
See also
Juilliard school of music. New York
MUSIC shells. See Orchestra shells
MUSIC teachers
Teaching music in the self-contained class-
room. E. M. Badger; E. M. Covell. il NEA J
55:16-18 My '66
MUSIC therapy
Arts in therapy. M. F. Thompson. il Parks
& Rec 1:712-14 S '66
MUSIC writing. See Composition (music)
MUSICAL accompaniment
Music for dancers; relationship between mu-
sician and dancer; reprint. Dance Mag 40:
60-1+ O '66
MUSICAL arrangement
Trivia market; canned classics. A. Rich. il
Opera N 31:8-11 D 24 '66
MUSICAL boxes. See Music boxes
MUSICAL comedies, revues, etc.
Reviewer's notebook. T. Lewis. America 114:
813-14 Je 4 '66
Show goes on, and production perks. Ad-
miral's new color tube plant. il Bsns W
p 122-4 Ap 16 '66
See also
Musical comedy, revue, etc.
Phonograph records—Musical comedies, re-
vues, etc.

MUSICAL comedies, revues, etc.—*Continued*

Criticisms, plots, etc.

Annie get your gun
America 114:882 Je 25 '66
Commonweal 84:393-4 Je 24 '66
Dance Mag 40:27+ Jl '66
Life il 60:47 Je 10 '66

Apple tree
America 115:786 D 10 '66
Commonweal 85:167 N 11 '66
Nation 203:493-4 N 7 '66
New Yorker 42:95 O 29 '66
Newsweek il 68:98 O 31 '66
Sat R 49:47 N 5 '66
Time il 88:90 O 28 '66
Vogue 148:161 D '66

At the drop of another hat
New Yorker 42:78 Ja 7 '67
Newsweek 69:71 Ja 9 '67
Sat R 50:98 Ja 14 '67
Time il 89:69 Ja 6 '67

Breakfast at Tiffany's
Newsweek 68:45 D 26 '66

Cabaret
America 116:25 Ja 7 '67
Commonweal 85:326 D 16 '66
Dance Mag il 41:26+ Ja '67
Life 62:16 Ja 13 '67
Life il 62:82-3 Ja 13 '67
Nation 203:651-2 D 12 '66
New Yorker 42:155-6 D 3 '66
Newsweek il 68:96 D 5 '66
Sat R 49:64 D 10 '66
Time il 88:84 D 2 '66
Vogue 149:52 Ja 1 '67

La grosse valise
Dance Mag 40:14-15+ F '66

Guys and dolls
Dance Mag 40:59 Jl '66
Life 60:18 Je 17 '66

Hooray! ! it's a glorious day... and all that
New Yorker 42:163-4 Mr 19 '66

How to succeed in business without really
trying
Dance Mag il 40:22 Je '66
Life 60:18 Je 17 '66

I do! I do!
Commonweal 85:402-3 Ja 13 '67
Life 62:16 Ja 13 '67
Life il 62:82-5 Ja 13 '67
Nation 204:29-30 Ja 2 '67
New Yorker 42:117 D 17 '66
Newsweek il 68:106 D 19 '66
Sat R 49:61+ D 24 '66
Time il 88:87 D 16 '66

Illya darling
Look il 31:66-71 Ja 24 '67

It's a bird, it's a plane, it's Superman
America 114:704 My 14 '66
Commonweal 84:156 Ap 22 '66
Dance Mag 40:25 My '66
Life il 60:25 Mr 11 '66
New Yorker 42:81 Ap 9 '66
Newsweek 67:94 Ap 11 '66
Sat R 49:62 Ap 16 '66
Time il 78:81 Ap 8 '66

Joyful noise
New Yorker 42:45 D 24 '66
Newsweek 68:45 D 26 '66

Let's sing Yiddish
Dance Mag il 41:25 Ja '67

Mad show
Commonweal 84:228 My 13 '66
Harper 232:114-15 My '66
Life il 60:24-5 Mr 11 '66
New Repub 154:36-7 Ja 29 '66
Time 87:65+ F 18 '66
Vogue 147:94 Mr 1 '66

Mame
America 115:79-80 Jl 16 '66
Commonweal 84:369-70 Je 17 '66
Dance Mag il 40:25-7 Jl '66
Life il 60:88-92+ Je 17 '66
New Yorker 42:75 Je 4 '66
Newsweek 67:89 Je 6 '66
Sat R 49:34 Je 11 '66
Time il 87:71 Je 3 '66
Vogue 148:28 Jl '66

Man of La Mancha
Life il 60:47-8+ Ap 8 '66
Nat R 18:1062-3 O 18 '66

Man with a load of mischief
New Yorker 42:178+ N 19 '66

Mardi gras
America 115:140 Ag 6 '66
Sat R 49:48 Jl 30 '66

Minstrel show, or Civil rights in a cracker
barrel
Nation 202:276-8 Mr 7 '66

Most happy fella
Dance Mag 40:25 Jl '66
Life 60:18 Je 17 '66

Oklahoma
Dance Mag 40:14-15+ F '66

Pousse-café
Dance Mag 40:24 My '66
New Yorker 42:120 Mr 26 '66
Newsweek 67:88 Mr 28 '66

Show boat
America 115:140-1 Ag 6 '66
Dance Mag 40:34+ S '66
Sat R 49:34 Ag 6 '66

Skyscraper
America 114:180 Ja 29 '66
Life il 60:90-2 F 4 '66

Sweet Charity
America 114:452 Ap 2 '66
Commonweal 84:57 Ap 1 '66
Dance Mag il 40:24 My '66
Life il 60:99-100 Mr 25 '66
Nation 202:248-9 F 28 '66
New Yorker 41:84 F 5 '66
Newsweek 67:88 F 14 '66
Sat R 49:44 F 12 '66
Time il 87:46 F 4 '66
Vogue 147:58 Mr 15 '66

Time for singing
America 114:881-2 Je 25 '66
Commonweal 84:370 Je 17 '66
Dance Mag 40:25 Jl '66
New Yorker 42:79 My 28 '66
Newsweek 67:89 Je 6 '66
Sat R 49:34 Je 11 '66

US
New Yorker 42:208+ D 3 '66
Newsweek il 68:98+ O 31 '66
Time il 88:61 O 21 '66

Wait a minim!
America 114:604 Ap 23 '66
Commonweal 84:154 Ap 22 '66
Dance Mag il 40:24 My '66
Life 61:26 O 14 '66
Nat R 18:1062-5 O 18 '66
Nation 202:374 Mr 28 '66
New Yorker 42:160 Mr 19 '66
Newsweek 67:98 Mr 21 '66
Sat R 49:45 Mr 26 '66
Time il 87:80 Mr 18 '66
Vogue 147:145 My '66

Walking happy
Dance Mag 41:76-7 Ja '67
Nation 204:29 Ja 2 '67
Newsweek 68:100 D 12 '66
Time il 88:60 D 9 '66

Where's Charley?
Dance Mag 40:27 Jl '66
Life 60:18 Je 17 '66

MUSICAL comedy production. See Theatrical
production

MUSICAL comedy, revue, etc.
Goings on about town. See issues of New
Yorker
Look, girls, there's the man with our tap
shoes! A. Laurents. il N Y Times Mag pt2
p42-3+ S 11 '66
To the love song, with love. R. Rodgers. il
Sat Eve Post 240:36-7 Ja 28 '67
Trouble in a musical paradise; Broadway
musicals. T. Prideaux. Life 62:16 Ja 13 '67

MUSICAL composition. See Composition (music)

MUSICAL education
They shall have music; project at Horace
Mann elementary school, Bellflower, Calif.
C. L. Herbert. il Am Ed 2:22 O '66

MUSICAL festivals. See Music festivals

MUSICAL instruments
Giving the gift of music. F. Bowers. House
& Gard 130:32+ D '66
How to choose a musical instrument for your
child. Bet Hom & Gard 44:42+ Mr '66
Music goes round and round, and comes out
over yonder. A. Whitman. il Pop Mech
126:100-1 S '66
See also names of musical instruments.
e.g. Guitar

MUSICAL instruments, Electronic
Electronic soxophone debut; Varitone. il Pop
Electr 25:48 N '66
Lumemin steals the show. L. Garner. il Pop
Electr 24:56-9+ Ja '66
Switching on; Varitone, Selmer's new sax-
ophone. H. Saal. Newsweek 68:100 O 10 '66

MUSICAL instruments, Mechanical
See also
Player piano

MUSICAL literature. See Music literature

MUSICAL parody. See Parody (music)

MUSICAL prodigies. See Children as musicians

MUSICAL recitals
Death of the recital. B. Boretz. Nation 203:
125-7 Ag 8 '66
See also
Organ recitals

MUTSCHLER, Herbert F.
Library education and the talent shortage. por Library J 91:1772-3 Ap 1 '66
MUTUAL assistance, Pacts of. See International security
MUTUAL defense assistance control act. See International security
MUTUAL funds. See Investment trusts
MUTUAL induction. See Inductance
MUTUAL security act of 1951. See Military assistance, American
MUTUAL shares corporation
Thriving on rewards of patience. il Bsns W p 134+ Ag 6 '66
MUTUAL trust funds. See Investment trusts
MUYDERMAN, E. A.
Bearings; with biographical sketch. Sci Am 214:20, 60-6+ biblog(p 143) Mr '66
MUZZLE loading shotguns. See Shotguns
MWALILINO, Olive
Terrible moments. Newsweek 68:68 O 24 '66
MY brand new mother-in-law; story. See Cave, H.
MY daughter's name is Sarah; story. See Beagle, P.
MY father and the fighter; story. See Mayer, T.
MY heart belongs to: (A) (B) (C) (D) (other) story. See Bayer, A.
MY sweet Charlie; drama. See Westheimer, D.
MY young and truly love; story. See Alexander, R. W.
MYCOPLASMA. See Microorganisms, Pathogenic
MYCOTOXICOSES. See Fungi
MYCOTOXINS. See Toxins and antitoxins
MYDANS, Carl
Expedition to an idyll. Life 60:56+ F 4 '66
With mind and heart and a magic box. por Life 61:64-6+ D 23 '66
MYELOMA proteins. See Proteins
MYERS, Bernard
Art and emotion; excerpts. Design 68:35-7 N '66
Fine arts and graphic design; excerpt from Book of art. Design 68:23-6 S '66
MYERS, Bob
Atlanta 500. Motor T 18:72-4 Je '66
McQuagg firecracks his first! Motor T 18: 65-6+ S '66
Peach Blossom 500. Motor T 18:70-1 Je '66
Rebel 400! Motor T 18:44-6 Jl '66
Stock talk. Motor T 18:82+ Ap; 76+ My; 80+ Ag '66
Two big D's, Dieringer wins at Darlington's Southern 500. Motor T 18:58-9+ D '66
Virginia 500! Motor T 18:42-3 Jl '66
Who lit the fuse on Dieringer's Comet? Motor T 18:68-70 O '66
World 600! Motor T 18:60-1+ Ag '66
(ed) See Petty, R. Richard Petty tells how he stokes the stockers
MYERS, Carl E.
Aerial adventures of Carlotta, the lady aeronaut. P. R. Bassett. il Am Heritage 17: 64-7 Ag '66
MYERS, Charles A.
Behavioral sciences for personnel managers. biblog f Harvard Bsns R 44:154-6+ Jl '66
MYERS, Chauncie Kilmer, bp
Bishop for California. il por Newsweek 68: 76 S 26 '66
Successor for Pike. por Time 88:62 S 23 '66
MYERS, Dafford Wayne
It's great to be alive. R. Armstrong. il pors Sat Eve Post 239:21-6 Je 4 '66; Same abr. with title Pilot is down! Read Digest 89:42-8 Ag '66
MYERS, David H.
Notes (faster) on the way (faster) to a lemon squash (faster) Esquire 66:50 Ag '66
MYERS, Fred
Movies (cont) Christian Cent 83:655-6 My 18 '66
Pressures on students. NEA J 55:31 S '66
MYERS, Joe I.
People-to-people. Américas 18:37-8 Ja '66
MYERS, M. Scott
Conditions for manager motivation. biblog f Harvard Bsns R 44:58-71 Ja '66
—See Gomersall, E. R. jt. auth.
MYERS, Mary Breed (Hawley)
Aerial adventures of Carlotta, the lady aeronaut. P. R. Bassett. il Am Heritage 17:64-7 Ag '66
MYERSON, Alan
Improvisation bit. J. Novick. Nation 203:614-15 D 5 '66
MYNAHS
Does Petey Boy talk dirty? Smithsonian zoo's dilemma. J. Neary. il Life 60:105-6 Je 24 '66
Morals of mynahs: troubles at Washington zoo. Reporter 34:16+ My 19 '66

MYOELECTRICITY. See Electrophysiology
MYOPATHIES. See Muscles—Diseases
MYOSIN
Actin-myosin interaction: inhibition of the myosin adenosine triphosphatase by actin. S. Barron and others. biblog il Science 151: 1541-2 Mr 25 '66
Synthetic myosin filaments. B. Kaminer and A. L. Bell. biblog il Science 151:323 Ja 21 '66
MYOTONIA
Myotonic response induced by inhibitors of cholesterol biosynthesis. N. Winer and others. biblog il Science 153:312-13 Jl 15 '66
MYRDAL, Alva
Two decades in the world of social science. UNESCO Courier 19:40-4 Jl '66
MYRDAL, Gunnar
FAO: the imperative of altruism; adaptation of address. Nation 203:666-70 D 19 '66
Swedish way to happiness. N Y Times Mag p 14-15+ Ja 30 '66
World is heading for a collision; excerpt from address, November 1965. UNESCO Courier 19:21-3 F '66
MYRDAL, Jan
Mood of the writer. por Sat R 49:15-16+ Ag 13 '66
Reshaping of Chinese society. Bul Atomic Sci 22:76-9 Je '66
MYRICA pensylvanica. See Bayberry
MYRICK, Frank B.
BDSA tells trade binders about shortages. Pub W 191:99 Ja 2 '67
MYSTERY at Tumble inn; drama. See Lello, E.
MYSTERY plays. See Miracle, morality and mystery plays
MYSTERY stories. See Detective stories
MYSTERY writers of America
Contenders for MWA honors. Pub W 189:32 Ap 11 '66
MWA Edgar and Raven awards. Pub W 189: 87 Ap 25 '66
MWA elects John Creasey as president. Pub W 189:42 Mr 14 '66
MYSTIC seaport museum, Mystic, Conn.
Mystic seaport. il U S Camera 29:48-9 My '66
Whaling in Old Mystic. B Zino. il Sch Arts 65:33-5 Ap '66
MYSTICISM
Mysticism in the lab; drug-induced mysticism. il Time 88:62 S 23 '66
See also
Cabala
MYTHOLOGY
Mephistopheles and the androgyne, by M. Eliade. Review
Commonweal 84:315-16 Je 3 '66. W. Arnold
Time 87:68+ F 11 '66
Myth and literature; ed. by J. B. Vickery. Review
Sat R 49:28-9 Ag 20 '66. T. H. Gaster
MYTHS. See Mythology
MYXOBACTERIUM. See Bacteria, Pathogenic
MYXOMA, infectious
Diseased fleas brought to bug rabbits; attack on Australian rabbit problem. Sci N 90:121 Ag 20 '66
MYXOMYCETES
Anaphase delay after inhibition of protein synthesis between late prophase and prometaphase. J. E. Cummins and others. biblog il Science 154:1343-4 D 9 '66

N

NAACP. See National association for the advancement of colored people
NACS. See National association of college stores
NACSAC. See National Catholic social action conference
NAE. See National academy of engineering
NAFBRAT. See National association for better radio and television
NAHB. See National association of home builders
NALC. See Negro American labor council
NAM. See National association of manufacturers
NARCO. See United States—Public health service hospital, Lexington, Ky.
NASA. See United States—National aeronautics and space administration

NASSP. See National association of secondary-school principals
NATO. See North Atlantic treaty organization
NAVA. See National audio-visual association
NAVOCEANO. See United States naval oceanographic office, Suitland, Md.
NAWAPA. See North American water and power alliance
NBA. See National book awards
NBAA. See National business aircraft association
NBC. See National book committee
NCAA. See National collegiate athletic association
NCC. See National council of the churches of Christ in the United States of America
NCCIJ. See National Catholic conference for interracial justice
NCCW. See National council of Catholic women
NCEA. See National Catholic educational association
NCGE. See National council for geographic education
NCPT. See National congress of parents and teachers
NCSS. See National council for the social studies
NCTE. See National council of teachers of English
NCWC. See National Catholic welfare conference
NDEA (National defense education act) See Libraries and state
NDEA institutes. See Teachers institutes
NDEA institutes for school librarians. See Library institutes and workshops
NDP (National democratic party) See Political parties—Germany (Federal Republic)
NEA. See National education association
NECEC. See New England Catholic education center
NERVA (nuclear engine for rocket vehicle application) See Rockets, Atomic powered
NESA. See National electric sign association
NET. See National educational television and radio center
NFIB. See National federation of independent business
NFL. See National football league
NFW. See National farm workers association
NFWA. See National farm workers' association
NHL. See National hockey league
NICB. See National industrial conference board
NIT (negative income tax) See Economic assistance, Domestic
NLRB. See United States—National labor relations board
NLW. See National library week
NMSE. See United States—Navy department—Naval material support establishment
NODC. See United States—National oceanographic data center
NORAD. See North American air defense command
NRA. See National recreation and park association
NRECA. See National rural electric cooperative association
NRMA. See National retail merchants association
NRPA. See National recreation and park association
NSA. See United States—National security agency: United States national student association
NSBRO. See National service board for religious objectors
NSC. See United States—National security council
NSF. See United States—National science foundation
NSSFNS. See National scholarship service and fund for Negro students
NSU-Wankel engines. See Automobile engines
NTL. See National training laboratory in group development
NYCLU (New York chapter of American civil liberties union) See American civil liberties union
NYFOA. See New York forest owners association, incorporated
NYLA. See New York library association
NYPL. See New York public library
NYSE (New York stock exchange) See Stock exchange—New York (city)
NYU. See New York university

NABB, Edward H.
  Preview: inboard power for '67. Motor B 118:80-7 N '66
NABOKOV, Dmitri
  (tr) See Nabokov, V. Affair of honor
NABOKOV, Vladimir
  Affair of honor; story, tr. by D. Nabokov. New Yorker 42:37-42 S 3 '66
    about
  All about Vladimir. G. Hicks. Sat R 50:27-8 Ja 7 '67
  From rubies to Lolita. E. Weeks. Atlan 219:115-16 Ja '67
  Nabokov. P. Gilliatt. il pors Vogue 148:224-9+ D '66
  Nabokov in time. Q. Anderson. New Repub 154:23-8 Je 4 '66
  Nabokov's look back; a national loss. J. Updike. Life 62:9+ Ja 13 '67
  Nabokov's puppet show. A. Appel, jr. New Repub 156:27-30 Ja 14; 25-8+ Ja 21 '67
  Reality of the past. il por Time 89:84 Ja 20 '67
NABRIT, James M. Jr
  Security council again extends U.N. peace force in Cyprus; statement, December 17, 1965. Dept State Bul 54:210-11 F 7 '66
  U.N. assumes responsibility for South West Africa; statement, October 27, 1966. Dept State Bul 55:870-1 D 5 '66
  U.N. urges no interference with right of peoples to self-determination; statements, November 9, 30, 1966. Dept State Bul 56:29-32 Ja 2 '67
  U.S. supports U.N. membership of Botswana and Lesotho; statement, October 14, 1966. Dept State Bul 55:758-9 N 14 '66
NACO. See National association of counties
NADAR
  Nadar's pantheon. F. V. Grunfeld. il Opera N 30:28-31 F 26 '66
NADER, Claire
  Technical expert in a democracy. Bul Atomic Sci 22:28-30 My '66
NADER, Ralph
  Coming struggle for auto safety; excerpt from Unsafe at any speed. Consumer Rep 31:84-91 F '66
  Safer cars: time for decision. Consumer Rep 31:194-7 Ap '66
  Seven safety features cars need most. por Sci Digest 60:75-9 Ag '66
    about
  Accusers: Detroit botches its job. C. Welles. il Life 60:40+ Mr 25 '66
  And now, pipelines. Newsweek 68:74 Jl 11 '66
  Auto safety author spurs new congressional hearings. Pub W 189:49 Mr 21 '66
  Auto safety: Nader vs. General motors. E. Langer. por Science 152:47-50 Ap 1 '66
  Car safety: another view of science; letter. H. H. Wakeland. Science 152:452 Ap 22 '66
  Dick. J. Ridgeway. New Repub 154:11-13 Mr 12 '66
  Drive for safer cars. D. Chu. Sr Schol 89:34+ O 21 '66
  GM and harassment. L. L. L. Golden. Sat R 49:56 Ag 13 '66
  GM comes clean. J. Ridgeway. New Repub 154:8-9 Ap 2 '66
  GM hired the dick. New Repub 154:8 Mr 19 '66
  Muckraking, 1966. Nation 202:316 Mr 21 '66
  Nader caper. por Newsweek 67:83 Mr 21 '66
  Nader file; G.M. apologizes. Sr Schol 88:21-2+ Ap 15 '66
  One man who mattered. H. Brandon. Sat R 49:9-10 My 28 '66
  Private eyes and public hearings. il por Newsweek 67:77-8 Ap 4 '66
  Ralph Nader sues GM for $26 million. Pub W 190:35 N 28 '66
  Restraining the snoopers. Christian Cent 83:452-3 Ap 13 '66
  Spartan life; invasion of privacy suit. por Newsweek 68:88+ N 28 '66
  Spies who were caught cold. il por Time 87:79 Ap 1 '66
  Trade winds; question of harassment. J. G. Fuller. il Sat R 49:8+ My 14 '66
NADIEN, David
  Distinguished fraternity. il por Time 88:92+ O 21 '66
NADLER, Charles F. and Hughes, C. E.
  Chromosomal aberrations in a population of ground squirrels. bibliog Science 151:579-80 F 4 '66
NADLER, Paul S. See Furniss, J. P. jt. auth.
NAESS, Ragnar D.
  How to handle your money now; interview. por U S News 60:58-62 Ja 31 '66
NAFZIGER, Ralph H. See Speidel, D. H. jt. auth.

NAGAS. See India—Native races
NAGASAKI
Day of Trinity, by L. Lamont. Review
Bul Atomic Sci 22:35-7 F '66. B. T. Feld
NAGASAWA, Hiroshi
Trace element partition coefficient in ionic
crystals. bibliog Science 152:767-9 My 6 '66
NAGASHIMA, Shusuke
Japan's defense rests on U.S. technology.
Tech W 19:32-3 D 5 '66
Sounding rockets fundamental to Japan's
space success. Tech W 19:34+ S 12 '66
Two dress rehearsals slated before Japanese
scientific shot. Tech W 19:34-5 O 17 '66
NAGEL, Charles
National portrait gallery. Antiques 90:642-6
N '66
about
Public faces. R. Lynes. il Harper 232:26+
Je '66
NAGEL, Isabel Tellez-. See Tellez-Nagel, I.
NAGY, Sibyl Moholy-. See Moholy-Nagy, S.
NAHUEL HUAPI NATIONAL PARK. See Na-
tional parks and reserves—Argentina
NAHUMCK, Nadia Chilkovsky
Pliés please. C. Conner. il pors Am Ed 2:
28-32 Je '66
NAILS
Nailing tips to lengthen life of your new
redwood siding. il Pop Mech 126:153 D '66
NAIRN, Ronald C.
American intellectual; address, June 1, 1966.
Vital Speeches 32:667-70 Ag 15 '66
NAIROBI press institute
Toward a native press. il Time 88:46 Jl 15
'66
NAISMITH, Grace
Common sense and the femininity pill. Read
Digest 89:99-102 S '66
NAITOH, Yutaka
Reversal response elicited in nonbeating cilia
of paramecium by membrane depolariza-
tion. bibliog Science 154:660-2 N 4 '66
NAKANO, Masayasu, and Braun, Werner
Fluctuation tests with antibody-forming
spleen cell populations. bibliog Science 151:
338-40 Ja 21 '66
NAKASA, Nathaniel
Aftermath. R. Jenkins. Esquire 65:16+ Je
'66
NAKATANI, Hiroshi, and others
N-cyclohexyl linoleamide: metabolism and
cholesterol-lowering effect in rats. bibliog
Science 153:1267-9 S 9 '66
NAKEDNESS. See Nudism
NAKIAN, Reuben
I'm on the satyr's side; Museum of modern
art show. il por Newsweek 68:83 Jl 4 '66
In praise of reason. T. B. Hess. il por Art N
65:22-5+ Sum '66
Nakian: Eros and grief. H. Rosenberg. il
pors Vogue 148:64-5+ Jl '66
NAM Ngum power project. See Hydroelectric
plants
NAMATH, Joe Willie
Joe, Joe, you're the most beautiful thing
in the world! J. Skow. il pors Sat Eve
Post 239:99-103 D 3 '66
Namath the game. G. Astor. il pors Look 30:
115-18 N 29 '66
Sweet life of swinging Joe. D. Jenkins. il
pors Sports Illus 25:42-4+ O 17 '66
NAMBOODIRI Brahmans (caste) See Caste
NAME of coins. See Coins—Names
NAMES
See also
Corporations—Names
Nicknames
NAMES, Asian
Asian name game. S. Karnow. Sat R 49:84
My 7 '66
NAMES, Constellation. See Constellations—
Names
NAMES, French
Name-dropping; law changed Newsweek 67:
60 My 23 '66
NAMES, Geographical
Geographical names; provisional agenda for
the United Nations conference on the
standardization of geographical names to
be held in 1967. UN Mo Chron 3:68 My '66
NAMES, Lunar
Lunar names proposed. Sci N 90:290 O 15 '66
NAMES, Personal
History in the telephone book; surnames in
the Manhattan directory. C. M. Matthews.
il Horizon 9:105-11 Wint '67
Name-dropping; law changed in France.
Newsweek 67:60 My 23 '66
's' vonderful; concerning request to add von
to a name. New Repub 155:7 Ag 27 '66

What's in a name; legal aspects regarding
use of name same as that of a famous
person. Time 87:81-2 My 13 '66
What's in a name? names of operatic char-
acters and composers. J. W. Stedman and
G. McElroy. il Opera N 30:6-7 F 12 '66
See also
Nicknames
NAMES of boats. See Boats—Names
NAMES of plants. See Botany—Nomenclature
NANKING, China
Reporter at large. H. Koningsberger. New
Yorker 42:99-100+ Ap 30 '66
NANTUCKET ISLAND
Going places, finding things in Nantucket.
il House & Gard 129:194-9+ Ap '66
NAPA VALLEY, Calif.
Old mill and a forest park are hiding in
the Napa Valley. il Sunset 137:39 Ag '66
NAPIER, B. Davie
Faith & learning at Stanford. il por Time 88:
100 N 25 '66
NAPIER, Jeff. See Stone, R. jt. auth.
NAPLES
Music
Naples. W. Weaver. il Opera N 30:36 Ap 2
'66
Naples, Rome. F. Nuzzo. Opera N 31:32 D 31
'66
Notes from our correspondents. W. Weaver.
Hi Fi 16:12+ F '66
NAPOLEON I, emperor of the French
Austerlitz, by C. Manceron. Review
Time il por 87:108 Mr 4 '66
NAPOLEON, Dorothy
Face to face. por Seventeen 25:141 Mr '66
NAPRAVNIK, Eduard
On records; Dubrovsky. Opera N 30:34 F 26
'66
NARAHASHI, Toshio, and others
Tetrodotoxin does not block excitation from
inside the nerve membrane. bibliog Science
153:765-7 Ag 12 '66
NARCISSUS
Double daffodils. M. J. Dietz. il Flower
Grower 53:36 O '66
Three plant garden. B. Black. il Flower
Grower 53:32-3+ N '66
NARCOLEPSY
Silas Marner diagnosed; hero's ailments. Sci
N 90:410 N 12 '66
NARCOTIC addicts
Addict program launched. P. McBroom. Sci
N 90:313 O 15 '66
Boy and girl; case of C. Crenshaw and R.
Friede. il Newsweek 67:31B F 21 '66
Britain's R for our drug addicts. J. Kobler.
il Sat Eve Post 239:74-8 Ag 13 '66
Congress: a new option for addicts; a look
at LSD. J. Walsh. Science 152:1726+ Je
24 '66
Death of a hooked heiress; case of C. Cren-
shaw and R. Friede, condensation. D.
Schaap. il Look 30:19-25 Jl 26 '66
Exiles from the American dream: the junkie
and the cop. B. Jackson. Atlan 219:44-51
Ja '67
Goof-ball set: addiction in the suburbs; prob-
lem in Long Island. M. Schram. il Nation
203:242-5 S 19 '66
High inhibitor: cyclazocine. il Time 87:85
Mr 18 '66
Logistics of junk. D. Lyle. il Esquire 65:
59-67+ Mr '66
Mix-up on drugs. R. Coles. New Repub 155:
23-5 S 17 '66
New hope for drug addicts. F. R. Schreiber
and M. Herman. il Sci Digest 60:15-17 Jl
'66
No mercy, no haven for addicts. Christian
Cent 83:577 My 4 '66; Discussion. 83:865-6
Jl 6 '66
No way out? drugs and therapeutic com-
munity programs. il Newsweek 68:77-8 O 10
'66
Ours is the addicted society. L. H. Farber.
il N Y Times Mag p43+ D 11 '66; Reply.
F. A. Seixas. p 15 Ja 8 '67
Psychedelic sentence; T. F. Leary and
daughter. Newsweek 67:35 Mr 21 '66
Rockefeller and the drug plan. W. F. Buck-
ley, jr. Nat R 18:257 Mr 22 '66
Speaking out; give drugs to addicts so we
can be safe. J. J. Goldstein. il Sat Eve
Post 239:12+ Jl 30 '66
Stoned on methadone; disagreement over
Dole-Nyswander treatment; with excerpts
from interview with Synanon staff. L. Ya-
blonsky. New Repub 155:14-16 Ag 13 '66;
Discussion. 155:28-9 S 3; 37-8 S 17 '66
Today's drug addicts. Sci N 89:432 Je 4 '66
Treating addicts humanely. Christian Cent
83:131-2 F 2 '66

NARCOTIC addicts—*Continued*
  Visit to Narco; Federal addiction treatment center, Lexington, Ky. G. Samuels. il N Y Times Mag p32-3+ Ap 10 '66
NARCOTIC habit
  Answer to youthful drug addiction. C. B. Luce. McCalls 93:70+ Mr '66
  Donna and the sugar cube; increasing use of LSD. il Newsweek 67:100 Ap 18 '66
  Drugs and youth. il Sr Schol 88:4-7 Ap 29 '66
  Drugs in the Great society. P. Turkel. Cath World 203:265-9 Ag '66
  Drugs on campus: turned on & tuned out. M. B. Freedman and H. Powelson. il Nation 202:125-7 Ja 31 '66
  Drugs on the campus. R. Goldstein. il Sat Eve Post 239:40-4+ My 21; 34-8+ Je 4 '66
  Menace of drug abuse. J. L. Goddard. il Am Ed 2:4-7 My '66
  Mix-up on drugs. R. Coles. New Repub 155: 23-5 S 17 '66
  Pills, glue and kids: an American tragedy. E. Selby and A. Selby. Read Digest 88: 66-70 Je '66
  Special island; Palisades high school students and narcotics. Newsweek 67:40 Ap 11 '66
  Teen-age drinking and drug addiction. J. H. Pollack. il NEA J 55:8-12 My '66
  White-collar pill party. B. Jackson. Atlan 218:35-40 Ag '66
NARCOTIC laws
  Doctor Leary's conviction. Commonweal 84:95 Ap 15 '66
  Kick; government agencies efforts to stamp out drugs. New Repub 154:10 Ap 16 '66; Discussion. 154:33-6 Ap 30; 34-6 My 7 '66
  Pot penalties too severe. P. McBroom. Sci N 90:270 O 8 '66
NARCOTIC trade. See Narcotics, Control of
NARCOTIC traffic. See Narcotics, Control of
NARCOTICS
  Drugs: a student report. A. Lake. Seventeen 25:170-1+ S '66
  Drugs and youth. il Sr Schol 88:4-7 Ap 29 '66
    See also
  Drugs
  Marihuana
  Morphine
  Opium
  United Nations—Permanent central opium board
NARCOTICS, Control of
  Crackdown on bootleg drugs; campaign to end traffic in counterfeit drugs. T. Irwin. il Todays Health 45:18-19+ Ja '67
  Hide and seek; conflict between the Mexican government and Mexican poppy growers. il Newsweek 67:60 Mr 14 '66
  Logistics of junk. D. Lyle. il Esquire 65: 59-67+ Mr '66
  Rockefeller and the drug plan. W. F. Buckley, jr. Nat R 18:257 Mr 22 '66
  Silver snuffbox; Dr Leary & daughter Susan. Time 87:85 Mr 18 '66
  U.S. Mexico discuss illicit traffic in narcotic drugs. Dept State Bul 55:968 D 26 '66
    See also
  Narcotic addicts
NARKISSOS; ballet. See Ballets—Criticisms
NARROW gage railroads. See Railroads, Narrow gage
NASCIMENTO, Edson Arantes do. See Arantes do Nascimento, E.
NASH, Gene
  Help fight heartache. America 114:835-6 Je 11 '66
NASH, Hugh
  Let us preserve its aged grandeur. por Parks & Rec 1:497-500 Je '66
NASH, Jim
  Kansas City gets a kid to build a dream on. W. Leggett. por Sports Illus 25:60-1 Ag 29 '66
NASH, Lyman M.
  Don't laugh at hiccups! Todays Health 44: 26-7 Ag '66
NASH, Ogden
  Darkest half hour; poem. New Yorker 42:26 Ja 7 '67
  Entrapment of John Alden; or, We paint the lily, we beard Mr Longfellow; poem. Atlan 218:118 S '66
  Fables Bulfinch forgot: narcissus and the treacherous vowel; poem. Vogue 147:101 Mr 15 '66
  Ill-met by fluorescence; poem. New Yorker 42:36 F 26 '66
  Never was I born to set them right; poem. Sat R 49:4 Ap 23 '66
  Notes for the chart in 306; poem. New Yorker 42:30 Je 25 '66
  Poems. McCalls 93:96-7 S '66

Precious string of Perelman pearls. Life 61: 11 S 23 '66
  Romantic age; poem. McCalls 94:181 O '66
  Short-order cocktail, or one cook to take out; poem. Sat Eve Post 239:24 My 21 '66
  Stilly night: a soporific reflection; poem. McCalls 93:148 Je '66
  Taste buds, en garde! poem. Harper 234:95 Ja '67
  Very nice, Rembrandt, but how about a little more color? poem. Sat R 49:4 Ag 13 '66
  Visitor from Porlock; but, alas, no xanadu; poem. New Yorker 42:60 N 12 '66
  Who put that spokesman in my wheel? poem. New Repub 155:24 S 17 '66
  You are old, Father Bertrand; poem. Reporter 36:58 Ja 12 '67
NASH, Stephen, pseud.
  Speaking out. Sat Eve Post 239:10+ Mr 12 '66
NASHER, Raymond D.
  From shops to city near Dallas. il por Fortune 73:162+ Je '66
NASHVILLE, Tenn.
  Churches
  Epistle to the First Baptist churches in Nashville; invitation for Negro and white Baptists to unite. Christian Cent 83:102 Ja 26 '66
  Music
  Country music snaps its regional bounds. il Bsns W p96-8+ Mr 19 '66
  Gold guitars; country-music. il Newsweek 67:96+ Ap 4 '66
  That new sound from Nashville. C. Portis. il Sat Eve Post 239:30-4+ F 12 '66
  Street traffic
  Metro Nashville starts area-wide street-sign program. J. Chronister. il Am City 81:116+ Jl '66
NASSAU COUNTY, N.Y.
  County park system grows up. R. R. Gamble. il Parks & Rec 1:316-18 Ap '66
  Don't stop when the sun goes down; Blue golf course. C. M. Alston. il Am City 81: 114-16 My '66
  Hospitals
  From site plan to sutures: planning the computerized hospital; Public general hospital. il Arch Rec 140:199-203 O '66
NASSAU COUNTY library association
  Librarians protest new N.Y. anti-smut laws. Pub W 189:79-80 Ap 18 '66
NASSAU library system
  Sample projects, title III, ESEA; school-public library project. D. S. Lindauer. il Library J 91:1024-8 F 15 '66
NASSER, Gamal Abdel
  Anti-colonial imperialist; Tanzania visit. Newsweek 68:45 O 3 '66
  As troubles pile up for another dictator. J. Law. il por U S News 60:70-2 Je 20 '66
  Back to the balcony. Time 87:42 Mr 4 '66
  Call to Mecca; Feisal's projected Islamic summit meeting. il por Time 88:45 S 30 '66
  Classicists. Newsweek 67:48 Mr 7 '66
  How much is Nasser worth? P. Seale and I. Beeson. New Reub 154:12-13 Je 4 '66
  Leader alone. por Newsweek 68:40-1+ Ag 8 '66
  Nasser speaks out: interview; ed. by G. P. Hunt. por Life 60:70A+ Mr 11 '66
  Nasser's tightrope begins to fray. il por Bsns W p86-7+ My 21 '66
  Of life & death; sniffing out subversion. Time 88:32 S 2 '66
  Will Britain's loss be Nasser's gain? il por U S News 60:91-3 Mr 28 '66
NASTUK, William L. and Liu, J. H.
  Muscle postjunctional membrane: changes in chemosensitivity produced by calcium. bibliog Science 154:266-7 O 14 '66
NASUTION, Abdul Haris
  New men at Indonesia's helm. por Sr Schol 88:24 Ap 1 '66
  Struggle for power in Indonesia. D. Kirk. il Reporter 34:40 F 24 '66
NATALIE, Sister
  Face to face with a girl who is becoming a nun. Seventeen 25:117+ Je '66
NATANSON, Maurice
  Epistemological self. Commentary 42:100-2 N '66
NATHAN, Abie
  Flight into Egypt. il por Newsweek 67:50+ Mr 14 '66
NATHAN, Jason R.
  New York's attack on design mediocrity. E. Goble. Arch Rec 140:9 N '66

NATHAN, John
I am a garish man with garish tastes. Life 61:28-31 S 2 '66
World's most expressive puppets. N Y Times Mag p34-5+ Mr 13 '66
NATHAN, Leonard E.
In disheartening rain before the Parthenon; Annunciation; poems. Poetry 109:14-16 O '66
Like us, maybe; poem. New Repub 154:23 My 14 '66
NATHAN, Marc A. See Smith, O. A. jr, jt. auth.
NATHAN, Paul
Rights and permissions. See issues of Publishers' weekly
NATICK, Mass.
Maximum flexibility for a junior high. il Arch Rec 139:170-3 F '66
NATION, Carry Amelia (Moore)
Vessel of wrath, by R. L. Taylor. Review Sat R 49:53 D 24 '66. J. F. Fixx
NATION, J. L. and Robinson, F. A.
Gibberellic acid: effects of feeding in an artificial diet for honeybees. bibliog Science 152:1765-6 Je 24 '66
NATIONAL academy of engineering
NAE names twenty-seven members. Sci N 89:325 Ap 30 '66
NATIONAL academy of religion and mental health. See Academy of religion and mental health
NATIONAL academy of sciences
Abstracts of papers presented at meeting, 1966. Science 152:672-8; 154:417-30 Ap 29, O 21 '66
By sharing knowledge. F. Seitz. il Sat R 49:65-7 My 7 '66
Campus computers: NAS panel calls for more federal aid. L. J. Carter. Science 151:969+ F 25 '66; Discussion. 152:591, 153:814+ Ap 29, Ag 19 '66
Civil defense: notes on Project Harbor. H. Margolis. Bul Atomic Sci 22:19-21 F '66
From new NAS report: an assessment of relative strength of U.S. physics; excerpts. Science 151:1354 Mr 18 '66
National academy: annual meeting includes elections and awards. Science 152:630-1 Ap 29 '66
NAS elects members. Sci N 89:338 My 7 '66
NAS, ICSU statements on international meetings; October 1966. Science 154:369 O 21 '66
NAS report finds physics strong, but serious strains developing. J. Walsh. il Science 151:1363+ Mr 18 '66
NAS urges solar observatory work; step-up in Orbiting solar observatory and Radio astronomy explorer. H. M. David. Miss & Roc 18:15 F 7 '66
Scope of astrophysics today; excerpt from report. Sky & Tel 31:272-3 My '66
Smale aftermath: ICSU and academy urge ban on politics at meetings. D. S. Greenberg. Science 154:368-70 O 21 '66
Weather modification: panels want greater federal effort. L. J. Carter. Science 141:428-31 Ja 28 '66

Space science board
Biomedical space technology lagging. Miss & Roc 18:18 F 21 '66
NATIONAL advisory commission on libraries. See United States—National advisory commission on libraries
NATIONAL advisory council on International monetary and financial policies. See United States—National advisory council on international monetary and financial policies
NATIONAL advisory council on the arts. See United States—National council on the arts
NATIONAL aeronautic association
See also
Collier trophy
NATIONAL aeronautics and space administration. See United States—National aeronautics and space administration
NATIONAL affairs, Bureau of. See Bureau of national affairs, incorporated
NATIONAL air races. See Airplane racing
NATIONAL airport, Washington, D.C. See Washington, D.C.—Airports
NATIONAL airways corporation. See Airlines—New Zealand
NATIONAL amateur athletic union. See Amateur athletic union of the United States
NATIONAL archives. See United States—National archives
NATIONAL association for better radio and television
Children's hours; shows recommended for children. Newsweek 67:47 F 7 '66

NATIONAL association for the advancement of colored people
Now, Negro attack on black power. US News 61:14 O 24 '66
Steel giants face a blast on bias; NAACP blames USW. Bsns W p81-2 Je 11 '66
NATIONAL association of business economists
More expansion still gets majority vote; with editorial comment. il Bsns W p37-8, 196 O 1 '66
NATIONAL association of college stores
College stores meet in Chicago; annual meeting. il Pub W 189:30-43 My 16 '66
Edwin Howard elected president of NACS. Pub W 189:30 Ap 11 '66
NACS gives annual awards for merchandising programs. Pub W 189:69-70 My 16 '66
NACS panels examine problems of management; summary of discussions. il Pub W 189:51-4 My 30 '66
NACS plans three new programs for books. il Pub W 189:31-2 Ap 11 '66
NACS regional meeting stresses new image; report of Eastern regional meeting in Albany, N.Y. il Pub W 190:18-22 N 28 '66
NACS sounds an alert: order fall textbooks soon! C. B. Grannis. Pub W 189:37 My 2 '66
NACS views special problems of college store operation; summary of discussions at NACS annual meeting. il Pub W 189:42-50 My 30 '66
Pioneers and guinea pigs: NACS bookselling seminar; report. il Pub W 190:28-33 Ag 15 '66
Survey shows the larger the college store, the smaller the net profit. il Pub W 190:66-7 N 21 '66
NATIONAL association of colored women's clubs
Oldest women's organization. il Ebony 22:72-4+ N '66
NATIONAL association of counties
New look. K. B. Pomeroy. Am For 72:7 S '66
NATIONAL association of Evangelicals
See also
Evangelical foreign missions association
NATIONAL association of home builders
Homebuilding sinks to a postwar low; tight money situation. il Bsns W p46 N 26 '66
NATIONAL association of independent schools
NAIS presents books awards at annual meeting. Pub W 189:43-4 Mr 14 '66
NATIONAL association of manufacturers
Big business do-gooders: private war on poverty. T. G. Harris. il Look 30:15-19 Ag 9 '66
NAM is playing by a new set of rules. il Bsns W p 114-16+ D 17 '66
U.S. firms promised gains by establishing branches abroad. W. S. Beller. Tech W 19:17-18 O 17 '66
NATIONAL association of photo-lithographers
800 attend 34th NAPL convention award. Pub W 190:118-19 N 7 '66
NATIONAL association of rocketry
Birds in the hand. il Time 88:49 Ag 26 '66
NATIONAL association of secondary-school principals
Meeting, 1966. Sr Schol 88:sup2 F 25 '66
NATIONAL association of teachers in colored schools. See American teachers association
NATIONAL audio-visual association
Washington report; 27th annual convention and exhibit. J. Lloyd. Sr Schol 89:sup 18 S 23 '66
NATIONAL Audubon society
Convention views our environment; with excerpts from address. J. Vosburgh. il Audubon Mag 68:42-6 Ja '66
Reporter at large; wild and captive whooping cranes. F. McNulty. il New Yorker 42:31-6+ Ag 6 '66
See also
Audubon nature centers
NATIONAL automation commission. See United States—National commission on technology, automation, and economic progress
NATIONAL automobile dealers association
Putting the chips on '66. il Bsns W p27-8 Ja 22 '66
NATIONAL ballet
Coppélius in the capital. F. Merkling. il Opera N 30:16 Ja 29 '66
National ballet, Brooklyn academy of music. M. Marks. Dance Mag 40:75 Ap '66
NATIONAL banks. See Banks and banking—United States
NATIONAL baseball hall of fame and museum
Casey and Ted. Sports Illus 25:9 Ag 8 '66

NATIONAL basketball association
Lame and the fat; hectic race for first-place honors in the Eastern division. Newsweek 67:83 F 28 '66
NATIONAL better business bureaus. See Better business bureaus
NATIONAL boat show. See Boats—Exhibitions
NATIONAL book awards
Annual book awards. J. Foster. Sr Schol 88: sup 12 Ap 15 '66
Does the bookstore benefit from national book events? Pub W 189:74-5 My 23 '66
Early leaders reported in 1966 NBA race. Pub W 189:73 Ja 31 '66
Four authors are given National book awards. il Pub W 189:47-8 Mr 21 '66
Judges announced for 18th annual National book awards. Pub W 190:33-4 N 28 '66
Judges announced for 1967 National book awards. il Library J 92:119 Ja 1 '67
National book award judges name twenty-nine leading contenders. Library J 91:910 F 15 '66; Same. Wilson Lib Bul 40:647 Mr '66
National book awards. Wilson Lib Bul 40: 688 Ap '66; Same. il Library J 91:1874-5 Ap 1 '66
NBA 1966; awards. il Newsweek 67:105-6 Mr 28 '66
1966 NBA awards: ceremonies at Philharmonic Hall; symposium. il Pub W 189:28-35 Mr 28 '66
NATIONAL book committee
National book committee elects officers for 1967. Library J 92:42-3 Ja 1 '67
National book committee, Ford foundation bring books to VISTA, other programs. Library J 91:5721+ N 15 '66
NBC's twelfth annual meeting. Wilson Lib Bul 41:458+ Ja '67
Nichols named chairman of Nat'l book committee. Pub W 190:29 D 12 '66
Two anti-poverty book projects undertaken. Pub W 190:40-1 Ag 15 '66
See also
National medal for literature
NATIONAL budget. See Budget—United States
NATIONAL bureau of economic research
Inflation isn't easy to measure; BLS chief urges five-year study. il Bsns W p54+ Je 4 '66
Watching the way a giant grows. US economic growth; with charts. Bsns W p86-8+ O 15 '66
NATIONAL bureau of standards. See United States—Standards, National bureau of
NATIONAL business aircraft association
NBAA meeting focuses on management problems. Aviation W 85:89+ O 10 '66
Traffic pattern; NBAA eye-opener. il Flying 79:14 D '66
NATIONAL business conference, New York. See Business conferences
NATIONAL cash register company
Machine that kept them honest. G. Carson. il Am Heritage 17:50-9+ Ag '66
Sears catalogue in postcard size? Bsns W p48 D 3 '66
NATIONAL cathedral. See Washington, D.C.—Churches
NATIONAL Catholic conference for interracial justice
Project equality. W. G. Pippert. Christian Cent 83:723+ Je 1 '66
NATIONAL Catholic educational association
Meeting, 1966. il Sr Schol 88:sup 1-2 My 6 '66
Washington report; meeting. J. Lloyd. Sr Schol 88:sup4 My 6 '66
NATIONAL Catholic office for motion pictures
Catholic film awards. America 114:247 F 19 '66
Church's word to the film industry. M. Boyd. Christian Cent 83:305-6 Mr 9 '66
Fear, games and Virginia Woolf; criteria for judging films. G. Wead. America 115:325-9 S 24 '66
Films; questioning the rating of Loves of a blonde. M. Walsh. America 115:812-13 D 17 '66
NATIONAL Catholic social action conference
Gap between religion and life. America 115: 243 S 10 '66
NATIONAL Catholic welfare conference
Another plus for CRS; problem of getting food to starving India. America 116:33 Ja 14 '67
NCWC: new life and vigor; meeting of Catholic bishops in Washington. America 115:643 N 19 '66

Refugee is still with us. America 115:198 Ag 27 '66
Statement for Labor day, 1966; plea for social awareness by Social action department, NCWC. America 115:220 S 3 '66
NATIONAL cemeteries
United States
Gravedoggle: veterans' battle for expansion of national cemeteries, for all veterans and their families. E. Drew. New Repub 155:6-7 N 26 '66
See also
Arlington, Va.—National cemetery
NATIONAL center for school and college television
Center for ITV. E. Cohen. il Am Ed 2:22-4 Je '66
NATIONAL championship air races. See Airplane racing
NATIONAL childrens book week. See Book week
NATIONAL cleanest town achievement contest
Awards spark clean-up campaign. il Am City 81:92-4 Je '66
NATIONAL collegiate athletic association
Eeny, meeny, miney, mo. . . college basketball NCAA tournament. F. Deford. il Sports Illus 24:32-4+ Mr 14 '66
In and out; USC declared ineligible for the Rose bowl. Sports Illus 25:11 D 12 '66
It's one point six pick up sticks; NCAA vs Ivy League, controversy over academic standards of athletes. D. Jenkins. Sports Illus 24:30-1 Mr 21 '66
N.C.A.A. go home; Ivy defection. Time 87: 72 Mr 18 '66
Sad music from a Stradivarius; T. Smith in NCAA track and field championships. G. S. Brown. il Sports Illus 24:64-5 Je 27 '66
NATIONAL collegiate basketball championship. See Basketball tournaments
NATIONAL commission on food marketing. See United States—National commission on food marketing
NATIONAL commission on technology, automation, and economic progress. See United States—National commission on technology, automation, and economic progress
NATIONAL committee for a sane nuclear policy
As SANE goes marching on. Nat R 18:504+ My 31 '66
NATIONAL company of the Metropolitan opera. See Metropolitan opera national company
NATIONAL computer center, Martinsburg, W. Va. See United States—Internal revenue service
NATIONAL conference of Catholic bishops
Bishops meet. Commonweal 85:245-6 D 2 '66
Bishops request change in mass; change in the abstinence laws and add a plea for peace. America 115:727-8 D 3 '66
Democracy for bishops; meeting of U.S. Roman Catholic bishops. il Time 88:98 N 25 '66
Did the bishops blunder? condemnation of government's welfare and foreign aid programs. Christian Cent 83:1464 N 30 '66
News and views. J. Leo. Commonweal 85:244 D 2 '66
They step out into space. America 115:675 N 26 '66
To the bishops; annual meeting scheduled. J. O'Gara. Commonweal 85:96 O 28 '66
Tree grows in Washington. T. N. Davis. America 115:732 D 3 '66
Voice of the bishops; national conference of bishops to reform the American church. il Newsweek 68:94-5 N 28 '66
NATIONAL conference on air pollution
Air pollution crisis demands new R&D. Tech W 19:44 D 19 '66
NATIONAL conference on library statistics. See Libraries—Statistics
NATIONAL conference on outdoor recreation
Sea of troubles; report on the third conference. K. B. Pomeroy. Am For 72:34+ D '66
NATIONAL congress for recreation and parks. See Congress for recreation and parks
NATIONAL congress of parents and teachers
Forecast for '67. J. Moorhead. PTA Mag 61:2-3 Ja '67
PTA in Washington. C. Ryan. PTA Mag 61: 29-30 O '66
Resolutions adopted at the 1966 convention. PTA Mag 61:2+ S '66
NATIONAL conventions (political)
Our national nominating conventions are a disgrace. D. D. Eisenhower. il Read Digest 89:76-80 Jl '66

NATIONAL council for geographic education
Meeting, 1966. Sr Schol 89:sup5-6+ D 9 '66
Preview: Thanksgiving convention. Sr Schol 89:sup4+ N 18 '66
NATIONAL council for the social studies
Meeting, 1965 Sr Schol 87:sup9-10 Ja 7 '66
Meeting, 1966. Sr Schol 89:sup2-3+ D 9 '66; sup 18+ Ja 6 '67
Preview: Thanksgiving convention. Sr Schol 89:sup2+ N 18 '66
NATIONAL council of Catholic women
NCCW's new Pentecost; convention at Miami Beach, October 5-8, 1966. America 115:370 O 1 '66
NATIONAL council of churches. See National council of the churches of Christ in the United States of America
NATIONAL council of independent schools. See National association of independent schools
NATIONAL council of Negro women
Three-horned dilemma facing Negro women; ed. by J. L. Noble. L. Horne. il Ebony 21:118-22+ Ag '66
NATIONAL council of senior citizens
Let's stop exploiting people over sixty-five! K. O. Gilmore. Read Digest 89:229-30+ S '66
NATIONAL council of state garden clubs, incorporated
Improving the garden club's image. D. P. Watson. il Horticulture 44:14-15 D '66
NATIONAL council of teachers of English
CBC-NCTE to cooperate in teacher training. Pub W 190:53 O 3 '66
Meeting, 1965 (cont) Sr Schol 87:sup 10 Ja 7 '66
Meeting, 1966. Sr Schol 89:sup4+ D 9 '66; sup21-2 Ja 6 '67
National study of high school English programs. J. R. Squire. il Sr Schol 88:sup 16-17 F 11 '66
Preview: Thanksgiving convention. Sr Schol 89:sup2+ N 18 '66
What's happening in English; new NCTE publications. H. R. Finch. Sr Schol 88:sup 10 F 11; 89:sup43 S 23 '66
NATIONAL council of the churches of Christ in the United States of America
Courtship in Miami; seventh General assembly. Newsweek 68:70 D 19 '66
Curbing the Delta ministry. Time 87:84 Je 10 '66
Delta data. Christian Cent 83:325 Mr 16 '66
Delta ministry approved. Christian Cent 83:794 Je 22 '66
Evangelism & involvement; triennial assembly. Time 88:63+ D 16 '66
N.C.C. general board takes peace-oriented action. Christian Cent 83:293 Mr 9 '66
N.C.C. holding operation; seventh triennial General assembly. K. Haselden. Christian Cent 83:1562-4 D 21 '66; Discussion. 84:81 Ja 18 '67
Of many things; meeting in Miami Beach. T. N. Davis. America 115:816 D 24 '66
Priority program on peace? of NCC. P. Peachey. Christian Cent 83:959-61 Ag 3 '66
Proof and Daniel Poling: NCC research specialists analyze D. Poling's poll of ministerial opinion. L. Whitman and G. Trimble. Christian Cent 83:1350+ N 2 '66
Rigging the consensus; NCC in favor of admission of Communist China to United Nations. Christian Cent 83:768, 1200-1 Je 15, O 5 '66
That the world may know . . . seventh triennial General assembly. Christian Cent 83:1466 N 30 '66
See also
North American conference on church and family

Broadcasting and film commission
Church's word to the film industry. M. Boyd. Christian Cent 83:305-6 Mr 9 '66
NATIONAL council on marine resources and engineering development. See United States—National council on marine resources and engineering development
NATIONAL council on the arts. See United States—National council on the arts
NATIONAL crime commission. See United States—National crime commission
NATIONAL dairy products corporation

Sealtest foods division
Ja, das ist ein Sealtest; Austria. il Newsweek 68:100-1 D 19 '66
NATIONAL dance teachers guild
Is this the time? convention at New York's 92nd st. YM-YWHA. S. J. Cohen. il Dance Mag 40:26-7 F '66

NATIONAL debt (United States) See Debts, Public—United States
NATIONAL defense
See also
Civil defense
Preparedness, Military
United States—Defenses
NATIONAL defense education act. See Libraries and state
NATIONAL democratic party. See Political parties—Germany (Federal Republic)
NATIONAL early American glass club
Early American glass club program. Hobbies 71:96 N '66
NATIONAL earthquake information center. See United States—Environmental science services administration
NATIONAL education association
Are teachers workers? R. D. Batchelder's polemic against the AFT. New Repub 154:7 F 19 '66; Discussion. 154:36 Mr 12 '66
Conflict issues in negotiations; excerpt from address. W. A. Wildman. Mo Labor R 89:617-20 Je '66
Editor interviews; ed. by M. S. Fenner. I. Applegate. NEA J 55:81-2 O '66
Focus on bargaining/negotiating. Sr Schol 89:sup2 D 2 '66
Look between the covers; NEA publications. il NEA J 55:47-54 N '66
Meet the candidates, 1966. il NEA J 55:50 My '66
NEA-ATA unification. W. N. Ridley. il NEA J 55:49-50 S '66
NEA lists 1,600 teachers to ease teacher shortage. il Sch & Soc 94:439-41 D 10 '66
NEA relationships. J. H. Starie. NEA J 56:55 Ja '67
NEA's panic button; reply. C. Cogen. Nation 202:inside cover F 14 '66
NEA's role in the improvement of instruction. NEA J 56:17-20 Ja '67
Proposed amendments to NEA bylaws and rules. NEA J 55:46+ Ap '66
Rains came; Miami convention; NEA state affiliates integration issues. J. M. Russin. il Newsweek 68:82-3 Jl 11 '66
Resolutions, 1966. il NEA J 55:46-8 S '66
Response from the NEA. A. W. Wolpert. Mo Labor R 89:621-2 Je '66
Signs of a maturing profession. S. M. Lambert. NEA J 55:52-5 D '66
Study plus action; NEA development project. S. Jacobson. NEA J 55:41-2+ N '66
Summary financial report to members. il NEA J 55:61 O '66
Teachers choose the NEA; representation elections. D. Dashiell. il NEA J 55:43 S '66
Unionism versus professionalism in teaching. R. D. Batchelder. NEA J 55:18-20 Ap '66
What is the professional services campaign? A. M. West. il NEA J 55:27-8 F '66
See also
American association of school administrators

Meeting, 1966
Convention by the sea; Miami Beach, host: Capsule convention program and list of hotels with rates. il NEA J 55:10-11 F '66
Convention roundup. Sr Schol 89:sup2-3 S 16 '66
Message to Miami Beach convention delegates. R. D. Batchelder. il NEA J 55:32-3 My '66
Three R's=billions; Miami convention. il Newsweek 68:72-4 Jl 11 '66

Department of elementary school principals
DESP convention; report. Sr Schol 88sup6 Ap 15 '66
NATIONAL education week. See American education week
NATIONAL educational television and radio center
Fast relief; give consumer a fair look at what he is spending his money on. Newsweek 67:94+ Ap 4 '66
Net gains. il Newsweek 67:47 F 7 '66
ST interview; ed. by P. Dilts. J. F. White. Sr Schol 88:sup 14 F 18 '66
NATIONAL electric sign association
You have a cluttered mess; NESA meeting. il Time 87:82 Mr 25 '66
NATIONAL emergency committee of clergy concerned about Vietnam
Clergy concerned about Vietnam; with list of members. Christian Cent 83:99-100 Ja 26 '66
On the antiwar front. Christian Cent 83:132 F 2 '66

NATIONAL endowment for the humanities. See National foundation for the arts and humanities

NATIONAL environmental satellite center. See United States—Environmental science services administration

NATIONAL faith and order colloquium. See Ecumenical movement

NATIONAL farm workers association
Farm union reaps first California victory; recognition by Schenley and Christian brothers vineyards. il Bsns W p 158+ Ap 16 '66

Farm vote; vote on union to represent them in California. il Newsweek 68:83 S 12 '66

Grape strike. J. L. Vizzard. Commonweal 84: 295-6 My 27 '66

Labor comes to life in the grape fields. New Repub 154:6-7 Ap 23 '66

March of migrants. il Life 60:93-4 Ap 29 '66

Monopoly in the vineyards; grapes of wrath strike; loss of anti-poverty grant. J. P. Degnan. Nation 202:151-4 F 7 '66

Schenley surrenders; migrant workers vs California grape growers. Christian Cent 823:315-16 Ap 27 '66

Victory at Delano. America 114:579 Ap 23 '66

Viva la huelga! T. N. Davis. America 114: 589-90 Ap 23 '66

Viva la huelga! Schenley corp. recognizes NFWA as sole bargaining agent. il Newsweek 67:42+ Ap 18 '66

NATIONAL farmers' union. See Farmers' educational and cooperative union of America

NATIONAL federation of independent business
Sargent Shriver remains unimpressed. Nat R 18:452+ My 17 '66

NATIONAL football league
After Foss: a hotter pro war. E. Shrake. Sports Illus 24:44-5 Ap 18 '66

Big dollar in pro football. E. Selby. il Read Digest 89:111-15 N '66

Calling the NFL's biggest plays; Commissioner Rozelle. il Bsns W p72-6 O 29 '66

Here's how it happened; ed. by T. Maule. T. Schramm. il Sports Illus 24:14-19 Je 20 '66

Merger that ends an expensive rivalry. U S News 60:10 Je 20 '66

Quid pro quo. Newsweek 67:61-2 Je 20 '66

Seven times four equals one. Time 87:68 Je 17 '66

Super bowl's superman. P. O'Neill. il Life 62: 75-6+ Ja 13 '67

Superend. Sports Illus 26:5 Ja 9 '67

NATIONAL foreign policy conference for educators, Washington, D.C.
National foreign policy conference for educators; Washington, D.C. June 16-17, 1966; with introd. by R. I. Phillips; symposium. Dept State Bul 55:71-109 Jl 18 '66

NATIONAL forest service. See United States—Forest service

NATIONAL forests
Ancient bristlecone pine forest; Inyo national forest. R. W. Cermak. il Nat Parks Mag 40:4-8 Jl '66

Attractions for vacationers in national forests. il Good H 162:177 Je '66

Friendly debate between two professionals; how much land for national forest recreation? letters. C. Granger; B. L. Orell. Am For 72:30-1+ Ja; 12+ F '66

Into Puerto Rico's rain forest; Caribbean national forest. il Sunset 137:55-6 S '66

Mike Frome. M. Frome. Am For 72:3+ O '66

Page Teddy Roosevelt or, here we go again; bad features of Senator Moss's bill. C. H. Reidel. il Outdoor Life 137:4+ F '66

Preserving a forest for recreation. R. C. Byrd. il Am For 72:18-20 S '66

Self-reliant forest; Green Mountain national forest. C. E. Randall. il Am For 72:4-7+ Ja '66

Sierra lakes for early fishing; Eldorado national forest, Calif. il Sunset 136:45 Je '66

Spruce Knob-Seneca Rocks national recreation area; in Monongahela national forest of West Virginia. R. C. Byrd. il Nat Parks Mag 40:8-10 D '66

Stanislaus. C. E. Randall. il Am For 72: 38-41+ Ag; 30-2+ S '66
See also
National parks and reserves—United States

NATIONAL foundation for the arts and humanities
Educational TV; NSF and arts foundation speak out. L. J. Carter. Science 154:1309-10 D 9 '66

First humanities grant; MLA receives $300,000; fund allocated to Center for editions of American authors. Pub W 190: 39-40 Ag 8 '66

Government and the arts: how much to whom? il Newsweek 68:56-60 Jl 18 '66

Humanities grant to American historical assn. Pub W 190:54 O 3 '66

Schism in American scholarship; address, November 6, 1965. J. Higham. bibliog f Am Hist R 72:1-21 O '66

Sciences, the humanities, and the federal government. G. T. Seaborg. il Am Ed 2: 8-11 S '66

Taxpayer as a patron. Sci Am 215:102 S '66

NATIONAL gallery of art, Washington, D.C.
Amateurs, Frakturs and elegant young ladies; Garbisch collection of American watercolors and pastels at the National gallery, Washington, D.C. W. P. Campbell. il Art N 65:50-3+ O '66

Celebration of masterpieces; three of the paintings lent to the National gallery of art by Mr and Mrs P. Mellon and Mrs M. Bruce. J. Walker. il Vogue 147:94-5 Mr 15 '66

Family reunion; French paintings from collections of Andrew Mellon's children. il Newsweek 67:99-100 Mr 21 '66

Four miracles, and a masterpiece; how the National gallery came into being. J. A. Michener. il Read Digest 89:158-65 N '66

French paintings from the collection of Mrs Mellon Bruce and Mr and Mrs Paul Mellon; twenty-fifth anniversary. D. Farr. il Antiques 89:556-63 Ap '66

Garden party at the National; loans of Paul Mellon's and Mrs Ailsa Mellon Bruce. il Time 87:66-9 Mr 25 '66

Glory that was France; paintings loaned by Mrs Mellon Bruce and Mr and Mrs Paul Mellon for 25th anniversary. R. Goldwater. il Art N 65:40-2+ Mr '66

Golden loans for a silver anniversary; French impressionist and post-impressionist works lent by Andrew Mellon's children. K. Kuh. il Sat R 49:45-51 Mr 19 '66

National gallery of art USA 1966; recipients of awards for distinguished service to education in art. J. W. Cataldo. il Sch Arts 65:2-3 Je '66

National gallery; preview of an anniversary exhibition; Mellons' collections. A. Saarinen. il McCalls 93:93-103+ Ap '66

National gallery turns twenty-five; Paul Mellon and Mrs Mellon Bruce collections. F. Getlein. New Repub 154:34-5 Ap 2 '66

Our American Louvre; Andrew W. Mellon collection. E. T. Folliard. America 114:544 Ap 16 '66

Pageant of painting from the National gallery of art, ed. by H. Cairns and J. Walker. Review
Life 61:22 S 23 '66. E. Stevens

Parnassus on Potomac; 25th anniversary. W. Walton. il Art N 65:36-9+ Mr '66

Rare twosome; gifts of works by Vermeer and Rogier van der Weyden. il Time 87: 88-9 My 20 '66

Throwing a party; twenty-fifth anniversary exhibits lent by Andrew Mellon's children. H. Brandon. Sat R 49:18+ Mr 19 '66

Uncle Sam and the arts. il Sr Schol 88: 2-3 Mr 11 '66

Vermeer painting; A lady writing, given to National gallery. il Am Artist 30:6 S '66

NATIONAL geographic atlas of the world. See Atlases

NATIONAL geographic magazine
To Gilbert Grosvenor; monthly monument twenty-five miles high. F. G. Vosburgh. il Nat Geog Mag 130:445-87 O '66

NATIONAL geographic society
Special publications. M. B. Grosvenor. il Nat Geog Mag 129:408-17 Mr '66

NATIONAL goals. See United States

NATIONAL guard (United States) See United States—National guard

NATIONAL health foundation
Amazing facts about a crusade that can hurt your health. R. L. Smith. il Todays Health 44:30-5+ O '66

NATIONAL health service (Great Britain) See Great Britain—National health service

NATIONAL heart institute. See United States—National heart institute

NATIONAL hockey league
Cold cash; expansion teams. Newsweek 67: 88+ F 21 '66

Habs hold a torch bien haut; Montreal Canadiens win their 13th Stanley cup. M. Kane. il Sports Illus 24:38-40+ My 16 '66

NATIONAL hockey league—*Continued*
High price for fresh northern ice; B. Orr, NHL's most ballyhooed and highest-paid rookie. F. Deford. il Sports Illus 25:60-2 O 17 '66
Mayhem on ice; Canada's specialty. D. Mac-Donald. il Read Digest 88:17-18+ Mr '66
NATIONAL horse show. See Horse shows
NATIONAL hot rod association
NHRA Winternationals; Pomona, Calif, February 18:20, 1966. S. Kelly. il Motor T 18:53 My '66
National scene. See issues of Hot rod
NATIONAL housewares manufacturers association
Design winners. il House & Gard 130:62 N '66
NATIONAL humane center. See Humane society of the United States
NATIONAL humanities endowment fund. See National foundation for the arts and humanities
NATIONAL industrial conference board
Business sees a new role for itself. Bsns W p 164 Ap 30 '66
More moms on payroll; highlights of NICB study. Bsns W p59 D 31 '66
NICB steps into the limelight; convocation in New York to examine The future of capitalism. il Bsns W p54-5 S 24 '66
New look at investments abroad; NICB survey of investment policies of leading U.S. companies. il Bsns W p92-4+ Mr 26 '66
Overseas pilot without a chart; E. B. Lovell's study of Changing role of the international executive. Bsns W p 185-6+ S 24 '66
Playing a civic role; NICB survey. il Bsns W p 100+ Ap 30 '66
'67: what kind of a year; forecast by twelve top economists; symposium. il U S News 62:72-9 Ja 9 '67
Where is it going? 50th anniversary convocation. il Newsweek 68:80-1 O 3 '66
NATIONAL institute of mental health. See United States—National institute of mental health
NATIONAL institutes of health. See United States—National institutes of health
NATIONAL inter-religious conference on peace. See Peace conferences
NATIONAL inventors council. See United States—National inventors council
NATIONAL key deer refuge. See Wildlife sanctuaries
NATIONAL labor relations board. See United States—National labor relations board
NATIONAL league of women voters. See League of women voters of the United States
NATIONAL library week
Does the bookstore benefit from national book events? Pub W 189:74-5 My 23 '66
Events highlight nationwide library week observance. Pub W 189:85-7 Ap 25 '66
Johnson message on libraries begins National library week. Library J 91:2442 My 15 '66
NLW and the cult of reading. J. Shera Wilson Lib Bul 40:767 Ap '66
NLW: British style. G. R. Davies. Library J 91:2435-6 My 15 '66
Out of the ivory tower into the grease pit; Ossining, N.Y, public library. E. Sclar. il Library J 91:2162-4+ Ap 15 '66
Rising tide on the continental (book) shelf. Sr Schol 88:28 Ap 15 '66
Slogans announced for tenth library week. Pub W 190:29 D 12 '66
NATIONAL lotteries. See Lotteries
NATIONAL manufacturers association. See National association of manufacturers
NATIONAL maritime day
National maritime day, 1966; proclamation. L. B. Johnson. Dept State Bul 54:619 Ap 18 '66
NATIONAL medal for literature
Edmund Wilson. Nation 202:733 Je 20 '66
Edmund Wilson wins National literature medal. Pub W 189:188-9 Je 6 '66
NATIONAL medal of science
Eleven scientists honored. Sci N 91:43 Ja 14 '67
President presents Medal of science awards; remarks, February 10, 1966. L. B. Johnson. Science 151:804 F 18 '66
NATIONAL mediation board. See United States—National mediation board
NATIONAL minorities. See Minorities
NATIONAL monuments
Humans, plants and animals in Florida's Fahkahatchee Strand. M. A. Finn. il Nat Parks Mag 40:13 Jl '66
Islandia proposal. Nat Parks Mag 40:22 Ap '66

Keeping Islandia isolated. R. H. Boyle. il Sports Illus 25:80+ O 17 '66
Mountain of the stone fishes; Fossil Butte in Wyoming. G. F. Stucker. il Nat Parks Mag 40:4-9 S '66
Wealth of Jersey's Barrens. J. T. Cunningham. il Audubon Mag 68:250-8 Jl '66
See also names of national monuments, e.g. Craters of the Moon National Monument
NATIONAL morale. See Morale, National
NATIONAL municipal league
See also
All-America cities
NATIONAL museum of anthropology, Mexico city. See Mexico (city)—Galleries and museums
NATIONAL music league
Mephisto's musings. Hi Fi 16:MA2+ Jl '66
NATIONAL oceanographic council (proposed) See United States—National oceanographic council (proposed)
NATIONAL oceanographic data center. See United States—National oceanographic data center
NATIONAL organization of mothers of twins clubs. See Twins
NATIONAL outdoor leadership school. See Physical education and training
NATIONAL park rangers. See United States—National park service
NATIONAL park service. See United States—National park service
NATIONAL parks and reserves

Maps

New guide to your vacationlands. H. E. Paine. il Nat Geog Mag 130:94-7, sup(folded map) Jl '66

Roads

Beauty or the bulldozer? issues involving Great Smoky Mountains National Park and Blue Ridge Parkway. M. Frome. il Am For 72:6-9+ F '66; Discussion. 72:2-3 Ap '66
Cross-country vehicle restriction; traffic prohibited in Sequoia and Inyo national forests, Calif. Liv Wildn 30:31 Sum '66
Detour for park roads? Nat Parks Mag 40:22 S '66
Great Smokies park and the wilderness act. il Liv Wildn 29:20-4 Aut '65
Is the National park service obliged to complete the north shore road? letter to George Marshall, March 31, 1966. R. W. Jasperson. il Liv Wildn 30:31-5 Spr '66
Mike Frome: hearings on road plan for the Smokies. M. Frome. Am For 72:5+ Ag '66
Trail and campfire country: an editorial. A. W. Smith. Nat Parks Mag 40:2 S '66
What alternate proposal? highway through Smokies; letter to the editor. E. T. Scoyen. Am For 72:4-5+ Ag '66; Reply. E. M. Dickerman. 72:5 N '66

Argentina

Nahuel Huapi, Tiger Island of Argentina; Nahuel Huapi National Park. E. J. Wilhelm, jr. il Nat Parks Mag 40:14-17 Mr '66

Bahama Islands

New park safeguards flamingos. C. W. Buchheister. il Audubon Mag 68:72 Mr '66

Canada
See also
Algonquin Provincial Park

Florida
See also
Everglades National Park

Germany (Federal Republic)

Mike Frome; Luneberger Heide. M. Frome. Am For 72:6+ Mr '66

New Zealand

Hiking out from the Hermitage; Mount Cook National Park. il Sunset 137:53-4 N '66

South Africa
See also
Kruger National Park

Tanganyika

Animals running free; two weeks in the Serengeti. M. Gellhorn. il Atlan 217:70-6 F '66

Tanzania

Reporter at large: Serengeti and Ngorongoro Crater reserve. A. Moorehead. New Yorker 42:154+ O 29 '66

NATIONAL parks and reserves—*Continued*

United States

Airports in parks. P. M. Tilden. Nat Parks Mag 40:2 My '66

At last a Redwood National Park is in the making. What sort of park will it be? il Sunset 136:44-6+ Mr '66

Conservation docket. See issues of National parks magazine

Economics of Redwood Park. Nat Parks Mag 40:2 F '66

End in sight to the battle over America's giant redwoods? il U S News 60:116+ Je 13 '66

Experts look at water in the national parks; U.S. geological survey. W. J. Shneider. il Nat Parks Mag 40:20-1 Ag '66

Fifty years of housekeeping; maintenance of national parks. R. K. Olsen. il Parks & Rec 1:648-50 Ag '66

Firm for Redwoods park. Am For 71:11 O '65

For your best vacation ever. R. Charles. il Parents Mag 41:82-7+ Mr '66

Formula for mediocrity; proposed Great Basin National Park. V. L. Fischer. il Am For 72:16-17+ Ja '66

Frontierland frolic. L. M. Rhodes. il Travel 125:47-9 Ap '66

Great redwoods controversy. P. Friggens. Read Digest 89:91-6 D '66

Guarding our outdoor heritage; ninety-first annual meeting of the American forestry association. J. B. Craig. il Am For 72:14-17+ D '66

How many new parks this year? objectives for '66. C. H. Callison. Audubon Mag 68:93 Mr '66

Hunting in parks. P. M. Tilden. Nat Parks Mag 40:2 My '66

Improvement or impairment; editorial. Am For 72:9 Ag '66

Joint study team submits its report on the North Cascades; recommendations presented by Park service and Forest service representatives. il Nat Parks Mag 40:20 Mr '66

Look at the North Cascades. J. B. Craig. il Am For 72:12-15+ Mr '66

National parks and the ecology of beauty. D. Goldman. il Am For 72:18-21+ N '66

One man's view; letter to President Johnson outlining views on redwoods in California. L. S. Rockefeller. Am For 72:6-7 Je '66

Our new parklands. C. H. Callison. il Audubon Mag 68:462-3 N '66

Over the years with Great Basin Park. D. Lambert. bibliog f il Nat Parks Mag 40:12-16 Je '66

Park and site proposals. Nat Parks Mag 40:20 D '66

Park for the North Cascades? meeting the test of national park eligibility. C. F. Brockman. il Am For 72:8-11+ S '66

Parks, or more people? W. H. Draper, jr. il Nat Parks Mag 40:10-13 Ap '66

Parkscape U.S.A. G. B. Hartzog, jr. il Nat Geog Mag 130:48-93 Jl '66

Progress in the redwoods. C. W. Buchheister. il Audubon Mag 68:140 My '66

Quickening tick of the conservation clock. J. B. Craig. il Am For 72:10-13+ N '66

Race for (recreation) space. il Newsweek 67:99-100 Je 20 '66

Raising the sights for the redwoods; address, August 17, 1966. A. W. Smith. il Nat Parks Mag 40:17-19 N '66

Redwood Park hearing. Nat Parks Mag 40:20 O '66

Redwood Park proposals. Natur Hist 75:4 Je '66

Redwood pot begins to boil. J. B. Craig. il Am For 72:38-9+ Ja '66; Reply. D. E. Osgood. 72:4 Ap '66

Reformation of Old Red. F. E. Dominy. il Parks & Rec 1:314-15+ Ap '66

Report of president and general counsel to the general membership of National parks association, May 19, 1966. A. W. Smith. Nat Parks Mag 40:I-IV My '66

Rush hour in the wilderness. il Time 88:60 Jl 22 '66

See our district national parks! il Parks & Rec 1:634-5+ Ag '66

Sonoran Desert National Park; proposal to combine Organ Pipe Cactus National Monument and the Cabeza Prieta game range. W. F. Heald. il Nat Parks Mag 40:4-9 Ap '66

Southwestern side trips. T. B. Lesure. il Travel 126:28-32+ S '66

Spirit of the mountain. S. A. Cain. il Américas 18:1-8 Mr '66

Teen travel talk; parks are part of the fun: Arista student travel association. il Seventeen 25:73-4 My '66

Telling the park story; interpretation program. H. Wharton. il Parks & Rec 1:622-4+ Ag '66

To protect parks from people. C. W. Buchheister. Audubon Mag 68:392 N '66

Today and tomorrow in our national parks. M. B. Grosvenor. il Nat Geog Mag 130:1-5 Jl '66

Trees don't vote; President's special conservation message to Congress. Newsweek 67:26 Mr 7 '66

Unspoiled areas U.S. wants for parks. il U S News 60:76-7 F 14 '66

Vacation U.S.A. a Redbook guide to the national parks. R. Kirk. Redbook 126:43-50 Ap '66

Wave of the future; activities of the Short course in the administration of national parks, by University of Michigan and the National park service. G. W. Sharpe and others. il Am For 72:20-1+ F '66

See also

National forests

National monuments

United States—National park service

also names of national parks and reserves, e.g. Big Bend National Park

NATIONAL parks association

NPA protests C&O Canal hunting suggestion. Nat Parks Mag 40:24-5 My '66

Report of president and general counsel, May 19, 1966. A. W. Smith. Nat Parks Mag 40:I-IV My '66

Wilderness in the Smokies; statements. June 13, 15, 1966. A. W. Smith. Nat Parks Mag 40:I-IV Ag '66

NATIONAL periodical publications, incorporated

Friend of Batman. R. Levy. il Duns R 87:51-2 Mr '66

Trade winds; confusion over copyright on Superman. J. Beatty, jr. Sat R 49:6 Ap 23 '66

NATIONAL planning

National planning of science and technology in France; adaptation of address, October 1964. J. B. Quinn; discussion. Science 151:517, 1330+ F 4, Mr 18 '66

NATIONAL portrait gallery. See Smithsonian Institution—National portrait gallery

NATIONAL program for acquisitions and cataloging. See United States—Library of Congress—National program for acquisitions and cataloging

NATIONAL recreation and park association

Fellow pioneers. L. S. Rockefeller. Parks & Rec 1:13 Ja '66

Let's look ahead. C. L. Wirth. Parks & Rec 1:955 D '66

Lifetime sports grant to NRPA. il Parks & Rec 1:312-13 Ap '66

NRPA news. See issues of Recreation (cont as) Parks & recreation

New National recreation and park association. Parks & Rec 1:621 Ag '66

Personal thank you; NRA staff and length of service. J. Prendergast. Parks & Rec 1:711 S '66

Recent board meetings. Parks & Rec 1:27+ Ja '66

Revival of confidence. J. A. Smith. Parks & Rec 1:45-6 Ja '66

Service to the American people. J. H. Evans. Parks & Rec 1:137+ F '66

Voice of the recreator. S. Lutzin. Parks & Rec 1:895-6 N '66

See also

Lifetime sports foundation

Volunteer division

Road to unity; excerpts from address. L. Gulick. Parks & Rec 1:309 Ap '66

NATIONAL recreation association. See National recreation and park association

NATIONAL recreation congress. See National congress for recreation and parks

NATIONAL research corporation

Cold comfort from outer space; NRC space blanket. il Consumer Rep 31:322-3 Jl '66

NATIONAL research council of Canada

Canada tests noise. Sci N 90:335 O 22 '66

NATIONAL responsibility. See Responsibility

NATIONAL retail merchants association

Europe's stores gear up for more free spenders; meeting in Milan. il Bsns W p80-2 Je 4 '66

NATIONAL review
American dissent. by J. Hart. Review
Nat R 18:536-7 My 31 '66. M. S. Evans
Linus Pauling takes the stand; excerpts
from proceedings. Nat R 18:459-66 My
17 '66
Linus Pauling: TKO; his suit for libel.
Nat R 18:403 My 3 '66
National review vindicated; Linus Pauling
case thrown out; Court's opinion, and
Obiter dicta, by National review. Nat R
18:404-7 My 3 '66
O'Bryan revolution. il Nat R 18:1218-21 N 29
'66
NATIONAL rifle association
Aimless; opponents of federal legislation to
control firearms. il Time 88:25 S 9 '66
Big shoot; gun-restricting legislation. R. G.
Sherrill. il Nation 202:260-4 Mr 7 '66
We need a firearms-control law, now! A.
Barth. Read Digest 90:22+ Ja '67
NATIONAL rural electric cooperative associa-
tion
Another co-op crutch; administration's plan
for a federal bank for rural electric sys-
tems. R. Moley. Newsweek 67:98 My 30 '66
NATIONAL scholarship service and fund for
Negro students
Equality of educational opportunity for Ne-
groes. Sch & Soc 94:32 Ja 22 '66
NATIONAL science fair. See Science fairs
NATIONAL science foundation. See United
States—National science foundation
NATIONAL secretaries association
Ladies, bless 'em, of the executive suite; an-
nual convention. il Newsweek 68:68-9+
Ag 1 '66
NATIONAL security agency. See United States
—National security agency
NATIONAL security council. See United States
—National security council
NATIONAL self-determination. See Self-de-
termination, National
NATIONAL service board for religious objec-
tors
In good conscience. Christian Cent 83:791-2
Je 22 '66
NATIONAL shooting dog championship. See
Field trials (dogs)
NATIONAL ski patrol system
Patrol chief of the ski slopes; C. Haskins.
il Ebony 22:84-6+ D '66
Samaritans of the ski slopes. E. H. Matthew.
il Am For 72:34-7 Ja '66
NATIONAL songs
United States
See also
Star-spangled banner (song)
NATIONAL student association. See United
States national student association
NATIONAL survival. See Survival of nations
NATIONAL tea company
After the marathon; violation of Clayton
act. Time 87:80+ Mr 25 '66
NATIONAL teacher corps. See United States
—National teacher corps
NATIONAL technical services association
Job shops profit from technology boom. R. G.
Barnhart. Tech W 19:34-5 Ag 29 '66
NATIONAL theater. See Theater, Municipal
and national
NATIONAL traffic safety agency. See United
States—National traffic safety agency
NATIONAL training laboratory in group de-
velopment
Where executives tear off the masks; NTL's
training labs. il Bsns W p76-8+ S 3 '66
NATIONAL university (proposed) See United
States—National university (proposed)
NATIONAL university extension association
Training 30,000 Head Start teachers. S. J.
Drazek. Sch & Soc 94:130-1 Mr 5 '66
NATIONAL university of Mexico. See Colleges
and universities—Mexico
NATIONAL urban league
How we integrated the urban league; adap-
tation of address. W. M. Young, jr. Har-
per 233:114 D '66
Leading the league; annual convention.
Newsweek 68:23 Ag 15 '66
NATIONAL watershed congress
Crisis in the countryside. il Am For 72:26-7
Jl '66
13th watershed congress. Nat Parks Mag
40:25 My '66
NATIONAL youth conference on natural beauty
and conservation
Accent on youth. I. Moore. il Am For 72:22-5
Ag '66

NATIONAL zoological park, Washington, D.C.
Come on over to the zoo. T. H. Reed. il Parks
& Rec 1:692-4+ S '66
NATIONALISM
Nationalism and ideology, by B. Ward. Re-
view
Sat R 49:27-8 Ag 20 '66. J. Real
Nationalism vs. economic growth. J.
Amuzegar. For Affairs 44:651-61 Jl '66
See also
Patriotism
Self-determination, National
also subhead Nationalism under names
of continents, countries, etc. e.g. Vietnam
(Republic)—Nationalism
NATIONALITY. See Citizenship
NATIONALMUSEUM. See Stockholm—Galler-
ies and museums
NATIONS
Nations of the world; table (cont) Sr Schol
89:pt2 27-30 S 23 '66
Passions & perils of nationhood; Time essay.
Time 87:38-9 Mr 11 '66
NATIONS, Survival of. See Survival of nations
NATION'S business (periodical)
We can get anybody a job. Nations Bsns 55:
35 Ja '67
NATIVE races
See also subhead Native races under
names of countries, continents. etc. e.g.
Africa. West—Native races
NATIVITY groups. See Christmas cribs
NATIVITY of Christ. See Jesus Christ—
Nativity
NATIVITY of Christ in art. See Jesus Christ
—Art
NATSUME, Kinnosuke. See Natsume, S.
NATSUME, Sōseki
Three-cornered world; excerpts from Kusa
makura (Pillow of grass) tr. by A. Turney.
UNESCO Courier 19:26-7 O '66
about
Soseki: most popular writer in Japan; with
excerpts from Three-cornered world, tr. by
A. Turney. bibliog por UNESCO Courier
19:25-7 O '66
NATURAL areas. See Wilderness areas
NATURAL BRIDGES NATIONAL MONU-
MENT
Tomorrow the tourists will come flooding. il
Sunset 137:6-8 S '66
NATURAL disaster warning system (proposed)
See United States—Weather bureau
NATURAL forms
Forms and shapes in nature; design in nature.
L. Boykin. il Sch Arts 66:19-20 S '66
NATURAL gas. See Gas, Natural
NATURAL history
Nature note. See issues of Science news
Study and teaching
See also
Moving pictures—Natural history films
Nature study
United States
See also
Geology—United States
NATURAL immunity; story. See White. V. R.
NATURAL resources
Expert group on resource surveys; five-year
programme of surveys designed as a con-
tribution to the development decade. UN
Mo Chron 3:54 My '66
Searching for buried riches. il Newsweek 68:
86-8+ O 17 '66
Sovereignty over natural resources; UN Gen-
eral assembly adopts resolution. UN Mo
Chron 3:76-7 D '66
See also
Conservation of resources
Marine resources—International aspects
Power resources
Water resources development
Wildlife conservation
Bibliography
Reading about resources. M. Bush. See is-
sues of American forests
Vocational guidance
Careers in conservation. New Repub 155:7-8
S 10 '66
Alaska
Mike Frome; trip in Alaska. M. Frome. Am
For 72:5+ S '66
Bolivia
Bolivia. R. E. Crist. bibliog il Focus 16:1-6
Mr '66

NATURAL resources—*Continued*

Cameroon Republic
Cameroon. J. I. Clarke. bibliog il Focus 16:1-6 Ap '66

Canada
Big rush is on to tap Canada's wealth. il U S News 61:92-4 Jl 25 '66

Germany (Democratic Republic)
East Germany; Soviet-occupied zone of Germany. N. J. G. Pounds. bibliog il Focus 17:1-6 O '66

Guyana
Guyana: rich potential with a spice of risk. il Bsns W p 132+ My 28 '66

Kenya
Kenya. D. N. McMaster. bibliog il Focus 16:1-6 F '66

Latin America
New conquistadors in the Amazon jungle. E. P. Hanson; reply with rejoinder. J. H. Norton. Américas 18:48 F '66

Mexico
Mexico. D. D. Brand. bibliog il Focus 16: 1-6 Je '66

Russia
Mike Frome; Soviet Union's management of its resources. M. Frome. Am For 72:6+ N '66

Saudi Arabia
Saudi Arabia. J. S. Haupert. bibliog il Focus 16:1-6 My '66

Sudan
Sudan. J. R. Randell. bibliog il Focus 17:1-6 S '66

United States
Land misuse: a theological concern. R. A. Baer, jr. Christian Cent 83:1239-41 O 12 '66; Discussion. 83:1445, 1480 N 23-30 '66
Natural resources, conservation and use. W. W. Porter, 2d. il Am For 72:28-31+ Ap '66
Washington lookout. A. G. Hall. See issues of American forests
Why I'm for a department of natural resources; address, February 7, 1966. F. E. Moss. il Am For 72:16-17+ Mr '66
You can be a conservationist. C. E. Randall. il Am For 72:17-27 Ap '66
See also
Water supply—United States

Venezuela
Venezuela: there's more to it than oil; ore, power, and new industry lure U.S. companies. il Bsns W p 178-80+ N 12 '66

NATURAL satellites. See Satellites
NATURAL scenery. See Landscape
NATURAL science camps. See Nature camps
NATURAL selection
Survival of fittest no longer holds true. Sci N 89:442 Je 4 '66
NATURALISM (philosophy)
Legitimacy of rational inquiry. L. D. Streiker. Christian Cent 83:458-60 Ap 13 '66
NATURALISTS
People and plant names. D. S. Manks. il Horticulture 44:18-21 Ag '66
See also
James, E.
NATURALIZATION
See also
Citizenship
NATURE
Biggest tree of all. M. Bush. Am For 72:35-6 D '66
Where nothing ever happens. E. A. Autry. il Audubon Mag 68:111 Mr '66
See also
Man—Influence on nature

Bibliography
Books. A. Clampitt. See issues of Audubon magazine to January 1966
Books in review. See issues of Natural history incorporating Nature magazine
Books in review: a foursome on nature. R. C. Murphy. Natur Hist 75:6+ Ag '66
Naturalist's bookshelf; gifts for inquisitive young minds. J. Goodwin. Audubon Mag 68:480 N '66

Philosophy
What I have learned: strategy for the war with nature. E. Hoffer. Sat R 49:27-9+ F 5 '66

NATURE (aesthetics)
From nature to art. K. Kuh. Sat R 49:56-7 S 24 '66
NATURE (periodical)
John Maddox: crusading science editor. J. Lear. Sat R 49:67-9 N 5 '66
Nature's way; John Maddox; new editor. Time 87:43 F 11 '66
NATURE, Balance of. See Balance of nature
NATURE, Human. See Human nature
NATURE and art. See Nature (aesthetics)
NATURE camps
Starting a natural science camp program. R. G. Dawson. bibliog il Parks & Rec 1: 220-2+ Mr '66
NATURE centers
Nature center education. Liv Wildn 30:30 Sum '66
Nature center for New York city? Staten Island's high rock park. J. J. Shomon. il Audubon Mag 68:54 Ja '66
Wilderness nature center for Ontario. J. J. Shomon. Audubon Mag 68:307 S '66
You can sell a nature center. J. J. Shomon. Audubon Mag 68:218-19 Jl '66
NATURE in art
Macro-drawing from nature. E. Adams. il Sch Arts 66:22-6 N '66
See also
Birds in art
Fruit in art
NATURE in poetry
Some uses of landscape. R. Loewinsohn. Poetry 109:123-6 N '66
NATURE literature

Illustrations
See Illustrations of books and periodicals
NATURE of man. See Man
NATURE photography
Fresh viewpoints with a camera. Natur Hist 75:48-51 F '66
Large camera technique for 35mm color; ed. by P. Caulfield. B. Randall. il Mod Phot 30:62-5 Je '66
Nature in your back yard. il Sci Digest 61: 79-81 Ja '67
Return to the classic scenic. P. Caulfield. il Mod Phot 30:54-63+ O '66
Spectacular scenic. M. Orovan. il U S Camera 29:46-51+ N '66
See also
Photography of animals
Photography of birds
NATURE study
Enjoying nature. il Audubon Mag 68:370-1, 472-5 S, N '66
Heritage to discover; training park rangers. G. B. Hartzog, jr. il Am Ed 2:15-19 Jl '66
Little learning; knowledge of outdoors. T. Trueblood. il Field & S 70:26+ Mr '66
Make nature study a family hobby. E. T. Hall. il Suc Farm 64:63+ Je '66
Nature courses star in city's schools; urban centers need nature teaching. C. W. Buchhesiter. Audubon Mag 68:140-1 My '66
See also
Audubon nature centers
Bird study
Nature centers
NATURE trails. See Trails
NATWAR-SINGH, K.
Return passage to India. Sat R 49:43 Mr 5 '66
NAUDE, Virginia N.
Lemon Hill revisited. Antiques 89:578-9 Ap '66
NAUGHTON, Francis P.
Merchantry of books. Wilson Lib Bul 41: 219-22 O '66
NAUMANN, Jack L.
Down the Mississippi. il Yachting 120:54-6+ N '66
To Florida via the Gulf. il Yachting 120: 52-4+ D '66
NAUTA method. See Stains and staining (biology)
NAUTICAL astronomy
And a star to steer her by. W. S. Kals. Motor B 118:36-7 Jl '66
NAUTICAL charts
New charts. E. S. Maloney. See issues of Motor boating
To chart a course. Holiday 40:106 Jl '66
Where to get ... Motor B 117:100-2+ Ap '66

NAUTICAL instruments
See also
Automatic pilot (boats)

NAUTILUS
Isotopic evidence on the early life history of nautilus pompilius. Linné. R. Eichler and H. Ristedt. bibliog il Science 153:734-6 Ag 12 '66

NAVAHO Indians
Plague and war, 1966, even in U.S. D. Lyle. il Esquire 66:158-63+ S '66
Three cultures of New Mexico. W. T. Le Viness. il Américas 18:8-15 Je '66
Where the real poverty is: plight of American Indians. il U S News 60:104-8 Ap 25 '66

NAVAJO Indian reservation. See Indians of North America—Reservations

NAVAJO Indians. See Navaho Indians

NAVAL architecture
See also
Hulls (naval architecture)

NAVAL battles
See also
United States—History—Revolution—Naval operations
World war, 1939-1945—Naval operations

NAVAL chaplains. See Chaplains, Military

NAVAL craft. See United States—Navy—Boats

NAVAL material support establishment. See United States—Navy department—Naval material support establishment

NAVAL museums
Bath marine museum: an enviable record. R. Davidson. il Antiques 89:636+ My '66
Figures and figureheads: the maritime collection at the State Street bank and trust company, Boston. W. D. Garrett. il Antiques 90:816-23 D '66
Maritime museum for the Chesapeake. E. Horan. il Yachting 119:158-9 Mr '66

NAVAL observatory (United States) See United States—Naval observatory

NAVAL ordnance. See Ordnance, Naval

NAVAL ordnance test station. See Navy yards and naval stations

NAVAL power. See Sea power

NAVAL research
Navy presses deep-sea probes; search for H-bomb sunk off Spain. il Bsns W p72-4+ Mr 12 '66
See also
United States naval oceanographic office, Suitland, Md.

NAVAL research laboratory. See United States —Naval research laboratory

NAVASKY, Victor S.
Advertising is a science, an art, a business? N Y Times Mag p52-3+ N 20 '66
Happy heretic. Atlan 218:53-7 Jl '66
Notes on cult; or, How to join the intellectual establishment. N Y Times Mag p28-9+ Mr 27 '66
Yales vs. the Harvards (legal division) N Y Times Mag p47-9+ S 11; p42 O 2 '66

NAVASSA (island)
Unluckiest island. H. R. Kaplan. il Motor B 117:193-5 Mr '66

NAVIES
See also
Sea power
also subhead Navy under names of countries, e.g. United States—Navy

NAVIGATION
Four dollar fog. W. Richards. il Motor B 117:30-2+ Je '66
Outboards in shallow water. B. Whittier. il Yachting 119:118-19+ Ja '66
Piloting, seamanship and small boat handling, by C. F. Chapman. Review. Motor B il 117:75+ F '66
Rough-water boat handling. J. A. Emmett. il Outdoor Life 139:76-7 Ja '67
Two navigational sides; toughest Bermuda race ever sailed. A. F. Loomis. il Yachting 120:35+ Ag '66
See also
Artificial satellites—Navigational applications
Nautical astronomy
Radio in navigation
Sailing
Voyages

Competitions
APBA action report; log schedules. J. D. Paris. il Motor B 117:140-1+ Mr '66
Control points. M. L. Hersey. See issues of Yachting
Powerboats in competition. M. L. Hersey. il Yachting 119:67-9+ F '66

NAVIGATION (space flight)
Charts may guide return from moon. Sci N 89:515 Je 25 '66
Man-computer interface studied for space navigation and guidance. Aviation W 84:196-7 Je 20 '66
Manned-Apollo flight to test optics. J. Mercer. Miss & Roc 18:18 Ja 24 '66
New timetables for planetary tours. il Time 88:39 D 30 '66

NAVIGATION, Aerial
BOAC plans new navigation system test. B. Miller. il Aviation W 85:41+ O 3 '66
See also
Airplanes—Piloting
Airplanes, Jet propelled—Piloting
Inertial guidance systems
Loran
Radio in aviation
Tacan

NAVIGATION aids
ESSA and the skipper. il Motor B 119:104-6+ Ja '67
See also
Electronics in navigation
Television in navigation

NAVION aircraft corporation
Used aircraft pilot report: the Navion. J. Gilbert. il Flying 78:54-8 Ap '66

NAVONE, John J.
Memories make the future. Cath World 204:149-53 D '66

NAVY cargo vessels. See United States—Navy —Boats

NAVY navigation satellite system. See Artificial satellites—Navigational applications

NAVY yards and naval stations
Navy's top handyman; civilian technical director of the U.S. naval ordnance test station; interview, ed. by J. Riley. W. B. McLean. il Life 62:31-2+ Ja 6 '67
Vietnam spurs navy weapons advances; research at Naval ordnance test station. Aviation W 84:28-9 Mr 21 '66

NAWAPA. See North American water and power alliance

NAWRACAJ, Edward. See Forman, F. jt. auth.

NAYARS (caste) See Caste

NAYUDU, P. R. V. and Moog, Florence
Intestinal alkaline phosphatase: regulation by a strain-specific factor in mouse milk. bibliog Science 152:656-7 Ap 29 '66

NAZARENES (Mandaeans) See Mandaeans

NAZI war criminals. See World war, 1939-1945 —War criminals

NAZISM. See Fascism—Germany; Fascism— Germany (Federal Republic)

NE Win
Burma: a study in how to stop progress. R. P. Martin. il por U S News 60:116+ My 16 '66
LBJ hosts Asians. il por Sr Schol 89:19 S 30 '66
200 per cent neutral. il por Time 88:41-2 S 16 '66
When China spits, we swim. R. K. McCabe. il pors N Y Times Mag p26-7+ F 27 '66

Visit to United States, 1966
Tour of a neutral; why Ne Win set U.S. visit. por U S News 61:21 S 12 '66

NEAL, Donald L.
Heterodyne vegetation meter. W. B. Morse. il por Pop Electr 26:72+ Ja '67

NEAL, Lee R.
Heterodyne vegetation meter. W. B. Morse. il Pop Electr 26:72+ Ja '67

NEAL, Patricia
Gift of love. McCalls 94:72 D '66

NEAR EAST. See Middle East

NEAR the Straits of Mackinac; story. See Woiwode. L.

NEARCTIC halictine bees. See Bees

NEARY, John
Does Petey Boy talk dirty? Life 60:105-6 Je 24 '66
His life with Lydia has given him a high threshold of surprise; the Katzenbachs. Life 60:54-5 My 6 '66
On an assignment with the age of the bugging business. Life 60:44-7 My 20 '66

NEBEL, Long John
From photography to flying saucers. S. M. Teller. il por U S Camera 29:60-1+ N '66

NEBLETTE, C. B.
Should you study photography in college? Mod Phot 31:130+ Ja '67

NEBRASKA
   See also
   Geology—Nebraska
   Hunting—Nebraska
NEBULAE
   Organic compounds in carbonaceous chon-
     drites. M. H. Studier and others; discus-
     sion. Science 152:102-7 Ap 1 '66
   Origin of planetaries. G. S. Mumford. Sky &
     Tel 32:333 D '66
NEBULAE, Photography of. See Astronomical
   photography
NEBULAR hypothesis
   See also
   Cosmogony
NECKERMANN, Josef
   Success of Neckermann's pig. por Time 88:
     106+ O 21 '66
NECKING. See Dating
NECROSIS
   Mast cells and necrosis. H. Selye. il Science
     152:1371-2 Je 3 '66
   Protective action of polycyclic hydrocarbons
     against induction of adrenal necrosis by di-
     methylbenzanthracene. P. H. Jellinck and
     B. Goudy. bibliog il Science 152:1375-6 Je 3
     '66
NECTAR
   Crossroads of the insect world. J. W. Mac-
     Swain. il Nat Geog Mag 130:844-57 D '66
NEEDHAM packing company
   Butchers of Sioux City. il Fortune 74:318 Jl
     15 '66
NEEDLEMAN, Samuel
   Exposure problems. U S Camera 29:44-5+ N
     '66
NEEDLEPOINT
   Needlepoint. il House & Gard 129:128-31+
     F '66
NEEDLEWORK
   Needlework: fancy stitches done easily. J.
     LemMon. il Suc Farm 64:102-3 S '66
     See also
   Applique work
   Crocheting
   Smocking
NEEL, Alice
   Curator of souls: show at New York's Gra-
     ham gallery. il por Newsweek 67:82 Ja 31
     '66
   Portrait and its double. T. Berrigan. il Art N
     64:30-3+ Ja '66
NEELY, Keith K.
   Divers' communications improved. Science
     153:321 Jl 15 '66
NEFF, George
   Let's have a tiger for dinner. bibliog por Sch
     Arts 66:5-9 N '66
NEFF, Hildegarde
   Knef. por Newsweek 67:115+ My 16 '66
NEFF, Muriel
   Kabul confluence. Art N 64:26-7+ F '66
NEFF, Philip
   Technological developments: address, May 11,
     1966. Vital Speeches 32:543-4 Je 15 '66
NEGAHBAN, Ezat O.
   Masterpieces from a lost kingdom. il UNESCO
     Courier 19:16-21 Je '66
NEGATIVE income tax. See Income
NEGATIVES, Photography. See Photography—
   Negatives
NEGEV
   Reclamation of Israel's desert; with photo-
     graphs by P. Merom. Natur Hist 75:30-3
     F '66
NEGI, Sushil S. and Olmo, H. P.
   Sex conversion in a male vitis vinifera L. by
     a kinin. bibliog Science 152:1624 Je 17 '66
NEGISHI, K. and Svaetichin, G.
   Oxygen dependence of retinal S-potential-
     producing cells. bibliog Science 152:1621-3
     Je 17 '66
NEGLIGENCE
   See also
   Liability (law)
NEGOTIABLE instruments
   What makes the boom in commercial paper.
     il Bsns W p76+ N 26 '66
NEGOTIATION, International. See Arbitration,
   International; International relations
NEGRO actors and actresses
   Carol Cole. il Ebony 21:114-16+ Jl '66
   Integration on the stage. T. Lewis. Amer-
     ica 115:213-14 Ag 27 '66
   Negro actors in dramatic roles. T. Lewis.
     America 115:298-300 S 17 '66
   See also
   Nichols, N.
NEGRO air pilots
   Death of a navy pilot. S. Booker. il Ebony
     22:25-8+ Ja '67

NEGRO ambassadors
   Our man in Damascus. T. Eigeland. il Ebony
     22:29-32+ D '66
NEGRO American labor council
   Negro unionists try a new tack; broader
     cooperation with AFL-CIO. il Bsns W
     p 140-2 Je 4 '66
NEGRO art. See Art, Negro
NEGRO artists. See Artists, Negro
NEGRO athletes
   Everyone's keen on Keino. C. E. Brown. il
     Ebony 21:100-2+ My '66
   Southern U; new kings of track. il Ebony
     21:69-70+ Jl '66
   Sports as an integrator. R. L. Tobin. Sat R
     50:32 Ja 21 '67
NEGRO authors
   Racial reality and American dream. G. Hicks.
     Sat R 49:27-8 F 12 '66
   See also
   Baldwin, J.
   Ellison, R.
   Hurston, Z. N.
   Yerby, F. G.
NEGRO businessmen
   Leading the league; J. Robinson. il Time
     88:79 Jl 8 '66
   Negro business feels stresses of success; white
     companies competing for their skilled em-
     ployees. il Bsns W p70-2+ Ap 9 '66
   Negro gets toehold in Harlem retailing. il
     Ebony 21:149-52 Mr '66
   Problem solver for corporate giants; W. A.
     Rutherford. il Ebony 21:62-4+ O '66
   Triumph of a stay-at-home. il Ebony 21:
     32-4+ F '66
NEGRO cabinet officers. See Cabinet officers
NEGRO career girls. See Business and profes-
   sional women
NEGRO children
   Discarded third; unstable family life. D. P.
     Moynihan. il Look 30:27-9 My 17 '66
   How to survive childhood. M. Polner. Na-
     tion 203:523 N 14 '66
   I get one more U, my mother goin' to beat
     me till it rains. O. Ryan. il N Y Times
     Mag p27-9+ F 13 '66
   Of many things: Negro slum child. T. N.
     Davis. America 115:102 Jl 30 '66
   When I draw the Lord he'll be a real big
     man; excerpt from Courage and fear in the
     South. R. Coles. il Atlan 217:69-72+ My '66
   See also
   Socially handicapped children
NEGRO civil rights organizations. See Civil
   rights organizations
NEGRO clergy
   Bishop Harold Perry; man of many firsts.
     E. B. Thompson. il Ebony 21:62-6+ F '66
   Historic action in the church. C. W. Thomas.
     Negro Hist Bul 29:65-6 D '65
NEGRO college presidents. See College presi-
   dents
NEGRO colleges. See Negroes in the United
   States—Education
NEGRO comedians
   Comedy row's top ten. il Ebony 21:105-8+
     Ap '66
   Good-by, Mr Bones. J. Boskin. il N Y Times
     Mag p30-1+ My 1 '66
NEGRO commentators. See Television broad-
   casting—News
NEGRO composers
   Negro composers of opera. J. Duncan. bibliog
     Negro Hist Bul 29:79-80+ Ja '66
NEGRO conductors. See Conductors (music)
NEGRO congressmen
   George Henry White: a militant Negro con-
     gressman in the age of Booker T. Wash-
     ington. W. Katz. bibliog Negro Hist Bul
     29:125-6+ Mr '66
   Long void is filled at last. S. McBee. il
     Life 62:32-32B Ja 13 '67
   See also
   Brooke, E. W.
NEGRO costume designers. See Costume de-
   signers
NEGRO cowboys. See Cowboys
NEGRO criminals. See Negroes in the United
   States—Crime
NEGRO dancers
   American dancer, Negro. H. Jackson. il
     Dance Mag 40:35-42 O 8 '66; Discussion. 40:
     35 D '66
   Dance career: Alvin Ailey's. A. Fatt. il Dance
     Mag 40:52-9 O '66
NEGRO divers. See Diving, Submarine
NEGRO drama
   See also
   Theater, Negro

NEGRO students—*Continued*
Wonderful trip to see the king; Chicago Negro students' Swedish tour. il Life 60:18-25 Ja 28 '66
NEGRO students in Scandinavia. See Foreign students in Scandinavia
NEGRO suffrage. See Negroes in the United States—Politics and suffrage
NEGRO teachers
Displaced Negro teachers. Sch & Soc 94:176 Ap 2 '66
It takes courage; Operation Reclaim, recruiting teachers from the South, displaced by desegregation. L. Rich and J. Rich. il Am Ed 2:5-8 Je '66
NEA's panic button; reply. C. Cogen. Nation 202:inside cover F 14 '66
Next step; teacher integration. P. A. Janssen. il Reporter 35:32-4 N 3 '66
Teacher victims of integration. America 114:433 Ap 2 '66
NEGRO theater. See Theater, Negro
NEGRO umpires. See Umpires (sports)
NEGRO visitors in Denmark. See Foreign visitors in Denmark
NEGRO visitors in Scandinavia. See Foreign visitors in Scandinavia
NEGRO visitors in Sweden. See Foreign visitors in Sweden
NEGRO voters, Registration of. See Voters, Registration of
NEGRO-white intermarriage. See Intermarriage of races
NEGRO-white relations. See Race relations
NEGRO women
Are Negro girls getting prettier? il Ebony 21:25-8+ F '66
Negro woman in retrospect; blueprint for the future. A. A. Shockley. bibliog il Negro Hist Bul 29:55-6+ D '66
Negro woman; symposium, with introd. by J. H. Johnson. Ebony 21:25+ Ag '66
Style setters of 1966. il Ebony 21:48-50+ My '66
See also
National council of Negro women
Single women

Employment
Long thrust toward economic equality; Negro women fastest advancing group. il Ebony 21:38-40+ Ag '66
See also
Married women—Employment
NEGRO women and politics. See Women and politics
NEGRO women as athletes. See Women as athletes
NEGRO women as college professors and instructors. See Women as college professors and instructors
NEGRO women as lawyers. See Women as lawyers
NEGRO womens clubs and societies. See National association of colored women's clubs
NEGRO youth
Fifteen years of trouble; Gail White at Livingston school for girls, N.Y. il Look 30:40-3 S 20 '66
Watch out whitey; Negro youth gangs and violence. L. Yablonsky; discussion. New Repub 154:29-30 Ja 22; 37-8 F 19 '66
See also
Negro students
NEGROES

Folklore
See Folklore, Negro

History
Aspect of bibliography and research in Negro history; address, October 22, 1965. C. H. Wesley. Negro Hist Bul 29:52-2+ D '65
Ignored by historians; concerning Negro heritage library publications. W. Katz. Sat R 49:67-8 Jl 16 '66
See also
Association for the study of Negro life and history

Intelligence
See Intelligence levels—Negroes
NEGROES, Catholic. See Catholic church—Negroes
NEGROES and Jews. See Jews and Negroes
NEGROES in Africa
Return to the bush. E. T. Chase. Nation 203:712-13 D 26 '66
See also
South Africa—Race problems
NEGROES in automobile racing. See Automobile racing

NEGROES in business. See Negro businessmen
NEGROES in Canada
Willie Fleming hits pay dirt. il Ebony 22:77-8+ Ja '67
NEGROES in Europe
Black man in Europe. J. A. Williams. il Holiday 41:8+ Ja '67
NEGROES in France
Memphis Slim: la vie est bonne. il Ebony 21:56-8+ Je '66
NEGROES in Germany
Journey into the past. H. J. Massaquoi. il Ebony 21:91-4+ F; 102-4+ Mr '66
NEGROES in Great Britain
Negro in Britain. R. Hodkinson. bibliog il Negro Hist Bul 29:77-8+ Ja '66
NEGROES in India
Industry to India, a Yank helps out. il Ebony 21:83-4+ Mr '66
NEGROES in literature
Black comedy with purifying laughter. R. Schickel. Harper 232:103-4+ My '66
Ebony book shelf. See issues of Ebony
Expression of the Negro experience. G. Hicks. Sat R 50:79-80 Ja 14 '67
NEGROES in South Africa
Other side of the South Africa story; address, 1966. H. L. T. Taswell. il U S News 60:70-2 Je 27 '66
See also
South Africa—Race problems
NEGROES in television. See Television broadcasting—Performers
NEGROES in the United States
An Animal views America. E. Burdon. il Ebony 22:160-2+ D '66
As Negro unrest continues to spread—. il U S News 61:30 Jl 25 '66
Crisis of color '66; survey findings. il Newsweek 68:20-32+ Ag 22 '66
Historical notes. C. W. Thomas. Negro Hist Bul 29:48, 71-2, 120+ N-D '65, F '66
Home, by L. Jones. Review
New Repub 154:23-5 My 28 '66. F. Berry
Is brotherhood enough? proposals to improve attitude towards Negroes. N. Wright. Cath World 204:234-8 Ja '67
Negro as immigrant. America 114:347 Mr 12 '66
Opinion: on Negro aims; open letter to LeRoi Jones. J. Meyer. Mlle 62:84+ Ap '66
Progress report for 1966. il Ebony 22:34-6+ Ja '67
Turning point; white backlash. il Time 88:29-30 O 7 '66
Two worlds of Thomas Holman. W. Rogers. il Look 31:60-3 Ja 10 '67
What the Negro has and has not gained; Time essay. Time 88:32-3 O 28 '66; Same abr. Read Digest 90:70-4 Ja '67
Why Negroes are still angry. V. H. Bernstein. il Redbook 127:54-5+ Jl '66; Reply. C. E. Silberman. 127:194 O '66
See also
Back-to-Africa movements
Freedmen
National association for the advancement of colored people
National urban league
Race relations
Slavery—United States
United States—History—Civil war—Negro troops
also subhead Negroes under names of cities, e.g. Los Angeles—Negroes

Civil rights
Absolute conflict seen. Sci N 90:172 S 10 '66
At the breaking point; struggle between moderate and radical elements. il Time 88:15-16 Jl 15 '66
Backlash in Congress; Negro rioting blamed. il Bsns W p50+ O 8 '66
Beyond the riots. Nat R 18:758-60 Ag 9 '66
Black power and the American Christ. V. Harding. Christian Cent 84:10-13 Ja 4 '67
Black power: divisive slogan; with viewpoints. il Sr Schol 89:17-18 S 16 '66
Black power for whom? ideological split in civil rights movement. Christian Cent 83:903-4 Jl 20 '66
Black power must be defined. Life 61:4 Jl 22 '66
Black power rhubarb. Nation 203:68 Jl 25 '66
Can Negroes do more to help themselves? excerpts from report. B. C. Porter. U S News 61:13 S 19 '66
Civil rights' dim prospects; bill of 1966. A. M. Bickel. New Repub 155:17-18 S 17 '66
Civil rights drive: where to from here? with press comments. il Sr Schol 88:6-10+ My 13 '66

NEGROES in the United States—Civil rights
—*Continued*
Civil rights must be legal rights. Christian
Cent 83:904 Jl 20 '66
Civil rights: untangling the race problem.
il Sr Schol 89:9-14 O 21 '66
Crisis in civil rights leadership. C. T. Rowan.
il Ebony 22:27-30+ N '66
Doctor King's case for nonviolence. Ameri-
ca 115:578 N 12 '66
Enlisting community support for civil rights;
address, January 20, 1966. B. DeHaan.
Vital Speeches 32:272-5 F 15 '66
For civil rights: a different theme. il U S
News 62:47 Ja 9 '67
For the long tomorrow; Kentucky's governor
signs state civil rights bill. il Time 87:27
F 4 '66
Freedom, when? by J. Farmer. Review
Sat R 49:37+ Ap 23 '66. G. Samuels
U S News il 60:46-7 Mr 7 '66
Freedom's crisis: last steep ascent. M. L.
King, jr. il Nation 202:288-92 Mr 14 '66
Frontier for '66. Newsweek 67:28-9 My 9 '66
Full equality: what it really means. D.
Lawrence. U S News 61:120 S 19 '66
Here lies integration. Nat R 18:1305-6 D 27
'66
Integration has failed. M. Halsey. Christian
Cent 83:1596-7 D 28 '66
Is Meredith right? violent or non-violent
policy? Nation 202:765 Je 27 '66
Let no drum be muffled; John F. Kennedy
award dinner; address, February 22, 1966.
T. C. Sorensen. Christian Cent 83:328-31
Mr 16 '66
Let's be unreasonable; Rusk's son on civil
rights; excerpts from address, 1966. D.
Rusk. U S News 61:11 Ag 15 '66
Long, hot summer of race trouble ahead?
with interview with F. B. McKissick. il
U S News 60:34-8+ My 23 '66
LBJ's civil rights bill. A. M. Bickel. New
Repub 154:12-14 My 21 '66
Major turning point against Negro movement;
concerning New York times survey. U S
News 61:46 O 3 '66
Morgan's crusade for Negro jurors. J. B.
Cumming, jr. Reporter 34:39-40 F 10 '66
Much yet to overcome. W. Katz. Sat R 49:
26-7 Ag 13 '66
Mutual aid and the Negro. J. Slawson. bib-
liog f Commentary 41:43-50 Ap '66
Negro congressman talks about black power;
interview. A. C. Powell. il U S News 61:
38-41 Ag 15 '66
Negro cry: black power! what does it mean?
il U S News 61:52 Jl 11 '66
Negro leader's advice to members of his
race; excerpts from address, May 29, 1966.
A. C. Powell. U S News 60:14 Je 13 '66
Negro leaders dividing: the effect; with ex-
cerpts from address by R. Wilkins. il U S
News 61:31-4 Jl 18 '66
Negro revolution: a new phase. F. S. Meyer.
Nat R 18:998 O 4 '66
Negro rights: the laws already on the books.
U S News 60:36 My 9 '66
Negroes and Vietnam; the two Souths. H.
Zinn. Commonweal 83:519-80 F 18 '66
Negroes tell Congress: poverty war on—.
il U S News 61:31 D 19 '66
Negroes want power. Commonweal 84:381-2
Je 24 '66
New civil rights bill; Titles IV and V at
stake. Commonweal 84:490-1 Ag 5 '66
New Negro mood. Life 60:4 Je 10 '66
New racism; emphasis on black power. il
Time 88:11-13 Jl 1 '66
Nonviolence: the only road to freedom. M. L.
King, jr il Ebony 21:27-30+ O '66
Pattern of revolution. R. Moley. Newsweek
68:84 Ag 8 '66
Petitioners, by L. Miller. Review
Sat R 49:32 Ja 29 '66. B. D. Diamon-
stein
Plotting a war on whitey; extremists set for
violence. R. Sackett. il Life 60:100-100B+
Je 10 '66
Politics and the Warren court, by A. M.
Bickel. Review
Commentary 41:106+ Ap '66. M. L. Wulf
Politics: the white backlash, 1966. il News-
week 68:27-8 O 10 '66
Race: fact and feeling. F. M. Cordasco. Sat R
49:40 Mr 12 '66
Requiem or revival? what's next for the
civil-rights movement. T. B. Morgan. il
Look 30:70-3+ Je 14 '66
Rights bill dead. Sr Schol 89:16-17 O 7 '66

Rights of man. il Ebony 21:142-3 O '66
Round three; President's third civil rights
bill. il Time 87:24 My 6 '66
Speaking out; Negroes have a right to fight
back. J. O. Killens. Sat Eve Post 239:10+
Jl 2 '66
Stokely Carmichael: architect of black pow-
er. L. Bennett, jr. il Ebony 21:25-8+ S '66
Temporary surgery; administration's 1966
civil rights bill. Christian Cent 83:975-6 Ag
10 '66
Time to be black. B. Detwiler. New Repub
155:19-22 S 17 '66; Reply. J. N. Miller. 155:
28-9 O 15 '66
Two minds about Carmichael. R. Coles. New
Repub 155:19-21 N 12 '66
Urgent new reach to be equal. J. K. Jessup.
il Life 60:88-90+ Je 3 '66
Voter backlash over race issue? il U S News
61:34-6 S 19 '66
What happened to the civil rights movement?
C. V. Woodward. il Harper 234:29-37 Ja '67
What's ahead for the Negro. il Newsweek
68:30-1 N 28 '66
Who speaks for the Negro? by R. P. Warren.
Review
Nation 202:134-6 Ja 31 '66. M. M. Kar-
patkin
Who won the election? the Negro or white
bigotry? Christian Cent 83:1369 N 9 '66
See also
Civil rights act of 1964
Civil rights demonstrations
Race relations
White House conference on civil rights, 1966

Caricatures and cartoons
As cartoonists see it. Sr Schol 88:9 My 13 '66

History
Freedom bound, by H. Buckmaster. Review
Negro Hist Bul 29:41 N '65. B. H. Nelson
Petitioners, by L. Miller. Review
Nation 202:529-30 My 2 '66. E. H. Norton

Crime
Rise in crime: what the police records show.
il U S News 61:103 S 12 '66

Economic conditions
Black power. N. Wright, jr. Cath World 204:
46-51 O '66
Negro middle class is right in the middle.
D. Cordtz. il Fortune 74:174-80+ N '66
Of dollars and sense; reprint. il Ebony 21:
56-7 S '66
See also
Negroes in the United States—Migration

Education
Achievements of the Negro colleges. B. E.
Mays. Atlan 217:90-2 F '66
Angry parents of I.S. 201. R. Gustaitis. il
Reporter 35:30-4 N 17 '66
Are all men equal? address, November 30,
1965. R. Jones. Vital Speeches 32:271-2 F
15 '66
Blueprint for education. H. Howe. 2d. il
Parents Mag 41:58-61+ O '66
Children of the South. by M. Anderson. Re-
view
New Repub 155:17-19 S 24 '66. R. Coles
Education; the racial gap; findings of James
Coleman's study. C. Jencks. New Repub
155:21-6 O 1 '66; Reply. F. McKissick. 155:
33-6 D 3 '66
History is not enough. il Ebony 21:40-1 F '66
Integration: Negro college hires an impatient
Briton. L. J. Carter. il Science 152:481-5 Ap
22 '66
I.S. 201: center of bitterness and ill will.
New Yorker 42:44-5 O 1 '66
Making up for the past; school-aid measure,
Lowndes County, Ala. New Repub 154:10-11
Mr 19 66
New direction for Negro colleges. H. Zinn.
Harper 232:75-81 My '66; Discussion. 233:4+
Jl '66
School 201: Board of education and parents
assured a voice. Commonweal 85:44 O 14 '66
Searchlight on high schools in the South.
W. W. Geier. Christian Cent 83:186-8 F 9
'66
Segregation fence: a young mother gets in-
volved; teacher in a southern city. M.
Jaynes. il Redbook 126:8+ Mr '66
South's revenge. S. Alsop. il Sat Eve Post
239:18 S 24 '66; Same abr. Read Digest 89:
79-81 D '66

NEGROES in the United States—Education—
Conitinued
What makes integration work. F. Morley. il
Nations Bsns 54:27-8 D '66
See also
American teachers association
Colleges and universities—Desegregation
Miles college, Birmingham, Ala.
Parochial schools, Catholic—Desegregation
Public schools—Desegregation
Segregation in education
West Virginia State college, Institute, W.Va.

History
Dunbar story (1870-1955) Review
Negro Hist Bul 29:117 F '66. L. Langborne
How Supreme court overcame its racism;
excerpts from The petitioners. L. Miller.
il Ebony 21:57-62+ Mr '66

Employment
Are all men equal? address, November 30,
1965. R. Jones. Vital Speeches 32:271-2
F 15 '66
Big target; protests at segregated facilities
in U.S. steel corp. il Newsweek 67:93+ Je
20 '66
Boost up job ladder for Negroes; Newport
News shipbuilding pact with federal agency. Bsns W p 130+ Ap 23 '66
Gains by Negroes in incomes, jobs. U S News
60:13 F 7 '66
Good Newport News; agreement against discrimination. Reporter 34:14-15 Ap 21 '66
Great American cities; role of private industry in solving unemployment problem; address, November 14, 1966. A. J. Cervantes.
Vital Speeches 33:176-9 Ja 1 '67
Job gap. H. P. Miller. il N Y Times Mag
p30-1+ My 8 '66; Reply. J. H. Scheuer.
p41 Je 5 '66
Negroes zero in on steel industry; U.S. steel
the prime target of civil rights groups.
Bsns W p 156+ D 10 '66
New drive to fulfill these rights; emphasis on
local efforts by business, labor, and gov-
ernment. il Bsns W p38-40 My 28 '66
New push for hiring of Negroes. U S News
60:110 Mr 14 '66
Newport News goes color-blind. America 114:
575 Ap 23 '66
Of dollars and sense; reprint. il Ebony 21:
56-7 S '66
Poverty areas of our major cities. J. R.
Wetzel and S. S. Holland. il Mo Labor R
89:1105-10 O '66
Power of the dollar; Operation breadbasket
in Chicago. Newsweek 68:62 D 26 '66
Unemployables; hard-core Negro joblessness.
il Newsweek 68:84-6 N 7 '66
See also
Negro American labor council
Negro government employees
Negro women—Employment
United States—President's equal employment
opportunity commission

Folklore
See Folklore, Negro

History
Aspect of bibliography and research in Negro
history; address, October 22, 1965. C. H.
Wesley. Negro Hist Bul 29:51-2+ D '65
Foreword to the pictorial history of the
American Negro; reprint. C. H. Wesley.
Negro Hist Bul 29:105-6 F '66
Longest journey; A. C. Sam's back-to-Africa
movement. A. J. Lane. Nation 202:530-1 My
2 '66
Much yet to overcome. W. Katz. Sat R 49:
26-7 Ag 13 '66
Mutual aid and the Negro. J. Slawson. bib-
liog f Commentary 41:43-50 Ap '66
Negro history in the public schools; trends
and prospects. W. F. Brazziel. Negro Hist
Bul 29:35-6+ N '65
Negro in modern American history textbooks,
comp. by I. Sloan. P. Schrag. Sat R 50:74
Ja 21 '67
Old South had something worth saving. H.
Carter. il N Y Times Mag p50-1+ D 4 '66
Race image improved; effect of Negro history
education. P. McBroom. Sci N 90:318 O 22
'66
Treatment of the Negro in American history
school textbooks. S. Axelrod. bibliog Negro
Hist Bul 29:135-6+, 167 Mr-Ap '66
What the historian owes the Negro. B.
Quarles. Sat R 49:10-13 S 3 '66
See also
Association for the study of Negro life and
history
Slavery—United States

Housing
Frontier for '66. Newsweek 67:28-9 My 9 '66
Housing and urban development; address.
August 1, 1966. R. C. Weaver. Vital
Speeches 32:674-8 S 1 '66
King in Chicago. B. Cook. Commonweal 84:
175-7 Ap 29 '66
Open housing: here's why. J. D. Ban. Chris-
tian Cent 83:1031 Ag 24 '66
Reston, Va; new design for an ideal city. il
Ebony 22:90-2+ D '66
Still King; open housing agreement be-
tween Chicago Freedom movement and
Chicago political, civic and social service
organizations. Christian Cent 83:1071 S 7
'66
That word ghetto. Fortune 74:102 S '66
Truce in Chicago; freedom march cracks the
ghetto's limits. il Bsns W p36-8 S 3 '66
White House camp-in. Newsweek 67:38 Ap 15
'66
See also
Discrimination in housing
Housing—Desegregation

Migration
As Negroes leave South; the outlook by 1970.
U S News 61:15 D 19 '66
Longest journey; A. C. Sam's back-to-Africa
movement. A. J. Lane. Nation 202:530-1
My 2 '66
Negro cities, white suburbs; it's the prospect
for year 2000. il U S News 60:72-3 F 21 '66
South's revenge. S. Alsop. il Sat Eve Post
239:18 S 24 '66; Same abr. Read Digest 89:
79-81 D '66
Time for tents; mobile church for a mobile
age. Christian Cent 83:639-40 My 18 '66

Occupations
Speaking of people. See issues of Ebony

Politics and suffrage
Alabama vote; Wallace still strong but some
Negroes win. il U S News 60:8 Je 13 '66
Alabama's new era; the Negro votes. il News-
week 67:25-30 My 16 '66
Alabama's restoration; sword in the heart of
Dixie; significance of the gubernatorial
primary. J. Beecher. il Nation 202:611-14
My 23 '66
Atlantic report; Negro electorate. Atlan 217:
4+ My '66
Black ballot. il Time 87:26 Ap 15 '66
Black power. F. Millspaugh. Commonweal
84:500-3 Ag 5 '66
Black power (cont) L. Bennett, jr. il Ebony
21:127-30+ F; 121-4+ Ap; 58-60+ Jl; 152-
4+ O; 22:146-8+ D '66; 114-16+ Ja '67
Black power and coalition politics. B. Rustin.
Commentary 42:35-40 S '66
Black power; politics of frustration. il News-
week 68:26+ Jl 11 '66
Constitutional disenfranchisement of the
Negro in Louisiana, 1898. G. E. Cunning-
ham. bibliog Negro Hist Bul 29:147-8+ Ap
'66
Corner turned; Alabama's Negroes at the
polls. il Time 87:23-4 My 13 '66
Crisis in civil rights leadership. C. T. Rowan.
il Ebony 22:27-30+ N '66
Crisis of color '66; survey findings. il News-
week 68:20-32+ Ag 22 '66
Despite Negro opposition, a Negro might
make it; running for sheriff in Alabama.
J. Beecher. New Repub 155:11-12 Jl 2 '66
Divided Negro vote; southern Africa. Time
87:30 Ap 29 '66
In defense of black power. D. Danzig. Com-
mentary 42:41-6 S '66
In first big test of the Negro vote; Ala-
bama's primary. il U S News 60:37-9 My
16 '66
Julian Bond; Georgia's uppity legislator. H.
Shapiro. il Nation 202:145-8 F 7 '66
Lair of the Black Panther; Lowndes County
Negroes form political party in Alabama. A.
Kopkind. New Repub 155:10-13 Ag 13 '66
Negro politics, old style and new; Chicago
and Mississippi. R. Cotton; H. Hurt. il Re-
porter 35:21-3+ Ag 11 '66
Negro strategy. Commonweal 84:626-7 S 30
'66
New face of politics in Alabama. il Life 60:
40-42A My 13 '66
Night, what of the watchman? reactions to
H. McCaskill's filing for office. Nation 202:
766 Je 27 '66
One black plum; result of Negroes' election
drive in Alabama. il Newsweek 67:44 Je 13
'66

NEIGHBORHOOD youth corps. See United States—Youth corps

NEIGHBORS, R. J.
Up-to-the-minute management information reports. Am City 81:102-4 Ag '66

NEIGHBORS
Ann's next-door neighbors were troublemakers. D. C. Disney. Ladies Home J 83: 22+ Ag '66

NEIGHBORS; story. See Dixon, S.

NEILANDS, J. B. See Komai, H. jt. auth.

NEISSER, Edith G.
Many meanings of money. Parents Mag 41: 25-9+ O '65
Problem preschoolers. Parents Mag 41:43-5+ Mr '66
—See Bernstein, H; Delano J. G. jt. auths.

NEIZVESTNYI, Ernst
Familiars of death. J. Berger. Nation 203: 553-7 N 21 '66

NELMS, Joyce
Digging for ideas. Writer 79:27-8 Mr '66

NELOY, Eddie
Inexact but incorporated. il por Time 88:63 Ag 19 '66

NELSON, Alexander. See Bowman, R. L. jt. auth.

NELSON, B. H.
Book review. Negro Hist Bul 29:41 N '65

NELSON, Betty Jean. See Hall, J. E. jt. auth.

NELSON, Bryan
Man-o'-war bird. Natur Hist 75:32-9 My '66

NELSON, C. A. See Cloud, P. E. jr, jt. auth.

NELSON, Claud D. See Kelley, D. M. jt. auth.

NELSON, D. J. and others
High-purity calcium carbonate in freshwater clam shell. bibliog Science 152:1368-70 Je 3 '66

NELSON, Dale
O rare! poem. New Yorker 42:48 Mr 5 '66

NELSON, Don. See Skadberg, M. jt. auth.

NELSON, Esther
Who can teach pre-school children, and why? por Dance Mag 40:64-6 Je '66

NELSON, Gaylord Anton
American highway scandal; address, February 3, 1966. Vital Speeches 32:329-32 Mr 15 '66

about
Systems approach: political interest rises. L. J. Carter. Science 153:1222-4 S 9 '66

NELSON, George
New Haven and its mayor. Holiday 39:62-3+ My '66

NELSON, J. Robert
COSMOS in conference. Christian Cent 83: 1433-5 N 23 '66
Ecumenical escalation. Christian Cent 83:858 Jl 6 '66
Movies. Christian Cent 83:335 Mr 16 '66
Oh, Henry! Christian Cent 83:295 Mr 9 '66
Romano, ma non troppo. Christian Cent 83: 825-6 Je 29 '66

NELSON, Jack L. See Gross, M. G. jt. auth.

NELSON, John W. Jr
Organize your operators. Am City 81:86-8 N '66

NELSON, Katherine Metcalf
San Francisco. Art N 65:59+ O '66

NELSON, Kay Shaw
Mushroom cook book. House & Gard 130: 131+ Ag '66

NELSON, Lee H.
Restoration in Independence Hall: a continuum of historic preservation. Antiques 90:64-8 Jl '66

NELSON, Lindsey, and Hirshberg, Al
Stadium inside a studio; excerpt from Backstage at the Mets. Sports Illus 24:38-40+ Mr 28 '66

NELSON, Marion John
Indigenous characteristics in American art pottery. Antiques 89:846-50 Je '66

NELSON, Oliver
Old blues dressed up fit to kill. C. Harman. Life 60:10 Mr 11 '66

NELSON, Oliver E. See Tsai, C. Y. jt. auth.

NELSON, P. G. See Burke, R. E. jt. auth.

NELSON, Ralph
Remodeling: hard work but worth it. Farm J 90:52-3 Ag '66

NELSON, Roy Paul
Less than saintly. Christian Cent 83:1473 N 30 '66

NELSON, William Rockhill, gallery of art. See William Rockhill Nelson gallery of art, Kansas City, Mo.

NELSON gallery of art. See William Rockhill Nelson gallery of art, Kansas City, Mo.

NEMATOCYSTS
Disulfide-linked collagenous protein of nematocyst capsules. F. Blanquet and H. M. Lenhoff. bibliog il Science 154:152-3 O 7 '66

NEMATODES
Cilia in nematode sensory organs. D. R. Roggen and others. bibliog il Science 152: 515-16 Ap 22 '66
Light sense in nematodes. P. A. G. Wilson. bibliog il Science 151:337-8 Ja 21 '66
Nematodes; what they are and how to control them. L. Pyenson. il Horticulture 44:30-1 Je '66

NEMEROV, Howard
At the airport; poem. New Yorker 42:66 N 12 '66
Grace to be said at the supermarket; poem. Nation 202:397 Ap 4 '66
Marriage of heaven and earth; poem. New Yorker 42:146 D 10 '66
View; poem. New Yorker 42:64 O 29 '66

NEMEROVSKI, Howard N.
To be a citizen. por Am Ed 2:21-3 Ap '66

NENES
Where to see the rare ney-ney. il Sunset 137:20 Jl '66

NEO-FASCISM. See Fascism—Germany

NEO-HUMANISM. See Humanism

NEON
Neon gas used by aquanauts. il Sci N 89:287 Ap 23 '66
Times square of the mind; sculpture. il Time 87:100-1 Mr 18 '66

NEOPRENE. See Rubber, Artificial

NEPAL
Sherpaland, my Shangri-La. D. Doig. il Nat Geog Mag 130:544-77 O '66
See also
Americans in Nepal
Economic assistance in Nepal
Hunting—Nepal

Description and travel
Well traveled camera. H. Keppler. il Mod Phot 30:28+ My; 32+ Je; 32+ Jl '66
Yaks and yeti. V. Gilmore. il Sat R 49:51-2 Ap 30 '66

NEPHRITIS
Beta-1C-globulin: metabolism in glomerulonephritis. C. A. Alper and others. bibliog il Science 153:180-2 Jl 8 '66
Drugs add to success of kidney transplants; preventing glomerulonephritis. Sci N 90:347 O 29 '66

NEPTUNE (planet)
Triton is doomed. il Time 88:66 O 14 '66

Satellites
See Satellites

NERO, emperor of Rome
Madman and his Bacchanal. il por Life 60: 62-3 Je 3 '66

NERUDA, Pablo
Ode to my socks; Funeral in the East; poems. tr. by R. Bly. Nation 203:53-4 Jl 11 '66

about
Day with Pablo Neruda. S. Rodman. pors Sat R 49:16-18 Jl 9 '66
Pablo Neruda: the poet in New York. J. Yglesias. Nation 203:52-5 Jl 11 '66

NERVE cells
Cell size and rate of protein synthesis in ventral horn neurones. R. P. Peterson. bibliog il Science 153:1413-14 S 16 '66
Key to nerve cell seen; theory explaining link between electricity and chemistry in nervous system function. P. McBroom. Sci N 90:347 O 29 '66
Marking single neurons by staining with intracellular recording microelectrodes. R. C. Thomas and V. J. Wilson. bibliog il Science 151:1538-9 Mr 25 '66
Nerve axon. P. F. Baker. il Sci Am 214: 74-82 Mr '66
Neurosecretory cell: capable of conducting impulse in rats. K. Yagi and others. bibliog il Science 154:778-9 N 11 '66
Neurosecretory cells: daily rhythmicity in leiobunum longipes. D. J. Fowler and C. J. Goodnight. bibliog il Science 152: 1078-80 My 20 '66
Rate of movement and redistribution of stainable neurosecretory granules in hypothalamic neurons. A. Jasinski and others. bibliog il Science 154:776-8 N 11 '66
Regeneration in spinal neurons: proteosynthesis following nerve growth factor administration. D. Scott, jr. and others. bibliog il Science 152:787-8 My 6 '66

NERVE cells—*Continued*
Release of coordinated behavior in crayfish by single central neurons. D. Kennedy and others. bibliog il Science 154:917-19 N 18 '66
Secretion into the cerebrospinal fluid by caudal neurosecretory neurons. G. Fridberg and R. S. Nishioka. bibliog il Science 152:90-1 Ap 1 '66
Synapses of horizontal cells in rabbit and cat retinas. J. E. Dowling and others. bibliog il Science 153:1639-41 S 30 '66
NERVE gases. See Gases, Asphyxiating and poisonous
NERVES
Dieldrin: interaction with nerve components of cockroaches. F. Matsumura and M. Hayashi. bibliog il Science 153:757-9 Ag 12 '66
See also
Nerve cells
Olfactory nerves
Synapses
NERVOUS fatigue. See Fatigue
NERVOUS system
Inhibition in the central nervous system. V. J. Wilson. il Sci Am 214:102-7+ bibliog(p 148) My '66
Key to nerve cell seen; theory explaining link between electricity and chemistry in nervous system function. P. McBroom. Sci N 90:347 O 29 '66
Perineural epithelium: a new concept of its role in the integrity of the peripheral nervous system. T. R. Shanthaveerappa and G. H. Bourne. bibliog il Science 154:1464-7 D 16 '66
Test in the crib; red ball dangling. Newsweek 67:79 Je 20 '66
United States-Japan committee on scientific cooperation: neurochemistry conference; report on conference on the function and metabolism of the nervous system. Y. Tsukada and A. Lajtha. Science 152:801-3 My 6 '66
See also
Chemoreceptivity
Shock
Synapses

Diseases
Ashkenazic inheritance. il Time 88:62 Ag 12 '66
Biting sickness; study findings on Nyhan's disease. Newsweek 68:52 S 5 '66
Glial responses to degenerating cerebellar cortico-nuclear pathways in the cat. R. P. Eager and P. R. Eager. bibliog il Science 153:553-5 Jl 29 '66
Metachromatic leucodystrophy: isolation and chemical analysis of metachromatic granules. K. Suzuki and others. bibliog il Science 151:1231-3 Mr 11 '66
Points for the virus theory; kuru reproduced in animals. Time 87:55 Ap 1 '66
See also
Ataxia

Surgery
Microscope reduces risks in neurosurgery. Sci N 90:166 S 3 '66
See also
Spinal cord—Surgery
NERVOUS system, Sympathetic
Anteroventral cochlear nucleus: wave forms of extracellularly recorded spike potentials. R. R. Pfeiffer. bibliog il Science 154:667-8 N 4 '66
Electron microscopy: tight junctions in synapses of the chick ciliary ganglion. A. J. D. De Lorenzo. bibliog il Science 152:76-8 Ap 1 '66
Inhibition of the carotid sinus reflex by stimulation of the inferior olive. O. A. Smith, jr. and M. A. Nathan. bibliog il Science 154:674-5 N 4 '66
Lithium's failure to replace sodium in mammalian sympathetic ganglia. A. J. Pappano and R. L. Volle. bibliog il Science 152:85-7 Ap 1 '66
Postsynaptic versus presynaptic inhibition in antagonistic stretch reflexes. D. G. Green and J. O. Kellerth. bibliog il Science 152:1097-9 My 20 '66
Sweating exercise stimulation during circulatory arrest. W. Van Beaumont and R. W. Bullard. bibliog il Science 152:1521-3 Je 10 '66
Sympathetic outflows from cervical spinal cord in the dog. G. G. Wiesman and others. bibliog il Science 152:381-2 Ap 15 '66
NERVOUS tension. See Stress (physiology)

NESBIT, E.
Pirates and explorers; excerpt from Long ago when I was young. Horn Bk 42:87-92 F '66
NESBITT, Dorothy
Invitation to the dance. por Parks & Rec 1:724-5+ S '66
NESS, Norman F.
Earth's magnetic field: a new look; address, December 26, 1965. bibliog Science 151:1041-52 Mr 4 '66
NESS, LOCH, Scotland
New evidence spurs hunt for Loch Ness monster. D. Scott. il Pop Sci 189:112-15+ N '66
NESTS
Nesting observation. J. Hancock. il Natur Hist 75:32-3 Je '66
Soft blanket, tough nest. E. M. White. Audubon Mag 68:124 Mr '66
NET book agreement. See Books—Prices
NETBOY, Anthony
Retreat of the Atlantic salmon. Am For 71:25-9+ O '65
Use of high country in Switzerland. Am For 72:6-7+ O '66
NETHERLANDS
See also
Airlines—Netherlands
Americans in the Netherlands
Amsterdam
Architecture, Domestic—Netherlands
Catholic church in the Netherlands
Cities and towns—Netherlands
Education—Netherlands
Music festivals—Netherlands

Description and travel
Touring the Dutch countryside. il Sunset 136:61-2+ Mr '66

Economic conditions
Leaky dikes. Time 88:112 O 7 '66
See also
Wages—Netherlands

Foreign relations
China (People's Republic)
Diplomatic corpse; death of Hsu Tzu-tsai in The Hague. Time 88:31 Ag 5 '66
Mystery of the locked legation; who killed Mr Hsu? R. Chelminski. il Life 61:30B Ag 19 '66

History
Bibliography
Articles and other books received; comp. by P. Rosenfeld. See issues of American historical review

Royal family
Though the heavens fall; Princess Beatrix wedding; anti-German demonstrations. il Newsweek 67:46-7 Mr 21 '66
NETHERLANDS WEST INDIES
See also
Curacao (island)
NETS, Fishing. See Fishing nets
NEUBAUER, John
Day they chased the sun. Pop Phot 58:72-3+ My '66
How'd you like to sell/buy your home on TV? Pop Phot 60:87 Ja '67
LBJ: he's turned the other cheek. Pop Phot 60:118-19+ Ja '67
Navy plans Vietnam exhibit. Pop Phot 59:42+ Jl '66
World's press was on hand August 6 when Luci Baines wed Patrick Nugent. il Pop Phot 59:86+ D '66
NEUBERT, Christine
Children's dance is serious fun. J. Anderson. il pors Dance Mag 40:68-70 My '66
NEUFELD, John
Extensive supplements needed; letter to the editor. Library J 91:4049 S 15 '66
NEUGASS, Fritz
Auction season in review. Art N 65:18-19 S '66
NEUHAUS, Richard
Voices in the vanguard. Christian Cent 83:778-80 Je 15 '66
NEUMAN, Robert W. See Hill, W. E. jr. jt. auth.
NEUMANN, Gerhard
G.E.'s hard-driving jockey in the jet-engine race. J. Mecklin. il por Fortune 74:116-18+ Jl 1 '66
NEURAIRTOME. See Surgical instruments and apparatus

NEURALGIA, Trigeminal
Most severe pain; relief from carbamaze-
pine. Time 87:56 Je 24 '66
Severe face pain helped by experimental
drug; trigeminal neuralgia or tic doulou-
reux. Sci N 89:514 Je 25 '66
NEURONS. See Nerve cells
NEUROPHYSIOLOGY. See Nervous system
NEUROSECRETORY cells. See Nerve cells
NEUROSES
    See also
Phobias
NEUROSPORA
Neurospora; report on third Neurospora
information conference. R. H. Davis. Sci-
ence 153:1553-4+ S 23 '66
Protoperithecia in neurospora crassa: tech-
nique for studying their development. H.
Rothschild and S. R. Suskind. bibliog il
Science 154:1356-7 D 9 '66
NEUROSURGERY. See Nervous system—Sur-
gery
NEUSTADT, Richard Elliott
John F. Kennedy school: helping government's
in-and-outers B. Nelson. il por Science 154:
135-8 O 7 '66
NEUTRA, Richard
Books. Arch Forum 125:88-9+ Jl '66
NEUTRAL salts. See Salts
NEUTRALITY
Waiting for the end; four-day meeting of the
nonaligned statesman in New Delhi. il
Newsweek 68:62-3 N 7 '66
    See also subhead Neutrality under names
of countries, e.g. Cambodia—Neutrality
NEUTRINOS
Neutrino: ghost particle of the atom, by
I. Asimov. Review
Nat R 18:1003-5 O 4 '66. F. Leiber
Neutrinos from the atmosphere and beyond.
F. Reines and J. P. F. Sellschop. il Sci Am
214:40-8 bibliog(p 138) F '66
NEUTRONS
Combination neutron experiment for remote
analysis. R. L. Caldwell and others. bibliog
il Science 152:457-65 Ap 22 '66
    See also
Neutrinos
NEVADA
    See also
Hunting—Nevada
Law—Nevada

Antiquities
    See Indians of North America—Antiqui-
ties—Nevada

Parks and reserves
Close call at Lake Tahoe; Lake Tahoe state
park. D. B. Alexander. il Parks & Rec
1:146-8 F '66

Politics and government
Feds, sharpers and politics in Nevada. E. F.
Sherman. New Repub 155:12-13 O 29 '66
Nevada: the end of the casino era. E. F.
Sherman. il Atlan 218:112-16 O '66
Nevada: the rotten borough: use made of
power in the Senate. G. M. Ostrander. il
Nation 202:452-5 Ap 18 '66
NEVADA. University, Reno
Back to school; course for trial judges at
the University of Nevada. Time 88:49 Ag
19 '66
NEVADA'S petrified forest. See Petrified for-
ests
NEVENZEL, Judd C. and others
Lipids of the living coelacanth, latimeria
chalumnae. bibliog Science 152:1753-5 Je 24
'66
NEVES, Irene
Khadejha: the girl who started it. Life 61:
147-8 S 16 '66
NEVEU, Ginette
Brief candles. H. Goldsmith. por Hi Fi 16:
54+ F '66
NEVILLE, Elizabeth
Amateur scientist; experiment in animal be-
havior. Sci Am 215:135-6 D '66
NEVILLE, Phoebe
Meredith Monk and Phoebe Neville; Judson
memorial church. J. Maskey. Dance Mag
41:69 Ja '67
NEVIN, David
Charlie Whitman: the eagle scout who grew
up with a tortured mind. Life 61:28D-31
Ag 12 '66
Dissent; it questions and attacks U.S. in-
volvement in Vietnam; interviews. Life 60:
56B-60+ F 25 '66
People out for stars, not peanuts. Life 61:50+
Jl 1 '66

NEVINS, Allan
Oral history: how and why it was born.
Wilson Lib Bul 40:600-1 Mr '66
Place of Franklin D. Roosevelt in history;
address, May 1965. Am Heritage 17:12-15+
Je '66
Presidency: power and purpose. Sat R 49:40-
1 D 3 '66
NEW ALBANY, Ind.
Parking decals serve overtime parkers. G.
Inman. Am City 81:134 O '66
NEW American library of world literature,
incorporated
Fast thinking and action on NAL's blackout
quickie; Night the lights went out. il Pub
W 189:122-3 F 7 '66
NEW BEDFORD, Mass.
Hold back the sea. F. C. Gray, jr. il Yacht-
ing 120:54+ Jl '66
NEW BEDFORD, Mass, free public library
Automated library in New England. J. S.
Healey. Wilson Lib Bul 41:411-13+ D '66
NEW BRITAIN (island)

Native races
Blowgun hunters of the South Pacific; the
Kaulong and the Sengseng. J. C. Goodale;
A. Chowning. il Nat Geog Mag 129:792-817
Je '66
NEW BRITAIN museum of American art, New
Britain, Conn.
New Britain museum of American art. C.
B. Ferguson. il Antiques 90:668-72 N '66
NEW BRUNSWICK, Canada
    See also
Saint John River
NEW business enterprises. See Business enter-
prises, New
NEW CALEDONIA
Travel's picture portfolio. Travel 125:50-5 My
'66
NEW CASTLE, Pa.
Keeping kids out of trouble. W. F. Burmester.
il Parents Mag 41:50-1+ F '66
NEW Catholic encyclopedia
Milestone in religious publishing. E. A. Weis.
America 115:586-7 N 12 '66
NEW cities. See New towns
NEW deal. See United States—History—1933-
1945
NEW DELHI, India
Preview; New Delhi civic center. il Arch
Forum 125:97 S '66
NEW DELHI conference of non-aligned na-
tions, 1966. See International conferences
NEW ENGLAND
New England yachting; symposium. il Yacht-
ing 120:50-61+ Jl '66
Power politics in New England; importing
low-cost power from Canada. V. Maerki.
New Repub 154:10 Ja 29 '66
    See also
Gardens—New England
Northeastern states
Theater—New England

Description and travel
Four family-planned circle tours. N. Kuehnl
and P. Lindberg. il Bet Hom & Gard 44:
70-1 Je '66
New England yachting. B. Robinson. Il
Yachting 120:51-3+ Jl '66

Industries
New England's big comeback: latest success
story. il U S News 60:72-5 F 14 '66

Intellectual life
New England saint; concerning A. Warren's
studies of prominent figures. S. Paul. Nation 203:647-8 D 12 '66

Religious institutions and affairs
New England saint; concerning A. Warren's
studies of prominent figures. S. Paul. Nation 203:647-8 D 12 '66

Social life and customs
    See also
Colonial life and customs
NEW ENGLAND book show. See Book exhibits
NEW ENGLAND Catholic education center
Catholic schools and educational publishing;
a dialog about the future. il Pub W 190:
18-23 D 12 '66
NEW ENGLAND cookery. See Cookery, Amer-
ican
NEW ENGLAND glass company. See Glass
manufacture
NEW ENGLAND town meeting. See Town
meeting

NEW ENGLANDERS
New England saint; concerning A. Warren's studies of prominent figures. S. Paul. Nation 203:647-8 D 12 '66

NEW eyes for the needy (organization) See Eyeglasses

NEW GUINEA
Margaret Mead answers questions about: housekeeping in the field. M. Mead. Redbook 127:38+ O '66

See also
Birds—New Guinea
Missions—New Guinea
New Britain (island)

Native races
Letter from the field; report of changes on fourth trip to study the Manus. M. Mead. Redbook 127:30+ My '66
Mission to the stone age; Nancy and Dennis Cochrane among the Dunas. E. Nadel. il Look 31:30-4 Ja 24 '67

NEW GUINEA, TERRITORY OF
Rights of primitive peoples; Papua-New Guinea: a crucial instance. M. Mead. il For Affairs 45:306-9 Ja '67

NEW HAMPSHIRE
See also
Education—New Hampshire
Franconia Notch

Description and travel
New Hampshire out of season. N. T. Di Giovanni. il Atlan 217:114-16 My '66

Politics and government
Primary mix; H. R. Thyng's Senate nomination. New Repub 155:7-8 S 24 '66

NEW HAMPSHIRE lottery. See Lotteries

NEW HAVEN, Conn.

City planning
City survey that saves. A. Landino. il Am City 81:94-5+ D '66
New Haven and its mayor. G. Nelson. Holiday 39:62-3+ My '66
Symbolic bells in Dixwell. M. Hommann. il Arch Forum 125:54-9 Jl '66

Education
Flexible structure for progressive primary school. il Arch Rec 139:174-5 F '66

Music
New-music journeys in the U.S.A. E. Salzman. Hi Fi 16:MA12-13+ Ag '66

Theater
Theater; Long Wharf theatre; summer presentations. H. Hewes. Sat R 49:38 Ag 27 '66
Theater; production of Chekhov's The three sisters. H. Hewes. Sat R 49:69 D 3 '66

NEW HAVEN, Conn. free public library
From supermarket to superlibrary. W. Cahn and R. Cahn. il Parents Mag 41:47-9+ Je '66
Little miracle on Chapel street. H. T. Drennan. il Am Ed 2:1-5 Jl '66
No glass boxes for New Haven; Mitchell branch. M. Bloss. il Library J 91:5869-71 D 1 '66
Take a giant step: New Haven library neighborhood center. M. Bloss; C. T. Schreiber; J. Coyne. il Library J 91:323-31 Ja 15 '66; Reply. M. B. Zimmerman. 91:2120 Ap 15 '66

NEW HAVEN railroad. See New York, New Haven and Hartford railroad company

NEW HOPE auto show. See Automobiles—Collectors and collecting

NEW JERSEY
See also
Airports—New Jersey
Architecture, Domestic—New Jersey
Booksellers and bookselling—New Jersey
Crime and criminals—New Jersey
Education—New Jersey
Hunting—New Jersey
Libraries—New Jersey
Mullica River

Historic houses, etc.
Highwaymen come to Morristown; Interstate highway system. J. Skow. il Sat Eve Post 239:68-75 Ap 9 '66

Parks and reserves
Dedicated to liberty; Liberty State Park being developed. Parks & Rec 1:643 Ag '66

Politics and government
Who needs progress? sales tax; Hughes new goal. Time 87:25B Ap 1 '66

NEW JERSEY branch of the American civil liberties union. See American civil liberties union

NEW JERSEY PINE BARRENS NATIONAL MONUMENT (proposed) See National monuments

NEW JERSEY turnpike. See Roads—New Jersey

NEW mathematics. See Mathematics

NEW MEXICO
Three cultures of New Mexico. W. T. Le Viness. il Américas 18:8-15 Je '66
See also
Education—New Mexico
Geology—New Mexico
Hunting—New Mexico
Paleontology—New Mexico
Pecos National Monument
Pueblo Indians
Skis and skiing—New Mexico

Description and travel
Last glowing isolation; countryside that inspired D. H. Lawrence. D. Pryce-Jones. Reporter 34:49-50 F 10 '66

NEW MEXICO state library, Santa Fe
Territorial for New Mexico. D. J. Watkins. il Library J 91:5867-8 D 1 '66

NEW ORLEANS
Lessons learned from hurricane Betsy. il Am City 81:93-6 Ap '66

City planning
Threat to New Orleans' famed quarter? il U S News 60:10 F 28 '66

Description
Through old New Orleans by banquette and a streetcar named St Charles. R. Dunlop. il Todays Health 44:40-5+ F '66

Economic conditions
New New Orleans; comeback of a southern city. il U S News 61:78-80 Jl 25 '66
New Orleans: throes of change. il Newsweek 67:76-7+ F 28 '66

Housing
Dixie Zeckendorf runs for cover; New Orleans developer S. J. Recile. il Bsns W p78-9 D 31 '66

Industries
New New Orleans; comeback of a southern city. il U S News 61:78-80 Jl 25 '66
New Orleans: throes of change. il Newsweek 67:76-7+ F 28 '66

International trade mart
New Orleans pins its trade hopes on a tower. il Bsns W p34-5 My 7 '66

Libraries
See also
New Orleans public library
Tulane university, New Orleans—Libraries

Music
Our footloose correspondents. W. Balliett. il New Yorker 42:128+ Je 11 '66
Profiles; Red Allen. W. Balliett. il New Yorker 42:33-6+ Je 25 '66
See also
New Orleans opera house association

Streets
Famous old street gets a new traffic look; Canal street. J. F. Exnicios. il Am City 81:107-8 N '66

Zoological park
See Audubon park zoo

NEW ORLEANS Mardi gras. See Carnival

NEW ORLEANS opera house association
Floyd's Markheim caps the season. H. W. McCraw. il Hi Fi 16:124-5 Je '66
New Orleans. J. Belsom. Opera N 30:31 F 5; 31 Ap 9; 28 Je 4; 31:24 N 19 '66
New Orleans; production of Lucia di Lammermoor and Bohème. J. Belsom. Opera N 31:31 D 24 '66
New Orleans; Strauss' Elektra. J. Belsom. Opera N 31:30 D 31 '66
New Orleans; world premiere of C. Floyd's Markheim. J. Belsom. il Opera N 30:22 My 7 '66

NEW ORLEANS philharmonic-symphony orchestra
Music to my ears; first performance in Carnegie Hall. I. Kolodin. Sat R 49:32 Mr 5 '66
Musical events; concert in Carnegie Hall, conducted by W. Torkanowsky. W. Sargeant. New Yorker 42:74 F 26 '66

NEW YORK (city)—*Continued*

Bibliography

New York, New York. ALA Bul 60:574-5 Je '66

Bookstores

See Booksellers and bookselling—New York (state)

Budget

Painful step toward solvency; meeting at Governor's mansion in Albany. il Time 87:29 Je 24 '66

Taxpayers' money; interview. E. Becker. New Yorker 42:42-3 Mr 26 '66

Buildings, Department of

Lady fights back. J. Horwitz. il Look 30:32+ O 4 '66

Carnegie Hall

Music to my ears; new Carnegie. I. Kolodin. Sat R 49:76 N 19 '66

Chief medical examiner

Routine murder in New York. M. Mayer. Esquire 66:88+ S '66

Chinatown

Chinese lack delinquency. Sci N 90:200 S 17 '66

Churches

Beatitudes at Judson memorial church. S. Kempton. il Esquire 65:106-9+ Mr '66

Church shining in the squalor; Church of the Resurrection, East Harlem. il Fortune 73:157 F '66

Judson revivals: a festival benefit; Judson memorial church. J. Anderson. Dance Mag 40:30-1+ Jl '66

Neighborhood church as focus for renewal; Church of the Resurrection, Harlem. J. Bailey. il Arch Forum 124:48-53 Ja '66

Wall Street Gothic; Trinity church. il Time 88:78 S 2 '66

See also

New York (city)—St John the Divine, Cathedral of

City planning

Framework for lower Manhattan. D. Canty. il Arch Forum 125:48-53 Jl '66

Metro North; a slum community's plan for creating its own new environment. il Arch Rec 139:166-7 Ja '66

New York report calls for single planning agency to operate on decentralized basis. Arch Rec 140:36 N '66

New Yorkers without a voice; a tragedy of urban renewal; excerpt from Faces of poverty. A. R. Simon. Atlan 217:54-9 Ap '66; Discussion. 217:42+ Je; 218:34 Jl '66

City unversity of New York

See New York (city) City university of New York

Civil defense

See New York (city)—Defenses

Clubs

Full house; the thanatopsis pleasure and inside straight club. H. H. Broun. il Am Heritage 18:64-7 D '66

Lotos of New York. Esquire 65:148-9+ Ap '66

Commission on human rights

Reporter at large. E. Iglauer. New Yorker 42:188-92+ S 24 '66

Community centers

Making friends with music; School of the arts of St James' community center. Harlem. O. Evans. il Opera N 31:15-17 N 5 '66

Courts

Judge with disciplined indignation; B. Botein. G. Samuels. il N Y Times Mag p38-40+ Ja 15 '67

Crime

Boy and girl; case of C. Crenshaw and R. Friede. il Newsweek 67:31B F 21 '66

By the numbers; statistics of police department. Newsweek 67:44 Ap 18 '66

Case in point; E. Gallashaw voted not guilty. Newsweek 68:46 O 24 '66

Death of a hooked heiress; case of C. Crenshaw and R. Friede, condensation. D. Schaap. il Look 30:19-25 Jl 26 '66

Detective; G. Barrett, hunter of men. J. Mills. il Read Digest 88:219-23+ F '66

Routine murder in New York; chief medical examiner. M. Mayer. Esquire 66:88+ S '66

Two commissioners; interview. V. L. Broderick. New Yorker 42:33-5 Mr 5 '66

Defenses

Sense in civil defense; Office of civil defense and disaster control. Nation 202:509 My 2 '66

Description

In the land of promise; lower East side exhibition at the Jewish museum. A. Werner. il Reporter 35:50-2 O 6 '66

New Yorker's New York. il ALA Bul 60:567-73 Je '66

Our footloose correspondents; spring walk around shoreline of Manhattan. A. Bailey. il New Yorker 42:142+ Ap 23 '66

Sentimental journey to the Lower East side. H. Swados. il N Y Times Mag p52-3+ S 18 '66

Through native eyes; symposium. il Library J 91:3075-88 Je 15 '66

See also

New York (city)—Streets

Economic conditions

Financial woes of wealthy New York. il U S News 60:14 Ja 31 '66

Is New York's new mayor solving the city's problems? il U S News 61:66-8 Ag 15 '66

Education

Angry parents of I.S. 201. R. Gustaitis. il Reporter 35:30-4 N 17 '66

College readiness program of east Harlem; Benjamin Franklin high school. K. K. Waller. il Sat R 49:90-1+ Ap 16 '66

Down the down staircase; parents, teachers, and public authorities. A. Kopkind. New Repub 155:11-14 O 22 '66

Fifteen years of trouble; Gail White at Livingston school for girls. il Look 30:40-3 S 20 '66

Harlem's besieged showpiece; Intermediate school 201. J. Bailey. il Arch Forum 125:48-51 N '66

High school of performing arts; N.Y. school of printing auditorium. J. Maskey. Dance Mag 40:66 Jl '66

I get one more U, my mother goin' to beat me till it rains. O. Ryan. il N Y Times Mag p27-9+ F 13 '66

Inheritance comes to P.S. 83; Primus-Borde dance troupe performing in a New York school. N. Hentoff. il Am Ed 2:28-32 F '66

I.S. 201; center of bitterness and ill will. New Yorker 42:44-5 O 1 '66

It takes courage; Operation Reclaim, recruiting teachers from the South, displaced by desegregation. L. Rich and J. Rich. il Am Ed 2:5-8 Je '66

Juliet on a ladder; performance at Benjamin Franklin high school. B. Waknin. Commonweal 84:96-7 Ap 15 '66

Normal day in P.S. 200; excerpt from Schoolchildren: growing up in the slums. M. F. Greene and O. Ryan. il McCalls 93:96-7+ Mr '66

Now, black power to run schools? I.S. 201. il U S News 61:16 O 3 '66

Our children are dying, by N. Hentoff. Review

Sat R 50:76 Ja 21 '67. R. Coles

Parent power; Negro parents attempt to influence school policy in New York. Newsweek 68:74-5 O 3 '66

Preschool boom; its pressures and rewards. L. Smith. il Newsweek 67:109-10+ My 16 '66

Profiles; E. Shapiro, principal of P.S. 119 and its replacement P.S. 92, Harlem. N. Hentoff. New Yorker 42:52-4+ My 7 '66

School of tomorrow, today; PS 219, Flushing. il Sr Schol 89:sup2 O 28 '66

School 201. Commonweal 85:44 O 14 '66

Schoolchildren: growing up in the slums, by M. F. Greene and O. Ryan. Review

Reporter 34:47-8 My 5 '66. P Herrera

Sat R 49:100 Ap 16 '66. J. F. Warner

Sorry struggle of I.S. 201. il Time 88:77 S 30 '66

Way it was; move from old PS 31 to modern PS 137, the John L. Bernstein school. New Yorker 42:47-8 O 22 '66

See also

Bank street college of education

Free university of New York

New York (city) City university of New York—City college

Public education association, New York

NEW YORK (city)—*Continued*

Education, Board of

Education board asks delay on Kingsport injunction. Pub W 189:29-30 Ap 4 '66
Judge enjoins school board in Kingsport strike case. Pub W 189:46-7 Mr 28 '66
N.Y. Board of education to vote on union plea; proposal to discontinue buying books manufactured at Kingsport press. Pub W 189:50 Mr 21 '66
NYC orders textbooks for parochial schools. Pub W 190:109 S 26 '66
N.Y.C. schools enjoined from Kingsport boycott. Pub W 190:27 O 24 '66
New York schools asked to boycott Kingsport press. Pub W 189:152 F 21 '66
Unions drop NLRB charges against Kingsport press. Pub W 189:45-6 Je 20 '66

Elections

Campaign by consensus; 17th congressional district, Manhattan. il Time 87:28-9 F 4 '66
Gracious race; seventeenth congressional district. il Newsweek 67:31A F 21 '66
Making of the surrogate. il Time 88:19-20 Jl 8 '66
New York; moderates or ultras? W. F. Buckley, jr. Nat R 18:201 Mr 8 '66
Winning non-candidate; Manhattan surrogate court's primary result. il Newsweek 68:25 Jl 11 '66

Empire state building

Solid gold skyscraper. R. Levy. il Duns R 88:45-6 Jl '66

Employees

Big city slowdown: the battle of bureaucracy. B. D. Blank. il Nation 203:632-7 D 12 '66
Civil service unionism; how to avert another strike. T. J. Cooney. Nation 202:88-9 Ja 24 '66
Sic transit; improvement needed in machinery for negotiating with government workers. Reporter 34:14+ Ja 27 '66

Finance

Federal vs. local; need for federal money. H. C. Wallich. Newsweek 67:80 Je 27 '66
$50 billion minus $25; letter to Mayor Lindsay. G. Ace. il Sat R 49:10 S 24 '66
Money at work; plan to use municipal treasury to deposit funds in banks located in slums. New Repub 156:9 Ja 21 '67
See also
New York (city)—Budget
New York (city)—Taxation
Stock exchange—New York (city)

Fires

See Fires

Foreign population

In the land of promise; lower East side exhibition at the Jewish museum. A. Werner. il Reporter 35:50-2 O 6 '66
Little milk, a little honey; New York's Lower East side. D. Boroff. il Am Heritage 17:12-14+ O '66
See also
Puerto Ricans in the United States

Galleries and museums

Cornucopia; autumn shows. il Newsweek 68:107 O 24 '66
New York, New York, it's a backwater town; major exhibitions slated to bypass city. Time 88:83 N 11 '66
Reviews and previews. See issues of Art news
Summer without smoke. L. Lastra. il Américas 18:40-1 O '66
See also
Museum of illustration art
Museum of modern art
Museum of primitive art
Whitney museum of American art, New York

Gardens

See also
New York botanical garden

Gracie mansion

Mayor's mansion; interview. M. Lindsay. New Yorker 42:47-8 O 15 '66

Greenwich Village

Children's village. il Newsweek 67:114-15+ My 23 '66
Locus: Washington square. W. Bower. il Sat R 49:23-5 Je 4 '66

New Bohemia. W. J. Smith. Commonweal 85:102-3 O 28 '66
New Bohemia, by J. Gruen. Review
  Sat R 49:42+ O 15 '66. D. Hales
Notes and comment. New Yorker 42:19 Ag 13 '66
Notes and comment; changes. New Yorker 42:51-2 N 12 '66
Wakin' up in an empty bed; report on the teen-agers. R. Kotlowitz. il Harper 233:145-7 N '66

Hall of science

Existing structure. New Yorker 42:43-4 O 1 '66

Harbor

See also
Statue of Liberty

Harlem

Big-star stomp through oldtime Harlem; H. Belafonte's production. Strollin' twenties; with report by K. Gouldthorpe. il Life 60:70-4+ F 4 '66
Black ghetto; photographs. Newsweek 68:49-56 Ag 22 '66
Corner; oratory on southwest corner of 125th street and Seventh avenue. New Yorker 42:19-21 Ja 7 '67
Fine arts school; cultural center. il Ebony 21:80-2+ My '66
Harlem, by G. Osofsky. Review
  Newsweek 67:86+ Ja 31 '66
  Sat R il 49:38-9 F 12 '66. E. Ginzberg
Harlem haven; concerning Ribicoff's subcommittee hearings. K. Crawford. Newsweek 68:28 S 12 '66
Harlem's besieged showpiece; Intermediate school 201. J. Bailey. il Arch Forum 125:48-51 N '66
Harlem's immortal five per cent; growing band of young Negro militants. T. M. Gannon. America 115:208-10 Ag 27 '66
Industry builds a showcase in the slums; U.S. gypsum's experiment. il Bsns W p40-1 F 26 '66
Judy Lewis reaches people. I. Mothner. il Look 30:68-72 D 27 '66
Making friends with music; School of the arts of St James' community center. O. Evans. il Opera N 31:15-17 N 5 '66
Menchildren speak; Ribicoff's Senate subcommittee hearings. il Time 88:21-2 S 9 '66
Metro North: a slum community's plan for creating its own new environment; Another east Harlem project. il Arch Rec 139:166-9 Ja '66
Metro North moves mountains; accomplishments of the Citizens committee. G. R. Metcalf. il Reporter 35:24-9 N 17 '66
Neighborhood church as focus for renewal. J. Bailey. il Arch Forum 124:48-53 Ja '66
Profiles; E. Shapiro, principal of P.S. 119 and its replacement P.S. 92. N. Hentoff. New Yorker 42:52-4+ My 7 '66
Relating to the community; Freedom national bank. il Time 87:80+ Ja 28 '66
Voices from the ghetto; Ribicoff's subcommittee hearings. il Newsweek 68:25-6 S 12 '66

Historic houses, etc.

Architecture; Cavaglieri's plans for Astor library. E. Galantay. Nation 202:500-2 Ap 25 '66
Great landmarks fight; private loss vs. public gain. S. D. Smith. il N Y Times Mag p 108+ Mr 27 '66
Must landmarks go? excerpts from The living end. R. Starr. il Horizon 8:48-59 Sum '66
See also
New York (city)—Gracie mansion

Hospitals

Community hospital in the ghetto; Lincoln hospital's new service and plans. M. Renek. New Repub 155:9 D 10 '66
Conundrums of causation; Doctors hospital settles negligence case. il Time 88:39 Jl 29 '66
Sickness in the hospitals; resignation threat by public health nurses. Newsweek 67:78 My 30 '66
Sisters of the poor; owners and operators of St Francis hospital. New Yorker 42:24-7 D 31 '66
Surgery for sick hospitals. il Newsweek 67:66 Mr 7 '66

Hotels, restaurants, etc.

Any number can eat; La fonda del sol and Chauveron restaurants. C. W. Morton. Atlan 219:105-6 Ja '67

NEW YORK (city)—Hotels, restaurants, etc.
—*Continued*
Arms against Venus; topless waitresses. G.
Ace. Sat R 49:16 D 10 '66
Around the world in Manhattan. C. Paddle-
ford. il Library J 91:3089-90 Je 15 '66
Closing a hotel, at a profit; British commer-
cial property administration sells furnish-
ings of Sheraton East hotel. il Bsns W
p64-6 Jl 23 '66
Dining in/out; Clos Normand and Le Manoir.
C. H. McBride. Esquire 65:75+ My '66
Dining in/out with Esquire; the Tower suite.
Esquire 67:54 Ja '67
Fifty-five New York restaurants of special
interest to visitors. S. Spitzer and H. Spit-
zer. Holiday 40:79 Jl '66
Fountain café: Central park at the Bethesda
fountain. New Yorker 42:50 S 17 '66
Fountain cafe in Central park: new life for a
landmark. il Arch Rec 140:140-1 D '66
From the academy; grand hotels. R. Kirk.
Nat R 18:730 Jl 26 '66
Goings on about town. See issues of New
Yorker
Ground floor. C. H. McBride. il Esquire 65:
94-5 Mr '66
King; H. Soulé's Le Pavillon. il Time 87:52
F 4 '66
Long-winded lady; episode at the Adano
restaurant. New Yorker 42:20-1 Ag 6 '66
Manhattan catches up; topless waitresses.
Newsweek 68:52 N 21 '66
Moriarty's trap; carriage advertising. P. J.
Moriarty's restaurant; interview. F. Smith.
New Yorker 42:38-40 My 7 '66
Princely suite; Prince Philip's suite in the
Hotel Pierre. il McCalls 93:74-5 Jl '66
Restaurants; abroad in New York. N. S.
Hazelton. Nat R 18:419+ My 3 '66
Well worth paying for: Coach house, and
Cedars of Lebanon. N. S. Hazelton. Nat R
18:841+ Ag 23 '66
See also
Night clubs

Housing
Blue Moerdler; war on slumlords and offi-
cials' in-laws. Newsweek 67:36+ Mr 28 '66
Bright landmarks on a changing urban scene;
New York university project. C. Robinson.
il Arch Forum 125:21-9 D '66
Extending Manhattan; Waterside, projected
complex jutting into East River. il Time
88:24 D 30 '66
High-density housing: a limited profit middle-
income project breaks the pattern. il Arch
Rec 140:200-1 Jl '66
Hopeful experiments in rehabilitation. il
Fortune 73:177 Ap '66
Lady fights back. J. Horwitz. il Look 30:
32+ O 4 '66
Landscape architect Paul Friedberg creates
handsome public spaces for Lower East
Side public housing. il Arch Rec 140:197-8
Jl '66
Metro North moves mountains; accomplish-
ments of the Citizens committee. G. R.
Metcalf. il Reporter 35:24-9 N 17 '66
New Yorkers without a voice: a tragedy of
urban renewal; excerpt from Faces of pov-
erty. A. R. Simon. Atlan 217:34-9 Ap '66;
Discussion. 217:42+ Je; 218:34 Jl '66
Private way; rehabilitation of a Manhattan
east Harlem ghetto. il Time 87:89 Je 3 '66
R for slums? U.S. gypsum project. Newsweek
68:68 Jl 25 '66
Riis plaza: design with keen understanding
of human needs. il Arch Rec 140:134-5 D
'66
Riis plaza: three acres filled wih life. J. M.
Dixon. il Arch Forum 125:68-73 Jl '66
Senator Kennedy's slum plan. New Repub
155:7 O 22 '66
Speaking out; we need more slumlords. J.
Kahn. Sat Eve Post 239:8+ D 17 '66
Swift slum clearance; new approach to re-
habilitation of tenements. Sci Am 214:56+
My '66
See also
Committee on civil rights in metropolitan
New York

Immigrants
See New York (city)—Foreign population

Industries
Industry chokes on its own lifeline; garment
industry choked to death by transportation.
il Bsns W p 104-6+ Ap 9 '66

Jacques Tiffeau: sauvage of Seventh avenue.
S. Brownmiller. il N Y Times Mag p36-7+
Ja 15 '67

Intellectual life
Notes on cult; or, How to join the intellec-
tual establishment. V. S. Navasky. il N Y
Times Mag p28-9+ Mr 27 '66
See also
New York (city)—Recreation and cultural af-
fairs administration

Libraries
New York's other libraries. L. Ash. il Library
J 91:3101-7 Je 15 '66
See also
Brooklyn public library
New York public library

Madison Square Garden
Arena rises atop buvied rail terminal. il Pop
Sci 188:80-1 My '66
Garden built for tomorrow. il Sports Illus
26:36-7 Ja 2 '67
Hiram at the horse show; National horse
show. New Yorker 42:54-6 N 5 '66

Mayors
Unmaking of a mayor, by W. F. Buckley, jr.
Review
Newsweek il 68:110+ O 17 '66. S. K.
Oberbeck
See also
Lindsay, J. V.

Metropolitan museum of art
See Metropolitan museum of art

Monuments, statues, etc.
Down with Mary Poppins; objections to
a life-size statue of Mary Poppins in
Central park. Sports Illus 25:16 O 24 '66

Moral conditions
Cleanup on the Square? il Newsweek 67:47-8
Ap 18 '66
See also
New York (city)—Crime

Music
Baroque flourishes. P. H. Lang. Opera N 31:
16-17 N 19 '66
Concert opera. Donizetti and Britten. G.
Movshon. il Hi Fi 16:127+ Mr '66
Death of the recital. B. Boretz. Nation 203:
125-7 Ag 8 '66
Debuts & reappearances. See issues of High
fidelity incorporating Musical America
Fiddlers four. S. Fleming. Hi Fi 16:132-3 F
'66
Golden age is now. M. Mayer. il N Y Times
Mag pt2 p 16+ S 11 '66
Heifetz-Piatigorsky, unlimited; Carnegie Hall
concerts. A. Chasins. il Hi Fi 16:MA7 D '66
Jeunesses musicales. S. Fleming. Hi Fi 16:
MA8 Jl '66
Magical month of Mozart; twenty-six Mozart
concerts in Philharmonic Hall. H. Gold-
smith. Hi Fi 16:MA7+ N '66
Met: Giovanni, Chénier return. C. L. Os-
borne. il Hi Fi 16:142-3+ Ap '66
Metropolitan opera presents summer concerts
at Lewisohn stadium; calendar (cont) Opera
N 30:16-17 Je 4 '66
Music; current concert season. B. Boretz.
Nation 202:111-12 Ja 24 '66
Music to my ears. I. Kolodin. See issues of
Saturday review
Musical events. W. Sargeant. See issues of
New Yorker
New York. R. D. Daniels; F. Stevenson. Opera
N 30:25-6 Je 4 '66
New York: Madama Butterfly at the Juilliard
school of music: Mozart Impresario and
Purcell's Dido and Aeneas at Manhattan
school of music. R. Schlein. Opera N 31:31
Ja 21 '67
Notes from our correspondents (cont) P. G.
Davis. Hi Fi 16:20+ Mr; 16+ Je; 30+ S; 22
D '66
Pianists, new encounters and old; New York
concerts. H. Goldsmith. Hi Fi 16:126+ Mr
'66
Safe with sound; public concerts in Central
park. Time 88:50 Ag 19 '66
Tannhäuser, Parsifal, and a cloud of prom-
ises. G. Movshon. il Hi Fi 16:113+ Je '66
Three Latins in Manhattan; New York con-
certs. A. Chasins. il Hi Fi 16:138+ Ap '66

NEW YORK (city)—Music—*Continued*
Three Mahler symphonies. B. Jacobson. Hi Fi 16:131 F '66
See also
Juilliard school of music
Lincoln Center for the performing arts
Little orchestra society
Manhattan opera company
Metropolitan opera company
Metropolitan opera house
New York city opera company
New York pro musica antiqua (organization)
Philharmonic symphony society of New York

History

They played the Metropolitan; opera house served as concert hall. F. Merkling and others. il Opera N 30:8-13 F 5 '66

Negroes

Black ghetto; photographs. Newsweek 68:49-56 Ag 22 '66
Corner: oratory on southwest corner of 125th street and Seventh avenue. New Yorker 42:19-21 Ja 7 '67
Frustrated minority: the Negro and New York city politics of the 1880s as typified by the mayoralty election of 1886. R. W. Gardner. bibliog Negro Hist Bul 29:83-4+ Ja '66
To whom it may concern: report from occupied territory; Harlem Negroes and the police. J. Baldwin. il Nation 203:39-43 Jl 11 '66
See also
Committee on civil rights in metropolitan New York

Newspapers

Missing readers; circulation figures. Newsweek 68:100+ O 17 '66
New show, old cast. il Time 87:63 Ap 22 '66
Picking up the pieces; World journal tribune's Frank Conniff's plans. il Newsweek 68:63 Ag 29 '66
Third strike. W. V. Shannon. Commonweal 84:216-17 My 13 '66
See also
Daily news, New York
El Diario-la Prensa
New York herald tribune
New York times
Newspapers—Consolidations and mergers
Strikes—United States—Newspapers
Worker (newspaper)
World journal tribune

Parks, Department of

Happening called Hoving. B. Weinraub. il N Y Times Mag p 10-11+ Jl 10 '66

Parks and playgrounds

Architects of Riis plaza promote park streets to link their project with nearby park. il Arch Rec 140-198-9 Jl '66
Beauty and horror: tour of Murray Hill, Lower East side, Chelsea, Hell's Kitchen, and Harlem; remarks. T. P. F. Hoving. New Yorker 42:28-31 My 28 '66
Bicycle hours; roads inside Central park. New Yorker 42:22 Jl 23 '66
Experiment in urban park design; Samuel Paley plaza. il Am City 81:45 Mr '66
Fountain café: Central park at the Bethesda fountain. New Yorker 42:50 S 17 '66
Hoving is a happening in the parks. Life 61:4 S 9 '66
Kept off the grass; protests against proposed Adele Levy memorial park. il Arch Forum 124:31 Je '66
Kites restored: weekends in Sheep Meadow, Central park. New Yorker 42:24-5 Ag 27 '66
Last sail; old man with model sailboat on Conservatory pond, Central park. New Yorker 42:51-2 N 26 '66
Mr Moomgimoops; summer drama program. M. Polsky. il Parks & Rec 1:322 Ap '66
Outdoor rooms; Jacob Riis plaza on Manhattan's Lower East side. il Time 87:52 Je 3 '66
Outdoorsman of the big city; interview, ed. by S. Davis. J. Hoving. il Life 60:39-40+ Ap 29 '66
Parking space; plaza park. il Newsweek 67:60 F 14 '66
Peopling the parks; concerning the work of T. Hoving. il Time 88:48 S 2 '66
Riis plaza: design with keen understanding of human needs. il Arch Rec 140:134-5 D '66
Riis plaza: three acres filled with life. J. M. Dixon. il Arch Forum 125:68-73 Jl '66
Safe with sound; public concerts in Central park. Time 88:50 Ag 19 '66

Summer romance; Commissioner Hoving's transformation programs. il Newsweek 68:26 Jl 18 '66
Swim-skate pool; Central park. il Parks & Rec 1:403-4 My '66
Think big about small parks. T. P. F. Hoving. il N Y Times Mag p 12-13+ Ap 10 '66
Two commissioners; interview. T. P. F. Hoving. New Yorker 42:35-7 Mr 5 '66
Vest-pocket parks, or piazzas up-to-date. E. Goble. Arch Rec 139:9 Mr '66
Waistcoat parks; plans for park on Stork club site. Time 87:57 F 11 '66
See also
New York zoological park

Police

By the numbers; statistics of police department. Newsweek 67:44 Ap 18 '66
Detective; G. Barrett, hunter of men. J. Mills. il Read Digest 88:219-23+ F '66
Do the big-city police have popular support? interview; ed. by F. Clinton. D. Mahoney. il Nat R 18:880-2 S 6 '66
Finest could be finer. T. R. Brooks. il N Y Times Mag p28-9+ Ap 3 '66
Fuzz with a buzz; motor scooter. il Time 89:39 Ja 13 '67
New York's finest. T. R. Brooks; discussion. Commentary 40:22+ N '65; 41:16+ F; 42:20 Jl '66
Notes and comment; prevention of possible riot July 23 in East New York. New Yorker 42:17-18 Ag 6 '66
Policing the police. il Newsweek 67:27-8 Mr 7 '66
Politics and police. R. Moley. Newsweek 67:104 Mr 7 '66
To whom it may concern: report from occupied territory; Harlem Negroes and the police. J. Baldwin. il Nation 203:39-43 Jl 11 '66

Police department

Backlash in Brooklyn; why the Review board failed. J. J. Graham. Commonweal 85:287-91 D 9 '66; Reply. R. P. Kennedy. 85:384 Ja 6 '67
Breakthrough in crime prevention? use of motor scooters. il U S News 60:14 F 14 '66
Civilian review of the police. Life 61:4 O 21 '66
Election night; defeat of Civilian review board. New Yorker 42:50-1 N 19 '66
Making the best use of the police force. A. M. Bickel. New Repub 154:8-9 Mr 12 '66
Man of that board; Civilian complaint review board. J. Corry. il N Y Times Mag p32-3+ N 6 '66
No honeymoon. il Time 87:29B Mr 18 '66
No! says the P.B.A; Patrolmen's benevolent association campaign against Civilian review board. T. R. Brooks. il N Y Times Mag p36-7+ O 16 '66; Reply. C. Ballon. p 139 O 30 '66
Not exactly a Jimmy Cagney cop: Police commissioner Leary. B. Weinraub. il N Y Times Mag p28-9+ O 30 '66
Of many things; question of the Civilian review board. T. N. Davis. America 115:469 O 22 '66
Scooter patrol puts zip in police work. Am City 81:45 Je '66
Speaking out; civilians shouldn't judge cops. W. Arm. Sat Eve Post 239:12+ My 7 '66
Symbol of the backlash; question of the Civilian review board. Nation 203:468 N 7 '66
T.S.U: Tactical scooter units. New Yorker 41:31-2 F 5 '66
Towaways: Pier 74, at Thirty-fourth street and the North River. New Yorker 42:52-4 N 12 '66
Two commissioners; interview. V. L. Broderick. New Yorker 42:33-5 Mr 5 '66
Vote of confidence; police review board. R. Moley. Newsweek 68:116 N 7 '66
Who will protect the police? with excerpts from address by V. Broderick. J. P. McFadden. Nat R 18:311-13+ Ap 5 '66

Politics and government

Behind closed doors, by E. N. Costikyan. Review
Sat R 49:96-7 My 7 '66. W. D. Ogdon
Costly confusion; gubernatorial candidates. il Time 88:31 N 4 '66
Fun city: life with Lindsay. il Newsweek 68:33-4 D 12 '66
Governing the ungovernable. il Time 88:30-1 D 16 '66

NEW YORK (city)—Politics and government
—Continued
Great mayor, that bum? R. Reeves. il N Y Times Mag p6-7+ Ja 1 '67
Is New York's new mayor solving the city's problems? il U S News 61:66-8 Ag 15 '66
Lindsay, the first six months. W. V. Shannon. New Repub 155:16-19 Jl 16 '66
Man of that board; Civilian complaint review board. J. Corry. il N Y Times Mag p32-3+ N 6 '66
No honeymoon. il Time 87:29B Mr 18 '66
No! says the P.B.A; Patrolmen's benevolent association campaign against Civilian review board. T. R. Brooks. il N Y Times Mag p36-7+ O 16 '66; Reply. C. Ballon. p 139 O 30 '66
Pow! zonk! blam! Lindsay and Price activities. il Newsweek 67:23 Ja 31 '66
Singular silk-stocking 17th. T. Buckley. il N Y Times Mag p52+ F 6 '66
Speaking out; civilians shouldn't judge cops. W. Arm. Sat Eve Post 239:12+ My 7 '66
That tired feeling. Newsweek 67:29 Mr 14 '66
This Lindsay takes on that city. R. J. Whalen. il Fortune 73:126-9+ Je '66
Tweed ring, by A. B. Callow, jr. Review New Repub 156:35-6 Ja 14 '67. M. Renek
Unlimited visibility; borough president of Manhattan. C. B. Motley. New Yorker 42: 48-50 S 17 '66
Unmaking of a mayor, by W. F. Buckley, jr. Review
Nat R 18:1171-4 N 15 '66. C. B. Luce
See also
New York (city)—Elections

History
Frustrated minority: the Negro and New York city politics of the 1880s as typified by the mayoralty election of 1886. R. W. Gardner. bibliog Negro Hist Bul 29:83-4+ Ja '66

Poor
Poorhouse state, by R. M. Elman. Review New Repub 155:28+ N 5 '66. M. Renek

Public buildings
Armory: demolition of the old 8th regiment armory. New Yorker 42:37-9 My 14 '66

Public officers
Big city slowdown: the battle of bureaucracy. B. D. Blank. il Nation 203:632-7 D 12 '66

Radio City music hall
How high the corn at Radio City. W. Como. il Dance Mag 40:36-41 Ag '66
Line. New Yorker 42:25-6 D 24 '66

Rapid transit
Fares
15-senselessness. Nat R 18:610 Je 28 '66

Recreation
Park dance program. C. H. Starke. il Parks & Rec 1:34-5+ Ja '66
See also
New York (city)—Parks and playgrounds
New York (city)—Recreation and cultural affairs administration

Recreation and cultural affairs administration
Libraries linked to cultural institutions. Wilson Lib Bul 41:460 Ja '67
Libraries to get attention of N.Y. cultural council. Library J 92:43 Ja 1 '67

Religious institutions and affairs
See also
Protestant council of the city of New York

Restaurants
See New York (city)—Hotels, restaurants, etc.

Riots
Very fine boy; Eric Dean death sparks riots. il Newsweek 68:27 Ag 8 '66

Rockefeller Center
Unity and harmony at Rockefeller Center D. Haskell. il Arch Forum 124:42-7 Ja '66

St John the Divine, Cathedral of
Dome for the Divine. il Time 88:78 D 2 '66
Leave the copestone to posterity. Christian Cent 83:1528-9 D 14 '66

School board
See New York (city)—Education, Board of

Schools
See New York (city)—Education

Scientific and technical advisory council
New York's new mayor enlists a panel of scientific advisers. J. Walsh. Science 151: 967-8 F 25 '66

Shops
See New York (city)—Stores

Social conditions
Books. N. Hentoff. New Yorker 42:237-8+ N 19 '66
Model noncommunity: J. P. Lyford's analysis of Manhattan's upper West Side. il Newsweek 68:103-4 S 12 '66
This is civilization? A. H. Sypher. il Nations Bsns 54:31-2 My '66
See also
New York (city)—Harlem
New York (city)—Poor

Social life and customs
Disenchanted: girls in the city. H. F. Waters. il N Y Times Mag p28-30+ F 6 '66
New Bohemia, by J. Gruen. Review
Sat R 49:42+ O 15 '66. D. Hales
Party roundup. New Yorker 42:52-5 O 29 '66
Where the singles are; enclave of bars on New York's midtown East side. il Newsweek 68:113 S 26 '66
Young, single, and a stranger in New York singles parties. I. Taves. il Look 30:88-94 Ag 23 '66

Stores
Menswear: opening of shop at Bonwit Teller. New Yorker 42:48-9 O 15 '66
New York, London, Paris collect. L. Lerman. Mlle 63:102-4 Je '66
See also
Abercrombie and Fitch company
Cartier, incorporated

Street traffic
Computer catches a traffic violator. il Am City 81:128 Mr '66
How to stretch city streets. H. A. Barnes. il Am City 81:115 D '66
Industry chokes on its own lifeline; garment industry choked to death by transportation. il Bsns W p 104-6+ Ap 9 '66
This automatic parking has tight revenue controls; Brooklyn civic center. il Am City 81:145-6 S '66
Traffic control New York style. il Am City 81: 114 Je '66

Streets
Notes and comment: Broadway, Seventh and Sixth avenues. New Yorker 42:25 S 3 '66

Taxation
Hearing: five-hundred-and-twenty-million-dollar tax increase plan. New Yorker 42: 40-1 My 7 '66
In a troubled city, still higher taxes. U S News 60:8 Je 27 '66
Just how high can city taxes go? il U S News 60:82 Mr 21 '66
Money riddle; new agreement. il Newsweek 67:32 Je 27 '66
Taxing problem solved: window tax proposal. A. Kennerly and M. Kennerly, jr. Sat R 49:6 Mr 19 '66
Wall Street balks at mayor's tax scheme. il Bsns W p44+ Mr 12 '66
Who pays the freight? Nation 202:477 Ap 25 '66

Telephone directory
See Telephone directories

Theater
Architecture: Cavaglieri's plans for Astor library; winter home of Shakespeare festival. E. Galantay. Nation 202:500-2 Ap 25 '66
Beginnings of salvation: American place theater. G. P. Gates. Holiday 40:178+ D '66
Bests of the 1965-1966 theater. H. Hewes. il Sat R 49:35-7 Je 11 '66
New York's best new theater group? American place theatre. R. Schickel. il Harper 233:92-4+ N '66
Notes; new plays on and off Broadway. H. Clurman. Nation 202:194-5 F 14 '66
Off-Broadway trio. G. Weales. il Reporter 34:47-8 F 24 '66

NEW YORK (state)—*Continued*

Parks and reserves

Beach construction in a state park; Robert Moses state park near Massena. H. S. Conover. il Parks & Rec 1:420-1+ My '66

Off-season; surf-casting at Robert Moses state park, Fire Island. New Yorker 42: 50-1 O 8 '66

Pool and ice rink in one area; Great Neck park district, Long Island. il Am City 81: 75-7 Je '66

Politics and government

Donkey beats himself. J. Desmond. il Nation 203:379-81 O 17 '66

Doorbells: politics of activism. W. Meyers. il Nation 202:581-3 My 16 '66

Election night; celebrations at Governor Rockefeller's campaign headquarters. New Yorker 42:47-50 N 19 '66

Eye to eye; N. Rockefeller and other candidates. il Time 87:25A Ap 1 '66

Happy warrior; Rockefeller campaign. il Newsweek 68:36+ O 31 '66

Kennedys at home have a few problems; unpopularity of Democratic party reform. M. F. Nolan. New Repub 154:10-11 Je 25 '66

Men who . . . scramble for gubernatorial nomination. Newsweek 67:46 My 23 '66

More zig than zag; Democrats announce candidacies for gubernatorial race. Time 87: 32-3 My 20 '66

Parties in chaos: New York guerrillas; Democratic divisions. J. Desmond. il Nation 202:355-7 Mr 28 '66

Return of Rockefeller. E. J. Hughes. Newsweek 68:23 O 17 '66

Rocky redivivus. il Time 88:35 O 7 '66

Rocky's roughest round. G. Astor. il Look 30: 52-4+ O 18 '66

Three men behind Rockefeller; W. Pfeiffer, campaign chairman; G. Hinman, personal emissary; W. Ronan, idea-and-issues man. T. Buckley. il N Y Times Mag p34-5+ O 30 '66

Tweedleham & Tweedlesam; rival candidates for the Republican nomination for Congress from the 28th district. il Time 87:21 My 27 '66

Very conventional; gubernatorial contest. Reporter 35:20+ S 22 '66

Winning non-candidate; R. F. Kennedy and others. il Newsweek 68:25 Jl 11 '66

Suffrage

See Suffrage—United States

NEW YORK airways, incorporated

N.Y. airways reduces Pan Am heliport trips. Aviation W 84:43 My 16 '66

Problems retard progress of helicopters and V/STOLs. D. A. Brown. il Aviation W 85: 134-5+ O 31 '66

NEW YORK aquarium. See Aquariums

NEW YORK automobile show. See Automobiles—Exhibitions

NEW YORK avant-garde festival. See Music festivals—New York (state)

NEW YORK botanical garden

Flowers: reception celebrating publication of first volume of Wild flowers of the United States. New Yorker 42:49-50 O 8 '66

Caricatures and cartoons

Botanical garden. Stevenson. New Yorker 42:46-9 My 14 '66

NEW YORK central railroad

Jetting down the track; Central's plans to replace long-distance trains with high-speed shuttles. il Bsns W p81 Jl 30 '66

Renaissance for rails? long-haul runs to end; plans. il Newsweek 68:52-3 Ag 8 '66

Toward the end of the twentieth century. il Time 88:84 Ag 5 '66

NEW YORK central railroad-Pennsylvania merger. See Railroads—Consolidations and mergers

NEW YORK chapter of American civil liberties union. See American civil liberties union

NEW YORK city ballet

Caution: choreographer at work. H. Saal. il N Y Times Mag pt2 p 18-19+ S 11 '66

Music to my ears; current presentation. I. Kolodin. Sat R 49:85 My 7 '66

Musical events; opening of spring season at the State theatre. W. Sargeant. New Yorker 42:162 Ap 9 '66

Musical events; performances of Apollo, Guirlande de Campra and Liebeslieder walzer. W. Sargeant. New Yorker 42:200-1 D 10 '66

Musical events; performance of Balanchine's Don Quixote. W. Sargeant. New Yorker 42: 106-7 My 21 '66

Musical events; performance of Balanchine's Midsummer night's dream. W. Sargeant. New Yorker 42:127-8 Ap 16 '66

Musical events; performance of Balanchine's Variations. W. Sargeant. New Yorker 42: 164 Ap 9 '66

Musical events; performance of Brahms-Schoenberg quartet. W. Sargeant. New Yorker 42:132 Ap 30 '66

Poetry of space; spring season. D. Hering. il Dance Mag 40:48-50+ Jl '66

Reviews; production of The nutcracker at New York state theatre. J. Maskey. Dance Mag 40:61-2 F '66

Toe to toe; four new ballets. il Newsweek 67:94-5 My 2 '66

Two premieres: NYC ballet; New York state theater. D. Hering. il Dance Mag 41:32+ Ja '67

NEW YORK city commission on human rights. See New York (city)—Commission on human rights

NEW YORK city employees. See New York (city)—Employees

NEW YORK city in literature

New York in fiction. J. F. Hopkins. Library J 91:3097-9 Je 15 '66

New York: two poetic impressions. A. Bartra. il Américas 18:14-22 O '66

NEW YORK city in poetry. See New York city in literature

NEW YORK city newspaper merger. See Newspapers—Consolidations and mergers

NEW YORK city opera company

At City opera, a Handel hit; New York stage premiere of Giulio Cesare. C. L. Osborne. il Hi Fi 16:MA8-10 D '66

Creating Don Rodrigo. F. Stevenson. il Opera N 30:14-16 F 26 '66

Music to my ears; housewarming at Lincoln Center's state theater. I. Kolodin. Sat R 49:44+ Mr 12 '66

Musical events; comparison with Metropolitan opera company. W. Sargeant. New Yorker 42:236-7 O 22 '66

Musical events; performance of A. Ginastera's Don Rodrigo. W. Sargeant. New Yorker 42:154-6 Mr 5 '66

Musical events; performance of Händel's Julius Caesar. W. Sargeant. New Yorker 42:119-20 O 8 '66

Musical events; performance of Poulenc's Dialogues of the Carmelites. W. Sargeant. New Yorker 42:163-4+ Mr 12 '66

Musical events; performance of R. Strauss's Capriccio. W. Sargeant. New Yorker 42: 165-6+ Ap 2 '66

Musical events; performance of Verdi's La Traviata. W. Sargeant. New Yorker 42:232 N 5 '66

Musical events; performance of von Einem's Danton's death. W. Sargeant. New Yorker 42:196-7 Mr 19 '66

New York. F. Merkling. il Opera N 30:30-1 Mr 26 '66

New York; production of Handel's Giulio Cesare, Puccini's La Bohème, and Kurt Schwitters' Class struggle opera. F. Merkling; R. D. Daniels; G. Fitzgerald. il Opera N 31:22-3 N 5 '66

New York; production of La Traviata. R. R. Schlein. il Opera N 31:27 D 3 '66

New York; The magic flute and Tosca. F. Merkling; R. D. Daniels. il Opera N 31: 22-3 N 19 '66

New York's other opera company; review of first season in New York state theater. R. Gelatt. il Reporter 34:43-4+ Ap 21 '66

Of the people; New York city opera moves from Mecca temple to Lincoln Center. M. Mayer. il Opera N 30:8-13 F 26 '66

On records; New York city opera. Opera N 30:34 F 26 '66

Other company; new beginning at New York state theater, Lincoln Center. il Newsweek 67:88-9 Mr 7 '66

Rudel and company in the new house. C. L. Osborne. Hi Fi 16:128+ My '66

Sense of adventure; move to New York state theater. Time 87:75 Mr 4 '66

Song of the scaffold; Poulenc's Carmelites staged in New York city. J. W. Freeman. il Opera N 30:14-15 Mr 5 '66

Words, music, and sweet eroticism. R. Kotlowitz. Harper 232:105-6 Je '66

NEW YORK city primaries. See Primaries

NEW YORK city transit authority
Socialism, U.S. style. H. Hazlitt. Newsweek 68:83 Jl 18 '66

NEW YORK civil liberties union. See American civil liberties union

NEW YORK curb exchange. See American stock exchange

NEW YORK daily news. See Daily news, New York

NEW YORK drama critics circle
Unofficial winner; Drama critics' voting, 1966. H. Hewes. Sat R 49:51+ Je 18 '66

NEW YORK film festival. See Moving picture festivals

NEW YORK flower show. See Flower exhibits

NEW YORK forest owners association, Incorporated
Forest riddle of New York. H. Kernan. il Am For 72:21 S '66; Reply. D. H. Hanaburgh. 72:8 D '66

NEW YORK Giants (football club) See Football clubs

NEW YORK graphic society
Time inc. purchases the New York graphic society. Pub W 190:29-30 D 12 '66

NEW YORK herald tribune
Battle of Paris; Times and Trib. il Time 88: 50 D 16 '66
Big bad Wolfe? concerning D. Macdonald article in New York review of books. il Newsweek 67:60 Ja 31 '66
Death in the afternoon. N. Kent. Am Artist 30:3+ O '66
Death of the Herald tribune. J. G. Smart. Nation 203:270-1 S 26 '66
Herald tribune. Nation 203:173 S 5 '66
Herald-tribune. T. Buckley. New Repub 155:8 Ag 27 '66
Herald tribune vs. Times; war of the Paris editions. W. B. Kerr. il Sat R 49:104-5 N 12 '66
Last blood from a pale stone; crippling of New York's newspapers. Time 87:79 Ap 29 '66
Media; N.Y. herald tribune comes to an end. Pub W 190:43 Ag 22 '66
Mercy killing. il Time 88:42-3 Ag 26 '66
Paris-herald-post. il Newsweek 68:56 Ag 15 '66
Struck paper, famous and needed, goes down. J. Breslin. il Life 61:26-9 Ag 26 '66
Very special paper. il Newsweek 68:90-1 Ag 22 '66
When unions killed a major newspaper. il U S News 61:70-2 Ag 29 '66
Who killed cock robin? R. L. Tobin. Sat R 49:67-8 S 10 '66
See also
Book week (periodical)

NEW YORK herald tribune children's spring festival awards
Backstage with the judges; the Herald tribune children's book awards. E. Geller. il Library J 91:2604-8 My 15 '66

NEW YORK hi-fi show. See Audio fairs

NEW YORK Jets (football club) See Football clubs

NEW YORK library association
NYLA opposes anti-obscenity bill passed by New York legislature. Library J 91:3666-7 Ag '66

NEW YORK Mets (baseball) See Baseball clubs

NEW YORK, New Haven and Hartford railroad company
Goats and the New Haven. il Fortune 74:294 Jl 15 '66
Keeping New Haven on tracks; new plan endorsed by governors of N.Y. and Conn. Bsns W p 148 O 1 '66

NEW YORK newspaper strike. See Strikes—United States—Newspapers

NEW YORK philharmonic. See Philharmonic-symphony society of New York

NEW YORK port authority. See Port of New York authority

NEW YORK post
Hello Dolly! Newsweek 68:102 S 19 '66

NEW YORK pro musica antiqua (organization)
Achievement of Noah Greenberg. G. P. Elliott. Commentary 42:67-71 Jl '66
Pro musica in retrospect. P. L. Miller. Sat R 49:48-9 Je 25 '66
Recordings. M. Mayer. Esquire 65:28 Ap '66

NEW YORK public library
Macmillan's author files, 1892-1960; gift to the NYPL. il Pub W 190:21-4 O 24 '66
NYPL launches experiments in use of large-type books. Library J 91:3895 S 1 '66

Noted acquisitions; recipient of the author files of the Macmillan company. Wilson Lib Bul 41:363 D '66
Trade winds; plight of the library. J. Beatty, jr. Sat R 49:12 F 12 '66
See also
Lincoln Center for the performing arts, New York—Library and museum of the performing arts

Branches
Boy, this place sure has changed! North Manhattan library center project of the Countee Cullen regional branch. M. Robbins. il Wilson Lib Bul 41:186-9 O '66
Saturday's children; Countee Cullen story; North Manhattan project. L. LaFleur; M. Robbins. bibliog il Library J 91:1581-90 Mr 15 '66

NEW YORK Rangers (hockey team) See Hockey teams

NEW YORK review of books (periodical)
Big bad Wolfe? concerning D. Macdonald article. il Newsweek 67:60 Ja 31 '66

NEW YORK Shakespeare festival
Summer camp; Central park presentations. H. Hewes. Sat R 49:48 Jl 30 '66

NEW YORK society for ethical culture. See Ethical culture society

NEW YORK state commission against discrimination. See New York (state)—Commission against discrimination

NEW YORK state in literature
Stars fell on York state. J. K. Hutchens. Sat R 49:45-6 D 24 '66

NEW YORK state library association. See New York library association

NEW YORK state museum, Albany
Oldest and largest state museum. J. L. Stoutenburgh. il Hobbies 71:110 N '66

NEW YORK state primaries. See Primaries

NEW YORK state safety car project. See Automobiles—Safety devices and measures

NEW YORK state theater. See Lincoln Center for the performing arts, New York—New York state theater

NEW YORK state university
Antioch to publish for State university of N.Y. Pub W 189:106 F 14 '66
How to lower the higher learning. R. Kirk. Nat R 18:686 Jl 12 '66
New York's late-blooming State university. R. Gross and J. Murphy. il Harper 233: 87-90+ D '66
Performance criteria; a system of communication for mobilizing building industry resources. R. G. Jacques. il Arch Rec 139:191-5 My '66

Agricultural and technical institute at Farmingdale, Long Island
Walk into springtime at Planting fields; Planting fields arboretum, Oyster Bay. il Flower Grower 53:40-1 My '66

Albany campus
Architecture; E. D. Stone's design. E. Galantay. il Nation 202:629-30 My 23 '66

Long Island center, Stony Brook
Concrete for complex forms of a lecture hall. il Arch Rec 140:142-3 N '66

Regents
Human experimentation; New York verdict affirms patient's rights. E. Langer. Science 151:663-6 F 11 '66; Discussion. 152:448+, 865 Ap 22, My 13 '66

NEW YORK state's forest preserve. See Forests, State

NEW YORK stock exchange. See Stock exchange—New York (city)

NEW YORK, Susquehanna and western railroad company
Susquehanna, anyone? Irving Maidman puts on sale. il Newsweek 68:76-7 S 5 '66

NEW YORK taxicabs. See Taxicabs

NEW YORK theological seminary. See Theological schools

NEW YORK times
All the handouts fit to print; New York times story concerning U.S. policy toward Communist China. Time 87:48 Ap 8 '66
Battle of Paris; Times and Trib. il Time 88:50 D 16 '66
Change of cast? plan to interchange arts critics. Newsweek 67:93 My 23 '66
Fast thinking and action on NAL's blackout quickie; Night the lights went out. il Pub W 189:122-3 F 7 '66

NEW YORK times—*Continued*
  Helping hands: editorials, reports, letters
    supporting admission of Communist China
    to the UN. Nat R 18:302-4 Ap 5 '66
  Herald tribune vs. Times: war of the Paris
    editions. W. B. Kerr. il Sat R 49:104-5
    N 12 '66
  Letter from Paris; coverage of the war in
    Viet Nam attacked; text of letter, excerpts.
    F. E. Nolting, jr. Time 88:79 N 4 '66
  Man & his Times; editorial line on Viet
    Nam. Time 87:64-5 Mr 11 '66
  News unfit to print? inside story of coverage
    of events leading to Bay of Pigs invasion.
    il Newsweek 67:101 Je 13 '66
  No news; SANE peace rally. Nation 203:692 D
    26 '66
  Parting shots; A. Krock retirement. News-
    week 68:98 O 10 '66
  Penance of Matthews. Nation 203:437-8 O 31
    '66
  Pomp and circumstance; concerning G.
    Talese's Esquire article. Newsweek 68:76
    O 24 '66
  Recent libel decision expands Times case
    doctrine. H. F. Pilpel. Pub W 189:43-5 My
    9 '66
  Scholarship virus; concerning authority for
    article on U.S.-China accord. Reporter 34:
    10+ Ap 7 '66
  Sons & mothers: the Harlem six; T. Nel-
    son's accusations against in The torture
    of mothers. J. Meyer. Nation 202:496-8 Ap
    25 '66
  Supercritic; hiring of W. Kerr. Newsweek
    68:94-5 S 12 '66
  Times' contention it was not present in Ala-
    bama upheld. H. F. Pilpel. Pub W 190:31-2
    N 28 '66
  Winners and sinners; realignment of power.
    Newsweek 69:81-2 Ja 16 '67
  Working press, by R. Adler. Review
    Sat R 49:57 Ag 13 '66. A. Balk
NEW YORK times book review
  Screening books for review; selecting and
    reviewing childrens and teen-agers books.
    G. Woods. il Wilson Lib Bul 41:168-72 O '66
  Times book review selects fifty best children's
    books. Pub W 189:58+ My 23 '66
NEW YORK transit strike. See Strikes—
  United States—Transportation workers
NEW YORK university
  Bright landmarks on a changing urban scene.
    C. Robinson. il Arch Forum 125:21-9 D '66
  Shimkin's NYU gift may aid training for
    publishing. il Pub W 190:35-6 N 28 '66
  Toward urban excellence; residential and
    library plans. il Time 87:94 Ap 1 '66
NEW YORK university bookstore. See College
  bookstores
NEW YORK yacht, launch and engine company
  Old New York yacht, launch & engine co.
    G. A. Taylor. il Motor B 118:36-7+ D '66
NEW YORK Yankees (baseball) See Baseball
  clubs
NEW YORK zoological park
  Wait till next year; takins at Bronx zoo.
    il Life 61:66A Jl 15 '66
  World of darkness; Bronx zoo. il Parks &
    Rec 1:405-6 My '66

    Childrens zoo
  Zoo nursery. B. L. David. il Look 30:M14-16
    My 17 '66
NEW YORKER (periodical)
  New Yorker lists at this season some books
    by its contributors published during the
    year. New Yorker 42:232-3 D 10 '66
NEW YORKERS
  Images of elegant New York; conversation
    pieces; portfolio. L. Auchincloss. Am
    Heritage 17:48-65 O '66
  Long-winded lady (cont) New Yorker 42:
    22-3 Jl 30; 20-1 Ag 6 '66
  Manner of speaking. J. Ciardi. Sat R 49:16-17
    F 12 '66
  Notes and comment. New Yorker 42:51-2 N
    12 '66
  Notes and comment: Broadway, Seventh and
    Sixth avenues. New Yorker 42:25 S 3 '66
  Other events; Krishna consciousness in
    Tompkins Square park. R. Adler. New
    Yorker 42:122+ N 12 '66
  Social dropout. F. Eberstadt. il Look 31:70-1
    Ja 10 '67
NEW ZEALAND
  Letter from Down Under. E. M. von Kueh-
    nelt-Leddihn. Nat R 18:310 Ap 5 '66
    See also
    Airlines—New Zealand
    Censorship—New Zealand
    Elections—New Zealand
    Fishing—New Zealand
    National parks and reserves—New Zealand
    Queenstown
    Zoology—New Zealand

    Native races
  Last of the Maoris. B. L. Burman. il Read
    Digest 89:210-12+ O '66

    Religious institutions and affairs
  World around us (cont of) News of the
    Christian world. Christian Cent 83:1484 N
    30 '66
NEW ZEALAND flax. See Phormium
NEWARK, N.J.

    Negroes
  Notes and comment; world première of
    Troublemakers, movie about Newark com-
    munity union project. New Yorker 42:47-8
    D 10 '66

    Social conditions
  Notes and comment; world première of
    Troublemakers, movie about Newark com-
    munity union project. New Yorker 42:47-8
    D 10 '66

    Stores
  Art over the counter; Gallery of the masters
    at Bamberger's. K. Kuh. Sat R 49:38-9 D 31
    '66
NEWARK, N.J. in art
  Henry Gasser's paintings of Newark. H.
    Gasser. il Am Artist 30:48-53+ N '66
NEWARK, N.Y.
  Greenspan program. J. J. Shomon. il Audu-
    bon Mag 68:414 N '66
NEWBERY medal
  ALA names book award winners. Sr Schol
    88:sup4 Mr 25 '66
  Elizabeth Borton de Trevino. C. Costello. il
    Library J 91:1592-3 Mr 15 '66
  Newbery and Caldecott medal books: 1956-
    1965. E. S. Ross. Horn Bk 42:186-7 Ap '66
  Newbery-Caldecott winners. il Wilson Lib
    Bul 40:688 Ap '66
  Treviño, Hogrogian: Newbery and Caldecott
    winners. il Pub W 189:30-2 Mr 14 '66
NEWBORN infants. See Infants. Newborn
NEWBURY, Mass.

    Historic houses, etc.
  Highfields and its heritage. L. W. Watkins.
    il Antiques 90:204-7 Ag '66
NEWCOMB, Robinson
  Will tight money get tighter? Nations Bsns
    54:38-9 N '66
NEWELL, Homer E.
  Surveyor: candid camera on the moon. por
    Nat Geog Mag 130:578-92 O '66
NEWEY, W. E.
  Conversation piece; poem. Commonweal 85:
    230 N 25 '66
NEWFIELD, Jack
  Bobby phenomenon. Nation 203:505-7 N 14
    '66
NEWFOUNDLAND dogs
  Big family dog: Warren family's Hardy at
    ASPCA dog-training school. I. Taves. il
    Look 30:M12-14+ Je 14 '66
NEWGREN, E. A.
  Multiple solutions through central micro-
    filming. Am City 81:146+ F '66
NEWHALL, Suzanne
  Departmental libraries and the problem of
    autonomy. por ALA Bul 60:721-2 Jl '66
  Science library cooperation in three colleges.
    ALA Bul 60:380-1 Ap '66
NEWHOUSE, D. L.
  Battle for wilderness in New York state's
    forest preserve. Liv Wildn 30:11-19 Sum '66
NEWHOUSE, Samuel I.
  Sam hits 21. Time 88:47 Jl 15 '66
  Victory in Springfield. por Time 87:49 Ap 8
    '66
NEWINGTON, Conn.
  Debut of a children's theater. C. Lemire. il
    Parks & Rec 1:142-4 F '66
NEWLIN, Dika
  Again. Mahler symphonies by Leinsdorf and
    Bernstein; the Sixth and Seventh. Am
    Rec G 33:114-16+ O '66
  Vanguard offers a stereo première of the
    Mahler Seventh from Salt Lake City. Am
    Rec G 32:950-1 Je '66
NEWMAN, Barbara. See Newman, J. jt. auth.
NEWMAN, Barnett
  Fourteen stations of the cross, 1958-1966.
    Art N 65:26-8+ My '66

    about
  Art; Guggenheim museum show. M. Kozloff.
    Nation 202:598 My 16 '66
  Of a different stripe. por Time 87:82 Ap
    29 '66

NEWMAN, Barnett—about—*Continued*
People are talking about... il por Vogue 147:
110-11 Ap 15 '66
Unanswerable question; show at the Guggenheim, New York. il por Newsweek 67:
100 My 9 '66
NEWMAN, Charles
Lesson of the master: Henry James and James Baldwin. Yale R 56:45-59 O '66
NEWMAN, David
More unseemly chronicles. Esquire 66:52 Ag '66
—and Benton, Robert
Fat power. Esquire 66:212-15 D '66
From Weehawken with love. Esquire 65:86-7 My '66
Good-bye to all that. Esquire 66:127 S '66
Man talk. See issues of Mademoiselle
Remember the sixties? Esquire 66:109-14 Ag '66

about
De senectute or old age, as Newmanized and Bentonated. A. Gingrich. Esquire 66:6 S '66
NEWMAN, Deborah
Long ago in Bethlehem; drama. Plays 26:44-8 D '66
Prince and the pauper; dramatization of story by M. Twain. Plays 26:81-95 O '66
Stolen heart; drama. Plays 25:85-8, 96 F '66
NEWMAN, Francis William
Newman brothers, by W. Robbins. Review America 115:139 Ag 6 '66. J. Pick
NEWMAN, Gemma
Greatness of Mary Cassatt. Am Artist 30:42-9+ F '66
NEWMAN, Harold
Ceramic kettles with stands. Antiques 89:240-4 F '66
NEWMAN, J. Nicholas. See Herreshoff, H. C. jt. auth.
NEWMAN, James, and Newman, Barbara
Why not try camping this summer? PTA Mag 60:15-17 My '66
NEWMAN, John Henry, cardinal
Sight of Christ; poem. Christian Cent 83:355 Mr 23 '66

about
If Newman had been at Vatican II; excerpt. J. Coulson. Commonweal 83:596 F 25 '66
Newman brothers, by W. Robbins. Review America 115:139 Ag 6 '66. J. Pick
Newman, Vatican I and II, and the church today. E. E. Kelly. Cath World 202:291-7 F '66
NEWMAN, Jon Ormond
Open file. il por Time 88:62 S 30 '66
NEWMAN, Marvin E.
Fabulous world of Florida golf; photographs. Sports Illus 24:30-7 Ja 24 '66
Shelters on a scalloped shore; photographs. Sports Illus 24:46-51 Mr 28 '66
NEWMAN, Nick
Alaska smokejumper. Field & S 71:60-2 Je '66
NEWMAN, Oscar
New campus. Arch Forum 124:30-55 My '66
NEWMAN, Paul
Cool hand Paul. por Newsweek 69:95-95A Ja 23 '67
Paul Newman makes a western. R. W. Lewis. il pors N Y Times Mag p38-9+ N 6 '66
NEWMAN, Paul Baker
Mood of Chopin; poem. Christian Cent 83:1265 O 19 '66
NEWMAN, Ralph G.
Appraisals and revenooers; excerpts from address. Am Heritage 17:82-4 Je '66
NEWMAN clubs
Nun enters the Newman apostolate. Sister M. Michael. Cath World 203:293-6 Ag '66
Present position of Catholics in English universities. R. Butler. Cath World 204:37-41 O '66
NEWMARK, Esther
New boat, a new venture (cont) il Yachting 119:114-16+ Ja '66
Offshore cruiser ventures inland. il Yachting 120:41-3+ S '66
NEWMARK, J. I.
Sound for silent films. U S Camera 29:72-3+ Ag '66
NEWPORT, R.I.
Metropolitan opera presents summer concerts at Newport, R.I. calendar. G. Sauls. Opera N 30:16-17 Je 4 '66

City planning
Least-known Newport revived. il Fortune 73:165 F '66

Historic houses, etc.
Newport, Rhode Island. il Antiques 90:532-3 O '66

NEWPORT, R.I. jazz festival. See Music festivals—Rhode Island
NEWPORT-Bermuda race. See Yacht racing
NEWPORT NEWS, Va.
See also
Mariners museum
NEWPORT NEWS shipbuilding and dry dock company
Boost up job ladder for Negroes. Bsns W p 130+ Ap 23 '66
Good Newport News; agreement against discrimination. Reporter 34:14-15 Ap 21 '66
NEWQUIST, Roy
Behind the scenes of a shocking movie. McCalls 93:86-9+ Je '66
(ed) See Andrews, J. Julie Andrews
NEWS
It's what's happening; attention span of public mind on any news story and New York strike. Nat R 18:507-8 My 31 '66
News is where you find it. R. L. Tobin. Sat R 49:135-6 Mr 12 '66; Discussion. 49:60 Ap 9 '66
See also
Current events
Government and the press
Radio broadcasting—News
Reporters and reporting
Television broadcasting—News
NEWS agencies
News from home; Hotaling's and other New York city sources. M. C. Blackman. Sat R 49:118 O 8 '66
See also
Associated press
NEWS broadcasts. See Radio broadcasting—News
NEWS commentators. See Television broadcasting—News
NEWS conferences. See Press conferences
NEWS dealers. See Newspaper vendors
NEWS letters
Departmental newsletters, they aren't worth it! Phoenix, Ariz. R. Coop. il Am City 81:157-8 Ag '66
NEWS magazines. See Periodicals
NEWS photographers. See Photographers
NEWS photography. See Photography, Journalistic
NEWS vendors. See Newspaper vendors
NEWSDAY (newspaper)
Captain takes command. il Time 88:80-1 N 4 '66
NEWSMAGAZINES. See Periodicals
NEWSOM, Sir John
Educational values and goals; address, January 21, 1966. Vital Speeches 32:244-8 F 1 '66
NEWSPAPER and periodical wholesalers
See also
Bureau of independent publishers and distributors
NEWSPAPER columns. See Newspapers—Sections, columns, etc.
NEWSPAPER correspondents. See Reporters and reporting
NEWSPAPER court reporting
Armored lady; C. Mossler trial; brings out ham. il Time 87:43 F 4 '66
Courts and the press; recommended rules to control publicity of proceedings. New Repub 155:8-9 O 15 '66
News on trial; Chicago tribune's attack on Reardon committee recommendations. Newsweek 68:100 O 17 '66
Open court & fair press. R. Spangler. il Nation 202:421-4 Ap 11 '66
Public and the court; free press and fair trials; address, January 6, 1966. A. Schaleben. Vital Speeches 32:268-70 F 15 '66
Stale Candy; news coverage of the Mossler trial. il Newsweek 67:64 Mr 14 '66
NEWSPAPER dealers. See Newspaper vendors
NEWSPAPER editorials. See Editorials
NEWSPAPER mergers. See Newspapers—Consolidations and mergers
NEWSPAPER publishing
At the grass roots; B. Sagan's weeklies. Newsweek 68:76 O 24 '66
Bertie and Cissy. il Newsweek 67:60+ Mr 7 '66
Houston's shackled press. B. H. Bagdikian. Atlan 218:87-8+ Ag '66; Discussion. 218:44+ O '66
If you want a paper ... il Newsweek 67:62+ Je 20 '66

NEWSPAPER publishing—*Continued*
So you want to own a weekly. W. Keifer. il
Sat R 49:69-70 My 14 '66; Reply. A. L.
Schafer. 49:60-1 Jl 9 '66
See also
Minneapolis star and tribune company
NEWSPAPER strikes. See Strikes—United
States—Newspapers
NEWSPAPER vendors
News from home; Hotaling's and other New
York city sources. M. C. Blackman. Sat R
49:117-18 O 8 '66
NEWSPAPERS
New field generals; battle of Europe. News-
week 68:76 S 26 '66
So you want to own a weekly. W. Keifer.
il Sat R 49:69-70 My 14 '66; Reply. A. L.
Schafer. 49:60-1 Jl 9 '66
See also
Freedom of the press
News
Religious newspapers and periodicals
Reporters and reporting

Advice columns
Behind the advice column. A. Landers. il
Sat R 49:108-10 N 12 '66
Getting over Glenda. T. Meehan. il Sat Eve
Post 239:18 N 5 '66
How to get some action. Newsweek 68:76 Ag
1 '66
Second decade for the Ann Landers style.
J. M. Flagler. il Look 30:66+ O 18 '66

Anecdotes, facetiae, satire, etc.
Hooboy advisor. J. Skow. il Sat Eve Post
239:14 D 31 '66
Winter of the small wildcats. J. Skow. il
Sat Eve Post 239:22 F 26 '66

Business news
See also
Business and the press

Columns
See Newspapers—Sections, columns, etc.

Consolidations and mergers
Collector's item; possibility of Times of Lon-
don merging with Sunday Times. News-
week 68:98 O 10 '66
Combo jumbo; merging of World-telegram,
Journal-American, and Herald tribune. S. J.
Adamo. America 114:566 Ap 16 '66
Divorce Chattanooga style. il Newsweek 68:
54 S 5 '66
Dynastic journalism dies in New York;
Herald-Journal-Telegram merger. A. H.
Raskin. Sat R 49:62-3+ Ap 9 '66
How a newspaper can be suppressed; state-
ment, April 22, 1966. J. H. Whitney. U S
News 60:37 My 2 '66
Labor disputes of merging newspapers; from
sixteen circulation English-language news-
papers in Manhattan, now there are four.
Mo Labor R 89:III-IV Ag '66
Last drop? New York city's three way
merger delay; staff contract agreements
dispute. il Newsweek 67:96 My 2 '66
Merger, Miami-style; Miami herald and the
Miami news. Time 88:34-5 Ag 12 '66
Merger, Paris-style; Paris herald tribune and
Washington post. il Time 88:34 Ag 12 '66
New York compromise; World journal trib-
une, inc. il Newsweek 67:68-70 Ap 4 '66
New York's new mix; three-way merger. il
Time 87:72 Ap 1 '66
Other spiral; New York newspaper merger.
Nation 202:380 Ap 4 '66
Paris herald-post; joint publication of Inter-
national edition of the New York herald
tribune-the Washington post. il Newsweek
68:56 Ag 15 '66
Picking up the pieces; World journal trib-
une's Frank Conniff's plans. il Newsweek
68:63 Ag 29 '66
Rumor comes true for New York dailies;
merger of Tribune, Journal and Telegram.
il Bsns W p51 Mr 26 '66
Sex, sin and synergism; result of San Francisco chronicle and Examiner merger. il
Newsweek 67:70 Ap 18 '66
Slow-motion merger in New York; Trib,
Telegram and Journal. il Time 87:37 Mr 25
'66
Three major N.Y. papers announce merger
plans. Pub W 189:45-6 Mr 28 '66
3,700 jobs or none; the stake in New York
newspaper strike. il U S News 60:97-9
My 9 '66
Why are we striking? case of N.Y. city
newspapers. G. Merlis. Nat R 18:532-4 My
31 '66

Why the decrease in big-city papers; proposed
merger; New York herald tribune, Journal-
American and World-Telegram and sun.
il U S News 60:12 Ap 4 '66

Crime reporting
Code for crime coverage; Toledo blade and
Toledo times. Time 88:76 S 2 '66
Crime and puzzlement; reactions to Supreme
court decisions on rights of suspects. News-
week 68:54+ S 5 '66
Ethics code for newspapers. America 115:217
S 3 '66
Headlines and checkbooks, Chicago press cov-
erage. il Newsweek 68:76 Ag 1 '66
See also
Crime and the press

Employees
Exodus; impact of strike on World journal
tribune. Newsweek 67:62 Je 6 '66
Last drop? New York city's three way
merger delay; staff contract agreements
dispute. il Newsweek 67:96 My 2 '66

Readers
Read all about it; world statistics. Newsweek
68:60+ Jl 18 '66
Spreading suburban daily. il Time 87:43-4 F 4
'66

Sections, columns, etc.
Feeding the food editor. N. S. Hazelton. Nat
R 18:1164 N 15 '66
Freedom and the old heave-ho. C. W.
Morton. il Atlan 218:138 N '66
International provocateur. Time 88:86 O 21
'66
Kraftsmanship; J. Kraft's column, Insight
and outlook. il Newsweek 68:54 Jl 4 '66
Loner; T. Lewis' Capitol stuff. il Time 88:48
D 16 '66
Muckraker; D. Pearson's Washington merry-
go-round. il Newsweek 67:87 Je 27 '66
No. 1 society snooper; interview, ed. by D.
Lurie. A. Mehle. il Life 61:59-60+ N 11 '66
Personal poverty program; R. Brougham. il
Time 87:51 Ap 15 '66
Zealots of the middle; political column, In-
side report. il Time 88:76-7 D 2 '66
See also
Newspapers—Advice columns

Social aspects
Racial news gap. A. Balk. Sat R 49:53-4 Ag
13 '66

Society page
No. 1 society snooper; interview, ed. by D.
Lurie. A. Mehle. il Life 61:59-60+ N 11
'66

Sports news
See Sports journalism

Study and teaching
How to teach a unit on newspapers. S.
Cochell. Sr Schol 89:sup63 S 23 '66

Travel news
Successful techniques for newspaper travel
articles. H. D. Steward. Writer 79:31-3 N
'66

Argentina
General's mustache. Newsweek 68:45 Ag 8
'66

China (People's Republic)
Paper that spreads the cult of Mao; Jenmin
Jih Pao, the People's daily of Peking. I.
Stewart. il N Y Times Mag p26-7+ D 18 '66

Cuba
Cuba's press today. G. A. Geyer. il Sat R
49:106-7+ N 12 '66

France
Value of privacy; France Dimanche fined over
Philipe family photographs. Time 87:72 Ap
'66
See also
Paris—Newspapers

Germany (Federal Republic)
Germany's Jewish watchdog; Allgemeine
unabhängige jüdische wochenzeitung (General independent Jewish weekly) Time 88:41
D 30 '66

Great Britain
English press; nasty, obsolete, the best in
the world. K. E. Meyer. il Esquire 66:56-7+
Jl '66

NEWSPAPERS—Great Britain—*Continued*
Guardian going down? Newsweek 69:62 Ja 9
'67
Squeeze on Fleet Street. Time 88:45 D 23 '66
Trouble on Fleet Street; Peter Jenkins report. il Newsweek 69:101-2 Ja 23 '67
See also
Newspapers—Consolidations and mergers
Times, London

Israel
Big noise from Tel Aviv; weekly newspaper
Ha'olam Hazeh. il Newsweek 67:72 F 7 '66

Portugal
Report on the press in Spain and Portugal.
V. Dabney. Sat R 49:50-1 Jl 9 '66

South Africa
Crusader pays: reports of prison brutality in
the Rand daily mail. Newsweek 67:38 F 7
'66
Doctor's conscience in South Africa; G.
Dean's charges of police and prison warders
brutality. New Repub 154:17-18 Ja 29 '66

Spain
Pressing toward freedom; press law. Time
87:27-8 Mr 25 '66
Report on the press in Spain and Portugal.
V. Dabney. Sat R 49:50-1 Jl 9 '66

United States
At the grass roots. Newsweek 68:76 O 24 '66
Dixie flamethrowers; Mississippi papers. il
Time 87:64 Mr 4 '66
English lesson; H. Fairlie surveys reading
papers. il Newsweek 67:60-2 Je 6 '66
I protest, by E. W. Scripps. Review
Sat R 49:73 Je 11 '66. N. S. Finney
Praise and panning from Britain; criticism
by H. Fairlie. Time 87:76 Je 3 '66
Suburban daily: new power in publishing.
J. N. Bell. Sat R 50:118+ Ja 14 '67
Today in Florida; Gannett group's new daily
aims at Brevard County, Fla. il Newsweek
67:82 Mr 28 '66
Underground alliance; shoestring papers of
the strident left. il Time 88:57 Jl 29 '66
Where and tear; question of publishing
names and addresses. Newsweek 67:64 Mr
14 '66
Where small news spells big profits; suburban
newspapers. il Bsns W p 127-8 Ag 27 '66
Winds of change for newspapers. il U S
News 60:67-9 Ap 25 '66
See also
American newspaper publishers association
also names of newspapers. e.g. Houston
chronicle; *also* subhead Newspapers under
names of cities e.g. New York (city)—
Newspapers

Foreign language press
Sparks & machete blows; El Diario and El
Tiempo. il Time 87:41-2 F 18 '66
See also
El Diario-la Prensa

Yugoslavia
Brash & frank in Yugoslavia. il Time 88:
101-2 N 18 '66
NEWSPAPERS, Childrens. See Childrens newspapers
NEWSPAPERS, Communist. See Communist
newspapers
NEWSPAPERS, Publishing of. See Newspaper publishing
NEWSPAPERS as textbooks
Newspapers: living textbooks. I. Solie. Sr
Schol 89:sup9 Ja 13 '67
NEWSWEEK (periodical)
News and views. J. Leo. Commonweal 85:4
O 7 '66
NEWSWRITERS. See Reporters and reporting
NEWTON, Blake T. Jr
What every young father should know about
life insurance. Parents Mag 41:71+ O '66
NEWTON, Douglas
Technology in publishing. por Wilson Lib
Bul 41:66-8+ S '66
NEWTON, Sir Isaac
In what year did Newton die? letter. W. H.
Crew. Science 153:1336 S 16 '66
NEWTON, Niles, and others
Parturient mice; effect of environment on
labor. bibliog Science 151:1560-1 Mr 25 '66
NEWTON, Robert C.
Kyanite-andalusite equilibrium from 700°
to 800°C. bibliog Science 153:170-2 Jl 8 '66
Kyanite-sillimanite equilibrium at 750°C.
bibliog Science 151:1222-5 Mr 11 '66

NEWTON, Vernon
Not power; for Sandro Botticelli; poem.
Commonweal 85:343 D 23 '66
NEWTON family
Newton coat-of-arms. H. K. Eilers. il Hobbies 71:124 O '66
NEWTON, Mass.
Education
Pointers on paperbacks; selling paperbacks
in a school library. E. Hall. il Library J
91:2589-91 My 15 '66
NEWTON, N.J.
Grass-roots facelifting. D. Whitman, jr. il
Am City 81:96-7 O '66
NEY, Edward P.
Night-sky phenomena photographed from
Gemini 9. Sky & Tel 32:276-7 N '66
—and Huch, W. F.
Optical environment in Gemini space flights.
Science 153:297-9 Jl 15 '66
NEY, John
Best place. il Newsweek 68:124+ N 21 '66
NEY, Richard
Ney sayer. il por Newsweek 67:87-8 Ap 4 '66
NEY, Robert L. and others
Heterogeneity of template RNA in adrenal
glands. bibliog Science 153:896-7 Ag 19 '66
NEYLAND, Leedell W.
Free Negro in Florida. bibliog por Negro
Hist Bul 29:27-8+ N '65
NEZ Percé Indians
Nez Percé Indians and the opening of the
Northwest, by A. M. Josephy. Review
Nation 202:493-4 Ap 25 '66. D. McNickle
NGO Tuong
Death at prayers; killing of Ap Quang Nam's
mayor. il por Time 87:31-2 F 25 '66
Obituary
Nat R 18:610 Je 28 '66. P. T. Duggan
NGUGEN-van-Gam
U.S.-Vietnamese team to expand education.
il por Sch & Soc 94:316+ O 15 '66
NGUYEN-cao-Ky
Ky's plan for final victory, invade North
Vietnam; interview. pors U S News 61:
22-4 Ag 1 '66
—See Rusk, D. jt. auth.

about
Another surprise from the tough, unpredictable Ky. por Life 60:32-32A My 27 '66
Central figures in the struggle for leadership
of Vietnam. il por U S News 60:14 Mr 28
'66
Coppered bets. il Newsweek 67:39 My 9 '66
Hawaii conference. il por Time 87:19-20 F 11
'66
In the eye of the storm. Time 87:21 Ap 15 '66
Invade North Vietnam? Ky's plan sparks debate; concerning interview in August 1
issue of U.S. news & World report. por U S
News 61:10 Ag 8 '66
Ky makes it harder for U.S. il Bsns W p44
My 21 '66
Letter from Saigon. R. Shaplen. New Yorker
42:155-62+ Ap 16 '66
Letter from South Vietnam. R. Shaplen.
New Yorker 42:142-4+ Je 4 '66
Loss of face. il Newsweek 67:56+ My 16 '66
LBJ in Hawaii: a look and a promise with
excerpts from Ky's opening statement. il
por Newsweek 67:24-7 F 21 '66
New realism; Honolulu conference. il por
Time 87:19-21 F 18 '66
Pilot with a mission. il pors Time 87.26-31
F 18 '66
Portrait of Premier Ky; candor and confusion; interview, ed. by E. J. Hughes.
por Newsweek 67:26 My 2 '66
Question of survival. il por Newsweek 67:
26-8 Ap 18 '66
Success & a promise. Time 87:34 My 13 '66
Syngman Ky? Newsweek 68:30-1 Ag 8 '66
Uses of power. il por Newsweek 68:36 Jl 11
'66
Vietnam must choose. New Repub 154:5-6 Ap
16 '66
Walk, don't run. New Repub 154:5-6 My 21
'66
What comes next in Vietnam war? il por
U S News 60:27-9 My 30 '66
Whole year. Time 87:40 Je 24 '66
Young generals who run the country. F. Mc-
Culloch. il por Life 60:52B+ F 25 '66
NGUYEN-cao-Ky, Mme
New angles. por Time 88:24-5 D 23 '66
Women of Vietnam. L. Bergquist. il pors
Look 30:17-21 D 27 '66

NGUYEN-chanh-Thi
War crisis: as General Thi sees it; interview. por U S News 60:22 Ap 25 '66

about
Bitter Thi. Newsweek 67:40 Mr 21 '66
Buddhists again. il por Newsweek 67:40 Mr 28 '66
Central figures in the struggle for leadership of Vietnam. il por U S News 60:14 Mr 28 '66
General Thi: his backers sided with demonstrators. por U S News 60:21 Ap 18 '66
How much power does Tri Quang want? background to March-April crisis. D. Warner. Reporter 34:11-14 My 5 '66
Letter from Saigon. R. Shaplen. New Yorker 42:157-62+ Ap 16 '66
Question of survival. il por Newsweek 67:26-8 Ap 18 '66
Saigon Thi party. Time 87:33 Mr 18 '66
Young generals who run the country. F. McCulloch. il por Life 60:52B+ F 25 '66

NGUYEN-huu-Thin
Is North Vietnam weakening? interview, ed. by G. C. Troelstrup. por U S News 61:54 D 12 '66

NGUYEN-ngoc-Loan
Maneuvers before Manila. Time 88:34-5 O 28 '66

NGUYEN-quang-Le
Diary of a soldier; ed. by F. Sully. Newsweek 67:36+ My 9 '66

NGUYEN-van-Thieu
Response [to remarks by President Johnson, February 6, 1966] Dept State Bul 54:303-4 F 28 '66
—and others
Declaration of Honolulu; text, February 7, 1966. Cur Hist 50:238-9+ Ap '66

NHAT Hanh
Thich Nhat Hanh; interview. New Yorker 42:21-3 Je 25 '66

NHI, Mai-hong-. See Mai-hong-Nhi

NI Gusti Raka
Bali revisited: 1966. J. Coast. il pors Dance Mag 40:46-9+ N '66

NIACIN
Vitamin therapy urged; promoted by Schizophrenics anonymous. P. McBroom. Sci N 89:199 Mr 26 '66

NIAGARA FALLS, N.Y.
Niagara Falls reduced to a trickle. il Life 61:139-40 N 25 '66

NIBLOCK, Robert W.
Memo from the publisher. J. Claar. il por Miss & Roc 18:5 Ap 4 '66

NICARAGUA
See also
Medical relief work—Nicaragua

Foreign relations
President Schick of Nicaragua visits Washington; texts of greetings exchanged, June 9. 1966. L. B. Johnson; R. Schick-Gutiérrez. Dept State Bul 55:14-17 Jl 4 '66

Politics and government
Constitutional way; new president. Time 88:34 Ag 19 '66

NICE, France
Revisiting the Riviera. A. Waugh. Nat R 18:368+ Ap 19 '66

NICHELS, Ray
Ray Nichels tells how he stiffens the stockers. pors Motor T 18:38-41 Mr '66

NICHOLAS, George P.
Insure, but insure wisely. Motor T 18:86 N '66

NICHOLAS, H. G.
Oxford looks beneath the ivy. Reporter 34:30-2 Je 16 '66

NICHOLS, Beverley
Twisted marriage of Somerset Maugham; excerpts from A case of human bondage. Look 30:32-7 O 18 '66

NICHOLS, Henry A.
Streamlining management; excerpts from address. Parks & Rec 1:919+ N '66

NICHOLS, Jeannette
Halfway; poem. Sat R 50:107 Ja 7 '67
Hidden in hair; poem. Sat R 49:63 My 14 '66
Road; poem. Sat R 49:51 Ag 27 '66
Wind in the wells; poem. Sat R 49:40 Mr 19 '66
Wonder's shoes; poem. Sat R 49:29 My 21 '66

NICHOLS, Mike
Mike Nichols talks about Barbara Harris. por Life 61:106-7 D 16 '66

about
Elizabeth Taylor and Richard Burton: the night of the brawl. J. Roddy. il por Look 30:42-8 F 8 '66
Mike Nichols director as star. M. Gussow. il pors Newsweek 68:95-9 N 14 '66
New faces. H. Alpert. por Sat R 49:12 D 24 '66

NICHOLS, Nichelle
New star in the TV heavens. il pors Ebony 22:70-2+ Ja '67

NICHOLS, Roberta
To the children with love, from Leo Politi. Horn Bk 42:218-22 Ap '66

NICHOLS, Roy F.
Profiles of ethics: a tribute to Lewis Miller Stevens. Ann Am Acad 363:1-3 Ja '66

NICHOLS, William I.
Let's not panic at the new morality; excerpt from address, January 26, 1966. Read Digest 89:75-8 Ag '66

about
Nichols named chairman of Nat'l book committee. por Pub W 190:29 D 12 '66

NICHOLSON, Jessie
Beau for Nora; drama. Plays 25:1-14 Mr '66

NICHOLSON, Margaret
Duty and copyright problems in importing books and sheets; summary of address at meeting of publishers, March 29, 1966. Pub W 189:40-1 My 9 '66

NICHOLSON, R. W. and others
Wet air oxidation of sewage sludge. Am City 81:97-9+ Ap '66

NICHOLSON, Thomas D.
Sky reporter. See issues of Natural history incorporating Nature magazine
Spectacle in the sky. Parents Mag 41:38-9+ Ag '66
This year earth passes through Saturn's ring plane three times. Natur Hist 75:36-9 Ap '66

NICKEL, Herman
West Germany minds its booming business. N Y Times Mag p54-5+ Mr 27 '66

NICKEL
Nickel orthouronate: high-pressure synthesis. A. P. Young. bibliog il Science 153:1380-1 S 16 '66
Pseudo-fivefold symmetry in carbonyl process nickel. G. L. Downs and J. D. Braun. il Science 154:1443-4 D 16 '66
See also
International nickel company
International nickel company of Canada

NICKEL cadmium batteries. See Storage batteries

NICKERSON, Albert Lindsay
Proprietary interest. por Time 88:92 D 16 '66

NICKLAUS, Jack
Awful putt showed me how to win; 1966 Masters. Sports Illus 24:36-8+ Ap 25 '66
Golf. See issues of Sports illustrated
Stopwatches are not the answer. Sports Illus 25:25 Jl 11 '66

about
Is the Masters fixed? G. S. Brown. il pors Sports Illus 24:58-9 Ap 4 '66
Jack plays too good. il por Newsweek 67:62 Ap 25 '66
Master. por Time 87:67 Ap 22 '66
Missing links. il por Newsweek 68:54-5 Jl 18 '66
Smiling Jack wins a rough one. A. Wright. pors Sports Illus 25:20-3 Jl 18 '66
Sporting scene. A. Cooke. New Yorker 42:171-2+ N 5 '66
Sporting scene. H. W. Wind. New Yorker 42:134+ Ap 30; 100+ Ag 13 '66
Three was a crowd. A. Wright. il pors Sports Illus 24:36-43 Ap 18 '66
Victory at Verdun. il por Time 88:40 Jl 15 '66
When two were twice as good. A. Wright. il por Sports Illus 25:40-1 D 19 '66

NICKNAMES
Nature of nicknames. H. A. Smith. il Holiday 40:24+ O '66

NICOLAYSEN, Mary
How preschoolers learn to give and take. Parents Mag 41:48-9+ My '66
Living with a four-year-old and loving it. Parents Mag 41:62-3+ D '66

NICOLIN, Curt René
Sweden's ASEA jolts electricity's future. il por Bsns W p80-4 Ag 27 '66

NICOLSON, Sir Harold
Childe Harold. S. Kauffmann. New Repub 155:22+ N 12 '66
Cultivated mind. il por Time 89:98 Ja 6 '67
Diary of a U-man. L. Kronenberger. por Atlan 218:131-2+ N '66

NICOLSON, Sir Harold—*Continued*
  Harold Nicolson, ed. by N. Nicolson. Review
    Reporter 35:42-4 D 29 '66. A. Fremantle
  Price of peace was war. L. Edel. por Sat R
    49:53-4 D 3 '66
NICOLSON, Nigel
  Art of keeping a diary. Esquire 66:28+ D '66
NICOTINAMIDE-adenine dinucleotidase. See
    Enzymes
NICOTINE
  Nicotine can stimulate or depress smokers.
    Sci N 89:292 Ap 23 '66
NICOTINIC acid. See Niacin
NIDER, Nick
  Sanitize your dog kennel. Field & S 71:114-
    15+ Ja '67
NIEBUHR, Reinhold
  Interview with Reinhold Niebuhr; ed. by
    J. Cogley. por McCalls 93:90-1+ F '66
  Interview with Reinhold Niebuhr; ed. by P.
    Granfield. Commonweal 85:315-21 D 16 '66
  Reinhold Niebuhr discusses the war in Viet-
    nam. New Repub 154:15-16 Ja 29 '66
        about
  Crisis continues. il Time 87:56 F 25 '66
NIEBURG, H. L.
  JPL story. Bul Atomic Sci 22:35-8 O '66
  Profits of war: putsch against McNamara.
    Nation 203:696-701 D 26 '66
  R&D and the contract state: throwing away
    the yardstick; excerpt from Science, stagna-
    tion, and the contract state. Bul Atomic
    Sci 22:20-4 Mr '66
NIEDERHOFFER, Victor
  Onomatopoetic roulette. il por Time 87:72 F
    25 '66
NIEH, Hua-ling
  Several blessings of Ta-nien Wang; story.
    Atlan 218:91-4 D '66
NIEHUIS, Charles C.
  Snowmobiles to high-lake fishing. Field & S
    71:37-9+ D '66
NIELSEN, A. C. company
  TV ratings stay clean; Nielsen system. Bsns
    W p46 S 10 '66
NIELSEN, Carl
  Four fruits of the Carl Nielsen centenary.
    J. W. Barker. il por Am Rec G 32:471-5 Ja
    '66
  Nielsen's Fourth symphony, it makes a
    splendid sound. H. Goldsmith. il Hi Fi 16:
    67 Jl '66
NIELSEN, Charles M.
  Seminary of the future. Christian Cent 83:
    1053-5 Ag 31 '66
NIELSEN, Christen B. See Feigen, G. A.
    jt. auth.
NIELSEN, Knut Schmidt-. See Schmidt-
    Nielsen, K.
NIELSEN, Niels C. Jr
  (ed) See Murray, M. E. Dialogue with Mrs
    O'Hair
NIELSEN rating system. See Television broad-
    casting—Program rating
NIEMANN-PICK disease
  Diagnosis of Gaucher's disease and Niemann-
    Pick disease with small samples of venous
    blood. J. P. Kampine and others. bib-
    liog il Science 155:86-8 Ja 6 '67
NIEPCE, Joseph Nicéphore
  All at once, a moment can be caught for-
    ever. il Life 61:32-50 D 23 '66
NIERENGARTEN, Phil
  Maintenance of public-use areas. por Parks
    & Rec 1:249-50 Mr '66
NIEUW Amsterdam trio. See Trios, Instru-
    mental
NIGERIA
        See also
  Colleges and universities—Nigeria
  Economic assistance in Nigeria
  Kano
        Economic conditions
  Nigeria: coup on a tightrope; corruption and
    economic inequalities. Nation 202:144-5 F 7
    '66
        Native races
  Massacre in Kano. il Time 88:44+ O 14 '66
  Nigeria: smashed showcase in a troubled
    Africa. il U S News 61:51-2 O 17 '66
  On the razor's edge; three tribes contest
    for political supremacy. il Newsweek 68:
    44 Ag 15 '66
  Tribal turmoil wracks Nigeria. il Sr Schol
    89:4 O 28 '66
        Politics and government
  Africa's officers take command. W. A. Lewis.
    Reporter 34:33-6 Mr 24 '66
  And now Nigeria. America 114:163-4 Ja 29 '66
  Another coup. Time 88:33 Ag 5 '66

Can Nigeria catch up with its reputation?
  C. Sterling. il Reporter 34:39-42 My 19
  '66
Cracks in Africa's show window. Bsns W
  p34 Ag 13 '66
Daily bonus. Newsweek 68:70 Ag 22 '66
Death in Nigeria. E. Huxley. Nat R 18:163-4
  F 22 '66; Reply with rejoinder. R. J. Pal-
  meri. 18:390+ My 3 '66
Drama in two acts; Hausa-Ibo feud. il News-
  week 68:54+ O 17 '66
Getting tough. il Newsweek 67:50 Je 6 '66
Good words & brave. Time 87:34+ F 4 '66
Grisly record; Gowon's plans. Time 88:43 D
  9 '66
Man must whack. il Time 88:45 O 7 '66
Men of Sandhurst. il Time 87:21-3 Ja 28 '66
Military governors. il Newsweek 67:48 Mr 21
  '66
New chance in Nigeria? unity or tribal pol-
  itics. H. K. Flad. Commonweal 83:525-6
  F 4 '66
New Ironsides; army coup. Newsweek 67:43
  Ja 31 '66
New realism. Newsweek 67:38 F 7 '66
Nigeria: smashed showcase in a troubled
  Africa. il U S News 61:51-2 O 17 '66
Nigeria, the pulling apart of a nation. New
  Repub 155:13 N 5 '66
Nigeria: troubled giant. il U S News 60:69
  Ja 31 '66
On the razor's edge. il Newsweek 68:44 Ag
  15 '66
Question of speed; coup attempt. Newsweek
  68:34-5 Ag 8 '66
Secret furies. il Time 87:45-6 Je 10 '66
Showcase shaken. il Sr Schol 88:15 F 4 '66
Three years to go. Time 87:33 Je 3 '66
Toward disintegration? il Time 88:27-8 Ag
  12 '66
Tribal turmoil wracks Nigeria. il Sr Schol
  89:4 O 28 '66
Why black Africa's richest nation is crum-
  bling. il U S News 61:8 Ag 15 '66
    See also
Political parties—Nigeria
NIGERIAN fiction
  Nigeria's new man; Chinua Achebe. R.
    Green. Nation 202:465-6 Ap 18 '66
NIGHT blindness
  Night blindness. J. E. Dowling. il Sci Am
    215:78-84 O '66
NIGHT-blooming cereus; story. See Deal, B. H.
NIGHT clubs
  A go-go girls. il Ebony 21:142-6 Ap '66
  Bundled in bond; Milwaukee's International
    exports, ltd. il Time 88:65 O 28 '66
  Cheetah gives youth rebellion a place to
    howl; Chicago branch caters to big market
    under twenty-five. il Bsns W p40-1 O 29
    '66
  El Morocco. F. Morton. il Holiday 39:78-80+
    F '66
  Entertainment; Fr Boyd at the hungry 1,
    San Francisco. L. Kinsolving. Christian
    Cent 83:1244 O 12 '66; Reply. E. D. Napier.
    83:1411 N 16 '66
  Europe by night. W. Murray. il Holiday 41:
    58-71+ Ja '67
  Filmotheques. R. Christgau. il Pop Phot 60:
    80+ Ja '67
  Las Vegas scene; Flamingo hotel. W. Como.
    il Dance Mag 40:14-15+ Jl '66
  Las Vegas scene; Tropicana's version of
    Folies Bergere. W. Como. il Dance Mag
    40:20-1 My '66
  Mr Playboy of the western world. C. Tom-
    kins. il Sat Eve Post 239:96-101 Ap 23 '66
  Murray the K's world. New Yorker 42:44-5
    Ap 16 '66
  Night on the wiggy scene; Cheetah a total-
    environment nightclub. T. Meehan. il Sat
    Eve Post 239:34-9 O 22 '66
  Nightclub priest; Father Boyd. S. Alexander.
    Life 61:29 O 28 '66
  Oasis dries up; Moscow American club. il
    Newsweek 69:51 Ja 16 '67
  Playboy holds key to night club success. il
    Bsns W p88-90 Ja 28 '67
  Playing the Piper; Piper club, Rome. il
    Newsweek 69:31 Ja 9 '67
  Roar of the Cheetah, the look of the
    crowd; Manhattan's Cheetah. il Time 87:
    52-3 My 6 '66
  Slipped disc; Manhattan discothèque craze
    going. Newsweek 68:108+ N 7 '66
  Starry soiree salutes the Lido. il Life 62:76-7
    Ja 6 '67
  Two for the show; M. Boyd's nightclub
    preaching. il Newsweek 68:68 O 3 '66
  Wild new flashy bedlam of the discothèque.
    il Life 60:72-6 My 27 '66

NIGHT driving, Automobile. See Automobile driving
NIGHT of the dunce; drama. See Gagliano, F.
NIGHT photography. See Photography, Night
NIGHT-sea journey; story. See Barth, J.
NIGHT vision
    See also
    Night blindness
NIGHTCLUBS. See Night clubs
NIGHTINGALE, E. M.
    Incident before Troy; drama. Plays 26:86-90 N '66
NIGHTINGALE, Earl
    On motivating the disadvantaged child; address, August 8, 1966. Vital Speeches 33:18-24 O 15 '66
NIGHTMARES. See Dreams
NIGHTQUEST; story. See Walker, P.
NIGRELLI, Ross F.
    Sea treasure; interview. New Yorker 42:22-3 Ag 27 '66
NIKE-X. See Guided missiles—Defenses
NIKOLAIS, Alwin
    Alwin in wonderland. il Time 87:86 My 20 '66
    Galaxy, Hunter college playhouse. M. Marks. Dance Mag 40:61 Mr '66
NIKON cameras. See Cameras
NILE RIVER
    See also
    Aswan High Dam

                    History
Nile; with photographs by E. Elisofon. Kinross. Horizon 8:80-99 Sum '66
NILE VALLEY
Nile; with photographs by E. Elisofon. Kinross. Horizon 8:80-99 Sum '66
NILSSON, Birgit
    Double Nilsson Tannhäuser. I. Kolodin. Sat R 49:45 Ap 2 '66
    Great artists of our time. I. Kolodin. il pors Sat R 49:47-9+ F 26 '66
    Musical events; performance of both Venus and Elisabeth in Wagner's Tannhäuser. W. Sergeant. New Yorker 42:176-7 Mr 26 '66
    Profiles. W. Sargeant. por New Yorker 42:66-70+ O 29 '66
    Two sopranos: both Wagnerians, both Scandinavians. P. L. Miller. por Am Rec G 32:516-17 F '66
NILSSON, Carl
    Some doubts about the earth's dust cloud. bibliog Science 153:1242-6 S 9 '66
NILSSON, Sven Erik C. See Crescitelli, F. jt. auth.
NIMBUS (satellite) See Artificial satellites—Meteorological applications
NIMITZ, Chester William
    Admiral Chester Nimitz, RIP. A. Burke. Nat R 18:256 Mr 22 '66
    Home is the sailor. il por Time 87:33 Mr 4 '66
    Two bites to a dog. il por Newsweek 67:30+ Mr 7 '66
NIMRUD
    Mallowans; interview. A. Christie; M. E. L. Mallowan. New Yorker 42:51-2 O 29 '66
    Nimrud and its remains, by M. E. L. Mallowan. Review
        Natur Hist 76:68+ Ja '67. C. H. Gordon
        Sat R 49:25-6 Jl 9 '66. L. Poole and G. Poole
NIMS, John Frederick
    Epitaph for a light lady; poem. Sat R 49:55 Mr 5 '66
    5:00 p.m; poem. Atlan 217:81 F '66
    1520; poem. Sat R 49:67 Ap 30 '66
    With fingering hand; poem. Sat R 50:82 Ja 14 '67
NIN, Anaïs
    Life without father. L. Edel. il por Sat R 49:91 My 7 '66
    Traffic island. pors Newsweek 67:104+ My 2 '66
NINETEEN hundred and forty-one
    That unforgettable month: December 1941. S. A. Mix. il Todays Health 44:12-15 D '66
    Where were you? conditions before Pearl Harbor. il Newsweek 68:36-8 D 12 '66
NINETEEN hundred and forty-seven
    20th anniversary issue: a special report; oh, how your life has changed! il Changing T 21:6-14 Ja '67
NINETEEN hundred and forty-two
    That unforgettable month: December 1941. S. A. Mix. il Todays Health 44:12-15 D '66

NINETEEN hundred and sixteen
    Those were the days; fifty years ago. Hi Fi 16:75-6 D 15 '66
NINETEEN hundred and sixties
    Remember the sixties? D. Newman and R. Benton. il Esquire 66:109-14 Ag '66
NINETEEN hundred and sixty-five
    Our top ten education stories of 1965. il Sr Schol 87:sup 1 Ja 7 '66
NINETEEN hundred and sixty-seven
    Letter from Paris; new year prediction by some of France's female fortune-tellers. Genêt. New Yorker 42:109-10 Ja 14 '67
    Opinion. W. V. Shannon. Mlle 64:14-15 Ja '67
    Predictions '67. Seventeen 26:89 Ja '67
    '67: what kind of a year? il U S News 62:21-30+ Ja 9 '67
    What's new about the year? D. Lawrence. U S News 62:100 Ja 16 '67
NINETEEN hundred and sixty-six
    Esquire's sixth annual dubious achievement awards. il Esquire 67:52-9 Ja '67
    Lively arts; a backwards glance at 1966. M. Ronan; P. Hudson; R. Hemming. il Sr Schol 89:28-9 D 9 '66
    1966: another year of change. America 115:821 D 24 '66
    Notes and comment. New Yorker 42:23 D 31 '66
    Route '66: a selective review and commentary on the (mostly American) library scene and its events of the past year. E. Moon. il Library J 92:51-63 Ja 1 '67
    Shape of events from one year to next. Life 62:4 Ja 6 '67
NINETEEN hundred and thirties
    Making the 1930s pay off, at last. il Bsns W p 128-30+ Ag 20 '66
NINETEEN hundred and thirty-three
    1933, by H. Feis. Review
        Sat R 49:37 Ap 2 '66. L. J. Walinsky
NINETEEN hundred and twenties
    There was something about the twenties. A. MacLeish. Sat R 49:10-13 D 31 '66
NINETEENTH century
    Nil, by R. M. Adams. Review
        Nation 204:26-7 Ja 2 '67. H. R. Wolf
NISBET, Robert A.
    Artist as prophet. Commentary 42:76-7 Jl '66
NISHIMURA, H. See Miller, R. W. jt. auth.
NISHIOKA, Richard S. See Fridberg, G. jt. auth.
NISHIZUKA, Yasutomi, and others
    Cancer research: U.S.-Japan cooperative science program; report on symposium. Science 152:1524-6 Je 10 '66
NISKAYUNA, N.Y.
    Team teaching: how it works in Niskayuna; Van Antwerp junior high school. L. Cerri. il Sr Schol 88:sup 16 Mr 25 '66
NISSAN motor company. See Automobile industry and trade—Japan
NISSENBAUM, A. See Kaplan, I. R. jt. auth.
NITELLA. See Characeae
NITRATES
                Physiological effects
    When to suspect nitrate poisoning in your cattle. D. Malena. Suc Farm 64:54A N '66
NITRIFYING bacteria. See Bacteria, Nitrifying
NITROGEN
    Denitrification rates in an island bay in the equatorial Pacific Ocean. J. J. Goering and R. C. Dugdale. bibliog il Science 154:505-6 O 28 '66
                Fixation
    Nitrogen fixation; report on informal colloquium. C. C. Delwiche. Science 151:1565-6 Mr 25 '66
NITROGEN, Liquid
    Produce sleeps and stays fresh. il Bsns W p49-50 Ja 29 '66
NITROQUINOLINE N-oxide. See Cancer producing substances
NITZE, Paul H.
    Image; summary of address, September 29, 1966. New Repub 155:5-6 N 19 '66
    Issues of world power; address, November 8, 1966. Vital Speeches 33:98-103 D 1 '66
NIXON, Raymond B. See Lindsay, R. jt. auth.
NIXON, Richard Milhous
    Academic freedom; address, June 5, 1966. Vital Speeches 32:550-2 Jl 1 '66; Same with title Academic freedom today. por(p433) Sch & Soc 94:451-4 D 10 '66
    Four academic freedoms. Sat R 49:12-13+ Ag 27 '66
    Hard lines and guidelines; address, December 3, 1965. Vital Speeches 32:194-7 Ja 15 '66

NIXON, Richard Milhous—*Continued*
If mob rule takes hold in U.S; a warning from Richard Nixon. por U S News 61: 64-5 Ag 15 '66
Issue was the Johnson Congress; interview. por U S News 61:56+ N 21 '66
Let's give business a square deal. por Nations Bsns 54:46-7+ Ap '66
Notes and comment; summary of statement. New Yorker 42:41 Mr 19 '66
Outlook for Republicans now; interview. por U S News 61:59-60+ O 3 '66

about

Answer please, Mr Nixon. Nat R 18:196 Mr 8 '66; Discussion. 18:294+, 304 Ap 5 '66
Availability of Richard Nixon. J. Witcover. por Reporter 35:27-9 Ag 11 '66
Can Romney stop Nixon in '68? por U S News 61:31 Jl 25 '66
Long-distance runner. T. Wicker. Atlan 217: 76 Ap '66
Mr Nixon advises Mr Kennedy. Nat R 18: 1146 N 15 '66
Mr Nixon back in business. M. McGrory. America 115:647 N 19 '66
Mr Nixon comes to town. M. McGrory. America 115:273 S 17 '66
Nixon and the GOP; comeback? il por Newsweek 68:30-5 O 10 '66
Nixon: '66 campaigner with '68 in mind. por U S News 61:12 S 5 '66
Old pro in action. il por Newsweek 68:18-19 S 5 '66
Operation withdrawal; remarks by L. B. Johnson. por Time 88:28 N 11 '66
Outsider's report. W. V. Shannon. Commonweal 85:8 O 7 '66
Plowing on with Richard Nixon. Nat R 18: 916+ S 20 '66
Polls '66: Nixon or Romney? P. Gennoy. Nat R 18:1084 N 1 '66
Pro's-eye view. R. Moley Newsweek 68:126 O 24 '66
White sound of Richard Nixon. E. J. Hughes. Newsweek 68:19 Ag 22 '66
Will it be Nixon vs. LBJ in '68? il pors U S News 61:54-8 O 3 '66

NIXON, Robert E. and Welch, M. S.
How to begin the treasure hunt for your real self. Seventeen 25:140-1+ O '66
Your Christmas moods. Seventeen 25:126-7+ D '66

NJEGOŠ, Petar Petrovič. See Petar II. prince bishop of Montenegro

NKRUMAH, Kwame
African game: who's leader of what? il por U S News 60:12 Mr 14 '66
African revolt that pleased the U.S. il por U S News 60:8 Mr 7 '66
And now Nkrumah: generals & the future of Africa. J. K. Sale. il por Nation 202:317-22 Mr 21 '66
Atlantic report. Atlan 217:12+ My '66
Back from the brink of communism in Ghana. A. J. Meyers. il por U S News 61: 88-9 Ag 22 '66
Clay-foot redeemer. America 114:344 Mr 12 '66
Cocoa curtain comes down. il por Sr Schol 88:16 Mr 11 '66
Exit Nkrumah, an old dreamer; enter Ankrah, a new realist. L. Garrison. il N Y Times Mag p32-3+ Ap 3 '66
Fall of Nkrumah. P. Crane. America 114:383 Mr 19 '66
Fount of honor. pors Newsweek 68:44+ Jl 11 '66
Ghana: communism's major defeat in Africa. D. Reed. Read Digest 88:75-80 Je '66
Ghana gets a second chance. C. Sterling. il Reporter 34:23-7 Ap 21 '66
Ghana without The Redeemer. R. W. Howe. New Repub 154:9-11 Mr 12 '66; Reply with rejoinder. A. W. Wolfe. 154:36+ Ap 2 '66
Ghana's burst of joy over a tyrant's fall. il Life 60:28-31 Mr 11 '66
Goodbye to the aweful. il Time 87:34-5 Mr 4 '66
Kwame Nkrumah. C. L. Sanders. il por Ebony 21:138-40+ S '66
Longing for home. il Time 87:30 Mr 11 '66
Macbeth in Africa. Commonweal 83:653 Mr 11 '66
My country is yours. il por Newsweek 67: 57-8 Mr 14 '66
Myth is broken. il por Newsweek 67:43-4 Mr 7 '66
Nkrumah-charisma fails. P. E. Sigmund. Commonweal 84:50-2 Ap 1 '66
On the beach. Time 89:31 Ja 6 '67
Revenant Lumumba; earlier association. Nat R 18:306-7 Ap 5 '66
Rope that hanged Nkrumah. E. Huxley. Nat R 18:268-70 Mr 22 '66

NO medal for Sonny; story. See Wilner, H.
NO one but me; story. See Blyth, M.

NOAH, Harold J.
Personal report. Sat R 49:99 Ap 16 '66

NOAKES, Edward H.
Making libraries useable. por Wilson Lib Bul 40:851-3 My '66

NOBEL, Alfred Bernhard
Nobel's hits and errors. D. Fleming. Atlan 218:53-9 O '66

NOBEL, Joel
Max, the lifesaver; Dr J. Nobel's. cart. il pors Life 60:31-2+ Ja 28 '66

NOBEL prizes
Belated recognition; 1966 Nobel prize in physiology and medicine. il Time 88:77 O 21 '66
Cancer fighters. il Newsweek 68:78+ O 24 '66
France considers significance of Nobel awards. V. K. McElheny; reply. L. Badash. Science 151:634 F 11 '66
Lauded at last; chemistry and physics awards. il Time 88:88 N 11 '66
1966 Nobel laureates in medicine or physiology. P. Talalay; G. Williams-Ashman; W. R. Bryan. il Science 154:362-5 O 21 '66
Nobel peace prize: acceptance speech, December 10, 1965. H. R. Labouisse. il UN Mo Chron 3:99-102 Ja '66
Nobel prize; for literature. B. Souvarine. Nat R 18:1148 N 15 '66
Nobel prize winners; A. Kastler wins physics prize, and R. S. Mulliken receives prize in chemistry. il Sci N 90:400 N 12 '66
Nobel prize-winners; 1966. R. Alter; G. C. Schwebell. il Sat R 49:44-7 D 10 '66
Nobel prizes. Sci Am 215:56-7 D '66
Nobels for 1966; literature award to two Jewish writers S. Maloff. Newsweek 68:112 O 31 '66
Nobel's hits and errors; survey of prizes, winners and speculation on 1966 winners. D. Fleming. Atlan 218:53-9 O '66
Practical theorists; prizes in physics and chemistry. il Newsweek 68:73 N 14 '66
Shmuel Agnon, Nelly Sachs win Nobel literature prize. Pub W 190:56-7 O 31 '66
Two share Nobel prize; prize for medicine and physiology to two American scientists. il Sci N 90:319 O 22 '66
See also
Kastler, A.
Mulliken, R. S.

NOBILE, Philip
Crisis in Louvain. Cath World 203:233-5 Jl '66

NOBILITY
See also
Titles of honor and nobility
also subhead Nobility under names of countries, e.g. Great Britain—Nobility

NOBLE, Hubert C.
Teaching about religion. Christian Cent 83: 621 My 11 '66

NOBLE, Jeanne L.
(ed) See Horne, L. Three-horned dilemma facing Negro women

NOBLE, Joseph V.
Athenian vase painters; excerpt from Technique of painted attic pottery. Am Artist 30:30-6+ F '66
Workshop: the Greek black glaze; excerpts from Techniques of painted attic pottery. Craft Horiz 26:37-9+ Mr '66

NOBLE, Mary
New way to have bigger camellias that bloom earlier. il Flower Grower 53:41 N '66

NOBLE, Norman W.
Highground haven. Am For 72:30-1+ Je '66

NOBLE gases. See Gases, Rare
Les NOCES; ballet. See Ballets—Criticisms
NOCTILUCA miliaris. See Dinoflagellates

NOCTURNES (music)
See also
Phonograph records—Nocturnes (music)
NODULE bacteria. See Bacteria, Nitrifying

NOËL HUME, Ivor
Mathews manor. Antiques 90:832-6 D '66
Mugs, jugs, and chamber pots. il Antiques 90:520-2 O '66
Ornamental glass bird fountains of the eighteenth century. Antiques 90:208-10 Ag '66

NOETHER, Emiliana P.
(comp) Articles and other books received; Italy. See issues of American historical review

NOGACZ, Filimon
Artificial kidney saves accident victim. Todays Health 44:72 My '66

NOISE
How to quiet down a noisy house. il Bet Hom & Gard 44:120 Mr '66
Sounds nobody wants. H. Downs. Sci Digest 59:95-7 Ap '66
When noise annoys; Time essay. Time 88: 24-5 Ag 19 '66
See also
Airplanes—Noise
Airports—Noise

Physiological effects
Assault on the ear; city dweller. Newsweek 67:70 Ap 4 '66
Direct test of the power function for loudness. L. E. Marks and A. W. Slawson. bibliog il Science 154:1036-7 N 25 '66
Noise. L. L. Beranek. il Sci Am 215:66-74+ D '66
Noise: how much more can we take? S. Blum. il McCalls 94:48-9+ Ja '67
Noise menace threatens man; hearing and sanity may be affected. B. J. Culliton. il Sci N 90:297-9 O 15 '66

Psychological effects
Noise. L. L. Beranek. il Sci Am 215:66-74+ D '66
Noise menace threatens man; hearing and sanity may be affected. B. J. Culliton. il Sci N 90:297-9 O 15 '66
Psychological reactions to aircraft noise. K. D. Kryter. bibliog il Science 151:1346-55 Mr 18 '66; Reply. P. K. Holmes. 152:865 My 13 '66

NOISE, Radio. See Radio interference
NOISE generator. See Sound—Apparatus
NOISE measurement. See Sound measurement
NOISE production by fishes. See Sound production by fishes

NOLAN, Hugh J.
Book review. America 115:72 Jl 16 '66

NOLAN, Martin F.
Draft by lottery? New Repub 155:9-10 Jl 30 '66
Junior senator from Massachusetts. Reporter 35:46+ D 1 '66
Kennedys at home have a few problems. New Repub 154:10-11 Je 25 '66
Negro stake in Washington home rule. Reporter 35:18-21 Ag 11 '66
New (sob!) trends in the comics. Reporter 35:32-3 D 29 '66
Teddy and Eddie revisited. Reporter 35:33-5 S 8 '66
Where the Pentagon gets its voice. Reporter 34:41-3 Ap 7 '66

NOLAN, Paul T.
Practical program in literary research. Sr Schol 89:sup 16 O 14 '66
Tree to the sky; drama. Plays 25:27-39 My '66
Trial of Peter Zenger; drama. Plays 25:13-25 Ap '66

NOLAND, A. W. Jr
Annual contracts solve everyday problems. Am City 81:107+ F '66

NOLAND, Kenneth
Art. M. Kozloff. Nation 202:370-2 Mr 28 '66
Green mountain boys. A. Solomon. il pors Vogue 148:104-9+ Ag 1 '66

NOLAND, Lloyd U. Jr
Think small, sell big. il por Duns R 87:55+ Mr '66

NOLL, A. Michael
Choreography and computers. Dance Mag 41: 43-5 Ja '67

NOLL, Hans
Chain initiation and control of protein synthesis. bibliog Science 151:1241-5 Mr 11 '66

NOLTING, Frederick E. Jr
Letter from Paris; excerpts. por Time 88:79 N 4 '66

NOMAD, Max, pseud.
Popular front for protest. Sat R 49:45-6 Je 4 '66

NOMBRE de Dios mission. See Florida—Missions

NOMENCLATURE. See subhead Nomenclature under various subjects, e.g. Biology—Nomenclature

NOMINATION expenditures. See Campaign funds

NON-ALIGNED nations, Conferences of. See International conferences

NON-COMBATANTS, Compensation of. See Vietnamese war, 1957- —Compensation of non-combatants

NON-COMMISSIONED officers. See United States—Army—Non-commissioned officers

NONCONFORMITY. See Conformity

NONCONFORMITY (religion) See Dissenters, Religious

NONDESTRUCTIVE testing. See Testing

NONDUGL, New Guinea. See Bird sanctuaries

NONESUCH press
Sir Francis Meynell lectures in New York; summaries of addresses; ed. by P. A. Bennett. F. Meynell. il Pub W 189:86-9+ Ap 4 '66

NONFAT dry milk. See Milk, Dried

NONFERROUS metals. See Metals, Nonferrous

NONGRADED classes. See Ungraded classes

NONINTERVENTION. See Intervention

NON-LETHÁL gases in warfare. See Gases in warfare

NON-MILITARY compulsory service. See Service, Compulsory non-military

NON-MUSICAL phonograph records. See Phonograph records—Spoken records

NONOMURA, Y. and others
Tetrodotoxin and manganese ions; effects on electrical activity and tension in taenia coli of guinea pig. bibliog Science 152: 97-9 Ap 1 '66

NONPROFIT corporation. See Corporations, Nonprofit

NONRESIDENT borrowers. See Libraries—Registration

NONRETURNABLE bottles. See Bottles

NONSTICK cookware. See Kitchen utensils

NONSUCH palace, England
Very pearl of the realm. M. Cable. il Horizon 8:108-15 Wint '66

NON-WAGE payments
Changing structure of compensation. A. Strasser. il Mo Labor R 89:953-8 S '66
Fringe benefits now rising twice as fast as wages. il Nations Bsns 54:50-2 Ag '66
Fringe binge: it costs more every year. il U S News 60:76-8 My 2 '66
Now a pattern for wages and fringes in 1967; General electric settlement. il U S News 61:76-7 O 31 '66
Personal business; executive fringe benefits. Bsns W p 101-2 Jl 30 '66
Personal business; executive job contract. Bsns W p 175-6 S 17 '66
When the worker is king, industry's big hunt for talent. il U S News 60:98+ F 14 '66
White-collar pay supplements. V. J. Sheifer. il Mo Labor R 89:496-502 My '66

NOONAN, John T. Jr
Contraception and the council. Commonweal 83:657-62 Mr 11 '66
Contraception; interview. Cath World 203: 153-6 Je '66

NORAD. See North American air defense command

NORADRENALIN. See Adrenalin

NORBERG, Fredrika
Man vs. machine, Elwood loses! Motor T 18:22 N '66

NORDLAND, Gerald
Gene Davis paints a picture. Art N 65:46-9+ Ap '66

NOREPINEPHRINE
Electron-microscopic autoradiography of rat hypothalamus after intraventricular H^3-norepinephrine. G. K. Aghajanian and F. E. Bloom. bibliog il Science 153:308-10 Jl 15 '66
Inhibition of insulin release by norepinephrine in man. D. Porte, Jr. and R. H. Williams. bibliog il Science 152:1248-50 My 27 '66
Norepinephrine methylation in fetal rat adrenals. F. L. Margolis and others. bibliog il Science 154:275-6 O 14 '66
Tritiated norepinephrine; release from brain slices by electrical stimulation. R. J. Baldessarini and I. J. Kopin. bibliog il Science 152:1630-1 Je 17 '66

NORFOLK, Ill.
Great mail crisis of Norfolk, Illinois. J. Crittenden. Atlan 219:106+ Ja '67

NORFOLK, Va.

Banks
Credit au go-go: look what's happened to bankers; First national. T. G. Harris. il Look 30:26-9 Ap 5 '66

City planning
One good civic center doesn't make a city. il Arch Rec 139:157-62 F '66

Police
Multi-channel network keeps the air waves clear. il Am City 81:50 O '66

NORFOLK, Va.—*Continued*

Street traffic

How to get the most out of a city's street system; with outline of plan. F. G. Jordan, jr. il Am City 81:77-9+ N '66

NORFOLK and Western railway-Chesapeake and Ohio merger. See Railroads—Consolidations and mergers

NORFOLK ISLAND pine

Christmas tree to grow indoors. Mrs W. B. Jolly. Flower Grower 53:41 D '66

NORFOLK music festival. See Music festivals —Connecticut

NORGE division, Borg-Warner corporation. See Borg-Warner corporation

NORINS, Leslie C. See Cohen, I. R. jt. auth.

NORLANDER, Everett

From the Tribune's ivory tower. New Repub 154:39-40 F 26 '66

NORMAN, Charles

Leafy air; poem. New Yorker 42:42 Ap 9 '66

NORMAN, Dorothy

Mrs Indira Gandhi, prime minister of India. Vogue 147:146-7+ Mr 1 '66

NORMAN, Jennifer

Wish; poem. Horn Bk 42:751 D '66

NORMAN, Philip

Prevalence of hobbits. N Y Times Mag p30-1+ Ja 15 '67

NORMAN, Richard S.

Rotation technique in radially symmetric electron micrographs: mathematical analysis. bibliog Science 152:1238-9 My 27 '66

NORMANDY

Beaches of pleasure, beaches of pain. H. Sutton. Sat R 49:38-9+ Jl 16 '66

Our highwayman in France. H. Sutton. il Sat R 49:37-8 Ag 6 '66

History

Norman conquest. K. M. Setton. il Nat Geog Mag 130:206-51 Ag '66

NORODOM Sihanouk, king of Cambodia (abdicated 1955)

Atlantic report; reply. Norodom Sihanouk. Atlan 217:44 Je '66

Ave ave. Time 88:28 Ag 19 '66

Hitting the Sihanouk Trail. il Time 87:33-4 My 13 '66

Letter from Cambodia. R. Shaplen. New Yorker 42:186+ S 17 '66

Man on a tightrope. il por Newsweek 68:30+ S 12 '66

NORRIS, Bobbe

Treatment. il por Time 88:69 Jl 8 '66

NORRIS, Harold

Fifty dinosaurs restyling the states: constitutions: the politics of power. Nation 203:472-5 N 7 '66

NORRIS, Kathleen (Thompson)

Obituary

Pub W 189:78 Ja 31 '66

NORRIS, Kenneth S. See Lang, T. G. jt. auth.

NORRIS, William C.

When a whiz kid grows up. por Bsns W p30 Jl 30 '66

NORRIS-Thermador corporation

Boom head. il Newsweek 67:79 Mr 14 '66

NORSGAARD, Campbell

Nature in your back yard. il pors Sci Digest 61:79-81 Ja '67

NORSTAD, Lauris

Excerpt from testimony, May 6, 1966. Cong Digest 45:253+ O '66

NORTH, Bill

Trick of putting a submarine in a bottle. Pop Mech 127:158-61+ Ja '67

NORTH, Jessica Nelson

Marion Strobel Mitchell. Poetry 108:264-5 Jl '66

NORTH, Lowell

Lowell North on sails; interview, ed. by K. Krüger. por Yachting 119:77-9+ Mr '66

NORTH, Sandie

Justice Douglas' twenty-three-year-old bride talks about her marriage. Ladies Home J 83:92+ N '66

NORTH, Sterling

Pet news; excerpt from Raccoons are the brightest people. Ladies Home J 83:57-8 O '66

NORTH AMERICA

See also

Birds—North America

NORTH AMERICAN air defense command

Early operational status expected for new Norad center; combat operations center. P. J. Klass. il Aviation W 84:74-5+ Ja 24 '66

Guardian mountain of our continent. J. G. Hubbell. il Read Digest 88:149-52+ Je '66

Mountain of preparedness; new combat operations center. il Time 87:52-3 Ja 28 '66

NORTH AMERICAN aviation, incorporated

Path to the future. W. J. Coughlin. Tech W 19:50 Ag 8 '66

Sabreliner: T-39 in civvies. B. Rogers. il Flying 78:40-7 My '66

NORTH AMERICAN conference on church and family

Church and the sexual crisis. Christian Cent 83:823-4 Je 29 '66; Discussion. 83:986 Ag 10 '66

NORTH AMERICAN Indians. See Indians of North America

NORTH AMERICAN water and power alliance

Bold water planning urged. Sci N 90:187 S 10 '66

North American water colossus. T. E. Stimson. il Pop Mech 126:80-1+ Ag '66

NORTH ATLANTIC council. See North Atlantic treaty organization

NORTH ATLANTIC treaty organization

Alliance under fire. Sr Schol 88:18 Mr 11 '66

Ami, go home; history behind de Gaulle policies. P. Ben. New Repub 154:10-11 Ap 9 '66

As France sees it. Time 87:37 Ap 29 '66

Atlantic alliance; southeast Asia; address, September 13, 1966. B. K. Holloway. Vital Speeches 33:11-14 O 15 '66

Atlantic report: de Gaulle and NATO. Atlan 217:24+ My '66

Bilateral programs gain European favor. Aviation W 84:96+ Mr 7 '66

Bridging the channel; Anglo-German summit conference. Newsweek 67:43-4 Je 6 '66

Can the President square the circle? J. Burnham. Nat R 18:106 F 8 '66

Change of command; French departure. Time 88:22-3 Jl 8 '66

Cliff-hanger; the perils of NATO; U.S. antide Gaulle crusade backfires. il Newsweek 67:32+ My 2 '66

Closer tie with Soviets seen behind de Gaulle's NATO move. Aviation W 84:36 Mr 14 '66

Conservation of tension. J. Burnham. Nat R 18:408 My 3 '66

Cost of moving; de Gaulle's ultimatum. il Time 87:51 Mr 18 '66

Dean Acheson's word for de Gaulle: nonsense; excerpts from interview. D. Acheson. U S News 60:79 Ap 18 '66

De Gaulle is not alone: the view from Europe. A. De Borchgrave. il Newsweek 67:40-1 Ap 25 '66

De Gaulle: no nation has friends, only interests. U S News 61:46 S 19 '66

DeGaulle sets forth to change the face of Europe. C. J. V. Murphy. il Life 61:18-25 Jl 8 '66; Same abr. with title What is de Gaulle up to? Read Digest 89:134-8 S '66

De Gaulle threatens NATO, U.S. with loss of bases in France. Aviation W 84:24 F 28 '66

Despite de Gaulle NATO is still needed. Life 61:4 Jl 8 '66

Doctor de Gaulle; eviction notice. K. Crawford. Newsweek 67:39 Mr 28 '66

Europe's new mood: its meaning for U.S. il U S News 60:39-41 Je 20 '66

For a new Atlantic alliance; address, June 1966. H. A. Kissinger. il Reporter 35:18-27 Jl 14 '66

Fourteen NATO nations declare alliance essential to common security; text of joint declaration; March 18, 1966. Dept State Bul 54:536 Ap 4 '66

France and NATO; address, April 14, 1966. M. Couve de Murville. Vital Speeches 32:450-3 My 15 '66

France hands NATO an eviction notice. Bsns W p42+ Mr 19 '66

France opts out; intention to pull out from NATO. Newsweek 67:42+ Mr 21 '66

French foreign affairs; address, November 3, 1966. M. Couve de Murville. Vital Speeches 33:106-11 D 1 '66

General's pronouncement; de Gaulle's threat to withdraw from NATO. E. Taylor. Reporter 34:16+ Mr 10 '66

Germany; address, May 25, 1966. L. Erhard. Vital Speeches 32:552-4 Jl 1 '66

Germany's new army; no. 1 in Europe again. il U S News 61:69-70 S 12 '66

House hunt; objections to Casteau-Chièvres area. Newsweek 68:40 S 5 '66

Hunting new quarters; Belgian town of Chièvres. il Time 88:26-7 Ag 12 '66

I think we have done damned well; excerpts from address before Senate foreign relations committee. M. Bundy. il Newsweek 68:40 Jl 4 '66

NORTH ATLANTIC treaty organization—Meetings, 1966—*Continued*
East and West: puzzle in common. il Newsweek 67:39 Je 20 '66
Steaming into Paris; R. S. McNamara's part. Newsweek 68:32+ Ag 8 '66
Tattered and torn. Newsweek 67:46-7 Je 27 '66

Multilateral force (proposed)
Nuclear weapons: a liability. J. Silard. il Bul Atomic Sci 22:15-20 S '66

NORTH CAROLINA
See also
Fishing—North Carolina
Labor and laboring classes—North Carolina
United States—History—Colonial period
Wilderness areas—North Carolina

Description and travel
Land of tumbling waters. M. J. Dunn. 3d. il Travel 126:37-42 O '66

Industries
Research park thrives in academic neighborhood; North Carolina's Research triangle park. il Bsns W p 184-5+ D 10 '66

NORTH CAROLINA forest fire. See Forest fires

NORTH CAROLINA mutual life insurance company
N.C. mutual reaches the heights. il Ebony 21:151-2+ Je '66

NORTH CAROLINA. University, Chapel Hill
Chapel Hill. F. G. Patton. il Holiday 40:54-63+ Ag '66
Coy chancellor: WRAL-TV attack on instructor. Nation 203:469 N 7 '66
Coy mistress caper; furor over assignment to rephrase A. Marvell's 17th century love poem. il Life 61:99-102 N 11 '66
Speaker ban: controversy is revived at U.N.C. L. J. Carter. Science 152:50-2 Ap 1 '66
Speaker ban: suit asserts a right to listen. L. J. Carter. Science 152:330 Ap 15 '66

NORTH CASCADES. See Cascade Range

NORTH CASCADES NATIONAL PARK (proposed) See National parks and reserves—United States

NORTH CASCADES primitive area. See Wilderness area—Northwestern states

NORTH DAKOTA
See also
Hunting—North Dakota

Antiquities
See Indians of North America—Antiquities—North Dakota

NORTH EASTON, Mass. See Easton, Mass.

NORTH KOREA. See Korea (People's Democratic Republic)—Army

NORTH PLATTE RIVER
Sick river is returned to health. R. Gannon. il Read Digest 89:29-30+ Jl '66

NORTH SEA
All that gas in the North Sea. T. Alexander. il Fortune 74:110-15+ Ag '66

NORTH Shore friends of opera, incorporated
North Shore friends: opera puts down roots on Long Island. A. M. Lingg. il Opera N 30:14-15 F 5 '66

NORTH VIETNAM. See Vietnam (Democratic Republic)

NORTH Vietnamese missile sites. See Guided missile bases

NORTHCOTT, Cecil
Anti-Semitism's taproot. Christian Cent 83:1049 Ag 31 '66
Cleaner of St Paul's. Christian Cent 83:238 F 23 '66
Graham crusade: abdication of evangelism. Christian Cent 83:673-5 My 25 '66

NORTHEAST airlines, incorporated
Watch the yellow birdie. il Time 88:102+ O 7 '66
Wiser presses improvements to Northeast. W. Wright. Aviation W 84:41-2 My 23 '66

NORTHEAST corridor project. See Transportation, High speed

NORTHEAST regional ballet festival. See Dance festivals

NORTHEASTERN states
Election trends: in thirty-four states; still no signs of big change. il U S News 61:59-60 O 24 '66
See also
Hunting—Northeastern states

NORTHERN Baptist convention. See Baptists in the United States

NORTHERN Europeans. See Europeans

NORTHERN IRELAND
Captain O'Neill and the anti-Papist. J. H. Huizinga. il Reporter 35:43-4 O 20 '66
Ecumenical backlash; report on rioting when Protestant extremists and Catholics clashed. E. McKiernan. America 115:31-3 Jl 9 '66
Ireland's hot summer. D. Fisher. Commonweal 84:555-6 S 2 '66
Paisley's pattern. il Time 88:23 Jl 29 '66
Thaw in the Irish cold war; antagonism between north and south. W. R. Rodgers. il N Y Times Mag p30-1+ F 27 '66
Unholy war of preacher Paisley. H. Moffett. il Life 61:35-6+ Ag 19 '66
See also
Protestant churches—Northern Ireland

NORTHERN RHODESIA. See Zambia

NORTHMEN
See also
Vikings

NORTHPARK, Dallas. See Dallas—Stores

NORTHROP, Birdsey Grant
Schools and communism. Sch & Soc 94:355-7 O 29 '66

NORTHROP corporation
Riding the Little Tiger; F-5. il Time 88:97-8 N 11 '66

NORTHRUP, Marguerite
(ed) Christmas story, from the Gospels of Matthew and Luke; excerpts from the Metropolitan museum of art's current book. McCalls 94:59-65 D '66

NORTHWEST
Greening North. A. Swensson. il Sat R 49:54+ O 8 '66
See also
Fishing—Northwestern states
Hunting—Northwestern states
Puget Sound Region
Skis and skiing—Northwestern states
Water supply—Northwestern states
Wilderness areas—Northwestern states

Economic conditions
Forgotten West comes into its own; Pacific Northwest. il U S News 61:62-7 N 7 '66

Social conditions
Forgotten West comes into its own; Pacific Northwest. il U S News 61:62-7 N 7 '66

NORTHWEST Indians. See Indians of North America

NORTHWEST TERRITORIES, Canada
Last frontier; new hunting country. R. M. Hobbs. il Outdoor Life 137:44-7+ Mr '66
Rugged place for a picnic. D. Barnes. il Sports Illus 24:78-80+ My 2 '66
See also
Thelon River

NORTHWESTERN Pacific railroad
Fight for the Rock Island. D. Cordtz. il Fortune 73:140-3+ Je '66
Western railroads collide on mergers; Union Pacific and North Western make strong bids for Rock Island. il Bsns W p 130-1+ Mr 19 '66

NORTHWESTERN university, Evanston, Ill.
Nation's first clinical professor; experimental program at School of education. Sch & Soc 94:116+ Mr 5 '66

Medill school of journalism
Urban renewal. Newsweek 67:93 My 16 '66

NORTON, Eleanor Holmes
End of a period. Nation 202:529-30 My 2 '66

NORTON, Jessica
Finish line vigil. Yachting 119:102-4+ Je '66

NORTON, W. W, and company
Norton to publish M.I.T. physics texts. Pub W 190:199 Jl 11 '66
W. W. Norton co. gives its authors a 5 per cent bonus. Pub W 189:72 Ja 31 '66

NORTON-TAYLOR, Duncan
Catholic layman confronts his changing church. Fortune 74:172-5+ D '66
Private world of the class of '66. Fortune 73:128-32+ F '66
Roger Stevens, a performing art. Fortune 73:152-3+ Mr '66
What the U.S. can do about world hunger. Fortune 73:110-14+ Je '66
World's fastest art market. Fortune 74:134-46+ S '66

NORVELL, Aubrey James
How guilty is the South? W. F. Buckley, jr. Nat R 18:611 Je 28 '66
March Meredith began. il Newsweek 67:28-31 Je 20 '66
Race issue inflamed again: aftermath of a shooting; J. Meredith, with editorial comment. il por U S News 60:36-8, 112 Je 20 '66
Surprise package. Newsweek 68:32 D 5 '66

NORVELL, Cynthia
Young woman in the white world. il pors Ebony 21:69-70+ Ag '66
NORWALK, Conn.
Education
Norwalk plan: team teaching is a privilege; interview, ed. by W. K. Richards. H. A. Becker. il Sr Schol 88:sup 13-15 Mr 25 '66
NORWAY
See also
Aluminum industry and trade—Norway
Bergen
Fishing—Norway
Merchant marine—Norway
Zoology—Norway
Description and travel
Norway. C. Kentfield. il Holiday 40:52-61+ N '66
Purple cow. P. L. Adams. il Atlan 217:109-13 Ap '66
Politics and government
Atlantic report; coalition aims. Atlan 217: 32+ Mr '66
Religious institutions and affairs
See also
Lutheran church in Norway
NORWAY rats. See Rats
NORWEGIAN America line, Incorporated
Profiles; maiden voyage of the Sagafjord. L. Ross. il New Yorker 42:65-8+ N 19 '66
NORWEGIAN cranes. See Cranes (birds)
NORWOOD, William R.
Trust Territory of the Pacific Islands; statement, June 27, 1966. Dept State Bul 55:388-400 S 12 '65
NORWORTH, Jack
John Blauer acquires the Jack Norworth miniature museum. S. A. Parvin. il Hobbies 71:122-3+ O '66
NOSE
See also
Olfactory nerves
NOSE cones. See Guided missiles
NOSSAL, Frederick
Canada's bold defense experiment. Reporter 34:36-8 Mr 24 '66
NOSSITER, Bernard D.
Awakening of a new Europe. New Repub 155: 11-13 Jl 16 '66
Getting tough with poor nations. New Repub 155:12-14 D 3 '66
Inside stories. Commentary 41:98-100 Mr '66
Success story. Commentary 41:95-7 Je '66
NOT like the others; story. See Shyer, M. F.
NOTABLE books council. See American library association—Adult services division
NOTABLES. See Celebrities
NOTE paper. See Stationery
NOTEBOOKS
On keeping a notebook. J. Didion. il Holiday 40:10+ D '66
NOTHING in excess; story. See Hazzard, S.
NOTHING personal; story. See Delius, A.
NOTHING to be thankful for; drama. See Hark, M. and McQueen, M.
NOTIONS (merchandise)
Girl in a paper dress; National notion association's semiannual trade show. New Yorker 42:20-1 Je 25 '66
NOTO, Mario T.
Travel and domestic controls. Ann Am Acad 367:73-84 S '66
NOTRE DAME, Ind. University
That legend is loose again; Notre Dame winning in Rockne-Leahy tradition. D. Jenkins. il Sports Illus 25:70-2+ N 7 '66
NOTROM, Henry B.
Doctoring a dunked motor. Pop Mech 126: 125-8+ Jl '66
In's and out's of electric starting. Pop Mech 125:170-3 Ap '66
Lowdown on lower units. Pop Mech 125:158-61+ My '66
Perfect marine plug. Pop Mech 126:144-7+ Ag '66
Right way to store your outboard. Pop Mech 126:162-5+ N '66
Stow-aboard tool kit for outboards. Pop Mech 125:158-60 Mr '66
Troubleshooting remote controls. Pop Mech 125:141-4 Je '66
NOTTINGHAM, England, public library
Why not work in England next year? K. F. Kister. il ALA Bul 61:72-6 Ja '67

NOTTINGHAMSHIRE COUNTY, England, library
Why not work in England next year? K. F. Kister. il ALA Bul 61:72-6 Ja '67
NOURSE, Louis M.
Charles Herrick Compton, 1880-1966. ALA Bul 60:723-6 Jl '66
NOVA, Lou
Fighter. M. Kram. il pors Sports Illus 25: 66-8+ D 12 '66
NOVA SCOTIA
See also
Cape Breton Island
Paleontology
NOVAE. See Stars, New
NOVAES, Gulomar
Music to my ears; appearance with the New York philharmonic orchestra. I. Kolodin. Sat R 49:28 Mr 19 '66
NOVAK, James F.
Designing a ducted-port bass-reflex enclosure. Electr World 75:25-8+ Ja '66
NOVAK, Michael
Catholic professors on the secular campus. por America 115:323 S 24 '66
New directions. Commonweal 85:400-2 Ja 13 '67
New kind of Catholicism. Sat R 49:48-9 Je 4 '66
New nuns. Sat Eve Post 239:21-7+ Jl 30 '66
What's right with Christmas. McCalls 94: 149 D '66
NOVAK, Robert
Zealots of the middle. por Time 88:76-7 D 2 '66
—See Evans, R. jt. auth.
NOVAKOVA, V.
Weaning of young rats: effect of time on behavior. bibliog Science 151:475-6 Ja 28 '66
NOVELISTS
First novelists, spring-summer, fall, 1966; statements by the writers. ed. by I. E. Stokvis. Library J 91:722-37, 2883-93, 4707-17 F 1, Je 1, O 1 '66
Minor novelist. W. Sheed. Commonweal 83: 638-40 Mr 4 '66
True lie-minded man. W. H. Gass. Nation 203:453-4 O 31 '66
What's happening to fiction? O. Prescott. Sat R 49:21-2 N 26 '66
NOVELISTS, American
Time to murder and create, by J. W. Aldridge. Review
Commentary 42:60-2 Ag '66. P. Rahv
Life 60:8+ Ap 29 '66. W. Sheed
Sat R 49:38 Ap 30 '66. M. Green
Truth about fiction. G. P. Elliott. Holiday 39:84-5+ Mr '66
World elsewhere, by R. Poirier. Review
New Repub 155:35-6 N 26 '66. G. A. Wolff
See also
Barth, J.
Capote, T.
Ellison, R.
Faulkner, W.
Hemingway, E.
Susann, J.
Updike, J.
NOVELISTS, English
See also
Lessing, D. M.
Waugh, E.
NOVELISTS, French
My life is the new novel; concerning meetings with authors of Le nouveau roman. V. Mercier. Nation 202:434-6 Ap 11 '66
See also
Destouches, L. F.
Robbe-Grillet, A.
Sagan, F. pseud.
NOVELISTS, German
See also
Grass, G.
NOVELISTS, Italian
See also
Moravia, A.
NOVELISTS, Japanese
See also
Mishima, Y. pseud.
Natsume, S.
NOVELISTS, Russian
See also
Turgenev, I. S.
NOVELS. See Fiction; also American fiction; Russian fiction; etc.
NOVICK, Joe
Smelt fever. Field & S 70:10-12 Ap '66
NOVICK, Julius
Improvisation bit. Nation 203:613-15 D 5 '66
Stratford and Ypsilanti. Nation 203:259-62 S 19 '66

NOVICK, Julius—*Continued*
Subtle sensualist. Hi Fi 16:55-8 Ag '66
Theater. Nation 203:427-8 O 24 '66
[Theatre across America] Nation 202:626-9, 689-93, 755-8; 203:27-30, 130-3; 195-8 My 23, Je 6, 20, Jl 4, Ag 8, S 5 '66

NOVOCAINE
Phony fountain of youth. R. L. Smith. il Todays Health 44:27-9+ F '66

NOYES, Douglas. See Smith. R. jt. auth.

NOYES, Eliot
Architectural details. il Arch Rec 139:121-32 Ja '66

NOYES, Judith
Head Start program: choosing books for the pre-school, underprivileged child. Pub W 190:220-1 Jl 11 '66

NOYES, Polly
West coast wanderings. See issues of Travel

NOZZLES, Rocket engine. See Rocket engines

NU, 1907-
Freedom now for Nu. por Time 88:36 N 4 '66

NUCLEAR bombs. See Atomic bombs

NUCLEAR carriers. See Aircraft carriers, Atomic powered

NUCLEAR counters. See Counters (electrons, ions, etc)

NUCLEAR energy. See Atomic power

NUCLEAR excavation. See Atomic blasting

NUCLEAR fusion
Hopes brighten for fusion. A. Ewing. il Sci N 90:565 D 31 '66
Progress toward fusion power. T. K. Fowler and R. F. Post. il Sci Am 215:21-31 bibliog(p 154) D '66

NUCLEAR laboratories. See Atomic research laboratories

NUCLEAR medicine. See Radiology, Medical

NUCLEAR physics
Odd or even? International congress on high energy physics. Newsweek 68:66 S 19 '66
See also
Atomic nuclei
Cosmic rays
Positrons
Quantum electrodynamics
Time reversal
Transmutation (chemistry)

NUCLEAR power plants. See Atomic power plants

NUCLEAR propulsion. See Rockets, Atomic powered

NUCLEAR reactors
Breeders move front and center. C. Behrens. il Sci N 90:563 D 31 '66
New British nuclear research reactor drawn. Sci N 90:184 S 10 '66

NUCLEAR reactors, Portable
Portable reactors urged. Sci N 89:320 Ap 30 '66

NUCLEAR research. See Atomic research

NUCLEAR rockets. See Rockets, Atomic powered

NUCLEAR test ban. See Atomic bombs—Testing, Suspension of

NUCLEAR test ban treaty, 1963
Three years after test ban: nuclear race speed up. il U S News 61:50-2 Jl 18 '66
U.S. marks third anniversary of limited test ban treaty; statement August 6, 1966. D. Rusk. Dept State Bul 55:268 Ag 22 '66
U.S. rejects Soviet allegations on air accident in Spain; aide memoire, February 25, 1966. Dept State Bul 54:397 Mr 14 '66

NUCLEAR warfare. See Atomic warfare

NUCLEAR weapons. See Atomic weapons

NUCLEI, Atomic. See Atomic nuclei

NUCLEIC acid purines. See Purines

NUCLEIC acids
Circular dichroism of biological macromolecules. S. Beychok. bibliog il Science 154:1288-99 D 9 '66
Examination of transfer of learning by nucleic acid. M. Luttges and others. bibliog il Science 151:834-7 F 18 '66
Nucleic acid and protein chemistry. R. D. Cole and C. A. Dekker. Science 153:92-4 Jl 1 '66
Nucleotide sequence of a nucleic acid. R. W. Holley. il Sci Am 214:30-9 bibliog(p 138) F '66
Protein and nucleic acid synthesis in escherichia coli: pressure and temperature effects. J. V. Landau. bibliog il Science 153:1273-4 S 9 '66
See also
Deoxyribonucleic acid

NUCLEOHISTONES. See Nucleoproteins

NUCLEOLUS. See Cells

NUCLEOPROTEINS
Cell-free protein synthesis: effects of age and state of ribosomal aggregation. L. D. Moore and others. bibliog il Science 154:1350-3 D 9 '66
Electron microscopic autoradiography of rabbit reticulocytes active and inactive in protein synthesis. A. Miller and A. B. Maunsbach. bibliog il Science 151:1000-1 F 25 '66
Immunochemical characterization of polyribonucleotides. J. Panijel and others. bibliog il Science 152:773-5 My 6 '66
Nature of the packing of ribosomes within chromatoid bodies. R. S. Morgan and B. G. Uzman. bibliog il Science 152:214-16 Ap 8 '66
Nucleohistone dissociation by ganglioside micelles. M. H. Meisler and R. H. McCluer. bibliog il Science 154:896-7 N 18 '66
Polyribosome disaggregation during metaphase. M. D. Scharff and E. Robbins. bibliog il Science 151:992-5 F 25 '66
Polysomes and protein synthesis in cells infected with a DNA virus. R. J. Sydiskis and B. Roizman. bibliog il Science 153:76-8 Jl 1 '66
Polysomes extracted from escherichia coli by freeze-thaw-lysozyme lysis. E. Z. Ron and others. bibliog il Science 153:1119-20 S 2 '66
Protein synthesis by heart muscle ribosomes: an effect of insulin independent of substrate transport. W. S. Stirewalt and I. G. Wool. bibliog il Science 154:284 O 14 '66
Reovirus-specific polyribosomes in infected L-cells. L. Prevec and A. F. Graham. bibliog il Science 154:522-3 O 28 '66
Ribosomes from pear fruit. L Ku and R. J. Romani. bibliog il Science 154:408-10 O 21 '66
Zonal ultracentrifuge for the separation of ribosomal subunits. E. S. Klucis and H. J. Gould. bibliog il Science 152:378 Ap 15 '66
See also
Interferon

NUCLEOTIDES
Cyclobutane-type pyrimidine dimers in polynucleotides. R. B. Setlow. bibliog il Science 153:379-86 Jl 22 '66
Nucleotide formation as a determinant of 5-fluorouracil response in mouse leukemias. D. Kessel and others. bibliog il Science 154:911-13 N 18 '66
Nucleotide sequence of a yeast tyrosine transfer RNA. J. T. Madison and others. bibliog il Science 153:531-4 Jl 29 '66
Nucleotide sequence repetition: a rapidly reassociating fraction of mouse DNA. M. Waring and R. J. Britten. bibliog Science 154:791-4 N 11 '66
Oligoribonucleotides: improvement in chromatographic separation. H. Ishikura and others. bibliog il Science 153:300-1 Jl 15 '66

NUCLEUS, Cellular. See Cells

NUDE culture. See Nudism

NUDE in art
Drexler's dialectical nudes. M. Benedikt. il Art N 64:50-1+ F '66
See also
Human figure in art

NUDE in photography. See Human figure in photography

NUDISM
Free beach; San Gregorio beach, Calif. il Time 88:50 Ag 26 '66
Naked as a..: housewives who go naked. Newsweek 68:58 Ag 1 '66

NUGENT, Elliott
Days of roses followed by rain. J. K. Hutchens Sat R 49:35 Mr 5 '66

NUGENT, Gerard
Pat Nugent's parents tell how to be a White House in-law. F. R. Schreiber. il por Ladies Home J 83:110-12 Ag '66

NUGENT, Joel
Saints and symphonies. Holiday 40:66-7+ O '66

NUGENT, Patrick
Approaching wedding of Pat and the President's daughter. il pors Life 61:76-8 Jl 15 '66
Behind the scenes at the big wedding. por U S News 61:12-13 Ag 22 '66
First family suitors: their military status. il por U S News 60:22 Ap 25 '66
Great American wedding. J. Neubauer; B. Brown; F. Ward. il pors Pop Phot 59:85-9+ D '66
It's wedding week at the White House. il por U S News 61:36-7 Ag 8 '66

NUGENT, Patrick—*Continued*
Luci Johnson and Pat Nugent talk about life without father. M. Means. por Ladies Home J 83:73+ Ag '66
Pat Nugent's parents tell: how to be a White House in-law. F. R. Schreiber. il Ladies Home J 83:110-12 Ag '66
Splendor of Luci's wedding. il pors Life 61:20-7 Ag 19 '66
Three-ring wedding. il pors Time 88:19-23 Ag 5 '66
Wedding in Washington. il pors Newsweek 68:17-21 Ag 15 '66
Who are the 400? wedding invitations. il por Newsweek 68:22-3 Jl 18 '66
Wonderful, terrible life of the President's daughters. il por Newsweek 67:36-8+ My 23 '66

NUGENT, Tillie
Pat Nugent's parents tell: how to be a White House in-law. F. R. Schreiber. il por Ladies Home J 83:110-12 Ag '66

NUMBER sense. See Harmonic analysis

NUMBERS, Symbolism of. See Symbolism of numbers

NUMBERS game. See Lotteries

NUMERIC identification. See Identification

NUMERICALLY controlled machine tools. See Machine tools—Control

NUMEROLOGY. See Symbolism of numbers

NUMISMATICS, Ancient
Scientific numismatics. D. D. Kosambi. il Sci Am 214:102-8+ bibliog(p 139) F '66
Thus coins began. C. French. Hobbies 71:102 Mr '66

Anecdotes, facetiae, satire, etc.
Worth of a shekel. M. Brooke. il Atlan 217:126-9 Ap '66

NUNAMIUTS. See Eskimos

NUNIVAK ISLAND
Reporter at large. P. Matthiessen. il New Yorker 41:94+ F 5 '66

NUNN, G. Raymond
Libraries and publishing in mainland China; excerpts from Publishing in mainland China. bibliog f Library J 91:3327-32 Jl '66

NUNN, McClinton
Toledo's biggest landlord. il pors Ebony 21:111-12+ Je '66

NUNNERIES. See Convents and nunneries

NUNS. See Convents and nunneries; Sisterhoods

NUNS as nurses. See Nurses and nursing

NUNS as teachers. See Women as teachers

NUOTIO, Pekka
Northern lights; interview, ed. by M. W. Cushing. por Opera N 31:27 D 24 '66

NUREEV, Rudolf
For the Jung in heart. il Time 88:56 Jl 1 '66
Report from Vienna. L. Zamponi. il Dance Mag 40:23+ Jl '66

NUREMBERG trials
Trial of the Germans: Nuremberg 1945-1946, by E. Davidson. Review
Newsweek il 69:64+ Ja 9 '67. S. Maloff

NURMELA, Ilmo
Finland's chief merchandiser. por Fortune 74:100 D '66

NURSE training schools. See Nursing schools

NURSELOG trees. See Trees

NURSERIES (horticulture)
See also
Stark brothers nurseries and orchards company

NURSERY rhymes
See also
Mother Goose

NURSERY schools
How to start a cooperative nursery school. J. Adams. il Parents Mag 41:58-9+ F '66
Is nursery school necessary? E. Gilson. Sat R 49:94 N 19 '66
Jam starts at nursery school. I. Mothner. il Look 30:66+ Ap 5 '66
Planning preschool facilities. M. P. Berson and W. W. Chase. il Am Ed 2:7-11 D '65
Problem preschoolers: Virginia Frank child development center, Chicago. E. G. Neisser. Parents Mag 41:43-5+ Mr '66

NURSERY stock
Bare-root planting. il Flower Grower 53:40-1 F '66

NURSES
See also
Strikes—United States—Nurses

NURSES, Male. See Nurses and nursing

NURSES and nursing
Shocking shortage of nurses. S. Frank. il Good H 162:96-7+ Mr '66
Sisters of the poor; owners and operators of St Francis hospital. New Yorker 42:24-7 D 31 '66
Unforgettable Sister Winifred. L. Young. il Read Digest 88:173-4+ Mr '66
Your next nurse may be a man. H. G. Earl. il Todays Health 44:38-9+ F '66
See also
Negro nurses

Salaries, pensions, etc.
Nurses are being shortchanged. Life 61:6 S 23 '66
Sickness in the hospitals; resignation threat by public health nurses in New York city. Newsweek 67:78 My 30 '66

NURSES and nursing, Public health
Where doctors don't reach; University of Colorado school of medicine program to lighten the work loads of physicians. il Time 88:71-2 Jl 22 '66

NURSING homes
Coming, a guide to good nursing homes. Changing T 20:24 F '66
Earnings in nursing homes in April 1965. L. E. Lewis. il Mo Labor R 89:291-5 Mr '66
A look at the nursing homes of Europe. il U S News 60:52 Je 13 '66
New legislation puts fresh impetus behind nursing homes and housing for the elderly. W. B. Foxhall. il Arch Rec 139:151-8 Je '66
New problem for the medicare program. U S News 61:10 Ag 1 '66
Now: more help for old people; latest on medicare and its problems. il U S News 62:60-2 Ja 9 '67
Nursing home industry tools up. J. Horwitz. il N Y Times Mag p26-7+ My 1 '66
Nursing homes, just how much will medicare pay? Bet Hom & Gard 44:122-3 N '66
Nursing homes offer an investment lure; medicare expected to spark a nursing home boom. il Bsns W p 113-14 Jl 23 '66
Nursing homes: one more problem for medicare. il U S News 60:50-2 Je 13 '66

NURSING schools
Student nurse with heart; double amputee studying at Mercy hospital school of nursing in Charlotte, N.C. C. Brossard. il Look 30:M16-21 D 13 '66

NUSSDORF, Steven
Face to face with a painter who also models clothes, plays tournament tennis. pors Seventeen 25:277 Ag '66

NUT grinders, Electric. See Electric apparatus and appliances, Domestic

NUTCRACKER; ballet. See Ballets—Criticisms

NUTRITION
Let's talk about food; ed. by P. L. White. See issues of Today's health
Travel well. E. N. Dye. See issues of Travel
What it takes to feed your family well. G. McCarthy. il Parents Mag 41:94-5+ N '66
See also
Athletes—Nutrition
Breakfasts
Children—Nutrition
Diet
Food
Proteins
Vitamins

NUTRITION problems
Asia
High-protein biscuit for Asian children. Sci N 89:514 Je 25 '66

NUTRITION research
Cheese biscuit may aid health in Asia. Sci N L 89:104 F 12 '66
High-protein biscuit for Asian children. Sci N 89:514 Je 25 '66

NUTS
See also
Cookery—Nuts

NUTS (machinery) See Bolts and nuts

NUUAN, Francis
Trust Territory of the Pacific Islands; statement. June 27, 1966. Dept State Bul 55:400-1 S 12 '66

NUVEEN, John
Facts of life. Christian Cent 83:983-6 Ag 10 '66

NYACK, N.Y.
Where did Frank's building go? il Nations Bsns 54:36-7 Ja '66

NYERERE, Julius Kambarage
Rhodesia in the context of southern Africa.
For Affairs 44:373-86 Ap '66
NYHAN, William Leo, 1926-
Biting sickness. Newsweek 68:52 S 5 '66
NYLON sails. See Sails
NYMPHS, Artificial. See Fishing lures, flies, etc.
NYQUIST, E. B.
Three R's in New York; address, July 1966.
por ALA Bul 60:1134-8 D '66

O

OAO (orbiting astronomical observatory) See Artificial satellites—Astronomical applications
OAS. See Organization of American states
OASDI. See Old age, survivors' and disability insurance trust fund
OAU. See Organization of African unity
O beautiful for spacious skies; story. See Roth, P.
OCAS. See Organization of Central American states
ODECA (Organizacion de estados centro-americanos) See Organization of Central American states
OECD. See Organization for economic cooperation and development
O, feast of Happy Mari; story. See Llewellyn, R.
OGO (orbiting geophysical observatory) See Artificial satellites—Astronomical applications
O. J. Hazeltine; story. See Cousins, M.
OSSA. See United States—National aeronautics and space administration—Space science and applications, Office of
OAHU (island)
Wet walk from Hanauma to Blow Hole. il Sunset 137:35-6 Ag '66
OAHU oceanarium. See Aquariums
OAK

Diseases and pests
Are the oaks next to disappear from our forests? E. J. Duda. il Horticulture 44:32-5+ Jl '66
OAK BROOK horse show. See Horse shows
OAK decline. See Oak—Diseases and pests
OAK wilt. See Oak—Diseases and pests
OAKES, Theresa
White sweater; story. Parents Mag 41:62-4 F '66
OAKLAND, Calif.
Trouble in an "All America city." S. Stern. il N Y Times Mag p20-2+ Jl 10 '66; Reply. W. F. Knowland. p 12 S 4 '66

Galleries and museums
Terraces in Oakland. il Arch Forum 125: 65-5 O '66

Negroes
Alinsky and Oakland. New Repub 154:7-8 My 21 '66
New race trouble in California. il U S News 61:12:12 O 31 '66
Oakland: the flats are smoldering. E. Richey. Christian Cent 83:152-5 F 2 '66
OAKLAND roadster show. See Automobiles, Racing—Exhibitions
OAKLAND symphony orchestra
California; Oedipus Rex. A. Boucher. Opera N 31:31 Ja 21 '67
Mr Samuel and the Rockefeller premieres. K. D. Wallace. il Hi Fi 16:MA26+ Jl '66
OAKLAND university, Rochester, Mich.
Case study at Oakland: recruitment of college students to librarianship. M. Ricking. ALA Bul 60:731 Jl '66
Point of increasing returns; Student library committee. J. Howey and E. McKenney. il Library J 91:6039-42 D 15 '66
OANCIA, David
Covering the Red guards. por Newsweek 69: 101 Ja 23 '67
OATES, Joyce Carol
Building tension in the short story. Writer 79:11-12+ Je '66
In the region of ice; story. Atlan 218:78-85 Ag '66

OATHS (profanity) See Swearing
OATS

Disease and pest resistance
Benefits of sowing wild oats; new wild oat resists rusts. il Time 88:82 O 28 '66
OBEDIENCE
How to get obedience; reprint. E. Aronson. il Sci Digest 60:54-9 Jl '66
OBEDIENCE (canon law)
DuBay at bay. Christian Cent 83:1023 Ag 24 '66; Discussion. 83:1216, 1348 O 5, N 2 '66
Due process for DuBay and for the church. America 115:200 Ag 27 '66; Discussion. 115: 304-5 S 24 '66
Loyal opposition in the church. J. G. Milhaven. America 114:622-4 Ap 30 '66; Discussion. 114:760, 844 My 28, Je 18 '66
OBER, William B.
Speaking out. por Sat Eve Post 239:14+ O 8 '66
OBERAMMERGAU passion play
Time for a new vow at Oberammergau; anti-Semitism of play. Christian Cent 83:1328-9 N 2 '66
OBEROI, Mohan S.
India's grandest hotel. H. Sutton. il Sat R 49:54+ Ap 16 '66
OBERON, Merle
In Acapulco: a pavilion by the sea. il House & Gard 131:98-103 Ja '67
OBESITY. See Corpulence
OBITUARIES
Mr Bad News. G. Talese. il Esquire 65:88-9+ F '66
OBJECTIVES in education. See Education—Aims and objectives
OBJECTS, Miniature. See Miniature objects
OBOE music
See also
Phonograph records—Oboe music
OBOLER, Eli M.
Constitutional crisis in the ALA? ALA Bul 60:384-6 Ap '66
OBOTE, Milton
Coup of convenience. por Time 87:35 Mr 4 '66
End of King Freddie. E. Huxley. Nat R 18: 569 Je 14 '66
Merely self-defense. il por Newsweek 67:44+ Mr 7 '66
O'BOYLE, Lenore
Middle class in western Europe, 1815-1848. bibliog f Am Hist R 71:826-45 Ap '66
O'BOYLE, Patrick A. abp
Gap between religion and life. America 115: 243 S 10 '66
OBREGON, Mauricio
FAI explained; ed. by J. Gilbert. por Flying 79:64-7 D '66
O'BRIEN, Conor Cruise
Africa's answer to Schweitzer. Atlan 217: 68-71 Mr '66
Irishman at large in the U.S.A. Sat R 49:59-60+ Mr 12 '66

about
Superstars. il por Newsweek 68:68 O 17 '66
O'BRIEN, George
Report on residential interior design. Arch Rec 139:29+ mid-My '66
O'BRIEN, James M. and others
Pricing library materials for insurance purposes. ALA Bul 60:729-30 Jl '66
O'BRIEN, Justin
Cats and casseroles. Reporter 35:59-60 O 20 '66
Man absent from himself. Reporter 34:50 Mr 10 '66
Observer of the human comedy. Sat R 49:26-7 Jl 9 '66
(tr) See Sartre, J. P. Condemned of Altona (Les séquestrés d'Altona)
O'BRIEN, Lawrence Francis
Bill of rights; address, July 1, 1966. Vital Speeches 32:646-9 Ag 15 '66
U.S. mails; address, February 8, 1966. Vital Speeches 32:290-1 Mr 1 '66

about
How to float on a sea of red ink. il por Newsweek 69:56-8 Ja 2 '67
JFK legatees. Newsweek 67:31A-31B F 21 '66
Larry O'Brien: the pro takes on the post office. D. R. Maxey. il pors Look 30:30-2+ F 8 '66
Resident professor of politics. H. Sidey. il por Life 61:50B O 14 '66

O'BRIEN, Leslie Kenneth
New man at Bank of England's helm. il por Bsns W p45 Je 18 '66

O'BRIEN, Robert
How to make the most in selling your car. Read Digest 88:93-6 Ap '66
Now you can bet on the weather and win, more often. Read Digest 88:125-8 Je '66
What's so different about CB antennas? Pop Electr 24:44-6+ My '66

O'BRIEN, Robert H.
O'Brien of MGM. H. Alpert. il por Sat R 49:17-19+ D 24 '66

O'BRIEN, William V.
War and peace and the American Catholic. Cath World 202:331-5 Mr '66

O'BRYAN, James
O'Bryan revolution. il por Nat R 18:1218-21 N 29 '66

OBSCENE literature. See Immoral literature and pictures

OBSCENE telephone calls. See Telephone calls

OBSCENITY (law)
Arbitration hearings called for promiscuity handbook; Housewife's handbook on selective promiscuity. Pub W 189:59 My 30 '66
Author-editor group hits Ginzburg conviction. Pub W 189:29-30 Ap 11 '66
Bad news for smut peddlers; Ginzburg, Mishkin and Fanny Hill; Supreme court decisions. il Time 87:56+ Ap 1 '66
Blocked exit; treatment of Last exit to Brooklyn in Great Britain. Time 88:34 D 30 '66
California booksellers attack Proposition 16. Pub W 190:57 O 31 '66
California LA resolves to fight CLEAN, inc. anti-obscenity bill. Library J 91:3368 Jl 1 '66
Censorship and obscenity: what's happened to taste? with press comments. D. Reische. il Sr Schol 89:12-15 O 14 '66
Censorship panel approved by N.J. legislators. Pub W 189:60 My 30 '66
CLEAN amendment: Proposition 16; California league enlisting action now, letter to the editor. J. Smith. ALA Bul 61:15 Ja '67
CLEAN down the drain; California league enlisting action now. E. T. Moore. il Library J 92:53-5 Ja 1 '67
Cleveland bookman arrested: police fascism charged; Asphodel bookshop, Cleveland. Pub W 191:57-8 Ja 16 '67
Confusion on obscenity. America 114:430 Ap 2 '66
Court declines to review two censorship convictions; R. Ginzburg and E. Mishkin. Pub W 189:49 My 9 '66
Court stirs a hornet's nest; obscenity rulings. Christian Cent 83:451-2 Ap 13 '66
Decisions, decisions: what's smut, what isn't? opinions in Ginzburg case and Fanny Hill case; excerpts. Newsweek 67:20 Ap 4 '66
Dissent to the High court's harsh verdict; R. Ginzburg case. L. Wainwright. Life 60:26 Ap 22 '66
End of the boom in smut? U S News 60:69 Ap 4 '66
Ginzburg & pornography; Supreme court's ruling. Nat R 18:346 Ap 19 '66
Ginzburg appeal argued; awaits ruling by Court. Pub W 190:108 Je 18 '66
Ginzburg appeal protests Supreme court trap. Pub W 189:82 Ap 25 '66
Ginzburg as precedent; concerning R. A. Klor's films. il Time 88:46 Jl 22 '66
Ginzburg petitions for rehearing; urges federal censorship board. Library J 91:2440+ My 15 '66
High court won't rule on N.Y. anti-smut youth laws. Pub W 190:54 O 31 '66
How not to read a dirty book. America 114:614 Ap 30 '66
Implications of the Ginzburg affair; address, April 20, 1966. K. Molz. il Wilson Lib Bul 40:941-7 Je '66
Is love, sweet love, a crime? case of R. Ginzburg. J. Skow. il Sat Eve Post 239:82-4+ F 12 '66
Judge orders Love book to be returned for sale; San Francisco booksellers. Pub W 191:58 Ja 16 '67
Keeping California clean: would you believe it? concerning California league enlisting action now. R. H. Smith. Pub W 190:41 Ag 8 '66
Last exit to Brooklyn enjoined in Connecticut. Pub W 190:76 N 14 '66
Last exit to Brooklyn found obscene in London. Pub W 191:34 Ja 2 '67

Legal bridge should exist between privacy and obscenity. H. F. Pilpel. Pub W 190:54-5 D 26 '66
Librarians protest new N.Y. anti-smut laws. Pub W 189:79-80 Ap 18 '66
May it please the Court. A. Kopkind; reply. D. Macdonald. New Repub 154:37 Ja 29 '66
Meaning of obscenity in California; proposition. il Time 88:64 S 30 '66
Naked in Nashville; nude photographs of husband and wife sent through mail by club. Time 87:44+ Je 3 '66
New Jersy obscenity bill vetoed by governor. Pub W 189:275 Ja 24 '66
Notes and comment; Ginzburg case. New Yorker 42:31 Ap 9 '66
Obscene premises bill passes N.Y. assembly. Pub W 189:49 My 9 '66
Obscene premises bill vetoed in New York. R. H. Smith. Pub W 190:46 Ag 15 '66
Obscenity and the law; recent decisions by Supreme court. New Repub 154:5-6 Ap 2 '66; Reply with rejoinder. S. Kipperman. 154:28 Ap 23 '66
Obscenity and the rights of children. H. F. Pilpel. Pub W 189:41-2 Mr 28 '66
Obscenity and the Supreme court. G. R. Blakey. America 115:152-6 Ag 13 '66
Obscenity business; analysis of Supreme court's ruling. J. Epstein. Atlan 218:56-60 Ag '66; Same. Library J 91:4566-71 O 1 '66
Obscenity ruling. Commonweal 84:94-5 Ap 15 '66
Obscenity test; legal poser. il Newsweek 67:19+ Ap 4 '66
Out of the bookstore kids! N.Y. bill. R. H. Smith. Pub W 189:47 Mr 14 '66
Police nail Mishkin in raid on Times square bookstore; Square books. Pub W 189:79 Ap 18 '66
Problem of censorship and youth. R. H. Smith. Pub W 189:91 Ap 25 '66
Pro-censorship Prop. 16 stays on Calif. ballot. Pub W 190:53-4 O 3 '66
Route '66: of obscenity and such. E. Moon. il Library J 92:53-5 Ja 1 '67
San Francisco police arrest booksellers; sale of book of poems entitled The love book. Pub W 190:27-8 D 12 '66
Society's lack of confidence in itself. R. H. Smith. Pub W 189:41 Ap 4 '66
Spring harvest festival; Mishkin, Ginzburg, and Fanny Hill. E. J. Gaines. ALA Bul 60:551-2 Je '66
Supreme court OK's Fanny Hill; Ginzburg and Mishkin get jail, with editorial comment. Library J 91:2016, 2020 Ap 15 '66
Supreme court rulings on obscenity cases. Wilson Lib Bul 40:795+ My '66
Times square book stores raided by cleanup squad. Pub W 190:47 S 19 '66
Trial by jury in an obscenity case? H. F. Pilpel. Pub W 190:307 Ag 29 '66
U.S. Supreme court rules pro-censorship in two of three cases involving books. Pub W 189:43-4 Mr 28 '66
Voyeurism not a point of view. America 114:187 F 5 '66
What is dirty? the Court fogs it up. Life 60:4 Ap 1 '66
What's obscene for the country; question of national standards in sexual expression. Time 88:39 Jl 29 '66

L'OBSÉDÉ; drama. See Roche, F.

OBSERVATIONS, Astronomical. See Astronomy —Observations

OBSERVATORIES
AMOS may feed new ABM designs; ARPA mid-course optical observatory station on Mt Haleakala. M. Getler. Tech W 18:20 Je 13 '66

OBSERVER, Texas. See Texas observer

OBSTETRICS
Disgraceful facts about infant deaths in the U.S; with list of 376 American hospitals where childbirth is safest. R. Brecher and E. Brecher. McCalls 93:82-3+ F '66
Expectant mother; pediatricians in the delivery room. M. J. Bulfin and D. Z. Meilach. Redbook 128:16 Ja '67
What really happens when your obstetrician is late. P. H. Brenner and R. L. Brenner. Ladies Home J 83:42+ Je '66
Why some mothers reject their babies; hospital practices. R. Brecher and E. Brecher. il Redbook 127:48-9+ My '66

OCAMPO, Victoria
Voice of the Algarrobo. Américas 18:1-7 S '66

OCCIDENTAL petroleum corporation
Putting food to sleep; inert nitrogen process. C. Welles. il Life 60:71-2 F 18 '66

OCCLUSAL rehabilitation. See Dentistry

OCCULT sciences
    See also
    Cabala

OCCULTATIONS
    Equipment for timing extreme grazing occultations. E. Halbach. il Sky & Tel 33:52-6 Ja '67
    Martian atmosphere: the Mariner occultation experiment. J. W. Chamberlain and M. B. McElroy. bibliog il Science 152:21-5 Ap 1 '66
    Occultation highlights. D. W. Dunham. il Sky & Tel 31:186, 382; 32:242; 33:62 Mr, Je, O '66, Ja '67
    Occultation supplement. il Sky & Tel 32:283-90 N '66

OCCUPATION, Free choice of. See Free choice of employment

OCCUPATIONAL aptitude tests. See Aptitude tests

OCCUPATIONAL guidance. See Vocational guidance

OCCUPATIONAL mobility
    Adaptation of labor resources to changing needs; excerpt from Manpower planning in a free society. R. A. Lester. Mo Labor R 89:245-9 Mr '66

OCCUPATIONAL rehabilitation. See Vocational rehabilitation

OCCUPATIONAL therapy
    Occupational therapy. B. Locher. Wilson Lib Bul 40:849-50+ My '66
    See also
    Garden therapy

OCCUPATIONS
    Boom in jobs for 1966 graduates. U S News 60:123 Je 13 '66
    Butcher, the baker, and the missilemaker; new edition of Dictionary of occupational titles. Mo Labor R 80:III-IV My '66
    Career barometer. C. Peet. See issues of Popular mechanics
    How can I be me? G. Zimmermann. il Look 30:52-7 S 20 '66
    Jobs in the future; where opportunties are best. il U S News 60:91-2 F 28 '66
    Manpower projections: some conceptual problems and research needs. S. Swerdloff. il Mo Labor R 89:138-43 F '66
    Military and civilian occupational structures; excerpt from Military specialist: specialized manpower requirements and resources of the armed forces. H. Wool. il Mo Labor R 89:29-33 Ja '66
    New careers, students' dilemma. il Sci Digest 60:22-4 O '66
    Pressures that push children into the wrong careers. S. Grafton. il McCalls 93:66-7+ Je '66
    Tomorrow's jobs, where the best will be. Changing T 20:7-11 F '66
    Tug-of-war over Ken. D. C. Disney. Ladies Home J 83:40+ O '66
    What can a child expect to earn in his chosen career? Bet Hom & Gard 44:30+ Ag '66
    Where job chances will be best in the years just ahead. il U S News 62:44-5 Ja 2 '67
    Where the jobs will be in 1975. il U S News 61:85-6 O 3 '66
    Working one's way through tomorrow. B. Michael and E. Weinstein. il Am Ed 2:29-32 D '65
    See also
    Agriculture as a profession
    Airlines—Employees
    Business

OCCUPATIONS, Choice of. See Occupations; Vocational guidance

OCCUPATIONS for children
    Are you using your most valuable asset? Junior ranges force program, Boulder, Colo. D. Miller. il Parks & Rec 1:494-5 Je '66
    Take a tip from Tom Sawyer; help with household chores. J. Graham. il Parents Mag 41:40-1+ Jl '66

OCEAN
    Antipodal location of continents and oceans. C. G. A. Harrison. bibliog il Science 153:1246-8 S 9 '66
    Promise of the seas' bounty; why oceans' riches should be placed under U.N. administration. C. M. Eichelberger. il Sat R 49:21-3 Je 18 '66
    See also
    Arctic Ocean
    Coast changes
    International oceanographic congress, Moscow. 1966
    Marine biology

    Oceanographic research
    Pacific Ocean
    Sea level changes
    Seashore
    Tides
    Waves

    Economic aspects
    See Marine resources

OCEAN bottom
    Age of the ocean floor; with discussion. E. Orowan. bibliog Science 154:413-16 O 21 '66
    Ages of horizon A and the oldest Atlantic sediments. J. Ewing and others. bibliog il Science 154:1125-32 D 2 '66
    Deep-sea iron deposit from the South Pacific. E. Bonatti and O. Joensuu. bibliog il Science 154:643-5 N 4 '66
    Found in the Pacific; carved rock columns and 800-mile crack in the ocean floor. B. Tufty. il Sci N 89:239 Ap 9 '66
    Layer of abnormally cold bottom water over southern Aves ridge. A. L. Gordon and others. bibliog il Science 151:1525-6 Mr 25 '66
    Lithology and paleontology of the reflective layer horizon A. T. Saito and others. bibliog il Science 154:1173-6 D 2 '66
    Lower Cretaceous rocks, Neocomian-Albian dredged from Blake escarpment. B. C. Heezen and R. E. Sheridan. bibilog il Science 154:1644-7 D 30 '66
    Lower cretaceous sediments from the Northwest Pacific. M. Ewing and others. bibliog il Science 152:751-5 My 6 '66
    Magnetic anomalies over the Pacific-Antarctic ridge. W. C. Pitman, 3d. and J. R. Heirtzler. bibliog il Science 154:1164-6+ D 2 '66
    Manganese pavements on the Blake plateau. R. F. Pratt and P. F. McFarlin. il Science 151:1080-2 Mr 4 '66
    Manganese road found in ocean. il Sci N 90:127 Ag 20 '66
    Marine geotechnique; report on first International research conference on marine geotechnique. W. Harrison. Science 153:326+ Jl 15 '66
    Sea fossils indicate movements of sea floor. Sci N 89:184 Mr 19 '66
    Soviets disclose new ocean floor maps. W. S. Beller. Tech W 18:19 Je 13 '66
    Spreading of the ocean floor: new evidence. F. J. Vine. bibliog il Science 154:1405-15 D 16 '66
    Tertiary sediment from the Mid-Atlantic ridge. T. Saito and others. bibliog il Science 151:1075-9 Mr 4 '66
    Unearthly world at the bottom of the sea. R. Platt. il Read Digest 89:241-2+ O '66
    See also
    Continental shelf
    Faults (geology)
    Submarine geology

OCEAN currents
    Ocean mysteries revealed. Sci N 90:85 Ag 6 '66
    Shaping of the continental rise by deep geostrophic contour currents. B. C. Heezen and others. bibliog il Science 152:502-8 Ap 22 '66
    Tidal currents. W. S. Kals. il Motor B 117:32-3+ Ap '66
    See also
    Gulf Stream

OCEAN life. See Marine biology

OCEAN liners
    Here comes the Pushkin; Russian effort to crash North Atlantic travel market. il Newsweek 67:74 My 9 '66
    Profiles; maiden voyage of the Sagafjord. L. Ross. il New Yorker 42:65-8+ N 19 '66
    Reds' sails in the sunset; Pushkin's maiden voyage. J. Lieber. il Sat R 49:41-2+ My 28 '66
    Venerable Queen sails into a new role; Queen Elizabeth, of Cunard line, converted to cruise business. il Bsns W p52-3 Ap 2 '66
    See also
    Ocean travel

OCEAN sounds
    See also
    Sound production by fishes

OCEAN systems, incorporated
    Industries combine talents for offshore oil. Tech W 19:29 S 26 '66

OCEAN temperature
    Gulf Stream wall charted for ASW; antisubmarine warfare environmental prediction service. R. W. Niblock. il Miss & Roc 18:40-1 My 9 '66

OCEAN temperature—*Continued*
Layer of abnormally cold bottom water over southern Aves ridge. A. L. Gordon and others. bibliog il Science 151:1525-6 Mr 25 '66

OCEAN travel
Europe, under their own steam; excerpts from Europe à go-go; life and love aboard a student ship. J. Fox. il Mlle 63:122-3+ Je '66
Mass culture on the high seas. D. E. Smucker. Christian Cent 83:805-6 Je 22 '66
Run away to sea: the fun of freighter travel. G. R. Boardman. Mlle 63:185-7 O '66
Traveler, beware! beat-up cruise ships, phony charter flights endanger your money, and your life. il Changing T 20:7-12 Ap '66
See also
Cruising
Ocean liners
Voyages

OCEAN yacht racing. See Yacht racing

OCEANAUTS. See Aquanauts

OCEANIA
See also
Islands of the Pacific

OCEANIC flights. See Aviation—Transoceanic flights

OCEANOGRAPHERS
See also
Bascom, W.

OCEANOGRAPHIC buoys
Sea eyes: an ocean of buoys. J. Eberhart. il Sci N 91:34-5 Ja 14 '67
Ship named FLIP; floating instrument platform. il UNESCO Courier 19:18-19 O '66

OCEANOGRAPHIC instruments
Foreign equipment sales may outstrip space product exports: American oceanographic products at the World trade center, Frankfurt, Germany. W. Buedeler. Tech W 19:44 N 14 '66
On-site processing needed for data boom. R. Pay. il Tech W 19:26+ O 3 '66
See also
Oceanographic buoys

OCEANOGRAPHIC research
AIAA meeting told of ASW problems. J. F. Judge. Tech W 19:50+ Ag 15 '66
Computers forecast tidal wave dangers; Pacific tsunami warning system. il Tech W 19:24-5 S 12 '66
Concept of a sea-grant university; address, October 28, 1965. A. Spilhaus. Vital Speeches 32:212-16 Ja 15 '66
Congress goading sea science. C. A. Betts. Sci N 90:418-19 N 19 '66
Continental shelf survey promising. R. W. Niblock. Miss & Roc 18:35 Mr 21 '66
Florida bids for ESSA's East coast site. K. Voss. Tech W 19:40 D 5 '66
Greater oceanographic effort fostered by Senate committee. H. M. David. Miss & Roc 18:14 Ja 24 '66
IEEE told of its undersea challenges. Miss & Roc 18:14 Mr 28 '66
International oceanography; way scientific co-operation develops. K. N. Fedorov. il UN Mo Chron 3:28-37 Mr '66
Is there a gold mine out in the ocean? money in underwater engineering. il Bsns W p90-2+ Ap 9 '66
Let's go after the neglected treasures beneath the seas; letter. J. Steinbeck. Pop Sci 189:84-7 S '66
New frontiers for the U.S: untold riches in the sea; interview. O. D. Waters, jr. il U S News 61:66-9 Ag 22 '66
North Atlantic deep-sea fertility. R. O. Fournier. bibliog il Science 153:1250-2 S 9 '66
Ocean adventure; condensation. G. Soule. il Pop Sci 189:88-93 S '66
Ocean secrets probed by fast-paced computer; laboratory on board research ship Oceanographer. Sci N 89:374 My 14 '66
Oceanography in Britain: significant new support. V. K. McElheny. Science 153:727-8 Ag 12 '66
Oceanography nears high tide: biggest government-sponsored research program. il Bsns W p51-2 Ag 6 '66
Oceanography; PSAC panel calls for setting up new agency. D. S. Greenberg. Science 153:391-3 Jl 22 '66
Oceanography study detailed. Tech W 19:28+ Jl 25 '66
Our deep and wide ocean. R. S. Dietz. Science 153:1423-4+ S 16 '66
Pair of lubbers takes to the sea: women oceanographers. il Ebony 21:112-14+ Ap '66
Sharing the seas' riches. C. M. Eichelberger. Sat R 49:18 Ag 13 '66

Ship to explore the oceans and their riches. U S News 61:12 Jl 25 '66
Soviet ministry speeds fishing technology. W. S. Beller. il Tech W 19:24-5+ Ag 22 '66
Special report on oceanology; symposium. il Tech W 19:16-19+ S 26 '66
Taylor Pryors' ocean adventure: Sea life park and Oceanic institute for research. V. Lawford. il Vogue 148:208-11+ N 1 '66
Trailbreaker of the deeps; activities of W. Bascom. P. O'Neil. il Life 61:108-10+ S 30 '66
Underwater harvest; Senate bill hopes. Atlan 217:8 Mr '66
Unearthly world at the bottom of the sea. R. Platt. il Read Digest 89:241-2+ O '66
U.S. lags in ocean plans. il Sci N 89:494 Je 18 '66
See also
Bathyscaphe
Institute of marine resources, La Jolla, Calif.
United States—Commerce, Department of—Institute of oceanography
United States—National council for marine sciences
United States—National oceanograhic data center

Equipment
Big business takes a dive in the ocean. H. Fantel. il Pop Mech 125:80-3+ Je '66
Deep-sea effort rivals space program. W. E. Wilks. il Miss & Roc 18:32-3+ Ap 11 '66
Diving saucers and sea-going laboratories. il UNESCO Courier 19:14-17 O '66
Foreign equipment sales may outstrip space product exports: American oceanographic products at the World trade center, Frankfurt, Germany. W. Buedeler. Tech W 19:44 N 14 '66
New ocean tools needed. Sci N L 89:50 Ja 22 '66
Ocean engineering takes the plunge. T. Alexander. il Fortune 73:144-7+ Je '66
On-site processing needed for data boom. R. Pay. il Tech W 19:26+ O 3 '66
Our newest frontier is underwater! R. F. Crossley. il Pop Mech 125:94-8+ My '66
Profits under the sea. G. Berkwitt. il Duns R 87:32-3+ Je '66
See also
Submarine boats
Underwater laboratories

OCEANOGRAPHY
At the gates of the depths. il Time 88:54-5 Ag 19 '66
Concept of a sea-grant university; address, October 28, 1965. A. Spilhaus. Vital Speeches 32:212-16 Ja 15 '66
Congress goading sea science. C. A. Betts. Sci N 90:418-19 N 19 '66
Oceanography; report of International congress in Moscow. R. H. Charlier. Science 153:1421-3 S 16 '66
Oceanology called growth stock area; report from third Space congress. J. Rhea. Miss & Roc 18:18 Mr 14 '66
Tropical oceanography; report on international conference. F. F. Koczy. bibliog Science 153:557-9 Jl 29 '66
See also
Marine resources
United States—Interagency committee on oceanography

Instruments
See Oceanographic instruments

Study and teaching
Learning about life at sea: graduate students from City college of New York. J. A. Osmundsen. il Look 30:M16-18+ D 27 '66
Sea-grant colleges: idea gains adherents. L. J. Carter. Science 152:1358-60 Je 3 '66

OCEANOLOGY. See Oceanography

OCHOTA, Leszek
What is the clinical evidence? New Repub 154:21-2 My 14 '66

OCKERSE, R. and others
Hormone-induced repression of a peroxidase isozyme in plant tissue. bibliog Science 151:452-3 Ja 28 '66

O'CONNELL, Jeffrey
Car maker and safety; address, June 18, 1966. Vital Speeches 32:656-60 Ag 15 '66
Double talk from Detroit. America 115:507-10 O 29 '66
Now the Tiger wears a seatbelt. N Y Times Mag p27+ O 2 '66

O'CONNELL, Richard
Brazilian happenings; poems. New Yorker 42:58 S 17; 60 O 22; 62 N 19 '66

O'CONNELL, Robert J.
Secular city revisited. America 114:545-8 Ap 16 '66

O'CONNOR, Arthur L. See Munsinger, G. M. jt. auth.

O'CONNOR, Bradford
Luck of the Yukon. Outdoor Life 138:20-3+ Jl '66

O'CONNOR, Edwin
Book fair. Atlan 218:124-5 Jl '66

about

Book of the month. G. Roy. Cath World 204: 180-1 D '66
Politics, Mr O'Connor, and the family novel. H. M. Jones. Atlan 218:117-18+ O '66

O'CONNOR, Flannery
Displaced person; dramatization. See Dawkins, C.

about

Added dimension: the art and mind of Flannery O'Connor, ed. by M. J. Friedman and L. A. Lawson. Review Christian Cent 83:1575-6 D 21 '66. J. D. Kellogg
Everything that rises must converge. J. M. Kann. por Cath World 204:154-9 D '66
Holy kind of horror. G. Hicks. Sat R 49:21-2 Jl 2 '66

O'CONNOR, Frank
All the Olympians. Sat R 49:30-2+ D 10 '66
Corkerys; story. New Yorker 42:45-51 Ap 30 '66
My father's wife. Sat Eve Post 239:84-6+ F 26 '66
School for wives; story. New Yorker 42:59-66 N 5 '66
Three hand reel; adaptation. See Mayer, P. A.

about

Obituary
Pub W 189:53 Mr 21 '66

O'CONNOR, Frank Daniel
Man from Queens. il por Newsweek 68:17-18 Ag 29 '66
O'Connor. New Yorker 42:50-1 O 15 '66
One of the boys. por Time 88:14-15 Ag 26 '66
Out of the fight into the fire. Time 88:20 Jl 15 '66
Rocky redivivus. il Time 88:35 O 7 '66

O'CONNOR, Jack
Bold, bad tiger of Ghatpiparia. pors Outdoor Life 137:36-9+ Mr '66
Getting the range. See issues of Outdoor life
Shooting. See issues of Outdoor life
Shots heard round the world. Outdoor Life 138:48-9+ Jl '66

O'CONNOR, James
Agit-prop pop opera. Nation 203:716-17 D 26 '66
Marxist heavyweight division. Nation 202: 749-50 Je 20 '66
New left: beyond the burning moral thing. Nation 203:20-2 Jl 4 '66

O'CONNOR, John
Russian revisionism in Africa. America 114: 773-5 My 28 '66
Sudan tragedy. America 114:171-2 Ja 29 '66

O'CONNOR, John Joseph, 1904-
History (cont) America 114:668-70; 115:700+ My 7, N 26 '66

O'CONNOR, W. J.
Bed fishing for bass. por Outdoor Life 137: 40-1+ Mr '66

O'CONNOR, William Van
Poems of Howard Baker. Poetry 109:187-9 D '66

OCTA-calcium phosphate. See Calcium phosphate

OCTAHEDRAL research satellite. See Artificial satellites—Use in research

OCTOPUS
Invertebrate learning. M. J. Wells. il Natur Hist 75:34-41 bibliog(p68) F '66
Octopus rasslin' is hand-to-hand-to-hand-to-hand. W. L. High. il Pop Mech 125:102-3 My '66

ODD lot sales. See Stocks—Odd lot sales

ODE to spring; drama. See Hark, M. and McQueen, N.

O'DELL, Betty Young
Heading off the problems of the loner. Todays Health 44:46-9 Ag '66

ODEN, Thomas C.
Christian ethics amid pietistic culture-Protestantism. Christian Cent 83:525-6+ Ap 27 '66

ODENBURG, Austria. See Sopron, Hungary

ODEND'HAL, Stewart, and Poulter, T. C.
Pressure regulation in the middle ear cavity of sea lions: a possible mechanism. bibliog Science 153:768-9 Ag 12 '66

ODER-Neisse line. See Germany (Democratic Republic)—Boundaries; Poland—Boundaries

ODETS, Clifford
How a playwright triumphs; interview, ed. by A. Wagner. Harper 233:64-70+ S '66

about

Country girl. Criticism
Nation 203:398 O 17 '66

ODINGA, Oginga
Another sweep for Jomo. il por Time 88:33 Jl 8 '66
Clipped wings. il por Newsweek 67:48+ My 9 '66
Double O naturel. por Newsweek 68:62 O 24 '66
Exit double O. por Newsweek 67:46 Ap 25 '66
Trouble with Odinga. il por Time 87:28 Mr 25 '66

O'DOHERTY, Brian
Life movie review (cont) Life 60:22 My 20 '66

O'DONNELL, Kenneth
Kenny comes home. il por Time 87:20 Ja 28 '66
Out of the fight into the fire. Time 88:20 Jl 15 '66

O'DONNELL, Walter E.
It's harder and harder to tell the truth. McCalls 93:91+ Ap '66

O'DONOGHUE, Joseph
CCD—R.I.P? Commonweal 84:573-4 S 16 '66

ODORS
Actinomycete: isolation and identification of agent responsible for musty odors. J. D. Dougherty and others. bibliog il Science 152:1372-3 Je 3 '66
Burn up those lift-station odors; Crystal, Minn. D. McKenzie. il Am City 81:80-2 N '66
Center established for research in odor; Olfactronics and odor sciences center. Sci N 89:463 Je 11 '66
Odor discrimination in pigeons. W. W. Henton and others. bibliog il Science 153:1138-9 S 2 '66
Paddle away manure odors. Farm J 90:H14 N '66
Voodoo lily. B. J. D. Meeuse. il Sci Am 215:80-8 Jl '66
War on smell: Bishop processing company, Selbyville. Del ordered to deodorize. Newsweek 67:23-4 Ja 31 '66
X-ray detection by the olfactory system: ozone as a masking odorant. E. L. Gasteiger and S. A. Helling. bibliog il Science 154:1038-41 N 25 '66
See also
Gardens, Fragrant
Perfumery
Smell

OEHSER, Paul H.
Crusader's hymnal. Liv Wildn 29:29-30 Wint '65

OERTLE, V. Lee
Load-equalizing hitch. Yachting 120:54-5+ S '66
Roam sweet home. Motor T 18:64-5 Ap '66
Room at the top! Motor T 18:74-5 Jl '66
Tips for touring. Motor T 18:28-30 Ag '66

OETTINGER, Anthony G.
Uses of computers in science; with biographical sketch. Sci Am 215:46, 160-6+ bibliog (p312+) S '66

O'FAOLAIN, Sean
Dividends; story. McCalls 93:114-15 S '66
Heat of the sun; story. Atlan 218:70-5 S '66
Jungle of love; story. Sat Eve Post 239:54-63 Ag 13 '66
Operation rosebud; story. Redbook 127:58-60 Ag '66

OFEK, Uriel
Books of a pioneer culture. por Library J 91:5706-8 N 15 '66

OFF-campus undergraduate centers. See Colleges and universities—Off-campus centers

OFFENBACH, Jacques
On records; Contes d'Hoffmann. Opera N 30:34 F 12 '66
Subtle sensualist. J. Novick. il por Hi Fi 16: 55-8 Ag '66

OFFICE appliances
General office machines. il Duns R 88:pt2 134-5+ S '66
Giving office gear the torture test: Buyers laboratory provides testing service. il Bsns W p 110-12 Mr 12 '66
See also
Cash registers

OFFICE buildings
Building types study. il Arch Rec 140:159-82 N '66
Chicago skyline adds a new dimension: John Hancock center, combination apartment and office building. il Bsns W p36 Ap 2 '66
N.C. mutual reaches the heights. il Ebony 21:151-2+ Je '66
Stone builds GM an urban amenity; new Manhattan headquarters. il Bsns W p 126 O 8 '66
Total design on a grand scale; CBS building, New York, and American republic insurance building, Des Moines; with report by C. Welles. il Life 60:50-7+ Ap 29 '66
Traveling to work by elevator; multipurpose buildings. il Bsns W p37-8 Ap 2 '66
Uplifting the skylines; new office space. il Time 87:89 Ap 8 '66
Urban building: hotels vs. offices. G. A. Christie. Arch Rec 140:44 Ag '66
See also
Bank buildings

Designs and plans
Charles center's latest; downtown Baltimore. il Arch Rec 140:173-8 S '66
Five small office buildings. J. S. Hornbeck. il Arch Rec 139:147-56 My '66
Moretti and Nervi's Place Victoria. il Arch Rec 139:141-6 Mr '66
Multi-level concourse connects multiple uses. il Arch Rec 140:162-5 N '66
Office designs that break the pattern. il Arch Rec 140:171 N '66
Orange County office building and courthouse, Goshen, N.Y. il Arch Rec 139:137-9 Je '66
Tale of two towers; CBS building in Manhattan and Brunswick building, Chicago. il Arch Forum 124:28-37 Ap '66

Lighting
Lighting troffer design for changing space needs. il Arch Rec 140:197-8 N '66
OFFICE decoration
Distinguished interior architecture for CBS; New York headquarters. il Arch Rec 139:129-34 Je '66
OFFICE for library education. See American library association—Office for library education
OFFICE furniture
Distinguished interior architecture for CBS; New York headquarters. il Arch Rec 139:129-34 Je '66
OFFICE holders. See Public officers
OFFICE machines. See Office appliances
OFFICE management
Office services. il Duns R 88:pt2 157-8+ S '66
Streamlining management; an outline for action! excerpts from address. H. A. Nichols Parks & Rec 1:919+ N '66
Transformation in the office. H. E. Klein. il Duns R 87:pt2 124-5+ Mr '66
OFFICE of business economics. See United States—Business economics, Office of
OFFICE of economic opportunity. See United States—Economic opportunity, Office of
OFFICE of education. See United States—Education, Office of
OFFICE of general aviation affairs. See United States—Federal aviation administration
OFFICE workers
Office services. il Duns R 88:pt2 157-8+ S '66

Salaries
Metropolitan area pay levels and trends in 1965. K. J. Hoffmann. il Mo Labor R 89:22-8 Ja '66
Payment by the hour? the week? the year? for life? A. H. Raskin. il N Y Times Mag p6-7+ S 4 '66
Trends in white-collar salaries, 1961-66. H. F. Zeman. il Mo Labor R 89:1250-4 N '66
Where salaries are heading in private business; clerical workers. il U S News 61:79 D 5 '66
White-collar pay supplements. V. J. Sheffer. il Mo Labor R 89:496-502 My '66
White-collar salaries in February-March 1965. L. E. Badenhoop. il Mo Labor R 88:1455-9 D '65
OFFICERS, Military. See United States—Armed forces—Officers
OFFICERS, Retired. See Retired military officers
OFFICES
Do you want an office or guest room or both? il Bet Hom & Gard 44:48-9 Ag '66

Find space for a farm home office. J. Lem-Mon. il Suc Farm 64:98-101 Ap '66
How to make an office right at home. il Bet Hom & Gard 44:126+ O '66
It's their disappearing office; home office measures. il Sunset 137:123 O '66
OFFICIAL entertaining. See Government entertaining
OFFICIAL grievance man. See Administrative remedies
OFFICIAL residences
Be it ever so humble; vice presidential mansion bill deferred. Newsweek 67:34 Mr 28 '66
OFFICIAL secrets
Blabbermouthism; violations of confidence at highest levels of government. N. Cousins. Sat R 49:34-5 D 10 '66
Washington: who leaked to whom? attack on oil installations around Hanoi and Haiphong. Newsweek 68:22-3 Jl 11 '66
See also
Government and the press
OFFICIALISM. See Bureaucracy
OFFSET printing. See Printing, Offset
OFFSHORE oil well drilling. See Oil well drilling, Submarine
OFFSHORE oilfields. See Petroleum in submerged lands
OFFSHORE platforms. See Artificial islands
O'GARA, James
All things considered. See issues of Commonweal
No more seaweed. Commonweal 85:283 D 9 '66
OGBURN, Charlton, Jr
Down, boy, down, blast you! Read Digest 88:121-4 Je '66
How the West was lost, and why. New Repub 154:34-6 Je 25 '66
Letter to Walter. Read Digest 89:193-4+ O '66
OGDEN, Warner
Man who wouldn't law with Uncle Sam. Read Digest 88:39+ F '66
OGDON, William D.
Tammany side of the story. Sat R 49:96-7 My 7 '66
OGILVIE, Elisabeth
Background; the most important character. Writer 79:11-14 Jl '66
OGLE, Alice
Facts about the aging poor. America 115:651+ N 19 '66
Plight of migrant America. America 115:33-4 Jl 9 '66
O'GORMAN, Ned
Bathing place; poem. Nation 202:724 Je 13 '66
Dark angel. New Repub 154:25-7 Mr 12 '66
War; poem. Nation 204:28 Ja 2 '67
OGRE MOUNTAIN. See Eiger (mountain) Switzerland
OH Lord, remember me; story. See Lord, R. K.
OH, my darling daughter; story. See Mackey, E.
O'HAIR, Madalyn E. Murray. See Murray, M. E.
O'HANLON, Daniel J.
Books. Commonweal 85:61-3, 202 O 14, N 18 '66
Critique of the council at Rome. Sat R 49:55-6 N 12 '66
What can Catholicism learn from the free churches? Cath World 203:81-5 My '66
O'HANLON, James F. Jr
Adrenaline and noradrenaline: relation to performance in a visual vigilance task. bibliog Science 150:507 9; 151:710 O 22 '65, F 11 '66
O'HANLON, Thomas
Atomic bomb in the land of coal. Fortune 74:132-3 S '66
Con Edison: the company you love to hate. Fortune 73:122-7+ Mr '66
Good thing in the Irish sweepstakes, for the owners. Fortune 74:170-3 N '66
Perilous prosperity of Anaconda. Fortune 73:116-21+ My '66
O'HARA, Frank
Frank O'Hara, 1926-1966. J. Ashbery. il por Art N 65:45+ S '66
From woodcarver to wordcarver. R. Roseliep. Poetry 107:326 F '66
O'HARA, James B.
Common beliefs; address, January 25, 1966. Vital Speeches 32:358-9 Ap 1 '66
O'HARA, John
Afternoon waltz; story. Sat Eve Post 239:56-60 Ap 23 '66
Fatimas and kisses; story. New Yorker 42:44-53 My 21 '66

O'HARA, John—*Continued*
Jama; story. Sat Eve Post 239:58-60 O 22 '66
Leonard; story. New Yorker 42:33-7 F 26 '66
On cars and snobbism. Holiday 40:52-3 Ag '66
Private people; story. Sat Eve Post 239:56-8 D 17 '66
Whistle stop. Holiday 40:16+ S: 34+ O: 20+ N; 22+ D '66; 41:24+ Ja '67
Yostie; story. Sat Eve Post 239:46-8 Je 4 '66

O'HARE, Tom
Little boy who plays Vietcong; with report by D. Sider. il pors Life 61:50B-52+ Ag 5 '66

O'HEARN, Robert
How I see The woman without a shadow. il Opera N 31:48-51 S 17 '66

OHIO
See also
Booksellers and bookselling—Ohio
Fishing—Ohio
Hunting—Ohio
Libraries—Ohio

Industries
Go-go in Ohio. il Time 89:63 Ja 13 '67

Politics and government
Great-grandson race; battle for First congressional district. il Time 88:32-3 O 21 '66
Ohio: can Bob Taft make a comeback? J. A. Maxwell. il Reporter 35:31-2 O 20 '66
Wonderful world of Governor Rhodes. A. S. Zaidan. il Reporter 35:44-6 O 6 '66

OHIO oil company. See Marathon oil company

OHIO RIVER
Ohio River Heritage cruise; glorious gateway to the West. J. Gribbins. il Motor B 118:38-43 S '66

History
Ohio River Heritage cruise; glorious gateway to the West. J. Gribbins. il Motor B 118:38+ S '66

OHIO state university, Columbus
Hard way; exam cheating. Newsweek 68:86 Jl 25 '66
Head start liaison. E. S. Ross. il Library J 91:337 Ja 15 '66

OHIO university press
Founding of a university press. T. Culbert. Sat R 49:47 Je 11 '66

OHKAWARA, Akira
Scientists discover secret of skin color. il pors Ebony 22:85-6+ Ja '67

OHLES, John F.
Berkeleyitis: a second look. Sch & Soc 94:66 F 5 '66

OHMMETERS
See also
Voltohmmeters

OHNO, Susumu, and Morrison, Martin
Multiple gene loci for the monomeric hemoglobin of the hagish (eptatretus stoutii) bibliog Science 154:1034-5 N 25 '66
—and others
Hexose-6-phosphate dehydrogenase found in human liver. bibliog Science 153:1015-16 Ag 26 '66

OHTSUKI, H. See Yoshida, M. jt. auth.

OIKAWA, Yoichi
Our junior high PTA makes a difference. NEA J 56:29-30 Ja '67

OIL. See Petroleum

OIL companies. See Petroleum industry and trade

OIL filters
How to keep those filters filtering. M. J. Schultz. il Pop Mech 126:217 N '66

OIL fires
Assault on a pillar of fire; exploratory well at Tang-e-Bijar; with report by L. Hall. il Life 60:24-31 F 18 '66

OIL industries
See also
Petroleum industry and trade
Standard oil company (New Jersey)

OIL lands
Bonanza in Colorado: who gets it? J. Duscha. il Atlan 217:82-6 Mr '66
Shale oil: the sleeping giant. R. Fleming. Nation 204:49-50 Ja 9 '67

OIL pollution on rivers, harbors, etc.
Our dying waters. J. Bird. il Sat Eve Post 239:29-35+ Ap 23 '66

OIL refineries
See also
Petroleum refineries

OIL shales
Exploiting Brazil's shale oil; international race to tap country's billions of tons of oil-rich rock. Bsns W p 192 Mr 12 '66

Future oil from rocks. B. Tufty. il Sci N L 89:71 Ja 29 '66
Now we're mining oil from mountains; deposits in the Rockies. J. N. Bell. il Pop Mech 126:142-5+ N '66
Occurrence of isoprenoid fatty acids in the Green River shale. G. Eglinton and others. bibliog il Science 153:1133-5 S 2 '66
Oil shale and the public lands. P. M. Tilden. il Nat Parks Mag 40:2 Ag '66
Oil-shale question; Green River resources. Natur Hist 75:5-6 Je '66
Oil-shale research. Nat Parks Mag 40:20 Jl '66
Shale oil: the sleeping giant. R. Fleming. Nation 204:49-50 Ja 9 '67
Tar sands and oil. shales. N. De Nevers. il Sci Am 214:21-9 F '66

OIL tankers. See Tank ships

OIL well drilling
Sweetening the oil; France's E.R.A.P. contractor to Iran. Time 88:106 O 14 '66

OIL well drilling, Submarine
Industries combine talents for offshore oil. Tech W 19:29 S 26 '66
Ocean is expansive oil field. C. A. Betts. il Sci N 89:372-3 My 14 '66
See also
Artificial islands
Petroleum in submerged lands

OILS, Lubricating. See Lubrication and lubricants

OILS and fats, Edible
Luncheon meats, sausage, frankfurters, hamburger; sources of high fat intake. il Consumer Bul 49:22-7 Je '66
New facts about fats in your diet; saturated vs. polyunsaturated. A. Hamilton. il Sci Digest 59:53-6 Je '66

OILSEED plants
Farmers grow crambe, a new oilseed crop. il Farm J 90:42 My '66
See also
Crambe abyssinica

OINTMENTS
Protection for baby's skin. M. B. Keiser. il Parents Mag 41:36+ Mr '66

OISTRAKH, Igor
New York concert. S. Fleming. Hi Fi 16:132-3 F '66

OJAI festival. See Music festivals—California

OJEDA, Fabricio
End of Lt. Hilton. Newsweek 68:49 Jl 4 '66

OJHA, Ishwer Chandra
Sino-American confrontation: Communist Chinese perspectives. bibliog f Cur Hist 51:147-52+ S '66

OKA, Takashi
Other regime in South Vietnam. N Y Times Mag p8-9+ Jl 31 '66

OKANAGAN helicopters, limited
Turbine, crane helicopters sought by Okanagan of Canada. R. G. O'Lone. il Aviation W 85:86-7+ D 19 '66

O'KEEFE, John A. and others
Lunar ring dikes from Lunar Orbiter I. bibliog Science 155:77-9 Ja 6 '67

O'KEEFE, Sister Maureen, and Evoy, J. J.
Personal fulfillment in man and woman; excerpt from Man and woman. America 115:582-6 N 12 '66

OKINAWA
Appealing to a power higher than Uncle Sam; concerning the prayer at the inauguration of Lieutenant General Ferdinand T. Unger as U.S. high commissioner for the Ryukyus. Christian Cent 83:1464 N 30 '66
See also
Recreation—Okinawa

OKLAHOMA
See also
Justice, Administration of—Oklahoma

History
Land! R. E. Cunningham. il Am Heritage 17:48-55+ F '66

OKLAHOMA; musical comedy. See Musical comedies, revues. etc.—Criticisms, plots. etc.

OKLAHOMA Christian college, Oklahoma City
Automated electronic learning center opened at Oklahoma Christian college. Library J 91:914 F 15 '66
Oklahoma City, center of education. il Esquire 66:174-5 D '66

OKLAHOMA CITY

Theater
[Theatre across America] J. Novick. Nation 202:693 Je 6 '66

OKLAHOMA CITY—*Continued*

Transportation

Meeting public-transportation problems head on. Am City 81:23 N '66

OKLAHOMA CITY civic ballet. See Ballet companies

OKLAHOMA TERRITORY

Land! R. E. Cunningham. il Am Heritage 17:48-55+ F '66

OKLAHOMA. University

College of fine arts

Giselle comes to the University of Oklahoma. J. Anderson. il Dance Mag 40:57-9 N '66

OKUDZHAVA, Bulat

Unperson sings to the Russians. M. Mihajlov. il por N Y Times Mag p26-7+ My 15 '66

OKUN, Arthur M.

Official size-up of the business outlook; excerpts from address, May 10, 1966. por U S News 60:78-9 My 23 '66

OLANA (historic house) See New York (state) —Historic houses, etc.

OLD age

Sadness, loneliness seen senility roots. Sci N 90:394 N 12 '66
  See also
Aged
Aging

OLD age homes

New legislation puts fresh impetus behind nursing homes and housing for the elderly. W. B. Foxhall. il Arch Rec 139:151-8 Je '66
  See also
Nursing homes
Retirement. Places of

OLD age pensions
  See also
Pensions, Industrial
Retirement income

United States

Ascertaining your social security benefits. Consumer Rep 32:23 Ja '67
Easier rules for self-pensioning? U S News 60:98 Je 6 '66
Now an LBJ plan to raise pensions. il U S News 61:120+ O 24 '66
Pension limits: misunderstood. U S News 61:94 N 7 '66
Social security keeps building momentum; with editorial comment. il Bsns W p44-5. 200 O 22 '66
  See also
Social security act amendments

OLD age, survivors' and disability insurance trust fund

Disability benefits under private pension plans. S. S. Sacks. il Mo Labor R 89:389-95 Ap '66

OLD airplanes

Collectors and collecting
  See Airplanes—Collectors and collecting

OLD automobile museums. See Automobile museums

OLD automobiles

Collectors and collecting
  See Automobiles—Collectors and collecting

OLD DEERFIELD. See Deerfield. Mass.

OLD farmer's almanac. See Almanacs

OLD LYME, Conn.

Landscape at New London; American art colony. F. Getlein. New Repub 154:34-5 Mr 12 '66

OLD Milwaukee days. See Festivals—Wisconsin

OLD Order Amish. See Mennonites

OLD people. See Aged

OLD STURBRIDGE VILLAGE, Mass.

Thompson bank at Old Sturbridge Village. J. O. Curtis. il Antiques 90:510-13 O '66
Traveling through history. M. Goodman. Redbook 127:125-6 S '66

OLD WESTBURY gardens. See Gardens—Long Island

OLD whalers' festival. See Festivals—New York (state)

OLDENBURG, Claes

Big-city boy; show at New York's Janis gallery. il por Newsweek 67:100 Mr 21 '66
Climbing Mt Oldenburg. H. Rosenstein. il por Art N 64:21-5+ F '66

OLDENDORPH, O. F.

Elephant tree. Nat Parks Mag 40:11-12 My '66
Monument Valley: a Navajo tribal park. Nat Parks Mag 40:4-8 Ag '66

OLDER man; story. See Lardner, S.

OLDEROGGE, Dimitri A.

Ancient scripts from the heart of Africa. UNESCO Courier 19:25-9 Mr '66

OLDFIELD, Barney

When a corporation turns toward sociology; address, April 18, 1966. Vital Speeches 32:427-9 My 1 '66

OLDHAM, C. H. G.

Science and education. Bul Atomic Sci 22:41-50 Je '66

OLDS, Glenn A.

Widening campus horizons. Sat R 49:67-8 Ag 20 '66

OLDSMOBILE division. See General motors corporation—Oldsmobile division

OLDUVAI gorge. See Tanzania

O'LEARY, Dillon

Canada guards its water against our big thirst. Reporter 34:36-8 Ja 27 '66
Quebec: separatism in a new guise. Nation 203:6-8 Jl 4 '66

OLENSKA, Chrystya

Midas touch. J. A. Zill. il pors Look 30:40-2 Jl 26 '66

OLEOMARGARINE. See Margarine

OLFACTORY nerves

Intracellular absorption difference spectrum of limulus extra-ocular photolabile pigment. G. C. Murray. bibliog il Science 154: 1182-3 D 2 '66
Odor discrimination in pigeons. W. W. Henton and others. bibliog il Science 153:1138-9 S 2 '66
Olfactory discrimination in the rabbit olfactory glomerulus. J. Leveteau and P. MacLeod. bibliog il Science 153:175-6 Jl 8 '66
What science is learning about smell. A. Hamilton. il Sci Digest 60:81-4 N '66

OLFSON, Lewy

Black Indies; dramatization of story by J. Verne. Plays 25:81-91 Ap '66
Through the looking-glass; dramatization of story by L. Carroll. Plays 25:95-105 My '66

OLGA, princess of Greece. See Paul, princess of Yugoslavia

OLGA Fedorovitch, Sister. See Fedorovitch, O.

OLIGOPOLY. See Monopolies

OLIGORIBONUCLEOTIDES. See Nucleotides

OLIM, Ellis G.

Children's ways of thinking. PTA Mag 61: 20-2 bibliog(p34) Ja '67

OLIN Mathieson chemical corporation

Winchester-Western division

Executives go hunting but sons cop prizes; Winchester-Western shooting seminar. il Bsns W p 132-3 O 15 '66

OLIPHANT, Mark

Over pots of tea; excerpts from a diary of a visit to China. Bul Atomic Sci 22: 36-43 My '66

OLITSKI, Jules

Green mountain boys. A. Solomon. il pors Vogue 148:104-9+ Ag 1 '66

OLIVA, Tony

Three in a row? il por Time 88:62 Ag 19 '66

OLIVE, Milton Lee, 3d

Heroes and history. por Ebony 21:160-1 Je '66
Hero's courage on a nameless trail. L. Wainwright. Life 60:32 My 6 '66
Highest decision. il por Newsweek 67:18 My 2 '66

OLIVE fruit flies

Bugged; Spain's eating-olive crop. il Time 88:90 Ag 5 '66
Sterile flies used to combat dacus; enemy of olives subjected to radioisotope technique. D. Whitney. il Natur Hist 75:30-5 Mr '66

OLIVE industry and trade

Bugged; Spain's eating-olive crop. il Time 88:90 Ag 5 '66

OLIVEIRA SALAZAR, António de. See Salazar, A. de O.

OLIVER, Dean

Dean of the faceless men. H. Peterson. il por Sports Illus 26:40-3 Ja 16 '67

OLIVER, Edith

Current cinema (cont) New Yorker 42:112 Je 11: 110 Je 18: 55 Je 25: 64-5 Jl 2 '66
Off Broadway. See issues of New Yorker

OLIVER, J. H. Jr. See Lanier, G. N. jt. auth.

OLIVER, Jack

Earthquake prediction. Science 153:1024-6 Ag 26 '66

OLIVER, Thelma

New girl on Broadway. il pors Ebony 21:52+ O '66

OLIVES
 All about olives. il Bet Hom & Gard 44:90-1
  O '66
 O is for olives. il Ladies Home J 83:112 Ap '66
OLIVIER, Sir Laurence
 Olivier and the Moor. N. Kallet. Holiday 39:
  143-4 Ap '66
OLIVINE
 Vacuum welding of olivine. P. R. Bell. bib-
  liog il Science 153:410-11 Jl 22 '66
OLMEC Indians. See Indians of Mexico
OLMO, Harold P. See Negi, S. S. jt. auth.
OLMSTED, Richard W.
 Pediatric outpatient department. Science 153:
  1026 Ag 26 '66
OLSEN, Bertha F.
 Will your child eat lunch at school? por
  Parents Mag 41:84-5+ S '66
OLSEN, Charles Oluf
 Into wild places; poem. Liv Wildn 29:14
  Wint '65
OLSEN, Leif H.
 Fiscal and monetary policy; address, Septem-
  ber 12, 1966. Vital Speeches 33:24-8 O 15 '66
OLSEN, Otto H.
 When sugar was king. Nation 202:754-5 Je
  20 '66
OLSEN, Russell K.
 Fifty years of housekeeping. Parks & Rec
  1:648-50 Ag '66
OLSON, Charles
 Maximus, in Gloucester Sunday, LXV; poem.
  Poetry 108:185-6 Je '66

about

 Foot is to kick with. R. Creeley. Poetry
  109:40-3 O '66
OLSON, Gary
 Riding the TV DX trail. Pop Electr 25:73-4+
  Jl '66
OLSON, Lynn
 Make a stained window. Sch Arts 66:9-11
  D '66
OLSON, Otmar O. and Klingenberg, John
 Aerated sewage lagoon. Am City 81:94-5 N
  '66
OLSON, Ted
 Oracles never give a straight answer; poem.
  Sat R 49:38 F 26 '66
OLSON, Willard C.
 Ability grouping: pros and cons. PTA Mag
  60:24-6 bibliog(p33) Ap '66
OLSSON, C. N. and Smith, A. G.
 Decametric radio pulses from Jupiter; char-
  acteristics. bibliog Science 153:289-90 Jl 15
  '66
OLYMPIC airways. See Airlines—Greece,
 Modern
OLYMPIC country club course. See Golf cour-
 ses
OLYMPIC games, 1964
 164 cameramen film athletes of ninety-four
  nations. H. V. Fondiller. il Pop Phot 59:
  82-3 N '66
OLYMPIC games, 1968
 Altitude no handicap. Sci N 90:267 O 8 '66
 Dissenters; International Olympic commit-
  tee's selection of Mexico city as site of the
  1968 games. Sports Illus 24:12 My 2 '66
 Friends in high places; move riding com-
  petition from Mexico city. Time 88:44 D 30
  '66
 Planning for 1968 Olympic games. Parks &
  Rec 1:851 O '66
 Up in the air; International Olympic com-
  mittee restriction on altitude training.
  Sports Illus 24:11-12 Je 27 '66
 Way up high and out of breath; Little Olym-
  pics trial run for the 1968 games. J. Under-
  wood. il Sports Illus 25:30-1+ O 31 '66
OLYMPIC games, 1972
 Bird watchers triumph; International Olym-
  pic committee selecting sites for 1972. B.
  Ottum. Sports Illus 24:68-9 My 9 '66
 No games in Banff Park; 1972 Olympic winter
  games. Nat Parks Mag 40:24 Ag '66
OLYMPIC NATIONAL PARK
 Call of the open trial. G. W. Martin. il
  Parks & Rec 1:630-2 Ag '66
 Cleavage on Olympic; logging proposal to
  improve boundaries. Liv Wildn 29:2 Wint
  '65
 Hands off Olympic Park! A. W. Smith. Nat
  Parks Mag 40:2 N '66
 Rain forest; excerpt from Olympic rain for-
  est. R. Kirk. il Audubon Mag 68:314-27 S
  '66
OLYMPIC rain forest. See Olympic National
 Park
OLYMPICS; ballet. See Ballets—Criticisms
OLZENDAM, Roderic Marble
 Keeping America green. Am For 72:8-11 Je
  '66

OMAHA, Neb.

Education

 Why the school bus doesn't stop; battle over
  amendment proposing local options for the
  transportation of non-public school children. R. T. Reilly. il America 116:21-3 Ja 7
  '67

Politics and government

 Silly hall no more. il Time 87:24 Ap 15 '66

Religious institutions and affairs

 Church breakthrough; film produced by
  Augustana Lutheran church. A. Knight.
  Sat R 49:65 N 19 '66

Riots

 Neighborhood. il Newsweek 68:24-5 Jl 18 '66
 Now, race riots in Nebraska and Iowa. il U S
  News 61:10 Jl 18 '66
O'MALLEY, Robert Emmett
 Gallantry on the line. il por Newsweek 68:
  23 D 19 '66
O'MALLEY, Walter
 King of the jungle. J. Mann. por Sports
  Illus 24:114-16+ Ap 18 '66
 Sandy Koufax story; my salary fights; ex-
  cerpts from Koufax, ed. by E. Linn. S.
  Koufax. il por Look 30:95-6+ Je 14 '66
OMAN, Charles
 English brass chandeliers in American
  churches. Antiques 90:192-4 Ag '66
O'MARA, Richard
 Church in Argentina. Commonweal 84:612-14
  S 23 '66
 Snap jobs and cheap money; Uruguay's
  double inflation. Nation 204:50-2 Ja 9 '67
OMBU
 Worth of a tree. W. L. Maughan. il Américas
  18:34-6 D '66
OMBUDSMAN. See Administrative remedies
OMEGA. See Radio in navigation
OMISSION, Criminal. See Criminal law
OMMAYA, Ayub K. and others
 Cerebral concussion in the monkey; an ex-
  perimental model. bibliog Science 153:211-12
  Jl 8 '66
OMORI, Minoru
 Hanoi's feuding friends. New Repub 155:9-10
  O 15 '66
OMPHACITE. See Pyroxenes
ONASSIS, Aristotle Socrates
 Aristotle the airman. il por Time 87:102+
  Je 10 '66
 Duel in the sun; economic dictatorship over
  Monte Carlo. il por Newsweek 68:42 Jl 18 '66
101st airborne division. See United States—
 Army
ONE moment to cherish; story. See Rodgers,
 M. A.
ONE more promise; story. See Soman, F. J.
ONE-of-a-kind regatta. See Regattas
ONE out of seven; story. See Shyer, M. F.
ONE ton cup competition. See Yacht racing
O'NEIL, James R. and Epstein, Samuel
 Oxygen isotope fractionation in the system
  dolomite-calcite-carbon dioxide. bibliog
  Science 152:198-201 Ap 8 '66
O'NEIL, Paul
 Flourishing legend of the greatest robbery.
  Life 60:102-6+ Ap 8 '66
 It wasn't no hullabillusion, said the farmer,
  and fifty-two agreed. Life 60:28-9 Ap 1
  '66
 Nick the Greek's last roll. Life 62:58-61 Ja 6
  '67
 Splendid blow to save our world. Life 60:
  85-6 Je 3 '66
 Super bowl's superman. Life 62:75-6+ Ja 13
  '67
 Trailbreaker of the deeps. Life 61:108-10+
  S 30 '66
 Unlikeliest poet. Life 61:48-70+ Jl 22 '66
O'NEILL, Gerard K.
 Particle storage rings; with biographical
  sketch. Sci Am 215:29, 107-16 N '66
O'NEILL, Michael
 Four myths about parochial schools. Amer-
  ica 116:82-6 Ja 21 '67
O'NEILL, Terence Marne
 Captain O'Neill and the anti-Papist. J. H.
  Huizinga. il Reporter 35:43-4 O 20 '66
O'NEILL, William D.
 O'Neill receives the American city aid-to-
  education award. il por Am City 81:10 N
  '66
ONETO, Clarence N.
 We put guts in our purchasing program. Am
  City 81:124-5 My '66

ONG, Walter J.
Only through time. Poetry 108:265-8 Jl '66
ONGANIA, Juan Carlos
Armor-plated hare. il por Time 88:47-8 N 18 '66
General's mustache. Newsweek 68:45 Ag 8 '66
Last coup? il por Newsweek 68:52 Jl 11 '66
Long drift. por Time 88:28 Ag 12 '66
No form chart. Newsweek 68:50 S 12 '66
No. 31. il por Time 88:21 Jl 8 '66
ONIKI, Saburou. See Fields, C. H. jt. auth.
ONIONS
See also
Cookery—Vegetables
Shallots
ONLY the lucky ones; story. See Stanton, W.
ONTARIO
See also
Algonquin Provincial Park
Geology—Ontario
Hospitals—Ontario
Libraries—Ontario
Paleontology—Ontario
Timmins
ONTOGENY
Phylogeny and ontogeny of behavior. B. F. Skinner. bibliog Science 153:1205-13 S 9 '66
ONTOLOGY
Religious slum-dwellers. D. Callahan. Commonweal 84:530-3 Ag 19 '66; Discussion. 84: 625+; 85:5+, 86-7 S 30-O 7, 21 '66
OONA O'; story. See Gallagher, T.
OORT, Jan Hendrik
Dutch astronomer honored. G. S. Mumford. Sky & Tel 32:333 D '66
OP art. See Modernism (art)
OPAL phytoliths in soil. See Soils—Silica content
OPDYKS, N. D. and others
Paleomagnetic study of Antarctic deep-sea cores. bibliog Science 154:349-57 O 21 '66
OPEN air theater. See Theater, Open air
OPERA
Before Broadway; musical comedy has an ancestor in opéra comique. M. Cooper. il Opera N 30:8-12 Ap 9 '66
Decline of the diva. M. J. Matz. il Opera N 30:12-16 Mr 12 '66
Opera companies: foreign. Hi Fi 16:262-7 D 15 '66
Profiles: B. Nilsson. W. Sargeant. New Yorker 42:66-70+ O 29 '66
Real poet; Giordano's Chénier. L. Kleine-Ahlbrandt. Opera N 30:22-3 F 5 '66
Unanswered question; music or words first. R. Berges. il Opera N 30:6-7 Mr 26 '66
See also
Libretto

Anecdotes, facetiae, satire, etc.
Aunt Ulrica answers your questions. J. Mathewson. Opera N 30:6 F 26 '66

Appreciation
Irrepressible spirit; Rossini's carefree Barber. S. Hughes. il Opera N 30:24-5 Mr 19 '66
See Music—Appreciation

Chorus
Voice of the people. K. Adler. il Opera N 31:8-12 Ja 14 '67

History and criticism
Aglow with life; singer's art keeps Donizetti's Elixir effervescent. H. Klein. il Opera N 30:24-5 My 5 '66
Along the way. H. W. Simon. il Opera N 31: 24-6 D 24 '66
Burning question. V. Thomson. Opera N 30:8-11 Mr 5 '66
Enter the hero; Lohengrin. E. Gerken. Opera N 31:6 Ja 31 '67
Fatal meeting; emotional drama of Lucia builds toward the celebrated sextet. K. McDonald. il Opera N 30:24-5 F 19 '66
Feel of reality; personal involvement is the key to La Bohème. E. Downes. il Opera N 30:24-5 Ap 16 '66
First love; Manon Lescaut set pattern for Puccini heroines. H. E. Phillips. Opera N 30:24-5 Mr 12 '66
Golden age is now. M. Mayer. il N Y Times Mag pt2 p 16+ S 11 '66
Great singers, by H. Pleasants. Review
Reporter 35:36+ D 29 '66. R. Gelatt
Is the ensemble dead? J. Wechsberg. il Opera N 30:10-12 F 12 '66
Kaleidoscope: The woman without a shadow reflects many facets of music and humanity. S. Jenkins, jr. Opera N 31:25-7 D 17 '66

New richness: Verdi's Un ballo in Maschera. O. Lehmann. Opera N 30:24-5 F 26 '66
Night music; smallest role in Die Meistersinger contributes to the magic of the whole. J. Kerman. Opera N 31:24-5 Ja 14 '67
Of timeless passions; collaboration of Strauss and Hofmannsthal. R. Breuer. il Opera N 31:24-5 D 10 '66
Sitting pretty; reasons for Faust's popularity. R. Lawrence. Opera N 30:24-5 Ap 9 '66
Strong beginning; balance between words and music with the Dresden Tannhäuser. T. H. Mulligan. il Opera N 30:24-5 Mr 26 '66
Transfigured knight: Parsifal. J. Honig. il Opera N 30:26-7 Ap 2 '66
Victorian Gothic; preview of Carlisle Floyd's Markheim. il Opera N 30:16-17 Ap 2 '66

Instruction and study
Traveling salesman; Popper, of U.C.L.A.'s opera workshop. E. Gerken. il Opera N 30: 6 Mr 12 '66

Stage lighting
Golden age memories; productions at the Metropolitan. R. P. Conkling. il Opera N 30:28-9 Ap 9 '66
Painting with light; projection techniques. Q. Eaton. il Opera N 30:28-31 Ap 2 '66

Stage mechanism
Giant stage that shifts for itself. C. Peet. il Pop Mech 126:110-13+ D '66
Met's amazing stage. il Arch Rec 140:156-60 S '66
New house. F. Stevenson. il Opera N 31:20-1 N 19 '66

Stage scenery
Art & artisans; stage designs. il Opera N 31:52-3 S 17 '66
How I see The woman without a shadow. R. O'Hearn. il Opera N 31:48-51 S 17 '66
Interopera; clearing house for productions. Q. Eaton. il Opera N 30:32 F 12 '66
New house. R. Stevenson. il Opera N 31:26-7 D 10 '66

Canada
Opera: U.S. & Canada. Hi Fi 16:200 D 15 '66
See also
Canadian opera company

Denmark
Denmark. S. A. K. Roewade. Opera N 30: 32 Mr 5 '66

Europe, Western
Eating with opera. S. Hughes. il Opera N 31:8-12 N 19 '66

France
What's going on in Paris? R. Kotlowitz. Harper 234:103 Ja '67

Germany (Federal Republic)
Germany. H. Koegler. Opera N 31:27 N 5 '66
Hanover, Brunswick. J. H. Sutcliffe. Opera N 31:28 N 19 '66

Great Britain
Other side; Glyndebourne and Covent Garden productions. T. Heinitz. Sat R 49:47 Jl 16 '66

Italy
Afloat in a sea of troubles; Rome-Naples-Florence. W. Weaver. il Hi Fi 16:144-5 Mr '66
Troubled waters; difficulties in Italy's opera houses. P. Elvins. il Opera N 31:8-11 D 10 '66
Wanted: real pasta. Time 87:65 Je 17 '66
See also
Television broadcasting—Operas

Netherlands
Great opera houses: Holland. P. Cronheim. il Opera N 30:26-9 F 5 '66

United States
Across the land. R. D. Daniels. Opera N 31:28-9 N 5 '66
Contemporary opera and the foundations; a plea to support recording of operas. Hi Fi 16:39 Je '66
Going full blast; five major companies open within four weeks. H. Kupferberg. il Opera N 31:9-11 S 10 '66
Metropolitan opera spring tour casts. Opera N 30:inside back cover Mr 26 '66
National company takes its stand. C. L. Osborne. il Hi Fi 16:122-5 F '66

OPERA—United States—*Continued*
Opera in the Lone Star state; productions in Dallas, Houston, San Antonio, and Fort Worth. R. C. Marsh. il Hi Fi 16:121-2 Je '66
Opera: U.S. & Canada. Hi Fi 16:198-200 D 15 '66
Operatic ups and downs. C. J. McNaspy. America 114:395 Mr 19 '66
U.S. calendar (cont) Opera N 31:36 S 10; 69-70 S 17; 35-7 O 31; 32-3 N 5; 32-3 N 19; 36-7 D 3; 36 D 10; 36 D 17; 36 D 24; 36 D 31 '66; 36 Ja 14 '67
U.S. opera survey: classics to the fore. F. Merkling. il Opera N 31:13-15 N 19 '66
What makes opera run. E. Leinsdorf. Atlan 217:53-8 Mr '66
  See also
American opera society
Central opera service
Connecticut opera association
Dallas civic opera company
Fort Worth opera association
Kentucky opera association
Metropolitan opera company
Metropolitan opera house, New York
Metropolitan opera national company
New York city opera company
North Shore friends of opera, incorporated
Opera, American
Opera company of Boston
Opera guilds
Opera society of Washington
Pittsburgh opera company
San Francisco opera company
Santa Fe opera association
Tri-Cities opera
OPERA, American
Met opens in the blaze of its new home. il Life 61:32-42 S 30 '66
New wine in new bottles; S. Barber's Antony and Cleopatra and G. Schuller's The visitation. R. Gelatt. il Reporter 35:57-9 N 17 '66
OPERA, Czech
Edge of truth. J. W. Freeman. il Opera N 31:6-7 N 19 '66
OPERA, French
Before Broadway; musical comedy has an ancestor in opéra comique. M. Cooper. il Opera N 30:8-12 Ap 9 '66
Souvenirs of French opera. A. Favia-Artsay. il Hobbies 71:35 Ag '66
OPERA, German
Richard Strauss, by W. Mann. Review
  Am Rec G 32:890-1 My '66. G. L. Mayer
  Hi Fi il 16:MA24-5 Ag '66. P. J. Smith
  See also
Phonograph records—German opera
OPERA, Russian
Unknown world of Prokofiev's operas; with discography. G. Pugliese. il Hi Fi 16:44-50+ Je '66
OPERA audiences. See Audiences
OPERA broadcasts. See Radio broadcasting—Music
OPERA club, Metropolitan. See Metropolitan opera club
OPERA company of Boston
Boston. H. Rogers. il Opera N 30:30 Ap 9; 23 My 7 '66
Boston; American premiere of Schoenberg's Moses and Aaron. F. Merkling. il Opera N 31:26-7 D 31 '66
Doing the undoable; Moses and Aron. il Time 88:95 D 9 '66
Music to my ears; premiere for Moses and Aron. I. Kolodin. Sat R 49:41 D 17 '66
Musical events: American première of A. Schönberg's Moses and Aron. W. Sargeant. New Yorker 42:198+ D 10 '66
Opera in the Back Bay theater. M. Steinberg. il Hi Fi 16:MA22-3 Jl '66
Rameau in Boston. H. Rogers. il Opera N 30:6-7 Ap 9 '66
Voice in the wilderness; performance of Schönberg's Moses and Aron. J. W. Freeman. il Opera N 30:14-15 My 7 '66
OPERA conducting. See Conducting (music)
OPERA critics. See Critics
OPERA guilds
Affiliated guilds report (cont) il Opera N 30: 28-9 My 7 '66
OPERA house, Lincoln Center. See Lincoln Center for the performing arts, New York —Opera house
OPERA houses
Berlin, Dresden; East Berlin's Komische oper. J. H. Sutcliffe. il Opera N 31:32-3 Ja 14 '67
Dortmund. J. H. Sutcliffe. il Opera N 30:30-1 Ap 16 '66

Eating with opera. S. Hughes. il Opera N 31:8-12 N 19 '66
Far-out opera uproar Down Under; new house in Sydney. D. Moser. il Life 62: 62-4+ Ja 6 '67
Going places finding things: Europe's opera houses. D. Walker. il House & Gard 129: 52-5+ Mr '66
Great opera houses: Holland. P. Cronheim. il Opera N 30:26-9 F 5 '66
Great opera houses: Lisbon; Teatro nacional de São Carlos. F. Teixeira Direito. il Opera N 31:26-9 Ja 14 '67
Mass and the opera; Milan cathedral and Teatro alla Scala. V. Sheean. il Opera N 30:8-13 Ap 2 '66
New house, old problems; Warsaw report. P. Heyworth. Hi Fi 16:146 F '66
Sydney opera house; engineer's view. il Arch Rec 139:175-80 Ja '66
  See also
Metropolitan opera house, New York
OPERA patronage. See Music patronage
OPERA singers
Acting in opera. L. Donath. Opera N 30:6-7 Ap 16 '66
Back to bel canto. il Time 89:42 Ja 20 '67
Decline of the diva. M. J. Matz. il Opera N 30:12-16 Mr 12 '66
Great singers, by H. Pleasants. Review
  Reporter 35:36+ D 29 '66. R. Gelatt
Is the ensemble dead? J. Wechsberg. il Opera N 30:10-12 F 12 '66
Metropolitan opera 1966-67; repertory and roster. Opera N 31:42+ S 17 '66
Singer's challenge; excerpt from The great singers. H. Pleasants. il Opera N 31:6-9 O 15 '66
Singing, with love & garlic; fads, phobias and superstitions. il Time 88:63 N 18 '66
Sound versus fury. E. Leinsdorf. il Atlan 217: 82-4+ Ap '66
Troubled waters; difficulties in Italy's opera houses. P. Elvins. il Opera N 31:8-11 D 10 '66
  See also names of opera singers, e.g. B. Nilsson
Photographs
Steichen gallery. Opera N 31:12-15 D 24 '66
OPERA society of Washington
Washington F. C. Smith. Opera N 30:30 F 19; 26 Je 4 '66
Washington; production of Haydn's Infedelta delusa. F. C. Smith. Opera N 31:30 D 31 '66
OPERAKÄLLAREN (restaurant) See Stockholm—Hotels, restaurants, etc.
OPERAS
Operas that survive; selected by Erich Leinsdorf. Atlan 217:59 Mr '66
  See also
Birds in music
Phonograph records—Operas

Bibliography
Musical events; several books on Tristan und Isolde. W. Sargeant. New Yorker 42:200-2 D 3 '66

Criticisms, plots, etc.
  See name of composer for full entry
Abduction from the seraglio. J. C. W. A. Mozart
Aida. G. Verdi
Amerika. R. Haubenstock-Ramati
Andrea Chénier. U. Giordano
Anna Bolena. G. Donizetti
Antony and Cleopatra. S. Barber
Arlecchino. F. Busoni
Ballad of Baby Doe. D. Moore
Un ballo in maschera. See Masked ball, below
Barber of Seville. G. Rossini
Il barbiere di Siviglia. See Barber of Seville, above
Bassarids. H. W. Henze
La Bohème. G. Puccini
Boris Godunov. M. P. Musorgskii
Burning fiery furnace. B. Britten
Capriccio. R. Strauss
Carmen. G. Bizet
Carry Nation. D. S. Moore
Coronation of Poppaea. C. Monteverdi
Danton's death. G. von Einem
Daughter of the regiment. G. Donizetti
Dialogues of the Carmelites. F. Poulenc
Dido and Aeneas. H. Purcell
Don Giovanni. J. C. W. A. Mozart
Don Pasquale. G. Donizetti
Don Rodrigo. A. Ginastera
Elektra. R. Strauss
L'elisir d'amore. See Elixir of love, below
Elixir of love. D. Donizetti
Falstaff. G. Verdi
Faust. C. F. Gounod

OPERAS—Criticisms, plots, etc.—*Continued*
Fille du regiment. See Daughter of the regiment, above
Die Fledermaus. J. Strauss, jr
Die frau ohne schatten. See Woman without a shadow, below
La Gioconda. A. Ponchielli
Giulio Cesare. See Julius Caesar, below
Good soldier Schweik. R. Kurka
Hippolyte et Aricie. J. P. Rameau
Hoosier tale. W. Kaufmann
Idomeneo. J. C. W. A. Mozart
Incidents in connection with a crash landing. B. Blacher
L'incoronazione di Poppea. See Coronation of Poppaea, above
Julius Caesar. G. F. Händel
Lohengrin. R. Wagner
Love on trial. G. Rossini
Lucia di Lammermoor. G. Donizetti
Magic flute. J. C. W. A. Mozart
Manon Lescaut. G. Puccini
Markheim. C. Floyd
Masked ball. G. Verdi
Mathis der maler. P. Hindemith
Mefistofele. A. Boito
Die Meistersinger von Nürnberg. R. Wagner
Mines of sulfur. R. R. Bennett
Moses and Aron. A. Schönberg
Parsifal. R. Wagner
Peer Gynt. W. Egk
Pelléas et Mélisande. C. Debussy
Pique dame. See Queen of spades, below
Porgy and Bess. G. Gershwin
Queen of spades. P. I. Tchaikovsky
Rape of Lucretia. B. Britten
Rigoletto. G. Verdi
Der Rosenkavalier. R. Strauss
Samson and Delilah. C. Saint-Saëns
Taming of the shrew. V. Giannini
Tannhäuser. R. Wagner
La Traviata. G. Verdi
Tristan und Isolde. R. Wagner
Triumph of honor. A. Scarlatti
Trojan men. See Les Troyens, below
Les Troyens. H. Berlioz
Turandot. F. Busoni
Turandot. G. Puccini
Turn of the screw. B. Britten
Visitation. G. Schuller
Woman without a shadow. R. Strauss
OPERATIC acting. See Acting
OPERATIC characters. See Characters in opera
OPERATIC composition. See Composition (music)
OPERATIC costume. See Costume, Theatrical
OPERATIC production
And this from Wagner's grandson! E. Helm. il N Y Times Mag p68-9+ Je 5 '66
Antony and Cleopatra; scenic and costume designs. il Opera N 31:28-30 S 17 '66
Balance regained; Mozart's Don Giovanni. S. Hughes. Opera N 30:24-5 Ja 29 '66
Barber, the bard, and the barge. H. Kupferberg. il Atlan 218:126+ S '66
Birth of an opera; S. Barber's Antony and Cleopatra. H. Klein. il N Y Times Mag p32-3+ Ag 28 '66
Craftsman; interview. ed. by C. N. Welsh. G. von Einem. Opera N 30:29 Mr 12 '66
Creating Don Rodrigo; in City Center. F. Stevenson. il Opera N 30:14-16 F 26 '66
Culture's big super-event; Antony and Cleopatra at the new Met. S. Alexander. Life 61:30B S 30 '66
Daughter of Agamemnon; photographs of Elektra. Opera N 31:21-3 D 10 '66
Evoking an era; La Scala's Aida; photographs. Opera N 30:21-3 F 12 '66
Golden age memories; productions at the Metropolitan. R. P. Conkling. il Opera N 30:28-9 Ap 9 '66
Hopeless love; photographs of Manon Lescaut. Opera N 30:21-3 Mr 12 '66
How I see The woman without a shadow. R. O'Hearn. il Opera N 31:48-51 S 17 '66
In a strange land. J. Gielgud. Opera N 30:8-9 F 12 '66
In rehearsal; Metropolitan opera house rehearsal department. F. Stevenson. il Opera N 30:28-31 F 12 '66
In search of the ideal; scenes from Don Giovanni; photographs. Opera N 30:21-3 Ja 29 '66
Is the ensemble dead? J. Wechsberg. il Opera N 30:10-12 F 12 '66
King's confidant; photographs of Masked ball. Opera N 30:21-3 F 26 '66
Love in a garret; photographs of Met's La Bohème. Opera N 30:21-3 Ap 16 '66

Love potion; photographs of L'elisir d'amore. Opera N 30:21-3 Mr 5 '66
Mad scene; Metropolitan production. il Opera N 30:21-3 F 19 '66
Make mingle with our tambourines; collaboration on Antony and Cleopatra; interviews. S. Barber; F. Zeffirelli; T. Schippers. Opera N 31:31-5 S 17 '66
Man from Iran; interview. ed. by F. Stevenson. L. Mansouri. Opera N 30:11 F 19 '66
Met opens in the blaze of its new home. il Life 61:32-42 S 30 '66
New directions for the Ring. J. Culshaw. il Hi Fi 16:65-8 N '66
Painting with light; projection techniques. Q. Eaton. il Opera N 30:28-31 Ap 2 '66
Persuader; interview. T. Capobianco. il Opera N 31:18 N 19 '66
Phantom of the Festspielhaus; imaginary conversation between Richard and Wieland Wagner; comp. by R. McMullen; with editorial comment. Hi Fi 16:59-64 N '66
Pilgrim's progress; photographs of Tannhäuser. Opera N 30:21-3 Mr 26 '66
Preview; working rehearsal for supporting members. N. Ross. il Opera N 30:26-8 Mr 12 '66
Pure fool; photographs of Parsifal. Opera N 30:23-5 Ap 2 '66
Redeemed; photographs of Faust. Opera N 30:21-3 Ap 9 '66
Reign of terror; Giordano's Andrea Chénier; photographs. Opera N 30:21 F 5 '66
Singing lesson; photographs of Barber of Seville. Opera N 30:21-3 Mr 19 '66
Sound versus fury. E. Leinsdorf. il Atlan 217:82-4+ Ap '66
Strauss vs. Wagner A. M. Lingg. il Opera N 31:6 D 10 '66
Swan knight; photographs of Lohengrin. il Opera N 31:21-3 Ja 21 '67
Trial song; Die Meistersinger, photographs. Opera N 31:21-3 Ja 14 '67
Two women; photographs of Frau ohne schatten. Opera N 31:21-4 D 17 '66
Voice of violence; photographs of Metropolitan's Turandot. Opera N 31:21-3 D 3 '66
Walpurgis night; photographs of La Scala's Faust. Opera N 31:21-3 D 24 '66
World of Wieland Wagner. E. Salzman. il Opera N 31:8-15 Ja 21 '67
See also
College operas, revues, etc.
Opera—Chorus
OPERATIC production, Cost of
Footing the bill; can opera's sources of support keep pace with its soaring deficits? R. W. Hall. il Opera N 31:8-12 D 17 '66
OPERATIC stage directors. See Theatrical directors
OPERATING engineers, International union of. See International union of operating engineers
OPERATION Reclaim. See New York (city)—Education
OPERATION rosebud; story. See O'Faolain. S.
OPERATION SEEK. See New York (city) City university of New York
OPERATIONAL analysis. See Operations research
OPERATIONS, Surgical. See Surgery
OPERATIONS research
Technique ranks space objectives; Honeywell's planning assistance through technical evaluation of relevance numbers. W. S. Beller. il Miss & Roc 18:22-4 F 7 '66
See also
Systems engineering
OPHTHALMOLOGISTS
Should eye doctors sell glasses? I. Ross. Read Digest 89:75-8 D '66
OPHTHALMOLOGY
And in Haiti. Focus: Foreign ophthalmological care. il Todays Health 44:25 Jl '66
Eye's electrical current warns of disease. Sci N 90:150 S 3 '66
Ultimate in research; Jules Stein eye institute. il Time 88:66+ N 11 '66
ÖPIK, Ernst J.
Martian surface. bibliog Science 153:255-65 Jl 15 '66
OPINION, Public. See Public opinion
OPINION, Student. See Student opinion
OPINION research. See Public opinion polls
OPIUM
Analgesic drugs. M. Gates. il Sci Am 215:131-6 bibliog(p 160) N '66

OPIUM trade
Logistics of junk. D. Lyle. il Esquire 65:
59-67+ Mr '66

Mexico

Hide and seek; conflict between the Mexican
government and Mexican poppy growers. il
Newsweek 67:60 Mr 14 '66
OPIUM war, 1840-1842. See China—History—
War of 1840-1842
OPOSSUMS
Extinct pigmy possum found live in Aus-
tralia. il(p317) Sci N 90:322 O 22 '66
OPPEN, George
Third path. T. Enslin. Poetry 108:339-41 Ag
'66
OPPENHEIM, Arthur, and Wasserman, Sey-
mour
Reverberant rooms: their design and use.
por Electr World 75:34-6 Ap '66
OPPENHEIM, Ronald W.
Amniotic contraction and embryonic motility
in the chick embryo. bibliog Science 152:
528-9 Ap 22 '66
OPPENHEIMER, Carl H.
Marine biology. Science 152:108 Ap 1 '66
OPPENHEIMER, George
Celebrity circuit. H. A. Smith. por Sat R 49:
39+ Ap 9 '66
OPPENHEIMER, Jane
Books in review. Natur Hist 75:4-10 My '66
OPPENHEIMER, Julius Robert
With Oppenheimer, on an autumn day; in-
terview, ed. by T. B. Morgan. pors Look
30:61+ D 27 '66

about

Doctor Oppenheimer retires. por Sci N 90:20
Jl 9 '66
Honor to Oppenheimer. por Newsweek 67:
64-5 Je 27 '66
OPTICAL art. See Modernism (art)
OPTICAL diffractometers. See Optical instru-
ments
OPTICAL glass fibers. See Fiber optics
OPTICAL illusions
Approach with care. R. L. Kuhlman. il Fly-
ing 78:88-90 Ap '66
Tricks played on hand & eye. il UNESCO
Courier 19:14-15 My '66
Visual disappearances caused by form sim-
ilarity. D. C. Donderi. bibliog il Science
152:99-100 Ap 1 '66
OPTICAL instruments
Laser as light source for optical diffrac-
tometers: Fourier analysis of electron mi-
crographs. J. E. Berger and others. bibliog
il Science 153:168-70 Jl 8 '66
Putting optical devices to work; precision
measuring devices getting wider applica-
tion on production lines. il Bsns W p 116-
18 O 8 '66
See also
Collimators
Microscope and microscopy
Schlieren apparatus
OPTICAL reading machines. See Reading
machines
OPTICAL scanners. See Reading machines
OPTICAL society of America
Techniques tomorrow; future potentials. B.
Sherman. il Mod Phot 30:44+ Jl '66
OPTICAL stimulus. See Stimulus and response
OPTICALLY active products. See Polarization
(light)
OPTICS
See also
Fiber optics
Photographic optics
OPTICS, Physiological. See Eye
OPTIMISM
Is it possible to be an optimist? N. Cousins.
Sat R 49:26 N 5 '66
On optimism and the optimists. G. Wills.
Nat R 18:360-1 Ap 19 '66
OPUS Dei
Opus Dei pursues power; institute's growing
role in Spain. Christian Cent 83:100-1 Ja
26 '66; Discussion. 83:338-9, 660 Mr 16, My
18 '66
ORAISON, Marc
Issue of imprimatur. por Time 88:74 Ag 19 '66
ORAL contraceptives. See Contraceptives
ORAL history
Symposium on oral history. bibliog il Wilson
Lib Bul 40:599-608+ Mr '66
Tape recorder as historian. J. Lieber. il Sat
R 49:98-9 Je 11 '66; Discussion. 49:60 Ag 13
'66

ORAL history recordings. See Tape record-
ings
ORAL Roberts university, Tulsa, Okla.
Oral Roberts favors futuristic. W. W.
Jernigan. il Library J 91:5889-91 D 1 '66
ORAL surgery
Radical new technique; jaw-splitting pro-
cedures for correcting malformations. il
Time 88:46 Jl 1 '66
ORANGE, A. S. See Brace, W. F. jt. auth.
ORANGE Blossom trail. See Florida—Descrip-
tion and travel
ORANGE coast pilot (newspaper)
Suburban daily; new power in publishing. J.
N. Bell. Sat R 50:118+ Ja 14 '67
ORANGE COUNTY, Calif.
Little piece of America. il Newsweek 68:32+
N 14 '66
ORANGE juice
Orange juice vs. the whole orange. Consumer
Bul 49:32-3 O '66
ORANGE juice, Frozen. See Fruit juices,
Frozen
ORANGE pie. See Pie
ORANGES
Reporter at large. J. McPhee. il New Yorker
42:142+ My 7; 144+ My 14 '66
See also
Cookery—Fruit
Orange juice
ORATORIOS
See also
Phonograph records—Oratorios
ORATORY, Outdoor. See Street speaking
ORAZEM, Ed
Jeep patrol tour. Travel 126:43-5 N '66
ORBELO, William R.
Pepperbox pistol. Hobbies 71:126-7 Ag '66
United States pistol model 1816. Hobbies 71:
125 Ap '66
ORBITAL rendezvous (space flight)
Agena ready for Gemini 8 rendezvous. H.
Taylor. il Miss & Roc 18:17 Mr 14 '66
Agena stabilizes in near-circular orbit. il
Aviation W 84:25-8 Mr 28 '66
Apollo plans change; Gemini 8 probed; re-
port by H. Taylor and J. Mercer. il Miss &
Roc 18:12-13 Mr 21 '66
Banner year for Geminis. il Sr Schol 87:3
Ja 7 '66
Color shows Gemini 8 docking, emergency;
photographs. Aviation W 84:99-101 Ap 11
'66
Crew adaptability chief yield of Gemini 9.
W. J. Normyle. il Aviation W 84:31-4 Je
13 '66
Curtailment of Gemini 8 to affect Apollo.
W. J. Normyle. Aviation W 84:30-2 Mr 21
'66
Double troubles; Gemini missions and Apollo
moonship tests. il Newsweek 67:58 My 30
'66
Final Gemini flights assume critical role. E. J.
Bulban. il Aviation W 85:48-9+ Jl 4 '66
Gemini-Apollo rendezvous studied. il Miss &
Roc 18:13 Mr 28 '66
Gemini docking in space. R. N. Watts, jr. il
Sky & Tel 31:274-5 My '66
Gemini 8 launched. J. Eberhart. Sci N 89:
195 Mr 26 '66
Gemini 8's troubled triumph; Agena docking;
rolling; photographs. Time 87:89-92 Ap 1
'66
Gemini flight speedup sought; GT-10 achieve-
ments detailed. il Tech W 19:13-14+ Jl 25
'66
Gemini rendezvous versatility boosted; with
editorial comment. H. Taylor and J. Mer-
cer. il Tech W 18:14-15, 54 Je 13 '66
Gemini 10 crew responsibility increased. W. J.
Normyle. Aviation W 85:37 Jl 11 '66
Gemini 10 goes walking and docking. Sci N
90:71 Jl 30 '66
Heavy traffic in orbit; Gemini 8-Agena mission. il Newsweek 67:94 Mr 21 '66
High tension over the astronauts; Gemini
8-Agena docking. il Life 60:34-5 Mr 25 '66
How to meet in orbit; photographs. Sci Di-
gest 59:20-3 F '66
I docked in space. K. V. Brown. il Pop
Mech 125:114-17+ Mr '66
Moment of the first docking in space; Gemini
8 and the Agena. il Life 60:88-91 Ap 1 '66
Space rendezvous; milestone on the way to
the moon. K. F. Weaver. il Nat Geog Mag
129:538-53 Ap '66
Third rendezvous added to Gemini 9. J. Mercer. Miss & Roc 18:15 Ap 18 '66

ORBITAL rendezvous (space flight)—*Continued*
Walk around the world; Gemini 9 schedule.
Newsweek 67:67 My 16 '66
See also
Space flight—Manned flights—Armstrong-Scott flight, 1966
Space flight—Manned flights—Conrad-Gordon flight, 1966
Space flight—Manned flights—Lovell-Aldrin flight, 1966
Space flight—Manned flights—Stafford-Cernan flight, 1966
Space flight—Manned flights—Young-Collins flight, 1966

ORBITING astronomical observatory. See Artificial satellites—Astronomical applications
ORBITING geophysical observatory. See Artificial satellites—Astronomical applications
ORBITING radio astronomy observatory. See Artificial satellites—Astronomical applications
ORBITING solar observatory. See Artificial satellites—Astronomical applications

ORBITS
Why are all our planets in approximately the same orbital plane? I. Asimov. Sci Digest 59:92-4 Ap '66
ORBITS of artificial satellites. See Artificial satellites—Orbits
ORBITS of communications satellites. See Communications satellites—Orbits

ORCHESTRA shells
Musical shell game. il Fortune 73:160 F '66
ORCHESTRAL conductors. See Conductors (music)
ORCHESTRAL music
See also
Phonograph records—Orchestral music
ORCHESTRAS
Bargaining prospects for major symphony orchestras. L. E. Lunden. Mo Labor R 89:481-4 My '66
City in a hurry; Sao Paulo report. B. R. Marks. Hi Fi 16:MA17+ Ag '66
Elite eleven; U.S. symphony orchestras. il Time 87:62+ Ap 8 '66
Flying the coop. il Time 88:54+ O 7 '66
Lists: international reference guide. Hi Fi 16:256-62 D 15 '66
Lists: North American reference guide; musical organizations throughout the United States (including Puerto Rico) and Canada. Hi Fi 16:182-97 D 15 '66
Mehta's Tosca in the Place des arts; Montreal report. C. L. Osborne. Hi Fi 16:154-5 Ap '66
Music to my ears; Monte-Carlo national orchestra, in Carnegie Hall. I. Kolodin. Sat R 49:73 Ap 16 '66
Orchestras U.S.A, the season's forecast. Hi Fi 16:MA7-10 S '66
Tuning out the tin; Bolivian national symphony. il Time 88:92 S 16 '66
See also
American symphony orchestra league
also names of orchestras. e.g. Israel philharmonic orchestra
ORCHID cactus. See Cactus
ORCHIDS
For April visitors to southern California, the largest orchid show ever held anywhere; World orchid conference show. il Sunset 136:108-9 Ap '66
Orchid for a winter window. J. Kramer. il Flower Grower 53:38 S '66
Protect your orchids from pests and diseases. J. W. Williams. il Horticulture 44:22-3 D '66
These are wild orchids. il Sunset 136:269-70 Ap '66
See also
Ladys slippers
ORD, Edward Otho Cresap
Tale of a table. M. A. Benjamin; reply. Am Heritage 17:100 Je '66
ORDAZ, Gustavo Diaz. See Diaz Ordaz. G.
ORDNANCE
See also
American ordnance association
Gun carriages
Weapons systems
ORDNANCE, Naval
NOTS pressed to meet urgent Viet needs. C. M. Plattner. il Aviation W 85:46-7+ mid-D '66
Vietnam spurs navy weapons advances; research at Naval ordnance test station. Aviation W 84:28-9 Mr 21 '66
ORDNANCE research
Hindsight for progress; Project Hindsight, DOD study of weapons systems. il Sci N 90:473 D 3 '66

ORE deposits
See also
Mines and mineral resources
ORE dressing
Ore-processing seminar. UN Mo Chron 3:22 Mr '66
ORE treatment. See Ore dressing
O'REAR, Eleanor Offutt
Living with antiques. Antiques 89:851-5 Je '66
OREGON
See also
Architecture, Domestic—Oregon
Booksellers and bookselling—Oregon
Cascade Range
Colleges and universities—Oregon
Fishing—Oregon
Forests and forestry—Oregon
Hell's Canyon
Hunting—Oregon
Roads—Oregon
Skis and skiing—Oregon
Waldo Lake

Description and travel
Up and down Oregon's Rogue. il Sunset 136:76-85 Je '66

Politics and government
Dissenter; M. O. Hatfield vs R. B. Duncan. W. J. Cook. Newsweek 68:30 O 3 '66
Monsoon season; race for U.S. Senate seat. Time 88:32 N 4 '66
Morse code. il Newsweek 67:29 Mr 21 '66
Morse of a different color. Reporter 34:9 My 5 '66
Viet Nam race. il Time 88:36 O 14 '66
OREGON flood. See Floods—United States
OREGON university cooperative. See College bookstores
O'REILLY, John
Fishing. Sports Illus 24:70+ Je 6 '66
ORELL, Bernard L.
Friendly debate between two professionals; letter. por Am For 72:31+ Ja; 12+ F '66
ORENSTEIN, Grace Manning
Up Kilimanjaro. Atlan 218:128-31 Jl '66
ORENTREICH, Norman
Science tackles the baldness problem. F. Warshofsky. Read Digest 88:87-91 F '66
—See Berger, R. A. jt. auth.
ORES
See also
Ore dressing
ORESTEIA; drama. See Aeschylus
ORFILA REYNAL, Arnaldo
Mexican uproar. M. Tejada. Nation 202:inside cover, 100 Ja 24 '66
ORGAN
Meet the Mini-organ. W. S. Gohl. il Pop Electr 24:70-1 F '66
ORGAN, Color. See Color organ
ORGAN piece; story. See Morgan, B.
ORGAN PIPE CACTUS NATIONAL MONUMENT
Sonoran Desert National Park: proposal to combine Organ Pipe Cactus National Monument and the Cabeza Prieta game range. W. F. Heald. il Nat Parks Mag 40:4-9 Ap '66
ORGAN recitals
Musical events; performance of Wolfgang von Karajan organ ensemble in Town Hall. W. Sargeant. New Yorker 41:114-15 F 12 '66
Pipe line; unique three-organ ensemble at New York's Town hall. Newsweek 67:90 F 14 '66
ORGANELLES
Protoperithecia in neurospora crassa: technique for studying their development. H. Rothschild and S. R. Suskind. bibliog il Science 154:1356-7 D 9 '66
ORGANIC compounds
Chemical fossils. G. Eglinton and M. Calvin. il Sci Am 216:32-43 Ja '67
Organic compounds in carbonaceous chondrites. M. H. Studier and others; discussion. Science 152:102-7 Ap 1 '66
See also
Electroorganic chemistry
ORGANIC crystals. See Crystallography
ORGANIC evolution. See Evolution
ORGANIC photochemistry. See Photochemistry
ORGANIZATION charts
How to read an organization chart for fun and survival. D. Winks. il Harper 234:38-41 Ja '67

ORGANIZATION for economic cooperation and development
Beating a growth goal; report issued by OECD. Bsns W p98 O 8 '66
Fifteen new centers urged for advanced study. Sci N L 89:67 Ja 29 '66
Growth till '70; Europe's size-up. il U S News 61:90 N 21 '66
OECD ministerial council meets at Paris; texts of statements, November 24, 25; with text of communique issued November 25, 1966. E. V. Rostow. Dept State Bul 56:19-28 Ja 2 '67
President hails OECD progress; text of message, September 28, 1966. L. B. Johnson. Dept State Bul 55:675 O 31 '66
Revamping overseas tax treaties. Bsns W p66 Ja 22 '66

Development assistance committee
Trying harder to feed the poor; DAC to co-ordinate national aid policies. il Bsns W p33-4 Jl 23 '66
World food and population crisis: DAC's fifth annual high-level meeting; statement by Secretary Rusk; remarks by Vice President Humphrey, July 20; statement by O. L. Freeman and message from President Johnson; with texts of communique and recommendation on food problems of less developed countries, July 21, 1966. Dept State Bul 55:199-212 Ag 8 '66

ORGANIZATION for European nuclear research. See European organization for nuclear research

ORGANIZATION of African unity
Cooperation for order in Africa. V. McKay. Cur Hist 50:129-34+ Mr '66
Disarray in Addis. Time 87:31 Mr 11 '66
LBJ on Africa; delegates White House visit. Newsweek 67:24-5 Je 6 '66
Message to OAU assembly; November 5, 1966. Thant. UN Mo Chron 3:75 D '66
Setback for the African left; summit conference. C. Sterling. il Reporter 35:21-3 D 1 '66

ORGANIZATION of American states
Drafting a new charter. G. de Zéndegui. il Américas 18:1-3 Ap '66
[Editorial; OAS/OCAS agreement] G. de Zéndegui. Américas 18:inside cover S '66
Inaugural message; excerpts, ed. by G. de Zéndegui. E. R. Aislán. Américas 18: inside cover D '66
Labor meeting; Permanent technical committee on labor affairs (COTPAL) G. Meek. il Américas 18:45-6 N '66
Non-alignment and poor nations. Commonweal 84:189-90 My 6 '66
OAS in action. See issues of Américas
Santo Domingo; labyrinth of policy; perils of an international force. T. Mockler. il Nation 202:154-7 F 7 '66
Toward new dimensions for the OAS: second special Inter-American conference; with excerpts from statements by delegates. G. Meek. il Américas 18:1-14 Ja '66
See also
Inter-American commission of women
Inter-American cultural council
Inter-American economic and social council

ORGANIZATION of Central American states
[Editorial; OAS/OCAS agreement] G. de Zéndegui. Américas 18:inside cover S '66
OAS council; agreement with ODECA. Américas 18:43 Mr '66
Progress of Central American regional integration hailed; statement, October 14, 1966. L. Gordon. Dept State Bul 55:716 N 7 '66

ORGANIZED crime. See Crime and criminals—United States

ORGANIZERS, Labor. See Trade unions—Officials

ORGANOPHOSPHORAMIDE compounds. See Phosphorus compounds

ORGANS, Artificial. See Prosthesis

ORIENT. See Asia; Far East

ORIENT and Occident. See East and West

ORIENTAL astronomy. See Astronomy, Oriental

ORIENTAL dancing. See Dancing, Oriental

ORIENTAL flowering cherry
Washington's flowering cherries. C. W. Heine. il Horticulture 44:30-1+ Ap '66

ORIENTAL Olympics. See Asiad (games)

ORIENTATION
Homing ability strong in some Trinidad bats. Sci N 89:331 My 7 '66
Mice may navigate by moon and stars. Sci N 89:237 Ap 9 '66

Navigation of penguins. J. T. Emlen and R. L. Penney. il Sci Am 215:104-13 O '66
Navigation of single homing pigeons: airplane observations by radio tracking. M. C. Michener and C. Walcott. bibliog il Science 154:410-13 O 21 '66
North sky guides birds. P. McBroom. Sci N 90:152 S 3 '66
Time and space in the life of the bee. M. Renner. il Natur Hist 75:52-7 O '66

ORIGIN of life. See Life (biology)

ORIGIN of man. See Man—Origin and antiquity

ORIGIN of species. See Evolution

ORIGINAL sin. See Sin

ORILLIA, Ontario

Historic houses, etc.
He left us laughing; Stephen Leacock memorial home. E. Logan. Sr Schol 88:sup6 Mr 18 '66

ORIOLES
Soft blanket, tough nest. E. M. White. Audubon Mag 68:124 Mr '66

ORIOLES (baseball) See Baseball clubs

O'RIORDAN, J. L. H. and others
Thyrocalcitonin: ultracentrifugation in gradients of sucrose. bibliog Science 154:885-6 N 18 '66

ORISKANY fire. See Aircraft carriers—Fires and fire protection

ORLANDO, Fla.
Use LP gas and save. J. E. Pipkin. il Am City 81:88-9 Je '66

Music
Orlando. M. E. Peltz. Opera N 30:31 Mr 26 '66

ORLÉANS, François Ferdinand Philippe Louis Marie d', prince de Joinville. See Joinville, F. F. P. L. M. d'O.

ORLEANS, Leo A.
Dealing with population problems. Bul Atomic Sci 22:22-6 Je '66

ORLINSKY, Harry M.
Revelation in translation. Sat R 49:46 D 3 '66

ORLOV, Alexander
How Stalin relieved Spain of $600,000,000. Read Digest 89:37-8+ N '66

ORLOV, Vladimir
USSR libraries: a status report; excerpts from editorial from Biblioteki SSSR. ALA Bul 60:648-50 Je '66

ORMANDY, Eugene
And we quote . . ; ed. by C. L. Osborne. por Hi Fi 16:MA11+ N '66

ORME, Frank
TV for children. il Parents Mag 41:54-5+ F '66

ORMOND BEACH, Fla.
Continuous-flow refuse collection. G. F. Althouse. il Am City 81:90-1 D '66

ORMSBEE, Thomas H.
Antiques: questions & answers. See issues of House & garden incorporating Living for young homemakers

ORMSBY, Virginia H.
Vacation with typewriter and drawing board. NEA J 55:36 My '66

ORMSBY GORE, Jane Teresa Denyse. See Rainey, J. T. D. O. G.

ORNAMENTAL cookery. See Cookery, Ornamental

ORNAMENTAL glass. See Glass, Ornamental

ORNAMENTAL plants. See Plants, Ornamental

ORNAMENTS (printing) See Printing—Design

ORNAMENTS, Christmas tree. See Christmas decorations

ORNE, Jerrold
Library education and the talent shortage. por Library J 91:1763-4 Ap 1 '66

ORNITHINE transcarbamylase enzymes. See Enzymes

ORNITHINE-urea cycle enzymes. See Enzymes

ORNITZ, Don
Big splash. il U S Camera 29:62-3 S '66
Crazy goings-on behind the picture. il U S Camera 29:62-4 Jl '66

ORÓ, J. and Han, J.
High-temperature synthesis of aromatic hydrocarbons from methane. bibliog Science 153:1393-5 S 16 '66
—and others
Alkanes in fungal spores. bibliog Science 154: 399-400 O 21 '66

ORPHANS and orphan asylums
Environment important; study and follow-up study of orphans. Sci N 90:248 O 1 '66

ORR, Bobby
Boston's Bobby. il por Newsweek 68:77 N 21 '66
High price for fresh northern ice. F. Deford. il por Sports Illus 25:60-2 O 17 '66

ORTH, Franklin L.
Excerpt from testimony, May 21, 1965. Cong Digest 45:305+ D '66

ORTH, Penelope
Data on data. Mlle 64:104-5+ Ja '67

ORTHAIRTOME. See Surgical instruments and apparatus

ORTHODONTICS
What parents ask about corrective dentistry. J. A. Carey. il Todays Health 44:28-31 Mr '66

ORTHODOX Eastern church
Ecumenical shift in the Middle East; reflections on Protestant-Orthodox relations. C. S. Calian. Christian Cent 83:1140-2 S 21 '66

ORTHODOX Eastern church, Russian
Open letters of protest and their aftermath. America 115:267 S 17 '66
Orthodoxy in Russia; concerning open letter to the patriarch and the presidium of the supreme Soviet. J. R. Nelson. Christian Cent 83:1170-1 S 28 '66
Two who dared to protest. America 114:820 Je 11 '66

ORTHODOX Eastern church in the Near East
Ecumenical shift in the Middle East; reflections on Protestant-Orthodox relations. C. S. Calian. Christian Cent 83:1140-2 S 21 '66

ORTHOPEDIA
Metal implants help hip victims walk better. F. Marley. il Sci N 90:321 O 22 '66

ORTHOPEDIC apparatus
Light leg designed; new device replaces heavy metal braces. Sci N 90:190 S 10 '66

ORTHOPEDIC walkers. See Walkers, Orthopedic

ORTHOPTERA
Nature note; straight wings. Sci N 89:254 Ap 9 '66
See also
Stick insects

ORTIZ, Carlos
Cops and robbers in Mexico city. M. Kram. il por Sports Illus 25:26-9 O 31 '66
Lightweight decision. il Newsweek 68:94-5 N 7 '66

ORTUÑO, René Barrientos. See Barrientos Ortuño, R.

ORVILLE, Richard E.
High-speed, time-resolved spectrum of a lightning stroke. bibliog Science 151:451 Ja 28 '66

ORWELL, George, pseud.
Crystal spirit, by G. Woodcock. Review Reporter 35:54+ O 6 '66. R. Mayne
I wasn't born for an age like this, was Smith? was Jones? were you? G. Woodcock. por Esquire 66:142-5+ S '66

OSAKA international festival. See Music festivals—Japan

OSBORN, Fairfield
Wildlife conservation. por Parks & Rec 1: 646-7+ Ag '66

OSBORN, M. Sheldon
Corporate goals & the outside expert. Duns R 87:pt2 108-9+ Mr '66

OSBORN, Rebecca M.
College stress and illness. Sci Digest 60:22-4 D '66

OSBORN, Robert Chesley
American way of love. il Sat Eve Post 239: 28-9 D 31 '66

about
Second fame: good food. N. Lyon il por Vogue 147:148-50 Mr 15 '66

OSBORN, Robert T.
Sex and the single God. Christian Cent 83: 1078-80 S 7 '66

OSBORNE, Conrad L.
At Caramoor: Curlew river, Escorial. Hi Fi 16:MA14-15 S '66
At City opera, a Handel hit. Hi Fi 16:MA8-10 D '66
At the Met, Mehta, Tucci, Tebaldi, Caballe. Hi Fi 16:122-3+ Mr '66
Cav & Pag, Karajan/La Scala style. Hi Fi 16:124-5 O '66
Columbia's Falstaff: it goes at once to the windswept summit. Hi Fi 16:79-80 D '66
Completion of London's Ring; a Walküre to fulfill all promise. Hi Fi 16:93-4+ N '66
Lohengrin in its entirety, with the full forces of Boston. Hi Fi 16:83-4 S '66
Mehta's Tosca in the Place des arts. Hi Fi 16:154-5 Ap '66
Met: Giovanni, Chénier return. Hi Fi 16: 142-3+ Ap '66

National company takes its stand. Hi Fi 16:122-5 F '66
New Met, a progress report. Hi Fi 16:MA11+ Jl '66
Rameau as master of lyric tragedy. Hi Fi 16:65-6 Jl '66
Rudel and company in the new house. Hi Fi 16:128+ My '66
Summer opera new and nervy. Hi Fi 16:MA16-17+ N '66
Tape underground. Hi Fi 16:44-8 Ag '66
Too much too soon. Opera N 31:6-7 D 24 '66
Verdi's Don Carlo. Hi Fi 16:83-5 Ap '66
Wagner operas on records. Hi Fi 16:78-82+ N: 26+ D '66

OSBORNE, John, 1907-
Evelyn Waugh faces Life and vice versa. Atlan 218:114-15 D '66
How to keep school segregation. New Repub 154:16-18 Mr 12 '66

OSBORNE, John, 1929-
Bond honoured; adaptation of play by L. de Vega. Criticism
Vogue 148:206 S 1 '66
Inadmissible evidence. Criticism
Commentary 41:75 Mr '66
Harper 232:125 Ap '66
Nat R 18:325-7 Ap 5 '66
Notes and comment. New Yorker 42:47 O 8 '66

OSBORNE, Karl
Follow the drum beat. por Outdoor Life 137: 50-1+ Ap '66
Midwinter specktacle. Outdoor Life 137:60-1+ F '66

OSBORNE, M. Sheldon
Design at the top. Duns R 88:135-6 N '66

OSCARS (prizes) See Academy awards (moving picures)

OSCILLATORS
Build light-to-sound translator; code practice oscillators. L. Vicens. il Pop Electr 24:74-5+ Je '66
Selecting a sweep frequency generator. S. C. Allen. il Electr World 76:88-92 N '66
See also
Multivibrators
Pulse generators

OSCILLOGRAPHS
Designing an oscilloscope vertical attenuator. D. R. Hicke. il Electr World 76:94-6 S '66
Oscilloscope probes. W. H. Buchsbaum. il Electr World 76:46-8 Ag '66
Sampling oscilloscope displays 12,400-MHz r.f. il Electr World 76:66 O '66
Sampling oscilloscopes. S. L. Silver. il Electr World 75:47-9+ Je '66

OSCILLOSCOPE calibrators. See Calibrators

OSCILLOSCOPES. See Oscillographs

OSER, Bernard L.
How safe are the chemicals in our food? Todays Health 44:61-4 Mr '66

OSHIN, Edith Sonn
How to work with a kitchen planner. House & Gard 130:240-1+ O '66
Is it any of their business? N Y Times Mag p 121+ My 1 '66
Parent and child (cont) N Y Times Mag p97-8 Mr 27 '66

OSLO
Architecture
Norwegian terrace housing: high-density on an unbuildable hillside. il Arch Rec 139: 162-3 Ja '66

OSMIUM black. See Stains and staining (microscopy)

OSMOSIS
Osmosis purifies water; using reverse osmosis. Sci N 89:290 Ap 23 '66
See also
Biological transport

OSSIFICATION. See Bone

OSSINING, N.Y. public library
Out of the ivory tower into the grease pit. E. Sclar. il Library J 91:2162-4+ Ap 15 '66

OSTEN, J. J.
What, if anything, is wrong with American wives? Mlle 63:175+ My '66

OSTEOLATHYRISM. See Lathyrism

OSTEOLYTIC sterols. See Sterols

OSTRACODS
Mummified pleistocene ostracods in Alaska. R. A. M. Schmidt and P. V. Sellmann. bibliog il Science 153:167-8 Jl 8 '66

OSTRANDER, Gilman M.
Nevada: the rotten borough. Nation 202: 452-5 Ap 18 '66

OSTRANDER, Sheila
Canada's birthday party. Mlle 64:120 Ja '67

OSTREM, Walter M.
Ruhr university Bochum library. bibliog Wilson Lib Bul 41:418-20 D '66

OSTRIKER, Alicia
Anti-critic. Commentary 41:83-4 Je '66

OSTROFF, Anthony
Asking about the beggars; poem. Sat R 49:55 Je 25 '66

OSTROFF, Eugene
Restoration of photographs by neutron activation. bibliog Science 154:119-23 O 7 '66

OSTROW, Ronald J.
New controversy involving Justice Douglas; reprint from Los Angeles times, October 16, 1966. U S News 61:66-8 O 31 '66

O'SULLIVAN, A. Don
Griffiths' gift; story. Mlle 62:139 F '66

OSWALD, James R.
Novel movie effects. U S Camera 29:74-5 S '66
Try rear-illuminated titles! U S Camera 30:70-1 Ja '67

OSWALD, Lee Harvey
Assassination syndrome fits Lee Oswald. Sci N 90:229 S 24 '66
Deep and growing doubts. Newsweek 68:36+ O 10 '66
Failure of the Warren report. A. M. Bickel. Commentary 42:31-9 O '66
Mother in history, by J. Stafford. Review Sat R 49:33-4 Mr 5 '66. G. Hicks
Rush to judgment, by M. Lane. Review Newsweek 68:30-3 Ag 15 '66
Truth about Kennedy assassination; with theories by A. Specter. il pors U S News 61:44-50+ O 10 '66
Warren commission: the critics and the law; theories of E. J. Epstein and M. Lane. K. Goodall; A. L. Goodhart. Reporter 35:44-8+ D 15 '66

OSWALD, Marguerite
Mother in history, by J. Stafford. Review New Repub 154:22-3 Mr 26 '66. P. Richard
Sat R 49:33-4 Mr 5 '66. G. Hicks

OSWALD, Marina
Forgotten widows of the Kennedy tragedy. L. A. Harris. il pors Good H 162:94-7+ Ap '66

OTHELLO; drama. See Shakespeare, W.—Plays

OTIS, Denise
Fresh spring of ideas bubbling in an ancient land. House & Gard 130:178-83+ D '66
Going places, finding things in Hawaii. House & Gard 130:25+ Ag '66

O'TOOLE, Peter
Steal-scening with Hepburn & O'Toole. V. Leduc. por Vogue 147:172-3+ Ap 1 '66

OTT, John F.
Story of Esther. Sat R 49:79+ O 15 '66

OTTAVIANI, Alfredo, cardinal
Letter from Rome. por Newsweek 68:99 S 19 '66

OTTAWAY, David. See Braestrup, P. jt. auth.

OTTEN, Alan L. and Seib, C. B.
Minor masterpiece of Ray C. Bliss. Reporter 34:35-8 F 10 '66

OTTERMAN, Joseph, and Bronner, F. E.
Martian wave of darkening: a frost phenomenon? bibliog Science 153:56-60 Jl 1 '66

OTTERS
Otter that uses its head. il Sci Digest 60:56 Ag '66

OTTIANO, John W.
Artist-teacher. Sch Arts 65:27-32 F '66

OTTO, archduke of Austria
Habsburg happening. il por Time 88:36 N 11 '66

OTTO, John
John Otto: letter writer extraordinary. C. Foley. il por Am For 72:40-2 Ap '66

OTTO, Rosina Maria Francesca. See Dakin, R. M. F. O.

OTTUM, Bob
Motor sports (cont) Sports Illus 25:58-9 N 7 '66
Olympic games. Sports Illus 24:68-9 My 9 '66
Skiing (cont) Sports Illus 24:52-5 Mr 7 '66
Three names and a barrel of money. Sports Illus 26:52-8 Ja 16 '67

OUDES, Bruce J.
Food for freedom: paradox of foreign aid. Nation 203:120-4 Ag 8 '66

OUFKIR, Mohammed
L'affaire Ben Barka. il por Time 87:33 Ja 28 '66
Ben Barka affair. C. Sterling. il Reporter 34:22-8 Mr 10 '66
Ben Barka is dead. A. Werth. Nation 202:350-2 Mr 28 '66
Diminished fifth. por Newsweek 67:44+ Ja 31 '66

Enter the CIA. il por Newsweek 67:32 F 7 '66
Fine French scandal over a missing Moroccan. il Life 60:30-32B F 4 '66
Silent witnesses. Time 87:32 F 4 '66
Trial begins. Newsweek 68:46+ S 19 '66

OULAHAN, Richard
Case of the missing H-bomb. Life 60:106A-106B+ F 25 '66
Life movie review (cont) Life 61:12 Jl 29 '66

OUMANSKY, Valentina
It's never enough just to imitate. V. H. Swisher. por Dance Mag 40:30-1 Je '66

OUT of print books. See Books—Out of print books

OUT-of-town newspaper stands. See Newspaper vendors

OUTBOARD boating club of San Diego. See Boat clubs

OUTBOARD electric engines. See Electric engines, Outboard

OUTBOARD motor boat racing. See Motor boat racing

OUTBOARD motors. See Gas and oil engines, Outboard

OUTDOOR Christmas decorations. See Christmas decorations, Outdoor

OUTDOOR cookery. See Cookery, Outdoor

OUTDOOR education
See also
Outward bound schools

OUTDOOR fireplaces. See Fireplaces, Outdoor

OUTDOOR furniture. See Furniture, Outdoor

OUTDOOR games. See Games

OUTDOOR kitchens. See Kitchens, Outdoor

OUTDOOR life
Camper, go home! C. B. Colby. Outdoor Life 137:18-20+ F '66
We take to the woods. C. Chilman. il Parents Mag 41:56-8+ Je '66
What every new camper should know. C. Conley. il Field & S 71:50-3+ Je '66
What's happening to camping? C. B. Colby. Outdoor Life 137:24+ Mr '66
See also
Camping
House boats
Hunting
Sierra club
Survival (after airplane accidents, shipwrecks, etc)
Tents
Vacations
Walking

Anecdotes, facetiae, satire, etc.
Outdoors. T. Williams. il Esquire 66:31-2+ O '66

OUTDOOR lighting. See Lighting, Outdoor

OUTDOOR meals
Party throw-aways. il House & Gard 129:146-7+ Je '66
Simple but elegant back-yard party. K. Smith. il Pop Gard 17:46-9+ Ag '66
Take-along foods for traveling families; with recipes. il Redbook 126:97-9+ Ap '66
There's a hot lunch in each knapsack il Sunset 136:152 F '66
Tucson: partying poolside. il Ladies Home J 83:120+ O '66
See also
Barbecue cookery
Cookery, Outdoor
Picnics

OUTDOOR recreation. See Recreation

OUTDOOR rooms
And here's a yard full of outdoor living! il Bet Hom & Gard 44:50-1 Ag '66
Build a care-free concrete patio. J. H. Ingersoll. il Pop Gard 17:46-7 Mr '66
Cavalier residence, Marin County, California. il Arch Rec 139:56-9 mid-My '66
Extend your living space with a deck. D. Huff. il Pop Sci 188:137-41+ Ap '66
How to build a flagstone terrace. J. J. Simpkins. il Flower Grower 53:50-1 Je '66
How to ring an old style-setter with up-to-date delights. il House & Gard 130:96-9 Ag '66
It's the deck that makes this garden. il Sunset 137:189 S '66
Lyman residence, Dover, Massachusetts. il Arch Rec 139:90-5 mid-My '66
Make room for summer; three patio substitutes. il Pop Mech 125:154-8 Ap '66
More garden for less work. A. W. Wood. il Farm J 90:122-3 Mr '66
Neuman residence, Baltimore County, Maryland. il Arch Rec 139:84-7 mid-My '66
New carport is also a party court. il Sunset 136:104-5 Ap '66

OUTDOOR rooms—*Continued*
New family room looks out on a new terrace, new veranda overlooks the pool. il Sunset 136:114-15 My '66
New terrace for an old house. il Flower Grower 53:34 N '66
New wing+new landscaping=a perfect about-face. il House & Gard 130:86-7 Ag '66
Outdoor hobby of an interior decorator. W. Radcliffe. il Pop Gard 17:26-9 My '66
Outside room the whole family can enjoy. il Pop Gard 17:74-5+ My '66
Patio and garden pool for summer living. M. P. Borman. il Flower Grower 53:30-1 Je '66
Terrace for people who like flowers. S. Stewart. il Pop Gard 17:6 Mr '66
Terrace to live in. E. B. McClure. il Pop Gard 17:10 D '66
They simply did over the outside. il Sunset 136:110-12 Ap '66
This is the year to build a wood deck. il Pop Gard 17:24-7 Mr '66
This old Victorian in San Francisco now opens up for private outdoor living. il Sunset 136:82-3 Mr '66
Time for fall maintenance. il Pop Gard 17: 58-9 D '66
2,000 square feet of comfort and convenience. N. Seney. il Bet Hom & Gard 44:60-3 S '66
With the new deck it's a different house. il Sunset 136:90 F '66
See also
Breezeways
Courtyards
Screens (sun)

Lighting
Patio lights for spring nights. il Pop Gard 17:34-9+ My '66

Snow melting systems
Double your outdoor living time. il Pop Gard 17:8+ Mr '66
OUTDOOR speaking. See Street speaking
OUTDOOR theater. See Theater. Open air
OUTER MONGOLIA. See Mongolia
OUTER space. See Space, Outer
OUTLAWS
See also
Brigands and robbers
OUTLER, Albert C.
Council, one year later. Commonweal 85:368-9 Ja 6 '67
Reflections of a council observer; interview, ed. by E. M. Gaffney. por Cath World 203: 353-60 S '66
OUTPATIENT service. See Hospitals—Outpatient service
OUTPUT of workers. See Labor productivity
OUTWARD bound schools
Babes in the woods; first girls' Outward bound program in this hemisphere. B. La Fontaine. il Sports Illus 25:60-2+ Jl 11; 44-6+ Jl 18 '66
Outward bound! twenty-four girls at Minnesota outward bound school, August 1966. G. Caesar. il Seventeen 25:92-3+ Jl '66
Rugged camps turn boys into iron men; Outward bound camps. J. R. Berry. il Pop Mech 125:116-19+ My '66
OVARIAN tumors. See Tumors
OVEN dinners. See Dinners and dining
OVENS, Smoke. See Smoke ovens
OVER-the-counter market. See Stocks—Marketing
OVERBECK, Adriaen van. See Overbeke, A. van
OVERBEKE, Adriaen van
Gallery for young people. C. B. Johnson. il Sch Arts 66:42 D '66
OVERBREATHING. See Respiration
OVERDUE books. See School libraries—Circulation, loans, etc.
OVERHAGE, Carl F. J.
Command-and-control problems; reply to address by V. M. Clapp. Library J 91:1171 Mr 1 '66
Plans for Project Intrex. bibliog Science 152: 1032-7 My 20 '66
OVERHEAD projectors. See Projection apparatus
OVERMYER, Daniel Harrison
Fourth network. R. L. Shayon. Sat R 49:39 Ag 27 '66
Wizard of the warehouse. R. Levy. il por Duns R 87:49-50 My '66
OVERPOPULATION. See Population—Overpopulation
OVERSEAS employees. See Americans in foreign countries—Employment

OVERSEAS spending. See Investments, Foreign
OVERSEAS weekly (newspaper)
Stars and stripes forever. il Newsweek 68: 63 Jl 18 '66
OVERTIME
Leisure and the long workweek. P. Henle. il Mo Labor R 89:721-7 Jl '66
Overtime hours and premium pay, May 1965. J. R. Wetzel. il Mo Labor R 89:973-7 S '66
OVERWEIGHT. See Corpulence
OVULATION
See also
Estruation
OWATONNA, Minn.
Chalet and a footbridge. R. Pecore and R. Rano. il Am City 81:118-19 Ap '66
OWEN, Allen
4-foot-11 marine to be looked up to. il pors Life 60:113-14 My 6 '66
OWEN, D. F.
Polymorphism in pleistocene land snails. bibliog Science 152:71-2 Ap 1 '66
OWEN, Jean Z.
Ten pitfalls and how to avoid them. Writer 79:15-17+ Jl '66
OWEN, Mickey
I've been living with it a long time. W. C. Heinz. il pors Sat Eve Post 239:112-17 O 8 '66
OWEN, Richard
Crucifixion; poem. Christian Cent 83:395 Mr 30 '66
OWEN, Robert
Angel in the forest, by M. Young. Review
New Repub 154:25-7 Mr 12 '66. N. O'Gorman
OWEN, Thomas
Make a low cost slave tripper. Pop Mech 127: 173+ Ja '67
OWEN, Wilfred
Fable of the American cities; address, September 13, 1966. U S News 61:77-8 O 3 '66
Grateful society: an urban fable. Arch Forum 125:92 O '66
OWENS, Rochelle
Beclch. Criticism
Sat R 50:111 Ja 7 '67
OWENS, W. H.
Hong Kong a thirsty city. UNESCO Courier 19:24-6 F '66
New patterns of transport for Africa. UNESCO Courier 19:11-15 Ja '66
OWENS, William A.
We had us some Christmas! story; excerpt from This stubborn soil. Ladies Home J 83: 100-1 D '66
OWENS-Illinois, incorporated
Warm glow at O-I; ventures in plywood, TV tubes, and plastics. il Bsns W p82-3 Ap 2 '66
OWLS
Owl in the kitchen; great horned owl, in home of P. and M. Dayton (Teacher of the year, 1966) D. Chapman. il Look 30:100+ D 13 '66
OXATHIIN
Fungicide selective for basidiomycetes. L. V. Edgington and others. il Science 153: 307-8 Jl 15 '66
Systemic fungicidal activity of 1,4-oxathiin derivatives. B. Von Schmeling and M. Kulka. il Science 152:659-60 Ap 29 '66
OXENFELDT, Alfred R.
Product line pricing. Harvard Bsns R 44:137-44 Jl '66
OXENHOPE; story. See Warner, S. T.
OXFAM. See Oxford committee for famine relief
OXFORD AND ASQUITH, Herbert Henry Asquith, 1st earl of
Asquith, by R. Jenkins. Review
New Repub 154:29-31 My 7 '66. J. F. Golay
OXFORD committee for famine relief
Drought knows no frontiers; Africa and India; aid measures. G. Ash. il UNESCO Courier 19:10-15 Ap '66
OXFORD University
Just a guy at Oxford; Princeton basketball star B. Bradley. J. Mann. il Sports Illus 24:52-8+ F 7 '66
Letter from abroad; American woman in an English-university community. D. Trilling. il McCalls 93:36+ Jl '66
Oxford looks beneath the ivy. H. G. Nicholas. il Reporter 34:30-2 Je 16 '66
R for Oxford; Franks commission reform proposals. Newsweek 67:98-9 My 23 '66
Seating a poet. Time 87:31 F 11 '66
What's wrong with Oxford? report by seven top Oxford scholars. Time 87:73-4 My 20 '66
See also
Rhodes scholars and scholarships

OXFORD university players
Liz launches 1,000 ships; the Burtons play Faustus at Oxford; with report by M. Smith. il Life 60:78-9+ Mr 4 '66
OXIDATION, Electrolytic
Synthetic electroorganic chemistry. S. Wawzonek. bibliog il Science 155:39-44 Ja 6 '67
OXIDATION ditches. See Sewage disposal
OXIDATION reduction reaction
Oxidation of graphitic carbon in certain soils. E. A. Shneour. bibliog il Science 151: 991-2 F 25 '66
Photochemical evolution of oxygen from certain aqueous solutions. B. Behar and G. Stein. bibliog Science 154:1012-13 N 25 '66
Retrograde melting in the system Mg-Fe-Si-O. D. H. Speidel and R. H. Nafziger. bibliog il Science 152:1367-8 Je 3 '66
Reversible inactivation of aged solutions of indolyl-3-acetic acid. A. A. Bitancourt. bibliog il Science 154:1327-9 D 9 '66
See also
Reduction, Electrolytic
OXYGEN
AF probes fires in 100 per cent oxygen. Miss & Roc 18:31-2 Mr 7 '66
Oxygen as a primary species in radiolysis of water. M. Daniels and E. Wigg. bibliog il Science 153:1533-4 S 23 '66
Role of oxygen. L. V. Berkner and L. C. Marshall. il Sat R 49:30-4 My 7 '66
See also
Hyperbaric oxygenation
Space vehicles—Cabin atmospheres

Isotopes

Isotopic evidence on the early life history of nautilus pompilius. Linné. R. Eichler and H. Ristedt. bibliog il Science 153:734-6 Ag 12 '66
Isotopic paleotemperatures. C. Emiliani. bibliog il Science 154:851-7 N 18 '66
Oxygen and carbon isotopic composition of limestones and dolomites, Bikini and Eniwetok atolls. M. G. Gross and J. I. Tracy, jr. bibliog il Science 151:1082-4 Mr 4 '66
Oxygen isotope fractionation in the system dolomite-calcite-carbon dioxide. J. R. O'Neil and S. Epstein. bibliog il Science 152:198-201 Ap 8 '66
Oxygen isotope studies of Ivory Coast tektites and impactite glass from the Bosumtwi crater, Ghana. H. P. Taylor, jr. and S. Epstein. bibliog il Science 153:173-5 Jl 8 '66
Quartz and magnetite: oxygen-18-oxygen-16 fractionation in metamorphosed Biwabik iron formation. E. C. Perry, jr. and B. Bonnichsen. bibliog il Science 153:528-9 Jl 29 '66

Physiological effects

Cyanide intoxication: protection with oxygen. J. L. Way and others. bibliog il Science 152:210-11 Ap 8 '66
OXYGEN deficiency. See Anoxemia
OXYGEN in rocks. See Gases in rocks
OXYGEN in the body
Blood gases: continuous in vivo recording of partial pressures by mass spectrography. S. Woldring and others. bibliog il Science 153: 885-7 Ag 19 '66
Lactate dehydrogenase isozymes of chick embryo: response to variations of ambient oxygen tension. S. Lindy and M. Rajasalmi. bibliog il Science 153:1401-3 S 16 '66
Oxygen consumption of a flying bird. V. A. Tucker. bibliog il Science 154:150-1 O 7 '66
Oxygen dependence of retinal S-potential-producing cells. K. Negishi and G. Svaetichin. bibliog il Science 152:1621-3 Je 17 '66
Survival of mammals breathing organic liquids equilibrated with oxygen at atmospheric pressure. L. C. Clark, jr. and F. Gollan. bibliog il Science 152:1755-6 Je 24 '66
OXYGEN process. See Steel metallurgy
OXYGENATION, Hyperbaric. See Hyperbaric oxygenation
OXYTOCIN
Deamino-oxytocin and 1-γ-mercaptobutyric acid-oxytocin: X-ray crystallographic data. B. W. Low and C. C. H. Chen. bibliog il Science 151:1552-3 Mr 25 '66
OYSTER BAY, N.Y.

Sanitary affairs

Smile, your incinerator is on TV. V. J. Cerniglia and A. Friedland. il Am City 81:110-12 Ap '66

OYSTER culture
New program in bays: aquaculture of oysters. Sci N L 89:72 Ja 29 '66
OYSTERS
See also
Pearls

Diseases and pests

Fluorescent-antibody studies of haplosporidian parasites of oysters in Chesapeake and Delaware Bays. J. H. Barrow, jr. and B. C. Taylor. bibliog il Science 153:1531-3 S 23 '66
Minchinia nelsoni n. sp. (haplosporid. haplosporidiidae) causative agent of the Delaware Bay oyster epizoötic. H. H. Haskin and others. bibliog il Science 153:1414-16 S 16 '66
Spores give clues to oyster killer; Delaware Bay disease, caused by MSX parasite. Sci N 90:424 N 19 '66
Sporulation of minchinia nelsoni, haplosporida, haplosporidiidae, in crassostrea virginica, gmelin. J. A. Couch and others. bibliog il Science 153:1529-31 S 23 '66

Parasites

See Parasites—Mollusks
OZACHROME. See Photography—Films
OZARK air lines
Trend seen in merger of Ozark, Central. H. D. Watkins. Aviation W 85:41 S 26 '66
OZARKS, LAKE OF. See Lake of the Ozarks
OZITE corporation
Now you can have a wall-to-wall lawn; all-synthetic carpeting for poolsides, patios, sidewalks and supermarkets. il Bsns W p88-90+ Jl 16 '66
OZMON, Ray
Boost sale weights 150 lbs. per calf. il Farm J 90:70-1 Mr '66
OZONE
Ozone and sulfur dioxide synergism: injury to tobacco plants. H. A. Menser and H. E. Heggestad. bibliog il Science 153:424-5 Jl 22 '66
Ozone-induced chemiluminescence of organic compounds. R. L. Bowman and N. Alexander. bibliog il Science 154:1454-6 D 16 '66
Ozone: nonlinear relation of dose and injury in plants. W. W. Heck and others. bibliog il Science 151:577-8 F 4 '66; Reply. F. D. H. Macdowall and others. 153:1552 S 23 '66

P

PAGEOS (passive geodetic earth orbiting satellite) See Artificial satellites—Mapping applications
PCM (pulse code modulation) See Space telemetry
PEN club
Events leading up to the banquet; International congress, New York. D. Dempsey. Sat R 49:28-9 Je 4 '66
500 writers to attend P.E.N. congress in New York. Pub W 189:58-9 My 30 '66
International P.E.N. congress in New York; report of 34th international congress. il Pub W 190:30-40 Jl 18 '66
Mightier than the sword; 34th international PEN congress. Nat R 18:665-6 Jl 12 '66
Pablo Neruda: the poet in New York. J. Yglesias. Nation 203:52-5 Jl 11 '66
P.E.N. club panel decides: pornography is here to stay; summary of discussion. Pub W 189:72-3 F 28 '66
P.E.N. congress continues to evoke global politics: Soviet and Cuban responses. Pub W 190:37-8 Ag 8 '66
P.E.N. pals; congress convenes in New York. il Newsweek 67:96+ Je 27 '66
Role of P.E.N; regenerating the morale of the writer. A. Miller. il Sat R 49:16-17 Je 4 '66
S.E.X. and the P.E.N; American center monthly meeting discusses pornography. D. Dempsey. Sat R 49:31 Mr 12 '66
View from the East. I. Boldizsar. Nation 203:55-9 Jl 11 '66
Writer as independent spirit; history of club. L. Galantière. Sat R 49:30+ Je 4 '66
PERT (program evaluation and review technique) See Criticial path analysis
P. F. Collier and son corporation. See Collier, P. F. and son, corporation
Ph.D. degrees. See Degrees, Academic

PIA. See Printing industries of America, incorporated

PKI (Indonesian Communist party) See Communist party (Indonesia)

PKU. See Phenylketonuria

PLA. See American library association—Public library association

PLA (People's liberation army) See China (People's Republic)—Armed forces

PMA. See Pacific maritime association

POAU. See Protestants and other Americans united for separation of church and state

PPA. See Publishers' publicity association

PR newswire association, incorporated
Broad tape gets a competitor; PR newswire competing against Dow Jones' news service. il Bsns W p 147-8+ My 21 '66

PRN. See PR newswire association, incorporated

PTA. See Parents and teachers associations

PX. See United States—Armed forces—Post exchanges

PX-15. See Submarine boats

PACE, N. R. and Spiegelman, S.
In vitro synthesis of an infectious mutant RNA with a normal RNA replicase. bibliog Science 153:64-7 Jl 1 '66

PACEMAKER, Heart. See Medical instruments and apparatus

PACIFIC airways. See Airways

PACIFIC books
Pacific books sold to Henry Pontleithner. Pub W 190:49 Jl 18 '66

PACIFIC cables. See Cables, Submarine

PACIFIC Coast opera company
Los Angeles. A. Goldberg. il Opera N 30: 28 Je 4 '66

PACIFIC Coast states. See Northwest; West

PACIFIC countries
Future of the Pacific community; address, November 15, 1966. D. Rusk. Dept State Bul 55:838-43 D 5 '66

PACIFIC economic community (proposed)
Pacific trade winds blow. America 115:475 O 22 '66

PACIFIC GROVE, Calif.
Conference center in a resort setting; Asilomar hotel and conference grounds. il Arch Rec 140:128-9 Ag '66

PACIFIC ISLANDS. See Islands of the Pacific

PACIFIC maritime association
1966 West coast longshore negotiations. M. D. Kossoris. Mo Labor R 89:1067-75 O '66

PACIFIC NORTHWEST. See Northwest

PACIFIC OCEAN
Found in the Pacific; carved rock columns and 800-mile crack in the ocean floor. B. Tufty. il Sci N 89:239 Ap 9 '66
Lower cretaceous sediments from the Northwest Pacific. M. Ewing and others. bibliog il Science 152:751-5 My 6 '66
Pacific science congress; report. R. S. Dietz. Science 154:1365-6 D 9 '66
See also
South Sea Islands

PACIFIC school of religion, Berkeley, Calif.
Word for the world; Earl lectures pastoral conference. E. T. Culver. Christian Cent 83: 246-8 Mr 16 '66

PACIFIC science center. See Seattle—Pacific science center

PACIFIC science congress
Pacific science congress; report. R. S. Dietz. Science 154:1365-6 D 9 '66

PACIFIC SOUTHWEST airlines
PSA accelerates flight school operation. Aviation W 84:61-2 My 16 '66

PACIFIC TRUST TERRITORY. See Trust Territory of the Pacific Islands

PACIFIC Western regional ballet festival. See Dance festivals

PACIFICA stations. See Radio stations

PACIFISM
Pacifism: an historical and sociological study, by D. A. Martin. Review
Christian Cent 83:963-4 Ag 3 '66. C. Chatfield
Peace and the Catholic conscience. C. L. Palms. Cath World 203:145-52 Je '66
Priority program on peace? of NCC. P. Peachey. Christian Cent 83:959-61 Ag 3 '66
Russia's other peace movement. A. Parry. Nation 203:142-5 Ag 22 '66

Theology of nonresistance. V. Eller. Christian Cent 83:1534-7 D 14 '66; Discussion. 84:80-1 Ja 18 '67
See also
Conscientious objectors
Passive resistance to government
Peace
Vietnamese war, 1957- —Protests, demonstrations, etc. against

PACIFISTS. See Pacifism

PACK, Robert
Old man; poem. Sat R 49:29 Ap 2 '66
To the muse; Locked; poems. Poetry 109:97-9 N '66

PACK transportation
Backpacking family style. R. J. Kelsey. il Field & S 70:56-9 F '66

PACKAGE foods
No time to cook; with menu. il McCalls 94: 29 Ja '67
See also
Meat—Prepackaging

PACKAGED mixes. See Food mixes

PACKAGES, Wrapping of. See Wrapping of packages

PACKAGING
Defeat for packaging. New Repub 155:8 O 8 '66
International infant? R. E. Graham. il Duns R 88:151-4 N '66
One-step way to turn out plastic packages; Eastoflow process. il Bsns W p73-4+ My 7 '66
Package design. J. C. Bott. il Design 68: 27-9 N '66
Packaged truth. Commonweal 83:652 Mr 11 '66
Packaging '67; symposium. Duns R 88:131+ N '66
Potato-chip thinking behind today's higher prices. Consumer Rep 31:246-8 My '66
See also
Government investigations—Packaging
Wrapping of packages

Laws and regulations

Congresswoman charges: Washington consumer aid is deceptive packaging; interview. C. May. il Nations Bsns 54:54-6+ My '66
This month's feature: Congress & consumer protection moves. Cong Digest 45:163-92 Je '66
Truth about truth-in-packaging. Nations Bsns 54:75 O '66

Materials

Sophisticated materials. il Duns R 88:144-7 N '66
Upgrading the industrial package. J. P. Frank. Duns R 88:145 N '66

PACKARD, Vance
Don't tell it to the computer. N Y Times Mag p44-5+ Ja 8 '67
Seven steps to greater personal freedom. Read Digest 88:123-7 Ap '66

PACKARD, Walter
Obituary
Nation 203:532-3 N 21 '66

PACKARD, William
(tr) See Racine, J. B. Phédre

PACKER, Nancy Huddleston
Man who hated cigarettes. Reporter 35:50+ S 22 '66

PACKING for shipment
Here is help as you wrap gifts for mailing. il Sunset 137:110+ D '66
How to pack for mail order shipping; excerpt from Successful selling of antiques by mail. C. H. Laestar and M. E. Laestar. Hobbies 71:34 Ag '66
Packaging and the distribution grind. W. J. Taylor. il Duns R 88:148-50 N '66
Packing a trophy. C. Conley. il Field & S 71: 32+ My '66
Plastic container sealer cuts costs at H-M plant. Pub W 190:116 Ag 1 '66
Your own flowers going east by air. il Sunset 137:170 D '66

PACKING Industry. See Meat industry and trade

PACKING of luggage
What's this all about? beauty care items to pack in the summer suitcase. Redbook 127: 84-5+ Je '66

PACTS of mutual assistance. See International security

PADAR, James R.
Fledgling perfection. Flying 79:77 Jl '66

PADDLEFORD, Clementine
Around the world in Manhattan. por Library
J 91:3089-96 Je 15 '66
PADGETT, Ron
Artist accompanies himself with his Rays.
Art N 65:51-3+ N '66
PADOVANO, Anthony T.
Celibacy and the church's new generation.
Cath World 203:276-83 Ag '66
Theology of poverty. por Cath World 204:
219-24 Ja '67
PADOVER, Saul K.
France's superpatriot. Sat R 49:65-6 N 12 '66
Gallic paradox. Sat R 49:29-31 Ag 6 '66
PADRE ISLAND
Many faces of Padre Island. W. M. Hall. il
Am For 72:30-2+ O '66
PADRE ISLAND NATIONAL SEASHORE
Many faces of Padre Island. W. M. Hall. il
Am For 72:30-2+ O '66
PAGE, Irvine H.
Medical ethics. Science 153:371 Jl 22 '66
PAGE, Joseph A.
Civic action in Latin America. New Repub
155:31+ N 5 '66
Health hazards in food and drink. New Repub
154:29-30 Je 25 '66
Still unsafe at any speed. New Repub 155:
32+ Jl 30 '66
PAGE, Lotta S.
Mama breaks the reading barrier. NEA J 55:
62-3 D '66
PAGE, Thomas Jefferson
Remarkable voyage of the Water Witch. R.
Wood. il Américas 18:4-9 Ap '66
PAGE, Thornton
Notes on South American astronomy. il Sky
& Tel 32:335-40 D '66
Observational aspects of cosmology; report
on conference. Science 151:1411-14+ Mr 18
'66
PAGE, Tim
Invitation to Tinh Hoi pagoda. G. P. Hunt.
il Life 60:3 Je 3 '66
Unbowed Brit. il por Time 88:39-40 Ag 19
'66
PAGE, Warren
Big Red's jaguar. por Field & S 71:44-5+
Ja '67
Herds of Hardangervidda. Field & S 71:38-
41 Ag '66
Lion hunters are nuts. por Field & S 71:64-5
N '66
Mixed bag in the chateau country. Field & S
71:60-1 O '66
Perfect boats for hunters. Field & S 71:30-
1+ Ja '67
(ed) Shooting. See issues of Field & stream
(ed) Shooting questions (cont) Field & S
70:140 Ap; 71:145 My '66
Two for the book. Field & S 71:23-5+ Jl '66
Wolves ain't so smart. Field & S 70:65-7+
Mr '66
PAGEANT books, Incorporated
FTC order curbs vanity claims of Pageant
press. Pub W 190:58 O 31 '66
PAGEANTS
Festa italiana, Madison Square Garden. J.
Maskey. Dance Mag 40:34 N '66
Hellzapoppin, Roman style; Landi's Festa
italiana at Madison Square Garden. il Time
88:80 O 7 '66
Why communities dramatize history; excerpts
from reprint. G. McCalmon and C. Moe.
Parks & Rec 1:778+ S '66

Anecdotes, facetiae, satire, etc.
Religious transvestitism; thirteen bearded
ladies of da Vinci's The last supper. Chris-
tian Cent 83:447 Ap 6 '66
PAGES, Supreme court. See United States—
Supreme court—Pages
PAGH, Mogens
Commander of the Danish Armada. por For-
tune 73:70 My '66
PAGLIARONI, Jim
Semi-continental Mr Pagliaroni. Sports Illus
25:9 Ag 22 '66
PAHLEVI, Mohammed Reza, shah of Iran. See
Mohammed Reza Pahlevi
PAHLMANN, William
Constant adventure. il por House & Gard
129:110-13 F '66
PAHUTOXIN. See Toxins and antitoxins
PAID hunting. See Farmer-hunter relations
PAIN
Advice eases patients' minds about post-
surgery pain. il Todays Health 45:11 Ja '67
Congenital indifference to pain very rare.
Sci N 89:466 Je 11 '66
Martyrs may not feel pain. P. McBroom. Il
Sci N 89:505-6 Je 25 '66

New surgery substitute relieves obstinate
pain; percutaneous chordotomy. Sci N 89:
395 My 21 '66
Pain: one mystery solved. H. K. Beecher.
Science 151:840-1 F 18 '66; Reply. R. Zen-
hausern and others. bibliog 152:1645 Je 17 '66
Painful subject; quiz. J. Daugherty and M.
Daugherty. il Sci Digest 60:89-91 Jl '66
Some thoughts on pain. H. Downs. Sci Digest
59:96-8 F '66
Temporary abolition of pain in man. P. D.
Wall and W. H. Sweet. bibliog Science
155:108-9 Ja 6 '67
What you don't know about pain can hurt
you. J. E. Gibson. il Todays Health 44:36-7
My '66
See also
Analgesia
Suffering
PAIN of possession; story. See McInerny, R.
PAINE, Howard E.
New guide to your vacationlands. Nat Geog
Mag 130:94-7 Jl '66
PAINE, Thomas H.
Impact of economic growth on employee
benefit planning; address, November 1965.
Vital Speeches 32:206-10 Ja 15 '66
PAINE, Wingate Holmes
Wingate Paine: in a class by himself. C.
Reynolds. il por Pop Phot 60:114-17+ Ja
'67
PAINT
How to buy paint. House & Gard 130:156-7+
S '66
New paints galore. il Changing T 20:45-7 Je
'66
Paintings of Franklin Jones; polymer paint-
ing. F. Whitaker. il Am Artist 30:24-9+
D '66
Right paint for your purpose. il Good H 162:
146+ F '66
What to know about latex paint for the out-
side of your house. Bet Hom & Gard 44:
110 My '66

Removal
Best finishes for wood; paint removal, how to
do it right. J. Hand. il Pop Sci 188:150-3+
Ap '66
PAINT, Heat resisting
Silicate paints proving thermal stability. W.
S. Beller. il Tech W 19:24-5 O 31 '66
PAINT, Protective
Paint for pre-coated plywood. T. C. Patton.
il Arch Rec 139:233-4 Ap '66
PAINT and varnish factories

Wages and hours
Wages in paint, candy, and southern saw-
mill industries. il Mo Labor R 89:881-4
Ag '66
PAINT brushes
How to clean paint-caked brushes. il Sunset
136:132 My '66
Make a brush. R. Reinholtz. il Sch Arts 65:
29-30 Je '66
Paint brush & roller cleaners. il Consumer
Rep 31:380-3 Ag '66
Right paint brush. il Sunset 136:139-40+ Mr
'66
PAINT mixing
Multi-action paint shaker. M. Banister. Il Pop
Mech 125:174-7+ My '66
PAINT rollers
Paint brush & roller cleaners. il Consumer
Rep 31:380-3 Ag '66
PAINT sprayers. See Spraying apparatus
PAINT spraying
Joy of push button painting. il Motor B 117:
133+ Mr '66
Painting with a spray can. Sunset 137:150+
N '66
PAINTED glass. See Glass painting and
staining
PAINTED trilliums. See Trilliums
PAINTER, Charlotte
Perfect day-care home for Tommy. por Ladies
Home J 83:72+ O '66
PAINTER, Harold W.
Iowa farm life vs. Walnut Creek. A. B.
Haines. Christian Cent 83:378-80 Mr 23 '66
Painter case to Supreme court. America 114:
403 Mr 26 '66
Question of custody. J. Mitford. il pors Mc-
Calls 93:96-7+ My '66
Should this father raise his son? J. West;
P. Engle. il por Ladies Home J 83:88-9+
My '66

PAINTER, Mark
Battle for a little boy. il pors Life 60:101-2 Mr 4 '66
Fathers and small sons. S. Alexander. Life 60:20 Mr 11 '66
Manner of speaking. J. Ciardi. Sat R 49:26+ Mr 26 '66; Discussion. 49:27 Ap 16 '66
Question of custody. J. Mitford. il por Mc-Calls 93:96-7+ My '66
Should this father raise his son? J. West; P. Engle. il por Ladies Home J 83:88-9+ My '66

PAINTING
Questions to Stella and Judd; interview, ed. by L. R. Lippard. B. Glaser; F. Stella; D. Judd. il Art N 65:55-61 S '66
See also
Artists
Frescoes
Impressionism (art)
Mural painting and decoration
Paint
Realism in art

Exhibitions
See Art—Exhibitions

Study and teaching
Action painting in the classroom. J. Zahniser. il Sch Arts 65:27-8 My '66
Art lesson in oil painting. R. Seidel. il Sch Arts 66:29 S '66
Motor-oil painting. T. Heidt. il Design 68:16-17 S '66

Materials
Shoe polish painting; elementary school. P. Smith. il Sch Arts 66:40 O '66

Technique
Brooms and prisms. J. Ashbery. il Art N 65:58-9+ Mr '66
Doctor Riggio; the art of an extractionist. J. W. Riggio. il Am Artist 30:44-9+ Mr '66
Gene Davis paints a picture. G. Nordland. il Art N 65:46-9+ Ap '66
Manet's mental museum. H. G. Gardiner. il Art N 65:48-50+ N '66
New dimension of Douglas Gorsline. F. Whitaker. il Am Artist 30:38-43+ My '66
Painting technique of John McCrady. J. Kelly. il Am Artist 30:50-5+ F '66
Paintings of Franklin Jones; polymer painting. F. Whitaker. il Am Artist 30:24-9+ D '66
Solid anti-geometry. E. C. Baker. il Art N 65:56-7+ Mr '66

PAINTING, Abstract. See Art, Abstract

PAINTING, American
Amateurs, Frakturs and elegant young ladies; Garbisch collection of American watercolors and pastels at the National gallery, Washington, D.C. W. P. Campbell. il Art N 65:50-3+ O '66
American art and the Whitney museum. L. Goodrich. il Antiques 90:655-62 N '66
Art galleries; exhibition: 250 years of American art, at Corcoran gallery of art, Washington, D.C. R. M. Coates. New Yorker 42:137-41 My 7 '66
Art news from nowhere. il Esquire 67:124-7 Ja '67
Background to systemic; exhibition at the Guggenheim museum. L. Alloway. il Art N 65:30-3 O '66
Early American painters and patrons; anonymous artists of the Upper Hudson Valley. il Antiques 91:22+ Ja '67
Egyptian motifs in nineteenth-century American painting and sculpture. W. H. Gerdts. il Antiques 90:495-501 O '66
From Pollock to pop; twenty years of painting and sculpture. H. Rosenberg. il Holiday 39:96-105+ Mr '66
Guide for the unperplexed; anxiety of modern art. H. Rosenberg. Art N 65:46-7+ S '66
In the museums; paintings. R. Davidson. il Antiques 89:194+ F '66
Landscapes of Frederic Edwin Church, by D. C. Huntington. Review
Sat R il 49:43+ Ap 16 '66. W. Andrews
Museum of early southern decorative arts; the paintings and prints. F. L. Horton. il Antiques 91:96-101 Ja '67
New Britain museum of American art, New Britain, Conn. C. B. Ferguson. il Antiques 90:668-72 N '66
Peales get together; works of the Peale family of artists. E. P. Birk. il Antiques 91:18 Ja '67
Portrait of the artist as a person. G. H. Hamilton. il Sat R 49:89-90 Ap 9 '66

Reviving Edward Church; Hudson River school. F. Getlein. New Repub 154:34-5 Mr 5 '66
Romantic of Olana; three events focused on F. E. Church. H. Cohen. Reporter 34:51-2 Ap 7 '66
Worcester art museum, Worcester, Mass. D. C. Rich and L. Dresser. il Antiques 90:647-54 N '66
Yankee doodlers; Garbisch collection on view at National gallery. il Newsweek 68:102-4 O 31 '66
See also
Adams, W. S.
Albers, J.
American water color society
Audubon, J. J.
Avery, M.
Aylon, H.
Bellows, G. W.
Birch, T.
Bishop, J.
Bradley, J.
Cassatt, M.
Catlin, G.
Champney, J. W.
Cloar, C.
Copley, J. S.
Custis, G. W. P.
Davis, G.
Di Gioia, F.
Ferren, J.
Frankenthaler, H.
Georges, P.
Glackens, W. J.
Gonzalez, A.
Gorsline, D.
Gottlieb, A.
Graham, J. D.
Grooms, R.
Hicks, E.
Hofmann, H.
Homer, W.
Indiana, R.
Johns, J.
Johnson, L.
Kanovitz, H.
Kensett, J. F.
Koch, J.
Lang, W.
Lukin, S.
McCrady, J.
Maciver, L.
Palmer, W. C.
Parrish, M.
Porter, J. E.
Prendergast, M. B.
Rattner, A.
Rauschenberg, R.
Ray, M.
Reinhardt, A.
Rivers, L.
Rockwell, N.
Russell, C. M.
Sirugo, S.
Spencer, F. R.
Spencer, N.
Steinberg, S.
Stuart, G.
Tchelitchew, P.
Thiebaud, W.
Warhol, A.
Watkins, F.
Waugh, F. J.
Whitney museum of American art, New York
Wyeth, A.
Wyeth, N. C.

PAINTING, Argentine
Image and imagination. J. R. Brest. il Américas 18:31-3 N '66
See also
Le Parc, J.

PAINTING, Belgian
See also
Folon, J. M.
Margritte, R.

PAINTING, British
Landscape of light; J. M. W. Turner's style. il Time 87:66-9 Ap 1 '66
See also
Bacon, F.
Bartlett, W. H.
Beardsley, A. V.
Lowry, L. S.
Moynihan, R.
Turner, J. M. W.

PAINTING, Canadian
Generous example; gift of R. and S. Mc-Michael to Ontario government. Am Artist 30:4+ F '66

PAINTING, Ceylonese
Sigiriya; palace of a god-king. M. M. Brown. il Sat R 49:48+ N 26 '66

PAINTING, Childrens. See Childrens art

PAINTING, Colombian
See also
Botero, F.
PAINTING, Czech
See also
Kokoschka, O.
PAINTING, Dutch
Age of Lowland giants; loan show for San Francisco, Toledo and Boston. H. K. Gerson. il Art N 65:28-32+ N '66
Golden age of Rembrandt. A. Werner. il Reporter 35:34-6 D 29 '66
Golden age; The age of Rembrandt, at San Francisco's Palace of the Legion of honor. il Newsweek 68:90-3 N 7 '66
See also
Hals, F.
Mondriaan, P. C.
Vermeer, J.
PAINTING, English. See Painting, British
PAINTING, European
Worcester art museum, Worcester, Mass. D. C. Rich and L. Dresser. il Antiques 90:647-54 N '66
PAINTING, Flemish
Flemish eye; portfolio of details from Flemish paintings. M. B. Davidson. Horizon 8:96-105 Wint '66
Flowering of Flemish art. J. Canaday. il Horizon 8:84-95 Wint '66
See also
Brueghel, P.
Overbeke, A. van
Rubens, P. P.
PAINTING, French
Dandy at the helm; P. Guillaume collection on exhibit at the Orangerie, Paris. F. Cachin. il Art N 65:36-8+ Ap '66
Family reunion; French paintings from collections of Andrew Mellon's children. il Newsweek 67:99-100 Mr 21 '66
French paintings from the collection of Mrs Mellon Bruce and Mr and Mrs Paul Mellon; twenty-fifth anniversary of the National gallery of art. D. Farr. il Antiques 89:556-63 Ap '66
French paintings in the English royal collection. O. Millar. il Antiques 89:706-8 My '66
Gauguin: the hidden tradition. il Art N 65:26-9 Sum '66
Glory that was France; paintings loaned by Mrs Mellon Bruce and Mr and Mrs Paul Mellon for 25th anniversary. R. Goldwater. il Art N 65:40-2+ Mr '66
Golden loans for a silver anniversary; French impressionist and post-impressionist works lent by Andrew Mellon's children. K. Kuh. il Sat R 49:45-51 Mr 19 '65
Letter from Paris; exhibition of great modern artists displayed by Alex Maguy in his Rue du Faubourg gallery. Genêt. New Yorker 42:116+ Ag 13 '66
National gallery: preview of an anniversary exhibition; Mellons' collections. A. Saarinen. il McCalls 93:96-103+ Ap '66
Romance of reality; benefit show at Wildenstein gallery. il Art N 65:28-30+ Ap '66
Thirteen colorplates; French pictures in the collections of Mrs Mellon Bruce and Mr and Mrs Paul Mellon. il Art N 65:43-50 Mr '66
Wild men of Paris; les Fauves; excerpt from Architectural record of May 1910. G. Burgess. il Arch Rec 140:237-40 Jl '66
See also
Arman
Boudin, E. L.
Cézanne, P.
Dallegret, F.
Dubuffet, J.
Dunoyer de Segonzac, A.
Dupuy, J.
Fantin-Latour, H.
Hoffbauer, C.
Ingres, J. A. D.
Manet, E.
Matisse, H.
Morisot, B.
Poussin, N.
Rousseau, H.
Sisley, A.
Staël, N. de
Watteau, J. A.
PAINTING, German
See also
Ernst, M.
PAINTING, Greek
See also
Vases, Greek

PAINTING, Industrial and practical
Painting secrets from a pro. T. Philbin, jr. il Pop Sci 188:168-9+ Je '66
See also
Automobiles—Painting
House painting
Wood finishing
PAINTING, Israeli
See also
Agam, Y.
PAINTING, Italian
See also
Angelico, F.
Correggio
Leonardo da Vinci
Modigliani, A
Tiepolo, G. B.
PAINTING, Japanese
See also
Foujita, T.
PAINTING, Latin American
From the pampas to Fifth avenue; Latin American painters and painting in the 1960's; Guggenheim museum show. F. Getlein. New Repub 154:33-4 Je 25 '66
PAINTING, Modern. See Modernism (art)
PAINTING, Norwegian
See also
Munch, E.
PAINTING, Peruvian
See also
Gil de Castro, J.
Portrait painting
PAINTING, Religious. See Christian art and symbolism
PAINTING, Romantic. See Romanticism
PAINTING, Russian
See also
Kandinsky, W.
PAINTING, Spanish
See also
Miró, J.
Picasso, P.
PAINTING, Swedish
See also
Fahlström, Ö.
PAINTING, Swiss
See also
Rederer, F. J.
PAINTING, Yugoslav
Village of painters: Hlebine, Yugoslavia. A. Werner. Reporter 35:49-50 S 8 '66
PAINTING as recreation. See Recreation—Activities
PAINTING on glass. See Glass painting and staining
PAINTINGS
In the museums; paintings. R. Davidson. il Antiques 89:416+, 878+; 90:700+ Mr, Je, N '66
Masters in the art news. il Art N 65:22-3 N; 22-5 D '66
Ponce art museum. R. Taylor. il Antiques 90:681-5 N '66
See also
Art—Expertising

Appreciation
See Art—Appreciation

Cleaning
How not to clean a painting. E. Zukowski. Am Artist 30:8 Ap '66

Collections
See Art—Galleries and museums; Art—Private collections

Prices
See Art—Prices
PAINTINGS, Photography of. See Photography of works of art
PAINTINGS, Theft of. See Art thefts
PAINTS. See Paint

PAIS, Bambos
Man who said no to Princess Margaret; with recipes. S. Robinson. por McCalls 94:95+ Ja '67
PAISLEY, Ian
Captain O'Neill and the anti-Papist. J. H. Huizinga. il Reporter 35:43-4 O 20 '66
Ecumenical backlash. E. McKiernan. America 115:31-3 Jl 9 '66
Paisley's pattern. il por Time 88:23 Jl 29 '66
Unholy war of preacher Paisley. H. Moffett. il pors Life 61:35-6+ Ag 19 '66
PAIUTE Indians
Paiute trail; or, Collecting in Nevada. C. Miles. Hobbies 71:113-14 S '66
PAK, Chung Hi. See Park, C. H.

PAKISTAN
Pakistan feels the pains of division; autonomy movement in East Pakistan. M. H. Zim. il Reporter 36:40-2 Ja 12 '67
See also
Airports—Pakistan
Architecture—Pakistan
Book industries and trade—Pakistan
Economic assistance in Pakistan
Kashmir

Antiquities
See also
Mohenjo-daro

Commercial treaties and agreements
United States and Pakistan sign cotton textile agreement; Department announcement with text of U.S. note; November 21, 1966. Dept State Bul 55:937-41 D 19 '66

Description and travel
Problems of a two-part land. B. Keating. il Nat Geog Mag 131:1-47 Ja '67

Economic conditions
Problems of a two-part land. B. Keating. il Nat Geog Mag 131:1-47 Ja '67

Foreign relations
Affair cools; friendship with China. Newsweek 68:46 Jl 11 '66
Bellyful of what? il Time 87:36 Ap 8 '66

Nationalism
Pakistan's search for national identity. D. D. Anderson. Yale R 55:552-69 Je '66

Politics and government
Bad marriage; East Pakistan vs. West Pakistan. il Time 87:41 Je 17 '66
Bellyful of what? il Time 87:36 Ap 8 '66
Maintaining the peace; Lahore opposition leaders arrested. Time 87:32 F 25 '66
Medical discharge. Time 88:30 Jl 1 '66
Pakistan feels the pains of division; autonomy movement in East Pakistan. M. H. Zim. il Reporter 36:40-2 Ja 12 '67
Pakistan's search for national identity. D. D. Anderson. Yale R 55:552-69 Je '66

Popular culture
Pakistan's search for national identity. D. D. Anderson. Yale R 55:552-69 Je '66

PAKISTANIS
Problems of a two-part land. B. Keating. il Nat Geog Mag 131:1-47 Ja '67

PALACES
Alla Turca; royal apartments in the Seraglio. il Vogue 148:186-7 D '66
Letter from Paris; Grand Trianon, Versailles. J. Flanner. New Yorker 42:109-11 Ag 27 '66
Royal pavilion, Brighton. C. Musgrave. il Antiques 90:74-9, 320-5 Jl, S '66
View of the water: American palaces by the sea. J. T. Maher. il Holiday 40:48-53+ Jl '66
See also
Nonsuch palace, England
Versailles, Palace of

PALATABILITY. See Taste

PALEOBIOCHEMISTRY
Chemical fossils. G. Eglinton and M. Calvin. il Sci Am 216:32-43 Ja '67

PALEOBOTANY
Corn of Coxcatlán. V. Bourjaily. bibliog il Horizon 8:50-5 Spr '66

Pleistocene
Late Pleistocene vegetation and degree of pluvial climatic change in the Chihuahuan Desert. P. V. Wells. bibliog il Science 153:970-5 Ag 26 '66

PALEOLITHIC period. See Stone age

PALEONTOLOGY
New clues to life's beginning; discovery of Precambrian fossils. D. Cohen. il Sci Digest 59:24-6 F '66
See also
Algae, Fossil
Animals, Extinct
Brachiopods, Fossil
Foraminifera, Fossil
Mammoths
Man, Prehistoric
Mastodon
Micropaleontology

Cambrian
Phanerozoic-cryptozoic and related transitions: new evidence. P. E. Cloud, jr. and C. A. Nelson. bibliog il Science 154:766-70 N 11 '66

Cretaceous
Lithology and paleontology of the reflective layer horizon A. T. Saito and others. bibliog il Science 154:1173-6 D 2 '66

Devonian
Ancient fishes of Escuminac Bay; specimens from late Devonian. D. L. Dineley. il Natur Hist 76:40-5 bibliog(p73) Ja '67

Eocene
Early eocene bat from Wyoming. G. L. Jepsen. bibliog il Science 154:1333-9 D 9 '66

Pleistocene
Pacific pleistocene cores: faunal analyses and geochronology. A. Blackman and B. L. K. Somayajulu. bibliog il Science 154:886-9 N 18 '66
Paleohunters in America: origins and diffusion. H. Müller-Beck. bibliog il Science 152:1191-210 My 27 '66
Pleistocene age determinations from California and Oregon. H. G. Richards and D. L. Thurber. bibliog il Science 152:1091-2 My 20 '66
Polymorphism in pleistocene land snails. D. F. Owen. bibliog il Science 152:71-2 Ap 1 '66

Pre-Cambrian
Drifting organisms in the Precambrian sea. D. Milton. bibliog Science 153:293-4 Jl 15 '66
Microorganisms three billion years old from the Precambrian of South Africa. E. S. Barghoorn and J. W. Schopf. bibliog il Science 152:758-63 My 6 '66

Triassic
Triassic fish found in West. il(p580) Sci N 90:572 D 31 '66

Alaska
Cross-dating the archeology of northwestern Alaska. J. L. Giddings. bibliog il Science 153:127-35 Jl 8 '66

Australia
Drifting organisms in the Precambrian sea. D. Milton. bibliog Science 153:293-4 Jl 15 '66

California
Phanerozoic-cryptozoic and related transitions: new evidence. P. E. Cloud, jr. and C. A. Nelson. bibliog il Science 154:766-70 N 11 '66
Precambrian mollusc-like fossils from Inyo County, California. M. E. Taylor. bibliog il Science 153:198-201 Jl 8 '66

California, Lower
Fossil mammals from Baja California: new evidence on early tertiary migrations. W. J. Morris. bibliog il Science 153:1376-8 S 16 '66

France
Man's oldest dwelling: H. De Lumley's discovery in Nice. il Time 87:102 F 25 '66

Great Plains
Paleo-Indian bison kill. J. B. Wheat. il Sci Am 216:44-52 Ja '67

Mongolia
Gobi's treasure of bones. il Time 88:75 Jl 22 '66

New Mexico
Correlation of archeological and palynological data. A. J. Jelinek. bibliog il Science 152:1507-9 Je 10 '66

Nova Scotia
Fluorine content of microsaur teeth from the carboniferous rocks of Joggins, Nova Scotia. J. S. Stevenson and L. S. Stevenson. bibliog il Science 154:1548-50 D 23 '66

Ontario
Grizzly bear skull: site of a find near Lake Simcoe. W. M. Tovell and R. E. Deane. Science 154:158 O 7 '66

South Africa
Microorganisms three billion years old from the Precambrian of South Africa. E. S. Barghoorn and J. W. Schopf. bibliog il Science 152:758-63 My 6 '66

Sudan
Fossil occurrence of murine rodent (nesokia indica) in the Sudan. P. Robinson. il Science 154:264 O 14 '66

PALEONTOLOGY—*Continued*
Wyoming
Early eocene bat from Wyoming. G. L. Jepsen. bibliog il Science 154:1333-9 D 9 '66
PALEONTOLOGY, Botanical. See Paleobotany
PALEOTEMPERATURE. See Earth temperature
PALERMO
Music
Palermo; Ernani. F. Nuzzo. Opera N 30:31-2 F 5 '66
PALESTINE
See also
Dead Sea
Antiquities
See also
Jordan—Antiquities
History
Jews in their land; ed. by D. Ben-Gurion. Review
Sat R il 49:26 Ag 20 '66. A. L. Sachar
Jewish-Arab problems
See Jewish-Arab relations
PALEVSKY, Max
How to succeed. il por Newsweek 67:73-4 Mr 28 '66
PALEY, William Samuel
How the wasteland began; early days of radio. C. Dreher. Atlan 217:53-8 F '66
Parking space. il por Newsweek 67:60 F 14 '66
PALHETA, Dom Francisco
Appetizing as sin. L. F. de Faro. il Américas 18:11-13 D '66
PALISADES park. See Amusement parks
PALLADIAN architecture. See Architecture, Italian
PALLADIO, Andrea
Palladio was not Palladian. P. Schneider. il Horizon 8:56-71 Spr '66
PALLAVICINI, Elvina Rospigliosi-. See Rospigliosi-Pallavicini, E.
PALLENBERG, Corrado
Day in the life of the Pope. Read Digest 89:64-9 Jl '66
PALM BEACH, Fla.
Best place. il Newsweek 68:124+ N 21 '66
PALMER, Arnold
Advice on weekend golf. pors Look 30:64-6+ Ag 9 '66
about
At Olympic: a summit of drama. A. Wright. il pors Sports Illus 24:22-7 Je 27 '66
Is the Masters fixed? G. S. Brown. il pors Sports Illus 24:60-1 Ap 4 '66
Palmer's jet aids golf, business schedule. D. A. Brown. il por Aviation W 84:107-9+ My 23 '66
Sporting scene. H. W. Wind. New Yorker 42:134+ Ap 30 '66
When two were twice as good. A. Wright. il por Sports Illus 25:40-1 D 19 '66
PALMER, Harvey E. See Beasley, T. M. jt. auth.
PALMER, Henry P. See Frost, A. D. jt. auth.
PALMER, Irene
Down-to-earth look at a growing problem; excerpts from letter. U S News 61:53 Ag 22 '66
PALMER, James A.
One-transistor muter for FM receivers. Electr World 75:79 F '66
Solid-state home temperature controller. Electr World 75:80-3 Je '66
PALMER, John D.
How a bird tells the time of day. Natur Hist 75:48-53 Mr '66
PALMER, Joseph, 1914-
United States role in a changing Africa; statement, May 10, 1966. Dept State Bul 54:898-9 Je 6 '66
about
Two appointments. New Repub 154:10 Mr 26 '66
PALMER, Norman D.
Challenge for aid in Asia. bibliog f Cur Hist 51:7-13+ Jl '66
PALMER, William Charles
Landscape paintings of William Palmer. L. Schmeckebier. il por Am Artist 30:50-5+ Je '66

PALMERSTON, Henry John Temple, 3d viscount
Palmerston, by D. Southgate. Review
Nat R 18:537-8 My 31 '66. S. Leslie
PALMORE, Ann
Perennial favorite. Flower Grower 53:35+ S '66
PALMQUIST, Jeanette, and LaChance, L. E.
Comparative mutagenicity of two chemosterilants, tepa and hempa, in sperm of bracon hebetor. bibliog Science 154:915-17 N 18 '66
PALMS, Charles L.
Peace and the Catholic conscience. Cath World 203:145-52 Je '66
(ed) See Dumpson, J. R. Philosophy of social welfare
PALMS
Magnificent palms. H. G. Yocum. il Horticulture 44:22-3+ Ap '66
PALOMAR, MOUNT, observatory. See Astronomical observatories
PALOMARES, Spain
Case of the missing H-bomb; Palomares search. R. Oulahan. il Life 60:106A-106B F 25 '66
H-bomb is missing and the hunt goes on. il Newsweek 67:55-7 Mr 7 '66
Little sub's big score; the H-bomb is found; drama of the bomb lost off Palomares. il Life 60:34-5 Ap 1 '66
Palomares learns to love the bomb. T. Szulc. il N Y Times Mag p22-3+ F 20 '66
PALSON, Lisa M.
Fisherman's song. Horn Bk 42:101 F '66
PALSY, Cerebral. See Paralysis
PALYI, Melchior
Canute at the Treasury. Nat R 18:579 Je 14 '66
PAMPAS
Worth of a tree; ombu. W. L. Maughan. il Américas 18:34-6 D '66
PAMPERING rooms. See Rooms
PAMPHLETS
Best in booklets. See issues of House & garden incorporating Living for young homemakers
Booklets about home repairs, plumbing. Consumer Bul 49:28 Mr '66
Booklets worth writing for. See issues of Good housekeeping
Dear sir, please send me all you have on Texas... R. G. Durnin. Sr Schol 89:sup42 S 23 '66
Sources of maintenance information. E. Horan. il Yachting 119:74+ Ap '66
Things to write for. See issues of Changing times
Write for these. See issues of Wilson library bulletin
Anecdotes, facetiae, satire, etc.
Merry crisis! happy solenoid! not getting nervous-breakdown from Easy instruction booklets. L. Rosten. il Look 31:10 Ja 10 '67
PAN-AFRICANISM
Russian revisionism in Africa. J. O'Connor. America 114:773-5 My 28 '66
PANAGRA. See Pan American Grace airways
PANAMA
Atmospheric gases and particulates in Panama. J. P. Lodge, jr. and J. B. Pate. bibliog il Science 153:408-10 Jl 22 '66
Antiquities
See Indians of Central America—Antiquities
PANAMA CANAL
Gone flying to Panama. L. L. Hallman. il Flying 79:52-6 Ag '66
PANAMA CANAL ZONE
Yankees welcome in Panama again. il U S News 61·89 S 5 '66
PAN AMERICAN conferences. See Inter-American conferences
PAN AMERICAN day and week
Pan American day. G. de Zéndegui. Américas 18:inside cover Ap '66
Pan American day and Pan American week, 1966; proclamation, April 6, 1966. L. B. Johnson. Dept State Bul 54:746-7 My 9 '66
Pan American week concerts. il Américas 18:38-9 My '66
PAN AMERICAN development foundation
Alliance for progress notes. Américas 18:47 Je '66
PAN AMERICAN Grace airways
Panagra acquisition approved. Aviation W 85:40 O 24 '66

PAN AMERICAN union
    Art. See issues of Américas
    Music. See issues of Américas
    Symbolic gift; unveiling of statue of Queen
        Isabella I. G. de Zéndegui. Américas 18:
        inside cover My '66
PAN AMERICAN world airways
    Atlantic tour fare agreement seen. J. W.
        Carter. Aviation W 85:35-6 D 5 '66
    Let's travel; Pan Am tours to Hawaii. il
        Mlle 63:199 My '66
    Pan Am, Aeroflot talks begin this week.
        D. C. Winston. Aviation W 85:47 N 14 '66
    Pan Am beginning Pacific navaid flights. K.
        J. Stein. Aviation W 85:43 S 19 '66
    Pan Am, Boeing set a new jet pace; Boeing
        747. il Newsweek 67:67-8 Ap 25 '66
    Pan Am opens mechanized cargo facility;
        cargo terminal at Kennedy international
        airport. il Aviation W 85:49-50 D 5 '66
    Pan American order for 747 opens new era
        in airline jet transport equipment; with
        editorial comment. W. H. Gregory. il Avia-
        tion W 84:21, 38-40 Ap 18 '66
    Pan Am prepares for automatic landings.
        P. J. Klass. Aviation W 85:35-6 Jl 18 '66
    Pan Am takes off with huge Boeing 747.
        Bsns W p46+ Ap 16 '66
    U.S. hopes for air pact soon in Pan Am talks
        with Aeroflot. J. W. Carter. Aviation W
        85:47 O 24 '66
PAN AMERICANISM. See Inter-American re-
    lations
PANCAKE houses. See Restaurants—United
    States
PANCAKES. See Griddle cakes
PANCREAS
                Diseases
        See also
    Cystic fibrosis
PANCREATIC fibrosis. See Cystic fibrosis
PANDAS
    Chi-Chi goes to Moscow. D. Cohen. il Sci
        Digest 59:10-15 Je '66
    Chi-Chi hates An-An but loves men; with re-
        ports by P. Young and R. Chelminski. il
        Life 61:93-4 N 11 '66
    Panda idyll hits a temporary snag. il Life
        61:66B Jl 15 '66
    Panda performs in Peking. il Natur Hist
        75:34-5 Ap '66
    Panderers; efforts to mate Chi Chi and An
        An. il Newsweek 68:46 S 26 '66
PANDOLFI, Frank
    Hartford story. R. D. Daniels. por Opera N
        31:20-1 O 15 '66
PANEL construction
        See also
    Sandwich construction
PANEL saws. See Saws
PANELING
    It's easier to install the new plasterboard;
        gypsum wallboard. H. Pfister. il Pop Sci
        189:164-8 S '66
    Many varieties of glass panels to control and
        diffuse light. C. W. Clarkson. il Arch Rec
        139:205-6 My '66
    Removable wall coverings. il House & Gard
        129:58-9 Mr '66
    Rough stuff: the big news in wall paneling.
        D. Huff. il Pop Sci 188:132-6+ Ap '66
    You can make your own paneling. R. Day. il
        Pop Sci 188:170-3 Mr '66
PANELS, Decorative
    Casting decorative panels in lightweight con-
        crete. il Sunset 137:92 S '66
PANICS
                1929
        See also
    Stock exchange—Crisis, October 1929
PANIJEL, Jacques, and others
    Immunochemical characterization of poly-
        ribonucleotides. bibliog Science 152:773-5
        My 6 '66
PANKHURST, K. V.
    Migration between Canada and the United
        States. bibliog f Ann Am Acad 367:53-62
        S '66
PANMUNJOM, Korea
    Pantomime at Panmunjom. B. Atkinson. il
        Sat R 49:61+ O 8 '66
PANNILL, William P.
    Will success spoil a poverty program? New
        Repub 154:10 F 26 '66
PANOFSKY, W. K. H. and others
    Electrons accelerated to the 10- to 20-gev
        range. Science 152:1353-5 Je 3 '66
PANSIES
    Colorful cousins: violas and pansies. il Sunset
        136:96-7 Mr '66

500 pansy plants for a pittance. Mrs S. A.
    Haley. Flower Grower 53:44 D '66
Time to start pansies from seed. C. Fer-
    guson. il Flower Grower 53:40 Jl '66
PANTER-DOWNES, Mollie
    Letter from London. See issues of New Yorker
PANTHERS
    Animal release in Everglades National Park.
        G. K. Zimmer. il Nat Parks Mag 40:22-3
        Ag '66
        See also
    Pumas
PANTOMIME

        Anecdotes, facetiae, satire, etc.
    Little louder, please. W. Allen. New Yorker
        42:39-41 My 28 '66
PANUSH, Naomi
    Science and technology: House subcommittee
        offers Capitol ideas. Science 154:993-4 N 25
        '66
PAOLA, Frank
    In rehearsal. F. Stevenson. il por Opera N
        30:28-31 F 12 '66
PAOLETTI, Rodolfo. See Kritchevsky, D. jt.
    auth.
PAPACY
        See also
    Popes
PAPAL encyclicals. See Encyclicals
PAPANDREOU, Andreas
    Behind the Aspida trial. K. Kyle. New Re-
        pub 156:17-18 Ja 21 '67
    One man's family. por Newsweek 69:45 Ja
        16 '67
PAPANDREOU, George
    One man's family. por Newsweek 69:45 Ja
        16 '67
PAPAZIAN, Pierre
    Old order and the new breed, or, Will auto-
        mation spoil Mel Dewey? ALA Bul 60:644-6
        Je '66
PAPER
    Basics concerning paper. S. Salter. Pub W
        190:135-7 O 3 '66
    Offset printing, paper reviewed at AIGA
        clinics. Pub W 189:126+ Mr 7 '66
        See also
    Waste paper

                Preservation
    History of the Barrow lab; or, The thirty
        years that revolutionized paper. il Pub W
        189:72-3+ Ap 4 '66
    Lab will seek solution to deterioration of
        paper. Pub W 191:102 Ja 2 '67
PAPER, Handmade. See Paper making and
    trade
PAPER, Waste. See Waste paper
PAPER bag players. See Theater, Childrens
PAPER books. See Paperback books
PAPER clothes. See Clothing and dress
PAPER clothing. See Paper textiles
PAPER dragon; novel. See Hunter, E.
PAPER dresses. See Clothing and dress
PAPER fabrics. See Paper textiles
PAPER making and trade
    Fine papermaking described by craftsman at
        Brentano's. il Pub W 190:120 Jl 4 '66
    Hand-made paper still flourishes; D. Howell.
        il Pub W 190:104+ S 5 '66; Correction. 190:
        146 O 3 '66; Discussion. 190:20 N 7 '66
        See also
    Kimberly Clark corporation
    Paper mills
PAPER mills
    They plant profits in economic deserts; Par-
        sons and Whittemore's overseas opera-
        tions. P. Deutschman. Read Digest 90:199-
        200+ Ja '67
PAPER money

                United States
    End of the road for the $2 bill. il U S
        News 61:10 Ag 22 '66
PAPER sculpture
    Paper sculpture. M. F. Sousa. il Sch Arts 65:
        29 Mr '66
PAPER textiles
    How soon will we wear paper clothes? D.
        Wharton. Read Digest 89:53-5 Ag '66
    Paper clothes: a wardrobe to throw away. il
        Bsns W p72-4 Jl 16 '66
    Paper dress caper. il Consumer Rep 31:
        426 S '66

PAPER work
Art of paper folding. il Design 67:32-3 My '66
Exquisite Christmas decorations with paper. E. Craster. il Bet Hom & Gard 44:70-1 N '66
Foldaway fairy-tale playhouses. il House & Gard 130:186-7+ D '66
See also
Papier-mâché

PAPERBACK book covers. See Book covers

PAPERBACK book jobbers. See Book jobbers

PAPERBACK books
Educators paperback service; Scholastic magazines, inc. il Sr Schol 89:sup21 S 30 '66
Is reading for everyone? the Ludington plan to make a slogan a reality; getting young people hooked on books. il Pub W 190:30-4 N 21 '66
Paperbacks. See issues of Publishers' weekly
Paperbacks, bound for success? il Sr Schol 88:20 Ap 15 '66
Role of paperbacks in libraries; summary of ALA's paperback sessions: The literate unreached. Pub W 190:32-6 Ag 8 '66
Space problems analyzed for paperbacks in schools; summary of discussions at conference at Teachers college, Columbia university. il Pub W 190:31-4 Jl 25 '66
Trade winds; paperbacks in classrooms. J. Beatty. jr. Sat R 49:20 N 19 '66
What's happening in education? use of paperbacks in school. W. D. Boutwell. PTA Mag 60:14 My '66
See also
Booksellers and bookselling—Paperback books
Libraries—Paperback books
Publishers and publishing—Paperback books

Bibliography
New paperbacks for social studies students. W. K. Richards. Sr Schol 89:sup 11 Ja 13 '67
New paperbacks for summer reading. J. Foster. Sr Schol 88:sup 12-13 My 20 '66
New paperbacks in and out of class. Sr Schol 88:sup38 Mr 4 '66
News of paperback books: summer, fall. il Pub W 189:161-87 Je 6 '66
Paperback bookshelf. See issues of Changing times
Paperbacks for supplementary reading. Sr Schol 87:sup 16 Ja 21 '66
Paperbacks to come; ed. by J. Putnam and K. Ahrens. Library J 91:4252-310 S 15 '66
Paperbacks to come; ed. by J. Putnam and J. Lindheim. Library J 91:368+, 2624+ Ja 15, My 15 '66
Paperbacks; what's in and what's basic. America 115:660-4 N 19 '66
Pick of the paperbacks. See issues of Saturday review
Pick of the paperbacks: best of the current season; juveniles. A. Currah. il Library J 91:2599-603 My 15 '66

Binding
Hardpaper book. A. Plotnik. bibliog Library J 91:2407-12 My 15 '66

Prices
FTC approves extra discount for premiums. Pub W 190:41 Ag 15 '66
Paperback price averages computed from PW listings. Pub W 189:106-7 F 14 '66

PAPERBOARD industry

Wages and hours
Wages in paperboard container and box plants. F. L. Bauer. il Mo Labor R 89:43-7 Ja '66

PAPERS of the presidents. See Archives—United States

PAPERWEIGHT snowstorm; story. See Clay, G. R.

PAPERWEIGHTS
Old glass paperweights. J. P. Boore. il Hobbies 71:98F-98G Je; 98L-98N N '66 (to be cont)
Outstanding French and American paperweights in the Wells collection. P. Hollister, jr. il Antiques 89:265-9 F '66

PAPIER-MÂCHÉ
Christmas with baubles and birds. il Ladies Home J 83:46+ D '66
Glistening ornaments you can make with instant papier-mâché. il House & Gard 130:164-5 D '66
Loving couples, likely and unlikely; suggestions for making pets. il McCalls 94:66-9+ D '66

Magic you make with papier-mâché. il Sunset 137:74-8 D '66
Midas touch. J. A. Zill. il Look 30:40-2 Jl 26 '66
Papier-mâché animals; project for primary grades. L. Werdegar. il Sch Arts 65:5-9 Mr '66
Really big shoe; project in Berwick, Pa. D. Shiner. il Design 67:13 My '66

PAPIKE, J. J. See Clark, J. R. jt. auth.

PAPON, Maurice
Papon to head Sud combine in French aerospace regrouping. Aviation W 86:35 Ja 16 '67

PAPP, Joseph
Architecture: Astor library acquisition. E. Galantay. Nation 202:500-2 Ap 25 '66

PAPPANO, Achilles J. and Volle, R. L.
Lithium's failure to replace sodium in mammalian sympathetic ganglia. bibliog Science 152:85-7 Ap 1 '66

PAPPAS, Lou Seibert
House & garden's Greek cook book. House & Gard 129:139+ F '66

PAPPAS, Thomas Anthony
Esso Pappas complex. il por Fortune 73:69-70+ F '66

PARACHUTE jumping. See Parachuting

PARACHUTE troops
Helluva way to grow up fast: paratrooper at Ft Benning, Ga. C. S. Wren. il Look 30:73-7 S 20 '66
See also
United States—Army—Parachute troops

PARACHUTES
Apollo land recovery tests continue. J. Mercer. Miss & Roc 18:24-5 F 28 '66
Mid-air parachutist recovery may be flier rescue boon. il Tech W 19:32+ S 19 '66
Sailwing; new gliding parachute. il Look 30:106+ N 29 '66
Wide use of mid-air retrieval plan seen. il Aviation W 85:107+ O 3 '66

Testing
'Chute popper; remote control guide. il Time 87:70 F 4 '66

PARACHUTING
Emergency 11 miles high; N. Piantanida mishap. il Newsweek 67:67 My 16 '66
Joys of falling through space; sky diving. il Sat Eve Post 239:82-5 Je 18 '66
Man set to dive 123,800 feet; N. Piantanida's fall, with report and editorial comment. il Life 60:3, 32-9 My 13 '66
Meet me in the middle of the air. J. Morris. il Esquire 65:110-13+ Ap '66
Way of life; death of D. Rutledge. Newsweek 68:57 N 21 '66

PARADES
Here comes Mr Parade. A. R. Roalman. il Pop Mech 125:84-7+ Je '66
Letter from Paris; Bastille day military parade. Genêt. New Yorker 42:68 Jl 30 '66
See also
Floats (parades)

PARADES in literature. See Literature—Themes

PARADISE, Ky.
Paradise is stripped. H. M. Caudill. il N Y Times Mag p26-7+ Mr 13 '66

PARADISE on Tuesday; story. See Levinson, N.

PARADISE parrot. See Parrots

PARAFFINIC hydrocarbons. See Hydrocarbons

PARAGLIDER. See Gliders (aeronautics)

PARALYSIS
Brain surgery by computer. S. Hopkins. il Pop Mech 126:94-7 D '66
Bullet through the window; young wife paralyzed from chest down. J. L. Block. il Good H 162:72+ Mr '66
Nerve cells and Parkinsonism; shaking palsy. P. McBroom. il Sci N 90:492 D 10 '66
New light on how certain amines act in the brain; report of symposium on Parkinson's disease. T. L. Campbell. il Science 152:232-6+ Ap 8 '66
Parkinson's disease linked with chemicals. Sci N 90:56 Jl 23 '66
Run away, little girl; condensation. M. M. Segal. il Read Digest 89:259-62+ N '66

PARAMECIA
Reversal response elicited in nonbeating cilia of paramecium by membrane depolarization. Y. Naitoh. bibliog il Science 154:660-2 N 4 '66

PARAMETERS
Hospital to benefit from space work. H. M. David. il Miss & Roc 18:26+ F 28 '66

PARAMETERS—*Continued*
Stokes parameters for 1665-megacycles-per-second emission from OH near source W3. M. L. Meeks and others. bibliog il Science 153:978-81 Ag 26 '66

PARAMOUNT pictures corporation
New star at Paramount. Time 87:73 Ap 22 '66

PARANA RIVER
Remarkable voyage of the Water Witch. R. Wood. il Américas 18:4-9 Ap '66

PARANOIA
Clean young Englishman, by J. Gale. Review New Repub 155:25-6 S 3 '66. L. Schaffer

PARANOV, Moshe
In the hall of the mountain king. Opera N 30:32-3 F 26 '66

PARAPROTEINEMIA. See Proteinemia

PARASAILS. See Parachutes

PARASITES
See also
Plasmodium (parasite)
Symbiosis
Worms, Intestinal and parasitic

Mammals
Hideaway for moths; symbiotic relationship with two- and three-toed sloths. R. S. Casebeer and C. L. Hogue. il Natur Hist 75:40-1 My '66

Mollusks
Fluorescent-antibody studies of haplosporidian parasites of oysters in Chesapeake and Delaware Bays. J. H. Barrow, jr. and B. C. Taylor. bibliog il Science 153:1531-3 S 23 '66
Minchinia nelsoni n. sp. (haplosporida, haplosporidiidae) causative agent of the Delaware Bay oyster epizoötic. H. H. Haskin and others. bibliog il Science 153:1414-16 S 16 '66
Spores give clues to oyster killer; Delaware Bay disease, caused by MSX parasite. Sci N 90:424 N 19 '66
Sporulation of minchinia nelsoni, haplosporida, haplosporidiidae in crassostrea virginica. gmelin. J. A. Couch and others. bibliog il Science 153:1529-31 S 23 '66

Oysters
See Parasites—Mollusks

PARASITIC diseases
See also
Schistosomiasis
Toxoplasmosis

PARASITIC plants
See also
Rafflesia

PARATHYROID hormones. See Hormones

PARATROOPERS. See Parachute troops; United States—Army—Parachute troops

Les PARAVENTS; drama. See Genêt, J.

PARCA, Gabriella
Italian men are lousy lovers. J. Bonfante. il pors Life 60:81-2+ F 4 '66

PARCEL post
Packages O'Brien; bill to double weight limit passed by House. Newsweek 68:74+ Jl 18 '66

PARCEL post rates. See Postal rates—United States

PARDEE, Lyall A.
Double-barreled clay-pipe sewer. Am City 81:82-3 D '66

PARENT and child (law)
Battle for a little boy; Iowa's custody case. il Life 60:101-2 Mr 4 '66
Choosing parents in Iowa; custody decision in Mark Painter case. il Time 87:45+ F 25 '66
Father and son; Iowa Supreme court decision. Newsweek 67:32 F 21 '66
Fathers and small sons; M. Painter custody case. S. Alexander. Life 60:20 Mr 11 '66
Iowa farm life vs. Walnut Creek; custody battle of five-year-old Mark Painter. A. B. Haines. Christian Cent 83:378-80 Mr 23 '66
Manner of speaking; Iowa: the Painter case. J. Ciardi. Sat R 49:26+ Mr 26 '66; Discussion. 49:27 Ap 16 '66
Painter case to Supreme court; effort to regain custody of son. America 114:403 Mr 26 '66
Question of custody: Mark Painter case. J. Mitford. il McCalls 93:96-7+ My '66
Should this father raise his son? Harold Painter case; pro and con discussion. J. West; P. Engle. il Ladies Home J 83:88-9+ My '66

PARENT-child relationship
Conversations parents never hear; fathers and sons. Look 30:M14-15 S 20 '66
Do you resent your children? J. Mendels. il Parents Mag 41:33-5+ Ag '66
Do you see your children as they really are? with quiz. W. Abraham. il PTA Mag 60:28-30 Je '66
Doctor Spock for parents? E. J. LeShan. il N Y Times Mag p76+ Ag 28 '66
Dream world, real world. C. Klein. il N Y Times Mag p 102+ O 16 '66
Early separations from mother cause anxiety. Todays Health 44:67 My '66
Happiness isn't being home for the holidays; questions and answers. A. Wood. Seventeen 25:174-5 D '66
How children react to praise and criticism. H. G. Ginott. il Parents Mag 41:46-7+ Ap '66
Inborn urge to grow. A. B. Auerbach. il Parents Mag 41:54-5+ Je '66
Is it any of their business? E. S. Oshin. il N Y Times Mag p 121+ My 1 '66
Juanita was an oversolicitous mother. D. C. Disney. Ladies Home J 83:30+ Je '66
Learning your baby's language. C. H. Turner. il Parents Mag 41:36-7+ Je '66
Look youth survey; are you a teen-ager? yeah. I'm afraid so. J. Shepherd. Look 30:44+ S 20 '66
Mothers & daughters; English Emma and her mother. C. MacInnes. Mlle 62:186-7+ Mr '66
Must my life be an open book? questions and answers. A. Wood. il Seventeen 25:148-9+ Ap '66
My father's wife. F. O'Connor. il Sat Eve Post 239:84-6+ F 26 '66
On being a father; personal account of elderly father and a young son. il Parents Mag 41:47-9+ D '66
Parents aren't enough. H. Milt. il Parents Mag 41:74-5+ O '66
Parents can help; excerpts from Prevention of failure. NEA J 55:39 Ap '66
Parents vs. children; frustrating games families play. J. L. Schimel. il Redbook 127:46-7+ Ag '66
Portfolio of American mothers and daughters. il McCalls 93:47-55 Jl '66
Preschoolers play favorites; excerpt from Growing up with children. M. W. Piers. il Parents Mag 41:64-5+ N '66
Speaking out; you force kids to rebel. S. Kelman. Sat Eve Post 239:12+ N 19 '66
Talks to teens. M. Lerner. Seventeen 25:162+ Mr '66
Thomas Woodrow Wilson; excerpts; with reply by A. Dulles. S. Freud and W. C. Bullitt. il Look 30:36-8+ D 13 '66; Discussion. 30:12 D 27 '66
Those teenage strangers. M. F. Farnham. il Parents Mag 41:33-5+ Je '66
Unlearning parental gobbledegook. W. Abraham. il Todays Health 44:12-13+ Jl '66
What parents should teach; with study-discussion program, by R. Strang. A. V. Keliher. bibliog il PTA Mag 60:14-16, 34 Mr '66
When it's hard to say good-bye; with group discussion program, by M. S. Smart. M. Brenton. il Parents Mag 41:42-3+, 92+ Ap '66
Why some mothers reject their babies; hospital practices. R. Brecher and E. Brecher. il Redbook 127:48-9+ My '66
Wonder is for sharing. A. Gordon. il Read Digest 88:159-60+ Je '66
See also
Family life
Fathers
Love, Maternal
Mothers
Youth—Management and training

PARENT-helpers. See Teachers aides

PARENT-teacher associations. See Parents and teachers associations

PARENT-teacher cooperation. See School and the home

PARENTHOOD, Planned. See Birth control

PARENTS
Doctor Spock for parents? E. J. LeShan. il N Y Times Mag p76+ Ag 28 '66
Help your child to a career. J. J. Cox. il Todays Health 44:29-31+ D '66
Learn to leave your student alone! W. F. Pillsbury. Bet Hom & Gard 44:20+ O '66
My father's wife. F. O'Connor. il Sat Eve Post 239:84-6+ F 26 '66
Parents with too much knowledge and too little confidence. E. J. LeShan. Redbook 126:49+ F '66
Report card on parents; results of McCall's questionnaire. L. Hershey. il McCalls 93:62+ My '66
See also
Family life
Fathers
School and the home

PARENTS and teachers associations
Child-centered planet; a Founders day feature. il PTA Mag 61:25-7 Ja '67
Forever strong and fair. J. Moorhead. il PTA Mag 60:2-3 F '66
Keeping pace with the PTA. See issues of PTA magazine
Local associations ask about. . . J. H. Starie. NEA J 55:42 Mr '66
Membership proclamation. J. Moorhead. PTA Mag 61:2-3 O '66
Our junior high PTA makes a difference. Y. Oikawa. NEA J 56:29-30 Ja '67
PTA year begins anew. J. Moorhead. PTA Mag 61:3 S '66
Truth about the PTA. PTA Mag 60:26-30 F; 10-13 Mr '66
See also
National congress of parents and teachers

PARENTS' magazine
Forty years and eighty-one million children later; fortieth anniversary; with letter from L. B. Johnson. G. J. Hecht. il Parents Mag 41:50 O '66
Librarian, educator win Parents' magazine awards. Pub W 190:59 O 31 '66
Parents' magazine seal found misleading by FTC. Pub W 190:31 D 12 '66
Parents' magazine's 1966 awards. il Parents Mag 46:57 D '66
See also
Youth group achievement awards
PARENTS school visiting. See School and the home
PARFAITS. See Ice cream, ices, etc.
PARIAN ware. See Pottery
PARICUTIN
Mexico's Paricutin is still worth a detour. il Sunset 137:38-9 N '66
PARIN, Vasilii Vasil'evich
Soviet seeks key to man's adaptation. W. S. Beller. il por Tech W 19:12-13 Jl 4 '66
PARIS, James D.
APBA action report. See issues of Motor boating
Four basic piloting problems. Motor B 117: 72+ My '66
PARIS
Letter from Paris. Genêt. New Yorker 42: 68+ Jl 30; 116 Ag 13; 199-204 O 22 '66

Architecture
Changing the skyline; proposed 55-story office building. il Time 88:115-16 N 18 '66
See also
United Nations educational, scientific and cultural organization—Headquarters

Art
Art news from Paris. See issues of Art news

Banks
Cashless, but not classless; Rothschild Frères cards. Time 89:94-5 Ja 6 '67

Clubs
Jockey of Paris. il Esquire 66:102-3+ Jl '66

Commune
See Paris—History

Description
Letter from abroad. J. Barry. il McCalls 93:62+ Mr '66
Paris by Penn. P. Coffin. il Look 30:46-57 Jl 26 '66
Travel notes. R. Joseph. Esquire 65:24+ Je '66
Traveler, consider my Paris; ed. by R. Joseph. L. Vaudable. il Esquire 65:114-15+ Je '66

Galleries and museums
Art; Guillaume-Walter collection at Musée de l'Orangerie and les Années 25 at the Musée des arts decoratifs. M. Grosser. Nation 202:531-3 My 2 '66
Double windfall; Marmottan musée, Paris, receives second Monet collection from son. il Newsweek 67:94+ Mr 28 '66
Monet's revenge; collection left to musée Marmottan. P. Schneider. il Horizon 8:28-33 Aut '66

History
Fall of Paris, by A. Horne. Review
Nation 202:786 Je 27 '66. G. Jackson
Fall of Paris; the siege and the Commune, 1870-71, by A. Horne. Review
Nat R 18:319-20 Ap 5 '66. G. F. Eliot

Hotels, restaurants, etc.
La belle epoque revisited; other eating establishments. H. Sutton. il Sat R 49:78+ Je 11 '66
Hilton invades Paris. H. Sutton. Sat R 49: 32+ Je 4 '66
Mr Hilton goes to Paris. il Newsweek 67:71 Ap 25 '66
Notes and comment; Guide Michelin omission of Relais de Porquerolles cause of restaurant owner's suicide. New Yorker 42: 47 D 3 '66
Paris encore. M. M. Davis. il Travel 126:62 Jl '66
Star-crossed; Relais de Porquerolles, Guide Michelin omission causes owner's suicide. Newsweek 68:67-8 O 24 '66
Travel notes; guides to Paris restaurants. R. Joseph. Esquire 65:24+ Je '66
See also
Night clubs

Intellectual life
Paris falls again, into this world. P. Zweig. Nation 202:557-9 My 9 '66

Libraries
For children only; new library at Clamart. il UNESCO Courier 19:16-19 Mr '66

Music
Music in the Marais. R. McMullen. il Hi Fi 16:69-72 My '66
Notes from our correspondents. R. McMullen. See issues of High fidelity incorporating Musical America
Paris. D. Stevens. il Opera N 30:31 Ap 16 '66
Paris; performance of Don Giovanni. D. Stevens. Opera N 31:31 D 10 '66
Tradition of the new; Domaine musical. Newsweek 68:102+ D 19 '66

Newspapers
Letter from Paris; news from Hanoi. Genêt. New Yorker 42:140+ S 10 '66
Newspaper de Gaulle has to read; Le Monde. H. R. Lottman. Harper 234:62-6 Ja '67
Reassurance of St Figaro. il Time 88:95-6 N 25 '66
Vive le sport! sports daily, L'Equipe. il Time 88:43 Ag 5 '66
See also
Newspapers—Consolidations and mergers

Social life and customs
Anecdotes, facetiae, satire, etc.
Paris in spring. W. Brandon. Sat R 49:4+ My 21 '66

Stores
New York, London, Paris collect. L. Lerman. Mlle 63:106 Je '66

Theater
European literary scene; production of Marcel Aymé's Passe-muraille. R. J. Clements. Sat R 50:29 Ja 7 '67
Letter from Paris; le Theatre de Poche-Montparnasse; summer program of one-act playlets by Arrabal and Ionesco. Genêt. New Yorker 42:145-6+ S 10 '66
Letter from Paris; production of La soifet la faim at the Comédie-Francaise. Genêt. New Yorker 42:101-2 Jl 16 '66
Performance from Poland. A. Freund. New Repub 155:35-6 Jl 30 '66
Theatre abroad; France. K. Tynan. New Yorker 42:120+ O 15 '66
See also
Comédie-Française
Music halls (variety theaters, cabarets, etc)

Views
See Paris—Description
PARIS air show. See Aviation—Exhibitions
PARIS edition, New York herald tribune. See New York herald tribune
PARIS edition, New York times. See New York times
PARIS herald
Merger, Paris-style; Paris herald tribune and Washington post. il Time 88:34 Ag 12 '66
PARIS Hilton. See Paris—Hotels, restaurants, etc.
PARIS-match (periodical) See Periodicals—France
PARIS opera. See Opera—France
PARIS peace conference, 1919. See Peace conference, 1919, Versailles

PARISE, Goffredo
  Traveler, consider my Venice; ed. by R.
    Joseph. pors Esquire 65:150-2 Ap '66
PARISHES
  Parish experiment; the Community of John
    XXIII. America 115:678 N 26 '66
  Reforming the parish; symposium. Common-
    weal 84:3-31 Mr 25 '66
PARK, Chung Hee
  Ready for take-off. il por Newsweek 67:36-7
    F 7 '66
  —See Johnson, L. B. jt. auth.
PARK, Kilho
  Deep-sea pH. bibliog Science 154:1540-2 D
    23 '66
PARK, Rosemary
  Women's higher education. Sch & Soc 94:35-9
    Ja 22 '66
PARK buildings
  Chalet and a footbridge; popular park in
    Owatonna, Minn. R. Pecore and R. Rano.
    il Am City 81:118-19 Ap '66
PARK maintenance equipment. See Municipal
  equipment
PARK rangers. See United States—National
  park service
PARK roads. See National parks and reserves
  —Roads
PARKE-Bernet galleries, incorporated
  Quick as a wink; G. David Thompson collec-
    tion auctioned. Newsweek 67:94 Ap 4 '66
  Reshuffling the goodies. il Esquire 65:72-5
    Mr '66
  Wilson of Sotheby's; interview. P. Wilson.
    New Yorker 42:48-50 D 3 '66
PARKER, Dixie
  Tutankhamen: a child's treasure far west of
    Thebes. Sch Arts 65:12-16 Je '66
PARKER, Donald, and Econopouly, Nicholas
  Teaching a unit of civil liberties: the case
    study method. Sr Schol 89:sup40-1 S 23 '66
PARKER, Donald H.
  Colonial Williamsburg. Horticulture 44:26-9+
    S '66
PARKER, Franklin
  1966 as a centennial year in the history of
    education. Sch & Soc 94:67 F 5 '66
  Rhodesia in crisis. por Negro Hist Bul 29:
    53-4+ D '65
  Robert Clifton Weaver; Secretary of housing
    and urban development. bibliog por Negro
    Hist Bul 29:75-6 Ja '66
  Unesco at twenty; swords and plowshares.
    Sch & Soc 94:411-14 N 26 '66
PARKER, Jerry
  Outdoor wiring that's easy and safe. Pop
    Sci 189:146-8+ Ag '66
PARKER, Julius A. See Tourtellotte, W. W.
  jt. auth.
PARKER, Lee E. A.
  Harassment for juries. Time 88:38 D 23 '66
PARKER, Maynard
  Americans in Thailand. Atlan 218:51-8 D '66
  Infrared cameras spotted enemy swarming in
    at night. Life 61:35 O 28 '66
  Squeeze play in Thailand? Reporter 35:16-18
    Ag 11 '66
PARKER, Mike
  Two views; the lab, the victim. W. Brad-
    bury. il pors Life 61:90-107 N 18 '66
PARKER, Patrick L. See Leo, R. F. jt. auth
PARKER, Sanford S. and others
  Business roundup. See issues of Fortune
PARKER, Stephen
  Landlord; poem. Nation 203:294 S 26 '66
  Winter in Étienburgh; poem. New Yorker
    41:40 F 5 '66
PARKER, William Henry
  Obituary
    Nat R 18:763 Ag 9 '66. B. Vaccariello
PARKING, Automobile. See Automobile park-
  ing
PARKING fines. See Fines (penalties)
PARKING meters
  Meters came back; Lima, Ohio. il Am City
    81:120 Jl '66
  Parking meters keep airport traffic moving;
    Seattle-Tacoma international airport. il Am
    City 81:148 S '66
  Vault-type meters stop vandals; Boston. T
    F. Carty. il Am City 81:123+ Mr '66
PARKINS, Phyllis V.
  Biosciences information service of biological
    abstracts. bibliog Science 152:889-94 My 13
    '66
PARKINSON, C. Northcote
  Mrs Parkinson's law. McCalls 93:104-5+ F '66
PARKINSON'S disease. See Paralysis
PARKS, Dennis
  Paul Soldner. Craft Horiz 26:20-3+ Ja '66
PARKS, Edgar L.
  From dream to reality. Motor B 119:94-7+
    Ja '67 (to be cont)

PARKS, Gordon
  I make my choice of weapons; excerpt from
    Choice of weapons. il pors Life 60:62-4+
    Ja 28 '66
  Redemption of the champion. il Life 61:76-
    7+ S 9 '66
            about
  Armed with a camera. il por Time 87:102+
    F 18 '66
  Camera as a sociological weapon. P. Stack-
    pole. U S Camera 29:16+ My '66
  No catch for the hawk. E. M. Yoder, jr.
    Sat R 49:40 F 12 '66
  Through a lens, darkly. il por Newsweek
    67:86 F 7 '66
PARKS, Isabel
  Welded metal sculpture. Sch Arts 65:21-3 F
    '66
PARKS, Joan W.
  Making the most of summer. Parents Mag
    41:42-3+ Ag '66
PARKS, John
  Talk about doves; interview. por Field & S
    71:56-7+ S '66
PARKS, Michael
  Cities on strike. America 115:455-7 O 15 '66
PARKS, Michael (actor)
  Who's Michael Parks? ed. by E. Miller. pors
    Seventeen 25:174-5+ S '66
PARKS, W. George
  Gordon research conferences: program for
    1966. Science 151:1249-64+ Mr 11 '66
PARKS, Wally
  Drags. por Motor T 18:45 Mr '66
PARKS
  Parks and recreation. See issues of Ameri-
    can city
            Fees
  See Recreation—Fees
            Finance
  Endowment management for parks. L. B.
    Houston. Parks & Rec 328-30+ Ap '66
            Lighting
  New lighting makes park a showplace;
    Thornden park, Syracuse, N.Y. il Am City
    81:124 Je '66
            Maintenance
  More maintenance per man-hour; Highland
    Park, Ill. D. H. Fritz. il Am City 81:96-8
    N '66
  Parks plans can simplify maintenance; Santa
    Clara, Calif. E. R. Carmichael. il Am City
    81:104-6 O '66
            Argentina
  See also
  National parks and reserves—Argentina
            South America
  Parks, plans, and people; how South Amer-
    ica guards her green legacy. M. Rocke-
    feller and L. Rockefeller. il Nat Geog Mag
    131:74-119 Ja '67
            United States
  Current trends in recreation and parks; ad-
    dress. G. H. Aull, jr. Parks & Rec 1:553-4
    Jl '66
  Looms weave by themselves; challenge of
    leisure time; excerpts from address. G. B.
    Hartzog, jr. il Parks & Rec 1:20-2 Ja '66
  Ventilating the crowded city. R. C. Weaver.
    Parks & Rec 1:893 N '66
  Where can a girl climb a tree? excerpts
    from article. Recreation magazine. Septem-
    ber 1945. W. T. Vanderlipp. Parks & Rec
    1:355-6 Ap '66
  Your town's open spaces, ways to save them.
    il Changing T 21:35-8 Ja '67
  See also
  National parks and reserves—United States
PARKSCAPE U.S.A. See United States—Na-
  tional park service
PARLIAMENTARY elections. See Elections—
  Great Britain
PARLIAMENTARY government
  Military origins of medieval representation.
    T. N. Bisson. bibliog f Am Hist R 71:
    1199-218 Jl '66
PARMA, Italy
  Forum for Verdi; Institute of Verdi studies
    of Parma; with introd. by J. W. Freeman.
    M. J. Matz. il Opera N 31:6-7 S 10 '66
  Singer vs. public; C. MacNeil and opera
    audience at Parma's Royal theater. A. M.
    Lingg. il Opera N 31:6-7 Ja 14 '67
PARMA, Ohio
            Recreation
  Summer baseball school. R. Bergstrom. il
    Parks & Rec 1:311+ Ap '66

PARMELEE, Grannis P.
Bells are back on the King's highway; El
Camino Real bells; reprint. Hobbies 71:
98O-98P N '66
PARMENTER, Ross
Elizabeth Borton de Treviño. Horn Bk 42:
412-18 Ag '66
PARMER, J. Norman
(ed) Peace corps. bibliog f Ann Am Acad 365:
1-146 My '66
PARNELL, Charles Stewart
Stag and hounds. por Newsweek 67:108+
Je 20 '66
PARNIS, Mollie
She has designs on three first ladies; ed.
by D. Lurie. pors Life 60:43-4+ Je 17 '66
PAROCHIAL schools
Are parochial schools racial escape valves?
Christian Cent 83:1298 O 26 '66
School v. family; survey of religious attitudes
and beliefs among parochial-school children.
Time 88:56 S 16 '66
  See also
Church schools

Federal aid
  See Federal aid to education
PAROCHIAL schools, Catholic
Analyzing the parochial schools. P. Deasy.
Commonweal 85:231-2 N 25 '66
Catholic schools in action: a report, ed. by
R. A. Neuwien. Review
  America 115:608 N 12 '66. E. J. Power
Degrees of devotion; results of survey of
U.S. parochial schools, N.O.R.C. il Time
88:49 Jl 29 '66
Education of Catholic Americans, by A. M.
Greeley and P. H. Rossi. Review
  Cath World 204:135-42 D '66. G. Moran
  Cath World 204:143-8 D '66. R. Robbins
Four myths about parochial schools. M.
O'Neill. America 116:82-6 Ja 21 '67
Greeley-Rossi report. R. D. Cross. Common-
weal 84:577-9 S 16 '66
Greeley-Rossi report on Catholic schools.
America 115:128 Ag 6 '66
Parochial benefits; concerning Greeley-Rossi
study. Newsweek 68:77 Ag 1 '66
Parochial pedagogy. R. L. Johnstone. Chris-
tian Cent 84:48 Ja 11 '67
Report card from Notre Dame. Time 88:65 S
2 '66
Report card; study by University of Notre
Dame. il Newsweek 68:59-60 S 5 '66
Report on the schools. M. P. Sheridan. Amer-
ica 115:245 S 10 '66
Using the Greeley-Rossi report. America 115:
150 Ag 13 '66
What's happening in education? Catholic
schools compared with public schools.
W. D. Boutwell. PTA Mag 61:11-12 D '66

Desegregation
Negroes in Catholic schools; de facto segrega-
tion? J. M. Cronin. Commonweal 85:13-16
O 7 '66
PARODIES
Spoofproof? Harvard Lampoon's parody of
Playboy. il Newsweek 68:102+ S 19 '66
PARODY (music)
By an unknown master. The Baroque Beatles
book. B. Jacobson. il Hi Fi 16:67 F '66
Prof's off on a Bach boff. R. Eyer. Life 60:
16 F 25 '66
  See also
Phonograph records—Musical parody
PAROUSIA (religion) See Second advent
PARR, Mary E.
Personalising process; address, January 26,
1966. Vital Speeches 32:341-4 Mr 15 '66
PARR, Michael
Two British chronicles. M. Bell. Poetry 107:
410 Mr '66
Two poems: Ram Aries; When I have slept.
Yale R 56:112-13 O '66
PARR, Richard S.
Capote sued for one-tenth of Cold blood
royalties. Pub W 189:60 My 30 '66
PARRA, Mariano
Mariano Parra ballet espanol. East 74th
street theatre. J. Maskey. Dance Mag 40:
65 F '66
PARRISH, Mrs Henry, 2d
Comfort is a whole way of life. il House &
Gard 131:80-7 Ja '67
PARRISH, Maxfield
Obituary
  Am Artist 30:3+ Je '66. N. Kent
PARRISH, Patrick
Day I really became a father. Parents Mag
41:56-7+ F '66
We live in the city and love it. Parents Mag
41:52-4+ My '66

PARROT; story. See Singer, I. B.
PARROTS
Extinct parrot found living in Australia;
paradise parrot. Sci N 90:372 N 5 '66
PARRY, Albert
Russia cracks jokes about China. N Y Times
Mag p 14:15+ Je 26 '66
Russians are computing. N Y Times Mag
p24-5+ Ag 28 '66
Russia's new bourgeois grows fat. N Y Times
Mag p44-5+ Je 5 '66
Russia's other peace movement. Nation 203:
142-5 Ag 22 '66
Soviet aid to Vietnam. Reporter 36:28-33 Ja
12 '67
PARRY, J. H.
Atahuallpa and the Spanish. Sat R 50:33-4
Ja 7 '67
Discoverers or desperados? Sat R 49:24-5
Jl 2 '66
PARRY, Jack
Fly to trophy fish on schedule. Field & S
71:48-9 Jl '66
PARRY, Stanley, and others
Hungary in revolt, November 1956; reprints
from November 1956 issue. Nat R 18:1105-10
N 1 '66
PARSEGHIAN, Ara
Who is the best now? por Life 61:100 D 2 '66
                    about
Psychologist on the sidelines. W. B. Fur-
long. il pors N Y Times Mag p56-7+ N
13 '66
That legend is loose again. D. Jenkins. il
por Sports Illus 25:70-2+ N 7 '66
PARSEGIAN, Vozcan Lawrence
Atomic transition, to what? Bul Atomic Sci
22:23-6 Ja '66
On the role of government laboratories. Bul
Atomic Sci 22:35-6 S '66
PARSIFAL; opera. See Wagner, R.
PARSONS, C. and Porter, K. R.
Muscle relaxation; evidence for an intra-
fibrillar restoring force in vertebrate stri-
ated muscle. bibliog Science 153:426-7 Jl
22 '66
PARSONS, Lindsley
Night of the santana. Yachting 120:48+ O '66
San Quintin: the forgotten harbor. Motor B
117:156-7+ My '66
PARSONS, Mary Ruth
Cookbook; text. Mlle 64:164-5+ N '66
PARSONS, Peter, and Simpson, M. V.
Biosynthesis of DNA by isolated mitochon-
dria: incorporation of thymidine triphos-
phate-2-C^{14}. bibliog Science 155:91-3 Ja 6
'67
PARSONS, Stuart O.
Election of AAAS officers. Science 153:1675-80
S 30 '66
PARSONS and Whittemore
They plant profits in economic deserts. P.
Deutschman. Read Digest 90:199-200+ Ja
'67
PARSONS college, Fairfield, Ia.
Wizard of flunk-out U; with report by J.
Frook. il Life 60:77-8+ Je 3 '66
PART time employment
New & better part-time jobs for women. il
Changing T 21:21-3 Ja '67
Work experience of the population in 1965.
F. A. Bogan and T. T. Swanstrom. bibliog f
il Mo Labor R 89:1372-7 D '66
  See also
Seasonal labor
PART time teachers. See Teachers, Part time
PARTHASARATHI, G.
Content in another country. Sat R 49:58
Jl 23 '66
PARTHENON
  See also
Elgin marbles
PARTIAL dentures. See Teeth, Artificial
PARTIALLY seeing children. See Blind
PARTICLE accelerators. See Accelerators
(electrons, etc)
PARTICLES
Purification and reconstitution of the periodic
fibril and unit structure of human amyloid.
G. G. Glenner and H. A. Bladen. bibliog
il Science 154:271-2 O 14 '66
PARTICLES (nuclear physics)
Back to symmetry. J. Reinert. Sci Digest
60:47 D '66
Current problems in particle physics; address,
December 27, 1965. E. M. McMillan. Sci-
ence 152:1210-15 My 27 '66
Death of a theory. M. L. Silbar. il Sci Digest
60:9-11 S '66

PARTICLES (nuclear physics)—*Continued*
Inner secret of matter. M. L. Silbar. il Sci Digest 60:66+ O '66
Invariance theory upset. A. Ewing. il(p 17) Sci N 90:18 Jl 9 '66
Odd or even? International congress on high energy physics. Newsweek 68:66 S 19 '66
Particles from sun may penetrate earth's belts. Sci N 90:394 N 12 '66
Quarks and the solar spectrum. G. S. Mumford. Sky & Tel 33:31 Ja '67
Quarks may be source of quasars' energy. Sci N L 89:83 F 5 '66
Tracks of charged particles in meteorites. G. S. Mumford. il Sky & Tel 31:144 Mr '66
What is a quark? J. Reinert. Sci Digest 60:87-8 Ag '66
   See also
Electrons
Mesons
Neutrinos
Protons

Acceleration

Broken mirror; Brookhaven experiment shatters Lee-Yang theory. Newsweek 68:52 Jl 4 '66
Polarized accelerator targets. G. Shapiro. il Sci Am 215:68-78 bibliog(p 131) Jl '66

Detection

Detection of relativistic particles. L. C. L. Yuan. bibliog il Science 154:124-30 O 7 '66
PARTICIPATION certificates. See Government lending
PARTICLES, Elementary. See Particles (nuclear physics)
PARTICLES, Interplanetary. See Matter, Interstellar
PARTIES. See Entertaining
PARTIN, Edward Grady
Hoffa decision. Nation 204:5-6 Ja 2 '67
How they got Jimmy Hoffa, or did they? excerpt from Crime war. R. M. Cipes. Atlan 218:118-22 N '66
PARTNERSHIP
   See also
Joint adventures
PARTNERSHIPS, Farm family. See Father-son farm operating agreements
PARTRIDGE shooting
Bird hunter's Shangri-la; chukars in Hell's Canyon. L. Miracle. il Outdoor Life 138:62-3+ N '66
More chukar hunters needed. C. Dickey. il Field & S 71:68-71+ S '66
Our most neglected gamebird; the chukar. C. Chatfield. il Outdoor Life 137:52-3+ F '66
PARTY favors
Party with pow! with recipes. il Seventeen 25:66-81+ Jl '66
PARTY for divorce; drama. See Kalcheim, L.
PARTY funds. See Campaign funds
PARTY menus. See Menus
PARTY platforms. See Platforms, Political
PARTY whips. See United States—Congress—Voting
PARVIN, Stuart A.
Miniaturia. See issues of Hobbies
PASADENA, Calif.

Music

Pasadena; lifeless Otello. A. Goldberg. Opera N 30:22 My 7 '66
PASADENA opera company
Pasadena. A. Goldberg. Opera N 30:30 Mr 12; 30:29 Ap 16 '66
PASARELL, Charles, 1943?-
Charlito moves to the head of the class. J. Jares. il por Sports Illus 24:50-1 F 28 '66
PASCIN, Jules
Unique affair. il Time 89:58-9 Ja 20 '67
PASCOE, Joyce
Pair of lubbers takes to the sea. il pors Ebony 21:112-14+ Ap '66
PASOLINI, Pier Paolo
Gospel according to St Matthew. M. Walsh. America 114:307-8 F 26 '66
Pasolini's passion. S. Kauffmann. New Repub 154:33-4 Mr 22 '66
PASOLLI, Robert
Blowup in Cincinnati. Nation 203:262 S 19 '66
Off-Broadway. Nation 202:310 Mr 14 '66
Off-off-Broadway. Nation 202:403-6 Ap 4 '66
Theatre. Nation 202:224, 597; 203:717-18 F 21, My 16, D 26 '66
PASQUEL, Jorge
Great Mexican war of 1946. F. Graham, jr. il Sports Illus 25:116-20+ S 19 '66

PASSAGEWAYS. See Breezeways; Halls
PASSENGER fares. See Airlines—Fares
PASSENGER traffic (railroads) See Railroads—Passenger traffic
PASSIN, Herbert
Japan joins the hipster international. Reporter 34:45-7 Ja 27 '66
PASSION music
What's the score? K. Penderecki's departure from the Passions of Bach and Telemann. il Time 88:55 O 14 '66
   See also
Phonograph records—Passion music
PASSION of Jesus Christ in art. See Jesus Christ—Art
PASSION plays
   See also
Oberammergau passion play
PASSIVE resistance to government
Civil disobedience: is it ever right to break the law? pro and con discussion. il Sr Schol 87:16-17 Ja 7 '66
Fruits of protest. C. Cohen; D. Krech. il Nation 202:357-64 Mr 28 '66
Neither blind obedience nor uncivil disobedience. S. Hook. il N Y Times Mag p52-3+ Je 5 '66
Protest, a right and a responsibility; round table discussion from 1966 student burgesses at Williamsburg. il Sr Schol 88:10-13+ My 6 '66
When conscience and government clash. il Sr Schol 89:2-5+ Ja 13 '67
PASSOVER
$475 bargain: B. Shahn's Haggadah. F. Getlein. New Repub 154:27-8 Ap 30 '66
PASSPORTS
Additional foreign passports valid beyond expiration date, Sudan and Viet Nam. P. B. Heymann. Dept State Bul 54:870 My 30 '66
Department announces revised passport regulations. Dept State Bul 55:723 N 7 '66
How to get a passport. Good H 162:182 Ap '66
Role of the State department in the administration and enforcement of the new immigration law. A. P. Schwartz. bibliog f Ann Am Acad 367:93-104 S '66
State, justice improve procedures on visas for conference guests. Dept State Bul 54:869 My 30 '66
   See also
United States—State, Department of—Passport division
PASTA. See Cookery, Italian; Macaroni
PASTEL drawing
Amateurs, Frakturs and elegant young ladies; Garbisch collection of American watercolors and pastels at the National gallery, Washington, D.C. W. P. Campbell. il Art N 65:50-3+ O '66
Erie Canal; a record in pastels by J. Erwin Porter. N. Kent. il Am Artist 30:42-7+ Je '66
PASTEUR Institute, Paris
Pasteur institute rebels lose a round. V. K. McElheny. Science 153:1226-8 S 9 '66
Pasteur institute scientists demand sweeping reform. V. K. McElheny. Science 151:809 F 18 '66
Pasteur institute takes the cure. il Bsns W p 132-4+ Ag 13 '66
PASTIMES. See Amusements
PASTORAL counseling. See Counseling
PASTORAL psychology. See Psychology, Pastoral
PASTORE, Arthur R. Jr
Switzerland's lakes. Travel 125:32-6 Ap '66
PASTRY
Colossal cream puff; with recipes. il Bet Hom & Gard 44:96 My '66
Compliant cream puff. P. Cannon. il Ladies Home J 83:98-9+ Je '66
For a try at French pastry. il Sunset 136:157 Je '66
Into the kitchen to make a tasty cream puff tree; with recipe. il Sunset 137:60-1 D '66
Pastry tricks in half an hour. il Bet Hom & Gard 44:102 Je '66
Puff pastry is child's play. P. Cannon. il Ladies Home J 83:102-3+ S '66
These swirls are snowballs; with recipe. il Sunset 137:152 D '66
PASTURES
Are pasture hogs best? J. Harvey. il Suc Farm 64:36-7 Je '66
PATAGONIA
Improving a wretched plain. B. F. Grossling. il Am For 72:26-7 N '66
Where the world ends. J. Kubic. il Newsweek 67:51-2 F 28 '66

PATCH, Sam
Wonderful leaps of Sam Patch; with excerpts from a children's book. R. M. Dorson. il pors Am Heritage 18:12-19 D '66
PATE, John B. See Lodge, J. P. jr. jt. auth.
PATENT laws and legislation
How to speed patents; Presidential commission recommended overhaul of the system. Bsns W p46 D 10 '66
Infringers beware! T. F. Kirby. il Pop Electr 25:75-6 Jl '66
Patent law change. F. Sartwell. Sci N 90:512 D 17 '66
    See also
Plant patents
PATENT office (United States) See United States—Patent office
PATENT rights. See Patent laws and legislation; Patents
PATENTS
Current U.S. patents. See issues of Science news
Get inventions off the shelf; concerning patent rights of the paid-to-invent inventor. C. E. Barnes. Harvard Bsns R 44:138-9 Ja '66
How Bert beat the bureaucrats: Supreme court rules government infringement of B. N. Adams patent. Time 87:61 Mr 4 '66
Inventions, teachers, and patents. C. E. Gauer. NEA J 55:52-3 S '66
Patent giveaway; Senate judiciary committee to consider bill. New Repub 154:9 My 7 '66
That mousetrap has to be better. Bsns W p42 F 26 '66
What's needed to keep new products coming; symposium. il Nations Bsns 53:42-3+ D '65
    See also
Drugs—Patents
Inventions
Patent laws and legislation
Plant patents
United States—Patent office

International aspects
Our international patent policy and the world patent crisis. H. J. Winter. bibliog f Dept State Bul 54:1006-12 Je 27 '66
Patent experts agree on dire need for international accord. W. S. Beller. Tech W 19:20 N 7 '66

Photographic reproduction and projection
    See also
Microfilms

United States
    See also
United States—Presidents commission on the patent system
PATENTS, Government owned
Industry-related bills on firing line; McClellan patent bill. Miss & Roc 18:15 Ap 11 '66
Senate battles over patents rights. F. Sartwell. Sci N 90:558 D 31 '66
PATERSON, William
William Paterson's copy of Louis XVI. P. W. Schmidtchen. il Hobbies 71:108-9 Ap '66
PATÉS. See Cookery—Meat
PATHOGENIC bacteria. See Bacteria, Pathogenic
PATHOLOGISTS
    See also
College of American pathologists
PATHOLOGY
    See also
Medicine, Preventive
PATHOLOGY, Animal. See Animals—Diseases and pests
PATHOLOGY, Comparative
Kinship of animal and human diseases. R. W. Leader. il Sci Am 216:110-16 bibliog(p 148) Ja '67
PATHS. See Garden walks
PATIALA, Yadavindra Singh, maharaja of. See Singh, Y.
PATIENCE
On patience as an American virtue; Time essay. Time 87:22-3 Mr 25 '66
PATIENT care. See Hospitals
PATIENTS, Hospital. See Sick, The
PATIENTS and physicians. See Physicians and patients
PATIO furniture. See Furniture, Outdoor
PATIOS. See Outdoor rooms
PATMAN, Wright
Patman pulls the veil from bank trust units. Bsns W p68 D 31 '66
Wright Patman: a lonely populist. il por Bsns W p51-2+ Jl 23 '66

PATNODE, Winton
Polarized beauty. il Natur Hist 75:24-5 Ap '66
PATRICK, James
Boat camping doubles your pleasure. Pop Sci 188:140-3 F '66
PATRICK, Peggy
Family work shops. Sch Arts 66:5-7 O '66
PATRICK, Ted
Parents for peace. il pors Ebony 21:72-4+ O '66
PATRICK Ann, Sister
Sixth graders express themselves in pictures. Sch Arts 65:33-4 F '66
PATRIOTISM
Enter patriotism? W. F. Buckley, jr. Nat R 18:764 Ag 9 '66
Ethics and the professional patriots. M. Q. Sibley. bibliog f Ann Am Acad 363:126-36 Ja '66
I am a tired American; reprint. A. McIntosh. U S News 60:120 F 14 '66
Inverted truth, subverted dream. Christian Cent 83:1591-2 D 28 '66
Patriotism: dead or alive? panel discussion. il Seventeen 25:160-1+ N '66
Patriotism; symposium. il NEA J 56:9-11+ Ja '67
Urge to serve in Washington can go too far. H. Sidey. Life 61:30B Jl 29 '66
    See also
Nationalism
PATRIOTISM; story. See Mishima, Y.
PATROL boats, Navy. See United States—Navy—Boats
PATROL cars. See Automobiles, Police
PATROL torpedo boats. See Torpedo boats
PATTEN, Karl
Deaf-mute picnic; poem. Commonweal 84: 637 S 30 '66
PATTERN (planning assistance through technical evaluation of relevance numbers) See Operations research
PATTERN making
    See also
Templets
PATTERNS (dress)
Fit the pattern to your figure. C. Houck. il Parents Mag 41:27 My '66
PATTERNS in design. See Design, Decorative
PATTERSON, Cissy. See Patterson, E. M.
PATTERSON, Eleanor Medill
Cissy Patterson, by A. A. Hoge. Review Newsweek il por 67:60+ Mr 7 '66
PATTERSON, Floyd
In defense of Cassius Clay; interview. ed. by G. Talese. Esquire 66:55-8 Ag '66

    about
Ringing in the old. Sports Illus 25:18 O 10 '66
PATTERSON, John Henry
Machine that kept them honest. G. Carson. il pors Am Heritage 17:50-9+ Ag '66
PATTERSON, Russell
Kansas City stock; interview, ed. by F. Merkling. por Opera N 31:13 S 10 '66
PATTERSON, William Allan
All in one lifetime: from crates to super jetliners; interview. por U S News 60:62-6 F 7 '66

    about
Exit pioneer Pat. por Time 87:99-100 My 6 '66
PATTERSON, William D.
Agenda for travel. Sat R 50:24+ Ja 7 '67
SR's businessman of the year. Sat R 50:74+ Ja 14 '67
SR's fourteenth annual advertising awards. Sat R 49:70-7 Ap 9 '66
PATTISON, E. Scott
Excerpt from testimony, April 30, 1965. Cong Digest 45:179+ Je '66
PATTON, Arch
Top executive pay: new facts & figures. Harvard Bsns R 44:94-7 S '66
PATTON, Eddie
Credit for time served. il por Time 88:46 S 2 '66
PATTON, Frances Gray
Chapel Hill. Holiday 40:54-63+ Ag '66
PATTON, James G.
Hell raisers' adieux. il por Time 87:20 Mr 25 '66
PATTON, Temple C.
Paint for pre-coated plywood. Arch Rec 139: 233-4 Ap '66
PAUGH, Tom
Mullica River. Motor B 118:28-9+ O '66

PAUL, Saint
Peter and Paul. V. P. McCorry. America 114:883 Je 25 '66

Teaching
Saint Paul, apostle to all men. E. O. Hauser. il Read Digest 89:146-50+ S '66

PAUL VI, pope
Religious value of the council; excerpt from address, December 6, 1965. Cath World 203:113-14 My '66
Two reactions to the new mass liturgy; address, March 17, 1965. Cath World 203:22-3 Ap '66
Warning from the Pope; its meaning; summary of address, November 16, 1966. U S News 61:15 N 28 '66
—and Athenagoras I, patriarch
Joint declaration Rome-Istanbul. Cath World 202:369-70 Mr '66

about
Archbishop at the Vatican. America 114:470 Ap 9 '66
Cardinal, Pope and war. Commonweal 85:391-2 Ja 13 '67
Contraception: toward decision. M. F. Vaente. Christian Cent 84:77-9 Ja 18 '67
Day in the life of the Pope. C. Pallenberg. il por Read Digest 89:64-9 Jl '66
Day with Pope Paul; excerpts from The Pope's backyard. C. G. Pepper. il por Mc-Calls 94:120-1+ O '66
Disappointing Marian development. S. Benko. Christian Cent 84:79-80 Ja 18 '67
Friend of peace, and the UN. M. McGrory. America 114:251 F 19 '66
Kiss of peace. il por Time 87:42 Ap 1 '66
Letter from Vatican City (cont) X. Rynne. New Yorker 42:140+ O 22 '66
Meaning of peace. America 115:438 O 15 '66
Paul VI on piety. America 114:820 Je 11 '66
Pope and birth control. Commonweal 85:157 N 11 '66
Pope and Jesuits: invitation and response. America 115:729-30 D 3 '66
Pope and Mr Gromyko. America 114:682 My 14 '66
Pope delays his decision. America 115:576-7 N 12 '66
Pope Paul on poverty. Commonweal 84:272 My 27 '66
Pope Paul's mournful November warning. Christian Cent 83:1497-8 D 7 '66
Pope's unsolvable problem. J. Roddy. por Look 30:120+ D 13 '66; Discussion. 31:16 Ja 24 '67
Real meaning of talks between the Pope and the Archbishop. il pors U S News 60:15 Ap 4 '66
Search for peace with justice. America 115:376 O 1 '66
Secret drama behind the Pope's momentous decision on birth control. L. R. Chevalier. por Ladies Home J 83:88-9+ Mr '66
Two leaders in drive for peace. por U S News 61:30 N 14 '66
Unity in truth. il por Newsweek 67:63 Ap 4 '66
Vatican peace initiatives. R. A. Graham. America 114:416 Mr 26 '66

Visit to New York (city) 1965
Pope's visit. M. Cartwright. il por Negro Hist Bul 29:33-4 N '65
U.N: one year later. J. Bel Geddes. Cath World 204:98-103 N '66

PAUL, princess of Yugoslavia
Family portrait. il por Vogue 147:122-3 Ap 15 '66

PAUL, Martin A. and Margrave, J. L.
Chemistry at high temperatures. Science 152:1113-14 My 20 '66

PAUL, Mimi
Why is a ballerina? interview. ed. by O. Maynard. pors Dance Mag 40:38-42 Ap '66

PAUL, Pearl, limited. See Pearl Paul, limited

PAUL, Sherman
For love of Chicago. Nation 202:657-9 My 30 '66
New England saint. Nation 203:647-8 D 12 '66
Pathology of undevelopment. Nation 202:102-3 Ja 24 '66
Seeing Williams with fresh eyes. Nation 203:356-7 O 10 '66

PAUL Bunyan and his blue ox; drama. See Cone, M.

PAUL Taylor dance company. See Dance companies

PAULIN, Lorna
First lady; libraries, readers and librarians in Great Britain. ed. by G. R. Davies. Library J 91:4052-3 S 15 '66

PAULING, Linus Carl
[Excerpts from testimony] Nat R 18:461-4 My 17 '66

about
Drawing the libel line. Newsweek 67:92 My 9 '66
Linus Pauling takes the stand; excerpts from proceedings. Nat R 18:459-61+ My 17 '66
Linus Pauling: TKO. Nat R 18:403 My 3 '66
National review vindicated. Nat R 18:404-7 My 3 '66
Pauling and libel. Commonweal 84:192 My 6 '66
Perils of being too public. il por Time 87:80 Ap 29 '66

PAULINGITE. See Zeolites

PAULLIN, Ellen Payne
Call me by my rightful number. Sat R 49:76 F 19 '66

PAULSON, F. M.
(ed) Boating. See issues of Field & stream
Boating: clear sailing ahead? Field & S 71:40-1+ Ja '67
Cruising Shasta Lake. Field & S 70:35-7+ F '66
Perfect boat for campers. Field & S 71:32-3+ Ja '67
Sacramento delta cruise. Field & S 71:42-3+ Je '66
Trek to treasure island. Field & S 70:53-5+ Ap '66

PAULSON, Joan
C is for cranberries. Ladies Home J 83:127 N '66
P is for peach. Ladies Home J 83:98 Ag '66

PAVAN, Crodowaldo, and Basile, Renato
Chromosome changes induced by infections in tissues of rhynchosciara angelae. bibliog Science 151:1556-8 Mr 25 '66

PAVEMENTS
How to get those impossible streets paved; Phoenix, Ariz. R. N. Taylor. il Am City 81:120-1 My '66
More and heavier trucks in residential areas. il Am City 81:39 Jl '66
Underfoot; look at eleven splendid kinds of garden paving. il Sunset 136:110-13 My '66
See also
Airports—Runways
Sidewalks

Maintenance and repair
How to guard a driveway from winter damage. R. Douglas. il Pop Sci 189:156 N '66
How to prevent scaling; Sioux City, Iowa. R. R. Fleming. il Am City 81:96-7 D '66
One-trip hole patching. L. Lowe. il Am City 81:38 O '66

Surface treatment
Paved surfaces and their construction; reprint. J. B. Clouston. il Parks & Rec 1:422-4+, 511-12+, 580-1, 752-3+ My-Jl, S '66
Seal coats and thin overlays. R. R. Fleming. bibliog il Am City 81:129-31+ S '66
Slurry seal cures spalled-concrete ills; Kenosha, Wis. D. K. Holland. il Am City 81:103 F '66
Why we add asbestos; St Louis, Mo. A. M. Johnson. il Am City 81:98-9 Mr '66
Why we switched to cationic emulsion; Bartlesville, Okla. D. Farrington. il Am City 81:104-5 N '66

PAVEMENTS, Asphalt
Design of modern asphalt pavements; Contra Costa County, Calif. V. W. Sauer. il Am City 81:113-16 Ap '66
Final shot of asphalt; Redwood City, Calif. D. Chester. il Am City 81:114-15 Ag '66
Why we add asbestos; St Louis, Mo. A. M. Johnson. il Am City 81:98-9 Mr '66

PAVEMENTS, Concrete
How to prevent scaling; Sioux City, Iowa. R. R. Fleming. il Am City 81:96-7 D '66
Pavement joints will disappear. il Am City 81:56 D '66

PAVIA, Phillip
Polemic on one-eye formats. Art N 65:28-31+ D '66
Stone notes: direct carving. Art N 65:50-1+ My '66

about
Art galleries; exhibition at the Martha Jackson. R. M. Coates. New Yorker 42:172+ D 10 '66
Art that makes its own light; Martha Jackson gallery show. K. Kuh. il Sat R 49:39-40 Je 25 '66
Two sculptors. J. Kroll. il por Newsweek 68:93 N 14 '66

PAVILION house. See Architecture, Domestic

PAVILIONS
From a bygone pool pavilion to newborn elegance. il House & Gard 130:88-91 Ag '66
Swim, sauna or just escape. il Sunset 136: 122-3 My '66

PAVLOV, Ivan Petrovich
Gap between sciences narrows to fine line. P. McBroom. Sci N 90:446 N 26 '66

PAVLOVA, Anna
Trial by celluloid; Museum of modern art program. R. Kotlowitz. Harper 232:127 Ap '66

PAWN shops. See Pawnbroking

PAWNBROKING
Only the rich go into hock. Time 87:54+ Ja 28 '66

PAWTUCKET, R.I.
Pawtucket's two-pronged attack. J. A. Keith. il Am City 81:108-9 Ag '66
Reconstruction and consolidation of a growing complex; Memorial hospital. il Arch Rec 139: 171 Mr '66

PAXTON, Glenn
Music to my ears; musical score for TV show. I. Kolodin. il Sat R 49:38 My 28 '66

PAXTON, Steve
Review. J. Anderson. Dance Mag 40:30 Mr '66

PAXTON, William H.
How to build and fly Chinese kites. Pop Sci 188:144-7 My '66

PAYMENTS, Balance of. See Balance of payments

PAYNE, Jack
Car-top boat for $20. Pop Sci 189:138-40 Ag '66

PAYNE, Lucile Vaughan
Teaching students to write. NEA J 55:28-30 N '66

PAYNE, Melvin M.
Preserving the treasures of Olduvai gorge. Nat Geog Mag 130:700-9 N '66

PAYROLL taxes. See Insurance, Unemployment—United States

PAYROLLS
Putting payroll on a paying basis; Salt Lake City. L. E. Holley. il Am City 81:154+ S '66

PAZ ESTENSSORO, Victor
Letter from La Paz. C. Rand. il New Yorker 42:36-40+ D 31 '66

PAZHWAK, Abdul Rahman
Human rights day 1966; message. UN Mo Chron 3:i-ii D '66

PEABODY, Endicott
Massachusetts mix-up. por Newsweek 68:30-1 O 17 '66

PEABODY, George
First great cheerful giver. G. T. Hellman. il por Am Heritage 17:28-33+ Je '66

PEABODY conservatory of music. See Peabody institute, Baltimore

PEABODY institute, Baltimore
Baltimore. G. M. Eby. il Opera N 30:26 Je 4 '66

PEACE
Artist's act of faith: a testimony of peace. il House & Gard 130:160-3 D '66
Assembly defers action until next session; question of the peaceful settlement of disputes. UN Mo Chron 3:36-8 Ja '66
Causes of peace; ineffectual peace movements. J. F. Wharton. Sat R 49:12-14+ Jl 2 '66
Christmas sermon. A. Waugh. Nat R 18:1312-14+ D 27 '66
Democracy and peace; address, May 24, 1966. Thant. UN Mo Chron 3:61-70 Je '66
Friend of peace, and the UN. M. McGrory. America 114:251 F 19 '66
Goal of a reliable peace: a survey of free-world progress; address, August 22, 1966. D. Rusk. Dept State Bul 55:362-8 S 12 '66
How do you make peace? D. Lawrence. U S News 60:124 F 28 '66
Meaning of peace. America 115:438 O 15 '66
New Year's prayer; reprint, January 2, 1942. D. Lawrence. U S News 62:76+ Ja 2 '67
Notes on the politics of peace. K. E. Boulding. Bul Atomic Sci 22:30-2 S '66
Peace and justice among nations: the agenda of the international community; address, May 2, 1966. A. J. Goldberg. Dept State Bul 54:798-802 My 23 '66
Peace and the bishops. J. O'Gara. Commonweal 85:338 D 23 '66
Peace and war, by R. Aron. Review
New Yorker 42:117-22 Ja 14 '67. G. Steiner
Peace begins in the minds of men; symposium. il UNESCO Courier 19:46-9 Jl '66
Peace comes of age. A. J. P. Taylor. il N Y Times Mag p 14-15+ Ag 14 '66

Peace, our most compelling task; remarks made at the lighting of the national Christmas tree, December 17, 1965. L. B. Johnson. Dept State Bul 54:51-2 Ja 10 '66
Peace, the modern approach; address, March 26, 1966. L. A. Ferre. Vital Speeches 32: 461-4 My 15 '66
Peace, war and the Vatican council. T. M. Finn. Cath World 203:270-5 Ag '66
Peacekeeping and peacemaking. L. P. Bloomfield. For Affairs 44:671-82 Jl '66
President Johnson lights the Nation's Christmas tree; remarks, December 15, 1966. L. B. Johnson. Dept State Bul 56:14 Ja 2 '67
Problems of peacemaking. W. V. Kennedy. America 114:855-7 Je 18 '66
Prospects of peace; excerpts from address. Chalfont. Bul Atomic Sci 22:2-4 My '66
Quest for peace; quotations. Sr School 88:8-9 Mr 11 '66
Religion and war. J. V. Schall. Commonweal 85:193-6 N 18 '66
Requirements for organizing the peace; address. October 12, 1966. D. Rusk. Dept State Bul 55:658-63 O 31 '66; Same with title Organizing the peace. Vital Speeches 33:67-71 N 15 '66
Revolution in peace education; Clark-Sohn plan and the World law fund. R. A. Falk. il Sat R 49:59-61+ My 21 '66
Roots of peace. B. V. A. Röling. il UNESCO Courier 19:22-6+ Ja '66
Search for peace with justice. America 115: 376 O 1 '66
Silent night, uneasy night. E. J. Hughes. Newsweek 68:13 D 26 '66
United Nations: a great chapter in man's pilgrimage toward peace; address, October 25, 1966. A. J. Goldberg. Dept State Bul 55:739-44 N 14 '66
U.N: one year later. J. Bel Geddes. Cath World 204:98-103 N '66
Vatican peace initiatives. R. A. Graham. America 114:416 Mr 26 '66
World peace through law; address, March 12, 1966. E. Warren. Vital Speeches 32:387-90 Ap 15 '66
See also
Aggression (international law)
Atomic power—International control
Disarmament
International education
International relations
International security
Pacifism
Vietnamese war, 1957- —Peace and mediation

PEACE, Pilgrim; drama. See Cable, H.

PEACE and education. See War and education

PEACE conference, 1919, Versailles
Great Britain and the African peace settlement of 1919. W. R. Louis. bibliog f Am Hist R 71:875-92 Ap '66

PEACE conferences
Christian peace conference's youth on record. R. Terrill. Christian Cent 83:1354-6 N 2 '66
Churches' concern for peace; National interreligious conference on peace. America 114: 434 Ap 2 '66
Doctor Hromadka and the will to peace; Communist peace propaganda through Christian peace conference; reply. J. C. Heidbrink. America 114:367 Mr 19 '66
Interreligious conference on peace. P. Peachey. Christian Cent 83:476-8 Ap 13 '66

PEACE corps. See United States—Peace corps

PEACE corps, Domestic. See Volunteers in service to America

PEACE movement. See Pacifism

PEACE societies
Causes of peace; ineffectual peace movements. J. F. Wharton. Sat R 49:12-14+ Jl 2 '66
See also
Catholic association for international peace

PEACE trees. See Trees

PEACEFUL uses of atomic power. See Atomic power—Economic aspects

PEACH BOTTOM, Pa, atomic power station. See Atomic power plants

PEACH seeds. See Seeds

PEACHES
P is for peach. J. Paulson. il Ladies Home J 83:98 Ag '66
See also
Cookery—Fruit

Handling
Can we get tree-ripe peaches to market? J. Bickers. il Farm J 90:28-9+ Ag '66

PEACHEY, Paul
Priority program on peace? Christian Cent 83:959-61 Ag 3 '66
PEACOCK plants. See Episcias
PEAKALL, David B. and East, Ben
Let's not kill ourselves. Outdoor Life 138:17-19+ Ag: 29-31+ S '66
PEALE, Norman Vincent
Letter to a well-intentioned parent. Read Digest 89:75-6 S '66
PEALE, Ruth Stafford
Adventure of being a wife. Read Digest 88: 71-4 Je '66
PEANUT butter
Popular, plentiful peanut butter; with recipes. Good H 162:244 Ap '66
PEANUT mold. See Fungi
PEANUTS
Much ado about peanuts; Tom's low calorie salted peanuts. Consumer Rep 31:425 S '66
PEARCE, John N.
Further comments on the lobate bowl form. Antiques 90:524-5 O '66
—and Pearce, L. W.
More on the Meeks cabinetmakers. Antiques 90:69-73 Jl '66
PEARCE, Lorraine W. See Pearce, J. N. jt. auth.
PEARCY, G. Etzel
Mainland China: geographic strengths and weaknesses. Dept State Bul 55:294-303 Ag 29 '66
PEARE, Catherine Owens
Writing juvenile biography. Writer 79:23-4+ Ap '66
PEARL, Milton A.
Public lands under review. por Parks & Rec 1:416-18 My '66
PEARL HARBOR, Atttack on, 1941
Admiral Kimmel: why was he not warned? excerpts from statement, 1966. H. E. Kimmel. U S News 61:20 D 19 '66
Dissent from an anti-revisionist. W. F. Rickenbacker. Nat R 19:34 Ja 10 '67
God, please get us out of this. S. B. Young. il Am Heritage 17:48-51+ Ap '66
Hawaii: taps at Pearl Harbor. J. Didion. il Sat Eve Post 239:22-9 D 17 '66
Lesson. D. Lawrence. U S News 61:104 D 19 '66
Memories still fresh. il Newsweek 68:38-42+ D 12 '66
Message spelled war. il Sr Schol 89:5 D 2 '66
Mystery of Pearl Harbor. H. E. Barnes; F. E. Beatty; P. Greaves. il Nat R 18:1260-72 D 13 '66
Notes and comment. New Yorker 42:23 D 24 '66
Robert West's second life. K. Wheeler. il Life 61:90-2+ D 16 '66
Sunday that seems like yesterday. R. Trumbull. il N Y Times Mag p 162+ D 4 '66
That Sunday twenty-five years ago I was on a tower overlooking all of Pearl Harbor. V. Adams. il Esquire 66:252+ D '66
Twenty-five years after Pearl Harbor; an attack that remade the world. il U S News 61:40-4+ D 12 '66
What really happened at Pearl Harbor; summary of Pearl Harbor: warning and decision. R. Wohlstetter. U S News 61:46-7 D 12 '66
Where were you? il Newsweek 68:36-8 D 12 '66
PEARL Paul, limited
Pearl Paul. ltd. reports swift production of books. Pub W 190:118 D 5 '66
PEARL S. Buck foundation
Born between East and West. M. Macmillan. Sat R 49:51 Jl 23 '66
PEARLS
Nature note; iridescent jewel: the pearl. Sci N 89:357 My 7 '66
PEARMAN, Robert
Arkansas prison farm: whip pays off. Nation 203:701-4 D 26 '66
PEARS
Ribosomes from pear fruit. L. Ku and R. J. Romani. bibliog il Science 154:408-10 O 21 '66
PEARSE, Benjamin H.
From Maine to California: revolution in summer schools. Am Ed 2:10-12 O '66
PEARSE, J. S.
Antarctic asteroid odontaster validus: constancy of reproductive periodicities. bibliog Science 152:1763-4 Je 24 '66
PEARSON, Andrall E.
Sales power through planned careers. Harvard Bsns R 44:105-16 Ja '66
PEARSON, Drew
Matter of ethics. S. Shaffer. il por Newsweek 67:29 Ap 11 '66
Muckraker. il por Newsweek 67:87 Je 27 '66
Pearson's hot potato. Nation 202:410 Ap 11 '66

PEARSON, John
Ian Fleming; excerpt from The life of Ian Fleming. Life 61:102-4+ O 7 '66
Rough rise of a dream hero; excerpt from The life of Ian Fleming. Life 61:112-14+ O 14 '66
about
Biographer of Ian Fleming. G. P. Hunt. por Life 61:7 O 7 '66
PEARSON, Lester Bowles
Man on the spot; Munsinger affair. il Time 87:44 My 20 '66
Preparing for change? Time 87:34 F 4 '66
PEARSON, Ronald
Metals; a discussion. por Craft Horiz 26:29-31 Je '66
PEAS
Five easy steps to planting peas. il Flower Grower 53:59-60 Mr '66
For fresh peas in December; planting peas. Sunset 137:187 S '66
See also
Cookery—Vegetables
PEASANT art. See Folk art
PEASANTRY
Social origins of dictatorship and democracy, by B. Moore, jr. Review
New Repub 156:34-6+ Ja 7 '67. J. Featherstone

Vietnam (Republic)
How goes pacification? joint effort by U.S. and South Vietnamese authorities to capture the loyalty of Vietnamese population. il Newsweek 68:58+ S 19 '66
Viet reds winning battle for rice. il U S News 61:41 O 3 '66
PEASE, Deborah
Doubt. New Yorker 42:186-7 S 24 '66
PEASE, R. F. W. and others
Electron microscopy of living insects. bibliog Science 154:1185-6 D 2 '66
PEAT
Radiocarbon dating of coastal peat, Barrow, Alaska. J. Brown and P. V. Sellmann. bibliog il Science 153:299-300 Jl 15 '66
PEAT, Marwick, Mitchell and company
Very private world of Peat, Marwick, Mitchell. T. A. Wise. il Fortune 74:88-91+ Jl 1 '66
PEAT moss
Peat moss fact & fiction. B. C. Kilvert, jr. il Flower Grower 53:63-6 My '66
PEBBLE mulch. See Mulching
PECCARY hunting
What's tough about javelina. B. W. Dalrymple. il Outdoor Life 138:52-3+ N '66
PECHMAN, Joseph A.
Income tax: how good? excerpts from Federal tax policy. U S News 61:115-16 S 26 '66
Planning the future of federal taxes. il por Bsns W p 147-8+ S 24 '66
Unmarried people are overtaxed. Life 61:8 S 30 '66
PECK, A. J. and Rabbidge, R. M.
Soil-water potential: direct measurement by a new technique. bibliog Science 151:1385-6 Mr 18 '66
PECK, Dallas L. See Waesche, H. H. jt. auth.
PECK, Don
Ross and his ram. Outdoor Life 138:34-5+ Ag '66
PECK, Gregory
Gregory Peck turns crusader. J. L. Block. il pors Good H 162:70+ My '66
PECK, Ruth L.
Do you recognize this? Sch Arts 65:18-19 My '66
PECK, Susan
Parent and child. N Y Times Mag p 118+ My 22 '66
PECK, Véronique
Gregory Peck turns crusader. J. L. Block. il por Good H 162:70+ My '66
PECKHAM, Morse
They lost religion but kept faith. Sat R 49: 62 Je 11 '66
PECORE, Robert, and Rano, Richard
Chalet and a footbridge. Am City 81:118-19 Ap '66
PECOS NATIONAL MONUMENT
Pecos National Monument. N. N. Dodge. il Nat Parks Mag 40:14-16 N '66
Trail guide to the Upper Pecos, by A. Montgomery and P. K. Sutherland. Review
Liv Wildn 29:27 Aut '65. E. S. Barker
PECTENS. See Scallops
PEDEN, Rachel
And the fulness thereof; excerpts from The land, the people. Farm J 90:65 N '66

PEDESTRIAN in the air; drama. See Ionesco, E.

PEDESTRIANS
Big step for pedestrians in Cincinnati. il Fortune 74:196 D '66

PEDIATRICIANS
Babies are my business. M. A. Wessel. il Parents Mag 41:66-7+ N '66

PEDIATRICS. See Children—Care and hygiene

PEEL, Robert
Reviewed protests. Christian Cent 83:1605 D 28 '66

PEER Gynt: opera. See Egk, W.

PEERCE, Jan
I was a teen-age beatle. por Seventeen 25: 170+ Ap '66
Working with Toscanini; ed. by B. H. Haggin. Atlan 218:75-9 D '66

about
Maestro's choice. L. Biancolli. por Opera N 30:26-7 Ja 29 '66

PEET, Creighton
Career barometer. See issues of Popular mechanics
Giant stage that shifts for itself. Pop Mech 126:110-13+ D '66

PEET, Doris S.
Love is a baby's best teacher. Parents Mag 41:58-9+ S '66

PEE WEE golf tournament. See Golf—Tournaments

PÉGUY, Charles Pierre
Charles Péguy, by M. Villiers. Review New Repub 154:23-6 Ap 16 '66. J. Featherstone
Hero of our time. M. Turnell. Commonweal 85:251-4 D 2 '66

PEI, Ieoh Ming
Jacqueline Kennedy goes public. L. Bergquist. il por Look 30:46+ Mr 22 '66

PEI, Mario
Challenge of linguistic realism. Sat R 49:27-8+ Ap 23 '66
English in its American fashion. Nation 203: 709-12 D 26 '66
Salame is salami is salamis. Nation 203:675-6 D 19 '66

PEIERLS, Rudolf E.
Books. Sci Am 216:137-40+ Ja '67

PEIPING. See Peking, China

PEIRCE, Neal R.
Electoral college goes to Court. Reporter 35: 34-7 O 6 '66
Financing our parties. Reporter 34:29+ F 10 '66

PEKING, China
Reporter at large. H. Koningsberger. New Yorker 42:57-8+ Ap 23 '66

PELE. See Arantes do Nascimento, E.

PELE. See Kilauea (crater)

PELETTA, Peter Paul
Dons are dreaming of sweet revenge. J. Jares. il por Sports Illus 24:53-4+ F 14 '66

PELIKAN, Jaroslav
Forbidden sacrament. Sat R 49:45-6 O 15 '66

PELLA, Greece (ancient city)
Pella: capital of ancient Macedonia. C. J. Makaronas. il Sci Am 215:98-105 D '66

PELLAPRAT, Henri Paul
Modern French culinary art; excerpts. Ladies Home J 83:102-3+ D '66

PELLÉAS et Mélisande; opera. See Debussy, C.

PELLEGRIN, Frank
Catholic higher education; address. April 16, 1966. Vital Speeches 32:567-71 Jl 1 '66

PELLOWSKI, Anne
Diamond and the parrot; aesthetics and ideology in children's literature. bibliog por Library J 91:5686-92 N 15 '66

PELTIER, Harvey
Pot of gold for a nervy Cajun. W. Tower. Sports Illus 25:112-13 S 19 '66

PELTON, Gerald W. Jr
Pacific Northwest. por Parks & Rec 1:634 Ag '66

PEN and ink drawing. See Pen drawing

PEN club. See PEN club

PEN drawing
Crow-quill pen. E. Emberley. il Horn Bk 42:553-5 O '66

PEN portraits. See Character sketches

PENAL law. See Criminal law

PENALTIES, Contractual
Major contracts keyed to performance. K. Johnsen. il Aviation W 84:101-2 F 21 '66

PENANCE, Sacrament of. See Confession

PENCIL drawing. See Drawing

PENCILS
See also
Scripto, incorporated

PENDERECKI, Krzysztof
New music of Poland. O. Daniel. Sat R 49: 52 Jl 30 '66
What's the score? il por Time 88:55 O 14 '66

PENDLETON, Camp. See Military training camps

PENELOPE, pride of the pickle factory; drama. See Huff, B. T.

PENG, Chen
One down, more to go. Newsweek 67:53 Je 13 '66
Punished by history. Time 87:40 Je 10 '66
Raging storm. il por Newsweek 67:48-9 Je 20 '66

PENGUIN books, limited
Houghton & Penguin books terminate sales agreement. Pub W 189:31 Ap 4 '66

PENGUINS
Nature's most delightful parade; fairy penguins on Phillip Island. il Sci Digest 60: 86-7 S '66
Navigation of penguins. J. T. Emlen and R. L. Penney. il Sci Am 215:104-13 O '66

PENICILLIN
New look for penicillins; Ampicillin and Hetacillin. Sci N 90:531 D 24 '66
Penicillin kills bacteria by stealing enzyme. Sci N 89:377 My 14 '66
Rare reaction in blood caused by penicillin. Sci N L 89:103 F 12 '66

PENIS. See Generative organs

PENKOVSKII, Oleg Vladimirovich
Joining father's outfit. S. L. Sharp. Nation 202:186-7 F 14 '66
My spy can lick your spy. M. Frankel. il Atlan 217:103-4+ Ap '66
Spy who came in from the cold war. H. Schwartz. por R 49:36-7 Ja 29 '66

PENMAN, Sheldon, and others
Ribosomal RNA synthesis and processing in a particulate site in the HeLa cell nucleus. bibliog Science 154:786-9 N 11 '66

PENN, Irving
Estremadura gypsies by Penn; photographs. Vogue 148:114-15+ Ag 15 '66
Paris by Penn; photographs. Look 30:46-57 Jl 26 '66
Penn photographs the foods of France. il Vogue 148:250-5+ O 1 '66

PENN foundation for mental health, incorporated. See Psychiatric clinics

PENN-nuclear corporation
Pulverizing process gives titanium an in. Bsns W p82 O 22 '66

PENN relay. See Running

PENNEL, John
Champions of winter. il por Sports Illus 24: 12-13+ F 7 '66
Victory over pain. il por Time 87:71 F 18 '66

PENNELL, C. Dan
Peonies. Horticulture 44:20-1+ My '66

PENNELL, Herb
Ponies. New Yorker 41:23-4 Ja 29 '66

PENNELL, Maynard L.
Master at building the big ones. por Bsns W p44 D 24 '66

PENNEY, J. C, company
Penneys recalls some radios. Consumer Rep 31:320 Jl '66

PENNEY, Richard L. See Emlen, J. T. jt. auth.

PENNINGTON, Harriet D.
Lost art of storytelling. Parents Mag 41:48-9+ Ag '66

PENNOCK, J. Liddon
Garden lighting. Horticulture 44:32 Je '66

PENNSYLVANIA
See also
Booksellers and bookselling—Pennsylvania
Crime and criminals—Pennsylvania
Fishing—Pennsylvania
Gardens—Pennsylvania
Hunting—Pennsylvania
Insurance, Unemployment—Pennsylvania
Trials—Pennsylvania
Unemployment—Pennsylvania

Boundaries
See also
Mason and Dixon's line

Description and travel
Pennsylvania revisited. G. Ade. il Travel 125:42-4 Je '66

Economic conditions
Coal country digs out from under. il Bsns W p96-8 My 21 '66

PENNSYLVANIA—*Continued*

Historic houses, etc.
See also
Bryn Mawr, Pa.—Historic houses, etc.
Whitemarsh, Pa.—Historic houses, etc.

History
Pennsylvania boyhood; memoir. J. N. Culbertson. il Am Heritage 18:80-8 D '66

Politics and government
Candidate ex machina; gubernatorial race. Time 88:32 N 4 '66
Cashkrieg; gubernatorial campaign. il Time 88:31-2 O 21 '66
Hopeless case of Milton Shapp; winner of gubernatorial primary. R. B. Stolley. il Life 60:68A-68D+ My 27 '66
Old class; D. L. Lawrence. Time 88:28-9 D 2 '66
$1 million winner; Democratic gubernatorial nomination. Newsweek 67:27-8 My 30 '66
Pennsylvania story; Shafer vs. Shapp. I. Bay. Nat R 18:1041-2 O 18 '66
Starting at the top; M. Shapp nominated for governor. Time 87:20-1 My 27 '66
Upset in Pennsylvania; M. J. Shapp's gubernatorial primary victory. Nation 202:637 My 30 '66

PENNSYLVANIA Dutch. See Pennsylvania Germans

PENNSYLVANIA German cookery. See Cookery, American

PENNSYLVANIA Germans
Plain 'n' fancy fair; annual Pennsylvania Dutch fair, Kutztown, Pa. C. J. Burgess. Sr Schol 88:sup24 Ap 15 '66

PENNSYLVANIA railroad
Is the sky the limit for the Pennsy? denies entering the airline business, Johnson flying service. il Bsns W p 106-8+ D 10 '66
Man who met the Pennsy's bills; D. C. Bevan. il Bsns W p62-4 Jl 16 '66

PENNSYLVANIA railroad-New York central merger. See Railroads—Consolidations and mergers

PENNSYLVANIA. University
Chemical reaction; controversy over classified investigations into gas and germ warfare. Newsweek 68:34 S 19 '66
Secret research at Penn. Time 88:62 S 16 '66

Wharton school of finance and commerce
Forecast for 1967, no pause in the expansion; Wharton school's computer prediction. il Bsns W p36-7 D 3 '66
Plenty of zip for the economy; Wharton school's econometric model prediction; with editorial comment. il Bsns W p53-4+. 160 S 3 '66

PENOBSCOT BAY
Summers in Penobscot country; with photographs. E. Porter. Natur Hist 75:34-43 Ag '66

PENROSE annual
Penrose annual 1966; ed. by H. Spencer. Review
Pub W 190:92-3+ Ag 1 '66. C. B. Grannis

PENS
Crow-quill pen. E. Emberley. il Horn Bk 42:553-5 O '66
New look in writing instruments. il Consumer Bul 49:37-40 S '66
Report on soft-tip pens. J. Reinert. il Sci Digest 60:81-2 O '66

PENSION funds. See Pensions—Finance

PENSIONS
See also
Old age pensions—United States
Teachers—Pensions
Vietnamese war, 1957- —Compensation of noncombatants

Finance
ABC's of pension funding. C. L. Trowbridge. il Harvard Bsns R 44:115-26 Mr '66
Pension fund investment: both sides of the coin. H. R. Bartell, jr. Mo Labor R 89: 128-9 F '66
Pension funds sniff a bargain; trend toward common stock. il Bsns W p 153-4 O 15 '66
Pension funds still want stocks. C. J. Loomis. il Fortune 73:130-1+ Je '66
Private pension funds zooming. U S News 61:69 Jl 4 '66
Report on some pension funds. Fortune 74: 241 D '66
Retirement benefits and teacher mobility. R. L. Lillywhite and M. L. Ware. NEA J 55: 15-16 Ap '66

Laws and regulations
Pinch on pensions? Treasury proposes nondiscriminatory plans. Bsns W p52 O 8 '66
Taking a cut at executive pensions; revision of hundreds of pension plans. il Bsns W p 180+ N 26 '66

PENSIONS, Industrial
Changes in pension plans for salaried employees. R. C. Joiner. il Mo Labor R 89: 381-4 Ap '66
Disability benefits under private pension plans. S. S. Sacks. il Mo Labor R 89:389-95 Ap '66
Early retirement plan meets goals. Bsns W p 120 Mr 5 '66
Private pension plans in danger? il U S News 61:64-5 O 10 '66
Study of pension funding. J. Krislov. il Mo Labor R 89:638-42 Je '66
Taking a cut at executive pensions; revision of hundreds of pension plans. il Bsns W p 180+ N 26 '66
See also
Government investigations—Industrial pensions

PENTAGON building, Arlington, Va.
Day with the army. S. Havens. il Library J 91:894-900 F 15 '66

PENTATEUCH. See Bible—Old Testament—Pentateuch

PENTECOST
Holy Spirit our helper; message from the presidents of the World council of churches. Christian Cent 83:671 My 25 '66
Pentecost in our lives. G. M. McCrossin. America 114:770-2 My 28 '66
Pentecostal triad. V. P. McCorry. America 114:786-7 My 28 '66

PENTHOUSES. See Apartments

PENTOBARBITAL
Pentobarbital sodium: variation in toxicity. H. A. Lindsay and V. S. Kullman. bibliog il Science 151:576-7 F 4 '66; Discussion. 152:671. 1282-3 Ap 29. My 27 '66

PENTYLENETETRAZOL. See Tetrazols

PENZER, Mark
Donzi's 1-2-3 the Long Island marathon. il Motor B 118:94-5+ S '66
Equipment you have to have. Motor B 117: 50-2+ My '66
Gold cup regatta. Motor B 118:85+ Ag '66
Miami-Nassau: Wynne and wind. Motor B 117:154-5+ Je '66
Mist+flip =a hectic Hudson. il Motor B 118: 81+ Ag '66

PEONIES
Peonies. C. D. Pennell. il Horticulture 44: 20-1+ My '66
Peonies up to date. M. Price. il Flower Grower 53:36-7 S '66
Why peonies don't bloom. H. Tinnappel. il Horticulture 44:42 O '66

PEOPLE-to-people program
People-to-people. J. I. Myers. il Américas 18:37-8 Ja '66

PEOPLE'S daily. See Newspapers—China (People's Republic)

PEOPLES gas, light and coke company
High cost of war. Newsweek 68:71 Ag 8 '66

PEOPLE'S liberation army. See China (People's Republic)—Armed forces

PEORIA, Ill.

Negroes
Enlisting community support for civil rights; address, January 20, 1966. B. DeHaan. Vital Speeches 32:272-5 F 15 '66

PEP pills. See Amphetamines

PEPIN, Eugène
Space flight and the rule of law. UNESCO Courier 19:17-18+ My '66

PEPPER, Curtis G.
Day with Pope Paul; excerpts from The Pope's backyard. McCalls 94:120-1+ O '66

PEPPER boxes (small arms) See Pistols

PEPPERRELL family
Louisburg and the Pepperrell silver. B. W. F. Trafton, jr. il Antiques 89:366-7 Mr '66

PEPPERS
See also
Cookery—Vegetables

PEPSI-COLA company
Pepsi generation, R.I.P. new slogan. Newsweek 68:94 O 24 '66

PEPTIC ulcers
Milk, enzymes & ulcers. il Time 87:60 Mr 25 '66
To freeze or not to freeze? stomach freezing as a treatment of duodenal ulcers. Time 87:50 Ja 28 '66
Ulcer operation value questioned. Sci N 89: 481 Je 18 '66

PEPTIDES

Allelic antigenic factor inv(a) of the light chains of human immunoglobulins: chemical basis. C. Baglioni and others. bibliog il Science 152:1517-19 Je 10 '66

Co-linearity of β-galactosidase with its gene by immunological detection of incomplete polypeptide chains. A. V. Fowler and I. Zabin. bibliog il Science 154:1027-9 N 25 '66

Cytokinin activity: localization in transfer RNA preparations. F. Skoog and others. bibliog il Science 154:1354-6 D 9 '66

Electrophoretic heterogeneity of polypeptide chains of specific antibodies. R. A. Reisfeld and P. A. Small, jr. bibliog il Science 152:1253-5 My 27 '66

Electrophoretic heterogeneity of the polypeptide chains of human G-myeloma proteins. W. D. Terry and others. bibliog il Science 152:1628-30 Je 17 '66

Evolution of immunoglobulin polypeptide chains: carboxy-terminal of an IgM heavy chain. R. F. Doolittle and others. bibliog il Science 154:1561-2 D 23 '66

Formation of hydroxyproline in collagen. S. Udenfriend. bibliog il Science 152:1335-40 Je 3 '66

Formylmethionine codon AUG as an initiator of polypeptide synthesis. R. E. Thach and others. bibliog il Science 153:416-18 Jl 22 '66

Hydroxylation of proline and the intracellular accumulation of a polypeptide precursor of collagen. K. Juva and others. bibliog il Science 152:92-4 Ap 1 '66

Hypotensive peptides; report on international symposium. E. G. Erdos. Science 152:1284-5 My 27 '66

Inhibitory and facilitatory effect of two related peptides on extinction of avoidance behavior. B. Bohus and D. De Wied. bibliog il Science 153:318-20 Jl 15 '66

Lobster hemocyanin: properties of the minimum functional subunit and of aggregates. S. M. Pickett and others. bibliog il Science 151:1005-7 F 25 '66

Multiplicity of hemoglobins in the genus chironomus, tendipes. P. E. Thompson and D. S. English. bibliog il Science 152:75-6 Ap 1 '66

Plasma kinins and cortisol: a possible explanation of the anti-inflammatory action of cortisol. M. J. Cline and K. L. Melmon. bibliog il Science 153:1135-8 S 2 '66

Polypeptide chains of immunoglobulins from the smooth dogfish (mustelus canis) J. Marchalonis and G. M. Edelman. bibliog il Science 154:1567-8 D 23 '66

Sea cucumber sibling species: polypeptide chain types and oxygen equilibrium of hemoglobin. C. Manwell. bibliog il Science 152:1393-6 Je 3 '66

Sex conversion in a male vitis vinifera L. by a kinin. S. S. Negi and H. P. Olmo. bibliog il Science 152:1624 Je 17 '66

Subclasses of human immunoglobulin A based on differences in the alpha polypeptide chains. J. P. Vaerman and J. F. Heremans. bibliog il Science 153:647-9 Ag 5 '66

Synthesis of insulin. P. G. Katsoyannis. bibliog il Science 154:1509-14 D 23 '66

PERCEPTION

Perceptual grouping produced by changes in orientation and shape. J. Beck. bibliog il Science 154:538-40 O 28 '66

Perception of temporal order and relative visual latency. R. Rutschmann. bibliog il Science 152:1099-101 My 20 '66

Shape perception in infants. Sci Am 214:56 My '66
    See also
Space perception
Time perception

PERCEPTION, Extrasensory. See Extrasensory perception

PERCH

Fish for all seasons: yellow perch. W. Davis. il Outdoor Life 138:54-6+ Ag '66

PERCH fishing

Big perch by jiggers; through the ice of Conesus Lake, N.Y. R. L. Estes. il Outdoor Life 138:58-61+ D '66

Midwinter specktacle. K. Osborne. il Outdoor Life 137:60-1+ F '66

Pike strike back; Ontario lake. J. O. Cartier. il Outdoor Life 137:48-9+ Je '66

350 miles of walleyes; Mississippi River. A. W. Prince. il Outdoor Life 138:40-1+ Jl '66

PERCIVAL, John

Report from London. Dance Mag 40:22 Jl '66

PERCY, Charles Harting

Republican future. por Sat R 49:19-21 O 29 '66
    about
American nightmare. il por Newsweek 68:22-3 O 3 '66

Backlash in the Percy campaign. R. C. Wade. por Reporter 36:37-40 Ja 12 '67

Boy wonder grows up. P. M. Deuel. por Nation 203:374-6 O 17 '66

Percy vs. Douglas; the blighted campaign. S. Alsop. il pors Sat Eve Post 239:26-9 N 5 '66

Second campaign. il por Newsweek 68:42 O 24 '66

What I must do. Time 88:36 O 14 '66

Whiz kid switches to politics. por Bsns W p71-2 N 26 '66

PERCY, Sharon Lee

Winning ticket. por Time 88:29 D 9 '66

PERCY, Valerie Jeanne

American nightmare. il por Newsweek 68:22-3 O 3 '66

Beyond grief. il por Time 88:22-4 S 30 '66

Who could kill Valerie Percy? il por Life 61:47 S 30 '66

PERCY, Walker

Last gentleman; novel; excerpts. Harper 232:54-6 My '66
    about
Elegant quest for ordinariness. W. Goodman. Life 60:20 Je 24 '66

PERDUE, James E.

Analytic and the synthetic; address, May 14, 1966. Vital Speeches 32:638-40 Ag 1 '66

PÈRE Bise restaurant. See Restaurants— France

PÈRE David deer. See Deer

PERELLA, Nicolas J.

Great poet, a continuing task. Poetry 107:333-7 F '66

PERELMAN, Sidney Joseph

Anna Trivia pluralized. New Yorker 42:53-5 N 26 '66

Hey, what's wriggling around that caduceus? New Yorker 42:32-5 Je 18 '66

Let a snarl be your umbrella. New Yorker 42:26-7 Ja 14 '67

Muddler on the roof. New Yorker 41:32-4 F 19 '66

Rape of the drape. New Yorker 42:56-8 S 24 '66

Too many undies spoil the crix. New Yorker 42:53-5 O 22 '66
    about
Precious string of Perelman pearls. O. Nash. Life 61:11 S 23 '66

PERENNIALS

Add some new perennial plants to your garden. E. Henderson. il Horticulture 44:20-3 Jl '66

New plants for your flower border. J. Fanning. il Pop Gard 17:52-4 My '66

Perennials that stand up to summer. H. V. Wilson. il Flower Grower 53:46-7+ My '66
    See also
Dahlias
Yarrows

PERÉNYI, Eleanor

Apostle of the compost heap. Sat Eve Post 239:30-3 Jl 16 '66

PERERA, Consuela B. and Frumin, A. M.

Hemagglutination by fava bean extract inhibited by simple sugars. bibliog Science 151:821 F 18 '66

PERERA, Padma

Mauna. New Yorker 42:205-10+ O 29 '66

PEREZ, Michael, Jr

Boy who found the sun. J. Robbins and J. Robbins. por Redbook 128:48-9+ D '66

PERFECTION

Can man perfect himself? tr. by D. T. LeFort. K. Rahner. Cath World 203:138-44 Je '66

PERFORMANCE standards

Components of skilled performance. M. I. Posner. bibliog il Science 152:1712-18 Je 24 '66

PERFORMING animals. See Animals—Training

PERFORMING arts

Arts and communications in recreation and park programs. S. H. Frieswyk. Parks & Rec 1:976-7+ D '66

As large as life. il Sr Schol 88:13-15 Ap 15 '66

Building for the arts, or, A house is not a home. T. P. De Gaetani. il Dance Mag 40:36-9+ N '66

PERFORMING arts—*Continued*
Cultural arts in recreation. M. B. Spector. il Parks & Rec 1:230-2 Mr '66
Exploding the explosion; conclusions from study by the Twentieth century fund. Time 88:64+ D 2 '66
How big is the boom in culture? summary of Performing arts: the economic dilemma, W. J. Baumol and W. G. Bowen. il U S News 61:14 N 28 '66
Lively arts; a backwards glance at 1966. M. Ronan; P. Hudson; R. Hemming. il Sr Schol 89:28-9 D 9 '66
Looking around with Zinsser. W. K. Zinsser. il Look 31:14 Ja 24 '67
Performing arts—the economic dilemma, by W. J. Baumol and W. G. Bowen. Review
    Newsweek 68:112-14 D 5 '66. S. Schmidt
SR/1967 world travel calendar. T. L. Christie. Sat R 50:77-82 Ja 7 '67

Finance

Culture booms and busts. America 115:768 D 10 '66

Study and teaching

Fine arts school; cultural center in Harlem. il Ebony 21:80-2+ My '66
Lincoln Center reaches out to New York state; educational program. il Sr Schol 87:sup4 Ja 14 '66
Why not every child? Irvington, N.J. cultural program. E. L. Raichle. il PTA Mag 60:35-6 Je '66

PERFORMING dogs. See Dogs—Training
PERFUMERY
By George! what will they think of next? J. Devaney. il Redbook 128:91+ N '66
Christmas in the air. il Seventeen 25:154-5 N '66
His for Christmas. il Seventeen 25:92-3 D '66
Jasmine perfume components synthesized. Sci N 89:292 Ap 23 '66
Perfume: the secret garden. il Mlle 64:154-7+ N '66
Reading list: colognes, after-shaves. Vogue 148:39 N 15 '66
S.C.E.N.T: a game of clues to you and your fragrance. il Seventeen 25:156-7+ My '66
Scents of summer. il Mlle 63:132-3+ My '66
Tell us, ladies, how should a man smell? symposium. il Esquire 67:128-9 Ja '67
Vogue's ready beauty; French designers' perfumes. Vogue 147:152-3 Mr 15 '66
PERFUSION apparatus
Versatile perfusion chamber for living cells and organs. P. R. White. bibliog il Science 152:1758-60 Je 24 '66
PERGAMON press
To halt the retreat. il Time 88:112+ N 19 '66
PERHAM, John
Business and Vietnam. Duns R 87:40-2+ Ap '66
Entrepreneur in Ireland. Duns R 87:65 F '66
Second look at municipal bonds. Duns R 87:45-6+ Mr '66
Where are tomorrow's executives? Duns R 87:36-7+ Je '66
PERHAM, Richard, and others
Light chains of mouse myeloma proteins: partial amino acid sequence. bibliog Science 154:391-3 O 21 '66
PERILLO, A. Dorothy, and St Clair, Jean
Crash program plus give-aways; with bibliography. Library J 91:340 Ja 15 '66
PERINE, Thomas J.
Lakemaker. il por Time 88:67 S 23 '66
PERINEURAL epithelium. See Epithelium
PERIODICAL advertising. See Advertising mediums—Periodicals
PERIODICAL covers
O'Bryan revolution. il Nat R 18:1218-21 N 29 '66
PERIODICAL literature
How to earn money writing for the European market; exchange of letters. E. L. Horwitz; S. Buchman; A. Wysard. Writer 79:25-7 Ag '66
How to research articles by mail; facts to build magazine articles. M. Gunther. Writer 79:13-16 Ap '66
How to submit poems. R. C. Swain. Writer 79:4 Je '66
Magazine articles as art. A. Balk. Sat R 49:57 Jl 9 '66; Reply. G. Walker. 49:60 Ag 13 '66
Magic sentence. B. Lang. Writer 79:20-1+ O '66

Ten article ideas that pay off. L. McLaughlin. Writer 79:18-20 Je '66
Three common errors in article writing. S. S. Baker. Writer 79:14-16 D '66
    See also
Fiction in periodicals and newspapers
PERIODICALS
Quarterlies: special report; In brief: annotated list of single issues. G. Davenport; G. Tullock. Nat R 18:627-8 Je 28 '66
Stories for Modern romances. H. P. Malmgreen. Writer 79:26-9 D '66
    See also
Blind, Periodicals for the
Childrens periodicals
Libraries—Periodical collections
Photography, Journalistic
    also subhead Periodicals under various subjects, e.g. Science—Periodicals; *also* names of periodicals, e.g. Technology week (periodical)

Bibliography

Magazines; ed. by B. Katz. Library J 92:91-2 Ja 1 '67
New periodicals. See issues of Library journal to December 15, 1966
    See also
Union list of serials

Directories

    See also
Standard periodical directory

Letters to the editor

Missives/missiles; letters in the diocesan press. S. J. Adamo. America 115:40-1 Jl 9 '66

Prices

Price indexes for 1966: US periodicals. H. M. Welch. il Library J 91:3339-41 Jl '66

Reprints

Motherlode; Kraus reprint corp. bringing back complete files of ground-breaking little mags. S. Maloff. il Newsweek 68:74-5 D 26 '66

Sections, columns, etc.

Travel notes; a look backward to when this column started. R. Joseph. il Esquire 66:74+ D '66

Titles

See Titles of periodicals

Transportation

KLM speeds magazine shipments. il Aviation W 84:29 F 28 '66
Publisher's memo. E. D. Muhlfeld. Flying 78:6 My '66

Europe

Impact of fact; European newsmagazines. Time 87:43 My 6 '66

France

Inventing neo-nazism; hoax of Paris match. il Time 88:49 Jl 8 '66
Literary newspapers and book reporting media in France. H. R. Lottman. Pub W 189:51-3 My 23 '66

Great Britain

English madness; Weekend literary competitions. P. Rowlett. Commonweal 84:475-6 Jl 22 '66
How to earn money writing for the European market; exchange of letters. E. L. Horwitz; S. Buchman; A. Wysard. Writer 79:25-7 Ag '66
Magazines: chaotic, imitative, the liveliest anywhere. il Esquire 66:58-9 Jl '66
    See also
Countryman (periodical)
Encounter (periodical)
Nature (periodical)
Penrose annual
Private eye (periodical)

Peru

Explorations in the apolitical; concerning bilingual literary journal, Quena. C. Eshleman. Nation 203:285-7 S 26 '66

Russia

Bread, salt and truth; Novy mir. il Newsweek 69:51-2 Ja 16 '67
Fair exchange? Sputnik in the U.S. il Newsweek 69:47 Ja 23 '67
New Russian journal in genetics; letter. H. J. Muller. Science 151:938+ F 25 '66
Russia cracks jokes about China. A. Parry. il N Y Times Mag p 14-15+ Je 26 '66
Russian digest; Sputnik. Time 89:35 Ja 6 '67

PERIODICALS—*Continued*

Spain

Shocking news from Spain; forced resignation of editor of Cuadernos para el diálogo. America 115:819 D 24 '66

Tunisia

Voice of the third world; Jeune Afrique (Young Africa) il Time 88:79 N 4 '66

United States

Black Christmas. il Time 88:44 D 23 '66

Fat days for the how-to publishers; special interest magazines. il Bsns W p50+ Jl 30 '66

Finding a market for your story. F. A. Rockwell. Writer 79:21-5 Je '66

God makes the news weeklies. Nation 202:443 Ap 18 '66

How to be rejected. L. Conger. Writer 79: 7-8 My '66

Lumps for the little ones; excuse for little magazine. Time 87:74+ Je 3 '66

Thunder on the left; new publications. il Newsweek 67:67 F 21 '66

Trade winds; three new magazines of the twenties. H. R. Mayes. Sat R 50:16 Ja 21 '67

Where to sell manuscripts. See issues of Writer

Why editors use form rejection slips. Writer 79:28-33 O '66

Youth magazines in the United States. M. Fuller. Horn Bk 42:110+ F '66
    See also
Catholic press
Periodicals for women
    also names of periodicals, e.g. Christianity and crisis

Yugoslavia

More arrests in Yugoslavia; magazine in opposition to regime. Time 88:76 D 2 '66

Publish and perish; Mihajlov arrested. Newsweek 68:71 Ag 22 '66

Strong constitution; M. Mihajlov's plan to publish oppositional magazine. il Newsweek 68:42+ Ag 15 '66

PERIODICALS, Publishing of

Still climbing; profits. Time 88:35 Ag 12 '66

Trade-technical magazines forge international chain. Pub W 190:41 Jl 25 '66

What's in a loophole? tax-exempt periodicals. il Time 88:62+ O 7 '66

PERIODICALS, Trade. See Trade journals

PERIODICALS for men

Sharp look at the men's magazines. M. Mannes. McCalls 94:18+ O '66
    See also
Esquire (periodical)
Playboy (periodical)

PERIODICALS for women
    See also
Good housekeeping (periodical)
McCall's (periodical)

Anecdotes, facetiae, satire, etc.

How fragile is your marriage? A. Buchwald. Ladies Home J 83:68 S '66

PERIODICITY

Activity rhythms and adiurnal light-dark control. M. L. R. Goff and F. W. Finger. bibliog il Science 154:1346-9 D 9 '66

Antarctic asteroid odontaster validus: constancy of reproductive periodicities. J. S. Pearse. bibliog il Science 152:1763-4 Je 24 '66

Bats used for rhythm studies. il Sci N 90:87 Ag 6 '66

Body has twenty-four-hour clock. Sci N 90: 152 S 3 '66

Circadian rhythm for tryptophan pyrrolase activity and its circulating substrate. M. I. Rapoport and others. bibliog il Science 153: 1642-4 S 30 '66

Circadian rhythm in pineal tyrosine hydroxylase. E. G. McGeer and P. L. McGeer. bibliog il Science 153:73-4 Jl 1 '66

Circadian rhythms in rats; effects of random lighting. D. L. Holmquest and others. bibliog il Science 152:662-4 Ap 20 '66; Reply with rejoinder. C. Heckrotte. 154:158-9 O 7 '66

Circadian rhythms: variation in sensitivity of isolated rat atria to acetylcholine. R. P. Spoor and D. B. Jackson. bibliog il Science 154:782 N 11 '66

Corals as paleontological clocks. S. K. Runcorn. il Sci Am 215:26-33 bibliog(p 150) O '66

Death in the afternoon; studies of circadian rhythms of insects and effectiveness of insecticides. Sci N 91:12 Ja 7 '67

Drugs rely on rhythms; body rhythms and susceptibility to drugs. Sci N 91:10 Ja 7 '67

Entrainment of circadian rhythms by sound in passer domesticus. M. Menaker and A. Eskin. bibliog il Science 154:1579-81 D 23 '66

Fire freed man from dictatorial clock; twenty-four hour cycle. Sci N 90:362 O 29 '66

Geographic variation in ovarian cycles and clutch size in cnemidophorus tigris (teiidae) C. J. McCoy and G. A. Hoddenbach. bibliog il Science 154:1671 D 30 '66

How a bird tells time of day; study of biological clocks. J. D. Palmer. il Natur Hist 75:48-53 Mr '66

If transatlantic flight has upset your biorhythm, relax! E. N. Dye. Travel 126:65-6 Jl '66

Internal clocks and insect diapause. P. L. Adkisson. bibliog il Science 154:234-41 O 14 '66

Neurosecretory cells; daily rhythmicity in leiobunum longipes. D. J. Fowler and C. J. Goodnight. bibliog il Science 152:1078-80 My 20 '66

Periodicity of desert rodent activity. N. R. French and others. bibliog il Science 154: 1194-5 D 2 '66

Those built-in clocks that run your body. C. R. Hicks. il Pop Mech 126:134-7+ O '66

What time is it? the body's clock knows. G. G. Luce and J. Segal. il N Y Times Mag p30-1+ Ap 3 '66

PERIODONTAL disease. See Gums (anatomy) —Diseases

PERIOPHTHALMUS. See Gobies

PERIPATUS

Nature note; shy velvet worm. Sci N L 89:63 Ja 22 '66

PERIPHERAL nervous system. See Nervous system

PERITZ, René

Changing world of Malaysia. bibliog f Cur Hist 52:29-35+ Ja '67

PERKIN-Elmer corporation

Management's rule-breakers; the ways of the winners. J. B. Weiner. Duns R 87: 36+ Ja '66

PERKINS, Carl D.

New Chairman Perkins; Powell's opposite. por U S News 62:14 Ja 23 '67

PERKINS, Dallas

Liquorville. il por Newsweek 67:77 F 14 '66

PERKINS, James A.

Foreign aid and the brain drain. For Affairs 44:608-19 Jl '66

    about

Jet-set prexy. il por Newsweek 67:82 Ap 25 '66

PERKINS, Lawrence A.

Lucifer; poem. Cath World 203:360 S '66

PERKINS, Ramona Sue

Relaxed, ranch style entertaining. pors Farm J 90:90-1+ My '66

PERKINSON, Jesse D. Jr

Science and development. Américas 18:inside cover N '66

PERLMAN, D.

Antimicrobial agents and chemotherapy. Science 152:108-9; 154-1591 Ap 1, D 23 '66

PERLMAN, I. See Hollander, J. M. jt. auth.

PERLMANN, Peter. See Lundkvist, U. jt. auth.

PERMA starch. See Starch (for clothes)

PERMANENT central opium board. See United Nations—Permanent central opium board

PERMANENT technical committee on labor affairs. See Organization of American states

PERNOUD, Régine

Age of Charlemagne. bibliog Horizon 8:16-22+ Spr '66

PEROMYSCUS. See Mice, White footed

PERÓN, Isabel

Red Ridinghood & the wolf. il por Time 87:34 Mr 11 '66

PERÓN, Juan Domingo

Another putsch in the Argentine? R. Peter. Nat R 18:469 My 17 '66

Blood feud. Newsweek 67:55 My 30 '66

How much longer? il Time 87:35 F 11 '66

Shadow of Peron. J. Potenze. Commonweal 83:662-3 Mr 11 '66

Trouble with Argentina. J. Gunther. por Read Digest 89:103-8 S '66

PERONISM. See Argentina—Politics and government

PEROXIDASES
Peroxidase and resistance to ceratocystis in sweet potato increased by volatile materials. B. Clare and others. bibliog il Science 153:62-3 Jl 1 '66

PERRAULT, Charles
Sleeping beauty; dramatization of story. See Thane, A.

PERREAULT, John
Modigliani's subject of desire. Art N 65:42-3+ O '66

PERRELLA, Vera C. and Waldman, Elizabeth
Out-of-school youth two years later. Mo Labor R 89:860-6 Ag '66

PERRETT, Patrick
Try camping afloat. Pop Mech 125:124-6+ My '66

PERRIN, Noel
Lamentations of Neo-Jeremiah. New Yorker 42:157-8 Mr 12 '66

PERRIN, Norman
Quest simplified. Christian Cent 83:273-4 Mr 2 '66

PERRIN, Richard W. E.
Log houses in Wisconsin. Antiques 89:867-71 Je '66

PERROUX, Carlo Alberto
Final win for the Blue. il por Sports Illus 24:34-6+ My 23 '66

PERRY, E. C. Jr, and Bonnichsen, B.
Quartz and magnetite: oxygen-18-oxygen-16 fractionation in metamorphosed Biwabik iron formation. bibliog Science 153:528-9 Jl 29 '66

PERRY, Eleanor
Everywoman's village stirs up the housewives. Life 60:46+ Mr 25 '66; Same abr. with title Housewives' school to beat the boredom. Read Digest 88:41-2+ Je '66
Goliath of a book on a modern David. Life 62:10 Ja 6 '67
Life movie review (cont) Life 60:8 F 4; 61:10 Ag 5; 10 O 28 '66

PERRY, Gaylord Jackson
Magic on the mound. il por Time 88:44 Ag 26 '66

PERRY, Geoffrey
Secret of Plesetsk. il por Time 88:38 D 30 '66

PERRY, Harold Robert, bp
Bishop Harold Perry: man of many firsts. E. B. Thompson. il pors Ebony 21:62-6+ F '66
La. Negro priest appointed bishop. C. W. Thomas. por Negro Hist Bul 29:65-6 Jl '65

PERRY, John Holliday, 1917-
Long-time leader in computerized type tools up for book work. il Pub W 189:90-1+ Mr 7 '66

PERRY, Lynn
Look of Japan's gardens. Flower Grower 53:30-1 Mr '66

PERRY, Margaret
Christmas card magic. il Flower Grower 53:22-3+ D '66

PERRY, Richard E.
Where the innocent die; ed. by R. J. Levin. por Redbook 128:46-7+ Ja '67

PERRY, Robert P.
Nucleolus: structure and function. Science 153:214-15+ Jl 8 '66

PERRY, Stephen Joseph
Father Perry's expedition to Kerguelen Island. J. Ashbrook. il por Sky & Tel 31:340-1 Je '66

PERRY, Thomas L. and others
Homocystinuria; excretion of a new sulfur-containing amino acid in urine. bibliog Science 152:776-8 My 6 '66
Homolanthionine excretion in homocystinuria. bibliog Science 152:1750-2 Je 24 '66

PERRY, William C.
Minimizing cracks in on-grade slabs. Arch Rec 139:197-8+ F '66

PERRY publications, incorporated
Long-time leader in computerized type tools up for book work. il Pub W 189:90-1+ Mr 7 '66

PERSECUTION
Annihilation in China & U.S. indifference. W. F. Buckley, jr. Nat R 18:1259 D 13 '66
Persecution in Sudan. Commonweal 84:272 My 27 '66
See also
Inquisition
Jews—Persecutions
Martyrs

PERSECUTION in literature. See Religion in literature

PERSEIDS. See Meteors

PERSEPOLIS
Persepolis: procession across the centuries. il UNESCO Courier 19:36-40 D '66

PERSHALL, T. W.
Cotton fires up Little Smoky. D. Barnes. il por Sports Illus 24:28-33 Ja 31 '66

PERSHING, John Joseph
Why no statue of Pershing? E. T. Folliard. America 114:850 Je 18 '66

PERSIA. See Iran

PERSIAN GULF
Vest-pocket states of Arabia. A. Higbee. il Newsweek 67:50+ Mr 28 '66

PERSIAN rugs. See Rugs and carpets, Oriental

PERSIMMONS
Persimmon and pomegranate, pick of the winter fruits. il Bet Hom & Gard 44:99 N '66

PERSING, Robert F.
Transistorized auto-light minder. Pop Electr 24:65-7 Ap '66

PERSONAL airplanes. See Airplanes—Private ownership

PERSONAL beauty. See Beauty, Personal

PERSONAL credit. See Credit

PERSONAL liberty. See Liberty

PERSONAL loans. See Loans, Personal

PERSONAL names. See Names, Personal

PERSONAL opinions. See Attitudes

PERSONAL property. See Property

PERSONAL responsibility. See Responsibility

PERSONALISM
Romantic generation. P. F. Drucker. Harper 232:12+ My '66

PERSONALITY
African personality. D. O. Ajala. il Negro Hist Bul 29:157-8 Ap '66
Do you act your part? reprint. M. Scheerer. Read Digest 89:211-12+ N '66
Personalising process; address. January 26, 1966. M. E. Parr. Vital Speeches 32:341-4 Mr 15 '66
Preschool personality patterns; with study-discussion program, by R. Strang. G. O. Dickinson. bibliog il PTA Mag 61:21-3, 35-6 O '66
See also
Individuality

PERSONALITY, Disorders of
See also
Autism

PERSONALITY tests
How to beat personality tests, by C. Alex. Review
New Repub 154:31-2 F 26 '66. J. Ridgeway
Job game; about psychological job tests and how to pass them. S. Birmingham. il McCalls 93:76-7+ Jl '66
Psychological testing and the invasion of privacy. D. Wolfle; reply. J. W. Hamblen. Science 151:1174 Mr 11 '66
Tests violate privacy. Sci N 90:198 S 17 '66

PERSONNEL management
Affluent organization; excerpts from address, April 8, 1966. R. E. Miles. bibliog f Harvard Bsns R 44:106-14 My '66
Behavioral sciences for personnel managers. C. A. Myers. bibliog f Harvard Bsns R 44:154-6+ Jl '66
Better management of managers' careers. L. L. Ferguson. bibliog f il Harvard Bsns R 44:139-52 Mr '66
Describing men to machines; computerized personnel system. il Bsns W p 113-14 Je 4 '66
Deterioration of work standards. C. W. Graves. il Harvard Bsns R 44:117-22+ S '66
Happy factory that sired a social ethic: Cocoa works and Rowntree & co, ltd. il Bsns W p 126+ Je 25 '66
How to keep key executives. J. G. Mason. Nations Bsns 54:75 Ag '66
Problem of executive dropout. L. S. Bickmore. il Duns R 87:34-5+ Ap '66
So your employees don't like you. R. Dreyfack. il Nations Bsns 54:74-6 Mr '66
See also
Communication in management
Profit sharing
Psychology, Industrial

PERSONNEL selection. See Employment systems

PERSONNEL service in education
Classroom incident: concerning girl who doesn't believe in God. NEA J 55:55+ S '66
College conundrum: how to choose. P. Janssen. il Am Ed 2:24-7 S '66
Guidance and counseling in groups. B. Cohn. NEA J 55:38-9 O '66
Teachers with the guidance point of view. R. M. Kaufman and M. Richstone. il NEA J 55:32-4 O '66
Wise old hand at a new calling: H. Gammons of Westfield, Mass. high school. il Life 61:39-40+ N 4 '66

PETERSON, Esther—*Continued*
Pennywise teenagers. por Am Ed 2:24-8 Ap '66
Things go better with consumer education. PTA Mag 60:7-9 My '66

about
Guardian of the gullible. por Time 87:29 Ap 29 '66

PETERSON, Harold
Baseball's week. Sports Illus 24:108-9 My 16 '66
Long ride home. Sports Illus 25:35-7 Ag 1 '66

PETERSON, Karin
Kitten's Christmas; poem. il Horn Bk 42: 750 D '66

PETERSON, Lloyd R.
Short-term memory; with biographical sketch. Sci Am 215:15, 90-5 bibliog(p 131) Jl '66

PETERSON, M. N. A.
Calcite: rates of dissolution in a vertical profile in the central Pacific. bibliog Science 154:1542-4 D 23 '66

PETERSON, Patricia
Let it fall. N Y Times Mag p48-9 My 29 '66

PETERSON, R. Price
Cell size and rate of protein synthesis in ventral horn neurones. bibliog Science 153: 1413-14 S 16 '66

PETERSON, Richard C.
CB radio call monitor. Pop Electr 26:54-6 Ja '67

PETERSON, Rudolph Arvid
Balance of payments; address, December 1, 1965. Vital Speeches 32:216-19 Ja 15 '66
New dynamics in U.S. foreign trade; address, October 31, 1966. Vital Speeches 33: 149-52 D 15 '66

about
Biggest bank's uncommon asset. il por Time 88:50-1 D 30 '66

PETERSON, Virgilia
ABPC annual meeting: literature of the future; excerpts from address, May 25, 1966. por Pub W 189:86-7 Je 13 '66
Fact of the matter. Reporter 35:57-8 O 20 '66
Pity and to love. Reporter 34:56-7 F 10 '66
Prejudice and hope. Reporter 35:34-6 Ag 11 '66

about
Obituary
Pub W por 191:42 Ja 9 '67

PETIOT, Fernand
Bloody-Mary man. il por Newsweek 69:6 Ja 2 '67

PETITIONS
Petition game: look before signing; Time essay. Time 88:39 O 14 '66

PETKOF, Benjamin
Gem stones. Consumer Bul 49:11-14 Je '66

PETRA, Jordan
T.R.B. from Petra. New Repub 154:4 Je 4 '66

PETRARCA, Francesco. See Petrarch, F.

PETRARCH, Francesco
Letters of Petrarch; selection, tr. by M. Bishop. Horizon 9:42-5 Wint '67
Letters from Petrarch, tr. by M. Bishop.
Review
Sat R 50:39 Ja 21 '67. M. Musa

PETREAT, Russell
Carbonless paper. por Am City 81:120+ Ag '66

PETRIE, A. F.
First integrated-circuit phonograph. Electr World 76:28-9+ D '66

PETRIE, Paul
Ancestors; poem. Sat R 49:71 My 14 '66
During the Christmas season; poem. New Yorker 42:30 D 31 '66
Murderer; poem. New Yorker 42:51 My 7 '66

about
Three poets. P. Weiss. Poetry 108:57-9 Ap '66

PETRIE, Robert M.
R. M. Petrie: Canadian astorphysicist. A. B. Underhill. por Sky & Tel 32:25 Jl '66

PETRIE, Vincent
As I see it. E. Hannigan. U S Camera 29:40+ Mr '66

PETRIFIED forests
Detour to Nevada's ancient fossil forest. il Sunset 137:50 N '66

PETROCHEMICALS. See Petroleum chemicals

PETROGLYPHS
Rock carvings at Chalcacingo; bas-reliefs add to knowledge of ancient Olmec culture in Mexico. C. T. E. Gay. il Natur Hist 75:56-61 Ag '66

PETROLEUM
See also
Bituminous sand
Oil shales

Chemistry
Terpenoid precursors of hydrocarbons from the gasoline range of petroleum. B. J. Mair and others. bibliog il Science 154: 1339-41 D 9 '66

International aspects
And more taxes to pay overseas. il Bsns W p49 O 8 '66
Oilmen rush to get their feet wet. il Bsns W p 104-6+ Je 4 '66
U.S. shipowners formally notified of ban on Rhodesian oil shipments; letter, May 4, 1966. T. C. Mann. Dept State Bul 54:859 My 30 '66
See also
Petroleum industry and trade—Middle East

Pipe lines
Pipelines. E. J. Jensen ad H. S. Ellis. il Sci Am 216:62-70+ bibliog(p 146) Ja '67

Production methods
See Petroleum engineering

Prospecting
North Sea petroleum. Sci Am 214:58 Mr '66
Ocean is expansive oil field. C. A. Betts. il Sci N 89:372-3 My 14 '66
Oilmen rush to get their feet wet. il Bsns W p 104-6+ Je 4 '66

Transportation
See also
Petroleum—Pipe lines
Tank ships

Alaska
Tycoons of Tyonek. il Time 88:19 Jl 1 '66

Alberta
See Petroleum—Canada

Arabia
See Petroleum—Middle East

Australia
Bonanza Down Under. il Time 87:102 Je 10 '66

California
Neighborhood well; Los Angeles drilling rigs beautified. il Newsweek 68:89-90+ O 10 '66

Canada
Oil bonanza in Canada and the excitement grows; Calgary and Rainbow Lake, Alberta. il U S News 60:71-2+ My 16 '66
Tiger by the tail; Rainbow well's race to beat thaw. Newsweek 67:87 Ap 11 '66

China (People's Republic)
Fill 'er up. il Newsweek 68:71 N 21 '66

Libya
Libya. R. S. Harrison. bibliog il Focus 17:1-6 N '66

Middle East
Sparks fly around world's biggest pool of oil; oil-rich Arabs are raising the ante again. il U S News 62:66-8 Ja 2 '66

PETROLEUM chemicals
What puts zip in petrochemicals. il Bsns W p40-3 D 17 '66

PETROLEUM engineering
Atom aims for role as prospector; nuclear test shots may unlock vast oil and gas fields. il Bsns W p83-4+ D 17 '66
Now we're mining oil from mountains; deposits in the Rockies. J. N. Bell. il Pop Mech 126:142-5+ N '66
See also
Oil well drilling, Submarine

PETROLEUM in submerged lands
North Sea bonanza. Newsweek 67:86 Ap 18 '66
Oilmen rush to get their feet wet. il Bsns W p 104-6+ Je 4 '66
See also
Oil well drilling, Submarine

PETROLEUM industry and trade

Exhibitions
New faces, new gear steal petroleum show; Tulsa's international oil exposition. il Bsns W p72-3 My 21 '66

PETROLEUM industry and trade—*Continued*

History

Photographer to oildom; Titusville, Pa; with photographs by J. A. Mather. E. C. Miller and T. K. Stratton. Am Heritage 17:38-45+ O '66

International aspects

See Petroleum—International aspects

Taxation

And more taxes to pay overseas. il Bsns W p49 O 8 '66

Europe, Western

Gas-pump war. il Fortune 75:62+ Ja '67

Germany (Federal Republic)

Bonn sends up warning on U.S. investments; curtailing Texaco-Deutsche Erdoel negotiations. Bsns W p36 My 7 '66

Playing for big stakes in West German oil. il Bsns W p 126+ Ap 16 '66

Iraq

Pumping under pressure; demanding more. il Time 88:94+ D 16 '66

Middle East

Mideast oil lands demand a bigger bite. il Bsns W p38-9 D 17 '66

Pumping under pressure; demanding more. il Time 88:94+ D 16 '66

Texas

Texas oil industry project; University archives in Eugene C. Barker Texas history center. C. V. Kielman. il Wilson Lib Bul 40:616-18 Mr '66

United States

Food for tomorrow; address, September 12, 1966. J. E. Swearingen. Vital Speeches 33: 61-4 N 1 '66

Gushing profits. Time 88:90+ N 4 '66

Just plain H. L. Hunt. T. Buckley. il Esquire 67:64-9+ Ja '67

Oil woes: fight over imports at home; petrochemical makers scrambling for special feedstock allotments. Bsns W p48 O 8 '66

Oilmen wary of aerospace promises; with editorial comment. Tech W 19:27, 78 S 26 '66

Soft sell for beauty; First lady's persuasion is adding impetus. il Bsns W p33 F 19 '66

U.S. companies tap a new source of European cash. il Fortune 75:64 Ja '67

See also names of oil companies, e.g. Sinclair oil corporation

Venezuela

Friction in oil. il Time 87:84 Ja 28 '66

Zambia

Hell run. il Time 87:39 F 25 '66

PETROLEUM mulch. See Mulching

PETROLEUM pipe lines. See Petroleum—Pipe lines

PETROLEUM refineries

Jersey Standard goes West again: refinery to be on site of historic Benicia arsenal, California. il Bsns W p 110-12+ O 1 '66

Wages and hours

Wages in industrial chemicals and petroleum refining. il Mo Labor R 89:994-9 S '66

PETROLEUM supply

Rhodesia

Challenge at sea; how to stop Rhodesia-bound oil . il Time 87:38 Ap 15 '66

Hot cargoes; oil bound for Rhodesia. Time 87:34 Ap 22 '66

Security council authorizes U.K. to use force to divert oil shipments bound for Rhodesia; statement, April 9, 1966; with text of resolution. A. J. Goldberg. Dept State Bul 54: 713-18 My 2 '66

Sit-ins; UN upholds British embargo on oil shipments to Rhodesia. Newsweek 67:56+ Ap 18 '66

Troubled waters; second blockade-runner flees. Newsweek 67:45 Ap 25 '66

Zambia

U.S. airlift to Zambia ends. Dept State Bul 54:783 My 16 '66

PETRY, Terence M.
Independence for Guyana. America 114:854 Je 18 '66

PETS

Happiness is a pocket kangaroo: gerbil. il Time 87:67 Ap 15 '66

How to avoid losing a pet. Good H 162:171 My '66

Nature note; gerbils make good pets. il Sci N 90:285 O 8 '66

Pet news. See issues of Ladies' home journal

Pet's gazette; news from the ark mart. il House & Gard 129:86+ Ap '66

Redbook's guide to family pets. M. S. Welch. il Redbook 127:88-96 S '66

Wolves social as dogs. P. McBroom. il Sci N 90:174-5 S 10 '66

See also names of animal pets, e.g. Cats

Care

How to keep pets healthy and happy in hot weather. Bet Hom & Gard 44:89 Jl '66

Importance of good pet grooming. il Good H 162:179 Mr '66

Equipment and supplies

Pet news; excerpt from Bears in the ladies room. B. Gilbert. Ladies Home J 83:12 S '66

PETS, Stealing of. See Animal thefts

PETTINGILL, Olin Sewall, jr
Bird finding. See issues of Audubon magazine

Coto Doñana. Audubon Mag 68:304-306A S '66

PETTY, H. B.
How to identify and control corn insects. Suc Farm 64:71+ Mr '66

PETTY, Richard
Richard Petty tells how he stokes the stockers; ed. by B. Myers. por Motor T 18:42-4 Mr '66

about

Return of the exile was rich and racy. T. C. Brody. il por Sports Illus 24:24-5 Mr 7 '66

PETUNIAS
Go togethers; petunias & pots. L. Burgess. il Flower Grower 53:32-3 Jl '66

PEW, J. Howard
Should the church meddle in civil affairs? Read Digest 88:49-54 My '66; Same. Farm J 90:28+ Jl '66

about

Century and Mr Pew. Christian Cent 83: 864-5 Jl 6 '66

Uncomfortable Pew. Christian Cent 83:607-8 My 11 '66

PEWTER
American silver and pewter. R. Davidson. il Antiques 91:128 Ja '67

PEYOTE
LSD may become legal if it gets religion. Sci N 90:22 Jl 9 '66

PEYRE, Henri
New France; changes in French society and culture. bibliog f Cur Hist 50:193-200+ Ap '66

PEYSER, Joan
New music. Vogue 147:176+ F 1 '66

PFAFF, William
Foreign affairs (cont) Commonweal 83:492-3, 654-5; 84:70-1, 248-9, 351-2, 456-7, 571-2; 85:45-6 Ja 28, Mr 11, Ap 8, My 20, Je 17, Jl 22, S 16, O 14 '66
—See Kahn, H. jt. auth.

PFALTZGRAFF, Robert L. Jr
Atlantic technological imbalance. New Repub 156:19-21 Ja 21 '67

PFEFFER, Leo
Constitutional confrontation in New York state. Christian Cent 83:885-7 Jl 13 '66

Supreme court and the Bill of rights. Nation 203:315-18, 351-4, 385-8 O 3-17 '66

What price federal aid? Sat R 50:59-60+ Ja 21 '67

PFEIFFER, John
How they'll rate your bonds. Am City 81:174+ O '66

PFEIFFER, John Edward
Man through time's mists. Sat Eve Post 239:40-4 D 3 '66

When homo erectus tamed fire, he tamed himself. N Y Times Mag p58-9+ D 11 '66

PFEIFFER, Russell R.
Anteroventral cochlear nucleus; wave forms of extracellularly recorded spike potentials. bibliog Science 154:667-8 N 4 '66

PFISTER, Herbert R.
It's easier to install the new plasterboard. Pop Sci 189:164-8 S '66

Repairing basement leaks. Pop Sci 189:121 Jl '66

Saw that speeds your plywood projects. Pop Sci 189:150-5+ N '66

PFITZER, Albert
Nazi past. Newsweek 68:62+ O 24 '66

PFIZER, Beryl
Planned aunthood. McCalls 94:94+ O '66

PFIZER, Charles, and company
FTC rules in tetracycline case; Pfizer & co. obtained patent by making false and misleading statements. Bsns W p46+ D 10 '66
Protection for baby's skin. M. B. Keiser. il Parents Mag 41:36+ Mr '66

PFLEIDERER, J. and Grewing, M.
Inverse Compton effect: some consequences for quasars. bibliog Science 154:1452-3 D 16 '66

PFLIEGER, Elmer F.
Civic education from sea to shining sea. NEA J 56:56-8 Ja '67

PHACELIA
Nature of seed dormancy in phacelia tanacetifolia. S. S. C. Chen and K. V. Thimann. bibliog il Science 153:1537-9 S 23 '66

PHALON, Richard A.
Insider and the SEC. Duns R 88:38-40+ S '66
Memo from an angry business writer. Duns R 87:38-9+ Ja '66

PHAN-quang-Dan
Diagnosis: murder; attempted assassination. Time 89:25-6 Ja 6 '67
Murky waters; assassination attempt. Newsweek 69:26 Ja 9 '67
Vietnam prepares for the elections. D. Warner. Reporter 35:12-15 Ag 11 '66

PHAN-trong-Chinh
Ky question. Tran van Dinh. New Repub 156:21-2 Ja 21 '67

PHANTOMS. See Apparitions

PHARMACEUTICAL industry. See Drug trade

PHARMACOLOGY
Clinical pharmacology: present status and future development; report on discussions of a small group of university scientists. L. Lasagna. Science 152:388-91 Ap 15 '66
Drug appraisal asked. Sci N 89:289 Ap 23 '66
  See also
Drugs

PHARMACOPOEIAS
  See also
Drugs

PHARMACY
  See also
Drugs
Pharmacology
Prescriptions

PHEASANT shooting
Feel free to hunt. C. Chatfield. il Outdoor Life 138:70-1+ N '66
New gamebird for the South. G. X. Sand. il Outdoor Life 137:40-1+ Je '66
Pheasant is a clever bird. T. Trueblood. il Field & S 71:64-7+ S '66
Ringnecks, humbler of hunters. J. Madson. il Farm J 90:50B-50C+ N '66

PHEASANTS
New pheasant for southern gunners. F. C. Hibben. il Field & S 70:30 F '66

PHÈDRE; drama. See Racine, J. B.

PHELAN, James
Can Reagan win California? Sat Eve Post 239:89-93 Je 4 '66
Case of the missing millionaire. Sat Eve Post 239:85-91 D 17 '66
Invisible billionaire. Reporter 35:57-8 Jl 14 '66
When I looked in those files, my eyes popped. Sat Eve Post 239:23-9 S 10 '66

PHELPS, Anthony
New plastic layer cages. Farm J 90:80 F '66

PHELPS, Flora L.
Mexico builds. Américas 18:26-9 My '66

PHELPS, Horace
Leslie. Criticism
Commonweal 85:141-2 N 4 '66

PHELPS, McAndrew
Washington front (cont) America 114:408, 644, 869 Mr 26, My 7, Je 25 '66

PHENOBARBITAL
Immunochemical studies of submicrosomal membranes from liver of normal and phenobarbital-treated rats. U. Lundkvist and P. Perlmann. bibliog il Science 152: 780-2 My 6 '66
Phenobarbital controls newborn jaundice case. Sci N 89:500 Je 18 '66

PHENYLALANINE
Phenylalanine: transplacental concentrations in rhesus monkeys. G. R. Kerr and H. A. Waisman. bibliog il Science 151:824-5 F 18 '66

PHENYLKETONURIA
Cure that fails? il Newsweek 69:40 Ja 2 '67
Phenylalanine: transplacental concentrations in rhesus monkeys. G. R. Kerr and H. A. Waisman. bibliog il Science 151:824-5 F 18 '66
Unnecessary menace to young brains: PKU. G. G. Greer. Bet Hom & Gard 44:25 F '66
You and your diet; diet and mental retardation. il Good H 162:177-9 F '66

PHEROMONES
Pheromone: evidence in a decapod crustacean. E. P. Ryan. bibliog il Science 151:340-1 Ja 21 '66
Trails of the leafcutters. J. C. Moser. il Natur Hist 76:32-5 bibliog(p73) Ja '67

PHILADELPHIA
Alarm horns cut false fire calls. J. J. McCarey. il Am City 81:50 N '66

Architecture
Private building respects public site; Philadelphia's Independence mall. il Arch Rec 139:141-8 Ja '66

City planning
Philadelphia's giant shopping machine; Market street east. D. Canty. il Arch Forum 125:34-43 N '66
Urban renewal, the Philadelphia story. J. Bookbinder. il Sch Arts 65:11-16 Ap '66

Education
Philadelphia schools sue eleven publishers on pricing. Pub W 190:55 Jl 4 '66
Project Get Set; prekindergarten program. A. Harding. il NEA J 55:16-18 O '66

Free library
Beatrix Potter lives in Philadelphia's Free library. E. Shaffer. il Horn Bk 42:401-5 Ag '66

Library for the blind
Day at a library for the blind. S. Havens. il Library J 91:3333-8 Jl '66

Galleries and museums
  See also
American museum of photography

Gardens
Neighborhood gardens in Philadelphia; special report. R. C. Hands. il Horticulture 44:34-5+ Mr '66

Historic houses, etc.
Lemon Hill revisited. V. N. Naude. il Antiques 89:578-9 Ap '66
Living with antiques: Pennsylvania home of Mr and Mrs John W. Batdorf. L. H. Solis-Cohen. il Antiques 90:224-7 Ag '66
Philadelphia story continued. B. Snow. il Antiques 89:546-7 Ap '66
  See also
Independence Hall, Philadelphia

Hotels, restaurants, etc.
Victor café. L. Saltzman. il Opera N 30:6-7 F 19 '66

Lighting
Ben Franklin's street lights make a comeback. il Am City 81:126 Je '66

Music
Baltimore, Philadelphia. M. De Schauensee. Opera N 30:31 Mr 12 '66
Debuts & reappearances. Hi Fi 16:MA12-13+ D '66
Notes from our correspondents. P. G. Davis. il Hi Fi 16:18+ F '66
Philadelphia. M. DeSchauensee. Opera N 30: 27 Je 4 '66
Philadelphia; productions by Lyric and the Grand opera companies. M. De Schauensee. Opera N 31:27 D 31 '66
  See also
Philadelphia lyric opera company

Negroes
Anatomy of a riot; case study by American Jewish committee. Christian Cent 83:164-5 F 9 '66
Out to get SNCC. P. Good. il Nation 203: 534-8 N 21 '66

Police
Dogs patrol the subways; policeman-dog teams. il Am City 81:95 Jl '66

Police department
How to handle demonstrations; civil-disobedience squad. il Time 88:57 D 9 '66

PHILADELPHIA—*Continued*

Riots

Anatomy of a riot; case study by American Jewish committee. Christian Cent 83:164-5 F 9 '66

Sanitary affairs

Better way to clean catch basins. R. E. Doyle. il Am City 81:102-3 Ap '66

Schools

See Philadelphia—Education

Streets

Big trees moved with speed and safety; by crane-and-clam technique. il Am City 81:92-3 F '66

Theater

Broadway postscript; Theatre of the living arts, second season. H. Hewes. Sat R 49:55 Mr 5 '66

End as a woman; Theater of the living arts production of Beclch. H. Hewes. Sat R 50:111 Ja 7 '67

[Theatre across America] J. Novick. Nation 203:29-30 Jl 4 '66

Theater; Theater of the living art's production of Room service. H. Hewes. Sat R 49:64 D 10 '66

Water supply

Dialogue on water resources; interview. ed. by E. F. Spitzer. S. S. Baxter. il Am City 81:97-9+ My '66

PHILADELPHIA booksellers association

Laura L. Brookman, president, Phila. booksellers assn. il Pub W 190:76-7 O 31 '66

PHILADELPHIA dance academy. See Dance schools

PHILADELPHIA free library. See Philadelphia—Free library

PHILADELPHIA grand opera company

Philadelphia; opera season. M. De Schauensee. Opera N 31:29 D 3 '66

PHILADELPHIA, here I come! drama. See Friel, B.

PHILADELPHIA lyric opera company

Philadelphia. M. De Schauensee. Opera N 30:28 F 19 '66

Philadelphia; opera season. M. De Schauensee. Opera N 31:29 D 3 '66

PHILADELPHIA orchestra

Flying the coop. il Time 88:54+ O 7 '66

Music to my ears; first collaboration in Philharmonic Hall of Eugene Ormandy and his peerless personnel. I. Kolodin. Sat R 50:96 Ja 14 '67

Music to my ears; Mexico city concert. I. Kolodin. Sat R 49:35-6 Jl 2 '66

PHILADELPHIA 76ers (basketball team) See Basketball teams

PHILADELPHIA society (organization)

Our man at the Golliwog lounge; second annual meeting. J. J. Kilpatrick. Nat R 18:258+ Mr 22 '66

PHILADELPHIA symphony orchestra. See Philadelphia orchestra

PHILANTHROPIC foundations. See Foundations, Charitable and educational

PHILANTHROPY. See Giving

PHILATELY. See Postage stamps

PHILBIN, Tom, Jr

Painting secrets from a pro. Pop Sci 188:168-9+ Je '66

PHILCO corporation

Can he turn on Philco? J. B. Weiner. Duns R 88:39-40 Ag '66

Henry Ford and his electronic can of worms. P. Siekman. il Fortune 73:116-19+ F '66

PHILCO-Ford corporation

Why they call it Philco-Ford. Bsns W p48+ O 15 '66

PHILHARMONIC Hall. See Lincoln Center for the performing arts, New York—Philharmonic Hall

PHILHARMONIC-symphony society of New York

Music; current season. B. Boretz. Nation 203:461-2 O 31 '66

Music; Stravinsky festival review. B. Boretz. Nation 203:165-6 Ag 22 '66

Music to my ears; Bernstein's reign. I. Kolodin. Sat R 49:76 N 19 '66

Music to my ears; final program of Festival of Stravinsky. I. Kolodin. Sat R 49:34 Ag 6 '66

Music to my ears; L. Bernstein's Philharmonic program. I. Kolodin. Sat R 49:41 F 26 '66

Music to my ears; Mitropoulous international competition winners show their wares. I. Kolodin. Sat R 49:34 F 5 '66

Music to my ears; New York philharmonic under W. Steinberg. I. Kolodin. Sat R 49:70 D 10 '66

Musical events:
Concert in Philharmonic Hall. W. Sargeant. New Yorker 42:232 O 29 '66
Performance of Beethoven's Ninth symphony, conducted by L. Maazel. W. Sargeant. New Yorker 42:229-30 N 19 '66
Performance of compositions by D. Diamond. W. Sargeant. New Yorker 42:128 My 7 '66
Performance of Haydn's Creation. W. Sargeant. New Yorker 42:111 My 21 '66

PHILIP II, king of Spain

King's prayer factory. H. R. Trevor-Roper. il por Horizon 8:66-75 Wint '66

PHILIP, consort of Elizabeth II, queen of Great Britain

Fanciful chronicle of a royal visit. R. Searle. il Look 30:50-2 Ap 5 '66

Inflation is a royal nuisance. Life 61:4 S 9 '66

Leisure. Sports Illus 24:12 Mr 28 '66

People are talking about. . . por Vogue 147:86-7 Mr 15 '66

Philip; prince with a purpose. F. Drake and K. Drake. por Read Digest 88:86-91 Mr '66

Prince for all seasons. R. Godden. il pors Ladies Home J 83:100+ Mr '66

Princely tour with a proper sell. il pors Bsns W p40-1 Mr 19 '66

PHILIPPINES

Bewildering collision; modern hopes and ancient habits. S. Karnow. il Sat R 49:41-2+ O 8 '66

New voice in Asia. il Time 88:38-42+ O 21 '66; Same abr. with title Marcos of Manila, new voice in Asia. Read Digest 90:101-6 Ja '67

Philippines. A. Campbell. New Repub 154:21-4 Mr 12 '66

Philippines; contour and perspective. D. T. Sternberg. For Affairs 44:501-11 Ap '66

Philippines; freedom's Pacific frontier. R. De Roos. il Nat Geog Mag 130:301-51 S '66

See also
Arts and crafts—Philippines
Colleges and universities—Philippines
Communism—Philippines
Crime and criminals—Philippines
Finance—Philippines
Hukbalahaps
Strikes—Philippines
World war, 1939-1945—Philippines

Description and travel

Going places, finding things in the Philippines. P. K. Brooks. il House & Gard 130:36-8+ N '66

Return to the Rock. H. Sutton. Sat R 49:70-2 D 3 '66

Foreign relations

Asian leader explains America's role to Americans; address, September 15, 1966. F. E. Marcos. il U S News 61:114-16+ O 3 '66; Same. Dept State Bul 55:534-47 O 10 '66; Same with title Philippines and the United States. Vital Speeches 33:2-10 O 15 '66

Formula from the Philippines. il Time 88:22-3 S 23 '66

Mutual admiration alliance; Washington visit of President and Mrs Marcos. il Life 61:133-4 S 30 '66

President Marcos of the Philippines visits the United States; exchanges of greetings and toasts, September 14, 1966; with joint communique, September 15, 1966. L. B. Johnson; F. Marcos. Dept State Bul 55:526-34 O 10 '66

U.S. and Philippines; drawing closer? il U S News 60:84-5 Ap 4 '66

What an ally sees ahead for U.S. in Asia; interview. ed. by K. M. Chrysler. F. E. Marcos. U S News 61:66-9 S 19 '66

History

Return to the Rock. H. Sutton. Sat R 49:70-2 D 3 '66

Japanese raids

See World war, 1939-1945—Philippines

Politics and government

Crusade in Manila; campaign against corruption. il Time 87:37 F 4 '66

Philippines and its president. E. J Hughes. il Newsweek 67:51-3 Ap 25 '66

Philippines: ray of hope? R. L. Deats. Christain Cent 83:283-6 Mr 2 '66

PHILIPPINES—Politics and government—*Cont.*
President Marcos and the Huk resurgence. D.
Warner. il Reporter 35:28-31 N 3 '66
Sex & the sleuths; Central investigation
service. Time 87:25 Mr 25 '66
Time for toughness. il Newsweek 67:42+ F
14 '66

Religious institutions and affairs
World around us (cont) Christian Cent 83:
596-7, 1192 My 4, S 28 '66
PHILIPPINES and the United States
Bewildering collision; modern hopes and an-
cient habits. S. Karnow. il Sat R 49:41-2+
O 8 '66
Elements of the Philippine-American partner-
ship; address. February 24, 1966. W. P.
Bundy. Dept State Bul 54:444-51 Mr 21 '66
Philippine veterans benefits signed into law;
statements, September 30 and October 11,
1966. L. B. Johnson. Dept State Bul 55:
684-6 O 31 '66
Philippines. A. Campbell. New Repub 154:
21-4 Mr 12 '66
Philippines: contour and perspective. D. T.
Sternberg. For Affairs 44:501-11 Ap '66
PHILISTINISM
How are things with the Philistines? R.
Lynes. il Harper 233:26+ Jl '66
PHILLIPPS, F. A.
Isle of Jersey's venerable master; Edmund
Blampied. Am Artist 30:40-5+ O '66
PHILLIPS, Alan
Canadian Rockies, lords of a beckoning land.
por Nat Geog Mag 130:352-93 S '66
PHILLIPS, Anthony
Turning a surface inside out; with biographi-
cal sketch. Sci Am 214:18, 112-20 bibliog
(p 148) My '66
PHILLIPS, Carleton A.
Combination RC substitution box. Pop Electr
24:82-3 Ja '66
PHILLIPS, David C.
Three-dimensional structure of an enzyme
molecule; with biographical sketch. Sci
Am 215:29, 78-90 bibliog(p 160) N '66
PHILLIPS, Don. See Belveal, D. jt. auth.
PHILLIPS, Duncan
Double loss. il por Time 87:88+ My 20 '66
Duncan Phillips, a guiding force. K. Kuh.
por Sat R 49:29 Je 11 '66
Intermediaries. il por Newsweek 67:100 My
23 '66
Obituary
Art N 65:8 Sum '66. H. LaFarge
PHILLIPS, Harry L.
New dimension. por Am Ed 2:15-20 Ap '66
—and others
(ed) Gadfly of the Education act. Library J
91:1020-4 F 15 '66
PHILLIPS, Harvey E.
First love. Opera N 30:24-5 Mr 12 '66
PHILLIPS, Jackson
Trend of business. See issues of Dun's review
and modern industry
PHILLIPS, John A.
Bonhoeffer in brief. Christian Cent 83:1603-4
D 28 '66
PHILLIPS, Norman
In the wake of Cortez. il Motor B 118:22-4+
D '66
Take 'em aboard to ride 'em ashore. Motor
B 117:82-4 Ja '66
PHILLIPS, Norman (bookkeeper)
When I looked in those files, my eyes popped.
J. Phelan. il por Sat Eve Post 239:23-9 S
10 '66
PHILLIPS, Pauline Esther (Friedman) See
Van Buren, A. pseud.
PHILLIPS, Peter
Hybrid. New Yorker 42:35-6 Ap 30 '66
Pollsters began with kits, questionnaires, no
know-how. il por Life 60:72 My 20 '66
PHILLIPS, Thomas L.
Raytheon's quicker pulse. il pors Bsns W
p72-4+ Jl 9 '66
PHILLIPS, Wendell
Great lam. il por Time 88:110+ S 30 '66
PHILLIPS, William
But is it good for literature? Commentary
41:77-80 My '66
PHILLIPS academy, Andover, Mass. See Pri-
vate schools
PHILLIPS collection. See Art—Private collec-
tions
PHILOSOPHERS
American philosophy is dead; decline from
golden age to an academic cult. L. S.
Feuer. il N Y Times Mag p30-1+ Ap 24
'66; Discussion. p22+ My 8 '66
Is philosophy dead too? N. S. Care. New
Repub 154:23-6 My 21 '66
See also
Buber, M.

PHILOSOPHY
Confessions of a reformed reformer. R.
Moses. Sat R 50:18-21+ Ja 7 '67
Ecumenism and philosophy. G. F. Kreyche.
bibliog f Christian Cent 83:521-4 Ap 27 '66
Future of philosophy. R. O. Johann. America
115:207 Ag 27 '66
Is philosophy dead too? N. S. Care. New
Repub 154:23-6 My 21 '66
Philosophy in the Catholic university. J.
Donceel. America 115:330-1 S 24 '66; Dis-
cussion. 115:470-1; 116:99+ O 22 '66, Ja 21
'67
Trade winds. J. G. Fuller. Sat R 49:16-17
Jl 16 '66
Where has all philosophy gone? T. J. Cun-
ningham. America 114:496-9 Ap 9 '66
See also
Christianity
Ethics
God
Life
Man
Metaphysics
Ontology
Optimism
Pragmatism
Rationalism
Reality
Religion
Subjectivism
Theism
Will
also subhead under various subjects,
e.g. Education—Philosophy

History
Patterns of history. W. L. Gundersheimer.
Reporter 34:50-2 Ap 21 '66

Study and teaching
Teaching of philosophy in universities of the
United States, by H. E. Davis and H. A.
Durfee. Review
Américas 18:40-2 N '66. S. Lipp
PHILOSOPHY, American
American philosophy is dead; decline from
golden age to an academic cult. L. S.
Feuer. il N Y Times Mag p30-1+ Ap 24
'66; Discussion. p22+ My 8 '66
PHILOSOPHY, Brazilian. See Philosophy, Latin
American
PHILOSOPHY, French
French thought in Latin America. J. L.
Martí. il Américas 18:8-15 S '66
PHILOSOPHY, German
See also
Jaspers, K.
Spengler, O.
PHILOSOPHY, Jewish
Martin Buber and the Jews; his interpreta-
tion of and path to Hasidism. C. Potok.
Commentary 41:43-9 Mr '66; Discussion.
42:20+ S '66
PHILOSOPHY, Latin American
Current trends in Brazilian philosophy. L.
W. Vita. Américas 18:32-6 Ag '66
French thought in Latin America. J. L.
Martí. il Américas 18:8-15 S '66
PHILOSOPHY and religion
Secular city and God. J. V. Schall. Cath
World 204:20-6 O '66
Ultimate meaning. R. O. Johann. America
114:260 F 19 '66
What can the church demand? Q. L. Quade
and J. M. Rhodes. Cath World 204:162-9
D '66
PHILPOTT, Gladys Oakes
Three-R war in Vietnam. R. S. Knowles.
Read Digest 90:172-4 Ja '67
PHINIZY, Coles
Lost pets that stray to the labs. Read Digest
88:131-4 Ap '66
PHINNEY, Bernard O. See Spector, C. jt.
auth.
PHIPPS, Allan R.
Browns of New Zealand. Outdoor Life 138:
58-61+ N '66
PHIPPS, David, and Wright, J. P.
Indy '66: can the Offy make a comeback
with supercharging? Pop Sci 188:65-8+ My
'66
PHLEGER, Fred B. and Bradshaw, J. S.
Sedimentary environments in a marine
marsh. bibliog Sciece 154:1551-3 D 23 '66
PHLOX
Phlox stand-by of summer. M. A. Roche.
il Pop Gard 17:12-13+ Ag '66
PHOBIAS
What psychiatry can do about phobias. F.
R. Schreiber and M. Herman. il Sci Digest
60:10-13 O '66
When a child's afraid of school. J. Wiener.
il Parents Mag 41:72-3+ S '66

PHOENICIA
See also
Byblos
PHOENIX, Ariz.
Departmental newsletters, they aren't worth
  it! R. Coop. Am City 81:157-8 Ag '66

Public buildings
Let all the audience see what's showing;
  council chamber. R. H. Sullivan. il Am
  City 81:90-1 N '66

Streets
How to get those impossible streets paved.
  R. N. Taylor. il Am City 81:120-1 My '66
PHOENIX art museum
Phoenix art museum. R. D. A. Puckle. il
  Antiques 90:673-80 N '66
PHOLIDOSTROPHID brachiopods. See Brach-
  iopods, Fossil
PHONE-a-larm. See Burglar alarms
PHONIC method. See Reading—Study and
  teaching
PHONO amplifiers. See Amplifiers
PHONOCARDIOSCAN. See Medical instruments
  and apparatus
PHONOGRAPH
Compact phonograph systems. Consumer Rep
  31:229-32 D '66
Look at new tape recorders and record play-
  ers. R. H. Burgert. Sr Schol 89:sup8 N 11
  '66
Music here and now. H. Fantel. Opera N
  31:33 S 10 '66
Sound ideas. L. Zide. See issues of American
  record guide
  See also
Automobiles—Phonograph equipment

High fidelity sound systems
New sound for '67: the fi is hi-er than ever.
  R. M. Benrey. il Pop Sci 189:148-52+ O '66

History
Edison's sound predictions. T. Schwartz.
  Pop Phot 59:34 Jl '66
1900 account of the phonograph; excerpt
  from Progress of invention in the nineteenth century. E. W. Byrn. il Hobbies 71:
  38-9 Ag; 37-8+ S; 37-8 O '66

Pickup
Trackability. H. Fantel. Opera N 31:37 D 24
  '66
  See also
Phonograph—Stereophonic pickup

Record changers
This changer pampers your records. il Pop
  Sci 189:117 S '66
Twelve record-changer troubles you can cure.
  W. G. Salm. il Pop Mech 126:170-3 Ag '66

Repairing
Twelve record-changer troubles you can cure.
  W. G. Salm. il Pop Mech 126:170-3 Ag '66

Stereophonic equipment
Compact phonograph systems. il Consumer
  Rep 31:384-7 Ag '66
Inexpensive integrated solid-state stereo
  record player. J. E. Rohen. il Pop Electr
  25:51-2 Jl '66
New equipment: turntables, arms, and cart-
  ridges. Hi Fi 16:95-6 O '66
Rustle of spring. H. Fantel. Opera N 30:32
  Mr 19 '66
Stereo phonographs. il Consumer Bul 50:6-10
  Ja '67

Stereophonic pickup
Best buy ceramic pickup. Consumer Rep 31:
  368 Ag '66
Build hi-fi amplifier for solid-state phono
  cartridge. A. Trauffer. il Pop Electr 25:65-7
  O '66
In a merry stereomobile. il Time 88:58+ Ag 5
  '66
New sights on stereo arms. I. M. Fried. il
  Hi Fi 16:60-4 D '66
Stero cartridges in '66. E. F. McIntyre. il
  Hi Fi 16:45-9+ F '66

Testing
Testing; test record for better listening. H.
  Frantel. Opera N 30:32 F 5 '66

Tone arm
New sights on stereo arms. I. M. Fried. il
  Hi Fi 16:60-4 D '66
War on skating. H. Fantel. il Pop Electr 25:
  66-8+ S '66

Turntables
Heavy-duty phonograph turntables. W. R.
  Moran. Hobbies 70:35 F '66
PHONOGRAPH, Automobile. See Automobiles
  —Phonograph equipment
PHONOGRAPH, Portable
First integrated-circuit phonograph. A. F.
  Petrie. il Electr World 76:28-9+ D '66
New portables. il House & Gard 129:28+ Je
  '66
PHONOGRAPH amplifiers. See Amplifiers
PHONOGRAPH in education
How I use records to teach; school in Wagga
  Wagga, Australia. D. G. Dufty. Sr Schol
  88:sup5 Ap 1 '66
Records & tapes issues; symposium. il Sr
  Schol 89:sup8+ N 11 '66
  See also
Phonograph records—Language teaching
  records
PHONOGRAPH record covers
School for annotators; or The case of the
  multiple liner notes. L. Haber. il Hi Fi 16:
  59-60+ Mr '66
PHONOGRAPH record industry
Low-price revolution; three new labels. R.
  Gelatt. Reporter 35:52-3 O 6 '66
Melvin and the little people. G. Lees. Hi Fi
  16:120 D '66
Originality and success; Nonesuch and
  Elektra records. H. Kupferberg. il Atlan
  217:150+ Mr '66
  See also
Audio fidelity records, incorporated
Blue note records, incorporated
Motown record corporation

Great Britain
Other side; Decca and CBS releases. T.
  Heinitz. Sat R 49:52 F 12 '66
Other side; effects of bargain-disc prices.
  T. Heinitz. Sat R 49:58 F 26 '66

Italy
Russians (and Italians) are coming. Hi Fi
  16:166 N '66

Poland
Notes from our correspondents. E. Helm. Hi
  Fi 16:20+ Ap '66

Russia
Russians (and Italians) are coming. Hi Fi
  16:166 N '66

Spain
Notes from our correspondents. R. Angus.
  Hi Fi 16:18+ Ap '66
PHONOGRAPH record libraries
New long-playing libraries. D. Dachs. Sat R
  49:49-51+ Ja 29 '66
PHONOGRAPH records
About Seraphim, angels of the highest order.
  J Lyons. il Am Rec G 33:14-16 S '66
And for the collector's own archive: souvenirs
  of the cylinder era: opera, song, drama.
  P. L. Miller. il Am Rec G 32:678-9 Ap '66
Berg, Bernstein, Britten, Bach, and the
  Beatles. H. Kupferberg. Atlan 217:125-6
  F '66
Brave new generation; season's releases. R.
  Gelatt. il Reporter 34:50-1 Ja 27 '66
Building your own record library; with
  discography, ed. by R. Hemming. il Sr
  Schol 88:21-4 My 6 '66
Catch up with; LP's, all sorts. L. Lerman.
  Mlle 63:112 O '66
Concert records (cont) D. Watt. New Yorker
  42:235-7 N 5; 232+ N 19 '66
Crossroads, Seraphim, World series; three
  brand-new economy labels. R. Freed. Sat
  R 49:83-4 S 24 '66
DISCussions. R. Hemming. See issues of
  Senior scholastic
Ev and Bob; Wild thing. Newsweek 69:69
  Ja 9 '67
Favorite pioneer recording artist. J. Walsh.
  See issues of Hobbies
From CRI and Desto: on six releases, eleven
  Americans. A. Cohn. Am Rec G 32:684-7
  Ap '66
From the editor: 1966 a good year for record
  collectors. J. Lyons. Am Rec G 33:299 D
  '66
Historical records. A. Favia-Artsay. See issues
  of Hobbies
Lighter side. J. S. Wilson. See issues of
  High fidelity incorporating Musical America
Lively arts. R. Hemming. Sr Schol 89:29 D
  9 '66

PHONOGRAPH records—*Continued*
Living heritage of Bruno Walter. J. Lyons.
il Am Rec G 32:1107 Ag '66
Mid-month recordings. See issues of Saturday
review
Midsummer miscellany. R. Gelatt. Reporter
35:38-40 Ag 11 '66
Music in the round. Discus. See issues of
Harper's magazine
Music of our time. H. Kupferberg. il Atlan
217:118-20 My '66
Music today via Angel, a superlative HMV
project; Boulez, Messiaen, and Koechlin.
A. Cohn. Am Rec G 32:780-1 My '66
New record releases from Folkways/Scholas-
tic; discography. Sr Schol 88:sup6 Ap 1 '66
New records in review. B. H. Haggin. See
issues of Yale review
New releases, what's ahead for classical
records; company-by-company preview. Hi
Fi 16:63-7 S '66
On the record; Music (cont of) Recorded
music. P. L. Miller. See issues of Library
journal
Other reviews; including stereo. See issues of
American record guide
Other side. T. V. Heinitz. See occasional
issues of Saturday review
Parable by Britten: Curlew River. J. Diether.
il Am Rec G 32:1034-6 Jl '66
Phonograph records. W. F. Grueninger. See
issues of Consumer bulletin
Popular records (cont) D. Watt. New Yorker
42:200-2+ Mr 19; 197-9 D 17 '66
Prospects in audio L. Marcus. il Hi Fi 16:
64-7+ Ap '66
Record notes. R. Gelatt. Reporter 34:49-50 F
24 '66
Record reviews. See issues of Consumer re-
ports
Record reviews. H. Kupferberg. See issues
of Atlantic
Recordings. M. Mayer. See issues of Esquire
Recordings in review. I. Kolodin. See issues
of Saturday review
Recordings reports: miscellaneous LPs. I.
Kolodin. See issues of Saturday review
Records. B. H. Haggin. See issues of New
republic
Records (cont) B. Boretz. Nation 202:533-4,
564-6; 203:364+, 428-9, 557-8, My 2-9, O 10,
24, N 21 '66
Records in review. See issues of High fidelity
incorporating Musical America
Records: 1966. B. Boretz. Nation 203:681-3
D 19 '66
Sounds in season! Seventeen 25:1256+ D '66
Spotlight! popular; classical. E. Miller. See
issues of Seventeen
Time listings. See issues of Time
Toscanini recordings: recommended by B. H.
Haggin. Atlan 218:76 D '66
Year's best recordings: comp. by R. Freed.
Sat R 49:76-9+ N 26 '66
You Wild thing, you; humanizing Bobby
Kennedy. Time 89:42 Ja 13 '67
See also
Libraries—Phonograph and phonograph rec-
ords

American music
Mostly from Missouri; current releases. O.
Daniel. Sat R 49:51 F 26 '66
Star spangled keyboard; current recordings
of American music. O. Daniel. Sat R 49:74+
D 10 '66

Arias
Bellini and Donizetti by Montserrat Caballé.
P. L. Miller. Am Rec G 32:512 F '66
Four IRCC programs of gilt and glister from
opera's Golden age. P. L. Miller. il Am
Rec G 32:1040-3 Jl '66
Gigli across thirty years. P. L. Miller. Am
Rec G 32:688-9 Ap '66
In retrospect, Richard Crooks. J. Maclain.
Am Rec G 32:819+ My '66
In Telefunken's historical series mementoes
of the Berlin opera in its golden age.
C. J. Luten. Am Rec G 32:592-4 Mr '66
On records:
  Apollo Granforte. Opera N 30:34 Mr
    26 '66
  Arias. Opera N 30:34 F 19 '66
  Bruno Prevedi. Opera N 30:34 F 5 '66
  Dusolina Giannini. M. De Schauensee.
    Opera N 30:34 Mr 5 '66
  Four tenors: Jan Peerce, Mario del
    Monaco, James McCracken, Richard
    Tucker. Opera N 30:38 Ap 2 '66
  Frances Alda. Opera N 30:34 Mr 26 '66
  Frieda Hempel. Opera N 30:34 Mr 19 '66
  George London sings Wagner. Opera N
    30:38 Ap 2 '66

Gerhard Husch. Opera N 30:34 Mr 19 '66
Grace Bumbry. Opera N 30:34 Mr 12 '66
Karl Erb. Opera N 30:34 Mr 19 '66
Leontyne Price sings Strauss. Opera N
  30:38 Ap 2 '66
Lotte Lehmann. Opera N 30:34 Mr 19 '66
McCracken and Warfield. Opera N 30:34
  Mr 5 '66
Maria Callas. Opera N 30:34 F 12 '66
Maria Ivogun; Elizabeth Schumann. Opera
  N 30:34 Ap 16 '66
Marilyn Horne. Opera N 30:34 Ja 29; 30 Je
  4 '66
Mirella Freni. Opera N 30:34 Mr 12 '66
Montserrat Caballé. Opera N 30:34 F 19
  '66
Richard Crooks. Opera N 30:34 Mr 26 '66
Richard Tauber. Opera N 30:34 Mr 19 '66
Souvenirs of opera and song. Opera N
  30:30 My 7 '66
Opening nights at the Met. P. L. Miller. Am
Rec G 33:122-3 O '66
Records:
  American singers. Opera N 31:34 D 24 '66
  Armand Tokatyan. Opera N 31:34 D 24 '66
  Göta Ljungberg; Gina Cigna. Opera N
    31:34 Ja 14 '67
  Montserrat Caballé. Opera N 31:32 O 15 '66
  Opening nights at the Met. Opera N 31:
    66 S 17 '66
  Richard Tucker, arias from Carmen,
    Manon. Opera N 31:66 S 17 '66
  Rita Streich; Titta Ruffo; Emilio de
    Gogorza. Opera N 31:34 Ja 21 '67
Sounds of the old Met, and a piece of its
curtain; opening nights at the Met. Hi Fi
16:134 O '66
Souvenir of a golden era; Marilyn Horne.
G. L. Mayer. Am Rec G 32:690-1 Ap '66
Souvenirs of French opera. Opera N 31:34
D 10 '66
Two voices from the past: Thill and Teyte.
P. L. Miller. il Am Rec G 32:422-4 Ja '66

Ballet music
Le diable à quatre. G. L. Mayer. il Am
Rec G 32:591 Mr '66
Fairy's kiss: Baiser de la fée. C. J. Luten.
Am Rec G 32:804-5 My '66
For younger balletomanes, another order of
enchantment; Walt Disney presents great
ballets and their stories. Am Rec G 32:805
My '66

Band music
Sweet and swing. F. Reynolds. See issues
of American record guide

Baroque music
Baroque on the Time-Life plan; literature
and recordings. P. H. Lang. Sat R 49:62-3
Ap 30 '66; Reply with rejoinder. W. J.
Gold. 49:62-3 Jl 30 '66
Decca's special joy; Baroque Christmas.
J. W. Barker. Am Rec G 33:309 D '66
Early German opera from the Goosemarket,
and other music of the baroque. J. W.
Barker. il Am Rec G 32:606-11 Mr '66
Handel makes the scene. R. Gelatt. Reporter
35:41 D 1 '66
New in Telefunken's Das alte werk series:
the whole sweep of the baroque era. J. W.
Barker. il Am Rec G 32:418-20 Ja '66

Blues music
See Phonograph records—Negro music

Cantatas
Concert records; Hodie (This day) by
Vaughan Williams. D. Watt. New Yorker
42:235-7 N 5 '66
For the holidays: V. W.'s Hodie. J. Diether.
Am Rec G 33:300-2 D '66
On Decca, Noah Greenberg's last recording.
J. W. Barker. Am Rec G 32:795 My '66

Care
How to make your records last longer. Bet
Hom & Gard 44:45 My '66
Phonograph records. il Consumer Bul 49:23 D
'66

Catalogs
March, 1901, catalog of Edison concert
cylinders. J. Walsh. il Hobbies 71:37-8+
N; 37-8+ D '66; 37-8+ Ja '67
Yours for the asking; new records catalogs.
J. Muri. il Sr Schol 89:sup 13 N 11 '66

Cello music
See Phonograph records—Violoncello
music

Chamber music
Pride of the BSO, its first-desk players take
a chamber bow. S. Fleming. il Hi Fi 16:
81-2 D '66

PHONOGRAPH records—*Continued*

Childrens records

Back to school, and all like that. C. A. Luten. Am Rec G 33:26-7 S '66
Christmas records for the young. 1966. A. Franklin. Sat R 49:78-80 D 3 '66
On and off the avenue. New Yorker 42:222+ D 10 '66
Records for young people; ed. by J. L. Limbacher (cont) Library J 91:1596-8, 5139-41 Mr 15, O 15 '66
Talking books tell stories by record on finger-powered phonograph. il Pop Sci 188: 117 Ap '66

Chinese music

Lyrichord's superb Chinese series. W. L. Purcell. il Am Rec G 32:432 Ja '66

Choral music

In the service of Heinrich Schütz, choral masterworks revealed. B. Jacobson. il Hi Fi 16:73+ Mr '66
On Everest, Gustav Holst; some rare and beautiful music: Choral fantasia. J. Diether. Am Rec G 32:952-3 Je '66
On records; Stabat Mater. Opera N 30:34 Mr 5 '66

Christmas music

Music of yuletides long, long past. J. W. Barker. Am Rec G 33:312-13 D '66
Nowell from Vaughan Williams and Joan Baez. I. Kolodin. Sat R 49:60-1 D 17 '66

Church music

Records:
  Souvenirs of French opera. Opera N 31:34 D 10 '66
  See also
Phonograph records—Motets

Collectors and collecting

Da capo; S. Rachmaninoff discography. S. Smolian. il Am Rec G 33:154-5 O '66
Lively arts; classics at bargain prices. R. Hemming. Sr Schol 89:24-5 O 21 '66
Record, record, who's got the record? P. T. Jackson. il Am Rec G 32:676-8 Ap '66

Concertos

Also, Bellini not for singing. D. Heckman. Am Rec G 32:513-14 F '66
Beethoven by Arrau; searching, satisfying. R. Kammerer. Am Rec G 32:1061 Jl '66
Compelling craftsmanship; Starer's Concerto for viola, strings and percussion and Sonata for piano. A. Cohn. Am Rec G 33: 350+ D '66
Elgar's violin concerto, as played by Menuhin today and by Menuhin yesterday. B. Jacobson. il Hi Fi 16:86-7 S '66
First recording of the sixteen Bach-Vivaldi concerti. S. Sell. il Am Rec G 32:1037 Jl '66
Great Mozart concerto marathon; on Epic, all the way with Lili Kraus. S. Sell. il Am Rec G 32:598-9 Mr '66
Louisville, from strength to strength. Am Rec G 32:798-803 My '66
Masterpieces galore; Mozart concertos played by L. Kraus, G. Anda and R. Serkin. R. Gelatt. Reporter 34:40+ My 5 '66
Puccini concerto; two recordings. R. Freed. Sat R 49:85 N 26 '66
Repeat performance at fifty; Y. Menuhin records Elgar violin concerto. E. Greenfield. il Hi Fi 16:24+ Ap '66

Dance music

Records for teachers. E. LeMone. See issues of Dance magazine
Sweet and swinging. F. Reynolds. See issues of American record guide
  See also
Phonograph records—Ballet music

Double bass music

Bass revelations; Contrabass recital. J. Diether. Am Rec G 32:1150 Ag '66

Educational applications

See Phonograph in education

Electronic music

How to get a joint raided, and other electronic music. A. Cohn. il Am Rec G 32: 1114-15+ Ag '66

English music

Delightful release: the cries of London. J. W. Barker. il Am Rec G 32:999 Je '66

Handel makes the scene: R. Gelatt. Reporter 35:40-1 D 1 '66
New sound in British music. E. Salzman. il Hi Fi 16:71-2 Mr '66

Fados

Fado; with discography. J. M. Reed. Am Rec G 32:1044-7 Jl '66

Folk music

Country music snaps its regional bounds; Nashville's Grand old opry, for nationwide taste. il Bsns W p96-8+ Mr 19 '66
Folk music. Hi Fi 16:136+ D '66
Folk music. H. Yurchenco. See issues of American record guide
Folk music (cont) O. B. Brummell. Hi Fi 16: 38+ Mr; 50+ My; 26+ Jl; 52 S; 42 N '66
Recommended recordings, Christmas 1966, mainly mainstream; comp. by S. Dance; M. Williams; L. Cohn. Sat R 49:61 D 17 '66
Recordings reports: folk and blues LPs (cont) L. Cohn. Sat R 49:80 N 26 '66
Singing their way West. R. L. Tobin. Sat R 49:48 F 12 '66

French music

Music of the birds and beasts; recordings of works by C. Koechlin, O. Messiaen, and P. Boulez. O. Daniel. Sat R 49:68-9 Mr 26 '66

German opera

On records; Early German opera from the Goose market. Opera N 30:30 My 7 '66

Harpsichord music

Musical panorama of the Elizabethan age; Fitzwilliam virginal book. E. Salzman. il Hi Fi 16:85-6 My '66
On Epic, another outstanding recital by Igor Kipnis; Italian baroque music for harpsichord. J. W. Barker. Am Rec G 32:683 Ap '66
  See also
Phonograph records—Concertos

Hebrew music

Art of the cantor. B. Rabb. Am Rec G 33: 310-11 D '66

Hindu music

Music of India, the music of Japan. W. L. Purcell. il Am Rec G 32:430-2 Ja '66
Via Odeon, a windfall, nineteen LPs from India. W. L. Purcell. Am Rec G 32:433+ Ja '66

History

Early Zon-o-phone record catalogs (cont) J. Walsh. il Hobbies 71:36+ Mr; 38-9 Ap '66
March, 1901, catalog of Edison concert cylinders. J. Walsh. il Hobbies 71:37-8+ N; 37-8+ D '66; 37-8+ Ja '67

Instrumental music

Another from the New York pro musica. J. W. Barker. Am Rec G 32:421 Ja '66
Decca's Nieuw Amsterdam trio. A. Cohn. Am Rec G 33:142 O '66
On Decca: an appealing collection of pages from the Little clavier book for Anna Magdalena Bach. J. W. Barker. il Am Rec G 32:1112-13 Ag '66

Irish music

Men that God made mad; Irish uprising celebrated on record. R. L. Tobin. il Sat R 49:61 O 15 '66

Japanese music

Music of India, the music of Japan. W. L. Purcell. il Am Rec G 32:430-2 Ja '66

Jazz music

Art Farmer, a natural evolution. B. Korall. il Sat R 49:68-9 Ap 16 '66
Catching up with a colleague; recent recordings. M. Williams. Sat R 49:55 Je 25 '66
Coltrane up to date. M. Williams. Sat R 49:67 Ap 30 '66
Dancing world of Coon-Sanders. H. Shultz. il Sat R 49:57+ My 14 '66
Forty years of Hawk's mighty honk; Coleman Hawkins' sax. C. Harman. Life 61:8 Jl 22 '66
Illya woodwind blows good; McCallum and the woodwinds. K. Gouldthorpe. Life 60: 12 Ap 29 '66
Jazz. J. S. Wilson. See issues of High fidelity incorporating Musical America
Jazz notes. E. Larrabee. See issues of Harper's magazine
Jazz records. W. Balliett. New Yorker 41: 108+ Ja 15 '66

PHONOGRAPH records—Jazz music—*Cont.*
Month's jazz. D. Heckman. See issues of
American record guide
More of the Ellington era. M. Williams.
Sat R 49:53 Jl 30 '66
Mostly about pianists. M. Williams. Sat R
49:130 Mr 12 '66
Mostly modernists. M. Williams. Sat R 49:
53 D 31 '66
Old blues dressed up fit to kill. C. Harman.
Life 60:10 Mr 11 '66
Ornette Coleman in Stockholm. M. Williams.
Sat R 49:83+ Je 11 '66
Problematic Mr Shepp. M. Williams. Sat R
49:90 N 12 '66
Recommended recordings, Christmas 1966,
mainly mainstream; comp. by S. Dance;
M. Williams; L. Cohn. Sat R 49:61 D 17 '66
Recordings reports: jazz LPs. S. Dance. See
issues of Saturday review

Korean music
Korea, vocal and instrumental music. W. L.
Purcell. il Am Rec G 32:429 Ja '66

Language teaching records
American language and culture: a selected
discography. K. W. Axthelm. il Library J
91:206-10 Ja 15 '66

Madrigals
Delightful release: The cries of London. J. W.
Barker. il Am Rec G 32:999 Je '66

Mass
Awesome, superlative: Klemperer's Missa
solemnis. G. L. Mayer. il Am Rec G 33:
8-9 S '66
Homage to Saint Cecilia: St Cecilia mass.
P. L. Miller. il Am Rec G 32:853 My '66
On records: St Cecilia mass. Opera N 30:
34 F 12 '66
Records: Missa solemnis. Opera N 31:32 O
15 '66

Medieval music
From Telefunken, Vox. Turnabout. Music
guild, Vanguard-Bach guild, Nonesuch,
Dover, and Westminster, music of the
renaissance and beforee. J. W. Barker. il
Am Rec G 32:518-23 F '66

Mexican music
Taping history in Mexico. H. Yurchenco. il
Am Rec G 33:4-7+ S '66

Motets
Heinrich Schütz; Cantiones sacrae. J. W.
Barker. il Am Rec G 33:216-20+ N '66

Moving picture music
Recordings reports: stage and screen. R.
Sherman. Sat R 49:70 Ap 30 '66
Shakespeare wallah: original soundtrack. J.
Lyons. Am Rec G 32:1108 Ag '66

Musical comedies, revues, etc.
From Lincoln Center, a joyous Annie and a
soggy Show boat. M. Kreuger. il Am Rec G
33:186-8 O '66
Recordings reports: stage and screen. R.
Sherman. Sat R 49:70 Ap 30 '66

Musical parody
Musical satire from Vanguard and Elektra:
P.D.Q. Bach, The baroque Beatles book.
J. Diether. il Am Rec G 32:508-10 F '66

Negro music
Big, happy, beating heart of the Detroit sound;
Motown's records. R. R. Lingeman. il N Y
Times Mag p48-9+ N 27 '66
Blues turned blue-eyed; Righteous brothers.
C. Welles. Life 61:18 Jl 1 '66
Recordings reports: folk and blues LPs (cont)
L. Cohn. Sat R 49:80 N 26 '66

Nocturnes (music)
For Chopin, the voices of poets: pianists. I.
Moravec and T. Vásáry. H. Goldsmith. il
Hi Fi 16:85 S '66

Oboe music
Four fine virtuosos of the honorable oboe.
B. Jacobson. il Hi Fi 16:87-8 My '66
Great Gomberg. V. N. Jackson. Am Rec G
32:771 My '66

Operas
And still they come, forty-five years after
his death: Caruso, new and otherwise. P.
L. Miller. Am Rec G 32:956-7 Je '66

Berlioz or Crespin? Les Troyens. R. Law-
rence. Sat R 49:52+ Ja 29 '66
Bernstein's first opera recording: Verdi's Fal-
staff, with Fischer-Dieskau. W. Weaver.
il Hi Fi 16:14+ Je '66
Bluebeard's castle; London edition. C. J.
Luten. il Am Rec G 33:100-1 O '66
Britten's Midsummer's night makes its stereo
debut. E. Greenfield. Hi Fi 16:16+ D '66
Caballé as Lucrezia Borgia. H. Weinstock.
Sat R 49:54 D 31 '66
Caruso on records, by A. Favia-Artsay. Re-
view
Am Rec G 32:1000-2 Je '66. P. L. Miller
Cav & Pag, Karajan/La Scala style. C. L.
Osborne. il Hi Fi 16:124-5 O '66
Cav 'n' Pag from La Scala; with editorial
comment. P. L. Miller. Am Rec G 33:336-7
D '66
Child of the baroque; J. P. Rameau available
as opera composer. R. Lawrence. il Sat R
49:53 Je 25 '66
Christmas opera by Rimsky-Korsakov;
Christmas eve. P. L. Miller. Am Rec G
33:314 D '66
Columbia's Falstaff. P. L. Miller. Am Rec G
33:202-3 N '66
Columbia's Falstaff: it goes at once to the
windswept summit. C. L. Osborne. il Hi Fi
16:79-80 D '66
Completion of London's Ring; a Walküre to
fulfill all promise. C. L. Osborne. Hi Fi 16:
93-4+ N '66
Concert records; Verdi's Luisa Miller. D.
Watt. New Yorker 42:232+ N 19 '66
Concert records; Wagner's Lohengrin, and
The art of Maria Callas. D. Watt. New
Yorker 42:235-7 N 5 '66
Contemporary opera and the foundations: a
plea to support recording of operas. Hi Fi
16:39 Je '66
Donizetti: Lucia di Lammermoor. Opera N
31:34 S 10 '66
Donizetti's Campanello. R. Jacobson. Sat R
49:65 O 29 '66
Donizetti's Lucrezia Borgia; RCA Victor.
P. L. Miller. Am Rec G 33:292-3 D '66
Early German opera from the Goosemarket,
and other music of the baroque. J. W.
Barker. il Am Rec G 32:606-11 Mr '66
Die entführung aus dem serail; satisfactory
recording. G. L. Mayer. il Am Rec G 33:
104-6 O '66
Falstaff from Vienna. I. Kolodin. il Sat R
49:49 D 31 '66
First complete recording of a Wagner opera
ever made in the U.S.A; Lohengrin. P. L.
Miller. il Am Rec G 32:1104-6 Ag '66
Five operas. H. Kupferberg. il Atlan 217:
136-8 Ap '66
Fritzi Scheff and others on IRCC. A. Favia-
Artsay. il Hobbies 71:35+ Mr '66
From L'Oiseau-Lyre, the first recording of
Rameau's Hippolyte et Aricie. J. W.
Barker. il Am Rec G 32:946-8 Je '66
G&S: after the carpets; Washington's Lyric
theater company's recordings. J. Ardoin.
Sat R 49:69+ Ap 16 '66
Gilbert and Sullivan: two views; new re-
cording issued by English Decca and RCA
Victor. J. Ardoin. Sat R 49:127+ Mr 12 '66
High notes; Rossini's Semiramide and
Donizetti's Lucrezia Borgia. R. Gelatt. Re-
porter 35:38 D 29 '66
Katerina Ismailova; Shostakovich's opera,
Lady Macbeth of the Mtsensk district. G.
L. Mayer. il Am Rec G 32:1116-19 Ag '66
Let there be light (operas) R. Lawrence.
Sat R 49:55 Jl 30 '66
Lohengrin in its entirety, with the full forces
of Boston. C. L. Osborne. il Hi Fi 16:83-4 S
'66
London's Don Carlo. P. L. Miller. il Am Rec
G 32:680-2 Ap '66
Los Angeles in Carthage; Purcell's Dido and
Aeneas. R. Jacobson. Sat R 49:63 D 17 '66
Lucia and the LP; new version, featuring
Anna Moffo and Carlo Bergonzi. J. Ardoin.
Sat R 49:57 My 28 '66
Mediterranean Götterdämmerung; Les Troyens
discs. R. Gelatt. Reporter 34:50+ Mr 24 '66
Middling Verdi; Don Carlo, Covent Garden
production on London record. R. Gelatt.
Reporter 34:39-40 Je 16 '66
Mozart and opera seria. H. Weinstock. Sat R
49:67-8 Mr 26 '66
Mozart with (and for) a song; Turnabout
bargains. I. Kolodin. Sat R 49:72 D 10 '66
Nabucco; first stereo edition. P. L. Miller. il
Am Rec G 33:110-11 O '66
New tenants for Bluebeard's castle. R. Ja-
cobson. Sat R 49:82 S 24 '66

PHONOGRAPH records—Operas—*Continued*
One slick modern; one masterpiece. Discus.
  il Harper 233:101-2 Ag '66
Opera notes; Lohengrin, Nabucco, and Cav.
  & Pag. R. Gelatt. Reporter 35:50-2 S 8 '66
Operas from EMI, Elisir and Butterfly.
  W. Weaver. Hi Fi 16:20+ N '66
Other side; Glyndebourne and Covent Garden
  productions. T. Heinitz. Sat R 49:47 Jl 16
  '66
Powerfully persuasive Don Carlo. I. Kolodin.
  Sat R 49:65 Ap 30 '66
Prince Igor premiered in stereo. R. McMullen.
  il Hi Fi 16:26+ S '66
Prokofiev's operas on records. Hi Fi 16:49+
  Je '66
RCA Victor's Orfeo ed Euridice. P. L. Miller.
  il Am Rec G 32:792-4 My '66
Rameau as master of lyric tragedy; Hippolyte
  et Aricie. C. L. Osborne. il Hi Fi 16:65-6
  Jl '66
Ring completed; London records new set. R.
  Lawrence Sat R 49:70-1+ O 29 '66
Rossini's Moses. H. Weinstock. Sat R 49:62
  Ja 29 '66
Sadler's Wells Hansel and Gretel; does Angel
  have the dark horse of the season's operatic
  recordings? J. Maclain. Am Rec G 32:546
  F '66
Summer's crop of star-strewn operas; RCA's
  recording in Rome. W. Weaver. il Hi Fi
  16:11-12+ O '66
Tristan and Isolde; Deutsche grammophon
  issue. C. J. Luten. il Am Rec G 33:284-8 D
  '66
Tristan und Isolde direct from the Festspiel-
  haus; Bayreuth. P. G. Davis. il Hi Fi 16:
  16+ N '66
Two triumphs: London records. Wagner's
  Ring of the Nibelungen. Discus. Harper
  234:104 Ja '67
Verdi: Don Carlo. Opera N 31:34 S 10 '66
Verdi's Don Carlo. C. L. Osborne. Hi Fi 16:
  83-5 Ap '66
Verdi's Nabucco revealed. H. Weinstock. il
  Sat R 49:50 Ag 27 '66
Verrett-Fasano Orfeo. R. Lawrence. Sat R
  49:69 Ap 30 '66
Via Philips, the first recording of Rossini's
  Mosè. P. L. Miller. il Am Rec G 32:504-6 F
  '66
La vida breve; Victoria de los Angeles.
  P. L. Miller. Am Rec G 33:206-7 N '66
La vida de los Angeles; new recording of
  Manuel de Falla's La vida breve. R. Law-
  rence. Sat R 49:80-1 S 24 '66
Wagner operas on records; a discography.
  C. L. Osborne. Hi Fi 16:78-82+ N; 26+
  D '66
Die Walküre; London's outstanding record-
  ing. H. Glass. il Am Rec G 33:196-9 N '66
  See also
Tape recordings—Operas

Oratorios
Authentic Messiah. B. Jacobson. Hi Fi 16:
  56-9 D '66
Bach passions and oratorios; discography. N.
  Broder. il Hi Fi 16:46-7+ Jl '66
Belated birthday greetings to Sir Malcolm;
  Mendelssohn's Elijah. M. Maxwell. Am Rec
  G 33:43+ S '66
Dream of Gerontius. M. Maxwell. Am Rec G
  32:796-7+ My '66
For the holidays: Robert Shaw's Messiah. J.
  Diether. il Am Rec G 33:302-4+ D '66
From DGG, Bach not so P.D.Q. but extra-
  ordinary. H. Glass. Am Rec G 32:511 F '66
From Philips, an exciting new Messiah. Am
  Rec G 33:92-3+ O '66
Handel makes the scene; new Messiah re-
  cordings. R. Gelatt. Reporter 35:40-1 D 1
  '66
On records:
  Belshazzar; Judas Maccabaeus. Opera N
  30:34 F 19 '66
Records:
  Christ on the Mount of Olives. Opera N
  31:34 D 24 '66
  Christmas oratorio. Opera N 31:34 D 17
  '66
Stokowski's Messiah. R. Jones. Am Rec G
  33:308 D '66
Two centuries of Messiah; Colin Davis and
  Robert Shaw interpretations. H. Weinstock.
  Sat R 49:73 D 10 '66
Two triumphs: Mercury recording of Han-
  del's Messiah. Discus. Harper 234:104-5 Ja
  '67

Orchestral music
Exaggeration of virtues and a wow, the
  Pictures in London's phase 4 stereo; Mus-
  sorgsky-Stokowski. A. Cohn. il Am Rec G
  32:604-5 Mr '66

For Crossroads' debut, a true Czech Smetana:
  Má vlast. P. Hart. il Hi Fi 16:94 N '66
For its 53rd spring, a superb 26th recording
  of Stravinsky's Rite; P. Boulez on None-
  such. W. Botsford. il Am Rec G 32:500-3
  F '66
Game of multiple choice; Boulez. Van
  Beinum, or Wenzinger; Water music. N.
  Broder. Hi Fi 16:96 N '66
Mozart with (and for) a song. I. Kolodin. Sat
  R 49:72-3 D 10 '66
Now that other American giant; Carl Ruggles.
  A. Cohn. il Am Rec G 32:588-90 Mr '66
Recordings reports: orchestral LPs. I.
  Kolodin. See issues of Saturday review
Stravinsky's Rite, in the Boulez Manner,
  frozen, immobile, violently precise. E. Salz-
  man. il Hi Fi 16:68 F '66

Passion music
Bach passions and oratorios; discography. N.
  Broder. il Hi Fi 16:46-7+ Jl '66
Bach's St John, a noble ideal nobly attempted.
  N. Broder. il Hi Fi 16:73-4 Ag '66
Finally, the race is over, three complete
  recordings of Musique de table. J. W.
  Barker. Am Rec G 32:812-15 My '66

Periodicals
  See also
American record guide (periodical)

Piano music
Absolutely hypnotic Chopin; recital by Jeanne-
  Marie Darré. S. Sell. Am Rec G 32:710
  Ap '66
At last, The years of pilgrimage on Odeon.
  R. Kammerer. Am Rec G 32:1138 Ag '66
Complete, on Vox, Chabrier's piano works:
  the very heart of his art. C. J. Luten. il
  Am Rec G 32:949+ Je '66
Connoisseur society edition of Chopin's
  Nocturnes by Ivan Moravec. S. Sell. Am
  Rec G 32:954-5 Je '66
Demus: spirit, drive, technique, and in-
  telligence; Goldberg variations. S. Sell. Am
  Rec G 32:620-1 Mr '66
Famous prodigy revisited: Philippa Schuyler.
  R. Kammerer. Am Rec G 32:726 Ap '66
Fascinatingly offbeat recital by Hilde Somer;
  Latin-American piano music. S. Sell. Am
  Rec G 33:328 D '66
Golden art of Sergei Rachmaninoff; with dis-
  cography. R. Kammerer. Am Rec G 33:156-
  65 O '66
Haydn by two grandes dames of the key-
  board; Sophie Svirsky and Nadia Reisen-
  berg. S. Sell. il Am Rec G 33:210-11 N '66
Julius Katchen finishes the complete Brahms
  piano music. S. Sell. Am Rec G 32:706-9
  Ap '66
More keyboard giants of the past. R. Kam-
  merer. il Am Rec G 32:806-9 My '66
Piano notes; new recordings. Discus. Harper
  232:128+ Ap '66
Recordings from piano rolls; valid history,
  rewarding artistry. H. Goldsmith. il Hi Fi
  16:82+ D '66
Records: operatic Liszt. Opera N 31:30 N 19
  '66
Schoenberg revealed by Gould. A. Rich. il
  Sat R 49:78 S 24 '66
Serkin. S. Sell. il Am Rec G 32:786-9 My '66
Star spangled keyboard: current recordings
  of American music. O. Daniel. Sat R 49:74+
  D 10 '66
Still incomparable: George Copeland. R. Kam-
  merer. Am Rec G 32:712 Ap '66
Three via London imports: by far the best
  piano-roll transfers. R. Kammerer. Am Rec
  G 33:296-8 D '66
  See also
Phonograph records—Concertos

Poetry
  See Phonograph records—Spoken records

Polish music
New music of Poland. O. Daniel. Sat R 49:
  51-2+ Jl 30 '66

Prices
For a song; top-class, inexpensive classical
  records. il Newsweek 68:88 N 21 '66
Gift records that sell cheap. Changing T 20:
  16 D '66
Latest in low-price records. il Changing T
  20:43-4 My '66
Lively arts; classics at bargain prices. R.
  Hemming. Sr Schol 89:24-5 O 21 '66
Low-price revolution; three new labels. R.
  Gelatt. Reporter 35:52-3 O 6 '66
Originality and success: Nonesuch and
  Elektra records. H. Kupferberg. il Atlan
  217:150+ Mr '66

PHONOGRAPH records—Prices—*Continued*
Records at half price; Crossroads, Seraphim, and World series. H. Kupferberg. il Atlan 218:128-30 D '66
Seraphim: Angel's entry in the low-price lists. P. G. Davis. Hi Fi 16:166-7 O '66

Recording

Bernstein eruption, new Rosenkavalier; London report. E. Greenfield. il Hi Fi 16:MA28-9 Jl '66
Britten's Midsummer's night makes its stereo debut. E. Greenfield. Hi Fi 16:16+ D '66
Caballé records her first complete opera. W. Weaver. il Hi Fi 16:99-102 O '66
Isaac Stern in a new role; first recordings with the soloist as conductor. E. Greenfield. il Hi Fi 16:20+ S '66
More Stravinsky by Stravinsky, and Ivesian explorations. W. Malloch. il Hi Fi 16:12+ Ag '66
Nice groove; recording of I spy for the F.B.I. New Yorker 42:27-8 F 26 '66
Ovations for Bernstein's Falstaff. W. Weaver. il Hi Fi 16:126-7 Je '66
Sonic showcase. R. D. Darrell. See issues of High fidelity incorporating Musical America
Summer's crop of star-strewn operas; RCA's recording in Rome. W. Weaver. il Hi Fi 16:11-12+ O '66
Taping history in Mexico. H. Yurchenco. il Am Rec G 33:4-7+ S '66
Vanguard's Gluck, and Handel from RCA; in Vienna. K. Blaukopf. Hi Fi 16:24+ O '66

Unauthorized recording

Piracy on the high C's; recording at concerts and operas. R. Freed. il Sat R 49:55-6+ Mr 26 '66

Reissues

Attention foundations and university presses: here is a new way of getting those deletions back. D. Hall. Am Rec G 32:944-5+ Je '66
Comic mask of Fats Waller. M. Williams. il Sat R 49:63 Mr 26 '66
Dancing world of Coon-Sanders. H. Shultz. il Sat R 49:57+ My 14 '66
Mozart with (and for) a song; Turnabout bargains. I. Kolodin. Sat R 49:72 D 10 '66
On records:
Historical reissues. Opera N 30:30 Je 4 '66
Other side: Hess tribute from HMV. T. Heinitz. Sat R 49:71 Ap 16 '66
Pseudo-stereo performances. W. F. Grueninger. Consumer Bul 49:24-5 Ag '66
Repeat performance. P. G. Davis. Hi Fi 16:106-8 My; 94-5 Je; 89-90 Jl; 99-100 Ag; 116-17 S; 166-7 O; 50+ N; 116+ D '66
Two notable reissue projects; a permanent door to the past; Columbia and RCA Victor, with discography. M. Kreuger. Am Rec G 33:272-5 N '66
World series; a budget line from Philips. H. Goldsmith. Hi Fi 16:169 O '66

Religious records

Britten's Curlew River burnished bronze solemnity. A. Frankenstein. il Hi Fi 16:69-70 Je '66
Performing arts; A. Ginsberg's Kaddish and M. Boyd's prayers. R. Kotlowitz. Harper 233:134-5 O '66
Records and risks. J. K. Waters. America 114:839-41 Je 11 '66

Requiems

On records: Requiem. Opera N 30:34 F 12; 34 Ap 16; 30 My 7; 31:30 N 19 '66

Sonatas

Compelling craftsmanship; Starer's Concerto for viola, strings and percussion and Sonata for piano. A. Cohn. Am Rec G 33:350+ D '66
Magnificent: Piatigorsky and Firskusny. A. Cohn. Am Rec G 32:1132 Ag '66
New on CRI: the diverse excellence of six Americans: Sessions, Mayer, Binkerd, Bacon, Gutché, La Montaine. A. Cohn. il Am Rec G 32:600-2 Mr '66

Songs

And still they come, forty-five years after his death: Caruso, new and otherwise. P. L. Miller. Am Rec G 32:956-7 Je '66
Anthology of American art song. P. L. Miller. Am Rec G 32:784-5 My '66
Ballads are for singing; with discography. W. W. Combs. il Sr Schol 88:sup 10-11 Ap 1 '66
Beautiful singing, lieder by Fritz Wunderlich. H. Glass. Am Rec G 33:106-7 O '66

Bob Dylan, a far cry from Aristotle. O. B. Brummell. il Hi Fi 16:125 O '66
Caruso on records, by A. Favia-Artsay. Review
Am Rec G 32:1000-2 Je '66. P. L. Miller
Gorgeous Strauss; Four last songs, by Elisabeth Schwarzkopf. H. Glass. Am Rec G 33:117 O '66
Historical bonanza on LP. A. Favia-Artsay. il Hobbies 71:36+ O '66
Lou Rawls lives. K. Gouldthorpe. Life 60:18 My 20 '66
Measure of Sinatra. B. Korall. Sat R 49:58-9 O 15 '66
Mildred; M. Bailey's three LP's. R. Gehman. il Sat R 50:104-5 Ja 14 '67
Must for all Mahler lovers: Angel's Des knaben wunderhorn. J. Diether. Am Rec G 33:212-15 N '66
Nice groove; recording of I spy for the F.B.I. New Yorker 42:27-8 F 26 '66
On Angel and Westminster, recital of songs by Francis Poulenc. P. L. Miller Am Rec G 33:346-8 D '66
On records:
Art of Tito Gobbi. Opera N 30:34 F 5 '66
Elena Gerhadt; Kirsten Flagstad. Opera N 30:34 Ap 16 '66
Julian Bream in concert. Opera N 30:34 Ja 29 '66
Music for voice and guitar. Opera N 30:34 Ja 29 '66
Schoenberg; Gurrie-lieder. Opera N 30:34 Ja 29 '66
Songs. Opera N 30:34 Mr 12 '66
Victoria de los Angeles. Opera N 30:34 Ap 9 '66
Recordings. M. Mayer. Esquire 66:30+ Ag '66
Records:
Deutsche vokslieder. Opera N 31:34 Ja 21 '67
Eighteen songs. Opera N 31:34 D 24 '66
Four last songs. Opera N 31:66 S 17 '66
Maggie Teyte and Madeleine Grey. Opera N 31:34 D 3 '66
Songs. Opera N 31:30 N 19 '66
Songs by Schubert and Schumann; Songs by Wolf and Pfitzner. Opera N 31:34 D 3 '66
Schubert by Souzay; Die schöne müllerin. A. Sperber. Am Rec G 32:425 Ja '66
Two sopranos; both Wagnerians, both Scandinavians: K. Flagstad and B. Nilsson. P. L. Miller. il Am Rec G 32:516-17 F '66
Two voices from the past: Thill and Teyte. P. L. Miller. il Am Rec G 32:422-4 Ja '66
Unlikely corners. E. Jablonski. See issues of American record guide to July 1966
Le véritable Maurice. H. Kupferberg. Atlan 219:111-13 Ja '67
Vocal contrasts on LP; electrical recordings. A. Favia-Artsay. il Hobbies 71:37+ Jl '66

Spoken records

American language and culture; a selected discography. K. W. Axthelm. il Library J 91:206-10 Ja 15 '66
Back to school, and all like that. C. A. Luten. Am Rec G 33:26-7 S '66
For children or grown-ups. S. Potter. Am Rec G 33:347 D '66
Four poets and one actor. J. Ciardi. Sat R 49:49 F 12 '66
From Folkways, Brecht by Bentley; Exception and the rule. S. Potter. Am Rec G 32:746-7 Ap '66
How to make a record collection really complete. Bet Hom & Gard 44:90 S '66
LSD; words only. S. Potter. il Am Rec G 33:24-5 S '66
Marat/Sade. S. Potter. il Am Rec G 32:790-1+ My '66
Men that God made mad; Irish uprising celebrated on record. R. L. Tobin. il Sat R 49:61 O 15 '66
Mist in the eye; best selling record, Day of decision. il Time 87:58 Je 3 '66
Much ado about nothing; three recorded productions. J. Diether. Am Rec G 32:816-18 My '66
Murrow in London, you can hear him now. R. Gelatt. il Hi Fi 16:123 O '66
Murrow remembers. R. L. Tobin. Sat R 49:87 N 26 '66
New records. Sr Schol 88:sup 18 F 11 '66
New records. J. Muri. il Sr Schol 87:sup27 Ja 14; 88:sup 12-13 Ap 1; sup24-5 Ap 29; sup 12 My 13 '66
On the record; Words (cont of) Recorded word. J. L. Limbacher. See issues of Library journal

PHONOGRAPH records—Spoken records—_Cont._
Performing arts; A. Voznesensky poems and T. Capote's excerpts from In cold blood. R. Kotlowitz. Harper 233:134 O '66
Recorded word. J. L. Limbacher. See second issue of each month of Library journal
Recordings for young people; ed. by J. L. Limbacher. il Library J 91:5139-41 O 15 '66
Records & tapes issue; symposium. il Sr Schol 89:sup8+ N 11 '66
Records for young people; ed. by J. L. Limbacher (cont) Library J 91:1596-8 Mr 15 '66
Voznesensky, and more Yevtushenko. Am Rec G 33:62 S '66
Words only. S. Potter. See issues of American record guide
See also
Talking books

Stereophonic records
Mozart by Rudolf, et al. H. Glass. Am Rec G 33:47-8 S '66
Other reviews; including stereo. See issues of American record guide
Phonograph records. W. F. Grueninger. See issues of Consumer bulletin
Record reviews. See issues of Consumer reports
Where to sit. H. Fantel. Opera N 30:33 F 19 '66
World label; compatible stereo at bargain prices! J. Lyons. il Am Rec G 33:20-2 S '66

String quartet music
Boccherini con Polo. C Farrell. Am Rec G 32:702-4 Ap '66
Brahms string quartets, and a great Schumann quintet; Serkin-Budapest and the Wellers. H. Glass. il Am Rec G 32:603 Mr '66
From the U.S.A., Austria, and Hungary, three superb string quartets. H. Glass. il Am Rec G 33:10-12 S '66
In a vox box, five French string quartets. A. Cohn. Am Rec G 32:447 Ja '66
On Epic: the Fourth quartet of David Diamond, magnificent creativity. A. Cohn. Am Rec G 32:507 F '66
Recordings. M. Mayer. Esquire 66:40+ S '66

Symphonies
After thirty-eight years, a landmark: the Thomson Symphony on a hymn tune. C. J. Luten. il Am Rec G 32:596-7 Mr '66
Again, Mahler symphonies by Leinsdorf and Bernstein; the Sixth and Seventh. D. Newlin. Am Rec G 33:114-16+ O '66
Another first from Louisville; B. Martinu's Fifth symphony. C. J. Luten. Am Rec G 33:221 N '66
By Bernstein, Mahler's Ten, minus one; with the New York philharmonic. P. G. Davis. Hi Fi 16:22 D '66
Concert records; Ives' Fourth symphony. D. Watt. New Yorker 42:235-6 N 19 '66
Erich Leinsdorf at his very best; Prokofiev's Symphony no. 6. A. Cohn. Am Rec G 32:553 F '66
Finest Sibelius Fifth, Leonard Bernstein's. J. Diether. Am Rec G 32:557 F '66
Five symphonies by Hans Werner Henze. A. Cohn. Am Rec G 33:118-20 O '66
From RCA Victor: after sixty-eight years, the first symphony of Chas. E. Ives. A. Cohn. il Am Rec G 32:1032-3 Jl '66
Gustav Mahler: the Ninth was not impassable. J. Bruck. il Am Rec G 32:412-16 Ja '66
Gustav Mahler, the unfinished Tenth quickened to vibrant life. W. Malloch. Hi Fi 16:65-6 F '66
Mahler (and Cooke's) No. 10. I. Kolodin. Sat R 49:55 Ja 29 '66
Mehta: glorious and blazing Bruckner, Symphony no. 9. J. Diether. Am Rec G 32:515 F '66
Music for, and of, our century: Hans Werner Henze's five symphonies. P. G. Davis. Hi Fi 16:74-5 Ap '66
New stereo discs for a further look at Ivesian questions and answers. E. Salzman. il Hi Fi 16:70-1 Je '66
Nielsen's Fourth symphony, it makes a splendid sound. H. Goldsmith. il Hi Fi 16:67 Jl '66
Previn's masterly Shostakovich Fifth; and an enthralling First from Prague. J. Diether. Am Rec G 32:692-3 Ap '66
Records:
Beethoven: symphony no. 9. Opera N 31:34 D 24 '66

Schmidt-Laserstedt's Ninth, the most satisfying in ten years. M. N. Kanny. il Am Rec G 33:208-9 N '66
Seven of Sibelius. E. Salzman. Sat R 49:68-9 O 29 '66
Sibelius symphonies by Akeo Watanabe; superlative. J. Diether. Am Rec G 33:112-13+ O '66
Sun treader, the work of an American radical, in its first American hearing. P. Yates. il Hi Fi 16:85-6 Ap '66
Two Nonesuch releases provide a new look at Franz Berwald. A. Cohn. Am Rec G 32:1038-9 Jl '66
Vanguard offers a stereo première of the Mahler Seventh from Salt Lake City. D. Newlin. Am Rec G 32:950-1 Je '66

Test records
Testing; test record for better listening. H. Fantel. Opera N 30:32 F 5 '66

Vietnamese music
Music of Viet Nam. W. L. Purcell. il Am Rec G 342:426-9 Ja '66

Violin music
Menuhin's Elgar: intimacy and bravura. J. Diether. Am Rec G 33:38 S '66

Violoncello music
Important new soloist in a belated Delius first; Jacqueline du Pfe. M. Maxwell. il por Am Rec G 32:539 F '66
In Bach's cello suites, playing with cerebral and passionate. B. Jacobson. Hi Fi 16:87 Ap '66
Pablo Casals: a discography; playing and conducting. Sat R 49:45-6+ D 31 '66

Zarzuelas
Not merely estimable. P. L. Miller. Am Rec G 32:1043 Jl '66
PHONOGRAPH repair. See Phonograph—Repairing
PHORMIUM
It's a bundle of sword leaves; New Zealand flax. il Sunset 137:196-7 S '66
PHOSPHATASES
Drosophila melanogaster: inheritance of a deficiency of alkaline phosphatase in larvae. F. M. Johnson. il Science 152:361-2 Ap 15 '66
Glucose-6-phosphatase in tubular endoplasmic reticulum of hepatocytes. S. I. Rosen and others. bibliog il Science 152:352-4 Ap 15 '66
Inactive alkaline phosphatase in duodenum of nursling mouse: immunological evidence. M. E. Etzler and F. Moog. bibliog il Science 154:1037-8 N 25 '66
Intestinal alkaline phosphatase: regulation by a strain-specific factor in mouse milk. P. R. V. Navudu and F. Moog. bibliog il Science 152:656-7 Ap 29 '66
Patterns of alkaline phosphatase in developing drosophila. H. Schneiderman and others. bibliog il Science 151:461-3 Ja 28 '66
PHOSPHATES
Imidonitrogen in chlorella polyphosphate. D. L. Correll. bibliog il Science 151:819-21 F 18 '66
Phosphate uptake in an obligately marine fungus: a specific requirement for sodium. P. A. Siegenthaler and others. bibliog il Science 155:93-4 Ja 6 '67
Precipitate formation in the strontium-phosphate system. R. L. Collin. bibliog il Science 151:1386-8 Mr 18 '66
See also
Carbamyl phosphate
PHOSPHATES in the body
1,2-propanediol-2-phosphate in ascaris lumbricoides. J. Kubištovà and D. Seth. bibliog Science 154:1461 D 16 '66
PHOSPHATIDES
Staphylococcal alpha-toxin: effects on artificial lipid spherules. G. Weissmann and others. bibliog il Science 154:772-4 N 11 '66
PHOSPHINE oxide
Growth-inhibiting action of tris(1-aziridinyl)-phosphine oxide in grasses. T. W. Holmsen and J. K. Leasure. bibliog il Science 153:1659 S 30 '66
PHOSPHOLIPIDS. See Lipides
PHOSPHORAMIDES
Fungicidal phthalimidophosphonothionates; novel type of organophosphoramide compound. H. Tolkmith and others, bibliog il Science 155:85-6 Ja 6 '67

PHOSPHORUS compounds
Fungicidal phthalimidophosphonothionates; novel type of organophosphoramide compound. H. Tolkmith and others. bibliog il Science 155:85-6 Ja 6 '67
PHOSPHORYLASES
Phosphorylase kinase of the liver: deficiency in a girl with increased hepatic glycogen. G. Hug and others. bibliog il Science 153:1534-5 S 23 '66
PHOSPHORYLATION
Nonphosphorylating respiration of mitochondria from brown adipose tissue of rats. R. E. Smith and others. bibliog il Science 154: 653-4 N 4 '66
Phosphorylation of nuclear protein early in the course of gene activation in lymphocytes. L. J. Kleinsmith and others. bibliog il Science 154:780-1 N 11 '66
PHOTO aerial reconnaissance. See Aerial reconnaissance
PHOTOCELLS. See Photoelectric cells
PHOTOCHEMISTRY
Air pollution: photochemical aspects; report on symposium. A. P. Altshuller. Science 151:1105-6 Mr 4 '66
Interpretation of some organic photochemistry. H. E. Zimmerman. bibliog il Science 153:837-44 Ag 19 '66
Solution photochemistry of thymine and uracil. A. A. Lamola and J. P. Mittal. bibliog il Science 154:1560-1 D 23 '66
PHOTOCHROMICS. See Microphotography
PHOTOCOMPOSING machines
Photocomposing studied at R&E council seminar. il Pub W 191:101 Ja 2 '67
PHOTOCOPYING. See Photography—Copying; Photomechanical processes
PHOTOELECTRIC cells
How and why of photocells; use in street lights. R. A. Farrall. il Am City 81:114+ N '66
Li'l Atlas defies gravity; using electromagnetic photoelectric cell. W. J. Price. il Pop Electr 24:67-70+ My '66
Lumemin steals the show. L. Garner. il Pop Electr 24:56-9+ Ja '66
PHOTOFLASH lamps. See Electric lamps, Flashlight
PHOTOGRAMMETRY
Mapmaking goes far afield; techniques of cartographers aiding surgeons, archaeologists, dentists. C. Behrens. il Sci N 91: 38-9 Ja 14 '67
PHOTOGRAMS. See Shadowgrams
PHOTOGRAPHERS
All at once, a moment can be caught forever. il Life 61:32-50 D 23 '66
Anywhere, everywhere for the story, for the news, the meaning, the drama. H. Moffett. il Life 61:120B-120C+ D 23 '66
Are you one of photography's true believers? C. Reynolds. il Pop Phot 58:47-9+ F '66
Cops and blockers; CBS and NBC camera crews; bodyguards in troubled areas. il Newsweek 68:66 O 3 '66
Flying photographer. See issues of Flying
Four photographers; celebrities. J. Morris. il U S Camera 29:60-3+ F '66
Increase stock picture price, day rates for photographers. Pub W 190:115 Ag 1 '66
Stuff of dreams and billions; fashion and commercial photography. il Newsweek 67: 74-7 F 14 '66
Whose Hall of fame? J. Deschin. Pop Phot 58:24+ Ap '66
See also
News photographers
Women as photographers
    also names of photographers, e.g. W. Evans

Public relations
Artist & agent. M. Orovan. il U S Camera 29: 54-7+ Ap '66
PHOTOGRAPHIC apparatus industry and trade
Brave new photo items excite camera market. il Bsns W p77 D 24 '66
Nikon crowds into Leica's picture; discussion. Mod Phot 30:20+ Jl '66
See also
Eastman Kodak company
PHOTOGRAPHIC chemistry
Foto facts; a formula for a divided developer. P. Farber. U S Camera 29:22+ Ag; 32-3 D '66
Testing films & prints for residual hypo. C. W. Kennedy. il Pop Phot 60:54+ Ja '67
Wolfman on printing; print flattening solutions. A. Wolfman. il Mod Phot 30:44+ Ag '66
PHOTOGRAPHIC Christmas cards. See Christmas cards

PHOTOGRAPHIC composing machines. See Photocomposing machines
PHOTOGRAPHIC copying. See Photography—Copying
PHOTOGRAPHIC equipment. See Photography—Apparatus and supplies
PHOTOGRAPHIC humor. See Humor, Pictorial
PHOTOGRAPHIC illustration. See Illustration of books and periodicals
PHOTOGRAPHIC industry. See Photographic apparatus industry and trade
PHOTOGRAPHIC laboratories
Rise of mediocrity. A. Franckevich. Pop Phot 59:26 N '66
Third member of the team. G. P. Hunt. il Life 61:8 D 23 '66
PHOTOGRAPHIC lenses. See Lenses, Photographic
PHOTOGRAPHIC measurements. See Photogrammetry
PHOTOGRAPHIC murals
Home murals from your favorite photos. E. H. Ortner. il Pop Sci 189:124-7+ S '66
PHOTOGRAPHIC notes. See Photographic records
PHOTOGRAPHIC optics
DSSP requirements hasten underwater photo-optics efforts: deep submergence systems project. W. E. Wilks. Tech W 19:39-40 O 24 '66
See also
Perspective
PHOTOGRAPHIC paper
Agfa #6 is all paper grades? il Mod Phot 30:70-3+ Mr '66
Printing paper cost too much? N. Rothschild. il Pop Phot 59:86-7+ Jl '66
Wolfman on printing; enlarging papers. A. Wolfman. il Mod Phot 30:24+ N '66
PHOTOGRAPHIC plates. See Photography—Plates
PHOTOGRAPHIC prints. See Photographs
PHOTOGRAPHIC records
Notes on taking notes. D. B. Eisendrath, jr. Pop Phot 58:14+ Ap '66
PHOTOGRAPHIC reproduction. See Photography—Copying
PHOTOGRAPHIC reproduction and projection
See also
University microfilms, Ann Arbor, Mich.
PHOTOGRAPHIC slides. See Transparencies
PHOTOGRAPHIC surveying. See Photogrammetry
PHOTOGRAPHS
Album of family fun. il Life 61:80-9 D 23 '66
Black & white & gray. il Pop Phot 59:67-70 N '66
Nine days; Photokina. B. Pierce. il Pop Phot 60:93-5+ Ja '67
1967 U.S. camera world annual; preview. il U S Camera 29:56-9 N '66
Portfolio: ISFTPOBAWP shows its true colors. il Pop Phot 59:80-5 S '66
Power of seeing; portfolio of twenty contemporary photographs. Life 61:135-54 D 23 '66
Small gallery. il Pop Phot 60:122-7 Ja '67
See also
Daguerreotypes
    also subhead Photographs under various subjects, e.g. Animals—Photographs

Collections
Brief exposures for holiday giving. M. R. Weiss. il Sat R 49:36-7 D 3 '66
Discovered: new Weston letter! concerning plan for making series of photographs of the West. J. Deschin. Pop Phot 59:16+ N '66

Collectors and collecting
Great collector, Fred Mazzulla. N. C. Lipton. il Pop Phot 58:84-5+ Je '66

Conservation and restoration
Restoration of photographs by neutron activation. E. Ostroff. bibliog il Science 154:119-23 O 7 '66

Prices
How much should you charge for a picture? A. Goldsmith. Pop Phot 58:70-2+ Ap '66
Survey reveals pricing practices. Pop Phot 58:73 Ap '66

Trimming, mounting, etc.
Crop the square anywhere. M. Edelson. il U S Camera 29:58-9 Mr '66
Dry mounting with a dryer. R. E. Largent. il U S Camera 29:72-3+ My '66

Washing
Wolfman on printing. A. Wolfman. Mod Phot 30:24+ O '66

PHOTOGRAPHS, Judging of. See Photography
—Criticism
PHOTOGRAPHS in books and periodicals. See
Illustrations of books and periodicals
PHOTOGRAPHY
Camera angles (cont) il Sr Schol 88:16 Mr 25
'66
Camera cues. R. Pinney. il Parents Mag
41:14+ Ag '66
Five picture spoilers, and what to do about
them. E. H. Ortner. il Pop Sci 188:114-
15+ Mr '66
Foto facts. P. Farber. See issues of U.S.
camera & travel
Hanson, Rothschild, Pierce report. N. Roths-
child; W. Hanson; B. Pierce. See issues
of Popular photography
Hattersley class: how to make a left turn
off the beaten path. il Pop Phot 59:67-70
D '66
Hattersley class: you and ideas. Pop Phot
58:106 Ag '66
How an amateur thinks out his photographs!
P. Draper. il Mod Phot 30:66-71 F '66
In the darkroom: planning backward. A.
Francekevich. il Pop Phot 59:18 Jl '66
It's done in the darkroom. il U S Camera
29:54-5 Jl '66
Lewis Jacobs: film-maker, director, author,
teacher; interview, ed. by J. Deschin. L.
Jacobs. Pop Phot 58:12+ F '66
[Life: 30th anniversary; special double issue]
il Life 61:6-8+ D 23 '66
Man Ray on the future! interview, ed. by E.
Hirsch and B. Zar. M. Ray. il Pop Phot
60:98-9 Ja '67
Oops! Modern's editors make some of the
most common photo mistakes. il Mod Phot
30:122+ O '66
Photo-boating, a sport within a sport. G.
K. Gould. il Motor B 118:40-1 Jl '66
Photo tips. See issues of Popular photography
Photo tips. E. Rickman. il Hot Rod 19:76 Ap
'66
Photography for inept sophisticates. H. Wolf.
il Mod Phot 30:54-5+ Jl '66
Portfolio: 1SFTPOBAWP shows its true
colors. il Pop Phot 59:80-5 S '66
Quick cuts & action shots. J. R. Gregory.
See issues of U.S. camera & travel to
May 1966
Seeing beyond the obvious; interview. A.
Goldsmith. il U S Camera 29:48-9+ Mr '66
Shoot now, think later? H. M. Kinzer. Pop
Phot 58:65+ My '66
Taking 250 pictures on one negative! Multiplex
recording photography. W. S. Bacon. il
Pop Sci 188:100-1+ F '66
To take and to tape; some random and
differing thoughts by the editors on record-
ing your trip with camera and recorder.
M. S. Fenner; W. A. Graves; M. B.
Tucker. il NEA J 56:62-4 Ja '67
Tony Karp on 35mm. T. Karp. Mod Phot 30:
84+ Je '66
Tony Karp on 35mm; how to beat camera
motion. T. Karp. il Mod Phot 30:18+ F '66
Tony Karp on 35mm; man against the ele-
ments. T. Karp. Mod Phot 30:22+ Ag '66
Tools & techniques. C. W. Kennedy. See
issues of Popular photography
Travel & camera. See issues of U.S. camera
& travel
Travel tips for photographers. U S Camera
29:47 My '66
Traveling with a camera. E. Bush. il Horti-
culture 44:38-9+ Je '66
Vagabond camera. W. Lane. See issues of
Travel
Well traveled camera. See issues of Modern
photography to July 1966
See also
Astronomical photography
Daguerreotypes
Electronics in photography
Human figure in photography
Lenses, Photographic
Montage
Photographs
Shadowgrams
Television—Photographic aspects
Vietnamese war, 1957- —Photography

Apparatus and supplies
Behind the scenes. See issues of Modern pho-
tography
Bleaching and etching prints. C. W. Ken-
nedy. il Pop Phot 59:22+ D '66
Brave new photo items excite camera mar-
ket. il Bsns W p77 D 24 '66
Buying in the surplus market. P. Stackpole.
U S Camera 29:26+ D '66
Call it a safelight, or whatever you want.
P. Farber. il U S Camera 29:52-3+ N '66

Catch 'em unawares; trigger that permits
wild animals to take their own pictures.
C. Sorenson, jr. il U S Camera 29:38+
Je '66
Crazy goings-on behind the picture. il U S
Camera 29:62-4 Jl '66
Dan Wynn's tricks of the trade. D. S. Gelatt.
il Pop Phot 59:70-5 S '66
Dry mounting with a dryer. R. E. Largent.
il U S Camera 29:72-3+ My '66
Dyes that hit the spot. C. W. Kennedy. il
Pop Phot 59:54+ N '66
Enlarging meters compared. T. Karp. il Mod
Phot 30:54-7+ Mr '66
Exclusive! T. Karp. il Mod Phot 30:82+ My
'66
From what we hear. il U S Camera 29:40-1+
Ap '66
Get a good grip on anything; visegrip as
camera-steadying device. R. Morse. il Pop
Phot 58:68-9+ F '66
Great show: what does it total up to?
symposium. il Pop Phot 60:134-7 Ja '67
Hanson, Rothschild, Pierce report. N. Roths-
child; W. Hanson; B. Pierce. See issues of
Popular photography
Heat-beating tricks. D. B. Eisendrath, jr.
Pop Phot 59:18+ Ag '66
Hitch any camera to a flashcube, if you can
find one. L. Samuels. il Pop Mech 126:180-1
O '66
How to get the most out of lens extenders.
C. W. Kennedy. il Pop Phot 58:68-9+ Ap '66
In the darkroom; equivalents in photography.
A. Francekevich. Pop Phot 59:30+ O '66
Instant adapters. D. Rickett. il U S Camera
29:68-9+ Mr '66
Large camera: darkroom equipment. A. Fein-
inger. Mod Phot 30:80+ Ag '66
Large camera; savers in my own darkroom.
A. Feininger. il Mod Phot 30:92+ S '66
Meyers on technique; Photokina. E. Meyers.
il Mod Phot 31:41 Ja '67
Modern photography's Photokina product
guide. il Mod Phot 31:85+ Ja '67
Modern tests. See issues of Modern photog-
raphy
New photography. il Pop Phot 58:67-71+
Je '66
New products. See issues of U.S. camera &
travel
1966, a new-product bust year? il Pop Phot
58:98-103+ Ap '66
1966 preview. il Mod Phot 30:66-71+ Je '66
1967 photography directory & buying guide. il
il Pop Phot 59:131-93 O; 139-201 N; 135-66
D '66
Old & new news you may have missed. D. B.
Eisendrath, jr. Pop Phot 59:16+ O '66
Photo tips. See issues of Popular photo-
graphy
Sensible advice on cameras and equipment.
R. Pinney. il Parents Mag 41:58-9+ My
'66
Simon says; buying equipment. N. Simon.
Mod Phot 30:72 D '66
Simon says: what will be shown at the 1966
Photokina. N. Simon. il Mod Phot 30:12+
Ag '66
Speed Magny 100; Polaroid adapter for the
Nikon F. P. Schleifer and I. Shirley. il
U S Camera 29:26+ O '66
Super close-ups with your SLR. T. Karp.
il Mod Phot 30:50-4+ F '66
Test reports. See issues of Popular photog-
raphy
35mm techniques; more on bidding & buying
in the surplus market. P. Stackpole. U S
Camera 30:24+ Ja '67
Tony Karp on 35mm. T. Karp. Mod Phot 30:
84+ Je '66
Tony Karp on 35mm; CdS meter batteries.
T. Karp. Mod Phot 30:16+ Jl '66
Tony Karp on 35mm; gadgets made for some
other purpose, adapted for photographic
use. T. Karp. il Mod Phot 30:18+ O '66
Tools & techniques. C. W. Kennedy. See
issues of Popular photography
Trouble testers for photographers. F. P.
Fritz. il Pop Mech 125:171-4+ Mr '66
Two heads are better than one, when one
is the Omega variable-contrast head. B.
Hoffman. il Pop Phot 59:112-13 D '66
U.S. camera & travel test reports. See issues
of U.S. camera & travel
Water cure; using Micronyl water filter. P.
Farber. il U S Camera 29:12+ S '66
Whiz-brrr tick-tock. P. Farber. il U S
Camera 29:58-9+ Jl '66
Wolfman on printing; darkrooms in small
spaces; how to test your safelight. A.
Wolfman. il Mod Phot 30:28+ Jl '66

PHOTOGRAPHY—Apparatus and supplies
—*Continued*
Wolfman on printing; enlarging meters. A.
 Wolfman. Mod Phot 30:26 Mr '66
Wolfman on printing; stabilization proces-
 sors. A. Wolfman. Mod Phot 31:58+ Ja '67
 See also
Camera tripods
Electric lamps, Flashlight
Exposure meters
Lenses, Photographic
Photography—Plates
Reflectors

Testing
Modern tests; how? T. Karp. il Mod Phot
 30:58-61+ Je '66

Bibliography
Books. See issues of U.S. camera & travel
Books in review. See issues of Modern
 photography
Don't miss these books. P. Caulfield. il Mod
 Phot 30:62-5 F '66
Photographic reading. U S Camera 29:32
 Ag '66

Christmas cards
See Christmas cards

Cold weather conditions
Opportunities and precautions for cold
 weather. A. Rothstein. U S Camera 29:14-
 15+ D '66
Winter shooting. M. Edelson. il U S Camera
 30:48-51+ Ja '67

Competitions
As I see it. E. Hannigan. U S Camera 29:
 40+ S; 44 D '66
Contests & exhibits. See issues of U.S.
 camera & travel
Monthly contest. See issues of Modern photog-
 raphy
1966 photo prize winners: a gallery; with re-
 port by M. R. Weiss and list of prizewin-
 ners. il Sat R 50:84-90+ Ja 7 '67
1966 Scholastic photography awards. il Sr
 Schol 88:13, 26+ My 20 '66
Photographers of the year: two for the title.
 M. R. Weiss. il Sat R 49:72-3 My 14 '66
Plan a prize-winning tour. L. Barry. il Pop
 Phot 58:40+ Je '66

Composition
See Composition (photography)

Copying
B&W slides from B&W negatives. L. Mulve-
 hill. il U S Camera 29:26 S '66
Copying & close-up equipment. il Pop Phot
 59:2C-5C D '66
Duplicating slides can be a snap. P. Farber.
 il U S Camera 29:36 Mr '66
Great copying boom; pioneers and their
 methods. J. Tebbel. il Sat R 49:62-3 My 14
 '66
Reproduction vs. preservation; excerpt from
 Care and preservation of books. J. Alden.
 Library J 91:5319-22 N 1 '66
Techniques tomorrow. B. Sherman. Mod Phot
 30:36 Mr '66
 See also
University microfilms, Ann Arbor, Mich.

Anecdotes, facetiae, satire, etc.
KOPY/CHAT; manuscript found when Lincoln Center was being demolished to build
 a parking garage. Library J 91:6045-6
 D 15 '66

Criticism
Color critique (cont) il U S Camera 29:62-3
 Ap; 46-7+ Ag '66
Critics at large. See issues of Popular
 photography
Critic's choice. il Pop Phot 59:100-1+ O; 100-
 1 D '66; 60:120-1 Ja '67

Developing and developers
Alphabet of soups; a personal evaluation of
 popular developers. B. Pierce. il Pop Phot
 58:68-9+ My '66
Brooks instant load developing kit. P. Far-
 ber. il U S Camera 29:67+ Je '66
Developers. Pop Phot 59:27C-28C+ D '66
E-4 may open new color era. J. S. Forney.
 Pop Phot 60:66+ Ja '67
Evaluation of Ethol LPD paper developer.
 P. Farber. il U S Camera 30:30+ Ja '67
Everything but the kitchen sink; how to
 develop your own color slides. P. Farber.
 il U S Camera 29:58-9+ D '66
Flies in your soup. J. S. Forney. il Pop Phot
 58:66-7+ My '66

Foto facts. P. Farber. U S Camera 29:24 F '66
Great stop-bath squabble. W. Hanson. il Pop
 Phot 58:84-5+ Mr '66
How to keep your hands out of photography.
 H. Shaman. il Pop Phot 58:90-1+ Ap '66
How to save water in the darkroom. B.
 Pierce. il Pop Phot 58:114-15 Mr '66
Is one developer enough? B. Pierce. il Pop
 Phot 58:34+ Ap '66
Large camera; 4 x 5-in. negatives. A. Fein-
 inger. il Mod Phot 30:96+ O '66
Merits of mixing your own. P. Farber. U S
 Camera 29:28+ My '66
1966 film-developer roundup; ed. by T. Hill.
 J. Wolbarst. il Mod Phot 30:62-7+ Mr '66
One-thousand and one, one-thousand and two,
 etc, etc, etc, etc, etc. P. Farber. il U S
 Camera 29:46-7 Ap '66
Solving the water problem. P. Farber. U S
 Camera 29:24+ Je '66
Talk with Tatem. A. Francekevich. il Pop
 Phot 58:30+ Je '66
Tony Karp on 35mm; how to get the most
 quality from 35mm. T. Karp. il Mod Phot
 30:10+ My '66
Tony Karp on 35mm; monobath. T. Karp.
 Mod Phot 30:30+ N; 22+ D '66
 See also
Photographic chemistry

Testing
Autofine. P. R. Farber. il U S Camera 30:
 23+ Ja '67
Paper developers. P. Farber. il U S Camera
 29:46-9+ S '66

Distortion
Scheichenbauer's created women. il Mod Phot
 30:48-53 Mr '66

Drying (films and prints)
Dry 'em fast! P. Farber. il U S Camera 29:
 72-3+ Ap '66
Wolfman on printing; low-cost, foolproof
 methods. A. Wolfman. Mod Phot 30:40+ My
 '66
Wolfman on printing; print dryers. A. Wolfman. il Mod Phot 30:30+ Je '66

Enlarging
Beseler's motorized marvel. H. Zucker. il Pop
 Phot 59:98-9 D '66
Contact photomicrography in the ultra-violet
 on high-resolution plates. F. P. McWhor-
 ter and C. M. Leach. il Science 152:757-8
 My 6 '66
Enlargers. il Pop Phot 59:19C-26C D '66
Most in enlargers. M. A. Matzkin. il Mod
 Phot 30:80-3 Ag '66
That first enlargement. P. Farber. il U S
 Camera 29:50-1+ F '66
Wolfman on printing; enlarging papers. A.
 Wolfman. il Mod Phot 30:24+ N '66

Equipment
See Photography—Apparatus and supplies

Exhibitions
Chim: shadow of violence; D. Seymour ex-
 hibit at the Israel museum, Jerusalem.
 M. R. Weiss. il Sat R 50:128-9 Ja 14 '67
Come to the photo fair; fourth International
 photography fair in New York. E. H.
 Ortner. il Pop Sci 188:104-5+ My '66
Contests & exhibits. See issues of U.S.
 camera & travel
Encore at the Louvre: Henri Cartier-Bresson.
 M. R. Weiss. il Sat R 49:23-8 N 26 '66
From the pampas to Fifth avenue; Cornell
 Capa's profiles of Latin American artists.
 F. Getlein. New Repub 154:33-4 Je 25 '66
Great show; what does it total up to? sym-
 posium. il Pop Phot 60:134-7 Ja '67
Innocent eye; F. B. Johnston show at Museum
 of modern art. New York. H. Cohen. il
 Reporter 34:45-8 Mr 10 '66
Kathleen Haven on hanging picture shows;
 interview, ed. by J. Deschin. K. Haven.
 il Pop Phot 59:46+ S '66
L. Fritz Gruber: statesman in photography;
 director of Photokina. C. Reynolds. il Pop
 Phot 59:74-7+ Ag '66
Lens explosion; Photokina. P. Leonian. il
 U S Camera 30:58-9+ Ja '67
Letter from Paris; one-man show in the
 Louvre. by H. Cartier-Bresson. Genêt.
 New Yorker 42:113-14 Ja 14 '67
Modern photography's Photokina product
 guide. il Mod Phot 31:85+ Ja '67
Navy plans Vietnam exhibit. J. Neubauer.
 il Pop Phot 59:42+ Jl '66
Nine days; Photokina, symposium. il Pop
 Phot 60:93-105+ Ja '67

PHOTOGRAPHY—Exhibitions—*Continued*
Photokina 1966. il U S Camera 30:52-7+ Ja '67
Place in the sun; P. Fink show at Art institute of Chicago. M. R. Weiss. il Sat R 49:16-17 Ag 27 '66
Recording life-in-process; D. Lange show at Museum of modern art. M. R. Weiss. il Sat R 49:50-1 Mr 5 '66
Riboud's camera covers China; Asia House exhibition. M. R. Weiss. il Sat R 49:89-91 D 10 '66
Salon calendar. See issues of Modern photography
Simon says; what will be shown at the 1966 Photokina. N. Simon. il Mod Phot 30:12+ Ag '66
Technical progress and creativity; Photokina 1966. A. Rothstein. U S Camera 30:12+ Ja '67
Thoughts in a German cathedral; Photokina. J. Durniak. Pop Phot 60:90+ Ja '67
What's new that's good? photo industry meets in Cleveland. il Pop Phot 58:102-10+ Je '66

Exposure
Case for close metering. il U S Camera 29:62-3 Je '66
Caulfield on color; Kodak master photoguide. P. Caulfield. il Mod Phot 30:34+ F '66
Caulfield on color; shutter speed. P. Caulfield. il Mod Phot 30:40 Ag '66
Caulfield on color; solutions for exposure errors. P. Caulfield. Mod Phot 30:14 Jl '66
Caulfield on color; through lens meters. P. Caulfield. il Mod Phot 30:22+ My '66
Color exposure guaranteed! D. B. Eisendrath, jr. Pop Phot 59:122-3+ N '66
Diary of an experiment; latensification exposure. B. Pierce. il Pop Phot 60:25+ Ja '67
Electronic exposure: more & better. C. W. Kennedy. il Pop Phot 60:96-7 Ja '67
Exposure problems. S. Needleman. il U S Camera 29:44-5+ N '66
Exposure problems? who hasn't got 'em? symposium. il Mod Phot 30:58-71 Jl '66
Exposures for close-ups. D. B. Eisendrath, jr. il Pop Phot 58:24+ Je '66
It ain't reciprocity so... P. Farber. U S Camera 29:30+ Ap '66
Meter, meter, where are you? H. Keppler. il Mod Phot 30:50-1 Jl '66
Pushing film speed. W. Hanson. il Pop Phot 59:98-101+ Ag '66
Those rubber ratings; instruction sheets. W. Hanson. il Pop Phot 58:32+ Ap '66
See also
Exposure meters

Films
Biggest film change? high speed Ektachrome type B. H. Keppler. il Mod Phot 30:78-83+ N '66
Black & white still films. Pop Phot 59:9C-13C D '66
Color clinic: how new or improved? D. B. Eisendrath. jr. Pop Phot 59:13+ Mr '66
Color exposure guaranteed! C. B. Eisendrath, jr. Pop Phot 59:122-3+ N '66
Color still films. Pop Phot 59:14C-15C D '66
Come back, little silver; use in film. W. Hanson. Pop Phot 58:60 Ap '66
Directory of color films. U S Camera 29:56-7+ S '66
Higher speeds for color film. A. Rothstein. U S Camera 29:26+ My '66
How to get the most out of Agfachrome. N. Rothschild. il Pop Phot 59:80-3+ Ag '66
How to get the most out of Plus-X pan. C. W. Kennedy. il Pop Phot 59:72-3+ Ag '66
How to get the most out of the Anscochromes. N. Rothschild. il Pop Phot 58:58-61+ F '66
How to get the most out of the Ektachromes. N. Rothschild. il Pop Phot 58:80-3+ Mr '66
Iffy world of films. N. Rothschild. Pop Phot 59:69+ Ag '66
Kodacolor-X: rerated, but unchanged. D. B. Eisendrath, jr. Pop Phot 59:22+ S '66
Kodacolor-X: serious film or only for snapshots? H. Keppler. il Mod Phot 30:64-7 My '66
Medium-speed color films. H. C. Birnbaum. il U S Camera 29:44-7+ O '66
Meyers on technique; fast color films. E. Meyers. Mod Phot 30:59 O '66
1966 film-developer roundup; ed. by T. Hill. J. Wolbarst. il Mod Phot 30:62-7+ Mr '66
1966/67 color films compared! comp. by D. L. Miller. Mod Phot 30:64-5 O '66
Pink Kodachrome disease & what to do. P. Caulfield. il Mod Phot 30:72-3+ F '66
Polacolor film as a medium for creative art. A. Rothstein. U S Camera 29:20+ S '66

Pushing film speed. W. Hanson. il Pop Phot 59:98-101+ Ag '66
Should you switch to the tan box? Dynachrome 64. H. Keppler. il Mod Phot 30:40-1 O '66
Sixty-second answers to Polaroid problems. P. Wahl. il Pop Sci 189:144-7 Jl '66
Slow-fast film catches both the brightest and the faintest stages of a nuclear blast; XR film. il Life 61:112-13 D 23 '66
Super 35. coming soon? H. Zucker. il Pop Phot 59:40+ S '66; Discussion. 59:4+ D '66
Tony Karp on 35mm; how to get the most quality from 35mm. T. Karp. il Mod Phot 30:10+ My '66
Tungsten color films. M. Edelson. il U S Camera 29:52-7+ F '66
Whose hue? PS guide to color films. P. Wahl. il Pop Sci 188:63-5+ Je '66
Wizard of Ozachrome. P. R. Farber. il U S Camera 30:46-7+ Ja '67
See also
Cameras—Loading
Moving picture films

Storage
Why should you store your film. and how? D. B. Eisendrath. jr. Pop Phot 59:94-5+ Ag '66

Testing
Is it true? H. N. Todd and R. D. Zakia. Pop Phot 58:62 My '66

Fixing
Tony Karp on 35mm; monobath. T. Karp. Mod Phot 30:30+ N '66

Focusing
Can you control a lens's definition? reprint from Here's how. J. W. McFarlane. il Mod Phot 30:74-7+ Je '66
For long legs, a short lens. P. Gowland. il Pop Phot 59:26+ S '66
Hold it! H. Shaman. il Pop Phot 59:100-1 N '66
Normal lens for wide angle. H. Keppler. il Mod Phot 30:62-3 Ap '66
Out is in; fuzzy pictures. R. M. Hattersley. il Pop Phot 58:50-3+ F '66
See, take tele. P. Caulfield. il Mod Phot 30:58-67 Ag '66
Sharp look at focusing. C. W. Kennedy. il Pop Phot 59:23+ O '66
Tricks of the trade. R. Pinney. il Parents Mag 41:14+ Ag '66
When you zoom, stop at wide-angle. M. A. Matzkin. il Mod Phot 30:84 Ap '66
Wide-angle. C. Reynolds. il Pop Phot 59:82-9+ O '66
Wide: from not so to very. H. Keppler. il Mod Phot 30:50-9 Ap '66

Galleries and museums
Gallery that's on the go; Underground gallery, New York. M. Orovan. il U S Camera 30:38+ Ja '67
See also
American museum of photography

History
Concise history of photography, by H. Gernsheim and A. Gernsheim. Review
Mod Phot il 30:62-3 My '66 D. L. Miller
Discovered: new Weston letter! concerning plan for making series of photographs of the West. J. Deschin. Pop Phot 59:16+ N '66
[Life: 30th anniversary; special double issue] il Life 61:6-8+ D 23 '66

Bibliography
Which history of photography is best? D. E. Halberstich. Pop Phot 59:75+ Jl '66

Landscapes
Dramatic light to make dramatic scenics. P. Caulfield. il Mod Phot 30:48-53 My '66
Return to the classic scenic. P. Caulfield. il Mod Phot 30:54-63+ O '66
Spectacular scenic. M. Orovan. il U S Camera 29:46-51+ N '66

Light
Beauty of open shade. il U S Camera 29:60-1 S '66
Black & white & gray. il Pop Phot 59:67-70 N '66
Creative color; temperature control. A. Rothstein. U S Camera 29:12+ F '66
Dramatic light to make dramatic scenics. P. Caulfield. il Mod Phot 30:48-53 My '66
Foto facts. P. Farber. U S Camera 29:14+ Jl '66
How to handle the sun. P. Caulfield. il Mod Phot 30:78-81 S '66

PHOTOGRAPHY—Light—*Continued*
Light does it! H. M. Keppler. il Pop Phot 59: 114-19 N '66
Nature and the camera; using polarized light. D. Linton. Natur Hist 75:66-7 Je '66
Paul Caponigro. P. Caulfield. il Mod Phot 31:62-5 Ja '67

Lighting

As I see it. E. Hannigan. U S Camera 29: 42+ N '66
I'd rather, three way, switch than fight. P. Farber. il U S Camera 29:46-7+ Je '66
Pictures from students. il Pop Phot 58:46 My '66
What's your favorite light? il U S Camera 29:42-3 Mr '66
See also
Photography, Flashlight

Marines

Big splash. il U S Camera 29:62-3 S '66
On the water. il U S Camera 29:66-7+ O '66

Negatives

Creative color; negative-positive versus positive-positive. A. Rothstein. U S Camera 29:30+ Mr '66
In search of the quality negative. P. Farber. il U S Camera 29:56-7+ My '66
Large camera. A. Feininger. Mod Phot 30: 92+ Ap '66
Large camera; 4 x 5-in. negatives. A. Feininger. il Mod Phot 30:96+ O '66
Negative personality. P. Farber. il U S Camera 29:52-3+ Mr '66
Testing films & prints for residual hypo. C. W. Kennedy. il Pop Phot 60:54+ Ja '67
Too thin negative; how to get the most out of it. B. Hoffman. il Pop Phot 59:92-3+ Ag '66
Wolfman on printing; how good is color negative film for black & white printing. A. Wolfman. il Mod Phot 30:14+ S '66

News

See Photography, Journalistic

Plates

Taking 250 pictures on one negative! W. S. Bacon. il Pop Sci 188:100-1+ F '66

Portraits

Beauty of open shade. il U S Camera 29:60-1 S '66
Behold the lowly flashcube. D. L. Miller. il Mod Phot 30:72-3 Je '66
Crazy goings-on behind the picture. il U S Camera 29:62-4 Jl '66
Diffused Jane Fonda. U S Camera 29:60-1 Jl '66
Discovery. P. Caulfield. il Mod Phot 30:70-1+ Ap '66
Eisenstaedt: faces of our time. A. Eisenstaedt. Life 61:110B-114+ S 16 '66
Eisenstaedt. witness to our time, by B. Holme. Review
Mod Phot il 30:66-7 N '66. H. Keppler
Empathy; fakirs. W. Cheney. il U S Camera 29:50-1 S '66
Estremadura gypsies by Penn. I. Penn. Vogue 148:114-15+ Ag 15 '66
Girl next door. Pop Phot 60:71-4 Ja '67
Halsman talks portraits; excerpts from address. P. Halsman. il Pop Phot 59:102-3+ O '66
Hattersley class: seeing faces. R. Hattersley. il Pop Phot 58:78 F '66
How to shoot the group. M. Orovan. il U S Camera 29:68-9+ Je '66
Is this a portrait? S. Plachy. Pop Phot 58: 92-3 My '66
Len Steckler's girls. Pop Phot 58:84-7+ My '66
Living faces; Easter Islanders. C. Mydans. il Life 60:50-3 F 4 '66
[Monthly column] P. Gowland. See issues of Popular photography
Nadar's pantheon; portraits of composers. F. V. Grunfeld. Opera N 30:28-31 F 26 '66
Novelist Henry Miller. P. Gowland. il Pop Phot 58:66-7+ Mr '66
Picture profile: the ship's photographer. G. Pyle. il Pop Phot 58:70-1+ Mr '66
Posed. unposed controversy. B. Downes. Pop Phot 58:16 Mr '66
Pretty as a picture: will the camera be smiling at you? il Seventeen 25:22 S '66
Scheichenbauer's created women. il Mod Phot 30:48-53 Mr '66
Secrets of a society photographer. il U S Camera 29:44-5+ Ap '66
Show of color. M. R. Weiss. Sat R 49:45-52 S 24 '66

Sneaky photographer; candid pictures of people. P. Farber. il U S Camera 29:52-3+ Ag '66
To see this world as it is. il Pop Phot 60: 106-7 Ja '67
Ursula. il U S Camera 29:64-5 Ag '66
With mind and heart and a magic box; how you should take pictures. C. Mydans. il Life 61:64-6+ D 23 '66
See also
Daguerreotypes

Printing materials

Been printing on paper? now try: aluminum, copper, linen, etc. B. G. Wels. il U S Camera 29:60-1+ My '66

Printing processes

Analyzing color prints; Mullan color print analyzer. M. Morrison. il U S Camera 29: 46-7+ Mr '66
Creative color; negative-positive versus positive-positive. A. Rothstein. U S Camera 29:30+ Mr '66
Dorothea Lange and her printer. J. Deschin. il Pop Phot 59:28+ Jl '66
Keep cleaning it up. A. Francekevich. Pop Phot 59:104+ S '66
Keppler on the SLR; how sharp and grainless should your SLR pictures be? H. Keppler. il Mod Phot 30:42+ O '66
Large camera. A. Feininger. Mod Phot 30: 96+ Mr '66; 31:123+ Ja '67
Large camera; small tricks. A. Feininger. Mod Phot 30:152+ D '66
Meyers on technique; color print making. E. Meyers. Mod Phot 30:34 N '66
Ultimate black and white; working with litho film. A. Francekevich. il Pop Phot 58:22+ Mr '66
Which print was made in 15 seconds? D. S. Gelatt. il Pop Phot 59:78-81+ Jl '66
Wolfman on printing. A. Wolfman. See issues of Modern photography

Retouching

Bleaching and etching prints. C. W. Kennedy. il Pop Phot 59:22+ D '66
Dyes that hit the spot. C. W. Kennedy. il Pop Phot 59:54+ N '66

Safety devices and measures

Tony Karp on 35mm; safety hazards. T. Karp. il Mod Phot 30:13-14+ Mr '66

Scientific applications

Analysis of complex vascular systems in plants: optical shuttle method. M. H. Zimmermann and P. B. Tomlinson. bibliog il Science 152:72-3 Ap 1 '66
Indispensable camera. R. B. Stolley. il Life 61:90A-90B+ D 23 '66
See also
Photography in archeology
Photomicrography

Social aspects

Indispensable camera. R. B. Stolley. il Life 61:90A-90B+ D 23 '66

Societies

See also
Professional photographers of America. incorporated

Still life

Along the Lehigh River. H. M. Kinzer. il Pop Phot 58:80-3 Je '66
Hattersley class: photographing food. il Pop Phot 58:92 Mr '66
Hattersley class: variations on a theme. il Pop Phot 59:51-4 S '66
Photo sculpture. A. Dorn. il U S Camera 29:54-5+ S '66
Photographing food; pictures from students. Pop Phot 58:55 Je '66

Studios and darkrooms

Apartment studio. C. W. Kennedy. il Pop Phot 58:80 F '66
Darkroom for every garage. K. Biggs. il Pop Phot 59:110-11 O '66
It's done in the darkroom. il U S Camera 29:54-5 Jl '66
Keep cleaning it up. A. Francekevich. Pop Phot 59:38 S '66
Large camera. A. Feininger. il Mod Phot 30: 91+ My; 90+ Jl '66
Rise of mediocrity. A. Francekevich. Pop Phot 59:26 N '66
Tony Karp on 35mm; safety hazards. T. Karp. il Mod Phot 30:13-14+ Mr '66

PHOTOGRAPHY—Studios and darkrooms
—Continued
Wolfman on printing. A. Wolfman. il Mod
Phot 30:46+ Ap '66
Wolfman on printing; darkrooms in small
spaces; how to test your safelight. A.
Wolfman. il Mod Phot 30:28+ Jl '66

Study and teaching

Anyone for college photo courses? Mod Phot
30:76+ D '66
Catfish-eating society; short courses. J.
Durniak. Pop Phot 58:56 Mr '66
Hattersley class. See issues of Popular pho-
tography
Improving color techniques at the Syracuse
workshop. A. Rothstein. U S Camera 29:
14-15 O '66
Should you study photography in college?
C. B. Neblette. Mod Phot 31:130+ Ja '67

Themes

All at once, a moment can be caught forever.
il Life 61:32-50 D 23 '66
Circus parade; Old Milwaukee days. il U S
Camera 29:56-7+ Jl '66
Guy with an eye. il U S Camera 29:50-1 Mr
'66
Hattersley class: reflections. il Pop Phot
58:43-5 My '66
Interplay. M. Orovan. il U S Camera 29:
66-9 My '66
Parade; Tournament of roses, Pasadena,
Calif. G. Long. il U S Camera 30:74 Ja '67
Swedish subway. il U S Camera 29:52-3 My
'66
Why didn't I see that? K. Poli. il Pop Phot
59:104-9 O '66
PHOTOGRAPHY, Aerial
Coast guard discovers that AN/AAR-33
Sperry iceberg tracker system aids map-
ping. K. Voss. il Tech W 20:38-9+ Ja 16
'67
Day they chased the sun. J. Neubauer. il
Pop Phot 58:72-3+ My '66
Flying photographer. See issues of Flying
Hans Herman Hugo Ernest Wilhelm Von
Groenhoff. E. D. Muhlfeld. il Flying 80:64-
9 Ja '67
Panoramic camera designed for low-level
operations; Minipan camera. R. D. Hibben.
il Aviation W 84:104-5+ My 9 '66
Picture yourself shooting panoramas from
gasbag. W. Lane. il Travel 126:66 S '66
See also
Aerial reconnaissance
Photogrammetry
Photography in archeology
Vietnamese war, 1957—Photography
PHOTOGRAPHY, Artistic
Beautiful image. il Pop Phot 59:86-91 Ag '66
Color abstractions for release from realism. A.
Rothstein. U S Camera 29:14-15+ Ap '66
Formagrams. E. Meyers. il Mod Phot 30:
70-1 Ag '66
Good subject, good idea. il Pop Phot 59:102-
11 D '66
Holiday lights. N. Rothschild. il Pop Phot
60:108-9 Ja '67
Out is in; fuzzy pictures. R. M. Hattersley.
il Pop Phot 58:50-3+ F '66
Who needs a camera? D. L. Miller. il Mod
Phot 31:70-1 Ja '67
PHOTOGRAPHY, Astronomical. See Astronom-
ical photography
PHOTOGRAPHY, Close-up
Closeups the easy way. il Mod Phot 30:74-
5+ Jl '66
Copying & close-up equipment. il Pop Phot
59:2C-5C D '66
Exposures for close-ups. D. B. Eisendrath,
jr. il Pop Phot 58:24+ Je '66
Go way out for movie close-ups. M. A. Matz-
kin. il Mod Phot 30:84-5 F '66
New front lenses: two easy ways to close-ups.
N. Rothschild. il Pop Phot 59:78-9+ Ag '66
Not so close close-ups. il Mod Phot 30:55+
F '66
Super close-ups with your SLR. T. Karp. il
Mod Phot 30:50-4+ F '66
PHOTOGRAPHY, Commercial
Color odds are ten to one against Tom Mc-
Carthy. il Pop Phot 59:88-97+ Jl '66
Dan Wynn's tricks of the trade. D. S. Gelatt.
il Pop Phot 59:70-5 S '66
David B. Eisendrath: photography's man for
all seasons. D. S. Gelatt. il Pop Phot 59:
66-9+ S '66
How did they make that commercial? H. V.
Fondiller. il Pop Phot 58:124-6+ Mr '66
How much should you charge for a picture?
A. Goldsmith. Pop Phot 58:70-2+ Ap '66
How to turn an editor into a friend; tips
on selling pictures to publications. Ullman.
U S Camera 29:16+ O '66

LBJ: he's turned the other cheek. J. Neu-
bauer. il Pop Phot 60:118-19+ Ja '67
Pie in the sky. il U S Camera 30:62-3 Ja '67
Where is the money in photography. J. G.
Morris. il Pop Phot 59:75-9+ O '66
See also
Advertising art
Photography as a profession
Photography in advertising

Anecdotes, facetiae, satire, etc.

Unpaid, uncomplaining, but not unappreci-
ated: a wife, the best photo assistant of
them all. A. Bosworth. il U S Camera 29:
40+ Ag '66
PHOTOGRAPHY, Composite. See Photomon-
tage
PHOTOGRAPHY, Documentary
As I see it; ship burning. E. Hannigan. U S
Camera 29:40+ Mr '66
Camera as a sociological weapon. P. Stack-
pole. U S Camera 29:16+ My '66
Concise history of photography, by H.
Gernsheim and A. Gernsheim. Review
Mod Phot il 30:62-3 My '66. D. L. Miller
Eisenstaedt, witness to our time, by B.
Holme. Review
Mod Phot il 30:62-9+ N '66. H. Keppler
Gettysburg; movement in photographs. il U S
Camera 29:64-5 Ap '66
Great American wedding; you are invited to
see how it was covered. J. Neubauer; B.
Brown; F. Ward. il Pop Phot 59:85-9+ D
'66
He builds in color; F. Maroon's pictures. il
Pop Phot 58:78-83 My '66
Images of the Great society. il U S Camera
29:52-3 Jl '66
John Albok, tailor-photographer. J. Deschin.
il Pop Phot 58:32+ Je '66
Portrait of a school year; picture document-
ary as a master's thesis. il Pop Phot 58:50
Ap '66
Profiles in poverty. il U S Camera 29:42-7
F '66
Recreating old photos. L. Mulvehill. il U S
Camera 29:20 Jl '66
Restless camera of George Holton. L. Barry.
il Pop Phot 58:86-95+ Je '66
This is the way it is, look at it! look at it!
interview; ed. by J. Deschin. D. Lange.
il Pop Phot 58:58+ My '66
Violent, gentle life of D. D. Duncan. J.
Durniak. il Pop Phot 59:90-7 D '66
PHOTOGRAPHY, Electronic
Electronic exposure: more & better. C. W.
Kennedy. il Pop Phot 60:96-7 Ja '67
Electrons: how good are those fast little
devils. N. Goldberg. Pop Phot 60:132+ Ja
'67
Plug-togetherness; modular system makes
eight photo aids. W. F. Wilson. il Pop
Phot 58:74 My '66
PHOTOGRAPHY, Fashion
Wide on women. il U S Camera 29:54-5 N '66
PHOTOGRAPHY, Flashlight
Electronic flash problems exposed. D. B.
Eisendrath, jr. Pop Phot 60:16+ Ja '67
How to bounce a cube. C. W. Kenney. il
Pop Phot 58:14+ Je '66
Look, ma! no reflectors! il Pop Phot 58:64-7+
Ap '66
Meyers on technique: guide numbers for
direct flash. E. Meyers. Mod Phot 30:40 S
'66
Secrets of using flash for better color pic-
tures. P. Wahl. il Pop Sci 188:140-3+
My '66
Tony Karp on 35mm: electronic flash. T.
Karp. il Mod Phot 31:14+ Ja '67
PHOTOGRAPHY, High speed
Sky's the limit; Jay Shuttleworth shoots
while he falls. il U S Camera 29:34 Mr '66
PHOTOGRAPHY, Infrared
IR photos yield data on natural resources.
W. S. Beller. il Tech W 19:24+ Ag 15 '66
Past; present; future. il Life 61:106-9 D 23
'66
PHOTOGRAPHY, Journalistic
Camera on the spot as a tragedy of the sea
unfolds. il Life 61:120D-125 D 23 '66
Chim; shadow of violence: D. Seymour ex-
hibit at the Israel museum. Jerusalem.
M. R. Weiss. il Sat R 50:128-9 Ja 14 '67
Dick Meek: color, real & unreal. il Pop Phot
59:90-5+ S '66
Eisenstaedt lens. K. Poli. il Pop Phot 59:
102-11 N '66
Eisenstaedt, witness to our time, by B.
Holme. Review
Mod Phot il 30:62-9+ N '66. H. Keppler
Eulogy: Vytas Valaitis. M. Orovan. il U S
Camera 29:54-7+ Mr '66
Garry Winogrand. M. Orovan. il U S Camera
29:70-3+ F '66.

PHOTOGRAPHY, Journalistic—*Continued*

Great unknown photographer; W. Eugene Smith. D. Vestal. il Pop Phot 59:114-17+ D '66

LBJ: he's turned the other cheek. J. Neubauer. il Pop Phot 60:118-19+ Ja '67

Man with a camera; D. D. Duncan. il Newsweek 68:100+ N 14 '66

Miami news photogs shoot it long and wide ... il U S Camera 29:64-7 S '66

Notes and comment; role of the camera as hero in the events it records. New Yorker 42:41 Ap 23 '66

Out of the frying pan; Image East, a photo agency. il U S Camera 29:48-51+ Ag '66

Pope in a teapot; how visit of Pope Paul VI was handled by Life. P. Caulfield. il Mod Phot 30:78-9 F '66

Portfolio; James Stanfield. Pop Phot 58:72-7+ Je '66

Restless camera of George Holton. L. Barry. il Pop Phot 58:86-95+ Je '66

Riboud's camera covers China; Asia House exhibition. M. R. Weiss. il Sat R 49:89-91 D 10 '66

Right? right! J. Durniak. Pop Phot 59:82 D '66

Talent for candids. P. Stackpole. U S Camera 29:26+ Je '66

They must be doing something right in Milwaukee. G. A. Young. il Pop Phot 59:98-101+ Jl '66

Violent, gentle life of D. D. Duncan. J. Durniak. il Pop Phot 59:90-7 D '66

See also

News photographers

Study and teaching

Cliff Edom: the man in Missouri. J. G. Morris. il Pop Phot 59:96-7+ S '66

Reporting an intense awareness of things as they are. E. Leos. il Sch Arts 66:14-18 S '66

PHOTOGRAPHY, Medical

Help diagnose cancer by thermography. Sci N 89:490 Je 18 '66

PHOTOGRAPHY, Military

See also

Aerial reconnaissance

PHOTOGRAPHY, Night

Moonlight. J. T. Taylor. il U S Camera 29:42-3 S '66

Night colors. N. Rothschild. il Pop Phot 59:90-3+ O '66

PHOTOGRAPHY, Rotation. See Photomicrography

PHOTOGRAPHY, Space. See Space photography

PHOTOGRAPHY, Submarine

Boy, oh, buoy! use of Johnson air buoy. K. Poli. il Pop Phot 59:96-7+ Ag '66

Camera that thinks it's a duck. M. V. Korda. il Pop Phot 58:62-5+ Mr '66

DSSP requirements hasten underwater photo-optics efforts; deep submergence systems project. W. E. Wilks. Tech W 19:39-40 O 24 '66

Equipment binds undersea photography. R. W. Niblock. il Tech W 18:24-5 Je 20 '66

How to take pictures at ten fathoms. S. James. il Pop Mech 127:110-13 Ja '67

Real fisheye, fisheye. H. Keppler. il Mod Phot 30:64-5 Ap '66

Sh-sh-sh-shark and other underwater festival goodies. P. Gowland. il Pop Phot 59:128-9 Ag '66

Techniques tomorrow; deeper ocean. B. Sherman. Mod Phot 30:30+ D '66

Underwater. P. J. Tzimoulis. il U S Camera 29:58-9+ My '66

Underwater color now easier with modern cameras and films. A. Rothstein. U S Camera 29:30-1 Ag '66

See also

Moving picture photography, Submarine

PHOTOGRAPHY, Theatrical

It began with photograms. J. Deschin. il Pop Phot 60:38+ Ja '67

Pleasure, pain, & the performers; taking circus pictures. il Pop Phot 59:86-9+ S '66

PHOTOGRAPHY, Three dimensional. See Stereophotography

PHOTOGRAPHY, Time-lapse

Nature and the camera; time-lapse photography. W. G. Smith, jr. il Natur Hist 75:73-4 Ag '66

PHOTOGRAPHY, Trick

Hattersley class: spacemanship. il Pop Phot 59:63-6 O '66

Kaleidoscope. il U S Camera 29:56-7 D '66

Killed by roses. H. Keppler. il Mod Phot 30:56-61 F '66

Making things you know that ain't. H. Keppler. il Mod Phot 30:58-61 Mr '66

Reflections in my hubcaps. M. Morrison. il U S Camera 30:6 Ja '67

Sexy sandwich. il U S Camera 29:62-5 O '66

PHOTOGRAPHY and art. See Art and photography

PHOTOGRAPHY as a profession

His way of working. B. Roddey. il U S Camera 29:40+ D '66

Wingate Paine: in a class by himself. C. Reynolds. il Pop Phot 60:114-17+ Ja '67

PHOTOGRAPHY clubs. See Camera clubs

PHOTOGRAPHY in advertising

Bechtold formula. K. Poli. il Pop Phot 60:110-11 Ja '67

Delectations; food photography. N. S. Hazelton. Nat R 18:1046+ O 18 '66

Gentle persuasion. M. R. Weiss. il Sat R 49:76-7 S 10 '66

Into the sun; campaign for Bain de soleil. F. Bez. il U S Camera 29:44-5+ Jl '66

Joe Weitz. il Pop Phot 58:74-7+ Mr '66

René Groebli's variations. N. Rothschild. il Pop Phot 59:94-5 O '66

Schulze and Schulze. il Pop Phot 58:76-81 Ap '66

What makes Gigli click? W. Rodarmor. il Pop Phot 59:96-7+ O '66

PHOTOGRAPHY in archeology

Indians and Eskimos prompt photography; aerial photography to detect signs of early habitation. Sci N 90:88 Ag 6 '66

PHOTOGRAPHY in science. See Photography—Scientific applications

PHOTOGRAPHY in traffic regulation

Computer and camera may unsnarl traffic. il Am City 81:150 My '66

PHOTOGRAPHY of animals

Alaska portfolio. T. Balog. il Field & S 71:46-7 D '66

Catch 'em unawares. C. Sorenson, jr. il U S Camera 29:38+ Je '66

Challenge; bull elk in Montana. E. A. Bauer. il Outdoor Life 137:60-1 Mr '66

How these photographs were taken; mountain sheep photography. J. C. Holroyd. Field & S 71:32+ Ag '66

Its intense and total cowness. D. Vestal. il Pop Phot 59:100-1 D '66

Mexican freetail bats; photography. H. E. Edgerton and others. il Science 153:201-3 Jl 8 '66

Photo safaris are fine, but your zoo is closer. W. Lane. il Travel 126:68 O '66

Photo trap lets you bring 'em back in pictures. E. Cesar. il Pop Sci 189:136-7 N '66

Waterhole photography. D. Beatie. il Nat Parks Mag 40:10-11 Je '66

See also

Animals—Photographs

PHOTOGRAPHY of birds

Beach babies. W. D. Griffin. il U S Camera 29:42-3+ Ap '66

Egg Island adventure. J. J. Stophlet. il Nat Parks Mag 40:9-12 Mr '66

How to shoot eagles. K. Botty. il Field & S 71:60-1 Ja '67

PHOTOGRAPHY of buildings and structures

Discovery. P. Caulfield. il Mod Phot 30:74-5+ Mr '66

PHOTOGRAPHY of children

Almost calculated disorder. J. Deschin. il Pop Phot 60:120-1 Ja '67

Child has 10,000 faces. K. Poli. il Pop Phot 58:78-9 Je '66

Good skates. il U S Camera 29:42-3 Je '66

Hattersley class: seeing the family. il Pop Phot 59:45-8 Ag '66

How to take better Christmas pictures. H. Arnold. il Pop Mech 126:146-8+ D '66

I like kids ... even my own. J. Taylor. il U S Camera 29:44-5 S '66

I was struck by those eyes! R. W. Brown. il Pop Phot 59:100-1+ O '66

Jennifer's first flight. il U S Camera 29:32 O '66

Jump, jump, jump. D. L. Miller. il Mod Phot 30:82-3 O '66

Magic lake. il U S Camera 29:54-5 My '66

Mirror, mirror on the wall. il U S Camera 29:26 Mr '66

My daughter the model. il U S Camera 29:56-9 O '66

Take them in action. R. Pinney. il Parents Mag 41:17 O '66

Those little darlings. E. Stone. il U S Camera 29:50-1+ Jl '66

Tips on how to take better pictures of your children. P. Young. il Parents Mag 41:56-7+ My '66

Trim little tale. D. Spirduso. il U S Camera 29:36 Ag '66

See also

Children—Photographs

PHOTOGRAPHY of eclipses. See Astronomical photography

PHOTOGRAPHY of emotions
Grateful and those with only grief. il Life 61:124-5 D 23 '66

PHOTOGRAPHY of fishes
Portrait of a living fossil; the coelacanth. il Life 61:64-6 Jl 22 '66

PHOTOGRAPHY of flowers, plants, trees, etc.
Photographing wild flowers. D. B. Eisendrath, jr. il Pop Phot 59:22+ Jl '66
Preserve the beauty and color of flowers in spring. A. Rothstein. U S Camera 29:12+ Je '66
Take photographs in your garden. S. H. Gottscho. il Horticulture 44:26-7+ F '66

PHOTOGRAPHY of food
Delectations; food photography. N. S. Hazelton. Nat R 18:1046+ O 18 '66

PHOTOGRAPHY of moving objects
Jump, jump, jump. D. L. Miller. il Mod Phot 30:82-3 O '66
Mexican freetail bats: photography. H. E. Edgerton and others. il Science 153:201-3 Jl 8 '66
Mulvehill, the great experimenter. H. M. Kinzer. il Pop Phot 58:96-101 Je '66
Photo tips. E. Rickman. Hot Rod 19:118 Mr '66
What to do about group action... P. Caulfield. il Mod Phot 30:74-7 S '66

PHOTOGRAPHY of nature. See Nature photography

PHOTOGRAPHY of nebula. See Astronomical photography

PHOTOGRAPHY of planets. See Astronomical photography

PHOTOGRAPHY of snow, ice, etc.
Caulfield on color; winter scenics. P. Caulfield. Mod Phot 30:14+ D '66
Winter's art. D. Shiner. il Design 68:16-18 N '66

PHOTOGRAPHY of sports
Dick Meek: color, real & unreal. il Pop Phot 59:90-5+ S '66
Get with the action. W. Wolf. il U S Camera 30:16 Ja '67
Horse in Ireland, or anywhere; taking pictures at a race meet. P. James. il U S Camera 29:46-7 My '66
Whir of the camera, the roar of the crowd. il U S Camera 29:66-7+ Jl '66
See also
Baseball—Photographs

PHOTOGRAPHY of the human figure. See Human figure in photography

PHOTOGRAPHY of works of art
Impact in chiaroscuro and color. G. H. Hamilton. il Sat R 49:24-7 Ag 27 '66

PHOTOGRAVURE
Photogravure used for MOMA photography books. il Pub W 189:104 Ap 4 '66

PHOTOJOURNALISM. See Photography, Journalistic

PHOTOKINA. See Photography—Exhibitions

PHOTOMECHANICAL processes
Copying dilemma: hazardous results of photo-copying by machines not made for the book: letter to the editor. G. L. Annan. Library J 91:3802+ S 1 '66
Toad beneath the harrow knows; Copyright revision bill and photocopying. E. Janeway. il Library J 91:887-91 F 15 '66; Correction. 91:2740 Je 1 '66

PHOTOMETERS
Why meter readings vary. C. W. Kennedy. il Pop Phot 59:42+ Ag '66

PHOTOMETRY
Automation of steroid analysis. I. E. Bush. bibliog il Science 154:77-83 O 7 '66

PHOTOMETRY, Astronomical
American pioneer in photoelectric astronomy. A. E. Whitford. il Sky & Tel 31:268-9 My '66
New image tubes for space astronomy. il Sky & Tel 32:207-8 O '66

PHOTOMICROGRAPHY
Analysis of complex vascular systems in plants: optical shuttle method. M. H. Zimmermann and P. B. Tomlinson. il bibliog il Science 152:72-3 Ap 1 '66
Beginning of a life; egg. il Life 61:115 D 23 '66
Contact photomicrography in the ultraviolet on high-resolution plates. F. P. McWhorter and C. M. Leach. il Science 152:757-8 My 6 '66
Polarized beauty: micra flakes reveal inner forms. W. Patnode. il Natur Hist 75:24-5 Ap '66
Rotation technique in radially symmetric electron micrographs: mathematical analysis. R. S. Norman. bibliog il Science 152:1238-9 My 27 '66

PHOTOMONTAGE
Anyone for paper dolls? R. E. Paley. il Mod Phot 30:16 Ag '66
How to put the Grand Canyon in a studio. J. S. Forney. il Pop Phot 58:78-9+ Mr '66
Photo-montage murals. C. Clements. il Sch Arts 66:25-7 O '66

PHOTOMURALS. See Photographic murals

PHOTONS
See also
Quantum electrodynamics

PHOTOPERIODISM. See Light—Physiological effects; Plants, Effect of light on

PHOTORECEPTORS. See Eye (crustacea)

PHOTOSENSITIZING compounds. See Light sensitization

PHOTOSYNTHESIS
Insight to evolution. Sci N 90:527 D 24 '66
Role of oxygen. L. V. Berkner and L. C. Marshall. il Sat R 49:30-4 My 7 '66

PHOTOTYPESETTING machines. See Photocomposing machines

PHRASING of questions. See Questioning

PHYCOMYCES
Light responses of phycomyces. E. S. Castle. bibliog il Science 154:1416-20 D 16 '66

PHYLOGENY
Phylogeny and ontogeny of behavior. B. F. Skinner. bibliog Science 153:1205-13 S 9 '66

PHYSALIA. See Portuguese man-of-war

PHYSARUM. See Myxomycetes

PHYSICAL astronomy. See Astrophysics

PHYSICAL directors
All the credentials; B. Russell. il Time 87:104+ Ap 29 '66
Baron's runts; A. Rupp of University of Kentucky. il Time 87:60 F 4 '66
Big little men; University of Kentucky. il Newsweek 67:82+ Mr 7 '66
The Brat and The Lip. J. Lake; P. Hager. il Newsweek 67:72-3 Ap 4 '66
Bravo for the baron; A. Rupp's undefeated Kentucky Wildcats. F. Deford. il Sports Illus 24:20-3+ Mr 7 '66
Carruthers have a fighter; J. Pittman. G. Ronberg. il Sports Illus 25:52-3 O 10 '66
Coach Russell. il Newsweek 67:72-3 My 2 '66
Double reverse; L. Saban. Newsweek 68:47 D 26 '66
Glory, frustration and a gamut of emotions; college football coaches; photographs. Sports Illus 25:36-52+ S 19 '66
He goes after scholars who can also shoot well; V. Bubas. il Life 60:52B Ja 28 '66
How to get the job done; Ed Emory, football coach at Wadesboro high school in Wadesboro. N.C. Sports Illus 25:14 O 3 '66
I have never broken a contract; ed. by M. Hyman. P. Dietzel. il Sports Illus 25:44-7 S 19 '66
I'll tell you about football; ed. by J. Underwood. P. Bryant. il Sports Illus 25:52-8+ Ag 15; 28-30+ Ag 22; 26-8+ Ag 29; 28-30+ S 5:98-100+ S 12 '66
Last puritan; G. Halas' dispute with the Rams. W. B. Furlong. il Sports Illus 24:12-17 Ja 31 '66
New role for Bill Russell. il Ebony 22:60-1+ Ja '67
Night they learned to forget the coach; LSU defeats P. Dietzel's South Carolina football team. G. Ronberg. il Sports Illus 25:56-7 S 26 '66
Nose to chin whiskers; Philadelphia 76ers. il Time 89:51 Ja 13 '67
Poison ivy in the Ivy league; Cornell's hockey team. M. Mulvoy. il Sports Illus 26:44-6 Ja 2 '67
Pro pecunia sunt; V. Lombardi. il Time 88:44 D 30 '66
Psychologist on the sidelines; Notre Dame's Parseghian. W. B. Furlong. il N Y Times Mag p56-7+ N 13 '66
Ralph Miller of Iowa; prophet of pressure; Hawkeye basketball coach. F. Deford. il Sports Illus 24:14-17 Ja 24 '66
They're only no. 2; J. T. Prothro of the U.C.L.A. Bruins. il Time 88:78-9 O 7 '66
Tiger in the Ivy; Princeton's Van Breda Kolff. Time 89:68 Ja 20 '67
Toughest bird in Baltimore; H. Bauer. J. R. McDermott. Life 61:48A-48B Jl 8 '66
See also
Billingsley, H. S.
Hannum, A.
Retherford, C.
Schaeffler, W.

PHYSICAL education and training
Lessons in adventure: National outdoor leadership school. M. E. Horn, jr. il Parks & Rec 1:704-5+ S '66

PHYSICAL education and training—*Continued*
Out of the cellar but not in the first division.
America needs more than spring training.
S. Musial. il Am Ed 2:28-30 S '66
See also
Sports

PHYSICAL education and training of women
In my opinion; our muscle mania has gone
too far. R. Holsapple. Seventeen 25:448
Ag '66

PHYSICAL examinations
And now, preventicare; Kaiser foundation
health plan. Time 88:85 S 30 '66
Check up before you check out. E. N. Dye.
Travel 126:20-1+ D '66
Enter the robot M.D; Neuberger's subcom-
mittee discusses multiphasic screening. il
Newsweek 68:92 O 3 '66
Health program for sisters; Chicago arch-
diocese program. America 115:642 N 19 '66
How are your medical manners? E. R. Conger.
il Todays Health 44:8-10 S '66
Now the automated physical checkup; Per-
manente center, Oakland, Calif. L. A.
Stevens. Read Digest 89:95-8 Jl '66
Your health-insurance checkup. Todays
Health 44:6+ Je '66
See also
Air pilots—Physical examinations
Children—Care and hygiene

PHYSICAL exercise. See Exercise

PHYSICAL fitness. See Health; Men—Health
and hygiene; Military service—Physical and
mental fitness

PHYSICAL geography
See also
Continents
Earth
Man—Influence on nature
Plains
Volcanoes

United States
See also
Geology—United States

PHYSICAL science. See Science

PHYSICALLY handicapped. See Handicapped

PHYSICIANS
British medicine: doctors carry on but show
new militancy. J. Walsh. Science 154:365-8
O 21 '66
Day with papa; country-doctor father. N. P.
Britton. il Todays Health 44:30-3+ F '66
Doctors, by M. L. Gross. Review
New Repub 155:28+ O 8 '66. E. T. Chase
Time 88:112+ N 4 '66
Doctor's image is sickly. W. Goodman. il
N Y Times Mag p38-9+ O 16 '66; Discus-
sion. p 12+ O 30; 12+ N 6; 42+ N 13 '66
Doctors who profit from prescriptions; doctor-
merchants probed by Senate antitrust and
monopoly subcommittee. Consumer Rep 31:
234-8 My '66
Great debate about your family doctor; ex-
cerpt from The doctors. M. L. Gross. il
Good H 162:90-1+ Je '66
Ṛ from the patient: physician, heal thyself;
Time essay. Time 87:46-7 My 13 '66
Specializing in the family. Time 88:77-8 O 21
'66
Tomorrow's family doctor. Changing T 20:34
O '66
Your family doctor: how to use him; key
to better care at less cost. A. Johnson
and C. Witten. il Changing T 20:33-4 Ap
'66
See also
American medical association
Interns (medicine)
Medical education
Medical ethics
Medical service
Medicine—Practice
Pediatricians
Surgeons

Fees
See Medical service, Cost of

Supply and demand
Congress, health and medical schools. America 116:37 Ja 14 '67
Doctor shortage studied. Sci N 90:337 O
22 '66
Fugitive British doctors. R. Kirk. Nat R
18:1113 N 1 '66
Keys to M.D.'s for your town. H. Earl. il
Todays Health 44:30-1+ Je '66
New emigrés: British doctors head for U.S.
in large numbers. J. Walsh. Science 154:
494-6 O 28 '66
Our backward medical schools; cause of
shortage. S. M. Creel. Atlan 217:46-50 My
'66; Discussion. 218:30+ Jl '66

Shortages medicare will face. U S News 60:
35 My 30 '66
Why crisis in medical care keeps growing.
il U S News 62:60-4 Ja 23 '67

PHYSICIANS and patients
Breach of confidence? question of how the
Texas revelations on Whitman case will
affect student-doctor relations. il News-
week 68:89 Ag 22 '66
Frank talk on how to choose, use, abuse
your doctor; symposium. ed. by G. E. Max-
well. il Todays Health 44:50-5+ O '66
How to help your doctor help you. Sister M.
Ferdinand. il Todays Health 44:74-6 Ap '66
I prescribe... J. D. Wassersug. Sci Digest
60:55-60 O; 67-71 N; 79-83 D '66; 61:82-6
Ja '67
It's harder and harder to tell the truth.
W. E. O'Donnell. il McCall 93:91+ Ap '66
Just between you and your doctor. Bet Hom
& Gard 44:76-7+ N '66
Student doctor learns to care; University of
Kansas medical school. R. H. Berg. il
Look 30:24-9 F 8 '66
Tell truth to dying. Sci N L 89:55 Ja 22 '66
Your family doctor: how to use him; key to
better care at less cost. A. Johnson and
C. Witten. il Changing T 20:33-4 Ap '66

PHYSICISTS
Questioners: physicists and the quantum the-
ory, by B. L. Cline. Review
New Yorker 42:174+ Ap 16 '66. J. Bern-
stein
See also
Bohr, N. H. D.
Kastler, A.

PHYSICS
U.S. must pay to keep physics leadership.
Sci N 89:221 Ap 2 '66
See also
Astrophysics
Fluids
Magnetism
Molecules
Nuclear physics
Quantum theory
Relativity (physics)

Experiments
Amateur scientist; a rain gauge, a fluid flip-
flop, a sundial and a way of seeing crystals as they grow. il Sci Am 214:128-30+
My '66
Curiosity and the kitchen sink. M. Bauer.
il Am Ed 2:8-10 Jl '66

History
Physics in the last twenty years; adaptation
of address, December 27, 1965. E. Segrè.
Science 151:1052-5 Mr 4 '66
Physics just before Einstein; adaptation of
address, December 29, 1964. A. M. Bork.
bibliog il Science 152:597-603 Ap 29 '66

Research
From new NAS report: an assessment of
relative strength of U.S. physics; excerpts.
Science 151:1364 Mr 18 '66
NAS report finds physics strong, but serious
strains developing. J. Walsh. il Science
151:1363+ Mr 18 '66

Study and teaching
His bag of tricks makes physics fun. W. S.
Griswold. il Pop Sci 188:95-9 My '66
Secret of Plesetsk; physics teacher and stu-
dents of Kettering grammar school, Eng-
land, discover location of rocket-launching
site in Russia. il Time 88:38 D 30 '66
Softer physics teaching. Sci N 91:27 Ja 7 '67

PHYSIOLOGICAL apparatus
Airflow control by auditory feedback: respira-
tory mechanics and wind instruments. A.
Bouhuys. bibliog il Science 154:797-9 N 11
'66
Cerebral concussion in the monkey: an ex-
perimental model. A. K. Ommaya and
others. bibliog il Science 153:211-12 Jl 8
'66
See also
Heart, Artificial
Perfusion apparatus
Transducers

PHYSIOLOGICAL chemistry. See Biochemistry

PHYSIOLOGICAL data transmission. See
Telemeter (physiological apparatus)

PHYSIOLOGICAL effects of alcohol. See Alcohol—Physiological effects

PHYSIOLOGICAL effects of noise. See Noise—
Physiological effects

PHYSIOLOGICAL research
Human sexual response; plans for research in 1967. R. L. Breeling. Todays Health 45: 40 Ja '67
See also
Space flight—Physiological aspects
PHYSIOLOGICAL specimens. See Anatomical specimens
PHYSIOLOGY
Physiological sciences; report on International congress of physiological sciences. H. S. Mayerson. Science 152:1770+ Je 24 '66
See also
Electrophysiology
Nervous system
Psychology, Physiological
Respiration
Sleep
Underwater physiology
Weight (physiology)

Nomenclature
Terminology of cell-water relations. P. J. Kramer and others. bibliog Science 153: 889-90 Ag 19 '66
PHYSOSTIGMINE. See Eserine
PHYTOHEMAGGLUTININS. See Agglutinins
PIANISTS
More keyboard giants of the past. R. Kammerer. il Am Rec G 32:806-9 My '66
Pianists, new encounters and old; New York concerts. H. Goldsmith. Hi Fi 16:126+ Mr '66
What makes a good pianist? F. Bowers. il House & Gard 130:35+ N '66
See also
Ashkenazy, V.
Ellington, D.
Hines, E.
Horowitz, V.
Kraus, L.
Larrocha, A. de
Lateiner, J.
Lewenthal, R.
Lupu, R.
Serkin, P.
Watts, A.
PIANO
How to choose a new piano. Bet Hom & Gard 44:164 O '66
Smoke rings from Baldwin: the SD-10. il Time 88:82 S 9 '66
See also
Player piano
PIANO competitions. See Music—Competitions
PIANO industry and trade
See also
Baldwin company
Steinway and sons, New York
PIANO music
See also
Concertos
Phonograph records—Piano music

Interpretation (paraphrasing, dynamics, etc)
Who's afraid of Lucrezia Borgia? opera paraphrases, once the stock in trade of virtuoso pianists. R. Lewenthal. il Opera N 31:8-12 D 31 '66
PIANO players, Mechanical. See Player piano
PIANTANIDA, Nick
Emergency 11 miles high. il por Newsweek 67:67 My 16 '66
Man set to dive 123,800 feet; with report and editorial comment. il pors Life 60:3, 32-9 My 13 '66
PIATIGORSKY, Gregor
Heifetz-Piatigorsky, unlimited. A. Chasins. il por Hi Fi 16:MA7 D '66
Master class. il por Time 87:64 My 13 '66
PIATIGORSKY, Jacqueline
In chess Piatigorsky is tops. R. Cantwell. il pors Sports Illus 22:22-4+ S 5 '66
PIATIGORSKY chess tournament. See Chess
PIAZZA, Tony
Fathers and small sons. S. Alexander. Life 60:20 Mr 11 '66
PIAZZAS. See Plazas
PICARD, Nicole
Why 1101=13; new approaches to mathematics teaching. UNESCO Courier 19:22-9 Je '66
PICASSO, Claude
People are talking about... por Vogue 147: 82-5 Mr 15 '66
PICASSO, Pablo
Force of nature; exhibition by French Ministry of culture. il Newsweek 68:102 N 28 '66

Letter from Paris; exhibitions at the Grand and the Petit Palais. Genêt. New Yorker 42:158+ N 5 '66
Letter from Paris; exhibitions in the Grand and the Petit palais and in Bibliotheque nationale. Genêt. New Yorker 42:214-16+ D 3 '66
Minotaur & the maze. il Time 88:72 D 2 '66
Perpetual president of modern art. J. Russell. il pors N Y Times Mag p28-31+ O 23 '66
Picasso kiss and tell. G. R. Swenson. Art N 64:19+ Ja '66
Quietly eighty-five. por Time 88:76 N 4 '66
Windy city windfall; sculpture for Chicago. il Time 88:73 S 23 '66
PICASSO, Paloma
People are talking about... por Vogue 147: 82-5 Mr 15 '66
PICCADILLY world match play tournament. See Golf—Tournaments
PICCARD experimental 15. See Submarine boats
PICHAT, Jean Bourgeois-. See Bourgeois-Pichat, J.
PICK, Hella
Reporter on the UN beat. Nation 202:648-50 My 30 '66
PICK, John
Book review. America 115:139 Ag 6 '66
PICKERING, James S.
Backyard astronomer. Natur Hist 76:58+ Ja '67
Backyard astronomer; choice of telescopes. Natur Hist 75:56+ N '66
PICKERING, William Hayward
New ways to explore the planets. UNESCO Courier 19:20-4 O '66
Personality of the month. A. Hamilton. il pors Sci Digest 59:12-17 Mr '66
PICKETING
Right to replace; inept handling of New York transit strike. H. Hazlitt. Newsweek 67:74 Ja 31 '66
PICKETT, S. M. and others
Lobster hemocyanin; properties of the minimum functional subunit and of aggregates. bibliog Science 151:1005-7 F 25 '66
PICKLES and relishes
How to pickle perfectly; with recipes. il Redbook 127:102-3+ S '66
September's the time to make old-fashioned dill pickles; with recipe. il Sunset 137:150 S '66
Treasure trove of gifts to make; with recipes. il Ladies Home J 83:78-9+ D '66
PICKREL, Paul
New books. Harper 232:98-100 Je '66
PICKUP trucks. See Motor trucks
PICNIC baskets, boxes, etc.
Picnic in style. J. Gillies. il Farm J 90:102 My '66
PICNICS
At this easy-going Mexican picnic you eat tacos with your fingers. il Sunset 136:154-5 Je '66
Early start, then breakfast on the road. il Sunset 136:188-9 My '66
Low-cal picnic. il Mlle 63:138-9 My '66
October is autumn's picnic month; with recipes. il Sunset 137:178-9 O '66
Open season for entertaining; lavish picnic; with recipes. il McCalls 93:110-11+ My '66
Safety tips for picnickers. il Good H 162:183 Je '66
See also
Clambakes
PICO, Fernando A.
Problem with non-Puerto Ricans. America 115:114-15 Jl 30 '66
PICTORIAL humor. See Humor, Pictorial
PICTORIAL maps. See Maps, Pictorial
PICTURE books
Albert Skira's reflections on making and publishing art books. Pub W 190:108 Ag 1 '66
Eisie does a book; interview, ed. by J. Deschin. A. Eisenstaedt; B. Holme. il Pop Phot 59:28+ D '66
Near 1¢ life. W. Ting. il Art N 65:38-9+ My '66
PICTURE books for children
Artist and the picture book; excerpts from address. E. Mathiesen. il Horn Bk 42:93-7 F '66
Ezra Jack Keats on collage as an illustrative medium. E. J. Keats. il Pub W 189: 94-5 Ap 4 '66
Profiles; M. Sendak. N. Hentoff. New Yorker 41:39-40+ Ja 22 '66
See also
Caldecott medal
PICTURE books for the blind. See Blind, Books for the

PICTURE collections
See also
Photographs—Collectors and collecting
PICTURE frames
Creative ways to mat pictures. il Parents Mag 41:84 Jl '66
Picture framing is fun. B. G. Wadsworth. il Parents Mag 41:90 F '66
Restoring a plaster frame. il Sunset 136:133-4 Mr '66
PICTURE of success; story. See Soman, F. J.
PICTURE tubes. See Television receiving apparatus—Picture tubes
PICTURED ROCKS NATIONAL LAKESHORE
Park system expands. Nat Parks Mag 40:18 D '66
PICTURES
Pick your picture; wild flowers into wall flowers. R. Kells. il Seventeen 26:120 Ja '67
Framing
See Picture frames
PICTURES, Glass. See Glass painting and staining
PICTURES, Hanging of
Decorating wrongs made right; picture groupings. il Bet Hom & Gard 44:40 Ap '66
Kathleen Haven on hanging picture shows; interview, ed. by J. Deschin. K. Haven. il Pop Phot 59:46+ S '66
Place to display pictures. il Sunset 137:112 N '66
PICTURES, Immoral. See Immoral literature and pictures
PICTURES, Photography of. See Photography of works of art
PICTURES, Study of. See Art—Appreciation
PICTURES, Theft of. See Art thefts
PICTURES of the year competition. See Photography—Competitions
PICTURES on glass. See Glass painting and staining
PIDGEON, R. T. and others
Uranium and lead isotopic stability in a metamict zircon under experimental hydrothermal conditions. bibliog Science 154:1538-40 D 23 '66
PIE
Boston cream pie. M. F. Williams. il Good H 162:190 Mr '66
Bride makes hot mince pie with rum sauce; with recipe. il McCalls 94:54 D '66
Bride makes lemon chiffon pie; with recipe. il McCalls 93:34 Je '66
Cantaloupe pie, there's a new idea! il Bet Hom & Gard 44:68+ Ag '66
Grape pies! il Bet Hom & Gard 44:85 S '66
How to make the pie on our cover. il Bet Hom & Gard 44:112 Je '66
Orange pie, meringue or chiffon. il Sunset 136:186 My '66
Pumpkin pie! B. Zache. il Bet Hom & Gard 44:88 N '66
Redbook's Christmas cookbook. il Redbook 128:103-6 D '66
Strawberry pie with a twist of lemon! with recipe. il Bet Hom & Gard 44:78-9 My '66
Susan makes cartwheel tuna pie. M. F. Williams. il Good H 162:206 Ap '66
Things your mother never taught you. il Ladies Home J 83:16 N '66
When is a chocolate chiffon pie perfect? with recipe. il Bet Hom & Gard 44:90 Jl '66
Yuletide pies. il Bet Hom & Gard 44:81-2 D '66
PIE in the morning; story. See Robinson, B.
PIEH, Robert J.
Outward bound! G. Caesar. il Seventeen 25:92-3+ Jl '66
PIEL, Gerard
Federal funds and science education; adaptation of statement, January 25, 1966. Bul Atomic Sci 22:10-15 My '66
PIEL brothers, Incorporated
Tap beer goes home for profit. il Bsns W p63-4 O 22 '66
PIELOU, E. C. and Arnason, A. N.
Correction to one of MacArthur's species-abundance formulas. bibliog Science 151:592 F 4 '66
PIÉRARD, André
Control of the activity of escherichia coli carbamoyl phosphate synthetase by antagonistic allosteric effectors. bibliog Science 154:1572-3 D 23 '66
PIERCE, Bill
Hanson, Rothschild, Pierce report. See issues of Popular photography
PIERCE, Edith Lovejoy
Slaughter of the innocents; poem. Christian Cent 83:1498 D 7 '66

PIERCE, John Robinson
Transmission of computer data; with biographical sketch. Sci Am 215:45, 144-50+ bibliog(p312) S '66
PIERCE, Ponchitta
Mission of Marian Wright. Ebony 21:94-7+ Je '66
Problems of the Negro woman intellectual. Ebony 21:144-9 Ag '66
What's not so funny about the funnies. Ebony 22:48-50+ N '66
PIERCE, Wendell H.
States and education; interview. por Sr Schol 89:sup21-2+ S 23 '66
about
Conant compact. Time 87:74+ Je 24 '66
William H. Pierce named to head states' Compact for education. Science 152:739 My 6 '66
PIERLEONI family
Popes from the ghetto, by J. Prinz. Review Sat R 49:37 Je 18 '66. A. H. Friedlander
PIERPOINT, Robert
(ed) See Moyers, B. White House rebuttal to Vietnam critics
PIERS, Maria W.
Preschoolers play favorites; excerpt from Growing up with children. Parents Mag 41:64-5+ N '66
PIERS
See also
Wharves
PIERSON, Robert M.
New ALA officer. ALA Bul 60:715-17 Jl '66
PIES, Vegetable. See Cookery—Vegetables
PIETY
Christian ethics amid pietistic culture-Protestantism. T. C. Oden. Christian Cent 83:525-6+ Ap 27 '66
Paul VI on piety. America 114:820 Je 11 '66
PIEZ, Gladys T.
IATUL: what it is and what it does. ALA Bul 60:712-13 Jl '66
Library technology. See issues of ALA bulletin
PIGEON; story. See Mountzoures, H. L.
PIGEON as food. See Cookery—Poultry
PIGEON shooting
Bandtail flyby. J. Mears. il Outdoor Life 138:46-7+ S '66
Pigeons vs. pints. E. Zern. il Field & S 71:64-5+ My '66
PIGEONS
Navigation of single homing pigeons; airplane observations by radio tracking. M. C. Michener and C. Walcott. bibliog il Science 154:410-13 O 21 '66
Pigeons everywhere, alas! reactions to San Francisco's bird purge. J. Fincher. il Life 61:149-50 D 9 '66
Stimulus control in pigeons based on proprioceptive stimuli from floor inclination. D. C. Riccio and others. bibliog il Science 153:434-6 Jl 22 '66
PIGMENTS
Maya blue: a clay-organic pigment? H. Van Olphen. Science 154:645-6 N 4 '66
PIGMENTS (biology)
Intracellular absorption difference spectrum of limulus extra-ocular photolabile pigment. G. C. Murray. bibliog il Science 154:1182-3 D 2 '66
Pigment protein complex from gonyaulax. D. J. Haidak and others. bibliog il Science 152:212-13 Ap 8 '66
Terminology of vertebrate melanin-containing cells: 1965. T. B. Fitzpatrick and others. bibliog Science 152:88-9 Ap 1 '66
See also
Porphyrins
PIGMIES. See Pygmies
PIGNATELLI, Luciana, princess
Pretty as a . . .; fashion show. por Newsweek 68:58 Ag 1 '66
Princess turns pro. il pors Life 61:70+ S 9 '66
PIGS. See Swine
PIGSKIN club. See Washington, D.C.—Clubs
PIGTAILED monkeys. See Monkeys
PIKE, Douglas
How strong is the NLF? Reporter 34:20-4 F 24 '66
PIKE, James Albert, bp
One clergyman's views on the death of God; excerpts from interview. U S News 60:57 Ap 18 '66
about
American bishop's search for a space-age God. C. S. Wren. il pors Look 30:25-9 F 22 '66

PIKE, James Albert, bp—about—*Continued*
Big event at Wheeling. Christian Cent 83: 1529 D 14 '66
Bishop on trial. por Time 88:69 O 21 '66
Bishop Pike and Advent in New York. M. Hyer. Christian Cent 84:28-30 Ja 4 '67
Bishop Pike's last diocesan battle. L. Kinsolving. Christian Cent 83:726+ Je 1 '66
Case of heresy? il por Newsweek 68:66 N 7 '66
Episcopal blunders. Christian Cent 83:1559-60 D 21 '66
Farewell from Pike. por Newsweek 68:99 S 19 '66
From pulpit to think tank. J. Cogley. il pors N Y Times Mag p 16-17+ Ag 14 '66
Heretic or prophet? il pors Time 88:56-8+ N 11 '66
In defense of heresy. A. Towne. Christian Cent 84:44-7 Ja 11 '67
Trial by rhetoric. por Time 88:53 N 4 '66
Worker-bishop. por Time 87:95 My 20 '66

PIKE, Marion
Letter from the publisher. B. M. Auer. il por Time 88:27 O 7 '66

PIKE, Otis G.
Excerpt from statement, February 23, 1966. Cong Digest 45:150 My '66

PIKE, Zebulon Montgomery
Pathfinder on the wrong path. J. A. Hawgood. por Sat R 49:33 S 3 '66

PIKE
New nurseries for pike; Fruitport, Mich. G. Laycock. il Field & S 70:10-12+ Mr '66

PIKE fishing
Jackfish country; Manitoba's Lake Vandekerckhove. E. A. Bauer. il Outdoor Life 138:50-2+ Ag '66
North of Nakina. W. W. Callender. il Outdoor Life 137:33-5+ My '66
Pike strike back; Ontario lake. J. O. Cartier. il Outdoor Life 137:48-9+ Je '66

PIKES PEAK race. See Automobile racing

PILCHER, K. S. See Craig, J. M. jt. auth.

PILCHER, Wayland
Corpus Christi's squad car lawyer. J. Biery. il Reporter 36:43-5 Ja 12 '67

PILEATED woodpeckers. See Woodpeckers

PILEGGI, Nicholas
Bugging the bedroom. Esquire 65:96-7+ My '66

PILES (disease) See Hemorrhoids

PILFERING. See Stealing

PILLOWS
For pillow-philes. il House & Gard 130:318-19 N '66
How to buy bed pillows. il Consumer Rep 31:114-16 Mr '66

PILLSBURY, Donald M.
How teen-age skin problems should be treated, and how they shouldn't. por(p34) Ladies Home J 84:42 Ja '67

PILLSBURY, Wilbur F.
Learn to leave your student alone! Bet Hom & Gard 44:20+ O '66

PILLSBURY company
Pillsbury finds a new mix that pays. il Bsns W p 176-8+ Je 25 '66

PILOT ejection seats, capsules etc. See Airplanes—Escape devices

PILOT lights, Electric. See Electric lamps

PILOT training. See Air pilots—Training

PILOT whales. See Whales

PILOTS and pilotage
Four basic piloting problems. J. D. Paris. il Motor B 117:72+ My '66
Piloting, seamanship and small boat handling, by C. F. Chapman. Review
    Motor B il 117:75+ F '66
Shoal water shambles. J. D. Williamson. il Motor B 117:120+ Mr '66

PILPEL, Harriet F.
But can you do that? See occasional issues of Publishers' weekly

PIMENTEL, George C.
Chemical lasers; with biographical sketch. Sci Am 214:20, 32-9 bibliog(p 140) Ap '66

PINBALL machines
Mother is a pinball machine; Sportland, Newark, N.J. T. Buckley. il Esquire 66:84-5+ Ag '66

PINCAS, Julius. See Pascin, J.

PINCH hitters. See Baseball players

PINCIAN gate; story. See Spencer, E.

PINCK, Dan C.
Contemporary ancestors. Reporter 34:58+ My 19 '66

PINCKNEY, Cathey, and Pinckney, Edward
Can I have one? Sat R 49:61-2 F 12 '66

PINCKNEY, Edward. See Pinckney, C. jt. auth.

PINCUS, Gregory
Control of conception by hormonal steroids; address, 1965. bibliog Science 153:493-500 Jl 29 '66

about
Three men who made a revolution. L. Lader. il por N Y Times Mag p8-9+ Ap 10 '66

PINCUS, Walter
Fight over money. Atlan 217:71-5 Ap '66
Mystery in the countinghouse. Atlan 218:71-5 O '66

PINE
Ancient bristlecone pine forest; Inyo national forest. R. W. Cermak. il Nat Parks Mag 40:4-8 Jl '66
Common pine, eighteen ways to improve its beauty. J. Hand. il Pop Sci 188:136-9+ Je '66
Incident in the Snake range; oldest bristlecone tree destroyed. Natur Hist 75:4-5 Je '66
Living ghosts of the Inyos. il Am For 72: 6-7 D '66
Portugal's pines; pinus pinaster, or maritime pine. C. E. Randall. il Am For 71:32-5+ O '65
World's oldest tree is found and felled; bristlecone pine. Nat Parks Mag 40:21 Ap '66

PINE MOUNTAIN wilderness (proposed) See Wilderness areas—Arizona

PINEAL body
Light-induced changes in pineal hydroxyindole-O-methyltransferase: abolition by lateral hypothalamic lesions. J. Axelrod and others. bibliog il Science 154:898-9 N 18 '66
LSD and the third eye; theories on the role of the pineal organ and its chemicals. J. N. Bleibtreu. Atlan 218:64-9 S '66

PINEAL gland. See Glands

PIÑEIRO, Armando Alonso. See Alonso Piñeiro, A.

PINES, Maya
Pressure cooker for four-year-old minds. Harper 234:55-61 Ja '67

PING, Charles J.
Idea of a Christian college. Sat R 49:90-1+ N 19 '66

PING pong. See Table tennis

PINGS, Vern M.
Crisis in research libraries. por Library J 91:3876-82 S 1 '66

PINILLA, Gustavo Rojas. See Rojas Pinilla, G.

PININFARINA, Battista
Homage to Pininfarina. D. Bartley. il Esquire 66:109-15 N '66

PINK bollworms. See Bollworms, Pink

PINKS
See also
Sweet williams

PINNEY, Roy
Camera cues. Parents Mag 41:14+ Ag '66
Sensible advice on cameras and equipment. Parents Mag 41:58-9+ My '66
Water fun for everyone. Parents Mag 41:44-6+ Jl '66

PINSON, Gerald. See Moyers, C. jt. auth.

PINSON, Penelope
Books for parents. See issues of Parents' magazine and better homemaking

PINTAURO, Joseph
Priest as many things including kings and surf buffs; poem. Commonweal 85:350 D 23 '66
This rain; poem. Commonweal 84:201 My 6 '66

PINTER, Harold
Homecoming. Criticism
    New Yorker 42:48 Ja 14 '67
    Newsweek il 69:93 Ja 16 '67
    Sat R 50:51 Ja 21 '67
    Time il 89:43 Ja 13 '67

PINUS aristata. See Pine

PINUS pinaster. See Pine

PIONE, Albert
Holiday bass. Field & S 71:42-3+ D '66

PIONEER library system. See Libraries—New York (state)

PIONEER life. See Frontier and pioneer life—United States

PIONEER probes. See Space probes

PIONEERING. See Frontier and pioneer life—United States

PIONEERS
Last of the mountain men; S. Hart in Big Five Mile Creek primitive area, Idaho. H. Peterson. il Sports Illus 25:84-8+ O 3 '66
See also
Frontier and pioneer life—United States

PIONS. See Mesons

PIPE fittings
Pipefitting job becomes threadless snap. il Bsns W p 134+ F 19 '66

PIPE laying
Dewatering by wells; solution to high-water-table problem on a sewer-construction project; Westport, Conn. J. E. Czel. jr. il Am City 81:80-1 Je '66
Speed with dependability; El Dorado Hills, Calif. il Am City 81:112-13 Ag '66

PIPE lines
And now, pipelines; R. Nader's new safety target. Newsweek 68:74 Jl 11 '66
Pipelines: coming of age. il Duns R 87:pt2 140-1+ My '66
See also
Gas, Natural—Pipe lines
Solids—Pipe lines

PIPER, Otto A.
In what direction? Christian Cent 83:306-7 Mr 9 '66

PIPER aircraft corporation
Boom town. il Flying 78:16+ Je '66

PIPER club. See Night clubs

PIPES, Plastic
Long-term tests on plastic pipe; park irrigation, San Antonio, Tex. R. L. Frazer and L. C. Schmidt. il Am City 81:84-5 Jl '66
Pipes of plastic. R. Yoshioka. il Sci N 90: 90-1+ Ag 6 '66

PIPKIN, J. E.
Use LP gas and save. Am City 81:88-9 Je '66

PIPPETT, Aileen
Prince was maid for a day. Sat R 49:38 Ap 9 '66
Unjustifiable violation. Sat R 49:30-1 Jl 16 '66

PIRANDELLO, Luigi
Right you are. Criticism
Nation 203:651 D 12 '66
New Repub 156:41-2 Ja 7 '67
Newsweek 68:96+ D 5 '66
Time 88:84 D 2 '66

PIRANESI, Giovanni Battista
Along the wayside of the past; memorials to law and power, victory and bloodshed; etchings. Life 60:38-9 Mr 11 '66

PIRATED editions. See Copyright—Unauthorized reprints

PIRATES (baseball) See Baseball clubs

PIRELLI, Leopoldo
How to insulate. por Time 87:100+ Ap 8 '66

PIRELLI group. See Italy—Industries

PIRIE, N. W.
Books. Sci Am 215:131-2+ Mr '66
Leaf protein as a human food. bibliog Science 152:1701-5 Je 24 '66

PIRONE, Thomas P. See Barnett, C. B. jr, jt. auth.

PISA
Campanile (leaning tower)
Tilt! J. Bryan, 3d. il Holiday 41:80-1+ Ja '67

PISAC, Peru
Speaking up for Pisac. L. Barry. il Pop Phot 59:50+ D '66

PISMO BEACH, Calif.
Pismo; long beach, the white dunes, the delicious clams. il Sunset 136:62-7 F '66

PISTOLETTO, Michelangelo
Talking of Michelangelo. J. Ashbery. il Art N 65:42-3+ Sum '66

PISTOLS
Colt model of 1911, automatic pistol .45 caliber. C. Worman. il Hobbies 71:122-3 Je '66
Deadly zip gun for the missile age; R. Meinhardt's miniature rockets and launchers. il Life 60:45-8 My 27 '66
Government expresses interest in small-arms rocket family; solid-propellant Gyrojet, Lancejet and Microjet projectiles. F. G. McGuire. il Tech W 18:34+ Je 13 '66
New England underhammer pistols. C. G. Worman. il Hobbies 71:126 S '66
Pepperbox pistol. W. R. Orbelo. il Hobbies 71:126-7 Ag '66
United States pistol model 1816. W. R. Orbelo. il Hobbies 71:125 Ap '66

PISTON engines. See Automobile engines

PISTON rings
Rings-a groovy subject. J. McFarland. il Hot Rod 19:60-3 O '66

PISTORIUS, Carl W. F. T.
Quenchable high-pressure polymorph of zinc selenate. bibliog Science 151:1003 F 25 '66

PITCHERS, Baseball. See Baseball players

PITCHFORD, Kenneth
Presences; poem. Yale R 55:390 Mr '66
La virginité sous le domino couleur d'invisible; poem. Sat R 49:44 My 14 '66

PITCHING. See Baseball

PITMAN, W. C. 3d, and Heirtzler, J. R.
Magnetic anomalies over the Pacific-Antarctic ridge. bibliog Science 154:1164-6+ D 2 '66

PITT, Patricia C.
Art and the emerging elementary curriculum. Sch Arts 65:25-6 F '66

PITTMAN, Jim
Carruthers have a fighter. G. Ronberg. il por Sports Illus 25:3 O 10 '66

PITTSBURGH

Crime
Pandemonium in Pittsburgh; convicts set out to goad judge into declaring mistrial. il Time 88:38 D 23 '66

Description
Personal business; Pittsburgh: bragging once again. Bsns W p 161 O 29 '66

Education
Council on higher education. Sch & Soc 94:444 D 10 '66
Morning devotional period in schools. Sch & Soc 94:145 My 19 '66
Pittsburgh philosophy; Sydney P. Marland's plans. Time 87:69-70 Mr 4 '66
Pittsburgh school story: a city's quest for racial equality. B. Fielding. il NEA J 55: 42-4 My '66
Pittsburgh: the virtues of candor. P. Schrag. il Sat R 49:82-4+ N 19 '66
See also
Schools, Experimental

Education, Board of
Pittsburgh: the virtues of candor. P. Schrag. il Sat R 49:82-4+ N 19 '66

Libraries
See also
Carnegie library of Pittsburgh

Music
Music where the rivers meet; Pittsburgh report. R. Croan. Hi Fi 16:152-3 My '66
Pittsburgh. R. J. Croan. Opera N 30:35 Ap 2 '66
See also
Pittsburgh opera company

Negroes
Pittsburgh school story: a city's quest for racial equality. B. Fielding. il NEA J 55: 42-4 My '66

School board
See Pittsburgh—Education, Board of

Theater
Tarnish on the golden triangle? Playhouse's financial crisis. H. Hewes. Sat R 49:28 D 17 '66
[Theatre across America] J. Novick. Nation 202:690-2 Je 6 '66
Theatre; production of Midsummer night's dream at Playhouse. T. Lewis. America 115:786 D 10 '66

Transportation
Transit expressway promises relief for medium-density cities. il Am City 81:141-2+ F '66

PITTSBURGH diocese. See Catholic church—Dioceses

PITTSBURGH opera company
Pittsburgh. R. J. Croan. Opera N 30:30 F 19 '66
Pittsburgh: production of Verdi's Otello. R. Croan. Opera N 31:31 Ja 21 '67

PITTSBURGH Pirates (baseball) See Baseball clubs

PITTSBURGH steel company
Better diet for oxygen steelmakers; more scrap, less pig iron. Bsns W p 178 Je 18 '66

PITTSBURGH Steelers (football club) See Football clubs

PITTSBURGH symphony orchestra
Musical events; concert Carnegie Hall. W. Sargeant. New Yorker 42:127-8 N 26 '66

PITTSBURGH. University
Editing text electronically; Computation and data processing center. C. R. T. Bacon. il Pub W 190:92-4 Jl 4 '66
New pilot for Pitt. Time 89:65 Ja 20 '67
Pilot for Pitt: W. W. Posvar appointed chancellor. Newsweek 69:64 Ja 23 '67

PITTSBURGH. University—*Continued*
Pittsburgh: the rocky road to academic excellence. D. S. Greenberg. il Science 151: 549-52, 658-62, 799-801 F 4-18 '66
Rich, risky life of a university trustee. R. Sheehan. il Fortune 75:124-7+ Ja '67

PITUITARY body
Retention of the biological potency of human pituitary growth hormone after reduction and carbamidomethylation. J. S. Dixon and C. H. Li. bibliog il Science 154:785-6 N 11 '66
See also
Gonadotropin

PITUITARY cancer. See Cancer

PITUITARY hormones. See Hormones

PITZ, Henry C.
Alan E. Cober: artist of the year '65. Am Artist 30:36-41+ Je '66
Brandywine tradition. Am Artist 30:43-9+ D '66
Resurgence of Robert Riggs. Am Artist 30: 50-5+ My '66

PIUS XII, pope
Latest charges against Pius XII. R. A. Graham. America 114:733-6 My 21 '66
One pope, 860,000 Jews. Newsweek 67:68 My 9 '66
Pius' silence. il Time 87:63 Je 3 '66
Pius XII and the Third Reich; excerpts. ed. by R. Leiber. S. Friedländer. il por Look 30:36-8+ My 17 '66
Was silence the only solution? G. Lewy. Sat R 49:26-7 My 21 '66

PIVEN, Frances Fox, and Cloward, R. A.
Desegregated housing. New Repub 155:17-22 D 17 '66
—See Cloward, R. A. jt. auth.

PIVER, Arthur
Trimaran in a tempest. il Motor B 118:30-1+ Ag '66

PIVIK, Terry, and Foulkes, David
Dream deprivation: effects on dream content. bibliog Science 153:1382-4 S 9 '66

PIZER, Vernon
Man with 8000 miracles. Read Digest 88:112-16 F '66

PIZZA. See Cookery, Italian

PLACEMENT bureaus. See Employment agencies

PLACENTA
Fascinating story of life before birth. M. Liley and B. Day. il Parents Mag 41:62-3+ O '66

PLACES of retirement. See Retirement, Places of

PLACHY, Sylvia
Is this a portrait? Pop Phot 58:92-3 My '66

PLAGUE
Plague and war. 1966. D. Lyle. il Esquire 66:158-63+ S '66
Plague on both houses; bubonic plague in Vietnam. Time 88:61 S 2 '66
Prairie dogs can cause bubonic plague. Sci N 90:57 Jl 23 '66

PLAIN brown bird; story. See Wilson, M.

PLAIN dealer. See Cleveland plain dealer

PLAINFIELD, N.J.
Gardens
Tribute garden. Mrs G. Smith. il Horticulture 44:49 O '66

PLAINS
Nature note; flood plains. Sci N 90:414 N 19 '66

PLAINS Indians. See Indians of North America

PLANARIANS
Unconditioned response to electric shock; mechanism in planarians. J. B. Best and E. Elshtain. bibliog il Science 151:707-9 F 11 '66

PLANCHÉITE. See Copper silicates

PLANCK'S law. See Quantum theory

PLANÇON, Pol
Odor of sanctity. R. D. Daniels. por Opera N 30:26-7 F 12 '66

PLANETARIUMS
Mark Smith planetarium in Georgia. A. B. Domingos, jr. il Sky & Tel 32:142-3 S '66
New skies for a new city; Dow planetarium, Montreal. D. D. Davis. il Sky & Tel 31:196-8 Ap '66
Planetarium notes. Sky & Tel 32:148-51 S '66
Want a planetarium? Adler planetarium and astronomical museum. R. I. Johnson. bibliog il Parks & Rec 1:831-3+ O '66

PLANETS
Astronomy. J. Stokley. See issues of Science news
New ways to explore the planets. W. H. Pickering. il UNESCO Courier 19:20-4 O '66

Sun, moon, and planets this month. See issues of Sky and telescope
See also
Interplanetary communication
Life on other planets
Orbits
Satellites
also names of planets, e.g. Mars (planet)

Radiation
See also
Jupiter (planet)—Radiation

Rotation
Rotation of the planet Mercury. W. H. Jefferys. bibliog Science 152:201 Ap 8 '66
See also
Jupiter (planet)—Rotation

PLANETS, Photography of. See Astronomical photography

PLANING hulls. See Hydrofoils

PLANING machines
See also
Shapers

PLANING mills
Wages and hours
Wages in paint, candy, and southern sawmill industries. il Mo Labor R 89:885-6 Ag '66

PLANKTON
See also
Diatoms

PLANNED parenthood. See Birth control

PLANNING
See also
Economic planning

PLANNING, Educational. See Educational planning

PLANNING, Industrial. See Industrial management and organization

PLANNING of cities. See City planning

PLANT, Elizabeth Davenport
Final freedom. Vogue 147:40 Je '66

PLANT, Richard
Where dreams ended, terror began. Sat R 49:29 My 21 '66

PLANT boxes. See Flower boxes, planters, etc.

PLANT catalogs. See Catalogs, Seed and plant

PLANT cells and tissues
Cell wall of melampyrum lineare seed: carbohydrate components. E. J. C. Curtis and J. E. Cantlon. bibliog il Science 151:580-1 F 4 '66
Cylindrical inclusions in the cytoplasm of leaf cells infected with tobacco etch virus. J. R. Edwardson. bibliog il Science 153:883-4 Ag 19 '66
Intracellular localization of growth hormones in plants. S. H. Liao and R. H. Hamilton. bibliog il Science 151:822-4 F 18 '66
Intranuclear microtubules. O. Behnke and A. Forer. bibliog il Science 153:1536-7 S 23 '66
Mitotic waves in laticifers of euphorbia marginata. P. Mahlberg and P. Sabharwal. bibliog il Science 152:518-19 Ap 22 '66
Plasmadesmata between hyphal cells of geotrichum candidum. B. T. Kirk and J. B. Sinclair. bibliog il Science 153:1646 S 30 '66
Proliferation of cells in the central cylinder of the reduced mutant in lanceolate tomato. J. L. Caruso and E. G. Cutter. bibliog il Science 154:1021-3 N 25 '66
Protoplasts: preparation from higher plants. A. W. Ruesink and K. V. Thimann. bibliog il Science 154:280-1 O 14 '66
Structure and organization of the living mitotic spindle of haemanthus endosperm. A. Bajer and R. D. Allen. bibliog il Science 151:572-4 F 4 '66

Culture
Single cells, coconut milk, and embryogenesis in vitro. W. Halperin. bibliog il Science 153:1287-8 S 9 '66

PLANT communities
Vegetation: identification of typal communities. R. Daubenmire. bibliog il Science 151: 291-8 Ja 21 '66; Discussion. 152:546-7 Ap 22 '66

PLANT cuttings. See Plant propagation

PLANT diseases. See Plants—Diseases and pests

PLANT distribution. See Geographical distribution of animals and plants

PLANT equipment. See Factories—Equipment

PLANT evolution. See Evolution

PLANT growth. See Growth (plants)

PLANT growth hormones. See Growth promoting substances (plants)

PLANT growth regulators. See Growth inhibiting substances (plants); Growth promoting substances (plants)
PLANT holders. See Flower boxes, planters, etc.
PLANT hormones. See Hormones, Plant
PLANT labels
Give a gardener some labels. il Sunset 137:192 D '66
PLANT lice
It's a happy sight to see ladybugs lunching away on aphids. il Sunset 136:108-9 Mr '66
Nature note; pine-sucking aphids. Sci N 90:94 Ag 6 '66
Stylet-borne virus: active probing by aphids not required for acquisition. C. B. Barnett, jr. and T. P. Pirone. bibliog il Science 154:291 O 14 '66
PLANT location. See Location in business and industry
PLANT lore
See also
Trees in religion, folklore, etc.
PLANT names. See Botany—Nomenclature
PLANT patents
Plant patents; Townsend-Purnell act. B. Black. Horticulture 44:26-8 Ag '66
PLANT pathology. See Plants—Diseases and pests
PLANT propagation
Fuchsia cuttings in plastic bags. il Sunset 136:252 My '66
Gardens for free; bathe simple cuttings in electrically controlled mist. K. Warner. il Pop Mech 125:104-6 Je '66
How to grow plants from cuttings. il Good H 162:170 My '66
Root cuttings in a plastic bag. G. Logsdon. il Farm J 90:76 Mr '66
Take a leaf; rooting an African violet. K. M. Bova. il Flower Grower 53:26+ N '66
Time to start pansies from seed. C. Ferguson. il Flower Grower 53:40 Jl '66
See also
Seeds
PLANT proteins
Leaf protein as a human food. N. W. Pirie. bibliog il Science 152:1701-5 Je 24 '66
PLANT research. See Botanical research
PLANTAIN lilies
Perennial that flowers in shade. M. Lillie. Flower Grower 53:38 D '66
PLANTERS (farm machines)
Faster planting on fertilized ridges. il Farm J 90:42-5 Mr '66
Planter hitches that save trips. C. F. Marley. il Farm J 90:66B Ap '66
See also
Seeding machinery
PLANTERS (flower boxes) See Flower boxes, planters, etc.
PLANTIN-Moretus museum, Antwerp
Plantin-Moretus museum in Antwerp. H. R. Lottman. il Pub W 190:78-9+ S 5 '66
PLANTING. See Gardening; Landscape gardening; Plants, Space arrangement of; Shrubs—Planting; Transplanting
PLANTING fields arboretum, Oyster Bay. See New York state university—Agricultural and technical institute at Farmingdale, Long Island
PLANTING of corn. See Corn—Seeding
PLANTS
Best plants; symposium. See occasional issues of Flower grower. the home garden
Caring for your gift plants. Sunset 138:144 Ja '67
[Month] in your garden. See issues of Sunset
Plants that solve problem spots. il Flower Grower 53:40-1 Ap '66
They're all handsome, and all space-savers. Sunset 136:250 Mr '66
This is my favorite. See issues of Popular gardening & living outdoors
Try these new plants for 1966. il Horticulture 44:38-40+ F '66
See also
Annuals (plants)
Biennials (plants)
Bulbs
Flowers
Garden borders
Gardening
Herbs
House plants
Nursery stock

All America selections
All-America roses for 1967. Flower Grower 53:23 Jl '66
All-America winners 1966. il Pop Gard 17:57 Mr '66
Here come golden jubilee, San Francisco, and foxy; 1967 All-America selections. il Sunset 138:125 Ja '67

New plants for your garden. il Horticulture 45:18-21+ Ja '67
Roses 1967. il Horticulture 44:32-3 Jl '66

Diseases and pests
H&G's 1966 guide to plant protection. C. Westcott. House & Gard 129:94-7+ Ap '66
If the deer are breakfasting on your favorite garden plants; advise. il Sunset 137:74-7 S '66
Plant pathology and human welfare. A. J. Riker. bibliog il Science 152:1027-32 My 20 '66
Protection from the birds. il Sunset 137:274 O '66
Ways to protect gardens for animals. il Good H 162:182 Je '66
See also
Fungi
Nematodes
Powdery mildew

Drought resistance
Drought, and what to do about it. W. A. Mitcheltree. il Horticulture 44:36-7 Je '66

Electrophysiology
See Electrophysiology of plants

Evolution
Chromosomal variation and evolution; address, December 30, 1965. G. L. Stebbins. bibliog il Science 152:1463-9 Je 10 '66

Hardiness
Lack of hardiness from too rapid growth. P. H. Wright. Horticulture 45:15 Ja '67

Metabolism
Excretion and heartwood formation in living trees. C. M. Stewart. bibliog il Science 153:1068-74 S 2 '66
Respiration of a forest measured by carbon dioxide accumulation during temperature inversions. G. M. Woodwell and W. R. Dykeman. bibliog il Science 154:1031-4 N 25 '66
Voodoo lily. B. J. D. Meeuse. il Sci Am 215:80-8 Jl '66

Mineral content
Tabashir: an opal of plant origin. L. H. P. Jones and others. bibliog il Science 151:464-6 Ja 28 '66

Nutrition
When leaves turn a sickly yellow. Sunset 137:136 Ag '66

Odors
See Odors

Physiology
See Botany—Physiology

Pruning
See Pruning

Respiration
Respiration of a forest measured by carbon dioxide accumulation during temperature inversions. G. M. Woodwell and W. R. Dykeman. bibliog il Science 154:1031-4 N 25 '66
Respiratory control: loss in mitochondria from diseased plants. H. Wheeler and P. J. Hanchey. bibliog il Science 154:1569-71 D 23 '66

Species
See Species

Translocation
Auxin effects on the mobility of kinetin in the plant. A. K. Seth and others. bibliog il Science 151:587-8 F 4 '66
Cherries and apples handy source of water. Sci N 90:218 S 24 '66
Excretion and heartwood formation in living trees. C. M. Stewart. bibliog il Science 153:1068-74 S 2 '66
Phosphate uptake in an obligately marine fungus: a specific requirement for sodium. P. A. Siegenthaler and others. bibliog il Science 155:93-4 Ja 6 '67

Transpiration
Calibration of β gauges for determining leaf water status. P. G. Jarvis and R. O. Slatyer. bibliog il Science 153:78-9 Jl 1 '66
Convection plumes from ulmus americana. L. E. B. Peterson and A. W. H. Damman. discussion. Science 149:764; 150:783, 1629; 152:387 Ag 13, N 5, D 17 '65, Ap 15 '66

PLANTS—Transpiration—*Continued*
Gaseous-diffusion porometer for continuous measurement of diffusive resistance of leaves. R. O. Slatyer and P. G. Jarvis. bibliog il Science 151:574-6 F 4 '66
Isopiestic technique: measurement of accurate leaf water potentials. J. S. Boyer. bibliog il Science 154:1459-60 D 16 '66
Relative turgidity of leaves: temperature effects in measurement. B. D. Millar. bibliog il Science 154:512-13 O 28 '66
Root pressure and leaf water potential. H. D. Barrs. bibliog il Science 152:1266-8 My 27 '66

Water requirements
Little water and little work. il Sunset 137: 226-7 N '66

PLANTS, Aquatic. See Aquatic plants

PLANTS, Artificial
I remember mama nature. M. Bennett. Atlan 217:119-20 F '66

PLANTS, Edible
He finds food in the oddest places; with excerpts from Stalking the healthful herbs. il Life 61:45-6 S 23 '66
Soloist survives on a bouillabaisse of seaweeds and fantasies of candy; testing E. Gibbons' theories. S. Davis. il Life 61:48-9 S 23 '66

PLANTS, Effect of air pollution on
Grapes, beans developed to resist air pollution. Sci N 89:395 My 21 '66

PLANTS, Effect of drought on. See Plants—Drought resistance

PLANTS, Effect of light on
Brassica campestris L.: floral induction by one long day. D. J. C. Friend and V. A. Helson. bibliog il Science 153:1115-16 S 2 '66
Light responses of phycomyces. E. S. Castle. bibliog il Science 154:1416-20 D 16 '66
Photoperiodism in lemna: reversal of night-interruption depends on color of the main photoperiod. W. S. Hillman. bibliog il Science 154:1360-2 D 9 '66

PLANTS, Effect of radiation on
Better forests from blue ribbon trees: Rhinelander station. Wis. E. S. Hurd. il Am For 72:12-14+ Je '66

PLANTS, Effect of temperature on
Light reaction in green plant photosynthesis: a method of study. W. Arnold. bibliog il Science 154:1046-9 N 25 '66

PLANTS, Effect of ultrasonic waves on
Amateur scientist: stimulating plant growth with ultrasonic vibrations. E. Horowitz. il Sci Am 215:100-2 Ag '66

PLANTS, Flowering of
Auxin-induced ethylene formation: its relation to flowering in the pineapple. S. P. Burg and E. A. Burg. bibliog il Science 152:1269 My 27 '66
Photoperiodism in lemna: reversal of night-interruption depends on color of the main photoperiod. W. S. Hillman. bibliog il Science 154:1360-2 D 9 '66

PLANTS, Food
Among the plants men live by; proposals for increasing research on food plants; excerpt from report. K. Thimann. Sat R 50: 118-20 Ja 7 '67
Japanese food plants. S. N. Swain. il Horticulture 44:16-19 Jl '66
Leaf protein as a human food. N. W. Pirie. bibliog il Science 152:1701-5 Je 24 '66
Plant pathology and human welfare. A. J. Riker. bibliog il Science 152:1027-32 My 20 '66

PLANTS, Fossil. See Paleobotany

PLANTS, Geographical distribution of. See Geographical distribution of animals and plants

PLANTS, Indoor. See House plants

PLANTS, Marsh. See Marshes

PLANTS, Medicinal. See Botany. Medical

PLANTS, Ornamental
How to plant in a narrow space. il Pop Gard 17:55 My '66
In living plants, the look of sculpture. C. Deame. il House & Gard 130:126-7+ Ag '66
Plants in offices. K. Berggrav. il Horticulture 44:32-5+ F '66
  See also
Columnea

PLANTS, Poisonous. See Poisonous plants

PLANTS, Potted
Add color with containers. il Pop Gard 17:28-31 Mr '66
Basket bounty to deck a summer garden. il House & Gard 129:134-5 Je '66
Best three plants for hanging baskets and how to grow them. il House & Gard 129: **172-4 Je '66**

Brave and bold. il Sunset 136:236-7 Je '66
Growing ferns in hanging wire baskets. il Sunset 136:246 Ap '66
Plants in offices. K. Berggrav. il Horticulture 44:32-5+ F '66
  See also
Flower boxes, planters, etc.
House plants

PLANTS, Protection of
Journey into winter. B. Black. Pop Gard 17:65+ D '66
Winter protection, why? il Flower Grower 53:28-30 D '66
  See also
Frost protection
Mulching

PLANTS, Rock garden
Choice small bulbs. R. Murfitt. il Horticulture 44:16-17+ S '66
  See also
Gardens, Rock

PLANTS, Sex in
Sex conversion in a male vitis vinifera L. by a kinin. S. S. Negi and H. P. Olmo. bibliog il Science 152:1624 Je 17 '66
  See also
Fungi, Sex in

PLANTS, Space arrangement of
How I decided to go narrow row, even on a rented farm; ed. by W. J. Fletcher. L. Jelm. il Suc Farm 64:46-7+ Mr '66
Narrow rows pay off; corn growers in Illinois. L. E. Zeman and R. J. Reiman. il Suc Farm 64:36-7+ Ap '66
Narrow rows: will it be thirty-inches or twenty-inches. D. Seim. il Farm J 90:40-1+ F '66
Switch to narrow-row corn? when to change. B. Brantley and P. B. Jones. il Suc Farm 64:48-9+ F '66
Twin-row corn makes more silage; ed. by R. D. Wennblom. il Farm J 90:30-1+ Je '66
What farm managers think about narrow row corn; symposium, ed. by H. D. Guither. Farm J 90:50V S '66
Why not solid-stand soybeans? D. Hagen. il Farm J 90:32-3+ My '66

PLANTS, Training of
Espaliers. J. A. Eaton. il House & Gard 130:268-71+ N '66

PLANTS in house decoration
How to dress up your doorway. il Pop Gard 17:36-9 Ag '66

PLAQUES, plaquettes
Interesting hobby: pictures in plaster. D. Rustebakke. il Farm J 90:120 Ap '66
Plaques: as easy as icing a cake! M. Garrity. il Bet Hom & Gard 44:52 N '66

PLASMA (ionized gases)
Many UFOs are identified as plasmas. P. J. Klass. il Aviation W 85:54-5+ O 3 '66
Plasma theory may explain many UFOs. P. J. Klass. il Aviation W 85:48-50+ Ag 22 '66; Discussion. 85:130 O 10 '66
Progress toward fusion power. T. K. Fowler and R. F. Post. il Sci Am 215:21-31 bibliog (p 154) D '66
Scientific explanation for the UFOs? J. Lear. il Sat R 49:67-9 O 1 '66
UCLA to build satellite for plasma study. Sci N 90:339 O 22 '66

PLASMA membranes
Phospholipids of bacteria with extensive intracytoplasmic membranes. P. O. Hagen and others. bibliog il Science 151:1543-4 Mr 25 '66
Surface area of human erythrocyte lipids: reinvestigation of experiments on plasma membrane. R. S. Bar and others. bibliog il Science 153:1010-12 Ag 26 '66

PLASMA rocket engines. See Rocket engines

PLASMODESMATA. See Plant cells and tissues

PLASMODIUM (parasite)
Malaria: infection (plasmodium lophurae) changes in free amino acids. I. W. Sherman and J. B. Mudd. bibliog il Science 154:287-9 O 14 '66
Plasma replacement for in vitro culture of plasmodium knowlesi. Q. M. Geiman and others. bibliog il Science 153:1129-30 S 2 '66

PLASMODIUM Infection. See Malaria

PLASMONIC waves. See Radio waves

PLASTER board. See Wallboard

PLASTER casts
So I went up to see Mae West. P. Gowland. il Pop Phot 59:32+ Jl '66

PLASTIC artificial organs. See Prosthesis

PLASTIC arts school, Cuba. See Art schools

PLASTIC coating
New skins for anything and everything: fluidized bed coating. R. Gannon. il Pop Mech 125:112-15+ Ap '66

PLASTIC dinnerware. See Tableware. Plastic
PLASTIC dome. See Domes
PLASTIC drawers. See Drawers
PLASTIC hearts. See Heart, Artificial
PLASTIC houses. See Houses, Plastic
PLASTIC milk bottles. See Milk bottles
PLASTIC molds. See Molds (for casting)
PLASTIC mulch. See Mulching
PLASTIC pipes. See Pipes, Plastic
PLASTIC sewer pipes. See Sewer pipes
PLASTIC surgery. See Surgery, Plastic
PLASTIC tableware. See Tableware. Plastic
PLASTIC teeth. See Teeth, Artificial
PLASTIC tents. See Tents
PLASTICS
    Contact lenses get a softer touch; hydron,
        a soft plastic developed in Czechoslovakia.
        il Bsns W p 147-8 Ap 30 '66
    Low-cost plastic greenhouses. il Farm J 90:
        69 Mr '66
    Plastic: look what it's doing to home build-
        ing. Bet Hom & Gard 44:126-31 S; 30+ O
        '66
    Why Sedalia selected plastic: media for the
        trickling filters. G. C. Higgins. bibliog il
        Am City 81:112-13+ S '66

Molding
    Plastics mold new auto uses. il Bsns W p 180
        Je 18 '66
PLASTICS, Reinforced
    NASA, AF funding Avco multidirectional
        reinforced plastics. J. F. Judge. il Tech W
        19:28-9 O 31 '66
PLATES (dishes) See Tableware
PLATES (photography) See Photography—
    Plates
PLATES, Printing. See Printing plates
PLATFORM boats. See Boats and boating
PLATFORMS, Mobile. See Artificial islands
PLATFORMS, Political
    Cooling the convention; suggest informal
        platform-drafting convention. Time 87:29A
        Mr 18 '66
    Platform, anyone? W. F. Buckley, jr. Nat R
        18:455 My 17 '66
    Story of two letters: effect on Romney
        chances; with letter by G. W. Romney,
        reply by B. M. Goldwater, and with ex-
        cerpts from other documents. il U S News
        61:62-70 D 19 '66
PLATH, Sylvia
    Daddy; poem. Time 87:118 Je 10 '66
    Inhabited by a cry: last poetry of Sylvia
        Plath. P. Davison. por Atlan 218:76-7
        Ag '66
        about
    Blood jet is poetry. il pors Time 87:118+
        Je 10 '66
    Russian roulette. il por Newsweek 67:109A+
        Je 20 '66
    Warnings from the grave. S. Spender. New
        Repub 154:23+ Je 18 '66
PLATING
        See also
    Chromium plating
    Metal coating
PLATO
    Plato's Republic. K. Rexroth. Sat R 49:33
        F 19 '66
PLATON, Nikolas
    Reporter at large. J. Alsop. New Yorker 42:
        34-8+ Ag 13 '66
PLATON, Sosso
    Reporter at large. J. Alsop. New Yorker 42:
        34-8+ Ag 13 '66
PLATT, Dorothy B. See Goldstein, L. jt.
    auth.
PLATT, James J.
    Tokyo trout; fisherman abroad. pors Outdoor
        Life 139:38-41+ Ja '67
PLATT, John R.
    Changing human nature; excerpts from Step
        to man. Science 152:1573 Je 17 '66
    Diversity; excerpts from address. Science
        154:1132-9 D 2 '66
    —See Rich, A. jt. auth.
PLATT, Marc
    How high the corn at Radio City. W. Como.
        il pors Dance Mag 40:36-41 Ag '66
PLATT, Rutherford
    My five favorite trees. por Am For 72:10-12+
        My '66
    Unearthly world at the bottom of the sea.
        Read Digest 89:241-2+ O '66
PLATYCODON. See Balloonflowers

PLAUT, Thomas
    You can't send a girl there! Mlle 63:34-6 Jl '66
PLAUT, Walter Newman
    Sales & marketing. J. F. Olesky. por Duns R
        87:55-7 Ja '66
PLAY
        See also
    Education of children
    Toys
PLAY accidents. See Accidents
PLAY apparatus. See Playgrounds—Equipment
PLAY houses. See Playhouses
PLAY of Daniel. See Drama, Medieval
PLAY of Herod. See Drama, Medieval
PLAY pens. See Furniture, Childrens
PLAY production. See Theatrical production
PLAY writing. See Drama—Technique
PLAYBOY (periodical)
    Hugh Hefner: I am in the center of the
        world; interview, ed. by O. Fallaci. H. Hef-
        ner. il Look 31:54-7 Ja 10 '67
    Spoofproof? Harvard Lampoon's parody. il
        Newsweek 68:102+ S 19 '66
    Turning green; Playboy's and Esquire's
        Christmas issues. R. A. Schroth. America
        115:777 D 10 '66
PLAYBOY clubs. See Night clubs
PLAYER, Gary
    Hit it my way. Sports Illus 24:32-41 Mr 21 '66
        about
    Gary and his beloved country. J. Underwood.
        il pors Sports Illus 24:82-6+ My 23 '66
    Is the Masters fixed? G. S. Brown. il pors
        Sports Illus 24:62-3 Ap 4 '66
    Some thin tempers among friendly enemies.
        A. Wright. il Sports Illus 25:74-6 O 17 '66
    Sporting scene. A. Cooke. New Yorker 42:
        171-2+ N 5 '66
PLAYER piano
    Old piano roll man. il Ebony 21:125-6+
        My '66
PLAYER piano rolls
    Recordings from piano rolls: valid history,
        rewarding artistry. H. Goldsmith. il Hi Fi
        16:82+ D '66
PLAYERS; story. See Rogin, G.
PLAYGROUND activities
    On the playground. M. Polsky. il Parks &
        Rec 1:322 Ap '66
PLAYGROUND apparatus. See Playgrounds—
    Equipment
PLAYGROUNDS
    Parks and recreation. See issues of Amer-
        ican city
        See also
    Parks
    School grounds
        also subhead Parks and playgrounds un-
        der names of cities, e.g. San Francisco—
        Parks and playgrounds

Equipment
    Community action: a children's dragon
        comes to life; Mercer Island woods,
        Washington. il Sunset 137:72-3 S '66
    Of the wayward bus, the tattered tarp, and
        other surplus things; playground equipment
        at Stephen F. Austin elementary school
        in San Angelo, Tex. L. Lewis. il Am Ed 2:
        1-3 S '66
    Playscape prototypes; plastics in playground
        equipment. il Parks & Rec 1:973 D '66
    Putting the play in playgrounds. C. L. Mee,
        jr. il N Y Times Mag p 112+ N 6 '66
        See also
    Swings
PLAYGROUNDS, Home

Equipment
    Captive copter you can build right in your
        own back yard. R. L. Brown and H. Wal-
        ton. il Pop Sci 188:148-53 Je '66
        See also
    Playhouses
PLAYGROUNDS, School. See School grounds
PLAYHOUSES
    A is for A-frame, and a lot of fun. il Bet
        Hom & Gard 44:126 My '66
    Another tree house without a tree. il Sunset
        136:156 My '66
    Foldaway fairy-tale playhouses. il House &
        Gard 130:186-7+ D '66
    Here's a playhouse that folds. R. A. Henry,
        jr. il Pop Gard 17:78-9 My '66

PODHORETZ, Norman
Passion for ideas. por Time 87:56+ My 20 '66

POE, Edgar Allan, awards. See Mystery writers of America

POEL, W. E.
Pituitary tumors in mice after prolonged feeding of synthetic progestins. bibliog Science 154:402-3 O 21 '66

POETIC inspiration. See Inspiration

POETICS
American outsider; The sixties magazine and books of the Sixties press. P. Zweig. Nation 203:517-19 N 14 '66
How not to rate a poet. H. Carruth. Sat R 49:21+ F 12 '66
On English and American poetry. S. Spender. Sat R 49:19-20+ Ap 23 '66
On Milton's poetry. R. Fraser. Yale R 56: 172-96 D '66
Poets of reality, by J. H. Miller. Review Nation 202:659-61 My 30 '66. E. W. Said
Poet's workshop. D. Holmes. Writer 79:25-8 My; 24-7+ Jl; 21-4 S; 27-30 N '66
Poet's workshop (cont) R. Stone. Writer 79: 24-6+ Mr '66
Problems and delights of revision. M. Sarton. Writer 79:20-2 D '66
  See also
Versification

POETRY
Double dactyl; with examples of poems. A. Hecht. Esquire 65:109 Je '66
I hear America singing slightly off-key; with examples of poems. A. Hecht. Esquire 66: 170 S '66
Manner of speaking: definition of poetry. J. Ciardi. Sat R 49:10+ S 17 '66
Poetry place. Mlle 62:112 F; 116 Mr '66
Shoe in the shark; national poetry. M. Goldman. Nation 202:246-8 F 28 '66
Some coordinates of modern literature. F. Lentricchia, jr. Poetry 108:65-7 Ap '66
Talk with Andrei Voznesensky; discussion. A. Voznesensky. Atlan 218:49+ Jl '66
  See also
Childrens poetry
Christmas poetry
Clerihews
College verse
Computers—Literary applications
Epic poetry
Love poetry
Poetics
Poets
Political poetry
War poetry
  also Canadian poetry; Latin American poetry; etc.

Appreciation
Truth and experience become one; excerpt from Journey toward poetry. J. Burden. Mlle 63:181+ O '66
Two books of criticism. R. Watson. Poetry 107:332-3 F '66

Authorship
Auden on poetry; a conversation with S. Kunitz. W. H. Auden; S. Kunitz. Atlan 218: 94-102 Ag '66
My wonderful lousy poem. B. Schulberg. Read Digest 89:67-9 Ag '66

Bibliography
All-American muse. D. Jaffe. Sat R 49:29-30 O 15 '66
Immortal bard and others. J. Slater. Sat R 49:24-5 D 31 '66
Muses are herd. R. J. Clements. Sat R 49: 30-1 My 21 '66
New books of poems. W. J. Smith. Harper 233:89-90+ Ag '66
Of education and poetry. J. Foster. il Sr Schol 89:sup 18-19 N 18 '66
Other voices, other rhythms. R. D. Spector. Sat R 49:42-4 F 19 '66
Poetry on the campus. R. J. Clements. Sat R 49:68-9 Je 11 '66

Memorizing
See Memorizing

Periodicals
American outsider: The sixties magazine and books of the Sixties press. P. Zweig. Nation 203:517-19 N 14 '66

Study and teaching
Age of overwrite and underthink. S. Spender. Sat R 49:21-3+ Mr 12 '66
Ideas for teaching poetry. A. S. Dunning. Sr Schol 88:sup 12 Mr 11 '66

Teaching poetry: the five-step method. T. Williams. Sr Schol 89:sup 13 N 18 '66
Using records to teach poetry; with poems written by seventh-graders of Middlesex junior high school, Darien, Conn. C. L. Reed. il Sr Schol 89:sup 16 N 11 '66

Technique
See Poetics

Themes
See Literature—Themes

POETRY (periodical)
Announcement of prize awards for 1966. Poetry 109:130-1 N '66

POETRY and art. See Art and literature

POETRY and science. See Literature and science

POETRY and war. See War and literature

POETRY editors. See Editors and editing

POETRY for periodicals. See Periodical literature

POETRY magazines. See Poetry—Periodicals

POETRY phonograph records. See Phonograph records—Spoken records

POETRY prizes. See Rewards, prizes, etc.

POETRY readings. See Dramatic readings

POETS
Poets of reality, by J. H. Miller. Review Nation 202:659-61 My 30 '66. E. W. Said

POETS, American
Hope for poetry. K. Rexroth. Holiday 39: 147-9+ Mr '66
Maryland, my Maryland; G. Wenk's crusade to strip V. G. Burns of state Poetry society's posts. Newsweek 68:41-2 O 10 '66
  See also
American poetry
Ammons, A. R.
Bunting, B.
Carruth, H.
Coxe, L.
Crane, H.
Creeley, R.
Dickey, J.
Frost, R.
Humphries, R.
Lindsay, V.
Louchheim, K. S.
Lowell, R.
Merrill, J.
Moore, M.
Olson, C.
Plath, S.
Pound, E.
Robinson, E. A.
Roethke, T.
Sanders, E.
Schwartz, D.
Spicer, J.
Stevens, W.
Williams, W. C.

POETS, Canadian
  See also
Canadian poetry
Finnigan, J.

POETS, Chilean
  See also
Neruda, P.

POETS, Chinese
  See also
Sie Thao

POETS, Danish
  See also
Hein, P.

POETS, English
  See also
Auden, W. H.
Davies, W. H.
Eliot, T. S.
Gascoyne, D.
Graves, R.
Heath-Stubbs, J.
Keats, J.
Muir, E.
Silkin, J.
Tomlinson, C.

POETS, French
  See also
French poetry
Péguy, C. P.

POETS, German
  See also
Brecht, B.

POETS, Israeli
Poetry in Israel. R. Alter; discussion. Commentary 41:19-20 Mr; 22+ Je '66

POETS, Italian
  See also
Dante Alighieri
Leopardi, G.

POETS, Russian
Yevtushenko and the underground poets. S. Karlinsky. Nation 203:549-53 N 21 '66
  See also
Evtushenko, E. A.
Maiakovskii, V. V.
Mandel'shtam, O. E.
Marshak, S.
Okudzhava, B.
Russian poetry
Voznesenskii, A.
POETS, Senegalese
  See also
Senghor, L. S.
POETS, Spanish
  See also
García Lorca, F.
POETS, Vietnamese
  See also
Ho-chi-Minh
POETS, essayists, novelists club. See PEN club
POGO shoes. See Shoes
POGROMS
  See also
Jews in Russia
POGUE, Forrest C.
George C. Marshall oral history project. por Wilson Lib Bul 40:606-8+ Mr '66
POHL, Herbert A. and Hawk, Ira
Separation of living and dead cells by dielectrophoresis. bibliog Science 152:647-9 Ap 29 '66
POI
Poi can save lives of allergic infants. Sci N 89:368 My 14 '66
POINSETT, Alex
Despised minority. Ebony 21:48-50+ Ag '66
Pitfalls of credit buying. Ebony 21:67-8+ Ap '66
$65 billion gold mine. Ebony 21:88-90+ Jl '66
POINSETTIAS
Crimson for Christmas. P. Friggens. il Read Digest 89:146-9 D '66
New dwarf poinsettias! il Bet Hom & Gard 44:54-5 D '66
Poinsettia fields south of Los Angeles. il Sunset 137:34 D '66
POINT REYES NATIONAL SEASHORE
Quickening tick of the conservation clock. J. B. Craig. il Am For 72:10-13+ N '66
POINTERS (dogs)
All-purpose dog. C. Dickey. il Field & S 71:110-12+ Ag '66
Fish dog. C. Ford. il Field & S 71:6+ Je '66
Pete. C. E. Gillham. il Field & S 71:50-2+ S '66
POIRIER, Normand
Plead insanity and skip three turns. Sat Eve Post 239:16 Ag 27 '66
POISON arrow frogs. See Frogs
POISON ivy
New & old cures for poison ivy. il Changing T 20:19-20 Ag '66
Travel well. E. N. Dye. Travel 126:58+ S '66
POISONING. See Poisons
POISONOUS gases in warfare. See Gases in warfare
POISONOUS mushrooms. See Mushrooms
POISONOUS plants
Osmotic pressure influence in germination tests for antibiosis. R. C. Anderson and O. L. Loucks. bibliog il Science 152:771-3 My 6 '66
Plant contact poisoning. C. J. Potthoff. Todays Health 44:76 My '66
  See also
Poison ivy
POISONS
How to combat poisons; major factor in canine mortality. P. Czura. il Field & S 71:176-7+ My '66
Make sure your child won't be a poison victim. il Consumer Bul 49:20-1 F '66
Pills as poisoner; accidental poisonings among children; oral contraceptives. Time 87:60 Mr 25 '66
  See also
Antidotes
Curare
Cyanide poisoning
Food poisoning
Lead poisoning
POKER
Full house: the thanatopsis pleasure and inside straight club. H. H. Broun. il Am Heritage 18:64-7 D '66

Anecdotes, facetiae, satire, etc.
Poker. J. Richardson. Esquire 65:74+ Ap; 66: 46+ D '66

POL, Heinz
Two views of two Germanys. Nation 203: 457-8 O 31 '66
POLACOLOR films. See Photography—Films
POLAND
Poland: on the treadmill. B. van Voorst. il Newsweek 69:32-4 Ja 9 '67
  See also
Automobile industry and trade—Poland
Church and state in Poland
Communism—Poland
Communist party (Poland)
Concentration camps—Poland
Foreign visitors in Poland
Phonograph record industry—Poland
Poles
Regional planning—Poland
Theater—Poland
Warsaw
Wroclaw

Boundaries
Church breaks a taboo. F. Lüpsen. Christian Cent 83:188-90 F 9 '66; Reply. W. C. Schmauch. 83:442-5 Ap 6 '66
Europe's unsettled borders: Oder-Neisse line. E. M. von Kuehnelt-Leddihn. Nat R 18:678 Jl 12 '66

Intellectual life
Trade winds: aims of the Polish institute of arts and sciences in America. J. G. Fuller. Sat R 49:14+ F 5 '66
  See also
Warsaw—Intellectual life

Politics and government
Beginnings of the cold war, by M. F. Herz. Review
  Sat R 49:42 Ap 2 '66. F. Altschul
No place for chitchat. Time 88:28 D 23 '66
  See also
Communist party (Poland)

Religious institutions and affairs
  See also
Catholic church in Poland

Riots
Two days that shook the Communist world. F. Lewis. il N Y Times Mag p25+ Je 12 '66
POLAND and Germany. See Germany and Poland
POLAND and the United States
United States and Poland: strengthening traditional bonds; address, October 16, 1966. L. B. Johnson. Dept State Bul 55:712-15 N 7 '66
POLAR bear hunting. See Bear hunting
POLAR bears. See Bears
POLAR exploration. See Arctic exploration
POLAR ice. See Ice—Polar Regions
POLAR REGIONS
Theory of ice ages III. W. L. Donn and M. Ewing. bibliog il Science 152:1706-12 Je 24 '66
POLAR research
Arctic current watched. Sci N 89:398 My 21 '66
New research stations probe Antarctica's ice. Sci N L 89:105 F 12 '66
On a floating island; U.S. Arctic drifting stations. V. P. Hessler. il Science 151:1360-2 Mr 18 '66
Similarity to space beckons scientists; using Antarctica for simulation of lunar and planetary environments. R. Lindsey. il Tech W 19:34+ D 5 '66
POLARIS missiles. See Guided missiles— Launching from submarine boats
POLARIS submarines. See Submarine boats, Atomic powered
POLARIZATION (light)
Mechanism of lunar polarization. J. J. Hopfield. bibliog il Science 151:1380-1 Mr 18 '66
Meteorites: optical activity in organic matter. W. G. Meinschein and others. bibliog il Science 154:377-80 O 21 '66
Nature and the camera; using polarized light. D. Linton. Natur Hist 75:66-7 Je '66
Polarization of the light of long-period variables. G. S. Mumford. Sky & Tel 32:198 O '66
Stokes parameters for 1665-megacycles-per-second emission from OH near source W3. M. L. Meeks and others. bibliog il Science 153:978-81 Ag 26 '66
POLARIZATION of rays
Galactic depolarization of the 21-centimeter-wavelength radiation of extragalactic sources. J. M. Bologna and others. bibliog il Science 154:1656-8 D 30 '66
POLARIZED light. See Polarization (light)

POLAROID color film. See Photography—Films
POLAROID corporation
Instant photography: the impossible that happened. il Pop Sci 189:130-1 O '66
Polaroid trains lens on quickie ID cards. il Bsns W p 132-4 O 1 '66
Singular growth of Polaroid corp. il Fortune 74:314 Jl 15 '66
POLAROID Land cameras
Instant photography: the impossible that happened. il Pop Sci 189:130-1 O '66
Sixty-second answers to Polaroid problems. P. Wahl. il Pop Sci 189:144-7 Jl '66
Through Europe with a Polaroid color pack camera. W. Hayum. il U S Camera 29:18+ S '66
POLAROID Land film. See Photography—Films
POLES
Report from a surrealist capital. K. Botsford. il N Y Times Mag p58-9+ S 11 '66; Reply. A. N. Oakes. p 122 O 23 '66
With Stravinsky in Warsaw; excerpt from Table talk. R. Craft. Harper 232:66-70+ F '66
POLESNY, B.
Public observatory in Czechoslovakia. Sky & Tel 32:138-9 S '66
POLI, Kenneth
Why didn't I see that? Pop Phot 59:104-9 O '66
POLICE
See also
Detectives
Secret service

Equipment and supplies
Coming: fantastic devices to end riots. R. Zacks. il Nations Bsns 54:62-4 Jl '66; Reply. J. C. Evans. Christian Cent 83:1203 O 5 '66

Public relations
Exiles from the American dream: the junkie and the cop. B. Jackson. Atlan 219:44-51 Ja '67
Mobile exhibit brings police story to the public. il Am City 81:53 Ap '66

Anecdotes facetiae, satire, etc.
Manner of speaking; a brush with the law. J. Ciardi. Sat R 49:12-13 Je 4 '66

Quotations, maxims, etc.
Men in blue; comp. by E. F. Murphy. il N Y Times Mag p52 Mr 6 '66

Great Britain
Trouble with Harry; manhunt for H. M. Roberts. il Time 88:30 S 2 '66
See also
London—Police

Philippines
See also
Manila—Police

Russia
See also
Secret service—Russia

United States
Behind those police brutality charges. F. E. Inbau. Read Digest 89:41-6 Jl '66
Can riots be stopped? the next move; with article by B. Shipp. il U S News 61:38-43 Ag 8 '66
Civilian review of the police. Life 61:4 O 21 '66
Cop watching; need for code to guide the police. New Repub 155:9 D 3 '66
Corpus Christi's squad car lawyer. J. Biery. il Reporter 36:43-5 Ja 12 '67
Court versus the cops; reactions to the Supreme court's recent ruling on criminal confessions. il Sat Eve Post 239:82 Jl 30 '66
Crisis facing the nation's police. il U S News 61:82-6 O 17 '66
Latest moves against crime in streets. il U S News 60:38-40 Ap 11 '66
Let's have justice for non-criminals, too! effect of Supreme court decision on police authority and safeguarding civil rights. E. H. Methvin. Read Digest 89:53-60 D '66
New rules for police rooms. il Time 87:53-4 Je 24 '66
Now policemen are joining teamsters. U S News 62:86 Ja 16 '67
Policing the police. il Newsweek 67:27-8 Mr 7 '66
Policing the police: are civilian review boards the answer? pro and con discussion. il Sr Schol 89:7-8 O 21 '66
Summer '66: cops on the spot. il Newsweek 67:22-6+ Je 27 '66
Surprise: desire to see police protection strengthened, not weakened; Ribicoff hearings. Nat R 18:918 S 20 '66

Talk about police brutality ... B. Shipp. Read Digest 89:111-12 O '66
Things are looking up in Logan Heights; police-Negro relations. H. Ellsberg. Read Digest 89:217+ N '66
See also subhead Police under names of states, cities, etc. e.g. Chicago—Police
POLICE, State

Training
School for tin stars with lead feet; California highway patrol academy. S. Kelly. il Motor T 18:24-6+ Ag '66
POLICE automobiles. See Automobiles, Police
POLICE communication systems
All the alarms in one console; system used in Middletown Township, N.J. il Am City 81:50 S '66
For emergency calls only; fire and police emergency calls; Greensboro, N.C. S. H. Smith. il Am City 81:153-4+ O '66
Multi-channel network keeps the air waves clear; Norfolk, Va. il Am City 81:50 O '66
POLICE dogs
Dogs patrol the subways; policeman-dog teams in Philadelphia. il Am City 81:95 Jl '66

Anecdotes, facetiae, satire, etc.
Query to a literary agent; story of a sentry dog. T. R. Fehrenbach. Esquire 66:122+ D '66
POLICE motor scooters. See Motor scooters, Police
POLICE power
After the arrest; interrogation and the right to counsel. A. M. Bickel. New Repub 154: 14-16 F 12 '66; Discussion. 154:36-7 Mr 5; 37 Mr 19 '66
POLICE state. See Totalitarianism
POLICEMEN. See Police
POLICY planning council. See United States —State, Department of—Policy planning council
POLIKOFF, Barbara
All in good time; story. McCalls 94:50-1 Ja '67
POLING, Daniel A.
Proof and Daniel Poling. L. Whitman and G. Trimble. Christian Cent 83:1350+ N 2 '66; Correction. 83:1446 N 23 '66
Rigging the consensus. Christian Cent 83: 768, 1200-1 Je 15, O 5 '66
POLING, David
Secular saints. Sat R 49:61-2 N 12 '66
Urban renewal of religion. Sat R 49:30-1+ My 14 '66
POLING, James
Invasion by lie detector. Read Digest 88: 109-13 My '66
POLIOMYELITIS

Prevention and control
More vaccines promised. F. Marley. Sci N 90:423 N 19 '66

Vaccines
Breakthrough, by R. Carter. Review Newsweek il 67:102+ Mr 28 '66
More vaccines promised. F. Marley. Sci N 90: 423 N 19 '66
New Salk vaccine produced in Canada. Sci N 89:168 Mr 12 '66
POLISH art. See Art, Polish
POLISH composers. See Composers, Polish
POLISH dancing. See Dancing, Polish
POLISH institute of arts and sciences in America
Trade winds; aims of the institute. J. G. Fuller. Sat R 49:14+ F 5 '66
POLISH poetry

Translations into English
To the heart: tr by V. Contoski. T. Rozenwicz. Nation 203:24 Jl 4 '66
POLISH theater. See Theater—Poland
POLISHERS, Electric
Electric shoe polishers. il Consumer Bul 49: 14-17 Mr '66
POLISHING machines
See also
Floor machines
POLISHING materials
Silver polishes. Consumer Bul 50:26 Ja '67
POLISHING of furniture. See Furniture—Care
POLITE, Frank
Manservant; poem. Poetry 109:23 O '66
POLITENESS. See Etiquette

POLITI, Leo
 To the children with love, from Leo Politi. R. Nichols. il por Horn Bk 42:218-22 Ap '66
POLITICAL activators. See Pressure groups
POLITICAL advertising. See Advertising, Political
POLITICAL asylum. See Asylum, Right of
POLITICAL attitudes
 They don't dig this security jazz. P. Lisagor. il Nations Bsns 54:19-20 Ag '66
POLITICAL bosses. See Boss rule
POLITICAL campaigns
 Anti-Vietnam politics; peace candidates in Oregon, California. A. Kopkind. New Repub 154:15-18 Je 4 '66
 Backlash in the Percy campaign. R. C. Wade. Reporter 36:37-40 Ja 12 '67
 Best man's wife; Mrs George Wallace. J. Richardson. il Esquire 66:68-71+ Jl '66
 Bobby phenomenon; Kennedy tour. il Newsweek 68:30+ O 24 '66
 Campaign mud. Reporter 35:20+ N 17 '66
 Campaign trail in the homestretch; races across the country. il Newsweek 68:30-2+ N 7 '66
 Charisma, calluses & cash. il Time 88:37-8 O 14 '66
 Close look at election trends. il U S News 61:37-40 O 17 '66
 Coattails of bigotry; backlash candidates in Chicago. H. W. De Zutter. New Repub 155:8-9 N 5 '66
 Color of the campaign. il Newsweek 68:31-3 O 24 '66
 Colorful campaign. Newsweek 68:29 O 17 '66
 Coming crisis; Vietnam policy as a campaign issue. Nation 203:67-8 Jl 25 '66
 Congress runs almost alone in midterm. J. N. Eller. America 115:445 O 15 '66
 Dirty politics and backlash. Life 61:8 O 7 '66
 Dirty politics. by B. L. Felknor. Review Commentary 42:99-102 D '66. A. Hacker New Repub 155:26-8 O 8 '66. T. Wicker New Yorker 49:100-1 O 8 '66. D. Young
 Every man for himself; war in Vietnam and the congressional campaigns. Newsweek 68: 21 Jl 25 '66
 Ezra's way; President Johnson campaigns in New York city. il Time 88:29 O 21 '66
 Happy warrior; New York and California gubernatorial campaigns. il Newsweek 68: 36+ O 31 '66
 How federal benefits figure in the election; excerpts from Congressional record. J. R. Hansen. U S News 61:13 O 31 '66
 In my opinion; experience of a teen-age volunteer worker. S. Sponzilli. Seventeen 25:246 N '66
 Johnson gamble; President to campaign on loyalty issue. Nation 203:139-40 Ag 22 '66
 Kennedy campaigning. by M. B. Levin. Review Sat R 49:100-1 O 8 '66. D. Young
 Kennedy chemistry; campaigning in West Virginia. Newsweek 68:21 O 3 '66
 Letter from Washington; issues to be debated in the fall campaigns. R. H. Rovere. New Yorker 42:167-74 My 21 '66
 L.B.J. reaches out (ouch!) to rally his consensus; New England tour; with report by R. B. Stolley. il Life 61:12-21 S 2 '66
 Making of the president, 1972? Newsweek 68: 17-18 S 5 '66
 Mealy-mouthed campaign; 1966 congressional campaign. S. Alsop. Sat Eve Post 239:20 N 19 '66
 Nixon and the GOP; comeback? 4,000 mile road show. il Newsweek 68:30-5 O 10 '66
 Off and running; the 1966 campaign. il Newsweek 68:28-30 S 19 '66
 Off-year election with a difference. K. Wheeler. il Life 61:61-4+ N 4 '66
 On Election day. New Repub 155:7-8 N 5 '66
 Operational withdrawal; cancellation of campaign plans by L. B. Johnson. il Time 88: 27-8 N 11 '66
 Outlook in ten key races. il U S News 61:38-9 N 7 '66
 Outsider's report. W. V. Shannon. Commonweal 85:8 O 7 '66
 Party politics and race. Nation 203:371-2 O 17 '66
 Perfect candidate; H. Evry's techniques for getting elected to public office. R. Wernick. il Life 60:41-2+ Je 3 '66
 Political paradox; Vietnam war indirect issue. K. Crawford. Newsweek 68:62 Ag 22 '66
 Reagan in the wilderness; and other major candidates for governorship. il Newsweek 67:30-3 Mr 28 '66

 Reagan vs. Brown; how to succeed with the backlash. C. McWilliams. il Nation 203: 438-42 O 31 '66
 Robert Kennedy on tour. J. Witcover. New Repub 155:9-10 O 1 '66
 Rules of the game. Nat R 18:1086 N 1 '66
 Senate races. W. V. Shannon. Commonweal 85:127-8 N 4 '66
 Wallace's skirt-tail victory. il Newsweek 67: 26-30 My 16 '66
 Warming up for November 8. P. M. Deuel; G. Hill; J. Desmond. il Nation 203:374-81 O 17 '66
 Welcome to the vineyard; L. B. Johnson tour. il Newsweek 68:38-9 O 24 '66
  See also
 Campaign funds
 Campaign literature
 Candidates, Political
 Presidential campaigns
 Television in politics
  also subhead Politics and government under names of countries, states, cities, e.g. California—Politics and government

Australia
 Vietnam issue; parliamentary election campaign. Newsweek 68:66+ N 21 '66

Brazil
 Solid brass candidate; terrorists target in Recife. il Newsweek 68:45 Ag 8 '66

Dominican Republic
 Heard but not seen. Newsweek 67:55 My 30 '66

Great Britain
 Atlantic report. Atlan 217:30+ Je '66
 Labor is the favorite. il Bsns W p48-9 Mr 26 '66
 Last lap. il Time 87:34 Ap 1 '66
 Sticking to the issues; Heath-Wilson activities. il Newsweek 67:47 Mr 28 '66

Japan
 What the gods provide. Newsweek 69:42 Ja 23 '67

Spain
 How Generalissimo Franco got his consensus. D. Searl. New Repub 156:12-13 Ja 14 '67
POLITICAL candidates. See Candidates, Political
POLITICAL cartoons. See Caricatures and cartoons
POLITICAL clubs and associations
 Beer blast; dropping of action against Anheuser-Busch by antitrust division. Newsweek 68:24+ Jl 25 '66
 Bipartisan finks; Young Republican national federation. Nat R 18:146+ F 22 '66
 Busch league; contributions to President's club. Time 88:21-2 Jl 22 '66
 Democrats who talk back; National committee's actions against College young Democrats. New Repub 155:7 D 24 '66
 LBJ's club, the whiff of scandal. J. Deakin. New Repub 155:13-14 O 1 '66
 President's club; what $1,000 brings. il U S News 61:6 Ag 1 '66
 Who won? analysis of 1966 elections. Nat R 18:1200-2 N 29 '66
  See also
 Free society association
POLITICAL conventions
 Parties need attention. J. N. Eller. America 115:7 Jl 2 '66
 Political almanack for the year 1966; state nominating conventions. il U S News 60: 42-3 Ag 18 '66
  See also
 National conventions (political)
POLITICAL corruption. See Politics, Corruption in
POLITICAL education
  See also
 Political science—Study and teaching
POLITICAL ethics
 Keep the faith, baby; case of Adam Clayton Powell. W. More. America 116:80 Ja 21 '67
 Law, love and politics; learning to live with tension. B. Wicker. Commonweal 85:218-21 N 25 '66
 LBJ's credibility; or, What happened to no comment? J. Deakin. New Repub 154:23-4 Ja 29 '66
 Rules of the game. Nat R 18:1086 N 1 '66
 Unethical behavior in government; symposium, ed. by J. C. Charlesworth. Ann Am Acad 363:12-51 Ja '66
 What new federal ethics code means to business. J. Kluttz. il Nations Bsns 54: 108+ O '66
  See also
 Patriotism
 Politics, Corruption in

POLITICAL forecasts
Ax-handle trauma. K. Crawford. Newsweek 68:38 O 17 '66
Democratic slippage; L. Harris survey findings. Newsweek 67:29 Mr 21 '66
Dim future. Commonweal 85:213-14 N 25 '66
Election '66; picking the winners. Newsweek 68:33 N 7 '66
GOP desert. New Repub 155:4 O 15 '66
Mathematics of consensus. L. H. Bean. Nation 203:573 N 28 '66
Politics and a poll. J. O'Gara. Commonweal 84:411 Jl 1 '66
Pro's-eye view; R. M. Nixon's forecast. R. Moley. Newsweek 68:126 O 24 '66
Question of how big; Republican gain. Time 88:31 N 4 '66
Republicans battle for gains in West, mood of voters; survey. il U S News 61:83-4+ O 10 '66
What the polls say. Time 88:33 O 21; 31 O 28 '66
Who will win on November 8? il U S News 61:35-9 N 7 '66
Worries of Washington; predicting the November elections. il Newsweek 67:37 Ap 18 '66
See also
Public opinion polls
POLITICAL independence. See Self-determination, National
POLITICAL interest groups. See Pressure groups
POLITICAL kidnapping. See Kidnapping
POLITICAL liberty. See Liberty
POLITICAL literature
Face to face with a successful political writer; ed. by C. Schwalberg. S. Kelman. Seventeen 25:169 D '66
POLITICAL novels. See Politics in literature
POLITICAL obligations. See Citizenship
POLITICAL parties
See also
Communist parties
Platforms, Political
Political conventions

Brazil
Quite the contrary & above all; new two-party system. Time 87:32+ F 11 '66

Canada
Socialism in Saskatchewan. A. Morrison. Yale R 56:256-70 D '66
See also
Conservative party (Canada)

Chile
Nationalism and communism in Chile, by E. Halperin. Review
  Commonweal 84:181-2 Ap 29 '66. D. D. Ranstead

Colombia
Threat of daggers. il Time 87:36 Ap 1 '66

Finland
Strange redmates; new four-party coalition government. Time 87:45 Je 10 '66

France
Atlantic report. Atlan 217:30+ Ap '66
Le front populaire; left-wing parties form new alliance. il Newsweek 69:27 Ja 2 '67
Pact of the left. il Time 88:19 D 30 '66

Germany (Federal Republic)
Comeback for Nazis in Germany? National democratic party. il U S News 61:54 N 28 '66
End of the affair. W. S. Schlamm. Nat R 18:1316-18 D 27 '66
Germany; the quickest coalition. il Newsweek 68:37 D 5 '66
Germany's radical right; Nationaldemokratische partei. A. Schalk. Commonweal 84:609-11 S 23 '66
Grand coalition. il Time 88:32 D 2 '66
In spite of himself; C.D.U. chairmanship and Erhard. Time 87:30 F 11 '66
Neo-Nazis or good Germans? National Democratic party. il Newsweek 68:38-9 D 5 '66
New worry over possible Nazi comeback; second election gain by National democratic party (NPD) U S News 61:12 D 5 '66
No fun in Bavaria; emergence of the National democratic party. C. Amery. Nation 203:637-9 D 12 '66
No. 2 man; R. Barzel, chairman of the Christian democratic union. il Time 87:35 Je 24 '66
Quiet is shattered on Bonn front; Kiesinger picked by CDU to replace Erhard. il Bsns W p44-5 N 19 '66

Real danger; concern over NDP success. Nation 203:596 D 5 '66
Reshuffle in Bonn. H.-B. Moeller. Commonweal 85:281-2 D 9 '66
Rumbling on the German right; National democratic party of Germany. J. D. Shand. America 115:803-4 D 17 '66
Straws in the wind; rehabilitation of Hitlerism? A. Werth. Nation 202:442 Ap 18 '66
Ugly echoes; NDP expansion. Newsweek 67:61-2 Ap 18 '66
W. German shakeup. Sr Schol 89:25 D 9 '66
What price Germany, now? E. Stillman. il N Y Times Mag p54-7+ D 4 '66
Willy's return; Dortmund convention of Social democratic party. il Time 87:40 Je 17 '66

Great Britain
Britain: labor's chance to govern. il Newsweek 67:46+ Ap 11 '66
Britain under socialism. O. Gass. bibliog f Commentary 41:65-72 F '66
Labor's victory; changing images of parties. H. Brandon. Sat R 49:11 Ap 23 '66
Muddling through chaos. T. Roszak. Nation 202:428-31 Ap 11 '66
See also
Conservative party (Great Britain)
Labor party (Great Britain)

History
Financing of the Whig party organization, 1783-1793. D. E. Ginter. bibliog f il Am Hist R 71:421-40 Ja '66

India
Congress party after Nehru. S. Rajan. il Reporter 35:33-5 O 20 '66
India for the Hindus, says the Jan Sangh; All-India people's party. J. A. Lukas. il N Y Times Mag p20-1+ Ag 14 '66
New manifesto; problems within the Congress party. il Time 88:42+ O 7 '66
See also
Indian national congress

Indonesia
Atlantic report. Atlan 219:12+ Ja '67
Indonesia's unfinished revolution. D. Warner. il Reporter 35:28-9+ Jl 14 '66

Israel
Atlantic report. Atlan 217:24+ F '66

Italy
Non-crisis in Italy. E. A. Bayne. For Affairs 45:353-62 Ja '67
Reunion near Rome; Nenni's Socialists reunited with Social democratic party. Time 88:41 N 4 '66
Special road to socialism. Time 87:34 F 4 '66
Unlocking the vise; Socialist party patches up quarrels. Newsweek 68:44+ N 14 '66
See also
Socialist party (Italy)

Japan
New left in Japan. P. G. Altbach. Christian Cent 83:333-4 Mr 16 '66

Latin America
Christian democracy in Latin America. America 115:645 N 19 '66

Nigeria
Nigeria: coup on a tightrope. V. L. Allen. Nation 202:143-5 F 7 '66

Norway
Atlantic report; coalition aims. Atlan 217:32+ Mr '66

Portugal
Salazar's Portugal; anniversary on thin ice. R. H. Chilcote. il Nation 202:638-41 My 30 '66

Russia
See also
Communist party (Russia)

Singapore
Singapore: one-party democracy. A. Josey. Nation 203:661-3 D 19 '66

United States
Liberty and discipline; living under elected tyranny until 1966 election. R. Moley. Newsweek 68:136 N 21 '66
Needed: party responsibility. D. Lawrence. U S News 61:140 N 21 '66
New politics in California. Nation 203:372-3 O 17 '66; Reply. M. Burnstein. 203:466 N 7 '66

POLITICAL parties—United States—*Continued*
Party leaders analyze the vote, look ahead; interviews and excerpts from news conferences. il U S News 61:55-6+ N 21 '66
Political party officials: responsiveness to the public. I. Hinderaker. Ann Am Acad 363: 28-35 Ja '66
Politics heats up; election outlook now; congressional and gubernatorial races. U S News 60:42-4 Mr 28 '66
Third party taking shape; how it might swing election. il U S News 61:44-5 O 3 '66
See also
Communist party (United States)
Democratic party
Progressive labor party
Republican party

Venezuela
One war that the Communists are losing; defeat of Armed forces of national liberation. il U S News 61:86-8 N 14 '66

Vietnam
Vietcong, by D. Pike. Review
New Repub 155:18-19 N 19 '66. S. Karnow
POLITICAL philosophy
Flirtation with fascism: American pragmatic liberals and Mussolini's Italy. J. P. Diggins. Am Hist R 71:487-505 Ja '66
Private acts & public goals: ideological vacuum. H. S. Kariel. il Nation 202:449-52 Ap 18 '66
See also
Communism and democracy
Conservatism
Democracy
Liberalism
Racism
POLITICAL platforms. See Platforms. Political
POLITICAL poetry
Poetry and politics: 1900-1960, by C. M. Bowra. Review
New Repub 155:29-30+ S 17 '66. G. Daniels
POLITICAL posters. See Posters
POLITICAL power. See Power (political science)
POLITICAL pressure. See Pressure groups
POLITICAL prisoners
Annihilation in China & U.S. indifference. W. F. Buckley, jr. Nat R 18:1259 D 13 '66
Death on a train; Mott case. Sr Schol 88:5 F 25 '66
Deepening mystery; case of N. Mott. Newsweek 67:34-5 F 7 '66
Journey's end; case of N. Mott. il Newsweek 67:44 Ja 31 '66
Russian mystery: an American's death; Mott case. il U S News 60:12 F 7 '66
South Africa: daily life in a police state; with report of M. Benson's and others experiences. New Repub 154:11-13 Je 11 '66
POLITICAL psychology
See also
Nationalism
Propaganda
POLITICAL reporting. See Reporters and reporting
POLITICAL responsibility. See Responsibility
POLITICAL rights. See Civil rights
POLITICAL rights of women. See Woman— Equal rights
POLITICAL science
Middlingness, by V. E. Starzinger. Review
Nat R 18:369 Ap 19 '66. R. Kirk
Social origins of dictatorship and democracy, by B. Moore, jr. Review
Time 88:113+ N 11 '66
Stages of political development, by A. F. K. Organski. Review
New Repub 154:23-4 Ap 23 '66. A. Campbell
See also
Citizenship
Civilization
Communism
Democracy
Federal government
Liberalism
Majorities
Minorities
Monarchy
Nationalism
Nations
Pluralism (political science)
Political ethics
Socialism
State, The
Tribes and tribal system

Bibliography
See also
Political science literature

Study and teaching
Political education; activities of the Taft institute. R. Moley. Newsweek 67:108 Mr 28 '66
POLITICAL science, Academy of. See Academy of political science
POLITICAL science literature
Literature of American government. O. Gass. bibliog f Commentary 41:67-72 Je '66
POLITICAL thought
Common thread; address, May 3, 1966. H. Ford, 2d. Vital Speeches 32:495-8 Je 1 '66
Future pattern for our political thinking. F. Morley. Nations Bsns 54:27-8 F '66
POLITICIANS
Ideas in action; relations between the academic community and elected representatives; address, December 4, 1965. S. Horn. Vital Speeches 32:283-8 F 15 '66
POLITICS
Politics of modernization, by D. E. Apter. Review
Nation 202:723-4 Je 13 '66. T. M. Franck
See also
Conservatism
Liberalism
Political ethics
Political parties—United States
Political science
Politicians
Scientists—Political activities
Television in politics
United States—Politics and government
Women and politics
World politics

Terminology
Key words in government. Sr Schol 88:22 F 18 '66
POLITICS, Corruption in
Dirty politics, by B. L. Felknor. Review
Commentary 42:99-102 D '66. A. Hacker
Housecleaning; scandal in Jacksonville City. Newsweek 68:34+ S 26 '66
When a state tries to clean itself up; Massachusetts. il U S News 60:46-8 F 7 '66
See also
Boss rule
Bribery
Campaign funds
Conflict of interests (public office)
Misconduct in office
POLITICS and art. See Art and politics
POLITICS and authors. See Authors and politics
POLITICS and business. See Business—Political aspects
POLITICS and Christianity. See Church and politics
POLITICS and education
Politics, propaganda, and pedagogy. W. W. Brickman. Sch & Soc 94:55 F 5 '66
See also
College students—Political activities
POLITICS and food. See Food supply—Political aspects
POLITICS and industry. See Industry and state
POLITICS and religion. See Church and politics
POLITICS and science. See Science and state
POLITICS in literature
Hogans goat; interview, ed. by D. L. Flaherty. W. Alfred. il America 114:378-81 Mr 19 '66
P.E.N. politics and literature: summary of address. A. Miller. Pub W 190:32-3 Jl 18 '66
Politics as romance. S. Kauffmann. New Repub 155:14+ O 15 '66
POLK, William R.
Scholar and the administrator in international affairs. Bul Atomic Sci 22:2-8 Mr '66
POLL tax
Coup de grâce; outlawed at the state level. Newsweek 67:22 Ap 4 '66
How Supreme court is making itself obsolete. F. Morley. il Nations Bsns 54:27-8 My '66
R.I.P. Supreme court outlaws. Time 87:25B Ap 1 '66
POLLACK, Gerald L.
Solid noble gases; with biographical sketch. Sci Am 215:16, 64-74 bibliog(p 150) O '66
POLLACK, Herman
Interaction of science and technology and foreign affairs; statement, April 19, 1966. Dept State Bul 54:946-9 Je 13 '66

POLLACK, Jack Harrison
Astonishing truth about girl dropouts. Parents Mag 41:66-7+ S '66
Teen-age drinking and drug addiction. NEA J 55:8-12 My '66
Wheels of justice. Sat R 50:32-3 Ja 7 '67

POLLARD, Spencer D.
Science in the saddle. Sat R 49:36 O 29 '66

POLLEN
Crossroads of the insect world. J. W. MacSwain. il Nat Geog Mag 130:844-57 D '66

POLLEN, Fossil
Correlation of archeological and palynological data. A. J. Jelinek. bibliog il Science 152:1507-9 Je 10 '66

POLLOCK, Francis
Junkets to apartheid: America's press on safari. Nation 203:479-81 N 7 '66

POLLS, Public opinion. See Public opinion polls

POLLSTERS. See Public opinion polls

POLLUTION, Air. See Air pollution

POLLUTION, Water. See Water pollution

POLLUTION of lakes. See Water pollution

POLLUTION of streams. See Water pollution

POLNER, Murray
How to survive childhood. Nation 203:523 N 14 '66
Qualified optimism. Christian Cent 84:14-15 Ja 4 '67

POLO, Marco
Marco Polo. K. Rexroth. Sat R 49:41 Ag 27 '66

POLO
Long trip and a good try; U.S. defeat in Argentina international polo matches. W. Tower. il Sports Illus 25:85-8 D 5 '66
Steamed up for a charge into the past; photographs by T. Evans; with account by P. Jennings. il Sports Illus 24:36-41 F 14 '66

POLO ponies
Ponies. New Yorker 41:23-4 Ja 29 '66

POLONIUM
Source of lead-210 and polonium-210 in tobacco. T. C. Tso and others. bibliog il Science 153:880-2 Ag 19 '66

Isotopes
Lead-210 and polonium-210 in biological samples from Alaska. T. M. Beasley and H. E. Palmer. bibliog il Science 152:1062-4 My 20 '66
Polonium-210 content of human tissues in relation to dietary habit. C. R. Hill. il Science 152:1261-2 My 27 '66

POLSKY, Milton
On the playground. Parks & Rec 1:322 Ap '66

POLYANDRY
War widow. Newsweek 68:40+ N 7 '66

POLYCYCLIC hydrocarbons. See Hydrocarbons

POLYETHYLENE
Surface recrystallization of polyethylene extended-chain crystals. B. Wunderlich and L. Melillo. bibliog il Science 154:1329-30 D 9 '66

POLYGRAPH
Polygraph. B. M. Smith. il Sci Am 216:25-31 bibliog(p 146) Ja '67
Truth and deception, by J. E. Reid and F. E. Inbau. Review
Sat R 49:20-1 D 31 '66. I. Younger
See also
Lie detectors

POLYMERIZATION
Acrylonitrile polymerization in a miniaturized high-pressure optical cell. V. M. Zhulin and others. bibliog il Science 153:649-50 Ag 5 '66

POLYMERS
Morphology of nascent Ziegler-Natta polymers. P. Blais and R. S. Manley. bibliog il Science 153:539-41 Jl 29 '66

POLYMORPHISM
High-pressure polymorphism in sodium chloride: a reinvestigation. Q. Johnson. bibliog il Science 153:419 Jl 22 '66
Molybdenum diselenide: rhombohedral high pressure-high temperature polymorph. L. C. Towle and others. bibliog il Science 154:895-6 N 18 '66
Polymorphism of shock loaded Fe-Mn and Fe-Ni alloys. T. R. Loree and others. bibliog il Science 153:1277-8 S 9 '66
Quenchable high-pressure polymorph of zinc selenate. C. W. F. T. Pistorius. bibliog il Science 151:1003 F 25 '66

POLYMORPHISM (biology)
Chromosomal polymorphism in the white-throated sparrow, zonotrichia albicollis (gmelin) H. B. Thorneycroft. bibliog il Science 154:1571-2 D 23 '66

Hemoglobin polymorphism in macaca nemestrina. M. H. Crawford. bibliog il Science 154:398-9 O 21 '66
Polymorphism in pleistocene land snails. D. F. Owen. bibliog il Science 152:71-2 Ap 1 '66
Polymorphism in some nearctic halictine bees. G. Knerer and C. E. Atwood. bibliog il Science 152:1262-3 My 27 '66
Polymorphism of heavy-chain genes in immunoglobulins of wild mice. R. Lieberman and M. Potter. bibliog il Science 154:535-7 O 28 '66

POLYNESIA
Island of memories. M. Petersen. il Motor B 118:89+ Ag '66
Isles neath the wind. M. Petersen. il Motor B 118:25+ D '66
See also
Marquesas Islands

POLYNESIAN dancing. See Dancing, Polynesian

POLYNESIANS
See also
Fijians

POLYNUCLEOTIDES. See Nucleotides

POLYOMA virus. See Tumor viruses

POLYPEPTIDES. See Peptides

POLYPHOSPHATES. See Phosphates

POLYPS (tumors) See Tumors

POLYRIBONUCLEOTIDES. See Nucleoproteins

POLYRIBOSOMES. See Nucleoproteins

POLYSACCHARIDES
Galactosamine glycan of chondrococcus columnaris. J. L. Johnson and W. S. Chilton. bibliog il Science 152:1247-8 My 27 '66
Mucopolysaccharide from patients with cystic fibrosis of the pancreas. C. U. Lowe and others. bibliog il Science 153:1124-5 S 2 '66
Mucopolysaccharides: N-acetylglucosamine- and galactose-6-sulfates from keratosulfate. V. P. Bhavanandan and K. Meyer. bibliog Science 151:1404-5 Mr 18 '66
Protein-polysaccharide loss during endochondral ossification: immunochemical evidence. A. Hirschman and D. D. Dziewiatkowski. bibliog il Science 154:393-5 O 21 '66

POLYSOMES. See Nucleoproteins

POLYSULFIDE sealants. See Sealing compositions

POLYUNSATURATED fats. See Oils and fats, Edible

POMARE, Eleo, dance company. See Dance companies

POMEGRANATES
Persimmon and pomegranate, pick of the winter fruits. il Bet Hom & Gard 44:99 N '66

POMERANCE, Harriet
Weaving of Crete. Craft Horiz 26:32-5+ S '66
about
Reporter at large. J. Alsop. New Yorker 42:33-8+ Ag 13 '66

POMERANCE, Leon
Reporter at large. J. Alsop. New Yorker 42:33-8+ Ag 13 '66

POMEROY, Kenneth B.
New look. Am For 72:7 S '66
Sea of troubles. Am For 72:34+ D '66
Workshop in the woods, 31 centuries! il por Am For 72:16-21+ O '66
—and Dixon, Dorothy
These are the champs. Am For 72:14-35 My '66

POMEROY, Ralph
Down from the forked hill unsullied. R. Wallace. Poetry 108:124 My '66

POMEROY, Ruth Fairchild
Mrs Johnson talks about her love for the White House. Redbook 127:72-8+ Jl '66

POMONA, Calif, public library
Three patios in Pomona. R. M. Holt. il Library J 91:5859-61 D 1 '66

POMONA college, Claremont
See also
Associated colleges at Claremont, Calif.

POMPANO BEACH, Fla.
Water supply
Not just for hurricanes; auxiliary engine in the water plant. R. C. Mills. il Am City 81:100-1 Ap '66

POMPANO fishing
Power rods for pomps. G. X. Sand. il Field & S 71:136-8 O '66

POMPEII
Whispers of Pompeii; with report by R. Espinosa. il Life 60:56-71+ Mr 25 '66

POMPIAN, Lillian
Minister in the marketplace. Read Digest 88: 29-30+ Je '66

POMPIDOU, Georges
Call me Georges. il por Time 88:31-2 Jl 15 '66
Letter from Paris; concerning interview on television. Genêt. New Yorker 42:151 O 8 '66

PONCE, Puerto Rico

Galleries and museums
Museum grows in Puerto Rico. S. W. Rich. il Sat R 49:24-5 F 12 '66
Old masters in Puerto Rico; Museum of fine arts. L. Lastra. il Américas 18:11-16 N '66
Ponce art museum. R. Taylor. il Antiques 90:681-5 N '66
Ponce: design for a temperate climate. il Arch Rec 139:196-9 Ap '66
Puerto Rico's newest art museum. il Fortune 73:169-70 Ap '66

PONCHIELLI, Amilcare
La Gioconda. Criticism
  Dance Mag 40:29-30 D '66
  Hi Fi 16:MA14 D '66
  New Yorker 42:208 O 1 '66
  Sat R 49:20+ O 8 '66

PONDERAL index
How to figure your ponderal index. il Sci Digest 60:71 Jl '66

PONDS
Birth and death of a pond. C. P. Meacham. il Nat Parks Mag 40:14-18 Jl '66
Fishing ponds. unlimited. J. P. Jackson. il Am For 71:36-7+ O '65
Henry Hawkins' fish farm. B. Schley. il Am For 72:34-5+ Ap '66

PONDS, Pollution of. See Water pollution

PONIES, Polo. See Polo ponies

PONSOT, Claude
Paintings of Claude Ponsot. L. A. Lonergan. il Cath World 203:191-2 Je '66

PONTOON boats. See Boats and boating

POOL, Joe
House loses patience with HUAC. D. Rapoport. il Reporter 35:35-6 D 1 '66
Joe Pool of HUAC. L. L. King. por Harper 233:61-5 N '66

POOL (game) See Billiards

POOL rooms
Pool-rink complex. il Parks & Rec 1:750+ S '66

POOLE, Gray. See Poole, L. jt. auth.

POOLE, Lynn, and Poole, Gray
Room in ancient Assyria. Sat R 49:25-6 Jl 9 '66

POOLE, Stafford
Book review. America 115:664-6 N 19 '66

POOLS. See Garden pools

POOLS (gambling) See Gambling—Great Britain

POOR, Henry Varnum
Art news from nowhere. il por Esquire 67: 126 Ja '67

POOR
See also
Charities
Legal aid
Poverty
Public welfare
Slums

Asia
Escalation of policy: L. B. Johnson's promises. Nation 203:530-1 N 21 '66

Canada
Canadian bishop on poverty. America 115:308-9 S 24 '66

Puerto Rico
La vida: a Puerto Rican family in the culture of poverty—San Juan and New York, by O. Lewis. Review
  Atlan 218:138+ D '66. O. Handlin
  Nation 204:22-3 Ja 2 '67. E. Bendiner
  New Repub 155:23-5 D 3 '66. M. Renek
  Newsweek il 68:131-2 N 21 '66. S. Maloff
  Sat R 49:58-9 D 10 '66. B. D. Diamonstein
  Time il 88:133+ N 25 '66

United States
After Vietnam, abolish poverty? S. Alsop. il Sat Eve Post 239:12 D 17 '66
America's poor; symposium. il Nations Bsns 54:33-41+ S '66
Big business do-gooders: private war on poverty. T. G. Harris. il Look 30:15-19 Ag 9 '66
Bum's rush for the poor. America 115:149-50 Ag 13 '66

Children Santa didn't forget after all; cases of seventeen children. H. Markel. il Ladies Home J 83:26+ My '66
City is the frontier, by C. Abrams. Review New Repub 154:42+ My 14 '66. W. Thabit
Communicating research on the poor; the problem of telling it like it is; some ways of telling it; address. L. P. Jackson, jr. bibliog Negro Hist Bul 29:151-2+ Ap '66
Dangerous poor. S. Alsop. il Sat Eve Post 239: 18 Jl 16 '66
Dialogue in Washington; excerpts from Senate hearings. Arch Forum 125:38-40+ O '66
Dream city (almost) H. Cox. Commonweal 85:426-7 Ja 20 '67
Finding jobs for the poor. E. Moscovitch. New Repub 155:16-19 N 5 '66
First congress of the poor. R. A. Cloward and R. M. Elman. il Nation 202:148-51 F 7 '66; Reply. J. L. Erlich. 202:inside cover. 241 F 28 '66
How to help the ones at the bottom. J. Smith. New Repub 154:13-15 F 5 '66
Is poverty a sin? Christian Cent 83:357 Mr 23 '66
Moral basis of the war on poverty. S. Shriver. Christian Cent 83:1531-3 D 14 '66
Now: a tax plan that pays people; negative income tax. il U S News 60:63 F 14 '66
Plight of the rural poor. B. Kovach and N. Caldwell. il Reporter 34:27+ Ap 21 '66
Poor are human; morals of the protest. Nation 202:508 My 2 '66
Poor find a friend in court; ABA pushing program to supply legal aid with federal anti-poverty funds. il Bsns W p92-4+ D 10 '66
Poverty as a crime; carefully hedged rights of the poor. I. Silver Commonweal 85:74-6 O 21 '66
Poverty, injustice and the welfare state. R. A. Cloward and R. M. Elman. il Nation 202: 230-5, 264-8 F 28-Mr 7 '66
Poverty: public enemy number one. W. C. McWilliams. Sat R 49:48-9+ D 10 '66
Poverty U.S. style. H. C. Wallich. Newsweek 68:76 Jl 11 '66
Prices in poor neighborhoods; Bureau of labor statistics report. P. Groom. il Mo Labor R 89:1085-90 O '66
Profiles in poverty. il U S Camera 29:42-7 F '66
Strength through misery. il Time 87:28-9 Mr 18 '66
Studies in the grocery; Bureau of labor statistics study confirms that the poor pay more. J. Ridgeway. New Repub 154:9-10 Je 25 '66
Weight of the poor: strategy to end poverty. R. A. Cloward and F. F. Piven. il Nation 202:510-17 My 2 '66
Welfare industry; social work & the life of the poor. R. Lubove. il Nation 202:609-11 My 23 '66
What poverty does to the mind. R. Coles. Nation 202:746-8 Je 20 '66
See also
Anti-poverty program, 1964-
Church and social problems
    also subhead Poor under names of cities.
e.g. New York (city)—Poor; *also* subhead Social conditions under names of states,
e.g. Mississippi—Social conditions

POOR Bitos; drama. See Anouilh, J.

POOR laws
See also
Public welfare

POOR relief. See Public welfare

POOR whites. See Poor—United States

POP art. See Modernism (art)

POPCORN
How to put the pop in popcorn! il Bet Hom & Gard 44:98 O '66

POPE, Martin
Electric currents in organic crystals; with biographical sketch. Sci Am 216:22, 86-97 bibliog(p 146) Ja '67

POPE, R. M.
2.0-mgd water plant built in 2½ months; address. April 14. 1966. por Am City 81:82-3 Jl '66

POPES
Day with Pope Paul; excerpts from The Pope's backyard. C. G. Pepper. il McCalls 94:120-1+ O '66
Popes from the ghetto, by J. Prinz. Review Sat R 49:37 Je 18 '66. A. H. Friedlander

POPKIN, Henry
Life theater review. Life 60:17 F 18 '66
Opinion: on the east European theatre. por Mlle 64:120+ N '66

POPLAR
Hybrid poplars. R. C. Davids. il Farm J 90:60 Mr '66

POPOVERS. See Bread

POPPER, Jan
Traveling salesman. E. Gerken. il por Opera N 30:6 Mr 12 '66

POPPIES
Poppy planting time. B. Brinhart. il Flower Grower 53:24-5 Ag '66
Shirley poppies. R. Roe. il Horticulture 44: 41 F '66
Silken Shirley poppy. il Flower Grower 53:36 F '66

See also
Opium

POPPY seed bread. See Bread

POPULAR culture
Emperor's new clothes; or, The underground is for sleeping. J. Arbuckle. Mlle 63:234 S '66
Sontag sensibility. P. Velde. Commonweal 84: 390-2 Je 24 '66
When is it in, and when is it sick? J. Crist. Ladies Home J 83:26 S '66
See also
United States—Popular culture

POPULAR music. See Music, Popular (songs, etc)

POPULAR names of plants. See Botany—Nomenclature

POPULAR singers. See Singers

POPULAR songs. See Music, Popular (songs, etc)

POPULATION
To be or not to be that will be the question; implications of population growth. B. R. Sen. il UNESCO Courier 19:10-15 F '66
To establish an equilibrium; excerpt from address at FAO conference, November 2, 1959. A. Toynbee. UNESCO Courier 19:12 F '66
World population prospects; new United Nations study. UN Mo Chron 3:57 N '66
See also
Birth control
Malthusianism
also subhead Population under names of countries, states, cities, e.g. United States —Population

Overpopulation
Banquet of life. J. O'Gara. Commonweal 84: 170 Ap 29 '66
Committee of experts on fertility. UN Mo Chron 3:40 O '66
How many Americans will be too many? T. K. Burch. Cath World 203:213-19 Jl '66
Many worry about population explosion. Sci N L 89:137 F 26 '66
No more seaweed. J. O'Gara. Commonweal 85:283 D 9 '66; Reply. S. H. Hutner. 85:385 Ja 6 '67
Overpopulation: dilemma for U.S. aid. T. E. Dow, jr. bibliog f il Cur Hist 51:65-71+ Ag '66
Population explosion: what it means for the U.S. il Sr Schol 89:4-7+ N 4 '66
Tax on babies to limit population? U S News 60:11 Ja 31 '66
Twin war: hunger and population. Sci N 91: 18 Ja 7 '67
See also
Population, Increase of

Anecdotes, facetiae, satire, etc.
Shape of things practically here; fable, with paintings by G. Liebmann based on those by T. Cole. O. Jensen. il Am Heritage 17:44-9 Je '66

Statistics
Demographic yearbook, 1965. UN Mo Chron 3:57-8 N '66
Pop. 6,000,000,000; interview. M. Macura; I. Singh. New Yorker 42:47-9 S 10 '66
Tales of many cities. il UNESCO Courier 19:16-19 F '66

POPULATION, Increase of
Can man domesticate himself? R. Revelle. Bul Atomic Sci 22:2-7 F '66
Coordination of policy on population matters; statement, April 11, 1966. T. C. Mann. Dept State Bul 54:784-7 My 16 '66
Facts of life; Thomas Malthus was right, birth control is urgent. J. Nuveen. Christian Cent 83:983-6 Ag 10 '66
Food: population trends move U.S. to tie aid to self help. J. Walsh. Science 152:732-4 My 6 '66
If world population doubles by the year 2000; interview. H. Brown. il U S News 62:51-4 Ja 9 '67

Our multiplying families. Changing T 20:6 My '66
Our shrinking planet; adaptation of U.N. radio programmes. E. N. Valters. UNESCO Courier 19:4-9 F '66
Parks, or more people? W. H. Draper, jr. il Nat Parks Mag 40:10-13 Ap '66
Pop!!ulation; address, November 29, 1965. D. T. Rice. bibliog Vital Speeches 32:376-81 Ap 1 '66
Population clock approaches midnight. Christian Cent 83:1592-3 D 28 '66
Population growth and development. J. Bourgeois-Pichat. bibliog f il Int Concil 556: 5-79 Ja '66
300,000,000 Americans would be wrong. D. E. Lilienthal; discussion. N Y Times Mag p75 Ja 30; 12+ F 20 '66
U.S. presents views on population growth and economic development; statement, December 15, 1965. J. Roosevelt. Dept State Bul 54:175-8 Ja 31 '66
Where your markets and manpower will change most. il Nations Bsns 54:78-9 Jl '66
See also
Population—Overpopulation

POPULATION pressure. See Population—Overpopulation

PORCELAIN. See Pottery

PORCELAIN figurines. See Figurines

PORCH furniture. See Furniture, Outdoor

PORET, Clifton Alton
In the shadow of the chair. il por Time 88:78 Ag 26 '66

PORGY
See also
Cookery—Fish

PORGY and Bess; opera. See Gershwin, G.

PORK
See also
Cookery—Meat

PORNOGRAPHY. See Immoral literature and pictures; Obscenity (law)

POROMETERS. See Botanical apparatus

PORPHYRINS
Recording microfluorospectrophotometer. W. J. Runge. bibliog il Science 151:1499-506 Mr 25 '66

PORPOISES. See Dolphins (mammals)

PORT authority of New York. See Port of New York authority

PORT of New York authority
Lindsay challenges the Port authority; controversy over World trade center project. E. T. Chase. il Reporter 34:23-6 Je 30 '66; Discussion. 35:6 Ag 11 '66
Reporter at large; Basic essential skills training or BEST. F. C. Shapiro. New Yorker 42: 181-98 O 22 '66
World trade center: Manhattan's Tower of Babel. D. Smith. il Nation 202:235-8 F 28 '66

PORT TOWNSEND, Wash.
Traveler's choice. E. D. Sandvig. Travel 126:15 S '66

PORTABLE electric tools. See Electric tools, Portable

PORTABLE phonograph. See Phonograph, Portable

PORTABLE radio receivers. See Radio receiving apparatus, Portable

PORTABLE television receiving apparatus. See Television receiving apparatus, Portable

PORTABLE typewriters. See Typewriters

PORTE, Daniel, Jr, and Williams. R. H.
Inhibition of insulin release by norepinephrine in man. bibliog Science 152:1248-50 My 27 '66

PORTER, Bryce C.
Can Negroes do more to help themselves? excerpts from report. U S News 61:13 S 19 '66

PORTER, Cole
Cole Porter, my most unforgettable character. G. Eells. por Read Digest 89:79-83 Ag '66
Not one but two books (both full of misinformation) about Cole Porter. M. Kreuger. Am Rec G 33:56-60 S '66

PORTER, Eliot
Summers in Penobscot country; with photographs. Natur Hist 75:34-43 Ag '66

PORTER, Fairfield
Art and knowledge. il Art N 64:30-2+ F '66
Prendergast anomaly. Art N 65:36—9+ N '66

PORTER, J. Erwin
Erie Canal; a record in pastels. N. Kent. il Am Artist 30:42-7+ Je '66

PORTER, J. R.
Drawing water from wastes. Sat R 49:48 My 7 '66

PORTER, John H.
In wheels. Mlle 62:160-1+ F '66

PORTER, Katherine Anne
Letters to a nephew. Mlle 62:189+ Ap '66
Winners' press conference; remarks, March 15, 1966. por Pub W 189:30-2 Mr 28 '66

about

Four authors are given National book awards. por Pub W 189:47-8 Mr 21 '66
NBA 1966. por Newsweek 67:105 Mr 28 '66
Univ. of Maryland to receive Katherine Anne Porter papers. Pub W 191:36 Ja 2 '67
PORTER, Keith R. See Parsons, C. jt. auth.
PORTER, Marina Oswald. See Oswald, M.
PORTER, Sylvia
Spending your money; questions and answers. See issues of Ladies' home journal
PORTER, by William W. 2d
Public domain: heart of the Republic. Am For 72:12-15+ Ja; 26-9+ F; 34-5+ Mr; 28-31+ Ap '66
PORTERS
Early organization of red caps 1937-1938. P. Romero. bibliog Negro Hist Bul 29:101-2+ F '66
PORTILLO, Chile
Let's travel: to ski. il Mlle 64:191 N '66
PORTIS, Charles
That new sound from Nashville. Sat Eve Post 239:30-4+ F 12 '66
Traveling light; story. Sat Eve Post 239:54-5 Je 18; 48-50 Jl 2 '66
PORTISCH, Hugo
China: behind the upheaval. Sat R 49:24-9+ D 10 '66
Chinese-Soviet gap widens. Sat R 49:8-12 Jl 2 '66
Chinese talk belligerently, act cautiously; interview, ed. by A. Kucherov. por U S News 61:50-4 S 12 '66
Eyewitness in red China; excerpt from Red China, today. Sat R 49:14-21+ Ap 30; 31 Je 4 '66
PORTLAND, Ore.
Painting Portland's picture. P. D. Elmon. il Am City 81:126+ D '66

Description

Concrete cascade. D. Lyndon. il Arch Forum 125:74-9 Jl '66

Education

Speech is English too. M. Zollinger. Sr School 89:sup52 S 23 '66

Religious institutions and affairs

Portland's interfaith testimony for peace; successive prayer services. R. Rumsey. Christian Cent 83:1554 D 14 '66
PORTMAN, John C.
John Portman. J. Barnett. il Arch Rec 139: 133-40 Ja '66
PORTMANN, Adolf
Portmann's thought; adaptation of address, August 1965. M. Grene; discussion. Commentary 41:6+ Mr '66
PORTRAIT drawing
Children in motion. L. Lew. il Sch Arts 66: 14-16 D '66
I draw in my pocket; subway riders. E. Hibbard. il Am Artist 30:48-9 Je '66
Interpretive portraits of Fred Steffen; with commentary by the editors. il Am Artist 31:38-43+ Ja '67
PORTRAIT drawings
Portrait drawings: brief review of a recent exhibition; Galleries of portraits incorporated. N. Kent. il Am Artist 30:50-5 S '66
PORTRAIT painting
Drawn by I. Bradley from Great Britton. M. C. Black and S. P Feld. il Antiques 90: 502-9 O '66
News of art. il Horizon 9:74-5 Wint '67
News of art: Latin American painter-patriot; J. Gil de Castro. il Horizon 8:90-1 Aut '66
Portrait and its double. T. Berrigan. il Art N 64:30-3+ Ja '66
Powerful art of Franz Rederer. J. Lovoos. il Am Artist 30:42-7+ N '66
Sterne: line and likeness; exhibition at the Parsons gallery, N.Y. L. Campbell. il Art N 64:28-9+ F '66
See also
Copley, J. S.
PORTRAITS
Family portraits; where you can enjoy them. R. Martens. il Farm J 90:117 Ap '66
See also
Photography—Portraits
Portrait painting

Exhibitions

Portrait drawings: brief review of a recent exhibition; Galleries of portraits incorporated. N. Kent. il Am Artist 30:50-5 S '66

PORTRAITS, American
French gentleman and the Washington portraits of 1776. C. C. Sellers. il Antiques 89:248-55 F '66
Gabriel Manigault & Mrs Gabriel Manigault (Margaret Izard) C. B. Johnson. il Sch Arts 65:39 Je '66
Glen-Sanders portraits of Scotia, New York. B. Etchison. il Antiques 89:245-7 F '66
Images of elegant New York; conversation pieces; portfolio. L. Auchincloss. Am Heritage 17:48-65 O '66
Museum of early southern decorative arts; the paintings and prints. F. L. Horton. il Antiques 91:96-101 Ja '67
National portrait gallery, Washington, D.C. C. Nagel. il Antiques 90:642-6 N '66
Portraits by Gauntt. E. Gaines. il Antiques 89:238-9 F '66
PORTRAITS, Pen. See Character sketches
PORTRAITURE. See Photography—Portraits
PORTS
Committee on ports; Inter-American economic and social council. G. Meek il Américas 18:44-5 Ag '66
PORTUGAL
See also
Fátima
Festivals—Portugal
Forests and forestry—Portugal
Music festivals—Portugal
Newspapers—Portugal
Political parties—Portugal
Tourist trade—Portugal
United Nations—Portugal
United States—Foreign relations—Portugal

Colonies

Portugal's African provinces. G. Martelli. il Reporter 35:17-19 D 29 '66
Salazar's Portugal: anniversary on thin ice; emergent nationalism in Africa. R. H. Chilcote. il Nation 202:638-41 My 30 '66
See also
Macao

Commercial treaties and agreements

U.S. and Portugal amend cotton textiles agreement; Department announcement; with text of U.S. note; August 17, 1966. Dept State Bul 55:356-7 S 5 '66

History
Bibliography

Articles and other books received; comp. by C. J. Bishko. See issues of American historical review

Politics and government

Salazar's Portugal: anniversary on thin ice. R. H. Chilcote. il Nation 202:638-41 My 30 '66
Who murdered General Delgado? S. De Gramont. il Sat Eve Post 239:49-51 Ja 1 '66; Correction. 239:6 F 12 '66
PORTUGUESE in Africa
Portugal's African provinces. G. Martelli. il Reporter 35:17-19 D 29 '66
PORTUGUESE language in Brazil
It's in the potato. P. Rónai. il Américas 18:17-23 N '66
PORTUGUESE man-of-war
Beware the deadly man-of-war! F. Warshofsky. il Read Digest 88:81-4 Je '66
PORTUGUESE pottery. See Pottery, Portuguese
PORTUGUESE wines. See Wine
PORTZ, John
So you're going to an NDEA institute. NEA J 55:30-1 My '66
PORTZ, Mary
Indomitable Mrs Portz. J. Gillies. il pors Farm J 90:92-3+ F '66
POSIN, Dan Q.
We'll build a city on the moon. Todays Health 44:30-5 My '66
POSITION, Social. See Social status
POSITIONS, Applications for. See Applications for positions
POSITRONS
Basic constant of atom measured for first time. Sci N L 89:104 F 12 '66
POSNER, Aaron S. See Termine, J. D. jt. auth.
POSNER, David
Birds: poem. New Yorker 42:139 Je 4 '66
Townsend's Japanese rock garden; poem. Sat R 50:105 Ja 7 '67
POSNER, Michael I.
Components of skilled performance. bibliog Science 152:1712-18 Je 24 '66
POSSESSION (law)
See also
Real property

POSSONY, Stefan T.
How safe is America? Nat R 18:691-4 Jl 12
'66
Secret of August 1914. Nat R 18:1176-8 N
15 '66
POSSUMS. See Opossums
POST, Ben. See Rudman, R. jt. auth.
POST, Richard F. See Fowler, T. K. jt. auth.
POST, Washington. See Washington post and
Times herald
POST cards
Indiana sesquicentennial. B. Finnegan. il
Hobbies 71:120-1+ Jl; 118-19+ S; 120-1 O '66
Military leaders of World war 1. B. Finne-
gan. il Hobbies 70:124-5 F '66

History
Divided back on the post card. B. Finnegan.
Hobbies 71:125 Mr '66
POST exchanges. See United States—Armed
forces—Post exchanges
POST libraries. See United States—Army—
Libraries
POST-MORTEM examiners. See Medical ex-
aminers (law)
POST office department (United States) See
United States—Post office department
POSTAGE stamps
Big boom in JFK stamps. E. Dunbar. il Look
30:52-4 N 29 '66
Horticultural/botanical stamps. G. H. M.
Lawrence. il Horticulture 44:24-5 Ag '66
Opera's many homes. M. Stahl. il Opera N
30:17 Ja 29 '66
Stamp of UNESCO. il UNESCO Courier 19:
50-1 Jl '66
Stamps. H. Herst. jr. See issues of Hobbies
Stamps around the world; grill impressions.
H. Herst, jr. Hobbies 71:99+ Ja '67
Stamps around the world; Sir Rowland's in-
vention. H. Herst, jr. Hobbies 71:99 D '66

Collectors and collecting
Fight over philately; Henry Harris wins case
against Panama Canal Zone officials. il
Time 87:51 F 11 '66
Stamp news. H. Herst, jr. il Hobbies 71:
99+ Jl '66
Stamps around the world. H. Herst, jr. Hob-
bies 71:99 Mr; 99 Ap '66
Stamps around the world; rigged issue.
H. Herst, jr. Hobbies 71:98H S '66
Stamps around the world; the mistake of
approaching your hobby as speculative eco-
nomic investments. H. Herst, jr. Hobbies
71:99 Ag '66
Touring the world with stamps; philatelic
garden tour. E. Englert. Horticulture 44:
36-7+ Ag '66
Who's a stamp collector? who is a philatelist?
H. Herst, jr. Hobbies 71:99+ My '66
POSTAL employees
Day the mails stopped; Chicago's problems.
C. Remsberg. Sat R 49:21-4 D 17 '66
Super postmen; L.A. and Chicago upgrading
racial minorities. il Ebony 22:48-50+ D '66
POSTAL rates
United States
Untying parcel post; uniform rules for fourth-
class service. Bsns W p32 F 19 '66
POSTAL savings banks
End to postal savings. Nation 202:349 Mr 28
'66
POSTAL service
Question the world over: what's wrong with
the mails? il U S News 61:95-6 O 24 '66
See also
Air mail service
Mail handling

Laws and regulations
Untying parcel post; uniform rules for fourth-
class service. Bsns W p32 F 19 '66

Brazil
Innocents abroad. P. Dursin. il Seventeen 25:
146-7+ Mr '66

Great Britain
British have their problems, too. Bsns W p47
N 5 '66
Russia
Behind the hair curtain; foreign visitors mail.
H. B. Jacobs. Sat R 49:6+ O 8 '66

United States
Breakdown ahead in mail service? with ex-
cerpts from address by D. B. Brewster. il
U S News 61:52-4 N 7 '66

Crisis in the post office; reform aims. J. N.
Miller. il Read Digest 88:127-32 Mr '66
Danger of breakdown in mail service? il
U S News 60:58-9+ Mr 14 '66
How to float on a sea of red ink. il News-
week 69:56-8 Ja 2 '67
Insider explains mail breakdown. il U S News
61:50-1 D 5 '66
Mail must go through, but how? il Bsns W
p46-7 N 5 '66
Neither snow, nor rain; bad service. Nation
203:500 N 14 '66
To make the mails go through faster. il U S
News 60:12 Ja 31 '66
U.S. mails; address, February 8, 1966. L. F.
O'Brien. Vital Speeches 32:290-1 Mr 1 '66
Your mail service, what's coming. Changing
T 20:6 O '66
Zip code sprints to deadline. Bsns W p64+
O 15 '66
See also
Mail handling
Parcel post
Postal employees
United States—Post office department
POSTERS
Design technique of visual persuasion. L.
Klaschik. il Design 67:8-11 Ja '66
Handwriting on the walls and streets; pro-
liferating posters, red China. il Time 89:
25 Ja 20 '67
Photo posters in junior high school. J. Lid-
stone. il Sch Arts 66:27-30 N '66
Posters in Europe. il Opera N 31:14-16 D 10
'66
Collectors and collecting
Poster passion. M. Levin. il Travel 125:39-41
F '66
POSTGRADUATE work. See Colleges and uni-
versities—Graduate work
POSTMASTERS
Insider explains mail breakdown. il U S News
61:50-1 D 5 '66
Super postmen; L.A. and Chicago upgrading
racial minorities. il Ebony 22:48-50+ D '66
POSTMEN

Anecdotes, facetiae, satire, etc.
Postman. B. Venables. Esquire 66:20+ Jl '66
POSTMORTEMS. See Autopsy
POSTNATAL treatment. See Obstetrics
POSTURE
See also
Stature
POSVAR, Wesley W.
New pilot for Pitt. por Time 89:65 Ja 20 '67
Pilot for Pitt. por Newsweek 69:64 Ja 23 '67
POTASSIUM
Potassium:rubidium ratio in ultramafic rocks;
differentiation history of the upper mantle.
A. M. Stueber and V. R. Murthy. bibliog
il Science 153:740-1 Ag 12 '66
POTASSIUM in the body
Association between potassium concentration
and serological type of sheep red blood
cells. B. A. Rasmusen and J. G. Hall. il
Science 151:1551 Mr 25 '66
POTATOES
Minimum tillage cuts potato costs. W. A.
Hayes and C. Roy. il Farm J 90:66P Ap
'66
See also
Cookery—Vegetables
POTEMKIN, Grigorii Aleksandrovich, kníaz'
Catherine's boat ride. M. Durant. il Horizon
8:98-104 Aut '66
POTENTIOMETERS
Variable resistors; symposium. il Electr World
75:37-60 Ap '66
POTENZE, Jaime
Shadow of Peron. Commonweal 83:662-3 Mr
11 '66
POTIER, Robert
Brayer rubbings. Design 67:30-4 Mr '66
POTOK, Chaim
Martin Buber and the Jews. Commentary
41:43-9 Mr; 24+ S '66
POTOMAC RIVER
C&O canal association favors national park.
Nat Parks Mag 40:19 Jl '66
Issues on the Potomac. A. W. Smith. Nat
Parks Mag 40:2 O '66
Potomac tragedy; editorial. A. W. Smith.
bibliog f Nat Parks Mag 40:2+ F '66
POTOSI, Bolivia
Imperial city of Potosi. G. Mendoza. il
Américas 18:1-6 Jl '66
POTS and pans. See Kitchen utensils
POTTER, Beatrix
Beatrix Potter. R. Godden. il por Horn Bk
42:391-8 Ag '66
Beatrix Potter lives in Philadelphia's Free
library. E. Shaffer. il Horn Bk 42:401-5
Ag '66

POTTER, Beatrix—*Continued*
Celebrating a century of Peter Rabbit. A. Pryce-Jones. Harper 233:109-10 S '66
Centenary of Beatrix Potter's birth marked by publication and exhibits. Library J 91:4240 S 15 '66
Journal of Beatrix Potter; a review. M. Sendak. il por Pub W 190:130-3 Jl 11 '66
Journal of Beatrix Potter from 1881 to 1897, by L. Linder. Review
  Horn Bk il 42:399-400 Ag '66. R. H. Viguers
Leslie Linder. B. Brandenburger. il Horn Bk 42:686-9 D '66
Letter from London, centenary exhibition at National book league. M. Panter-Downes. New Yorker 42:115 Ag 20 '66
Peter Rabbit's mother. il por Time 88:82+ Ag 26 '66
Three faces of Beatrix Potter. G. Bott. por Sr Schol 89:sup29 O 28 '66

POTTER, Michael. See Lieberman, R. jt. auth.

POTTER, Raymond I.
Which oil is best for your engine? interview, ed. by J. Dunne. por Pop Sci 189:98-102 S '66

POTTER, Ryerson
Cincinnati paperback shop stresses poetry and art books. Pub W 189:66-8 Mr 21 '66
Foreign publications are a specialty of St Louis shop. Pub W 189:82-4 F 7 '66
Pages & prints; a paperback shop that is educationally-oriented. Pub W 189:86-9 F 28 '66

POTTER, Stephen
LSD; words only. Am Rec G 33:24-5 S '66
Marat/Sade. Am Rec G 32:790-1+ My '66
Uncle Samsmanship and other games. Sat R 49:64-6 Mr 12 '66
Words only. See issues of American record guide

POTTER, Van R. See Blobel, G. jt. auth.

POTTERY
Adams-Emery wing at the Cincinnati art museum. il Antiques 89:400-3 Mr '66
Banded creamware. S. Van Rensselaer. il Antiques 90:337-41 S '66
Casual china strong on style! il Bet Hom & Gard 44:80-1 Je '66
Ceramic kettles with stands. H. Newman. il Antiques 89:240-4 F '66
Christmas dangles; ceramic Christmas tree ornaments. il Seventeen 25:200 N '66
Redbook's guide to contemporary dinnerware. il Redbook 128:82-90 N '66
Room divider; use of ceramics and wood. W. Skinner. il Sch Arts 66:6-9 S '66

Competitions

Faenza: International ceramics competition. N. Caruso. il Craft Horiz 26:20-1 S '66

Decoration

Indigenous characteristics in American art pottery. M. J. Nelson. il Antiques 89:846-50 Je '66
Redbook's guide to provincial dinnerware; 18th-century-European pottery. il Redbook 127:82-90 O '66

Exhibitions

Ceramics today; three major exhibitions. D. McKinley; H. Giambruni; J. Pugliese. il Craft Horiz 26:10-30+ N '66
Parian ware exhibit; biscuit ware. il Hobbies 71:92 Ag '66

Technique

Experiment A; natural clay from an eroded bank. R. Simpson. il Design 67:12-15 Ja '66
Importance of being classical. M. Frimkess. il Craft Horiz 26:18-21+ Mr '66
Stoneware; an ancient art makes an exciting comeback. W. Radcliffe. il Pop Gard 17:58-61 Ag '66

POTTERY, American
Ceramics, East coast; symposium. il Craft Horiz 26:20-4+ Je '66
Ceramics today; three major exhibitions. D. McKinley; H. Giambruni; J. Pugliese. il Craft Horiz 26:10-30+ N '66
Ceramics, West coast; a discussion. P. Voulkos; P. Soldner. il Craft Horiz 26:25-8+ Je '66
Hugh Cornwall Robertson and the Chelsea period. L. E. Hawes. il Antiques 89:409-13 Mr '66
Indigenous characteristics in American art pottery. M. J. Nelson. il Antiques 89:846-50 Je '66
Paul Soldner. D. Parks. il Craft Horiz 26:20-3+ Ja '66
Potters of Poughkeepsie. J. P. Remensnyder. il Antiques 90:90-5 Jl '66

Redbook's guide to early American china, silver and glass. il Redbook 127:66-74 Je '66
Three California ceramists. J. Lovoos. il Am Artist 30:50-5+ D '66

POTTERY, Ecuadorian
Japanese in B.C. America? Jomon-like pottery unearthed at Valdivia, Ecuador. il Sci N L 89:53 Ja 22 '66

POTTERY, English
Carborundum grinds at faster clip; acquisition of W. T. Copeland & sons, manufacturer of Spode china. il Bsns W p58-62 Jl 23 '66
Examination of English eighteenth-century porcelains by transmitted light. J. L. Dixon. il Antiques 90:214-17 Ag '66
Mugs, jugs, and chamber pots; taking issue with some of Dr Boney's findings. I. N. Hume. il Antiques 90:520-2 O '66

POTTERY, European
Redbook's guide to provincial dinnerware; 18th-century-European pottery. il Redbook 127:82-90 O '66

POTTERY, German
Adding to a Meissen collection. I. Bischoff. il Antiques 89:535-9 Ap '66
Of Meissen men. il Newsweek 67:74+ Je 6 '66

POTTERY, Greek
See also
Vases, Greek

POTTERY, Japanese
Japanese in B.C. America? Jomon-like pottery unearthed at Valdivia, Ecuador. il Sci N L 89:53 Ja 22 '66

POTTERY, Peruvian
Peruvian chronicles in clay. il UNESCO Courier 19:12-13 Mr '66

POTTERY, Portuguese
Pottery of Barcelos. N. Flowers. il Natur Hist 75:44-51 Je '66

POTTERY dating. See Radioactive dating

POTTERY industry
Potters of Poughkeepsie. J. P. Remensnyder. il Antiques 90:90-5 Jl '66

POTTHOFF, Carl J.
First aid. See issues of Today's health

POUGHKEEPSIE, N.Y.
Organize your operators; battle against snow and ice. J. W. Nelson, jr. il Am City 81:86-8 N '66

POULENC, Francis
Dialogues of the Carmelites. Criticism
  New Yorker 42:163-4+ Mr 12 '66
  Opera N 30:34 Ap 2 '66
  Opera N il 30:14-15 Mr 5 '66
  Opera N il 31:24 S 10 '66
For children or grown-ups. S. Potter. Am Rec G 33:347 D '66
On Angel and Westminster, recitals of songs by Francis Poulenc. P. L. Miller. por Am Rec G 33:346-8 D '66

POULTER, Thomas C. See Odend'hal, S. jt. auth.

POULTRY
Ever go to a rooster crow? Rooster crowing contest, Rogue River, Ore. J. Lowe, sr. Farm J 90:64X F '66
News. See issues of Farm journal
Talk about chicken. Parents Mag 41:73-7 F '66
What's new. See issues of Successful farming
See also
Carving (meat, etc)

Egg production

How to make extra money with layers. D. Seim. Farm J 90:36A Ag '66
Poultry production. W. O. Wilson. il Sci Am 215:56-62+ bibliog(p 131) Jl '66

POULTRY cages. See Poultry houses—Equipment

POULTRY houses
Cleaning
How to prepare for chicks. Suc Farm 64:100A Mr '66
Layer houses that don't need cleaning. B. Hardy. il Farm J 90:40-1+ Mr '66

Equipment
New plastic layer cages. A. Phelps. il Farm J 90:80 F '66

Litter
Tetrachloroanisol; a source of musty taste in eggs and broilers. C. Engel and others. Science 154:270-1 O 14 '66

POULTRY industry and trade
Broiler growers bargain for better contracts. Farm J 90:72 F '66
Poultry picture brighter. D. Hagen. Farm J 90:50D S '66

POULTRY industry and trade—*Continued*
Poultry production. W. O. Wilson. il Sci Am
  215:56-62+ bibliog(p 131) Jl '66
  See also
  Turkeys
POUND, Ezra
  Image as style; poem. Sat R 49:56 Ap 9 '66

  about
  Ezra Pound and the great style. H. Carruth.
    por Sat R 49:21-2+ Ap 9 '66
  Ezra Pound at eighty. M. de Rachewiltz.
    pors Esquire 65:114-16+ Ap '66
POUND sterling. See Money—Great Britain
POUNDS, Norman J. G.
  East Germany. bibliog Focus 17:1-6 O '66
POUSSE-café; musical comedy. See Musical
  comedies, revues, etc.—Criticisms, plots,
  etc.
POUSSIN, Nicolas
  Luminous logician. il Time 88:68-9 Jl 22 '66
POUT fishing. See Bullhead fishing
POVERTY
  Culture of poverty. O. Lewis. il Sci Am 215:
    19-25 bibliog(p 150) O '66
  Faces of poverty. by A. Simon. Review
    Christian Cent 83:761-2 Je 8 '66. A. A.
    Gross
  On helping the poor. America 115:272 S 17 '66
  Oscar Lewis and the Puerto Rican family. J.
    P. Fitzpatrick. il America 115:778-9 D 10
    '66
  Pope Paul on poverty. Commonweal 84:272
    My 27 '66
  Poverty gap is big and growing. America
    115:472 O 22 '66
  Privilege and poverty; two worlds on one
    planet. N. Keyfitz. il Bul Atomic Sci 22:
    9-14 Mr '66; Reply. D. Felix. 22:29-30 D '66
    See also
  Anti-poverty program, 1964-
  Poor
  Public welfare
  Slums
POVERTY (virtue)
  Theology of poverty. A. T. Padovano. Cath
    World 204:219-24 Ja '67
POVERTY, Voluntary
  Voluntary austerity: the necessary art; vital
    to welfare of underprivileged men. D. A.
    Goulet. Christian Cent 83:748-52 Je 8 '66
POWDER puff derby. See Airplane racing
POWDERED titanium. See Titanium, Pow-
  dered
POWDERMAKER, Hortense
  Anthropologists in the field. M. Mead. Holi-
    day 40:113-15 Jl '66
  Many ways of man. M. Haynes. Sat R 49:
    59-60 Jl 23 '66
POWDERY mildew
  Powdery mildew you should act now. il Sun-
    set 137:198 S '66
POWELL, Adam Clayton, 1908-
  Negro congressman talks about black power;
    interview. por U S News 61:38-41 Ag 15 '66

  about
  Adam cast out. il Newsweek 69:28-9 Ja 23
    '67
  Adam's fall. por Newsweek 68:29-30 O 3 '66
  Armed Powell defends his hideout; with re-
    port by M. Acoca. il por Life 61:101-2+
    D 9 '66
  Bigger than Adam. Nation 203:300 O 3 '66
  Black power advocate in a powerful post. por
    U S News 61:8 Ag 1 '66
  Cliffhanger. Reporter 35:16-17 D 15 '66
  Curse of Adam. il por Time 89:13-14 Ja 13
    '67
  Disarming Powell. New Repub 155:7-8 O 1 '66
  Even on Sundays. il por Newsweek 68:28 D
    12 '66
  Green power. Newsweek 68:41 O 10 '66
  Growing troubles of Chairman Powell. il por
    U S News 62:10 Ja 2 '67
  Hands off Adam! il Time 89:17 Ja 6 '67
  House committee studies treatment of
    minorities in text and library books; report
    of hearings. il Pub W 190:34-40 S 19 '66
  House hearings hit textbooks on grounds of
    racial bias Pub W 190:39-40 S 5 '66
  Keep the faith, baby. W. More. America
    116:30 Ja 21 '67
  Keeping the faith; barred from Congress.
    il por Time 89:15-16 Ja 20 '67
  Maid in Bimini. Newsweek 69:20 Ja 2 '67
  Must Adam leave Eden? il pors Newsweek
    69:24-8 Ja 16 '67
  Negro leader's advice to members of his
    race; excerpts from address. May 29, 1966.
    por U S News 60:14 Je 13 '66

New Chairman Perkins; Powell's opposite.
  U S News 62:14 Ja 23 '67
Out of Powell case: reforms in Congress?
  with excerpts from report. il por U S
  News 62:29-30 Ja 16 '67
Outlaw in the House. il Time 88:29 D 9 '66
Powell and black bravado. A. Kopkind. New
  Repub 156:13-15 Ja 21 '67
Powell and the power of prejudice. America
  116:9 Ja 7 '67
Powell case. Commonweal 85:416 Ja 20 '67
Powell is sacked by his peers. il pors Life
  62:34B-34C Ja 20 '67
Powell: one more try. W. F. Buckley, jr. Nat
  R 18:975 O 4 '66
Problems of Adam Clayton Powell. por U S
  News 61:19 D 19 '66
Put the whole house in order! Christian
  Cent 84:69 Ja 18 '67
Reform hits Capitol hill: Powell is pushed
  aside; with reprint from Washington post,
  January 9, 1967 by R. Harwood. il pors
  U S News 62:32-4+ Ja 23 '67
Reverend Powell sees it through. Nat R 18:
  1308 D 27 '66
Revolt in the House. por Sr Schol 89:19-20 O
  14 '66
Slap at Adam Clayton Powell; but not much
  sting. il pors U S News 61:26+ O 3 '66
Snakes in Adam's Eden. il por Time 88:13
  D 30 '66
What to do about Adam Powell? Life 62:6
  Ja 13 '67
POWELL, Anthony
  Reference for Lady Chatterley's lover; story.
    Vogue 148:126-7 D '66
POWELL, Bud
  In memoriam, Bud Powell. M. Williams. por
    Sat R 49:51 Ag 27 '66
  Notes and comment. New Yorker 42:25 Ag 20
    '66
POWELL, Daniel
  Nation's first clinical professor. Sch & Soc
    94:116+ Mr 5 '66
POWELL, Dick
  Egos and actors. J. O'Hara. il Holiday 40:34+
    O '66
POWELL, J. L. and DeLong, S. E.
  Isotopic composition of strontium in volcanic
    rocks from Oahu. bibliog Science 153:
    1239-42 S 9 '66
POWELL, Lawrence Clark
  Library named at UCLA for Lawrence C.
    Powell. Library J 92:46 Ja 1 '67
POWELL, Peter John
  Chicago's Indian priest. il por Newsweek
    69:91 Ja 23 '67
POWELL, Ralph L.
  Military affairs of Communist China. bib-
    liog f Cur Hist 51:140-6+ S '66
POWELL, Watson, Jr
  How it feels to live in total design. C.
    Welles. il Life 60:59+ Ap 29 '66
POWELL, Yvette Diago
  Growing troubles of Chairman Powell. il por
    U S News 62:10 Ja 2 '67
POWELL, LAKE. See Lakes, Artificial
POWELSON, Harvey. See Freedman, M. B.
  jt. auth.
POWER, Edward J.
  Book review. America 115:608 N 12 '66
POWER, Eugene Barnum
  Power resigns from U. of Michigan, cites
    conflict of interest opinion. Library J 91:
    2020-1 Ap 15 '66
  University microfilms head resigns Michigan
    post. Pub W 189:47-8 Mr 28 '66
  Wagman blasts Michigan student paper, de-
    fends Power against conflict charge; ex-
    cerpts from letter. F. H. Wagman. Li-
    brary J 91:2296-7 My 1 '66
  Weak arm of the law. Nation 202:350 Mr 28
    '66
POWER (mechanics)
  Energy for the future. P. H. Abelson. Sci-
    ence 154:1607 D 30 '66
POWER (political science)
  New coalition, wave of the future. L. Harris.
    Newsweek 68:24 Jl 25 '66
  Pattern of revolution; black power gimmick;
    leaders use to hold personal power. R.
    Moley. Newsweek 68:84 Ag 8 '66
  World politics of responsibility. O. Gass; dis-
    cussion. Commentary 41:12+ Ap '66
POWER (psychology)
  Psychology of power, by R. V. Sampson. Re-
    view
    Nation il 203:581-6 N 28 '66. C. Lasch
POWER amplifiers. See Amplifiers
POWER bicycles. See Motor scooters
POWER boat racing. See Motor boat racing
POWER boats. See Motor boats

POWER equipment. See Electric machinery
POWER lawn mowers. See Lawn mowers
POWER lines. See Electric lines
POWER plants
  See also
  Atomic power plants
  Electric plants
  Hydroelectric plants
POWER politics. See Power (political science)
POWER pools. See Electric plants—Interconnection
POWER resources
  Report pussyfoots on issues; government report on energy resources. Sci N 90:417 N 19 '66
POWER saws. See Saws
POWER steering. See Automobiles—Steering gear
POWER supply. See Electric power
POWER tools. See Electric tools, Portable
POWER transmission
  Amazing new cone drive is clutch, transmission, differential. H. Walton. il Pop Sci 188:59-62+ Je '66
POWERS, Barbara Gay (Moore)
  Barbara Powers: she married a sky spy. D. Cort. Nation 202:101 Ja 24 '66
POWERS, Charles F. and Robertson, Andrew
  Aging Great Lakes; with biographical sketches. Sci Am 215:29, 94-100+ bibliog (p 160) N '66
POWERS, Dennis
  Vietnam: no place for people. Sat R 49:41 Ap 2 '66
POWERS, Francis Gary
  Barbara Powers: she married a sky spy. D. Cort. Nation 202:101 Ja 24 '66
  Going to see Gary. O. Demaris. il pors Esquire 65:88-91+ My '66
POWERS, Melvin
  Aunt Candy. il por Newsweek 67:26 Ja 31 '66
  Candy trial. il Newsweek 67:35 Mr 14 '66
  Mesmerism in Miami. por Time 87:66 Mr 18 '66
  Trials of Candy and Mel. L. H. Lapham. il por Sat Eve Post 239:28-32+ Ag 27; 32-6+ S 10 '66
POWERS, Stefanie
  Stefanie Powers: the U.N.C.L.E. doll. I. Mothner. il pors Look 30:42+ O 18 '66
POWILLS, Dorothy
  Playing cards. See issues of Hobbies
POWLEDGE, Fred
  If I get up from here and do a little bit, a little bit more's going to come to me. Redbook 127:66-7+ S '66
  Segregation, northern style. Am Ed 3:1-5 D '66
POZNAN, Poland
  Two days that shook the Communist world. F. Lewis. il N Y Times Mag p25+ Je 12 '66
PRACTICAL jokes
  Caution! genius at play. J. N. Bell. il Pop Mech 125:120-3+ Mr '66; Same abr. with title Look out! genius at play. Read Digest 88:201-4 My '66
PRADELLI, Francesco Molinari-. See Molinari-Pradelli, F.
PRADES festivals. See Music festivals—France
PRAEGER, Frederick A, incorporated
  Britannica buys Frederick A. Praeger, inc. Pub W 189:31-2 My 2 '66
PRAEGER, R. Q. and Waterbury, J. W.
  Convertibility. Am City 81:100-1 Ag '66
PRAGMATISM
  How I bet my life; Spinozist who became a pragmatist. H. M. Kallen. Sat R 49:27-30+ O 1 '66
PRAGUE
  Prague in metamorphosis. R. J. Gerber. America 115:480-2 O 22 '66; Discussion. 115:636; 116:30-1 N 19 '66, Ja 14 '67
    Description
  Kafka's Prague. S. Bullaty and A. Lomeo. il Horizon 9:88-99 Wint '67
    Intellectual life
  Letter from Prague. J. Yglesias. Nation 204: 59-61 Ja 9 '67
    Music
  Midseason superlatives. W. Weaver. il Hi Fi 16:162-3 Ap '66
  Prague. P. Eckstein. il Opera N 30:33 Mr 12 '66
  Prague; Benjamin Britten's Albert Herring and Prokofiev's Betrothal in a monastery. P. Eckstein. il Opera N 30:25 My 7 '66

    Theater
  Reports from abroad. H. Koegler. il Dance Mag 40:18+ Ap '66
  Theatre, Apparition theatre of Prague. J. McCarten. New Yorker 42:155 D 3 '66
PRAIRIE CREEK REDWOODS STATE PARK. See California—Parks and reserves
PRAIRIE schooners. See Wagons
PRANGE, Gordon W.
  Master spy; condensation. Read Digest 90: 209-12+ Ja '67
PRATER, Yvonne
  Washington high trails. Liv Wildn 29:28 Aut '65
PRATO, Lou
  New medical schools: building up for tomorrow's patients. Todays Health 44:36-41 N '66
PRATT, Charles
  Its intense and total cowness. D. Vestal. il Pop Phot 59:100-1 D '66
PRATT, Jonathan
  Girl on a dark road; story. Sat Eve Post 239: 66-8 D 3 '66
PRATT, Richard M. and McFarlin, P. F.
  Manganese pavements on the Blake plateau. Science 151:1080-2 Mr 4 '66
PRATT, Theodore
  English as spoken in Scandinavia. Atlan 217: 122-3 Je '66
PRATT and Whitney aircraft division. See United aircraft corporation—Pratt and Whitney aircraft division
PRAYER
  Person and the people. V. P. McCorry. America 114:861-2 Je 18 '66
  Speaking out: our prayers are meaningless. M. Boyd. Sat Eve Post 239:10+ Ag 27 '66
  That problem again. V. P. McCorry. America 116:127-8 Ja 21 '67
PRAYER in the schools. See Public schools and religion
PRAYERS
  Appealing to a power higher than Uncle Sam; concerning the prayer at the inauguration of Lieutenant General Ferdinand T. Unger as U.S. high commissioner for the Ryukyus. Christian Cent 83:1464 N 30 '66
  See also
  Lord's prayer
PRAYERS, Table. See Grace (at meals)
PREACHING
  Learning a Sunday punch; Catholic university of America preaching workshop. Newsweek 68:82 Jl 4 '66
  See also
  Sermons
PREAMPLIFIERS. See Amplifiers
PREBINDING. See Bookbinding
PREBIOTIC synthesis. See Synthesis
PREBISCH, Raúl
  Some fundamental problems of world trade; excerpts from a statement, January 26, 1966. UN Mo Chron 3:44-52 F '66
PRECAMBRIAN period. See Geology, Stratigraphic—Precambrian; Paleontology—Precambrian
PRECAST concrete. See Concrete, Precast
PRECIOUS metals
  Unique fabricator: Handy and Harman, New York. T. J. Murray. il Duns R 87:41-3+ F '66
PRECIOUS stones
  Gem stones. B. Petkof. il Consumer Bul 49:11-14 Je '66
PRECIPITATION (meteorology)
  See also
  Rain and rainfall
PRECOGNITION. See Extrasensory perception
PRE-COLLEGE guidance. See Educational guidance
PRE-COLUMBIAN art. See Art, Pre-Columbian
PREDATOR and rodent control. See United States—Fish and wildlife service
PREDATORY animals. See Animals, Predatory
PREDATORY birds. See Birds of prey
PREDICTIONS. See Forecasts (economics)
PREDNISOLONE
  Glucocorticoid-induced resistance to deoxycholate lysis in HeLa cells. G. Melnykovych. bibliog il Science 152:1086-7 My 20 '66
PREDOEHL, Martin C.
  Antarctic pack ice: boundaries established from Nimbus I pictures. Science 153:861-3 Ag 19 '66
PRE-EMPLOYMENT testing. See Employment systems
PRE-ENGINEERED buildings. See Buildings, Prefabricated

PREFAB fireplaces. See Fireplaces

PREFABRICATED buildings. See Buildings, Prefabricated

PREFABRICATED houses. See Houses, Prefabricated

PREFERRED stocks. See Stocks

PREGNANCY
Advantage of pregnancy? case of Mrs Marvin Glidden. with a transplanted kidney. il Time 88:72 O 7 '66
Barbra Streisand talks about her million-dollar baby; interview. ed. by G. Steinem. B. Streisand. Ladies Home J 83:64+ Ag '66
Catecholamine concentrations: changes in plasma of rats during estrous cycle and pregnancy. R. D. Green, 3d. and J. W. Miller. bibliog il Science 151:825-6 F 18 '66
Eating for two. V. Apgar. il Todays Health 44:12+ F '66
Expectant mother: breast changes during pregnancy and after. J. W. Huffman. Redbook 127:28+ Ag '66
Expectant mother: how the blood system responds to pregnancy. G. J. Vosburgh and B. R. Boylan. Redbook 127:40+ My '66
Expectant mother: should a woman work during pregnancy? D. Cavanagh and D. Z. Meilach. Redbook 128:40+ D '66
Expectant mother: vocabulary of pregnancy and childbirth. R. A. Kimbrough. Redbook 126:42+ Mr '66
Expectant mother: where the unborn baby grows; ed. by D. Meilach. E. A. Friedman. Redbook 127:35-6 S '66
Expectant mother: why do I feel so tired? K. P. Russell and others. Redbook 127:38+ Je '66
I was the world's most expectant mother; mother of quadruplets; ed. by M. Bloom and S. Bloom. S. Sklar. il Redbook 126:56-7+ Mr '66
Pregnancy among husbands quite common. Todays Health 44:6 S '66
Progesterone retards postpartum involution of the rabbit myometrium. F. R. Goodall. bibliog il Science 152:356-8 Ap 15 '66
Smokers show decreased toxemia in pregnancy. Sci N 89:392 My 21 '66
Smoking & pregnancy. Time 87:72 My 13 '66
What doctors are discovering now about pregnancy and infancy: a special section; symposium. il Ladies Home J 83:44+ Ag '66
What every mother-to-be should know (cont) V. Apgar. il Todays Health 44:6+ Mr; 8+ Ap; 16+ My; 16+ Je '66
Woman on her way to a miracle; ed. by E. Graves. M. Falk. il Life 61:48-61+ Jl 22 '66
See also
Abortion
Childbirth
Fetus
Obstetrics
Prenatal influences
Sex determination and control

PREGNANCY, Complications of
Expectant mother: extrauterine pregnancy. B. Word and B. R. Boylan. Redbook 127:20+ O '66
Expectant mother: warning signals during pregnancy. J. E. Hall and B. J. Nelson. Redbook 128:50+ N '66
How pregnancy affects your health; ed. by P. Deutsch and R. Deutsch. W. G. Slate. Redbook 126:54+ Ap '66

PREGNANCY diet. See Diet

PREHISTORIC astronomy. See Astronomy, Prehistoric

PREHISTORIC man. See Man, Prehistoric

PREJUDICE
Day I learned about prejudice; mob murder. E. A. Morrison. Mlle 63:122+ S '66
See also
Race prejudice

PRE-KINDERGARTEN schools. See Nursery schools

PREMATURE infants. See Infants, Premature

PREMINGER, Otto
Profiles. L. Ross. por New Yorker 41:42-6+ F 19 '66

PREMIUMS
See also
Trading stamps

PRENATAL influences
Maternal effect in dental traits of the house mouse. P. Tenczar and R. S. Bader. bibliog il Science 152:1398-400 Je 3 '66
Parturient mice: effect of environment on labor. N. Newton and others. bibliog il Science 151:1560-1 Mr 25 '66
Stimulation of the proliferation of cortical neurons by prenatal treatment with growth hormone. S. Zamenhof and others. bibliog il Science 152:1396-7 Je 3 '66

What expectant mothers need to know; interview. D. Harting. il U S News 60:54-6+ F 14 '66

PRENATAL sex determination. See Sex determination and control

PRENDERGAST, Joseph
Personal thank you Parks & Rec 1:711 S '66

PRENDERGAST, Maurice Brazil
Prendergast anomaly. F. Porter. il Art N 65:36-9+ N '66

PRENTICE-Hall, incorporated
Prentice-Hall receives president's E award. il Pub W 189:81 Ap 18 '66

PREPACKAGED meat. See Meat—Prepackaging

PREPARATION for college. See Colleges and universities—Entrance requirements

PREPARATORY schools. See Private schools

PREPARED mustard. See Mustard, Prepared

PREPAREDNESS, Military
Plain facts of war and peace. D. Lawrence. U S News 60:128 My 16 '66
Worldwide defense expenditures. il Bul Atomic Sci 22:44-8 S '66
See also
Armaments
also subhead Defenses under names of countries, e.g. France—Defenses

PRERECORDED video tape. See Video tape recorders and recording

PRESBYTERIAN church in Canada
Presbyterian church in Canada assembly. D. H. Rayner. Christian Cent 83:921-2 Jl 20 '66

PRESBYTERIAN church in the United States. See United Presbyterian church in the United States of America

PRESBYTERIAN church in the United States (South)
Move toward union. Christian Cent 83:197-8 F 16 '66
Southerners for aggiornamento? America 114:684 My 14 '66
Southerners step forward; General assembly. Time 87:76+ My 6 '66

PRESBYTERIAN general assembly. See United Presbyterian church in the United States of America

PRESCHOOL children
Anxious child can learn, but what? with study-discussion program, by R. Strang. E. J. LeShan. bibliog il PTA Mag 61:8-10, 35 D '66
Emotional problems of preschoolers; with study-discussion program, by R. Strang. S. M. Finch. bibliog il PTA Mag 60:15-17, 32 Ap '66
How preschoolers learn to give and take. M. Nicolaysen. il Parents Mag 41:48-9+ My '66
Preschool boom: its pressures and rewards; New York city's problems. L. Smith. il Newsweek 67:109-10+ My 16 '66
Preschool personality patterns; with study-discussion program, by R. Strang G. O. Dickinson. bibliog il PTA Mag 61:21-3, 35-6 O '66
Problem preschoolers; Virginia Frank child development center, Chicago. E. G. Neisser. il Parents Mag 41:43-5+ Mr '66
Who can teach pre-school children, and why? E. Nelson. il Dance Mag 40:64-6 Je '66
See also
Child study
Nursery schools
Socially handicapped children

Education
Mother of childhood schooling; New York's Bank Street college of education. il Time 88:94-5 O 7 '66

PRESCHOOL education. See Education of children; Nursery schools; Preschool children

PRESCOTT, Katherine
Book week in braille. Library J 91:4197-9 S 15 '66

PRESCOTT, Orville
All for love of Abelard. Sat R 50:83 Ja 14 '67
Caesars' last stand. Sat R 49:46-7 D 24 '66
Mixture of logic and magic. Sat R 49:58 C 22 '66
Mystic maid of Orleans. Sat R 49:56 D 3 '66
Opinion: on reading fiction. por Mlle 63:68+ S '66
What's happening to fiction? Sat R 49:21-2 N 26 '66

PRESCOTT, R. G. W.
Estrous cycle in the rat: effects on self-stimulation behavior. bibliog Science 152:796-7 My 6 '66

PRESCOTT, Ariz.
Mile-high Prescott. il Sunset 137:40-5 Jl '66

PRESCRIPTIONS

Doctors who profit from prescriptions; doctor-merchants probed by Senate antitrust and monopoly subcommittee. Consumer Rep 31:234-8 My '66

Uneasy balance, ethics vs profits; physicians who profit from prescribed medications. K. Wheeler and W. Lambert. il Life 60:86-8+ Je 24 '66

PRESENT, The

Today and tomorrow. V. P. McCorry. America 115:468-9 O 15 '66

PRESERVATION of food. See Canning and preserving

PRESERVATION of landmarks, scenery, etc.

See also
Historic houses, etc.

United States

Design for Washington state; citizens go into action. il Parks & Rec 1:834-5 O '66

Knights of the golden horseshoe; Germanna. H. D. Crawford. il Am For 72:28-31+ N '66

Philadelphia story continued. B. Snow. il Antiques 89:546-7 Ap '66

They bring back magic yesterdays; preservationists. K. Detzer. il Read Digest 88:160-5 Mr '66

They're saving America's priceless seashore. D. Wharton. il Read Digest 89:181+ Ag '66

See also
United States—Historic houses, etc.

PRESERVATION of paper. See Paper—Preservation

PRESERVATION of vegetables. See Food preservation and preservatives

PRESERVES. See Jelly, jam, etc.

PRESERVES, Game. See Game preserves

PRESIDENTIAL advisers. See Public officers

PRESIDENTIAL airplanes. See Airplanes, Government

PRESIDENTIAL campaigns

L.B.J. isn't really the master politician everybody thinks he is. H. Sidey. il Life 61:30B Jl 15 '66

See also
Campaign funds
Presidential candidates

1960

My hero LBJ. L. L. King. il Harper 233:58-61 O '66

With Kennedy, by P. Salinger. Review Newsweek il 68:86 Jl 25 '66

1964

Romney-Goldwater clash; storm signal for '68. il U S News 61:14 D 12 '66

Story of two letters: effect on Romney chances; with letter by G. W. Romney, reply by B. M. Goldwater, and with excerpts from other documents. il U S News 61:62-70 D 19 '66

PRESIDENTIAL candidates

Kennedy in '68? H. H. Miller. New Repub 155:11-13 O 15 '66

Robert Kennedy and the what if game. D. Kiker. il Atlan 218:66-70 O '66

Unlike old soldiers, labels never fade away. P. Lisagor. il Nations Bsns 54:21-2 S '66

See also
Campaign funds

1964

How Goldwater views '68, and '64: interview. B. M. Goldwater. U S News 61:22 S 12 '66

1968

Alabama's Wallace: aiming at presidency? interview. il U S News 60:23 My 16 '66

As Republican governors look over the ranks for '68. il U S News 61:37-8 D 26 '66

Availability of Richard Nixon. J. Witcover. Reporter 35:27-9 Ag 11 '66

Best Republican for '68. S. V. Roberts. il Esquire 65:84-5+ Mr '66

Can Romney stop Nixon in '68? il U S News 61:31 Jl 25 '66

Consensus by any other name. il Time 88:21-2 D 2 '66

Dorado summit. il Newsweek 68:30-1 D 5 '66

Four hearties of the good ship G.O.P. W. Weaver, jr. il N Y Times Mag p50-1+ N 27 '66

Front-runner; Harris survey. Newsweek 68:31 N 28 '66

Governors to the front; Republicans. R. Moley. Newsweek 68:76 D 26 '66

GOP: it's Romney vs. Nixon; with report by J. Lindsay. il Newsweek 67:23 Je 6 '66

How Goldwater views '68, and '64; interview. B. M. Goldwater. U S News 61:22 S 12 '66

How the future looks to Republicans now. il U S News 61:36+ Jl 4 '66

It's like running against God. S. Alsop. il Sat Eve Post 239:20 O 22 '66

Lonesome George; Romney is gearing up. Newsweek 68:20-1 Jl 4 '66

A look ahead. Nation 203:562 N 28 '66

LBJ vs. which Republican in '68? il U S News 61:50-2 N 21 '66

Making of president Robert Kennedy. W. V. Shannon. il Harper 233:62-8 O '66

Memo from Washington: who will control the GOP in 1968? W. Rogers. Look 31:76 Ja 24 '67

Mr Nixon comes to town. M. McGrory. America 115:273 S 17 '66

Next president. K. Crawford. Newsweek 68:24 S 5 '66

1968 already. Nat R 18:450 My 17 '66

Nixon and the GOP: comeback? 4,000 mile road show. il Newsweek 68:30-5 O 10 '66

Nobody's rumpled, nobody's real; Romney-Percy-Reagan images. H. Sidey. Life 61:56 D 9 '66

Nuts in the basket. Time 88:20 D 23 '66

Plot to steal the GOP. W. A. Rusher. il Nat R 18:668-71 Jl 12 '66

Political realignment. W. Lippmann. Newsweek 69:13 Ja 2 '67

Polls '66: Nixon or Romney? P. Gennoy. Nat R 18:1084 N 1 '66

Republican challenge. H. Brandon. Sat R 49:10+ D 3 '66

Romney victory gilds his chances for '68. Bsns W p44-5 N 12 '66

Romney's chances to head ticket in '68. il U S News 61:29-30 D 5 '66

Sorensen looks at '68: not a single state safe for Democrats; excerpts from address, December 12, 1966. T. C. Sorensen. U S News 61:10 D 26 '66

Stop me if you've heard this. Nat R 18:1202+ N 29 '66

Two for the future; Republicans. il Time 87:18 Je 3 '66

Who'll take on LBJ? il Newsweek 68:34-7 N 21 '66

1972

Bobby phenomenon. il Newsweek 68:30+ O 24 '66

Front runners for '72. W. Weaver, jr. il N Y Times Mag p26-7+ My 22 '66

Making of the president, 1972? Newsweek 68:17-18 S 5 '66

PRESIDENTIAL conventions. See National conventions (political)

PRESIDENTIAL duties. See Presidents—United States—Powers and duties

PRESIDENTIAL entertaining. See Government entertaining

PRESIDENTIAL government. See Presidents—United States

PRESIDENTIAL papers. See Archives—United States

PRESIDENTIAL planes. See Airplanes, Government

PRESIDENTIAL polls. See Public opinion polls

PRESIDENTIAL scholars. See High school students, Mentally superior

PRESIDENTS

United States

America's political dynasties, by S. Hess. Review Newsweek 68:124 O 10 '66. R. Moley

Great American presidents; address, February 3, 1966. J. A. Farley. Vital Speeches 32:393-6 Ap 15 '66

Impressions of Johnson, the Kennedys, and today's government; interview. A. Krock. il U S News 61:44-9 D 19 '66

A look at the inner workings of the White House; interview. B. D. Moyers. il U S News 60:78-85 Je 13 '66

My hero LBJ. L. L. King. il Harper 233:51-61 O '66

Our way with heroes: hot-and-cold public whim. K. Crawford. Newsweek 69:22 Ja 2 '67

Presidents and their spending: million once was a lot of money. il U S News 60:52-3 F 14 '66

Presidentville, U.S.A.; pre-White House roles; cartoon. Am Heritage 17:6-7+ O '66

Public crises take no vacations. P. Lisagor. il Nations Bsns 54:23-4 My '66

Truman presidency, by C. Phillips. Review Newsweek il 67:100 Je 6 '66

Unlike old soldiers, labels never fade away. P. Lisagor. il Nations Bsns 54:21-2 S '66

PRESIDENTS—United States—*Continued*
Wealth of presidents. H. F. Graff. il Am Heritage 17:4-5+ O '66
White House style-makers; L. B. Johnson vs. J. F. Kennedy. C. Fritchey. Harper 232: 47-9 Ap '66
See also
United States—Executive office of the president
White House

Election

Sloppy elections do not a Great society make. F. Morley. il Nations Bsns 54:25-6 Ja '66
See also
Electoral college
Presidential campaigns
Presidential candidates

Families

Homecoming for the kin of presidents. il U S News 61:10 D 12 '66
Living White House. L. Aikman. il pors Nat Geog Mag 130:593-643 N '66

Health
See also
Johnson, L. B.—Health

Messages

Cautious, candid & conciliatory; State of Union address. il Time 89:13-14 Ja 20 '67
Lying low; impending State of the Union address. Time 89:12 Ja 13 '67
LBJ trims sail to do all we can; highlights of State of the Union address. il Newsweek 69:22-4 Ja 23 '67
No staying power? reactions to State of the Union message. New Repub 156:7-8 Ja 21 '67
Reminder of the grandeur of office. H. Sidey. il Life 62:34D Ja 20 '67
Run just to stand still; speculation about LBJ's State of the Union message. il Newsweek 69:21 Ja 16 '67
Snarled state of the union. E. J. Hughes. Newsweek 69:19 Ja 23 '67
State of the Union messages of the presidents, 1790-1966; ed. by F. I. Israel. Review
    Sat R 49:40-1 D 3 '66. A. Nevins

Poetry

Three presidents; A. Jackson, T. Roosevelt, J. F. Kennedy. R. Bly. Nation 202:108 Ja 24 '66

Powers and duties

Four centers of U.S. foreign policy; government departments and the President's position. N. Cousins. Sat R 49:16-18 Jl 2 '66
Gray capital, gray debate; sweep of presidential power in foreign affairs. E. J. Hughes. Newsweek 67:23 F 21 '66
Heresy at Omaha; concerning L. B. Johnson's remarks about rights and duties of the President. W. Lippmann. Newsweek 68:17 Jl 18 '66
LBJ and Lincoln; the agonies of decision; to bomb or not to bomb North Vietnam. U S News 60:6 F 7 '66
Presidency; most powerful elected office in the world. il Sr Schol 88:8-9 F 18 '66
Presidency: power & paradox. J. M. Burns. il Sat R 49:30-1 F 5 '66
Presidential government, by J. M. Burns. Review
    Nat R 18:222-3 Mr 8 '66. M. S. Evans
    New Repub 154:24 F 5 '66. R. L. Strout
    Sat R 49:38 F 5 '66. F. Freidel
President's conduct of foreign policy. D. Lawrence. U S News 61:84 Jl 4 '66
Reminder of the grandeur of office. H. Sidey. il Life 62:34D Ja 20 '67
Traitors to their constituents. Nation 203: 405 O 24 '66
Wedge of dissent: Democratic rebels in Congress. R. G. Sherrill. Nation 203:341-6 O 10 '66

Protection

Questions of security on the LBJ flight. il U S News 60:14 F 21 '66

Public relations

Atlantic report; L. B. Johnson's self-imposed isolationism. D. Kiker. Atlan 218:6+ S '66
Consensus that isn't; voters against the President. Nation 202:282 Mr 14 '66
Doctor Lyndon B. Fell. S. Alsop. il Sat Eve Post 239:16 Jl 30 '66
Exit Goldman, enter Roche: can LBJ and intellectuals be friends? B. Nelson. Science 153:1505-7 S 23 '66
Government by public opinion polls. E. Roper. Sat R 49:18 My 28 '66
Lonely quest, by R. Rienow and L. T. Rineow. Review
    Sat R 49:43 Ap 16 '66. W. Johnson

LBJ at Princeton: some words about intellectuals and government. D. S. Greenberg. il Science 152:1223-5 My 27 '66
LBJ's fading consensus. il Bsns W p37-8 Je 18 '66
Mr Johnson's problem; pretense and deception. Nation 203:370 O 17 '66
Pity the poor President. S. Alsop. Sat Eve Post 239:18 Jl 2 '66
Pity the President? K. Crawford. Newsweek 68:27 Ag 1 '66
Poll pains of a living, breathing contradiction. H. Sidey. Life 60:38B Je 24 '66
Press, the President and foreign policy. J. B. Reston. For Affairs 44:553-73 Jl '66; Same abr. Read Digest 89:69-73 S '66
State of the consensus. il Sat Eve Post 239: 90 Ja 29 '66
That fragile thing, political popularity. P. Lisagor. il Nations Bsns 54:21-2 Mr '66
Town's troubled mood as a war comes home; Massillon, Ohio questions administration's position. il Life 61:50-7 Ag 12 '66
Truth and power: the intellectuals and the Johnson administration. H. J. Morgenthau. New Repub 155:8-14 N 26 '66; Discussion. 155:35-6 D 24 '66; 156:42-3 Ja 7 '67
Uncle Ezra's legacy. M. Ascoli. Reporter 35: 14+ N 3 '66
Washington desk. J. R. Slevin. Duns R 87: 5-6 Mr '66
When friends fall out. P. Lisagor. Nations Bsns 54:23-4 Je '66
White House in transition; L. B. Johnson's mystifying image. H. Brandon. Sat R 49: 10 Je 11 '66
Why Democrats are losing ground; size-up by nation's governors. il U S News 61:37-9 Jl 18 '66

Relations with Congress

As Congress starts new term; LBJ's wishes, his chances. il U S News 60:32-3 Ja 31 '66
As LBJ asks more and more laws. il U S News 60:25-6 Ap 4 '66
Changing mood of Congress: how outlook is shifting. il U S News 60:28-30 My 2 '66
Congress and LBJ: a widening split. U S News 60:8 My 9 '66
Congress fights for defense policy role. G. C. Wilson. il Aviation W 84:26-7 My 23 '66
Creative tension between President & Senate; Time essay. Time 87:30-1 Mr 18 '66
Go slow session? Sr Schol 89:14 Ja 13 '67
How LBJ's programs fare in Congress. il U S News 61:8 S 19 '66
In the new Congress: a go slow mood. il U S News 62:34-5 Ja 9 '67
Larry O'Brien: the pro takes on the post office. D. R. Maxey. il Look 30:30-2+ F 8 '66
LBJ and Congress: a new ball game. U S News 61:34 N 28 '66
LBJ and Congress: why the magic is gone. il U S News 60:53-5 Mr 21 '66
LBJ's great Congress: rubber stamp or creativity? B. Nelson. Science 154:620-2 N 4 '66
Now beginning: the cautious Congress. U S News 62:27-8 Ja 16 '67
Rough winds force Johnson to new tack; outlook for '67. il Bsns W p 19-20 D 31 '66
Senate lets L.B.J. down. H. Hamilton. America 115:56 Jl 16 '66
Senate revolt: protesting U.S. overcommitment abroad. B. Nelson. Science 154:751-3 N 11 '66
State of the Union. R. Hotz. Aviation W 86: 21 Ja 16 '67
Time to catch breaths and mend fences. P. Lisagor. il Nations Bsns 53:21-2 D '65
War in Washington: the temper of the capital. M. Greenfield. il Reporter 34:29+ Mr 10 '66
Wedge of dissent: Democratic rebels in Congress. R. G. Sherrill. Nation 203:341-6 O 10 '66
What new laws Congress will pass; interviews. G. R. Ford; C. Albert. Nations Bsns 54:62-4+ Ja '66
White House in transition; L. B. Johnson's mystifying image. H. Brandon. Sat R 49:10 Je 11 '66
Who could ask for anything more? P. Lisagor. il Nations 54:23-4 N '66

Relations with the press
See Government and the press

State of the Union messages
See Presidents—United States—Messages

Succession

While LBJ was under surgery. U S News 61: 15 N 28 '66

PRESIDENTS, Company. See Executives

PRESIDENT'S club. See Political clubs and associations

PRESIDENT'S commission on heart disease, cancer and stroke; President's council on physical fitness; etc. See United States—President's commission on heart disease, cancer and stroke; United States—President's council on physical fitness; etc.

PRESIDENT'S cup regatta. See Motor boat racing

PRESIDENTS press conferences. See Press conferences

PRESIDENTS representatives. See Public officers

PRESQUE ISLE, Maine
Presque Isle points the way. H. Tupper. Read Digest 88:31-2+ Mr '66

PRESS, Frank, and Brace, W. F.
Earthquake prediction bibliog Science 152: 1575-84 Je 17 '66

—and Harkrider, David
Air-sea waves from the explosion of Krakatoa. bibliog Science 154:1325-7 D 9 '66

PRESS, Sylvia
Book review of a very limited edition. M. Muggeridge. il Esquire 65:94+ My '66

PRESS. See Newspapers

PRESS, Catholic. See Catholic press

PRESS agencies. See News agencies

PRESS agents
Diving horses, and a three-sheet on a downtown corner; interview. B. Doll. New Yorker 42:20-1 Jl 2 '66

PRESS and crime. See Crime and the press

PRESS and government. See Government and the press

PRESS associations. See News agencies

PRESS conferences
Atlantic report: Washington; President Johnson's press conferences. D. Kiker. Atlan 218:4+ D '66
Behind the bureaucratic curtain; contrast between covering the news in Washington and London. A. Howard. il N Y Times Mag p34-5+ O 23 '66
LBJ meets the press...sort of. R. L. Strout. New Repub 154:13-14 Ap 16 '66
Once more, with feeling; LBJ's double-header news conference. Newsweek 68:54 Jl 4 '66
Press views LBJ: fearsome antagonist. C. Roberts. Nation 203:406-11 O 24 '66

PRESS photographers. See Photographers

PRESS relations. See Publicity

PRESSED flowers and leaves. See Flowers, Dried

PRESSING of garments
Questionable traveling companion; Westinghouse steam-press valet. il Consumer Rep 32:6-8 Ja '67

PRESSMAN, D. See Roholt, O. A. jt. auth.

PRESSURE
High-pressure polymorphism in sodium chloride: a reinvestigation. Q. Johnson. bibliog il Science 153:419 Jl 22 '66
Melting of tin telluride at high pressures. W. Klement, jr. and L. H. Cohen. bibliog il Science 154:1176-7 D 2 '66
Molybdenum diselenide: rhombohedral high pressure-high temperature polymorph. L. C. Towle and others. bibliog il Science 154:895-6 N 18 '66
Nickel orthouronate: high pressure synthesis. A. P. Young. bibliog il Science 153:1380-1 S 16 '66
Pressure-induced phase of sulfur-selenium. S. Geller and M. D. Lind. il Science 155: 79-80 Ja 6 '67
Pressure-induced phases of sulfur. S. Geller. bibliog il Science 152:644-6 Ap 29 '66
See also
Compression

PRESSURE, Political. See Pressure groups

PRESSURE, Root. See Roots

PRESSURE cooker
Good cooking with a pressure cooker. H. S. Sharpe. il Parents Mag 41:61-4+ Ag '66

PRESSURE groups
Doorbells: politics of activism; need for peace candidates. W. Meyers. il Nation 202:581-3 My 16 '66
Entering the lists. Reporter 35:14 D 1 '66
Establishment game: Nicholas Murray Butler rides again; New York's foreign policy syndicate and its influence on conduct of U.S. foreign policy. P. Seabury. Reporter 34:24-6 My 19 '66; Correction. 34:5 Je 2 '66
See also
Lobbying

PRESSURE of population. See Population—Overpopulation

PRESSURE suits
Cocoon of air for shock victims. il Life 61:73-4 O 7 '66
See also
Astronauts—Clothing

PRESSURIZED containers. See Aerosols

PRESTIGE
Prestige. R. P. Lister. il Atlan 218:125-6 Jl '66

PRESTRESSED concrete institute
First runway over water wins an award; LaGuardia airport. Am City 81:42 N '66

PRE-TEEN-age singers. See Singers

PRETENDERS, Royal
Pretender's cabinet; Spain's D. J. de Borbón y Battenberg. Time 87:41 Je 17 '66

PRÊTRE, Georges
Recordings. M. Mayer. Esquire 65:54 Mr '66

PRE-TRIAL practice. See Procedure (law)

PREVALLET, Sister Elaine Marie
Meaning of virginity. America 115:93-5 Jl 23 '66

PREVEC, L. and Graham, A. F.
Reovirus-specific polyribosomes in infected L-cells. bibliog Science 154:522-3 O 28 '66

PREVENTICARE. See Insurance, Health—United States

PREVENTION of accidents. See Accidents—Prevention

PREVENTION of crime. See Crime prevention

PREVENTION of cruelty to animals. See Animals—Treatment

PREVENTIVE medicine. See Medicine, Preventive

PREVIN, André
Almost like Bernstein. por Time 88:62 Jl 15 '66
Previn's masterly Shostakovich Fifth. J. Diether. por Am Rec G 32:692-3 Ap '66

PREWITT, Lena B.
Need for quality instruction; address, July 17, 1966. Vital Speeches 33:49-50 N 1 '66

PRIBILOF ISLANDS
Sealing the future. il Newsweek 67:38+ Je 27 '66
See also
Geology—Pribilof Islands

PRICE, Arnold H.
(comp) Articles and other books received; Germany, Austria and Switzerland. See issues of American historical review

PRICE, Charles
Golf (cont) Esquire 66:44+ S '66
Golfer, go abroad. Esquire 65:120-1+ Ap '66
How to be a golf champion. N Y Times Mag p34-5+ Ag 28 '66

PRICE, Don K. 1910-
Federal money and university research. bibliog Science 151:285-90 Ja 21 '66
Text of the new lesson; science and human freedom; excerpt from Scientific estate. Sat R 49:54-7 Ap 2 '66

about

Head keeper of the new cathedral. J. Langone. por Sat R 49:53-4 Ap 2 '66
John F. Kennedy school: helping government's in-and-outers. B. Nelson. il por Science 154: 135-8 O 7 '66
Price: an effect, not a cause. F. Sartwell. por(p 1) Sci N 91:17 Ja 7 '67

PRICE, Edison
Man of many lights. il por Fortune 73:170+ Ap '66

PRICE, Leontyne
Laurel; poem. McCalls 93:80 Je '66

about

Diva sang for the old Met ghosts. il pors Life 61:38-9 S 30 '66
Diva's date with destiny. il pors Ebony 22: 184-6+ D '66
Price's Ballo, Grist and Lorengar debuts. M. Mayer. il por Hi Fi 16:134+ My '66
Stars at home. il pors Opera N 30:14-16 F 12 '66
Tony and Cleo. il por Newsweek 68:98 S 26 '66

PRICE, Molly
In pursuit of the rainbow. Flower Grower 53:24-7 Je '66
Peonies up to date il Flower Grower 53:36-7 S '66

PRICE, Monroe
By their own bootstraps Am Ed 2:6-8 N '66

PRICE, Nancy
Books; poem. Horn Bk 42:44 F '66
Cardinals; poem. America 114:262 F 19 '66
Christmas letter to a friend on Mars; Flight; poems. Reporter 35:52-3 D 15 '66

PRICES—United States—*Continued*
Price pressure. Newsweek 68:80 D 5 '66
Price rise: no end in sight. il U S News 61: 48 D 12 '66
Prices: a wage question. il Fortune 74:20+ Ag '66
Prices and profits: tearing down the guide-posts. New Repub 155:7 Ag 27 '66
Prices in poor neighborhoods; Bureau of labor statistics report. P. Groom. il Mo Labor R 89:1085-90 O '66
Recommendation for periodic evaluation of guideposts. Mo Labor R 89:1122 O '66
Rising prices: how long, how high? with report by H. C. Wallich il Newsweek 68: 69-75 S 5 '66
Takes more cash to make ends meet; with analysis by W. W. Heller. il Life 61:26-31 S 9 '66
Trend is up. Newsweek 67:81 Mr 14 '66
Up, up, up. il Time 88:69-70 S 2 '66
White House delays a tax-boost decision; prices rising. Bsns W p46 Mr 26 '66
   See also
Cost of living—United States
Index numbers
Price discrimination
Price indexes
Price regulation by government—United States
   also subhead Prices under various sub-jects, e.g. Food—Prices

PRICHARD, M. I.
Across the Potomac on London bridge: ad-dress, April 17, 1966. Vital Speeches 32: 464-6 My 15 '66

PRIDE, Cheryl
Brown beauty with courage. il pors Ebony 21:102+ O '66

PRIDEAUX, Tom
Arias and tears in the old tradition. Life 60: 30-3 Ap 29 '66
Life book review. Life 62:12 Ja 20 '67
Life theater review. See issues of Life

PRIEST workers. See Worker priests

PRIESTHOOD. See Priests

PRIESTLEY, John Boynton
Light in a thousand dark places. Horizon 8:32-7 Wint '66
   about
COMSA and DISCUS. E. Moon. por Sat R 49:50-1 F 5 '66

PRIESTLEY, Mike
Lively Lotus-Cortina. Pop Mech 126:36+ N '66

PRIESTMAN, Brian
And we quote...; ed. by S. Fleming. por Hi Fi 16:MA17 D '66
George Frideric Handel. Opera N 31:32 D 10 '66

PRIESTS
Austin Ripley and alcoholic priests. H. A. Hammett. America 115:831 D 24 '66
Celibacy in Holland; excerpts. L. van Wersch and H. Suér. Cath World 204:177-9 D '66
Challengers of their church. il Life 60:72-4+ Je 24 '66
Clerical trade union. Nation 202:255 Mr 7 '66
Cody in Chicago; priests' group formed. J. Leo. Commonweal 84:334-6 Je 10 '66; Reply. J. Fitzgerald. 84:452 Jl 22 '66
De Pauw's departure; openly challenged church policy. Time 87:70 Ja 28 '66
Disappearing priesthood. R. E. McNally. America 114:877-8 Je 25 '66; Discussion. 115:64+, 107, 221 Jl 16, 30, S 3 '66
Father DuBay's union; labor union for priests. Commonweal 83:654 Mr 11 '66; Dis-cussion. 84:43+, 244 Ap 1, My 20 '66
Father takes a wife. Time 88:45 Jl 1 '66
Genius of the apostolate, by E. C. Kennedy and P. F. D'Arcy. Review
   America 114:751 My 21 '66. R. J. Willmes
History of sacerdotal celibacy in the Christian church, by H. C. Lea. Review
   Sat R 49:45-6 O 15 '66. J. Pelikan
Learning a Sunday punch; Catholic university of America preaching workshop. Newsweek 68:82 Jl 4 '66
Marrying kind? survey of clerical opinion in U.S. Newsweek 68:72 D 19 '66
More priests and why. America 114:216 F 12 '66
Optional celibacy? priestly marriages. il Newsweek 68:86 Jl 18 '66
Priest: celibate or married, by P. Hermand. Review
   America 114:524+ Ap 9 '66. R. J. Willmes
Priestly celibacy: keeping the issues clear. America 115:88 Jl 23 '66; Discussion. 115: 180-1 Ag 20 '66

Priests as witnesses. R. W. Hovda. Common-weal 83:532-4 F 4 '66
Prophets to the world: priests and laymen. America 114:218 F 12 '66
Reforms that priests want. F. Canavan. America 114:582-5 Ap 23 '66
Rejecting Rome; Father C. Davis. Newsweek 69:51 Ja 2 '67
Renewed priesthood. E. C. Bianchi. America 116:48-50+ Ja 14 '67
Retirement for 200 bishops; resignation. il Time 88:93 S 30 '66
Return of Father DePauw. Newsweek 67: 76-7 F 7 '66
Rights of priests. J. D. Conway. Common-weal 84:197-200 My 6 '66
Speaking out; I am a priest, I want to marry. S. Nash. il Sat Eve Post 239:10+ Mr 12 '66
That celibacy survey. J. H. Fichter. America 116:92-4 Ja 21 '67
Theologian defects; Rev. C. Davis. il Time 88:42 D 30 '66
Timely psychoanalysis; disturbed priests and nuns. America 115:87 Jl 23 '66
Union for priests? J. O'Gara. Commonweal 84:72 Ap 8 '66
When a priest marries. il Newsweek 67:83 Ap 25 '66
Which way does the priest face? America 114:822 Je 11 '66
Wounded priest, wounded church. America 116:8-9 Ja 7 '67
   See also
American federation of priests
Association of Chicago priests
Chaplains, Military
Clergy
Theological students
Women as priests
Worker priests

Salaries, allowances, etc.
Priest's income. J. J. Kavanaugh. America 114:585-7 Ap 23 '66; Discussion. 114:714-15 My 21 '66

PRIMARIES
Alabama vote: Wallace still strong but some Negroes win. il U S News 60:8 Je 13 '66
Alabama's new era: the Negro votes. il News-week 67:25-30 My 16 '66
Analyzing the vote and its lessons; Alabama gubernatorial primary. L. Harris. il News-week 67:27 My 16 '66
Another Virginia. New Repub 155:7-8 Jl 30 '66
At issue: Viet Nam; Oregon primary. il Time 87:17 Je 3 '66
Big Jim's comeuppance; Alabama primary. Time 87:19 Je 3 '66
Changes ahead? what primaries tell. il U S News 61:39-40 S 26 '66
Hopeless case of Milton Shapp; winner of gubernatorial primary. R. B. Stolley. il Life 60:68A-68D+ My 27 '66
In first big test of the Negro vote; Alabama's primary. il U S News 60:37-9 My 16 '66
In the governor's race, Lurleen sweeps on toward a Wallace dynasty. il Life 60:42-42A My 13 '66
Letting George do it; Alabama primary. il Sr Schol 88:6 My 20 '66
Man vs. machine: Michigan; Idaho; Tennes-see results. il Newsweek 68:22-3 Ag 15 '66
One man, one vote, no Smith; Virginia's Democratic primary. W. More. America 115:110 Jl 30 '66
$1 million winner; Pennsylvania's Demo-cratic gubernatorial nomination. Newsweek 67:27-8 My 30 '66
Other places, other races. il Newsweek 67: 30-1 My 16 '66
Political almanack for the year 1966. il U S News 60:42-3 Ap 18 '66
Prevailing winds; harbingers of what the voters will do in November. il Newsweek 68:30-2 S 26 '66
Primaries; opening day for '66 politics. il U S News 60:18 My 16 '66
Primaries '66: spring training for the big race. il Sr Schol 88:16-19 My 6 '66
Primary mix. New Repub 155:7-8 S 24 '66
Real reconstruction; first Alabama Negro to win a Democratic nomination for sheriff. Time 87:38 Je 10 '66
Signs of a protest vote: trends in primaries and polls. il U S News 61:36-7 Ag 22 '66
Tantamount to election: South Carolina: Chicago; results. Newsweek 67:33+ Je 27 '66
Test of the tide; New York Republican congressional primary, contest on Long Island's North Shore. il Newsweek 67:33 Je 27 '66

PRIMARIES—*Continued*
Three contests: Manhattan, 19th congressional district, Nassau County. Nat R 18:664 Jl 12 '66
Three primaries with a white backlash. il U S News 61:16 O 10 '66
Two mistakes too many; Florida's Democratic primary. Time 87:18-19 Je 3 '66
Two primaries; what the results mean: Oregon and Florida. il U S News 60:12 Je 6 '66
Upset for two of old guard in Congress; Virginia's Democratic primary election. il U S News 61:15 Jl 25 '66
Was the war the issue? Oregon; Florida; Oklahoma results. il Newsweek 67:24 Je 6 '66
Why Republican hopes are rising; California primary. il U S News 60:31-2 Je 20 '66
PRIMARY elections. See Primaries
PRIMATES
Antigenic correspondence of serum albumins among the primates. A. S. Hafleigh and C. A. Williams, jr. bibliog il Science 151: 1530-5 Mr 25 '66
Lemur social behavior and primate intelligence. A. Jolly. bibliog il Science 153:501-6 Jl 29 '66
PRIME ministers conferences
Mr Wilson squeaks through; Commonwealth conference communiqué on Rhodesia. C. Sterling. Reporter 35:32-3 O 6 '66
Wrangling over Rhodesia: Commonwealth's venture into controversy. R. W. Howe. New Repub 155:8-9 O 1 '66
PRIME of Miss Jean Brodie; drama. See Allen, J. P.
PRIMITIVE and early church. See Church history—Primitive and early church
PRIMITIVE art. See Art, Primitive
PRIMITIVE hunting. See Hunting, Primitive
PRIMITIVE man. See Man, Primitive
PRIMITIVE sculpture. See Sculpture, Primitive
PRIMITIVE society. See Society, Primitive
PRIMITIVES, American. See Painting, American
PRIMROSES
In late winter a white flower carpet. il Sunset 137:272 O '66
Primulas. E. Hasko. il Horticulture 44:22-5+ My '66
PRIMULAS. See Primroses
PRIMUS, Pearl
Inheritance comes to P.S. 83. N. Hentoff. il pors Am Ed 2:28-32 F '66
PRINA, Lee Lorick
Parent and child. N Y Times Mag p78+ Ja 8 '67
PRINCE, Alain Wood
350 miles of walleyes. Outdoor Life 138:40-1+ Jl '66
PRINCE, Harold Smith
Broadway's Prince Charming. G. P. Gates. por Holiday 39:99-104+ Ap '66
PRINCE; story. See Jonas, G.
PRINCE EDWARD COUNTY, Va.
Lost years. J. P. Blank. il Look 30:71-2+ N 29 '66
Midnight raid. Time 88:82 D 9 '66
They closed their schools, by B. Smith. Review
Nation 203:521-2 N 14 '66. K. Jackson, jr
PRINCE and the pauper; drama. See Newman, D.
PRINCE GEORGES COUNTY, Md.
See also
Maryland-National capital park and planning commission
PRINCE GEORGES COUNTY memorial library, Hyattsville, Md.
Computer potential in Maryland. E. B. Hage. Wilson Lib Bul 41:401-3 D '66
PRINCES ISLANDS
Princes' Islands: Kinali and others in the Sea of Marmara. P. L. Meras. Travel 125: 48-9 Je '66
PRINCESS and the dragon; drama. See Wolfys, N
PRINCETON institute for advanced study. See Institute for advanced study, Princeton, N.J.
PRINCETON meeting on renewal. See Religious conferences
PRINCETON university
Princeton; excerpts from Tiger in the ivy; the Princeton man and his university, 1900-1967. J. Davies. il Horizon 9:57-66+ Wint '67
Teaching the big men on campus: college presidents learn managerial techniques in one-week course at Princeton. il Bsns W p 152-4+ Jl 9 '66

Art museum
Morrison collection of silver at Princeton, New Jersey. E. P. Birk. il Antiques 90:608+ N '66
PRINT lending. See Prints—Circulation, loans, etc.
PRINT shops. See Workshops
PRINTED circuits
Circuitry that bends takes a sales upturn. il Bsns W p 150-2+ F 12 '66
Computer PC salvage. P. H. Fuge. il Pop Electr 24:66 Je '66
How to etch professional printed circuit boards. J. A. Gupton, jr. il Pop Electr 24:54-9+ Mr '66
PRINTERS
More than just a businessman; illustrious printers. P. W. Schmidtchen. il Hobbies 71:104-5+ D '66
See also
Strikes—United States—Printers
PRINTING
Grouping of similar formats could help in production crisis. M. A. Friedman. Pub W 189:114-15 Mr 7 '66
Printing monks of Venice; Armenian Catholic monks of the Mechitarian order, printers of Books in Armenian. H. R. Lottman. Pub W 190:110-11 D 5 '66
Shallow relief plates may make letterpress competitive with offset; excerpts from panel discussion. il Pub W 190:96-7+ S 5 '66
Sir Francis Meynell lectures in New York; summaries of addresses; ed. by P. A. Bennett. F. Meynell. il Pub W 189:86-9+ Ap 4 '66
Trade book clinic hears a pitch for letterpress. Pub W 189:109 Ap 4 '66
See also
Block printing
Color printing
Computers—Printing applications
Lithography
Photogravure
Photomechanical processes
Type and typefounding

Design
Fleuron for PW. il Pub W 191:62 Ja 2 '67
Freeman Craw, graphic designer. E. M. Ettenberg. il Am Artists 30:32-7+ Mr '66
See also
Type and typefounding

History
More than just a businessman; illustrious printers. P. W. Schmidtchen. il Hobbies 71:104-5+ D '66

Legibility
Conventional type, enlarged, best for poor eyesight. il Pub W 189:107 Ap 4 '66
NYPL launches experiments in use of large-type books. Library J 91:3895 S 1 '66
Royal college of art begins investigation of legibility. Pub W 191:103 Ja 2 '67

Private presses
Ascending Spiral. R. Lynes. il Harper 232: 24+ My '66
Blotter press. M. Kerr. il Sch Arts 66:14-17 N '66
Spiral press honored with exhibit at Morgan library; with editorial comment. P. A. Bennett. il Pub W 189:97-101+ F 7 '66
PRINTING (photography) See Photography—Printing processes
PRINTING, Offset
More about web offset for books; excerpts from panel discussion. il Pub W 190:70+ Ag 1 '66
Offset printing, paper reviewed at AIGA clinics. Pub W 189:126+ Mr 7 '66
Why web offset for books? summary of address. P. L. Brink. Pub W 190:98+ Jl 4 '66
PRINTING industries of America, incorporated
Litho platemakers meet, adopt trade customs. Pub W 190:123-4 D 5 '66
Printers are urged to specialize; report of 80th and advertising awards. il Pub W 190:82+ N 7 '66
PIA computer section holds first annual meeting. Pub W 190:117 Ag 1 '66
Publishers and printers win PIA graphic arts and advertising awards. il Pub W 190:82+ N 7 '66

Graphic arts marketing information service
New PIA division will study marketing information. Pub W 191:103 Ja 2 '67

PRINTING industries of metropolitan New York, incorporated
See also
Franklin award for distinguished service

PRINTING industry
Future of printing in a data-hungry society; summary of address. L. C. Deighton. Pub W 189:55-60 Ja 31 '66
Mondadori expands sales efforts in the U.S.A. il Pub W 191:76+ Ja 2 '67
Printers are urged to specialize; report of 80th annual convention. il Pub W 190:70-1+ N 7 '66
Vail-Ballou has second plant in full operation. il Pub W 190:116+ O 3 '66
See also
International printing pressmen's and assistants' union of North America
Strikes—United States—Printers

Consolidations and mergers
Turck & Reinfeld bought by Adams group, printers. Pub W 191:56 Ja 16 '67

Statistics
Census of manufactures: book publishing and printing figures reported for 1958, 1963; with excerpts.. Pub W 189:39-44 Mr 7 '66
Printing and publishing data: excerpts from U.S. industrial outlook 1966. Pub W 189:97 F 7 '66

PRINTING machinery
Electrostatic printing is being tried on book work. il Pub W 190:96-8 N 7 '66
How to set up a home print shop. J. Burroughs. il Pop Sci 189:124-8+ Jl '66

PRINTING plates
Shallow relief plates may make letterpress competitive with offset; excerpts from panel discussion. il Pub W 190:96-7+ S 5 '66

PRINTING presses, Hand
Build a tabletop printing press. M. Banister. il Pop Mech 126:152-6+ N; 150-2+ D '66

PRINTS
See also
Shadowgrams

Circulation, loans, etc.
Original print; loans to patrons of Cary memorial library, Lexington, Mass. R. E. Cain. il Library J 91:5323-6 N 1 '66

Collectors and collecting
Collecting original art prints. M. Elkoff. il Holiday 39:101-6 F '66

Exhibitions
Fifteen and still going strong; National print exhibition, Brooklyn museum. K. Kuh. il Sat R 49:43-4 F 26 '66
Museum of early southern decorative arts: the paintings and prints. F. L. Horton. il Antiques 91:96-101 Ja '67
Printmaking since Goya; Prints: 1800-1945 assembled by Minneapolis institute of arts. F. Getlein. New Repub 154:27-8 Ap 23 '66

Technique
Blotter press. M. Kerr. il Sch Arts 66:14-17 N '66
Crepe paper prints. S. Gruenberg. il Sch Arts 65:20-1 My '66
Ink & tempera prints. M. E. Kerns. il Sch Arts 65:17-20 F '66

PRINTS. Bird. See Birds in art
PRINTS, Black-and-white See Photographs
PRINTS, Drying of. See Photography—Drying (films and prints)
PRINTS, Photographic. See Photographs

PRIORIES
Community for Benedictine sisters; St Bedes priory. il Arch Rec 140:112-14 Ag '66

PRIORITIES and allocations, Industrial
What about priorities? constructive projects cut back for defense spending. Nation 203:403-4 O 24 '66

PRIP, John
Metals; a discussion. por Craft Horiz 26:29-31 Je '66

PRISENDORF, Anthony
National data center: computer vs. the Bill of rights. Nation 203:449-52 O 31 '66

PRISON camps
Parable from prison; L. Gilkey's memoir of life in a Japanese prison camp Time 88:78+ S 2 '66

PRISON escapes. See Escapes
PRISON farms. See Farms, Prison

PRISON libraries
Prison libraries below standard according to AHIL-ACA inventory. Library J 91:1189 Mr 1 '66

PRISON reform. See Prisons
PRISON schools. See Education of prisoners

PRISONERS
Cells as second homes. K. Lamott. il Holiday 39:12+ F '66
Dangerous poor. S. Alsop. il Sat Eve Post 239:18 Jl 16 '66
Malaria wins round two. C. P. Gilmore. il N Y Times Mag p44-5+ S 25 '66
No room in the jail; District of Columbia jail. R. Goldfarb. New Repub 154:12-14 Mr 5 '66
See also
Prisons

Law
See Criminal law

Rehabilitation
How to rescue America from plumbers, carpenters, and people like that. J. Fischer. Harper 234:14+ Ja '67
Meeting prisoner father helps children adjust. Sci N 90:89 Ag 6 '66
Plastic surgery goes to prison. C. Remsberg and B. Remsberg. il Todays Health 44:38-41 Ap '66
Prisoners also are people. America 114:344 Mr 12 '66
What life is like in today's federal prisons; work release program; interview. M. E. Alexander. il U S News 61:98-102 Jl 11 '66
See also
Education of prisoners

Religion
Judges v. jailers; case of W. Howard at Virginia state prison. Time 88:69 S 16 '66

Treatment
Arkansas prison farm; whip pays off: Cummins and Tucker farms. R. Pearman. il Nation 203:701-4 D 26 '66
Union stripes; San Francisco inmates committee. Nation 203:437 O 31 '66
Violence in prison. J. P. Conrad. Ann Am Acad 364:113-19 Mr '66

China (People's Republic)
Call for release of American prisoners held by Communist China; address, May 7, 1966. W. P. Bundy. Dept State Bul 54:866-9 My 30 '66
Dissent on China. C. P. Tung. Christian Cent 83:1183 S 28 '66

Germany (Democratic Republic)
Ransomed; Bonn crack down on Westerners seeking to assist in escapes of East Berliners. il Time 87:30-1 F 11 '66

PRISONERS, Discharged
Uproar as confessed rapists and murderers go free; with report by D. Jackson. il Life 61:34-41 O 21 '66

PRISONERS, Education of. See Education of prisoners
PRISONERS, Political. See Political prisoners

PRISONERS of war
How they should be treated, Geneva convention. U S News 61:21 Ag 1 '66
See also
Vietnamese war, 1957- —Prisoners and prisons

PRISONERS of war, Returned

Rehabilitation
Children, by C. Blackstock. Review Sat R 49:42+ N 26 '66. I. Halperin

PRISONERS of war in China
Aftermath; cake that took six months to bake. K. F. Mulder. Esquire 65:70-2 My '66

PRISONERS of war in Korea
American defector comes home; why I quit China; ed. by R. Moskin. M. R. Wills. il Look 30:84-8+ F 22 '66
Why I chose China; ed. by J. R. Moskin. M. R. Wills. il Look 30:75-80+ F 8 '66

PRISONS
See also
Reformatories

Arkansas
Arkansas prison farm; whip pays off; Cummins and Tucker farms. R. Pearman. il Nation 203:701-4 D 26 '66

California
Violence in prison. J. P. Conrad. Ann Am Acad 364:113-19 Mr '66
See also
San Francisco—Prisons and reformatories

PRISONS—*Continued*

Cuba

American in Cuba; tour of political prisons.
E. R. John. il Nation 202:296-7 Mr 14 '66

Florida

Gideon's ironic impact; crime wave following
Clarence Gideon's victory in the U.S. Supreme court. Time 87:46 Je 3 '66

Germany

Last prisoner of Spandau; R. Hess. P.
Shabecoff. il N Y Times Mag p28-9+ Ag 28
'66

Great Britain

Away they go! Time 88:28 D 23 '66
Great escape; jail-break by G. Blake. W. F.
Buckley, jr. Nat R 18:1150 N 15 '66
Holiday exodus. il Time 89:30 Ja 6 '67
Letter from London; problem of security.
M. Panter-Downes. New Yorker 42:100 Ja
14 '67
Open-door policy. Newsweek 69:34 Ja 9 '67

South Africa

Crusader pays; reports of prison brutality
in the Rand daily mail. Newsweek 67:38
F 7 '66
Doctor's conscience in South Africa; G. Dean's
charges of police and prison warders brutality. New Repub 154:17-18 Ja 29 '66
Immaculate confinement; H. Strachan another
2½ years. Time 87:34 F 4 '66

United States

Cells as second homes. K. Lamott. il Holiday
39:12+ F '66
Violence in prison. J. P. Conrad. Ann Am
Acad 364:113-19 Mr '66
What life is like in today's federal prisons;
interview. M. E. Alexander. il U S News
61:98-102 Jl 11 '66
  See also subhead Prisons and reforma-
tories under names of cities, e.g. Atlanta—
Prisons and reformatories

PRITCHARD, James B.
Rampart against the Romans. Sat R 49:39 N
26 '66

PRITCHETT, Victor Sawdon
Denmark. Holiday 40:68-75+ N '66
Honeymoon; story. Harper 232:59-65 F '66
Skeleton; story. New Yorker 42:44-50 Mr 5
'66

PRITTIE, Terence
Der Alte replies to history. New Repub 154:
32-4 My 21 '66
Bailiffscourt. Atlan 219:109-10 Ja '67
Requiem for potheen. Atlan 217:116-17 My '66

PRIVACY
Are we all in the fishbowl? il Sr School 88:
9-11 F 11 '66
Battle of the book; Manchester's The death
of a President. il Time 88:15-18 D 23 '66
Burgeoning Big brotherism; fight to halt a
subtle, persistent growth in violations of
the individual's right to privacy. E. V.
Long. Christian Cent 83:645-7 My 18 '66
Chains of plastic; dropping of Budget bureau's plan for file of information on U.S.
citizens. Newsweek 68:27 Ag 8 '66
Chapter II, or finis? Manchester book. il Time
88:10-12 D 30 '66
Child's right to privacy; excerpt from Life
among the giants. L. R. Young. McCalls
93:57+ Mr '66
Continuing assault on privacy; social survey
for 1970 census. Nat R 18:608-9 Je 28 '66
Data vampire; concerning proposed National
data center. Time 88:46+ Ag 5 '66
Freedom to publish and the right of privacy;
N.Y. bill. R. H. Smith. Pub W 189:47 Mr 14
'66
Government watch on 200 million Americans?
il U S News 60:56-9 My 16 '66
In defense of privacy; Time essay. Time 88:
38-9 Jl 15 '66
Jacqueline B. Kennedy. plaintiff. il News-
week 68:39-43 D 26 '66
Kennedy book. Commonweal 85:360-1 Ja 6 '67
Kennedy-Manchester book controversy; sym-
posium. il Sat R 50:18-29 Ja 21 '67
Legal bridge should exist between privacy
and obscenity. H. F. Pilpel. Pub W 190:
54-5 D 26 '66
Let me alone! right to privacy. Christian Cent
83:1135-6 S 21 '66; Reply. M. Hamilton. 83:
1347 N 2 '66
Libel and the right of privacy. H. F. Pilpel.
Pub W 189:41 Mr 28 '66
March of science on privacy in the home.
Life 60:4 My 20 '66

Must my life be an open book? questions and
answers. A. Wood. il Seventeen 25:148-9+
Ap '66
National data center; computer vs. the Bill
of rights; C. E. Gallagher hearings. A.
Prisendorf. il Nation 203:449-52 O 31 '66
N.Y. bill would exempt books from privacy
invasion suits. Pub W 189:37 Mr 14 '66
Now, official word on bugging. il U S News
61:53 Jl 25 '66
Papa's troubled legacy; Hemingway-Hotch-
ner decision leaves unresolved legal prob-
lems. J. Tebbel. il Sat R 49:30-1+ Ap 9 '66
Pragmatic view of privacy; approved govern-
ment use of informers and certain elec-
tronic eavesdropping. il Time 88:36+ D 23
'66
Privacy and libel again; case concerning
Massachusetts physician's objection to his
name being used in connection with na-
tional advertising campaign. H. F. Pilpel.
Pub W 189:55-6 My 30 '66
Privacy cases versus freedom of expression.
H. F. Pilpel. Pub W 189:42 Mr 28 '66
Privacy for Nazis. Time 89:80+ Ja 6 '67
Privacy v. free press; the Hills sue Time,
inc. il Time 87:74 My 6 '66
Private eyes and public hearings; J. R.
Roche and R. Nader before Ribicoff's
traffic-safety subcommittee. il Newsweek
67:77-8 Ap 4 '66
Research in America; illegality of tests on
New York city children; with letter by
C. Isler. J. Lear. il Sat R 49:64-5 F 5 '66;
Discussion. 49:68 Mr 5; 57-8 Ap 2 '66
Restraining the snoopers; GM's invasion of
the privacy of R. Nader. Christian Cent
83:452-3 Ap 13 '66
Snooping industry. Nation 202:412 Ap 11 '66
Tests violate privacy. Sci N 90:198 S 17 '66
To balance individual rights and community
interests; Afro-American publishing co. inc.
vs. Eli Jaffe. H. F. Pilpel. Pub W 190:51-3
O 31 '66
Vote for the press over privacy; case of
James Hill and his family. il Time 89:56 Ja
20 '67
You ought to be left alone. E. V. Long. Es-
quire 65:102-3 My '66
  See also
Wire tapping

PRIVATE airplanes. See Airplanes—Private
ownership

PRIVATE detectives. See Detectives

PRIVATE enterprise. See Free enterprise

PRIVATE eye (periodical)
Beyond the fringe; benefit show to pay libel
suits. Newsweek 67:93 My 23 '66

PRIVATE flying
Bearcat professor; Yale's N. R. Hanson;
philosopher, scholar and wildman. J. Gil-
bert. il Flying 78:52-6 Mr '66
Buying an airliner instead of a ticket. il
Bsns W p 160-2+ Jl 9 '66
Gone flying; the route of the island traders.
H. Groenhoff. il Flying 79:86-9+ Jl '66
Gone flying to Mexico. R. Mock. il Flying
78:46-51 Ap '66
Gone flying to Panama. L. L. Hallman. il
Flying 79:52-6 Ag '66
Gone flying to Russia. J. Gilbert. il Flying
79:46-53+ D '66
Gone flying USA. J. Fricker. il Flying 78:
48-52 F '66
Haldeman way. J. N. Haldeman. il Flying
78:50-4 Je '66
How to fly to Europe without buying a
ticket. E. M. Iger. il Esquire 67:70-5 Ja '67
I'll take the high camp. K. Connes. il Flying
79:85-7 S '66
Jet in my windshield. J. Haley. il Flying
78:108 F '66
Palmer's jet aids golf, business schedule.
D. A. Brown. il Aviation W 84:107-9+ My
23 '66
Washington clipboard; Office of general avi-
ation affairs. R. Burkhardt. Flying 79:28-9
O '66
Weekend pilot. F. K. Smith. See issues of
Flying
  See also
Airplanes in business

PRIVATE helicopters. See Helicopters—Private
ownership

PRIVATE libraries. See Libraries, Private

PRIVATE ownership. See Property

PRIVATE people; story. See O'Hara, J.

PRIVATE property See Property

PRIVATE school buildings. See School buildings

PRIVATE schools
Boarding-school mystique. J. Steinberg. Mlle 63:176-7+ My '66
Face to face with a prep school romantic; Negro student at Andover. B. Reid. Seventeen 25:169 N '66
Garland of girls' schools. M. Durant. il Holiday 40:68-73+ O '66
Girls' school planned for future change; Hutchison school. il Arch Rec 139:176-7 F '66
Gospel according to St Paul's. J. Brackman. il Esquire 65:92-4+ Je '66
Just testing, testing, test—. A. P. Eliasberg. il N Y Times Mag p 109+ Mr 20 '66
Memo to the Corinthians: is Zak Starr entered for Eton? G. Frazier, 4th. Esquire 66:191-4 O '66
Mystery of St Mark's: arson investigation at St Mark's school, Southboro, Mass. il Newsweek 67:101 Ap 18 '66
Profiles: F. L. Boyden, headmaster of Deerfield academy. J. McPhee. New Yorker 42:57-8+ Mr 19 '66
Public or private school? some pros and cons. D. Klein. Seventeen 25:215-16+ Ag '66
Should your child go to a private school? D. Barr. il Parents Mag 41:74-7+ S '66
Steps down to the sea. il Arch Forum 125:44-7 D '66
See also
Education and state

PRIVATE secretaries. See Secretaries

PRIVETS
Privet hedges; good looking, fast growing, inexpensive. D. Wyman. il Flower Grower 53:32+ Ap '66

PRIVILEGED class; story. See Bradshaw, G.

PRO; story. See Updike, J.

PRO musica (organization) See New York pro musica antiqua (organization)

PRO quarterback (game). See Games

PROBATE law and practice
Art of avoiding probate. Time 88:65-7 Jl 8 '66
(Conflict of interest)²; newsmen on the appraisers list, Cincinnati. Newsweek 68:66 D 19 '66
How to follow a hunch; appointments of appraisers; Cincinnati. Time 88:48+ D 16 '66
Mess in our probate courts. M. T. Bloom. Read Digest 89:102-5 O '66
Probate bonanza; concerning N. Dacey's book How to avoid probate. il Newsweek 67:78 Je 27 '66
Probate fuss; concerning How to avoid probate! by N. F. Dacey. T. B. Morgan. il Look 30:36-8+ N 29 '66
See also
Wills

PROBES, Space. See Space probes

PROBLEM children
Children in conflict. B. Culliton. il Sci N 90:122-3+ Ag 20 '66
Emotional disturbance in the classroom. T. M. Miller; I. N. Berlin; J. F. Ott. il Sat R 49:76-9+ O 15 '66; Discussion. 49:80 N 19 '66
Fifteen years of trouble; Gail White at Livingston school for girls. il Look 30:40-3 S 20 '66
Our disturbed children: who is to care for them? W. Ryan. il Nation 202:775-80 Je 27 '66
Problem preschoolers; Virginia Frank child development center, Chicago. E. G. Neisser. il Parents Mag 41:43-5+ Mr '66
Robert finds a friend; Teacher-Mom programs. J. N. Miller. il PTA Mag 60:4-7 Je '66; Same abr. Read Digest 89:89-93 Jl '66
See also
Child guidance clinics
Runaway boys and girls

PROBLEM drinking. See Alcoholism

PROBLEM solving
And now, the captive consultant. J. Weingarten. il Duns R 88:57-8+ N '66
Heuristic programs for decision making. J. D. Wiest. bibliog f il Harvard Bsns R 44:129-43 S '66
Methods of problem solving; ideas presented at the tenth Institute for recreation administrators, on creative problem solving. J. J. Bannon. Parks & Rec 1:917-18 N '66
Shake-up of conventional economics. il Bsns W p 186+ Je 25 '66
Sharpen your number sense; statistical data, figures, interpreting reports on operations. R. A. Golde. il Harvard Bsns R 44:73-83 Jl '66

Solving problems by organized action; interview. M. A. Wright. il Nations Bsns 54:44-5+ My '66
Stretch your mind! mental exercises. R. W. Samson. il Read Digest 88:37+ Mr '66

PROBOSCIDEA
See also
Mammoths
Mastodon

PROBY, P. J.
Old mod: home from England. por Newsweek 67:95 Ap 18 '66

PROCACCI, Ugo
Sleuthing behind the wall. il por Time 88:78 S 9 '66

PROCAINE. See Novocaine

PROCEDURE (law)
Backlash for the A.B.A; reactions to proposed curbs on trial by newspaper. il Time 88:72+ O 14 '66
Confrontation; R. Speck's right to fair trial compromised? il Newsweek 68:26 Ag 1 '66
Judges go back to school; Sentencing institutes. G. Samuels. il N Y Times Mag p36-7+ N 6 '66
Law and warfare, ed. by P. Bohannan. Review
  Newsweek il 69:96+ Ja 23 '67. S. K. Oberbeck
Learning by trying; trial training. il Time 87:67 Ap 8 '66
Open file; J. O. Newman's disclosure of prosecution's evidence to defense counsel. il Time 88:62 S 30 '66
Peek at the pros; Michigan's annual advocacy institute. il Time 87:43-4 Mr 25 '66
See also
Criminal procedure

PROCTOR, Antonio
Free Negro in Florida. L. W. Neyland. bibliog Negro Hist Bul 29:43+ N '65

PROCTER and Gamble company
Detergent tailored for baby's wash. M. B. Keiser. il Parents Mag 41:26+ Ap '66
Period to protraction. Time 87:82 Mr 25 '66

PROCTOR-Silex corporation
Toaster doesn't pop? fix it yourself, mom. il Bsns W p42 Ja 7 '67

PROCUREMENT, Military. See United States—Armed forces—Procurement

PRODIGAL fool; story. See Singer, I. B.

PRODIGIES. See Children, Gifted

PRODIGIES, Musical. See Children as musicians

PRODUCE exchanges. See Exchanges

PRODUCT liability. See Liability (law)

PRODUCTION
Production under pressure. W. Skinner. Harvard Bsns R 44:139-46 N '66
See also
Efficiency, Industrial
Gross national product
Labor productivity
Technocracy

PRODUCTION, Agricultural
See also
Food supply

PRODUCTION, Theatrical. See Theatrical production

PRODUCTION code, Motion picture. See Moving picture censorship

PRODUCTION control
Designed decay; products and systems constructed to last the shortest feasible time. H. M. Case. il Harvard Bsns R 44:126-31 Ja '66
Productivity management. D. Sirota. Harvard Bsns R 44:111-16 S '66
See also
Critcal path analysis
Factory management

PRODUCTION line method. See Assembly line methods

PRODUCTION standards
See also
Work measurement

PRODUCTIVITY, Labor. See Labor productivity

PRODUCTS, New
Advanced technology (cont of) Products and processes. See issues of Missiles and rockets (cont as) Technology week
Case of the product priority; excerpts from Cases in marketing management. E. C. Bursk. il Harvard Bsns R 44:6-8+ Mr '66
Chosen one hundred; exhibition of Hundred most significant technical products at the New York Hilton. New Yorker 42:43-4 D 17 '66
Innovative imitation. T. Levitt. il Harvard Bsns R 44:63-70 S '66
Inventions, patents, processes. See issues of Science digest

PRODUCTS, New—*Continued*
New products. See issues of Business week
New products. See issues of Popular electronics
New products for the house. il Arch Rec 139:123-4+ mid-My '66
Product development speeds up. Bsns W p 130 O 15 '66
Products and processes. See issues of Missiles and rockets
Small companies can pioneer new products. A. C. Cooper. il Harvard Bsns R 44:162-4+ S '66
What's newest. See issues of Newsweek
PRODUCTS, Quality of. See Quality of products
PROFANITY. See Swearing
PROFESSION, Choice of. See Vocational guidance
PROFESSIONAL basketball players. See Basketball players
PROFESSIONAL education
Education of educators; Carnegie corporation study. F. G. Jennings. Sat R 49:79-80 N 19 '66
See also
Library schools and education
PROFESSIONAL ethics
See also
Legal ethics
Librarians, Professional ethics for
Medical ethics
Scientists, Professional ethics for
Teachers ethics
PROFESSIONAL football clubs. See Football clubs
PROFESSIONAL football players. See Football players
PROFESSIONAL golfers' association championship. See Golf—Tournaments
PROFESSIONAL photographers of America, incorporated
Whose Hall of fame? J. Deschin. Pop Phot 58:24+ Ap '66
PROFESSIONAL women. See Business and professional women
PROFESSIONAL workers
New class. D. T. Bazelon. Commentary 42:48-53 Ag '66

Supply and demand

Scientific personnel and the professions. T. J. Mills. bibliog f il Ann Am Acad 367:33-42 S '66
PROFESSIONS
See also
Occupations
Self employed
PROFESSORS. See College professors and instructors
PROFIT
American industry; function of profits; address, February 24, 1966. D. L. Jordan. Vital Speeches 32:381-4 Ap 1 '66
Buck's being passed to you. il Nations Bsns 54:40-1 Je '66
Misevaluation of investment center performance. J. J. Mauriel and R. N. Anthony. bibliog f il Harvard Bsns R 44:98-105 Mr '66
Ominous swipe at profits. Fortune 73:103-4 Je '66
Record profits. Fortune 73:36+ My '66
See also
Corporations—Finance
Risk
PROFIT sharing
Big payoff in sharing profits; retirement checks. il Bsns W p52-3 D 24 '66
PROFITEERING
See also
Black markets
PROGESTERONE
Pituitary tumors in mice after prolonged feeding of synthetic progestins. W. E. Poel. bibliog il Science 154:402-3 O 21 '66
Progesterone retards postpartum involution of the rabbit myometrium. F. R. Goodall. bibliog il Science 152:356-8 Ap 15 '66
PROGESTIN. See Progesterone
PROGRAM evaluation and review technique. See Critical path analysis
PROGRAMMED teaching
Computer-tutor. J. Ridgeway. New Repub 154:19-22 Je 4 '66
Electronic instruction; blessing or curse? Christian Cent 83:1201 O 5 '66; Reply. D. E. Engel. 83:1388 N 9 '66
Gabbernot has got me. S. Alexander. Life 61:38 S 16 '66
Programed instruction; an evaluation. P. K. Komoski. Sr Schol 8:sup 13 F 11 '66

Sullivan's crusade; schools without pain; California. J. Poppy. il Look 30:37-40 Je 28 '66
Survey of programed materials; table. Sr Schol 88:sup 14 F 11 '66
Technology is knocking at the schoolhouse door. C. E. Silberman. il Fortune 74:120-5+ Ag '66
See also
Teaching machines
PROGRAMMERS, Computer. See Computer workers
PROGRAMMING (computers)
Computer programming; today's high-pay career. J. F. Williams. il Sci Digest 59:50-5 My '66
Software gap, a growing crisis for computers; shortage of programmers. il Bsns W p 126-8+ N 5 '66
System analysis and programming. C. Strachey. il Sci Am 215:112-18+ bibliog (p312) S '66
You can't enjoy a computer without a program. il Fortune 74:140-1 O '66
PROGRAMMING languages (computers)
Square language designed for computers. Sci N 90:31 Jl 9 '66
System analysis and programming; CPL, ALGOL, and FORTRAN programming languages. C. Strachey. il Sci Am 215:112-18+ bibliog(p312) S '66
This article is written in FASE; fundamentally analyzable simplified English. il Sci Digest 60:40-1 S '66
PROGRAMS, School. See School programs
PROGRESS
See also
Civilization
Reform
Science and civilization
Social progress
PROGRESSIVE education
At last, some progress in progressive education. F. Morley. Nations Bsns 54:23-4 Ag '66
Name of progressive education taken in vain. T. M. Carter. Sch & Soc 94:102-3 F 19 '66
PROGRESSIVE labor movement. See Progressive labor party
PROGRESSIVE labor party
Chinese communism, U.S.A. D. McReynolds. Commonweal 83:528-31 F 4 '66
PROHIBITED books
See also
Index librorum prohibitorum
PROHIBITION

Mississippi

Bourbon borealis; governor urges law repeal. Time 87:24 F 11 '66
Moonshine on the rocks; ban on liquor dropped. Time 88:34 N 4 '66
Sobering thought. Newsweek 67:30 F 14 '66

United States

Those wild, wild getaway cars! violating the Volstead act. D. MacDonald. il Motor T 18:72-4 O '66
PROJECT Apollo. See Space flight to the moon
PROJECT Camelot
Camelot affair. G. E. Lowe. Bul Atomic Sci 22:44-8 My '66
PROJECT CUE (culture, understanding, and enrichment) See New York (state)—Education department
PROJECT Gemini. See Space flight—Manned flights
PROJECT Harbor. See Civil defense
PROJECT Head Start
Accommodating whites; Child development group of Mississippi. C. Jencks. New Repub 154:19-22 Ap 16 '66
Children and politics; Child development group of Mississippi. Nation 203:501 N 14 '66
Compromise in the Delta; Child development group of Mississippi and the O.E.O. Christian Cent 84:3 Ja 4 '67
False start for Head Start in Michigan. R. Kirk. Nat R 18:886 S 6 '66
Head Start is a banner project. I. Ross. il PTA Mag 60:20-3 Mr '66; Same abr. with title Head Start for America's youngsters. Read Digest 88:156-8+ Ap '66
Head Start liaison; Ohio state university. E. S. Ross. il Library J 91:337 Ja 15 '66
Head Start or false start? C. S. Carleton. il Am Ed 2:20-2 S '66
Head Start program; choosing books for the pre-school, underprivileged child; with book list by the Chinook bookshop, Colorado Springs. J. Noyes. Pub W 190:220-1 Jl 11 '66

PROJECT Head Start—*Continued*
Head Start report. Sr Schol 88:sup2 Mr 18 '66
Head Start to what? I Kraft. il Nation 203: 179-82 S 5 '66
How do you fight it? Child development group of Mississippi; mismanagement jeopardizes program. A. Kopkind. New Repub 155:6-7 S 3 '66
Not enough head start? question of whether preschool training makes a difference in later formal schooling. il Newsweek 68:100 N 7 '66
Preschool boom: its pressures and rewards; New York city's problems. L. Smith. il Newsweek 67:109-10+ My 16 '66
Project keep moving. America 115:763 D 10 '66
Shriver comes across; Child development group of Mississippi wins fight for funds from OEO. New Repub 156:10-11 Ja 7 '67
Shriver drops CDGM. New Repub 155:7 O 15 '66; Discussion. 155:35-8 O 29 '66
Shriving Shriver. Christian Cent 83:1431-2 N 23 '66
Small start in Mississippi. R. L. Shayon. Sat R 50:99 Ja 14 '67
Training 30,000 Head Start teachers. S. J. Drazek. Sch & Soc 94:130-1 Mr 5 '66
Washington report. J. Lloyd. Sr Schol 88: sup4 F 25 '66
What Sonny learned. il Newsweek 67:87 F 21 '66
Which way Head Start? interview; ed. by T. L. Moses. E. W. Gordon. Sr Schol 88: sup2+ My 13 '66
PROJECT immortality; drama. See Mandel, L.
PROJECT Intrex. See Information storage and retrieval systems
PROJECT MATCH Box. See Boston children's museum
PROJECT Mohole. See Mohole project
PROJECT SLEDGE. See Balloons—Use in research
PROJECTION, Light. See Light projection
PROJECTION, Television. See Television projection
PROJECTION apparatus
Buypoints: slide projectors. M. Grennan. il Pop Phot 59:163-72 O '66
Caulfield on color; table viewer-projectors. P. Caulfield. Mod Phot 30:96+ Je '66
Messraster. M. Orovan. il U S Camera 29: 20+ Je '66
Movie test reports. il Pop Phot 58:104-5 F '66
Overhead projector progress at Willow Glen h.s. F. Hale. il Sr Schol 87:sup20-1 Ja 14 '66
Six-way theater wall. il Pop Mech 126:164-9+ O '66
Slide projectors. Consumer Rep 31:272-9 D '66
Slide viewers. il Pop Phot 59:175-8 O '66
Super 8/Single 8 movie projectors. il Consumer Rep 31:437-41 S '66
See also
Television projection
PROJECTS (teaching)
MATCH Boxes; project in Boston. il Am Ed 3:9 D '66
PROKOF'EV, Sergei Sergeevich
Erich Leinsdorf at his very best. A. Cohn. Am Rec G 32:553 F '66
Magnificent: Piatigorsky and Firskusny. A. Cohn. Am Rec G 32:1132 Ag '66
Records:
Love for three oranges: Betrothal in a monastery; Story of a real man. Opera N 31:34 D 31 '66
Unknown world of Prokofiev's operas; with discography. G. Pugliese. Hi Fi 16:44-50+ Je '66
PROLOGUE to the last day; story. See Crabb, A. L.
PROMENADE concerts, London. See London—Music
PROMISCUITY. See Sexual ethics
PROMISE of heat; story. See Ayer, E.
PROMISES
Anecdotes, facetiae, satire, etc.
Keep off these promises. W. Stanton. Look 30:47 Ag 9 '66
PROMOTERS and promoting
Delayed payday for Cleve; C. Williams-C. Clay fight. E. Shrake and M. Sharnik. il Sports Illus 25:34-6 D 5 '66
Group; C. Clay's Louisville sponsoring group. Sports Illus 25:20 N 14 '66
Superfan and super achiever. J. Mann. il Sports Illus 24:52-60 Ja 24 '66

Three names and a barrel of money; J. K. Cooke. B. Ottum. il Sports Illus 26:52-8 Ja 16 '67
See also
Impresarios
PROMOTIONAL games. See Sales promotion
PROMS, School. See Student activities
PRONGHORN hunting
Pronghorns in the pasture. D. Hamilton. il Outdoor Life 137:54-5+ F '66
PRONGHORNS
Antelope play in Florida. C. Elliott. il Outdoor Life 137:52-5+ My '66
Sheep fences or antelope? concerning fencing on public land in Wyo. B. Milek. Field & S 71:10-12+ S '66
PRONICHEV, Dina Mironovna
Dina Mironovna Pronichev remembers Babi Yar; excerpt from novel, Babi Yar. A. Kuznetsov. N Y Times Mag p45+ D 11 '66
PROOFREADING
Five with enterprise; girl owned proofreading firm. P. Rifield. il Mlle 63:146 S '66
PROPAGANDA
Do we really want to be brainwashed? F. Morley. Nations Bsns 54:25-6 S '66
Propaganda, by J. Ellul; tr. by K. Kellen and J. Lerner. Review
Nation 202:397-8 Ap 4 '66. C. Lasch
See also
Communication (speech, writing, etc)
Moving pictures—Propaganda
Radio broadcasting—Propaganda
Vietnamese war, 1957- —Propoganda
Voice of America (radio program)
PROPAGANDA, Anti-Jewish. See Anti-Semitism
PROPAGANDA, Communist
We're helping the Communists win the propaganda war. C. T. Rowan. Read Digest 89:106-10 N '66
PROPAGANDA, Korean (North Korean)
North Koreans accused of forging Bibles; counterfeit issues of some 1000 publications. Pub W 189:103 F 14 '66
PROPAGANDA, Russian
Peace questionnaire; Soviets seek views of U.S. scientists. E. Langer. Science 153: 276-7 Jl 15 '66; Discussion. 153:1335-6; 154:338 S 16, O 21 '66
Russians faked it. D. Cohen. il Nation 203: 445-7+ O 31 '66
PROPAGANDA, South African
Junkets to apartheid; America's press on safari; free trips to South Africa to improve image in U.S. F. Pollock. Nation 203:479-81 N 7 '66
PROPAGANDA, Vietnamese
Vietnam: the ordeal of pacification; Revolutionary development program. D. Warner. il Reporter 35:24-8 D 1 '66
PROPAGATION of plants. See Plant propagation
PROPANEDIOL. See Propylene glycol
PROPELLERS
Repairing
Pour your own pitch block. E. G. Sandrock. il Pop Mech 125:154-5 Mr '66
PROPER motion of the stars. See Stars—Motion
PROPERTY
Conditioning the comrades; Lenin's prohibition. Time 88:30 S 2 '66
See also
Alien property
Estates, Decedents
Joint tenancy
PROPERTY, Intellectual
Authors of Trivia sue Pocket books, Metromedia. Pub W 190:32 Ag 1 '66
Court says Peyton Place is intangible property interest. H. F. Pipel. Pub W 189:66+ Ja 31 '66
It depends on what kind of idea it is. H. F. Pipel. Pub W 189:64 F 28 '66
Permission to quote; use of original documents, letters, etc. E. L. Bernays. Writer 79:20-2 Ap '66
PROPERTY rights. See Real property
PROPERTY tax
Heating the property tax battle; concerning Brookings Institution book Economics of the property tax. Bsns W p 179-80+ Mr 12 '66
100 percenter; California. Newsweek 68:80 N 7 '66
Property tax reform; irregularities in three California cities. R. Moley. Newsweek 68:96 Jl 11 '66
Property tax scandal; conditions in California. Nation 204:68-9 Ja 16 '67

PROPERTY values. See Land values
PROPHECIES
Gift of prophecy, by Ruth Montgomery. Christian Cent 83:995 Ag 10 '66
Prophetic principle; counterweight to the institutional. B. G. Murchland. Commonweal 84:171-5 Ap 29 '66; Reply with rejoinder. T. S. Hanrahan. 84:381+ Je 24 '66
See also
Astrology
Fortune telling
PROPOSED religions. See Religions (proposed, universal, etc)
PROPRIETY. See Decency
PROPST, Howard B.
And how we can make money with it; address. Farm J 90:68W Mr '66
PROPULSION, Jet. See Jet propulsion
PROPYLENE glycol
1,2-propanediol-2-phosphate in ascaris lumbricoides. J. Kubištová and D. Seth. bibliog Science 154:1461 D 16 '66
PROSPECTING
Atomic signals from silver; U.S. geological survey scientists silver snooper. il Time 87: 53 My 13 '66
Gold in mountains? large survey underway. il(p97) Sci N L 89:101 F 12 '66
How I search for lost gold mines, and why. E. S. Gardner. il Pop Sci 188:100-5 Mr '66
Searching for buried riches. il Newsweek 68: 86-8+ O 17 '66
See also
Petroleum—Prospecting
PROSPERITY
Can we manage prosperity? E. L. Dale, jr. il N Y Times Mag p24-5+ Mr 6 '66
Economic growth; key to the good life for all. il Sr Schol 89:15-17 O 21 '66
Government and the economy; planning for prosperity. il Sr Schol 88:6-7 Ap 1 '66
Government and the economy; tricky business of managing prosperity. il Sr Schol 89:11-13 D 9 '66
Prosperity wears an uneasy smile. il Bsns W p43-5 Mr 26 '66
See also
Business conditions
United States—Economic conditions
PROSTAGLANDIN
Prostaglandin synthesized; dihydro-PGE 1. il Sci N 89:481 Je 18 '66
PROSTATE gland
Cryosurgery vs. cancer. il Newsweek 69:84 Ja 16 '67
PROSTHESIS
Hope and help for handicapped children; UCLA child amputee prosthetics project; ed. by A. Hamilton. M. Brooks. il Todays Health 44:60-3+ N '66
More spare parts for humans. T. Berland. il Todays Health 44:42-5+ Jl '66
Motor-driven limbs. R. L. Breeling. il Todays Health 45:40 Ja '67
Muscle from a wink or twitch; myoelectric control applied to artificial limbs. Sci N 90:501 D 10 '66
New hands muscled by motors. il Life 61: 58A-58B+ Ag 19 '66
Nonthrombogenic plastic surfaces. R. I. Leininger and others. bibliog il Science 152: 1625-6 Je 17 '66
See also
Artificial limbs
PROSTITUTION
Apologia pro verbis suis; expression of regret over recent remarks about moral conditions in Saigon. Time 87:70 My 27 '66
Back to the brothel; discussion in Senate foreign relations committee hearings of conditions in Saigon. Time 87:29 My 20 '66
Body politic; Chile. Time 88:28 Ag 12 '66
Disneyland east; brothel quarter built exclusively for American soldiers. il Time 87: 29-30 My 6 '66
PROSTRATION, Heat. See Heatstroke
PROTACTINIUM
Manganese nodules; thorium-230; protactinium-231 ratios. W. M. Sackett. bibliog il Science 154:646-7 N 4 '66
PROTECTION against radioactivity. See Radioactivity—Safety devices and measures
PROTECTION from frost. See Frost protection
PROTECTION of animals. See Animals—Protection
PROTECTION of birds. See Birds—Protection
PROTECTION of books. See Books—Conservation and restoration
PROTECTION of plants. See Plants, Protection of

PROTECTIVE coatings
Instant cure for coatings. il Bsns W p 176 Je 11 '66
See also
Plastic coating
PROTECTIVE mechanisms (biology) See Defense mechanisms (biology)
PROTEIN-polysaccharides. See Polysaccharides
PROTEIN synthesis. See Proteins
PROTEINEMIA
Paraproteinemia and reticulum cell sarcoma in an inbred mouse strain. H. J. Wanebo and others. bibliog il Science 154:901-3 N 18 '66
PROTEINS
Acute phase protein in serum of women using hormonal contraceptives. G. F. B. Schumacher. bibliog il Science 153:901-2 Ag 19 '66
Anaphase delay after inhibition of protein synthesis between late prophase and prometaphase. J. E. Cummins and others. bibliog il Science 154:1343-4 D 9 '66
Antimicrobial specificity of leukocyte lysosomal cationic proteins. H. I. Zeya and J. K. Spitznagel. bibliog il Science 154:1049-51 N 25 '66
Arrested protein synthesis in polysomes of cultured chick embryo cells. R. Soeiro and H. Amos. bibliog il Science 154:662-5 N 4 '66
Cell size and rate of protein synthesis in ventral horn neurones. R. P. Peterson. bibliog il Science 153:1413-14 S 16 '66
Chain initiation and control of protein synthesis. H. Noll. bibliog il Science 151: 1241-5 Mr 11 '66
Circular dichroism of biological macromolecules. S. Beychok. bibliog il Science 154:1288-99 D 9 '66
Civic meeting, Anchorage; signing fish protein concentrate act, excerpts from remarks, November 2, 1966. L. B. Johnson. Dept State Bul 55:809 N 28 '66
Clue to tissue repair in mysterious protein. Sci N L 89:120 F 19 '66
Continuity of protein synthesis through cleavage metaphase. P. R. Gross and B. J. Fry. bibliog il Science 153:749-51 Ag 12 '66; Reply. H. Timourian. 154:1055 N 25 '66
Dairy proteins from none. Sci Am 215:42+ Ag '66
Disulfide-linked collagenous protein of nematocyst capsules. R. Blanquet and H. M. Lenhoff. bibliog il Science 154:152-3 O 7 '66
Electrochromatography with reversing electrophoretic field. S. Raymond and J. Broome. bibliog il Science 153:1381-2 S 16 '66
Electrophoretic heterogeneity of the polypeptide chains of human G-myeloma proteins. W. D. Terry and others. bibliog il Science 152:1628-30 Je 17 '66
Encephalitogenic activity of bovine basic proteins. M. W. Kies and others. bibliog il Science 151:821-2 F 18 '66
Genetic code; aspects of organization. A. L. Goldberg and R. E. Wittes. bibliog il Science 153:420-4 Jl 22 '66
Heme stimulation of globin synthesis in a cell free system. C. L. Hammel and S. P. Bessman. bibliog il Science 152:1080-2 My 20 '66
Hemes and hemoproteins; report on colloquium. B. Chance and others. Science 152: 1409-11 Je 3 '66
Human protein synthesized. Sci Am 214:50 Ap '66
Immunoglobulin structure; variation in the sequence of Bence Jones proteins. K. Titani and others. bibliog il Science 152:1513-16 Je 10 '66
Inhibition of protein synthesis; a mechanism for the production of impaired iron absorption. N. J. Greenberger and R. D. Ruppert. bibliog il Science 153:315-16 Jl 15 '66
Leaves provide protein. Sci N 90:43 Jl 16 '66
Light chains of mouse myeloma proteins; partial amino acid sequence. R. Perham and others. bibliog il Science 154:391-3 O 21 '66
Low-molecular-weight proteins related to Bence Jones proteins in multiple myeloma. A. Solomon and others. bibliog il Science 151:1237-9 Mr 11 '66
Noncollagenous nature of the proteins of shark enamel. P. T. Levine and others. bibliog il Science 154:1192-4 D 2 '66
Nucleic acid and protein chemistry. R. D. Cole and C. A. Dekker. Science 153:92-4 Jl 1 '66
Nucleotide sequence of a nucleic acid. R. W. Holley. il Sci Am 214:30-9 bibliog(p 138) F '66
One cell protein from oil. Sci N 91:40 Ja 14 '67
Polysomes and protein synthesis in cells infected with a DNA virus. R. J. Sydiskis and B. Roizman. bibliog il Science 153:76-8 Jl 1 '66

PROTEINS—*Continued*
Protein and nucleic acid synthesis in escherichia coli: pressure and temperature effects. J. V. Landau. bibliog il Science 153:1273-4 S 9 '66
Protein conformations in the plasma membrane. A. H. Maddy and B. R. Malcolm; reply with rejoinder. J. L. Kavanau. Science 153:213 Jl 8 '66
Protein shortage seen solved by natural gas. Sci N 90:56 Jl 23 '66
Protein synthesis by heart muscle ribosomes: an effect of insulin independent of substrate transport. W. S. Stirewalt and I. G. Wool. bibliog il Science 154:284 O 14 '66
Protein synthesis in micrometres of the sea urchin egg. M. Spiegel and A. Tyler. bibliog il Science 151:1233-4 Mr 11 '66
Proteins linked to cancer. P. McBroom. il Sci N 89:283 Ap 23 '66
Proteins start here. Sci Am 215:102 S '66
Puromycin and cycloheximide: different effects on hippocampal electrical activity. H. D. Cohen and others. bibliog il Science 154:1557-8 D 23 '66
Rate of protein synthesis: regulation during first division cycle of sea urchin eggs. W. H. Sofer and others. bibliog il Science 153:1644-5 S 30 '66
Release of catecholamines and specific protein from adrenal glands. N. Kirshner and others. bibliog il Science 154:529-31 O 28 '66
Sweet-sensitive protein from bovine taste buds: isolation and assay. F. R. Dastoli and S. Price. bibliog il Science 154:905-7 N 18 '66
Transverse gradient electrophoresis: protein homogeneity test and subfractionation technique. C. A. Dubbs. bibliog il Science 151:463-4 Ja 28 '66
See also
Collagen
Grain—Protein content
Interferon
Lipoproteins
Milk—Protein content
Plant proteins
Tryptophan

PROTEST songs. See Music, Popular (songs, etc)

PROTESTANT church-owned publishers' association
Protestant publishers urged to think in terms of 2000 A.D. Pub W 189:36 Mr 14 '66

PROTESTANT churches
See also
Catholic church—Relations—Protestant churches
Church unity
Ecumenical movement
Liturgical movement—Protestant churches
Protestantism

Clergy
See Clergy

Relations
Catholic church
To genuflect or not to genuflect? distinctions between Roman Catholic and Protestant worship as expressions of churches' growth toward unity. il Time 87:95-6 My 20 '66

Orthodox Eastern Church
Ecumenical shift in the Middle East; reflections on Protestant-Orthodox relations. C. S. Calian. Christian Cent 83:1140-2 S 21 '66

England
Thou better not; reactions to Sex and morality report. Newsweek 68:66 O 31 '66
See also
British council of churches

Germany
See also
Evangelical church in Germany

India
India. V. Koilpillai. Christian Cent 83:1458 N 23 '66
See also
Church of south India

Ireland
Protestantism in the land of St Patrick. E. Best. Christian Cent 83:1453-6 N 23 '66

Northern Ireland
Protestantism in the land of St Patrick. E. Best. Christian Cent 83:1453-6 N 23 '66

United States
Negro worship and universal need. H. H. Mitchell. Christian Cent 83:396-8 Mr 30 '66; Discussion. 83:780+ Je 15 '66

Protestant mergers. J. L. C. Ford. America 115:486-90 O 22 '66
Protestants united; Dallas meeting of Consultation on church union. il Newsweek 67:103 My 16 '66
Worldly parish; Protestant ministers revitalize parishes. il Time 87:76 Mr 11 '66

PROTESTANT churches and race problems. See Church and race problems

PROTESTANT churches and social problems. See Church and social problems

PROTESTANT colleges. See Denominational colleges

PROTESTANT council of the city of New York
Name change, neighborhood basis; to drop the word Protestant. E. C. Parker. Christian Cent 83:602 My 4 '66

PROTESTANT dissenters. See Dissenters, Religious

PROTESTANT Episcopal church
Big event at Wheeling; interim report from a special committee appointed to study the role of women in the ministry. Christian Cent 83:1529 D 14 '66
Bishop on trial; demand for heresy trial of J. A. Pike. il Time 88:69 O 21 '66
Bishop Pike's last diocesan battle; relinquishing leadership of the Protestant Episcopal church's diocese of California. L. Kinsolving. Christian Cent 83:726+ Je 1 '66
Case of heresy? concerning Bishop Pike. il Newsweek 68:66 N 7 '66
Episcopal blunders; Episcopal house of bishops vs. J. A. Pike. Christian Cent 83:1559-60 D 21 '66
In defense of heresy. A. Towne. Christian Cent 84:44-7 Ja 11 '67
Trial by rhetoric; concerning Bishop Pike. il Time 88:53 N 4 '66
See also
Church of England

Clergy
Part-time priesthood; Episcopal laymen with full-time jobs trained to be part-time priests. il Newsweek 68:72 Ag 15 '66

PROTESTANT film commission. See National council of the churches of Christ in the United States of America—Broadcasting and film commission

PROTESTANT ministerial association. See Religious cooperation

PROTESTANT reformation. See Reformation

PROTESTANTISM
Braaten brouhaha; idea of return to Roman Catholic church. Christian Cent 83:1296-7 O 26 '66
Christian ethics amid pietistic culture-Protestantism. T. C. Oden. Christian Cent 83:525-6+ Ap 27 '66
Freedom today, by H. Küng. Review
Christian Cent 83:716-17 Je 1 '66. R. E. Wentz
From churches to church. Christian Cent 83:1231-2 O 12 '66; Reply. R. W. Huston. 83:1446 N 23 '66
Henry VIII and the Protestant triumph. L. B. Smith. bibliog f Am Hist R 71:1237-64 Jl '66
Impact of Vatican II on Protestantism; address, October 13, 1966. V. D. Rogers. Vital Speeches 33:91-4 N 15 '66
Lutherans and back to Rome. America 115:370 O 1 '66
Protestant hara-kiri; C. E. Braaten's idea of returning to Roman Catholic church. Christian Cent 83:794 Je 22 '66; Discussion. 83:1011 Ag 17 '66
Protestantism in transition, by C. W. J. Kegley. Review
Christian Cent 83:306-7 Mr 9 '66. O. A. Piper

Anecdotes, facetiae, satire, etc.
Seminary of the future. C. M. Nielsen. Christian Cent 83:1053-5 Ag 31 '66; Discussion. 83:1307 O 26 '66

PROTESTANTS and other Americans united for separation of church and state
P.O.A.U. proof-texting. Christian Cent 83:1459 N 23 '66
Vatican council and POAU. America 114:188 F 5 '66

PROTESTANTS in Spain
Changing law. J. F. Drane. America 114:870-2 Je 25 '66
Changing mood. R. Cornwall. America 114:873-5 Je 25 '66

PROTESTANTS in the United States
Oh, Henry! concerning editorial in Christianity today. J. R. Nelson. Christian Cent 83:295 Mr 9 '66; Reply. L. S. Lunardini. 83:590 My 4 '66
Protestantism and the American labor movement: the Christian spirit in the gilded age; excerpts from address, April 1965. H. G. Gutman. bibliog f Am Hist R 72:74-101 O '66

PROTESTS against Vietnamese war. See Vietnamese war, 1957- —Protests, demonstrations, etc. against

PROTHRO, James Thompson, jr
They're only no. 2. il por Time 88:78-9 O 7 '66

PROTOCOLS of the wise men of Zion
Myth of the Jewish world-conspiracy; excerpt from Warrant for genocide. N. Cohn. Commentary 41:35-42 Je '66; Discussion. 42:10+ D '66

PROTON accelerators. See Accelerators (electrons, etc)

PROTON synchrotron. See Synchrotron

PROTON whistlers (radio waves) See Radio waves

PROTONS
Sun protons affect moon. Sci N 89:510 Je 25 '66

PROTOPERITHECIA. See Organelles

PROTOPLASMIC streaming
Energy balancing in nitella cells treated with dinitrophenol. C. E. Barr and T. C. Broyer. bibliog il Science 151:1245-6 Mr 11 '66

PROTOPLASTS. See Plant cells and tissues

PROTOPTERUS aethiopicus. See Lungfishes

PROTOZOA
Cilia isolated from tetrahymena after membrane stabilization by 1,5-difluoro-2,4-dinitrobenzene. J. R. Culbertson. bibliog il Science 153:1390-1 S 16 '66
Protozoology; report on second international conference. R. W. Hull. Science 151:596-7 F 4 '66

PROULX, E. A.
Thief; story. Seventeen 25:128-9 O '66

PROUST, Marcel
Proust and the tartar relation. M. Curtis. Nation 202:160-3 F 7 '66

PROUTY, Winston L.
Exceptional children, the neglected legion. NEA J 55:25 Mr '66
Excerpt from debate, August 19, 1965. Cong Digest 45:87+ Mr '66

about
Prouty's pride. por Time 82:27B Mr 18 '66

PROVENCE
Two kitchens in Provence. M. F. K. Fisher. New Yorker 42:29-36 Ag 27 '66

PROVENCHER, Pierre
Young amputee's new grip on the future. il por Life 61:58B+ Ag 19 '66

PROVERBS
See also
Maxims

PROVIDENCE, R.I.
Hurricane protection; Fox Point Hurricane Dam project. il Am City 81:78 Jl '66

Housing
Beneficent house, Providence, R.I. il Arch Rec 139:144-5 Je '66

PROVIDENCE college, Providence, R.I.
Combined library and study facility. il Arch Rec 140:218 S '66

PROVINCETOWN, Mass.
Pilot report: gone flying to Provincetown in the new Cherokee 235B. R. B. Weeghman. il Flying 79:76-80 O '66

Galleries and museums
In and out with art; Chrysler museum's four movement installation. K. Kuh. il Sat R 49:42-3 Ag 27 '66

PROVINCIALISM
Provincialism is dead, long live regionalism! Time essay. Time 88:36-7 O 21 '66

PROVING grounds
ASW facility readied for March use; Barking Sands underwater test range. R. Pay. il Tech W 19:23-5 O 17 '66
MILA launch site readied for first Saturn V vehicle. il Miss & Roc 18:15 My 16 '66
Munitions test group mission will expand; Eglin AFB, Fla. Aviation W 85:38 mid-D '66
No major expansion seen necessary for ETR launches. K. Voss. Miss & Roc 18:57 My 30 '66

Reconnaissance hardware gets realistic test at Eglin site. il Tech W 19:24-6 N 7 '66
Switching job refined at ETR by Westrex; air force Eastern test range. K. Voss. Tech W 19:33-4 O 10 '66
Way station to the moon; Mississippi test facility. il Bsns W p62+ Ap 2 '66
WTR build-up under way for MOL, Titan III-C in '68. W. Wilks. Miss & Roc 18:58 My 30 '66

PROWN, Jules David
John Singleton Copley: a balanced view; excerpts from introduction. Antiques 89:380-3 Mr '66

PROXMIRE, William
Congress tries new focus on economics. por Bsns W p22+ D 24 '66

PRPIC, George J.
Book reviews. America 115:99 Jl 23 '66

PRUITT, Eleanor
Open house at Tongue Point; with bibliography. Library J 91:332-4+ Ja 15 '66

PRUITT, William O. jr
Ghost of the North. Audubon Mag 68:470-1 N '66

PRUNING
Barbered trees: fruit trees. G. Lorang and J. Snyder. il Farm J 90:68T Mr '66
Character pruning with small container plants. il Sunset 137:60-1 Ag '66
Chemical pruning of plants. H. M. Cathey and others. bibliog il Science 153:1382-3 S 16 '66
Guide to spring pruning. il Pop Gard 17:64-5+ My '66
How to prune a tree. il Pop Gard 17:83 My '66
How to prune old roses. A. Murphy. Flower Grower 53:66 Mr '66
Shape up your flowering shrubs. il Flower Grower 53:50-1+ My '66
Spray speeds up pruning; chemical growth regulator helps prune plants. Sci N 90:251 O 1 '66
When you know how, rose pruning is so simple. M. Costigan. il Flower Grower 53:42-4 F '66
Why you should cut back, what to cut back, and how to cut back. Sunset 137:129 Ag '66
See also
Fruit trees, Training of
Trees, Training of

PRUNUS ilicifolia. See Hollyleaf cherry

PRUNUS lyonii. See Islands cherry

PRYCE-JONES, Alan
Celebrating a century of Peter Rabbit. Harper 233:109-10 S '66
How to be nice. Commonweal 84:579-81 S 16 '66
Late transplant: why I left London for New York. Harper 233:11-12+ Ag '66
Opinion: young men's looks. por Mlle 62:84-5 F '66
Youngest romantics. Vogue 148:248+ D '66

PRYCE-JONES, David
Last glowing isolation. Reporter 34:49-50 F 10 '66

PRYOR, Andrew J.
Home fire alarms. Consumer Bul 50:35-8 Ja '67

PRYOR, Hubert
(ed) See Hornig, D. F. Science in your life

PRYOR, Karen. See Lang. T. G. jt. auth.

PRYOR, Samuel F.
Samuel F. Pryor Christmas exhibit of dolls at National geographic society, 1965. J. A. Douglass. il Hobbies 71:40+ Ja '67

PRYOR, Taylor
Taylor Pryors' ocean advantage. V. Lawford. il pors Vogue 148:208-11+ N 1 '66

PRYOR, Mrs Taylor
Taylor Pryors' ocean advantage. V. Lawford. il pors Vogue 148:208-11+ N 1 '66

PSEUDO medicine. See Quacks and quackery

PSEUDOSCORPIONS. See Book scorpions

PSORIASIS
Psoriasis: the pesky scaling disease. C. Baker. Todays Health 44:61+ My '66

PSYCHEDELIC art. See Hallucinogenic. drugs and art

PSYCHIATRIC clinics
Snake pits give way to the new clinics; Penn foundation for mental health, inc. il Bsns W p 190-2 N 5 '66
See also
Child guidance clinics

PSYCHIATRIC insurance. See Insurance, Mental health

PSYCHIATRIC research
Assassination syndrome fits Lee Oswald. Sci N 90:229 S 24 '66

PSYCHIATRIC schools. See Special classes and special schools

PSYCHIATRISTS
Problems in psychotherapy: the vacation period; excerpt from Why you need analysis. R. Clurman. il N Y Times Mag p26+ Je 26 '66

PSYCHIATRY
Breakthrough in psychiatry: revolutionary treatment of the mentally ill; Delaware Valley mental health foundation, Doylestown, Pa. C. Brossard. il Look 30:30-4+ Ap 5 '66
Doctor Berne plays the celebrity game. J. Langguth. il N Y Times Mag p 10-11+ Jl 17 '66; Discussion. p22 Ag 28 '66
Games people play at Christmas. E. Berne. il McCalls 94:82-3+ D '66
Inside psychiatry today. F. R. Schreiber and M. Herman. See issues of Science digest
Parents vs. children: frustrating games families play. J. L. Schimel. il Redbook 127:46-7+ Ag '66
Psychiatrist's notebook: questions and answers. T. I. Rubin. McCalls 93:50+ S; 94:93+ O '66
Psychiatrists under attack; rebellious Dr Szasz; America's drift toward the therapeutic state. E. M. Schur. Atlan 217:72-6 Je '66; Discussion. 218:31-2 Ag '66
U.S.S.R. vs U.S. psychiatry. Sci N 90:342 O 29 '66
See also
Child psychiatry
Mental illness
Psychoanalysis
Psychology, Pathological
Social psychiatry

PSYCHIATRY, Forensic. See Forensic psychiatry

PSYCHIATRY, Social. See Social psychiatry

PSYCHIATRY and religion
Bible's timeless and timely insights. S. Blanton. Read Digest 89:93-6 Ag '66
Can ministers and psychiatrists work together? W. F. Lynch. Redbook 128:52-3+ D '66
Ecumenics and psychiatry; world Consultation for psychiatrists and theologians at Chateau de Bossey. T. G. Oden. Christian Cent 83:689-90 My 25 '66
Importance of Freud. Sister Marie Michael. Cath World 204:212-18 Ja '67
Sin, illness and guilt; reservations regarding O. H. Mowrer's quasi-religious, sin-centered approach to psychotherapy. R. J. Becker. Christian Cent 83:1007-9 Ag 17 '66
See also
Church and social problems

PSYCHOANALYSIS
Freud, friend or enemy? S. Rubenfeld. New Repub 154:30+ Mr 19 '66
Freud saw it coming. D. Callahan. Commonweal 84:312-13 Je 3 '66; Discussion. 84:405+, 483-4 Jl 1, 22 '66
Importance of Freud. Sister Marie Michael. Cath World 204:212-18 Ja '67
Monks in psychoanalysis. Time 88:80 D 2 '66
Psychoanalysis and morality. L. H. Farber; discussion. Commentary 41:23+ Mr; 6+ Ap '66

PSYCHOANALYSIS and religion. See Psychiatry and religion

PSYCHOBIOLOGY
Mind, brain, and humanist values. R. W. Sperry. Bul Atomic Sci 22:2-6 S '66

PSYCHODRAMA
Mock murder to cool Watts; street pantomimes given, to promote better understanding between races. il Life 61:85-6 Ag 19 '66

PSYCHOLOGICAL examinations
Challenge to unconcerned bystanders; experiment to measure the willingness of subjects to report a dangerous situation. L. Wainwright. Life 61:32 S 23 '66
Research in America; illegality of tests on New York city children; with letter by C. Isler. J. Lear. il Sat R 49:64-5 F 5 '66; Discussion. 49:68 Mr 5; 57-8 Ap 2 '66
See also
Personality tests

PSYCHOLOGICAL measurement. See Psychometrics

PSYCHOLOGICAL societies
See also
American psychological association

PSYCHOLOGICAL stress. See Stress (physiology)

PSYCHOLOGICAL warfare
See also
Terrorism

PSYCHOLOGY
See also
American psychological association
Attitudes

Behavior (psychology)
Brain
Child study
Complexes (psychology)
Fighting (psychology)
Intelligence
Personality
Psychiatry
Psychoanalysis
Psychobiology
Retention (psychology)
Sleep
Will
also subhead Psychology under various subjects, e.g. Advertising—Psychology

Experiments
Psychology experiments without subjects' consent; letters. S. E. Miller; M. Rokeach. Science 152:15 Ap 1 '66; Discussion. 152:1455-6 Je 10 '66

Industrial applications
See Psychology, Industrial

Measurement
See Psychometrics

PSYCHOLOGY, Applied
See also
Human engineering

PSYCHOLOGY, Comparative
See also
Animals—Habits and behavior

PSYCHOLOGY, Criminal. See Criminal psychology

PSYCHOLOGY, Educational
Editor interviews; ed. by M. S. Fenner. E. T. Hall. NEA J 56:87-8 Ja '67
Focus on success instead of failure. B. Haldane. NEA J 55:32 Ap '66
Prevention of failure. W. B. Waetjen; K. W. Clarke. il NEA J 55:37-40 Ap '66
Sensitivity training in the classroom. D. Simon; D. Sarkotich. NEA J 56:12-13 Ja '67
See also
Learning, Psychology of
Transfer of training

PSYCHOLOGY, Experimental
Components of skilled performance. M. I. Posner. bibliog il Science 152:1712-18 Je 24 '66
Man may learn to be ill. P. McBroom. Sci N 89:331 My 7 '66

PSYCHOLOGY, Forensic
See also
Forensic psychiatry

PSYCHOLOGY, Industrial
Famous firsts: measuring minds for the job. il Bsns W p60+ Ja 29 '66

PSYCHOLOGY, Pastoral
Pastoral care and public ministry. D. Browning. Christian Cent 83:1175-7 S 28 '66; Reply. A. D. Jorjorian. 83:1345 N 2 '66

PSYCHOLOGY, Pathological
Four-letter men; Gilles de la Tourette syndrome. Time 88:46 Ag 26 '66
See also
Hysteria
Psychotherapy

PSYCHOLOGY, Physiological
Physiological insight grows. P. McBroom. Sci N 90:555 D 24 '66
See also
Conditioned response
Human engineering
Mind and body
Movement, Psychology of
Pain
Psychology, Experimental
Time perception

PSYCHOLOGY of learning. See Learning, Psychology of

PSYCHOMETRICS
Metric for the social consensus. S. S. Stevens. bibliog il Science 151:530-41 F 4 '66

PSYCHOSES
Psychedelic state fluid. Sci N 90:238 S 24 '66
Similar psychoses found. Sci N 89:378 My 14 '66

PSYCHOSOMATIC medicine. See Medicine, Psychosomatic

PSYCHOTHERAPY
Back to the womb in a pool; L. Wiener's hydropsychotherapy treatments. il Life 60:61-3 Je 10 '66
Games keeper; Transactional analysis; E. Berne's theories. il Newsweek 68:56 Ag 8 '66
Prenatal weightlessness at the Beverly Hilton. H. Downs. il Sci Digest 60:88-92 S '66
Problems in psychotherapy: the vacation period; excerpt from Why you need analysis. R. Clurman. il N Y Times Mag p26+ Je 26 '66

PSYCHOTHERAPY—*Continued*
Psychotherapy improves patient's earning power. Sci N 90:253 O 1 '66
Sin, illness and guilt; reservations regarding O. H. Mowrer's quasi-religious, sin-centered approach. R. J. Becker. Christian Cent 83:1007-9 Ag 17 '66
See also
Group psychotherapy
Psychiatry and religion
PSYCHOTROPIC drugs
See also
Hallucinogenic drugs
PSYCHROMETERS. See Hygrometers
PSYCOPATHS. See Insane, Criminal and dangerous
PTERIDINES
Pteridines in the fat body of a mutant of drosophila melanogaster. C. P. Wright and E. W. Hanly. bibliog il Science 152:533-5 Ap 22 '66
PTERIDOPHYTA. See Ferns
PUBERTY
See also
Adolescence
PUBLIC address amplifiers. See Amplifiers
PUBLIC address microphones. See Microphones
PUBLIC-address systems. See Loud speaking apparatus
PUBLIC bank of Detroit. See Detroit—Banks
PUBLIC buildings
See also
Art in public buildings
Courthouses
Library architecture
also subhead Public buildings under names of cities, e.g. New York (city)—Public buildings
PUBLIC corporations. See Government corporations
PUBLIC debt (United States) See Debts, Public—United States
PUBLIC decency. See Decency
PUBLIC defenders
Justice in the courtroom, can the poor get it? G. Samuels. Sat R 49:25+ Ja 29 '66
Saga of the Little green pig; scheme for selling vacuum cleaners at several times their worth. R. L. Smith. il Reporter 35:39-40+ N 3 '66
PUBLIC domain. See Public lands
PUBLIC education association, New York
Seven decades, 1895-1965; exhibition at ten galleries. New Yorker 42:37-8 My 7 '66
PUBLIC employees. See Government employees
PUBLIC health
Appeal abroad of American medicine and public health; address; with questions and answers. L. L. Terry. Ann Am Acad 366:78-88 Jl '66
See also
Air pollution
Food adulteration and inspection
Medicine, Preventive
Rats as carriers of infection
Vaccination
Water pollution

International aspects
Ethics for an international health profession. C. E. Taylor. bibliog Science 153:716-20 Ag 12 '66
Exporting the Great society; funds are a limiting factor. J. Walsh. Science 152:45-7 Ap 1 '66
International education and health; message to the Congress; February 2, 1966. L. B. Johnson. Dept State Bul 54:328-35 F 28 '66; Same. abr. with title Proposed international education act of 1966; excerpts. Sch & Soc 94:186-9 Ap 2 '66

India
See also
Calcutta—Sanitary affairs

Kansas
They're country doctors no longer; Kansas rural health plan. H. Earl. il Todays Health 44:24-9 Je '66

Underdeveloped areas
Medical problems of the developing countries. R. E. Brown. bibliog il Science 153:271-5 Jl 15 '66
Western health methods not needed everywhere. Sci N 90:377 N 5 '66

United States
Advise aid to sick, aged. Sci N L 89:61 Ja 22 '66

America's unhealthy children: an emerging scandal. R. Tunley. Harper 232:41-6 My '66; Discussion. 233:4 Jl; 8 Ag '66
Health of the American people. F. E. Linder. il Sci Am 214:21-9 bibliog(p 144) Je '66
NIH: demand increases for applications of research. J. Walsh. Science 153:149-52 Jl 8 '66
Pollution: everybody's adversary; symposium. il Today Health 44:37-65 Mr '66
Public health and drug safety; address, October 14, 1965. H. S. Ingraham. Vital Speeches 32:231-4 F 1 '66
White House gifts said to trigger health law; multimillion dollar heart disease, cancer and stroke law. Sci N 90:136 Ag 27 '66
See also
United States—Public health service
also subhead Public health under names of cities, e.g. Boston—Public health

Vietnam (Republic)
U.S. physicians face great odds in war. Sci N 89:169 Mr 12 '66
PUBLIC health centers. See Health centers
PUBLIC health service (United States) See United States—Public health service
PUBLIC health service hospital, Lexington, Ky. See United States—Public health service hospital, Lexington, Ky.
PUBLIC houses (France) See Bars and barrooms
PUBLIC houses (Great Britain) See Bars and barrooms
PUBLIC interest (periodical)
Middle-aged meliorists. il Time 87:64 Mr 4 '66
PUBLIC land law review commission. See United States—Public land law review commission
PUBLIC lands

United States
Friendly debate between two professionals; how much land for national forest recreation? letters. C. Granger; B. L. Orell. Am For 72:30-1+ Ja; 12+ F '66
Maintenance of public-use areas. P. Nierengarten. Parks & Rec 1:249-50 Mr '66
People and the out-of-doors; crisis of natural and open areas. T. J. Rillo. il Am For 72:8+ Mr '66
Public domain: heart of the Republic. W. W. Porter. 2d. il Am For 72:12-15+ Ja; 26-9+ F; 34-5+ Mr; 28-31+ Ap '66; Reply to January and February issues. E. L. Campbell. 72:4 Ap '66
Sheep fences or antelope? concerning fencing on public land in Wyo. B. Milek. il Field & S 71:10-12+ S '66
See also
Homesteads
National forests
National parks and reserves—United States
United States—Land management, Bureau of
United States—Public land law review commission
PUBLIC libraries. See Libraries
PUBLIC library association. See American library association—Public library association
PUBLIC meetings
See also
Assembly, Right of
PUBLIC officers
After Moyers leaves; the key men at the White House. il U S News 61:12 D 26 '66
America's political dynasties, by S. Hess. Review
Newsweek 68:124 O 10 '66. R. Moley
Arrogance of dissent: views of G. McGee. K. Crawford. Newsweek 68:27 Jl 18 '66
Atlantic report: musical chairs; search for a new man to replace Bill D. Moyers as presidential press secretary. D. Kiker. Atlan 218:10 D '66
Blabbermouthism; violations of confidence at highest levels of government. N. Cousins. Sat R 49:34-5 D 10 '66
Bobby Kennedy's shadow cabinet. S. V. Roberts. il Esquire 66:168-9+ S '66
Bone weariness brought on by a driving boss and the sleep gap. H. Sidey. il Life 60:48 Je 10 '66
Brain pickers. il Newsweek 68:30-1 S 19 '66
By the way; new appointments to State department. il Newsweek 68:20-1 O 3 '66
Even LBJ's right arm can't juggle everything. P. Lisagor. il Nations Bsns 55:21-2 Ja '67
Greener pastures: notable men in government turn to big think. C. Fritchey. Harper 232:50 Ap '66

PUBLIC officers—*Continued*
Johnsonization of Washington; exodus of intellectuals and Establishmentarians. S. Alsop. Sat Eve Post 239:20 F 26 '66
LBJ makes some changes. il U S News 61:39 O 3 '66
LBJ's foreign policy: mirror of the man. il Bsns W p38-40 Jl 9 '66
LBJ's tight reins; on advisers. Atlan 218:12-13 Jl '66
Need for scholars; address, May 11, 1966. L. B. Johnson. Vital Speeches 32:482-4 Je 1 '66
New link; J. R. Roche. il Time 88:31 S 16 '66
Old characters in new roles. C. Fritchey. Harper 233:34 Jl '66
Pecksniffs squeeze the fun from a joyless bunch. H. Sidey. il Life 60:40B Je 17 '66
Playing all the bases; two new White House aides. il Time 87:25 Ap 8 '66
Revolving door at 1600; why the rapid turnover? il Newsweek 67:26-7 My 9 '66
Shortage of liberals. W. V. Shannon. Commonweal 84:46-7 Ap 1 '66
Shrinking inner circle; resignations. Time 87:21-2 My 6 '66
Sorry, wrong number; W. M. Watson's critics. Newsweek 67:21 Ja 31 '66
Spring and that tired feeling. il Newsweek 67:17-18 Ap 4 '66
State's new team. Time 88:24 S 30 '66
Switching squads; changeover in foreign-policy establishment. Time 87:29-30 My 20 '66
T.R.B. from Washington; five interesting men in public life. New Repub 154:4 My 7 '66
Those who sniff at the hem of power. P. Lisagor. il Nations Bsns 54:23-4 F '66
Turnover in the Johnson old guard. il U S News 60:12 My 9 '66
Unfortunate standoff: Johnson versus the intellectuals. H. Sidey. il Life 61:42D S 23 '66
Urge to serve in Washington can go too far. H. Sidey. Life 61:30B Jl 29 '66
Utility men: new members of White House team. Newsweek 67:28 Ap 11 '66
Washington: ten of its most powerful men. il pors Vogue 148:150-3 N 15 '66
White House in transition. H. Brandon. Sat R 49:10 Je 11 '66
White House staff. New Repub 154:8-9 Ap 16 '66
See also
Conflict of interests (public office)
Governors
Legislators
Negro public officers
Women as public officers
also subhead Public officers under names of cities, e.g. Richmond, Va.—Public officers

Appointment, qualifications, tenure, etc.
Anti-intellectualism in the government. W. W. Brickman. Sch & Soc 94:437 D 10 '66
It's the idea that offends; electing movie stars. S. Alexander. Life 61:17 Jl 8 '66
Perfect candidate; H. Evry's techniques for getting elected to public office. R. Wernick. il Life 60:41-2+ Je 3 '66
State of affairs; perils of staying in government too long. H. Brandon. Sat R 50:16+ Ja 14 '67

Gifts
Dodd dinners; disclosures by Drew Pearson and Jack Anderson. il Newsweek 67:19-20 My 2 '66
Is Dodd dead? New Repub 154:7 Ap 30 '66

Germany (Federal Republic)
Nazi past. Newsweek 68:62+ O 24 '66
PUBLIC opinion
About marriage; CBS telecast. Feedback: marriage, a game for kids? America 116:34-5 Ja 14 '67
Attitude formation and public opinion. D. Katz. bibliog f il Ann Am Acad 367:150-62 S '66
Crisis of color '66; survey findings. il Newsweek 68:20-32+ Ag 22 '66
World opinion: does it really count? pro and con discussion. Sr Schol 87:10-11 Ja 21 '66
See also
Petitions
Public opinion polls
Student opinion
Vietnamese war, 1957- —Public opinion
also subhead Foreign opinion under names of countries, e.g. Germany (Federal Republic)—Foreign opinion

Asia
Who's afraid of China? A. Campbell. New Repub 154:12-16 Ap 9 '66
See also
United States—Foreign opinion—Asian

Australia
Australia votes to stay in Vietnam. D. Warner. il Reporter 35:29-31 D 29 '66
Sinister word; reactions to conscription for Vietnam. il Newsweek 67:44+ My 16 '66
See also
United States—Foreign opinion—Australian

China (People's Republic)
Great leap outward: four who fled; interviews, ed. by S. Liu. il Newsweek 68:57-60 O 24 '66

Communist countries
Polling the proletariat; Soviet Union and Eastern Europe. il Newsweek 67:40 F 21 '66
See also
Europe, Western
United States—Foreign opinion—European
Vietnamese war, 1957- —Public opinion

France
New style; indifference toward C. de Gaulle on northern provincial tour. Newsweek 67:42+ My 9 '66
See also
United States—Foreign opinion—French
Vietnamese war, 1957- —Public opinion

Germany (Federal Republic)
Smell of change; mounting criticism of Erhard's failure. Newsweek 68:33-4 Ag 29 '66

Great Britain
See also
United States—Foreign opinion—British

India
See also
United States—Foreign opinion—Indian

Japan
See also
United States—Foreign opinion—Japanese

Rhodesia
Atlantic report. A. Lewis. Atlan 218:12+ D '66

Russia
Moscow: the defense does not rest; case of Sinyavsky and Daniel. D. Brown. il Reporter 35:43-5 S 22 '66
Russia's other peace movement. A. Parry. Nation 203:142-5 Ag 22 '66
See also
China (People's Republic)—Foreign opinion—Russian
Vietnamese war, 1957- —Public opinion

United States
Atlantic report: LBJ and the polls. Atlan 217:26+ My; 218:6+ Jl '66
Boom times, unhappy people, why? results of a nationwide survey. il U S News 60:64-8+ Mr 21 '66
Can LBJ reverse the polls? il U S News 60:33 Je 20 '66
Democratic slippage; L. Harris survey findings. Newsweek 67:29 Mr 21 '66
Division street: America, by S. Terkel. Review
    Sat R 49:65 D 24 '66. R. L. Shayon
Election near: mood of voters. il U S News 61:50-2+ O 24 '66
Good case of the poll sniffles; President Johnson impressed by polls. W. H. Honan. il N Y Times Mag p34-5+ Ag 21 '66; Reply with rejoinder. J. Belden. p 12+ S 18 '66
Government and the boom; executive opinion. Sat R 49:29 Mr 5 '66
Growing drama in U.S. politics: new front runner? il U S News 61:15 Ag 29 '66
Hail, Harry Golden; American skepticism about foreign policy. K. Crawford. Newsweek 68:27 D 26 '66
How things are changing for LBJ. il U S News 60:40-3 Je 6 '66
How you voted; with editorial comment. il Farm J 90:33+, 98 N '66
Major turning point against Negro movement; concerning New York times survey. U S News 61:46 O 3 '66
Mood of Americans at this time: interview. G. Gallup. il U S News 61:50-4 S 19 '66
Neither blind obedience nor uncivil disobedience. S. Hook. il N Y Times Mag p52-3+ Je 5 '66

PUBLIC opinion—United States—_Continued_
Next two years. New Repub 155:5-6 D 3 '66
Our way with heroes; hot-and-cold public whim. K. Crawford. Newsweek 69:22 Ja 2 '67
Party leaders analyze the vote, look ahead; interviews and excerpts from news conferences. il U S News 61:55-6+ N 21 '66
Poll pains of a living, breathing contradiction. H. Sidey. Life 60:38B Je 24 '66
Polls and more polls: what they are showing. U S News 61:18 O 3 '66
Press, the President and foreign policy. J. B. Reston. For Affairs 44:553-73 Jl '66; Same abr. Read Digest 89:69-73 S '66
Signs of a protest vote: trends in primaries and polls. il U S News 61:36-7 Ag 22 '66
View from Jakarta; public reaction to the Indonesian crisis. Nation 202:171 F 14 '66
What Americans really think of business; and why college students are disenchanted; L. Harris survey. il Newsweek 67:84-6+ My 2 '66
What's bothering Americans, as told to Congress. il U S News 61:56-9 Ag 15 '66
Where consensus breaks down; Great society. H. J. Morgenthau; discussion. New Repub 154:34+ F 19 '66
      See also
India—Foreign opinion—American
United States—Foreign opinion
Vietnamese war, 1957- —Public opinion

Vietnam (Republic)
People, resigned; interviews with Vietnamese people, ed. by F. Sully. il Newsweek 67:33-4 Ap 18 '66
Thich Nhat Hanh; interview. Nhat Hanh. New Yorker 42:21-3 Je 25 '66
      See also
United States—Foreign opinion—Vietnamese

PUBLIC opinion polls
Fallible priesthood. il Time 88:28 D 16 '66
Government by public opinion polls. E. Roper. Sat R 49:18 My 28 '66
May I ask you a few questions about love? Elmo Roper's opinion poll. S. Brown. il Sat Eve Post 239:24-7 D 31 '66
New computerized age: town meeting reborn. V. F. Miller. Sat R 49:34-5 Jl 23 '66
New space poll; Trendex poll. W. J. Coughlin. Miss & Roc 18:46 Mr 21 '66
Poll with a purpose; Edina, Minn; ed. by P. D. Elmon. il Am City 81:171-2+ S '66
Polling the proletariat: Soviet Union and Eastern Europe. il Newsweek 67:40 F 21 '66
Polls and the war. W. Lippmann. Newsweek 68:13 Jl 4 '66
Pollsters at work; firms and their operators. il Newsweek 68:42-4 O 31 '66
Proof and Daniel Poling; NCC research specialists analyze D. Poling's poll of ministerial opinion. L. Whitman and G. Trimble. Christian Cent 83:1350+ N 2 '66; Correction. 83:1446 N 23 '66
Were the polls wrong? E. Roper. Sat R 49:33 D 10 '66
      See also
Scholastic research center

PUBLIC ownership. See Government ownership

PUBLIC relations
Perfect candidate; H. Evry's techniques for getting elected to public office. R. Wernick. il Life 60:41-2+ Je 3 '66
Public relations. L. L. L. Golden. See second issue of each month of Saturday review
      See also
Customer relations
Moving pictures in public relations
      also subhead Public relations under various subjects, e.g. Banks and banking —Public relations

Bibliography
Books in communications. A. Balk. See issues of Saturday review

PUBLIC relations directors
On being a no man. L. L. L. Golden. Sat R 49:64 F 12 '66

PUBLIC roads, Bureau of. See United States—Public roads, Bureau of

PUBLIC school libraries. See School libraries
PUBLIC school teachers. See Teachers
PUBLIC schools

Accreditation
School system that failed; with discussion group program, by M. S. Smart. W. Hartley and E. Hartley. il Parents Mag 41:26, 52-3+ Mr '66

Appraisal
See Evaluation (education)

Attendance
See School attendance

Desegregation
Attacked in court; northern segregation. U S News 61:9 Ag 1 '66
Back to school, a long way. il Newsweek 68:21-2 S 12 '66
Bending the guidelines; new federal law proposed. Time 87:25-6 F 25 '66
Bridging two worlds; Negro students bussed to suburbs. il Time 88:60 O 28 '66
Charade on Goat Hill; G. Wallace's bill to reject federal aid. Newsweek 68:20 S 5 '66
Children of the South, by M. Anderson. Review
      Life 61:22 O 21 '66. R. Stolley
      New Repub 155:17-19 S 24 '66. R. Coles
      Sat R 49:90 S 17 '66. K. Taylor
Civil rights' dim prospects; bill of 1966. A. M. Bickel. New Repub 155:18 S 17 '66
Civil rights guidelines. J. Lloyd. Sr Schol 88:sup5 Mr 25 '66
Computerized integration; school district 65, Evanston, Ill. Christian Cent 83:1367-9 N 9 '66
Desegregation in the North; developing power in the ghetto. G. Grant. il Sat R 49:75-6+ D 17 '66
Desegregation in the South; deliberate speed of title VI. J. Leeson. Sat R 49:74+ D 17 '66
Do we really want equality? J. Cass. Sat R 49:65-7 D 17 '66
Down the down staircase: parents, teachers, and public authorities. A. Kopkind. New Repub 155:11-14 O 22 '66
Education; racial controversy dogs U.S. commissioner. L. J. Carter. Science 154:242-3+ O 14 '66
ESEA deferred in over 200 districts; Alabama passes anti-guidelines law. Library J 91:5142 O 15 '66
Equal educational opportunity act of 1967; excerpts from proposals. Sat R 49:66+ D 17 '66
Failure in the schools? Commonweal 84:406 Jl 1 '66
Federal dictatorship? D. Lawrence. U S News 61:112 D 12 '66
Federal money in public schools; interview. H. Howe, 2d. U S News 61:68-74 D 5 '66
Federal steps vs. school desegregation. Sch & Soc 94:261 Sum '66
Forcing desegregation through Title VI; new guidelines. A. M. Bickel. New Repub 154:8-9 Ap 9 '66; Reply. C. White. 154:29-30 Ap 23 '66
Government's plan to desegregate the suburbs. il U S News 61:76-8 O 10 '66
Harlem's beseiged showpiece; Intermediate school 201. J. Bailey. il Arch Forum 125:48-51 N '66
How to keep school segregation. J. Osborne. New Repub 154:16-18 Mr 12 '66
Howe of integration; House rules committee grill commissioner. il Newsweek 68:74 O 24 '66
I guess we're just impatient; PRIDE projects. Volusia County, Fla. P. Mann. il Am Ed 2:5-7 Mr '66
In defense of the guidelines; statement, September 27, 1966, with editorial comment. H. Howe, 2d. Library J 91:5002+ O 15 '66
Integration vendetta in a northern town; New Rochelle after five years. K. Wheeler. il Life 60:94-6+ My 6 '66
Intruders in the dust; Negro children attacked at schools; Grenada, Miss. il Time 88:26 S 23 '66
Is bussing self-defeating? Time 87:73 Ap 29 '66
Is federal aid helping to end neighborhood schools? il U S News 61:49-50 S 5 '66
Lesson in bias; H. E. Garrett's pamphlet, How classroom desegregation will work. Newsweek 67:63 My 30 '66
Malverne; integration is not enough. B. J. De Noie. Nat R 18:679-81 Jl 12 '66
Mr Howe and his racial views; center of controversy. U S News 61:24 O 17 '66
Mixed classes; a report as schools open; South. il U S News 61:12 S 12 '66
Negro shortage; seeking more Negro students in Great Neck, N.Y. Newsweek 67:82 F 28 '66
New crackdown on local schools. il U S News 60:25-7 My 2 '66
New integration targets; northern cities and suburbs. il U S News 61:47-8 Jl 4 '66

PUBLIC utilities—*Continued*

Securities

Opportunities in utilities. il Duns R 87:85-6 My '66

PUBLIC welfare

First congress of the poor: total participation of the poor; aim of Syracuse convention. R. A. Cloward and R. M. Elman. il Nation 202:148-51 F 7 '66; Reply. J. L. Erlich. 202:inside cover. 241 F 28 '66

Law

See Social legislation

California

Watts: where welfare bred violence. E. Selby and A. Selby. Read Digest 88:67-71 My '66

Canada

How to fight poverty. New Repub 155:4 D 24 '66

Kansas

When a county tried to cut relief bill; Dickson County. Il U S News 60:44-7 Ja 31 '66

New York (state)

Honor thy father & thy mother; modification in regulations. Nation 203:4 Jl 4 '66

United States

Poverty as a crime; carefully hedged rights of the poor. I. Silver. Commonweal 85:74-6 O 21 '66

Poverty: public enemy number one. W. C. McWilliams. Sat R 49:48-9+ D 10 '66

Size of the jungle; Great society killing charitable activities of service clubs; discussion. Christian Cent 83:239 F 23 '66

Weight of the poor: strategy to end poverty. R. A. Cloward and F. F. Piven. il Nation 202:510-17 My 2 '66

Welfare backlash. America 115:680-1 N 26 '66

When everybody is on welfare. il U S News 61:72 Ag 1 '66

PUBLIC works

Germany (Federal Republic)

Germany's spending spree; government spending on public works, subsidies, and social services. il Fortune 74:72+ Ag '66

PUBLICITY

Biting the handout they feed you; Florida business leader treats handouts as ad-insertion orders. Time 88:41 Ag 19 '66

See also
Advertising
Booksellers and bookselling—Publicity
Press agents

PUBLISHERS and libraries. See Libraries and publishers

PUBLISHERS and publishing

Again, an agenda for action: publisher-bookseller relationships. C. B. Grannis. Pub W 189:59 Je 20 '66

The book revolution, by R. Escarpit. Review
Pub W 190:24-6 D 12 '66. D. Melcher

Designer-publisher relations. S. Salter. Pub W 189:166+ Je 13 '66

Publishing and bookselling, two worlds, or one? C. B. Grannis. Pub W 189:200 Je 6 '66

Translating books for newly developing countries; excerpt from Guide to book publishing. D. C. Smith, jr. Pub W 190: 22-6 Ag 1 '66

See also
American newspaper publishers association
Authors and publishers
Books
Books—Advertising
Books—Prices
Booksellers and bookselling
Copyright
International publishers association
Newspaper publishing
Periodicals. Publishing of
University presses

Catholic literature

Elbowroom for the mind; with editorial comment. J. G. Lawler. America 116:28, 41-3 Ja 14 '67

Milestone in religious publishing. E. A. Weis. America 115:586-7 N 12 '66

Childrens literature

Are books overpriced? publishers' library bindings. D. Melcher. Library J 91:2542+ My 15 '66

Big business, a big problem. C. B. Grannis. Pub W 189:155 F 21 '66

Children's book field. il Pub W 190:212-19 Jl 11 '66

Children's book needs in a changing society; summary of addresses at conference in Tarrytown, N.Y. Pub W 190:35-8 Jl 25 '66

Children's books. il Pub W 189:60 Mr 14; 68 My 9; 118-19 Je 13; 190:48 Ag 8; 63 O 10; 52-3 N 7; 77-8 D 26 '66

Price-fixing of library-bound books? Senate hearings in Washington. E. Geller. il Library J 91:2570-8 My 15 '66

Publication of children's books far outweighs adult fiction; with charts. Library J 91: 1048-9 F 15 '66

Publishers accused of price fixing; librarians testify before senators, excessive prices for juveniles in publisher's library bindings. Library J 91:2292+ My 1 '66

Real and the unreal; address, October 13, 1965. J. Karl. il Wilson Lib Bul 41:162-7 O '66

Xerox: a new string to the bow; University microfilms enters children's book market. D. Dempsey. Sat R 49:39-40 F 19 '66

See also
Lion press

Computer installations

Bible society will install IBM 360 in new headquarters. il Pub W 189:102-3 F 14 '66

Golden books reports it has mastered its Univac computer; automated distribution system. il Pub W 190:45-50 O 3 '66

Magnetic tape unit helps law publisher meet growth problem; Michie co, Charlottesville, Va. W. O. Lewis and A. G. Colley, jr. il Pub W 189:24-5 Ap 4 '66

M.I.T. press demonstrates its computer system. il Pub W 190:73-5 N 14 '66

PBA hears views on impact of new technology; excerpts from address, Ma 27, 1966. R. Kaplan. Pub W 189:73-4 Je 27 '66

R&E council is briefed on new tools from IBM. il Pub W 189:82-5 My 2 '66

Technology in publishing. D. V. Newton. il Wilson Lib Bul 41:66-8+ S '66

Consolidations and mergers

Mergers and changes in French publishing. H. R. Lottman. Pub W 189:38-42 Mr 21 '66

S&S and Regents publishing in merger negotiations. Pub W 190:37 Ag 1 '66

History

Book publishing in America, by C. A. Madison. Review
Pub W 190:49-51 O 31 '66. J. T. Winterich

International aspects

Keys to successful co-publishing: communication and organization. il Pub W 189: 118-20 F 7 '66

New subsidiary right: European premium editions. Pub W 190:40 Ag 8 '66

Prentice-Hall receives president's E award. il Pub W 189:81 Ap 18 '66

Paperback books

Ante zooms for reprint rights. il Bsns W p45-6 F 12 '66

Books without number; publishers' book numbers. D. Melcher. Pub W 190:52 Jl 18 '66

Bookseller suit challenges ID franchise on paperbacks. Pub W 190:106 S 26 '66

No Noonday paperbacks in Great Britain. R. W. Straus, jr. Pub W 190:17 O 24 '66

Paperback revolution hits France. H. R. Lottman. il Pub W 190:41-4 Jl 18 '66

Paragraphics, artists' medium in large-size quality paperback; published by Grossman. il Pub W 190:116-17 S 5 '66

Religious literature

Out of the ghetto of churchiness. C. B. Grannis. Pub W 189:112 F 14 '66

Protestant publishers urged to think in terms of 2000 A.D; annual meeting of the Protestant church-owned publishers' association. Pub W 189:36 Mr 14 '66

Scientific literature

Science, technology: November-March high spots. il Pub W 190:44-72 N 14 '66

Scientific & technical book notes. Pub W 190: 89-94 N 14 '66

Securities

Book publishing stock prices: a monthly report. See first issue of each month of Publishers' weekly

Statistics

American book title output January through June 1966. Pub W 190:89 Jl 4 '66

ATPI statistical charts, 1965. Pub W 189:30-3 My 30 '66

PUBLISHERS and publishing—Statistics—*Cont.*
Census of manufactures: book publishing and
printing figures reported for 1958, 1963;
with excerpts. Pub W 189:39-44 Mr 7 '66
General book sales increased 10 per cent
in 1965; with table. Pub W 190:37-40 Ag
15 '66
Printing and publishing data; excerpts from
U.S. industrial outlook 1966. Pub W 189:
97 F 7 '66
See Jim read the book; production explosion.
P. H. Kendall. Reporter 34:37-8 Je 30 '66
Trends in net sales of books, 1958-1965, based
on reports of 145 publishers; chart. Pub W
189:74-5 Je 13 '66
   See also
Book industries and trade—Statistics

Study and teaching
Career-building at Radcliffe; publishing pro-
cedures course. D. Dempsey. Sat R 49:29
My 14 '66

Taxation
Publishers study situation on state and local
taxation; summary of one-day workshop
by the American textbook publishers institute. Pub W 189:55-7 F 7 '66

Technical literature
Book publishing, and bookkeeping. D. N.
Fischel. Science 152:871-5 My 13 '66
Science, technology: November-March high
spots. il Pub W 190:44-72 N 14 '66
Scientific & technical book notes. Pub W
190:89-94 N 14 '66

Textbooks
ATPI prepares for new changes in educa-
tion; report of 24th annual meeting. il
Pub W 189:24-36 My 30 '66
College market textbook problems analyzed
by publishers, suppliers; report of ATPI
conference. il Pub W 191:44-8 Ja 16 '67
House hearings called on minority groups
in texts. Pub W 190:56 Ag 22 '66
Implications of the Powell hearings. R. H.
Smith. Pub W 190:50 S 19 '66
Powell committee considers treatment of mi-
nority groups in school books. Library J 91:
5720 N 15 '66
We will leave no worm unturned; address
at the opening of the Textbook show 1966;
April 6, 1966. L. C. Deighton. Pub W 189:
26-9 My 2 '66
   See also
Textbooks

Asia
Reading habits and book publishing in Asia;
adaptation of address, May 1966. I. Insha.
il UNESCO Courier 19:12-16 N '66

China (People's Republic)
Libraries and publishing in mainland China;
excerpts from Publishing in mainland
China. G. R. Nunn. bibliog f il Library J
91:3327-32 Jl '66

Europe, Eastern
Publisher as diplomat. D. Dempsey. Sat R
49:33 S 17 '66

Europe, Western
Education by remote control: report on DI-
DACTA: 8th European educational mate-
rials fair. E. V. Epstein. Pub W 190:37-8
S 5 '66

France
Crime, violence, espionage: 1000 volumes of
Série noire. H. R. Lottman. il Pub W 189:
44-8 Mr 7 '66
French publishers cope with state censorship.
H. R. Lottman. Pub W 189:51-4 F 7 '66
Letter from Paris: five of seven annual De-
cember book prizes won by Grasset. Genêt.
New Yorker 42:65-6 D 31 '66
Mergers and changes in French publishing.
H. R. Lottman. Pub W 189:38-42 Mr 21 '66
New imprint in Paris; Editions Christian
Bourgois. H. R. Lottman. Pub W 190:34-6
N 21 '66
New role for French literary agents? H. R.
Lottman. Pub W 190:27-9 Ag 1 '66
Paperback revolution hits France. H. R.
Lottman. il Pub W 190:41-4 Jl 18 '66
Pléiade library. H. R. Lottman. Pub W 191:
49+ Ja 16 '67
Time, inc. buys 46 per cent share of Edi-
tions Laffont, Paris. Pub W 190:58 O 31
'66

Germany (Federal Republic)
I've got a sixth sense; A. Springer's empire.
Newsweek 67:98+ Ap 11 '66
West Germany's publishing powerhouse; A.
Springer's empire. J. Tebbel. Sat R 50:125-6
Ja 14 '67

Great Britain
British books to be numbered beginning this
month. D. Melcher. Pub W 191:28-30 Ja 2
'67
British title production increased by 204 in
1965. il Pub W 189:276 Ja 24 '66
Postmark: Pall Mall. G. R. Davies. Pub W
190:60-2 S 12 '66
Transatlantic view (cont) L. Kramer. Pub
W 189:61-4 Ja 31; 61-3 F 28 '66

Italy
La Dolce vita: Italian publishers discover
Rome. H. R. Lottman. Pub W 191:31-2 Ja
2 '67
Mondadori expands sales efforts in the U.S.A.
il Pub W 191:76+ Ja 2 '67

Mexico
Mexican uproar. M. Tejada. Nation 202:
inside cover, 100 Ja 24 '66

Taiwan
Solution for Taiwan book piracy proposed.
Pub W 190:56-7 Jl 4 '66

United States
Best title of all; impact of Title II of the
Elementary and secondary education act.
D. Dempsey. Sat R 49:50 O 1 '66; Re-
ply. D. Lacy. 49:26 O 29 '66
Book publishing and the new technologies.
H. S. Bailey, jr. il Sat R 49:41-3 Je 11
'66
Book publishing in America, by C. A. Madi-
son. Review
  New Repub 155:24+ N 5 '66. S. Kauffmann
  Pub W 190:49-51 O 31 '66. J. T. Wint-
erich
Books without number; publishers' book num-
bers. D. Melcher. Pub W 190:52 Jl 18 '66
Books without number; some of the history
of proposals for an industry book numbering system. D. Melcher. Pub W 190:24-7 Ag
15 '66
Cerfit of riches. il Time 88:100-2+ D 16 '66
Christmas offer mystique; booksellers orders
for Christmas stock. M. Bacon. il Pub W
190:50-1 Ag 8 '66
Collect calls; sampling of policies. Pub W 190:
48-9 N 28; 53 D 5 '66
College store and the publisher. C. B. Grannis. Pub W 189:54 My 16 '66
Continuing comments on the production
crisis. C. B. Grannis. Pub W 189:39 Mr
7 '66
Copyright and government; need for definition of publication of the United States
government. C. G. Benjamin. il Library
J 91:881-6 F 15 '66
Education and the copyright law. J. Cass.
Sat R 49:53-4 My 21 '66
Environment in which the fortuitous accident
can happen; summary of panel discussion
at dinner seminar, on subject of independent publishers, April 14, 1966. il Pub W
189:20-5 My 2 '66
Future of printing in a data-hungry society;
summary of address. L. C. Deighton. Pub
W 189:55-60 Ja 31 '66
Grouping of similar formats could help in
production crisis. M. A. Friedman. Pub W
189:114-15 Mr 7 '66
House committee studies treatment of minorities in text and library books: report of
hearings. il Pub W 190:34-40 S 19 '66
In praise of publishers and their Christmas
offers. R. B. Campbell. Pub W 190:60-1
S 5 '66
Inordinate delays between delivery and payment; getting institutions to pay their
bills. C. B. Grannis. Pub W 190:81 N 14 '66
Is the industry prepared for the crush of
school orders? R. H. Smith. Pub W 189:
69 F 7 '66
Major promotions for January books. il
Pub W 190:34-48 O 31 '66
Net prices, library editions; Senate hearings
reviewed. Pub W 190:26-30 Jl 25 '66
New responsibilities for publishing; summary
of address, June 13, 1966. D. Lacy. il Pub
W 190:39-40 Jl 4 '66
Philadelphia schools sue eleven publishers on
pricing Pub W 190:55 Jl 4 '66
Problems in bookseller-publisher relations;
summary of panel discussion. Pub W 189:
58+ Je 27 '66

PUBLISHERS and publishing—United States
—*Continued*
Production crisis: it grows worse. Pub W 190:
74-6 S 5 '66
Publisher as diplomat. D. Dempsey. Sat R
49:33 S 17 '66
Publishers see crisis in production; responses
to PW questionnaire.   Pub W 189:50-4
Ja 31 '66
Publishers study impact of U.S. school-aid
funds; ABPC meeting on Changing nature
and scope of the school and library mar-
ket; summary of conference. il Pub W
189:28-50 My 23 '66
Publishing explosion. il Newsweek 68:118+ O
10 '66
Publishing's unagonizing reappraisal. D.
Dempsey. New Repub 154:23-6 My 14 '66;
Reply with rejoinder. B. Cerf. 154:28-9 My
28 '66
Release dates debated at PPA club luncheon.
Pub W 189:39-40 Mr 14 '66
Rush for the finish line seen under ESEA
programs; summary of ABPC-ATPI meet-
ing. Pub W 189:58-60 F 7 '66
Sales conference blazes winning path. Ad-
club told. Pub W 189:57 Mr 7 '66
Senate committee to study library edition
pricing. Pub W 189:48 Mr 21 '66
Senate ends net-price study; grand jury
starts inquiry. Pub W 189:55-6 My 23 '66
Senators hear complaints on net prices to
libraries. Pub W 189:26-7 Ap 4 '66
Some fall books postponed to 1967. Pub W
190:49-50 N 28; 53 D 5 '66
Stockholders' support for copyright revision.
R. H. Smith. Pub W 189:36 Ap 11 '66
Teaching machines: the impact of new de-
vices on educational publishing; summary
of addresses at January meeting of the
Master printers section, Graphic arts in-
stitute of New England, inc. Pub W 189:
103-5+ Mr 7 '66
Tomorrow's printing processes and the human
element; excerpts from address. J. Kelly.
Pub W 189:98-9+ Mr 7 '66
Trends in Catholic publishing. P. K. Cuneo.
America 114:263-4 F 19 '66
USIA to disclose subsidies to publishers. Pub
W 190:37 O 17 '66
While we wait: further thoughts on the
Lasser report; publishers' distribution
methods. M. Bacon. Pub W 189:49-50 Mr
7 '66
Year the writers broke the bank; high-
bidding publishers desperate for big names.
Fortune 73:156-8 Ap '66
See also
Authors
University presses
also names of publishers, e.g. Random
house, incorporated
PUBLISHERS' book numbers. See Book num-
bers
PUBLISHERS newspaper syndicate
Field now full owner of newspaper syndicate.
Pub W 190:199 Jl 11 '66
PUBLISHERS' publicity association
PPA hears views on impact of new technol-
ogy; excerpts from address, May 27, 1966.
R. Kaplan. Pub W 189:73-4 Je 27 '66
PPA's press conferences; summary. Pub W
189:36 Mr 28 '66
PUBLISHERS' weekly
Fleuron for PW. il Pub W 191:62 Ja 2 '67
PUBLISHING of periodicals. See Periodicals.
Publishing of
PUBS (Great Britain) See Bars and barrooms
PUCCINI, Domenico Vincenzo Maria
Puccini concerto. R. Freed. Sat R 49:85 N 26
'66
PUCCINI, Giacomo
Here's your letter, asking me; poem, tr. by
J. W. Freeman. Opera N 31:17 D 3 '66

about
La Bohème. Criticism
Opera N il 30:17-21 Ap 16 '66
Opera N il 30:24-5 Ap 16 '66
Manon Lescaut. Criticism
Opera N 30:24-5 Mr 12 '66
Opera N il 30:17-20 Mr 12 '66
On records; Manon Lescaut. Opera N 30:34
Mr 12 '66
On records; Turandot; La Bohème. Opera N
30:34 Ap 16 '66
Turandot. Criticism
Opera N 31:29 D 17 '66
Opera N il 31:18-20 D 3 '66
Opera N il 31:24-5 D 3 '66
Unfinished symphony. R. Lawrence. il Opera
N 31:24-5 D 3 '66
PUCINSKI, Roman C.
Excerpt from address, January 25, 1966. Cong
Digest 45:86+ Mr '66

PUCKLE, R. D. A.
Phoenix art museum. Antiques 90:673-80 N '66
PUDDINGS
Plum pudding and fruitcake, faster than ever.
il Bet Hom & Gard 44:70-1+ D '66
Pudding full of plums; with recipes. il Look
30:112-13 N 29 '66
Successful recipes; bread puddings. il Suc
Farm 64:89-90 O '66
PUEBLA festival. See Music festivals—Mexico
PUEBLO Indians
Pueblo parade. H. P. Chapman. il Travel 126:
42-5 Ag '66
Three cultures of New Mexico. W. T. Le
Viness. il Américas 18:8-15 Je '66
PUERTO RICAN art. See Art, Puerto Rican
PUERTO RICAN cookery. See Cookery, Puerto
Rican
PUERTO RICAN students in the United States.
See Foreign students in the United States
PUERTO RICANS in Chicago. See Puerto Ric-
ans in the United States
PUERTO RICANS in the United States
Chicago riot: venganza! il Newsweek 67:23
Je 27 '66
Culture of poverty. O. Lewis. il Sci Am 215:
19-25 bibliog(p 150) O '66
Division lesson: problems of Chicago's Puer-
to Rican community. il Time 87:30-1 Je 24
'66
No hablo ingles; police blamed for Puerto
Rican riots. New Repub 154:7 Je 25 '66
Oscar Lewis and the Puerto Rican family.
J. P. Fitzpatrick. il America 115:778-9 D 10
'66
La vida: a Puerto Rican family in the culture
of poverty—San Juan and New York, by
O. Lewis. Review
Atlan 218:138+ D '66. O. Handlin
Nation 204:22-3 Ja 2 '67. E. Bendiner
New Repub 155:23-5 D 3 '66. M. Renek
Newsweek il 68:131-2 N 21 '66 S. Maloff
Sat R 49:58-9 D 10 '66. B. D. Diamon-
stein
Time il 88:133+ N 25 '66
La vida; excerpt. O. Lewis. Commentary 42:
44-7 Ag '66
PUERTO RICO
See also
Art—Puerto Rico
Ponce
Poor—Puerto Rico

Description and travel
Picture islands. J. Durniak; L. Barry. il Pop
Phot 59:94-9+ N '66
Pretty Puerto Rico. L. Mulvehill. il U S
Camera 29:62-3+ Ag '66

Economic conditions
Puerto Rico moves forward. C. T. Goodsell. il
Cur Hist 51:321-6 D '66

Economic policy
Demi-developed society; Roberto Sánchez
Vilella's program. il Time 87:27 F 25 '66

Moral conditions
La vida: a Puerto Rican family in the culture
of poverty—San Juan and New York, by O.
Lewis. Review
Atlan 218:138+ D '66. O. Handlin
Nation 204:22-3 Ja 2 '67. E. Bendiner
New Repub 155:23-5 D 3 '66. M. Renek
Newsweek il 68:131-2 N 21 '66. S. Maloff
Sat R 49:58-9 D 10 '66. B. D. Diamon-
stein
Time il 88:133+ N 25 '66

Politics and government
Puerto Rico: how much independence does it
want? Commission on the status of Puerto
Rico to meet. M. M. Karpatkin. New
Repub 154:12-15 My 7 '66
Puerto Rico moves forward. C. T. Goodsell. il
Cur Hist 51:321-6 D '66
Puerto Rico's future. F. Canavan. America
115:111-15 Jl 30 '66

Social conditions
Culture of poverty. O. Lewis. il Sci Am 215:
19-25 bibliog(p 150) O '66
Oscar Lewis and the Puerto Rican family.
J. P. Fitzpatrick. il America 115:778-9 D 10
'66
La vida; excerpt. O. Lewis. Commentary 42:
44-7 Ag '66
See also
Poor—Puerto Rico
PUERTO RICO and the United States
Puerto Rico moves forward. C. T. Goodsell.
il Cur Hist 51:321-6 D '66

PUEYRREDÓN, Juan Martín de
  Voice of the Algarrobo. V. Ocampo. il Américas 18:3-7 S '66
PUEYRREDÓN, Mariquita (Telle Echea)
  Voice of the Algarrobo. V. Ocampo. il Américas 18:3-7 S '66
PUGET SOUND
  Island hopping by auto. A. H. Carhart. il Travel 125:52-6 Mr '66
    See also
  San Juan Islands, Wash.
PUGET SOUND REGION
  Pugetopolis; bursting with new industry. il Time 87:90 My 27 '66
PUGLIESE, Giuseppe
  Unknown world of Prokofiev's operas. Hi Fi 16:44-8+ Je '66
PUGLIESE, Joseph
  Ceramics from Davis. Craft Horiz 26:26-9 N '66
PUGWASH conferences on science and world affairs
  Pugwash XV. Bul Atomic Sci 22:42-7 Ap '66
PULCINELLA. See Punch and Judy
PULESTON, Dennis
  In the land of the Maya. Audubon Mag 68: 146-50 My '66
PULITZER prizes
  Fifty years of Pulitzer prizes. J. Hohenberg. il Sat R 49:73-4+ My 7 '66
  1966 Pulitzer prizes: drama award omitted for ninth time. il Pub W 189:46-7 My 9 '66
  Prize complaints; selection process criticized; R. M. Bendiner charges. Newsweek 67:96-8 My 2 '66
  Pulitzer book juries will have three members each. Pub W 189:43 Mr 14 '66
  Schlesinger, Porter get Pulitzers; no prize for drama again this year. Library J 91: 2787 Je 1 '66
  Three for AP. il Newsweek 67:92-3 My 16 '66
  Truth about the Pulitzer prize awards. R. Bendiner. il McCalls 93:82-3+ My '66
PULLMAN porters. See Porters
PULMONARY emphysema. See Emphysema
PULMONARY histoplasmosis. See Histoplasmosis
PULP mills. See Paper mills
PULSE counters. See Medical instruments and apparatus
PULSE generators
  Pulse generator. D. Lancaster. il Pop Electr 24:60-2 Ap '66
PULSE techniques (electronics)
  Nanosecond pulses: techniques & applications. D. E. Lancaster. il Electr World 75:37-9+ F '66
PUMA hunting
  Cattle slayers of Shiwishi-win S. E. Brock. il Outdoor Life 138:66-9+ N '66
  Harder they come; ed. by B. East. C. Atwood. il Outdoor Life 138:64-7+ O '66
  Lion hunters are nuts; cougar chasing in Zion National Park. W. Page. il Field & S 71:64-5 N '66
PUMAS
  Cougar in our national parks and monuments. F. Weddle. il Nat Parks Mag 40: 4-7 My '66
PUNCH (beverage)
  Best Holiday beverages. il Bet Hom & Gard 44:96 D '66
  Canapé cake and pink sham-pagne; with recipes. il Seventeen 25:122-3+ Je '66
  Drinks for the big party. J. A. Beard. House & Gard 129:204+ Ap '66
  Four long cool formulas. A. Treacher. il Esquire 66:84-5 Jl '66
  Instant hospitality; with recipes. il McCalls 94:92-3+ D '66
  Party punches. il Bet Hom & Gard 44:93-4 My '66
PUNCH and Judy
  Notes fom a European diary: 1963-64; Punch and Judy and Pulcinella. E. Wilson. New Yorker 42:57-8+ My 28 '66
  Punch and Judy; drama. M. T. Leech. Plays 26:91-8 N '66
PUNCH and Judy; drama. See Leech. M. T.
PUNCHED card systems
  Accounting machines & punched-card DP. il Duns R 88:pt2 138-9+ S '66
PUNISHMENT
  Crime and punishment. V. P. McCorry. America 115:122 Jl 30 '66
  Implications of laboratory studies of aggression for the control and regulation of violence. R. H. Walters. bibliog f Ann Am Acad 364:60-72 Mr '66
    See also
  Capital punishment
  School discipline

PUNISHMENT of children. See Children—Management and training
PUNJAB, India
  Flames in Punjab; Sikhs and Hindus. il Time 87:32 Mr 25 '66
    Politics and government
  After freedom; Sikh state plan causes riots. Newsweek 67:49-50 Mr 28 '66
  Housework; Sikh state in Punjab to be created. il Newsweek 67:48 Mr 21 '66
PUNKE, Harold H.
  Homework in American school and community. Sch & Soc 94:327-30 O 15 '66
PUPIL (eye)
  Pupil diameter and load on memory. D. Kahneman and J. Beatty. bibliog il Science 154:1583-5 D 23 '66
  Pupillograph to aid pupil size research. Sci N 89:467 Je 11 '66
PUPIL progress records. See School reports and records
PUPPETS and puppet plays
  Art of making puppets. C. J. Alkema. il Design 68:29-33 S '66
  Doll masters; New York debut of the Japanese Bunraku puppet theater. il Newsweek 67:88 Mr 28 '66
  Finger puppets. il House & Gard 130:242-3 O '66
  Hansel and Gretel go back to school. G. Creegan. Plays 25:89-92 F '66
  Let's have a tiger for dinner. G. Neff. bibliog il Sch Arts 66:5-9 N '66
  Million-dollar quiz show. S. E. Janey. Plays 25:92-5 Ap '66
  Miraculous marionettes; Salzburg's famed troupe tours the U.S. F. Stevenson. il Opera N 30:26-8 Mr 5 '66
  Princess and the dragon. N. Wolfys. Plays 25:81-5 Mr '66
  Puppet shows promote classic children's books. il Pub W 189:104-6 F 21 '66
  Quarreling pair; text. J. Bowles. il Mlle 64: 116-17 D '66
  World's most expressive puppets; Japanese Bunraku puppets. J. Nathan. il N Y Times Mag p34-5+ Mr 13 '66
    See also
  Moving pictures—Puppet films
  Punch and Judy
PUPPY love; drama. See Miller. H. L.
PURCELL, Carl
  Teach me! excerpts. il Sat R 49:72-3 D 17 '66
PURCELL, Henry
  Celebration of Henry Purcell. J. Haskins. il Hi Fi 16:MA9 Ag '66
  Dido and Aeneas. Criticism
    Sat R 49:49+ Je 18 '66
PURCELL, William L.
  Music of Viet Nam. Am Rec G 32:426-9 Ja '66
PURCHASING
    See also
  Consumers
  Instalment plan
  Shopping and shoppers
    also subhead Purchasing under various subjects, e.g. Airplanes—Purchasing
PURCHASING, County
  We merged city and county purchasing; Louisville, Ky. and Jefferson County, Ky. R. S. Greer. il Am City 81:114-15 O '66
PURCHASING, Government
    See also
  Contracts, Government
  United States—General accounting office
PURCHASING, Household
    See also
  Food—Prices
  Quality of products
PURCHASING, Library. See Library purchasing
PURCHASING, Military
  Arm-twisting arms salesmen. Nation 202:732 Je 20 '66
  Helping hand; U.S. probably bought steel manufactured in Communist China. Newsweek 69:30+ Ja 2 '67
  Pandora's ammunition box; U.S. policies. J. A. Morris, jr. il Nation 203:109-12 Ag 8 '66
  U.S. supplier of weapons to the world; with list of 1962-1965 sales. E. J. McCarthy. il Sat R 49:13-15 Jl 9 '66
    See also
  United States—Armed forces—Procurement
PURCHASING, Municipal
  Annual contracts solve everyday problems; Bakersfield, Calif. A. W. Noland, jr. il Am City 81:107+ F '66
  Good ethics result in better purchasing. A. C. Shepherd. il Am City 81:132+ S '66

PURCHASING Municipal—_Continued_
Joint purchasing in review; excerpts from report. C. T. Hardwick. Am City 81:144+ Mr '66
Partnerships in purchasing. M. Leff and others. il Am City 81:145-6 Je '66
Sell the salesman on city hall; informative brochure encourages vendors to bid, and tells the procedures; San Diego County, Calif. V. O. Gehringer. Am City 81:90-1 Jl '66
Small communities can have centralized purchasing. J. G. White. Am City 81:162 N '66
We merged city and county purchasing; Louisville, Ky. and Jefferson County, Ky. R. S. Greer. il Am City 81:114-15 O '66
We put guts in our purchasing program; Milford, Conn. C. M. Oneto. il Am City 81:124-5 My '66

PURCHASING power
Why there's less left to spend. il Bsns W p48-9 N 26 '66
See also
Wages

Russia
U.S.S.R. worktime requirements for consumer purchases. E. Nash. il Mo Labor R 89:772-3 Jl '66

PURDUE university, Lafayette, Ind.
Publisher's memo; Purdue's self-instruction program. E. D. Muhlfeld. il Flying 79:6 Jl '66

PURDY, James
Malcolm; dramatization. See Albee, E.

PURDY, Ken W.
Better roads, worse drivers. Atlan 218:123-4 D '66
—See Stevenson, C. jt. auth.

PURGE, Russian. See Russia—Politics and government

PURIFICATION of air. See Air purification

PURIFICATION of water. See Water purification

PURIFIERS, Air. See Air purifiers

PURINES
Conditions for purine synthesis; did prebiotic synthesis occur at low temperatures? R. Sanchez and others. bibliog il Science 153:72-3 Jl 1 '66
Hydrogen bonding specificity of nucleic acid purines and pyrimidines in solution. Y. Kyogoku and others. bibliog il Science 154:518-20 O 28 '66

PURITAN cookery. See Cookery, American

PURITANISM
Revolution of the saints; a study in the origins of radical politics, by M. Walzer. Review
Nation 202:216-17 F 21 '66. W. W. Wager

PURNELL, Karl H.
Peace for Vietnam; GOP's nettle of success. Nation 202:94-6 Ja 24 '66

PUROMYCIN
End-organ effects of thyroid hormones; subcellular interactions in cultured cells. E. Siegel and C. A. Tobias. bibliog il Science 153:763-5 Ag 12 '66
Puromycin analogs; action of adrenocorticotropic hormone and the role of glycogen. L. D. Garren and others. bibliog il Science 152:1386-8 Je 3 '66
Puromycin and cycloheximide; different effects on hippocampal electrical activity. H. D. Cohen and others. bibliog il Science 154:1557-8 D 23 '66
Puromycin effect on successive phases of memory storage. S. H. Barondes and H. D. Cohen. bibliog il Science 151:594-5 F 4 '66

PURPLE MOUNTAIN observatory. See Astronomical observatories—China (People's Republic)

PUSEY, Nathan M.
Doubts & the Divinity school; summary of address. por Time 88:94 O 7 '66

PUSH pin studios
Milton Glaser of Push pin studios. D. Waugh. il Am Artist 30:56-61+ Je '66

PUSHKIN (ship) See Ocean liners

PUSHKOV, Nicolai, and Silkin, Boris
Years of the quiet sun. UNESCO Courier 19:22-8 S '66

PUTNAM, Arthur James
Obituary
Pub W 189:109 F 14 '66

PUTNAM, Judith
(ed) Books to come. Library J 92:139-40+ Ja 1 '67
(ed) Business books to come. Library J 91:5433-40+ N 1 '66
(ed) Scientific, technical, and medical books to come. Library J 91:5441-90 N 1 '66
—and Ahrens, Kathleen
(eds) Books to come. Library J 91:2894-6+, 4718-24+ Je 1, O 1 '66
34-80 Jl '66
(eds) Business books to come. Library J 91:
(eds) Paperbacks to come. Library J 91:4252-310 S 15 '66
(eds) Religious books to come. Library J 91:3978-93 S 1 '66
(eds) Scientific, technical, and medical books to come. Library J 91:3481-524+ Jl '66
—and Lindheim, Judy
(eds) Books to come. Library J 91:740-854 F 1 '66
(eds) Business books to come (cont) Library J 91:1254-63 Mr 1 '66
(eds) Paperbacks to come. Library J 91:368+, 2624+ Ja 15, My 15 '66
(eds) Scientific, technical, and medical books to come (cont) Library J 91:1264-313 Mr 1 '66

PUTNAM, Leon J.
Blaine on religion and youth. Christian Cent 83:1310-13 O 26 '66

PUTNEY graduate school of education, Putney, Vt. See Antioch college, Yellow Springs, Ohio

PUTSCH, J. W.
Excerpt from statement, June 29, 1965. Cong Digest 45:57+ F '66

PUTTING (golf)
Awful putt showed me how to win; 1966 Masters. J. Nicklaus. il Sports Illus 24:36-8+ Ap 25 '66
Casper on the putter. B. Casper, jr. il Esquire 65:118-19 Ap '66
Hit short when preparing to play long. J. Nicklaus. il Sports Illus 26:51 Ja 16 '67
Outrageous suggestion about putting. J. Nicklaus. il Sports Illus 25:81-2 O 3 '66

PUYA
Giants of the puna; bromeliad of the Peruvian highlands. F. D. Ayres. il Natur Hist 75:54-7 Mr '66

PUYE ruins, New Mexico. See Cities and towns, Ruined, extinct, etc.

PUZZLES
Betty Thomson's 'puzzles. W. Accorsi. il Craft Horiz 26:24-7 Ja '66
Floors can be fun with jigsaw puzzles underfoot. J. Peter. il Look 30:57+ N 29 '66
Puzzle fun for everyone. il Parents Mag 41:162-3+ N '66
See also
Crossword puzzles

PYE, Lucian W.
China in context. For Affairs 45:229-45 Ja '67
Coming dilemmas for China's leaders. For Affairs 44:387-402 Ap '66

PYENSON, Louis
Control plant pests indoors. il Horticulture 45:22-3+ Ja '67
Nematodes. il Horticulture 44:30-1 Je '66
Spraying or dusting? Horticulture 44:38-9 Ap '66

PYGMIES
Outsider; study of Mbuti; interview. C. Turnbull. New Yorker 42:26-7 Ag 20 '66

PYGMY stars. See Stars, Subdwarf

PYLE, Gene
Picture profile; the ship's photographer. il Pop Phot 58:70-1+ Mr '66

PYLE, Howard
Brandywine tradition. H. C. Pitz. il Am Artist 30:49+ D '66

PYNCHON, Thomas
Journey into the mind of Watts. N Y Times Mag p34-5+ Je 12 '66

PYNE, Joe
Joe Pyne; anatomy of a TV bully. B. Rollin. il pors Look 30:M8-11 O 4 '66
Killer Joe. por Time 88:30 Jl 29 '66

PYRACANTHA. See Firethorns

PYRAMID LAKE, Nev.
Look what is just minutes from Reno. il Sunset 136:40-2 Je '66

PYRAMIDS
Exploration with radiation; X-ray technique, to discover unfound burial chambers in Pharaohs' pyramids. Sci N 90:7 Jl 2 '66
Peering into the pyramids; use of cosmic rays. il Time 89:84 Ja 6 '67

PYRIDINE
Enzyme-coenzyme complexes of pyridine nucleotide-linked dehydrogenases. H. F. Fisher and D. G. Cross. bibliog il Science 153:414-15 Jl 22 '66

PYRIMIDINES
Cyclobutane-type pyrimidine dimers in polynucleotides. R. B. Setlow. bibliog il Science 153:379-86 Jl 22 '66
Hydrogen bonding specificity of nucleic acid purines and pyrimidines in solution. Y. Kyogoku and others. bibliog il Science 154: 518-20 O 28 '66
Pyrimidine dimers: effect of temperature on photoinduction. R. O. Rahn. bibliog il Science 154:503-4 O 28 '66

PYROGENICS. See High temperature engineering

PYRON, Joseph H.
Gibberellic acid makes the difference in camellias. Horticulture 44:20-1+ S '66

PYROPHOSPHATES
Inorganic pyrophosphate: formation in bacterial photophosphorylation. H. Baltscheffsky and others. bibliog il Science 153: 1120-2 S 2 '66

PYROXENES
Eclogitic pyroxenes, ordered with P2 symmetry. J. R. Clark and J. J. Papike. bibliog il Science 154:1003-4 N 25 '66

PYRRHO, pseud.
Liberals' new fundamentalism. Nat R 18: 219 Mr 8 '66
Obituary
Nat R 18:454 My 17 '66

PYRUVATES
Pyruvate inhibition of lactate dehydrogenase activity in human tissue extracts. A. L. Latner and others. bibliog il Science 154: 527-9 O 28 '66
Pyruvate oxidation and the permeability of mitochondria from blowfly flight muscle. C. C. Childress and B. Sacktor. bibliog il Science 154:268-70 O 14 '66

PYTHONS
Thermoregulation in a brooding female Indian python, python molurus bivittatus. V. H. Hutchison and others. bibliog il Science 151:694-6 F 11 '66

PYTKOWICZ, R. M. and others
Magnesium ions: activity in seawater. bibliog Science 152:640-2 Ap 29 '66

Q

QUACKS and quackery
Amazing facts about a crusade that can hurt your health. R. L. Smith. il Todays Health 44:30-5+ O '66
Doctor Abrams, dean of machine quacks. J. Kaplan. il Todays Health 44:20-1+ Ap '66
Face burners. R. L. Smith. il Todays Health 44:20-3+ Je '66
Fighting space-age quackery; symposium. il Todays Health 44:50-3+ D '66

QUADE, Quentin L. and Rhodes, J. M.
What can the church demand? Cath World 204:162-9 D '66

QUADRUPLETS
I was the world's most expectant mother; ed. by M. Bloom and S. Bloom. S. Sklar. il Redbook 126:56-7+ Mr '66
Mother's questions about raising quadruplets; questions of Mrs H. Sklar. B. Spock. Redbook 126:22+ Mr '66

QUAGGAS
Science reports; the vanished quagga. D. P. Willoughby. il Natur Hist 75:60-3 F '66

QUAIL shooting
Bobwhites teach me a lesson. T. Janes. il Outdoor Life 138:54-5+ D '66
Each man kills the thing he loves. S. Alsop. il Sat Eve Post 239:20 My 21 '66
Ozark quail with a twist. D. Duffey. il Outdoor Life 139:68-9+ Ja '67
Shooting on Mr Bud's place; L. B. Maytag's plantation in Union Springs, Ala. V. Kraft. il Sports Illus 25:50-4 N 21 '66
Truth or consequences quail. P. Czura. il Field & S 71:47-9 S '66
Very easy birds to miss; valley quail. T. Trueblood. il Field & S 71:28-30+ N '66

QUAKER CITY tournament. See Basketball tournaments

QUAKERS. See Friends, Society of

QUALIFICATIONS of librarians. See Librarians—Qualifications

QUALITY control
Does zero defects really work? G. Berkwitt. il Duns R 88:24-6+ Ag '66; Discussion. 88: 15+ O '66
Traffic lights for quality control; customer is the boss at Ex-cell-o corporation. il Bsns W p 196+ O 22 '66

USAF readies reliability center; Rome air development center. Aviation W 84:105 Je 13 '66
Western's quality control features inspection unit; Western printing and lithographing co. il Pub W 191:95 Ja 2 '67
See also
Automobile industry and trade—Quality control
Electronic circuits—Quality control

QUALITY of products
Bilking the public; Fairchild publications findings. Nation 202:476 Ap 25 '66
Branding on trial. T. Levitt. bibliog f Harvard Bsns R 44:20-2+ Mr '66
Buying guide issue (cont) il Consumer Rep 31:1-447 D '66
Case of the fishy no. Consumer Rep 31:456 S '66
Consumer's stake in standards. Consumer Bul 49:29-32 F '66
Designed decay: products and systems constructed to last the shortest feasible time. H. M. Case. il Harvard Bsns R 44:126-31 Ja '66
Do you really get what you pay for? M. Mayer. Bet Hom & Gard 44:7 N '66
Look out for lemons in new home appliances. Consumer Bul 49:30-1 Ag '66
Personal business; getting defective merchandise during Christmas shopping. Bsns W p 169-70 N 19 '66
Speaker for the house. C. Montgomery. See issues of Good housekeeping
Yacht safety bureau. C. F. Kelley. il Yachting 119:87-9+ Ap '66
See also
Quality control
Testing

QUANG, Dang-van-. See Dang-van-Quang

QUANT, Mary
Young will not be dictated to; excerpts from Quant by Quant. Vogue 148:86-8 Ag 1 '66
about
Switched on. il por Newsweek 68:114B+ S 19 '66

QUANTITY cookery. See Cookery, Quantity

QUANTUM electrodynamics
Development of quantum electrodynamics; address, May 6, 1966. S. Tomonaga. bibliog Science 154:864-8 N 18 '66
Development of the space-time view of quantum electrodynamics; address, December 11, 1965. R. P. Feynman. Science 153: 699-708 Ag 12 '66

QUANTUM field theory
Relativistic quantum field theory. J. Schwinger. bibliog Science 153:949-53 Ag 26 '66

QUANTUM mechanics. See Quantum theory

QUANTUM theory
Conceptual development of quantum mechanics, by M. Jammer. Review
Sci Am 216:137-40+ Ja '67. R. E. Peierls
Kinetic isotope effects and organic reaction mechanisms. M. J. Goldstein. bibliog il Science 154:1616-21 D 30 '66
Questioners: physicists and the quantum theory. by B. L. Cline. Review
New Yorker 42:174+ Ap 16 '66. J. Bernstein
See also
Quantum electrodynamics
Quantum field theory
Time reversal

QUARANTINE
Plastic quarantine envelope proposed; precautionary measures against contamination from moon-type organisms. H. M. David. Tech W 19:28-30 Ag 1 '66

QUARKS. See Particles (nuclear physics)

QUARLES, Benjamin
Frederick Douglass: bridge-builder in human relations. por Negro Hist Bul 29:99-100+ F '66
What the historian owes the Negro. Sat R 49:10-13 S 3 '66

QUARRELING pair; puppet play. See Bowles, J.

QUARRELS
Our kids settle their own squabbles. M. Treichler. il Parents Mag 41:50-1+ Je '66

QUARRIES and quarrying
See also
Granite industry and trade

QUARRY, Jerry
Jab that wiped out a smile. M. Kram. il por Sports Illus 24:28-9 Je 6 '66
Quarry who likes to hunt. T. Maule. il pors Sports Illus 24:20-3 Mr 14 '66
Sudden rush of new heavies. T. Maule. il por Sports Illus 24:14-17 F 21 '66

QUARTER horses. See Horses

QUARTERBACKS. See Football players

QUARTZ crystals
Stimulated Brillouin and Raman scattering in quartz at 2.1° to 293° Kelvin. P. E. Tannenwald and J. B. Thaxter. bibliog il Science 154:1319-20 D 9 '66

QUARTZSITE, Ariz.
Hottest town. il Travel 126:40-1 Ag '66

QUASARS. See Radio astronomy

QUASI-stellar objects. See Radio astronomy

QUASI-stellar radio sources. See Radio astronomy

QUASIMODO, Salvatore
European literary scene. R. J. Clements. Sat R 49:51 O 1 '66

QUAYLE, Oliver
Good case of the poll sniffles. W. H. Honan. il pors N Y Times Mag p34-5+ Ag 21 '66

QUEALY, Michael Joseph
Chaplain's death. por Time 88:82 N 18 '66

QUEBEC (province)
See also
Gaspé Peninsula
Libraries—Quebec (province)

Politics and government
Liberal defeat. Time 87:42 Je 17 '66
Moving backward? Quebec's provincial elections. il Newsweek 67:48B Je 20 '66
Quebec changes governments. C. Ryan. For Affairs 45:148-61 O '66
Quebec: separatism in a new guise. D. O'Leary. il Nation 203:6-8 Jl 4 '66
University of Montreal: where the two Canadas meet. L. J. Carter. il Science 154:868-72 N 18 '66

QUEEN Elizabeth (ship) See Ocean liners

QUEEN of spades; opera. See Tchaikovsky, P. I.

QUEENAN, John T.
How doctors heal the unborn. A. Lake. il Sat Eve Post 239:39-42 F 12 '66

QUEENS, N.Y.
Housing
Lefrak way of life. G. Steinem. il N Y Times Mag p 18-20+ Jl 31 '66
When black and white live together; Rochdale village. H. Swados. il N Y Times Mag p47+ N 13 '66
Stores
Multi-level store with wrap-around parking, Macy's Rego Park branch. il Arch Rec 139:168-70 Ap '66

QUEENS borough public library
Convenience in Queens. H. W. Tucker and V. M. Shea. il Library J 91:5855-8 D 1 '66
Crash program plus give-aways; picture book Head start program; with bibliography. A. D. Perillo and J. St Clair. il Library J 91:340 Ja 15 '66

QUEENS of France; drama. See Wilder, T.

QUEENSTOWN, New Zealand
Catch your breath in New Zealand's Queenstown. il Sunset 137:24-6 D '66

QUENA (periodical) See Periodicals—Peru

QUENNELL, Peter
Casanova in England. Horizon 8:34-7 Aut '66

QUESTIONING
Ask, don't tell. N. R. Campion. il Read Digest 89:49-52 Ag '66

QUESTIONS, Childrens. See Childrens questions

QUESTIONS and answers; story. See Gallant, M.

QUETZALCOATL and the lady; story. See Farrell, P.

QUICKSILVER. See Mercury

QUIET girl; story. See Cleaver, V. and Cleaver, B.

QUIGLEY, Harold S.
Toward perspective on Vietnam. Christian Cent 83:104-6 Ja 26 '66

QUIGLEY, Thomas E.
Exchange peace corps. America 114:834-5 Je 11 '66

QUILL, Michael Joseph
Lad from Gourtloughera. il por Time 87:29 F 4 '66
Lindsay, Quill & the transit strike. T. R. Brooks. Commentary 41:50-7 Mr '66

QUILL pens. See Pens

QUIMBY, David. See Lynds, R. C. jt. auth.

QUINCY, Mass.
Education
New approach to teaching social studies; use of materials are developed by Educational services, inc. (ESI) K. Jorgensen. il Sr Schol 89:sup9 N 4 '66

QUININE
Frontier malaria fighter. H. E. Dark. il Todays Health 44:28-9+ My '66

QUINN, Anthony
Life and suspiciously hard times of Anthony Quinn. H. Lawrenson. pors Esquire 66: 93-5+ O '66

QUINN, James Brian
Technological competition: Europe vs. U.S. Harvard Bsns R 44:113-16+ Jl '66

QUINN, John Robert
In England; poem. Christian Cent 83:653 My 18 '66

QUINN, William John
Presidential turntable. por Time 88:105 O 21 '66

QUINTUPLETS
Africa's only living quintuplets; Tukutese quintuplets. il Ebony 22:106-8+ D '66
And now they are three; Fischer quints. il Sat Eve Post 239:30-5 S 24 '66
They couldn't have a baby, and then quintuplets! Lawson babies. B. Day. il McCalls 93:82-3+ Je '66

QUISLING, Vidkun
Quisling: phophet without honour, by R. Hewins. Review
Newsweek il por 67:101+ F 21 '66

QUITO, Ecuador
Description
Equatorial Quito. S. Clark. il Travel 126:40-4 D '66

QUIZ shows. See Television broadcasting—Quiz programs

QUIZZES. See Information tests

QUMRAN scrolls. See Dead Sea scrolls

QUOIREZ, Françoise. See Sagan, F. pseud.

QUOTA controls. See Agricultural administration—United States

QUOTAS, Immigration. See Immigration and emigration—United States

QUOTAS, Import. See Import quotas

QUOTATIONS
Quotable quotes. See issues of Reader's digest
See also
Bible—Quotations
Children—Sayings
Marriage—Quotations, maxims, etc.

R

RAF. See Great Britain—Royal air force

RCA. See Radio corporation of America

RCA-Hertz merger. See Business consolidations and mergers

RCA Victor. See Radio corporation of America—RCA Victor division

RCA'S aviation equipment department. See Radio corporation of America

RDF (radio direction finders) See Radio in navigation

REA. See United States—Rural electrification administration

REA express. See Railway express agency, incorporated

REM (rapid eye movement) sleep. See Sleep

RES. See Reticulo-endothelial system

RFE. See Radio free Europe

RFP (request for proposal) See Contracts, Government

Rh factors
Conquest of death before birth; intrauterine transfusion. J. D. Ratcliff. Read Digest 88:107-11 Ap '66
How doctors heal the unborn. A. Lake. il Sat Eve Post 239:39-42 F 12 '66
Pre-birth transfusions save Rh-negative infants. Sci N 90:56 Jl 23 '66
Rh factor: prevention of isoimmunization and clinical trial on mothers. V. J. Freda and others. bibliog il Science 151:828-30 F 18 '66
Rh incompatibility controlled? Sci Am 214: 58 Mr '66
See also
Erythroblastosis

RNA. See Ribonucleic acid

RPI. See Rensselaer polytechnic institute, Troy, N.Y.

R. R. Bowker company. See Bowker, R. R, company

RA, Sun. See Sun Ra

RABANNE, Paco
Pieced in plastic. il por Time. 87:53 Ap 8
'66
RABB, Bernard
Art of the cantor. Am Rec G 33:310-11 D '66
RABB, Miriam
North Carolina's trail riding. Travel 125:32-
5 My '66
RABBAN, Elana
Elementary paperback: a trial run; with
bibliography. por Library J 91:2591-8 My
15 '66
RABBIDGE, R. M. See Peck, A. J. jt. auth.
RABBIT hunting
Comfort in cold covers. B. Elliot. il Outdoor
Life 139:56-7+ Ja '67
Cottontails or snowshoes? J. Chiappetta. il
Field & S 71:50-2+ Ja '67
Grandest hunting of all; cottontail. H. Brad-
shaw. il Field & S 71:66-7+ N '66
Hitting the hot line; hunting rabbits with a
beagle. H. Bradshaw. il Outdoor Life 137:
56-8+ F '66
New place for rabbits. N. Karas. il Outdoor
Life 138:70-1+ O '66
Rabbits the hard way. H. F. Blaisdell. il
Field & S 71:55 D '66
RABBIT who refused to run; drama. See
Miller, H. L.
RABBITS and hares
Easter rabbits are symbol of renewed life.
il(p209) Sci N 89:212 Ap 2 '66
Olfactory discrimination in the rabbit olfac-
tory glomerulus. J. Leveteau and P. Mac-
Leod. bibliog il Science 153:175-6 Jl 8 '66
Overbreeding Down Under. il Time 88:120+
N 18 '66
See also
Cookery—Game

Diseases and pests
See also
Myxoma, Infectious
RABE, Olive. See Fisher, A. jt. auth.
RABIES
Rabies: the growing threat. P. Czura. il
Field & S 70:162-3+ Mr '66
RABIES vaccine
Rabies: the growing threat. P. Czura. il
Field & S 70:162-3+ Mr '66
Rabies vaccine approved for preinfection use.
Sci N L 89:104 F 12 '66
Two new rabies vaccines reported from
Canada. Sci N L 89:136 F 26 '66
RABINOFF, Max
Obituary
Opera N 30:32 Je 4 '66
RABINOWITCH, Eugene
New year's thoughts 1966. Bul Atomic Sci
22:3-7+ Ja '66
Offense is the worst defense. Bul Atomic Sci
22:32-4 O '66
Second challenge. Bul Atomic Sci 22:25-7
My '66
about
Rabinowitch awarded Kalinga prize. A. K.
Smith. Science 153:1627 S 30 '66
RABINOWITZ, Michael
Classroom documented. H. P. Raleigh. il Sch
Arts 66:21-3 D '66
RABINOWITZ, Shalom
Echoes of Sholom Aleichem. por Sat R 49:
61-2 O 1 '66
RABINOWITZ, Victor
To solve at paradox. Nation 204:27-9 Ja 2 '67
RABORN, William Francis, 1905-
What's CIA? interview. por U S News 61:74-
80 Jl 18 '66
about
Pro for CIA. Time 87:24 Je 24 '66
RABSON, Alan S. and others
Virus: mixed infection with herpes simplex
and simian virus 40. bibliog Science 151:
1535-6 Mr 25 '66
RACCOON hunting
All about coonhounds. D. M. Duffey. il Out-
door Life 138:158-60+ N '66
Born to tree coon. D. J. Anderson. il Field
& S 71:52-3+ N '66
Dog hunters. G. Logsdon. il Farm J 90:68Q
Mr '66
Longest coon hunt. M. Mudd. il Outdoor Life
137:44-7+ My '66
RACCOONS
Pet news; excerpt from Raccoons are the
brightest people. S. North. Ladies Home J
83:57-8 O '66
RACE attitudes. See Attitudes
RACE car drivers. See Automobile drivers
RACE differences. See Racial differences

RACE discrimination
Arthur Ashe thing; Dallas country club in-
vitational tennis tournament canceled.
Sports Illus 24:8 F 21 '66
Pastoral letter of the South African bishops,
July 25. 1966. Cath World 204:240-1 Ja '67
Psychologists face ethical dilemma. Sci N
89:259 Ap 16 '66
See also
Discrimination in education
Discrimination in employment
International convention on the elimination
of all forms of racial discrimination
Race prejudice
RACE equality. See Equality
RACE horses
All in the family; ten horses from seven dif-
ferent countries in the 15th international.
il Time 88:58 N 18 '66
All out for the roses: Abe's Hope and
Graustark. il Time 87:54 My 6 '66
Bret's revenge was sweet; Bret Hanover
won his second race with Cardigan Bay.
R. Cantwell. Sports Illus 24:72+ Je 13 '66
Buck stopped here: 1:32 3/5; Arlington clas-
sic. W. Tower. il Sports Illus 25:18-21 Jl 4
'66
Buckpasser: a three grows in Brooklyn.
W. Tower. Sports Illus 25:40 Ag 1 '66
Comeuppance; Bret Hanover and Cardigan
Bay. Time 87:50 My 27 '66
Debut of the Derby dandy from Darby Dan;
Graustark and Buckpasser. W. Tower. il
Sports Illus 24:45 Ja 31 '66
French and the Phippses; Washington, D.C.
international at Laurel, Md. and 2-year-old
championship at New Jersey's Garden
state park. W. Tower. il Sports Illus 25:28-
31 N 21 '66
Hail the magnificent chestnut. W. Tower.
Sports Illus 24:82 Ap 25 '66
Hopes go up and some come down; confused
result of the Florida Derby. W. Tower. il
Sports Illus 24:24-7 Ap 11 '66
Hot tip: don't bet against Bret Hanover.
B. Surface. il N Y Times Mag p36-7+ S
25 '66
Hot tip; get rid of their soreness with
saunas. Newsweek 68:92 N 14 '66
Little bit of luck; Graustark. il Time 87:44
Ja 28 '66
Mother was a sport; Graustark. il Newsweek
67:84 Mr 7 '66
Race that scrambled the Derby; Graustark
loses to Abe's Hope at Keeneland. W.
Tower. il Sports Illus 24:22-7 My 9 '66
Race track. A. Minor. See issues of New
Yorker
Search for some sleepers; Graustark's future
uncertain. W. Tower. il Sports Illus 24:56-7
Mr 7 '66
Short and sweet; quarter-horse. il Newsweek
68:64 S 12 '66
Trotter, P. C. Welsh. il Am Heritage 18:30-49
D '66
Two down, one to go; Kauai King. Time 87:
50 My 27 '66
Two out of three came back; Kentucky
Derby favorites. W. Tower. il Sports Illus
24:107-9 Ap 18 '66
Young at heart; Cardigan Bay. il Newsweek
68:47 D 26 '66
See also
Horse racing
RACE prejudice
African queen complex; Negro resentment
towards white female civil rights workers.
il Newsweek 67:94-5 My 23 '66
Bridging the prejudice gap. K. D. Fish-
man. il N Y Times Mag p 114+ O 23 '66
General assembly adopts four resolutions;
with texts. UN Mo Chron 3:48-53 N '66
Integration: Negro colleges' newest challenge.
il Ebony 21:36-8+ Mr '66
Portrait of a Klansman: R. Cranford. S.
Alsop. il Sat Eve Post 239:23-7 Ap 9 '66
Prejudice and progress. D. Danzig. Sat R
49:26+ Mr 12 '66
Pride of color; reprint from August 23. 1957
issue. D. Lawrence. U S News 61:100 Jl
25 '66
Race: fact and feeling. F. M. Cordasco. Sat
R 49:40 Mr 12 '66
What's not so funny about the funnies. P.
Pierce. il Ebony 22:48-50+ N '66
White northerner: pride and prejudice. R.
Coles. Atlan 217:53-7 Je '66
See also
Racism
RACE problems
Mandate for white Christians, by K. Hasel-
den. Review
Christian Cent 83:1448 N 23 '66. J. M.
Dabbs
See also
Church and race problems
Minorities

RACE problems—See also—*Continued*
  Negroes in Africa
  Negroes in the United States
  Race prejudice
  Race relations
    also subhead Race problems under
    names of continents, countries, etc, e.g.
    South Africa—Race problems
RACE problems in literature
  Child's world of difference. Z. Sutherland.
    Sat R 49:60–2 O 22 '66
  Goliath of a book on a modern David. E.
    Perry. Life 62:10 Ja 6 '67
RACE relations
  Apartheid for America? black power. Nat R
    18:716–17 Jl 26 '66
  Black power and the American Christ. V.
    Harding. Christian Cent 84:10–13 Ja 4 '67
  Black power; divisive slogan; with view-
    points. il Sr Schol 89:17–18 S 16 '66
  Black power for whom? ideological split in
    civil rights movement. Christian Cent 83:
    903–4 Jl 20 '66
  Black power: politics of frustration. il News-
    week 68:26+ Jl 11 '66
  Black power speech that has Congress
    aroused; excerpts from address, August 5,
    1966. S. Carmichael. U S News 61:6 Ag 22
    '66
  Bleak promise of black power. E. J. Hughes.
    Newsweek 68:15 Jl 25 '66
  Crisis of color '66; survey findings. il News-
    week 68:20–32+ Ag 22 '66
  How to solve racial problems; varying views
    of Negro leaders; excerpts from televised
    panel discussion. il U S News 61:14 S 5
    '66
  Inside story of black power and Stokely
    Carmichael. il U S News 61:12 Ag 15 '66
  Josie; friendship between African and white
    American. P. Clingerman. Mlle 64:101+ D
    '66
  Negro congressman talks about black power;
    interview. A. C. Powell. U S News 61:
    38–41 Ag 15 '66
  Negro cry: black power! what does it mean?
    il U S News 61:52 Jl 11 '66
  Negro leaders dividing; the effect; with ex-
    cerpts from address by R. Wilkins. il U S
    News 61:31–4 Jl 18 '66
  New racism; emphasis on black power. il
    Time 88:11–13 Jl 1 '66
  Not black power, but human power; inter-
    view, ed. by G. B. Leonard. L. Smith.
    Look 30:40+ S 6 '66
  Peace corps volunteers on race relations.
    Sch & Soc 94:56+ F 5 '66
  Pride of color; reprint from August 23, 1957
    issue. D. Lawrence. U S News 61:100 Jl
    25 '66
  Primarily a guy; television series I spy.
    C. H. Simonds. Nat R 18:1007–8 O 4 '66
  Professor; interview with owner of National
    memorial African bookstore in New York
    city. L. Michaux. New Yorker 42:28–9 S 3
    '66
  Profiles; interracial relations between Mex-
    icans, Japanese, Negroes, whites in Los
    Angeles. C. Rand. New Yorker 42:64–6+
    O 15 '66
  Race tension worldwide; thoughts from Ge-
    neva. D. Kitagawa. Christian Cent 83:
    1220–3 O 5 '66
  Revolution of color. by T. P. Melady. Review
    Cath World 203:52–3 Ap '66. B. V.
    Mtshali
  Summer uproar. il Sat Eve Post 239:88 Jl 16
    '66
  Thoughts to remember. R. J. Cushing. Good
    H 162:240 My '66
  Time to be black. B. Detwiler. New Repub
    155:19–22 S 17 '66; Reply. J. N. Miller. 155:
    28–9 O 15 '66
  Turning point; white backlash. il Time 88:
    29–30 O 7 '66
  Voter backlash over race issue? il U S News
    61:34–6 S 19 '66
  What I learned from Negroes; white coed in
    Atlanta's Negro community. S. Bady. il
    Ebony 21:58–60+ S '66
  When white girls go South as civil-rights
    workers. U S News 60:10 My 30 '66
  Where the backlash was felt. il U S News
    61:65 N 21 '66
  White House conference on whites. il Ebony
    21:86–7 Jl '66
    See also
  Race prejudice
RACE riots. See Riots
RACE tracks
  Anything goes in the bush; Hidden Valley; no
    holds barred, no rules enforced. J. Olsen.
    il Sports Illus 25:60–2+ O 31 '66
  Glorious Goodwood; photographs by J. Cooke;
    with account by M. Richardson. Sports Il-
    lus 25:26–31 Jl 25 '66

RACHEWILTZ, Mary de
  Ezra Pound at eighty. Esquire 65:114–16+
    Ap '66
RACHMANINOFF, Sergei
  Da capo. S. Smolian. il por Am Rec G 33:154–
    5 O '66
  Golden art of Sergei Rachmaninoff. R. Kam-
    merer. por Am Rec G 33:156–65 O '66
RACIAL differences
  Equality; a geneticist's view; reprint. T.
    Dobzhansky. il Cath World 204:104–12 N
    '66
  Races of mankind; quiz. J. Daugherty and
    M. Daugherty. il Sci Digest 60:85–7 O '66
  Science on race; recognizing genetic dif-
    ferences. P. McBroom. Sci N 91:44 Ja 14
    '67
RACIAL discrimination. See Race discrimina-
    tion
RACIAL equality. See Equality
RACINE, Jean Baptiste
  Phèdre; tr. by W. Packard. Criticism
    Commonweal 83:699 Mr 18 '66
    New Yorker 41:130 F 19 '66
RACING. See Airplane racing; Horse racing;
    and similar headings
RACING car models. See Automobile models
RACING cars. See Automobiles, Racing
RACISM
  Is Mormonism reformable on race? Mormon
    view of Negro. Christian Cent 83:576 My 4
    '66
  Mr White Backlash; L. Maddox of Georgia.
    R. Cleghorn. il N Y Times Mag p27–9+ N
    6 '66
  Southerner, by C. L. Weltner. Review
    Sat R 49:97–8 My 7 '66. B. Galphin
    See also
  Race prejudice
RACKETEERING
    See also
  Black markets
RACKS, Magazine. See Magazine stands, racks,
    etc.
RADAR
  Signatures in the sky; Radar signature analy-
    sis. il Time 88:112 O 21 '66
    See also
  Pulse techniques (electronics)
  Surveillance radar

    Antenna and scanning mechanisms
  Distant galaxies caught in a steel mesh;
    Arecibo radio-radar telescope, Puerto Rico.
    il UNESCO Courier 19:8–9 Ja '66
  Phased-array design trims weight, cost.
    P. J. Klass. il Aviation W 84:88–91 My
    9 '66

    Meteorological applications
    See Radar meteorology

    Military applications
  ALTAIR antenna promises missile defense
    improvement; Advanced research projects
    agency long-range tracking and instru-
    ment radar. Tech W 20:38 Ja 2 '67
  Army orders lightweight, portable radar. il
    Aviation W 85:81–3 Ag 1 '66
  Bids due soon on new Nike-X radar; multi-
    function array radar. R. Barnhart. il Miss
    & Roc 18:14–15 My 30 '66
  Man-pack radars readied for evaluation.
    P. J. Klass. il Aviation W 84:56–7+ Ap 11
    '66
  New radar system to aid ECM design; in-
    vestigating vulnerability of missile systems
    to electronic countermeasures. R. Pay. Miss
    & Roc 18:36–7 Mr 7 '66
  New tactical radar system ready for army;
    portable short-range surveillance radar.
    C. D. LaFond. il Tech W 19:39 Ag 1 '66
  Radar may alter point defense plans; hard-
    point demonstration array radar. M. Getler.
    Miss & Roc 18:15 Mr 14 '66
  Spying on the sky; black art of radar signa-
    ture analysis. J. Eberhart. il Sci N 90:
    226–7 S 24 '66
  Surveillance needs systems approach. J. F.
    Judge. il Miss & Roc 18:110–12 Mr 28 '66
  Tactical radar homing programs pushed. B.
    Miller. il Aviation W 84:78–9+ Mr 21 '66
  Units chosen for reliability effort. P. J. Klass.
    il Aviation W 85:32 O 10 '66
    See also
  Radar defense networks
RADAR beacons. See Radar in aviation
RADAR defense networks
  DEWline marks tenth anniversary. il(p365)
    Sci N 90:370 N 5 '66
  Sea-launched ballistic missile warning net
    development set. il Miss & Roc 18:16–17
    Ja 24 '66

RADIO advertising
TV overseas: the U.S. hard sell. H. I. Schiller. il Nation 203:609-12 D 5 '66
Why radio is here to stay; with list of top ten advertisers and agencies. R. L. Tobin. il Sat R 49:47-8 Jl 9 '66
RADIO aids to aviation. See Radio in aviation
RADIO aids to navigation. See Radio in navigation
RADIO announcers. See Radio broadcasting—Announcing
RADIO antennas
Antenna boom. R. Cornell. il Pop Electr 24:39-43+ My '66
Antenna placement does make a difference. R. L. Ruyle. il Pop Electr 25:64-5+ N '66
Build an 80/40 meter bandswitching vertical. L. Dezettel. il Pop Electr 25:73-4 O '66
Digital links, millimeter waves studied. W. S. Beller. il Miss & Roc 18:70+ Ja 31 '66
NASA seeks bids on 30-ft. ATS erectable satellite antenna study. Aviation W 85:33 Jl 25 '66
New giant tracking antenna at Goldstone. il Sky & Tel 31:342-3 Je '66
SWL antennas for the forgotten man. Pop Electr 24:47 My '66
Technician band antenna coupler. E. H. Leftwich. il Pop Electr 25:87-8 Ag '66
What's so different about CB antennas? R. O'Brien. il Pop Electr 24:44-6+ My '66
See also
Radio telescope
RADIO apparatus
Build the Modbox; adapter takes the guesswork out of monitoring modulation. G. J. Whalen. il Pop Electr 25:41-5+ Ag '66
See also
Microphones
Radio instruments
RADIO apparatus industry and trade
Why radio is here to stay. R. L. Tobin. il Sat R 49:47-8 Jl 9 '66
RADIO apparatus on aircraft
Short count: servicing of aviation radios. R. B. Parke. Flying 80:28 Ja '67
See also
Radio telephone on aircraft
RADIO apparatus on ships, boats, etc.
See also
Radio telephone on ships, boats, etc.
RADIO astronomy
Absence of short-term variability of CTA 102. J. M. Bologna and others. bibliog il Science 153:294-5 Jl 15 '66
Are quasars the products of peculiar galaxies? H. Arp theory. il Time 87:88+ Ap 1 '66
Are quasars truly remote? G. S. Mumford. Sky & Tel 31:338 Je '66
Birth and life of the universe; observations through the Hale telescope at Palomar observatory. C. P. Gilmore. il N Y Times Mag p26-7+ Je 12 '66
Blue objects in sky number some 400,000. Sci N 89:245 Ap 9 '66
Brightness distributions of radio sources at 2-centimeter wavelength. S. H. Zisk. bibliog il Science 153:1107-9 S 2 '66
Cosmic X-ray sources observed. il Sky & Tel 32:12 Jl '66
Cosmology, 1966. B. Frisch. il Sci Digest 59:66-72 My '66
Do comets really break down to produce meteor showers? T. D. Nicholson. il Natur Hist 75:50-2 D '66
Doppler interpretation of quasar red shifts. H. S. Zapolsky. bibliog il Science 153:635-8 Ag 5 '66
Doubt cast on quasars. Sci N 89:215 Ap 2 '66
Energy spectra of a number of celestial X-ray sources in the energy range from 2 to 60 kiloelectron volts. K. G. McCracken. bibliog il Science 154:1000-2 N 25 '66
Exciting new world of X-ray astronomy; reprint. H. Simons. il Sci Digest 59:60-6 Je '66
Friedman on X-ray stars. Sci N 91:10 Ja 7 '67
Galaxies, quasars, and the expanding universe. T. D. Nicholson. il Natur Hist 76:36-9 Ja '67
Gas clouds speed to earth. Sci N 90:103 Ag 13 '66
Greatest explosion of them all; discoveries spark debate among astronomers over origin of universe. E. Ubell. Read Digest 88:123-7 F '66
Helium from a fireball. Sci Am 214:54+ My '66
Hunt for quarks goes on. Sci N 89:335 My 7 '66
Identification of the X-ray source in Scorpius. H. Gursky. il Sky & Tel 32:252-5 N '66

Interplanetary radio scintillation. il Sky & Tel 31:142 Mr '66
Interstellar hydroxyl radio emission. N. H. Dieter and others. il Sky & Tel 31:132-6 Mr '66
Inverse Compton effect: some consequences for quasars. J. Pfleiderer and M. Grewing. bibliog il Science 154:1452-3 D 16 '66
Locating radio sources with the moon. R. W. Clarke. il Sci Am 214:30-41 Je '66
Long-base-line interferometer at Jodrell Bank. A. D. Frost and H. P. Palmer. il Sky & Tel 32:21-4 Jl '66
Long look back to creation. M. Gunther. il Sat Eve Post 239:23-5 Mr 12 '66
Man on the mountain; M. Schmidt; quasars and theories of the universe. L. Jaroff. il Time 87:80-4 Mr 11 '66
Mercury: anomalous absence from the 3.4-millimeter radio emission of variation with phase. E. E. Epstein. bibliog il Science 151:445-7 Ja 28 '66
Observational aspects of cosmology. L. C. Green. il Sky & Tel 31:199-202 Ap '66
Observational aspects of cosmology; report on conference. T. Page. Science 151:1411-14+ Mr 18 '66
Origin of cosmic rays. G. Burbidge. il Sci Am 215:32-8 Ag '66
Peculiar galaxies and radio sources. H. Arp. bibliog il Science 151:1214-16 Mr 11 '66
Peculiar galaxies and radio sources. H. Arp. bibliog il Science 151:1214-16 Mr 11 '66; Reply. B. Hoffmann. 152:671 Ap 29 '66
Problem of the quasi-stellar objects. G. Burbidge and F. Hoyle. il Sci Am 215:40-52 D '66
Quasar clues. Sci Am 215:54 Jl '66
Quasars. New Yorker 42:37-8 My 21 '66
Quasars. Sci Am 214:50-1+ F '66
Quasars and quarks are objects of studies. Sci N 90:162 S 3 '66
Quasars: lagging left-outs. A. Ewing. Sci N L 89:83 F 5 '66
Quasars may be abundant in cosmos. il Sci N 90:29 Jl 9 '66
Quasars remain puzzling. Sci N 90:126 Ag 20 '66
Quasi-stellar objects: possible local origin. J. Terrell. bibliog Science 154:1281-8 D 9 '66
Radio astronomers detect cosmic helium emission. Sky & Tel 32:123 S '66
Radio astronomy aired at IEEE. C. D. LaFond. il Miss & Roc 13:31-2+ Ap 4 '66
Radio astronomy and the galactic system. B. J. Bok. il Sky & Tel 32:271-4, 341-3 N-D '66
Radio astronomy: surveying the unquiet universe. C. Sheridan. il Pop Electr 24:39-44+ Ja '66
Radio observations of Uranus and Neptune. Sky & Tel 31:346 Je '66
Radio sources: angular size from scintillation studies. M. H. Cohen and others. bibliog il Science 153:745-6 Ag 12 '66
Raise space mileage. Sci N 89:366 My 14 '66
Soviet X-ray studies. R. N. Watts, jr. il Sky & Tel 32:141 S '66
Space X-rays from star. Sci N 90:86 Ag 6 '66
Spectra of quasars. il Sky & Tel 31:344 Je '66
Spectrum and distance of source Sco XR-1. H. Friedman and others. bibliog il Science 153:1527-8 S 23 '66
Supernova remnant W-44: obesrvations at 8350 megacycles per second. J. P. Hollinger and R. W. Hobbs. bibliog il Science 153:1633-4 S 30 '66
World astronomers checking crazy quasar. Sci N 90:121 Ag 20 '66
X-ray galaxies. Sci Am 214:50 Ap '66
X-ray sky. Sci Am 215:44 O '66..
See also
Radio telescope
RADIO astronomy explorer (satellite) See Artificial satellites—Astronomical applications
RADIO attenuators
Designing an oscilloscope vertical attenuator. D. R. Hicke. il Electr World 76:94-6 S '66
Resistive attenuators and pads. C. F. Scott. il Electr World 75:35-7+ My '66
Symmetrical attenuator pad nomograms. M. H. Applebaum. il Electr World 76:27 S '66
RADIO-autography. See Autoradiography
RADIO batteries. See Storage batteries
RADIO broadcasting

Advertising applications
See Radio advertising

RADIO broadcasting—*Continued*

Announcing

Stadium inside a studio; excerpt from Back-stage at the Mets. I. Nelson and A. Hirshberg. il Sports Illus 24:38-40+ Mr 28 '66

Conversation programs

Air pollution, new style; Los Angeles programs. B. Vaccariello. Nat R 18:270-1 Mr 22 '66

Dandy Dan in Africa; visit to publicize the fifth anniversary of Peace corps. New Yorker 42:38-9 Ap 30 '66

From photography to flying saucers. S. M. Teller. il U S Camera 29:60-1+ N '66

Hello, there! you're on the air. J. Mitford. Harper 232:47-53 My '66

Killer Joe; J. Pyne. Time 88:30 Jl 29 '66

Logorrhea in Los Angeles; radio station KNX. il Newsweek 67:65 Mr 7 '66

Trade winds; WCAU and WNBC telephone talk-jockey shows. J. C. Fuller. il Sat R 49:12-13 Mr 5 '66

White sound, black sound; program Family line; WAOK, Atlanta. il Time 88:76-7 S 9 '66

Drama

Theater of the ear; presentations by WRVR. R. L. Shayon. Sat R 49:52 Ap 9 '66

See also
Radio plays

Educational applications

See Radio in education

Frequency modulation

See Radio frequency modulation

History

How the wasteland began; early days of radio. C. Dreher. Atlan 217:53-8 F '66

Illegal applications

See also
Radio stations, Illegal

International aspects

U.S. and Mexico begin talks on new radio agreement. Dept State Bul 55:465 S 26 '66

U.S. and Mexico extend radio agreement. Dept State Bul 54:720 My 2 '66

Multiplex system

Automatic stereo multiplex demodulator. D. R. Von Recklinghausen. il Electr World 76:32-3+ Jl '66

Correspondence school by radio: Educasting. J. R. Berry. il Pop Mech 126:96-8+ S '66

Music

Boudoir Bob; CBS's Music 'til dawn. il Time 88:30 Jl 29 '66

FM radio has to change its tune; rock-'n'-roll displaces the quartets. il Bsns W p 173-4+ S 24 '66

Gold guitars; country-music. il Newsweek 67:96+ Ap 4 '66

TV Italian style. W. Weaver. il Opera N 31: 14-15 O 31 '66

Texaco-Metropolitan opera radio network. Opera N 31:32 D 3 '66

That new sound from Nashville; Grand ole opry. C. Portis. il Sat Eve Post 239:30-4+ F 12 '66

Verismo in the air. A. Ronnie. il Opera N 31:6-7 D 3 '66

See also
Disc jockeys

Negro programs

Negro radio; WDIA in Memphis, all-Negro oriented station. R. S. Kahlenberg. bibliog Negro Hist Bul 29:127-8+ Mr '66

News

Code for crime coverage; WMCA's policy. R. L. Shayon. il Sat R 49:46 N 5 '66

Last big voice; news analyst, E. P. Morgan. Newsweek 68:98 S 19 '66

Opera

See Radio broadcasting—Music

Programs

Antiques take to the airways on Cape Cod. il Hobbies 71:96 Ag '66

Look and listen. P. Dilts. See issues of Senior scholastic

Looking and listening. P. Dilts. See issues of Senior scholastic

Mike fright; attacked while on the air. Newsweek 67:21 F 7 '66

Radio's golden age, by B. Owen and F. Buxton. Review
Sat R 50:132 Ja 14 '67. A. Balk

Propaganda

Foundation pipe lines: the beneficent CIA; funneling money to shape foreign policy; Group research findings. R. G. Sherrill. Nation 202:542-4+ My 9 '66

Sounds of the right; extremist broadcasters programs and stations. il Newsweek 68:80-1 Jl 4 '66

See also
Radio free Europe

Short wave

See Radio broadcasting, Short wave

Sports

Responsibility; Yankees fire R. Barber. Sports Illus 25:17 O 10 '66

Some series! Koufax fans the Babe; 1966 dream world series. S. Moore Life 61:27 O 7 '66

Sportscasting, anyone? interview, ed. by H. L. Masin. J Simpson. il Sr Schol 88:20 F 11 '66

Stadium inside a studio; excerpt from Back-stage at the Mets. L. Nelson and A. Hirshberg. il Sports Illus 24:38-40+ Mr 28 '66

Time signals

See Time signals, Radio

Weather forecasts

Weather when you want it. R. Humphrey. il Motor B 119:107-8+ Ja '67

United States

Out of the bag. il Time 87:77-8 F 18 '66

Radio: hitting it big on the comeback trail. P. Dilts. il Sr Schol 88:26 My 6 '66

Why radio is here to stay. R. L. Tobin. il Sat R 49:47-8 Jl 9 '66

RADIO broadcasting, Short wave

Long and short of short wave. R. Gelatt. il Hi Fi 16:69-71 D '66

South of the border with Telefunken. I. Kolodin. Sat R 49:44-5 Jl 16 '66

RADIO broadcasting stations, Amateur. See Radio stations, Amateur

RADIO City. See New York (city)—Rockefeller Center

RADIO City music hall. See New York (city)—Radio City music hall

RADIO communication

Supersensitive communications systems. J. Kyle. il Electr World 75:41-4 F '66; Reply with rejoinder. A. L. Marc. 76:6+ Jl '66

See also
Cipher and telegraph codes
Communications satellites
Intercommunicating systems
Radio in navigation
Space flight—Communication problems

Interference

See Radio interference

International aspects

Enthusiasm grows for global Comsats. C. D. LaFond. il Miss & Roc 18:46-7+ Ja 31 '66

RADIO communication, Military

Army to propose billion-dollar overhaul; Project Mallard. M. Getler. Tech W 19:13 O 10 '66

Bendix-developed AF radio may find inter-service use. R. Barnhart. il Tech W 19: 35+ S 19 '66

Jungle soak-up of radio in Viet Nam. Sci N 89:316 Ap 30 '66

Soundless, languageless radio; jungle message encoder-decoder. Sci Digest 59:24 Mr '66

Units chosen for reliability effort. P. J. Klass. il Aviation W 85:32 O 10 '66

See also
Communications satellites—Military applications
United States—Air force—Communication systems

RADIO communication in aviation. See Radio apparatus on aircraft

RADIO control

See also subhead Radio control under various subjects, e.g. Cranes, derricks, etc.—Radio control

RADIO converters

Build a GC-2 Deluxe converter. H. B. Smith. il Pop Electr 25:41-7 N '66

RADIO corporation of America
Hertz, too, becomes a no. 2; merger with RCA. Time 88:99-100 O 28 '66
Into the back seat; Hertz merger. Newsweek 68:79 O 31 '66
New tricks from the old dog; RCA's aviation equipment department. A. Trammell. il Flying 78:53-5 F '66
RCA and Random directors approve deal for merger. Pub W 189:38 Mr 14 '66
Random house stockholders approve merger with RCA. Pub W 189:57 My 23 '66
Salute to David Sarnoff. Electr World 76:8 O '66

RCA Victor division
Recordings. M. Mayer. Esquire 66:40+ S '66
Summer's crop of star-strewn operas; RCA's recording in Rome. W. Weaver. il Hi Fi 16:11-12+ O '66

RADIO direction finders. See Radio in navigation

RADIO direction finding stations. See Radio in navigation

RADIO free Europe
Struggle for the world's airwaves and men's minds. il Sr Schol 87:7-9+ Ja 21 '66

RADIO frequency
Digital links, millimeter waves studied. W. S. Beller. il Miss & Roc 18:70+ Ja 31 '66
UHF changes behavior; effects of UHF radiation. Sci N 90:394 N 12 '66
VHF, marine radio's new horizon. R. Humphrey. Electr World 75:50-2 Ja '66

RADIO frequency modulation
Button, button, which has the answer? FM radio educational broadcasting. il Bsns W p 188+ Je 18 '66
See also
Radio stations, Frequency modulation

RADIO frequency signal generators. See Signal generators

RADIO generators. See Signal generators

RADIO in agriculture
Calling all villagers; Radio rural forums. il UNESCO Courier 19:25 Ap '66

RADIO in aviation
Aircraft-satellite link antennas readied. K. J. Stein. il Aviation W 85:60-1+ D 26 '66
Airlines plan communication satellites. Electr World 75:74 My '66
Airlines seek less costly VOR change; visual omnirange. Aviation W 85:50 O 10 '66
Arinc studies domestic airline satellite; nationwide microwave network evaluated. K. Johnsen. Aviation W 85:49 S 26 '66
Collins to show new all-solid-state line. P. J. Klass. il Aviation W 85:100-1+ O 10 '66
New techniques may reduce VOR errors. P. J. Klass. il Aviation W 85:71+ Ag 1 '66
Pilots given new eyes; Microvision. C. A. Betts. il Sci N 89:222-3 Ap 2 '66
See also
Radio apparatus on aircraft
Tacan

RADIO in education
Button, button, which has the answer? FM radio educational broadcasting. il Bsns W p 188+ Je 18 '66
Correspondence school by radio; Educasting. J. R. Berry. il Pop Mech 126:96-8+ S '66
Educational broadcasting in Asia; summary of UNESCO meeting. UN Mo Chron 3:81 Je '66
Inventor of the month; Educasting system. S. V. Jones. il Sci Digest 60:11 Ag '66

RADIO in navigation
All-weather, long range electronic pelorus; RDF. F. E. Lawton. il Motor B 117:78-81+ Ja '66
Global navigation net three-eighths ready; Omega. Sci N 90:95 Ag 6 '66
See also
Loran

RADIO in politics
See also
Radio broadcasting—Propaganda

RADIO in tracking and trailing
Trailing Yellowstone's grizzlies by radio. F. Craighead, jr. and J. Craighead. il Nat Geog Mag 130:252-67 Ag '66

RADIO in traffic control
Citizen-band radio aids city traffic flow; Detroit. il Am City 81:121 N '66
Radio traffic surveillance gets aired in San Jose. A. R. Turturici. il Am City 81:130 Ag '66

RADIO industry. See Radio apparatus industry and trade

RADIO instruments
CB radio call monitor. R. C. Peterson. il Pop Electr 26:54-6 Ja '67
See also
Wavemeters

RADIO interference
How to spot and eliminate mobile radio noise. R. L. Ruyle. il Pop Electr 24:45-50 Je '66
Interstation hiss suppressor for FM tuners. J. T. Samuelson. il Pop Electr 24:60 Je '66
Receiver noise measurements. I. Math. il Electr World 76:24+ Ag '66

RADIO liberty (agency) See American committee for liberation

RADIO operators
Licenses
First license, and before. H. E. Church. il Pop Electr 24:54-5+ Ja '66

RADIO operators, Amateur
Amateur radio. H. S. Brier. See issues of Popular electronics
How to get the most out of your key and bug. M. Lincoln. il Pop Electr 25:68-71 Jl '66
Short-wave listening. H. Bennett. See issues of Popular electronics

RADIO oscillators. See Oscillators

RADIO plays
Merry Christmas; dramatization of Little women by L. M. Alcott. W. Hackett. Plays 26:88-96 D '66
Prince and the pauper; dramatization of story by M. Twain. D. Newman. Plays 26:81-95 O '66
Tale of two cities; dramatization of novel by C. Dickens. W. Hackett. Plays 26:99-111 N '66
Through the looking-glass; dramatization of story by L. Carroll. L. Olfson. Plays 25:95-105 My '66
Treasure Island. M. A. York. Plays 25:87-94 Mr '66
See also
Radio broadcasting—Drama

RADIO programs. See Radio broadcasting—Programs

RADIO receiving apparatus
AM table radios. il Consumer Rep 31:348-51 Jl '66
FM/AM radios. Consumer Rep 31:237-47 D '66
FM/AM table radios. il Consumer Rep 31:482-5 O '66
Identifying surplus crystals. I. Math. il Electr World 76:57 Ag '66
Is plasmonics for the birds? picking up fish talk on homemade hydronics receiver. J. D. Drummond. il Pop Electr 25:63-5 Jl '66
Penneys recalls some radios. Consumer Rep 31:320 Jl '66
Small radios; '67 table models or portables. il Consumer Bul 49:2+ N '66
Sure-shot Q5-er hookup. B. J. Thompson. il Pop Electr 25:87 Jl '66
See also
Automobiles—Radio equipment

Control
Crystal-saving frequency synthesized. F. P. Smith. il Electr World 76:46-8+ D '66

Frequency modulation receivers
Crystal-saving frequency synthesizer. F. P. Smith. il Electr World 76:46-8+ D '66
FM/AM table radios. il Consumer Rep 31:482-5 O '66
Music wherever; portables; with survey table. I. Berger. Sat R 49:60-1 Jl 30 '66
One-transistor muter for FM receivers. J. A. Palmer. il Electr World 75:79 F '66

Phonograph combination
Compact phonograph systems. il Consumer Rep 31:384-7 Ag '66

Transistor receivers
Build a one-transistor autogen radio. J. D. Amorose. il Pop Mech 126:169-70 S '66
Build time-signal-only receiver. C. Caringella. il Pop Electr 25:41-6+ O '66
Turn your portable into a clock radio. S. Rothfeld. il Pop Sci 188:120 Je '66
Wake up to music while traveling; miniature transistor radio. Consumer Rep 31:522-3 N '66
World's first single chip integrated circuit radio. J. A. Cacciola and E. Q. Carr. il Electr World 76:44-6 N '66

Tuning
Interstation hiss suppressor for FM tuners. J. T. Samuelson. il Pop Electr 24:50 Je '66

RADIO receiving apparatus, Portable
Music, Moscow, and transistors; with list. I. Berger. Sat R 49:56-7 Je 25 '66
New portables. il House & Gard 129:28+ Je '66

RAGHU, K. and MacRae, I. C.
Biodegradation of the gamma isomer of benzene hexachloride in submerged soils. bibliog Science 154:263-4 O 14 '66

RAHM, Neal M.
Salmon: River of No Return. Nat Parks Mag 40:8-10 My '66

RAHMAN, Abdul, tunku
Letter from Singapore. R. Shaplen. New Yorker 42:60+ Ja 14 '67
Rupture in Malaysia. C. P. Bradley. bibliog f Cur Hist 50:98-105 F '66

RAHN, Ronald O.
Pyrimidine dimers: effect of temperature on photoinduction. bibliog Science 154:503-4 O 28 '66

RAHNER, Karl
Can man perfect himself? tr. by D. T. Le-Fort. Cath World 203:138-44 Je '66
Paul, apostle for our times; excerpt from Christian in the marketplace. Cath World 203:331-4 S '66

RAHV, Philip
Critical view. Commentary 42:60-2 Ag '66

RAICHLE, Elaine L.
Why not every child? PTA Mag 60:35-6 Je '66

RAIL mergers. See Railroads—Consolidations and mergers

RAIL shooting
Chincoteague clappers. M. Rosko. il Outdoor Life 138:52-3+ O '66
High-tide tidbit. C. Robinson. il Field & S 71:53-5+ S '66

RAILINGS. See Hand railings

RAILROAD board of mediation. See United States—National mediation board

RAILROAD clubs
Frimbo's frolic: excursion arranged by the Electric railroaders association; interview. E. M. Frimbo. New Yorker 42:22-5 Ja 14 '67

RAILROAD consolidation. See Railroads—Consolidations and mergers

RAILROAD law
Presidential unit asks revised labor act. K. Johnsen. Aviation W 85:40-1 S 5 '66
See also
United States—Interstate commerce commission

RAILROAD management. See Railroads—Management

RAILROAD models
Steamy day at an auction of engines; Christie's auction of models of locomotives, ships and steam engines. il Life 61:69-70+ D 9 '66
There's something about a steam engine. il Pop Mech 127:116-17 Ja '67
See also
Railroads, Toy

RAILROAD passengers. See Railroads—Passenger traffic

RAILROAD porters. See Porters

RAILROAD presidents. See Railroads—Presidents

RAILROAD stations. See Railroads—Stations

RAILROAD stocks. See Railroads—Securities

RAILROAD strikes. See Strikes—United States —Railroads

RAILROAD strikes (Canada) See Strikes—Canada

RAILROAD tracks. See Railroads—Track

RAILROAD travel
Drive your own locomotive. H. Fast. Esquire 65:36+ My '66
Long live the railroads. P. Lyon. il Holiday 39:50-61+ My '66
Rail route to a more mobile America. E. K. Faltermayer. il Fortune 74:106-9+ Jl 1 '66
Sugar tongs and the gush of steam; cross-country trip with a five-year-old. S. Alexander. Life 61:39 D 9 '66
U.S.A, Canada, and Mexico; up, down, and sideways by railroad tour. il Sunset 138:41 Ja '67
Vanishing choo-choo trains. Holiday 39:136-7 My '66
See also
Railroads—Passenger traffic

RAILROAD workers. See Railroads—Employees

RAILROADS

Accidents
Biggest day in Flushing; excerpt from Situation in Flushing. E. G. Love. il Read Digest 88:69-74 F '66

Automatic train control
Automatic train control for Chicago transit. il Am City 81:59 Ag '66

Cars
BART: the trains and tracks. J. Bailey. il Arch Forum 124:44-7 Je '66
Booms, rails and ACF. J. Weingarten. Duns R 87:49-50 Mr '66

Consolidations and mergers
Eastern rail mergers' bumpy track; ICC recommendation to add three small Eastern lines to proposed Norfolk and Western-Chesapeake and Ohio merger. Bsns W p49 D 31 '66
Erie toils to make a match. il Bsns W p60-2+ Ag 6 '66
Fight for the Rock Island. D. Cordtz. il Fortune 73:140-3+ Je '66
Go east, stop west. il Time 87:91-2 My 6 '66
Green light for biggest rail merger, meaning for others: new Penn Central. il U S News 60:64-5 My 9 '66
ICC lays out the route; merger of Pennsylvania and New York central. il Bsns W p35-7 Ap 30 '66
Investors stay off the rails; result of ICC rail merger decisions. il Bsns W p 139-40 My 7 '66
Let them eat cake. Time 89:60 Ja 13 '67
Merger rivals tell it to the ICC; fight over Union Pacific-Rock Island merger. il Bsns W p 135-6+ My 14 '66
Mergers that unions can live with; Pennsy-Central combine. il Bsns W p83-4+ My 14 '66
Merging at milk-train speed; Pennsylvania railroad and the New York central. Time 88:100+ O 14 '66
More & more mergers. Time 87:88 Je 17 '66
New Penn Central, a precedent. Life 60:4 My 13 '66
Pennsy-Central merger, the biggest ever. America 114:687 My 14 '66
Pennsy-Central: one big happy railroad. D. Smith. il Nation 202:184-5 F 14 '66
Pennsy-Central: the biggest merger. il Newsweek 67:78-80 My 9 '66
Rail merger okayed: Pennsylvania and New York central. il Sr Schol 88:17 My 13 '66
Transportation outlook; rail mergers. Bsns W p71 My 28 '66
Western railroads collide on mergers; Union Pacific and North Western make strong bids for Rock Island. il Bsns W p 130-1+ Mr 19 '66

Employees
Mergers that unions can live with Pennsy-Central combine. il Bsns W p83-4+ My 14 '66
Rail firemen to get jobs back? U S News 60:74 Ap 4 '66
See also
Porters
Strikes—United States—Railroads
United States—National mediation board

Equipment and supplies
Railroads slam brakes on outlays next year: slash budgets for new equipment in wake of tax-credit. il Bsns W p 153-4 D 3 '66

Finance
Man who met the Pennsy's bills: D. C. Bevan. il Bsns W p62-4 Jl 16 '66
Pennsy-Central: one big happy railroad. D. Smith. il Nation 202:184-5 F 14 '66
Vanishing railroads. W. V. Shannon. Commonweal 84:517-18 Ag 19 '66
See also
Railroads—Securities

Freight cars
Freight-car builders hit full throttle. il Bsns W p 102+ Jl 16 '66
Freight cars can change an industry. Bsns W p 129 S 24 '66
Great boxcar shortage. Time 87:80+ Ap 1 '66
Look what's happening to freight cars! H. B. Comstock. il Pop Mech 126:138-41+ O '66

Freight service
Railroads: on the express track. R. Rutter. il Duns R 87:pt2 115-17+ My '66

Government regulations
See Railroads and state

History
Erie toils to make a match. il Bsns W p60-2+ Ag 6 '66
Frimbo's frolic: excursion arranged by the Electric railroaders association; interview. E. M. Frimbo. New Yorker 42:22-5 Ja 14 '67

RAILROADS—*Continued*

Management

Big business takes the management track. Bsns W p 104+ Ap 30 '66
See also
Railroads—Finance

Passenger service

Flying low; Canadian national railways. Time 87:93 My 27 '66
Jetting down the track; Central's plans to replace long-distance trains with high-speed shuttles. il Bsns W p81 Jl 30 '66

Passenger traffic

New trend in passenger-train service; move to discontinue long-haul trains. il U S News 61:12 Ag 8 '66
Toward the end of the twentieth century; New York central plans. il Time 88:84+ Ag 5 '66

Presidents

Presidential turntable; shifting of presidents. il Time 88:105 O 21 '66

Public relations

BART: planning and persuasion. J. Bailey. il Arch Forum 124:54-61 Je '66

Regulation

See Railroads and state

Safety devices and measures

See also
Air brakes

Securities

Investors stay off the rails; result of ICC rail merger decisions. il Bsns W p 139-40 My 7 '66

Stations

BART: architecture along the line. J. Bailey. il Arch Forum 124:48-53 Je '66
Is gate automation the ticket? il Bsns W p76+ N 19 '66
Station closed; with water colors by R. Bye. W. Buehr. Am Heritage 17:33-41 F '66

Strikes

See Strikes—United States—Railroads

Tickets

Is gate automation the ticket? il Bsns W p76+ N 19 '66

Track

BART: the trains and tracks. J. Bailey. il Arch Forum 124:44-7 Je '66

Train speed

Agency delivers transportation report. Tech W 19:17 O 10 '66
Budd-built cars to trim N.Y.-Wash. time. R. Barnhart. Tech W 20:25 Ja 9 '67
Fastest train in America. H. B. Comstock. il Pop Mech 126:89-92+ N '66
Jet railcar viewed as shuttle possibility; Budd railcar used in speed trials. J. W. Carter. il Aviation W 85:31-2 Ag 1 '66
Jetting down the track; Central's plans to replace long-distance trains with high-speed shuttles. il Bsns W p81 Jl 30 '66
Look at the old iron horse now; Budd passenger car, equipped with two G.E. turbojet aircraft engines. il Sci Digest 60:91 O '66
125-mph trains will make appearance. il Am City 81:46 S '66
Renaissance for rails? il Newsweek 68:52-3 Ag 8 '66
Shape of trains to come; high-speed ground transportation project. Bsns W p 142 My 14 '66
Would you have jumped? J. W. Cox. il Sci Digest 59:77-81 Je '66

Trains

Budd-AiResearch turbine railcar to begin trial runs this summer. R. D. Hibben. il Aviation W 84:65+ Ap 18 '66
Budd-built cars to trim N.Y.-Wash. time. R. Barnhart. Tech W 20:25 Ja 9 '67
Fastest train in America. H. B. Comstock. il Pop Mech 126:89-92+ N '66
Super-trains planned for Italy by 1969. Sci N 90:228 S 24 '66

Argentina

No way to run a... Newsweek 67:60 Mr 14 '66

Canada

Adding up the bill; railroads moving again. il Time 88:99 S 9 '66
See also
Canadian national railways

France

See also
Railroads and state—France
Transportation, High speed

Italy

Super-trains planned for Italy by 1969. Sci N 90:228 S 24 '66

Japan

How a railway gets speed from diversity; Hankyu empire. il Bsns W p 116-18+ Mr 19 '66
On the New Tokaido line. C. Stinnett. Holiday 39:28+ Ap '66

Mexico

Mexico's railroad in the sky; Ferrocarril Chihuahua al Pacifico. G. S. Wells. il McCalls 93:29-30+ F '66
Narrow gauge to Ozumba. E. J. Wojtas. il Travel 126:46-9 N '66
Wildest railroad in the West; Chihuahua al Pacifico. R. Dunlop. il Pop Mech 126:82-5+ Jl '66

Switzerland

In Switzerland try the train. il Sunset 137:34 N '66

United States

Long live the railroads. P. Lyon. il Holiday 39:50-61+ My '66
Moving the goods is getting tougher; nation's transportation capacity. il Bsns W p64+ Ap 16 '66
Rail route to a more mobile America. E. K. Faltermayer. il Fortune 74:106-9+ Jl 1 '66
Reshaping our national transportation policy; railroads must be allowed to compete; address, January 19, 1966. S. T. Saunders. Vital Speeches 32:237-9 F 1 '66
Speakers or spectators; address, February 9, 1966. E. S. Marsh. Vital Speeches 32:439-42 My 1 '66
Vanishing railroads. M. V. Shannon. Commonweal 84:517-18 Ag 19 '66
See also
Railroads—Consolidations and mergers
Railroads—History
Railroads, Short line
United States—Interstate commerce commission

Vietnam (Republic)

Rail splitters; Viet Cong target, incidents. il Time 87:31 F 4 '66

RAILROADS, Cable. See Cable railroads

RAILROADS, Electric. See Electric railroads

RAILROADS, Elevated. See Elevated railroads

RAILROADS, Narrow gage

Narrow gauge to Ozumba. E. J. Wojtas. il Travel 126:46-9 N '66

RAILROADS, Short line

To Apache Springs and back by steam; White Mountain scenic railroad, Ariz. il Sunset 136:53-4 Je '66
Where the steam engines still roll the rails. il Changing T 20:40 Jl '66
See also
Reader railroad

RAILROADS, Single rail

French put Aerotrain onto a faster track; high-speed train that rides on cushion of air, guided by a monorail. il Bsns W p50-1 D 31 '66
On the right track, 1887; forerunner of monorail in East Cambridge, Mass. il Am Heritage 17:16-17 Je '66
Son of monorail; aerotrain. il Time 88:96 D 16 '66

RAILROADS, Toy

It's an outdoor train table. il Sunset 137:73 Jl '66

RAILROADS and state

France

Timetable for SNCF; out of the red by '72; Europe's most efficient state-owned railroads. il Bsns W p72-4+ N 5 '66

United States

Speakers or spectators; address, February 9, 1966. E. S. Marsh. Vital Speeches 32:439-42 My 1 '66
See also
Railroad law
United States—Interstate commerce commission

RAILS (birds)

Bird believed extinct discovered on island. Sci N 89:477 Je 11 '66

RAILWAY express agency, Incorporated

Parcel post; opposition to new bill. Newsweek 68:74+ Jl 18 '66

RAILWAY labor acts. See Railroad law
RAILWAY regulation. See Railroads and state
RAILWAY tickets. See Railroads—Tickets
RAIMI, Ralph A.
Cheating in college. Harper 232:68-70+ My '66
RAIN and rainfall
Big rain that eased the drought. il U S News 61:10 S 26 '66
Israel's new prophet; long-range winter rainfall forecasts for eastern Mediterranean area. il Time 88:77 D 16 '66
Magnesium-28 in rain; produced by cosmic rays. L. Husain and P. K. Kuroda. bibliog il Science 154:1180-1 D 2 '66
See also
Droughts
RAIN forests
Jungle journal. J. Liedloff. Esquire 65:44+ My '66
Olulaau O Kauai (the forest of Kauai) R. Wenkham. il Audubon Mag 68:430-5 N '66
See also
Olympic National Park
RAIN making
Can we change the weather? seeding explodes a cloud. B. Frisch. il Sci Diges 60:76-82 S '66
Current status of rainmaking. G. S. Mumford. Sky & Tel 31:214 Ap '66
Rain may come to desert. B. Tufty. Sci N 89:374 My 14 '66
Rainmakers focus on the thirsty West; cloud seeding. il Bsns W p96+ Ap 9 '66
Rainmaking; it works; National academy of sciences report recommendations. il Newsweek 67:77 Ja 31 '66
Shepherding the wind. J. Lear. il Sat R 49:49-52 Ap 2 '66; Discussion. 49:43 My 7 '66
RAINBOW terrace; drama. See Gorelik, M.
RAINBOW trout fishing. See Trout fishing
RAINER, Yvonne
Review. J. Anderson. Dance Mag 40:30 Mr '66
RAINEY, Froelich, and Ralph, E. K.
Archeology and its new technology. bibliog Science 153:1481-91 S 23 '66
RAINEY, Jane Teresa Denyse (Ormsby Gore)
Now the miniwedding. il por Newsweek 68:56 O 10 '66
RAINIER, Mount
See also
Mount Rainier National Park
RAINNIE, William O.
How we found the missing H-bomb. por Pop Mech 126:72-8+ Ap '66
RAISED beds. See Landscape gardening
RAJA Rao
Irish interlude. Sat R 49:32+ Je 25 '66
RAJA and Shala (dancers) See Shala and Raja (dancers)
RAJAGOPALACHARI, Chakravarti
What man cannot know. por Sat R 49:19-21+ Ap 16 '66
RAJAN, Sundar
Congress party after Nehru. Reporter 35:33-5 O 20 '66
RAJASALMI, Matti. See Lindy, S. jt. auth.
RAJASTHAN DESERT
Rain may come to desert. B. Tufty. Sci N 89:374 My 14 '66
RAJEWSKY, M. F. and others
Liver carcinogenesis by diethylnitrosamine in the rat. bibliog Science 152:83-5 Ap 1 '66
RAKOSI, Carl
Lying in bed on a summer morning; poem. Poetry 108:239-40 Jl '66
RALE, Janet. See Davidson, M. jt. auth.
RALEIGH, Henry P.
Classroom documented. Sch Arts 66:21-3 D '66
RALEIGH, Sir Walter
Let valor be my end! P. W. Schmidtchen. pors Hobbies 71:105-6 N '66
RALPH, Elizabeth K. See Rainey, F. jt. auth.
RALSTON, Richard M.
Quest for silence; address. August 17, 1966. Vital Speeches 32:726-31 S 15 '66
RALSTON Purina company
Ralston ties on a bigger feedbag; revamps both structure and outlook. il Bsns W p76-8+ D 3 '66
RAM, Charat
New generation sets the pace. il por Bsns W p82-4 D 24 '66
RAM wing vehicles. See Ground effect machines
RAMA RAU, Santha
It's a long, long way from old Camp Shawnee. N Y Times Mag p52-3+ N 13 '66

Oranges, birds and crystals. Reporter 34:54+ Mr 24 '66
Traveling with Mlle; travel, temples, and tolerance. Mlle 64:132-4 D '66
RAMALHO, Rosa
Pottery of Barcelos. N. Flowers. il Natur Hist 75:44-51 Je '66
RAMATI, Roman Haubenstock-. See Haubenstock-Ramati, R.
RAMEAU, Jean Philippe
Child of the baroque. R. Lawrence. il por Sat R 49:53 Je 25 '66
From L'Oiseau-Lyre, the first recording of Rameau's Hippolyte et Aricie. J. W. Barker. il por Am Rec G 32:946-8 Je '66
Hippolyte et Aricie. Criticism
Opera N 30:7 Ap 9 '66
Opera N il 30:24 Je 4 '66
Rameau as master of lyric tragedy. C. L. Osborne. il por Hi Fi 16:65-6 Jl '66
Records:
Hippolyte et Aricie. Opera N 31:34 Ja 14 '67
RAMEY, James T.
Atom and the law; address, April 28, 1966. Vital Speeches 32:731-6 S 15 '66
RAMJET propulsion. See Jet propulsion
RAMOS, Sugar
Cops and robbers in Mexico city. M. Kram. il por Sports Illus 25:26-9 O 31 '66
Lightweight decision. il Newsweek 68:94-5 N 7 '66
RAMPART DAM (proposed) See Dams—Alaska
RAMPARTS (periodical)
Bomb in every issue. il Time 89:35 Ja 6 '67
Rampartisanship; indictment of Michigan state university's technical-assistance program in support of Ngo Dinh Diem's regime in Saigon. il Newsweek 67:78 Ap 25 '66
Spies beside the red cedar; Ramparts' indictment of MSU expedition to Saigon. R. Kirk. Nat R 18:630 Je 28 '66
With cap & cloak in Saigon. il Time 87:20 Ap 22 '66
RAMPS, Airport. See Airports—Equipment
RAMRAS, Sandy
Baseball's week. Sports Illus 24:114-15 Je 13; 76-7 Je 20; 84-5 Je 27; 25:77 Jl 18; 64-5 Jl 25; 56-7 Ag 1; 68-9 Ag 15; 103 O 3 '66
RAMS (football club) See Football clubs
RAMSEY, Alf
Sporting scene. A. Reid. New Yorker 42:166+ S 10 '66
RAMSEY, Arthur Michael, abp
Archbishop at the Vatican. America 114:470 Ap 9 '66
Kiss of peace. il por Time 87:42 Ap 1 '66
Real meaning of talks between the Pope and the Archbishop. il por U S News 60:15 Ap 4 '66
Unity in truth. il por Newsweek 67:63 Ap 4 '66
RAMSEY, Diane
Information and control processes in living systems. Science 152:1285-6 My 27 '66
RAMSEY, Paul
Farewell to Christian realism. America 114:618-22 Ap 30 '66
Saints; poem. Commonweal 84:31 Mr 25 '66
Vietnam: dissent from dissent. Christian Cent 83:909-13 Jl 20 '66
RAMSEY, Ronald
Hanoi Harry. il Newsweek 67:23 F 14 '66
This is Granny Goose. Sr Schol 88:5 F 25 '66
RAMSEY, Stewart
Covering the Moscow beat. Sat R 49:72-3+ S 10 '66
RAMUS, Michael
Variations on a four-letter word; drawings. Horizon 8:98-103 Spr '66
RANCH life
Their hearts are as big as their country; farm and ranch vacations for city children at McKay ranch, Ore. W. B. Morse. il Am For 72:30-1+ Ag '66
RANCHES
Fly-in ranch; Medford, N.J. il Travel 126:6 S '66
RAND, Austin L.
Snipe rediscovered. Audubon Mag 68:351-4 S '66
RAND, Christopher
Letter from La Paz. New Yorker 42:35-40+ D 31 '66
Profiles (cont) New Yorker 42:56-60+ O 1; 64-6+ O 8; 64-6+ O 15 '66
RAND, Lester
Where teenage money goes. PTA Mag 61:8-10 bibliog (p37) O '66
RAND, Paul
Paul Rand receives medal of AIGA. Pub W 189:118 My 2 '66
RAND corporation
Top hand at Rand. Time 88:25 Ag 5 '66

RANDAL, Judith
Wasteful duplication in our hospitals. Reporter 35:35-8 D 15 '66
RANDALL, Betty
Large camera technique for 35mm color; ed. by P. Caulfield. Mod Phot 30:62-5 Je '66
RANDALL, Bo
Knives for astronauts and everyone. G. X. Sand. il por Pop Mech 127:144-7+ Ja '67
RANDALL, Charles Edgar
Portugal's pines. Am For 71:32-5+ O '65
Self-reliant forest. Am For 72:4-7+ Ja '66
Stanislaus. Am For 72:38-41+ Ag; 30-2+ S '66
You can be a conservationist. Am For 72:17-27 Ap '66
RANDALL, Darrell
U.S. aid in Africa. bibliog f Cur Hist 51:20-7 Jl '66
RANDALL, Florence Engel
Filing cabinet. Writer 79:11-13 F '66
RANDALL, Julia
Five poets. M. McCloskey. Poetry 108:274 Jl '66
RANDALL, W. D. Jr
Christmas list; holiday greeting. J. Fischer. Harper 233:23-4+ D '66
RANDAZZO, Frank
Misprision: crime of omission; first winner of New York city citizenship responsibility award. por Time 87:62 Mr 4 '66
RANDELL, John R.
Sudan. bibliog Focus 17:1-6 S '66
RANDOLPH, Jennings
Senator Randolph's blind businessmen. R. B. Scott. il por Todays Health 44:73-6 O '66
RANDOM house, incorporated
Cerfit of riches. il Time 88:100-2+ D 16 '66
Dictionary project: leading Random house event to date; Random house dictionary of the English language. il Pub W 189:61 My 30 '66
How one publisher aids Italian flood victims. Pub W 190:62 D 26 '66
Overruling an obsession: Court of appeals permits distribution of Howard Hughes biography. Newsweek 68:63 Ag 29 '66
Piracy or champerty? H. Hughes piracy lawsuit. il Newsweek 68:54-5 Ag 8 '66
RCA and Random directors approve deal for merger. Pub W 189:38 Mr 14 '66
Random house asks court to void Hughes injunction. Pub W 190:39-40 Ag 8 '66
Random house enjoined on Hughes biography. Pub W 190:193-4 Jl 11 '66
Random house stockholders approve merger with RCA. Pub W 189:57 My 23 '66
Some precedents in the Howard Hughes verdict. R. H. Smith. Pub W 190:312 Ag 29 '66
Stuart, Random et al. vs. Hughes, Rosemont, etc. concerning biographies of H. Hughes. Pub W 189:47-8 My 16 '66
U.S. court voids injunction on biography of Hughes. Pub W 190:308-9 Ag 29 '66
RANDOM house dictionary of the English language. See English language—Dictionaries
RANDOM processes. See Sampling (statistical methods)
RANGE finders. See View finders
RANGERS, Park. See United States—National park service
RANGES, Kitchen. See Electric stoves; Stoves
RANK, Peter
D.A.'s assistant wins the point race. C. Goren. il Sports Illus 24:58 F 21 '66
RANKIN, Allen
Great Mont Blanc tunnel. Read Digest 88:207-10+ My '66
—See Goodwin, G. A. jt. auth.
RANKIN, Jeannette
Woman against war. il pors Newsweek 67:12 F 14 '66
RANKOVIĆ, Aleksandar
Beyond the halfway house. il por Time 88:28+ Jl 15 '66
Going gets rough in Yugoslavia. P. Ben. New Repub 155:15-16 S 3 '66
Kid glove purge. Newsweek 68:36-8 Jl 18 '66
RANO, Richard. See Pecore, R. jt. auth.
RANSOM, Harry Howe
Cause of war, conditions for peace. Sat R 49:53 Je 11 '66
Containing Central intelligence. New Repub 153:12-15 D 11 '65; 154:38 F 5 '66
What are our foreign affairs? Sat R 49:32-3 My 14 '66
RANSTEAD, Charlotte
Nido de Aguilas. Sch Arts 65:5-8 F '66
RANSTEAD, Donald D.
Arms race in Latin America. Commonweal 85:313-14 D 16 '66
Evolution or revolution in Frei country? Commonweal 84:181-2 Ap 29 '66

RANUNCULUS. See Buttercups
RAO, Lakshmanasandra Srikanta
Taking the waters. il Newsweek 67:48 Je 27 '66
RAO, M. N. and others
Mass-yield distribution of the fission products in fallout from the 14 May 1965 nuclear explosion. bibliog Science 153:633-5 Ag 5 '66
RAO, Raja. See Raja Rao
RAPE
Justice for Franca; challenging Mafia traditions by prosecuting her abductor in Sicily. il Newsweek 69:37 Ja 2 '67
RAPE of Lucretia; opera. See Britten, B.
RAPER, John R. See Koltin, Y. jt. auth.
RAPHAEL (Raffaelo Sanzio d'Urbino)
Raphael's St Jerome punishing Sabinian. C. Gould. bibliog il Art N 65:44-6+ Sum '66
RAPHIOLEPIS
One of the plants you can build a garden around. il Sunset 136:238-9 Je '66
RAPID reading. See Speed reading
RAPID transit
As tangled cities turn to rapid transit. il U S News 60:75-7 My 23 '66
Don't sell on a strike. Am City 81:9 F '66
Free mass transit; First international conference on urban transportation. bibliog il Am City 81:124+ Ap '66
Mass transit. See issues of American city
Personal car for roads and rails; StaRRcar combines mobility of automobiles and efficiency of rapid-transit systems. M. J. Pedersen. il Pop Mech 126:61A Ag '66
Speeding urban transit. Bsns W p 162 F 12 '66
Strong voice is raised for integrated transportation planning; International conference on urban transportation, Pittsburgh. M. F. Schmertz. Arch Rec 139:125+ Ap '66
Transit expressway promises relief for medium-density cities; Pittsburgh. il Am City 81:141-2+ F '66
See also
Transportation, High speed
also subhead Rapid transit under names of cities, e.g. San Francisco—Rapid transit
RAPIDS shooting. See Boats and boating
RAPOPORT, Daniel
House loses patience with HUAC. Reporter 35:35-6 D 1 '66
RAPOPORT, Morton I. and others
Circadian rhythm for tryptophan pyrrolase activity and its circulating substrate. bibliog Science 153:1642-4 S 30 '66
RAPP, Fred, and Melnick, J. L.
Footprints of tumor viruses; with biographical sketches. Sci Am 214:20, 34-41 bibliog(p 143) Mr '66
RAPP, Gene
Triple-deck bunks. Pop Mech 126:122-3 Ag '66
RAPP, George
Angel in the forest, by M. Young. Review New Repub 154:25-7 Mr 12 '66. N. O'Gorman
Pros and cons of paradise. C. Walsh. Sat R 49:36-7 Jl 30 '66
RARE books. See Book rarities
RARE earths. See Earths, Rare
RARE gases. See Gases, Rare
RARITAN BAY, N. J.
Stench from New Jersey. J. Ridgeway. New Repub 155:13-15 Jl 16 '66
RAS, Norberto
Society, technology, and development. bibliog Américas 18:14-23 D '66
RASCO, José Ignacio. See Ignacio Rasco, J.
RASCOE, Judith
For garden country; rally on the right. Atlan 218:88-91 S '66
RASCOVICH, Mark
Day the giant tuna died. Field & S 71:56-7+ My '66
Eagles; story, excerpt from Eagle and his egg. Sat Eve Post 239:54-6 Ja 29 '66
Haunted battleground; story. Sat Eve Post 239:50-2 F 12 '66
RASKIN, A. H.
Dynastic journalism dies in New York. Sat R 49:62-3+ Ap 9 '66
Great society; address, April 21, 1966. Vital Speeches 32:554-9 Jl 1 '66
Labor's political frustrations. Reporter 34:26-8+ Ap 7 '66
Making strikes obsolete. Atlan 217:47-52 Je '66
Open door to inflation? Reporter 35:24-7 S 8 '66

RASKIN, A. H.—*Continued*
Payment by the hour? the week? the year? for life? N Y Times Mag p6-7+ S 4 '66
Yesterday's Berkeley rebel says: I'm just here to study. N Y Times Mag p 12-13+ Ja 30 '66
RASMUSEN, B. A. and Hall, J. G.
Association between potassium concentration and serological type of sheep red blood cells. Science 151:1551 Mr 25 '66
RASMUSSEN, Boyd Lester
BLM gets third director in five years; editorial. E. Linford. Am For 72:13 S '66
RASMUSSEN, C. Douglas
Carrier generator for SSB reception. Electr World 76:25 D '66
RASMUSSEN, H. P. and Bukovac, M. J.
Naphthaleneacetic acid: localization in the abscission zone of the bean. bibliog Science 152:217-18 Ap 8 '66
RASPBERRIES
Cane berry year begins in February. il Sunset 136:208-9 F '66
RASPBERRY, William
Right to riot? U S News 60:128 Ap 25 '66
RASPONI, Lanfranco
Tough guy and the jet set. H. Frankel. por Sat R 49:33+ S 24 '66
RASPUTIN, Grigorii Efimovich
I killed Rasputin; excerpt from Lost splendor. F. F. Iusupov. il Read Digest 88:133-7 Mr '66
Princes and the pauper. M. K. Argus. Sat R 49:6+ Mr 12 '66
RAT liver. See Liver
RATCLIFF, John Drury
Conquest of death before birth. Read Digest 88:107-11 Ap '66
Daring floating-pipeline gamble. Read Digest 88:225-6+ My '66
Do traces of metal decide our fate? Todays Health 44:34-6+ Mr '66; Same abr. with title Metals within us. Read Digest 88:109-13 Mr '66
Everything is Mitsui's business. Read Digest 89:255-8 O '66
Here come the sea giants. Read Digest 89:193-4+ S '66
New facts about human reproduction. Read Digest 89:119-22 D '66
New life for failing hearts. Read Digest 88:181-2+ F '66
Out through the bamboo curtain. Read Digest 89:149-50+ Ag '66
Radiation: saving more lives than ever. Todays Health 45:52-3+ Ja '67; Same abr. with title Unfolding miracle of X rays. Read Digest 90:205-8 Ja '67
RATCLIFFE, Jane
How to turn discards into dollars. Read Digest 89:25-6+ Ag '66
RATHEL, Otis
Chicago cop faces crime. il pors Ebony 21:48-50+ Ap '66
RATHGEB, Marlene
Mlle's tips for savvy skiers. Mlle 64:190+ N '66
RATIA, Armi
Black lace lingerie isn't our food. por Life 60:71 Je 24 '66
That little dress goes over big. il por Bsns W p88-90 D 10 '66
RATING. See subhead Rating under various subjects, e.g. Gasoline—Rating
RATIONALISM
Legitimacy of rational inquiry. L. D. Streiker. Christian Cent 83:458-60 Ap 13 '66
RATISHER, Carol
In my opinion. por Seventeen 25:178 O '66
RATS
Rats. S. A. Barnett. il Sci Am 216:78-85 Ja '67
Weaning of young rats: effect of time on behavior. V. Nováková. bibliog il Science 151:475-6 Ja 28 '66

Extermination
Rat! public enemy no. 1! B. Tufty. il Sci N 89:318-19 Ap 30 '66
RATS as carriers of infection
Rat! public enemy no. 1! B. Tufty. il Sci N 89:318-19 Ap 30 '66
RATTE, John
Books (cont) Commonweal 85:82-4 O 21 '66
RATTI, John
Fire; poem. Poetry 108:19 Ap '66
RATTLESNAKES
Day on snake mountain; snake-hunting. W. B. Allen, jr. il Outdoor Life 137:40-3+ F '66
Once too often. C. E. Kuschel. il Outdoor Life 138:42-5+ Jl '66

RATTNER, Abraham
Art galleries; exhibition at the Downtown. R. M. Coates. New Yorker 42:152+ Mr 12 '66
RAU, Santha Rama. See Rama Rau, S.
RAUP, Henry A.
Sleeping Bear Dunes National Lakeshore. Nat Parks Mag 40:10-14 F '66
RAUS, Jüri
CIA above the law. Nation 202:541 My 9 '66
Undercover slander. New Repub 154:5-6 My 14 '66
RAUSCH, Howard
Russian moon lander yields data on lunar soil firmness, density. Aviation W 86:81+ Ja 16 '67
RAUSCHENBERG, Robert
Artist as playwright and engineer. R. Kostelanetz. il pors N Y Times Mag p32-3+ O 9 '66
New techniques and images illustrate Abrams Inferno. il Pub W 189:106-7 Ap 4 '66
RAUSCHENBUSCH, Walter
Rauschenbusch; letter. E. T. Dahlberg. Christian Cent 83:806 Je 22 '66
RAUSHENBUSH, Esther
Still not a casual experience. Sat R 49:71-2 My 21 '66
RAVEL, Maurice
On records; L'heure espagnole. Opera N 30:34 F 5 '66
RAVEN award. See Mystery writers of America
RAVETZ, Jerome R.
Origins of the Copernican revolution; with biographical sketch. Sci Am 215:16, 88-95+ bibliog(p 152) O '66
RAVIOLI. See Cookery, Italian
RAW materials
Cyclical stocks with a plus. il Duns R 87:91-2 Mr '66
New co-prosperity sphere; Japan signs agreements to guarantee industrial raw materials. Time 87:98 F 25 '66
See also
Strategic materials
RAWE, Marcella
Time for purpose; drama. Plays 25:27-38 F '66
When the lotus-eating days are done. NEA J 55:37-8 My '66
RAWLINGS, John
Fashionable figure; photographs, excerpts from The photographer and his model. U S Camera 29:50-1 O '66
Good nudes: Rawlings is back. H. Keppler. il Mod Phot 31:74-5 Ja '67
RAWLS, Lou
Lou Rawls, live! il pors Ebony 22:140-2+ N '66
Superb blues man goes pop. K. Gouldthorpe. Life 60:18 My 20 '66
RAWSKI, Conrad H.
Bibliographic organization in the humanities. bibliog por Wilson Lib Bul 40:738-50 Ap '66; Correction. 41:26 S '66
RAY, David
Committee; poem. Atlan 217:90 Mr '66
Homecoming; poem. Nation 203:226 S 12 '66
Hospitality; poem. Nation 203:487 N 7 '66
Mid-evening; poem. Nation 202:658 My 30 '66
RAY, Gordon N.
Future of the book: address July 10, 1966. bibliog f por ALA Bul 60:783-93 S '66
RAY, Man
Artist accompanies himself with his Rays. R. Padgett. il Art N 65:51-3+ N '66
Man Ray on the future! interview, ed. by E. Hirsch and B. Zar. pors Pop Phot 60:98-9 Ja '67
RAY, Michael L. and Webb, E. J.
Speech duration effects in the Kennedy news conferences. bibliog Science 153:899-901 Ag 19 '66
RAY, Satyajit
Music of Satyajit Ray. J. Ivory. il por Am Rec G 32:1109-11 Ag '66
RAY, Shreela
Remembering Michelangelo's David; Manner of attachment; poems. Poetry 107:378-9 Mr '66
RAYBURN House office building. See Washington, D.C.—Public buildings
RAYETTE-Faberge, Incorporated
Rayette Sabreliner gives on-call service. D. A. Brown. il Aviation W 84:103+ My 30 '66
RAYLEIGH fractionation. See Separation (technology)
RAYMAR book company
Raymar is doing well on West coast. il Pub W 190:26-9 D 5 '66

RAYMOND, Jack
It's a dirty war for correspondents, too. N Y Times Mag p32-3+ F 13 '66
RAYMOND, Nicholas, and Carty, W. P.
Elections in Brazil: the revolution digs in. Reporter 35:42-4 S 8 '66
RAYMOND, Samuel, and Broome, John
Electrochromatography with reversing electrophoretic field. bibliog Science 153:1381-2 S 16 '66
—and others
Lipoprotein patterns in acrylamide gel electrophoresis. bibliog Science 151:346-7 Ja 21 '66
RAYMOND, Steve
Great Cascades debate. Field & S 71:10-12+ N '66
RAYMOND M. Hilliard center, Chicago. See Housing projects, Government
RAYNAUD'S disease
Peculiar viscosity. il Time 88:58 N 25 '66
RAYNER, DeCourcy H.
Presbyterian church in Canada assembly. Christian Cent 83:921-2 Jl 20 '66
RAYNOR, Vivien
4,000 paintings and 1,500 sculptures. N Y Times Mag p52-5+ N 27 '66
RAYONIER, incorporated
Can cash flow be turned on? interview. R. F. Erickson. Duns R 88:32 Jl '66
RAYS (fishes)
First baby bat rays doing well in captivity. il(p 145) Sci N 90:148 S 3 '66
RAYS, Molecular. See Molecular beams
RAYSSE, Martial
Times square of the mind. il Time 87:100-1 Mr 18 '66
RAYTHEON company
Raytheon completes D.C. Heath acquisition. Pub W 190:37 Ag 1 '66
Raytheon's quicker pulse. il Bsns W p72-4+ Jl 9 '66
RAZOR blades
Stainless-steel razor blades. il Consumer Bul 50:11-12 Ja '67
RAZORS
Battery operated shaver as a second shaver. il Consumer Bul 49:15-16 N '66
Build a stick-shift electric shaver. R. Wilson. il Pop Electr 25:90 O '66
Men's electric shavers. il Consumer Bul 49:11-15 N '66
New safety razors with ribbon blades. il Consumer Bul 50:13 Ja '67
Women's electric shavers. Consumer Rep 31:249 My '66
Women's electric shavers. il Consumer Bul 49:37-8 D '66
See also
Schick safety razor company
REA, Charles D.
ABC's of flight control. por Am Ed 2:4-7 Ap '66
REA, Gardner
Obituary
Pub W 191:42 Ja 9 '67
REACTANCE coils. See Electric reactors
REACTIONS, Chemical. See Chemical reactions
REACTORS, Electric. See Electric reactors
REACTORS, Nuclear. See Nuclear reactors
READ, David
Aeneas; poem. Commonweal 84:282 My 27 '66
READER guidance. See Libraries—Readers advisory service
READER railroad
Possum trot! Reader to Waterloo, Ark. E. J. Wojtas. il Travel 126:48-9 D '66
Reader railroad: Reader to Waterloo, Ark. il U S Camera 29:24 My '66
READERS and libraries. See Libraries and readers
READER'S digest
Reader's digest humor; excerpt from introd. to Laughs and chuckles. Writer 79:23 Mr '66
READER'S digest association, incorporated
Sylvania eyes school sales with Reader's digest link. Pub W 189:34 Ap 4 '66
READERS of newspapers. See Newspapers—Readers
READINESS for school
What every first grader needs to know. C. E. Hammil. il Parents Mag 41:44-7 Ag '66
See also
School age
READING, Mass.
Equipment-replacement plan. P. Welch. il Am City 81:84-5 D '66
READING, Pa.

Lighting

Teamwork produces modern lighting. il Am City 81:139 O '66

READING
See also
Books and reading
International reading association

Remedial teaching

Is your child a reluctant reader? V. Bartel. il Parents Mag 41:38-9+ Jl '66
Teacher is a teen-ager; New York's MFY program. il Newsweek 68:89-90 Ag 22 '66
See also
Speed reading

Adults

Swans into Larks; project of LARK (Literacy and related knowledge) foundation. H. Gilbert. il Library J 91:2780-2 Je 1 '66

Study and teaching

Culturally disadvantaged children can be helped; self-directive dramatization. L. Carlton and R. H. Moore. il NEA J 55:13-14 S '66
Dropouts anonymous. D. Weldon. il Parents Mag 41:44-5+ My '66
Fierce phonics war; Sheridan, Wyo. R. Kirk. Nat R 18:936 S 20 '66
Giving disadvantaged Negro children a reading start. E. J. Josey. Negro Hist Bul 29:155-6 Ap '66
How to teach reading skills in social studies classes. I. E. Aaron. Sr Schol 87:sup 15 Ja 21 '66
New reading materials for high school students. H. Finch. il Sr Schol 87:sup22-3 Ja 21 '66
Reaching the culturally deprived. T. Borton. il Sat R 49:77-8+ F 19 '66
Reading-go-round. D. V. Gunderson. il Am Ed 2:26-7 D '65
Reading is for the birds. M. A. Brandon. il Sr Schol 89:sup22-3 O 28 '66
See Jim read the book. P. H. Kendall. Reporter 34:37-8 Je 30 '66
Some Johnnies just can't; dyslexia. il Time 87:56+ My 13 '66
Sound over sight in reading; programmed learning. il Time 87:42-3 Ja 28 '66
Sullivan's crusade: schools without pain; California. J. Poppy. il Look 30:37-40 Je 28 '66
Teaching the dyslexic child: new hope for non-readers; McGlannan school method. C. Ellingson and J. Cass. il Sat R 49:82-5+ Ap 16 '66
Unsound reading systems in American education. il Sch & Soc 94:459-60 D 10 '66
Violence: a neglected mode of behavior. B. Bettelheim. bibliog f Ann Am Acad 364:50-9 Mr '66
Why don't they teach phonics? R. Kirk. Nat R 18:1169 N 15 '66

Anecdotes, facetiae, satire, etc.

Logical extreme reading method; textbooks cutting across all three socio-economic levels. M. Bennett. Pub W 189:33-5 Mr 14 '66
Mama breaks the reading barrier. L. S. Page. il NEA J 55:62-3 D '66
READING, Choice of. See Books and reading
READING air show. See Aviation—Exhibitions
READING aloud. See Books and reading—Reading aloud
READING and moving pictures. See Moving pictures and reading
READING by children. See Childrens reading
READING lists
Book news roundup. J. Foster. Sr Schol 89:sup 16 S 30 '66
Books to read while the grass grows green. R. Girson. il Sat R 49:33-5+ Ap 16 '66
Pow! zam! zowie! or, Down with summer reading lists. L. Russ. Pub W 189:47-9 Ap 25 '66
Revised summer reading list for secondary schools. G. R. Smith. Pub W 189:224-9 Je 6 '66
You need books at hand; roundup of new books; ed. by J. Foster. il Sr Schol 89:sup 10-14+ O 28 '66
READING machines
Blind read by machine; Visotactor. P. McBroom. il Sci N L 89:99 F 12 '66
Braille-reading machine. A. P. Grunwald. il Science 154:144-6 O 7 '66
From one machine: 100 days' work in eight hours; optical scanner. il U S News 61-11 Ag 22 '66
Reading machines for the blind; report on sixth technical conference. H. Freiberger and E. F. Murphy. Science 152:679-80 Ap 29 '66

READING of maps. See Map reading

READING readiness
When should a child learn to read? R. E. Krebs and M. C. Krebs. il Parents Mag 41: 54-5+ Ap '66

READING to children. See Books and reading —Reading aloud

READINGS, Dramatic. See Dramatic readings

REAGAN, Michael D.
Washington should pay taxes to the poor. N Y Times Mag p24-5+ F 20 '66

REAGAN, Ronald
Atlantic report. Atlan 218:22+ Ag '66
People feel they've been regimented; interview. por U S News 61:55-6 N 21 '66

about
Action on the set. il por Time 88:33 D 16 '66
Barbecues and other trivia. G. Hill. il por Nation 203:377-9 O 17 '66
Battle over a budget. por Time 89:64 Ja 20 '67
Berkeley: new crisis breaks out on California campus. D. S. Greenberg. Science 154:1304-6 D 9 '66
California: Ronnie to the rescue. J. Roddy. il pors Look 30:51-2+ N 1 '66
California: the final battle? M. Ryskind. Nat R 18:1094-7+ N 1 '66
Can Reagan win California? J. Phelan. il pors Sat Eve Post 239:89-93 Je 4 '66
Citizen-politician. il por Sr Schol 89:20 D 2 '66
Conservative tide. il por Newsweek 67:31-2 Je 20 '66
Giant rocks block road for Reagan. il por Bsns W p70-1 N 26 '66
Grandpa vs. the dude. Newsweek 68:61-2 Ag 22 '66
Notes from the land of political pop. H. Gold. il por N Y Times Mag p48-9+ D 11 '66
Once and future governor? Christian Cent 83:1323 O 26 '66
Parkinson's law. il por Time 87:20 My 27 '66
Political fun and games in California. J. Langguth. il pors N Y Times Mag p27-9+ O 16 '66
Reagan campaign purring. Nat R 18:818 Ag 23 '66
Reagan for president? New Repub 155:4 Jl 2 '66
Reagan in the wilderness. il pors Newsweek 67:30-3 Mr 28 '66
Reagan saga. M. Ryskind. Nat R 18:616 Je 28 '66
Reagan vs. Brown: how to succeed with the backlash. C. McWilliams. il Nation 203:438-42 O 31 '66
Reagan vs. Brown: see how they run! J. Bonfante. il pors Life 61:43-6 O 14 '66
Ronald for real. il pors Time 88:31-5 O 7 '66
Ronald Reagan: a light in the West. F. Clinton. il Nat R 18:613-15 Je 28 '66
Ronald Reagan, star. Commonweal 84:383 Je 24 '66
Ronald Reagan to the rescue! J. Murray. il Esquire 65:76-8+ F '66
Story of Ronald Reagan. il pors U S News 62:30-6 Ja 2 '67
Take two; swearing in. Newsweek 69:21 Ja 9 '67
Trek to the East. il por Newsweek 67:32-3 Je 27 '66
Two key men in a top '66 contest. il por U S News 60:19-20 Je 20 '66
Up from Death Valley. il por Time 87:24-5 Je 17 '66
Why Republican hopes are rising. por U S News 60:31-2 Je 20 '66
Will California stand Pat? J. Duscha. il Reporter 35:40-2 S 22 '66

REAL, James
Fragmented world. Sat R 49:27-8 Ag 20 '66

REAL estate. See Real property

REAL estate business
Bored by retirement, he builds an empire; Coral Ridge properties, inc, Fla. il Bsns W p 162-4+ F 26 '66
Dealer who's remaking Houston: combination of financial acumen and architectural knowhow. il Bsns W p 170-2+ D 3 '66
Dixie Zeckendorf runs for cover; New Orleans developer S. J. Recile. il Bsns W p78-9 D 31 '66
Europe breeds new colonizers; Britons, Scandinavians, and Germans rush to build or invest in Bahamas, Florida, and Hawaii. il Bsns W p 155-6+ Je 4 '66
House doctor; L. Jaffe, Los Angeles real-estate man. il Newsweek 67:75 Mr 7 '66
How'd you like to sell/buy your home on TV? J. Neubauer. il Pop Phot 60:87 Ja '67

Lakemaker; T. J. Perine. il Time 88:67 S 23 '66
Making of a compleat realtor. Fortune 73: 164+ My '66
Our island paradise; retirement at the age of thirty. S. Beamish. il Redbook 127:50-1+ Ag '66; Same abr. with title We retired at age thirty. Read Digest 89:108-12 D '66
Veteran fighter engages a new foe; E. Ball of du Pont estate in Florida, vs U.S. law. Bsns W p 184-6+ S 17 '66

Anecdotes, facetiae, satire, etc.
When the great developer became extinct. J. Skow. il Sat Eve Post 239:29 O 8 '66

REAL property
Man who wouldn't law with Uncle Sam; case of W. Metcalf and government suit. W. Ogden. Read Digest 88:39+ F '66
What about real estate as an investment now? questions and answers. il U S News 60:58-62 Je 20 '66
See also
Joint tenancy
Land values
Mortgages

Anecdotes, facetiae, satire, etc.
My slice of the real-estate pie; land in New York city. M. Kitman. il Sat Eve Post 240:16 Ja 14 '67

Valuation
Buy your own hunk of the outdoors. D. N. Keller. il Field & S 71:8-11+ Ja '67
See also
Assessment

REAL property and taxation
Needed, property tax reform. Am City 81:38 D '66

REALISM
See also
Idealism
Naturalism (philosophy)

REALISM in art
Talking of Michelangelo. J. Ashbery. il Art N 65:42-3+ Sum '66

REALISM in drama. See Realism in literature

REALISM in literature
Challenge of linguistic realism; dilemmas in drama and literature. M. Pei. Sat R 49:27-8+ Ap 23 '66
Substance and fantasy. L. Alexander. il Library J 91:6157-9 D 15 '66
Truth in fiction. J. Stafford. il Library J 91: 4557-65 O 1 '66

REALITY
Coping with reality; with study-discussion program by the authors. C. Smallenburg and H. Smallenburg. PTA Mag 60:18-20 bibliog (p36-7) F '66
Does anyone know reality? J. F. Wharton. Sat R 49:21-3 D 3 '66

REALS, Lucile Farnsworth
More about the glass of Emil Larsen. Hobbies 71:98 S '66

REAPPORTIONMENT. See Apportionment (election law)

REARDEN, Jim
Bear are crazy. Field & S 71:34-5+ Ag '66
Haystack bear. por Outdoor Life 137:44-6+ Je '66

REASON, Joseph H.
New ALA officer. R. M. Pierson. por ALA Bul 60:715-17 Jl '66

REASON
See also
Rationalism

REASONER, Harry
Letter from the publisher; excerpts from broadcasts on CBS program Dimension. Time 88:7 Ag 26 '66

REASONING
See also
Problem solving
Thought and thinking

REASSESSMENT. See Assessment

REAVEY, George
(tr) See Evtushenko, E. A. Babi Yar

REAY, Devon
Strawberries. Horticulture 45:53 Ja '67

REBA, Imants
Applications of the Coanda effect; with biographical sketch. Sci Am 214:16, 84-92 Je '66

REBEKAH Harkness foundation dance festival. See Dance festivals

REBERDY, Janet L.
On a weathered bronze crucifix; poem. Christian Cent 83:170 F 9 '66

REBHAN, John R.
New look in near-the-house planting. Flower Grower 53:34-6+ Mr '66

RECEPTORS, Retinal. See Retina

RECESSION, Business. See Business depression

RECESSIONAL; story. See Duprey, R. A

RECHCIGL, M. Jr
Czechoslovak science. Science 154:924-6 N 18 '66

RECHY, John
Conduct unbecoming. Nation 202:204-8 F 21 '66

RECILE, Sam
Dixie Zeckendorf runs for cover. por Bsns W p78-9 D 31 '66
Sam's suits. il Newsweek 68:91-2 D 12 '66

RECIPES. See Cookery

RECITALS, Musical. See Musical recitals

RECLAMATION of land
Frail lands; advanced stages of erosion. G. L. Turcott. il Am For 72:16-19 F '66
Politics of conservation, by F. E. Smith. Review
Sat R 50:90-2 Ja 14 '67. W. Stegner
Public land, private profits; conflicts between California and Idaho. Reporter 34:18 My 19 '66
Strip mining, reclamation, and the public interest. D. B. Brooks. il Am For 72:18-19+ Mr '66
Wetlands, wildlife and the army engineers; adaptation of address, October 2, 1965. J. S. Gottschalk. il Audubon Mag 68:116-18 Mr '66

Libya
Asphalt agriculture; upgrading marginal land by undercoating sandy soils to retain rainfall. Sci Am 216:60 Ja '67

RECLASSIFICATION. See Classification

RECLUSE; drama. See Foster, P.

RECLUSES
See also
Eccentrics and eccentricities

RECOGNITION machines. See Reading machines

RECOGNITIONS; story. See Miller, A.

RECOIL (gunnery) See Gunnery

RECOMMENDATIONS for positions
Anecdotes, facetiae, satire, etc.
This to recommend, well . . .me. J. R. De Foe. il Sat Eve Post 240:18 Ja 28 '67

RECONNAISSANCE airplanes. See Airplanes, Military

RECONSTRUCTION (Civil war)
Black power (cont) L. Bennett, jr. il Ebony 21:127-30+ F; 121-4+ Ap; 58-60+ Jl; 152-4+ O; 22:146-8+ D '66; 114-16+ Ja '67

RECONSTRUCTION (Vietnamese war, 1957-)
Refugees
See Refugees—Resettlement

RECONSTRUCTION (World war, 1939-1945)
See also
Germany (Federal Republic)—Reconstruction

RECORD changers. See Phonograph—Record changers

RECORD players. See Phonograph

RECORDED sound collections. See Collectors and collecting

RECORDER (musical instrument)
Pipe with a pedigree; the recorder. il Time 88:62-3 Jl 15 '66

RECORDING instruments
Amateur scientist; inexpensive machine to record observational data automatically; scanner servo-recorder. T. W. Maskell. il Sci Am 215:114-18 Jl '66
Helium-neon laser; thermal high-resolution recording. C. O. Carlson and others. il Science 154:1550-1 D 23 '66

RECORDS
In the future, less government secrecy. U S News 61:14 Jl 18 '66
Shackled historian. H. Feis. For Affairs 45:332-43 Ja '67
Under all that paper, there's the government. il U S News 61:16 N 7 '66
See also
Farm records
Fishing records
School reports and records

Preservation
See Archives

RECORDS, Phonograph. See Phonograph records

RECORDS, Preservation of. See Archives

RECORDS, School. See School reports and records

RECORDS, Sports. See Sports records

RECREATION
See also
Amusements
Leisure

Activities
Arts and communications in recreation and park programs. S. H. Frieswyk. Parks & Rec 1:976-7+ D '66
Creative programming in commercial recreation; address, 1965. B. H. Chetkow. il Parks & Rec 1:696-8 S '66
Cultural arts in recreation. M. B. Spector. il Parks & Rec 1:230-2 Mr '66
Far-out weekending. il Newsweek 67:96+ Je 6 '66
Into the wild blue yonder; Flying for recreation program, White Plains, N.Y. B. M. Dille. il Parks & Rec 1:332-3 Ap '66
Invitation to the dance; program of Wilmington, N.C. recreation department. D. Nesbitt. il Parks & Rec 1:724-5+ S '66
Looms weave by themselves; challenge of leisure time; excerpts from address. G. B. Hartzog, jr. il Parks & Rec 1:20-2 Ja '66
New programs under the sun; industrial arts program of New Castle recreation commission, Chappaqua, N.Y. D. R. Griffin. Parks & Rec 1:550 Jl '66
Painting the waterfront. H. Gasser. il Parks & Rec 1:558-60 Jl '66
Recreation and the job corps. R. Kraus. il Parks & Rec 1:898-900+ N '66
See also
Music as recreation

Administration
City management speaks out; excerpts from address. K. A. Murdoch. Parks & Rec 1:413+ My '66
Current trends in recreation and parks; address. G. H. Aull, jr. Parks & Rec 1:553-4 Jl '66
Innovation in management; excerpts from How to build your management skills. J. G. Mason. Parks & Rec 1:170-1 F '66
Local cooperation means strength; North Jeffco metropolitan recreation and park district, Arvada, Colo. Parks & Rec 1:897 N '66
Merger, what now! F. Vaydik. Parks & Rec 1:211 Mr '66
Methods of problem solving; ideas presented at the tenth Institute for recreation administrators, on creative problem solving. J. J. Bannon. Parks & Rec 1:917-18 N '66
Use operation & administration manuals; Recreation and park department organization, Alameda, Calif. S. Silver. Parks & Rec 1:44+ Ja '66

Aims and objectives
Blind umpire. F. Stark. Parks & Rec 1:202-3 Mr '66

Bibliography
Books. Parks & Rec 1:59-60 Ja '66

Economic aspects
Economics of recreation. N. Berkeley, jr. Parks & Rec 1:549-50 Jl '66

Equipment and supplies
Buyer's guide. il Parks & Rec 1:65-7+ Ja '66

Exhibitions
Exhibits at Washington congress. Parks & Rec 1:691 S '66

Fees
Golden passport to keep America beautiful; Federal recreation area entrance permit. Field & S 71:148 My '66
Golden passports. Liv Wildn 29:43 Wint '65

Finance
Fees and charges; a legitimate source of revenue; address. B. G. Memmel. Parks & Rec 1:152-3 F '66
Making the budget work; reprint. T. Lantz. Parks & Rec 1:744-5 S '66

Public relations
Green grass from grass roots. D. B. Alexander. Parks & Rec 1:902-3 N '66
Publicize, publicize; how to utilize local communications media. J. L. Kennison. Parks & Rec 1:699+ S '66

Study and teaching
Recreation enrollment growth reported. H. D. Sessoms. il Parks & Rec 1:867-9 O '66

RECREATION—*Continued*

Japan

Recreation Nippon-style. M. M. Meehan. il Parks & Rec 1:132 F '66

Okinawa

Youth activities on Okinawa. R. F. McKeta. il Parks & Rec 1:156-8 F '66

Switzerland

Use of high country in Switzerland; North Cascades debate continues using Switzerland as yardstick. A. Netboy. il Am For 72:6-7+ O '66

United States

Don't let the eagle lay an egg; Land and water conservation fund bill, administered by Bureau of outdoor recreation. G. H. Gillelan. Outdoor Life 138:24+ N '66

Forester meets recreationists. A. B. Hafer. Liv Wildn 29:25-6 Aut '65

Highground haven; Lake Fork recreation area, Colo. N. W. Noble. il Am For 72:30-1+ Je '66

Reaching our goals. F. G. McInnis. Parks & Rec 1:401 My '66

Research. bibliog Parks & Rec 1:516-17 Je '66

Rivers, recreation, and you; interview. F. Church. il Field & S 71:10-13+ Jl '66

Should wildlife refuges become public playgrounds? question for the Leopold committee. C. H. Callison. il Audubon Mag 68:312-13 S '66

See also

Lifetime sports foundation

National conference on outdoor recreation

Parks—United States

also subhead Recreation under names of cities, e.g. Parma, Ohio—Recreation

RECREATION activities. See Recreation—Activities

RECREATION and cultural affairs administration, New York city. See New York (city)—Recreation and cultural affairs administration

RECREATION and state

1965 legislative roundup; laws of interest to parks and recreation agencies; comp. by K. Smithee. Parks & Rec 1:14-16 Ja '66

RECREATION areas

Entrance permits available. Nat Parks Mag 40:22 Mr '66

For the greatest number; ski resort at California's Mineral King Valley. Sports Illus 25:25 D 19 '66

Greenspan program. O. L. Freeman. il Parks & Rec 1:829-30 O '66

Highground haven; Lake Fork recreation area, Colo. N. W. Noble. il Am For 72:30-1+ Je '66

Injun country nature area; Waterloo, Ia. park department. L. T. Katoski. il Parks & Rec 1:251-3 Mr '66

Maintenance of public-use areas. P. Nierengarten. Parks & Rec 1:249-50 Mr '66

National recreation areas. J. Jaeger, jr. il Parks & Rec 1:629+ Ag '66

New county recreation center in action; Lucas County recreation center, Maumee, Ohio. A. G. Morse. il Parks & Rec 1:720-1+ S '66

New trends and designs in construction (title varies) il Parks & Rec 1:403-8, 738-9+ My, S '66

Parasols and spirals for a Michigan park; structures for the Bald Mountain recreational area. il Arch Rec 140:98-9 Ag '66

Preserving a forest for recreation. R. C. Byrd. il Am For 72:18-20 S '66

Race for (recreation) space. il Newsweek 67:99-100 Je 20 '66

Recreation; fresh opportunities for inventive design; building types study. il Arch Rec 140:133-48 D '66

Seesaw in the Sawtooth. V. Fischer. il Am For 72:36-9+ N '66

Spruce Knob-Seneca Rocks national recreation area; in Monongahela national forest of West Virginia. R. C. Byrd. il Nat Parks Mag 40:8-10 D '66

Utilizing the great river. C. Hayden. il Parks & Rec 1:501+ Je '66

RECREATION associations

Foundation of a new era. C. L. Wirth. Parks & Rec 1:485-6 Je '66

See also

League of federal recreation associations

RECREATION buildings

New trends and designs in construction (title varies) il Parks & Rec 1:403-8, 738-9+ My, S '66

Recreation; fresh opportunities for inventive design; building types study. il Arch Rec 140:133-48 D '66

RECREATION centers

Japanese design finds favor; San Jose, Calif. il Parks & Rec 1:722-3+ S '66

Show goes on; Seattle park department capitalizes on its World's fair legacy. D. Brink. il Parks & Rec 1:561-2 Jl '66

See also

Library buildings as social centers

Recreation areas

RECREATION conferences

Coming events. See issues of Recreation (cont as) Parks & recreation

Executive development; eleventh national institute. W. C. Sutherland. il Parks & Rec 1:515 Je '66

Penn state conference. il Parks & Rec 1:172 F '66

See also

Congress for recreation and parks

RECREATION departments

Department accreditation plan; innovation developed by Indiana outdoor recreation council. B. McGinnis. Parks & Rec 1:217 Mr '66

RECREATION for the aged

Act provides activity; Older Americans act. Sci N 89:446 Je 4 '66

Craftmobile for seniors; Cleveland division of recreation. H. Goldstein. il Parks & Rec 1:719 S '66

Creative aging. A. B. Stough. Parks & Rec 1:910-11 N '66

Hoosier senior citizens camp; project in Indiana. B. McGinnis. il Parks & Rec 1:419+ My '66

Longevity in San Francisco; senior center. M. E. Segal. il Parks & Rec 1:455+ My '66

Outdoor facilities for the aged or disabled. E. M. Avedon. bibliog il Parks & Rec 1:426-9+ My '66

RECREATION for the handicapped

Adventure in creative volunteering; programs of the Highlights club. John J. Kane hospital. Allegheny County, Pa. H. Ryman. il Parks & Rec 1:36-8 Ja '66

How to teach handicapped children to swim. J. Streva. il Parks & Rec 1:502-3 Je '66

Mentally retarded need recreation. J. U. Stein. bibliog Parks & Rec 1:574-5+ Jl '66

Outdoor facilities for the aged or disabled. E. M. Avedon. bibliog il Parks & Rec 1:426-9+ My '66

Spot billiards for the cerebral palsied. C. T. Jones. il Parks & Rec 1:159 F '66

Teenagers provide recreation for the mentally retarded. J. Lavker and N. Rosett. Parks & Rec 1:487 Je '66

See also

Sports for the handicapped

RECREATION maintenance men. See Maintenance men

RECREATION workers

People in the news. See issues of Recreation (cont as) Parks & recreation

Personnel standards; excerpts from Personnel standards in community recreation leadership. Parks & Rec 1:258 Mr '66

Training

Summer internship program; Topeka, Kan. J. J. Bannon. Parks & Rec 1:321+ Ap '66

RECREATIONAL therapy

Arts in therapy. M. F. Thompson. il Parks & Rec 1:712-14, 858+, 926 S-N '66

Place for recreation in mental health. P. Haun. Parks & Rec 1:906-8, 974-5+ N-D '66

Therapeutic recreation in a federal maze. E. M. Avedon. Parks & Rec 1:840-1 O '66

RECRUITING and enlistment

See also

United States—Armed forces—Recruiting and enlistment

United States—Army—Recruiting and enlistment

RECRUITING for business and industry. See Employment systems

RECRUITING of air pilots. See Air pilots—Recruiting

RECRUITING of engineers. See Engineers—Supply and demand

RECRYSTALLIZATION. See Crystallization

RECTIFIERS. See Electric current rectifiers

RECTUM, Cancer of the. See Cancer

RED blood cells. See Blood

RED cross; drama. See Shepard, S.

RED guard. See Youth movement—China (People's Republic)

RED hot poker plants. See Torch lilies
RED mangrove. See Mangrove
RED SEA
  Isotopic composition and origin of the Red
    Sea and Salton Sea geothermal brines. H.
    Craig. bibliog il Science 154:1544-8 D 23 '66
RED-tailed hawks. See Hawks
RED tape. See Bureaucracy
RED water mites. See Mites
RED Wings (hockey team) See Hockey teams
REDCAPS (porters) See Porters
REDDICK, Anne, and Roesel, C. E.
  Rubella virus: growth and cytopathic effect
    in primary cultures of cells of rabbit em-
    bryos. bibliog Science 151:1405-6 Mr 18 '66
REDDISH, V. C.
  Twin 16-inch photometric reflectors at Edin-
    burgh. Sky & Tel 32:124-6 S '66
REDDY, John
  TV's killer Diller. Read Digest 89:90-4 N '66
REDEMPTION. See Salvation
REDERER, Franz Joseph
  Powerful art of Franz Rederer. J. Lovoos.
    il por Am Artist 30:42-7+ N '66
REDEVELOPMENT, Urban. See City planning
REDEVELOPMENT programs. See Economic
    assistance, Domestic
REDEYE (rocket) See Guided missiles
REDFIELD, Malissa
  Sense of happiness; story. Ladies Home J 83:
    63-70 Jl '66
REDFIELD, William
  Night Elizabeth Taylor said so what? and
    Richard Burton kicked the television set in.
    Esquire 67:108-9+ Ja '67
REDFISH (bass) fishing. See Bass fishing
REDFORD, Polly
  In vinos felicitas. Atlan 218:128+ O '66
  Victory in Miami: a follow-up report. Harper
    233:30 Ag '66
  Where the roads end. Atlan 217:130-2+ Ap
    '66
REDFORD, Robert
  Reflections of a secret soldier of fortune; ed.
    by E. Miller. por Seventeen 25:126-7+ F
    '66
REDGRAVE, Lynn
  Lynn, the reluctant Redgrave; interview, ed.
    by R. Chelminski. pors Life 61:61-2+ N
    18 '66
              about
  People are talking about. . . il por Vogue 149:
    92-3 Ja 1 '67
REDGRAVE, Michael, family
  First family. il Newsweek 67:102-3 My 23
    '66
REDGRAVE, Vanessa
  Laertes' daughter. por Time 87:82+ My 27
    '66
  Shakespearean turned sexpot. J. Hicks. il
    pors Life 61:79-80+ Jl 1 '66
REDLANDS, Calif.
  Biggest dollar's worth of sewage treatment.
    il Am City 81:83-6 Mr '66
REDLICH, Don
  Brief biography. S. Goodman. pors Dance
    Mag 40:56-7 D '66
  Don Redlich dance concert, Henry street
    settlement playhouse. M. Marks. Dance
    Mag 40:33+ D '66
REDLICH, Norman
  Justice Black at eighty: common sense of
    freedom. Nation 202:322-6 Mr 21 '66
REDMANN, M. Esther
  My year with the fifth grade; poem. America
    114:695 My 14 '66
REDMOND, James Francis
  Change in Chicago. Newsweek 67:98 My 23
    '66
  New start in Chicago. por Time 87:72-3 My 20
    '66
REDNER, M.
  Opinion: on decadence. por Mlle 63:58+ O '66
REDOUBT, MOUNT
  Lava, smoke and ash spew from Mt Redoubt.
    Sci N L 89:88 F 5 '66
REDUCING. See Corpulence
REDUCING diet. See Diet
REDUCING exercises. See Exercise
REDUCING preparations. See Weight reducing
    preparations
REDUCTASES
  Autoradiography with tritiated methotrexate
    and the cellular distribution of folate re-
    ductase. Z. Darzynkiewicz and others. bib-
    liog il Science 151:1528-30 Mr 25 '66

REDUCTION, Electrolytic
  Electrolytic reduction of CO_2 promising;
    changing carbon dioxide into breathable
    oxygen and carbon powder. Tech W 19:45
    D 5 '66
  Synthetic electroorganic chemistry. S.
    Wawzonek. bibliog il Science 155:39-44 Ja
    6 '67
REDWOOD
  Coast redwoods: struggle over national park
    proposals. B. Nelson. il Science 153:1620-3
    S 30 '66; Reply. G. R. Fahnestock. 154:
    1117 D 2 '66
  Discovery: tallest tree in world; Sequoia
    sempervirens. il Audubon Mag 68:303 S '66
  End in sight to the battle over America's
    giant redwoods? il U S News 60:116+ Je
    13 '6
  Great redwoods controversy. P. Friggens.
    Read Digest 89:91-6 D '66
  Great redwoods controversy. il Fortune 74:
    134-41 Ag '66
  One man's view; letter to President Johnson
    outlining views on redwoods in California.
    L. S. Rockefeller. Am For 72:6-7 Je '66
  Redwood murder case. R. Starnes. Field &
    S 70:14-16+ F '66
  Redwood Park hearing. Nat Parks Mag 40:
    20 O '66
  Redwoods Park grant; state highway not
    to invade tract of redwoods. Nat Parks
    Mag 40:20 F '66
  Redwoods to the sea. D. H. Clausen. il Am
    For 72:22-5+ N '66; Correction. 72:9 D
    '66
  Redwoods win protection. B. Tufty. il Sci N
    89:264-6 Ap 16 '66
  Rushing to save redwoods; White House
    backs emergency bill. Bsns W p45-6 S
    10 '66
REDWOOD CITY, Calif.
              Streets
  Final shot of asphalt. D. Chester. il Am
    City 81:114-15 Ag '66
REDWOODS NATIONAL PARK (proposed)
    See National parks and reserves—United
    States
REED, Anna
  When a county tried to cut relief bill. il
    U S News 60:44-7 Ja 31 '66
REED, Cecilia L.
  Using records to teach poetry. Sr Schol 89:
    sup 16 N 11 '66
REED, Christopher
  Most kids avoid discussions with adults; ed.
    by H. F. Waters. il pors Newsweek 67:67
    Mr 21 '66
REED, David
  Ghana: communism's major defeat in Africa.
    Read Digest 88:75-80 Je '66
  White vs. black in Rhodesia. Read Digest
    89:125-31 O '66
  With the quiet heroes of Vietnam. Read Di-
    gest 88:103-7 Mr '66
REED, David, 1941?-
  Study in black and white. S. Alsop. por Sat
    Eve Post 239:16 N 5 '66
REED, Donald
  Black Tiger of Mang Buk. S. Booker. il pors
    Ebony 21:68-70+ S '66
REED, John M.
  Fado. Am Rec G 32:1044-7 Jl '66
REED, Kenneth M.
  McNally is in touch. America 115:84 Jl 23 '66
REED, Kit
  Writing dialogue. Writer 79:16-17 Ag '66
REED, Pem
  Niobe; poem. Christian Cent 83:110 Ja 26 '66
REED, Rex
  Lady known as Lenya. N Y Times Mag p
    128+ N 20 '66
REED, Roy
  Another face of Orval Faubus. N Y Times
    Mag p44-5+ O 9 '66
REED, Sarah R.
  Federal government and professional library
    education. ALA Bul 60:163-6 F '66
REED, Theodore H.
  Come on over to the zoo. por Parks & Rec
    1:692-4+ S '66
REED, Willis
  Pro basketball's tall men. W. J. McKean. il
    pors Look 31:34+ Ja 24 '67
REED college, Portland, Ore.
  Informal wood frame campus buildings. H.
    Weese. il Arch Rec 139:184-8 My '66
  Reed's woes. il Newsweek 67:92 My 2 '66
REEDER, Norm, and Braun, Dick
  Road ahead has fewer bumps for dairymen.
    Farm J 90:A4+ Jl '66
REEDY, George E.
  Revolving door at 1600. il Newsweek 67:26-7
    My 9 '66

REEDY, John Louis
Chicago dud. S. J. Adamo. America 115:395-6 O 1 '66

REEDY, William
P.R. with a touch of magic. J. Deschin. por Pop Phot 59:24+ O '66

REEFS, Coral. See Coral reefs and islands

RE-ENTRY problems (space flight) See Space vehicles—Atmospheric entry

REEVES, Nancy
For each her own tiny revolt. Nation 203: 490-2 N 7 '66

REEVES, Richard
Great mayor, that bum? N Y Times Mag p6-7+ Ja 1 '67

REEVES, Rosser
Sell hard, live soft. por Newsweek 67:83 F 21 '66

REEVES, Thomas C.
Foundations in blinders: cool billions. Nation 202:381-5 Ap 4 '66

REFEREES. See Umpires (sports)

REFERENCE books
Grolier diversifies with big new books; Book of art, and the New book of knowledge. il Pub W 190:188-92 Jl 11 '66
Useful reference books; with list of publishers. W. T. Johnston. Consumer Bul 49: 2+ Je '66
What's new in reference works? aids for teachers and students. H. R. Finch. Sr Schol 88:sup 14-15+ F 4 '66
Your foot-long reference shelf; classroom reference-book collection. L. Dobler. il Sr Schol 88:sup 13 F 4 '66
    See also
Dictionaries
Encyclopedias
        Bibliography
All the facts and where to find them. D. M. Glixon. il Sat R 49:34-8+ Mr 19 '66
Current reference books. F. N. Cheney. See issues of Wilson library bulletin
Reference books of 1965; recommendations of a committee of the Reference services division of the American library association. J. Bartling. il Library J 91:1987-94 Ap 15 '66
With reference to. D. M. Glixon. il Sat R 49:49-52+ N 19 '66

REFERENCE for Lady Chatterley's lover; story. See Powell, A.

REFERENCE librarians. See Librarians

REFERENCE services division. See American library association—Reference services division

REFERENCE work. See Libraries—Reference work

REFERENDUM
Confusing clutter. Time 88:32-3 N 18 '66

REFINERIES. See Petroleum refineries

REFINISHING furniture. See Furniture—Finishing

REFLECTOMETERS
Time domain reflectometry; measuring transmission-line characteristics by means of step generator and oscilloscope. J. D. Lenk. il Electr World 76:48-50+ S '66

REFLECTOR blankets. See Blankets

REFLECTORS
I'd rather, three way, switch than fight. P. Farber. il U S Camera 29:46-7+ Je '66

REFLECTORS, Telescope. See Mirrors for telescopes

REFLEXES
Visceral reflex activity: development in postnatal rabbit. W. E. Bradley and F. S. Wright. bibliog il Science 152:216 Ap 8 '66
    See also
Conditioned response

REFLEXOMETERS. See Electronic apparatus and appliances

REFORESTATION
Israel, land of milk and honey. A. Hamilton. il Am For 71:20-4+ O '65

REFORM
Rise of nopanaceism. C. W. Griffin, jr. Atlan 218:76-7 S '66

REFORM Judaism. See Judaism

REFORMATION
Celebrating the 450th year of the reformation; in East Germany. Christian Cent 83: 1370 N 9 '66

REFORMATORIES
Chance on the outside: MDTA project at Lorton youth center. T. R. Sard. il Am Ed 2:29-32 Ap '66

REFORMED church in America
Move toward union. Christian Cent 83:197-8 F 16 '66
Reformed-Lutheran conversations. T. G. Tappert. Christian Cent 83:412-14 Mr 30 '66

REFORMED church in South Africa
Giving aid and comfort. Christian Cent 83: 1259 O 12 '66

REFORMERS
Rebel in a wing collar; march on Washington: J. Coxey and his Commonweal army, 1894. G. A. Gipe. il Am Heritage 18:24-9+ D '66

REFREGIER, Anton
Anton Refregier designs a tapestry; interview. il pors Am Artist 30:46-51+ O '66

REFRIGERATED motor trucks. See Motor trucks, Refrigerated

REFRIGERATION and refrigerating machinery
    See also
Freezers
Refrigerators

REFRIGERATION on boats
Refrigeration, it's wonderful. Z. Taylor. il Motor B 117:36-9 F '66

REFRIGERATOR desserts. See Desserts

REFRIGERATORS
Two-door, top freezer refrigerators. il Consumer Rep 31:372-9 Ag '66

REFRIGERATORS, Electric
Coolest place in the house! il Bet Home & Gard 44:64-5 N '66
Italy finds a bonanza in Europe's kitchens; dominates refrigerator market. il Bsns W p 104-5+ O 8 '66
Refrigerator-freezers. Consumer Rep 31:36-53 D '66
Refrigerator-freezers. il Consumer Rep 31:476-81 O '66

REFUELING of airplanes. See Airplanes—Refueling

REFUGEES
Continuity of refugee and migration policies; address, March 22, 1966. W. J. Crockett. Dept State Bul 54:704-6 My 2 '66
Refugee problems today; address, October 24, 1966. J. Wine. Dept State Bul 55:751-5 N 14 '66
Refugees. R. F. Smith. bibliog f il Ann Am Acad 367:43-52 S '66
Review of United States refugee policy; statement, July 14, 1966. D. Rusk. Dept State Bul 55:235-40 Ag 15 '66
    See also
United Nations—High commissioner for refugees
United Nations relief and works agency for Palestine refugees in the Near East
Vietnamese war, 1957- —Refugees
        Resettlement
Saigon: the impact of the refugees; national and international projects. E. B. Marks. il Reporter 36:33-6 Ja 12 '67

REFUGEES, Arab
Arab refugees: a Zionist view. M. Syrkin; reply with rejoinder. R. S. Goldman. Commentary 41:6+ Je '66
    See also
United Nations relief and works agency for Palestine refugees in the Near East

REFUGEES, Argentine
Footnote to the Argentine crisis: a letter from American scientists. L. Berkner and others. Science 154:992 N 25 '66

REFUGEES, Chinese
Exodus; Indonesia's Chinese. E. Behr. Newsweek 68:60+ O 24 '66
Great leap outward: four who fled; interviews, ed. by S. Liu. il Newsweek 68:57-60 O 24 '66
Out through the bamboo curtain. J. D. Ratcliff. il Read Digest 89:149-50+ Ag '66
Reporter at large: findings of the China watchers or Pekinologists in Hong Kong. R. Shaplen. New Yorker 41:41-2+ F 12 '66

REFUGEES, Cuban
Airlift anniversary. Time 88:44 D 9 '66
Cuban refugee airlift completes first year of operation. Dept State Bul 55:966-7 D 26 '66
Cubans in Miami. B. O. Walsh. America 114: 286-9 F 26 '66
Cubans in Miami. C. K. Yearley; reply. B. O. Walsh. Commonweal 83:651+ Mr 11 '66
Cuba's new refugees get jobs fast; opportunities in the U.S. Bsns W p69 Mr 12 '66
Do-it-yourself airlift. Time 87:36 Ap 8 '66
Door stays open. Newsweek 67:55 Je 6 '66
Freedom flood: statistics. Time 87:34+ Ap 1 '66

REFUGEES, Cuban—*Continued*
New procedures to admit Cuban refugees from third countries; joint announcement issued by the Departments of state and justice. May 31, 1966. Dept State Bul 54: 1005 Je 27 '66
New shuttle. Time 89:31 Ja 6 '67
Other Cuba: Cuban exiles in the U.S. il Sr Schol 88:11-13 My 13 '66
Permanent resident application fees for Cuban refugees waived: statement. L. B. Johnson. Dept State Bul 55:967 D 26 '66
Review of movement of Cuban refugees and hemisphere policy toward Cuba: statement, March 23, 1966. R. M. Sayre. Dept State Bul 54:707-13 My 2 '66
Those amazing Cuban emigres. T. Alexander. il Fortune 74:144-9 O '66

REFUGEES, European
This way out; escapes from eastern Europe. Time 88:38 S 9 '66
We came as children, ed. by K. Gershon. Review
New Repub 155:20-4 N 26 '66. L. Segal

REFUGEES, German
Bodies for sale; purchasing prisoners from the Communists. Newsweek 67:36+ F 14 '66
Never again; cold-blooded murder; two escape. Newsweek 67:55 F 21 '66
Waltzing bulldozer. Time 88:38 S 23 '66
We are scarcely James Bond ladies; interview, ed. by J. Robbins and J. Robbins. I. Cook; L. Cook. il McCalls 93:104-5+ S '66

REFUGEES, Vietnamese
See also
Vietnamese war, 1957- —Refugees

REFUGES, Wildlife. See Wildlife sanctuaries

REFUSE, Utilization of
Garbage in, merchandise out. Sci Am 216: 58 Ja '67
Solid-waste disposal: incineration and composting. R. R. Fleming. bibliog il Am City 81:94-6 F '66

REFUSE and refuse disposal
All that glitters; constructive attitudes toward litter. C. W. Burgener. il Parks & Rec 1: 573 Jl '66
Continuous-flow refuse collection; Ormond Beach, Fla. G. F. Althouse. il Am City 81: 90-1 Jl '66
Dave Lee takes a poke at pollution. D. B. Lee. Am City 81:101-4 S '66
Environmental pollution; 133rd AAAS meeting, Washington, D.C. H.B. Stewart, jr. il Science 154:1056-7 N 25 '66
European refuse-disposal. J. A. Fife. il Am City 81:125-8 S '66
If you burn trash outdoors. Consumer Bul 49:31 O '66
Pawtucket's two-pronged attack. J. A. Keith. il Am City 81:108-9 Ag '66
Polipollutionists: movement for the survival of pollution. J. K. Galbraith. Atlan 219:52-4 Ja '67
Pollution: NAS report examines dual aspect of the problem; with editorial comment. J. Walsh. Science 152:297. 329-31 Ap 15 '66
Pollution of man's environment. E. R. Fosdick. il Nat Parks Mag 40:16-20 S '66
Refuse collection and disposal. See issues of American city
Solid-waste disposal (cont) R. R. Fleming. bibliog il Am City 61:94-6 F '66
Solid wastes: every day, another 800 million pounds. S. A. Mix. il Todays Health 44:46-9 Mr '66
Two roads to cleanliness; street-sweeping and refuse-collecting programs. Claremont, Calif. W. Glickman and G. Ford. il Am City 81:110-11 My '66
Waste-disposal frustrations. Am City 81:8 S '66

See also
Refuse, Utilization of
Refuse grinders
Sewage disposal
Trade waste
Water pollution

Cost
Rates periodically adjusted to meet expenses; San Bernadino, Calif. il Am City 81:26 N '66

Federal aid
First field grants for refuse disposal. Am City 81:36 D '66

REFUSE collection. See Refuse and refuse disposal

REFUSE collection trucks
Big transfer trailer; Winter Park. Fla. R. G. Simmons. il Am City 81:108-9 O '66

REFUSE containers. See Refuse receptacles

REFUSE grinders
Electric waste disposers. House & Gard 130: 38+ S '66
Food waste disposers. il Consumer Rep 31: 117-23 Mr '66
Good riddance! il McCalls 93:52+ Mr '66
No cover material needed for converted refuse; Wheatley, Oxfordshire, England. il Am City 81:18 F '66

REFUSE incinerators
Change the landscape to sell the incinerator; Ft. Lauderdale. J. Lewis. il Am City 81:26 Jl '66
Smile, your incinerator is on TV; Oyster Bay, N.Y. V. J. Cerniglia and A. Friedland. il Am City 81:110-12 Ap '66
Solid-waste disposal: incineration and composting. R. R. Fleming. bibliog il Am City 81:94-6 F '66
Swiss engineers explain incinerator income. il Am City 81:24 Je '66

REFUSE receptacles
Copolymer plastic refuse-can liners. il Am City 81:100-1 Je '66
Good riddance! il McCalls 93:52+ Mr '66
It straddles the car's hump; tote box. il Sunset 137:89 Jl '66
New lights make a city garbage-pail conscious; Long Beach, N.Y. F. E. Vogel. il Am City 81:111 Jl '66

REGAN, Phil
Vulture. por Newsweek 68:73 O 3 '66

REGATTAS
Bermuda's Whartons are sunfish sovereigns. F. Rohr. il Motor B 117:136-7+ F '66
Founding the Frostbite fleet; 36th annual regatta. il Newsweek 69:8 Ja 9 '67
Month in yachting. See issues of Yachting
Now there's even a regatta for houseboats; International houseboat regatta, Ohio River, Louisville, Ky. P. Hadley. il Pop Sci 189:142-5 O '66
Old-timers race on San Francisco Bay; Master mariners' regatta. il Sunset 136:62+ My '66
One-of-a-kind regatta; special report. B. Robinson. il Yachting 119:55-64+ My '66
Out island regatta is in. R. W. Carrick. il Motor B 117:114-17+ Ja '66
Regatta circuit. il Yachting 120:36-40+ O '66
Regatta results. See issues of Yachting
Salty centennial at Copenhagen. E. F. Haylock. il Motor B 118:32-3+ Ag '66
Southern cruising almanac; Florida and Bahamas events. il Motor B 118:22-5 O '66
Sporting scene; Henley royal regatta. R. Angell. New Yorker 42:92+ Ag 27 '66
Sporting show for Henley and Harvard; Henley royal regatta il Life 61:30-1 Jl 15 '66
Then and now, yachting on the Chesapeake. W. L. Henderson. il Yachting 119:66-7+ Mr '66
They sail to win; reflections on the One-of-a-kind races. B. Bavier. il Yachting 119:62-3+ Je '66
Transatlantic skippers toast the centenary of the Royal Danish yacht club. il Motor B 118:78-9 D '66

REGENERATION (biology)
Hemopoietic colony-forming units in regenerating mouse liver; suppression by anticoagulants. M. L. Varon and L. J. Cole. bibliog il Science 153:643-4 Ag 5 '66
Regeneration in spinal neurons: proteosynthesis following nerve growth factor administration. D. Scott, jr. and others. bibliog il Science 152:787-8 My 6 '66

REGENTS American publishing corporation
Merger terms set for S&S, Regents publishing Pub W 190:39 O 17 '66
S&S and Regents publishing in merger negotiations. Pub W 190:37 Ag 1 '66

REGER, Max
Max Reger festival. P. J. Korn. por Hi Fi 16:MA20-1 Ag '66

REGIONAL airlines. See Local service airlines

REGIONAL campuses. See Colleges and universities—Off-campus centers

REGIONAL high schools. See Consolidated schools

REGIONAL libraries. See Libraries, Regional

REGIONAL planning
Design for Washington state; citizens go into action. il Parks & Rec 1:834-5 O '66
How Washington would remake the map of the U.S. il Nations Bsns 54:31-3+ Jl '66
Keeping suburbia green; the land trust. Newsweek 68:33 N 28 '66
Old steel valley starts to shake off its grime; mill towns along Monongahela. il Bsns W p72-3+ Ja 22 '66
Shaping the community in an era of dynamic social change; with introd. by M. F. Schmertz. il Arch Rec 140:189-206 Jl '66

REISS, Alvin H.
Lincoln Center syndrome. Esquire 66:94+ **Ag** '66

REISS, Franklin J.
Is now the time to buy farmland? Suc Farm 64:48H Jl '66

REISS, George R.
Flying clubs. Flying 78:111 F '66

REISSUES of phonograph records. See Phonograph records—Reissues

REIST, Benjamin A.
Life in the old boys yet! Christian Cent 83:1179-80 S 28 '66

REITH, Marian
800 volunteers and an upright idiot. R. Lynes. il Harper 234:24-6 Ja '67

REITZ, Charles J.
Pacific Southwest. por Parks & Rec 1:634 Ag '66

REJECTED manuscripts. See Editors and editing

REJECTEES, Rehabilitation of. See Military service—Physical and mental fitness

REJECTIONS, Army. See Military service—Physical and mental fitness

REJUVENATION
Stay young with ions. T. W. Hill. il Sci Digest 61:74-7 Ja '67

RELATIVES
Shake hands with my yafney; new words for in-laws. H. A. Smith. McCalls 93:144 Mr '66

RELATIVISTIC quantum field theory. See Quantum field theory

RELATIVITY (physics)
Proving Einstein right; Stanford experiment to orbit perfect gyroscope. il Time 87:58-9 Ap 22 '66
Relativity in 500 words. I. Asimov. Sci Digest 59:82-3 My '66
Soviets disclose orbiting of atomic clock; Cosmos 97 to check Einstein's theory of relativity. Aviation W 85:36 N 21 '66
Test theory of relativity. Sci N 89:309 Ap 30 '66
See also
Light—Velocity
Quantum field theory
Quantum theory

RELAXACIZOR. See Exercising equipment

RELAY running. See Running

RELAY transmitters. See Radio relay systems

RELAYS
See also
Electric relays

RELIABILITY control. See Quality control

RELIABILITY of products. See Quality of products

RELIEF work
See also
Charities
Food relief
International voluntary workcamps
Medical relief work
Vietnamese war, 1957- —Relief work

Vietnam (Republic)
See also
Medical relief work—Vietnam (Republic)

RELIGION
Beyond the new orthodoxy; unorthodox notions of Father Boyd. il Time 88:85-6 O 7 '66
Business, social progress and religion; address October 27, 1966. R. Moreell. Vital Speeches 33:119-25 D 1 '66
Can organized religion be unethical? P. C. Empie. Ann Am Acad 363:70-8 Ja '66
Entertainment; Fr Boyd at the hungry i, San Francisco. L. Kinsolving. Christian Cent 83:1244 O 12 '66; Reply. B. D. Napier. 83:1411 N 16 '66
Nightclub priest: Father Boyd. S. Alexander. Life 61:29 O 28 '66
Opinion: on living religion. M. Boyd. Mlle 64:34+ D '66
Youth and the hazards of affluence, by G. B. Blaine, jr. Review
Christian Cent 83:1310-13 O 26 '66. L. J. Putnam
See also
Atheism
Authority (religion)
Christian life
Christianity
Faith
God
Humanism
Life
Mysticism
Mythology
Philosophy
Piety
Public schools and religion

Rationalism
Religions
Revelation
Secularism
Supernatural
Television broadcasting—Religious programs
Theism
Theology
Women and religion
Worship
Youth—Religion

Bibliography
Books to come; ed. by J. Putnam. Library J 92:139-40+ Ja 1 '67
Religious books; some spring highspots January-May. il Pub W 189:63-90 F 14 '66
Religious books to come; ed. by J. Putnam and K. Ahrens. Library J 91:3978-93 S 1 '66
See also
Catholic literature—Bibliography

Study and teaching
Faith & learning at Stanford. il Time 88:100 N 25 '66
Studying God on campus. il Time 87:72+ F 4 '66
Teaching the facts of faith. il Time 88:61 D 23 '66
See also
Chicago. University—Federated theological faculty

RELIGION and art. See Art and religion

RELIGION and business. See Business ethics

RELIGION and communism. See Communism and religion

RELIGION and education. See Public schools and religion

RELIGION and higher education. See Church and education

RELIGION and labor. See Church and labor

RELIGION and medicine. See Medicine and religion

RELIGION and philosophy. See Philosophy and religion

RELIGION and politics. See Church and politics

RELIGION and psychiatry. See Psychiatry and religion

RELIGION and science
Clergy-scientist dialogue. K. A. Leach. Christian Cent 83:244 F 23 '66
Fresh look at man; excerpt from Teilhard de Chardin and the mystery of Christ. C. F. Mooney. Sat R 49:20-4 F 26 '66
Galileo, science and the church, by J. J. Langford. Review
Commonweal 85:144+ N 4 '66. T. P. McTighe
Life in a test tube. P. R. Gastonguay. Cath World 204:27-31 O '66
Reflections on biological engineering. G. M. Schurr. Christian Cent 83:1300-3 O 26 '66
Science and contemporary theology. R. B. McLaren. Bul Atomic Sci 22:25-6 Mr '66
What modern science offers the church. E. G. Mesthene. Sat R 49:29-31+ N 19 '66

RELIGION and sex. See Sex and religion

RELIGION and social problems. See Church and social problems

RELIGION and sociology
See also
Sociology, Christian

RELIGION and state. See Church and state

RELIGION and war. See War and religion

RELIGION in fiction. See Religion in literature

RELIGION in literature
Japanese—Catholic novel; persecution of Catholics in Japan, theme of The silence. M. Gallagher. Commonweal 85:136-8 N 4 '66

RELIGION in the public schools. See Public schools and religion

RELIGIONS
Profile of world religions: where does religion end and politics begin? il Sr Schol 89:pt2 11-12 S 23 '66
See also
Christian Science
Ethical culture society
Hinduism
Zoroastrianism

RELIGIONS (proposed, universal, etc)
Religions of the future. America 115:793 D 17 '66

RELIGIOUS advertising
No spot for God: refusal of Chicago's WBBM-TV to run National council of churches' spot announcements. il Newsweek 68:84 Jl 25 '66
See also
Church advertising

RELIGIOUS advertising—*Continued*

Anecdotes, facetiae, satire, etc.

O oikoumene! Christian Cent 83:1395 N 9 '66

RELIGIOUS architecture. See Church architecture

RELIGIOUS art. See Christian art and symbolism

RELIGIOUS bigotry. See Toleration

RELIGIOUS books. See Religious literature

RELIGIOUS conferences

Bible-whackers in Berlin; World congress on evangelism. il Newsweek 68:62 N 14 '66

Catholic inter-American program. G. F. Hall. Christian Cent 83:248-50 F 23 '66

Contemporary theological institute; third annual meeting, report. A. Padovano. Christian Cent 83:1062-4 Ag 31 '66

Evangelical congress on worldwide mission; Wheaton, Ill. college campus April 9-16, 1966. M. Shelly. Christian Cent 83:695-7 My 25 '66

From churches to church; International convention of Christian churches, Dallas. Christian Cent 83:1231-2 O 12 '66; Reply. R. W. Huston. 83:1446 N 23 '66

From handholding to engagement; Consultation on church union. il Time 87:86 My 13 '66

Methodists and the urban scene; fourth quadrennial convocation on urban life. A. P. Klausler. Christian Cent 83:348-50 Mr 16 '66

Notre Dame conference; international conference on the theological issues of Vatican II. J. O'Gara. Commonweal 84:98 Ap 15 '66

Princeton meeting on renewal. G. Fackre. Christian Cent 83:1095-8 S 7 '66

Protestantism at Notre Dame conference; conference on theological issues of Vatican council II. W. B. Blakemore. Christian Cent 83:506-10 Ap 20 '66

Protestants united; Dallas meeting of Consultation on church union. il Newsweek 67:103 My 16 '66

St Xavier symposium on theological tasks. Christian Cent 83:562+ Ap 27 '66

Spree was grey; World congress on evangelism. H. O. J. Brown. Nat R 18:1324-5 D 27 '66

S.D.S. camps on the old campground; North Iowa Methodist annual conference. P. B. Mather. Christian Cent 83:1251-2 O 12 '66

See also

Asian faith and order conference

Conference of religious, philosophic and ethic nonconformists

Consultation on church union

World council of churches

RELIGIOUS contemplation. See Meditation

RELIGIOUS cooperation

Baptist-Catholic dialogue; plans for pastoral talks. Christian Cent 83:769 Je 15 '66

Baptist students select Catholic adviser; Christian association council at Meredith college, Raleigh, N.C. Christian Cent 84:5 Ja 4 '67

Changing mood. R. Cornwall. America 114:873-5 Je 25 '66

Channel opening for East-West church study. M. Bourdeaux. Christian Cent 83:1482 N 30 '66

Ecumenical high school. O. J. Murdick. America 115:780-1 D 10 '66

Ecumenical spirit. Easter, 1966. Life 60:4 Ap 8 '66

Ecumenical way of learning; Manhattan's Protestant union theological seminary and Fordham university exchange projects. Time 87:86 Mr 4 '66

Four for St Mark's; first joint Protestant-Roman Catholic congregation; Kansas City, Mo. il Time 88:65 Jl 22 '66

I joined the ministerial education. E. E. Ryan. America 115:158-9 Ag 13 '66

Inter-communion barrier. Time 87:56 F 25 '66

MUST; project for urban service. D. M. Lindsey. Christian Cent 83:1041-2 Ag 24 '66

Opportunity knocks. il Newsweek 68:105 O 24 '66

Plan ecumenical theology center; Catholic seminary foundation of Indianapolis and the Christian theological seminary of the Christian churches. Christian Cent 83:1529 D 14 '66

Portland's interfaith testimony for peace; successive prayer services. R. Rumsey. Christian Cent 83:1554 D 14 '66

Princeton meeting on renewal. G. Fackre. Christian Cent 83:1095-8 S 7 '66

Road between Rome and Jerusalem. S. Sandmel. Sat R 49:42-3 D 3 '66

Something new in ecumenism; Seattle, Wash. America 115:533 N 5 '66

Speaking out; don't try to sell me your religion. H. Singer. il Sat Eve Post 240:10+ Ja 28 '67

See also

International conference of Christians and Jews

Bibliography

Renewal. G. Fackre. Christian Cent 84:50+ Ja 11 '67

RELIGIOUS discussion. See Discussion

RELIGIOUS drama

Whitney, jazz and folk; E. Bonnemere's Missa hodierna, mass in jazz. C. J. McNaspy. America 115:465-7 O 15 '66

See also

Drama, Medieval

Miracle, morality and mystery plays

RELIGIOUS education

Declaration on Christian education. Sch & Soc 94:284-7 Sum '66

Religion and the schools. E. Wakin. Sat R 49:85-6 Mr 19 '66

Statement on teaching religion. America 116:16-20 Ja 7 '67

See also

Catechetics

Catholic church—Education

Church schools

Confraternity of Christian doctrine

Denominational colleges

Sunday schools

Theological education

RELIGIOUS faith. See Faith

RELIGIOUS films. See Moving pictures—Religious films

RELIGIOUS freedom. See Religious liberty

RELIGIOUS institutions and affairs

World around us. See issues of Christian century

See also subhead Religious institutions and affairs under names of countries, e.g. Japan—Religious institutions and affairs

RELIGIOUS intermarriage. See Marriages, Mixed

RELIGIOUS liberty

Conscience and orthodoxy. D. Callahan. Commonweal 84:53-5 Ap 1 '66; Discussion. 84:240-1, 320-1 My 13, Je 3 '66

Declaration on religious freedom: its deeper significance; address. J. C. Murray. America 114:592-3 Ap 23 '66

Ecumenical symposium. A. P. Klausler. Christian Cent 83:376-8 Mr 23 '66

Freedom, authority, community. J. C. Murray. America 115:734-7+ D 3 '66

Freedom today, by H. Kung. Review Cath World 202:371 Mr '66. J. B. Sheerin

Freedom under church law; excerpt from address, October 16, 1965. T. M. Cunningham. Cath World 202:348-53 Mr '66

Judges v. jailers; case of W. Howard at Virginia state prison. Time 88:69 S 16 '66

Liberty within the Catholic church. P. Blanshard. Cath World 203:335-40 S '66

Of many things; final passage of the Spanish draft law. T. N. Davis. America 116:1 Ja 7 '67

Personal freedom and community responsibility. C. R. McCarthy. Cath World 203:165-8 Je '66

Religion in Spain. Commonweal 85:392-3 Ja 13 '67

Religious liberty: an end and a beginning. ed. by J. C. Murray. Review Nat R 18:1228-30 N 29 '66. W. Herberg

Religious liberty: toward consensus. D. M. Kelley and C. D. Nelson. Christian Cent 83:651-3 My 18 '66

Spain finds an excuse. S. I. Stuber. Christian Cent 83:1246 O 12 '66

See also

Institute for freedom in the Church

RELIGIOUS literature

Media spokesmen tell how religious books make news; summary of panel discussion. Pub W 190:39-40 N 7 '66

Religious books are news. C. B. Grannis. Pub W 190:112 S 26 '66

Religious books: some fall highspots, September-December (cont) il Pub W 190:65-94 S 26 '66

See also

Booksellers and bookselling—Religious literature

Publishers and publishing—Religious literature

RELIGIOUS music. See Church music

RELIGIOUS newspapers and periodicals
Baltimore sets an example; how a diocesan newspaper makes itself relevant to its readers and its region. America 115:87 Jl 23 '66
See also
Associated church press (organization)
Dialogue (periodical)
Katallagete (periodical)
Liturgical arts quarterly
Motive (periodical)
RELIGIOUS orders
See also
Sisterhoods
Vocation (in religion)
RELIGIOUS persecution. See Persecution
RELIGIOUS poetry
See also
Hymns
RELIGIOUS poverty. See Poverty (virtue)
RELIGIOUS publishers group. See American book publishers council—Religious publishers group
RELIGIOUS records. See Phonograph records—Religious records
RELIGIOUS schools. See Church schools; Sunday schools
RELIGIOUS services. See Church services
RELIGIOUS statistics
See also
Church statistics
RELIGIOUS supplies. See Church supplies
RELIGIOUS theater. See Theater
RELIGIOUS vocation. See Vocation (in religion)
RELISHES. See Pickles and relishes
REMARRIAGE
Marriage, divorce and remarriage. F. R. Schreiber and M. Herman. il Sci Digest 60: 24-7 N '66
Rocky road to remarriage; excerpts from The world of the formerly married. M. M. Hunt. il Mc Calls 94:126-7+ O '66
REMBRANDT Hermanszoon van Rijn
Golden age of Rembrandt; loan exhibition. A. Werner. il Reporter 35:34-6 D 29 '66
REMEDIAL reading. See Reading—Remedial teaching
REMEDIAL teaching
See also
Reading—Remedial teaching
REMEDIES (in medicine) See Therapeutics
REMEMBER Charlie Mock? story. See Cochrane, S. G.
REMENSNYDER, John P.
Potters of Poughkeepsie. Antiques 90:90-5 Jl '66
REMICK, Lee
Lee Remick soars in a sightless role. D. Chapman. il pors Look 30:112-13+ My 17 '66
REMINDERS. See Memorandums
REMINGTON, Phil
Phil Remington, man of many talents. R. Brock. il pors Hot Rod 19:79-81 D '66
REMINGTON arms company
Happy birthday. W. Page. il Field & S 70: 130-3 Ap '66
REMINISCENCE
Life for life. R. Price. Esquire 66:246 D '66
Reflections of a non-travel writer. J. O'Hara. il Holiday 41:24+ Ja '67
Secret; a recollection. T. Torres. Commonweal 85:345-8 D 23 '66
Some things I miss. C. Ford. il Todays Health 44:26-7 S '66
REMMERT-Werner, incorporated
Eastern moving to diversification with Remmert-Werner acquisition. D. A. Brown. Aviation W 85:41 S 19 '66
Foes of Eastern-Remmert cloud airline diversification. Aviation W 85:33 O 17 '66
REMODELED airplanes. See Airplanes, Remodeled
REMODELED buildings. See Buildings, Remodeled
REMODELED houses. See Houses, Remodeled
REMODELING (architecture)
Art moves into an old railroad station; Maryland institute, College of art, Baltimore. il Fortune 73:170 My '66
Artist's act of faith: a testimony of peace. il House & Gard 130:160-3 D '66
Industry builds a showcase in the slums; U.S. gypsum's experiment in Harlem. il Bsns W p40-1 F 26 '66
Look what happened to their old garage. il Sunset 136:76-7 F '66
Old city hall gets a new face; Lamesa, Tex. C. A. Taylor. il Am City 81:91 Mr '66

Remodeling's rewards. il House & Gard 130: 79-99 Ag '66
Renovate or rebuild? Hollidaysburg, Pa. J. M. Mitchell. il Am City 81:147-8+ O '66
Station saved for art's sake; B&O's Mt Royal station into an art school. J. Bailey. il Arch Forum 125:52-7 S '66
See also
Buildings, Remodeled
Houses, Remodeled
REMOTE control
Carrier-current remote-control system. R. Zarr. il Pop Electr 26:50-3 Ja '67
REMOVAL of paint. See Paint—Removal
REMSBERG, Bonnie. See Remsberg, C. jt. auth.
REMSBERG, Charles
Day the mails stopped. Sat R 49:21-4 D 17 '66
—and Remsberg, Bonnie
Plastic surgery goes to prison. Todays Health 44:38-41 Ap '66
Wooing the dimply, pimply. N Y Times Mag p 100-2 Je 5 '66
RENAISSANCE
Renaissance and revolution. by J. A. Mazzeo. Review
Nation 202:788-9 Je 27 '66. A. Heiserman Sat R 49:34-5 Mr 12 '66
RENAULT automobile company. See Automobile industry and trade—France
RENDEZVOUS (space) See Orbital rendezvous (space flight)
RENEK, Morris
Boss Tweed's dynasty. New Repub 156:35-6 Ja 14 '67
Community hospital in the ghetto. New Repub 155:9 D 10 '66
Down and out. New Repub 155:28+ N 5 '66
New windows on poverty. New Repub 155: 23-5 D 3 '66
RENEWAL movement. See Religious cooperation
RENIN
Increased cardiovascular reactivity to angiotensin caused by renin. G. M. C. Masson and others bibliog il Science 153:1002-4 Ag 26 '66
RENNER, Max
Time and space in the life of the bee. Natur Hist 75:52-7 O '66
RENNER, Richard R.
NSF fellowships to foreign scientists. Sch & Soc 94:146+ Mr 19 '66
RENO, Nev.
Description
Changeover. M. F. K. Fisher. New Yorker 42:43-5 My 14 '66
RENOIR, Auguste
Diary of a Paris art dealer; excerpts from Diary of an art dealer. R. Gimpel. Vogue 148:275+ O 1 '66
RENSHAW cells. See Spinal cord
RENSSELAER polytechnic institute, Troy, N.Y.
Supermice of another Troy; RPI football. H. Weiskopf. Sports Illus 25:63-4 O 3 '66
RENSTROM, Richard
Honda Grand prix four. Hot Rod 19:84-6 S '66
Trail bikes for sportsmen. Field & S 71:48-51+ D '66
RENSVOLD, Verna
Midwest. por Parks & Rec 1:635 Ag '66
RENT
Looking for a place to rent? il Changing T 20:35-7 N '66
RENTAL services
Villa vacations; renting houses abroad through agents in the U.S. C. Meyer. House & Gard 129:72+ My '66
You name it, we rent it. H. Manchester. il Read Digest 89:114-16 Jl '66
See also subhead Renting under various subjects, e.g. Motor vehicles—Renting
RENTON, Wash. public library
Renton bridges a river. M. Hillgen. il Library J 91:5864-6 D 1 '66
RENZELMAN, Marilyn
Poems: Cinderella revisited; Convalescent. Good H 162:189 My '66
REORGANIZATION (business) See Business management and organization
REORGANIZED church of Jesus Christ of Latter day saints
Other saints. il Time 87:74 Ap 29 '66
REOVIRUSES. See Viruses
REPAIR parts
How to make money out of obsolescence; replacement parts for obsolete electrical apparatus. il Bsns W p80-2 F 5 '66

REPAIR shops
  See also
  Automobile service stations
REPAIRING
  Simple confession; author's war with the inanimate. A. Gingrich. il Esquire 65:82-3+ Mr '66
  See also
  Calking
  Houses—Maintenance and repair
  also subhead Repairing under various subjects, e.g. Clocks—Repairing
REPARATION
  Break for the victim; cases of the Criminal injuries compensation board in England. Time 87:78+ Je 10 '66
  Indemnifying the victims. New Repub 154:6 F 26 '66
  Victim-induced criminality; proposals for compensation of victims. M. Fooner. bibliog Science 153:1080-3 S 2 '66
REPARATIONS (European war, 1914-1918) See European war, 1914-1918—Reparations
REPARTEE. See Conversation
REPELLENTS, Deer. See Deer repellents
REPERTORY companies. See Theater—United States
REPERTORY theater. See Theater
REPERTORY theater of Lincoln Center for the performing arts. See Lincoln Center repertory theater company
REPKE, Doris I. See Katz, A. M. jt. auth.
REPLACEMENT parts. See Repair parts
REPORT; story. See Gallant, M.
REPORTERS and reporting
  All the way with LBJ; covering the Pacific trip. il Newsweek 68:68 O 31 '66
  Camera obscura; disparate readings of Hawaiian conference. Time 87:41 F 18 '66
  Communicating research on the poor; the problem of telling it like it is; some ways of telling it; address. L. P. Jackson, jr. bibliog Negro Hist Bul 29:151-2+ Ap '66
  Crime reporting; need for professionals; address, February 14, 1966. N. deB. Katzenbach. Vital Speeches 32:351-2 Mr 15 '66
  Distorted cry? U.S. press and projection of black power. Newsweek 68:54 Ag 8 '66
  Errors of our ways. J. O'Hara. il Holiday 40:22+ D '66
  Good times in Texas; White House press corps welcomed to San Antonio. il Time 87:77 Mr 18 '66
  Help wanted; American newspaper publishers association recruitment campaign. il Newsweek 68:68+ O 31 '66
  Hot on the line; H. Romanoff. Time 88:56-7 Jl 29 '66
  Instinct for the Orient; R. S. Elegant. il Time 88:68+ S 9 '66
  Junkets to apartheid; America's press on safari; free trips to South Africa. F. Pollock. Nation 203:479-81 N 7 '66
  Letter from the publisher; coverage of Johnson's southeast Asia trip. B. M. Auer. Time 88:23 N 4 '66
  Mollenhoff cocktail. il Time 88:35 Ag 12 '66
  Newsman's lot. F. Cormier; S. Ramsey. il Sat R 49:70-3+ S 10 '66
  Operation disparagement; Washington correspondents. Nation 202:349 Mr 28 '66
  Opinionmakers, by W. L. Rivers. Review Commentary 41:98-100 Mr '66. B. D. Nossiter
  Personal voice and the impersonal eye; how to raise reporting to an art. D. Wakefield. il Atlan 217:86-90 Je '66
  Please don't steal my reporters. F. B. Gilbreth. Sat R 49:119-20+ O 8 '66
  Pollycassandra; reporters, chroniclers and pundits usually wrong or absurd or both. J. Burnham. Nat R 18:720 Jl 26 '66
  Pops and boppers; pop beat of R. Goldstein. il Newsweek 68:66 D 19 '66
  Press in Washington, by R. E. Heibert. Review Sat R 49:80 Ap 9 '66. J. F. Fixx
  Racial news gap. A. Balk. Sat R 49:53-4 Ag 13 '66
  Reporter on the UN beat. H. Pick. il Nation 202:648-50 My 30 '66
  Responsible muckraker: J. Ridgeway. il Time 87:74 Ja 28 '66
  Soviet self-criticism; Soviet journalists. Time 88:74 O 28 '66
  Surgical spectacular; reporting the DeBakey operation on Marcel DeRudder. Nation 202:540 My 9 '66
  Sweetheart of Sigma delta chi; concerning R. H. Fleming's remarks. Time 87:79 Ap 29 '66

  Trials of statehouse journalism. T. Littlewood. Sat R 49:82-3 D 10 '66
  Use & misuse of politicians. Time 88:92+ N 11 '66
  Where are today's muckrakers? A. Weinberg and L. Weinberg. Sat R 49:54-5 Jl 9 '66
  See also
  Crime and the press
  Foreign correspondents
  Higgins, M.
  Interviewing
  News
  Newspaper court reporting
  Newspapers—Crime reporting
  Press conferences
  Radio broadcasting—Sports
  Sports journalism
  Women as reporters
REPORTS
  Behind the color; a new frankness; annual reports. il Bsns W p 123-4+ Ap 2 '66
  How to give a really good report on a meeting. L. Lane. Farm J 90:95 O '66
  Tips you can dig out of financial reports. il Changing T 20:29-31 Mr '66
REPORTS, Library. See Library reports
REPPERT, John E.
  Hutch-style planter for the wall. Pop Sci 189:178-9 O '66
REPRESENTATIVE government and representation
  See also
  Apportionment (election law)
  Parliamentary government
REPRESENTATIVES, Congressional. See Congressmen
REPRESENTATIVES, Presidential. See Public officers
REPRINTS. See Periodicals—Reprints
REPRODUCTION
  Antarctic asteroid odontaster validus; constancy of reproductive periodicities. J. S. Pearse. bibliog il Science 152:1763-4 Je 24 '66
  Control systems in bird reproduction; hypothalamus regulates avian breeding activity. D. S. Farner. il Natur Hist 75:22-7 Ag '66
  New facts about human reproduction. J. D. Ratcliff. Read Digest 89:119-22 D '66
  Reproduction in lizards; influence of temperature on photoperiodism in testicular recrudescence. P. Licht. bibliog il Science 154:1668-70 D 30 '66
  Reproductive failure; report on first conference on Comparative aspects of reproductive failure. E. S. E. Hafez. Science 154:546+ O 28 '66
  Solid sex-education program; L. Smith's sixth grade class on human reproduction, University City, Mo. il Look 30:24-5 Mr 8 '66
  Tree shrews; unique reproductive mechanism of systematic importance. R. D. Martin. bibliog il Science 152:1402-4 Je 3 '66
  See also
  Estruation
  Fertility
  Fertility, Human
REPRODUCTIONS of works of art
  See also
  Prints—Circulation, loans, etc.
REPTILES
  Cutaneous water loss in reptiles. P. J. Bentley and K. Schmidt-Nielsen. bibliog il Science 151:1547-9 Mr 25 '66; Discussion. 152:1523 Je 10 '66
  See also
  Alligators
  Chameleons
  Horned toads
  Snakes
REPTILES, Fossil
  See also
  Dinosaurs
REPUBLIC aviation division. See Fairchild Hiller corporation
REPUBLIC-Florida collision. See Collisions at sea
REPUBLIC of the Philippines. See Philippines
REPUBLICAN clubs. See Political clubs and associations
REPUBLICAN party
  All quiet on the western front; Republican governors conference. Nat R 18:1303-4 D 27 '66
  Analyzing the swing to the right wing; California primary. il Newsweek 67:32 Je 20 '66
  Another Democratic Congress, but by less; gain by GOP, likely. il Bsns W p42-3 S 10 '66
  Answer please, Mr Nixon. Nat R 18:196 Mr 8 '66; Discussion. 18:294+, 304 Ap 5 '66

REPUBLICAN party—*Continued*

As Republican governors look over the ranks for '68. il U S News 61:37-8 D 26 '66
Back to Goldwater? A. Kopkind. New Repub 155:12-13 S 17 '66
Back to the middle way. il Bsns W p39-40 N 12 '66
Best Republican for '68. S. V. Roberts. il Esquire 65:84-5+ Mr '66
Big Republican opportunity; address, March 20, 1966. R. R. Spitzer. Vital Speeches 32:472-7 My 15 '66
Big three among Republican governors, what they urge; In the Senate, accent on newcomers. il U S News 62:17-18 Ja 16 '67
Business and the G.O.P. J. Berry; reply. B. Goldwater. Duns R 87:16 Ja '66
Challenge of change, by E. W. Brooke. Review
    Reporter 35:46+ D 1 '66. M. F. Nolan
    Sat R 49:46-7 Ap 23 '66. L. L. L. Golden
Consensus by any other name; G. Romney & N. Rockefeller in Puerto Rico. il Time 88: 21-2 D 2 '66
Consensus government and the opposition role; economic program for Republicans; address, March 21, 1966. J. K. Javits. Vital Speeches 32:391-3 Ap 15 '66
Conservative tide; California's gubernatorial primaries. il Newsweek 67:31-2 Je 20 '66
Conservatives. si. M. S. Evans. Nat R 18: 1091-3+ N 1 '66
Cooling the convention; suggest informal platform-drafting convention. Time 87:29A Mr 18 '66
Coordinating the GOP; Coordinating committee takes over the preliminaries of framing party issues. R. Moley. Newsweek 69:72 Ja 9 '67
Counting chickens; chance of GOP regaining presidency. K. Crawford. Newsweek 68:35 D 12 '66
Dawk talk; Viet Nam as an election issue. il Time 88:20 S 30 '66
Death of the New deal. W. D. Burnham. Commonweal 85:284-7 D 9 '66
Dilemma in Dixie. Time 87:21-2 Ap 22 '66
Dorado summit. il Newsweek 68:30-1 D 5 '66
Elephant is tempted. Nation 203:498 N 14 '66
Elephant lives. il Sat Eve Post 239:92 D 17 '66
Four hearties of the good ship G.O.P. W. Weaver, jr. il N Y Times Mag p50-1+ N 27 '66
Governors; Republican sweep. il U S News 61:45-6 N 21 '66
Governors to the front. R. Moley. Newsweek 68:76 D 26 '66
GOP and the UN. Nat R 18:819 Ag 23 '66
GOP backs a new kind of candidate; younger, more attractive, more positive than the old guard. il Bsns W p45-7 O 8 '66
GOP in the South. R. Moley. Newsweek 67: 108 My 9 '66
GOP: it's Romney vs. Nixon; with report by J. Lindsay. il Newsweek 67:23 Je 6 '66
GOP '66; back on the map; election results, with table. il Newsweek 68:31-4 N 21 '66
G.O.P. stars who came on strong. il Life 61:44-44B N 18 '66
GOP's hopes come up to the test. il Bsns W p35-6 O 29 '66
Grand old players; New York state legislators receive coaching in vote-getting art. G. Ace. Sat R 49:8 Ag 20 '66
How the future looks to Republicans now. il U S News 61:36+ Jl 4 '66
How to succeed; successful failures. K. Crawford. Newsweek 68:28 D 19 '66
Ideas in action; relations between the academic community and elected representatives; address. December 4, 1965. S. Horn. Vital Speeches 32:283-8 F 15 '66
Importance of Reagan. F. S. Meyer. Nat R 18:1315 D 27 '66
Is there a Republican party? il Sat Eve Post 239:98 Mr 12 '66
Issues that will tip the '66 elections. C. B. Seib. il Nations Bsns 54:38-9+ Mr '66
Key Republicans with new stature. il U S News 61:26-7 N 21 '66
Letter from Washington. R. H. Rovere. New Yorker 42:197-201 N 19 '66
Life in the elephant. Nation 202:444 Ap 18 '66
LBJ vs. which Republican in '68? il U S News 61:50-2 N 21 '66
Man of the year for Republicans. U S News 60:16 F 7 '66
Memo from Washington; who will control the GOP in 1968? W. Rogers. Look 31:76 Ja 24 '67
Minor masterpiece of Ray C. Bliss. A. L. Otten and C. B. Seib. Reporter 34:35-8 F 10 '66

Must Republicans be cannibals? Nat R 18: 146 F 22 '66
Never again? conservatives, stronger than ever. Newsweek 68:24 S 12 '66
New hope for Republicans. A. Kopkind. New Repub 154:15-18 Mr 5 '66
1968 already. Nat R 18:450 My 17 '66
90th Congress; the men; the issues. il Bsns W p41-4 N 12 '66
90th girds for battle. il Newsweek 69:24-7 Ja 23 '67
Nixon and the GOP: comeback? il Newsweek 68:30-5 O 10 '66
Order of battle; a Republican's call to reason, by J. K. Javits. Review
    New Repub 155:20-2 S 3 '66. G. W. Johnson
Party for all; election results. il Time 88: 23-8 N 18 '66
Party that lost its head, by G. F. Gilder and B. K. Chapman. Review
    New Repub 154:27-9 Je 25 '66. G. W. Johnson
Peace for Vietnam; GOP's nettle of success. K. H. Purnell. Nation 202:94-6 Ja 24 '66
Plea for positivism; views of E. Brooke. Time 87:18 Mr 25 '66
Plot to steal the GOP. W. A. Rusher. il Nat R 18:668-71 Jl 12 '66
Politics of equivocation; two faces of the GOP. M. Viorst. Nation 203:630-2 D 12 '66
Polls '66; Nixon or Romney? P. Gennoy. Nat R 18:1084 N 1 '66
Pragmatic Republicans; R. Finch's progressive ideas. R. Moley. Newsweek 67:108 Mr 14 '66
Race issue jolts GOP in South. il Bsns W p45-6 O 15 '66
Republican answer to LBJ's program; interview. G. R. Ford. U S News 62:10 Ja 23 '67
Republican comeback? K. Crawford. Newsweek 67:32 F 21 '66
Republican future. C. H. Percy. Sat R 49:19-21 O 29 '66
Republican plan; Laird plan of tax sharing. K. Crawford. Newsweek 68:35 N 28 '66
Republican rebound. America 115:638 N 19 '66
Republicans battle for gains in West, mood of voters; survey. il U S News 61:83-4+ O 10 '66
Republicans win key contests. il Sr Schol 89:23 N 18 '66
Responsibles vs. influentials. Life 60:6 Ap 15 '66
Romney's chances to head ticket in '68. il U S News 61:29-30 D 5 '66
Rowdies and dowdies of the right. Life 60:4 My 20 '66
Semantic tyranny. R. Moley. Newsweek 68: 120 N 28 '66
Squandering Republicans. E. J. Hughes. Newsweek 67:17 Je 27 '66
State of the GOP. D. S. Broder; W. Pincus; T. Wicker. il Atlan 217:64-80 Ap '66
State of the Union; address, January 17, 1966. E. M. Dirksen. Vital Speeches 32:258-9 F 15 '66
State of the Union; address, January 17, 1966. G. R. Ford. Vital Speeches 32:259-61 F 15 '66
State of the Union as Republicans see it; excerpts from addresses, January 17, 1966. M. Dirksen; G. R. Ford. il U S News 60: 72-3 Ja 31 '66
Stop me if you've heard this. Nat R 18:1202+ N 29 '66
T.R.B. from Washington; switch toward the war. New Repub 154:4 F 12 '66
That fragile thing, political popularity. P. Lisagor. il Nations Bsns 54:21-2 Mr '66
Those twenty-five GOP governors; propositions which bear upon the conference, December 9-10. R. Moley. Newsweek 68:116 D 5 '66
Trustee for tomorrow; J. K. Javits. il Time 87:25-9 Je 24 '66
Two for the future; fund-raising dinner for the Nassau County G.O.P. il Time 87:18 Je 3 '66
Two-party system is back. Life 61:4 N 18 '66
Vietnam: the Republican performance. F. S. Meyer. Nat R 18:316 Ap 5 '66
War issue; what it can do for candidates in November election. K. Crawford. Newsweek 68:34 Jl 11 '66
Washington desk; GOP's prospects and campaign issues. J. R. Slevin. Duns R 87:5-6 My '66
What's wrong with the Republican party. E. W. Brooke. il Pub W 189:37-8 Mr 28 '66
Where Republicans hope for gains in November. il U S News 61:28-30 S 5 '66
Who won? analysis of 1966 elections. Nat R 18:1200-2 N 29 '66

RESEARCH—Federal aid—*Continued*
Research policy: trumpets on Capitol hill.
D. S. Greenberg. Science 153:278 Jl 15 '66
Research: the midas touch. H. S. Reuss;
reply with rejoinder. P. Siekevitz. Nation
202:196 F 21 '66
Role of applied science. E. Teller. il Bul
Atomic Sci 22:15-19 Mr '66
Science budget decreased. Sci N L 89:84 F
5 '66
Share the wealth: LBJ directive beginning to
show some effects. D. S. Greenberg. Science
154:1628-9 D 30 '66
Vietnam needs cloud advanced projects; with
table. C. Brownlow. Aviation W 84:16-21
Ja 31 '66
Where the brains are. R. E. Lapp. il For-
tune 73:154-6+ Mr '66
Where the R&D funds are headed. il Bsns
W p 110-12 N 12 '66

International aspects
See Science—International aspects

Study and teaching
That ghastly term paper! D. Klein. il Seventeen 25:162+ D '66

Canada
See also
National research council of Canada

China (People's Republic)
China's push to catch up in science; report
for National science foundation, by C. Y.
Cheng. il Bsns W p 116-20 F 5 '66
First for China; synthesis of insulin by
Chinese researchers. Newsweek 68:70 S 26
'66

Czechoslovakia
Research and industry in Czechoslovakia; In-
stitute of macromolecular chemistry. V. K.
McElheny. Science 153:620-2 Ag 5 '66

Latin America
Organizing scientific research. R. V. Garcia.
Bul Atomic Sci 22:12-15 S '66

Russia
For world science: a bear hug; third Inter-
national congress on metallic corrosion in
Moscow's Sovetskaya hotel. il Bsns W p92+
Je 4 '66
Kapitsa's visit to England. V. K. McElheny.
Science 153:725-7 Ag 12 '66
Science in U.S. far ahead, says top Russian;
nuclear physicist. P. Kapitsa. il Bsns W
p74-5 D 24 '66
Yakovlev urges more integration of Russian
research, production; excerpts from Izvestia
article. A. S. Yakovlev. Aviation W 84:
83+ Ap 25 '66
See also
Atomic research—Russia

United States
Allocating federal support for basic research.
C. Kaysen. Bul Atomic Sci 22:16-22 Ja '66
Allocating support for basic research and
the importance of practical applications.
G. B. Kistiakowsky. Bul Atomic Sci 22:12-
18 F '66
Basic research still strong. F. Marley. Sci N
90:147 S 3 '66
Basic science; quiet progress. R. Yoshioka.
Sci N 90:546 D 24 '66
California: the first mass aristocracy anytime,
anywhere. T. G. Harris. il Look 30:42+ Je
28 '66
Editor comments on space, basic research,
and an International science foundation.
E. Rabinowitch. Bul Atomic Sci 22:2-3 O
'66
Policy shifts mark science's year. W. Korn-
berg. Sci N 90:545 D 24 '66
Pressure on basic research. P. H. Abelson.
Science 153:11 Jl 1 '66
R&D, 1967: $23.8 billion. Sci N 91:40 Ja 14
'67
Research in America. See issues of Saturday
review
Role of applied science. E. Teller. il Bul
Atomic Sci 22:15-19 Mr '66
Science, choice, and human values; address,
October 1965. A. M. Weinberg. il Bul Atomic
Sci 22:8-13 Ap '66
Standards lab broadens its bailiwick; moves
to Gaithersburg, Md. il Bsns W p96-8+ Je
18 '66
See also
Carnegie institution of Washington
Colleges and universities—Research
Government research
Hudson institute, incorporated

Institute for defense analyses
Stanford research institute
United States—National science foundation
United States—Naval research laboratory

RESEARCH, Cooperative
Industry research plan. Sci N 89:279 Ap 16
'66

RESEARCH and engineering council of the
graphic arts industry, incorporated
Photocomposing studied at R&E council
seminar. il Pub W 191:101 Ja 2 '67
R&E council is briefed on new tools from
IBM. il Pub W 189:82-5 My 2 '66
R&E seminar on automation for control in
graphic arts; summary of addresses. Pub
W 189:116+ Mr 7 '66
Systems approach to automation is explained
to R&E council; annual conference. Pub W
189:154-6+ Je 13 '66

RESEARCH and industry. See Industrial research

RESEARCH corporation
Science studies get help. Sci N 89:458 Je
11 '66

RESEARCH in colleges. See Colleges and universities—Research

RESEARCH laboratories
Laboratory as a machine; Standard oil. il
Arch Forum 124:40-7 Ap '66
Small lab has to be different; Bjorksten re-
search laboratories. il Bsns W p90-2+ Ag 27
'66
See also
Atomic research laboratories
Bell telephone laboratories
Corporations, Nonprofit
United States—National aeronautics and
space administration—Electronics research
center

RESEARCH librarians. See Libraries—Reference work

RESEARCH libraries
Crisis in research libraries. V. M. Pings. il
Library J 91:3876-82 S 1 '66; Reply. P. M.
Strain. 91:5282+ N 1 '66

RESEARCH ships. See Ships, Research

RESERPINE
Reserpine: inhibition of olfactory blockage
of pregnancy in mice. C. J. Dominic. bibliog Science 152:1764-5 Je 24 '66

RESERVE forces (United States) See United
States—Armed forces—Reserves

RESERVOIRS
Gigantic reservoir floats a decorous pool; Cin-
cinnati's century-old Eden Park reservoir.
T. M. Taylor. il Am City 81:87-90+ O '66

RESETTLEMENT of refugees. See Refugees—
Resettlement

RESIDENCE halls. See Dormitories

RESINOUS products
See also
Teflon

RESISTANCE in insect control. See Insects,
Injurious and beneficial—Resistance to control

RESISTANCE to drugs. See Drugs, Resistance to

RESISTANCE to government. See Government,
Resistance to; Passive resistance to government

RESISTANCE to Negro segregation. See
Negroes in the United States—Segregation,
Resistance to

RESISTORS, Electric. See Electric resistors

RESNICK, Joseph Yale
Inventor of the month; inventor is a congressman. S. V. Jones. por Sci Digest 59:
21 Je '66

RESNIK, Henry
Hobbit-forming world of J. R. R. Tolkien.
Sat Eve Post 239:90-2+ Jl 2 '66

RESNIK, Regina
Plus one; interview, ed. by J. W. Freeman.
por Opera N 31:13 D 10 '66

RESOLUTIONS
See also
New Year's resolutions

RESORT hotels. See Summer resorts

RESORTS. See Summer resorts; Winter resorts

RESOURCES, Conservation of. See Conservation of resources

RESOURCES, Natural. See Natural resources

RESOURCES and technical services division. See American library association—
Resources and technical services division

RESPIRATION
Airflow control by auditory feedback;
respiratory mechanics and wind instruments. A. Bouhuys. bibliog il Science 154:
797-9 N 11 '66
Anatomy for the ballet teacher; proper
breathing; ed. by W. Como. R. Gelabert.
il Dance Mag 40:78-9 My '66

RESPIRATION—*Continued*
Anxiety and tension may cause over-breathing; hyperventilation. Sci N 90:243 O 1 '66
Nonphosphorylating respiration of mitochondria from brown adipose tissue of rats. R. E. Smith and others. bibliog il Science 154:653-4 N 4 '66
Organic fluids can be breathed by animals. Sci N 90:23 Jl 9 '66
Survival of mammals breathing organic liquids equilibrated with oxygen at atmospheric pressure. L. C. Clark, jr. and F. Gollan. bibliog il Science 152:1755-6 Je 24 '66
Swallowed air causes false angina symptoms. Sci N 90:89 Ag 6 '66
See also
Asphyxia

RESPIRATION, Artificial
Artificial respiration: would you be ready? il Bet Hom & Gard 44:154 Je '66

RESPIRATORY allergy. See Allergy

RESPIRATORY apparatus
Learning to breathe; pressure-limited respirator. il Newsweek 68:57 Ag 1 '66
Lifesaving fog; fog machines aid respiration. T. Berland. il Todays Health 44:22-4+ D '66
Portable resuscitator used by rescue squad. Sci N 89:200 Mr 26 '66

RESPIRATORY organs
See also
Lungs

Diseases
New vaccine reduces respiratory illness. Sci N 89:348 My 7 '66
There's a lot of it going around; acute respiratory disease. Changing T 20:23 F '66
Thing that's going around. B. Davidson. il Sat Eve Post 239:88-90 My 7 '66
See also
Bronchitis
Cold (disease)
Hyaline membrane disease
Influenza
Pneumothorax

RESPONSES to stimuli. See Stimulus and response

RESPONSIBILITY
Former justice warns: return to law, or face anarchy; address, April 12, 1966. C. E. Whittaker. U S News 60:58-60+ Ap 25 '66
From Grenada, Mississippi, a minister warns Christians: stand up or get out! C. B. Burt. il Look 30:34+ D 27 '66
Needed: party responsibility. D. Lawrence. U S News 61:140 N 21 '66
Personal freedom and community responsibility. C. R. McCarthy. Cath World 203:165-8 Je '66
Quotes of the week; ed. by D. Lawrence. U S News 61:96 Ag 22 '66
Reduction of human misery; address, January 15, 1966. H. Ford, 2d. Vital Speeches 32:278-80 F 15 '66

RESPONSIBILITY (law) See Liability (law)

RESS, Paul Evan
Tennis. Sports Illus 24:80+ Je 13 '66

REST homes. See Nursing homes

RESTAURANT guide books. See Guidebooks

RESTAURANTS
See also subhead Hotels, restaurants, etc. under names of cities, e.g. New York (city)—Hotels, restaurants, etc.

Automation
Computerburgers hit the assembly line; an automated drive-in restaurant. C. B. Hicks. il Pop Mech 126:80-3 S '66
Dining in/out with Esquire; Jay's Brookdale drive-in Brooklyn center, Minneapolis, Minn. Esquire 66:215-16 S '66
Inventor of the month; everything is automated but the carhop. S. V. Jones. il Sci Digest 60:32 N '66

Designs and plans
Five restaurants. il Arch Rec 140:161-8 O '66

Drive-in and curb services
See Drive-in and curb services

Finance
Restaurant business: what it's really like. il Changing T 20:13-16 Mr '66

Music
Victor café; Philadelphia's famous operatic restaurant. L. Saltzman. il Opera N 30:6-7 F 19 '66

Europe, Western
Europe's finest restaurants 1967. S. Spitzer and H. Spitzer. il Holiday 41:82-6+ Ja '67
Gourmet's guide to Europe: N. Newnham-Davis's book. C. W. Morton. il Atlan 217:140-1 Mr '66

France
Père Bise and the swans. M. J. Kempner. il Harper 232:86-7 Je '66
Snack v. la grande cuisine; Wimpy chain, France. Time 87:102 My 6 '66
See also
Paris—Hotels, restaurants, etc.

Hong Kong
Lox on lye; Lindy's East. Newsweek 68:67 Ag 1 '66

Italy
Eating surprises in Italy. il Sunset 136:176+ Mr '66

United States
Fortune in flapjacks. R. Levy. il Duns R 87:53-4 Je '66
Holiday's choice of American restaurants. Holiday 40:74-9 Jl '66
Joys of country dining; with a list of restaurants. il Time 88:67-8 S 23 '66
Not just food, gastrodomes. il Newsweek 67:72-4 My 30 '66
Vive les surgelés! frozen food for Howard Johnson chain. il Time 88:100+ O 28 '66

RESTIF DE LA BRETONNE, Nicolas Edme
Restif de la Bretonne. K. Rexroth. Sat R 49:25 Ap 2 '66

RESTITUTION claims
U.S. agency preparing claims relating to Gut Dam. Dept State Bul 54:207 F 7 '66

RESTON, James Barrett
New light on why U.S. is in Vietnam; excerpts from television broadcast, January 17, 1966. U S News 60:16 Ja 31 '66
Press, the President and foreign policy. For Affairs 44:553-73 Jl '66; Same abr. Read Digest 89:69-73 S '66

—and Hutchison, Bruce
Canada: test of the American conscience; discussion. Read Digest 89:189-90+ Jl '66

about
Voices of dissent. Newsweek 67:32+ Ja 31 '66

RESTON, Richard
Atlantic report. Atlan 218:4+ O '66

RESTON, Scotty. See Reston, J. B.

RESTON, Va.
Architecture. E. Galantay. il Nation 203:652-4 D 12 '66
Creating a new town. R. Atcheson. Holiday 39:121+ F '66
Dream city (almost) H. Cox. Commonweal 85:426-7 Ja 20 '67
How do you want to live? M. Mannes. McCalls 93:20+ Je '66
Reston, Va: new design for an ideal city. il Ebony 22:90-2+ D '66

RESTORATION of books. See Books—Conservation and restoration

RESTORATION of buildings. See Architecture—Conservation and restoration

RESTORATION of works of art. See Art—Conservation and restoration; Art objects—Conservation and restoration

RESTORED airplanes. See Airplanes, Restored

RESTORED churches. See Churches, Restored

RESTORED villages. See Villages, Restored

RESTRAINT of trade
Another trade wall crumbles; European Court of justice decision resulting from Grundig-Consten case. Bsns W p32 Jl 23 '66
Blow for freer competition; EEC opinion on Consten-Grundig case. Time 88:66 Jl 29 '66
Open season; discount-house car sales. Time 87:94 My 6 '66
See also
Exclusive agencies

RESTREPO, Carlos Lleras. See Lleras Restrepo, C.

RESTRICTIONS on travel. See Travel regulations

RÉSUMÉS of employment. See Applications for positions

RESURRECTION
See also
Immortality

RESURRECTION of João Jacinto; story. See Cronin, A. J.

RESUSCITATION
Frozen Christian: cryogenic interment. R. C. W. Ettinger; discussion. Christian Cent 82:1550+; 83:183-4 D 15 '65, F 9 '66
Heart cart may save your life. H. Fantel. il Pop Sci 189:54-7 Jl '66
Look out! it's hot! with first aid for shock victims. C. Sheridan. il Pop Electr 24:51-5+ Je '66
See also
Cardiac resuscitation

RESUSCITATION apparatus. See Respiratory apparatus

RETAIL credit. See Credit

RETAIL prices. See Prices

RETAIL trade
Closing the pocketbook. il Fortune 74:30+ S '66
English unorthodoxy of Marks & Spencer. J. Ross-Skinner. il Duns R 88:45-7+ O '66
Europe's stores gear up for more free spenders; computers in retail merchandising. il Bsns W p80-2 Je 4 '66
Make way for *le super-marche;* French retailing today. il Fortune 74:39-40+ Jl 1 '66
New ways to bigger profits; use of electronic data processing. B. L. Carter. il Nations Bsns 54:44-5+ D '66
No letup in rush to buy. Bsns W p37-8 Mr 19 '66
Powering the boom: the urge to buy. il U S News 61:63-4+ O 24 '66
Ratios of retailing; with table (cont) Duns R 88:52-3 S '66
Retailers' happy hunting ground. il Bsns W p 186 Mr 26 '66
Shoppers' spree goes on unabated. il Bsns W p32-4 S 3 '66
See also
Bargain sales
Christmas business
Department stores
Discount houses (retail trade)
Drugstores
Grocery trade
Mail order business
Returned goods

RETAIL, wholesale, and department store union
Union cards were phony: case of the Washington area Drug fair chain. il Nations Bsns 54:100-1+ Mr '66

RETAIL workers

Wages and hours
Employee earnings and hours in retail trade. A. Bauman. il Mo Labor R 89:754-9 Jl '66
Wages and hours, 1962 and 1965. A. Bauman. il Mo Labor R 89:877-80 Ag '66

RETAINING walls
Wood strips face the wall. il Sunset 136:248-9 Mr '66

RETARDED children. See Slow learning children

RETENTION (psychology)
High-speed scanning in human memory. S. Sternberg. bibliog il Science 153:652-4 Ag 5 '66
List differentiation with varied trials on both lists. E. Winograd and W. S. Smith. bibliog il Science 152:1101-2 My 20 '66
Pentylenetetrazol enhances memory function. S. Irwin and A. Benuazizi. bibliog il Science 152:100-2 Ap 1 '66
Puromycin effect on successive phases of memory storage. S. H. Barondes and H. D. Cohen. bibliog il Science 151:594-5 F 4 '66

RETHERFORD, Claude
Pair of sparklers in poky. F. Deford. il por Sports Illus 24:52+ F 21 '66

RETICULAR formation, Brain. See Brain

RETICULOCYTES. See Erythrocytes

RETICULO-ENDOTHELIAL system
Erythropoietic and reticuloendothelial function in bone marrow in dogs. M. L. Greenberg and others. bibliog il Science 152:526-8 Ap 22 '66

RETICULUM cell sarcoma. See Sarcoma

RETINA
Comparison of the effects of striate cortex and retinal lesions on visual acuity in the monkey. L. Weiskrantz and A. Cowey. bibliog il Science 155:104-6 Ja '6 '67
Oxygen dependence of retinal S-potential-producing cells. K. Negishi and G. Svaetichin. bibliog il Science 152:1621-3 Je 17 '66
Specialized receptive fields of the cat's retina. J. Stone and M. Fabian. bibliog il Science 152:1277-9 My 27 '66

Spectral sensitivity of the scallop pecten maximus; study of photoreceptor process. J. R. Cronly-Dillon. bibliog il Science 151:345-6 Ja 21 '66
Synapses of horizontal cells in rabbit and cat retinas. J. E. Dowling and others. bibliog il Science 153:1639-41 S 30 '66
Visual receptive fields in the cat's retina; complications. D. N. Spinelli. bibliog il Science 152:1768-9 Je 24 '66; Reply with rejoinder. H. B. Barlow and others. 154:920-1 N 18 '66

RETIRED military officers
Brass pyramid. R. G. Sherrill. il Nation 203:49-51 Jl 11 '66

RETIRED skippers' race. See Sailboat racing

RETIREMENT, Places of
Europe breeds new colonizers; Britons, Scandinavians, and Germans rush to build or invest in Bahamas, Florida, and Hawaii. il Bsns W p 155-6+ Je 4 '66

RETIREMENT from business, etc.
Advice to businessmen on health and retirement; interview. H. J. Johnson. il U S News 60:62-7 Mr 7 '66
Attraction of retirement. America 114:540 Ap 16 '66
Big year of executive change; retirement of top executives of prominent corporations. il Bsns W p76-8 Ja 7 '67
Decision to retire: a canvass of possibilities. Mo Labor R 89:III-IV Ja '66
Health insurance coverage for workers on layoff. W. W. Kolodrubetz. Mo Labor R 89:851-5 Ag '66
Our island paradise; retirement at the age of thirty. S. Beamish. il Redbook 127:50-1+ Ag '66; Same abr. with title We retired at age thirty. Read Digest 89:108-12 D '66
Second test for early retirement; steelworkers. il Bsns W p74-5 Jl 2 '66
Will you avoid these retirement pitfalls? Bet Hom & Gard 44:8+ My '66
See also
Pensions, Industrial

RETIREMENT housing. See Aged—Housing

RETIREMENT income
Money enough to retire on. il Changing T 20:7-12 Jl; 27-32 Ag; 24-30 S '66

RETIREMENT systems. See Pensions, Industrial

RETREATS, Spiritual
Campus corner; regarding long-established compulsory retreat policies and religious changes among students. M. P. Sheridan. America 115:543 N 5 '66
What's with lay retreats? America 115:5-6 Jl 2 '66

RETRIEVERS
See also
Labrador dogs

RETTALIATA, John T.
Future of the private university. Sch & Soc 94:348-9 O 29 '66

RETURNED goods
Many happy returns; Christmas gift returns. Time 89:34 Ja 13 '67

REUNIFICATION question, German. See Germany—Union (proposed)

REUSS, Henry S.
Excerpt from debate, June 29, 1965. Cong Digest 45:26+ Ja '66
Excerpt from statement, February 21, 1966. Cong Digest 45:144+ My '66
Research: the midas touch. Nation 202:69-71, 196 Ja 17, F 21 '66
Two Chinas. Commonweal 84:251-4 My 20 '66
—and Anderson, S. V.
Ombudsman: tribune of the people. bibliog f Ann Am Acad 363:44-51 Ja '66

about
Research policy: trumpets on Capitol hill. D. S. Greenberg. Science 153:278 Jl 15 '66

REUTER, Richard W.
World's food and population problems: address, November 12, 1966. Dept State Bul 55:862-6 D 5 '66

REUTHER, Walter Philip
Building the Great society: address, January 17, 1966. Vital Speeches 32:432-5 My 1 '66
Walter Reuther's widening goal; interview. U S News 61:104 D 12 '66

about
Auto union maps road for future. il por Bsns W p 158-60 My 21 '66
Breaking ranks at the top. por Bsns W p 149 Je 18 '66
Conflicts shake labor's house. Bsns W p 110 Je 25 '66
Different worlds. Newsweek 67:69-70 Je 27 '66

REUTHER, Walter Philip—about—*Continued*
Look out for 1967: what unions have in mind. il por U S News 60:84+ My 23 '66
Meany vs. Reuther: split widens in the AFL-CIO. U S News 61:82-3 N 28 '66
Reuther: more UAW ahead, less AFL-CIO. il por Bsns W p46+ N 19 '66
Rift at the top; feud with George Meany. Time 88:23 D 2 '66
When Reuther crosses Meany. U S News 60:94 Je 27 '66
Yeps have it. Nat R 18:1204 N 29 '66

REVEILLE (periodical)
Reveille in Arizona; new magazine. Newsweek 67:67 F 21 '66

REVELATION
Apex of revelation. V. P. McCorry. America 115:758 D 3 '66
Catechsis of revelation. by G. Moran. Review America 115:288 S 17 '66. A. Murphy
Common goal. P. J. Hallinan. America 116: 11-14 Ja 7 '67
Council and the word; Constitution on divine revelation. America 114:283 F 26 '66
Event and prophet. V. P. McCorry. America 115:718 N 26 '66
Post-biblical Christianity. D. Callahan. Commonweal 85:291-3 D 9 '66; Discussion. 85: 359+ Ja 6 '67
Revelation and history. V. P. McCorry. America 115:669-70 N 19 '66
Theology of revelation, by G. Moran. Review Commonweal 84:591-2 S 16 '66. A. Dulles
Two consider revelation. R. E. Koenig. Christian Cent 83:808-10 Je 22 '66

REVELLE, Roger
Can man domesticate himself? Bul Atomic Sci 22:2-7 F '66
Role of the oceans. Sat R 49:39-41 My 7 '66

REVENUE
See also
United States—Revenue

REVENUE, Municipal. See Municipal finance
REVENUE, State. See State finance
REVENUE bill. See Taxation—United States
REVENUE bonds. See Bonds, Revenue
REVERBERATION. See Acoustics, Architectural
REVERE, Paul
Series of historical paintings. A. L. Ripley. il pors Am Artist 30:44-9+ My '66
REVERSAL of time. See Time reversal
REVERSE osmosis. See Osmosis
REVIEW board, Civilian. See New York (city)
—Police department
REVIEWS of books. See Book reviews
REVIN, Valentin A.
Soviet science aide ousted by United States. D. S. Greenberg. il por Science 153:1500 S 23 '66

REVISED standard version of the Holy Bible. See Bible—Versions
REVISION, Literary. See Authorship
REVIVALS
See also
Evangelistic work
REVLON, incorporated
Putting a new face on father: Revlon's Braggi collection of men's grooming products. il Bsns W p74+ N 12 '66
REVOLUTION, Social. See Social revolution
REVOLUTIONARY war (United States) See United States—History—Revolution
REVOLUTIONS
American nightmare: why we fear peasants in revolt. B. Moore, jr. Nation 203:271-4 S 26 '66
Bankruptcy of the liberals; address, November 27, 1965. C. Oglesby; discussion. Commonweal 83:400-1, 547+ Ja 7, F 11 '66
Insurgency and counterinsurgency: new myths and old realities. C. Wolf, jr. Yale R 56:225-41 D '66
Revolutions: the big problem in the world today. D. Lawrence. U S News 60:112 Mr 7 '66
U.S. the Communists, and wars of national liberation. il Sr Schol 89:12-13+ O 7 '66
REVOLVERS
James Reid and friend. C. G. Worman. il Hobbies 71:122 Jl '66
REWALD, John
How New York became the capital of 19th-century Paris; excerpts from preface to the Knoedler catalogue for the Impressionist treasures show Art N 64:34-6+ Ja '66
REWARDS, prizes, etc.
Anglo-American book award finds no winner. Pub W 189:277 Ja 24 '66
Awards. See issues of Wilson library bulletin

French literary prizes confound, somewhat, their critics. H. R. Lottman. il Pub W 190: 43-7 D 26 '66
Grants, fellowships, and awards. See issues of Science
Juvenile literary awards, 1965. Library J 91:1623 Mr 15 '66
Misprision; crime of omission: F. Randazzo, first winner of New York city citizenship responsibility award. Time 87:62 Mr 4 '66
Nominations invited for ALA awards. Library J 91:6176 D 15 '66
Nominations sought for 1967 ALA awards. Library J 91:6052-3+ D 15 '66
Prize offers and awards. See issues of Writer
Prizes and awards. See issues of Publishers' weekly
Top ten; men of the year. il Am City 81: 169 Je '66
Twenty-one winners. G. P. Hunt. il Life 60:3 My 6 '66
Vietnam hero salutes his teacher; Golden key award. D. Chapman. il Look 30:68+ F 22 '66
See also
New York drama critics circle
Scholastic magazines. incorporated
also names of awards, e.g. Newbery medal

Anecdotes, facetiae, satire, etc.
Honor roll, 1966. il Art N 65:27 D '66
REWARDS and punishments in education. See Incentives in education
REXROTH, Kenneth
Classics revisited. See issues of Saturday review
Dimanche bleu; Parity; Education; Confusion of the senses; poems. Poetry 109:172-4 D '66
Hapax; or, The same poem over and over. Commonweal 84:229 My 13 '66
Hope for poetry. Holiday 39:147-9+ Mr '66
Phaedo; poem. Sat R 49:58 O 22 '66
Yin and yang poem. Harper 233:58 Ag '66

about
Compared with me. S. Eimerl. Reporter 34: 60+ My 19 '66
Last Bohemian. il por Time 87:108 F 25 '66
Rexroth: citizen of Bohemia. L. Kriegel. Nation 202:688-9 Je 6 '66
Sad of mind but glad at heart. E. Capouya. Sat R 49:29-30 F 12 '66
REYER, Randall W. and others
Lens differentiation. Science 154:1682-4+ D 30 '66
REYES, Alfonso
Alfonso Reyes. J. W. Robb. il pors Américas 18:17-23 Ap '66
REYNAL, Arnaldo Orfila. See Orfila Reynal, A.
REYNAUD, Paul
Obituary
New Yorker 42:154-6 O 8 '66. Genêt.
REYNOLDS, Fred
Sweet and swinging. See issues of American record guide
REYNOLDS, Paul R.
Hollywood screen writers. Sat R 49:52-3+ Jl 9 '66
Literary agent: his function, life, and power. Sat R 49:113-14 O 8 '66
REYNOLDS, Richard Samuel, 1908-
Being an innovator; interview. pors Nations Bsns 54:66-70+ F '66
REYNOLDS, Robert V.
Washington clipboard. R. Burkhardt. por Flying 79:28-9 O '66
REYNOLDS, Robert W. and Meeker, M. R.
Thiosemicarbazide injection followed by electric shock increases resistance to stress in rats. bibliog Science 151:1101-2 Mr 4 '66
REYNOLDS metals company
Being an innovator; interview. R. S. Reynolds, jr. il Nations Bsns 54:66-70+ F '66
REZNIKOFF, Charles
Failure of contempt. H. Carruth. Poetry 107: 396-7 Mr '66
RHEA, John
Oceanology called growth stock area. Miss & Roc 18:18 Mr 14 '66
RHEINFELDER, W. A.
Phono equalizer uses FET's. Electr World 75:32-3+ Ap '66
Substituting FET's for tubes in hi-fi amplifiers. Electr World 75:42-3 Mr '66
RHEOSTATS
General-purpose rheostats. H. Levy. il Electr World 75:47-9 Ap '66
RHESUS monkeys. See Monkeys
RHETT, Leigh C.
Independent study and the campus crisis. Sat R 49:62-4 Jl 16 '66

RHEUMATISM
Arthritis & rheumatism. il Time 87:71-2
Je 17 '66
See also
Arthritis

RHEUMATOID arthritis. See Arthritis

RHINE, Charles E.
New saw blade for cutting dovetails. Pop
Sci 188:128-30 My '66

RHINE, Joseph Banks
ESP: science or delusion? D. Cohen. il Nation 202:550-3 My 9 '66

**RHINELANDER station, Wis. See Institute of
forest genetics**

RHINOCEROS
Nature note; one-horned rhino. Sci N 89:470
Je 11 '66
Rhinoceros at bay. P. Brooks. il Horizon 9:
14-21+ Wint '67

RHINOPLASTY. See Surgery, Plastic

RHIZOPHORA. See Mangrove

RHOADES, Jonathan
Grandfather and the racquet-tailed drongo.
Sports Illus 24:60-4+ F 28 '66

RHODE ISLAND
See also
Block Island
Music festivals—Rhode Island

Politics and government
Colonel & the senator. il Time 88:15 Ag
26 '66

Social conditions
Rhode Island's misspent youth; irregularities
in youth corps projects. J. M. Berry. il
Reporter 34:29+ Ja 27 '66

**RHODE ISLAND school of design. Providence,
R.I.**
R.I.S.D. hypotheses. D. Manzella; reply. H.
S. Paston Sch Arts 65:40 Je '66

**RHODE ISLAND State Great swamp wildlife
reservation. See Wildlife sanctuaries**

RHODES, James Allen
Wonderful world of Governor Rhodes. A. S.
Zaidan. il Reporter 35:44-6 O 6 '66

RHODES, James M. See Quade, Q. L. jt. auth.

RHODES, Lynwood Mark
Frontier land frolic. Travel 125:47-9 Ap '66
Sunrise serenade: Guam. Travel 126:38+ S '66
Virgin Islands: our Caribbean treasure. To-
days Health 44:44-9 D '66

RHODES, Samuel
Death of the recital. B. Boretz. Nation 203:
125-7 Ag 8 '66

RHODES (island)
Living like a knight; summer retreat by
Beatrice Monti. B. Plumb. il N Y Times
Mag p72-3 Je 12 '66

RHODES scholars and scholarships
Sixty-three years of Yanks at Oxford. R.
Harrity. il Look 30:80-3+ O 4 '66

RHODESIA
Pretoria's view. J. Burnham. Nat R 18:1310
D 27 '66
U.S. and Zambia hold talks on Rhodesian
situation; joint communique. December 27,
1965. D. Rusk. Dept State Bul 54:85 Ja 17
'66
See also
Americans in Rhodesia
Foreign visitors in Rhodesia
Great Britain—Foreign relations—Rhodesia
Petroleum supply—Rhodesia
United Nations—Rhodesia
United States—Commerce—Rhodesia
United States—Foreign relations—Rhodesia
Zoology—Rhodesia

Economic conditions
Africa; gasoline situation. Time 87:31 Mr 11
'66
Britain's showdown in Africa; where sanc-
tions aren't working. il U S News 60:38-9
Ap 18 '66
Crisis in Southern Rhodesia; address, Jan-
uary 28, 1966. G. M. Williams. Dept State
Bul 54:265-70 F 21 '66
Great oil leak. Newsweek 67:46 F 28 '66
How long can Rhodesia last? J. L. Cefkin.
il Reporter 34:42+ F 10 '66
How Rhodesian whites are riding out a block-
ade; interview, ed. by A. J. Meyers. I.
Smith. il U S News 60:77-8 My 9 '66
Report from Rhodesia. il Fortune 74:73-4+
N '66
Tobacco curtain. Time 87:32 Ap 8 '66

Economic relations
Churches and sanctions. America 116:75 Ja 21
'67

Masquerade at sea fails for Rhodesia; Britain
scuttles oil ship to Rhodesia. Bsns W p41-2
Ap 16 '66
Rhodesia's woes mount; Britain preparing
new mandatory economic sanctions. Bsns W
p44 D 10 '66
We can go forever with sanctions as they
are. il Life 60:24-5 My 27 '66

Industries
Auction in Rhodesia; tobacco auction. Newsweek 67:52 Ap 11 '66

Politics and government
Address in General assembly, December 16,
1965; summary. H. Wilson. UN Mo Chron
3:73-5 Ja '66
Admission of failure; failure of British policy.
il Time 88:35-6 D 16 '66
Budging Rhodesia. New Repub 155:9 D 24 '66
Cock of the walk; constitutional rule; rebuff
to Britain. il Newsweek 68:55-6 O 10 '66
College crackdown in Rhodesia; Operation In-
tellect at University college of Rhodesia.
I. Henderson. New Repub 155:15-16 N 19
'66
Confident Rhodesians. New Repub 155:15-16
S 17 '66
Crackdown on Rhodesia; another country for
U.S. to rescue? il U S News 62:28-9 Ja 2 '67
Crisis in Southern Rhodesia; address, Jan-
uary 28, 1966. G. M. Williams. Dept State
Bul 54:265-70 F 21 '66
Crush Rhodesia resolution. Nat R 18:564+ Je
14 '66
Dialogue of the deaf; Harold Wilson au-
thorizes exploratory talks. il Newsweek 67:
45 My 9 '66
Dramatic meeting· between H. Wilson and
I. Smith. Time 88:41-2 D 9 '66
Footnote on Wilson. C. Brogan. Nat R 18:
149 F 22 '66
How long can Rhodesia last? J. L. Cefkin.
il Reporter 34:42+ F 10 '66
How Rhodesian whites are riding out a
blockade; interview, ed. by A. J. Meyers.
I. Smith. il U S News 60:77-8 My 9 '66
Ian Smith's inescapable crisis. Life 60:4 My
27 '66
Kicking the gong around. il Time 88:50 N 18
'66
Last thread; cutting of last thread to
London. Time 88:16 D 30 '66
Letter from London (cont) M. Panter-
Downes. New Yorker 42:54-5 D 24 '66
Letter from Salisbury. C. Trillin. il New
Yorker 42:139-40+ N 12 '66
Man on the Tiger. J. M. Cameron. Common-
weal 85:394-5 Ja 13 '67
Mission to London. Time 87:44+ My 20 '66
Mr Wilson squeaks through; Commonwealth
conference communiqué on Rhodesia. C.
Sterling. Reporter 35:32-3 O 6 '66
Naked emperor economic sanctions. E. Hux-
ley. Nat R 18:877-8 S 6 '66
No-progress report; British talks to resume.
il Newsweek 68:69 Ag 22 '66
Off again; British peace talks. Newsweek 68:
44 S 5 '66
Queen's pawns. Time 87:22 Ja 28 '66
Rhodesia: a taste of clover. R. W. Howe.
New Repub 154:9-10 My 14 '66
Rhodesia and the world's conscience. G.
Klein. Christian Cent 83:156-8 F 2 '66
Rhodesia. cross-currents in a turbulent con-
tinent. il Sr Schol 87:6-9+ Ja 14 '66
Rhodesia in crisis. F. Parker. il Negro Hist
Bul 29:53-4+ D '65
Rhodesia in the context of southern Africa.
J. K. Nyerere. For Affairs 44:373-86 Ap '66
Rhodesia: the fight goes on. il Newsweek 68:
33+ D 19 '66
Rhodesia through the looking glass: Smith's
declaration of white independence. K. Kyle.
New Repub 155:10-12 D 24 '66
Rhodesian declaration of independence; pro-
clamation, November 11, 1965. I. D. Smith.
Cur Hist 50:174-7 Mr '66
Rhodesia's enduring rebellion. J. Morris. il
Sat Eve Post 239:74-7 Jl 30 '66
Rhodesia's face of defiance; with report by
L. Hall. il Life 60:22-31 My 27 '66
Riding the tiger; Wilson and Smith meet.
Newsweek 68:54+ D 12 '66
Salisbury talks. N. M. Shamuyarira. Nation
203:5-6 Jl 4 '66
Score at half time; results of economic
sanctions. Nat R 18:196-8 Mr 8 '66
Seven days' humiliation; concerning Rhodesian
debate at Commonwealth prime ministers'
conference. E. Huxley. Nat R 18:989 O 4
'66
Shadows' shadow. Newsweek 67:45-6 F 14 '66
Something burning; issue in Commonwealth
dispute. Time 88:40 S 16 '66

RHODESIA—Politics and government—*Cont.*
Southern Rhodesia: the time for action. T. P. Melady. Cath World 204:230-3 Ja '67
Terror? Zimbabwe African nationalist's kill white settlers. Newsweek 67:52 My 30 '66
Test of loyalty; Queen Elizabeth commutes death sentences of two African prisoners. Sr Schol 88:16 F 4 '66
Will sanctions work? time is on our side; interview, ed. by P. Webb. I. D. Smith. Newsweek 68:43 D 19 '66
Will the lion bite? outburst in Lusaka precedes exploratory talks with Britain. Newsweek 67:50+ My 16 '66
Wishes & reality; talks resumed with Britain. Time 87:35 My 6 '66
Wrangling over Rhodesia: Commonwealth's venture into controversy. R. W. Howe. New Repub 155:8-9 O 1 '66
Yes. but how? break-up of Commonwealth conference. Time 88:37 S 23 '66

Race problems
Atlantic report. A. Lewis. Atlan 218:12+ D '66
College crackdown in Rhodesia: Operation Intellect at University college of Rhodesia. I. Henderson. New Repub 155:15-16 N 19 '66
Restriction in Rhodesia. Christian Cent 83:1316 O 26 '66
Southern Rhodesia: the time for action. T. P. Melady. Cath World 204:230-3 Ja '67
We and they in Rhodesia. M. Cable. New Yorker 41:36-41 F 19 '66
White vs. black in Rhodesia. D. Reed. il Read Digest 89:125-31 O '66

Religious institutions and affairs
See also
Christians in Rhodesia
RHODESIA, NORTHERN. See Zambia
RHODIN, Eric
Ugly man; story. Seventeen 25:114-15 O '66
RHODIZITE
Absence of neutral alkali atoms in rhodizite. G. Donnay and others. bibliog il Science 154:889-90 N 18 '66
Rhodizite: structure and composition. M. J. Buerger and K. Taxer. bibliog il Science 152:500-2 Ap 22 '66
RHODODENDRONS
Here are the spectacular tree rhododendrons. il Sunset 136:276-7 My '66
He's making a rhododendron standard. il Sunset 136:244 Ap '66
How to grow rhododendrons where rhododendrons won't grow. Sunset 136:216 F '66
RHYNCHOSCIARA angelae. See Diptera
RHYTHM
They shall have music: project at Horace Mann elementary school, Bellflower, Calif. C. L. Herbert. il Am Ed 2:22 O '66
RHYTHM and blues singers. See Singers
RHYTHMIC phenomena. See Periodicity
RIBBENTROP, Joachim von
Pius XII and the Third Reich; excerpts, ed. by R. Leiber. S. Friedländer. il por Look 30:36-8+ My 17 '66
RIBICOFF, Abraham
Car stealing made simple! por Pop Mech 126:57-9+ Jl '66
Our chaotic traffic laws. Read Digest 88:101-2 Mr '66
Traffic safety; address, October 24, 1966. Vital Speeches 33:104-6 D 1 '66

about
Automotive safety. R. Moley. Newsweek 67:100 F 14 '66
Bonfire of discontent; Subcommittee on executive reorganization hearings. il por Time 88:9-10 Ag 26 '66
Letter from Washington. R. H. Rovere. New Yorker 42:108+ S 10 '66
Ribicoff is a cautious crusader. J. F. Welsh. il pors N Y Times Mag p32-3+ Je 12 '66
Vision or television? Reporter 35:8-9 D 29 '66
RIBMAN, Ronald
Journey of the fifth horse; dramatization of story by I. S. Turgenev. Criticism
Commonweal 84:283 My 27 '66
Nation 202:661 My 30 '66
New Repub 154:31+ My 7 '66
New Yorker 42:79 Ap 30 '66
RIBONUCLEIC acid
Actinomycin D: inhibition of respiration and glycolysis. J. Laszlo and others. bibliog il Science 151:1007-10 F 25 '66
Aflatoxin B₁: binding to DNA in vitro and alteration of RNA metabolism in vivo. M. B. Sporn and others. bibliog il Science 151:1539-41 Mr 25 '66

Arrested protein synthesis in polysomes of cultured chick embryo cells. R. Soeiro and H. Amos. bibiog il Science 154:662-5 N 4 '66
Cell-free protein synthesis; effects of age and state of ribosomal aggregation. L. D. Moore and others. bibliog il Science 154:1350-3 D 9 '66
Chain initiation and control of protein synthesis. H. Noll. bibliog il Science 151:1241-5 Mr 11 '66
Cytokinin activity: localization in transfer RNA preparations. F. Skoog and others. bibliog il Science 154:1354-6 D 9 '66
Formylmethionyl-tRNA dependence of amino acid incorporation in extracts of trimethoprim-treated escherichia coli. J. Eisenstadt and P. Lengyel. bibliog il Science 154:524-7 O 28 '66
Gene-specific messenger RNA: isolation by the deletion method. E. K. F. Bautz and E. Reilly. bibliog il Science 151:328-30 Ja 21 '66
Heterogeneity of template RNA in adrenal glands. R. L. Ney and others. bibliog il Science 153:896-7 Ag 19 '66
In vitro synthesis of an infectious mutant RNA with a normal RNA replicase. N. R. Pace and S. Spiegelman. bibliog il Science 153:64-7 Jl 1 '66
Inside the molecules of the mind. L. Lessing. il Fortune 74:100-5+ Jl 1 '66
Isopycnic centrifugation for the isolation of DNA strands coding for ribosomal RNA. P. F. Davison. bibliog il Science 152:509-12 Ap 22 '66
Magnesium pemoline: enhancement of brain RNA polymerases. A. J. Glasky and L. N. Simon. bibliog il Science 151:702-3 F 11 '66
Memory still elusive. il Sci N 91:9 Ja 7 '67
Memory transfer unlikely; testing RNA-injected animals for learning transfer. P. McBroom. Sci N L 89:151 Mr 5 '66
Native and renatured transfer ribonucleic acid. T. Lindahl and A. Adams. bibliog il Science 152:512-14 Ap 22 '66
New RNA chemical found. il Sci N 90:35 Jl 16 '66
Nucleotide sequence of a yeast tyrosine transfer RNA. J. T. Madison and others. bibliog il Science 153:531-4 Jl 29 '66
Pill that helps you remember; Cylert. S. M. Spencer. il Sat Eve Post 239:64-6+ S 24 '66
Pills to help us remember? Cylert. I. Asimov. il N Y Times Mag p38-9+ O 9 '66
Rapid and marked inhibition of rat-liver RNA polymerase by aflatoxin B₁. H. V. Gelboin and others. bibliog il Science 154:1205-6 D 2 '66
Reovirus-specific polyribosomes in infected L-cells. L. Prevec and A. F. Graham. bibliog il Science 154:522-3 O 28 '66
Replication of the RNA of bacteriophage f2. H. F. Lodish and N. D. Zinder. bibliog il Science 152:372-8 Ap 15 '66
RNA composition and base pairing. W. Traub and D. Elson. bibliog il Science 153:178-80 Jl 8 '66
RNA structure revealed. Sci N 89:306 Ap 30 '66
RNA vaccine postulated. Sci N 90:459 N 26 '66
Ribosomal RNA synthesis and processing in a particulate site in the HeLa cell nucleus. S. Penman and others. bibliog il Science 154:786-9 N 11 '66
Synthesis of nonribosomal RNA by lymphocytes: a response to phytohemagglutinin treatment. H. L. Cooper and A. D. Rubin. bibliog il Science 152:516-18 Ap 22 '66
Understanding memory. P. McBroom. il Sci N 89:186-7 Mr 19 '66
RIBONUCLEOPROTEINS. See Nucleoproteins
RIBOSOMES. See Nucleoproteins
RIBOUD, Marc
Panda performs in Peking; photographs. Natur Hist 75:34-5 Ap '66

about
Riboud's camera covers China. M. R. Weiss. il Sat R 49:89-91 D 10 '66
RICALTON, James
How we know about James Ricalton. G. P. Hunt. por Life 61:5 O 14 '66
RICARD, Paul
Making much of a mess. il por Time 87:98 F 25 '66
RICCI, Robert
Vogue's ready beauty. por Vogue 147:153 Mr 15 '66
RICCIO, David C. and others
Stimulus control in pigeons based on proprioceptive stimuli from floor inclination. bibliog Science 153:434-6 Jl 22 '66

RICKEY, George
Engineer of movement. il por Time 88:76-7
N 4 '66
RICKING, Myrl
Recruitment (cont) ALA Bul 60:665-9, 731
Je-Jl '66
RICKMAN, Eric
Rooster tales. See issues of Hot rod
RICKMAN, R. W. and others
Compact subsoil can be harmful to plant
growth. Parks & Rec 1:334-5 Ap '66
RICKOVER, Hyman G.
Rickover vs. McNamara on a nuclear navy;
excerpts from testimony. June 23, 1966. U S
News 61:10-11 Jl 4 '66
RICKS, Christopher
Literary style of L.B.J. Esquire 66:117+ N
'66
RICKS, Horace
Guardians of the Viet Nam coastline. il pors
Ebony 22:129-30+ D '66
RIDD, J. Carl
Message from Bonhoeffer. Christian Cent
83:827-9 Je 29 '66
RIDGE, William G.
Sewer within a sewer. Am City 81:112-13 O '66
RIDGEWAY, James F.
Advising Congress. New Repub 155:17-18 Jl
30 '66
Attack on Kodak. New Repub 156:11-13 Ja 21
'67
Back to electric cars? New Repub 155:9-10
Ag 13 '66
Birth and non-birth. New Repub 155:38-40
N 26 '66
Black mischief. New Repub 155:14-16 D 24 '66
Computer-tutor. New Repub 154:19-22 Je
4 '66
Dirty deal in small loans. New Repub 155:
11-12 O 8 '66
Girls in white. New Repub 154:10-12 F 19 '66
How to take a test. New Repub 154:31-2
F 26 '66
More on auto insurance. New Repub 156:21-
3 Ja 14 '67
New cities are big business. New Repub 155:
15-17 O 1 '66
Out of business, by FTC order. New Repub
154:13-14 F 12 '66
Rebuilding the slums. New Repub 156:22-5 Ja
7 '67
Responsible muckraker. por Time 87:74 Ja
28 '66
Simulating poverty: input and output. New
Repub 154:9-10 Je 11; 155:35+ Jl 2 '66
Stench from New Jersey. New Repub 155:
13-15 Jl 16 '66
Studies in the grocery. New Repub 154:9-
10 Je 25 '66
Underground war on auto insurance. New
Repub 155:19-21 D 3 '66
—and Wiggins, David
Cheap life insurance. New Repub 155:11-12
N 12 '66
—See Kopkind, A. D. jt. auth.
about
Art of finding out. il por Newsweek 67:80 My
30 '66
RIDGWAY, John
We rowed across the North Atlantic; ed. by
J. Atwater. pors Sat Eve Post 239:30-6+
N 5 '66
about
Heroes reward. Newsweek 68:56 S 19 '66
RIDGWAY, Matthew B.
Pull-out, all-out, or stand fast in Vietnam?
por Look 30:81-2+ Ap 5 '66
RIDGWAY, Sam H. and Johnston, D. G.
Blood oxygen and ecology of porpoises of
three genera. bibliog Science 151:456-8 Ja
28 '66
RIDLEY, Walter N.
NEA-ATA unification. NEA J 55:49-50 S '66
RIECKER, Robert E. and Rooney, T. P.
Weakening of dunite by serpentine dehydra-
tion. bibliog Science 152:196-8; 153:1287 Ap
8, S 9 '66
RIEGER, James
Back to work in California. New Repub 155:
8-9 D 17 '66
RIEKE, William O.
Lymphocytes from thymectomized rats: im-
munologic, proliferative, and metabolic
properties. bibliog Science 152:535-8 Ap 22
'66
RIESSMAN, Frank
Styles of learning. NEA J 55:15-17 Mr '66
—and Alberts, Frank
Digging the mans language. Sat R 49:80-1+
S 17 '66
RIETH, Marian
Acts of Corporal Charity: story. Seventeen
25:90-1 Jl '66

RIFAMYCINS. See Antibiotics
RIFIELD, Phyllis
Five with enterprise. Mlle 63:144-7 S '66
Wanted volunteers who mean it. Mlle 64:
118-19+ D '66
RIFLE practice. See Trap shooting
RIFLE sights. See Firearms—Sights
RIFLE targets. See Targets
RIFLES
Accuracy? W. Page. il Field & S 71:78-81 D
'66
Add another 6.5 round. W. Page. il Field &
S 71:82-5 Jl '66
Aim for safety. R. Rood. il Parents Mag 41:
50-1+ Ag '66
All-American game rifle. W. Page. il Field
& S 71:98-100+ S '66
Elegant sporter. J. O'Connor. il Outdoor Life
138:86+ D '66
Good ole thutty-thutty. J. O'Connor. il Out-
door Life 138:70+ S '66
Model 1866 Winchester. C. Worman. il Hob-
bies 71:124-5 My '66
Mossberg sporter; bolt-action hunting rifle.
Field & S 70:130 Mr '66
Number one single shot. W. Page. il Field
& S 71:88-92 O '66
Plating solves headspace. E. Bogedal. il Out-
door Life 137:131 Mr '66
Ruger no. 1 single shot rifle. J. O'Connor.
il Outdoor Life 138:76+ O '66
Sharps buffalo rifle. C. G. Worman. il Hob-
bies 71:127+ O '66
.22 caliber autoloading rifles. Consumer Rep
31:292-5 D '66
History
Guns of the 7th cavalry. C. G. Worman. il
Hobbies 71:126-7 N '66
RIFT valleys
Cracks in a continent; east Africa. B. H.
Baker. il UNESCO Courier 19:11-15 Je '66
RIGGAN, Byron
Where they think about the unthinkable.
Horizon 8:40-4+ Sum '66
RIGGIO, John W.
Doctor Riggio: the art of an extractionist.
il por Am Artist 30:44-9+ Mr '66
RIGGS, Robert
Resurgence of Robert Riggs. H. C. Pitz. il
Am Artist 30:50-5+ My '66
RIGHT and left (political science)
Age of innocents; new left. A. M. Greeley.
Reporter 35:52-4 S 8 '66
Battle for your child's mind. R. D. Bat-
chelder. Parents Mag 41:40+ Mr '66
Birchism at the grass roots; Birch watchers
retaliatory group. A. Forster. il Nation
203:73-6 Jl 25 '66
Criticism sans action. P. Lathrop. Nation 203:
23-5 Jl 4 '66
European right, ed by H. Rogger and E.
Weber. Review
Nat R 18:172-3 F 22 '66. F. D. Wilhelmsen
Extremism: danger to our schools; address,
June 30, 1966. E. H. Methvin. Vital
Speeches 32:694-700 S 1 '66
Extremism; excerpts from address, June 23,
1965. E. Duff. Library J 91:619-23+ F 1 '66
Fallacy of balance in public library book
selection; excerpts from address, October
1965. R. A. Landor. il Library J 91:629-32
F 1 '66; Discussion. 91:1952+. 2734 Ag 15,
Je 1 '66
Feud among the radicals. S. Kelman. Harper
232:67-72+ Je '66
For garden country: rally on the right; New
England rally for God, family & country.
J. Rascoe. Atlan 218:88-91 S '66
Gideon's army and Moynihan's pros. P. Sea-
bury. New Repub 154:23-5 Mr 19 '66; Re-
ply. E. Prange. 154:38 Ap 2 '66
Left and right meet. R. Hamowy. New Re-
pub 154:14-16 Mr 12 '66
Left in Europe since 1789, by D. Caute. Re-
view
Nation 202:784-6 Je 27 '66. J. J. Kaplow
Mystical militants. M. Harrington. New Re-
pub 154:20-2 F 19 '66
National temper; new rightist realism. E. J.
Hughes. Newsweek 68:15 S 5 '66
New direction in the U.S: right? R. Kirk. il
N Y Times Mag p20-1+ Ag 7 '66
New left: a spook out of the past. J. Dos
Passos. Nat R 18:1037-9 O 18 '66
New left: beyond the burning moral thing.
J. O'Connor. Nation 203:20-2 Jl 4 '66
New left, by P. A. Luce. Review
Nat R 18:687-8 Jl 12 '66. M. S. Evans
New left in the U.S: what the radicals want.
il U S News 60:53-4 Ja 31 '66
New left: what does it mean? E. M. Keating.
Sat R 49:25-7+ S 24 '66

RIGHT and left (political science)—*Continued*
New right: what does it seek? J. J. Kilpatrick. Sat R 49:29-31+ O 8 '66
Old left & the new: emancipation from dogma. H. Zinn. il Nation 202:385-9 Ap 4 '66
Persistent danger. J. Moorhead. PTA Mag 60:2-3 My '66
Politics of extremism; address, May 24, 1966. R. H. Hinckley. Vital Speeches 32:599-604 Jl 15 '66
Popular front for protest; the new left. M. Nomad. Sat R 49:45-6 Je 4 '66
Problem of the new left. T. Kahn. Commentary 42:30-8 Jl '66; Discussion. 42:7-8+ N '66
Profiles; right-wing extremism in Los Angeles. New Yorker 42:100+ O 14 '66
Prophetic minority, by J. Newfield. Review New Repub 155:28-30 D 10 '66. A. Kopkind
Newsweek il 68:111+ N 14 '66. S. Schmidt
Radical papers, ed. by I. Howe. Review Atlan 217:145-7 Ap '66
Right and left. W. Pfaff. Commonweal 83:654-5 Mr 11 '66
Search for community. R. Coles. New Repub 154:12-14 F 26 '66
Spokesman for the new left. J. Corry. il N Y Times Mag p 12-13+ Ja 23 '66
Steady work by I. Howe. Review Sat R 50:47 Ja 21 '67. M. R. Konvitz
Thunder on the left; new publications. il Newsweek 67:67 F 21 '66
Violence on the fanatical left and right. A. Forster. bibliog f Ann Am Acad 364:141-8 Mr '66
Weird warriors in war on poverty. il Nations Bsns 54:42-3+ My '66
See also
Conservatism
Free university of New York
Liberalism
South—Politics
Bibliography
Extreme right in American politics; comp. by Adult services division of ALA. Wilson Lib Bul 40:933-6 Je '66
RIGHT and wrong. See Ethics
RIGHT ascension and declination (astronomy) See Astronomy, Spherical and practical
RIGHT of assembly. See Assembly, Right of
RIGHT of asylum. See Asylum, Right of
RIGHT of conquest. See Conquest, Right of
RIGHT of counsel. See Right to counsel
RIGHT of privacy. See Privacy
RIGHT to counsel
Torture of mothers, by T. Nelson. Review Nation 202:496-8 Ap 25 '66. J. Meyer
Where to after Gideon? misdemeanors. Time 88:81 D 16 '66
RIGHT to strike of government employees. See Strikes—United States—Government employees
RIGHT to travel. See Travel regulations
RIGHT to work laws. See Labor laws and legislation—United States
RIGHT wing (politics) See Right and left (political science)
RIGHT you are; drama. See Pirandello, L.
RIGHTEOUS brothers. See Singers
RIGHTS, Bill of (United States) See United States—Constitution—Bill of rights
RIGHTS, Civil. See Civil rights
RIGHTS, Personal. See Civil rights
RIGHTS of conscience. See Liberty of conscience
RIGHTS of women. See Woman—Equal rights
RIGOLETTO; opera. See Verdi, G.
RIIS houses. See New York (city)—Housing
RIKER, A. J.
Plant pathology and human welfare. bibliog Science 152:1027-32 My 20 '66
RIKHOFF, Jean
Short story or novel? Writer 79:11-15 O '66
RIKLIS, Meshulam
Master of arts. por Newsweek 68:84+ S 12 '66
RILEY, Art
Birth of a bridge. Am Artist 30:39-41+ F '66
RILEY, Nord
How to shoot the bird of peace. Outdoor Life 138:34-5+ Jl '66
RILEY, Robert
Miniature tapestry. Craft Horiz 26:11-15 Mr '66

RILEY, Vernon
Spontaneous mammary tumors: decrease of incidence in mice infected with an enzyme-elevating virus. bibliog Science 153:1657-8 S 30 '66
RILLO, Thomas J.
People and the out-of-doors. Am For 72:8+ Mr '66
RIMBAUD, Arthur. See Rimbaud, J. N. A.
RIMBAUD, Jean Nicolas Arthur
Works of Rimbaud. K. Rexroth. Sat R 50:34+ Ja 14 '67
RIMOIN, David L. and others
Growth-hormone deficiency in man: an isolated, recessively inherited defect. bibliog Science 152:1635-7 Je 17 '66
RIMSKII-KORSAKOV, Nikolai Andreevich
Christmas opera by Rimsky-Korsakov. P. L. Miller. Am Rec G 33:314 D '66
On records; Xmas eve; Sadko, and Le coq d'or. Opera N 30:34 Mr 26 '66
RINFRET, Pierre A.
Vietnam's economic lesson: peace can yield fatter profits than war. T. G. Harris. il por Look 30:44+ My 31 '66
RING-necked pheasants. See Pheasants
RING of the Nibelung; operas. See Wagner, R.
RINGGENBERG, Harold
Ever use a paddle in art? Design 68:12-15 S '66
String along with Ring. Design 67:26-7 Mr '66
RINGLAND, Arthur C.
Their constituents are the next generation. Am For 72:8 Ag '66
RINGLING brothers circus. See Circus
RINGO, Roy
On strengthening the U.N. Bul Atomic Sci 22:30-1 D '66
RINGOLD, Evelyn S.
Parent and child. N Y Times Mag p69-70+ Ja 15 '67*
RINGS
Diamond for the day you dream of; Tiffany, New York. il Seventeen 25:28 My '66
Gold funeral rings. J. D. Kernan. il Antiques 89:568-9 Ap '66
RIO DE JANEIRO
Description
Carnival in Rio. M. Miller. il Holiday 39:40-53+ F '66
RIO GRANDE
Travel far and near; Rio Grande canoe trip. R. W. Schery. Natur Hist 75:58+ Ap '66
U.S, Mexico announce proposals on Rio Grande salinity problem. Dept State Bul 54:118 Ja 24 '66
U.S, Mexico to join in solving Rio Grande salinity problem; statement, with text of telegram to President G. Diaz Ordaz, September 19, 1966. L. B. Johnson. Dept State Bul 55:686-7 O 31 '66
RIORDAN, William F.
Sporting scene. H. W. Wind. New Yorker 42:136+ Mr 12 '66
RIOS, Simplicio
I'm proud to be poor; interview, ed. by O. Lewis. Commentary 42:44-7 Ag '66
RIOT control
Coming: fantastic devices to end riots. R. Zacks. il Nations Bsns 54:62-4 Jl '66; Reply. J. C. Evans. Christian Cent 83:1203 O 5 '66
Request for a riot cure. il Ebony 22:144-5 D '66
RIOT prevention. See Riot control
RIOTOUS life; story. See Stanton, W.
RIOTS
City riots, a worldwide plague. Read Digest 88:175-6+ F '66; Discussion. Harper 232:8+ Mr '66
See also
Mob violence
Riot control
also subhead Riots under names of countries, cities, etc. e.g. United States—Riots
RIOUX, J. William
At the teacher's right hand. por Am Ed 2:5-6 D '65
RIP Van Winkle; drama. See Thane, A.
RIPLEY, A. Lassell
Series of historical paintings. il Am Artist 30:44-9+ My '66
RIPLEY, Austin
Austin Ripley and alcoholic priests. H. A. Hammett. America 115:831 D 24 '66
RIPLEY, Daniel C.
Glassware patents by the Daniel C. Ripleys. A. G. Peterson. il Hobbies 71:98B-98C S; 84+ O '66

RIPLEY, S. Dillon
Perspective of the Smithsonian program in ecology; excerpt from address, March 15, 1966. Nat Parks Mag 40:10-13 O '66

about
Profiles: Smithsonian institution. G. T. Hellman. New Yorker 42:67-8+ D 3; 100+ D 17 '66
Smithsonian: more museums in slums, more slums in museums? B. Nelson. Science 154:1152-4 D 2 '66
RIPON society. See Political clubs and associations
RISK
Rewards of risking it. J. K. Lagemann. Read Digest 90:191+ Ja '67
See also
Hedging
RISORGIMENTO. See Italy—History
RISOTTO. See Cookery—Rice
RISK capital. See Capital
RISTAU, Harland
September always dies before the heart; poem. Christian Cent 83:1145 S 21 '66
RISTEDT, H. See Eichler, R. jt. auth.
RITE of spring; ballet. See Ballets—Criticisms
RITES and ceremonies

Vietnam
Incest of Tieng and Aang who had a common ancestor fifteen generations ago; excerpt from Nous avons mangé la forêt de la Pierre-Génie Gôo, tr. by V. Bordaz. G. Condominas. il Natur Hist 75:13-19 Je '66
RITSCHL, Albrecht Benjamin
Life in the old boys yet! B. A. Reist. Christian Cent 83:1179-80 S 28 '66
RITTER, Jay
Lee raised his hat. Negro Hist Bul 29:59-60 D '65
RITTER, Lawrence S.
Glory of their times; excerpt. Sat Eve Post 239:36-40+ Ag 13 '66
RITUAL. See Catholic church—Liturgy and ritual; Liturgies; Rites and ceremonies
RITUAL murder. See Blood accusation
RIVER boats. See Steamships and steamboats
RIVER trips
Cruising Florida's cricks. M. Hunn. il Motor B 117:180+ Mr '66
Down the Mississippi; passage from Lake Michigan to New Orleans. J. L. Naumann. il Yachting 120:54-6+ N '66
Dream come true; expedition down the Colorado. B. M. Goldwater. il McCalls 93:64+ Mr '66
Enjoying the ancient Apalachicola. E. White. il Motor B 118:34-6+ O '66
Of lost days on a river; Mexico's Usumacinta River. C. Phinizy. il Sports Illus 24:62-4+ Mr 28 '66
Spring cruising in the Delta; Sacramento-San Joaquin Delta. il Sunset 136:94-103 My '66
Wilderness trip with the Kennedys; a run down the rivers of Dinosaur National Monument. D. Connelly. il McCalls 93:66+ My '66
Wyoming's Snake River float trip. T. B. Lesure. il Travel 125:36-8 My '66
See also
Canoe trips
Congo River
RIVERA, Diego, museum. See Mexico (city)—Galleries and museums
RIVERS, Joan
Hot potato. por Time 88:61-2+ O 21 '66
RIVERS, Larry
Rivers: boy painter. B. Kaufman. Commonweal 84:400 Je 24 '66
Rivers paints himself into the canvas. G. Glueck. il pors N Y Times Mag p34-5+ F 13 '66
RIVERS, Lucius Mendel
Congressman Rivers on the rampage. Christian Cent 84:70 Ja 18 '67
Muckraker; D. Pearson's Washington merry-go-round. il Newsweek 67:87 Je 27 '66
Now it's Rivers vs. McNamara. por U S News 60:15 Je 27 '66
Vote for non-leadership. por Time 87:24 Je 24 '66
RIVERS
River meanders. L. B. Leopold and W. B. Langbein. il Sci Am 214:60-70 Je '66
River spoilers; fate of Florida's Kissimmee, Caloosahatchee. Pearce and Oklawaha. S. Trumbull. il Audubon Mag 68:102-10 Mr '66

Wild rivers bill lacks teeth; National scenic riverways. C. H. Callison. Audubon Mag 68:92 Mr '66
See also
Alluvium
Erosion
Water pollution
also names of rivers, e.g. Rio Grande

Regulation
Our wild rivers. E. S. Helfman. il Liv Wildn 30:24-9 Sum '66
See also
Colorado River
Dams
Mississippi River—Regulation
RIVERSIDE, Calif.

Newspapers
Digging by the Riverside; morning Enterprise and evening Press. il Newsweek 68:71 S 12 '66
RIVIERE, Bill
Map reading for fun. Field & S 71:76 S '66
RIVKIN, Arnold
International agencies for development. bibliog f Cur Hist 51:96-101+ Ag '66
RIZZO, Francis
Stravinsky. Opera N 31:7 Ja 14 '67
ROACHES. See Cockroaches
ROAD accidents. See Traffic accidents
ROAD construction. See Highway engineering
ROAD guards. See Roads—Safety guards
ROAD traffic
Automobiles & highways: getting there is twice the effort. il Sr Schol 89:4-7 Ja 6 '67
ROADS
See also
Automobiles and roads
National parks and reserves—Roads
Snow and ice removal
Toll roads

Finance
Why the biggest tax-exempt failed; New Jersey turnpike's record $440-million issue. il Bsns W p 143-4+ Mr 26 '66
See also
Toll roads

Foundations
Plastic highways, by Caesar! foam plastic provides protection from frost damage. C. B. Hicks. il Pop Mech 125:78-9 Je '66

Lighting
Why keep safety in the dark? Life 61:4 S 2 '66

Location
Highway location, a socio-economic problem. R. M. Whitton. il Parks & Rec 1:24-6+ Ja '66

Materials
Plastic highways, by Caesar! foam plastic provides protection from frost damage. C. B. Hicks. il Pop Mech 125:78-9 Je '66

Safety devices and measures
Automotive safety. R. Moley. Newsweek 67:88 F 7 '66
How to stay alive on the turnpikes. E. D. Fales, jr. il Pop Mech 126:63-7+ Ag '66
Let's abolish traffic danger spots. B. Schapper. il Todays Health 44:18-21 O '66
LBJ and auto safety; Traffic safety act of 1966; proposals. R. Moley. Newsweek 67:112 Mr 21 '66
Make our neighborhood roads safer now. J. N. Miller. Read Digest 89:129-33 S '66
Safety myths that mess up your driving. J. F. Pearson. il Pop Mech 126:96-7 N '66
Wanted: new safety for older roads. J. N. Miller. Read Digest 89:215-16+ D '66
Why keep safety in the dark? Life 61:4 S 2 '66

Safety guards
Quick way to divide a roadway; Louisiana department of highways. il Am City 81:98-9 O '66

Africa
New patterns of transport for Africa. W. H. Owens. il UNESCO Courier 19:11-15 Ja '66

Alaska
See also
Alaska highway

Arizona
Community action: desert nature drive. il Sunset 137:68+ O '66

ROADS—*Continued*

Brazil

Roads start to tame Brazil's green hell. il Bsns W p 192-4+ S 10 '66

California

Bells are back on the King's highway; El Camino Real bells; reprint. G. P. Parmelee. il Hobbies 71:98O-98P N '66

Old road was like this; Beale's Cut. il Sunset 138:20 Ja '67

San Francisco still says no. Time 87:48 Ap 1 '66

Canada

See also
Alaska highway

Florida

Orange Blossom trail. J. H. Winchester. il Travel 125:35-8 F '66

Louisiana

Quick way to divide a roadway. il Am City 81:98-9 O '66

Massachusetts

Last hitch in the Inner belt; Boston's Inner belt highway through Cambridge. J. M. Dixon. il Arch Forum 124:68-71 My '66

New Jersey

Why the biggest tax-exempt failed; New Jersey turnpike's record $440-million issue. il Bsns W p 143-4+ Mr 26 '66

Oregon

McKenzie pass before snow flies; old McKenzie highway. il Sunset 137:64+ O '66

Willowdale red rock. H. D. Brown. Hobbies 71:117 N '66

Peru

Peruvian politics stalls Belaúnde's reforms. S. Rodman. il Reporter 35:37-40 Jl 14 '66

Texas

Chamizal highway to symbolize U.S.-Mexican friendship; statement, November 8, 1966. L. B. Johnson. Dept State Bul 55:882 D 12 '66

United States

Abolish the highways! J. B. Jackson. Nat R 18:1213-17 N 29 '66

Concrete Juggernaut. W. G. Wing. il Audubon Mag 68:266-72, 294, 360-7 Jl-S '66

Highway system; address, July 21, 1966. H. Ford, jr. Vital Speeches 32:690-4 S 1 '66

Make our neighborhood roads safer now. J. N. Miller. Read Digest 89:129-33 S '66

Traffic jam; Arthur D. Little, inc. questions goals of Interstate highway system. Reporter 34:14+ Ap 7 '66

See also
Express highways
Toll roads

ROADS and automobiles. See Automobiles and roads

ROADSIDE improvement

Abolish the highways! J. B. Jackson. Nat R 18:1213-17 N 29 '66

Keynote address: America the beautiful; with editorial comment. R. E. Train. il Am For 71:11, 16-19+ O '65

Natural beauty, the follow through. J. B. Craig. il Am For 71:12-15+ O '65

Screen the junkyards. D. Wyman. il Horticulture 44:24-7+ Ap '66

See also
Billboards

ROADSIDE planting. See Roadside improvement

ROADSTERS. See Sports cars

ROALMAN, A. R.

Antiques, what are they worth? Bet Hom & Gard 44:146-7 Mr '66

Here comes Mr Parade. Pop Mech 125:84-7+ Je '66

ROANOKE ISLAND

British-America's birthplace. H. D. Crawford. il Am For 72:14-17+ S '66

ROASTING. See Cookery—Meat

ROBARDS, Jason, 1922-

Send the script to Jason. T. Thompson. il pors Life 60:83-4+ F 18 '66

ROBB, James Willis

Alfonso Reyes. Américas 18:17-23 Ap '66

ROBBE-GRILLET, Alain

Istanbul; city tinged with blood and gold; tr. by A. Foulke. Vogue 147:58-9+ F 1 '66

about

Books. N. Bliven. New Yorker 42:165-8 Ap 9 '66

Nothing new. S. Kauffmann. New Repub 156: 26+ Ja 14 '67

Who is Robbe-Grillet? M. Chapsal. il Reporter 35:54-7 Jl 14 '66

ROBBERIES and assaults

Deer snatchers. C. Robinson. il Field & S 70:50-2+ Ap '66

Flourishing legend of the greatest robbery; England's train robbery. P. O'Neil. il Life 60:102-6+ Ap 8 '66

Anecdotes, facetiae, satire, etc.

First federal savings bank grand prix; drivers of getaway cars. il Sports Illus 24:34-6+ F 21 '66

ROBBERS. See Brigands and robbers

ROBBERSON, Elbert

Automatic pilots. Yachting 119:79-81+ Ja '66

Electronic maintenance. Yachting 119:76+ Ap '66

ROBBERSON, Winifred

Boating business. See Issues of Yachting

ROBBINS, Elliott. See Scharff, M. D. jt. auth.

ROBBINS, Jhan

(ed) See Cook, I. We are scarcely James Bond ladies

—and Robbins, June

Beatrice and Brendan Behan; love remembered. Redbook 126:60-1+ Mr '66

Boy who found the sun. Redbook 128:48-9+ D '66

Nice girls who ran away. McCalls 94:114-15+ N '66

One city that cares enough to make every mother's day care dream come true. Ladies Home J 83:71+ Jl '66

ROBBINS, June

(ed) See Cook, I. We are scarcely James Bond ladies

—See Robbins, Jhan, jt. auth.

ROBBINS, Margaret

Boy, this place sure has changed! Wilson Lib Bul 41:186-9 O '66

No roses for Harry. bibliog Library J 91: 1587-90 Mr 15 '66

ROBBINS, Richard M.

Continuing debate about Catholic schools. Cath World 204:143-8 D '66

ROBBINS, Sidney J. and others

When cancer is only skin deep. Todays Health 44:31+ Jl '66

ROBERSON, John R.

Tape it. Holiday 40:111-16 O '66; Same abr. with title Why not tape it? Read Digest 89:231-2+ D '66

ROBERT, Lawrence W.

(ed) See Garner, J. N. Garner: he couldn't be elected without our Lyndon

ROBERT C. Scull collection. See Art—Private collections

ROBERT Joffrey ballet. See City Center Joffrey ballet

ROBERT Moses state park. See New York (state)—Parks and reserves

ROBERTS, Brigham Henry

Cliffhanger. Reporter 35:16-17 D 15 '66

ROBERTS, C. F. See Mandell, N. jt. auth.

ROBERTS, Charles

Press views LBJ; fearsome antagonist. Nation 203:406-11 O 24 '66

ROBERTS, Gene

From freedom high to black power. N Y Times Mag p27-9+ S 25 '66

Remarkable thing is happening in Wilcox County, Ala. N Y Times Mag p26-7+ Ap 17 '66

ROBERTS, Harry Maurice

Harry's hideaway. Newsweek 68:58 N 28 '66

Trouble with Harry. il Time 88:30 S 2 '66

ROBERTS, Henry J.

(comp) Recent books on international relations. See issues of Foreign affairs

ROBERTS, Jo

Thoughts in verse on the tide's reverse; poem. Motor B 117:164 Ap '66

ROBERTS, Marjorie S. See Terry, W. D. jt. auth.

ROBERTS, Millard George

Wizard of flunk-out U; with report by J. Frook. il por Life 60:77-8+ Je 3 '66

ROBERTS, Stanley

TV spy in the sky. Pop Mech 125:127 Ap '66

ROBERTS, Steven V.

Best Republican for '68. Esquire 65:84-5+ Mr '66

Bobby Kennedy's shadow cabinet. Esquire 66:168-9+ S '66

ROCHE, James Michael
Private eyes and public hearings. il por Newsweek 67:77-8 Ap 4 '66
Rattles in the engine. il pors Time 87:100-2+ My 20 '66

ROCHE, John P.
Exit Goldman, enter Roche: can LBJ and intellectuals be friends? B. Nelson. por Science 153:1505-7 S 23 '66
New group leader. Nation 203:301 O 3 '66
New link. il por Time 88:31 S 16 '66

ROCHE, Mary Alice
Choose flowers to put bright color into summer borders. Pop Gard 17:34-5 Ag '66
Church with an indoor garden. il Flower Grower 53:54-5 Mr '66
Enjoy spectacular color two ways. Pop Gard 17:48-50 My '66
Japanese garden, Maine-style. il Flower Grower 53:26-8 Jl '66

ROCHEFORT, Christiane
Notes from a European diary: 1963-64. E. Wilson. New Yorker 42:79-80+ My 21 '66

ROCHEFORT, Henri
Henri Rochefort, by R. L. Williams. Review Newsweek 68:114-15 D 5 '66. S. K. Oberbeck

ROCHEFORT-LUÇAY, Victor Henri, marquis de. See Rochefort, H.

ROCHESTER, N.Y.
ID cards for forty-three cents each. E. C. Traugott. il Am City 81:45 Jl '66

Churches
St Luke's Episcopal church. il Arch Rec 139:178-9 Ap '66

Music
Artistic climate revamped. H. Southgate. Hi Fi 16:133 Mr '66

Negroes
Attack on Kodak: FIGHT dispute. J. Ridgeway. New Repub 156:11-13 Ja 21 '67

Sanitary affairs
Ingram filter provides secondary treatment; Greece, N.Y. F. J. Cramer. il Am City 81:94-5 O '66

Streets
Instead of big bulky trees. J. Gerling. il Am City 81:105-7 Ag '66

ROCHESTER, N.Y. University
Rich, risky life of a university trustee. R. Sheehan. il Fortune 75:124-7+ Ja '67

ROCK, John
Three men who made a revolution. L. Lader. il por N Y Times Mag p8-9+ Ap 10 '66

ROCK borders. See Garden borders
ROCK carvings. See Petroglyphs
ROCK climbing. See Mountaineering
ROCK creek; story. See Mazor, J.
ROCK dolls. See Dolls
ROCK garden plants. See Plants, Rock garden
ROCK gardens. See Gardens, Rock
ROCK ISLAND railway. See Chicago, Rock Island and Pacific railway
ROCK ISLAND-Union Pacific merger. See Railroads—Consolidations and mergers

ROCK 'n' roll music
An Animal views America. E. Burdon. il Ebony 22:160-2+ D '66
Daddy is a hippy. R. Lemon. il Sat Eve Post 239:22 Jl 2 '66
Don't knock the rock. J. A. Michener. il Read Digest 88:157-60+ F '66
From Bach to rock: accent's on youth. il Sr Schol 88:20 My 6 '66
Hip star in Harvard yard. il Life 60:110 Je 3 '66
In my opinion; rock and roll outpoints classical music on every count. D. Dunn. Seventeen 25:192 D '66
Lovin' Spoonful: rock 'n' roll sweetner. B. Rollin. il Look 30:77-81 N 1 '66
Moppets: college ladies of rock. J. Morschauser. il Look 30:56+ Je 14 '66
New troubadours; takeover of the folk rockers. il Time 88:92+ O 28 '66
Nitty-gritty sound; San Francisco sound. il Newsweek 68:102 D 19 '66
Nubes; marketing angles aimed at pre-teens. il Time 87:60+ Mr 11 '66

ROCK 'n' roll songs. See Music, Popular (songs, etc)
ROCK of Cashel. See Cashel, Ireland
ROCK sculpture. See Mountain sculpture

ROCKEFELLER, David
Culture and the corporation; address, September 20, 1966. Vital Speeches 33:14-18 O 15 '66

Population problem and economic progress; address, February 14, 1966. Vital Speeches 32:366-70 Ap 1 '66
What private enterprise means to Latin America. For Affairs 44:403-16 Ap '66

ROCKEFELLER, Jeannette Edris
Mental health and counseling. Todays Health 44:52-3 D '66

ROCKEFELLER, John Davison, 1906-
Greatest challenge of our time. Read Digest 89:85-90 O '66

ROCKEFELLER, John Davison, 1938?-
Improbable bachelor life of John D. Rockefeller IV. G. Greene. il por Ladies Home J 83:108-9+ N '66
John D. 4th campaigns as a Democrat; with report by S. McBee. il pors Life 60:41-2+ Ap 1 '66
Turncoat Rockefeller. C. Boiarsky. New Repub 154:9 F 26 '66
Winning ticket. por Time 88:29 D 9 '66

ROCKEFELLER, Laurance S.
Business and beauty; address, December 2, 1965. Vital Speeches 32:219-21 Ja 15 '66;
Same. il Audubon Mag 68:112-15 Mr '66
Fellow pioneers. por Parks & Rec 1:13 Ja '66
Golden anniversary and a golden opportunity. por Parks & Rec 1:613 Ag '66
One man's view; letter. Am For 72:6-7 Je '66

about
Introducing Laurance Rockefeller. por Parks & Rec 1:18-19+ Ja '66
Mauna Kea, one on the isle. C. Stinnett. Holiday 39:26+ Mr '66
—See Rockefeller, M. jt. auth.

ROCKEFELLER, Mary, and Rockefeller, L. S.
Parks, plans, and people. pors Nat Geog Mag 131:74-119 Ja '67

ROCKEFELLER, Nelson Aldrich, 1908-
Election has shown wide points of view; excerpts from news conference, November 9, 1966. por U S News 61:61 N 21 '66
We honor our teachers. por Parents Mag 41:38 My '66

about
Consensus by any other name. il por Time 88:21-2 D 2 '66
Donkey beats himself. J. Desmond. il por Nation 203:379-81 O 17 '66
Dorado summit. il por Newsweek 68:30-1 D 5 '66
Election night. New Yorker 42:47-50 N 19 '66
Eye to eve. il Time 87:25A Ap 1 '66
Happy warrior. il por Newsweek 68:36+ O 31 '66
Innocent bystander. R. Moley. Newsweek 67:104 Ap 4 '66
Obscene premises bill vetoed in New York. R. H. Smith. Pub W 190:46 Ag 15 '66
Polar elephants. T. Wicker. Atlan 217:80 Ap '66
Return of Rockefeller. E. J. Hughes. Newsweek 68:23 O 17 '66
Rockefeller. New Yorker 42:50 O 22 '66
Rockefeller and the drug plan. W. F. Buckley, jr. Nat R 18:257 Mr 22 '66
Rocky redivivus. il por Time 88:35 O 7 '66
Rocky road to art. il por Newsweek 68:90 Jl 18 '66
Rocky's roughest round. G. Astor. il pors Look 30:52-4+ O 18 '66
Three men behind Rockefeller. T. Buckley. il pors N Y Times Mag p34-5+ O 30 '66

ROCKEFELLER, Winthrop
Opportunity regained. il pors Time 88:24-8 D 2 '66

ROCKEFELLER Center. See New York (city)—Rockefeller Center

ROCKET engines
New TVC development uses free air. R. Lindsey. il Miss & Roc 18:35-6 Mr 14 '66
Plug nozzles regain popularity after earlier GE groundwork. J. F. Judge. il Tech W 19:19 D 12 '66
Tiny whipcrack rocket to launch bigger rocket. Sci N 90:86 Ag 6 '66
U.S. rocket motors; specifications (cont) Aviation W 84:219-23 Mr 7 '66
UTC to show hybrid engine thrust scaling. Tech W 19:40 O 3 '66
Water can oxidize fuel in rocket engine. Sci N 90:86 Ag 6 '66

See also
Liquid propellant rockets
Solid propellant rockets
Space vehicles—Propulsion systems

Design
P&W designs extendible skirt for RL20 rocket engine; telescoping nozzle skirt extension. G. Alexander. il Aviation W 85:60-1+ S 19 '66

ROCKET engines—*Continued*

Materials

Airborne missiles get new winter overcoat.
Sci N 90:224 S 24 '66
Roll-extruded rocket cases move into production stage. il Tech W 18:38 Je 13 '66
Thiokol hydroburst test shows reliability of 156-in. motor case; glass fiber motor case.
il Tech W 19:42-3 D 12 '66

Testing

Firing of 156-in. Thiokol motor completes air force test series. H. D. Watkins. Aviation W 84:29 My 23 '66
GE's plasma engine nears flight testing. M. L. Yaffee. il Aviation W 85:101+ S 5 '66
Rocket testers guard people's eardrums. Sci N 89:388 My 21 '66
Test labs hold space secrets. J. Eberhart. il Sci N 89:391 My 21 '66

Transportation

Titan III-C performance validates solid motor transportation methods. il Miss & Roc 18:27-8 F 14 '66

ROCKET fuel. See Rockets—Fuel

ROCKET launchers
See also
Pistols

ROCKET models
Birds in the hand; national meet of the National association of rocketry. il Time 88:49 Ag 26 '66
U.S. rocketeers rip the iron curtain; first international model rocketry meet. B. Gunn. il Pop Mech 126:152-3 O '66

ROCKET motor cases

Materials

See Rocket engines—Materials

ROCKET pistols. See Pistols

ROCKET power, incorporated
RPI sees F-111 escape rocket proving ability. J. F. Judge. il Tech W 19:25+ Jl 18 '66

ROCKET propulsion
GE's plasma engine nears flight testing. M. L. Yaffee. il Aviation W 85:101+ S 5 '66
Tide rising in rocket propulsion market. M. L. Yaffee. il Aviation W 85:123+ Jl 11 '66
UTC to show hybrid engine thrust scaling. Tech W 19:40 O 3 '66
See also
Rockets, Atomic powered
Solid propellant rockets

ROCKET research corporation
Rocket research studies using manned vehicle waste for fuel; Monex W. J. F. Judge. il Tech W 20:30+ Ja 2 '67

ROCKET sleds
New Sandia track to test Mach 5. R. Pay. il Tech W 19:26+ Jl 4 '66
Torture rides the desert rails. J. Eberhart. Sci N 90:533 D 24 '66

ROCKETS
World missile/space encyclopedia 1966. il Tech W 19:42-8+ Jl 25 '66
See also
Guided missiles
Liquid propellant rockets
Solid propellant rockets

Fuel

Fuel with fizz; liquid hydrogen. Newsweek 68:88 Jl 18 '66
Gemini 10 crew explains fuel consumption. il Tech W 19:18 Ag 8 '66
Rocket research studies using manned vehicle waste for fuel; Monex W. il Tech W 20:30+ Ja 2 '67
Taming liquid hydrogen. il Time 88:57 Jl 15 '66
Taming the tiger in Apollo's tank; controlling liquid hydrogen. il Bsns W p66+ Jl 16 '66
Uprated Saturn flight confirms. S-4B role. G. Alexander. il Aviation W 85:32-3 Jl 11 '66
Waste of space; way to use human waste as a source of rocket fuel. Time 88:43 D 23 '66

Launching

Coon gun launcher saves fuel. il(p437) Sci N 90:444 N 26 '66
Launch operations accelerate at Thumba. Aviation W 84:91-2 My 23 '66

Materials

MSFC testing beryllium for structural use. Miss & Roc 18:32 Ja 24 '66
Thin booster walls yield payload hike. il Tech W 19:35 D 12 '66

Testing

See also
Space vehicles—Propulsion systems—Testing

Transportation

Crawling toward the moon; Saturn 5 rocket moved to launch pad. il Time 87:42 Je 3 '66
Moon rocket rolls out; Saturn V mock-up moved to pad. il Life 60:32-7 Je 10 '66

Use in research

Chemical releases at high altitudes. N. W. Rosenberg. bibliog il Science 152:1017-27 My 20 '66
French launching probes from Antarctica. W. C. Wetmore. il Aviation W 85:55+ D 26 '66
Infrared sky scanning from a rocket. il Sky & Tel 31:208-9 Ap '66
U.S. research rockets; specifications (cont) Aviation W 84:229 Mr 7 '66
Venus flytrap rocket to collect space dust; air force to study Leonid meteor shower. Sci N 90:401 N 12 '66
X-ray spectra from three cosmic sources. R. J. Grader and others. bibliog il Science 152:1499-504 Je 10 '66

ROCKETS, Atomic powered
Nuclear rocket for Mars. Sci N 90:327 O 22 '66
Preparing to go past the moon; testing nuclear rocket system for deep space probes. il Bsns W p 136+ F 12 '66
Saturn nuclear stage seen possible in '75. H. M. David. il Tech W 19:118+ N 28 '66
Seaborg presses nuclear case at WESCON. C. D. LaFond. Tech W 19:18-19 Ag 29 '66
Stainless steel exhaust duct scheduled for NERVA firing. il Tech W 18:36-7 Je 20 '66
Webb sees nuclear rocket by 1975; $1 billion needed. Miss & Roc 18:36 My 23 '66

Testing

First experimental rocket firings slated. H. Taylor. il Tech W 19:15-16 N 7 '66
Full-thrust NERVA firing may slip a week. Miss & Roc 18:17 F 21 '66
Nerva breadboard engine system achieves full power in test run. R. G. O'Lone. il Aviation W 84:101-2 Mr 21 '66

ROCKETS, Sounding
Dornier tests guided integral paraglider. W. C. Wetmore. il Aviation W 84:57-8 F 7 '66
French Centaure to carry German particle collector. Miss & Roc 18:25 F 28 '66
French launching probes from Antarctica. W. C. Wetmore. il Aviation W 85:55+ D 26 '66
Launch operations accelerate at Thumba. Aviation W 84:91-2 My 23 '66
Sounding rockets fundamental to Japan's space success. S. Nagashima. il Tech W 19:34+ S 12 '66
Systems approach to sounding rockets benefits Thiokol unit. il Tech W 19:25+ S 12 '66

ROCKFORD, Ill.

Streets

Penny test for Dutch elm disease. A. Grimm. il Am City 81:122-3 My '66

ROCKS
Electrical resistivity changes in saturated rock under stress. W. F. Brace and A. S. Orange. bibliog il Science 153:1525-6 S 23 '66
Kyanite-sillimanite equilibrium at 750°C. R. C. Newton. bibliog il Science 151:1222-5 Mr 11 '66
Save those rocks. il Pop Gard 17:70-1 My '66
Shock-lithification of unconsolidated rock materials. N. M. Short. bibliog il Science 154:382-4 O 21 '66

Collectors and collecting

Be an independent rockhound. H. D. Brown. il Hobbies 71:117 My '66
Thoughts of an amateur mineralogist; give me my West. H. D. Brown. il Hobbies 71:117 D '66

ROCKS, Gases in. See Gases in rocks

ROCKS, Igneous
Deep-sea iron deposit from the South Pacific. E. Bonatti and O. Joensuu. bibliog il Science 154:643-5 N 4 '66
Isotopic composition of strontium in volcanic rocks from Oahu. J. L. Powell and S. E. DeLong. bibliog il Science 153:1239-42 S 9 '66
Oxygen fugacities directly measured in magmatic gases; Makaopuhi lava lake, Kilauea volcano, Hawaii. M. Sato and T. L. Wright. bibliog il Science 153:1103-5 S 2 '66

ROCKS, Sedimentary
Molecules crack rocks. il(p65) Sci N 90:69 Jl 30 '66
Submarine lithification of carbonate sediments. J. D. Milliman. bibliog il Science 153:994-7 Ag 26 '66

ROCKS, Water in. See Water in rocks
ROCKVILLE, Md.

City planning
Rockville's multi-level mini-core. J. Bailey.
    il Arch Forum 125:56-61 D '66
ROCKWELL, F. A.
Finding a market for your story. Writer 79:
    21-5 Je '66
ROCKWELL, Mabel M.
Instant odyssey. Travel 126:33-6 D '66
ROCKWELL, Norman
Man on the moon; paintings. Look 31:39-42
    Ja 10 '67

about
Norman Rockwell: silent film star. C. Mor-
    rison. il pors Look 30:40+ Mr 8 '66
Peace corps: JFK's bold legacy. il Look
    30:34-9 Je 14 '66
ROCKWELL, Willard Frederick, 1914-
Rockwell-Standard's jet-age management. T.
    J. Murray. il Duns R 87:28-31+ Je '66
ROCKWELL manufacturing company
Rockwell bets on its own name. il Bsns W
    p85 Ap 23 '66
ROCKWELL-Standard corporation
Rockwell-Standard's jet-age management. T.
    J. Murray. il Duns R 87:28-31+ Je '66
ROCKY MOUNT, N.C.
Hermetically sealed transformer cuts utility
    costs. C. Bateman. il Am City 81:104 Ag '66
ROCKY MOUNTAIN sheep. See Mountain
    sheep
ROCKY MOUNTAINS
Four family-planned circle tours. N. Kuehnl
    and P. Lindberg. il Bet Hom & Gard 44:
    72-3 Je '66
See also
Hell's Canyon
Mission Range

Canadian Rockies
Canadian Rockies, lords of a beckoning land.
    A. Phillips. il Nat Geog Mag 130:352-93 S '66
RODALE, Jerome Irving
Apostle of the compost heap. E. Perényi. il
    por Sat Eve Post 239:30-3 Jl 16 '66
RODARMOR, William
What makes Gigli click? Pop Phot 59:96-7+
    O '66
RODD, Thomas Whitney
Four ways to go: Tommy Rodd went to jail.
    B. Weinraub. por Esquire 66:124+ S '66
RODDEY, Barbara
His way of working. U S Camera 29:40+ D
    '66
RODDEY, Phil
His way of working. B. Roddey. il por U S
    Camera 29:40+ D '66
RODE, Alex
Henry Miller: the novelist as liberator.
    Américas 18:41-3 Ja '66
RODELL, Fred
It is the Earl Warren court. N Y Times Mag
    p30-1+ Mr 13 '66
RODENTS
See also
Pocket mice
Rats
RODENTS as carriers of infection
Search for the invisible killer; Bolivian
    hemorrhagic fever in the village of San
    Joaquín. T. Armbrister. il Sat Eve Post
    239:92-4+ D 3 '66
See also
Plague
Rats as carriers of infection
RODEOS
Charros of Monterrey. il Sunset 137:38 Jl '66
Dean of the faceless men; rodeo circuit cow-
    boys. H. Peterson. il Sports Illus 26:40-3
    Ja 16 '67
RODGERS, Mary Augusta
One moment to cherish; story. Good H 162:
    78-9 F '66
This time last year; story. Redbook 128:48-9
    Ja '67
RODGERS, Richard
To the love song, with love. Sat Eve Post
    240:36-7 Ja 28 '67
RODGERS, Rod A.
Men and the dance: why do we question the
    image? por Dance Mag 40:35-6 Je '66
RODGERS, W. R.
Thaw in the Irish cold war. N Y Times
    Mag p30-1+ F 27 '66
RODIA, Simon
Legacy of Simon Rodia. L. Barry. il Pop
    Phot 59:34 O '66
RODMAN, Selden
Day with Pablo Neruda. Sat R 49:16-18 Jl
    9 '66
Peruvian politics stalls Belaúnde's reforms.
    Reporter 35:37-40 Jl 14 '66

Why Balaguer won. New Repub 154:17-21
    Je 18 '66
RODRIGUES, Amália
Joys of suffering; U.S. concert debut. il por
    Time 87:62-3 Je 24 '66
RODRIGUEZ, Mario
Guatemala in perspective. bibliog f Cur Hist
    51:338-43+ D '66
RODRIGUEZ VILLAR, Antonio
World press institute. Américas 18:2-7 Je '66
RODY, M. J.
Cooperation built a market plaza. Am City
    81:104-5 Ap '66
ROE, Jim
Rendezvous at Little Current. Motor B 118:
    44-5+ Jl '66
So you have bought a new cruiser. Yachting
    119:80-2+ Je '66
ROE, Kenneth A.
Desalting methods, their costs and promise.
    Am City 81:126-8 My '66
ROE, Richard D.
Color when you least expect it. Flower
    Grower 53:44-5 Mr '66
Fall crocus. Horticulture 44:30+ S '66
Shirley poppies. il Horticulture 44:41 F '66
ROE, Yale
High noon in Bakersfield. R. L. Shayon.
    Sat R 49:22 Ag 20 '66
ROEDER, Kenneth D.
Auditory system of noctuid moths; excerpts
    from address, April 27, 1966. bibliog Sci-
    ence 154:1515-21 D 23 '66
Differential anemometer for measuring the
    turning tendency of insects in stationary
    flight. Science 153:1634-6 S 30 '66
ROENTGEN, Wilhelm Konrad. See Röntgen,
    W. K.
ROEPKE, Wilhelm
Dollar seen from Geneva. Nat R 18:216-18
    Mr 8 '66
Obituary
    Nat R 18:200 Mr 8 '66. L. Von Mises
ROESEL, Catherine E. See Reddick, A. jt.
    auth.
ROETGER, R. C.
110 volt AC A-OK aboard. Motor B 118:32-5+
    D '66
ROETHKE, Theodore
Roethke in his prose. K. Hoskins. Poetry
    107:400-1 Mr '66
Roethke memorial plans. J. Ciardi. Sat R
    49:16 Ap 9 '66
Roethke: the lost son. S. Spender. New
    Repub 155:23-5 Ag 27 '66
ROFFEY, Jack
Hostile witness. Criticism
    America 114:365 Mr 12 '66
    Newsweek il 67:87 F 28 '66
    Time 87:101 F 25 '66
    Vogue 147:64 Ap 15 '66
ROFFWARG, Howard P. and others
Ontogenetic development of the human sleep-
    dream cycle. bibliog Science 152:604-19 Ap
    29 '66
ROGERS, Bennett
Sabreliner: T-39 in civvies. Flying 78:40-7
    My '66
ROGERS, David
Sign: poem. Cath World 203:308 Ag '66
ROGERS, Frank
Sweet talk from Old Wool. D. Jenkins. por
    Sports Illus 24:67-8 My 30 '66
ROGERS, Gary
Salt seekers. Sci N 90:249-50 O 1 '66
ROGERS, Harold
Rameau in Boston. Opera N 30:6-7 Ap 9 '66
ROGERS, John
Building a different kind of tree house. il
    por Sports Illus 25:56-9 O 17 '66
ROGERS, Millard F. Jr
Living with antiques. Antiques 90:350-3 S '66
New England glass company marks. Antiques
    89:724-9 My '66
ROGERS, Paul
Sparse oceanology funding criticized; sum-
    mary of address, ed. by R. W. Niblock.
    Miss & Roc 18:18 Ap 25 '66
ROGERS, Robert, and Yates, Ted
Undeclared war in Guatemala. Sat Eve Post
    239:30-3 Je 18 '66
ROGERS, Roy
Roy Rogers goes north. W. E. A. Anderson.
    il pors Outdoor Life 137:52-5+ Ap '66
ROGERS, Vance D.
Impact of Vatican II on Protestantism; ad-
    dress, October 13, 1966. Vital Speeches 33:
    91-4 N 15 '66
ROGERS, Walter
Excerpt from January 15, 1966, newsletter
    to his constituents. Cong Digest 45:142+
    My '66
ROGERS, Will
I never met a man I didn't like. por Sr Schol
    89:3 N 4 '66

ROGERS, William P.
Principles of international law concerning friendly relations and cooperation among states; statement. December 8, 1965. Dept State Bul 54:168-75 Ja 31 '66
ROGGEN, D. R. and others
Cilia in nematode sensory organs. bibliog Science 152:515-16 Ap 22 '66
ROGIN, Gilbert
Indoor and watcher; story. New Yorker 42:40-4 Ap 2 '66
Players; story. New Yorker 42:40-3 Ap 30 '66
Uncompleted investigation; story. New Yorker 42:22-4 Jl 9 '66
ROGIN, Michael
Politics of outrage. Commonweal 84:99-102 Ap 15 '66
ROGOFF, Gordon
Investigation: unbroken silence. New Repub 155:42-4 N 26 '66
Writer as enemy. New Repub 155:32-3+ D 17 '66
ROGUE RIVER, Ore.
Up and down Oregon's Rogue. il Sunset 136:76-85 Je '66
ROHE, Ludwig Mies van der. See Mies van der Rohe, L.
ROHEN, James E.
Inexpensive integrated solid-state stereo record player. Pop Electr 25:51-2 Jl '66
ROHMER, Sax, pseud.
Truth in fiction. J. Stafford. il por Library J 91:4557-65 O 1 '66
ROHOLT, O. A. and Pressman, D.
Antibody molecules: discontinuous heterogeneity of heavy chains. bibliog Science 153:1257-9 S 9 '66
ROHR, Frank
Bermuda's Whartons are sunfish sovereigns. Motor B 117:136-7+ F '66
Coast guard re-shapes its saving ways. Motor B 117:22-5+ F '66
Crushing race on a cruel sea. il Motor B 117:132-6 Ap '66
Fresh landfalls in the Out Islands. il Motor B 118:39-42 O '66
Sail care without tears. Motor B 117:28-9+ Je '66
Thunderbird soars to Bermuda win. por Motor B 118:82-3+ Ag '66
Vamp X, new victor on southern seas. il Motor B 117:174-9 My '66
ROHRBACH, Heinrich
Hardy heather. Horticulture 44:20-1+ Ap '66
ROIG, Arturo Andrés
Amadeo Jacques. Américas 18:7-13 Jl '66
ROIZEN, Joseph
Ampex home video recorder. Electr World 75:52-4 My '66
ROIZMAN, Bernard. See Sydiskis. R. J. jt. auth.
ROJAS PINILLA, Gustavo
Threat of daggers. il por Time 87:36 Ap 1 '66
RÖLING, Bert V. A.
Roots of peace. UNESCO Courier 19:22-6+ Ja '66
ROLLEI cameras. See Cameras
ROLLEI SL 66. See Single-lens reflex cameras
ROLLERS, Paint. See Paint rollers
ROLLING hotel. See Motor buses
ROLLING MEADOWS, Ill.
Don't trade that police car. J. McFeggan. il Am City 81:100-2 F '66
ROLLINS, Howard A. Jr
Apple growing fence. il Flower Grower 53:34-5+ F '66
ROLLS. See Bread
ROLLS-Royce (automobile) See Automobiles.
ROLLS-Royce, limited
Flying high with Rolls; bought out Bristol Siddeley engines ltd. il Time 88:99-100 S 9 '66
Passion for perfection. Holiday 40:96-7 Ag '66
Rolls explores third-generation lift jets. H. J. Coleman. il Aviation W 84:54-5+ Ap 18 '66
Rolls mystique. L. Beebe. il Horizon 8:40-8 Wint '66
Rolls plans multiple versions of RB.178. H. J. Coleman il Aviation W 85:40-1 Jl 18 '66
Rolls Royce materials work stresses filament composites. J. F. Judge. il Miss & Roc 18:26+ Mr 7 '66
ROLO, Charles J.
Market à go go. N Y Times Mag p26-7+ My 8 '66
ROLOFF, Michael
(tr) See Sachs, N. O the chimneys
ROLVAAG, Karl Fritjof
Down with youth. por Time 88:25 S 23 '66
Minnesota's Democrats try to dump their governor. R. Steele. il Reporter 34:29-31 Je 2 '66

Out of the fight into the fire. Time 88:20 Jl 15 '66
Poll vault; gubernatorial primary contenders. Reporter 35:10 Ag 11 '66
Smiling through. Newsweek 67:30+ Mr 14 '66
Statehouse to woodshed. il por Newsweek 68:20 Jl 4 '66
To the woodshed. il Time 88:15-16 Jl 1 '66
ROMAN, Robert C.
Jessie Matthews. Dance Mag 40:66-71 S '66
ROMAN, Stephen Boleslav
Biggest and best speculator in Canada. J. L. Schecter. por Fortune 74:67 S '66
ROMAN aqueducts. See Aqueducts
ROMAN Catholic church. See Catholic church
ROMAN civilization. See Rome—Civilization
ROMAN curia. See Catholic church—Roman curia
ROMAN emperors
Caesars. il Life 60:56-74+ Je 3 '66
Crucible of Christendom. E. Kern. il Life 60:77-8+ Je 17 '66
See also
Aurelius Antoninus, M.
ROMAN empire. See Rome
ROMAN legions. See Rome—Army
ROMAN republic. See Rome—History—Republic, B.C. 510-30
ROMAN walls
Great Britain
Wall to mark the northern reaches; Hadrian's wall. il Life 60:72-3 Je 17 '66
ROMANI, Roger J. See Ku, L. jt. auth.
ROMANOFF, Harry
Hot on the line. Time 88:56-7 Jl 29 '66
ROMANTIC love. See Love
ROMANTICISM
Mondrian and romanticism; excerpt from catalogue of Toronto show. R. Rosenblum. il Art N 64:33-7+ F '66
ROME
Lead among the Romans; lead poisoning. il Time 88:79 S 23 '66
Romans. il Life 60:56-74+ Mr 4; 36-46+ Mr 11; 50-64+ Mr 18; 56-71+ Mr 25; 56-74+ Je 3; 66-79 Je 10; 58-78+ Je 17 '66
See also
Education—Rome

Antiquities
Feats in concrete raised colossal structures; baths of Caracalla; construction technique. il Life 60:60-3 Mr 18 '66
Romans; legacy of stone and spirit. il Life 60:58-78+ Je 17 '66
Romans; 1300 years; great men and their deeds. il Life 60:36-9 Mr 11 '66
See also
Baalbek, Lebanon

Army
Craftsmen in the art of war; Roman legions. il Life 60:54-9 Mr 18 '66

Civilization
Mask of love, by S. Barr. Review
Sat R 49:46-7 D 24 '66. O. Prescott
Roman culture, ed. with introds. by G. Wills. Review
Nat R 18:938-9+ S 20 '66. H. Kenner
Romans. il Life 60:56-74+ Mr 4; 36-46+ Mr 11; 50-64+ Mr 18; 56-71+ Mr 25; 56-74+ Je 3; 66-79 Je 10; 58-78+ Je 17 '66

History
Imperial America; similarity to Roman empire. T. Molnar. Nat R 18:409-11 My 3 '66; Discussion. 18:554+ Je 14 '66
Mask of love, by S. Barr. Review
Sat R 49:46-7 D 24 '66. O. Prescott
Romans. il Life 60:56-74+ Mr 4; 36-46+ Mr 11; 50-64+ Mr 18; 56-71+ Mr 25; 56-74+ Je 3; 66-79 Je 10; 58-78+ Je 17 '66
Theodor Mommsen; neglected master of Roman history. W. H. Chamberlin. Sat R 49:18-19+ My 21 '66

Republic, B.C. 510-30
Stormy road to grandeur; with historical chart showing great events. E. Kern. il Life 60:40-6+ Mr 11 '66

Social conditions
Swinging hub of the world. E. Kern. il Life 60:67-71 Je 10 '66

Social life and customs
Swinging hub of the world. E. Kern. il Life 60:72-9 Je 10 '66
Whispers of Pompeii; with report by R. Espinosa. il Life 60:56-71+ Mr 25 '66

ROME (city)
Personal business; corporate headquarters in the Eternal City. Bsns W p 121 Ag 27 '66

Architecture
Marriage Italian style. B. Zevi; G. de Carlo. il Arch Forum 124:62-7 My '66

Art
Art news from Rome. M. Gendel. il Art N 65:22+ Mr; 54 Sum '66

Description
Regal Rome. M. M. Davis. il Travel 126:56-60 Jl '66

Galleries and museums
Rome's gallery girls; directors and dealers. il Newsweek 68:85-6 Ag 15 '66

Hotels, restaurants, etc.
See also
Night clubs

Music
Naples. Rome. F. Nuzzo. Opera N 31:32 D '66
Notes from our correspondents (cont) W. Weaver. Hi Fi 16:20+ N '66
Rome. F. Nuzzo. il Opera N 30:32 F 19; 36 Ap 2; 32-3 Ap 16 '66

Social life and customs
Letter from abroad. A. Menen. il McCalls 93:76+ Ap '66

Street traffic
Roman roulette. A. Menen. il N Y Times Mag p24-5+ Ja 30 '66

Traffic problem
See Rome (city)—Street traffic

ROMEO and Juliet; ballet. See Ballets—Criticisms

ROMERO, Patricia
Early organization of red caps 1937-1938. bibliog Negro Hist Bul 29:101-2+ F '66
Look at Supreme court Justice William O. Douglas. Negro Hist Bul 29:129-30+ Mr '66

ROMEY, David
Sephardim. Américas 18:48 Je '66

ROMNES, Haakon Ingolf
A.T.&T.'s new boss. il por Time 88:52-3 D 30 '66
Lot to learn. por Newsweek 69:54 Ja 2 '67
New top man for the AT&T. por U S News 62:11 Ja 2 '67

ROMNEY, George, 1907-
People lack confidence in Washington; interview. por U S News 61:59-60 N 21 '66
Romney: I urged repudiation of extremists; letter, December 21, 1964. U S News 61:66-70 D 19 '66; Summary. Time 88:28 D 9 '66
We need a new capitalism in America. por Nations Bsns 54:34-5+ Jl '66
Where Romney stands on major issues; statements. U S News 61:61 S 5 '66

about

All-American boy. T. Wicker. Atlan 217:78 Ap '66
Auditioning for '68. il por Newsweek 68:21 Jl 18 '66
Back for a checkup. Nat R 18:716 Jl 26 '66
Boost for Romney: Scranton bows out. il U S News 60:22 Je 13 '66
Can Romney stop Nixon in '68? por U S News 61:31 Jl 25 '66
Consensus by any other name. il por Time 88:21-2 D 2 '66
Conservative-progressive-liberal. Time 88:17 Jl 1 '66
Dogma of the South. R. Kirk. Nat R 19:38 Ja 10 '67
Dorado summit. il por Newsweek 68:30-1 D 5 '66
Holy George. New Repub 155:4 D 3 '66
It's like running against God. S. Alsop. il pors Sat Eve Post 239:20 O 22 '66
Letter to Barry. Newsweek 68:27 D 12 '66
Lonesome George. Newsweek 68:20-1 Jl 4 '66
Polls '66: Nixon or Romney? P. Gennoy. Nat R 18:1084 N 1 '66
Ready for Romney. Time 89:17 Ja 6 '67
Romney-Goldwater clash; storm signal for '68. por U S News 61:14 D 12 '66
Romney-Javits ticket for Republicans? il pors U S News 60:20 Je 6 '66
Romney on the road. il por Newsweek 68:22-3 D 19 '66
Romney: Republican hope for '68? profile of a candidate. il por U S News 61:54-61 S 5 '66
Romney victory gilds his chances for '68. por Bsns W p44-5 N 12 '66

Romney's chances to head ticket in '68. il por U S News 61:29-30 D 5 '66
Romney's letter. Nat R 18:1257 D 13 '66
See how he runs. il por Time 88:32 D 16 '66
Story of two letters: effect on Romney chances. por U S News 61:62-5 D 19 '66

ROMNEY, George, family
George Romney family: all aboard for the White House! E. Havemann. il pors Ladies Home J 83:176-8+ O '66

RON, Eliora Z. and others
Polysomes extracted from escherichia coli by freeze-thaw-lysozyme lysis. bibliog Science 153:1119-20 S 2 '66

RÓNAI, Paulo
It's in the potato. Américas 18:17-23 N '66

RONAN, Margaret
Following the films. See issues of Senior scholastic
ST at the movies. Sr Schol 88:sup 16+ Mr 4 '66

RONBERG, Gary
College football. Sports Illus 25:56-7 S 26; 52-3 O 10; 58-9 O 24 '66
Hockey. Sports Illus 24:53-4 F 28; 25-71-3 N 28 '66; 26:46-7 Ja 16 '67

RONETTES (singers) See Negro singers

RONGELAP atoll
Golden lining. Reporter 34:16+ F 24 '66

RONNIE, Art
Verismo in the air. Opera N 31:6-7 D 3 '66

RONNING, C. Neale
Brazil's revolutionary government. Cur Hist 51:296-300+ N '66

RONSHAUSEN, E. J.
Hike to lost lake. Nat Parks Mag 40:9 Jl '66

RÖNTGEN, Wilhelm Konrad
Practical use of X-ray made on discovery. Sci N 89:293 Ap 23 '66

RONY, Abdul
(comp) Articles and other books received; south Asia. Am Hist R 71:774-5 Ja '66

ROOD, Ronald
Aim for safety. Parents Mag 41:50-1+ Ag '66
Despised one, la cucaracha. Aububon Mag 68:426-9 N '66
Everybody profits but the starfish. NEA J 55:34-5 My '66

ROOF gardens
Gardening on a deck, terrace or even on a roof. il Sunset 136:236-8+ Ap '66
How to insure a triumphant spring show. il House & Gard 129:184-5 Ap '66

ROOF heliports. See Heliports

ROOFING
New roofing with a timeless look. il House & Gard 130:82+ O '66

ROOFS
Building movement can damage built-up roofing systems. W. H. Gumpertz. il Arch Rec 140:221-4 S '66
House whose strength is in the roof. il Arch Rec 139:215-18 Ap '66
How materials react to solar energy. J. I. Yellott. il Arch Rec 139:196-8 My '66
Leak-free roof for underground garage. K. A. Gruber. il Arch Rec 140:163-4 D '66
New theory for what's behind built-up roofing failures. K. Tator. il Arch Rec 140:190-2 N '66
Private residence, Martha's Vineyard Island, Massachusetts. il Arch Rec 139:46-9 mid-My '66
See also
Gutters (roof)

ROOKERY BAY wildlife sanctuaries. See Wildlife sanctuaries

ROOKS, Dorothy (Maynor) See Maynor, D.

ROOM; story. See Vivante, A.

ROOM air conditioners. See Air conditioning equipment

ROOM furnishings. See Household furnishings

ROOM painting. See Painting, Industrial and practical

ROOMS
Growing boy needs a growing room. il Bet Hom & Gard 44:36 My '66
Maurice Medcalfe's bathing pillar. il Vogue 148:168-71 S 15 '66
Pampering room. il House & Gard 131:88-93 Ja '67
Place to workout, or just work. il Bet Hom & Gard 44:136 My '66
Take-it-easy rooms. il House & Gard 129:102-13 Je '66
Two very special rooms! one his, one hers. il Bet Hom & Gard 44:46-7 Ag '66
See also
Bedrooms
House decoration
Kitchens

ROOMS—See also—*Continued*
  Laundries
  Libraries (rooms)
  Outdoor rooms
  Sewing rooms
ROOMS; drama. See Mann, S.
ROOMS, Miniature
  Little rooms created for fun. S. A. Parvin. il Hobbies 71:122-3+ Mr; 122-3 Ap '66
ROOMS, Remodeled. See Houses, Remodeled
ROONEY, Thomas P. See Riecker, R. E. jt. auth.
ROOSEN, Willem
  New York to Nantucket by day sailer. Motor B 118:34+ Jl '66
ROOSEVELT, Eleanor (Roosevelt)
  Wise and warm thoughts from Eleanor Roosevelt; excerpts from Common sense wisdom of three first ladies, ed. by B. Adler. por Good H 162:95 Je '66

about

In new book: story of an FDR romance; concerning Time between the wars, by J. Daniels. por U S News 61:13 Ag 22 '66
Memorial ceremony; monument dedicated at United Nations headquarters, April 23, 1966. il UN Mo Chron 3:69-70 My '66
ROOSEVELT, Franklin Delano, 1882-1945
  Day a generation wept; excerpts from The last 100 days. J. Toland. il Ladies Home J 83:60+ Je '66
  First New deal, by R. Moley. Review
    Newsweek il pors 68:109+ D 12 '66. R. Moses
    Sat R 49:49-51+ D 24 '66. D. Young
    Time il por 88:54 D 30 '66
  F.D.R. & Lucy. Time 88:13 Ag 26 '66
  F.D.R.'s secret romance. A. Schlesinger, jr. por Ladies Home J 83:66+ N '66
  Great American love story; concerning J. Daniels' book. il por Newsweek 68:60-1 Ag 22 '66
  Great romance. por Time 88:23 Ag 19 '66
  In new book: story of an FDR romance; concerning Time between the wars, by J. Daniels. por U S News 61:13 Ag 22 '66
  Mystery of Pearl Harbor. P. Greaves. il Nat R 18:1266-72 D 13 '66
  New light on the thinking of FDR and Churchill. por U S News 61:6 D 26 '66
  Old wives' tale; concerning J. Daniels book. R. Moley. Newsweek 68:76 Ag 29 '66
  Place of Franklin D. Roosevelt in history; address, May 1965. A. Nevins. il por Am Heritage 17:12-15+ Je '66
  Romantic footnote to an era; with report by J. Daniels. il pors Life 61:44-9 S 2 '66
  Roosevelt as friend of France. J. M. Haight, jr. bibliog f For Affairs 44:518-26 Ap '66
  Roosevelt legacy: facing the realities of our time; remarks, August 21, 1966. L. B. Johnson. Dept State Bul 55:371-2 S 12 '66
ROOSEVELT Franklin Delano, 1914-
  Roosevelt tells how government will press for equal employment; letter. por Nations Bsns 53:10+ D '65

about

F.D.R. jr, the last race. W. V. Shannon. Commonweal 84:550-1 S 2 '66
Rise, fall and...of F.D.R. jr. M. Levitas. il pors N Y Times Mag p27+ O 23 '66
Roosevelt candidacy that helps Republicans? por U S News 61:14 S 19 '66
ROOSEVELT, James
  U.N. development program, a new effort in peacebuilding; statement, January 11, 1966. Dept State Bul 54:420-6 Mr 14 '66
  U.N. extends World food program; statement, December 10, 1965. Dept State Bul 54:130-3 Ja 24 '66
  U.N. Security council extends peace force in Cyprus; statement, March 16, 1966. Dept State Bul 54:718-19 My 2 '66
  U.S. presents views on population growth and economic development; statement, December 15, 1965. Dept State Bul 54:175-8 Ja 31 '66
ROOSEVELT memorial. See Washington, D.C.—Monuments, statues, etc.
ROOSTERS. See Poultry
ROOT, Howard F.
  Brighter future for children with diabetes; ed. by D. W. Lord. Parents Mag 41:70-1+ N '66
ROOTS
  Morphogenetic substance in legume nodule formation. A. G. Schaffer and M. Alexander. bibliog il Science 152:82-3 Ap 1 '66
  Root pressure and leaf water potential. H. D. Barrs. bibliog il Science 152:1266-8 My 27 '66

ROPE
  How to make the Melin tail splice. H. deFontaine. il Yachting 119:200-1 F '66
  Many uses of stretch rope. F. M. Paulson. il Field & S 71:76-80 Jl '66
  Stowing the anchor rode. J. F. Jayne. il Motor B 117:152+ Mr '66
  Throwing a bowline. J. E. Weber. il Motor B 118:38 Jl '66
    See also
  Knots and splices
ROPE ladders. See Ladders
ROPER, Elmo
  Adlai Stevenson: a new vision. Sat R 49:20 Jl 9 '66
  Government by public opinion polls. Sat R 49:18 My 28 '66
  How culturally active are Americans? Sat R 49:22-3 My 14 '66
  Were the polls wrong? Sat R 49:33 D 10 '66
ROPER, Hugh Redwald Trevor-. See Trevor-Roper, H. R.
ROQUEFORT cheese. See Cheese
ROREM, Ned
  From a composer's journal; excerpts from Music from inside out. Commentary 42:82-7 N '66
  Is new music new? Am Rec G 32:776-9+ My '66
RORIMER, James Joseph
  Double loss. il por Time 87:88+ My 20 '66
  Intermediaries. il por Newsweek 67:100 My 23 '66
  Obituary
    Art N 65:8 Sum '66. H. LaFarge
    Sat R il por 49:36-7 Je 4 '66. K. Kuh
ROSE, Barbara
  Reinhardt. Vogue 148:183 N 1 '66
ROSE, Billy
  Bantam Barnum. por Newsweek 67:68 F 21 '66
  Competitor. il pors Time 87:77 F 18 '66
  Many careers of Billy Rose. por Read Digest 88:117-24 My '66
  Obituary
    Life il por 60:38 F 18 '66
    Subject is Rose's; trouble over burial. il Time 88:49 Ag 19 '66
ROSE, Dixie E.
  Alpine buttercup. Horticulture 44:50 D '66
ROSE, Lloyd
  Curl up and read. Seventeen 25:190 My '66
ROSE, Richard G. and Wilson, A. C.
  Peafowl lactate dehydrogenase: problem of isoenzyme identification. bibliog Science 153:1411-13 S 16 '66
ROSE, Robert H.
  Yosemites of the Kings River. Nat Parks Mag 40:4-9 O '66
ROSE, Stephen C.
  Protestant manifesto. Newsweek 67:86-7 Mr 7 '66
ROSE Latulippe; ballet. See Ballets—Criticisms
ROSE tattoo; drama. See Williams, T.
ROSE white and rose red; story. See Jaffe, R.
ROSEBUD reservaion, S. D. See Indians of North America—Reservations
ROSECRANS, William Starke
  Obituary
    Am For por 71:3 O '65
ROSELIEP, Raymond
  All that glitters; poem. Christian Cent 83:1601 D 28 '66
  By what is not the world. Poetry 107:394-6 Mr '66
  From woodcarver to wordcarver. Poetry 107:326-30 F '66
  In the dry light; Tar roof; Eight haiku; In extremis; poems. Poetry 108:294-300 Ag '66
  Like Swinburne to Sappho; poem. Nation 203:286 S 26 '66
  Tree, lake, moon: and man. Poetry 108:54-7 Ap '66
  Walk in woods; poem. Nation 203:326 O 3 '66

about

Five poets. M. McCloskey. Poetry 108:273 Jl '66
ROSEMAN, Alvin
  Foreign aid under Lyndon Johnson. Cur Hist 50:335-41+ Je '66
ROSEMONT enterprises, incorporated
  Random house enjoined on Hughes biography. Pub W 190:193-4 Jl 11 '66
  U.S. court voids injunction on biography of Hughes. Pub W 190:308-9 Ag 29 '66
ROSÉN, Carin
  Annals of espionage: Wennerström case. T. Whiteside. New Yorker 42:115-18+ Ap 2 '66
ROSEN, Gerald R.
  Bobby Kennedy and the businessmen. Duns R 88:32-3+ O '66

ROSEN, Roslyn
He never said good-bye. Ladies Home J 83: 49+ Jl '66
ROSEN, Sidney I. and others
Glucose-6-phosphatase in tubular endo-plas-mic reticulum of hepatocytes. bibliog Science 152:352-4 Ap 15 '66
ROSENAU, William A.
Supplementary feeding. Horticulture 44:38-9+ Jl '66
Testing soil. Horticulture 44:26-7+ Mr '66
ROSENBERG, Harold
Eulogy. February 20, 1966. Art N 65:21 Ap '66
From Pollock to pop: twenty years of painting and sculpture. Holiday 39:96-105+ Mr '66
Guide for the unperplexed. Art N 65:46-7+ S '66
Image as counterforce. Art N 64:48-9+ F '66
Is there a Jewish art? excerpt from address. Commentary 42:57-60 Jl '66; 42:20+ Discussion. O '66
Leisure and the split man. Vogue 147:142-3+ F 1 '66
Nakian: Eros and grief. Vogue 148:64-5+ Jl '66
Saul Steinberg's art world. Art N 65:51-4+ Mr '66
Steinberg. Vogue 149:96-9+ Ja 1 '67
Virtuosos of boredom. Vogue 148:296-7+ S 1 '66
ROSENBERG, Julius and Ethel, case
After seventeen years. Nation 203:203-4 S 12 '66
Atomic bomb secret, fifteen years later. Bul Atomic Sci 22:2-3+ D '66
Case of Morton Sobell; new queries from the defense. E. Langer. il Science 153:1501-5 S 23 '66; Discussion. 154:962 N 25 '66
End of a mystery? A-bomb sketch release; M. Sobell appeal. il Newsweek 68:22 Ap 15 '66
Invitation to an inquest, by W. Schneir and M. Schneir. Review
Commentary 41:69-70+ Ja '66. A. M. Bickel; Discussion. 41:8+ Je '66
ROSENBERG, L. T. See Caren, L. D. jt. auth.
ROSENBERG, Leon E.
Cystinuria: genetic heterogeneity and allelism. bibliog Science 154:1341-3 D 9 '66
ROSENBERG, N. W.
Chemical releases at high altitudes. bibliog Science 152:1017-27 My 20 '66
ROSENBERGER, Carol
Girl with the unreasonable dream. E. M. Wylie. il por Redbook 126:76-7+ Ap '66
ROSENBLATT, Herta
By grace of pain; poem. Cath World 204: 205 Ja '67
Song came late that year; poem. Cath World 204:142 D '66
ROSENBLATT, Jay S. See Roth, L. L. jt. auth.
ROSENBLATT, Rand
Something new in Britain. New Repub 155: 9-10 D 17 '66
ROSENBLUM, Robert
Mondrian and romanticism; excerpt from catalogue of Toronto show. Art N 64:33-7+ F '66
ROSENFELD, Albert
Space law for man, and anybody else out there. Life 61:30-1 Ag 5 '66
Superplan to cut years off the war. Life 61: 108+ N 18 '66
Vital facts about the drug and its effects. Life 60:30-30A Mr 25 '66
ROSENFELD, Barbara
I had my baby in Moscow. por Redbook 127: 52-3+ Jl '66
ROSENFELD, Isaac
Artist in his skin. G. Dennison. Commentary 42:102-4 N '66
ROSENFELD, Mordecai
Investing in mutual funds. New Repub 155: 13-15 Jl 2 '66
Laying down some rules for mutual funds. New Repub 156:13-14 Ja 7 '67
ROSENFELD, Paul
(comp) Articles and other books received; Low Countries. See issues of American historical review
ROSENFIELD, Isadore, and Rosenfield, Zachary
Board approach to planning for medical education. Arch Rec 139:164-7 Mr '66
ROSENFIELD, Zachary. See Rosenfield, I. jt. auth.
ROSENHOUSE, Leo
Floor-level garden pool. il Flower Grower 53:18-19 Jl '66
Der **ROSENKAVALIER**; opera. See Strauss, R.

ROSENSTEIN, Harris
Black pastures. Art N 65:33-5+ N '66
Climbing Mt Oldenburg. Art N 64:21-6+ F '66
Gottlieb at the summit. Art N 65:42-3+ Ap '66
Ideologue in Lotosland. Art N 65:36-8+ O '66
ROSENTHAL, Gerald
Public pays the bill. Atlan 218:107-10 Jl '66
ROSENTHAL, Harold
Mediterranean. Opera N 30:14-15 Ap 2 '66
ROSENTHAL, Jamie Gould
Vincent Millay; poem. Mlle 63:322 Ag '66
ROSENTHAL, M. L.
Delmore Schwartz. Poetry 109:181-3 D '66
To think of time; Winter without Danny; Love song; poems. Poetry 107:308-9 F '66
ROSENTHAL, Raymond
(tr) See Babel, I. Sunset
ROSES
Fashions in roses, 1966. R. C. Allen. il Pop Gard 17:54-8 Mr '66
Four pretty roses for next year. il House & Gard 130:158 S '66
Fragrant roses are back in style. C. Westcott. il Flower Grower 53:32-3+ F '66
Grow better roses. C. P. Dawson. il Horticulture 44:44-5 Ap '66
Handful of pretty roses. il House & Gard 129:160-1+ F '66
How to make the most of a half-dozen roses. il Bet Hom & Gard 44:115 Je '66
My first rose garden. B. Gerson. il Flower Grower 53:40-1+ Mr '66
1967 roses. il Sunset 138:130+ Ja '67
Old roses for small gardens. M. Helleiner. il Horticulture 45:42-3 Ja '67
Plan to use roses in new ways. M. Bassity. il Horticulture 44:30-1+ D '66
Roses: planting, pruning, feeding, mulching. il Pop Gard 17:90-1 Mr '66
Roses that do a real landscaping job. il Bet Hom & Gard 44:66-71 F '66
Trio of old roses. A. Murphy. il Flower Grower 53:46-7 F '66
See also
Plants—All America selections

All America selections
See Plants—All America selections
ROSETT, Nancy. See Lavker, J. jt. auth.
ROSEVEARE, R. W.
How to install loop detectors. Am City 81: 120-1 Ap '66
ROSKO, Milt
Chincoteague clappers. Outdoor Life 138:52-3+ O '66
ROSLAVLEVA, Natalia
Lopukhov and his Tanzsymphonia; excerpt from Era of the Russian ballet. Dance Mag 41:72-4 Ja '67
ROSPIGLIOSI-PALLAVICINI, Elvina, princess
Zagarolo. P. Dallas. Atlan 218:145-7 N '66
ROSS, Arthur M.
Forecast for high schoolers. PTA Mag 60: 18-19 My '66
ROSS, Bertram
Bertram Ross and dance company, 92nd street Y. J. Maskey. Dance Mag 40:59 Mr '66
Bertram Ross and dance company, 92nd street Y. M. Marks. Dance Mag 40:29 Mr '66
ROSS, Diana
Off the record with the Supremes; ed. by E. Miller. pors Seventeen 25:280-1+ Ag '66
ROSS, Elaine
Big party cook book. House & Gard 129:205+ Ap '66
Tart and tartlet cook book. House & Gard 130:249+ O '66
ROSS, Eulalie Steinmetz
Heat start liaison. Library J 91:337 Ja 15 '66
Newbery and Caldecott medal books; 1956-1965. Horn Bk 42:186-7 Ap '66
Summer storytelling in Ohio. Horn Bk 42: 279-81 Je '66
ROSS, Gertrude
How to treat the handicapped. Good H 162: 242 Ap '66
ROSS, Irwin
Head Start is a banner project. PTA Mag 60:20-3 Mr '66; Same abr. with title Head Start for America's youngsters. Read Digest 88:156-8+ Ap '66
His goal is full employment. Read Digest 89:119-23 S '66
Scrappy, happy James J. Saxon. Fortune 73: 162-4+ Ap '66
Should eye doctors sell glasses? Read Digest 89:75-8 D '66
What coffee really does to you. Sci Digest 60:79-83 Jl '66
ROSS, James William, Jr. See Frant, M. S; Thompson, M. E. jt. auths.

ROSS, Kenneth
Genesis: last chapter; poem. Am For 72:43
Ag '66

ROSS, Kevin
Few notes about the Arabian oryx; story.
Seventeen 25:98-9 Je '66

ROSS, Lillian
Books. New Yorker 42:236-8+ D 10 '66
Profiles; maiden voyage of the Sagafjord.
New Yorker 42:65-8+ N 19 '66
Profiles: O. Preminger. New Yorker 41:42-
6+ F 19 '66

about

Mrs Stanley, I presume; concerning Talk
stories. G. Culligan. Reporter 34:57-8 My 19
'66
Woman's eye on New York. M. Gattis. Sat R
49:39 Ap 30 '66

ROSS, Michael H. and Long, I. R.
Contractile cells in human seminiferous
tubules. bibliog Science 153:1271-3 S 9 '66

ROSS, Nancy Wilson
Preview. Opera N 30:26-8 Mr 12 '66
Self as a dangerous delusion. Sat R 49:23+
D 31 '66

ROSS, Russell, and Greenlee, T. K. Jr
Electron microscopy: attachment sites between connective tissue cells. bibliog Science 153:997-9 Ag 26 '66

ROSS, Wallace C.
Modern sail handling. Yachting 120:45-7+
Jl; 44-6+ Ag '66 (to be cont)

ROSS, Walter B.
RC waveshaping. Electr World 75:78 F '66

ROSS, William A.
Submarine doctor. il pors Ebony 22:112-14+
N '66

ROSS SEA, Antarctica. See Antarctic Regions

ROSSI, Lawrence J.
Medicine thinks big on the prairie. C. Smith.
il Read Digest 88:149-52 Ap '66

ROSSI, Peter Henry
Greeley-Rossi report. R. D. Cross. Common-
weal 84:577-9 S 16 '66
Greeley-Rossi report on Catholic schools.
America 115:128 Ag 6 '66
Using the Greeley-Rossi report. America 115:
150 Ag 13 '66
—See Greeley, A. M. jt. auth.

ROSSINI, Gioacchino
Barber of Seville (Il barbiere di Siviglia)
Criticism
Opera N il 30:17-20 Mr 19 '66
Opera N il 30:24-5 Mr 19 '66
Byron & Rossini. L. A. Marchand. il Opera
N 30:6-7 Mr 19 '66
Love on trial. Criticism
Opera N 30:31 Ja 29 '66
Music to my ears; concert version of Mosè.
H. Weinstock. Sat R 49:92 N 12 '66
On records; Il barbiere di Siviglia. Opera N
30:34 Mr 19 '66
On records; Mosè. il Opera N 30:34 Mr 19 '66
On records; Stabat Mater. Opera N 30:34
Mr 5 '66
Records:
Semiramide. Opera N 31:34 Ja 14 '67
Rossini's Moses. H. Weinstock. Sat R 49:62
Ja 29 '66
Via Philips, the first recording of Rossini's
Mosè. P. L. Miller. il Am Rec G 32:504-6
F '66

ROSSNICK, Julian
VOM range splitter. Pop Electr 26:70-1+ Ja
'67

ROSSOFF, Martin
Forgotten key: independent research a myth?
por Library J 91:5126-8+ O 15 '66

ROSTEN, Leo
More than meets the eye: excerpt from The
story behind the painting. Read Digest 88:
213-15 Ap '66
They made our world (cont) Look 30:74-5 Mr
8; 48-9 Je 14 '66
Wallop von horse with a parachute. Look
30:16 Mr 8 '66; Same abr. with title Please
pardon my French, German, Italian, etc.
Read Digest 89:143-6 Ag '66
World of Leo Rosten. See issues of Look

ROSTEN, Norman
Ones who wait. Sat Eve Post 239:62-5 D 31
'66

ROSTEN, Samuel C.
My father died. L. Rosten. il Look 30:14+
Je 28 '66

ROSTORFER, Ronald
Ronald Rostorfer on the art of covering.
Yachting 119:55+ Mr '66

ROSTOW, Eugene Victor
OECD ministerial council meets at Paris;
texts of statements. November 24, 25, 1966.
Dept State Bul 56:19-28 Ja 2 '67

about

LBJ makes some changes. il por U S News
61:39 O 3 '66
State's new team. por Time 88:24 S 30 '66

ROSTOW, Walt Whitman
Problems and constructive trends on the
world scene; excerpt from address, June
16, 1966. Dept State Bul 55:78-83 Jl 18 '66
Sharing of the good life; adaptation of
address, February 15, 1966. Dept State Bul
54:803-11 My 23 '66
United States and the new Asia; address,
November 16, 1966. Dept State Bul 55:910-
14 D 19 '66

about

Hawk-eyed optimist. por Time 88:18-19 Jl
15 '66
Idea man. por Newsweek 68:19-20 Ag 8 '66
Playing all the bases. por Time 87:25 Ap 8 '66
Utility men. Newsweek 67:28 Ap 11 '66
White House staff. New Repub 154:8-9 Ap 16
'66

ROSZAK, Theodore
Muddling through chaos. Nation 202:428-31
Ap 11 '66

ROTARIAN (periodical)
Some facts for writers about The Rotarian
magazine. K. K. Krueger. Writer 79:25 Ap
'66

ROTARY periodicals
See also
Rotarian (periodical)

ROTATING combustion engines. See Automobile engines; Gas and oil engines

ROTATION of stars. See Stars—Rotation

ROTATION of the plan of polarization. See
Polarization (light)

ROTATORS, Antenna. See Television antennas

ROTE, Kyle
Language of pro football. Look 30:148 O 18
'66

ROTH, Arnold
Roth waxes spring training. il Sports Illus
24:34-41 F 28 '66

ROTH, Arthur Thomas
Swank bank. il por Newsweek 67:88 My 2 '66

ROTH, Henry
Surveyor; story. New Yorker 42:22-30 Ag 6
'66

ROTH, Lorraine L. and Rosenblatt, J. S.
Mammary glands of pregnant rats: development stimulated by licking. bibliog Science
151:1403-4 Mr 18 '66

ROTH, Louis M. See Dateo, G. P. jt. auth.

ROTH, Marc, and others
Allure of the female mosquito; with biographical sketches. por Natur Hist 75:4-5, 26-31
bibliog(p70) D '66

ROTH, Philip
In trouble; story; excerpt from When she
was good. Atlan 218:72-9 N '66
O beautiful for spacious skies; story; excerpt from When she was good. Harper
233:66-78 N '66

ROTH, Richard
Associated practice: ground rules and variations. Arch Rec 140:101 N '66

ROTH, Thomas F. and Hayashi, Masaki
Allomorphic forms of bacteriophage φX-174
replicative DNA. bibliog Science 154:658-60
N 4 '66

ROTH, William M.
Johnson trade policy; excerpts from address.
bibliog f Dept State Bul 54:856-9 My 30 '66

ROTHENBERG, Jerome
For sharing. J. L. Weil. Poetry 109:196-7
D '66
Seven books by eight poets. A. R. Ammons.
Poetry 108:191-3 Je '66

ROTHENSTEIN, Guy G.
In-factory or on-site for concreting? Arch
Rec 139:221-3 Ap '66

ROTHENSTEIN, Sir John
Charmed life. E. Weeks. Atlan 217:141 Ap
'66
Home among the masterpieces. D. C. Rich.
Sat R 49:90 Ap 9 '66
Within the madding crowd. J. Jacobs. Re-
porter 34:44+ My 5 '66

ROTHER, Ellie
Drawing caricatures. il pors Design 67:12-15
Mr '66

ROTHFELD, Solomon
Turn your portable into a clock radio. Pop
Sci 188:120 Je '66

ROTHFUSS, Edwin L.
Beneath the surface. Parks & Rec 1:715-16+
S '66

ROTHMAN, Esther
Case for educatonal parks. Arch Rec 139:
180-1 F '66

ROTHROCK, George A.
Early mapping of the land and sea. Natur
Hist 75:24-9 bibliog(p68) F '66
ROTHSCHILD, Edmond, baron de
New House of Rothschild. il por Newsweek
67:62 F 7 '66
ROTHSCHILD, Henry, and Suskind, S. R.
Protoperithecia in neurospora crassa: tech-
nique for studying their development. bib-
liog Science 154:1356-7 D 9 '66
ROTHSCHILD, Norman
Hanson, Rothschild, Pierce report. See issues
of Popular photography
ROTHSCHILD, Pauline, baronne de
Notes on Leningrad. Vogue 148:142-3+ O
15 '66
Worldly retreat. il pors Vogue 148:144-7 O
15 '66
ROTHSCHILD Frères cards. See Credit cards
ROTHSTEIN, Arthur
Creative color. See issues of U.S. camera
& travel
            about
Photo safari. il U S Camera 29:60-1 Ap '66
ROTHWELL, Evelyn
Music to my ears: Carnegie Hall appearance
with the Houston symphony orchestra. I.
Kolodin. Sat R 49:28 Ap 9 '66
ROTIFERA
Nuclear number in the rotifer asplanchna:
intraclonal variation and environmental
control. C. W. Birky, jr. and B. Field.
bibliog il Science 151:585-7 F 4 '66
Rotifer ecology and embryological induction.
J. J. Gilbert. bibliog il Science 151:1234-7
Mr 11 '66
ROTIFERS. See Rotifera
ROTORS
Honeycomb rotor blade patching cuts Viet
helicopter downtime. il Aviation W 85:57
Jl 4 '66
New supersonic compressors under test. M. L.
Yaffee. il Aviation W 84:29-30 Ap 11 '66
Rotor blade radar array to undergo test.
P. J. Klass. il Aviation W 85:67-9 Jl 4 '66
ROTORS (helicopters)
Vertol to build, flight test boron filament
rotor blade. B. K. Thomas, jr. il Aviation W
85:40-1+ Ag 29 '66
ROTTERDAM
            Architecture
New concert hall in Rotterdam. M. Seif. il
Sat R 49:45+ Jl 16 '66
ROUAULT, Georges
Relating to Rouault. G. Haddad. il Sch Arts
65:41 Mr '66
ROUECHÉ, Berton
Annals of medicine (cont) New Yorker 42:
198+ N 12 '66
            about
Curl up and read. J. Stone. il Seventeen
25:38 Mr '66
Our far-flung correspondents. New Yorker
42:98+ O 22 '66
ROUEN, France
            Description
Spring in Normandy. H. Sutton. Sat R 49:42+
Je 18 '66
ROUKES, Nicholas
Signs and symbols. Sch Arts 66:15-19 O '66
ROUND buildings. See Buildings, Round
ROUNDS, George
Down to the sea with DLP. Motor B 119:80+
Ja '67
ROUQUETTE, Robert
Working priests in France. Cath World 203:
161-4 Je '66
ROUS, Francis Peyton
Belated recognition. il por Time 88:77 O 21
'66
Cancer fighters. il por Newsweek 68:78+ O
24 '66
1966 Nobel laureates in medicine and physiol-
ogy. W. R. Bryan. por Science 154:364-5
O 21 '66
Two share Nobel prize. por Sci N 90:319 O
22 '66
ROUS, Peyton. See Rous, F. P.
ROUS sarcoma. See Sarcoma
ROUSE, Anthony Gerald Roderick
Consul-general; interview. New Yorker 42:
27-8 Je 18 '66
ROUSE, James W.
Architecture. E. Galantay. Nation 203:714-16
D 26 '66
Master builder with a new concept. il por
Bsns W p 106+ Ag 20 '66

ROUSON, W. Ervin
Testing results of preschoolers from some
predominantly disadvantaged neighborhoods
in St Petersburg, Fla. bibliog por Negro
Hist Bul 29:111+ F '66
ROUSSEAU, Henri
Still life with tropical fruit; Real life with
tropical fruit; with painting. M. Kaytor.
Look 30:70-1+ Mr 22 '66
ROUSSEAU, Jean Jacques
Jean Jacques Rousseau, by J. Guéhenno.
Review
Time 88:124 O 21 '66
ROUSSELOT, John Harbin
Whose hand to shake? W. F. Buckley, jr. Nat
R 18:352 Ap 19 '66
ROUTING machines
Now everyone can afford a router. C. E.
Rhine. il Pop Sci 188:196-8 Ap '66
Routermatic; attachment for electric drill.
R. J. De Crisotforo. il Pop Sci 189:119
Ag '66
ROUX, Ambroise
Pathfinder for French industry. por Fortune
74:74 Ag '66
ROUX, Edmonde Charles-. See Charles-Roux,
E.
ROVERE, Richard H.
Books (cont) New Yorker 42:224+ N 26 '66
Letter from Washington. See issues of New
Yorker
ROVNER, Jerome S.
Courtship in spiders without prior sperm in-
duction. bibliog Science 152:543-4 Ap 22 '66
ROW spacing of plants. See Plants, Space ar-
rangement of
ROWAN, Carl Thomas
Crisis in civil rights leadership. por Ebony
22:27-30+ N '66
Education in the post-modern world. NEA
J 55:19 F '66
Metamorphosis of Jomo Kenyatta. Read Di-
gest 88:119-23 Mr '66
Problems of the new Negro elite. pors Ebony
21:43-6+ F '66
Thailand fights for freedom. Read Digest 89:
217-18+ S '66
We're helping the Communists win the
propaganda war. Read Digest 89:106-10 N
'66
ROWAN, Robert L.
Inventor of the month; it started with an
article. S. V. Jones. por Sci Digest 59:26
My '66
ROWAN, Yetta
Inventor of the month; it started with an
article. S. V. Jones. por Sci Digest 59:26
My '66
ROWE, Alleen
Alleen Rowe had a thing about death. D.
Moser. il Life 60:80D+ Mr 4 '66
ROWE, David Nelson
China problem today in United States policy-
making. Nat R 18:515-20 My 31 '66
ROWELL, John
Bugbear of school library education. por Li-
brary J 91:5123-5 O 15 '66
Total book selection process. por Wilson Lib
Bul 41:190-6 O '66
ROWING
Final escape; David Johnstone and John
Hoare missing in battle to cross Atlantic
by rowboat. il Newsweek 68:54 O 31 '66
Heroes' reward; row from Cape Cod to
Ireland's Aran Islands. Newsweek 68:56 S
19 '66
Joe Burk's blinking black box; electronic
gadget designed by Pennsylvania's rowing
coach. T. C. Brody. il Sports Illus 24:65-7
Je 6 '66
Putting on the old Indian sign; Intercollegiate
rowing association championships. P.
Stewart. il Sports Illus 24:66+ Je 27 '66
We rowed across the North Atlantic; ed. by
J. Atwater. J. Ridgway. il Sat Eve Post
239:30-6+ N 5 '66
Wizard of ugh; Penn's prompter. il Time 87:
92 My 20 '66
Yes, that good; victories of Harvard varsity
crew. il Time 87:61 Je 24 '66
    See also
Regattas
ROWLETT, Frank Byron
Other guy's mail. il por Newsweek 67:28
Mr 14 '66
ROWLETT, Peter
English madness. Commonweal 84:475-6 Jl
22 '66
ROWNTREE, Benjamin Seebohm
Happy factory that sired a social ethic. il
por Bsns W p 126+ Je 25 '66
ROY, Gregor
Book of the month. Cath World 204:180-1 D
'66
Play of the month (cont) Cath World 203:
254-6, 319-20 Jl-Ag '66

ROY, Jessie Hailstock
  Colored judges (cont) por Negro Hist Bul 29:
    37-8, 85-6 N '65, Ja '66
ROY, P. See Fahimi, H. D. jt. auth.
ROYAL academy of dancing
  Royal academy of dancing. L. Browne. Dance
    Mag 40:63-4+ D '66
ROYAL air force. See Great Britain—Royal
    air force
ROYAL art collections. See Art—Private collec-
    tions
ROYAL botanic gardens, Kew
  Queen's beasts invite you to the Royal
    botanic gardens at Kew. il Sunset 136:54+
    My '66
ROYAL botanical gardens, Hamilton, Ontario.
    See Botanical gardens
ROYAL collection, Great Britain. See Art—
    Private collections
ROYAL college of physicians, London
  Ceremonial modern for the establishment. il
    il Arch Rec 140:179-84 S '66
ROYAL Danish ballet
  Royal Danish ballet, New York state theater.
    D. Hering. Dance Mag 40:20-2 F '66
ROYAL Danish yacht club. See Yacht clubs
ROYAL Dutch airlines. See Airlines—Nether-
    lands
ROYAL Dutch-Shell group
  Shell shows Hungarians how to fill 'er up.
    il Bsns W p 102-3 Jl 9 '66
ROYAL family of Great Britain. See Great
    Britain—Royal family
ROYAL Hellenic air force. See Greece, Modern
    —Air force
ROYAL highland fusiliers. See Great Britain—
    Army—Scottish regiments
ROYAL hunt of the sun; drama. See Shaffer, P.
ROYAL observatory, Edinburgh. See Astro-
    nomical observatories—Scotland
ROYAL pavilion, Brighton. See Palaces
ROYAL pretenders. See Pretenders, Royal
ROYALS (basketball team) See Basketball
    teams
ROYALTIES
  Book publishing, and bookkeeping. D. N.
    Fischel. Science 152:871-5 My 13 '66
  Copying caper. il Newsweek 68:76 Ag 8 '66
  Licensing system: making copies of material
    from books and periodicals on royalty basis;
    proposal by Authors league of America, inc.
    il Library J 91:892-3 F 15 '66; Reply.
    J. Weatherford. 91:2784 Je 1 '66
ROYKO, Mike
  Love & hate in Chicago. il por Time 88:50
    Jl 1 '66
RÓŻE, Marie
  First opera singer recording. H. Birdoff. il
    por Hobbies 71:37-8+ Je '66
ROZELLE, Alvin Ray
  Calling the NFL's biggest plays. il por Bsns
    W p72-6 O 29 '66
  Super bowl's superman. P. O'Neil. il pors
    Life 62:75-6+ Ja 13 '67
ROZELLE, Pete. See Rozelle, A. R.
ROZEWICZ, Tadeusz
  To the heart; poem. tr. by V. Contoski.
    Nation 203:24 Jl 4 '66
ROZZANO, Italy
  Cemetowers. il Newsweek 67:49-50 Mr 14 '66
RUARK, Gibbons
  For my wife in her great good time: Muse's
    answer; poems. Poetry 108:376-7 S '66
RUAULT, Edouard. See Barclay, E.

RUBBER
                Stockpiling
    See Stockpiling
RUBBER, Artificial
  Amazing new world of silicone rubber. J.
    Hand. il Pop Sci 188:158-61+ Je '66
  Liquid handyman; liquid neoprene. B. Behme.
    il Field & S 71:66+ My '66
  Neoprene sheet for waterproofing structures.
    il Arch Rec 139:193-4 Mr '66
  Silicone rubber: a new diffusion property
    useful for general anesthesia. J. Folkman
    and others. bibliog il Science 154:148-9 O
    7 '66
  Space age product may pave roads; thermo-
    plastic rubber. Sci N 90:180 S 10 '66
RUBBER footwear. See Shoes, Rubber, plastic,
    etc.
RUBBER gloves. See Gloves, Rubber
RUBBER industry and trade
  New selling program cuts down the bounce;
    U.S. decision to unload rubber stockpile
    draws protests. Bsns W p46 My 14 '66
    See also
  Tire industry and trade

                Securities
  Tire prospects. Fortune 73:211-12+ My '66
RUBBER manufacturers association
  Be kind to trailer tires. Consumer Rep 31:268
    Je '66
RUBBER rafts. See Rafts
RUBBINGS
  Brayer rubbings. R. Potier. il Design 67:30-4
    Mr '66
  New England tombstone rubbings. T. Mc-
    Guire. il Sch Arts 65:21-3 Je '66
RUBEL, John H.
  On a project basis; interview. New Yorker
    42:19-21 Ag 13 '66
RUBELLA
  German measles. L. Z. Cooper. il Sci Am
    215:30-7 bibliog(p 130) Jl '66
  Rubella vaccine needs several year's study.
    Sci N 89:349 My 7 '66
  Rubella virus: growth and cytopathic effect
    in primary cultures of cells of rabbit em-
    bryos. A. Reddick and C. E. Roesel. bibliog
    Science 151:1405-6 Mr 18 '66
  Test reassures women exposed to rubella.
    Sci N 90:401 N 12 '66
  Vaccine against German measles. il Time 87:
    60 My 6 '66
  Vaccine for German measles Sci Am 214:55 Je
    '66
  Vaccine still in future; vaccination of girls
    against German measles. Sci N 90:423 N 19
    '66
RUBEN, Samuel
  Inventor of the month. S. V. Jones. por Sci
    Digest 60:28 Jl '66
  Inventor of the year worked on pacemaker.
    Sci N 89:307 Ap 30 '66
RUBENFELD, Seymour
  Freud, friend or enemy? New Repub 154:30+
    Mr 19 '66
  Psychiatry and existentialism. New Repub
    154:25-7 Je 25 '66
RUBENS, Sir Peter Paul
  How to smell a Rubens; strange case of the
    Judgment of Paris. il Time 88:88-91 S
    16 '66
  Rubens' sacrifice of Abraham. R. T. Coe.
    il Art N 65:36-9+ D '66
  Triple rediscovery of Rubens. il Life 61:103-
    7 O 14 '66
RUBENSTEIN, Richard E.
  Speaking out. por Sat Eve Post 239:10+ F
    12 '66
RUBENSTEIN, Richard L.
  Who are the true children of God's election?
    Commonweal 84:420-1 Jl 1 '66
RUBIDIUM
  Potassium:rubidium ratio in ultramafic rocks:
    differentiation history of the upper mantle.
    A. M. Stueber and V. R. Murthy. bibliog il
    Science 153:740-1 Ag 12 '66
RUBIN, Albert L. See Stenzel, K. H. jt. auth.
RUBIN, Arnold D. See Cooper, H. L. jt. auth.
RUBIN, Barney
  (tr) See Agnon, S. J. Fable of the goat
RUBIN, Ernest
  Demography of immigration to the United
    States. Ann Am Acad 367:15-22 S '66
  Statistical overview of Americans abroad.
    Ann Am Acad 368:1-10 N '66
RUBIN, Isadore
  Sex and morality: a challenging point of
    view. Redbook 127:68-9+ O '66
RUBIN, Jerome S.
  Art and taxes. Horizon 8:4-15 Wint '66
RUBIN, Joan Alleman
  Staking out a new world of film. Mlle 62:
    170-1+ Mr '66
  Student and film. Mlle 62:172 Mr '66
RUBIN, Lionel F. and Mattis, P. A.
  Dimethyl sulfoxide: lens changes in dogs
    during oral administration. Science 153:
    83-5 Jl 1 '66
RUBIN, Robert T. and others
  Corticosteroid responses to limbic stimula-
    tion in man: localization of stimulus sites.
    bibliog Science 153:767-8 Ag 12 '66
RUBIN, Ronald I.
  Looking at Lyndon. Christian Cent 83:1276-7
    O 19 '66
RUBIN, Theodore Isaac
  Advice to dieters from a formerly fat
    psychiatrist; excerpts from The Thin book.
    por Todays Health 44:35+ Jl '66
  How to lose weight, and stay thin; excerpt
    from The thin book by a formerly fat
    psychiatrist. Read Digest 89:124-7 S '66
  Psychiatrist's notebook; questions and an-
    swers. por McCalls 93:50+ S; 94:93+ O;
    52+ N; 40+ D '66; 38+ Ja '67
RUBINSTEIN, Anton Grigor'evich
  Great Rubinstein road show. M. Goldin. il
    Hi Fi 16:60-2 S '66

RUBINSTEIN, Artur
Undeniable romantic. il pors Time 87:84-8 F 25 '66; Same abr. with title He lives life from miracle to miracle. Read Digest 88: 57-61 Je '66
RUBINSTEIN, Helena
Beautician's booty. il por Time 87:82-5 Ap 29 '66
RUBLES. See Money—Russia
RUBOTTOM, R. Richard, Jr
Assessment of current American influence in Latin America. Ann Am Acad 366:117-25 Jl '66
RUBY, Jack
Exit Jack Ruby, a nobody with one big moment. L. Wainwright. Life 62:18 Ja 13 '67
Last wish. Time 88:12 D 30 '66
Nonentity for history. il Time 89:16-17 Ja 13 '67
Objection sustained. il Newsweek 68:31 O 17 '66
Trial of Jack Ruby, by J. Kaplan and J. R. Waltz. Review
  Commentary 41:83-5+ F '66. M. Mayer
Who can understand? il por Newsweek 69: 28-9 Ja 16 '67
RUBY, Jack, trial. See Trials (murder)
RUBY MOUNTAINS
Detour into Nevada's Ruby Mountains. il Sunset 137:44+ O '66
RUBY trial. See Trials (murder)
RUCH, Jim
All-season big game. Field & S 71:48-9+ Ag '66
RUCHKIN, D. S. and John, E. R.
Evoked potential correlates of generalization. bibliog Science 153:209-11 Jl 8 '66
RUDD, Hughes
Close-up look at today's Russians; excerpts from radio broadcasts. U S News 61:66-8 Jl 11 '66
        about
Sardonic man in Moscow. por Time 87:69 My 27 '66
RUDDLE, Frank H. See Ledley, R. S. jt. auth.
RUDEL, Julius
Other company. il por Newsweek 67:88-9 Mr 7 '66
Sense of adventure. por Time 87:75 Mr 4 '66
RUDIN, Harry R.
Political rivalry in the Congo. Cur Hist 50: 159-64+ Mr '66
RUDINSKY, Julius A.
Scolytid beetles associated with Douglas fir; response to terpenes. bibliog Science 152: 218-19 Ap 8 '66
RUDMAN, Reuben, and Post, Ben
Carbon tetrachloride: a new crystalline modification. bibliog Science 154:1009+ N 25 '66
RUDNICKI comet. See Comets
RUDNIK, Raphael
Lady in the barbershop; poem. New Yorker 42:38 D 31 '66
RUDOLPH, Lillian
Free; poem. Ladies Home J 83:112 Ag '66
RUDOLPH, Paul Marvin
Paul Rudolph's elaborated spaces: six new projects. il Arch Rec 139:135-50 Je '66
RUE, Eloise
Economy in the catalog. por Library J 91: 5130-1 O 15 '66
RUECKERT, William H.
Burke's other life. Nation 203:648-9 D 12 '66
RUECKRIEGEL, Helmut
Goethe on private confession. America 115: 210 Ag 27 '66
RUEFF, Jacques
Is the strongest economy in the world going bankrupt? interview. por U S News 61: 60-3 O 17 '66
RUESINK, Albert W. and Thimann, K. V.
Protoplasts: preparation from higher plants. bibliog Science 154:280-1 O 14 '66
RUETHER, Rosemary
Catholicism's celibacy crisis. Christian Cent 83:1268-70 O 19 '66
RUFFNER, Frederick G. Jr
FASGROLIA. Newsweek 67:94+ Mr 14 '66
RUGBY football
Gentlemanly game for ruffians; University of California in Berkeley. J. Jares. il Sports Illus 24:30-5 Ap 4 '66
RUGGLES, Carl
Carl Ruggles festival; Brunswick report. S. Fleming. Hi Fi 16:158 Ap '66
Music. B. Boretz. Nation 202:278-80 Mr 7 '66
Music of our time. H. Kupferberg. il Atlan 217:118-20 My '66
Now that other American giant; Carl Ruggles. A. Cohn. il por Am Rec G 32:588-90 Mr '66
Season in the sun. por Newsweek 67:80 F 7 '66

Sun treader, the work of an American radical, in its first American hearing. P. Yates. il por Hi Fi 16:85-6 Ap '66
RUGGLES, Melville J.
National advisory commission gets staff director from CLR. por Library J 91:5908+ D 1 '66
Ruggles named director Library advisory committee. por Pub W 190:77 N 14 '66
RUGGLES, Rudy L. jr. See Smalter, D. J. jt.
RUGH, Douglas
American outpost for recreation. por Parks & Rec 1:166-7 F '66
RUGS and carpets
Carpeting vs. resilient floor coverings. il Consumer Bul 49:29-30 Mr '66
Carpets & rugs are better than ever! il Good H 162:116-23 F '66
Fashion on the floor. il Seventeen 25:162+ O '66
GH guide to carpet fibers. Good H 162: 152 F '66
Indoor-outdoor carpets; polypropylene fiber carpets. Consumer Bul 49:22-3 Ag '66
Is carpet practical? carpets for libraries. M. Van Buren; discussion. Library J 90:5320+; 91:462+ D 15 '65. F 1 '66
Now you can have a wall-to-wall lawn; all-synthetic carpeting for poolsides, patios, sidewalks and supermarkets. il Bsns W p88-90+ Jl 16 '66
        Care
Care and safekeeping of rugs and carpets. House & Gard 129:6+ F; 36+ Mr '66
RUGS and carpets, Oriental
Fabulous Oriental rug collection. R. N. Gregg. il Hobbies 71:36-7 Je '66
Persian palace rugs in Oshkosh. R. N. Gregg. il Antiques 89:718-23 My '66
RUHR VALLEY
New Ruhr; Germany's industrial heartland. W. Hangen. il Sat Eve Post 239:30-4+ My 7 '66
RUINED cities. See Cities and towns, Ruined, extinct, etc.
RUIZ-GIMENEZ, Joaquin
Shocking news from Spain. America 115:819 D 24 '66
RUKEYSER, Muriel
Crystal for the metaphysical. Sat R 49:52-3+ O 1 '66
RULE, Bruce H. See Bowen, I. S. jt. auth.
RULE of law
If mob rule takes hold in U.S; a warning from Richard Nixon. R. M. Nixon. U S News 61:64-5 Ag 15 '66
Rule of law in an unruly world; address, May 18, 1966. A. J. Goldberg. Dept State Bul 54:936-44 Je 13 '66
RUM
Rum coolers. P. S. Brown. House & Gard 130:22-3+ Ag '66
RUMANIA
Third communism. il Time 87:34-48 Mr 18 '66
        See also
Ballet—Rumania
Communist party (Rumania)

        Foreign relations
Eroding barriers. il Time 88:38 S 9 '66

        Russia
Rumania and Russia. V. Zorza. New Repub 154:10-11 Je 4 '66
Rumania rocks the boat; N. Ceausescu's latest bid for independence. il Newsweek 67:46+ My 30 '66

        Nationalism
Rumania rocks the boat; N. Ceausecul's latest bid for independence. il Newsweek 67:46+ My 30 '66

        Politics and government
Man battering at the Kremlin wall; Ceausescu of Rumania. D. Binder. il N Y Times Mag p 10-11+ My 29 '66
Rumanian Gaullists. P. Ben. New Repub 155: 20 Ag 27 '66
RUMANIAN dancing. See Dancing, Rumanian
RUMANIAN fiction
Ideological framework for fiction. R. L. Stilwell. il Sat R 49:61-3 S 10 '66
RUMANIAN folk ballet. See Ballet—Rumania
RUMFORD, Sir Benjamin Thompson
Count Rumford of Woburn, Mass, by W. J. Sparrow. Review
  Harper 233:92 Jl '66. J. D. Carr
  Sat R 49:45 F 5 '66. R. B. Morris

RUMICS, Elizabeth
Oral history; defining the term. bibliog por Wilson Lib Bul 40:602-5 Mr '66

RUMINANTS
Hyperphagia in ruminants induced by a depressant. C. A. Baile and J. Mayer. bibliog il Science 151:458-9 Ja 28 '66

RUNAWAY boys and girls
Drinking man's diet; Bill Waddell and David Harvey rescued after freight car incarceration. il Newsweek 67:23-4 My 2 '66
Nice girls who ran away. J. Robbins and J. Robbins. il McCalls 94:114-15+ N '66

RUNCORN, S. K.
Corals as paleontological clocks; with biographical sketch. Sci Am 215:16, 26-33 bibliog(p 150) O '66

RUNGE, Walter J.
Recording microfluorospectrophotometer. bibliog Science 151:1499-506 Mr 25 '66

RUNNELS, L. K.
Ice; with biographical sketch. Sci Am 215:16, 118-24+ bibliog(p 156) D '66

RUNNING
America's gritty guinea pig. G. S. Brown. il Sports Illus 25:40-2 Jl 11 '66
Chasing girls through a park; National AAU women's cross-country championship in St Louis. J. Underwood. il Sports Illus 25:30-3 D 5 '66
Crowd pleaser; national championship outdoor race at Downing stadium. il Newsweek 68:80 Jl 11 '66
Ethiopia's modern Pheidippides: A. Bikila. il Ebony 21:128-33 Mr '66
Game girl in a man's game; R. G. Bingay of Boston. G. S. Brown. il Sports Illus 24:67-8+ My 2 '66
Hats off; K. Keino. il Newsweek 67:84 F 14 '66
Hurry-up-and-wait game; Australia's R. Clarke beaten by New Zealand's B. Baillie. G. S. Brown. il Sports Illus 24:18-19 F 21 '66
Jim Ryun first 3:50 miler? il Life 60:81-2+ My 20 '66
Just perfect; J. Ryun's record mile. il Newsweek 68:74-5 Ag 1 '66
Kama for the Angelenos; K. Keino. G. S. Brown. il Sports Illus 24:18-19 Ja 31 '66
Lonely tribe of long-distance runners; Mexico's Tarahumare Indians. E. Shrake. il Sports Illus 26:56-62+ Ja 9 '67
Miniature Snell to quicken the indoor pulse; half-miler. T. Farrell. il Sports Illus 24:49-51 Ja 24 '66
Outrunning the rabbits; J. Ryun's record-smashing victory. il Time 88:34 Jl 29 '66
People vs. Flowers. il Newsweek 67:83 F 28 '66
Punishment of the long-distance runner. R. Bannister. il N Y Times Mag p76-7+ S 18 '66
Puzzling prodigy; J. Ryun. il Time 87:68 Je 17 '66
Queen of the marathon; Boston marathon. il Time 87:104 Ap 29 '66
Ready for the goal; the mythical 3:50 mile. J. Olsen. il Sports Illus 24:64-9+ Je 20 '66
Second fastest ever; 19-year-old Kansas freshman. J. Ryun. G. S. Brown. il Sports Illus 24:26-9 Je 13 '66
Special brand of fame: J. Ryun, winner of 3:51-3 mile world record. G. S. Brown. il Sports Illus 25:20-1+ Ag 1 '66
Storm of bright promises; Penn and Drake relays. G. S. Brown. Sports Illus 24:74-5 My 9 '66
Teen-agers take charge: nineteen-year-old J. Ryun. G. S. Brown. il Sports Illus 24:69-70 My 23 '66
3:50 miler? il Newsweek 67:82-3 My 30 '66
Time to remember: 3:51.3; new world mile record won by J. Ryun. A. Verschoth. il Sports Illus 25:10-13 Jl 25 '66
Track: what limit to human achievement? International games. il Newsweek 68:53-5 Jl 25 '66
Way up high and out of breath; Little Olympics trial run for the 1968 games. J. Underwood. il Sports Illus 25:30-1+ O 31 '66
World's finest miler? J. Ryun. E. Linn. il Sat Eve Post 239:90+ Ap 23 '66

Anecdotes, facetiae, satire, etc.
Road runner's bonanza; or, Has anybody seen Kelley? H. Higdon. il Sports Illus 25:58-60+ S 5 '66

RUNNING aground (boats) See Boats and boating—Accidents

RUNNING foxes; story. See Stranger, J.

RUNWAYS, Airport. See Airports—Runways

RUNYON, Damon
Runyonese, by J. Wagner. Review Nation 203:456-7 O 31 '66. D. W. Maurer

RUPEES. See Money—India

RUPERT, Anthony Edward
Missionaries or mercenaries? address, May 9, 1966. Vital Speeches 32:754-60 O 1 '66

RUPP, Adolph
Baron's runts. il por Time 87:60 F 4 '66
Big little men. il por Newsweek 67:82+ Mr 7 '66
Bravo for the baron. F. Deford. il pors Sports Illus 24:20-3+ Mr 7 '66

RUPPENTHAL, Karl M.
Pilot shortage. Nation 203:481-4 N 7 '66

RUPPERT, Richard D. See Greenberger, N. J. jt. auth.

RUPTURE. See Hernia

RURAL areas development program. See Rural planning

RURAL development program. See Rural planning

RURAL economics. See Agriculture—Economic aspects

RURAL electric cooperatives. See Cooperative associations

RURAL electrification administration. See United States—Rural electrification administration

RURAL life. See Farm life

RURAL medical service. See Medical service, Rural

RURAL planning
Plight of the rural poor. B. Kovach and N. Caldwell. il Reporter 34:27+ Ap 21 '66

RURAL press. See Country newspapers

RURAL-urban conflict. See City and country

RUSH, Cyndy
Mile makes more of four G.E.s. pors Mlle 63:274-9 Ag '66

RUSH, Hazel S.
Clowns. Design 67:20-1 My '66

RUSH, Myron
Fallen ruler. Commentary 42:135-7 O '66

RUSH, Phillip D.
Walk through medicine's past. il Todays Health 45:46-51 Ja '67

RUSHER, William A.
Plot to steal the GOP. Nat R 18:668-71 Jl 12 '66

RUSHMER, Robert F. and others
Skin. bibliog Science 154:343-8 O 21 '66

RUSHMORE, Robert
Singing voice: first sounds. Opera N 31:24-7 Ja 21 '67

RUSK, David Patrick
Let's be unreasonable; Rusk's son on civil rights; excerpts from address, 1966. por U S News 61:11 Ag 15 '66

RUSK, Dean
As Secretary Rusk looks ahead; excerpts from news conference, January 21, 1966. por U S News 60:8 Ja 31 '66
As told by Secretary Rusk; why U.S. fights in Vietnam; statement before the Senate foreign relations committee, February 18, 1966. por U S News 60:76-8+ F 28 '66
Background of U.S. policy in southeast Asia; statement, May 9, 1966. bibliog f Dept State Bul 54:830-4 My 30 '66
Battle over U.S. policy in Vietnam; excerpts from testimony, February 17 and 18, 1966. por U S News 60:40-2 F 28 '66
Central treaty organization meets at Ankara; opening statement, April 20, remarks at the dedication of the CENTO microwave telecommunications system and transcript of press conference, April 22, 1966; with text of final communique. Dept State Bul 54:775-81 My 16 '66
Chain of common interest uniting the United States and Mexico; remarks, February 10, 1966. Dept State Bul 54:365-7 Mr 7 '66
East-West trade relations act of 1966; letter of transmital, May 11, 1966. bibliog f Dept State Bul 54:838-43 My 30 '66
Excerpt from testimony, April 18, 1966. Cong Digest 45:201+ Ag '66
Excerpt from testimony, February 18, 1966, before Senate committee on foreign relations. Cong Digest 45:113-18 Ap '66
Excerpt from testimony, June 16, 1966. Cong Digest 45:235+ O '66
Food for freedom act of 1966; statements, March 7, 14, 1966. Dept State Bul 54:496-503 Mr 28 '66
Foreign assistance program for 1967; statement, March 17, 1966. Dept State Bul 54:628-34 Ap 18 '66

RUSK, Dean—*Continued*
Future of the Pacific community; address, November 15, 1966. Dept State Bul 55:838-43 D 5 '66
Goal of a reliable peace: a survey of free-world progress; address, August 22, 1966. Dept State Bul 55:362-8 S 12 '66
How the Secretary of state spends his time; excerpt from Open end interview; April 3, 1966. Dept State Bul 54:652-4 Ap 25 '66
International defense commitments of the United States; statement, August 25, 1966. Dept State Bul 55:377-81 S 12 '66
Is our China policy changing? excerpts from testimony. Nat R 18:398 My 3 '66
Keeping our commitment to peace; address, March 14, 1966. Dept State Bul 54:514-21 Ap 4 '66
Nonproliferation of nuclear weapons; statement, February 23, 1966. Dept State Bul 54:406-10 Mr 14 '66
North Atlantic council meets at Brussels; statement, June 4, 1966. Dept State Bul 54:1001 Je 27 '66
Official U.S. stand on dealing with the Viet Cong; excerpts from statement, January 23, 1966. por U S News 60:14 F 7 '66
Organizing the peace for man's survival; address, May 24, 1966; with questions and answers. Dept State Bul 54:926-34 Je 13 '66
Outlook for freedom; address, September 21, 1966. Dept State Bul 55:586-90 O 17 '66
Progress toward a decent world order; address, June 14, 1966. Dept State Bul 55:44-9 Jl 11 '66
Report on the NATO meeting at Brussels; statement, June 16, 1966. Dept State Bul 55:7-9 Jl 4 '66
Requirements for organizing the peace; address, October 12, 1966. Dept State Bul 55: 658-63 O 31 '66; Same with title Organizing the peace. Vital Speeches 33:67-71 N 15 '66
Review of United States foreign and military policy; transcript of press conference, August 25, 1966; with questions and answers. Dept State Bul 55:413-17, 421-4 S 19 '66
Review of United States refugee policy; statement, July 14, 1966. Dept State Bul 55:235-40 Ag 15 '66
Rusk: power has not corrupted American people; excerpts from remarks, May 8, 1966. por U S News 60:121-2 My 23 '66
Rusk tells student leaders: why America is in the Vietnam war; questions and excerpts from answers. por U S News 62:16 Ja 16 '67
Secretary comments on Peiping's militancy in southeast Asia; transcript of an interview for the television program, Red China: year of the gun? on April 27, 1966. Dept State Bul 54:772-5 My 16 '66
Secretary gets new responsibility for conduct of foreign affairs; texts of a White House announcement and a message, March 4, 1966. Dept State Bul 54:506-9 Mr 28 '66
Secretary Rusk answers questions on NATO issues and Viet-Nam; interview by Paris-match. Dept State Bul 54:695-9 My 2 '66
Secretary Rusk interviewed:
Canadian broadcasting corporation. December 30, 1965. Dept State Bul 54:86-9 Ja 17 '66
Face the Nation program, March 20, 1966. Dept State Bul 54:565-70 Ap 11 '66
Secretary Rusk meets with Asian leaders; statements on various occasions during the trip, transcripts of news conferences; with texts of communiques released after the meetings at Canberra and Kyoto; June 26-July 9, 1966. Dept State Bul 55:169-84 Ag 1 '66
Secretary Rusk, Secretary McNamara, Mr McCloy meet with President Johnson; excerpts from press briefing, November 23, 1966. Dept State Bul 55:919-21 D 19 '66
Secretary Rusk's news conference:
January 21, 1966. Dept State Bul 54:189-97 F 7 '66
January 31, 1966. Dept State Bul 54:223-9 F 14 '66
March 25, 1966. Dept State Bul 54:557-64 Ap 11 '66
May 17, 1966. Dept State Bul 54:882-7 Je 6 '66
May 27, 1966. Dept State Bul 54:918-25 Je 13 '66
July 12, 1966. Dept State Bul 55:162-8 Ag 1 '66
August 5, 1966. Dept State Bul 55:258-65 Ag 22 '66
September 16, 1966. Dept State Bul 55: 478-83 O 3 '66
November 18, 1966. Dept State Bul 55:844-51 D 5 '66

Twelfth anniversary of SEATO; statement, September 8, 1966. Dept State Bul 55:454-5 S 26 '66
U.S. commitment in Viet-Nam; fundamental issues; statement, February 18, 1966. bibliog f Dept State Bul 54:346-56 Mr 7 '66
U.S.-Japan scientific committee holds sixth annual meeting; remarks, October 10, 1966. Dept State Bul 55:682-3 O 31 '66
U.S. marks third anniversary of limited test ban treaty; statement, August 6, 1966. Dept State Bul 55:268 Ag 22 '66
United States policy toward Communist China; statement; March 16, 1966. Dept State Bul 54:686-95 My 2 '66
University campus and foreign policy; address, November 14, 1966. Dept State Bul 55:914-18 D 19 '66
Where NATO stands; statement, June 13, 1966. Dept State Bul 54:998-1001 Je 27 '66
Why the U.S. fights; Rusk and Taylor; excerpts from Fulbright committee hearings. por Newsweek 67:19-20 F 28 '66
World food and population crisis; DAC's fifth annual high-level meeting; statement, July 20, 1966. Dept State Bul 55:199-202 Ag 8 '66
—and Malik, Adam
Indonesian foreign minister meets with Secretary Rusk; joint statement, September 27, 1966. Dept State Bul 55:652 O 24 '66
—and Nguyen-cao-Ky
Secretary Rusk and Vietnamese premier restate basic positions; joint communique, January 16, 1966. Dept State Bul 54:155-6 Ja 31 '66

about

Dean Rusk: cool man in a hot world. J. R. Moskin. il pors Look 30:14-21 S 6 '66
Exhaustive, explicit & enough. il Time 87: 22-3 F 25 '66
Franklin award for distinguished service; citation. Dept State Bul 54:198-9 F 7 '66
International cop? concerning statements. il por Newsweek 68:22-3 S 12 '66
Messenger. il por Newsweek 68:34 Jl 18 '66
Mr Dove and Mr Hawk. S. Alsop. por Sat Eve Post 239:18 Je 18 '66
On hawks and doves. M. Ascoli. Reporter 34: 24 Mr 24 '66
Room at the top. il por Newsweek 67:30-1 My 23 '66
Rusk doctrine. New Repub 154:5-7 Mr 5 '66
Rusk's Francophobia; de Gaulle and NATO. R. D. Masters. Commonweal 84:431-3 Jl 8 '66
Rusk's problem in Europe; trying to explain Vietnam. por U S News 60:22 Je 13 '66
String runs out. il por Time 87:21-6 F 4 '66
Washington: ten of its most important men. por Vogue 148:153 N 15 '66
Whose history? New Repub 154:7 Mr 12 '66

RUSK, Howard A.
Gift of love. McCalls 94:146 D '66
Other war in Vietnam. Read Digest 89:108-12 Jl '66

RUSKAUFF, Bob
Westward ho! See issues of Motor boating

RUSS, Lavinia
Author, stay 'way from my door. Pub W 189: 37-8 My 30 '66
For me? children's books to give adults. Pub W 190:38-9 O 10 '66
Letter from limbo, or, WNBC-TV I love you. Pub W 191:42-3 Ja 16 '67
Pow! zam! zowie! or, Down with summer reading lists. Pub W 189:47-9 Ap 25 '66
What gift of prophecy? or promising juvenile titles for bookstores. Pub W 190:46-8 Ag 22 '66

RUSSEL, Andy
Much maligned wolverine. Field & S 71:74+ N '66

RUSSELL, Bertrand Russell, 3d earl
Lord Russell and Lord Amberley. P. Toynbee. New Repub 156:32-3+ Ja 21 '67
Trial of LBJ. por Newsweek 68:42 Ag 15 '66
You are old, Father Bertrand; poem. O. Nash. Reporter 36:58 Ja 12 '67

RUSSELL, Bill
All the credentials. il por Time 87:104+ Ap 29 '66
Coach Russell. il por Newsweek 67:72-3 My 2 '66
New role for Bill Russell. il pors Ebony 22: 60-1+ Ja '67

RUSSELL, Charles Marion
Russell gallery at Great Falls. J. Meyer. il por Am Artist 30:26-9+ N '66

RUSSELL, Dorothy
Motivations for children's art. Sch Arts 65:40 My '66

RUSSELL, Francis
Breslau revisited. Horizon 9:46-56 Wint '67
Doubts about Dallas. Nat R 18:887-8+ S 6 '66
More secrets of the White House. Nat R 18: 1052-3 O 18 '66
Movies (cont) Nat R 18:124-6, 542-4, 793; 19: 47+ F 8, My 31, Ag 9 '66, Ja 10 '67
Passing scene (cont) Nat R 18:430-2 My 3 '66
(ed) See Doe, W. Apples of wrath

RUSSELL, Franklin
Why we should behave like animals. Life 60: 8+ Je 3 '66

RUSSELL, John, 1919-
Art news from London. See issues of Art news
Perpetual president of modern art. N Y Times Mag p28-31+ O 23 '66

RUSSELL, John R.
Attack on incentive system seen in rising debate on contracting; address. Aviation W 84:119+ My 23 '66

RUSSELL, John Robert, 13th duke of Bedford. See Bedford, J. R. R.

RUSSELL, John, viscount Amberley. See Amberley, J. R.

RUSSELL, Keith P. and others
Expectant mother. Redbook 127:38+ Je '66

RUSSELL, Richard Brevard
Excerpt from address, February 25, 1966. Cong Digest 45:125-6 Ap '66
Senator Russell on Vietnam: go in and win, or get out; interview. por U S News 60: 56-7 My 2 '66

about
Checking on CIA. New Repub 154:7-8 My 28 '66
Dissent & defeat. il Time 87:24 Mr 11 '66
Russell of Georgia: old guard at its shrewdest. D. Kiker. Harper 233:101-4+ S '66
Senator Russell of Georgia. N. F. Busch. por Read Digest 89:150-2+ D '66
Victory for Russell: Fulbright loses CIA wrangle. U S News 61:19 Jl 25 '66
War in Vietnam: which way now? por U S News 62:11 Ja 16 '67
Washington: ten of its most powerful men. il por Vogue 148:156 N 15 '66

RUSSELL, Roger, H.
Enclosures for high-compliance loudspeakers. Electr World 76:25-8+ Ag '66

RUSSELL, Rosalind
Frank Sinatra's $25,000 weekend. por Ladies Home J 84:48+ Ja '67

RUSSELL, W. H.
Book review. America 115:73-4 Jl 16 '66

RUSSELL, William Felton. See Russell, B.

RUSSIA
Russia at the crossroads. R. Sherrod. il Sat Eve Post 239:28-33 Mr 26 '66
Soviet Union, 1966: symposium. bibliog f il Cur Hist 51:193-232+ O '66
See also
Agricultural colonialization—Russia
Airlines—Russia
Airplane industry and trade—Russia
Atomic research—Russia
Automobile industry and trade—Russia
Azerbaijan
Ballet—Russia
Censorship—Russia
Chemical industries—Russia
Children—Russia
Childrens literature—Russia
Colleges and universities—Russia
Crime and criminals—Russia
Customs service—Russia
Earthquakes—Russia
Education—Russia
Foreign visitors in Russia
Georgia
Industrial management and organization—Russia
Jews in Russia
Juvenile delinquency—Russia
Kazakhstan
Labor supply—Russia
Leningrad
Libraries—Russia
Liquor problem—Russia
Medical service—Russia
Medicine—Russia
Merchant marine—Russia
Money—Russia
Moscow
Moving pictures—Russia
Natural resources—Russia
Periodicals—Russia
Phonograph record industry—Russia
Postal service—Russia
Public opinion—Russia
Research—Russia
Russians
Schools—Russia
Science—Russia
Secret service—Russia
Space research—Russia
Sports—Russia
Tourist trade—Russia
Trials—Russia
Youth—Russia

Antiquities
Russia's buried treasure; art treasures on exhibit at The Hague's Gemeentemuseum. il Newsweek 68:106 O 24 '66

Armed forces
See also
Russia—Navy

Forces in Europe
Must all those troops stay? Soviet troops in eastern Europe. Time 87:36 My 27 '66

Boundaries
Bordering on madness; Russia and China. il Time 88:38 D 2 '66
Sino-Soviet border comrades up in arms. il Sr Schol 88:14-16 Mr 18 '66

Climate
Truth is winter. E. S. Staples. il Reporter 34:43-5 Mr 10 '66

Commerce
Close-up: talk with Leon M. Herman; interview, ed. by J. Berry. L. M. Herman. il Duns R 88:8-9+ S '66
Communist cut-rates; campaign to acquire foreign money. il Newsweek 68:76 S 5 '66
See also
Russia—Industries

Cultural relations
See also
Exchange of persons programs

Defenses
Arms and the Soviet Union. V. Zorza. New Repub 156:13-15 Ja 14 '67
Defusing an arms race: administration persuading Russia not to deploy an anti-missile system. il Bsns W p 13-14 D 24 '66
Is Soviet arms race starting again? Russians' anti-missile system raises Pentagon fears. il Bsns W p38-40 N 19 '66
Joint chiefs fear Soviet technical coup; with editorial comment. G. C. Wilson. Aviation W 84:11, 16-17 F 28 '66
McNamara says Soviets err on ABM. M. Getler. Miss & Roc 18:12-14 My 2 '66
New arms race. New Repub 155:8-9 D 24 '66
New heat in the missile killer race. il U S News 61:12 N 21 '66
Russia talks of peace, builds up missiles, navy. il U S News 61:70-2 N 21 '66
Soviet ABM deployment expected in year. M. Getler. il Tech W 19:10-12 N 21 '66
Soviet ICBM report awesome; summary of address, June 2, 1966. F. J. Larsen. Tech W 18:10 Je 6; 11 Je 13 '66
Soviet ICBM strength; letter to the editor. A. Sylvester. Tech W 18:8 Je 13 '66
Soviet missile efforts emphasize concealment, mobility, anti-ICBM. Aviation W 84:90 Mr 7 '66
Soviets show details of various missiles; photographs. Aviation W 85:58-9+ N 28 '66
Soviets trying to close strategic gap. M. Getler. Tech W 18:14-15 Je 27 '66
USSR to put multiple warheads on ICBM's. M. Getler. Tech W 19:13-14 D 12 '66
See also
Russia—Navy

Description and travel
Gone flying to Russia. J. Gilbert. il Flying 79:46-53+ D '66
Soviet Union's 50th: is Russia a tourist country? M. Kalb. il Sat R 50:51-2+ Ja 7 '67

Diplomatic and consular service
Consular treaty, next bridge to Russia. Life 61:4 N 18 '66

Economic conditions
Auspicious rise of the Soviet consumer. G. Burck. il Fortune 74:130-3+ Ag '66
Close-up: talk with Leon M. Herman; interview, ed. by J. Berry. L. M. Herman. il Duns R 88:8-9+ S '66
Importance of sufficiency. il Time 87:41 Je 10 '66

RUSSIA—Economic conditions—*Continued*
Latest from inside Russia. J. Fromm. il U S News 60:60-5 Mr 28 '66
New Soviet plan: guns still before butter. T. Sosnovy. il For Affairs 44:620-32 Jl '66
Soviet growth: still a lag behind U.S. il U S News 60:12 F 14 '66

See also
Food supply—Russia
Russia—Industries
Wages—Russia

Economic history
Soviet economy. A. W. Wright. bibliog f il Cur Hist 51:218-25+ O '66

Economic policy
Antonov urges cost accounting in USSR; excerpts from article. O. K. Antonov. il Aviation W 84:103+ Mr 21 '66
Communist capitalism: will it work? G. W. Trivoli. Nat R 18:265-7 Mr 22 '66
Economic revolution in the Soviet Union. M. I. Goldman. For Affairs 45:319-31 Ja '67
How the Baltic republics fare in the Soviet Union. V. S. Vardys. For Affairs 44:512-17 Ap '66
How the new men run Russia. il Bsns W p 138-42+ Jl 23 '66
Inside Libermanism; profit motive. il Time 88:75 Jl 1 '66
Labor aspects of the economic reform in the Soviet Union. E. Nash. Mo Labor R 89:597-602 Je '66
Little realism; new five-year plan. Time 87: 36+ Mr 4 '66
New Soviet plan: guns still before butter. T. Sosnovy. il For Affairs 44:620-32 Jl '66
Russia upgrades its managers; growing management movement; with editorial comment. Bsns W p76+, 196 Ap 16 '66
Russia's new bourgeois grows fat. A. Parry. il N Y Times Mag p44-5+ Je 5 '66
Soviet economy. A. W. Wright. bibliog f il Cur Hist 51:218-25+ O '66
Soviet five-year plan comes down to earth. Bsns W p37 F 26 '66
Soviet Union's eighth five-year plan; summary of draft directives published by Tass, February 21, 1966. Cur Hist 51:238-40 O '66
Soviets' new profit lure. Bsns W p 115 S 17 '66
Time for caprice. il Time 88:41 O 14 '66
Toughest management job in the world. G. Burck. il Fortune 74:72-9+ Jl 1 '66
Why fight? ruble-dollar road to peace. R. C. Garretson. il Nation 202:576-81 My 16 '66

Economic relations
Japan
Sharing the wealth: Japan's economic dealings with Russia. Time 87:86 Mr 25 '66
Syria
Russia cozies up to Syria, too. Bsns W p90 My 21 '66

Foreign relations
China watchers; Soviet strategy. H. Brandon. Sat R 49:18+ F 5 '66
Don't fence Mao in. Time 87:22 Ja 28 '66
On the road again: state visits: Kosygin to United Arab Republic, Brezhnev to Rumania. Nat R 18:506-7 My 31 '66
Time to split the old act? America 114: 848-9 Je 18 '66
U.S.S.R. and the West. D. T. Cattell. bibliog f Cur Hist 51:193-9+ O '66
What is Russia's game now? with report by F. B. Stevens. il U S News 60:39-41 Ja 31 '66

See also
Communist strategy
Cuban crisis, 1962
Russia—Boundaries

Africa
Peking's stake in Africa: battleground in ideological war against the USSR. P. Lessing. Nat R 18:262-4 Mr 22 '66
Russian revisionism in Africa. J. O'Connor. America 114:773-5 My 28 '66
Setback for the African left; revision of strategy. C. Sterling. il Reporter 35:23 D 1 '66

See also
Austria
Austria—History—Allied occupation, 1945-1955

China (People's Republic)
Chinese threat seen focused on Soviets. C. Brownlow. Aviation W 85:29 N 14 '66
C.P.S.U. statement on China: text of statement, August 31, 1966. Cur Hist 51:237-8+ O '66

How communism split: communism divided, or multiplied? Sr Schol 89:9-10 N 11 '66
Moscow-Peiping feud: rift grows wider. U S News 60:6 Ap 4 '66
Profile of the Sino-Soviet split. il Sr Schol 89:pt2 5-6 S 23 '66
Red romance that went sour; with reports. il Life 60:26-35 Ap 8 '66
Russia vs. China: the end of revolutionary communism; interview. M. Garder. U S News 61:50 N 7 '66
Sino-Soviet conflict. K. L. London. bibliog f Cur Hist 51:206-12+ O '66
Who's containing now? Commonweal 83:490 Ja 28 '66

Egypt
Defining the limit. il Newsweek 67:48 My 30 '66
New caution: restraining Nasser. Time 87: 36 My 27 '66
Price of penury. il Time 87:42 My 20 '66

Europe
Sparring for positions: Soviet diplomatic offensive. Time 87:39 My 13 '66

Europe, Eastern
Rumania and Russia. V. Zorza. New Repub 154:10-11 Je 4 '66
Soviet relations with east Europe. S. S. Anderson. Cur Hist 51:200-5 O '66

Finland
Small hello: Kosygin reception. il Newsweek 67:47 Je 27 '66

France
French mission to Moscow: what de Gaulle is up to. F. B. Stevens. U S News 60:68 My 2 '66
Kosygin in Paris: differences within amity. A. Werth. Nation 203:693-6 D 26 '66
Lively robot; A. Kosygin. il Time 88:38+ D 16 '66
Marxist mellowed; Kosygin's visit to France. il Newsweek 68:50 D 19 '66
Wait until spring; Kosygin visit to France. il Newsweek 68:52 D 12 '66

Hungary
See also
Hungary—History—Revolution, 1956

Italy
Visitor; Gromyko's visit. il Newsweek 67:54 My 2 '66

Japan
Red carpet for Gromyko; Tokyo visit. il Newsweek 68:35 Ag 8 '66

Middle East
Price of penury. il Time 87:42 My 20 '66
What the Russians are up to in the Middle East; interview, ed. by J. Law. Hussein. il U S News 61:39-42 D 26 '66

Spain
How Stalin relieved Spain of $600,000,000. A. Orlov. il Read Digest 89:37-8+ N '66

Turkey
Appointment in Ankara; visit of Kosygin. il Newsweek 69:26 Ja 2 '67

United States
After the cold war; prospective issues of U.S.-Soviet relations. C. O. Lerche, jr. il Nation 202:673-6 Je 6 '66
Bolshevik invasion of the West, by L. F. Budenz. Review
Nat R 18:475+ My 17 '66. E. Lyons
Calculated chill; taking advantage of three unpleasant incidents involving Americans. Newsweek 68:57-8 S 26 '66
Canada's role in East-West relations; address, March 11, 1966. P. Martin. Vital Speeches 32:409-14 Ap 15 '66
Detente rides again. A. Weill-Tuckerman. Nation 203:402-3 O 24 '66
Ending the cold war; Vietnam need not slow the thaw. W. C. McWilliams. Commonweal 85:363-5 Ja 6 '67
Is a deal with Russia stirring? with analysis by F. B. Stevens. il U S News 61:46-9 N 7 '66
Mutual trust? Sr Schol 89:20-1 O 21 '66
Neither liberty nor safety, by N. F. Twining. Review
Nat R 18:923 S 20 '66. J. Burnham
Pax Russo-Americana? Sino-Soviet dispute. G. Lichtheim. Commentary 41:60-5 Ap '66
Proliferation and Soviet-American relations. R. C. Tucker. Bul Atomic Sci 22:14-18 O '66

RUSSIA—Foreign relations—United States
—*Continued*
Russian dilemma; how to resume détente. il
Newsweek 67:40+ Je 20 '66
Thaw; accentuating the positive; cordial week
of Soviet-American talks. il Newsweek 68:
55-6 O 24 '66
U.S. views on developments in Viet-Nam
given to U.S.S.R; Russian charges of US
threat to Soviet merchant vessels; texts of
U.S. note, July 23 and Soviet note, July 9,
1966. Dept State Bul 55:213-14 Ag 8 '66
Up the back stairs. il Time 88:33-4 O 21 '66

Vietnam (Democratic Republic)
Kremlin's move? is Moscow preparing to es-
calate support of Hanoi and Vietcong?
J. Burnham. Nat R 18:822 Ag 23 '66
Russian equation. il Time 88:11-12 S 2 '66

Yugoslavia
One step backward; Tito and Brezhnev talks.
il Newsweek 68:48 O 3 '66

History
Soviet Union's 50th. M. Kalb. il Sat R 50:51-
2+ Ja 7 '67
Bibliography
Articles and other books received; comp.
by R. V. Allen. See issues of American
historical review
Recent developments in the history of the
Soviet Union and eastern Europe. R. V.
Allen. bibliog f Ann Am Acad 365:147-60
My '66
Historiography
Current Soviet theory of history; new trends
or old? A. P. Mendel. bibliog f Am Hist R
72:50-73 O '66
Recent developments in the history of the
Soviet Union and eastern Europe. R. V.
Allen. bibliog f Ann Am Acad 365:147-60
My '66

Industries
Changing Soviet Union; address, February 7,
1966. J. Scott. Vital Speeches 32:469-72 My
15 '66
How Russia really lives; getting the goods;
ed. by R. Littell. Newsweek 67:47-8 My 2
'66
I was a Soviet manager. G. Ryapolov. Harvard
Bsns R 44:117-25 Ja '66
Russia bets its future on computer know-
how; Five year plan in computer develop-
ment. il Bsns W p92+ Ag 13 '66
Russia upgrades its managers; growing
management movement; with editorial
comment. Bsns W p76+. 196 Ap 16 '66
Toughest management job in the world.
G. Burck. il Fortune 74:72-9+ Jl 1 '66
Why Russia is lagging in technology race.
il U S News 60:90-1 Ap 25 '66
See also
Automobile industry and trade—Russia
Machine tool industry and trade

Intellectual life
Art, politics, & the Soviet writer. T. Fran-
kel. bibliog f Commentary 41:52-9 My '66
On trial, by M. Hayward. Review
Sat R 49:25 Ag 6 '66. M. MacDuffie
Unperson sings to the Russians; B. Okudzava,
a balladeer. M. Mihajlov. il N Y Times
Mag p26-7+ My 15 '66
See also
Russian literature

Maps
Map of Russia (cont) Sr Schol 89:pt2 20 S
23 '66

Military policy
Arms and the Soviet Union. V. Zorza. New
Repub 156:13-15 Ja 14 '67
See also
Russia—Defenses

Navy
Cold wet war. R. Moley. Newsweek 68:104
Ag 22 '66
Russia talks of peace, builds up missiles.
navy. il U S News 61:70-2 N 21 '66

Submarine service
Soviet missile subs patrol off U.S. M. Getler.
Miss & Roc 18:12 Ap 4 '66

Politics and government
A. N. Shelepin on the rise. America 114:
471-2 Ap 9 '66
Art, politics, & the Soviet writer. T. Frankel. bibliog f Commentary 41:52-9 My '66
Brezhnev and Kosygin; the cult of impersonality. P. Grose. il N Y Times Mag
p34-7+ O 9 '66

How the new men run Russia. il Bsns W
p 138-42+ Jl 23 '66
Looking aghast at Soviet Russia. G. Feifer.
Nation 202:624 My 23 '66
No changes. il Time 88:25 Ag 12 '66
Russian summer; worried vacationists; Viet-
namese war causing anxiety. A. Werth.
Nation 203:176-9 S 5 '66
Soviet politics and interest groups. B. B.
Green. bibliog f Cur Hist 51:213-17+ O '66
Thirty years after Stalin's great purge. B.
Wolfe. il N Y Times Mag p66-7+ S 18 '66
See also
Communism—Russia
Communist party (Russia)

Popular culture
From the *kasatchok* to the twist. R. Symont.
il Horizon 8:78-85 Spr '66

Relations (diplomatic)
Catholic church
See Catholic church—Relations (diplo-
matic)—Russia

Religious institutions and affairs
Religion in Russia. Commonweal 83:685-6 Mr
18 '66
Religion in the Soviet Union. T. N. Davis
and E. K. Culhane. America 114:252-5+
F 19 '66
See also
Orthodox Eastern church, Russian

Social conditions
How Russia really lives; ed. by R. Littell.
il Newsweek 67:36+ My 2 '66
Russia's new bourgeois grows fat. A. Parry.
il N Y Times Mag p44-5+ Je 5 '66
See also
Children—Russia
Communism—Russia
Jews in Russia
Youth—Russia

Social life and customs
American in Moscow. T. T. Hammond. il Nat
Geog Mag 129:297-351 Mr '66

Treaties
Space treaty; a step forward. il Newsweek
68:21 D 19 '66
RUSSIA, Asiatic
How the East was won; Virgin lands de-
velopment. R. J. Korengold. Newsweek
68:58-9 O 10 '66
RUSSIA and China
Wisdom in watermelons; Soviet press ri-
diculing the red Chinese. Time 87:40-1 Je
10 '66
RUSSIA and Europe
Thaw in east Europe's ice age. E. Stillman.
il N Y Times Mag p27+ Ag 21 '66
RUSSIA and the United States
Cultural exchange as the Soviets use it. G.
Bailey. il Reporter 34:20-5 Ap 7 '66; Discus-
sion. 34:6+ My 19 '66
Iorn curtin; survey of children's knowledge
about Russia or the Soviet Union; report.
B. Appel. Library J 91:2174-5 Ap 15 '66
New U.S.-Russian link, by air. il U S News
61:93 N 14 '66
Visitors; decade of cultural exchange. M.
Mayer. il Sat R 49:53-5+ O 29 '66
RUSSIA and the West. See World politics,
1945-
RUSSIA-United States air agreement. See
Aviation—International aspects
RUSSIAN authors. See Authors, Russian
RUSSIAN bonds. See Bonds, Government—
Russia
RUSSIAN Communist party. See Communist
party (Russia)
RUSSIAN cookery. See Cookery, Russian
RUSSIAN culture. See Russia—Intellectual life
RUSSIAN dancing. See Dancing, Russian
RUSSIAN economic assistance. See Economic
assistance, Russian
RUSSIAN fiction
Dostoevsky and romantic realism, by D.
Fanger. Review
Nation 203:164-5 Ag 22 '66. S. Karlinsky
RUSSIAN humor. See Humor, Russian
RUSSIAN Jews. See Jews in Russia
RUSSIAN librarians. See Librarians
RUSSIAN literature
Chekhov and his prose, by T. Winner. Re-
view
Nation 202:684-6 Je 6 '66. D. Fanger
Ivan Turgenev; romantic humanist. W. H.
Chamberlin. Sat R 49:24-5+ Je 18 '66

RUSSIAN literature—*Continued*
Trial of two Soviet writers; case of Y. Daniel and A. Tertz. G. Bailey. il Reporter 34: 34-8 F 24 '66
See also
Authors, Russian
RUSSIAN military assistance. See Military assistance, Russian
RUSSIAN Orthodox church. See Orthodox Eastern church, Russian
RUSSIAN poetry
Eloquent new voice in Russia; A. Voznesensky. P. Young. il Life 60:69-71 Ap 1 '66

Bibliography
Yevtushenko and the underground poets. S. Karlinsky. Nation 203:549-53 N 21 '66

Translations into English
Autumn in Sigulda; tr. by W. H. Auden. A. Voznesensky. Sat R 49:17 My 21 '66
Babi Yar; tr. by G. Reavey. Y. Yevtushenko. N Y Times Mag p44 D 11 '66
Give me peace; tr. by M. Hayward. A. Voznesensky. Nation 203:162 Ag 22 '66
Last train to Malakhovka; poem, tr. by J. Garrigue. A. Voznesensky. New Repub 154:26 Ap 30 '66
My Achilles heart; Striptease; Ballad of the full stop; tr. by S. Kunitz. A. Voznesensky. Life 60:72 Ap 1 '66
My Achilles heart; tr. by W. H. Auden. A. Voznesensky. Newsweek 68:93 Jl 11 '66
Performing arts; A. Voznesensky on record. R. Kotlowitz. Harper 233:134 O '66
Six poems by Andrei Voznesensky; with introduction by R. Lowell. A. Voznesensky. New Repub 154:28-9 Ap 16 '66
Surging outcry against repression: The city of yes and the city of no; tr. by G. Dutton. E. A. Evtushenko. Life 61:118 N 18 '66
Two poems; tr. by S. Kunitz. A. Voznesensky. Atlan 218:50 Jl '66

RUSSIAN poets. See Poets, Russian
RUSSIAN propaganda. See Propaganda, Russian
RUSSIAN RIVER
Canoeing on the Russian River. il Sunset 136:84+ My '66
RUSSIAN scientists. See Scientists, Russian
RUSSIAN space probes. See Space probes, Russian
RUSSIAN spies. See Spies
RUSSIAN youth. See Youth—Russia
RUSSIANS
Eagles of Kazakhstan. E. S. Staples. Atlan 219:92-5 Ja '67
From the *kasatchok* to the twist. R. Symont. il Horizon 8:78-85 Spr '66
From two Americans: a close-up look at today's Russians. H. Rudd; F. C. Painton. il U S News 61:66-8 Jl 11 '66
How America lives: the Malones in Moscow. L. Benjamin. Ladies Home J 83:99-101+ S '66
See also
Humor, Russian
RUSSIANS in Egypt
Homesick for Russia in Aswan. R. J. Korengold. il Newsweek 67:52-3 My 23 '66
RUSSIANS in France
Russia on the Seine; White Russian colony of Paris. il Newsweek 67:39-40 F 14 '66
RUSSIANS in Vietnam
Soviet aid to Vietnam. A. Parry. il Reporter 36:28-33 Ja 12 '67
RUSSO, Michael
Area vocational schools. Am Ed 2:15-19 Je '66
RUSSO-German war, 1941-1945. See World war, 1939-1945—Campaigns and battles—Russia
RUST. See Corrosion and anticorrosives
RUSTAVELI, Shota
Rustaveli and the knight in the tiger's skin. I. Abashidze. il por UNESCO Courier 19:28-30 O '66
RUSTEBAKKE, Dorothy
Interesting hobby: pictures in plaster. Farm J 90:120 Ap '66
RUSTIN, Bayard
Black power and coalition politics. Commentary 42:35-40 S '66
Manifesto; excerpt from address, December 6, 1966. New Repub 156:23 Ja 7 '67
Watts manifesto & the McCone report. Commentary 41:29-35 Mr; 42:10+ Ag '66
Why don't Negroes. . . America 114:796-9 Je 4 '66
RUSTPROOFING of trucks. See Motor trucks —Care

RUTENBURG, Alexander M. See Smith, E. E. jt. auth.
RUTGERS university, New Brunswick, N.J.
Report from Rutgers. J. K. Hutchens. Sat R 49:44-5 Je 11 '66
RUTGERS university press
Report from Rutgers. J. K. Hutchens. Sat R 49:44-5 Je 11 '66
Rutgers university press marks 30th anniversary. W. Sloane. il Pub W 190:52-4 Jl 4 '66
RUTHERFOORD, Jim
New ideas in prefab cabins. Field & S 71: 64-6+ Je '66
RUTHERFORD, Ernest
How the newer alchemy was received. L. Badash. il por Sci Am 215:88-95 bibliog (p 116) Ag '66
RUTHERFORD, William A.
Problem solver for corporate giants. il pors Ebony 21:62-4+ O '66
RUTHERFURD, Lucy Page (Mercer)
F.D.R. & Lucy. por Time 88:13 Ag 26 '66
F.D.R.'s secret romance. A. Schlesinger, jr. por Ladies Home J 83:66+ N '66
Great American love story; concerning J. Daniels' book. il por Newsweek 68:60-1 Ag 22 '66
Great romance. Time 88:23 Ag 19 '66
In new book; story of an FDR romance; concerning Time between the wars, by J. Daniels. il U S News 61:13 Ag 22 '66
Old wives' tale; concerning J. Daniels book. R. Moley. Newsweek 68:76 Ag 29 '66
Romantic footnote to an era; with report by J. Daniels. il pors Life 61:44-9 S 2 '66
RUTLAND, Robert A.
Strenuous life of California politics. New Repub 154:11-12 Ap 16 '66
RUTLEDGE, Carl A.
Way of life. Newsweek 68:57 N 21 '66
RUTLEDGE, Dana
Way of life. por Newsweek 68:57 N 21 '66
RUTMAN, Robert J. and others
Bipiperidyl mustard, a new obesifying agent in the mouse. bibliog Science 153:1000-2 Ag 26 '66
RUTSCHMANN, Ruth
Perception of temporal order and relative visual latency. bibliog Science 152:1099-101 My 20 '66
RUTTER, Richard
Railroads: on the express track. Duns R 87: pt2 115-17+ My '66
RUTTING season. See Sex behavior
RUYLE, Robert L.
Antenna placement does make a difference. Pop Electr 25:64-5+ N '66
How to spot and eliminate mobile radio noise. Pop Electr 24:45-50 Je '66
RYAN, Charlotte
PTA in Washington. PTA Mag 61:29-30 O '66
RYAN, Clare E.
For whom does the bell toll? letter to the editor. Library J 91:4048 S 15 '66
RYAN, Claude
Quebec changes governments. For Affairs 45: 148-61 O '66
RYAN, Cornelius
How Germany was partitioned. por(p37) Pub W 189:39 Mr 28 '66
Last battle; excerpt. Read Digest 88:189-92+ Mr; 241-6+ Ap; 239-42+ My '66

about
Author. J. Beatty, jr. por(cover) Sat R 49:31 Mr 26 '66
RYAN, Edward Parsons
Pheromone: evidence in a decapod crustacean. bibliog Science 151:340-1 Ja 21 '66
RYAN, Eugene E.
I joined the ministerial association. America 115:158-9 Ag 13 '66
RYAN, James W. and others
Antibodies affecting metabolism of chicken erythrocytes: examination of schizophrenic and other subjects. bibliog Science 151:1408-10 Mr 18 '66
RYAN, Joseph T. abp
Poorest diocese in the U.S.A. J. Morris. America 114:549-50 Ap 16 '66
RYAN, Josephine MacDonald
Contraception fulfills nature. Cath World 203:207-12 Jl '66
RYAN, Mary Perkins
Church to die in or to live in? Cath World 203:17-21 Ap '66
Priest as witness. America 114:587-9 Ap 23 '66
RYAN, Orletta
I get one more U, my mother goin' to beat me till it rains. N Y Times Mag p27-9+ F 13 '66
—See Greene, M. F. jt. auth.

RYAN, Patricia
  Golf. Sports Illus 24:78+ Ap 11; 25:56-8 Jl 4
    '66
  Harness racing (cont) Sports Illus 24:70-1 My
    30; 25:52-3 Ag 22 '66
  Midsummer fairy tale for old folks. Sports
    Illus 25:26-7+ Jl 18 '66
  Perils of paralysis. Sports Illus 25:22-5+
    Jl 11 '66
  Return of the littlest tiger. Sports Illus 25:
    32-4+ Ag 15 '66
RYAN, William
  Our disturbed children: who is to care for
    them? Nation 202:775-80 Je 27 '66
RYAN aeronautical company
  Magical flight of Ryan aeronautical. Fortune
    74:350 Jl 15 '66
RYAN homes, incorporated
  Homebuilder bucks ebbing sales tide. il
    Bsns W p68-70+ O 8 '66
RYAPOLOV, Gregory
  I was a Soviet manager. Harvard Bsns R 44:
    117-25 Ja '66
RYCROFT, Sir Benjamin William
  Corneal transplants. Sci N 89:396-7 My 21 '66
RYDER, David Warren
  Day they killed the Constitution. Nat R 18:
    838 Ag 23 '66
RYDER, Norman B. and Westoff, C. F.
  Use of oral contraception in the United
    States, 1965. Science 153:1199-205 S 9 '66
RYE bread. See Bread
RYMAN, Helen
  Adventure in creative volunteering. por Parks
    & Rec 1:36-8 Ja '66
RYNNE, Xavier, pseud.
  Letter from Vatican City (cont) New Yorker
    42:140+ O 22 '66
RYSKIND, Morrie
  California: the final battle? Nat R 18:1094-
    7+ N 1 '66
RYUKYU ISLANDS
  Ryukyu's legislature to elect chief executive;
    statement, December 20, 1965; with execu-
    tive order. L. B. Johnson. Dept State Bul
    54:66 Ja 10 '66
RYUN, Jim
  Doleful day for Ryun: 3:58-6. G. S. Brown.
    il por Sports Illus 25:22-4 Jl 4 '66
  Jim Ryun first 3:50 miler? il pors Life 60:
    81-2+ My 20 '66
  Just perfect. il por Newsweek 68:74-5 Ag 1
    '66
  Outrunning the rabbits. il por Time 88:34
    Jl 29 '66
  Puzzling prodigy. il por Time 87:68 Je 17
    '66
  Ready for the goal. J. Olsen. il por Sports
    Illus 24:64-9+ Je 20 '66
  Second fastest ever. G. S. Brown. il pors
    Sports Illus 24:26-9 Je 13 '66
  Special brand of fame. G. S. Brown. il pors
    Sports Illus 25:20-1+ Ag 1 '66
  Sportsman of the year. por Sports Illus 25:
    46-7 D 19 '66
  Teen-agers take charge. G. S. Brown. il por
    Sports Illus 24:69-70 My 23 '66
  3:50 miler? il por Newsweek 67:82-3 My 30
    '66
  Time to remember: 3:51.3.   A. Verschoth.
    il pors Sports Illus 25:10-13 Jl 25 '66
  Track: what limit to human achievement? il
    pors Newsweek 68:53-5 Jl 25 '66
  World's finest miler? E. Linn. il pors Sat
    Eve Post 239:90+ Ap 23 '66

S

S and H. See Sperry and Hutchinson company
SA Les forges de Zeebrugge. See Munitions in-
    dustries—Belgium
SAAB. See Airplane industry and trade—Swe-
    den
SAMPE. See Society of aerospace materials
    and process engineers
SAR (search and rescue) See United States—
    Coast guard
SBA. See United States—Small business ad-
    ministration
SBIC. See Small business investment com-
    panies
SCLC. See Southern Christian leadership con-
    ference
SCM corporation
  Inventor who still won't quit: E. E. Klein-
    schmidt. il Bsns W p 154-6+ S 3 '66
SCR (silicon controlled rectifiers) See Electric
    current rectifiers

SDS. See Scientific data systems incorporated;
    Students for a democratic society (organi-
    zation)
SEATO. See Southeast Asia treaty organiza-
    tion
SEC. See United States—Securities and ex-
    change commission
SEC vidicon. See Television cameras
S. G. Warburg and company. See London—
    Banks
SEEK (search for education, elevation, and
    knowledge) See New York (city) City uni-
    versity of New York
SHAPE. See Supreme headquarters, Allied
    powers, Europe
SINA. See Society for indecency to naked ani-
    mals
SLA. See Special libraries association
SLEDGE (simulating large explosive detonable
    gas experiment) See Balloons—Use in
    research
SLR cameras. See Single-lens reflex cameras
SLR lenses. See Lenses, Photographic
S-meters. See Electric meters
SMSG. See School mathematics study group
SNCC. See Student nonviolent coordinating
    committee
SNCF (Société nationale des chemins de fer
    Francais) See Railroads and state—France
SNPO. See United States—Space nuclear
    propulsion office
SOL (sequence operated lock) See Locks and
    keys
SOS (organization)
  Help me, I'm alone; divorcees helping each
    other to fight loneliness and despair. B.
    Davidson. il Sat Eve Post 239:74-5 S 10 '66
SPET (solid propellant electric thruster) See
    Solid propellant rockets
SPF (specific pathogen-free program) See
    Swine—Diseases and pests
SRAM (short-range attack missile) See Guided
    missiles—Launching from airplanes
S. S. Kresge company. See Kresge, S. S. Com-
    pany
SSRS. See Society for social responsibility in
    science
STOL airplanes. See Airplanes, Short take-off
    and landing
SUB. See Supplemental unemployment benefits
SUNY (State university of New York) See
    New York state univeristy
SV40
  Susceptibility of human diploid fibroblast
    strains to transformation by SV40 virus.
    G. J. Todaro and others. bibliog il Sci-
    ence 153:1252-4 S 9 '66
SAAL, Hubert
  Caution: choreographer at work. N Y Times
    Mag pt2 p 18-19+ S 11 '66
SAARI, John M. and Shorthill, R. W.
  Hot spots on the moon. pors Sky & Tel 31:
    327-31 Je '66
SAARINEN, Aline B.
  He saw architecture as the permanent stage
    set of an age. Life 61:103-4+ S 16 '66
  National gallery: preview of an anniversary
    exhibition. McCalls 93:96-103+ Ap '66
SAARINEN, Eero
  Saarinen's CBS skyscraper. D. Jacobs. Holi-
    day 39:124-6 Je '66
SABAN, Louis
  Double reverse. Newsweek 68:47 D 26 '66
SABBATICAL leave. See Leave of absence;
    Teachers—Leaves of absence
SABHARWAL, Pritam. See Mahlberg, P. jt.
    auth.
SABINA and the herd; story. See Auchincloss,
    L.
SACCO-Vanzetti case
  Protest: Sacco-Vanzetti and the intellectuals,
    by D. Felix. Review
    Nat R 18:734-5 Jl 26 '66. W. H. Chamber-
      lin
    New Repub 154:23-4+ Ap 2 '66. A. M.
      Bickel; Discussion. 154:36-7 Je 4 '66
SACHAR, Abram L.
  People's span. Sat R 49:26 Ag 20 66
  Victims of a pious cruelty. Sat R 49:36-7 Je 18
    '66
SACHS, Gunther
  Fun couples. por Newsweek 68:58 Jl 25 '66
SACHS, Nelly
  O the chimneys; poem, tr. by M. Roloff. Sat
    R 49:47 D 10 '66
            about
  Nelly Sachs. G. C. Schwebell. por Sat R 49:
    46-7 D 10 '66
  Shmuel Agnon, Nelly Sachs win Nobel litera-
    ture prize. Pub W 190:56-7 O 31 '66

SACHS, Paul Joseph
Friend of the Fogg. il por Time 89:54 Ja 13 '67
SACK, John
M; account of one company of American soldiers. Esquire 66:79-86+ O '66
Publisher's page. A. Gingrich. Esquire 66:6 O '66
SACKETT, Gene P.
Monkeys reared in isolation with pictures as visual input: evidence for an innate releasing mechanism. Science 154:1468+ D 16 '66
SACKETT, Russell
Plotting a war on whitey. Life 60:100-100B+ Je 10 '66
Whitey in the Negro underground. G. P. Hunt. por Life 60:3 Je 10 '66
SACKETT, William M.
Manganese nodules: thorium-230: protactinium-231 ratios. bibliog Science 154:646-7 N 4 '66
SACKTOR, Bertram. See Childress, C. C. jt. auth.
SACRAMENT of penance. See Confession
SACRAMENTO, Calif.
Inn at city crossroads; Mansion inn hotel. il Arch Rec 140:136 Ag '66

Newspapers
See also
Sacramento union (newspaper)
SACRAMENTO, Calif. state college
Lost book campaign at Sacramento. P. D. Morrison. il Wilson Lib Bul 40:526-9 F '66
SACRAMENTO COUNTY, Calif.
Cast-in-place drainage pipe. T. E. Campbell. il Am City 81:100-2 D '66
How to make traffic signals super safe. J. C. Ray. il Am City 81:130 O '66
SACRAMENTO national wildlife refuge. See Wildlife sanctuaries
SACRAMENTO union (newspaper)
Competition in Sacramento. il Time 88:48-9 Jl 8 '66
SACRAMENTS
Mutual sacraments; suspicion between Roman Catholics and Protestants. Time 88:70 Ag 5 '66
Word as sacrament. E. Gibson. Christian Cent 83:1172-5 S 28 '66
See also
Marriage
SACRE du printemps; ballet. See Ballets—Criticisms
SACRED cows. See Cows in religion, folklore, etc.
SACRED dolphins. See Dolphins (mammals)
SACRED music. See Church music
SACRIFICE
See also
Suffering
SADE, Donatien Alphonse François, comte de
Wicked Mister Six. por Time 87:108+ Mr 4 '66
SADHUS
In search of the seekers of truth: holy men of India. K. Singh. il N Y Times Mag p42-3+ Ja 8 '67
SADLER, Barry
Senior scholastic interviews; ed. by J. Nickerson. por Sr Schol 88:3+ Mr 4 '66

about
Hail to Green Berets; with report by D. Martin. il pors Life 60:93-4+ Mr 4 '66
No time for sergeanting. il por Time 87:84-6 Ap 15 '66
Selling the green berets. il por Newsweek 67:101A My 2 '66
Vietnam blues. por Newsweek 67:91A F 21 '66
SADLER, Christine
Luci Johnson's engagement. McCalls 93:104-5+ Mr '66
SADOVY, John
Jump, jump, jump. D. L. Miller. il Mod Phot 30:82-3 O '66
SADUSK, Joseph F. Jr
Support for a shake-up. il Time 87:55 Ap 1 '66
SAFDIE, Moshe
Habitat 67. D. Jacobs. il por Horizon 9:70-3 Wint '67
SAFELIGHTS. See Photography—Apparatus and supplies
SAFETY belts
Children's auto harnesses. il Consumer Rep 31:113 Mr '66
Double-shoulder harness gives best protection. Sci N 90:183 S 10 '66
Fasten your seat belt; failure to use a seat belt may bar recovery in a personal-injury suit. Time 88:46 Jl 22 '66

Rockabye, hot rods, to the federal safety lullaby. A. H. Sypher. il Nations Bsns 54:27-8 Jl '66
Seat-belt retractors. il Consumer Rep 31:496-7 O '66
Seat belts and protective caps. Consumer Bul 49:9 O '66
SAFETY devices and measures
How to survive, anywhere. C. C. Trobest. il Pop Sci 189:62-5+ Ag '66
Safety in science projects. F. L. Snakenberg. il Sci N L 89:90-1 F 5 '66
See also
Accidents—Prevention
Traffic regulations
also subhead Safety devices and measures under various subjects, e.g. Automobiles—Safety devices and measures
SAFETY glass. See Glass, Safety
SAFETY guards. See Roads—Safety guards
SAFETY razors. See Razors
SAFETY stud tires. See Tires, Automobile
SAFRAN printing company
McCall corp. may acquire Safran printing. Detroit. Pub W 189:88 Ap 25 '66
Some new thoughts on color printing; summary of discussion at second seminar on Color in print, 1966. Pub W 191:92-3 Ja 2 '67
SAGA of Patsy and Oscar; story. See Manchester. H.
SAGAFJORD (ship) See Ocean liners
SAGAN, Bruce
At the grass roots. Newsweek 68:76 O 24 '66
SAGAN, Carl
Saucerian cult; with excerpt from Intelligent life in the universe. Sat R 49:50-2 Ag 6 '66
SAGAN, Françoise, pseud.
Un certain succès. por Time 88:108 O 14 '66
Le cheval évanoui (Fainting horse) Criticism New Yorker 42:179 O 1 '66
Toujours tristesse. S. Kauffmann. New Repub 155:21+ O 29 '66
SAGE, Tom
Seducers of the Emerald Coast. Nat R 18:992-4 O 4 '66
Who' afraid of Dr Faustus? Nat R 18:1319-20 D 27 '66
SAGE grouse. See Grouse
SAGE hens. See Grouse
SAGENDORPH, Robb
Old faithful goes out on a limb. il pors Life 61:147-8 N 18 '66
SAGINAW, Mich.
Roethke memorial plans. J. Ciardi. Sat R 49:16 Ap 9 '66
SAGUARO. See Cactus
SAGUARO NATIONAL MONUMENT
Decline of the saguaro. L. W. Robinson. il Am For 72:46+ My '66
SAHARA DESERT
Sahara song: the last legions, the first art; in Spanish Sahara. F. V. Grunfeld. il Reporter 35:48-50 Jl 14 '66
Water under the Sahara. R. P. Ambroggi. il Sci Am 214:21-9 My '66
SAHL, Mort
Onward! and downward! with Mort Sahl. Nat R 18:760 Ag 9 '66
SAID, Edward W.
Configuration of themes. Nation 202:659-61 My 30 '66
SAID, Sami I. and others
Metabolism of alveolar cells: histochemical evidence and relation to pulmonary surfactant. bibliog Science 152:657-9 Ap 29 '66
SAIGON
Along PX alley; black market. il Newsweek 68:68+ N 28 '66
Bonfire in PX alley. il Time 88:39 N 25 '66
Boy-state; sense of community in slum; District 8. il Time 88:24 S 2 '66
Encircled city; V.C. activity around Saigon. Time 88:23-4 S 2 '66
Nobody move! dramatic attempt to disrupt South Vietnam's National day parade. il Newsweek 68:54 N 14 '66
Saigon: at night, war flares and road checks; corruption and profiteering. S. Angeloff. il Life 60:47-52A F 25 '66
Saigon: stained pearl of the Orient. S. Castan. il Look 30:70-4+ My 17 '66
Securing Saigon; Operation Cedar Falls. il Time 89:23 Ja 20 '67
Suburban warfare. F. Sully. Newsweek 68:29 S 5 '66
Tragedy of Saigon. F. FitzGerald. il Atlan 218:59-67 D '66

Mayors
Overworked mayor; arrest by American MPs. Time 88:36 D 16 '66

SAIGON—*Continued*

Riots

Insurrection inside the war. il Life 60:28-33 Ap 22 '66

Storm breaks; war in the streets. il Time 87: 28-9 Ap 15 '66

Turmoil in Vietnam: war within a war? il Newsweek 67:24-5 Ap 18 '66

U.S. holds firm in wobbly Vietnam; Buddhist anti-government demonstrations and riots shake Saigon regime. il Bsns W p39-40 Ap 16 '66

Social conditions

Apologia pro verbis suis; J. W. Fulbright expresses regret over recent remarks. Time 87:70 My 27 '66

Back to the brothel; discussion in Senate foreign relations committee hearings. Time 87:29 My 20 '66

Brothels and hair spray. il Newsweek 67:30 My 23 '66

Water supply

Design, build, operate and train; water-treatment plant. W. T. McPhee and J. F. Lenard. il Am City 81:100-3 O '66

SAILBOAT building. See Boatbuilding

SAILBOAT models. See Ship and boat models

SAILBOAT racing

Always on Sunday; Tri club yacht racing association. B. Wisner. il Motor B 117:40-3+ Je '66

Can you handle extreme conditions? J. Sutphen. il Yachting 119:90-1+ Ap '66

Dyer dhow derby; seaport's fall finale. il Motor B 117:112 Ja '66

Geriatric a-go-go; Maine's annual Retired skippers' race. P. Loring. il Yachting 120: 60-1+ Jl '66

Meanest vamp at sea; fiber-glass Cal-40 sailboat. H. Whall. il Sports Illus 24:56-7 Mr 28 '66

Report from a racing sailor. K. Lamott. il Holiday 40:8+ Jl '66

Skipper's test; North American men's sailing championships. il Time 88:50+ S 9 '66

Storm in a calm over Tempest; England's Olympic candidate challenges Star class in One-of-a-kind regatta at Tampa Bay. H. Whall. Sports Illus 24:96-8 Ap 4 '66

Strangest yachting crowd; Grand Turk. T. J. King. il Yachting 119:224-5 Mr '66

They sail to win. il Yachting 119:55+ Mr '66

They sail to win; team racing. W. Brown. il Yachting 120:28-9+ N '66

With the racing classes. B. Robinson. See issues of Yachting

SAILBOATS

Great American sailboats; story of Baruna. il Motor B 117:44-5 F '66

1967 sailboats. il Motor B 119:148-57 Ja '67

Sailboats, 1966. il Motor B 117:154-61+ Ja '66

Selecting a sailboat. F. M. Paulson. il Field & S 71:100-2+ Je '66

They sail to win; making a Finn go fast. P. Barrett. il Yachting 120:36-7+ Jl; 23+ Ag '66

See also

Trimarans

Ballast

See Ballast (boats)

Design

And then there were two; IYRU selection committee recommends development of two new classes. B. Bavier. il Yachting 120:58-9+ N '66

Designs. W. H. DeFontaine. il Yachting 119: 120-6+ Ja '66

Duckling for the deep; Cal-40. il Time 88: 40+ Jl 15 '66

Gilbert (Gil) M. Smith, a great South Bay legend. W. H. deFontaine and P. Bigelow. il Yachting 119:244-7 Mr '66

Man and his boat, Star Song. B. D. Burrill. il Yachting 119:95-7+ Ap '66

Shields class sloop. il Motor B 117:47+ Ap '66

Storm in a calm over Tempest; England's Olympic candidate challenges Star class in One-of-a-kind regatta at Tampa Bay. H. Whall. Sports Illus 24:96-8 Ap 4 '66

They never say die! Cape Cod baby Knockabout. D. I. Crossley. il Yachting 119:222-3 Mr '66

Equipment

Yachting's boat show. il Yachting 119:127-30+ **Ja '66**

Materials

New lightning construction in glass. B. Cobb, jr. il Yachting 119:73-5+ Ja '66

Safety devices and measures

Spinnakers and safety at sea. B. D. Barker, 3d. il Yachting 119:69-71+ Je '66

SAILFISH fishing

Fly rod over the deep blue. L. Wulff. il Esquire 66:253-5+ D '66

SAILING

Bosun's mate, J. G; Richie Boyd. C. Morrison. il Look 30:M6-8 Jl 26 '66

Can you handle extreme conditions? J. Sutphen. il Yachting 119:90-1+ Ap '66

Ives sings a song of the sea; interview, ed. by G. Sloane. B. Ives. il Motor B 117:42-3 Mr '66

Joys of cruising in a 19 footer. I. Schildroth. il Yachting 119:108-9+ Ja '66

Modern sail handling. W. C. Ross. il Yachting 120:45-7+ Jl; 44-6+ Ag '66 (to be cont)

New England yachting; symposium. il Yachting 120:50-61+ Jl '66

Salty sailor of Park avenue. C. Phinizy. il Sports Illus 25:32-4+ Jl 11 '66

See how de mainsail sets. J. C. Kozlick. il Motor B 118:43+ O '66

They sail to win. See issues of Yachting

See also

Sailboat racing

Study and teaching

Instructional slides for juniors. K. Morgan. il Yachting 120:33 D '66

Junior sailing; Newport Beach, Calif. L. J. Kennedy. il Yachting 120:40-1+ Ag '66

Sail trainer; dry land instruction for the novice. E. F. Haylock. il Motor B 117:102 F '66

Shopwalk; Sloane school of sailing, Oyster Bay, N.Y. J. Bruce. Sports Illus 25:16 S 19 '66

Teaching executives sailsmanship; Ardell sailing school, Newport Beach, Calif. il Bsns W p78-9 Je 4 '66

They sail to win; Jimmy DeWitt conducts a sailing symposium. M. Wiley. il Yachting 120:31+ D '66

They sail to win; Peter Barrett and the USISA symposium. E. Horan. il Yachting 119:52-3+ F '66

Where sailing is all; Noroton yacht club. W. Roberts. il Yachting 119:70-2+ F '66

SAILING ships. See Sailing vessels

SAILING vessels

Great American sailboats; new Yankee for the old world. R. Stephens. il Motor B 117:40-1+ Mr '66

Saga of a ship, the Yankee. L. Marden. il Nat Geog Mag 129:262-9 F '66

Through a glass darkly. A. W. Moffat. Yachting 119:194 F '66

Yankee sails again. il Motor B 117:36-9 Mr '66

See also

Schooners

SAILING yachts. See Yachts and yachting

SAILPLANES. See Gliders (aeronautics)

SAILS

Is this the sailcloth secret? Australian sailcloth for 1967 America's cup challenge. L. D'Alpuget. il Yachting 119:102-3+ Ja '66

Lowell North on sails; interview, ed. by K. Krüger. L. North. il Yachting 119:77-9+ Mr '66

Modern sail handling. W. C. Ross. il Yachting 120:45-7+ Jl; 44-6+ Ag '66

Sail means only a sale to Sol; dacron and nylon sails. H. Whall. il Sports Illus 24: 26-9 Ja 24 '66

Spinnakers and safety at sea. B. D. Barker, 3d. il Yachting 119:69-71+ Je '66

Steadying sails. J. Emmett. il Yachting 120: 50+ S '66

Repairing

Sail care without tears. F. Rohr. il Motor B 117:28-9+ Je '66

ST ANNE'S maternity hospital. See Los Angeles—Hospitals

ST AUGUSTINE, Fla.

St Augustine: city of artists, 1883-1895. F. A. Sharf. il Antiques 90:220-3 Ag '66

St Augustine, nation's oldest city, turns 400. R. L. Conly. il Nat Geog Mag 129:196-229 F '66

Churches

Our oldest mission; symbol of peace; new votive church at Nombre de Dios mission. V. P. McCorry. America 114:625 Ap 30 '66

ST CHARLES seminary, Overbrook, Pa. See
Theological schools
ST CLAIR, Jean. See Perillo, A. D. jt. auth.
ST DENIS, Ruth
Open letter about Isadora Duncan. Dance
Mag 40:26 N '66
ST JAMES' community center, Harlem.   See
New York (city)—Community centers
ST JOHN ISLAND
Through a snorkeler's mask; marine life in
Caneel Bay. V. B. Moore. il Read Digest 89:
133-8 Ag '66
SAINT JOHN RIVER
U.S. and Canada to negotiate for develop-
ment of Saint John River; department an-
nouncement; with texts of notes exchanged.
Dept State Bul 54:67-8 Ja 10 '66
ST JOHN-STEVAS, Norman
Abortion laws. Commonweal 85:163-6 N 11
'66
ST JOHN the Divine, Cathedral of. See New
York (city)—St John the Divine, Cathedral
of
ST JOHN'S college, Annapolis, Md.
St John's college of Annapolis P. Janssen.
il Am Ed 2:13 O '66
ST JOHN'S seminary, Brighton, Mass. See
Theological schools
ST JOHN'S university, Collegeville, Minn.
Concrete trees in St John's. B. J. Stein and
U. J. Steiner. il Library J 91:5880-3 D 1 '66
ST JOHN'S university, Jamaica, N.Y.
Academic disorder at St John's. R. Kirk.
Nat R 18:116 F 8 '66; Reply. J. Morressy.
18:138 F 22 '66
Academic freedom and St John's. America
115:795 D 17 '66; Discussion. 116:68+ Ja 21
'67
Academic freedom: lessons from the crisis
at St John's. L. J. Carter. Science 154:1428-
30 D 16 '66
Church and the university. America 114:165
Ja 29 '66; Discussion. 114:230-1 F 12 '66
Crisis at St John's. E. Wakin. Sat R 49:
93 Ap 16 '66
In the vulgate; reply. T. F. Mader. Nat R
18:94+ F 8 '66
Join the picket line! concerning letter from
union to librarians to boycott annual con-
gress. J. N. Berry. 3d. il Library J 91:
1782-7 Ap 1 '66
Not with a bang but a fizzle. Nat R 18:199
Mr 8 '66
Reflections on the St John's case. J. Hitch-
cock. Cath World 203:24-8 Ap '66
St John's strike. Commonweal 83:571-2 F 18
'66
St John's university. America 114:684 My 14
'66
St John's university: the issues. F. Canavan;
discussion. America 114:241, 276-7 F 19-26
'66
St John's; university violated its own laws.
F. Griffith. Commonweal 83:647 Mr 4 '66;
Reply with rejoinder. H. R. Horvat. 84:67+
Ap 8 '66
Strike at St John's. J. Leo. Commonweal
83:500+ Ja 28 '66; Reply. S. Poole. 83:705
Mr 18 '66
Strike at St John's: why the professors
picket. M. R. Berube. il Nation 202:172-4
F 14 '66
Time bomb in Catholic education. R. Horch-
ler. il Look 30:23-5 Ap 5 '66
Victory for St John's. Commonweal 84:382 Je
24 '66; Discussion. 84:596-7; 85:67+ S 16,
O 21 '66
ST LAURENT, Yves Mathieu
Vogue's ready beauty. por Vogue 147:152 Mr
15 '66
ST LAWRENCE RIVER
See also
Thousand Islands
ST LAWRENCE SEAWAY
Adding five lakes to the seven seas. il Sr
Schol 88:2 Ap 22 '66
Sailing the eighth sea: Great Lakes. J. D.
Scott. Redbook 126:49 Mr '66
Toll tempest on the Seaway; 10 per cent
boost in tolls proposed. il Bsns W p 120+
Jl 23 '66
ST LOUIS, Mo.
Suit against the unions; attempt to enforce
the nondiscrimination clause. E. C. Gott-
schalk. New Repub 154:7-8 Mr 12 '66

Architecture
Soaring St Louis. il Travel 125:34-5 Je '66

Courts
Spiral to a gun. M. Gellhorn. Harper 233:
69-73 O '66

Crime
Spiral to a gun. M. Gellhorn. Harper 233:
69-73 O '66
Description
Soaring St Louis. il Travel 125:34-5 Je '66
Galleries and museums
See also
St Louis city art museum
Hospitals
Diagnostic tower has convertible self-care,
office and nursing floors; Queeny tower of
the Barnes hospital. il Arch Rec 140:214-16
O '66
Housing
Where D(3) helped wipe out a slum; St
Louis' 12-acre La Clede town. il Bsns W
p 162-4+ D 17 '66
Labor and laboring classes
Administration hardens stand against job
bias; St Louis scene of labor walkout. il
Bsns W p94+ F 12 '66
Monuments, statues, etc.
Gateway arch. Holiday 39:137 My '66
Highest arch in the U.S; Gateway to the
West. il Sci Digest 59:9 F '66
Sanitary affairs
Best value; goal of St Louis sewage purifica-
tion system. G. D. Simpson and W. G.
Shifrin. il Am City 81:75-8 Jl '66
Streets
Why we add asbestos. A. M. Johnson. il Am
City 81:98-9 Mr '66
ST LOUIS Cardinals (football club) See Foot-
ball clubs
ST LOUIS city art museum
City art museum of Saint Louis.   C. E.
Buckley. il Antiques 90:686-91 N '66
ST LOUIS encephalitis. See Encephalitis.
Epidemic
ST LOUIS Hawks (basketball team) See Bas-
ketball teams
ST LOUIS review. See Catholic press
ST MALO tidal dam. See Dams—France
ST MARKS chrondrite. See Meteorites
ST MARK'S school, Southboro, Mass. See Pri-
vate schools
ST MARTIN (island)
Beach bumming south of Nassau in a great
new bonanza. R. B. Weeghman. il Flying
79:34-40 S '66
ST MARY'S hospital, Evansville. See Evans-
ville, Ind.—Hospitals
ST MICHAELS, Md.
Maritime museum for the Chesapeake. E.
Horan. il Yachting 119:158-9 Mr '66
SAINT MICHEL, MONT, France. See Mont
Saint Michel, France
SAINT on earth; story. See Coffer. H. L.
ST PAUL
New twin cities; cultural appetite. B. Hersh.
il Holiday 39:50-5+ Je '66
Twins that dominate the northern plains. il
Bsns W p74-6+ My 21 '66
Architecture
Convent and home for girls; Home of the
Good Shepherd. il Arch Rec 140:108 Ag '66
Music
St Paul; production of Tales of Hoffmann.
A. B. Cutts. il Opera N 31:29 D 31 '66
ST PAUL'S school, Concord, N.H. See Private
schools
ST PETERSBURG times
Youth among the oldsters; summer jobs at
the St Petersburg times. il Time 88:50+ Jl 1
'66
ST PHALLE, Niki de
Calico dames in a frolic of art. il por Life
60:58-60+ Ap 1 '66
ST REGIS hotel. See New York (city)—Hotels,
restaurants, etc.
SAINT-SAENS, Camille
Samson and Delilah. Criticism
Opera N 30:29 Ap 16 '66
ST THOMAS ISLAND
Desalted sea water for St Thomas. R. E.
Cannard. il Am City 81:104-6 F '66
ST VINCENT college, Latrobe, Pa.
Confrontation at Latrobe. Nation 203:404-5
O 24 '66
How to sabotage a seminar; demonstrations
over inviting Herbert Aptheker as speaker.
America 115:530 N 5 '66

SAINTENY, Jean
Where are they now? il pors Newsweek 68:16
D 19 '66
SAINTPAULIA ionantha. See African violets
SAINTS
Handle (truth) with care. V. P. McCorry.
America 115:562-3 N 5 '66
See also
Martyrs
SAITO, Tsunemasa, and others
Lithology and paleontology of the reflective
layer horizon A. Science 154:1173-6 D 2 '66
Tertiary sediment from the Mid-Atlantic
ridge. bibliog Science 151:1075-9 Mr 4 '66
SAIZ, Víctor
Multiple guilt; story. Américas 18:34-7 Je '66
SAKS, Katia
Doll; story. Américas 18:28-30 S '66
SALAD dressings
Classic salad dressings; with recipes. il Red-
book 127:82-4 Ag '66
Successful recipes: salad dressings. il Suc
Farm 64:73-4 Je '66
See also
Mayonnaise
SALADS
Apple salads. il Bet Hom & Gard 44:95-6
S '66
Avocado and crab, the happy companions.
il Sunset 136:188-9 Ap '66
Best hot salads. il Bet Hom & Gard 44:93-4
My '66
Big bean salad. il Ladies Home J 83:86-7+
Ag '66
Bride serves Caesar salad; recipe. il McCalls
93:34 Jl '66
Caesar salad as summer entrée; with recipe.
il Sunset 137:156 S '66
Choice summer salads for a crowd; with rec-
ipes. Good H 162:240 Ap '66
He likes to cook. P. Knowlton. il Bet Hom
& Gard 44:82 My '66
Holiday salad molds. il Bet Hom & Gard 44:
81-2 D '66
Jeweled Christmas salads; with recipes. il
McCalls 94:104-5+ D '66
Meet the summer cook's friend. il Sunset
136:178-9 My '66
Midwinter surprises, two summery salads
using fresh fruits and vegetables. il Sunset
136:78-9 F '66
Salad with a briny bite; herring salad; with
menu and recipes. E. Graves. il Life 61:72-
3+ Ag 12 '66
Salads double as desserts. il Bet Hom & Gard
44:73-4 Ag '66
Sparkling summer salads; with recipes. il
McCalls 93:92-3+ Jl '66
Summer salads with rice; with recipes. il
Sunset 137:138 Jl '66
Supper's ready and waiting in a mold. il
Farm J 90:60 Je '66
Susan makes springtime chicken salad. M.
F. Williams. il Good H 162:160 My '66
Swiss salad with Swiss cheese. il Sunset
136:198+ Je '66
This superb salad could make you famous.
il Bet Hom & Gard 44:82-3+ O '66
Toss these when you throw a barbecue! il
Bet Hom & Gard 44:109 Je '66
Winter salads, good looking, tasty; with
recipes. il Sunset 138:92 Ja '67
SALANDINI, Victor
Decision at Di Giorgio. America 115:415+
O 8 '66
SALANT, Richard S.
Bad days at Black Rock. il por Newsweek
67:62-3 F 28 '66
SALANT, Walter S.
Other side of the gold and dollar story; in-
terview. por U S News 61:76-8 O 24 '66
SALARIES
What can a child expect to earn in his
chosen career? Bet Hom & Gard 44:30+ Ag
'66
See also
Non-wage payments
also subhead Salaries under various sub-
jects, e.g. Librarians—Salaries
SALAZAR, António de Oliveira
Salazar's Portugal: anniversary on thin ice.
R. H. Chilcote. il Nation 202:638-41 My 30
'66
SALB, Jesse
Teen-age scientist, a college drop-out, reports
on virus research. Todays Health 44:13 S
'66
SALE, J. Kirk
And now Nkrumah: generals & the future of
Africa. Nation 202:317-22 Mr 21 '66
Bridge nuts, doubled and redoubled. N Y
Times Mag p32-3+ My 8 '66
SALES, Art. See Art sales

SALES, Bargain. See Bargain sales
SALES, Book. See Book sales
SALES agencies. See Exclusive agencies
SALES conferences
Sales conference blazes winning path. Ad-
club told. Pub W 189:57 Mr 7 '66
SALES management
Sales power through planned careers. A. E.
Pearson. il Harvard Bsns R 44:105-16 Ja
'66
SALES managers
Sales manager's alter ego. M. A. Brice. il
Duns R 88:59+ N '66
SALES policies
Bride business; techniques employed by mer-
chants. il Newsweek 67:100 My 2 '66
Think small, sell big. il Duns R 87:55+ Mr
'66
SALES promotion
How to get salesmen through the doorway;
pre-selling tactics. il Bsns W p84+ Je 4
'66
Playing the games; Esso's promotional game,
Tigerino. New Repub 156:10 Ja 21 '67
See also
Competitions
Trading stamps
SALES talk. See Salesmen and salesmanship
SALES tax
See also
Stock transfer tax
SALES techniques. See Salesmen and sales-
manship
SALESMANSHIP. See Salesmen and sales-
manship
SALESMEN, Insurance. See Insurance agents
SALESMEN and salesmanship
Bride business; techniques employed by
merchants. il Newsweek 67:100 My 2 '66
Can salesmen be tested? L. Rich. il Duns R
87:40-1+ Mr '66
Controversy in sales quotas. L. Rich. il
Duns R 87:47-8+ My '66
Goodbye Hong Kong, hello Acapulco; Gibson's
free travel as sales incentive. il Time 88:
106 S 30 '66
Nightfight with the nicest guy in town;
auto salesmen's techniques. M. Greenfield.
Reporter 35:35-7 Jl 14 '66
Profile of tomorrow's salesman; address, July
6, 1966. F. K. Doscher. Vital Speeches 32:
764-8 O 1 '66
Sales power through planned careers. A. E.
Pearson. il Harvard Bsns R 44:105-16 Ja
'66
Sell more with fewer salesmen. R. N.
Mc-Murry. il Nations Bsns 54:96-8+ Je '66
Spreading the message with tape. il Bsns
W p87 Jl 9 '66
See also
Advertising
Automobile dealers
Booksellers and bookselling
Sales promotion

Study and teaching
Ins and outs of sales training. L. Rich. il
Duns R 88:35+ Ag '66
Marketing outlook; new ways to grow sales-
men. Bsns W p 181 My 14 '66
SALESWOMEN. See Clerks (retail trade)
SALIDA, Colo.
Jeep patrol tour; trip sponsored by the Salida
chamber of commerce. E. Orazem. il Travel
126:43-5 N '66
SALIK, Charles Eliot
Thinking big about small business. il por
Bsns W p 123-4+ Ja 7 '67
SALINGER, J. D.
Cup of consecrated chicken soup. M. Ely.
Cath World 202:298-301 F '66
SALINGER, Pierre
Salinger tells how Kennedy tried to hide
Vietnam build-up; excerpts from With
Kennedy. por U S News 61:103 S 12 '66
about
President and the press secretary. M. W.
Childs. New Repub 155:16-17 S 10 '66
SALISBURY, Harrison E.
History, politics, and opinion. Sat R 49:52
Je 11 '66
about
Behind enemy lines. il por Newsweek 69:61-
2 Ja 9 '67
Civilian bit. Nat R 19:11 Ja 10 '67
Flak from Hanoi. il por Time 89:13-14 Ja 6
'67
Storm over Viet Nam bombings. il Sr Schol
89:12-13 Ja 13 '67

SALISBURY, Harrison E.—about—*Continued*
Times and the signs. W. J. Coughlin. Tech W 20:50 Ja 2 '67
Winners and sinners. Newsweek 69:81-2 Ja 16 '67

SALISBURY, Winfield W.
Generation of light from free electrons. Science 154:386-8 O 21 '66

SALISBURY, Md.
Sporting scene; United States indoor tennis championships. H. W. Wind. New Yorker 42:135-6+ Mr 12 '66

SALISIAN, Steve
Three California ceramists. J. Lovoos. il por Am Artist 30:54-5+ D '66

SALIVA
Salivary secretion; report on International conference on mechanisms of salivary secretion and their regulation. L. H. Schneyer. Science 155:115+ Ja 6 '67
Severe impairment of heat-induced saliva-spreading in rats recovered from lateral hypothalamic lesions. F. R. Hainsworth and A. N. Epstein. bibliog il Science 153:1255-7 S 9 '66

SALK, Jonas Edward
Breakthrough; the saga of Jonas Salk. by R. Carter. Review
     Life 60:10 F 25 '66. A. Rosenfeld
     New Repub 154:38-9 My 14 '66. M. Alderman
     Newsweek il por 67:102+ Mr 28 '66
Landmark for medical research. J. Peter il por Look 31:52-3 Ja 10 '67

SALK institute for biological studies, San Diego, Calif.
Landmark for medical research. J. Peter il Look 31:52-3 Ja 10 '67

SALK vaccine. See Poliomyelitis—Vaccines

SALM, Walter G.
TV shows when you want them. Sci Digest 59:73-8 My '66
Tomorrow's color TV. Sci Digest 60:63-8 Ag '66
Twelve record-changer troubles you can cure. Pop Mech 126:170-3 Ag '66

SALMON, Stephen R.
ISAD: off to a flying start; letter to the editor. ALA Bul 60:753-4 S '66

SALMON
Clostridium botulinum type F; isolation from salmon from the Columbia River. J. M. Craig and K. S. Pilcher. bibliog il Science 153:311-12 Jl 15 '66
Lo, the poor salmon; Chinook salmon of the Pacific Northwest. il Newsweek 67:22 F 7 '66
Retreat of the Atlantic salmon. A. Netboy. il Am For 71:25-9+ O '65
     See also
Cookery—Fish

SALMON, Canned. See Canned food

SALMON fishing
Bus ride to Atlantic salmon. J. Brooks. il Outdoor Life 138:46-9+ O '66
First report: salmon succeed in Great Lakes. J. Chiappetta. il Field & S 71:10-15 D '66
High-flying landlock. W. Davis. il Outdoor Life 137:82+ Ap '66
Kokanee comes east. J. Hayes. il Outdoor Life 137:29-31+ Je '66
Line of scrimmage. C. R. Hull. il Outdoor Life 138:58-61+ O '66
Misplaced salmon of Hosmer Lake: Atlantic salmon from Oregon lake. T. Trueblood. il Field & S 70:49-51+ Mr '66
New Atlantic salmon fishing; Whale River. M. G. Treziev. il Outdoor Life 137:33-5+ Ap '66
Royal domain for kingly salmon; Norway. il Life 61:46-57 Ag 19 '66
Silver from the sea. L. Miracle. il Outdoor Life 138:50-2+ Jl '66
Spring on the Miramichi. T. Janes. il Outdoor Life 137:48-9+ My '66

SALMON RIVER
Now it's traffic jams on the last frontier. il U S News 61:56-9 Ag 29 '66
Salmon: River of No Return. N. M. Rahm. il Nat Parks Mag 40:8-10 My '66

SALMONELLA. See Bacteria, Pathogenic

SALMONELLOSIS
Timely warning for parents. M. J. E. Senn. McCalls 93:40+ Mr '66

SALOM, Georgine Sachs. See Aaron, J. jt. auth.

SALOMON, I. L.
Response to a question at a convocation; poem. Commonweal 85:73 O 21 '66
(tr) See Campana, D. Three Florentine girls walk

SALT
High-pressure polymorphism in sodium chloride; a reinvestigation. Q. Johnson. bibliog il Science 153:419 Jl 22 '66
Phosphate uptake in an obligately marine fungus: a specific requirement for sodium. P. A. Siegenthaler and others. bibliog il Science 155:93-4 Ja 6 '67
Salt seekers; solar evaporation of sea water at San Francisco Bay area's salt farms. G. Rogers. il Sci N 90:249-50 O 1 '66

Physiological effects
Mast cells and necrosis. H. Selye. il Science 152:1371-2 Je 3 '66

SALT farms. See Salt industry and trade

SALT glaze ware
Mugs, jugs, and chamber pots; taking issue with some of Dr Boney's findings. I. N. Hume. il Antiques 90:520-2 O '66

SALT industry and trade
Salt seekers; solar evaporation of sea water at San Francisco Bay area's salt farms. G. Rogers. il Sci N 90:249-50 O 1 '66

SALT LAKE. See Great Salt Lake

SALT LAKE CITY
Putting payroll on a paying basis. L. E. Holley. il Am City 81:154+ S '66

Intellectual life
Saints and symphonies. J. Nugent. Holiday 40:66-7+ O '66

SALT marsh caper; story. See Brodeur. P.

SALT marshes
Sedimentary environments in a marine marsh. F. B. Phleger and J. S. Bradshaw. bibliog il Science 154:1551-3 D 23 '66

SALT water fishing
Day the giant tuna died. M. Rascovich. il Field & S 71:56-7+ My '66
Drifters make good. G. Heinold. il Outdoor Life 138:72-3+ N '66
Far-out fishing camp; operated from unique floating resort in the Keys. E. A. Bauer. il Outdoor Life 138:42-5+ D '66
Fly rod over the deep blue. L. Wulff. il Esquire 66:253-5+ D '66
Follow the drum beat. K. Osborne. il Outdoor Life 137:50-1+ Ap '66
For better fishing go fly a kite. E. A. Bauer. il Field & S 70:64-5+ Ap '66
He stalks sharks by kayak. G. X. Sand. il Pop Mech 125:120-2 My '66
Little boats for big fish. P. Kalman. il Field & S 70:57-9+ Mr '66
Mystique of surf fishing. B. Brower. il Holiday 40:46-7+ Jl '66
New angle for an old sport. D. Barnes. Sports Illus 25:56-7 Jl 11 '66
New billfish discovery. R. F. Burgess. il Field & S 71:58-9+ S '66
Off-season; surf-casting at Robert Moses state park, Fire Island. New Yorker 42:50-1 O 8 '66
Party boat bonanza. R. S. Mikkelsen. il Outdoor Life 137:62-4+ Je '66
Plenty of fish in the sea? long-lining depleting world stock of tuna, marlin and swordfish. M. Kane. il Sports Illus 24:20-2+ Ja 31 '66
Salt water. G. Heinold. See issues of Outdoor life
Sportfishing (title varies) N. Benedict. See issues of Yachting
Troubled waters in paradise; reefs off Florida Keys. J. O'Reilly. Sports Illus 24:70+ Je 6 '66
Twin bill: sailfish and marlin. G. Heinold. il Outdoor Life 137:62-4+ Mr '66
     See also
Bonefish fishing
Dolphin fishing
Shark fishing
Tarpon fishing
Tuna fishing

SALTER, Stefan
Designer's corner. por Pub W 189:113-15 My 2; 166+ Je 13; 190:109+ Jl 4; 98+ Ag 1; 111-13 S 5; 135-7 O 3; 100+ N 7; 112-13 D 5 '66

SALTON SEA
Isotopic composition and origin of the Red Sea and Salton Sea geothermal brines. H. Craig. bibliog il Science 154:1544-8 D 23 '66

SALTON SEA race. See Motor boat racing

SALTONSTALL family
Saltonstall coat-of-arms. H. K. Eilers. il Hobbies 71:126-7 Je '66

SALTS
Structure-disrupting ions: detection of qualitative change in an enzyme. J. C. Warren and D. M. Peterson. bibliog il Science 152:1245-6 My 27 '66

SALTS, Marine
See also
Sea water
SALTZMAN, Leopold
Victor café. Opera N 30:6-7 F 19 '66
SALTZMAN, Pauline
More phantoms of the opera. Opera N 31:6-7 D 31 '66
SALVADOR, Brazil
Bahia. J. Egan. il Holiday 40:80-6+ S '66
SALVAGE
Found: missing H-bomb. Sr Schol 88:22 Ap 1 '66
¡La bomba recuperada! recovery of bomb lost off Spanish coast. il Time 87:27 Ap 15 '66
Rescue and unveiling of an H-bomb. il U S News 60:11 Ap 18 '66
Sigh of relief; hydrogen bomb recovery off coast of Spain. il Newsweek 67:62-3 Ap 18 '66
SALVAGE (barges) See Salvage (ships)
SALVAGE (ships)
Ancient ship uncovered; probable Turkish warship discovered at the mouth of Acre harbor. Sci N 90:573 D 31 '66
Navy details rescue, salvage systems. J. F. Judge. il Tech W 19:30+ S 26 '66
Saving a city from a cloud of death; salvaging lost chlorine barge. T. Irwin. il Pop Sci 188:108-11+ Ap '66
SALVAGE archeology. See Archeology
SALVATION
Sharing in redemptive anguish; excerpt from Even so, believe. C. A. Pennington. Christian Cent 83:291 Mr 9 '66
This time of salvation, by B. Häring. Review America 114:859-60 Je 18 '66. R. A. McCormick
SALVATION army
Just what is the Salvation army? Good H 162:181 Mr '66
With a prayer, Upland goes on the block; sold to Salvation army. il Bsns W p 194-6+ N 5 '66
SALWAK, Stanley F.
Academic common market. Sat R 49:72-3+ Je 18 '66
SALZBURG
Over a drawbridge to the past; Schloss Sighartstein. M. Leatherbee. Life 61:42-42A S 2 '66

Hotels, restaurants, etc.
Christmas list; holiday greeting; food-and-drinkery, Franziskanerkeller. J. Fischer. il Harper 233:20+ D '66

Social life and customs
Christmas eve supper in Salzburg; with recipes. il Look 30:58-9 D 27 '66
SALZBURG festival
Operatic contrasts: Henze, Bizet, Mozart. P. G. Davis. il Hi Fi 16:MA2+ O '66
Salzburg. F. J. Warnke; E. Davidson; T. Goth. il Opera N 31:28 O 15 '66
SALZBURG seminar in American studies
America in Salzburg. M. Mannes. il Harper 232:91-5 F '66
SALZMAN, Eric
Footnote on some footnotes. Sat R 49:56-7 D 31 '66
Maazel, classicist. Sat R 49:51 D 31 '66
Musical panorama of the Elizabethan age. Hi Fi 16:85-6 My '66
New-music journeys in the U.S.A. Hi Fi 16:MA12-13+ Ag '66
New sound in British music. Hi Fi 16:71-2 Mr '66
New stereo discs for a further look at Ivesian questions and answers. Hi Fi 16:70-1 Je '66
Seven of Sibelius. Sat R 49:68-9 O 29 '66
Stravinsky's Rite, in the Boulez manner, frozen, immobile, violently precise. Hi Fi 16:68 F '66
World of Wieland Wagner. Opera N 31:8-15 Ja 21 '67
SAM, Alfred C.
Longest journey. A. J. Lane. Nation 202:530-1 My 2 '66
SAM Griffith memorial race. See Motor boat racing
SAMARAS, Lucas
Art; Pace gallery exhibition. M. Kozloff. Nation 203:525-6 N 14 '66
Samaras: reliquaries for St Sade. D. Waldman. il Art N 65:44-6+ O '66
SAMARITANS
Superior Samaritans; Jericho cave remains challenges the Bible. Time 87:42 Ap 1 '66
SAMOA, AMERICAN. See American Samoa

SAMOA, WESTERN
Coming of the jet age in Samoa. H. Sutton. il Sat R 49:42-3 F 12 '66
Tea and sympathy; failure to get aid. il Newsweek 68:59-60 O 10 '66
SAMOAN architecture. See Architecture, Samoan
SAMORE, Theodore
Federal legislation and programs to assist academic libraries. ALA Bul 60:156-9 F '66
SAMPLES (merchandising)
Big marketing man on campus; Guest Pac corp. il Time 87:94 Mr 4 '66
SAMPLEY, Arthur M.
Riders; poem. Christian Cent 83:801 Je 22 '66
SAMPLING (statistical methods)
Stratigraphic sections, bedding sequences, and random processes. D. D. Carr and others. bibliog il Science 154:1162-4 D 2 '66
SAMPSON, Anthony
His cherubic smile seemed to say, it's all so simple. Life 61:42D S 16 '66
SAMS, Howard W, and company
ITT plans to acquire Howard W. Sams & co. Pub W 189:54-5 My 23 '66
Sams board approves its merger proposal. Pub W 190:198 Jl 11 '66
Sams school division grows with third acquisition. Pub W 189:80 Ap 18 '66
Sams stockholders agree on acquisition by ITT. Pub W 190:52 O 10 '66
SAMSON, Richard W.
Stretch your mind! Read Digest 88:37+ Mr '66
SAMSON and Delilah; opera. See Saint-Saëns, C.
SAMSON et Dalila; opera. See Saint-Saëns, C.
SAMSTAG, Nicholas
Dreams of a man-god. Sat R 50:86 Ja 14 '67
What to do with leftover millions. Sat R 49:41-2 Ap 16 '66
SAMUEL, Gerhard
Mr Samuel and the Rockefeller premieres. K. D. Wallace. il por Hi Fi 16:MA26+ Jl '66
SAMUELS, Charles Thomas
Contra Sontag. Nation 202:219-21 F 21 '66
He made the books and he died. Nation 203:220-2 S 12 '66
Spirit of Hawthorne's prose. Commonweal 84:504-6 Ag 5 '66
SAMUELS, Gertrude
Chance to catch up to equality. Sat R 49:37+ Ap 23 '66
Fight for civil liberties never stays won. N Y Times Mag p 14-15+ Je 19 '66
Judge with disciplined indignation. N Y Times Mag p38-40+ Ja 15 '67
Judges go back to school. N Y Times Mag p36-7+ N 6 '66
Justice in the courtroom, can the poor get it? Sat R 49:25+ Ja 29 '66
Man of Sde Boker. N Y Times Mag p42+ O 16 '66
Visit to Narco. il N Y Times Mag p32-3+ Ap 10 '66
SAMUELS, H. J.
Wagons ho! Travel 126:37-9+ Ag '66
SAMUELS, Len
Hitch any camera to a flashcube, if you can find one. Pop Mech 126:180-1 O '66
SAMUELSON, James T.
Interstation hiss suppressor for FM tuners. Pop Electr 24:60 Je '66
SAMUELSON, Paul Anthony
Economics of war. por Newsweek 68:107 N 21 '66
Open letter to LBJ. por Newsweek 69:59 Ja 2 '67
Raising 1967 tax rates. por Newsweek 68:94 D 12 '66
Requiem for a scourge. por Newsweek 68:96 O 10 '66
Science and stocks. por Newsweek 68:92 S 19 '66
State of the economy. por Newsweek 69:81 Ja 23 '67
Tight money. por Newsweek 68:90 O 31 '66
about
Tax credit that business may lose. por U S News 60:102+ My 9 '66
SAN AGUSTIN, Columbia
Jungle gods of San Agustín. G. Reichel-Dolmatoff. il Natur Hist 75:42-9 D '66
SAN ANTONIO, Tex.
Good times in Texas; White House press corps welcomed. il Time 87:77 Mr 18 '66

Parks and playgrounds
Long-term tests on plastic pipe; park irrigation. R. L. Frazer and L. C. Schmidt. il Am City 81:84-5 Jl '66

SAN ANTONIO, Tex—*Continued*
Water supply
Rate increase offered the best solution. Am City 81:148 N '66
SANASARDO, Paul
Paul Sanasardo dance company, 92nd street Y. J. Maskey. Dance Mag 40:71+ Ap; 80-1 Je '66
Paul Sanasardo dance company, 92nd street Y. M. Marks. Dance Mag 40:63 Mr; 34-5 My '66
SAN BERNARDINO, Calif.
Rates periodically adjusted to meet expenses. il Am City 81:26 N '66
Staggered starting hours; for sweeper operators, loaders and mechanics. H. Vaile and M. Cornelison. il Am City 81:82-3 Je '66
SANCHEZ, George I.
Autonomy of the university. Sch & Soc 94:147-9 Mr 19 '66
SANCHEZ, R. and others
Conditions for purine synthesis: did prebiotic synthesis occur at low temperatures? bibliog Science 153:72-3 Jl 1 '66
Cyanoacetylene in prebiotic synthesis. bibliog Science 154:784-5 N 11 '66
SANCTIONS (International law)
Britain's showdown in Africa: where sanctions aren't working. il U S News 60:38-9 Ap 18 '66
Confident Rhodesians; ten months of sanctions. New Repub 155:15-16 S 17 '66
Masquerade at sea fails for Rhodesia; Britain scuttles oil ship to Rhodesia. Bsns W p41-2 Ap 16 '66
Naked emperor; economic sanctions in Rhodesian crisis. E. Huxley. Nat R 18:877-8 S 6 '66
Oil of discord; African effort to force Britain to embark on crusade against South Africa. Nation 202:477-8 Ap 25 '66
Pretoria's view. J. Burnham. Nat R 18:1310 D 27 '66
Report from Rhodesia. il Fortune 74:73-4+ N '66
Reporter at large; economic sanctions in Rhodesian crisis. J. Kramer. il New Yorker 42:142-4+ Ap 2 '66
Rhodesia: the fight goes on. il Newsweek 68:33+ D 19 '66
Rhodesia's woes mount; Britain preparing new mandatory economic sanctions. Bsns W p 44 D 10 '66
Sanctions against Rhodesia. Time 88:27 D 23 '66
Sanctions: the hollow weapon. Time 88:27 D 23 '66
Sanctions voted; U.N. vs. Rhodesia. Sr Schol 89:15 Ja 6 '67
Score at half time; results of economic sanctions. Nat R 18:196-8 Mr 8 '66
U.N. vs. Rhodesia. il Newsweek 68:30 D 26 '66
See also
Embargo
SANCTUARIES, Bird. See Bird sanctuaries
SANCTUARIES, Wildlife. See Wildlife sanctuaries
SAND, George X.
Florida sure-shot for tarpon. Field & S 71:128-30+ Je '66
He stalks sharks by kayak. Pop Mech 125:120-2 My '66
Knives for astronauts and everyone. Pop Mech 127:144-7+ Ja '67
New gamebird for the South? Outdoor Life 137:40-1+ Je '66
Power rods for pomps. Field & S 71:136-8 O '66
SAND
See also
Bituminous sand
SAND boxes. See Sandboxes
SAND casting. See Molds (for casting)
SAND dunes
Up and over the Algodones dunes. il Sunset 137:22+ N '66
SAND sculpture
On the beach, with sculpture. A. Kleihauer. il Sch Arts 65:9-13 F '66
Sand castling. il Sunset 137:54-5 Ag '66
Sophistication of the sand box; Sandcraft tournament; Austin, Tex. il Parks & Rec 1:323 Ap '66
SANDAGE, Allan Rex
Quasars. New Yorker 42:37-8 My 21 '66
SANDALWOOD
Olulaau O Kauai (the forest of Kauai) R. Wenkham. il Audubon Mag 68:430-5 N '66
SANDBOXES
Sandboxes look to the future; serve as garden well. il Pop Gard 17:6 My '66

SANDBURG, Carl
Carl Sandburg, my father. H. Sandburg. il por Redbook 126:60-1+ F '66
SANDBURG, Helga
Carl Sandburg, my father. por Redbook 126:60-1+ F '66
SANDEEN, Ernest
Nearing winter; poem. New Yorker 42:149 N 5 '66
SANDERS, Charles L.
Cold weather, warm hearts. Ebony 21:27-30+ Ap '66
Escape from the rat race. Ebony 22:132-4+ N '66
SANDERS, Doug
Dandiest swinger on the fairway; interview, ed. by D. Fales. pors Life 60:53-4+ Je 10 '66
about
Win or lose, Doug Sanders is a pop artist's dream. D. Jenkins. pors Sports Illus 24:86-7 Ap 25 '66
SANDERS, Ed
Eyes and I. R. Duerden. Poetry 108:126-30 My '66
SANDERS, Harland
Chicken colonel. il por Newsweek 68:79 Jl 25 '66
SANDERS, Irwin T.
American professionals overseas. Bul Atomic Sci 22:40-5 D '66
SANDERS, Joan
Getting into historical fiction. Writer 79:18-22 Ag '66
SANDERS, Marion K.
Case for a National service corps. N Y Times Mag p 16-17+ Ag 7 '66
Several worlds of American Jews. Harper 232:53-62 Ap '66
SANDERS, Paul
Gospel is in the verb. Christian Cent 83:400 Mr 30 '66
SANDERS, Ralph
Autumn of power: the scientist in the political establishment. Bul Atomic Sci 22:22-5 O '66
SANDERS, Thomas G.
Books. Commonweal 85:430-2 Ja 20 '67
SANDIA laboratory
How they found the bomb: calculation by Sandia scientists of location of bomb missing off Spain. il Time 87:53 My 13 '66
New Sandia track to test at Mach 5. R. Pay. il Tech W 19:26+ Jl 4 '66
SAN DIEGO, Calif.

Description
Seventy-mile beach. C. Stinnett. Holiday 40:32+ Jl '66
Music
San Diego. S. A. Desick. Opera N 31:24 S 10 '66
San Diego; performances of Aida. S. A. Desick. Opera N 31:28 D 10 '66
Negroes
Parents for peace; Volunteer parents organization. il Ebony 21:72-4+ O '66
Things are looking up in Logan Heights; police-Negro relations. H. Ellsberg. Read Digest 89:217+ N '66
Police
Things are looking up in Logan Heights; police-Negro relations. H. Ellsberg. Read Digest 89:217+ N '66
SAN DIEGO-Acapulco race. See Yacht racing
SAN DIEGO ballet. See Ballet companies
SAN DIEGO COUNTY, Calif.
Sell the salesman on city hall; informative brochure encourages vendors to bid, and tells the procedure. V. O. Gehringer. Am City 81:90-1 Jl '66
SAN DIEGO Mesa college, Calif.
Catalog-first theory; letter to the editor. K. P. Anderson. Library J 91:5506+ N 15 '66
SANDING
Best finishes for wood; sanding is the start that makes the finish. J. Hand. il Pop Sci 189:124-8 Ag '66
SANDING machines
Band sander for your bench saw. R. Shoberg. il Pop Mech 126:160-2 Ag '66
Double-duty-sander-setup. R. J. De Cristoforo. il Pop Mech 125:176-8 Ap '66
SANDLER, Irving H.
Sugarman makes a sculpture. Art N 65:34-7 My '66
SANDLER, Steve
(Hand) ball of fire! H. L. Masin. il por Sr Schol 89:40 D 9 '66

SANDMEL, Samuel
Road between Rome and Jerusalem. Sat R
49:42-3 D 3 '66
SANDOZ, Mari
Grisly epilogue. Am Heritage 17:73 Ap '66

about

Obituary
Pub W 189:53 Mr 21 '66
SANDOZ, Incorporated
Drug tests: integrity and courage; letter. P.
Lowinger. Science 153:121 Jl 8 '66; Reply.
C. Henze. 153:688 Ag 12 '66
SANDPAPER
Best finishes for wood: sanding is the start
that makes the finish. J. Hand. il Pop Sci
189:124-8 Ag '66
Rub 'er down right; boat refinishing sand-
paper guide. N. Meiners. Motor B 117:35+
Mr '66
SANDROCK, E. G.
Pour your own pitch block. Pop Mech 125:
154-5 Mr '66
SANDS, Leo G.
Hi-fi and TV for your boat. Motor B 117:38-
9+ Je '66
SANDVIG, Earl D.
Traveler's choice. Travel 126:15 S '66
SANDWICH construction
IBM improves board laminating technique;
multi-layer interconnection boards. il Avi-
ation W 85:82-3 Jl 11 '66
SANDWICHES
Canapé cake and pink sham-pagne; with
recipes. il Seventeen 25:122-3+ Je '66
Have a Mexican torta. il Sunset 137:110 Ag
'66
Hot sandwich makes an evening meal; with
recipes. il Sunset 137:142-3 Jl '66
Hot sandwiches for hungry men; with
recipes. Farm J 90:79-80 O '66
Hot sandwiches with meat, cheese; with reci-
pe. il Sunset 137:144 D '66
Sensational salad sandwiches! with recipes.
R. Holmberg. il Bet Hom & Gard 44:66-
71+ Jl '66
Switch to hot sandwiches. il Suc Farm 64:88
S '66
World in a sandwich; with recipes. il Ladies
Home J 83:116-17+ My '66

Anecdotes, facetiae, satire, etc.
Yes, but can the steam engine do this?
W. Allen. New Yorker 42:52-3 O 8 '66
SANDY, Stephen
Hunter's moon; poem. New Yorker 42:195 O
8 '66
Et quid amabo nisi quod aenigma est; poem.
New Yorker 42:54 D 3 '66
SANE (organization) See National committee
for a sane nuclear policy
SANFORD, Charles L.
Where the stakes are real. Nation 203:426-7
O 24 '66
SANFORD, David
Admen in orbit. New Repub 155:13-15 D 17
'66
Come right in colonel, admiral, or whoever.
New Repub 154:11-13 F 12 '66
Damming the Grand Canyon for a thirsty
Southwest. New Repub 154:9 Ap 30 '66
Excor-iating the airlines. New Repub 156:12-
13 Ja 7 '67
Gamesmanship in the supermarkets. New
Repub 155:14-16 N 12 '66
Keeping an eye on tourists. New Repub
154:9-10 Ap 9 '66
SAN FRANCISCO
Golden Gate. H. Gold. il Sat R 49:51-2+ O
8 '66

Airports
San Francisco may need regional airport.
R. G. O'Lone. il Aviation W 85:55+ N 21
'66

Anti-poverty program
View from Hunters Point: no way downtown.
D. Bess. il Nation 203:606-9 D 5 '66

Art
Art news from San Francisco. K. Metcalf
il Art N 64:46-7 F; 65:55 Sum '66
San Francisco. K. M. Nelson. il Art N 65:
59+ O '66
San Francisco's cultural donnybrook. R.
Lynes. il Harper 232:31-2+ Mr '66

City planning
Systems approach to city planning. C. C.
Herrmann. il Harvard Bsns R 44:71-80 S '66

Crime
Death no. 3; suicide of fund administrator of
the Brotherhood of painters, decorators
and paperhangers. Time 87:22 My 27 '66
Death of a wild man; Wilson-Green murders.
il Newsweek 67:87 My 23 '66
Painters in blood. Time 87:30-1 My 20 '66

Description
Going places, finding things in San Fran-
cisco. J. Wilson. il House & Gard 130:18+
Jl '66
San Francisco: photographyville. L. Barry.
il Pop Phot 59:14+ Jl '66

Earthquake and fire, 1906
1906 disaster post cards. B. Finnegan. il Hobbies 71:120-1+ Ap '66

Education
Schools and race: integration for excellence.
R. W. Major. Nation 203:213-15 S 12 '66

Galleries and museums
See also
M. H. De Young memorial museum, San
Francisco

Hospitals
Independent outpatient annex looks to the
future; Mt Zion hospital and medical
center. il Arch Rec 139:172-3 Mr '66

Hotels, restaurants, etc.
Naked luncheon. G. Berriault. il Esquire 65:
96-7+ Mr '66
West passes the topless test. A. Levy. il
Life 60:79-80+ Mr 11 '66

Intellectual life
San Francisco's cultural donnybrook. R.
Lynes. il Harper 232:31-2+ Mr '66

Moral conditions
West passes the topless test. A. Levy. il Life
60:79-80+ Mr 11 '66

Music
Majesty restored. R. Lawrence. Opera N 31:
9+ N 5 '66
San Francisco. A. Boucher. Opera N 30:29
Ap 16; 31:25-6 S 10 '66
Spring opera 1966, triumph and trouble. K. D.
Wallace. il Hi Fi 16:MA8+ Ag '66
See also
Oakland symphony orchestra
San Francisco opera company

Newspapers
See also
Newspapers—Consolidations and mergers

Parks and playgrounds
Handkerchief-size demonstration garden in
San Francisco's Golden Gate park; Japa-
nese-style garden. il Sunset 137:132-3 S '66
Tree of light; eucalyptus trees in Golden Gate
park, Presidio, and Sutro forest; excerpt
from Natural world of San Francisco. H.
Gilliam. il Natur Hist 75:54-9 D '66

Prisons and reformatories
Union stripes; County jail no. 2; inmates
activities committee. Nation 203:437 O 31 '66

Rapid transit
BART: the Bay area takes a billion-dollar
ride. J. Bailey. il Arch Forum 124:38-61 Je
'66
Bay area previews new rapid-transit car.
il Am City 81:46 Jl '66
Bay area rapid transit: advance into yesterday. M. Harris. il Nation 202:679-83 Je 6 '66
City's splendid plan hurt by myopia; Bay
area rapid transit difficulties. Life 61:6 O
14 '66
Relational complexes in architecture. C. Alexander and others. il Arch Rec 140:185-90 S
'66

Religious institutions and affairs
Two for the show; M. Boyd's night club
preaching. il Newsweek 68:68 O 3 '66

Riots
San Francisco riot. Hunter's Point and Fill-
more. il Newsweek 68:28-9 O 10 '66
Why the new round of Negro rioting. il U S
News 61:13-14 O 10 '66

Social conditions
View from Hunters Point: no way downtown.
D. Bess. il Nation 203:606-9 D 5 '66

SAN FRANCISCO—*Continued*

Stores

Going places, finding things in San Francisco. J. Wilson. il House & Gard 130:18+ Jl '66

Shopping; along Clement street. il Sunset 137:32-4 O '66

Streets

Shopping; along Clement street. il Sunset 137:32-4 O '66

Theater

Actor's workshop is dead. F. H. Gardner. Nation 203:256-7 S 19 '66

Agit-prop pop opera; Romeo and Pagliacci. J. O'Connor. Nation 203:716-17 D 26 '66

Improvisation bit; the Committee. J. Novick. Nation 203:613-15 D 5 '66

Sinking feeling; Actors workshop. Newsweek 68:82 Ag 1 '66

Surprise in the wings. L. Zimpel. Nation 202:276-8 Mr 7 '66

Transportation

Where city transit is fueled by nostalgia; San Francisco's colorful cable cars. il Bsns W p 182-4 O 22 '66

SAN FRANCISCO BAY
Opening day on S.F. Bay; yacht parade. D. Selby. il Motor B 117:27+ My '66

SAN FRANCISCO BAY REGION
BART; the Bay area takes a billion-dollar ride. J. Bailey. il Arch Forum 124:38-61 Je '66

Bay area previews new rapid-transit car. il Am City 81:46 Jl '66

Offshore cruiser ventures inland. E. Newmark. il Yachting 120:41-3+ S '66

Transit tube to link San Francisco and Oakland. il Am City 81:52 My '66

SAN FRANCISCO children's zoo. See Zoological gardens

SAN FRANCISCO Giants (baseball) See Baseball clubs

SAN FRANCISCO international airport. See San Francisco—Airports

SAN FRANCISCO international film festival. See Moving picture festivals

SAN FRANCISCO mime troupe. See San Francisco—Theater

SAN FRANCISCO opera company
Golden Gate opera. H. Saal. il Newsweek 68:66+ N 28 '66

San Francisco (cont) A. Boucher. il Opera N 31:23-4 N 5; 26 D 3; 28 D 10 '66

San Francisco; American premiere of Leos Janácek's Makropoulos case. A. Boucher. il Opera N 31:30 D 24 '66

SAN FRANCISCO state college
Do-it-yourself U; experimental college. il Newsweek 68:100+ N 7 '66

SAN FRANCISCO Warriors (basketball team) See Basketball teams

SANGER, Clyde
Transformation of Jomo Kenyatta. Reporter 34:37-9 Mr 10 '66

SANGER, Margaret
Every child a wanted child. il pors Time 88:96+ S 16 '66

Obituary
Christian Cent 83:1139 S 21 '66
Pub W 190:48 S 19 '66
Rebel with a cause. il por Newsweek 68:34+ S 19 '66

SAN GORGONIO wilderness area. See Wilderness areas—California

SANITARY affairs. See subhead Sanitary affairs under names of countries, states, cities, e.g. South Milwaukee, Wis.—Sanitary affairs

SANITARY engineering
See also
Filters and filtration

SAN JORGE RIVER
Mystery of an engineering wonder. J. Reinert. il Sci Digest 60:8-9 O '66

SAN JOSE, Calif.

Recreation

Japanese design finds favor. il Parks & Rec 1:722-3+ S '66

Street traffic

Computer-controlled traffic moves faster. il Am City 81:154 My '66

Radio traffic surveillance gets aired in San Jose. A. R. Turturici. il Am City 81:130 Ag '66

SAN JUAN, Puerto Rico

Libraries

Expansion set for Casa del libro, Puerto Rico. Pub W 190:58+ Ag 22 '66

Social conditions

Fabulous Doña Felisa. S. Seegers and K. Seegers. il Read Digest 89:145-8+ Jl '66

SAN JUAN ISLAND NATIONAL HISTORICAL PARK
U.S.-Canadian friendship symbolized by new park; statement, September 9, 1966. L. B. Johnson. Dept State Bul 55:499 O 3 '66

SAN JUAN ISLANDS, British Columbia
Island-hopping holiday. C. West. il Motor B 119:88-9+ Ja '67

SAN JUAN ISLANDS, Wash.
Verdant ysles. Sports Illus 25:16 N 28; 11-13 D 12 '66

SAN LEANDRO, Calif.
City that said: no thanks to Washington. il Nations Bsns 54:64-7 S '66

SAN MARTIN, José de
Sweeping the Spanish from Spanish America. il por Sr Schol 88:2 F 25 '66

Voice of the Algarrobo. V. Ocampo. il Americas 18:5-7 S '66

SAN MATEO, Calif.
Woodlake: a small community complete within itself. il Arch Rec 139:164-5 Ja '66

Gardens

How San Mateo got its new Japanese garden. il Sunset 137:178-9 D '66

SAN MATEO COUNTY, Calif.
Fighting mental illness on home ground. P. Deutsch and R. Deutsch. il Todays Health 44:20-1+ S '66; Same abr. with title San Mateo shows the way to treat mental illness. Read Digest 89:185-6+ S '66

SANQUINI, R. L. See Vonderschmitt, B. V. jt. auth.

SAN QUINTIN, Mexico
San Quintin; the forgotten harbor; Cinco de mayo classic. L. Parsons. il Motor B 117:156-7+ My '66

SAN SEBASTIAN film festival. See Moving picture festivals

SANSOM, William
Amsterdam. Holiday 40:82-9+ D '66
Frankfurt. Holiday 41:74-9+ Ja '67
Letter from abroad. McCalls 93:48+ My '66

SANTA ANA winds. See Winds

SANTA calls a conference; drama. See Miller, H. L.

SANTA CLARA, Calif.

Parks and playgrounds

Parks plans can simplify maintenance. E. R. Carmichael. il Am City 81:104-6 O '66

Streets

Street signs that drivers can't miss. F. T. Shreve. il Am City 81:126 F '66

SANTA FE, N.Mex.

Architecture

Capitol in the round; new state capitol. il Time 88:84 D 16 '66

SANTA FE opera association
Santa Fe; production of Berg's Wozzeck. B. Haddad. il Opera N 31:24 O 15 '66

SANTANA, Manuel
Manolo is king, and a king is queen. J. Lovesey. il por Sports Illus 25:50+ Jl 11 '66

Numero uno. il por Time 88:39 Jl 8 '66

SANTANAS. See Winds

SANTIAGO, Chile

Education

Nido de Aguilas; art program. C. Ranstead. il Sch Arts 65:5-8 F '66

SANTIAGO, Spain
Santiago de Compostela. J. D. Scott. il Holiday 41:30+ Ja '67

SANTIAGO de Compostela, Spain. See Santiago, Spain

SANTORIN (island) See Thera (island)

SANTOS-DUMONT, Alberto
Magnificent Brazilian in his flying machine. P. De Paulo. il pors Américas 18:16-22 S '66

SÃO PAULO (city), Brazil

Description

São Paulo, Brazil's paradise for marketers. il Bsns W p92-4+ Je 11 '66

Industries

São Paulo, Brazil's paradise for marketers. il Bsns W p92-4+ Je 11 '66

Music

City in a hurry. B. R. Marks. Hi Fi 16:MA 17+ Ag '66

SÃO PAULO biennial. See Art—Exhibitions

SÃO PAULO philharmonic orchestra. See Orchestras

SÃO SALVADOR. See Salvador, Brazil

SAPERS, Carl M.
Suggestions by another attorney on reform of state licensing laws. Arch Rec 140:108 N '66

SAPPHO
Some fragments; Parting; Absent friend. tr. by C. M. Bowra. Horizon 8:109 Spr '66
Some fragments; Throned in splendor; Some say a host: Peer of immortal Gods. tr. by P. Green. Horizon 8:109 Spr '66

about

From the Greek. G. Davenport. Poetry 108:416 S '66
In search of Sappho. P. Green. il Horizon 8:104-8+ Spr '66
Sappho, poems and fragments, by G. Davenport. Review
Nat R 18:279-81 Mr 22 '66. G. Wills

SAPPINGTON, John
Frontier malaria fighter. H. E. Dark. il Todays Health 44:28-9+ My '66

SARAH, waiting; story. See Hunt, J.

SARASOTA, Fla.
Florida rococo; Asolo theater brought from Italy. T. Hoffman. il Opera N 30:6-7 F 5 '66

Description

Sarasota. E. Scully. il U S Camera 30:72-3+ Ja '67

Theater

Florida flourishes; Asolo theatre; season's repertoire. H. Hewes. Sat R 49:39 Ag 20 '66

SARATOGA performing arts center
Arts in Saratoga: Performing arts center. Holiday 39:112 Je '66
Arts outdoors in Saratoga. il Hi Fi 16:MA16 O '66
Dancing in the rain. il Newsweek 68:80 Ag 1 '66
New center at Saratoga. I. Kolodin. il Sat R 49:49-50+ Jl 30 '66
New life at the old spa; Saratoga performing arts center. il Parks & Rec 1:404-5 My '66
Opera evenings at Saratoga. I. Kolodin. Sat R 49:52 S 10 '66
Place, a show, a win. il Time 88:56-9 Jl 22 '66
Saratoga! G. Fitzgerald. il Opera N 31:14-17 S 10 '66
Saratoga, Lake George. F. Merkling. il Opera N 31:23 O 15 '66
Saratoga on a new track. T. Prideaux. il Life 61:89-90 Jl 22 '66
Summer opera, new and nervy; Saratoga & Lake George. C. L. Osborne. Hi Fi 16:MA16-17+ N '66
Tired old spa tries serving up culture. il Bsns W p32-3 Jl 16 '66

SARCIONE, Edward J. and Bogden, A. E.
Hepatic synthesis of alpha₂ acute phase-globulin of rat plasma. bibliog Science 153:547-8 Jl 29 '66

SARCOMA
Complement-fixing antigens in hamster tumors induced by the Bryan strain of Rous sarcoma virus. M. J. Casey and others. bibliog il Science 151:1086-8 Mr 4 '66

1-Adamantanamine hydrochloride: inhibition of rous and esh sarcoma viruses in cell culture. A. M. Wallbank and others. bibliog il Science 152:1760-1 Je 24 '66

Paraproteinemia and reticulum cell sarcoma in an inbred mouse strain. H. J. Wanebo and others. bibliog il Science 154:901-3 N 18 '66

SARD, Thomas R.
Chance on the outside. por Am Ed 2:29-32 Ap '66

SARDINIA
Sardinia. P. Dallas. il Atlan 217:145-6+ Mr '66
Seducers of the Emerald Coast. T. Sage. il Nat R 18:992-4 O 4 '66

See also
Crime and criminals—Sardinia

SARDINIAN bronzes. See Bronzes

SARDINIAN sculpture. See Sculpture, Italian

SARDIS
Dig confirms Herodotus' tales. il Sci N 90:426 N 19 '66

SARGEANT, Winthrop
Musical events. See issues of New Yorker
Profiles (cont) New Yorker 42:66-70+ O 29 '66

SARGENT, E. N.
Things; poem. New Yorker 42:50 Mr 12 '66
Three poems: Paradise; Break; Child. New Yorker 41:33 Ja 22 '66

SARGENT, John Singer
John Singer Sargent in his studio. W. James, jr. il por Atlan 217:91-2 Mr '66

SARGENT, Sir Malcolm
Birthday party. il Newsweek 68:57 Ag 15 '66

SARGENT, T. D.
Background selections of geometrid and noctuid moths. Science 154:1674-5 D 30 '66

SARGENT and company
You've never seen a key like this! il Pop Mech 125:165 F '66

SARICH, Vincent M. and Wilson, A. C.
Quantitative immunochemistry and the evolution of primate albumins: micro-complement fixation. bibliog Science 154:1563-6 D 23 '66

SARIN
Dealkylation and loss of capacity for reactivation of cholinesterase inhibited by sarin. L. W. Harris and others. bibliog il Science 154:404-7 O 21 '66

SARKISSIAN, Igor V. See McDaniel, R. G. jt. auth.

SARKO, A. and Marchessault, R. H.
Crystal structure of amylose triacetate: a nonintegral helix. bibliog Science 154:1658-9 D 30 '66
56:12-13 Ja '67

SARKOTICH, Diane
Sensitivity training in the classroom. NEA J

SARNOFF, David
Envisioning the future; interview. pors Nations Bsns 54:60-1+ Je '66
No life untouched. Sat R 49:21-2 Jl 23 '66
TV revolution ahead! Read Digest 88:66-70 Mr '66

about

David Sarnoff, by E. Lyons. Review
Nat R 18:322-3 Ap 5 '66. M. S. Evans
Nation 202:332-5 Mr 21 '66. C. Dreher
Sat R il por 49:36 Mr 5 '66. P. G. Hoffman
How the wasteland began; early days of radio. C. Dreher. Atlan 217:53-8 F '66
Man of the future. il por Time 88:106 O 7 '66
Salute to David Sarnoff. por Electr World 76:8 O '66
Sarnoff at seventy-five. J. Tebbel. por Sat R 49:138-9 Mr 12 '66
Televisionary. il por Newsweek 68:84 O 10 '66

SARNOFF, Robert W.
Communications; address, June 5, 1966. Vital Speeches 32:670-2 Ag 15 '66

SAROYAN, Aram
From Sled hill voices; poem. Poetry 108:380-1 S '66
Sentence; poem. Nation 202:250 F 28 '66

SAROYAN, Lucy
Face to face; with a dresser with dreams. pors Seventeen 25:137 F '66

SAROYAN, William
Our greatest man. Sat Eve Post 239:80-1 Mr 12 '66

SARRIS, Andrew
Gloom at San Sebastian. Sat R 49:63 Jl 23 '66
Hollywood-haters. Sat R 49:23-5 D 24 '66

SARTON, May
Problems and delights of revision. Writer 79:20-2 D '66
Five poets. A. Freeman. Poetry 109:192 D '66

SARTRE, Jean Paul
Condemned of Altona (Les séquestrés d'Altona) tr. by J. O'Brien. Criticism
America 114:272-3 F 19 '66
Nation 202:222-4 F 21 '66
New Repub 154:42-3 F 26 '66
New Yorker 41:110+ F 12 '66
Newsweek 67:88 F 14 '66
Sat R 49:52 F 19 '66
Time 87:67 F 18 '66
Vogue 147:58 Mr 15 '66
Jean-Paul Sartre: Christian theist? J. B. Mow. Christian Cent 83:1437-9 N 23 '66; Reply. S. Keen. 83:1578 D 21 '66
Sartre vs. Lévi-Strauss; who are the radicals today? L. Abel. Commonweal 84:364-8 Je 17 '66

SARTWELL, Frank
Man and his science. Sci N 90:496; 91:17 D 10 '66, Ja 7 '67
Patent law change. Sci N 90:512 D 17 '66

SARVIS, Shirley
Cool cooking in a skillet. Farm J 90:59+ Je '66
Four superb sauces for fish. Farm J 90:107 Mr '66

SASAKI, Takeru, and others
Stable complex of fibrinogen and fibrin. bibliog Science 152:1069-71 My 20 '66

SASHES, Window. See Window sashes

SASKATCHEWAN
Socialism in Saskatchewan. A. Morrison. Yale R 56:256-70 D '66

SASS, Samuel
Persecuted minority. Library J 91:3126-7 Je 15 '66

SATELLITE and space communications systems, incorporated
Comsat patent claims itemized by firm. Tech W 19:41-2 Ag 1 '66
Comsat systems monopolized? Tech W 19:24+ Jl 25 '66

SATELLITE states. See Europe, Eastern

SATELLITES
New moon over Saturn. Time 89:56 Ja 13 '67
Satellites of Uranus. G. S. Mumford. il Sky & Tel 32:127 S '66
Tenth moon of Saturn. il Sci N 91:33 Ja 14 '67
Triton on collision path; Neptune's moon may form ring around planet. Sci N 90:310 O 15 '66
See also
Artificial satellites
Moon

SATIE, Erik
Pierrot of Paris. M. Cooper. por Opera N 30:6-7 My 7 '66

SATIRE
Saturnalia, satire, and utopia. R. C. Elliott. Yale R 55:521-36 Je '66
See also
Caricatures and cartoons
also subhead Anecdotes, facetiae, satire, etc. under various subjects, e.g. Apartments—Anecdotes, facetiae, satire, etc.

SATISFACTION
Personal fulfillment in man and woman; excerpt from Man and woman. M. O'Keefe and J. J. Evoy. America 115:582-6 N 12 '66

SATISFACTION in work. See Job satisfaction

SATO, Eisaku
Black mist. il por Newsweek 68:58 O 31 '66
Black mist & banana skins. Time 88:37 N 4 '66
Divided & conquerable. Time 88:38 D 16 '66
First test for Sato. il Time 89:26 Ja 6 '67
Old face, new wrinkle. por Time 88:38 D 2 '66
Seconds for Sato. Time 88:43-4 D 9 '66

SATO, Motoaki, and Wright, T. L.
Oxygen fugacities directly measured in magmatic gases. bibliog Science 153:1103-5 S 2 '66

SATTER, David A.
West side story. New Repub 155:15-19 Jl 2 '66

SATTERFIELD, David Edward, 1920-
Excerpt from February 25, 1966, statement to the press. Cong Digest 45:158 My '66

SATURDAY evening post
Headlines and checkbooks; concerning scramble for C. Amurao's story of nurses slayings. il Newsweek 68:76 Ag 1 '66

SATURDAY night; story. See Maropis, P. S.

SATURDAY people; story. See Madocs, R.

SATURDAY review
College literary magazine contest. Sat R 49:38 D 31 '66
Just by writing a letter; readers and the Science and humanity supplement. J. Lear. il Sat R 49:70-2 My 7 '66
SR's fourteenth annual advertising awards. W. D. Patterson. il Sat R 49:70-7 Ap 9 '66; Discussion. 49:61 My 14 '66
Where the action is; aims of SR's Education supplement. J. Cass. Sat R 49:69 O 15 '66
See also
Anisfield-Wolf awards
Loveman award

SATURN (planet)
Recent observations of Saturn. il Sky & Tel 33:58-9 Ja '67
Saturn; a 1966 spectacle. il Sky & Tel 31:374-5 Je '66
This year earth passes through Saturn's ring plane three times. T. D. Nicholson. il Natur Hist 75:36-9 Ap '66

Satellites
See Satellites

SATURN booster. See Space vehicles—Propulsion systems

SATURN launch vehicles. See Space vehicles—Propulsion systems

SATURNALIAN festivals. See Festivals

SAUCEPANS. See Kitchen utensils

SAUCERS, Flying. See Flying saucers

SAUCES
Fish sauce is the secret. il Sunset 136:171-3 Je '66

Four superb sauces for fish. S. Sarvis. il Farm J 90:107 Mr '66
Ice cream sauces. R. Hanna. il Suc Farm 64:106-7 S '66
Work wonders with sauce mixes; with recipes. il Ladies Home J 84:82+ Ja '67
World's best spaghetti sauce; with recipe and menu. G. Schremp. il Life 60:124-5+ Ap 15 '66

SAUDI ARABIA
King Faisal: Saudi Arabia's modern monarch. G. Gaskill. il Read Digest 90:117-22 Ja '67
King-size question. Newsweek 67:54+ Je 27 '66
Revolution from the throne. il Time 87:45 Je 24 '66
See also
Natural resources—Saudi Arabia
United Nations—Saudi Arabia

Economic conditions
Desert kingdom that is beginning to stir. il U S News 60:66-8 Je 27 '66

Foreign relations
Leader alone; King Faisals efforts towards Arab unity. Newsweek 68:44 Ag 8 '66
President Johnson and King Faisal of Saudi Arabia exchange views on matters of common interest; exchange of greetings, exchange of toasts, June 21; with text of joint communique, June 22, 1966. L. B. Johnson; Feisal. Dept State Bul 55:38-42 Jl 11 '66

Industries
Saudi Arabia. J. S. Haupert. bibliog il Focus 16:1-6 My '66

Politics and government
Desert kingdom that is beginning to stir. il U S News 60:66-8 Je 27 '66

SAUDI ARABIAN airlines. See Airlines—Saudi Arabia

SAUER, Carl Ortwin
Author. W. Hogan. Sat R 49:25 Jl 2 '66

SAUER, Jean Claude
Paris fall styles full of surprises; photographs. Life 61:60-3+ S 2 '66
about
Fashion story was like a cleansing shower. G. P. Hunt. il por Life 61:3 S 2 '66

SAUER, Louis W.
Your child's health. See issues of PTA magazine

SAUER, Victor W.
Design of modern asphalt pavements. Am City 81:113-16 Ap '66

SAUERKRAUT
Pinnacle for a peasant dish; choucroute garni from Alsace; with recipes and menu by E. Graves. il Life 62:88-9+ Ja 20 '67

SAUL, Ralph Southey
Amex hires its critic. por Bsns W p36 Ag 20 '66
Can he trade up Amex's image. il por Bsns W p 150+ O 29 '66
Hiring the harasser. por Time 88:68 Ag 26 '66
New man at Amex. por Newsweek 68:56 Ag 29 '66
Ralph Saul of the American exchange. por Fortune 74:47 O '66

SAULNIER, Raymond J.
We can fight inflation without controls; interview. pors Nations Bsns 54:33-5+ Mr '66

SAULS, Glen
Metropolitan opera presents summer concerts at Lewisohn stadium; calendar. Opera N 30:16-17 Je 4 '66

SAUNDERS, Earl W.
Parallelogram. Christian Cent 83:1577-8 D 21 '66

SAUNDERS, George C. and King, D. W.
Antibody synthesis initiated in vitro by paired explants of spleen and thymus. bibliog Science 151:1390-1 Mr 18 '66

SAUNDERS, John
Mary French told of digging the grave; A. Rowe death. D. Moser. Life 60:82+ Mr 4 '66

SAUNDERS, John W. jr
Death in embryonic systems. bibliog Science 154:604-12 N 4 '66

SAUNDERS, Stuart Thomas
Reshaping our national transportation policy; address, January 19, 1966. Vital Speeches 32:237-9 F 1 '66

SAUROMATUM
Nature note; voodoo lily. Sci N 90:386 N 5 '66
Voodoo lily. B. J. D. Meeuse. il Sci Am 215:80-8 Jl '66

SAUSAGE
See also
Cookery—Meat
SAVAGE, John
Getaway; story. Sat Eve Post 239:76-7 My 7 '66
SAVAGES. See Man, Primitive
SAVANNAH, Ga.
History
Who's got Button's bones? R. M. Williams. il Am Heritage 17:28-32+ F '66
SAVANYU, Jean Marie
Mlle's guest editors: '66. por Mlle 63:246-7 Ag '66
SAVING and savings
Borrowing and saving. M. Mayer. Bet Hom & Gard 44:6 O '66
Can you actually make those years-ahead financial goals? Bet Hom & Gard 44:10+ N '66
How long will your savings last? il Changing T 20:24-5 Ap '66
Latest on what your savings can earn. il U S News 60:60-1 Mr 21 '66
Penny saved is a penny wanted; battle for savers' favor. il Time 87:97 Je 10 '66
Saving money; campaign for all kinds of saving. M. L. Silberstein. New Repub 155: 36-7 D 17 '66
War against personal thrift; address, November 21, 1966. A. S. Murphy. Vital Speeches 33:169-73 Ja 1 '67
War for savings heats up. Bsns W p21-2 Jl 2 '66
Will tight money get tighter? R. Newcomb. Nations Bsns 54:38-9 N '66
See also
Christmas clubs
Investments
SAVINGS and loan associations
Action to help savings & loans. U S News 60:88 Je 27 '66
California S&Ls see some sunlight. il Bsns W p75-6+ D 17 '66
Financial engineering. H. C. Wallich. Newsweek 68:92 D 5 '66
Getting money for a home; why it's tough. the outlook; interview. J. E. Horne. il U S News 61:82-5 Ag 8 '66
Hidden clause; savings-and-loan associations use escalation clauses to boost rates. il Newsweek 68:80 O 17 '66
Hounding the S&Ls' own watchdog; J. E. Horne. Bsns W p51-2+ Ag 20 '66
House of troubles. il Time 87:97-8 Je 10 '66
How scramble for savings is hurting savings & loans. il U S News 60:75-7 My 30 '66
Money is heading to lusher pastures; S&L losing out to stiff bank competition. il Bsns W p 147-8+ My 28 '66
New rules on interest; meaning for savers. borrowers. il U S News 61:101-2 O 3 '66
Rates up, money vanishing, and new troubles for borrowers. U S News 61:85-7 Ag 22 '66
Savings and loan; easy lenders; associations problem loans in California. M. Harris. il Nation 203:152-4 Ag 22 '66
S&Ls hold their own in battle for savings. il Bsns W p48 Jl 9 '66
Savings & loans; western report. U S News 61:85-6 S 5 '66
See also
Credit unions
Securities
Savings and loan; easy lenders; associations problem loans in California. M. Harris. il Nation 203:152-4 Ag 22 '66
SAVINGS banks
War against personal thrift; address, November 21, 1966. A. S. Murphy. Vital Speeches 33:169-73 Ja 1 '67
See also
Savings deposits
SAVINGS bonds. See Bonds, Government
SAVINGS certificates. See Savings deposits
SAVINGS deposits
Taxation
Tax due now on savings accounts. U S News 60:115-16 Mr 14 '66
SAVIO, Mario
Uncertain future of the multiversity. Harper 233:88-90+ O '66
SAVITZ, David
Gas and guerrillas, a word of caution. New Repub 154:13-14 Mr 19 '66
SAVORY, Theodore H.
False scorpions; with biographical sketch. Sci Am 214:22, 95-100 Mr '66
SAW stands. See Machinery—Stands
SAWADA, Kyoichi
Combat photographer. il por U S Camera 29: 48-9 O '66

SAWALLISCH, Wolfgang
Music to my ears; guest conductor of the Philadelphia orchestra. I. Kolodin. Sat R 49:51+ Mr 26 '66
SAWMILL waste. See Wood waste
SAWMILLS
Wages and hours
Wages in paint, candy, and southern sawmill industries. il Mo Labor R 89:885-6 Ag '66
SAWS
Add an electric brake to your saw. J. D. Griffith. il Pop Mech 125:194+ Mr '66
AMT's new price bustin' radial-arm saw. A. Lees. il Pop Mech 126:160-1+ S '66
Brand new contractors' trim saw. H. Silken. il Pop Mech 126:192-3+ N '66
Double-insulated portable saber saw; Rockwell Porter-cable model 60. il Consumer Rep 31:100-1 Mr '66
Four new saws for home shops. il Pop Sci 189:144 Ag '66
Jig-of-all-work for your table saw. R. J. De Cristoforo. il Pop Sci 189:180-4 O '66
New chain saw has electric starter. il Pop Sci 189:169 O '66
New saw blade for cutting dovetails. C. E. Rhine. il Pop Sci 188:128-30 My '66
Pee-wee saws make hard jobs easy; slitting and slotting saws. W. E. Burton. il Pop Mech 125:186-8 F '66
Rockwell's new 10-in. table saw. A. Lee. il Pop Mech 126:194-5+ O '66
Saw that speeds your plywood projects; panel saw. H. Pfister. il Pop Sci 189:150-5+ N '66
Selection and use of chain saws for the nonprofessional user. L. W. Hooker. il Consumer Bul 49:14-16 O '66
Two handsome new radial-arm saws. R. J. De Cristoforo. il Pop Sci 189:144-9 N '66
SAWTOOTH national recreation area, Idaho (proposed) See Recreation areas—Idaho
SAWTOOTH primitive area. See Wilderness areas—Idaho
SAWYER, Grant
Nevada: the end of the casino era. E. F. Sherman. il Atlan 218:112-16 O '66
SAX, Martin. See Pletcher, J. jt. auth.
SAXÉN, Lauri
Drug-induced teratogenesis in vitro; inhibition of calcification by different tetracyclines. bibliog Science 153:1384-7 S 16 '66
SAXITOXIN. See Toxins and antitoxins
SAXON, James J.
At it again. por Time 87:72-3 Ap 22 '66
Bank merger fight begins. Bsns W p 136+ Ap 9 '66
Saxon races a deadline; term expires in six months. por Bsns W p 170+ Mr 26 '66
Saxon's farewell. il por Newsweek 68:86 N 7 '66
Scrappy, happy James J. Saxon. I. Ross. il por Fortune 73:162-4+ Ap '66
Undoing Saxon's rules. Bsns W p24 D 24 '66
SAXON, O. Glenn, jr
Annual headache; the stockholder's meeting. Harvard Bsns R 44:132-7 Ja '66
SAXOPHONE, Electronic. See Musical instruments, Electronic
SAXTON, Pa.
Small town solves a big water problem. P. S. Siebert, jr. il Am City 81:83-5 N '66
SAY something African; story. See Gordimer, N.
SAYERS, Gale
Chicago's dream Gale. H. L. Masin. il por Sr Schol 89:22 O 21 '66
SAYINGS. See Aphorisms and apothegms; Quotations
SAYLOR, John P.
Excerpt from remarks, August 30, 1966. Cong Digest 45:299+ D '66
Many-headed dragon. por Audubon Mag 68. 52-3 Ja '66
SAYRE, Robert M.
Review of movement of Cuban refugees and hemisphere policy toward Cuba; statement, March 23, 1966. Dept State Bul 54:707-13 My 2 '66
SAYRE, Ruth Buxton
Will Russia's farmers decide her future? por Farm J 90:99+ Mr '66
SCACCHETTI, Richard V.
Professionalization of management; address, November 11, 1966. Vital Speeches 33:137-41 D 15 '66
SCALAPINO, Robert A.
We cannot accept a Communist seizure of Vietnam. N Y Times Mag p46-7+ D 11 '66
SCALES (weighing instruments)
Farm scales do pay. D. Malena. il Suc Farm 64:38-9 Ag '66

SCALLOPS
Spectral sensitivity of the scallop pecten maximus. J. R. Cronly-Dillon. bibliog il Science 151:345-6 Ja 21 '66
See also
Cookery—Fish

SCALZO, Joe
Circle track, its men and machinery. Hot Rod 19:34-40+ Jl '66
Foyt vs Jones. Motor T 18:40 Jl '66
Ten off the top. Motor T 18:28-9 Mr '66

SCANDINAVIA
Scandinavia; symposium. il Holiday 40:8+ N '66
See also
Foreign students in Scandinavia
Foreign visitors in Scandinavia
Youth—Scandinavia

Description and travel
Enjoying Scandinavia. N. Barry. il Holiday 40:117-22 N '66
Scandinavia's secret season. A. Chamberlin. Vogue 148:56+ S 15 '66
When the racing is done. F. R. Smith. il Sports Illus 25:46-7 Jl 4 '66

Moral conditions
Sex in the classroom; Scandinavian systems. Newsweek 68:83 Jl 11 '66

SCANDINAVIAN cookery. See Cookery, Scandinavian

SCANDINAVIAN languages
Speaking Scandinavian. G. Jennings. il Holiday 40:8+ N '66

SCANLON, David G.
Aid to African education. por Sch & Soc 94:447 D 10 '66

SCANNER servo-recorder. See Recording instruments

SCANNING devices, Optical. See Reading machines

SCANNING electron microscope. See Electron microscope and microscopy

SCANU, A.
Serum high-density lipoprotein: effect of change in structure on activity of chicken adipose tissue lipase. bibliog Science 153:640-1 Ag 5 '66

SCARBOROUGH campus. See Toronto. University—Scarborough campus

SCAREDY cat; drama. See Boiko. C.

SCARFE, Gerald
Vision of cosmic disgust. il por Time 88:46-7 Jl 15 '66

SCARLATTI, Alessandro
Triumph of honor. Criticism
Opera N 31:26 S 10 '66

SCARSDALE, N.Y.

Education
Elementary paperback: a trial run; Edgewood elementary school. E. Rabban. il Library J 91:2591-4 My 15 '66

SCATES, Alice Y.
Women moving ahead. por Am Ed 2:1-4 Mr '66

SCATTERING (physics)
Stimulated Brillouin and Raman scattering in quartz at 2.1° to 293° Kelvin. P. E. Tannenwald and J. B. Thaxter. bibliog il Science 154:1319-20 D 9 '66

SCATTERING of particles and rays
See also
Compton effect

SCELOPORUS occidentalis. See Lizards

SCENE designing. See Theater—Stage scenery

SCENERY. See Landscape

SCENERY, Stage. See Theater—Stage scenery

SCENIC areas. See Preservation of landmarks, scenery, etc.

SCENT. See Perfumery

SCENT of birds. See Odors

SCHAAP, Dick
Death of a hooked heiress. Look 30:19-25 Jl 26 '66

SCHAEFER, Paul
Adirondack trails; reprint. Liv Wildn 29:36-7 Aut '65
Bob Marshall, Mount Marcy, and the wilderness. il Liv Wildn 30:6-9 Sum '66
Unmapped Adirondack Lake. Liv Wildn 30:10 Sum '66

SCHAEFER, Vincent J.
Amateur scientist. Sci Am 214:120-4+ Mr '66
Ice nuclei from automobile exhaust and iodine vapor. bibliog Science 154:1555-7 D 23 '66

SCHAEFFLER, Willy
Peak performance. por Newsweek 67:93 Mr 21 '66

SCHAELING, Marianne
Happening; story. Seventeen 25:168-9 My '66

SCHAETZEL, J. Robert
Necessary partnership. For Affairs 44:417-33 Ap '66

SCHAFER, Irwin A. and others
Vitamin C-induced increase of dermatan sulfate in cultured Hurler's fibroblasts. bibliog Science 153:1008-10 Ag 26 '66

SCHAFER, Roger
Happy householders of Halen. Arch Forum 124:80-5 Je '66

SCHAFFER, A. G. and Alexander, M.
Morphogenetic substance in legume nodule formation. bibliog Science 152:82-3 Ap 1 '66

SCHAFFER, Leslie
Shape of madness. New Repub 155:25-6 S 3 '66

SCHAFFNER, Gerald
Varactor diodes. por Electr World 76:53-6 Jl '66

SCHALEBEN, Arville
Public and the court; address, January 6, 1966. Vital Speeches 32:268-70 F 15 '66

SCHALK, Adolph
Cardinal and commissar. Commonweal 84:497-9 Ag 5 '66
Germany's radical right. Commonweal 84:609-11 S 23 '66

SCHALL, James V.
Censorship in the church. Commonweal 83:601-3 F 25 '66
Religion and war. Commonweal 85:193-6 N 18 '66
Secular city and God. Cath World 204:20-6 O '66

SCHALLER, George B.
Serengeti lion. por Life 62:58+ Ja 20 '67
Tiger and its prey. Natur Hist 75:30-7 O '66

SCHAPIRO, Shawn, and others
Maturation of a stress-activated mechanism inhibiting induction of tyrosine transaminase. bibliog Science 152:1642-3 Je 17 '66

SCHAPPER, Beatrice
Let's abolish traffic danger spots. Todays Health 44:18-21 O '66

SCHARDT, Arlie
Georgia: Lester Maddox and the mad Democrats. Reporter 53:29-30 O 20 '66
Mississippi mayor fights the Klan. Reporter 34:39-40 Ja 27 '66

SCHARF, Kurt, bp
Scharf succeeds Dibelius. F. Lüpsen. Christian Cent 83:311-12 Mr 9 '66

SCHARFF, Matthew D. and Robbins, Elliott
Polyribosome disaggregation during metaphase. bibliog Science 151:992-5 F 25 '66

SCHECHNER, Richard
Pornography and the new expression. Atlan 219:74-8 Ja '67

SCHECTER, Jerrold
Beatles under wraps in Tokyo. Life 61:72-4 Jl 15 '66
Golf. Sports Illus 25:67-8 N 21 '66
Inji goes to Fuji for speed and art. Sports Illus 25:38-9 O 17 '66

SCHEER, Roberta
Change of face. il pors Mlle 63:140-1 Je '66

SCHEERER, Maud
Do you act your part? reprint. Read Digest 89:211-12+ N '66

SCHEFF, Fritzi
Fritzi Scheff and others on IRCC. A. Favia-Artsay. il por Hobbies 71:35+ Mr '66

SCHEFFEL, R. L.
Indian pipe's secret. Audubon Mag 68:224-5 Jl '66

SCHEICHENBAUER, Franco
Scheichenbauer's created women. il Mod Phot 30:48-53 Mr '66

SCHEJBAL, Jaroslav
Christmas list; holiday greeting. J. Fischer. Harper 233:30 D '66

SCHELIN, Eric
Pre-cruise check-up. Motor B 117:152+ Ap '66

SCHELLHASE, Dave
Unknown wonder. H. L. Masin. por Sr Schol 88:20 F 4 '66

SCHEMANSKY, Norbert
Looking for a lift. M. Kram. il por Sports Illus 25:128-30+ S 12 '66

SCHENK, Gretchen Knief
(ed) Extending library service. See issues of Wilson library bulletin

SCHEPMAN, Robert G.
Take a broad view. Flying 80:63 Ja '67

SCHERF, Margaret
One cow, one vote. Harper 232:103-9 Ap '66

SCHERMAN, Harry
Birthday-of-the-month. H. Frankel. por Sat R 49:31+ Ap 16 '66

SCHERY, Robert W.
Common sense lawn care. Flower Grower
53:30-1+ Ap '66
Lawns. Horticulture 44:34-6 S '66
Steps to assure a good lawn. House & Gard
130:146-7+ Ag '66
Travel far and near; Rio Grande canoe trip.
Natur Hist 75:58+ Ap '66
Where you can't have a lawn. Horticulture
45:26+ Ja '67

SCHEUER, Paul J. See Boylan, D. B. jt. auth.

SCHEVILL, James
Mailman and das ewig weibliche; poem. Nation 203:429 O 24 '66

about

Seven poets. T. Clark. Poetry 108:408-11 S '66

SCHICK, Frank L. and Trezza, A. F.
National conference on library statistics.
ALA Bul 60:499-500 My '66

SCHICK-GUTIÉRREZ, René
President Schick of Nicaragua visits Washington; texts of greetings exchanged, June
9, 1966. Dept State Bul 55:15-17 Jl 4 '66

about

Obituary
Américas 18:47 S '66

SCHICK safety razor company
Trying to dull Gillette's edge. Bsns W p78
N 12 '66

SCHICKEL, Richard
Black comedy with purifying laughter. Har-
per 232:103-4+ My '66
Hal Holbrook tonight! Holiday 40:103-5 Ag
'66
Life movie review. See issues of Life
New York's best new theater group? Harper
233:92-4+ N '66
Scandinavian screen. Holiday 40:156+ N '66
Why young people are seeking new values.
Redbook 127:73+ My '66

SCHICKELE, Peter
Musical satire from Vanguard and Elektra:
P.D.Q. Bach, The baroque Beatles book.
J. Diether. il Am Rec G 32:508-10 F '66
Prof's off on a Bach boff. R. Eyer. Life 60:16
F 25 '66

SCHIDLOVSKY, G. See Toplin, I. jr. auth.

SCHIERMAN, L. W. See McBride, R. A. jt.
auth.

SCHIFF, Dorothy
Hello Dolly! por Newsweek 68:102 S 19 '66

SCHILDKRAUT, Joseph J.
Antidepressant drugs. Science 154:1058+ N
25 '66

SCHILDROTH, Irmgard
Joys of cruising in a 19 footer. Yachting
119:108-9+ Ja '66

SCHILL, Bert. See Schill, Bill. jt. auth.

SCHILL, Bill, and Schill, Bert
Trailer cruise in the Keys. il Yachting 120:
45+ N '66

SCHILLER, Herbert I.
TV overseas: the U.S. hard sell. Nation 203:
609-12 D 5 '66

SCHILLER, Peter H. and Chorover, S. L.
Metacontrast: its relation to evoked potentials. bibliog Science 153:1398-400 S 16 '66

SCHILLING, Jean-Guy, and Winchester, J. W.
Rare earths in Hawaiian basalts. Science
153:867-9 Ag 19 '66

SCHILLING, John
Case for the small college. C. Wren. il pors
Look 30:25-7 O 4 '66

SCHILTZ, Michael E.
Catholics and the Chicago riots. Commonweal 85:159-63, 321-4 N 11, D 16 '66
Facing outward. Commonweal 84:14-16 Mr
25 '66

SCHIMEL, John L.
Parents vs. children: frustrating games
families play. Redbook 127:46-7+ Ag '66

SCHIOP, Pauline E. See Stansly, P. G. jt.
auth.

SCHIPPERS, David J.
Two against the mob. H. Bruno. Newsweek
67:44+ My 23 '66

SCHIPPERS, Thomas
Make mingle with our tambourines; interview. por Opera N 31:34-5 S 17 '66

SCHIRRA, Walter Marty, 1923-
Astronauts Schirra and Borman make Far
Eastern tour. Dept State Bul 54:364-5 Mr 7
'66
Heart of the matter; statement. por UNESCO
Courier 19:4 My '66

SCHISGALL, Lillian, and Schisgall, Oscar
UNICEF: tomorrow must be better. Read
Digest 90:151-2+ Ja '67

SCHISGALL, Oscar
Are you a self-starter? Read Digest 89:99-
102 Jl '66

How to beat the high cost of college. PTA
Mag 61:11-13 S '66; Same abr. Read Digest
89:141-4 S '66
Vicar wanted to travel. Read Digest 89:
187-8+ O '66
—See Schisgall, L. jt. auth.

SCHISTOSOMIASIS
Drug for schistosomiasis. Sci N L 89:51 Ja
22 '66
Unconquered plague. J. M. Weir. il Bul
Atomic Sci 22:46-8 O '66

SCHIZOPHRENIA
Acquisition of imitative speech by schizo-
phrenic children. O. I. Lovaas and others.
bibliog il Science 151:705-7 F 11 '66
Antibodies affecting metabolism of chicken
erythrocytes: examination of schizophrenic
and other subjects. J. W. Ryan and others.
bibliog il Science 151:1408-10 Mr 18 '66
Disturbed mute children can learn to speak.
Sci N L 89:151 Mr 5 '66
One of the great mystery stories of medicine.
L. Galton. il N Y Times Mag p34-5+ N 6
'66; Discussion. p41 N 20; 42+ N 27 '66
Schizophrenia clue found. Sci N 90:166 S 3
'66
Schizophrenics may have too much copper.
Sci N 89:200 Mr 26 '66
That old chemical complex, the human mind.
I. Asimov. il N Y Times Mag p 12-13+ Jl
3 '66
Vitamin therapy urged. P. McBroom. Sci N
89:199 Mr 26 '66

Diagnosis
Diagnosis by fungus. Sci N 89:199 Mr 26 '66

SCHIZOPHYLLUM commune
Schizophyllum commune: new mutations in
the B incompatibility factor. Y. Koltin and
J. R. Raper. bibliog il Science 154:510-11 O
28 '66

SCHLAMM, William S.
End of the affair. Nat R 18:1316-18 D 27 '66
New Yorker profile of the West. Nat R 18:
117-19 F 8 '66
Surprise for Karl Jaspers. Nat R 18:620 Je 28
'66
Whose decline? Nat R 18:427-8+ My 3 '66

SCHLEGEL, Gail
Informal bookstore in Honolulu. Pub W 190:
54-6 O 17 '66

SCHLEH, Edward C.
Dangerous supervisory gap. Duns R 87:57-8+
F '66

SCHLEIFER, Peter, and Shirley, Isabel
Speed Magny 100. U S Camera 29:26+ O '66

about

To hell with instructions. H. Keppler. il por
Mod Phot 30:64+ D '66

SCHLEISNER, Doris G.
Birth of a butterfly. Flower Grower 53:34+
Jl '66

SCHLESINGER, Arthur, 1917-
America in transition. Sat R 49:36-7 Ap 23
'66
Arthur M. Schlesinger, jr. on history.
por(p31) Pub W 189:32-3 Mr 28 '66
F.D.R.'s secret romance. Ladies Home J 83:
66+ N '66
Informal history of love U.S.A. Sat Eve Post
239:30-2+ D 31 '66
Katharine Graham. Vogue 149:108-9 Ja 1 '67
Mark Twain, or the ambiguities. Atlan 218:
61-4 Ag '66
Middle way out of Vietnam. N Y Times Mag
p47-9+ S 18; 98 O 16 '66
Movies. Vogue 148:59 Ag 1; 162 O 1; 151 N 1;
166 D '66
Speaking out. por Sat Eve Post 239:10+ Ag
13 '66
Strangulation by federal contract. Life 61:8
S 9 '66
Vietnam: what should we do now? por Look
30:31 Ag 9 '66

about

Four authors are given National book
awards. por Pub W 189:47-8 Mr 21 '66
NBA 1966. por Newsweek 67:106 Mr 28 '66
Should historians write contemporary history?
H. S. Commager. il Sat R 49:18-20+ F 12
'66
Superstars. il por Newsweek 68:68 O 17 '66

SCHLESINGER, Ina
Soviet education in 1965. bibliog f Sch & Soc
94:270-2 Sum '66

SCHLESINGER, James R.
Strategic consequences of nuclear proliferation. Reporter 35:36-8 O 20 '66

SCHLEY, Ben
Henry Hawkins' fish farm. Am For 72:34-5+
Ap '66

SCHLIEMANN, Heinrich
One passion, two loves, by L. Poole and G.
Poole. Review
Sat R il 49:38 N 26 '66. F. G. Brattton
SCHLIEMANN, Sophia
One passion, two loves, by L Poole and G.
Poole. Review
Sat. R il 49:38 N 26 '66. F. G. Bratton
SCHLIEREN apparatus
Ultracentrifuge schlieren photographs: auto-
matic analysis. R. Moore and others. il
Science 152:1509-11 Je 10 '66
SCHLOSSBACH, Ike
One horse airport. J. Gilbert. il por Flying
78:54-7 My '66
SCHLUMBERGER, Eveline
Victor Hugo, decorator. Vogue 147:224-31+
My '66
SCHMALE, Jack
Action-packed '66 program promises un-
limited thrills. Motor B 117:150-2 Je '66
Northern Cal roundup. Motor B 118:122 O;
110 N; 100 D '66
SCHMECKEBIER, Laurence
Landscape paintings of William Palmer. Am
Artist 30:50-5+ Je '66
SCHMID, Charles Howard, Jr
Growing up in Tucson; death sentence. il
por Time 87:28 Mr 11 '66
Killing for kicks. il por Newsweek 67:35+
Mr 14 '66
Pied Piper of Tucson; with report by D.
Moser. il pors Life 60:18-24A+ Mr 4 '66
SCHMID, Peter
Letter from Tokyo. Commentary 42:49-53 O
'66
SCHMIDT, Albert C.
Estival festival foolishness. Reporter 35:50-
1 O 20 '66
SCHMIDT, Beverly
Beverly Schmidt; the Bridge theatre. M.
Marks. Dance Mag 40:30 Ap '66
SCHMIDT, Gerald L.
See here, specialist Schmidt. por Time 87:67
Ap 8 '66
SCHMIDT, Glen H.
Interview with a milking expert; ed. by J. R.
Borcherding. por Suc Farm 64:32-3 D '66
SCHMIDT, Harold
Picture profile: the ship's photographer. G.
Pyle. il Pop Phot 58:70-1+ Mr '66
SCHMIDT, Laverne C. See Frazer, R. L. jt.
auth.
SCHMIDT, Maarten
Birth and life of the universe. C. P. Gil-
more. il por N Y Times Mag p26-7+ Je 12
'66
Man on the mountain. L. Jaroff. il pors Time
87:80-4 Mr 11 '66
SCHMIDT, Ruth A. M. and Sellmann, P. V.
Mummified pleistocene ostracods in Alaska.
bibliog Science 153:167-8 Jl 8 '66
SCHMIDT, William J.
Apostrophe; poem. Cath World 204:179 D '66
Hour cometh; poem. Christian Cent 83:1498
D 7 '66
SCHMIDT-NIELSEN, Knut, and Bentley, P. J.
Desert tortoise gopherus agassizii: cutaneous
water loss. Science 154:911 N 18 '66
—See Bentley, P. J. jt. auth.
SCHMIDTCHEN, Paul W.
Books. See issues of Hobbies
William Paterson's copy of Louis XVI. Hob-
bies 71:108-9 Ap '66
SCHMITT, Hans A.
Ludwig Erhard: another Bismarck? bibliog
f Cur Hist 50:257-62+ My '66
SCHMITT, Marshall L.
Learning the art of industry. por Am Ed 2:
8-11 My '66
SCHMITT, R. A. and others
Chainpur-like chondrites: primitive pre-
cursors of ordinary chondrites? bibliog
Science 153:644-7 Ag 5 '66
SCHMOKEL, Wolfe W.
Germany in the underdeveloped world. Cur
Hist 50:281-8+ My '66
SCHNAUFER, Pete
Response from the AFT. Mo Labor R 89:620
Je '66
SCHNEEMANN, Carolee
Water light; water needle, St Mark's church-
in-the-Bowery. D. Hering. Dance Mag 40:
31-2 My '66
SCHNEIDER, Gerald
Confessions of a conservationist. Am For
72:8+ Ap '66
Conservation education for people. Am For
72:72+ S '66
Philosophy of conservation. Am For 72:10+
Jl '66
SCHNEIDER, John A.
Bad days at Black Rock. il por Newsweek
67:62-3 F 28 '66
Casting at CBS. por Newsweek 67:84 F 21 '66
Sounding brass. il Time 87:64 F 25 '66

SCHNEIDER, Pierre E.
Monet's revenge. Horizon 8:28-33 Aut '66
Palladio was not Palladian. Horizon 8:56-71
Spr '66
What we can't cover with plants, we'll paint
N Y Times Mag p 18-19+ Ag 14 '66
SCHNEIDER, Ronald M.
U.S. policy in Latin America. bibliog f Cur
Hist 51:257-63 N '66
SCHNEIDER, William J.
Experts look at water in the national parks.
Nat Parks Mag 40:20-1 Ag '66
Water and the Everglades. Natur Hist 75:32-
41 N '66
SCHNEIDER and company. See France—In-
dustries
SCHNEIDERMAN, Herbert, and others
Patterns of alkaline phosphatase in develop-
ing drosophila. bibliog Science 151:461-3 Ja
28 '66
SCHNEIER, Arthur
Time runs out for Russia's Jews; ed. by J.
Star. por Look 30:100+ N 29 '66
SCHNEIRLA, T. C.
Books in review. Natur Hist 75:16+ D '66
SCHNETZLER, C. C. and others
Rubidium-strontium age of the Bosumtwi
crater area, Ghana, compared with the age
of the Ivory Coast tektites. bibliog Science
151:817-19 F 18 '66
SCHNEYER, Leon H.
Salivary secretion. Science 155:115+ Ja 6 '67
SCHNITZER, M. and Kodama, H.
Montmorillonite: effect of pH on its absorp-
tion of a soil humic compound. bibliog
Science 153:70-1 Jl 1 '66
SCHOEN, Barbara
Identity crisis; story. Seventeen 25:134-5 F '66
SCHOEN, Elin
Traveling with Mlle: skdl, et al. Mlle 63:
351+ Ag '66
SCHOENBERG, Arnold. See Schönberg, A.
SCHOENBERNER, Franz
False prophet of the blond beast. Sat R 49:
32-3 Mr 19 '66
Historical interpretation of horror. Sat R 49:
40+ F 5 '66
SCHOENBRUN, David
Cassandra tradition. Sat R 49:32-3 Ap 23
'66
Red tape road to Berlin. Sat R 49:30-2 Mr 26
'66
They both served France. Sat R 49:31 Ag
6 '66
Tragic course in Vietnam. Sat R 49:23-4 My
28 '66
SCHOENMAECKERS, Ernest
Dutch bishops speak. America 115:414 O 8 '66
SCHOENSTEIN, Ralph
Shaggy-dog story. il Newsweek 68:68 N 28
'66
SCHÖFFER, Nicolas
Sculptures in motion; with report by D.
Bourdon. il Life 61:41-3+ Ag 12 '66
SCHOLARS
Need for scholars; address, May 11, 1966.
L. B. Johnson. Vital Speeches 32:482-4
Je 1 '66
Scholar and the administrator in interna-
tional affairs. W. R. Polk. il Bul Atomic
Sci 22:2-8 Mr '66
Scholar and the alienated generation; ad-
dress, May 16, 1966. A. C. Baird. Vital
Speeches 32:590-3 Jl 15 '66
See also
College professors and instructors
SCHOLARS, Russian. See Russia—Intellectual
life
SCHOLARSHIPS and fellowships
Anniversary of the Fulbright act; Interna-
tional education act now in Congress. J.
Cass. Sat R 49:47-8 Ag 20 '66
As long as you're up, get me a grant. Es-
quire 65:87+ Je '66
Boothbay's scholarship fund. C. B. Norwood.
NEA J 56:85-6 Ja '67
Choosing graduate fellows. D. Wolfle. Sci-
ence 154:1279 D 9 '66
Deadline in Dixie; athletic scholarships.
Sports Illus 24:11 Je 6 '66
In darkest Fulbright; the Fulbright pro-
gram. R. Kostelanetz. Nation 202:725-6 Je
13 '66; Reply. O. Handlin. 203:434+ O 31
'66
Maybe he can become a doctor. C. Carner.
il Todays Health 44:22-3+ My '66
Nominations invited for ALA awards. Library
J 91:6176 D 15 '66
Nominations sought for 1967 ALA awards.
Library J 91:6052-3+ D 15 '66
Off-the-job training; scholarships for experi-
enced journalists. il Time 87:74 Je 3 '66

SCHOLARSHIPS and fellowships—*Continued*
Speaking out; colleges short-change their football players. M. Shaara. Sat Eve Post 239:10+ N 5 '66
View from the top; White House fellows program. il Newsweek 67:62 Ap 4 '66
Year at the top; the White House fellows. T. W. Carr. il Am Ed 2:1-3 F '66
See also
Carnegie corporation of New York
College students—Aid
Rhodes scholars and scholarships
United Nations institute for training and research
United States—National science foundation
United States—State, Department of—Foreign scholarships, Board of

SCHOLASTIC ability. See Ability

SCHOLASTIC achievements. See Student achievements

SCHOLASTIC institute of student opinion. See Scholastic research center

SCHOLASTIC magazines, incorporated
Art and photography award winners chosen. il Sr Schol 88:sup 12 My 6 '66
At our corner; Fiction for young adults awards program; Educators paperback service; Folkways/Scholastic records. il Sr Schol 89:sup21 S 30 '66
At our corner; field operations program. il Sr Schol 89:sup22 O 7 '66
At our corner; M. Asch, consultant for new Folkways Scholastic records program. Sr Schol 89:sup22 N 11 '66
At our corner; social studies series. Sr Schol 89:sup22 D 2 '66
National advisory council. il Sr Schol 88:sup 14 My 13 '66
Presenting the 1966 Scholastic awards. il Sr Schol 88:12-20+ My 20 '66
Scholastic and Disney sign book agreement. il Pub W 189:30-1 Ap 4 '66
Scholastic 'round the world. Sr Schol 88:sup22 F 25 '66
Scholastic teacher travel awards. Sr Schol 88:sup 17-18+ Ap 15 '66
Student's work is published; concerning sketch in Scholastic scope. M. A. Elliott. il Sr Schol 89:sup47-8 S 23 '66

SCHOLASTIC magazines and books services (firm)
Scholastic offers $11,000 prizes for new fiction. Pub W 190:43 Ag 15 '66

SCHOLASTIC research center
At our corner; Scholastic research center & Institute of student opinion. il Sr Schol 87:sup 14 Ja 7 '66
National service corps for young Americans; poll by Scholastic magazine's Institute of student opinion. Sr Schol 89:26 D 9 '66

SCHOLASTIC teacher. See Senior scholastic (periodical)

SCHOLEM, Gershom
Jews and Germans; excerpt from address at World Jewish congress, 1966; tr. by W. J. Dannhauser. Commentary 42:31-8 N '66
about
Cosmic religion. M. Eliade. Commentary 41:95-6+ Mr '66

SCHOLES, Robert
Confessions of a reformed bibliomaniac; summary of address. Pub W 190:30-1 Ag 1 '66

SCHOLL, David W. and others
Exposure of basement rock on the continental slope of the Bering Sea. bibliog Science 153:992-4 Ag 26 '66

SCHOLL, S. E.
Two toadstools and a wall of water. Am City 81:94-5 Mr '66

SCHOLL, Sharon
Music for dancers. Dance Mag 40:60-1+ O '66

SCHOLZ, Lucile
Mansion: an old doll house. Hobbies 71:122 Ag '66

SCHON, Donald A.
New regionalism. Harvard Bsns R 44:30-2+ Ja '66

SCHÖNBERG, Arnold
Moses and Aron. Criticism
Life 62:18 Ja 20 '67
New Yorker 42:198+ D 10 '66
Opera N il 30:14-15 My 7 '66
Opera N il 31:26-7 D 31 '66
Sat R 49:41 D 17 '66
Time il 88:95 D 9 '66
On records: Gurre-lieder. Opera N 30:34 Ja 29 '66
Schoenberg revealed by Gould. A. Rich. il Sat R 49:78 S 24 '66
Schoenberg still ascendant. Discus. Harper 232:120-2 F '66

SCHONBERG, Harold C.
Artist behind the Steinbergian mask. N Y Times Mag p48-51+ N 13 '66
Greatest single influence on today's conductors. N Y Times Mag p46-7+ Ja 8 '67
Phantom of the opera. N Y Times Mag p 10-11+ F 6 '66

SCHOOL activities. See Student activities

SCHOOL administration. See School management and organization

SCHOOL administrators. See School superintendents and principals

SCHOOL age
School at age four. Sch & Soc 94:345 O 29 '66

SCHOOL and social and economic problems
Doctor Daniel Fader: a child without books is impoverished; summary of address. June 6, 1966. D. N. Fader. il Pub W 189:33-5 Je 20 '66
Harlem childhood. J. O'Gara. Commonweal 84:353 Je 17 '66
Lesson from Watts: it can happen here. C. C. Trillingham. il PTA Mag 61:12-14 O '66
Our children are dying, by N. Hentoff. Review
Nation 203:520-1 N 14 '66. M. R. Berube
Profiles; E. Shapiro, principal of P.S. 119 and its replacement P.S. 92, Harlem. N. Hentoff. New Yorker 42:52-4+ My 7 '66
Schoolchildren: growing up in the slums, by M. F. Greene and O. Ryan. Review
Commonweal 84:371-3 Je 17 '66. N. Hentoff
Reporter 34:47-8 My 5 '66. P. Herrera
See also
Socially handicapped children—Education

SCHOOL and society (periodical)
Status of School and society, 1965-66. W. W. Brickman. Sch & Soc 94:310 O 15 '66

SCHOOL and the community
Art & human planning issue; symposium. bibliog il Sch Arts 65:5-22 Ap '66
Roots of failure. K. C. Cotter; M. W. Hass; J. E. Mizer. il NEA J 55:33-6 Ap '66
School system that failed; with discussion group program, by M. S. Smart. W. Hartley and E. Hartley. il Parents Mag 41:26, 52-3+ Mr '66

SCHOOL and the home
Homework in American school and community. H. H. Punke. Sch & Soc 94:327-30 O 15 '66
How parents feel; survey of attitudes toward schools, made for the Charles F. Kettering foundation. Time 87:51 Je 3 '66
Open house adds up. NEA J 55:56 S '66
Parents can help their children succeed in school. G. G. Unruh. il NEA J 55:14-16 D '66
See also
Home study

SCHOOL annuals. See High school annuals

SCHOOL architecture. See School buildings

SCHOOL assemblies. See School programs

SCHOOL athletics
Don't rush kids into organized sports. W. Sloan and D. West. il Parents Mag 41:78-9+ S '66
See also
Basketball
Physical education and training

SCHOOL attendance
Financial status of public schools, 1966. B. V. Bechdolt and J. M. Flanigan. il NEA J 55:55-6 O '66
See also
Dropouts

SCHOOL boards
Response from a school board member. J. G. Solberg. Mo Labor R 89:622-3 Je '66

SCHOOL books. See Textbooks

SCHOOL breakfasts. See Breakfasts

SCHOOL buildings
Circle and square for an Indiana school; Lincoln elementary school, Columbus, Ind. il Arch Rec 140:95-7 Ag '66
Cluster of huts: Swiss high school. il Arch Forum 124:86-91 Ja '66
Harlem's besieged showpiece: Intermediate school 201. J. Bailey. il Arch Forum 125:48-51 N '66
Hooded roofs reaching for the sky; Columbus, Ind. il Arch Forum 125:48-53 D '66
John W. Chorley elementary school, Middletown, N.Y. il Arch Rec 139:148-50 Je '66
Little red schoolhouse goes modern. A. Hamilton. il Read Digest 89:164-6+ O '66
New school has three kinds of flexible space; Candlewood junior high school, Long Island, N.Y. il Arch Rec 140:225-6 S '66
Planning preschool facilities. M. P. Berson and W. W. Chase. il Am Ed 2:7-11 D '65

SCHOOL buildings—*Continued*
Schools: building types study. il Arch Rec 139:163-82 F '66
Shape of schools: today and tomorrow. S. Miller. il Todays Health 44:58-63 S '66
Steps down to the sea; private school in Spain. il Arch Forum 125:44-7 D '66
Tomorrow's schools are here today. A. Hamilton. il PTA Mag 61:4-7 O '66; Same with title Little red schoolhouse goes modern. Read Digest 89:164-6+ O '66
What's new in urban school buildings? C. W. Brubaker. il NEA J 55:26-9 D '66

SCHOOL bus transportation. See School children—Transportation

SCHOOL buttons. See Schools—Insignia

SCHOOL children
Children's school complaints; with study-discussion program, by E. Harris and D. Harris. bibliog il PTA Mag 60:4-6, 36-7 My '66
Forgotten youth in today's America: the "just average" majority. il U S News 60:52-4+ F 21 '66
Sex makes a difference; complication in teaching. il Time 88:114+ D 16 '66
    See also
Intelligence tests
Problem children
School age
School lunches
Teachers and students

Adjustment
When a child's afraid of school. J. Wiener. il Parents Mag 41:72-3+ S '66
    See also
Problem children

Grading and promotion
See Grading and marking (students)

Photographs
Teach me! excerpts. C. Purcell. Sat R 49:72-3 D 17 '66

Punishment
See School discipline

Reading
See Childrens reading

Transportation
Why the school bus doesn't stop; battle over amendment proposing local options for the transportation of non-public school children in Omaha, Neb. R. T. Reilly. il America 116:21-3 Ja 7 '67

SCHOOL children and strangers. See Children and strangers

SCHOOL childrens boners. See Blunders

SCHOOL clubs. See Student activities

SCHOOL construction. See School buildings

SCHOOL counselors. See Personnel service in education

SCHOOL dances. See Student activities

SCHOOL discipline
Discipline isn't dated; with study-discussion program. R. Strang. bibliog il PTA Mag 61:26-8, 34 N '66
Hair-do's, and don'ts; faculty-student squabbles over hair and dress styles. il Newsweek 68:94 O 3 '66
Hairsplitting; senior suspended because of length of hair; Unionville, Pa. il Time 87:55-6 My 27 '66
Long hair and mini-skirts; styles in the classroom. P. Woodring. Sat R 50:55-6 Ja 21 '67

SCHOOL districts
Impact impasse; Stanford report on assistance to school districts with federal government installations. Reporter 34:14+ Mr 24 '66
Local districts react with bold proposals; project proposals for supplementary education centers and services. Sr Schol 87:sup4 Ja 21 '66
Neighborhood school? P. Schrag. Sat R 49:84 D 17 '66
Some children the schools have never served. R. Coles. il Sat R 49:58-60 Je 18 '66

SCHOOL drama. See College and school drama

SCHOOL entrance age. See School age

SCHOOL excursions
Age of discovery. V. Wagner. il Parks & Rec 1:904-5 N '66
Whaling in Old Mystic. B. Zino. il Sch Arts 65:33-5 Ap '66

SCHOOL finance
Characteristics of good school financing. W. R. Fulton and J. C. Moffitt. PTA Mag 60:14 F '66
Education and the bond market. See issues of American education
    See also
Colleges and universities—Finance
Education—Economic aspects

Statistics
Financial status of public schools, 1966. B. V. Bechdolt and J. M. Flanigan. NEA J 55:55-6 O '66

SCHOOL for scandal; drama. See Sheridan, R. B. B.

SCHOOL for wives; story. See O'Connor, F.

SCHOOL furniture, equipment, etc.
Teacher-opinion poll: who provides school supplies? il NEA J 55:44 N '66

SCHOOL grading and promotion. See Grading and marking (students)

SCHOOL grounds
Of the wayward bus, the tattered tarp, and other surplus things; playground equipment at Stephen F. Austin elementary school in San Angelo, Tex. L. Lewis. il Am Ed 2:1-3 S '66
School landscaping in Dublin; Nielsen school, Dublin, Calif. il Sunset 137:230 N '66

SCHOOL houses. See School buildings

SCHOOL laboratories

Equipment
Some current trends in school laboratory design. il Arch Rec 140:188-9 N '66

SCHOOL laws and legislation
PTA in Washington. Mrs E. F. Ryan. PTA Mag 61:24 Ja '67

Arkansas
    See also
Evolution—Laws and legislation

United States
Equal educational opportunity act of 1967; excerpts from proposals. Sat R 49:66+ D 17 '66
How to get into the acts. il Sr Schol 89:sup 17-19 O 21 '66
Library education; Title XI of the National defense education act. P. P. Price and H. A. Carl. ALA Bul 61:27-8 Ja '67
1966 NDEA institutes announced in advanced school library study; also education courses. Library J 91:354+ Ja 15 '66
Promises fulfilled; progress under Title I of the Elementary and secondary education act of 1965. R. Goff. il Am Ed 2:10-17 F '66
When Wisconsin pine went to college; Morrill land-grant college act of 1862. establishment of Cornell. E. Swift. il Am For 72:8-9+ Ja '66
    See also
Federal aid to education

SCHOOL leaving. See Dropouts

SCHOOL librarians
Educating school librarians. F. K. Johnson. Library J 91:4894-6 O 15 '66
School librarians; address, July 11, 1966. J. E. Fogarty. Vital Speeches 32:682-4 S 1 '66
School libraries today; interview, ed. by W. D. Boutwell. M. V. Gaver. Sr Schol 88:sup 1-3 My 20 '66
Why not listen to the librarian? E. R. Christine; discussion. ALA Bul 60:99-100, 211-13 F. Mr '66
    See also
American association of school librarians

Supply and demand
Washington report. J. Lloyd. Sr Schol 88:sup8 Ap 15 '66

SCHOOL librarians institutes. See Library institutes and workshops

SCHOOL libraries
Arts, the humanities, and the school library; symposium, ed. by E. E. Ahlers. il ALA Bul 60:899-908+ O '66
Books persist. H. Borland. il Am Ed 2:8-12 Mr '66
Education act: off the ground; symposium. il Library J 91:1009-32+ F 15 '66
80 per cent for library resources; Title II of the Elementary and secondary education act. R. H. Smith. Pub W 189:280 Ja 24 '66
Elementary school library collection, ed. by M. V. Gaver. Review
    Library J 90:5492-4 D 15 '65. D. M. Broderick; Discussion. 91:1601-4 Mr 15 '66

SCHOOL libraries—*Continued*
Federal legislation and programs to assist school libraries. M. H. Mahar. ALA Bul 60:153-6 F '66
Freeing kids for learning. G. K. Hodenfield. il PTA Mag 60:8-10 Je '66
Highlights of 1965. Library J 91:360 Ja 15 '66
Instant access to students' reading levels; University of Chicago laboratory school. E. L. Thomas. il Library J 91:2165-8 Ap 15 '66
School libraries today; interview, ed. by W. D. Boutwell. M. V. Gaver. Sr Schol 88:sup 1-3 My 20 '66
Suburbia: the target area; paucity of books dealing with social problems: adaptation of address, May 1966. P. Evarts. il Wilson Lib Bul 41:173-6+ O '66
Twenty-seven tips for the new librarian. H. Wheeler. il Library J 91:6164-5 D 15 '66
Vote for flexible scheduling; visits by individual students and class groups throughout the school day. il Library J 91:4192-6+ S 15 '66
See also
High school libraries
Knapp school libraries project
Libraries and schools

Acquisitions
Book bind tight as ESEA nears deadline; difficulties of manufacturers, publishers, and wholesalers in filling school orders. Library J 91:2612-13 My 15 '66
Suppose butter; problems in spending federal money. J. Weatherford. Library J 91:3366 Jl '66

Administration
See Library administration

Censorship
March hare mother; excerpt from America and Americans. J. Steinbeck. Library J 91:6169 D 15 '66
N.J. governor vetoes antismut bill; school librarians' influence cited. Virginia librarians confronted with immoral classics. sex books. il Library J 91:1043-5 F 15 '66
Not on the list; Hanover County, Va. ALA Bul 60:691+ Jl '66
Sex education and the censor. E. Geller. Library J 91:2118 Ap 15 '66
Virginia book ban controversy grows. Library J 91:1632+ Mr 15 '66

Circulation, loans, etc.
Circulation procedures: catching overdues; letter to the editor. F. Heinritz. Library J 91:5666+ N 15 '66

Designs and plans
Learning center focuses on multi-use library; Eaglebrook school, Deerfield, Mass. il Arch Rec 139:164-7 F '66

Extension work
See School library extension

Hours of opening
School library extension service: real or imagined? report of survey of selected California schools. E. R. Christine. ALA Bul 60:623-6 Je '66

Paperback books
Elementary paperback: a trial run; Edgewood elementary school, Scarsdale, N.Y.; with bibliography. E. Rabban. il Library J 91:2591-8 My 15 '66
Paperback boom seen for future school libraries. Library J 91:4238-9 S 15 '66; Discussion. 91:5666 N 15 '66
Pointers on paperbacks; selling paperbacks in a school library, Newton, Mass. E. Hall. il Library J 91:2589-91 My 15 '66
Space problems analyzed for paperbacks in schools; summary of discussions at conference at Teachers college, Columbia university. il Pub W 190:31-4 Jl 25 '66

Periodical collections
How to start with long-term subscriptions; Oceana high school, Pacifica, Calif. G. J. Figgins. il Library J 91:2168-9 Ap 15 '66

Standards
New standards: revision by AASL. E. Geller. Library J 91:4154+ S 15 '66

Technical processes
Is central processing for you? services in Montgomery County, Md. R. L. Darling. Library J 91:6153-6 D 15 '66

Work with blind
Card catalog for the blind; Arkansas school for the blind, Little Rock, Ark. il Wilson Lib Bul 40:830-1 My '66
School library program for the blind; Lakeland school district, Mohegan Lake, N.Y. S. M. Mahoney and L. Z. Stokes. Wilson Lib Bul 40:829+ My '66
SCHOOL libraries and art; School libraries and publishers; etc. *See* Libraries and art; Libraries and publishers; etc.
SCHOOL library architecture. *See* Library architecture
SCHOOL library catalogs. *See* Catalogs, Library
SCHOOL library extension
School library extension service: real or imagined? report of survey of selected California schools. E. R. Christine. ALA Bul 60:623-6 Je '66
SCHOOL lunches
My kids love the school lunch; with recipes. K. Kuperstock. il Parents Mag 41:86-7+ S '66
School lunches: the changes proposed. U S News 60:9 Mr 28 '66
Will your child eat lunch at school? B. F. Olsen. il Parents Mag 41:84-5+ S '66
SCHOOL management and organization
Crisis in the administration of inner city schools. D. U. Levine. Sch & Soc 94:322-4 O 15 '66
Current issues facing leadership in the school library field; adaptation of address, July 1966. H. G. Shane. ALA Bul 60:923-6 O '66
Regional approaches to educational problems. P. F. Johnston. NEA J 55:27-8+ Ap '66
What educational plan for the in-between-ager? the six-three-three plan and others. W. M. Alexander. il NEA J 55:30-2 Mr '66
See also
Cheating in schoolwork
School discipline
School districts
School superintendents and principals

Teacher participation
Professional negotiation for improving education. C. J. Hannan. il NEA J 55:56-7 D '66
School administrators view professional negotiation; excerpts. NEA J 56:23-5 Ja '67
SCHOOL mathematics study group
Mathematics curriculum: new study; letter. E. G. Begle. Science 151:632 F 11 '66
SCHOOL music
See also
Musical education
SCHOOL of American ballet, incorporated
Three California brothers; report on 1964-65 Ford foundation national scholarship program. M. Moseley. il Dance Mag 40:32-3 Mr '66
SCHOOL of the arts of St James' community center, Harlem. *See* New York (city)—Community centers
SCHOOL organization. *See* School management and organization
SCHOOL playgrounds. *See* School grounds
SCHOOL plays. *See* College and school drama
SCHOOL prayer. *See* Public schools and religion
SCHOOL prayer decision. *See* United States —Supreme court—Decisions
SCHOOL programs
Tragedy of the tombs; art assembly program; Alex G. Barret junior high school in Louisville. R. Friedman. il Sch Arts 65:36-8 My '66
SCHOOL projects. *See* Projects (teaching)
SCHOOL reports and records
Parents and report cards; with study-discussion program, by E. Harris and D. Harris. E. Klemm. bibliog il PTA Mag 61:24-6, 36 O '66
Should teachers see student records? J. Wellington; C. B. Wellington; E. Lawton. il NEA J 55:35-7 O '66
What good are report cards? P. K. McCauley. il Parents Mag 41:42-3+ Je '66
SCHOOL research. *See* Research
SCHOOL sessions. *See* School year
SCHOOL statistics. *See* Education—Statistics
SCHOOL subjects. *See* Courses of study
SCHOOL superintendents and principals
Change in Chicago. Newsweek 67:98 My 23 '66
Collective bargaining: a primer for superintendents. L. B. Ball. il Sat R 50:70-1+ Ja 21 '67

SCHOOL superintendents and principals—*Cont.*
Needed: a new breed of school superintendent. A. R. Talbot. Harper 232:81-2+ F '66; Discussion. 232:14+ Ap; 11 My '66
See also
National association of secondary-school principals
National education association—Department of elementary school principals

SCHOOL supplies. See School furniture, equipment, etc.

SCHOOL surveys. See Educational surveys

SCHOOL teachers. See Teachers

SCHOOL teaching. See Teaching

SCHOOL terms. See School year

SCHOOL-to-school program
Foreign aid: school to school. J. Daniel. Read Digest 88:65-8 F '66
New idea in foreign aid. J. Daniel. il PTA Mag 60:7-9+ F '66; Same abr. with title Foreign aid: school to school. Read Digest 88:65-8 F '66
Project Sam; Tipton, Iowa and Samororo, Guatemala. O. Bay. il Farm J 90:66 My '66
School-to-school; a partnership in understanding. J. Vaughn. Parents Mag 41:30+ Je '66
Thousand partnerships. G. E. Bradley. il Am Ed 2:1-4 Je '66
Upper Darby senior high builds a school in Africa. R. Hoopes. il Seventeen 25:98-9+ Ap '66

SCHOOL visitations. See School and the home

SCHOOL year
Why not year-round schools? J. Engh. il Sat R 49:82-4 S 17 '66; Same abr. with title Case for year-round schools. Read Digest 89:141-4 D '66

SCHOOLS
See also
High schools
Kindergarten
Nursery schools
Parochial schools, Catholic
School buildings
Sunday schools
Textbooks

Insignia
School buttons. D. F. Brown. il Hobbies 71:50-1 Ap '66

Statistics
See Education—Statistics

Cuba
American in Cuba; visit to Ciudad Camille Cienfuegos, a school-city. E. R. John. il Nation 202:297-9 Mr 14 '66

England
See also
Public schools (endowed)—England

Guatemala
Project Sam. O. Bay. il Farm J 90:66 My '66

Russia
Question of quality. Time 88:33 D 30 '66

United States
See also
Education—United States
Public schools—United States

SCHOOLS, Experimental
Moment of learning; Fifteenth street school, New York. G. B. Leonard. il Look 30:24-30 D 27 '66
This amazing new school; Pittsburgh learning research & development center. R. C. Davids. il Farm J 90:32-3+ S '66
See also
Special classes and special schools

SCHOOLS, Medical. See Medical colleges

SCHOOLS, Traveling
See also
Colleges and universities, Traveling

SCHOOLS and libraries. See Libraries and schools

SCHOOLS and social and economic problems. See School and social and economic problems

SCHOOLS for dogs. See Dogs—Training

SCHOOLS of nursing. See Nurses and nursing—Training

SCHOONER racing. See Yacht racing

SCHOONERS
They couldn't beat Bluenose. D. MacDonald. il Read Digest 89:118-22 O '66

SCHOONOVER, Shirley
Finland. Holiday 40:62-7+ N '66

SCHOPF, J. William. See Barghoorn, E. S. jt. auth.

SCHOPP, Walter W.
Cryogenic liquid level controls. Electr World 76:36-8+ D '66

SCHOR, Resia
Jewelry by Resia Schor. R. Howard. il Craft Horiz 26:8-11+ Jl '66

SCHORR, Alvin L.
Program for the social orphans. N Y Times Mag p32-3+ Mr 13 '66

SCHORR, Daniel
He brought Berlin back to life. Sat R 49:30-1 My 28 '66

SCHORSKE, Carl
Profess with a passion. il por Time 87:83 My 6 '66

SCHOTT, Webster
Life book review. Life 61:14 S 16; 8 O 21; 8+ N 18 '66
Shriek from wasted women. Life 61:17 D 16 '66

SCHRAG, Peter
Boston: education's last hurrah. Sat R 49: 56-8+ My 21 '66
Irrelevance of Dick and Jane. Nation 202: 335-7 Mr 21 '66
New pedagogy. Reporter 35:58-60 S 22 '66
Pittsburgh: the virtues of candor. Sat R 48:82-4+ N 19 '66
Voices in the classroom. Sat R 49:85-6 S 17; 87 O 15; 97 N 19; 84 D 17 '66; 50:74 Ja 21 '67

SCHRAGE, Chuck
USPS is 54! Yachting 119:61+ Ja '66
With the power squadrons. See issues of Yachting

SCHRAM, Martin
Goof-ball set: addiction in the suburbs. Nation 203:242-5 S 19 '66

SCHRAMM, B. J.
Poor man's back-yard whirlybird. K. V. Brown. il por Pop Mech 126:132-3 D '66

SCHRAMM, Tex
Here's how it happened; ed. by T. Maule. por Sports Illus 24:14-19 Je 20 '66

SCHRAMM, Wilbur
Social and educational implications of communication satellites; adaptation of address, December 6-10, 1965. Sch & Soc 94:346-8 O 29 '66
What TV is doing to our children; summary of The effects of television on children and adolescents. Sr Schol 88:sup9-10 F 18 '66

SCHREIBER, Carol T.
Intellectual gymnasium. Library J 91:326-8 Ja 15 '66

SCHREIBER, Flora Rheta
Pat Nugent's parents tell: how to be a White House in-law. Ladies Home J 83:110-12 Ag '66
Watching Johnny's memory grow. Todays Health 44:22-4+ O '66
—and Herman, Melvin
ESP enters the laboratory. Sci Digest 60: 48-54 O '66
Inside psychiatry today. See issues of Science digest

SCHREMP, Gerry
Great dinners. Life 61:89+ S 9 '66
World's best spaghetti sauce. Life 60:124-5+ Ap 15 '66

SCHRIEVER, Bernard A.
Quiet retirement. il por Time 88:24 S 9 '66
Salute to a general. W. J. Coughlin. Tech W 19:50 S 5 '66

SCHRIFTGIESSER, Karl
Keeping watch on the economy. Sat R 49: 65-6+ Ja 8; 27 F 26 '66

SCHROEDER, Gerald L. and others
Lithium-drifted germanium detectors: applications to neutron-activation analysis. Science 151:815-17 F 18 '66

SCHROEDER, Henry Alfred
Cadmium & blood pressure. il por Time 88:61-2+ N 4 '66
Killer cadmium. il por Newsweek 68:73 N 7 '66

SCHROEDER, M. R.
Architectural acoustics. bibliog Science 151: 1355-9 Mr 18 '66

SCHROEDER, R. J.
Etc (cont) Commonweal 83:696-7; 85:139-41 Mr 18. N 4 '66

SCHROTEL, Stanley
Policing the grocery store. por Time 88:111 S 16 '66

SCHROTH, Raymond A.
...And get back a man. America 115:382-4 O 1 '66
Between the lines (cont) America 114:356, 699; 115:98, 284, 550, 777 Mr 12, My 14, Jl 23, S 17, N 5, D 10 '66
Ecumenical encounter. America 114:552-3 Ap 16 '66

SCHROTH, Raymond A.—*Continued*
New books. Cath World 204:182-4 D '66
Of many things; the human church in Los
Angeles. America 115:236 S 10 '66

SCHUBART, Joachim
Comet Tempel-Tuttle: recovery of the long-
lost comet of the November meteors. bibliog
Science 152:1236-7 My 27 '66

SCHUBERT, Franz Peter
Records:
Die schöne müllerin. Opera N 31:32 O
15 '66
Schubert by Souzay. A. Sperber. Am Rec
G 32:425 Ja '66

SCHUBERT, Jack
Chelation in medicine; with biographical
sketch. Sci Am 214:16, 40-50 My; 215:6 Jl
'66

SCHUBERT, Terrence
Schubert's shards. A. Thorpe. il Craft Horiz
26:18-19 Ja '66

SCHUBERTH, Christopher J.
Hudson's six geologies; with biographical
sketch. Natur Hist 76:7, 46-55 bibliog(p73)
Ja '67

SCHUCHMAN, Robert M.
Obituary
Nat R 18:307 Ap 5 '66. W. F. Buckley,
jr

SCHUESSLER, Raymond
Painting still-life. Design 67:16-17 Ja '66

SCHULBERG, Budd
My wonderful lousy poem. Read Digest 89:67-
9 Ag '66
West coast of Mexico. Holiday 39:46-59+
Ap '66
about
Screenwriter in the ghetto. il por Time 88:
53 Jl 22 '66

SCHULER, Graham, and others
Low-noise, interference-resistant amplifier
suitable for biological signals. Science 154:
1191-2 D 2 '66

SCHULER, Stanley
Bright young men choose business careers.
Nations Bsns 54:46-7+ Je '66

SCHULKE, Flip
How to take pictures at ten fathoms. S.
James. il Pop Mech 127:110-13 Ja '67

SCHULLER, Gunther
In the third stream. por Newsweek 68:108
O 24 '66
Music to my ears. I. Kolodin. Sat R 49:45
Ap 2 '66
Out of Ellison into Kafka. H. W. Heins-
heimer. il por Sat R 49:86-7 N 12 '66
Visitation. Criticism
Hi Fi il 16:MA28-9 D '66
Reporter 35:58-9 N 17 '66
Time il 88:92 O 21 '66

SCHULTZ, Morton J.
Go ahead, do your own body work! Pop Mech
127:178-81+ Ja '67
Saturday mechanic. See issues of Popular
mechanics
Where even Santa gets ideas. Pop Mech 126:
76-9+ D '66
Wild new weapons for Vietnam. Pop Mech
127:95-8+ Ja '67
Winter tune-up for your cycle (cont) Pop
Mech 125:170-3+ F '66

SCHULTZ, Robert S.
Understanding economic growth. Harvard
Bsns R 44:32-4+ N '66

SCHULTZ, Sheila
1965-66 music season. Hi Fi 16:65-9 D 15 '66

SCHULTZE, Charles Louis
Close-up; interview, ed. by J. Berry. pors
Duns R 87:8-9+ Je '66
Inside view of the new budget; interview.
pors Nations Bsns 55:42-3+ Ja '67
about
Research policy: trumpets on Capitol hill.
D. S. Greenberg. Science 153:278 Jl 15 '66

SCHULTZE, Mildred
Art experiences and divergent thinking. Sch
Arts 65:37-40 Mr '66

SCHULZ, Charles M.
Peanuts festival; excerpts from Peanuts
books. il McCalls 93:106-11 S '66

SCHULZ, Theodore E.
Mental health trap. Nat R 18:510-12+ My 31
'66

SCHULZE, Fred
Schulze and Schulze. il Pop Phot 58:76-81
Ap '66

SCHULZE, K. L.
Can fish farms clean our polluted waters? Sat
R 49:62-3 Je 4; 51 Jl 2 '66

SCHULZE, Marti
Schulze and Schulze. il Pop Phot 58:76-81
Ap '66

SCHUMACHER, Anne W. See Cavonus, C. R. jt.
auth.

SCHUMACHER, E. F.
Growing pains. Commentary 42:137-40+ O '66

SCHUMACHER, G. F. B.
Acute phase protein in serum of women
using hormonal contraceptives. bibliog Science 153:901-2 Ag 19 '66

SCHUMANN, Robert Alexander
Brahms string quartets, and a great
Schumann quintet; Serkin-Budapest and
the Wellers. H. Glass. il Am Rec G 32:
603 Mr '66
Musical events; performance of Scenes from
Faust, by Boston symphony orchestra with
soloists and chorus. W. Sargeant. New
Yorker 42:168 Mr 12 '66

SCHUR, Edwin M.
Abortion on demand. Nation 203:492-3 N 7
'66
Psychiatrists under attack: rebellious Dr
Szasz. Atlan 217:72-6 Je '66

SCHURR, George M.
Reflections on biological engineering. Christian Cent 83:1300-3 O 26 '66
Why bother about life beyond death? Christian Cent 83:424-6 Ap 6 '66

SCHURR, J. M. and McLaren, A. D.
Enzyme action: comparison on soluble and insoluble substrate. bibliog Science 152:1064-
6 My 20 '66

SCHUSTER, M. Lincoln
Schuster's statement on the sale of his S&S
stock. Pub W 189:100 F 14 '66

SCHUSTERMAN, Ronald J. and others
Underwater vocalization by sea lions: social
and mirror stimuli. bibliog Science 154:540-
2 O 28 '66

SCHUTZ, George
Putting the art before the war horse. il por
Time 88:83 S 9 '66
Sound sellers. Newsweek 67:88 F 28 '66

SCHÜTZ, Heinrich
Heinrich Schütz: Cantiones sacrae. J. W.
Barker. il Am Rec G 33:216-20+ N '66
In the service of Heinrich Schütz, choral
masterworks revealed. B. Jacobson. il Hi Fi
16:73+ Mr '66

SCHWAB, Fred
Fred Schwab: Synanon photographer. P.
Gowland. il por Pop Phot 59:28+ O '66

SCHWAB, Matty
Swardsmanship. il Newsweek 67:86 Je 6 '66

SCHWALBERG, Carol
(ed) See Harris, G. 3d. Face to face with a
writer-producer-director-actor
(ed) See Kelman, S. Face to face with a
successful political writer

SCHWARTZ, Abba P.
Role of the State department in the adminis-
tration and enforcement of the new immi-
gration law. bibliog f Ann Am Acad 367:93-
104 S '66
about
Knifing of Abba Schwartz. New Repub 154:
12-13 Mr 19 '66
Quietly dropped. New Repub 154:8 My 28 '66
Shortage of liberals. Commonweal 84:46-7
Ap 1 '66
Storm at State. il por Newsweek 67:27 Mr
21 '66
Trouble in four syllables. Time 87:27B-28 Mr
18 '66
Truth about the Abba Schwartz case. C.
Fritchey. Harper 232:33-4+ Je '66

SCHWARTZ, Alvin
Rainy day fun for kids. Parents Mag 41:40-
1+ Ap '66

SCHWARTZ, Benjamin
Chinese visions & American policies. Commentary 41:53-9 Ap '66

SCHWARTZ, David C.
Science of crisis diplomacy. H. Pryor. il Sci
Digest 59:33-6 Ap '66

SCHWARTZ, Delmore
Delmore Schwartz. M. L. Rosenthal. Poetry
109:181-3 D '66

SCHWARTZ, Edward L.
Caveats on estate planning. bibliog f Harvard Bsns R 44:48-50+ Mr '66

SCHWARTZ, Fred
Crafts in education. Craft Horiz 26:7-8 Ja '66

SCHWARTZ, Harry
Spy who came in from the cold war. Sat R
49:36-7 Ja 29 '66
Survival of the Soviet synagogue. Sat R 49:
42 N 26 '66

SCHWARTZ, Jonathan
Fine silk thread; story. Redbook 127:70-1 S '66
Singular honor; story. Redbook 128:68-9 N '66

SCHWARTZ, Maurice L.
Fluorescent tracer: transport in distance and depth in beach sands. bibliog Science 151:701 F 11 '66

SCHWARTZ, Simon M.
Drylot. Farm J 90:56R O '66

SCHWARTZ, Tony
Exhibition of sound. Pop Phot 58:22 Ap '66
Sound for photographers. See issues of Popular photography

SCHWARTZ, William F.
VD: wages of ignorance; excerpt from address. PTA Mag 61:14-17 S '66

SCHWEBELL, Gertrude C.
Nelly Sachs. Sat R 49:46-17 D 10 '66

SCHWEID, Bernard
Bookseller's Christmas memory. Pub W 190:79 D 26 '66

SCHWEITZER, Albert
Africa's answer to Schweitzer. C. C. O'Brien. Atlan 217:68-71 Mr '66; Reply. E. Olssen. 217:44 Je '66
Is Schweitzer dead? Albert Schweitzer international convocation, Aspen, Colo. C. Scipio. Atlan 218:41-4 Ag '66; Discussion. 218:48 O; 44 D '66
Schweitzer convocation at Aspen. H. A. Jack. Christian Cent 83:840-1 Je 29 '66

SCHWEITZER, Louis
Train of clients. H. Bowser. Sat R 49:26 Ap 16 '66

SCHWEITZER, N. Tina
Is the Job corps conservation program working? Am For 72:18-21+ Ag '66

SCHWEITZER, Pierre Paul
It's an uphill fight for monetary reform. il Bsns W p73-4+ S 24 '66
Muddy road to monetary reform. il Bsns W p40-1 O 1 '66

SCHWEIZER soaring school. See Aviation schools

SCHWINGER, Julian
Relativistic quantum field theory. bibliog Science 153:949-53 Ag 26 '66

SCIENCE
Books in review; the meaning of science. J. Oppenheimer. Natur Hist 75:4-10 My '66
Bringing the public to science; address, October 25, 1965. P. Weiss. Vital Speeches 32:221-4 Ja 15 '66
Goals in understanding science; excerpts from remarks, October 19, 1966. G. T. Seaborg. Sci N 90:354-6 O 29 '66
In the name of science, by H. L. Nieburg. Review
   Bul Atomic Sci 22:22-3 N '66. B. I. Spinrad
Look at twenty-five years of STS; address, March 7, 1966. G. T. Seaborg. il Sci N 89:181-2+ Mr 19 '66
Physical sciences notes. Sci N 90:471, 493, 510, 534, 564; 91:36 D 3-31 '66, Ja 14 '67
Please explain; questions and answers. See issues of Science digest
Russian and U.S. science: another view of the gap. Science 151:432 Ja 28 '66
Science forecast by HHH; excerpts from address. H. H. Humphrey. Sci N 90:52 Jl 23 '66
Science forecast for 1967. Sci N 91:20-1 Ja 7 '67
Science in a world of widening horizons; address, January 17, 1966. G. T. Seaborg. Dept State Bul 54:280-8 F 21 '66
Science of science. Sci Am 214:58 Je '66
   See also
American association for the advancement of science
Communication in science
Meteorology
Religion and science
Technology

Bibliography
Book reviews. See issues of Science
Books about science. D. Wolfle. Science 151:943 F 25 '66
Science and the common reader. E. Larrabee. Commentary 41:43-8 Je '66
Science, technology: high spots. il Pub W 189:50-78 Ap 18 '66
Science, technology: November-March high spots. il Pub W 190:44-72 N 14 '66
Scientific and technical books of 1965; one hundred outstanding titles for a general collection; comp. by R. L. Snyder. il Library J 91:1147-54 Mr 1 '66
Scientific, technical, and medical books to come; ed. by J. Putnam. Library J 91:5441-90 N 1 '66
Scientific, technical, and medical books to come; ed. by J. Putnam and K. Ahrens. Library J 91:3481-524+ Jl '66

Scientific, technical, and medical books to come; ed. by J. Putnam and J. Lindheim (cont) Library J 91:1264-313 Mr 1 '66

Exhibitions
Art in science; exhibit at 1965 annual meeting of the AAAS. D. G. Barry; discussion. Science 151:1170; 152: 1011-12 Mr 11, My 20 '66

Experiments
Safety in science projects. F. L. Snakenberg. il Sci N L 89:90-1 F 5 '66
   See also
Physics—Experiments

Federal aid
See Research—Federal aid

Fiction
See Science fiction

History
History of American science, a field finds itself; excerpts from address, December 1964. A. H. Dupree. bibliog f Am Hist R 71:863-74 Ap '66
Science in history, by J. D. Bernal. Review
   Sci Am 214:131-2+ Mr '66. N. W. Pirie

Information services
Information services: a guide to federal offerings. M. Zeiger. Science 153:722-4 Ag 12 '66

International aspects
Angled money; Senate hearings on methods for supervising research-spy money. Nation 203:140 Ag 22 '66
Anthropologists' debate: concern over future of foreign research. B. Nelson. Science 154:1525-7 D 23 '66
Capitol hill: science among nations. F. Sartwell. Sci N 90:566 D 31 '66
CERN and Serpukhov prepare for collaboration; European center for nuclear research and Soviet Union. V. K. McElheny. Science 153:622 Ag 5 '66
Congenital malformations and cancer: United States-Japan cooperative science program; report from meeting in Tokyo. R. W. Miller and H. Nishimura. Science 151:357-8 Ja 21 '66
Franco-Russian collaboration in science: De Gaulle's visit. V. K. McElheny. Science 153:43-5 Jl 1 '66
Hornig committee: beginning of a technological Marshall plan? B. Nelson. Science 154:1307-9 D 9 '66
International meetings. P. H. Abelson. Science 154:341 O 21 '66
International science activities: some new vistas open. J. Walsh. Science 152:1605-7 Je 17 '66; Reply. L. C. Mitchell. 153:483 Jl 29 '66
International scientific cooperation: an American view; reprint. G. C. McGhee. Dept State Bul 54:369-78 Mr 7 '66
Kapitsa's visit to England. V. K. McElheny. Science 153:725-7 Ag 12 '66
New outposts of science. E. Fedorov. il UNESCO Courier 19:14-18+ Jl '66
ONR London: two decades of scientific quid pro quo. J. Walsh. Science 154:623-5 N 4 '66
Peace questionnaire: Soviets seek views of U.S. scientists. E. Langer. Science 153:276-7 Jl 15 '66; Discussion. 153:1335-6; 154:338 S 16, O 21 '66
Research and the munitions list: scientific exchange not always easy. E. Langer. Science 154:625-6 N 4 '66
Transatlantic cooperation on research: new U.S. moves. V. K. McElheny. Science 152:190-1 Ap 8 '66
Two decades in the world of science. R. Calder. il UNESCO Courier 19:8-14 Jl '66
UNESCO: stress on development brings parity for science. J. Walsh. Science 154:990-3 N 25 '66
   See also
International geophysical year
Joint United States-Japan committee on scientific cooperation
Project Camelot
United States—State, Department of—International scientific and technological affairs, Office of

Juvenile literature
See Scientific literature for children

Periodicals
New Russian journal in genetics: letter. H. J. Muller. Science 151:938+ F 25 '66
   See also
Nature (periodical)
Worm runner's digest

SCIENCE—*Continued*

Philosophy

Aspects of scientific explanation and other essays in the philosophy of science, by C. G. Hempel. Review
　Sci Am 214:129-30+ F '66. S. Toulmin; Reply with rejoinder. E. Nagel. 214:8-11 Ap '66
　See also
Naturalism (philosophy)

Religious aspects

See Religion and science

Scholarships and fellowships

Grants, fellowships, and awards. See issues of Science
Tea leaves or the record? P. H. Abelson. Science 151:783 F 18 '66

Social aspects

Ethical basis of science; excerpt from Science and ethical values. B. Glass; discussion. Science 151:935; 152:294; 153:362+; 154:846-7 F 25, Ap 15, Jl 22, N 18 '66
It's two-thirds of a century; we've made it, so far. E. E. Morison. il N Y Times Mag p34-5+ Ap 24 '66
Other U.S. S. Dedijer. Bul Atomic Sci 22:28-30 F '66
Partners in progress; address, April 22, 1966. G. T. Seaborg. il Sci N 89:339-40+ My 7 '66
Science, choice, and human values; address, October 1965. A. M. Weinberg. il Bul Atomic Sci 22:8-13 Ap '66
Step to man, by J. R. Platt. Review
　Sat R 49:36 Ag 13 '66. S. Chase
Technical expert in a democracy. C. Nader. Bul Atomic Sci 22:28-30 My '66
Third culture. N. Cousins. il Sat R 49:42 My 7 '66
Where responsibility lies. J. G. Dash. Bul Atomic Sci 22:35-7 Ja '66
　See also
Society for social responsibility in science

Study and teaching

College scene. il Sci Digest 60:22-9 O; 42-7 N; 20-9 D '66; 61:39-40 Ja '67
Elementary science: a new scheme of instruction. R. M. Gagné; discussion. Science 151:1033; 152:1186 Mr 4, My 27 '66
New Jersey chicken trial: verdict for science. E. Langer. Science 152:479-81 Ap 22 '66
Science education in Africa. G. Burkhardt. Bul Atomic Sci 22:46-8 F '66
Science studies: a gathering of the clan in Edinburgh; report on International science studies seminar. J. Walsh. Science 154:1150-1 D 2 '66
Start early in science. F. L. Snakenberg. il Sci N 89:367-8 My 14 '66
　See also
Physics—Study and teaching

Projects

Safety in science projects. F. L. Snakenberg. il Sci N L 89:90-1 F 5 '66

Terminology

Do they dig you, daddio? communication between scientist and layman, adaptation of address; reprint. R. G. Lynch. Am For 72: 30-1+ F '66

Argentina

Crisis of Argentine science. T. Tellez. Bul Atomic Sci 22:32-4 D '66

Brazil

Science for development, a view from Latin America. J. L. Lopes. Bul Atomic Sci 22: 7-11 S '66

China (People's Republic)

China's science growing. Sci N L 89:91 F 5 '66
Chinese science: it's not a paper atom. J. M. H. Lindbeck. il N Y Times Mag p38-9+ Ja 8 '67
Over pots of tea: excerpts from a diary of a visit to China. M. Oliphant. Bul Atomic Sci 22:36-43 My '66; Reply. B. T. Feld. 22: 33-4 S '66
Science and education. C. H. G. Oldham. Bul Atomic Sci 22:41-50 Je '66

Czechoslovakia

Czechoslovak science; report on panel discussion at meeting of Czechoslovak society of arts and sciences in America, inc. M. Rechcigl, jr. Science 154:924-6 N 18 '66

Europe, Western

How quickly will Europe close the science spending gap? V. K. McElheny. il Science 151:976-8 F 25 '66

France

France considers significance of Nobel awards. V. K. McElheny; reply. L. Badash. Science 151:634 F 11 '66
National planning of science and technology in France; adaptation of address, October 1964. J. B. Quinn; discussion. Science 151: 517, 1330+ F 4, Mr 18 '66

Great Britain

Bolder policies for British technology? V. K. McElheny. Science 152:741-4 My 6 '66
Management gap; present state and prospects. A. Simmons. il Newsweek 68:34-5 Jl 25 '66
Squeeze threatens U.K. science. Sci N 90: 427 N 19 '66

India

Science and the problems of development; address. H. J. Bhabha. Science 151:541-8 F 4 '66; Discussion. 151:1485; 152:865-6 Mr 25, My 13 '66

Italy

Appeal judges cut Ippolito's sentence in half. V. K. McElheny. Science 152:54-5 Ap 1 '66
Cabinet reshuffle changes Italy's science minister. V. K. McElheny. Science 152: 336-7 Ap 15 '66

Russia

Russian and U.S. science: another view of the gap. Science 151:432 Ja 28 '66
Soviet biologists push revolt against old boss. Bsns W p72 F 26 '66
Soviet science appraised. J. Turkevich. For Affairs 44:489-500 Ap '66

United States

See Science

SCIENCE (periodical)

Instructions for contributors (cont) Science 152:xix-xx; 153:xix-xx; 154:xviii-xix Je 24, S 30, D 30 '66
Science, and the scientific community. P. H. Abelson. Science 153:1473 S 23 '66

SCIENCE, Ethics of. See Scientists, Professional ethics for

SCIENCE adviser, Office of. See United States —State. Department of—International scientific and technological affairs. Office of

SCIENCE and art. See Art and science

SCIENCE and civilization

Breakthrough: the saga of Jonas Salk, by R. Carter. Review
　New Repub 154:38-9 My 14 '66. M. Alderman
Commitment to science. D. Wolfle. Science 153:1339 S 16 '66
Future of capitalism. R. L. Heilbroner. Commentary 41:23-35 Ap '66; Discussion. 42: 6+ Jl; 14+ Ag '66
Government, science, and public policy; adaptation of address, January 25, 1966. C. P. Snow. Science 151:650-3 F 11 '66
History of American science, a field finds itself; excerpts from address, December 1964. A. H. Dupree. bibliog f Am Hist R 71:863-74 Ap '66
Homi Bhabha and the underdeveloped nations. F. Seitz. Science 151:1039 Mr 4 '66
Identity of man, by J. Bronowski. Review
　Nation 202:559-61 My 9 '66. F. H. Gardner
Inner nature of science; excerpts from address, October 14, 1965. W. Weaver. UNESCO Courier 19:34 Ja '66
Limits of American capitalism, by R. L. Heilbroner. Review
　Sat R 49:36 O 29 '66. S. D. Pollard
Logic & limits of technology. H. Wheeler; B. V. B. Bowden. il Nation 204:9-21 Ja 2 '67
Science and engineering; address, November 2, 1966. J. H. Hollomon. Vital Speeches 33: 111-15 D 1 '66
Science and technology need careful watching. Sci N 90:345 O 29 '66
Science and the problems of development; address. H. J. Bhabha. Science 151:541-8 F 4 '66; Discussion. 151:1485; 152:865-6; 153: 249-50; 688 Mr 25, My 13, Jl 15, Ag 12 '66

SCIENCE and civilization—*Continued*
Science in a world of widening horizons; address, January 17, 1966. G. T. Seaborg. Dept State Bul 54:280-8 F 21 '66
Science in your life; interview, ed. by V. Block and H. Pryor. D. F. Hornig. il Sci Digest 60:72-80 O '66
Scientific-government-industrial machine. E. Clark. New Repub 155:32-5 Ag 27 '66
Sociobiology and man. A. M. Guhl; reply. J. P. Scott. Bul Atomic Sci 22:33-4 F '66
With Oppenheimer, on an autumn day; interview, ed. by T. B. Morgan. J. R. Oppenheimer. il Look 30:61+ D 27 '66

SCIENCE and industry
See also
Industrial research

SCIENCE and literature. See Literature and science

SCIENCE and religion. See Religion and science

SCIENCE and society. See Science and civilization

SCIENCE and state
Appeal judges cut Ippolito's sentence in half. V. K. McElheny. Science 152:54-5 Ap 1 '66
Autumn of power: the scientist in the political establishment. R. Sanders. Bul Atomic Sci 22:22-5 O '66
Basic research: the political tides are shifting. D. S. Greenberg. Science 152:1724-6 Je 24 '66
Bootlegging: it holds a firm place in conduct of research. D. S. Greenberg. Science 153: 848-9 Ag 19 '66; Reply. L. B. Williams. 153:1596 S 30 '66
Capitol hill: science among nations. F. Sartwell. Sci N 90:566 D 31 '66
Congress and science; congressional subcommittee emphasizes need for methods of utilizing technical knowledge. Sci Am 215: 57-8 D '66
Damaging criticism; letter. E. W. Price. Science 152:447 Ap 22 '66; Reply with rejoinder. J. L. Fischer. 153:480-1 Jl 29 '66
Government, science, and public policy; adaptation of address, January 25, 1966. C. P. Snow. Science 151:650-3 F 11 '66
Hindsight: DOD study examines return on investment in research. D. S. Greenberg. il Science 154:872-3 N 18 '66
Information services: a guide to federal offerings. M. Zeiger. Science 153:722-4 Ag 12 '66
New Congress and science. A. Ewing. Sci N 90:429 N 19 '66
Science and the common reader. E. Larrabee. Commentary 41:43-8 Je '66
Science in your life; interview, ed. by V. Block and H. Pryor. D. F. Hornig. il Sci Digest 60:72-80 O '66
Science policy and national goals. P. H. Abelson. Science 151:521 F 4 '66
Science policy: when Congress looks for a leader NSF is usually nominated. J. Walsh. Science 152:184-5 Ap 8 '66
Scientific advice in the State department. E. B. Skolnikoff. bibliog Science 154:980-5 N 25 '66
Scientific estate, by D. K. Price. Review Sci Am 214:131-2+ Ap '66. K. E. Boulding
Scientific-government-industrial machine. E. Clark. New Repub 155:32-5 Ag 27 '66
Scientists as advisors and consultants in Washington. B. T. Eiduson. Bul Atomic Sci 22:26-31 O '66
Tea leaves or the record? P. H. Abelson. Science 151:783 F 18 '66
Text of the new lesson; science and human freedom; excerpt from Scientific estate. D. K. Price. il Sat R 49:54-7 Ap 2 '66
Why our scientists are about to be dragged, moaning, into politics. J. Fischer. Harper 233:16+ S '66; Discussion. 233:8+ N '66
See also
Government spending policy
Research—Federal aid
United States—National science foundation

SCIENCE and the humanities
Computer, the eye, the soul; excerpts from Of molecules and men. F. Crick. Sat R 49: 53-5 S 3 '66
Confessions of a scientist-humanist. W. Weaver. Sat R 49:12-15 My 28 '66
Partners in progress; address, April 22, 1966. G. T. Seaborg. il Sci N 89:339-40+ My 7 '66

SCIENCE aptitude tests. See Aptitude tests

SCIENCE as a profession
How to get a science job at home. J. A. Kraft, jr. Sci Digest 59:77-9 F '66

SCIENCE books for children. See Scientific literature for children

SCIENCE city. See Akademgorodok, Siberia

SCIENCE clubs
Science club news. Sci N 89:218+, 253, 277, 300, 365, 453, 471, 497 Ap 2-23, My 14, Je 4-18 '66

SCIENCE clubs of America
Science clubs of America. Sci N 90:158 S 3 '66
See also
Science talent search

SCIENCE fairs
Dallas: center of science; host city of International science fair. il Sci N 89:363-5 My 14 '66
Fairs: international, national, local. il Sci N 90:157 S 3 '66
On to Dallas for science fair! 17th International science fair. S. Moore. il Sci N 89:216-18 Ap 2 '66
Science fair in Connecticut. Sci N 89:301 Ap 23 '66
Science fair winners exhibit at AMA meeting. Sci N 90:24 Jl 9 '66
Top winners at ISF. il Sci N 89:409-16+ My 28 '66

SCIENCE fiction
Astounding story! about a science fiction writer. G. Smith. il N Y Times Mag p28-9+ Mr 6 '66
Fantastic voyage. I. Asimov. il Sat Eve Post 239:40-4 F 26; 56-60+ Mr 12 '66
From out of this world; contemporary scene. G. Hicks. Sat R 49:23-4 Ag 20 '66
From Terra to TANSTAAFL. T. Sturgeon. Nat R 18:1278+ D 13 '66
Other worlds to conjure. M. R. Hillegas. Sat R 49:33-4 Mr 26 '66
Simplicity in scientific writing. L. DeBakey. Writer 79:25-6 S '66
See also
Moving pictures—Science fiction

Bibliography
Science fiction basics. D. Knight. il Library J 91:2777-9 Je 1 '66
Science fiction for the space age; how to stimulate supplementary reading among students of all ability levels. S. Solomon. il Sr Schol 87:sup20-1 Ja 21 '66

Single works
Computer that sweated. H. Downs. il Sci Digest 59:88-93 Je '66

SCIENCE in fiction. See Science fiction; Science in literature

SCIENCE in literature
Science is where the action is. A. Rosenfeld. Life 61:16 Jl 29 '66

SCIENCE information. See Communication in science

SCIENCE literature. See Scientific literature

SCIENCE news
Late science news. See issues of Science digest
Public understanding of science; AAAS meeting, Washington, D.C. E. Kurtz. il Science 154:800-1 N 11 '66
Science critics; excerpts from address, October 19, 1966. R. Dubos. Science 154:595 N 4 '66
Science newsfront. W. S. Bacon. See issues of Popular science monthly

SCIENCE of life: story. See Berriault, G.

SCIENCE projects. See Science—Study and teaching—Projects

SCIENCE service, incorporated
Science service president and director announced. il Sci N 89:332 My 7 '66
Science youth program. Sci N 90:158 S 3 '66
See also
Science talent search

SCIENCE students
Biologist top winner. il Sci N 89:179+ Mr 19 '66
Science talent search winners. Sci N L 89: 85-6 F 5 '66
Winners favor teamwork. Sci N 89:163 Mr 12 '66
See also
Science talent search

SCIENCE talent search
Look at twenty-five years of STS; address, March 7, 1966. G. T. Seaborg. il Sci N 89: 181-2+ Mr 19 '66
Science talent search. il Sci N 90:156 S 3 '66
STS alumni speak. M. P. Meyers; P. E. Teschan. Sci N 89:180+ Mr 19 '66
Talent search has 25th year. il Sci N L 89: 149-50 Mr 5 '66

SCIENCE talent search—*Continued*
1966 (25th)
Anniversary remarks. H. S. Kaltenborn. Sci N 89:182 Mr 19 '66
Biologist top winner. il Sci N 89:179+ Mr 19 '66
Science talent search winners. Sci N L 89:85-6 F 5 '66
1967 (26th)
Talent hunt tests on. Sci N 90:541 D 24 '66
Talent search vital. Sci N 90:209 S 17 '66
SCIENCE teachers
Japanese science education centers. B. Glass. Science 154:221-8 O 14 '66
SCIENCE teaching. See Science—Study and teaching
SCIENCE writing. See Scientific literature
SCIENTIFIC and technical advisory council, New York. See New York (city)—Scientific and technical advisory council
SCIENTIFIC apparatus and instruments
Instrument issue; symposium. il Science 154: 84-98+ O 7 '66
See also
Astronomical instruments
Oceanographic instruments
Optical instruments
Recording instruments
   also names of scientific apparatus and instruments, e.g. Telescope
SCIENTIFIC committee on the effects of atomic radiation. See United Nations—Scientific committee on the effects of atomic radiation
SCIENTIFIC conferences
International meetings. P. H. Abelson. Science 154:341 O 21 '66
Meetings. See issues of Science
NAS, ICSU statements on international meetings; October 1966. Science 154:369 O 21 '66
Ninety-four years of progress? excerpts from article of 1871; letter. D. W. Jacobs and W. N. Tavolga. Science 154:725 N 11 '66
Science studies: a gathering of the clan in Edinburgh; report on International science studies seminar. J. Walsh. Science 154:1150-1 D 2 '66
Smale aftermath: ICSU and academy urge ban on politics at meetings. D. S. Greenberg. Science 154:368-70 O 21 '66
When and where. See issues of Missiles and rockets
SCIENTIFIC data systems, incorporated
Fast computer draws bead on two markets; new Sigma 7 line. il Bsns W p79 Mr 19 '66
How to succeed; Sigma 7 unveiled. il Newsweek 67:73-4 Mr 28 '66
SCIENTIFIC education
China's push to catch up in science; report for National science foundation, by C. Y. Cheng. il Bsns W p 116-20 F 5 '66
Japanese science education centers. B. Glass. Science 154:221-8 O 14 '66
See also
Science—Study and teaching
SCIENTIFIC exchanges. See Exchange of persons programs; Exchanges, Literary and scientific
SCIENTIFIC expeditions
See also
Anthropological expeditions
SCIENTIFIC information. See Communication in science
SCIENTIFIC libraries
Departmental libraries and the problem of autonomy; science library, Haverford college. Pa. S. K. Newhall. ALA Bul 60:721-2 Jl '66
Science library cooperation in three colleges; Bryn Mawr, Haverford, and Swarthmore, Pa. S. Newhall. ALA Bul 60:380-1 Ap '66
SCIENTIFIC literature
Bibliographic organization in the physical sciences. J. C. Shipman. bibliog il Wilson Lib Bul 40:706-13 Ap '66; Correction. 40: 911 Je '66
Flood; problem of keeping worthless material. W. J. Coughlin. Tech W 19:50 O 3 '66
National document-handling systems in science and technology; federal government's responsibilities. L. F. Carter. bibliog Science 154:1299-304 D 9 '66
Science writing ancient. Sci N 90:291 O 15 '66
See also
Publishers and publishing—Scientific literature
Science—Bibliography
SCIENTIFIC literature for children
Experiment in cooperative reviewing by scientists and librarians. P. L. Moulton. Horn Bk 42:345-9 Je '66

From first grade to graduate level; scientific books. C. B. Grannis. Pub W 189:86 Ap 18 '66
Producing concepts in science. il Pub W 189:108-12 My 2 '66
Prose imagination. I. Adler. Library J 91: 6160-1 D 15 '66
Some sci-tech titles for children. il Pub W 189:42-5 Ap 18 '66
Views on science books. I. Asimov. See issues of Horn book magazine

Bibliography
Christmas survey of new books about science for younger children. P. Morrison and P. Morrison. Sci Am 215:141-6+ D '66
Natural history's 1966 survey of science books for young people. Natur Hist 75:24-5+ N '66
SCIENTIFIC management. See Industrial management and organization
SCIENTIFIC management, international congress. See International congress for scientific management
SCIENTIFIC personnel, Government. See Government employees
SCIENTIFIC photography. See Photography—Scientific applications
SCIENTIFIC research. See Research
SCIENTIFIC socialism. See Socialism
SCIENTIFIC societies
International scientific cooperation: an American view; reprint. G. C. McGhee. Dept State Bul 54:369-78 Mr 7 '66
See also names of scientific societies, e.g. American philosophical society

History
Accademia dei Lincei; its founding in 1603 and later history; address, December 28, 1965. S. Drake. Science 151:1194-200 Mr 11 '66
SCIENTIFIC terms. See Science—Terminology
SCIENTIFIC toys. See Toys
SCIENTIFIC writing. See Scientific literature
SCIENTISTS
Beginning of the commonsense. H. M. Meyer. Bul Atomic Sci 22:23-5 F '66
Nurturing new scientists; address, May 13, 1966. G. T. Seaborg. il Sci N 89:417+ My 28 '66
Scientists were kids, too, once; need for the non-specialist. H. Downs. Sci Digest 60: 90-3 Ag '66
See also
Mathematicians
Naturalists
Physicists
Women as scientists

Political activities
Autumn of power: the scientist in the political establishment. R. Sanders. Bul Atomic Sci 22:22-5 O '66
Careers, science, and politics. D. MacRae, jr. Bul Atomic Sci 22:26-8 F '66
NAS, ICSU statements on international meetings; October 1966. Science 154:369 O 21 '66
Scientists as advisors and consultants in Washington. B. T. Eiduson. Bul Atomic Sci 22:26-31 O '66
Scientists in politics and out. M. J. Moravcsik. Bul Atomic Sci 22:32-4 Ja '66
Smale aftermath: ICSU and academy urge ban on politics at meetings. D. S. Greenberg. Science 154:368-70 O 21 '66

Supply and demand
Brain drain. Commonweal 85:190 N 18 '66
Brain drain. D. Wolfle. Science 154:965 N 25 '66
Brain-drain from Latin America. America 115: 109 Jl 30 '66
Brain drain starts to hurt; Britain and Europeans, worried about siphoning off of scientific and technical talent to the U.S. il Bsns W p 122+ D 10 '66
From the other side: a European view. B. Thomas. bibliog f il Ann Am Acad 367: 63-72 S '66
Manpower: output of scientists and engineers may exceed goals set by White House committee. L. J. Carter. il Science 151:666-8 F 11 '66
Migrant scientists. Sci Am 215:49 Jl '66
Projections of manpower supply in a specific occupation. N. Rosenthal. il Mo Labor R 89:1262-6 N '66
Scientific personnel and the professions. T. J. Mills. bibliog f il Ann Am Acad 367: 33-42 S '66
Trained manpower: British studies call for better use of the supply. J. Walsh. Science 154:1425-7 D 16 '66

SCIENTISTS—Supply and demand—*Continued*
Where the brains are. R. E. Lapp. il Fortune 73:154-6+ Mr '66
Where the jobs are. Sci Am 214:57-8 Mr '66
Why not a draft for applied research? letter. N. S. Radin. Science 154:1276 D 9 '66
SCIENTISTS, American
Where responsibility lies. J. G. Dash. Bul Atomic Sci 22:35-7 Ja '66
Where the jobs are. Sci Am 214:57-8 Mr '66
SCIENTISTS, British
Trained manpower: British studies call for better use of the supply. J. Walsh. Science 154:1425-7 D 16 '66
SCIENTISTS, Chinese
China's push to catch up in science; report for National science foundation, by C. Y. Cheng. il Bsns W p 116-20 F 5 '66
Chinese science: it's not a paper atom. J. M. H. Lindbeck. il N Y Times Mag p38-9+ Ja 8 '67
SCIENTISTS, Exchange of. See Exchange of persons programs
SCIENTISTS, French
Pasteur institute rebels lose a round. V. K. McElheny. Science 153:1226-8 S 9 '66
SCIENTISTS, Latin American
Brain-drain from Latin America. America 115:109 Jl 30 '66
Latin American brain drain; emigration of trained personnel to the United States. Américas 18:40-1 Ap '66
SCIENTISTS, Professional ethics for
Ethics of science evolved with man. Sci N 89:299 Ap 23 '66
Luna IX pictures: a question of ethics; letter. D. C. Krause; with reply by B. Lovell. Science 151:1477 Mr 25 '66
Technical expert in a democracy. C. Nader. Bul Atomic Sci 22:28-30 My '66
SCIENTISTS, Russian
New class divided. by A. Parry. Review Sci Digest il 60:42-3 S '66. J. Reinert
SCIENTISTS as astronauts. See Astronauts
SCILLY ISLANDS
Tresco Abbey gardens. C. Chowins. il Horticulture 44:32-4+ O '66
SCINTILLATION counters. See Counters (electrons, ions, etc)
SCINTILLATION of stars. See Stars—Scintillation
SCIPIO, Cornelius
Is Schweitzer dead? Atlan 218:41-4 Ag '66
SCLAR, Elaine
Out of the ivory tower into the grease pit; with bibliography. Library J 91:2162-4+ Ap 15 '66
SCLEROSIS, Multiple
Multiple sclerosis clue significant. Sci N 89: 258 Ap 16 '66
Multiple sclerosis: correlation between immunoglobulin-G in cerebrospinal fluid and brain. W. W. Tourtellotte and J. A. Parker. bibliog il Science 154:1044-6 N 25 '66
MS may lurk for years. Sci N 90:344 O 29 '66
Multiple sclerosis: serum factor producing reversible alterations in bioelectric responses. J. A. Cerf and G. Carels. bibliog il Science 152:1066-8 My 20 '66
MS study uses frogs. Sci N 89:451 Je 4 '66
Possible virus-MS link. Sci N 89:507 Je 25 '66
Tonsillectomy linked to multiple sclerosis. Sci N L 89:51 Ja 22 '66
SCOFIELD, John
Freedom speaks French in Ouagadougou. il Nat Geog Mag 130:153-203 Ag '66
SCOFIELD, Paul
Introverted Englishman. il pors Time 89:68 Ja 6 '67
SCOGGIN, Margaret C.
(comp) Outlook tower. See issues of Horn book magazine
SCOLYTID beetles. See Bark beetles
SCOOTERS. See Motor scooters
SCOPE calibrators. See Calibrators
SCOPES, John Thomas
Day the Bible beat the monkeys; with report by W. Warga. il pors Life 61:97-8 D 9 '66
SCOPES, Wilfred
New theological college in the Caribbean. A. J. Hunter. Christian Cent 83:1488 N 30 '66
SCOPES. See Oscillographs
SCOPES trial. See Tennessee evolution controversy
SCORE project. See United States—Small business administration
SCORING (sports) See Sports officiating
SCORPIONS
Nature note; stinging scorpion. Sci N L 89: 142 F 26 '66

SCORPIONS, False. See Book scorpions
SCORPIUS (constellation) See Constellations
SCOTCH in Bechuanaland
Scottish mother for an African tribe. N. Mitchison. il Harper 233:86-8+ S '66
SCOTCHGARD. See Textile fabrics—Protection
SCOTLAND
See also
Astronomical observatories—Scotland
Clans and clan system
Ness, Loch
Religious institutions and affairs
Specter of bishops; suggested talks between Church of Scotland and Episcopal church in Scotland. C. Northcott. Christian Cent 83:770 Je 15 '66
World around us (cont of) News of the Christian world. Christian Cent 83:155-6, 600-1, 1190-1 F 2, My 4, S 28 '66
See also
Church of Scotland
Iona community
Social conditions
Slums and the remedy. I. Logan. Christian Cent 83:1582 D 21 '66
SCOTLAND, Md. See Montgomery County, Md.
SCOTLAND, Church of. See Church of Scotland
SCOTT, Chester F.
Resistive attenuators and pads. Electr World 75:35-7+ My '66
SCOTT, Christine E.
Then came the good harvest; drama. Plays 26:70-4 N '66
SCOTT, David H.
New look in pilot licenses. Flying 79:45 Jl '66
Scott's corner (cont) Flying 79:91-2 S; 103 O; 121 N; 82+ D '66; 80:88 Ja '67
SCOTT, David Q.
Tidewater sketches. il Yachting 119:71-3 Mr '66
SCOTT, David R.
See also
Space flight—Manned flights—Armstrong-Scott flight, 1966
—See Armstrong, N. A. jt. auth.
SCOTT, Donald, Jr, and others
Regeneration in spinal neurons: proteosynthesis following nerve growth factor administration. bibliog Science 152:787-8 My 6 '66
SCOTT, Donald C. See Weber, J. B. jt. auth.
SCOTT, Donald F. and Bickford, R. G.
Electrophysiologic studies during scanning and passive eye movements in humans. bibliog Science 155:101-2 Ja 6 '67
SCOTT, Foresman and company
Scott, Foresman to buy William Morrow & co. Pub W 190:26 O 24 '66
SCOTT, Geoffrey
King Kam and the Isle of love. Sat R 49: 68-9 O 22 '66
SCOTT, George
Year of the tape measure. il por Time 87: 92+ My 20 '66
SCOTT, Harley A. Jr. See Kenshalo, D. R. jt. auth.
SCOTT, Harold
How to beat the Japanese beetle. Flower Grower 53:44-5 Ag '66
SCOTT, Herbert
Crow box; poem. Harper 233:88 Ag '66
SCOTT, Hugh
Excerpt from address, January 26, 1966. Cong Digest 45:145+ My '66
Excerpt from statement, January 10, 1966. Cong Digest 45:81+ Mr '66
SCOTT, Jack Denton
Adventures in pasta. Holiday 40:74-6 O '66
Sailing the eighth sea. Redbook 126:49 Mr '66
Santiago de Compostela. Holiday 41:30+ Ja '67
Woodland wonderworld. Read Digest 89: 175-7+ Jl '66
SCOTT, John
Changing Soviet Union; address. February 7, 1966. Vital Speeches 32:469-72 My 15 '66
SCOTT, John Dick
Buchan and the British Guermantes. New Repub 154:23-4 Ap 30 '66
SCOTT, John Finley
Marriage is not a personal matter. N Y Times Mag p27+ O 30 '66
Parent and child. N Y Times Mag p 119-20+ N 20 '66
SCOTT, John Paul
That old-time aggression. Nation 204:53-4 Ja 9 '67
SCOTT, John William Robertson-. See Robertson-Scott, J. W.

SCOTT, Johnie
Bad news; poem; excerpt. Time 88:54 Jl 22 '66
How it is: my home is Watts. Harper 233: 47-8 O '66; Correction. 234:92 Ja '67
SCOTT, Joseph, and Scott, Lenore
Calorie game. McCalls 93:94-5+ Ag '66
SCOTT, Laurie
Pilgrimage to pet Marjory country. Horn Bk 42:589-90 O '66
SCOTT, Lenore. See Scott, J. jt. auth.
SCOTT, Louise
Climb to sunrise: Rincon Mountains, Arizona; poem. Liv Wildn 30:23 Sum '66
SCOTT, Marion
Marion Scott and dance company; 92nd street Y. J. Maskey. Dance Mag 40:64 Jl '66
SCOTT, Meredith A.
Pangs of ICW traffic. Motor B 118:32-3+ S '66
SCOTT, Nathan Alexander, 1925–
Wasteland observed. Newsweek 68:84 Jl 25 '66
SCOTT, Peter Dale
Vietnam: importance of January. Nation 204: 74-7 Ja 16 '67
SCOTT, R. F. See Jaffe, L. D. jt. auth.
SCOTT, Ruth Boyer
Senator Randolph's blind businessmen. To-days Health 44:73-6 O '66
SCOTT, Thomas D.
Peace corps and the private sector: the failure of a partnership. Ann Am Acad 365:93-104 My '66
SCOTT, Vernon
Nancy Sinatra talks about life with father. Ladies Home J 83:82-3+ S '66
Step by step: Lynda Bird Johnson's Hollywood beauty treatment. Ladies Home J 83:62+ Jl '66
SCOTT, Wendell
Stock car racer reaches bigtime. il pors Ebony 21:61-2+ My '66
SCOTT, Winfield Townley
Roethke; For an old Sunday painter; Gudhjem on Bornholm; Orchard burial; Sprague Smith studio; Once off England . .; At Jaffrey center; poems. Poetry 108:287-93 Ag '66
SCOTTISH clans. See Clans and clan system
SCOTTISH tartans. See Tartans
SCOTTSDALE, Ariz, All-Arabian horse show. See Horse shows
SCOURING powders. See Cleaning compositions
SCOUTING, Basketball. See Basketball scouting
SCOUTING, Football. See Football scouting
SCOVILL manufacturing company
Scovill responds to classic remedies; new president using textbook management methods. il Bsns W p 190-2+ O 22 '66
SCOYEN, E. T.
What alternate proposal? letter to the editor. Am For 72:4-5+ Ag '66
SCRAMJET airplanes. See Airplanes, Jet propelled
SCRANTON, William Warren
Boost for Romney; Scranton bows out. por U S News 60:22 Je 13 '66
Hamlet of Harrisburg. T. Wicker. Atlan 217:78-9 Ap '66
William Tecumseh Scranton; an irrevocable statement. por Time 87:37-8 Je 10 '66
SCRAPPING of automobiles. See Automobiles—Wrecking
SCREEN writers. See Dramatists
SCREEN writing. See Moving picture authorship
SCREENS (furniture)
Room divider; use of ceramics and wood. W. Skinner. il Sch Arts 66:6-9 S '66
SCREENS (sun)
How materials react to solar energy. J. I. Yellott. il Arch Rec 139:197-8 Je '66
If trees are too slow try man-made shade. il Pop Gard 17:38-41 Mr '66
Intercept the sun outside the glass. il Sunset 136:128+ My '66
Modern ways to use building blocks. il Pop Gard 17:44-7 D '66
Peripheral corridor provides sun control. il Arch Rec 140:172-3 N '66
Shady way to expand outdoor living; cantilevered screen. il Bet Hom & Gard 44:150 My '66
This screen hides a garden. il Sunset 137: 277 O '66
SCREENS; drama. See Genet. J.
SCREENS, Moving picture. See Moving picture screens
SCREENS, Projector. See Projection apparatus

SCREW threads
Pipefitting job becomes threadless snap. il Bsns W p 134+ F 19 '66
SCREW worms. See Screwworms
SCREWWORMS
Last of the screwworm fly. Sci Am 215:44+ O '66
U.S. and Mexico to cooperate in screw-worm eradication plan; statement, July 27, 1966. L. B. Johnson. Dept State Bul 55:232 Ag 15 '66
SCRIPT writing. See Television authorship
SCRIPTO, Incorporated
Rewriting the script for Scripto; C. N. Singer. il Bsns W p 168+ D 17 '66
SCRIPTURES. See Bible
SCROLLS (decorative design)
Master scrolls unroll in New York; exhibition of scroll paintings from the Sung, Yüan, Ming and Ch'ing dynasties. H. La Farge. il Art N 65:30+ Sum '66
SCROLLS from the Dead Sea. See Dead Sea scrolls
SCUBA diving. See Diving, Submarine
SCULL, Ethel
Casting of Ethel Scull. il por Time 87:69 Ap 1 '66
Profiles; R. C. Scull. J. Kramer. New Yorker 42:64-6+ N 26 '66
SCULL, Robert Cooper
Profiles; J. Kramer. por New Yorker 42:64-6+ N 26 '66
SCULL, Robert C, collection. See Art—Private collections
SCULLY, Vincent
America's architectural nightmare: the motorized megalopolis. Holiday 39:94-5+ Mr '66
about
Profess with a passion. il por Time 87:80-1 My 6 '66
SCULPTORS
E=MC² à go-go: ten painters and sculptors of the Park Place gallery, New York. D. Bourdon. il Art N 64:22-5+ Ja '66
Movement movement; kinetic artists. il Time 87:64-9 Ja 28 '66
See also
Sculptors guild
Sculpture
SCULPTORS guild
Art galleries; twenty-sixth annual exhibition at Lever house. R. M. Coates. New Yorker 42:150+ N 5 '66
SCULPTURE
Are they trying to tell us something? Primary structures. J. Jacobs. il Reporter 34: 38-9 Je 16 '66
Market research art; consumer-determined sculpture by G. Laing and P. Phillips. il Life 60:71-2+ My 20 '66
Profiles; R. C. Scull, collector of pop art. J. Kramer. New Yorker 42:64-6+ N 26 '66
Sculptors in the factory; sponsorship of Long Beach state college, Calif. il Fortune 73: 140-5 Ap '66
Sculptures in motion; with report by D. Bourdon. il Life 61:40-7+ Ag 12 '66
Tech style; electronic gadgets. il Time 88:84 D 9 '66
Ultimate She; a gargantuan work at Stockholm's Museum of modern art. il Time 87:92+ Je 17 '66
See also
Bronzes
Carving (art industries)
Metal sculpture
Mountain sculpture
Wood carving
Exhibitions
Are they trying to tell us something? Primary structures at New York's Jewish museum. J. Jacobs. il Reporter 34:38-9 Je 16 '66
Art galleries; exhibition of modern sculptures: Primary structures at the Jewish museum. R. M. Coates. New Yorker 42: 177-9 My 21 '66
Art; Primary structures at the Jewish museum. M. Kozloff. Nation 202:693-4 Je 6 '66
Engineer's esthetic; exhibition at Jewish museum in Manhattan. il Time 87:64-5+ Je 3 '66
New druids; Anglo-U.S. show at New York's Jewish museum. il Newsweek 67:104-5 My 16 '66
Please don't feed the sculpture. il Time 87: 70 Je 10 '66
Poetic emptiness; New York's Whitney museum annual. il Time 88:51 D 23 '66

SCULPTURE—*Continued*

Private collections

See Art—Private collections

Study and teaching

Creating plaster sculpture; program at Lincoln junior high, La Crosse, Wis. R. Sherin. il Sch Arts 66:11-14 O '66

Materials

Branches, rags and plaster. R. DeAngelo. il Design 67:4-7 My '66

Sculpture in homemade clay. Sister Mary Alice. il Design 68:32-4 N '66

SCULPTURE, American

Art galleries; 1966 sculpture and prints annual at the Whitney. R. M. Coates. New Yorker 42:84-6 Ja 7 '67

Casting of Ethel Scull; and husband. il Time 87:69 Ap 1 '66

Controlled: exhibition at the Whitney museum. New Yorker 42:41-2 Ap 16 '66

Egyptian motifs in nineteenth-century American painting and sculpture. W. H. Gerdts. il Antiques 90:495-501 O '66

From Pollock to pop; twenty years of painting and sculpture. H. Rosenberg. il Holiday 39:96-105+ Mr '66

See also

Bufano, B. B.
Calder, A.
Gabo, N.
Hall, J.
Jonas, L. P
King, W. D.
Mallary, R.
Nakian, R.
Pavia, P.
Rickey, G.
Robus, H.
Sculptors guild
Shonnard, E.
Smith, D.
Smith, T.
Sugarman, G.
Trova, E
Ziolkowski, K.

SCULPTURE, Animal. See Animal sculpture

SCULPTURE, Architectural. See Decoration and ornament, Architectural

SCULPTURE, British

Hybrid: "the ideal art object" of G. Laing and P. Phillips. New Yorker 42:35-6 Ap 30 '66

See also

Caro, A.
Dalwood, H.
Leon, D.

SCULPTURE, Chinese

Han army spectacularly unearthed in mainland China. H. N. Ho. il Art N 65:36-7 Sum '66

SCULPTURE, French

See also

Duchamp-Villon, R.
St Phalle, Niki de

SCULPTURE, German

Welding their way up; work of B. Meier-Denninghoff & M. Matschinsky. il Time 88:88 O 7 '66

SCULPTURE, Greek

See also

Elgin marbles

SCULPTURE, Italian

Bronze miniatures from ancient Sardinia. A. Borio. il UNESCO Courier 19:16-21 S '66

See also

Bernini, G. L.
Manzu, G.
Marini, M.

SCULPTURE, Metal. See Metal sculpture

SCULPTURE, Pre-Columbian

Relics show their merits: Dr Weisman's collection of medical figures of the pre-Columbian era. F. Marley. il Sci N 90:396-7 N 12 '66

SCULPTURE, Primitive

Of artists and owls; Taino sculpture. D. Suro. il Américas 18:21-8 Mr '66

See also

Sculpture, Pre-Columbian

SCULPTURE, Russian

See also

Neizvestnyi, E.

SCULPTURE, Swiss

See also

Giacometti, A.

SEA. See Ocean

SEA anemones

Disulfide-linked collagenous protein of nematocyst capsules. F. Blanquet and H. M. Lenhoff. bibliog il Science 154:152-3 O 7 '66

SEA change; story. See Teall, K. M.

SEA coasts. See Coast changes

SEA cucumbers. See Holothurians

SEA food

Coastal seafood. S. Spitzer. il Holiday 40:70-3+ Jl '66

Food for our future from pastures of the sea; excerpt from The living world of the sea. W. J. Cromie. il Todays Health 44:48-53+ N '66

Grilled shrimp scampi style; with menu and recipes by G. Schremp. il Life 61:86-7+ S 9 '66

Out of the deep. C. Claiborne. il N Y Times Mag p35 S 4 '66

Sea food exhaustible. Sci N 90:84 Ag 6 '66

See also

Cookery—Fish

SEA-girls; story. See Wheelis, A.

SEA-grant colleges. See Oceanography—Study and teaching

SEA gulls. See Gulls

SEA hares

Grazing mollusks in the weeds. D. Linton. il Natur Hist 75:58-61 Mr '66

SEA horses

She's admiring her sea horse. il Sunset 136:135-6 My '66

SEA level. See Sea level changes

SEA level changes

World seas rising from melting ice. Sci N 89:311 Ap 30 '66

SEA life park, Hawaii. See Aquariums

SEA lions. See Seals (animals)

SEA nettles. See Jellyfish

SEA planes. See Seaplanes

SEA power

East of Suez. R. Moley. Newsweek 68:96 Jl 25 '66

Total wet war; address, May 2, 1966. J. S. McCain. Vital Speeches 32:514-18 Je 15 '66

SEA products. See Marine resources

SEA salt. See Salt

SEA shells. See Shells (conchology)

SEA shore. See Seashore

SEA stars. See Starfishes

SEA tides; story. See Hoffman, W.

SEA urchins

Cilia regeneration in the sea urchin embryo: evidence for a pool of ciliary proteins. W. Auclair and B. W. Siegel. bibliog il Science 154:913-15 N 18 '66

Protein synthesis in micromeres of the sea urchin egg. M. Spiegel and A. Tyler. bibliog il Science 151:1233-4 Mr 11 '66

See also

Embryology—Echinoderms

SEA water

Calcite: rates of dissolution in a vertical profile in the central Pacific. M. N. A. Peterson. bibliog il Science 154:1542-4 D 23 '66

Calcium in sea water by electrode measurement. M. E. Thompson and J. W. Ross, jr. bibliog il Science 154:1643-4 D 30 '66

Chromium-51 in sea water: chemistry. N. Cutshall and others. bibliog il Science 152:202-3 Ap 8 '66

Concentration of dissolved amino acids from saline waters by ligand-exchange chromatography. A. Siegel and E. T. Degens. il Science 151:1098-101 Mr 4 '66

Deep-sea pH. K. Park. bibliog il Science 154:1540-2 D 23 '66

Denitrification rates in an island bay in the equatorial Pacific Ocean. J. J. Goering and R. C. Dugdale. bibliog il Science 154:505-6 O 28 '66

Diagenesis of carbonate sediments: interaction of magnesium in sea water with mineral grains. R. A. Berner. bibliog il Science 153:188-91 Jl 8 '66

Isotopic composition and origin of the Red Sea and Salton Sea geothermal brines. H. Craig. bibliog il Science 154:1544-8 D 23 '66

Magnesium in sea water: an electrode measurement. M. E. Thompson. bibliog il Science 153:866-7 Ag 19 '66

Magnesium ions: activity in seawater. R. M. Pytkowicz and others. bibliog Science 152:640-2 Ap 29 '66

Desalting

Dead Sea isn't dead anymore. G. Gaskill. il Read Digest 89:157-8+ Jl '66

Desalinization benefits. Nat Parks Mag 40:20 F '66

SEA water—Desalting—*Continued*
Desalted sea water for St Thomas. R. E. Cannard. il Am City 81:104-6 F '66
Desalting methods, their costs and promise. K. A. Roe. il Am City 81:126-8 My '66
Key West gets largest desalting plant. Am City 81:22 Jl '66
Method to desalt water uses minerals, gravity. Sci N L 39:63 Ja 22 '66
Nuclear fueled desalting power plant planned. Sci N 90:130 Ag 27 '66
Osmosis purifies water; using reverse osmosis. Sci N 89:290 Ap 23 '66
Scientific magic and economic development. R. Solo. Bul Atomic Sci 22:25-6 N '66
Study completed on large-scale power-desalting plant for Israel. Dept State Bul 54:494 Mr 28 '66

SEA water temperature. See Ocean temperature

SEA waves. See Waves

SEA waves. Seismic. See Seismic sea waves

SEABEE (airplane) See Airplanes, Amphibious

SEABOARD world airlines
Cargo carriers seek more charter rights. H. D. Watkins. Aviation W 86:31-2 Ja 2 '67
Seaboard unveils cargo terminal; Kennedy international airport. J. W. Carter. il Aviation W 85:39 O 10 '66

SEABORG, Glenn T.
Goals in understanding science; excerpts from remarks, October 19, 1966. Sci N 90:354-6 O 29 '66
Look at twenty-five years of STS; address, March 7, 1966. Sci N 89:181-2+ Mr 19 '66
Nurturing new scientists; address, May 13, 1966. Sci N 89:417+ My 28 '66
Partners in progress; address, April 22, 1966. Sci N 89:339-40+ My 7 '66
Science in a world of widening horizons; address, January 17, 1966. Dept State Bul 54:280-8 F 21 '66
Sciences, the humanities, and the federal government. Am Ed 2:8-11 S '66

about
Seaborg presses nuclear case at WESCON. C. D. LaFond. Tech W 19:18-19 Ag 29 '66

SEABURY, Paul
Establishment game: Nicholas Murray Butler rides again. Reporter 34:24-6 My 19 '66; Correction. 34:5 Je 2 '66
Gideon's army and Moynihan's pros. New Repub 154:23-5 Mr 19 '66

SEAFOOD. See Sea food

SEAGER, Laura
Mother, mother! story. Mlle 62:84-5 Ja '66

SEAGRAM, Joseph E, and sons
Bronfmans: an instinct for dynasty. P. Siekman. il Fortune 74:144-9+ N; 176-9+ D '66

SEAGREN, Bob
Bittersweet taste of success. il Time 87:72 Mr 18 '66

SEAGULLS. See Gulls

SEAHORSES. See Sea horses

SEAL hunting
Bad luck *oogruk*. C. E. Gillham. il Field & S 70:46-8+ Mr '66

SEAL sounds. See Sound production by animals

SEALAB projects. See Underwater laboratories

SEALE, Douglas
Baltimore, on center. H. Hewes. Sat R 49:40 My 28 '66

SEALE, Patrick, and Beeson, Irene
Babies along the Nile. New Repub 154:10-11 My 7 '66
How much is Nasser worth? New Repub 154:12-13 Je 4 '66
Rival Arabs. New Repub 155:11 Ag 27 '66

SEALING compositions
Caulking, a guide to the new sealants. M. E. Dowd. il Pop Mech 126:170-5+ O '66
Dow Corning silicone wins annual product award. il Tech W 19:20+ N 21 '66
How to specify polysulfide sealants. M. Sitter. il Arch Rec 140:153-4 Ag '66

SEALS (animals)
Arterial constrictor response in a diving mammal. K. M. Bron and others. bibliog il Science 152:540-3 Ap 22 '66
Maximum diving capacities of the Weddell seal, leptonychotes weddelli. G. L. Kooyman. bibliog il Science 151:1553-4 Mr 25 '66
Pressure regulation in the middle ear cavity of sea lions: a possible mechanism. S. Odend'hal and T. C. Poulter. bibliog il Science 153:768-9 Ag 12 '66
Underwater vocalization by sea lions: social and mirror stimuli. R. J. Schusterman and others. bibliog il Science 154:540-2 O 28 '66

SEALS (numismatics)
See also
United States—Seals

SEALTEST foods division. See National dairy products corporation—Sealtest foods division

SEAMAN, John
Between shadow and light. G. Astor. il pors Look 30:20-3 Ag 9 '66

SEAMANS, Robert C. Jr
Achievement of space; address, March 15, 1966. Vital Speeches 32:527-33 Je 15 '66

SEAMEN
Future of maritime manpower. A. W. Warner. Mo Labor R 89:268-71 Mr '66
Idle fleet; seamen out on strike. Time 87:36+ My 27 '66

Wages and hours
All aboard again; end to seamen's strike; Great Britain. Time 88:28 Jl 8 '66

SEAPLANES
Cherokee Six floatplane handles easily. K. J. Stein. il Aviation W 85:84-5+ O 10 '66
Cool world of seaplanes. J. Gilbert. il Flying 78:40-7 Je '66

Design
Old photos used in rebuilding of seaplane. il Aviation W 85:86-7 Ag 1 '66

Floats
Cessna 150, it floats. R. B. Weeghman. il Flying 80:30-5 Ja '67
Training boom swelling Cessna 150 sales. E. J. Bulban. il Aviation W 85:101+ Ag 8 '66

Testing
Pilot report; Cherokee six-300. J. Gilbert. il Flying 79:108-11 N '66

SEAPORTS. See Ports

SEARCH and rescue (service) See United States—Coast guard

SEARCH for a future; story. See Miller, A

SEARCH for J. Kruper; story. See Berriault, G.

SEARCHES and seizures
Baltimore finds the Constitution; judge-signed warrants before searching private homes needed by police. il Time 88:65 Jl 8 '66
Frisk & find; concerning stop-and-frisk laws. il Time 88:45 Jl 22 '66

SEARL, David
How Generalissimo Franco got his consensus. New Repub 156:12-13 Ja 14 '67

SEARLE, G. D, and company
Searle mixes a new prescription. il Bsns W p 103-4+ N 5 '66

SEARLE, Ronald
Fanciful chronicle of a royal visit. il Look 30:50-2 Ap 5 '66

SEARS, Roebuck and company
Company man; G. M. Metcalf. Newsweek 68:88 N 14 '66
Pick of the rack. il Time 88:101 N 11 '66
Sears's profitable alianza; Latin American growth. il Time 87:96 Mr 4 '66
Vincent Price: he likes what he knows; interview. V. Price. il Design 67:18-22 Ja '66

SEASCAPE; story. See Seitter, J.

SEASHORE
American seashore; symposium. il Holiday 40:8+ Jl '66
Mike Frome; saving our coastal islands. M. Frome. Am For 72:7+ Je '66
Public seashores: their administration. W. Frederickson. jr. il Parks & Rec 1:638-40 Ag '66
Shore in human hands; excerpts from Atlantic shore. J. Hay and P. Farb. il Audubon Mag 68:162-6 My '66
They're saving America's priceless seashore. D. Wharton. il Read Digest 89:181+ Ag '66
Transmigration of shoals; new Mediterranean fishing problem. D. Behrman. il UNESCO Courier 19:23-4 Mr '66
See also
Beaches
Coast changes

SEASHORE ecology
Disappearing seacoast. A. Bester. il Holiday 40:56-69+ Jl '66

SEASHORE houses. See Beach architecture

SEASHORE protection. See Shore protection

SEASHORE vegetation
If you garden near the sea. il Sunset 136:272-3 My '66

SEASIDE resorts
Hunt of the sun; life at beach communities. il Time 88:62 Jl 8 '66

SEASONAL industries
Reducing seasonal unemployment; in construction industry. Mo Labor R 89:990-3 S '66
SEASONAL labor
It's a most unseasonal summer. il Newsweek 68:67 Jl 25 '66
Youthpower! summer jobs for teens. A. Gonzalez and G. Gonzalez. il Seventeen 25:156-7+ Mr '66
SEASONINGS
Seeds for a gourmet touch. Redbook 128:95 Ja '67
See also
Garlic
Herbs
SEASONS
See also
Autumn
Spring
SEASON'S end; story. See Goldman, H. S.
SEAT belts. See Safety belts
SEATON, Esta
Faustus: in the summer of '65; poem. Christian Cent 83:611 My 11 '66
SEATON, S. L.
We take a cruise to Bermuda. Motor B 117:26-7+ Je '66
SEATTLE

Airports

Parking meters keep airport traffic moving; Seattle-Tacoma international airport. il Am City 81:148 S '66

Century 21 exposition, 1962

Aftermath in Seattle: visit to site of World's fair. R. Lynes. il Harper 232:22+ F '66

Music

See also
Seattle opera company

Pacific science center

Dubos wins science award. il Sci N 90:292 O 15 '66
Personality of the month; Arches of science award to Dr Dubos. Sci Digest 60:37 D '66

Recreation

Show goes on; Seattle park department capitalizes on its World's fair center facilities. D. Brink. il Parks & Rec 1:561-2 Jl '66

Religious institutions and affairs

Sephardim: Spanish-speaking Jew. J. Dash; reply. D. Romey. Américas 18:48 Je '66

Sanitary affairs

How to save on sewer maintenance. H. T. Thornquist. il Am City 81:104-5 My '66
SEATTLE boat show. See Boats—Exhibitions
SEATTLE opera company
Seattle (cont) F. J. Warnke. il Opera N 30:30 Mr 12; 28 Je 4; 31:24 N 5 '66
Seattle: production of Cavalleria rusticana and Pagliacci. F. J. Warnke. Opera N 31:30 D 24 '66
SEATTLE public library
Seattle: sensitive and unaggressive; Magnolia and Lake City branches. R. Mostar. il Library J 91:5878-9 D 1 '66
Welcome gift; Journal of Negro history presented to Yesler branch's Negro life and history collection. J. A. Welsh. il Negro Hist Bul 29:156+ Ap '66
SEAVER, Stanley K.
Consumer holds the veto; excerpts from address, ed. by D. Hanson. Suc Farm 64:6+ Ap '66
SEAWEED
Seaweed supplies low. Sci N 89:497 Je 18 '66
See also
Kelp
SEAWRIGHT, James
Tech style. il por Time 88:84 D 9 '66
SEBASTIAN, John
Lovin' Spoonful: rock 'n' roll sweetner. B. Rollin. il pors Look 30:77-81 N 1 '66
SECADES, Rolando Cubela. See Cubela Secades, R.
SECHELT rapids. See Georgia, Strait of
SECOND advent
Celibacy problem: discipline in the light of eschatology. L. Dewart. Commonweal 84:146-50 Ap 22 '66; Discussion. 84:344-5 Je 10 '66
SECOND baby; story. See Cave, H.
SECOND career; story. See Harington, D.
SECOND committee of the General assembly. See United Nations—Economic and financial committee

SECONDARY boycott. See Boycott
SECONDARY school teachers. See Teachers
SECRET; story. See Greene, G.
SECRET; story. See Vivante, A.
SECRET by the pond; story. See Brown, J.
SECRET journal of Waring Stohl; story. See Auchincloss, L.
SECRET of the Roman stairs; drama. See Heshmati, L. B.
SECRET police, Russian. See Secret service—Russia
SECRET service
See also
World war, 1939-1945—Secret service

France

L'affaire Ben Barka. il Time 87:33 Ja 28 '66
Atlantic report: Ben Barka scandal and other cloak-and-dagger affairs. Atlan 217:30+ Ap '66
Beards; the special cops. New Repub 154:7 F 5 '66
Ben Barka affair. C. Sterling. il Reporter 34:22-8 Mr 10 '66
De Gaulle and l'affaire; Ben Barka scandal. A. Werth. Nation 202:200-4 F 21 '66
Diminished fifth; l'affaire Ben Barka erupts into scandal. il Newsweek 67:44+ Ja 31 '66
Fine French scandal over a missing Moroccan. il Life 60:30-32B F 4 '66
Silent witnesses; Ben Barka affair. Time 87:32 F 4 '66

Russia

Licensed to kill in real life; murders of two Ukrainian nationalist leaders. E. Lyons. il Nat R 18:259-61 Mr 22 '66
Soviet tourist traps; KGB's interest in foreign tourists. L. M. Taubinger. Nat R 18:575 Je 14 '66

United States

See also
United States—Central intelligence agency

Anecdotes, facetiae, satire, etc.

I spy for the C.I.A. Esquire 65:80-3 My '66

Yugoslavia

Fading fear; UDBA. Time 88:32 S 9 '66
SECRET societies
See also
Ku Klux klan
Mafia
SECRETARIAL publishing company
Secretarial pub. co. to issue business books. Pub W 190:46 N 21 '66
SECRETARIAL schools. See Business education
SECRETARIAT of the United Nations. See United Nations—Secretariat
SECRETARIES
Ladies, bless 'em, of the executive suite; annual convention of National secretaries association. il Newsweek 68:68-9+ Ag 1 '66
Man talk; village of the damned. D. Newman and R. Benton. Mlle 62:112+ Mr '66
Personal business; how to find an executive secretary. Bsns W p 117-18 Ja 7 '67
State of the secretary. D. Klein. Seventeen 25:228-30 Mr '66
SECRETARIES (furniture) See Desks
SECRETARIES of defense (United States)
See also
McNamara, R. S.
SECRETARIES of state (United States)
How the Secretary of state apportions his time; study prepared in the Bureau of public affairs; with excerpt from interview with Secretary Rusk on Open end, April 3, 1966. Dept State Bul 54:651-4 Ap 25 '66
Secretary gets new responsibility for conduct of foreign affairs; texts of a White House announcement and a message, March 4, 1966. D. Rusk. Dept State Bul 54:506-9 Mr 28 '66
See also
Rusk, D.
SECRETARY General of the United Nations. See United Nations—Secretary General
SECRETIONS
Defensive secretions of arthropods. T. Eisner and J. Meinwald. bibliog il Science 153:1341-50 S 16 '66
D-Gluconic acid: isolation from the defensive secretion of the cockroach eurycotis decipiens. G. P. Dateo and L. M. Roth. bibliog il Science 155:88-9 Ja 6 '67
Insects speak in chemicals. B. Tufty. il Sci N 90:271 O 8 '66

SECRETIONS—*Continued*
Major components in the exocrine secretion of a male butterfly, lycorea. J. Meinwald and others. bibliog il Science 151:583-5 F 4 '66
1,2-dialkyl-4(3H)-quinazolinones in the defensive secretion of a millipede (glomeris marginata) Y. C. Meinwald and others. bibliog il Science 154:390-1 O 21 '66
Pahutoxin: a fish poison. D. B. Boylan and P. J. Scheuer. bibliog il Science 155:52-6 Ja 6 '67
Tanning of grasshopper eggs by an exocrine secretion. T. Eisner and others. bibliog il Science 152:95-7 Ap 1 '66
See also
Saliva

SECRETS, Official. See Official secrets

SECRETS, Trade. See Trade secrets

SECTIONALISM
See also
Provincialism

SECTS
Miss Velma descends. A. B. Haines. Christian Cent 83:992+ Ag 10 '66
Swinging sermon; Los Angeles's World church. il Newsweek 68:62+ N 14 '66
See also
Church of God
Church unity
Churches of Christ
Mennonites
Mormons and Mormonism

SECULAR institutions
See also
Opus Dei

SECULARISM
Essentiality of tradition. K. Hamilton. Christian Cent 83:707-10 Je 1 '66
Is the world a problem? T. Merton. Commonweal 84:305-9 Je 3 '66
Now man is dead. America 114:609 Ap 30 '66
Prophet of the future God; F. Gogarten. il Time 88:63 D 16 '66
Puritanism moribundus; concerning Cox's The secular city. J. Hart. Nat R 18:847-50 Ag 23 '66
Secular city revisited. R. J. O'Connell. America 114:545-8 Ap 16 '66
Sell-out or the well acculturated Christian. R. E. Fitch. Christian Cent 83:202-5 F 16 '66; Discussion. 83:;370-2 Mr 23 '66

SECULARIZATION
Secularization of Christianity, by E. L. Mascall. Review
Commonweal 84:642-3 S 30 '66. R. L. Richard
Nat R 18:370 Ap 19 '66. H. O. J. Brown

SECURITIES
See also
Bonds
Investments
Investments, Foreign
Municipal bonds
Stock exchange
Stocks
also subhead Securities under various subjects, e.g. Airlines—Securities

Advertising
SEC watchmen prowl a new beat; investigates Genesco and Georgia-Pacific cases. il Bsns W p53-4+ My 7 '66

Marketing
Huge profits out of tiny margins; art of arbitrage. il Bsns W p 114+ My 28 '66

SECURITIES, Fraudulent
Preaching and profit; S.E.C. accuses Y. L. Anthony of unregistered bonds sales. Newsweek 67:85-6 Ap 11 '66

SECURITIES, Tax exempt
How much is tax exemption worth? table. Duns R 87:46 Mr '66
Second look at municipal bonds. J. Perham. il Duns R 87:45-6+ Mr '66
Tax-exempt bonds and the small investor. il Changing T 20:21-3 My '66
Why the biggest tax-exempt failed; New Jersey turnpike's record $440-million issue. il Bsns W p 143-4+ Mr 26 '66

SECURITIES and exchange commission. See United States—Securities and exchange commission

SECURITY. See International security; Social and economic security

SECURITY analysts. See Investments—Advisers

SECURITY and consular affairs, Bureau of. See United States—State, Department of —Security and consular affairs, Bureau of

SECURITY and insecurity (psychology)
Sure sources of that sensation of warmth and security. Mim. McCalls 93:105 Jl '66
When it's hard to say good-bye; with group discussion program, by M. S. Smart. M. Brenton. il Parents Mag 41:42-3+, 92+ Ap '66

SECURITY classification (government records)
Shackled historian. H. Feis. For Affairs 45: 332-43 Ja '67

SECURITY council of the United Nations. See United Nations—Security council

SECURITY measures in industry. See Industry —Security measures

SECURITY service. See Secret service

SEDALIA, Mo.
Why Sedalia selected plastic; media for the trickling filters. G. C. Higgins. bibliog il Am City 81:112-13+ S '66

SEDIMENTARY rocks. See Rocks, Sedimentary

SEDIMENTATION and deposition
Anomalous carbon-isotope ratios in nonvolatile organic material; coastal plain of southern Israel. I. R. Kaplan and A. Nissenbaum. bibliog il Science 153:744-5 Ag 12 '66
Branched-chain fatty acids in sediments. R. F. Leo and P. L. Parker. bibliog il Science 152:649-50 Ap 29 '66
Deep flowing currents deposited ocean shelves. il Sci N 89:495 Je 18 '66
Deep layer of sediments in Alpine Lake in the tropical mid-Pacific. A. H. Woodcock and others. bibliog il Science 154:647-8 N 4 '66
Diagenesis of carbonate sediments: interaction of magnesium in sea water with mineral grains. R. A. Berner. bibliog il Science 153:188-91 Jl 8 '66
Fluorescent tracer: transport in distance and depth in beach sands. M. L. Schwartz. bibliog il Science 151:701 F 11 '66
Kodiak seamount not flat-topped. E. L. Hamilton and R. E. Von Huene. bibliog il Science 154:1323-5 D 9 '66
Manganese nodules: thorium-230: protactinium-231 ratios. W. M. Sackett. bibliog il Science 154:646-7 N 4 '66
Sediment movement on the Continental shelf near Washington and Oregon. M. G. Gross and J. L. Nelson. bibliog il Science 154:879-80+ N 18 '66
Sedimentary environments in a marine marsh. F. B. Phleger and J. S. Bradshaw. bibliog il Science 154:1551-3 D 23 '66
Sediments from the lower Columbia River and origin of graywacke. J. T. Whetten. bibliog il Science 152:1057-8 My 20 '66
Shaping of the continental rise by deep geostrophic contour currents. B. C. Heezen and others. bibliog il Science 152:502-8 Ap 22 '66
Soviets disclose new ocean floor maps. W. S. Beller. Tech W 18:19 Je 13 '66
See also
Rocks, Sedimentary

SEE, Elliot M. Jr
Lives of good brave men. W. J. Coughlin Miss & Roc 18:54 Mr 14 '66
Perfectly paired Gemini team falls to earth R. Morse. il por Life 60:34 Mr 11 '66
Rendezvous in St Louis. il por Time 87:27 Mr 11 '66
Safety above, risk below? il por Newsweek 67:68 Mr 14 '66

SEE the moon? story. See Barthelme, D.

SEE you in the funnies; drama. See Dias, E. J.

SEED drills. See Seeding machinery

SEED trade
Make way for spring; flowers. il Time 87: 68-71 Mr 18 '66

SEEDING
Direct seeding. W. Berry. il Horticulture 44: 30-1+ Mr '66
See also
Corn—Seeding
Seeding machinery

SEEDING machinery
Drills a sorghum-sudan hybrid into pasture sod. R. C. Black. il Farm J 90:380 Je '66

SEEDLINGS
See also
Tree seedlings

SEEDS
Dormancy regulation in peach seeds. W. N. Lipe and J. C. Crane. bibliog il Science 153: 541-2 Jl 29 '66
Home garden notebook. J. B. Brimer. il Flower Grower 53:57-8 Mr '66
Seed lipids. I. A. Wolff. bibliog il Science 154:1140-9 D 2 '66
See also
Seed trade

SEEDS—*Continued*
Germination
See Germination
SEEGERS, Kathleen. See Seegers, S. jt. auth.
SEEGERS, Scott, and Seegers, Kathleen
Fabulous Doña Felisa. Read Digest 89:145-8+ Jl '66
Mike's revolution. Américas 18:30-5 Ap '66; Same abr. with title One-man revolution on the Amazon. Read Digest 88:185-8+ My '66
One-man revolution on the Amazon. Read Digest 88:185-8+ My '66
SEELEY, Beverly
Dieter's clipboard; letters. por Seventeen 25:130 Jl; 310 Ag; 212 S; 174 O; 136 D '66
SEELEY, Maxwell H.
What every U.S. pilot should know about flying in Canada. Flying 78:118-19 Je '66
SEEMAN, Elizabeth
And the books came tumblin' in. S. C. Gross. il Sr Schol 88:sup 10 My 6 '66
SEEMAN, Ernest
And the books came tumblin' in. S. C. Gross. il Sr Schol 88:sup9-10 My 6 '66
SEGAL, George, 1924-
Casting of Ethel Scull. il Time 87:69 Ap 1 '66
One for the road. il Time 88:60 Ag 26 '66
SEGAL, Julius
Latest on sleep: what research shows; interview. por U S News 61:60-4 Ag 29 '66
—See Luce, G. G. jt. auth.
SEGAL, Lore
No longer refugees. New Repub 155:20-4 N 26 '66
about
From exile to exile. E. Wiesel. Nation 202:494-5 Ap 25 '66
SEGAL, Marilyn M.
Run away, little girl; condensation. Read Digest 89:259-62+ N '66
SEGAL, Martin E.
Longevity in San Francisco. Parks & Rec 1:455+ My '66
SEGAL, Stanton. See Cuatrecasas, P. jt. auth.
SEGONZAC, André Dunoyer de. See Dunoyer de Segonzac, A.
SEGRÈ, Emilio
Physics in the last twenty years; adaptation of address, December 27, 1965. Science 151:1052-5 Mr 4 '66
SEGREGATION, Social
See also
Discrimination in housing
SEGREGATION in education
Failure of gradualism; concerning H. Howe's address at School administrators' conference, New York. Newsweek 68:80 Jl 4 '66
Risk being fired; law students may aid OEO's integration plan. New Repub 155:8 Jl 2 '66
Separation means unequal; statistical proof that the Nation's public schools are still segregated. Time 88:54 Jl 22 '66
South reports education gains. Sr Schol 88:sup3+ F 4 '66
See also
Parochial schools, Catholic—Desegregation
SEGREGATION of libraries. See Libraries and Negroes
SEGREGATION of Negroes. See Negroes in the United States—Segregation
SEIB, Charles B.
Issues that will tip the '66 elections. Nations Bsns 54:38-9+ Ap '66
—See Otten, A. L. jt. auth.
SEIB, Kathleen Hurst
Bit much; story. Seventeen 25:143 Mr '66
SEIBERT, Russell J.
Longwood gardens. Horticulture 44:46-50 Ap '66
SEIDEL, Frederick
Young reporter; Black Sappho; poems. Poetry 108:87-9 My '66
SEIDEL, Ruth
Art lesson in oil painting. Sch Arts 66:29 S '66
SEIDL, Anthony E.
Costs of Catholic education. America 114:375 Mr 19 '66
SEIDLER, David
Independence? Fiji isn't sure. N Y Times Mag p50-1+ N 20 '66
SEIF, Morton
London's world of dance. Sat R 49:67-8+ S 24 '66
New concert hall in Rotterdam. Sat R 49:45+ Jl 16 '66
SEINGALT, Giacomo Girolamo Casanova de. See Casanova de Seingalt, G. G.

SEISMIC sea waves
Air-sea waves from the explosion of Krakatoa. F. Press and D. Harkrider. bibliog il Science 154:1325-7 D 9 '66
Computers forecast tidal wave dangers; Pacific tsunami warning system. il Tech W 19:24-5 S 12 '66
Nature note; tsunami. Sci N 90:77 Jl 30 '66
SEISMOLOGY
Earth viscosity. D. L. Anderson. bibliog il Science 151:321-2 Jl 21 '66
Earthquake prediction. J. Oliver. Science 153:1024-6 Ag 26 '66
Earthquake prediction. F. Press and W. F. Brace. bibliog il Science 152:1575-84 Je 17 '66
SEITTER, Jean
Seascape; story. Mlle 63:294-5 Ag '66
SEITZ, Frederick
By sharing knowledge. Sat R 49:65-7 My 7 '66
Homi Bhadha and the underdeveloped nations. Science 151:1039 Mr 4 '66
Science and the space program; address, March 31, 1966. Science 152:1719-21 Je 24 '66
SELBY, Anne. See Selby, E. jt. auth.
SELBY, Don
Opening day on S.F. Bay. Motor B 117:27+ My '66
SELBY, Earl
Big dollar in pro football. Read Digest 89:111-15 N '66
Farewell to loafers' paradise. Read Digest 89:161-2+ S '66
—and Selby, Anne
New grab for federal power; unemployment benefits. Read Digest 88:56-9 F '66
Pills, glue and kids; an American tragedy. Read Digest 88:66-70 Je '66
Proud demonstration at Anadarko. Read Digest 88:229-30+ Ap '66
Watts: where welfare bred violence. Read Digest 88:67-71 My '66
SELBY, Hubert, Jr
Blocked exit. por Time 88:34 D 30 '66
Last exit to Brooklyn enjoined in Connecticut. Pub W 190:76 N 14 '66
Last exit to Brooklyn found obscene in London. Pub W 191:34 Ja 2 '67
SELDEN, Armistead Inge, 1921-
Excerpt from debate, July 27, 1966. Cong Digest 45:273+ N '66
SELDEN, William K.
AAU, higher education's enigma. Sat R 49:76-8 Mr 19 '66
SELDES, Gilbert
Public entertainment and the subversion of ethical standards. Ann Am Acad 363:87-94 Ja '66
SELECTION of librarians. See Librarians—Selection and appointment
SELECTIVE service, Military. See Military service, Compulsory
SELENIUM
Pressure-induced phase of sulfur-selenium. S. Geller and M. D. Lind. il Science 155:79-80 Ja 6 '67
See also
Umangite
SELF
See also
Satisfaction
SELF assurance. See Self reliance
SELF confidence. See Self reliance
SELF culture
Can man perfect himself? tr. by D. T. Le-Fort. K. Rahner. Cath World 203:138-44 Je '66
How to succeed in business? pre-packaged personal success and self-improvement. il Newsweek 67:84-6 Ap 4 '66
Personal freedom and community responsibility. C. R. McCarthy. Cath World 203:165-8 Je '66
SELF defense
Right and duty of self-defense. F. S. Meyer. Nat R 18:471 My 17 '66
SELF defense for women
In defense of women. Time 87:67 Ap 15 '66

Anecdotes, facetiae, satire, etc.
Lady be good (and so will I) W. K. Zinsser. il Sat Eve Post 239:20 S 24 '66
SELF dependence. See Self reliance
SELF depreciation
Don't sell yourself short. G. Burgess. Read Digest 88:114-16 My '66

SELF-determination, National
General assembly adopts resolution; prohibition of the use of force: with text. UN Mo Chron 3:55-63 D '66
Self-determination in the western Indian Ocean. P. M. Allen. bibliog f il Int Concil 560:4-74 N '66
U.N. urges no interference with right of peoples to self-determination; statements. November 9, 30; with text of resolution adopted, November 30 1966. J. M. Nabrit, jr. Dept State Bul 56:29-33 Ja 2 '67

SELF discipline. See Discipline

SELF employed
Easier rules for self-pensioning? U S News 60:98 Je 6 '66
Open for business: baedeker for the girl who wants to be her own boss. A. Grant. il Mlle 63:142-3+ S '66
See also
National federation of independent business

SELF evaluation
Interpersonal barriers to decision making. C. Argyris. il Harvard Bsns R 44:84-97 Mr '66
Not all the disadvantaged are poor; with study-discussion program, by R. Strang. W. J. Congreve. bibliog il PTA Mag 60:15-17, 35 F '66
Open generation: we want self-identity before it's too late. Look 30:105-6+ S 20 '66
Take stock of yourself. J. D. Weinland. il Nations Bsns 54:106-7 Ap '66
Where bosses fail; excerpt from Management's self-inflicted wounds; a formula for executive self-analysis. C. F. Austin. il Nations Bsns 54:60+ O '66

SELF expression. See Personality

SELF feeders, Cattle. See Cattle self feeders

SELF government in education
College honor systems: can they work? J. Shepherd. Look 31:25 Ja 24 '67
Self-scheduled examinations under an honor system. W. E. Cadbury, jr. Sch & Soc 94:68-70 F 5 '66
Student self-government. America 115:443-4 O 15 '66

SELF help. See Self reliance

SELF improvement. See Self culture

SELF knowledge. See Self evaluation

SELF murder. See Suicide

SELF realization
See also
Satisfaction

SELF reliance
Alone and not afraid. G. Mayer and M. Hoover. il Redbook 127:58-9+ Je '66
Are you a self-starter? O. Schisgall. Read Digest 89:99-102 Jl '66
Letter to a well-intentioned parent. N. V. Peale. Read Digest 89:75-6 S '66

SELF respect
Books to make them proud. B. B. Washingtin. il NEA J 55:20-2 My '66
Bringing up children in an age of disenchantment. B. Spock. Redbook 126:20+ F '66
Child's right to dignity; excerpt from Life among the giants. L. R. Young. McCalls 94:62+ O '66

SELF service gas stations. See Automobile service stations

SELF service stores. See Stores. Self service

SELIGMAN, Daniel
Why the stock market acts that way. Fortune 74:154-7+ N '66

SELIGMANN, Maxime, and others
Antigenic determinants common to human immunoglobulins G and M: importance of conformational antigens. bibliog Science 154:790-1 N 11 '66

SELL, Stephen
Connoisseur society edition of Chopin's Nocturnes by Ivan Moravec. Am Rec G 32:954-5 Je '66
Great Mozart concerto marathon; on epic, all the way with Lili Kraus. Am Rec G 32:598-9 Mr '66
Haydn by two grandes dames of the keyboard. Am Rec G 33:210-11 N '66
Julius Katchen finishes the complete Brahms piano music. Am Rec G 32:706-9 Ap '66
Serkin. Am Rec G 32:786-9 My '66

SELL, Stewart
Immunoglobulin M allotypes of the rabbit: identification of a second specificity. bibliog Science 153:641-3 Ag 5 '66

SELLARS, Mary
Exit smiling; story. Seventeen 25:150-1 N '66

SELLER, Mary J.
Erythrocyte chimerism after injection of spleen cells into anemic mice of the W-series. bibliog Science 155:90-1 Ja 6 '67

SELLERS, Charles Coleman
French gentleman and the Washington portraits of 1776. Antiques 89:248-55 F '66

SELLING. See Marketing; Salemen and salesmanship

SELLMAN, Paul V. See Brown, J; Schmidt, R. A. M. jt. auths.

SELLSCHOP, J. P. F. See Reines, F. jt. auth.

SELMA, Ala.
Selma revisited; primary contenders. il Newsweek 67:25-6 Ap 25 '66

SELTZER, Louis Benson
Why I went West, and stayed there. por Sat R 49:68-9+ Ap 9 '66

SELYE, Hans
Mast cells and necrosis. Science 152:1371-2 Je 3 '66

SELZNICK, Gene
Another big Selznick production. J. Jares. por Sports Illus 24:72 My 23 '66

SEMANTICS
Warning, danger, loaded words ahead! il Sr Schol 88:5-7 Mr 11 '66

SEMEN
Fatherhood in deep freeze. H. Wray-McCann. Sci Digest 60:12-14 Jl '66
Toward a sperm bank. Newsweek 67:101 Ap 18 '66

SEMICONDUCTOR diodes. See Diodes

SEMICONDUCTORS
Application of high-resolution semiconductor detectors in X-ray emission spectrography. H. R. Bowman and others. bibliog il Science 151:562-8 F 4 '66; Reply with rejoinder. T. Hall. 153:320-1 Jl 15 '66
Insulated gate transistor. D. E. Lancaster. il Electr World 76:34-6+ Jl '66
Semiconductor revolution in nuclear radiation counting. J. M. Hollander and I. Perlman. bibliog il Science 154:84-93 O 7 '66
Transit-time semiconductors. il Electr World 75:80-1 F '66
See also
Electric current rectifiers

Testing
Audible continuity and semiconductor checker. J. B. Frost and R. W. Bailey. il Electr World 76:86+ O '66
TX concept to raise component reliability; military-quality semiconductors. P. J. Klass. il Aviation W 85:75+ D 19 '66

SEMINAR in American studies. See Salzburg seminar in American studies

SEMINARIANS. See Theological students

SEMINARIES. See Theological schools

SEMINARS
Seminar on resources for investment; United Nations. UN Mo Chron 3:39 O '66
See also
Freedom studies center

SEMINOLE Indians
Painting among the Seminoles. J. Hutchinson. il Am Artist 30:52-7+ Ap '66

SEMIPERFECT man; story. See Shyer, M. F.

SEMI-PRECIOUS stones. See Precious stones

SEMONIN, Paul F.
Killing them definitively. Nation 202:129-32 Ja 31 '66

SEMPÉ, Jean Jacques
Nation's midsummer madness; sketches. Sports Illus 25:60-72+ Ag 22 '66

SEN, Binay Ranjan
To be or not to be that will be the question. UNESCO Courier 19:10-15 F '66

SENATE ethics committee. See United States—Congress—Senate—Standards and conduct. Committee on

SENATE foreign relations committee. See United States—Congress—Senate—Foreign relations committee

SENATORIAL candidates. See Candidates, Political

SENATORIAL primaries. See Primaries

SENATORS
In the Senate, accent on newcomers. U S News 62:17-18 Ja 16 '67
Record of the Senate; 89th Congress. New Repub 155:19 O 22 '66
Senate revolt: protesting U.S. overcommitment abroad. B. Nelson. Science 154:751-3 N 11 '66

Election
How '66 Senate races look. il U S News 60:43 Mr 28 '66
Senate races: who won, who lost. U S News 61:42 N 21 '66
When you vote for a senator. F. Morley. il Nations Bsns 54:27-8 N '66

SEND a patrol car to Spartanburg; story. See Hudson, H.

SENDAK, Maurice
Journal of Beatrix Potter; a review. Pub W 190:130-3 Jl 11 '66

about

Maurice Sendak is a success at Hathaway house. Wellesley. il por Pub W 189:91 Je 27 '66
Profiles. N. Hentoff. por New Yorker 41: 39-40+ Ja 22 '66

SENDEROFF, S. and Mellors, G. W.
Coherent coatings of refractory metals. bibliog Science 153:1475-81 S 23 '66

SENECA Indians
Tribal lands vanish; Kinzua Dam. Nat Parks Mag 40:24 My '66

SENEGAL
President Senghor of Senegal visits the United States; exchange of greetings; with exchange of toasts. September 28, 1966. L. S Senghor; L. B. Johnson. Dept State Bul 55:649-52 O 24 '66
Senghor of Senegal: philosopher president. C. J. McNaspy. il America 115:516-17 O 29 '66

See also
Festivals—Senegal

SENEGALESE art. See Art, Senegalese

SENESI, Mauro
Dog for Rock; story. Atlan 218:125-7 N '66

SENFT, Craig T.
Library trustees and the literate society. ALA Bul 60:942-5 O '66

SENGHOR, Léopold Sédar
Hidden force of black African art; tr. by A. Foulke. Vogue 148:236-9+ D '66
President Senghor of Senegal visits the United States; exchange of greetings; with exchange of toasts. September 28, 1966. Dept State Bul 55:649-52 O 24 '66

about

Senghor of Senegal: philosopher president. C. J. McNaspy. il por America 115:516-17 O 29 '66
Within the show's excitement, the deeper issue of négritude. B. Farrell. il Life 60: 88A-88B Ap 22 '66

SENGSENG. See New Britain (island)—Native races

SENILITY. See Old age

SENIOR scholastic (periodical)
At our corner; Scholastic teacher celebrates 20th anniversary. il Sr Schol 89:sup64 S 23 '66
At our corner; Scholastic teacher's special issue on federal aid. il Sr Schol 89:sup26 O 21 '66
Communication: two-way street; Scholastic teacher. W. D. Boutwell. Sr Schol 89:sup9 S 16 '66
Memo from the editor: about Senior scholastic's editorial policy. R. Hemming. Sr Schol 88:sup 10 My 20 '66
1966 editorial advisory board for Senior scholastic. M. R. Robinson. il Sr Schol 88: sup6 My 13 '66
Scholastic sponsors P.E. workshop; Weehawken high school, N.J. il Sr Schol 87: sup32 Ja 14 '66

SENIORITY, Employee
Seniority as security: a rationale. F. Meyers. Mo Labor R 89:127-8 F '66

SENIUS, Felix
Historical records. A. Favia-Artsay. Hobbies 71:38+ My '66

SENN, Milton J. E.
Autism: a medical mystery. McCalls 93:40+ Ap '66
Children's eyes. McCalls 93:26+ Jl '66
Intestinal parasites: the enemy within. McCalls 93:46+ Je '66
Medical problems of adolescents. McCalls 94: 64+ N '66
Our growing knowledge about cancer in children. McCalls 93:40+ F '66
Timely warning for parents. McCalls 93:40+ Mr '66

SENSE of happiness; story. See Redfield, M.

SENSE of humor. See Humor

SENSE organs
See also
Chemoreceptivity

SENSES and sensation
See also
Hearing
Pain
Sight
Smell
Stimulus and response
Taste

SENSORY aid for the blind. See Blind, Apparatus for the

SENSORY deprivation
Study shows biochemical link. Sci N 90:425 N 19 '66

SENTENCE, Imposing of. See Justice, Administration of

SENTER, Raymond D. pseud.
Arms race, a spiral of fear. New Repub 154: 17-18 My 7 '66
Russia and the moon. New Repub 155:14-15 S 10 '66

SENTRY dogs. See Dogs, War use of

SENTRY insurance companies
Whole staff has a voice in running Sentry. il Bsns W p 112-14 Jl 30 '66

SEPARATION (chemistry)
New chemical separation principle developed. Sci N L 89:155 Mr 5 '66
Zonal centrifuges and other separation systems. N. G. Anderson. bibliog il Science 154:103-12 O 7 '66

SEPARATION (religion) See Dissenters, Religious

SEPARATION (technology)
Garnet zoning: an interpretation based on the Rayleigh fractionation model. L. S. Hollister. bibliog il Science 154:1647-51 D 30 '66

SEPHARDIM
Sephardim. J. Dash; reply. D. Romey. Américas 18:48 Je '66

SEPULCHRAL monuments
New England tombstone rubbings. T. McGuire. il Sch Arts 65:21-3 Je '66
See also
Pyramids

SEQUEIRA, Domingos Antonio de
Portuguese plate. C. Bracegirdle. il Antiques 89:834-7 Je '66

Les SÉQUESTRES d'Altona; drama. See Sartre, J. P.

SEQUOIA
See also
Redwood

SERBIN, Max
Fiddlers on the roof. Am Rec G 32:766-70 My '66
Massive documentation of Byrd's technique. Am Rec G 33:60-1 S '66

SERENGETI NATIONAL PARK. See National parks and reserves—Tanganyika

SERETSE Khama. See Khama, S.

SERGEANT major. See United States—Army—Non-commissioned officers

SERJEANT Musgrave's dance; drama. See Arden, J.

SERKIN, Peter
Music to my ears; performance in Carnegie Hall with the Cleveland orchestra. I. Kolodin. Sat R 49:32 Mr 5 '66
Wonder kid. J. Egan. il por Holiday 40:81-5 Ag '66

SERKIN, Rudolf
Masterpieces galore. R. Gelatt. Reporter 34: 42-3 My 5 '66
Serkin, S. Sell. por Am Rec G 32:786-9 My '66

SERMONS
Pulpit platitudes. E. R. Fallon. America 114: 548 Ap 16 '66
See also
Preaching

SEROTONIN
Schizophrenia clue found. Sci N 90:166 S 3 '66

SERPENTINE
Weakening of dunite by serpentine dehydration. R. E. Riecker and T. P. Rooney. bibliog il Science 152:196-8 Ap 8 '66; Reply with rejoinder. C. B. Sclar and L. C. Carrison. 153:1285-7 S 9 '66

SERRA international
Serrans in St Louis: 24th annual convention. America 115:23 Jl 9 '66

SERREULLES, Claude
Wizardry of Oise. V. Lawford. il Vogue 148: 256-9+ O 1 '66

SERUM
Antiserum to lymphocytes: prolonged survival of canine renal allografts. A. F. Monaco and others. bibliog il Science 153: 1264-7 S 9 '66
Beta-glucuronidase activity in serum increased by coronary-artery atherosclerosis. B. F. Miller and others. bibliog Science 152:775-6 My 6 '66
Blood groups of the I system in pigs: association with variants of serum amylase. E. Andresen. bibliog il Science 153:1660-1 S 30 '66
Homoreactant: a naturally occurring autoantibody in rabbits. W. J. Mandy and L. C. Kormeier. bibliog il Science 154:651-2 N 4 '66

SERUM—*Continued*

Inherited variations of human serum α₁ antitrypsin. F. Kueppers and A. G. Bearn. bibliog il Science 154:407-8 O 21 '66

Serum concentration: effects on cycle and X-ray sensitivity of mammalian cells. G. M. Hahn and M. A. Bagshaw. bibliog il Science 151:459-61 Ja 28 '66

Transplants prolonged; testing anti-lymphocyte serum. F. Marley. Sci N 90:357 O 29 '66

See also
Serotonin

SERUM albumins. See Blood—Proteins

SERUM globulins

Allelic antigenic factor inv(a) of the light chains of human immunoglobulins: chemical basis. C. Baglioni and others. bibliog il Science 152:1517-19 Je 10 '66

Alpha globulin injections and decreased gamma globulin production in chickens. B. B. Kamrin. bibliog il Science 153:1261-2 S 9 '66

Antibody active sites and immunoglobulin molecules. S. J. Singer and R. F. Doolittle. bibliog il Science 153:13-25 Jl 1 '66

Antigenic determinants common to human immunoglobulins G and M: importance of conformational antigens. M. Seligmann and others. bibliog il Science 154:790-1 N 11 '66

Antigenic heterogeneity of human immunoglobulin A proteins. W. D. Terry and M. S. Roberts. bibliog il Science 153:1007-8 Ag 26 '66

Antiserum to immunoglobulin A: inhibition of cell-mediated demyelination in tissue culture. G. F. Winkler and B. G. Arnason. bibliog il Science 153:75-6 Jl 1 '66

Beta-1C-globulin: metabolism in glomerulonephritis. C. A. Alper and others. bibliog il Science 153:180-2 Jl 8 '66

Evolution of immunoglobulin polypeptide chains: carboxy-terminal of an IgM heavy chain. R. F. Doolittle and others. bibliog il Science 154:1561-2 D 23 '66

Hepatic synthesis of alpha₁ acute phase-globulin of rat plasma. E. J. Sarcione and A. E. Bogden. bibliog il Science 153:547-8 Jl 29 '66

Immunoglobulin M allotypes of the rabbit: identification of a second specificity. S. Sell. bibliog il Science 153:641-3 Ag 5 '66

Immunoglobulin structure: variation in the sequence of Bence Jones proteins. K. Titani and others. bibliog il Science 152:1513-16 Je 10 '66

Immunoglobulin synthesis in vitro by established human cell lines. J. L. Fahey and others. bibliog il Science 152:1259-61 My 27 '66; Reply. G. E. Moore and others. 153:212-13 Jl 8 '66

Multiple sclerosis: correlation between immunoglobulin-G in cerebrospinal fluid and brain. W. W. Tourtellotte and J. A. Parker. bibliog il Science 154:1044-6 N 25 '66

Natural human antibodies to gram-negative bacteria immunoglobulins G, A, and M. I. R. Cohen and L. C. Norins. bibliog il Science 152:1257-9 My 27 '66

Polymorphism of heavy-chain genes in immunoglobulins of wild mice. R. Lieberman and M. Potter. bibliog il Science 154:535-7 O 28 '66

Polypeptide chains of immunoglobulins from the smooth dogfish (mustelus canis) J. Marchalonis and G. M. Edelman. bibliog il Science 154:1567-8 D 23 '66

Subclasses of human immunoglobulin A based on differences in the alpha polypeptide chains. J. P. Vaerman and J. F. Heremans. bibliog il Science 153:647-9 Ag 5 '66

SERUM proteins. See Blood—Proteins

SERVICE, Community. See Community service

SERVICE, Compulsory non-military

Alternate service. Commonweal 84:303 Je 3 '66

Anything goes; concerning Secretary McNamara's Montreal address. F. S. Meyer. Nat R 18:629 Je 28 '66

Case for drafting all boys and girls. M. Mead. Redbook 127:40+ S '66

Draft for nonmilitary service? il Changing T 20:41-2 D '66

More pressure for universal service. U S News 61:8 N 28 '66

National service corps for young Americans; poll by Scholastic magazine's Institute of student opinion. Sr Schol 89:26 D 9 '66

National service proposal. J. M. Swomley, jr. Christian Cent 84:40-3 Ja 11 '67

National service to replace the draft? pro and con discussion. Sr Schol 89:16-17+ O 14 '66

SERVICE, Volunteer. See Volunteer service

SERVICE corps of retired executives. See United States—Small business administration

SERVICE industries

Kinney spreads umbrella wider; expanding service, from autos to funerals. il Bsns W p 101-2+ Ap 16 '66

No place like; house calls. il Newsweek 67:95-6 Mr 14 '66

Training in service occupations; excerpt from Manpower development and training act. il Mo Labor R 89:523-7 My '66

See also
Courtesy associates

SERVICE men

Pay, allowances, etc.

See United States—Armed forces—Pay, allowances, etc.

Recreation

See United States—Armed forces—Recreation

SERVICE men, Discharged

Benefits

GI benefits: bigger and better. il U S News 61:92 N 28 '66

Join the army and buy a home; new bill provides educational loan and hospital benefits. Time 87:23 F 18 '66

Latest benefits for GI's: who will be helped. il U S News 60:50-1 F 21 '66

Philippine veterans benefits signed into law; statements, September 30 and October 11, 1966. L. B. Johnson. Dept State Bul 55:684-6 O 31 '66

Education

Cold war G.I. bill. America 114:278 F 26 '66

Continued evaluation of veterans' careers as a function of education. R. J. Anderson and others. il Sch & Soc 94:357-8 O 29 '66

GI bill: answers to questions. U S News 60:50 Mr 21 '66

GI is a GI; new GI bill of rights. Newsweek 67:28 F 14 '66

Latest benefits for GI's: who will be helped; GI bill for veterans with service after the Korean war. il U S News 60:50-1 F 21 '66

Latest GI bill, what you get. il Changing T 20:33-4 Ag '66

Why the draft won't hurt your labor supply. il Nations Bsns 54:35-7+ N '66

You and the new G.I. bill. F. K. Smith. Flying 79:80-1 S '66

Employment

Continued evaluation of veterans' careers as a function of education. R. J. Anderson and others. il Sch & Soc 94:357-8 O 29 '66

SERVICE mens benefits. See Service men, Discharged—Benefits

SERVICE mens entertainments. See United States—Armed forces—Recreation

SERVICE mens families

Phone pollution; obscene calls to families of men serving in Vietnam. Nation 202:445 Ap 18 '66

Waiting wives of Schilling Manor. A. Whitman. il Look 30:66+ N 15 '66

Youth activities on Okinawa. R. F. McKeta. il Parks & Rec 1:156-8 F '66

SERVICE mens graves

Not all the Yanks can go home; Normandy American cemetery. A. H. Sypher. il Nations Bsns 54:31-2 O '66

SERVICE mens wives

Wives alone; wives of U.S. civilians in Vietnam. L. Martin. il Newsweek 68:29-30 S 5 '66

Women who wait; husbands in Vietnam. M. Frady. il Good H 162:100-1+ My '66

SERVICE of reconciliation. See Volunteer service, International

SERVICE stations. See Automobile service stations

SERVICE women, Negro. See Negro service men and women

SERVICES, Farm. See Farm services

SERVING baskets. See Baskets

SERVING carts

How to make a party cart. il Ladies Home J 83:128 O '66

Meals in motion! il Bet Hom & Gard 44:66-7 N '66

Party à la cart. il Ladies Home J 83:124+ O '66

Seven slaves on wheels; service carts all. il Pop Mech 125:149-55+ F '66

SERVING trays. See Trays

SERVO-recorder. See Recording instruments
SESHAN, K. R. and Ittycheriah, P. I.
Iphita limbata stal.: components of neurosecretory material. bibliog Science 153:427-8 Jl 22 '66
SESPE country. See Wilderness areas—California
SESSIONS, Roger
Music to my ears; Trial of Lucullus performed by Juilliard opera theater. I. Kolodin. Sat R 49:38 Je 4 '66
SESSLER, Andrew M. See Laslett, L. J. jt. auth.
SESSOMS, H. Douglas
Recreation enrollment growth reported. Parks & Rec 1:867-9 O '66
SÈTE, France
Movie-set Sète. C. Stinnett. il Holiday 41:40+ Ja '67
SETH, A. K. and others
Auxin effects on the mobility of kinetin in the plant. bibliog Science 151:587-8 F 4 '66
SETH, D. See Kubištová, J. jt. auth.
SETLOW, R. B.
Cyclobutane-type pyrimidine dimers in polynucleotides. bibliog Science 153:379-86 Jl 22 '66
SETON, Cynthia
Must everything be ugly? Redbook 127:59+ S '66
SETTERS
Aging gun dog. G. B. Evans. il Field & S 71:146-7+ N '66
Don't count out the Irish. D. M. Duffey. il Outdoor Life 137:150-2+ Ap '66
See also
Pointers (dogs)
SETTLE, Jane Anne
English is to enjoy. Sr Schol 88:sup20 F 11 '66
SETTLES, Gary S.
Amateur scientist. Sci Am 215:120-4+ O '66
SETTLING in; story. See Benchley, N.
SETTON, Kenneth M.
Norman conquest. por Nat Geog Mag 130:206-51 Ag '66
SEVAREID, Eric
(ed) See Fulbright, J. W. Why our foreign policy is failing
SEVEN whiteface; story. See Morgan, B.
SEVENTEEN (periodical)
Seventeen at my fingertips; first braille edition. M. E. Earls. Seventeen 26:22 Ja '67
SEVENTEEN-nation disarmament conference, Geneva, 1962-. See Conference of the Eighteen-nation committee on disarmament. Geneva, 1962-
SEVENTH avenue. See New York (city)—Streets
SEVENTH day Adventists
Adventists' advantage; few deaths due to lung cancer. Time 88:68 O 28 '66
Basic training; conscientious objectors. Newsweek 68:54 S 12 '66
SEVENTH fleet. See United States—Navy
SEVERAL blessings of Ta-nien Wang; story. See Nieh, H. L.
SEVERIN, Kurt
Just to change the subject. Outdoor Life 138:72-3 O '66
SEVERN RIVER
Suspension bridges cross a new frontier; Severn River bridge linking England and south Wales. il Bsns W p 104-5 S 10 '66
SEVERO, Richard
What's news at CBS? New Repub 154:29+ Mr 12 '66
SEVERSON, John
I won't ever punch the clock; interview. ed. by H. Wingo. por Life 61:42 S 9 '66
about
Riding the crest of surfing's wave. il pors Life 61:37-8+ S 9 '66
SEVIGNY, Pierre
Finding Gerda's goat. Newsweek 67:50 Mr 21 '66
Gerda cooks up a Canadian stew. il por Life 60:105-6 Mr 25 '66
Munsinger affair. il por Time 87:54 Mr 18 '66
Not very romantic. il por Newsweek 67:71 My 23 '66
Suspended degradation. por Newsweek 67:58 Mr 28 '66
SEVILLE, Jack
Before you button-up the engine. Motor B 118:38-9 N '66
SEVILLE, Spain
Letter from abroad; Holy week. W. Sansom. il McCalls 93:48+ My '66

SEWAGE
See also
Water pollution
SEWAGE aeration. See Sewage disposal—Activated sludge method
SEWAGE disposal
And not a drop to drink. L. Kavaler. il Redbook 126:80-1+ Ap '66
Oxidation ditch; sewage-purification process. W. L. Berk. il Am City 81:120-1+ S '66
Sewerage and sewage purification. See issues of American city
Wet air oxidation of sewage sludge; South Milwaukee, Wis. R. W. Nicholson and others. il Am City 81:97-9+ Ap '66
See also
Trade waste
Water pollution

Activated sludge method
Aerobic treatment in a ditch; Pasveer method. R. Smith and D. Noyes. il Am City 81:25 O '66
Old units form basis of new plant; Excelsior, Minn. S. A. Friedman. il Am City 81:90-1 F '66

Filtration
Biggest dollar's worth of sewage treatment; Redlands, Calif. il Am City 81:83-6 Mr '66
Kansas City's West side story. L. W. Weller il Am City 81:108-11 F '66
More vacuum filtration of raw sewage sludge. il Am City 81:13 Ag '66
Why Sedalia selected plastic; media for the trickling filters. G. C. Higgins. bibliog il Am City 81:112-13+ S '66

Phosphate removal
New sewage treatment reduces growth of algae; controlling phosphates in sewage. Sci N 90:250 O 1 '66

SEWAGE disposal plants
Best value; goal of St. Louis sewage purification system. G. D. Simpson and W. G. Shrifrin. il Am City 81:75-8 Jl '66
Biggest dollar's worth of sewage treatment; Redlands, Calif. il Am City 81:83-6 Mr '66
Labor and material requirements for sewer works construction. R. V. Murray. il Mo Labor R 89:288-90 Mr '66
No storm-water bypass; Milwaukee's new sewage-purification plant. R. D. Leary. il Am City 81:93-5 Ag '66
One plant, two processes; Estes Park, Colo. R. G. Crabtree. il Am City 81:118-19 My '66
Report on present status of a new simple low-cost coal sewage treatment. E. R. Fosdick. il Nat Parks Mag 40:18-19 Ap '66
SR research; East Lansing methods. K. L. Schulze. Sat R 49:62-3 Je 4 '66; Reply with rejoinder. J. R. Hanson. 49:51 Jl 2 '66
Sewerage and sewage purification. See issues of American city
Sick river is returned to health; North Platte. R. Gannon. il Read Digest 89:29-30+ Jl '66
Sludge-disposal solution: thicken, filter, dry and burn; Holyoke, Mass. E. J. Bayon. il Am City 81:95-7 Je '66
Two plants in one remove 97.5 percent BOD; Sioux Falls, S.D. R. Jackson and R. Wieting. il Am City 81:158+ O '66
Wet air oxidation of sewage sludge; South Milwaukee, Wis. R. W. Nicholson and others. il Am City 81:97-9+ Ap '66
SEWAGE gas. See Gas as fuel
SEWAGE lagoons
Aerated sewage lagoon; Harvey, N.D. O. O. Olson and J. Klingenberg. il Am City 81:94-5 N '66
SEWAGE sludge. See Sewage disposal—Activated sludge method
SEWAGE systems. See Sewerage
SEWAGE treatment plants. See Sewage disposal plants
SEWELL, Elizabeth
Science and literature; adaptation of address. Commonweal 84:218-21 My 13 '66
SEWELL, W. R. Derrick, and White, G. F.
Lower Mekong. bibliog f pors(back cover) Int Concil 558:5-63 My '66
SEWER cleaning
Better way to clean catch basins; Philadelphia. R. E. Doyle. il Am City 81:102-3 Ap '66
SEWER inspection
How to save on sewer maintenance; Seattle, Wash. H. T. Thornquist. il Am City 81:104-5 My '66
SEWER pipe laying. See Pipe laying

SEWER pipes
British engineer's attitude toward plastic pipe. C. E. Tiffen. il Am City 81:108-9 Ap '66
Cast-in-place drainage pipe; Sacramento County, Calif. T. E. Campbell. il Am City 81:100-2 D '66
Double-barreled clay-pipe sewer; Los Angeles, Calif. L. A. Pardee. il Am City 81:82-3 D '66
How to tap prestressed-concrete pipe. il Am City 81:87 Mr '66
New sewer system sparks new industry; Gadsden. Ala. il Am City 81:66 My '66
Sewer within a sewer; Minneapolis. W. G. Ridge. il Am City 81:112-13 O '66

SEWERAGE
Labor and material requirements for sewer works construction. R. V. Murray. il Mo Labor R 89:288-90 Mr '66

SEWING
See also
Dressmaking

SEWING centers. See Sewing rooms

SEWING equipment

Collectors and collecting
Sewing circle. D. F. Brown. il Hobbies 70:50-1 F '66

SEWING machines
Beware of these sewing machine rackets. il Good H 162:179 Ap '66
How to care for your sewing machine. il Bet Hom & Gard 44:138+ O '66
Sewing machine. Consumer Bul 49:22 O '66
Sewing machines. il Consumer Rep 31:68-73 F '66
Singer 600E sewing machine. il Consumer Bul 49:31-2 Mr '66
See also
Singer company

SEWING rooms
Find space for a sewing center. J. LemMon. il Suc Farm 64:104-5 S '66
Give your wife a break; step-saving work center. H. Clark. il Pop Mech 126:124-5 S '66
It's her sewing and laundry room. il Sunset 137:126+ S '66

SEX
Sex and your teen-ager. M. S. Calderone. Farm J 90:90-1 F '66
Sex is dead! E. H. Brill. Christian Cent 83:957-9 Ag 3 '66; Reply. H. B. Berg. 83:1146 S 21 '66
Who killed sex? Earl H. Brill comment. Newsweek 68:93 Ag 22 '66

SEX (biology)
Pheromone; evidence in a decapod crustacean. E. P. Ryan. bibliog il Science 151:340-1 Ja 21 '66
See also
Estruation

SEX, Change of. See Change of sex

SEX and religion
British churches' report on sex. America 115:503 O 29 '66
Total gift. J. T. Culliton. America 115:770-3 D 10 '66
See also
Sex in the Bible

SEX attractants (insects) See Insect sex attractants

SEX behavior
Adolescent sex in America; reprint. il Sci Digest 60:45-8 S '66
Church and the sexual crisis. Christian Cent 83:823-4 Je 29 '66; Discussion. 83:986 Ag 10 '66
Human sexual response, by W. H. Masters and V. E. Johnson. Review
Life 60:8+ Ap 22 '66. A. Rosenfeld
Sci Am 215:107-10+ Ag '66. F. A. Beach
Human sexuality explored. P. McBroom. Sci N 89:323 Ap 30 '66
Inhibitory centers in sexual behavior in the male rat. R. D. Lisk. bibliog il Science 152:669-70 Ap 29 '66; Reply with rejoinder. F. A. Beach. 153:769-70 Ag 12 '66
Italian men are lousy lovers; concerning G. Parca's book The sultans. J. Bonfante. il Life 60:81-2+ F 4 '66
Margaret Mead answers questions about: study by W. H. Masters and V. E. Johnson on physiology of sex. M. Mead. Redbook 127:36+ O '66
Mites on a substrate; study of mating behavior. S. Radinovsky. il Natur Hist 75:38-43 Je '66
My secret life. Review
Time il 88:54+ D 30 '66
Problems of sex; Masters-Johnson research. il Time 87:51 Ap 29 '66
Response to response; Masters-Johnson book. Human sexual response. il Newsweek 67:94 My 23 '66

Seasonal variation in mating behavior in cats after desensitization of glans penis. L. R. Aronson and M. L. Cooper. bibliog il Science 162:226-30 Ap 8 '66
Sex and the college student, by the Committee on the college student group for the advancement of psychiatry. Review
Cath World 204:182-4 D '66. R. A. Schroth
Sat R 49:71-2 My 21 '66
Sex and the person. D. Sullivan. Commonweal 84:460-4 Jl 22 '66; Discussion. 84:548-9+ S 2 '66
Sex becomes a brand-new problem. K. D. Fishman. il N Y Times Mag p69+ Mr 13 '66
Sex goes public; interview, ed. by D. Dury. H. Miller. il Esquire 65:118-21+ My '66
Sex in the laboratory; concerning books in response to Masters-Johnson study. G. Krupp. Sat R 49:38-9 N 19 '66
Sex study raises ruckus. il Sci Digest 60:29-30 Jl '66
Sex under scrutiny; concerning W. Masters and V. Johnson's study of the sex act. il Newsweek 67:80 Ap 25 '66
Sexual-response study; concerning book by W. H. Masters and V. E. Johnson. Sci Am 214:54 Je '66
Should this sex research be allowed to go on? L. R. Chevalier. Ladies Home J 83:26+ My '66
Today's children and sex; excerpts from panel discussion of Child study association of America meeting. il Changing T 20:7-12 Je '66; Discussion. 20:21-3 S '66
Trouble between the sexes. Time 88:68 D 9 '66
Wild spectacle; bighorn rams in rutting season. J. C. Holroyd. il Field & S 71:31-3+ Ag '66
See also
Courtship of insects

SEX crimes
Sex criminal: I don't know why I did it. J. Kobler. il Sat Eve Post 240:23-9+ Ja 28 '67
Society and the sex criminal; excerpt from How many more victims? G. D. Shultz. Read Digest 89:139-46 N '66
Uncontrollable vegetable; case of Albert De-Salvo. il Newsweek 69:30+ Ja 23 '67

SEX determination and control
Baby's sex predicted by prenatal fluid test. Sci N 90:276 O 8 '66
Predicting sex. Time 88:72 O 7 '66
Sex-ratio condition; unusual mechanisms in bark beetles. G. N. Lanier and J. H. Oliver, jr. bibliog il Science 153:208-9 Jl 8 '66

SEX differences
Sex differences in the brain. S. Levine. il Sci Am 214:84-90 Ap '66

SEX education. See Sex instruction

SEX hormones. See Hormones, Sex

SEX in art
Eros in polyester; show at Sidney Janis gallery called Erotic art 66. il Newsweek 68:102-3 O 10 '66
Pornography and the new expression. R. Schechner. Atlan 219:74-8 Ja '67
Wilfred Lang: artist, critic of today's church. D. Devereux. Christian Cent 83:1515-19 D 7 '66

SEX in literature
Apology for pornography. P. Michelson. New Repub 155:21-4 D 10 '66
Pornography and the new expression. R. Schechner. Atlan 219:74-8 Ja '67

SEX in moving pictures. See Moving pictures —Moral aspects

SEX in the Bible
Sex and the single God. R. T. Osborn. Christian Cent 83:1078-80 S 7 '66; Discussion. 83:1245-6 O 12 '66

SEX instruction
Are parents the best sex educators? with study-discussion program, by E. Harris and D. Harris. F. R. Wake. bibliog il PTA Mag 61:8-10, 35 N '66
Controversy over sex education; with study-discussion program by E. G. Neisser. B. B. Gotthold. il Parents Mag 41:20+, 68-70+ O '66
Defense of love and morality. W. H. Masters and V. E. Johnson. McCalls 94:102-3+ N '66
Dialogue with mothers. B. Bettelheim. Ladies Home J 83:36-7 Je '66
Every sixth teen-age girl in Connecticut—; will become pregnant out of wedlock before her 20th birthday. R. Brecher and E. Brecher. il N Y Times Mag p6-7+ My 29 '66; Discussion. p22+ Je 12 '66
Goodbye to the birds and the bees; an approach; adaptation of address. M. S. Calderone. il Am Ed 2:17-18 N '66

SEX instruction—*Continued*
Goodbye to the birds and the bees; what's happening. E. Ferber **and** J. H. Sofokidis. il Am Ed 2:16+ N '66
Home, the school, and sex education. M. A. Hinrichs and R. Kaplan. Todays Health 44:16+ F '66
Let's call a stork a stork. N. C. Hooper. il Read Digest 89:139-40 S '66
~ Planning for sex education, a community-wide responsibility; with discussion. M. S. Calderone. NEA J 56:26-9 Ja '67
Sex among teen-agers; letters to the editor. W. G. Cowan; I. Rubin. N Y Times Mag p90+ Mr 27 '66; Reply. p22 Ap 24 '66
Sex and your teen-ager. M. S. Calderone. Farm J 90:90-1 F '66
Sex becomes a brand-new problem. K. D. Fishman. il N Y Times Mag p69+ Mr 13 '66
Sex education and the censor. E. Geller. Library J 91:2118 Ap 15 '66
Sex education and the very young child. M. S. Calderone il PTA Mag 61:16-18 O '66
Sex education comes of age. L. Gross. il Look 30:20-3 Mr 8 '66
Sex education: the common denominator; Boston public library, with bibliography. J. Manthorne. il Library J 91:319-22 Ja 15 '66
Sex in the classroom; Scandinavian systems. Newsweek 68:83 Jl 11 '66
Sex without secrets; interview. M. Calderone. il Seventeen 25:106-7+ Jl '66
Solid sex-education program; L. Smith's sixth grade class on human reproduction, University City, Mo. il Look 30:24-5 Mr 8 '66
Sweden's new battle over sex. J. R. Moskin. il Look 30:36-42 N 15 '66
Teaching young teenagers about sex. J. A. Matz. il Parents Mag 41:60-1+ Mr '66
Today's children and sex; excerpts from panel discussion of Child study association of America meeting. il Changing T 20:7-12 Je '66; Discussion. 20:21-3 S '66

SEX organs. See Generative organs

SEX perversion
See also
Homosexuality

SEX psychology
Sex and the person. D. Sullivan. Commonweal 84:460-4 Jl 22 '66; Discussion. 84:548-9+ S 2 '66

SEX relations
Antidotes for the new puritanism; dilemmas of sex and love. R. May. Sat R 49:19-21+ Mr 26 '66
Calculus of sex. C. Dowling and P. Fahey. il Esquire 65:122-3+ My '66
Human sexual response, by W. H. Masters and V. E. Johnson. Review
Life 60:8+ Ap 22 '66. A. Rosenfeld
Last word: the public fantasy versus the private act. M. Magid. Esquire 65:128-9 My '66
Response to response; Masters-Johnson book, Human sexual response. il Newsweek 67:94 My 23 '66
Sex in the laboratory; concerning books in response to Masters-Johnson study. G. Krupp. Sat R 49:38-9 N 19 '66
Sex kick, by T. Coffin. Review
Sat R 49:36-7 N 26 '66. R. J. Levin
Sex study raises ruckus. il Sci Digest 60:29-30 Jl '66
Sex under scrutiny; concerning W. Masters and V. Johnson's study of the sex act. il Newsweek 67:80 Ap 25 '66
Should this sex research be allowed to go on? L. R. Chevalier. Ladies Home J 83:26+ My '66
Single girl and the married man. G. Dickerson. Mlle 62:154-5+ F '66
Two sex researchers on the firing line; interview, ed. by W. Bradbury. W Masters and V. Johnson. il Life 60:43-4+ Je 24 '66

Anecdotes, facetiae, satire, etc.
Some day he'll come along, the man I love. W. Goodhart. il Esquire 65:124-7 My '66

SEX-role inversion. See Change of sex

SEX surgery. See Generative organs—Surgery

SEXTON, Anne
Flee on your donkey; poem. New Yorker 42:44-5 My 7 '66
Pain for a daughter; poem. New Yorker 42:50 Mr 26 '66
Your face on the dog's neck; poem. New Yorker 42:40 S 3 '66

SEXTON, John
How to make a landfill attractive. Am City 81:92-3 N '66

SEXTON, Owen J. and others
Anolis carolinensis: effects of feeding on reaction to aposematic prey. Science 153:1140 S 2 '66

SEXTON, Peggy
To kill a whooping crane. por Library J 91:5327-32 N 1 '66

SEXUAL diseases. See Venereal diseases

SEXUAL ethics
California classic: the Berkeley girl. J. Shepherd. il Look 30:78-80+ Je 28 '66
Defense of love and morality. W. H. Masters and V. E. Johnson. McCalls 94:102-3+ N '66
Every sixth teen-age girl in Connecticut—; will become pregnant out of wedlock before her 20th birthday. R. Brecher and E. Brecher. il N Y Times Mag p6-7+ My 29 '66; Discussion. p22+ Je 12 '66
Free-sex movement; growth on campuses. il Time 87:66 Mr 11 '66
How important is premarital chastity? dialogue between a mother and daughter. F. M. Bruce. Good H 162:16+ Je '66
Hugh Hefner: I am in the center of the world; interview, ed. by O. Fallaci. H. Hefner. il Look 31:54-7 Ja 10 '67
Let's not panic at the new morality; excerpt from address, January 26, 1966. W. I. Nichols. Read Digest 89:75-8 Ag '66
Modern morals in a muddle. R. A. McCormick. America 115:116 Jl 30 '66
Pill: how it is affecting U.S. morals, family life. il U S News 61:62-5 Jl 11 '66
Roman holidays for students. R. Kirk. Nat R 18:472 My 17 '66
Sex and morality; a challenging point of view. I. Rubin. il Redbook 127:68-9+ O '66
Sex and the college student, by the Committee on the college student group for the advancement of psychiatry. Review
Cath World 204:182-4 D '66. R. A. Schroth
New Repub 154:21-3 My 28 '66. R. Coles
Sex and the teen-age girl. D. Sugarman and R. Hochstein. Read Digest 88:119-22 F '66
Sex goes public; interview, ed. by D. Dury. H. Miller. il Esquire 65:118-21+ My '66
Sex without secrets; interview. M. Calderone. il Seventeen 25:106-7+ Jl '66
Sexual revolution. K. Mehlinger. il Ebony 21:57-60+ Ag '66
Situation sex; report published by a committee of the British council of churches. Time 88:44 O 28 '66
Sweden's new battle over sex. J. R. Moskin. il Look 30:36-42 N 15 '66
That new morality. R. Kirk. Nat R 18:165 F 22 '66
Thou better not; reactions to Sex and morality report. Newsweek 68:66 O 31 '66
Unstructured relations; students living together. il Newsweek 68:78 Jl 4 '66
~ What sex means to college girls today. M. Lerner. il Redbook 127:51+ Je '66
What should I tell my son? A. Silberman. Read Digest 88:103-6 My '66
See also
Illegitimacy
Incest
Marriage
Sex and religion
Sex instruction
Sex relations

SEXUAL sterilization. See Sterilization, Sexual

SEYBOLT, George Crossan
Red devil bites off a new market. il pors Bsns W p66+ Je 18 '66

SEYCHELLES (islands)
Seychelles. L. Millar. il Natur Hist 75:48-51 O '66

SEYMOUR, David
Chim: shadow of violence. M. R. Weiss. il Sat R 50:128-9 Ja 14 '67

SEYMOUR, James Patrick
Babes in wonderland. il por Time 88:50-2+ O 28 '66

SEYNES, Philippe de
Trends and objectives of the world economy; statement, October 4, 1966. UN Mo Chron 3:133-46 N '66

SHAARA, Michael
In the midst of life. por Sat Eve Post 239:79-83 Ag 27 '66
Speaking out. por Sat Eve Post 239:10+ N 5 '66

SHABECOFF, Alice
Parent and child. N Y Times Mag p 179-80+ N 13 '66

SHABECOFF, Philip
Country cousin of the Berlin wall. N Y Times Mag p8-9+ Jl 10 '66
Last prisoner of Spandau. N Y Times Mag p28-9+ Ag 28 '66

SHABOS nahamu: story. See Babel, I.

SHAD fishing
Fishing the shad runs. G. Heinold. il Outdoor Life 137:10+ My '66
Hickory shad on the Susquehanna. N. Karas. il Field & S 70:66-7+ Ap '66

SHADE
See also
Screens (sun)

SHADES. See Window shades

SHADES of Shakespeare: drama. See Dias, E. J.

SHADOW stick. See Astronomical instruments

SHADOWGRAMS
Photograms. S. Blake. il Design 67:23-5 Ja '66

SHAFER, Raymond Philip
Cashkrieg. il por Time 88:31-2 O 21 '66
Pennsylvania story. I. Bay. Nat R 18:1041-2 O 18 '66

SHAFER, Ronald G.
Confessions of a car salesman. Pop Mech 126:59-61+ S '66

SHAFFER, Ellen
Beatrix Potter lives in Philadelphia's Free library. Horn Bk 42:401-5 Ag '66

SHAFFER, N. Manfred
Sudan: Arab-African confrontation. bibliog f Cur Hist 50:142-6+ Mr '66

SHAFFER, Peter
Royal hunt of the sun. Criticism
Sat R 49:72 N 19 '66

SHAHN, Ben
$475 bargain. F. Getlein. New Repub 154:27-8 Ap 30 '66

SHAKER furniture. See Furniture, American

SHAKERS
Movers and Shakers; Shaker community, Hancock, Mass. R. Lynes. il Harper 233:34+ D '66

SHAKESPEARE, William
Much ado about nothing. J. Diether. Am Rec G 32:816-18 My '66
On writing a children's play. B. Quint. Horn Bk 42:181-5 Ap '66
Shakespeare wallah; original soundtrack. J. Lyons. Am Rec G 32:1108 Ag '66

Characters
Hamlet's hamartia: Aristotle or St Paul? R. L. Cox. Yale R 55:347-64 Mr '66

Criticism and interpretation
Hamlet's hamartia: Aristotle or St Paul? R. L. Cox. Yale R 55:347-64 Mr '66

Plays
Hamlet
Shakespeare's Hamlet, by R. Mamoulian. Review
Sat R 49:43-4 Mr 5 '66. P. Burton

Henry VI
Stratford and Ypsilanti. J. Novick. Nation 203:259-60 S 19 '66

Macbeth
Macbeth. K. Rexroth. Sat R 49:17 Je 25 '66

Measure for measure
Summer camp: Central park production. H. Hewes. Sat R 49:48 Jl 30 '66

Midsummer night's dream
Theatre; production at the Pittsburgh playhouse, in Pittsburgh, Pa. T. Lewis. America 115:786 D 10 '66

Othello
Olivier and the Moor. N. Kallet. Holiday 39:143-4 Ap '66

Tempest
Classics revisited. K. Rexroth. Sat R 49:57+ S 24 '66

Translations
Shakespeare's Hamlet, by R. Mamoulian. Review
Sat R 49:43-5 Mr 5 '66. P. Burton

SHAKESPEARE (game) See Games

SHAKESPEARE festival, Stratford, Ontario
Oh what a lovely tsar; season's productions. H. Hewes. Sat R 49:35 Ag 6 '66
Stratford and Ypsilanti. J. Novick. Nation 203:259-61 S 19 '66

SHAKESPEARE festivals
See also
American Shakespeare festival theatre and academy. Stratford, Conn.
Great Lakes Shakespeare festival
New York Shakespeare festival
Shakespeare festival, Stratford, Ontario

SHAKESPEARE library, Washington. See Folger Shakespeare library, Washington, D.C.

SHAKING palsy. See Paralysis

SHALA and Raja (dancers)
Shala and Raja; 92nd street Y. M. Marks. Dance Mag 41:68 Ja '67

SHALE
Rare earths in European shales: a redetermination. M. A. Haskin and L. A. Haskin. bibliog il Science 154:507-9 O 28 '66

SHALE oil. See Oil shales

SHALES, Oil. See Oil shales

SHALIT, Amos de
Remarks on nuclear structure. Science 153:1063-7 S 2 '66

SHALIT, Gene
Good grief! a computer picks the partners for a high school dance. Seventeen 25:124-5 D '66
What's happening. Ladies Home J 84:116+ Ja '67

SHALLOTS
Good cook can grow her shallots. Sunset 136:240+ Mr '66
See also
Cookery—Vegetables

SHALOM of Safed
Grandpa Moses. il por Newsweek 67:86 My 30 '66

SHAMBURGER, Page
Nuts to fashion. Flying 79:88 O '66

SHAMUYARIRA, N. M.
Salisbury talks. Nation 203:5-6 Jl 4 '66

SHAN, Hwui. See Hwui Shan

SHAND, James D.
Rumbling on the German right. America 115:803-4 D 17 '66

SHANE, Dorothy
You can take it with you. Audubon Mag 68:55-6 Ja '66

SHANE, Harold G.
Current issues facing leadership in the school library field; adaptation of address. July 1966. por ALA Bul 60:923-6 O '66

SHANE, Jeffrey
Draft those reservists? New Repub 155:14-15 S 17 '66

SHANE, Ted
Roamer's ramblings. See issues of Travel

SHANGHAI
Description
Reporter at large. H. Koningsberger. New Yorker 42:104+ Ap 23 '66

Industries
Shanghai's repentant capitalists. R. Guillain. il Reporter 34:38-41 Ap 7 '66

SHANKAR, Ravi
Raga man. P. D. Zimmerman. il por Newsweek 69:65-6 Ja 2 '67

SHANNON, George M.
All about bonds for investment; interview. por U S News 61:64-6+ S 26 '66

SHANNON, James A.
General of the war on disease. il pors Bsns W p88-90 D 31 '66

SHANNON, William V.
Campaign dollars. Commonweal 84:385-6 Je 24 '66
Dam site. Commonweal 84:329-30 Je 10 '66
End of Johnson's Congress? Commonweal 84:433-4 Jl 8 '66
Enough is enough. Commonweal 85:191-2 N 18 '66
Lindsay, the first six months. New Repub 155:16-19 Jl 16 '66
Making of president Robert Kennedy. Harper 233:62-8 O '66
National affairs. See issues of Commonweal
Opinion. por Mlle 64:14-15 Ja '67
Shortage of liberals. Commonweal 84:46-7 Ap 1 '66
Southern politics. Commonweal 85:69-70 O 21 '66
Texas sojourn. Commonweal 84:273-4 My 27 '66
Third strike. Commonweal 84:216-17 My 13 '66
Transportation tangle. Commonweal 84:574-5; 84:263+ F 18, My 20 '66

SHANTHAVEERAPPA, T. R. and Bourne, G. H.
Perineural epithelium: a new concept of its role in the integrity of the peripheral nervous system. bibliog Science 154:1464-7 D 16 '66

SHAPE perception. See Perception

SHAPERS
Popular science salutes Stanley for its Surform tools. il Pop Sci 189:140-1 S '66

SHAYS' rebellion, 1786-1787
Horrid and unnatural rebellion of Daniel Shays. A. T. Vaughan. il Am Heritage 17:50-3+ Je '66
SHAZAR, Shneor Zalman
U.S. and Israel reaffirm ties of friendship; toast at state dinner, August 2, 1966. Dept State Bul 55:347 S 5 '66
SHEA, Donald R.
Preparation of Peace corps volunteers for overseas service: challenge and response. bibliog f Ann Am Acad 365:29-45 My '66
SHEA, Joseph
Boy who wanted to die. Time 87:57+ Mr 11 '66
SHEA, Margaret
Curl up and read. Seventeen 25:182 F '66
SHEA, Virginia M. See Tucker, H. W. jt. auth.
SHEAR flow. See Hydrodynamics
SHEARER, William M.
Speech: behavior of middle ear muscle during stuttering. bibliog Science 152:1280 My 27 '66
SHEARS, Russ
Metal sculpture of Russ Shears. J. Lovoos. il pors Am Artist 30:38-42+ Mr '66
SHECTER, Leonard
Can't anyone here use Kanehl? Sports Illus 25:54-6+ Ag 8 '66
(ed) See DeCausey, B. Our neighbors helped us rebuild out of the ashes
SHEDESKY, Pat
Biennials make the early summer garden. Flower Grower 53:24-5 Jl '66
Friendly look with vines. Flower Grower 53:32-3+ Ag '66
SHEEAN, Vincent
Mass and the opera. Opera N 30:8-13 Ap 2 '66
SHEED, Wilfrid
Hemingway si, papa no. Commonweal 84:221-3 My 13 '66
Life book review. Life 60:8+ Ap 29 '66
Life theater review. Life 60:17 F 4 '66
Stage. See issues of Commonweal
SHEEHAN, Edward R. F.
Cities of the dreadful night. Nation 202:300-2 Mr 14 '66
It's still the heart of darkness. il N Y Times Mag p30-3+ O 30 '66
SHEEHAN, Ethna
Best books of the season for children. America 115:551 N 5 '66
Summer reading for children. America 115:14-16 Jl 2 '66
SHEEHAN, Neil
Not a dove, but no longer a hawk. N Y Times Mag p27+ O 9 '66
SHEEHAN, Robert
Monty Spaght's Royal Dutch treat. Fortune 73:154-6+ Je '66
Rich, risky life of a univeristy trustee. Fortune 75:124-7+ Ja '67
There's plenty of privacy left in private enterprise. Fortune 74:224-5+ Jl 15 '66
Way they think at TRW. Fortune 74:153-7+ O '66
SHEEHAN, Susan
Reporter at large. New Yorker 42:62-6+ S 10; 137-8+ N 5 '66
SHEEN, Fulton John, bp
Compassion for punks too much, says Bishop Sheen; excerpts from statement. por U S News 62:16 Ja 23 '67
Hope. Vogue 148:216-17 D '66

about

Charity or duplicity? Christian Cent 83:1167 S 28 '66
SHEEP
What's new. See issues of Successful farming

Performance records and registration

Tested rams pay these sheepmen. il Farm J 90:38A Je '66
SHEEP farms
Twenty rules for sheep raisers. Suc Farm 64:100E Mr '66
SHEEP fences. See Fences
SHEEP herding
Basque sheepherders, lonely sentinels of the American West. R. Laxalt. il Nat Geog Mag 129:870-88 Je '66
SHEERIN, John B.
Book of the month. Cath World 204:55-6 O '66
Editorial. See issues of Catholic world

SHEET metal work
Sheet metal former. M. Banister. il Pop Mech 125:190-5+ F '66
SHEFTER, Eli, and Kennard, Olga
Crystal and molecular structure of acetyl-selenocholine iodide. bibliog Science 153:1389-90 S 16 '66
SHEHAN, Lawrence Joseph, cardinal
Overriding moral issues of modern warfare; pastoral letter, June 28, 1966. Cath World 203:365-7 S '66

about

Cardinal on war; excerpts from pastoral letter. J. O'Gara. Commonweal 84:459 Jl 22 '66
SHEIL, Bernard James, abp
No-nonsense archbishop. Time 87:96 My 20 '66
SHELBURNE FALLS, Mass.

Gardens

Garden on a bridge. il Horticulture 44:28-9 O '66
SHELBURNE museum, Shelburne, Vt.
Traveling through history. M. Goodman. il Redbook 127:97+ S '66
SHELBY, Carroll Hall
School for speed teaches you expert car handling. J. P. Norbye. il Pop Sci 189:94-8+ Jl '66
SHELBY Williams industries, Incorporated
Sitting pretty in contract furniture. il Bsns W p62+ My 7 '66
SHELDON, Carol M.
Glacier ice for cocktails. M. Wiley. il por Yachting 120:44-5+ O '66
SHELDON, Oliver
Happy factory that sired a social ethic. il por Bsns W p 126+ Je 25 '66
SHELEPIN, Aleksandr Nikolaevich
A. N. Shelepin on the rise. America 114:471-2 Ap 9 '66
SHELL houses. See Architecture, Domestic; Houses, Prefabricated
SHELLAC
Best finishes for wood; the smart ways to use shellac. J. Hand. il Pop Sci 189:172-4 O '66
SHELLFISH
See also
Cookery—Fish
SHELLFISH fisheries
See also
Oyster culture
SHELLS (architectural engineering)
Space frame costs less than $4 a square foot; Pauley pavilion at U.C.L.A. il Arch Rec 139:181-4 Mr '66
SHELLS (conchology)
Carrier shells. A. G. Melvin. il Hobbies 70:130 F '66
Elusive music volute. A. G. Melvin. il Hobbies 71:130 D '66
Emerald snail. A. G. Melvin. il Hobbies 71:130 O '66
Fascinating cone shells. A. G. Melvin. il Hobbies 71:130+ Mr '66
Packing sea-shells for mailing. A. G. Melvin. il Hobbies 71:130 My '66
Pholidostrophiid brachiopods: origin of the nacreous luster. K. M. Towe and C. W. Harper, jr. bibliog il Science 154:153-5 O 7 '66
Radiocarbon content of marine shells from the California and Mexican West coast. R. Berger and others. bibliog il Science 153:864-6 Ag 19 '66
Sea-shells that have color. A. G. Melvin. il Hobbies 71:130 N '66
Shell tower. A. G. Melvin. il Hobbies 71:130+ Je '66
What is a strombus? A. G. Melvin. il Hobbies 71:130+ Ap '66
See also
Cowries

Collectors and collecting

Collecting seashells. K. Y. Johnstone. il Holiday 40:99-104 Jl '66
SHELLS (structural engineering)
Bucky's biggest bubble; Crystal palace, U.S. pavilion at Canada's Expo 67. il Arch Forum 124:74-9 Je '66
Mobile shell for outdoor concerts. il Arch Rec 139:228 Ap '66
Out of the theory class into the realistic: thin-shell structures in limitless shapes and space frames with almost no limit on size. il Arch Rec 140:158-9 Jl '66
SHELLS, Orchestra. See Orchestra shells

SHELTERS
Chain saw is all you need to build this rustic storage shelter. il Pop Mech 125:140-7 Ap '66
Infra-red heaters bring bus riders back; Detroit street railways passenger shelters. il Am City 81:52 O '66
To enjoy the view without the wind. il Sunset 137:94 Jl '66
SHELTERS, Atomic bomb. See Atomic bomb shelters

SHELTON, C. W.
I shot Big Red. il por Outdoor Life 139:44-5+ Ja '67

SHELTON, Harrietta W.
Baltimore corners its commuters. Library J 91:5892-4 D 1 '66

SHELTON, Robert M. Jr
Operation contempt. T. Catchpole. Nat R 18: 152 F 22 '66
Wiz that was. Time 88:27 S 23 '66

SHELTON, William
How Andy McGhee got a better job. Fortune 75:116-17+ Ja '67
Russians mean to win the space race. Fortune 73:140-3+ F '66

SHELVES
Shelf insert in a child's wall. il Sunset 137: 124 S '66

SHENANDOAH NATIONAL PARK
Last of the Shenandoah settlers: Mrs A. Shenk. I. Moore. il Am For 72:10-11+ F '66; Discussion. 72:3-4 Ap; 2 Jl '66

SHENK, Annie Lee
Last of the Shenandoah settlers. I. Moore. il por Am For 72:10-11+ F '66; Discussion. 72:3-4 Ap; 2 Jl '66

SHEPARD, Francis P.
Meander in valley crossing a deep-ocean fan. bibliog Science 154:385-6 O 21 '66

SHEPARD, Marietta Daniels
Report on Latin American libraries. Wilson Lib Bul 40:538-42 F '66

SHEPARD, Paul
Virtues of anonymity. por Sat R 49:77 S 17 '66

SHEPARD, Sam
Chicago. Criticism
Nation 202:405 Ap 4 '66
Red cross. Criticism
Nation 202:224 F 21 '66
TV and radio; plays broadcast on WRVR. R. L. Shayon. Sat R 49:52 Ap 9 '66

SHEPARDSON, Charles N.
Debt-financed binge, an official warning; excerpts from address. January 29, 1966. U S News 60:90 F 14 '66

SHEPHERD, A. C.
Good ethics result in better purchasing. Am City 81:132+ S '66
Some facts you should know about guaranteed maintenance. Am City 81:92-3 D '66

SHEPHERD, Jean
Opinion: on the hero myth. por Mlle 63:18+ Jl '66

SHEPHERD, Tryon M.
Mr Knickerbocker's Staffordshire. Hobbies 71:28-9+ O '66

SHEPP, Archie
New jazz. il por Newsweek 68:104+ D 12 '66
Problematic Mr Shepp. M. Williams. por Sat R 49:90 N 12 '66

SHEPPARD, Carl F.
Findings of the National assn. of state boating law administrators. Yachting 119: 77-8 F '66

SHEPPARD, Peggy
Your garden's first gift to the table, asparagus. Farm J 90:104-5+ Ap '66

SHEPPARD, Samuel
Doctor Sam's reprise. il por Newsweek 68: 43-4 N 7 '66
Press on trial. il por Time 87:64 Mr 11 '66
Press v. the accused. il por Time 87:66 Je 17 '66
Trial by headline. il por Newsweek 67:64 Je 20 '66
Wheels of justice. J. H. Pollack. por Sat R 50:32-3 Ja 7 '67

SHEPPARD trial. See Trials (murder)

SHERA, Jesse H.
(ed) Bibliographic organization. bibliog Wilson Lib Bul 40:703-20+ Ap '66
What is past is prologue: beyond 1984. bibliog f por ALA Bul 61:35-47 Ja '67
Without reserve. See issues of Wilson library bulletin

SHERATON, Mimi
Sunday cooks. Harper 233:95-7 Ag '66

SHERATON East hotel. See New York (city)— Hotels, restaurants, etc.

SHERFIELD, Roger Mellor Makins, 1st baron
Daring & the elite. por Time 88:73 Ag 19 '66

SHERIDAN, Michael P.
Campus corner. America 115:543, 802; 116:87 N 5, D 17 '66, Ja 21 '67

Of many things. America 115:264 S 17 '66
Razz-ma-tazz in the drug industry. Nation 202:425-7, 683 Ap 11, Je 6 '66
Report on the schools. America 115:245 S 10 '66
Student rights in higher education. America 114:731-2 My 21 '66
Students rate their professors. America 115: 593-4 N 12 '66

SHERIDAN, Monica
Art of Irish cooking; excerpts. Ladies Home J 83:112-13+ Mr '66

SHERIDAN, Richard Brinsley Butler
School for scandal. Criticism
America 116:25-6 Ja 7 '67
Nation 203:651 D 12 '66
New Repub 156:41-2 Ja 7 '67
Newsweek 68:96+ D 5 '66

SHERIDAN, Robert E. See Heezen, B. C. jt. auth.

SHERIDAN, Wyo.
Fierce phonics war. R. Kirk. Nat R 18:936 S 20 '66

SHERIN, Ray
Creating plaster sculpture. Sch Arts 66:11-14 O '66

SHERMAN, Allie
Roar of the crowd. il por Time 88:35 D 23 '66

SHERMAN, Edward F.
Feds, sharpers and politics in Nevada. New Repub 155:12-13 O 29 '66
Nevada: the end of the casino era. Atlan 218:112-16 O '66

SHERMAN, Harry
We went underground to find beauty. Am City 81:126+ Ag '66

SHERMAN, Irwin W. and Mudd, J. B.
Malaria infection (plasmodium iophurae): changes in free amino acids. bibliog Science 154:287-9 O 14 '66

SHERMAN, Jimmy
Th' workin' machine; poem. Time 88:54 Jl 22 '66

SHERMAN, William D.
One American family in ten. PTA Mag 61: 14-16 Ja '67

SHERPAS
Sherpaland, my Shangri-La. D. Doig. il Nat Geog Mag 130:544-77 O '66

SHERRILL, Robert G.
Brass pyramid. Nation 203:49-51 Jl 11 '66
Family next door in the big White House. N Y Times Mag p6-7+ Jl 31 '66
Foundation pipe lines: the beneficent CIA. Nation 202:542-4+ My 9 '66
Politics on the king's ranch. N Y Times Mag p43+ Je 5 '66
Republican Turks: draft under fire. Nation 202:285-8 Mr 14 '66
Schools in the South: guidelines to frustration. Nation 204:69-74 Ja 16 '67
Wedge of dissent: Democratic rebels in Congress. Nation 203:341-6 O 10 '66
White House conference: bubble of unreality. Nation 202:734-7 Je 20 '66

SHERRIS, Roma
Last of the suffragettes; story. Ladies Home J 83:82-3 My '66

SHERROD, Robert
Russia at the crossroads. Sat Eve Post 239: 28-33 Mr 26 '66

SHERRY, Gerard E.
Sherry's new port. S. J. Adamo. America 114:676-7 My 7 '66

SHERWOOD, Kenneth
Negro gets toehold in Harlem retailing. il pors Ebony 21:149-52 Mr '66

SHERWOOD, Sidney
India; address. January 17, 1966. Vital Speeches 32:305-7 Mr 1 '66

SHETLER, Richard L.
Letter from the publisher. B. M. Auer. por Time 87:21 Ap 29 '66

SHIBBOLETH (term)
Flourishing shibboleth. America 115:170-1 Ag 20 '66

SHIDELER, Mary McDermott
Coup de grâce. Christian Cent 83:1499-502 D 7 '66
God speaks to a godless world. Christian. Cent 83:676-80 My 25 '66

SHIELDING (heat)
Apollo heat shield evaluated; photographs. Aviation W 84:30-1 Ap 4 '66
Early data indicate success for Apollo re-entry system. il Miss & Roc 18:33 Mr 7 '66
First Saturn IB launch will test Apollo heat shield design. J. Mercer. Miss & Roc 18: 16 F 7 '66
Heat shield verified in first Apollo test. G. Alexander. il Aviation W 84:92-3+ Mr 14 '66
Isotope radiation used to measure ablation changes. Miss & Roc 18:37 Mr 7 '66

SHIELDING (radiation)
　Dogs test Soviet radiation shield in 22-day flight of Cosmos 110. il Aviation W 84:34 Mr 21 '66
　　See also
　Guided missiles—Shielding (radiation)
SHIELDS, Cornelius
　Shields class sloop. il Motor B 117:47+ Ap '66
SHIFRIN, Walter G. See Simpson, G. D. jt. auth.
SHIMKIN, Leon
　Glottologist's new edition; Simon & Schuster and Pocket books. por Time 88:80 Jl 8 '66
　Leon Shimkin: the businessman as publisher. J. Tebbel. il por Sat R 49:74-5+ S 10 '66
　Shimkin's NYU gift may aid training for publishing. il por Pub W 190:35-6 N 28 '66
SHIMOFF, Karel
　Brief biography. S. Goodman. il por Dance Mag 41:50-1 Ja '67
SHINER, Don
　Opening for a young man. il Outdoor Life 137:62-4 Ap '66
　Really big shoe. Design 67:13 My '66
　Winter's art. Design 68:16-18 N '66
SHIP and boat models
　Last sail; old man with model sailboat on Conservatory pond, Central park. New Yorker 42:51-2 N 26 '66
　Trick of putting a submarine in a bottle. B. North. il Pop Mech 127:158-61+ Ja '67
SHIP building. See Shipbuilding
SHIP libraries. See Libraries, Ship
SHIP propulsion
　Down to the sea by jet power; gas turbine engines for ships. il Bsns W p 152+ Ja 22 '66
　　See also
　Gas turbines, Marine
SHIP radio operators. See Radio operators
SHIP subsidies
　Recommendation for maritime labor relations policies. Mo Labor R 89:19-21 Ja '66
SHIPBUILDING
　Annals of the sea; Argincourt by Armstrong, Whitworth & co. R. Hough. il New Yorker 42:41-4+ Ag 20 '66
　At the eye of the shipping storm; building ships abroad. Bsns W p 132+ Je 18 '66
　Giants of the ocean grow bigger still; Japan's shipyards, preparing for 300,000-tonners. il Bsns W p 114-16+ Ap 16 '66
　Here come the sea giants; Japan, world's largest shipbuilder. J. D. Ratcliff. il Read Digest 89:193-4+ S '66
　Navy pushing more multi-year purchases. Tech W 19:14-15 Ag 22 '66
　New ways; U.S. speed contest to produce navy FDLS. il Newsweek 68:67 Ag 15 '66
　On the ways; East Germany. il Time 89:65 Ja 13 '67
　United States looks at Swedish shipbuilding technology. V. K. McElheny. il Science 153:850-1 Ag 19 '66
　U.S. shipbuilding: mighty no more. il U S News 60:47 Je 27 '66
　Why it's made in Japan on big ships. il U S News 61:92-3 S 19 '66
　Wide gains for shipbuilding seen in FDLS. M. Getler. il Tech W 19:14-16 Ag 15 '66
　　See also
　Newport News shipbuilding and dry dock company
　Shipyards
SHIPMAN, Joseph C.
　Bibliographic organization in the physical sciences. bibliog por Wilson Lib Bul 40:706-13 Ap '66
SHIPMENT, Packing for. See Packing for shipment
SHIPMENT of books. See Books—Transportation
SHIPMENT of goods
　Methods and rules of shipping; excerpt from Successful selling of antiques by mail. C. H. Laestar and M. E. Laestar. Hobbies 71:76+ S '66
　Warehouses and distribution centers. il Arch Rec 140:121-5 D '66
　　See also
　Air freight service
　Distribution of goods
　Materials handling
SHIPMENT of periodicals. See Periodicals—Transportation
SHIPP, Bill
　Police brutality vs. people brutality; reprint. U S News 61:43 Ag 8 '66; Same. Read Digest 89:111-12 O '66
SHIPP, Robert E.
　Southwest. por Parks & Rec 1:635 Ag '66
SHIPPEE, William R.
　Simplified tremolo. Electr World 76:88 O '66

SHIPPING
　Shipping in UNCTAD: dynamic approach. C. H. J. Amaratunga. UN Mo Chron 3:75-80 Ag '66
　　See also
　Marine transport lines, incorporated
　Ports
International aspects
　Diplomatic adjustment by the maritime nations. P. F. Geren. Dept State Bul 54:78-85 Ja 17 '66
　　See also
　Intergovernmental maritime consultative organization
Rates
　Cargo rates run into heavy seas; competitive bidding for military cargoes. Bsns W p82 Jl 30 '66
　Diplomatic adjustment by the maritime nations. P. F. Geren. Dept State Bul 54:78-85 Ja 17 '66
Africa
　New patterns of transport for Africa. W. H. Owens. il UNESCO Courier 19:11-15 Ja '66
Great Britain
　　See also
　Merchant marine—Great Britain
United States
　Our leaky pipeline to Vietnam. L. Velie. il Read Digest 89:113-18 D '66
　　See also
　Inland water transportation
　Merchant marine—United States
Vietnam (Republic)
　How big a shipping jam in Vietnam? il U S News 60:11 F 21 '66
SHIPPING, Inland water. See Inland water transportation
SHIPPING companies
　　See also
　American export and Isbrandtsen lines
　Matson navigation company
SHIPS
　　See also
　Aircraft carriers
　Dry docks
　Galleys (ships)
　Ocean liners
　Sailing vessels
　Salvage (ships)
　Tank ships
　Transports
　Whalers
Fires and fire protection
　Fire at sea, and new safety questions; Viking Princess. U S News 60:11 Ap 18 '66
　Fire drill that proved its worth; Viking Princess. il Life 60:36-7 Ap 22 '66
　Miracle at sea; Viking Princess fire. il Newsweek 67:50+ Ap 18 '66
　Safety at sea: crackdown on foreign ships? il U S News 60:12 My 2 '66
　Tale of two ships; fire on Viking Princess. il Time 87:27 Ap 15 '66
　U.S. and European officials discuss fire safety of ships; Department statement, April 25, 1966. Dept State Bul 54:782 My 16 '66
　U.S. asks international action on passenger-ship fire safety; statement, May 3, 1966. W. A. Harriman. Dept State Bul 54:952-4 Je 13 '66
Registration and transfer
　　See also
　Yachts—Registration
Safety devices and measures
　U.S. welcomes IMCO action on passenger-ship safety. Dept State Bul 55:965 D 26 '66
SHIPS, Atomic powered
　　See also
　Aircraft carriers, Atomic powered
　Warships, Atomic powered
SHIPS, Hospital. See Hospital ships
SHIPS, Model. See Ship and boat models
SHIPS, Research
　Aluminum catamaran planned for ocean study. il Sci N 90:15 Jl 2 '66
　First civilian vessel navigates by satellite; Vema. Sci N 90:287 O 8 '66
　North Atlantic deep-sea fertility; University of Rhode Island's Trident. R. O. Fournier. bibliog il Science 153:1250-2 S 9 '66

SHIPS, Research—*Continued*
Ship to explore the oceans and their riches.
U S News 61:12 Jl 25 '66
Soviet ministry speeds fishing technology;
Akademik Kurtshatov. W. S. Beller. il
Tech W 19:24-5+ Ag 22 '66
SHIPS, Troop. See Transports
SHIPS in bottles. See Ship and boat models
SHIPS logs. See Logbooks
SHIPS papers
See also
Logbooks
Yachts—Registration
SHIPWORKERS
Boost up job ladder for Negroes; Newport
News shipbuilding pact with federal agency.
Bsns W p 130+ Ap 23 '66
SHIPWRECKED king; drama. See Slattery,
M. E.
SHIPWRECKS
Camera on the spot as a tragedy of the sea
unfolds. il Life 61:120D-125 D 23 '66
Death on wine-dark waters; sinking of the
ferry, Heraklion in the Aegean Sea. Time
88:42 D 16 '66
Moonport site lies near treasure run. Sci N
90:387 N 5 '66
Passage through a sea gone berserk; Michel-
angelo damage. il Life 60:34-5 Ap 29 '66
Pounds of prevention; freighter Daniel J.
Morrell disaster. Time 88:30 D 9 '66
Static and silence; Greek ferry, Heraklion.
Newsweek 68:49 D 19 '66
Where do sunken ships go? I. Asimov. il Sci
Digest 61:87-8 Ja '67
See also
Collisions at sea
Salvage (ships)
Titanic (steamship)
SHIPYARD employees. See Shipworkers
SHIPYARDS
Setting shipyards on a new course; navy
prods builders to update and automate
their facilities. il Bsns W p 186+ O 22 '66
Shipyard for all seasons; Arendal of Sweden.
il Fortune 74:44+ Jl 1 '66
See also
Shipbuilding
SHIRLEY, Isabel. See Schleifer, P. jt. auth.
SHIRLEY, John W.
Problems involved in cooperation between
universities and government agencies. bib-
liog f Sch & Soc 94:222-7 Ap 16 '66
SHIRLEY, Robin
Uric acid dihydrate: crystallography and
identification. bibliog Science 152:1512-13
Je 10 '66
SHIRLEY poppies. See Poppies
SHIRTS
CPO shirts; country-wide fad. I. Bauer. il
Look 30:M13 My 17 '66
Men's T-shirts. il Consumer Bul 49:10-14 S
'66
Permanent-press shirts (cont) il Consumer
Rep 31:232-3 My '66
SHIVELY, Daniel
On survival. Bul Atomic Sci 22:34 S '66
SHNEOUR, Elie A.
Oxidation of graphitic carbon in certain
soils. bibliog Science 151:991-2 F 25 '66
SHOALS. See Seashore
SHOBAKEN, Bruce
Artist and teacher. il pors Sch Arts 65:21-5
Ja '66
SHOBERG, Ray
Band sander for your bench saw. Pop Mech
126:160-2 Ag '66
Build this $2 battery polarity tester. Pop
Mech 126:166-7 N '66
SHOCK
Cocoon of air for shock victims. il Life 61:
73-4 O 7 '66
First aid. C. J. Potthoff. Todays Health 44:
64 Jl '66
Shock treatment. Sci Digest 60:36 D '66
See also
Electric shock
SHOCK-lithification. See Rocks
SHOCK waves
Buildings and the sonic boom. R. S. Lanier.
il Arch Forum 125:54-5+ D '66
Near-field criteria give SST required trans-
onic boom level. Aviation W 86:38-9 Ja 16
'67
Rocket testers guard people's eardrums. Sci
N 89:388 My 21 '66
Sonic boom tests seek forecast data. C. M.
Plattner. Aviation W 84:55-7 Je 20 '66
SST called technically feasible; noise, boom
still pose problems. Aviation W 84:43 My
2 '66

SHOCKLEY, Ann Allen
Negro woman in retrospect: blueprint for the
future. bibliog Negro Hist Bul 29:55-6+ D
'65
SHOE industry. See Shoes—Trade and manu-
facture
SHOE makers. See Shoemakers
SHOE polishers, Electric. See Polishers, Elec-
tric
SHOE stores
See also
Edison brothers stores, incorporated
SHOEMAKERS
Second greatest shoeshine. G. Frazier. il
Esquire 66:147-52 N '66
SHOES
C'est chic, la plastique; R. Vivier creations.
il Time 87:52 F 4 '66
Eight points to check when you buy new
shoes. il Good H 162:188 Mr '66
Pogo shoes give you a lift. J. Wiley. il Pop
Mech 125:157 Je '66

Care
Second greatest shoeshine; six establishments
where you can get the best shines. G.
Frazier. il Esquire 66:147-52 N '66

Trade and manufacture
Footwear plant earnings in April 1965. G. L.
Stelluto. il Mo Labor R 89:296-9 Mr '66
New shine for a master retailer; Edison
brothers stores. il Bsns W p 110+ Ap 16
'66
Output per man-hour in the footwear indus-
try. F. T. Moss. il Mo Labor R 89:401-4 Ap
'66
SHOES, Rubber, plastic, etc.
Art of wading. A. J. McClane. il Field & S
71:112-16+ S '66
Boots with in-and-out insulation. C. Conley.
il Field & S 71:95 Ja '67
Footgear for campers. G. B. Colby. il Out-
door Life 138:112+ S '66
SHOES; story. See Mawhinney, P. E.
SHOLOKHOV, Mikhail Aleksandrovich
Sholokhov and the Nobel prize. E. J. Brown.
Nation 203:160-4 Ag 22 '66
SHOMON, Joseph J.
Cavalcade of the caribou. il Outdoor Life 137:
46-7+ Je '66
Greenspan program. Audubon Mag 68:414 N
'66
Nature center for New York city? il Audu-
bon Mag 68:54 Ja '66
Wilderness nature center for Ontario. Audu-
bon Mag 68:307 S '66
You can sell a nature center. Audubon Mag
68:218-19 Jl '66
SHONFIELD, Andrew
Britain needs a second industrial revolution.
N Y Times Mag p32-3+ Ag 21 '66
Limits of innovation. Commentary 42:91-2+
N '66
SHONNARD, Eugenie Frederica
Sculpture of Eugenie Shonnard. E. Bell. il
por Am Artist 30:62-7+ Je '66
SHOOK, Edgar. See Bowen, W. jt. auth.
SHOOTING
Economy hand trap to improve your shoot-
ing. P. Czura. il Field & S 70:133 Mr '66
Honk's life insurance; expert marksmen
through growing up with guns. R. Starnes.
Field & S 71:16+ N '66
Shooting. J. O'Connor. See issues of Outdoor
life
Shooting; ed. by W. Page. See issues of
Field & stream
Shooting questions (cont) W. Page. Field
& S 70:140 Ap '66
Topgunmanship. R. Starnes. Field & S 70:
14+ Ap '66
See also
Gunnery
Skeet (game)
Targets
Trap shooting
also Duck shooting; and similar headings

Accidents and injuries
Aim for safety. R. Rood. il Parents Mag
41:50-1+ Ag '66

Anecdotes, facetiae, satire, etc.
How to shoot the bird of peace. N. Riley.
il Outdoor Life 138:34-5+ Jl '66
What is good shooting? J. O'Connor. il Outdoor Life 139:28+ Ja '67

SHOW windows
Matching the window to the event; New York bookshops. il Pub W 190:72-3+ Jl 4 '66
Packaged window displays are available for small bookstores. il Pub W 190:55-6 N 7 '66

SHOWERS (parties) See Entertaining

SHRAKE, Edwin
Boxing (cont) Sports Illus 24:74+ My 23 '66
Pro football (cont) Sports Illus 24:44 Ja 24; 25:74+ N 28 '66

SHRAWDER, John F.
Paradise nearly lost. Audubon Mag 68:228-9 Jl '66

SHREVE, Ronald L.
Sherman landslide, Alaska. bibliog Science 154:1639-43 D 30 '66

SHREVEPORT, La.
New museum for Louisiana; R. W. Norton art gallery. R. Davidson. il Antiques 90:436 O '66

SHRIMPS
Salt transport organelle in artemia salenis (brine shrimp) E. Copeland. bibliog il Science 151:470-1 Ja 28 '66
See also
Cookery—Fish

SHRIMPTON, Jean Rosemary
Jean Shrimpton: star model makes her movie bow. J. Hamilton. il pors Look 30:44-6+ N 29 '66

SHRINE of the book. See Jerusalem—Israel museum

SHRIVER, Robert Sargent, 1915-
Change of emphasis for the poverty war? summary of news conference, November 22, 1966. por U S News 61:10 D 5 '66
Excerpt from address, December 6, 1965. Cong Digest 45:80+ Mr '66
First-hand report on poverty war; interview. por U S News 60:64-9 F 28 '66
Five years with the Peace corps. pors Sat R 49:14+ Ap 23 '66
Moral basis of the war on poverty. Christian Cent 83:1531-3 D 14 '66

about
By or for the poor? New Repub 154:5-6 Ap 30 '66
Grilled Shriver. il por Time 87:21 Ap 22 '66
Hard truth. Newsweek 67:24 Ap 25 '66
Little by little, less and less of the OEO. New Repub 155:10-11 D 10 '66
One man, one job. Newsweek 67:22-3 Ja 31 '66
Sargent Shriver and the role of the poor. B. Carter. il Reporter 34:17-20 My 5 '66
Sargent Shriver remains unimpressed. Nat R 18:452+ My 17 '66
Shriver under fire. Sr Schol 88:14 Ap 29 '66
Shriver leaves the Peace corps. America 114:186 F 5 '66
Shriver's last stand? por Newsweek 69:20 Ja 2 '67
Shriver's limited war. S. Lens. Commonweal 84:412-14 Jl 1 '66
Shriving Shriver. Christian Cent 83:1431-2 N 23 '66
Six-star Sargent. il Time 87:28 Mr 18 '66
Too many abuses in a big poverty project? U S News 61:14-15 N 7 '66
Two-armed Sargent. New Repub 154:9 Ja 29 '66
War within the war. il por Time 87:25-9 My 13 '66

SHRUBS
Plant for privacy. il Flower Grower 53:34-6 Je '66
Summer-blooming shrubs? R. P. Korbobo. il Horticulture 44:16-17+ Ag '66
See also
Evergreens
Hedges
Holly
Pruning
Roadside improvement
Witch hazel
also names of shrubs, e.g. Viburnums

Planting
Shrubs to frame your picture window. G. Taloumis. il Pop Gard 17:26-9 D '66

Pruning
See Pruning

SHUBIK, Philippe. See Toth, B. jt. auth.

SHUFFLEBOARD
Back-yard shuffleboard. il Pop Gard 17:76-7 My '66
Build a shuffleboard in your backyard. il Sunset 136:137 Ap '66

SHULDINER, Herbert
Batman's Batmobile. Pop Sci 189:46-7+ Jl '66
Your new mower, safest one yet. Pop Sci 189:130-2 Jl '66

SHULTZ, Gladys Denny
Society and the sex criminal; excerpt from How many more victims? Read Digest 89:139-46 N '66

SHULTZ, Herb
Dancing world of Coon-Sanders. Sat R 49:57+ My 14 '66

SHUMAN, Charles Baker
Should we take the wraps off production? por Farm J 90:31+ S '66

SHUMAN, Helen Glossner
Red hot poker. Flower Grower 53:37+ My '66

SHUR-guide steering control. See Automobiles —Steering gear

SHURTLEFF, Mal
Report on maize dwarf mosaic. Suc Farm 64:62 F '66

SHUSTER, George Nauman
Planning for a better world. Sat R 50:42+ Ja 21 '67

SHUSTER, Joe
Trade winds. J. Beatty, jr. Sat R 49:6 Ap 23 '66

SHUTTERS
Louvered shutter. il House & Gard 129:78-9 Ap '66
Which house shutters: wood, plastic, aluminum? A. J. Hand. il Pop Sci 189:164-5 N '66

SHUTTERS, Camera. See Camera shutters

SHYER, Marlene Fanta
Big evening; story. Redbook 127:56-7 My '66
Not like the others; story. Redbook 127:68 Ag '66
One out of seven; story. Redbook 128:60-1 N '66
Semiperfect man; story. Redbook 127:50-1 Jl '66

SIALIC acids
Nucleohistone dissociation by ganglioside micelles. M. H. Meisler and R. H. McCluer. bibliog il Science 154:896-7 N 18 '66
Sialic acid binding sites: role in hemagglutination by mycoplasma gallisepticum. B. Gesner and L. Thomas. bibliog il Science 151:590-1 F 4 '66

SIAMESE twins
Masha and Dasha: rare study of Siamese twins in Soviet. il Life 60:67-8+ Ap 8 '66
United unto death: Mary & Margaret Gibb (1949) il Time 89:50 Ja 20 '67

SIBELIUS, Jean Julius Christian
Finest Sibelius Fifth. Leonard Bernstein's. J. Diether. Am Rec G 32:557 F '66
Seven of Sibelius. E. Salzman. Sat R 49:68-9 O 29 '66
Sibelius symphonies by Akeo Watanabe: superlative. J. Diether. Am Rec G 33:112-13+ O '66

SIBERIA
Sharing the wealth; Japan's economic dealings with Russia. Time 87:86 Mr 25 '66
See also
Akademgorodok

Description and travel
Siberia; with report by R. Brigham. il Life 60:54-67+ Ap 22 '66

Industries
Siberian dilemma: a country of riches, but nobody wants to live there. il U S News 61:110-12 Jl 18 '66

SIBLEY, Agnes
Paradox and poetic truth; address, November 17, 1965. Vital Speeches 32:344-51 Mr 15 '66

SIBLEY, Celestine
Celebrities at Rich's: authors and assorted; excerpt from Dear store. Pub W 191:50-1 Ja 9 '67

SIBLEY, Hi
Portable ice-fishing house. Field & S 71:54-5 D '66

SIBLEY, Mulford J.
Ethics and the professional patriots. bibliog f Ann Am Acad 363:126-36 Ja '66

SIBLINGS
Bobby's new baby; brand-new little sister. il Good H 162:52+ My '66
Dialogue with mothers; jealousy in the younger sibling. B. Bettelheim. Ladies Home J 83:39-40 Jl '66
My kid sister. J. Wescott. Seventeen 25:22 D '66
Oh, brother! questions and answers. A. Wood. Seventeen 25:28+ Jl '66
Our kids settle their own squabbles. M. Treichler. il Parents Mag 41:50-1+ Je '66

SICILIAN cookery. See Cookery, Italian

SICK, The
De hospitalibus excelsior: hospitalization procedure. J H. Slate. il Atlan 218:122-3 Jl '66
It's a miracle that we save any of them; remodeling plans for Georgetown hospital. Wash. W. R. Young. il Life 61:102-4+ D 2 '66
On being a patient. S. Becker. Atlan 218: 95-101 Jl '66
Will they, won't they? question of overcrowding hospitals with medicare patients. New Repub 155:10 Jl 2 '66
See also
Occupational therapy

Anecdotes, facetiae, satire, etc.
Hospitality; being admitted to a hospital. G. Ace. Sat R 49:8 O 15 '66

SICKELS, Robert J.
Survival of the gerrymander. New Repub 155:9 D 3 '66

SICKLE cell anemia. See Anemia

SICKLEMIA. See Anemia

SICKNESS
See also
Diagnosis
Sick, The

SICKNESS absence. See Absenteeism

SICKNESS benefit plans. See Employees benefit plans

SICRE, José Gómez-. See Gómez-Sicre, J.

SICURO, N. A.
University branches: solution for college crush. Sch & Soc 94:458-9 D 10 '66

SIDAY, Eric
Swurpledeewurpledeezeech! il por Time 88: 68 N 4 '66

SIDE-looking sonar. See Sonar

SIDEL, Victor W. See Mayer, J. jt. auth.

SIDER, Don
It's done the boy a world of good. Life 61: 54 Ag 5 '66

SIDEREAL time. See Time measurements

SIDEWALKS
Sidewalks and street lights. Am City 81:6 Je '66

SIDEY, Hugh
He makes a truce with a man he came almost to hate. L.B.J. Life 61:38-9 N 18 '66
Presidency. See issues of Life

about
Life's third regular columnist. G. P. Hunt. por Life 60:3 My 27 '66

SIDNEY LANIER, LAKE. See Lakes, Artificial

SIE Thao
I am a thought of you. M. Kennedy. Vogue 147:66 Ap 1 '66

SIEBERT, Paul S. Jr
Small town solves a big water problem. Am City 81:83-5 N '66

SIEGEL, Abraham J.
Shifting concepts of worker security. Mo Labor R 89:126 F '66

SIEGEL, Alvin, and Degens, E. T.
Concentration of dissolved amino acids from saline waters by ligand-exchange chromatography. bibliog Science 151:1098-101 Mr 4 '66

SIEGEL, Barry W. See Auclair, W. jt. auth.

SIEGEL, Benjamin
In the beginning; story. Redbook 128:147 D '66

SIEGEL, Bernard J.
Some recent developments in studies of social and cultural change. bibliog f Ann Am Acad 363:137-53 Ja '66

SIEGEL, Dorothy
How will you have your baby? Parents Mag 41:46-7+ F '66
Play it cool with your baby. Parents Mag 41:28-9 Jl '66

SIEGEL, Edward, and Tobias, C. A.
End-organ effects of thyroid hormones: subcellular interactions in cultured cells. bibliog Science 153:763-5 Ag 12 '66

SIEGEL, Jeanne
Why Spiral? Art N 65:48-51+ S '66

SIEGEL, Jerry
Trade winds. J. Beatty, jr. Sat R 49:6 Ap 23 '66

SIEGEL, Jules
Surf, wheels & free souls. Sat Eve Post 239:32-7 N 19 '66
Well, what have we here? Sat Eve Post 239:32-6+ Jl 30 '66

SIEGEL, Morris
Welcome to the country club, you misfortunates. Nations Bsns 54:75 Je '66

SIEGEL, Robert
Fish; poem. America 115:514 O 29 '66

SIEGELMAN, Ellen
Quick lesson in every language. Travel 125: 65-7 F '66

SIEGENTHALER, Paul André, and others
Phosphate uptake in an obligately marine fungus: a specific requirement for sodium. bibliog Science 155:93-4 Ja 6 '67

SIEKMAN, Philip
Bronfmans: an instinct for dynasty. Fortune 74:144-9+ N; 176-9+ D '66
Henry Ford and his electronic can of worms. Fortune 73:116-19+ F '66
In electronics, the big stakes ride on tiny chips. Fortune 73:120-5+ Je '66
On lovable Madison avenue with Mary, Dick, and Stew. Fortune 74:142-6+ Ag '66

SIEPI, Cesare
Cesare means emperor of bassos. H. Klein. il pors N Y Times Mag p44+ Mr 20 '66
Music to my ears: recital in New York. I. Kolodin. Sat R 49:28 Ap 9 '66

SIERRA club
Battle of the wilderness. il Newsweek 68:108 O 3 '66
Conservationists and the IRS. New Repub 155:7 D 3 '66
Fall from grace. il Newsweek 69:24-5 Ja 9 '67
Senator Goldwater vs. the Sierra club: statement. B. M. Goldwater. Nat R 18:918-20 S 20 '66

SIERRA NEVADA, Calif.
Glaciation about 3,000,000 years ago in the Sierra Nevada. R. R. Curry. bibliog il Science 154:770-1 N 11 '66
See also
Kings Canyon National Park
Yosemite National Park

SIGAFOOS, Mary D. See Sigafoos, R. S. jt. auth.

SIGAFOOS, Robert S. and Sigafoos, M. D.
Flood history told by tree growth. Natur Hist 75:50-5 Ag '66

SIGEL, Efrem
Peace corpsman looks back. Reporter 35:12-16 D 29 '66

SIGHT
Adrenaline and noradrenaline: relation to performance in a visual vigilance task. J. F. O'Hanlon, jr; reply with rejoinder. A. H. Anton. bibliog Science 151:709-10 F 11 '66
Human visual acuity measured with colored test objects. C. R. Cavonus and A. W. Schumacher. bibliog il Science 152:1276-7 My 27 '66
Infants see shape early. Sci N 90:116 Ag 20 '66
Metacontrast: its relation to evoked potentials. P. H. Schiller and S. L. Chorover. bibliog il Science 153:1398-400 S 16 '66
More than meets the eye: why we see things as we are: excerpt from The story behind the painting. L. Rosten. il Read Digest 88: 213-15 Ap '66
Slant perception and shape constancy in infants. T. G. R. Bower. bibliog il Science 151:832-4 F 18 '66
Visual excitation and blood clotting. G. Wald; reply. W. H. Seegers. bibliog Science 151:841 F 18 '66
Visual world of infants. T. G. R. Bower. il Sci Am 215:80-4+ D '66
See also
Blindness
Night blindness
Space perception

SIGHT (animals)
Interaction of cortex and superior colliculus in mediation of visually guided behavior in the cat. J. M. Sprague. bibliog il Science 153:1544-7 S 23 '66
Light sense in nematodes. P. A. G. Wilson. bibliog il Science 151:337-8 Ja 21 '66
Optomotor responses by echolocating bats. R. A. Suthers. bibliog il Science 152:1102-4 My 20 '66
Receptive fields of directionally selective units in the optic nerve of the ground squirrel. C. R. Michael. bibliog il Science 152:1092-5 My 20 '66
Receptive fields of opponent color units in the optic nerve of the ground squirrel. C. R. Michael. bibliog il Science 152:1095-7 My 20 '66
Visual acuity in a stumptail macaque. M. Yarczower and others. bibliog il Science 152:1392-3 Je 3 '66

SIGHT (insects)
Color vision in the adult female two-spotted spider mite. W. D. McEnroe and K. Dronka. bibliog il Science 154:782-4 N 11 '66

SIGHTS for firearms. See Firearms—Sights

SIGIRIYA, Ceylon
Sigiriya: palace of a god-king. M. M. Brown. il Sat R 49:48+ N 26 '66

SIGMAN, Carl T.
Five ways to fly the American flag. Pop Sci 189:122-3 Jl '66
How to live happily without an entrance hall. Pop Sci 188:154-7 F '66
Seven smart ways to gain living space in the home. Pop Sci 189:142-8 S '66

SIGMOIDOSCOPY. See Cancer—Diagnosis

SIGMUND, Paul E.
Nkrumah-charisma fails. Commonweal 84:50-2 Ap 1 '66

SIGN language
Sign talk analyzed. Sci N 90:473 D 3 '66

SIGNAL generators
Carrier-current remote-control system; radio-frequency signal to control electrical devices. R. Zarr. il Pop Electr 26:50-3 Ja '67
Color-tv signal generators. L. Solomon. il il Electr World 76:31-3+ D '66
CB radio call monitor. R. C. Peterson. il Pop Electr 26:54-6 Ja '67
High-quality square-wave generator. C. J. Ulrick. il Electr World 76:43+ N '66
Selecting a sweep frequency generator. S. C. Allen. il Electr World 76:88-92 N '66
Square deal audio generator. D. Lancaster. il Pop Electr 25:59-63 N '66
Square-wave generator. M. J. Moss. il Electr World 75:75-7 F '66
Square-wave testing. J. F. Kennedy. il Electr World 75:94-5 Mr '66
V.H.F. ham band scanner. il Electr World 76:82 D '66

SIGNALS and signaling
Mayday. A. Trammell. Flying 78:76-8 Ap '66

SIGNATURES (writing)
See also
Autographs

SIGNS and signboards
Airports urged to standardize terminal signs. il Aviation W 85:63+ N 14 '66
See also
Billboards
Electric signs

Anecdotes, facetiae, satire, etc.
Inglish spocken here. J. Bryan, 3d. il Holiday 40:56-7 O '66

SIHANOUK, Norodom. See Norodom Sihanouk

SIK, A. E.
Long lurid life of hurricane Betsy. Motor B 118:38-40+ Ag '66

SIK, Ota
Toward market economics. il por Time 88:42-3 N 11 '66

SIKA deer hunting. See Deer hunting

SIKES, Robert L. F.
Excerpt from debate, August 3, 1966. Cong Digest 45:271+ N '66
Import-export statistics off the beam; address, February 8, 1966. Vital Speeches 32:325-7 Mr 15 '66
about
Old hole-in-the-head. P. D. Smith. il pors Outdoor Life 138:62-3 D '66

SIKHS
Dilemma in the Punjab. il Time 89:29 Ja 6 '67
Flames in Punjab; Sikhs and Hindus. il Time 87:32 Mr 25 '66
Housework; Sikh state in Punjab to be created. il Newsweek 67:48 Mr 21 '66
Standing fast. il Newsweek 69:30-1 Ja 9 '67

SIKKIM
Queen of Sikkim: an intimate portrait. A. Kandell. il Redbook 127:52-5+ Je '66

SIKORSKI, Tomasz
New music of Poland. O. Daniel. Sat R 49:52 Jl 30 '66

SIKORSKY, Igor I.
It's a bird, it's a plane, it's the Riesenflugzeug of W.W.I. il por Esquire 66:115 O '66

SIKORSKY aircraft division. See United aircraft corporation—Sikorsky aircraft division

SILAGE
Fourteen tons of low-moisture alfalfa silage. il Suc Farm 64:40-1 Ag '66
Should you enrich your corn silage? B. Hardy. il Farm J 90:26-7+ Ag '66

SILAGE handling
Make hay and silage with less help. il Farm J 90:30-1 Jl '66

SILARD, John
Nuclear weapons: a liability. Bul Atomic Sci 22:15-20 S '66

SILAS Marner (literary character) See Characters in literature

SILBAR, Margaret L.
Biggest synchrotron ever—why? Sci Digest 60:69-74 Ag '66
Death of a theory. Sci Digest 60:9-11 S '66
Inner secret of matter. Sci Digest 60:66+ O '66

SILBERMAN, Arlene
Pregnant bride. il Redbook 128:58-9+ N '66
What should I tell my son? Read Digest 88:103-6 My '66

SILBERMAN, Charles E.
Business can live with the labor shortage. Fortune 73:112-15+ My '66
Is technology taking over? Fortune 73:112-15+ F '66
Technology is knocking at the schoolhouse door. Fortune 74:120-5+ Ag '66

SILBERSTEIN, Murray L.
Saving money. New Repub 155:36-7 D 17 '66

SILBERSTEIN, Paula E.
Festival of Stratford. Sr Schol 88:sup 14 Ap 15 '66

SILENT song; story. See Clark, D.

SILHOUETTES
Hattersley class: transformations. il Pop Phot 59:53-6 Jl '66

SILICATE paint. See Paint, Heat resisting

SILICATES
Silicate paints proving thermal stability. W. S. Beller. il Tech W 19:24-5 O 31 '66
See also
Serpentine

SILICON
More spare parts for humans. T. Berland. il Todays Health 44:42-5+ Jl '66

SILICON controlled rectifiers. See Electric current rectifiers

SILICON counters. See Radiation—Measurement

SILICON diodes. See Diodes

SILICONE rubber. See Rubber, Artificial

SILICONE rubber molds. See Molds (for casting)

SILICONE sealants. See Sealing compositions

SILICON solar batteries. See Solar batteries

SILICON transistors. See Transistors

SILK
Good care advice for silk fabrics. il Good H 162:171 My '66

SILKEN, Howard
Brand new contractors' trim saw. Pop Mech 126:192-3+ N '66

SILKIN, Boris. See Pushkov, N. jt. auth.

SILKIN, Jon
Three younger poets. R. J. Mills, jr. Poetry 109:114-15 N '66
Two British chronicles. M. Bell. Poetry 107:411-12 Mr '66

SILLIMANITE
Kyanite-sillimanite equilibrium at 750°C. R. C. Newton. bibliog il Science 151:1222-5 Mr 11 '66

SILLOWAY, Stuart Furbish
New chiefs lead IDS back into the race. il por Bsns W p 152-4+ Je 25 '66

SILLS, Beverly
Going for baroque. H. Saal. il Newsweek 68:100 O 10 '66

SILLS, Paul
Improvisation bit. J. Novick. Nation 203:614 D 5 '66

SILOS
Don't write off bunker silos. W. J. Fletcher. il Suc Farm 64:54B My '66
How to seal silo walls, old or new. il Farm J 90:58T My '66
Sealed silo for $24 a ton. il Farm J 90:68L Mr '66

SILURIAN period. See Geology, Stratigraphic—Silurian

SILVA, Artur da Costa e
Brazil's new head. por Sr Schol 89:18-19 O 21 '66
Brazil's new leader: inherits old problems. por U S News 61:24 O 17 '66
Making of a president. il por Time 87:40 Ap 29 '66
Making of a president-elect. il por Time 88:46+ O 7 '66
Next president? por Newsweek 67:54 Ja 31 '66
Solid brass candidate. il por Newsweek 68:45 Ag 8 '66
Some unpleasant business. il por Time 89:30 Ja 13 '67
Sure winner. por Newsweek 68:65 O 10 '66
Top brass in Brazil. M. J. Kubic. New Repub 155:11-13 S 10 '66

SILVA, Michel
Friendly enemies who live bumper-to-bumper. Life 61:134+ O 14 '66
Grisly evidence brings twenty-nine charges of cruelty. Life 60:26-7 F 4 '66

about

It was rougher in the horse-and-buggy days. G. P. Hunt. por Life 60:5 Ap 15 '66

SILVER, Isidore
Confession and the Court. Commonweal 84: 435-7 Jl 8 '66
Poverty as a crime. Commonweal 85:74-6 O 21 '66

SILVER, Nathan
Model A spirit. Nation 203:357-9 O 10 '66

SILVER, Norman
Garden lighting. Flower Grower 53:10+ My '66

SILVER, Raymond S.
Automate mass-transit fare sales. Am City 81:83-5 F '66

SILVER, Sidney L.
Electromechanical choppers. Electr World 76: 42-5+ Ag '66
Meter-relay devices. Electr World 75:36-8+ Mr '66
Sampling oscilloscopes. Electr World 75:47-9+ Je '66

SILVER, Stanley
Use operation & administration manuals. por Parks & Rec 1:44+ Ja '66

SILVER
See also
Silverware

Prices
Is the shiny metal's luster only skin deep? il Bsns W D 110 Ag 6 '66

SILVER All-America awards. See Sports illustrated silver anniversary All-America

SILVER alloys
Unique fabricator: Handy and Harman, New York. T. J. Murray. il Duns R 87:41-3+ F '66

SILVER as money
Silver coin hoarding. Nat R 18:104 F 8 '66
Who's hiding all the half-dollars? il Changing T 21:33-4 Ja '67
Wooden nickels, by W. F. Rickenbacker. Review
Nat R il 18:579 Je 14 '66. M. Palyi

SILVER plate. See Silverware
SILVER polishes. See Polishing materials
SILVER prospecting. See Prospecting
SILVER question. See Silver as money

SILVERBERG, Robert
Rise and fall of Sir Stamford Raffles: colonialist, naturalist. Natur Hist 76:18+ Ja '67
William Halsted: tragic figure, great surgeon; excerpt from The great doctors. Todays Health 45:62-7 Ja '67

SILVERMAN, Betsy Marden
Teenagers make good ambassadors. Parents Mag 41:38-9+ Ap '66

SILVERMAN, Ronald H.
Art for the disadvantaged. bibliog NEA J 55:29-31 Ap '66

SILVERMAN, Rosemary
Heroes and lovers; story. Redbook 128:44-5 Ja '67

SILVERMAN, Samuel J.
Making of the surrogate. por Time 88:20 Jl 8 '66
Winning non-candidate. il por Newsweek 68:25 Jl 11 '66

SILVERMAN, Victor
Men behind the camera. E. Bennett. por U S Camera 29:34+ Ag '66

SILVERSMITHING
Portuguese plate: service plate presented by the Prince Regent of Portugal to the first Duke of Wellington. C. Bracegirdle. il Antiques 89:834-7 Je '66

SILVERSMITHS
Corrected attribution. F. J. Dallett. il Antiques 89:734-5 My '66
F. Hoffmann, Philadelphia silversmith. E. Gaines. il Antiques 89:385 Mr '66

SILVERSTEIN, Arthur M. and others
Immunologic maturation in utero: kinetics of the primary antibody response in the fetal lamb. bibliog Science 154:1675-7 D 30 '66

SILVERSTEIN, Elliot
New faces. A. Knight. il por Sat R 49:22 D 24 '66

SILVERSTEIN, Josef
Military rule in Burma. Cur Hist 52:41-7 Ja '67

SILVERSTEIN, Robert M. and others
Sex attractants in frass produced by male ips confusus in ponderosa pine. bibliog Science 154:509-10 O 28 '66

SILVERTON, Michael
Cowgirl ball; poem. Nation 203:526 N 14 '66

SILVERWARE
Adams-Emery wing at the Cincinnati art museum. il Antiques 89:404-5 Mr '66
American silver and pewter. R. Davidson. il Antiques 91:128 Ja '67
Classic is to cherish: sterling for your table. il Seventeen 25:132-3 Ap '66
English inkstands in silver and Sheffield plate. J. Stone. il Antiques 90:342-6 S '66
English plated silver. R. Davidson. il Antiques 90:100+ Jl '66
English silver pocket nutmeg grater. E. B. Miles. il Antiques 90:828-31 D '66
Further comments on the lobate bowl form. J. N. Pearce. il Antiques 90:524-5 O '66
Louisburg and the Pepperrell silver. B. W. F. Trafton, jr. il Antiques 89:366-7 Mr '66
Morrison collection of silver at Princeton, New Jersey. E. P. Birk. il Antiques 90:608+ N '66
Museum acquisitions in silver. R. Davidson. il Antiques 90:851+ D '66
Portuguese plate: service plate presented by the Prince Regent of Portugal to the first Duke of Wellington. C. Bracegirdle. il Antiques 89:834-7 Je '66
Redbook's guide to early American china, silver and glass. il Redbook 127:66-74 Je '66
Silver and silversmiths of Strasbourg in the eighteenth century. H. Haug. il Antiques 89:564-7 Ap '66
Silver manners. il Seventeen 25:146-7+ N '66
Sterling Christmas. il Seventeen 25:192 N '66

See also
Tankards

Exhibitions
Brent Kington's wheeling world. il Craft Horiz 26:43-5 N '66
China trade silver: exhibition at Robert Bennet Forbes House museum, Milton, Mass. J. D. Kernan. il Antiques 90:195-9 Ag '66
Five hundred years of British craftsmanship; traveling exhibition arranged by the Goldsmiths' company. E. P. Birk. il Antiques 90:412 O '66

SILVESTRI, George
Where even Santa gets ideas. M. J. Schultz. il Pop Mech 126:76-9+ D '66

SIMIAN virus. See Cancer viruses; SV40

SIMISON, Frank M. and Harvey, John
Market ten pigs per litter. Suc Farm 64:40-1 My '66

SIMMONS, Charles
George Plimpton is different from you and me. N Y Times Mag p48+ Ja 8 '67
Please re-pot the sauerkraut. Sat Eve Post 239:22 Ja 29 '66; Same abr. Read Digest 88: 21-2+ Ap '66
Who ate father's scarf? Sat Eve Post 239: 22 My 7 '66

SIMMONS, Dykes
Until proven innocent. por Time 88:87-8 O 28 '66

SIMMONS, Joseph Edgar
Begin and end with water music in Ireland; poem. Yale R 55:389 Mr '66

SIMMONS, R. G.
Big transfer trailer. Am City 81:108-9 O '66
City hall that mirrors the city it serves. Am City 81:118-19 Ag '66

SIMMONS, Roscoe Conkling
Roscoe Conkling Simmons: the golden voiced politico. M. H. Boulware. bibliog Negro Hist Bul 29:131-2 Mr '66

SIMON, André L.
Epicure reminisces. Holiday 40:34+ D '66

SIMON, Arthur R.
New Yorkers without a voice: a tragedy of urban renewal; excerpt from Faces of poverty. Atlan 217:54-9 Ap '66

SIMON, Benjamin
Aboard a flying saucer; excerpt from The interrupted journey. J. G. Fuller. il por Look 30:44-8+ O 4; 111-14+ O 18 '66

SIMON, Dan
Sensitivity training in the classroom. NEA J 56:12 Ja '67

SIMON, Henry W.
Along the way. Opera N 31:24-6 D 24 '66

SIMON, Herbert Alexander
Shake-up of conventional economics. il Bsns W D 186+ Je 25 '66

SIMON, Joe
How to keep sows and pigs healthy; interview, ed. by J. Harvey. Suc Farm 64:44-5+ Ap '66
SIMON, John
Books. Commonweal 83:669-70+ Mr 11 '66
Tragedy of American theater. Holiday 39: 76-83+ Mr '66
(tr) See Kästner, E. Young man: five a.m.
SIMON, Lionel N. See Glasky, A. J. jt. auth.
SIMON, Mina Lewiton
Fugue in three voices; story. New Yorker 42:133-4 O 1 '66
SIMON, Nathan
Simon says. por Mod Phot 30:12+ Ag; 44+ N; 72 D '66; 31:110+ Ja '67
SIMON, Neil
B for comedy. Writer 79:23-4 My '66
about
Human comedian. il por Newsweek 69:70 Ja 9 '67
Simon says thumbs up. G. Weales. Reporter 34:36+ Je 2 '66
Star-spangled girl. Criticism
New Yorker 42:59 D 31 '66
Newsweek 69:66 Ja 2 '67
Sat R 50:98 Ja 14 '67
Time il 88:45 D 30 '66
SIMON, Norton
Shuffle & cut; relinquishing post of board chairman of Wheeling steel. por Time 88: 88+ D 2 '66
Simon creates a new riddle. por Bsns W p52 N 26 '66
Simon says it with a broad brush. il pors Bsns W p62-4+ My 14 '66
SIMON, Paul
Two about Lincoln. Christian Cent 83:176 F 9 '66
SIMON, Paul (singer)
Simon & Garfunkel, young poets of folk-rock. B. Rollin. il pors Look 30:M14-16 N 29 '66
SIMON, Robert Edward, 1914–
Architecture. E. Galantay. il Nation 203:652-4 D 12 '66
Dream city (almost) H. Cox. Commonweal 85: 426-7 Ja 20 '67
SIMON, Seymour
Scholastic teacher reviews: conservation-books for all ages. Sr Schol 88:sup 19 Ap 29 '66
SIMON, Sidney B. See Harmin, M. jt. auth.
SIMON and Schuster, incorporated
Leon Shimkin describes the new Simon & Schuster. il Pub W 190:58-60 Jl 4 '66; Reply. L. Shimkin. 190:44-5 Ag 22 '66
Merger terms set for S&S, Regents publishing. Pub W 190:39 O 17 '66
Shimkin to own all of S&S, merge it with Pocket books. Pub W 189:72-3 Ja 31 '66
S&S and Regents publishing in merger negotiations. Pub W 190:37 Ag 1 '66
S&S to sell its holdings in Western publishing co. Pub W 190:30 D 12 '66
SIMONDS, C. H.
Children's books; a medley. Nat R 18:1284-6 D 13 '66
TV in review. Nat R 18:584+, 1007-8 Je 14, O 4 '66
Where the theater is. Nat R 18:223-4+ Mr 8 '66
SIMONS, Ellen Louise
Balaguer takes over. Commonweal 84:437-40 Jl 8 '66
SIMONS, Francis, bp
Consensus ethics. Time 88:91-2 D 9 '66
SIMONS, George F.
Atlanta statement; commentary. Cath World 202:302-5 F '66
SIMONS, Howard
Exciting new world of X-ray astronomy; reprint. Sci Digest 59:60-6 Je '66
Great Dane. New Repub 155:28+ D 3 '66
Spies that can't feel the cold. Esquire 65: 104-5+ My '66
SIMONSON, Harold P.
Grierson: a strange fish. Nation 203:226-7 S 12 '66
SIMONT, Marc
It's bigger than bingo; drawings. Sports Illus 24:56-9 My 16 '66
SIMPKINS, John J.
How to build a flagstone terrace. Flower Grower 53:50-1 Je '66
SIMPLICIA, Sister M. See M. Simplicia, Sister
SIMPSON, Claude M. Jr
New world ballads. Sat R 49:53 F 12 '66
SIMPSON, Dale R.
Apatite and octa-calcium phosphate: effects of carbon dioxide and halogens on formation. bibliog Science 154:1660-1 D 30 '66

SIMPSON, Fred
Adventure aboard a square-rigger. Yachting 119:212-14 F '66
SIMPSON, George D. and Shifrin, W. G.
Best value. Am City 81:75-8 Jl '66
SIMPSON, George Gaylord
Biological nature of man. bibliog Science 152: 472-8; 154:1120 Ap 22, D 2 '66
SIMPSON, Jim
Sportscasting, anyone? interview, ed. by H. L. Masin. por Sr Schol 88:20 F 11 '66
SIMPSON, Larry
Toxic impurities in nalgene filter units. Science 153:548 Jl 29 '66
SIMPSON, Louis
Indolence; poem. Sat Eve Post 239:43 D 31 '66
Making of a soldier USA. Harper 232:76-80 F '66
On a veranda; poem. Harper 233:86 O '66
Why are you walking? poem. Nation 202:690 Je 6 '66
about
What we are, and are not. B. Cutler. Poetry 108:270 Jl '66
SIMPSON, Melvin V. See Parsons, P. jt. auth.
SIMPSON, Richard
Experiment A. Design 67:12-15 Ja '66
SIMPSON, Robert Henry
Mental health trap. T. E. Schulz. Nat R 18:510-12+ My 31 '66
SIMPSON, Robert Tennent
Recusation in Alabama. por Time 88:81 D 16 '66
SIMPSON, Smith
Rise of the CIA: how foggy bottom lost its spies; excerpt from Anatomy of the State department. Nation 204:38-42 Ja 9 '67
SIMROSS, Lynn
Dogs. Sports Illus 25:50-1 Jl 25 '66
Heave ho, lock in and rock. Sports Illus 25: 40-1 O 17 '66
SIMULATORS
Eighteen days on the moon. il Sci Digest 60:9 Jl '66
First real man-made tornado generated. Sci N 89:310 Ap 30 '66
Hurricanes made to order; Wave and current lab of the Netherlands ship model basin. il Sci Digest 59:57 Ap '66
Martin builds guidance research facility; duplicating operational environment of missile or aircraft. il Aviation W 84:191+ Je 20 '66
Missile guidance simulator for tests; electro-optical guidance simulator. il Sci N 89:309 Ap 30 '66
New navy facility to better ASW ability. R. Pay. il Tech W 19:20+ Ag 1 '66
On the moon eighteen days but still on earth; test chamber Lunex II. Sci N 89:195 Mr 26 '66
Undersea air supply; utilizing sea water to regenerate breathing mixtures. H. P. Vind. bibliog il Science 153:873-5 Ag 19 '66
SIMULATORS, Flight. See Flight simulators
SIMULATORS, Warfare. See War games
SIN
Adam, Eve and the Pope; contemporary concepts of original sin; Catholic scholars report. il Newsweek 68:93 Ag 22 '66
Office of the keys. Christian Cent 83:227 F 23 '66
See also
Salvation

Anecdotes, facetiae, satire, etc.
New seven deadly sins; portfolio. Esquire 66:190-5 D '66
SINATRA, Frank
Boy meets girl. G. Ace. Sat R 49:6 Ag 13 '66
Frank Sinatra has a cold. G. Talese. pors Esquire 65:89-98+ Ap '66
Frank Sinatra's $25,000 weekend. R. Russell. il por Ladies Home J 84:48+ Ja '67
Fun couples. por Newsweek 68:58 Jl 25 '66
Measure of Sinatra. B. Korall. por Sat R 49: 58-9 O 15 '66
Mia to Mrs in four minutes. il por Life 61: 46A-46B Jl 29 '66
Nancy Sinatra talks about life with father. V. Scott. por Ladies Home J 83:82-3+ S '66
Sinatra special that's very; Sinatra's spectacular revisited. J. M. Ferrer, 3d. Life 61:24 D 9 '66
SINATRA, Nancy
Daughter of the chairman. il por Newsweek 67:100 My 16 '66
Nancy: another swinging Sinatra. D. Chapman. il pors Look 38:58-63 Jl 12 '66
Nancy Sinatra talks about life with father. V. Scott. por Ladies Home J 83:82-3+ S '66

SINCERITY
Turned-on and super-sincere in California. R. Todd. il Harper 234:42-7 Ja '67
See also
Truthfulness

SINCLAIR, James B. See Kirk, B. T. jt. auth.

SINCLAIR oil corporation
Sinclair breaks the clamp on its profits; chairman E. L. Steiniger refines company's goals. il Bsns W p64-6+ Ag 27 '66

SINGAPORE
Letter from Singapore. R. Shaplen. il New Yorker 42:57-8+ Ja 14 '67
Rupture in Malaysia. C. P. Bradley. bibliog f Cur Hist 50:98-105 F '66

Armed forces
Dismissed. Time 87:29-30 F 11 '66

Commercial treaties and agreements
U.S. and Singapore reach cotton textiles understanding; Department announcement, August 30, 1966; with letter from government of Singapore and Singapore cotton textile industry restraint schedule. il Dept State Bul 55:509-13 O 3 '66

Description and travel
Maughamland revisited. H. Sutton. Sat R 50:52-3 Ja 21 '67
Singapore, reluctant nation. K. MacLeish. il Nat Geog Mag 130:268-300 Ag '66

Foreign relations
Singapore and Malaysia: a divorce of inconvenience. D. Warner. Reporter 34:44-6 Ap 7 '66

Politics and government
See also
Political parties—Singapore

SINGAPORE national library. See Libraries—Singapore

SINGER, Aubrey E.
Science broadcasting in Britain; excerpts from address, February 16, 1966. Science 154:743-5 N 11 '66

SINGER, Carl N.
Rewriting the script for Scripto. il por Bsns W p 168+ D 17 '66

SINGER, Howard
Speaking out. por Sat Eve Post 240:10+ Ja 28 '67

SINGER, Isaac Bashevis
Boudoir; story. Vogue 147:148-9 Ap 1 '66
Dreamers. Reporter 35:45-6 Jl 14 '66
First shlemiel; story. Commentary 42:45-8 Jl '66
Mixed-up feet and the silly bridegroom; story. Commentary 42:43-5 Jl '66
Parrot; story, tr. by R. Whitman. Harper 232:59-66 Je '66
Prodigal fool; story. Sat Eve Post 239:64-6 F 26 '66
Snow in Chelm; story. Commentary 42:41-3 Jl '66

about
God in the ghetto. Newsweek 67:106-7 My 2 '66
In the shtetl of Bilgoray. J. Chametzky. Nation 203:392-3 O 17 '66
Other Singer. I. Howe. Commentary 41:78+ Mr '66
People are talking about... por Vogue 147:146-7 Ap 1 '66
Rabbis, angels and demons. A. H. Friedlander. Sat R 49:91 My 7 '66

SINGER, Israel Joshua
Other Singer. I. Howe. Commentary 41:78+ Mr '66

SINGER, S. J. and Doolittle, R. F.
Antibody active sites and immunoglobulin molecules. bibliog Science 153:13-25 Jl 1 '66

SINGER, Susanne
Photographed by; Susanne Singer. M. P. R. Thomas. il U S Camera 29:50-3 D '66

SINGER company
Aid to home sewing. M. B. Keiser. il Parents Mag 41:22+ Je '66

SINGERS
Artists in the kitchen; favorite foods and recipes of some opera singers. P. Gravina. il Opera N 30:26-9 Mr 19 '66
Benchley's Bushmen. R. Gehman. Sat R 49:59+ O 15 '66
Biggest cat; James Brown show. il Time 87:75 Ap 1 '66
Blues turned blue-eyed; Righteous brothers. C. Welles. Life 61:18 Jl 1 '66
Debuts & reappearances: New York concerts. See issues of High fidelity incorporating Musical America

France's long-haired Donnybrook: the imitable Antoine, and rival, Edouard. R. Chelminski. il Life 61:12 Ag 19 '66
In my opinion; with a few marvelous exceptions, folk rock is terrible. M. Medeiros. Seventeen 25:250 F '67
Life from the hearthside; Beers family. il Time 89:38+ Ja 6 '67
Lovin' Spoonful. il Newsweek 68:80 S 5 '66
Musical whirl; photographs. See issues of High fidelity incorporating Musical America
New sparrow stirs France. il Life 60:115-16 Je 10 '66
New troubadours; takeover of the folk rockers. il Time 88:92+ O 28 '66
Nubes; pre-teen rock 'n' roll groups. il Time 87:60+ Mr 11 '66
Romp! romp! the Monkees. il Newsweek 68:102 O 24 '66
Singing voice: first sounds. R. Rushmore. il Opera N 31:24-7 Ja 21 '67
Sonny & Chér: they're what's happening, baby. P. Bogdanovich. il Sat Eve Post 239:46-50+ Ap 23 '66
Sonny talks about Chér; interview, ed. by P. Bogdanovich. S. Bono. il Vogue 148:137-8 N 15 '66
Starting at the top; Bobbe Norris. il Newsweek 67:88-9 Je 27 '66
TV's swinging Monkees. B. Rollin. il Look 30:93-6 D 27 '66
These are the Mamas; Mamas and the Papas, pop group; with report by G. Moore. il Life 61:77-8+ S 30 '66
Under the lemon trees; Mamas and the Papas. il Newsweek 68:78 Ag 8 '66
What ever happened to the Andrews sisters? oddball names. Time 88:78 D 16 '66
When four nice boys go ape! NBC Monday night show, The Monkees. R. W. Lewis. il Sat Eve Post 240:74-6+ Ja 28 '67
See also
American guild of musical artists
Beatles
Opera singers
Singing
also names of singers, e.g. N. Wilson

SINGH, Inderjit
Pop. 6,000,000,000; interview. New Yorker 42:47-9 S 10 '66

SINGH, K. Natwar-. See Natwar-Singh, K.

SINGH, Khushwant
In search of the seekers of truth. N Y Times Mag p42-3+ Ja 8 '67
We've never had it so bad. N Y Times Mag p5+ Ja 23 '66
Women of India. N Y Times Mag p24-5+ Mr 13 '66

SINGH, Sir Yadavindra, maharaja of Patiala
Maharajah's mangoes. il por Newsweek 67:93 Je 20 '66

SINGING
Back to bel canto. il Time 89:42 Ja 20 '67
Do the things you love; opera singing. A. Moffo. Seventeen 25:172+ N '66
Phantom of the opera; voice amplification. H. C. Schonberg. il N Y Times Mag p 10-11+ F 6 '66; Discussion. p 19+ F 20 '66
Singer's challenge; excerpt from The great singers. H. Pleasants. il Opera N 31:6-9 O 15 '66
Who's afraid of Lucrezia Borgia? opera paraphrases, once the stock in trade of virtuoso pianists. R. Lewenthal. il Opera N 31:8-12 D 31 '66
See also
Opera singers
Singers
Voice

Competitions
Broncobuster in Moscow; Tchaikovsky international competition. il Newsweek 68:84 Jl 11 '66
Diva derby; Metropolitan audition winners. il Newsweek 67:96 Ap 11 '66

SINGLE, age twenty-five; story. See Hobson, L. Z.

SINGLE-lens reflex cameras
At last: Rollei has an SLR. E. H. Ortner. il Pop Sci 189:138-9 N '66
Here it is: first instant-loading SLR. N. Rothschild. il Pop Phot 59:80-1+ O '66
Keppler looks over the SLR's. H. Keppler. Mod Phot 30:67+ Je '66
Keppler on the SLR. H. Keppler. See issues of Modern photography
Keppler on the SLR; behind-the-lens meter SLR cameras. H. Keppler. Mod Phot 30:18+ Je '66
New SLR alphabet: CTL, SL, TTL, FT, VX. N. Rothschild. il Pop Phot 60:102-5 Ja '67
Rollei goes SLR! N. Rothschild. il Pop Phot 59:89-93+ N '66

SINGLE-lens reflex cameras—Continued
Rollei SL 66. il U S Camera 29:32 N '66
Simon says; Rollei SLR. N. Simon. Mod
Phot 30:44+ N '66
Single-lens-reflex cameras. il Consumer Bul
49:6-9 S '66
SLR cameras compared. D. L. Miller. il Mod
Phot 30:48-57 Ag '66
SLR's coming on strong. N. Rothschild. il
Pop Phot 58:30+ Ap '66
Super close-ups with your SLR. T. Karp. il
Mod Phot 30:50-4+ F '66
Techniques tomorrow; 2 1/4 single-lens re-
flex. B. Sherman. Mod Phot 31:22+ Ja '67
2¼ Rollei SLR! A. Mannheim. il Mod Phot
30:84-5+ N '66
What's new that's good. N. Rothschild. il
Pop Phot 58:112+ Je '66

Loading
Keppler on the SLR; quick loading systems.
H. Keppler. il Mod Phot 30:10+ Mr '66

SINGLE men
Eligible bachelors. il Ebony 21:132-4+ Je '66
Most unhappy fellow; report findings. News-
week 67:104+ Ap 11 '66
Where the singles are; enclave of bars on
New York's midtown East side. il News-
week 68:113 S 26 '66
Young, single, and a stranger in New York;
singles parties. I. Taves. il Look 30:88-94
Ag 23 '66
SINGLE rail railroads. See Railroads, Single
rail
SINGLE sideband system. See Radio transmis-
sion—Single sideband system
SINGLE women
Bachelor girl; Negro girls in nation's capital.
R. Lantz. il Ebony 21:102-4+ Ag '66
For the single girl: a new way of life in
California; South Bay club, in a Los
Angeles suburb. G. Greene. il Ladies
Home J 83:58-9+ Jl '66
Life and the single woman. M. Mannes.
McCalls 93:20+ My '66
Life insurance for single women. il Chang-
ing T 20:33-5 D '66
My mother said I should give it a try; hunt
for a husband in Catskills. W. Kloman. il
Sat Eve Post 239:36-41 O 8 '66
Single girl and the married man. G. Dicker-
son. Mlle 62:154-5+ F '66
Where the singles are; enclave of bars on
New York's midtown East side. il News-
week 68:113 S 26 '66
Young, single and a stranger in New York;
singles parties. I. Taves. il Look 30:88-94
Ag 23 '66
SINGULAR honor; story. See Schwartz, J.
SINÍAVSKII, Andrei D. See Tertz, A. pseud.
SINKIANG province, China
Sino-Soviet border comrades up in arms. il
Sr Schol 88:14-16 Mr 18 '66
SINKING of land. See Land sinking
SINKS

Anecdotes, facetiae, satire, etc.
Wrong mash. W. McQuade. il Arch Forum
125:76 D '66
SIOUX CITY, Ia.

Streets
How to prevent scaling. R. R. Fleming il
Am City 81:96-7 D '66
SIOUX FALLS, S.D.

Sanitary affairs
Two plants in one remove 97.5 percent BOD.
R. Jackson and R. Wieting. il Am City
81:158+ O '66
SIQUEIROS, David Alfaro
Man needs space. il por Newsweek 68:69 Ag
29 '66
SIRE, Glen, and Sire, Jane
Girl in the green hat; story. McCalls 94:106-
7 N '66
SIRE, Jane. See Sire, G. jt. auth.
**SIRIKIT Kitiyakara, consort of Bhumibol Adul-
yadej, king of Thailand**
Holder of the kingdom, strength of the land.
il pors Time 87:28-30+ My 27 '66
SIRKIS, Nancy
Young gourmet. il Look 30:M14-16 Ap 19 '66
SIROTA, David
Productivity management. Harvard Bsns R
44:111-16 S '66
SIRUGO, Salvatore
Private worlds of Sal Sirugo. N. Edgar. il
Art N 65:42-3+ N '66
SISCO, Joseph J.
Fresh look at the United Nations; address,
April 2, 1966. Dept State Bul 54:646-50 Ap
25 '66

Hard work ahead for the United Nations;
address, March 18, 1966. Dept State Bul
54:571-6 Ap 11 '66
Power and responsibility; address, November
12, 1966. Dept State Bul 55:856-61 D 5 '66
Rising hopes for international cooperation;
address, September 7, 1966. Dept State Bul
55:458-63 S 26 '66
Unfinished business of the U.N. and the
world; address, September 8, 1966. Dept
State Bul 55:487-91 O 3 '66
U.S. calls for peaceful settlement of Middle
East disputes; urges U.S.S.R. to move for
peace in Viet-Nam; texts of statements,
July 29, August 3, 1966. Dept State Bul
55:313-17 Ag 29 '66
SISLEY, Alfred
Art galleries; exhibition at the Wildenstein.
R. M. Coates. il New Yorker 42:193-5 N 19
'66
Unknown Sisley. J. Ashbery. il Art N 65:
44-5+ N '66
SISSMAN, L. E.
Chamber music. Bar Harbor, off-season;
poem. Atlan 217:139 Mr '66
Day in the city; poem. New Yorker 42:64 D 3
'66
Elegy; E. W. New Yorker 42:36 My 28 '66
In and out; poem. New Yorker 42:50-1 My 14
'66
Museum of comparative zoology; poem. Atlan
219:108 Ja '67
On the island; poem. New Yorker 41:32-3
Ja 29 '66
Two happenings in Boston; poem. New
Yorker 42:58 O 8 '66
West forties; morning, noon, and night;
poem. New Yorker 42:42-3 Mr 5 '66
SISTER schools. See School-to-school program
SISTER students. See College students, Women
SISTERHOODS
Archbishop and the sisters; Glenmary
sisters. J. O'Gara. Commonweal 85:47 O 14
'66
Face to face with a girl who is becoming
a nun. Sister Natalie. il Seventeen 25:117+
Je '66
Health program for sisters; Chicago arch-
diocese program. America 115:642 N 19 '66
New nuns. M. Novak. il Sat Eve Post 239:
21-7+ Jl 30 '66
Nun enters the Newman apostolate. Sister
M. Michael. Cath World 203:293-6 Ag '66
Nuns in the inner city; force for freedom
and creativity. P. Barrett. Christian Cent
83:1050-3 Ag 31 '66
Putting sisters in their place. S. Kelly; dis-
cussion. America 114:329-30 Mr 5 '66
Restive nuns; steady loss among sisters. il
Time 89:66+ Ja 13 '67
Shackling the sisters; restrictions on the
Glenmary sisters. Commonweal 85:5-6 O 7
'66; Reply. K. J. Alter. 85:93+ O 28 '66
Sisters of the poor; owners and operators of
St Francis hospital. New Yorker 42:24-7 D
31 '66
Timely psychoanalysis; disturbed priests and
nuns. America 115:87 Jl 23 '66
Why did sister change her name? America
115:444 O 15 '66
See also
Vocation (in religion)
SITE planning. See Housing projects—Site
planning
SITE values. See Land values
SITES, James N.
Why bureaucrats can't run a business. Na-
tions Bsns 54:35+ O '66
SITES, Historic. See United States—Historic
houses, etc.
SITKA, Alaska
Rebuilding St Michael's; Russian Orthodox
church in Alaska. Christian Cent 83:1003
Ag 17 '66
SITTER, Matt
How to specify polysulfide sealants. Arch Rec
140:153-4 Ag '66
SITWELL, Sir George, family
Montegufoni. E. De Lanux. New Yorker 42:
198+ S 10 '66
SIX, Robert Forman
Arms & men at Continental. Time 88:71-2 Jl
1 '66
Six's biggest gamble. il por Newsweek 68:88
N 14 '66
SIX-three-three plan. See School management
and organization
SIXTH avenue. See New York (city)—Streets
SIXTH committee of the General assembly. See
United Nations—Legal committee
SIZE
Manner of speaking; impulse to confuse
physical dimension with the dimension of
idea. J. Ciardi. Sat R 49:6 Jl 2 '66

SIZER, Theodore Ryland
Pressing problems and national assessment; excerpt from address. PTA Mag 61:18+ N '66

SJOGREN, William L. See Mulholland. J. D. jt. auth.

SKADBERG, Marvin, and Nelson, Don
How much is cattle shrink costing you? Suc Farm 64:78 S '66

SKATING
Champions of winter; P. Fleming, figure skater. il Sports Illus 24:14-15 F 7 '66
Delicacy at Davos; world championships. P. Fleming triumph. il Time 87:70 Mr 11 '66
High-altitude triumph for a tough little miss; women's world figure-skating championship. G. Gross. il Sports Illus 24:58-9 Mr 7 '66
Icemen cometh; ice skating's popularity. il Newsweek 67:95 F 21 '66
I'm someone else when I skate. P. Fleming. il Seventeen 25:118-19+ D '66
Paris fling for a teen queen; World figure skating champion. il Sports Illus 24:30-3 My 2 '66
Peggy at seventeen; 1966 championship at Davos, Switzerland. il Newsweek 67:92 Mr 14 '66
Peggy Fleming's triumph on ice; World figure skating championships. il Life 60:93-4 Mr 11 '66

SKATING rinks
Hot-flooded ice rinks. B. L. Wrede. Parks & Rec 1:760+ S '66
Pool and ice rink in one area; Great Neck park district, Long Island, N.Y. il Am City 81:75-7 Je '66
Pool-rink complex. il Parks & Rec 1:750+ S '66
Swimming and ice skating team up. C. R. Hoaglund. il Am City 81:17 F '66

SKEET (game)
Guns for hire. il Newsweek 68:110 N 28 '66
See also
Trap shooting

SKEHAN, Patrick W.
Capriccio Allegro; or, How not to learn in ten years. Christian Cent 83:1211-13 O 5 '66

SKELETON; story. See Pritchett. V. S.

SKELTON, Robin
Canadian chronicle. Poetry 109:53-8 O '66

SKENE, Don
Telegrams. R. L. Tobin. Sat R 49:8+ Jl 30 '66

SKEPTICISM
See also
Belief and doubt

SKETCHING. See Drawing

SKEWER cookery. See Cookery

SKI boats. See Motor boats

SKI clothing. See Clothing and dress—Sports clothes

SKI jumping. See Skis and skiing

SKI lifts
Portable ski tow: easy to make, fun to use. E. F. Muehlmatt. il Pop Sci 189:166-8 N '66

SKI rack, Automobile. See Automobiles—Equipment

SKI resorts. See Winter resorts

SKI tows. See Ski lifts

SKIBBINS, Gerald J. and Weymar, C. S.
Right to work controversy. bibliog f Harvard Bsns R 44:6-8+ Jl '66

SKIDDING of airplanes. See Airplanes—Skidding

SKIERS
Wild watusi weekend on the Snowball Special; Union Pacific from Los Angeles to Sun Valley. B. Ottum. il Sports Illus 24:50-2+ Mr 14 '66

SKIING. Water. See Water skis and skiing

SKILLED labor
Brain drain: a U.S. dilemma. H. G. Grubel. bibliog Science 154:1420-4 D 16 '66
From the other side: a European view. B. Thomas. bibliog f il Ann Am Acad 367:63-72 S '66
Still in short supply; Bureau of labor statistics report. il Bsns W p92+ O 29 '66

SKILLED performance. See Performance standards

SKIM boats. See Ground effect machines

SKIN
It's your skin. L. Galton. il Pop Sci 188:69-71 My '66
Light-stimulated electrical responses from skin. H. E. Becker and R. A. Cone. bibliog il Science 154:1051-3 N 25 '66

Skin. R. F. Rushmer and others. bibliog il Science 154:343-8 O 21 '66
See also
Color of man

Care and hygiene
Beauty bulletin; beauty care with electrical current. il Vogue 148:86-9 Jl '66
Beauty life: self-preservation: never too soon. il Mlle 62:140-1+ Mr '66
Beauty life: the masked heroine. il Mlle 63: 74-5 Jl '66
How to know when to do what to your face. il Vogue 147:158-61 Mr 1 '66
Sensible sunning. L. D. Kirk. il Parents Mag 41:78 Je '66

Diseases
It's your skin. L. Galton. il Pop Sci 188:69-71 My '66
See also
Allergy
Psoriasis

Papillary ridges
See Dermatoglyphics

SKIN, Color of. See Color of man

SKIN cancer. See Cancer

SKIN diving. See Diving, Submarine

SKIN grafting. See Transplantation of organs, tissues, etc.

SKIN ointments. See Ointments

SKIN patterns. See Dermatoglyphics

SKINNER, Burrhus Frederic
Phylogeny and ontogeny of behavior. bibliog Science 153:1205-13 S 9 '66

SKINNER, Constance Lindsay, award. See Constance Lindsay Skinner award

SKINNER, Cornelia Otis
Hope; poem. por McCalls 93:81 Je '66
Technically speaking, I can't. Read Digest 88:174-6+ Je '66

SKINNER, George
Trade winds; telephone talk-jockey show. J. C. Fuller. il Sat R 49:12-13 Mr 5 '66

SKINNER, Lloyd E.
Consumer; address, December 6, 1966. Vital Speeches 33:189-92 Ja 1 '67
Excerpt from testimony, May 6, 1965. Cong Digest 45:187+ Je '66

SKINNER, Wayne
Room divider. il Sch Arts 66:6-9 S '66

SKINNER, Wickham
Production under pressure. Harvard Bsns R 44:139-46 N '66

SKIRA, Albert
Albert Skira's reflections on making and publishing art books. Pub W 190:108 Ag 1 '66
Book as display; exhibition at Hallmark gallery. F. P. Naughton. il Wilson Lib Bul 41:331-3 N '66
Skira art book exhibit on display in New York. il por Pub W 190:48 Jl 18 '66
Skira plans U.S. exhibits, new art book projects. por Pub W 189:34 Ap 4 '66

SKIS and skiing
Allez, France! with skis and water pistols; French captured the Werner cup at the Sun Valley lodge. D. Jenkins. Sports Illus 24:88-9 Ap 4 '66
Amputees on skis; Amputee slalom race, Mount Hood, Ore. E. H. Matthew. il Todays Health 45:12-13 Ja '67
Found: a pretty Penny; performance of U.S. girls at World ski championships, Portillo, Chile. B. Ottum. il Sports Illus 25:12-15 Ag 15 '66
France has a picnic in Vermont; U.S. Alpine championships at Stowe. D. Jenkins. il Sports Illus 24:30-3 Mr 28 '66
French snowball; World Alpine ski championships, Portillo, Chile. il Time 88:62 Ag 19 '66
Gallic gauntlet on the snow; World ski championships in Portillo. Chile won by France. B. Ottum. il Sports Illus 25:24-5 Ag 22 '66
He built his own hill for skiing! B. Brantley. il Suc Farm 64:114 Mr '66
It's fun time on the slopes. D. Williamson. Sat R 49:4+ N 19 '66
Junior jumps into the family act. il Life 60:95-6 F 4 '66
No-snow slope to nonsport; ski resorts along Mason-Dixon line. B. Gilbert. il Sports Illus 24:62-6+ F 21 '66
Peak performance; Denver university coach W. Schaeffler. Newsweek 67:93 Mr 21 '66
Ski time in Sun Valley and Jackson Hole. G. E. Maxwell. il Todays Health 44:42-7+ N '66

SKIS and skiing—*Continued*

Skiing on sawdust; field testing and experimentation by U.S. forest service. R. K. Peter. il Parks & Rec 1:245+ Mr '66

Skiing the Rockies: the high-powered life in the West. J. Skow. il Sat Eve Post 239:26-31 Mr 12 '66

Skiing's darling of derring-do: J. C. Killy of France. D. Jenkins. il Sports Illus 24:20-2+ F 21 '66

Soaring week for the nervy Norse; FIS Nordics B. Ottum. il Sports Illus 24:52-5 Mr 7 '66

Stein Eriksen: Horatio Alger on skis. T. F. Smith. il Harper 232:87-90 Mr '66

Sun spot for skiing; Mt Baldy in San Bernardino Mountains. il Travel 126:64 Ag '66

Teen travel talk; one of American youth hostels in Rochester, Vt. il Seventeen 25:80 N '66

Traveling with Mlle: skimanship; symposium. Mlle 64:185+ N '66

Turboprop to a glacier; flying to ski in the French Alps. F. R. Smith. il Sports Illus 24:36-43 F 7 '66

U.S. leaders take to the slopes. il Life 62:28-28A Ja 6 '67

Wild watusi weekend on the Snowball Special; Union Pacific from Los Angeles to Sun Valley. B. Ottum. il Sports Illus 24:50-2+ Mr 14 '66

Year of Billy the Kidd. D. Jenkins. il Sports Illus 24:10-13 Ja 24 '66

See also
National ski patrol system
Ski lifts
Water skis and skiing

Accidents and injuries

Patrol chief of the ski slopes. il Ebony 22:84-6+ D '66

Anecdotes, faceticae, satire, etc.

Confessions of a wounded skier. B. Brower. il Holiday 39:62-7+ F '66

Shtepping around with Hoobert. J. Olsen. il Sports Illus 24:46-52 Ja 31 '66

Equipment

Backsliding on the slopes: stolen skis. il Time 87:84 F 18 '66

Releasable ski bindings. il Consumer Rep 31:560-5 N '66

Study and teaching

Ski parallel in one day. S. James. il Pop Mech 126:126-9+ D '66

Ski school; Edmonds, Wash. program. A. May. il NEA J 55:43 F '66

California

West Face KT-22, Squaw Valley. B. Ottum. il Sports Illus 25:64-5 N 14 '66

Colorado

Riva ridge, Vail. B. Ottum. il Sports Illus 25:56-7 N 14 '66

Ruthie's run, Aspen. B. Ottum. il Sports Illus 25:68-9 N 14 '66

Idaho

Warm Springs, Sun Valley. B. Ottum. il Sports Illus 25:62-3 N 14 '66

Italy

Mickey Mouse Olympics; American skiers at World university winter games, Sestriere. B. Ottum. il Sports Illus 24:43-6 F 28 '66

New Mexico

Al's run, Taos. B. Ottum. il Sports Illus 25:58-9 N 14 '66

Northwestern states

Green Valley, Crystal Mountain. B. Ottum. il Sports Illus 25:66-7 N 14 '66

Making the ski scene. il Newsweek 68:50-6 D 26 '66

Oregon

Mount Ashland's unusual attraction. il Sunset 136:48 F '66

United States

America's best ski runs. B. Ottum. il Sports Illus 25:52-69 N 14 '66

Fast off the slopes. il Time 89:62-7 Ja 6 '67

Utah

Into Utah's Treasure Mountains. il Sunset 138:22+ Ja '66

Payday, Park City; Chartreuse trail, Alta. B. Ottum. il Sports Illus 25:61 N 14 '66

Vermont

Glades, Sugarbush. B. Ottum. il Sports Illus 25:60 N 14 '66

Nose dive, Stowe. B. Ottum. il Sports Illus 25:54-5 N 14 '66

SKLAR, Robert

Dos Passos' restless times. Nation 204:87-8 Ja 16 '67

Humdrum epic. Reporter 36:56+ Ja 12 '67

SKLAR, Sheila

I was the world's most expectant mother. ed. by M. Bloom and S. Bloom. por Redbook 126:56-7+ Mr '66

SKOLNIKOFF, Eugene B.

Scientific advice in the State department. bibliog Science 154:980-5 N 25 '66

SKOOG, Folke, and others

Cytokinin activity: localization in transfer RNA preparations. bibliog Science 154:1354-6 D 9 '66

SKOOGFORS, Judy

Metalworkers of Europe. Craft Horiz 26:36-41+ S '66

SKOOKUMCHUCK rapids. *See* Georgia, Strait of

SKOPLJE, Yugoslavia

Skopje rebuilds. il UN Mo Chron 3:57-62 Ap '66

SKORYNA, Stanley

Expedition to an idyll. C. Mydans. il Life 60:56+ F 4 '66

SKOW, John

Black man leading a G.O.P. march on Washington. Sat Eve Post 239:82-7 S 10 '66

Has TV gasp! gone Batty? Sat Eve Post 239:93-7 My 7 '66

Highwaymen come to Morristown. Sat Eve Post 239:68-75 Ap 9 '66

Hooboy advisor. Sat Eve Post 239:14 D 31 '66

"If I had to practice cannibalism. . ." Sat Eve Post 239:28-31 Jl 30 '66

Is love, sweet love, a crime? Sat Eve Post 239:82-4+ F 12 '66

Joe, Joe, you're the most beautiful thing in the world! Sat Eve Post 239:99-103 D 3 '66

Skiing the Rockies: the high-powered life in the West. Sat Eve Post 239:26-31 Mr 12 '66

When the great developer became extinct. Sat Eve Post 239:29 O 8 '66

Winter of the small wildcats. Sat Eve Post 239:22 F 26 '66

SKROWACZEWSKI, Stanislaw

Music to my ears. I. Kolodin. Sat R 49:41 F 26 '66

Recordings. M. Meyer. Esquire 66:16 Jl '66

Young Pole in the Midwest. Hi Fi 16:126 My '66

SKULL

See also
Jaws

Surgery

Paste plugs hole in skull. Sci N 90:68 Jl 30 '66

SKUNK cabbages

Western skunk cabbage. M. M. Taylor. il Horticulture 44:18-19 F '66

SKY diving. *See* Parachuting

SKY writing. *See* Skywriting

SKYCARS. *See* Cableways

SKYLIGHT filters. *See* Light filters

SKYSCRAPER; musical comedy. *See* Musical comedies, revues, etc.—Criticisms, plots, etc.

SKYSCRAPERS

New context for the office tower. il Arch Rec 140:160-1 N '66

New structural systems and analysis make a whole new concept in skyscraper design possible and practical for one hundred or more. il Arch Rec 140:154-5 Jl '66

New wind tests devised; study of oscillatory behavior of two skyscrapers for World trade center. il Sci N L 89:86 F 5 '66

See also
New York (city)—Empire state building
Office buildings

SKYWRITING

Sky has to be big enough: Stinis air service; interview. A. Stinis. New Yorker 42:52-4 S 24 '66

SLACK, Jack

How to find sunken treasure, and keep it. L. Steckler. il Pop Mech 126:124-7+ N '66

SLACK, Kenneth T.

Oasis in Arizona. Library J 91:5883-5 D 1 '66

SLACKS, Womens. *See* Clothing and dress

SLAMECKA, Vladimir

Teaching machines. Science 153:1289-90 S 9 '66

SLANDER. See Libel and slander

SLANG
G-eye view of Vietnam. J. B. Treaster. il N Y Times Mag p 100+ O 30 '66
Trade winds; concerning Stuart Flexner's supplement to the Dictionary of American slang. J. Beatty, jr. Sat R 49:14 D 3 '66
See also
Jargon

SLAPSTICK moving pictures. See Moving pictures—Comedy

SLAPSTICK tragedy; drama. See Williams, T.

SLATE, George L.
Grapes for your garden. Horticulture 44:16-17+ N '66

SLATE, John
Build your own home atom-smasher. Sat Eve Post 239:24 O 22 '66

SLATE, John H.
Decapitation revisited (all tumbrils are go) Atlan 218:117-18 S '66
De hospitalibus excelsior. Atlan 218:122-3 Jl '66

SLATE, William G.
How pregnancy affects your health; ed. by P. Deutsch and R. Deutsch. Redbook 126:54+ Ap '66

SLATE floors. See Floors, Slate

SLATER, Joseph
Immortal bard and others. Sat R 49:24-5 D 31 '66

SLATER, Lavina
Costumes by Christine. Sch Arts 65:9-11 My '66

SLATTED floors (swine houses) See Swine houses—Floors

SLATTERY, Margaret E.
Shipwrecked king; drama. Plays 25:55-61 My '66

SLATYER, R. O. and Jarvis, P. G.
Gaseous-diffusion porometer for continuous measurement of diffusive resistance of leaves. bibliog Science 151:574-6 F 4 '66
—See Jarvis, P. G. jt. auth.

SLAUGHTER, L. W.
On time. See issues of Hobbies

SLAVE trade
Delaware's amazon outlaw. M. B. Duda. il Negro Hist Bul 29:153-4 Ap '66

SLAVERY
World built on slavery; Roman empire. J. Stuart. il Life 60:74+ Mr 4 '66

Africa
Smugglers of flesh; Kenya and Tanzania. il Time 87:35-6 My 6 '66

United States
Motive was economic; why freed Negroes remained isolated after Civil war. H. Hansen. Sat R 49:71-2 Je 11 '66
Political economy of slavery, by E. D. Genovese. Review
  Commentary 42:73-5 Jl '66. S. Elkins
See also
Slave trade

Fugitive slaves
Free Negro in Florida. L. W. Neyland. bibliog Negro Hist Bul 29:27-8+ N '65

SLAVIK. See Vasiliev, V.

SLAVITT, David R.
Apres l'opera; poem. Harper 233:80 S '66
Cape Cod house; poem. Reporter 34:39 Je 2 '66
Pruning; poem. Yale R 56:274 D '66

SLAWSON, A. Wayne. See Marks, L. E. jt. auth.

SLAWSON, John
Mutual aid and the Negro. bibliog f Commentary 41:43-50 Ap '66

SLAYTON, William L.
Do you understand your new clients? interview. ed. by E. Goble. Arch Rec 140:9-10 Ag '66

SLED dog racing. See Dog racing

SLED dogs
See also
Dog racing

SLEDS
Bike skis. il Pop Mech 125:168 F '66
Tob-sled. J. Simack and G. Hoffman. il Pop Mech 125:163 F '66
See also
Motor sleds

SLEDS, Rocket. See Rocket sleds

SLEEP
Anatomy of slumber; rapid eye movement or dream sleep. P. McBroom. il Sci N 90:254-5 O 1 '66

Carotid body chemocaptors; physiological role in buffering fall in blood pressure during sleep. M. Guazzi and others. bibliog il Science 153:206-8 Jl 8 '66
Dream deprivation; effects on dream content; rapid-eye-movement sleep. T. Pivik and D. Foulkes. bibliog il Science 153:1282-4 S 9 '66
Dreaming is ancient tool; study of rapid eye movement stage of sleep. Sci N 90:154 S 3 '66
Dreaming sleep in man; changes in urine volume and osmolality. A. J. Mandell and others. bibliog il Science 151:1558-60 Mr 25 '66
Good unrestful slumber; R.E.M; with report by V. Lee. il Life 60:111-12+ My 20 '66
Infant's dreams useful; study of rapid eye movement. P. McBroom. Sci N 89:369 My 14 '66
Instant sleep; will the ancient dream come true? ed. by V. Cohn. P. Wright. Ladies Home J 83:24 Ap '66
Latest on sleep; what research shows; interview. J. Segal. il U S News 61:60-4 Ag 29 '66
Mind thinks in two ways; study of sleep associated with dreaming and rapid eye movement sleep. Sci N 89:135 F 26 '66
Ontogenetic development of the human sleep-dream cycle. H. P. Roffwarg and others. bibliog il Science 152:604-19 Ap 29 '66
Perchance to dream. Sci N 89:70 Ja 29 '66
Response during sleep with intervening waking amnesia. F. J. Evans and others. bibliog Science 152:666-7 Ap 29 '66
Simultaneous changes in visual separation threshold and voltage of cortical alpha rhythm. J. Anliker. bibliog il Science 153:316-18 Jl 15 '66
Sleep deprivation and brain acetylcholine. M. B. Bowers, jr. and others. bibliog Science 153:1416-17 S 16 '66
Sleep deprivation in the rat. R. A. Levitt. bibliog il Science 153:85-7 Jl 1 '66
Sleep, from alpha to delta. G. G. Luce and J. Segal. il N Y Times Mag p28-9+ Ap 17 '66; Same abr. with title What happens when you sleep. Read Digest 89:84-8 Ag '66
Sleep, perchance to REM. Newsweek 67:104 My 23 '66
Sleep; suppression of rapid eye movement phase in the cat after electroconvulsive shock. H. B. Cohen and W. C. Dement. bibliog il Science 154:396-8 O 21 '66
Sleepless children. Sci Digest 60:30-1 Jl '66
What scientists really know about sleep. il Good H 162:161 F '66
What time is it? the body's clock knows. G. G. Luce and J. Segal. il N Y Times Mag p30-1+ Ap 3 '66
When children sleep. G. Luce and J. Segal. il Redbook 128:50-1+ Ja '67
Year of the bed. M. C. Burke. House & Gard 130:96-7 O '66
Your hidden life asleep; excerpt. il Sci Digest 60:62-73 S '66
See also
Insomnia
Narcolepsy

SLEEPER, Frank
Winter sports. Sports Illus 26:52-4 Ja 9 '67

SLEEPERS (clothing) See Clothing and dress—Children

SLEEPING BEAR NATIONAL PARK (proposed) See National parks and reserves—United States

SLEEPING beauty; drama. See Thane, A.

SLEEPING sickness
Winter resort for viruses. il Time 88:62 Ag 12 '66

SLEEPING sickness, African. See Trypanosomiasis

SLEEPLESSNESS. See Insomnia

SLEEPWALKING. See Somnambulism

SLESINGER, Tess
From the depths of the thirties. M. Kempton. New Repub 155:25-8 N 5 '66
Young in the thirties. L. Trilling. Commentary 41:43-51 My '66

SLIDE projectors. See Projection apparatus
SLIDE viewers. See Projection apparatus
SLIDES; story. See Richmond, J.
SLIDES, Color. See Transparencies
SLIDES, Microscopic. See Microscopic slides
SLIDING doors. See Doors, Sliding
SLIDING screens. See Doors, Sliding
SLIME molds. See Myxomycetes

SLIP covers
Answers to your questions on slipcovers. il Good H 162:196 Mr '66

SLIPS of the tongue. See Blunders

SLITTING saws. See Saws

SLIVKA, Rose
Craft horizons: 25th anniversary. Craft Horiz
26:13+ Je '66

SLOAN, Alfred Pritchard, 1875-1966
Mr Sloan. il pors Time 87:92+ F 25 '66
Organization man. por Newsweek 67:79 F
28 '66
Sloan touch. L. L. L. Golden. Sat R 49:78 Ap
Ap 9 '66

SLOAN, Richard K.
Scientific experiments of Mariner IV; with
biographical sketch. Sci Am 214:16, 62-72
bibliog(p 146-7) My '66

SLOAN, William, and West, Daphene
Don't rush kids into organized sports. Parents Mag 41:78-9+ S '66

SLOANE, Eric
Natural ice. Am Heritage 17:82-3 Ag '66

about

Joyous sound of freedom. T. J. Fleming. il
Read Digest 88:19-20+ Je '66

SLOANE, Gloria
Marina life in St Thomas V.I. Motor B 118:
46-7+ D '66
(ed) See Ives, B. Ives sings a song of the
sea

SLOANE, William
Rutgers university press marks 30th anniversary por Pub W 190:52-4 Jl 4 '66

SLOOP racing. See Yacht racing

SLOT-car racing. See Automobile models—
Racing

SLOTHS
Hideaway for moths; symbiotic relationship
with two- and three-toed sloths. R. S. Casebeer and C. L. Hogue. il Natur Hist 75:
40-1 My '66

SLOTNICK, Burton M. and Jarvik, M. E.
Deficits in passive avoidance and fear conditioning in mice with septal lesions. bibliog Science 154:1207-8 D 2 '66

SLOTTING saws. See Saws

SLOVAK, Mira
Toughest chicken afloat. H. Whall. por Sports
Illus 25:110-11 S 19 '66

SLOW learning children
Diagnosis, retarded. P. Deutsch and R.
Deutsch. il Parents Mag 41:56-7+ Mr '66
Retardation: a grave challenge to parents.
il Todays Health 44:92 Mr '66
Some retarded children are not. P. Deutsch
and R. Deutsch. Read Digest 88:92-6 Mr
'66

Education

Russians test failures. Sci N 90:3 Jl 2 '66
Who is this child? E. F. Lehman and R. E.
Hall. il Am Ed 2:10-12 Ap '66

SLOYAN, Gerard S.
Debate on the eucharist. Commonweal 84:
357-61 Je 17 '66
Parish as educator. Commonweal 84:20-3 Mr
25 '66

SLUM children. See Socially handicapped children

SLUM clearance. See Slums; Urban renewal

SLUMGULLION slide, Colo. See Landslides

SLUMS
Boston's powerful model for rebuilders; Ed
Logue administrator of housing and plan-
ning program. il Bsns W p 152-4 N 26 '66
Doctor King carries fight to northern slums;
Chicago. il Ebony 21:94-6+ Ap '66
Doing something about slums. H. J. Gans.
Commonweal 83:688-93 Mr 18 '66
Manny Gelder: slumlord; excerpt from Poor-
house state. R. M. Elman. il Atlan 218:128-
30 N '66
Money at work; plan to use municipal
treasury to deposit funds in banks located
in slums. New Repub 156:9 Ja 21 '67
R for slums? U.S. gypsum project. Newsweek
68:68 Jl 25 '66
Rebuilding the slums. J. Ridgeway. New
Repub 156:22-5 Ja 7 '67
Renewal without the bulldozer; renovating
slum dwellings without tearing them down.
il Bsns W p 173-4 D 10 '66
Senator Kennedy's slum plan. New Repub 155:
7 O 22 '66
Smithsonian: more museums in slums, more
slums in museums? B. Nelson. Science 154:
1152-4 D 2 '66
Speaking out: we need more slumlords. J.
Kahn. Sat Eve Post 239:8+ D 17 '66
What to do about the cities. M. McGrory.
America 115:203 Ag 27 '66

Where D(3) helped wipe out a slum: St Louis'
12-acre La Clede town. il Bsns W p 162-4+
D 17 '66
White slumlord confesses. B. Dahl. il Esquire
66:92-4+ Jl '66

SLURRY seal. See Pavements—Surface treatment

SLUTZ, Donald
This traffic safety expert has an idea! interview, ed. by D. Gregg. Bet Hom & Gard
44:18+ S '66

SMALE, Stephen
Smale aftermath: ICSU and academy urge
ban on politics at meetings. D. S. Greenberg. Science 154:368-70 O 21 '66
Smale case: NSF and Berkeley pass through
a case of jitters. D. S. Greenberg. il por
Science 154:130-3 O 7 '66; Discussion. 154:
1395-6 D 16 '66

SMALL, Parker A. Jr. See Reisfeld, R. A.
jt. auth.

SMALL business
Big business can help you be your own boss.
L. Velie. Read Digest 88:141-4 My '66
Helping to shore up small business; Tech-
nical services act of 1965. il Bsns W p 146-
8 Ja 22 '66
Hunting for action, in small business; busi-
ness school student interest in the small-
business jobs. il Bsns W p82-4 Ap 9 '66
Riding to the rescue of small businessmen.
il Bsns W p 118+ F 12 '66
Small companies can pioneer new products.
A. C. Cooper. il Harvard Bsns R 44:162-4+
S '66
See also
Exclusive agencies
National federation of independent business
Self employed

SMALL business administration. See United
States—Small business administration

SMALL business investment companies
SBIC's road back. Fortune 74:194+ Ag '66
Thinking big about small business; C. E.
Salik of ECC. il Bsns W p 123-4+ Ja 7 '67

SMALL race. See Airplane racing

SMALLENBURG, Carol, and Smallenburg,
Harry
Coping with reality. PTA Mag 60:18-20 bib-
liog(p36-7) F '66

SMALLENBURG, Harry
Pressures on students. NEA J 55:28-9 S '66
—See Smallenburg, C. jt. auth.

SMALLEY, I. J.
Drumlin formation: a rheological model. bibliog Science 151:1379 Mr 18 '66

SMALLMOUTH fishing. See Bass fishing

SMALLPOX
Smallpox cure foreseen. Sci N 90:82 Ag 6 '66
Two faces of smallpox. il Time 87:50+ My 20
'66
See also
Vaccination

SMALTER, Donald J. and Lancey, R. C.
P/E analysis in acquisition strategy. Harvard Bsns R 44:85-95 N '66
—and Ruggles, R. L. Jr
Six business lessons from the Pentagon. Harvard Bsns R 44:64-75 Mr '66

SMART, James G.
Death of the Herald tribune. Nation 203:270-1
S 26 '66

SMART, John
Miniatures by John Smart. D. Foskett. il
Antiques 90:354-7 S '66

SMART set (periodical)
Smart set. by C. R. Dolmetsch. Review
Atlan 219:118-19 Ja '67. O. Handlin
New Repub 155:24+ D 24 '66. S. Kauff-
mann
Something wonderful happened. G. Hicks.
Sat R 49:41-2 D 10 '66

SMARTT, Lucien E.
Amish in Iowa; letter. Commonweal 83:707 Mr
18 '66

SMEARS, Political. See Political campaigns

SMELL
Nostalgic smells. E. Janeway. House & Gard
129:106-7 F '66
What science is learning about smell. A.
Hamilton. il Sci Digest 60:81-4 N '66
See also
Olfactory nerves

SMELT fishing
Smelt fever. J. Novick. il Field & S 70:10-12
Ap '66

SMELTING
Evidence of early pyrometallurgy in the
Kerman Range in Iran; copper smelting
in the fifth milennium B.C. R. C. Dougherty
and J. R. Caldwell. bibliog il Science 153:
984-5 Ag 26 '66
See also
Blast furnaces

SMERK, George M.
Who's in the driver's seat? America 115:688-9 N 26 '66

SMETANA, Bedřich
For Crossroads' debut, a true Czech Smetana: Má vlast. P. Hart. il Hi Fi 16:94 N '66

SMIGHT, Jack
New faces. A. Knight. por Sat R 49:19 D 24 '66

SMILANSKY, Moshe
Fighting deprivation in the promised land. Sat R 49:82+ O 15 '66

SMITH, A. Robert
Senator Morse's advice and dissent. N Y Times Mag p24-5+ Ap 17 '66

SMITH, Aaron, and Burklund, C. W.
Dominant hemispherectomy: preliminary report on neuropsychological sequelae. bibliog Science 153:1280-2 S 9 '66

SMITH, Adolph E. and Bellware, F. T.
Dehydration and rehydration in a prebiological system. bibliog Science 152:362-3 Ap 15 '66

SMITH, Alex G. See Olsson, C. N. jt. auth.

SMITH, Alice Kimball
Rabinowitch awarded Kalinga prize. Science 153:1627 S 30 '66

SMITH, Mrs Anson Howe
Arrangements for spring. Horticulture 44:28-9+ Mr '66

SMITH, Anthony Wayne
Raising the sights for the redwoods; address, August 17, 1966. Nat Parks Mag 40:17-19 N '66
Wilderness in the Smokies; statements, June 13, 15, 1966. Nat Parks Mag 40:I-IV Ag '66
—and Hart, W. J.
Wilderness plan for Craters of the Moon National Monument and the surrounding region. Nat Parks Mag 40:4-9 N '66

SMITH, Bernard Brussel-. See Brussel-Smith, B.

SMITH, Beverly Bush
Breast feeding: facts and fallacies. Todays Health 44:36-7+ F '66
Lunches kids like. Parents Mag 41:104 F; 122 Mr; 102 Ap; 108 My; 90 Je; 82 Jl '66
—See DeLee, S. T. jt. auth.

SMITH, Burke M.
Polygraph; with biographical sketch. Sci Am 216:21, 25-31 bibliog(p 146) Ja '67

SMITH, C. Lavett
Descending the Andros Reef. Natur Hist 75:38-43 O '66

SMITH, C. R.
Riding high in a new era; interview. pors Nations Bsns 54:42-4+ Mr '66

SMITH, Carlton
Medicine thinks big on the prairie. Read Digest 88:149-52 Ap '66

SMITH, Carol H.
Eliot as playwright. Nation 203:325-8 O 3 '66

SMITH, Carol J.
Beacon of beauty. Parks & Rec 1:636-7+ Ag '66

SMITH, Clydelle Talbot
Day I nearly turned in my apron. Farm J 90:87+ F '66

SMITH, Dale
Sea at sunset; poem. Horn Bk 42:101 F '66

SMITH, Dan Throop
Financial variables in international business. Harvard Bsns R 44:93-4+ Ja '66

SMITH, Datus C. Jr
Interview with Datus C. Smith, jr; ed. by K. Molz. por Wilson Lib Bul 40:532-7 F '66
Translating books for newly developing countries; excerpt from Guide to book publishing. por Pub W 190:22-6 Ag 1 '66

SMITH, David
Art galleries; memorial exhibition at the Fogg museum, Cambridge, Mass. R. M. Coates. New Yorker 42:93-4+ O 22 '66
Giant Smithy. il por Time 88:60-1+ Ag 26 '66

SMITH, David W. E.
Mutagenicity of cycasin aglycone methylazoxymethanol, a naturally occuring carcinogen. bibliog Science 152:1273-4 My 27 '66

SMITH, Desmond
Breakfast with Sukarno. Nation 202:553-5 My 9 '66
On media trouble. Nation 202:402-3 Ap 4 '66
Pennsy-Central: one big happy railroad. Nation 202:184-5 F 14 '66
Saigon: drowning in dollars. Nation 203:602-5 D 5 '66
World trade center: Manhattan's Tower of Babel. Nation 202:235-8 F 28 '66

SMITH, Dido
Artist and/in the electronic environment. Craft Horiz 26:42+ N '66

SMITH, Donald L. and others
Mechanism for intercalation of kaolinite by alkali acetates. bibliog Science 153:741-3 Ag 12 '66

SMITH, Dorothy M.
Traveler's choice. Travel 126:9 N '66

SMITH, E. Norbert
Oscilloscope preamplifier. Electr World 75:84+ F '66

SMITH, Edgar E. and Rutenburg, A. M.
Starch-gel electrophoresis of human tissue enzymes which hydrolyze L -leucyl-β-naphthylamide. bibliog Science 152:1256-7 My 27 '66

SMITH, Edmund Ware
Hellhole fishing. Field & S 71:26-8+ Jl '66
Legend of the Pink Lady. Field & S 70:54-6+ Mr '66

SMITH, F. Patterson
Crystal-saving frequency synthesizer. por Electr World 76:46-8+ D '66

SMITH, Floyd W. and Zeman, L. E.
How to fertilize for high-yield, high-quality wheat. Suc Farm 64:52-3 S '66

SMITH, Frank
Moriarty's trap; interview. New Yorker 42:38-40 My 7 '66

SMITH, Frank Kingston
Weekend pilot. See issues of Flying
You and the new G.I. bill. Flying 79:80-1 S '66

SMITH, Fred R.
Sporting look. Sports Illus 25:50-1 Ag 8 '66

SMITH, G. Roysce
Revised summer reading list for secondary schools. Pub W 189:224-9 Je 6 '66

SMITH, Mrs Garret
Tribute garden. il Horticulture 44:49 O '66

SMITH, Gene
Some day it will all be just wonderful. Sat Eve Post 239:34-7 Ja 29 '66
Technical representative. Electr World 76:40-1+ Ag '66
Would you believe Don Adams? Sat Eve Post 239:32-3 Je 4 '66

SMITH, George E.
Charges dismissed. Newsweek 67:24 Ap 25 '66
Out of action. Commonweal 84:45-6 Ap 1 '66
Out of limbo. Nation 202:509 My 2 '66
Two GI's in limbo. H. W. Ernst. il Nation 202:294-5 Mr 14 '66

SMITH, Gerald L. K.
Monument to himself. Time 88:23 Jl 22 '66

SMITH, Gilbert M.
Gilbert (Gil) M. Smith, a great South Bay legend. W. H. deFontaine and P. Bigelow. il por Yachting 119:244-7 Mr '66

SMITH, Gladys V.
Tiger, the Brahman, and the jackal; dramatization of an Indian folk tale. Plays 26:75-8 N '66

SMITH, Godfrey
Astounding story! about a science fiction writer! N Y Times Mag p28-9+ Mr 6 '66
Outline of H. G. Wells. N Y Times Mag p30-1+ Ag 21 '66

SMITH, Goldwin
One man's opinion about the present. Sat R 49:34 F 12 '66

SMITH, Gordon S.
Stoppers! Motor B 118:41 Ag '66

SMITH, H. A. P. See Lang, T. G. jt. auth.

SMITH, H. Allen
Celebrity circuit. Sat R 49:39+ Ap 9 '66
Conquest of the jar lid. Look 30:M20 N 1 '66
Good or bad, it's a record. Holiday 40:28+ D '66
Nature of nicknames. Holiday 40:24+ O '66
Shake hands with my yafney. McCalls 93:144 Mr '66

SMITH, Harold W.
Landmark; poem. New Yorker 42:185 Ap 23 '66

SMITH, Hartland B.
Build a GC-2 Deluxe converter. Pop Electr 25:41-7 N '66

SMITH, Hedrick
Watermelon Village races against time. il N Y Times Mag p30-1+ Ag 28 '66

SMITH, Helen
These, too, are our children. Farm J 90:115 F '66

SMITH, Hilary
Main Street: a job for the church. America 114:689-91 My 14 '66

SMITH, Holland M.
Marine named Smith. por Newsweek 69:36-7 Ja 23 '67

SMITH, Howard Worth
Call for courage in handling unrest; excerpts from address, July 25, 1966. por U S News 61:14 Ag 8 '66
Elder statesman looks at U.S. today; interview. por U S News 61:50-4 O 31 '66

SMITH, Howard Worth—*Continued*

about

Congress: old guard's leader is beaten. L. J. Carter. il por Science 153:512-15 Jl 29 '66
Fourth branch down. K. Crawford. Newsweek 68:30 Jl 25 '66
New dominion. il por Time 88:22 Jl 22 '66
Trial of Judge Smith. Time 88:16-17 Jl 1 '66

SMITH, Ian Douglas

How Rhodesian whites are riding out a blockade; interview, ed. by A. J. Meyers. por U S News 60:77-8 My 9 '66
Rhodesian declaration of independence; proclamation, November 11, 1965. Cur Hist 50:174-7 Mr '66
Will sanctions work? time is on our side; interview, ed. by P. Webb. por Newsweek 68:43 D 19 '66

about

Admission of failure. il por Time 88:35-6 D 16 '66
Britain's showdown in Africa: where sanctions aren't working. il por U S News 60:38-9 Ap 18 '66
Dramatic meeting; between H. Wilson and I. Smith. Time 88:41-2 D 9 '66
Ian is like a wounded buffalo. L. Hall. il pors Life 60:30-1 My 27 '66
Letter from Salisbury. C. Trillin. il New Yorker 42:139-40+ N 12 '66
Man on the Tiger. J. M. Cameron. Commonweal 85:394-5 Ja 13 '67
Reporter at large. J. Kramer. il New Yorker 42:138+ Ap 2 '66
Rhodesia: the fight goes on. il por Newsweek 68:33+ D 19 '66
Riding the tiger; Wilson and Smith meet. Newsweek 68:54+ D 12 '66
Storm signals on Rhodesia. A. Lejeune. Nat R 18:1309-10 D 27 '66
Unrelenting fighter: Rhodesia's Ian Smith. U S News 61:20 D 19 '66

SMITH, J. Austin

Revival of confidence. Parks & Rec 1:45-6 Ja '66

SMITH, J. Richard

Adult education: daytime, nighttime, Saturday, too. NEA J 55:40-1 Mr '66

SMITH, Jack

Of nuts and bolts. Read Digest 89:156B Jl '66

SMITH, Jack P.

Death in the Ia Drang Valley. Sat Eve Post 240:80-5 Ja 28 '67

SMITH, James Oscar. See Smith, Jimmy

SMITH, Jean

How to help the ones at the bottom. New Repub 154:13-15 F 5 '66

SMITH, Jean Edward

Two Germanys and two Chinas. Reporter 34:36-8 My 19 '66

SMITH, Jimmy

Electric organ blues. M. Williams. por Sat R 49:53 D 31 '66

SMITH, Joan Merriam

Pair of aces. R. B. Parke. Flying 78:34 F '66

SMITH, John

Tomorrow's new foods; interview, ed. by V. Block. por Sci Digest 61:65-9 Ja '67

SMITH, Joseph J.

Community hospital in the ghetto. M. Renek. New Repub 155:9 D 10 '66

SMITH, Kelly Miller

Epistle to the First Baptist churches in Nashville. Christian Cent 83:102 Ja 26 '66

SMITH, Kirk

Art of game cookery. Pop Gard 17:54-6 D '66
Cookouts that come from the sea. Pop Gard 17:44-7 My '66
Simple but elegant back-yard party. Pop Gard 17:46-9+ Ag '66

SMITH, Lacey Baldwin

Henry VIII and the Protestant triumph. bibliog f Am Hist R 71:1237-64 Jl '66
King is dead, long live the king! Horizon 8:90-7 Spr '66

SMITH, Larry

Smith to remember. por Sports Illus 25:60 S 19 '66

SMITH, LeRoi

Doin' what comes automatically. Hot Rod 19:52-6 N '66
Hangin' doors in glass. Hot Rod 19:55-7 D '66
MT road test: Dart GT road test. Motor T 18:54-5 My '66
MT road test: Electra 225. il Motor T 18:56-7 My '66
Super shift for the Satellite! Motor T 18:48 Ap '66
Universal mounts. il Hot Rod 19:56-7 O '66

SMITH, Levi, family

Family of Levi Smith. B. Villet and G. Villet. il pors Life 61:72-86+ N 25 '66
Levi Smith's bonus, fifteen grandchildren. B. Villet and G. Villet. il pors Life 61:80-94 D 9 '66
Three sons of Levi Smith. B. Villet and G. Villet. il pors Life 61:68-82 D 2 '66
Youngest of the Smiths. B. Villet and G. Villet. il pors Life 61:60-71 D 16 '66

SMITH, Lillian

Not black power, but human power; interview, ed. by G. B. Leonard. pors Look 30:40+ S 6 '66

about

Herald of the dream. por Time 88:36-7 O 7 '66
Obituary
  Pub W 190:53 O 10 '66
One less friend in Georgia. Christian Cent 83:1234 O 12 '66
You do it because you love somebody. G. P. Brockway. por Sat R 49:53-4 O 22 '66

SMITH, Liz

Desert is Arizona's ocean. Sports Illus 26:36-9 Ja 16 '67

SMITH, McGregor, Jr

Canalizers; poem. Audubon Mag 68:106 Mr '66
Straight from the shoulder; poem. Christian Cent 83:295 Mr 9 '66

SMITH, Marie Stalker

Maureen. NEA J 55:62+ F '66

SMITH, Marshall

His lifetime record, won: 700, lost: 1. Life 60:92-4+ Ap 1 '66
Jack Dreyfus: Maverick wizard behind the Wall Street lion. Life 60:70-2+ F 11 '66
Please, lady, get off my golf course. Life 60:105-6+ Je 17 '66

about

From exercise boy to dramatic bleeder. G. P. Hunt. il por Life 60:3 F 11 '66

SMITH, Michael E.

Honor's judo defense of honor. Life 60:127-8 My 20 '66
Oxonians find Burton short but gorgeous. Life 60:80A Mr 4 '66

SMITH, Morgan K.

Book industry needs annual planning; adaptation of address, September 29, 1966. por Pub W 190:18-20 O 24 '66
Government-backed library buying not alone responsible for book surge; excerpts from address, September 29, 1966. Library J 91:4910+ O 15 '66

about

Morgan Smith's plea. C. B. Grannis. pub W 190:61 O 31 '66

SMITH, Mortimer

CBE and the fine arts. Sch & Soc 94:132 Mr 5 '66

SMITH, Ned

Weasel at our fingertips. Field & S 71:38 Je '66

SMITH, Norman S.

Instant indexing. U S Camera 29:16-18+ F '66

SMITH, Orville A. Jr, and Nathan, M. A.

Inhibition of the carotid sinus reflex by stimulation of the inferior olive. bibliog Science 154:674-5 N 4 '66

SMITH, Page

Some advice on sex, dress and manners; excerpts from memorandum. U S News 60:14-15 Je 6 '66

SMITH, Patricia Ann

Negro cowboys. bibliog por Negro Hist Bul 29:107 F '66

SMITH, Patricia Marie

Healing the Montagnards. il por Time 89:52 Ja 13 '67

SMITH, Patrick

Bird on light; poem. America 115:70 Jl 16 '66

SMITH, Patrick J.

New York opera; current Met production of Die frau ohne schatten. Hi Fi 16:MA15+ D '66
Strauss operas, judiciously surveyed. Hi Fi 16:MA24-5 Ag '66

SMITH, Paul D.

Old hole-in-the-head. Outdoor Life 138:62-3 D '66

SMITH, Perry Edward

In cold blood, by T. Capote. Review
  Commentary 41:77-80 My '66. W. Phillips
  Harper 232:110+ F '66. R. West
  Nat R 18:226-9 Mr 8 '66. J. G. Dunne
Two faces and.., a landscape. T. Capote. il por Vogue 147:144-9 F 1 '66

SMITH, Peter
Shoe polish painting. Sch Arts 66:40 O '66
SMITH, Philip E. L. See Young, T. C. jr, jt.
auth.
SMITH, Ralph A.
Aesthetic dimension of environmental respon-
sibility. bibliog Sch Arts 65:20-2 Ap '66
SMITH, Ralph Lee
Amazing facts about a crusade that can hurt
your health. Todays Health 44:30-5+ O '66
Face burners. Todays Health 44:20-3+ Je '66
Million-dollar trinket. Nation 203:354-5 O 10
'66
Phony fountain of youth. Todays Health
44:27-9+ F '66
Saga of the Little green pig. Reporter 35:
39-40+ N 3 '66
Showdown on vitamins. Nation 203:578-80 N
28 '66
SMITH, Randolph, and Noyes, Douglas
Aerobic treatment in a ditch. Am City 81:
25 O '66
SMITH, Ray
Orozco in Guadalajara; poem. Poetry 109:22
O '66
about
Tree, lake, moon: and man. R. Roseliep.
Poetry 108:54 Ap '66
SMITH, Richard
And now: Top. il por Time 87:58-9 F 11 '66
SMITH, Richard Bensted-. See Bensted-Smith,
R.
SMITH, Richard Ferree
Refugees. bibliog f Ann Am Acad 367:43-52
S '66
SMITH, Robert Benjamin
Quiet one. il por Newsweek 68:32 N 28 '66
Slaughter in the college of beauty. Time 88:
33 N 18 '66
SMITH, Robert C.
New museum of tiles in Lisbon. il Antiques
89:828-33 Je '66
SMITH, Robert E. and others
Nonphosphorylating respiration of mitochond-
ria from brown adipose tissue of rats. bib-
liog Science 154:653-4 N 4 '66
SMITH, Robert L.
Man who couldn't be bought. W. Goodman.
il pors Redbook 128:66-7+ N '66
SMITH, Ruth B.
(comp) Calendar of coming events. See is-
sues of Motor boating
SMITH, Sandy. See Davidson, B. jt. auth.
SMITH, Sanford H.
For emergency calls only. Am City il 81:153-
4+ O '66
SMITH, Sherwin D.
Great landmarks fight. N Y Times Mag p
108+ Mr 27 '66
SMITH, Sherwood. See Plumb, R. jt. auth.
SMITH, Stevie
Easy; poem. Atlan 218:55 Ag '66
SMITH, Terence F.
Stein Eriksen: Horatio Alger on skis. Harper
232:87-90 Mr '66
SMITH, Thurston Twigg-. See Twigg-Smith, T.
SMITH, Timothy L.
New approaches to the history of immigra-
tion in twentieth-century America. bibliog
f Am Hist R 71:1265-79 Jl '66
SMITH, Tommie
Sad music from a Stradivarius. il por Sports
Illus 24:64-5 Je 27 '66
SMITH, Tony
Old master at the new frontier. S. Burton.
il por Art N 65:52-5+ D '66
Two sculptors. J. Kroll. il por Newsweek 68:
93 N 14 '66
SMITH, W. Eugene
One whom I admire. Dorothea Lange (1895-
1965) Pop Phot 58:86-8 F '66
about
Great unknown photographer. D. Vestal. il
pors Pop Phot 59:114-17+ D '66
SMITH, William G. jr
Nature and the camera. il Natur Hist 75:73-4
Ag '66
SMITH, William James
New Bohemia. Commonweal 85:102-3 O 28 '66
SMITH, William Jay
New books of poems. Harper 233:89-90+ Ag
'66
(tr) See Voznesenskiĭ, A. Her shoes; Of
Stalin do not sing
about
Choice and range. X. J. Kennedy. Poetry
109:184-5 D '66

SMITH, William S. See Winograd, E. jt. auth.
**SMITH, Hinchman and Grylls associates, in-
corporated**
New design department puts all disciplines
to work on building concepts. Arch Rec
139:153 F '66
Reorganization for better design; with introd.
by R. F. Hastings. il Arch Rec 140:177-88
O '66
SMITH, Kline and French laboratories
Aiding developing nations; foreign fellow-
ships. L. L. L. Golden. Sat R 49:71 My 14
'66
Happy pillmaker. Fortune 74:353 Jl 15 '66
SMITHEE, Kenneth
(comp) 1965 legislative roundup. Parks &
Rec 1:14-16 Ja '66
(comp) 1966 legislative roundup. por Parks
& Rec 1:960-1+ D '66
SMITHERS, Jan
Sometimes I feel like dropping out; ed. by
H. F. Waters. il pors Newsweek 67:66 Mr
21 '66
SMITHIES, Arthur
Effect abroad of American private enter-
prise; address; with questions and an-
swers. Ann Am Acad 366:51-9 Jl '66
SMITHSON, James
Profiles: Smithsonian institution. G. T.
Hellman. New Yorker 42:68+ D 3 '66
SMITHSONIAN institution
Dinosaurs and fossil reptile exhibits. H. D.
Brown. Hobbies 71:117 S '66
Laying in the vintage. Time 88:56 Ag 12 '66
Perspective of the Smithsonian program in
ecology; excerpt from address, March 15,
1966. S. D. Ripley. il Nat Parks Mag 40:
10-13 O '66
Profiles. G. T. Hellman. New Yorker 42:66-
8+ D 3; 64-6+ D 10; 58-62+ D 17 '66
Science chases dust from nation's attic. the
Smithsonian; expands and rejuvenates its
exhibits. il Bsns W p 110-12+ My 21 '66
Smithsonian: more museums in slums, more
slums in museums? B. Nelson. Science 154:
1152-4 D 2 '66
You own $10,000,000 worth of gems; Hall of
gems and minerals. D. J. Cooper. il Esquire
66:181-5+ D '66

Astrophysical observatory
Smithsonian geodetic studies. R. N. Watts,
jr. il Sky & Tel 32:140 S '66

Hall of medical sciences
Walk through medicine's past. P. D. Rush.
il Todays Health 45:46-51 Ja '67

National portrait gallery
National portrait gallery, Washington D.C.
C. Nagel. il Antiques 90:642-6 N '66
Public faces. R. Lynes. il Harper 232:26+
Je '66

Traveling exhibition service
Fabulous Oriental rug collection. R. N.
Gregg. il Hobbies 71:36-7 Je '66
SMOCKING
Add smocking to your sewing skills. C.
Houck. il Parents Mag 41:100 Ag '66
SMOG
Danger in the air: what caused it. il U S
News 61:8 D 5 '66
Smog predicted to be fatal in urban areas.
Sci N 89:236 Ap 9 '66
Western wind, when wilt thou blow? grimy
pall from Boston to Baltimore. il Time 88:
29 D 2 '66
SMOKE
See also
Smog
SMOKE ovens
Smoke oven right in the kitchen. il Sunset
137:107-8 S '66
SMOKE prevention
See also
New York (city)—Air pollution
SMOKELESS-powder cartridge. See Cartridges
SMOKING
Is there a best way to stop smoking? il Good
H 162:165-7 My '66
Schools, parents included in anti-smoking
program. Sci N 90:53 Jl 23 '66
Stop smoking plan begun. Sci N 90:266 O 8
'66
See also
Cigarettes
Tobacco—Physiological effects
SMOKING, Cigarette. See Cigarettes
SMOKY MOUNTAINS. See Great Smoky
Mountains
SMOLE, Janko
Canceling the rubber stamp. Time 88:28 D 23
'66

SMOLIAN, Steven
Da capo. Am Rec G 33:154-5 O '66
SMOTHERS, Dick
Smothers brothers, crazy for wheels. W. S.
Griswold. il pors Pop Sci 188:104-6 F '66
SMOTHERS, Tom
Smothers brothers, crazy for wheels. W. S.
Griswold. il pors Pop Sci 188:104-6 F '66
SMUCKER, Donovan E.
Mass culture on the high seas. Christian
Cent 83:805-6 Je 22 '66
SMUGGLING
Good bad man; D. H. Walcott in Bombay's
prison. il Time 87:36 F 11 '66
Long finger of the law; diamonds smuggled
out of the Congo. Time 88:42+ N 25 '66
On smuggling. F. Stark. il Holiday 40:8+ O
'66
Sparrow and Hawke: indictment in munitions
exports. il Newsweek 67:29-30 My 9 '66
Tantalizing tantalite; four Americans held in
Brazil. Newsweek 68:49-50 Ag 15 '66
Tobacco road: North Carolina to New York
cigarette traffic. il Newsweek 67:32 My 9 '66
Wacky spy caper; or, The case of the
bumbling Hawke, the mysterious sparrow
and the seven wandering birds. B. L.
Collier. il Sat Eve Post 239:97-101 Jl 2 '66
Why big money is slipped abroad. U S News
61:90 Jl 25 '66
SMUIN, Michael
Many careers of Michael Smuin. J. Anderson.
il pors Dance Mag 40:18-19+ Ag '66
SMYLIE, Lucille Irwin
Why I feel sorry for Lurleen Wallace and
Alabama. Ladies Home J 83:64+ S '66
SMYLIE, Robert E.
Ironic defeat. Time 88:12-13 Ag 12 '66
SMYTH, Peter R.
Meander down the Marne. Travel 126:31-6
Ag '66
SMYTHE, Hugh Heyne
Our man in Damascus. T. Eigeland. il pors
Ebony 22:29-32+ D '66
SNACK bars
Snack bar for the kitchen. T. B. Shearer.
il Pop Sci 188:163 F '66
SNACKS
Easy summer snacks from Let's start to
cook. N. B. Nichols. il Farm J 90:54-5 Jl '66
For a quick snack party; with recipes. il
Seventeen 25:150-3+ O '66
Leisure stirs rush to snacks. il Bsns W p 102
F 26 '66
SNAIL fever. See Schistosomiasis
SNAILS, Fossil
Polymorphism in pleistocene land snails. D.
F. Owen. bibliog il Science 152:71-2 Ap 1
'66
SNAITH, Bill
Comments and asides on ocean racing. Yacht-
ing 119:69-71+ My '66
about
Salty sailor of Park avenue. C. Phinizy. por
Sports Illus 25:32-4+ Jl 11 '66
SNAKE bite. See Venom
SNAKE charmers
Department of amplification; use of snake
charmers to remove snakes from United
States embassy grounds. J. K. Galbraith.
New Yorker 42:50+ Ja 14 '67
SNAKE RIVER
Ordeal in Hell's Canyon; expedition of
Astor's fur traders, under W. P. Hunt,
1810-12. A. M. Josephy, jr. il Am Heritage
18:72-9+ D '66
Way along the lonely Snake. il Sunset 136:
73-4 My '66
Wyoming's Snake River float trip. T. B.
Lesure. il Travel 125:36-8 My '66
SNAKES
Locomotion without limbs. C. Gans. il Natur
Hist 75:10-17 bibliog(p68) F; 36-41 Mr '66
Our far-flung correspondents; snake farm at
Gosford, north of Sydney, Australia. A.
Moorehead. New Yorker 42:186-91 N 19 '66
Shedding king snake. il Natur Hist 76:56-7
Ja '67
Snakes on buttons. D. F. Brown. il Hobbies
71:52-3+ Je '66
Strangers in paradise; snakes in Hawaii.
Sports Illus 25:13-14 Ag 22 '66
See also
Copperhead snakes
Pythons
Rattlesnakes
SNAPDRAGONS
Snapdragon fable. J. Wilson. il Flower
Grower 53:37 D '66
SNAPPER fishing
How to catch snapper blues. G. Heinold. il
Outdoor Life 138:10-11+ Ag '66

SNAPSHOTS. See Photographs
SNEAD, William, Jr
Air academy's cheating scandal; ed. by J.
Shepherd. Look 31:23-5 Ja 24 '67
SNEEZING
Nothing to sneeze about; June Clark's ordeal,
a world record. il Newsweek 67:80 Mr 28 '66
Shocks to stop sneezes; case of June Clark.
Time 87:72 Je 17 '66
Still sneezing; J. Clark. il Time 87:52 Ap 22
'66
SNELLING family
Snelling coat-of-arms. H. K. Eilers. il Hob-
bies 71:124-5 Ag '66
SNIDER, Arthur J.
Progress of medicine. See issues of Science
digest
SNIPES
Snipe rediscovered; Wilson snipe. A. L. Rand.
il Audubon Mag 68:351-4 S '66
SNOBS and snobbishness
Snob cure. S. Wilson. il Read Digest 88:185-
8 Mr '66

Anecdotes, facetiae, satire, etc.

Put up your dukes. J. O'Hara. il Holiday 40:
20+ N '66
SNODGRASS, W. D.
Leaving the motel; poem. Sat Eve Post 239:
43 D 31 '66
SNOOK fishing
Rough-and-ready snook. G. Heinold. il Out-
door Life 137:14+ Mr '66
SNORING
Is there a snorer in the house? A. Van
Buren. il Read Digest 89:114-16 S '66
SNOW, Brian C.
Breakthrough! old-state car voltage regula-
tor. Pop Electr 24:39-44+ Je '66
SNOW, Charles Percy, baron Snow of Lei-
cester. See Snow of Leicester, C. P. S.
SNOW, Edgar
China and Vietnam. New Repub 155:12-14
Jl 30 '66
Man alongside Mao. New Repub 155:15-18 D
3 '66
Tree of many branches. Nation 202:303-4 Mr
14 '66
SNOW, Pamela Hansford (Johnson) baroness.
See Johnson, P. H.
SNOW of Leicester, Charles Percy Snow,
baron
Government, science, and public policy;
adaptation of address, January 25, 1966.
Science 151:650-3 Fl 11 '66
about
Let's all be eggheads. H. Downs. por Sci
Digest 59:90-3 My '66
Snow returns to writing. V. K. McElheny.
Science 152:745 My 6 '66
Third culture. N. Cousins. il Sat R 49:42 My
7 '66
SNOW
Amateur scientist; preserving the shapes of
snow crystals by catching snowflakes in
dissolved plastic. V. J. Schaefer. il Sci Am
214:120-4+ Mr '66
SNOW, Artificial
No-snow slope to nonsport; ski resorts along
Mason-Dixon line. B. Gilbert. il Sports
Illus 24:62-6+ F 21 '66
SNOW and ice removal
Balance plows and routes; Bloomington,
Minn. A. S. Michalik. il Am City 81:110-11
S '66
Combating snow and ice. il Consumer Bul
49:28-30 D '66
Equipment-replacement plan; Reading, Mass.
P. Welch. il Am City 81:84-5 D '66
Getting ready for the storm; excerpts from
addresses. R. R. Fleming. bibliog il Am
City 81:96-9 Ag '66
Heated highways. il Sci Digest 59:26-7 Mr
'66
Ice- and snow-melting devices. il Consumer
Bul 49:2+ F '66
Job-matched units spur snow-fighting; De-
catur, Ill. W. D. Kirby. il Am City 81:98-9
F '66
Organize your operators; battle against snow
and ice in Poughkeepsie, N.Y. J. W. Nel-
son, jr. il Am City 81:86-8 N '66
Snow removal. See issues of American city
Tandem plowing clears snow curb-to-curb;
Westchester, Ill. H. Witcher. il Am City
81:92-3 O '66
SNOW blowers, throwers, etc.
Better than a snow shovel; Toro Snow Pup.
il Consumer Rep 31:520 N '66
Combating snow and ice. il Consumer Bul 49:
28-30 D '66

SNOW blowers, throwers, etc.—*Continued*
Finally, a snow shovel your wife can use. J. Liston. il Pop Mech 127:56+ Ja '67
Succor for the snowbound. il House & Gard 130:324-6 N '66
Which snow thrower should you buy? il Pop Sci 189:140-3 N '66

SNOW cycles. See Sleds

SNOW fences
Saving trout from drought; Lake Creek Water Yield Improvement project, Colo. R. Cantwell. il Sports Illus 25:66-7 O 24 '66

SNOW in Chelm; story. See Singer, I. B.

SNOW leopards. See Leopards

SNOW melting. See Snow and ice removal

SNOW-on-the-mountain
Mitotic waves in laticifers of euphorbia marginata. P. Mahlberg and P. Sabharwal. bibliog il Science 152:518-19 Ap 22 '66

SNOW plows
Balance plows and routes; Bloomington, Minn. A. S. Michalik. il Am City 81:110-11 S '66
New kind of snow remover; Toro Snow Pup. il Consumer Bul 49:33 Mr '66

SNOW removal equipment
Have you heard? il Flower Grower 53:36-7 N '66

SNOW removal equipment, Municipal
Getting ready for the storm; excerpts from addresses. R. R. Fleming. bibliog il Am City 81:96-9 Ag '66
Melting takes the spotlight at snow conference; sixth annual North American snow conference. Am City 81:52 Je '66

SNOW storms. See Snowstorms

SNOW throwers. See Snow blowers, throwers, etc.

SNOW tire studs. See Tires, Automobile

SNOW tires. See Tires, Automobile

SNOW White's rescue; drama. See Creegan, G. R.

SNOWBIRDS. See Juncos

SNOWCAT. See Snowmobiles

SNOWDON, Antony Charles Robert Armstrong-Jones, 1st earl of
Gale of shock rips across the British stage; photographs. Life 60:88-97 My 20 '66

about
Alice in wonderland; photographs. J. Miller. Vogue 148:240-7+ D '66
New essay by Lord Snowdon. G. P. Hunt. por Life 60:3 My 20 '66
White tie and tails; party at the Waldorf. R. Lynes. Harper 232:28+ F '66

SNOWFLAKES. See Snow

SNOWMOBILES
Cops, dogs and snowmobiles without snow; trip from Vancouver, B.C. to South Portland, Me. F. Sleeper. il Sports Illus 26:52-4 Ja 9 '67
Snowmobiles to high-lake fishing. C. C. Niehuis. il Field & S 71:37-9+ D '66

SNOWS of Minnesota; story. See Williams, T.

SNOWSHOE hare hunting. See Rabbit hunting

SNOWSTORMS
Belial unbound; blizzard of '66. il Time 87:22 F 11 '66
Blizzard of '66; eastern United States. il Newsweek 67:24+ F 14 '66
Blizzard of '66; its cause and cost. il U S News 60:8 F 14 '66
Like a lion; Dakotas and western Minnesota. il Newsweek 67:29 Mr 14 '66
Unscheduled stop in a blizzard; North Dakota. il Life 60:40-2 Mr 18 '66
See also
Aviation—Storm hazards

SNYDER, Frederick
Dreaming is ancient tool. Sci N 90:154 S 3 '66

SNYDER, Gary
Six poems: How to make stew in the Pinacate Desert, recipe for Locke & Drum; Work to do toward town; Up at dawn; Twelve hours out of New York after twenty-five days at sea; For the boy who was Dodger Point Lookout fifteen years ago; August on Sourdough, a visit from Dick Brewer. Holiday 40:40-1 Ag '66
Three worlds, three realms, six roads; excerpts from Mountains and rivers without end; poems. Poetry 109:147-52 D '66

SNYDER, John. See Lorang, G. jt. auth.

SNYDER, L. C. and others
Transient free radicals; report of International symposium on free radicals. Science 154:802+ N 11 '66

SNYDER, Louis L.
Hitler was his only master. Sat R 49:37+ Mr 5 '66
Short trip down the Styx. Sat R 49:23 My 21 '66
Toward a united Europe. Sat R 49:42-3 Ap 2 '66

SNYDER, Mary. See Szuba, E. jt. auth.

SNYDER, Richard L.
(comp) Scientific and technical books of 1965. por Library J 91:1147-54 Mr 1 '66

SOAP
Detergent bar for skin care; Dove beauty bar. M. B. Keiser. il Parents Mag 41:20+ Ag '66
Rub-a-dub-dub, what's in the tub? il Mlle 62:196-7 Ap '66

SOAP box oratory. See Street speaking

SOAP bubbles and films
Effect of temperature on the life of soap bubbles, and their solidification at low temperature. A. V. Grosse. bibliog il Science 153:894-5 Ag 19 '66

SOAP dishes, trays, etc.
Pretty holders for pretty soaps. il House & Gard 129:26+ My '66

SOAP industry and trade

Advertising
Justice in a lather over soap ad outlays; investigating advertising spending in the packaged soap and detergent industry. Bsns W p44-5 N 5 '66

SOAP operas. See Television broadcasting—Drama

SOAPBOXERS. See Street speaking

SOARING (aeronautics) See Gliding and soaring

SOBEL, Jael S.
DNA synthesis and differentiation in embryonic kidney mesenchyme in vitro. bibliog Science 153:1387-9 S 16 '66

SOBELL, Morton
After seventeen years. Nation 203:203-4 S 12 '66
Case of Morton Sobell; new queries from the defense. E. Langer. il por Science 153:1501-5 S 23 '66
Dead secret. Sci Am 215:43-4 O '66
End of a mystery? il Newsweek 68:22 Ag 15 '66
Nagging Sobell case. A. Kopkind. New Repub 155:13-14 S 24 '66

SOBILOFF, Hy
Cut; Shall I tell you how I feel; Drying a memory; Hummingbird; Never having been a lizard; Ant without a hill; Shapeless folds; True storm; poems. Poetry 107:386-93 Mr '66

SOBRINHO, João Barbosa
Diamonds are forever. Newsweek 68:36 Ag 29 '66

SOCCER
Bongo! for the golden cup; world soccer championship in England. T. Maule. il Sports Illus 25:32-5 Jl 25 '66
Consolation from the cup; World cup for England. il Time 88:52 Ag 5 '66
England, England; wins World cup. il Newsweek 68:74 Ag 8 '66
Flying finale for soccer's World cup; with report by M. Acoca. il Life 61:84-9+ Ag 26 '66
Getting their kicks; World cup. il Newsweek 68:74 Ag 1 '66
Global fever; World cup. il Time 88:24 Jl 29 '66
It was like V-E day revisited; England's victory over Germany. T. Maule. il Sports Illus 25:14-19 Ag 8 '66
Sporting scene; World cup competition. A. Reid. New Yorker 42:152+ S 10 '66
USF wins one for the U.N; University of San Francisco soccer squad has Asian, European, South and Central American backgrounds. J. Jares. il Sports Illus 25:24-5 D 12 '66

SOCCER players
Freezing dagger; Portuguese soccer players jolted by electric shock in pool. Newsweek 68:64 D 19 '66
It was like V-E day revisited; England's victory over Germany. T. Maule. il Sports Illus 25:14-19 Ag 8 '66
Most famous athlete in the world; E. Arantes de Nascimento of Brazil. P. Axthelm. il Sports Illus 25:76-8+ O 24 '66
USF wins one for the U.N; University of San Francisco soccer squad has Asian, European, South and Central American backgrounds. J. Jares. il Sports Illus 25:24-5 D 12 '66

SOCCER pools. See Gambling—Great Britain

SOCHOR, Eugene
    International campaign against illiteracy. Sch
    & Soc 94:76+ F 5 '66

SOCIAL action department. See National Catholic welfare conference

SOCIAL adjustment. See Adjustment, Social

SOCIAL agencies
    Services to the handicapped: a list of professional agencies and directories. Wilson Lib
    Bul 40:844-8 My '66

SOCIAL and economic council of the United
    Nations. See United Nations—Economic and
    social council

SOCIAL and economic security
    Abundance in perspective: should men compete with machines? R. Theobald. il Nation
    202:544-50 My 9 '66
    Changing structure of compensation. A.
    Strasser. il Mo Labor R 89:953-8 S '66
    Economics of optimism. J. F. Becker. Nation
    202:751-2 Je 20 '66; Reply. J. H. G. Pierson.
    203:202+ S 12 '66
    How unions are signing them up. W. Wingo.
    il Nations Bsns 54:36-7+ S '66
    Poverty, injustice and the welfare state.
    R. A. Cloward and R. M. Elman. il Nation
    202:230-5, 264-8 F 28-Mr 7 '66
    Program for the social orphans: next step in
    social security. A. L. Schorr. il N Y Times
    Mag p32-3+ Mr 13 '66; Reply. D. Ferraro.
    p21+ My 1 '66
    Responsibility of government; trading in our
    constitutional republic for the welfare
    state; address, January 28, 1966. M. F.
    Caldwell. Vital Speeches 32:536-40 Je 15 '66
        See also
    Insurance, Health
            Sweden
    Life in a Great society; what one country
    finds. A. Zanker. il U S News 60:58-60
    F 7 '66
    Swedish way to happiness. G. Myrdal. il
    N Y Times Mag p 4-15+ Ja 30 '66; Discussion. p 14 F 20 '66
    Welfare state. K. Crawford. Newsweek 67:
    41 Je 27 '66

SOCIAL aspects of art. See Art and society

SOCIAL aspects of science. See Science—Social
    aspects

SOCIAL attitudes. See Attitudes; Moral attitudes

SOCIAL behavior of animals. See Animals—
    Habits and behavior

SOCIAL change
    Anatomy of change 1939/1966. J. Brooks. il
    Horizon 8:48-55 Aut '66
    California; symposium, ed. by G. B. Leonard
    and J. Poppy. il Look 30:28-40+ Je 28 '66
    Changing human nature; excerpts from Step
    to man. J. R. Platt. Science 152:1573 Je 17
    '66
    Changing pattern of American life; excerpts
    from address. D. Gray. Parks & Rec 1:212-
    14+ Mr '66
    Christian function in a technological culture.
    M. B. Bloy, jr. bibliog f Christian Cent
    83:231-4 F 23 '66
    Dynamics of modernization, by C. E. Black.
    Review
        Sat R 49:34+ O 15 '66. C. Brinton
    Elder statesman looks at U.S. today; interview. H. W. Smith. U S News 61:50-4
    O 31 '66
    Extremism; excerpts from address. June 23,
    1965. E. Duff. Library J 91:619-23+ F 1
    '66
    Great change-overs for you. M. McLuhan.
    Vogue 148:62-3+ Jl '66
    Insurgency and counterinsurgency; new
    myths and old realities. C. Wolf, jr.
    Yale R 56:225-41 D '66
    Manpower development and incentives to
    change. Mo Labor R 89:1123-5 O '66
    New class. D. T. Bazelon. Commentary 42:
    48-53 Ag '66
    Peaceful social and economic change; address, August 18, 1966. K. Brandt. Vital
    Speeches 32:712-17 S 15 '66
    Politics of modernization, by D. E. Apter.
    Review
        Nation 202:723-4 Je 13 '66. T. M. Franck
    Reflections on the Great society. C. Malik.
    Sat R 49:12-15 Ag 6 '66
    Report on world social situation; concerning
    new publication of UN. UN Mo Chron 3:
    29-31 Ap '66
    Rights of primitive peoples. M. Mead. il
    For Affairs 45:304-18 Ja '67
    Shaping the community in an era of dynamic
    social change; with introd. by M. F.
    Schmertz. il Arch Rec 140:189-206 Jl '66

Sharing of the good life; adaptation of address, February 15, 1966. W. W. Rostow.
    Dept State Bul 54:803-11 My 23 '66
Some recent developments in studies of social and cultural change. B. J. Siegel. bibliog f Ann Am Acad 363:137-53 Ja '66
Step to man, by J. R. Platt. Review
    Sat R 49:36 Ag 13 '66. S. Chase
Surfeit your money and honey; swinging England. il Bsns W p 148– Jl 16 '66
Things aren't that simple. B. Hope. Seventeen 25:130+ D '66
Three worlds of development: the theory and
    practice of international stratification, by
    I. L. Horowitz. Review
        Commentary 42:137-40+ O '66. E. F.
        Schumacher
Tomorrow's agenda. Z. Brzezinski. For Affairs 44:662-70 Jl '66
Twenty-five years after Pearl Harbor; an attack that remade the world. il U S News
    61:40-4+ D 12 '66
Understanding Canada and sundry other
    matters; interview. M. McLuhan. Mlle 64:
    114-15+ Ja '67
        See also
    Educational sociology
    Social progress
    Social revolution

SOCIAL commission of the United Nations.
    See United Nations—Social commission

SOCIAL conditions
        See also
    Civilization
    Poverty
        also subhead Social conditions under
        names of countries, states, cities, etc. e.g.
        United States—Social conditions

SOCIAL conflict
    City riots, a worldwide plague. Read Digest
    88:175-6+ F '66; Discussion. Harper 232:
    8+ Mr '66
    Prejudice and progress. D. Danzig. Sat R
    49:26+ Mr 12 '66
    Primitive rebels, by E. J. Hobsbawm. Review
    Nation 202:625-6 My 23 '66. R. K. Webb

SOCIAL democrats (Germany) See Political
    parties—Germany (Federal Republic)

SOCIAL development. See Social progress

SOCIAL diseases. See Venereal diseases

SOCIAL drinking. See Liquor problem

SOCIAL education
        See also
    Citizenship, Education for
    Sex education
    Social sciences—Study and teaching

SOCIAL ethics
    Oxford conference on the new morality. D. E.
    Smucker. Christian Cent 83:729-30 Je 1 '66
    Should the code of ethics in public life be
    absolute or relative? E. C. Blake. Ann Am
    Acad 363:4-11 Ja '66
        See also
    Business ethics
    Christian ethics
    Church and race problems
    Political ethics
    Sexual ethics

SOCIAL evolution. See Social change; Social
    progress

SOCIAL group work
    Judy Lewis reaches people, and is reached.
    I. Mothner. il Look 30:68-72 D 27 '66

SOCIAL history
        See also
    Urbanization

SOCIAL, humanitarian and cultural committee
    of the United Nations. See United Nations
    —Social, humanitarian and cultural committee

SOCIAL hygiene. See Venereal diseases

SOCIAL isolation
    Cabin fever. F. Dufresne. il Field & S 71:
    62-3+ D '66
    Heading off the problems of the loner. B. Y.
    O'Dell. il Todays Health 44:46-9 Ag '66
    Of many things; concerning suicide of young
    wife of an African UN delegate. T. N.
    Davis. America 115:inside cover O 29 '66

SOCIAL justice
        See also
    Sociology, Christian

SOCIAL legislation
        See also
    Pensions—Laws and regulations
            United States
    Congress slows down the Great society. U S
    News 61:33-4 S 12 '66
    For the record; excerpts from address. D.
    Cater. Reporter 35:24-6 D 15 '66
    Poverty as a crime; carefully hedged rights
    of the poor. I. Silver. Commonweal 85:74-6
    O 21 '66

SOCIAL legislation—United States—*Continued*
Poverty, injustice and the welfare state. R. A. Cloward and R. M. Elman. il Nation 202:230-5, 264-8 F 28-Mr 7 '66
What Congress did, and some things it didn't do. il U S News 61:44-5 O 31 '66
See also
Old age pensions—United States

SOCIAL life and customs. *See* Manners and customs; *also* subhead Social life and customs under names of countries, states, cities, e.g. New York (city)—Social life and customs

SOCIAL planning

United States
Architecture. E. Galantay. Nation 203:714-16 D 26 '66
See also
United States—Social policy

SOCIAL policy
See also
United States—Social policy

SOCIAL problems
California effort is key to growth area. H. D. Watkins. il Aviation W 84:79+ F 7 '66
Ones who wait. N. Rosten. il Sat Eve Post 239:62-5 D 31 '66
See also
Church and social problems
Crime and criminals
Divorce
Homosexuality
Illegitimacy
Juvenile delinquency
Libraries and social and economic problems
Liquor problem
Marriage
Narcotic habit
Public welfare
Race problems
School and social and economic problems
Slums
Sociology, Christian
Suicide
Technology and civilization
Unemployables
War

SOCIAL problems and art. *See* Art and society
SOCIAL problems in literature
American writer and the great depression, ed. by H. Swados. Review
Sat R 49:23-4 My 21 '66. G. Hicks
Lesson of the master: Henry James and James Baldwin. C. Newman. Yale R 56: 45-59 O '66
Powell committee considers treatment of minority groups in school books. Library J 91:5720 N 15 '66
Return to Durango street; address, July 1966. F. Bonham. il Library J 91:4188-91 S 15 '66

SOCIAL progress
Business, social progress and religion; address, October 27, 1966. B. Moreell. Vital Speeches 33:119-25 D 1 '66
Foreign aid and the brain drain. J. A. Perkins. For Affairs 44:608-19 Jl '66
Future of capitalism. R. L. Heilbroner. Commentary 41:23-35 Ap '66; Discussion. 42: 6+ Jl; 14+ Ag '66
Vatican II on social progress. B. L. Masse. America 114:776-8 My 28 '66
See also
Social change

SOCIAL psychiatry
Mental health ethic; community psychiatry. T. S. Szasz. Nat R 18:570-2 Je 14 '66; Correction. 18:598 Je 28 '66
New job for psychiatry; General systems theory applied to society. Sci N 89:426 My 28 '66

SOCIAL psychology
Escalation of violence through legitimation. W. A. Westley. bibliog f Ann Am Acad 364: 120-6 Mr '66
Violence: a neglected mode of behavior. B. Bettelheim. bibliog f Ann Am Acad 364:50-9 Mr '66
See also
Attitudes
Common man
Hysteria (social psychology)
Morale, National
Public opinion
Race prejudice
Social psychiatry

SOCIAL reformers. *See* Reformers
SOCIAL responsibility. *See* Responsibility
SOCIAL revolution
Primitive rebels, by E. J. Hobsbawm. Review
Nation 202:625-6 My 23 '66. R. K. Webb

Social origins of dictatorship and democracy, by B. Moore, jr. Review
New Republic 156:34-6+ Ja 7 '67. J. Featherstone

SOCIAL science and state
See also
United States—National science foundation

SOCIAL science literature
Bibliographic organization in the social sciences. D. Bergen. bibliog il Wilson Lib Bul 40:751-8 Ap '66

Translating
See Translations and translating

SOCIAL science research
Government support for social science. D. Wolfle. Science 153:485 Jl 29 '66
Physiological insight grows. P. McBroom. Sci N 90:555 D 24 '66
Scholar and the administrator in international affairs. W. R. Polk. il Bul Atomic Sci 22:2-8 Mr '66
Social problems and social science. D. Wolfle. Science 151:1177 Mr 11 '66
Social sciences: problems examined by Senate panel. L. J. Carter. Science 153:154-6 Jl 8 '66
Social sciences: where do they fit in the politics of science? L. J. Carter. Science 154:488-91 O 28 '66

SOCIAL sciences
Schism in American scholarship; address, November 6, 1965. J. Higham. bibliog f Am Hist R 72:1-21 O '66
Social sciences notes. Sci N 90:476, 502, 516, 538; 91:42 D 3-24 '66, Ja 14 '67
See also
Behavioral sciences
Economics
Geography
Political science
United States—National science foundation

Bibliography
At our corner; Scholastic publications. Sr Schol 89:sup22 D 2 '66
New paperbacks for social studies students. W. K. Richards. Sr Schol 89:sup 11 Ja 13 '67
New social studies books. Sr Schol 88:sup 18-19 Mr 25 '66
New social studies books. W. K. Richards. il Sr Schol 89:sup6-7 Ja 6 '67
What's new in social studies; summaries of articles and reports, ed. by H. L. Hurwitz. Sr Schol 88:sup21 F 11; sup20-1 Mr 25; 89: sup39 S 23 '66

International aspects
Two decades in the world of social science. A. Myrdal. il UNESCO Courier 19:40-4 Jl '66

Research
See Social science research

Study and teaching
Hannibal and Jefferson and LBJ; what does this mean for your college work? D. Klein. Seventeen 25:102-4 My '66
New approach to teaching social studies; use of materials are developed by Educational services, inc. (ESI) K. Jorgensen. il Sr Schol 89:sup9 N 4 '66
Social studies and English combine in humanities approach; Gunn high school, Palo Alto, Calif. R. Goben. Sr Schol 88:sup8 Ap 22 '66
Spotlight on the social studies. J. S. Gibson. Sr. Schol 88:sup 11+ Ap 22 '66
Teaching the new social studies in secondary schools, by E. Fenton. Review
Sat R 49:80-1+ O 15 '66
Sr Schol 89:sup39 S 23 '66. H. L. Hurwitz
World affairs in our schools and in teacher education, panel discussion; excerpts. Dept State Bul 55:99-107 Jl 18 '66
See also
Citizenship, Education for
Current events—Study and teaching
National council for the social studies

Textbooks
Literary monstrosities: throw them out! summary of address. November 1966. R. W. Edgar. Sr Schol 89:sup 16 D 9 '66
SOCIAL security. *See* Insurance, Social; Social and economic security
SOCIAL security act amendments
Answers you need on the new social security laws. F. Bailey, jr. Suc Farm 64:46-7+ Ap '66
Free ride starts in social security. U S News 60:94-5 Mr 28 '66
Prouty's pride; proposal to extend social security benefits. Time 87:27B Mr 18 '66

SOCIALLY handicapped children—Education—
—*Continued*
Reaching the culturally deprived. T. Borton.
   il Sat R 49:77-8+ F 19 '66
Schoolchildren, by M. F. Greene and O. Ryan.
   Review
      Commonweal 84:371-3 Je 17 '66. N. Hen-
      toff
      Nation 202:335-7 Mr 21 '66. P. Schrag
Skid row child bypassed. Sci N 89:167 Mr
   12 '66
Some children the schools have never served.
   R. Coles. il Sat R 49:58-60 Je 18 '66
Special learning problems of deprived chil-
   dren. I. N. Berlin. il NEA J 55:23-4 Mr '66
Subtler significance of urban unrest. Am City
   81:8 O '66
Teach them the arts of freedom. L. C.
   Howard. il Sat R 49:66-7+ Je 18 '66
Upgrading. il Sch & Soc 94:441 D 10 '66
Upward bound: a summer romance? M. Levy.
   il Reporter 35:41-3 O 6 '66
Urban education studies; series published
   by John Day. E. Geller. il Library J 91:
   1036-7 F 15 '66
With schools reopening: a new era in educa-
   tion. il U S News 61:42-4 S 5 '66
SOCIÉTÉ Wassmer. See Airplane industry and
   trade—France
SOCIETIES
In vinos felicitas: first international conven-
   tion of the Wine and food societies of the
   world. P. Redford. il Atlan 218:128+ O '66
SOCIETY. See Debutantes; *also* subhead Social
   life and customs under names of countries,
   states, cities, e.g. Washington, D.C.—Social
   life and customs
SOCIETY, High. See Upper classes
SOCIETY, Primitive
In search of the primitive, by L. Cotlow.
   Review
      Newsweek il 69:66 Ja 9 '67. S. K. Ober-
      beck
Primitive life of Vietnam's mountain people.
   G. Condominas. il Natur Hist 75:8-13 Je
   '66
Report from Africa: a people apart; Ik tribe.
   C. M. Turnbull. il Natur Hist 75:8-10+ O
   '66
Rights of primitive peoples. M. Mead. il For
   Affairs 45:304-18 Ja '67
Vanishing Ainu of north Japan. S. Takakura.
   il Natur Hist 75:16-25 O '66
   See also
Indians of North America—Culture
Man, Primitive
Taboo
Tribes and tribal system
SOCIETY and art. See Art and society
SOCIETY and literature. See Literature and
   society
SOCIETY and the individual. See Individual
   and society
SOCIETY for indecency to naked animals
Trade winds; Alan Abel's stunt. J. Beatty,
   jr. Sat R 49:14 Je 18 '66
SOCIETY for social responsibility in science
Beginning of the commonsense. H. M. Meyer.
   Bul Atomic Sci 22:23-5 F '66
SOCIETY for the prevention of cruelty to ani-
   mals
New Jersey chicken trial: verdict for science.
   E. Langer. Science 152:479-81 Ap 22 '66
SOCIETY ISLANDS
Travel's picture portfolio: French Polynesia.
   Travel 125:50-5 F '66
SOCIETY news. See Newspapers—Society page
SOCIETY of aerospace materials and process
   engineers
SAMPE blankets reinforced composites. J.
   F. Judge. il Tech W 19:24-5+ N 21 '66
SOCIETY of Friends. See Friends, Society of
SOCIETY of illustrators
High technical level in illustrators '66; eighth
   annual exhibition. il Pub W 189:110-12 Mr
   7 '66
Twenty-eight artists boycott Illustrators '67.
   Pub W 190:142 O 3 '66
SOCIETY of Jesus. See Jesuits
SOCIETY of photographer and artist repre-
   sentatives
Creative islands and new officers at SPAR;
   summary of panel discussion. Pub W 189:
   110-11 Ap 4 '66
SOCIETY page. See Newspapers—Society page
SOCIODRAMA. See Psychodrama
SOCIO-ECONOMIC status of students. See Stu-
   dents—Social and economic status
SOCIOLOGY
Academy urged to study heredity-slum mys-
   tery. Sci N 90:353 O 29 '66
Human brokers recommended. Sci N 90:424 N
   19 '66

Some social functions of violence. L. A.
   Coser. bibliog f Ann Am Acad 364:8-18
   Mr '66
   See also
Age groups
Attitudes
Culture
Public welfare
SOCIOLOGY, Animal. See Animals—Habits and
   behavior
SOCIOLOGY, Christian
Christian social relations; address, June 6,
   1966. W. W. Wirtz. Vital Speeches 32:546-
   50 Jl 1 '66
Church and social progress, by B. L. Masse.
   Review
      America 114:878 Je 25 '66. D. R. Campion
Evangelism & involvement; triennial assem-
   bly of the NCC. Time 88:63+ D 16 '66
Vatican II on social progress. B. L. Masse.
   America 114:776-8 My 28 '66
   See also
Christianity and economics
Church and social problems
SOCIOLOGY, Educational. See Educational so-
   ciology
SOCIOLOGY, Urban
Negro today is like the immigrant yesterday.
   I. Kristol. il N Y Times Mag p50-1+ S 11
   '66; Discussion. p24+ S 25 '66
Studying the urban revolution; urban univer-
   sities. il Time 89:59 Ja 6 '67
Urban America conference; excerpts from pro-
   ceedings. il Arch Forum 125:39+ O '66
   See also
Cities and towns—United States
Urban renewal
Urbanization
SOCIOLOGY and literature. See Literature and
   society
SOCIOLOGY and science. See Science—Social
   aspects
SOCOLOW, Susan M.
Uruguay today. Cur Hist 51:270-5 N '66
SODAS, ice cream. See Beverages
SODDY, Frederick
How the newer alchemy was received. L.
   Badash. il por Sci Am 215:88-95 bibliog
   (p 116) Ag '66
SODIUM bicarbonate
Bicarbonate for dairy cows. Suc Farm 64:
   54E My '66
SODIUM chloride. See Salt
SODIUM in the body
Lithium's failure to replace sodium in mam-
   malian sympathetic ganglia. A. J. Pappano
   and R. L. Volle. bibliog il Science 152:85-7
   Ap 1 '66
Tetrodotoxin does not block excitation from
   inside the nerve membrane. T. Narahashi
   and others. bibliog il Science 153:765-7 Ag
   12 '66
SODIUM pentobarbital. See Pentobarbital
SODIUM sulfides
Stibnite (Sb_2S_3) solubility in sodium sulfide
   solutions. R. H. Arntson and others. bibliog
   il Science 153:1673-4 S 30 '66
SOEIRO, Ruy, and Amos, Harold
Arrested protein synthesis in polysomes of
   cultured chick embryo cells. bibliog Science
   154:662-5 N 4 '66
SOFAS
Best seats in the house. il McCalls 93:68-73
   Jl '66
SOFER, W. H. and others
Rate of protein synthesis: regulation during
   first division cycle of sea urchin eggs. bib-
   liog Science 153:1644-5 S 30 '66
SOFIAN, Naid
(comp) SR's check list of the week's new
   books. See issues of Saturday review
SOFOKIDIS, Jeanette H. See Ferber E. jt.
   auth.
SOFT drink bottling industry. See Bottling
   industry
SOFT drinks. See Beverages
SOFT-tip pens. See Pens
SOFTENING agents
Germ warfare in the laundry. il Consumer
   Rep 32:5-6 Ja '67
Ways to keep clothing looking like new. R.
   Hoefgen. il Parents Mag 41:18 O '66
SOHIO. See Standard oil company (Ohio)
SOHN, Louis B.
Reorganization of the United Nations; inter-
   view, ed. by C. L. Palms. Cath World 203:
   347-52 S '66
SOHO. See London
La SOIF et la faim; drama. See Ionesco, E.
SOIKE, Kenneth. See Allen, M. jt. auth.

SOIL conservation
New rules on soil conserving bases. Suc
Farm 64:62+ My '66
Walls for wandering farms. A .Whitman. il
Pop Mech 125:95-7+ Je '66
SOIL disinfection
How and when to use soil sterilants. E. P.
Sylvester. Suc Farm 64:88-9 Mr '66
Soil sterilization. C. O. Dean. Horticulture
45:47 Ja '67
SOIL fertility
Now or spring? il Flower Grower 53:29+
O '66
Wake up your soil. il Flower Grower 53:32-3
Mr '66
SOIL moisture
Asphalt may help relieve food shortage: keep-
ing water from seeping down through the
sand. Sci N 90:229 S 24 '66
Paving the way for more food; asphalt-
layered soil to trap rain water. il Time 88:
69 O 7 '66
Soil-water potential: direct measurement by
a new technique. A. J. Peck and R. M.
Rabbidge. bibliog il Science 151:1385-6 Mr
18 '66
Testing
Tracers determine movement of soil moisture
and evapotranspiration. U. Zimmermann
and others. il Science 152:346-7 Ap 15 '66
SOIL sterilization. See Soil disinfection
SOILS
Compact subsoil can be harmful to plant
growth. R. W. Rickman and others. il
Parks & Rec 1:334-5 Ap '66
Montmorillonite: effect of pH on its adsorp-
tion of a soil humic compound. M. Schnit-
zer and H. Kodama. bibliog il Science 153:
70-1 Jl 1 '66
Soils. F. E. Bear. il Horticulture 44:40-1+
Ap '66
What's new. See issues of Successful farm-
ing
See also
Alluvium
Fertilizers and manures
Analysis
Here's a quick course in soil science. J.
Threlkeld. il Pop Gard 17:60-1+ Mr '66
Testing soil. W. A. Rosenau. Horticulture
44:26-7+ Mr '66
Carbon content
Oxidation of graphitic carbon in certain
soils. E. A. Shneour. bibliog il Science 151:
991-2 F 25 '66
Silica content
Tabashir: an opal of plant origin. L. H. P.
Jones and others. bibliog il Science 151:
464-6 Ja 28 '66
Water content
See Soil moisture
SOKA Gakkai (sect)
Reporter at large. J. M. Flagler. New Yorker
42:137-8+ N 26 '66
Soka Gakkai enters Japanese politics. G. K.
Chapman. Christian Cent 83:1546-8 D 14
'66
War of the sects; leaders of other religious
sects band together to wage war on the
Soka Gakkai. il Newsweek 67:86 Mr 7 '66
SOKAL, Robert R.
Numerical taxonomy; with biographical
sketch. Sci Am 215:16, 106-16 bibliog(p 155)
D '66
SOKOLOW, Anna
Anna Sokolow in Japan. E. Stodelle. il por
Dance Mag 41:40-2+ Ja '67
SOLAR atmosphere. See Sun—Atmosphere
SOLAR batteries
High-energy demands press technology. W. E
Wilks. Tech W 19:14-15 O 3 '66
Solar cells heal selves. Sci N 90:127 Ag 20 '66
Solar-electric propulsion potential grows. B.
Miller. il Aviation W 84:103+ Mr 28 '66
SOLAR cells. See Solar batteries
SOLAR corona. See Sun—Corona
SOLAR division. See International harvester
company
SOLAR eclipses. See Eclipses, Solar
SOLAR energy
See also
Solar batteries
SOLAR flares
Implantation in interplanetary dust of rare-
gas ions from solar flares. D. Tilles. bib-
liog il Science 153:981-4 Ag 26 '66

NASA solar flare patrol. G. S. Mumford. il
Sky & Tel 31:265 My '66
Radio observations of a solar flare. Sky &
Tel 32:13 Jl '66
Weather report from the sun; to aid Apollo
moon mission. il Time 87:70-1 F 4 '66
SOLAR heat. See Solar radiation
SOLAR heating
Density-current plumes. D. T. Mason. bib-
liog il Science 152:354-6 Ap 15 '66
SOLAR magnetic field. See Magnetic field
(cosmic physics)
SOLAR neutrinos. See Neutrinos
SOLAR photography. See Astronomical pho-
tography
SOLAR probes. See Space probes
SOLAR radiation
Earth's magnetic field: a new look; address
December 26, 1965. N. F. Ness. bibliog
Science 151:1041-52 Mr 4 '66
How materials react to solar energy. J. I.
Yellott. il Arch Rec 139:196-8 My; 197-8
Je '66
Solar wind seen cause of red glow on moon.
Sci N 90:329 O 22 '66
Space waves give new information about sun.
Sci N 89:388 My 21 '66
Spectral distribution of solar radiation at
the earth's surface. D. M. Gates. bibliog
il Science 151:523-9 F 4 '66
Violent sun. H. Friedman. il Read Digest
88:167-8+ Mr '66
What are solar winds? Sci Digest 59:94 Ap
'66
See also
Solar flares
Solar heating
Sunspots
SOLAR research. See Sun
SOLAR spectrum. See Spectrum, Solar
SOLAR system
Books. J. Bernstein. New Yorker 42:117-20+
My 28 '66
Proto-solar system. Sci N 90:527 D 24 '66
See also
Earth
Planets
SOLAR telescope. See Telescope
SOLAR tides. See Tides
SOLAR time. See Time measurements
SOLBERG, James G.
Response from a school board member. Mo
Labor R 89:622-3 Je '66
SOLDERING apparatus
Soldering tools. il Consumer Rep 32:48-52 Ja
'67
SOLDIERS, Negro
Black Tiger of Mang Buk; lieutenant living
among Montagnards. S. Booker. il Ebony
21:68-70+ S '66
Soldier is buried in Charleston. C. Brossard.
il Look 30:72-6 My 31 '66
See also
United States—Army—Negroes
United States—History—Civil war—Negro
troops
World war, 1939-1945—Negroes
SOLDIERS equipment. See United States—
Army—Equipment and supplies
SOLDIERS graves. See Service mens graves
SOLDIERS monuments. See War memorials
SOLDIERS publications
See also
Overseas weekly (newspaper)
Stars and stripes (newspaper)
SOLDIERS slang. See Slang
SOLDNER, Paul
Ceramics. West coast; a discussion. por Craft
Horiz 26:25-8+ Je '66
Craftsmen USA '66; Northwest Region. Craft
Horiz 26:72-4 Je '66
about
Paul Soldner. D. Parks. il por Craft Horiz
26:20-3+ Ja '66
SOLE (fish) See Cookery—Fish
SOLID gases. See Gases, Solidified
SOLID noble gases. See Gases, Solidified
SOLID propellant rockets
Aerojet to build alternate Phoenix motor. il
Tech W 19:19 Ag 8 '66
Big solids given steady support; propulsion
test plant near completion. J. F. Judge.
il Tech W 19:108-10+ N 28 '66
Control for burning rate believed found.
Aviation W 85:33 N 21 '66

SOLID propellant rockets—*Continued*
Government expresses interest in small-arms rocket family; solid-propellant Gyrojet, Lancejet and Microjet projectiles. F. G. McGuire. il Tech W 18:34+ Je 13 '66
LPC test-fires big solid-solid system. W. E. Wilks. il Tech W 20:34-5 Ja 16 '67
Scientist reports new lightweight rocket; solid propellant electric thruster. Sci N 90: 352 O 29 '66
Slight fund hike predicted for solids. R. F. Cottrell. Miss & Roc 18:15 My 9 '66
Surveyor retro-rocket nozzle redesigned. il Aviation W 84:103+ My 16 '66
Titan III-C strap-on performance detailed. J. F. Judge. il Tech W 19:26-8 Ag 1 '66

Manufacture
Hercules enters tactical missile field. J. F. Judge. il Tech W 19:28-9 N 7 '66

Testing
Controllable solid claimed. Tech W 19:12-13 S 26 '66
Full-length big solid firing backed. il Miss & Roc 18:16 Mr 7 '66
Proving the reliability of solid fuel. il Bsns W p 104 Mr 5 '66
Space solid performance revealed. J. F. Judge. il Miss & Roc 18:22 F 14 '66

SOLID state amplifiers. See Amplifiers
SOLID wastes. See Refuse and refuse disposal
SOLIDS

Pipe lines
Pipelines. E. J. Jensen and H. S. Ellis. il Sci Am 216:62-70+ bibliog(p 146) Ja '67

Transportation
See also
Solids—Pipe lines
SOLIE, Iris
Newspapers: living textbooks. Sr Schol 89: sup9 Ja 13 '67
SOLIS-COHEN, Lita H.
Living with antiques. Antiques 89:573-7; 90: 224-7 Ap, Ag '66
SOLITUDE
Just thinking. P. Wylie. Read Digest 88: 137-8 F '66
See also
Loneliness
SOLO, Robert
Scientific magic and economic development. Bul Atomic Sci 22:25-6 N '66
SOLOMON, Alan, and others
Low-molecular-weight proteins related to Bence Jones proteins in multiple myeloma. bibliog Science 151:1237-9 Mr 11 '66
SOLOMON, Alan R.
Green mountain boys. Vogue 148:104-9+ Ag 1 '66
SOLOMON, Anthony M.
Problems resulting from the internationalization of business; statement, April 21, 1966. Dept State Bul 54:820-5 My 23 '66
United States trade policy after the Kennedy round: helping the developing countries help themselves; address, November 2, 1966. Dept State Bul 55:784-9 N 21 '66; Same with title United States trade policy. Vital Speeches 33:115-19 D 1 '66
SOLOMON, Leslie
Ferrite beads. Electr World 76:42-3 O '66
SOLOMON, Robert
Where the Fed gets its bold new ideas. por Bsns W p 101-2+ D 10 '66
SOLOMON, Stanley
Science fiction for the space age. Sr Schol 87:sup20-1 Ja 21 '66
SOLOMON ISLANDS, Battle of, 1942
See also
Guadalcanal, Battle of, 1942-1943
SOLOMON R. Guggenheim museum, New York
Background to systemic; exhibition at the Guggenheim museum. L. Alloway. il Art N 65:30-3 O '66
SOLT, Mary Ellen
Flowers in concrete; poem. Poetry 107:380 Mr '66
SOLUTION (chemistry)
See also
Heat of solution
SOLUTION, Heat of. See Heat of solution
SOLUTIONS
Very fast reactions in solution. G. G. Hammes. bibliog il Science 151:1507-11 Mr 25 '66
SOLVAY conference
Report on thirteenth conference. J. E. Mayer. Science 152:393 Ap 15 '66
SOMALIA
War in the desert. Newsweek 68:46 Jl 25 '66
See also
Education—Somalia

SOMALILAND, FRENCH
Costly choice. il Time 88:46 S 30 '66
Incident in Djibouti; visit of C. de Gaulle. il Time 88:29 S 2 '66
Ultimate weapon; independence vote; France's threat. Newsweek 68:46 O 3 '66
SOMAN, Florence Jane
One more promise; story. Good H 162:82-4 Je '66
Picture of success; story. Good H 162:71-3 F '66
SOMAN, Shirley Camper. (See Blum, S. jt. auth.
SOMATIC hybrids. See Hybridization
SOMAYAJULU, B. L. K. See Blackman, A. jt. auth.
SOME thoughts on the meaning of life; story. See Adams, J.
SOMEONE in the kitchen; story. See Holland, B.
SOMEONE to love; story. See Robinson, B.
SOMERLOTT, Robert
Magnificent trifles. Writer 79:16-19 O '66
SOMERS, Florence
New movies. See issues of Redbook
SOMERVILLE, Ronald L.
Tryptophan operon of escherichia coli: regulatory behavior in salmonella typhimurium cytoplasm. bibliog Science 154:1585-7 D 23 '66
SOMETHING happened; novel. See Heller, J.
SOMMERS, F. J.
Close by my side; story. Good H 162:84-6 Je '66
SOMMERS, Nancy, and Ridgeway, James
Can a woman be feminine forever? New Repub 154:15-16 Mr 19 '66
SOMNAMBULISM
Patter of little sleepwalking feet. il Life 60:112 My 20 '66
Sleepwalker not dreaming. Sci N 89:508 Je 25 '66
SONAR
Auditory system of noctuid moths; excerpts from address, April 27, 1966. K. D. Roeder. bibliog il Science 154:1515-21 D 23 '66
Huzza porpoise. T. H. Lineaweaver. 3d. Holiday 40:20+ Jl '66
Low-noise, interference-resistant amplifier suitable for biological signals. G. Schuler and others. il Science 154:1191-2 D 2 '66
Monaco: the shallow continental shelf. H. E. Edgerton and O. Leenhardt. il Science 152:1106-7 My 20 '66
Sonic detection of a fresh water-salt water interface. H. E. Edgerton. il Science 154: 1555 D 23 '66
Sound waves used to map ocean floor; side-looking sonar. Sci N 90:135 Ag 27 '66
Ultrasonic sensitivity: a tympanal receptor in the green lace wing chrysopa carnea. L. A. Miller and E. G. MacLeod. bibliog il Science 154:891-3 N 18 '66
SONAR fishing devices. See Fishing—Implements and appliances
SONATAS
See also
Phonograph records—Sonatas
SONDERMEYER, J. C. See Gold, R. D. jt. auth.
SONDHEIMER, Ernest, and others
Composition of combustible concretions of the alewife, alosa pseudoharengus. bibliog Science 152:221-3 Ap 8 '66
SONED, Leonard
How to shoot the group. M. Orovan. il U S Camera 29:68-9+ Je '66
SONG at twilight; drama. See Coward, N.
SONG of Roland
Song of Roland; excerpt, tr. by F. B. Luquiens. il Horizon 8:22-3 Spr '66
SONG of the earth; ballet. See Ballets—Criticisms
SONG publishing. See Music publishing
SONG writers. See Composers
SONGS
Mr American music: I. Berlin's counterpoint songs. H. Hewes. Sat R 49:36+ O 1 '66
See also
Copyright—Music
Hymns
Phonograph records—Songs
SONGS, American
Anthology of American art song. P. L. Miller. Am Rec G 32:784-5 My '66
Whatever happened to love songs? singing of Bill in Showboat; with report by T. Prideaux. il Life 61:61-2+ S 16 '66
See also
Star spangled banner (song)
SONGS, Popular. See Music, Popular (songs, etc)
SONGS of birds. See Birds—Song

SONIC boom. See Shock waves

SONIC detection. See Sonar

SONNY (singer) See Bono, S.

SONORAN DESERT NATIONAL PARK (proposed) See National parks and reserves—United States

SONS and fathers. See Parent-child relationship

SONTAG, Susan
Avant-garde and contemporary literature; excerpts from address, October 28, 1965. por Wilson Lib Bul 40:930-2+ Je '66
Role of the writer as critic. por Pub W 189: 36-7 Mr 28 '66

about

Anti-critic. A. Ostriker. Commentary 41:83-4 Je '66
Books. A. Goldman. Vogue 147:110 Ap 1 '66
Contra Sontag. C. T. Samuels. Nation 202: 219-21 F 21 '66
People are talking about... il por Vogue 147:96-7 Je '66
Sensational Susan Sontag. M. Ellmann. por Atlan 218:59-63 S '66
Sontag sensibility. P. Velde. Commonweal 84: 390-2 Je 24 '66

SONY corporation. See Japan—Industries

SOOD, R. Raman, and Stager, R. A.
Pressure-induced dehydration reactions and transitions in inorganic hydrates. bibliog Science 154:388-90 O 21 '66

SOOTHSAYERS. See Fortune telling

SOPRANO recorders. See Physiological apparatus

SOPRON, Hungary
Revanche. R. Berczeller. New Yorker 42: 200+ N 5 '66

SOPRON-Ödenburg, Austria-Hungary. See Sopron, Hungary

SORA rail shooting. See Rail shooting

SORCERY. See Witchcraft

SORE throat. See Throat—Diseases

SOREL, Edward
Awards for excellence in marriage; Order of the culinary heart; Home-on-time trophy; Ever-loving cup; Croix de paix; Best supporting role; Confessional medal of honor; poems. Good H 162:44+ F '66

SORELL, Walter
With Mary Wigman in the Ticino. por Dance Mag 40:40-2 N '66

SORENSEN, Alexander Vergman
Silly hall no more. il por Time 87:24 Ap 15 '66

SORENSEN, Theodore Chaikin
Close-up: interview. pors Duns R 88:8-9 Jl '66
Importance of being civil. Sat R 49:30 N 26 '66
Let no drum be muffled; John F. Kennedy award dinner; address, February 22, 1966. Christian Cent 83:328-31 Mr 16 '66
(comp) Looking-glass war of words. Sat R 49:19 Ag 20 '66
New and future clergy. Sat R 49:24-5 Ap 30 '66
Notes from a world tour; questions asked abroad. Sat R 49:31 O 1 '66
Public obligations and the private corporation. Sat R 49:24+ My 14 '66
Rate of dissent. Sat R 49:26 Ap 2 '66
Reforming Congress. Sat R 49:22 Jl 16 '66
Scrooge and the students. Sat R 50:66 Ja 14 '67
Sorensen looks at '68: not a single state safe for Democrats; excerpts from address, December 12, 1966. por U S News 61:10 D 26 '66
Stars at night but no electric light. Sat R 49: 35 Je 18 '66

about

Should historians write contemporary history? H. S. Commager. il Sat R 49:18-20+ F 12 '66

SORENSON, Cloyd, Jr
Catch 'em unawares. U S Camera 29:38+ Je '66

SORGE, Richard
Career of Richard Sorge. K. Lamott. Nation 202:687-8 Je 6 '66
Case of Richard Sorge, by F. W. Deakin and G. R. Storry. Review
Atlan 217:130-1 My '66. O. Handlin
Master spy; condensation. G. W. Prange. il Read Digest 90:209-12+ Ja '67

SORGHUM
Weeds in grain sorghum, how to control them. O. C. Burnside. Suc Farm 64:112 Mr '66
See also
Milo

Hybrids
Drills a sorghum-sudan hybrid into pasture sod. R. C. Black. il Farm J 90:380 Je '66

SORIA, Dorle J.
Artist life. See issues of High fidelity incorporating Musical America

SOROKA, Diane
Food Q's and A's. Parents Mag 41:24 Mr; 91 Je; 154 N '66

SORORITIES, College. See College fraternities

SORRENTINO, Gilbert
The perfect fiction; poem; excerpt. Poetry 107:369-72 Mr '66
Words are . . . not mocked. Poetry 108:134-5 My '66

SORROW
See also
Bereavement

SŌSEKI, Natsume. See Natsume, S.

SOSNOVY, Timothy
New Soviet plan: guns still before butter. For Affairs 44:620-32 Jl '66

SOSS, Wilma
Queen of corporate gadflies. il pors Life 60: 115-16+ Mr 18 '66

SOTER, Steven L.
Mercury: infrared evidence for nonsynchronous rotation. bibliog Science 153:1112-13 S 2 '66

SOTHEBY and company
Wilson of Sotheby's; interview. P. Wilson. New Yorker 42:48-50 D 3 '66
World's fastest art market; with portfolio of art objects. D. Norton-Taylor. il Fortune 74:134-46+ S '66

SOTHERN, Ann
All she ever heard while she was growing up is how beautiful she was; interview. por Esquire 67:78-81 Ja '67

SOTO, Jesús Raphael
People are talking about... il por Vogue 147: 194 My '66

SOTOBAYASHI, Takeshi, and Koyama, Seitaro
Strontium-90 fallout from surface and underground nuclear tests. bibliog Science 152:1059-60 My 20 '66

SOUFFLÉ glacé. See Desserts

SOUFFLÉS
Fabulous cheese soufflé. il McCalls 93:26 F '66
It's a dessert soufflé; with recipe. il Sunset 137:155 S '66
Ready and waiting: soufflés; with recipes. il McCalls 94:82-3+ Ja '67

SOULE, Gardner
Ocean adventure; condensation. Pop Sci 189: 88-93 S '66
—and Armagnac, A. P.
Fabulous machines that recovered our lost H-bomb. Pop Sci 188:86-90+ Je '66

SOULÉ, Henri Remy
Obituary
Time il por 87:52 F 4 '66
One of a kind. il por Newsweek 67:54 F 7 '66

SOULES, Jack A.
Do lectures teach? Sci Digest 60:26 O '66

SOUND
Audio peak factor. Electr World 75:71 Je '66
See also
Acoustics, Architectural
Noise
Vibration
Voice

Apparatus
Accessories; gadgets, known as audio accessories. E. Fantel. Opera N 31:32 Ja 21 '67
Device clarifies helium speech from Sealab II; vocoder. Sci N 89:482 Je 18 '66
Exhibition of sound; New York's Gallery of modern art. T. Schwartz. Pop Phot 58:22 Ap '66
Phono equalizer uses FET's. W. A. Rheinfelder. il Electr World 75:32-3+ Ap '66
Receiver noise measurements. I. Math. il Electr World 76:24+ Ag '66
Sound for photographers. T. Schwartz. See issues of Popular photography
See also
Amplifiers
Earphones
Loud speaking apparatus
Magnetic recorders and recording
Megaphones
Microphones
Moving picture cameras—Sound equipment
Phonograph
Sonar

SOUND—*Continued*

Recording and reproducing

Exhibition of sound; New York's Gallery of modern art. T. Schwartz. Pop Phot 58:22 Ap '66

Sound. J. Wesson. See issues of U.S. camera & travel

Sound advice. W. J. Weaver. See occasional issues of Modern photography

Sound for photographers. T. Schwartz. See issues of Popular photography

Sound of travel. il Travel 125:9+ Ap '66

See also

Magnetic recorders and recording

Stereophonic recording and reproducing

Audio. H. Fantel. See issues of Opera news

Derived center-channel stereo system. D. Hafler. il Electr World 75:76-7 Ap '66

Stereo vs. hi fi: that eternal, irritating question. J. Wesson. U S Camera 29:34+ Jl '66

When stereo is not stereo. J. Wesson. U S Camera 29:32+ S '66

See also

Stereophonic sound systems

SOUND measurement

Canada tests noise. Sci N 90:335 O 22 '66

See also

Decibels

SOUND production by animals

Coldest swim in the world; diving under Antarctica's ice field to record sounds of the Weddell seal. D. Lavallee. il Pop Mech 126:70-4 Jl '66

Communication between dolphins in separate tanks by way of an electronic acoustic link. T. G. Lang and H. A. P. Smith; reply with rejoinder. R. J. Schusterman. Science 152: 387 Ap 15 '66

Marine bioacoustics; report on symposium. W. N. Tavolga. Science 153:771+ Ag 12 '66

Underwater vocalization by sea lions; social and mirror stimuli. R. J. Schusterman and others. bibliog il Science 154:540-2 O 28 '66

SOUND production by fishes

Sounds of the sea; interview. W. N. Tavolga. New Yorker 42:50-2 D 3 '66

SOUND production by insects. See Insect sounds

SOUND waves

Generation and detection of coherent elastic waves at 114,000 Mc/sec. J. Ilukor and E. H. Jacobsen. bibliog il Science 153:1113-14 S 2 '66

Medical applications

Sound waves diagnose abnormal blood vessels. Sci N 89:234 Ap 9 '66

SOUNDING and soundings

New radar device probes Antarctic ice. Sci N L 89:152 Mr 5 '66

SOUNDING rockets. See Rockets, Sounding

SOUNDPROOFING

How to furnish your rooms for quiet. il House & Gard 131:132-5 Ja '67

Quiet home. R. Charles. il Parents Mag 41: 78-83+ Ap '66

SOUP mixes. See Food mixes

SOUPS

Come to an open house soup supper. il Sunset 137:174-5 N '66

Icy lemon soup; with menu and recipes by E. Graves. il Life 60:116-17+ Je 17 '66

It's a happy marriage of flavors; maritata; with recipe. il Sunset 138:104 Ja '67

It's a soup which makes a dinner; onion soup; with recipes. il Sunset 137:174+ O '66

Jumbo gumbo. C. Claiborne. il N Y Times Mag p68 D 18 '66

Long, happy history of minestrone. il Sunset 137:56-7 Ag '66

Marrowbone soup; with recipe. M. Kaytor. il Look 30:40-1 My 31 '66

Oriental introductions. C. Claiborne. il N Y Times Mag p62 F 27 '66

Select soups. il Ebony 21:118+ F '66

Start them with a mug of soup. il Sunset 137:209+ N '66

Summer soups; cool, quick, company special; with recipes. il Bet Hom & Gard 44:76 Jl '66

Super supper soups; with recipes. il McCalls 94:80-1+ Ja '67

These are really knife-and-fork soups. il Sunset 136:156-7 F '66

Too good to ignore; with recipes. C. Claiborne. il N Y Times Mag p 177 N 13 '66

Winter melon soup; with recipe. il Sunset 138:103 Ja '67

See also

Campbell soup company

Chowder

SOUSA, Mary Pfaff

Paper sculpture. Sch Arts 65:29 Mr '66

SOUSTER, Raymond

Thaw: Bed from Holland; Night raider; poems. Poetry 108:17-18 Ap '66

about

Canadian chronicle. R. Skelton. Poetry 109: 55-6 O '66

SOUTH

Who speaks for the South. by J. M. Dabbs. Review

Negro Hist Bul 29:40 N '65. J. H. Franklin

See also

American literature—Southern states

Education—Southern states

Hunting—Southern states

Justice, Administration of—Southern states

Liquor laws and regulations—Southern states

Negroes in the United States—South

Wages—Southern states

Description and travel

Ghostly Gullah country. M. Davis. Holiday 40:54-5+ Jl '66

Economic conditions

South on the rise; success story. il U S News 61:54-8 Ag 22 '66

History

See also

Ku Klux klan

Negroes in the United States—History

Reconstruction (Civil war)

Industries

Booming South. Newsweek 67:72-3 Ja 31 '66

See also

Intellectual life

American literature—Southern states

Politics

As election nears: how much of a two-party South this year? il U S News 61:62-3 O 31 '66

Bavaria, U.S.A. Nation 203:467-8 N 7 '66

Blue notes from Dixie. P. Good. il Nation 203:570-5 N 28 '66

Conservativism in the South; address, April 1, 1966. S. Thurmond. Vital Speeches 32: 420-3 My 1 '66

From toehold to foothold; election results. il Time 88:29-30 N 18 '66

GOP in the South. R. Moley. Newsweek 67: 108 My 9 '66

Race issue jolts GOP in South. il Bsns W p45-6 O 15 '66

Southern politics. W. V. Shannon. Commonweal 85:69-70 O 21 '66

Southerner, by C. L. Weltner. Review

Sat R 49:97-8 My 7 '66. B. Galphin

Still a painful issue. M. McGrory. America 115:506 O 29 '66

Why Republicans see new hope in the new South. U S News 61:53 Ag 1 '66

See also

Southern governors conference

History

Minor states: the vote revolt that failed. L. Bennett, jr. il Ebony 21:58-60+ Jl '66

Politics and suffrage

America at the crossroads; bargain of 1877. L. Bennett, jr. il Ebony 22:114-16+ Ja '67

Popular culture

Anecdotes, facetiae, satire, etc.

Dogma of the South. R. Kirk. Nat R 19:38 Ja 10 '67

Race problems

See Negroes in the United States—South

Religious institutions and affairs

God and man in the South; church's indifference to civil rights movement. M. Frady. il Atlan 219:37-42 Ja '67

Social conditions

How guilty is the South? wounding of J. Meredith by A. J. Norvell. W. F. Buckley, jr. Nat R 18:611 Je 28 '66

South on the rise; success story. il U S News 61:54-8 Ag 22 '66

South's many moods. W. G. Carleton. Yale R 55:623-40 Je '66

Social history

Society turned bottom side up; social changes in reconstruction era. L. Bennett, jr. il Ebony 21:152-4+ O '66

See also

Slavery—United States

SOUTH AFRICA

Great white laager. il Time 88:18-22+ Ag 26 '66

Missionaries or mercenaries? address, May 9. 1966. A. E. Rupert. Vital Speeches 32:754-60 O 1 '66

Pretoria's view. J. Burnham. Nat R 18:1310 D 27 '66

Prospects for southern Africa. F. M. G. Willson. il Cur Hist 50:165-71+ Mr '66

South Africa: an unhysterical report. C. B. Marshall. il Nat R 18:724-9 Jl 26 '66

South Africa: an unsentimental journey. P. L. Buckley. il Nat R 19:18-25 Ja 10 '67

South West Africa case: what happened? E. A. Gross. For Affairs 45:36-48 O '66

See also
Architecture—South Africa
Church and race problems in South Africa
Civil rights—South Africa
Elections—South Africa
Foreign visitors in South Africa
Gold mines and mining—South Africa
Investments, Foreign (in South Africa)
Justice, Administration of—South Africa
Kruger National Park
Paleontology—South Africa
Transkei
Trials—South Africa
United Nations—South Africa
United   States—Foreign   relations—South Africa
Zambia

Cultural relations

See also
Exchange of persons programs

Economic conditions

Only real industrial complex south of Milan. J. Davenport. il Fortune 74:180-5+ D '66

Other side of the South Africa story; address, 1966. H. L. T. Taswell. il U S News 60:70-2 Je 27 '66

Economic policy

Story of race and progress in Africa's richest nation; interview, ed. by A. J. Meyers. B. J. Vorster. il U S News 61:94-6+ N 14 '66

Foreign relations

Kennedy reception. New Repub 154:13-14 Je 11 '66

Summit of sorts; Verwoerd & Chief Jonathan. il Time 88:37 S 9 '66

History

See also
Zulu war, 1879

Industries

Only real industrial complex south of Milan. J. Davenport. il Fortune 74:180-5+ D '66

Native races

Brief reprieve; eviction plan for Cape Coloreds of Cape Town's District 6. il Newsweek 68:54-5 O 10 '66

When God threw the dice they fell wrong for us; South Africa's Cape coloreds. J. Lelyveld. il N Y Times Mag p24-5+ My 15 '66

See also
South Africa—Race problems

Politics and government

After assassination; future of white Africa. il U S News 61:57-8 S 19 '66

Balthazar Vorster; with excerpts from 1962 article by W. F. Buckley, jr. Nat R 18:971-2 O 4 '66

Death of the architect. il Time 88:38-40 S 16 '66

Minority of one in South Africa's Parliament. J. Lelyveld. il N Y Times Mag p34-5+ Mr 20 '66

More of the same. il Newsweek 68:56-7 S 26 '66

Security man; B. J. Vorster. il Time 88:34+ S 23 '66

South Africa: daily life in a police state; with report of M. Benson's and others experiences. New Repub 154:11-13 Je 11 '66

South Africa gets a new warden. A. Delius. il Reporter 35:38-40 O 6 '66

South Africa under its new leader. New Repub 155:10-11 O 29 '66

Successor? six strong men in the running. il Newsweek 68:42-3 S 19 '66

Tougher racial policy from a tough new leader? il U S News 61:24 S 26 '66

Violent end for the apostle of apartheid; with report by A. Sampson. il Life 61:40-3 S 16 '66

What Verwoerd's successor faces. Bsns W p48 S 10 '66

White man's fears in South Africa: a bishop's size-up; excerpts from radio interview. C. E. Crowther. U S News 61:132 S 26 '66

Race problems

Africa and the American right: question of who originated the study, Apartheid and United Nations collective measures. V. McKay. New Repub 154:13-16 Mr 26 '66

Afrikaner feels lonely in the world. J. Lelyveld. il N Y Times Mag p9+ F 6 '66

Another race official banned. J. Squire. Christian Cent 83:783-4 Je 15 '66

Apartheid: catalyst in the U.N; World court's unfavorable verdict in regard to South West Africa. A. A. D'Amato. Christian Cent 83:1303-6 O 26 '66

Apartheid's symbol. il Sr Schol 89:18-19 S 23 '66

Brief reprieve; eviction plan for Cape Coloreds of Cape Town's District 6. il Newsweek 68:54-5 O 10 '66

Death of apartheid? New Repub 155:9 S 17 '66

Financing racism. Christian Cent 83:1495-6 D 7 '66; Reply. J. I. Miller. 84:18 Ja 4 '67

Giving aid and comfort. Christian Cent 83:1259 O 12 '66

Great white laager. il Time 88:18-22+ Ag 26 '66

Hendrik Verwoerd, RIP. Nat R 18:920 S 20 '66

ICJ South-West Africa judgment: U.S. appraises legal situation; Department statement. Dept State Bul 55:231 Ag 15 '66

Judgement in South West Africa cases. UN Mo Chron 3:67-74 Ag '66

Minority of one in South Africa's Parliament. J. Lelyveld. il N Y Times Mag p34-5+ Mr 20 '66

Monitoring the Monitor; concerning ad titled Economic giant of Africa, in the Christian Science monitor. J. C. Evans. Christian Cent 83:796 Je 22 '66

Only real industrial complex south of Milan. J. Davenport. il Fortune 74:180-5+ D '66

Pastoral letter of the South African bishops, July 25, 1966. Cath World 204:240-1 Ja '67

Racial scene; distribution of M. L. King's speech in South Africa. Christian Cent 83:930 Jl 27 '66

Shock from The Hague; World court dismisses case on Southwest Africa policy. il Newsweek 68:42+ Ag 1 '66

South Africa: an unsentimental journey. P. L. Buckley. il Nat R 19:18-25 Ja 10 '67

South Africa's dilemma. Christian Cent 83:952 Ag 3 '66

South Africa's stud book. America 115:85 Jl 23 '66

South of the Zambezi: white man's Africa? Rhodesia, South Africa, Angola and Mozambique. A. J. Meyers. il U S News 61:40-3 D 19 '66

South West Africa: World court's ticklish case. il Nation 202:389-93 Ap 4 '66

Story of race and progress in Africa's richest nation; interview, ed. by A. J. Meyers. B. J. Vorster. il U S News 61:94-6+ N 14 '66

Suppose God is black. R. F. Kennedy. il Look 30:44-6+ Ag 23 '66

Vorster on Vorster, and race; interview, ed. by P. Webb. B. J. Vorster. il Newsweek 68:55 O 17 '66

Vote on apartheid; case dismissed by World court. Time 88:22 Jl 29 '66

When God threw the dice they fell wrong for us; South Africa's Cape coloreds. J. Lelyveld. il N Y Times Mag p24-5+ My 15 '66

Where 78 per cent of the people are the others J. Lelyveld. il N Y Times Mag p 10-11+ Je 19 '66

White man's fears in South Africa; a bishop's size-up; excerpts from radio interview. C. E. Crowther. U S News 61:132 S 26 '66

Why did Bram Fischer choose jail? N. Gordimer. il N Y Times Mag p30-1+ Ag 14 '66

Why foster apartheid? D. W. Hornbeck and others. Christian Cent 83:1506-7 D 7 '66

Withdrawal protest reaches $22 million. Christian Cent 84:69-70 Ja 18 '67

World court's non-decision; South West Africa case. New Repub 155:7 Ag 13 '66

See also
Church and race problems in South Africa
United Nations—Special committee on the policies of apartheid of the government of the Republic of South Africa

Race relations

U.S. rejects South African charge of interference; text of aide memoire, September 21, 1966. Dept State Bul 55:567-8 O 10 '66

SOUTH AFRICA—*Continued*

Religious institutions and affairs

World around us (cont of) News of the Christian world. Christian Cent 83:279-80, 966+, 1158, 1484+ Mr 2, Ag 3, S 21, N 30 '66

See also

Christian council of South Africa

SOUTH AFRICA and the United States

Junkets to apartheid; America's press on safari. F. Pollock. Nation 203:479-81 N 7 '66

New bridge of understanding and cooperation. F. S. Loescher. Sch & Soc 94:126-8 Mr 5 '66

SOUTH AFRICAN music. See Music, South African

SOUTH AFRICAN political prisoners. See Political prisoners

SOUTH AFRICAN propaganda. See Propaganda, South African

SOUTH AFRICAN students

Kennedy reception. New Repub 154:13-14 Je 11 '66

Senator Kennedy crosses the color line. A. P. Goller. Commonweal 84:455-6 Jl 22 '66

We shall overcome; anti-government demonstrations over I. Robertson's arrest. Newsweek 67:48+ My 30 '66

SOUTH AFRICANS

Afrikaner feels lonely in the world. J. Lelyveld. il N Y Times Mag p9+ F 6 '66

South Africa: an unsentimental journey. P. L. Buckley. il Nat R 19:18-25 Ja 10 '67

South African tragedy, by A. Paton. Review Esquire 65:44+ Mr '66

SOUTH AFRICA'S Cape coloreds. See South Africa—Native races

SOUTH AMERICA

See also

Parks—South America

Patagonia

Defenses

See Latin America—Defenses

Description and travel

Better homes and gardens tour: South America. il Bet Hom & Gard 45:27 Ja '67

Parks, plans, and people; how South America guards her green legacy. M. Rockefeller and L. Rockefeller. il Nat Geog Mag 131:74-119 Ja '67

Economic conditions

See Latin America—Economic conditions

Education

See Education—Latin America

History

See also

Incas

Native races

See Indians of South America

Politics

See Latin America—Politics

SOUTH AMERICAN Indians. See Indians of South America

SOUTH BEND, Ind.

Politics took a second place; selection of a water-works control system. H. R. Goodhew. il Am City 81:177+ S '66

South Bend comes out from under; recovers from Studebaker shutdown. il Bsns W p58-60+ F 19 '66

SOUTH CAROLINA

See also

Hunting—South Carolina

SOUTH CAROLINA forest fire. See Forest fires

SOUTH DAKOTA

State vs. the Predator; case history. G. Charles. il Audubon Mag 68:436-42 N '66

See also

Birds—South Dakota

Hunting—South Dakota

Antiquities

See Indians of North America—Antiquities—South Dakota

Industries

Gold from lead; Homestake mining co. il Time 87:88 Mr 11 '66

SOUTH HAVEN, Mich.

7,000 flowering trees. L. J. Harris. il Am City 81:34 S '66

SOUTH MILWAUKEE, Wis.

Sanitary affairs

Wet air oxidation of sewage sludge. R. W. Nicholson and others. il Am City 81:97-9+ Ap '66

SOUTH PACIFIC championship drags. See Automobile racing

SOUTH SEA ISLANDS

See also

Guam

Marquesas Islands

Micronesia

Midway (islands)

New Caledonia

Polynesia

Tahiti

Trobriand Islands

Tuamotu Islands

Description and travel

Resort isles of the future. M. Atwater. il Travel 125:57-9 Mr '66

Ten enchanted evenings; Orient and South Pacific. R. Joseph. il Esquire 66:96-105 Ag '66

Travel notes; Orient and South Pacific tours. R. Joseph. Esquire 66:40-2+ Ag '66

SOUTH VIETNAM. See Vietnam (Republic)

SOUTH WARNER wilderness area. See Wilderness areas—California

SOUTH WEST AFRICA. See Southwest Africa

SOUTHAM, Chester M.

Do we need new rules for experiments on people? J. Lear. il Sat R 49:63-70 F 5 '66

Research and responsibility. Nation 202:284-5 Mr 14 '66

SOUTHAMPTON, N.Y.

Happening at the Hamptons. il Time 88:42+ Ag 19 '66

SOUTHEAST ASIA. See Asia, Southeastern

SOUTHEAST ASIA treaty organization

Half life; eleventh ministerial council. il Newsweek 68:46+ Jl 11 '66

Keeping our commitment to peace; address, March 14, 1966. D. Rusk. Dept State Bul 54:514-21 Ap 4 '66

Letter from Washington. R. H. Rovere. New Yorker 42:167-72 Mr 19 '66

President Johnson holds talks with SEATO Secretary General. Dept State Bul 54:748-9 My 9 '66

Secretary Rusk meets with Asian leaders; statement before SEATO ministerial council, June 27; with text of SEATO council communique, June 29, 1966. D. Rusk. Dept State Bul 55:169-74 Ag 1 '66

Twelfth anniversary of SEATO; statement, September 8, 1966. D. Rusk. Dept State Bul 55:454-5 S 26 '66

SOUTHEASTERN MASSACHUSETTS technological institute, North Dartmouth

Architecture that gives a campus the unity of a single building; with account by J. Barnett. il Arch Rec 140:145-60 O '66

SOUTHEASTERN regional ballet festival. See Dance festivals

SOUTHERN AFRICA. See Africa, Southern

SOUTHERN Baptist convention. See Baptists in the United States

SOUTHERN Baptists. See Baptists in the United States

SOUTHERN Christian leadership conference

We have got to deliver nonviolent results; annual convention. il Newsweek 68:58-9 Ag 22 '66

SOUTHERN cookery. See Cookery, American

SOUTHERN 500. See Automobile racing

SOUTHERN forest fire prevention conference

When the South marched! efforts of southern states to reduce timber losses caused by forest fires. J. E. Mixon and J. H. Kitchens, jr. il Am For 72:36-41 Mr '66

SOUTHERN governors conference

Whistlin' Dixie; the southern governors in caucus. J. H. Ford. Atlan 218:80-2+ D '66

SOUTHERN ILLINOIS university

Edwardsville campus

Handsome beginning for Southern Illinois' new Edwardsville campus. il Arch Rec 140:111-20 D '66

SOUTHERN mountaineers. See Mountaineers (southern states)

SOUTHERN ocean racing conference. See Yacht racing; Sailboat racing

SOUTHERN Presbyterian church. See Presbyterian church in the United States (South)

SOUTHERN states. See South

SOUTHERN states, incorporated

Anatomy of inflation; effect on production. il Newsweek 67:66-8 Mr 28 '66

SOUTHERN university and agricultural and mechanical college, Baton Rouge, La.

See Southern run. il Time 87:67 Ap 22 '66

Southern U; new kings of track. il Ebony 21:69-70+ Jl '66

SOUTHERNERS
South's many moods. W. G. Carleton. Yale R 55:623-40 Je '66

SOUTHFIELD, Mich.
Clustered units expand existing school. il Arch Rec 139:168-9 F '66

SOUTHGATE, Harvey
Artistic climate revamped. Hi Fi 16:133 Mr '66

SOUTHWEST
Mexican-Americans: new wind from the Southwest. J. W. Moore and R. Guzman. il Nation 202:645-8 My 30 '66
See also
Education—Southwestern states
Fishing—Southwestern states
Hunting—Southwestern states
Water supply—Southwestern states

Description and travel
Southwestern side trips. T. B. Lesure. il Travel 126:28-32+ S '66

History
See also
Oklahoma—History

SOUTHWEST AFRICA
Apartheid: catalyst in the U.N; World court's unfavorable verdict in regard to South West Africa. A. A. D'Amato. Christian Cent 83:1303-6 O 26 '66
Prospects for southern Africa. F. M. G. Willson. il Cur Hist 50:165-71+ Mr '66
Realities of South-West Africa. Fortune 74:134 D '66
Shock from The Hague. il Newsweek 68:42+ Ag 1 '66
South Africa's victory. Nation 203:107-8 Ag 8 '66
South West Africa case: what happened? E. A. Gross. For Affairs 45:36-48 O '66
South West Africa: World court's ticklish case. il Nation 202:389-93 Ap 4 '66
World court's non-decision. New Repub 155:7 Ag 13 '66
See also
United Nations—Southwest Africa

SOUTHWEST water plan. See Colorado River

SOUTHWORTH family
At the sign of the crest. H. K. Eilers. il Hobbies 71:118-19+ D '66

SOUVANNA Phouma, prince of Laos
President Johnson confers with the Prime Minister of Laos; statement at news conference. October 13, 1966. Dept State Bul 55:667 O 31 '66
about
Fragile web. il Time 89:24+ Ja 13 '67

SOUVARINE, Boris
Nobel prize. Nat R 18:1148 N 15 '66

SOUVENIRS
Silly souvenirs and how they sell. il Changing T 20:13-15 Jl '66

SOUZA, João Gonçalves de. See Gonçalves de Souza, J.

SOVA, Carl R.
Lactate dehydrogenase activity: effect in vitro of some pesticidal chemicals. bibliog Science 154:1661-2 D 30 '66

SOVIET education. See Education—Russia
SOVIET government. See Russia—Politics and government
SOVIET literature. See Russian literature
SOVIET reporters. See Reporters and reporting
SOVIET UNION. See Russia
SOVIET writers. See Authors, Russian
SOVIET youth. See Youth—Russia

SOWDER, A. M.
What is the best Christmas tree? Horticulture 44:26-7+ D '66

SOWING asphodel; story. See Litvinoff, I.

SOYBEANS
Commotion in the bean pit. il Time 88:77-8 Jl 8 '66
How to figure what it costs to grow soy beans. J. Russell. Farm J 90:38D Je '66
Should you gear-up for more soybeans? J. Bickers. il Farm J 90:40B Ag '66
Soybeans move up on the menu. il Bsns W p82+ Jl 23 '66
U.S. to grow more rice; response to President Johnson's message on Food for freedom. Sci N 89:158 Mr 5 '66
What's ahead for soybeans? W. E. Swegle. Suc Farm 64:31 O '66
Who'll be the 1966 soybean champ? D. Seim. il Farm J 90:44H+ D '66
Why not solid-stand soybeans? D. Hagen. il Farm J 90:32-3+ My '66

Why they call those soybeans golden. W. Bowen and E. Shook. il Fortune 74:126-9+ Ag '66
World's best soybean grower; University of Illinois soybean yield contest. D. Seim. il Farm J 90:81-2 F '66
See also
Cookery—Vegetables

Diseases and pests
Weed-free soybeans all season; new ways to put on weed killers. G. W. Wormley. il Farm J 90:32-3+ My '66

SPAAK, Paul Henri
Mr Europe. por Time 88:31 Ag 5 '66

SPACE (architecture)
Space around us. Fortune 73:162+ Mr '66

SPACE, Outer
It does not matter who reaches the moon first; what counts is the benefit to man. A. Blagonravov. il UNESCO Courier 19:7-12 My '66
Three unknowns found in orbit; debris or accessories from U.S. spacecraft. Aviation W 85:29 N 7 '66

International control
Assembly adopts resolution; peaceful uses of outer space; with text of resolution. UN Mo Chron 3:39-42 Ja '66
Carving up the universe. Nat R 18:1307-8 D 27 '66
Disarmament on the moon: the prospects look good. E. Langer. Science 153:153-4 Jl 8 '66
International cooperation in outer space; statement, December 18, 1965. A. J. Goldberg. Dept State Bul 54:163-7 Ja 31 '66
President Johnson hails U.N. accord on treaty governing exploration of outer space; statement, December 8, 1966; with text of treaty. L. B. Johnson. Dept State Bul 55:952-5 D 22 '66
Space treaty: a step forward; U.S. and Soviet Union ban on nuclear weapons. il Newsweek 68:21 D 19 '66
Space treaty: a step in easing U.S.-Soviet tensions. B. Nelson. Science 154:1430-1 D 16 '66
Space treaty starts coming down to earth; U.S. and Russia appear close to agreement. il Bsns W p70-1 Jl 23 '66

Law
See Space law

SPACE age
Man's limitless mind; excerpts from comments. E. B. Fitzgerald. Electr World 75:6 Mr '66

SPACE and time
Gravitational collapse and the death of a star (cont) K. S. Thorne; reply with rejoinder. W. J. Luyten. Science 153:366+ Jl 22 '66
See also
Time reversal

SPACE arrangement of plants. See Plants, Space arrangement of

SPACE biology
Antarctica studied to learn about Mars. Sci N 90:449 N 26 '66
Automatic chemical processor tested. H. M. David. il Miss & Roc 18:34 Ap 18 '66
Biological specimen preservation during space flight to be studied. Aviation W 85:69 S 5 '66
Bios-1 orbits thirteen biological experiments. G. Alexander. Aviation W 85:23 D 19 '66
Gemini unit includes biological panels; collecting micro-organisms in space and measuring effect of radiation on earth-born organisms. il Aviation W 84:91+ Je 13 '66
New IBM lab will attack variety of space problems. Tech W 20:41 Ja 16 '67
Procedures for lunar surface sampling outlined by scientists. Miss & Roc 18:28+ Ja 24 '66
Special report on space bio-science; with editorial comment. D. E. Fink. il Aviation W 85:21, 54-65+ Ag 15 '66

SPACE blanket. See Blankets

SPACE cabin atmospheres. See Space vehicles—Cabin atmospheres

SPACE docking. See Orbital rendezvous (space flight)

SPACE environment chamber. See Testing laboratories

SPACE flight
Chronology of fiscal 1966. Tech W 19:136-44 Jl 25 '66
Deadlines press the space race. il Bsns W p36-7 Je 4 '66

SPACE flight—*Continued*
NASA discloses new planetary schedule. H.
  Taylor. il Tech W 19:18-19 S 12 '66
New timetables for planetary tours. il Time
  88:39 D 30 '66
Pioneers of astronautics. il UNESCO Courier
  19:10-11 My '66
Space activity projected for FY 2001. W. S.
  Beller. Miss & Roc 18:17 Mr 21 '66
Space report: U.S. steps up its timetable. il
  U S News 60:66-7 Je 20 '66
Space science: congressmen want larger voice.
  L. J. Carter. Science 153:615+ Ag 5 '66
Tomorrow, which world? W. J. Coughlin.
  Miss & Roc 18:46 Ja 24 '66
What comes after the moon; ideas for put-
  ting the U.S. more deeply into space. il
  Bsns W p 130-1+ D 10 '66
  See also
Ground support systems (space flight)
International astronautical federation
Orbital rendezvous (space flight)
United States—National aeronautics and
  space administration

Astronomical observations

Night-sky phenomena photographed from
  Gemini 9. E. P. Ney. il Sky & Tel 32:
  276-7 N '66
Optical environment in Gemini space flights.
  E. P. Ney and W. F. Huch. il Science 153:
  297-9 Jl 15 '66
Stargazing is not easy. Sci N 90:71 Jl 30
  '66
Stellar ultraviolet spectra from Gemini 10.
  K. G. Henize and L. R. Wackerling. il Sky
  & Tel 32:204-5 O '66

Communication problems

Laser potential in deep-space link grows.
  B. Miller. il Aviation W 84:71+ Ja 31 '66
Messages from space. J. Reinert. il Sci Di-
  gest 59:53-7 F '66
Radiation advances redundancy cutting. K.
  Voss. il Tech W 19:34-5 Ag 8 '66
X-ray of moon suggested; translunar radio
  communication. Sci N 90:206 S 17 '66

Economic aspects

But what comes after the moon? excerpt
  from address, November 11, 1966. R. E.
  Lapp. New Repub 155:10-12 N 19 '66
Space request erases Apollo fund pad. E. H.
  Kolcum. Aviation W 84:23-4 Ja 31 '66

Food problems

Mars flight goal of bio-science research. il
  Aviation W 85:88-90+ Ag 15 '66
What do astronauts eat in space? I. Asimov.
  il Sci Digest 59:82-3 Je '66

International aspects

Blessings and evils of space travel. M. Born.
  Bul Atomic Sci 22:12-14 O '66
Comparison of U.S. and Soviet efforts to ex-
  plore Mars. B. C. Murray and M. E. Davies.
  bibliog il Science 151:945-54 F 25 '66
Disarmament on the moon: the prospects
  look good. E. Langer. Science 153:153-4
  Jl 8 '66
International activity in space. R. N. Watts,
  jr. il Sky & Tel 31:203-5 Ap '66
Man and space: symposium. il UNESCO
  Courier 19:4-37 My '66
Peaceful space treaty. F. Sartwell. Sci N 90:
  530 D 24 '66
Treaty called key arms control measure.
  Aviation W 85:72 D 19 '66
United States and Spain conclude agreements
  on space cooperation. Dept State Bul 54:
  787-8 My 16 '66
United States calls for treaty on exploration
  of the moon; statement, May 7, 1966, with
  letter. L. B. Johnson; A. J. Goldberg. Dept
  State Bul 54:900-1 Je 6 '66
U.S. emphasizes need to reserve outer space
  and celestial bodies for peaceful activities;
  statement, July 12, 1966. A. J. Goldberg.
  Dept State Bul 55:249-52 Ag 15 '66
U.S. notes progress of negotiations on peaceful uses of outer space, the moon, and
  other celestial bodies; statement, August 3,
  1966. A. J. Goldberg. Dept State Bul 55:
  321-5 Ag 29 '66
  See also
United Nations—Committee on peaceful uses
  of outer space

Laws and legislation
  See Space law

Manned flights

After Apollo, a void? R. Hotz. Aviation W
  85:21 O 10 '66

Agena-powered climb to 750 mi. included in
  Gemini 11 flight plan. Aviation W 85:27-8
  Ag 15 '66
All systems are ho-hum; lack of excitement
  over later flights. L. Wainwright. Life 61:
  30 D 2 '66
Ambitious Gemini 9 flight set for May 17.
  W. J. Normyle. Aviation W 84:27 My 2 '66
Apollo applications leading victim in first
  manned space fund cut. W. J. Normyle.
  il Aviation W 84:24-6 Ja 31 '66
AAP goals outlined; experiment pallet out.
  H. Taylor. Tech W 19:16 Ag 29 '66
Astronaut bail-out system uses foldable heat
  shield, foam structure. W. J. Normyle. il
  Aviation W 85:72-3+ S 12 '66
Astronauts named; first manned Apollo mis-
  sion and Gemini 11. Sci N 89:241 Ap 9 '66
Beating the perils of manned space flight.
  W. Von Braun. il Pop Sci 188:118-20 Ap
  '66
Beginnings. W. J. Coughlin. Tech W 19:50
  N 21 '66
Calm in the void; crew for the first manned
  flight of the Apollo. Newsweek 67:67 Ap
  4 '66
Charts may guide return from moon. Sci N
  89:515 Je 25 '66
Dog tired; ailments of Soviet mutts, Blackie
  and Breezy. il Newsweek 67:58 My 30 '66
Final Gemini 11 flight plan likely in ten
  days; exercises detailed. H. Taylor. il
  Tech W 19:16-17 Ag 1 '66
Final Gemini flights assume criticial role.
  E. J. Bulban. il Aviation W 85:48-9+ Jl 4
  '66
First manned MOL flight may slip into early
  1970. Miss & Roc 18:13 My 9 '66
Gemini 8 set for Mars. 15 launch; docking
  target still to be decided. E. H. Kolcum.
  Aviation W 84:27 F 7 '66
Gemini 11 to create artificial gravity. Tech
  W 18:18 Je 6 '66
Gemini flight record. Tech W 19:14 N 21 '66
Gemini 9 to try third-orbit rendezvous. W. J.
  Normyle. il Aviation W 84:32-3 My 16 '66
Gemini 10 flight profile reviewed to exploit
  past data, experience. Aviation W 84:32
  Je 27 '66
Gemini 10 may dock with two Agenas. J.
  Mercer. il Miss & Roc 18:15+ Mr 7 '66
Gemini 10 to include dual Agena docking,
  spacewalks. H. Taylor. Tech W 18:18 Je 20
  '66
Gemini's last mission is a lulu, now on to
  the moon. R. Bailey. il Life 61:40-1 D 2 '66
Interplanetary vehicle proposals studied.
  Aviation W 85:131-2 Ag 15 '66
Late January manned Apollo flight likely. H.
  Taylor. il Tech W 19:20 N 14 '66
Lockheed, Martin are picked for AAP sys-
  tems definition; Apollo applications pro-
  gram. Tech W 18:19 Je 6 '66
Long elliptical Gemini orbit proposed. Tech
  W 18:20 Je 27 '66
Longer manned flights now seen safe. H. M.
  David. Miss & Roc 18:31 Mr 21 '66
Manned-Apollo flight to test optics. J. Mer-
  cer. Miss & Roc 18:18 Ja 24 '66
Manned flight planning gap delays Saturn
  development. G. Alexander. il Aviation W
  85:58-9+ Ag 8 '66
NASA nearing critical Gemini decisions. W.
  J. Normyle. Aviation W 84:25 F 21 '66
NASA official details current plans for pre-
  lunar Apollos. J. Mercer. Tech W 19:17 O
  31 '66
NASA ponders Apollo team future. H. Tay-
  lor. il Miss & Roc 18:16 Ap 25 '66
NASA switches to ATDA for Gemini 9; augmented target docking adapter. G. Alexander. Aviation W 84:30-1 My 23 '66
National debate: post-Apollo goals of the
  space program. W. J. Coughlin. Tech W 18:
  50 Je 20 '66
New Gemini objectives transcend Apollo sup-
  port role. W. J. Normyle. il Aviation W
  85:16-18 Ag 1 '66
New Soviet manned flights expected soon.
  Tech W 19:13-14 O 24 '66
No Gemini program delay foreseen. H. Tay-
  lor. il Miss & Roc 18:17-18 My 23 '66
Of glory & gliches; plans for Gemini 11.
  il Time 88:80-1 Ag 5 '66
Optical environment in Gemini space flights.
  E. P. Ney and W. F. Huch. il Science
  153:297-9 Jl 15 '66
Report urges increased attention to planets
  during next fifteen years. W. J. Normyle.
  Aviation W 84:71+ Ja 24 '66
Requirements for manned flights near Mars,
  Venus to be studied. Aviation W 85:65+
  S 19 '66
Review of Gemini 9 flight plan scheduled.
  W. J. Normyle. il Aviation W 84:22-5 Mr
  28 '66

SPACE flight—Manned flights—Stafford-Cernan flight. 1966—*Continued*
In space, a triumph and a big disappointment; Surveyor I and Gemini-9. il Bsns W p62+ Je 11 '66
Spectacularly routine; Gemini 9 mission. il Newsweek 67:76-9 Je 20 '66

Young-Collins flight, 1966

After Gemini X, the moon in 1968? il U S News 61:28-9 Ag 1 '66
Closing in on the moon; Gemini 10 mission. il Newsweek 68:52-4 Ag 1 '66
Fattening the record book. il Time 88:28-9 Jl 29 '66
Gemini flight speedup sought; GT-10 achievements detailed. il Tech W 19:13-14+ Jl 25 '66
Gemini 10 advances technology for EVA. W. J. Normyle. Aviation W 85:28-30 Jl 25 '66
Gemini 10 attains apogee, docking goals. E. J. Bulban. Aviation W 85:26-7 Jl 25 '66
Gemini 10 crew describes EVA problems. E. J. Bulban. il Aviation W 85:32-3 Ag 8 '66
Gemini 10 goes walking and docking. Sci N 90:71 Jl 30 '66
Gemini-10 lifts U.S. closer to the moon. Bsns W p28-9 Jl 23 '66
Gemini 10 mission shows problem areas. E. J. Bulban. il Aviation W 85:124-5+ Ag 15 '66
No escape in space? scheduled flight of Gemini 10. il Newsweek 68:82 Jl 25 '66
Of glory & gliches. il Time 88:80-1 Ag 5 '66

Meteor hazards

Micrometeorite data challenges theories. R. D. Hibben. il Aviation W 85:54-5+ S 5 '66
These spacecraft say ouch! W. Von Braun. il Pop Sci 189:76-7+ Jl '66

Military applications

Cold war in space. W. Ley. il Pop Sci 189:41-5+ Ag '66
Future programs considered hinged to MOL performance. H. Taylor. il Miss & Roc 18:32-3+ My 30 '66
Lessons from Gemini: next, the military spaceman. il U S News 61:74-5 S 26 '66
Man's utility in space stressed at AIAA; special report; with editorial comment. C. LaFond and others. il Tech W 19:18+, 54 D 5 '66
Military set to face key space issues. M. Getler. il Miss & Roc 18:24-6+ My 30 '66
Space war on ground. J. Eberhart. il Sci N 90:393 N 12 '66
Treaty called key arms control measure. Aviation W 85:72 D 19 '66

Physiological aspects

Angel of mercy to the astronauts. il Ebony 21:49-50+ Je '66
Dog-carrying Cosmos includes many experiments. Miss & Roc 18:44 Mr 14 '66
Dog tired. il Newsweek 67:58 My 30 '66
Dogged determination; Cosmos 110. Time 87:39 Mr 25 '66
Dog's life; Soviet dogs after twenty-two days in orbit. Newsweek 67:62 Mr 28 '66
Finding life in outer space. J. R. Thomson and K. W. Dockter. il Todays Health 44:42-5 Ap '66
Health prediction during orbit studied. Tech W 18:32+ Je 6 '66
Heavy traffic in orbit; dogs in orbit; next project. il Newsweek 67:94-5 Mr 21 '66
In the bag; lower body negative pressure device. il Time 89:50 Ja 20 '67
Long-term monkey orbit study begun. Sci N 90:385 N 5 '66
Longer manned flights now seen safe. H. M. David. Miss & Roc 18:31 Mr 21 '66
NASA, DOD join in planning long primate vestibular test; two advanced biosatellite flight experiments. Tech W 19:38+ N 14 '66
Nitrogen- and helium-induced anoxia: different lethal effects on rye seeds. R. L. Latterell. bibliog il Science 153:69-70 Jl 1 '66
Of dogs, men and moons; Russia's Cosmos series satellites carrying dogs. il Newsweek 67:85 Mr 7 '66
Russians refine training of space dogs. Tech W 19:37-8 O 31 '66
Scanner to examine chromosome changes. R. D. Hibben. il Aviation W 85:95+ D 5 '66
Space cabin contaminant study spurred by environment tests. H. M. David. Tech W 19:20+ Jl 4 '66
Space doctors advised to stay on earth. Sci N 90:377 N 5 '66
Space monkey study to add detailed data. Sci N 89:404 My 21 '66

Special report on space bio-science; with editorial comment. D. E. Fink. il Aviation W 85:21, 54-65+ Ag 15 '66
Tricks played on hand & eye. il UNESCO Courier 19:14-15 My '66
USSR sees gains in manned space tests. W. C. Wetmore. Aviation W 85:30-2 O 24 '66
Year-long orbital primate flight planned. W. J. Normyle. Aviation W 85:28-9 O 17 '66
See also
Astronauts
Life support systems (space environment)
Space flight—Radiation hazards
Space medicine
Space vehicles—Cabin atmospheres
Weightlessness

Psychological aspects

Mars trip like POW camp. Sci N 89:274 Ap 16 '66

Radiation hazards

Dogs test Soviet radiation shield in 22-day flight of Cosmos 110. il Aviation W 84:34 Mr 21 '66
What's up with Veterok & Ugolyok; dogs in Cosmos 110. Time 87:81 Mr 4 '66

Social aspects

Science and the space program; address, March 31, 1966. F. Seitz. Science 152:1719-21 Je 24 '66

Terminology

Speaking of space. Time 88:60 Jl 1 '66
Speaking of space. D. McNeill. bibliog il Science 152:875-80 My 13 '66; Discussion. 153:480+, 692+, 1468 Jl 29, Ag 12, S 23 '66

SPACE flight simulators

Altitude test successful. il Sci N 90:222 S 24 '66
Ames flight simulation lab to be operational in January. il Miss & Roc 18:28 My 23 '66
Apollo training stresses operations. E. H. Kolcum. il Aviation W 86:16-17 Ja 2 '67
Assembly and launching elements proof-tested by 500F vehicle. Aviation W 84:115+ Je 20 '66
Douglas cites test results of simulated zero-G study. H. M. David. il Miss & Roc 18:40-1+ My 16 '66
Effort focuses on man's judgment utility in space systems. W. E. Wilks. il Tech W 19:64-6+ N 28 '66
Flexible simulator flies varied missions. D. A. Brown. il Aviation W 84:68-75 My 2 '66
Herzfeld praises potential of gas gun at new GM plant. W. E. Wilks. Tech W 19:38 S 12 '66
I docked in space. K. V. Brown. il Pop Mech 125:114-17+ Mr '66
Lunar module simulators enter checkout at Cape, MSC. C. D. LaFond. il Tech W 20:35-6+ Ja 16 '67
MSC gets advanced docking simulator. il Miss & Roc 18:38-9 F 7 '66
Practicing a moon landing on earth; training with lunar landing research vehicle. W. Von Braun. il Pop Sci 188:98-9+ F '66
Scale models simulate Apollo module docking. il Aviation W 85:53 Jl 4 '66
Simulator may help define EVA problems. H. M. David. il Tech W 19:37-8 O 10 '66
Simulator readied for Apollo lunar flight. il Aviation W 84:150-1+ Je 20 '66
Space cabin contaminant study spurred by environment tests. H. M. David. Tech W 19:20+ Jl 4 '66
Super wind tunnel. Sci Digest 60:18 O '66
USAF research seeks methods to extend man's capacity for long-term space flight; studies form basis for manned orbiting laboratory program. il Aviation W 85:110-11+ Ag 15 '66

SPACE flight to Jupiter

Jupiter probe, 1971 Mariner top NASA budget prospects. H. Taylor. Tech W 20:18 Ja 16 '67

SPACE flight to Mars

Budget uncertainty delays Voyager rfp. Tech W 19:16 N 14 '66
Chuting for Mars; parachute to land payload on Mars. Newsweek 68:59 S 12 '66
Comparison of U.S. and Soviet efforts to explore Mars. B. C. Murray and M. E. Davies. bibliog il Science 151:945-54 F 25 '66
For sale: men to Mars. B. Frisch. il Sci Digest 59:67-70 Mr '66
GE designing two-module bus for Voyager/Mars vehicle. M. L. Yaffee. il Aviation W 85:36-7 Ag 22 '66
High hoist to Martian skies. il Life 61:55-6+ O 21 '66

SPACE flight to Mars—*Continued*

Jupiter probe, 1971 Mariner top NASA budget prospects. H. Taylor. Tech W 20:18 Ja 16 '67

Manned Mars trip, space station sought. J. Mercer. il Tech W 19:56-8+ N 28 '66

Mars flight goal of bio-science research. il Aviation W 85:88-90+ Ag 15 '66

Mars tests may double; automated biological laboratory, possible payload for the Voyager. Sci N 89:434 Je 4 '66

Mars trip like POW camp. Sci N 89:274 Ap 16 '66

Miniature laboratory will probe life on Mars; Automated biological laboratory. il Sci N 90:367 N 5 '66

NASA will reopen competition for orbiter on Mars Voyager. Aviation W 84:40 My 30 '66

Nuclear rocket for Mars. Sci N 90:327 O 22 '66

Soft landing on Mars. R. N. Watts, jr. il Sky & Tel 31:346-7 Je '66

Voyager development awaiting word on funding, management. Tech W 19:137 N 28 '66

Voyager of Mariner IV. J. N. James. il Sci Am 214:42-52 bibliog(p 143) Mr '66

See also
Space probes

SPACE flight to the moon

After we land on the moon: what? J. A. Osmundsen. il Look 30:134 D 13 '66

Apollo delayed. Sci N 90:449 N 26 '66

Apollo lunar surface package to carry seven measurement devices. W. J. Normyle. Aviation W 84:63 F 7 '66

Beating the perils of manned space flight. W. Von Braun. il Pop Sci 188:118-20 Ap '66

Blocks or spines? il Sci N 90:465 D 3 '66

Closer and closer now: a U.S. landing on the moon. il U S News 61:8 S 26 '66

Eight years of moon shots. Sci N 90:420 N 19 '66

Houston gets AAP earth resources task. Tech W 19:15-16 D 12 '66

Industry will study improved lunar personnel, cargo delivery. Aviation W 85:71+ Ag 29 '66

Libration point useful; may be used as stopping point in space. Sci N 90:351 O 29 '66

Moonbird. J. Eberhart. il Sci N 90:106-7+ Ag 13 '66

NASA details first manned Apollo flight. H. Taylor. il Tech W 19:14-15 Ag 8 '66

NASA plans 1968 manned lunar landing. W. J. Normyle. Aviation W 85:26-7 Ag 15 '66

New target date for man on the moon: 1968; Apollo plans. il U S News 60:41-3 Je 13 '66

On the way to the moon. J. Eberhart. Sci N 90:550-1 D 24 '66

Plastic quarantine envelope proposed; precautionary measures against contamination from moon-type organisms. H. M. David. Tech W 19:28-30 Ag 1 '66

Russia and the moon. R. D. Senter. New Repub 155:14-15 S 10 '66

Two steps toward the moon. il Time 88:118 N 18 '66

United States calls for treaty on exploration of the moon; statement, May 7, 1966, with letter. L. B. Johnson; A. J. Goldberg. Dept State Bul 54:900-1 Je 6 '66

Weather report from the sun; to aid Apollo moon mission. il Time 87:70-1 F 4 '66

We'll build a city on the moon. D. Q. Posin. il Todays Health 44:30-5 My '66

What we'll do on the moon. W. Von Braun. il Pop Sci 189:90-2+ N '66

See also
Lunar probes
Orbital rendezvous (space flight)

Economic aspects

Trouble ahead in moon industry? il U S News 61:29-32 Ag 1 '66

International aspects

After Gemini X, the moon in 1968? il U S News 61:28-9 Ag 1 '66

Handicapping the moon. Reporter 34:16 F 24 '66

Year when Russia will try to put a man on the moon? il U S News 62:32-3 Ja 9 '67

Luna flights

Birth of the moon; Luna 10; preliminary findings and U.S. theories. il Newsweek 67:71 My 2 '66

Control achievements stressed on Luna 9; with editorial comment. D. Winston. il Aviation W 84:21, 29-33 F 14 '66

Eye on the moon; Soviet Union's Luna 9. il Newsweek 67:54-6 F 14 '66

Inhospitable moon; Moscow discloses Luna 9's findings. il Time 87:52 F 18 '66

Luna 9 photos indicate surface erosion. W. C. Wetmore. Aviation W 84:34+ My 23 '66

Lunar landscape; Soviets land softly. il Time 87:42 F 11 '66

Lunar 9's double success. il Sky & Tel 31: 131+ Mr '66

Manned landing plans boosted by Luna 13 photos, data. il Aviation W 86:22-4 Ja 2 '67

Measure of achievement; Luna 9. il Newsweek 67:60-1 F 21 '66

Moonscape close-up; Luna 9. il Sr Schol 88: 23 F 18 '66

Orbiting of Soviets' Luna 10 widens USSR lead to moon. il Miss & Roc 18:13 Ap 11 '66

Right down on the moon; Russia's Luna 9; with British and Soviet photographs. Life 60:26-30 F 11 '66

Ring around the moon; Luna 10's path. Newsweek 67:90-1 Ap 18 '66

Robot on the moon; Luna 9 and how B. Lovell took pictures. J. Lear. il Sat R 49:57-65 Mr 5 '66

Russian moon lander yields data on lunar soil firmness, density. H. Rausch. Aviation W 86:81+ Ja 16 '67

Russians receive Luna 12 photos of moon, press for spectacular. il Aviation W 85:34 N 7 '66

Say-it-isn't-so! syndrome; John Campbell syndrome. J. W. Campbell; L. Mallan. Nat R 18:412-16+ My 3 '66

Soviet lunar probe achieves soft landing. Miss & Roc 18:9 F 7 '66

Soviet TV lands on moon. il Sci N L 89:114-15 F 19 '66

Soviet view of lunar surface reported. W. S. Beller. Miss & Roc 18:14-15 My 23 '66

What Lunar 9 proves, and doesn't. D. Cohen. il Sci Digest 59:10-12 Ap '66

What Russia found on the moon. il U S News 60:9 F 14 '66

What U.S. learns from moon landing. il Bsns W p 134-5 F 12 '66

Manned flights

And now, Apollo. il Sci Digest 60:9-11 D '66

Apollo system maturing despite problems. il Aviation W 85:18-20 D 26 '66

Gemini ends: next, the moon. il U S News 61: 29 N 28 '66

Gemini paves the way to moon for Apollo. il Bsns W p41 N 19 '66

Go-ahead sought with fiscal '68 funding; Apollo applications program. il Tech W 19: 128-9+ N 28 '66

Man on the moon in '68? interview. W. Von Braun. il U S News 61:62-7 D 12 '66

Officials cautious about achieving lunar landing on first moon-capable flight; Apollo program. il Tech W 19:152+ N 28 '66

Problems spur Apollo schedule review. Aviation W 85:29 N 7 '66

Success caps Gemini; next stop: moon. il Sr Schol 89:18-19 D 2 '66

USSR may aim to settle and farm moon. H. M. David. Tech W 20:18-19 Ja 2 '67

Orbiter 1 and Orbiter 2 flights

Around the moon; Lunar Orbiter 1. il Time 88:54 Ag 19 '66

Dual cameras map lunar landing sites. I. Stone. il Aviation W 85:34-6 N 28 '66

Fifth Pioneer being added to solar series. Tech W 19:17 Ag 15 '66

Finding a toe-hold for man. il Bsns W p76+ Ag 20 '66

Flying photo lab lights astronauts' way to the moon; Orbiter II's mission yields 422 pictures of lunar surface. il Bsns W p 100-2 D 3 '66

Historic first photo of earth; Lunar Orbiter. il U S News 61:6 S 5 '66

Lunar exploration; Orbiter 2 readied for Nov. 19 activation. Tech W 19:16 N 14 '66

Lunar Orbiter goes into good early orbit. R. Pay. Tech W 19:19-20 Ag 22 '66

Lunar Orbiter 1 begins photo mission. B. Miller. Aviation W 85:20-1 Ag 22 '66

Lunar Orbiter ranging data: initial results. J. D. Mulholland and W. L. Sjogren. bibliog il Science 155:74-6 Ja 6 '67

Lunar Orbiter surveys the moon. R. N. Watts, jr. il Sky & Tel 32:192-7 O '66

Lunar Orbiter: tracking data indicate properties of moon's gravitational field. W. H. Michael, jr. and others. Science 153:1102 S 2 '66

Moon beamed; Lunar Orbiter's photo reconnaissance mission. il Newsweek 68:88 Ag 22 '66

SPACE flight to the moon—Orbiter 1 and Orbiter 2 flights—*Continued*

Moon from perilune. Newsweek 68:80 N 21 '66
NASA puts Pioneer 7 into orbit around sun; period is 403 days. Aviation 85:23 Ag 22 '66
New Lunar Orbiter assigned thirteen prime photo target areas. Tech W 19:17 N 7 '66
Orbiter: flying photo lab. Sci N 90:503 D 10 '66
Orbiter has own darkroom. B. Culliton. il Sci N 90:133 Ag 27 '66
Orbiter launched toward moon to photograph nine Apollo sites. G. Alexander. il Aviation W 85:34 Ag 15 '66
Orbiter-2 starts journey around the moon. Aviation W 85:34 N 14 '66
Overhead satellite rare. Sci N 90:162 S 3 '66
Photo mission finished; report on findings from Orbiter 1 and Luna 11. il(p 169) Sci N 90:176 S 10 '66
Results from Lunar Orbiter 2. R. N. Watts, jr. and J. Ashbrook. il Sky & Tel 33:22-6 Ja '67
75 per cent achievement of Orbiter goals seen. I. Stone. il Aviation W 85:16-19 Ag 29 '66
Unearthly vista. il Sci N 90:494-5 D 10 '66

Surveyor flight, 1966

Along the Apollo belt; Surveyor on the moon. il Newsweek 67:32-4 Je 13 '66
First Surveyor ready for limited mission. H. D. Watkins. il Aviation W 84:79+ Mr 28 '66
Fund cuts, technical troubles slow Surveyor, Voyager programs. J. Walsh. il Science 151:305-7 Ja 21 '66
How the first soft landing on the moon was achieved. L. A. DuBridge. il Read Digest 89:100-5 D '66
In space, a triumph and a big disappointment; Surveyor I and Gemini-9. il Bsns W p62+ Je 11 '66
Lunar rocks loom as hazard to Apollo. H. D. Watkins. il Aviation W 84:26-30 Je 13 '66
Morning for Surveyor. Time 88:57 Jl 15 '66
Payoff was perfection. il Time 87:60-1 Je 10 '66
Pictures from the moon. R. N. Watts, jr. il Sky & Tel 32:16-19 Jl '66
Procedures for lunar surface sampling outlined by scientists. Miss & Roc 18:28+ Ja 24 '66
Project Surveyor. il U S News 60:43 Je 13 '66
Sad end for a Surveyor. il Time 88:114 S 30 '66
Soft moon landing successful. J. Eberhardt. il Sci N 89:457 Je 11 '66
Soft touch. il Sci Am 215:50 Jl '66
Some Surveyor findings. Sky & Tel 32:63+ Ag '66
Surveyor: an embarrassing success. D. Cohen. il Sci Digest 60:8-10 Ag '66
Surveyor: candid camera on the moon. H. E. Newell. il Nat Geog Mag 130:578-92 O '66
Surveyor, Gemini poised for launch. H. Taylor. il Miss & Roc 18:16 My 30 '66
Surveyor may survive lunar night; next launch scheduled; with editorial comment. R. Pay. il Tech W 18:16-17, 54 Je 13 '66
Surveyor mission rigidly controlled. il Tech W 18:44+ Je 6 '66
Surveyor I: preliminary results; report by the Surveyor scientific evaluation and analysis team. bibliog il Science 152:1737-50 Je 24 '66; Reply. E. A. Whitaker. 153:1550-1 S 23 '66
Surveyor I prompts confidence, caution. H. D. Watkins. il Aviation W 84:60-1+ Je 27 '66
Surveyor program leapfrogs ahead. R. Pay. il Tech W 18:14-16 Je 6 '66
Surveyor readied for moon flight. Aviation W 84:39 My 30 '66
Surveyor sits softly on the moon. il Life 60:38-9 Je 10 '66
Surveyor success to alter future flights. W. J. Normyle. il Aviation W 85:94-6 Jl 11 '66
Surveyor's honor roll. R. Hotz. Aviation W 85:21 Jl 25 '66
Surveyor's pictures bolster LEM plans. il Aviation W 84:26-9 Je 6 '66
Surveyor's smashing success. R. Hotz. Aviation W 85:21 Jl 18 '66

SPACE flight to Venus
NASA report to Congress details planetary alternatives for future; emphasis on Venus. W. J. Normyle. Aviation W 85:91+ S 19 '66
See also
Space probes

SPACE industry. See Aerospace industries
SPACE jargon. See Space flight—Terminology

SPACE law
Keeping law & order in space; Time essay. Time 88:26-7 S 30 '66
Men on the moon will need laws. Life 60:6 Je 17 '66
Peace in outer space; Geneva meeting. Nation 203:141 Ag 22 '66
Peaceful space treaty. F. Sartwell. Sci N 90:530 D 24 '66
Space flight and the rule of law. E. Pepin. il UNESCO Courier 19:17-18+ My '66
Space law for man, and anybody else out there. A. Rosenfeld. il Life 61:30-1 Ag 5 '66
Space treaty. Sci Am 216:54 Ja '67
Space treaty starts coming down to earth; U.S. and Russia appear close to agreement. il Bsns W p70-1 Jl 23 '66
U.N. comes to grips with space; international treaty on outer space; with editorial comment. Bsns W p 14, 100 D 24 '66
U.S. Russia near accord on space pact. L. L. Doty. Aviation W 85:21-2 Ag 1 '66
Young man, be a space lawyer. J. Boolittle. Esquire 65:118-19 Je '66

SPACE medicine
Biomedical space technology lagging. Miss & Roc 18:18 F 21 '66
Chronic exposure to low lunar magnetism considered harmful. Tech W 18:38 Je 27 '66
Gemini medical data gives confidence in Apollo, MOL. il Aviation W 85:56-8+ Ag 15 '66
New IBM lab will attack variety of space problems. Tech W 20:41 Ja 16 '67
Russians refine training of space dogs. Tech W 19:37-8 O 31 '66
Russians release new biology reports. H. M. David. Miss & Roc 18:26-7 Ap 11 '66
Soviet seeks key to man's adaptation. W. S. Beller. il Tech W 19:12-13 Jl 4 '66
Space medicine trade agreed on by US-USSR. Sci N 89:185 Mr 19 '66
USSR finds drugs vital in space. D. E. Fink. Aviation W 85:30-1 O 17 '66
USSR sees gains in manned space tests; cosmonauts using twenty different drugs. W. C. Wetmore. Aviation W 85:30-2 O 24 '66
See also
Biomedical engineering
Space flight—Physiological aspects
Weightlessness

SPACE navigation. See Navigation (Space flight)
SPACE nuclear propulsion office. See United States—Space nuclear propulsion office
SPACE ordnance systems, incorporated
Lasers, fiber bundles yield rfi-immune explosive initiator; laser-energized explosive device system. R. Pay. il Tech W 19:33+ N 14 '66

SPACE people. See Life on other planets
SPACE perception
Binocular disappearance of monocular symmetry. B. Julesz. il Science 153:657-8 Ag 5 '66
Eyes see depth as lag in time. Sci N 89:491 Je 18 '66
Visual-cliff preference by infant rats; effects of rearing and test conditions. J. M. Eichengreen and others. bibliog il Science 151:830-1 F 18 '66
Visual world of infants. T. G. R. Bower. il Sci Am 215:80-4+ D '66

SPACE photography
Along the Apollo belt; Surveyor on the moon. il Newsweek 67:32-4 Je 13 '66
Ampex device to cut waste in ATS photos; applications technology satellite B. Tech W 19:34 N 7 '66
ATS-1 data point to commercial payoffs. W. S. Beller. il Tech W 20:28-30 Ja 16 '67
ATS photos reflect weather patterns. il Aviation W 85:19-21 D 19 '66
Around the moon; Lunar Orbiter 1. il Time 88:54 Ag 19 '66
Dual cameras map lunar landing sites. I. Stone. il Aviation W 85:34-6 N 28 '66
Earth from orbit. P. D. Lowman, jr. il Nat Geog Mag 130:644-71 N '66
Earth from the moon. il Sci Am 215:42 O '66
Final Orbiter photos under interpretation; Soviets seen studying photos from Luna 11. il Aviation W 85:32 S 5 '66
Finding a toe-hold for man. il Bsns W p76+ Ag 20 '66
First Lunar Orbiter clears tests en route to TV mission. il Tech W 19:14-15 Ag 1 '66
Gemini 11 photos. il Aviation W 85:30-4 S 26 '66

SPACE photography—*Continued*
Geography lesson by Gemini 11. il Life 61: 102-6 S 30 '66
High-flying Gemini 11. R. N. Watts, jr. il Sky & Tel 32:264-5 N '66
How Surveyor did it. il U S Camera 29:36+ S '66
How the moon color photographs were made. G. P. Hunt. il Life 61:3 Jl 1 '66
Is there life on earth? G. S. Mumford. Sky & Tel 31:213-14 Ap '66
JPL abandons Surveyor photo attempts. il Aviation W 85:28 Jl 18 '66
Luna photos encouraging for Surveyor; with editorial comment. R. Pay. il Miss & Roc 18:12-14, 46 F 14 '66
Lunar Orbiter flight revised by Surveyor. W. J. Normyle. Aviation W 85:30 Ag 8 '66
Lunar Orbiter 1 begins photo mission. B. Miller. Aviation W 85:20-1 Ag 22 '66
Lunar Orbiter photographs earth and moon. il Sky & Tel 32:346-7+ D '66
Lunar Orbiter surveys the moon. R. N. Watts, jr. il Sky & Tel 32:192-7 O '66
Lunar rocks loom as hazard to Apollo. H. D. Watkins. il Aviation W 84:26-30 Je 13 '66
Lunar view of a socked-in earth; photograph taken by Lunar Orbiter. Life 61:34B-34C S 9 '66
Mars pictures year old. Sci N 90:59 Jl 23 '66
Moon beamed; Lunar Orbiter's photo reconnaissance mission. il Newsweek 68:88 Ag 22 '66
Orbiter: flying photo lab. Sci N 90:503 D 10 '66
Orbiter has own darkroom. B. Culliton. il Sci N 90:133 Ag 27 '66
Orbiter launched toward moon to photograph nine Apollo sites. G. Alexander. il Aviation W 85:34 Ag 15 '66
Orbiter photo quality heightened by gridding technique. il Aviation W 85:28-31 O 10 '66
Photo mission finished; report on findings from Orbiter 1 and Luna 11. il(p 169) Sci N 90:176 S 10 '66
Photo spacecraft to circle moon. W. Von Braun. il Pop Sci 188:92-3+ Je '66
Photographs from Mariner IV. R. B. Leighton. il Sci Am 214:54-68 bibliog(p 140) Ap '66
Pictures from the moon. R. N. Watts, jr. il Sky & Tel 32:16-19 Jl '66
Planet earth by dawn's early light; views from Gemini 10. Life 61:24-8 Ag 5 '66
Quarter earth in the sky; Lunar Orbiter's photos. Time 88:45 S 2 '66
Russians receive Luna 12 photos of moon, press for spectacular. il Aviation W 85:34 N 7 '66
Self-portrait; earth from the moon. il Newsweek 68:78 S 5 '66
Soviet TV lands on moon. il Sci N L 89:114-15 F 19 '66
Soviets still hoping for Venus 2 photos. D. Winston. Aviation W 84:34-5 Mr 14 '66
Space age prospecting; geological patterns seen on satellite photographs. C. I. Taggart. il Sat R 49:64-5 Je 4 '66
Suiting up; earth from Gemini 11. il Newsweek 68:62-4 O 3 '66
Surveyor: candid camera on the moon. H. E. Newell. il Nat Geog Mag 130:578-92 O '66
Surveyor may endure second lunar night. il Tech W 19:18 Jl 18 '66
Surveyor I prompts confidence, caution. H. D. Watkins. il Aviation W 84:60-1+ Je 27 '66
Surveyor program leapfrogs ahead. R. Pay. il Tech W 18:14-16 Je 6 '66
Surveyor's last job? taking pictures of the lunar sunset. Bsns W p70 Jl 16 '66
Surveyor's bolster LEM plans. il Aviation W 84:26-9 Je 6 '66
Surveyor's smashing success. R. Hotz. Aviation W 85:21 Jl 18 '66
Techniques tomorrow: new photographic equipment to help Gemini astronauts. B. Sherman. Mod Phot 30:26+ F '66
Tools to reach beyond the boundaries of man's action. il Life 61:104-5 D 23 '66
U.S. intercepts, translates Luna 9 signals. W. J. Normyle. Aviation W 84:33-5 F 14 '66
View from out there. il Sci Digest 60:10-11 N '66
What Luna 9 told us about the moon; tr. by A. Boyko. Y. N. Lipsky. il Sky & Tel 32:257-60 N '66
See also
Moon—Photographs, maps, etc.
SPACE physics laboratory. See Aerospace corporation
SPACE poll. See Public opinion polls
SPACE power systems. See Space vehicles—Power supply

SPACE probes
Atmospheric probe stressed for Mars; experiments for the '73 Voyager mission. W. S. Beller. il Miss & Roc 18:16-17 Ap 4 '66
Automatic chemical processor tested. H. M. David. il Miss & Roc 18:34 Ap 18 '66
DSIF antenna to extend Pioneer life. R. Pay. il Tech W 18:25-6+ Je 13 '66
Dual trip to Venus, sun is studied for Pioneer. Miss & Roc 18:18 F 28 '66
Experiments for 1969 Mars flight to be picked by May. R. Pay. Miss & Roc 18:18 F 28 '66
Fifth Pioneer being added to solar series. H. Taylor. Tech W 19:17 Ag 15 '66
Fund cuts, technical troubles slow Surveyor, Voyager programs. J. Walsh. il Science 151:305-7 Ja 21 '66
Funds considered for Mars '69 landing probe. H. M. David. Miss & Roc 18:13 Mr 7 '66
Mariner IV: developing the scientific experiment. G. A. Reiff. bibliog il Science 151: 413-17 Ja 28 '66
Mariner 4 heard from again. Sky & Tel 32: 3 Jl '66
Mariner '69 support RFP imminent. H. Taylor. Miss & Roc 18:14 Ap 4 '66
Mariner Venus craft lacks power for TV. Miss & Roc 18:33-5 F 14 '66
Mars next space target. Sci N L 89:116 F 19 '66
Martian atmosphere: the Mariner occultation experiment. J. W. Chamberlain and M. B. McElroy. bibliog il Science 152:21-5 Ap 1 '66
NASA discloses new planetary schedule. H. Taylor. il Tech W 19:18-19 S 12 '66
NASA drops Mariner support plans. H. Taylor. il Miss & Roc 18:16 My 2 '66
NASA ponders Pioneer shot to Venus. H. Taylor. Miss & Roc 18:13 Ap 18 '66
NASA puts Pioneer 7 into orbit around sun; period is 403 days. Aviation W 85:23 Ag 22 '66
Pioneer 6 orbits the sun. R. N. Watts, jr. il Sky & Tel 31:152-3 Mr '66
Planetary probe stabilization unit sought. Aviation W 85:34 S 19 '66
Report urges increased attention to planets during next fifteen years. W. J. Normyle. Aviation W 84:71+ Ja 24 '66
Scientific experiments of Mariner IV. R. K. Sloan. il Sci Am 214:62-72 bibliog(p 146-7) My '66
Single-purpose concept credited with pioneer 6 success. R. G. O'Lone. il Aviation W 84: 88-9+ Ap 11 '66
Study Mars with photos. Sci N 89:215 Ap 2 '66
Unified earth-sensor orbiter considered. W. J. Normyle. Aviation W 86:28-9 Ja 16 '67
Unmanned planetary missions stressed. Miss & Roc 18:15-16 Ja 24 '66
Voyage of Mariner IV. J. N. James. il Sci Am 214:42-52 bibliog(p 143) Mr '66
Voyager impact pegged at 2,000 g's. Miss & Roc 18:32-3 Ap 18 '66
SPACE probes, Russian
Apollo and Venus. il Sr Schol 88:19 Mr 18 '66
Luna photos encouraging for Surveyor; with editorial comment. R. Pay. il Miss & Roc 18:12-14, 46 F 14 '66
Meeting Venus; Venus III. Time 87:34 Mr 11 '66
Russia beats us to Venus. D. Cohen. Sci Digest 59:44-5 My '66
Russians reach Venus. J. Eberhart. Sci N 89:165 Mr 12 '66
Soviet space shot: a scientific blunder? Venus III. il U S News 60:18 Mr 14 '66
Soviets still hoping for Venus 2 photos. D. Winston. Aviation W 84:34-5 Mr 14 '66
Venus unobserved; Venus 3 probe. Newsweek 67:68-9 Mr 14 '66
See also
Lunar probes, Russian
SPACE propulsion. See Space vehicles—Propulsion systems
SPACE quarantine. See Quarantine
SPACE radiation. See Cosmic rays
SPACE rescue work
AF considering study awards for two space-rescue modes. H. M. David. Tech W 20:16 Ja 9 '67
Astronaut bail-out system uses foldable heat shield, foam structure. W. J. Normyle. il Aviation W 85:72-3+ S 12 '66
Hybrid maneuvering unit design progresses. H. M. David. il Tech W 19:36-7 O 17 '66
Lifeboats in space. W. Von Braun. il Pop Sci 189:96-7+ S '66

SPACE rescue work—*Continued*
NASA to begin space rescue study. Miss &
Roc 18:13 Ap 4 '66
No escape in space? scheduled flight of
Gemini 10. il Newsweek 68:82 Jl 25 '66
Space rescue problems. R. Hotz. Aviation W
85:11 Ag 22 '66

SPACE research
Chronology of fiscal 1966. Tech W 19:136-44
Jl 25 '66
Man and space; symposium. il UNESCO
Courier 19:4-37 My '66
Nth country's problem in space exploration.
N. E. Golovin. il Bul Atomic Sci 22:13-18
D '66
On the way to the moon. J. Eberhart. Sci N
90:550-1 D 24 '66
Orbiting potato. J. Lear; discussion. Sat R
48:92 D 4 '65; 49:72 F 5 '66
Some results from space studies. R. N. Watts,
jr. il Sky & Tel 32:140-1 S '66
See also
Artificial satellites—Use in research
International council of scientific unions—
Committee on space research
United Nations—Committee on the peaceful
uses of outer space

Economic aspects

How space agency expects to fund OART
and OTDA. H. Taylor. il Miss & Roc 18:
16-17 F 14 '66
Webb's space warning; excerpts from testimony before Senate appropriations subcommittee. J. E. Webb. Aviation W 84:21
My 23 '66

International aspects

First ESRO satellite readied for launch;
NASA international cooperation program.
H. J. Coleman. il Aviation W 86:79-81 Ja
16 '67
Launch operations accelerate at Thumba;
joint rocket research project sponsored by
U.N. Aviation W 84:91-2 My 23 '66
Man and space; symposium. il UNESCO
Courier 19:4-37 My '66
Man's utility in space stressed at AIAA; spe-
cial report; with editorial comment. C.
LaFond and others. il Tech W 19:18+, 54 D
5 '66
Reporter at large; seventeenth annual con-
gress of International astronautical federa-
tion. D. Lang. Nw Yorker 42:37-40+ D 24
'66
Science and the space program; address,
March 31, 1966. F. Seitz. Science 152:1719-21
Je 24 '66
Space club's roster goes international; Madrid
meeting of international space scientists. il
Bsns W p 112+ O 22 '66
Space exploration, a new dimension in U.S.-
European cooperation; excerpts from ad-
dress, January 14, 1966. G. C. McGhee.
Dept State Bul 54:460-3 Mr 21 '66
Space treaty starts coming down to earth;
U.S. and Russia appear close to agreement.
il Bsns W p70-1 Jl 23 '66
Time for decisions. W. J. Coughlin. Miss &
Roc 18:46 My 23 '66
Treaty for peace in space: its meaning. U S
News 61:8 D 19 '66
USSR spectacular would spur U.S. space pro-
gram. Sci N 90:185 S 10 '66
U.S. now has dimming hopes for space pact
with Europe. H. Taylor. Miss & Roc 18:
16 My 9 '66
U.S. presents draft treaty on exploration of
the moon and other celestial bodies to
U.N. committee; text of letter to the chair-
man of the U.N. committee on the peaceful
uses of outer space, with text of the U.S.
draft treaty, June 16, 1966. A. J. Goldberg.
Dept State Bul 55:60-2 Jl 11 '66
See also
United Nations—Committee on peaceful uses
of outer space

Military applications

Military space program; address, April 26,
1966. D. J. Fink. Vital Speeches 32:518-21
Je 15 '66
Special report: military space; symposium;
with editorial comment. il Miss & Roc 18:
24-6+, 94 My 30 '66
Treaty for peace in space: its meaning. U S
News 61:10 D 19 '66

Europe, Eastern

Technology need inspires east Europe to
space work. il Aviation W 84:198-206 Je 20
'66

Europe, Western

ELDO crisis possible despite cost move.
W. C. Wetmore. Aviation W 84:73-5 Je 27
'66
Europe's growing stake in space science;
ESRO and ELDO and other organizations
programs. P. Auger. il UNESCO Courier
19:24-6 My '66
See also
European space research organization
Eurospace

Germany (Federal Republic)

Space exploration, a new dimension in U.S.-
European cooperation; excerpts from ad-
dress, January 14, 1966. G. C. McGhee.
Dept State Bul 54:460-3 Mr 21 '66

Great Britain

Britain pressured to stay in ELDO. W. S.
Beller. il Tech W 18:20 Je 20 '66

Japan

Two dress rehearsals slated before Japanese
scientific shot. S. Nagashima. il Tech W
19:34-5 O 17 '66

Russia

Comparison of U.S. and Soviet efforts to ex-
plore Mars. B. C. Murray and M. E. Davies.
bibliog il Science 151:945-54 F 25 '66
Council compiles list of space firsts. Aviation W 84:100 My 16 '66
Dog's life; dogs after twenty two days in
orbit. Newsweek 67:62 Mr 28 '66
Heavy traffic in orbit; dogs in orbit; next
project. il Newsweek 67:94-5 Mr 21 '66
Letter from the editor. W. J. Coughlin. Tech
W 19:58 D 19 '66
M=1. W. J. Coughlin. Tech W 19:58 S 19
'66
1966 to reveal extent of Soviet efforts. D. E.
Fink. il Aviation W 84:130-1+ Mr 7 '66
No second best. W. J. Coughlin. Miss & Roc
18:46 My 2 '66
Russians faked it; concerning L. Mallan's
articles and theories. D. Cohen. il Nation
203:445-7+ O 31 '66
Russians mean to win the space race. W.
Shelton. il Fortune 73:140-3+ F '66
Russians seen cutting U.S. lead in unmanned
space exploration. M. L. Yaffee. Aviation W
84:59-61 F 7 '66
Soviet seeks key to man's adaptation. W. S.
Beller. il Tech W 19:12-13 Jl 4 '66
Soviet space effort. J. Turkevich. Cur Hist
51:226-32+ O '66
Soviets revamp lunar space plan. D. C.
Winston. Aviation W 85:22-3 N 28 '66
Space race pace. W. J. Coughlin. Miss &
Roc 18:46 Mr 7 '66
USSR sees gains in manned space tests.
W. C. Wetmore. Aviation W 85:30-2 O 24
'66
What's up with Veterok & Ugolyok; dogs
in Cosmos 110. Time 87:81 Mr 4 '66

United States

After Apollo, a void? R. Hotz. Aviation W
85:21 O 10 '66
Are the tame cats in charge? omens of Or-
well. P. Abelson; discussion. Sat R 49:71
F 5 '66
Beginnings. W. J. Coughlin. Tech W 19:50
N 21 '66
Bonanzas on the way to the moon. W. Von
Braun. il Pop Sci 188:106-7+ Mr '66
Case for space; excerpts from address. E. Q.
Daddario. Aviation W 84:21 Je 13 '66
Comparison of U.S. and Soviet efforts to ex-
plore Mars. B. C. Murray and M. E. Davies.
bibliog il Science 151:945-54 F 25 '66
Council compiles list of space firsts. Avia-
tion W 84:100 My 16 '66
Despite failures, search goes on for new
ways to spend on space. il U S News 60:36
Mr 28 '66
Editor comments on space, basic research,
and an International science foundation.
E. Rabinowitch. Bul Atomic Sci 22:2-3 O
'66
House asks decision on future space aims.
Tech W 19:23 Ag 15 '66
House committee urges AAP merger into
MOL program. H. M. David. Miss & Roc
18:14 Mr 21 '66
Houston gets AAP earth resources task.
Tech W 19:15-16 D 12 '66
Humphrey: space program is here to stay: in-
terview. H. H. Humphrey. il Tech W 19:
12-13 S 5 '66
In-house work trend emerging at NASA. Avi-
ation W 85:80 S 12 '66

SPACE research—United States—*Continued*
International cooperation in outer space; statement, December 18, 1965. A. J. Goldberg. Dept State Bul 54:163-7 Ja 31 '66
Letter from the editor. W. J. Coughlin. Tech W 19:58 D 19 '66
Lockheed, Martin are picked for AAP systems definition; Apollo applications program. Tech W 18:19 Je 6 '66
M—1. W. J. Coughlin. Tech W 19:58 S 19 '66
Man's utility in space stressed at AIAA; special report; with editorial comment. C. LaFond and others. il Tech W 19:18+, 54 D 5 '66
NASA post-Apollo plan urged by Dec. 1. G. C. Wilson. Aviation W 85:26 Ag 8 '66
NASA's war against secrecy. J. Eberhart. il Sci N 89:492-3 Je 18 '66
National debate; post-Apollo goals of the space program. W. J. Coughlin. Tech W 18:50 Je 20 '66
No second best. W. J. Coughlin. Miss & Roc 18:46 My 2 '66
Opportunities vast, budget confining. J. E. Webb. Tech W 19:44 N 28 '66
Post-Apollo lag angers Congress. Aviation W 84:314-15 Mr 7 '66
Rallying point. W. J. Coughlin. Tech W 19:50 Ag 22 '66
Remarks at Cape Kennedy, Fla, September 27, 1966. L. B. Johnson. Dept State Bul 55:581-3 O 17 '66
Saturn V successors squelched at AIAA. C. LaFond and others. il Tech W 19:24-5+ D 12 '66
Science and the space program; address, March 31, 1966. F. Seitz. Science 152:1719-21 Je 24 '66
Sciences take brunt of space fund slash. D. E. Fink. il Aviation W 84:27-8 Ja 31 '66
Scientific space program to show stability. Aviation W 84:137+ Mr 7 '66
Scientist-astronauts: only the perspicacious need apply. L. J. Carter. Science 154:133-5 O 7 '66
Second-generation spacecraft; excerpts from remarks. E. Konecci. Aviation W 85:21 Ag 8 '66
Similarity to space beckons scientists; using Antarctica for simulation of lunar and planetary environments. R. Lindsey. il Tech W 19:34+ D 5 '66
Space: caution prevails on post-Apollo commitments. D. S. Greenberg. Science 153:1221-2 S 9 '66
Space council, House panel press for post-lunar plans. Miss & Roc 18:13 My 16 '66
SPL probes solar, atmospheric features. R. Pay. il Tech W 19:24-6+ O 24 '66
Space program may swamp planes of future. Sci N 89:501 Je 18 '66
Space race pace. W. J. Coughlin. Miss & Roc 18:46 Mr 7 '66
Space request erases Apollo fund pad. E. H. Kolcum. Aviation W 84:23-4 Ja 31 '66
Space research plans; Woods Hole report. Sky & Tel 31:255+ My '66
Technological war. W. J. Coughlin. Tech W 19:54 N 14 '66
United States space program and its international significance; address; with questions and answers. A. W. Frutkin. Ann Am Acad 366:89-98 Jl '66
Webb's space warning; excerpts from testimony before Senate appropriations subcommittee. J. E. Webb. Aviation W 84:21 My 23 '66
We'll build a city on the moon. D. Q. Posin. il Todays Health 44:30-5 My '66
What comes after the moon? il Bsns W p36-8 Jl 2 '66
What comes after the moon; ideas for putting the U.S. more deeply into space. il Bsns W p 130-1+ D 10 '66
What next in space? excerpts from remarks. J. E. Karth. Aviation W 85:11 Ag 1 '66
See also
United States—National aeronautics and space administration
SPACE science and applications, Office of. See United States—National aeronautics and space administration—Space science and applications, Office of
SPACE science board. See National academy of sciences—Space science board
SPACE-simulation chambers. See Testing laboratories
SPACE speak. See Space flight—Terminology
SPACE station simulators
GE facility to study zero-G performance. K. Voss. il Tech W 20:17 Ja 2 '67
USAF research seeks methods to extend man's capacity for long-term space flight; studies form basis for manned orbiting laboratory program. il Aviation W 85:110-11+ Ag 15 '66

SPACE stations
Astronomical, lunar surface stations eyed. M. Getler. il Tech W 19:48-52 N 28 '66
Douglas lists major MOL subsystem contractors. Miss & Roc 18:15 Ap 4 '66
First manned MOL flight may slip into early 1970. Miss & Roc 18:13 My 9 '66
Five orbital shots planned in MOL tests. W. J. Normyle. Aviation W 85:33-4 S 12 '66
Forty-six stations may orbit. il(p383) Sci N 89:391 My 21 '66
Future programs considered hinged to MOL performance. H. Taylor. il Miss & Roc 18:32-3+ My 30 '66
House committee urges AAP merger into MOL program. H. M. David. Miss & Roc 18:14 Mr 21 '66
Instrumentation needs low; majority are tied to MOL. C. D. LaFond and others. il Miss & Roc 18:58+ My 30 '66
IBM urges three core labs for AAP. Miss & Roc 18:47 My 16 '66
Lessons from Gemini: next, the military spaceman; manned orbiting laboratory, MOL. il U S News 61:74-5 S 26 '66
McDonnell to build airlock for Apollo spent-stage test; using empty hydrogen tank as a manned space laboratory. il Tech W 19:19 Ag 29 '66
McNamara outlines MOL schedule; summary of statement; ed. by M. Getler. R. S. McNamara. Miss & Roc18:14-16 F 28 '66
Manned Mars trip, space station sought. J. Mercer. il Tech W 19:56-8+ N 28 '66
MOL dummy does stunts in space; Titan IIIC hoists mockup lab into near-perfect orbit. il Bsns W p 115 N 12 '66
NASA adapting S-4B for space station. W. J. Normyle. Aviation W 85:34 S 5 '66
NASA plans space station. Tech W 19:12 S 26 '66
NASA studying space station funding needs for FY 1968. H. Taylor. Tech W 19:16 O 10 '66
New space station concept study planned. W. J. Normyle. Aviation W 85:28 O 24 '66
Orbital launching of S-2 stages studied. D. E. Fink. il Aviation W 84:52-3+ Ja 24 '66
Post-Apollo programs focusing on multipurpose earth-orbiter. W. J. Normyle. Aviation W 85:17 D 26 '66
Post-Apollo station plans altered. W. J. Normyle. Aviation W 85:22-3 D 5 '66
S-IVB stage may become space station. J. Mercer. il Miss & Roc 18:17 Ap 25 '66
Space war on ground. J. Eberhart. il Sci N 90:393 N 12 '66
Spectacular Titan III-C flight results bode well for MOL. Tech W 19:15 N 14 '66
USAF research seeks methods to extend man's capacity for long-term space flight; studies form basis for manned orbiting laboratory program. il Aviation W 85:110-11+ Ag 15 '66
SPACE suits. See Astronauts—Clothing
SPACE technology
Gravity, electric power plague planners. W. S. Beller. il Tech W 19:102-4+ N 28 '66
NASA will study EVA procedures for building antennas in space. Aviation W 85:132+ Ag 15 '66
Space activity projected for FY 2001. W. S. Beller. Miss & Roc 18:17 Mr 21 '66
Space to keep large market potential. il Aviation W 84:103-5 Mr 7 '66
Special report on space bio-science; with editorial comment. D. E. Fink. il Aviation W 85:21, 54-65+ Ag 15 '66
Wide planetary effort is seen by 2000. R. D. Hibben. il Aviation W 84:64-5+ Ap 4 '66

Study and teaching
UCLA may become first college with complete satellite project. W. E. Wilks. Tech W 19:36 D 12 '66
SPACE telemetry
Apollo PCM subsystems come of age. il Miss & Roc 18:36+ F 28 '66
Biosatellite mission objectives detailed. R. Pay. il Tech W 18:24-5+ Je 27 '66
CIF incorporates time plot curve display. il Aviation W 84:138+ Je 20 '66
DEI monitor may have myriad new uses. Tech W 19:38 Ag 1 '66
Messages from space. J. Reinert. il Sci Digest 59:53-7 F '66
Radiation advances redundancy cutting. K. Voss. il Tech W 19:34-5 Ag 8 '66
SPACE tools. See Space vehicles—Maintenance and repair
SPACE vehicle models
Model venture thrives on space; scale models of Mercury and Gemini space capsules. il Bsns W p 177 Mr 19 '66

SPACE vehicles—Equipment—*Continued*
NASA considers facsimile camera. R. Barnhart. il Miss & Roc 18:35-6 My 23 '66
New ECU problem postpones AS-204; environment control unit. Aviation W 85:33 D 12 '66
New Nimbus avionics interface transmits infrared on APT link; automatic picture transmission. K. J. Stein. il Aviation W 84:77+ My 2 '66
Space trash, and an inventory of hardware in orbit. Life 61:29 Ag 5 '66
Unified earth-sensor orbiter considered. W. J. Normyle. Aviation W 86:28-9 Ja 16 '67
Waste treatment plant to improve system. H. M. David. il Tech W 20:28 Ja 9 '67
See also
Life support systems (space environment)
Magnetic recorders and recording—Space flight applications
Space vehicles—Fuel tanks
Telescope on space vehicles

Escape devices

Chute planned for escape from Saturn 5. G. Alexander. il Aviation W 84:65-6 F 28 '66
For astronauts in trouble, this way out. W. Von Braun. il Pop Sci 188:72-4+ My '66
Hard shelter to protect Apollo crew. K. Voss. il Tech W 18:39 Je 20 '66
Space rescue problems. R. Hotz. Aviation W 85:11 Ag 22 '66

Fuel

See Rockets—Fuel

Fuel tanks

Silicon strain gauge to pinpoint Apollo system fuels in zero-G. R. Pay. il Tech W 19:40-1 D 12 '66
Tank problems may delay Apollo. W. J. Normyle. il Aviation W 85:26-7 N 14 '66

Inspection

Personality of the month; man who looks for trouble; M. R. Comer, jr. L. B. Taylor. il Sci Digest 60:40-3 Jl '66

Landing systems
Mars

NASA begins drop tests of Mars lander parachutes. il Tech W 19:17 Ag 29 '66
NASA drops Mariner support plans. H. Taylor. il Miss & Roc 18:16 My 2 '66
Parachutes seen still feasible for Mars. Aviation W 84:103 Ap 11 '66
Quest for Martian life re-emphasized. W. Wilks and R. Pay. il Tech W 18:26-8 Je 6 '66
Soft landing on Mars. R. N. Watts, jr. il Sky & Tel 31:346-7 Je '66
Voyager impact pegged at 2,000 g's. Miss & Roc 18:32-3 Ap 18 '66

Moon

Apollo landing may come early in '68. il Tech W 19:14-15 Jl 11 '66
Control achievements stressed on Luna 9; with editorial comment. D. Winston. il Aviation W 84:21, 29-33 F 14 '66
ECS elements for LEM nearing delivery. R. D. Hibben. il Aviation W 84:76-7+ My 30 '66
Geological survey aiding NASA in landing site determination. R. Lindsey. il Tech W 20:40 Ja 9 '67
Grumman refining lunar module design. M. L. Yaffee. il Aviation W 85:56-9+ O 24 '66
Latest configuration of Apollo lunar module near delivery. R. Barnhart. il Tech W 19:40 O 17 '66
Luna photos encouraging for Surveyor; with editorial comment. R. Pay. il Miss & Roc 18:12-14, 46 F 14 '66
LEM rendezvous decision expected. J. Mercer. Miss & Roc 18:17 My 30 '66
Lunar surface can support Apollo LEM. il Tech W 18:17 Je 20 '66
Man on the moon; with paintings by N. Rockwell. J. A. Osmundsen. Look 31:39-42 Ja 10 '67
Practicing a moon landing on earth; training with lunar landing research vehicle. W. Von Braun. il Pop Sci 188:98-9+ F '66
Ready for new strides on pathway to moon; lunar module. il Bsns W p80-1+ N 26 '66

Robot on the moon; Luna 9 and how B. Lovell took pictures. J. Lear. il Sat R 49:57-65 Mr 5 '66
See also
Space flight to the moon—Surveyor flight, 1966

Launching

Apollo gets nearer its target. il Bsns W p 102-4 Mr 5 '66
Blast off; photographs. Sci N 89:242-3 Ap 9 '66
Chute planned for escape from Saturn 5. G. Alexander. il Aviation W 84:65-6 F 28 '66
Deadlines press the space race. il Bsns W p36-9 Ja 4 '66
First Lunar Orbiter clears tests en route to TV mission. il Tech W 19:14-15 Ag 1 '66
Ground-based guidance problem stymies launch of Gemini 9A. Aviation W 84:40 Je 6 '66
Lunar Orbiter flight revised by Surveyor. W. J. Normyle. Aviation W 85:30 Ag 8 '66
No problems for next Saturn-Apollo. J. Mercer. Miss & Roc 18:22 Mr 14 '66
Orbital launching of S-2 stages studied. D. E. Fink. il Aviation W 84:52-3+ Ja 24 '66
Revised program may save time and money. Sci N 89:484 Je 18 '66
Roster of space activity. R. N. Watts, jr. il Sky & Tel 33:28-30 Ja '67
Soviet failure, mystery orbiters disclosed. H. Taylor. Tech W 19:16 O 31 '66
Surveyor, Gemini poised for launch. H. Taylor. il Miss & Roc 18:16 My 30 '66
Unmanned launch goals still uncertain. Aviation W 84:173 Je 20 '66
Varied checkout requirements spur new philosophies. E. H. Kolcum. il Aviation W 84:126-7+ Je 20 '66
See also
Artificial satellites—Launching
Communications satellites—Launching

Launching pads

Crawler, tower embody mobile concept. il Aviation W 84:110-13+ Je 20 '66
Launch areas 34,37 to be ready for full Apollo vehicle in 1967. Aviation W 85:73 Ag 29 '66
Lessons from first pad alter KSC pad B. Tech W 20:20 Ja 2 '67

Launching sites

Control center reflects mobile concept. il Aviation W 84:121-3+ Je 20 '66
Kennedy center gears for Apollo, future. il Aviation W 84:75-80 Je 20 '66
Meanwhile, NASA builds a moonport; portfolio. Fortune 73:144-9 F '66
Secret of Plesetsk; physics teacher and students of Kettering grammar school, England, discover location of rocket-launching site in Russia. il Time 88:38 D 30 '66

Maintenance and repair

Air force studies elastomers to plug micrometeorite holes. Aviation W 84:59 Je 27 '66
Astronauts get a tool kit. W. Von Braun. il Pop Sci 189:146-7+ O '66
Low-torque tools evolve for orbit use. il Aviation W 85:84-5+ Ag 15 '66

Manufacture

Cold welding dangerous. Sci N 90:371 N 5 '66
New method may solve mismatch. il Miss & Roc 18:31 My 23 '66
Non-vacuum electron beam welder to get Saturn tasks. il Tech W 19:18-20 Jl 4 '66
Trend seen in impending Voyager transfer. W. J. Normyle. Aviation W 85:32 N 21 '66

Materials

AF probes fires in 100 per cent oxygen. Miss & Roc 18:31-2 Mr 7 '66
Air force studies elastomers to plug micrometeorite holes. Aviation W 84:59 Je 27 '66
Aluminum-steel plate bests titanium. J. F. Judge. Miss & Roc 18:26+ Ap 25 '66
Ceramic beats heat. Sci N 90:39 Jl 16 '66
Hexagonal crystal structure will enhance bearing alloys. il Tech W 19:36 Ag 22 '66
Micrometeorite data challenges theories. R. D. Hibben. il Aviation W 85:54-5+ S 5 '66
See also
Shielding (heat)

Orbits

Long elliptical Gemini orbit proposed. Tech W 18:20 Je 27 '66

Parts

See Space vehicle parts

Power supply

DOD seeks more orderly development. W. S. Beller. il Miss & Roc 18:83-4+ My 30 '66
Dynamic liquid-metal plants practical. J. F. Judge. il Miss & Roc 18:22-3+ My 9 '66

SPACE vehicles—Power supply—*Continued*
Fuel cell/nuclear combination proposed. K. Voss. Tech W 20:37 Ja 9 '67
Gravity, electric power plague planners. W. S. Beller. il Tech W 19:102-4+ N 28 '66
Ion devices move toward useful space applications. R. Pay. il Miss & Roc 18:43-4 Mr 14 '66
Marquardt developing composite engines. M. L. Yaffee. il Aviation W 85:93+ D 12 '66
NASA, AF enthusiastic about solar-electric powerplants. Miss & Roc 18:36-7 F 14 '66
Solar-electric propulsion potential grows. B. Miller. il Aviation W 84:103+ Mr 28 '66

Propulsion systems

Apollo systems developed concurrently. G. Alexander. il Aviation W 84:82-4+ Je 20 '66
Big Burner II buys foreseen. Tech W 19:36 Ag 8 '66
Blast off; photographs. Sci N 89:242-3 Ap 9 '66
Building blocks reaching payoff stage. J. F. Judge. il Miss & Roc 18:50-2+ My 30 '66
Buildup of Titan 3 shown at Kennedy complex; photographs. Aviation W 84:86-9 Je 13 '66
Centaur flight to test stage's in-orbit re-ignition capability. Tech W 19:15 O 24 '66
Changing concepts key to design of future Saturn family; Saturn launch vehicles. W. J. Normyle. il Aviation W 84:106-9+ Mr 7 '66
Cruise/launch vehicle guidance studied. I. Stone. il Aviation W 84:93-5+ My 9 '66
Decision near on target vehicle for Gemini 8 flight. il Miss & Roc 18:14 F 7 '66
Delivery of refurbished Atlas boosters begins this month. il Tech W 19:18 Jl 11 '66
ELDO to provide Comsat launcher. W. S. Beller. il Tech W 19:20 Jl 18 '66
Family of small engines planned for space. M. L. Yaffee. il Aviation W 85:82-3+ Ag 8 '66
Flight of Saturn IB will test J-2 engine. I. Stone. il Aviation W 84:53+ F 14 '66
Heat shield verified in first Apollo test. G. Alexander. il Aviation W 84:92-3+ Mr 14 '66
In a single launching, a belt of satellites; Titan III-C rocket. il U S News 60:10 Je 27 '66
Launch vehicle changes trigger expansion. K. Voss. il Tech W 19:62-3 N 28 '66
Lightened EOS electric unit clears full flight-type test. il Tech W 19:35 O 24 '66
LMSC foresees steady Agena demand. R. Lindsey. Tech W 19:29 S 5 '66
Manned flight planning gap delays Saturn development. G. Alexander. il Aviation W 85:58-9+ Ag 8 '66
Marquardt developing composite engines. M. L. Yaffee. il Aviation W 85:93+ D 12 '66
Moonbird. J. Eberhart. il Sci N 90:106-7+ Ag 13 '66
Move to long-tank Delta made to boost comsat capability. H. M. David. Tech W 19:19 S 12 '66
NASA considering radio guidance study. I. Stone. il Aviation W 84:95+ Je 13 '66
NASA considers new launcher for TV, planet orbiter payloads. Aviation W 85:29 D 12 '66
NASA, North American pressing S-2 systems qualification effort. Aviation W 85:112 Jl 25 '66
NASA seeks simpler, more flexible J-2. G. Alexander. il Aviation W 85:60-1+ Ag 29 '66
NASA switches to ATDA for Gemini 9; augmented target docking adapter. G. Alexander. Aviation W 84:30-1 My 23 '66
New funds to maintain Saturn IB line. Miss & Roc 18:17 My 9 '66
New launch vehicle study proposals due. Tech W 19:18 Ag 1 '66
New NASA satellite projects may demand new boost stages. Tech W 19:15 D 5 '66
New Titan III-C procurement planned. M. Getler. Miss & Roc 18:14 Ap 18 '66
No static firing scheduled for Gemini 8 Agena target. R. Lindsey. il Miss & Roc 18:31-2 Ja 24 '66
Precision plan marks lunar system mating. il Aviation W 84:100-1+ Je 20 '66
Reusable Saturns may mean 75 per cent savings. K. Voss. il Tech W 19:36+ O 24 '66
S-II stage due at Cape early in maneuver to gain time. Tech W 20:20 Ja 16 '67
Saturn/Apollo delay reports discounted. K. Voss. Tech W 19:20 S 12 '66

Saturn 1B proving Saturn 5 control unit. G. Alexander. il Aviation W 84:107+ Ap 18 '66
Saturn set to lift heaviest satellite; lunar IMP slated. il Tech W 18:19 Je 27 '66
Saturn V successors squelched at AIAA. C. LaFond and others. il Tech W 19:24-5+ D 12 '66
78-lb. payload seen for orbital Athena. B. K. Thomas, jr. Aviation W 85:103+ Jl 18 '66
Surveyor retro-rocket nozzle redesigned. il Aviation W 84:103+ My 16 '66
Thin booster walls yield payload hike. il Tech W 19:35 D 12 '66
Titan failure with satellites probed. M. Getler. il Tech W 19:18 S 5 '66
Titan III-C strap-on performance detailed. J. F. Judge. il Tech W 19:26-8 Ag 1 '66
Titan III-C successfully launches IDCSP; Initial defense communications satellite program. C. D. LaFond. il Tech W 18:16-17 Je 27 '66
U.S. launch vehicles; International launch vehicles; specifications (cont) Aviation W 84:197-8 Mr 7 '66
USAF presses Atlas-ATDA preparation; augmented target docking adapter. G. Alexander. Aviation W 84:38-9 My 30 '66
USAF pushes advanced motors for manned orbital vehicles. Aviation W 85:27-8 N 14 '66
UTC chief sees tighter rocket market. R. Lindsey. Miss & Roc 18:22-3 Ap 18 '66
Vacuum freezing effects probed. J. F. Judge. il Miss & Roc 18:22-3 Mr 21 '66
VAB key to fast Apollo/Saturn assembly and launch. il Aviation W 84:92-4+ Je 20 '66
Voyager, planet probe technology in hand. R. Pay. il Tech W 19:95-8+ N 28 '66

See also
Liquid propellant rockets
Rocket engines
Solid propellant rockets

Design

Aerospike, multi-chamber designs considered for advanced vehicle. I. Stone. il Aviation W 85:70+ S 19 '66
Study of advanced air-breathing launch vehicles sought by NASA. Aviation W 85:77+ S 19 '66

Testing

AC-9 demonstrates Centaur versatility. G. Alexander. Aviation W 85:33 N 7 '66
Apollo gets nearer its target. il Bsns W p 102-4 Mr 5 '66
Apollo/Saturn 5 assembly begins for flight in 1967. il Aviation W 85:38-9 O 24 '66
AS-202 bolsters manned Apollo schedule. G. Alexander. Aviation W 85:33 S 5 '66
Apollo success paves way for first manned mission. H. Taylor. il Tech W 19:16-17 S 5 '66
Big solids given steady support; propulsion test plant near completion. J. F. Judge. il Tech W 19:108-10+ N 28 '66
Effects of retro-rocket exhaust studied in Arnold test cell. il Tech W 19:28 Ag 8 '66
First Apollo-Saturn 1B readied for verification flight Feb. 23. Aviation W 84:30 F 21 '66
J-2 engine parts show little wear after thirty test-firings. il Tech W 20:36-7 Ja 2 '67
LPC test-fires big solid-solid system. W. E. Wilks. il Tech W 20:34-5 Ja 16 '67
Manned Apollo to fly this year; Apollo/Saturn 1B-201 mission. H. Taylor. il Miss & Roc 18:14 Mr 7 '66
MILA launch site readied for first Saturn V vehicle. il Miss & Roc 18:15 My 16 '66
MOL dummy does stunts in space; Titan IIIC hoists mockup lab into near-perfect orbit. il Bsns W p 115 N 12 '66
New Apollo/Saturn schedule may delay first manned flight. H. Taylor. Miss & Roc 18:14 Ap 11 '66
No problems for next Saturn-Apollo. J. Mercer. Miss & Roc 18:22 Mr 14 '66
Of dogs, men and moons; flight test of Saturn IB booster. il Newsweek 67:85 Mr 7 '66
Rocket research studies using manned vehicle waste for fuel; Monex W. il Tech W 20:30+ Ja 2 '67
S-2 faces critical firing tests. Aviation W 85:33 O 3 '66
Saturn IB-Apollo awaits first test. il Miss & Roc 18:16-17 F 21 '66
Saturn IB-Apollo may finish early. H. Taylor. Miss & Roc 18:17 F 28 '66
Space war on ground. J. Eberhart. il Sci N 90:393 N 12 '66

SPACE vehicles—Propulsion systems—Testing
—*Continued*
Spectacular Titan III-C flight results bode well for MOL. Tech W 19:15 N 14 '66
Tank problems may delay Apollo. W. J. Normyle. il Aviation W 85:26-7 N 14 '66
Thiokol hydroburst test shows reliability of 156-in. motor case; glass fiber motor case. il Tech W 19:42-3 D 12 '66
Titan 3C passes sixth test, furnishes MOL support. Aviation W 85:30 N 14 '66
Trial & triumph; Saturn IB test. il Time 87: 81 Mr 4 '66
Unmanned Apollo test represents critical lunar landing milestone. W. J. Normyle. Aviation W 85:22 Ag 22 '66
Way station to the moon; Mississippi test facility. il Bsns W p62+ Ap 2 '66
Wyle facility will supply on-line Saturn V analysis. R. G. Pay. il Miss & Roc 18:37+ My 16 '66
Wyle tests S-2 stage structural parts. G. Alexander. il Aviation W 85:69-71 D 19 '66

Quarantine
See Quarantine

Recovery
Astronauts may return to land, not sea; new terminal landing system. il Sci N 90: 203 S 17 '66
How to get a good man down. K. V. Brown. il Pop Mech 126:80-3 D '66
Lifting-body program may surpass X-15; flights of M2-F2 and HL-10. C. M. Plattner. Aviation W 85:105+ Jl 25 '66
Manned flight tests to seek lifting-body technology. W. J. Normyle. il Aviation W 84: 64-5+ My 16 '66
NASA plans powered flight of lifting bodies in 1967. Miss & Roc 18:14 My 2 '66
Reusable Saturns may mean 75 per cent savings. K. Voss. il Tech W 19:36+ O 24 '66
Rotor re-entry system studied. il Tech W 19:35 Ag 22 '66
Space ferry patented; lifting body, or wing-less spacecraft. il Sci N 90:380 N 5 '66
USAF seeks parachute stations as targets for JC-130 pickups. Aviation W 85:61 O 24 '66

Safety devices and measures
Built-in fire fighter; burning rates reduced by weightlessness. Time 88:76-7 D 16 '66
How to get a good man down. K. V. Brown. il Pop Mech 126:80-3 D '66
See also
Space vehicles—Escape devices

Seats
Bean bag may replace astronauts' couches. Sci N 89:324 Ap 30 '66

Shielding from heat
See Shielding (heat)

Stability and stabilizers
Launch set for gravity-gradient vehicle. R. D. Hibben. il Aviation W 85:109+ S 26 '66
Planetary probe stabilization unit sought. Aviation W 85:34 S 19 '66
Satellite would wed merits of spin, active stabilization. il Tech W 20:35 Ja 9 '67
See also
Gyroscope

Sterilization
Germs and the space age. J. Eberhart. il Sci N 89:312-13 Ap 30 '66
Soviet spacecraft sterilization methods aired at COSPAR. W. S. Beller. Miss & Roc 18:17-18 My 16 '66

Testing
ACE brain of complex Apollo checkout. P. J. Klass. il Aviation W 84:131+ Je 20 '66
All Apollo programs to be going by June. il Sci N 89:165 Mr 12 '66
Failure analysts fight tight schedule. il Aviation W 84:167-8 Je 20 '66
McDonnell to build airlock for Apollo spent-stage test; using empty hydrogen tank as a manned space laboratory. il Tech W 19: 19 Ag 29 '66
New Apollo/Saturn schedule may delay first manned flight. H. Taylor. Miss & Roc 18: 14 Ap 11 '66
Saturn IB-Apollo awaits first test. il Miss & Roc 18:16-17 F 21 '66

Tracking
Advanced deep-space dish readied. R. Pay. il Miss & Roc 18:34 My 2 '66
Apollo ship, aircraft elements readied. S. Butler. il Miss & Roc 18:24-6 Ja 24 '66
Bringing credit to Jodrell bank. Time 87:52 Ap 15 '66

Control center reflects mobile concept. il Aviation W 84:121-3+ Je 20 '66
DSIF antenna to extend Pioneer life. R. Pay. il Tech W 18:25-6+ Je 13 '66
Gemini control success may boost mission flexibility. E. J. Bulban. il Aviation W 84:64-5+ Ja 24 '66
Gemini 9A data link bypass successful. il Aviation W 84:183+ Je 20 '66
Getting a word to outer space; Goldstone complex. Bsns W p 168 My 7 '66
Instrumentation needs low; majority are tied to MOL. G. D. LaFond and others. il Miss & Roc 18:58+ My 30 '66
New giant tracking antenna at Goldstone. il Sky & Tel 31:342-3 Je '66
Our secret eye on space; Space defense center at Ent AFB in Colorado Springs. D. Robinson. il Look 30:94-6+ N 15 '66
Probe tracking antenna will follow men to Pluto. Sci N 89:334 My 7 '66
Real-time tracking data concept pushed. B. Miller. il Aviation W 84:99-103 My 23 '66
Russians tracking space probes optically. W. C. Wetmore. Aviation W 84:83+ My 30 '66
Secret of Plesetsk; physics teacher and students of Kettering grammar school, England, discover location of rocket-launching site in Russia. il Time 88:38 D 30 '66

Transportation
Crawler, tower embody mobile concept. il Aviation W 84:110-13+ Je 20 '66
Improved crawler undergoes first trial. G. Alexander. il Aviation W 84:51+ F 21 '66
Precision plan marks lunar system mating. il Aviation W 84:100-1+ Je 20 '66
Saturn V crawler trouble cleared up. S. Butler. Miss & Roc 18:34-5 F 7 '66
Storm tests launch mobility concept. il Aviation W 84:175 Je 20 '66

Water supply
Astronauts' water problem could ruin whole mission. Sci N 90:425 N 19 '66
Mars flight goal of bio-science research. il Aviation W 85:88-90+ Ag 15 '66
Waste treatment plant to improve system. H. M. David. il Tech W 20:28 Ja 9 '67

SPACE vehicles, Russian
Moscow display reveals Luna 9 details; photographs. Aviation W 84:82-3 My 23 '66
Soviet failure, mystery orbiters disclosed. H. Taylor. Tech W 19:16 O 31 '66
Soviets reveal new data on spacecraft; Voskhod 2 and Cosmos 110. W. C. Wetmore. Aviation W 84:26-7 My 16 '66

SPACELABS, incorporated
Hospital to benefit from space work. H. M. David. il Miss & Roc 18:26+ F 28 '66

SPACEMEN. See Astronauts

SPACESUITS. See Astronauts—Clothing

SPACEWALK. See Space flight—Manned flights—Extravehicular activity

SPACKS, Barry
At thirty-five; poem. Nation 203:260 S 19 '66
Freshmen; poem. New Yorker 42:48 O 1 '66
October; Recommendations; poems. Poetry 108:98-9 My '66
Virtue intense, most bright and active grace. Poetry 108:337-9 Ag '66

SPADEFOOT toad. See Toads

SPAGHETTI. See Macaroni

SPAGHT, Monroe Edward
Monty Spaght's Royal Dutch treat. R. Sheehan. il por Fortune 73:154-6+ Je '66

SPAHN, Warren Edward
El Spahnie of los Tigres. M. Cope. il por Sports Illus 25:26-8+ Jl 4 '66
N.Y.'s top court upholds Spahn on biography. Pub W 190:33 N 7 '66

SPAIN, David M.
Atherosclerosis; with biographical sketch. Sci Am 215:10, 48-56 bibliog(p 114) Ag; 8 D '66

SPAIN
See also
Airlines—Spain
Architecture, Domestic—Spain
Birds—Spain
Censorship—Spain
Church and state in Spain
Colleges and universities—Spain
Escorial
Gardens—Spain
Gipsies in Spain
Guernica
Labor laws and legislation—Spain
Newspapers—Spain
Periodicals—Spain

SPAIN—See also—*Continued*
Phonograph record industry—Spain
Political campaigns—Spain
Private schools—Spain
Santiago
Seville
Strikes—Spain
Tourist trade—Spain
Villena

Antiquities
Gypsy's treasure; discovery of ancient trove of gold near Villena. B. Wason. il Horizon 9:102-4 Wint '67

Army
Foreign legion
Sahara song; the last legions, the first art. F. C. Grunfeld. il Reporter 35:48-50 Jl 14 '66

Church history
See also
Inquisition

Colonies
Spanish seaborne empire, by J. H. Parry. Review
Sat R 49:36 Jl 9 '66. J. A. Crow
See also
Latin America—History
Mexico—History—Spanish colony, 1540-1810

Commercial treaties and agreements
U.S. and Spain amend cotton textiles agreement; Department announcement; with text of U.S. note, September 14, 1966. Dept State Bul 55:509 O 3 '66

Constitution
After him, the deluge? il Newsweek 68:40+ D 5 '66
Si! il Newsweek 68:32-4 D 26 '66
Si. il Time 88:26 D 23 '66
Spain's new constitution. il Sr Schol 89:13-14 Ja 13 '67
Umbrella of monarchy. Time 88:32-3 D 2 '66

Description and travel
Falling in love with Spain. J. M. Flecke. Sr Schol 88:sup28 Ap 15 '66

Economic conditions
Franco's peace: Spain thirty years after the insurrection. S. F. Wexler. Yale R 56:25-44 O '66
Spaniards say *si* to department stores; Galerias' chain of sixteen stores is being followed by Federated, Sears and Woolworth. il Bsns W p 176-8 My 28 '66
Spanish temper heats up; economy out of balance. il Bsns W p78-9+ Ag 6 '66
Wrinkles on my lady. P. Crumpet. Nat R 18:827-8 Ag 23 '66

Foreign relations
Great Britain
Will Spain win out in fight for Rock? il Bsns W p36-7 Mr 5 '66
Writing on the Rock; Anglo-Spanish conference. N. Mostert. Reporter 34:28-31 Je 30 '66

History
Spanish seaborne empire, by J. H. Parry. Review
Sat R 49:36 Jl 9 '66. J. A. Crow

Bibliography
Articles and other books received; comp. by C. J. Bishko. See issues of American historical review

Arab period, 711-1492
Where both sides gained; Spanish history in art. il Time 88:76-81 O 28 '66

Civil war, 1936-1939
How Stalin relieved Spain of $600,000,000. A. Orlov. il Read Digest 89:37-8+ N '66
Spain and Vietnam; comparing two civil wars. W. C. McWilliams and D. Hale. Commonweal 84:575-7 S 16 '66

Civil war, 1936-1939—Bibliography
Spanish civil war booklist. Nation 203:100 Jl 25 '66

Civil war, 1936-1939—Fiction
Body testing the slogans. A. Guttmann. Nation 204:90-1 Ja 16 '67

Civil war, 1936-1939—Poetry
Song of the little death; tr. by R. Humphries; reprint. F. G. Lorca. Nation 203:92 Jl 25 '66

Civil war, 1936-1939—Volunteers
International brigades, by V. Brome. Review
Nation 203:91-4 Jl 25 '66. J. Herbst
New Repub 154:27-8 Mr 12 '66. S. Weintraub
Spanish war. O. Handlin. Atlan 218:140 S '66

Industries
See also
Olive industry and trade
Wine trade

Intellectual life
Heat in Spain; new protests. G. Jackson. Commonweal 84:327-9 Je 10 '66

Politics and government
After Franco, the generalissimo's plans. il U S News 61:16 D 5 '66
Franco's peace: Spain thirty years after the insurrection. S. F. Wexler. Yale R 56:25-44 O '66
Libertad, libertad! students strikes. Newsweek 67:52 My 16 '66
Now the priests; protest about police brutality against imprisoned student. Newsweek 67:59-60 My 23 '66
Of many things. T. N. Davis. America 115: 787 D 17 '66
Spain faces the future. B. van Voorst. il Newsweek 67:46-8 Je 20 '66
Spain: no homage allowed! demonstration at Homage to Machado. Nation 202:462-4 Ap 18 '66
See also
Spain—Constitution

Religious institutions and affairs
Church in Spain; Pope Paul's reform efforts and outcome of Spanish Episcopal conference. il Newsweek 67:86-7 Mr 28 '66
See also
Catholic church in Spain
Protestants in Spain

Social conditions
Wrinkles on my lady. P. Crumpet. Nat R 18:827-8 Ag 23 '66

Social life and customs
Anecdotes, facetiae, satire, etc.
Keeping up with the caballeros; letter writing preferable to telephoning. P. Crumpet. Nat R 18:365-7 Ap 19 '66

Territorial expansion
Rock that does not roll to Franco's beat; Gibraltar. R. W. Howe. New Repub 156:16-17 Ja 21 '67

SPAIN and the United States
Case of the missing H-bomb; Palomares search. R. Oulahan. il Life 60:106A-106B F 25 '66

SPALDING, John Lancaster
Life of John Lancaster Spalding, by D. F. Sweeney. Review
America 114:265 F 19 '66. F. X. Curran

SPALDING, Joseph A.
Americans not everybody knows. PTA Mag 60:11-13 Je '66

SPANDAU prison. See Prisons—Germany

SPANG, Joseph Peter, 3d
Wells-Thorn house in Deerfield, Massachusetts. Antiques 89:730-3 My '66

SPANGLER, Raymond
Open court & fair press. Nation 202:421-4 Ap 11 '66

SPANIARDS
Turismo! in a little Spanish town; Alcudia, Majorca. A. S. Mehdevi. il N Y Times Mag p6-7+ Jl 24 '66

SPANIELS
Something different in dogs; Jagdterrier and Boykin spaniel. D. M. Duffey. il Outdoor Life 138:108-11 Ag '66

SPANISH. See Spaniards

SPANISH AMERICAN history. See Latin America—History

SPANISH AMERICAN poetry. See Latin American poetry

SPANISH AMERICANS in the United States. See Latin Americans in the United States

SPANISH colonies in America. See Spain—Colonies

SPANISH cookery. See Cookery, Spanish

SPANISH dancing. See Dancing, Spanish

SPANISH department stores. See Department stores

SPANISH designers. See Costume designers

SPANISH foreign legion. See Spain—Army—Foreign legion

SPANISH inquisition. See Inquisition

SPANISH-language press. See Newspapers—United States—Foreign language press

SPANISH MAIN
Early Spanish Main, by C. O. Sauer. Review Sat R 49:24-5 Jl 2 '66. J. H. Parry

SPANISH missions in California. See California—Missions

SPANISH missions in Florida. See Florida—Missions

SPANISH poetry

Translations into English
Song of the little death; tr. by R. Humphries; reprint. F. G. Lorca. Nation 203:92 Jl 25 '66

SPANISH Sahara. See Sahara Desert

SPANISH students
Revolt and repression in Spain's universities. E. Cary. Reporter 34:43-5 My 19 '66

SPANISH suit; story. See Miller, W.

SPARE parts. See Repair parts

SPARE time. See Leisure

SPARGER, Rex
TV ratings stay clean. por Bsns W p46 S 10 '66
Tripped on the riggings. il Time 88:60+ Jl 15 '66

SPARGUR, Ronn
Sonnets on the seven last words. Christian Cent 83:399 Mr 30 '66

SPARK, Muriel
Brontës as teachers. New Yorker 41:30-3 Ja 22 '66
Canaan; poem. New Yorker 42:48 Ap 16 '66
Chrysalis; poem. Ladies Home J 83:122 F '66
House of the famous poet; story. New Yorker 42:46-50 Ap 2 '66
Prime of Miss Jean Brodie; adaptation. See Allen, J. P.

SPARK plugs
Get out from behind this eight ball! M. J. Schultz. il Pop Mech 126:154-8 Ag '66
Perfect marine plug. H. B. Notrom. il Pop Mech 126:144-7+ Ag '66
Plug pointin'. J. McFarland. il Hot Rod 19:92-3 D '66
Spark plug analysis. L. Heiner. il Yachting 120:52-3+ Ag '66

SPARKMAN, John
Two men who are expected to move into top spots in Congress. por U S News 61:19 Jl 25 '66

SPARKPLUGS. See Spark plugs

SPARROW (guided missile) See Guided missiles—Launching from airplanes

SPARROWS
Chromosomal polymorphism in the white-throated sparrow, zonotrichia albicollis (gmelin) H. B. Thorneycroft. bibliog il Science 154:1571-2 D 23 '66
Entrainment of circadian rhythms by sound in passer domesticus. M. Menaker and A. Eskin. bibliog il Science 154:1579-81 D 23 '66
Nature note; English sparrow. Sci N 90:339 O 22 '66

SPARTANS industries, incorporated
Korvette gets a new driver; company to be run by Spartans. Bsns W p50 S 17 '66

SPATIAL orientation. See Orientation

SPAULDING, Jean
Universal education for four-year-olds? NEA J 55:11 N '66

SPAULDING, Robert L.
Common blocks of learning. PTA Mag 61:28-30 bibliog(p35) S '66

SPEAKING
See also
Voice

SPEAKING machines. See Reading machines

SPEARS, Harold
Spears on education; interview, ed. by W. K. Richards. por Sr Schol 88:supl+ Ap 22 '66

SPECIAL classes and special schools
Bobby joins his world; 5 million brain-damaged children can be helped; unique private school, Vanguard, Haverford, Pa. C. Mangel. il Look 30:84-6+ N 15 '66
Children in conflict; treatment at Hillcrest children's center, Washington, D.C. B. Culliton. il Sci N 90:122-3+ Ag 20 '66
Outlook for special education. W. Abraham. NEA J 55:50-1 D '66
Robert finds a friend; Teacher-Mom programs. J. N. Miller. il PTA Mag 60:4-7 Je '66; Same abr. Read Digest 89:89-93 Jl '66

Teaching the dyslexic child; new hope for non-readers; McGlannan school method. C. Ellingson and J. Cass. il Sat R 49:82-5+ Ap 16 '66
See also
Slow learning children—Education

SPECIAL collections in libraries. See Libraries—Special collections

SPECIAL committee of twenty-four on colonialism. See United Nations—Special committee on the situation with regard to implementation of declaration on granting of independence to colonial countries and peoples

SPECIAL days, weeks and months
Coming events. Parks & Rec 1:11, 135, 209 Ja-Mr '66
How the Swedes celebrate the longest day; midsummer. il Sunset 136:158-60 Je '66
We honor our teachers; Teacher recognition day. N. A. Rockefeller. Parents Mag 41:38 My '66
See also names of special days, weeks, and months, e.g. National library week

SPECIAL forces of the United States army. See United States—Army—Special forces

SPECIAL libraries. See Libraries, Special

SPECIAL libraries association
Ad and promotion standards set by ABPC-SLA committee. Pub W 190:198 Jl 11 '66
Redundancy and feedback; report of convention. J. Berry. il Library J 91:3346-54 Jl '66
Russian library delegation on U.S. study tour. Pub W 189:74 Ja 31 '66
SLA awards. Library J 91:3374 Jl '66
SLA receives $80,530 NSF grant to index scientific translations. Library J 91:3374 Jl '66

SPECIALISTS
Foreign aid and the brain drain; drain of foreign specialists to fill important jobs in the U.S. J. A. Perkins. For Affairs 44:608-19 Jl '66

SPECIALIZATION in agriculture. See Farm management

SPECIALIZATION in medicine
Specialization keeps medicine up-to-date. Todays Health 44:88 O '66

SPECIATION. See Species

SPECIES
Polyteny; a source of cryptic speciation among copepods. I. A. McLaren and others. bibliog il Science 153:1641-2 S 30 '66
Speciation in flowering plants. H. Lewis. bibliog Science 152:167-72 Ap 8 '66

SPECIFIC gravity
Where do sunken ships go? I. Asimov. il Sci Digest 61:87-8 Ja '67

SPECIFIC pathogen-free program. See Swine—Diseases and pests

SPECIFICATIONS
See also subhead Specifications under various subjects, e.g. Automobiles—Specifications

SPECIMENS, Anatomical. See Anatomical specimens

SPECK, Richard
Confrontation. il por Newsweek 68:26 Ag 1 '66
Headlines and checkbooks. il Newsweek 68:76 Ag 1 '66
Man who liked liquor, woman and knives. il por Life 61:24 Jl 29 '66
One by one. por Time 88:21 Jl 22 '66
Speck: handled with care. Life 61:4 Jl 29 '66
They are all dead! il por Newsweek 68:20 Jl 25 '66
Twenty-four years to page one. il Time 88:15-17 Jl 29 '66

SPECTACLES. See Eyeglasses

SPECTER, Arlen
Overwhelming evidence Oswald was assassin; interview. por U S News 61:48-50+ O 10 '66

about
Confusion compounded. Nat R 18:1032-3 O 18 '66

SPECTOR, Calvin, and Phinney, B. O.
Gibberellin production; genetic control in the fungus gibberella fujikuroi. bibliog Science 153:1397-8 S 16 '66

SPECTOR, Minnette B.
Cultural arts in recreation. Parks & Rec 1:230-2 Mr '66

SPECTOR, Robert Donald
Other voices, other rhythms. Sat R 49:42-4 F 19 '66

SPECTOR, Stanley, and Moore, J. H.
China conference; the dragon; myths and realities. Nation 202:256-60 Mr 7 '66

SPECTROGRAPH
Amateur scientist; making of an inexpensive diffraction-grating spectrograph. S. Epstein. il Sci Am 215:277-8+ S '66

SPECTROPHOTOMETERS
Recording microfluorospectrophotometer. W. J. Runge. bibliog il Science 151:1499-506 Mr 25 '66

SPECTROSCOPY. See Spectrum analysis

SPECTRUM
Absorption spectra
See Absorption spectra

Fluorescence spectra
Recording microfluorospectrophotometer. W. J. Runge. bibliog il Science 151:1499-506 Mr 25 '66

SPECTRUM, Infrared
Infrared spectra from fine particulate surfaces. J. R. Aronson and others. bibliog il Science 152:345-6 Ap 15 '66

SPECTRUM, Solar
Silicon absorption effects in the solar ultra-violet. il Sky & Tel 31:208 Ap '66
Spectral distribution of solar radiation at the earth's surface. D. M. Gates. bibliog il Science 151:523-9 F 4 '66

SPECTRUM analysis
Application of high-resolution semiconductor detectors in X-ray emission spectrography. H. R. Bowman and others. bibliog il Science 151:562-8 F 4 '66; Reply with rejoinder. T. Hall. 153:320-1 Jl 15 '66
Frequency or wavelength? letter. G. Wald; discussion. Science 151:400+ Ja 28 '66
High-speed, time-resolved spectrum of a lightning stroke. R. E. Orville. bibliog il Science 151:451 Ja 28 '66
Semiconductor revolution in nuclear radiation counting. J. M. Hollander and I. Perlman. bibliog il Science 154:84-93 O 7 '66
System aids RF spectrum surveillance; identifying and analyzing unknown electromagnetic signals. il Aviation W 86:61+ Ja 9 '67
See also
Absorption spectra
Stars—Spectra

SPECULATION
How big is the binge on Wall Street? stock market's speculative action. il Bsns W p 122+ Ap 30 '66
Wall Street: Aunt Jane's high flyers. il Newsweek 67:83 My 2 '66
See also
Arbitrage
Hedging
Investments
Investments, Foreign
Stock exchange

SPEECH
Body dances to speech. P. McBroom. Sci N 89:483 Je 18 '66
Speech and development. Sci N 90:392 N 12 '66
See also
Conversation

Study and teaching
See Speech education

SPEECH, Freedom of. See Free speech

SPEECH education
Speech is English too; Portland, Ore. public schools. M. Zollinger. Sr Schol 89:sup52 S 23 '66

SPEECH research
Feedback of speech muscle activity during silent reading; rapid extinction. C. D. Hardyck and others. il Science 154:1467-8 D 16 '66
Speech duration effects in the Kennedy news conferences. M. L. Ray and E. J. Webb. bibliog il Science 153:899-901 Ag 19 '66

SPEECH therapy
Acquisition of imitative speech by schizophrenic children. O. I. Lovaas and others. bibliog il Science 151:705-7 F 11 '66
Disturbed mute children can learn to speak. Sci N L 89:151 Mr 5 '66

SPEECHES, addresses, etc.
See also
Baccalaureate addresses

SPEED
See also
Automobiles—Speed

SPEED boats. See Motor boats

SPEED indicators
See also
Accelerometers
Tachometers

SPEED of birds. See Birds—Flight

SPEED of light. See Light—Velocity

SPEED reading
Feedback of speech muscle activity during silent reading; rapid extinction. C. D. Hardyck and others. il Science 154:1467-8 D 16 '66

Anecdotes, facetiae, satire, etc.
Notes (faster) on the way (faster) to a lemon squash (faster) D. H. Myers. Esquire 66:50 Ag '66

SPEED ways. See Speedways

SPEEDWAYS
Inji goes to Fuji for speed and art. J. Schecter. il Sports Illus 25:38-9 O 17 '66
Place to run in the sun! Stardust international raceway. J. Ethridge. il Motor T 18:20+ Ag '66
Salt in a pinch; Bonneville race course. J. McFarland. il Hot Rod 19:62-4+ S '66

SPEIDEL, David H. and Nafziger, R. H.
Retrograde melting in the system Mg-Fe-Si-O. bibliog Science 152:1367-8 Je 3 '66

SPEISER, Jean
Unseen world of Kentucky's Mammoth cave. Nat Parks Mag 40:4-9 F '66

SPELEOLOGY. See Caves

SPELLING
Spelling the words they need today. K. Larson and J. Swan. NEA J 55:51-2 F '66

SPELLMAN, C. L.
Psycho-social retardation in education. Sch & Soc 94:101-2 F 19 '66

SPELLMAN, Francis Joseph, cardinal
Fatima's 50th; the day the sun danced. Sat R 50:70+ Ja 7 '67

about
Cardinal, Pope and war. Commonweal 85:391-2 Ja 13 '67
Cardinal Spellman, Charles Davis. J. M. Cameron. Commonweal 85:417-18 Ja 20 '67
Cardinal Spellman's holy war. Christian Cent 84:36 Ja 11 '67
Cardinal under fire: Spellman's views irk reds. por U S News 62:14 Ja 9 '67
Cardinal's mistake. Nation 204:69 Ja 16 '67
New Yorkers hail their Cardinal. America 114:762 My 28 '66
News and views. J. Leo. Commonweal 85:4 O 7 '66
Spellman of New York; 50th anniversary of ordination. il por Newsweek 67:61-2 My 30 '66

SPENCER, Elizabeth
Absence; story. New Yorker 42:53-4 S 10 '66
Pincian gate; story. New Yorker 42:50-2 Ap 16 '66
Those Bufords; story. McCalls 94:76-7 Ja '67

SPENCER, Eric W. and others
Electrophoresis; an accident and some precautions. Science 152:1722-3 Je 24 '66

SPENCER, Frederick Randolph
Little-noted aspect of Spencer's art. L. B. Goodrich. il por Antiques 90:361-3 S '66

SPENCER, Herbert R. Jr
Open-window theory of executive conferences. Duns R 88:34-5 O '66

SPENCER, Lyle M.
New social-industrial complex; address, July 13, 1966. Vital Speeches 32:721-5 S 15 '66

SPENCER, Niles
Art galleries; exhibition at the Whitney museum. R. M. Coates. New Yorker 42:93+ Mr 5 '66

SPENCER, Samuel
Interstate practice; legal and accounting problems. Arch Rec 140:104-5+ N '66

SPENCER, Shirley. See Constella

SPENCER, Steven M.
Crib deaths; search for a mystery killer. Sat Eve Post 239:78-80+ N 19 '66
Pill that helps you remember. Sat Eve Post 239:64-6+ S 24 '66

SPENCER gifts, incorporated. See Mail order business

SPENDER, Stephen
Age of overwrite and underthink. Sat R 49:21-3+ Mr 12 '66
On English and American poetry. Sat R 49:19-20+ Ap 23 '66
Roethke: the lost son. New Repub 155:23-5 Ag 27 '66
Warnings from the grave. New Repub 154:23+ Je 18 '66

SPENGLER, Oswald
False prophet of the blond beast. F. Schoenberner. por Sat R 49:32-3 Mr 19 '66
Whose decline? W. S. Schlamm. Nat R 18:427-8+ My 3 '66

SPENO, Edward J.
New York car: design for survival. W. D. Gardner. il Nation 202:489-92 Ap 25 '66

SPERACIO, Mario
Easter again; poem. Good H 162:272 Ap '66
SPERBER, Ann
Berg sans context. Am Rec G 32:901-3 My '66
SPERM. See Semen
SPERM banks. See Semen
SPERMATOZOA
Comparative mutagenicity of two chemo-sterilants, tepa and hempa, in sperm of bracon hebetor. J. Palmquist and L. E. LaChance. bibliog il Science 154:915-17 N 18 '66
Substructure of certain cytoplasmic micro-tubules: an electron microscopic study. P. R. Burton. bibliog il Science 154:903-5 N 18 '66
SPERRY, Roger W.
Mind, brain, and humanist values. Bul Atomic Sci 22:2-6 S '66
SPERRY and Hutchinson company
How green their stamps; prospectus filed for first public sale of stock. Newsweek 67:89 Ap 11 '66
Lifting the veil on S&H; sell 10 per cent of holdings. Bsns W p 112+ Ap 2 '66
What's big and green and hard to classify? Fortune 74:286 Jl 15 '66
SPERRY attitude gyro. See Gyroscope
SPERRY autopilots. See Automatic pilot (air-planes)
SPERRY gyroscope company
Laser unit challenges conventional gyros. P. J. Klass. il Aviation W 85:103+ S 12 '66
SPERRY Rand corporation
At Sperry Rand a conglomerate finally works to one purpose; headed in happier profit direction. il Bsns W p 180-2+ Mr 19 '66
See also
Sperry gyroscope company
SPESSIVTZEVA, Olga
Sleeping ballerina, by A. Dolin. Review
Dance Mag 40:28+ N '66. J. Anderson
SPETZ, Marseille
Allergies: ecological approach. Science 153: 903 Ag 19 '66
SPHERES
Turning a surface inside out. A. Phillips. il Sci Am 214:112-20 bibliog(p 148) My '66
SPICE cake. See Cake
SPICE racks
Two ways to add spice to your life. il Pop Mech 127:162-5 Ja '67
SPICER, Jack
Words are . . . not mocked. G. Sorrentino. Poetry 108:134-5 My '66
SPIDER webs
Evolution of the web. B. J. Kaston. il Natur Hist 75:26-33 Ap '66
SPIDERS
Courtship in spiders without prior sperm induction. J. S. Rovner. bibliog il Science 152:543-4 Ap 22 '66
Nature note; friendly spiders. Sci N L 89:159 Mr 5 '66
Nature note: wolf spider. Sci N 89:174 Mr 12 '66
SPIEGEL, Melvin, and Tyler, Albert
Protein synthesis in micromeres of the sea urchin egg. bibliog Science 151:1233-4 Mr 11 '66
SPIEGELMAN, S. See Pace, N. R. jt. auth.
SPIELMAN, Andrew, and Williams, C. M.
Lethal effects of synthetic juvenile hormone on larvae of the yellow fever mosquito, aedes aegypti. bibliog Science 154:1043-4 N 25 '66
SPIES
Annals of espionage; Wennerström case. T. Whiteside. New Yorker 42:58-60+ Mr 26: 51-2 Ap 2; 92+ Ap 9 '66
Faceless ones; arrest of H. Boeckenhaupt. Time 88:33 N 11 '66
In the cold war, new charges of spying. il U S News 61:12 Jl 25 '66
Never forget! arrest in Prague of V. Kazan-Komarek. Newsweek 68:52+ N 28 '66
Penkovskiy papers, by O. Penkovskiy. Review
Nation 202:186-7 F 14 '66. S. L. Sharp
Red hot week for the spy business; with report and interview, ed. by S. McBee. il Life 61:20-7 Jl 22 '66
Sergeant's revenge; arrest of H. Boeckenhaupt. il Newsweek 68:37-8 N 14 '66
Way down; W. Whalen indictment. il Newsweek 68:22-3 Jl 25 '66
Way up; double agent Mrkva. Newsweek 68:23 Jl 25 '66
See also
Blake, G.
Espionage
Rosenberg, Julius and Ethel, case
Sorge, R.
Wennerström, S.

Caricatures and cartoons
From Weehawken with love. D. Newman and R. Benton. Esquire 65:86-7 My '66
SPIES, Industrial
Auto safety: Nader vs. General motors E. Langer. Science 152:47-50 Ap 1 '66
Ferreting out the spies in business; Senate subcommittee investigation of industrial espionage. il Bsns W p51 Ap 2 '66
Hunting industry spies; electronic protection devices. il Bsns W p42-3 O 1 '66
SPIES in literature
Book review of a very limited edition. M. Muggeridge. il Esquire 65:94+ My '66
007: the gentleman in decline. B. Cook. Cath World 203:169-74 Je '66
How James Bond destroyed my husband; interview, ed. by L. Hannon. A. G. C. Fleming. il Ladies Home J 83:158+ O '66
Rough rise of a dream hero. J. Pearson. il Life 61:112-14+ O 14 '66
Who is the real James Bond anyhow? J. Hamilton. il Look 30:50-4+ N 15 '66
SPIESMAN, Mildred C.
(comp) Dance magazine's 1966 directory of dance in colleges and universities. Dance Mag 40:43-6 F '66
SPIKE, Robert W.
Churchman and civil rights leader murdered. Christian Cent 83:1330 N 2 '66
SPIKER, LaRue
Blanket over homicide. Nation 202:483-6 Ap 25 '66
SPILHAUS, Athelstan
Concept of a sea-grant university; address, October 28, 1965. Vital Speeches 32:212-16 Ja 15 '66
Resourceful waste management; address, June 7, 1966. Sci N 89:486-8+ Je 18 '66
SPILLER, Robert E.
American studies abroad: culture and foreign policy; address; with questions and answers. bibliog f Ann Am Acad 366:1-16 Jl '66
Standards for setting standards. Sat R 49: 28-9+ Je 25 '66
SPINA bifida. See Spine—Abnormities and deformities
SPINACH
See also
Cookery—Vegetables
SPINAL cord
Ascending and descending cholinergic fibers in cat spinal cord: histochemical evidence. D. G. Gwyn and J. H. Wolstencroft. bibliog il Science 153:1543-4 S 23 '66
Electron microscopy: two major synaptic types on spinal motoneurons. D. Bodian. bibliog il Science 151:1093-4 Mr 4 '66
Noradrenaline and inhibition of Renshaw cells. T. J. Biscoe and D. R. Curtis. bibliog il Science 151:1230-1 Mr 11 '66
Sympathetic outflows from cervical spinal cord in the dog. G. G. Wiesman and others. bibliog il Science 152:381-2 Ap 15 '66
Surgery
New surgery substitute relieves obstinate pain; percutaneous chordotomy. Sci N 89: 395 My 21 '66
SPINAL fluid. See Cerebrospinal fluid
SPINAL meningitis. See Meningitis
SPINARD, Bernard I.
Why not national laboratories? Bul Atomic Sci 22:20-3 Ap '66
SPINDEL, Bernard Bates
On an assignment with the age of the bugging business. J. Neary. il pors Life 60:44-7 My 20 '66
SPINDLE fibers. See Plant cells and tissues
SPINDLE mitosis. See Cell division (biology)
SPINE
Abnormities and deformities
Donna Dill's victory; victim of spina bifida. D. C. Davis. il Todays Health 45:26-7+ Ja '67
SPINELLI, D. N.
Visual receptive fields in the cat's retina: complications. bibliog Science 152:1768-9; 154:921 Je 24, N 18 '66
SPINELLO, Matt P.
On the citizens band. See issues of Popular electronics
SPINGARN, Lawrence P.
Philatelic lessons: the German collection; poem. New Yorker 42:58 S 10 '66
SPINNAKERS. See Sails
SPINNING
How to work a spinning wheel. A. W. Lees. il Pop Mech 125:182-3+ Mr '66

SPINNING reels. See Fishing tackle

SPINNING tackle. See Fishing tackle

SPINNING wheels
Doctor of spinning wheels. W. Waltner and E. Waltner. il Pop Mech 125:110-12 Mr '66
How to work a spinning wheel. A. W. Lees. il Pop Mech 125:182-3+ Mr '66
Reproduce this prized antique on your lathe; ed. by A. W. Lees. E. R. Haan. il Pop Mech 125:176-81+ Mr '66

SPINRAD, Bernard I.
In the name of science. Bul Atomic Sci 22: 22-3 N '66

SPINSTERS. See Single women

SPIRAL press. See Printing—Private presses

SPIRDUSO, Don
Trim little tale. U S Camera 29:36 Ag '66

SPIRIT, Holy. See Holy Spirit

SPIRITS. See Ghosts

SPIRITUAL life
See also
Religion
Retreats, Spiritual

SPIRITUAL retreats. See Retreats, Spiritual

SPIRO, Herbert J.
Foreign policy and political style. Ann Am Acad 366:139-48 Jl '66

SPITTLE insects. See Froghoppers

SPITZER, Edward
Snorkel that goes on loan. Am City 81:117 Ap '66

SPITZER, Robert R.
Big Republican opportunity; address, March 20, 1966. Vital Speeches 32:472-7 My 15 '66

SPITZER, Silas
Coastal seafood. Holiday 40:70-3+ Jl '66

SPITZNAGEL, J. K. See Zeya, H. I. jt. auth.

SPIVACK, Kathleen
Mythmaking; poem. Poetry 109:163-4 D '66
Nerved up; poem. Atlan 218:75 Ag '66

SPLEEN
Erythrocyte chimerism after injection of spleen cells into anemic mice of the W-series. M. J. Seller. bibliog il Science 155: 90-1 Ja 6 '67

SPLEEN cells. See Cells

SPLICES. See Knots and splices

SPOCK, Benjamin
[Monthly column] See issues of Redbook
about
Not the Dr Spock! R. K. Massie. il pors Sat Eve Post 239:80-2+ My 7 '66

SPODE pottery. See Pottery, English

SPOHNHOLZ, Conrad
Explorations in the apolitical. C. Eshleman. Nation 203:285-7 S 26 '66

SPOILING of children. See Children—Management and training

SPOKANE, Wash.
Water supply
Like a lighted fountain. G. A. Yake. il Am City 81:147-8+ Ag '66

SPOKEN phonograph records. See Phonograph records—Spoken records

SPOLETO festival. See Festivals—Italy

SPONGES
Sponge: effect on the form of reef corals. T. F. Goreau. bibliog il Science 151:343-4 Ja 21 '66

SPONSORS, Advertising. See Television advertising

SPONZILLI, Sue
In my opinion. por Seventeen 25:246 N '66

SPOON (fishing lure) See Fishing lures, flies, etc.

SPOONFUL of nothing; story. See Toperoff, S.

SPOONS
Apostle spoons. M. Alves. il Hobbies 71:116 N '66
Stirring up the past; Apostle spoons. il Time 89:76+ Ja 6 '67

SPOOR, R. P. and Jackson, D. B.
Circadian rhythms: variation in sensitivity of isolated rat atria to acetylcholine. bibliog Science 154:782 N 11 '66

SPORES (botany)
Alkanes in fungal spores. J. Oró and others. bibliog il Science 154:399-400 O 21 '66

SPORN, Michael B. and others
Aflatoxin B₁: binding of DNA in vitro and alteration of RNA metabolism in vivo. bibliog Science 151:1539-41 Mr 25 '66

SPORT buses. See Station wagons

SPORT fisheries and wildlife, Bureau of. See United States—Fish and wildlife service

SPORTING goods
What's new. See issues of Outdoor life
See also
Abercrombie and Fitch company
Hunting outfits
Exhibitions
Coliseum hour: Sport and camping show. New Yorker 42:44-5 Mr 12 '66

SPORTS
Life-saving sports; study of former students health status. Sci Digest 60:23 S '66
SR/1967 world travel calendar. T. L. Christie. Sat R 50:77-82 Ja 7 '67
Southern cruising almanac; Florida and Bahamas events. il Motor B 118:22-5 O '66
See also
Physical education and training
Radio broadcasting—Sports
School athletics
Sports journalism
Television broadcasting—Sports
also names of sports, e.g. Tennis

Accidents and injuries
Little league shoulder bothers young pitchers. Sci N 90:105 Ag 13 '66
See also
Baseball—Accidents and injuries
Football—Accidents and injuries

Bibliography
Abercrombie & Fitch enters book publishing; facsimiles and reprints of classics in the field of sports and adventure. Pub W 189: 96-7 Je 13 '66

International aspects
Stop the world, the U.S. is on; major international sports. D. Jenkins. il Sports Illus 24:26-9 My 2 '66

Psychological aspects
Why people play football. F. R. Schreiber and M. Herman. il Sci Digest 60:12-16 S '66

Records
See Sports records

Africa
Africa: sport in the emerging nations. il Sports Illus 25:56-77 D 19 '66

Asia
See also
Asiad (games)

Brazil
See also
Soccer

Canada
See also
Hockey

Caribbean Region
Sportsman's tip sheet on the West Indies. R. Joseph. il Esquire 67:120-3+ Ja '67
Travel notes. R. Joseph. il Esquire 67:8+ Ja '67

China (People's Republic)
Half-time show in the China bowl; Second national games. il Life 60:72-4+ Mr 11 '66

England
See also
Soccer

Kenya
Everyone's keen on Keino. C. E. Brown. il Ebony 21:100-2+ My '66
Very welcome redcoat; J. Velzian, British coach of the Kenya national track team. M. Kane. il Sports Illus 25:78-82 D 19 '66

Mexico
Great Mexican war of 1946; Mexican league baseball. F. Graham, jr. il Sports Illus 25: 116-20+ S 19 '66
See also
Bullfights

Russia
Poet against the destroyers. Y. Yevtushenko. il Sports Illus 25:104-8+ D 19 '66

United States
For the record. See issues of Sports illustrated
Sports. See issues of Newsweek
Sports. H. L. Masin. See issues of Senior scholastic

SPORTS car club of America. See Automobile clubs

SPORTS car racing. See Automobile racing

SPORTS cars
Cars a la carte. il Motor T 18:74+ S '66
Cool cars for young and young at heart. il
Ebony 22:96-9 Ja '67
Cord 8/10 drivescription. J. Ethridge. il
Motor T 18:70-2 Jl '66
Rally 'round the roadsters. J. McFarland.
il Hot Rod 19:30-3 D '66
Sports car camping. R. Barlow. il Field & S
70·53-5 F '66
Sports cars of the world. J. P. Norbye. il Pop
Sci 189:46-53 Ag '66
Street roadsters. B. Lang. il Hot Rod 19:
34-8+ D '66
  See also
Automobiles, Racing

Testing
Star among fast friends: photographs by
James Drake; with account by S. Mc-
Queen, ed. by K. Rudeen. Sports Illus 25:
34-42 Ag 8 '66
Super street Chevelle. E. Dahlquist. il Hot
Rod 19:30-3+ F '66
SPORTS cars, Foreign. See Automobiles, For-
eign
SPORTS columns. See Newspapers—Sections,
columns, etc.
SPORTS equipment. See Sporting goods
SPORTS fans
England's posh house of pow; photographs by
J. Alexander and J. Cooke; account by J.
Lovesey. il Sports Illus 25:40-5 O 31 '66
Enjoy, enjoy! how to watch a football game.
H. L. Masin. Sr Schol 89:31 O 28 '66
Four-legged halfbacks and friendly wolves;
the Kansas City Chiefs and fans. E.
Shrake. il Sports Illus 25:74+ N 28 '66
Texas football: fierce, frantic, fabulous. M.
Cope. il Sat Eve Post 239:83-7 S 24 '66
SPORTS for the handicapped
Amputees on skis; Amputee slalom race,
Mount Hood, Ore. E. H. Matthew. il To-
days Health 45:12-13 Ja '67
SPORTS illustrated (periodical)
Sportsman of the year. il Sports Illus 25:46-
50+ D 19 '66
SPORTS illustrated silver anniversary All-
America
Never to be the same; 1966 Silver anniversary
All-America team. R. Cantwell. il Sports
Illus 25:88-90+ D 19 '66
SPORTS journalism
Letter from the publisher; requirements for
reporters of Sports illustrated. G. Valk.
Sports Illus 25:4 N 7 '66
Lots of fun with a poison pen. F. Deford.
il Sports Illus 25:56-8 O 3 '66
SPORTS officiating
  See also
Baseball—Organization and administration

Anecdotes, facetiae, satire. etc.
Untroubled sport for those who play VAAGG;
Van Alen's answer to grief in golf. J. Van
Alen. il Sports Illus 25:48-50+ N 28 '66
SPORTS promoting. See Promoters and pro-
moting
SPORTS records
Hit records: baseball. H. L. Masin. il Sr
Schol 88:32-3 My 20 '66
Hockey's biggest moment: no. 51; B. Hull of
Black Hawks broke the record. M. Kane. il
Sports Illus 24:26-9 Mr 21 '66
Onward and upwards: track. H. L. Masin. il
Sr Schol 88:34 My 6 '66
Why all the new records in sports? V. Block.
il Todays Health 44:22-5+ S '66
SPORTS shelters. See Shelters
SPORTSMANS park, St Louis. See Stadiums
SPORTSMANSHIP
International trophies for sportsmanship; sec-
ond annual International fair play trophies.
il UNESCO Courier 19:30-1 Je '66
SPORTSMEN
Awakening giant; sportsmen's part in politics.
T. Trueblood. il Field & S 71:26-7+ O '66
  See also
Hunters
SPORTSWOMEN. See Women as athletes
SPOT meters. See Exposure meters
SPOT welding. See Electric welding
SPOTLIGHTS
Homemade spot puts glamour in your pic-
tures. P. C. Yob. il Pop Mech 126:188-9+
N '66
SPOTONE retouching colors. See Photography—
Apparatus and supplies
SPOTSWOOD, Alexander
Knights of the golden horseshoe. H. D.
Crawford. il por Am For 72:28-31+ N '66

SPRAGUE, Clifton Albert Frederic
Battle off Samar. W. P. Deac. il por Am
Heritage 18:20-3+ D '66
SPRAGUE, James M.
Interaction of cortex and superior colliculus
in mediation of visually guided behavior in
the cat. bibliog Science 153:1544-7 S 23 '66
SPRAGUE, Rosemary
Biography: the other face of the coin. Horn
Bk 42:282-9 Je '66
SPRAGUE electric company
Sprague intensifies microcircuit efforts. P. J.
Klass. il Aviation W 84:95+ Mr 28 '66
SPRAY, Sally
Help me, I'm alone. B. Davidson. il por Sat
Eve Post 239:74-5 S 10 '66
SPRAY guns. See Spraying apparatus
SPRAY-on starch. See Starch (for clothes)
SPRAY painting. See Paint spraying
SPRAY-steam irons, Electric. See Electric irons
SPRAYING and dusting
Spraying or dusting? L. Pyenson. Horticul-
ture 44:38-9 Ap '66
  See also
Fungicides

Safety devices and measures
What to spray at, and what to spray with.
Sunset 136:234 Je '66
SPRAYING apparatus
Garden sprayers. Consumer Rep 31:195-200
D '66
Garden sprayers. il Consumer Rep 31:334-9
Jl '66
Hot-glue gun with lukewarm talents; Ther-
mogrip electric glue gun. il Consumer Rep
31:102-3 Mr '66
How to buy a paint sprayer and make it
pay. E. F. Lindsley. il Pop Sci 189:160-3
S '66
New ways to kill more weeds. il Farm J 90:
38-41 Ap '66
Sprayers for the home gardener. il Consumer
Bul 49:10-11 Ag '66
Stick 'em up! Thermogrip glue gun. il Pop
Mech 125:189 F '66
Which garden sprayer should you choose?
W. L. Meachem. il Pop Sci 189:84-6 Jl '66
  See also
Aerosols
SPREKELIA formosissima. See Jacobean lilies
SPRING, Bernard P.
Truth is in building, not talk. Arch Forum
124:74-80 Ap '66
SPRING
Changing face of spring. B. Tufty. il Sci N
89:170-1+ Mr 12 '66
Letter from... S. Delaplane. il Todays Health
44:11 Mr '66

Drama
Ode to spring. M. Hark and N. McQueen.
Plays 25:41-54 My '66
SPRING menus. See Menus
SPRINGBOKS. See Springbucks
SPRINGBUCKS
Springbok. R. C. Bigalke. il Natur Hist 75:
20-5 Je '66
SPRINGER, Axel
I've got a sixth sense. Newsweek 67:98+
Ap 11 '66
West Germany's publishing powerhouse. J.
Tebbel. Sat R 50:126-6 Ja 14 '67
SPRINGER, C. H.
Systems approach. Sat R 50:56+ Ja 14 '67
SPRINGER-verlag, West Germany. See Pub-
lishers and publishing—Germany (Federal
Republic)
SPRINGFIELD, Mass.

Newspapers
Victory in Springfield; publisher S. New-
house. Time 87:49 Ap 8 '66
SPRINGFIELD, Ohio

Parks and playgrounds
Hurry-up leaf pick-up. R. B. Spitler. il Am
City 81:47 N '66
SPRINGFIELD, Ore.
Practice waterskiing indoors. G. R. McGuire.
il Parks & Rec 1:754-5 S '66
Put teeth into compaction. G. K. Attig and
J. Clay. il Am City 81:88-90 Mr '66

Crime
Stranger at the door; the Charles Fawbush's
ordeal. J. P. Blank. il Read Digest 89:60-6
S '66
SPRINGFIELD Junior college, Springfield, Ill.
Springfield: small and intimate; Charles E.
Becker library. M. L. Zimmerman. il Li-
brary J 91:5900-1 D 1 '66

SPRINGS
See also
Hot springs
SPRINGS (mechanism)
See also
Automobiles—Springs and suspension
SPRINGTAILS
Nature note. Sci N 89:231 Ap 2 '66
SPRINKLERS
Carefree watering with a traveling sprinkler. il Flower Grower 53:41 Jl '66
Greenest lawn for the least water. J. Hand. il Pop Sci 189:134-9 Jl '66
Sprinkler intended for odd-shaped lawns. il Consumer Rep 31:368-9 Ag '66
Underground goes the sprinkler. M. J. Dietz. il Flower Grower 53:42 My '66
Water, water everywhere you want it. J. Threlkeld. il Pop Gard 17:62-3+ Ag '66
SPRINT missiles. See Guided missiles—Defenses
SPRINTING. See Running
SPRUCE KNOB-SENECA ROCKS national recreation area, W.Va. See Recreation areas
SPRUE
Soldiers may have hidden malnutrition. Sci N 90:40 Jl 16 '66
SPRUNT, Alexander, Jr
Bird walk to Japan. Audubon Mag 68:186-7 My '66
SPUHLER, J. N.
Human population genetics. Science 153:660-1 Ag 5 '66
SPURGEON, William H. 3d
Explorer scouts; address, December 6, 1965. Vital Speeches 32:314-20 Mr 1 '66
SPURIA irises. See Irises
SPURLOCK, Virginia
Our family goes for doubles. Parents Mag 41:46-7+ My '66
SPURR, Stephen H.
Rampart Dam: a costly gamble. por Audubon Mag 68:172-5+ My '66
SPURRIER, Steve
Bulldog answer to an S.O.S. J. Underwood. il por Sports Illus 25:30-5 N 14 '66
Golden Gator; Heisman trophy winner. il por Time 88:50 D 2 '66
He's out $1,000,000. il pors Life 61:113-14 O 21 '66
Mr Quarterback. il por Newsweek 68:77-8 N 21 '66
No greater Gator. H. L. Masin. il por Sr Schol 89:20 O 7 '66
SPUTNIK (periodical) See Periodicals—Russia
SPUZICH, Sandra
Up from the basement. por Time 88:40 Jl 15 '66
SPY programs (television) See Television broadcasting—Drama
SPY stories. See Spies in literature
SPYGLASS hill golf course, Calif. See Golf courses
SPYING. See Spies
SQUAB. See Cookery—Poultry
SQUARE dancing
Park dance program; development under New York city department of parks. C. H. Starke. il Parks & Rec 1:34-5+ Ja '66
SQUARE-wave generators. See Signal generators
SQUASH (game)
Knockout of a champion; S. Vehslage. R. Lardner. il Sports Illus 24:30-2 F 7 '66
Onomatopoetic roulette; National singles championship. il Time 87:72 F 25 '66
SQUASHES
See also
Cookery—Vegetables
SQUEALER; story. See Adarkar, V.
SQUIDS
Effects of tetrodotoxin on excitability of squid giant axons in sodium-free media. A. Watanabe and others. bibliog il Science 155:95-7 Ja 6 '67
SQUIRE, David F.
Idealistic industrialist. J. Berry. il por Duns R 87:46-7+ Je '66
SQUIRE, James R.
National study of high school English programs. Sr Schol 88:sup 16-17 F 11 '66
SQUIRREL hunting
Alone with the squirrels. C. Vinson. il Outdoor Life 138:62-3+ O '66
Snow hunt for stew. G. Heinold. il Outdoor Life 138:62-4+ S '66
SQUIRREL shrews
Taxonomic status of tree shrews. C. B. G. Campbell. bibliog Science 153:436 Jl 22 '66; Reply. M. Goodman. 153:1550 S 23 '66
Tree shrews: unique reproductive mechanism of systematic importance. R. D. Martin. bibliog il Science 152:1402-4 Je 3 '66

SQUIRRELS
Chromosomal aberrations in a population of ground squirrels. C. F. Nadler and C. E. Hughes. bibliog il Science 151:579-80 F 4 '66
Receptive fields of opponent color units in the optic nerve of the ground squirrel. C. R. Michael. bibliog il Science 152:1095-7 My 20 '66
SQUIRRU, Rafael
Books. B. Lugris. il Américas 18:41 Jl '66
Happening: art or jest? Américas 18:26-33 Je '66
STAATS, Elmer B.
Where government can cut spending; interview. pors Nations Bsns 54:42-3+ D '66
STABILE, Toni
Truth about magic ingredients in cosmetics; excerpt from Cosmetics: trick or treat. Todays Health 45:20-1+ Ja '67
STABILITY, Airplane. See Airplanes—Stability and stabilizers
STABILIZATION processors. See Photography —Apparatus and supplies
STABILIZERS. See Airplanes—Stability and stabilizers
STABLER, Elizabeth
French military police. bibliog f Cur Hist 50:232-7+ Ap '66
STACEY, J. W, incorporated
Stacey speeds delivery with new billing system. G. McCorkle il Pub W 189:46-9 Ap 18 '66
STACEY, Nicolas
Decline of the church in England. Harper 232:64-6+ Mr '66
STACK, John
Variable sweep vs. the fixed Delta. C. Welles. por Life 61:79+ O 28 '66
STACKHOUSE, Max L.
Guide to the ploys of some Catholics. Christian Cent 83:275-6 Mr 2 '66
STACKPOLE, Peter
35mm techniques. See issues of U.S. camera & travel
STACY, B. D. and Thorburn, G. D.
Chromium-51 ethylenediaminetetraacetate for estimation of glomerular filtration rate. bibliog Science 152:1076-7 My 20 '66
STADIUMS
Convertibility. R. Q. Praeger and J. W. Waterbury. il Am City 81:100-1 Ag '66
Gashouse full of memories; Sportsman's park in St Louis. il Sports Illus 24:28-9 My 9 '66
Simplicity produces a neat, inexpensive stadium; University of Massachusetts at Amherst. il Arch Rec 139:185-6 F '66
Sporting scene; Houston Astros in the Astrodome. R. Angell. New Yorker 42:125-6+ My 14 '66
Swardsmandship; groundskeepers and their fields. il Newsweek 67:86 Je 6 '66
University of Massachusetts. il Arch Rec 139:172-3 My '66
STAEL, Nicolas de
Art galleries; memorial exhibition at the Guggenheim museum. R. M. Coates. New Yorker 42:151-2 Mr 12 '66
Retrospective; exhibition at the Guggenheim. B. Kaufman. Commonweal 84:61-2 Ap 1 '66
STAFFORD, Ellen
Canadian justice: ordeal of Steven Truscott. Nation 202:614-17 My 23 '66
STAFFORD, Jean
Books. See issues of Vogue
Truth in fiction. por Library J 91:4557-65 O 1 '66
STAFFORD, Thomas P.
See also
Space flight—Manned flights—Stafford-Cernan flight, 1966
STAFFORD, William
At the level of love; poem. New Yorker 42:27 Ja 14 '67
Bill Watson's report from Canada; poem. Nation 202:159 F 7 '66
Farewell picture; poem. Nation 202:278 Mr 7 '66
In the airport at Denver; poem. Harper 234:37 Ja '67
Memorandum; poem. New Yorker 42:104 F 26 '66
Montana eclogue; poem. New Yorker 42:56 D 17 '66
Remembering Althea; poem. New Yorker 42:144 O 8 '66
Society column; poem. Nation 203:397 O 17 '66
Story; poem. Atlan 218:67 D '66
There yet remains what fashion cannot kill. Poetry 108:187-8 Je '66
Where we are; poem. Harper 232:83 Ap '66

STAFFORD, William—*Continued*
about
Country boy. S. Moss. New Repub 155:23-4 N 19 '66
STAFFORDSHIRE ware
Mr Knickerbocker's Staffordshire. T. M. Shepherd. il Hobbies 71:28-9+ O '66
STAG hunting. See Deer hunting
STAGE. See Theater
STAGE censorship. See Dramatic censorship
STAGE craft. See Theater—Stage scenery
STAGE lighting. See Opera—Stage lighting
STAGE photography. See Photography, Theatrical
STAGE props. See Operatic production; Theatrical production
STAGE robbers. See Brigands and robbers
STAGE scenery. See Opera—Stage scenery; Theater—Stage scenery
STAGER, R. A. See Sood, R. R. jt. auth.
STAGGERWINGS. See Airplane wings
STAINLESS steel blades. See Razor blades
STAINLESS steel tableware. See Tableware, Stainless steel
STAINPROOF textiles. See Textile fabrics—Protection
STAINS and staining
Best finishes for wood: how to use stains to get the color you want. J. Hand. il Pop Sci 189:170-6 N '66
See also
Wood finishing
STAINS and staining (biology)
Cytochemistry of synapses: selective staining for electron microscopy. F. E. Bloom and G. K. Aghajanian. bibliog il Science 154: 1575-7 D 23 '66
Marking single neurons by staining with intracellular recording microelectrodes. R. C. Thomas and V. J. Wilson. bibliog il Science 151:1538-9 Mr 25 '66
Neurofibrils and the Nauta method. R. D. Lund and L. E. Westrum. bibliog il Science 151:1397-9 Mr 18 '66
STAINS and staining (microscopy)
Staining tissue for light and electron microscopy by bridging metals with multidentate ligands. J. S. Hanker and others. bibliog il Science 152:1631-4 Je 17 '66
STAIRCASES. See Stairways
STAIRWAYS
Stairs should do more than get you up and down. il Sunset 137:113-14+ S '66
STALEY, Thomas F.
Books. Commonweal 83:645-6 Mr 4 '66
Waugh the artist. Commonweal 84:280-2 My 27 '66
STALIN, Iosif
Georgia on their minds. Time 88:38 N 11 '66
Ghost of Stalin; protests against refurbishing image. Newsweek 67:48 Mr 28 '66
Moscow congress: prudence and semantics. A. Ulam. Reporter 34:25-7 My 5 '66
Stalin at war. Newsweek 68:58 S 26 '66
STALVEY, Lois Mark
I can't ignore the boy next door. por Redbook 127:10+ S '66
Our three-story family. Read Digest 89:111-14 Ag '66
STAMFORD, Conn.
Churches
Exodus for Christ; Churches of Christ. il Time 89:66 Ja 20 '67
Housing
Stamford's attempt to integrate suburbia; scattered sites program. J. R. Wolf. il Reporter 35:20+ D 29 '66
STAMLER, Jeremiah
HUAS: Stamler's challenge draws academic support. E. Langer. Science 152:898 My 13 '66
STAMMERING
Speech: behavior of middle ear muscle during stuttering. W. M. Shearer. bibliog il Science 152:1280 My 27 '66
STAMP collecting. See Postage stamps— Collectors and collecting
STAMPS, James E.
Fifty years later. por Negro Hist Bul 29:31-2 N '65
STAMPS, Postage. See Postage stamps
STANCHIONS. See Barns and stables—Equipment
STANDARD airways, incorporated
Standard airways adds to jet fleet. **Aviation W** 85:52 D 19 '66

STANDARD and Poors corporation
Justice dept. ok's merger of McGraw-Hill and S&P. Pub W 189:53 Mr 7 '66
STANDARD of living
U.S. population stops exploding; with editorial comment. il Bsns W p 19-21, 96 Jl 2 '66
See also
Poverty
Purchasing power
STANDARD oil company (New Jersey)
Jersey Standard goes West again; refinery to be on site of historic Benicia arsenal, California. il Bsns W p 110-12+ O 1 '66
Jersey's board opens door to outsiders. il Bsns W p34+ F 12 '66
Statesman in the boardroom; E. Collado, Jersey Standard's executive vice-president. il Bsns W p 186-7+ N 26 '66
STANDARD oil company (Ohio)
Plan that put fire into Sohio's profits. il Bsns W p 106-7+ F 12 '66
STANDARD periodical directory
Supplementary story: letter. Z. F. Smith. Library J 91:3016+ Je 15 '66; Discussion. 91:4010+ S 15 '66
STANDARD time. See Time—Systems and standards
STANDARDS (ethics) See Ethics
STANDARDS, Library. See Libraries—Standards; School libraries—Standards
STANDARDS, National bureau of. See United States—Standards, National bureau of
STANDARDS in education. See Education—Standards
STANDARDS of living
See also
Cost of living
STANDEES, Opera. See Audiences
STANDING congressional committees. See United States—Congress—Committees
STANFIELD, James L.
Portfolio: James Stanfield. Pop Phot 58:72-7+ Je '66
STANFORD, Henry King
University and anti-Communist pressure. Sch & Soc 94:123-5 Mr 5 '66
STANFORD-Binet tests. See Intelligence tests
STANFORD research institute
Perils of running a nonprofit. S. Klaw. il Fortune 74:158-61+ N '66
Real causes and cures of auto accidents. il U S News 60:44-6 My 23 '66
STANFORD university, Stanford, Calif.
Drinking approved at Stanford. Sch & Soc 94:340-2 O 29 '66
Faith & learning at Stanford. il Time 88:100 N 25 '66
Good theater of Stanford. H. Hewes. Sat R 49:55 Je 4 '66
Rebel president; David Harris's campaign. Nation 202:573 My 16 '66
Stanford's Niemans; Professional journalism fellowships program. Newsweek 67:72 F 7 '66
Superhighway for electrons; Stanford's linear accelerator. il Time 88:74 Jl 22 '66
Twentieth century music and art, at Stanford; third annual Summer festival of the arts. il Sunset 136:69-70 Je '66
STANFORD university summer festival of the arts. See Music festivals—California
STANIFORTH, Maxwell
(tr) Aurelius, M. Reflections of a lonely ruler
STANISLAUS national forest, Calif. See National forests
STANKY, Eddie
The Brat and The Lip. J. Lake. il por Newsweek 67:72-3 Ap 4 '66
Two headliners take over Chicago. W. Leggett. il pors Sports Illus 24:26-8+ F 28 '66
STANLEY, David
Bible: new translations, new editions and commentaries. America 115:747-54 D 3 '66
Catholic professors on the secular campus. por America 115:322 S 24 '66
STANLEY, Wendell M.
Entertainer, two researchers honored by AMA. por Todays Health 44:17 Ag '66
STANLEY cup. See Hockey
STANLEY works (firm)
Stanley tries the faster track; program of acquisitions, borrowing and even TV advertising. il Bsns W p84-7 N 5 '66
STANNARD, Frank
Where time runs backward. Time 88:57-8 S 9 '66
STANS, Maurice
How honest is the U.S. budget? interview pors U S News 62:66-70 Ja 16 '67
STANSLY, Philip G. and Schlop, P. E.
Virus-induced murine leukemia: its inhibition and suppression by serum containing erythropoietin. bibliog Science 152:1082-3 My 20 '66

STANTON, Edward S.
  Religion (cont) America 114:662-3+; 115: 710-13 My 7, N 26 '66
STANTON, Frank
  How it feels to live in total design. C. Welles. il por Life 60:59+ Ap 29 '66
STANTON, Ron
  Las Vegas scene. W. Como. il por Dance Mag 40:20 S '66
STANTON, Will
  Butterfinger; story. Redbook 126:78-9+ Ap '66
  Human comedy. Sat Eve Post 239:20 Jl 16 '66
  I'm having all kinds of fun; story. Redbook 127:60-1 Je '66
  Just for laughs. Look 30:130 D 13 '66
  Keep off these promises. Look 30:47 Ag 9 '66
  Only the lucky ones; story. Redbook 126:58-9 F '66
  Riotous life; story. Redbook 127:48-9 Ag '66
  Secret thoughts of a first lady. Sat Eve Post 239:16 Je 4 '66
  Watch out for the wollypops. Sat Eve Post 239:22 F 12 '66
  Wrong is what you think up by yourself. Redbook 128:56-7+ D '66
STAPHYLOCOCCI
  New hope for control of staph infections. Sci N 90:346 O 29 '66
  Staphylococcal alpha-toxin: effects on artificial lipid spherules. G. Weissmann and others. bibliog il Science 154:772-4 N 11 '66
  Unusual tent aids fight against microbes. il Todays Health 44:14 My '66
STAPLERS, Surgical. See Surgical instruments and apparatus
STAPLES, Eugene S.
  Eagles of Kazakhstan. Atlan 219:92-5 Ja '67
  Truth is winter. Reporter 34:43-5 Mr 10 '66
STAR (research vehicle) See Submarine boats
STAR charts. See Astronomy—Charts, diagrams, etc.
STAR class race. See Sailboat racing
STAR clusters. See Stars—Clusters
STAR measurements. See Astronomical measurements
STAR of Bethlehem
  Christmas sky. F. M. Branley. il Redbook 128:45+ D '66
STAR spangled banner (song)
  Case for a new national anthem. R. B. Fisher. il Sat R 49:45-6+ Je 25 '66; Discussion. 49:57+ Jl 30 '66
  O, long may it wave! P. W. Schmidtchen. Hobbies 70:106+ F '66
STAR-spangled girl; drama. See Simon. N.
STARBUCK, George
  Extravaganza; poem. New Yorker 42:36 Jl 30 '66
  Poem issued by me to congressmen; Of late; poems. Poetry 109:30-9 O '66
  Two poems; Ballade of the golden rule; Beauty. Yale R 55:550-1 Je '66
  Well-trained English critic surveys the American scene; poem. Atlan 217:91 Je '66
STARCH (for clothes)
  Fabric finish or spray starch. il Consumer Bul 49:43+ Ag '66
  Spray starch. Consumer Bul 50:25 Ja '67
  Ways to keep clothing looking like new. R. Hoefgen. il Parents Mag 41:18 O '66
STARCH-gel electrophoresis. See Electrophoresis
STARCK, Walter A. 2d
  Marvels of a coral realm. il Nat Geog Mag 130:710-38 N '66
STARDUST International raceway. See Speedways
STARER, Robert
  Compelling craftsmanship. por A. Cohn. Am Rec G 33:350+ D '66
STARFISHES
  Compound ocellus of a starfish: its function. M. Yoshida and H. Ohtsuki. bibliog il Science 153:197 Jl 8 '66
  Deadly sea beasts or lifesavers? Crown-of-thorns starfish. il Sci N 90:498 D 10 '66
  Shellfish eat starfish, save Great Barrier Reef. Sci N 90:376 N 5 '66
  Ten-rayed sea star found in Pacific. Sci N 89:477 Je 11 '66
STARGAZER; story. See Madocs, R.
STARIE, John H.
  Local associations ask about. See issues of NEA journal
STARK, Freya
  On smuggling. Holiday 40:8+ O '66
STARK, Gail D.
  Cambodia beset. Nation 202:445-9 Ap 18 '66

STARK brothers nurseries and orchards company
  It all began with an apple. il Pop Gard 17: 76-7 Ag '66
  Weathervane. R. G. Miner. Flower Grower 53:8 S '66
STARKE, Charles H.
  Park dance program. por Parks & Rec 1:34-5+ Ja '66
STARKER, Janos
  Mephisto's musings. por Hi Fi 16:124+ My '66
STARNES, Richard
  [Monthly article on outdoor life] See issues of Field & stream
STARR, Bart
  Green Bay's constant Starr. G. Astor. il pors Look 30:74-6 S 6 '66
STARR, John T.
  Cabot trail. Am For 72:34-5+ Jl '66
  Would you throw trash in your bathtub? Am For 72:4-5+ Jl '66
STARR, Ringo
  Old Beatles, a study in paradox. M. Cleave. il por N Y Times Mag p 10-11+ Jl 3 '66
STARR, Roger
  Must landmarks go? excerpts from The living end. Horizon 8:48-59 Sum '66
  On the side of the cities; excerpt from The living end. Horizon 8:66-71 Aut '66
STARS
  Astronomy. J. Stokley. See issues of Science news
  Deep-sky wonders. W. S. Houston. See issues of Sky and telescope
  Gravitational collapse and the death of a star (cont) K. S. Thorne; reply with rejoinder. W. J. Luyten. Science 153:366+ Jl 22 '66
    See also
  Astrophysics
  Constellations
  Milky way
  Occultations
  Orbits
  Planets

Atmospheres
  Stellar chromospheres. O. C. Wilson. bibliog il Science 151:1487-98 Mr 25 '66

Brightness
  See Stars—Magnitudes

Catalogs
  Complete star catalog calculated by computer. Sci N 89:297 Ap 23 '66
  Deep-sky wonders: the Messier catalogue. W. S. Houston. il Sky & Tel 31:238-40 Ap '66

Clusters
  Composite pictures of five globular clusters. E. Robson and M. Robson. il Sky & Tel 32: 46-8 Jl '66

Distance
  Hertzsprung-Russell diagram today. M. Hack. il Sky & Tel 31:260-3, 332-6 My-Je '66
  Stellar distances refined. A. Ewing. Sci N 89:387 My 21 '66

Magnitudes
  Three variable star types are visible in the October sky. T. D. Nicholson. il Natur Hist 75:44-7 O '66

Measurements
  See Astronomical measurements

Motion
  Visual binary Krüger 60. J. F. Wanner. il Sky & Tel 33:16-17 Ja '67
    See also
  Stars—Catalogs

Observations
  Stars: near and dark. A. Ewing. il Sci N 90:470 D 3 '66
  Washington 6-inch transit circle. P. D. Hemenway. il Sky & Tel 31:72-7 F '66

Radiation
  Infrared stars. H. L. Johnson. bibliog il Sky & Tel 32:73-7 Ag '66

Rotation
  Synchronization in close binaries. S. S. Huang. il Sky & Tel 31:215-17 Ap '66

Scintillation
  Measuring stellar scintillation from an aircraft. il Sky & Tel 31:345 Je '66

STARS—*Continued*

Spectra

Analysis of a unique stellar spectrum. Sky & Tel 32:71 Ag '66
Experiments in infrared spectroscopy. il Sky & Tel 32:12 Jl '66
Hertzsprung-Russell diagram today. M. Hack. il Sky & Tel 31:260-3, 332-6 My-Je '66
Identification of the X-ray source in Scorpius. H. Gursky. il Sky & Tel 32:252-5 N '66
Spectrum of 10 Lacertae. il Sky & Tel 31:337 Je '66
Spectrum of 2 Andromedae. G. S. Mumford. Sky & Tel 31:264-5 My '66

Temperature

Infrared stars; observation of very cool stars. H. L. Johnson. bibliog il Sky & Tel 32:73-7 Ag '66

STARS, Double

Diameter of Antares; red super-giant. il Sky & Tel 32:13 Jl '66
Evolution of the W Ursae Majoris binaries. G. S. Mumford. Sky & Tel 32:275 N '66
Finding the combined magnitude of a double star. R. K. Marshall. Sky & Tel 31:180 Mr '66
KO Aquilae as a fission binary. G. S. Mumford. Sky & Tel 32:198 O '66
Orientations of eclipsing binary orbits. G. S. Mumford. Sky & Tel 31:213 Ap '66
Pulkovo double stars and J. H. Madler. J. Ashbrook. Sky & Tel 31:79 F '66
Synchronization in close binaries. S. S. Huang. il Sky & Tel 31:215-17 Ap '66
Unseen companion. A. Ewing. Sci N 89:296 Ap 23 '66
Unusual binary. G. S. Mumford. Sky & Tel 31:338 Je '66
Visual binary Krüger 60. J. F. Wanner. il Sky & Tel 33:16-17 Ja '67

STARS, Dwarf

Two pygmy stars. G. S. Mumford. Sky & Tel 33:31 Ja '67

STARS, Flare. See Stars, Variable
STARS, Magnetic. See Magnetism, Stellar

STARS, Multiple

Multiple system in Draco? Sky & Tel 31:345-6 Je '66

STARS, New

Distance of Tycho's supernova. Sky & Tel 31:344 Je '66
Expansion of supernova remnants. il Sky & Tel 31:209 Ap '66
Jean Richer and a possible nova in 1673. J. Ashbrook. Sky & Tel 32:79 Ag '66
One of dimmest stars is also among twenty-five closest. Sci N L 89:117 F 19 '66
Oriental records of novae and supernovae. J. Ashbrook. il Sky & Tel 33:3+ Ja '67
Star is born; R monocerotis may be surrounded by the beginnings of planetary system. il Time 88:43 D 23 '66
200 trillion trillion H-bombs; supernovae. il Time 88:80 Ag 5 '66

History

Ancient Oriental records of novae and supernovae; excerpts from address, 1964. tr. by K. S. Yang. Z. Z. Xi and S. J. Po. bibliog il Science 154:597-603 N 4 '66

STARS, Subdwarf

Pygmy stars: first pair. F. Zwicky. bibliog il Science 153:53-4 Jl 1 '66

STARS, Variable

Ex-variable star? il Sky & Tel 31:323+ Je '66
Origin of U Geminorum stars. G. S. Mumford. Sky & Tel 31:265 My '66
Periods of RR Lyrae variable stars. V. Zessevich. il Sky & Tel 32:199-202 O '66
Star flares again; Nova Persei. Sci N 90:153 S 3 '66
Star once variable now in stable state; Cepheid variable RU Camelopardalis. Sci N 89:459 Je 11 '66
Three variable star types are visible in the October sky. T. D. Nicholson. il Natur Hist 75:44-7 O '66

STARS and stripes (newspaper)

Stars and stripes forever. il Newsweek 68:63 Jl 18 '66

STARVATION
See also
Famines

STASHINSKII, Bogdan Nikolaevich
Licensed to kill in real life. E. Lyons. il Nat R 18:259-61 Mr 22 '66

STATE, The

Bureaucracy and freedom: N. M. Korkunov's theory of the state. G. L. Yaney. bibliog f Am Hist R 71:468-86 Ja '66
See also
Church and state

STATE, Heads of. See Heads of state

STATE aid to business. See Government aid to business

STATE aid to education. See Education and state

STATE aid to libraries. See Libraries and state

STATE and art. See Art and state

STATE and church. See Church and state

STATE and education. See Education and state

STATE and federal relations. See Federal and state relations

STATE and industry. See Industry and state

STATE and libraries. See Libraries and state

STATE and municipal relations

Chance for creative federalism; L. B. Johnson's program. Life 60:4 F 11 '66
Mayor tells how to modernize America's cities. H. W. Goldner. Nations Bsns 54:108-10+ Ap '66

STATE and science. See Science and state

STATE and the individual. See Individual and state

STATE and theater. See Theater and state

STATE bonds

How states voted on bond issues, taxes. il U S News 61:123-5 N 21 '66
Thumbs down on state bond plan. U S News 61:85 Ag 29 '66

STATE candidates. See Candidates, Political

STATE COLLEGE, Pa.

Town and gown in step. il Am City 81:132+ Jl '66

STATE colleges. See Colleges and universities, State

STATE constitutions. See Constitutions, State

STATE conventions, Political. See Political conventions

STATE court buildings. See Courthouses

STATE department (United States) See United States—State, Department of

STATE elections. See Elections—United States

STATE encouragement of science, literature, and art

Challenge of college dance education. J. Morrison. Dance Mag 40:34+ Mr '66
National endowment on the humanities. C. B. Grannis. Pub W 189:54 My 9 '66
Pay the piper, call the tune? government and the arts. Sr Schol 88:30 Ap 15 '66
Theater in the red. J. J. Greene. Cath World 202:364-8 Mr '66
See also
Art and state

STATE expenditures. See State finance

STATE fairs. See Agricultural exhibitions

STATE farm mutual automobile insurance company
State farm mutual sets an industry pace. il Bsns W p78-80+ F 26 '66

STATE finance

Aiding the states; the Heller plan. New Repub 55:4 D 3 '66
Plan for a tax transfusion; Heller plan. Life 61:6 D 9 '66
Sharing revenue: national taxes and local needs; W. Heller proposal to transfer federal revenue to individual states. R. A. Musgrave. Nation 204:78-80 Ja 16 '67
State of the states: troubled. il Newsweek 67:19-20 Ja 31 '66
State self-support. R. Moley. Newsweek 68:116 D 12 '66
Surplus for local governments? U S News 61:87 D 12 '66
Those lavish local spenders; state and local government spending. il Time 88:90 N 4 '66
See also
Taxation, State

STATE flowers

Your state flower; apple blossom. Arkansas & Michigan. L. Krelove. Flower Grower 53:42 O '66

STATE forest preserves. See Forests, State

STATE foresters. See Foresters

STATE governments

American squirearchy. J. Reichley. il Harper 232:98+ F '66
Creative localism; emphasis on reform. il Time 89:21 Ja 20 '67
Last chance for the states. J. D. Tydings. il Harper 232:71-4+ Mr '66

STATE governments—*Continued*
Octopus in the state house; report. T. Armbrister. il Sat Eve Post 239:25-9+ F 12 '66
Our changing state governments. Sr Schol 88:14-15 F 18 '66
See also
Constitutions, State
Governors

STATE labor legislation. See Labor laws and legislation—United States

STATE legislators. See Legislators

STATE legislatures
Dirksen's defeat; legislatures reapportionment. K. Crawford. Newsweek 67:24 My 2 '66
Legislatures: the 100-year lag. D. H. Beetle. il Nation 203:475-8 N 7 '66
Octopus in the state house; report. T. Armbrister. il Sat Eve Post 239:25-9+ F 12 '66
State legislatures: a battle for survival? Sr Schol 88:3-5 Mr 25 '66
Three-time loser; Dirksen proposal for reapportioning state legislatures fails again. Newsweek 67:19 My 2 '66
Trials of statehouse journalism. T. Littlewood. Sat R 49:82-3 D 10 '66

STATE libraries. See Libraries, State

STATE library consultants. See Library consultants

STATE library surveys. See Library surveys

STATE lotteries. See Lotteries

STATE medicine. See Medical service, State

STATE of the Union messages. See Presidents—United States—Messages

STATE ownership. See Government ownership

STATE parks and reserves
See also subhead Parks and reserves under names of states, e.g. Texas—Parks and reserves

Maps
New guide to your vacationlands. H. E. Paine. il Nat Geog Mag 130:94-7, sup(folded map) Jl '66

STATE police. See Police, State

STATE regulation of industry. See Industry and state

STATE rights
Cause not lost with Harry Byrd. Life 61:4 N 4 '66
Is the Constitution being abolished? D. Lawrence. U S News 60:120+ Mr 21 '66
See also
Federal and state relations

STATE socialism. See Socialism

STATE taxation. See Taxation, State

STATE universities. See Colleges and universities, State

STATE university of New York. See New York state university

STATEN ISLAND
Island in the Bay; with photographs by A. Austen. A. Robertson. Am Heritage 17:24-39+ Ag '66

STATES, Bert O.
Chekhov's dramatic strategy. Yale R 56: 212-24 D '66

STATES (United States)
Chart of the fifty states (cont) Sr Schol 89: pt2 30-1 S 23 '66
New regionalism; states and regions seeking economic growth. D. A. Schon. Harvard Bsns R 44:30-2+ Ja '66
See also
Constitutions, State
Interstate compacts
State governments

STATES, Ideal. See Utopias

STATES, New
See also
Underdeveloped areas

Politics
Passions & perils of nationhood; Time essay. Time 87:38-9 Mr 11 '66
Second round for Africa: independence on trial. S. Thompson. Atlan 218:79-83 O '66
Uhuru turns sour in Africa. Life 60:4 F 4 '66

STATES attorneys. See District attorneys

STATES rights. See State rights

STATESMEN
See also
Heads of state

STATION wagons
Comparing Ford-Chevy-Plymouth wagons. J. P. Norbye. il Pop Sci 188:75-9+ F '66
1967 cars. Changing T 20:30 D '66

Off-the-road luxury; $6000 jeep Wagoneer drivescription. J. Ethridge. il Motor T 18: 48-9 Je '66
Station wagons. Consumer Bul 49:29 My '66

Four wheel drive
Driving in sand. J. A. McNally. Field & S 70:40 Mr '66

Rating
Road-tests of family bus-wagons. il Consumer Rep 31:342-7 Jl '66

Specifications
MT tests and evaluates six wagons at six prices. il Motor T 18:56-62 S '66

Testing
MT tests and evaluates six wagons at six prices. il Motor T 18:56-62 S '66
1966 station wagons. il Consumer Rep 31:295-305 Je '66
Road-tests of family bus-wagons. il Consumer Rep 31:342-7 Jl '66

STATIONERY
Write-in campaign. il Seventeen 25:152-3 Je '66
See also
Envelopes (stationery)

STATIONS, Railroad. See Railroads—Stations

STATIONS in space. See Space stations

STATIONS of the Cross
Fourteen stations of the Cross, 1958-1966. B. Newman. il Art N 65:26-8+ My '66
Of a different stripe; B. Newman's paintings. Time 87:82 Ap 29 '66
Stations of the cross: a series of wood engravings by B. Brussel-Smith. N. Kent. il Am Artist 30:40-5 Ap '66

STATISTICAL commission of the United Nations. See United Nations—Statistical commission

STATISTICAL methods
Statistical method; letter. A. F. Johnson. Science 152:450+ Ap 22 '66

STATISTICAL yearbook. See United Nations statistical yearbook

STATISTICS
Not so vital statistics; comp. by H. Helfer. il N Y Times Mag p60 N 13 '66
See also
Economic statistics
United Nations—Statistical commission
United Nations statistical yearbook
also subhead Statistics under various subjects, e.g. Libraries—Statistics

STATUARY. See Statues

STATUE of Liberty
Hail Liberty! D. G. McCullough. il Am Heritage 17:22-3+ F '66

STATUES
Fallen idols. il Horizon 8:118-19 Aut '66
Little Squirt; most famous child's statue in the world; Manneken-Pis. J. Bryan, 3d Holiday 39:48-9 Je '66

STATURE
Advice to tall girls from a tall man. B. Gale. il Seventeen 25:206-7 Mr '66
Nightmare: how to stop the good big man. M. Hyman. il Sports Illus 25:71-3 D 5 '66
Pro basketball's tall men; W. Reed and W. Bellamy. W. J. McKean. il Look 31:84+ Ja 24 '67

STATUS. See Prestige

STATUS, Social. See Social status

STATUS of women, Commission on the. See United Nations—Commission on the status of women

STAUFFACHER, Jack Werner
Greenwood press, S.F. reopens after eleven years. Pub W 190:122 S 5 '66

STAUFFER chemical company
Management alchemy at Stauffer chemical. J. Perham. il Duns R 88:33-4+ Jl '66

STAVELEY, Gaylord, and East, Ben
Last days of the Colorado? Outdoor Life 138:24-7+ Jl '66

STAVIG, Richard T.
Why study abroad pays off. Sat R 49:82+ F 19 '66

STAVROPOULOS, Constantin A.
United Nations programme of assistance and exchange in the field of international law. UN Mo Chron 3:41-7 Ap '66

STEAD, Dom Julian
October hunting; poem. Commonweal 85:16 O 7 '66

STEADY dating. See Dating

STEAK. See Beef; Cookery—Meat

STEALING
Backsliding on the slopes: stolen skis. il Time 87:84 F 18 '66
Capsule history of jewel thievery. D. Dodge. Holiday 39:60-1 Ap '66
Larceny in everyday life: Time essay. Time 88:26-7 S 9 '66
Petty thieves in camp. C. B. Colby. il Outdoor Life 138:22+ D '66
See also
Animal thefts
Art thefts
Automobiles, Theft of
Book thefts
Burglary and burglars
Embezzlement
Shoplifting
STEAM automobiles. See Automobiles, Steam
STEAM engine models. See Railroad models
STEAM engines
Steamed up for a charge into the past; photographs by T. Evans; with account by P. Jennings. il Sports Illus 24:36-41 F 14 '66
STEAM engines, Automotive. See Automobile engines
STEAM polo. See Polo
STEAM-spray irons, Electric. See Electric irons
STEAMBOATS. See Steamships and steamboats
STEAMERS (ships) See Steamships and steamboats
STEAMING (cookery)
To cook with steam automatically. il Consumer Rep 31:521-2 N '66
STEAMSHIP lines
See also
American president lines
Cunard steamship company
Hudson River day lines
Norwegian American line. incorporated

Consolidations and mergers
Three or four from one & one; A.P.L. il Time 87:96 My 13 '66
STEAMSHIPS and steamboats
O Keewatin! trip on a real, old-fashioned passenger steamer. R. Bissell. il Holiday 40:42-51+ Ag '66
Whistle good-bye; excerpts from Farewell to steam. D. Plowden. il Am Heritage 18:54-63 D '66
See also
Ocean liners

Fire protection
See Ships—Fires and fire protection
STEBBINS, Doris E.
Caladium. Horticulture 45:48 Ja '67
STEBBINS, G. Ledyard
Chromosomal variation and evolution; address, December 30, 1965. bibliog Science 152:1463-9 Je 10 '66
STEBBINS, Joel
American pioneer in photoelectric astronomy. A. E. Whitford. il por Sky & Tel 31:268-9 My '66
STEBBINS, W. C. and others
Auditory sensitivity of the monkey. bibliog Science 153:1646-7 S 30 '66
STEBER, Eleanor
Is there a soprano in the house? H. Butler. il Harper 233:77-81 Ag '66
STECHLER, Gerald, and others
Attention in the newborn: effect on motility and skin potential. bibliog Science 151:1246-8 Mr 11 '66
STECHOW, Wolfgang
Cleveland's golden anniversary acquisitions. Art N 65:30-44+ S '66
STECKLER, Larry
Electronics' new gee-whiz kits. Pop Mech 125:180-4 My '66
How to find sunken treasure, and keep it. Pop Mech 126:124-7+ N '66
Put a guitar amplifier in your pocket. Pop Mech 126:198-9+ O '66
STECKLER, Len
Len Steckler's girls. il por Pop Phot 58:84-7+ My '66
STEDMAN, Jane W.
Tails you lose! Opera N 31:10-11 S 17 '66
(ed) See Bartoletti, B. High key
—and McElroy, George
What's in a name? Opera N 30:6-7 F 12 '66
STEEGMULLER, Francis
Our far-flung correspondents. New Yorker 42:160+ S 17 '66
STEEL, Ronald
Cold war myths. Commonweal 83:576-8 F 18 '66
Doubts of Europe. Commonweal 84:629-31 S 30 '66

Films at the Philharmonic. Christian Cent 83:1340-1 N 2 '66
Halle's applied philosophy. New Repub 154:28-30 My 14 '66
New books for social studies teachers. Sr Schol 87:sup 18 Ja 21 '66
STEEL
See also
Steel industry and trade

Prices
Business takes steel hike in stride. Bsns W p27-8 Ag 13 '66
Compromise: price rise. Sr Schol 87:15 Ja 21 '66
Labor costs up, then a price rise: latest story in steel. il U S News 61:71 Ag 15 '66
Peaceful price boosting. Bsns W p204 Mr 12 '66
Stainless steel has shiny new prices. Bsns W p43 N 19 '66
Steel price increase hits where it hurts: Inland steel's lead in price rise. Bsns W p28 Ag 6 '66
Steel prices up: planes still down. il Newsweek 68:61-2+ Ag 15 '66
Why not? Time 88:66+ Ag 12 '66
STEEL castings
See also
Continuous casting
STEEL company of Canada
Canada rolls back prices, too. Bsns W p56 S 24 '66
STEEL construction
Big steel: Chicago's civic center complete. il Arch Forum 125:33-7 O '66
Dark steel pavilion designed for export; Cummins engine co. plant, Darlington, England. il Arch Forum 125:82-7 O '66
New steel framing system promises major savings in high-rise apartments. il Arch Rec 139:191-6 Je '66
No painting required; Miami County, Ohio. il Am City 81:47 F '66
STEEL industry and trade
Too much steel in the world? il U S News 60:94 Ja 31 '66
See also
Allegheny Ludlum steel corporation
Steel workers
Steel works

Consolidations and mergers
Simon creates a new riddle; merger of Wheeling steel and Crucible steel co. of America. Bsns W p52 N 26 '66

Finance
Are steels a bargain or a dud? prices low for steel stocks. il Bsns W p 151-2 My 14 '66

International aspects
World battle for steel; special report. il Bsns W p58-64+ Je 4 '66

Securities
Are steels a bargain or a dud? prices low for steel stocks. il Bsns W p 151-2 My 14 '66

Wages and hours
Labor costs up, then a price rise: latest story in steel. il U S News 61:71 Ag 15 '66

China (People's Republic)
Steel for Peiping; a deal by U.S. allies. il U S News 60:6 Mr 28 '66

Europe, Western
Cold steel. Time 88:70+ Ag 12 '66
Trouble for steel. il Fortune 73:63-4+ My '66
See also
European coal and steel community

France
Surge to merge; USINOR to merge with Lorraine-Escaut. Newsweek 67:72+ Mr 7 '66

Germany (Federal Republic)
Return of the cartel? il Newsweek 67:82 Je 13 '66

Great Britain
Britain: the shadow of nationalization. Bsns W p73-4 Je 4 '66

Italy
Italy boosts steel output with modern plant in south. il Bsns W p68 Je 4 '66

Japan
Japan piles up impressive gains. il Bsns W p68+ Je 4 '66

STEEL industry and trade—*Continued*

United States

Billions build Chicago into a steel titan; nation's leading steelmaker. il Bsns W p68-75 N 19 '66

Defense buoys up steel. il Bsns W p43 Jl 9 '66

How steel is winning luster in Washington. il Bsns W p 146+ N 26 '66

Knocking on wood. il Time 88:69+ Jl 15 '66

Old steel valley starts to shake off its grime; mill towns along Monongahela. il Bsns W p72-3 Ja 22 '66

Steel buying surprises the experts. il Bsns W p30-1 F 12 '66

Steel is rebuilding for a new era. J. McDonald. il Fortune 74:130-7+ O '66

Steel sees record '66, slight slowdown ahead; autos are key, imports are worry, basic oxygen process is booming. il Bsns W p42-3 N 19 '66

Technology to the rescue. il Time 87:94-9 My 6 '66

See also

Titan industrial corporation

STEEL metallurgy

Better diet for oxygen steelmakers; more scrap, less pig iron. Bsns W p 178 Je 18 '66

Kaiser plans appeal in BOF case. il Bsns W p97 Jl 23 '66

Steel sees record '66, slight slowdown ahead; autos are key, imports are worry, basic oxygen process is booming. il Bsns W p42-3 N 19 '66

STEEL mills. See Steel works

STEEL sculpture. See Metal sculpture

STEEL workers

Negroes zero in on steel industry; U.S. steel the prime target of civil rights groups. Bsns W p 156+ D 10 '66

Second test set for early retirement. il Bsns W p74-5 Jl 2 '66

Steel's jobless press for relief; steelworkers from McKeesport, Pa. descend on Washington. il Bsns W p90-2 Ja 22 '66

Steelworkers on campus. H. J. Golatz. America 114:652-4 My 7 '66

See also

Steel industry and trade—Wages and hours

STEEL works

China goes west for steel mill; West Germany to build steel-finishing complex. il Bsns W p 105-6 Mr 26 '66

Steel and jasmine tea; proposed sale, by a European consortium of a steel plant to red China. il Fortune 73:73-4+ Je '66

See also

Inland steel company

STEELE, Edward

Arizona's mystery bird. Audubon Mag 68:167-71 My '66

STEELE, George P.

Books under water; library life aboard a Polaris submarine. por Library J 91:2281-5 My 1 '66

STEELE, Richard

Minnesota's Democrats try to dump their governor. Reporter 34:29-31 Je 2 '66

STEELE, W.

Help on the open road, or Have every licensee policed. Pop Electr 24:64 Ap '66

STEELE glacier, Canada. See Glaciers

STEELWORKERS union. See United steelworkers of America

STEER wrestling. See Rodeos

STEERING gear, Automobile. See Automobiles —Steering gear

STEFANILE, Felix

Profiles and presences. Poetry 109:198-200 D '66

Years; poem. Poetry 108:110 My '66

STEFFEN, Fred

Interpretive portraits of Fred Steffen. il por Am Artist 31:38-43+ Ja '67

STEFIANOS, Dimitri

Death of the architect. il por Time 88:38-40 S 16 '66

Hendrik Verwoerd, RIP. Nat R 18:920 S 20 '66

Letter from Cape Town. E. J. Kahn, jr. New Yorker 42:182+ N 5 '66

Man dies but not apartheid. il por Newsweek 68:40-2+ S 19 '66

Mind of an assassin. Newsweek 68:56+ O 31 '66

Tapeworm murder. Time 88:41 O 28 '66

STEGANOGRAPHY. See Cryptography

STEGNER, Wallace

Lake Powell. Holiday 39:64-9+ My '66

Legislating to save the land. Sat R 50:90-2 Ja 14 '67

To save the Grand Canyon. Sat R 49:20 Ag 20 '66

STEHLIN, Joseph

One cylinder success car. A. Rothenberg. il Look 30:M22+ N 15 '66

STEICHEN, Edward

Steichen gallery. il Opera N 31:12-15 D 24 '66

STEIN, Benjamin J. and Steiner, U. J.

Concrete trees in St John's. Library J 91:5880-3 D 1 '66

STEIN, Emanuel

Ethical aspects of union policy and conduct. bibliog f Am Ann Acad 363:117-25 Ja '66

STEIN, Gabriel. See Behar, B. jt. auth.

STEIN, Gerald

Have another cupcake, Jack; story. Redbook 127:79 My '66

STEIN, Jules

Ultimate in research. il por Time 88:66+ N 11 '66

STEIN, Julian U.

Mentally retarded need recreation. bibliog por Parks & Rec 1:574-5+ Jl '66

STEIN, Ralph

Ralph Stein on vintage cars. See issues of Motor trend

STEIN, Robert

Manifest destiny of change. Sat R 49:38 N 5 '66

STEIN, Ruth

Launching the new literate. Library J 91:5713-15 N 15 '66

STEINBECK, John

America and the Americans. Sat Eve Post 239:32-8+ Jl 2 '66; Same abr. with title What's happening to America? Read Digest 89:175-6+ O '66

Let's go after the neglected treasures beneath the seas; letter. por Pop Sci 189:84-7 S '66

March hare mother; excerpt from America and Americans. por Library J 91:6169 D 15 '66

My dear friend Genya. Read Digest 89:128 S '66

about

As simple as that; reply to Y. Yevtushenko. America 115:89 Jl 23 '66

Covici: Steinbeck's editor, collaborator, and conscience. C. A. Madison. Sat R 49:15-16 Je 25 '66

Eye of the veteran. il por Time 88:41 D 30 '66

STEINBERG, Alfred

Passenger trains that can turn a profit. Read Digest 89:249-50+ N '66

STEINBERG, Benjamin

Symphony of the New World. il pors Ebony 22:39-40+ N '66

STEINBERG, Jane

Boarding-school mystique. Mlle 63:176-7+ My '66

Going native, without culture shock. Mlle 64:62 N '66

Next: a sleep-in? Mlle 62:10+ Ap '66

Strangle of the apron strings? Mlle 63:342+ Ag '66

STEINBERG, Michael

Opera in the Back Bay theater. Hi Fi 16:MA22-3 Jl '66

STEINBERG, Saul

Art. M. Kozloff. Nation 203:683-4 D 19 '66

Artist behind the Steinbergian mask. H. C. Schonberg. il por N Y Times Mag p48-51+ N 13 '66

Lord of the line. D. L. Shirey. il por Newsweek 68:98 D 12 '66

Message in the medium. il por Time 87:76 Ap 15 '66

Saul Steinberg's art world. H. Rosenberg. il Art N 65:51-4+ Mr '66

Steinberg. H. Rosenberg. il por Vogue 149:96-9+ Ja 1 '67

STEINBERG, William

Music to my ears. I. Kolodin. Sat R 49:70 D 10 '66

STEINEM, Gloria

Lefrak way of life. N Y Times Mag p 18-20+ Jl 31 '66

Maurice Joseph Micklewhite, what's 'e got? N Y Times Mag p66-7 D 4 '66

(ed) See Streisand, B. Barbra Streisand talks about her million-dollar baby

STEINER, George

Books. New Yorker 42:238+ N 5 '66; 117-22 Ja 14 '67

STEINER, Jean François

Treblinka revisited. por Time 87:37-8 Ap 29 '66

STEINER, Nyle A.
Amateur scientist. Sci Am 215:102-4 Ag '66
STEINER, Urban J. See Stein, B. J. jt. auth.
STEINFELS, Peter
Oh, what a lovely dialogue. Commonweal 85:397-9 Ja 13 '67
U.S. and France. Commonweal 84:570-1 S 16 '66
STEINHAUER, Neal
Long shot. il Newsweek 69:89 Ja 23 '67
STEINIGER, Edward L.
Sinclair breaks the clamp on its profits. il por Bsns W p64-6+ Ag 27 '66
STEINMAN, Gary
Synthesis of amino acid residues with reactive side chains under simple conditions. bibliog Science 154:1344-6 D 9 '66
STEINMANN, Marion
Most exciting new development in image-making. Life 61:120A D 23 '66
STEINS. See Drinking vessels
STEINWAY and sons, New York
Great Rubinstein road show; selling Steinway pianos in the 1870s. M. Goldin. il Hi Fi 16:60-2 S '66
STELCO. See Steel company of Canada
STELLA, Frank
Questions to Stella and Judd; interview, ed. by L. R. Lippard. il por Art N 65:55-61 S '66
about
Art; show at Castelli gallery. M. Kozloff. Nation 202:370-2 Mr 28 '66
STELLAR atmospheres. See Stars—Atmospheres
STELLAR interferometers. See Interferometers
STELLAR magnetism. See Magnetism, Stellar
STELLAR motion. See Stars—Motion
STELLMACK, J. A. See Curl. R. L. jt. auth.
STENCIL work
Art of stenciling. il House & Gard 130:198-9+ S '66
Decorative stenciling the early American way. J. Hanks. il Farm J 90:86 O '66
STENDHAL, pseud. See Beyle, M. H.
STENGEL, Casey
Casey and Ted; induction into the Baseball hall of fame. Cooperstown, N.Y. Sports Illus 25:9 Ag 8 '66
STENGEL, Charles Dillon. See Stengel. C.
STENNIS, John Cornelius
Excerpt from address, February 17, 1966. Cong Digest 45:126-8 Ap '66
From a top senator: how Vietnam war grew, what to do now; excerpts from statement, January 27, 1966. por U S News 60:6 F 7 '66
George Washington wept here; remarks at presidential prayer breakfast, February 23, 1966. Christian Cent 83:635 My 11 '66
How high is the cost of the Vietnam war? excerpts from television interview. U S News 61:22 O 24 '66
Stennis vs. McNamara: how ready for combat are U.S. forces? excerpts from statements. por U S News 60:21 Ap 11 '66
We should buckle down and win; excerpts from address, November 30, 1966. por U S News 61:27 D 26 '66
about
Senate investigators urge TAC review. il por Aviation W 85:86-9+ Ag 22 '66
STENTOR coeruleus. See Ciliata
STENZEL, Kurt H. and Rubin, A. L.
Biosynthesis of gamma globulin: studies in a cell-free system. bibliog Science 153:537-9 Jl 29 '66
STEPHANOPOULOS, Stephanos
End of the string. Newsweek 69:27-8 Ja 2 '67
STEPHEN, John
It all started in London and it's making a smash here. il por Life 60:82B My 13 '66
STEPHEN Leacock memorial home. See Orillia. Ontario—Historic houses. etc.
STEPHENS, Cleo
But it's got to come out. Am For 72:44-5+ My '66
STEPHENS, Douglas W.
Finding the hidden causes of bad breath. Todays Health 44:4-5 D '66
STEPHENS, Elizabeth
Ding dong, the bells are gone. Seventeen 25: 410-11 Ag '66
STEPHENS, Geoff
Doodles and tenderness. il por Newsweek 69: 66 Ja 2 '67

STEPHENS, Roderick, Jr
Great American sailboats. Motor B 117:40-1+ Mr '66
(ed) See Mitchell, C. Great American sailboats: Finisterre
STEPHENS, William M.
Improbable mollusk. Natur Hist 75:44-5 Ag '66
STEPPARENTS
Will you be my daughter? R. Barenbaum. il Redbook 128:8+ Ja '67
STEPPING stones. See Garden walks
STEPS, Door. See Door steps
STERBA, Monica
Love and hate and Dr Tisch; story. Reporter 34:36-9 My 5 '66
STEREO amplifiers. See Amplifiers
STEREO cabinets. See Loud speaking apparatus—Cabinets
STEREO cartridges. See Phonograph—Stereophonic pickup
STEREO fluoricon. See Fluoroscopy
STEREO loud speakers. See Loud speaking apparatus
STEREOPHONIC phonograph records. See Phonograph records—Stereophonic records
STEREOPHONIC recorders. See Magnetic recorders and recording—Stereophonic recorders
STEREOPHONIC sound. See Sound—Stereophonic recording and reproducing
STEREOPHONIC sound systems
Cabinets, the new look in stereo housing; with editorial comment. N. Eisenberg. il Hi Fi 16:55, 56-9 S '66
New equipment. Hi Fi 16:94-8 O '66
Plus or minus 3dB. I. Berger. Sat R 49: 55-6 D 31 '66
Portfolio of stereo decor, 1966. il Hi Fi 16: 46-53 Mr '66
Stereo on wheels. il Hi Fi 16:103 O '66
STEREOPHONIC sound systems, Used
Second-hand stereo; a buyers and sellers guide to used equipment. L. Marcus. il Hi Fi 16:68-70 S '66
STEREOPHONIC television transmission. See Television broadcasting—Stereophonic transmission
STEREOPHOTOGRAMMETRY. See Photogrammetry
STEREOPHOTOGRAPHY
Those incredible holograms; amazing frozen light waves give first true 3D pictures. C. P. Gilmore. il Pop Sci 189:78-82+ Jl '66
STEREOSCOPIC television. See Television, Stereoscopic
STEREOTYPERS and electrotypers association
Several printing unions plan merger in 1967. Pub W 190:126 D 5 '66
STERILITY
Reproductive failure; report on first conference on Comparative aspects of reproductive failure. E. S. E. Hafez. Science 154:546+ O 28 '66
STERILITY in insects
Population flushing with sexually sterile insects. J. Monro. bibliog il Science 151:1536-8 Mr 25 '66
See also
Chemosterilants
STERILIZATION
Sterilization by electrohydraulic treatment. M. Allen and K. Soike. il Science 154:155-7 O 7 '66
See also
Soil disinfection
STERILIZATION. Sexual
Voluntary sterilization approved by majority. Sci N 90:277 O 8 '66
See also
Chemosterilants
STERILIZATION of defectives, criminals, etc.
Cruel and unusual? Judge Kearney's sterilization or jail decree in Santa Barbara court. il Newsweek 67:46 Je 13 '66
Jail or sterilization? sentence of Judge Kearney in Santa Barbara, Calif. il Time 87: 46 Je 3 '66
Sterilization sentiment focuses on the poor. Sci N 89:371 My 14 '66
Sterilize that woman! jail or sterilization. decree by Judge Kearney in Santa Barbara, Calif. W. F. Buckley, jr. Nat R 18:666 Jl 12 '66
Unfit: Denmark's solution. il U S News 60: 74 Mr 7 '66
STERILIZATION of water. See Water purifiers, Domestic
STERILIZING chemicals. See Chemosterilants
STERLING, Albert
Right connections. Hi Fi 16:108-9 O '66

STERLING, Claire
  Ben Barka affair. Reporter 34:22-8 Mr 10 '66
  Can Nigeria catch up with its reputation?
    Reporter 34:39-42 My 19 '66
  Ghana gets a second chance. Reporter 34:
    23-7 Ap 21 '66
  Houphouet-Boigny wins a bet. Reporter 34:
    27-9 Je 16 '66
  Mr Wilson squeaks through. Reporter 35:32-3
    O 6 '66
  Mystic mayor, and Fanfani outfoxed. Re-
    porter 34:34-6 Ja 27 '66
  Setback for the African left. Reporter 35:
    21-3 D 1 '666
  Strong medicine for Britain's economic ills.
    Reporter 35:47-9 N 17 '66
STERLING, Patricia Ann
  All she ever heard while she was growing up
    is how beautiful she was; interview. A.
    Sothern. por Esquire 67:78-81 Ja '67
STERLING, Thomas
  On being foreign. Holiday 39:16+ Ap '66
STERLING, Wallace
  Drinking approved at Stanford. por Sch &
    Soc 94:340-2 O 29 '66
STERLING (money) See Money—Great Britain
STERLING silver. See Silverware
STERN, Edith M.
  Life with grandma. Parents Mag 41:36-7+
    Jl '66
STERN, F.
  Testing and measuring resistors. Electr
    World 76:44-6 S '66
STERN, George G.
  Freshman myth. NEA J 55:41-3 S '66
STERN, H, comercio e industria. See Brazil—
  Industries
STERN, Hans
  In Brazil, it's breakfast at Stern's. il por
    Bsns W p 110-12+ My 14 '66
STERN, Isaac
  Isaac Stern in a new role; first recordings
    with the soloist as conductor. E. Green-
    field. il pors Hi Fi 16:20+ S '66
STERN, Richard Gustave
  Yarmolinsky & the cannibal. Nation 203:639-
    40 D 12 '66
STERN, Richard Martin
  Beginning; story. McCalls 93:68-9 Je '66
STERN, Robert K.
  Critical path to management control. Duns R
    87:pt2 137+ Mr '66
STERN, Sol
  Trouble in an "All America city." N Y Times
    Mag p20-2+ Jl 10 '66
STERN drives. See Marine engines
STERNBERG, David T.
  Philippines: contour and perspective. For
    Affairs 44:501-11 Ap '66
STERNBERG, Saul
  High-speed scanning in human memory. bib-
    liog Science 153:652-4 Ag 5 '66
STERNE, Hedda
  Sterne: line and likeness; exhibition at the
    Parsons gallery, N.Y. L. Campbell. il Art
    N 64:28-9+ F '66
STEROID hormones. See Hormones. Sex
STEROID oral contraceptives. See Contracep-
  tives
STEROLS
  Osteolytic sterol in human breast cancer.
    G. S. Gordan and others. bibliog il Science
    151:1226-8 Mr 11 '66
STESSIN, Lawrence
  Which way for the foreman? Duns R 87:45+
    Ap '66
STEVAS, Norman St John-. See St John-
  Stevas, N.
STEVEN, William Pickford
  Houston's shackled press. B. H. Bagdikian.
    Atlan 218:87-8+ Ag '66
STEVENS, Chris
  Build this CB intercom and keep track of
    your kids. Pop Mech 126:166-8+ S '66
STEVENS, David
  (ed) See Windgassen, W. Wandering minstrel
STEVENS, Earl
  Two-time loser. por Outdoor Life 137:36-9+
    My '66
STEVENS, Elisabeth
  Life art review. Life 61:22 S 23 '66
  Where comfort starts: the air around you.
    House & Gard 131:104-5 Ja '67
STEVENS, Frank A.
  Even break for the poor. por Library J 91:
    1010-13 F 15 '66
STEVENS, Jacques
  Portrait of a living fossil. il por Life 61:64-6
    Jl 22 '66
STEVENS, Leonard A.
  Now the automated physical checkup. Read
    Digest 89:95-8 Jl '66

STEVENS, Lewis Miller
  Profiles of ethics: a tribute to Lewis Miller
    Stevens. R. F. Nichols. Ann Am Acad 363:1-
    3 Ja '66
STEVENS, Richard E.
  Planning building exits that work. Arch
    Rec 140:225-6 O '66
STEVENS, Robert W.
  Wishful thinking on the balance of pay-
    ments. bibliog f Harvard Bsns R 44:6-8+
    N '66
STEVENS, Roger L.
  Arts, the humanities, and the federal govern-
    ment; adaptation of address, July 1966. por
    ALA Bul 60:900-3 O '66
  State of the arts: a 1966 balance sheet. Sat
    R 49:24-5+ Mr 12 '66

                    about
  Capital cultural crusader. H. Brandon. Sat R
    49:7 Ag 27 '66
  Government and the arts: how much to
    whom? il por Newsweek 68:56-60 Jl 18 '66
  Nobody ever loses on my deals. Fortune 73:
    197 Mr '66
  Roger Stevens, a performing art. D. Norton-
    Taylor. il por Fortune 73:152-3+ Mr '66
STEVENS, S. S.
  Metric for the social consensus. bibliog Sci-
    ence 151:530-41 F 4 '66
STEVENS, Sylvester Kirby
  Academic freedom for historians; text of
    announcement, July 22, 1966. por Sch & Soc
    94:461-3 D 10 '66
  Banning history: Frick vs. Stevens. E.
    Langer. Science 153:616 Ag 5 '66
  People's right to the past. Christian Cent
    83:1169 S 28 '66
  Stevens asks court to enjoin Frick suit.
    Pub W 190:49-50 O 10 '66
  Stevens countersues Frick, charges rights
    violation. Pub W 190:41-2 Ag 15 '66
  Stevens loses suit in federal court. Pub W
    190:26 O 24 '66
  Stevens presents case to U.S. Court of ap-
    peals. Pub W 190:58-60 D 26 '66
  Stevens takes case to U.S. Court of appeals.
    Pub W 190:38 N 28 '66
STEVENS, Thaddeus
  One hundred years ago. R. L. Strout. New
    Repub 154:17-18 F 12 '66
STEVENS, Wallace
  Hartford walker. S. Kunitz. New Repub 155:
    23-6 N 12 '66
  Letters of Wallace Stevens, ed. by H.
    Stevens. Review
    Newsweek il 68:114+ N 28 '66. J. Kroll
  Poet behind the desk. W. Y. Tindall. por Sat
    R 49:42 N 19 '66
  Wallace Stevens: business and a sonnet. A.
    W. Litz. Nation 204:85-7 Ja 16 '67
  Wallace Stevens: emergence of the poet. F.
    Lentricchia, jr. Poetry 109:201-3 D '66
STEVENS, William
  Munch in America. Art N 64:41-3+ Ja '66
STEVENSON, Adlai Ewing, 1900-1965
  Adlai Stevenson: letters from his mother;
    his reactions, ed. by A. Michaelis. McCalls
    93:58 My '66

                    about
  Adlai Stevenson: a new vision. E. Roper.
    Sat R 49:20 Jl 9 '66
  Adlai Stevenson's son releases father's letter
    to Viet critics. il por Sr Schol 87:20 Ja 14 '66
  Flaming arrows to the sky; excerpt from As
    we knew Adlai. G. W. Ball. Atlan 217:41-5
    My '66
  Portrait, with scratches: Adlai Stevenson. T.
    S. Matthews. Vogue 147:192-3+ My '66
  Stevenson wit, by B. Adler. Review
    Time 87:108+ F 4 '66

                 Photographs
  Speaking likeness. Sat R 49:96-7 Je 11 '66
STEVENSON, Adlai Ewing, 1931?-
  Adlai III: another Stevenson stirs Illinois
    politics. J. Star. il pors Look 30:28-31 O 4
    '66
STEVENSON, Adlai E. memorial fund. See
  Adlai E. Stevenson memorial fund
STEVENSON, Charles
  Big brother is here! Read Digest 89:81-6 N '66
  What price the Great society? Read Digest
    88:49-53 Mr '66
  What your vote can do for Congress. Read
    Digest 89:61-6 O '66
  —and Purdy, K. W.
  New approach in automobile repair. Read
    Digest 90:123-6 Ja '67

STEVENSON, Florence
Don Carlo and the Kirov in Greece. Hi Fi
16:MA24 O '66
In rehearsal. Opera N 30:28-31 F 12 '66
Miraculous marionettes. Opera N 30:26-8 Mr 5
'66
Opera in motion. Dance Mag 40:28-9+ F '66
STEVENSON, George Charles
Who may assist a surgeon? il por Time 88:
36 D 30 '66
STEVENSON, John S. and Stevenson, L. S.
Fluorine content of microsaur teeth from the
carboniferous rocks of Joggins, Nova Sco-
tia. bibliog Science 154:1548-50 D 23 '66
STEVENSON, Louise S. See Stevenson, J. S.
jt. auth.
STEVENSON, Robert Louis
Treasure Island; dramatization of novel. See
York, M. A.
STEVENSON, Robert P.
Shop talk. See issues of Popular science
monthly
STEW
Bride makes Hungarian goulash. il McCalls
94:88 O '66
French springtime stew delicious in our au-
tumn; lamb stew; with recipe. il Sunset
137:216-17 O '66
Lamb of a stew. C. Claiborne. il N Y Times
Mag p99 My 22 '66
STEWARD, Hal D.
Anatomy of a true adventure story. Writer
79:13-17 My '66
Successful techniques for newspaper travel
articles. Writer 79:31-3 N '66
STEWARDESSES, Air. See Airlines—Hostesses
STEWART, Bruce W.
Data processing in an academic library. por
Wilson Lib Bul 41:388-95 D '66
STEWART, Charles M.
Excretion and heartwood formation in living
trees. bibliog Science 153:1068-74 S 2 '66
STEWART, David C.
Intellectual recreation at mid-year. Sat R
49:79-80 Mr 19 '66
STEWART, Edward
Barefoot soprano; story. Esquire 65:112-15
Mr '66
STEWART, Harris B. Jr
Environmental pollution. Science 154:1065-7 N
25 '66
STEWART, Ian
Paper that spreads the cult of Mao. N Y
Times Mag p26-7+ D 18 '66
STEWART, J. George
Build he must. Newsweek 68:18 Jl 4 '66
Stewart's plot against the Capitol. C. Frit-
chey. Harper 233:40+ S '66
STEWART, Jackie
When you're no. 2 you drive harder. R. Daley.
il por Sports Illus 25:24-6+ Ag 15 '66
Yen for speed. il Newsweek 68:72 O 24 '66
STEWART, James
Th' respawnsibility of bein' J...Jimmy
Stewart. gosh! P. Bogdanovich. por Esquire
66:104-6+ Jl '66
STEWART, James R.
Strong, modern and bold. Am City 81:77-9
D '66
STEWART, Mary
Dropouts anonymous. D. Weldon. il Parents
Mag 41:44-5+ My '66
STEWART, Michael, 1906-
Reporter at large. J. Kramer. il New Yorker
42:138+ Ap 2 '66
STEWART, Paul
Rowing. Sports Illus 24:66+ Je 27 '66
Sporting look. Sports Illus 24:46-7 F 21; 62
Je 27 '66
STEWART, Robert
Jackhammer; poem. America 114:415 Mr 26
'66
STEWART, Robert Sussman
Vision of Franco Zeffirelli. N Y Times Mag
p 10-11+ S 4 '66
STEWART, Thomas
Music to my ears; Ford in Falstaff. I. Kolo-
din. Sat R 49:51 Mr 26 '66
STEWART, William Huffman
Conquering childhood diseases. por Am Ed
2:30-2 Mr '66
Experiments on humans, the growing debate:
invitation to open dialogue. Sat R 49:43-4
Jl 2 '66
STEWART-GORDON, James
Crazy over quarter horses. Read Digest 89:
124-7 Ag '66
Farmer Grösch and his singing birds. Read
Digest 88:205-6+ F '66
STEWS. See Stew
STIBECK, Ray
Hamburger university. N. Fraser. il por Life
61:100 O 21 '66

STIBITZ, Mildred T.
Library workshop for adults. ALA Bul 60:
937-41 O '66
STIBNITE
Stibnite (Sb$_2$S$_3$)solubility in sodium sulfide
solutions. R. H. Arntson and others. bib-
liog il Science 153:1673-4 S 30 '66
STICK insects
Insect you can't see. il Sci Digest 60:36 Jl
'66
See also
Walkingsticks (insects)
STICKEL, Lucille F. and others
Residues of DDT in brains and bodies of
birds that died on dosage and in survivors.
bibliog Science 151:1549-51 Mr 25 '66
STICKNEY, Ill.
Man who couldn't be bought; when Bob
Smith went into politics. W. Goodman. il
Redbook 128:66-7+ N '66
STIEGLITZ, Alfred
Alfred Stieglitz: photographer. H. M.
Kinzer. il Pop Phot 58:28 Je '66
STIGLER, George J.
Private enterprise and public intelligence.
Duns R 88:17+ O '66
STILL life painting
Painting still-life. R. Schuessler. il Design
67:16-17 Ja '66
Still life with tropical fruit; with painting
by H. Rousseau. M. Kaytor. Look 30:70-1
Mr 22 '66
STILL life photography. See Photography—
Still life
STILL waters; story. See Cousins, M.
STILLINGER, Elizabeth
Art and history in American toys. Antiques
90:837-9 D '66
STILLMAN, Edmund
Thaw in east Europe's ice age. N Y Times
Mag p27+ Ag 21 '66
What price Germany, now? N Y Times Mag
p54-7+ D 4 '66
STILLWELL, Joseph Warren. Jr
Cider Joe at sea. il por Time 88:24-5 Ag 5 '66
STILWELL, Robert L.
From sivas to civil servants. Sat R 49:42-3
S 24 '66
Ideological framework for fiction. Sat R 49:
61-3 S 10 '66
STIMAC, Michael
Africa. Flying 79:114-20 S '66
about
Flying monk. il por Newsweek 68:49 N 28 '66
STIMSON, Henry Lewis
Responsibilities of peace; address, August 20,
1966. G. W. Ball. Dept State Bul 55:373-5 S
12 '66
STIMSON, Thomas E.
500 eggs in one basket. Pop Mech 126:68-9+
S '66
New Alaskan gold rush. Pop Mech 126:148-
51+ O '66
(ed) See Madden, R. J. High explosives on
the highways
STIMULANTS
See also
Coffee
Liquors
STIMULATORS, Electronic. See Electronic ap-
paratus and appliances
STIMULUS and response
Circadian rhythms in rats: effects of random
lighting. D. L. Holmquest and others. bib-
liog il Science 152:662-4 Ap 29 '66
Conflict and arousal. D. E. Berlyne. il Sci Am
215:82-7 bibliog(p 116) Ag '66
Control of sensory fields by stimulation of
hypothalamus. M. F. MacDonnell and J. P.
Flynn. il Science 152:1406-8 Je 3 '66
Copulation-reward site in the posterior hypo-
thalamus. A. R. Caggiula and B. G. Hoebel. bibliog il Science 153:1284-5 S 9 '66
Corticosteroid responses to limbic stimulation
in man: localization of stimulus sites. R. T.
Rubin and others. bibliog il Science 153:767-
8 Ag 12 '66
Curiosity and exploration. D. E. Berlyne.
bibliog il Science 153:25-33 Jl 1 '66; Reply. J. M. Burgers. 154:1680-1 D 30 '66
Direct test of the power function for loudness. L. E. Marks and A. W. Slawson.
bibliog il Science 154:1036-7 N 25 '66
Estrous cycle in the rat: effects on self-stimulation behavior. R. G. W. Prescott. bibliog
il Science 152:796-7 My 6 '66
Evoked potential in relation to subsequent
alpha frequency. E. Levonian. bibliog il
Science 152:1280-2 My 27 '66
Evoked pressure responses in the rabbit
eye. C. C. Collins. bibliog il Science 155:
106-8 Ja 6 '67

STIMULUS and response—_Continued_
Imagery: effect of a concealed figure in a stimulus. M. Eagle and others. bibliog il Science 151:837-9 F 18 '66; Discussion. 152:230 Ap 8 '66
Inhibition of the carotid sinus reflex by stimulation of the inferior olive. O. A. Smith, jr. and M. A. Nathan. bibliog il Science 154: 674-5 N 4 '66
Light-stimulated electrical responses from skin. H. E. Becker and R. A. Cone. bibliog il Science 154:1051-3 N 25 '66
Long temporal gradient of retrograde amnesia for a well-discriminated stimulus. R. Kopp and others. bibliog il Science 153: 1547-9 S 23 '66
Metacontrast: its relation to evoked potentials. P. H. Schiller and S. L. Chorover. bibliog il Science 153:1398-400 S 16 '66
Neurosecretory cell: capable of conducting impulse in rats. K. Yagi and others. bibliog il Science 154:778-9 N 11 '66
Optomotor response in human infants to apparent motion: evidence of innateness. E. S. Tauber and S. Koffler. bibliog Science 152:382-3 Ap 15 '66
Rate of movement and redistribution of stainable neurosecretory granules in hypothalamic neurons. A. Jasinski and others. bibliog il Science 154:776-8 N 11 '66
Release of coordinated behavior in crayfish by single central neurons. D. Kennedy and others. bibliog il Science 154:917-19 N 18 '66
Response during sleep with intervening waking amnesia. F. J. Evans and others. bibliog Science 152:666-7 Ap 29 '66
Science is born: study of interaction between physical and psychological forces. H. Pryor. il Sci Digest 59:9-11 Mr '66
Sleep: suppression of rapid eye movement phase in the cat after electroconvulsive shock. H. B. Cohen and W. C. Dement. bibliog il Science 154:396-8 O 21 '66
Thiosemicarbazide injection followed by electric shock increases resistance to stress in rats. R. W. Reynolds and M. R. Meeker. bibliog il Science 151:1101-2 Mr 4 '66
Tritiated norepinephrine: release from brain slices by electrical stimulation. R. J. Baldessarini and I. J. Kopin. bibliog il Science 152:1630-1 Je 17 '66
Unconditioned response to electric shock: mechanism in planarians. J. B. Best and E. Elshtain. bibliog il Science 151:707-9 F 11 '66
Visual adaptation: increased efficiency resulting from spectrally distributed mixtures of stimuli. R. M. Boynton and S. R. Das. bibliog il Science 154:1581-3 D 23 '66
Visual world of infants. T. G. R. Bower. il Sci Am 215:80-4+ D '66
Visually evoked potentials: amplitude changes with age. R. E. Dustman and E. C. Beck. bibliog il Science 151:1013-15 F 25 '66

STINCHECUM, Theodore
Antigone. Criticism
  Nation 202:224 F 21 '66

STINIS, Anthony
Sky has to be big enough: interview. New Yorker 42:52-4 S 24 '66

STINNETT, Caskie
Speaking of travel. See issues of Holiday

STINSON, Christopher Hall
It's different, but not quite; poem. Horn Bk 42:357 Je '66

STINSON, George Arthur
Businessmen in the news. por Fortune 73:51 Ap '66

STIPENDS, Mass. See Mass stipends

STIREWALT, William S. and Wool, I. G.
Protein synthesis by heart music ribosomes: an effect of insulin independent of substrate transport. bibliog Science 154:284 O 14 '66

STITCHES. See Needlework

STIVER, Frank G.
Voltage-regulated battery power supply. Pop Electr 25:85-6+ N '66

STOBBE, Emily
Tagging the migratory monarch. Audubon Mag 68:343-6 S '66

STOCK. See Livestock

STOCK averages. See Stocks—Price indexes and averages

STOCK brokers. See Brokers

STOCK-car racing. See Automobile racing

STOCK control. See Stores or stock-room keeping

STOCK control (bookstores) See Booksellers and bookselling—Stock

STOCK exchange
Are stocks ready to move up? opinions of top security analysts and institutional investors. il Bsns W p 18-19 D 31 '66
Can mutual funds outguess the market? J. L. Treynor and K. K. Mazuy. il Harvard Bsns R 44:131-6 Jl '66
Changing outlook? stock market's influence on economy. H. C. Wallich. Newsweek 67: 76 My 30 '66
Critical look at the stock market; interview. M. F. Cohen. U S News 60:36-40 My 30 '66
How inflation baffles investment markets: U.S., Europe, Japan. il U S News 60:62-3 Mr 21 '66
Speculation: the big worry in the stock market. il U S News 60:92-3 My 2 '66
Speculative market; stringent set of rules. il Time 87:92+ Ap 29 '66
What the bears are worried about. Fortune 74:241 O '66
Why the stock market acts that way. D. Seligman. il Fortune 74:154-7+ N '66
  See also
Arbitrage
United States—Securities and exchange commission

Crisis, October 1929
Another '29 in sight? pro and con. il U S News 60:46-8 My 16 '66

Regulation
Floor traders learn to live with rules. il Bsns W p 114-16 Jl 16 '66
Personal business; margin buying. Bsns W p 141 Ap 30 '66
SEC has a little list; with editorial comment. C. J. Loomis. il Fortune 75:86, 110-15+ Ja '67
SEC watchmen prowl a new beat; investigates Genesco and Georgia-Pacific cases. il Bsns W p53-4+ My 7 '66

Europe, Western
Down their own street. Time 87:93 My 27 '66

Mexico (city)
Mexico's money men learn to lure capital; promise of fat dividends and growth. il Bsns W p 116-18+ N 26 '66

New York (city)
Big-block buyers may speak up. il Bsns W p 139-40 N 26 '66
Blue chips build hope; short selling. il Bsns W p43 O 22 '66
Brokers who ring up the records, are little known. il Bsns W p 160-2 Je 18 '66
Bulls take a breather. il Newsweek 67:70 Mr 7 '66
Corporate mistakes on Wall Street; a company's day-to-day relations with the financial community. T. J. Murray. il Duns R 88:36-8+ O '66
Curb for Wall Street? il Newsweek 68:94-6 D 19 '66
Day of the little bulls; Johnson's anti-inflation package. il Time 88:87 S 23 '66
Fear of credit crisis dulls investors' spirits. il Bsns W p36-7 Mr 12 '66
Floor traders learn to live with rules. il Bsns W p 114-16 Jl 16 '66
Funston's farewell. Newsweek 68:87 S 26 '66
GM puts on a brake and stocks skid. il Newsweek 67:73-4 My 16 '66
How big is the binge on Wall Street? stock market's speculative action. il Bsns W p 122+ Ap 30 '66
Investors tremble over indecision; Wall Street blames White House policymakers. il Bsns W p 158-9 Mr 19 '66
Is short selling bullish or bearish? il Bsns W p 129-30+ D 3 '66
Long look upward. il Time 88:66-70 Ag 19 '66
Man for everyman's capitalism; president to leave. il Time 88:88+ S 23 '66
Market à go go. C. J. Rolo. il N Y Times Mag p26-7+ My 8 '66
Reasons why; dark grey Monday on Wall Street. Time 88:83 Ag 5 '66
SEC enters a period of persuasion. Bsns W p94-6+ F 5 '66
Stocks near their own millennium. il Bsns W p 110-11+ Ja 29 '66
Tight-money market. il Time 87:89 Mr 18 '66
Too taxing? search for a new home. Newsweek 67:68 Mr 28 '66
Wall Street. See issues of Newsweek
Wall Street balks at mayor's tax scheme. il Bsns W p44+ Mr 12 '66
Wall Street establishment. P. B. Finney and J. S. Tompkins. il Esquire 65:95-7+ Je '66

STOCK exchange—New York (city)—*Cont.*
Wall Street takes a wary stand. il Bsns W
p32 Mr 5 '66
Wall St. talks. See occasional issues of Business week
Wall Street: the money market. il Sr Schol
88:13 Ap 1 '66
What does the plunge portend? il Bsns W
p35-6 My 14 '66
What the stock market is saying; with chart.
U S News 61:110-12 O 17 '66
What's going on in the stock market, and why. il U S News 60:32-3 My 23 '66
Will the big board leave the big town? il
Time 87:80 Mr 25 '66
Wiring odd lots for efficiency. il Bsns W p84-7
Jl 30 '66

STOCK exchange, American. See American
stock exchange

STOCK gambling. See Speculation

STOCK margin requirements. See Stock exchange—Regulation

STOCK market. See Stock exchange

STOCK market charts. See Stocks—Price indexes and averages

STOCK-room keeping.   See Stores or stockroom keeping

STOCK speculation. See Speculation

STOCK transfer tax
Wall Street balks at mayor's tax scheme. il
Bsns W p44+ Mr 12 '66
Wall Street: behind the transfer-tax spat.
Newsweek 67:84 Ap 11 '66
Will the big board leave the big town? il
Time 87:80 Mr 25 '66

STOCKBROKERS. See Brokers

STOCKER, Vera McPherson
Tribute to a teacher. Sr Schol 89:sup61 S 23
'66

STOCKHOLDERS
AT&T shareowners win a voice; protest FCC
probe of the Bell system. Bsns W p 158+
O 22 '66
Big-block buyers may speak up. il Bsns W
p 139-40 N 26 '66
Surprising sagacity of the small investor.
C. J. Loomis. Fortune 74:209 S '66
Voice of the investor. il Newsweek 68:78 S 12
'66

STOCKHOLDERS meetings
Annual headache: the stockholders' meeting.
O. G. Saxon, jr. Harvard Bsns R 44:132-7 Ja '66
General motors caps rite of spring. il
Bsns W p 112-13 My 28 '66
How companies are wooing investors abroad;
via Early bird and underwater cable. il
Bsns W p 154-5+ My 14 '66
Preserving corporate philanthropy; publicity-seeking characters at meetings. L. L. L.
Golden. Sat R 49:56 Jl 9 '66
Queen of corporate gadflies: W. Soss; with
report by N. Fraser. il Life 60:115-16+ Mr
18 '66
Reporter at large. J. Brooks. New Yorker
42:159-60+ O 8 '66

STOCKHOLM
City planning
Poet with a slide rule: P. Hein. J. Hicks. il
Life 61:55-6+ O 14 '66

Description
Sweden's atomic city: Farsta. S. Clark. il
Travel 126:41-3 Jl '66

Galleries and museums
Fit for a queen; Christina's collection on
show. il Newsweek 68:79 Ag 1 '66
Our far-flung correspondents: exhibition
called Christina, queen of Sweden, a personality of European civilization at The
Nationalmuseum. F. Steegmuller. il New
Yorker 42:160+ S 17 '66
Queen Christina of Sweden; exhibition of her
treasures. J. Stuart. il Antiques 90:164+ Ag
'66
Ultimate She; a gargantuan work at Stockholm's Museum of modern art. il Time 87:
92+ Je 17 '66
World of Queen Christina. F. Getlein. New
Repub 155:33-4 Ag 13 '66

Hotels, restaurants, etc.
Stockholm's opera cellar; Operakällaren at the
Royal opera. A. M. Swanson. il Opera N
31:14-15 Ja 14 '67

Music
Stockholm. K. Atterberg. il Opera N 30:31
F 5; 31:30 S 10 '66
Stockholm; Lohengrin. K. Atterberg. il Opera
N 30:33 Mr 12 '66

Theater
Depth and breadth in Sweden; Royal dramatic
theater productions. H. Hewes. Sat R 49:
51+ My 14 '66

STOCKHOLM festival. See Music festivals—
Sweden

STOCKING of streams, lakes, etc. See Fish culture

STOCKINGS. See Hosiery

STOCKLIN, William A.
For the record. See issues of Electronics
world

STOCKPILING
New selling program cuts down the bounce;
U.S. decision to unload rubber stockpile
draws protests. Bsns W p46 My 14 '66
Scraping the barrel for copper; U.S. releases
150,000 tons of stockpiled metal. Bsns W
p40 D 10 '66
Stockpile strategy. Sister Thomasine Cusack.
America 114:197-9 F 5 '66
Stockpiling and the future. Duns R 87:33 Ja
'66

STOCKS
Can you make money in stocks by using a
formula? Bet Hom & Gard 44:12 Ap '66
Easy & practical way to buy stocks. il
Changing T 20:16-20 F '66
Experts see for '67: a period of opportunity
for investors. il U S News 62:36-9 Ja 9 '67
How to do business with a stockbroker;
the machinery & the lingo. il Changing T
20:7-12 D '66
How to handle your money now; interview.
R. D. Naess. il U S News 60:58-62 Ja 31
'66
How to make money in science stocks. D. L.
Markstein. il Sci Digest 59:82-5 Ap '66
New issues reviving, but a difference. il Bsns
W p 120+ Ap 23 '66
Pension funds sniff a bargain; tend toward
common stock. il Bsns W p 153-4 O 15 '66
Racing to pick the winners. il Bsns W p 108+
Ag 27 '66
Relic of the 1920s returns: convertible participating preferred stock. il Bsns W p80+
Ag 13 '66
Stock for all reasons: Litton's convertible
preference stock, participating series. Newsweek 67:77 F 14 '66
Stocks start out of the cellar. Bsns W p41
O 15 '66
Stocks the big money likes best. Newsweek
67:69 Ja 31 '66
Timely ideas for investors. il Changing T
20:24-5 N '66
Wall Street:
Choice for '67. C. Morgello. Newsweek
68:63 D 26 '66
Convertible mirage. C. Morgello. il Newsweek 69:55 Ja 2 '67
Double-duty funds. C. Morgello. Newsweek 68:89 D 12 '66
How to gauge stock prices; price-earnings
ratios. il Newsweek 67:78 F 28 '66
Merger stocks. Newsweek 67:74 Ap 25 '66
New interest in new issues. il Newsweek
67:77 My 9 '66
Ogling the blue chips again; Harris,
Upham survey findings. il Newsweek
68:76 Jl 18 '66
Picking the winning stocks. Newsweek 68:
70 Ag 1 '66
Rewards of high risks; growth stocks
prospects. C. Morgello. il Newsweek
68:89 O 24 '66
What the experts favor now. C. Morgello. il Newsweek 67:87 Je 13 '66
Wall Street oracles foresee earnings drop;
price-earnings ratio. il Bsns W p 152+ S
24 '66
See also
Automobile industry and trade—Securities
Banks and banking—Securities
Bonds
Computers—Investment applications
Speculation
Stock exchange

Insider trading
Crying on the inside; SEC insider regulations.
Time 87:94 My 13 '66
Disclosure and insider investing; address.
H. H. Budge. Duns R 87:21-2+ Ja '66
In defense of insider trading; excerpts from
Insider trading and the stock market. H. G.
Manne. bibliog f Harvard Bsns R 44:113-22
N '66
Inside out; SEC lawsuit: decision on Texas
Gulf. Newsweek 68:58 Ag 29 '66
Love, honor, and report; SEC advises insiders. Bsns W p200 My 14 '66

STOCKTON, Calif.
Awards for volunteers. Parks & Rec 1:945 N '66
STODELLE, Ernestine
Anna Sokolow in Japan. Dance Mag 41:40-2+ Ja '67
College or career for dancers? University of Arkansas' answer. Dance Mag 40:56-9 F '66
College or career for dancers? University of Illinois' answer. Dance Mag 40:52-5 Ap '66
Turtle and the bee. Dance Mag 40:16-19 Mr '66
STOKES, Joseph, 3d
New profession within medicine? Sat R 49: 90-2 D 3 '66
STOKES, Joseph M.
Team teaching in college. Sat R 49:64-5 Jl 16 '66
STOKES, Liselotte Z. See Mahoney, S. M. jt. auth.
STOKES parameters. See Parameters
STOKLEY, James
Astronomy. See issues of Science news
STOKOWSKI, Leopold Anton Stanislaw
Musical events; concerts performed by American symphony orchestra in Carnegie Hall (cont) W. Sargeant. New Yorker 42: 107-8+ My 21 '66
Stoky's striplings. il pors Time 87:54 Je 3 '66
STOKVIS, Irene Ellen
(ed) First novelists: spring-summer, fall. 1966. Library J 91:722-37, 2883-93, 4707-17 F 1, Je 1, O 1 '66
STOLEN automobiles. See Automobiles, Theft of
STOLEN heart; drama. See Newman, D.
STOLLE, Fred
All-Aussie. Newsweek 68:78 S 26 '66
Forgotten Aussie refreshes the memory. F. Deford. il por Sports Illus 25:105-6+ S 19 '66
STOLLER, Robert
Reflections on the curtain wall; photographs. Horizon 8:100-3 Sum '66
STOLLEY, Richard
Bright career given up. Life 61:110 O 14 '66
Hopeless case of Milton Shapp. Life 60:68A-6RD+ My 27 '66
Indispensable camera. Life 61:90A-90B+ D 23 '66
Solemn event in a fiesta city, no miracle, but solid results. Life 61:31 N 4 '66
STOLOFF, Carolyn
Young man; poem. Nation 203:334 O 3 '66
STOLTZ, Jim
Amazing Janie D. Motor B 117:35 F '66
New look at planing hull design. Motor B 118:98-101+ S; 48-51 O; 46-9+ N; 48-50+ D '66
STOLZ, Robert K.
Executive development, new perspective. Harvard Bsns R 44:133-6+ My '66
STOMACH
Diseases
See also
Digestive system—Diseases
STONAKER, H. H.
What to breed for. Suc Farm 64:52-3 Mr '66
STONE, Edward Durell
Architecture. E. Galantay. il Nation 202:629-30 My 23 '66
Man with a billion on the drawing board. il por Bsns W p 124-6+ O 8 '66
Mogul modern. il Time 88:56 Ag 12 '66
STONE, Erika
Those little darlings. il U S Camera 29:50-1+ Jl '66
STONE, George Winchester, Jr
Lady in pursuit of enlightenment. Sat R 49:30-1 F 12 '66
STONE, I. F.
Why we fail as revolutionaries. New Repub 155:23-5 Jl 30 '66
STONE, James
Curl up and read. Seventeen 25:38 Mr '66
STONE, Jeremy J.
ABM, the next MLF? Bul Atomic Sci 22:20-1 S '66
General faces reality. New Repub 155:30-1 O 29 '66
McNamara story continues. Bul Atomic Sci 22:39-42 Ap '66
Minutes from Armageddon. New Repub 154: 28-30 Mr 5 '66
Nike-X: who needs it? New Repub 154:11-12 Je 18 '66
Waiting for an end of history. New Repub 155:30 Jl 2 '66
Why bomb North Vietnam? Commonweal 85: 339-41 D 23 '66

STONE, Jim
In my opinion. por Seventeen 25:284 My '66
STONE, Jonathan
English inkstands in silver and Sheffield plate. Antiques 90:342-6 S '66
—and Fabian, Miriam
Specialized receptive fields of the cat's retina. bibliog Science 152:1277-9 My 27 '66
STONE, P. W.
Odyssey of the Elgin marbles. Sat R 49:34+ O 22 '66
STONE, Robert
Farley the sailor; story. Sat Eve Post 240:42-4 Ja 14 '67
Thunderbolts in red, white, and blue; story. Sat Eve Post 240:62-4 Ja 28 '67
STONE, Ron, and Napier, Jeff
Great pollution pickle. Motor B 119:352-3+ Ja '67
STONE, Ruth
Poet's workshop (cont) Writer 79:24-6+ Mr '66
STONE, S. H. and others
Autoimmune encephalomyelitis and ocular lesions in monkeys sensitized during the neonatal period. bibliog Science 151:473-5 Ja 28 '66
STONE, William T.
Deep water Chesapeake. Yachting 199:64-5+ Mr '66
Washington report. See issues of Yachting
STONE age
Man's oldest dwelling; H. De Lumley's discovery in Nice. il Time 87:102 F 25 '66
Mud-walled village oldest in world; discovered in southern Kurdistan. Sci N 89: 268 Ap 16 '66
Prehistory of the Australian aborigine. D. J. Mulvaney. il Sci Am 214:84-91+ bibliog(p 143) Mr '66
STONE carving
Stone notes: direct carving. P. Pavia. il Art N 65:50-1+ My '66
See also
Carving (art industries)
STONE HARBOR, N.J.
No fly-by-night operation; Stone Harbor bird sanctuary. B. Gilbert. il Sports Illus 24:36-8+ Je 20 '66
STONE HARBOR bird sanctuary. See Bird sanctuaries
STONE implements and weapons
Cross-dating the archeology of northwestern Alaska. J. L. Giddings. bibliog il Science 153:127-35 Jl 8 '66
Folsoms, Clovisis, and the development of mankind. C. Miles. il Hobbies 71:112-15 N '66
Paleohunters in America: origins and diffusion. H. Müller-Beck. bibliog il Science 152:1191-210 My 27 '66
See also
Indians of North America—Implements
Stone age
STONE MOUNTAIN memorial
Great stone faces. il Time 88:66 Ag 5 '66
STONE sheep hunting. See Mountain sheep hunting
STONEBERG, Everett
Dollars and sense tips for buying feeder cattle. Suc Farm 64:54-5 S '66
STONEBURNER, Tony
Directions for a sculpture of the Holy Spirit; poem. Christian Cent 84:43 Ja 11 '67
STONEHENGE, England
Stonehenge decoded, by G. S. Hawkins and J. B. White. Review
Sky & Tel il 32:32-4+ Jl '66. T. M. Gates
Stonehenge revisited. B. Tufty. il Sci N 90: 514-15 D 17 '66

Anecdoes, facetiae, satire, etc.
Something was fishy about Stonehenge. E. Zern. il Sports Illus 25:44-6 Ag 22 '66
STONES, Barney V.
Camera that refused to die. U S Camera 29: 30+ Je '66
STONES, Flowering. See Flowering stones
STONEWARE. See Pottery
STONEWORK, Decorative. See Decoration and ornament, Architectural
STONG, C. L.
Amateur scientist. See issues of Scientific American
STONY BROOK campus, New York state university. See New York state university— Long Island center, Stony Brook
STOOLS
Simple stools for extra seating. il Sunset 137:134+ O '66
STOPHLET, John J.
Egg Island adventure. il Nat Parks Mag 40: 9-12 Mr '66

STORAGE
See also
Boats—Storage
Garden houses, shelters. etc.
Garden tools, equipment and supplies—Storage

STORAGE batteries
Back to electric cars? more federal activity urged in research. J. Ridgeway. New Repub 155:9-10 Ag 13 '66
Better battery care means better boating. J. Weber. il Motor B 117:36-7+ Je '66
Breakthrough! solid-state car voltage regulator. B. C. Snow. il Pop Electr 24:39-44+ Je '66
Eterna VTVM C cell; substituting nickel-cadmium battery for flashlight cell. G. Boross. il Pop Electr 24:66 My '66
New spark for old electrics: Ford builds a better battery. il Life 61:74A-74B+ O 21 '66
Plug-in cars will give commuters a charge. J. Eberhart. il Sci N 90:293-4 O 15 '66
Poised for a comeback: electric autos. il U S News 61:10-11 O 17 '66
Sealed lead-acid batteries. E. T. DeBlock and J. R. Thomas. il Electr World 75:32-4 Je '66
Voltswagen? major breakthrough for the electric car. il Newsweek 68:88-9 S 26 '66
Which battery to use? types for transistor radios. il Consumer Bul 49:15-17 F '66
See also
Electric storage battery company

Charging
Check out your charging system. L. Heiner. il Motor B 117:34-5+ Ap '66

Testing
Build this $2 battery polarity tester. R. Shoberg. il Pop Mech 126:166-7 N '66

STORAGE battery chargers
Automobile battery chargers. il Consumer Rep 31:537-9 N '66
Lantern battery charger. C. Conley. il Field & S 71:149 My '66

STORAGE cabinets. See Cabinets (furniture)

STORAGE elements (computers) See Magnetic memory (computers); Memory devices (computers)

STORAGE in boats. See Boats—Equipment

STORAGE in the home
Changing western home. il Sunset 136:89 F '66
Comfort for a triple life. il House & Gard 131:112-15 Ja '67
Conquest of space. il Seventeen 25:182 Ap '66
Convenient stow-aways. il Farm J 90:64 S '66
Houseful of storage. J. Gillies. il Farm J 90:72-3+ O '66
How to get storage where there isn't place. il Bet Hom & Gard 44:128 Mr '66
Ingenious new storage for the dining room. il Bet Hom & Gard 44:82+ Ap '66
Make the most of kitchen storage. J. LemMon. il Suc Farm 64:79-83+ O '66
Put every inch of space to work; built-in storage. J. LemMon. il Suc Farm 64:64-5 Je '66
Solved: the toughest problems any house can have! il Bet Hom & Gard 44:60-81 Mr '66
Space-making storage. il Seventeen 25:142-3 Ap '66
Space-saving furniture. J. LemMon. il Suc Farm 64:64-5 Jl '66
Storage ideas for every room in the house. il Bet Hom & Gard 44:42+ F '66
Store it where you use it, that's the new way. il Pop Sci 188:144-8 Ap '66
Twenty-five marvelous ideas for Sunday artists, over half our panel, and collectors almost everyone. il House & Gard 130:98-101 Jl '66
See also
Kitchen cabinets

STORAGE of bulbs. See Bulbs—Storage

STORAGE of fruit. See Fruit—Storage

STORAGE shelters. See Shelters

STORAGE walls
Organizing storage in the kitchen walls. il Sunset 137:89 N '66
Prefab this storage wall in your workshop. D. Jordan. il Bet Hom & Gard 44:70-1 O '66
Six-way theater wall. il Pop Mech 126:164-9+ O '66

STORE decorations. See Christmas decorations

STORES
Building types study. Arch Rec 139:149 Ap '66
See also
Antiques shops
Retail trade
also subhead Stores under names of cities, e.g. Dallas—Stores

STORES, Self service
Word of honor; supermarkets honor-system checkout, Switzerland. il Time 87:98 Mr 18 '66

STORES or stock-room keeping
Stock control in bookselling; condensation of pamphlet. G. Bartlett. il Pub W 190:68-72 Jl 18; 62-6 Jl 25 '66

STORIES. See Short stories

STORM, Alex
Who gets the gold? il por Newsweek 67:64 Ap 18 '66

STORM KING (mountain)
Storm King. New Yorker 42:17-19 Ja 7 '67

STORM KING hydroelectric project. See Hydroelectric plants

STORM waves. See Waves

STORMS
Night of the santana. L. Parsons. il Yachting 120:48+ O '66
Passage through a sea gone berserk; Michelangelo. il Life 60:34-5 Ap 29 '66
Squalls and frustration; 1966 Bermuda race. B. D. Barker. 3d. il Yachting 120:36+ Ag '66
Trimaran in a tempest. A. Piver. il Motor B 118:30-1+ Ag '66
See also
Aviation—Storm hazards
Rain and rainfall
Snowstorms
Tornadoes
Winds

STORY of Jorkel Hayforks; story. See Brown, G. M.

STORY of pink jade; story. See Lederer, W. J.

STORY telling
Build me a story, daddy. J. Boyd. il Farm J 90:72 My '66
Lost art of storytelling. H. D. Pennington. il Parents Mag 41:48-9+ Ag '66
Summer storytelling in Ohio. E. S. Ross. Horn Bk 42:279-81 Je '66

STORY telling records. See Phonograph records—Childrens records

STORYTELLING. See Story telling

STOUGH, Ada Barnett
Creative aging. Parks & Rec 1:910-11 N '66

STOUT, Ellis
Make gates last longer. il Suc Farm 64:124 Mr '66
164 bushels of milo/acre. Suc Farm 64:36-7+ My '66

STOUT, Rex
Murderer's milieu. Sat R 49:29-30 O 29 '66

STOUTENBURG, Adrien
Tree service; poem. New Yorker 42:165 My 21 '66

STOUTENBURGH, John L. Jr
Museum world. See issues of Hobbies

STOVES
Range-top units that read your mind. il Good H 162:132-3 My '66
Ranges revisited. il McCalls 93:56+ S '66
See also
Camp stoves
Electric stoves

History
Art of keeping warm. J. M. Dennis. il Antiques 89:374-9 Mr '66

STOVES, Earthenware
Art of keeping warm. J. M. Dennis. il Antiques 89:374-9 Mr '66

STOWE, Shirley
Look to the East. Library J 91:3645 Ag '66

STOWELL, Jack
Tuckaway camper cabana. Pop Mech 126:130-1 Ag '66

STRACHAN, Harold
Crusader pays. Newsweek 67:38 F 7 '66
Immaculate confinement. Time 87:34 F 4 '66

STRACHEY, Christopher
System analysis and programming; with biographical sketch. Sci Am 215:45, 112-18+ bibliog(p312) S '66

STRACKE, Dick
Recreation in space. por Parks & Rec 1:28-9+ Ja '66

STRAIGHT, Michael
Spanish tragedy. New Repub 155:28+ N 12 '66

STRAIGHT wings. See Orthoptera

STRAIN gages
Silicon strain gauge to pinpoint Apollo system fuels in zero-G. R. Pay. il Tech W 19:40-1 D 12 '66

STRAINS and stresses
Building movement can damage built-up roofing systems. W. H. Gumpertz. il Arch Rec 140:221-4 S '66

STRAINS and stresses—*Continued*
Electrical resistivity changes in saturated rock under stress. W. F. Brace and A. S. Orange. bibliog il Science 153:1525-6 S 23 '66
Stress-corrosion failure. P. R. Swann. il Sci Am 214:72-81 F '66
See also
Strain gages

STRAITS of Florida. See Florida, Straits of

STRAKA, Ronald M. See Castelli, J. P. jt. auth.

STRAND, Harold P.
Temperature sentry guards against freeze-up. Pop Mech 126:159-60 N '66

STRAND, Kaj Aage
Stars: near and dark. A. Ewing. il Sci N 90: 470 D 3 '66

STRAND, Mark
Dead; poem. Atlan 218:108 D '66
Man in black; poem. New Yorker 42:34 Ag 6 '66
Suicide; poem. New Yorker 42:158 Mr 12 '66

STRANG, Charles D.
To Slovak/Tahoe Miss. the Governor's cup. Motor B 118:41+ N '66

STRANG, Ruth
Discipline isn't dated. PTA Mag 61:26-8 bibliog(p34) N '66

STRANGER, Joyce
Running foxes; story. Sat Eve Post 239:50-5 My 7 '66

STRASSER, Judith
Something to talk about on campus. Mlle 63: 324+ Ag '66

STRATEGIC intelligence. See Military intelligence

STRATEGIC materials
Metal shortages forcing delivery delays. M. L. Yaffee. Aviation W 85:31-2 S 19 '66

STRATEGIC space plans. See Space flight—Military applications

STRATEGY
As top strategists see it: U.S. role in a changing world; report. M. S. Johnson. U S News 61:45 Jl 18 '66
Deterrence and strategy, by A. Beaufre. Review
Bul Atomic Sci 22:38-40 S '66. R. D. Masters
See also
Korean war, 1950-1953—Strategy
Military art and science
Vietnamese war, 1957- —Strategy

STRATEGY, Communist. See Communist strategy

STRATFORD, Hugh
Jennifer's first flight. il U S Camera 29:32 O '66

STRATFORD, Virginia Tyler
Jacqueline Kennedy's new life. Ladies Home J 83:70+ F '66

STRATFORD, Conn, Shakespeare festival. See American Shakespeare festival theatre and academy, Stratford, Conn.

STRATFORD, Ontario, Shakespeare festival. See Shakespeare festival, Stratford, Ontario

STRATTON, T. K. See Miller, E. C. jt. auth.

STRAUS, R. Peter
Straus scores Hershey. Christian Cent 83:325 Mr 16 '66

STRAUS, Roger W. Jr
No Noonday paperbacks in Great Britain. Pub W 190:17 O 24 '66
Noonday paperbacks in the U.S. and the U.K. Pub W 190:36 O 10 '66

STRAUSS, Claude Lévi-. See Lévi-Strauss, C.

STRAUSS, Eduard
Music to my ears; Carnegie Hall debut. I. Kolodin. Sat R 49:51 N 5 '66

STRAUSS, Franz, 1897?-
Strauss vs. Wagner. A. M. Lingg. il Opera N 31:6 D 10 '66

STRAUSS, Franz Josef
Time to start U.S. pullback in Europe? interview; ed. by R. Haeger. por U S News 60:68-70+ Ap 18 '66

STRAUSS, Johann, 1825-1899
Die fledermaus. Criticism
Sat R 49:52 S 10 '66
Sat R 50:34 Ja 21 '67
Waltz king and his ancestors. R. Breuer. por Sat R 49:126-7 Mr 12 '66

STRAUSS, Richard
Capriccio. Criticism
New Yorker 42:165-6+ Ap 2 '66
Elektra. Criticism
New Yorker 42:231 N 5 '66
Opera N 30:30 F 5 '66
Opera N il 31:18-20 D 10 '66
Opera N il 31:24-5 D 10 '66
Sat R 49:76 N 12 '66
Gorgeous Strauss; Four last songs, by Elisabeth Schwarzkopf. H. Glass. Am Rec G 33: 117 O '66

Records: Four last songs. Opera N 31:66 S 17 '66
Richard Strauss, by W. Mann. Review
Am Rec G 32:890-1 My '66. G. L. Mayer
New Yorker 42:166+ Ap 2 '66. W. Sargeant
Opera N 30:32 My 7 '66. J. Honig
Der Rosenkavalier. Criticism
Sat R 49:52 S 10 '66
Unanswered question. R. Berges. il Opera N 30:6-7 Mr 26 '66
Woman without a shadow (Die frau ohne schatten) Criticism
Hi Fi 16:MA15+ D '66
New Yorker 42:233-4 O 15 '66
Opera N 31:25-7 D 17 '66
Opera N il 31:17-20 D 17 '66
Sat R 49:56+ O 15 '66
Sat R 49:58 N 26 '66
Sat R 50:26 Ja 7 '67
Time il 88:50 O 14 '66

STRAUSZ-HUPÉ, Robert
Restoration Europe and world politics. Yale R 55:488-99 Je '66

STRAVINSKY, Igor Fedorovich
Music and the statistical age; interview. Commentary 42:49-52 S '66
—and Craft, Robert
Perfect total; excerpts from Themes and episodes. por Seventeen 25:304+ Ag '66

about
California. A. Boucher. Opera N 31:31 Ja 21 '67
Fairy's kiss. C. J. Luten. por Am Rec G 32:804-5 My '66
Footnote on some footnotes; concerning book Themes and episodes. E. Salzman. Sat R 49:56-7 D 31 '66
For its 53rd spring, a superb 26th recording of Stravinsky's Rite; P. Boulez on Nonesuch. W. Botsford. il Am Rec G 32:500-3 F '66
Music. B. Boretz. Nation 203:165-6 Ag 22 '66
Music to my ears; New York Philharmonic celebrates eighty-fourth birthday. I. Kolodin. Sat R 49:48 Jl 16 '66
Sacre du Stravinsky; concerning latest book. Time 88:92+ S 16 '66
Stravinsky and the dance, Philharmonic Hall. M. Marks. Dance Mag 40:32+ S '66
Stravinsky, by E. W. White. Review
Opera N 31:7 Ja 14 '67. F. Rizzo
Stravinsky, his heritage and his legacy. B. Jacobson. por Hi Fi 16:MA9+ O '66
Stravinsky on record. Discus. Harper 232: 116-17 My '66
Stravinsky's new Requiem canticles. B. Jacobson. Hi Fi 16:MA11 D '66
Stravinsky's Rite, in the Boulez manner, frozen, immobile, violently precise. E. Salzman. il Hi Fi 16:68 F '66
Twentieth-century models; Pulcinella and Agon. Harper 233:136+ O '66
View from the top. Time 87:67 My 6 '66
With Stravinsky in Warsaw; excerpt from Table talk. R. Craft. Harper 232:66-70+ F '66

STRAWBERRIES
Red-ripe strawberries; treat them right. il Bet Hom & Gard 44:108 Ap '66
Strawberries. D. Reay. Horticulture 45:53 Ja '67
See also
Cookery—Fruit

STREAM pollution. See Water pollution

STREET, Donald M. Jr
Crazy capers of the Caribbean charter fleet. Yachting 120:50-1+ N '66

STREET accidents. See Traffic accidents

STREET car museums
Motorman's friends; trolley museums. il Time 87:94+ Je 24 '66

STREET cleaning
Staggered starting hours; for sweeper operators, loaders and mechanics; San Bernardino, Calif. H. Vaile and M. Cornelison. il Am City 81:82-3 Je '66
Street cleaning. See issues of American city
Two roads to cleanliness; street-sweeping and refuse-collecting programs, Claremont, Calif. W. Glickman and G. Ford. il Am City 81:110-11 My '66
See also
Refuse and refuse disposal
Snow and ice removal

STREET cleaning apparatus
No more dumping on the street; two new sweepers. Kalamazoo, Mich. D. H. Swets. il Am City 81:92-3 Mr '66
Street cleaning. See issues of American city

STREET cleaning apparatus—*Continued*

Testing

Tests rate cleaning efficiencies of sweeper brooms. il Am City 81:92-4 Jl '66

STREET lighting

New lights make a city garbage-pail conscious; Long Beach, N.Y. F. E. Vogel. il Am City 81:111 Jl '66

Outdoor lighting. See issues of American city

Sidewalks and street lights. Am City 81:6 Je '66

See also subhead Lighting under names of cities, e.g. Philadelphia—Lighting

STREET lighting fixtures

Aerial platform solves tall-order lighting problem. il Am City 81:128 Je '66

Ben Franklin's street lights make a comeback. il Am City 81:126 Je '66

STREET musicians

Blackstone on gutbucket: the trials of William Brown and Charles Bandy in New York. J. D. Zirin. il Reporter 35:48-9 O 6 '66

STREET parades. See Parades

STREET paving. See Pavements

STREET railroads

See also

Cable railroads

STREET shows. See Theater, Open air

STREET signs

Metro Nashville starts area-wide street-sign program. J. Chronister. il Am City 81:116+ Jl '66

Street signs that drivers can't miss; Santa Clara, Calif. F. T. Shreve. il Am City 81: 126 F '66

STREET speaking

Corner: oratory on southwest corner of 125th street and Seventh avenue. New Yorker 42:19-21 Ja 7 '67

Gripe corner; Hamburg's Theodor Heuss Platz. il Newsweek 67:50 Mr 14 '66

STREET traffic

Car ban for cities? pro and con discussion. il Sr Schol 89:14-15 O 7 '66

What happened to Caesar. il Am City 81: 132 Ag '66

See also

Automobile parking

Road traffic

also subhead Street traffic under names of cities, e.g. Hamburg—Street traffic

STREETER, Edward

Fine art of making money. Sat R 49:51-2 D 24 '66

STREETER, Thomas Winthrop

Streeter books to be sold at Parke-Bernet auctions. Pub W 190:42 O 17 '66

STREETS

See also

Arcades

Sidewalks

STREIKER, Lowell D.

Boundary lines. Christian Cent 83:1012+ Ag 17 '66

Honest to Robinson. Christian Cent 83:1449 N 23 '66

Legitimacy of rational inquiry. Christian Cent 83:458-60 Ap 13 '66

STREISAND, Barbra

Barbra Streisand talks about her million-dollar baby; interview, ed. by G. Steinem. Ladies Home J 83:64+ Ag '66

about

Barbra. por Newsweek 67:92 Mr 28 '66

Fan letter to Streisand. G. Ace. Sat R 49: 15 Ap 16 '66

Flip-side Streisand. il por Time 87:61 Ap 8 '66

Girl who catches the light. por Vogue 147: 144-5 Ap 1 '66

Instant Barbra. P. Devlin. il pors Vogue 147:68-73+ Mr '66

Not so funny girl; reactions to Paris haut couture. il por Time 87:56-7 F 11 '66

Poifect. por Time 88:64 Ag 19 '66

Superbarbra. T. B. Morgan. il pors Look 30:54-61+ Ap 5 '66

Tears of Barbra Streisand; with report by D. Lurie. il pors Life 60:95-96B+ Mr 18 '66

STRENGTH of materials

Designing strength into materials; fiber-reinforced composite materials. il Bsns W p91-2+ D 17 '66

See also

Strains and stresses

STRENS, Roger G. J. See Burns, R. G. jt. auth.

STREPTOCOCCI

Against streptococcus; experimental vaccine shows promise. Sci Am 215:65 D '66

Cell-free protein synthesis: effects of age and state of ribosomal aggregation. L. D. Moore and others. bibliog il Science 154: 1350-3 D 9 '66

Rheumatic-like cardiac lesions in mice. W. J. Cromartie and J. G. Craddock. bibliog il Science 154:285-7 O 14 '66

Transformation of auxotrophic mutants of group H streptococci. C. G. Leonard and others. bibliog il Science 152:1255-6 My 27 '66

STREPTOCOCCUS sore throat. See Throat—Diseases

STRESHINSKY, Shirley G.

Does it run in the family? Parents Mag 41: 61-3+ N '66

STRESS (physiology)

Adrenocorticotrophin-releasing hormone in peripheral blood: increase during stress. E. Anderson. bibliog il Science 152:379-80 Ap 15 '66

High strung; Hugo Schmale study of factors affecting orchestral musicians. Newsweek 68:80 S 5 '66

It's what's bugging them; restlessness of college students. W. C. McFadden. America 114:502-3 Ap 9 '66

Maturation of a stress-activated mechanism inhibiting induction of tyrosine transaminase. S. Schapiro and others. bibliog il Science 152:1642-3 Je 17 '66

Personal business; back to the rat race: tensions. Bsns W p 169-70 S 10 '66

Pressures on students; symposium. NEA J 55:28-31 S '66

Racial reaction pattern studied. Sci N 90: 475 D 3 '66

Stress and the brain. Sci N 91:9 Ja 7 '67

Stress causes rise in hormone output. Sci N 89:371 My 14 '66

Thiosemicarbazide injection followed by electric shock increases resistance to stress in rats. R. W. Reynolds and M. R. Meeker. bibliog il Science 151:1101-2 Mr 4 '66

Turning points of life; crises in women's lives. G. Caplan and V. Cadden. McCalls 94:114-15+ O '66; Same abr. with title How to deal with a crisis. Read Digest 90:80-3 Ja '67

What stress does. F. R. Schreiber and M. Herman. Sci Digest 59:18-20 Je '66

What to do about tension. J. Brothers. Good H 162:60+ Ap '66

STRESS- corrosion. See Corrosion and anti-corrosives

STRESSES. See Strains and stresses

STRETCH, Bonnie Barrett

Experiment that worked. Sat R 49:60-1+ Ag 20 '66

STRETCH fabrics. See Textile fabrics, Synthetic

STRETCH rope. See Rope

STREVA, Joe

How to teach handicapped children to swim. Parks & Rec 1:502-3 Je '66

STRICK, Joseph

Joycensors beware. il Newsweek 68:110+ S 19 '66

STRIDULATION. See Insect sounds

STRIKES

Qantas, pilots, government deadlocked in labor dispute. Aviation W 85:37 D 12 '66

Qantas pilots reject appeal to end strike. Aviation W 85:40 D 5 '66

Qantas pilots threaten walkout; strike at Air Canada continues. Aviation W 85:41 N 28 '66

Strikes are breaking out all over. il U S News 60:71-3 My 30 '66

See also

Hunger strikes

Economic aspects

Airline strike clips the wings of tourism. il Bsns W p31 Ag 13 '66

Bookshop business dropped during N.Y. transit strike. Pub W 189:307 Ja 24 '66

How the strike has been hurting; airline strike. Bsns W p30 Ag 6 '66

Strike cost $93 million revenue in July. Aviation W 85:45 O 3 '66

Subsonic, supersonic transport orders reflect blow of strike. J. W. Carter. Aviation W 85:41 S 12 '66

Law

See Labor laws and legislation—United States

Statistics

Review of work stoppages during 1965. E. D. Onanian. il Mo Labor R 89:749-53 Jl '66

STRIKES—*Continued*

Belgium

In poor health; doctors strike threatened. il Newsweek 67:35-6 F 14 '66

Canada

Adding up the bill; railroads moving again. il Time 88:99 S 9 '66

Back from sclerosis; Canada's coast-to-coast railroad strike. il Newsweek 68:50-1 S 12 '66

Canada getting set for a rough year; labor to press hard for greater gains. il Bsns W p51-2+ Ja 7 '67

Canada's rail unions pull the cord. il Bsns W p 128+ S 3 '66

How Canada halted rail strike. U S News 61:78 S 12 '66

How government stepped in when a rail strike tied up Canada. U S News 61:70 S 5 '66

Strikes hit Canadian, Philippine carriers. Aviation W 85:41 N 21 '66

30 percenters; rail workers. Newsweek 68:49 S 5 '66

Europe, Western

Butcher, the baker. . . il Newsweek 67: 72 F 14 '66

Strikes plague Europe's airlines. Bsns W p 109-10 Je 25 '66

France

Letter from Paris; 1936 sitdown strikes. Genêt. New Yorker 42:118-20 Ag 13 '66

Letter from Paris; transport strike: fifth this year. Genêt. New Yorker 42:199-200 O 22 '66

Great Britain

All aboard again; end to seamen's strike. Time 88:28 Jl 8 '66

Britain gets a $1-billion breather; seamen's strike threatens balance-of-payments. Bsns W p44-5 Je 18 '66

Britain's big shipping strike; labor vs. a labor government. U S News 60:74 My 30 '66

British losses in ship strike. U S News 61:80 Jl 11 '66

Hint of hope; Harold Wilson's approach to six-week-old shipping strike. Time 88:33 Jl 1 '66

How a strike hurt Britain; shipping strike. U S News 60:93 Je 20 '66

How reds kept a strike going; seamen's strike. U S News 61:63-4 Jl 4 '66

How will Wilson get out of this one? seamen's strike. B. Wenham. New Repub 154: 10-11 Je 18 '66

Idle fleet; seamen out on strike. Time 87: 36+ My 27 '66

Invisible impact; shipping strike. Time 87:45 Je 10 '66

Letter from London; shipping strike. M. Panter-Downes. New Yorker 42:81-2+ Jl 9 '66

Ready for emergency; merchant seamen's strike. Time 87:27 Je 3 '66

Rule Britannia, without a ship at sea? economic effects. il Newsweek 67:38+ Je 6 '66

Still landlocked. il Newsweek 67:44A Je 20 '66

Strike fever; merchant seamen strike. il Newsweek 67:68 My 30 '66

Ireland

Closing the banks; among other strikes. il Time 87:111+ My 20 '66

Latin America

Where politics causes strikes. U S News 60:75 Ap 4 '66

Philippines

Strikes hit Canadian, Philippine carriers. Aviation W 85:41 N 21 '66

Spain

Coming alive. il Time 89:28+ Ja 13 '67

Labor pains. Newsweek 69:44 Ja 16 '67

United States

After airline strike, a new wave of labor trouble? U S News 61:68 Ag 8 '66

How we create strikes. H. Hazlitt. Newsweek 68:70 Ag 15 '66

Impasse over mutual trust issue; UAW vs. Allis-Chalmers plant in Pittsburgh. il Bsns W p86-7 D 24 '66

Making strikes obsolete. A. H. Raskin. Atlan 217:47-52 Je '66

Parity with their peers; strikes by public employees. il Time 88:87 Ag 5 '66

Strike fever. il Newsweek 67:68 My 30 '66

Strike fever and the public; with reports by J. Breslin and B. Farrell. il Life 61: 24-36B Ag 26 '66

Strikes and the public interest. il Sr Schol 87:4-6+ Ja 21 '66

Union rejects $8.59 an hour; five month strike goes on; New York. U S News 62:45 Ja 2 '67

What the right to strike means. il U S News 61:23-5 Ag 15 '66

Why big strikes aren't stopped. il U S News 61:17-19 Ag 1 '66

Will 1967 be the year of the big strikes? U S News 62:65-6 Ja 9 '67

Work stoppages; tables. See issues of Monthly labor review

Agricultural workers

See Strikes—United States—Farm labor

Airlines

Aid pact will fail to meet strike loss. H. D. Watkins. Aviation W 85:24-5 Ag 22 '66

Air strike agreement has a rough landing. il Bsns W p31 Ag 20 '66

Air strike; machinists ground five lines. il Newsweek 68:22 Jl 18 '66

Airline strike. Commonweal 84:515-16 Ag 19 '66

Airline strike signals new labor struggle. il Aviation W 85:34-6+ Jl 18 '66

Airline strike: the impact, the cost. il U S News 61:10 Jl 25 '66

Airlines stay poised for flight. il Bsns W p25-6 Jl 30 '66

Back to work through an open gate. il Time 88:66-8 Ag 26 '66

Caught at the crest. il Time 88:80-3+ Jl 22 '66

Comic connotations. Time 88:19 Ag 19 '66

Congress pressing to end airline strike. Aviation W 85:30 Ag 1 '66

Getting upstaged by the union wasn't in the scenario; L. B. Johnson intervention. H. Sidey. il Life 61:32 Ag 12 '66

Grounded; machinists strike against airlines. il Time 88:16-17 Jl 15 '66

Hot-potato game. il Time 88:65-6 Ag 12 '66

How to fly; scheme and lie; strike effects on public. il Newsweek 68:63 Ag 15 '66

IAM cool to proposed airline settlement; July 5 strike threat. J. W. Carter. Aviation W 84:45 Je 13 '66

Is sky the limit on wage raises? il U S News 61:34-5 Ag 29 '66

Mr Johnson's labor problem. Nation 203: 106-7 Ag 8 '66

Steel prices up; planes still down. il Newsweek 68:61-2+ Ag 15 '66

Strike clogs airline reservations systems. Aviation W 85:41-3 Jl 25 '66

Strike clouds airlines' economic future; with editorial comment. H. D. Watkins. Aviation W 85:25-6 Ag 29 '66

Strike economic, social impact deepens. il Aviation W 85:40-2 Ag 8 '66

Strike jolts July trunk earnings. Aviation W 85:41 S 5 '66

Strike losers: airlines, travelers, hotels, industries, workers. U S News 61:69-70 Ag 8 '66

Strike socks in the airlines; five carriers grounded. il Bsns W p28-9 Jl 16 '66

Strikebound, but flying high; machinists' strike at United, TWA, Northwest, Eastern and National airlines. il Newsweek 68:74-5+ Jl 25 '66

Taking the lid off wages? mechanics reject settlement. il Newsweek 68:17-18 Ag 8 '66

2-billion-dollar strike: who's hurt by airline shutdown? with excerpts from letter by D. P. Babson. il U S News 61:70-3 Ag 22 '66

Up in the air; no settlement. Newsweek 68:64 Ag 1 '66

What other unions learned from the airline strike. il U S News 61:67-9 S 5 '66

When a union struck five major airlines; Machinists union. il U S News 61:105-6 Jl 18 '66

When Congress and President try to get a strike settled. U S News 61:72-4 Ag 15 '66

Why it's hard to stop strikes against the public. U S News 61:70-1 Jl 25 '66

Woodshed solution. il Time 88:17-18 Ag 5 '66

Anecdotes, facetiae, satire, etc.

Three strikes and you're in. Nat R 18:869-70 S 6 '66

Coal mines and mining

Striking miners foggy over issues. Bsns W p 132 Ap 23 '66

STRIKES—United States—*Continued*

Cotton workers

Strike that failed; Mississippi tent city. D. R. Maxey. il Look 30:26-9 Mr 8 '66

Electric workers

Electrical brotherhood makes its power play; IBEW bid for prestige. il Bsns W p50+ N 5 '66

Farm labor

Church and Delano. J. Wolf. Commonweal 84: 168-9 Ap 29 '66

Dispute in Delano. Commonweal 83:491 Ja 28 '66

Farm union reaps first California victory; recognition by Schenley and Christian brothers vineyards. il Bsns W p 158+ Ap 16 '66

From Delano to Sacramento. America 114: 430 Ap 2 '66

Grape pickers' strike; war in California. A. Kopkind. New Repub 154:12-15 Ja 29 '66

Grape strike. M. Novak; reply. V. Salandini. Commonweal 83:683+ Mr 18 '66

Labor comes to life in the grape fields. New Repub 154:6-7 Ap 23 '66

March of migrants. il Life 60:93-4 Ap 29 '66

Monopoly in the vineyards; grapes of wrath strike. J. P. Degnan. il Nation 202:151-4 F 7 '66

Schenley surrenders; migrant workers vs California grape growers. Christian Cent 83: 515-16 Ap 27 '66

Victory in the vineyards; support given to farm workers in Calif. il Time 87:59 Ap 15 '66

Vineyards of strife. Sr Schol 88:18 Mr 18 '66

Viva la huelga! Schenley corp. recognizes NFWA as sole bargaining agent. il News-week 67:42+ Ap 18 '66

Viva la huelga! T. N. Davis. America 114: 589-90 Ap 23 '66

Firemen

Firemen to end no-strike policy? U S News 62:68 Ja 9 '67

What does a city do when firemen go on strike? Atlanta. il U S News 61:86+ S 19 '66

Government employees

Cities on strike. M. Parks. America 115:455-7 O 15 '66

Coming: unionized government; interview. J. Wurf. U S News 61:96-9 S 26 '66

See also

Strikes—United States—Municipal employees

Government intervention

Administration hardens stand against job bias; St Louis scene of labor walkout. il Bsns W p94+ F 12 '66

Congress pressing to end airline strike. Avia-tion W 85:30 Ag 1 '66

Forced arbitration? H. Hazlitt. Newsweek 68:58 Ag 29 '66

Getting upstaged by the union wasn't in the scenario. L. B. Johnson intervention. H. Sidey. il Life 61:32 Ag 12 '66

Johnson draws bead on GE fight; wins two-week delay in nationwide strike. il Bsns W p 145-7 O 8 '66

Johnson moves to curb public interest strikes; amending Taft-Hartley and the Railway labor act. il Bsns W p39-40 D 10 '66

Not off the ground yet; airline machinists force Congress to take action. il Bsns W p30 Ag 13 '66

Steel prices up; planes still down. il News-week 68:61-2+ Ag 15 '66

When Congress and President try to get a strike settled. U S News 61:72-4 Ag 15 '66

Why tolerate the excesses of unions. Life 61:4 Ag 26 '66

Municipal employees

Another headache for cities: strikes by public workers. il U S News 61:78-9 Ag 1 '66

Cities on strike. M. Parks. America 115:455-7 O 15 '66

Civil service unionism; how to avert another strike. T. J. Cooney. Nation 202:88-9 Ja 24 '66

It's getting popular to strike against city hall. il U S News 60:91-2 Je 20 '66

Public employees ask for a better shake; rethinking of rules under which essential workers bargain. il Bsns W p92+ D 3 '66

See also

Strikes—United States—Firemen

Newspapers

Another big city learns what it's like with-out newspapers; Boston. il U S News 60: 76-8 Ap 11 '66

Blackout in Boston. Newsweek 67:82 Mr 28 '66

Boston loses its newspapers, finds bitterness in the strike. il Bsns W p 120 Mr 12 '66

Doing without the dailies; ending of Boston's month-old newspaper strike. il Time 87: 48 Ap 8 '66

Guild strike ends; who gets what, New York. U S News 61:107 Jl 18 '66

How not to negotiate in New York; World journal tribune. Time 87:43 My 6 '66

How the Constitution was violated: news-paper strike, New York city, December 1953 and interference with right to publish; reprint. D. Lawrence. U S News 61:136+ S 26 '66

Kheel hauled? strike against New York city's newspaper merger. Newsweek 67:92 My 16 '66

Labor disputes of merging newspapers; from sixteen circulation English-language news-papers in Manhattan, now there are four. Mo Labor R 89:III-IV Ag '66

Last blood from a pale stone; crippling of New York's newspapers. Time 87:79 Ap 29 '66

Last lap? World journal tribune. il Newsweek 68:87 Jl 25 '66

Long ninety minutes. Time 88:43 Ag 5 '66

Notes and comment; New York newspaper strike. New Yorker 42:37 My 7 '66

Printers rise again; shut down of Boston's five dailies. il Time 87:77 Mr 18 '66

Proud, the powerless; New York city's merged papers strike over layoffs. il Newsweek 67:92 My 9 '66

Stride toward settlement; World journal trib-une. Time 88:48 Jl 8 '66

Stymied by seniority; strikebound World journal tribune. il Time 87:56 My 20 '66

Tenuous franchise; effect on readers. R. Moley. Newsweek 68:92 S 5 '66

Third strike. W. V. Shannon. Commonweal 84:216-17 My 13 '66

3,700 jobs or none: the stake in New York newspaper strike. il U S News 60:97-9 My 9 '66

When unions killed a major newspaper; New York herald tribune. il U S News 61:70-2 Ag 29 '66

Who won what in 135-day strike? New York newspaper strike of 1966. U S News 61:90 S 19 '66

Why are we striking? case of N.Y. city newspapers. G. Merlis. Nat R 18:532-4 My 31 '66

Nurses

Now, it's strike moves by nurses. U S News 61:72 Jl 25 '66

When nurses go on strike; San Francisco. U S News 61:80 S 12 '66

Printers

Allied Kingsport unions refile unfair labor charges. Pub W 190:194-5 Jl 11 '66

Composing room workers strike Haddon craftsmen; members of the Scranton typo-graphical union, Pa. Pub W 189:110 Ap 4 '66

Kingsport press upheld against union charges. Pub W 190:45 S 19 '66

N.Y. Board of education to vote on union plea; proposal to discontinue buying books manufactured at Kingsport press. Pub W 189:50 Mr 21 '66

N.Y.C. schools enjoined from Kingsport boy-cott. Pub W 190:27 O 24 '66

New York schools asked to boycott Kings-port press. Pub W 189:152 F 21 '66

Printers settle; New York's World journal tribune. Time 87:69 My 27 '66

Unions drop NLRB charges against Kings-port press. Pub W 189:45-6 Je 20 '66

Railroads

Dead issue comes to life: why firemen went on strike. U S News 60:79 Ap 11 '66

Featherbedding again. Newsweek 67:86 Ap 11 '66

Festering fight on the rails; brotherhood continues battle for jobs that carriers and arbitrators call obsolete. il Bsns W p 144+ Ap 9 '66

No fires to stoke; firemen strike. Sr Schol 88:14-15 Ap 29 '66

Nothing but trouble. Time 87:23 Ap 15 '66

Strike that split rail unions: firemen's strike. U S News 60:79 My 2 '66

Walking the rails; largest U.S. railway walk-out since 1946. Time 87:27 Ap 8 '66

STRIKES—United States—Railroads—*Cont.*
Whiskey rebellion; walk out on Long Island rail road to protest executive drinking. Newsweek 67:87 My 23 '66

Social workers

Chicago social workers' strike. D. G. Cater. Christian Cent 83:842-3 Je 29 '66

Teachers

And gladly strike? J. S. LeSure. Sat R 49:79 F 19 '66
For 194 striking teachers: dismissal; Ecorse. Detroit suburb. U S News 60:95 Je 27 '66
It's getting popular to strike against city hall; cases in Michigan. il U S News 60:91-2 Je 20 '66
Should teachers strike? P. Friggens. Read Digest 89:95-9 N '66
Teacher-opinion poll; should teachers strike? il NEA J 55:54 My '66
Teacher strikes delay schools; cases in Michigan. U S News 61:90 S 19 '66
What's happening in education? W. D. Boutwell. PTA Mag 61:17-18 Ja '67

Transportation workers

Backfires follow the strike. Bsns W p32 Ja 22 '66
Bookshop business dropped during N.Y. transit strike. Pub W 189:307 Ja 24 '66
Don't sell on a strike. Am City 81:9 F '66
Lindsay, Quill & the transit strike. T. R. Brooks. Commentary 41:50-7 Mr '66
Mediator: N. P. Feinsinger and the New York transit strike. New Yorker 41:21-4 Ja 22 '66
Moving again; New York transit. Sr Schol 88:15-16 F 4 '66
New boy survives a hazing; New York transit strike. J. K. Jessup. Life 60:17 Ja 28 '66
Right to replace; inept handling of New York transit strike. H. Hazlitt. Newsweek 67:74 Ja 31 '66
Road to catastrophe: New York transit strike. il Sat Eve Post 239:92 F 12 '66
Sic transit; improvement needed in machinery for negotiating with government workers. Reporter 34:14+ Ja 27 '66
Striking down the strike; Condon-Waldin act violation; G. Weinstein's suit. il Time 87:50 F 18 '66
Traffic jams and aching feet; New York transit strike. il Sr Schol 87:14-15 Ja 21 '66

Transportation workers—Anecdotes, facetiae, satire, etc.

Two wheeler; middle-aged man on a bicycle. R. Lynes. il Harper 232:36+ Ap '66

Truck drivers

As Hoffa's deadline nears; a strike deadline too. il U S News 62:85-7 Ja 16 '67

Vietnam (Republic)

On the waterfront; Saigon dock workers union. il Time 89:25 Ja 6 '67
Vietnam strike that hurt the U.S. war effort; civilian longshoremen. il U S News 62:8 Ja 9 '67

STRINE (dialect) See English language—Dialects

STRING quartets
Award-winning quartet; Beaux-arts chamber ensemble. Hi Fi 16:126 My '66
Brothers four; de Pasquale string quartet. il Time 87:67 My 6 '66
See also
Phonograph records—String quartet music

STRING quintets
See also
Phonograph records—String quintet music

STRINGED instruments
See also names of stringed instruments, e.g. Guitar

STRINGFELLOW, William
News and views; the Great society myth. Commonweal 85:188 N 18 '66
What's right with Christmas. McCalls 94:149 D '66

STRINGS, Tennis racket
Restring a tennis racket like a pro. J. A. Kraft, jr. il Pop Sci 188:140-3 Je '66

STRIP coal mining. See Coal mines and mining—Stripping operations

STRIP mine dumps, Reclamation of. See Reclamation of land

STRIP mining. See Coal mines and mining—Stripping operations

STRIPED bass fishing. See Bass fishing

STRIPER fishing. See Bass fishing

STRIPTEASE acts. See Vaudeville

STRNAD, J.
Atomic nuclei: moments of inertia and quadrupole moments. bibliog Science 154:259-61 O 14 '66

STROBEL, Marion
Marion Strobel Mitchell. J. N. North. Poetry 108:264-5 Jl '66

STRODE, Bill
Photographers of the year. M. R. Weiss. il por Sat R 49:72-3 My 14 '66

STROEBEL, Daniel
Helluva way to grow up fast. C. S. Wren. il pors Look 30:73-7 S 20 '66

STROHM, John
Mexico closes the food gap. Read Digest 88:165-8+ Je '66

STROKES, Apoplectic. See Cerebral hemorrhage

STROKES, Cardiovascular. See Heart—Diseases

STROMBUS shells. See Shells (conchology)

STRONG, Lydia
Obituary
Consumer Rep por 31:156 Ap '66

STRONTIUM
Precipitate formation in the strontium-phosphate system. R. L. Collin. bibliog il Science 151:1386-8 Mr 18 '66

Isotopes

Isotopic composition of strontium in volcanic rocks from Oahu. J. L. Powell and S. E. DeLong. bibliog il Science 153:1239-42 S 9 '66
Strontium isotopes in deep-sea sediments. E. J. Dasch and others. bibliog il Science 153:295-7 Jl 15 '66
Strontium-90 fallout: comparison of rates over ocean and land. W. S. Broecker and others. bibliog il Science 152:639-40 Ap 29 '66
Strontium-90 fallout from surface and underground nuclear tests. T. Sotobayashi and S. Koyama. bibliog il Science 152:1059-60 My 20 '66

STRONTIUM in the body
Strontium incorporation into dental enamel. A. R. Johnson and others. bibliog il Science 153:1396-7 S 16 '66
Strontium 90 reduced by alginate in diet. Sci N 89:371 My 14 '66
Strontium uptake in rates on alginate-supplemented diet. G. E. Harrison and others. bibliog il Science 152:655-6 Ap 29 '66

STROTHER, Edward D.
Blacksmith for the horsey set. il pors Ebony 21:83-4+ S '66

STROTHER, Robert S.
Business booms on the waterways. Read Digest 88:213-14+ F '66
City sinking in a sea of mud. Read Digest 89:99-103 Ag '66

STROUP, Herbert
Service; the churches and government. Christian Cent 83:938-9 Jl 27 '66

STROUSE, Norman Hulbert
Adman with a difference. il por Bsns W p 112-14+ Je 18 '66

STROUT, Donald E. and Strout, R. B.
Placement situation 1965 (with a preview of 1966) Library J 91:3117-26 Je 15 '66

STROUT, Richard L.
American roulette. New Repub 154:24 F 5 '66
LBJ meets the press. . .sort of. New Repub 154:13-14 Ap 16 '66
One hundred years ago. New Repub 154:17-18 F 12 '66

STROUT, Ruth B. See Strout, D. E. jt. auth.

STRUCTURAL engineering

Study and teaching

Dome; study by Children's art lab, University of Oregon. J. Burgner. il Design 67:34-7 My '66

STRUCTURAL glass. See Glass, Structural

STRUCTURES, Underground. See Underground structures

STRUCTURES, Underwater. See Underwater structures

STRUNG, Norman
Month the Madison goes mad. Field & S 71:54-5+ Je '66

STRUVE, Otto
Otto Struve memorial symposium. B. J. Bok. il por Sky & Tel 32:68-71 Ag '66

STRYK, Lucien
Torero; poem. Sat R 49:16 F 26 '66

about

Four poets. L. Mueller. Poetry 109:50 O '66

STUART, Dabney
Home room; Ties; poems. Poetry 107:243-4 Ja '66
Student; poem. Poetry 109:17 O '66

STUART, Dick
My son the outfielder, and my major-leaguer, Dick Stuart. M. Kitman. il Sat Eve Post 239:20 S 10 '66

STUART, Gilbert
Gabriel Manigault & Mrs Gabriel Manigault (Margaret Izard) C. B. Johnson. il Sch Arts 65:39 Je '66

STUART, James
Letter from London. See issues of Antiques

STUART, Jesse
Accident; story. Sat Eve Post 239:54-6 N 19 '66
Autumn here and there; poem. il Am For 72: 44-5 N '66
Resurrection; poem. Am For 72:45 Ap '66
Thoughts afield. por Am For 72:22-5+ Ja '66

STUART, Jozefa
World built on slavery. Life 60:74+ Mr 4 '66

STUART, Lawrence
Saving the Allagash. Parks & Rec 1:352-4 O '66

STUART, Lyle
Lyle Stuart buys University books, Mystic arts club. Pub W 190:69 S 12 '66
Stuart, Random et al. vs. Hughes, Rosemont, etc. Pub W 189:47-8 My 16 '66

STUART-STUBBS, Basil
Square miles, love, and money: academic libraries. por Library J 91:5529-32 N 15 '66

STUBBS, Basil Stuart-. See Stuart-Stubbs, B.

STUBBS, John Heath-. See Heath-Stubbs, J.

STUBER, Stanley I.
Council, one year later. Commonweal 85:371-2 Ja 6 '67
Religious freedom in Spain; letter. America 115:1 Jl 2 '66
Spain finds an excuse. Christian Cent 83:1246 O 12 '66
Two-way responsibility. Christian Cent 83: 686-7 My 25 '66

STUCKER, Gilbert F.
Mountain of the stone fishes. Nat Parks Mag 40:4-9 S '66

STUCKI, Lorenz
China looks weaker than two years ago; interview, ed. by A. Zanker. por U S News 61:54-6 S 12 '66

STUDEBAKER corporation
Encore the Avanti! D. Ash. il Esquire 65: 140-1+ Ap '66
Final departure: out of auto business. Time 87:90 Mr 11 '66
South Bend comes out from under; recovers from Studebaker shutdown. il Bsns W p58-60+ F 19 '66
Tender invitation; G. W. Murphy's offer. Time 87:92+ F 18 '66
Ugly duckling; moving smartly. il Newsweek 67:73 F 28 '66

STUDENT achievements
Helping students who should do better. il Good H 162:184 Mr '66
International project for the evaluation of educational achievement. Sch & Soc 94:105-6 F 19 '66
Junior college: social experiment; relationship between social status and academic success. M. Fallows. Commonweal 85:9-13 O 7 '66
School success and satisfaction. Sch & Soc 94:442 D 10 '66
Special feature on the failing student; symposium. il NEA J 55:33-40 Ap '66
Why bright children get poor marks; excerpt from Underachievers: how they can be helped. B. Fine. il Redbook 127:72-3+ S '66

STUDENT activities
Campus '66; activism on the wane? il Newsweek 68:72 O 10 '66
Getting-involved-for-good club. H. T. Gott and M. L. Hurlburt. NEA J 55:15-16 S '66
Good grief! a computer picks the partners for a high school dance. G. Shalit. il Seventeen 25:124-5 D '66
Important aid to teachers: San Jose high school's A-V club. M. V. Chatton. il Sr Schol 87:sup22-3 Ja 14 '66
Moods & mores; new responsibility, dampening of protest. il Time 88:95-6+ N 18 '66
Prize-winning proms. Farm J 90:97 My '66
Something to talk about on campus. J. Strasser; M. L. Goodfriend. il Mlle 63:324-7 Ag '66

Summertime; decrease in activism. il Newsweek 67:60 Je 27 '66
See also
College and school drama
College and school journalism
College libraries—Student advisory committees
College students—Political activities
High school students—Political activities
School athletics
Student unions

STUDENT advisory committees. See College libraries—Student advisory committees

STUDENT aid
Dollars, decisions, and diplomas. J. L. Bowman. il Am Ed 2:30-2 My '66
Maybe he can become a doctor. C. Carner. il Todays Health 44:22-3+ My '66
Money for all somewhere. il Time 88:112+ O 14 '66
See also
College students—Aid
Graduate students
Scholarships and fellowships
Student loans

STUDENT assistants
See also
Library assistants

STUDENT clubs. See Student activities

STUDENT committees. See Self government in education

STUDENT conferences
While school keeps; National high school students conference on education. J. Cass. Sat R 49:75 Mr 19 '66
Who should be drafted? conference at Antioch. L. Grauman, Jr. New Repub 155: 11-12 D 10 '66

STUDENT councils. See Self government in education

STUDENT counselors. See Personnel service in education

STUDENT demonstrations
Berkeley: new crisis breaks out on California campus. D. S. Greenberg. Science 154:1304-6 D 9 '66
Berkeley, 1966. Commonweal 85:337 D 23 '66
Berkeleyitis; a second look. J. F. Ohles. Sch & Soc 94:66 F 5 '66
Campus protest yes, violence no. Life 61:4 D 2 '66
Politics of outrage; notes on the student left. M. Rogin. Commonweal 84:99-102 Ap 15 '66
Turbulence on the campus. J. E. Hoover. il PTA Mag 60:4-6 F '66
Turmoil in Boston; St John's seminary, Brighton, Mass. Commonweal 84:68-70 Ap 8 '66
University turmoil in Tanzania; reaction to the National service system. America 115: 806-7 D 17 '66
Vietnam: growing war and campus protests threaten student deferments. E. Langer; reply. B. M. Vetter. Science 151:517-18 F 4 '66
What's behind the student demonstrations. F. Morley. Nations Bsns 54:25-6 Mr '66

History
History of college student unrest. Sch & Soc 94:56 F 5 '66

STUDENT drinking. See Liquor problem—United States

STUDENT employment
Employment of school age youth, October 1965. F. A. Bogan. il Mo Labor R 89: 739-43 Jl '66
Long & short of jobs; summer employment. Time 87:81 Je 17 '66
Memories of a mother's summertime helper: Anita Poluga's experience. J. Hamilton. il Look 30:74-8 O 4 '66
Rush for summer jobs. il Sr Schol 88:14-15 My 6 '66
Summer among the savages; college students' summer jobs in Yellowstone National Park. il Seventeen 25:96-7 Je '66
Summer baby sitter. S. Peck. il N Y Times Mag p 118+ My 22 '66
Working their way through summer. C. Himber. il N Y Times Mag p59+ F 27 '66
See also
College students—Employment

STUDENT enrollment. See School attendance

STUDENT exchange programs. See Students, Interchange of

STUDENT forums. See Forums (discussion and debate)

STUDENT government. See Self government in education

STUDENT health. See College students—Health and hygiene

STUDENT life
Campus community: experiment in living. A. M. Greeley. America 115:588-91 N 12 '66
Catholic students and parietal hours. America 115:767-8 D 10 '66
Europe, under their own steam; excerpts from Europe à go-go; life and love aboard a student ship. J. Fox. il Mlle 63:122-3+ Je '66
A look back at college. L. B. Johnson. McCalls 94:68-9+ Ja '67
Princeton; excerpts from Tiger in the ivy; the Princeton man and his university, 1900-1967. J. Davies. il Horizon 9:57-66+ Wint '67
Sex and the college student, by the Committee on the college student of the group for the advancement of psychiatry. Review New Repub 154:21-3 My 28 '66. R. Coles
Unstructured relations; students living together. il Newsweek 68:78 Jl 4 '66
See also
College students
Student activities

STUDENT loans
Campus cash squeeze; banks reluctant to lend money for college tuition. Bsns W p 114 S 10 '66
Dollars, decisions, and diplomas, J. L. Bowman. il Am Ed 2:30-2 My '66
Latest on borrowing for a college education. il U S News 61:96-7 D 19 '66
Money for all somewhere. il Time 88:112+ O 14 '66
New ways to pay for college. Farm J 90:50M N '66
Now, education loans for everybody. Changing T 20:36-7 O '66

STUDENT newspapers. See College and school journalism

STUDENT nonviolent coordinating committee
Behind the image. il Newsweek 68:32 S 19 '66
Black power. F. Millspaugh. Commonweal 84:500-3 Ag 5 '66
Black-power brokers; staff meeting. Newsweek 68:21-2 D 26 '66
Black power! Carmichael's new politics. il Newsweek 67:36 Je 27 '66
Black power in the red. il Time 88:21 Jl 8 '66
Black power; new emphasis on self-determination. New Repub 154:5-6 Je 18 '66
Black power: politics of frustration. il Newsweek 68:26+ Jl 11 '66
Brilliancy of black. B. Weinraub. il Esquire 67:130-5 Ja '67
From freedom high to black power. G. Roberts. il N Y Times Mag p27-9+ S 25 '66; Reply. S. Carmichael. p98+ O 16 '66
Future of black power: a movement in search of a program; report on Catskills meeting, December 1966. A. Kopkind. New Repub 156:16-18 Ja 7 '67
Growl of the Panther; new voice of SNCC. Newsweek 67:33+ My 30 '66
Inside story of black power and Stokely Carmichael. il U S News 61:12 Ag 15 '66
Mr Charlie's puzzle; new hard line. Nation 202:669 Je 6 '66
No seat for the Negro who won; concerning J. Bond. R. Cleghorn. New Repub 154:11-12 Ja 29 '66
Out to get SNCC: a tale of two cities; Philadelphia and Atlanta. P. Good. il Nation 203:534-8 N 21 '66
Thinking big. Time 87:22 My 27 '66
White look at black power. P. Good. il Nation 203:112-17 Ag 8 '66
White reflections on black power. C. E. Fager. Christian Cent 83:980-3 Ag 10 '66
Who's Carmichael? Christian Cent 83:1000-1 Ag 17 '66

STUDENT opinion
Children's school complaints; with study-discussion program, by E. Harris and D. Harris. bibliog il PTA Mag 60:4-6, 36-7 My '66
Five college students speak out; questions and answers, ed. by L. F. McKernan. Cath World 204:198-204 Ja '67
Student attitudes at Lafayette, 1964-65. K. R. Bergethon. Sch & Soc 94:74-6 F 5 '66
What students think about college. Changing T 20:42-3 F '66

STUDENT personnel work. See Personnel service in education

STUDENT program of Lincoln Center. See Lincoln Center fund for education and artistic advancement

STUDENT publications. See College and school journalism

STUDENT rating of teachers. See College professors and instructors—Rating by students

STUDENT selection
Tips for college-bound youngsters. A. H. Witten and G. W. Daigler. il Parents Mag 41:50-1+ Mr '66

STUDENT self government. See Self government in education

STUDENT self-support. See College students—Employment

STUDENT service, International. See International student service

STUDENT sisters. See College students, Women

STUDENT teachers
Teacher is a teen-ager: New York's MFY program. il Newsweek 68:89-90 Ag 22 '66

STUDENT tours. See Travel study courses

STUDENT travel. See Travel

STUDENT tutors. See Tutors and tutoring

STUDENT union buildings. See College architecture

STUDENT unions
Reed college community center. il Arch Rec 139:186-8 My '66
Student center for a school: contemporary for Cotswold; Pierpont student activities center, Avon old farms school, Avon, Conn. il Arch Rec 140:144-5 D '66
Up from the Red lion inn. T. Thomas. il Am Ed 2:16-23 Mr '66

STUDENT volunteer service. See Volunteer service

STUDENT withdrawals. See Dropouts

STUDENTS
Fourth R, the rat race; schools as high-pressure learning factories. J. Holt. il N Y Times Mag p46-7+ My 1 '66; Discussion. p 12+ My 15; 21+ My 22 '66
See also
Catholic students
Chinese students
College students
High school students
Jewish students
Negro students
South African students

Employment
See Student employment

Social and economic status
Junior college: social experiment; relationship between social status and academic success. M. Fallows. Commonweal 85:9-13 O 7 '66

STUDENTS, Interchange of
Busmen's holiday for medical students. Sch & Soc 94:343 O 29 '66
See also
American field service
Experiment in international living (organization)

STUDENTS, Mentally superior. See High school students, Mentally superior

STUDENTS, Women. See College students, Women

STUDENTS and teachers. See Teachers and students

STUDENTS for a democratic society (organization)
S.D.S. camps on the old campground; North Iowa Methodist annual conference. P. B. Mather. Christian Cent 83:1251-2 O 12 '66

STUDENTS socio-economic status. See Students—Social and economic status

STUDIER, Martin H. and others
Organic compounds in carbonaceous chondrites. bibliog Science 149:1455-9, 152:102-7 S 24 '65, Ap 1 '66

STUDIES (rooms)
See also
Libraries (rooms)

STUDIOS
Found space for studios. il House & Gard 130:86-9 Jl '66

STUDIOS, Dance. See Dance studios

STUDY
See also
Home study
Independent study

STUDY tours. See Travel study courses

STUEBER, Alan M. and Murthy, V. R.
Potassium:rubidium ratio in ultramafic rocks: differentiation history of the upper mantle. bibliog Science 153:740-1 Ag 12 '66

STUFFING. See Cookery—Poultry

STULBERG, Louis
On the heels of a giant. por Bsns W p54+ Jl 16 '66

STUMP, Al
Last, triumphant ride of Johnny Longden. Sat Eve Post 239:74-6+ Je 4 '66

SUBMARINE diving. See Diving, Submarine
SUBMARINE geology
Atlantic deep-sea stratigraphy: extension of absolute chronology to 320,000 years; thorium-230 measurements. T. L. Ku and W. S. Broecker. bibliog il Science 151: 448-50 Ja 28 '66
Deep-sea authigenic calcite and dolomite. E. Bonatti. bibliog il Science 153:534-7 Jl 29 '66
Extension of northeastern-Pacific fracture zones. H. W. Menard. bibliog il Science 155:72-4 Ja 6 '67
Manganese nodules: their evolution. M. Bender and others. bibliog il Science 151: 325-8 Ja 21 '66
Meander in valley crossing a deep-ocean fan. F. P. Shepard. bibliog il Science 154:385-6 O 21 '66
Pacific science congress; report. R. S. Dietz. Science 154:1365-6 D 9 '66
Paleomagnetic study of Antarctic deep-sea cores. N. D. Opdyke and others. bibliog il Science 154:349-57 O 21 '66
Uplift of the continental margin and possible continental accretion off Oregon. J. V. Byrne and others. bibliog il Science 154: 1654-6 D 30 '66

SUBMARINE mines. See Mines, Submarine
SUBMARINE models. See Ship and boat models
SUBMARINE moving picture photography. See Moving picture photography, Submarine
SUBMARINE oil well drilling. See Oil well drilling, Submarine
SUBMARINE photography. See Photography, Submarine
SUBMARINE research. See Oceanographic research
SUBMARINE structures. See Underwater structures
SUBMARINE target simulators. See Simulators
SUBMARINE warfare
AIAA meeting told of ASW problems. J. F. Judge. Tech W 19:50+ Ag 15 '66
ASW demands retain top DOD priority; advanced weapon system components for the navy's anti-submarine warfare package. C. Brownlow. il Aviation W 85:62-3 Jl 4 '66
Martell confirms delay in VSK program. Tech W 20:14 Ja 2 '67
Navy seeks quantum ASW improvements. C. Brownlow. il Aviation W 84:22-4 Je 27 '66
Radar/sonar monitor tested for ships: ASW destroyer escorts. R. Pay. il Miss & Roc 18:39-40 Ap 4 '66
See also
Guided missiles—Launching from submarine boats
SUBMERGED lands
See also
Gold in submerged lands
SUBMERSIBLE boats. See Submarine boats
SUBMERSIBLE heaters. See Water heaters
SUBMERSION
See also
Underwater physiology
SUBMICROSOMAL membranes. See Membranes (biology)
SUBSCRIPTION audiences. See Audiences
SUBSIDIES
Government by totem pole. il Nations Bsns 54:36-7+ O '66
See also
Agricultural administration—United States
Economic assistance, Domestic
also subhead Federal aid under various subjects, e.g. Hospitals—Federal aid
SUBSONIC engines. See Gas turbines, Aircraft
SUBSTITUTE products
Great, phony, outdoors. il Newsweek 67:92 My 30 '66
SUBSTITUTE teachers
More and better substitutes: Wilmington public schools and the AAUW substitute workshop. J. H. Jenny. NEA J 55:15 O '66
SUBSTITUTES
See also
Food substitutes
SUBTILISIN. See Enzymes
SUBURBAN newspapers. See Newspapers—United States
SUBURBAN schools
Suburbia: the target area; paucity of books dealing with social problems; adaptation of address, May 1966. P. Evarts. il Wilson Lib Bul 41:173-6+ O '66
SUBURBS
Education and society in disadvantaged suburbia. W. E. Kuschman. il Sch & Soc 94: 386-7 N 12 '66

Feud between city and suburb. Life 61:4 Jl 1 '66
One person, one vote; suburbs the real gainers. il U S News 60:66-7 F 14 '66
Speaking out; I hate the suburbs. J. Breslin. il Sat Eve Post 239:10+ S 24 '66
Suburbs again show biggest crime increase. il Am City 81:22 D '66
Suburbs: made to order for crime. J. R. Moskin. il Look 30:20-7 My 31 '66
Sweden's atomic city: Farsta. S. Clark. il Travel 126:41-3 Jl '66
We can cope with the coming suburban explosion. E. K. Faltermayer. il Fortune 74: 147-51+ S '66
See also
Regional planning
SUBVERSIVE activities
Profiles: Los Angeles. New Yorker 42:100+ O 15 '66
See also
Communism—United States

Anecdotes, facetiae, satire, etc.
Wake up, America! it can happen here! il Esquire 65:92-3+ My '66

Egypt
Balanced docket; trials against opponents of regime. Newsweek 68:44 S 5 '66
Of life & death; sniffing out subversion; Egypt. Time 88:32 S 2 '66

SUBVOCAL speech. See Speech research
SUBWAY stations
Spitting punishable by fine of $50.00; New York city's clammy stations. W. McQuade. il Arch Forum 125:90 S '66
SUBWAYS
See also
Montreal—Subways
Rapid transit
SUCCESS
Dropout who made it to the top. P. Gallico. Read Digest 89:121-6 N '66
Envisioning the future; interview. D. Sarnoff. il Nations Bsns 54:60-1+ Je '66
Focus on success instead of failure. B. Haldane. NEA J 55:32 Ap '66
Foolproof formula for success. A. Gordon. Read Digest 89:88-90 D '66
How young wives can help their husbands succeed. S. Blum and S. C. Soman. Redbook 127:47+ My '66
I was a teen-age beatle; turns on the road. J. Peerce. Seventeen 25:170+ Ap '66
Special feature on the failing student; symposium. il NEA J 55:33-40 Ap '66
Spotting the seed of success; interview. W. E. Heller. Nations Bsns 54:78-80+ Ap '66
See also
Ability
Business
Self reliance
SUCCESSION tax. See Inheritance tax
SUCCESSION to the crown. See Great Britain—Royal family
SUCCULENT plants
Enchanting plants that are easy to grow. il Pop Gard 17:8-9 Ag '66
Succulents offer variety of color and form. L. Cutak. il Horticulture 44:14-15+ N '66
See also
Flowering stones
Kalanchoes
SUCROSE. See Sugars
SUD aviation. See Airplane industry and trade—France
SUDAN
Sudan: Arab-African confrontation. N. M. Shaffer. bibliog f Cur Hist 50:142-6+ Mr '66
See also
Law—Sudan
Natural resources—Sudan
Paleontology—Sudan

History
Sudan. J. R. Randell. bibliog il Focus 17:1-6 S '66

Native races
Proud primitives, the Nuba people. O. Luz. il Nat Geog Mag 130:672-99 N '66

Politics and government
Atlantic report. Atlan 219:20+ Ja '67
Family affair; El Mahdi family. Time 88: 32 Ag 5 '66

Race problems
Control of the Red Sea. A. Ford. il Nat R 18:314-15 Ap 5 '66
Sudan: Arab-African confrontation. N. M. Shaffer. bibliog f Cur Hist 50:142-6+ Mr '66

SUDAN—*Continued*

Religious institutions and affairs

Hope in the Sudan; relations between Muslims and Christians. America 115:308 S 24 '66
See also
Catholic church in Sudan

SUDAN grass

Hybrids
See also
Sorghum—Hybrids

SUDAR, Dan D.
Three levels of library education. bibliog por Library J 91:4899-903 O 15 '66

SUÉR, Henk. See Wersch, L. van. jt. auth.

SUEZ CANAL
Atlantic report; ten years after crisis. Atlan 218:6+ Ag '66
It works; earnings vital to Egypt. Time 88:79 Jl 15 '66

SUEZ crisis. See Egypt—History—Invasion, 1956

SUFFERING
Suffering with Christ. C. Davis. America 115: 157 Ag 13 '66
See also
Pain

SUFFOLK cooperative library system, Patchogue, N.Y.
Sample projects, title III, ESEA. W. W. Curley. il Library J 91:1029-31 F⁵ 15 '66

SUFFOLK sun (newspaper)
Out of the roaring '20s; birth pangs. Newsweek 68:100 D 5 '66
Sun rise in Suffolk. il Newsweek 68:85 N 21 '66
Youthful dreams on Long Island. il Time 88:76 D 2 '66

SUFFRAGE
See also
Voters. Registration of
Voting

United States
Old enough to vote; recommendation to make eighteen the voting age. America 114:189-90 F 5 '66
Responsible electorate. by V. O. Key, jr. and M. C. Cummings, jr. Review
Commentary 42:62-4 Ag '66. W. Berns; Discussion. 42:16+ N '66
See also
Negroes in the United States—Politics and suffrage
Woman suffrage—United States

SUGAR

Prices
Sugar: a sticky mess in Congress. P. Findley. Read Digest 88:88-92 Je '66

SUGAR act of 1937. See Sugar industry and trade

SUGAR beets
Uncle Sam finds hot potato in beet field; Aroostook County, Me. il Nations Bsns 54: 58-9+ N '66

SUGAR industry and trade
Cuba, Castro and the United States. P. W. Bonsal. For Affairs 45:260-76 Ja '67
Sugar: a sticky mess in Congress. P. Findley. Read Digest 88:88-92 Je '66
Sugar blues; Cuba's crop. Time 87:38+ Ap 15 '66

SUGAR lobby. See Lobbying

SUGAR maple. See Maple

SUGAR substitutes
Overuse of sugary, starchy foods. Consumer Bul 49:35-6 Ag '66

SUGARMAN, Daniel, and Hochstein, Rollie
Inferiority. Seventeen 25:158-9+ S '66
Sex and the teen-age girl. Read Digest 88: 119-22 F '66
What it means to be a girl now! Seventeen 25:172-3+ My '66

SUGARMAN, George
Sugarman makes a sculpture. il pors Art N 65:34-7 My '66

SUGARS
Phytohemagglutinin: inhibition of the agglutinating activity by N-acetyl-D-galactosamine. H. Borberg and others. bibliog il Science 154:1019-20 N 25 '66
Selection of sucrose-dependent escherichia coli to obtain envelope mutants and fragile cultures. G. Mangiarotti and others. bibliog il Science 153:892-4 Ag 19 '66
Transport of sugars and amino acids in the intestine: evidence for a common carrier. F. Alvarado. bibliog il Science 151:1010-13 F 25 '66
See also
Glucose

SUGRUE, Thomas
My most unforgettable character. D. Agee. il Read Digest 88:95-100 Je '66

SUHARTO, 1921?-
Talk with General Suharto; interview; ed. by B. Krisher. por Newsweek 68:43 S 5 '66
about
Emergency time. il Time 87:25 Mr 25 '66
From Sukarno to Suharto. America 114:402 Mr 26 '66
Indonesia: change at the top. por Newsweek 67:42 Mr 21 '66
Indonesia: complete overhaul. B. Krisher. il por Newsweek 67:48+ Ap 4 '66
Indonesia: generation of '66. R. Littell. il por Newsweek 67:36+ My 16 '66
New men at Indonesia's helm. por Sr Schol 88:24 Ap 1 '66
Now you see him... il por Time 87:33 Mr 18 '66
Vengeance with a smile. il por Time 88:22-6 Jl 15 '66

SUICIDE
Aftermath; death of N. Nakasa. R. Jenkins. Esquire 65:16+ Je '66
College suicides. America 115:502 O 29 '66
Fiery rebellion; self immolations in South Vietnam. il Newsweek 67:48-9 Je 13 '66
Immolations and consensus: the justification of innocence. A. Towne; discussion. Christian Cent 83:276 Mr 2 '66
Last testament; R. Wishnetsky. Newsweek 67:32 F 28 '66
Light that failed; self immolations in Viet Nam. il Time 87:39 Je 10 '66
Morphinist; incident at Hospital of the city of Vienna, 1928. R. Berczeller. New Yorker 42:141-2+ Ap 16 '66
On suicide; Time essay. Time 88:48-9 N 25 '66
Rescue, incorporated. America 116:6 Ja 7 '67
Special report on a growing social problem: when the cry for help comes; suicide prevention centers. J. N. Bell. Good H 162: 108-9+ Je '66
Student suicides. Sci N 91:45 Ja 14 '67
Suicidal tendencies. Sci N 90:513 D 17 '66
Suicidal tendencies; college student. Time 88: 114 O 14 '66
Suicide; a new attack against an old killer. J. Star. il Look 30:60+ Ag 23 '66
Suicide among teenagers. il Sci Digest 60:42 Ag '66
Suicide can't be eliminated. A. Herzog. il N Y Times Mag p32-3+ Mr 20 '66
When listening means life; the Samaritans and other suicide prevention groups. R. J. Levin. Sat R 49:65 O 1 '66

SUICIDE prevention center, Los Angeles
Fake suicide calls. Sci N 89:278 Ap 16 '66
Suicide; a new attack against an old killer. J. Star. il Look 30:62+ Ag 23 '66

SUIT making. See Tailoring

SUITS, Mens. See Clothing and dress—Men

SUITS at law. See Actions and defenses

SUKARNO, 1901-
Album of romantic memories for a fallen dictator. il pors Life 60:32B-33 Ap 1 '66
As Indonesia tries military rule. il por U S News 60:46 Mr 28 '66
Asian flu. il Newsweek 68:42+ S 5 '66
Bloodbath with reds on receiving end. il U S News 60:34 Ja 31 '66
Breakfast with Sukarno. D. Smith. il Nation 202:553-5 My 9 '66
Bung's bounce; new cabinet. il por Time 87: 40 Mr 4 '66
Counter-counterattack. il por Newsweek 67: 46 Mr 7 '66
Dilemma in Djakarta. Newsweek 68:34-5 D 26 '66
Eclipse. Newsweek 68:38+ Jl 18 '66
Emergency time. il Time 87:25 Mr 25 '66
End of the line for Sukarno; more power for his successor. il por U S News 61:20 Jl 18 '66
Final drive? por Time 89:26 Ja 20 '67
Forward to chaos. Newsweek 67:35 F 7 '66
From Sukarno to Suharto. America 114:402 Mr 26 '66
Getting rid of Sukarno. R. Butwell. New Repub 155:12-13 O 8 '66
Indonesia: change at the top. por Newsweek 67:42 Mr 21 '66
Indonesia: generation of '66. R. Littell. il por Newsweek 67:36+ My 16 '66
Indonesia: night of terror, dawn of hope. C. W. Hall. il por Read Digest 89:275-8+ O '66
Indonesia: the plot that failed. L. M. Taubinger. por Nat R 18:160 F 22 '66

SUKARNO, 1901—*Continued*
Indonesia's unfinished revolution. D. Warner.
il Reporter 35:28-9+ Jl 14 '66
King of kings. il Newsweek 67:59 My 2 '66
Now you see him... il Time 87:33 Mr 18 '66
Pride and fall. Nation 202:346 Mr 28 '66
Reducing the aura. Time 87:36 Ap 22 '66
Sentence of death, a sentence of advice. Time
89:26+ Ja 6 '67
Situation normal. il Newsweek 67:48-9 Mr 28
'66
Small price to pay. il por Newsweek 69:42+
Ja 23 '67
Struggle for power in Indonesia. D. Kirk.
il Reporter 34:38-40 F 24 '66
Students boot out the Communists. H. C.
Atyeo. Nat R 18:458 My 17 '66
Temper tantrum. Newsweek 68:34 Ag 8 '66
Thousand cuts. il Newsweek 68:42 Jl 4 '66
Tightening the noose. il Time 87:27 My 27 '66
Turmoil rules in Indonesia. Bsns W p44 Mr
19 '66
Ultimatum for Sukarno? Newsweek 69:31 Ja
9 '67
Uncertain balance. il Time 87:35 My 13 '66
Unmaking of a president. il por Time 88:
29-30 Jl 1 '66
Vengeance with a smile. il pors Time 88:22-6
Jl 15 '66
Where the girls were. por Newsweek 68:40
S 12 '66
SUKARNO, Mme
Father Sukarno, reduced to just a figure-
head, with the help of his no. 1 wife. il
pors Life 61:30-1 Jl 1 '66
SULFATES
Mucopolysaccharides: N-acetylglucosamine-
and galactose-6-sulfates from keratosulfate.
V. P. Bhavanandan and K. Meyer. bibliog
Science 151:1404-5 Mr 18 '66
SULFIDES
Gamma-A cold agglutinin: importance of
disulfide bonds in activity and structure.
B. R. Andersen. bibliog il Science 154:281-
3 O 14 '66
See also
Djerfisherite
SULFONES
See also
Diaminodiphenyl sulfone
SULFUR
Anomalous carbon-isotope ratios in non-
volatile organic material; coastal plain of
southern Israel. I. R. Kaplan and A. Nis-
senbaum. bibliog il Science 153:744-5 Ag 12
'66
Pressure-induced phase of sulfur-selenium.
S. Geller and M. D. Lind. il Science 155:79-
80 Ja 6 '67
Pressure-induced phases of sulfur. S. Geller.
bibliog il Science 152:644-6 Ap 29 '66
Prices
Price wrangle approaches a climax. il Bsns
W p 126-7+ Je 18 '66
Sulfur prices head up again; increases of $5
ton. Bsns W p33 Ja 22 '66
SULFUR dioxide
Ozone and sulfur dioxide synergism: injury to
tobacco plants. H. A. Menser and H. E.
Heggestad. bibliog il Science 153:424-5 Jl 22
'66
SULFUR mines and mining
Canada
See also
Texas Gulf sulphur company
United States
Price wrangle approaches a climax. il Bsns
W p 126-7+ Je 18 '66
Sulfur prices head up again; increases of $5
ton. Bsns W p33 Ja 22 '66
SULICH, Vassili
Las Vegas scene. W. Como. il pors Dance
Mag 40:20-1 My '66
SULIOTIS, Elena
Gift of the Greeks; interview. ed. by G.
McElroy. por Opera N 31:14 N 5 '66
SULKIN, S. Edward, and others
Isolation of St Louis encephalitis virus from
bats (Tadarida b. mexicana) in Texas. bib-
liog Science 152:223-5 Ap 8 '66
SULKIN, Sidney
College folklore and fact. New Repub 154:
11-13 Mr 26 '66
SULLENGER, Don B. and Kennard, C. H. L.
Boron crystals; with biographical sketches.
Sci Am 215:15, 96-107 bibliog(p 132) Jl '66
SULLIVAN, Aloysius Michael
Reviewing stand. See issues of Dun's review
and modern industry
SULLIVAN, Dan
Sex and the person. Commonweal 84:460-4,
564-5 Jl 22, S 2 '66

SULLIVAN, Frank
Greetings, friends; poem. New Yorker 42:31
D 24 '66
SULLIVAN, Fred R.
Professional. il por Newsweek 68:74 Jl 4 '66
SULLIVAN, James
Incredible position of General Poisson; poem.
Commonweal 84:256 My 20 '66
SULLIVAN, Kevin
Ireland rehearses the future. Nation 203:485-
6 N 7 '66
SULLIVAN, Leonor K.
Citizen's role in furthering consumer in-
terests; address, April 21, 1966. Vital
Speeches 32:498-501 Je 1 '66
SULLIVAN, Louis Henry
Drawings by Louis Sullivan. Arch Rec 139:
147-54 Mr '66
SULLIVAN, Maurice William
Sound over sight in reading. il por Time
87:42-3 Ja 28 '66
Sullivan's crusade: schools without pain. J.
Poppy. il pors Look 30:37-40 Je 28 '66
SULLIVAN, Nancy
Pop poems. Sat R 49:39 Ap 30 '66
about
Four poets. L. Mueller. Poetry 109:48-50 O
'66
SULLIVAN, Pamela Wylie
Survivors; story. Seventeen 25:164-5 My '66
SULLIVAN, Peggy
Knapp high schools and the ALA standards.
por Library J 91:2609-11 My 15 '66
SULLIVAN, R. H.
Let all the audience see what's showing. Am
City 81:90-1 N '66
SULLIVAN, Richard Howard
Reed's woes. il por Newsweek 67:92 My 2 '66
SULLIVAN, Terry
Hot draft card. D. Feeley. New Repub 155:38
Ag 27 '66
SULLIVAN, Walter
Goodbye to infection; reprint. Sci Digest
59:71-4 Mr '66
What earthly use is the moon? N Y Times
Mag p39+ Ag 28 '66
SULLY, François
Journey through China. por Newsweek 67:
54-8 Je 13 '66
SULTANIAN, I. V. and Freeman, G.
Enhanced growth of human embryonic cells
infected with adenovirus 12. bibliog Science
154:665-7 N 4 '66
SULZBERGER, Cyrus L.
International provocateur. Time 88:86 O 21
'66
Man & his Times. por Time 87:64-5 Mr 11 '66
SUMBERG, M. S.
Selecting a P. A. amplifier. Electr World 75:
39-42+ Je '66
SUMMER
Waves of summers past and present. L.
Wainwright. Life 61:22 Ag 12 '66
Quotations, maxims, etc.
Where has it gone?, comp. by R. Block. il
N Y Times Mag p38 S 18 '66
SUMMER; drama. See Weingarten, R.
SUMMER camps. See Camps
SUMMER cookery. See Cookery
SUMMER drinks. See Beverages
SUMMER entertaining. See Entertaining
SUMMER furniture. See Furniture, Outdoor
SUMMER homes
Breuer and Wise summer houses. M. Breuer.
il Arch Rec 140:134-6 N '66
How the Morgans roughed it; Camp Uncas,
J. P. Morgans' Adirondack retreat. B.
Plumb. il N Y Times Mag p74-5+ Ag 21 '66
Personal business; second home. Bsns W
p 167-8 My 21 '66
Ship of shingles; cottage on canal. B. Plumb.
il N Y Times Mag p72-3+ My 15 '66
SUMMER institute of linguistics
Mission to the stone age; Nancy and Dennis
Cochrane among the Dunas of New Guinea.
E. Nadel. il Look 31:30-4 Ja 24 '67
Progress in literacy; Mexico. A. Zambrano.
Christian Cent 83:1061 Ag 31 '66
SUMMER institutes. See Teachers institutes
SUMMER jobs. See Seasonal labor
SUMMER jobs for college students. See College
students—Employment
SUMMER jobs for students. See Student em-
ployment
SUMMER reading projects. See Libraries,
Childrens—Projects

SUMMER resorts
Best U.S. golf resorts. T. B. Lesure. il Travel 125:24-8+ Mr '66
See also
Seaside resorts

SUMMER schools
Farm kids focus on a career; Iowa program. R. C. Davids. il Farm J 90:36-7+ My '66
From Maine to California: revolution in summer schools. B. H. Pearse. il Am Ed 2:10-12 O '66
Ideas for teen-age summers; college programs for high school students. J. Cass. Sat R 49:81 F 19 '66
1966 Summer study guide: at home and abroad. il Sr Schol 88:sup8-10+ F 25 '66
Summer art in northern New York. R. Plumb and S. Smith. il Sch Arts 66:36-9 O '66
Summer school: it can benefit most students. il Good H 162:180 Je '66
Tom and Huck just wouldn't believe it. Sr Schol 88:sup3 My 6 '66
Union men take to the campus; curriculum ranging from pensions and politics. il Bsns W p64+ Ag 13 '66
USOE announces NDEA summer institutes: School library personnel; Educational media. Library J 91:6172-3 D 15 '66
See also
Salzburg seminar in American studies
University extension

SUMMER vacations. See Vacations

SUMMERILL, Frederick
Phenomenal career. Hobbies 71:40 My: 40-1+ Je: 38+ Jl '66

SUMMERS, F. William
Library education and the talent shortage. por Library J 91:1767-8 Ap 1 '66

SUMMERS, Hollis
Snapshots of the four grandchildren; poem. Atlan 217:113 My '66

SUMMERS, John E.
Toward a safer baby bed. Consumer Bul 49: 43+ Ap '66

SUMMERTON, S. C.
How to keep school segregation. J. Osborne. New Repub 154:16-18 Mr 12 '66

SUMMIT conferences. See International conferences

SUMMO, Anthony J.
Psychologist views the new liturgy. Cath World 202:272-7 F '66

SUN, Kuan-han
Doctor Sun & the moon. il por Time 88:82 O 28 '66

SUN Ra
New jazz. il por Newsweek 68:106+ D 12 '66

SUN
James Croll and solar evolution. N. J. Woolf. il Sky & Tel 31:150-1 Mr '66
Sun, moon, and planets this month. See issues of Sky and telescope
Violent sun. H. Friedman. il Read Digest 88:167-8+ Mr '66
See also
Eclipses, Solar
International years of the quiet sun
Sunspots

Atmosphere
Stellar chromospheres. O. C. Wilson. bibliog il Science 151:1487-98 Mr 25 '66

Corona
Problems of the solar corona. D. E. Billings. il Sky & Tel 33:18-21 Ja '67

Influence on weather
See Sun and meteorology

Observations
Coming eclipse will receive unprecedented data coverage. W. S. Beller. il Tech W 19:28+ S 19 '66
Solar observing with a broad-band filter. il Sky & Tel 32:262-3 N '66
Some hints for observing the sun. il Sky & Tel 31:241-3 Ap '66

Spectrum
See Spectrum, Solar

SUN, Photography of. See Astronomical photography

SUN and cancer. See Cancer—Causes

SUN and meteorology
Abbot: cycles and sub-cycles; solar influence on weather. F. Sartwell. Sci N 90:496 D 10 '66

SUN CITY, Ariz.
Death in Sun City. C. Davis. il Esquire 66: 134-7 O '66

SUN dials. See Sundials

SUN domes. See Garden houses, shelters, etc.

SUN glasses
Choose the right sunglasses, design and workmanship are important. il Consumer Bul 49:32-4 Ag '66
How to choose; how to use sunglasses. Todays Health 44:67-8 Jl '66
New sound in sunglasses; Spectra radio sunglasses. il Consumer Rep 31:158-9 Ap '66
Shadow of her smile. il Time 87:70 My 13 '66
Take a fresh squint at sunglasses. il Changing T 20:23-4 Jl '66

SUN into darkness; ballet. See Ballets—Criticisms

SUN screens. See Screens (sun)

SUN tan. See Tan

SUN tan preparations. See Cosmetics

SUN VALLEY, Idaho
Gone flying to Sun Valley. A. F. Edwards, jr. il Flying 78:66-70 Mr '66
Ski time in Sun Valley and Jackson Hole. G. E. Maxwell. il Todays Health 44:42-7+ N '66
Sun Valley in summer. C. W. Casewit. il Travel 125:45-7 Je '66
Teen travel talk. il Seventeen 25:74 My '66

SUNCOAST cup regatta. See Motor boat racing

SUNDAY schools
What good is Sunday school? N. M. Lobsenz. il Redbook 127:60-1+ O '66

SUNDIALS
How to make a sun-dial fire pit. J. S. Lorr. il Pop Sci 188:132-5 Je '66
Results of sundial competition. H. Egger. il Sky & Tel 32:256 N '66
Sundials to adorn your garden. il House & Gard 130:290-3+ O '66

SUNFISH fishing
Belligerent bluegill. G. Gresham. il Field & S 70:73-5+ Ap '66
Bluegills by the bushel. H. G. Tapply. il Field & S 71:54 Ag '66
New way to find winter bluegills. J. O. Cartier. il Outdoor Life 137:36-7+ F '66

SUNGLASSES. See Sun glasses

SUNKEN treasure. See Treasure trove

SUNSET (periodical)
Three old-timers off to a fresh start; American institute of architects-Sunset magazine Western home awards. il Sunset 136: 78-85 Mr '66

SUNSET; drama. See Babel, I.

SUNSET Strip. See Los Angeles—Streets

SUNSPOTS
Toward a new astronomical imagination. R. S. Richardson. il Sky & Tel 32:344-5 D '66

SUPER 8 cameras. See Moving picture cameras

SUPER stock nationals. See Automobile racing

SUPER 35 films. See Photography—Films

SUPERCHARGERS
See also
Automobile engines—Superchargers

SUPERCONDUCTIVE magnets. See Magnets

SUPERCONDUCTIVITY
Josephson effects. D. N. Langenberg and others. il Sci Am 214:30-9 bibliog(p 146) My '66
Superconductivity of alpha-uranium and the role of 5f electrons. T. H. Geballe and others. bibliog il Science 152:755-7 My 6 '66
Superconductivity of beta-uranium. B. T. Matthias and others. bibliog il Science 151: 985-6 F 25 '66; Reply with rejoinder. B. W. Howlett. 154:542-3 O 28 '66

SUPERINTENDENTS, School. See School superintendents and principals

SUPERMARKETS
Behind the boycotts: why prices are high. il Time 88:89 N 4 '66
Boycotts and prices. M. Friedman. Newsweek 68:92 N 28 '66
Gamesmanship in the supermarkets. D. Sanford. New Repub 155:14-16 N 12 '66
Grocers' answer on prices: if women really want a change it can be arranged; elimination of games, gimmicks and extra services. il U S News 61:110+ N 14 '66
Housewives' chain reaction; boycott. il Newsweek 68:79 N 7 '66
Housewives' revolt. Sr Schol 89:18-19 N 11 '66
MRCA gets rich supermarket data. Bsns W p 134 Ap 30 '66
Prices: picketers and the picketed. il Newsweek 68:78-80 N 14 '66
Researchers snap up supermarket secrets; chains sell records of merchandise movement to market researchers. Bsns W p83 Mr 5 '66

SUPERMARKETS—*Continued*
See-through meat trays. il Consumer Rep 31: 330-1 Jl '66
Word of honor; supermarkets honor-system checkout, Switzerland. il Time 87:98 Mr 18 '66
See also
Kroger company

SUPERNATURAL
Tension and tensions. V. P. McCorry. America 115:234-5 S 3 '66
See also
Apparitions
Ghosts

SUPERNOVAE. See Stars, New

SUPERREALISM (art) See Surrealism (art)

SUPERSONIC aerodynamics. See Aerodynamics, Supersonic

SUPERSONIC airplane engines. See Jet airplane engines

SUPERSONIC airplanes. See Airplanes, Supersonic

SUPERSONIC combustion ramjet. See Jet propulsion

SUPERSONIC compressor rotors. See Rotors

SUPERSONIC engines. See Gas turbines, Aircraft

SUPERSONIC wind tunnels. See Wind tunnels

SUPERSTITION
Knock on wood and cross your fingers? il Sr Schol 88:5 My 13 '66
Palmy days in Japan. il Newsweek 68:96+ D 19 '66
Some of the nicest people are superstitious; superstitions of celebrities. W. Wolfe. il Good H 162:100-1+ Mr '66
See also
Astrology
Witchcraft

SUPERTANKERS. See Tank ships

SUPERVIA, Conchita
Conchita Supervia. A. Favia-Artsay. por Hobbies 71:38 My '66

SUPERVISORS
See also
Foremen

SUPERVISORS, Library. See Library administration

SUPPERS
Blaze-of-glory suppers; with recipes. il Ladies Home J 84:80-1+ Ja '67
Come to an open house soup supper. il Sunset 137:174-5 N '66
Cool cooking in a skillet. S. Sarvis. il Farm J 90:59+ Je '66
Dallas: charity supper, plus. il Ladies Home J 83:92-3+ O '66
For a late supper party, here are entrée ideas; with recipes. il Sunset 138:106-7 Ja '67
Minneapolis: a party in three acts. il Ladies Home J 83:106-9+ O '66

SUPPES, Patrick
Computer and excellence. Sat R 50:46+ Ja 14 '67
Plug-in-instruction; excerpt from The computer in American education. Sat R 49:25+ Jl 23 '66
Uses of computers in education; with biographical sketch. Sci Am 215:51, 206-8+ S '66

SUPPLEMENTAL unemployment benefits
Financial aspects of SUB plans. E. H. Beier. il Mo Labor R 89:385-9 Ap '66

SUPPLEMENTARY employment
Making ends meet, by moonlight. T. Irwin. N Y Times Mag p73+ Ap 3 '66
Multiple jobholders in May 1965. F. A. Bogan and T. E. Swanstrom. il Mo Labor R 89:147-54 F '66

SUPPLY and demand of teachers. See Teachers—Supply and demand

SUPREME court of the United States. See United States—Supreme court

SUPREMES (singers) See Negro singers

SURAN, J. J.
Functional designing; excerpts from remarks. por Electr World 75:46-9+ Mr '66

SURF fishing. See Salt water fishing

SURF riding
Beach bite; California's tax plan. Newsweek 67:99 Je 6 '66
Charger sinks the dancer; 1966 world championship of surfing. B. Ottum. il Sports Illus 25:26-9 O 10 '66
Is J.J. really king of the surf? J. Bonfante. il Life 60:81-2 Je 10 '66
Is surfing too tough for girls? J. Hoffman. il Seventeen 25:88-9+ Jl '66
Joyce Hoffman: number one in the surf. S. Gordon. il Look 30:92-3+ My 3 '66

New wave; world championships. il Newsweek 68:64+ O 17 '66
Riding the wave of the East coast's surfing boom. B. Ottum. il Sports Illus 25:30-2+ Jl 18 '66
Shoo-in surf champ; world championships. il Life 61:141-2+ O 14 '66
Surfer's cross; German iron cross. il Time 87: 81 Ap 22 '66
Surfers' feet chip. Sci N 90:87 Ag 6 '66

SURFACE, Bill
Hot tip: don't bet against Bret Hanover. N Y Times Mag p36-7+ S 25 '66
If you're thinking of moving. Read Digest 89:134-8 N '66
Keen private eye. N Y Times Mag p 121-2+ D 11 '66
Planned bankruptcy: the racket that cheats us all. Read Digest 88:125-9 My '66

SURFACE chemistry
Infrared spectra from fine particulate surfaces. J. R. Aronson and others. bibliog il Science 152:345-6 Ap 15 '66
Sonic detection of a fresh water-salt water interface. H. E. Edgerton. il Science 154: 1555 D 23 '66

SURFACE contamination
Meseran contamination measurer. il Tech W 19:37 Jl 4 '66

SURFBOARDS
Surfboard for sand and sea. M. J. Pedersen. il Pop Mech 125:98-9 Ap '66

SURFER magazine
Riding the crest of surfing's wave. il Life 61:37-8+ S 9 '66

SURFING. See Surf riding

SURGAIRTOME. See Surgical instruments and apparatus

SURGEONS
Diary of a Russian surgeon. N. M. Amosov. il Harper 233:79-86 D '66
See also
American college of surgeons

SURGERY
Help for hemophiliacs; safe surgery with factor VIII. il Newsweek 67:58 F 28 '66
New surgical advances that can save your life. Good H 162:155-7 F '66
Vietcong mortar shell inside a living soldier. il Life 61:98A-98B+ O 14 '66
Who may assist a surgeon? il Time 88:36 D 30 '66
See also
Amputation
Cryogenic surgery
Foreign bodies (surgery)
Surgeons
Sutures
Transplantation of organs, tissues, etc.
also subhead Surgery under names of organs and regions of the body, e.g. Heart—Surgery

History
See Medicine—History

SURGERY, Cosmetic. See Surgery, Plastic

SURGERY, Facial
Should I, or shouldn't I have my face lifted? with chart. il Vogue 148:147-9+ S 15 '66
See also
Chemosurgery

SURGERY, Plastic
New angles; Asian women. il Time 88:24-5 D 23 '66
Plastic surgery goes to prison. C. Remsberg and B. Remsberg. il Todays Health 44:38-41 Ap '66
What's up front: boom in rhinoplasty. il Newsweek 67:91 My 30 '66
See also
Surgery, Facial

History
First plastic surgery on nose a life-or-death matter. Todays Health 44:41 Ap '66

SURGICAL adhesives. See Adhesives

SURGICAL instruments and apparatus
New tools for surgery; searing heat and deep frost. J. R. Berry. il Pop Mech 126:64-7+ S '66
Stitch to save nine; auto suture stapler. il Time 88:61 S 2 '66
Tiny air turbines drive surgical tools to 100,000 r.p.m; Surgairtome, Neurairtome and Orthairtome. W. S. Bacon. il Pop Sci 189:82-3+ S '66
Upside-down surgery; table developed at the Retina foundation, Boston. il Life 60:63-4 Mr 11 '66
See also
Medical instruments and apparatus

SURGICAL research
See also
American college of surgeons
SURGICAL shock. See Shock
SURINAM
Three Guianas. T. Mathews. Cur Hist 51:
333-7+ D '66

Description and travel
Just beyond the Caribbean, the tranquil
Surinam jungle. il Sunset 136:58+ Je '66
Surinam. il U S Camera 29:70-1 Je '66
Surprising Surinam. I. C. Kuhn. il Travel 126:
30-4 N '66
SURNAMES. See Names, Personal
SURO, Dario
Of artists and owls. Américas 18:21-8 Mr '66
SUROWITZ, Dora
Stitch in time. Time 87:67 Mr 18 '66
SURPLUS food supply. See Food supply
SURPLUS products
Identifying surplus crystals. I. Math. il Electr
World 76:57 Ag '66
SURPLUS products, Agricultural
Why they're so rich on the farm. il Bsns W
p78+ S 17 '66
SURPRISE party; drama. See Dorand, J.
SURREALISM
Letter from Paris; A. Breton. Genêt. New
Yorker 42:202-4 O 22 '66
Philosophy of surrealism, by F. Alquié. Re-
view
Sat R 49:33-4 Mr 12 '66. A. Balakian
Search for the ideal absurdity. G. Hicks. Sat
R 49:21-2 S 3 '66
Surrealism in the round. J. Lanes. New
Repub 155:28+ D 17 '66
SURREALISM (art)
Art: Giacometti: 1901-1966. J. Berger. Na-
tion 202:341-2 Mr 21 '66
Art of the possibility; R. Magritte's New
York show. H. Cohen. Reporter 34:51 F 10
'66
Artist accompanies himself with his Rays. R.
Padgett. il Art N 65:51-3+ N '66
Now all artists are surrealists. M. Esslin.
il N Y Times Mag p32-3+ My 22 '66
See also
Dalí, S.
SURROGATE law. See Probate law and prac-
tice
SURTEES, John
Dry crucible for the hot ones. B. Ottum. il
por Sports Illus 25:32-4+ N 21 '66
Duel in the sun. il por Newsweek 68:66 N
14 '66
SURVEILLANCE radar
Army orders lightweight, portable radar;
short-range surveillance radar. il Avia-
tion W 85:81-3 Ag 1 '66
New tactical radar system ready for army.
C. D. LaFond. il Tech W 19:39 Ag 1 '66
SURVEYING
City survey that saves; New Haven, Conn.
A. Landino. il Am City 81:94-5+ D '66
SURVEYING, Aerial
Aerial survey pays big dividends; Florham
Park, N.J. J. M. DiMarzo. il Am City 81:
113-14 F '66
See also
Photogrammetry
SURVEYING, Photographic. See Photogram-
metry
SURVEYING instruments
See also
Theodolites
SURVEYOR (space vehicle) See Space vehicles
SURVEYOR; story. See Roth, H.
SURVEYOR flight. See Space flight to the
moon—Surveyor flight, 1966
SURVEYS
Too many surveys; letter. W. C. H. Prentice.
Science 151:1034+ Mr 4 '66; Reply. R. C.
Amara. 152:450 Ap 22 '66
SURVEYS, Educational. See Educational sur-
veys
**SURVIVAL (after airplane accidents, ship-
wrecks, etc)**
Anatomy of survival. E. Crimmin. il Sci Di-
gest 60:57-61 N '66
Flame-resistant jet fuel and fireproofed
people. il Life 60:38-9+ Ap 15 '66
How to survive an air crash. E. Crimmin. il
Sci Digest 60:44-6 O '66
How to survive, anywhere. C. C. Troebst. il
Pop Sci 189:62-5+ Ag '66
Unseaworthy? Boeing and FAA cooperating
on redesign studies. Newsweek 67:77 Ja 31
'66
SURVIVAL of nations
Doctor Jekyll and Mr Kahn. J. C. Fleck.
Christian Cent 83:680-3 My 25 '66

SURVIVAL of the fittest. See Natural selection
SURVIVORS; story. See Sullivan, P. W.
SUSANN, Jacqueline
Author goes to court over store's selling
policy. Pub W 189:51 Mr 21 '66
Happiness is being number 1. J. Howard. il
pors Life 61:68-70+ Ag 19 '66
SUSKIND, Sigmund R. See Rothschild, H.
jt. auth.
SUSPENSION bridges. See Bridges, Suspension
SUSPENSION cables. See Cables
SUSPENSION of atomic bomb testing. See
Atomic bombs—Testing, Suspension of
SUSSEX university. See Colleges and universi-
ties—England
SUSSKIND, David
Susskind network. il por Newsweek 68:90+
Jl 25 '66
SUSSMAN, Alfred S. See Fultz, S. A. jt.
auth.
SUSSMAN, M. V. and Chin, L.
Liquid water in frozen tissue: study by nu-
clear magnetic resonance. bibliog Science
151:324-5 Ja 21 '66
SUTCLIFFE, Alys
Plant groundcovers with bulbs. Horticulture
44:32-3+ N '66
SUTHERLAND, David A.
Michigan's harvest. Opera N 30:13-15 Mr 19
'66
SUTHERLAND, Dorothy B.
Trade winds. Sat R 49:16 Je 11 '66
SUTHERLAND, Ivan E.
Computer inputs and outputs; with bio-
graphical sketch. Sci Am 215:45, 86-96 S '66
SUTHERLAND, Joan
Music to my ears. I. Kolodin. Sat R 50:26
Ja 7 '67
Musical events; performance of Donizetti's
Lucia di Lammermoor. W. Sargeant. New
Yorker 42:50+ D 24 '66
Notes from our correspondents. E. Greenfield.
Hi Fi 16:16+ Ap '66
Sutherland as Donna Anna. I. Kolodin. Sat
R 50:34 Ja 21 '67
Sutherland as La Fille. T. Heinitz. Sat R
49:47 Jl 16 '66
SUTHERLAND, W. C.
Executive development. Parks & Rec 1:515
Je '66
SUTHERLAND, Zena
Books for young people. See issues of Sat-
urday review, October 22, 1966-
Stories for a Christmas morning. Sat R 49:56
D 10 '66
SUTHERS, Roderick A.
Optomotor responses by echolocating bats.
bibliog Science 152:1102-4 My 20 '66
SUTLIFF, Cal
Unofficial ambassadors. Sat R 49:58-9 Ag 20
'66
SUTOR, D. June. See Lonsdale, K. jt. auth.
SUTPHEN, Jack
Can you handle extreme conditions? Yacht-
ing 119:90-1+ Ap '66
SUTTER, Johann Augustus
Something of the utmost importance. il Sr
Schol 87:3 Ja 21 '66
SUTTON, Horace
Booked for travel. See issues of Saturday re-
view
Manila summit. Sat R 49:14+ N 12 '66
Mighty Mississippi: a full-length portrait.
McCalls 93:40+ Jl '66
People riding the riptide. Vogue 148:204-7+
N 1 '66
Turning the red, white, and blue into gold.
Sat R 49:50-1+ My 12 '66
What chance the tourist? Sat R 50:45+ Ja 7
'67
Young hangouts. Mlle 63:140+ My '66
SUTTON, Isaac
Intimate look at the champ. il por Ebony 22:
148-54+ N '66
SUTTON, Lee
Search for the instant library. Sat R 49:24-5
Ap 16 '66
SUTURES
Glue replaces stitches. Sci N 89:507 Je 25 '66
SUVOROV, Aleksandr Vasil'evich, kni͡az'
Art of victory: the life and achievements of
Field-Marshal Suvorov, by P. Longworth.
Review
Sat R 49:38 S 17 '66. H. Kohn
SUYDAM, Henry West, 1926-1966
In memory of Hank Suydam. G. P. Hunt. il
por Life 61:3 D 16 '66
SUYIN, Han
Reflections on social change. Bul Atomic
Sci 22:80-3 Je '66

SUYIN, Han—*Continued*

about

Tree of many branches. E. Snow. Nation 202: 303-4 Mr 14 '66
Woman scorned. E. Hahn. por Sat R 49:38 S 24 '66

SUZMAN, Helen G.
Minority of one in South Africa's Parliament. J. Lelyveld. il por N Y Times Mag p34-5+ Mr 20 '66

SUZUKI, Kunihiko, and others
Metachromatic leucodystrophy: isolation and chemical analysis of metachromatic granules. bibliog Science 151:1231-3 Mr 11 '66

SVAETICHIN, G. See Negishi, K. jt. auth.

SVETLOVA, Marina
Only the best. W. Como. il Dance Mag 40: 74-5 F '66

SVOBODA, William S.
Negative aspects of educational programs for the culturally deprived. Sch & Soc 94:388-9 N 12 '66

SWADOS, Harvey
Ambivalent scholars; Marx and shame: socialism today. Nation 203:347-51 O 10 '66
Death traps. Commentary 41:88-92 Je '66
Sentimental journey to the Lower East side. N Y Times Mag p52-3+ S 18 '66
When black and white live together. N Y Times Mag p47+ N 13 '66

SWAIN, Alma
March of the caterpillars. Audubon Mag 68: 158-9 My '66

SWAIN, Dwight V.
Fiction strategy; excerpts from Tricks and techniques of the selling writer. Writer 79:15-19 N '66

SWAIN, Raymond C.
River; poem. Am For 72:26-7 S '66

SWAIN, Su Zan Noguchi
Japanese food plants. Horticulture 44:16-19 Jl '66

SWALLOW, Alan
Obituary
Pub W 190:31-2 D 12 '66

SWALLOW-tailed gulls. See Gulls

SWALLOWED objects. See Accidents; Foreign bodies (surgery)

SWALLOWING
Difficulty in swallowing can be dangerous symptom. Todays Health 44:10 My '66

SWALM, Ralph O.
Utility theory, insights into risk taking. bibliog f Harvard Bsns R 44:123-36 N '66

SWAMPS. See Marshes

SWAN, James
Conservation joins the three R's. Audubon Mag 68:119-20+ Mr '66

SWAN, Jeanne. See Larson, K. jt. auth.

SWAN, Jon
Father father son and son; poem. New Yorker 42:204 N 19 '66
Winter; poem. Reporter 35:39 D 29 '66

SWAN, K. D.
1925-trip into the Missions. il Liv Wildn 29:3-8 Wint '65

SWAN lake; ballet. See Ballets—Criticisms

SWANKER, Esther. See Heidbreder, M. A. jt. auth.

SWANN, Donald
Aromatic spirits. H. Hewes. Sat R 50:98 Ja 14 '67
Light of heart. por Newsweek 69:71 Ja 9 '67
Maharajah & the cricket. por Time 89:69 Ja 6 '67
Popular records. D. Watt. New Yorker 42: 197-8 D 17 '66
Theatre. J. McCarten. New Yorker 42:78 Ja 7 '67

SWANN, Peter R.
Stress-corrosion failure; with biographical sketch. Sci Am 214:17, 72-81 F '66

SWANS
Nature note; trumpeter swan. Sci N 89:425 My 28 '66

SWANSON, Alan M.
Stockholm's opera cellar. Opera N 31:14-15 Ja 14 '67

SWANSON, Don R.
On improving communication among scientists. Bul Atomic Sci 22:8-11 F '66

SWANSON, Gloria
Hollywood sunset. Esquire 66:76-81 Ag '66

SWANSON, Steve
Sanctification; poem. Christian Cent 83:802 Je 22 '66
Withdrawal; poem. Christian Cent 83:110 Ja 26 '66

SWANSTROM, Edward Ernest, bp
Foreign aid and conscience. America 114: 762 My 28 '66

SWAP funds. See Investment trusts

SWAPPING. See Barter

SWARD, Robert
Concert; in Mexico; poems. Poetry 108:35-8 Ap '66

SWARTZ, Fred
Family Las Vegas: vacation jackpot. il Todays Health 44:44-9 O '66

SWARTZ, Roberta Teale
Thank you note to Wallace Stevens; poem. Sat R 49:33 Jl 30 '66

SWAYDUCK, Edward
Working with a capitalistic union. il por Nations Bsns 54:38-9+ Ja '66

SWAZILAND
See also
United Nations—Swaziland

SWEARING
Four-letter men; Gilles de la Tourette syndrome. Time 88:46 Ag 26 '66
Manner of speaking; taboo language. J. Giardi. Sat R 49:14-15 Ag 20 '66

SWEARINGEN, John E.
Food for tomorrow; address, September 12, 1966. Vital Speeches 33:61-4 N 1 '66

SWEATERS
Gimme those oldtime pinup sweaters; mini-Shetland. il Time 89:34 Ja 13 '67
Wool sweaters go into the washer. il Consumer Bul 49:21-3 S '66

SWEATING. See Perspiration

SWEAZEY, Patricia
Transparent color design. Sch Arts 65:18-20 Mr '66

SWEDEN
See also
Airplane industry and trade—Sweden
Booksellers and bookselling—Sweden
Education—Sweden
Gardens—Sweden
Labor supply—Sweden
Moving picture industry—Sweden
Music festivals—Sweden
Social and economic security—Sweden
Theater—Sweden
Tourist trade—Sweden

Defenses

Sweden goes underground. O. Clausen. il N Y Times Mag p23-5+ My '66

Description and travel

Sweden. A. Karlen. il Holiday 40:44-51+ N '66
Traveling with Mlle: *skål*, et al. E. Schoen. il Mlle 63:351+ Ag '66

Economic conditions

Inflation in Utopia. il Time 87:97 Ap 15 '66
Modern Sweden; address, November 9, 1965. T. Erlander. Vital Speeches 32:425-7 My 1 '66
Now the Swedes feel the pinch. il Bsns W p55-6 Je 25 '66
Where a business-labor partnership is in trouble. il U S News 61:95-7 S 10 '66
See also
Labor and laboring classes—Sweden
Wages—Sweden

Industries

Men of the iron mountain; mines of the Grängesberg company. M. Mayer. il Reporter 35:41-4 Jl 14 '66
Modern Sweden; address, November 9, 1965. T. Erlander. Vital Speeches 32:425-7 My 1 '66
Shipyard for all seasons; Arendal of Sweden. il Fortune 74:44+ Jl 1 '66
See also
Electric equipment industry

Labor policy

Sweden's manpower programs. S. Swerdloff. Mo Labor R 89:1-6 Ja '66

Moral conditions

Life in a Great society; what one country finds. A. Zanker .il U S News 60:58-60 F 7 '66
Sex, sin and salvation in Sweden. D. W. Ferm. Christian Cent 83:1142-6 S 21 '66; Discussion. 83:1343-5 N 2 '66

Religious institutions and affairs

See also
Lutheran church in Sweden

Social conditions

See also
Social and economic security—Sweden

SWEDEN—*Continued*

Social life and customs

Sweden's new battle over sex. J. R. Moskin. il Look 30:36-42 N 15 '66

Social policy

Can we afford to play follow the leader? A. H. Sypher. Nations Bsns 54:29-30 S '66

SWEDISH dancing. See Dancing, Swedish

SWEDISH literature
See also
Childrens literature—Sweden

SWEDISH spies. See Spies

SWEDISH students
Pupils into the breach; teachers strike; with report by B. Wise. il Life 61:65+ N 25 '66

SWEENEY, Ben
Accumulator versus the collector. Hobbies 71:124-5 Je '66

SWEENEY, James Johnson
Collectors' house: the De Menils' affair with art. Vogue 147:184-93+ Ap 1 '66

SWEENEY, Pat
Green air at evening; poem. America 115:339 S 24 '66

SWEEP generators. See Signal generators

SWEEPSTAKES. See Lotteries

SWEET, Waldo E.
Latina vivat. il Newsweek 68:64 D 5 '66

SWEET, William H. See Wall, P. D. jt. auth.

SWEET basil. See Basil

SWEET breads. See Bread

SWEET Charity; musical comedy. See Musical comedies, revues, etc.—Criticisms, plots, etc.

SWEET peas
New sweet pea is a two-footer. il Sunset 137:257 N '66

SWEET potatoes
Peroxidase and resistance to ceratocystis in sweet potato increased by volatile materials. B. Clare and others. bibliog il Science 152:62-3 Jl 1 '66
See also
Cookery—Vegetables

SWEET williams
Sweet william for colorful borders. il Sunset 137:207 S '66

SWEETENING agents. See Sugar substitutes

SWEEZY, Carl
Long way from the buffalo road; excerpt from The Arapaho way, ed. by A. Bass. il por Am Heritage 17:22-5+ O '66

SWEGLE, Wayne E.
Lake of the Ozarks. il Motor B 118:22-5 Ag '66

SWEIGARD, Dick
Harsh-voice fever. pors Outdoor Life 139:62-5+ Ja '67

SWENSON, G. R.
Horizons of Robert Indiana. Art N 65:48-9+ My '66
Picasso kiss and tell. Art N 64:19+ Ja '66
(ed) See Thek, P. Beneath the skin

SWENSON, May
April light; poem. Nation 202:434 Ap 11 '66
City garden in April; poem. New Yorker 42:48 Ag 23 '66
Little rapids; poem. New Yorker 42:141 My 7 '66
On handling some small shells from the Windward Islands; poem. New Yorker 42:232 N 12 '66
Out of the sea, early; poem. New Yorker 42:58 O 29 '66
Rain at Wildwood; poem. New Yorker 42:32 Jl 2 '66
Tall figures of Giacometti; poem. Nation 203:224 S 12 '66
Waking from a nap on the beach; poem. Sat R 49:34 Jl 9 '66

SWENSSON, Anne
Greening North. Sat R 49:54+ O 8 '66

SWETS, Donald H.
No more dumping on the street. Am City 81:92-3 Mr '66

SWIDLER, Arlene
Male church. Commonweal 84:387-9 Je 24 '66

SWIDLER, Leonard
Ecumenism in the parish? Commonweal 84:27-9 Mr 25 '66
Theology in the state university. Christian Cent 83:619-20 My 11 '66

SWIFT, Ernest
When Wisconsin pine went to college. Am For 72:8-9+ Ja '66

SWIFT, Lloyd W.
Black brant. Liv Wildn 29:28 Aut '65

SWIMMING
He makes a splash with a ripple; B. McKean of Pittsburgh. C. Phinizy. il Sports Illus 24:60-2+ My 16 '66
Kids keep going faster; A.A.U. meet at Lincoln, Neb. il Life 61:42C-42D S 2 '66
Water babies; U.S. championships. il Newsweek 68:62-3 S 5 '66
See also
Diving

Safety devices and measures

Drownproofing keeps you afloat till help comes. R. C. Wetmore. il Pop Sci 189:58-9 Jl '66

Study and teaching

How to teach handicapped children to swim. J. Streva. il Parks & Rec 1:502-3 Je '66
Johnny Weissmuller was a slow swimmer. K. Monroe. il N Y Times Mag p32-3+ D 18 '66

Caricatures and cartoons

Learning to swim. Stevenson. New Yorker 42:30-1 Ag 13 '66

SWIMMING clubs
Johnny Weissmuller was a slow swimmer. K. Monroe. il N Y Times Mag p32-3+ D 18 '66

SWIMMING pools
Build a swimming pool just for the fun of it. D. Wirkus. il Pop Mech 125:152-5 Je '66
Facts about backyard swimming pools. il Changing T 20:33-5 Jl '66
New look of swimming pools. il House & Gard 129:136-43 Je '66
Pool and ice rink in one area; Great Neck park district, Long Island, N.Y. il Am City 81:75-7 Je '66
Pool fits crosswise, and turns a corner. il Sunset 137:64-5 Ag '66
Will your banker help you build a swimming pool? Pop Gard 17:15 Mr '66
See also
Wading pools

Equipment

Taking care of pool plumbing. Sunset 136:150+ My '66

Safety devices and measures

Build a swimming pool splash alarm. F. Maynard. il Pop Electr 25:48-9+ Jl '66
Kidproofing the backyard pool. D. P. Webster. il Todays Health 44:34-7 Je '66
Swimming pool safety. Consumer Bul 49:12 Ag '66

SWIMMING pools, Municipal
Swimming and ice skating team up. C. R. Hoaglund. il Am City 81:17 F '66

SWINDLERS and swindling. See Fraud

SWINE
Animal health guide; ten steps that save baby pigs. J. Harvey. il Suc Farm 64:74 O '66
Hog extra; symposium. Farm J 90:H1-2+ N '66
How to keep sows and pigs healthy; interviews, ed. by J. Harvey. J. Simon; N. R. Underdahl. il Suc Farm 64:44-5+ Ap '66
News. See issues of Farm journal
Superswine! R. Carter. Esquire 66:264+ D '66
Swine in biomedical research; report on international symposium. L. K. Bustad and R. O. McClellan. Science 152:1526-8+ Je 10 '66
Thirty-three ideas that will save you more pigs. J. Harvey. il Suc Farm 64:48-9+ Mr '66
Tips if you expand in hogs. J. Harvey. Suc Farm 64:54D N '66
What's new. See issues of Successful farming

Care

Those critical five days. L. L. LeBeuf. il Suc Farm 64:54 O '66

Confinement methods

Confinement hog setups. J. Harvey. il Suc Farm 64:40-1 Jl '66

Diseases and pests

Diseases big problem facing hog producers. J. Harvey. Suc Farm 64:60 Mr '66
SPF plus performance. R. C. Black. il Farm J 90:H4-5+ N '66
See also
Hog cholera

SWINE—*Continued*

Feeding

Are pasture hogs best? J. Harvey. il Suc Farm 64:36-7 Je '66

Cuts sow costs with liquid feed. il Farm J 90:55D O '66

Ten ways to cut your hog feeding costs. G. R. Carlisle and J. Harvey. il Suc Farm 64:38-9 O '66

Trouble-free start for feeder pigs. D. Wolf. il Farm J 90:68G Mr '66

Grading and standardization

Bonus helps buy boars, improves feeder pigs; Wisconsin feeder pig marketing co-operative. D Hagen. Farm J 90:38H Jl '66

Boom in meat-type hogs. J. Bickers. il Farm J 90:50D N '66

Here are ten tips on buying feeder pigs. Suc Farm 64:54A My '66

Marketing

How to prevent marketing losses. H. Helms. Farm J 90:A12 Ag '66

How to sell your hogs for more money. D. Seim. il Farm J 90:38-9+ O '66

Prices

As market men see it, what's holding prices up? il Farm J 90:H19 N '66

Expect lively trade in hog futures. Farm J 90:68H Mr '66

Firm prices ahead on hogs. Suc Farm 64:50 Je '66

Price forecast. Farm J 90:A1-2 Ag '66

Price forecast. Farm J 90:H1-2 N '66

What's ahead now for hog prices. R. C. Black. Farm J 90:38N Je '66

Who's making prices? il Farm J 90:A15 Ag '66

Transportation

Four ideas for moving hogs. il Suc Farm 64:50 O '66

SWINE, Care of

Here are ten tips on buying feeder pigs. Suc Farm 64:54A My '66

SWINE, Cooling of. See Livestock. Cooling of

SWINE, Effect of temperature on

Hogs need your help in hot, humid weather. J. Harvey. il Suc Farm 64:14 Jl '66

SWINE as laboratory animals. See Laboratory animals

SWINE breeding

Breeding news and trends. D. Wolf. Farm J 90:H20 N '66

Pigs in the laboratory. L. K. Bustad. il Sci Am 214:94-100 bibliog(p 144) Je '66

They wean nearly every pig farrowed. D. Hagen. il Farm J 90:H12-13 N '66

Ultrasonics can improve your herd; Sonoray. J. Harvey. il Suc Farm 64:64 Mr '66
See also
Artificial insemination

SWINE farms

Don't write off hogs. R. C. Black. il Farm J 90:24+ Ag '66

500-hog setup for $7,500. E. Waltner and W. Waltner. il Farm J 90:50N+ S '66

High labor return producing feeder pigs. Suc Farm 64:48A Jl '66

Hog system that stretches the man. D. Seim. il Farm J 90:26-7+ Je '66

How I farm today. W. J. Conover. il Suc Farm 64:52-3 Mr '66

Two top-notch ways to manage a sow herd. E. Stout and J. Harvey. il Suc Farm 64:58-9+ S '66

Why the hog business isn't likely to move South. R. J. Amick. Farm J 90:38K Jl '66

Equipment

Adjustable chutes load hogs easier. il Farm J 90:A9 Ag '66

Problem: his hired man left. J. Harvey. il Suc Farm 64:44-5 Ag '66
See also
Swine—Confinement methods

SWINE farrowing crates and pens

Best farrowing plan I've ever had. J. Harvey. il Suc Farm 64:26-7+ Jl '66

Good ideas for handling hogs easier. il Farm J 90:36D Ag '66

How to fumigate a farrowing house. J. Harvey. il Suc Farm 64:62 O '66

How to get ready for new pigs. J. Harvey. il Suc Farm 64:44-5 F '66

Market ten pigs per litter. F. M. Simison and J. Harvey. il Suc Farm 64:40-1 My '66

Most unusual farrowing house we've seen. D. Hagen. il Farm J 90:38F Jl '66

They harnessed the sun's heat. W. J. Fletcher. il Suc Farm 64:30-1 D '66

They wean nearly every pig farrowed. D. Hagen. il Farm J 90:H12-13 N '66

Two low-cost farrowing ideas. J. Harvey. il Suc Farm 64:48G Jl '66

SWINE house floors. See Swine houses—Floors

SWINE houses

Best remodeling job I've seen! J. Harvey. il Suc Farm 64:48-9+ Ap '66

Hog system that stretches the man. D. Seim. il Farm J 90:26-7+ Je '66

New hog systems, how they work. il Suc Farm 64:25-7+ N '66

New kind of pig shelter. J. Harvey. il Suc Farm 64:46-7 Ap '66
See also
Swine—Confinement methods
Swine farrowing crates and pens

Cleaning

How to build deep, narrow gutters for hog houses. L. D. Van Fossen. il Suc Farm 64:54-5 F '66

Floors

How to pour slat floors in place. il Farm J 90:40F Ag '66

Slat floors: key to expansion in hogs. J. Russell. il Farm J 90:59H S '66

Slats slash labor load. J. Harvey. Suc Farm 64:57 N '66

SWING (golf)

Be sure you get the right slant. J. Nicklaus. il Sports Illus 24:78 My 9 '66

Bend your back when digging out of a ditch. J. Nicklaus. il Sports Illus 26:47 Ja 2 '67

Boros on the wedge. J. Boros. il Esquire 65:118 Ap '66

Hebert on the driver. J. Hebert. il Esquire 65:119 Ap '66

Know what your hands are up to. J. Nicklaus. il Sports Illus 24:66 Ap 11 '66

There is no pause that refreshes. J. Nicklaus. il Sports Illus 25:124 S 12 '66

Try using half a swing for the half-pitch shot. J. Nicklaus. il Sports Illus 24:60 F 14 '66

Try your footwork to waltz time. J. Nicklaus. il Sports Illus 24:62 My 30 '66

Woodsman's chop cuts through an impossible lie. J. Nicklaus. il Sports Illus 25:76 D 5 '66

SWINGER; story. See Boles, P. D.

SWINGS

Pedal-plane whiz-around. D. A. Gattis. il Pop Mech 126:134-7+ Ag '66

SWINK, Charles

Those who care; story. Good H 162:82-3 F '66

SWISHER, Viola Hegyi

It's never enough just to imitate. Dance Mag 40:30-1 Je '66

Meanwhile back at the pueblo. Dance Mag 40:41-4 D '66

Peter Gennaro works at what makes a special special. Dance Mag 40:20-1 D '66

Toumanova in Hollywood. Dance Mag 40:26-7 Mr '66

(ed) See Alexander, R. Rod Alexander: back where he is happy to belong

(ed) See Godkin, P. To thine own self be true

(ed) See Lanchester, E. Isadora Duncan had nothing to pass on to the future

(ed) See Montes, L. Lola Montes

SWISS watch; story. See Ustinov, P.

SWITCHES. See Wigs

SWITCHES, Electric. See Electric switches

SWITZERLAND
See also
Architecture—Switzerland
Architecture, Domestic—Switzerland
Education—Switzerland
Music—Switzerland
Music festivals—Switzerland
Railroads—Switzerland
Recreation—Switzerland

Description and travel

Switzerland's lakes. A. R. Pastore, jr. il Travel 125:32-6 Ap '66

History
Bibliography

Articles and other books received; comp. by A. H. Price. See issues of American historical review

Religious institutions and affairs

World around us (cont of) News of the Christian world. Christian Cent 83:836 Je 29 '66

SYRIA—*Continued*

Antiquities
Pre-neolithic village; Tell Mureybat. Sci Am 214:53 My '66
Village 9,500 years old unearthed in Syria; Tell Mureybat. Sci N 89:231 Ap 2 '66

Boundaries
Dangerous border. R. Chesnoff. il Newsweek 68:40+ Ag 15 '66

Foreign relations
Doctors of Damascus; Palestine front and Western oil interests. Newsweek 68:34 D 26 '66
Gunfire over Galilee. il Time 88:28 Ag 26 '66
Incident at Samu; Israel attack on Jordan rather than Syria. il Time 88:36 N 25 '66

Politics and government
Another coup. Sr Schol 88:19 Mr 18 '66
Classicists. Newsweek 67:46+ Mr 7 '66
Party affair; Hafez out after coup. il Time 87:42 Mr 4 '66
To the left, march. il Time 89:31-2 Ja 20 '67

SYRKIN, Marie
Arab refugees. Commentary 41:23-30 Je; 6+ Je '66

SYRUPS
Surprises from the syrup jug. il Ladies Home J 83:106 Je '66

SYSTEM analysis
About the systems system. J. Eberhart. il Sci N 91:19 Ja 7 '67
House space committee urges systems approach to pollution. H. M. David. Tech W 19:20 O 31 '66
Systems approach: political interest rises. L. J. Carter. Science 153:1222-4 S 9 '66

SYSTEM development corporation
Non-profit SDC expands market base. J. L. Trainor. il Miss & Roc 18:32-4 My 23 '66

SYSTEM simulation
See also
Computers—Simulation programs

SYSTEM theory. See System analysis

SYSTEMS engineering
California effort is key to growth area. H. D. Watkins. il Aviation W 84:79+ F 7 '66
System engineering aids social problems. H. D. Watkins. il Aviation W 84:52-3+ Ja 31 '66
Systems approach: political interest rises. L. J. Carter. Science 153:1222-4 S 9 '66
Systems approach to automation is explained to R&E council; annual conference. Pub W 189:154-6+ Je 13 '66
See also
Weapons systems

SYSTEMS management
Middle managers vs. the computer. G. Berkwitt. il Duns R 88:40-2+ N '66
Road to 1977. M. Ways. il Fortune 75:92-5+ Ja '67
Systems approach to city planning; San Francisco. C. C. Herrmann. il Harvard Bsns R 44:71-80 S '66
Systems approach to sounding rockets benefits Thiokol unit. il Tech W 19:25+ S 12 '66
Where the industries of the seventies will come from. L. Lessing. il Fortune 75:96-9+ Ja '67
See also
Systems engineering

SZABO, Emery
Selecting the right alternator for the job. Am City 81:156+ Mr '66

SZASZ, Thomas S.
Mental health ethic. Nat R 18:570-2 Je 14 '66; Correction. 18:598 Je 28 '66
Mental illness is a myth. N Y Times Mag p30-1+ Je 12; 4+ Jl 3; 2 Jl 10 '66
about
Doctor Szasz on abortion. America 115:476 O 22 '66
Psychiatrists under attack; rebellious Dr Szasz. E. M. Schur. por Atlan 217:72-6 Je '66; Discussion. 218:31-2 Ag '66
Psychoanalysis and morality. L. H. Farber; discussion. Commentary 41:23+ Mr; 6+ Ap '66

SZELL, George
Discovery of freshness. R. L. Shayon. Sat R 49:37 D 31 '66

SZUBA, Eugene, and Snyder, Mary
Motivations for children's art. Sch Arts 65:39 My '66

SZULC, Tad
Palomares learns to love the bomb. N Y Times Mag p22-3+ F 20 '66

T

T-groups. See Executives—Training

T-shirts. See Shirts

TFX. See Airplanes, Military—United States

TRW, incorporated
TRW to study land-use planning; studies on transportation, waste disposal, information systems and juvenile delinquency. Tech W 18:20 Je 6 '66
Way they think at TRW. R. Sheehan. il Fortune 74:153-7+ O '66
Where diversity is the tie that binds. il Bsns W p88-90+ S 24 '66

TRW systems. See TRW, incorporated

TUC. See Trades union congress

TV tape recorders. See Video tape recorders and recording

TVA. See Tennessee Valley authority

TWA. See Trans World airlines

TAAL, MOUNT. See Volcanoes

TABLE, The. See Table setting

TABLE decoration
I love breakfast! symposium. il Seventeen 25:190-3 S '66
Imaginative centerpieces. il House & Gard 129:232-3 My '66
Liveliest personal art: creative table settings. il House & Gard 130:92-5 Jl '66
One big beautiful splurge. il House & Gard 130:210-13 O '66
Party throw-aways. il House & Gard 129:146-7+ Je '66
Repertoire of centerpieces. il House & Gard 129:190-5 My '66
Sugarplum cookies; with recipes. il Seventeen 25:128-9+ D '66
Very easy sewing with felt! Christmas table decoration. il Bet Hom & Gard 44:62-3 D '66
When is a gathering an event? il Seventeen 25:156-7 S '66
See also
Party favors

TABLE linen
Tops for holiday tables. C. Houck. Parents Mag 41:80 D '66

TABLE manners. See Etiquette

TABLE saws. See Saws

TABLE setting
Little-party tables. il McCalls 94:108-13 N '66
Liveliest personal art: creative table settings. il House & Gard 130:92-5 Jl '66
New role for the place plate. il House & Gard 129:124-7 F '66
One big beautiful splurge. il House & Gard 130:210-13 O '66
Party strategy; tips from five great hostesses. il House & Gard 130:272-82 N '66
Set for the holidays. B. Plumb. il N Y Times Mag p70-1 D 18 '66
What's new in table settings? plenty! E. Craster. il Bet Hom & Gard 44:78-9 Je '66

TABLE silver. See Silverware

TABLE tennis
Bat about ping-pong. D. Miles. il Sports Illus 25:90-2+ O 17 '66

TABLECLOTHS. See Table linen

TABLES
Card-table sets. il Consumer Rep 31:566-9 N '66
Connoisseur's corner; cigarette and wine tables. il House & Gard 129:43-4 Mr '66
Good looking tables for fun and games. il House & Gard 130:24+ N '66
Put a pole-lamp table at your elbow. L. Samuels. il Pop Mech 126:160+ O '66
Six new fantasy finishes. il House & Gard 130:254-7 N '66
Very tricky table! il Bet Hom & Gard 44:117 Je '66
See also
Work tables

TABLEWARE
Complete guide to buying and using dinnerware. Bet Hom & Gard 44:118+ Je '66
Dishes for moppets; from six different countries. il House & Gard 130:280-1 O '66
Dishes; points to check before you buy. Changing T 20:38-40 Mr '66
Knife rests. Hobbies 71:28 Ag '66
New role for the place plate. il House & Gard 129:124-7 F '66
Photographs in dishes. A. G. Peterson. il Hobbies 71:96 My '66

TABLEWARE, Plastic
Melamine, more depth, more uses! il Bet Hom & Gard 44:82-3 Je '66
Plastic dinnerware. il Consumer Bul 49:6-9 Ag '66
TABLEWARE, Stainless steel
President modifies import duty on stainless-steel flatware; White House announcement; with text of proclamation. L. B. Johnson. il Dept State Bul 54:160-2 Ja 31 '66
Stainless-steel flatware. il Consumer Bul 49: 6-10 My '66
TABOO
Incest taboo uncovered. Sci N 90:111 Ag 13 '66
TABORSKY, Robert G. and others
6-Hydroxylation: effect on the psychotropic potency of tryptamines. bibliog Science 153: 1018-19 Ag 26 '66
TABS (boats)
Keep tabs on her running trim. A. L. Beal. il Motor B 118:36-7+ N '66
TACAN
F-4K/M Tacan set designed for improved reliability, maintenance. il Aviation W 85:79-80 Ag 1 '66
TACHOMETERS
Solid-state tachometer for CD or transistor ignition systems. M. Gellman. il Pop Electr 24:54-7 F '66
TACKETT, Stanford L. and others
Electrolytic dissolution of iron meteorites. bibliog Science 153:877-80 Ag 19 '66
TACTICAL air command. See United States—Air force—Tactical air command
TACTICAL air navigation. See Tacan
TACTICAL fighter, Experimental. See Airplanes, Military—United States
TACTICS
Army seeks to improve ground positioning; man-pack receiver version of Loran tactical radio navigation system. M. Getler. il Tech W 19:14-15 O 17 '66
    See also
Military art and science
TAFAWA BALEWA, Sir Abubakar. See Balewa, A. T.
TAFT, Philip
Violence in American labor disputes. bibliog f Ann Am Acad 364:127-40 Mr '66
TAFT, Robert, 1917-
Sense of history; address. PTA Mag 60:28-9 Mr '66
    about
Great-grandson race. il por Time 88:32-3 O 21 '66
Ohio: can Bob Taft make a comeback? J. A. Maxwell. il Reporter 35:31-2 O 20 '66
TAFT, Robert Alphonso, 1889-1953
Keeping Taft's memory alive. R. Kirk. Nat R 18:1276 D 13 '66
TAFT, William Howard, 1857-1930
Big Bill Taft. S. Hess. il pors Am Heritage 17:32-7+ O '66
TAFT-Hartley law. See Labor laws and legislation—United States—Taft-Hartley law
TAGGART, C. I.
Space age prospecting. Sat R 49:64-5 Je 4 '66
TAGGING of insects. See Insect tagging
TAGLIABUE, John
By a rich fast moving stream; poem. Nation 203:254 S 19 '66
Don't bomb human nature out of existence; poem. Harper 232:75 F '66
Six poems from a Greek journey. Poetry 108: 20-4 Ap '66
TAGUE, William H.
Mike Frome. Am For 72:5+ Ap '66
TAHITI
Boom times. il Newsweek 68:51-2 Jl 11 '66
Island of the lotus eaters; Djerba differences and similarities. A. Waugh. Nat R 18:470+ My 17 '66
Opening of the South Seas; excerpts from Fatal impact, an account of the invasion of the South Pacific 1767-1840. A. Moorehead. il Harper 232:39-48 F; 121-2+ Mr '66
Tahiti: golden outpost of France. M. Petersen. il Motor B 118:50+ N '66
TAHOE, LAKE
Boat campers' paradise, Lake Tahoe's Emerald Bay. H. Bottel. il Motor B 118:22-4 Jl '66
Close call at Lake Tahoe; Lake Tahoe state park. D. B. Alexander. il Parks & Rec 1:146-8 F '66
Keeping Tahoe alive. il Time 88:46-7 Ag 12 '66
Lake Tahoe: measured for pollution; letter. E. S. Deevey, jr. Science 154:68 O 7 '66

TAILORING
Men's suits, tailor-made, just $80. il Changing T 20:37-8 Ag '66
TAIPEI, Taiwan
Tempted in Taipei. C. Stinnett. Holiday 39: 24+ F '66
TAIRA, Osamu
Appealing to a power higher than Uncle Sam. Christian Cent 83:1464 N 30 '66
TAIWAN
Dissent on China. C. P. Tung. Christian Cent 83:1183 S 28 '66
Formosa betrayed, by G. H. Kerr. Review Atlan 217:131-2 F '66. O. Handlin
Taiwan: the other China. il Newsweek 67: 54+ Ap 11 '66
Taiwan: the other China. M. A. Plummer. bibliog f Cur Hist 51:165-71+ S '66
    See also
Agriculture—Taiwan
Publishers and publishing—Taiwan

Commercial treaties and agreements
U.S. and China amend cotton textile agreement; Department announcement, April 26; with text of U.S. note. April 22, 1966. il Dept State Bul 54:817-19 My 23 '66

Economic conditions
Formosa: Asia's heartening success story. K. Beech and C. W. Hall. il Read Digest 88: 139:44 F '66

Foreign relations
Orient: a problem of nonexistence; attitudes toward two Chinas. W. J. Thorbecke. Sat R 49:38-9 Mr 26 '66

History
Formosa betrayed, by G. H. Kerr. Review Nation 202:656-7 My 30 '66. C. P. Fitzgerald

Industries
Tiger in plastics. il Fortune 74:44 Jl 1 '66

Politics and government
Formosa: Asia's heartening success story. K. Beech and C. W. Hall. il Read Digest 88: 139:44 F '66
Formosa betrayed, by G. H. Kerr. Review Nation 202:656-7 My 30 '66. C. P. Fitzgerald
Martial law in free China. N. B. McLeod. Christian Cent 83:1040-1 Ag 24 '66
Other China; report on Taiwan. M. D. Zeik. Commonweal 85:129-31 N 4 '66
Problems of age; re-election of Chiang; and vice-president appointed. Time 87:30+ Ap 1 '66
Taiwan: myth, dream and nightmare. J. K. Fairbank. New Repub 154:11-13 F 5 '66; Reply. L. D. Huang. 154:37-8 Mr 26 '66
TAJ MAHAL
Well traveled camera. H. Keppler. il Mod Phot 30:22+ Mr '66
TAKAKURA, Shin'ichiro
Vanishing Ainu of north Japan. Natur Hist 75:16-25 O '66
TAKANO, Isoroku. See Yamamoto, I.
TAKEMOTO, Kenneth K. and others
Heat-labile serum factor required for immunofluorescence of polyoma tumor antigens. Science 153:1122-3 S 2 '66
TAKING the consequence; story. See Durrell, L.
TAKINS
Wait till next year; takins at Bronx zoo. il Life 61:66A Jl 15 '66
TALALAY, Paul, and Williams-Ashman, Guy
1966 Nobel laureates in medicine or physiology. Science 154:362-4 O 21 '66
TALAR landing system. See Airplanes—Landing
TALBOT, Allan R.
Boston's bristly Mr Logue. Harper 233:18+ N '66
Needed: a new breed of school superintendent. Harper 232:81-2+ F '66
TALBOT, Norman
Cactus; poem. Yale R 56:106-9 O '66
TALCOTT, Burt Lacklen
Excerpt from debate, June 29, 1965. Cong Digest 45:29+ Ja '66
Excerpt from remarks, January 25, 1966. Cong Digest 45:156+ My '66
TALE of two cities; drama. See Hackett, W.
TALENT associates, limited
Susskind network. il Newsweek 68:90+ Jl 25 '66
TALENTED children. See Children, Gifted
TALESE, Gay
Frank Sinatra has a cold. Esquire 65:89-98+ Ap '66

TALESE, Gay—*Continued*
Kingdoms, the powers, and the glories of the New York times. Esquire 66:91-5+ N '66
Mr Bad News. Esquire 65:88-9+ F '66
Silent season of a hero. Esquire 66:40-3+ Jl '66
(ed) See Patterson, F. In defense of Cassius Clay

about
Pomp and circumstance. Newsweek 68:76 O 24 '66

TALK. See Conversation

TALKING books
Talking book: a prelude to action. V. R. Boyles. il Library J 91:201-4 Ja 15 '66
See also
American printing house for the blind

TALKING typewriters. See Teaching machines

TALL boy; story. See Taylor, E.

TALL girls. See Stature

TALL men. See Stature

TALLAHASSEE, Fla.

Lighting
Lighting program that sells itself. il Am City 81:135 Ap '66

TALLEY, Truman M.
Weybright and Talley: new publishing firm. il Pub W 190:36-7 D 5 '66

TALMADGE, Herman E.
What has happened to the moral climate in America? remarks, June 8, 1966. por U S News 60:90-1 Je 27 '66

TALMEY, Allene
Theatre. Vogue 147:99 F 1 '66

TALOUMIS, George
Eat your avocado and grow it too. Pop Gard 17:82-3 Mr '66
Europe's grandest gardens. Travel 125:32-3+ Mr '66
Gardens at your windows. il Horticulture 44:16-19+ Ap '66
Grow lentils on your windowsill. il Flower Grower 53:47 D '66
Horticultural therapy achieves results. il Horticulture 44:26-7+ Jl '66

TAM Chau
Divided Buddhists of South Vietnam. D. Warner. Reporter 34:22-4 Je 16 '66

TAMALES. See Cookery, Mexican

TAMERLANE. See Timūr the Great

TAMING of the shrew; opera. See Giannini, V.

TAMIRIS, Helen
Obituary
Dance Mag por 40:6 S '66

TAMPA, Fla.

Airports
Tampa shortens the long voyage home. il Fortune 73:163-4 My '66
Two-part Tampa terminal to aid passengers. G. Alexander. il Aviation W 85:49+ N 28 '66

TAMPA International airport. See Tampa, Fla. —Airports

TAN
Be a sun-wise beauty! il Good H 162:96-7+ Je '66
Brown as a . . . il Newsweek 68:58-9 Ag 1 '66
License to tan. il Mlle 62:190-1 Ap '66
Sensible sunning. L. D. Kirk. il Parents Mag 41:78 Je '66

TANAKA, Shōji
Tanaka scandal. il por Newsweek 68:28+ Ag 29 '66

TANENBAUM, Marc H.
Is the ecumenical movement anti-Semitic? Christian Cent 83:1048 Ag 31 '66; Reply. J. C. Rylaarsdam. 83:1306 O 26 '66

TANG-e-BIJAR, Iran, oil well fire. See Oil fires

TANGANYIKA territory
See also
Kilimanjaro

TANGIER, Morocco
Captain's paradise. A. Waugh. Nat R 18:272+ Mr 22 '66

TANGLEWOOD music festival. See Berkshire symphonic festival

TANGUY, John
Corrected attribution. F. J. Dallett. il Antiques 89:734-5 My '66

TANIS, Norman E.
Preparation of the guidelines. ALA Bul 61: 54-5 Ja '67

TANK ships
Biggest ship; Idemitsu Maru of Japan's Ishikawajima-Harima heavy industries. il Newsweek 68:93+ S 19 '66

Giant life for cheaper oil; Japan's Tokyo Maru. il Fortune 73:152-3 My '66
Giants of the ocean grow bigger still; Japan's shipyards, preparing for 300,000-tonners. il Bsns W p 114-16+ Ap 16 '66
Here come the sea giants; Japan's Tokyo Maru. J. D. Ratcliff. il Read Digest 89: 193-4+ S '66
Liquified gas sails the seas; from Algeria to Britain. il Bsns W p 175-6+ F 19 '66
Masquerade at sea fails for Rhodesia; Britain scuttles oil ship to Rhodesia. il Bsns W p41-2 Ap 16 '66
Ship assembled at sea may carry million tons; Japanese tanker Idemitsu Maru. Sci N 90:311 O 15 '66
Time of leviathans. il Time 87:96+ Mr 18 '66

TANKARDS
One hundred years of American tankards. A. Wardwell. il Antiques 90:80-3 Jl '66

TANKERS. See Tank ships

TANKS, Military

Manufacture
1970 U.S.-German tank has problems already; question of using dimensions would be given in both inches or centimeters for nut and bolt sizes. Sci N 90:73 Jl 30 '66

TANNENWALD, P. E. and Thaxter, J. B.
Stimulated Brillouin and Raman scattering in quartz at 2.1° to 293° Kelvin. bibliog Science 154:1319-20 D 9 '66

TANNHÄUSER; opera. See Wagner, R.

TANTRUMS. See Temper

TANZANIA
University turmoil in Tanzania: reaction to the National service system. America 115: 806-7 D 17 '66
See also
Hunting—Tanzania
Technical assistance in Tanzania

Antiquities
Preserving the treasures of Olduvai gorge. M. M. Payne. il Nat Geog Mag 130:700-9 N '66

TAO, Chu
Likely candidate. il por Newsweek 68:58 N 28 '66

TAO, Tien-wen, and Uhr, J. W.
Primary-type antibody response in vitro. bibliog Science 151:1096-8 Mr 4 '66

TAP dancing

Study and teaching
Tap for young children (title varies) A. Gilbert. Dance Mag 40:72-5 My; 84-5 Je; 70-2 Jl; 68-9 Ag; 84 S; 96 O; 77 N; 70-1 D '66 (to be cont)

TAPE, Magnetic. See Magnetic tape

TAPE controlled machine tools. See Machine tools—Control

TAPE measures
New type of measuring tape. il Consumer Bul 49:30 S '66

TAPE memory. See Magnetic memory (computers)

TAPE recorder amplifiers. See Amplifiers

TAPE recorders and recording. See Magnetic recorders and recording

TAPE recordings
Basic tape library; list of tapes. R. C. Marsh. il Hi Fi 16:59-62+ Ag '66
New records and tapes. il Sr Schol 89:sup 14-15+ N 11 '66
New world of tape. I. Kolodin. Sat R 49:63-4 N 26 '66
Prospects in audio. L. Marcus. il Hi Fi 16:64-7+ Ap '66
Sound advice; historical records. W. J. Weaver. Mod Phot 30:91+ Ap '66
Tape deck. R. D. Darrell. See issues of High fidelity incorporating Musical America
Tape life. H. Fantel. Opera N 31:37 O 31 '66
Tape recorder as historian. J. Lieber. il Sat R 49:98-9 Je 11 '66
Ten years of the tape deck. R. D. Darrell. Hi Fi 16:73-4+ My '66
Tuning up cartridge volume. il Bsns W p78-80 Jl 2 '66
Twenty ways to get more out of your tape recorder. C. H. Lawrence. il Pop Mech 126:197-9+ N '66
See also
Oral history

Operas
Opera on reels. R. D. Darrell. il Hi Fi 16:108 Ag '66

TAPE recordings—*Continued*

Stereophonic recordings

Stereotape reviews. J. W. Barker and others. See issues of American record guide

TAPE-slide synchronizers. See Magnetic recorders and recording—Equipment

TAPER, Bernard
City that puts people first. McCalls 93:62+ Ap '66; Same abr. with title City remade for people. Read Digest 89:146-50 O '66

TAPESTRY
Adams-Emery wing at the Cincinnati art museum; De Bertier de Sauvigny tapestries. il Antiques 89:408 Mr '66
Anton Refregier designs a tapestry; interview. A. Refregier. il Am Artist 30:46-51+ O '66
Children of Chinaya and their tapestries. il House & Gard 130:58+ N '66
Miniature tapestry; exhibitions at New York's Museum of contemporary crafts. R. Riley. il Craft Horiz 26:11-15 Mr '66
See also
Bayeux tapestry
Gobelin tapestry

TAPESTRY, Bayeux. See Bayeux tapestry

TAPESTRY weaving
Anton Refregier designs a tapestry; interview. A. Refregier. il Am Artist 30:46-51+ O '66

TAPLINGER, Richard
Whatever happened to the American male? Sat R 49:29-31 Jl 30 '66

TAPPLY, H. G.
Sportsman's notebook. See issues of Field & stream

TAR sand. See Bituminous sand

TARAHUMARA Indians. See Indians of Mexico

TARCHER, Jeremy
Jeremy Tarcher, TV's Dick Clark co-producing books. Pub W 189:75 Ja 31 '66

TARG, William
Memoirs of a merchant-scholar. Sat R 49:59-60 O 22 '66

TARGA Florio. See Automobile racing

TARGAN, Barry
Harry Belten and the Mendelssohn violin concerto; story. Esquire 66:95-7 Jl '66

TARGEE, John
Corrected attribution. F. J. Dallett. il Antiques 89:734-5 My '66

TARGET airplanes. See Airplanes, Target

TARGET indicators. See Target locators

TARGET locators
USAF studies Saab miss-distance gear. W. C. Wetmore. il Aviation W 85:111+ Jl 18 '66

TARGET practice, Aerial
USAF studies Saab miss-distance gear. W. C. Wetmore. il Aviation W 85:111+ Jl 18 '66
See also
Airplanes, Target

TARGET simulators. See Simulators

TARGETS
Targets shoot back; testing efficiency of riflemen under fire. Sci N 90:311 O 15 '66

TARIFF
Kennedy round: down the homestretch. il Fortune 74:67-8+ Ag '66
Kennedy round: the final phase; address, September 28, 1966. W. M. Blumenthal. Dept State Bul 55:671-5 O 31 '66
New horizons in foreign trade. W. Diebold, jr. For Affairs 45:291-303 Ja '67
Tariff cutters get set for big push in Geneva; Kennedy round nears make-or-break phase. Bsns W p42-3 D 10 '66
United States trade policy after the Kennedy round: helping the developing countries help themselves; address, November 2, 1966. A. M. Solomon. Dept State Bul 55:784-9 N 21 '66; Same with title United States trade policy. Vital Speeches 33:115-19 D 1 '66
Will to agree; Kennedy round negotiations. Time 88:94 S 23 '66
See also
Free trade and protection
General agreement on tariffs and trade

Canada

U.S. and Canada sign agreement updating U.S. tariff concessions; announcement, with annex II of the agreement. il Dept State Bul 54:106-9 Ja 17 '66

Europe, Western

See also
European economic community

United States

Aid for the Kennedy round; reductions on watch movements and sheet glass. Newsweek 69:78 Ja 23 '67
Duty and copyright problems in importing books and sheets; summary of addresses at meeting of publishers, March 29, 1966. M. Nicholson; A. I. Demcy. Pub W 189:40-3 My 9 '66
Hearings to be held on new list of possible tariff concessions. Dept State Bul 55:375-6 S 12 '66
Lines shift in Swiss watch war; new opportunities for competition. Bsns W p107-8+ S 24 '66
President ends increased duty on clinical thermometers; White House announcement; with text of proclamation. L. B. Johnson. Dept State Bul 54:159-60 Ja 31 '66
President modifies import duty on stainless-steel flatware; White House announcement; with text of proclamation. L. B. Johnson. il Dept State Bul 54:160-2 Ja 31 '66
President reports on textured yarn tariffs; letter of transmittal, February 1, 1966. L. B. Johnson. Dept State Bul 54:293 F 21 '66
Rolling them back; reduction of duties on imported watch movements and sheet glass. Time 89:79 Ja 20 '67
Time grows short for freer trade; problems confronting Kennedy round tariff negotiators in Geneva. il Bsns W p30-2 My 7 '66
Trade legislation and adjustment assistance; benefits under the Trade expansion act. Mo Labor R 89:III-IV D '66
U.S. and Canada sign agreement updating U.S. tariff concessions; announcement, with annex II of the agreement. il Dept State Bul 54:106-9 Ja 17 '66
See also
Customs service—United States
Duty free importation
United States—Commercial treaties and agreements

TARIFF, Exemption from. See Duty free importation

TARKE, Betty, and Tarke, Louis
How to plan a home you'll always like; interview, ed. by R. Martens. pors Farm J 90:82+ N '66

TARKE, Louis. See Tarke, B. jt. auth.

TARKINGTON, Andrew Wilson
Tarkington of Conoco. il por Fortune 75:41 Ja '67

TARNISH preventives. See Polishing materials

TARO
See also
Poi

TARPAULINS
Ten years with the same tarp. F. W. Fleischhauer. il Motor B 118:45+ N '66

TARPON fishing
Florida sure-shot for tarpon. G. X. Sand. il Field & S 71:128-30+ Je '66
Group; or, Us old men and the sea; Boca Grande. R. Lynes. il Harper 233:30+ S '66
Small boats are tops for tarpon. M. Hunn. il Motor B 117:40-1+ Ap '66

TARR, David W.
Military abroad. bibliog f Ann Am Acad 368:31-42 N '66

TARR, Jeff
We're not taking the love out of love, we're making it more efficient. G. Shalit. il por Look 30:34-5 F 22 '66

TARSIS, Valerii
And don't come back. por Time 87:39 Mr 4 '66
Art and politics in the U.S.S.R. il por Newsweek 67:38+ F 21 '66
Dinner with Valery Tarsis. T. Molnar. Nat R 18:684 Jl 12 '66
Tarsis talks. por Newsweek 67:102+ Mr 14 '66
Valeriy Tarsis meets the press in New York. Pub W 189:49 My 16 '66

TARTANS
Clan tartan cards. D. Powills. il Hobbies 71:118-19 My '66

TARTAS, Joseph
How to select R.F. Chokes. Electr World 75:48-51+ My '66

TARTS
Tart and tartlet cook book. E. Ross. il House & Gard 130:249+ O '66

TASHKENT, Russia
Disaster in Tashkent. il Newsweek 68:46 Jl 25 '66

TASMANIAN tigers
Rare tiger trace seen; thylacine, or Tasmanian pouched wolf. il(p 113) Sci N 90:118 Ag 20 '66

TASTE
How science tricks your taste. J. H. Winchester. il Pop Sci 189:79-81+ S '66
Sweet-sensitive protein from bovine taste buds: isolation and assay. F. R. Dastoli and S. Price. bibliog il Science 154:905-7 N 18 '66

Anecdotes, facetiae, satire, etc.
Notes and comment; effects of synthetic flavors. New Yorker 42:27 Je 4 '66

TASTE (aesthetics) See Aesthetics

TASWELL, H. L. T.
Other side of the South Africa story; address, 1966. por U S News 60:70-2 Je 27 '66

TATE, James
Last letter from old Kampoukos; poem. Atlan 218:94 S '66
Lost pilot; poem. Atlan 218:127 N '66
Reapers of the water; poem. Atlan 219:43 Ja '67

TATEM, Mike
Talk with Tatem. A. Francekevich. il Pop Phot 58:30+ Je '66

TATLOW, Michael
Letter from Australia. Nat R 18:1208 N 29 '66
Vital election. Nat R 18:837+ Ag 23 '66

TATOR, Kenneth
New theory for what's behind built-up roofing failures. Arch Rec 140:190-2 N '66

TATSUMOTO, M.
Genetic relations of oceanic basalts as indicated by lead isotopes. bibliog Science 153:1094-101 S 2 '66

TATTLING. See Children—Management and training

TAUB, Edward, and others
Deafferentation in monkeys: effect on conditioned grasp response. bibliog Science 151:593-4 F 4 '66

TAUBE, Mortimer
Information technology: problems and promises; excerpts from address, May 27, 1965. por Library J 91:1155-8 Mr 1 '66

TAUBE, Myron
Kiss; story. Seventeen 25:164-5 S '66

TAUBER, Edward S. and Koffler, Sandra
Optomotor response in human infants to apparent motion: evidence of innateness. bibliog Science 152:382-3 Ap 15 '66

TAUBER, Richard
Historical records. A. Favia-Artsay. por Hobbies 71:41 My '66

TAUBINGER, Laszlo M.
Communist grab for African unions. Nat R 18:1222 N 29 '66
Indonesia: the plot that failed. Nat R 18:160 F 22 '66
Soviet tourist traps. Nat R 18:575 Je 14 '66

TAUBMAN, Howard
Shakespeare speaks to kids. Parents Mag 41:72-3+ O '66

TAVARD, George H.
Changing church. Cath World 202:267-70 F '66
Doctrinal development. Cath World 202:336-40 Mr '66
Evolution in moral theology. Cath World 203:29-32 Ap '66

TAVES, Isabella
Flower people. Look 30:87-8 Mr 22 '66

TAVOLGA, William N.
Marine bioacoustics. Science 153:771+ Ag 12 '66
Sounds of the sea; interview. New Yorker 42:50-2 D 3 '66

TAX agents. See Tax consultants

TAX collection
Good news for taxpayers. W. D. Mills. Nations Bsns 53:50-2+ D '65
Taxes on the double; Treasury extends twice-a-month collection system to more payrolls. Bsns W p21 D 24 '66
See also
Tax returns
United States—Internal revenue service
Withholding tax

TAX consultants
Electronic ally for the taxpayer; computerized tax preparation. il Bsns W p 167-8 Mr 26 '66
When I looked in those files, my eyes popped; California tax scandal. J. Phelan. il Sat Eve Post 239:23-9 S 10 '66

TAX deductions. See Income tax—Deductions

TAX evasion
How the collector is changing Latin America. il U S News 61:67-8 Jl 4 '66
Revenuer and the red in the red; Albert Deschenes' witch-hunt on R. G. Lenske. New Repub 155:9 N 19 '66
Tax wonderland; California. Newsweek 67:29-30 Mr 7 '66
Why big money is slipped abroad. U S News 61:90 Jl 25 '66
You have to be insane not to pay taxes. Time 89:80 Ja 6 '67
See also
Tax planning

TAX exempt securities. See Securities, Tax exempt

TAX exemption. See Taxation, Exemption from

TAX forms
Here come those tax forms again. il Changing T 21:19-20 Ja '67
Tax form that dispels own fog. il Bsns W p50 D 10 '66

TAX informers. See Informers (law)

TAX planning
How can you manage your money to pay less tax? N. Kuehnl and G. Bush. Bet Hom & Gard 44:7+ D '66
Personal business; tax selling can be dangerous. Bsns W p 149-50 D 3 '66

TAX reduction. See Taxation—United States

TAX returns
Born free. Commonweal 84:166-7 Ap 29 '66
How long should you save your old tax returns? Bet Hom & Gard 44:6 Ap '66
One return for all taxes? U S News 61:87 Ag 8 '66
Tax-appeal ordeal. W. R. Frye. Reporter 34:21-4 My '66
What are your rights if IRS audits your tax return? F. Bailey, jr. Suc Farm 64:41+ Mr '66
When an accountant can help on tax returns. Good H 162:182 Mr '66
Will the new tax computer get after you? il Farm J 90:28+ F '66
Your tax return may be questioned this year. il Changing T 20:21-3 Mr '66

TAX selling. See Tax planning

TAX write-off program. See Amortization deductions

TAXATION
See also
Assessment
Property tax
Stock transfer tax
also subhead Taxation under various subjects, e.g. Machinery—Taxation

California
Property tax scandal. Nation 204:68-9 Ja 16 '67

Great Britain
Britain's squeeze hurts. il Bsns W p40 S 3 '66
Callaghan's surprise. il Newsweek 67:76 My 16 '66
Jobs tax hits British booksellers. G. R. Davies. Pub W 189:39-41 My 30 '66
Out of the black case. il Time 87:101 My 13 '66
Payroll tax irks British churches. Christian Cent 83:737 Je 8 '66
Selective torment; Selective employment tax. il Time 88:112 S 16 '66
Taxing Peter to pay Paul; how Britain's new tax will work. il Bsns W p 103+ My 14 '66

Latin America
How the tax collector is changing Latin America. il U S News 61:67-8 Jl 4 '66

Liechtenstein
See also
Corporations—Taxation

United States
Administration's tax dilemma. Bsns W p 176 D 3 '66
After tax cuts: more prosperity, higher revenue. U S News 60:103 Je 13 '66
As the new tax picture rounds into shape. U S News 61:112+ S 26 '66
Avoiding overcure; inflation. il Time 87:93 My 13 '66
Boom now getting out of hand? il U S News 60:25-6 My 9 '66
Calculation and uses of spendable earnings series. il Mo Labor R 89:405-9 Ap '66
Case against a tax increase. E. L. Dale, jr. New Repub 154:11-13 Ap 2 '66; Discussion. 154:37-8 Ap 16; 18 Ap 23 '66

TAXATION—United States—*Continued*

Chances of a tax increase now. U S News 60:27 Ap 4 '66

Church-abetted favoritism; tax-exempt retirement homes. A. C. Hausske. Christian Cent 83:463-4 Ap 13 '66

Clear sailing for tax bill. Bsns W p49 S 24 '66

Congress lets LBJ call tune on tax hike. il Bsns W p27-8 Ap 9 '66

Congress opens a door to overseas investors; no tax on investment income under law aimed at aiding U.S. payments balance. il Bsns W p 102+ O 29 '66

Cost, loss and agony; L. B. Johnson asks for war tax. K. Crawford. Newsweek 69: 37 Ja 23 '67

Decision & delay; question of a tax increase. il Time 88:29-30 N 25 '66

Dose of taxes, but enough? tax bill to curb inflation. il Newsweek 67:66 Mr 28 '66

Drunken pyramid. il Time 87:92 Mr 4 '66

Effect of taxes on the CPI. J. C. Daugherty. il Mo Labor R 89:182-5 F '66

Experts turn against tax boosts; survey of 100 top men finds 60 per cent opposed. il Bsns W p 154-5+ My 28 '66

Fiscal flexibility. America 114:849 Je 18 '66

Foggy days. il Time 88:27 D 16 '66

Getting $6-billion more in revenues. il Bsns W p30-1 Ja 22 '66

Good news for taxpayers. W. D. Mills. Nations Bsns 53:50-2+ D '65

Guessing games on taxes. Time 88:26-7 D 9 '66

If Washington shares tax revenue with states. il U S News 61:86-7 D 5 '66

Is it really too late for a tax increase? hind-sight and foresight. Bsns W p 136 Ag 27 '66

Jockeying the budget; laying the groundwork for budget and taxes. il Bsns W p37-8 D 3 '66

Kick Johnson week; White House plan for funding Vietnam war. Newsweek 67:26-7 Mr 21 '66

Lesser of the evils; tax boost better anti-inflation weapon than guideposts. il Bsns W p 160+ My 28 '66

LBJ prepares to ask for a tax hike. il Newsweek 68:61 D 26 '66

LBJ's deadline for decision; concerning '67 tax boost. il Newsweek 68:79 N 28 '66

Making sense of transfer taxes. il Bsns W p98+ Jl 9 '66

Modified tax bill moves on to Senate; exemptions for devices to halt pollution, plus other changes. Bsns W p47 O 8 '66

New rash of tax laws on the way. il Nations Bsns 54:76-7+ S 24 '66

Newest idea about raising taxes; summary of interview. W. W. Heller. U S News 62: 96 Ja 16 '67

Now it's up to Congress; to slow inflation and ease strain on the money market. il Bsns W p35-8 S 17 '66

Open letter to LBJ. P. A. Samuelson. Newsweek 69:59 Ja 2 '67

Pay now. Nation 203:627-8 D 12 '66

Paying the (high) cost of government. il Sr Schol 88:20 F 18 '66

Planning the future of federal taxes; Brookings institution's study Federal tax policy. il Bsns W p 147-8+ S 24 '66

President revises designations under interest equalization tax; White House announcement; with text of Executive order. L. B. Johnson. Dept State Bul 55:27-8 Jl 4 '66

Public favor for tax sharing. il U S News 62:83 Ja 9 '67

Raising 1967 tax rates. P. A. Samuelson. Newsweek 68:94 D 12 '66

Republican plan; Laird plan of tax sharing. K. Crawford. Newsweek 68:35 N 28 '66

Senate sugars the tax bill. Bsns W p41-2 O 15 '66

Strong case for a new kind of tax; value added tax vs. a corporate income tax. Bsns W p 164 Ap 23 '66

Stronger dose to curb inflation? with editorial comment. il Bsns W p29-30, 140 Ap 2 '66

T.R.B. from Washington; crazy taxes. New Repub 155:4 D 17 '66

Tax boost; a flexible weapon. il Newsweek 69:69-70+ Ja 23 '67

Tax boost; pro, con, maybe. U S News 60: 114 My 16 '66

Tax boost; too late to help? il Newsweek 67:73 My 9 '66

Tax changes voted by Congress. U S News 61:87-9 O 31 '66

Tax credit has fans and foes 7 per cent investment credit; with editorial comment. il Bsns W p49-50, 200 Mr 26 '66

Tax hike bill goes on books; Congress tacks old-age pensions to Johnson's proposals. Bsns W p 160+ Mr 19 '66

Tax-hike decision is still a cliffhanger. il Bsns W p47 N 26 '66

Tax rise; it looks likely. U S News 61:35 Ag 1 '66

Taxation as discipline; sharing of federal personal-income-tax revenue. R. Moley. Newsweek 69:68 Ja 2 '67

Taxes; are you getting your money's worth? M. Mayer. Bet Hom & Gard 44:14 D '66

Taxes; to boost or not to boost? Newsweek 68:87 D 19 '66

Taxing the boom. Sr Schol 89:19-20 S 30 '66

10-billion-dollar tax rise coming? il U S News 61:26-8 Ag 15 '66

Too much of a good thing? increased withholding. il Newsweek 67:77-8 My 2 '66

Top seers urge a tax hike now; to help control inflation. il Bsns W p29-30 Ag 27 '66

What key congressmen say about a tax rise this year. il U S News 60:102+ My 23 '66

What's up with taxes. R. Lekachman. Atlan 218:65-6+ Ag '66

Where tax bills run the gauntlet; Joint committee on internal revenue taxation. il Bsns W p 106+ Je 11 '66

White House delays a tax-boost decision; prices rising. Bsns W p46 Mr 26 '66

Will higher taxes mean lower interest rates? concerning State-of-the-Union message. U S News 62:99-100 Ja 23 '67

Will there really be a tax increase? il U S News 60:33-5 Ap 11 '66

Willie's big whisper; amendment to Viet Nam tax bill passed. il Time 87:26 Mr 11 '66

Wrong tax increase; proposal to suspend investment tax credit. H. C. Wallich. Newsweek 68:90 O 3 '66

   See also

Income tax—United States

Inheritance tax

Property tax

Real property and taxation

Taxation, Exemption from

Taxation, State

United States—Internal revenue service

United States—Revenue

   also subhead Taxation under names of cities, e.g. New York (city)—Taxation; *also* subhead Taxation under various subjects, e.g. Transportation—Taxation

TAXATION, Double

Income tax protocol with Germany enters into force. Dept State Bul 54:90-1 Ja 17 '66

Supplementary tax convention signed with Canada. Dept State Bul 55:761 N 14 '66

Supplementary tax protocol signed with United Kingdom. Dept State Bul 54:549 Ap 4 '66

Supplementary tax protocol with U.K. enters into force. Dept State Bul 55:465-6 S 26 '66

Tax convention with Honduras to continue in force for 1966. Dept State Bul 54:91 Ja 17 '66

U.S. and Netherlands sign supplementary tax convention. Dept State Bul 54:91-2 Ja 17 '66

U.S.-Belgium income tax protocol enters into force. Dept State Bul 55:440 S 19 '66

U.S.-Netherlands tax convention enters into force. Dept State Bul 55:253 Ag 15 '66

TAXATION, Exemption from

Cc; IRS. Nat R 18:1205 N 29 '66

Companies rush for cheaper money; tax-exempt industrial development bonds. Bsns W p 114+ Je 11 '66

Fall from grace; Sierra club. il Newsweek 69:24-5 Ja 9 '67

Modern indulgences; question of tax exempt bonds. New Repub 155:4 O 15 '66

Of love, kisses & nudism; decisions. Time 88:58-9 Jl 15 '66

On the trail of runaway plants; tax-exempt bonds lure industry. il Bsns W p 114-16 Ag 6 '66

Public bonds and private profit. America 115:26 Jl 9 '66

Tax-free bonds under fire. U S News 60: 104-5 My 9 '66

What's in a loophole? tax-exempt periodicals. il Time 88:62+ O 7 '66

   See also

Church property—Taxation

Securities, Tax exempt

TAXATION, Municipal. See Local taxation

TAXATION, Progressive

Income-tax illusions; economists misgivings. H. Hazlitt. Newsweek 67:96 Je 20 '66

TAXATION, State
Are you overpaying your state taxes?
Changing T 20:17-18 Ag '66
How states voted on bond issues, taxes. il
U S News 61:123-5 N 21 '66
State, local tax rise steepens. U S News
61:87-8 Jl 11 '66
State taxes may reach a record. U S News
60:99-100 Mr 7 '66
States' surplus funds: a warning. U S News
62:51 Ja 2 '67
TAXATION of bonds, securities, etc.
See also
Taxation. Exemption from
TAXATION of corporations. See Corporations
—Taxation
TAXATION of foreign investments. See In-
vestments, Foreign—Taxation
TAXATION of insurance. See Insurance—
Taxation
TAXATION of legacies. See Inheritance tax
TAXATION of works of art
Art and taxes. J. S. Rubin. il Horizon 8:4-15
Wint '66
TAXER, Karlheinz. See Buerger, M. J. jt.
auth.
TAXICAB drivers
Five with enterprise, girl cab driver. P. Ri-
field. il Mlle 63:144 S '66
Taxi! taxi! John V. Lindsay's suggested
changes in the taxi system in New York
city. Newsweek 69:58 Ja 23 '67
Traffic jam in the taxi industry: troubles
in New York. T. Buckley. il N Y Times
Mag p8-9+ S 4 '66
TAXICABS
Are fleet cars a good buy? D. MacDonald. il
Motor T 18:37 Je '66
Traffic jam in the taxi industry: troubles
in New York. T. Buckley. il N Y Times
Mag p8-9+ S 4 '66
TAXICABS, Aerial. See Air taxi service
TAXIDERMY
Dioramas out of the deepfreeze. C. West.
il Pop Mech 125:126-9+ F '66
TAXONOMY. See Zoology—Classification
TAYLOR, A. J. P.
Peace comes of age. N Y Times Mag p 14-
15+ Ag 14 '66
TAYLOR, A. N. See Wasserman, R. H. jt.
auth.
TAYLOR, Barnard C.
Graphic designer in a college community. il
Am Artist 30:56-61+ S '66
TAYLOR, Bruce C. See Barrow, J. H. jr. jt.
auth.
TAYLOR, C. A.
Old city hall gets a new face. Am City 81:
91 Mr '66
TAYLOR, Carl E.
Ethics for an international health profession.
bibliog Science 153:716-20 Ag 12 '66
TAYLOR, Cecil
New jazz. il Newsweek 68:104+ D 12 '66
TAYLOR, Clif
Ski parallel in one day. S. James. il por
Pop Mech 126:126-9+ D '66
TAYLOR, Deems
Obituary
Opera N por 31:62 S 17 '66
TAYLOR, Desmond
Is Dewey dead? por Library J 91:4035-7 S 15
'66
TAYLOR, Duncan Norton-. See Norton-Taylor,
D.
TAYLOR, Edmond
Back from Vietnam. Reporter 34:23-6 Ja 27 '66
Long NATO crisis. Reporter 34:16-21 Ap 21
'66
TAYLOR, Elizabeth, 1912-
Devastating boys: story. McCalls 93:102-3
My '66
Tall boy: story. New Yorker 42:31-4 D 31 '66
TAYLOR, Elizabeth, 1932-
Bawd of Avon. por Time 87:58 Je 3 '66
Elizabeth Taylor and Richard Burton: the
night of the brawl. J. Roddy. il pors Look
30:42-8 F 8 '66
Liz launches 1,000 ships: Faustus at Oxford:
with report by M. Smith. il pors Life
60:78-9+ Mr 4 '66
Night Elizabeth Taylor said so what? and
Richard Burton kicked the television set
in. W. Redfield. il por Esquire 67:108-9+
Ja '67
Richard Burton to Liz: I love thee not . . .
R. Braddon. il pors Sat Eve Post 239:88-91
D 3 '66
Surprising Liz in a film shocker; with report
by T. Thompson. il pors Life 60:87-92+ Je
10 '66
Who's afraid of Dr Faustus? T. Sage. il Nat
R 18:1319-20 D 27 '66

TAYLOR, Floyd B. See Epstein, S. S. jt. auth.
TAYLOR, Frank J.
Friendly man from medicare. Read Digest
88:175-6+ Ap '66
TAYLOR, George E.
United States relations with Communist
China. Nat R 18:526-8 My 31 '66
TAYLOR, George W.
Close-up: talk with George W. Taylor; inter-
view. ed. by J. Berry. por Duns R 88:8-9+
O '66
TAYLOR, Glenn A.
Old New York yacht, launch & engine co.
Motor B 118:36-7+ D '66
TAYLOR, Harold C.
Coordination of manpower programs; ex-
cerpt. Mo Labor R 89:959-64 S '66
TAYLOR, Hugh P. jr, and Epstein, Samuel
Oxygen isotope studies of Ivory Coast tektites
and impactite glass from the Bosumtwi
crater, Ghana. bibliog Science 153:173-5 Jl
8 '66
TAYLOR, James R.
Precision non-wirewound trimmers; with
Potentiometer terms and definitions. Electr
World 75:37-9 Ap '66
TAYLOR, James W. and Dean, N. J.
Managing to manage the computer. Harvard
Bsns R 44:98-110 S '66
TAYLOR, Jay T.
I like kids. . . even my own. il U S Camera
29:44-5 S '66
Moonlight. il U S Camera 29:42-3 S '66
TAYLOR, Jim
Locks vs. Boom Boom. D. Jenkins. il
por(cover) Sports Illus 25:20-3 Ag 22 '66
TAYLOR, Katherine
Explosion in Clinton. Sat R 49:90 S 17 '66
TAYLOR, L. B.
Personality of the month. Sci Digest 60:40-3
Jl '66
TAYLOR, Leslie G.
Charges of reckless driving. il por Time 88:
68 Ag 12 '66
TAYLOR, Mark M.
Western skunk cabbage. Horticulture 44:18-19
F '66
TAYLOR, Maxwell Davenport
Battle over U.S. policy in Vietnam; excerpts
from testimony, February 17 and 18, 1966.
por U S News 60:40-2 F 28 '66
Excerpt from testimony, February 17, 1966,
before Senate committee on foreign rela-
tions. Cong Digest 45:110-13 Ap '66
General Taylor hits holding strategy, defends
Vietnam policy; excerpts from address,
February 3, 1966. por U S News 60:20 F
14 '66
1954 and 1966: is U.S. repeating French mistakes in Vietnam? interview. U S News
60:36-7 F 28 '66
Problems confronting us: address. December
3, 1965. Vital Speeches 32:264-8 F 15 '66
Top authority looks at Vietnam war and
its future: interview. por U S News 60:
38-42+ F 21 '66
U.S. commitment in Viet-Nam: fundamental
issues; statement, February 17, 1966. bib-
liog f Dept State Bul 54:356-62 Mr 7 '66
Why the U.S. fights: Rusk and Taylor; excerpts from Fulbright committee hearings.
por Newsweek 67:19-20 F 28 '66
about
Exhaustive, explicit & enough. il por Time
87:21-3 F 25 '66
Touch of psychology? Newsweek 67:40 Mr 21
'66
TAYLOR, Merle
Belly whopper to a take-out win. T. C.
Brody. il por Sports Illus 24:22-3 F 28 '66
TAYLOR, Michael E.
Precambrian mollusc-like fossils from Inyo
County, California. bibliog Science 153:198-
201 Jl 8 '66
TAYLOR, Paul
Down with choreography; excerpts from The
modern dance: seven statements of belief,
ed. by S. J. Cohen. Dance Mag 40:39-41
F '66
about
Barefoot boy with cheek. il por Time 89:38
Ja 6 '67
TAYLOR, Philip B. jr
Democracy for Venezuela? bibliog f Cur Hist
51:284-90+ N '66
TAYLOR, R. E.
Idea exchange. NEA J 55:60+ S '66
—See Long, S. V. jt. auth.
TAYLOR, Raymond L.
Eighth Washington meeting. Science 152:1117-
26+; 153:437-41 My 20, Jl 22 '66

TAYLOR, René
Ponce art museum. Antiques 90:681-5 N '66
TAYLOR, Richard N.
How to get those impossible streets paved.
Am City 81:120-1 My '66
TAYLOR, Telford
Battle to the end of war. Sat R 49:42 Mr
12 '66
Britannia ruled the skies. Sat R 49:48 Jl 23
'66
TAYLOR, Tom M.
Gigantic reservoir floats a decorous pool. Am
City 81:87-90+ O '66
TAYLOR, W. I.
Source of indole alkaloids. bibliog Science 153:
954-6 Ag 26 '66
TAYLOR, William Howland
Obituary
Yachting por 119:54 F '66
TAYLOR, William J.
Packaging and the distribution grind. Duns R
88:148-50 N '66

about

Booms, rails and ACF. J. Weingarten. por
Duns R 87:49-50 Mr '66
TAYLOR, Zack
Fishingest way south. Motor B 118:30-1+ O
'66
High time the boatman came into his own.
Motor B 117:46+ Ap '66
Refrigeration, it's wonderful. Motor B 117:
36-9 F '66
TAYLOR Allerdice high school. See Pittsburgh
—Education
TAZIEFF, Haroun
Hottest job on earth. G. Kent. il Read Digest
90:184-6+ Ja '67
TCHAIKOVSKY, Peter Ilyitch
On records:
Oprichnik; Maid of Orleans. Opera N 30:30
Je 4 '66
Queen of spades. Criticism
Opera N il 31:26 N 19 '66
TCHAIKOVSKY international competition. See
Music—Competitions
TCHELITCHEW, Paul
Letter from Paris; retrospective show at
the Galerie au Pont des arts. Genêt. New
Yorker 42:160+ N 5 '66
TCHISTIAKOV, Nikolai I. See Chistiakov, N.
I.
TEA
Step by step to sparkling iced tea. il Bet
Hom & Gard 44:92 Je '66
What makes tea black or oolong? Good H
162:179 Mr '66
TEA drinking. See Manners and customs
TEA parties. See Entertaining
TEA pots. See Teapots
TEACHER assignments. See Teaching assign-
ments
TEACHER corps. See United States—National
teacher corps
TEACHER education. See Teachers—Education
TEACHER grievances. See Teachers grievances
TEACHER-Mom programs. See Special classses
and special schools
TEACHER morale. See Morale
TEACHER participation in school administra-
tion. See School management and organiza-
tion—Teacher participation
TEACHER pupil relations. See Teachers and
students
TEACHER recognition day. See Special days,
weeks, and months
TEACHER shortage. See Teachers—Suppply
and demand
TEACHERS
Dear Miss O'Neill. L. Rosten. il Look 30:
19 S 20 '66
Fair deal for the teacher. J. Thomas. il
UNESCO Courier 19:4-6+ S '66
Federal aid: teachers lead the way; with
statements from education leaders. J.
Lloyd. Sr Schol 89:sup4 O 21 '66
Five finalists named for teacher awards. Sr
Schol 87:sup4 Ja 21 '66
For Samoa: a barefoot teacher from Okla-
homa. il Look 30:88+ My 31 '66
From the editor. Am Ed 2:inside cover F '66
Good teacher is a good teacher. S. J. Idzerda.
NEA J 55:14-16 N '66
High school classic: B. Kaufman's novel. il
Time 87:74 Mr 18 '66
Improving teachers' status world-wide. NEA
J 55:45-6 Ap '66
International Magna charta for teachers;
concerning the document, adopted unan-
imously by delegates to Unesco. W. G.
Carr. NEA J 55:42-4 D '66

New breed of teachers: igniting the individual pupil. il Newsweek 68:100-1+ S
26 '66
Plea for professional dignity; interview, ed.
by H. Ravis. B. Kaufman. il Sr Schol 89:
sup5 O 14 '66
Special feature on summer opportunities for
teachers; symposium. il NEA J 55:28-38 My
'66
Superior people are rejecting classroom
teaching. J. M. Harrer. il NEA J 55:20-2
N '66
Teacher benefits; fringe benefits and work-
ing conditions. Sr Schol 88:sup4 Mr 25 '66
Teacher insurance: who foots the bill? E. S.
Crowley. NEA J 55:51+ S '66
Teacher of the year: Mona Dayton's magical
classroom. D. Chapman. il Look 30:85-6+
Ap 19 '66
Tolstoi and teachers. H. Howe, 2d. NEA J
55:19 My '66
Tomorrow's teacher. R. F. Campbell. il Sat
R 50:60+ Ja 14 '67
Travel: of, by, and for teachers; ed. by L.
Jonckheere. il Sr Schol 89:sup 13-15 S 30 '66
Tribute to a teacher. V. M. Stocker. Sr
Schol 89:sup61 S 23 '66
Vietnam hero salutes his teacher; Golden key
award. D. Chapman. il Look 30:68+ F 22
'66
Washington report; National teacher of the
year award. J. Lloyd. Sr Schol 88:sup7
Ap 29 '66
What makes a good teacher? panel discus-
sion. il Seventeen 25:284-5+ Ag '66
What parents can do about bad teachers. A.
Toffler. Good H 162:84-5+ F '66
See also
Academic freedom
American teachers in foreign countries
Collective bargaining—Teachers
College professors and instructors
Dance teachers
Foreign teachers in the United States
Gifts for teachers
Music teachers
National education association
School and the home
School management and organiaztion—Teach-
er participation
Substitute teachers
Teachers unions
Teaching
Women as teachers

Adjustment

Plea from the ghetto; letter to Theodore
Sizer. A. Kovner. il Am Ed 3:12 D '66
Teacher from Appalachia. F. C. Mayer. Sch
& Soc 94:324-5 O 15 '66

Certification

Comments on teacher certification. C. L.
Melaro; D. Davies. NEA J 55:18-19 S '66

Contracts

Collective bargaining: a primer for superintendents. L. B. Bail. il Sat R 50:70-1+ Ja
21 '67

Dismissal

Ethics opinion: reasons for dismissal. NEA J
55:62 O '66

Duties

At the teacher's right hand. J. W. Rioux.
il Am Ed 2:5-6 D '65
Time to teach. J. H. Starie. NEA J 55:32
S '66

Education

Creative programs in teacher education. W.
E. Engbretson. il NEA J 55:45-7 D '66
Education of educators; Carnegie corpora-
tion study. F. G. Jennings. Sat R 49:79-80
N 19 '66
Federal aid for teachers. Sr Schol 88:sup2+
Mr 4 '66
Research in teacher education at University
of Texas; and at Stanford. Sch & Soc 94:
121-2 Mr 5 '66
Small colleges and teacher education. D.
Tyack. Sch & Soc 94:326-7 O 15 '66
Tax deductions for educational expenses. W.
W. Brickman. Sch & Soc 94:341 O 29 '66
Teaching sisters. America 116:76-7 Ja 21 '67
Tomorrow's teacher. R. F. Campbell. il Sat
R 50:60+ Ja 14 '67
Training 30,000 Head Start teachers. S. J.
Drazek. Sch & Soc 94:130-1 Mr 5 '66
See also
Colleges and universities—Education depart-
ments
Educational workshops
Summer schools
Teachers institutes

TEACHERS—*Continued*

Ethics

See also
Teachers ethics

Leaves of absence

Around the world on a sabbatical. J. B. Carr. il Sr School 89:sup 14-15 Ja 6 '67

Morale

See Morale

Oaths of allegiance, etc.

See Loyalty. Oaths of

Pensions

Retirement benefits and teacher mobility. R. L. Lillywhite and M. L. Ware. NEA J 55:15-16 Ap '66

Teachers must leave retirement benefits behind. L. E. Kraft. NEA J 55:50+ F '66

Political activities

His Honor is a teacher. M. W. Krey. NEA J 55:47+ Mr '66

Should teachers form their own political action groups? T. P. Lantos; H. Bain. NEA J 55:58-60 D '66
See also
College professors and instructors—Political activities

Qualifications

See also
Teachers—Certification

Rating

Good teaching. W. Weaver. Science 151:1335 Mr 18 '66; Discussion. 153:813-14; 154:1504-5 Ag 19, D 23 '66
See also
College professors and instructors—Rating by students

Reading

Teachers' reading and recreational interests; findings of questionnaire by NEA research division; tables. NEA J 55:17-19 N '66

Recreation

Local associations ask about: cultural activities. J. H. Starie. NEA J 55:23 N '66

Teachers' reading and recreational interests; findings of questionnaire by NEA research division; tables. NEA J 55:17-19 N '66

Salaries

Changes in teachers' salaries, 1963 to 1965. A. Sackley. il Mo Labor R 88:1460-4 D '65

Long term trends in urban teachers' compensation. A. Sackley. bibliog f il Mo Labor R 89:1223-9 N '66

No strike, but where will Chicago get money to pay teachers? U S News 62:74 Ja 23 '67

Teacher-opinion poll. il NEA J 55:29 O '66

Teachers' salaries in the twenty largest school systems in the United States; September-October, 1965; table. Sr School 88:sup3 F 4 '66

Teachers' salaries: where they stand. Sr School 89:sup2 O 14 '66
See also
College professors and instructors—Salaries
Strikes—United States—Teachers

Social status

International draft recommendation on teachers' status. Sch & Soc 94:175-6 Ap 2 '66

Statistics

Caught short; where the shortage is. il Newsweek 68:79 S 19 '66

Profile of the teacher of 1966. Sch & Soc 94:436 D 10 '66

Teachers' reading and recreational interests; findings of questionnaire by NEA research division; tables. NEA J 55:17-19 N '66

Supply and demand

Bigger teacher shortage. Time 88:43 S 23 '66

Filling the teacher gap. America 115:577 N 12 '66

NEA lists 1,600 teachers to ease teacher shortage. il Sch & Soc 94:439-41 D 10 '66

Next step; teacher integration. P. A. Janssen. il Reporter 35:32-4 N 3 '66

Schools make news; Partnership teaching program. Sat R 49:75 Mr 19 '66

Teacher shortage: is there one? why? Sr School 89:sup2 S 30 '66

Tenure

What parents can do about bad teachers. A. Toffler. Good H 162:84-5+ F '66

Training

See Teachers—Education

TEACHERS, Handicapped. See Vocational rehabilitation

TEACHERS, Interchange of

Teacher-opinion poll; domestic teacher exchange. NEA J 55:50 Mr '66

Teachers go abroad; Teacher exchange section. L. Jonckheere. il Sr School 89:sup 13 S 30 '66

Why not a domestic teacher exchange program? H. Lobdell. NEA J 55:15 F '66

TEACHERS, New. See Teachers—Adjustment

TEACHERS, Part time

Answer to shortage: part-time teachers. Sr School 89:sup4 O 28 '66

TEACHERS, Retired

See also
Teachers—Pensions

TEACHERS, Women. See Women as teachers

TEACHERS aides

At the teacher's right hand. J. W. Rioux. il Am Ed 2:5-6 D '65

Parents provide time to teach. Sr School 88:sup5+ Mr 25 '66

Teacher and his staff. G. W. Denemark. il NEA J 55:17-19+ D '66

Teachers' (adult) helpers. il Sr School 89: sup2+ Ja 6 '67

TEACHERS and libraries. See Libraries and schools

TEACHERS and students

Children's school complaints; with study-discussion program. by E. Harris and D. Harris. bibliog il PTA Mag 60:4-6, 36-7 My '66

Classroom incident. NEA J 56:58-9 Ja '67

Editor interviews; ed. by M. S. Fenner. E. T. Hall. NEA J 56:87-8 Ja '67

Establishing teacher-student rapport. Sister Marian Frances. NEA J 55:19-20 O '66

Maureen; a prize-winning true story. M. S. Smith. NEA J 55:62+ F '66

Of baseball and harmonicas. J. Woods. NEA J 55:57-9 Mr '66

Roots of failure. K. C. Cotter; M. W. Hass; J. E. Mizer. il NEA J 55:33-6 Ap '66

Teaching young teenagers about sex. J. A. Matz. il Parents Mag 41:60-1+ Mr '66

Virtues of anonymity. P. Shepard. Sat R 49: 77 S 17 '66

What your child can teach his teacher. G. B. Leonard. Look 30:29-30 D 27 '66

TEACHERS and the community

Professional relations. J. H. Starie. NEA J 55:64 D '66

TEACHERS attitudes. See Attitudes

TEACHERS certificates. See Teachers—Certification

TEACHERS ethics

Acceptance of gifts. NEA J 55:27 My '66

Ethics opinion: exchanging confidential information. NEA J 55:54 S '66

TEACHERS grievances

It burns me up. NEA J 56:79-81 Ja '67

What makes teachers burn? A. Mulford. NEA J 55:13-15 My '66

TEACHERS in colored schools, National association of. See American teachers association

TEACHERS institutes

English from the inside. E. Welty. Am Ed 2:18-19 F '66

Federal aid for summer institutes. Sr School 89:sup8 D 2 '66

Federal aid for summer study. Sr School 87: sup5 Ja 7 '66

1966 NDEA institutes announced in advanced school library study; also education courses. Library J 91:354+ Ja 15 '66

Opportunities for teacher education; programs under NDEA. il Am Ed 2:1-3 Ap '66

So you're going to an NDEA institute. J. Portz. NEA J 55:30-1 My '66

USOE announces NDEA summer institutes: School library personnel; Educational media. Library J 91:6172-3 D 15 '66

TEACHERS meetings

Perk up your faculty meeting. K. Winters. il NEA J 55:30-1 O '66

TEACHERS salaries. See Teachers—Salaries

TEACHERS strikes. See Strikes—United States—Teachers

TEACHERS unions

Editor's bookshelf. P. Woodring. Sat R 49: 89-90 S 17 '66

Join the picket line! concerning letter from union to librarians to boycott annual congress at St John's. J. N. Berry, 3d. il Library J 91:1782-7 Ap 1 '66

Progress toward mergers; affiliated associations now organized along racial lines. NEA J 55:53 D '66

TEACHERS unions—*Continued*
Representation among teachers. M. H. Moskow. il Mo Labor R 89:728-32 Jl '66
Strike at St John's: why the professors picket. M. R. Berube. il Nation 202:172-4 F 14 '66
Summer school short course in teacher negotiations. G. R. Potts. Mo Labor R 89:847-50 Ag '66
Teachers choose the NEA; representation elections. D. Dashiell. il NEA J 55:43 S '66
Time bomb in Catholic education; crisis at St John's. R. Horchler. il Look 30:23-5 Ap 5 '66
Unionism versus professionalism in teaching. R. D. Batchelder. NEA J 55:18-20 Ap '66
See also
American federation of teachers

TEACHERS vacations
Vacation with typewriter and drawing board. V. H. Ormsby. il NEA J 55:36 My '66
When the lotus-eating days are done. M. S. Rawe. il NEA J 55:37-8 My '66

TEACHERS workshops. See Educational workshops

TEACHERS' writing competition. See Literature—Competitions

TEACHING
Changing directions in American education; symposium. il Sat R 50:37-43+ Ja 14 '67
Curriculum molder; J. Zacharias. il Time 88:110+ D 16 '66
Don't stifle your students' nonconformity. K. Harris. il NEA J 55:24-6 O '66
Editor interviews; ed. by M. S. Fenner. L. C. Eiseley. NEA J 55:71-2 N '66
Education and the new technology; symposium. Sr Schol 89:sup 13 O 7 '66
Need for quality instruction; address, July 17, 1966. L. B. Prewitt. Vital Speeches 33:49-50 N 1 '66
New breed of teachers; igniting the individual pupil. il Newsweek 68:100-1+ S 26 '66
New ideas in high school teaching; with study-discussion program, by C. Smallenburg and H. Smallenburg. J. L. Trump. bibliog il PTA Mag 61:4-7. 36 N '66
Norwalk plan: team teaching is a privilege; interview, ed. by W. K. Richards. H. A. Becker. il Sr Schol 88:sup 13-15 Mr 25 '66
Panacea; teaching on Christian Island in Lake Huron. E. Beeson. il Sr Schol 88:sup 12-13 Mr 18 '66
Sex makes a difference; complication in teaching. il Time 88:114+ D 16 '66
Stop waiting for miracles; excerpt from address. M. Mayer. PTA Mag 61:19+ N '66
Teacher and his staff. G. W. Denemark. il NEA J 55:17-19+ D '66
Team teaching: how it works in Niskayuna; Van Antwerp junior high school. L. Cerri. il Sr Schol 88:sup 16 Mr 25 '66
Team teaching in college. J. M. Stokes. il Sat R 49:64-5 Jl 16 '66
Technology in education; team teaching. L. Edinger. bibliog il Wilson Lib Bul 41:73-5 S '66
Testing vs. your child. G. B. Leonard. il Look 30:63-4 Mr 22 '66
Today's innovations in teaching. B. Z. Friedlander. il NEA J 55:10-14 Mr '66
Toward a theory of instruction, by J. S. Bruner. Review
    Commentary 42:79-80 Jl '66. E. Z. Friedenberg
Volunteers in the field: teaching; Peace corps. A. Deutchman. bibliog f Ann Am Acad 365:72-82 My '66
Whirlwind of wonder. M. W. Dayton. il NEA J 55:8-10 S '66
Will the class please come to order! teachers learn from being students again in summer institute. E. Edwards. NEA J 55:11-12 S '66
    See also
Academic freedom
Adult education
Audio-visual instruction
Colleges and universities—Teaching
Education, Experimental
Individual instruction
Lecture method in teaching
Memorizing
Motivation (education)
Programmed teaching
Sunday schools
Teachers
Teachers—Education
    also subhead Study and teaching under various subjects, e.g. Reading—Study and teaching

Aids and devices
Changing directions in American education; symposium. il Sat R 50:37-43+ Ja 14 '67
Computer-tutor. J. Ridgeway. New Repub 154:19-22 Je 4 '66
Education by remote control: report on DIDACTA; 8th European educational materials fair. E. V. Epstein. Pub W 190:37-8 S 5 '66
Education technology teaches a hard lesson. il Bsns W p32-4 Ag 20 '66
Educational technology: an emerging market for systems-oriented firms. W. S. Beller. il Tech W 19:28-30+ O 10 '66
Evaluation of materials for teaching: a dilemma; report of ATPI annual industry conference. il Pub W 191:26-9 Ja 9 '67
Games in fabuland. J. Ridgeway. New Repub 155:17-18 Ag 27 '66
IED gets USOE grant for purchasing advice project; Educational products information exchange. Pub W 190:38 N 28 '66
Learning through games. J. S. Coleman. NEA J 56:69-70 Ja '67
List of lists: AASL bibliography; non-book materials; with directory of producers. Library J 91:1621-2 Mr 15 '66
Machines that can talk but have nothing to say; educational technology. R. H. Smith. Pub W 190:79 Ag 22 '66
New breed of teachers: igniting the individual pupil. il Newsweek 68:100-1+ S 26 '66
New educational materials. il Sr Schol 89:sup 16-17 O 7; sup8 D 9 '66
New products. Sr Schol 89:sup55 S 23; sup8 N 18 '66
Pedagogical futility in fun and games? I. Kraft. NEA J 56:71-2 Ja '67
Teaching machines: the impact of new devices on educational publishing; summary of addresses at January meeting of the Master printers section, Graphic arts institute of New England, inc. Pub W 189:103-5+ Mr 7 '66
Technology in the schools: educators are uneasy. L. J. Carter. il Science 153:1624-6 S 30 '66
Three R's=billions; companies dealing in educational services, teaching machines, textbooks and instructional aids. il Newsweek 68:72-4 Jl 11 '66
USOE scores sales zeal of educational materials firms; caution urged in drafting Title I proposals. Pub W 189:152-3 F 21 '66
What's happening in education? W. D. Boutwell. PTA Mag 61:15-16 N '66
What's happening in education? meaning of multi media. W. D. Boutwell. PTA Mag 60:17 Mr '66
Word maze. il Sci Digest 60:17 O '66
    See also
Audio-visual aids
Computers—Educational applications
Instructional materials centers
Magnetic recorders and recording—Educational applications
Moving pictures in education
Newspapers as textbooks
Phonograph in education
Radio in education
Tape recordings
Teaching machines
Telephone in education
Television in education

Bibliography
Look between the covers; NEA publications. il NEA J 55:47-54 N '66

TEACHING, Freedom of. See Academic freedom

TEACHING as a profession
International Magna charta for teachers: concerning the document, adopted unanimously by delegates to Unesco. W. G. Carr. NEA J 55:42-4 D '66

TEACHING assignments
Assignment and misassignment of teachers. M. P. Ford and W. C. Allen. NEA J 55:41-2 F '66

TEACHING-learning laboratory. See Chicago. University

TEACHING machines
Educational technology: an emerging market for systems-oriented firms. W. S. Beller. il Tech W 19:28-30+ O 10 '66
Oklahoma City, center of education. il Esquire 66:174-5 D '66
Our era of opportunity; methods for improving the quality of education; excerpt from address. J. L. Burns. il Sat R 50:38-9 Ja 14 '67
Teaching machines; report on fourth symposium on teaching machines. V. Slamecka. Science 153:1289-90 S 9 '66

TEACHING machines—*Continued*
Teaching machines: the impact of new devices on educational publishing; summary of addresses at January meeting of the Master printers section, Graphic arts institute of New England, inc. Pub W 189:103-5+ Mr 7 '66
See also
Programmed teaching

TEACH-ins
Hudson Valley teach-in on Vietnam; the host: Marist college, Poughkeepsie, N.Y. C. Austin. Christian Cent 83:503-5 Ap 20 '66
University government and the teach-ins. J. R. Johnston. Bul Atomic Sci 22:30-1 F '66

TEAGUE, Dorwin
Preparation for offshore racing. Yachting 119:84-6+ Ap '66

TEAKETTLES. See Kettles

TEAL, John
Reporter at large. P. Matthiessen. il New Yorker 41:94+ F 5 '66

TEALL, Kaye Moulton
Sea change; story. McCalls 93:74-5 My '66

TEAM bidding. See Contracts, Government

TEAM teaching. See Teaching

TEAMSTERS union. See International brotherhood of teamsters, chauffeurs, warehousemen and helpers of America

TEAPOTS
Teapots to make pouring a joy. il House & Gard 130:32 S '66

TEAS (parties) See Entertaining

TEATRO nacional de São Carlos, Lisbon. See Opera houses

TEBALDI, Renata
Recordings. M. Mayer. Esquire 65:39-40 Je '66

TEBBEL, John
Book-publishers' salvation? Sat R 49:32-3 Jl 23 '66
Fleet Street fortune at work: two seminars in understanding. Sat R 49:101-2 N 12 '66
Great copying boom. Sat R 49:62-3 My 14 '66
Journalism: public enlightenment or private interest? Ann Am Acad 363:79-86 Ja '66
Leon Shimkin: the businessman as publisher. Sat R 49:74-5+ S 10 '66
New look at Curtis. Sat R 49:94-5+ Je 11 '66
Papa's troubled legacy. Sat R 49:30-1+ Ap 9 '66
Sarnoff at seventy-five. Sat R 49:138-9 Mr 12 '66
Training for the journalist in Africa and Vietnam. Sat R 49:84-5+ D 10 '66
West Germany's publishing powerhouse. Sat R 50:125-6 Ja 14 '67
What are the journalism schools teaching? Sat R 49:48-50 Ag 13 '66
When a book hits the jackpot. Sat R 49:62-4 F 12 '66

TECHNICAL assistance
Blackett decries cuts: more financial and technical aid urged. Sci N 91:11 Ja 7 '67
Limited response; foreign Peace corps. il Newsweek 67:46-7 F 14 '66
See also
Underdeveloped areas

TECHNICAL assistance, American
Advancement of peace; remarks, January 20, 1966. L. B. Johnson. Dept State Bul 54:186-9 F 7 '66
American professionals overseas. I. T. Sanders. Bul Atomic Sci 22:40-5 D '66
Foreign aid; message to the Congress; February 1, 1966. L. B. Johnson. Dept State Bul 54:320-7 F 28 '66
Quality of aid. D. E. Bell. For Affairs 44:601-7 Jl '66
Role shock: an occupational hazard of American technical assistants abroad. F. C. Byrnes. bibliog f Ann Am Acad 368:95-108 N '66
Voluntary service for all youth; address, May 19, 1966. R. S. McNamara. Vital Speeches 32:484-8 Je 1 '66
What the U.S. can do about world hunger. D. Norton-Taylor. il Fortune 73:110-14+ Je '66
World impact of American technology; address; with questions and answers. B. Harvey. Ann Am Acad 366:41-50 Jl '66
See also
United States—Peace corps

TECHNICAL assistance, Canadian
Canada responds to Asia's need. America 114:371 Mr 19 '66

TECHNICAL assistance, German
Germany in the underdeveloped world. W. W. Schmokel. Cur Hist 50:281-8+ My '66

TECHNICAL assistance in Africa
U.S. aid in Africa. D. Randall. bibliog f il Cur Hist 51:20-7 Jl '66

TECHNICAL assistance in Argentina
Mineral search in the Andes; photographs. UN Mo Chron 3:45-52 Mr '66

TECHNICAL assistance in Asia
See also
Colombo plan

TECHNICAL assistance in India
Christian social action in India. America 114:866 Je 25 '66
Industry to India, a Yank helps out. il Ebony 21:83-4+ Mr '66

TECHNICAL assistance in Israel
Study completed on large-scale power-desalting plant for Israel. Dept State Bul 54:494 Mr 28 '66

TECHNICAL assistance in Jamaica
Water school hops to Jamaica. L. Caughran. il Am City 81:111 Mr '66

TECHNICAL assistance in Tanzania
First steps in a development project; development of the Pangani and Wami River basins; irrigated farming; photographs. UN Mo Chron 3:59-64 F '66

TECHNICAL assistance in the Congo
Technical co-operation in the Congo; assistance provided under the U.N. technical co-operation programme. UN Mo Chron 3:59 Jl '66

TECHNICAL assistance in Vietnam
Adding social reform to Vietnam arsenal; topics of Honolulu conference. il Bsns W p27-8 F 12 '66
General Greene tells the story of Vietnam war; interview. W. M. Greene, jr. il U S News 61:34-40 S 5 '66; Same abr. with title Vietnam: progress and prospects. Read Digest 89:175-8+ N '66
Letter from South Vietnam. R. Shaplen. il New Yorker 42:58-60+ Mr 12 '66
Mr Komer reports to President on civil programs in Viet-Nam; excerpts from report. R. W. Komer. Dept State Bul 55:128-9 Jl 25 '66
Pacification in Vietnam: here's how it's to be done. il U S News 60:34-6 F 21 '66
Real revolution; reorganization of villages. Time 88:26+ Jl 1 '66
Second front; U.S.-backed program of social, economic and political reforms. il Newsweek 67:35-6 F 21 '66
War at the grass roots: pacification in Vietnam; AID, as the main civilian instrument. il U S News 61:50-2 S 26 '66

TECHNICAL assistance in Vietnam (Democratic Republic)
Soviet aid to Vietnam. A. Parry. il Reporter 36:28-33 Ja 12 '67

TECHNICAL education
Junior college and technical education. Sch & Soc 94:340 O 29 '66
Project choose:
Correspondence schools. K. Gilmore. il Pop Electr 24:41-9 F '66
Technical education and society; the community college; address, May 12, 1966. E. J. Gleazer, jr. Vital Speeches 32:540-3 Je 15 '66
See also
Case institute of technology, Cleveland, Ohio
Engineering education
Illinois institute of technology, Chicago
Massachusetts institute of technology, Cambridge
Trade schools

TECHNICAL high schools. See Trade schools

TECHNICAL information
GE will market its knowhow commercially; venture, known as Empis. il Bsns W p 138 F 19 '66
Helping to shore up small business; Technical services act of 1965. il Bsns W p 146-8 Ja 22 '66
Information technology: problems and promises; excerpts from address, May 27, 1965. M. Taube. Library J 91:1155-8 Mr 1 '66

Anecdotes, facetiae, satire, etc.
Technically speaking, I can't. C. O. Skinner. il Read Digest 88:174-6+ Je '66

TECHNICAL innovations. See Technological innovations

TECHNICAL libraries
See also
Libraries—Technology departments

TECHNICAL literature
See also
Booksellers and bookselling—Technical literature
Publishers and publishing—Technical literature
Scientific literature

TECHNICAL processes in libraries. *See* Libraries—Technical processes

TECHNICAL representatives. *See* Consulting engineers

TECHNICIANS, Electronic. *See* Electric workers

TECHNICIANS, Medical. See Medical workers

TECHNICIANS in industry
    See also
    Electric workers

TECHNIQUE. See Fiction—Technique; Literature—Technique

TECHNOCRACY
Science and technology need careful watching. Sci N 90:345 O 29 '66

TECHNOLOGICAL aids in education. See Teaching—Aids and devices

TECHNOLOGICAL change
Artist and/in the electronic environment. D. Smith. Craft Horiz 26:42+ N '66
Economics of technological change. A. P. Carter. il Sci Am 214:25-31 bibliog(p 140) Ap '66
Hornig committee: beginning of a technological Marshall plan? B. Nelson. Science 154:1307-9 D 9 '66
Marshall McLuhan. R. Kostelanetz. Commonweal 85:420-6 Ja 20 '67
On the drawing board, a new America. il Nations Bsns 54:42-4+ S '66
Where the industries of the seventies will come from. L. Lessing. il Fortune 75:96-9+ Ja '67
Wrong question? T. R. Brooks. Duns R 87:59-61 Mr '66

TECHNOLOGICAL innovations
Maze in new technology. G. J. Berkwitt. il Duns R 87:46-8+ Ja '66
Technological competition de-emphasized: symposium on technology and world trade sponsored by the secretary of commerce. W. S. Beller. Tech W 19:38-9 D 5 '66
Technological competition: Europe vs. U.S. J. B. Quinn. il Harvard Bsns R 44:113-16+ Jl '66
Technological developments: the economic impact five years hence; address, May 11, 1966. P. Neff. Vital Speeches 32:543-4 Je 15 '66
You can argue with success. C. A. Cerami. il Nations Bsns 54:82-4+ F '66

TECHNOLOGICAL research. See Industrial research

TECHNOLOGICAL unemployment. See Unemployment, Technological

TECHNOLOGY
Can Europe catch up with U.S. technology? lucrative opportunities for U.S. business. il Bsns W p60+ O 29 '66
East-West exchanges of technology increase rapidly. V. K. McElheny. Science 153:156-8 Jl 8 '66
Impact of technology on world trade and economic development: addresses, November 16, 1966. J. T. Connor; H. H. Humphrey. Dept State Bul 55:956-65 D 26 '66
Management gap: problems in Great Britain. A. Simmons. il Newsweek 68:34-5 Jl 25 '66
Role of applied science. E. Teller. il Bul Atomic Sci 22:15-19 Mr '66
Technology in Britain: new moves. V. K. McElheny. Science 153:619-20 Ag 5 '66
Technology notes. Sci N 90:472, 497, 510, 532, 562; 91:36 D 3-31 '66, Ja 14 '67
Why Russia is lagging in technology race. il U S News 60:90-1 Ap 25 '66
    See also
    Inventions
    Space technology
    Technocracy
    Technological innovations

Bibliography
Science, technology: high spots. il Pub W 189:50-78 Ap 18 '66
Science, technology: November-March high spots. il Pub W 190:44-72 N 14 '66
Scientific and technical books of 1965; one hundred outstanding titles for a general collection; comp. by R. L. Snyder. il Library J 91:1147-54 Mr 1 '66
Scientific, technical, and medical books to come; ed. by J. Putnam and J. Lindheim (cont) Library J 91:1264-313 Mr 1 '66
Scientific, technical, and medical books to come; ed. by J. Putnam and K. Ahrens. Library J 91:3481-524+ Jl '66
Scientific, technical, and medical books to come; ed. by J. Putnam. Library J 91:5441-90 N 1 '66

International aspects
Atlantic technological imbalance. R. L. Pfaltzgraff, jr. New Repub 156:19-21 Ja 21 '67
Technological competition de-emphasized: symposium on technology and world trade sponsored by the secretary of commerce. W. S. Beller. Tech W 19:38-9 D 5 '66
U.S. answers allies' plea: the technology gap. Sci N 90:491 D 10 '66
Where U.S. is leaving Europe far behind. il U S News 61:69-70 Jl 18 '66

Terminology
Do they dig you, daddio? communication between scientist and layman, adaptation of address; reprint. R. G. Lynch. Am For 72:30-1+ F '66

TECHNOLOGY and civilization
Art, technology and education; excerpt from address, February 1966. A. I. Cox, jr. Christian Cent 83:862-4 Jl 6 '66
Can technology replace social engineering? address, 1966. A. M. Weinberg. Bul Atomic Sci 22:4-8 D '66
Christian function in a technological culture. M. B. Bloy, jr. bibliog f Christian Cent 83:231-4 F 23 '66
Computer and the poet. N. Cousins. Sat R 49:42 Jl 23 '66
Education and the new technology; symposium. Sr Schol 89:sup 13 O 7 '66
Great change-overs for you. M. McLuhan. Vogue 148:62-3+ Jl '66
Is technology taking over? philosophies of J. Ellul and M. McLuhan. C. E. Silberman. il Fortune 73:112-15+ F '66
It's two-thirds of a century: we've made it, so far. E. E. Morison. il N Y Times Mag p34-5+ Ap 24 '66
Logic & limits of technology. H. Wheeler; B. V. B. Bowden. il Nation 204:9-21 Ja 2 '67
Man in the technological society; symposium. bibliog il Wilson Lib Bul 41:40-75+ S '66
Myths of automation, by C. E. Silberman. Review
    Sat R 49:37-8 O 29 '66. J. Diebold
National planning of science and technology in France; adaptation of address, October 1964. J. B. Quinn; discussion. Science 151:517, 1330+ F 4, Mr 18 '66
New computerized age: whither personal privacy? J. Lear. il Sat R 49:36+ Jl 23 '66
Science and engineering; address, November 2, 1966. J. H. Hollomon. Vital Speeches 33:111-15 D 1 '66
Society, technology, and development. N. Ras. bibliog il Américas 18:14-23 D '66
Step to man, by J. R. Platt. Review
    Sat R 49:36 Ag 13 '66. S. Chase
    See also
    Social problems

Anecdotes, facetiae, satire, etc.
New technologies, old media; excerpt from Learn with book. J. R. Heathorn. Library J 91:6170 D 15 '66

TECHNOLOGY week (periodical)
Dow Corning silicone sealant wins annual product award. il Tech W 19:20+ N 21 '66
Memo from the publisher. A. C. Boughton. il Tech W 18:7 Je 6; 19:6 D 12 '66
Second decade. W. J. Coughlin. Tech W 18:56 Je 6 '66

TEDESCO, Samuel J.
We put new life in emergency reporting. Am City 81:112-13 Mr '66

TEEN-age book clubs. See Book clubs

TEEN-age buying. See Youth market

TEEN-age codes. See Discipline; Youth—Management and training

TEEN-age drinking. See Liquor problem—United States

TEEN-age drivers. See Automobile drivers

TEEN-age employment. See Youth—Employment

TEEN-age fads. See Fads

TEEN-age marriage. See High school students, Married

TEEN-age periodicals. See Periodicals

TEEN-age reading. See Books and reading; Reading lists

TEEN-age smoking. See Smoking

TEEN-age spending. See Budget, Personal

TEEN-agers. See Youth

TEEN-agers amusements. See Amusements

TEETH
Noncollagenous nature of the proteins of shark enamel. P. T. Levine and others. bibliog il Science 154:1192-4 D 2 '66

TEETH—*Continued*
Strontium incorporation into dental enamel. A. R. Johnson and others. bibliog il Science 153:1396-7 S 16 '66
Why oh why are there wisdom teeth? il Changing T 20:36 Je '66
World's most talkative tooth. il Todays Health 44:92 F '66
See also
Dental research
Dentistry

Care and hygiene
Dangers of do-it-yourself dentistry. il Good H 162:185 Je '66
Good teeth for life; proper care for children. D. Bressler. il Parents Mag 41:72-3+ N '66
Secret of keeping your teeth; how to avoid periodontal disease. D. Murray. Read Digest 88:63-5 Mr '66
What keeps dentists in steady business. il Bsns W p86+ N 26 '66
See also
Toothpicks, Electric

Diseases
Electronic dental spies are bugging teeth. Sci N 89:514 Je 25 '66
Fluorides for adults; prevention of tooth decay. il Time 87:47 Ap 8 '66
More comfort for you at the dentist's. R. Gannon. il Pop Mech 126:96-9+ Ag '66
New war on tooth decay. il Sci Digest 59:30-1 Je '66
Storage fat in teeth may be cause of decay. Sci N 90:105 Ag 13 '66
What keeps dentists in steady business. il Bsns W p86+ N 26 '66

Extraction
Wisdom of the third molar; impacted wisdom teeth. il Time 88:55 D 16 '66

TEETH (animals)
Maternal effect in dental traits of the house mouse. P. Tenczar and R. S. Bader. bibliog il Science 152:1398-400 Je 3 '66
Retention of potential to differentiate in long-term cultures of tooth germs. J. H. P. Main. bibliog il Science 152:778-80 My 6 '66

TEETH, Artificial
Contact lenses get a softer touch; hydron. a soft plastic developed in Czechoslovakia. il Bsns W p 147-8 Ap 30 '66
Dangers of do-it-yourself dentistry. il Good H 162:185 Je '66
Getting used to a new smile. R. O. Geissler. Todays Health 44:66-8 D '66
Steel tested on teeth; stainless variety for bridgework and caps. il Sci N 89:291 Ap 23 '66

TEFLON
How does Teflon work? J. Reinert. il Sci Digest 59:92 Ap '66
TEFLON-coated cookware. See Kitchen utensils
TEFLON-coated electric grills. See Electric grills

TEHACHAPI MOUNTAINS
Tehachapi country in May, snowy with apple blossoms. il Sunset 136:88+ My '66

TEHRANIAN, Majid
Politics of anti-Americanism. Nation 203:415-18 O 24 '66

TEHUACAN, Mexico
Digging up prehistoric America; discoveries of ancient cultivated corn solve prehistoric mystery. R. Claiborne. il Harper 232:69-74 Ap '66

TEICHMANN, Howard
By George S. Kaufman and... N Y Times Mag p64-5+ N 13 '66
TEIIDAE lizards. See Lizards
TEILHARD DE CHARDIN, Pierre
Fresh look at man; excerpt from Teilhard de Chardin and the mystery of Christ. C. F. Mooney. por Sat R 49:20-4 F 26 '66
On optimism and the optimists. G. Wills. Nat R 18:360-1 Ap 19 '66
Significance of Teilhard. T. E. Clarke. America 114:779 My 28 '66
Teilhard de Chardin and the mystery of Christ, by C. L. Mooney. Review
Sat R 49:49-50 Je 4 '66. C. Vollert
Teilhard de Chardin; the man and his meaning, by H. de Lubac. Review
Cath World 202:372-3 Mr '66. P. Hoheisel
Thought of Teilhard de Chardin, by M. H. Murray. Review
America 114:600 Ap 23 '66. D. A. Drennen
Voices of convergence; Teilhard, McLuhan and Brown. D. J. Leary. Cath World 204:206-11 Ja '67

TEIXEIRA DIREITO, F.
Great opera houses; Lisbon. Opera N 31:26-9 Ja 14 '67
TEKTITES
Are tektites terrestrial? G. S. Mumford. Sky & Tel 32:127 S '66
Oxygen isotope studies of Ivory Coast tektites and impactite glass from the Bosumtwi crater, Ghana. H. P. Taylor, jr. and S. Epstein. bibliog il Science 153:173-5 Jl 8 '66
Rubidium-strontium age of the Bosumtwi crater area, Ghana, compared with the age of the Ivory Coast tektites. C. C. Schnetzler and others. bibliog il Science 151:817-19 F 18 '66
Tektites are terrestrial. H. Faul. bibliog il Science 152:1341-5 Je 3 '66
TEL AVIV, Israel

Music
Tel-Aviv. A. Frankenstein. Opera N 30:32 Mr 12; 33 Ap 16; 31:27 N 19 '66
TELECASTING stations. See Television stations
TELECOMMUNICATION
See also
Communications satellites
Facsimile transmission
Telegraph, Wireless
TELEFAX. See Facsimile transmission
TELEGRAM from Mr Smooth; story. See Richards. C.
TELEGRAPH
See also
Radio telegraph
TELEGRAPH, Wireless
First license, and before. H. E. Church. il Pop Electr 24:54-5+ Ja '66
In the days of spark, a rescue at sea; sinking of the SS Republic. H. E. Church. il Pop Electr 25:57-8+ N '66
See also
Antique wireless association
TELEGRAPH codes. See Cipher and telegraph codes
TELEGRAPH companies
See also
American telephone and telegraph company
TELEGRAPH keys
Dit makers; keys on display in museum of American radio relay league, Newington, Conn. M. Lincoln. il Pop Electr 25:64-5 Ag '66
TELEKI, Geza
Geologist and his apple; reprint. Am For 72:6+ Ag '66
TELELECTURES. See Telephone in education
TELEMANN, Georg Philipp
Finally, the race is over, three complete recordings of Musique de table. J. W. Barker. por Am Rec G 32:812-15 My '66
In composer; with discography and editorial comment. B. Jacobson. il por Hi Fi 17:39 F '66
TELEMETER
Lonely sentinels in dirty jobs. M. J. Walker. Sci N 90:499 D 10 '66
See also
Space telemetry
TELEMETER (physiological apparatus)
Blood pressure responses of wild giraffes studied by radio telemetry. R. L Van Citters and others. bibliog il Science 152:384-6 Ap 15 '66
Pacemaker synchronization. C. E. Anagnostopoulos and others. il Science 153:1636 S 30 '66
Pill gives inside view; radio transmitters giving scientists data on basic body functions. P. McBroom. il Sci N 90:131 Ag 27 '66
TELEMETRY, Biological. See Biotelemetry
TELEMETRY, Space. See Space telemetry
TELEMETRY space. See Space telemetry
TELEPATHY. See Extrasensory perception
TELEPHONE
Direct line for emergencies; getting the operator without a coin on pay phones. Time 88:47 Ag 19 '66
Facsimile by phone offered by Xerox; Telecopier. Bsns W p76 My 7 '66
If you compare phone service in U.S. and abroad. il U S News 60:98-100 Mr 14 '66
Teen-ager and the telephone. E. J. Leshan. McCalls 93:84+ Mr '66
Those fancy phones. il Changing T 20:24 Je '66
See also
Emergency communication systems
Radio telephone on ships, boats, etc.

TELEPHONE—*Continued*

Anecdotes, facetiae, satire, etc.

Long-distance doesn't lend enchantment. R. Armour. Sat R 49:6+ S 10 '66

Apparatus and supplies

Magic box that calls you to the telephone; wired-wireless remote control. H. G. McEntee. il Pop Sci 188:116-19 Je '66

Computer combination

Electronic speechmaker; dial stock quotations from American stock exchange. il Electr World 75:68 Je '66

Intercommunicating systems

See Intercommunicating systems

Rates

Is there anything you can do about the phone bill? il Changing T 20:33-4 F '66

See also

Government investigations—American telephone and telegraph company

Statistics

Canadians use telephone more than other people. Sci N L 89:56 Ja 22 '66

Line is busy; survey of the world's phones. Newsweek 69:58 Ja 9 '67

Testing

Number freeze; environment test. il Sci Digest 60:85 N '66

Wire tapping

See Wire tapping

TELEPHONE cables
More talk underseas. Sci N 90:15 Jl 2 '66

U.S. and Venezuela inaugurate undersea telephone cable; remarks, August 3. 1966. R. Leoni and L. B. Johnson. Dept State Bul 55:274-5 Ag 22 '66

TELEPHONE calls
Dial-a-victim; Senate hearings on obscene telephone calls. Newsweek 67:36 My 30 '66

Girl from B.E.L.L; monitoring calls. il Time 88:27 S 23 '66

Phone pollution; obscene calls to families of men serving in Vietnam. Nation 202:445 Ap 18 '66

Ringing in the suspect; called-party holding device weapon against abusive calls. Time 87:53 Ap 8 '66

TELEPHONE companies
Thriving independents. Time 88:78 Jl 8 '66

See also

American telephone and telegraph company

Anecdotes, facetiae, satire, etc.

All tolled. W. Stanton. Look 30:130 D 13 '66

Employees

See also

Telephone companies—Wages and hours

Securities

Executive investor. Duns R 88:137-8 O '66

Wages and hours

Communications workers; wage rates in 1964. J. C. Bush. il Mo Labor R 88:1465-9 D '65

TELEPHONE directories
History in the telephone book; surnames in the Manhattan directory. C. M. Matthews. il Horizon 9:105-11 Wint '67

TELEPHONE in business
Coming next; push-button banking. il U S News 60:108-10 F 14 '66

TELEPHONE in education
Block Island; report on Projects to advance creativity in education. il Am Ed 2:9 N '66

TELEPHONE information service. See Information services

TELEPHOTO lenses. See Lenses, Photographic

TELEPUPPETS. See Automatons

TELESCOPE
Advanced large orbital telescope systems urged as astronomy goal. W. J. Normyle. Aviation W 84:61+ F 14 '66

Amateur astronomy. A. Bester. il Holiday 40:113-18 S '66

Backyard astronomer; choice of telescopes. J. S. Pickering. il Natur Hist 75:56+ N '66

Backyard astronomer; setting up a telescope. J. S. Pickering. il Natur Hist 76:58+ Ja '67

Birth and life of the universe; observations through the Hale telescope at Palomar observatory. C. P. Gilmore. il N Y Times Mag p26-7+ Je 12 '66

Construction of solar vacuum telescope begun. Sci N 89:370 My 14 '66

Gleanings for ATM's; ed. by R. E. Cox. See issues of Sky and telescope

Lunar 'scope to double known universe. Sci N 9:459 N 26 '66

Need more telescopes; use in solving the problem of the universe's birth. Sci N L 89:116 F 19 '66

New mechanical designs for large telescopes. Sky & Tel 32:208 O '66

New telescope to join 200-inch on Palomar. Sci N 89:419 My 28 '66

Palomar 60-inch photometric reflector. I. S. Bowen and B. H. Rule. il Sky & Tel 32:184-7 O '66

Starry-eyed; plans for 60-inch scope and observatory at Palomar. Newsweek 68:78 Jl 11 '66

Training of an astronomer; establishing telescopes in good climates. J. B. Irwin. Science 152:1597-9 Je 17 '66; Discussion. 153:934+; 154:1275-6 Ag 26, D 9 '66

Yale has new 40-inch telescope. il Sci N 89:499 Je 18 '66

See also

Mirrors for telescopes

Radio telescope

TELESCOPE mirrors. See Mirrors for telescopes

TELESCOPE on space vehicles
Apollo telescope mount RFP due soon. Miss & Roc 18:16 Mr 21 '66

Live mirror adapts itself to space. W. S. Beller. il Miss & Roc 18:24-5 Ap 25 '66

Marshall gets Apollo telescope task. Tech W 19:19 Jl 18 '66

Telescopes in orbit. Sci Am 214:48-9 Ap '66

TELEVISION

Color

See Television, Color

Photographic aspects

How did they make that commercial? H. V Fondiller. il Pop Phot 58:124-6+ Mr '66

Three-D home TV foreseen. A. Ewing. il Sci N 89:468-9+ Je 11 '66

Social aspects

See Television broadcasting—Social aspects

TELEVISION, Closed circuit
Closed circuit color TV beams vivid surgery pix. Sci N 90:361 O 29 '66

Playback; new aid in the ordeal of self-discovery; tool of Drs Peter Hogan and Ian Alger. D. Monaco. il Look 31:26-9 Ja 24 '67

Smile, your incinerator is on TV; Oyster Bay, N.Y. V. J. Cerniglia and A. Friedland. il Am City 81:110-12 Ap '66

See also

Television in education

TELEVISION, Color
Chroma circuits in color TV; Motorola. W. H. Buchsbaum. il Electr World 76:33-5+ S '66

Chroma demodulation in color sets; RCA. W. H. Buchsbaum. il Electr World 75:45-7+ My '66

Chroma synchronization in color sets; RCA. W. H. Buchsbaum. il Electr World 75:35-7+ Je '66

Color-TV broadcasting. il Electr World 76:21-4+ D '66

Colorful history of color TV. D. M. Costigan. il Pop Electr 25:45-7+ S '66

Great color explosion in television. F. Bowers. House & Gard 130:46-7 S '66

Incompatibly split; Europe's color TV. il Time 88:72 Ag 12 '66

Rosy hue for color TV in Europe. il Bsns W p94-6+ O 22 '66

Soviet color-TV system. L. Solomon. il Electr World 76:72 D '66

TV controversy rages; disagreement over a standard European color system. Sci N 90:100 Ag 13 '66

Three-D color TV. B. Grant. il Pop Mech 125:192 Ap '66

Tomorrow's color TV. W. G. Salm. il Sci Digest 60:63-8 Ag '66

TELEVISION, Stereoscopic
Three-D home TV foreseen. A. Ewing. il Sci N 89:468-9+ Je 11 '66

TELEVISION actors and actresses. See Television broadcasting—Performers

TELEVISION advertising
Breathes there a mouth; advertising of mouthwashes. il Time 88:74 D 9 '66

By the hair; men advertising hair spray. il Time 89:78 Ja 20 '67

Commercial success. il Newsweek 67:90-1 My 30 '66

TELEVISION advertising—*Continued*
Costly spectaculars score TV comeback. il Bsns W p86-7+ F 12 '66
Emasculation? Inserting commercials with movies. Newsweek 67:05 Mr 7 '66
Flying to that resort hideaway, Mr Bryant? filming of commercial for United air lines. New Yorker 42:43-5 Mr 26 '66
High noon in Bakersfield; KBAK; KERO: KLYD and the Television code. R. L. Shayon. Sat R 49:22 Ag 20 '66
How'd you like to sell/buy your home on TV? J. Neubauer. il Pop Phot 60:87 Ja '67
Keeping the sales pitch blurry; Mutual funds commercials severely restricted by SEC. il Bsns W p 129-30+ Je 4 '66
Madison medicine man on the move; sales pitches. G. Ace. Sat R 49:14-15 Mr 5 '66
Ooh, the head! filming of series of commercials for Anacin. New Yorker 42:28-31 Je 18 '66
Other events: exhibition of public-relations films and television commercials at Museum of modern art. R. Adler. New Yorker 42:128 N 12 '66
Rebellion that caught the mood of youth; Dodge rebellion a household word. il Bsns W p74 D 10 '66
TV overseas: the U.S. hard sell. H. I. Schiller. il Nation 203:609-12 D 5 '66

Anecdotes, facetiae, satire, etc.
Strange world of TV commercials. M. Mannes. McCalls 93:20+ Ap '66

TELEVISION advertising, Religious. See Religious advertising

TELEVISION and children. See Television broadcasting and children

TELEVISION antennas
Antenna boom. R. Cornell. il Pop Electr 24: 39-43+ My '66
Antenna rotators. il Consumer Rep 31:408-10 Ag '66
Big changes ahead in TV: a wider choice for watchers; community-antenna television or CATV. il U S News 60:92-3 Ap 4 '66
Coming cable TV war; community antennas. A. Warren. il Sat R 49:90+ Je 11 '66; Discussion. 49:47+ Ag 13 '66
CATV, a booming new industry. W. A. Stocklin. Electr World 75:6 My '66
CATV held liable for copyright infringement; broadcasts of copyrighted motion pictures to paying subscribers. Pub W 189:189-90 Je 6 '66
Compromise on CATV; FCC regulation. il Newsweek 67:67-8 F 28 '66
Designing an all-channel TV antenna. P. E. Mayes. il Electr World 75:45-8+ F '66
Growing dispute over a growing form of television; community antenna television (CATV) U S News 60:6 F 28 '66
How a broadcaster spreads its net; community antenna cable and microwave systems. il Bsns W p57-8+ D 3 '66
Low-profile U.H.F. antenna. Electr World 75:65 Je '66
New low-loss coax for TV; coaxial lead-in for color TV and U.H.F. L. Cantor. il Electr World 76:33 Ag '66
New U.H.F. TV antenna design. H. Harris. il Electr World 75:44-5 Mr '66
Pygmy of airwaves pushes to be a giant; community antenna television. il Bsns W p 100-2+ F 19 '66
Rotate to better television viewing. L. Steckler. il Pop Mech 125:188-91 Ap '66
Senate copyright hearings stall on issue of CATV. Pub W 190:57 Ag 22 '66
Tangled tower of CATV. C. Welles. il Life 61:53-4+ N 18 '66
Whither cable TV? CATV. R. L. Shayon. Sat R 49:63+ S 17 '66
Will CATV revolutionize your TV viewing habits? L. Cantor. il Pop Electr 25:48-52+ S '66

TELEVISION apparatus industry and trade
Big-screen color TV tunes down prices. Bsns W p 101 Je 11 '66
See also
Admiral corporation

TELEVISION auctions. See Auctions

TELEVISION authorship
Hollywood screen writers: who are they and how do they work? P. R. Reynolds. il Sat R 49:52-3+ Jl 9 '66
Saint on TV. L. Charteris. Writer 79:19-21+ F '66
Tallest dwarf in the world: ed. by E. Miller. W. Allen. il Seventeen 25:158-9+ My '66

TELEVISION awards. See Academy of television arts and sciences

TELEVISION broadcasting
Color-TV broadcasting. il Electr World 76:21-4+ D '66

Direct TV broadcasts forecast; home broadcasts via satellites. il Sci N 89:402 My 21 '66
Soviet color-TV system. L. Solomon. il Electr World 76:72 D '66
See also
Television stations

Advertising
See Television advertising

Animated cartoons
Digging Dudley Do-right. D. M. Davis. Holiday 39:150+ Ap '66

Art programs
Television and the mystery masterpiece. W. Dean. il Sch Arts 65:13-15 Mr '66

Baseball
See Television broadcasting—Sports

Book programs
Letter from limbo, or, WNBC-TV I love you; Children explore books. L. Russ. il Pub W 191:42-3 Ja 16 '67

Censorship
TV: no place for satire; controversy over Cleveland TV station WJW's Parma Place. R. Fischer. Nation 202:470 Ap 18 '66

Children, Effect on
See Television broadcasting and children

Childrens programs
Air; Alice through the looking glass. M. J. Arlen. New Yorker 42:220 N 26 '66
Air; Captain Kangaroo. M. J. Arlen. New Yorker 42:197-8 O 29 '66
Air; educational shows. M. J. Arlen. New Yorker 42:82-3 Ja 7 '67
Backstage with Captain Kangaroo. B. Keeshan. il Parents Mag 41:40-1+ Ag '66
Better than people; Stingray and adult serials. C. W. Morton. il Atlan 217:121-2 Ap '66
Mini-wasteland; conclusions of Boston's Foundation for character education. il Newsweek 69:92-4 Ja 23 '67
TV for children. F. Orme. il Parents Mag 41:54-5+ F '66
Theology of Batman. R. E. Terwilliger. Cath World 204:127-8 N '66
Time out for television. See issues of PTA magazine

Christmas programs
Christmas memory by T. Capote: filmed by ABC. il Look 30:79-83+ N 29 '66
No crib for their beds; Christmas and Bonanza and Run for your life. R. L. Shayon. Sat R 50:40 Ja 7 '67

Comedy
See Television broadcasting—Humor

Conversation programs
Air pollution, new style; Los Angeles programs. B. Vaccariello. Nat R 18:270-1 Mr 22 '66
Even better than Batman; Firing line. S. Alexander. Life 61:22 Ag 5 '66
Gingering man; W. F. Buckley's Firing line show. il Time 87:59 Je 17 '66
Gypsy Rose Lee: dowager stripper. J. Hamilton. il Look 30:58-9+ F 22 '66
Killer Joe; J. Pyne. Time 88:30 Jl 29 '66
Logorrhea in Los Angeles; TV station KTTV. il Newsweek 67:65 Mr 7 '66
Meet the Nation answers; Sunday interview shows. Newsweek 67:100 My 16 '66
Net gains; interviews with members of the Cabinet and others close to LBJ. il Newsweek 67:47 F 7 '66
Today's nice people. il Newsweek 67:67 My 9 '66

Crime programs
Exit Perry Mason. R. L. Shayon. il Sat R 49: 81 Je 11 '66
Morality building with the FBI. R. L. Shayon. Sat R 49:42 Jl 30 '66
Saint on TV. L. Charteris. Writer 79:19-21+ F '66

Dancing
Backstage at television's Hollywood palace. O. Maynard. il Dance Mag 40:36-8 F '66
Looking at television. A. Barzel. See issues of Dance magazine
Peter Gennaro works at what makes a special special; Stage 67's Rodgers and Hart today. V. H. Swisher. il Dance Mag 40:20-1 D '66

Documentary programs
Air: Channel 13 documentaries not noticeably better than network documentaries. M. J. Arlen. New Yorker 42:80+ Ja 7 '67

TELEVISION broadcasting—Documentary programs—*Continued*
Air; C.B.S. reports about prisons and N.B.C.
  special on civil rights. M. J. Arlen. New
  Yorker 42:196-7 O 29 '66
Automation and the Negro; ETV's History
  of the Negro people. R. L. Shayon. Sat R
  49:44 Ja 29 '66
Behind the myth the face of Norma Jean; TV
  film uncovers rare photos of Marilyn Monroe. R. Meryman. il Life 61:49-54 N 4 '66
Eyeful of song; Bell telephone hour to introduce documentary aspect. il Newsweek
  68:79 S 5 '66
Family's ordeal by heroin; Storm signal. D.
  Martin. Life 61:7 S 2 '66
Fine hours; Hill country; Lyndon Johnson's
  Texas. Time 87:85 My 20 '66
Glitch on Gemini 8 and viewer reaction to
  cancellation of Lost in space. America 114:
  430-1 Ap 2 '66; Reply. J. P. Hecker. 114:
  608 Ap 30 '66
Mob scene; Fred Freed's project on organ-
  ized crime in the U.S. Newsweek 68:67 Ag
  29 '66
NET and man at Yale; concerning To be a
  man. R. L. Shayon. Sat R 49:75 D 3 '66
Small start in Mississippi; Head Start in
  Mississippi. R. L. Shayon. Sat R 50:99
  Ja 14 '67
Television and Vietnam. il Sat Eve Post
  233:120 Mr 26 '66
Texas sojourn; Hill country; Lyndon John-
  son's Texas, NBC documentary. W. V.
  Shannon. Commonweal 84:273-4 My 27 '66
Two-edged sword; A time for burning. film
  on racial patterns in a Lutheran parish.
  America 115:643-4 N 19 '66
Where sociology meets journalism; reactions
  to Sixteen in Webster Groves. R. L.
  Shayon. Sat R 49:44 Ap 2 '66
You gettin' that deer? NBC's called Lyndon
  Johnson's Texas. Newsweek 67:97 Ap 18 '66

Drama

Air. M. J. Arlen. New Yorker 42:220+ N 26
  '66
Air; Stage 67. M. J. Arlen. New Yorker 42:
  219-20 O 1 '66
Better than people; Stingray and adult serials. C. W. Morton. il Atlan 217:121-2 Ap
  '66
Brains and action, with no jokes; Mission:
  impossible. J. M. Ferrer, 3d. Life 62:15
  Ja 13 '67
Can TV overcome? multiracial-story ap-
  proaches. R. L. Shayon. Sat R 49:24 O 29
  '66
Charlie Brown's all-stars; Peanuts people to
  be on TV again. il Good H 162:55-7 Je '66
Child of the city; Love song of Barney
  Kempinski to open Stage 67 series. il News-
  week 68:96+ Jl 18 '66
Death of a salesman. R. L. Shayon. il Sat R
  49:39 My 28 '66
Exalted theater; Death of a salesman. il
  Newsweek 67:74 My 23 '66
Fine hours; Death of a salesman. il Time
  87:82+ My 20 '66
Hawk folds its wings. il Newsweek 68:68
  D 5 '66
In the spell of Under milk wood. America
  114:405 Mr 26 '66
No crib for their beds; Christmas and Bon-
  anza and Run for your life. R. L. Shayon.
  Sat R 50:40 Ja 7 '67
Polymorph; Barefoot in Athens preview.
  Newsweek 68:99 O 10 '66
Promised wasteland. G. Ace. Sat R 49:12
  S 10 '66
Rights and permissions; adaptations of popu-
  lar books, stories and plays. P. Nathan.
  Pub W 189:95 Je 27 '66
Seven deadly daytime sins. il Time 87:61
  Ap 8 '66
Stampede for excellence. R. L. Shayon. Sat
  R 49:66 Jl 23 '66
Stefanie Powers; the U.N.C.L.E. doll. I.
  Mothner. il Look 30:42+ O 18 '66
TV; no place for satire; controversy over
  Cleveland TV station WJW's Parma Place.
  R. Fischer. Nation 202:470 Ap 18 '66
Trouble on Stage 67. R. L. Shayon. Sat R
  49:74 N 12 '66
Two-season season; 1966-67 preview. il News-
  week 68:99-99A+ Ag 22 '66
Vintage wine; Noon wine. il Time 88:64 D
  2 '66

Texts
See Television plays

Economic aspects

Costly spectaculars score TV comeback. il
  Bsns W p86-7+ F 12 '66

Educational applications
See Television in education

Election results

Evening of rash predictions. il Time 88:101
  N 18 '66
'Tain't the heat. P. Benchley. il Newsweek
  68:108-9 N 21 '66
Victorygraph: CBS election night program;
  interview. A. Westin. New Yorker 42:51-3
  N 5 '66

Financial news

Small-screen big board; Los Angeles' KWHY-
  TV. Newsweek 69:46 Ja 2 '67

Football
See Television broadcasting—Sports

Golf
See Television broadcasting—Sports

Government programs

Giving the doves a break; public hearings
  of the Senate foreign relations committee.
  R. L. Shayon. Sat R 49:55 Mr 5 '66

Humor

For sale; comedy and gimmicks. G. Ace.
  Sat R 49:16 Mr 26 '66
Gleason and Carney; a second honeymoon
  for The honeymooners. B. Rollin. il Look
  30:76-80+ N 15 '66
Good grief, Charlie Brown, don't you know
  anything about women? Peanuts television
  special. L. Tornabene. il Ladies Home J
  83:36 O '66
Good show quits while it's ahead; The Dick
  Van Dyke show. J. M. Ferrer, 3d. Life 60:
  15 Je 3 '66
Honeymoon that reran for ten years; plans
  to revive The honeymooners. J. McCarthy.
  Life 60:12 Mr 25 '66
Monkee do. il Time 88:84 N 11 '66
Pop of the news. il Newsweek 69:41 Ja 9 '67
Romp! romp! the Monkees shows. il Newsweek 68:102 O 24 '66
Second honeymoon; Gleason's new Honeymooners. il Time 88:108 O 14 '66
TV's swinging Monkees. B. Rollin. il Look
  30:93-6 D 27 '66
Uncle Miltie's back. il Newsweek 68:60 S 12
  '66
When four nice boys go ape! NBC Monday
  night show, The Monkees. R. W. Lewis.
  il Sat Eve Post 240:74-6+ Ja 28 '67

International aspects

TV overseas; the U.S. hard sell. H. I.
  Schiller. il Nation 203:609-12 D 5 '66

Medical programs

Failing the health test; concerning CBS's
  National health test. Newsweek 67:78 Ja 31
  '66

Moral aspects

Mission: immoral. R. L. Shayon. Sat R 49:
  34 N 19 '66
Teaching the screen arts. Brother DePaul.
  Cath World 203:109-12 My '66
    See also
Television broadcasting and children

Moving pictures

All nights at the movies. Newsweek 67:76
  Ja 31 '66
At the movies; Kwai showing and other deals.
  Newsweek 68:99 O 10 '66
Bombs away? films shown first on NBC's
  World premiere series. Newsweek 68:68 D
  5 '66
Can TV save the films? C. Champlin. il Sat R
  49:11-13 D 24 '66
Colonel Bogey's march. Time 88:80 O 7 '66
CATV held liable for copyright infringe-
  ment; broadcasts of copyrighted motion
  pictures to paying subscribers. Pub W 189:
  189-90 Je 6 '66
Emasculation? inserting commercials. News-
  week 67:65 Mr 7 '66
Fighting back; O. Preminger and G. Stevens
  law suits to protect works from the dep-
  redations of television. A. Knight. Sat R
  49:64-5 F 19 '66
Hollywood rides again. S. H. Brown. il
  Fortune 74:181-2+ N '66
Nonmovie movies; original TV-movies. il
  Time 89:42 Ja 13 '67
Profiles; case of O. Preminger vs CBS over
  TV showing of Anatomy of a murder.
  L. Ross. New Yorker 41:42-6+ F 19 '66
TV and Hollywood sing a new duet; movies
  made for TV. Bsns W p 106-8 Ap 16 '66

TELEVISION broadcasting—Moving pictures
—*Continued*
Wonderful world of wheels. B. Greene. il
Hot Rod 19:82-3 S '66
Wonderful world of wheels; semi-documen-
tary movie. il Motor T 18:52-3 S '66

Music

Bell ringer; Bell telephone hour. il Time 88:78
D 16 '66
Discovery of freshness; new Bell telephone
hour. R. L. Shayon. Sat R 49:37 D 31 '66
Eyeful of song; Bell telephone hour to in-
troduce documentary aspect. il Newsweek
68:79 S 5 '66
McLuhan effect; Mickie Finn's program.
R. L. Shayon. Sat R 49:54 Je 4 '66
Music to my ears; G. Paxton's Hill country
music. I. Kolodin. il Sat R 49:38 My 28 '66
Please dial again; new Bell telephone hour.
R. L. Shayon. Sat R 49:77 D 10 '66
Pop music on camera. N. Compton. Commen-
tary 42:60-3 Jl '66

News

Air; importance of voices. M. Arlen. New
Yorker 42:140+ D 10 '66
Air; NBC program The Vietnam weekly re-
view: The Manila report. M. J. Arlen.
New Yorker 42:196-7 N 12 '66
Air; networks coverage of elections and the
last Gemini space flight. M. J. Arlen. New
Yorker 42:219 N 26 '66
Anniversary talk with Huntley & Brinkley;
interview, ed. by J. F. Fixx. C. Huntley;
D. Brinkley. McCalls 94:56+ O '66
Bad days at Black Rock. il Newsweek 67:62-3
F 28 '66
Covering a massacre; Austin's KTBC's cov-
erage of the murder at the University of
Texas. il Time 88:34 Ag 12 '66
Dig, dig, dig; Are you safe in your hospital?
reflects new look in coverage by local sta-
tions. il Newsweek 67:84 Je 6 '66
Image; summary of address, September 29,
1966. P. H. Nitze. New Repub 155:5-6
N 19 '66
Making the most of the medium. il Time
88:76+ Jl 22 '66
Most intimate medium. il Time 88:56-8+ O
14 '66
Real Stokely Carmichael; presented image.
R. L. Shayon. Sat R 49:42 Jl 9 '66
Selecting the news; Gemini 9 coverage. News-
week 67:68 Je 20 '66
Star system and TV news; concerning Elmer
Davis memorial lecture address by D.
Brinkley. R. L. Tobin. Sat R 49:59-60 Ap
9 '66
TV news hens; Negro television newscasters.
il Ebony 21:44-6+ O '66
What's news at CBS? R. Severo. New
Repub 154:29+ Mr 12 '66
When the tail wags the dog; news for its
importance, or visual value? J. Kinkel.
Sat R 49:140+ Mr 12 '66
    See also
Television broadcasting—Election results

Operas

TV Italian style. W. Weaver. il Opera N 31:
14-15 D 31 '66

Performers

Can TV overcome? R. L. Shayon. Sat R 49:
24 O 29 '66
Color him funny; B. Cosby. il Newsweek
67:76 Ja 31 '66
From TV to Tiffany's in one wild leap;
M. T. Moore in Breakfast at Tiffany's. J.
Bowers. il Sat Eve Post 239:97-101 N 19 '66
Jes' rich folks; Andy Griffith, Jim Nabors
and their manager. il Newsweek 68:94 O
17 '66
Something special; dilemma of Negro performers. R. L. Shayon. Sat R 49:47 Mr
26 '66
Telepromptings. S. Kauffmann. New Repub
156:24+ Ja 21 '67
    See also names of television performers,
e.g. B. Walters

Political programs

See Television in politics

Program production

Alice in wonderland; dramatized for BBC
television. J. Miller. il Vogue 148:240-7+
D '66
At last, an Alice unspoiled; Alice in Wonder-
land dramatized for BBC television; with
account by H. Judson. il Life 61:96A-98
N 25 '66
Batman's Batmobile; Lincoln Futura. H.
Shuldiner. il Pop Sci 189:46-7+ Jl '66

Has TV gasp! gone Batty? Batman TV
program. J. Skow. il Sat Eve Post 239:93-7
My 7 '66
Hawk folds its wings; New York-based
shows. il Newsweek 68:68 D 5 '66
How they do those magic TV tricks. H.
Shuldiner and R. M. Benrey. il Pop Sci
189:56-61 Ag '66
TV madness; Hollywood gambling $30 mil-
lion on television pilot productions. B.
Davidson. il Sat Eve Post 239:114-19 Mr 26
'66
You watch a television show in the making.
il Sunset 136:43-4+ F '66

Program rating

How they stand; second Nielsens. Time 88:
84 N 4 '66
Man from N.I.E.L.S.E.N. security leak. News-
week 67:67 Mr 14 '66
Panic buttons; previews shown to off-the-
sidewalk critics. il Time 88:60 Jl 15 '66
Peeking order; Nielsen ratings. Newsweek 68:
102 O 24 '66
Rating rigger; rigging Nielsen ratings. News-
week 67:34 Ap 4 '66
Ratings rumble; inadequacies of A. C. Nielsen
company. R. L. Shayon. Sat R 49:44 Ap 23
'66
Sounds of aaaargh; first Nielsen ratings of
the season. Time 88:64 O 21 '66
TV-radio; Arbitron and Trendex figures.
Newsweek 68:99 O 10 '66
TV ratings stay clean; Nielsen system.
Bsns W p46 S 10 '66
TV spy in the sky; Airborne television audit.
S. Roberts. il Pop Mech 125:127 Ap '66
They kill you with silence. W. C. Heinz.
il Sat Eve Post 239:91-5 F 26 '66
Tripped on the riggings; Nielsen ratings.
il Time 88:60+ Jl 15 '66

Programming

Please, somebody, get smart; prime-time cannibalism. J. M. Ferrer, 3d. Life 60:22 My 6
'66
Take a letter. G. Ace. Sat R 49:12 N 12 '66

Programs

Air. M. Arlen. New Yorker 42:46+ D 24 '66
Air; importance of voices. M. Arlen. New
Yorker 42:140+ D 10 '66
Air; series programs Mission: impossible and
Batman. M. J. Arlen. New Yorker 42:
197 N 12 '66
All the way to the bank; Batman. R. L.
Shayon. Sat R 49:46 F 12 '66
At last, an Alice unspoiled; Alice in Wonder-
land dramatized for BBC television; with
account by H. Judson. il Life 61:96A-98
N 25 '66
At war with Batman. E. J. LeShan. il N Y
Times Mag p 112+ My 15 '66
Batman's backstage helper. il Ebony 21:40-
2+ Ap '66
Big-star stomp through oldtime Harlem; H.
Belafonte's production, Strollin' twenties;
with report by K. Gouldthorpe. il Life
60:70-4+ F 4 '66
Bill Cosby talks about life, laughter and the
pursuit of wonderfulness; interview, ed. by
J. Long. B. Cosby. il Seventeen 26:94-5+
Ja '67
Bright & early; Today show. il Time 89:55
Ja 20 '67
Costly spectaculars score TV comeback. il
Bsns W p86-7+ F 12 '66
Dog nights; new shows. il Time 88:85-6 S
16 '66
Don't change a hair for me, Batman; new
show. S. Alexander. Life 60:21 F 4 '66
Flip-side Streisand; second television special.
il Time 87:61 Ap 8 '66
For whom the gong tolls; original amateur
hour. il Time 88:58 Ag 5 '66
Funny thing; Jack Paar's A funny thing
happened on the way to the White House.
Time 87:84 My 27 '66
Good-chap sexuality; Avengers. il Newsweek
67:94 Ap 4 '66
Has TV gasp! gone Batty? Batman TV pro-
gram. J. Skow. il Sat Eve Post 239:93-7
My 7 '66
Here come capes and capers and genuine
Batman blood; commerce exploits cult. il
Life 60:26-26A Mr 11 '66
Holy flypaper! Batman. il Time 87:61 Ja 28 '66
Hornet's nest; Green hornet. il Newsweek
68:96 Jl 18 '66
How to avoid TV dinners while watching
TV; French chef J. Barthel. il N Y Times
Mag p30-1+ Ag 7 '66
Julia Child, the master chef; interview, ed.
by J. Howard. il Life 61:45-6+ O 21 '66

TELEVISION broadcasting—Programs—*Cont.*
Late late show? CBS 1967 plans. Newsweek 68:78 Ag 1 '66
Letter from London; BBC's production of Alice in Wonderland. M. Panter-Downes. New Yorker 42:103-4 Ja 14 '67
Life TV review. Life 60:15 Ja 21; 22 My 6; 15 Je 3; 61:7 S 2 '66; 62:15 Ja 13 '67
Lively arts. P. Hudson. il Sr Schol 89:28-9 D 9 '66
Look and listen. P. Hudson. See issues of Senior scholastic
Looking and listening. P. Hudson. See issues of Senior scholastic
Make Sammy shuffle? S. Davis' program. G. Ace. Sat R 49:22 F 5 '66
Mike Douglas show; he turns the stars on. C. Brossard. il Look 30:75-9 Ag 9 '66
Much more money for same old diet. il Bsns W p42-3 Je 18 '66
New power for broadcast consumers. Consumer Rep 31:321-2 Jl '66
New round; ABC Stage 67; interview. H. Robinson. New Yorker 42:50-2 S 17 '66
New shows on TV this fall. il Changing T 20:35-6 Ag '66
New tool for gun safety; TV firearms course. B. East. il Outdoor Life 138:74-5+ Jl '66
Of dogs and Monkees; criticism of the new offerings. il Newsweek 68:72 S 26 '66
Of many things; Batman and Robin. P. K. Cuneo. America 114:635 My 7 '66
Old moderately; Dean Martin show. il Time 87:60 Mr 11 '66
Previewing the '66-'67 season. P. Hudson. il Sr Schol 89:30. sup 15 S 16 '66
Primarily a guy; the series I spy. C. H. Simonds. Nat R 18:1007-8 O 4 '66
Second caesarian; catering to the twelve-year-old minds. G. Ace. Sat R 49:8 F 12 '66
Sinatra special that's very; Sinatra's spectacular revisited. J. M. Ferrer, 3d. Life 61:24 D 9 '66
Spotlight! E. Miller. See issues of Seventeen
Strato-camp; new programs based on comic books. Newsweek 67:96 F 21 '66
Summer of a malcontent. G. Ace. Sat R 49:6 Jl 9 '66
TV chronicle; end of season review. N. Compton. Commentary 41:82-6 Ap '66
TV-radio. See issues of Newsweek
TV sets stage for quality shows; ABC-TV will launch Stage 67. il Bsns W p83-4 My 21 '66
TV shows are not supposed to be good. D. Karp. il N Y Times Mag p6-7+ Ja 23 '66
TV solves Miranda; Felony squad. il Time 88:79 Ag 26 '66
TV while the sun shines. N. Compton. Commentary 42:95-6+ O '66
That's wonderland, baby! BBC's production of Cinderella and Alice in wonderland. Newsweek 69:46 Ja 2 '67
Those cool war heroes; shows dealing with World war II. il Newsweek 68:77 D 19 '66
Time listings. See issues of Time
Time out for television. See issues of PTA magazine
UHF breakthrough in Chicago? WFLD programs. R. L. Shayon. Sat R 49:55 Ag 13 '66
Underdose of talent. il Time 88:87 N 18 '66
Unloved ones; retirement list. Time 87:75 Ap 1 '66
Uplift and dragdown. C. H. Simonds. il Nat R 18:584+ Je 14 '66
Virtue is its own award; telecast of the Oscar awards. G. Ace. Sat R 49:10 My 21 '66
What the housewife sees. J. G. Dunne. New Repub 154:26-8 Mr 26 '66
Would you believe Don Adams? NBC's Get Smart. G. Smith. il Sat Eve Post 239:32-3 Je 4 '66
Yes, he can; the Sammy Davis show. R. L. Shayon. Sat R 49:38 My 21 '66
See also
Academy of television arts and sciences
National association for better radio and television
Television broadcasting—Dancing

Quiz programs
Games TV plays. il Newsweek 68:106+ N 7 '66
Testing, one, two, three; CBS and NBC programs. il Time 87:69 F 4 '66

Religious programs
Excitement on the tube. il Time 87:70 Ja 28 '66
Reformation in sixty minutes. Christian Cent 83:390 Mr 30 '66
TV as religion. R. L. Shayon. Sat R 49:74 O 22 '66

What's wrong with the church? unique telecast, Richmond, Va. S. Nichols. Christian Cent 83:597-8 My 4 '66

Scientific programs
Science broadcasting in Britain; excerpts from address, February 16, 1966. A. E. Singer. Science 154:743-5 N 11 '66
Science comes to TV. il Pop Electr 25:66 Ag '66

Social aspects
Electronic age. J. Wheeler. Sat R 49:21-2 Je 4 '66
Man is more than a statistic. J. W. Krutch. Sat R 49:14-16 My 21 '66
Television and society, by H. J. Skornia. Review Nation 202:337-8 Mr 21 '66. C. Koch
Theology of Batman. R. E. Terwilliger. Cath World 204:127-8 N '66
See also
Television broadcasting and children

Sound transmission
See also
Television broadcasting—Stereophonic transmission

Sports
Calling the NFL's biggest plays; Commissioner Rozelle. il Bsns W p72-6 O 29 '66
It's sport, it's money, it's TV; ed. by G. Rogin. R. Arledge. il Sports Illus 24:92-4+ Ap 25 '66
Responsibility; Yankees fire R. Barber. Sports Illus 25:17 O 10 '66
Roller derby, anyone? C. W. Morton. il Atlan 218:119 D '66
Seeing is disbelieving; Yankee rating below Mets. G. Ace. Sat R 49:12 N 5 '66
Sportscasting, anyone? interview, ed. by H. L. Masin. J. Simpson. il Sr Schol 88:20 F 11 '66
Television sports hoax; fall's sports coverage. R. L. Tobin. il Sat R 49:109-10 O 8 '66

Spy stories
See Television broadcasting—Drama

Stereophonic transmission
Soviet polar-modulation stereo. il Electr World 75:66 My '66

Study and teaching
Fleet Street fortune at work; two seminars in understanding; enterprises of the Thomson foundation. J. Tebbel. Sat R 49:101-2 N 12 '66

War news
Air; news about Vietnam war from television. M. J. Arlen. New Yorker 42:200-2 O 15 '66
Bringing the war home; reports of U.S. in Viet Nam on French TV screens. Time 88:29-30 Ag 19 '66
Escalating TV; in the U.S. and in South Viet Nam. Sr Schol 88:20 Mr 18 '66
Giving the doves a break; ways of presenting an evenly balanced picture. R. L. Shayon. Sat R 49:55 Mr 5 '66
Information war in Saigon; weaknesses in public-relations apparatus in Washington and Vietnam. H. W. Baldwin. il Reporter 34:29-31 F 24 '66

Anecdotes, facetiae, satire. etc.
Live from Vietnam. G. Ace. Sat R 49:14 Ap 2 '66

Weather forecasts
Weather or not. R. L. Tobin. il Sat R 49:95-6 N 12 '66; Discussion. 49:80-1 D 10 '66

Westerns
Anecdotes, facetiae, satire, etc.
Hero bullet and other related nonsense. J. Belck. il Atlan 217:142+ Mr '66

Canada
On media trouble; concerning the Fowler commission report. D. Smith. Nation 202:402-3 Ap 4 '66
Television; Seven days program. P. Gzowski. Nation 203:61-2 Jl 11 '66

Europe, Western
Incompatibly split; Europe's color TV. il Time 88:72 Ag 12 '66
TV controversy rages; disagreement over a standard European color system. Sci N 90:100 Ag 13 '66

TELEVISION broadcasting—*Continued*

France

Letter from Paris; TV première showing of La prise du pouvoir par Louis XIV (Taking of power by Louis XIV) Genêt. New Yorker 42:200-2 O 22 '66

Great Britain

Alice in Wonderland. J. Miller. il Vogue 148:240-7+ D '66
At last, an Alice unspoiled; Alice in Wonderland dramatized for BBC television; with account by H. Judson. il Life 61:96A-98 N 25 '66
Good-chap sexuality; Avengers. il Newsweek 67:94 Ap 4 '66
Letter from London; BBC's production of Alice in Wonderland. M. Panter-Downes. New Yorker 42:103-4 Ja 14 '67
Sex in the space age; B.B.C's Exit 19. il Newsweek 68:69-70 Ag 22 '66
That's Wonderland, baby! BBC's production of Cinderella and Alice in Wonderland. Newsweek 69:46 Ja 2 '67
   See also
British broadcasting corporation

United States

Fourth steps forth; fourth television network; Overmyer network. Sports Illus 25:9 Ag 15 '66
One infringement or many in a network telecast. H. F. Pilpel. Pub W 190:306-7 Ag 29 '66
Rerun industry. C. W. Morton. il Atlan 218:123-4 O '66
Television and society, by H. J. Skornia. Review
   Nation 202:337-8 Mr 21 '66. C. Koch
Top of my head. G. Ace. See issues of Saturday review
Where the action is? il Sr School 88:16-18 Ap 15 '66
   See also
Columbia broadcasting system
United States—Federal communications commission

Vietnam (Republic)

Escalating TV; in the U.S. and in South Viet Nam. Sr Schol 88:20 Mr 18 '66
TELEVISION broadcasting, Stereophonic. See Television broadcasting—Stereophonic transmission
TELEVISION broadcasting and children
At war with Batman. E. J. LeShan. il N Y Times Mag p 112+ My 15 '66
Morality building with the FBI. R. L. Shayon. Sat R 49:42 Jl 30 '66
Television for the pre-school child. H. R. Cassirer. il UNESCO Courier 19:4-11 N '66
TV vs homework; teacher-opinion poll. il NEA J 55:26 F '66
What TV is doing to our chldren; summary of The effects of television on children and adolescents. W. Schramm. il Sr Schol 88:sup9-10 F 18 '66
   See also
Television broadcasting—Childrens programs
TELEVISION broadcasting for children. See Television broadcasting—Childrens programs
TELEVISION broadcasting stations. See Television stations
TELEVISION cabinets
More ways to hide TV. il Sunset 136:135-6 F '66
TELEVISION cables
New low-loss coax for TV; coaxial lead-in for color-TV and U.H.F. L. Cantor. il Electr World 76:33 Ag '66
TELEVISION camera tubes. See Television cameras
TELEVISION cameras
Canoga camera modified for undersea use. W. E Wilks. il Tech W 19:44 D 5 '66
Laser TV system sees in the dark. il Pop Sci 188:119 F '66
Modern color-TV camera. il Electr World 76:30 D '66
Nighttime TV system gets Vietnam use; image-intensifier tubes and low-light-level vidicons in tactical warfare. R. Pay. il Tech W 19:26-7 D 19 '66
Plumbicon: a new approach to camera tubes. il Electr World 76:47 S '66
Televise in your home; first closed-circuit TV camera kit. il Pop Electr 24:52-3 My '66
TELEVISION circuits
Chroma circuits in color TV; Motorola. W. H. Buchsbaum. il Electr World 76:33-5+ S '66
Chroma circuits in color TV; Sylvania. W. H. Buchsbaum. il Electr World 76:34-5+ D '66

Convergence circuits of color sets; RCA. W. H. Buchsbaum. il Electr World 76:38-9+ Ag '66
Heath blazes trail with 25 inch color TV kit; automatic degaussing circuit, a feature. J. D. Drummond. il Pop Electr 24:62-3 My '66
Modern shadow-mask color-TV tube. R. K. Gessford. il Electr World 76:43-5+ D '66
TV set uses integrated circuit. il Electr World 75:28-9 Je '66
TELEVISION commentators. See Television broadcasting—News
TELEVISION commercials. See Television advertising
TELEVISION criticism
Most influential fellow; J. Gould. Newsweek 67:92+ My 9 '66
Take a letter. G. Ace. Sat R 49:12 N 12 '66
TELEVISION drama. See Television broadcasting—Drama
TELEVISION generators. See Signal generators
TELEVISION heroes
Opinion; on the hero myth. J. Shepherd. Mlle 63:18+ Jl '66
TELEVISION in education
Air; Channel 13 documentaries not noticeably better than network documentaries. M. J. Arlen. New Yorker 42:80+ Ja 7 '67
Battle line shifts on satellites; Comsat. AT&T join in opposing Ford foundation's TV plan. Bsns W p34 Ag 27 '66
Challenge of TV teaching. G. D. Davis. il NEA J 55:10-11+ Ap '66
Educational broadcasting in Asia; summary of UNESCO meeting. UN Mo Chron 3:31 Je '66
Educational satellites; proposed Broadcasters' non-profit satellite service. Sci Am 215:101-2 S '66
Educational TV and the classroom teacher. il Sr Schol 88:sup 12-13 F 18 '66
ETV; challenge to teachers. J. R. Lange. il Sr Schol 88:sup 12-13 F 18 '66
ETV communications satellites raise new copyright issues. R. H. Smith. Pub W 190:46 S 5 '66
ETV: Ford foundation calls for nonprofit satellite system. E. Langer. Science 153:962-4 Ag 26 '66
Educational television in the art room. K. K. Agee. il Sch Arts 66:24-5 D '66
Educational TV; NSF and arts foundation speak out. L. J. Carter. Science 154:1309-10 D 9 '66
ETV via satellites? H. E. Wigren. NEA J 55:52-4 O '66
Ford foundation, Comsat corp. clash over non-profit TV. Tech W 19:18 Ag 22 '66
Group to study educational TV for use in aid program; text of a memorandum, November 26, 1966. L. B. Johnson. Dept State Bul 56:15-16 Ja 2 '67
In the spell of Under milk wood. America 114:405 Mr 26 '66
New approach to educational TV. il Electr World 75:68 Mr '66
Return of the wizard; adult science series, Experiment. il Time 88:80 O 7 '66
Satellite built for TV; Toronto's Scarborough college. il Time 89:46-8 Ja 13 '67
Science comes to TV. il Pop Electr 25:66 Ag '66
Social and educational implications of communication satellites; adaptation of address, December 6-10, 1965. W. Schramm. Sch & Soc 94:346-8 O 29 '66
Technology in education. L. Edinger. bibliog il Wilson Lib Bul 41:73-5 S '66
Telepromptings. S. Kauffmann. New Repub 156:24+ Ja 21 '67
Televison and the mystery masterpiece. W. Dean. il Sch Arts 65:13-15 Mr '66
Unfulfilled promise of ITV. J. Murphy and R. Gross. il Sat R 49:88-9+ N 19 '66
What's wrong with ETV? America 115:199 Ag 27 '66
Who gets satellite profits? Bsns W p45 S 10 '66
   See also
National center for school and college television
Television stations, Educational
TELEVISION in medicine
Closed circuit color TV beams vivid surgery pix. Sci N 90:361 O 29 '66
TELEVISION in navigation
TV speeds ship traffic; Welland Canal, St Lawrence Seaway. Sci N 90:207 S 17 '66
TELEVISION in politics
Seeing spots; homestretch TV electioneering. il Newsweek 68:34+ N 7 '66
TV and youth; new style for politics. H. Mendelsohn. il Nation 202:669-73 Je 6 '66
   See also
Television broadcasting—Election results

TELEVISION in science
See also
Television broadcasting—Scientific programs
TELEVISION in sewer inspection. See Sewer inspection
TELEVISION in traffic control
See also
Television in navigation
TELEVISION industry
See also
Television apparatus industry and trade

Securities
Growth in the air. il Fortune 75:179-80 Ja '67

Europe, Western
Rosy hue for color TV in Europe. il Bsns W p94-6+ O 22 '66

United States
Noble networks; need for government subsidized network. New Repub 154:6 F 26 '66
They kill you with silence. W. C. Heinz. il Sat Eve Post 239:91-5 F 26 '66

TELEVISION interference
Correcting color signal distortion. il Electr World 75:66 F '66
TELEVISION laws and regulations
U.S. court sustains United church of Christ; petition challenging renewal of licenses for television stations in Jackson, Miss. Christian Cent 83:484 Ap 20 '66
See also
United States—Federal communications commission
TELEVISION lines. See Television cables
TELEVISION news photographers. See News photographers
TELEVISION performers. See Television broadcasting—Performers
TELEVISION photography. See Television—Photographic aspects
TELEVISION plays
Life of a salesman; a television epilogue. il Sat Eve Post 239:20 Je 18 '66
Play's the thing; NBC rights to Slow dance on the killing ground. Newsweek 68:79 S 5 '66
TELEVISION production. See Television broadcasting—Program production
TELEVISION program rating. See Television broadcasting—Program rating
TELEVISION programming. See Television broadcasting—Programming
TELEVISION programs. See Television broadcasting—Programs
TELEVISION projection
How they do those magic TV tricks. H. Shuldiner and R. M. Benrey. il Pop Sci 189:56-61 Ag '66
TELEVISION receiving apparatus
Case of the shrinking screen; FTC's new regulations. Bsns W p58-9 D 31 '66
Hi-fi and TV for your boat. L. G. Sands. il Motor B 117:38-9+ Je '66
Laser replaces TV tube. Bsns W p 123 O 8 '66
New rule on TV size designations. Consumer Rep 31:269 Je '66
'67 TV sets; color and black and white. il Consumer Bul 49:6-11 D '66
TV sets. Consumer Rep 31:203-6 D '66

Color receivers
Big-screen color TV tunes down prices. Bsns W p 101 Je 11 '66
Case of TV nerves; customers turning more selective. Bsns W p48 N 19 '66
Cheapest color set yet. R. M. Benrey. il Pop Sci 188:134-5 Mr '66
Chroma circuits in color TV: Motorola. W. H. Buchsbaum. il Electr World 76:33-5+ S '66
Chroma circuits in color TV: Sylvania. W. H. Buchsbaum. il Electr World 76:34-5+ D '66
Chroma demodulation in color sets: RCA. W. H. Buchsbaum. il Electr World 75:45-7+ My '66
Chroma synchronization in color sets: RCA. W. H. Buchsbaum. il Electr World 75:35-7+ Je '66
Convergence circuits of color sets; RCA. W. H. Buchsbaum. il Electr World 76:38-9+ Ag '66
Correcting color signal distortion. il Electr World 75:66 F '66
Fantastic new portable color TV. L. Steckler. il Pop Mech 125:90-4 F '66
G-E 11-inch color TV; the new look in color receivers. W. H. Buchsbaum. il Electr World 75:39-41+ Mr '66
GE's small-screen color TV set. il Consumer Rep 31:61 F '66

Great color explosion in television. F. Bowers. House & Gard 130:46-7 S '66
Heath blazes trail with 25 inch color TV kit. J. D. Drummond. il Pop Electr 24:62-3 My '66
Hue of all flesh. il Time 87:83 Mr 4 '66
Inside those easy-to-tune '67 color TVs. R. M. Benrey. il Pop Sci 189:110-13 S '66
Large-screen color TV. il Consumer Rep 32:9-13 Ja '67
New rectangular 25-inch color TV you build from a kit. H. Luckett. il Pop Sci 188:102-3 My '66
RCA gambles on chips; microcircuits to replace transistors in color and black-and-white TV. il Bsns W p27 F 5 '66
Rosy hue for color TV in Europe. il Bsns W p94-6+ O 22 '66
16-inch color TV for less than $300. il Consumer Rep 31:216 My '66
'67 TV sets; color and black and white. il Consumer Bul 49:6-11 D '66
Time to buy color TV? il Changing T 20:37-9 D '66

Control
Automatic TV brightness control. S. Hoberman. il Electr World 75:38 My '66

Picture tubes
Modern shadow-mask color-TV tube. R. K. Gessford. il Electr World 76:43-5+ D '66
They make the mask that makes color TV; Buckbee-Mears of St Paul, Minn. il Bsns W p 126-8+ N 12 '66
Tomorrow's color TV. W. G. Salm. il Sci Digest 60:63-8 Ag '66

Repairing
Repairman, spare that set; findings of a secret survey of repair shops. Newsweek 67:75 My 30 '66
Television repair records. il Consumer Rep 31:449-50 S '66

Transistor receivers
Fantastic new portable color TV. L. Steckler. il Pop Mech 125:90-4 F '66
Line-operated transistor TV sets: Emerson. W. H. Buchsbaum. il Electr World 75:40+ F '66
Line-operated transistor TV sets: G-E. W. H. Buchsbaum. il Electr World 76:29+ O '66
Line-operated transistor TV sets: Magnavox. W. H. Buchsbaum. Electr World 76:27+ N '66
Line-operated transistor TV sets: Sylvania. W. H. Buchsbaum. il Electr World 75:38+ Ja '66
Line-operated transistor TV sets: Westinghouse. W. H. Buchsbaum. il Electr World 75:34-5 Mr '66
Line-operated transistor TV sets: Zenith. W. H. Buchsbaum. il Electr World 75:90-1 Ap '66

Tuning
Inside those easy-to-tune '67 color TVs. R. M. Benrey. il Pop Sci 189:110-13 S '66
TELEVISION receiving apparatus, Portable
New portables. il House & Gard 129:28+ Je '66
Small-screen television sets. il Consumer Rep 31:104-7 Mr '66
TV under the trees; Sony TV-700 U 7-inch portable. Consumer Rep 31:520-1 N '66
See also
Television receiving apparatus—Transistor receivers
TELEVISION reception
Home TV via satellite. B. B. Underhill. il Electr World 75:39-41+ My '66
Riding the TV DX trail. G. Olson. il Pop Electr 25:73-4+ Jl '66
TELEVISION relay systems
See also
Communications satellites
TELEVISION repairing. See Television receiving apparatus—Repairing
TELEVISION script writing. See Television authorship
TELEVISION scripts. See Television authorship
TELEVISION stations
Consumers' rights; racism and Jackson, Miss, WLBT-TV. Nation 202:412 Ap 11 '66
Covering a massacre; Austin's KTBC's coverage of the murder at the University of Texas. il Time 88:34 Ag 12 '66
Fourth network. R. L. Shayon. Sat R 49:39 Ag 27 '66
High noon in Bakersfield; KBAK; KERO; KLYD and the Television code. R. L. Shayon. Sat R 49:22 Ag 20 '66

TELEVISION stations—*Continued*
Historic reversal for the FCC; Court of appeals rules FCC erred in renewing license of WLBT. R. L. Shayon. Sat R 49: 102 My 7 '66
How a broadcaster spreads its net; community antenna cable and microwave systems. il Bsns W p57-8+ D 3 '66
How CATV makes room for more. il Bsns W p 102 F 19 '66
Making the most of the medium; New Orleans' WDSU-TV. il Time 88:76+ Jl 22 '66
Small-screen big board; Los Angeles' KWHY-TV. Newsweek 69:46 Ja 2 '67
UHF breakthrough in Chicago? WFLD. R. L. Shayon. Sat R 49:55 Ag 13 '66
See also
Columbia broadcasting system
Trigg-Vaughn stations, incorporated
TELEVISION stations, Educational
ETV facts. Sr Schol 88:sup 12-13 F 18 '66
Fourth network; Ford foundation proposal that a nonprofit corporation operate a domestic satellite system for educational TV. J. Ridgeway. New Repub 155:13-14 S 17 '66
1966: the year ETV comes of age. Sr Schol 89:sup2 N 4 '66
People's dividend; Ford foundation proposal of a company for the Early bird. il Time 88:38+ Ag 12 '66
People's satellite; national ETV programs; opposition to Ford foundation proposals. il Newsweek 68:76-7 Ag 15 '66
Satellite static; critics complaints of Ford scheme. Newsweek 68:79 S 5 '66
TELEVISION towers
Pride in the sky. il Time 88:96 S 16 '66
World's tallest television tower. il UNESCO Courier 19:33 N '66
TELEVISION transmission
Direct TV broadcasts forecast; home broadcasts via satellites. il Sci N 89:402 My 21 '66
Wideband video in digital form transmitted over laser system. B. Miller. il Aviation W 85:61+ Ag 22 '66
See also
Television, Color
Television broadcasting—Stereophonic transmission
TELEVISION tubes. See Television receiving apparatus—Picture tubes
TELEVISION writing. See Television authorship
TELL al-Rimah excavations. See Iraq—Antiquities
TELLEFSEN, Robert N.
Dual-sensitivity field strength and absorption meter. Pop Electr 24:67-8 Ja '66
TELLER, Edward
Role of applied science. Bul Atomic Sci 22: 15-19 Mr '66
Will NATO survive? address, May 20, 1966. Vital Speeches 32:687-90 S 1 '66
about
Breakfast with Dr Teller. N. Cousins. Sat R 49:26+ Mr 19 '66
TELLER, Sanford M.
From photography to flying saucers. U S Camera 29:60-1+ N '66
TELLEZ, Theresa
Crisis of Argentine science. Bul Atomic Sci 22:32-4 D '66
TELLEZ-NAGEL, Isabel, and Harter, D. H.
Subacute sclerosing leukoencephalitis: ultrastructure of intranuclear and intracytoplasmic inclusions. bibliog Science 154:899-901 N 18 '66
TELLICO DAM (proposed) See Dams
TELLURIDES
Melting of tin telluride at high pressures. W. Klement, jr. and L. H. Cohen. bibliog il Science 154:1176-7 D 2 '66
TEMKIN, S. D.
Unitarian imbroglio. Christian Cent 83:1082-3 S 7 '66
TEMPEL-Tuttle comet. See Comets
TEMPER
Dialogue with mothers; coping with temper tantrums. B. Bettelheim. Ladies Home J 83:31-2 Ap '66
See also
Anger
TEMPERANCE
Urge revision of abstinence code. Christian Cent 83:1264 O 19 '66
TEMPERATURE
Isotopic paleotemperatures. C. Emiliani. bibliog il Science 154:851-7 N 18 '66
See also
Hot weather
Ocean temperature
Stars—Temperature
Thermistors

Measurement
See also
Thermometers and thermometry
Physiological effects
Pyrimidine dimers; effect of temperature, on photoinduction. R. O. Rahn. bibliog il Science 154:503-4 O 28 '66
Reproduction in lizards: influence of temperature on photoperiodism in testicular recrudescence. P. Licht. bibliog il Science 154:1668-70 D 30 '66
See also
Heat—Physiological effects
Heatstroke
Regulation
See also
Thermostats
TEMPERATURE, Animal and human
Sceloporus occidentalis: preferred body temperature of the western fence lizard. S. M. McGinnis. bibliog il Science 152:1090-1 My 20 '66
Thermoregulation in a brooding female Indian python, python molurus bivittatus. V. H. Hutchison and others. bibliog il Science 151:694-6 F 11 '66
See also
Thermometers, Clinical
TEMPERATURE, Atmospheric. See Atmospheric temperature
TEMPERATURE and business. See Weather and business
TEMPERATURE regulators. See Thermostats
TEMPERATURES, Low. See Low temperatures
TEMPERED glass. See Glass, Safety
TEMPEST; drama. See Shakespeare, W.—Plays
TEMPLATES. See Templets
TEMPLE, Henry John, 3d viscount Palmerston. See Palmerston, H. J. T.
TEMPLE, Shirley
Sex at the box office. McCalls 94:45+ Ja '67
about
Washington report; statement, ed. by J. Lloyd. Sr Schol 89:sup6 N 18 '66
TEMPLE university, Philadelphia
Temple university to open art school in Rome. il Design 67:35 Mr '66
TEMPLES
Egypt
What home for the temple? question of moving the Temple of Dendur to the United States. K. Kuh. il Sat R 49:56-7 N 26 '66
See also
Abu Simbel, Temples of
India
Terra-cotta temples of India. R. Bussabarger. il Craft Horiz 26:28-33 Ja '66
Traveling with Mlle: travel, temples, and tolerance. S. Rama Rau. il Mlle 64:132-4 D '66
TEMPLETON, Edith
Equality cake. New Yorker 42:56-67 N 12 '66
Talking of Count Sternborn. New Yorker 42: 54-63 O 15 '66
TEMPLETS
Templates make contour filing easy. W. E. Burton. il Pop Mech 127:176-7 Ja '67
TEMPORARY technical help agencies. See Employment agencies
TEN cents' worth of love; story. See Gerber, M. J.
TEN-pound box of candy; story. See Johnson, D. M.
TEN THOUSAND ISLANDS
Marco's millions; Marco Island development. il Travel 125:4 Mr '66
TENANTS. See Landlord and tenant
TENCZAR, Paul, and Bader, R. S.
Maternal effect in dental traits of the house mouse. bibliog Science 152:1398-400 Je 3 '66
TENEMENT houses
Industry builds a showcase in the slums; U.S. gypsum's experiment in Harlem. il Bsns W p40-1 F 26 '66
See also
Slums
TENG, Hsiao-ping
From a single spark. Newsweek 67:46 Je 27 '66
TENNESSEE
See also
Booksellers and bookselling—Tennessee
Cumberland Gap
Hunting—Tennessee
Wilderness areas—Tennessee

TENNESSEE—*Continued*

Politics and government

Machine v. style; Democratic gubernatorial primary. Time 88:12 Ag 12 '66

TENNESSEE evolution controversy
Day the Bible beat the monkeys; J. Scopes case; with report by W. Warga. il Life 61:97-8 D 9 '66
John T. Scopes redivivus. Christian Cent 84: 429 Ap 5 '67

TENNESSEE mountaineers. See Mountaineers (southern states)

TENNESSEE. University
See also
Agricultural research laboratory, Oak Ridge, Tenn.

TENNESSEE VALLEY authority
Second spring stirs the TVA. il Bsns W p 112-15+ O 29 '66
TVA chooses atom power. Bsns W p 150 Je 25 '66

TENNEY, A. Webster
This farming business. Am Ed 2:28-32 Jl '66

TENNIS
All-Aussie. Newsweek 68:78 S 26 '66
Australia wins an Indian war; Davis cup challenge round. K. Chapin. il Sports Illus 26:50-1 Ja 9 '67
Bounce-ball, anyone? Davis cup zone matches. il Newsweek 68:65-6 Ag 29 '66
Bright future for little Miss Bombshell; R. Casals of San Francisco. K. Chapin. il Sports Illus 25:68-70 O 24 '66
Charlito moves to the head of the class. J. Jares. il Sports Illus 24:50-1 F 28 '66
Duel on grass at 26 paces; B. J. King-N. Richey at Forest Hills. B. Collins. Sports Illus 25:54-5 S 5 '66
Forgotten Aussie refreshes the memory; Australians win the U.S. Davis cup. F. Deford. il Sports Illus 25:105-6+ S 19 '66
Handbook of dishonorable tennis. R. Lardner. il N Y Times Mag p36-7+ Ap 24 '66
Harvest without seeds; Forest Hills. il Time 88:80 S 23 '66
In their cups; Davis cup for the Aussies. il Newsweek 69:60-1 Ja 9 '67
Jaws; Aussies win Davis cup. il Time 89:73 Ja 6 '67
Lot of horses; Davis cup team. il Time 88: 44-5 Ag 26 '66
Man to lead the pros out of the darkness; W. Dill. F. Deford. il Sports Illus 24:58+ Je 20 '66
Manolo is king, and a king is queen; Wimbledon tournament. J. Lovesey. il Sports Illus 25:50+ Jl 11 '66
Missile v. computer; New York pro tournament. il Time 87:64 Ap 1 '66
Nothing like it; Van Alen simplified scoring system. Sports Illus 25:9 Ag 1 '66
Numero uno; Santana wins at Wimbledon. il Time 88:39 Jl 8 '66
Old game stages a rally; indoor tennis at Madison Square Garden. M. Kane. il Sports Illus 24:84-6 Ap 4 '66
Quick trip to Wicomico; National indoor championships. il Time 87:48+ Mr 4 '66
Reasons why the roof fell in; embarrassing defeat of U.S. Davis cup team in Brazil. W. Bingham. Sports Illus 25:73-4+ N 21 '66
Round one at Forest Hills; photographs by H. Knopf; with accounts by L. Smith and F. Deford. il Sports Illus 25:40-50 Ag 29 '66
Russian serves a warning; A. Metreveli upsets D. Ralston in the French nationals. P. Ress. il Sports Illus 24:80+ Je 13 '66
Sporting scene; 1966 United States lawn tennis championships. H. W. Wind. New Yorker 42:150+ O 1 '66
Sporting scene; United States indoor tennis championships. Salisbury, Md. H. W. Wind. New Yorker 42:135-6+ Mr 12 '66
Success for VASSS; new scoring system. il Time 87:61 Je 24 '66
To the ludicrous; U.S. Davis cup team beaten in preliminary interzone play. il Time 88:58 N 18 '66
What we can learn about tennis; memo from Down Under. H. Gordon. il N Y Times Mag p 185-7+ N 27 '66
Whatever happened to 40-love? Van Alen simplified scoring system. S. Moore. Life 61:10 Jl 8 '66

TENNIS, Table. See Table tennis

TENNIS courts
Missile v. computer; rubber surface at Madison Square Garden. il Time 87:64 Ap 1 '66

Lighting

Days aren't long enough; courts in Randolph park, Tucson, Ariz. H. L. Danforth. il Am City 81:56 Je '66

TENNIS courts, Indoor
Love indoors. Newsweek 68:110 O 10 '66
Old game stages a rally; indoor tennis at Madison Square Garden. M. Kane. il Sports Illus 24:84-6 Ap 4 '66

TENNIS players
Forgotten Aussie refreshes the memory; Australians win the U.S. Davis cup. F. Deford. il Sports Illus 25:105-6+ S 19 '66
Put a lion in your tank; African safari. B. Collins. il Sports Illus 25:36-8+ Jl 25 '66
Reasons why the roof fell in; embarrassing defeat of U.S. Davis cup team in Brazil. W. Bingham. Sports Illus 25:73-4+ N 21 '66
Richey kids; tennis is their business. C. Brossard. il Look 30:128-32+ O 18 '66
Riven to victory; the Richeys. il Time 88:35 Jl 29 '66
Sporting scene; 1966 United States lawn tennis championships. H. W. Wind. New Yorker 42:150+ O 1 '66
Sporting scene; United States indoor tennis championships. Salisbury, Md. H. W. Wind. New Yorker 42:135-6+ Mr 12 '66
What we can learn about tennis; memo from Down Under. H. Gordon. il N Y Times Mag p 185-7+ N 27 '66
See also
Ashe, A.

Salaries
See Athletes—Salaries

TENNIS racket strings. See Strings, Tennis racket

TENNYSON-D'EYNCOURT, Sir Eustace, 1st bart
Annals of the sea. R. Hough. il New Yorker 42:41-4+ Ag 20 '66

TENSION (psychology) See Fatigue; Stress (psychology)

TENT caterpillars
March of the caterpillars. A. Swain. il Audubon Mag 68:158-9 My '66

TENTING. See Camping

TENTS
Designed for camping. il Field & S 71:89 Jl '66
New shapes make news in tents. R. Gannon. il Pop Sci 188:154-9 My '66
Ray's $3 tent; plastic sheeting. H. G. Tapply. il Field & S 71:54 Ja '67
Revolution in tents. C. B. Colby. il Outdoor Life 138:12+ O '66
Selecting a tent. J. B. Miller. Consumer Bul 49:16-18 Je '66
Tent with a view. J. Peter. il Look 30:M18+ Ap 19 '66
Tents. T. Trueblood. il Field & S 71:16+ Jl '66
Tents for automobile camping. J. B. Miller. il Consumer Bul 49:32-6 Jl '66
What's new in tent frames, tent shapes, tent fabrics. il Sunset 137:70+ Ag '66

TENURE, Teacher. See Teachers—Tenure

TEPA. See Chemosterilants

TEPEES. See Tents

TERATOLOGY. See Abnormalities (animals)

TEREKHOV, Miguel
Giselle comes to the University of Oklahoma. J. Anderson. il pors Dance Mag 40:57-9 N '66

TER HORST, Jerald
Ballad of the green bow tie. Reporter 35:36-8 S 8 '66

TERMINAL buildings, Airport. See Airport buildings

TERMINE, John D. and Posner, A. S.
Infrared analysis of rat bone; age dependency of amorphous and crystalline mineral fractions. bibliog Science 153:1523-5 S 23 '66

TERMINOLOGY. See subhead Terminology under various subjects, e.g. Politics—Terminology

TERMITES
Termites? here's how to tell. Suc Farm 64: 69 My '66

TERMS and phrases. See English language—Terms and phrases

TERNS
Nature note; Arctic tern. Sci N 90:13 Jl 2 '66

TERPENES
Scolytid beetles associated with Douglas fir; response to terpenes. J. A. Rudinsky. bibliog il Science 152:218-19 Ap 8 '66

TERRACE, H. S.
Discrimination learning and inhibition. bibliog Science 154:1677-80 D 30 '66

TERRACE furniture. See Furniture, Outdoor

TERRACES (outdoor living areas) See Outdoor rooms

TERRAPIN
Isle of Hope; the terrapin's last stand. C. Stippett. il Holiday 40:24+ S '66

TERRELL, James
Quasi-stellar objects: possible local origin. bibliog Science 154:1281-8 D 9 '66
TERRELL, Tex.
What is Project Discovery discovering? J. A. Brill. il Sr Schol 89:sup8+ O 7 '66
TERRES, John K.
How high do birds fly? excerpt from Flashing wings; a story of bird flight. Audubon Mag 68:449-53 N '66
Search for the golden mouse. il por Audubon Mag 68:96-101 Mr '66
TERRESTRIAL magnetism. See Magnetism, Terrestrial
TERRESTRIAL rotation. See Earth—Rotation
TERRIERS
Something different in dogs; Jagdterrier and Boykin spaniel. D. M. Duffey. il Outdoor Life 138:108-11 Ag '66
TERRILL, Ross
China and Vietnam. New Repub 155:16-20 O 29 '66
TERRITORIAL expansion
See also
Conquest, Right of
TERRITORIALISM (animals) See Animals—Habits and behavior
TERRORISM
Brutality with a purpose; political weapon of the Viet Cong. Time 88:33 S 16 '66
Nobody move! dramatic attempt to disrupt South Vietnam's National day parade. il Newsweek 68:54 N 14 '66
Report from Thailand: Communists heating up a second front in Asia. S. W. Sanders. il U S News 61:42-4 Jl 18 '66
Speaking of killing civilians: look at what's happening to the South Vietnamese. il U S News 62:34-6 Ja 16 '67
TERRORISM, Telephone. See Telephone calls
TERRY, Alfred Howe
Grisly epilogue. M. Sandoz. Am Heritage 17: 73 Ap '66
TERRY, Fernando Belaúnde. See Belaúnde Terry, F.
TERRY, Luther L.
Appeal abroad of American medicine and public health; address; with questions and answers. Ann Am Acad 366:78-88 Jl '66
TERRY, Megan
Viet rock. Criticism
Nation 203:586-7 N 28 '66
Newsweek il 68:114 N 21 '66
Time 88:61 O 21 '66
Vogue 149:52 Ja 1 '67
TERRY, William D. and Roberts, M. S.
Antigenic heterogeneity of human immunoglobulin A proteins. bibliog Science 153:1007-8 Ag 26 '66
—and others
Electrophoretic heterogeneity of the polypeptide chains of human G-myeloma proteins. bibliog Science 152:1628-30 Je 17 '66
TERTIS, Lionel
Great musician at ninety. I. Kolodin. por Sat R 50:105 Ja 14 '67
TERTZ, Abram, pseud.
Accusers accused; protest raging in Russia. il Newsweek 68:52 N 28 '66
Art and politics in the U.S.S.R. il por Newsweek 67:38+ F 21 '66
Bit of fear. Time 87:33 F 25 '66
Moscow: the defense does not rest. D. Brown. il Reporter 35:43-5 S 22 '66
On trial, by M. Hayward. Review
Sat R 49:25 Ag 6 '66. M. MacDuffie
Time il 88:86 Ag 19 '66
Socialist legality on trial. A. Brumberg. il Reporter 34:34-6 Mr 10 '66
Trial and error. Newsweek 67:42+ F 28 '66
Trial begins. il Time 87:32 F 18 '66
Trial ends. J. L. Laber. New Repub 154:26-9 Mr 19 '66
Trial in Moscow. Commonweal 83:598 F 25 '66
Trial of Sinyavsky and Daniel; excerpt from the Paris-based Polish magazine Kultura, tr. by M. Hayward. il pors N Y Times Mag p20-3+ Ap 17 '66
Trial of two Soviet writers. G. Bailey. il Reporter 34:34-8 F 24 '66
West registers shock at Soviet writers' punishment. Pub W 189:151 F 21 '66
When Soviet writers dare to be critical. U S News 60:16 F 28 '66
Yes, they were subversive. Christian Cent 83:262 Mr 2 '66
TERWILLIGER, Robert E.
Theology of Batman. Cath World 204:127-8 N '66
TERYLENE sails. See Sails
TERZIEV, Marc G.
New Atlantic salmon fishing. il pors Outdoor Life 137:33-5+ Ap '66

TESCHAN, P. E.
STS alumni speak. Sci N 89:180+ Mr 19 '66
TEST anxiety. See Anxiety
TEST ban treaty. See Nuclear test ban treaty, 1963
TEST records. See Phonograph records—Test records
TESTES. See Testicles
TESTICLES
Contractile cells in human seminiferous tubules. M. H. Ross and I. R. Long. bibliog il Science 153:1271-3 S 9 '66
TESTIMONY. See Witnesses
TESTING
Non-destructive testing. J. R. Collins. il Electr World 75:33-6 F; 53-6+ Mr '66
See also subhead Testing under various subjects, e.g. Drugs—Testing
TESTING, Educational. See Educational tests and measurements
TESTING instruments
Army field calibration technicians; calibrating electronic test equipment used to maintain and check missiles. C. J. Diodati. il Electr World 76:80-2 S '66
Audible continuity and semiconductor checker. J. B. Frost and R. W. Bailey. il Electr World 76:86+ O '66
Measuring instruments for electronic components. F. Van Veen. il Electr World 76:36-8+ S '66
Popular science's nine-in-one troubleshooter. R. M. Benrey. il Pop Sci 188:114-17+ F; 138-40+ Mr; 192-4 Ap '66
Test equipment product report. See issues of Electronics world
Test measurements profile. J. H. Drummond. il Pop Electr 24:49-53 Ap '66
Trouble testers for photographers. F. P. Fritz. il Pop Mech 125:171-4+ Mr '66
Ultrasonics can improve your herd; Sonoray. J. Harvey. il Suc Farm 64:64 Mr '66
See also
Calibrators
TESTING laboratories
Consulting engineer's lighting laboratory. il Arch Rec 140:158 D '66
Effects of retro-rocket exhaust studied in Arnold test cell. il Tech W 19:28 Ag 8 '66
Giving office gear the torture test; Buyers laboratory provides testing service. il Bsns W p110-12 Mr 12 '66
Martin builds guidance research facility; duplicating operational environment of missile or aircraft. il Aviation W 84:191+ Je 20 '66
Martin missile guidance development center opening. C. D. LaFond. il Miss & Roc 18:32-3 My 2 '66
See also
Good housekeeping institute
Wyle laboratories, incorporated
TESTING machines
See also
Rocket sleds
TESTIS. See Testicles
TESTOSTERONE
Sex differences in the brain. S. Levine. il Sci Am 214:84-90 Ap '66
TESTS, Information. See Information tests
TETLEY, Glen
Glen Tetley and company, Hunter college playhouse. M. Marks. Dance Mag 40:63 My '66
TETRACHLOROANISOL. See Anisole
TETRACYCLINES
Drug-induced teratogenesis in vitro: inhibition of calcification by different tetracyclines. L. Saxén. bibliog il Science 153:1384-7 S 16 '66
FTC rules in tetracycline case; Pfizer & co. obtained patent by making false and misleading statements. Bsns W p46+ D 10 '66
TETRAETHYLAMMONIUM
Tetraethylammonium and tetrodotoxin: effects on cochlear potentials. Y. Katsuki and others. bibliog il Science 151:1544-5 Mr 25 '66
TETRAHYMENA pyriformis. See Protozoa
TETRALOGY of Fallot
Balloon to save a baby; Rashkind technique overcomes congenital heart defect. il Life 60:65-6 My 27 '66
Blue babies: bounce back. Newsweek 69:84 Ja 16 '67
TETRAZOLS
Pentylenetetrazol enhances memory function. S. Irwin and A. Benuazizi. bibliog il Science 152:100-2 Ap 1 '66
TETRODOTOXIN. See Toxins and antitoxins
TEWARI, K. K. and Wildman, S. G.
Chloroplast DNA from tobacco leaves. bibliog Science 153:1269-71 S 9 '66

TEXANS
Texas trademark: flair for the flamboyant. il Life 61:34-47 Jl 8 '66
Texas; with report by D. Nevin. il Life 61: 36-50+ Jl 1 '66

TEXAS
Texas sojourn; Hill country: Lyndon Johnson's Texas, NBC documentary. W. V. Shannon. Commonweal 84:273-4 My 27 '66
Texas trademark: flair for the flamboyant. il Life 61:34-47 Jl 8 '66
Texas; with report by D. Nevin. il Life 61: 36-50+ Jl 1 '66
See also
Architecture, Domestic—Texas
Big Bend National Park
Booksellers and bookselling—Texas
Botany—Texas
Educaton—Texas
Festivals—Texas
Fishing—Texas
Guadalupe Mountains National Park
Hunting—Texas
Law—Texas
Padre Island
Petroleum industry and trade—Texas
Roads—Texas

Anecdotes, facetiae, satire, etc.
Inside Texas. Christian Cent 83:415 Mr 30 '66

Description and travel
Cruising the Karankaway country. A. W. Lloyd. il Motor B 118:22-5+ N '66
Mrs LBJ country; ed. by M. Simons. C. A. T. Johnson. il Look 30:35-41 Jl 12 '66
Texas trails. P. Crittenden. il Travel 126:35-8 N '66
Texas triumph; Caddo Lake-Jefferson-Lake O' the Pines. A. Eason. il Travel 126:46-9 Ag '66

Economic conditions
LBJ country: from poverty to riches. il U S News 60:52-5 My 2 '66

Parks and reserves
Are arms being twisted to pay for LBJ park? U S News 61:15 O 31 '66
Good-neighbor policy; opposition to plan for state park across Pedernales from the President's land in Texas. il Newsweek 67: 30+ Mr 21 '66
New uproar over the LBJ state park. U S News 60:10 Mr 28 '66

Politics and government
Atlantic report; issues of concern. Atlan 218: 26+ O '66
Johnson-Connally axis. Nation 202:605 My 23 '66
Me for ma, and I ain't got a dern thing against pa; M. Ferguson as governor of Texas. R. S. Gallagher. il Am Heritage 17:46-7+ O '66
New Texas voters: Governor J. Connally's new law to avenge poll tax removal. Nation 202:381 Ap 4 '66
Politics on the king's ranch. R. Sherrill. il N Y Times Mag p43+ Je 5 '66
Quiet change; Negro office seekers win. il Time 87:31-2 My 20 '66
Two-party party. il Time 88:36 O 7 '66

TEXAS agricultural and mechanical university.
See Texas A&M university system, College Station—Texas A&M university, College Station

TEXAS A&M university system. College Station

Texas A&M university, College Station
Data processing in an academic library; circulation and serials systems. B. W. Stewart. il Wilson Lib Bul 41:388-95 D '66

TEXAS Gulf sulphur company
Cashing in on an inside tip; SEC vs. Texas Gulf sulphur company. M. Adams. New Repub 155:14-16 Jl 30 '66
Inside out; SEC lawsuit; decision. Newsweek 68:58 Ag 29 '66
New tack on insider trading. Bsns W p 150 D 10 '66
Ten without intent; accused of using insiders' information. Time 88:68 Ag 26 '66
Timmins bonanza reaches the surface; deposits of copper, zinc, silver, and lead. il Bsns W p92-4 N 26 '66
Where the Texas Gulf ruling could lead; court decision on insider trading case. il Bsns W p 112+ Ag 27 '66

TEXAS Instruments, Incorporated
Breakthrough in on-the-job training. E. R. Gomersall and M. S. Myers. il Harvard Bsns R 44:62-72 Jl '66

TEXAS observer
Eye on Texas. Newsweek 67:62 Mr 7 '66

TEXAS. University, Austin
New roundup? il Newsweek 67:101-2+ Ap 18 '66
Texas education. W. Morris. Commentary 42:23-32 Ag '66
Texas oil industry project; University archives in Eugene C. Barker Texas history center. C. V. Kielman. il Wilson Lib Bul 40:616-18 Mr '66
See also
Texas Western college, El Paso, Tex.

Libraries
LBJ library model unveiled in Texas. il Library J 92:37 Ja 1 '67
Ten-gallon stack. il Time 88:84 D 9 '66

TEXAS Western college, El Paso, Tex.
Conduct unbecoming; lieutenant on the peace line; case of H. H. Howe. J. Rechy. il Nation 202:204-8 F 21 '66; Reply. J. L. Howe. 202:346+ Mr 28 '66
Defense by a coyote caller. J. Jares. il Sports Illus 24:48-9 F 7 '66

TEXTBOOK censorship. See Censorship

TEXTBOOK publishers institute, American.
See American textbook publishers institute

TEXTBOOKS
ATPI statistical charts, 1965. il Pub W 189: 30-3 My 30 '66
Big drive for balance; multiracial textbook. il Time 88:53 Ag 19 '66
Evaluation of materials for teaching; a dilemma; report of ATPI annual industry conference. il Pub W 191:26-9 Ja 9 '67
House committee studies treatment of minorities in text and library books; report of hearings. il Pub W 190:34-40 S 19 '66
House hearings called on minority groups in texts. Pub W 190:56 Ag 22 '66
House hearings hit textbooks on grounds of racial bias. Pub W 190:39-40 S 5 '66
I.P.A. educational group meets during the fair. il Pub W 190:29-32 N 7 '66
Integrating the texts; the American Negro in U. S. textbooks. il Newsweek 67:93-4+ Mr 7 '66
Minority groups in texts and library books; hearings before the House ad hoc subcommittee on de facto school segregation. G. Krettek and E. D. Cooke. Wilson Lib Bul 41:235 O '66
Norton to publish M.I.T. physics texts. Pub W 190:199 Jl 11 '66
Publishers study impact of U.S. school-aid funds; ABPC meeting on Changing nature and scope of the school and library market; summary of conference. il Pub W 189: 28-50 My 23 '66
Textbook artist. il Design 67:4-7 Ja; 16-25 Mr '66
Textbooks and the child-benefit theory. America 116:36-7 Ja 14 '67
See also
Publishers and publishing—Textbooks
Social science—Textbooks
United States—History—Textbooks

Anecdotes, facetiae, satire, etc.
Logical extreme reading method; textbooks cutting across all three socio-economic levels. M. Bennett. Pub W 189:33-5 Mr 14 '66

Exhibitions
See Book exhibits

Central America
Free textbooks for Central American schools; Alliance project financed by Agency for international development. il Sch & Soc 94:342-3 O 29 '66

United States
See Textbooks

TEXTILE design
Happy rediscovery of Romanesque. il House & Gard 129:118-23 F '66
Textiles; symposium. il Craft Horiz 26:32-4 Je '66
See also
Weaving

Study and teaching
Leaf printing with textile paint. R. Wilcox. il Design 68:38-42 S '66

TEXTILE fabrics
Fabrics for elegance; party clothes. McCalls 94:52 O '66
Fabulous fabrics for your windows! P. Rumely and N. Cordts. il Bet Hom & Gard 44:78-83 N '66

TEXTILE fabrics—*Continued*
What's new with permanent press. J. Gillies and N. Bowden. Farm J 90:66-7 N '66
See also
Paper textiles
Silk
Textile finishing

Dyeing
See Dyes and dyeing

Finishing
See Textile finishing

Fireproofing
See Fireproofing of textiles

Protection
Stain-resistant fabric finishes you can apply. E. Taylor. il Good H 162:226 Je '66

Softening
See Softening agents

TEXTILE fabrics, Flammable
Clothing catches on fire. Consumer Bul 49:16 N '66

TEXTILE fabrics, Synthetic
GH reports on stretch fabrics and fashions. il Good H 162:178+ My '66
Great, phony, outdoors. il Newsweek 67:92 My 30 '66
Today's miracle fabrics, fibers, finishes and fashion. P. Rumely. il Bet Hom & Gard 44:46-59 My '66

TEXTILE fibers
See also
Fiber research

TEXTILE fibers, Synthetic
Indoor-outdoor carpets; polypropylene fiber carpets. Consumer Bul 49:22-3 Ag '66
Now you can have a wall-to-wall lawn; all-synthetic carpeting for poolsides, patios, sidewalks and supermarkets. il Bsns W p88-90+ Jl 16 '66
Too many fibers spoil the miracle; overcapacity putting pressure on prices and earnings. il Bsns W p 165-6+ O 29 '66
See also
Fiber research
Textile fabrics, Synthetic

TEXTILE finishing
Alteration aid for permanent press garments; Alter-ease. il Consumer Bul 49:43 S '66
At last: woolens you can wash by machine. J. A. Morris. Read Digest 89:233-7 O '66
Built-in press for your clothes; Koret of California revolutionized industry. D. Wharton. Read Digest 88:128-31 F '66
Graffiti with a grapefruit; chameleon cloth. P. Stewart. il Sports Illus 24:46-7 F 21 '66
Miracle fabrics and new equipment add up to easier laundering. R. Charles. il Parents Mag 41:89-92+ O '66
Permanent-press shirts (cont) il Consumer Rep 31:232-3 My '66
Pressed & impressed; permanent-crease process. Time 87:67 Ap 15 '66
What's the story on durable press? il Good H 162:195+ Ap '66

TEXTILE industry
See also
Textile finishing

Computer installations
Computers cultivate an eye for color; electronic monitors taking control of many variables in textile dyeing. il Bsns W p 106+ O 15 '66

Wages and hours
Earnings in synthetic textile mills, September 1965. C. M. O'Connor. il Mo Labor R 89:762-5 Jl '66
Wages in synthetic fibers, textile finishing, and dress manufacturing. il Mo Labor R 89:1255-61 N '66

India
New generation sets the pace; India's Charat Ram expands family's textile mills into new industrial areas. il Bsns W p82-4 D 24 '66

United States
Looming prosperity. il Time 87:94 Ap 8 '66
See also
Cotton industry and trade
Deering, Milliken and company

TEXTILE workers
See also
Cotton mills—Employees
Textile industry—Wages and hours

TEXTILE workers union of America
Jim Crow and 14-B. H. Golden. New Repub 155:16-18 N 12 '66

TEYSSÈDRE, Bernard
Largillere's portrait of Elizabeth Throckmorton. Art N 64:44-7+ Ja '66

THABIT, Walter
Cities of Charles Abrams. New Repub 154:42+ My 14 '66

THACH, R. E. and others
Formylmethionine codon AUG as an initiator of polypeptide synthesis. bibliog Science 153:416-18 Jl 22 '66

THACKRAY, John
Dilemma with directors. Duns R 88:48-9+ O '66

THAI, Vu-van-. See Vu-van-Thai
THAI dancing. See Dancing, Thai
THAI race
Most beautiful word in English? Bangkok says, progress. W. Warren. il N Y Times Mag p 18-19+ Ag 7 '66

THAILAND
See also
Americans in Thailand
Architecture, Domestic—Thailand
Ayutthaya
Bangkok
Communism—Thailand
Guerrillas—Thailand
United Nations—Thailand

Defenses
ARPA team aids Thailand in developing R&D capability. M. Getler. Tech W 19:17-18 D 19 '66
See also
United States—Armed forces—Forces in Thailand

Foreign relations
Memo from Thailand. S. Castan. Look 30:90+ Mr 22 '66
Thailand fights for freedom; policies and projects to combat communism. C. T. Rowan. il Read Digest 89:217-18+ S '66
U.S. and Thailand sign treaty of amity and economic relations. Dept State Bul 54:991-2 Je 20 '66
Vice President reviews Asian problems with Thai premier; joint communique. February 15, 1966. H. H. Humphrey and T. Kittikachorn. Dept State Bul 54:396-7 Mr 14 '66

History
Thailand: a second South Viet Nam? ed. by E. Sparn. il Sr Schol 88:7-10 F 25 '66

Native races
Living with Thailand's gentle Lua. P. Kunstadter. il Nat Geog Mag 130:122-52 Jl '66

Politics and government
Dragon train to Singapore; trip on Thailand-Singapore dragon train. W. Eastlake. il Nation 203:283-4 S 26 '66
Holder of the kingdom, strength of the land. il Time 87:28-30+ My 27 '66
Memo from Thailand. S. Castan. Look 30:90+ Mr 22 '66
Menace in the northeast; program to counter guerrillas. il Time 87:32 F 25 '66
Next on Peking's hit parade? S. Topping. il N Y Times Mag p30-1+ F 20 '66
Pictures in our minds; concerning NBC documentary The battle for Asia. New Repub 156:9-10 Ja 7 '67
Thailand fights for freedom; policies and projects to combat communism. C. T. Rowan. il Read Digest 89:217-18+ S '66
Thailand; is this something to fall back on? A. Campbell. New Repub 154:17-20 Mr 26 '66
Thailand: its meaning for the U.S. B. K. Gordon. bibliog f il Cur Hist 52:16-21+ Ja '67
Thailand: the anatomy of a domino. il Newsweek 67:35-6+ Ja 31 '66
Where we're a little ahead. il Time 88:22 Ag 12 '66
See also
Communism—Thailand

THAILAND and the United States
Most beautiful word in English? Bangkok says, progress. W. Warren. il N Y Times Mag p 18-19+ Ag 7 '66
Thailand; is this something to fall back on? A. Campbell. New Repub 154:17-20 Mr 26 '66

THAIS (people) See Thai race
THAL, Ron
Beauty of open shade. il U S Camera 29:60-1 S '66

THALER, Mike
All in line. il Opera N 30:12-14 Je 4 '66

THALIDOMIDE
Intravenous injection of thalidomide in pregnant rabbits. R. R. Fox and others. bibliog il Science 153:310-11 Jl 15 '66; Discussion. 154:1362 D 9 '66

THANE, Adele
King Alfred and the cakes; dramatization of an old English folktale. Plays 25:79-84 My '66
Rip Van Winkle; dramatization of story by W. Irving. Plays 25:53-61 Ap '66
Sleeping beauty; dramatization of story by C. Perrault. Plays 25:67-74 Mr '66
Three wishes; dramatization of An English folktale. Plays 25:69-74 Ap '66

THANK you, Miss Victoria; drama. See Hoffman, W.

THANKS. See Thanksgiving

THANKSGIVING
To God thanks; meditation. F. J. Mc Garrigle. America 115:690 N 26 '66

THANKSGIVING day
Now, the grateful society; excerpt from proclamation. il Time 88:27 O 28 '66
Thought for Thanksgiving. il Ebony 22:64-5 N '66
To God, thanks; meditation. F. J. Mc Garrigle. America 115:690 N 26 '66

Drama
Nothing to be thankful for. M. Hark and N. McQueen. Plays 26:53-62 N '66
Peace, Pilgrim. H. Cable. Plays 26:1-14 N '66
Then came the good harvest. C. E. Scott. Plays 26:70-4 N '66

THANKSGIVING dinners
Change-of-pace dishes in the Thanksgiving tradition; excerpts from The art of American Indian cooking. N. Nichols. il Farm J 90:70-1+ N '66
For Thanksgiving dinner. Redbook 28:106+ N '66
Season's fare. H. S. Witty. Flower Grower 53:8 N '66
Thanksgiving desserts, only the flavors are traditional. il Sunset 137:166+ N '66
Thanksgiving dinner with my European mother-in-law. il Sunset 137:72-7 N '66
Try a New England Thanksgiving; with recipes and menu. G. Maddox. il Todays Health 44:54-9 N '66

THANKSGIVING proclamations
Thanksgiving proclamation, 1966. Christian Cent 83:1367 N 9 '66

THANT, 1909-
Address to the Consultative assembly of the Council of Europe at Strasbourg, France, May 3, 1966. pors UN Mo Chron 3:51-60 Je '66
Appointment of Secretary General; statement, December 2, 1966. UN Mo Chron 3: 5-7 D '66
Assembly anniversary; message; January 7, 1966. UN Mo Chron 3:65-6 F '66
Democracy and peace; address, May 24, 1966. UN Mo Chron 3:61-70 Je '66
Development decade; summary of interim report. UN Mo Chron 3:36-7 Je '66
Human rights day 1966; message. UN Mo Chron 3:ii-iii D '66
International convention on the elimination of all forms of racial discrimination; statement. December 21, 1965. UN Mo Chron 3:103-4 Ja '66
Interview; BBC programme entitled People to watch, May 1, 1966. UN Mo Chron 3: 57-66 My '66
Introduction to the annual report of the Secretary-General on the work of the organization. UN Mo Chron 3:93-122 O '66
Message to British council; October 19, 1966. UN Mo Chron 3:75 D '66
Message to OAU assembly; November 5, 1966. UN Mo Chron 3:75 D '66
New Year message, 1966. UN Mo Chron 3:i-ii Ja '66
Press conference; January 20, 1966. UN Mo Chron 3:33-43 F '66
Press conference, September 19, 1966; summary. UN Mo Chron 3:30-2 O '66
Remarks to press on developments in Viet-Nam. UN Mo Chron 3:32 Ag '66
Secretary-General opens 1966 session; with summary of statement. March 8, 1966. UN Mo Chron 3:13-14 Ap '66
Special committee elects officers; with summary of statement by the Secretary-General. UN Mo Chron 3:13-14 Mr '66
Statement on second term; September 1, 1966. UN Mo Chron 3:37-9 Ag '66
Trip to Latin America; summary of talks, addresses, and press conferences. UN Mo Chron 3:36 Ag '66

United Nations day 1966; message. UN Mo Chron 3:i-ii O '66
Visit to Europe; summary of talks, addresses, and press conferences. UN Mo Chron 3:29-36 My; 29-33 Je; 24-7 Jl; 33-5 Ag '66
World bank's 20th anniversary; summary of message of congratulations. UN Mo Chron 3:57 Jl '66

about
Absolutely, Mr G! new five-year term. Newsweek 68:61 D 12 '66
Appointment of Secretary-General; appointment extended; with text of statement. UN Mo Chron 3:3-5 N '66
Appointment of Secretary-General; with summary of statement by A. R. Pazhwak, December 2, 1966. por UN Mo Chron 3:3-5 D '66
Frailest of them all. M. Ascoli. Reporter 35: 26 O 6 '66
Man for all nations. E. J. Hughes. por Newsweek 68:62-3 D 12 '66
Mood of resignation. por Newsweek 68:35-6 S 12 '66
New life, new crises for the United Nations. il por U S News 61:36+ D 19 '66
New Viet role for U Thant? Sr Schol 89:14-15 Ja 6 '67
Peace talks; U Thant gets go-ahead, but; summary of letter. A. J. Goldberg. por U S News 62:11 Ja 2 '67
Re-election of U Thant. Time 88:38+ D 9 '66
Re-election of U Thant. W. Lippmann. Newsweek 68:19 D 19 '66
750 million couches. Reporter 34:16 F 10 '66
Thanks to U Thant. Christian Cent 83:1527 D 14 '66
Time of frustration. por Time 88:38 S 9 '66
U Thant. N. Cousins. Sat R 49:32 O 1 '66
U Thant; another term, and more power in U.N? U S News 61:14 D 12 '66
U Thant, by J. Bingham. Review
  Sat R por 49:34 Je 18 '66. K. K. L. Kuliang
U Thant on war and peace. A. Weill-Tuckerman. Nation 203:38-9 Jl 11 '66
U Thant; the early years. J. Bingham. por (cover) Sat R 49:16-17 My 28 '66
U Thant's decision. New Repub 155:7-8 D 10 '66
U Thant's price. por Sat Eve Post 239:118 O 8 '66
U Thant's retirement; a helpful dilemma. D. Lawrence. U S News 61:128 O 3 '66
U Thant's secret. Commonweal 85:311-12 D 16 '66
United Nations at twenty-one. il pors Newsweek 68:35-9 O 3 '66
U.S. hopes U.N. will extend Secretary-General's term; statement, September 1, 1966. A. J. Goldberg. Dept State Bul 55:434-5 S 19 '66
U.S. pleased at reappointment of U.N. Secretary-General; text of letter from President Johnson, December 3 and statement by Ambassador Goldberg, December 2, 1966. L. B. Johnson; A. J. Goldberg. Dept State Bul 56:14-15 Ja 2 '67
Unmistakable reproach. Christian Cent 83: 1105 S 14 '66
What is a Secretary General? F. T. P. Plimpton. il por N Y Times Mag p58-9+ N 27 '66
Why U Thant is indispensable at the U.N. il por U S News 61:16 S 19 '66
World needs U Thant. Christian Cent 83:1168-9 S 28 '66

THAO, Sie. See Sie Thao

THAXTER, J. B. See Tannenwald, P. E. jt. auth.

THAYER, Charles W.
Don't shoot unless you're loaded. Sports Illus 25:96-102+ D 5 '66
Mongolia; odd prize in the red tug-of-war? Look 31:60+ Ja 24 '67

THAYER, Gertrude May (Wheeler)
Muzzy, by C. W. Thayer. Review
  Life 61:17 Jl 1 '66. E. Kimbrough

THEATER
Broadway postscript; plays without plots. H. Hewes. Sat R 49:43 Ap 23 '66
Engineers had all the fun; nine evenings; theatre and engineering, 69th Regiment armory. D. Hering. il Dance Mag 40:36-40 D '66
King; interview. M. Escande. New Yorker 42:29-31 F 26 '66
Modern theater or, the world as a metaphor of dread; Time essay. Time 88:34-5 Jl 8 '66
Other events; Nine evenings; Theatre and engineering, at the Sixty-ninth regiment armory. R. Adler. New Yorker 42:116+ N 12 '66

THEATER—*Continued*

Theater of cruelty. M. Esslin. il N Y Times Mag p22-3+ Mr 6 '66

Theater of mystery; from the absurd to the religious. P. Martin. Commonweal 84:582-5 S 16 '66

Third theater that is superb, gay and wild. R. Brustein. il N Y Times Mag p32-3+ S 25 '66; Discussion. p22+ O 16 '66

See also

Actors and actresses
Amateur theatricals
Comedy
Drama
Dramatic criticism
Opera
Pantomime
Vaudeville

Bibliography

See also

Theatrical literature

Censorship

See Dramatic censorship

Equipment

See Theatrical production

Finance

See also

Theatrical production

Moral and religious aspects

Theater of commitment; excerpt from address. E. Bentley. Commentary 42:63-72 D '66

Stage mechanism

See also

Opera—Stage mechanism

Stage scenery

Lights! camera! model rooms! B. Plumb. il N Y Times Mag p 106-7 Mr 20 '66

Mielziner: stage designs; interview. J. Mielziner. New Yorker 42:44-5 Mr 19 '66

Soviet scene. E. Elder. il Opera N 30:8-13 My 7 '66

Spoleto's choice; exhibition of Three centuries of theater design. S. Preston. il Opera N 31:20-3 S 10 '66

Stage design: bogged in tradition, startlingly new. il Esquire 66:64-5 Jl '66

Canada

Theater; Ontario's Shaw festival. H. Hewes. Sat R 49:38 Ag 27 '66

China

See also

Chinese drama

Czechoslovakia

See also

Prague—Theater

Europe, Eastern

Opinion; on the east European theatre. H. Popkin. Mlle 64:120+ N '66

France

See also

Comédie-Française
Paris—Theater

Germany (Federal Republic)

Broadway postscript; Munich Bavarian state theater at the New York city center. H. Hewes. Sat R 49:43 Ap 23 '66

European literary scene; new dramas. R. J. Clements. Sat R 49:29 Mr 26 '66

History onstage; documentary movement. il Newsweek 67:81-2 Ja 31 '66

Great Britain

Gale of shock rips across the British stage; with report by P. Gilliat and photographs by Lord Snowden. Life 60:88-98+ My 20 '66

Theatre: kinky, arrogant and frankly magnificent. R. Gilman. il Esquire 66:62-3+ Jl '66

See also

London—Theater

Ireland

See also

Dublin—Theater

Mexico

See also

Mexico (city)—Theater

New England

Theatre: New England. J. Novick. Nation 203:130-3 Ag 8 '66

Ontario

See Theater—Canada

Poland

Performance from Poland; Jerzy Grotowski's laboratory theatre of Wroclaw. A. Freund. New Repub 155:35-6 Jl 30 '66

Russia

Soviet scene. E. Elder. il Opera N 30:8-13 My 7 '66

Sweden

Swedish theater; subsidized and commercial enterprises. H. Hewes. Sat R 49:47 My 21 '66

See also

Stockholm—Theater

History

Mozart. Moliere. and cupid; Drottningholm court theatre. M. Moseley. il Dance Mag 40:56-61 S '66

United States

Completely off Broadway. J. L. Collier. Holiday 39:32+ Mr '66

Festivity and ritual: reflections on true theatre. H. Clurman. il Nation 202:583-7 My 16 '66

Good theater of Stanford. H. Hewes. Sat R 49:55 Je 4 '66

One for the road; Helen Hayes repertory company tour. G. Weales. Reporter 34:54-5 My 19 '66

Pacific coast; postwar resident professional theatres. J. Novick. Nation 202:755-8 Je 20 '66

Pisthetairos in Ypsi; Ypsilanti, Mich, home of America's first classic Greek repertory theater il Newsweek 68:85-6 Jl 11 '66

Summer repertory schedule, 1966. H. Hewes. Sat R 49:55 Je 4 '66

[Theatre across America] J. Novick. Nation 202:626-9, 689-93; 203:27-30, 130-3, 195-8 My 23, Je 6, Jl 4, Ag 8, S 5 '66

Theater in the red. J. J. Greene. Cath World 202:364-8 Mr '66

Tragedy of American theater. J. Simon. il Holiday 39:76-83+ Mr '66

Where the theater is. C. H. Simonds. Nat R 18:223-4+ Mr 8 '66

With a comic to the Catskills; interview. P. Foster. New Yorker 42:30-1 Je 11 '66

See also

College and school drama
Improvisation (acting)
Theater, Negro

also subhead Theater under names of cities, e.g. Fort Worth, Tex.—Theater

History

How a playwright triumphs; interview. ed. by A. Wagner. C. Odets. Harper 233:64-70+ S '66

Integration on the stage. T. Lewis. America 115:213-14 Ag 27 '66

What will happen next? M. Esslin. il N Y Times Mag pt2 p20-1+ S 11 '66

THEATER, Childrens

Debut of a children's theater; Newington, Conn. C. Lemire. il Parks & Rec 1:142-4 F '66

Guffawhaw, Paper bag players, Henry street settlement playhouse. M. Marks. Dance Mag 40:77 D '66

THEATER, Municipal and national

[Theatre across America] J. Novick. Nation 202:626-9, 689-93; 203:27-30, 130-3, 195-8 My 23, Je 6, Jl 4, Ag 8, S 5 '66

THEATER, Negro

Free Southern theatre. R. J. Schroeder. Commonweal 83:696-7 Mr 18 '66

Hand is on the gate. America 115:432 O 8 '66

Loving. healing kind of theater; Free Southern theater. T. Prideaux. Life 61:24 S 16 '66

Theatre; Hand is on the gate. J. McCarten. New Yorker 42:121-2 O 1 '66

THEATER, Open air

Family terrace: teen-age theatre; Virginia country theatre. il House & Gard 130:104-5+ Jl '66

Mexico's strolling players; teatro Trashumante (Nomadic theater) J. Linde. il Américas 18:34-7 N '66

Mock murder to cool Watts; street pantomimes given, to promote better understanding between races. il Life 61:85-6 Ag 19 '66

THEATER and children

Shakespeare speaks to kids; how to encourage natural interest. H. Taubman. il Parents Mag 41:72-3+ O '66

THEATER and engineering festival. See Festivals

THEATER and state
Letter from Paris; threat of subsidy cut, because of Genet's Les paravents (The screens) at Théâtre de France. Genêt. New Yorker 42:223-5 N 19 '66

THEATER Atlanta. See Atlanta—Theater

THEATER buildings
Florida flourishes; Asolo theater, Sarasota. H. Hewes. Sat R 49:39 Ag 20 '66
Florida rococo; Asolo theater brought from Italy to Sarasota, Fla. T. Hoffman. il Opera N 30:6-7 F 5 '66

THEATER festivals. See Drama festivals

THEATER in the street. See New York (city) —Theater

THEATER of cruelty. See Theater

THEATER of illusion. See Theater

THEATER of the absurd. See Theater

THEATRE of the living arts. See Philadelphia —Theater

THEATER photography. See Photography, Theatrical

THEATRICAL directors
How playwrights lose. W. Kerr. Harper 233: 75-80 S '66
In a strange land. J. Gielgud. Opera N 30: 8-9 F 12 '66
See also
Prince, H. S.
Zeffirelli, F.

THEATRICAL literature
Books in the field: drama. I. Deer. bibliog il Wilson Lib Bul 41:318-24 N '66

THEATRICAL make-up. See Make-up, Theatrical

THEATRICAL photography. See Photography, Theatrical

THEATRICAL production
Face to face: with a dresser with dreams. L. Saroyan. Seventeen 25:137 F '66
Face to face with a writer-producer-director-actor; ed. by C. Schwalberg. G. Harris, 3d. Seventeen 26:19 Ja '67
Festivity and ritual: reflections on true theatre. H. Clurman. il Nation 202:583-7 My 16 '66
From TV to Tiffany's in one wild leap; M. T. Moore in Breakfast at Tiffany's. J. Bowers. il Sat Eve Post 239:97-101 N 19 '66
He's Broadway today; D. Merrick's present and future shows. il Newsweek 67:96-7 Mr 21 '66
Hey, stupid, where's the glass? experiences of propman author of Agatha Sue, I love you; interview. A. Einhorn. New Yorker 42:54-5 N 12 '66
Marat/Sade: two front-row ticket holders get hated every night. J. Roddy. il Look 30: 110 F 22 '66
Melina Mercouri rehearses Never on Sunday for Broadway; new title: Illya darling. J. Hamilton. il Look 31:66-71 Ja 24 '67
Subject was faith; success of The subject was roses. J. P. Blank. il Read Digest 88: 144-7 Je '66
See also
College and school drama
Operatic production
Television broadcasting—Program production
Theatrical directors

THEATRICAL properties. See Theatrical production

THEATRICAL revues. See Musical comedies, revues etc

THEFT. See Embezzlement; Shoplifting; Stealing

THEISEN, Bonnie R.
Love. 1966; poem. America 115:514 O 29 '66

THEISM
Dewart on belief. G. Vahanian. Commonweal 85:257-9 D 2 '66

THEK, Paul
Beneath the skin; interview, ed. by G. R. Swenson. Art N 66:34-5+ Ap '66

THELON RIVER
Life along an Arctic river: excerpt from Downstream: a natural history of the river. J. Bardach. il Liv Wildn 29:14-19 Aut '65

THEMATIC apperception test. See Personality tests

THEME writing. See English language—Composition

THEN came the good harvest; drama. See Scott, C. E.

THEOBALD, Robert
Abundance in perspective: should men compete with machines? Nation 202:544-50 My 9 '66
Guaranteed income; address, May 21, 1966. Vital Speeches 32:573-6 Jl 1 '66
Higher education and cybernation. NEA J 55:26-9 Mr '66

THEODOLITES
New cinetheodolite enhances accuracy. D. A. Anderton. il Miss & Roc 18:42-5 My 9 '66
Theodolite, gyro combined for improved guidance accuracy; instrument using Barnes miniature electronic autocollimator. C. D. LaFond. il Tech W 19:32-3 N 14 '66

THEOLOGIANS
Contemporary continental theologians, by S. P. Schilling. Review
Christian Cent 83:833 Je 29 '66. C. W. Kegley
New theologian, by V. Mehta. Review
Sat R 49:56 N 12 '66. R. Muska

THEOLOGICAL education
Christian ethics amid pietistic culture-Protestantism. T. C. Oden. Christian Cent 83 525-6+ Ap 27 '66
Ecumenism and philosophy. G. F. Kreyche. bibliog f Christian Cent 83:521-4 Ap 27 '6
Letter from the fringe: a defense of the nonpastoral ministry. L. R. Lindsay. Christian Cent 83:1075-7 S 7 '66; Discussion. 83:1306 O 26 '66
Pre-seminary education, by K. R. Bridston and D. W. Culver. Review
Christian Cent 83:558-61 Ap 27 '66. R H. King
Time, tide and seminary priorities. W. D. Wagoner. Christian Cent 83:519-21 Ap 2 '66
See also
Theological schools

THEOLOGICAL schools
Ecumenical way of learning; Manhattan's Protestant union theological seminary and Fordham university exchange projects. Time 87:86 Mr 4 '66
He couldn't say no; New York theological seminary to specialize in urban ministry. il Time 88:70 Ag 5 '66
Liberal charges beset Baptist seminary; Berkeley Baptist divinity school. L. Kinsolving. Christian Cent 84:90+ Ja 18 '67
New seminaries in Europe. W. F. Jabusch. Commonweal 85:17-21 O 7 '66
New theological college in the Caribbean; United theological college of the West Indies. A. J. Hunter. Christian Cent 83:1488 N 30 '66
Not all is golden at Golden Gate. Christian Cent 83:672-3 My 25 '66
Philadelphia story; expulsion of five seminarians from St Charles seminary, Overbrook, Pa. S. J. Adamo. America 115:756-8 D 3 '66
Please reconsider, Cardinal Cushing! Christian Cent 83:453-4 Ap 13 '66
Poland's battle over seminaries. America 116:33 Ja 14 '67
Reform in the seminaries; carrying out new spirit of freedom in the Catholic church. il Time 87:60 Ap 15 '66
Revolt in the seminary; St John's seminary, Boston. il Newsweek 67:68-9 Ap 18 '66
Seminary for a Baptist college; Bethel college and seminary. il Arch Rec 140:110-11 Ag '66
Seminary: Protestant and Catholic. by W. D. Wagoner. Review
America 115:664-6 N 19 '66. S. Poole
Christian Cent 83:1602-3 D 28 '66. J. L. McKenzie
Commonweal 85:376 Ja 6 '67. R. E. McNally
Seminary town: Rome. il Time 88:94 O 14 '66
Turmoil in Boston; St John's seminary, Brighton, Mass. Commonweal 84:68-70 Ap 8 '66
See also
Chicago. University—Federated theological schools
Harvard university—Divinity school
Jewish theological seminary of America, New York

Cooperation
Toward seminary merger; possible forms of cooperation. J. L. Leavenworth. Christian Cent 83:527-8+ Ap 27 '66

Directories
Directory: seminary offerings. il Christian Cent 83:529-58 Ap 27 '66

THEOLOGICAL students
Dangerous mission. Christian Cent 83:641-2 My 18 '66
Of many things; seminarian's summer activities. M. P. Sheridan. America 115:264 S 17 '66
Please reconsider, Cardinal Cushing! Christian Cent 83:453-4 Ap 13 '66
Reform in the seminaries; carrying out new spirit of freedom in the Catholic church. il Time 87:60 Ap 15 '66

THEOLOGICAL students—*Continued*
Seminarians and service. R. P. Mohan. America 114:384-5 Mr 19 '66
What would John Wesley do about it? Union theological students vs. Methodist church's board of missions. Christian Cent 83:1264 O 19 '66; Reply. D. W. Hornbeck and others. 83:1506-7 D 7 '66

THEOLOGY
Christian ethics and contemporary philosophy, ed. by I. T. Ramsey. Review Christian Cent 84:84 Ja 18 '67. W. Hordern
Church to die in or to live in? M. P. Ryan Cath World 203:17-21 Ap '66
Contemporary theological institute; third annual meeting, report. A. Padovano. Christian Cent 83:1062-4 Ag 31 '66
Demythologizing the new theology. W. B. Glover. Christian Cent 83:882-4 Jl 13 '66; Discussion. 83:1085 S 7 '66
Evolution in moral theology. G. H. Tavard Cath World 203:29-32 Ap '66
Future of belief, by L. Dewart. Review Newsweek 68:67 N 7 '66. K. L. Woodward
God and the human mind, by F. J. Sheed. Review Commonweal 85:202 N 18 '66. D. J. O'Hanlon
Heresy by translation; Service book and hymnal used by National Lutheran council churches. C. R. McCormack. Christian Cent 83:437-8 Ap 6 '66
Heretic or prophet? il Time 88:56-8+ N 11 '66
Hermeneutical theology. J. M. Robinson. Christian Cent 83:579-82 My 4 '66
Learning church in a teaching world. E. C. Bianchi. Cath World 203:287-92 Ag '66
Life in the old boys yet! B. A. Reist. Christian Cent 83:1179-80 S 28 '66
Logic of religion. D. Callahan; reply. M. Barnes. Commonweal 83:565-6 F 11 '66
New Presbyterian creed; excerpts from the proposed Confession of 1967 approved May 24, 1966 by the General assembly of the United Presbyterian church. Cath World 203:307-8 Ag '66
Place and purpose of theology. H. Cox; discussion. Christian Cent 83:239 F 23 '66
Post-Vatican II theology. W. Herberg. Nat R 18:421-4 My 3 '66
Principles of Christian theology, by J. Macquarrie. Review Christian Cent 83:1243 O 12 '66. B. F. Wade
Radical theology and the death of God, by T. J. J. Altizer and W. Hamilton. Review Christian Cent 83:622-4 My 11 '66. F. Ferré
Radical theology; from honest-to-God to God-is-dead. R. P. McBrien. Commonweal 84:605-8 S 23 '66
Relational nature of theology. D. Callahan. Christian Cent 83:135-7 F 2 '66; Discussion. 83:372 Mr 23 '66
Stress on the Spirit. Time 88:69-70 Ag 5 '66
Theological asides (cont) C. Davis. America 114:445, 800 Ap 2, Je 4 '66
Theological historicism as an experiment in thought. G. D. Kaufman. Christian Cent 83:268-71 Mr 2 '66; Discussion. 83:439-40 Ap 6 '66
Theology in the living room; group discussions among Christians. il Time 88:50 Jl 8 '66
Torah and gospel; Jewish and Catholic theology in dialogue, ed. by P. Scharper. Review Cath World 203:309-10 Ag '66. G. Baum
What can Catholicism learn from the free churches? D. O'Hanlon. Cath World 203:81-5 My '66; Reply. E. Gibson. 204:225-9 Ja '67
See also
Authority (religion)
Catechetics
Christian life
Christianity
Death of God theology
Eschatology
God
Good and evil
Heresy
Love (theology)
Mary, Virgin—Theology
Protestantism
Rationalism
Religion
Religion and science
Revelation
Sacraments
Salvation
Secularism
Theism
Time (theology)
Worship

Bibliography
God and his men. W. R. Miller. New Repub 155:29-32 N 26 '66
Urban renewal of religion; the God is dead theologians and their books. D. Poling. Sat R 49:30-1+ My 14 '66; Discussion. 49:22+ Je 25 '66

Study and teaching
See also
Theological schools

THEOLOGY, Doctrinal
Doctrinal development. G. H. Tavard. Cath World 202:336-40 Mr '66

THERA (island)
How a civilization disappeared; Minoan civilization. Time 87:46+ My 6 '66
Serene Santorin. J. Meehan. il Travel 126:35-7 Jl '66
Volcano that shaped the western world; Santorini eruption: theories of A. Galanopoulos. J. Lear. il Sat R 49:57-60+ N 5 '66; Discussion. 49:93-4 D 3 '66

THERAPEUTIC abortion. See Abortion

THERAPEUTIC reading. See Bibliotherapy

THERAPEUTICS
Doctors who disagree. il Sci Digest 60:20-1 S '66
See also
Acupuncture
Chelation therapy
Drugs
Occupational therapy
Psychotherapy
Ultrasonic waves—Medical applications

THERE'S a camel in my cocktail; story. See Eastlake, W.

THÉRÈSE, Sister Mary. See Mary Thérèse, Sister

THERESIANS (organization)
Convention: the Theresians; organization of Catholic lay women to encourage religious vocations among Catholic girls. America 115:642 N 19 '66

THERMAL adaptation. See Adaptation (biology)

THERMAL conductivity. See Heat conductivity

THERMAL waters. See Hot springs

THERMIONIC converters
RCA tests thermal energy pipe. J. F. Judge. il Miss & Roc 18:36-8 F 21 '66

THERMISTORS
How to build a weather anticipator. R. M. Benrey. il Pop Sci 189:130-3 N '66
Static-free thermistorized aquarium heater. A. E. Donkin. il Pop Electr 25:73-5+ S '66

THERMO King corporation
Crash hits a company; Thermo King executives and top dealers in wreck of jetliner in Japan. il Bsns W p46 Mr 12 '66
Tragedy at Thermo King: air crash effects. Newsweek 67:83 Mr 21 '66

THERMOCHEMISTRY
See also
Heat of solution

THERMODYNAMIC equilibrium. See Equilibrium (thermodynamic)

THERMODYNAMICS
Organic compounds in carbonaceous chondrites. M. H. Studier and others; discussion. Science 152:102-7 Ap 1 '66

THERMOGRAPHY, Infrared. See Photography, Infrared

THERMOGRAPHY, Medical. See Photography, Medical

THERMOLUMINESCENT dating. See Radioactive dating

THERMOMETERS, Clinical
Clinical thermometers. il Consumer Rep 31:388-90 Ag '66
President ends increased duty on clinical thermometers; White House announcement; with text of proclamation. L. B. Johnson. Dept State Bul 54:159-60 Ja 31 '66
Rectal thermometer. Time 87:47 Ap 8 '66
Report on tests of fever thermometers. il Consumer Bul 49:16-20 S '66

THERMOMETERS, Cooking
Meat thermometers. il Consumer Rep 31:124-6 Mr '66

THERMOMETERS and thermometry
Air thermometers. il Consumer Rep 31:74-7 F '66
This gizmo warns: icy roads. R. M. Benrey. il Pop Sci 188:118 F '66

THERMONUCLEAR reactions. See Nuclear fusion

THERMONUCLEAR war. See Atomic warfare

THERMOPLASTIC rubber. See Rubber, Artificial

THERMOS containers
  Picnic jugs. il Consumer Bul 49:2+ Ag '66
  Testing the new Thermos thermos. C. Conley. il Field & S 71:127 O '66
THERMOSTATS
  Automatic thermostat booster. H. Hilton. il Pop Mech 126:160-1+ D '66
  How to build a weather anticipator. R. M. Benrey. il Pop Sci 189:130-3 N '66
  Solid-state home temperature controller. J. A. Palmer. il Electr World 75:80-3 Je '66
THESSALONIKI industrial complex. See Greece. Modern—Industries
THEY do not always remember; story. See Burroughs, W.
THI, Nguyen-chanh-. See Nguyen-chanh-Thi
THIAMINE pyrophosphate. See Cocarboxylase
THIBODEAU, Ralph
  Fiasco in church music. Commonweal 84:73-5+ Ap 8 '66
THICH Nhat Hanh. See Nhat Hanh
THICH Tam Chau. See Tam Chau
THICH Tri Quang. See Tri Quang
THIEBAUD, Wayne
  Thiebaud: eros in cafeteria. D. Waldman. il Art N 65:39-41+ Ap '66
THIEF; story. See Proulx, E. A.
THIELEN, Benedict
  Other islands, other reefs. Holiday 40:60-7+ D '66
THIESENHUSEN, William C.
  Latin American land reform; enemies of promise. Nation 202:90-4 Ja 24 '66
THIEU, Nguyen-van-. See Nguyen-van-Thieu
THIEVES
  Copper caper; thieves activities and preventive measures. Newsweek 68:64+ Ag 1 '66
  See also
  Burglary and burglars
  Stealing
THIMANN, Kenneth V.
  Among the plants men live by; excerpt from report. por Sat R 50:118-20 Ja 7 '67
  —and Krauss, R. W.
  AIBS: crisis in retrospect, and the outlook. Science 153:507 Jl 29 '66
  —See Chen, S. S. C; Ruesink, A. W. jt. auths.
THIN, Nguyen-huu-. See Nguyen-huu-Thin
THINKING. See Thought and thinking
THINKING machines. See Computers—Digital computers
THINNESS. See Weight (physiology)
THIOKOL chemical corporation
  Device mass-screens for heart defects. J. F. Judge. il Tech W 19:20+ Ag 8 '66
  How Thiokol weathered the storm; top-to-bottom reorganization. il Bsns W p98-100+ N 12 '66
  New space poll; Trendex poll. W. J. Coughlin. Miss & Roc 18:46 Mr 21 '66
  Systems approach to sounding rockets benefits Thiokol unit. il Tech W 19:25+ S 12 '66
THIRD committee of the General assembly. See United Nations—Social, humanitarian and cultural committee
THIRD party movement. See Political parties —United States
THIRD theater. See Theater
THIRST
  Anticholinergic blockade of centrally induced thirst. R. A. Levitt and A. E. Fisher. bibliog il Science 154:520-2 O 28 '66
35mm cameras. See Cameras
THIRTY-sixth brick; story. See Freeman, J. T.
THIS is the rill speaking; drama. See Wilson, L.
THIS newspaper here; story. See Barthelme, D.
THIS time last year; story. See Rodgers, M. A.
THOM, Robert
  Day it all happened, baby; story. Esquire 66:220-5 D '66
THOMAS More, Saint. See More, T.
THOMAS, Albert
  Albert Thomas: late congressman who supervised NSF budget had witty views on science and politics. D. S. Greenberg. por Science 151:1064-5 Mr 4 '66
THOMAS, Alexander. See Chess, S. jt. auth.
THOMAS, Bill
  Beautiful new Ohio. Outdoor Life 137:54-5+ Je '66
THOMAS, Brinley
  From the other side: a European view. bibliog f Ann Am Acad 367:63-72 S '66

THOMAS, Charles Walker
  Atlanta in retrospect; report on 50th annual meeting. Negro Hist Bul 29:29-30+ N '65
  Historic action in the church. Negro Hist Bul 29:65-6 D '65
  Historical notes. Negro Hist Bul 29:48, 71-2, 120+ N-D '65, F '66
  Negro history observances, 1966. Negro Hist Bul 29:123-4 Mr '66
THOMAS, Dallas L.
  Housecleaning. Newsweek 68:34+ S 26 '66
THOMAS, Danny
  Entertainer, two researchers honored by AMA. por Todays Health 44:17 Ag '66
THOMAS, Dorothy
  Joy cometh in the morning; story. Redbook 128:50-1 D '66
THOMAS, Dylan
  Letters: Dylan Thomas; excerpts from Selected letters of Dylan Thomas, ed. by C. FitzGibbon. Mlle 63:99-101+ Je '66
  Love letters from a poet to his wife; excerpts from Selected letters of Dylan Thomas, ed. by C. FitzGibbon. por McCalls 93:73+ F '66
  Poems; excerpts from The notebooks of Dylan Thomas, ed. by R. Maud. Mlle 63:84-6 Je '66
  Resolutions for 1934; excerpts from Selected letters of Dylan Thomas. Reporter 34:45-6 Mr 24 '66
  about
  Life of Dylan Thomas, by C. FitzGibbon. Review
    Commentary 41:89-93 Ap '66. J. Wain
    New Yorker 41:100-2 Ja 22 '66. N. Bliven
THOMAS, Ellen Lamar
  Instant access to students' reading levels. Library J 91:2165-8 Ap 15 '66
THOMAS, Ernest
  Deacons go north. Newsweek 67:20-1 My 2 '66
THOMAS, Gene
  Great antiques; the Curtiss Fledgling; ed. by B. Kieffer. Flying 80:52-5 Ja '67
THOMAS, George
  A nobody at the Open. J. Underwood. il pors Sports Illus 24:96-100+ Je 13 '66
THOMAS, Gwyn
  Harvest frenzy; story. Reporter 34:41-3 Ap 21 '66
THOMAS, Jack
  More of an individual. il por Newsweek 68:48 N 28 '66
THOMAS, Jean
  Fair deal for the teacher. UNESCO Courier 19:4-6+ S '66
THOMAS, John L.
  What did the council say on contraception? America 114:294-6 F 26 '66
THOMAS, John R. See DeBlock, E. T. jt. auth.
THOMAS, Lewis. See Gesner, B. jt. auth.
THOMAS, Lowell
  Felix von Luckner, RIP. Nat R 18:402 My 3 '66
  Keep an eye on your inner clock. por Read Digest 89:61-4 Ag '66
THOMAS, Norman
  President Johnson's great society. Christian Cent 83:300-3 Mr 9 '66
  about
  Dominican election and the role of the observers. J. Mendelsohn. Christian Cent 83:894-8 Jl 13 '66
THOMAS, R. C. and Wilson, V. J.
  Marking single neurons by staining with intracellular recording microelectrodes. bibliog Science 151:1538-9 Mr 25 '66
THOMAS, R. Murray
  Literacy by decree in Indonesia. bibliog f Sch & Soc 94:279-83 Sum '66
THOMAS, Trevor
  Up from the Red lion inn. por Am Ed 2:16-23 Mr '66
THOMAS, Veronica
  Witches of 1966. Atlan 218:119-25 S '66
  Wizard of Plockropool. Atlan 217:124-6 Je '66
THOMAS R. Coward memorial award
  Gavin Lambert wins first Thomas R. Coward award. Pub W 189:58 Mr 7 '66
THOMASINE Cusack, Sister
  Stockpile strategy. America 114:197-9 F 5 '66
THOMASTON, Me.
  Historic houses, etc.
  Lady Knox. D. Forbes-Robertson. il Am Heritage 17:76-9 Ap '66
THOMASVILLE, N.C.
  Recaning the chair city. P. D. Eimon. il Am City 81:134+ F '66

THOMISM
Philosophy in the Catholic university. J. Donceel. America 115:330-1 S 24 '66; Discussion. 115:470-1; 116:99+ O 22 '66, Ja 21 '67
THOMPSON, Sir Benjamin, count Rumford. See Rumford, B. T.
THOMPSON, Benjamin
Environment as design inspiration. Arch Rec 139:110-20 Ja '66
Let's make it real. por Arch Rec 139:107-9 Ja '66
THOMPSON, Betty
Lengthened shadow. Christian Cent 83:610-11 My 11 '66
Methodist women in quadrennial assembly. Christian Cent 83:784-6 Je 15 '66
THOMPSON, Bob
Obituary
Art N 65:13 S '66
THOMPSON, Dolphin G.
Tolson's gallery brings poetry home. Negro Hist Bul 29:69-70 D '65
THOMPSON, Donald E. See McClarren, R. R. jt. auth.
THOMPSON, Era Bell
Australia: its white policy and the Negro. Ebony 21:46-50+ Jl; 96-8+ S '66
Bishop Harold Perry: man of many firsts. Ebony 21:62-6+ F '66
Dean Dixon: conductor without a country. Ebony 21:78-80+ O '66
What weaker sex? Ebony 21:84-6+ Ag '66
THOMPSON, Eric
Questions and answers about conservatives. Esquire 66:88-9 Jl '66
THOMPSON, Hunter S.
Life styles: the cyclist. Esquire 67:57-63+ Ja '67
THOMPSON, Huston
Huston Thompson: a memoir. H. M. Albright. il por Nat Parks Mag 40:22 Je '66
Obituary
Nat Parks Mag 40:20 Ap '66
THOMPSON, J. Walter, company
Adman with a difference; N. H. Strouse. il Bsns W p 112-14+ Je 18 '66
J. Walter global. Time 88:65 D 23 '66
THOMPSON, James D.
Which glue is best for wood? Pop Mech 126: 138-40+ Ag '66
THOMPSON, James E.
Lath house for plants. Flower Grower 53:75 Mr '66
THOMPSON, James H. W.
House of the happy spirit. il Vogue 147:142-7 Mr 15 '66
THOMPSON, John
Vacancies of August; letter from the Greek islands. Commentary 42:41-51 N '66
THOMPSON, John Beauchamp
Accent; poem. Christian Cent 83:653 My 18 '66
Ikon; poem. Christian Cent 84:76 Ja 18 '67
THOMPSON, Kenneth W.
American education and the developing areas; address; with questions and answers. Ann Am Acad 366:17-32 Jl '66
United Nations on a divided planet. Sat R 49: 41-2 Mr 19 '66
THOMPSON, Llewellyn E. 1904-
United States and Soviet Union sign civil air transport agreement; statement. November 4, 1966; with a Department announcement and texts of the agreement and related documents. Dept State Bul 55: 791-800 N 21 '66

about
Old pros. por Time 88:34 O 14 '66
Return to Moscow for skilled negotiator. por U S News 61:23 O 17 '66
Three for the seesaw. G. Packard. il por Newsweek 68:28 O 17 '66
THOMPSON, Mary E.
Magnesium in sea water: an electrode measurement. bibliog Science 153:866-7 Ag 19 '66
—and Ross, J. W. Jr
Calcium in sea water by electrode measurement. bibliog Science 154:1643-4 D 30 '66
THOMPSON, Mickey
Session with Mickey; interview, ed. by J. McFarland. por Hot Rod 19:80-1 Ag '66
THOMPSON, Myrtle Fish
Arts in therapy. por Parks & Rec 1:712-14, 858+. 926 S-N '66
THOMPSON, Peter E. and English, D. S.
Multiplicity of hemoglobins in the genus chironomus, tendipes. bibliog Science 152: 75-6 Ap 1 '66

THOMPSON, Robert G.
Banned from Valhalla. Nation 202:171 F 14 '66
Beyond the pale. il por Newsweek 67:22+ F 7 '66
Blackballed from Arlington. Time 87:30 F 4 '66
THOMPSON, Sir Robert Grainger Ker
Fiercer tomcat. por Newsweek 67:36 Je 6 '66
THOMPSON, Sally Anne
Dogs. U S Camera 29:56-7 Ag '66
THOMPSON, Scott
Second round for Africa: independence on trial. Atlan 218:79-83 O '66
THOMPSON, Thomas
Hit team back in step. Life 60:102 Mr 25 '66
Music soaring in a darkened world. Life 61:54-6+ Jl 29 '66
Raw dialogue challenges all the censors. Life 60:92+ Je 10 '66
Send the script to Jason. Life 60:83-4+ F 18 '66
THOMPSON, Tracy
For rainy days; poem. Christian Cent 83: 752 Je 8 '66
THOMPSON, Warren M.
Soldier of my country; poem. por Am For 72: 43 S '66
THOMPSON, William Phelps
Layman leader. il Time 87:62 Je 3 '66
THOMPSON Ramo Wooldridge, incorporated. See TRW, incorporated
THOMPSONVILLE, Conn. See Enfield, Conn.
THOMS, Wayne
Behind the bedlam of the featherfoot fleet. Motor T 18:60-2 Mr '66
Make the demonstration ride pay off. Motor T 18:69 N '66
THOMSON, Betty
Betty Thomson's puzzles. W. Accorsi. il pors Craft Horiz 26:24-7 Ja '66
THOMSON, J. Richard, and Dockter, K. W.
Finding life in outer space. Todays Health 44:42-5 Ap '66
THOMSON, James Claude, 1931-
Ex-administration officials discuss U.S. policy in Asia. B. Nelson. por Science 154:988-90 N 25 '66
THOMSON, James Edward
Long look upward. il pors Time 88:66-70 Ag 19 '66
THOMSON, Jean C.
(comp) Children's paperbacks (cont) Library J 91:368+, 2624+, 4252-6 Ja 15, My 15, S 15 '66
(comp) New fall and winter books. Library J 91:5172-211 O 15 '66
(comp) New spring and summer books. Library J 91:1652-86 Mr 15 '66
THOMSON, Keith Stewart
Intracranial mobility in the coelacanth. bibliog Science 153:999-1000 Ag 26 '66
THOMSON, Roy Herbert, 1st baron Thomson of Fleet. See Thomson of Fleet, R. H. T.
THOMSON, Virgil
Burning question. por Opera N 30:8-11 Mr 5 '66
Distaste for music; excerpt from Virgil Thomson. por Vogue 148:292-5+ S 1 '66

about
After thirty-eight years, a landmark: the Thomson Symphony on a hymn tune. C. J. Luten. il pors Am Rec G 32:596-7 Mr '66
In the air of several worlds. H. Clurman. Nation 203:421-2 O 24 '66
Portraitist portrayed. R. Evett. New Repub 155:40-2 N 26 '66
Selective self-portrait. R. Craft. Harper 233: 120+ D '66
Self-portrait. H. Saal. por Newsweek 68:98 N 7 '66
Virgil Thomson's self portrait. R. McMullen. Hi Fi 16:MA21+ N '66
THOMSON of Fleet, Roy Herbert Thomson, 1st baron
Canada's 100th: the birthday party upstairs. Sat R 50:60+ Ja 7 '67

about
Collector's item. por Newsweek 68:98 O 10 '66
Fleet Street fortune at work. J. Tebbel. Sat R 49:102 N 12 '66
Guardian going down? Newsweek 69:62 Ja 9 '67
Lord Thomson adds a jewel to his coronet. il por Bsns W p56-8+ Ja 7 '67
Stealing his thunderer? por Newsweek 68:100 D 5 '66
Thomson takes the Times. Time 88:61 O 7 '66
THOMSON organisation, limited
Fleet Street fortune at work: two seminars in understanding. J. Tebbel. Sat R 49: 101-2 N 12 '66

THOMSON organization, limited—*Continued*
Lord Thomson adds a jewel to his coronet; expanding empire of newspaper, TV, radio, and book properties, acquires Times of London. il Bsns W p56-8+ Ja 7 '67
No Noonday paperbacks in Great Britain. R. W. Straus, jr. Pub W 190:17 O 24 '66
Noonday imprint changed to Sphere books, ltd. Pub W 190:59 O 31 '66
Noonday paperbacks in the U.S. and the U.K. R. W. Straus, jr. Pub W 190:36 O 10 '66

THORBECKE, William J.
Orient: a problem of nonexistence. Sat R 49: 38-9 Mr 26 '66
Search for a constructive peace. Sat R 49: 32-3 Ap 9 '66

THORBURN, G. D. See Stacy, B. D. jt. auth.

THORESEN, Otto
Tale of two ships. il por Time 87:27 Ap 15 '66

THORGERSON, Ring
Should boating be taught in public schools? E. Crimmin. il pors Motor B 117:32-5+ My '66

THORIUM
Manganese nodules: thorium-230: protactinium-231 ratios. W. M. Sackett. bibliog il Science 154:646-7 N 4 '66

THORIUM dating. See Radioactive dating

THORKELSON, Willmar L.
L.C.A. gives final push to L.C.U.S.A. Christian Cent 83:917+ Jl 20 '66

THORMAN, Donald J.
Today's layman: an uncertain Catholic. America 116:39-41 Ja 14 '67

THORNE, Kip S.
Gravitational collapse and the death of a star. bibliog Science 150:1671-9; 153:366+ D 24 '65, Jl 22 '66

THORNEYCROFT, H. B.
Chromosomal polymorphism in the white-throated sparrow, zonotrichia albicollis (gmelin) bibliog Science 154:1571-2 D 23 '66

THORNQUIST, H. T.
How to save on sewer maintenance. Am City 81:104-5 My '66

THORNTON, Wayne
And an Irishman takes a shelllacking at Shea. M. Kram. il por Sports Illus 24: 24-5 My 30 '66

THORON, Gray
Report on judicial ethics. bibliog f Ann Am Acad 363:36-43 Ja '66

THORP, Roderick
Private eye. il por Newsweek 68:89+ Jl 4 '66

THORPE, Azalea
Schubert's shards. Craft Horiz 26:18-19 Ja '66

THORPE, David
Mad mad models of David Thorpe. il U S Camera 29:50-1 Ap '66

THOSE Bufords; story. See Spencer, E.

THOSE who care; story. See Swink, C.

THOUGHT and language
Schools, styles, and systems in thinking; adaptation of address, September 25, 1965. B. Dearing. Sch & Soc 94:317-19+ O 15 '66

THOUGHT and thinking
Change and challenge; address, June 12, 1966. R. Drummond. Vital Speeches 32:660-3 Ag 15 '66
Children's ways of thinking; with study-discussion program, by R. Strang. E. G. Olim. bibliog il PTA Mag 61:20-2, 34 Ja '67
Fantasy life, the human condition, and deep thoughts or, no subject. J. Ciardi. Sat R 49:20-1 Mr 5 '66
Now hear this. il Nations Bsns 54:78-80 Ag '66
Qualities that should be encouraged in children's thinking; excerpts. E. W. Linderman. il Parks & Rec 1:925+ N '66
Schools, styles, and systems in thinking; adaptation of address, September 25, 1965. B. Dearing. Sch & Soc 94:317-19+ O 15 '66
Secrets of how we think and how we learn; reprint. Sci Digest 59:41-7 Mr '66
See also
Ideology
Metaphysics
Problem solving

THOUSAND ISLANDS
1000 Islands, then and now. il Motor B 118:34-7 Ag '66

THREADS, Screw. See Screw threads

THREE and the dragon; drama. See Fisher, A.

THREE bags full; drama. See Chodorov, J.

THREE-dimensional map construction. See Cartography

THREE dimensional photography. See Stereophotography

THREE-dimensional television. See Television, Stereoscopic

THREE hand reel; drama. See Mayer, P. A.

THREE SISTERS wilderness area. See Wilderness areas—Oregon

THREE-toed sloths. See Sloths

THREE-way lamps. See Electric lamps

THREE way switches. See Electric switches

THREE wishes; drama. See Thane, A.

THRELKELD, John
Here's a quick course in soil science. Pop Gard 17:60-1+ Mr '66
Water, water everywhere you want it. Pop Gard 17:62-3+ Ag '66

THRIFT
See also
Debt
Saving and savings

THROAT
Diseases
Strep throat vaccine here. Sci N 90:369 N 5 '66
Surgery
See also
Larynx—Surgery

THROMBOGENICITY. See Blood—Coagulation

THROMBOSIS
Abscess: coronary cause. F. Marley. il Sci N 90:391 N 12 '66

THRONE, Henry
Inquest on a premature burial. T. Buckley. il pors Esquire 65:75-81+ Je '66

THRONE in heaven; story. See Grossman, S.

THROUGH-lens meters. See Exposure meters

THROUGH the looking-glass; drama. See Olfson, L.

THROWERS, Snow. See Snow blowers, throwers, etc.

THUNDERBOLTS in red, white, and blue; story. See Stone, R.

THUNDERSTORMS
Thunderstorm electrification of hail and graupel by polar dribble. R. Gunn. il Science 151:686 F 11 '66
See also
Aviation—Storm hazards

THURBER, David L. See Richards, H. G. jt. auth.

THURBER, Helen W.
Self-portraits and self-appraisals by James Thurber; excerpts from the introduction to Thurber & company. Harper 233:44-5 Ag '66

THURBER, James
Owl who was God; excerpt from Thurber carnival. Read Digest 88:172C Mr '66
about
Self-portraits and self appraisals by James Thurber; excerpts from the introduction to Thurber & company. H. W. Thurber. il Harper 233:44-5 Ag '66

THURMOND, Strom
Conservatism in the South; address, April 1, 1966. Vital Speeches 32:420-3 My 1 '66
Excerpt from debate, August 17, 1965. Cong Digest 45:77 Mr '66

THYLACINE. See Tasmanian tigers

THYMIDINE
Synchronization of mammalian cells with tritiated thymidine. G. F. Whitmore and S. Gulyas. bibliog il Science 151:691-4 F 11 '66

THYMINE
Solution photochemistry of thymine and uracil. A. A. Lamola and J. P. Mittal. bibliog il Science 154:1560-1 D 23 '66

THYMUS gland
Immunological competence: alteration by whole body X-irradiation and shielding of selected lymphoid tissues. J. Miller. bibliog il Science 151:1395-7 Mr 18 '66
Lymphocytes from thymectomized rats: immunologic, proliferative, and metabolic properties. W. O. Rieke. bibliog il Science 152:535-8 Ap 22 '66
Useless gland that guards our health. A. Q. Maisel. Read Digest 89:229-30+ N '66

THYMUS gland, Transplantation of. See Transplantation of organs, tissues, etc.

THYNG, Harrison R.
Primary mix. New Repub 155:7-8 S 24 '66

THYROGLOBULIN. See Thyroproteins

THYROID extracts
Thyrocalcitonin: cytological localization by immunofluorescence. G. K. Hargis and others. bibliog il Science 152:73-5 Ap 1 '66
Thyrocalcitonin: effect on idiopathic hypercalcemia. G. Milhaud and J. C. Job. bibliog il Science 154:794-6 N 11 '66

THYROID extracts—*Continued*
Thyrocalcitonin inhibition of bone resorption induced by parathyroid hormone in tissue culture. M. A. Aliapoulios and others. bibliog il Science 151:330-1 Ja 21 '66
Thyrocalcitonin: ultracentrifugation in gradients of sucrose. J. L. H. O'Riordan and others. bibliog il Science 154:885-6 N 18 '66

THYROID gland
End-organ effects of thyroid hormones: subcellular interactions in cultured cells. E. Siegel and C. A. Tobias. bibliog il Science 153:763-5 Ag 12 '66
Thyroid hormone: effects on electron transport. J. R. Bronk. bibliog il Science 153: 638-9 Ag 5 '66
See also
Thyroxine

THYROPROTEINS
Thyro stops a production slump. L. A. Baker. il Farm J 90:A10 Jl '66
Thyroglobulin: evidence for crystallization and association. W. B. Jakoby and others. bibliog il Science 153:1671-2 S 30 '66

THYROXINE
How a tadpole becomes a frog. W. Etkin. il Sci Am 214:76-80+ My '66

TIBBETT, Lawrence
Lasting tribute: memorials to three great singers. il Opera N 31:30-1 O 15 '66

TIBERIUS, emperor of Rome
Tiberius a tormented man who spread terror from a sunny island. il por Life 60:60-1 Je 3 '66

TIBET
See also
United Nations—Tibet

Description and travel
Timely rain, by S. Gelder and R. Gelder. Review
Nation 202:304-6 Mr 14 '66. M. Young

TIBETANS
See also
Sherpas

TIBETANS in the United States
Tibetan New Year; formal party at the Plaza. New Yorker 42:41-4 Mr 19 '66

TIC douloureux. See Neuralgia, Trigeminal

TICE, George
Normal lens for wide angle. H. Keppler. il Mod Phot 30:62-3 Ap '66

TICKET on Skoronski; story. See Algren, N.

TICKETS
See also
Airlines—Tickets

TIDAL currents. See Ocean currents

TIDAL power. See Tide power

TIDAL waves. See Seismic sea waves

TIDE power
French harness tides for power; St Malo tidal dam. il Bsns W p 108-10 Ap 30 '66

TIDES
Was Columbus in Canada? lunar and solar tides in Bay of Fundy. P. Bilbao. il Américas 18:17-28 Jl '66

TIDWELL, Dolores
For Samoa: a barefoot teacher from Oklahoma. il pors Look 30:88+ My 31 '66

TIE-in merchandise. See Merchandising

TIEPOLO, Giovanni Battista
One last dramatic moment. il Time 88:70-3 S 23 '66
Tiepolo triumph at the Met. il Art N 65:34-5+ O '66

TIFFANY and company
Diamond for the day you dream of. il Seventeen 25:28 My '66
East meets West; holdup at Chicago branch. Newsweek 68:44+ O 31 '66

TIFFEAU, Jacques
Jacques Tiffeau: sauvage of Seventh avenue. S. Brownmiller. il pors N Y Times Mag p36-7+ Ja 15 '67

TIFFEN, C. E.
British engineer's attitude toward plastic pipe. Am City 81:108-9 Ap '66

TIGAR, Michael E.
Brennan v Tigar. A. Kopkind. New Repub 155:21-2 Ag 27 '66

TIGER, Dick
Champion. il Newsweek 68:47-8 D 26 '66
Shrinking poppy's nonbout with a reluctant Tiger. por Sports Illus 24:70-2 My 9 '66
Will and ability. Sports Illus 26:5 Ja 2 '67

TIGER catcher; drama. See McFarlan, E.

TIGER hunting
Bold, bad tiger of Ghatpiparia. J. O'Connor. il Outdoor Life 137:36-9+ Mr '66

TIGER, the Brahman, and the jackal; drama. See Smith. G. V.

TIGERFLOWERS
Weeks of summer brilliance from tigridias planted now. il Sunset 136:218+ F '66

TIGERS
Fascinating tiger; quiz. J. Daugherty and M. Daugherty. il Sci Digest 60:83-6 Ag '66
Man-eaters of Naini Tal. F. Turner. il Outdoor Life 138:67-81 D '66
Tiger and its prey. G. B. Schaller. il Natur Hist 75:30-7 O '66

Stories
Day grandfather tickled a tiger. R. Bond. il Read Digest 88:169-70+ F '66

TIGHTROPE walker; drama. See Lee, M.

TIGRIDIAS. See Tigerflowers

TIJERINA, Reies Lopez
Finders keepers. por Newsweek 68:40 N 7 '66

TIJUANA, Mexico
In Tijuana, shopping for Mexican gifts. il Sunset 137:53 D '66

TIKAL. See Mayas

TILDEN, Freeman
Seize the moment! por Parks & Rec 1:625+ Ag '66

TILDEN, Paul Mason
Singular metal from cinnabar. Natur Hist 75:26-31 Je '66
Washington newsletter (cont) Natur Hist 75: 4 Je; 68+ O '66

TILE floors. See Floors, Tile

TILE stoves. See Stoves, Earthenware

TILES
New museum of tiles in Lisbon; Museu do azulejo. R. C. Smith. il Antiques 89:828-33 Je '66

TILES, Floor
Newly versatile quarry tile. il House & Gard 129:170-3 Mr '66
They laid tile over tile. il Sunset 136:158+ Ap '66

TILL, Emmett
Has the Fifth amendment become a menace to human rights? P. Chamberlain. Nat R 18:362-4 Ap 19 '66

TILLAGE
Fall farming: best way to beat the spring labor shortage. A. J. Englehorn and J. C. Herman. il Farm J 90:40-1 O '66
Minimum tillage cuts potato costs. W. A. Hayes and C. Roy. il Farm J 90:66P Ap '66

TILLES, David
Atmospheric noble gases from extraterrestrial dust. bibliog Science 151:1015 F 25 '66
Implantation in interplanetary dust of raregas ions from solar flares. bibliog Science 153:981-4 Ag 26 '66

TILLES, Seymour
Strategies for allocating funds. bibliog f Harvard Bsns R 44:72-80 Ja '66

TILLETT, Gladys A.
Elimination of discrimination against women; report on 19th session Dept State Bul 55: 284-8 Ag 22 '66

TILLICH, Paul
Boundary lines. L. D. Streiker. por Christian Cent 83:1012+ Ag 17 '66
Man in estrangement, by G. Hammond. Review
Cath World 202:312-14 F '66. D. P. Gray

TILLINGHAST, Charles Carpenter, 1911-
Caught at the crest. il por Time 88:80-3+ Jl 22 '66

TILLINGHAST, Richard
Angels and ministers of grace; For a teacher's wife, dying of cancer; poems. Poetry 107:375-7 Mr '66
Europe for adventurous students. Holiday 41:133-40 Ja '67
Prizewinner, the real thing, and two others. Poetry 109:118-22 N '66
Reading late, in winter; poem. Atlan 219:54 Ja '67

TILT pins. See Gas and oil engines, Outboard

TIMBER
North Tongass timber sale; Juneau, Alaska. V. Metcalfe. Am For 72:10 Ja '66
Trees to sell? see a forester. J. E. Moore. il Am For 72:20-7 Mr '66

TIMBER connectors. See Connectors

TIMBER wolves. See Wolves

TIME
How to speed up time. H. Downs. Sci Digest 60:84-8 Jl '66
Is time dead? S. Minor. Nat R 18:456+ My 17 '66

TIME—*Continued*
What is time? I. Asimov. il Sci Digest 60:93-4 S '66
See also
Calendar
Periodicity
Present, The

Systems and standards
Time and time measurement. J. Evans. il Electr World 76:25-9+ Jl '66

TIME (periodical)
Letter from the publisher: average Time subscriber. B. M. Auer. Time 88:29 O 14 '66
Letter from the publisher; concerning Time essays B. M. Auer. Time 87:17 Ap 1 '66
Letter from the publisher; excerpts from broadcasts on CBS program Dimension. H. Reasoner. Time 88:7 Ag 26 '66
Letter from the publisher; good target for caricature. B. M. Auer. Time 88:15 Ag 5 '66
Letter from the publisher; third overseas news tour. B. M. Auer. il Time 88:24-5 N 11 '66

TIME (theology)
Discovery of time, by S. Toulmin and J. Goodfield. Review
Nation 202:561-3 My 9 '66. C. Johnson

TIME, Daylight saving. See Daylight saving

TIME, incorporated
Baroque on the Time-Life plan; literature and recordings. P. H. Lang. Sat R 49:62-3 Ap 30 '66; Reply with rejoinder. W. J. Gold. 49:62-3 Jl 30 '66
Letter from the publisher; Bureau of editorial reference. B. M. Auer. il Time 87:13 Mr 25 '66
Privacy v. free press; the Hills sue Time, inc. il Time 87:74 My 6 '66
Time, inc. buys 46 per cent share of Editions Laffont, Paris. Pub W 190:58 O 31 '66
Time inc. purchases the New York graphic society. Pub W 190:29-30 D 12 '66
Vote for the press over privacy; case of James Hill and his family. il Time 89:56 Ja 20 '67
See also
General learning corporation

TIME, Use of
How to manage your time. P. F. Drucker. il Harper 233:56-60 D '66

TIME domain reflectometry. See Reflectometers
TIME for purpose; drama. See Rawe, M.
TIME for singing; musical comedy. See Musical comedies, revues, etc.—Criticisms, plots, etc.
TIME-lapse photography. See Photography, Time-lapse
TIME-Life records. See Time, incorporated
TIME measurements
Time and time measurement. J. Evans. il Electr World 76:25-9+ Jl '66
Time scales & time measurements; including solar, universal, ephemeris, atomic, sidereal time. E. C. Wilson, 3d. il Electr World 75:42-3 Ja '66; Reply with rejoinder. K. E. Stone. 75:22-3 My '66

TIME off. See Leave of absence
TIME payment sales. See Instalment plan
TIME perception
Discovery of time, by S. Toulmin and J. Goodfield. Review
Nation 202:561-3 My 9 '66. C. Johnson
Simultaneous changes in visual separation threshold and voltage of cortical alpha rhythm. J. Anliker. bibliog il Science 153:316-18 Jl 15 '66
Voices of time, ed. by J. T. Fraser. Review
Sat R 49:34-5 Ja 29 '66. J. B. Lieberman

TIME reversal
Can time go backward? M. Gardner. il Sci Am 216:98-102+ bibliog (p 146+) Ja '67

TIME sharing computers. See Computers—Co-operative use
TIME signals, Radio
Build time-signal-only receiver. C. Caringella. il Pop Electr 25:41-6+ O '66

TIMES, London
Changing Times. Newsweek 67:98 Ap 11 '66
Collector's item: takeover by Thomson organization. Newsweek 68:98 O 10 '66
Fleet Street fortune at work; merger with Sunday Times. J. Tebbel. Sat R 49:102 N 12 '66
Letter from London; disappearance as an independent newspaper. M. Panter-Downes. New Yorker 42:100-2 Ja 14 '67

Lord Thomson adds a jewel to his coronet. il Bsns W p56-8+ Ja 7 '67
Old lady's new face; page one. il Time 87:77 My 13 '66
Passing of a fine front page. T. Green. Life 60:23 Je 10 '66
Stealing his thunderer? hope of Morris-Berry proposal to affect Monopolies commission rule on Thomson deal. Newsweek 68:100 D 5 '66
Thomson takes the Times. Time 88:61 O 7 '66
Times gets with the times; first-page format changed. Bsns W p38 My 7 '66

TIMES, Los Angeles
Enterprise in Los Angeles. il Time 87:76-7 My 13 '66
How to build an empire. il Newsweek 69:41-5 Ja 2 '67

TIMES, New York. See New York times
TIMES literary supplement, London
R. R. Bowker to reprint Times literary supplement. Pub W 190:45 S 19 '66

TIMES-Mirror company
Times Mirror acquires Harry N. Abrams, inc. Pub W 189:28 Ap 11 '66
Times-Mirror co: spreading into the knowledge industry. il Newsweek 69:44-5 Ja 2 '67

TIMES newspapers, limited
Collector's item; takeover by Thomson organization. Newsweek 68:98 O 10 '66

TIMES square, New York city. See New York (city)—Times square
TIMING devices
Semiconductor interval timer. D. E. Lancaster. il Electr World 75:82-4 My '66

TIMMINS, Ontario
Why Timmins takes it calmly. il Bsns W p94 N 26 '66

TIMUR the Great
Ibn Khaldūn: man of history; excerpts from radio program. B. Bray. il UNESCO Courier 19:4-10 Je '66

TIN
Melting of tin telluride at high pressures. W. Klement, jr. and L. H. Cohen. bibliog il Science 154:1176-7 D 2 '66

TIN cans
See also
American can company

TIN industry and trade
Tin council and U. S. officials discuss tin sales program. Dept State Bul 55:756 N 14 '66

TIN mines and mining

Bolivia
High flier; Barrientos' plans. il Newsweek 68:44 Jl 18 '66
Letter from La Paz. C. Rand. New Yorker 42:42+ D 31 '66

TINARI, Anne
African-violet; questions and answers. Flower Grower 53:27+ N '66

TINDALL, William Y.
Poet behind the desk. Sat R 49:42 N 19 '66

TING, Walasse
Near 1¢ life. Art N 65:38-9+ My '66

TINGUELY, Jean
Sculptures in motion; with report by D. Bourdon. il Life 61:40-1+ Ag 12 '66

TINKER, Frank
Air racing. il Flying 78:36-41 F '66

TINNAPPEL, Harold
Why peonies don't bloom. Horticulture 44:42 O '66

TINSLEY, Russell
Hunting's best-kept secret. por Field & S 71:25-7+ Ag '66
Jackpotful of bass. por Outdoor Life 138:48-9+ D '66

TINTED glass. See Glass
TINY Alice; drama. See Albee, E.
TIPPETT, Michael
Tippett premiere, Britten revivals. E. Greenfield. Hi Fi 16:160-1 Ap '66

TIPPING
Room 306 doesn't tip! W. P. Fox, jr. il Holiday 40:78-81+ D '66
Tips on tipping at the beauty salon. Good H 162:186 Ap '66

TIPPIT, Marie
Forgotten widows of the Kennedy tragedy. L. A. Harris. il pors Good H 162:94-7+ Ap '66

TIPTON, Stuart G.
New trends shaping policy for carriers; address, 1966. por Aviation W 85:100-1+ Jl 11 '66

TIRE industry and trade
Gas & rubber war; western European and American competition. il Time 88:112+ S 16 '66

TIREDNESS. See Fatigue
TIRES, Automobile
Are your tires safe enough? C. P. Gilmore. il Pop Sci 188:108-12+ Mr '66
Be kind to trailer tires. Consumer Rep 31:268 Je '66
Confusion in the tire industry. il Consumer Bul 49:37-40 Ap; 37-40 My '66
FTC takes aim at false tire claims. Consumer Rep 31:217 My '66
Fresh spin on tires; Armstrong rubber co. using glass fiber for cords. il Bsns W p70 Mr 12 '66
Has handling improved, or is it still an optional extra? il Motor T 18:33 S '66
Indy-style tires for your car? ed. by P. Bryan. M. Andretti. il Pop Sci 189:128-31 S '66
Lurking hazard with tubeless tires. Consumer Rep 31:157 Ap '66
Notes on tires. Sr Schol 88:37+ Ap 22 '66
Snow tires. Consumer Bul 49:31 N '66
Snow tires, chains & studs. il Changing T 20:11-13 O '66
Tire prospects. Fortune 73:211-12+ My '66
Tire standards for 1966. Consumer Rep 31:197 Ap '66
Tire studs catch on; snow tire studs. Bsns W p78 N 12 '66
Treading more surely; making tires safer. il Time 87:84 Je 17 '66

Prices
Shady sales methods in the tire trade may, at long last, be on their way out. il Consumer Bul 50:39-40 Ja '67

Testing
Ceramic tire studs, they really grab you! A. Markovich. il Pop Mech 126:148-51 N '66

TIRES, Motor truck
Fill first, then compact; way to protect the unreinforced rubber tires of loader; Buchanan, Mich. M. Hankila. il Am City 81:173-4 My '66
Rubber tires work well on sanitary landfills; use in Bismarck, N.D. E. Booth and E. Carlson. il Am City 81:98-9 Jl '66

TIROS (satellite) See Artificial satellites—Meteorological applications

TISHCHENKO, Boris
Russians are coming. il por Time 87:54+ Je 3 '66

TISSUE porphyrins. See Porphyrins

TISSUES
Contractile cells in human seminiferous tubules. M. H. Ross and I. R. Long. bibliog il Science 153:1271-3 S 9 '66
Liquid water in frozen tissue: study by nuclear magnetic resonance. M. V. Sussman and L. Chin. bibliog il Science 151:324-5 Ja 21 '66
Pyruvate inhibition of lactate dehydrogenase activity in human tissue extracts. A. L. Latner and others. bibliog il Science 154:527-9 O 28 '66
See also
Bone
Membranes (biology)

Culture
Amateur scientist; how to perform experiments with animal cells living in tissue culture. T. M. Fancolli. il Sci Am 214:122-4+ Ap '66
Antibody synthesis initiated in vitro by paired explants of spleen and thymus. G. C. Saunders and D. W. King. bibliog il Science 151:1390-1 Mr 18 '66
Antiserum to immunoglobulin A: inhibition of cell-mediated demyelination in tissue culture. G. F. Winkler and B. G. Arnason. bibliog il Science 153:75-6 Jl 1 '66
Cell-free protein synthesis: effects of age and state of ribosomal aggregation. L. D. Moore and others. bibliog il Science 154:1350-3 D 9 '66
Centromere: absence of DNA replication during chromatid separation in human fibroblasts. D. E. Comings. bibliog il Science 154:1463 D 16 '66
End-organ effects of thyroid hormones: subcellular interactions in cultured cells. E. Siegel and C. A. Tobias. bibliog il Science 153:763-5 Ag 12 '66
Establishment of four functional, clonal strains of animal cells in culture. Y. Yasumura and others. bibliog il Science 154:1186-9 D 2 '66
Neurosecretory cells: daily rhythmicity in leiobunum longipes. D. J. Fowler and C. J. Goodnight. bibliog il Science 152:1078-80 My 20 '66

One-way stimulation in mixed leukocyte cultures. F. H. Bach and N. K. Voynow. bibliog il Science 153:545-7 Jl 29 '66
Reaggregation of insect cells as studied by a new method of tissue and organ culture. D. R. Walters and C. M. Williams. bibliog il Science 154:516-17 O 28 '66
Rubella virus: growth and cytopathic effect in primary cultures of cells of rabbit embryos. A. Reddick and C. E. Roesel. bibliog Science 151:1405-6 Mr 18 '66
Vesicular stomatitis virus replication in human leukocyte cultures: enhancement by phytohemagglutinin. R. Edelman and E. F. Wheelock. bibliog il Science 154:1053-5 N 25 '66

TITAN industrial corporation
Titan makes the sidelines pay off. il Bsns W p88-90 Jl 2 '66

TITAN III-C (booster) See Space vehicles—Propulsion systems

TITANI, Koiti, and others
Immunoglobulin structure: variation in the sequence of Bence Jones proteins. bibliog Science 152:1513-16 Je 10 '66

TITANIC (steamship)
Disaster at sea. B. Finnegan. il Hobbies 71:120-1+ Je '66

TITANIUM
FAA to study titanium sparking problem. M. L. Yaffee. Aviation W 85:69+ Jl 25 '66
SST's skin bears watching. Sci N 90:559 D 31 '66
Titanium cracks when exposed to salt water. Sci N 90:61 Jl 23 '66

TITANIUM, Powdered
Pulverizing process gives titanium an in. Bsns W p82 O 22 '66

TITANIUM alloys
Boeing pushes titanium airframe effort. C. M. Plattner. il Aviation W 85:38-9+ D 26 '66
Interest grows in titanium alloy wheels. M. L. Yaffee. il Aviation W 84:69-71 My 23 '66
Lockheed plans three titanium alloys in SST. C. M. Plattner. il Aviation W 85:74-5+ D 5 '66

TITANIUM carbide
RIAS investigation of TiC crystal defects. il Tech W 20:25 Ja 16 '67

TITLER, Dale M.
Brief and to the point. Writer 79:28 Jl '66

TITLES, Moving pictures. See Moving pictures—Titles

TITLES of address. See Forms of address

TITLES of books, stories, etc.
Court says Peyton Place is intangible property interest. H. F. Pipel. Pub W 189:66+ Ja 31 '66
Label on the package. R. Armour. Writer 79:25-6 N '66

TITLES of honor and nobility
's' vonderful; concerning request to add von to a name. New Repub 155:7 Ag 27 '66

TITLES of periodicals
Periodical abbreviation center initiated by ASA Z39 committee. Library J 91:3891+ S 1 '66

TITMICE
Nature note; titmouse. il Sci N 89:321 Ap 30 '66

TITO
Beyond the halfway house. il por Time 88:28+ Jl 15 '66
Freedom for Djilas. Newsweek 69:34 Ja 9 '67
Limits of freedom. Time 88:28-9 Ag 19 '66
Policy of pardons. Time 89:29 Ja 6 '67
Purge, and new prestige for Tito. por U S News 61:20 Jl 18 '66
Tito's Yugoslavia: is it communism? with report by F. Y. Blumenfeld. il pors Newsweek 68:49-54 O 17 '66
Unmeritorious pardon. Time 88:42 D 16 '66

TITUS, Harold
(ed) Conservation. See issues of Field & stream
Custom-made hunters. Field & S 71:72-3+ N '66
Warbler of the jack pines. Field & S 71:51+ My '66

TITUSVILLE, Pa.
Photographer to oildom; with photographs by J. A. Mather. E. C. Miller and T. K. Stratton. Am Heritage 17:38-45+ O '66

TIV (African people) See Africa, West—Native races

TIZARD, Sir Henry Thomas
Tizard, by R. W. Clark. Review
Bul Atomic Sci 22:39-41 Ja '66. S. A. Lakoff

TJURS, José
Arithmetic in Brasilia. il por Time 87:94 My 27 '66

TO all a good night; story. See Loeser, K.

TO honor the harvest; story. See Crichton, R.

TO the moon; drama. See Fontaine, R.

TOADS
It could be a froad; maybe a trog; spadefoot. A. O. Wasserman. il Natur Hist 75:18-23 Ap '66

TOADSTOOLS. See Mushrooms

TOASTERS, Electric. See Electric toasters

TOBACCO
Ozone and sulfur dioxide synergism; injury to tobacco plants. H. A. Menser and H. E. Heggestad. bibliog il Science 153:424-5 Jl 22 '66
Replication of chloroplast DNA of tobacco. B. R. Green and M. P. Gordon. bibliog il Science 152:1071-4 My 20 '66
Source of lead-210 and polonium-210 in tobacco. T. C. Tso and others. bibliog il Science 153:880-2 Ag 19 '66
See also
Nicotine

Physiological effects
Filters give false hope. F. Marley. il Sci N 90:173 S 10 '66
Lead-210 and polonium-210 in tissues of cigarette smokers. R. B. Holtzman and F. H. Ilcewicz. bibliog il Science 153:1259-60 S 9 '66
No-smoking signs. il Newsweek 68:73-4 O 31 '66
Smoking and women. Newsweek 67:66 Mr 7 '66
To the cigarette makers: just the facts, please. L. M. Miller and J. Monahan. il Read Digest 89:61-7 N '66
Tobacco fungus causes emphysema in animals. Sci N 90:261 O 1 '66

Psychological effects
Smokers less agreeable. Sci N 90:266 O 8 '66

TOBACCO etch virus. See Viruses, Plant

TOBACCO fungus. See Fungi

TOBACCO industry and trade
Cat and dog food, too; diversification moves. il Newsweek 68:84 D 12 '66
Where there's smoke there's a BAT brand; British-American tobacco company. il Bsns W p72-4+ Je 18 '66
Yardley in a lather; British-American tobacco co. ltd. bid for Yardley & co. ltd. Time 89:65 Ja 13 '67
See also
American tobacco company
Cigarettes

Wages and hours
Earnings in cigarette manufacturing. C. M. O'Connor. il Mo Labor R 89:40-2 Ja '66

TOBACCO mosaic virus
Growth in microculture of single tobacco cells infected with tobacco mosaic virus. N. Chandra and A. C. Hildebrandt. bibliog il Science 152:789-91 My 6 '66

TOBACCO workers
See also
Tobacco industry and trade—Wages and hours

TOBAGO
Well traveled camera. il Mod Phot 31:26+ Ja '67

TOBIAS, Cornelius A. See Siegel, E. jt. auth.

TOBIN, Jack
Horse racing. Sports Illus 24:88-9+ Mr 21 '66
Pool. Sports Illus 24:74+ My 2 '66
Track and field (title varies) Sports Illus 24:74-6 My 16 '66

TOBIN, James
Check the boom? New Repub 155:9-14 S 3 '66

TOBIN, Richard L.
(ed) Communications. See issues of Saturday review
Machinations for a military mind. Sat R 49:59 O 22 '66
Murrow remembers. Sat R 49:87 N 26 '66
Observations of a rookie. Sat R 49:60-1 D 10 '66
Telegrams. Sat R 49:8+ Jl 30 '66

TOBOGGANS and tobogganing
See also
Sleds

TOBY, Jackson
Violence and the masculine ideal: some qualitative data; with excerpts from a tape-recorded interview with an imprisoned armed robber. bibliog f Ann Am Acad 364:19-27 Mr '66

TOCQUEVILLE, Alexis Charles Henri Maurice Clérel de
Who is the American man? excerpt from Fortnight in the wilds. Sat R 49:66 Mr 12 '66

TODARO, George J. and others
Susceptibility of human diploid fibroblast strains to transformation by SV40 virus. bibliog Science 153:1252-4 S 9 '66

TODAY, a woman went mad in the supermarket; story. See Wolitzer, H.

TODD, Hollis N. and Zakia, R. D.
Is it true? (cont) Pop Phot 58:62 My '66

TODD, John M.
England. 1966. Cath World 203:284-6 Ag '66

TODD, Paul Harold, 1921-
Kalamazoo to Calcutta. K. Crawford. Newsweek 68:27 Jl 4 '66

TODD, Richard
Turned-on and super-sincere in California. Harper 234:42-7 Ja '67

TOFFLER, Alvin
What parents can do about bad teachers. Good H 162:84-5+ F '66

TOGGLE switches. See Electric switches

TOGO
See also
United States—Treaties—Togo

Commercial treaties and agreements
Department supports commercial treaty with Togo; statement, September 12, 1966. W. C. Trimble. Dept State Bul 55:692-3 O 31 '66

Foreign population
Cornflake syndrome; scorning of local foods. S. Fuller. il Atlan 217:110-12 My '66

Politics and government
Coup no. 2. Time 89:32 Ja 20 '67
Togo does it again; military coup. Newsweek 69:47 Ja 23 '67

TOILET
See also
Beauty, Personal
Perfumery

TOILET preparations
Bulletin for women who take their men seriously; table. Vogue 148:174-7 N 15 '66
Something: men's toiletries. D. Erickson. il Esquire 65:111-13 Je '66
See also
Cosmetics

TOILET soap. See Soap

TOILET water. See Perfumery

TOILETS. See Water closets

TOKAIDO line. See Railroads—Japan

TOKATYAN, Armand
Armand Tokatyan. A. Favia-Artsay. pors Hobbies 71:36+ Ja '67

TOKENS
Hi-ho, silver! gaming tokens. il Time 87:51 Mr 25 '66

TOKLE, Art, Jr
Junior jumps into the family act. il pors Life 60:95-6 F 4 '66

TOKYO

Architecture
Love that bank; Fuji bank. Newsweek 68:86+ S 12 '66

Description
Metropolis mountain; Tokyo rock; photographs. Travel 125:49-51 Mr '66

Hotels, restaurants, etc.
Ah so, Maxim's. il Newsweek 68:94+ N 21 '66

Music
Western music: a flowering in the East. E. Cunningham. il Hi Fi 16:140-1 Mr '66

Stores
Thermometer. il Time 88:75 Ag 26 '66

Streets
Akihabara; Tokyo's radio row. J. Wandres. il Pop Electr 24:54-5 My '66

TOLAND, John
Day a generation wept; excerpts from The last 100 days. Ladies Home J 83:60+ Je '66

TOLBERT, Frank X.
Jim Hall speaks out. Motor T 18:32-3 Mr '66
World's oldest Chevy driver? 103 skiddoo! Motor T 18:93 Mr '66

TOLBERT, William R. Jr
Liberian Negro leads World Baptists. C. W. Thomas. por Negro Hist Bul 29:65 D '65

TOLEDANO, José
José Toledano, Town Hall. M. Marks. Dance Mag 40:33 N '66

TOLEDO, Ohio
Design for a dedication; ed. by P. D. Eimon. il Am City 81:142+ O '66

Galleries and museums
See also
Toledo, Ohio, museum of art

Housing
Toledo's biggest landlord. il Ebony 21:111-12+ Je '66

Newspapers
Code for crime coverage; Toledo blade and Toledo times. Time 88:76 S 2 '66

Parks and playgrounds
Passive park; George P. Crosby park. V. J. Wiersma. Am City 81:20 Ap '66

TOLEDO, Ohio, museum of art
Toledo museum of art. L. Bruner. il Am Artist 30:33-9+ Ap '66
What it takes to put on a $50-million art exhibit. il Bsns W p 112-14+ D 10 '66

TOLEDO, Ohio, public library
Dewey proportions; comparison of Toledo public library adult circulating book stock at main library and at typical Toledo branch library with Lj adult book review coverage. E. Moon. Library J 91:2783 Je 1 '66
How many copies are enough? reprint. R. D. Franklin. il Library J 91:4573-5 O 1 '66

TOLERANCE of pain. See Pain

TOLERATION
Murderous bigotry in Northern Ireland; Catholics vs Protestants. Christian Cent 83:929 Jl 27 '66

TOLKIEN, John Ronald Reuel
J. R. R. Tolkien talks about the discovery of middle-earth, the origins of elvish; interview, ed. by R. Plotz. por Seventeen 26:92-3+ Ja '67

about
Ace books reaches agreement with Tolkien. Pub W 189:37-8 Mr 14 '66; Reply. R. Unwin. 189:31 My 9 '66
Face to face; with R. D. Plotz, founder of Tolkien society of America. R. D. Plotz. Seventeen 25:153 Ap '66
Hobbit-forming world of J. R. R. Tolkien. H. Resnik. il por Sat Eve Post 239:90-2+ Jl 2 '66
Hobbit habit. J. Mathewson. il Esquire 66:130-1+ S '66
Hobbit habit. por Time 88:48+ Jl 15 '66
Prevalence of hobbits. P. Norman. il por N Y Times Mag p30-1+ Ja 15 '67
Tolkien's magic ring. P. S. Beagle. Holiday 39:128+ Je '66

TOLKMITH, Henry, and others
Fungicidal phthalimidophosphonothionates. bibliog Science 155:85-6 Ja 6 '67

TOLL roads
High roads & low. il Time 88:106+ S 16 '66

TOLSON, Melvin Beaunorus
Tolson's gallery brings poetry home. D. G. Thompson. Negro Hist Bul 29:69-70 D '65

TOM says it's that kids have more freedom these days; story. See Dillon, J.

TOMASI DI LAMPEDUSA, Giuseppe. See Lampedusa, G. di

TOMASSO, Victor E.
African-violets your own way. Flower Grower 53:38-9 O '66

TOMASSON, Helgi
Brief biography. S. Goodman. il pors Dance Mag 40:54-5 F '66

TOMATOES
Anti-freeze your tomatoes with ice. J. R. Sansregret. Pop Gard 17:85 D '66
Home garden notebook. B. C. Kilvert, jr. il Flower Grower 53:61-2 My '66
In praise of the tomato. W. A. Buck. il Pop Gard 17:66-8+ My '66
Proliferation of cells in the central cylinder of the reduced mutant in lanceolate tomato. J. L. Caruso and E. G. Cutter. bibliog il Science 154:1021-3 N 25 '66
Tomato. F. C. Coulter. il Horticulture 44:22-3 Ag '66
See also
Cookery—Vegetables

TOMBS
See also
Taj Mahal

TOMKIEVICZ, Shirley
Seek and (with luck) ye shall find. Horizon 8:94-7 Aut '66

TOMKINS, Calvin
Annals of law. New Yorker 42:105-6+ O 29 '66

Mr Playboy of the western world. Sat Eve Post 239:96-101 Ap 23 '66
Profiles; E. Hoffer. New Yorker 42:34-6+ Ja 7 '67
Ursus horribilis. New Yorker 42:42-3 My 7 '66
Village explainer. New Yorker 42:53-5 D 3 '66

TOMLINSON, Charles
Precision in two languages. T. Enslin. Poetry 109:112-14 N '66

TOMLINSON, Homer Aubrey, bp
Profiles. W. Whitworth. por New Yorker 42:67-70+ S 24 '66

TOMLINSON, P. B. See Zimmermann, M. H. jt. auth.

TOMOGRAPHY. See Radiography

TOMONAGA, Shin'ichiro
Development of quantum electrodynamics; address, May 6, 1966. bibliog Science 154:864-8 N 18 '66

TOMPKINS, Jerry R.
Monkey law unconstitutional. Sci N 89:461 Je 11 '66

TOMPKINS, John S. See Finney, P. B. jt. auth.

TOMPKINS, Phillip K.
In cold fact. Esquire 65:125+ Je '66

TOMPKINS, Warwick M.
Designer up a stick. Yachting 119:100-1+ Ja '66

TONE arm, Phonograph. See Phonograph—Tone arm

TONGUE, Ruth Lyndell
Witches of 1966. V. Thomas il Atlan 218:119-25 S '66

TONGUE
See also
Taste

TONKIN GULF, Battle of. See Vietnamese crisis, 1964

TONSOR, Stephen J.
Minerva's owl. Nat R 18:631-2 Je 28 '66

TOOKE, James C.
When I looked in those files, my eyes popped. J. Phelan. il por Sat Eve Post 239:23-9 S 10 '66

TOOKER, Elisabeth J.
Iroquois research. Science 51:712 F 11 '66

TOOL and die makers. See Machine shops—Employees

TOOL belts. See Garden tools, equipment and supplies

TOOL houses. See Garden houses, shelters, etc.

TOOL industry
See also
Stanley works (firm)

TOOLS
Handyman how-to time-savers! il Bet Hom & Gard 44:145-6+ Je '66
Roundup of new tools for the hardware show. il Pop Sci 189:198+ N '66
Shop talk. R. P. Stevenson. See issues of Popular science monthly
Shopping for tools. R. Howe. See issues of Popular mechanics
Special new tools for special jobs. il Pop Sci 189:141 Ag '66
Stow-aboard tool kit for outboards. H. B. Notrom. il Pop Mech 125:158-60 Mr '66
Tool chest for the lady of the house. il Changing T 20:16 Ag '66
Tools: old, new, and remembered. il Pop Electr 24:46-7 Ap '66
See also
Jigs
Shapers

Care
Beauty treatments for rusty tools. W. E. Burton. il Pop Mech 125:158-9 Je '66
Keeping tools like new. il Pop Sci 188:144-6 Je '66

Storage
Handy place for tool storage. il Sunset 137:93 Jl '66
See also
Garden tools, equipment and supplies—Storage

TOOMEY, Bill
What price what glory? il por Time 88:52-3 Ag 5 '66

TOOP, Nicole
Off to school with a good breakfast. Parents Mag 41:36 S '66

TOOTELL, Jack
Jonah; poem. Christian Cent 83:777 Je 15 '66

TOOTH decay. See Teeth—Diseases

TOOTHBRUSHES
Electric toothbrushes. il Consumer Rep 31:402-6 Ag '66

TOOTHPICKS, Electric
Companion for the toothbrush; electrically powered Water Pik. Consumer Rep 31:369 Ag '66

TOOTHPICKS, Electric—*Continued*
New aid for oral hygiene; Water Pik oral hygiene appliance. M. B. Keiser. il Parents Mag 41:48+ N '66

TOP art. See Modernism (art)

TOPCOATS. See Coats

TOPEKA, Kan.

Recreation
Summer internship program. J. J. Bannon. Parks & Rec 1:321+ Ap '66

Stores
My year in the five and ten; experience as a clerk at Duckwell's variety store. A. House. il Seventeen 25:162-3+ S '66

TOPEKA tornado, 1966. See Tornadoes

TOPEROFF, Sam
Spoonful of nothing; story. Atlan 218:50-5 Ag '66
Weaver of carpets; poem. Atlan 217:63 My '66

TOPLIN, I. and Schidlovsky, G.
Partial purification and electron microscopy of virus in the EB-3 cell line derived from a Burkitt lymphoma. bibliog Science 152:1084-5 My 20 '66

TOPOGRAPHICAL art. See Modernism (art)

TOPOLOGY
Turning a surface inside out. A. Phillips. il Sci Am 214:112-20 bibliog(p 148) My '66

TOPPING, Audrey R.
Through darkest red China N Y Times Mag p26-7+ Ag 28 '66

TOPPING, Seymour
Long live Chairman Mao! long live Lin Piao! N Y Times Mag p 18-19+ Jl 17 '66
Next on Peking's hit parade? N Y Times Mag p30-1+ F 20 '66

TORAH. See Bible—Old Testament—Pentateuch

TORCH lilies
Bulb for a cold window. V. Greiff. il Flower Grower 53:28 O '66
Red hot poker. H. G. Shuman. il Flower Grower 53:37+ My '66

TORDAY, Ursula. See Blackstock, C. pseud.

TORKANOWSKY, Werner
Musical events; concert in Carnegie Hall, performed by New Orleans philharmonic-symphony orchestra. W. Sargeant. New Yorker 42:74 F 26 '66

TORMÉ, Mel
Melvin and the little people. G. Lees. por Hi Fi 16:120 D '66

TORNABENE, Lyn
Bored housewife. Ladies Home J 83:97-9+ N '66
Good grief, Charlie Brown, don't you know anything about women? Ladies Home J 83:36 O '66

TORNADO simulators. See Simulators

TORNADOES
Aftermath of a tornado; Palm Sunday tornadoes, Elkhart County, Ind. M. Cohen. il Redbook 127:64-5+ O '66
Coming: better warnings on tornadoes. il U S News 60:14 Mr 14 '66
Curtain of destruction; Mississippi toll. Time 87:28 Mr 11 '66
Killer wind; quiz. J. Daugherty and M. Daugherty. il Sci Digest 60:83-5 S '66
Like a lion; Jackson, Miss. il Newsweek 67:29 Mr 14 '66
Luminous phenomena in nocturnal tornadoes. B. Vonnegut and J. R. Weyer. bibliog il Science 153:1213-20 S 9 '66; Discussion. 155:27+ Ja 6 '67
New twist in tornadoes; research by Chieh-chein Chang. il Time 87:52+ Ap 15 '66
Potawatomi revisited; Topeka's twister. il Time 87:28 Je 17 '66
Short circuit for tornadoes. Time 88:72 N 25 '66
Storm's incalculable energy. E. Kessler. il Natur Hist 75:12-17 Ap '66
Time of the twister; Topeka damage. Newsweek 67:34 Je 20 '66
Tornado photos needed. il Sci N 90:247 O 1 '66
Tornado season peak reached in spring. Sci N 89:205 Mr 26 '66
Tornado's black fury; Topeka, Kan. il Life 60:38-9 Je 24 '66
See also
Aviation—Storm hazards

TORNEK, Terry Eliot
DRIVE: teamsters in politics. Nation 203:663-5 D 19 '66

TORONTO

Architecture
Office buildings at the 100 per cent corner; Eaton centre. il Arch Rec 140:168-70 N '66

City planning
Canadian cities rebuild on a three-layer plan. il Bsns W p42-3 Mr 12 '66

Streets
Snow melting for 64 cents per ton. M. R. Browning. Am City 81:34 N '66

TORONTO Maple Leafs (hockey team) See Hockey teams

TORONTO. University

Scarborough campus
New campus. O. Newman. il Arch Forum 124:31-41+ My '66
Satellite built for TV. il Time 89:46-8 Ja 13 '67

TORPEDO boats
New designs seen for patrol boats. il Miss & Roc 18:79-81 Mr 28 '66

TORQUE
Let's torque about horsepower. J. McFarland. il Hot Rod 19:96 O '66

TORRE, Joe
Joe Torre: the last of the great catchers. M. Cope. il pors Sat Eve Post 239:84-6+ Jl 2 '66

TORRES, Camilo
Death of a rebel priest. A. W. Wilde. Commonweal 83:693-6 Mr 18 '66
Death of Camilo Torres. V. Andrade. America 114:355 Mr 12 '66; Discussion. 114:650-1 My 7 '66

TORRES, José
And an Irishman takes a shellacking at Shea. M. Kram. il Sports Illus 24:24-5 My 30 '66
Champion. por Newsweek 68:47-8 D 26 '66
Lost hero. P. Hamill. il pors Sat Eve Post 239:84-6+ My 21 '66
Will and ability; D. Tiger's defeat of J. Torres. Sports Illus 26:5 Ja 2 '67
Without honor in his own land. M. Kram. il por Sports Illus 25:30-1 O 24 '66

TORRES, Tereska
Secret. Commonweal 85:345-8 D 23 '66

TORRES BODET, Jaime
Hispanic chronicle. R. Howard. Poetry 107:338-9 F '66

TORS, Ivan
King of the beasts. il por Newsweek 67:96 F 21 '66

TORSION bar suspension. See Automobiles—Springs and suspension

TORT liability. See Liability (law)

TORTAS. See Sandwiches

TORTE. See Cake

TORTILLAS. See Cookery, Mexican

TORTOISES
Desert tortoise gopherus agassizii; cutaneous water loss. K. Schmidt-Nielsen and P. J. Bentley. il Science 154:911 N 18 '66

TORTURE
Addenda to De Sade; murder of S. M. Likens in Indianapolis. il Time 87:25 My 6 '66

TORY party (Great Britain) See Conservative party (Great Britain)

TOSCANINI, Arturo
Greatest single influence on today's conductors. H. C. Schonberg. il pors N Y Times Mag p46-7+ Ja 8 '67
This was Toscanini; excerpt. S. Antek. por Read Digest 89:103-17 Jl '66
Toscanini and the others. G. R. Marek. il Harper 233:40+ N '66
Toscanini recordings; recommended by B. H. Haggin. Atlan 218:76 D '66
Working with Toscanini; ed. by B. H. Haggin. W. Carboni; J. Peerce. por Atlan 218:72-9 D '66

TOSCANINI, Walfredo
(ed) See Harrison, W. K. Bridge to the future

TOTAL abstinence. See Temperance

TOTE bag. See Handbags

TOTEM poles
Alaska's vanishing art. K. Kuh. il Sat R 49:25-31 O 22 '66
Chain saw revives totem pole art. il Pop Mech 125:148 Ap '66

TOTALITARIANISM
Should the United States aid totalitarian countries? C. V. Crabb, jr. bibliog f Cur Hist 50:346-52+ Je '66

TOTH, Bela, and Shubik, Philippe
Mammary tumor inhibition and lung adenoma induction by isonicotinic acid hydrazide. bibliog Science 152:1376-7 Je 3 '66

TOUCH
Blindfolded seeing claimed to be peeking. Sci N L 89:152 Mr 5 '66
Dermo-optical perception; a peek down the nose. M. Gardner. bibliog Science 151:654-7 F 11 '66; Discussion. 152:1108-10 My 20 '66

TOUGALOO Southern Christian college, Tougaloo, Miss.
How to grow a campus. J. M. Dixon. il Arch Forum 124:56-61 Ap '66

TOULMIN, Stephen
Books. Sci Am 214:129-30+ F; 9-11 Ap '66

TOULOUSE-LAUTREC MONFA, Henri Marie Raymond de
Dining with Toulouse-Lautrec. Time 87:52+ Je 17 '66
Toulouse-Lautrec: his complete lithographs and drypoints, by J. Adhémar. Review Reporter 34:52+ Ap 21 '66. A. Werner

TOUMANOVA, Tamara
Toumanova in Hollywood. V. H. Swisher. il pors Dance Mag 40:26-7 Mr '66

TOUPIN, Elizabeth Ahn
Hawaii cookbook & backyard luau; excerpt. Ladies Home J 83:122-3+ N '66

TOUR: story. See Dikeman, M.

TOURÉ, Sékou
Africa's top nationalist, or Africa's prima donna? L. Garrison. il pors N Y Times Mag p 12-13+ Ja 1 '67

TOURGÉE, Albion Winegar
Carpetbagger's crusade, by O. H. Olsen. Review Nation 202:272-3 Mr 7 '66. A. Guttmann

TOURIST trade
American tourist. S. R. Waters. Ann Am Acad 368:109-18 N '66
Americans step up race for the sun. il Bsns W p46 D 17 '66
If you're planning a trip abroad: what to expect. il U S News 60:62-9 Ap 11 '66
If you're thinking of a winter vacation. il U S News 62:54-7 Ja 16 '67
It was the islands' wildest season. il Bsns W p52+ Mr 26 '66
Let's travel; summer news notes. Mlle 63:148-51 Je '66
New House of Rothschild; financing tourist business. il Newsweek 67:62 F 7 '66
1967: International tourist year. il UNESCO Courier 19:5-9 D '66
Traveler, beware! beat-up cruise ships, phony charter flights endanger your money, and your life. il Changing T 20:7-12 Ap '66
What chance the tourist? H. Sutton. Sat R 50:45+ Ja 7 '67
See also
Souvenirs
Travel—Economic aspects

Bahama Islands
ABC Bahama Baedeker. H. M. Winters. il Motor B 118:38+ O '66

Bay Islands
Delightful beaches, splendid fishing, room with meals $5 and up. il Sunset 137:46+ N '66

Bermuda
How Bermuda defuses the revels of spring; college week. il Bsns W p72-4 Ap 16 '66

Bulgaria
Big beat in the Balkans. Time 88:42 N 25 '66

Canary Islands
To Madeira and the Canaries. il Sunset 136:26+ F '66

Caribbean Region
It was the islands' wildest season. il Bsns W p52+ Mr 26 '66

Communist countries
Iron-curtain lands: what to see; what to avoid. U S News 60:69 Ap 11 '66

Denmark
Mayors, Moreno, and a marriage; how it is going to celebrate 800th anniversary of Copenhagen. M. Connelly. il Sat R 50:54+ Ja 7 '67

Europe
Personal business; still time to book into Europe. Bsns W p 169-70 My 14 '66

Hawaii
BAC-111, DC-9 competing in Island rivalry. R. G. O'Lone. il Aviation W 85:40-1+ N 7 '66
Going places, finding things in Hawaii. D. Otis. House & Gard 130:25+ Ag '66
Hawaii: its hotels, planes, restaurants. D. Messinesi. il Vogue 148:146-9 N 1 '66
Let's travel; Pan Am tours to Hawaii. il Mlle 63:199 My '66
Young hangouts. H. Sutton. il Mlle 63:140+ My '66

Madeira (island)
To Madeira and the Canaries. il Sunset 136:26+ F '66

Monaco
Duel in the sun. il Newsweek 68:42 Jl 18 '66
Putting Monaco back on the tourist's map; Prince Rainier vs Aristotle Onassis, the Greek shipping magnate. il Bsns W p28-9 Jl 30 '66

Portugal
Travel notes. R. Joseph. Esquire 66:28+ Jl '66

Russia
Another poor bargain; agreements for New York-Moscow air service. R. Hotz. Aviation W 85:21 N 7 '66
New U.S.-Russian link, by air. il U S News 61:93 N 14 '66
Soviet Union's 50th: is Russia a tourist country? M. Kalb. il Sat R 50:51-2+ Ja 7 '67

Spain
Travel notes. R. Joseph. Esquire 66:28+ Jl '66
Turismo! in a little Spanish town; Alcudia, Majorca. A. S. Mehdevi. il N Y Times Mag p6-7+ Jl 24 '66

Sweden
Three-day cruise across Sweden. il Sunset 136:70+ Ap '66

United States
Airline strike clips the wings of tourism. il Bsns W p31 Ag 13 '66
Big roundup: this year's prospects. Newsweek 67:84+ My 16 '66
Challenge of the travel boom. Life 61:4 Jl 22 '66
Foreign hands see employer's home base: cut-rate U.S. tour for IBM overseas workers. il Bsns W p78-9 Ag 13 '66
See also
United States—Travel service

Venezuela
Picture portfolio: Venezuela. Travel 126:55 Jl '66

Vietnam (Republic)
Pearl of the Orient. D. Fawcett. Sat R 49:70-2 O 8 '66

Virgin Islands
Pix mark the spots. L. Barry. il Pop Phot 59:31+ N '66

Yugoslavia
Yugoslavia; with report by M. Leatherbee. il Life 60:52-63 My 27 '66

TOURISTS. See Tourist trade; Travelers

TOURISTS and customs administration. See Customs service and tourists

TOURNACHON, Félix. See Nadar

TOURNAMENT players. See Bridge players

TOURNAMENTS
Rouster jouster; game of joutes, as practiced in southern France. il Travel 125:6 Je '66
See also
Basketball tournaments

TOURNAMENTS, Bridge. See Bridge tournaments

TOURS, European. See Europe, Western—Description and travel

TOURS, Garden. See Garden tours

TOURS, Industrial. See Industrial tours

TOURS, Package. See Travel

TOURTELLOTTE, Wallace W. and Parker, J. A.
Multiple sclerosis: correlation between immunoglobulin-G in cerebrospinal fluid and brain. bibliog Science 154:1044-6 N 25 '66

TOUSTER, Saul
Between Thoreau and me; poem. Nation 203:131 Ag 8 '66
Lunch hour idyll. Nation 203:360 O 10 '66

TOVELL, Walter M. and Deane, R. E.
Grizzly bear skull: site of a find near Lake Simcoe. Science 154:158 O 7 '66

TOWBOATS. See Tugboats

TOWE, Kenneth M. and Harper, C. W. Jr
Pholidostrophiid brachiopods: origin of the nacreous luster. bibliog Science 154:153-5 O 7 '66

TOWEL racks, rings, etc.
Flip-top towel rack. il House & Gard 129:187 Mr '66

TOWELL, William Earnest
Towell succeeds Hornaday. por Am For 72:
4 D '66

TOWER, John Goodwin
Excerpt from debate, July 15, 1965. Cong
Digest 45:19+ Ja '66

about

Three races. H. Alexander. Nat R 18:1043-5
O 18 '66

TOWER, Whitney
Horse racing. See issues of Sports illustrated
Polo. Sports Illus 25:85-8 S 5 '66

TOWER ISLAND. See Galápagos Islands

TOWER suite. See New York (city)—Hotels,
restaurants, etc.

TOWERS
Legacy of Simon Rodia; towers in the Watts
section of Los Angeles. L. Barry. il Pop
Phot 59:34 O '66
Maurice Medcalfe's bathing pillar. il Vogue
148:168-71 S 15 '66
See also
Television towers
Water towers

TOWHEES
Our wintering tailless towhee. T. A. McNett.
Audubon Mag 68:195 My '66

TOWING equipment. See Automobiles—Equipment

TOWLE, Laird C. and others
Molybdenum diselenide: rhombohedral high
pressure-high temperature polymorph. bibliog Science 154:895-6 N 18 '66

TOWN houses. See Architecture, Domestic

TOWN life. See City and town life

TOWN meeting
Basic democracy; New England. Newsweek
67:32+ Ap 4 '66

TOWN planning. See City planning

TOWNE, Anthony
In defense of heresy. Christian Cent 84:44-7
Ja 11 '67
My soul faints within me; poem. Christian
Cent 83:1331 N 2 '66

TOWNS. See Cities and towns

TOWNS, Models of. See Models of cities, towns,
etc.

TOWNS, New. See New towns

TOWNS, Restored. See Villages, Restored

TOWNSEND, Dwight D.
Excerpt from testimony, May 3, 1965. Cong
Digest 45:184+ Je '66

TOWNSEND, J. David
Righting a rite. Christian Cent 83:369 Mr 23
'66

TOWNSEND, James R.
Internal politics since 1956; excerpt from
New communisms. Bul Atomic Sci 22:58-
65 Je '66

TOWNSEND, Lynn Alfred
Idealism without illusions; address, June 11,
1966. Vital Speeches 32:626-9 Ag 1 '66
Investment abroad by U.S. companies; address, January 26, 1966. Vital Speeches 32:
280-3 F 15 '66

about

How Chrysler restyled its top. il por Bsns W
p70-1+ D 10 '66

TOWNSEND, Maurice Wilbur
Unique fabricator. T. J. Murray. il por
Duns R 87:41-3+ F '66

TOWNSHIPS
Man who couldn't be bought; when Bob
Smith went into politics. W. Goodman. il
Redbook 128:66-7+ N '66

TOXINS and antitoxins
Deadly sea beasts or lifesavers? il Sci N 90:
498 D 10 '66
Effects of tetrodotoxin on excitability of squid
giant axons in sodium-free media. A. Wat-
anabe and others. bibliog il Science 155:95-7
Ja 6 '67
Mycotoxicoses: toxic fungi in tobaccos. J.
Forgacs and W. T. Carll. il Science 152:
1634-5 Je 17 '66
Osmotic pressure influence in germination
tests for antibiosis. R. C. Anderson and
O. L. Loucks. bibliog il Science 152:771-3
My 6 '66
Pahutoxin: a fish poison. D. B. Boylan and
P. J. Scheuer. bibliog il Science 155:52-6
Ja 6 '67
Staphylococcal alpha-toxin: effects on arti-
ficial lipid spherules. G. Weissmann and
others. bibliog il Science 154:772-4 N 11 '66
Tetraethylammonium and tetrodotoxin: ef-
fects on cochlear potentials. Y. Katsuki
and others. bibliog il Science 151:1544-5
Mr 25 '66

Tetrodotoxin and manganese ions: effects on
electrical activity and tension in taenia coli
of guinea pig. Y. Nonomura and others.
bibliog il Science 152:97-9 Ap 1 '66
Tetrodotoxin does not block excitation from
inside the nerve membrane. T. Narahashi
and others. bibliog il Science 153:765-7 Ag
12 '66
Toxin causing mussel poisoning isolated:
saxitoxin. Sci N 89:490 Je 18 '66

TOXOPLASMOSIS
Parasite effect studied. Sci N 90:503 D 10 '66

TOY automobiles. See Automobiles, Toy

TOY chests. See Chests

TOY ferries. See Ferries, Toy

TOY houses. See Doll houses

TOY industry
Japan's toy men play it together; tiny
companies pooling facilities. il Bsns W
p 110-12 D 17 '66
Toys for fun and education; American toy
fair in New York city. il Consumer Bul 49:
12-15 D '66

TOY trains. See Railroads, Toy

TOYNBEE, Arnold Joseph
To establish an equilibrium; excerpt from
address, November 2, 1959. UNESCO
Courier 19:12 F '66

TOYNBEE, Philip
Churchill to his son. New Repub 155:28-9
D 24 '66
Lord Russell and Lord Amberley. New Repub
156:32-3+ Ja 21 '67
Victorian pornotopia. New Repub 155:19-20
S 3 '66

TOYOTA motor company. See Automobile industry and trade—Japan

TOYS
Artful toys. B. Plumb. il N Y Times Mag
p 126-7+ N 27 '66
Christmas (ka-pow!) again; war toys. W. H.
Honan. New Repub 155:7-8 D 17 '66
Computers for fun; two interesting new toys.
il Consumer Bul 49:43 N '66
Fabulous cardboard toys. il Bet Hom & Gard
44:56-7 D '66
Fun for junior mailmen. S. Ellingson. il Pop
Mech 125:174-6+ F '66
On and off the avenue (cont) New Yorker
42:203-4+ D 10 '66
Pop goes the pop-uppet. il Sunset 137:80+
D '66
Remote control toys. il Consumer Bul 50:20
Ja '67
This kind of toy should be banned; and we
may get a new law to do it; dangers of the
Sonic blaster. il Consumer Rep 31:266-7
Je '66
This year give baby an ego-expander. W. K.
Zinsser. Life 61:10 D 16 '66
Those unassembled Christmas toys! Con-
sumer Bul 49:31-2 D '66
Three pull-apart pull toys. W. Waltner and
E. Waltner. il Pop Mech 126:143-5 D '66
Today's toys; Mattel, inc.'s pre-school toys.
M. B. Keiser. il Parents Mag 41:46+ O '66
Toys of yesteryear; private collection of G.
William Holland. il Todays Health 44:25-8
D '66
Where even Santa gets ideas. M. J. Schultz.
il Pop Mech 126:76-9+ D '66
Wonderful toys any father can make for
Christmas; designed by Tomi Ungerer.
K. D. Fury. il Redbook 128:70-7 N '66
Your kids will get a bang! out of this: Big
Bertha cannon. H. W. Teter. il Pop Mech
126:141 Ag '66
See also
Alexander doll company
Christmas gifts for children
Dolls
Kites
Toy industry

Anecdotes, facetiae, satire, etc.

Bold new trend in plaything creation. D. L.
Goodrich. il Sat Eve Post 239:14 D 17 '66

Collectors and collecting

Art and history in American toys. E. Stillinger. il Antiques 90:337-9 D '66

History

History of toys, by A. Fraser. Review
New Yorker 42:233-4+ D 3 '66. N. Bliven
Some fine cast iron toys. il (p 1) Hobbies 71:
48 D '66

Storage

His miniature town and train just disappear.
il Sunset 136:139 F '66

TOYS—Storage—*Continued*
  What is it? It's a cupboard, a toy wall, a puppet theater. And if you are a woodworker, maybe it's for Christmas. il Sunset 137:78-9 N '66

TOYS for Santa; drama. See Robertson, O. J.

TRACE elements
  Trace element partition coefficient in ionic crystals. H. Nagasawa. bibliog il Science 152:767-9 My 6 '66

TRACERS, Radioactive. See Radioactive tracers

TRACEY, Andrew
  Songsters from a southern latitude; interview. New Yorker 42:27-9 Je 4 '66

TRACEY, Hugh, family
  Songsters from a southern latitude; interview. A. Tracey and P. Tracey. New Yorker 42:27-9 Je 4 '66

TRACEY, Joshua I. Jr. See Gross, M. G. jt. auth.

TRACEY, Paul
  Songsters from a southern latitude; interview. New Yorker 42:27-9 Je 4 '66

TRACHTENBERG, Alan
  City and the road. Nation 202:526-8 My 2 '66

TRACHTENBERG, Alexander
  Obituary
    Pub W 190:65-6 D 26 '66

TRACK athletes. See Athletes

TRACK athletes, Negro. See Negro athletes

TRACK athletics
  Are girl athletes really girls? sex inspections stir international furor. il Life 61:63-6 O 7 '66
  Doleful day for Ryun: 3:58.6. G. S. Brown. il Sports Illus 25:22-4 Jl 4 '66
  Emotion in motion; paintings. J. Jonson. Sports Illus 24:48-55 My 23 '66
  Everyone's keen on Keino. C. E. Brown. il Ebony 21:100-2+ My '66
  Fierce fight in the family; British empire and Commonwealth games. G. S. Brown. il Sports Illus 25:56-9 Ag 22 '66
  Great leap forward and back; European athletic championships in Budapest. J. Lovesey. il Sports Illus 25:40-1 S 12 '66
  If at first you don't succeed try thirty-three more times; UCLA beats its rival. USC. J. Tobin. il Sports Illus 24:74-6 My 16 '66
  Muddy day in East Berlin; Olympischer tag. J. Olsen. il Sports Illus 25:68-70+ Jl 18 '66
  Sad music from a Stradivarius; T. Smith in NCAA track and field championships. G. S. Brown. il Sports Illus 24:64-5 Je 27 '66
  See Southern run; Southern university. il Time 87:67 Ap 22 '66
  Soaring above snafus; AAU national indoor championships in Albuquerque. G. S. Brown. il Sports Illus 24:16-19 Mr 14 '66
  Southern U; new kings of track. il Ebony 21:69-70+ Jl '66
  Storm of bright promises; Penn and Drake relays. G. S. Brown. Sports Illus 24:74-5 My 9 '66
  Very welcome redcoat; J. Velzian, British coach of the Kenya national track team. M. Kane. il Sports Illus 25:78-82 D 19 '66
  What price what glory? decathlon. il Time 88:52-3 Ag 5 '66
    See also
  Running
  Vaulting (sport)

TRACKING and trailing
    See also
  Radio in tracking and trailing

TRACKING radar. See Radar in tracking and trailing

TRACKS, Railroad. See Railroads—Track

TRACTION (automobiles) See Automobiles—Traction

TRACTOR air filters. See Air filters

TRACTOR engines
  Turbocharge for more power? Suc Farm 64:54B Ag '66

Fuel
  Know your diesel. C. N. Hinkle and W. J. Fletcher. il Suc Farm 64:48 Ag '66

Maintenance and repair
  Know your diesel. C. N. Hinkle and W. J. Fletcher. il Suc Farm 64:94+ S '66

TRACTOR industry and trade
    See also
  Caterpillar tractor company

TRACTORS
  Bigger tractors, eight ways they pay. P. B. Jones. il Suc Farm 64:38-9 My '66
  How practical are garden tillers. J. Krill. il Flower Grower 53:56-7 Je '66
  It's a four-hour kit assembling the lawn mule. A. Mikesell. il Pop Mech 125:130-4 Je '66
  Lawn mule. A. Mikesell. il Pop Mech 125:68-9 Je '66
  Little tractor that can. J. Liston. il Pop Gard 17:50-3+ D '66
  Now: man-sized jobs for baby tractors. G. Logsdon. il Farm J 90:64R-64S F '66
  Small home tractor. il House & Gard 129:232-5 Ap '66
  Tractor revolution. il Flower Grower 53:60-3 Ap '66
    See also
  Crawler tractors

Loading and unloading
  See Loading and unloading

TRACTORS, Used
  How to buy a used tractor. D. Hull. il Suc Farm 64:42-3 Je '66

TRACY, Honor
  Greek in England. New Repub 154:37-8 F 26 '66
  Here we go gathering nuts. New Repub 155:27-8 D 10 '66

TRADE. See Commerce

TRADE acceptances. See Acceptances

TRADE agreements
  Air strike agreement has a rough landing. il Bsns W p31 Ag 20 '66
  Back to work through an open gate. il Time 88:66-8 Ag 26 '66
  Cooperation provisions in major agreements. T. L. Ellis. il Mo Labor R 89:283-7 Mr '66
  Developments in industrial relations. See issues of Monthly labor review
  Labor's rebellious rank and file. M. J. Gart. il Fortune 74:150-3+ N '66
  Major agreement expirations and reopenings. C. T. Ward. il Mo Labor R 88:1426-37 D '65
  Major collective bargaining settlements, 1965. L. M. David. il Mo Labor R 89:372-6 Ap '66
  Management rights provisions in major agreements. R. F. Groner and L. E. Lunden. il Mo Labor R 89:170-4 F '66
  New number to live by; General electric settlement with unions establishes 5 per cent as pattern for wage increases. il Bsns W p37-8 O 22 '66
  Steel contract puts Abel on spot; dissatisfaction within union. Bsns W p97-8 Ja 22 '66
  Wage calendar for 1967; with tables. C. Ward and W. Davis. Mo Labor R 89:1339-55 D '66
  Wage developments in manufacturing, 1965. G. Ruben. il Mo Labor R 89:871-6 Ag '66
  Who won in the GE settlement. il Bsns W p 149-50+ O 22 '66

TRADE associations
  New help in the race to stay ahead. il Nations Bsns 54:100-2+ Jl '66

TRADE balance. See Balance of payments

TRADE book clinic. See American institute of graphic arts—Trade book clinic

TRADE expansion act. See Tariff—United States

TRADE fairs. See Exhibitions

TRADE journals
  P.R. with a touch of magic; publications of Eastman Kodak company. J. Deschin. Pop Phot 59:24+ O '66

TRADE marks
  Monacan trade mark raid threatens nine publishers. Pub W 189:61 F 7 '66
  Story behind... See issues of Changing times
  What's in a name? trademark piracy. Newsweek 67:62+ F 7 '66

TRADE names
  Branding on trial. T. Levitt. bibliog f Harvard Bsns R 44:20-2+ Mr '66
  Name game. Read Digest 88:201-2+ F '66
  Story behind... See issues of Changing times

TRADE practices
  Regulation, by business or government? J. G. Van Cise. bibliog f Harvard Bsns R 44:53-63 Mr '66
    See also
  Restraint of trade
  Sales policies

TRADE regulation
  Regulation, by business or government? J. G. Van Cise. bibliog f Harvard Bsns R 44:53-63 Mr '66

TRADE schools
  Area vocational schools. M. Russo. il Am Ed 2:15-19 Je '66
  Post-high opportunity in DeKalb. Georgia. T. W. Hollingsworth. il NEA J 55:44-5 S '66

TRADE secrets
Unlocking corporate secrets: Paris-based company, known as Eurofinance. il Time 87: 99-100 Ap 8 '66

TRADE union congress. See Trades union congress

TRADE union leaders. See Trade unions—Officials

TRADE unions
Beating the system; tutoring school for union qualifying exams. Newsweek 69:56 Ja 16 '67
Foreign labor briefs. Mo Labor R 89:1000-1 S '66
    See also
Boycott
Collective bargaining
Industrial relations
Strikes

Communist activities
How reds kept a strike going; seamen's strike; Great Britain. U S News 61:63-4 Jl 4 '66

Constitutions
National union constitutions before and after LMRDA. il Mo Labor R 88:1451-4 D '65

Dues, fees, etc.
Dues and fees structure of local unions. L. Applebaum. il Mo Labor R 89:1236-40 N '66

Educational work
Touch of realism; California trucking association's teamsters' transportation opportunity program. Nation 203:597 D 5 '66
Union men take to the campus; curriculum ranging from pensions and politics. il Bsns W p64+ Ag 13 '66
What a union does to fill a shortage; helping sailors become marine engineers. il Bsns W p 105-6 Ap 2 '66

Elections
National union constitutions before and after LMRDA. il Mo Labor R 88:1451-4 D '65
Referendum elections of national union officers. D. L. Everette. il Mo Labor R 89: 856-9 Ag '66
Voting representation of local unions at national conventions. C. E. Skopic. Mo Labor R 88:1423-5 D '65

International aspects
Auto labor goes multinational. il Bsns W p74-6 Je 11 '66
Breaking ranks at the top; clash between Meany and Reuther over U.S. labor's boycott of ILO meeting at Geneva. Bsns W p 149 Je 18 '66
CIA-AFL-CIO; dissension over activities of J. Lovestone. Nation 202:700 Je 13 '66
International unions: how influential are they? reprint. Mo Labor R 89:518-19 My '66
Lovestone, Meany & State: American labor overseas. H. W. Berger. il Nation 204:80-4 Ja 16 '67
Lovestone's cold war: AFL-CIO has its own CIA. D. Kurzman. New Repub 154:17-22 Je 25 '66

Law
    See Labor laws and legislation—United States

Management
How union shop breeds corruption. il Nations Bsns 54:42-3+ F '66
Labor's rebellious rank and file. M. J. Gart. il Fortune 74:150-3+ N '66
Working with a capitalistic union; Amalgamated lithographers of America Local 1. il Nations Bsns 54:38-9+ Ja '66

Membership
Attitudes toward unionism of active and passive members. il Mo Labor R 89:175-7 F '66
Automation & white collar unionism. T. R. Brooks. Duns R 87:59-62 Ja '66
Farm workers: target in union drive. U S News 60:124 Je 13 '66
New militancy of labor. il Newsweek 68:93-5 S 26 '66
Pressures on labor: Vietnam, race and the unions. B. J. Widick. il Nation 203:545-8 N 21 '66
Trends and changes in union membership. H. P. Cohany. il Mo Labor R 89:510-13 My '66
Union cards were phony; case of the Washington area Drug fair chain. il Nations Bsns 54:100-1+ Mr '66
Unions: fast action, slow growth; despite accelerated organizing drives, no big gains. Bsns W p56-7 Ag 20 '66

Negro membership
Against union discrimination; NLRB victory against United rubber workers of America's Local 12. Time 88:60 D 2 '66
Early organization of red caps 1937-1938. P. Romero. bibliog Negro Hist Bul 29:101-2+ F '66
Jim Crow in building unions. Life 60:4 F 18 '66
Magnificent tokenism; Labor department requests federal action against the A.F.L.-C.I.O. Building trades council. Time 87: 19-20 Ja 28 '66
Suit against the unions; St Louis. E. C. Gottschalk. New Repub 154:7-8 Mr 12 '66
    See also
Negro American labor council

Officials
Adamant Mr Meany. Nation 202:764 Je 27 '66
Coal strike leaves discord in UMW ranks; lack of strong union leadership. il Bsns W p 122+ My 7 '66
Labor leaders, tough, remote, or feuding. B. Farrell. il Life 61:30-36B Ag 26 '66
Labor's rebellious rank and file. M. J. Gart. il Fortune 74:150-3+ N '66
Little room at top for labor's women; O. M. Madar, UAW's vice-president. Bsns W p62+ My 28 '66
Making strikes obsolete. A. H. Raskin. Atlan 217:47-52 Je '66
Pressures on labor: Vietnam, race and the unions. B. J. Widick. il Nation 203:545-8 N 21 '66
Referendum elections of national union officers. D. L. Everette. il Mo Labor R 89: 856-9 Ag '66
Winds of change ruffle unions' top executives; disunity and restiveness threatens invulnerability of union leaders. il Bsns W p71-2+ S 17 '66

Political activities
Air strike turns into political hot potato; legislators debate who should issue the back-to-work order. il Bsns W p29-31 Ag 6 '66
AFL-CIO heads for Johnson clash. il Bsns W p57-8 F 26 '66
Big losers in the election: union leaders. U S News 61:102-5 N 21 '66
DRIVE: teamsters in politics; Democrat Republican independent voter education. T. E. Tornek. il Nation 203:663-5 D 19 '66
How unions are signing them up. W. Wingo. il Nations Bsns 54:36-7+ S '66
How unions are trying to take over. il Nations Bsns 54:40 F '66
Labor's love lost; labor and the Democratic party. Time 87:25 Ap 1 '66
Labor's political frustrations. A. H. Raskin. il Reporter 34:26-8+ Ap 7 '66
Now it's the unions that are worrying LBJ. il U S News 60:86-8 F 28 '66
Political unions' woes. R. Moley. Newsweek 68:120 D 19 '66
Reuther's chance; AFL-CIO leaders reactions to election. Nation 203:595 D 5 '66
So politics comes first? D. Lawrence. U S News 61:100 Ag 15 '66
Strike curbs are labor's no. 1 issue; rallying cry of unions in congressional elections. il Bsns W p 104+ O 1 '66
Unions fail to deliver the goods. Bsns W p 103+ N 19 '66
Unions' split with LBJ: what will come out of it. il U S News 60:76-8 Mr 7 '66
Vanishing vote. Time 88:34 N 25 '66
What unions want in Congress and what they aren't getting. il U S News 60:120-2 Je 13 '66
Where will labor turn? legislative setbacks on Capitol hill. Bsns W p29-31 Je 4 '66
Yeps have it. Nat R 18:1204 N 29 '66
    See also
American federation of labor and Congress of industrial organizations—Committee on political education
Trade unions—Communist activities

Publications
Breaking labor's rules; Amalgamated lithographer's Lithopinion. il Time 87:78 Mr 18 '66

Representation elections
    See Trade unions—Elections

Africa
Communist grab for African unions. L. M. Taubinger. Nat R 18:1222 N 29 '66

TRADE unions—*Continued*

Brazil

U.S. labor launches road show in Rio; sponsorship of worker-to-worker program. il Bsns W p98-100 F 12 '66

Canada

International unions: how influential are they? reprint. Mo Labor R 89:518-19 My '66

Wage parity with U.S. will be Canadian issue; equal pay for equal jobs big factor in bargaining. il Bsns W p 153-4+ Mr 19 '66

See also

Strikes—Canada

Germany (Federal Republic)

I'm all right, Hans; unionization of West German army. Time 88:40+ N 18 '66

Great Britain

Chips are down for Harold Wilson. G. Bailey. il Reporter 34:31-4 Je 2 '66

Wilson and the unions. B. Wenham. New Repub 155:12 S 24 '66

See also

Trades union congress

Latin America

Labor's new weapon for democracy. E. H. Methvin. il Read Digest 89:21-2+ O '66

Latin America: labor between bread and revolution. S. Lens. il Nation 203:248-51 S 19 '66

Spain

Labor and the Spanish syndical system; excerpt from Labor policy and practices in Spain. F. Witney. Mo Labor R 89:867-70 Ag '66

United States

Boom gives labor its '67 leverage; economists fear wage-price spiral; with editorial comment. il Bsns W p40-1, 200 My 14 '66

Close-up: talk with George W. Taylor; interview, ed. by J. Berry. il Duns R 88: 8-9+ O '66

Developments in industrial relations. See issues of Monthly labor review

Ethical aspects of union policy and conduct. E. Stein. bibliog f Ann Am Acad 363:117-25 Ja '66

Labor month in review. See issues of Monthly labor review

Mood is militant. il Bsns W p47-9 S 24 '66

New militancy of labor; signs of unrest. il Newsweek 68:93-5 S 26 '66

Now it's union vs. union in bids for biggest raises. il U S News 61:78-9 D 19 '66

Pressures on labor: Vietnam, race and the unions. B. J. Widick. il Nation 203:545-8 N 21 '66

Push is on for fatter pay envelopes; bargaining issues of 1967; with charts. Bsns W p72-5 D 31 '66

Trouble ahead. Time 88:33 D 16 '66

Unions call 5 per cent a minimum for '67; win Wirtz's blessing. Bsns W p 163-4 N 26 '66

Unions press harder against the guideposts. il Bsns W p 117-18 Mr 5 '66

What other unions learned from the airline strike. il U S News 61:67-9 S 5 '66

What to do when the union knocks. W. Wingo. il Nations Bsns 54:42-5+ N; 40-1+ D '66; 55:82-5+ Ja '67

See also

Arbitration, Industrial—United States

Building trades unions

Strikes—United States

Trade unions—Officials

United States—Labor policy

also names of unions, e.g. United automobile, aerospace and agricultural implement workers of America

TRADE waste

Can fish farms clean our polluted waters? research project at Michigan state university. K. L. Schulze. Sat R 49:62-3 Je 4 '66; Reply with rejoinder. J. R. Hanson. 49:51 Jl 2 '66

City-industry treatment plant; Kalamazoo, Mich. Am City 81:26 F '66

How companies are cleaning the streams. Nations Bsns 53:75 D '65

Mile-deep well dug out of solid rock; world's deepest wastebasket. Sci N 89:267 Ap 16 '66

Report on present status of a new simple low-cost coal sewage treatment. E. R. Fosdick. il Nat Parks Mag 40:18-19 Ap '66

Resourceful waste management: address, June 7, 1966. A. Spilhaus. il Sci N 89:486-8+ Je 18 '66

Shredded secrets; Document distintegration, inc, Los Angeles. Newsweek 67:80 F 28 '66

See also

Wood waste

TRADE winds

Amateur scientist: study of the salty rain of Venezuela; periodic wind called alisio blows the calina fog away. G. Zuloaga. il Sci Am 215:136-8 D '66

TRADERS, Grain. See Grain trade

TRADES union congress

Thin margin for Harold; reluctant acquiescence to wage-price freeze. Time 88:40 S 16 '66

Wilson and the unions. B. Wenham. New Repub 155:12 S 24 '66

TRADING stamps

Different stamping: difficulties of trading-stamp industry. Time 87:92+ Ap 8 '66

Lifting the veil on S&H; sell 10 per cent of holdings. Bsns W p 112+ Ap 2 '66

Not licked yet. Time 89:89 Ja 6 '67

Stamps: taking a licking. il Time 88:97 N 11 '66

Trading stamps, bonus or bogus? pro and con discussion. il Sr Schol 89:10-11 Ja 13 '67

TRADING. See Barter

TRADITION

On tradition, or what is left of it; Time essay. Time 87:42-3 Ap 22 '66

TRADITION (theology)

Essentiality of tradition. K. Hamilton. Christian Cent 83:707-10 Je 1 '66

TRAFFIC. See Road traffic; Street traffic

TRAFFIC, Airline. See Airlines—Traffic

TRAFFIC accidents

American highway scandal; address, February 3, 1966. G. Nelson. Vital Speeches 32:329-32 Mr 15 '66

And sudden death; reprint. J. C. Furnas. Read Digest 89:153-7 O '66

Auto safety goes into high gear. il Newsweek 67:77-8+ F 21 '66

Auto safety: new study criticizes manufacturers and universities. E. Langer; discussion. Science 151:277-9+, 1480+ Ja 21, Mr 25 '66

Automotive safety (cont) R. Moley. Newsweek 67:90 Ja 31; 88 F 7; 100 F 14; 106 F 21 '66

Can you withstand 30 g's? H. Downs. il Sci Digest 60:88-90 O '66

Clip out these things you'd never think to do if involved in an accident. Bet Hom & Gard 44:38 My '66

Dick; investigation of author of Unsafe at any speed. J. Ridgeway. New Repub 154: 11-13 Mr 12 '66

For the fastest ride out of this world, take a motorbike. J. Contini. il Seventeen 25: 152-3+ N '66

Force on impact! il Sr Schol 89:37 O 21 '66

Growing slaughter on highways; what to do? il U S News 60:42-5 F 7 '66

Hazards of Roseville road. G. C. Maurer. il Pop Phot 58:60-2 Je '66

High highway accident rate: who's to blame? automobiles! highways! drivers! Sr Schol 89:10-11 Ja 6 '67

How can we stop the slaughter on our nation's highways? forum discussion; discussion. il Sr Schol 87:22-3 Ja 14 '66

If you have an accident. . il Sr Schol 88:30 Ap 22 '66

If you think driving in the U.S. is dangerous; driving in western Europe. il U S News 60:104-6 Je 20 '66

Let's abolish traffic danger spots. B. Schapper. il Todays Health 44:18-21 O '66

LBJ and auto safety; Traffic safety act of 1966; proposals. R. Moley. Newsweek 67:112 Mr 21 '66

Mayhem on motorcycles. il Time 88:33 Jl 29 '66

Morals of driving. America 114:278 F 26 '66

Motor deaths on the rise worldwide. il Am City 81:128+ D '66

Personal business. Bsns W p 125-6 Ag 6 '66

R for safety; fix nut behind the wheel. A. H. Sypher. il Nations Bsns 54:31-2 Ap '66

Real causes and cures of auto accidents; study from the Stanford research institute. il U S News 60:44-6 My 23 '66

Ribicoff is a cautious crusader. J. F. Welsh. il N Y Times Mag p32-3+ Je 12 '66

Rural accidents highly hazardous. il Todays Health 44:11 S '66

Safety myths that mess up your driving. J. F. Pearson. il Pop Mech 126:93-7 N '66

Set for safety; auto-safety bill. il Time 88: 106 S 16 '66

TRAFFIC accidents—*Continued*
Still unsafe at any speed. J. A. Page. New Repub 155:32+ Jl 30 '66
This traffic safety expert has an ideal interview, ed. by D. Gregg. D. Slutz. Bet Hom & Gard 44:18+ S '66
Urgent more coffins; Philippine bus accident worst road disaster in history. Newsweek 69:52 Ja 16 '67
Why cars must, and can, be made safer; Time essay. Time 87:26-7 Ap 1 '66; Same abr. with title Safer cars on the roads ahead? Read Digest 88:115-18 Je '66
World of Leo Rosten. L. Rosten. il Look 30:14 My 31 '66
Your child's health; motorcycle accidents and startling statistics. L. W. Sauer. il PTA Mag 61:29-30 N '66
    See also
Automobile driving
Automobiles—Safety devices and measures
Insurance, Automobile

Cases
Death watch in Washtenaw; two-man team of University of Michigan medical school professors. A. Rothenberg. il Look 30:38-9 Ap 19 '66

Prevention
See Traffic safety

TRAFFIC congestion. See Street traffic
TRAFFIC control, Airport. See Airports—Traffic control
TRAFFIC control, Airway. See Air traffic control
TRAFFIC courts
Instant justice; French and German roadside courts. il Newsweek 68:34-5 Ag 29 '66
TRAFFIC engineering
Some remedies for traffic chaos; Little Rock, Ark. H. M. de Noble. il Am City 81:106-8 D '66
Traffic engineer must be an educator; Atlanta, Ga. K. A. Bevins. il Am City 81:116-18 O '66
    See also subhead Street traffic under names of cities, e.g. New York (city)—Street traffic
TRAFFIC fines. See Fines (penalties)
TRAFFIC lights. See Traffic signals
TRAFFIC markings
Drivers get a lift from raised lane markers; Nimitz freeway near Oakland, Calif. il Am City 81:147 My '66
Home-made line striper that's versatile; Zanesville, Ohio. F. E. Hardy. il Am City 81:122 Jl '66
Performance is the best test for traffic paints. H. Cannon. Am City 81:168-9 O '66
TRAFFIC regulations
Custom channelization tames an intersection; Vermillion, Ohio. H. Lechner. il Am City 81:120+ F '66
Last speed trap? Coleman, Fla. Time 88:60 D 2 '66
Letter fom Paris; suspension of license and fining for reckless driving. J. Flanner. New Yorker 42:111-12+ Ag 27 '66
One-way streets for winter; Easton, Pa. W. Tomino. il Am City 81:24 Jl '66
Our chaotic traffic laws. A. Ribicoff. Read Digest 88:101-2 Mr '66
Real causes and cures of auto accidents; study from the Stanford research institute. il U S News 60:44-6 My 23 '66
Traffic control. See issues of American city
Traffic violators beware; taming Akron, Ohio's speeding motorists. V. A. Busson. il Am City 81:134+ Je '66
    See also
Automobile parking
Computers—Traffic control applications
Electronics in traffic control
Motor vehicles—Laws and regulations
Photography in traffic regulation
Traffic courts
TRAFFIC safety
Double talk from Detroit; which to believe, auto makers' ads or safety statements? J. O'Connell. America 115:507-10 O 29 '66; Discussion. 115:673-4 N 26 '66
How to stop highway slaughter. R. I. Brown. il Duns R 54:31-3 Ag '66
Should combine study of cars, drivers, roads. Sci N 89:504 Je 25 '66
Smoke dims drivers view. Sci N 90:224 S 24 '66
Traffic safety; federal coordination; address, October 24, 1966. A. Ribicoff. Vital Speeches 33:104-6 D 1 '66
Unsafer everywhere else. Sci Am 215:102+ S '66

Which way to safety? R. P. Crossley. il Motor T 18:66-9 Ap '66
Who's in the driver's seat? G. M. Smerk. America 115:688-9 N 26 '66
    See also
Roads—Safety devices and measures
TRAFFIC safety agency. See United States—National traffic safety agency
TRAFFIC shelters. See Shelters
TRAFFIC signals
Countdown to red. Time 88:80 O 21 '66
How to make traffic signals super safe; Sacramento County, Calif. J. C. Ray. il Am City 81:130 O '66

Control
How to install loop detectors; DeKalb County, Ga. R. W. Roseveare. il Am City 81:120-1 Ap '66
TRAFFIC signs
Signs that sell traffic safety; Hempstead, N.Y. M. A. Pancia. il Am City 81:122 N '66
Traffic safety made simple; with pictures. A. H. Sypher. Nations Bsns 54:31-2 N '66
TRAFTON, Burton W. F. Jr
Louisburg and the Pepperrell silver. Antiques 89:366-7 Mr '66
TRAGER, Frank N.
China (is; is not) an aggressive power; debate. por N Y Times Mag p28-9+ Mr 13; 6+ Ap 10 '66
Vietnam; peace on the 1954 terms? Nat R 18:778-81 Ag 9 '66
TRAIL bikes. See Motorcycles
TRAIL riders of the wilderness
North Carolina's trail riding. M. Rabb. il Travel 125:32-5 My '66
TRAILER camps. See Automobile trailer camps
TRAILER-size containers. See Container system (freight handling)
TRAILING of cattle. See Cattle driving
TRAILS
Call of the open trail. G. W. Martin. il Parks & Rec 1:630-2 Ag '66
High trails; a guide to the Cascade Crest trail, by R. H. Wills. Review
    Liv Wildn 29:28 Aut '65
Our need for bicycle trails. E. C. Crafts. il Parks & Rec 1:435+ My '66
Path through the mist forest. M. B. Mellinger. il Nat Parks Mag 40:21-3 My '66
Railways to pathways; Minnesota. A. Marshall. il Parks & Rec 1:978+ D '66
This mountain hike is adjustable; John Muir trail. il Sunset 137:20 S '66
Trails across the Nation. il Parks & Rec 1:632-3+ Ag '66
Walk to Blaney meadows; a hike to the gateway of the Sierra Nevada, Calif. il Sunset 137:24-5 Jl '66
Wilderness trails. Natur Hist 75:75-6 O '66
    See also
Apache trail
Appalachian trail
TRAIN, Russell E.
Keynote address; America the beautiful. Am For 71:16-19+ O '65
Storm King opinion; stunning conservation victory. Am For 72:10-11 Mr '66
TRAIN robberies. See Robberies and assaults
TRAIN speed. See Railroads—Train speed
TRAIN travel. See Railroad travel
TRAINED nurses. See Nurses and nursing
TRAINING, Transfer of. See Transfer of training
TRAINING of children. See Children—Management and training
TRAINING of dogs. See Dogs—Training
TRAINING schools for delinquents. See Reformatories
TRAINOR, James L.
Government use of nonprofit companies. Harvard Bsns R 44:38-40+ My '66
TRAINS, Model. See Railroad models
TRAINS, Toy. See Railroads, Toy
TRAITORS
    See also
Trials (treason)
TRAJAN, emperor of Rome
Warlike Spaniard sounded a call to conquest and a golden age. il por Life 60:64-5 Je 3 '66
TRAMMELL, Archie
Afterthoughts of a racing fan. il Flying 78:42-5 F '66
Great insurance mystery. Flying 78:62-3 Ap; 58-61 My '66
Mayday. Flying 78:76-8 Ap '66
New tricks from the old dog. Flying 78:53-5 F '66

TRAMMELL, Archie—*Continued*
  On ice. Flying 78:57-60 Mr '66
  Pilot report: the new Bellanca. Flying 78:
    48-52 My '66
  What's going on at Beech? Pilot report; the
    three Musketeers. Flying 78:34-9 Je '66
TRAN-thi-Xa, Mme
  Distaff delegate. por Time 88:42 O 14 '66
TRAN-van-Dinh
  Elections in Vietnam. New Repub 155:19-22
    Jl 2 '66
TRANQUILIZING drugs
    See also
  Chlorpromazine
  Meprobamates
TRANS-ACTION (periodical)
  Sociology in English. Time 88:102 S 16 '66
TRANSACTIONAL analysis. See Psycho-
    therapy
TRANSATLANTIC flights. See Aviation—
    Transatlantic flights
TRANS-ATLANTIC race. See Yacht racing
TRANSATLANTIC voyages. See Voyages
TRANSATLANTIC yacht race. See Yacht rac-
    ing
TRANS-AUSTRALIA airlines. See Airlines—
    Australia
TRANSCEIVERS. See Radio telephone
TRANSCEIVERS, Portable. See Radio tele-
    phone, Portable
TRANSCENDENTALISM
    See also
  Brook Farm
TRANSCONTINENTAL European politics. See
    Europe—Politics
TRANSCONTINENTAL passenger service. See
    Railroads—Passenger traffic
TRANSCONTINENTAL railroad trips. See
    Railroad travel
TRANSDUCERS
  Divers' communications improved. K. K.
    Neely. Science 153:321 Jl 15 '66
  Lipid films as transducers for detection of
    antigen-antibody and enzyme-substrate re-
    actions. J. Del Castillo and others. bibliog
    il Science 153:185-8 Jl 8 '66
TRANSEXUALISM. See Change of sex
TRANSFER of learning. See Transfer of train-
    ing
TRANSFER of training
  Memory transfer unlikely; testing RNA-
    injected animals for learning transfer. Sci
    N L 89:151 Mr 5 '66
  Transfer evidence found. Sci N 90:346 O 29
    '66
TRANSFER taxes. See Gifts—Taxation; In-
    heritance tax
TRANSFORMERS. See Electric transformers
TRANSISTOR circuits
  Automatic stereo multiplex demodulator.
    D. R. Von Recklinghausen. il Electr World
    76:32-3+ Jl '66
TRANSISTOR organ. See Organ
TRANSISTOR receivers. See Radio receiving
    apparatus—Transistor receivers
TRANSISTOR vibrators. See Multivibrators
TRANSISTORS
  Designing silicon-transistor hi-fi amplifiers.
    R. D. Gold and J. C. Sondermeyer. il Electr
    World 76:23-6+ S; 34-6+ O; 47-50+ N '66
  Insulated gate field effect transistor ampli-
    fier. R. L. Cechner. il Science 153:1549-50
    S 23 '66
  New equipment: solid core of stereo. Hi Fi
    16:94-5 O '66
  Phono equalizer uses FET's. W. A. Rhein-
    felder. il Electr World 75:32-3+ Ap '66
  Solid state. L. Garner. See issues of Popular
    electronics
  Substituting FET's for tubes in hi-fi ampli-
    fiers; field-effect transistors. W. A. Rhein-
    felder. il Electr World 75:42-3 Mr '66
  Transistor replacement problems. W. A.
    Stocklin. Electr World 75:6 F '66
  Transistors and the shape of things. I. B.
    Berger. il Sat R 49:53 Ja 29 '66
  Trends in transistors: progress report. Hi Fi
    16:57-8 Mr '66
  Whisker for transistor; resonant-gate tran-
    sistor. Sci N 90:143 Ag 27 '66
    See also
  Television receiving apparatus—Transistor
    receivers
      Testing
  Transistor failure predicted; study of ger-
    manium-alloy transistors. il Electr World
    75:27 Je '66
TRANSIT systems. See Rapid transit
TRANSITION in literature. See Fiction—Tech-
    nique
TRANSITIONAL metals. See Metals

TRANSKEI
  Tiger snarls; under K. Matanzima's power.
    P. Webb. il Newsweek 67:44 Ap 25 '66
TRANSLATING machines
  Braille-reading machine. A. P. Grunwald. il
    Science 154:144-6 O 7 '66
  Machine translation: committee skeptical over
    research support. B. Nelson Science 155:58-
    9 Ja 6 '67
TRANSLATIONS and translating
  Almost-English. S. Kauffmann. New Repub
    155:26+ D 10 '66
  English translations of foreign social sci-
    ence materials. C. Brock il Library J 91:
    1995-2002 Ap 15 '66; Reply. M. E. Sharpe.
    91:3804+ S 1 '66
  Hazardous art of mistranslation. A. R. Mac-
    Andrew. Harper 232:94-6+ Ap '66
  Heresy by translation; Service book and
    hymnal used by National Lutheran council
    churches. C. R. McCormack. Christian Cent
    83:437-8 Ap 6 '66
  Peripatetic reviewer. E. Weeks Atlan 219:115
    Ja '67
  Translating books for newly developing
    countries; excerpt from Guide to book
    publishing. D. C. Smith, jr. Pub W 190:22-6
    Ag 1 '66
TRANSMISSION, Automobile. See Automobiles
    —Transmission
TRANSMISSION lines. See Electric lines
TRANSMISSION of heat. See Heat transmission
TRANSMISSION of power. See Power trans-
    mission
TRANSMUTATION (chemistry)
  How the newer alchemy was received. L.
    Badash. il Sci Am 215:88-95 bibliog(p 116)
    Ag '66
TRANSOCEANIC flights. See Aviation—Trans-
    oceanic flights
TRANSONIC aerodynamics. See Aerodynamics,
    Supersonic
TRANSPACIFIC flights. See Aviation—Trans-
    pacific flights
TRANSPARENCIES
  B&W slides from B&W negatives. L. Mulve-
    hill. il U S Camera 29:2 S '66
  Canon/Kalvar system; slide-making system
    that works like magic. N. Rothschild. il
    Pop Phot 58:70-1 F '66
  Home-grown slide sets. J. L. Debes. Sr
    Schol 89:sup 18 O 7 '66
  Overhead transparencies; a new service for
    teaching; with editorial comment. F. R.
    McElwain. il Sr Schol 89:sup 7 S 16 '66
      Copying
  Slide duplicators. il Pop Phot 59:172-3 O '66
      Editing
  Editing your slides can produce augmented
    scenic effects. W. Lane. il Travel 125:62-3
    F '66
      Projection
  Caulfield on color; slide shows. P. Caulfield.
    Mod Phot 31:42+ Ja '67
  Caulfield on color; slides out of focus. P.
    Caulfield. Mod Phot 30:44+ O '66
  Caulfield on color; slide show problems
    solved. P. Caulfield. il Mod Phot 30:10+
    S '66
  Filmotheques. R. Christgau. il Pop Phot 60:
    80+ Ja '67
  Stopping popping; how to keep slides from
    buckling out of focus in the projector. N.
    Rothschild. il Pop Phot 59:70-1+ Ag '66;
    Reply. D. B. Eisendrath, jr. 59:16+ D '66
      Storage
  Caulfield on color. P. Caulfield. Mod Phot
    30:18 Mr '66
  Caulfield on color; 35mm slide storage. P.
    Caulfield. il Mod Phot 30:58+ N '66
  Slide trays, magazines. il Pop Phot 59:174-5
    O '66
      Trimming, mounting, etc.
  Caulfield on color. P. Caulfield. Mod Phot 30:
    94+ Ap '66
  Slide mounts. il Pop Phot 59:173-4 O '66
      Viewers
  Two unusual slide viewers. il Consumer Bul
    49:12-13 F '66
TRANSPLANTATION of organs, tissues, etc.
  Antiserum to lymphocytes: prolonged sur-
    vival of canine renal allografts. A. F.
    Monaco and others. bibliog il Science 153:
    1264-7 S 9 '66
  Chimeric and ex-parabiotic frogs, rana
    pipiens: specificity of tolerance. bibliog il
    Science 152:1250-3 My 27 '66

TRANSPLANTATION of organs, tissues, etc.
—*Continued*

Chimeric mice with donor-type liver cells. R. C. Hard, jr. and B. Kullgren. bibliog il Science 152:349-52 Ap 15 '66

Corneal transplants. B. Rycroft. il Sci N 89: 396-7 My 21 '66

Crossover for life; tissue transplants between R. F. Allen and H. T. Griffith. il Time 87: 44 Mr 11 '66

Drugs add to success of kidney transplants; preventing glomerulonephritis. Sci N 90:347 O 29 '66

Fingers from the dead; surgery performed by Russia's Dr Viktor Kalnberz. Time 87: 53 Je 10 '66

Genes affect transplants. F. Marley. Sci N L 89:147 Mr 5 '66

Girl receives third kidney. F. Marley. Sci N 90:307 O 15 '66

Increased incidence of lymphoma after injections of mice with cells differing at weak histocompatibility loci. R. L. Walford. bibliog il Science 152:78-80 Ap 1 '66

Local recognition of histocompatibility differences in skin grafts. P. B. Lambert and H. A. Frank. bibliog il Science 155:99-101 Ja 6 '67

Memory transfer. W. L. Byrne and others. Science 153:658-9 Ag 5 '66

Mothers' skin grafts better than fathers'. Sci N L 89:136 F 26 '66

No brain transplant seen to offset senile future. Sci N 89:447 Je 4 '66

Rejoined leg; Carl L. Larsen. il Time 87:51 F 4 '66

Replantation: saving severed limbs. G. E. Maxwell. il Todays Health 44:34-9+ S '66

Science tackles the baldness problem: punch graft technique. F. Warshofsky. Read Digest 88:87-91 F '66

Surgeons transplant earbones in cats. Sci N 90:424 N 19 '66

Thymus helps in cure. Sci N 89:227 Ap 2 '66

Tissue transplantation: scope and prospect; excerpts from addresses. R. E. Billingham. bibliog Science 153:266-70 Jl 15 '66

Too many miracles. Time 88:86 S 30 '66

Transplants prolonged; testing anti-lymphocyte serum. F. Marley. Sci N 90:357 O 29 '66

Upside-down valve; transplanted heart valve. Time 87:80 My 27 '66

TRANSPLANTING
Bare-root planting. il Flower Grower 53:40-1 F '66

TRANSPONDERS
Small radar transponder offers automatic altitude reporting. Aviation W 84:93 Mr 21 '66

TRANSPORT, Biological. See Biological transport

TRANSPORT workers
Unkindest cut; Chicago transit workers reject contract. Newsweek 67:68 Ja 31 '66

TRANSPORT workers union
American-TWU contract criticized. Aviation W 85:41 O 10 '66

TWU rejects board recommendations. Aviation W 85:45 N 7 '66

TRANSPORTATION
Trial by travel; modern transportation. M. Mannes. McCalls 93:16+ Ag '66
See also
Inland water transportation
Shipping
also subhead Transportation under various subjects, e.g. Farm produce—Transportation

Federal aid
We must stop choking our cities. J. N. Miller. Read Digest 89:37-41 Ag '66

History
Ancient heavy transport, methods and achievements. R. F. Heizer. bibliog il Science 153:821-30 Ag 19 '66

Private operations
Private carriage: the flourishing stepchild. J. Weingarten. il Duns R 87:pt2 133-5+ My '66

Research
System engineering aids social problems. H. D. Watkins. il Aviation W 84:52-3+ Ja 31 '66

Speed
See also
Transportation, High speed

Taxation
Airway user tax revision passage seen. G. C. Wilson. il Aviation W 85:39-40 S 12 '66

British Columbia
By boat to Alaska; Queen of Prince Rupert car ferry. il Time 87:44 My 27 '66

Great Britain
Czar for British freight? Mrs B. Castle. Bsns W p67 Ag 6 '66

She masterminds plans for British transport; B. Castle, Labor's Minister of transport. il Bsns W p90-2+ Mr 5 '66

Why bureaucrats can't run a business; British road and rail operations. J. N. Sites. Nations Bsns 54:35+ O '66

Japan
See also
Railroads—Japan

United States
Agony of getting anywhere. il Newsweek 69: 43-6+ Ja 9 '67

Comments on congestion. Aviation W 85:11 D 19 '66

Getting there is hardly ever half the fun; Time essay. Time 88:48-9 N 4 '66

Job for a new department: safer cars, fewer traffic jams, faster planes, better ships; summary of message, March 2, 1966. L. B. Johnson. il U S News 60:39-40 Mr 14 '66

Moving the goods is getting tougher; nation's transportation capacity. il Bsns W p64+ Ap 16 '66

Reshaping our national transportation policy; railroads must be allowed to compete; address, January 19, 1966. S. T. Saunders. Vital Speeches 32:237-9 F 1 '66

Speakers or spectators; address, February 9, 1966. E. S. Marsh. Vital Speeches 32:439-42 My 1 '66

Special report on transportation; symposium. il Duns R 87:pt2 104-14+ My '66

Transit snarl: is it back to the rails? C. Dreher. il Nation 203:11-15 Jl 4 '66

Transport crisis: fact or fancy? Sci N 90:405 N 12 '66

Transportation, changing fast. Changing T 20:6 Jl '66

Transportation jam. il Sr Schol 89:3-13 Ja 6 '67

Transportation tangle; President Johnson's request for cabinet-level Department of transportation. W. V. Shannon. Commonweal 83:574-5 F 18 '66; Reply with rejoinder. W. W. Belson. 84:245+ My 20 '66

What the President is proposing; new transportation dept. Bsns W p 158+ Ja 22 '66
See also
Air travel—United States
Roads—United States
United States—Transportation, Department of (proposed)
Waterways—United States

TRANSPORTATION, Automotive
Highway system; address, July 21, 1966. H. Ford, jr. Vital Speeches 32:690-4 S 1 '66

TRANSPORTATION, High speed
Forty-two minutes to anywhere; frictionless tubes for rapid intercontinental travel. il Sci N L 89:117 F 19 '66

France set to fund Aerotrain system. W. C. Wetmore. il Aviation W 85:114-15+ O 10 '66

French company speeding development of Aerotrain. W. C. Wetmore. il Aviation W 85:78-84 O 3 '66

French put Aerotrain onto a faster track; high-speed train that rides on cushion of air, guided by a monorail. il Bsns W p50-1 D 31 '66

More funds sought for NE corridor plans. W. S. Beller. Tech W 20:23-4 Ja 9 '67

Northeast corridor: transport project gains headway; high speed ground transport systems. L. J. Carter. Science 151:1065-7 Mr 4 '66

Ram wing studied as transit vehicle. M. L. Yaffee. il Aviation W 86:56-8+ Ja 2 '67

Renaissance for rails? high-speed ground transportation; Northeast corridor projects. il Newsweek 68:52-3 Ag 8 '66

Son of monorail: aerotrain. il Time 88:96 D 16 '66

Strong voice is raised for integrated transportation planning; International conference on urban transportation. Pittsburgh. M. F. Schmertz. Arch Rec 139:125+ Ap '66

To everywhere in 42 minutes; Paul Cooper's theory of subterranean tunnel travel at ballistic missile speed. il Time 87:42-3 F 11 '66

TRANSPORTATION, High speed—*Continued*
Tomorrow's commuter. J. Eberhart. il Sci
N L 89:138-9 F 26 '66
Transportation ten years from now? il Sr
Schol 89:12-13 Ja 6 '67
See also
Railroads—Train speed

TRANSPORTATION, Military
See also
Airplanes, Military transport
Transports
United States—Military airlift command
Vietnamese war, 1957- —Transportation

TRANSPORTATION equipment

Renting
Leasing: all systems go. il Duns R 87:pt2
136-9+ My '66

TRANSPORTATION of school children. See
School children—Transportation

TRANSPORTATION research
Research & development; the wondrous world
of tomorrow. J. Focarino. il Duns R 87:pt2
106-9+ My '66

TRANSPORTATION to airports. See Airports—
Transportation problems

TRANSPORTS
New ways; U.S. speed contest to produce
navy FDLS. il Newsweek 68:67 Ag 15 '66

TRANSUBSTANTIATION
See also
Catholic church—Eucharist

TRAN-van-Dinh
Ky question. New Repub 156:21-3 Ja 21 '67

TRAN-van-Van
Death in the morning. il por Time 88:36 D 16
'66
Funeral in Saigon. Newsweek 68:28 D 26 '66

TRANS WORLD airlines
Big grab-up of Howard Hughes's sell-off. il
Life 60:45 My 13 '66
Caught at the crest. il Time 88:80-3+ Jl 22
'66
Eccentric; H. Hughes to sell shares. il Time
87:89 Ap 15 '66
Howard Hughes's biggest surprise. J. Mc-
Donald. il Fortune 74:119-20+ Jl 1 '66
Howard Hughes's lucrative beating. il News-
week 67:75-6 Ap 18 '66
Pilot behind TWA's success; E. R. Breech.
il Bsns W p 102-4+ Ap 23 '66
TWA shortens ground training time in course
for DC-9 pilots. W. Wright. il Aviation W
84:58+ My 2 '66
TWA to press claim against Hughes tool.
Aviation W 84:33 Ap 18 '66
What's behind the big TWA sale. Bsns W
p 145-6+ Ap 16 '66

TRAP shooting
Best BB shooters in the world; International
BB-gun shooting championship. C. Conley.
il Field & S 71:58-61 D '66
Bogardus glass ball. A. G. Peterson. il Hob-
bies 71:88 D '66
Crazy quail. A. MacBain. il Field & S 71:43+
Jl '66
Devilish stroll in the woods; Laurel guns,
clay-target game. D. Barnes. il Sports
Illus 24:22-4+ F 14 '66
See also
Skeet (game)

TRAPASSI, Pietro. See Metastasio, P. A. D. B.

TRAPEZE performers. See Acrobats and acrobatism

TRAPPING
See also
Fur trade

TRAPS
Desert tragedy: caught in wolf trap. R. P.
Holland. il Field & S 71:72-3+ S '66

TRAPS, Insect. See Insect traps

TRASH. See Refuse and refuse disposal

TRASH cans. See Refuse receptacles

TRAUB, W. and Elson, D.
RNA composition and base pairing. bibliog
Science 153:178-80 Jl 8 '66

TRAUFFER, Art
Build hi-fi amplifier for solid-state phono
cartridge. Pop Electr 25:65-7 O '66

TRAVEL
ABC Bahamas Baedeker. H. M. Winters. il
Motor B 118:38+ O '66
Agenda for travel. W. D. Patterson. Sat R
50:24+ Ja 7 '67
Americans step up race for the sun. il
Bsns W p46 D 17 '66
Booked for travel. H. Sutton. See issues of
Saturday review
Dribbling, senile fool! Insult dictionary. Time
88:51 Ag 5 '66

Family travel. Bet Hom & Gard 44:94-5 Jl;
28 Ag; 28 S; 121-2+ O '66
Here and there. See issues of Holiday
Holiday planning for 1966. A. H. Hepburn.
il Sr Schol 87:sup 11 Ja 7 '66
Holiday travel; with questions and answers
(cont) A. H. Hepburn. Sr Schol 88:sup20-1
F 25 '66
How to take full advantage of package tour
bargains. Bet Hom & Gard 44:28 Ag '66
International tourist year 1967; symposium.
il Sat R 50:43-8+ Ja 7 '67
Last-minute travel thoughts. A. H. Hepburn.
Sr Schol 88:sup 14 My 20 '66
Let's travel; tips for student travelers. B.
Belford. Mlle 63:357-8 Ag '66
Let's travel; tour, weekend, and cruise ideas.
Mlle 63:188-90 O '66
Lizzie and me in a wagon-lit; or how I lost
my best friend traveling. L. Gottlieb. il
Mlle 63:197-9 S '66
[Month] travel in and beyond the West.
See issues of Sunset
More travel, less trouble. A. I. Currie; M.
Bouteiller. il NEA J 55:28-30 My '66
Musical rewards for the traveler. F. Bowers.
House & Gard 129:30+ Ap '66
My first trip; memories of a childhood ad-
venture, by six famous Americans. il Mc-
Calls 93:80+ Ap '66
1967: International tourist year. il UNESCO
Courier 19:5-9 D '66
Opinion: on getting out. A. Alvarez. Mlle
63:72+ Je '66
Personal business; 1967 travel plans. Bsns W
p 149-50 D 17 '66
Photo safari. il U S Camera 29:60-1 Ap '66
Place-dropper's guide. K. D. Fishman. il Mlle
63:145-7 Je '66
Roamer's ramblings. T. Shane. See issues of
Travel
Roaming the globe with Travel. See issues
of Travel
Speaking of travel. C. Stinnett. See issues
of Holiday
Teen travel talk; parks are part of the fun;
Arista student travel association. il Seven-
teen 25:73-4 My '66
To take and to tape; some random and dif-
fering thoughts by the editors on recording
your trip with camera and recorder. M. S.
Fenner; W. A. Graves; M. B. Tucker. il
NEA J 56:62-4 Ja '67
Tour for every taste; Spectours, inc. il Holi-
day 39:113 Je '66
Travel. See issues of Vogue
Travel. L. Barry. See issues of Popular
photography
Travel. il Life 60:74-86 F 25; 52-63 My 27;
61:34-42A S 2; 69-70 N 18 '66
Travel & camera. See issues of U.S. camera
& travel
Travel comforts collected by a cagey travel-
ler. D. Messinesi. Vogue 147:56-7 F 1 '66
Travel digest. See issues of Travel
Travel notes. R. Joseph. See issues of Esquire
Travel; of, by, and for teachers; ed. by L.
Jonckheere. il Sr Schol 89:sup 13-15 S 30 '66
Traveling with a camera. E. Bush. il Horti-
culture 44:38-9+ Je '66
Trial by travel; modern transportation. M.
Mannes. McCalls 93:16+ Ag '66
See also
Air travel
Automobile touring
Canoe trips
Cruising
Customs service and tourists
Guidebooks
Luggage
Ocean travel
Packing of luggage
Railroad travel
Tourist trade
Vacations
Youth hostels

Anecdotes, facetiae, satire, etc.
Down on the reservation. L. Haynes. Sat R
49:48-9 Ap 9 '66
Images of travel. L. Rosten. il Look 30:20
Ap 5 '66
Inglese spoken here. M. Bennett. Sat R 49:
64+ S 17 '66

Bibliography
Read now and enjoy it later. E. Hall. Sr
Schol 88:sup 10 Mr 4 '66
Travel information. A. H. Hepburn. Sr Schol
88:sup21 F 25 '66

Economic aspects
Solving the Nation's travel arithmetic. H.
H. Humphrey. il Sat R 49:52 Mr 12 '66

TRAVEL—Economic aspects—*Continued*
These travel tips can save your travel dollars. Bet Hom & Gard 44:94-5 Jl '66
Turning the red, white, and blue into gold. H. Sutton. il Sat R 49:50-1+ Mr 12 '66
See also
Tourist trade

Health aspects

Bon voyage, and fare well! O. Achtenhagen. il Todays Health 44:28-31 Ag '66
Ten health tips for overseas travel; reprint. il Sci Digest 59:74-6 Je '66
Travel well. E. N. Dye. See issues of Travel
When a U.S. traveler abroad became ill; care in Regional hospital, Dooradoyle, Limerick. il U S News 61:16 O 31 '66

Quotations, maxims, etc.

Hither and yon; some thoughts on the subject, pro and con. il N Y Times Mag p42 Ap 24 '66

Taxation

Airway user tax revision passage seen. G. C. Wilson. il Aviation W 85:39-40 S 12 '66
Charge it; airway user tax. R. B. Parke. Flying 79:36 N '66

TRAVEL (periodical)
See also
Mr Travel award

TRAVEL agencies
Green pastures; Tjaereborg travels, Denmark. il Time 88:66 Jl 29 '66
Traveler, beware! beat-up cruise ships, phony charter flights endanger your money, and your life. il Changing T 20:7-12 Ap '66
What makes a tour a photo tour? L. Barry. il Pop Phot 58:48+ My '66

TRAVEL clubs. See Clubs

TRAVEL guides. See Guidebooks

TRAVEL literature
Dear sir, please send me all you have on Texas... R. G. Durnin. Sr Schol 89:sup42 S 23 '66
See also
Guidebooks

TRAVEL news. See Newspapers—Travel news

TRAVEL photographs. See Photographs

TRAVEL posters. See Posters

TRAVEL regulations
Agenda for travel. W. D. Patterson. Sat R 50:24+ Ja 7 '67
Atlantic report; Washington's relaxed restrictions. R. Reston. Atlan 218:4+ O '66
Department liberalizes exceptions to travel bans. Dept State Bul 55:234-5 Ag 15 '66
Iron-curtain lands: where to see; what to avoid. U S News 60:69 Ap 11 '66
Legal status and problems of the American abroad. M. S. Madden and S. L. Cohn. bibliog f Ann Am Acad 368:119-31 N '66
No dollar wall; proposal to reduce gold drain by restricting travel abroad. W. D. Patterson. Sat R 49:30 Je 11 '66
Passport decision; student delegation to Cuba did not violate statute. Nation 202:508 My 2 '66
Passport please? Commonweal 84:67-8 Ap 8 '66
State department travel bans: are they justified? pro and con discussion. il Sr Schol 88:15-16 F 25 '66
T.R.B. from Washington; State department's bill. New Repub 154:4 My 21 '66
To fill it in or not, that's the question; with excerpts from address by B. Kooka at P.A.T.A. convention. H. Sutton. il Sat R 49:40-2+ Ap 9 '66
Travel and domestic controls. M. T. Noto. Ann Am Acad 367:73-84 S '66
Travel controls relaxed for doctors and medical scientists; Department statement, December 29, 1965. Dept State Bul 54:90 Ja 17 '66
Travel controls to restricted areas relaxed for scholars; Department statement concerning travel in Communist China. Dept State Bul 54:491 Mr 28 '66
Travel restraints seen unlikely this year. Aviation W 84:35-6 Ap 25 '66
U.S. chess team excepted from ban on travel to Cuba. Dept State Bul 55:723 N 7 '66
U.S. eases travel, reds clamp down. U S News 61:10 Jl 25 '66

TRAVEL study courses
Europe for the 2-S set. R. Joseph. Esquire 66:148-9 S '66
Europe, under their own steam; excerpts from Europe à go-go: life and love aboard a student ship. J. Fox. il Mlle 63:122-3+ Je '66

Fiskites win travel-study scholarships to Scandinavia. il Negro Hist Bul 29:94-6 Ja '66
International vacation study course in Scandinavia; report C. A. Lee. Negro Hist Bul 29:108 F '66
Ready, jet set, go; Foreign language league. W. Johnson. il Sr Schol 89:22+ S 30 '66
Teen travel talk; language work in classroom or homestay program, then touring. il Seventeen 25:389+ Ag '66
Travel notes. R. Joseph. Esquire 66:58+ S '66
Work with play in Europe; Foreign language league. W. Johnson. il Sr Schol 89:sup 17 D 2 '66
See also
Colleges and universities, Traveling
Experiment in international living (organization)

TRAVEL tax. See Travel—Taxation

TRAVEL with children
Animal bingo makes a trip go better. M. Garrity. il Bet Hom & Gard 44:42 My '66
Around the world on a sabbatical. J. B. Carr. il Sr Schol 89:sup 14-15 Ja 6 '67
Can your child qualify for airline discounts? il Bet Hom & Gard 44:28 S '66
En route to Christmas. H. Wilson. il Travel 126:30-2+ D '66
Game gifts for young travelers. il Sunset 137: 46+ D '66
Practical parents' guide to touring Europe with children. L. Hadley. il Holiday 39: 179-90 Mr '66
Taking baby abroad. A. Matell and R. Matell. il Travel 126:56-8+ N '66
Ten for the road; trip across the country. B. Hughes. il McCalls 94:54+ N '66

TRAVEL with pets
Travel care for dogs. D. M. Duffey. il Outdoor Life 138:136-8+ S '66

TRAVELERS
American tourist. S. R. Waters. Ann Am Acad 368:109-18 N '66
No holiday for guides. Bsns W p46 Je 11 '66
What chance the tourist? H. Sutton. Sat R 50:45+ Ja 7 '67

History

Capsule history of tourists. R. Collier. il Holiday 41:72-3 Ja '67

TRAVELERS checks
Day we lost $3,000. L. Barry. Pop Phot 59: 102-3+ Jl '66

TRAVELING bags. See Luggage

TRAVELING exhibitions. See Exhibitions, Traveling

TRAVELING light; story. See Portis, C.

TRAVELS
From Scotland to Silverado, by R. L. Stevenson, ed by D. Hart. Review
Sat R 49:34 S 3 '66. L. Edel
See also
Travel

TRAVERS, Pamela Lyndon
Elusive Mary Poppins author expansive for children's audience; statements. Library J 91:1640+ Mr 15 '66
Some friends of Mary Poppins; interview by group of American children. McCalls 93:32+ My '66
Visit with the real Mary Poppins; interview, ed. by J. Roddy. por Look 30:84+ D 13 '66

about

Visit with Mary Poppins and P. L. Travers. R. R. Lingeman. il por N Y Times Mag p 12-13+ D 25 '66

La TRAVIATA; opera. See Verdi, G.

TRAWLS and trawling
Way down deep; trolling. A. J. McClane. il Field & S 71:114-17 N '66

TRAYS
Easy to make walnut trays. il Sunset 137: 130 S '66
TV dinner tray. A. Kennedy. il Pop Sci 188: 162 F '66

TREACHER, Arthur
Four long cool formulas. pors Esquire 66:84-5 Jl '66

TREASON trials. See Trials (treason)

TREASTER, Joseph B.
G-eye view of Vietnam. N Y Times Mag p 100+ O 30 '66

TREASURE Island; drama. See York, M. A.

TREASURE trove
Florida state museum; custodian of all treasure found off the coast of Florida. J. L. Stoutenburgh. Hobbies 71:111 S '66

TREASURE trove—*Continued*
How to find sunken treasure, and keep it. L. Steckler. il Pop Mech 126:124-7+ N '66
Treasure finds could affect values. C. French. Hobbies 71:102 My '66
Who gets the gold? Chameau treasure. il Newsweek 67:64 Ap 18 '66
Yo ho ho! Florida's give-away program of its sunken treasure. Nation 203:629 D 12 '66

TREASURY department (United States) See United States—Treasury department

TREATIES
See also
North Atlantic treaty organization
Nuclear test ban treaty, 1963
also subhead Treaties under names of countries, e.g. United States—Treaties

TREATMENTS, Medical. See Medical service

TREATY of Moscow. See Nuclear test ban treaty, 1963

TREE breeding
Super trees will keep United States in paper. Sci N 90:159 S 3 '66
Sweet maples may be improved by breeding. il Sci N 89:361 My 14 '66

TREE farms. See Forest management

TREE felling
One-two-three and down she goes. il Pop Mech 125:149 Ap '66
Use proper form in felling trees. B. C. Kilvert jr. il Flower Grower 53:47 Ap '66

TREE ferns
Tree ferns indoors. A. Albohn. il Horticulture 44:12-13 D '66

TREE hoppers
Nature note. Sci N 89:301 Ap 23 '66

TREE lore. See Trees in religion, folklore, etc.

TREE planting
Big trees moved with speed and safety; by crane-and-clam technique; Philadelphia. il Am City 81:92-3 F '66
Plant a tree, but plant the right one. il Changing T 20:45-7 S '66
Super trees. il Am For 72:10-11 O '66
When you plant a specimen tree. il Sunset 137:281 O '66

TREE rhododendrons. See Rhododendrons

TREE rings
Growth-rings of trees: their correlation with climate; excerpts from address, December 27, 1965. H. C. Fritts. bibliog il Science 154:973-9 N 25 '66

TREE seedlings
Nurselog. R. Kirk. il Audubon Mag 68:320-7 S '66

TREE shrews. See Shrews

TREE shrews. See Squirrel shrews

TREE stumps. See Trees

TREE to the sky; drama. See Nolan, P. T.

TREEHOPPERS. See Tree hoppers

TREES
Arboreal pollution; tree-caused air pollution. il Time 88:57 S 9 '66
Date with a tree; reprint. F. B. Harris. Am For 72:15 O '66
Deciduous trees for the plains. G. Viehmeyer. il Horticulture 44:48-9+ Mr '66
My five favorite trees; white oak, sugar maple, aspen, white pine and canoe birch. R. Platt. il Am For 72:10-12+ My '66
Nurselog. R. Kirk. il Audubon Mag 68:320-7 S '66
Petrifying forest; emissions of terpenes and esters. Newsweek 68:59 S 12 '66
Plant for privacy. il Flower Grower 53:34-6 Je '66
Seattle's trees for peace, International friendship grove; photographs. Am For 72:34-7 Je '66
Specimen plants are for gardeners in a hurry. il Sunset 137:248+ O '66
Stump for beauty. M. Buttner. il Pop Gard 17:73 D '66
Tree detectives and ecology; AFA's social register of big tree champions. Am For 72:9 My '66
Trees make the difference. il Pop Gard 17:36-7 Mr '66
Trees that stay small. H. V. Wilson. il Flower Grower 53:46-7+ Mr '66
See also
Christmas trees
Forest conservation
Roadside improvement
Tree breeding
Tree felling
Tree planting
also names of trees, e.g. Elm

Deformities
See Abnormalities (plants)

Diseases and pests
See also
Tent caterpillars
also subhead Diseases and pests under names of trees, e.g. Elm—Diseases and pests

Growth
See Growth (plants)

Planting
See Tree planting

Pruning
See Pruning

Translocation
See Plants—Translocation

TREES, Age of
Living ghosts of the Inyos. il Am For 72:6-7 D '66
These are the champs. K. B. Pomeroy and D. Dixon. il Am For 72:14-35 My '66

TREES, Care of
But it's got to come out. C. Stephens. il Am For 72:44-5+ My '66
Trees of Williamsburg; reprint. M. Frome. il Am For 72:18-21+ D '66

TREES, Dwarf
Bonsai outdoors. C. E. Derderian. il Horticulture 44:22-3+ Je '66

TREES, Effect of climate on
Growth-rings of trees: their correlation with climate; excerpts from address, December 27, 1965. H. C. Fritts. bibliog il Science 154:973-9 N 25 '66

TREES, Effect of radiation on. See Plants, Effect of radiation on

TREES, Growth of. See Growth (plants)

TREES, Historic
Trees of Williamsburg; reprint. M. Frome. il Am For 72:18-21+ D '66

TREES, Training of
Espaliers. J. A. Eaton. il House & Gard 130:268-71+ N '66
Train trees on walls and fences. J. E. Dwyer. il Pop Gard 17:70-4 Mr '66
See also
Fruit trees, Training of

TREES in cities
Beautify America forum: trees bloom on Main Street. J. R. Downie. Flower Grower 53:26 F '66
Instead of big bulky trees; Rochester, N.Y. J. Gerling. il Am City 81:105-7 Ag '66
7,000 flowering trees; South Haven, Mich. L. J. Harris. il Am City 81:34 S '66
Tree time in Anaheim; community celebrations in Anaheim, Calif. P. A. Deimel. il Parks & Rec 1:218-19 Mr '66
We duck the Dutch elm disaster; Lincoln, Neb. D. Guinan. il Am City 81:102-3 Mr '66

TREES in religion, folklore, etc.
Folklore and nature; the immortal holly tree. D. Jacob. il Natur Hist 75:6+ D '66
Worth of a tree; ombu from Pampas of Argentina. W. L. Maughan. il Américas 18:34-6 D '66

TREGASKIS, Richard
Golden cities of the Rhine. Travel 126:33-7 S '66
Keiki the porpoise, our new underwater errand boy. Pop Sci 188:82-5+ Je '66

TREGUNNA, Bruce
Flavin mononucleotide control of glycolic acid oxidase and photorespiration in corn leaves. bibliog Science 151:1239-41 Mr 11 '66

TREHALASE
Trehalase from dictyostelium discoideum; purification and properties. C. Ceccarini. bibliog il Science 151:454-6 Ja 28 '66

TREICHLER, Martha
Our kids settle their own squabbles. Parents Mag 41:50-1+ Je '66

TREILLAGE. See Trellises

TREISTER, Kenneth
Project; a living community park. A. Hurwitz. il Sch Arts 65:17-19 Ap '66

TREJOS, José J.
Moles have it. Newsweek 67:57 F 21 '66
Two for the seesaw. Time 87:52 Mr 18 '66

TRELLISES
Treillage, delightful laciness, newly practical. il House & Gard 129:114-19 Je '66
Treillage indoors. il House & Gard 129:120-3 Je '66
Vines and shrubs on trellises, arches, posts, pyramids. il Sunset 136:102-3 Ap '66

TREMOLO. See Vibrato

TREMULIS, Alex Sarantos
Sarantos Dia Kosa. il Motor T 18:36-8 Ap '66

TRENDEX poll. See Public opinion

TRENHOLM, Harper Councill
In memoriam. por Negro Hist Bul 29:113 F
'66

TREPLEFF; story. See Harris, M.

TRESCO abbey
Subtropic flora thrives on 50th parallel. E.
Javorsky. il Natur Hist 75:18-23 F '66

TRESCO Abbey gardens. See Gardens—England

TRESPASS
Law, speech and disobedience; Ann Arbor
sit-in case and trespass law. C. Cohen. il
nation 202:357-62 Mr 28 '66
See also
Real property

TREVELYAN, Carlyle F.
Art of movie making. U S Camera 29:56-9
Je; 68-71 Ag '66
Entertainment film. U S Camera 29:70-3 O '66
Pins & needles. U S Camera 29:68-71+ D '66
Slapstick to satire. U S Camera 29:70-3 S
'66

TREVIÑO, Elizabeth (Borton)
Newbery award acceptance; address, July 12,
1966. Horn Bk 42:406-11 Ag '66

about
Elizabeth Borton de Treviño. C. Costello. il
Library J 91:1592-3 Mr 15 '66
Elizabeth Borton de Treviño. R. Parmenter.
por Horn Bk 42:412-14 Ag '66
Newbery-Caldecott winners. por Wilson Lib
Bul 40:688 Ap '66
Treviño, Hogrogian: Newbery and Caldecott
winners. il por Pub W 189:30-2 Mr 14 '66

TREVOR-ROPER, Hugh Redwald
King's prayer factory. Horizon 8:66-75 Wint
'66

TREYNOR, Jack L. and Mazuy, K. K.
Can mutual funds outguess the market?
Harvard Bsns R 44:131-6 Jl '66

TREZZA, Alphonse F. See Schick, F. L. jt.
auth.

TRI Quang
Ky's crackdown; interview. ed. by D. Perry.
il Newsweek 68:28 Jl 4 '66
Talk with Thich Tri Quang. Time 87:27 Ap
22 '66
Thich Tri Quang speaks out; interview, ed.
by E. G. Martin. por Newsweek 67:33+ Ap
25 '66

about
Buddhist leader Tri Quang: instigator of pro-
tests. por U S News 60:21 Ap 18 '66
Civil war within a war? with report by
M. D. Perry. il por Newsweek 67:38+ My
30 '66
Divided Buddhists of South Vietnam. D.
Warner. Reporter 34:22-4 Je 16 '66
How much power does Tri Quang want? D.
Warner. Reporter 34:11-14 My 5 '66
Just who are the Buddhists? por U S News
60:29-30 My 30 '66
Letter from Saigon. R. Shaplen. New Yorker
42:155-62+ Ap 16 '66
Letter from South Vietnam. R. Shaplen.
New Yorker 42:142-4+ Je 4 '66
Politician from the pagoda. il pors Time 87:
25-6+ Ap 22 '66
Question of survival. il por Newsweek 67:26-8
Ap 18 '66
Thich Tri Quang: Buddhist mystery man. il
por Sr Schol 88:8 My 6 '66

TRI club yacht racing association. See Yacht
clubs

TRIAD dance theatre. See Dance companies

TRIAL by jury. See Jury

TRIAL dockets. See Court calendars

TRIAL of Manfred the magician; drama. See
Baher, C. W.

TRIAL of Peter Zenger; drama. See Nolan,
P. T.

TRIAL practice. See Procedure (law)

TRIAL reporting. See Newspaper court reporting

TRIALS
Bobby Baker's big test, in court. U S News
62:31 Ja 23 '67
Case of the cancer cure; krebiozen trial.
il Newsweek 67:65-6 F 14 '66
Collector; Bobby Baker trial opens. il News-
week 69:35-6 Ja 23 '67
Flair for fund raising; Bobby Baker hearing
under way. Time 89:22 Ja 20 '67
Kafka goes to court; concerning J. Mar-
shall's book, Law and psychology in con-
flict. il Time 88:53 Jl 15 '66
Uncontrollable vegetable; case of Albert De-
Salvo. il Newsweek 69:30+ Ja 23 '67

Verdicts of history; with editorial comment.
T. J. Fleming. il Am Heritage 18:4-11+
D '66
What does a change of venue gain? Time
89:39-40 Ja 13 '67
What is felony murder? case of Marvin
Phillips in California. Time 87:67 Je 17 '66
See also
Jury
Newspaper court reporting

Cuba
Caning the students; R. Cubela-Secades not
to be executed. Time 87:54 Mr 18 '66
Plot to kill Castro; defendants sentences.
Newsweek 67:50 Mr 21 '66

Egypt
Balanced docket; trials against opponents
of regime. Newsweek 68:44 S 5 '66

France
Slight oversight; Ben Barka case adjourns
over Ahmed Dlimi surrender. il Newsweek
68:52+ O 31 '66
Surprise witness; Ben Barka trial. il Time
88:38 O 28 '66
Trial begins; Ben Barka case. Newsweek
68:46+ S 19 '66

Georgia
Protectors; trial of Klansmen accused of
harassing Negroes; Athens. Time 88:20 Jl
8 '66

Germany (Federal Republic)
Investigation; theme of P. Weiss's play.
R. J. Schroeder. Commonweal 85:139-41 N 4
'66
Worst that ever happened; with editorial
comment. S. Bedford. il Sat Eve Post 239:
29-33+, 112 O 22 '66

Great Britain
Moorland murders; verdicts. il Newsweek 67:
52 My 16 '66
Trial begins; Downey-Kilbride-Evans murders. il Newsweek 67:34 My 2 '66

Greece, Modern
Behind the Aspida trial; plot to carry out a
left-wing coup against the palace. K. Kyle.
New Repub 156:17-18 Ja 21 '67

Indonesia
Friend in need; Subandrio guilty of treason.
Time 88:37-8 N 4 '66
Naming names; Jusuf Muda Dalam con-
demned to death. Newsweek 68:58 S 26 '66
Whose coup? Subandrio trial. Newsweek 68:
56+ O 17 '66
Whose skin? death penalty for Subandrio.
Newsweek 68:61 N 7 '66

Israel
See also
Eichmann trial

Italy
School for scandal; sex quiz-obscenity case.
Newsweek 67:56 Ap 11 '66

Mexico
Until proven innocent. il Time 88:87-8 O 28
'66

Pennsylvania
Pandemonium in Pittsburgh; convicts set out
to goad judge into declaring mistrial. il
Time 88:38 D 23 '66

Russia
Authors league protests Sinyavsky-Daniel
trial. Pub W 189:68 F 28 '66
Backstage at a Moscow trial; Sinyavsky-
Daniel case. America 114:279-80 F 26 '66
Bit of fear; D. Sinyavsky and Y. Daniel
sentences. Time 87:33 F 25 '66
East and west from Paris; trial of Siniavsky
and Daniel. A. Werth. Nation 202:225 F
28 '66
Fact of the matter; Beiliss case of 1911. V.
Peterson. Reporter 35:57-8 O 20 '66
On trial, by M. Hayward. Review
Sat R 49:25 Ag 6 '66. M. MacDuffie
Socialist legality on trial; A. Sinyavsky-
Y. Daniel trial. A. Brumberg. il Reporter
34:34-6 Mr 10 '66
Soviet justice in action; injustice of the
trial of Andrei Sinyavsky and Yuli Daniel.
Reporter 34:8 My 5 '66
Trial begins; Y. Daniel and A. Sinyavsky.
il Time 87:32 F 18 '66
Trial in Moscow; conviction of Andrei D.
Sinyavsky. and Yuli Daniel. Commonweal
83:598 F 25 '66

TRIAL—Russia—_Continued_
Trial of Sinyavsky and Daniel; excerpt from the Paris-based Polish magazine Kultura, tr. by M. Hayward. il N Y Times Mag p20-3+ Ap 17 '66

South Africa
Doctor's conscience in South Africa; G. Dean's charges of police and prison warders brutality. New Repub 154:17-18 Ja 29 '66
Enemy of the state; A. Fischer's sentence. il Newsweek 67:54 My 23 '66
South Africa: daily life in a police state; with report of M. Benson's and others experiences. New Repub 154:11-13 Je 11 '66

Yugoslavia
One step backward; Mihajlov sentence. il Newsweek 68:48 O 3 '66

TRIALS (espionage)
After seventeen years; Rosenberg-Sobell trial. Nation 203:203-4 S 12 '66
Nagging Sobell case. A. Kopkind. New Repub 155:13-14 S 24 '66
See also
Rosenberg, Julius and Ethel, case

TRIALS (impeachment)
All the justice money can buy; Oklahoma cases. B. Bailey. New Repub 154:8-9 Je 11 '66
See also
Impeachments

TRIALS (libel)
Academic freedom for historians; text of announcement, July 22, 1966. Sch & Soc 94: 461-3 D 10 '66
Another clash between fundamental principles; Gilligan case. H. F. Pilpel. Pub W 189:64-5 F 28 '66
Drawing the libel line; W. F. Buckley suits. Newsweek 67:92 My 9 '66
Perils of being too public; Pauling v. National review. il Time 87:80 Ap 29 '66
Showdown in the Southwest; editor sues reader; McGaw-Webster case. il Time 87:44 F 11 '66
To balance individual rights and community interests; Afro-American publishing co. inc. vs. Eli Jaffe. H. F. Pilpel. Pub W 190:51-3 O 31 '66

TRIALS (murder)
Addenda to De Sade; murder of S. M. Likens in Indianapolis. il Time 87:25 My 6 '66
After a twelve-year fight; freedom for Dr Sheppard. U S News 61:16 N 28 '66
Alabaman condemns Alabama justice; E. Thomas acquitted of V. Liuzzo murder. Christian Cent 83:1233 O 12 '66
Armored lady; Mossler trial opens. il Time 87:43 F 4 '66
Aunt Candy; case of C. Mossler. il Newsweek 67:26 Ja 31 '66
Avenging Sylvia; death by torture of S. M. Likens. Time 87:22-3 My 27 '66
Boy who wanted to die; Joseph Shea, acquitted of M. Meslener death. Time 87: 57+ Mr 11 '66
Candy trial; case of C. Mossler. il Newsweek 67:35 Mr 14 '66
Case for the defense; Coppolino case. il Newsweek 68:27-8 D 19 '66
Case in point; E. Gallashaw voted not guilty. Newsweek 68:46 O 24 '66
Charlie's peers; Hunter brothers sentences. Time 87:26 F 25 '66
Coppolino case, 1. il Newsweek 68:22+ D 26 '66
Doctor Sam's reprise. il Newsweek 68:43-4 N 7 '66
Endure and conquer; Sheppard verdict. il News week 68:34-5 N 28 '66
Growing up in Tucson; C. Schmid, death sentence. il Time 87:28 Mr 11 '66
Grudging acquittal; B. H. Kinsey. Time 88: 62 S 30 '66
His lifetime record, won: 700, lost: 1; some P. Foreman cases. M. Smith. il Life 60:92-4+ Ap 1 '66
How can I tell them there's nothing left? case of Lucille Marie Maxwell Miller. J. Didion. il Sat Eve Post 239:38-42+ My 7 '66
How Sheppard won. il Time 88:56 N 25 '66
In another country; B. H. Kinsey's acquittal. Newsweek 68:40+ O 3 '66
In ghastly transcripts, a test of our times; murders by I. Brady-M. Hindley; with excerpts from trial. P. H. Johnson. il Life 61:62+ Ag 12 '66
Jury of their peers; defense attorneys in connection with 1964 murder of civil-rights workers seek to call off trial. Reporter 35:24 O 6 '66

Letter from Cape Town; trial of Verwoerd's assassin. E. J. Kahn, jr. New Yorker 42: 182+ N 5 '66
Maximum sentence; Brady and Hindley trial; Great Britain. Time 87:42 My 13 '66
Mesmerism in Miami; verdict in C. Mossler trial. Time 87:66 Mr 18 '66
Most unusual trial; trial of Ian Brady and Myra Hindley. il Time 87:36+ Ap 29 '66
New trial for Ruby. Sr Schol 89:19-20 O 21 '66
New turn? Alabama trials: Brewster, Liuzzo, and Reeb cases. Sr Schol 87:4-5 Ja 7 '66
Now, a chance of freedom for Jack Ruby. il U S News 61:16 O 17 '66
Objection sustained; to get new trial. il Newsweek 68:31 O 17 '66
One down; Coppolino acquittal in N.J. il Time 88:21-2 D 23 '66
Peace corps murder case. il Time 88:64+ S 16 '66
Press on trial; S. Sheppard case before Supreme court. il Time 87:64 Mr 11 '66
Press v. the accused; S. Sheppard's trial in 1954 declared unfair by Supreme court. il Time 87:66 Je 17 '66
Ruby revisited. Time 88:36 O 14 '66
Stale Candy; news coverage of the Mossler trial. il Newsweek 67:64 Mr 14 '66
Trial by headline; Sheppard trial ruled unfair by Supreme court. il Newsweek 67:64 Je 20 '66
Trial of Jack Ruby, by J. Kaplan and J. R. Waltz. Review
Commentary 41:83-5+ F '66. M. Mayer
Trial of Steven Truscott, by I. LeBourdais. Review
Esquire 66:12+ O '66. M. Muggeridge
Trials of Candy and Mel. L. H. Lapham. il Sat Eve Post 239:28-32+ Ag 27; 32-6+ S 10 '66
Verdicts of history: the Boston massacre. T. J. Fleming. il Am Heritage 18:6-11+ D '66
What does a change of venue gain? Ruby and Speck trials. Time 89:39-40 Ja 13 '67
Whitewashed court; cases involving the shooting and murder of civil rights workers on trial in Hayneville, Ala. Time 88:36 O 7 '66
Who issued the orders? Malcolm X assassination convictions. Newsweek 67:36 Mr 21 '66
See also
Sacco-Vanzetti case

TRIALS (perjury)
Machine wins; Gene Wirges; three year sentence. Time 87:44 F 11 '66

TRIALS (slander) See Trials (libel)

TRIALS (treason)
Conspiracy and trial of Aaron Burr; excerpts from Shackles of power. J. Dos Passos. il Am Heritage 17:4-7+ F '66; Reply with rejoinder. S. E. Burr, jr. 17:91 Ag '66

TRIALS in the press. See Newspaper court reporting

TRIANGLE; story. See Delman, D.

TRIBBETT, Miss.
Secret crisis in the Delta; Negro farm laborers. il Newsweek 67:28-9 Mr 7 '66

TRIBES and tribal system
Death in Nigeria. E. Huxley. Nat R 18:163-4 F 22 '66; Reply with rejoinder. R. J. Palmeri. 18:390+ My 3 '66
New chance in Nigeria? unity or tribal politics. H. K. Flad. Commonweal 83:525-6 F 4 '66
Turmoil in an African university; Nigeria's University of Lagos. S. B. Yesufu. America 114:200-3 F 5 '66
See also
Society, Primitive

TRIBOLIUM confusum. See Flour beetles

TRIBUNE (Chicago) See Chicago tribune

TRICHODERMA. See Fungi

TRI-CITIES opera
Binghamton. J. Browning. Opera N 31:24 N 19 '66

TRICK photography. See Photography, Trick

TRICONTINENTAL conference. Havana, 1966
Havana conference. P. D. Bethel. il Reporter 34:25-9 Mr 24 '66
U.S. joins other American republics in denouncing Havana Tricontinental conference; statement, January 24, 1966. W. P. Allen. Dept State Bul 54:383-5 Mr 7 '66

TRIDENT (ship) See Ships, Research

TRIEM, Eve
Hostage; Trees, near and far; poems. Poetry 108:241-2 Jl '66

about

Down from the forked hill unsullied. R. Wallace. Poetry 108:122-3 My '66

TRIGEMINAL neuralgia. See Neuralgia. Trigeminal

TRIGG-Vaughn stations, incorporated
Doubleday to acquire radio-TV station chain. Pub W 190:33 N 7 '66

TRIGGS, Matt
Excerpt from statement. June 2, 1965. Cong Digest 45:49+ F '66

TRIGLYCERIDES. See Glycerides

TRILLIN, Calvin
Barnett Frummer hears a familiar ring; story. New Yorker 42:22-4 Jl 2 '66
Barnett Frummer is an unbloomed flower; story. New Yorker 41:34-6 F 5 '66
Joy to the world and especially to Pickens. S. C. Esquire 66:242-3 D '66
Letter from Salisbury. New Yorker 42:139-40+ N 12 '66
Onward and upward with the arts. New Yorker 42:118+ Je 11; 126+ S 24 '66

TRILLING, Diana
Letter from abroad. McCalls 93:36+ Jl '66

TRILLING, Lionel
Young in the thirties. Commentary 41:43-51 My '66

TRILLINGHAM, C. C.
Lesson from Watts: it can happen here. PTA Mag 61:12-14 O '66

TRILLIUMS
Trillium triumph. H. S. Hull. il Flower Grower 53:38-9+ My '66
Trilliums. W. C. Curtis. Horticulture 44:40-1+ Mr '66

TRILOBITES
Trilobites. Hobbies 71:130 Ag '66

TRIM saws. See Saws

TRIM tabs. See Tabs (boats)

TRIMARANS
Florida's wild west coast. J. S. Doherty. il Yachting 120:52-3+ N '66
Trimaran in a tempest. A. Piver. il Motor B 118:30-1+ Ag '66

TRIMBLE, William C.
Department supports commercial treaty with Togo; statement, September 22, 1966. Dept State Bul 55:692-3 O 31 '66

TRIMESTER system. See College year

TRIMETHOPRIM
Formylmethionyl-tRNA dependence of amino acid incorporation in extracts of trimethoprim-treated escherichia coli. J. Eisenstadt and P. Lengyel. bibliog il Science 154:524-7 O 28 '66

TRINITY
In defense of heresy. A. Towne. Christian Cent 84:44-7 Ja 11 '67
Unreconstructed trinity. V. P. McCorry. America 114:814 Je 4 '66

TRINITY church. See New York (city)—Churches

TRIOS, Instrumental
Decca's Nieuw Amsterdam trio. A. Cohn. Am Rec G 33:142 O '66

TRIPLE crown. See Horse racing

TRIPODS, Camera. See Camera tripods

TRIPPE, Juan T.
Airlines' new role; excerpts from remarks. Aviation W 85:21 S 26 '66

TRISTAN und Isolde: opera. See Wagner, R.

TRITIUM
Incorporation of tritiated actinomycin D into drug-sensitive and drug-resistant HeLa cells. M. N. Goldstein and others. il Science 151:1555-6 Mr 25 '66

TRITOMAS. See Torch lilies

TRITON (satellite) See Satellites

TRIUMPH of honor; opera. See Scarlatti, A.

TRIVERI, Edgar A.
Latin America: search for a politics. Nation 203:182-5 S 5 '66

TRIVOLI, G. William
Communist capitalism: will it work? Nat R 18:265-7 Mr 22 '66

TRNKA, Jiri
Trnkaland. il Newsweek 67:99 Mr 28 '66

TROBRIAND ISLANDS
King Kam and the Isle of love. G. Scott. Sat R 49:68-9 O 22 '66

TROEBST, Cord Christian
How to survive, anywhere. Pop Sci 189:62-5+ Ag '66

TROGONS
Arizona's mystery bird. E. Steele. il Audubon Mag 68:167-71 My '66

TROJAN men; opera. See Berlioz, H.

TROLLEY museums. See Street car museums

TROLLING. See Trawls and trawling

TRONDHEIM, Norway
Trondheim. P. L. Adams. il Atlan 217:100-2+ F '66

TROOP ships. See Transports

TROPHIES
See also
Harmon international trophies

TROPHIES, Sport
Changing picture of whitetail trophies. W. Page. Field & S 71:50+ Jl '66
Hunt for the records: trophies to qualify for Boone and Crockett listings. A. F. Benson. il Outdoor Life 138:20-3+ Ag '66
International trophies for sportsmanship; second annual international fair play trophies. il UNESCO Courier 19:30-1 Je '66
Packing a trophy. C. Conley. il Field & S 71:32+ My '66
Pennsylvania trophy census. R. D. Parlaman. il Field & S 70:28 F '66

TROPICAL fishes. See Fishes

TROPICAL forests. See Forests and forestry—Tropics

TROPICAL oceanography. See Oceanography

TROPICAL winds. See Winds

TROPICANA, Las Vegas, Nev. See Night clubs

TROPICS
Atmospheric gases and particulates in Panama. J. P. Lodge, jr. and J. B. Pate. bibliog il Science 153:408-10 Jl 22 '66
See also
Forests and forestry—Tropics

Diseases and hygiene
See also
Sprue

TROPOMYOSIN. See Muscle

TROTTENBERG, A. D.
Colleges graduate visual illiterates. Sat R 49:73-5+ F 19 '66

TROTTERS. See Race horses

TROTTING races. See Harness racing

TROUBLE in outer space; drama. See Anderson, R. A.

TROUBLED children. See Problem children

TROUT
See also
Cookery—Fish

TROUT fishing
Ancient art of dapping. W. Davis. il Outdoor Life 138:102+ N '66
Angling paradise of the Apaches. R. B. Whitaker. il Outdoor Life 138:36-9+ S '66
Argentina: the grand tour. A. J. McClane. il Field & S 70:94-8 Mr '66
Big steelhead are back. J. Chiappetta. il Field & S 70:47-9+ Ap '66
Big trout controversy. E. Zern. il Field & S 70:69+ Ap '66
Browns of New Zealand. A. R. Phipps. il Outdoor Life 138:58-61+ N '66
Creek the crowds forgot. J. Mears. il Field & S 71:154-7+ My '66
Desert rainbows. F. H. Ames. il Outdoor Life 137:64+ My '66
Dream trip for fall trout. F. R. Martin. il Outdoor Life 138:24-7+ Ag '66
Dry flies for sundown. W. Davis. il Outdoor Life 137:66-8+ Je '66
Fall windfall. R. Attaway. il Outdoor Life 138:58-9+ S '66
Fly fishing for trout in lakes. T. Trueblood. il Field & S 71:24+ My '66
Grande Ronde; new steelhead paradise. R. R. Gerlach. il Field & S 71:30-3+ Jl '66
Hellhole fishing. E. W. Smith. il Field & S 71:26-8+ Jl '66
How to catch the smartest trout of all. D. Wendzel. il Outdoor Life 137:54-5+ Mr '66
How wild the Wolf? G. Laycock. il Outdoor Life 137:48-51+ F '66
Jigging for lake trout. G. Laycock. il Field & S 70:58-60+ Ap '66
Look to the lakes for trout. J. O. Cartier. il Outdoor Life 137:40-1+ Ap '66
Month the Madison goes mad. N. Strung. il Field & S 71:54-5+ Je '66
Opening for a young man. D. Shiner. il Outdoor Life 137:62-4 Ap '66
Pack-in ponds: Little Fish pond, in Adirondacks. N. Karas. il Field & S 71:34-5+ Jl '66
Patty's patience; opening day of trout season. C. Ford. il Field & S 70:6+ Ap '66
Rooftop river. C. Elliott. il Outdoor Life 138:32-3+ Jl '66
Sea-run cutthroats in Puget Sound. Sunset 137:60+ N '66
Tokyo trout; fisherman abroad. J. J. Platt. il Outdoor Life 139:38-41+ Ja '67
Trek to treasure island. F. M. Paulson. il Field & S 70:53-5+ Ap '66

TROUT fishing—*Continued*
Trophy browns of the Brule. J. O. Cartier. il Outdoor Life 138:40-1+ Ag '66
Trout that never hear traffic. P. Barrett. il Outdoor Life 137:36-9+ Je '66
Where the trout are. H. G. Tapply. il Field & S 70:78 Ap '66
Where the trout sleep late in the morning; Idaho's Teton River. J. Olsen. il Sports Illus 24:86-90+ My 16 '66
TROVA, Ernest
Uses of ingenuity. il por Time 89:76-7 Ja 6 '67
TROWBRIDGE, Alexander B.
Harmonizing East-West trade with U.S. national interests; address, November 23, 1965. Dept State Bul 54:59-65 Ja 10 '66
TROWBRIDGE, Charles L.
ABC's of pension funding. Harvard Bsns R 44:115-26 Mr '66
TROY, N.Y.

Water supply
We have the tools to do the job. J. P. Buckley. il Am City 81:86-9 F '66
Les TROYENS; opera. See Berlioz, H
TRUCIAL OMAN
See also
Abu Dhabi
TRUCIAL states
Vest-pocket states of Arabia. A. Higbee. il Newsweek 67:50+ Mr 28 '66
TRUCK drivers. See Motor truck drivers
TRUCK tires. See Tires, Motor truck
TRUCKING
If Jimmy Hoffa goes to jail. il U S News 61:65-6 D 26 '66
Industry chokes on its own lifeline; garment industry choked to death by transportation. il Bsns W p 104-6+ Ap 9 '66
Trucking: rounding a new bend. il Duns R 87:pt2 118-19+ My '66

Finance
Trucking stocks go into high. il Bsns W p 122+ Ja 22 '66

Private operations
Private carriage: the flourishing stepchild. J. Weingarten. il Duns R 87:pt2 133-5+ My '66

Rates
Truckers drive hard for new rate schedules. Bsns W p 125-6+ O 29 '66
TRUCKS
Build this beach dolly for your boat. E. Wobeck. il Pop Sci 189:100-1 Jl '66
See also
Motor trucks
TRUCKS, Toy. See Toys
TRUEBLOOD, D. Elton
Deeds and a few words. Christan Cent 83:914 Jl 20 '66
TRUEBLOOD, Ted, pseud.
[Monthly article on outdoor life] See issues of Field & stream
Pheasant is a clever bird. Field & S 71:64-7+ S '66
TRUEMAN, E. R.
Bivalve mollusks: fluid dynamics of burrowing. bibliog Science 152:523-5 Ap 22 '66
TRUESCHLER, Josephine
Youngest son; poem. Commonweal 84:611 S 23 '66
TRUFFAUT, François
Letter from Paris. Genêt. New Yorker 42:182-3 O 1 '66
TRUJILLO, Rafael, 1929-
Dick's in the act. Nation 203:237 S 19 '66
TRUJILLO MOLINA, Rafael Leonidas
Depraved legacy. il por Newsweek 68:86 Ag 1 '66
Overtaken by events, by J. B. Martin. Review
New Yorker 42:224+ N 26 '66. R. H. Rovere
Trujillo, by R. D. Crassweller. Review
Sat R por 49:28-9 Ag 13 '66. H. Lavine
TRUKHANOVSKY, V. G.
Soviet teaching of history and international understanding. Sch & Soc 94:152-5 Mr 19 '66
TRUMAN, Harry S.
Annals of legislation. R. Harris. New Yorker 42:29-38+ Jl 2 '66
Call for action; criticism of economic policy. il por Time 88:19-20 S 9 '66
Et tu, Harry? criticism of economic policy. il por Newsweek 68:23 S 12 '66
Fair chance against slums. por Sr Schol 89:2 Ja 6 '67
Life with grandfather. M. T. Daniel. il por McCalls 94:52-3+ Ja '67

Truman presidency, by C. Phillips. Review
Newsweek il por 67:100 Je 6 '66
Time il por 87:120+ Je 10 '66
Truman vs. Johnson: danger of a depression? criticism of high interest rates. por U S News 61:22 S 12 '66
TRUMAN, Margaret. See Daniel, M. T.
TRUMBULL, Robert
Sunday that seems like yesterday. N Y Times Mag p 162+ D 4 '66
TRUMBULL, Stephen
River spoilers. il Audubon Mag 68:102-10 Mr '66
TRUMP, J. Lloyd
New ideas in high school teaching. PTA Mag 61:4-7 bibliog(p36) N '66
TRUMPET music
Phenomenal career; E. White. F. Summerill. il Hobbies 71:40 My; 40-1+ Je; 38+ Jl '66
TRUMPETER swans. See Swans
TRUNKS of trees. See Trees
TRUONG, Dinh-long-. See Dinh-long-Truong
TRUSCOTT, Steven
Canadian justice: ordeal of Steven Truscott. E. Stafford. il Nation 202:614-17 My 23 '66
Trial of Steven Truscott, by I. LeBourdais. Review
Esquire 66:12+ O '66. M. Muggeridge
TRUSLOW, Frederick Kent
When disaster struck a woodpecker's home. il Nat Geog Mag 130:882-4 D '66
TRUST
Respect and trust; address, September 14, 1966. R. M. Vogel. Vital Speeches 33:46-9 N 1 '66
TRUST TERRITORY OF THE PACIFIC ISLANDS
America's paradise lost, by W. Price. Review
Atlan 217:132 F '66. O. Handlin
Pacific Isles under U.S.: they're in bad shape. il U S News 61:84-6+ N 21 '66
Reporter at large. E. J. Kahn, jr. il New Yorker 42:42-6+ Je 11; 42-4+ Je 18; 56+ Je 25 '66
Small islands. E. J. Kahn, jr. il Sat R 49:45-6 O 8 '66
Trust Territory of the Pacific Islands; statements, June 27, 1966. E. Anderson; W. R. Norwood; F. Nuuan. Dept State Bul 55:387-401 S 12 '66
TRUSTEES, Library. See Libraries—Trustees, boards, committees, etc.
TRUSTEES of colleges. See College trustees
TRUSTEESHIP council. See United Nations—Trusteeship council
TRUSTS, Charitable. See Charitable uses, trusts, foundations
TRUSTS, Industrial
See also
Business consolidations and mergers
Monopolies

International trusts
Antitrust: a double-edged blade for U.S. companies abroad; western Europe's tradition of cartelism. Bsns W p 113 My 7 '66
Cartels fence in European steel; steel producers form blocs to regulate competition and fend off U.S. giants. il Bsns W p94+ S 3 '66

Law
After the marathon; violation of Clayton act. Time 87:80+ Mr 25 '66
Antitrust: a tough new line; new ruling overturns merger of two California supermarket chains. il Newsweek 67:81 Je 13 '66
Antitrust and the apparel industry; address, June 17, 1966. P. R. Dixon. Vital Speeches 32:617-21 Ag 1 '66
Antitrust in an era of radical change. M. Ways. il Fortune 73:128-31+ Mr '66; Discussion. 73:92, 111-14 Ap '66
From the trustbusters: guidelines for businessmen. il U S News 61:46+ Jl 25 '66
Guidelines for fair competition; interview. D. F. Turner. il U S News 60:76-80+ F 21 '66
More and more power for the trustbusters; Brown shoe company case and the Supreme court. U S News 60:15 Je 20 '66
Period to protraction; concerning FTC order to Procter & Gamble. Time 87:82 Mr 25 '66
Trouble with antitrust; excerpts from address. M. A. Wright. il Duns R 88:50-1+ N '66

United States
See also
National cash register company
United States—Justice, Department of—Antitrust division

TRUSTS, Investment. See Investment trusts

TRUSTS and trustees
How life estates and trusts can save taxes.
B. Brantley. Suc Farm 64:45+ Jl '66

TRUTH
Of many things; church's attitude toward
truth and truthfulness. T. N. Davis. Amer-
ica 116:67+ Ja 21 '67
Paradox and poetic truth; beauty of life; ad-
dress, November 17, 1965. A. Sibley. Vital
Speeches 32:344-51 Mr 15 '66
Truth from others changes self-image. Sci N
89:491 Je 18 '66
See also
Belief and doubt
Metaphysics
Reality
Sincerity

TRUTHFULNESS
Of many things; church's attitude toward
truth and truthfulness. T. N. Davis. America 116:67+ Ja 21 '67

TRYPANOSOMIASIS
Wildlife and the tsetse fly in Rhodesia.
A. S. Mossman. il Nat Parks Mag 40:10-15
S '66

TRYPSIN
Enzyme action: comparison on soluble and
insoluble substrate. J. M. Schurr and A. D.
McLaren. bibliog il Science 152:1064-6 My
20 '66

TRYPTAMINE
6-Hydroxylation: effect on the psychotropic
potency of tryptamines. R. G. Taborsky
and others. bibliog il Science 153:1018-19
Ag 26 '66

TRYPTOPHAN
Circadian rhythm for tryptophan pyrrolase
activity and its circulating substrate. M. I.
Rapoport and others. bibliog il Science 153:
1642-4 S 30 '66
Coordinate synthesis of heme and apoenzyme in the formation of tryptophan pyrrolase. H. S. Marver and others. bibliog
il Science 154:501-3 O 28 '66
Tryptophan deficiency in rabbit reticulocytes:
polyribosomes during interrupted growth of
hemoglobin chains. M. Hori and others.
bibliog il Science 155:83-4 Ja 6 '67
Tryptophan operon of escherichia coli: regulatory behavior in salmonella typhimurium
cytoplasm. R. L. Somerville. bibliog il Science 154:1585-7 D 23 '66

TSAFENDAS, Dimitrio. See Stefianos, D.

TSAI, Chia-yin, and Nelson, O. E.
Starch-deficient maize mutant lacking adenosine diphosphate glucose pyrophosphorylase activity. bibliog Science 151:341-3 Ja
21 '66

TSAI, Gerald, Jr
Inscrutable Mr Tsai. por Newsweek 67:84
My 9 '66
New mutual fund starts scramble. il por
Bsns W p 126 F 12 '66

TSALICKIS, Mike
Mike's revolution. S. Seegers and K. Seegers.
il pors Américas 18:30-5 Ap '66; Same abr.
with title One-man revolution on the
Amazon. Read Digest 88:185-8+ My '66

TSARAPKIN, S. K.
Non-proliferation gambit out of Moscow. il
Nat R 18:254-5 Mr 22 '66

TSETSE flies
African wildlife destruction; control program
through elimination of big-game in Rho-
desia. Nat Parks Mag 40:21 F '66
See also
Trypanosomiasis

TSHOMBE, Moise
Stanleyville rescue: American policy in the
Congo. K. W. Grundy. Yale R 56:242-55
D '66

TSIEN, Hsue-shen
Chinese puzzle. W. J. Coughlin. Tech W 19:
50 N 7 '66

TSIOLKOVSKII, Konstantin Eduardovich
Pioneers of astronautics. il por UNESCO
Courier 19:10 My '66

TSO, T. C. and others
Source of lead-210 and polonium-210 in tobacco. bibliog Science 153:880-2 Ag 19 '66

TSUCHINSHAN observatory. See Astronomical
observatories—China (People's Republic)

TSUKADA, Yasuzo, and Lajtha, Abel
United States-Japan committee on scientific
cooperation: neurochemistry conference.
Science 152:801-3 My 6 '66

TSUNAMI. See Seismic sea waves

TU, Fu
Poetry of Tu Fu. K. Rexroth. Sat R 50:30
Ja 21 '67

TUAMOTU ISLANDS
Dangerous Low Archipelago. M. Petersen. il
Motor B 118:52+ O '66
That day in Mururoa. E. B. Miller. il Sat R
49:62+ O 8 '66

TUBA (musical instrument)
Harlem tuba player. il Ebony 22:82+ N '66

TUBERCULOSIS
TB outbreaks reported in navy. Sci N 89:
436 Je 4 '66
When TB strikes: Garden City Hansel and
Gretel day nursery epidemic. il Newsweek
67:78 Ja 31 '66

Prevention and control
Italians announce new antibiotic useful in
TB. Sci N 90:398 N 12 '66
When TB strikes. il Newsweek 67:78 Ja 31
'66

Vaccines
RNA vaccine postulated. Sci N 90:459 N 26 '66

TUBERCULOSIS bacilli
Nicotinamide-adenine dinucleotide in tubercle
bacilli exposed to isoniazid. A. Bekierkunst.
bibliog il Science 152:525-6 Ap 22 '66

TUBEROUS begonias. See Begonias

TUBOCURARINE
d-Tubocurarine chloride: effect on insects.
J. R. Larsen and others. bibliog il Science 152:225-6 Ap 8 '66

TUCCI, Gabriella
Life and art. E. R. Rizzo. por Opera N 30:14-
15 Ap 16 '66

TUCCI, Niccolò
Gypsy, gypsy, where are you? Vogue 148:
115-17+ Ag 15 '66

TUCHMAN, Barbara (Wertheim)
Israel: land of unlimited impossibilities. Sat
Eve Post 240:30-4+ Ja 14 '67
Mind behind the blitzkrieg. Reporter 34:52+
F 24 '66

TUCK, Jim
Mexico's Polynesian surprise. Travel 125:42-4

TUCK, William Munford
Excerpt from debate, July 26, 1966. Cong
Digest 45:275+ N '66

TUCKER, Harold W. and Shea, V. M.
Convenience in Queens. Library J 91:5855-8
D 1 '66

TUCKER, Marion B.
To take and to tape. NEA J 56:62-4 Ja '67

TUCKER, Martin
Odd fish in Iris Murdoch's kettle. New Repub 154:26-8 F 5 '66

TUCKER, R. K. See Crosby, D. G. jt. auth.

TUCKER, Richard
Tenor of the House. M. Kastendieck. por
Opera N 30:18-19 Je 4 '66

TUCKER, Robert C.
Proliferation and Soviet-American relations.
Bul Atomic Sci 22:14-18 O '66

TUCKER, Sophie
Obituary
Newsweek por 67:91B F 21 '66

TUCKER, Vance A.
Oxygen consumption of a flying bird. bibliog
Science 154:150-1 O 7 '66

TUCKERMAN, Anne Weill-. See Weill-Tuckerman, A.

TUCKERMAN, Frederick Goddard
American heart of darkness. B. Cutler. Poetry
107:401-3 Mr '66

TUCSON, Ariz.
City planning
COMB untangles Tucson; ed. by P. D.
Eimon. il Am City 81:144+ N '66

Crime
Growing up in Tucson; C. Schmid, death
sentence. il Time 87:28 Mr 11 '66
Pied Piper of Tucson; C. Schmid multiple
murderer; with report by D. Moser. il Life
60:18-24A+ Mr 4 '66

Description
Tucson sun country. il Sunset 138:46-57 Ja '67

Education
Noble experiment; opposition to School resource officer program. Reporter 35:14+ O
20 '66
On the classroom beat. il Newsweek 68:76-
7 Ag 8 '66
Tucson's dangerous alliance; school-police
liaison. Christian Cent 83:879-80 Jl 13 '66

Hotels, restaurants, etc.
Mexican eating in Tucson and Nogales. il
Sunset 138:58-9 Ja '67

TUDOR, Antony
Antony Tudor talks about his new ballets; ed. by J. Anderson. por Dance Mag 40:42-5 My '66

about

Evening of Tudor at the Met. I. Kolodin. Sat R 49:28 Ap 9 '66

TUESDAY (periodical) See Negro periodicals

TUFTS, Charles F. See Bodi, L. J. jt. auth.

TUG of war
Heave ho, lock in and rock; Hope college's annual tug of war. L. Simross. il Sports Illus 25:40-1 O 17 '66

TUGBOATS
Business booms on the waterways. R. S. Strother. il Read Digest 88:213-14+ F '66
Danger signals from a river towboat. W. Belvin and A. Klein. il Yachting 119:72-4+ Je '66

TUGGLE, Robert A.
Gift of enthusiasm. Opera N 30:12-13 Mr 5 '66

TUITION fees. See Colleges and universities—Finance

TULANE university, New Orleans

Libraries

New Orleans jazz archive at Tulane. R. B. Allen. il Wilson Lib Bul 40:619-23 Mr '66

TULCHIN, Joseph S.
Latin America: focus for U.S. aid. Cur Hist 51:28-35 Jl '66

TULLIUS, F. P.
Look at the spring suits. New Yorker 42:86+ F 26 '66
Out of the death bag in west Hollywood. New Yorker 42:57-8 N 5 '66
Season's greetings from West Hollywood. New Yorker 42:28-30 D 31 '66

TULSA, Okla.

Public buildings

Tulsa civic center moves toward completion. il Am City 81:211 S '66

TUMOR viruses
Footprints of tumor viruses. F. Rapp and J. L. Melnick. il Sci Am 214:34-41 bibliog(p 143) Mr '66
Heat-labile serum factor required for immunofluorescence of polyoma tumor antigens. K. K. Takemoto and others. il Science 153:1122-3 S 2 '66
Partial purification and electron microscopy of virus in the EB-3 cell line derived from a Burkitt lymphoma. I. Toplin and G. Schidlovsky. bibliog il Science 152:1084-5 My 20 '66
Viral neoplastic transformation of hamster pineal cells in vitro: retention of enzymatic function. S. A. Wells, jr. and others. bibliog il Science 154:278-9 O 14 '66
Virus induction of osteosarcomas in mice. M. P. Finkel and others. bibliog il Science 151:698-701 F 11 '66

TUMORS
Antagonism of purified asparaginase from guinea pig serum toward lymphoma. T. O. Yellin and J. C. Wriston, jr. bibliog il Science 151:998-9 F 25 '66
Biosynthesis and composition of histones in Novikoff hepatoma nuclei and nucleoli. L. S. Hnilica and others. bibliog il Science 152:521-3 Ap 22 '66
Dominant hemispherectomy: preliminary report on neuropsychological sequelae. A. Smith and C. W. Burklund. bibliog il Science 153:1280-2 S 9 '66
Increased incidence of lymphoma after injections of mice with cells differing at weak histocompatibility loci. R. L. Walford. bibliog il Science 152:78-80 Ap 1 '66
Mammary tumor inhibition and lung adenoma induction by isonicotinic acid hydrazide. B. Toth and P. Shubik. bibliog il Science 152:1376-7 Je 3 '66
Minute tumor found causing sudden death. Sci N 89:184 Mr 19 '66
Parathyroid hormone in plasma in adenomatous hyperparathyroidism, uremia, and bronchogenic carcinoma. S. A. Berson and R. S. Yalow. bibliog il Science 154:907-9 N 18 '66
Polyp, hernia like LBJ's not rare; vocal cord polyp. Sci N 90:393 N 12 '66
Pregnancy tumors found; benign ovarian tumors called luteomas. Sci N 90:259 O 1 '66
President's surgery no small matter. F. Marley. Sci N 90:443 N 26 '66
Transmigration of lymph nodes by tumor cells. B. Fisher and E. R. Fisher. bibliog Science 152:1397-8 Je 3 '66

Tumor found innocent; C. Whitman's brain tumor unrelated to headache pain causing rage. P. McBroom. Sci N 90:98 Ag 13 '66
See also
Sarcoma

TUNA fishing
Battling bluefin. G. Heinold. il Outdoor Life 137:16+ Je '66
Day the giant tuna died. M. Rascovich. il Field & S 71:56-7+ My '66

TUNG, Chi-ping
Dissent on China. Christian Cent 83:1183 S 28 '66
I was a student in red China; ed. by H. Evans. por Read Digest 89:189-90+ D '66

TUNG, S. T.
Fallacy of China scholars; address, April 27, 1966. Vital Speeches 32:629-31 Ag 1 '66

TUNGSTEN films. See Photography—Films

TUNING, Television. See Television receiving apparatus—Tuning

TUNIS, Edwin
Some problems of a writer-illustrator. Horn Bk 42:690-3 D '66

TUNIS, John R.
Battle for a library. Sat R 49:58-9 Jl 9 '66

TUNISIA
Tunisian way. H. Bourguiba. For Affairs 44:480-8 Ap '66
See also
Airlines—Tunisia
Periodicals—Tunisia
Women—Tunisia

Description and travel

Blue world of Tunisia; Sidi-Bou-Saïd, Tunis. D. R. Browne. Sat R 49:69-71 N 19 '66
Tunisia; extravagant space and serenity. D. Messinesi. Vogue 147:21+ F 15 '66

TUNLEY, Roul
America's unhealthy children; an emerging scandal. Harper 232:41-6 My; 233:4 Jl '66
Big package flap. Sat R 49:64+ Ap 9 '66

TUNNEL diodes. See Diodes

TUNNELS, Water. See Water tunnels

TUNNELS and tunneling
Great Mont Blanc tunnel. A. Rankin. il Read Digest 88:207-10+ My '66
Our far-flung correspondents; complete circuit of Mont Blanc by surrounding glacial passes and valleys before opening of tunnel. J. Bernstein. il New Yorker 42:148+ Mr 26 '66
To everywhere in 42 minutes; Paul Cooper's theory of subterranean tunnel travel at ballistic missile speed. il Time 87:42-3 F 11 '66

TUNNELS and tunneling, Underwater
Transit tube to link San Francisco and Oakland. il Am City 81:52 My '66
Tunnel: Richmond tunnel, aqueduct tunnel from Staten Island to Brooklyn; interview. M. J. Barkin. New Yorker 42:48-51 N 26 '66
See also
English Channel tunnel (proposed)

TUONG, Ngo. See Ngo Tuong

TUPPER, Harmon
Presque Isle points the way. Read Digest 88:31-2+ Mr '66

TURANDOT; opera. See Busoni, F.

TURANDOT; opera. See Puccini, G.

TURBINES
See also
Air turbines
Gas turbines, Aircraft
Gas turbines, Marine

TURBINES, Gas. See Gas turbines

TURBOFAN engines. See Gas turbines, Aircraft

TURBOJETS. See Gas turbines, Aircraft

TURBOPROP airplane engines. See Gas turbines, Aircraft

TURBULENCE
Turbulent-gas chromatography. J. C. Giddings and others. bibliog il Science 154:146-8 O 7 '66
See also
Atmospheric turbulence

TURCIOS LIMA, Luis Augusto
Red Robin Hood. M. J. Kubic. il por Newsweek 68:61 O 17 '66

TURCO, Lewis
From Pocoangelini; poem; excerpt. Poetry 108:230-4 Jl '66
School drawing; poem. Sat R 49:33 D 17 '66
Student; poem. Sat R 49:17 Jl 2 '66

TURCOTT, George L.
Frail lands. Am For 72:16-19 F '66

TUREENS
Tureens for the soup of the evening. il House & Gard 131:76-7 Ja '67
TURF. See Lawns
TURFGRASS. See Grasses
TURGENEV, Ivan Sergeevich
Journey of the fifth horse; dramatization. See Ribman, R.

about
Ivan Turgenev. W. H. Chamberlin. por Sat R 49:24-5+ Je 18 '66
TURKEL, Peter
Drugs in the Great society. Cath World 203:265-9 Ag '66
TURKEVICH, John
Soviet science appraised. For Affairs 44:489-500 Ap '66
Soviet space effort. Cur Hist 51:226-32+ O '66
—and Fujita, Y.
Methyl radicals: preparation and stabilization. bibliog Science 152:1619-21 Je 17 '66
TURKEY
See also
Earthquakes—Turkey
Education—Turkey
Golden Horn
Princes Islands

Antiquities
See also
Sardis

Description and travel
Sparking tomorrow's tourist explosion. il UNESCO Courier 19:13-15 D '66
Timeless Turkey. J. Lieber. il Travel 126:30-6 O '66
Turkey: its surprises, rough, tough and magnificent. D. Messinesi. il Vogue 148:162-5 D '66

Economic conditions
Why Turkey's economy is taking off. Bsns W p73 Ja 7 '67

Foreign relations
Russia
Appointment in Ankara; visit of Kosygin. il Newsweek 69:26 Ja 2 '67
Polite distance; visit of Kosygin. il Time 88:21 D 30 '66

United States
What has gone wrong in Turkey? E. O. Hauser. il Read Digest 88:130-4 My '66

History
Unremembered genocide; murder of Armenians in Turkey during 1915-1916. M. Housepian. Commentary 42:55-61 S '66; Discussion. 42:7-8+ D '66

Industries
Turkish tycoon rolls his own; V. Koc's industrial empire. il Bsns W p66-8+ Ja 7 '67

Politics and government
Polite distance. il Time 88:21 D 30 '66
What has gone wrong in Turkey? E. O. Hauser. il Read Digest 88:130-4 My '66

Religious institutions and affairs
Islamic revival in Turkey. America 114:369 Mr 19 '66

Social life and customs
Alla Turca; life once lived within the sultan's palace. L. Blanch. Vogue 148:266-7+ D '66
TURKEY hunting
Turkey are back. G. Laycock. il Field & S 71:70-1+ N '66
TURKEYS
Now it's feeder turkeys. J. Bickers. il Farm J 90:64V F '66
TURKEYS, Wild
Mountain notebook 1950. H. Broome. il Liv Wildn 29:3-13 Aut '65
Tiny transmitters help wild-turkey study. Field & S 71:112 O '66
See also
Turkey hunting
TURKISH art. See Art, Turkish
TURKISH cookery. See Cookery, Turkish
TURN of the screw; opera. See Britten, B.
TURNBULL, Colin M.
Outsider; interview. New Yorker 42:26-7 Ag 20 '66
Report from Africa; a people apart. Natur Hist 75:8-10+ O '66

TURNELL, Martin
Hero of our time. Commonweal 85:251-4 D 2 '66
TURNER, C.
Valentine for Janie; story. Good H 162:90-1 F '66
TURNER, Corbett H.
Learning your baby's language. Parents Mag 41:36-7+ Je '66
TURNER, Donald Frank
Antitrust chief dissents; summary of address. por Fortune 73:113-14 Ap '66
Guidelines for fair competition; interview. por U S News 60:76-80+ F 21 '66
about
Beer blast. por Newsweek 68:24+ Jl 25 '66
It pays to advertise, all right, but how much? il Fortune 74:66+ Jl 1 '66
Top trustbuster, scholarly and tough. il por Bsns W p 166+ Mr 12 '66
TURNER, Fitzhugh
Man-eaters of Naini Tal. Outdoor Life 138:67-81 D '66
TURNER, Frederick Jackson
Science and symbol in the Turner frontier hypothesis. W. Coleman. bibliog f Am Hist R 72:22-49 O '66
TURNER, Joseph Mallord William
Art galleries; exhibition at the Museum of modern art. R. M. Coates. New Yorker 42:155-8 Ap 9 '66
Blots, spots and silken stains. L. Campbell. il Art N 65:44-7+ My '66
By Turner. Am Artist 30:6 My '66
Conflagration in the soul; J. M. W. Turner show at Museum of modern art, New York. A. Werner. Reporter 34:47-8 Mr 24 '66
Landscapist of light; exhibition at Museum of modern art. il por Time 87:66-9 Ap 1 '66
Over-Turner; New York's museum of modern art show. il por Newsweek 67:92-5 Ap 18 '66
Painting set free. L. Gowing. il Vogue 147:166-7+ Ap 1 '66
True father of modern painting. H. Kramer. il por N Y Times Mag p30-1+ Mr 20 '66
Turner at the Modern. F. Getlein. New Repub 154:26-7 Ap 9 '66
Turner; exhibition at Museum of modern art, N.Y. M. Wheeler. il Look 30:42-6 Ap 5 '66
Turner's emissary; exhibition at Museum of modern art; interview. L. Gowing. New Yorker 42:36-7 Ap 2 '66
William Turner, watercolor's old master. N. Kent. il por Am Artist 30:34-5+ Je '66
TURNER, Robert E. 1939?-
Vamp X, new victor on southern seas. F. Rohr. il por Motor B 117:174-9 My '66
TURNEY, Alan
(tr) See Soseki, N. Three-cornered world
TURNING
How to get started in metal turning. W. C. Lammey. il Pop Mech 127:186-9+ Ja '67 (to be cont)
TURRETS, Gun
Army adopts Vulcan anti-aircraft vehicle. D. A. Brown. il Aviation W 84:88-9+ Mr 14 '66
TURRO, James C.
Book of the month. Cath World 203:184 Je '66
TURTLES
Two in the bush; animal adventures in Malaya. G. Durrell. il Harper 233:104+ O '66
See also
Terrapin
TURTLES, Green
Don't mock the turtle; green sea turtles. il Newsweek 68:59 S 12 '66
How to trace a turtle and follow a deer. D. Cohen. il Sci Digest 59:28-31 Mr '66
TUSIANI, Joseph
Agreement; poem. Cath World 203:103 My '66
Conjugal ode; poem. New Yorker 42:52 Ap 23 '66
Dante Alighieri. Cath World 203:301-6 Ag '66
New books. Cath World 203:317-18 Ag '66
Ornithology; footnote number 2; poem. Cath World 203:275 Ag '66
Perfect joy; poem. Cath World 204:239 Ja '67
TUSKEGEE, Ala.
Murder in Tuskegee: day of wrath in the model town. A. S. Kaufman. il Nation 202:118-25 Ja 31 '66
TUSKEGEE institute
Booker T. Washington and the white man's burden. L. R. Harlan. bibliog f Am Hist R 71:441-67 Ja '66
Murder in Tuskegee: day of wrath in the model town. A. S. Kaufman. il Nation 202:118-25 Ja 31 '66

TUSSAUD'S gallery of wax figures. See Wax figures
TUSSOCK moth. See Moths
TUTORS, Volunteer. See Volunteer workers in education
TUTORS and tutoring
Let the children teach; child-to-child tutoring. B. Asbell. il Redbook 126:52-3+ F '66
Schools make news; ineffectual coaching for college boards. Sat R 49:74-5 Mr 19 '66
Something more; student tutors. D. Mallery. il Sat R 49:70-1 Je 18 '66
TVARDOVSKII, Aleksandr Trifonovich
Bread, salt and truth. il por Newsweek 69: 51-2 Ja 16 '67
TWACHTMAN, John Henry
Quiet American. il Time 88:90-1 O 14 '66
TWAIN, Mark, pseud. See Clemens, S. L.
TWEED, William Marcy
Tweed ring, by A. B. Callow, jr. Review New Repub 156:35-6 Ja 14 '67. M. Renek
TWEED
Light new breed of Irish tweed. il Sports Illus 25:40-4 S 5 '66
TWEEDMAKERS. See Weavers
TWEEDSMUIR, John Buchan, 1st baron. See Buchan, J.
TWEETER speakers. See Loud speaking apparatus
TWELFTH wedding anniversary; story. See Brennan, M.
TWENTIETH century
Demythologizing the new theology. W. B. Glover. Christian Cent 83:882-4 Jl 13 '66; Discussion. 83:1085 S 7 '66
See also
Nineteen hundred and thirties
TWENTIETH century-Fox film corporation
Hollywood's new leader. il Bsns W p80-4+ Ja 7 '67
TWIGG-SMITH, Thurston
Century of stubbornness. il por Time 88:82 S 23 '66
TWIGGY (model)
Cockney kid. il por Time 88:49 N 11 '66
TWINING, Nathan F.
Military starts to speak out; excerpts from Neither liberty nor safety. por U S News 61:92-4 O 3 '66
about
General faces reality. J. J. Stone. New Repub 155:30-1 O 29 '66
TWINS
Blessed is the mother of twins; National organization of mothers of twins clubs. C. B. Hicks. il Todays Health 44:24-7 My '66
How I'm raising my twins; ed. by J. Heimlich. S. Glick. il Parents Mag 41:58-9+ D '66
Identical twins inherit coronary artery disease. Sci N L 89:51 Ja 22 '66
Our family goes for doubles. V. Spurlock. il Parents Mag 41:46-7+ My '66
See also
Siamese twins
TWISS, Robert
Boeing plans to let 60 per cent SST work. Tech W 20:13-15 Ja 9 '67
TWISTED Juniper. See Juniper
TWISTED trees. See Abnormalities (plants)
TWO dollar bills. See Paper money—United States
TWO-family living. See Family life
TWO masks; drama. See Greth, R.
TWO people and a clock on the wall; story. See Tyler, A.
TWO thousand (year)
Futurists: looking toward A.D. 2000; Time essay; professionals make prophecy an organized enterprise. Time 87:28-9 F 25 '66
If world population doubles by the year 2000; interview. H. Brown. il U S News 62:51-4 Ja 9 '67
My safari into darkest atrophy. R. Starnes. Field & S 71:14-15+ Ag '66
TWO-toed sloths. See Sloths
TWO-year colleges. See Junior colleges
TWOMBLY, Cy
Roman classic surprise. V. Lawford. il pors Vogue 148:182-7+ N 15 '66
TYACK, David
Small colleges and teacher education. Sch & Soc 94:326-7 O 15 '66
TYDINGS, Joseph D.
Last chance for the states. Harper 232:71-4+ Mr '66
TYHANIC, Elaine F.
What makes a Catholic conservative conservative? Cath World 203:11-16 Ap '66

TYLER, Albert. See Spiegel, M. jt. auth.
TYLER, Anne
As the earth gets old; story. New Yorker 42: 60-4 O 29 '66
Genuine fur eyelashes; story. Mlle 64:102-3 Ja '67
Two people and a clock on the wall; story. New Yorker 42:207-8 N 19 '66
about
[Mademoiselle's Merit award winner] por Mlle 62:46 Ja '66
TYLER, Edward T.
Control of unborn life. pors Todays Health 44: 58-62 Jl '66
TYLER, Ralph W.
Reactions. NEA J 55:28-9 Mr '66
TYNAN, Kenneth
Theatre abroad: France. New Yorker 42:120+ O 15 '66
about
Cold-blooded crossfire; critic of In cold blood. il por Time 87:48 Ap 15 '66
TYONEK, Alaska
Tycoons of Tyonek. il Time 88:19 Jl 1 '66
TYPE and typefounding
Amsterdam continental types; new Roman outline letter called Contura. Pub W 190: 112 Ag 1 '66
Dinner and exhibition climax Goudy centennial year. il Pub W 189:98+ Ap 4 '66
John Dreyfus: typographic advisor, editor, printing historian. P. A. Bennett. il Pub W 190:84-6+ S 5 '66
New typefaces chosen in world-wide contests; first International type face design competition. il Pub W 190:120+ S 5 '66
See also
Printing—Legibility
TYPESETTING
Instant typesetting. il Sci Digest 59:17 Ap '66
See also
Photocomposing machines
TYPESETTING machines
IBM Selectric composing units. il Pub W 190:132+ O 3 '66
New Photon sets hyphen-less lines. Pub W 190:140 O 3 '66
RCA introduces Videocomp, an electronic typesetter. Pub W 190:118-19 Jl 4 '66
Type casting, by electronics; Videocomp model. il Bsns W p 176 Je 11 '66
TYPEWRITERS
Portable typewriters. il Consumer Rep 31:524-9 N; 369-74 D '66
Shopping tips; typewriters. il Changing T 20: 41-2 S '66
Typewriter and I. R. Armour. Writer 79:21-2 My '66
TYPEWRITING
Study and teaching
Capsule course in touch typing. il Writer 79:52-6 Jl '66
TYPHACEAE. See Cattails
TYPHOID carriers. See Carriers of infection
TYPING. See Typewriting
TYPOGRAPHY. See Printing
TYRONE Guthrie theatre. See Minneapolis—Theater
TYROSINE
Circadian rhythm in pineal tyrosine hydroxylase. E. G. McGeer and P. L. McGeer. bibliog il Science 153:73-4 Jl '66
Maturation of a stress-activated mechanism inhibiting induction of tyrosine transaminase. S. Schapiro and others. bibliog il Science 152:1642-3 Je 17 '66
Nucleotide sequence of a yeast tyrosine transfer RNA. J. T. Madison and others. bibliog il Science 153:531-4 Jl 29 '66
TYUS, Verneda
If I get up from here and do a little bit, a little bit more's going to come to me. F. Powledge. il por Redbook 127:66-7+ S '66
TZIMOULIS, Paul J.
Underwater. U S Camera 29:58-9+ My '66

U

U-2 (airplane) See Airplanes, Military—United States
UAW. See United automobile, aerospace and agricultural implement workers of America
UCLA. See California, University—Los Angeles campus

UFO (unidentified flying object) See Flying saucers

UFWOC. See American federation of labor and Congress of industrial organizations—United farm workers organizing committee

UHF television stations. See Television stations

UMT (universal military training) See Military training

UMW. See United mine workers of America

UN. See United Nations

UNEF (United Nations emergency force) See United Nations—Armed forces

UNESCO. See United Nations educational scientific and cultural organization

UNHCR. See United Nations—High commissioner for refugees

UNICEF. See United Nations children's fund

UNIDO. See United Nations industrial development organization

UNITAR. See United Nations institute for training and research

UNRWA. See United Nations relief and works agency for Palestine refugees in the Near East

U.S. camera and travel (periodical)
U.S. camera achievement awards. il U S Camera 29:30-1 D '66

US; revue. See Musical comedies, revues, etc. —Criticisms, plots, etc.

USBE. See United States book exchange, incorporated

USES. See United States—Employment service

USIA. See United States—Information agency

USIA libraries. See American libraries abroad

USIS. See United States—Information service

USIS libraries. See American libraries abroad

USOE. See United States—Education, Office of

USOM (United States Operations Mission) See United States—Agency for international development

USPS. See United States power squadrons, incorporated

USSR (Union of the Soviet Socialist Republics) See Russia

UTA (Union de transports aeriens) See Airlines—France

UTC. See United aircraft corporation—United technology center

UWF. See United world federalists

UBELL, Earl
Coming, leprosy's end; reprint. Sci Digest 59:87-9 F '66
Greatest explosion of them all. Read Digest 88:123-7 F '66

UCHIDA, Genko
Technology in China; with biographical sketch. Sci Am 215:28, 37-45 N '66

UCHUPI, Elazar
Shallow structure of the Straits of Florida. bibliog Science 153:529-31 Jl 29 '66

UDALL, Stewart Lee
American as host. Sat R 49:54+ Mr 12 '66
Books in review. Natur Hist 75:6+ F '66
Open letter. por Parks & Rec 1:608-9 Ag '66

UDENFRIEND, Sidney
Catecholamine symposium. Science 151:481-2 Ja 28 '66
Formation of hydroxyproline in collagen. bibliog Science 152:1335-40 Je 3 '66

UGANDA
See also
Hunting—Uganda

Description and travel
Uganda. O. Achtenhagen. il Travel 125:56-60 F '66

Native races
Outsider: study of Ik; interview. C. Turnbull. New Yorker 42:26-7 Ag 20 '66
Report from Africa; a people apart; Ik tribe. C. M. Turnbull. il Natur Hist 75:8-10+ O '66

Politics and government
Battle of Mengo hill. il Time 87:30+ Je 3 '66
Coup of convenience. Time 87:35 Mr 4 '66
End of King Freddie. E. Huxley. Nat R 18:569 Je 14 '66
Merely self-defense. il Newsweek 67:44+ Mr 7 '66
Nothing to regret? seizure of the palace. Newsweek 67:50 Je 6 '66
Rolls, gold and ivory. il Newsweek 67:56 F 21 '66

UGLINESS. See Aesthetics

UGLY man; story. See Rhodin, E.

UHR. Jonathan W. See Tao, T. W. jt. auth.

UHRIG, J. William
Will it pay to dry corn this year? Suc Farm 64:60 S '66

UINTAS wilderness area (proposed) See Wilderness areas—Utah

UKRAINIAN dance company. See Dancing, Ukrainian

UKRAINIAN dancing. See Dancing, Ukrainian

ULAM, Adam
Moscow congress: prudence and semantics. Reporter 34:25-7 My 5 '66

ULANOV, Barry
Catholic professors on the secular campus. por America 115:319 S 24 '66
Play of the month (cont) Cath World 203:63-4 Ap '66

ULANOVA, Galina
Ulanova talks of American ballet theatre in USSR; interview, ed. by A. Ilupina. Dance Mag 40:28-9 Ag '66

ULCERATIVE colitis. See Colitis

ULCERS
See also
Peptic ulcers

ULLETT, Nic
Foftly, foftly blowf the gale. por Time 88:85 N 11 '66

ULLMAN, Barbara
How to turn an editor into a friend. U S Camera 29:16+ O '66

ULLMAN, Norm
Nice guy who learned to be troublesome. G. Ronberg. il Sports Illus 24:53-4 F 28 '66

ULLMAN, Samuel S.
Youth, Bolivar; drama. Plays 25:59-66 Mr '66

ULRICH, Roger. See Vernon, W. jt. auth.

ULRICK, C. J.
High-quality square-wave generator. Electr World 76:43+ N '66

ULTRACENTRIFUGE. See Centrifuges

ULTRA-HIGH frequency. See Radio frequency

ULTRA-HIGH frequency radiation. See Radiation

ULTRAMINIATURE cameras. See Cameras

ULTRASONIC alarms. See Alarms

ULTRASONIC test instruments. See Testing instruments

ULTRASONIC waves
Microwave ultrasonics. E. H. Jacobsen. bibliog il Science 151:1179-87 Mr 11 '66; Reply. T. A. Anderson. 152:1011 My 20 '66
See also
Plants, Effect of ultrasonic waves on

Medical applications
Ultrasonics in medicine. A. Kagan. il Electr World 75:25-9+ My '66

ULTRASONIC waves in dentistry
Inventor of the month; ultra sound for dentistry. S. V. Jones. Sci Digest 61:23 Ja '67
Ultrasonics detect cavities. il Sci N 90:381 N 5 '66

ULTRAVIOLET rays

Physiological effects
Cyclobutane-type pyrimidine dimers in polynucleotides. R. B. Setlow. bibliog il Science 153:379-86 Jl 22 '66

UMANGITE
Crystal structure of umangite, Cu_3Se_2. N. Morimoto and K. Koto. il Science 152:345 Ap 15 '66

UMBRELLAS
How to buy an umbrella. il Changing T 20:45-7 Ap '66

UMPIRES (sports)
Ashford arrives. il Ebony 21:65-6+ Je '66
Delayed call; first major league Negro appointed. il Newsweek 67:62 Ap 25 '66
Emmett Ashford: ultra ump. G. Shalit. il Look 30:92-5+ O 4 '66
Making it official; pro football officials. il Newsweek 69:60 Ja 9 '67

UN-AMERICAN activities committee. See United States—Congress—House of representatives—Un-American activities committee

UNASSEMBLED toys. See Toys

UNAUTHORIZED phonograph records. See Phonograph records — Recording — Unauthorized recording

UNAUTHORIZED reprints. See Copyright—Unauthorized reprints

UNAUTHORIZED tape recording. See Magnetic recorders and recording—Unauthorized recording

UNCLE Tom
In defense of Uncle Toms. G. Wills; reply with rejoinder. N. Hentoff. Commonweal 83:489+ Ja 28 '66

UNCLE Wiggily stories. See Garis, H. R.
UNCOMPLETED investigation; story. See Rogin, G.
UNDER the mount of Saturn; story. See Midwood, B.
UNDER the weather; drama. See Bellow, S.
UNDERACHIEVEMENT, Student. See Student achievements
UNDERCOVER man; drama. See Kennelly, N.
UNDERDAHL, Norman R.
How to keep sows and pigs healthy; interview, ed. by J. Harvey. Suc Farm 64:44-5+ Ap '66
UNDERDEVELOPED areas
American education and the developing areas; address; with questions and answers. K. W. Thompson. Ann Am Acad 366:17-32 Jl '66
Effect abroad of American private enterprise; address; with questions and answers. A. Smithies. Ann Am Acad 366:51-9 Jl '66
Expert group on forest products meets in Geneva. UN Mo Chron 3:56-7 N '66
Industrial development. UN Mo Chron 3:71-8 Je '66
International flow of capital; concerning report of study. UN Mo Chron 3:37-8 Je '66
Interrupted dialogue: address. November 1, 1966. B. K. Nehru. Vital Speeches 33:141-4 D 15 '66
Nationalism vs. economic growth. J. Amuzegar. For Affairs 44:651-61 Jl '66
Needs of underdeveloped economies. K. De Schweinitz, jr. Cur Hist 51:72-7+ Ag '66
Population problem and economic progress; address, February 14, 1966. D. Rockefeller. Vital Speeches 32:366-70 Ap 1 '66
Rights of primitive peoples. M. Mead. il For Affairs 45:304-18 Ja '67
Sharing of the good life; adaptation of address, February 15, 1966. W. W. Rostow. Dept State Bul 54:803-11 My 23 '66
Social effects of animal diseases in developing countries. M. Kaplan. il Bul Atomic Sci 22:15-21 N '66
Three worlds of development, by I. L. Horowitz. Review
Nation 203:252-4 S 19 '66. J. Gerassi
Trade, aid and world peace. America 114:580 Ap 23 '66
Trade and the war on world poverty. R. M. Fagley. Christian Cent 83:745-8 Je 8 '66
United States trade policy after the Kennedy round; helping the developing countries help themselves; address, November 2, 1966. A. M. Solomon. Dept State Bul 55:784-9 N 21 '66; Same with title United States trade policy. Vital Speeches 33:115-19 D 1 '66
World impact of American technology; address; with questions and answers. B. Harvey. Ann Am Acad 366:41-50 Jl '66
World is heading for a collision: proposals for food aid program; excerpt from address, November 1965. G. Myrdal. il UNESCO Courier 19:21-3 F '66
See also
Agriculture—Underdeveloped areas
Arts and crafts—Underdeveloped areas
Economic assistance in underdeveloped areas
Education—Underdeveloped areas
Food relief—Underdeveloped areas
Food supply—Underdeveloped areas
Medical relief work—Underdeveloped areas
Public health—Underdeveloped areas
United States—Commerce—Underdeveloped areas
UNDERGRADUATES. See College students
UNDERGROUND cables. See Electric cables, Underground
UNDERGROUND gallery, New York. See Photography—Galleries and museums
UNDERGROUND irrigation. See Irrigation, Underground
UNDERGROUND movies. See Moving pictures
UNDERGROUND sprinklers. See Sprinklers
UNDERGROUND structures
Sweden goes underground. O. Clausen. il N Y Times Mag p23-5+ My 22 '66
UNDERGROUND water. See Water, Underground
UNDERHILL, Anne B.
R. M. Petrie: Canadian astrophysicist. Sky & Tel 32:25 Jl '66
UNDERHILL, Bradford B.
Home TV via satellite. por Electr World 75:39-41+ My '66
UNDERPRIVILEGED children. See Socially handicapped children
UNDERSEA mountains. See Ocean bottom
UNDERSEA research vehicles. See Submarine boats

UNDERTAKERS and undertaking
Meat and mortality: butcher's feud with mortician in Italy. il Newsweek 67:42 F 28 '66
UNDERWATER laboratories
Ambitious Sealab III program planned. H. M. David. il Tech W 19:37+ S 26 '66
Living under the sea. J. B. MacInnis. il Sci Am 214:24-33 bibliog(p 143) Mr '66
Ocean engineering takes the plunge. T. Alexander. il Fortune 73:144-7+ Je '66
Sea lab: man's toe in the deep sea. il Todays Health 44:18-23 F '66
Undersea college lab launched; Florida Atlantic university. il Tech W 19:35 Jl 11 '66
Working for weeks on the sea floor; Conshelf three. J. Y. Cousteau. il Nat Geog Mag 129:498-537 Ap '66
UNDERWATER lighting. See Lighting, Underwater
UNDERWATER moving picture photography. See Moving picture photography, Submarine
UNDERWATER oil well drilling. See Oil well drilling, Submarine
UNDERWATER photography. See Moving picture photography, Submarine; Photography, Submarine
UNDERWATER physiology
Cardiovascular defense against asphyxia. R. Elsner and others. bibliog il Science 153:941-9 Ag 26 '66
Living under the sea. J. B. MacInnis. il Sci Am 214:24-33 bibliog(p 143) Mr '66
UNDERWATER structures
Aquarium for people. J. Gould. il Esquire 66:46-9 Jl '66
See also
Marine structures
UNDERWATER television cameras. See Television cameras
UNDERWATER tunnels and tunneling. See Tunnels and tunneling, Underwater
UNDERWEAR
New underworld. il Time 87:46 Mr 25 '66
See also
Foundation garments
UNDERWEIGHT. See Weight (physiology)
UNDERWOOD, John
College football (cont) Sports Illus 25:67-70 O 17 '66
Journey to chickcharney country. Sports Illus 24:80-4+ My 9 '66
UNDERWOOD, William, company
Red devil bites off a new market. il Bsns W p66+ Je 18 '66
UNEMPLOYABLES
Coming to grips with unemployment. S. A. Levitan and G. L. Mangum. il Reporter 35:44-6 N 17 '66
Finding jobs for the poor. E. Moscovitch. New Repub 155:16-19 N 5 '66
From relief rolls to rehabilitation; training program launched by Cook County department of public aid in association with Institute of technological training. il Am City 81:34+ Ag '66
UNEMPLOYED. See Unemployment
UNEMPLOYMENT
Foreign labor briefs. Mo Labor R 89:1126-7, 1389-90 O, D '66
See also
Unemployables

Relief measures
Industrial growth in areas of chronic unemployment. G. Iden. il Mo Labor R 89:485-90 My '66
See also
United States—Job corps

Statistics
Experimental study of repeated unemployment. L. Nixdorf. Mo Labor R 89:650-2 Je '66
Portrait of the unemployed. C. B. Kalish. Mo Labor R 89:7-14 Ja '66
Shrinking map of idleness; Labor dept.'s report. il Bsns W p64+ D 17 '66
Work experience of the population. S. Saben. Mo Labor R 89:155-63 F '66
Work experience of the population in 1965. F. A. Bogan and T. E. Swanstrom. bibliog f il Mo Labor R 89:1369-77 D '66

Great Britain
Problems of redeployment. Time 88:38+ O 28 '66

Illinois
New jobless count ups the figure; census in three Chicago poverty areas. il Bsns W p 160+ D 10 '66

UNEMPLOYMENT—*Continued*

Pennsylvania

Coal country digs out from under. il Bsns W p96-8 My 21 '66

United States

Coming to grips with unemployment. S. A. Levitan and G. L. Mangum. il Reporter 35:44-6 N 17 '66

Different unemployment problem. Bsns W p200 N 5 '66

Employed and unemployed; changes in counting the employed and unemployed. America 115:763 D 10 '66

His goal is full employment; W. Wirtz's goal. I. Ross. il Read Digest 89:119-23 S '66

More glorious war; S. Shriver's aims and schemes. New Repub 154:7-9 Mr 26 '66

Only slightly pregnant? il Newsweek 67:74 F 21 '66

Poverty areas of our major cities. J. R. Wetzel and S. S. Holland. il Mo Labor R 89:1105-10 O '66

Rebel in a wing collar; march on Washington: J. Coxey and his Commonweal army, 1894. G. A. Gipe. il Am Heritage 18: 24-9+ D '66

Recovery of depressed areas: a gazetteer. Mo Labor R 88:III-IV D '65

Structural unemployment and aggregate demand, by E. Gottesfocht Gilpatrick. Review Reporter il 35:54-6 O 20 '66. E. T. Chase

Unbenefited; youth and Negro labor. Reporter 34:18 F 24 '66

Unemployed; a new definition. U S News 61:82 D 5 '66

Unemployment; a problem that's down but not out. il Sr Schol 88:10-13 Mr 11 '66

See also

Unemployment—Relief measures

UNEMPLOYMENT, Technological

Automation commission's report on technological development. Mo Labor R 89:274-7 Mr '66

Canadian automation code; excerpt from address, September 1965. A. Balloch. Mo Labor R 89:520-2 My '66

Cost of change. Nation 202:444 Ap 18 '66

Great society; its impact of automation; address, April 21, 1966. A. H. Raskin. Vital Speeches 32:554-9 Jl 1 '66

Program for automated future; highlights of National commission on technology, automation, and economic progress report. Bsns W p30 F 5 '66

See also

Unemployment—United States

United States—National commission on technology, automation and economic progress

UNEMPLOYMENT benefits, Supplemental. See Supplemental unemployment benefits

UNEMPLOYMENT compensation. See Insurance, Unemployment

UNEMPLOYMENT insurance. See Insurance, Unemployment

UNESCO House. See United Nations educational, scientific and cultural organization—Headquarters

UNESCO institute for education. See United Nations educational, scientific and cultural organization—Institute for education

UNGAR, Elisabeth

Beauty bulletin. L Vogue 148:86-9 Jl '66

UNGER, Leonard, 1917-

United States and the Far East: problems and policies; address. February 18, 1966. Dept State Bul 54:451-9 Mr 21 '66

UNGER, Robert

Bohikee creek. Criticism

America 114:705 My 14 '66

New Yorker 42:120+ My 7 '66

UNGERLEIDER, J. Thomas, and Fisher, D. D.

LSD: research & joy ride. Nation 202:574-6 My 16 '66

UNGRADED classes

Ding dong, the bells are gone: Chippewa Valley high school, Mount Clemens, Mich. E. Stephens. Seventeen 25:410-11 Ag '66

Non-graded classes: a better start for your kids? G W Wormley. il Farm J 90:74 F '66; Same. 90:C5 Jl '66

Nongraded school. Sch & Soc 94:32+ Ja 22 '66

School of tomorrow, today: PS 219. Flushing. N.Y. il Sr Schol 89:sup2 O 28 '66

Teachers in the nongraded school. M. C. Hunter. il NEA J 55:12-15 F '66

UNHAPPY returns; story. See Glenday, A.

UNICORN

Rhinoceros at bay. P. Brooks. il Horizon 9: 14-21+ Wint '67

UNICORN plants

With capsules of the unicorn plant. il Sunset 137:173 D '66

UNIDENTIFIED flying objects. See Flying saucers

UNIFORMS

Raid on braid; craze in England. il Newsweek 68:72 D 19 '66

Regimental tie; outfitting employees with identical wardrobes. il Time 88:40 Jl 1 '66

UNILEVER, limited. See Lever brothers and Unilever, limited

UNION agreements. See Trade agreements

UNION carbide corporation

Man from UNCARB. R. Levy. Duns R 87:46-8 Je '66

Shining up to a European market. il Bsns W p 190+ My 14 '66

Linde division

Plating reclaims worn jet engine parts; Linde's flame plating operation. M. L. Yaffee. il Aviation W 85:63+ O 17 '66

UNION college and university, Schenectady, N.Y.

Curriculum revision at Union college. Sch & Soc 94:261-2 Sum '66

UNION list of serials

Third edition of serials list includes over 150,000 titles. Library J 91:649+ F 1 '66

Union list published: third and final edition. il Wilson Lib Bul 40:483-4 F '66

UNION of the Soviet Socialist Republics. See Russia

UNION Pacific railroad company

Fight for the Rock Island. D. Cordtz. il Fortune 73:140-3+ Je '66

Western railroads collide on mergers; Union Pacific and North Western make strong bids for Rock Island. il Bsns W p 130-1+ Mr 19 '66

UNION Pacific-Rock Island merger. See Railroads—Consolidations and mergers

UNION representation elections. See Trade unions—Elections

UNION theological seminary, New York

Across borderlines; cooperative program in graduate courses of theology. Christian Cent 83:562 Ap 27 '66

UNIONS, Teachers. See Teachers unions

UNIT construction

See also

Modular coordination (architecture)

UNITARIANISM

Preachers in purgatory, by L. Mondale. Review

Christian Cent 83:1082-3 S 7 '66. S. D. Temkin

UNITAS, Johnny

$1,000,000 fumble. T. Maule. il Sports Illus 25:34-9 D 19 '66

UNITED air lines

Exit pioneer Pat. Time 87:99-100 My 6 '66

Traffic spurs United, Continental orders. C. M. Plattner. Aviation W 84:35 Je 27 '66

United bows to in-flight movies. Bsns W p 150 O 1 '66

United moves to combat airport delays. J. W. Carter. il Aviation W 85:40-1 N 28 '66

UNITED aircraft corporation

Fastest train in America. H. B. Comstock. il Pop Mech 126:89-92+ N '66

Corporate systems center

UAC planing hull craft aimed at oilmen. R. W. Niblock. il Tech W 19:12-13 Ag 1 '66

Pratt and Whitney aircraft division

Maintainability becomes engine byword. M. L. Yaffee. il Aviation W 85:106-7+ O 31 '66

P&W designs extendible skirt for RL20 rocket engine. G. Alexander. il Aviation W 85: 60-1+ S 19 '66

Pratt & Whitney feels the pangs of success. il Bsns W p 138-9+ Ag 6 '66

P&W increases airflow for SST engine. M. L. Yaffee. il Aviation W 85:50+ Ag 29 '66

Sikorsky aircraft division

Ship-helicopter cargo operation offered. D. A. Brown. il Aviation W 84:58-9 My 16 '66

United technology center

Mach 4 AF target to use UTC Hybrid. il Tech W 19:20+ Jl 11 '66

UTC chief sees tighter rocket market. R. Lindsey. Miss & Roc 18:22-3 Ap 18 '66

UNITED ARAB airlines. See Airlines—Egypt

UNITED NATIONS—*Continued*

Administrative and budgetary committee
Estimates and appropriations. UN Mo Chron 3:86-90 D '66

Advisory committee on the application of science and technology to development
Committee on application of science and technology to development meets. UN Mo Chron 3:35-6 Ap '66
Science and technology; international plan of action. UN Mo Chron 3:51-2 My '66
Science and technology; sixth session. UN Mo Chron 3:55-6 N '66

Armed forces
Financing the United Nations emergency force; statement, December 20, 1965. P. H. B. Frelinghuysen. Dept State Bul 54:295-6 F 21 '66
Key questions in the United Nations; U.S. outlook; address, April 25, 1966. A. J. Goldberg. Vital Speeches 32:489-92 Je 1 '66
Peacekeeping and peacemaking. L. P. Bloomfield. For Affairs 44:671-82 Jl '66
Reorganization of force. UN Mo Chron 3:12 Mr '66
United Nations: crisis of confidence and will. C. W. Yost. For Affairs 45:19-35 O '66
U.S. urges better U.N. machinery for peaceful settlement; statement, November 24, 1965. A. J. Goldberg. bibliog f Dept State Bul 54:93-9 Ja 17 '66

Forces in Cyprus
Appeal for funds for UNFICYP. UN Mo Chron 3:12-13 Mr '66
Extension of quiet. Time 87:31 Mr 25 '66
Security council adopts resolution; with text of resolution. UN Mo Chron 3:3-9 Ap; 3-9 Jl '66
Security council again extends U.N. peace force in Cyprus; statement, December 17, 1965. J. M. Nabrit, jr. Dept State Bul 54:210-11 F 7 '66
U.N. peace force in Cyprus extended for six months; statement, June 16, 1966. A. J. Goldberg. Dept State Bul 55:63-4 Jl 11 '66
U.N. Security council extends peace force in Cyprus; statement, March 16, 1966. J. Roosevelt. Dept State Bul 54:718-19 My 2 '66

Budget
See United Nations—Finance

Capital development fund
Committee on capital development fund. UN Mo Chron 3:36-7 O '66

Charter
Principles of international law concerning friendly relations and cooperation among states; statement, December 8, 1965. W. P. Rogers. Dept State Bul 54:168-75 Ja 31 '66
World peace and the UN. America 114:342 Mr 12 '66

Commission on human rights
Conclusion of twenty-second session. UN Mo Chron 3:40-3 My '66
Twenty-second session. UN Mo Chron 3:24-7 Ap '66
United Nations and human rights; statement; March 21, 1966. M. Abram. Dept State Bul 54:636-40 Ap 18 '66
United States favors creation of a U.N. high commissioner for human rights; statements, March 25, 28, 30, 1966. M. Abram. Dept State Bul 54:1029-33 Je 27 '66

Commission on the status of women
Commission concludes session. UN Mo Chron 3:27-9 Ap '66
Elimination of discrimination against women; report on 19th session. G. A. Tillett. Dept State Bul 55:284-8 Ag 22 '66
Nineteenth session opens in Geneva. UN Mo Chron 3:24-5 Mr '66

Committee for development planning
Committee for development planning; first session. UN Mo Chron 3:35-6 Je '66

Committee for industrial development
Committee for industrial development; ended sixth session. UN Mo Chron 3:34-5 Je '66
Sixth session. UN Mo Chron 3:47-8 My '66

Committee of twenty-four
See United Nations—Special committee on the situation with regard to implementation of declaration on granting of independence to colonial countries and peoples

Committee on housing, building and planning
See United Nations—Economic and social council

Committee on the peaceful uses of outer space
Adoption of report of Working group. UN Mo Chron 3:25 My '66
Adoption of report to Assembly. UN Mo Chron 3:23-4 O '66
Carving up the universe. Nat R 18:1307-8 D 27 '66
Conference recommended. UN Mo Chron 3:5-7 F '66
Cooperation and arms control in outer space. B. G. Lall. Bul Atomic Sci 22:34-7 N '66
Great international venture. A. H. Abdel-Ghani. UNESCO Courier 19:5-6 My '66
International cooperation in space; statement, September 19, 1966. A. J. Goldberg. Dept State Bul 55:605-8 O 17 '66
Legal sub-committee fifth session. UN Mo Chron 3:31-2 Ag '66
Peace in outer space; Geneva meeting. Nation 203:141 Ag 22 '66
President Johnson hails U.N. accord on treaty governing exploration of outer space; statement, December 8, 1966; with text of treaty. L. B. Johnson. Dept State Bul 55:952-5 D 26 '66
Treaty called key arms control measure. Aviation W 85:72 D 19 '66
U.N. comes to grips with space; international treaty on outer space; with editorial comment. Bsns W p 14, 100 D 24 '66
U.S. emphasizes need to reserve outer space and celestial bodies for peaceful activities; statement, July 12, 1966. A. J. Goldberg. Dept State Bul 55:249-52 Ag 15 '66
U.S. presents draft treaty on exploration of the moon and other celestial bodies to U.N. committee; text of letter to the chairman of the U.N. committee on the peaceful uses of outer space, with text of the U.S. draft treaty, June 16, 1966. A. J. Goldberg. Dept State Bul 55:60-2 Jl 11 '66
U.S. Russia near accord on space pact. L. L. Doty. Aviation W 85:21-2 Ag 1 '66
U.S.-USSR accord foreseen on language of space treaty. Tech W 19:37-8 Ag 29 '66
U.S. urges early action on space treaty; statement, September 15, 1966. A. J. Goldberg. Dept State Bul 55:508 O 3 '66

Committees
Main committees of Assembly; election of officers. UN Mo Chron 3:11 O; 35 N '66

Councils, committees, etc.
Assembly fills vacancies; elections to councils. UN Mo Chron 3:69-70 Ja '66

Development program
First steps in a development project; development of the Pangani and Wami River basins; irrigated farming; photographs. UN Mo Chron 3:59-64 F '66
Foreign aid that works. J. Daniel. Read Digest 89:203-4+ S '66
Governing council meets. UN Mo Chron 3:85-6 D '66
Mineral search in the Andes; photographs. UN Mo Chron 3:45-52 Mr '66
New projects approved by UNDP governing council. UN Mo Chron 3:21-30 F; 27-35 Jl '66
1966 pledging conference. UN Mo Chron 3:53-4 N '66
U.N. development program, a new effort in peacebuilding; statement, January 11, 1966. J. Roosevelt Dept State Bul 54:420-6 Mr 14 '66
UNESCO and literacy; progress report. R. L. Tobin. Sat R 49:24 Jl 30 '66

Documents
See United Nations—Publications

Drama
Birthday party for UNICEF. A. Fisher and O. Rabe. Plays 26:47-58 O '66

Economic and financial committee
Second committee adopts two draft resolutions. UN Mo Chron 3:45-8 N '66
Second committee recommendations. UN Mo Chron 3:77-80 D '66
Trends and objectives of the world economy; statement, October 4, 1966. P. de Seynes. UN Mo Chron 3:133-46 N '66

Economic and social council
Assembly fills vacancies. UN Mo Chron 3:64 D '66

UNITED NATIONS—Economic and social council—*Continued*

Economic and social council; second part of its resumed thirty-ninth session. UN Mo Chron 3:85 Ja '66

Forty-first session resumed. UN Mo Chron 3: 83-5 D '66

Housing, building and planning. UN Mo Chron 3:37-9 O '66

Problems and challenges of the U.N. decade of development; statement, July 6, 1966. A. J. Goldberg. Dept State Bul 55:241-8 Ag 15 '66

Science and technology; international plan of action. UN Mo Chron 3:51-2 My '66

Special committee on co-ordination. UN Mo Chron 3:44-5 Je; 40 Jl '66

See also
United Nations—Social commission

Meetings, 1966

ECOSOC concludes session; fortieth session. UN Mo Chron 3:19-22 Ap '66

Economic and social council; fortieth session convened. UN Mo Chron 3:16-19 Mr '66

Summer session in Geneva seeks further development aid. UN Mo Chron 3:40-5 Ag '66

Economic commission for Asia and the Far East

Asian development bank. UN Mo Chron 3: 15-16 F '66

ECAFE: annual session. UN Mo Chron 3:31-2 Ap '66

ECAFE committee on trade. UN Mo Chron 3:15 F '66

1966 session concluded. UN Mo Chron 3:37-8 My '66

See also
Conference of the ministers of education of Asian member states of Unesco

Economic commission for Europe

Twenty-first session in Europe. UN Mo Chron 3:38-40 My '66

Emergency force

See United Nations—Armed forces

Employees

See also
United Nations—Secretariat

Finance

Ad Hoc committee of experts; summary of statement; March 25, 1966. M. Majoli. UN Mo Chron 3:36-7 Ap '66

Article 19 again. Reporter 34:12 Ap 21 '66

Budget estimates for 1967. UN Mo Chron 3: 58-64 N '66

Budget estimates for 1967. il UN Mo Chron 3:60-5 Ag '66

Budget estimates, 1965; estimates and appropriations. UN Mo Chron 3:88-94 Ja '66

Estimates and appropriations. UN Mo Chron 3:86-90 D '66

Expert committee on finances. UN Mo Chron 3:65-7 Ag '66

Meeting of Expert committee; with opening statement by the Secretary-General. UN Mo Chron 3:25-7 Mr '66

Secretary-General's report; analysis of United Nations finances. il UN Mo Chron 3:30-1 F '66

United States expresses views on 1966 U.N. budget estimates; statement, October 19, 1965. P. H. B. Frelinghuysen. Dept State Bul 54:69-74 Ja 10 '66

What does the U.S. want from the U.N.? G. J. Mangone. il Bul Atomic Sci 22:8-12 Ja '66

General assembly

Assembly anniversary; message. Thant. UN Mo Chron 3:65-6 F '66

Political influence in the General assembly. R. O. Keohane. bibliog f il Int Concil 557: 5-64 Mr '66

United Nations: crisis of confidence and will. C. W. Yost. For Affairs 45:19-35 O '66

Sessions (20th)

Conclusion of twentieth session. UN Mo Chron 3:3-4 Ja '66

Question of intervention in the domestic affairs of states; statement, December 10, 1965, with text of resolution, December 21, 1965. A. J. Goldberg. Dept State Bul 54:124-9 Ja 24 '66

Record of the month (cont) UN Mo Chron 3: 3-4, 11-98 Ja '66

Sessions (21st)

Agenda of twenty-first session of the U.N. General assembly. Dept State Bul 55:610-12 O 17 '66

Frustrated United Nations; U Thant's reference to the war in Vietnam and the problem of China. America 115:367 O 1 '66

General assembly twenty-first regular session: notes on the provisional agenda. UN Mo Chron 3:96-120 Ag; 132-4 O '66

General assembly 21st session; picture section. UN Mo Chron 3:41-4 O '66

General debate; summaries of representatives statements. UN Mo Chron 3:45-92 O; 67-132 N '66

Issues before the 21st General assembly. bibliog f il Int Concil 559:5-204 S '66

Keeping afloat; highlights. il Newsweek 69:30 Ja 2 '67

New session, old problems. il Sr Schol 89:16 O 7 '66

Opening of twenty-first session. UN Mo Chron 3:5-11 O '66

Provisional agenda, twenty-first session of U.N. General assembly. Dept State Bul 55: 353-6 S 5 '66

Record of the month. See issues of UN monthly chronicle

Storm signals on the East River. A. Weill-Tuckerman. Nation 203:298 O 3 '66

Topic A: how to bring peace to Vietnam. il Newsweek 68:54 O 10 '66

United Nations and chemical warfare. H. A. Jack. Christian Cent 84:60-2 Ja 11 '67

United Nations at twenty-one. il Newsweek 68:35-9 O 3 '66

Headquarters

Anecdotes, facetiae, satire, etc.

UN: marching orders. Nat R 18:1149 N 15 '66

High commissioner for refugees

Programme for refugees. UN Mo Chron 3:46-7 Je '66

United Nations day 1966: the world's refugees. Y. Zarjevski. il UNESCO Courier 19: 29-31 S '66

International law commission

Eighteenth session. UN Mo Chron 3:49-50 Je; 74 Ag '66

Election of International law commission. UN Mo Chron 3:94 D '66

Seventeenth session, second part. UN Mo Chron 3:32 F '66

Sixth committee recommendations. UN Mo Chron 3:64-5 N '66

Legal committee

Assembly adopts two resolutions; principles of international law concerning friendly relations and co-operation among states. UN Mo Chron 3:95-8 F 11 '66

Principles of international law concerning friendly relations and co-operation among states. UN Mo Chron 3:91-2 D '66

Sixth committee consideration; right of asylum. UN Mo Chron 3:65 N '66

Sixth committee recommendations; reports of the International law commission. UN Mo Chron 3:64-5 N '66

Technical assistance to promote international law. UN Mo Chron 3:92-3 D '66

Library

Dag Hammarskjold library's fifth year observed. Wilson Lib Bul 41:463 Ja '67

UN library celebrates its first five years Library J 92:37-8 Ja 1 '67

Membership

East German bid for U.N. status rejected by France, U.K., U.S; texts of a tri-partite communique, March 3, 1966; with letter to the president of the U.N. Security council from representatives of the three countries. Dept State Bul 54:640-1 Ap 18 '66

Notes and comment: small countries now independent and eligible for membership. New Yorker 42:19 Je 25 '66

Put out more flags: problem of mini-states. Newsweek 68:56+ N 7 '66

U.N. needs family planning. F. T. P. Plimpton. il N Y Times Mag p54-5+ S 18 '66

Permanent central opium board

Board reports to ECOSOC. UN Mo Chron 3:18-20 F '66

Political and security committee

Discussions in First committee; consideration of disarmament items. UN Mo Chron 3:35-8 N '66

Publications

Report on world social situation. UN Mo Chron 3:29-31 Ap '66

Trends and prospects analyzed; world economic survey. UN Mo Chron 3:37-8 Jl '66

UNITED NATIONS—Publications—*Continued*

Bibliography

Current U.N. documents: a selected bibliography. See occasional issues of Department of state bulletin

Documents: selected list. See issues of UN monthy chronicle

Recent publications: descriptive list. See issues of UN monthly chronicle

Scientific committee on the effects of atomic radiation

Effects of atomic radiation; sixteenth session concluded. UN Mo Chron 3:59-60 Jl '66

Secretariat

Composition of secretariat. UN Mo Chron 3: 90 D '66

Engine in the glass house. il Newsweek 68:38 O 3 '66

Secretary General

Appointment of Secretary-General; appointment extended; with text of Thant's statement. UN Mo Chron 3:3-5 N '66

Appointment of Secretary-General; with summary of statement by A. R. Pazhwak, December 2, 1966. UN Mo Chron 3:3-5 D '66

Mood of resignation; U Thant's decision to step down. Newsweek 68:35-6 S 12 '66

Thanks to U Thant. Christian Cent 83:1527 D 14 '66

U Thant; problems of his job. N. Cousins. Sat R 49:32 O 1 '66

U Thant's decision. New Repub 155:7-8 D 10 '66

U Thant's retirement; a helpful dilemma. D. Lawrence. U S News 61:128 O 3 '66

United Nations at twenty-one; U Thant's term. il Newsweek 68:35-9 O 3 '66

What is a Secretary General? F. T. P. Plimpton. il N Y Times Mag p58-9+ N 27 '66

Why U Thant is indispensable at the U.N. il U S News 61:16 S 19 '66

Security council

Assembly fills vacancies. UN Mo Chron 3:64 D '66

New roadblocks on the way to peace. il U S News 60:35-7 F 14 '66

Peacekeeping at the U.N. B. G. Lall. Bul Atomic Sci 22:43-5 O '66

Reporter at large; Rhodesian crisis. J. Kramer. il New Yorker 42:138+ Ap 2 '66

United Nations: crisis of confidence and will. C. W. Yost. For Affairs 45:19-35 O '66

U.N. needs family planning. F. T. P. Plimpton. il N Y Times Mag p54-5+ S 18 '66

U.N. votes Viet Nam debate. il Sr Schol 88: 24 F 18 '66

United States presents views on Security council procedures; letter, April 21, 1966. A. J. Goldberg. Dept State Bul 54:906-8 Je 6 '66

U.S. views on delay in calling Security council meeting; statement; April 8, 1966. Dept State Bul 54:715 My 2 '66

U.S. welcomes Security council views on Viet-Nam situation; statement, February 26, 1966. A. J. Goldberg. Dept State Bul 54:547-8 Ap 4 '66

Meetings, 1965

Record of the month:
Cyprus (cont) UN Mo Chron 3:4-11 Ja '66

Meetings, 1966

Record of the month:
Complaint of the Democratic Republic of the Congo against Portugal. UN Mo Chron 3:3-5 O '66
Congo; Palestine question. UN Mo Chron 3:5-19 N '66
Cyprus; admission of Guyana. UN Mo Chron 3:3-11 Jl '66
Cyprus. UN Mo Chron 3:3-9 Ap '66
Palestine question. UN Mo Chron 3:7-22 D '66
Palestine question; South Arabia incident. UN Mo Chron 3:3-21 Ag '66
Southern Rhodesia. UN Mo Chron 3:3-12 My: 3-15 Je '66
Viet-Nam. UN Mo Chron 3:3-10 Mr '66

Social commission

Conclusion of seventeenth session. UN Mo Chron 3:39-42 Je '66

Seventeenth session. UN Mo Chron 3:43-7 My '66

Social, humanitarian and cultural committee

General assembly adopts four resolutions; with texts. UN Mo Chron 3:48-53 N '66

Resolutions adopted by the General assembly; social and humanitarian questions. UN Mo Chron 3:80-5 Ja '66

Third committee discusses draft covenant. UN Mo Chron 3:80-3 D '66

Special committee of twenty-four on colonialism

See United Nations—Special committee on the situation with regard to implementation of declaration on granting of independence to colonial countries and peoples

Special committee on peace-keeping operations

Assembly adopts two resolutions; Peace-keeping operations; with texts of resolutions. UN Mo Chron 3:30-4 Ja '66

Committee considers draft resolutions. UN Mo Chron 3:66-70 D '66

Meetings of Special committee. UN Mo Chron 3:24-5 My; 15-17 Je; 11-13 Jl '66

Peacekeeping at the U.N. B. G. Lall. Bul Atomic Sci 22:43-5 O '66

Special committee approves report. UN Mo Chron 3:22-3 O '66

Special committee elects officers; with summary of statement by the Secretary-General. Thant. UN Mo Chron 3:13-14 Mr '66

Special committee on principles of international law concerning friendly relations and cooperation among states

Meetings of Special committee. UN Mo Chron 3:39-40 Ap '66

Peacekeeping at the U.N. B. G. Lall. Bul Atomic Sci 22:43-5 O '66

Special committee session concluded; with texts adopted. UN Mo Chron 3:55-6 My '66

Special committee on the policies of apartheid of the government of the Republic of South Africa

Committee discusses seminar report. UN Mo Chron 3:20-2 O '66

Meetings of Special committee. UN Mo Chron 3:10-13 Ap '66

Report to General assembly and Security council. UN Mo Chron 3:13-15 Jl; 21-4 Ag '66

Work of Special committee. UN Mo Chron 3:25-8 My '66

Special committee on the situation with regard to implementation of declaration on granting of independence to colonial countries and peoples

Assembly adopts resolution; concerning declaration on granting of independence to colonial countries and peoples; with text of resolution. UN Mo Chron 3:55-63 Ja '66

Conclusion of meetings in Africa; with texts of resolutions. UN Mo Chron 3:15-24 Jl '66

Meetings in Africa. UN Mo Chron 3:28-9 My '66

Reports to General assembly. UN Mo Chron 3:42-5 N: 71-5 D '66

Secretary-General opens 1966 session; with summary of statement, March 8, 1966. UN Mo Chron 3:13-19 Ap '66

Special committee of twenty-four; meetings in July and August. UN Mo Chron 3:24-9 Ag '66

Special committee of twenty-four; reports of meetings. UN Mo Chron 3:17-28 Je '66

Special committee of twenty-four; with texts of resolutions. UN Mo Chron 3:24-30 O '66

United Nations action in Security council and Special committee of twenty-four; with texts of resolutions. UN Mo Chron 3:12-24 My '66

Special fund

Assessment of seven years of Special fund aid. UN Mo Chron 3:85-6 Ja '66

Special political committee

Committee considers draft resolutions; consideration of question of peace-keeping operations. UN Mo Chron 3:66-70 D '66

Meetings of Special political committee; Palestine refugees. UN Mo Chron 3:38-42 N '66

Statistical commission

Statistical commission meets in Geneva. UN Mo Chron 3:55 N '66

UNITED NATIONS—*Continued*

Statistics

Wonderful world of UN statistics. Nat R 18: 1089 N 1 '66

Sub-commission on prevention of discrimination and protection of minorities

Sub-commission meets. UN Mo Chron 3:17-18 F '66

Technical assistance program

See also
United Nations—Development program

Trusteeship committee

Fourth committee begins consideration; Aden. UN Mo Chron 3:70 D '66
Fourth committee begins consideration; Portuguese territories. UN Mo Chron 3:71 D '66
Fourth committee's recommendations approved. UN Mo Chron 3:63-8 Ja '66

Trusteeship council

Thirty-third session. UN Mo Chron 3:48-9 Je; 41-4 Jl; 49-60 Ag '66
Trust Territory of the Pacific Islands; statements, June 27, 1966. E. Anderson; W. R. Norwood; F. Nuuan. Dept State Bul 55: 387-401 S 12 '66

Aden

Fourth committee begins consideration. UN Mo Chron 3:70 D '66
Question of Aden. UN Mo Chron 3:10 F '66
Secretary-General opens 1966 session. UN Mo Chron 3:15-19 Ap '66
Special committee of twenty-four. UN Mo Chron 3:21-6 Je '66

Africa

One-nation-one-vote; African bloc. Nat R 18:1033 O 18 '66

Austria

Address in General assembly, December 1, 1965; summary. J. Klaus. UN Mo Chron 3: 70-1 Ja '66

Barbados

Barbados admitted to United Nations; statement, December 7, 1966. A. J. Goldberg. Dept State Bul 56:28-9 Ja 2 '67

Basutoland

General assembly adopts resolutions; with text of resolution. UN Mo Chron 3:12-15 O '66
Special committee of twenty-four; meetings in July and August. UN Mo Chron 3:24-9 Ag '66

Bechuanaland

General assembly adopts resolution; with text of resolution. UN Mo Chron 3:12-15 O '66

Botswana

Assembly admits Botswana and Lesotho. UN Mo Chron 3:34 N '66
U.S. supports U.N. membership of Botswana and Lesotho; statement, October 14, 1966. J. M. Nabrit, jr. Dept State Bul 55:758-9 N 14 '66

Cambodia

Communications. UN Mo Chron 3:14-16 Mr '66
Communications; Cambodia; Thailand. UN Mo Chron 3:7-8 F '66
U.S. replies to Cambodian charges on frontier situation; letter to U Thant, January 8, 1966. A. J. Goldberg. Dept State Bul 54: 167-8 Ja 31 '66

China (People's Republic)

Assembly decision. UN Mo Chron 3:36-43 D '66
Four against the red China lobby; symposium; ed. with introd. by T. Lit. il Nat R 18: 513-28 My 31 '66; Correction. 18:598+ Je 28 '66
Helping hands; editorials, reports, letters supporting admission of Communist China to the UN in New York times. Nat R 18:302-4 Ap 5 '66
How firm a no? U.S. policy on admission of Peking. Newsweek 68:33 S 26 '66
In the U.N, a louder no to red China. il U S News 61:10-11 D 12 '66
Initiative for peace; statement. September 22, 1966. A. J. Goldberg. Dept State Bul 55:518-25 O 10 '66; Same with title Vietnam settlement. Vital Speeches 33:34-8 N 1 '66

Messenger; Rusk talks to Nationalists about admittance. il Newsweek 68:34 Jl 18 '66
Move to change representation of China in U.N. again rejected by the General assembly; statement, November 21, 1966; with texts of resolutions. A. J. Goldberg. Dept State Bul 55:926-9 D 19 '66
New debate on China. Newsweek 67:25-6 Mr 21 '66
No. New Yorker 42:50-1 D 10 '66
No admittance. Time 88:38 D 9 '66
No seat for Mao. America 115:762 D 10 '66
Our war with red China; in the United Nations. A. Harrigan. Nat R 18:207-8 Mr 8 '66
Problem of China. America 115:367 O 1 '66
Tale of two Chinas. Newsweek 68:39-40 D 5 '66
Two Chinas; Americans are ready for a new policy. H. S. Reuss. Commonweal 84:251-4 My 20 '66
See also
Committee of one million against the admission of Communist China to the United Nations

Congo (capital Kinshasa)

Complaint of the Democratic Republic of the Congo against Portugal. UN Mo Chron 3: 3-5 O '66
Security council adopts resolution; with text. UN Mo Chron 3:5-13 N '66
U.N. urges nations to refrain from interference in the Congo; statement, October 14, 1966; with text of resolution. A. J. Goldberg. Dept State Bul 55:759-60 N 14 '66

Cyprus

Security council adopts resolution; with text of resolution. UN Mo Chron 3:4-11 Ja '66
United Nations mediator resigns. UN Mo Chron 3:9-10 F '66
See also
United Nations—Armed forces—Forces in Cyprus

Fiji

Special committee of twenty-four. UN Mo Chron 3:17-21 Je '66
Special committee of twenty-four; with text of resolution. UN Mo Chron 3:24-6 O '66

Great Britain

Address in General assembly, December 16, 1965; summary. H. Wilson. UN Mo Chron 3:73-5 Ja '66

Guyana

Admission of new members; Guyana. UN Mo Chron 3:9-11 Jl '66
Security council recommends Guyana's admission to U.N; statement, June 21, 1966. A. J. Goldberg. Dept State Bul 55:188 Ag 1 '66

India

See also
United Nations—Kashmir

Indonesia

Resumption of membership. UN Mo Chron 3: 11-12 O '66

Israel

Israel condemned; Security council's censure for reprisal raids. New Repub 155:7 D 10 '66
Massive retaliation; Israeli army units in Jordan. il Newsweek 68:42 N 28 '66
Security council considers complaint against the Syrian Arab Republic. UN Mo Chron 3:13-19 N '66
Security council considers complaint against the Syrian Arab Republic; with text of resolution. UN Mo Chron 3:7-22 D '66
Security council considers dispute between Israel and the Syrian Arab Republic. UN Mo Chron 3:3-12 Ag '66
U.S.S.R. vetoes Security council resolution on Israel complaint; statements; with text of draft resolution vetoed November 4, 1966. A. J. Goldberg. Dept State Bul 55:969-74 D 26 '66
U.N. security council censures Israel for raid against Jordan; statement; with text of resolution adopted, November 25, 1966. A. J. Goldberg. Dept State Bul 55:974-8 D 26 '66

Jordan

Massive retaliation; Israeli army units in Jordan. il Newsweek 68:42 N 28 '66
U.N. Security council censures Israel for raid against Jordan; statement; with text of resolution adopted, November 25, 1966. A. J. Goldberg. Dept State Bul 55:974-8 D 26 '66

UNITED NATIONS—*Continued*

Kashmir

Address in General assembly, December 13, 1965; summary. M. Ayub Khan. UN Mo Chron 3:71-3 Ja '66
Completion of troop withdrawals. UN Mo Chron 3:10-11 Mr '66

Korea

Assembly adopts resolution; Korean question. UN Mo Chron 3:45-6 Ja '66

Lesotho

Assembly admits Botswana and Lesotho. UN Mo Chron 3:34 N '66
U.S. supports U.N. membership of Botswana and Lesotho; statement, October 14, 1966. J. M. Nabrit, jr. Dept State Bul 55:758-9 N 14 '66

Pakistan

See also
United Nations—Kashmir

Portugal

Complaint of the Democratic Republic of the Congo against Portugal. UN Mo Chron 3: 3-5 O '66
Fourth committee begins consideration. UN Mo Chron 3:71 D '66
Portuguese territories. UN Mo Chron 3:39 Ag '66

Rhodesia

Assembly adopts resolution; with text. UN Mo Chron 3:29-34 N; 43-7 D '66
Crackdown on Rhodesia; another country for U.S. to rescue? il U S News 62:28-9 Ja 2 '67
Double standard for U.N? action on Rhodesia, not on Vietnam. il U S News 60: 50+ Ap 25 '66
Reporter at large. J. Kramer. il New Yorker 42:138+ Ap 2 '66
Rhodesia's woes mount; Britain preparing new mandatory economic sanctions. Bsns W p44 D 10 '66
Sanctions against Rhodesia. Time 88:27 D 23 '66
Sanctions voted. il Sr Schol 89:15 Ja 6 '67
Security council authorizes U.K. to use force to divert oil shipments bound for Rhodesia; statement, April 9, 1966; with text of resolution. A. J. Goldberg. Dept State Bul 54: 713-18 My 2 '66
Security council considers situation. UN Mo Chron 3:3-15 Je '66
Special committee of twenty-four; meetings in Africa; text of resolution. UN Mo Chron 3:26-8 Je '66
United Nations action in Security council and Special committee of twenty-four; with texts of resolutions. UN Mo Chron 3:3-24 My '66
U.N. vs. Rhodesia. il Newsweek 68:30 D 26 '66
U.S. urges Security council unity on Rhodesian problem; statement, May 18, 1966. A. J. Goldberg. Dept State Bul 54:986-91 Je 20 '66

Saudi Arabia

Consensus on South Arabia incident. UN Mo Chron 3:12-21 Ag '66

South Africa

Assembly approves two resolutions; apartheid in South Africa; with texts of resolutions. UN Mo Chron 3:48-55 Ja '66
How irresponsible can you get? Nat R 18: 1145 N 15 '66
South West Africa case: what happened? E. A. Gross. For Affairs 45:36-48 O '66
South-West Africa: we rose to be counted. Life 61:4 N 11 '66

Southwest Africa

Assembly approves resolution; with texts of resolutions. UN Mo Chron 3:20-9 N '66
Assembly discusses draft resolution. UN Mo Chron 3:15-18 O '66
Committee appointed. UN Mo Chron 3:66 D '66
How irresponsible can you get? Nat R 18: 1145 N 15 '66
How the wind blows; African delegates request special session of General assembly. Nat R 18:820 Ag 23 '66
South West Africa case: what happened? E. A. Gross. For Affairs 45:36-48 O '66
South-West Africa mandate. T. P. Melady. il America 115:600-2 N 12 '66

South West Africa: the resolution and South Africa. Nation 203:691-2 D 26 '66
South-West Africa: we rose to be counted. Life 61:4 N 11 '66
Special committee of twenty-four; committee approves report. UN Mo Chron 3:27 O '66
Sticks and stones; question of South Africa's right to rule Newsweek 68:56 N 7 '66
U.N. assumes responsibility for South West Africa; statement with text of resolution, October 27, 1966. J. M. Nabrit, jr. Dept State Bul 55:870-2 D 5 '66
U.S. to serve on U.N. ad hoc committee on South West Africa; statement, November 21, 1966. A. J. Goldberg. Dept State Bul 55:937 D 19 '66
United States urges concrete U.N. action on South West Africa; statement, October 12, 1966. A. J. Goldberg. Dept State Bul 55: 690-1 O 31 '66

Swaziland

General assembly adopts resolution; with text of resolution. UN Mo Chron 3:12-15 O '66

Syria

Security council considers complaint against the Syrian Arab Republic. UN Mo Chron 3:13-19 N '66
Security council considers complaint against the Syrian Arab Republic; with text of resolution. UN Mo Chron 3:7-22 D '66
Security council considers dispute between Israel and the Syrian Arab Republic. UN Mo Chron 3:3-12 Ag '66
U.S.S.R. vetoes Security council resolution on Israel complaint; statements; with text of draft resolution vetoed November 4, 1966. A. J. Goldberg. Dept State Bul 55:969-74 D 26 '66

Thailand

Communications. UN Mo Chron 3:14-16 Mr '66
Communications; Cambodia; Thailand. UN Mo Chron 3:7-8 F '66

Tibet

Assembly adopts resolution; question of Tibet; with text of resolution. UN Mo Chron 3:42-5 Ja '66

United States

Adventures of Arthur Goldberg. A. Kopkind. New Repub 155:15-18 O 8 '66
Ambassador Goldberg submits Viet-Nam question to U.N. Security council; texts of two letters of January 31, 1966 and texts of two statements, February 1, 1966. A. J. Goldberg. Dept State Bul 54:229-39 F 14 '66
Coming of age of the U.N; address, September 5, 1966. A. J. Goldberg. Dept State Bul 55: 492-6 O 3 '66
Financing the United Nations emergency force; statement, December 20, 1965. P. H. B. Frelinghuysen. Dept State Bul 54:295-6 F 21 '66
Fresh look at the United Nations; address, April 2, 1966. J. J. Sisco. Dept State Bul 54:646-50 Ap 25 '66
Goldberg parallel center. Nat R 18:1086+ N 1 '66
Key questions in the United Nations; U.S. outlook; address. April 25, 1966. A. J. Goldberg. Vital Speeches 32:489-92 Je 1 '66
Mr Goldberg dissents. Nation 202:668 Je 6 '66
President reaffirms U.S. support for an effective United Nations; message, June 16, 1966. Dept State Bul 55:232-3 Ag 15 '66
Running hard to stand still; Chinese admission and Israel votes. A. Weill-Tuckerman. Nation 203:626-7 D 12 '66
Should U.S. aid be channeled through the U.N? M. H. McVitty. Cur Hist 51:102-7+ Ag '66
United Nations adopts convention on racial discrimination; statements; December 14 and 21, 1965. A. J. Goldberg; F. E. Willis. Dept State Bul 54:212-16 F 7 '66
United States announces pledge for Palestine refugees; statement, December 20, 1965. P. H. B. Frelinghuysen. Dept State Bul 54:212 F 7 '66
United States commitment to UNESCO; statement, October 27, 1966. C. Frankel. Dept State Bul 55:883-9 D 12 '66
United States expresses views on 1966 U.N. budget estimates; statement, October 19, 1965. P. H. B. Frelinghuysen. Dept State Bul 54:69-74 Ja 10 '66
U.S. hopes U.N. will extend Secretary-General's term; statement, September 1, 1966. A. J. Goldberg. Dept State Bul 55:434-5 S 19 '66

UNITED NATIONS—United States—*Continued*
U.S. participation in the U.N. during 1964;
text of message transmitting report, March
3, 1966. L. B. Johnson. Dept State Bul 54:
504-6 Mr 28 '66
U.S. peace efforts reported to members of
U.N; letter, January 4, 1966. A. J. Gold-
berg. Dept State Bul 54:117 Ja 24 '66
United States presents views on Security
council procedures; letter, April 21, 1966.
A. J. Goldberg. Dept State Bul 54:906-8 Je
6 '66
U.S. supports proposal for High commissioner
for human rights; statement, December 13,
1965. F. E. Willis. Dept State Bul 54:178-9
Ja 31 '66
U.S. views on delay in calling Security coun-
cil meeting; statement, April 8, 1966. Dept
State Bul 54:715 My 2 '66
What does the U.S. want from the U.N.?
G. J. Mangone. il Bul Atomic Sci 22:8-12
Ja '66

Vietnam (Republic)
After the pause: motion or progress? il
Newsweek 67:17-21 F 14 '66
Ambassador Goldberg reviews U.N. peace
efforts with President; statement, February
11, 1966. A. J. Goldberg. Dept State Bul
54:309 F 28 '66
Ambassador Goldberg submits Viet-Nam
question to U.N. Security council; texts
of two letters of January 31, 1966 and
texts of two statements, February 1, 1966.
A. J. Goldberg. Dept State Bul 54:229-39
F 14 '66
Ambassador Goldberg visits President John-
son to report on U.N. developments; state-
ment, November 7, 1966. A. J. Goldberg.
Dept State Bul 55:851-3 D 5 '66
Another peace offensive? New Repub 154:11
Mr 19 '66
Communications; concerning replies to let-
ter by A. Matsui to members of Security
Council. UN Mo Chron 3:9-10 Ap '66
Communications from permanent representa-
tive of United States. A. J. Goldberg. UN
Mo Chron 3:3-4 F '66
Double standard for U.N? action on Rho-
desia, not on Vietnam. il U S News 60:
50+ Ap 25 '66
Message to British council; October 19, 1966.
Thant. UN Mo Chron 3:75 D '66
New Viet role for U Thant? Sr Schol 89:14-15
Ja 6 '67
Peace talks: U Thant gets go-ahead, but;
summary of letter. A. J. Goldberg. il U S
News 62:11 Ja 2 '67
Press conference; January 20, 1966. Thant.
UN Mo Chron 3:33-43 F '66
Question inscribed on Council's agenda; with
summary of letter from president of Sec-
urity council. UN Mo Chron 3:3-10 Mr '66
Tragedy of errors; humiliation of the US in
the Security council. P. Ben. New Repub
154:8-10 F 19 '66
U.N. speak-in. Sr Schol 89:19 O 14 '66
U.S. letter to U.N. on Viet-Nam refused by
Soviet delegate; statement, July 12, 1966.
Dept State Bul 55:252 Ag 15 '66
U.S. replies to statements on Viet-Nam
proposals; statements, September 23, 28,
1966. A. J. Goldberg. Dept State Bul 55:609
O 17 '66
U.S. welcomes Security council views on
Viet-Nam situation; statement, February
26, 1966. A. J. Goldberg. Dept State Bul 54:
547-8 Ap 4 '66
Vietnam at the UN. A. Weill-Tuckerman.
Nation 202:169 F 14 '66
Vietnam: what role for the UN? R. J. Leng.
Nation 202:227-9 F 28 '66

UNITED NATIONS children's fund
Halloween's new spirit. il Parks & Rec 1:737
S '66
Nobel peace prize: acceptance speech. De-
cember 10, 1965. H. R. Labouisse. il UN Mo
Chron 3:99-102 Ja '66
UNICEF. B. Bernstein. il Dept State Bul 54:
271-80 F 21 '66
UNICEF celebrates its 20th birthday. C. L.
Bailey. il Parents Mag 41:44+ D '66
UNICEF executive board; 1966 session. UN
Mo Chron 3:46 Je '66
UNICEF: tomorrow must be better. L. Schis-
gall and O. Schisgall. il Read Digest 90:
151-2+ Ja '67

UNITED NATIONS cocoa conference
Resolution seeks reconvening of session later
in 1966; with text. UN Mo Chron 3:36
Jl '66
UN cocoa conference, 1966, opens session at
UN headquarters. UN Mo Chron 3:33-4
Je '66

**UNITED NATIONS conference on trade and
development**
Committee on capital development fund. UN
Mo Chron 3:36-7 O '66
Committee on invisibles and financing. UN
Mo Chron 3:87-8 Ja '66
Expert group on forest products meets in
Geneva. UN Mo Chron 3:56-7 N '66
Fourth session concluded; Trade and devel-
opment board. UN Mo Chron 3:33-6 O '66
Shipping in UNCTAD: dynamic approach.
C. H. J. Amaratunga. UN Mo Chron 3:75-
80 Ag '66
Trade and development; Assembly adopted
resolution. UN Mo Chron 3:77-8 Ja '66
Trade and development board. UN Mo Chron
3:13-14 F '66
Trade and development board; fourth session.
UN Mo Chron 3:45-9 Ag '66
Trade and development board; third session.
UN Mo Chron 3:19-21 Mr '66
Trade and development; report by a com-
mittee of experts on expansion of trade.
UN Mo Chron 3:50 My '66
UNCTAD committee on manufacturers; end
of first session. UN Mo Chron 3:23 Ap '66
UNCTAD commodity sub-committee. UN Mo
Chron 3:39 Jl '66
UNCTAD expert group on monetary issues.
UN Mo Chron 3:38 Jl '66

UNITED NATIONS correspondents. See Reporters and reporting

UNITED NATIONS day
Mr Kaiser named U.S. national chairman for
United Nations day; text of letter from
President Johnson, May 11, 1966. L. B.
Johnson. Dept State Bul 54:976 Je 20 '66
United Nations day 1966; message. Thant. UN
Mo Chron 3:i-ii O '66
United Nations day, 1966; proclamation, May
11, 1966. L. B. Johnson. Dept State Bul 54:
976 Je 20 '66
United Nations day 1966: the world's refu-
gees. Y. Zarjevski. il UNESCO Courier 19:
29-31 S '66

**UNITED NATIONS educational, scientific and
cultural organization**
Achievement of objectives by Unesco centers.
Sch & Soc 94:47-8 Ja 22 '66
Asia book conference opens in Tokyo, May
25. Pub W 189:57 My 23 '66
Birthday plans; twentieth birthday. D. Wolf-
le. Science 154:465 O 28 '66
Conserving man's cultural heritage; examples
of art saved by UNESCO's program. il UN
Mo Chron 3:49-56 Jl '66
Education for a new agricultural revolution.
il UNESCO Courier 19:23-4 Ap '66
That nations may know; L. B. Johnson
makes U.S. member of the Florence agree-
ment. W. Benton. Sat R 49:25+ D 3 '66
Twentieth anniversary of UNESCO: prola-
mation. August 31, 1966. L. B. Johnson.
Dept State Bul 55:463-4 S 26 '66
Two decades of Unesco. W. W. Brickman.
Sch & Soc 94:403 N 26 '66
Unesco and education. R. C. LeBlanc. il
NEA J 55:42-3 Ap '66
UNESCO and literacy; progress report. R. L.
Tobin. Sat R 49:24 Jl 30 '66
UNESCO at twenty; symposium. il Sch & Soc
94:403-30 N 26 '66
UNESCO celebrates its twenty years.
UNESCO Courier 19:41 D '66
UNESCO experimental literary projects. Sch
& Soc 94:120 Mr 5 '66
UNESCO in 1965. Sch & Soc 94:162-3 Mr 19
'66
UNESCO is twenty years old; symposium,
with questions and answers. il UNESCO
Courier 19:4-74 Jl '66
UNESCO: stress on development brings
parity for science. J. Walsh. Science 154:
990-3 N 25 '66
Unesco: two decades of dedication. il Li-
brary J 91:5716-17 N 15 '66
UNESCO's world literacy programme enters
operational phase. UNESCO Courier 19:33
Ap '66
United States commitment to UNESCO;
statement, October 27, 1966. C. Frankel.
Dept State Bul 55:883-9 D 12 '66
U.S. delegation to 14th UNESCO General
conference confirmed. Dept State Bul 55:
760 N 14 '66
What's happening to the E in UNESCO?
T. Gjesdal. il Sr Schol 89:sup 14-15 D 2 '66
See also
Conference of the ministers of education of
Asian member states of Unesco

UNITED STATES—*Continued*

Agriculture, Department of

Be happy, light up; film touting the pleasures of smoking. New Repub 154:8 Mr 5 '66

Bon appétit! concerning Food and home notes. service. Reporter 35:9 D 29 '66

Historic change on the farm; liberalizing restrictions on plantings. il Fortune 74:34+ S '66

Juiced for you; foreign film program. New Repub 155:7 S 10 '66

Smoke screen: Department of agriculture film to stimulate sales of U.S. tobacco abroad. Newsweek 67:19 F 7 '66

U.S. as others see us; reprint. il Nations Bsns 54:60 Ja '66

Wilderness regulations of the Department of agriculture. Liv Wildn 30:60-3 Spr '66

See also

United States—Agricultural research center, Beltsville, Md.

United States—Federal extension service

United States—Forest service

Forest service

See United States—Forest service

Air force

Air force, army agree on roles, missions. Aviation W 84:26-7 Ap 25 '66

Air force turning attention to better tactical support. C. D. LaFond. il Miss & Roc 18:105-8 Mr 28 '66

Bomb hunt: B-52 bomber collides over Spain. Nation 202:141-2 F 7 '66

Fallacy of the nuclear stalemate; address, March 24, 1966. J. P. McConnell. Vital Speeches 32:456-9 My 15 '66

Luftwaffe flies again, in Arizona skies; Luke air force base. il U S News 60:82-3 My 9 '66

Nonprofits: air force says we can't do without them. J. Walsh. Science 152:734-6 My 6 '66

Of 10,147 flying saucer sightings, there are rational explanations for all but 646. B. Wise. il Life 60:30-1 A pl '66

Services pushing for heavy increase in training of pilots. Aviation W 85:34 D 12 '66

UFO's: they're back in new sizes, shapes, colors. il U S News 61:59-60 Ag 22 '66

UFO's what a new investigation may reveal. D. Cohen. il Sci Digest 60:54-6+ D '66

USAF readies reliability center; Rome air development center. Aviation W 84:105 Je 13 '66

USAF seeks parachute stations as targets for JC-130 pickups Aviation W 85:61 O 24 '66

See also

Air bases

United States—Civil air patrol

Administration

Confessions of an ex-physicist; excerpts from remarks. H. Brown. Aviation W 84:21 My 9 '66

Air national guard

See United States—Air national guard

Air proving grounds

See Proving grounds

Appropriations and expenditures

AMSA shelved in fiscal 1968 budget plan; advanced manned strategic aircraft. C. Brownlow. Aviation W 84:22-5 My 2 '66

Air force research funding detailed. J. Ferguson. Aviation W 84:117 Ap 18 '66

Lack of funding worries air force. J. F. Judge and W. Wilks. il Miss & Roc 18:72-4+ My 30 '66

Communication systems

USAF planning space data link system. B. Miller. il Aviation W 84:65-6+ Ap 11 '66

USAF plans new Leap Frog flight test; two-way airground voice communication via Syncom 3 satellite. P. J. Klass. il Aviation W 84:79-82 Je 27 '66

Education

See also

Air pilots—Training

United States air force academy, Colorado Springs

Forces in Europe

Winging toward change. Time 87:35 Je 24 '66

Forces in Vietnam

Wall of lead; air losses over North increase. Newsweek 68:64 Ag 22 '66

Medical and sanitary affairs

Plan for an air force hospital provides light-care innovation; Composite medical facility, March air force base, Riverside, Calif. il Arch Rec 140:210-11 O '66

Military airlift command

See United States—Military airlift command

Procurement

AF considering study awards for two space-rescue modes. H. M. David. Tech W 20:16 Ja 9 '67

Air force moves to streamline contracts. il Aviation W 85:28-32 mid-D '66

Changes in store for AF non-profits; with editorial comment. M. Getler. Miss & Roc 18:14-15, 54 Ap 25 '66

FB-111 procurement to be hiked by 25 per cent. Tech W 19:19 S 19 '66

House unit drops non-profit investigation. K. Johnsen. Aviation W 84:29-30 Ap 25 '66

Improved total package concept sought. H. D. Watkins. Aviation W 84:95-7+ My 2 '66

Non-profit SDC expands market base. J. L. Trainor. il Miss & Roc 18:32-4 My 23 '66

Total procurement package; excerpts from remarks. G. F. Keeling. Aviation W 84:21 Ap 25 '66

USAF plans crucial AMSA bid in July; advanced manned strategic aircraft. C. Brownlow. Aviation W 84:28-9 My 16 '66

Strategic air command

Dunderball; H-bomb search off Spanish coast. il Time 87:33 F 4 '66

Real bomb; H-bomb, missing after B-52 and KC-135 collide. il Newsweek 67:50 Ja 31 '66

Systems command

Lab stresses non-nuclear weapons; Air force armament laboratory il Aviation W 85:39 mid-D '66

Quiet retirement; B. Schriever. il Time 88:24 S 9 '66

Tactical air command

House unit calls for improvement to fill gaps in tactical airlift. Aviation W 84:59 Je 6 '66

JATACS to answer joint tactical C&C requirements; joint advanced tactical command and control systems. W. Andrews. il Miss & Roc 18:115-16+ Mr 28 '66

Senate investigators urge TAC review. il Aviation W 85:86-9+ Ag 22 '66

Air force, Army

Air force, army agree on roles, missions. Aviation W 84:26-7 Ap 25 '66

War in Vietnam: Mohawk helps confirm army air concept. C. M. Plattner. il Aviation W 84:70-2+ F 28 '66

Education

See also

Air pilots—Training

Air force, Navy

E-2A controls navy North Vietnam strikes. C. Brownlow. il Aviation W 85:57+ Ag 1 '66

Navy moves to add Sparrow to F-111B. il Tech W 18:19 Je 29 '66

War in Vietnam: combat dictates shift in navy air tactics. C. M. Plattner. il Aviation W 84:64-72 F 7 '66

Education

See also

Air pilots—Training

Air national guard

Guard fighting airlines' pilot recruiting. Aviation W 84:60 Je 6 '66

Something for real; men who fly vital military cargo into Vietnam. il Newsweek 68:18-19 Jl 4 '66

Anti-Communist measures

See Communism—United States—Anti-Communist measures; United States—Foreign relations—Anti-Communist measures

Anti-poverty program

See Anti-poverty program, 1964-

Appalachian regional commission

Plight of the rural poor. B. Kovach and N. Caldwell. il Reporter 34:27+ Ap 21 '66

Appropriations and expenditures

Bad news for taxpayers: U.S. money troubles close in on LBJ. il U S News 62:82-3 Ja 9 '67

**UNITED STATES—Appropriations and expendi-
tures—***Continued*

Forestry in the federal budget; fiscal year ending June 30, 1967. il Am For 72:12 Jl '66

Great society priorities; military budget and Vietnam war funded at cost of social investments. S. Melman. Commonweal 84:494-7 Ag 5 '66

High cost of fighting. Nation 202:478 Ap 25 '66

How to slice a trillion dollar pie; symposium. il Nations Bsns 54:33-5+ Ja '66

Keep the lid on, fellows; concerning L. B. Johnson's address to members of appropriations committees. Newsweek 68:63 Ag 1 '66

No staying power? reactions to State of the Union message. New Repub 156:7-8 Ja 21 '67

President urges careful review of international agency budgets; statement, with texts of memorandums, March 15, 1966. L. B. Johnson. Dept State Bul 54:576-8 Ap 11 '66

Report on Washington; cutback in spending. Atlan 218:10+ Jl 16 '66

Spendthrifts; reasons for Congress's profligacy. Newsweek 67:32-3 My 16 '66

Two wars. Time 87:28 Mr 4 '66

What about priorities? constructive projects cut back for defense spending. Nation 203:403-4 O 24 '66

Who'll be helped, hurt by LBJ plans; concerning State-of-the-Union message. il U S News 62:27-30 Ja 23 '67

See also
Budget—United States
Government spending policy
United States—Armed forces—Appropriations and expenditures
United States—Economic policy

Architecture

See Architecture—United States

Area redevelopment administration

Proud demonstration at Anadarko; D. J. Greve's Sequoyah projects. E. Selby and A. Selby. Read Digest 88:229-30+ Ap '66

Armed forces

Imaginary weaknesses; review of U.S. defense capability. Time 87:24-5 Mr 11 '66

Military and civilian occupational structures; excerpt from Military specialist: specialized manpower requirements and resources of the armed forces. H. Wool. il Mo Labor R 89:29-33 Ja '66

New management and the new budget. il Miss & Roc 18:131-4+ Mr 28 '66

Up dating the world's biggest military machine; Time essay. Time 87:34-5 Je 3 '66

What does U.N. peacekeeping mean? A. M. Cox. Sat R 49:19-22 My 14 '66

See also
United States—Air force
United States—Defense, Department of
United States—Joint chiefs of staff
United States—Navy

Appropriations and expenditures

Congress fights for defense policy role. G. C. Wilson. il Aviation W 84:26-7 My 23 '66

Congressional protests escalating over defense budget procedures. G. C. Wilson. il Aviation W 84:39 Mr 21 '66

Defense budget rebellion moves to House. G. C. Wilson. Aviation W 84:30-1 My 9 '66

DOD likely to ask extra $7-8 billion. M. Getler. il Tech W 19:15 Jl 18 '66

FY '67 budget; with editorial comment. il Miss & Roc 18:13-18+. 82 Ja 31 '66

Fairy-tale figures on defense. il Bsns W p 182-4 O 29 '66

Growing burden of Vietnam. il Newsweek 67:67 My 30 '66

House group force-feeds DOD budget. H. M. David. Miss & Roc 18:14 My 9 '66

If you are worried about war's cost. il U S News 61:46 S 26 '66

McNamara outlines MOL schedule; summary of statement; ed. by M. Getler. R. S. McNamara. Miss & Roc 18:14-16 F 28 '66

McNamara scales down his buying. Bsns W p34 Jl 16 '66

McNamara's other war. il Newsweek 67:28 My 9 '66

More billions for defense, but. . . U S News 61:10 Jl 25 '66

New defense fund to be obligated by July. G. C. Wilson. Aviation W 84:35-6 Mr 28 '66

New management and the new budget. il Miss & Roc 18:131-4+ Mr 28 '66

New 1967 defense requests considered. G. Brownlow. Aviation W 84:18-20 F 28 '66

Now you see it. . . . Nation 202:141 F 7 '66

Pentagon cost-saving claims challenged. G. C. Wilson. il Aviation. W 85:26-8 Jl 18 '66

Pentagon escalates dollars for Vietnam. il Bsns W p38-9 Mr 12 '66

President signs supplemental military authorization bill; remarks, March 15, 1966. L. B. Johnson. Dept State Bul 54:578-9 Ap 11 '66

President urges action on funds for southeast Asia operations; text of letter, January 19, 1966. L. B. Johnson. Dept State Bul 54:254-5 F 14 '66

President's dilemma; inflationary problems; with editorial comment. il Bsns W p33-5, 200 Mr 19 '66

Senate group urges DOD fund increase. Miss & Roc 18:15 My 2 '66

70 million lives at stake; developing issue in defense. il U S News 60:48-50+ My 23 '66

Special budget report: Asian war may undermine budget hopes; with editorial comment. G. C. Wilson. il Aviation W 84:9, 14-31 Ja 31 '66

Tactical needs shape long-term outlook. il Aviation W 84:69-75 Mr 7 '66

$30 billion vs. 70 million U.S. lives. il U S News 61:30-3 N 28 '66

This month's feature: Congress and the war in Vietnam. Cong Digest 45:99-128 Ap '66

Three missiles figure in DOD request. M. Getler. Miss & Roc 18:13-14 Ja 24 '66

Top congressman's warning to Hanoi. U S News 61:11 Ag 1 '66

Viet supplemental to buy 2,900 aircraft. G. C. Wilson. il Aviation W 84:32-3 Ja 24 '66

Vote for non-leadership. Time 87:24 Je 24 '66

Where dollars go for the weapons. il Bsns W p 130-2+ Ja 22 '66

See also
Vietnamese war, 1957- —Economic aspects

Dental service

Dentists' offices got to Viet Nam in suitcases. Sci N 90:37 Jl 16 '66

Education

Three R's in the army. il Time 88:61-2 S 16 '66

Why the draft won't hurt your labor supply. il Nations Bsns 54:35-7+ N '66

Equipment and supplies

Lag in deliveries puts squeeze on Pentagon. il Bsns W p 18-19 D 24 '66

See also
United States—Army—Equipment and supplies
United States—Defense, Department of—Defense supply agency
Vietnamese war, 1957- —Equipment and supplies

Forces in Europe

Can U.S. troops in Europe be cut soon? outcome of Erhard's U.S. visit. il U S News 61:23 O 10 '66

More U.S. troops are protecting Europe than are fighting in Vietnam. U S News 60:37 F 14 '66

NATO: a question of survival; reactions to de Gaulle plan to oust foreign troops, bases, etc. il Newsweek 67:44+ Mr 28 '66

NATO and Vietnam; Erhard's Washington talks. New Repub 155:6 O 8 '66

NATO without France: de Gaulle forces U.S. to showdown in Europe; with analysis by M. S. Johnson. il U S News 60:44-6+ Mr 21 '66

Now that France is out of NATO. il U S News 61:46+ Jl 18 '66

Payments are the problem. Time 88:34 O 28 '66

Review of United States foreign and military policy; transcript of press conference, August 25, 1966. R. S. McNamara. Dept State Bul 55:417-18 S 19 '66

Time to start U.S. pullback in Europe? interview; ed. by R. Haeger. F. J. Strauss. il U S News 60:68-70+ Ap 18 '66

U.S. responsibilities toward Europe and Germany; address, July 14, 1966. G. C. McGhee. Dept State Bul 55:269-73 Ag 22 '66

When GIs come marching home; cut in spending could have major impact on companies here. il Bsns W p43-4 O 8 '66

When too many troops are too much. Bsns W p206 S 24 '66

UNITED STATES—Armed forces—*Continued*

Forces in foreign countries

Fairly peaceful world, except in Vietnam. il U S News 62:20-1 Ja 2 '67

Growing problem for U.S. shortage of trained troops. il U S News 61:44-5 S 19 '66

Military abroad. D. W. Tarr. bibliog f Ann Am Acad 368:31-42 N '66

Forces in Korea

Death of a patrol. il Newsweek 68:50+ N 14 '66

Forces in Laos

Laos report: gains in a forgotten war; team of Americans and Meo tribesmen. S. W. Sanders. il U S News 61:24-5 Jl 4 '66

Forces in Southeast Asia

Ring around Asia: putting Peking on notice. il Newsweek 67:40 Ja 31 '66

Forces in Thailand

Americans in Thailand; counterinsurgency activities of armed forces, USIS and AID. M. Parker. Atlan 218:51-8 D '66

Atlantic report. Atlan 217:17-18+ Ap '66

Pattern. Nation 203:299 O 3 '66

Forces in the Dominican Republic

Exit the Peace force. il Time 88:28 S 30 '66

Homeward bound. Newsweek 68:49 Jl 4 '66

Forces in Vietnam

Accent on the sloggers; the average American fighting man. E. T. Folliard. America 114: 320 Mr 5 '66

Amazing Americans. S. Alsop. il Sat Eve Post 240:12 Ja 14 '67

Americans at war; Operation Hastings. il Newsweek 68:28-32+ Ag 1 '66

As the GI's see it; interview, ed. by W. Cook. il Newsweek 67:36 Ap 25 '66

Beating reds at their own kind of war; with interviews with red prisoners; ed. by G. C. Troelstrup. W. S. Merick. il U S News 61:50-4 D 12 '66

Camranh Bay; address, October 26, 1966. L. B. Johnson. Vital Speeches 33:66-7 N 15 '66

Case for mobilization. H. W. Baldwin. il Reporter 34:20-3 My 19 '66

Charge of the Air Cav. il Time 88:31-2 S 23 '66

Crazy Horse; First Cavalry casualties. il Newsweek 67:34+ Je 6 '66

Day with Westmoreland. O. Elliott. il Newsweek 67:32 Ap 18 '66

Draft: the unjust vs. the unwilling; ed. by J. Sanders. il Newsweek 67:30-2+ Ap 11 '66

Flood of replacements to Vietnam. il U S News 60:6 My 30 '66

Gnawing debate. il Newsweek 67:25-6 Mr 14 '66

Honorable estate; boom in U.S.-Vietnamese marriages. il Newsweek 68:31 Ag 8 '66

How U.S. hopes to cut troop buildup in Asia. il Bsns W p38-9 D 3 '66

Integrated society. il Time 88:22 D 23 '66

Is Vietnam really a poor boys' war? il U S News 61:58-9 N 14 '66

Men who run the war. il Newsweek 68:53-5 D 5 '66

More U.S. troops are protecting Europe than are fighting in Vietnam. U S News 60:37 F 14 '66

New U.S. front in a widening war: the Delta: steamy, teeming heartland of the Vietcong. il Life 62:22-31 Ja 13 '67

Not a dove, but no longer a hawk. N. Sheehan. il N Y Times Mag p27+ O 9 '66

Numbers game; future estimates. Newsweek 68:64+ Ag 22 '66

On with the war and Operation Masher; and Operation Double Eagle; 1st Cavalry division activities with photographs by H. Huet. Life 60:20-24E F 11 '66

Resort to candor; summary of address on American withdrawal. K. Y. Lee. il Newsweek 68:30+ Jl 4 '66

Review of United States foreign and military policy; transcript of press conference, August 25, 1966. R. S. McNamara. Dept State Bul 55:418-19 S 19 '66

Saigon: at night, war flares and road checks; corruption and profiteering. S. Angeloff. il Life 60:47-52A F 25 '66

Saigon: stained pearl of the Orient; rest & recreation in Saigon. S. Castan. il Look 30 70-4+ My 17 '66

Secretary Rusk, Secretary McNamara, Mr McCloy meet with President Johnson; excerpts from press briefing, November 23, 1966. R. S. McNamara. Dept State Bul 55: 921-3 D 19 '66

Vietnam is like an oriental western. A. Carthew. il N Y Times Mag p8-9+ Ja 23 '66

Visit to Cam Ranh Bay; President's visit. il Newsweek 68:24-7 N 7 '66

Visitor; future plans. il Newsweek 68:51 O 24 '66

Wanted: more men in Viet Nam. Time 88: 39 N 18 '66

What it's like for the fighting man; excerpt from Vietnam: the confusing war. H Mulligan. Read Digest 89:68-73 N '66

What McNamara learned in Vietnam. il U S News 61:41-2 O 24 '66

What we are learning in Viet Nam. il Nations Bsns 54:35-7+ Je '66

Where the girls are; how and where GI's spend their rest and recuperation. il Newsweek 68:28+ Jl 18 '66

Why LBJ visited Vietnam; excerpt from address, October 26, 1966. L. B. Johnson. U S News 61:19 N 7 '66

With LBJ in Viet Nam. il Sr Schol 89:18 N 11 '66

You can tell 'em Buddy; report from Artillery Plateau. B. B. Fall. New Repub 156:17-20 Ja 14 '67

See also

United States—Air force—Forces in Vietnam

United States—Marine corps—Forces in Vietnam

Vietnamese war. 1957- —American participation

Forces in Vietnam—Recreation

See United States—Armed forces—Recreation

Leaves and furloughs

Quality of coming home. L. Wainwright. Life 61:22 Jl 1 '66

Medical and sanitary affairs

War on disease; a battle U.S. is winning in Vietnam. J. A. Wier. il U S News 61: 74-5 Jl 25 '66

Mobilization

Case for mobilization. H. W. Baldwin. il Reporter 34:20-3 My 19 '66

Negroes

Dilemma for Dr King. C. E. Fager. Christian Cent 83:331-2 Mr 16 '66

Great society, in uniform. il Newsweek 68: 46+ Ag 22 '66

Integrated society. il Time 88:22 D 23 '66

See also

United States—Army—Negroes

Officers

If you want to be an officer: programs and prospects. U S News 60:31 My 9 '66

Pay, allowances, etc.

GI benefits: bigger and better. il U S News 61:92 N 28 '66

Post exchanges

Companies scramble for space at the PX. il Bsns W p 182-4+ My 14 '66

Procurement

Controversial total package plan tested. il Aviation W 85:24+ Mid-D '66

Defense orders head for plateau. il Bsns W p50-2 S 24 '66

DOD, services gear to manage war. L. J. Curran and H. M. David. il Miss & Roc 18:132-4+ Mr 28 '66

DOD stressing life cycle costing plan. P. J. Klass. Aviation W 86:33-4 Ja 16 '67

DOD stressing procurement competition. C. Brownlow. il Aviation W 85:16-21 Mid-D '66

Military aerospace procurement proposals. fiscal 1967. Aviation W 84:15 Ja 31 '66

New 1967 defense requests considered. C. Brownlow. Aviation W 84:18-20 F 28 '66

Tactical needs shape long-term outlook. il Aviation W 84:69-75 Mr 7 '66

Recreation

Bright red bonus of the logistics; Leigh Ann Austin, entertains in Vietnam. il Life 60:42 F 25 '66

G-eye view of Vietnam. J. B. Treaster. il N Y Times Mag p 100+ O 30 '66

UNITED STATES—Armed forces—Recreation
—*Continued*
GI's best friend. T. Armbrister. il Sat Eve Post 239:93-7 Mr 12 '66
Over there; little-known entertainers touring G.I. bases in South Vietnam. il Time 89:69 Ja 6 '67
Where the girls are; how and where GI's spend their rest and recuperation. il Newsweek 68:28+ Jl 18 '66
   See also
United States—Marine corps—Recreation

Recruiting and enlistment
How not to get shot at; with editorial comment. S. Alsop. il Sat Eve Post 239:24, 118 O 8 '66
   See also
Military service, Compulsory—United States

Relations with civilians
Query to a literary agent; story of a sentry dog. T. R. Fehrenbach. Esquire 66:122+ D '66
Servicemen and the children; activities in South Vietnam. il NEA J 55:47 Ap '66

Reserves
Case for mobilization. H. W. Baldwin. il Reporter 34:20-3 My 19 '66
   See also
United States—Army—Reserves
United States—National guard

Training
See Military training

Womens services
Hershey favors drafting women. Christian Cent 83:1561 D 21 '66
In my opinion; girls should be drafted just as boys are. J. Stone. Seventeen 25:284 My '66
Speaking out; let's draft women too! C. Bird. il Sat Eve Post 239:10+ Je 18 '66

Armed forces, Industrial college of
See United States—Industrial college of the armed forces

Arms control and disarmament agency
Arms control in Congress, 1966. B. G. Lall. Bul Atomic Sci 22:35-7 D '66
Arms control; non-proliferation treaty; address, November 23, 1965. W. C. Foster. Vital Speeches 32:199-202 Ja 15 '66
International negotiations for arms control and disarmament; letter, February 15, 1966; with excerpt from annual report. bibliog f Dept State Bul 54:410-18 Mr 14 '66

Army
Abolish the draft? il Newsweek 68:23 D 19 '66
New multi-purpose U.S. army. C. J. V. Murphy. il Fortune 73:122-4+ My '66
Stennis vs. McNamara: how ready for combat are U.S. forces? excerpts from statements. R. S. McNamara; J. Stennis. il U S News 60:21 Ap 11 '66
Volunteer army. M. Friedman. Newsweek 68:100 D 19 '66
   See also
Military training camps

Chaplains
See Chaplains, Military

Communications
See Radio communication, Military

Corps of engineers
Corps of engineers: the pork-barrel soldiers. R. G. Sherrill. il Nation 202:180-3 F 14 '66
Essayons! construction feats in Vietnam. il Time 87:25 F 11 '66
Rampart Dam and the perpetual engineers. H. Titus. Field & S 71:34+ Je '66

Crimes and misdemeanors
Two GI's in limbo; Smith-McClure case. H. W. Ernst. il Nation 202:294-5 Mr 14 '66

Defense information school
Where the Pentagon gets its voice. M. F. Nolan. il Reporter 34:41-3 Ap 7 '66

Defense language institute
Sidearm for peace. J. Villaverde. il Américas 18:26-33 F '66

Education
See also
United States military academy, West Point

Enlistment
See United States—Army—Recruiting and enlistment

Equipment and supplies
Decorated military Americana. W. H. Guthman. il Antiques 90:60-3 Jl '66
Tiny weapons aid fighter. J. Eberhart. Sci N 89:511 Je 25 '66
   See also
Vietnamese war, 1957- —Equipment and supplies

Forces in Europe
Massive retaliation? Newsweek 68:52 O 31 '66

Forces in Vietnam
American army in Vietnam. E. M. von Kuehnelt-Leddihn. Nat R 18:359 Ap 19 '66
Americans at war; Warren Eichelberger's men of 101st airborne division. il Newsweek 68:28-32+ Ag 1 '66
Bloody checkerboard; Colonel Emerson's units. M. D. Perry. il Newsweek 67:64+ My 23 '66
Cupboard is bare; summary of article. H. W. Baldwin. Nat R 18:195 Mr 8 '66
Facts behind the Green beret myth. C. S. Wren. il Look 30:28-36 N 1 '66
G-eye view of Vietnam. J. B. Treaster. il N Y Times Mag p 100+ O 30 '66
Getting GI's ready for war in jungle: Fort Polk, La. il U S News 60:53-5 My 30 '66
He's winning our war in Vietnam. S. L. A. Marshall. il Look 31:57-9 Ja 10 '67
How U.S. troops really behave in Vietnam. G. C. Troelstrup. il U S News 60:57-8+ My 23 '66
New multi-purpose U.S. army. C. J. V. Murphy. il Fortune 73:122-4+ My '66
Pete Dawkins takes the field; with report by S. Angeloff. il Life 60:91-4+ Ap 8 '66
Tunnel rats and the red moles of Vietnam. il Read Digest 89:89-92 Ag '66
Tunnel rats: U.S. troops who explore tunnel complexes of the Reds. il Time 87:40-2 Mr 4 '66
Young commander went looking for trouble: Captain Carpenter's battle in the Dak Ta Kan River Valley. A. Zich. il Life 61:60+ Jl 8 '66

Infantry
New reliables: reincarnation of the 9th infantry division. il Time 87:31 My 20 '66

Libraries
Day with the army; Pentagon and post libraries. S. Havens. il Library J 91:894-900 F 15 '66
Modern army look: Kelley Hill branch, Fort Benning, Ga, Third United States army library system. A. L. Etchison. il Library J 91:5902-4 D 1 '66

Materiel command
Army develops future management tools. B. K. Thomas, jr. il Aviation W 85:50-3 Mid-D '66
Viet needs spur army industrial growth. E. J. Bulban. il Aviation W 85:54-7+ Mid-D '66

Medical and sanitary affairs
Angel of mercy to the astronauts. il Ebony 21:49-50+ Je '66

Negroes
Army and the Negro. G. Grove. il N Y Times Mag p4-5+ Jl 24 '66; Discussion. p 12 Ag 7 '66
   See also
World war, 1939-1945—Negroes

Non-commissioned officers
Noncom sir; Sergeant major. il Time 88:24 Jl 22 '66

Officers
Backbone class of '42; portfolio. C. G. Burck. il Fortune 73:125-9 My '66
   See also
Generals

Parachute troops
Birdmen with black rifles: Screaming Eagle paratroopers. il Ebony 21:37-42 O '66

Public relations
Information war in Saigon; weaknesses in public-relations apparatus in Washington and Vietnam. H. W. Baldwin. il Reporter 34:29-31 F 24 '66
   See also
United States—Army—Defense information school

UNITED STATES—Central intelligence agency
—*Continued*
I spy for the C.I.A. Esquire 65:80-3 My
'66
Michigan state and the CIA: a dilemma for
social science. I. L. Horowitz. Bul Atomic
Sci 22:26-9 S '66
No trespassing. New Repub 155:9 Jl 30 '66
Not so silent service. J. Burnham. Nat R
18:667 Jl 12 '66
Pro for CIA. Time 87:24 Je 24 '66
Rampartsanship; participation in Michigan
state university program. il Newsweek 67:
78 Ap 25 '66
Reader beware: sub rosa financing by the
CIA. Nation 202:701 Je 13 '66
Rise of the CIA: how foggy bottom lost its
spies; excerpt from Anatomy of the State
department. il Nation 204:38-42 Ja 9 '67
Secret seven's secrets: Senate foreign rela-
tions committee proposal that members be
added to Senate's review panel. il Newsweek 67:26-7 My 30 '66
Shake-up at CIA. il Newsweek 67:31-2 Je
27 '66
Sparrow and Hawke; alleged part in illegal
munitions exports. il Newsweek 67:29-30 My
9 '66
Suspicion and the CIA. Commonweal 84:214
My 13 '66
These men run the C.I.A. il Esquire 65:84-
5+ My '66
Tracking the iceberg; Foreign relations committee demand for creation of Committee
on intelligence operations. Time 87:19 My
27 '66
Undercover slander; case of Juri Raus. New
Repub 154:5-6 My 14 '66
Victory for Russell Fulbright loses CIA
wrangle. U S News 61:19 Jl 25 '66
Wacky spy caper; or, The case of the
bumbling Hawke, the mysterious sparrow
and the seven wandering birds. B. L.
Collier. il Sat Eve Post 239:97-101 Jl 2 '66
Watching the watchers; concerning the New
York times survey, with examples of cases.
il Newsweek 67:30-1 My 9 '66
What's CIA? interview. W. F. Raborn. il U S
News 61:74-80 Jl 18 '66
Why LBJ chose Helms to run the CIA. U S
News 61:14 Jl 4 '66
With cap & cloak in Saigon; participation
in Michigan state university program. il
Time 87:20 Ap 22 '66

Anecdotes, facetiae, satire, etc.
Just like in the movies. New Repub 154:7
Je 11 '66

Church history
History of religion in the United States, by
E. S. Gaustad. Review
Christian Cent 83:1148 S 21 '66. N. R.
Burr

Civil aeronautics board
Board alters scope in route investigations.
H. D. Watkins. Aviation W 85:28 D 26 '66
Board sets rules for transpacific case. Avia-
tion W 84:42 Je 6 '66
CAB may boost pressure on IATA. R. G.
O'Lone. Aviation W 85:41-2 O 24 '66
CAB views IATA; comments. C. S. Murphy.
Aviation W 85:17 N 28 '66
CAB zooms in on thriving airlines. il Bsns W
p 140+ F 26 '66
Nonsked airlines get a new flight plan;
CAB ruling giving supplemental airlines
new charter rights. il Bsns W p72-4+ My
28 '66
Safety in the air; no move to ground Boeing
727. New Repub 154:7 F 19 '66
Trouble with the 727. il Newsweek 67:84 F
28 '66

Civil air patrol
First twenty-five years of CAP. M. W.
Horowitz. il Flying 78:94-7 Ap '66

Civil service commission
Under fire: race check on federal workers.
il U S News 60:12 My 23 '66

Civilization
American civilization: its influence on our
foreign policy; symposium, ed. by J. C.
Charlesworth. bibliog f il Ann Am Acad
366:1-148 Jl '66
Asian revolution and American ideology. R. S.
Manglapus. bibliog f For Affairs 45:344-52
Ja '67
Impact of the American way; Time essay.
Time 88:38-9 Jl 22 '66

My safari into darkest atrophy. R. Starnes.
Field & S 71:14-15+ Ag '66
Packaged society. R. Lynes. Harper 233:18+
Ag '66
Policy-making in a world turned upside down.
T. L. Hughes. For Affairs 45:202-14 Ja '67
State of the Nation, ed. by D. Boroff. Review
Sat R 49:36-7 Ap 23 '66. A. M. Schle-
singer, jr
This almost chosen people, by R. B. Nye.
Review
Sat R 49:26-8 S 3 '66. D. B. Davis
Uncommitted: alienated youth in American
society, by K. Keniston. Review
Nation 202:245-6 F 28 '66. F. Zweig
See also
United States—Intellectual life
United States—Social conditions

Climate
Were old-time summers warmer? B. Frisch.
il Sci Digest 59:48-52 Je '66

Coast guard
Coast guard discovers that AN/AAR-33
Sperry iceberg tracker system aids map-
ping. K. Voss. il Tech W 20:38-9+ Ja 16
'67
Coast guard re-shapes its saving ways. F.
Rohr. il Motor B 117:22-5+ F '66
Decision at sea; rescue of crewmen from
Smith Voyager. J. J. Cadigan. il Read Di-
gest 90:50-4 Ja '67
Great rewards and great frustrations. J. F.
Hunt. il Motor B 117:54-5+ F '66
Lighthouse knee deep in sea. il Sci N 90:278+
O 8 '66
SAR; Coast guard search and rescue service.
E. Shrake. il Sports Illus 24:76-8+ My 30 '66
Science of searching. J. Gribbins. il Motor B
117:50-2+ Je '66

Boats
Unsinkable, high-powered rescue; coast
guard's latest 44-foot motor lifeboat. il Pop
Mech 125:146-7 Mr '66

Coast guard auxiliary
Coast guard auxiliary offers free boating
courses. E. A. Weinberg. il Motor B 118:
77 Ag '66
Under the blue ensign. B. Woodward. See
issues of Motor boating
U.S. Coast guard auxiliary. R. Birnn. See
issues of Yachting

Commerce
America in the market place, by P. H. Doug-
las. Review
Sat R 49:37+ O 15 '66. D. M. Keezer
Eroding bulwark; trade surplus. il Newsweek
68:80 N 14 '66
Exports feel the pinch; export-import gap
narrowing. il Bsns W p32 Ag 27 '66
Fourth annual review of the Long-term
cotton textile arrangement; statement,
September 27, 1966. G. R. Jacobs. Dept
State Bul 55:903-5 D 12 '66
Further steps taken to remove restrictions on
U.S. exports; Department announcement,
March 14, 1966; with lists of import liberal-
izations of Denmark; Finland; and Spain.
Dept State Bul 54:624-7 Ap 18 '66
Import-export statistics off the beam; ad-
dress, February 8, 1966. R. L. F. Sikes.
Vital Speeches 32:325-7 Mr 15 '66
Johnson trade policy; excerpts from address.
W. M. Roth. bibliog f Dept State Bul 54:
856-9 My 30 '66
New dynamics in U.S. foreign trade; ad-
dress, October 31, 1966. R. A. Peterson.
Vital Speeches 33:149-52 D 15 '66
New horizons in foreign trade. W. Diebold,
jr. For Affairs 45:291-303 Ja '67
Problems resulting from the internationali-
zation of business; statement, April 21, 1966.
A. M. Solomon. Dept State Bul 54:820-5
My 23 '66
Trade legislation and adjustment assistance;
benefits under the Trade expansion act. Mo
Labor R 89:III:IV D '66
U.S. and the world: it's trade or fade. il
S. Schol 88:20-1 Ap 1 '66
U.S. economy and the world; riding the wave
of global trade. il Sr Schol 89:19-21 D 9
'66

UNITED STATES—Commerce—*Continued*

United States trade policy after the Kennedy round; helping the developing countries help themselves; address, November 2, 1966. A. M. Solomon. Dept State Bul 55: 784-9 N 21 '66; Same with title United States trade policy. Vital Speeches 33:115-19 D 1 '66

See also

Import quotas

Merchant marine—United States

Tariff—United States

Waterways—United States

Canada

Balance of payment; address, April 27, 1966. W. E. McLaughlin. Vital Speeches 32:521-4 Je 15 '66

Communist countries

Businessmen appraise East-West trade; problems in review. M. I. Goldman and A. Conner. il Harvard Bsns R 44:6-8+ Ja '66

Communist trade: no bonanza yet. Bsns W p68+ O 29 '66

East-West relations: shaping a stable world; address, December 11, 1966. F. D. Kohler. Dept State Bul 56:6-11 Ja 2 '67; Excerpts. U S News 61:52-3 D 26 '66

Expanding trade with Communists. America 115:766-7 D 10 '66

Should we be trading with the reds? N. F. Busch. Read Digest 89:84-8 Jl '66

Storm over Rusk. Nation 202:635-6 My 30 '66

U.S. eases curbs. Sr Schol 89:5+ O 28 '66

We can trade with the Communists. H. J. Berman. il Nation 202:766-70 Je 27 '66

See also

United States—Commerce—Europe, Eastern

Europe, Eastern

Contracts, not contrasts. Time 88:112 N 18 '66

East-West trade: a realistic appraisal; address, March 31, 1966. G. C. McGhee. Dept State Bul 54:1019-26 Je 27 '66

East-West trade gets a lift; 400 items off the export control list. Bsns W p39 O 15 '66

East-West trade policy in a balanced strategy for peace; address, October 11, 1966. J. A. Greenwald. Dept State Bul 55:676-80 O 31 '66

East-West trade relations act of 1966; Department announcement, with letter of transmittal, May 11, 1966, and text of proposed legislation. bibliog f Dept State Bul 54:838-44 My 30 '66

Goodyear and Rumania; Time, inc. mission. New Repub 155:8 N 12 '66

Harmonizing East-West trade with U.S. national interests; address, November 23, 1965. A. B. Trowbridge. Dept State Bul 54:59-65 Ja 10 '66

Issues of East-West trade; address, December 9, 1966. N. deB. Katzenbach. Dept State Bul 56:2-5 Ja 2 '67

National affairs; new policy. E. Weintal. Newsweek 68:28-9 O 24 '66

Nyet to Nicolae; bill to liberalize trade. Time 87:29 My 20 '66

Private boycotts versus the national interset; text of Department of state pamphlet. Dept State Bul 55:446-52 S 26 '66

Report of the Special committee on U.S. trade with east European countries and the Soviet Union. Dept State Bul 54:845-55 My 30 '66

Report on Washington; trade with eastern Europe? Atlan 218:8+ Jl '66

Summary of proposed East-West trade relations act of 1966; with analysis of the principal features. Dept State Bul 55:140-2 Jl 25 '66

United States policy on East-West trade; address, June 8, 1966. E. M. Braderman. Dept State Bul 54:1013-19 Je 27 '66; Same. Vital Speeches 32:559-62 Jl 1 '66

Europe, Western

Military exports expected to remain high. C. Brownlow. Aviation W 85:26-7 O 3 '66

France

U.S. is prime Anglo-French export goal. H. J. Coleman. il Aviation W 83:33-5 mid-D '65

Japan

See also

Joint United States-Japan committee on trade and economic affairs

Rhodesia

All U.S. exports to Rhodesia to require validated licenses. Dept State Bul 54:466 Mr 21 '66

What U.S. crackdown on Rhodesia means. U S News 62:12 Ja 16 '67

Russia

Businessmen appraise East-West trade; problems in review. M. I. Goldman and A. Conner. il Harvard Bsns R 44:6-8+ Ja '66

Close-up: talk with Leon M. Herman; interview, ed. by J. Berry. L. M. Herman. il Duns R 88:8-9+ S '66

East-West trade relations act of 1966; Department announcement, with letter of transmittal, May 11, 1966, and text of proposed legislation. bibliog f Dept State Bul 54:838-44 My 30 '66

Private boycotts versus the national interest; text of Department of state pamphlet. Dept State Bul 55:446-52 S 26 '66

Report of the Special committee on U.S. trade with east European countries and the Soviet Union. Dept State Bul 54:845-55 My 30 '66

Summary of proposed East-West trade relations act of 1966; with analysis of the principal features. Dept State Bul 55:140-2 Jl 25 '66

Underdeveloped areas

Food for freedom: paradox of foreign aid. B. J. Oudes. il Nation 203:120-4 Ag 8 '66

Commerce, Department of

New puzzle: the LBJ plan for a business-labor merger; concerning State-of-the-Union message. il U S News 62:72-3 Ja 23 '67

Paradoxical predicament of John Connor. H. B. Meyers. il Fortune 73:150-2+ F '66

Second time around; L. B. Johnson's call for merger with Labor department. il Newsweek 69:75 Ja 23 '67

See also

United States—Business and defense services administration

Institute of oceanography

Administration, Congress boost civilian agency budget hopes. W. S. Beller. il Tech W 19:52+ S 26 '66

Commercial treaties and agreements

Cotton textile arrangement with Japan extended; Department announcement, January 14, 1966; exchange of notes, January 15, 1966. Dept State Bul 54:180-1 Ja 31 '66

Department supports commercial treaty with Togo: statement, September 12, 1966. W. C. Trimble. Dept State Bul 55:692-3 O 31 '66

King crab fishery agreement with Japan extended; text of U.S. note, November 29, 1966. D. Rusk. Dept State Bul 55:984 D 26 '66

U.S. and Canada exchange notes on automotive products agreement; Department announcement; with texts of notes, September 16, 1966. Dept State Bul 55:616 O 17 '66

U.S. and Canada sign agreement updating U.S. tariff concessions; announcement, with annex II of the agreement. il Dept State Bul 54:106-9 Ja 17 '66

U.S. and China amend cotton textile agreement; Department announcement, April 26; with text of U.S. note, April 22, 1966. il Dept State Bul 54:817-19 My 23 '66

U.S. and Colombia amend cotton textiles agreement; Department announcement; with texts of U.S. note and U.S. letter, June 24, 1966. Dept State Bul 55:58-9 Jl 11 '66

U.S. and Greece amend cotton textile agreement; Department announcement, with text of U.S. note, May 23, 1966. Dept State Bul 54:992-3 Je 20 '66

United States and Hong Kong sign cotton textiles agreement; Department announcement with texts of agreement and related documents. Dept State Bul 55:467-72 S 26 '66

U.S. and Israel amend cotton textiles agreement; Department announcement; with text of U.S. note, June 20, 1966. Dept State Bul 55:189 Ag 1 '66

U.S. and Japan sign agreement updating U.S. concessions; with list of concessions. Dept State Bul 55:466 S 26 '66

UNITED STATES—Commercial treaties and agreements—*Continued*
United States and Korea amend cotton textile agreement; Department announcement; with texts of U.S. note and letter, November 22, 1966. Dept State Bul 55:982-3 D 26 '66
United States and Pakistan sign cotton textile agreement; Department announcement with text of U.S. note; November 21, 1966. Dept State Bul 55:937-41 D 19 '66
U.S. and Portugal amend cotton textiles agreement; Department announcement; with text of U.S. note; August 17, 1966. Dept State Bul 55:356-7 S 5 '66
U.S. and Singapore reach cotton textiles understanding; Department announcement, August 30, 1966; with letter from government of Singapore and Singapore cotton textile industry restraint schedule. il Dept State Bul 55:509-13 O 3 '66
U.S. and Spain amend cotton textiles agreement; Department announcement; with text of U.S. note, September 14, 1966. Dept State Bul 55:509 O 3 '66
U.S. and U.K. sign agreement updating U.S. tariff concessions. Dept State Bul 54:719-20 My 2 '66

Committee for economic development
See Committee for economic development

Committee on libraries
Commission on libraries set up by President. Pub W 190:44 S 19 '66
LBJ names Committee on libraries and National advisory commission. Library J 91:4590 O 1 '66

Comptroller of currency, Office of
Camp chosen to succeed Saxon; as comptroller of the currency. Bsns W p 162 N 12 '66
Man to calm down the bankers; Camp to succeed James J. Saxon. Bsns W p66 N 19 '66

Congress
Congress: legislator, investigator, counsel. il Sr Schol 88:4-5+ F 18 '66
For a better Congress. R. Moley. Newsweek 68:114 O 17 '66
Repair? renew? revolt? J. N. Eller. America 115:823 D 24 '66
Some ethical problems of Congress. J. S. Clark. Ann Am Acad 363:12-22 Ja '66
What your vote can do for Congress. C. Stevenson. Read Digest 89:61-6 O '66
Young men who are remaking Congress. D. M. Davis. Holiday 39:60-1+ F '66
See also
Congresswomen
Legislation—United States
Presidents — United States — Relations with Congress

Committees
Congress: debate over science jurisdictions. L. J. Carter. Science 153:1364-6 S 16 '66
Congressional committees: dividing the legislative workload. il Sr Schol 88:6-7 F 18 '66
Debate in search of a forum; Vietnam congress. Reporter 34:16+ Ja 27 '66
Science and technology: House subcommittee offers Capitol ideas. N. Panush. Science 154:993-4 N 25 '66
Two men who are expected to move into top spots in Congress. il U S News 61:19 Jl 25 '66

Employees
Capitol hill classroom; summer as congressional interns. il Newsweek 68:46 Ag 29 '66
Robber in the House; inefficient police department. Time 87:25A Ap 1 '66

Joint committee on internal revenue taxation
Where tax bills run the gauntlet. il Bsns W p 106+ Je 11 '66

Joint economic committee
Congress' own economic adviser; J. W. Knowles. il Bsns W p 102+ Je 11 '66

Powers and duties
Congress & foreign policy: timid political will. E. A. Kolodziej. il Nation 202:292-4 Mr 14 '66
Congress and the undeclared war. Christian Cent 83:195-6 F 16 '66
New Congress will see if it reaped a whirlwind. P. Lisagor. il Nations Bsns 54:21-2 Ja '66
Reforming Congress. T. C. Sorensen. Sat R 49:22 Jl 16 '66

Too many blank checks? C. Fritchey. Harper 232:50 Ap '66
Traitors to their constituents. Nation 203:405 O 24 '66
When you vote for a senator. F. Morley. il Nations Bsns 54:27-8 N '66

Rules and practice
Congress: debate over science jurisdictions. L. J. Carter. Science 153:1364-6 S 16 '66
New rules in Congress? Bsns W p28 Jl 2 '66
Reforming Congress. T. C. Sorensen. Sat R 49:22 Jl 16 '66
Science and technology: House subcommittee offers Capitol ideas. N. Panush. Science 154:993-4 N 25 '66

Term of members
See Congressmen—Term

Voting
Teapot tempest; controversy over telling how each representative intended to vote. New Repub 154:9 Ap 16 '66

89th Congress
B+ Congress: key votes in the 89th. il New Repub 155:15-22 O 22 '66
Congress, health and medical schools. America 116:37 Ja 14 '67
89th closes shop. America 115:534-5 N 5 '66
89th in perspective. Commonweal 85:125-6 N 4 '66
Focus on Washington. Cato. Nat R 18:1143 N 15 '66
LBJ's great Congress heads home. Newsweek 68:36 O 31 '66
Reaching into the future. il Time 88:27-8 O 28 '66
T.R.B. from Washington; Barry's fabulous Congress. New Repub 155:4 O 29 '66
Ten days that shook the capital. A. Kopkind. New Repub 155:9-11 N 5 '66
Tensions and conservatism in American politics. O. Gass. bibliog f Commentary 42:63-70 N '66
What unions want in Congress and what they aren't getting. il U S News 60:120-2 Je 13 '66
Will Congress ram through costly new laws? voting records of individual senators and congressmen. il Nations Bsns 54:41+ F '66

89th Congress—2d session
As Congress heads home: decisions that affect everybody. il U S News 61:47-8 O 24 '66
As Congress starts new term; LBJ's wishes, his chances. il U S News 60:32-3 Ja 31 '66
As election nears. Congress speeds up. U S News 61:6+ O 17 '66
As LBJ asks more and more laws. il U S News 60:25-6 Ap 4 '66
Backlash jitters. New Repub 155:5-6 O 22 '66
Changing mood of Congress: how outlook is shifting. il U S News 60:28-30 My 2 '66
Congress. See issues of Newsweek
Congress. See issues of Time
Congress builds its own record. Bsns W p27-8 Jl 23 '66
Congress in no mood to curb spending; eyes on November. Bsns W p47-8 Mr 26 '66
Congress lets LBJ call tune on tax hike. il Bsns W p27-8 Ap 9 '66
Congress: productive year is seen despite Vietnam. L. J. Carter. Science 151:308-11 Ja 21 '66; Discussion. 151:1172+ Mr 11 '66
Congress races into the homestretch: bills watered down to speed them through. Bsns W p43 O 1 '66
Congress slows down the Great society. U S News 61:33-4 S 12 '66
Congress wraps up two busy years. Bsns W p38-9 O 22 '66
Debate in search of a forum; Vietnam congress. Reporter 34:16+ Ja 27 '66
89th Congress adjourned. G. Krettek and E. D. Cooke. Wilson Lib Bul 41:433+ D '66
Fabulous Congress? Sr Schol 89:17-18 N 4 '66
Focus on Washington: white backlash. Cato. Nat R 18:1031 O 18 '66
Friendly Congress turns sour; 14(b) hopes dying, threat of tough anti-strike laws. il Bsns W p47-8 F 5 '66
How LBJ's programs fare in Congress. il U S News 61:8 S 19 '66
Late great. Time 88:34 O 21 '66
LBJ and Congress: why the magic is gone. il U S News 60:53-5 Mr 21 '66

UNITED STATES—Congress—89th Congress—
2d session—*Continued*
LBJ's domestic plans face a cool Congress.
il Bsns W p28-30 Ja 22 '66
LBJ's great Congress: rubber stamp or creativity? B. Nelson. Science 154:620-2 N 4
'66
Month in Congress. Cong Digest 45:33-6,
65-6, 97-8, 129-30, 161-2 F-Je '66
Most ever for education from Congress. il Sr
Schol 89:sup2 N 11 '66
1966 legislative roundup: legislation of significance to the park and recreation field;
comp. by K. J. Smithee. Parks & Rec
1:960-1+ D '66
Playing fast and loose with democracy. il
Nations Bsns 54:38-9+ D '66
That fenced-in feeling: last couple of weeks
of the session. Time 88:34-5 O 14 '66
What Congress did, and some things it didn't
do. il U S News 61:44-5 O 31 '66
What new laws Congress will pass; inter-
views. G. R. Ford; C. Albert. Nations Bsns
54:62-4+ Ja '66
What's Congress doing? the Great society,
and the Vietnam war. New Repub 154:7-8
My 7 '66
Whiff of November. Time 87:23 Ap 15 '66

90th Congress
Another Democratic Congress, but by less:
gain by GOP likely. il Bsns W p42-3 S
10 '66
As Congress convenes: the agenda for 1967;
topics of concern to book publishing indus-
try. R. H. Smith. Pub W 191:60 Ja 16 '67
Computerized 90th Congress. H. Hamilton.
America 115:733 D 3 '66
Congress: a quiet year. Sci N 91:33 Ja 14
'67
Crucial struggle for forty-five congressional
seats. L. Lamont. il Fortune 74:124-7+
S '66
Debating session: more contention than con-
sensus. Time 89:14-15 Ja 20 '67
House will be its own master. il Bsns W
p36-9 Ja 7 '67
New Congress. New Repub 156:9-10 Ja 14
'67
New Congress and science. A. Ewing. Sci N
90:429 N 19 '66
New Congress: survey of congressional
opinion. il Newsweek 68:38+ N 21 '66
90th Congress: interlude for Democrats. J. N.
Eller. America 116:38 Ja 14 '67
90th Congress: the men; the issues. il Bsns
W p41-4 N 12 '66
90th girds for battle. il Newsweek 69:24-7
Ja 23 '67

No smorgasbord. Time 89:15 Ja 6 '67

90th Congress—1st session
Big issues in the new Congress. il Nations
Bsns 54:35-7+ D '66
Go slow session? Sr Schol 89:14 Ja 13 '67
In the new Congress: a go slow mood. il
U S News 62:34-5 Ja 9 '67
LBJ and Congress: a new ball game. U S
News 61:34 N 28 '66
Now beginning: the cautious Congress; Great
society programs, where they stand. U S
News 62:27-8 Ja 16 '67

House of representatives
Congressmen need four-year terms. Life 60:4
Ja 28 '66
Election proposal; extending the terms of
members of the House. H. Hazlitt. News-
week 67:84 Mr 14 '66
Four-year House. W. Lippmann. Newsweek
67:15 F 28 '66
Four-year term. New Repub 154:5-6 Mr 12
'66
Four-year term for House members? il U S
News 60:48 Ja 31 '66
House will be its own master. il Bsns W
p36-9 Ja 7 '67
Must Adam leave Eden? il Newsweek 69:
24-8 Ja 16 '67
New House: shifts in party strength. U S
News 61:41 N 21 '66
No time for haste; President Johnson's
proposal to extend term to four years. R. L.
Tobin. Sat R 49:26 Ja 29 '66
Powell and black bravado; A. C. Powell ex-
pulsion debate. A. Kopkind. New Repub
156:13-15 Ja 21 '67
Record of the Houes; 89th Congress. New
Repub 155:20-2 O 22 '66
Teapot tempest; controversy over telling how
each representative intended to vote. New
Repub 154:9 Ap 16 '66

This month's feature: question of a longer
House term. Cong Digest 45:131-9+ My '66
See also
Apportionment (election law)

*House of representatives—Administra-
tion committee*
Out of Powell case: reforms in Congress?
with excerpts from report. il U S News
62:29-30 Ja 16 '67

*House of representatives—Armed
services committee*
Vote for non-leadership. Time 87:24 Je 24 '66

House of representatives—Committees
House group aims to make space policy.
Miss & Roc 18:18+ Mr 28 '66
New Congress: Rules, ways and means, and
appropriations committees to feel impact
of Democratic losses. New Repub 156:9-10
Ja 14 '67
What the new Congress needs most; con-
cerning choice of chairmanships. R. Bolling.
Harper 234:79-81 Ja '67

*House of representatives—Education
and labor committee*
Adam cast out. il Newsweek 69:28-9 Ja 23 '67
Adam's fall. Newsweek 68:29-30 O 3 '66
Bigger than Adam. Nation 203:300 O 3 '66
Disarming Powell. New Repub 155:7-8 O 1
'66
Judgment of Daniel: powers of House educa-
tion and labor committee chairman. il Time
88:21-2 S 30 '66
Keeping the faith; A. Powell barred from
Congress. il Time 89:15-16 Ja 20 '67
New Chairman Perkins: Powell's opposite.
U S News 62:14 Ja 23 '67
Powell and black bravado; how A. C. Powell
used his power. A. Kopkind. New Repub
156:13-15 Ja 21 '67
Revolt in the House, reduction of power of
A. C. Powell. Sr Schol 89:19-20 O 14 '66
Slap at Adam Clayton Powell: but not much
sting; chairman of Committee on education
and labor. il U S News 61:26+ O 3 '66

House of representatives—Rules committee
Fourth branch down. K. Crawford. News-
week 68:30 Jl 25 '66
What the new Congress needs most; con-
cerning choice of chairmanships. R. Bolling.
Harper 234:79-81 Ja '67

*House of representatives—Science
and astronautics, Committee on*
Capitol hill: science among nations. F. Sartwell. Sci N 90:566 D 31 '66

*House of representatives—Un-American
activities committee*
Congnik uproar in the Congress. il Life 61:
38A Ag 26 '66
Contempt breeds contempt. Nation 203:171-2
S 5 '66
End of hearings on the Klan. America 114:343
Mr 12 '66
House loses patience with HUAC; criticism
during Pool bill debate. D. Rapoport. il
Reporter 35:35-6 D 1 '66
HUAC eyes the campus; ACLU urges resist-
ance against intimidation. Nation 203:628-
9 D 12 '66
HUAC: from pillory to farce; hostile witnesses disrupt hearing on bill to amend the
Internal security act. F. J. Donner. Nation
203:174-6 S 5 '66
HUAC hellzapoppin. New Repub 155:5-6 Ag
27 '66
HUAC: inquiry into peace movement has
ramifications in academia. E. Langer. Science 153:1087 S 2 '66
HUAC: Stamler's challenge draws academic
support. E. Langer. Science 152:898 My 13
'66; Discussion. 153:813; 154:330 Ag 19, O
21 '66
HUAC: Stamler's challenge draws academic
support. E. Langer. Science 152:898 My 13
'66; Reply. S. T. Martin. 153:813 Ag 19
'66
Hullabaloo at HUAC; excerpt from hearings
on J. Pool bill. il Newsweek 68:15-16 Ag
29 '66
In the camp of the enemy; HUAC hearings.
J. Burnham. Nat R 18:876 S 6 '66
Making bad matters worse; HUAC inquiry
into acts of violence. Christian Cent 83:
1399-400 N 16 '66

UNITED STATES—Constitution—*Continued*

Bill of rights

Bill of rights; address, July 1, 1966. L. F. O'Brien. Vital Speeches 32:646-9 Ag 15 '66

Burgeoning Big brotherism; fight to halt a subtle, persistent growth in violations of the individual's right to privacy. E. V. Long. Christian Cent 83:645-7 My 18 '66

Let me alone! right to privacy. Christian Cent 83:1135-6 S 21 '66; Reply. M. Hamilton. 83:1347 N 2 '66

Practical course in law. Sr Schol 89:sup 14-15 D 9 '66

Supreme court and the Bill of rights. L. Pfeffer. il Nation 203:315-18. 351-4. 385-8 O 3-17 '66

Teaching the Bill of rights. S. Cochell. il Sr Schol 88:sup 14 Ap 1 '66

Teaching the Bill of rights in California; Constitutional rights foundation programs. J. W. McKenney. il Sat R 49:68-9+ Mr 19 '66

Toward a general theory of the First amendment, by T. I. Emerson. Review
Nation 204:27-9 Ja 2 '67. V. Rabinowitz

Warren court and the Bill of rights. A. T. Mason. Yale R 56:197-211 D '66

Who's against prayer? Dirksen gains hearings on school-prayer decisions. K. Crawford. Newsweek 68:29 Ag 8 '66

Study and teaching

Practical course in law: fundamentals of the Bill of rights. Sr Schol 89:sup 14-15 D 9 '66

Teaching the Bill of rights. S. Cochell. il Schol 88:sup 14 Ap 1 '66

Constitutional convention, 1787

Miracle at Philadelphia, by C. D. Bowen. Review
Sat R 49:47-8 D 24 '66. M. L. Coit

1787. by C. Rossiter. Review
Nat R 18:539-40 My 31 '66. J. Lobdell
Sat R 49:38 Ap 2 '66. W. R. Jacobs

Constitutional history

See also
United States—Supreme court

Constitutional law

See also
United States—Supreme court

Council of economic advisers

Advisers should stick to advising. Fortune 74:130 N '66

Awash in affluence, but what next? history, policies, staff. il Newsweek 68:67-70+ Jl 18 '66

Boom gives labor its '67 leverage; economists fear wage-price spiral; with editorial comment il Bsns W p40-1, 200 My 14 '66

New role for CEA: economic fireman; troubleshooters for wage and price policies. Bsns W p30-1 Ap 2 '66

President's dilemma; inflationary problems; with editorial comment. il Bsns W p33-5. 200 Mr 19 '66

Six characters in search of a posture. il Bsns W p 152+ Mr 5 '66

Top seers urge a tax hike now; to help control inflation. il Bsns W p29-30 Ag 27 '66

Worried advisers; CEA chiefs past and present. il Newsweek 67:71-2 Mr 7 '66

Council on the arts
See United States—National council on the arts

Council on the humanities

Goof; appointment of M. Willson to Council on the humanities. Nation 202:477 Ap 25 '66

Courts
See Courts—United States

Crime commission
See United States—National crime commission

Cultural relations

American studies abroad: culture and foreign policy; address; with questions and answers. R. E. Spiller. bibliog f Ann Am Acad 366:1-16 Jl '66

Exploration in the apolitical; Instituto cultural peruano norteamericano. C. Eshleman. Nation 203:285-7 S 26 '66

Flow of ideas between Africa and America. W. S. Dillon. Bul Atomic Sci 22:23-6 Ap '66

Our cultural exchanges; one-way street? R. Marshall. Commonweal 84:150-3 Ap 22 '66

U.S. China policy is changing; travel comes first. B. G. Lall. Bul Atomic Sci 22:93-6 Je '66

U.S.-Japan cultural conference held at Tokyo. Dept State Bul 54:405 Mr 14 '66

See also
American libraries abroad
Exchange of persons programs
People-to-people program

Culture, Popular
See United States—Popular culture

Customs
See United States—Social life and customs

Declaration of independence
See also
Fourth of July

Defense, Department of

Arm-twisting arms salesmen. Nation 202:732 Je 20 '66

Cryogenic engine is latest DOD/NASA joint project. Miss & Roc 18:31-2 My 30 '66

Cutback on bases. Sr Schol 87:18 Ja 14 '66

DOD cost reduction aired. Tech W 19:32+ Jl 25 '66

DOD, services gear to manage war. L. J. Curran and H. M. David. il Miss & Roc 18:132-4+ Mr 28 '66

Hindsight: DOD study examines return on investment in research. D. S. Greenberg. il Science 154:872-3 N 18 '66

Hindsight for progress; Project Hindsight, DOD study of weapons systems. il Sci N 90:473 D 3 '66

Mission: impossible: Pentagon's chief spokesman. il Newsweek 69:81 Ja 16 '67

Project Hindsight. P. H. Abelson. Science 154:1123 D 2 '66

Service secretary: has he a useful role? E. M. Zuckert. For Affairs 44:458-79 Ap '66

Six business lessons from the Pentagon. D. J. Smalter and R. L. Ruggles, jr. il Harvard Bsns R 44:64-75 Mr '66

Tactical needs shape long-term outlook. il Aviation W 84:69-75 Mr 7 '66

Tensions rise in shortages investigation. G. C. Wilson. Aviation W 84:33 Mr 14 '66

U.S. supplier of weapons to the world with list of 1962-1965 sales. E. J. McCarthy. il Sat R 49:13-15 Jl 9 '66

Where the Vietnam pipeline begins. il Bsns W p 188+ Ap 16 '66

Where's the money going next? Defense marketing services. il Bsns W p86+ My 7 '66

Yea, team! team bidding on major defense systems. W. J. Coughlin. Miss & Roc 18:62 My 16 '66

See also
Pentagon building, Arlington. Va.
United States—Defense research and engineering. Director of
United States—Industrial college of the armed forces

Advanced research projects agency

AMOS may feed new ABM designs; ARPA mid-course optical observatory station on Mt Haleakala. M. Getler. Tech W 18:20 Je 13 '66

ARPA team aids Thailand in developing R&D capability. M. Getler. Tech W 19:17-18 D 19 '66

ALTAIR antenna promises missile defense improvement; Advanced research projects agency long-range tracking and instrument radar. Tech W 20:38 Ja 2 '67

Radar may alter point defense plans. M. Getler. Miss & Roc 18:15 Mr 14 '66

Appropriations and expenditures

Birthing a behemoth. Time 88:23 D 2 '66

Cry of the cities; Conference of mayors calls for Vietnam cutback. Nation 203:3-4 Jl 4 '66

Defense plans harsh R&D review to help meet Vietnam war costs. Aviation W 85:32 S 12 '66

DOD asks restoration of funds for guided missile destroyers. H. M. David. Tech W 19:17 Ag 8 '66

DOD cost reduction claims challenged. Tech W 19:16 Jl 18 '66

DOD '68 budget may exceed $65 billion. M. Getler. il Tech W 19:15-16 S 12 '66

UNITED STATES—Economic conditions—*Cont.*
Economics in action. il Sr Schol 89:8-9 S 16;
14-16 S 23; 8-11 O 7; 6-9 O 14; 15-17 O 21;
11-13 N 4 '66; 6-9+ Ja 13 '67
Economics in the news. See issues of Senior
scholastic to May 13, 1966
Economy: a soaring '66 if; economic report.
il Newsweek 67:59-61 F 7 '66
Economy: fair but cooler. il Newsweek 67:78-
9 My 23 '66
Economy looks up by cooling off. Newsweek
68:93 N 21 '66
Economy: what next? J. Perham. il Duns R
88:30-2+ S '66
Foggy days. il Time 88:27 D 16 '66
Future of U.S. boom as Europe sees it. il
U S News 60:62-4 My 2 '66
GM puts on a brake and stocks skid. il News-
week 67:73-4 My 16 '66
Inflationary recession. M. Friedman. News-
week 68:92 O 17 '66
Just right; Vietnam war; prop of current
prosperity. N. Cousins. Sat R 49:30 Mr 5
'66
Keep the lid on, fellows. Newsweek 68:63
Ag 1 '66
Labor month in review. See issues of Month-
ly labor review
Little anti-inflation tonic; how foreign bank-
ers size up health of the U.S. economy.
U S News 61:74 O 10 '66
A look at the national economy; excerpts
from Public interest of private enterprise;
annual report. R. Blough. il U S News
61:82-4 S 12 '66
Man in the middle: LBJ's economic aide. il
U S News 61:11 Ag 15 '66
No longer boiling but still hot. il Time 88:69
Jl 15 '66
Only slightly pregnant? il Newsweek 67:74
F 21 '66
Our economic soothsayers; confusing inter-
pretations of fluctuations. Reporter 34:13-
14 Ap 21 '66
Path still points up. il Bsns W p31-2 Je 25
'66
Prices going up. il Newsweek 68:13-14 Ag 29
'66
Prices: let us eat dumplings. il Newsweek
68:87 O 24 '66
Profits will feel the bite. il Bsns W p35-7
O 1 '66
Reading the consumer's crystal ball; findings
of University of Michigan's survey research
center. il Newsweek 67:69 Je 27 '66
Runaway boom? what business leaders think
now. il Nations Bsns 54:40-1+ Ap '66
Signs of overheating in the U.S. boom. il
U S News 60:81-2 Ja 31 '66
'67 balancing trick. il Bsns W p 13-15 D 31
'66
Soaring, and then some; with editorial com-
ment. il Bsns W p25-7. 152 Jl 16 '66
Soviet growth: still a lag behind U.S. il U S
News 60:12 F 14 '66
State of the economy. Commonweal 83:547-8
F 11 '66
State of the economy. New Repub 156:11-12
Ja 7 '67
State of the economy. P. A. Samuelson.
Newsweek 69:81 Ja 23 '67
State of the union: unfinished; state of the
union is sounder. Bsns W p 136 Ja 7 '67
Takes more cash to make ends meet; with
analysis by W. W. Heller. il Life 61:26-31
S 9 '66
Taking the expansion in stride; whopping
first-quarter rise in GNP. il Bsns W p31-3
Ap 23 '66
Talk with Thurman Arnold; interview. T.
Arnold. Duns R 88:10-11+ N '66
Tax those profits. New Repub 155:5-6 S
24 '66
Technological developments: the economic
impact five years hence; address. May 11.
1966. P. Neff. Vital Speeches 32:543-4 Je
15 '66
Things are looking up all over. il Newsweek
67:67 Ja 31 '66
Turn to prudence? Fortune 73:31-2 My '66
U.S. economy, 1966. O. Gass. Commentary
41:72-7 Ap '66; Reply R. L. Weissman.
42:12 Jl '66
U.S. economy, 1966; symposium. il Sr Schol
88:2-16+ Ap 1 '66
U.S. muffles its boom. il Newsweek 67:83
Je 20 '66
Vietnam's economic lesson: peace can yield
fatter profits than war. T. G. Harris. il
Look 30:44+ My 31 '66
War profiteering. New Repub 155:4 O 1 '66

Watching the weather vane. Time 87:87 My
27 '66
Well, hello there! W. F. Rickenbacker. Nat R
18:634-6 Je 28 '66
What they're saying: sampling of business-
men's opinions. Time 87:88 My 27 '66
What's happening to the boom. il Nations
Bsns 55:36-9+ Ja '67
When auto industry falters: the impact on
U.S. il U S News 61:44-6 Jl 11 '66
When does a boom become inflation? il News-
week 67:78+ Mr 21 '66
Where restraint begins; economy that keeps
on exuberantly expanding. il Time 88:59
Jl 29 '66
Where shortages are beginning to pinch. il
U S News 60:49-50 Mr 14 '66
Why one region outstrips another. il Bsns W
p78-80 F 12 '66
Woe is us. K. Crawford. Newsweek 68:46 O
31 '66
Year of tight money and where it will lead.
il Time 88:47-50+ D 30 '66
See also
Business conditions
Cost of living—United States
Debts, Public—United States
Food supply—United States
Labor and laboring classes—United States
Minimum wage—United States
Negroes in the United States—Economic
conditions
Prices—United States
Prosperity
Taxation—United States
Unemployment—United States
Wages—United States

Economic history

First New deal, by R. Moley. Review
Sat R 49:49-51+ D 24 '66. D. Young
Invisible scar, by C. Bird. Review
Nation 202:366-7 Mr 28 '66. J. F. Becker
Presidents and their spending: million once
was a lot of money. il U S News 60:52-3
F 14 '66
20th anniversary issue: a special report: oh,
how your life has changed! il Changing T
21:6-14 Ja '67
U.S. economy: what kind of ism is it? il Sr
Schol 89:14-16 S 23 '66
When money is tightened; what the record
shows. U S News 60:90-1 Ap 18 '66
See also
United States—Economic conditions

Economic opportunity, Office of

Antipoverty funds. Sr Schol 89:sup2+ N 11
'66
By or for the poor? Shriver's administrative
problems. New Repub 154:5-6 Ap 30 '66
Compromise in the Delta: Child development
group of Mississippi and the O.E.O. Chris-
tian Cent 84:3 Ja 4 '67
Coordination of manpower programs; excerpt.
H. C. Taylor. Mo Labor R 89:959-64 S '66
Cuts threaten OEO. il Sci N 90:409 N 12 '66
Facts about the aging poor. A. Ogle. Amer-
ica 115:651+ N 19 '66
How do you fight it? Child development
group of Mississippi; mismanagement jeo-
pardizes program. A. Kopkind. New Repub
155:6-7 S 3 '66
How goes the poverty war? B. L. Masse.
America 115:281-3 S 17 '66
Little by little, less and less of the OEO;
S. Shriver protests budget cutbacks. New
Repub 155:10-11 D 10 '66
Love is being needed: Foster grandparents
project. C. Brossard. il Look 30:67-71 Ag
23 '66
One man, one job. Newsweek 67:22-3 Ja 31 '66
Report on the poverty war. America 114:246
F 19 '66
Sargent Shriver and the role of the poor.
B. Carter. il Reporter 34:17-20 My 5 '66
Shriver's last stand? Newsweek 69:20 Ja 2
'67
Simulating poverty: input and output. J.
Ridgeway. New Repub 154:9-10 Je 11 '66;
Reply with rejoinder. E. C. Wilson. 155:
35+ Jl 2 '66
Six-star Sargent; presentation to House pov-
erty subcommittee. il Time 87:28 Mr 18 '66
Small business loans; part of the poverty
loan program to go to SBA. New Repub
155:9-10 S 24 '66
This month's feature: Congress & the John-
son poverty program. Cong Digest 45:67-96
Mr '66
Too many abuses in a big poverty project?
U S News 61:14-15 N 7 '66

UNITED STATES—Economic opportunity, Office of—*Continued*

War within the war. il Time 87:25-9 My 13 '66

What happened to Farmer? Center for community-action education. New Repub 154:7-8 Ap 2 '66

See also
Anti-poverty program, 1964-
United States—Job corps

Economic policy

Action at last; anti-inflation program. il Time 88:29-30 S 16 '66

Address on the State of the Union. America 116:78 Ja 21 '67

American economy: power and paradox. N. A. Bailey. Yale R 55:537-48 Je '66

And if peace should come? il Newsweek 68:73 Jl 18 '66

Another look at the new economics. E. L. Dale, jr. il N Y Times Mag p50-1+ S 18 '66

Big-brother state; concerning the annual Economic report. H. Hazlitt. Newsweek 67:80 F 28 '66

Boom; too good to last? il Newsweek 67:67 F 28 '66

Budget policy for a year of change. Bsns W p 176 D 17 '66

Building trades and guideposts. America 114:316 Mr 5 '66

Businessman's formula to head off inflation; excerpts from address, February 19, 1966. R. M. Blough. U S News 60:87-8 Mr 7 '66

Call for action. il Time 88:19-20 S 9 '66

Case against a tax increase. E. L. Dale, jr. New Repub 154:11-13 Ap 2 '66; Discussion. 154:37-8 Ap 16; 18 Ap 23 '66

Case for doing almost nothing. Fortune 74:113-14 O '66

Chances now for a tax increase; with excerpt from address by A. F. Burns. il U S News 61:27-9 D 12 '66

Congress' own economic adviser; J. W. Knowles of Joint economic committee. il Bsns W p 102+ Je 11 '66

Congress slows down the Great society. U S News 61:33-4 S 12 '66

Congressional investigations: business in the spotlight. il Nations Bsns 54:38-9+ F '66

Consensus government and the opposition role; economic program for Republicans; address, March 21, 1966. J. K. Javits. Vital Speeches 32:391-3 Ap 15 '66

Cooling off. il Time 88:64 D 23 '66

Day of the little bulls; Johnson's anti-inflation package. il Time 88:87 S 23 '66

Dead end for economic policy. Bsns W p 150 Jl 23 '66

Economic policy for 1967. Bsns W p92 D 31 '66

Economic report to Congress, January 27, 1966; excerpts. L. B. Johnson. Mo Labor R 89:278-82 Mr '66; il U S News 60:88-93 F 7 '66

Economic situation: public policy; address, May 23, 1966. W. B. Hickman. Vital Speeches 32:565-7 Jl 1 '66

Economics of self-restraint. B. L. Masse. America 115:222 S 3 '66

Economy: a soaring '66 if: economic report. il Newsweek 67:59-61 F 7 '66

Effects of November 8. H. Brandon. Sat R 49:20+ S 10 '66

Elder statesman looks at U.S. today; interview. H. W. Smith. U S News 61:50-4 O 31 '66

End to the agony of indecision; applying the new economics. Bsns W p202 S 17 '66

Field marshal directs a voluble war of persuasion; L. B. Johnson's campaign. H. Sidey. Life 60:36B Ap 29 '66

Finally, fiscal policy to the rescue. America 115:314 S 24 '66

Fiscal and monetary policy; address, September 12, 1966. L. H. Olsen. Vital Speeches 33:24-8 O 15 '66

Fiscal flexibility. America 114:849 Je 18 '66

Flaw in the new economics. W. F. Butler. il Duns R 88:41-2+ O '66

From mist to rain. il Time 87:15-16 Mr 25 '66

Genesis of the Great society; how the President planned to develop program. W. E. Leuchtenberg. il Reporter 34:36-9 Ap 21 '66

Goldilocks economy. Newsweek 69:52 Ja 9 '67

Government and the economy; planning for prosperity. il Sr Schol 88:6-7 Ap 1 '66

Government and the economy; tricky business of managing prosperity. il Sr Schol 89:11-13 D 9 '66

Great society and its future; a progress report; with excerpts from statements by L. B. Johnson. il U S News 61:32-5 D 19 '66

Guidelines for the guidelines. L. B. Johnson. il Newsweek 68:79 Ag 22 '66

Guidelines sag under new siege; President Johnson's wage-price policy is reeling. Bsns W p27 Ag 6 '66

Guiding the Nation's reluctant tigers. il Bsns W p 160+ Ap 23 '66

Guns and butter, too; concerning State-of-the-Union message. D. Lawrence. U S News 62:112 Ja 23 '67

Guns plus butter; State of the Union message. Sr Schol 88:17 F 4 '66

Hard lines and guidelines; surrender to Washington; address, December 3, 1965. R. M. Nixon. Vital Speeches 32:194-7 Ja 15 '66

High gear for LBJ programs. il Bsns W p32-3 Mr 5 '66

High-level help on economic guideposts; labor-management group to advise on how to maintain economic stability. il Bsns W p42-3 My 14 '66

How fast? H. C. Wallich. Newsweek 68:90 N 14 '66

How 1966 probably will unfold. il Bsns W p 104-6 Ja 29 '66

How the glow goes; businessmen's criticism of the President's economic policies. il Time 87:81 Je 3 '66

How to cheat the people. D. Lawrence. U S News 60:104 My 2 '66

Inflation: bugbear and battle cry; with excerpts from L. B. Johnson's addresses. il Newsweek 67:27-8 Ap 11 '66

Inflation; pro and con debate over LBJ's program. il Life 60:83-4+ Ap 15 '66

Inflation: the White House acts; five-point package. Newsweek 68:82+ S 19 '66

International economic policies for 1966; excerpts from Economic report of the President. L. B. Johnson. Dept State Bul 54:290-3 F 21 '66

International environment; address, October 6, 1966. L. B. Krause. Vital Speeches 33:50-2 N 1 '66

Johnson tries for a fresh formula: need for wage-price guidepost reinforcement. il Bsns W p25-6 Ag 13 '66

Johnson's new consensus; Business week survey of top executives; with editorial comment. il Bsns W p25-6, 172 Ap 9 '66

Keeping watch on the economy; meaning of 1946 Employment act. K. Schriftgiesser; reply with rejoinder. C. H. Madden. Sat R 49:27 F 26 '66

Keynes isn't enough; goal beyond full employment. L. J. Walinsky. New Repub 154:14-16 Ap 16 '66

Letter from Washington; concerning State of the Union message. R. H. Rovere. New Yorker 41:88+ Ja 22 '66

L.B.J. and his splintered guideposts. Life 61:4 Ag 19 '66

L.B.J. populist versus L.B.J. entrepreneur. H. Sidey. il Life 61:34D S 9 '66

LBJ stays on course. il Bsns W p25-6 Jl 23 '66

LBJ's economic baling wire; anti-inflation moves. il Newsweek 68:79 O 3 '66

Monetary policy+fiscal policy+politics=? il Sr Schol 89:6-9 O 14 '66

Must full employment mean inflation? G. Burck. il Fortune 74:120-3+ O '66

National economic policy, by J. Tobin. Review
New Repub 155:22-4 S 10 '66. R. N. Cooper

New dimensions of political economy, by W. W. Heller. Review
New Repub 155:26-8 D 17 '66. A. Campbell
Time 88:130+ N 25 '66

New economics. E. T. Chase. Commonweal 83:551-3 F 11 '66

New economics. H. C. Wallich. Newsweek 67:70 F 7 '66

New economics: a new shine on the dismal science? il Sr Schol 89:8-11 O 7 '66

New economics: what it is, how it's working; twentieth anniversary of the Employment act. il U S News 60:99-101 F 28 '66

New LBJ request on Great society plans. U S News 60:9 F 28 '66

Now beginning: the cautious Congress. U S News 62:27-8 Ja 16 '67

Now it's up to Congress; to slow inflation and ease strain on the money market. il Bsns W p35-8 S 17 '66

UNITED STATES—Economic policy—*Cont.*

OECD ministerial council meets at Paris; texts of statements, November 24, 25; with text of communique issued November 25, 1966. E. V. Rostow. Dept State Bul 56: 19-27 Ja 2 '67

Papers from a guidelines conference; excerpts il Mo Labor R 89:624-33 Je '66

People speak softly when government carries big stick. A. H. Sypher. il Nations Bsns 54:29-30 Ja '66

President and inflation. Farm J 90:110 O '66

Presidential instructor; concerning book by W. Heller. L. S. Martz. Newsweek 68:90 D 5 '66

President's package. il Fortune 74:31-2 O '66

Private enterprise and public intelligence. G. J. Stigler. Duns R 88:17+ O '66

Problems of prosperity. il Time 87:93-4 F 4 '66

Program for automated future; highlights of National commission on technology, automation, and economic progress report. Bsns W p30 F 5 '66

Protecting the family budget; address, September 4, 1966. G. Meany. Vital Speeches 32:749-51 O 1 '66

Questions of confidence; excerpts from editorials: Wall Street journal and Chicago tribune, January 19, 1966. U S News 60:100 Ja 31 '66

Racing into a looking-glass world; new language of economic policy likened to Carroll's Through the looking glass. il Bsns W p136+ Ap 2 '66

Rattles in the engine. il Time 87:100-2+ My 20 '66

Reaction: up & mixed: State of the Union message. il Time 89:73 Ja 20 '67

Republican answer to LBJ's program; interview. G. R. Ford. U S News 62:10 Ja 23 '67

Rise of the new economics. il Sr Schol 87: 12-16 Ja 14 '66

Soaring, and then some; with editorial comment. il Bsns W p25-7, 152 Jl 16 '66

State of the riposte; E. Dirksen and G. Ford criticize State of the Union message. il Newsweek 67:22 Ja 31 '66

State of the Union; address, January 17, 1966. G. R. Ford. Vital Speeches 32:259-61 F 15 '66

State of the Union; address, January 12, 1966. L. B. Johnson. Vital Speeches 32:226-30 F 1 '66; Excerpts. Dept State Bul 54:150-5 Ja 31 '66

State of the Union as Republicans see it. E. M. Dirksen; G. R. Ford. il U S News 60:72-3 Ja 31 '66

Step in the right direction? five-point anti-inflation program. il Newsweek 68:82+ S 26 '66

Stockpile strategy. Sister Thomasine Cusack. America 114:197-9 F 5 '66

T.R.B. from Washington; candid Mr Keyserling; private opulence and public squalor. New Repub 154:4 Mr 5 '66

T.R.B. from Washington; economic turnabout. New Repub 155:4 O 22 '66; Discussion. 155:38 N 12; 44-5 N 26 '66

Tax boost soon? adaptation of address, May 2, 1966. W. W. Heller. New Repub 154:9-11 My 21 '66

This nation is flourishing. Fortune 73:99+ F '66

Time to step on the brakes? il Time 87:89 F 18 '66

Time to touch the brakes. Time 87:27-27A Mr 18 '66

To spend more, to tax more or to economize? D. Lawrence. U S News 61:112 D 5 '66

Toward improved economic policy; address, February 23, 1966. T. B. Curtis. Vital Speeches 32:327-9 Mr 15 '66

Unions press harder against the guideposts. il Bsns W p 117-18 Mr 5 '66

Virtues of penny pinching. il Time 87:23-4 Ap 8 '66

War, taxes, Great society. Johnson's blueprint for '67; Statt-of-the-Union message. January 10, 1967. L. B. Johnson. il U S News 62:104-10 Ja 23 '67

We planned it that way: repeal of 7 per cent tax credit for investment in new plant and equipment. Nat R 18:968 O 4 '66

What comes after the guideposts? Bsns W p 148 Ag 13 '66

What comes after the new economics? with editorial comment. il Bsns W p 125-6, 128 F 5 '66

What Congress did, and some things it didn't do. il U S News 61:44-5 O 31 '66

What the President could do; former economic advisers statements at Washington symposium. il Time 87:91 Mr 4 '66

What's new about the year? D. Lawrence. U S News 62:100 Ja 16 '67

Where restraint begins; economy that keeps on exuberantly expanding. il Time 88:59 Jl 29 '66

Who'll be helped, hurt by LBJ plans; concerning State-of-the-Union message. il U S News 62:27-30 Ja 23 '67

Why fight? ruble-dollar road to peace. R. C. Garreston. il Nation 202:576-81 My 16 '66

Why not let the people know? D. Lawrence. U S News 61:120 O 10 '66

Wishful thinking on the balance of payments. R. W. Stevens. bibliog f il Harvard Bsns R 44:6-8+ N '66

With baling wire; latest anti-inflation moves. il Time 88:103 S 30 '66

Year of tight money and where it will lead. il Time 88:47-50+ D 30 '66

See also

Agricultural administration—United States
Budget—United States
Committee for economic development
Economic assistance, Domestic
Government spending policy
Income tax—United States
Price regulation by government—United States
Tariff—United States
Taxation—United States
United States—Appropriations and expenditures
United States—Council of economic advisers

Economic relations

Business-to-business exchange; Dillon mission to France. Bsns W p200 My 21 '66

Military power: the limits of persuasion. J. M. Gavin. Sat R 49:18-22+ Jl 30 '66

Outlook for freedom; address, September 21, 1966. D. Rusk. Dept State Bul 55:586-90 O 17 '66

This month's feature: Congress considers foreign aid for FY67. Cong Digest 45:193-224 Ag '66

See also

Economic assistance, American
United States—Commerce
United States—Commercial treaties and agreements

Argentina

U.S.-Argentine trade committee holds initial meeting; text of an announcement, May 20, 1966. Dept State Bul 54:944 Je 13 '66

Canada

See also
Joint United States-Canadian committee on trade and economic affairs

Europe, Eastern

After the big freeze, defrosting? summary of address. L. B. Johnson. Newsweek 68: 42+ O 17 '66

France

Advice to U.S. on blackmail. U S News 60: 105-6 My 23 '66

Japan

Expanding the fabric of U.S.—Japanese economic relations; address, July 8, 1966. J. T. Connor. Dept State Bul 55:215-21 Ag 8 '66

See also
Joint United States-Japan committee on trade and economic affairs

Latin America

See also
Inter-American economic and social council

Russia

Where now the Yankee trader? Nation 202: 636 My 30 '66

Education, Office of

Education pentagon. J. N. Berry, 3d. il Library J 91:195-200 Ja 15 '66; Reply. W. L. Morin. 91:1092 Mr 1 '66

Education: racial controversy dogs U.S. commissioner. L. J. Carter. Science 154:242-3+ O 14 '66

Guide to federal money for education; table. NEA J 55:55-6 N '66

Here's Harold Howe new education chief. il Sr Schol 87:sup2 Ja 14 '67

UNITED STATES—Federal bureau of investigation—*Continued*

Snooping industry. Nation 202:412 Ap 11 '66

Tapper's taint; U.S. government. Newsweek 68:27 D 12 '66

Who is being bugged, and on whose orders. il U S News 61:71-3 Jl 11 '66

Wiretap war: Kennedy, Johnson and the FBI. R. M. Cipes. New Repub 155:16-22 D 24 '66

Federal communications commission

AT&T case: what's ahead for the company now. il U S News 61:106-7 D 5 '66

AT&T masses its forces for FCC investigation. il Bsns W p38+ Je 4 '66

AT&T takes a hard look at its past and future; with editorial comment. il U S News 60:62-4, 100 Je 27 '66

Composite satellite, cable rate studied. K. Johnsen. Aviation W 85:32 O 3 '66

Compromise on CATV; FCC regulation. il Newsweek 67:67-8 F 28 '66

Contenders chafe over FCC comsat delay. il Tech W 20:13 Ja 2 '67

FCC blocking direct Comsat-DOD lease. il Aviation W 85:23 Jl 4 '66

FCC's expanding, demanding universe. il Fortune 73:150-3 Je '66

FM gets a shake-up; FCC decision to diversify radio programing. il Newsweek 68:107-8 N 28 '66

FM radio has to change its tune; rock-'n'-roll displaces the quartets. il Bsns W p 173-4+ S 24 '66

Figures of fun; E. Henry resigns. G. Ace. Sat R 49:8 My 7 '66

Green light for expansion by Comsat. il U S News 61:10 D 19 '66

Growing dispute over a growing form of television. U S News 60:6 F 28 '66

Historic reversal for the FCC; Court of appeals rules FCC erred in renewing license of WLBT. R. L. Shayon. Sat R 49:102 My 7 '66

New power for broadcast consumers. Consumer Rep 31:321-2 Jl '66

On media trouble; concerning the FCC 1964 annual report. D. Smith. Nation 202:402-3 Ap 4 '66

Pygmy of airwaves pushes to be a giant; community antenna television. il Bsns W p 100-2+ F 19 '66

Reluctant regulator heads the FCC. Bsns W p42 Je 25 '66

U.S. court sustains United church of Christ; petition challenging renewal of licenses for television stations in Jackson, Miss. Christian Cent 83:484 Ap 20 '66

Whither cable TV? CATV. R. L. Shayon. Sat R 49:63+ S 17 '66

Whole new system for TV? il U S News 61:82 Ag 15 '66

Federal convention

See United States—Constitutional convention, 1787

Federal extension service

These housewives polish up their homemaking skills; Extension homemakers councils. G. E. Maxwell. il Todays Health 44:8+ Mr '66

Federal home loan bank board

Federal savings bank bill; housing and mortgage market; address, February 21, 1966. J. E. Horne. Vital Speeches 32:363-6 Ap 1 '66

Hounding the S&Ls' own watchdog; J. E. Horne. Bsns W p51-2+ Ag 20 '66

Federal housing administration

Family money management; financing an older home. N. Kuehnl and G. Bush. Bet Hom & Gard 44:12+ Je '66

Stench at FHA. J. Barron. Read Digest 88:61-7 Ap '66

Federal mediation and conciliation service

Why the rank and file say no; terms fail to resolve issues of local memberships in Schenectady, N.Y. il Bsns W p59-60+ D 17 '66

Federal national mortgage association

Home building; a new support. U S News 61:88-9 D 12 '66

Federal power commission

FPC bars new pipeline into California market; denying Tenneco's bid to send natural gas into Los Angeles. Bsns W p26-7 Jl 30 '66

New power in the FPC; Chairman White. Bsns W p27 Jl 30 '66

Storm King opinion: stunning conservation victory. R. E. Train. Am For 72:10-11 Mr '66

Storm King project; licensing order set aside by United States Court of appeals. Nat Parks Mag 40:20 F '66

What's needed to prevent more power blackouts. il Consumer Rep 31:136-42 Mr '66

Federal reserve board

Cheers for Fed strategy; survey of leading financial economists. il Bsns W p83-4+ O 8 '66

Control the Fed? Atlan 217:10 F '66

Current monetary policy; Fed policy regarding quantity of money. M. Friedman. il Newsweek 69:59 Ja 9 '67

End to September; relief of bankers and businessmen. Time 89:88 Ja 6 '67

Fed flashes new signal easing tight money. Bsns W p22 D 31 '66

Fed holds a tiger by the tail. il Bsns W p62-3 Jl 9 '66

Fed looks to its impact. il Bsns W p70-2+ Mr 5 '66

Go-ahead for easier credit. U S News 62:84 Ja 9 '67

High cost of money is heading downward; Fed's policymakers easing of credit. il Bsns W p 15-16 D 24 '66

Is money tight, or isn't it? never been tighter since the 1920's. il Bsns W p96-8 Ag 6 '66

Learning to live with tight money; Fed tightens credit. il Bsns W p35-6 Je 11 '66

Mediator moves into the Fed. Bsns W p 124+ Mr 5 '66

Money turns a little easier; why Fed policy is changing. il Bsns W p35-6 D 10 '66

Outlook now; tighter credit, higher interest rates. il U S News 60:113-14 Mr 14 '66

Reviving bond market keeps eye on the Fed. il Bsns W p40 Ja 7 '67

Selectively tight. Time 87:86 Je 24 '66

Strain is on the banks. J. Davenport. il Fortune 74:96-9+ Jl 1 '66

Surprise choice; A. F. Brimmer. Newsweek 67:72 Mr 7 '66

There wasn't any panic at 23 Wall. J. McDonald. il Fortune 74:152-5+ D '66

What the Fed wants. il Fortune 74:40+ N '66

When should the Fed ease up? to continue the monetary freeze or allow bank reserves to grow again. Bsns W p200 O 8 '66

Where the Fed gets its bold new ideas; from new style of researcher. il Bsns W p 101-2+ D 10 '66

Year of the Fed. Fortune 75:85-6 Ja '67

Year of tight money and where it will lead. il Time 88:47-50+ D 30 '66

Federal trade commission

Anchor in the past; antitrust cases. il Time 87:85 Je 24 '66

Angry housewives win key skirmish; support from FTC against high food prices. il Bsns W p42 O 29 '66

Astounding changes seen from Robinson-Patman moves. Pub W 189:48-9 My 9 '66

FTC and co-op ads. Pub W 189:59 Je 20 '66

FTC approves extra discount for premiums. Pub W 190:41 Ag 15 '66

FTC attorneys, publishers discuss Robinson-Patman compliance; with editorial comment. Pub W 189:58-60, 75 F 28 '66

FTC examiner drops Calories charges vs. S&S. Pub W 190:49 Jl 18 '66

FTC hits at joint ventures; Phillips-National distillers agree to dissolve joint efforts in petrochemicals. Bsns W p33 Ag 13 '66

FTC order curbs vanity claims of Pageant press. Pub W 190:58 O 31 '66

FTC rules sales deception for Collier's encyclopedia. Pub W 190:30 D 12 '66

FTC takes aim at false tire claims. Consumer Rep 31:217 My '66

From the trustbusters: guidelines for businessmen. il U S News 61:46+ Jl 25 '66

Giants put on more muscle. il Bsns W p72-4+ Jl 23 '66

High court tightens the antitrust reins; FTC can stall mergers while legality is tested. il Bsns W p40-1 Je 18 '66

New rule on TV size designations. Consumer Rep 31:265-6 Je '66

On the way: rules for buy now, pay later. U S News 62:11 Ja 9 '67

UNITED STATES—Federal trade commission
—*Continued*
Out of business, by FTC order; Robinson-Patman act invoked on Southern California jobbers, inc. J. Ridgeway. New Repub 154: 13-14 F 12 '66
Palliatives but no cures; advertising claims for treatment of hemorrhoids. Time 89:52 Ja 13 '67
Parents' magazine seal found misleading by FTC. Pub W 190:31 D 12 '66
Split vision jumbles the merger picture; top antitrusters Paul Rand Dixon and Donald F. Turner. Bsns W p54 Mr 26 '66
Talks with Paul Rand Dixon; philosophies underlying the new FTC; interview, ed. by J. Berry. P. R. Dixon. il Duns R 87:44-5+ Ja '66
Testing the draw; cigarettes on trial. Bsns W p83 Ag 20 '66
To the cigarette makers: just the facts, please. L. M. Miller and J. Monahan. il Read Digest 89:61-7 N '66

Federal water pollution control administration
Industry joins battle to stem pollution tide. il Bsns W p76-7 D 31 '66
Water pollution: new agency moving from HEW to interior. L. J. Carter. Science 152: 736-8 My 6 '66

Fish and wildlife service
Concepts for conservation; address, September 21, 1965. S. A. Cain. Vital Speeches 32: 202-6 Ja 15 '66
Custom-made hunters: introducing waterfowl shooting; project by the Boston office of U.S. bureau of sport fisheries and wildlife. H. Titus. il Field & S 71:72-3+ N '66
FPC: nearing approval? B. J. Culliton. il Sci N 90:474 D 3 '66
State vs. the Predator; case history: South Dakota. G. Charles. il Audubon Mag 68: 436-42 N '66

Fisheries, Bureau of
See United States—Fish and wildlife service

Food and drug administration
Bit intemperate; attack on pharmaceutical industry. Time 87:92+ Ap 15 '66
Consumer's view of food controls. il Consumer Bul 49:19-24 Jl '66
Drug makers get a tough, new cop. Bsns W p72+ Mr 26 '66
Drug sales and tests: U.S. tightens stand. U S News 60:24-5 Mr 21 '66
Drug tests get the FDA needle; keeping three pain relievers: Measurin, Norgesic and Stendin off the market. Bsns W p 114+ N 19 '66
FPC: nearing approval? B. J. Culliton. il Sci N 90:474 D 3 '66
Fish flour: FDA approval likely on improved product. J. Ayres. Science 152:738-9 My 6 '66; Reply. D. M. Hadjimarkos. 152:1567 Je 17 '66
FDA, plus and minus. America 114:403 Mr 26 '66
FDA takes the offensive; Goddard's antidotes for drug abuses. Newsweek 67:100 Ap 18 '66
Food and drug administration: test for leadership vaccine. J. Walsh. Science 151:801-3 F 18 '66
FDA's edict: patients, not profits, come first; excerpts from address, April 6, 1966. J. L. Goddard. Science 152:332-3 Ap 15 '66
From the report on the Food and drug administration. Science 151:802 F 18 '66
Goddard at FDA: new rules for the game. E. Langer. Science 152:1487-90 Je 10 '66
Hard-nosed medic, policeman of all pills; interview, ed. by B. Paisner. il Life 61:60+ Ag 26 '66
He is shaking Food and drug well before using. G. A. W. Boehm. il N Y Times Mag p23+ My 15 '66
Investigating the investigator; FDA strikes physician's name from its approved list of researchers. Time 88:65 Ag 5 '66
Krebiozen case: what happened in Chicago. E. Langer. Science 151:1061-4 Mr 4 '66
Meet Dr Goddard, new FDA chief. T. Lewis. il Todays Health 44:6-7 Ap '66
Misuse of antibiotics: eighteen feed additives and food preservatives declared hazardous. Sci Am 215:44 O '66
More vigilance at FDA; new commissioner James L. Goddard. Bsns W p 170 Mr 12 '66
New firm hand at the old FDA. New Repub 154:10-11 Mr 26 '66

Prescription for the FDA: a new dose of courage. Consumer Rep 31:411-15 Ag '66
Razz-ma-tazz in the drug industry; lessons of the DMSO case. R. G. Sherrill. il Nation 202:425-7 Ap 11 '66; Reply with rejoinder. J. H. Brown. 202:666+ Je 6 '66
Safety of Symmetrel. Time 88:57 D 2 '66
Storm breaks over drug testing. il Bsns W p88-90+ F 19 '66
Support for a shake-up. il Time 87:55 Ap 1 '66
Testing, testing; J. L. Goddard's agency efficiency tasks. Newsweek 67:92 Mr 21 '66
This kind of toy should be banned, and we may get a new law to do it; dangers of the Sonic blaster. il Consumer Rep 31:266-7 Je '66
Vitamin crackdown. il Time 88:48+ Jl 1 '66

Foreign opinion
American scholarship and the cultural image abroad. W. W. Brickman. Sch & Soc 94:373 N 12 '66
Anatomy of anti-Americanism. il Sr Schol 88:6-8+ F 11 '66
As others see us. See issues of Saturday review
Australia's answer to the Vietnam critics; interview. H. Holt. Read Digest 89:67-72 D '66
Despite the uproar: does world really want U.S. to quit? il U S News 62:31-2 Ja 16 '67
Overseas image of American democracy; address; with questions and answers. G. V. Allen. Ann Am Acad 366:60-7 Jl '66
Speaking out; psst! I love America. J. Morris. Sat Eve Post 239:12+ O 22 '66
Teachers from abroad take a look at America. R. W. Lykes. il Am Ed 2:14-19 S '66
What the visitors really think. B. Wedge. il Sat R 49:98+ Mr 12 '66

African
View from Africa. C. Fritchey. Harper 233: 124+ N '66

Asian
How Asians view the Vietnam war. il U S News 62:6 Ja 2 '67

Australian
Johnson visit; a dissent from Australia. N. Brennan. Commonweal 85:215-16 N 25 '66; Reply. R. A. De Gregorio. 85:391+ Ja 13 '67

British
British support on Vietnam? with statements. J. Fletcher. Nat R 18:356-8 Ap 19 '66
U.S. as others see us; reprint. il Nations Bsns 54:60 Ja '66

European
America in Salzburg; Seminar in American studies. M. Mannes. il Harper 232:91-5 F '66
As Europe sees U.S. outlook: how much slowdown? American economy. A. Zanker. il U S News 61:43-4 S 26 '66
Doubts of Europe. R. Steel. Commonweal 84: 629-31 S 30 '66
Through European eyes: you're on your own. J. Blocker. Newsweek 68:34-5 O 31 '66
View from Germany; and western Europe. H. Brandon. Sat R 49:16 Ap 2 '66
What's eating our allies. New Repub 154:6 Ap 2 '66

French
Bringing the war home. Time 88:29-30 Ag 19 '66
It's your ball, chum. J. Burnham. Nat R 18:457 My 17 '66

German
Now the Germans. Nation 202:86-7 Ja 24 '66

Indian
Myths that divide India and us. L. Markel. il N Y Times Mag p29+ Ja 15 '67

Japanese
From Japan. P. Kuhn. Bul Atomic Sci 22:26-7 Mr '66
Kodomo's garden of American images; excerpt from Young Japan views Uncle Sam, by W. Barbe. il Sat R 49:96+ Mr 12 '66
Letter from Tokyo. P. Schmid. Commentary 42:49-53 O '66

UNITED STATES—Foreign opinion—*Continued*

Latin American

Cool cat against the reds' cherry bombs; interview, ed. by R. Hemming. P. Winter. il Sr Schol 87:2+ Ja 21 '66

Vietnamese

Vietnamese want GI's to stay. G. C. Troelstrup. il U S News 60:39 Ap 25 '66

Foreign population

See also
Immigration and emigration—United States
   also Irish in the United States; and similar headings

Foreign relations

American civilization: its influence on our foreign policy; symposium, ed. by J. C. Charlesworth. bibliog f il Ann Am Acad 366:1–148 Jl '66

American nightmare: why we fear peasants in revolt. B. Moore, jr. Nation 203:271–4 S 26 '66

American ordeal; need for a more normal range of American commitment. W. Lippmann. Newsweek 67:25 Ap 11 '66

Analogies & images: thoughtways of foreign policy. W. F. Whyte. Nation 202:641–5 My 30 '66

Appointment in Manila; L. B. Johnson's post conference plans. Newsweek 68:36 O 10 '66

Arrogance of power: a clash over U.S. policy; address, May 5, 1966. J. W. Fulbright. U S News 60:113–21 My 23 '66; Discussion. 60:121–4 My 23 '66

As world problems mount for LBJ. il U S News 61:6+ S 12 '66

Atlantic report (cont) Atlan 217:6 F: 6+ Ap; 22+ My '66

Atlantic report; President Johnson's approach. Atlan 217:6 F '66

Balance of world power: where the U.S. fits in; with charts. U S News 60:48–50 Ap 4 '66

Beyond isolation: has the U.S. gone too far? viewpoints. il Sr Schol 89:10–11 D 2 '66

Blabbermouthism; violations of confidence at highest levels of government. N. Cousins. Sat R 49:34–5 D 10 '66

Computers, program management and foreign affairs. J. Diebold. For Affairs 45:125–34 O '66

Congress & foreign policy: timid political will. E. A. Kolodziej. il Nation 202:292–4 Mr 14 '66

Coordination of policy on population matters; statement, April 11, 1966. T. C. Mann. Dept State Bul 54:784–7 My 16 '66

Dean Rusk: cool man in a hot world. J. R. Moskin. il Look 30:14–21 S 6 '66

De Gaulle, the U.S. and Russia: a look at the trends; interview, ed. by F. C. Painton. A. Grosser. U S News 60:42–3 Je 20 '66

Eisenhower speaks his mind; interview, ed. by P. Martin. D. D. Eisenhower. U S News 61:42–5 N 7 '66

End of either/or. M. Bundy. For Affairs 45:189–201 Ja '67

Escalating the war of words. J. N. Eller. America 114:479 Ap 9 '66

Establishment game: Nicholas Murray Butler rides again: New York's foreign policy syndicate and its influence. P. Seabury. Reporter 34:24–6 My 19 '66; Correction. 34:5 Je 2 '66

Fatal arrogance of power. J. W. Fulbright. il N Y Times Mag p28–9+ My 15 '66

Foreign policy and the crisis mentality. G. McGovern. Atlan 219:55–7 Ja '67

Foreign policy conference to be held for news media. Dept State Bul 55:789 N 21 '66

Foreign policy in Christian perspective, by J. C. Bennett. Review
   America 115:38 Jl 9 '66. E. Waldman

Four centers of U.S. foreign policy; government departments and the President's position. N. Cousins. Sat R 49:16–18 Jl 2 '66

Four fundamental facts of our foreign policy; excerpt of address, September 5, 1966. L. B. Johnson. Dept State Bul 55:453–4 S 26 '66

Free world colossus: a critique of American foreign policy in the cold war, by D. Horowitz. Review
   Nation 202:214–16 F 21 '66. A. S. Kaufman

Fulbright on camera. A. Campbell. New Repub 154:19–22 My 21 '66

Fulbright revolt. M. J. Goldbloom. Commentary 42:63–9 S '66

Fulbright the undecider. Life 60:4 My 13 '66

Global apartheid? question of recognizing or doing business with a minority government. J. Burnham. Nat R 18:1036 O 18 '66

Goal of a reliable peace: a survey of free-world progress; address, August 22, 1966. D. Rusk. Dept State Bul 55:362–8 S 12 '66

Goals for American power. R. D. Masters. Yale R 55:365–88 Mr '66

Hail, Harry Golden; American skepticism. K. Crawford. Newsweek 68:27 D 26 '66

High price of power. New Repub 155:5–6 S 10 '66

How U.S. leaders see today's world. il U S News 61:28–31 D 26 '66

Imperial America: similarity to Roman empire. T. Molnar. Nat R 18:409–11 My 3 '66; Discussion. 18:554+ Je 14 '66

Importance of being civil. T. C. Sorensen. Sat R 49:30 N 26 '66

Importance of obscurity; Time essay. Time 87:27 My 6 '66

International cop? concerning statements by D. Rusk. il Newsweek 68:22–3 S 12 '66

Issues of world power: place of the university; address, November 8, 1966. P. H. Nitze. Vital Speeches 33:98–103 D 1 '66

Johnson takes the slow road; no radical changes in either domestic or foreign policies. Bsns W p37–8 N 19 '66

Kennedy image, three years later. il Sr Schol 89:10–13+ N 18 '66

Lest we forget: isolationism: excerpts from editorial, Sept. 26, 1938; with comment. D. Lawrence. U S News 60:116+ Mr 28 '66

Lonely role of the U.S. U S News 61:119 O 17 '66

LBJ's balancing act: can it last? il U S News 60:31–2 F 28 '66

LBJ's foreign policy: mirror of the man. il Bsns W p38–40 Jl 9 '66

L.B.J.'s foreign policy successes. Life 60:4 Je 24 '66

McNamara's call for a new policy; its meaning and impact. U S News 60:14 My 30 '66

McNamara's new design for world peace and security; address, May 18, 1966. R. S. McNamara. il U S News 60:90–5 My 30 '66; Same with title Security in the contemporary world. Dept State Bul 54:874–81 Je 6 '66

Manila: is it only a gesture? E. Weintal. Newsweek 68:28–9 O 24 '66

Military power: the limits of persuasion. J. M. Gavin. Sat R 49:18–22+ Jl 30 '66

Mission for humanity. D. Lawrence. U S News 61:144 N 14 '66

Most urgent work of our time; epilog for the book, This America. L. B. Johnson. Dept State Bul 55:715–16 N 7 '66

National foreign policy conference for educators; Washington, D.C. June 16–17, 1966; with introd. by R. I. Phillips; symposium. Dept State Bul 55:71–109 Jl 18 '66

Neo-isolationism? W. Pfaff. Commonweal 84:351–2 Je 17 '66

Neutrality belt; new isolationism. M. Ascoli. Reporter 35:24 S 22 '66

Nonintervention vs. containment. B. G. Lall. Bul Atomic Sci 22:21–4 My '66

Not so ancient history; annual meeting of ADA. Nation 202:538 My 9 '66

Obligations of power; excerpt from address, May 11, 1966. L. B. Johnson. Dept State Bul 54:835–6 My 30 '66

Offense is the worst defense. E. Rabinowitch. Bul Atomic Sci 22:32–4 O '66

Organizing the peace for man's survival: address, May 24, 1966; with questions and answers. D. Rusk. Dept State Bul 54:926–34 Je 13 '66

Our place in the world. W. Lippmann. Newsweek 67:23 Je 20 '66

Outlook for freedom; address, September 21, 1966. D. Rusk. Dept State Bul 55:586–90 O 17 '66

Patriotism of dissent. J. W. Fulbright. Redbook 128:44+ N '66

Plain facts of war and peace. D. Lawrence. U S News 60:128 My 16 '66

Policy-making in a world turned upside down. T. L. Hughes. For Affairs 45:202–14 Ja '67

Politics. D. Macdonald. Esquire 67:26+ Ja '67

Power akin to freedom; Foreign relations committee hearing on foreign-aid bill. il Time 87:25 Ap 29 '66

UNITED STATES—Foreign relations—Asia
—*Continued*
Bright spirit; H. Humphrey on U.S. aims. il Time 87:21-5 Ap 1 '66
Can he be serious? concerning Fulbright's Asian policy speech. Nat R 18:757-8 Ag 9 '66
Case for realism. Time 87:17 Mr 25 '66
China in context. L. W. Pye. For Affairs 45:229-45 Ja '67
Dawn over Asia; address, October 6, 1966. C. P. Kim. Vital Speeches 33:42-6 N 1 '66
Eugene Black on ten-nation trip to discuss Asian development; White House announcement, October 13, 1966. Dept State Bul 55:669 O 31 '66
Ex-administration officials discuss U.S. policy in Asia. B. Nelson. il Science 154:988-90 N 25 '66
Four essentials for peace in Asia; address, July 12, 1966. L. B. Johnson. Dept State Bul 55:158-62 Ag 1 '66; Same with title United States Asian policy. Vital Speeches 32:610-13 Ag 1 '66
From Fulbright: a sweeping attack on LBJ's Asian doctrine. U S News 61:12 Ag 1 '66
Future of the Pacific community; address, November 15, 1966. D. Rusk. Dept State Bul 55:838-43 D 5 '66
Globe-trotting with the veep. il Newsweek 67:39-40 F 28 '66
How a French authority sees U.S. role in Asia; interview, ed. by F. C. Painton. R. Dabernat. il U S News 62:93-4+ Ja 23 '67
Japan: co-prosperity again; U.S.-Japan-China situation. A. Axelbank. il Nation 202:479-80 Ap 25 '66
Matter of understanding; L. B. Johnson defines policy. Reporter 35:8 Ag 11 '66
New appraisal of the old domino game. C. Fritchey. Harper 232:46 Ap '66
New realism; L. B. Johnson's position. Time 88:17-18 Jl 22 '66
Peking's threats; address, August 30, 1966. L. B. Johnson. Vital Speeches 32:706-8 S 15 '66; Same with title True meaning of patriotism. Dept State Bul 55:424-7 S 19 '66
Perspective on Asia; address, June 8, 1966. H. H. Humphrey. Dept State Bul 55:2-6 Jl 4 '66; Same. Vital Speeches 32:582-5 Jl 15 '66
Political gimmick? K. Crawford. Newsweek 68:38 N 14 '66
Secretary Rusk meets with Asian leaders; statements on various occasions during the trip, transcripts of news conferences; with texts of communiques released after the meetings at Canberra and Kyoto; June 26-July 9, 1966. D. Rusk. Dept State Bul 55:169-84 Ag 1 '66
Should U.S. fight a land war in Asia? views of military leaders. il U S News 60:21 Ap 25 '66
Story of U.S. and its stake in Asia. il U S News 60:33-8 F 28 '66
Talking at a distance; summary of statement. L. B. Johnson. il Newsweek 68:39+ Jl 25 '66
U.S. in Asia: is this the dawn of a new Pacific era? il Newsweek 68:30-4 O 31 '66
Vice President Humphrey reports to President on Asian trip; text of memorandum; March 6, 1966. H. H. Humphrey. Dept State Bul 54:489-91 Mr 28 '66
Where U.S. stands in Asia: a first-hand report; interview. R. P. Martin. il U S News 60:40-3 Je 27 '66

Asia, Southeastern
American intellectual; address, June 1, 1966. R. C. Nairn. Vital Speeches 32:667-70 Ag 15 '66
Asia trap: what do we do now? J. Mirsky. Nation 202:524-6 My 2 '66
Australia today; U.S. Asian policy; address, July 5, 1966. H. Holt. Vital Speeches 32:613-17 Ag 1 '66
Background of U.S. policy in southeast Asia; statement, May 9, 1966. D. Rusk. bibliog f Dept State Bul 54:830-4 My 30 '66
Changing face of southeast Asia, by A. Vandenbosch and R. Butwell. Review
  Sat R 49:43-4 N 5 '66. J. M. Allison
Containing China: a round-table discussion; ed. by N. Podhoretz. Commentary 41:23-41 My '66
Contemporary American influence in south and southeast Asia. W. A. Wilcox. bibliog f Ann Am Acad 366:108-16 Jl '66
How firmness in Vietnam is paying off; interview. W. E. Griffith. Read Digest 88:112-16 Ap '66

New building blocs for Asia. C. J. V. Murphy. Fortune 74:134+ D '66
Pedernales flows into the Pacific. H. Sidey. il Life 61:46 O 28 '66
Pictures in our minds; concerning NBC documentary The battle for Asia. New Repub 156:9-10 Ja 7 '67
Southeast Asia; how important, to whom? R. Butwell. bibliog f il Cur Hist 52:1-7 Ja '67
U.S. policy in southeast Asia: what's ahead? W. C. Johnstone. Cur Hist 50:106-11+ F '66
Vietnam: the war is worth winning. H. Donovan. il Life 60:27-31 F 25 '66
Viet-Nam witness 1953-66, by B. B. Fall. Review
  Sat R il 49:23-4 My 28 '66. D. Schoenbrun
Way red China can be stopped; interview. A. M. Halpern. il U S News 60:56-9 Mr 21 '66
World that waits. E. J. Hughes. Newsweek 67:28-9 Je 13 '66
  See also
Vietnamese crisis, 1964
Vietnamese war, 1957-

Australia
Australia takes a new look, and turns toward U.S. il U S News 60:74+ Ap 18 '66
President and Australian Prime Minister conclude talks; text of joint communique, July 14, 1966. Dept State Bul 55:212-13 Ag 8 '66

Austria
  See also
Austria—History—Allied occupation, 1945-1955

Burma
U.S. and Burma reaffirm bonds of friendship and cooperation; exchange of greetings, toast by President Johnson, September 8; with text of joint communique, September 9, 1966. L. B. Johnson; Ne Win. Dept State Bul 55:483-6 O 3 '66

Burundi
United States asks for recall of Burundi ambassador; statement, January 11, 1966. Dept State Bul 54:158 Ja 31 '66

Cambodia
Haunted voyage; concerning A. Harriman's proposed visit. Newsweek 68:28 Ag 29 '66
U.S. replies to Cambodian charges on frontier situation; letter to U Thant, January 8, 1966. A. J. Goldberg. Dept State Bul 54:167-8 Ja 31 '66

Canada
Canada: test of the American conscience; discussion. J. Reston and B. Hutchison. Read Digest 89:189-90+ Jl '66
Canada; with editorial comment. H. MacLennan. il Am Heritage 17:4, 6-45+ D '65; Correction. 17:100 Je '66
  See also
International joint commission (United States and Canada)

Chile
  See also
Project Camelot

China (People's Republic)
All the handouts fit to print; New York times story. Time 87:48 Ap 8 '66
American dealings with Peking. K. T. Young. For Affairs 45:77-87 O '66
Anti-anti; experiment in containment without isolation. M. Ascoli. Reporter 34:16 My 19 '66
Atlantic report; more flexible approach. R. Reston. Atlan 218:4+ O '66
Atlantic report; Senate foreign relations committee's hearings. Atlan 217:22 My '66
Be kind to China. K. Crawford. Newsweek 67:34 Ap 4 '66
Call for release of American prisoners held by Communist China; address, May 7, 1966. W. P. Bundy. Dept State Bul 54:866-9 My 30 '66
China and Vietnam. R. Terrill. New Repub 155:16-20 O 29 '66
China conference: the dragon: myths and realities. S. Spector and J. H. Moore. Nation 202:256-60 Mr 7 '66
China: dangers of misunderstanding. il Newsweek 67:35-8+ Mr 7 '66
China in context. L. W. Pye. For Affairs 45:229-45 Ja '67
China next. Nation 202:253 Mr 7 '66
China policy: Rusk's new 10-point plan. U S News 60:16 Ap 25 '66

UNITED STATES—Foreign relations—China
(People's Republic)—*Continued*
Containing China: a round-table discussion;
ed. by N. Podhoretz. Commentary 41:23-41
My '66; Discussion. 42:17-18 Ag; 28+ S '66
Defective vision. New Repub 154:5+ Mr
19 '66
Deflating the dragon. il Time 87:16-17 Mr 25
'66
Ex-administration officials discuss U.S. pol-
icy in Asia. B. Nelson. il Science 154:988-90
N 25 '66
Fallacy of China scholars; address. April 27,
1966. S. T. Tung. Vital Speeches 32:629-31
Ag 1 '66
Four against the red China lobby; sym-
posium; ed. with introd. by T. Lit. il Nat
R 18:513-28 My 31 '66; Correction. 18:598+
Je 28 '66
Gnawing debate. il Newsweek 67:25-6 Mr 14
'66
Great American reflex: anti-Communist
neurosis. Nation 202:378 Ap 4 '66
Hopeful shift in our China policy. Life 60:4
Ap 22 '66
How fierce the red dragon? China policy
debate. Sr Schol 88:6 Mr 25 '66
Is our China policy changing? excerpts from
testimony. D. Rusk. Nat R 18:398 My 3 '66
Issue is China. Christian Cent 83:355-7 Mr 23
'66; Discussion. 83:683-4 My 25 '66
Japan: co-prosperity again; appeal for softer
attitude. A. Axelbank. il Nation 202:479-80
Ap 25 '66
Must fear of China shackle our power in
Asia? F. V. Drake. Read Digest 88:53-6 Je
'66
New China policy. H. Brandon. Sat R 49:10
Jl 9 '66
New debate on China; Senate foreign rela-
tions committee's hearings on U.S. China
policy. Newsweek 67:25-6 Mr 21 '66
New thinking about China. J. K. Fairbank.
Atlan 217:77-8+ Je '66
No sanctuary. Commonweal 84:213-14 My 13
'66
Our war with red China; symposium. il
Nat R 18:204-9 Mr 8 '66
Peking's other enemy. Newsweek 67:47 Ap 4
'66
Quest for peace; address, March 25, 1966. A. J.
Goldberg. Dept State Bul 54:608-13 Ap 18
'66
Reading the dragon's mind; two opinions
from the academic community. Time 87:27A
Mr 18 '66
Scholarship virus; question of authority for
New York times article. Reporter 34:10+
Ap 7 '66
Secretary comments on Peiping's militancy in
southeast Asia; transcript of an interview
for the television program, Red China: year
of the gun? on April 27, 1966. D. Rusk.
Dept State Bul 54:772-5 My 16 '66
Secretary Rusk appears on Face the Nation,
March 20, 1966. D. Rusk. Dept State Bul 54:
565-70 Ap 11 '66
Secretary Rusk's news conference of March
25, 1966. D. Rusk. Dept State Bul 54:557-
8+ Ap 11 '66
Senator Javits and the Committee of one
million. Nat R 19:14+ Ja 10 '67
750 million couches; concerning U Thant's
views on Peking's nervous system. Re-
porter 34:16 F 10 '66
Sino-American confrontation: Communist
Chinese perspectives. I. C. Ojha. bibliog f
Cur Hist 51:147-52+ S '66
Slight thaw. Nation 202:700-1 Je 13 '66
Top-priority issue; need for hearings and de-
bate on China policy. Nation 202:199 F 21
'66
Two Chinas; Americans are ready for a new
policy. H. S. Reuss. Commonweal 84:251-4
My 20 '66
Underlining China; Fulbright hearings. Time
87:26 Ap 8 '66
United States and Communist China; ad-
dress, February 12, 1966. W. P. Bundy.
Dept State Bul 54:310-18 F 28 '66
U.S. China policy: conciliation or collision
course? B. Nelson. Science 154:245-8 O 14
'66
U.S. China policy is changing: travel comes
first. B. G. Lall. Bul Atomic Sci 22:93-6
Je '66
United States policy toward Communist
China; statement; March 16, 1966. D. Rusk.
Dept State Bul 54:686-95 My 2 '66
U.S. starts rethinking policies on red China.
Bsns W p41 Mr 12 '66

Voice of freedom. D. Lawrence. U S News
60:104 Ap 4 '66
War in Asia. W. Lippmann. Newsweek 67:23
Mr 14 '66
War with China? New Repub 154:7-8 Ja 29 '66
Way red China can be stopped; interview.
A. M. Halpern. il U S News 60:56-9 Mr
21 '66
What the draft might blow up. C. Fritchey.
Harper 233:29-30 Ag '66
When the U.S. negotiates with Peiping, in
Warsaw; interview, ed. by R. A. Haeger.
J. A. Gronouski, jr. il U S News 61:44-6
Jl 4 '66
Who's containing now? Commonweal 83:490
Ja 28 '66
Why Peking casts us as the villain. J. K.
Fairbank. il N Y Times Mag p30-1+ My 22
'66

Communist countries
. . . And why he will try to end the cold
war. Life 62:4 Ja 20 '67
Détente, or daydreaming? M. Ascoli. Reporter
35:18 D 15 '66
East-West relations: shaping a stable
world; address, December 11, 1966. F. D.
Kohler. Dept State Bul 56:6-11 Ja 2 '67
Small-step détente in Europe. Life 61:4 O 21
'66
Storm over Rusk. Nation 202:635-6 My 30 '66

Congo (Capital Kinshasa)
Stanleyville rescue: American policy in the
Congo. K. W. Grundy. Yale R 56:242-55
D '66

Cuba
Cuba, Castro and the United States. P. W.
Bonsal. For Affairs 45:260-76 Ja '67
New shuttle. Time 89:31 Ja 6 '67
U.S. calls on Cuba to prevent incursions into
Guantanamo base; Department statement,
May 28; with text of U.S. note, May 27,
1966. Dept State Bul 54:934-5 Je 13 '66
See also
Cuba—History—Invasion, 1961

Dominican Republic
Another U.S. problem that just will not go
away. H. Handleman. il U S News 60:52+
F 28 '66
Case of defamation: US intelligence versus
Juan Bosch. T. Draper. New Repub 154:16-
18 F 26 '66
Correspondence with Theodore Draper &
Commentary. appropriate & inappropriate.
T. Draper; J. B. Bender; P. Bethel. Nat R
18:823-7 Ag 23 '66
Dominican crisis; case study in American
policy. T. Draper; discussion. il Nat R 18:
99-100, 107-14 F 8 '66; Commentary 41:18+
Ap; 6+ My '66
Dominican dilemma. J. N. Goodsell. New
Repub 154:29-31 F 5 '66
Dominican Republic: burden of the past.
K. Wagenheim. il Nation 203:541-4 N 21 '66
Overtaken by events, by J. B. Martin. Re-
view
Nation 204:23-5 Ja 2 '67. W. A. Williams
New Repub 155:25-8 D 24 '66. S. Halper
New Yorker 42:224+ N 26 '66. R. H.
Rovere
Santo Domingo; labyrinth of policy; perils of
an international force. T. Mockler. il Na-
tion 202:154-7 F 7 '66
Santo Domingo: unfinished revolution. S.
Lens. Nation 202:520-3 My 2 '66
Truth about Santo Domingo. K. O. Gilmore.
Read Digest 88:93-8 My '66

Europe
Europe? where's that? New Repub 155:5-6 D
17 '66
NATO and U.S. foreign policy; excerpt from
address, July 22, 1966. N. Cousins. Sat R
49:18-19+ Ag 6 '66
President marks Poland's national millennium; calls for wider East-West contracts; remarks, with text of proclamation, May 3, 1966. L. B. Johnson. Dept
State Bul 54:794-7 My 23 '66

Europe, Eastern
After the big freeze, defrosting? summary
of address. L. B. Johnson. Newsweek 68:
42+ O 17 '66
Bridge builder; J. Gronouski. Time 87:37 Ap
15 '66
Continuing the search for areas of common
understanding with eastern Europe; remarks, June 15, 1966. L. B. Johnson. Dept
State Bul 55:56-8 Jl 11 '66

UNITED STATES—Foreign relations—Europe, Eastern—*Continued*
Making Europe whole: an unfinished task; address, October 7, 1966. L. B. Johnson. Dept State Bul 55:622-5 O 24 '66
Overtures to the East. il Time 88:27-8 D 9 '66
When the U.S. negotiates with Peiping. in Warsaw; interview, ed. by R. A. Haeger. J. A. Gronouski, jr. il U S News 61:45-6 Jl 4 '66

Europe, Western
As LBJ prepares for Asia trip: a formula for uniting Europe; excerpts from address, October 7, 1966. U S News 61:80 O 17 '66
Bygone notions. W. Lippmann. Newsweek 68:15 Ag 1 '66
Department presents views on Senate resolutions on closer relations among Atlantic nations; statement, March 24, 1966. J. M. Leddy. Dept State Bul 54:672-4 Ap 25 '66
East-West trade is stymied in Arkansas; trade in relation to future role of U.S. in Europe. Life 60:4 Je 3 '66
Europe's new mood: its meaning for U.S. il U S News 60:39-41 Je 20 '66
For a new Atlantic alliance; address, June 1966. H. A. Kissinger. il Reporter 35:18-27 Jl 14 '66
Is Europe pulling away from America? il U S News 60:41-3 My 9 '66
Larger meaning of the NATO crisis; address, April 29, 1966. G. W. Ball. Dept State Bul 54:762-8 My 16 '66; Same. Vital Speeches 32:492-5 Je 1 '66
Long NATO crisis. E. Taylor. il Reporter 34:16-21 Ap 21 '66
Making Europe whole: an unfinished task; address, October 7, 1966. L. B. Johnson. Dept State Bul 55:622-5 O 24 '66
Necessary partnership. J. R. Schaetzel. For Affairs 44:417-33 Ap '66
Now Europe is catching up with de Gaulle. U S News 62:57 Ja 2 '67
Our alternatives in Europe. H. Kahn and W. Pfaff. For Affairs 44:587-600 Jl '66
Rusk's Francophobia; de Gaulle and NATO. R. D. Masters. Commonweal 84:431-3 Jl 8 '66
U.S. policy and the new Europe. F. Church. For Affairs 45:49-57 O '66
U.S. policy on Atlantic union; statement, September 20, 1966. G. W. Ball. Dept State Bul 55:613-15 O 17 '66
U.S. policy toward NATO; statement, June 30, 1966. G. W. Ball. Dept State Bul 55:143-8 Jl 25 '66
U.S. responsibilities toward Europe and Germany; address, July 14, 1966. G. C. McGhee. Dept State Bul 55:269-73 Ag 22 '66
Why Europe is pulling away from the United States. il U S News 61:49-51 D 26 '66
Why Vietnam war worries U.S. allies. il U S News 60:38-9 Je 13 '66
See also
Atlantic community

Far East
Astronauts Schirra and Borman make Far Eastern tour. Dept State Bul 54:364-5 Mr 7 '66
Humphrey mission: questions abroad and in Congress. il U S News 60:16 F 28 '66
U.S. mission chiefs in Far East meet at Baguio, Philippines; joint statement. Dept State Bul 54:492-3 Mr 28 '66
Viet-Nam and U.S. objectives in the Far East; address, May 23, 1966. W. P. Bundy. Dept State Bul 54:965-70 Je 20 '66

France
Cliff-hanger: the perils of NATO; U.S. anti-de Gaulle crusade back fires. il Newsweek 67:32+ My 2 '66
Falsification of history; discrepancies between published and unpublished accounts by State department of Franco-American relations. Nation 203:235 S 19 '66
Opening duel; de Gaulle's decrees. Time 87:33 Ap 22 '66
Secretary Rusk answers questions on NATO issues and Viet-Nam; interview by Parismatch. D. Rusk. Dept State Bul 54:695-9 My 2 '66
Under Secretary Ball discusses U.S. views on Viet-Nam and NATO; interview, ed. by A. Fontaine. G. W. Ball. Dept State Bul 54:613-16 Ap 18 '66
Undiplomatic diplomats; philosophies behind NATO crisis; U.S. anti-de Gaulle offensive. E. Weintal. il Newsweek 67:39 Ap 25 '66

U.S. and France. P. Steinfels. Commonweal 84:570-1 S 16 '66
U.S. ready to consult with France and NATO on French demands; texts of aide memoire exchanged between United States and France; April 12 and March 29, 1966. Dept State Bul 54:699-703 My 2 '66
What U.S. has done for France. il U S News 60:36-8 Ap 4 '66

Germany (Federal Republic)
New leaders in Germany; meaning to U.S. alliance. il U S News 61:30-1 D 12 '66
President Johnson and Chancellor Erhard hold talks at Washington; exchange of toasts, December 20, 1966; with joint communique. L. Erhard; L. B. Johnson. Dept State Bul 54:46-51 Ja 10 '66
Time for a new look at Germany. Bsns W p 196 N 26 '66
United States and Germany reaffirm community of interest; exchange of toasts, September 26; with text of joint communique, September 27, 1966. L. B. Johnson; L. Erhard. Dept State Bul 55:578-80, 583-5 O 17 '66

Ghana
U.S. recognizes Ghana government of National liberation committee; Department statement, March 4, 1966. Dept State Bul 54:440 Mr 21 '66

Great Britain
President Johnson confers with British Prime Minister; exchange of toasts, July 29, 1966. L. B. Johnson; H. Wilson. Dept State Bul 55:265-8 Ag 22 '66
Wilson's mission: a test of U.S.-British partnership. il U S News 61:33-4 Ag 1 '66

Guinea
Flight 150 to Accra. il Newsweek 68:52 N 14 '66
Unhappy landing of Flight 150; international incident over a Pan American put down at Accra airport. il Time 88:41 N 11 '66
U.S. informs OAU of position on Ghana-Guinea dispute; text of note. Dept State Bul 55:790-1 N 21 '66
U.S. protests house arrest of Americans in Guinea. Dept State Bul 55:789 N 21 '66

Guyana
Prime Minister of Guyana visits the United States; exchange of greetings and exchange of toasts, July 21, 1966. L. B. Johnson; F. Burnham. Dept State Bul 55:229-31 Ag 15 '66
U.S. relinquishes 99-year lease to Atkinson field in Guyana. Dept State Bul 54:935 Je 13 '66

Haiti
Bailing out Duvalier; Inter-American development bank approves loan. R. D. Heinl, jr. New Repub 156:15-16 Ja 14 '67
Haiti: chaotic and corrupt. G. R. Latortue. il Nation 203:539-41 N 21 '66

India
America, India, and Pakistan; chance for a fresh start. S. S. Harrison. Harper 233:56-60+ Jl '66
New bloom; Mrs Gandhi's visit. il Time 87:25-6 Ap 8 '66
President Johnson and Prime Minister Gandhi of India confer at Washington; exchange of greetings; exchange of toasts; with joint communique, March 29, 1966. L. B. Johnson; I. Gandhi. Dept State Bul 54:598-605 Ap 18 '66
US, India and Pakistan: coming showdown over arms. New Repub 155:11 S 17 '66

Indonesia
Friends again? Sr Schol 88:18 My 13 '66
Indonesian foreign minister meets with Secretary Rusk; joint statement, September 27, 1966. D. Rusk and A. Malik. Dept State Bul 55:652 O 24 '66

Iran
Politics of anti-Americanism: in Iran. M. Tehranian. il Nation 203:415-18 O 24 '66

Israel
U.S. and Israel reaffirm ties of friendship; exchange of toasts, August 2, 1966. L. B. Johnson; Z. Shazar. Dept State Bul 55:346-7 S 5 '66

UNITED STATES—Foreign relations—*Cont.*

Japan

Alexis Johnson's new job in Japan. A. Axelbank. New Repub 155:19-20 Ag 27 '66

Bridge builder: E. O. Reischauer's part in mending broken dialogue. il Newsweek 68:20 Ag 8 '66

Dialogue restored: American ambassador to Tokyo. il Time 88:23 Ag 5 '66

Word from an expert. il Time 88:16-17 Ag 26 '66

Jordan

U.S. comments on sales of aircraft to Jordan; Department statement; April 2, 1966. Dept State Bul 54:663 Ap 25 '66

Korea (Republic)

Visits to Thailand and Korea; text of joint statement, November 2, 1966. L. B. Johnson and C. H. Park. Dept State Bul 55:777-80 N 21 '66

See also
Korean war, 1950-1953—American participation

Laos

President Johnson confers with the Prime Minister of Laos; statements at news conference, October 13, 1966. L. B. Johnson; Souvanna Phouma. Dept State Bul 55:667-9 O 31 '66

Latin America

Adjustable Linc; L. Gordon appointed Vaughn's successor. Newsweek 67:54 Ja 31 '66

Assessment of current American influence in Latin America. R. R. Rubottom, jr. Ann Am Acad 366:117-25 Jl '66

Challenge of the Americas; address, April 15, 1966. L. B. Johnson. Vital Speeches 32:418-20 My 1 '66; Same with title Address at dedication of Abraham Lincoln statue. Dept State Bul 54:727-31 My 9 '66

Correspondence with Theodore Draper & Commentary, appropriate & inappropriate. T. Draper; J. B. Bender; P. Bethel. Nat R 18:823-7 Ag 23 '66

Cry for progress. il Time 87:39 Ap 8 '66

Dominican crisis; case study in American policy. T. Draper; discussion. il Nat R 18:99-100, 107-14 F 8 '66

Foreign assistance program for Latin America in 1967; statement, May 2, 1966. L. Gordon. Dept State Bul 54:977-86 Je 20 '66

Latin America, to date. Commonweal 83:628-9 Mr 4 '66

Litany of woe; Robert Kennedy's Senate speech. Newsweek 67:71 My 23 '66

New boy at State: S. Linowitz. il Newsweek 69:53-4 Ja 16 '67

Panorama of challenge and response in Latin America; address, September 28, 1966. L. Gordon. Dept State Bul 55:644-8 O 24 '66

President hails fifth anniversary of the Alliance for progress; statement, March 14, 1966. L. B. Johnson. Dept State Bul 54:537-8 Ap 4 '66

Rocky road for the alliance. il Bsns W p 126+ Je 11 '66

Soldiers all; race for big arms. Newsweek 68:56 N 14 '66

Tensions in U.S.-Latin American relations. W. J. Hinson. Christian Cent 83:1004-7 Ag 17 '66

U.S. policy in Latin America. R. M. Schneider. bibliog f Cur Hist 51:257-63 N '66

Voice of Latin America, by W. Benton. Review
Nation 202:495-6 Ap 25 '66. J. Gerassi

Mexico

Chain of common interest uniting the United States and Mexico; remarks, February 10, 1966. D. Rusk. Dept State Bul 54:365-7 Mr 7 '66

Intuition's reward; President Johnson's visit to Mexico. il Time 87:19-20 Ap 22 '66

Mexican tonic; L. B. Johnson's visit. il Newsweek 67:22+ Ap 25 '66

Our debts to Mexico. H. E. Fey. Christian Cent 83:1594-5 D 28 '66

President Johnson visits Mexico city; remarks upon his arrival, April 14, 1966; address at dedication of Abraham Lincoln statue, remarks to the staff of the U.S. embassy, with text of joint statement, April 15, 1966. L. B. Johnson. Dept State Bul 54:726-33 My 9 '66

Middle East

Rival Arabs. P. Seale and I. Beeson. New Repub 155:11 Ag 27 '66

U.S. calls for peaceful settlement of Middle East disputes; urges U.S.S.R. to move for peace in Viet-Nam; texts of statements, July 29, August 3, 1966. J. J. Sisco. Dept State Bul 55:313-17 Ag 29 '66

Nicaragua

President Schick of Nicaragua visits Washington; texts of greetings exchanged, June 9, 1966. L. B. Johnson; R. Schick-Gutiérrez. Dept State Bul 55:14-17 Jl 4 '66

Pakistan

America, India, and Pakistan; chance for a fresh start. S. S. Harrison. Harper 233:56-60+ Jl '66

US, India and Pakistan; coming showdown over arms. New Repub 155:11 S 17 '66

Panama

Yankees welcome in Panama again. il U S News 61:89 S 5 '66

Philippines

Formula from the Philippines. il Time 88:22-3 S 23 '66

Johnson and Marcos. M. Meadows. New Repub 155:12 S 17 '66

President Marcos of the Philippines visits the United States; exchanges of greetings and toasts, September 14, 1966; with joint communique, September 15, 1966. L. B. Johnson; F. Marcos. Dept State Bul 55:526-34 O 10 '66

U.S. and Philippines; drawing closer? il U S News 60:84-5 Ap 4 '66

What an ally sees ahead for U.S. in Asia; interview, ed. by K. M. Chrysler. F. E. Marcos. U S News 61:66-9 S 19 '66

Poland

President marks Poland's national millennium; calls for wider East-West contracts; remarks, with text of proclamation, May 3, 1966. L. B. Johnson. Dept State Bul 54:794-7 My 23 '66

Portugal

Bombers for Portugal. Commonweal 85:68 O 21 '66; Reply with rejoinder. J. T. Curtin. 85:238-9 N 25 '66

Rhodesia

Crackdown on Rhodesia; another country for U.S. to rescue? il U S News 62:28-9 Ja 2 '67

Crisis in Southern Rhodesia; address, January 28, 1966. G. M. Williams. Dept State Bul 54:265-70 F 21 '66

Registration of Rhodesian agent implies no recognition by U.S. Department statement, February 12, 1966. Dept State Bul 54:318 F 28 '66

Rhodesia: cross-currents in a turbulent continent. il Sr Schol 87:6-9+ Ja 14 '66

Security council authorizes U.K. to use force to divert oil shipments bound for Rhodesia; statement, April 9, 1966. A. J. Goldberg. Dept State Bul 54:713-17 My 2 '66

Under fire: U.S. policy on Rhodesia; excerpts from letter. D. G. Acheson. U S News 61:13 D 26 '66

U.S. and U.K. hold talks on Southern Rhodesia; joint statement, December 1, 1966. Dept State Bul 55:965 D 26 '66

U.S. informs U.N. Security council of action on Rhodesian agent; letter to Security council, containing letter to H. J. C. Hooper, February 28, 1966. A. J. Goldberg. Dept State Bul 54:588-9 Ap 11 '66

U.S. moves to support sanctions against Southern Rhodesia; announcements of December 30, 1965; January 10, 1966. Dept State Bul 54:157 Ja 31 '66

U.S. urges Security council unity on Rhodesian problem; statement, May 18, 1966. A. J. Goldberg. Dept State Bul 54:986-91 Je 20 '66

Russia

After the big freeze, defrosting? summary of address. L. B. Johnson. Newsweek 68:42+ O 17 '66

After the cold war; prospective issues of U.S.-Soviet relations. C. O. Lerche, jr. il Nation 202:673-6 Je 6 '66

As LBJ prepares for Asia trip: a formula for uniting Europe; excerpts from address, October 7, 1966. U S News 61:80 O 17 '66

Bolshevik invasion of the West, by L. F. Budenz. Review
Nat R 18:475+ My 17 '66. E. Lyons

UNITED STATES—Foreign relations—Russia
—*Continued*
Canada's role in East-West relations; address, March 11, 1966. P. Martin. Vital Speeches 32:409-14 Ap 15 '66
Interview; reprint from America illustrated, September, 1966. L. B. Johnson. Dept State Bul 55:574-8 O 17 '66
Is a deal with Russia stirring? with analysis by F. B. Stevens. il U S News 61:46-9 N 7 '66
Mutual trust? Sr Schol 89:20-1 O 21 '66
Neither liberty nor safety, by N. F. Twining. Review
    Nat R 18:923 S 20 '66. J. Burnham
Pax Russo-Americana? Sino-Soviet dispute. G. Lichtheim. Commentary 41:60-5 Ap '66
Proliferation and Soviet-American relations. R. C. Tucker. Bul Atomic Sci 22:14-18 O '66
Russian equation; LBJ urges new spirit of common endeavor between Moscow and Washington. il Time 88:11-12 S 2 '66
Search for agreements in the cause of peace; address, August 26, 1966. L. B. Johnson. Dept State Bul 55:410-13 S 19 '66
Thaw: accentuating the positive; cordial week of Soviet-American talks. il Newsweek 68:55-6 O 24 '66
Thinker; Z. Brzezinski. por Newsweek 68:44 N 14 '66
U.S. rejects Soviet allegations on air accident in Spain; aide memoire, February 25. 1966. Dept State Bul 54:397 Mr 14 '66
U.S. views on developments in Viet-Nam given to U.S.S.R: Russian charges of US threat to Soviet merchant vessels; texts of U.S. note. July 23 and Soviet note. July 9. 1966. Dept State Bul 55:213-14 Ag 8 '66
Up the back stairs. il Time 88:33-4 O 21 '66
Voice of freedom. D. Lawrence. U S News 60:104 Ap 4 '66
Why Russia is our biggest danger; interview. W. E. Griffith. Read Digest 89:119-23 Ag '66
    See also
Cuban crisis. 1962
United States—Treaties—Russia

Saudi Arabia
President Johnson and King Faisal of Saudi Arabia exchange views on matters of common interest; exchange of greetings, exchange of toasts, June 21; with text of joint communique, June 22, 1966. L. B. Johnson; Feisal. Dept State Bul 55:38-42 Jl 11 '66

Senegal
President Senghor of Senegal visits the United States; exchange of greetings; with exchange of toasts; September 28, 1966. L. S. Senghor; L. B. Johnson. Dept State Bul 55:649-52 O 24 '66

South Africa
Africa and the American right; question of who originated the study, Apartheid and United Nations collective measures. V. McKay. New Repub 154:13-16 Mr 26 '66
Dubious dialogue. Nation 202:316 Mr 21 '66
Missionaries or mercenaries? address, May 9, 1966. A. E. Rupert. Vital Speeches 32:754-60 O 1 '66
South Africa. Commonweal 84:405-6 Jl 1 '66; Reply. L. Swidler. 84:569+ S 16 '66
South Africa: an unhysterical report. C. B. Marshall. il Nat R 18:724-9 Jl 26 '66
United States policy toward South Africa; statement, March 1, 1966. G. M. Williams. Dept State Bul 54:430-40 Mr 21 '66
U.S. rejects South African charge of interference; text of aide memoire. September 21, 1966. Dept State Bul 55:567-8 O 10 '66

Taiwan
Messenger; Rusk mission. il Newsweek 68:34 Jl 18 '66

Thailand
Advise and dissent. Newsweek 68:54 N 14 '66
Does intervention work? W. Pfaff. Commonweal 85:45-6 O 14 '66
Memo from Thailand. S. Castan. Look 30:90+ Mr 22 '66
President Johnson meets with Thai cabinet ministers; White House announcement. October 7, 1966. Dept State Bul 55:669 O 31 '66
Sinews on the Gulf; Thai bases. Time 88:26 Ag 19 '66
Thailand: its meaning for the U.S. B. K. Gordon. bibliog f il Cur Hist 52:16-21+ Ja '67

U.S. and Thailand sign treaty of amity and economic relations. Dept State Bul 54:991-2 Je 20 '66
Vice President reviews Asian problems with Thai premier; joint communique, February 15, 1966. H. H. Humphrey and T. Kittikachorn. Dept State Bul 54:396-7 Mr 14 '66

Vietnam
One step after another. New Repub 155:9 O 8 '66

Vietnam (Democratic Republic)
Establishing credibility; Administration's quest for peace. Commonweal 85:67-8 O 21 '66
Hawks and realists. W. Pfaff. Commonweal 83:492-3 Ja 28 '66; Reply. D. Sullivan. 84:86-7 Ap 8 '66

Vietnam (Republic)
Adlai Stevenson's son releases father's letter to Viet critics. il Sr Schol 87:20 Ja 14 '66
America and Britain: unity of purpose; address, March 4, 1966. A. J. Goldberg. Dept State Bul 54:539-43 Ap 4 '66
Analogies & images: thoughtways of foreign policy. W. F. Whyte. Nation 202:641-5 My 30 '66
Atlantic report. Atlan 217:6+ Je '66
Atlantic report. D. Kiker. Atlan 218:4. 8+ N '66
Camera obscura; disparate readings of Hawaiian conference in U.S. press. Time 87:41 F 18 '66
Carrot and stick; Honolulu conference. Commonweal 83:599 F 25 '66
Challenge came in Vietnam; address, November 15, 1966. E. G. Wheeler. Vital Speeches 33:130-3 D 15 '66
Chinese puzzle; if China enters the war. H. Brandon. Sat R 49:18 Mr 5 '66
Crisis of confidence; Vietnam; discussion between two senators and two student representatives. il Mlle 63:272-3+ Ag '66
Cross-purposes and crossed fingers; LBJ's views. il Newsweek 67:25-6 My 30 '66
Dawk talk. il Time 88:20 S 30 '66
Debate in search of a forum; Vietnam congress. Reporter 34:16+ Ja 27 '66
Dilemmas and agonies for all. N. Cousins. Sat R 49:32 F 5 '66
Dissent & defeat; administration's critics. il Time 87:24 Mr 11 '66
Dissent; it questions and attacks U.S. involvement in Vietnam; interviews, D. Nevin. il Life 60:56B-60+ F 25 '66
Does Vietnam need a supreme commander? D. Warner. il Reporter 34:11-15 Je 30 '66
Exhaustive, explicit & enough; Senate foreign relations committee proceedings on television. il Time 87:21-3 F 25 '66
Fishing for peace; M. Matsuda's ideas for U.S. paradise on earth. il Newsweek 67:46 Je 6 '66
Free world's stake in Viet-Nam; address, October 19, 1966. D. MacArthur, 2d. Dept State Bul 55:745-50 N 14 '66
Freedom to end freedom; latest Mansfield declaration. M. Ascoli. Reporter 34:10 My 5 '66
Getting in deeper. New Repub 154:5-6 F 19 '66
Goliath's dilemma; hypocrisy about our unselfish aims. Nation 202:474-5 Ap 25 '66
Grand alliance; views of Senator Fulbright and G. F. Kennan. Reporter 34:16 F 24 '66
Greatest drama. il Time 87:19-20 Ap 1 '66
Hawaii conference; criticism of Johnson's Vietnam approach. il Time 87:19-20 F 11 '66
Honolulu meeting, and after; with press comments. il Sr Schol 88:3-4 F 25 '66
Hung-up on Vietnam; President Johnson suspended between distasteful alternatives. il New Repub 155:5-6 D 10 '66
If America is asked to leave Vietnam. U S News 60:21 Ap 25 '66
If the American people lose heart. America 115:25 Jl 9 '66
If told to leave. Commonweal 84:142 Ap 22 '66
Importance of obscurity; Time essay. Time 87:27 My 6 '66
In the eye of the storm. Time 87:21 Ap 15 '66
Initiative for peace; statement, September 22, 1966. A. J. Goldberg. Dept State Bul 55:518-25 O 10 '66; Same with title Vietnam settlement. Vital Speeches 33:34-8 N 1 '66

UNITED STATES—Foreign service—*Continued*
Two-way communication with the education
community; excerpt from address, June
16, 1966. W. J. Crockett. Dept State Bul
55:72-5 Jl 18 '66
See also
Women as foreign service employees

Foreign service institute

Foreign service institute and the academic
community; excerpt from address, June 16,
1966. G. V. Allen. Dept State Bul 55:76-7
Jl 18 '66
Our man in Saigon, and how he got there.
L. Hydle. il Am Ed 3:6-8 D '66

Forest service

Forest service appointments. Nat Parks Mag
40:23 My '66
Forest service special areas. Nat Parks Mag
40:20 Je '66
Friendly debate between two professionals;
how much land for national forest recrea-
tion? letters. C. Granger; B. L. Orell. Am
For 72:30-1+ Ja; 12+ F '66
National forests come alive; new vistas
through VIS. D. B. Huyck. il Am For 72:12-
16 Ap '66
Page Teddy Roosevelt or, here we go again;
bad features of Senator Moss's bill. C. H.
Reidel. il Outdoor Life 137:4+ F '66
Skiing on sawdust; field testing and experi-
mentation by U.S. forest service. R. K.
Peter. il Parks & Rec 1:245+ Mr '66
Wilderness research, a start; studies on un-
manned registration stations at Three
Sisters wilderness area and the Mountain
Lakes wild area. W. B. Morse. il Am For
72:32-3+ Je '66

General accounting office

GAO may press probe of federal R&D. H. M.
David. Miss & Roc 18:15 F 21 '66
GAO report raps contractor operation of
business aircraft. Aviation W 85:33 S 19 '66
Profits of war; putsch against McNamara.
H. L. Nieburg. Nation 203:696-701 D 26 '66
Where government can cut spending; inter-
view. E. B. Staats. il Nations Bsns 54:42-
3+ D '66

General services administration

1967 and 1968 GSA standards. Consumer Rep
31:198 Ap '66

Government

See United States—Politics and government

Government property

Annals of law; Lewis and Clark case: United
States government's claim to field notes.
C. Tomkins. New Yorker 42:105-6+ O 29
'66

Government publications

See Government publications

Health, education and welfare, Department of

Act provides activity; Older Americans act.
Sci N 89:446 Je 4 '66
Confusion compounded; HEW's desegregation
guidelines. Reporter 35:16+ O 20 '66
Death of a taboo; creating deputy assistant
secretary for science and population. News-
week 67:32 My 16 '66
Gardner hews out the Great society. il News-
week 67:22-4+ F 28 '66
Gradualism at HEW; concerning discrimina-
tion of hospitals approved to participate in
medicare program. D. Sanford. New Repub
155:8-10 Ag 27 '66
HEW assaults air pollution in U.S. cities.
B. J. Culliton. Sci N 90:458 N 26 '66
HEW; Gardner proposes reorganization. E.
Langer. Science 154:1151-2 D 2 '66
HEW shakeup for payoffs. B. Culliton. Sci N
90:415 N 19 '66
Medicare bonanza. S. Greenberg. il Nation
203:513-16 N 14 '66; Discussion. 204:34+
Ja 9 '67
Prime mover of the Great society; Secretary
of health, education & welfare. J. W.
Gardner. il Bsns W p 130-2+ My 21 '66
Public health service to reorganize, expand.
Sci N 90:328 O 22 '66
Sense of what should be. il Time 89:16-21
Ja 29 '67
When everybody is on welfare. il U S News
61:72 Ag 1 '66

Appropriations and expenditures

HEW appropriation hearings under way. G.
Krettek and E. D. Cooke. ALA Bul 60:
328-9 Ap '66
$10.2 billion; how to spend it. il Newsweek
67:29 F 28 '66
White Wednesday; Senate debate on HEW's
desegregation guidelines. New Repub 155:5-6
O 8 '66

Historic houses, etc.

Fruits of the legacy; Vanderbilt houses. il
Am Heritage 17:12-13 Ap '66
Home & garden tours. House & Gard 129:
125-6 Mr '66
How to use landmarks in program. W. L.
Landahl. il Parks & Rec 1:642-3 Ag '66
Must landmarks go? excerpts from The liv-
ing end. R. Starr. il Horizon 8:48-59 Sum
'66
Neglected American treasures. M. Frome. il
Holiday 39:129-34 My '66
Tracking down a heritage; reblazing the
wilderness route of Lewis and Clark. D.
B. Alexander. il Parks & Rec 1:224-6 Mr
'66
See also
Henry Ford museum and Greenfield Village,
Dearborn, Mich.
Williamsburg, Va.
also subhead Historic houses, etc. under
names of states, cities, etc. e.g. New York
(state)—Historic houses, etc.

History

American primer, ed. by D. J. Boorstin.
Review
Sat R 49:35-6 N 5 '66. R. Walters, jr
Shackles of power, by J. Dos Passos. Review
Sat R 49:99 My 7 '66. H. Hansen
See also
Cities and towns—United States—History
Frontier and pioneer life—United States
Presidents—United States
United States—Church history
United States—Economic history
United States—Foreign relations—History
United States—Social history
also subhead History under names of re-
gions, states, etc. e.g. California—History

Art

See History in art

Bibliography

Articles and other books received; comp.
by W. Gray. See issues of American his-
torical review
New books on American history. H. L.
Hurwitz. Sr Schol 88:sup 12+ Mr 4; sup9-10
Mr 11 '66

Textbooks

History is a dangerous subject; findings of
Anglo-United States team survey of sec-
ondary school textbooks. R. A. Billington;
discussion. Sat R 49:68+ F 19 '66
Negro history in the public schools: trends
and prospects. W. F. Brazziel. Negro Hist
Bul 29:35-6+ N '65
Negro in modern American history text-
books, comp. by I. Sloan. P. Schrag. Sat
R 50:74 Ja 21 '67
Treatment of the Negro in American history
school textbooks. S. Axelrod. bibliog Negro
Hist Bul 29:135-6+, 167 Mr-Ap '66

Discovery and exploration

See also
America—Discovery and exploration

Colonial period

British-America's birthplace. H. D. Craw-
ford. il Am For 72:14-17+ S '66
New nation in a New World. W. R. Jacobs.
Sat R 49:35-6 N 26 '66
See also
Colonial life and customs

Revolution

Lady Knox. D. Forbes-Robertson. il Am
Heritage 17:46-7+ Ap '66
Practical revolutionaries. il Sat Eve Post
239:102 Jl 2 '66
See also
Boston massacre, 1770

Revolution—Bicentennial

Bicentennial commission established by Congress. Pub W 190:56 Ag 22 '66

UNITED STATES—History—*Continued*

Revolution—French participation

French volunteer. M. Bishop. il Am Heritage 17:46-9+ Ag '66

Revolution—Naval operations

Battle at Valcour Island: Benedict Arnold as hero. T. W. Hubbard. il Am Heritage 17:8-11+ O '66

I have not yet begun to fight. Sr Schol 89:5 S 23 '66

Constitutional period, 1789-1809

Conspiracy and trial of Aaron Burr; excerpts from Shackles of power. J. Dos Passos. il Am Heritage 17:4-7+ F '66; Reply with rejoinder. S. E. Burr, jr. 17: 91 Ag '66

Nineteenth century

House divides, by P. I. Wellman. Review Sat R 49:37 F 12 '66. H. Hansen

War with Mexico, 1845-1848

Our first foreign war; letters, ed. with introd. by W. F. Goetzmann. B. Upton. il Am Heritage 17:18-27+ Je '66

Civil war

Lee raised his hat. J. Ritter. Negro Hist Bul 29:59-60 D '65

Princely service; excerpts from Civil war album of paintings by the Prince de Joinville. A. Maurois. il Am Heritage 17:52-63+ Ap '66

See also

Reconstruction (Civil war)

Civil war—Bibliography

Lincolniana in 1965; the Civil war centennial. B. E. Wheeler. il Hobbies 70:28-9+ F '66

Civil war—Historiography

On writing about the Civil war. B. Catton. il Am Heritage 17:104-5 Ap '66

Civil war—Negro troops

Note on two Va. Negro Civil war soldiers: one Union, one Confederate. C. Cahill. il Negro Hist Bul 29:39-40 N '65

Civil war—Personal narratives

Harold Frederic's stories of York state; ed. by T. F. O'Donnell. Review Sat R 49:59+ Je 11 '66. R. H. Goldstone

1865-1898

See also

Little Big Horn, Battle of the. 1876
Reconstruction (Civil war)

1918-1941

Time between the wars, by J. Daniels. Review
Sat R 49:28 S 3 '66. H. Hansen

1933-1945

Place of Franklin D. Roosevelt in history; address, May 1965. A. Nevins. il Am Heritage 17:12-15+ Je '66

World war, 1939-1945
See World war, 1939-1945—United States

1941-

Great leap, by J. Brooks. Review
Sat R 49:38 N 5 '66. R. Stein

History, Naval

See also
United States—History—Revolution—Naval operations

House of representatives

See United States—Congress—House of representatives

Housing and home finance agency

Weaver's HUD. New Repub 154:8 Ja 29 '66

Housing and urban development, Department of

Are cities livable? J. O'Gara. Commonweal 83:656 Mr 11 '66

Cities need social plan; federal funds for Demonstration cities program. P. McBroom. Sci N 90:416 N 19 '66

First Negro Cabinet officer. Sr Schol 88:19 F 4 '66

Great society's advance man. il Bsns W p51-2+ Ja 22 '66

Hope for the heart; HUD's responsibilities. il Time 87:29-33 Mr 4 '66

HUD's troubles; new Department of transportation? Reporter 34:18-19 F 24 '66

Seven winners named for urban design excellence. il Am City 81:89 N '66

Urban renaissance, or boondoggle? Demonstration cities program. il Bsns W p 141-2 O 29 '66

Weaver's HUD. New Repub 154:8 Ja 29 '66

Immigration and naturalization service

Travel and domestic controls. M. T. Noto. Ann Am Acad 367:73-84 S '66

Indian affairs, Bureau of

Udall and the Indians. New Repub 154:8 Ap 30 '66

Where the real poverty is; plight of American Indians. il U S News 60:106-8 Ap 25 '66

See also
Indians of North America—Government relations

Industrial college of the armed forces

Where defense decision-makers learn the trade. il Bsns W p52-4 F 5 '66

Industries

Economics of technological change. A. P. Carter. il Sci Am 214:25-31 bibliog(p 140) Ap '66

Industry and the economy; the big squeeze. il Sr Schol 89:16-17 D 9 '66

Industry: will what's gone up come down? il Sr Schol 88:8-9 Ap 1 '66

Placing the bets; capital-spending plans. Newsweek 67:82 Mr 14 '66

Technological competition: Europe vs. U.S. J. B. Quinn. il Harvard Bsns R 44:113-16+ Jl '66

Technology gap; Europe's fear of falling victim to American economic conquest; Time essay. Time 89:18-19 Ja 13 '67

Three R's=billions; companies dealing in educational services, teaching machines, textbooks and instructional aids. il Newsweek 68:72-4 Jl 11 '66

Where the industries of the seventies will come from. L. Lessing. il Fortune 75:96-9+ Ja '67

See also
Industrial mobilization
Shipbuilding
United States—Economic conditions
West—Industries
   also subhead United States under names of industries, e.g. Aluminum industry and trade—United States

Information agency

Atlantic report. D. Kiker. Atlan 219:6+ Ja '67

Films from Uncle Sam. il Newsweek 67:109-10+ Ap 18 '66

Hidden ingredient: books that are midwived by USIA. Nation 203:373 O 17 '66

IMG liquidation plan being formulated. Pub W 190:55 O 31 '66

Of junkets & the USIA. Time 88:43 Ag 26 '66

Propaganda junkets; subsidized visits of European and Asian newsmen to Vietnam for pro-America propaganda. Nation 203:173 S 5 '66

USIA to disclose subsidies to publishers. Pub W 190:37 O 17 '66

Information service

Saigon follies? newsmen accuse USIS of withholding news. Newsweek 68:54+ Ag 15 '66

Institute for applied technology

Building from the idea out. Sci N 91:41 Ja 14 '67

Intellectual life

American philosophy is dead; decline from golden age to an academic cult. L. S. Feuer. il N Y Times Mag p30-1+ Ap 24 '66; Discussion. p22+ My 8 '66

American scholarship and the cultural image abroad. W. W. Brickman. Sch & Soc 94: 373 N 12 '66

Arts, the humanities, and the federal government: adaptation of address, July 1966. R. L. Stevens. ALA Bul 60:900-3 O '66

Life and times of Thomas Bailey; Aldrich: address, October 7, 1965. M. S. Cosgrave. bibliog il Horn Bk 42:223-32, 350-5, 464-73 Ap-Ag '66

UNITED STATES—Intellectual life—*Continued*
Speaking out; the courts must curb culture.
T. Wolfe. Sat Eve Post 239:10+ D 3 '66
Young in the thirties. L. Trilling. Commentary 41:43-51 My '66
See also
Books and reading
Colleges and universities—United States
Education—United States
New York (city)—Intellectual life
United States—Popular culture

Interagency committee on oceanography

ICO effort termed incomplete picture of national program. R. W. Niblock. Miss & Roc 18:23 Ap 4 '66

Interior, Department of

Leopold committee assignment; Advisory board on wildlife and game management. Nat Parks Mag 40:20 Je '66
Oceanography: Interior department bids for a major role. L. J. Carter. Science 154: 749-51 N 11 '66
Page Teddy Roosevelt or, here we go again; bad features of Senator Moss's bill. C. H. Reidel. il Outdoor Life 137:4+ F '66
Wilderness regulations of the Department of the interior. Liv Wildn 30:54-9 Spr '66
See also
United States—Federal water pollution control administration
United States—Fish and wildlife service
United States—Outdoor recreation, Bureau of

Internal revenue service

Appraisals and revenooers; gifts of books, letters or manuscripts to institutions or organizations; excerpts from address. R. G. Newman. il Am Heritage 17:82-4 Je '66
Computers get results on taxes. U S News 60:81-2 F 7 '66
Conservationists and the IRS. New Repub 155:7 D 3 '66
Educational deductions: IRS wants to tighten up. E. Langer. Science 153:845-6 Ag 19 '66
Electronic eyes are watching your tax returns; National computer center, Martinsburg, W.Va. T. Irwin. il Pop Mech 125: 94-8+ Mr '66
Green light ahead for swap funds. Bsns W p 174+ N 5 '66
IRS defines professional corporation for tax purposes. Arch Rec 139:154-5 F '66
Meet the Monster that checks your taxes. J. A. Morris. Read Digest 90:177-8+ Ja '67
Revenuer and the red in the red; Albert Deschenes' witch-hunt on R. G. Lenske. New Repub 155:9 N 19 '66
Tax-appeal ordeal. W. R. Frye. Reporter 34: 21-4 My 5 '66
Tax due now on savings accounts. U S News 60:115-16 Mr 14 '66
What are your rights if IRS audits your tax return? F. Bailey, jr. Suc Farm 64:41+ Mr '66
Your tax return may be questioned this year. il Changing T 20:21-3 Mr '66

Anecdotes, facetiae, satire, etc.
No taxee, no shirtee. J. G. Dunne. il Sat Eve Post 239:20 Ap 9 '66

Interoceanic canal commission

Progress of Interoceanic canal studies reported to Congress; text of White House announcement; with text of President Johnson's letter of transmittal, August 15, 1966. Dept State Bul 55:349-50 S 5 '66

Interstate commerce commission

Eastern rail mergers' bumpy track; ICC recommendation to add three small Eastern lines to proposed Norfolk and Western-Chesapeake and Ohio merger. Bsns W p49 D 31 '66
Green light for biggest rail merger, meaning for others. il U S News 60:64-5 My 9 '66
ICC lays out the route; merger of Pennsylvania and New York central. il Bsns W p35-7 Ap 30 '66
Investors stay off the rails; result of ICC rail merger decisions. il Bsns W p 139-40 My 7 '66
Merger rivals tell it to the ICC; fight over Union Pacific-Rock Island merger. il Bsns W p 135-6+ My 14 '66
New rules for household movers; mildly consumer-oriented. Consumer Rep 31:450-1 S '66

Transportation outlook; rail mergers. Bsns W p71 My 28 '66
Truckers drive hard for new rate schedules. Bsns W p 125-6+ O 29 '66

Job corps

Bad marks for Bismarck; reaction to job corps center. Christian Cent 83:293-4 Mr 9 '66
Conversations parents never hear. il Look 30:61 S 20 '66
Is the Job corps conservation program working? N. T. Schweitzer. il Am For 72:18-21+ Ag '66
Job corps on the job; Austin, Tex. parks and recreation department. W. G. Leddick. il Parks & Rec 1:839 O '66
Job; Gary job corps training center, San Marcos, Tex. C. S. Carleton. il Am Ed 2: 28-32 N '66
New social-industrial complex; address, July 13, 1966. L. M. Spencer. Vital Speeches 32: 721-5 S 15 '66
Open house at Tongue Point; library of Center in Astoria, Ore; with bibliography. E. Pruitt. il Library J 91:332-4+ Ja 15 '66
Out of the Job corps, into a job. il Bsns W p32-3 Ja 29 '66
Recreation and the job corps. R. Kraus. il Parks & Rec 1:898-900+ N '66
Reporter at large; Camp Kilmer, N.J. J. Bainbridge. New Yorker 42:112+ My 21 '66
This month's feature; Congress & the Johnson poverty program. Cong Digest 45:67-96 Mr '66
When a corporation turns toward sociology; address, April 18, 1966. B. Oldfield. Vital Speeches 32:427-9 My 1 '66
Where the action isn't; Camp Parks. Pleasanton. Calif. R. L. Hanlin. New Repub 155: 7-8 S 3 '66
See also
United States—Youth corps

Joint chiefs of staff

How to fight the war in Vietnam; growing differences between Pentagon and the President. il U S News 60:37 Ap 11 '66
Joint chiefs wear a different hat; administration's top military advisers. il Bsns W p68-72 Jl 30 '66

Justice, Department of

Alexander case; defense committee ordered to register. Nation 203:69 Jl 25 '66
Ameliorating hardships under the immigration laws. C. Gordon. bibliog f Ann Am Acad 367:85-92 S '66
Family affair; the Clarks. il Newsweek 68: 31 D 5 '66
From the trustbusters; guidelines for businessmen. il U S News 61:46+ Jl 25 '66
Government asks ban against Valachi memoirs. Pub W 189:56-7 My 23 '66
Now U.S. gets JFK autopsy photos. il U S News 61:81 N 14 '66
See also
United States—Federal bureau of investigation

Antitrust division
Anchor in the past; antitrust cases. il Time 87:85 Je 24 '66
Guidelines for fair competition; interview. D. F. Turner. il U S News 60:76-80+ F 21 '66
High court tightens the antitrust reins; FTC can stall mergers while legality is tested. il Bsns W p40-1 Je 18 '66
Justice in a lather over soap ad outlays; investigating advertising spending in the packaged soap and detergent industry. Bsns W p44-5 N 5 '66
Justice toughens line on price agreements; indictments in plumbing industry. Bsns W p43 O 15 '66
Split vision jumbles the merger picture; top antitrusters Paul Rand Dixon and Donald F. Turner. Bsns W p54 Mr 26 '66
Top trustbuster, scholarly and tough; D. F. Turner. Bsns W p 166+ Mr 12 '66

Labor, Department of

His goal is full employment; W. Wirtz's goal. I. Ross. il Read Digest 89:119-23 S '66
New puzzle; the LBJ plan for a business-labor merger; concerning State-of-the-Union message. il U S News 62:72-3 Ja 23 '67
Second time around; L. B. Johnson's call for merger with Commerce department. il Newsweek 69:75 Ja 23 '67

UNITED STATES—Labor, Department of —*Continued*
U.S. labor launches road show in Rio; sponsorship of worker-to-worker program. il Bsns W p98-100 F 12 '66
See also
United States—Employment security, Bureau of

Labor policy
Air strike turns into political hot potato; legislators debate who should issue the back-to-work order. il Bsns W p29-31 Ag 6 '66
Collapse of Washington's labor policy. Bsns W p 148 Ag 6 '66
End to paralysis? need for new procedure to settle labor disputes in public-service facilities. Time 87:20 Ja 28 '66
So politics comes first? D. Lawrence. U S News 61:100 Ag 15 '66
Steel prices up; planes still down. il Newsweek 68:61-2+ Ag 15 '66
What the right to strike means. il U S News 61:23-5 Ag 15 '66
Why big strikes aren't stopped. il U S News 61:17-19 Ag 1 '66
See also
Labor laws and legislation—United States
United States—National labor relations board

Land management, Bureau of
Bureau of land management campground listing. Field & S 71:97 Je '66
BLM gets third director in five years; editorial. E. Linford. Am For 72:13 S '66
Frail lands; advanced stages of erosion. G. L. Turcott. il Am For 72:16-19 F '66
Parks on paper? P. M. Tilden. Nat Parks Mag 40:2 Mr '66

Library of Congress
Annual report of the Librarian of Congress for the fiscal year ending June 30, 1965; summary. L. Q. Mumford. Wilson Lib Bul 40:893 Je '66; Same. Library J 91:2786 Je 1 '66
Are they getting their money's worth? Special recruit program. C. A. Goodrum. il Library J 91:2759-64 Je 1 '66
Late news: experiment in distribution of cataloging information on magnetic tapes. Wilson Lib Bul 41:363 D '66
Library of Congress assistance to the Nation's libraries. A. McCormick and H. A. Carl. ALA Bul 60:159-63 F '66
LC in NY: preconference institute; sponsored by the cataloging and classification section. N. C. Batts. Library J 91:3649-50 Ag '66; Reply. D. Gore. 91:4386 O 1 '66
LC launches MARC program; test tapes shipped in October. Library J 91:5912 D 1 '66
L.C. study tests machines at sending catalog data. Pub W 189:42 Mr 14 '66
Lj and LC win Edpress awards for excellence in educational journalism. il Library J 91:3370 Jl '66
Rare Chinese library materials returned to Taiwan by LC. Library J 91:216 Ja 15 '66
Washington report: from the Library of Congress. E. Hamer and A. McCormick. See issues of ALA bulletin

Automation
Automation at LC: philosophy, plans, progress. S. S. Snyder; reply. B. A. Custer. Library J 91:1746 Ap 1 '66

Division for the blind
Library services to the physically handicapped; bills to extend Books-for-the-blind program. E. Hamer and A. McCormick. ALA Bul 60:421-2 My '66

Legislative reference service
Advising Congress; Legislative reference service. J. Ridgeway. New Repub 155:17-18 Jl 30 '66
Research in America; excerpts from the Science policy research divisions study on federal agencies projects on environmental pollution. J. Lear. Sat R 49:86-7 D 3 '66

Manuscript division
Acquisitions by the manuscript division of the Library of Congress. K. V. Hostick. Hobbies 71:105 S '66
Advisory committee appointed by LC on photocopying foreign manuscripts. Library J 91:3138+ Je 15 '66
Lincoln papers in the Stern bequest; reprint. J. M. Ediestein. Hobbies 70:110-12 F; 71:106-7+ Mr '66
Quarterly notes; recent acquisitions. K. V. Hostick. Hobbies 71:107+ My; 107+ Je; 105 O; 104+ N; 108-9 D '66; 109+ Ja '67

National program for acquisitions and cataloging
International breakthrough: account of the operational beginnings of the Shared cataloging program. L. Q. Mumford. il Library J 92:79-82 Ja 1 '67

Shared cataloging program
See United States—Library of Congress—National program for acquisitions and cataloging

Literary landmarks
See Literary landmarks

Manners and customs
See United States—Social life and customs

Maps
New guide to your vacationlands. H. E. Paine. il Nat Geog Mag 130:94-7, sup(folded map) Jl '66

Marine corps
Marine tactical data system detailed; evaluation of air operations central. R. Pay. il Miss & Roc 18:24-6 F 21 '66
Rebirth of the 5th marines; training at Camp Pendleton; with report by L. Norman. il Newsweek 68:33-4 Jl 11 '66

Forces in Vietnam
General Greene tells the story of Vietnam war; interview. W. M. Greene, jr. il U S News 61:34-40 S 5 '66; Same abr. with title Vietnam: progress and prospects. Read Digest 89:175-8+ N '66
Marine comes home from Vietnam. C. S. Wren. il Look 30:30-2+ Mr 8 '66
Marine control of air tested in combat. C. M. Plattner. il Aviation W 84:90-1+ F 14 '66
Marines blunt the invasion from the North; action in the DMZ; with report by M. Parker. il Life 61:30-9 O 28 '66
Rockpile: marines capture the Razorback and Hill 400. il Time 88:40-1 O 7 '66
Small, hard war in the Delta. D. Warner. il Reporter 35:27-8+ D 15 '66

Recreation
Recreation with the marines in Vietnam. D. V. Joyce. il Parks & Rec 1:842-4 O '66

Training
See Military training

Maritime administration
At sea with Johnson. J. Ridgeway. New Repub 154:10 Mr 5 '66

Military air transport service
See United States—Military airlift command

Military airlift command
Air cargo shows what it can do. il Bsns W p96-8+ Jl 16 '66
Continental shapes Pacific growth aims. W. H. Gregory. il Aviation W 85:45+ Ag 8 '66
House unit calls for improvement to fill gaps in tactical airlift. Aviation W 84:59 Je 6 '66
Jet use to be urged on Logair, Quicktrans; modernization of Military airlift command. G. C. Wilson. Aviation W 84:25 F 7 '66
MAC awards total $341 million. Aviation W 85:52 Jl 11 '66
MAC charter needs spurred by Vietnam. Aviation W 84:34 Je 27 '66
MAC forecasts long-term charter need. C. Brownlow. il Aviation W 85:65+ O 31 '66

Military cooperation
See Military assistance, American

Military policy
Escalation and the nuclear option, by B. Brodie. Review
Reporter 36:63-4 Ja 12 '67. T. W. Wolfe
Joint chiefs wear a different hat; administration's top military advisers. il Bsns W p68-72 Jl 30 '66
Military power: the limits of persuasion. J. M. Gavin. Sat R 49:18-22+ Jl 30 '66
Planning our military forces. H. Brown. For Affairs 45:277-90 Ja '67
Review of United States foreign and military policy; transcript of press conference, August 25, 1966. D. Rusk; R. S. McNamara; W. S. Gaud. Dept State Bul 55:413-24 S 19 '66

UNITED STATES—Military policy—*Continued*
Yarmolinsky & the cannibal; concerning address at University of Chicago law school. R. Stern. Nation 203:639-40 D 12 '66
  See also
United States—Defenses

Moral conditions

Call of the wild; questions and answers. A. Wood. il Seventeen 25:148-9+ Mr '66
Corrupted land, by F. J. Cook. Review
  New Repub 154:29+ Ap 2 '66. R. Yoakum
Ethics in an affluent society. C. McWilliams. Christian Cent 83:797-802 Je 22 '66
Hugh Hefner: I am in the center of the world; interview, ed. by O. Fallaci. H. Hefner. il Look 31:54-7 Ja 10 '67
I am a tired American; reprint. A. McIntosh. U S News 60:120 F 14 '66
Let's not panic at the new morality; excerpt from address, January 26, 1966. W. I. Nichols. Read Digest 89:75-8 Ag '66
Sex kick, by T. Coffin. Review
  Sat R 49:36-7 N 26 '66. R. J. Levin
What has happened to the moral climate in America? remarks, June 8, 1966. H. E. Talmadge. U S News 60:90-1 Je 27 '66
  See also
Crime and criminals—United States

National academy of sciences
See National academy of sciences

National advisory commission
on libraries

Balancing the Commission. E. Moon. Library J 92:35 Ja 1 '67
Commission on libraries set up by President. Pub W 190:44 S 19 '66
LBJ names Committee on libraries and National advisory commission. Library J 91:4590 O 1 '66
National advisory commission gets staff director from CLR. Library J 91:5908+ D 1 '66
President names library commission. G. Krettek and E. D. Cooke. Wilson Lib Bul 41:235 O '66
Ruggles named director Library advisory committee. Pub W 190:77 N 14 '66

National advisory council on international
monetary and financial policies

Council on international monetary policies set up; executive order, February 14, 1966. L. B. Johnson. Dept State Bul 54:404 Mr 14 '66

National aeronautics and space
administration

Achievement of space; address, March 15, 1966. R. C. Seamans, jr. Vital Speeches 32:527-33 Je 15 '66
Admen in orbit; NASA and the advertisers. D. Sanford. New Repub 155:13-15 D 17 '66
Bogies and budgets; federal budget time. New Repub 155:10 S 24 '66
Cryogenic engine is latest DOD/NASA joint project. Miss & Roc 18:31-2 My 30 '66
Information processing in NASA's library. M. S. Day. il Wilson Lib Bul 41:396-400+ D '66
Joint enterprises are now a going concern in the exciting field of space research; NASA projects since 1958. A. W. Frutkin. UNESCO Courier 19:13-14+ My '66
Manned flight planning gap delays Saturn development. G. Alexander. il Aviation W 85:58-9+ Ag 8 '66
NASA centers. M. Getler. il Tech W 19:48-52+ N 28 '66
NASA discloses new planetary schedule. H. Taylor. il Tech W 19:18-19 S 12 '66
NASA-Intelsat conclude contract for Apollo communications work. Aviation W 84:33 Ap 4 '66
[NASA issue] ed. by H. Taylor. il Tech W 19:43-52+ N 28 '66
NASA nearing critical Gemini decisions. W. J. Normyle. Aviation W 84:25 F 21 '66
NASA offers to train European scientists for U.S. space missions. W. J. Normyle. Aviation W 84:23 F 28 '66
NASA ponders Apollo team future. H. Taylor. il Miss & Roc 18:16 Ap 25 '66
NASA ponders Pioneer shot to Venus. H. Taylor. Miss & Roc 18:13 Ap 18 '66
NASA post-Apollo plan urged by Dec. 1. G. C. Wilson. Aviation W 85:26 Ag 8 '66
NASA presses research on limited war. Aviation W 85:75 Jl 4 '66

NASA recruits spacemen. il Sci N 90:275 O 8 '66
NASA report to Congress details planetary alternatives for future. W. J. Normyle. Aviation W 85:91+ S 19 '66
NASA reshapes deep space plan; Goddard to direct two new probes. Aviation W 85:30 N 28 '66
NASA tightening incentive fee system. il Aviation W 85:150+ Ag 15 '66
NASA to begin space rescue study. Miss & Roc 18:13 Ap 4 '66
NASA will battle to regain funds. Aviation W 84:29 My 2 '66
NASA's war against secrecy. J. Eberhart. il Sci N 89:492-3 Je 18 '66
Post-Apollo programs focusing on multi-purpose earth-orbiter. W. J. Normyle. Aviation W 85:17 D 26 '66
Rallying point. W. J. Coughlin. Tech W 19:50 Ag 22 '66
Scientist-astronauts: only the perspicacious need apply. L. J. Carter. Science 154:133-5 O 7 '66
Test of time. W. J. Coughlin. Tech W 19:152 Jl 25 '66
Webb orders analysis of headquarters organization. Tech W 20:20 Ja 16 '67
What made Gemini a success. il Bsns W p 106+ S 17 '66
  See also
United States—Space nuclear propulsion office

Ames research center

Ames flight simulation lab to be operational in January. il Miss & Roc 18:28 My 23 '66
Ames researchers find Mars produces life forms. Miss & Roc 18:23 F 14 '66
Effort focuses on man's judgment utility in space systems; Ames research center's advanced development work. W. E. Wilks. il Tech W 19:64-6+ N 28 '66

Appropriations and expenditures

After Apollo, why? Nation 204:36 Ja 9 '67
AEC space funding stretched moderately. K. Johnsen. il Aviation W 84:22-3 Ja 31 '66
Biosatellite program faces budget hurdle. Tech W 19:13 O 17 '66
But what comes after the moon? excerpt from address, November 11, 1966. R. E. Lapp. New Repub 155:10-12 N 19 '66
$5 billion sought to launch AAP, Voyager. H. Taylor. il Tech W 19:45-7 N 28 '66
Fund cuts, technical troubles slow surveyor, Voyager programs. J. Walsh. il Science 151:305-7 Ja 21 '66
Funds considered for Mars '69 landing probe. H. M. David. Miss & Roc 18:13 Mr 7 '66
House space report to ask detail on fiscal 1968 advanced plans. W. J. Normyle. Aviation W 84:30 Ap 18 '66
How space agency expects to fund OART and OTDA. H. Taylor. il Miss & Roc 18:16-17 F 14 '66
Increase in Voyager funds proposed. Miss & Roc 18:15 Mr 21 '66
Johnson approves $5.05 billion for NASA. H. Taylor. Tech W 20:17 Ja 9 '67
Lunar, planetary funds reapportioned. H. M. David. il Miss & Roc 18:15 F 14 '66
LBJ seen inclined to grant '68 request. H. Taylor. Tech W 19:13 D 5 '66
NASA authorized $5 billion. Tech W 19:23-4 Jl 25 '66
NASA cutback. Sky & Tel 31:71+ F '66
NASA cutback perils moon schedule. il Miss & Roc 18:25-30 Ja 31 '66
NASA details plans for FY '67 money. H. Taylor. il Miss & Roc 18:12-14 F 7 '66
NASA estimates advanced plans funds. W. J. Normyle. Aviation W 85:20-1 Ag 29 '66
NASA offers FY '68 budget choice. H. Taylor. Tech W 19:16-17 Jl 4 '66
NASA request cut $25 million. Aviation W 84:32 Ap 11 '66
NASA spending to approach $100 million. H. Taylor. Tech W 19:18 O 3 '66
NASA studying space station funding needs for FY 1968. H. Taylor. Tech W 19:16 O 10 '66
NASA to ask $1 billion next year for Apollo applications program. W. J. Normyle. Aviation W 84:30-1 Ap 25 '66
Post-Apollo station plans altered. W. J. Normyle. Aviation W 85:22-3 D 5 '66
Senate rejects space, SST funding cuts. E. H. Kolcum. Aviation W 85:29-30 Ag 15 '66

UNITED STATES—National aeronautics and space administration—Appropriations and expenditures—*Continued*

Space science: congressmen want larger voice. L. J. Carter. Science 153:615+ Ag 5 '66

$3 billion annual manned program seen. il Aviation W 84:115+ Mr 7 '66

Tight budget, loose reins. W. J. Coughlin. Tech W 19:164 N 28 '66

Trend seen in impending Voyager transfer. W. J. Normyle. Aviation W 85:32 N 21 '66

Webb doubts possibility of 1973 Mars landing, urges lab delay. Aviation W 84:35 Mr 14 '66

What comes after the moon? il Bsns W p36-8 Jl 2 '66

Electronics research center

Building phase near at NASA Boston site; with summary of research objectives. K. J. Stein. il Aviation W 84:84-8 Ap 4 '66

Electronics investment climbing sharply; study at Electronics research center. R. Barnhart. il Tech W 19:74-6+ N 28 '66

Flight research center

Lifting body flight investigation moving into transonic regime; study at Flight research center. il Tech W 19:116-17 N 28 '66

Goddard space flight center

Focus to shift from cislunar to deep space; new developments planned by Goddard space flight center. C. D. LeFond. il Tech W 19:88-90+ N 28 '66

Impact of Goddard report spreads. W. J. Normyle. Aviation W 85:26-7 D 12 '66

It's just a game; GREMEX, Goddard research engineering management exercise. J. Eberhart. Sci N 90:256 O 1 '66

NASA panel sets new guidelines for observatories at Goddard center. H. Taylor. Tech W 19:16-17 D 12 '66

Jet propulsion laboratory
See Jet propulsion laboratory

John F. Kennedy space center

Kennedy space center; springboard to the moon; with editorial comment. il Aviation W 84:21, 71-80+ Je 20 '66

Launch vehicle changes trigger expansion; study at Kennedy space center. K. Voss. il Tech W 19:62-3 N 28 '66

PERT aids Saturn-Apollo site schedule. Tech W 19:40 Ag 15 '66

Langley research center

Gravity, electric power plague planners; space work of Langley research center. W. S. Beller. il Tech W 19:102-4+ N 28 '66

Lewis research center

Big solids given steady support; propulsion test plant near completion; booster development at Lewis research center. J. F. Judge. il Tech W 19:108-10+ N 28 '66

NASA/Lewis revives air-breather effort; emphasis on supersonic transport propulsion. M. L. Yaffee. il Aviation W 84:71+ Je 13 '66

Manned spacecraft center

Gemini control success may boost mission flexibility. E. J. Bulban. il Aviation W 84:64-5+ Ja 24 '66

Houston gets AAP earth resources task. Tech W 19:15-16 D 12 '66

Invitation to a spacecraft. J. Reinert. il Sci Digest 60:48-53 Ag '66

Manned Mars trip, space station sought; study at Manned spacecraft center. J. Mercer. il Tech W 19:56-8+ N 28 '66

Marshall space flight center

Astronomical, lunar surface stations eyed; study at Marshall space flight center. M. Getler. il Tech W 19:48-52 N 28 '66

In-house work trend emerging at NASA. Aviation W 85:80 S 12 '66

Marshall gets Apollo telescope task. Tech W 19:19 Jl 18 '66

NASA seeks simpler, more flexible J-2. G. Alexander. il Aviation W 85:60-1+ Ag 29 '66

Technique ranks space objectives. W. S. Beller. il Miss & Roc 18:22-4 F 7 '66

Procurement

Industry gets 81 per cent of NASA procurement. Tech W 19:19 O 24 '66

Industry, institutions, universities conduct NASA bio-sciences research. Aviation W 85:98-9 Ag 15 '66

Industry to share in Mariner task. H. Taylor. Miss & Roc 18:14 F 21 '66

Major Saturn 1B subcontractors listed. Aviation W 84:94-6 Mr 14 '66

NASA awards list shows incentives push. il Aviation W 84:55+ Je 27 '66

NASA lists top 100 contractors. il Aviation W 85:85-6+ N 7 '66

NASA procurement drops in FY '66. il Miss & Roc 18:18 My 30 '66

$25.6-million Gemini incentive seen for near-perfect effort. Aviation W 86:32 Ja 16 '67

Space science and applications, Office of

Unified earth-sensor orbiter considered. W. J. Normyle. Aviation W 86:28-9 Ja 16 '67

National archives

Kennedy assassination; photographs and X rays. New Repub 155:8 N 12 '66

Now U.S. gets JFK autopsy photos. il U S News 61:81 N 14 '66

National bureau of standards
See United States—Standards, National bureau of

National commission on food marketing

Fat cats in the food market: study by National commissin on food marketing. Consumer Rep 31:306-9 Je '66

Food report feeds controversy; results of National commission on food marketing study. il Bsns W p 173-4 My 28 '66

National council for marine sciences

Dry christening. W. J. Coughlin. Tech W 18:50 Je 27 '66

Freshening impetus for oceanology. R. W. Niblock. il Tech W 19:16-18 S 26 '66

Ocean commission named; Stratton appointed chairman. Tech W 20:42 Ja 16 '67

National commission on technology, automation, and economic progress

Automation report. R. Lekachman. il Commentary 41:65-71 My '66

Impact of automation. Sci Am 214:54-5 Mr '66

Job or subsidy for everybody? summary of report. U S News 60:102 F 14 '66

T.R.B. from Washington; swell report. New Repub 154:4 F 19 '66

Technology and employment; address, March 30, 1966. H. R. Bowen. Vital Speeches 32:435-9 My 1 '66

Those who stand at the queue's end; concern for socially and economically deprived revealed in government report: Technology and the American economy. C. P. Hall. Christian Cent 83:1271-3 O 19 '66

Verdict on automation. America 114:246 F 19 '66

National council on the arts

Farrar to publish first national arts anthology. Pub W 190:63 D 26 '66

National arts council awards $1.8 million. Pub W 190:67-8 S 12 '66

New grants and awards by National council on the arts. Pub W 191:36 Ja 9 '67

Roger Stevens, a performing art. D. Norton-Taylor. il Fortune 73:152-3+ Mr '66

State of the arts: a 1966 balance sheet. R. L. Stevens. Sat R 49:24-5+ Mr 12 '66

National forest service
See United States—Forest service

National foundation for the arts and humanities
See National foundation for the arts and humanities

National guard

Can riots be stopped? the next move. il U S News 61:38-42 Ag 8 '66

If war brings a call-up of the reserves; interview. W. P. Wilson. U S News 60:38-40 F 7 '66

See also
United States—Air national guard

National heart institute

Crash heart program out. Sci N 90:489 D 10 '66

UNITED STATES—*Continued*

National institute of mental health

Experimental approach to mental health needed; Appalachia. Sci N L 89:135 F 26 '66

Institute of mental health reorganized. Sci N 89:201 Mr 26 '66

National institutes of health

Biomedical policy: LBJ's query leads to an illuminating conference. D. S. Greenberg. Science 154:618-20 N 4 '66

General of the war on disease; J. A. Shannon, top man. il Bsns W p88-90 D 31 '66

House: increases for education, NIH a new formula for research funds. J. Walsh. Science 152:1355-8 Je 3 '66

Human population genetics; report on conference. J. N. Spuhler. Science 153:660-1 Ag 5 '66

Information exchange group no. 5; created by the National institutes of health; letter. S. Dray. Science 153:694-5 Ag 12 '66; Discussion. 153:332+ O 21 '66

Information exchange groups. P. H. Abelson. Science 154:727 N 11 '66

Information exchange groups to be discontinued; letter. E. A. Confrey. Science 154:843 N 18 '66

NIH budget hearings. P. H. Abelson. Science 153:579 Ag 5 '66

NIH: demand increases for applications of research. J. Walsh. Science 153:149-52 Jl 8 '66

Progress report on cures for the killer diseases. il U S News 60:60-1 My 2 '66

Public health service: reorganizing the doctors. E. Langer. Science 152:1607-9 Je 17 '66

Unplugging the muted trumpet: Senate says, NIH, blow your horn. B. Nelson. Science 154:491+ O 28 '66

National inventors council

More inventive America; excerpts of remarks, January 21, 1966. Sci N L 89:84 F 5 '66

National labor relations board

Against union discrimination; NLRB victory against United rubber workers of America's Local 12. Time 88:60 D 2 '66

Give a round to Darlington; NLRB examiner finds shutdown not illegal. Bsns W p62 Ag 20 '66

Is the labor board biased? an authority says this. H. L. Browne. U S News 61:72-4+ N 28 '66

Labor board gags your freedom of speech. J. A. Jenkins. il Nations Bsns 54:52-3+ Ap '66

NLRB and the duty to bargain. P. Ross. il Mo Labor R 89:1241-5 N '66

New facts and new law in the NLRB annual report. Mo Labor R 89:760-1 Jl '66

New labor law? a business view; recommendation to transfer the authority of NLRB or to abolish it. U S News 62:67 Ja 9 '67

New punishment for employers. U S News 60:76 Ap 4 '66

Significant decisions in labor cases. See issues of Monthly labor review

Tempest in a coffee cup; concerning raised prices in cafeterias in Westinghouse electric corp.'s Defense center at Maryland. Newsweek 67:61 F 7 '66

Union cards were phoney; case of the Washington area Drug fair chain. il Nations Bsns 54:100-1+ Mr '66

What to do when the union knocks. W. Wingo. il Nations Bsns 54:40-1+ D '66 (to be cont)

Who is unfair? Newsweek 68:87 S 19 '66

National mediation board

Public interest rides the rails; negotiations between carriers and railroad unions may get peaceful solution. il Bsns W p 156+ N 5 '66

National oceanographic council (proposed)

Oceanography; Congress wants cabinet council and study. L. J. Carter. Science 152: 1490-2 Je 10 '66

National oceanographic data center

Fund shortage threatens data center plan. H. Taylor. Tech W 19:50+ S 26 '66

National park service

Fifty years of housekeeping; maintenance of national parks. R. K. Olsen. il Parks & Rec 1:648-50 Ag '66

Golden anniversary and a golden opportunity. L. S. Rockefeller. Parks & Rec 1:613 Ag '66

Guarding our outdoor heritage; ninety-first Annual meeting of the American forestry association. J. B. Craig. il Am For 72:14-17+ D '66

Heritage to discover; training park rangers. G. B. Hartzog, jr. il Am Ed 2:15-19 Jl '66

Mission called 66. C. L. Wirth. il Nat Geog Mag 130:6-47 Jl '66

NPS reorganization continues. Nat Parks Mag 40:20 N '66

National parks and the ecology of beauty. D. Goldman. il Am For 72:18-21+ N '66

Notice of public hearing on Smokies wilderness; with data concerning proposals. il Liv Wildn 30:10-18 Spr '66

On such foundations. M. Frome. Am For 72:9 N '66

Open letter. S. L. Udall. Parks & Rec 1: 608-9 Ag '66

Park wilderness hearings. Nat Parks Mag 40:21 S '66

Parkscape U.S.A. il Audubon Mag 68:416-17 N '66

Parkscape U.S.A; conservation for natural and human resources. G. B. Hartzog, jr. il Parks & Rec 1:616-20 Ag '66

Some thoughts on future park policy. Nat Parks Mag 40:20 N '66

Telling the park story; interpretation program. H. Wharton. il Parks & Rec 1:622-4+ Ag '66

Wave of the future; activities of the Short course in the administration of national parks, by University of Michigan and the National park service. G. W. Sharpe and others. il Am For 72:20-1+ F '66

Wilderness hearings and reviews. Nat Parks Mag 40:23 My '66

National parks and reserves

See National parks and reserves—United States

National science foundation

Albert Thomas: late congressman who supervised NSF budget had witty views on science and politics. D. S. Greenberg. Science 151:1064-5 Mr 4 '66

Choosing graduate fellows. D. Wolfle. Science 154:1279 D 9 '66

Daddario study says NSF should be in forefront of policymaking. D. S. Greenberg; discussion. Science 152:292+ Ap 15 '66

Educational TV: NSF and arts foundation speak out. L. J. Carter. Science 154:1309-10 D 9 '66

Interaction of science and technology and foreign affairs; statement, April 19, 1966. H. Pollack. Dept State Bul 54:946-9 Je 13 '66

NSF fellowships to foreign scientists. R. R. Renner. Sch & Soc 94:146+ Mr 19 '66

National science policy. P. H. Abelson. Science 151:407 Ja 28 '66

Revised charter for the science foundation. E. Q. Daddario. Science 152:42-5 Ap 1 '66; Discussion. 152:869; 153:9 My 13, Jl 1 '66

Science policy: when Congress looks for a leader NSF is usually nominated. J. Walsh. Science 152:184-5 Ap 8 '66

Smale case: NSF and Berkeley pass through a case of jitters. D. S. Greenberg. il Science 154:130-3 O 7 '66; Discussion. 154:1395-6 D 16 '66

Social sciences: where do they fit in the politics of science? L. J. Carter. Science 154:488-91 O 28 '66

U.S. seeks wider base for science; NSF's centers of excellence program in Case and WRU. il Bsns W p60-2 S 3 '66

Where the R&D funds are headed. il Bsns W p 110-12 N 12 '66

National security agency

Other guy's mail. il Newsweek 67:28 Mr 14 '66

National security council

NSC reviews Viet-Nam problems; remarks, May 10, 1966. L. B. Johnson. Dept State Bul 54:834 My 30 '66

National service corps

See Volunteers in service to America

UNITED STATES—*Continued*

National teacher corps

Congress flunks. Reporter 35:18+ S 8 '66

Missionaries in the classroom. R. Van Doren. il Am Ed 3:10-11+ D '66

Odds against the teacher corps. J. Egerton. Sat R 49:71 D 17 '66

Teacher corps head speaks out; interview, ed. by J. Lloyd. R. Graham. il Sr Schol 89:sup2-3 Ja 13 '67

To school in a squad car; opposition endangers program. il Newsweek 68:77 Ag 1 '66

What's happening in education? W. D. Boutwell. PTA Mag 60:13 My '66

National traffic safety agency

Are auto standards too tough? safety standard for '68 cars. U S News 62:14 Ja 16 '67

Detroit gets the word; new standards for 1968 models. Bsns W p44+ D 3 '66

National traffic safety agency; address, November 29, 1966. W. Haddon, jr. Vital Speeches 33:179-84 Ja 1 '67

New federal safety czar's tough views on cars! R. W. Irvin. Motor T 18:42-4 D '66

Safety strictures; new safety regulations. Newsweek 68:84 D 12 '66

Scientist buckles the seat belt; W. Haddon, jr, chief of new Traffic safety agency. Bsns W p 120+ O 29 '66

Tiger in the tone; new set of safety-first standards. Newsweek 68:24 D 19 '66

Twenty-three rules. il Time 88:97-8 D 9 '66

Washington yields on standards; modification of Haddon proposals. Sci N 90:559 D 31 '66

National university (proposed)

National university; excerpts from address, November 13, 1965. R. D. Calkins. bibliog Science 152:884-9 My 13 '66
See also
United States—Advanced study center (proposed)

Naval materiel command

See United States—Navy—Naval materiel support establishment

Naval observatory

Stars: near and dark. A. Ewing. il Sci N 90:470 D 3 '66

Washington 6-inch transit circle. P. D. Hemenway. il Sky & Tel 31:72-7 F '66

Naval ordance test station, California

See Navy yards and naval stations

Naval research, Office of

ONR London: two decades of scientific quid pro quo. J. Walsh. Science 154:623-5 N 4 '66

Office of naval research: twenty years bring changes. L. J. Carter. il Science 153:397-400 Jl 22 '66

Naval research laboratory

High-precision 85-foot radio telescope. E. F. McClain. il Sky & Tel 32:4-6 Jl '66

Navy

ASW facility readied for March use. R. Pay. il Tech W 19:23-5 O 17 '66

Battle for a nuclear navy: will McNamara or Congress win? il U S News 60:44-6 Je 27 '66

Creation of a nuclear navy; address, January 17, 1966. C. Holifield. Vital Speeches 32:261-4 F 15 '66

Deep-sea effort rivals space program. W. E. Wilks. il Miss & Roc 18:32-3+ Ap 11 '66

Freshening impetus for oceanology. R. W. Niblock. il Tech W 19:16-18 S 26 '66

How the navy helps fight a jungle war; Seventh fleet. G. C. Troelstrup. il U S News 61:44-6 S 12 '66

Is U.S. stripping Atlantic defenses? il U S News 62:10 Ja 9 '67

Navy details rescue, salvage systems; deep submergence rescue vehicle. J. F. Judge. il Tech W 19:30+ S 26 '66

Navy seeks quantum ASW improvements. C. Brownlow. il Aviation W 84:22-4 Je 27 '66

Navy tightens management, places emphasis on incentive contracting. Aviation W 84:38 Mr 21 '66

Quality of coming home: Enterprise in San Francisco after tour of duty in the South China Sea. L. Wainwright. Life 61:22 Jl 1 '66
See also
Hospital ships
Naval research
United States—Air force, Navy
United States—Naval research laboratory
United States naval oceanographic office, Suitland, Md.
Warships—United States
World war, 1939-1945—Naval operations

Administration

Navy to strengthen central authority. R. W. Niblock. Miss & Roc 18:16 Mr 14 '66

Air force

See United States—Air force, Navy

Appropriations and expenditures

ASW demands retain top DOD priority; advanced weapon system components for the navy's anti-submarine warfare package. C. E. Q. Daddario. Science 152:42-5 Ap 1 '66;

DOD denies navy FY 1968 money for purchase of AS-12. M. Getler. il Tech W 20:18-19 Ja 9 '67

F-111 runs into new head winds; Congress moves to limit funds. Bsns W p84+ S 10 '66

Sparse oceanology funding criticized; inadequate undersea research vehicles; summary of address, ed. by R. W. Niblock. P. Rogers. Miss & Roc 18:18 Ap 25 '66

Boats

Navy rebuilds for limited war; thanks to researchers and to war in Vietnam. il Bsns W p 107-8 O 29 '66

River patrol boat for Viet Nam. B. Cobb, jr. il Yachting 120:65+ D '66

Skim boats: our new weapon in Vietnam. J. H. Winchester. il Pop Sci 189:122-5+ O '66

Wide gains for shipbuilding seen in FDLS; improved navy cargo vessels with long transoceanic range. M. Getler. il Tech W 19:14-16 Ag 15 '66
See also
Torpedo boats

Crimes and misdemeanors

Captain's paradise: alleged infractions by A. C. Kuntze in Vietnam. Newsweek 68:36 Ag 15 '66

Closed case: Kuntze's sentence. Newsweek 68:36 N 28 '66

Mayor: Captain A. Kuntze. il Time 88:21 Ag 12 '66

Paying for prowess; A. Kuntze. il Time 88:36 N 25 '66

Time of trial; concerning A. C. Kuntze. Newsweek 68:55 N 14 '66

Education

See also
United States naval academy, Annapolis

Equipment and supplies

See also
United States—Navy department—Naval material support establishment

History

Great white fleet, by R. A. Hart. Review Am Heritage 17:66-7 F '66. B. Catton

Medical and sanitary affairs

Fluorides for adults; prevention of tooth decay. il Time 87:47 Ap 8 '66
See also
Hospital ships

Procurement

Aerospace optimism quickens in-house ocean effort funding. W. E. Wilks and R. Barnhart. il Tech W 19:62-4+ S 26 '66

NOTS pressed to meet urgent Viet needs. C. M. Plattner. il Aviation W 85:46-7+ mid-D '66

Navy pushing more multi-year purchases. Tech W 19:14-15 Ag 22 '66

Setting shipyards on a new course; navy prods builders to update and automate their facilities. il Bsns W p 186+ O 22 '66
See also
United States—Navy department—Naval material support establishment

Navy department

Navy reorganization takes industry line. il Aviation W 84:99+ My 9 '66

UNITED STATES—Navy department—*Cont.*

Naval material command

Naval material support; address, January 20, 1966. I. J. Galintin. Vital Speeches 32:308-11 Mr 1 '66

Vietnam tests navy's systems concept. E. H. Kolcum. il Aviation W 85:42-3 mid-D '66

Neighborhood youth corps

See United States—Youth corps

Office of education

See United States—Education, Office of

Officials and employees

See Government employees

Outdoor recreation, Bureau of

Don't let the eagle lay an egg; Land and water conservation fund bill. G. H. Gillelan. il Outdoor Life 138:24+ N '66

Providing new dimensions; functions; aims. E. C. Crafts. il Parks & Rec 1:826-8+ O '66

Passport division

See United States—State. Department of —Passport division

Patent office

How to speed patents; Presidential commission recommended overhaul of the system. Bsns W p46 D 10 '66

Patent office: progress and change. F. Sartwell. Sci N 90:552 D 24 '66

Peace corps

Advice to future Peace corps volunteers. R. Hoopes. Seventeen 25:24+ My '66

All we had to give was ourselves; two Peace corps volunteers in leper colony; Bolivia. L. Elliott. il Redbook 127:58-9+ My '66

Business teaches the Peace corps. il Bsns W p 132-3+ O 22 '66

Dandy Dan in Africa; visit to publicize the fifth anniversary. New Yorker 42:38-9 Ap 30 '66

Fifth anniversary of the Peace corps; remarks, March 1, 1966. L. B. Johnson. Dept State Bul 54:441-3 Mr 21 '66

Five years of the Peace corps; a progress report. J. N. Wallace. il U S News 61:72-3 Jl 18 '66

Five years with the Peace corps. S. Shriver. il Sat R 49:14+ Ap 23 '66

It's a long, long way from old Camp Shawnee; volunteers being trained for service in India. S. Rama Rau. il N Y Times Mag p52-3+ N 13 '66

Job crises defined. Sci N 90:446 N 26 '66

Peace corps around the world; photographs. P. Conklin. Sat R 49:16-17 Ap 23 '66

Peace corps' daring new look. A. Kopkind. New Repub 154:15-20 F 5 '66

Peace corps highlights; excerpts from report. J. H. Vaughn. il Dept State Bul 55:278-9 Ag 22 '66

Peace corps: JFK's bold legacy; with paintings by N. Rockwell. Look 30:34-9 Je 14 '66

Peace corps: revolutions without blood. I. Mothner. il Look 30:40+ Je 14 '66

Peace corps; symposium, ed. by J. N. Parmer. bibliog f il Ann Am Acad 365:1-146 My '66

Peace corps volunteers on race relations. Sch & Soc 94:56+ F 5 '66

Peace corpsman looks back. E. Sigel. il Reporter 35:12-16 D 29 '66

President Johnson pays tribute to Peace corps volunteers; remarks, September 13, 1966. L. B. Johnson. Dept State Bul 55:496-9 O 3 '66

President transmits fourth annual report of Peace corps to Congress; March 14, 1966. L. B. Johnson. Dept State Bul 54:634-5 Ap 18 '66

Seminarians to the Peace corps? M. McGrory. America 114:167 Ja 29 '66

Toward a draft without guns; universal voluntary service. H. Wofford. Sat R 49:19-21+ O 15 '66

Western man at his best. A. Balk. il Sat R 49:15 Ap 23 '66

Yankee, don't go home! il Time 87:16-17 Ja 28 '66

You can't send a girl there! il Mlle 63:33-40 Jl '66

See also

School-to-school program

Politics and government

Affairs of state. S. Alsop. See issues of Saturday evening post

After elections: changes ahead; with excerpts from address by S. Lubell. il U S News 61:45-7 N 14 '66

American malaise. Commonweal 85:189-90 N 18 '66

America's political dynasties, by S. Hess. Review

New Repub 155:32+ S 17 '66. G. W. Johnson

Newsweek 68:124 O 10 '66. R. Moley

Atlantic report. Atlan 217:4+ My '66

Atlantic report: Washington. D. Kiker. See issues of Atlantic, November 1966-

Big brother is here! C. Stevenson. Read Digest 89:81-6 N '66

Can LBJ reverse the polls? il U S News 60:33 Je 20 '66

Consensus politics: end of an experiment. D. S. Broder. il Atlan 218:60-5 O '66

Critical look at U.S. U S News 61:23 O 10 '66

W. E. Griffith. Read Digest 89:119-23 Ag '66

Dim future. Commonweal 85:213-14 N 25 '66

Eisenhower speaks his mind; interview, ed. by P. Martin. D. D. Eisenhower. U S News 61:42-5 N 7 '66

Elder statesman looks at U.S. today; interview. H. W. Smith. U S News 61:50-4 O 31 '66

Empty society; excerpts from Massey lectures. P. Goodman. Commentary 42:53-60 N '66

End of an era? foreign affairs before domestic concerns. K. Crawford. Newsweek 68:46 O 24 '66

End of Johnson's Congress? conduct of the war in Vietnam. W. V. Shannon. Commonweal 84:433-4 Jl 8 '66

The establishment, USA. H. H. Miller. New Repub 156:23-5 Ja 14 '67

First New deal, by R. Moley. Review

Sat R 49:49-51+ D 24 '66. D. Young

Focus on Washington. Cato. See issues of National review

Foreign policy and political style. H. J. Spiro. il Ann Am Acad 366:139-48 Jl '66

Games Johnson plays: deeper and deeper into the credibility gap. J. Deakin. New Repub 156:10-11 Ja 14 '67

Government by public opinion polls. E. Roper. Sat R 49:18 My 28 '66

GOP '66: back on the map; election results, with table. il Newsweek 68:31-4 N 21 '66

How things are changing for LBJ. il U S News 60:40-3 Je 6 '66

Impressions of Johnson, the Kennedys, and today's government; interview. A. Krock. il U S News 61:44-9 D 19 '66

Invisible scar, by C. Bird. Review

Sat R 49:37-8 F 12 '66. B. H. Wilkins

Is the Great society just a barbecue? R. Flacks. New Repub 154:18-19+ Ja 29 '66

Johnson and Kennedy; the two thousand days. T. A. Bailey. il N Y Times Mag p30-1+ N 6 '66; Discussion. p22 D 4 '66

Johnson takes the slow road; no radical changes in either domestic or foreign policies. Bsns W p37-8 N 19 '66

Kennedy as statesman. G. Kateb. Commentary 41:54-60 Je '66; Discussion. 42:12+ N '66

Kennedy image, three years later. il Sr Schol 89:10-13+ N 18 '66

Letter from Washington. R. H. Rovere. See issues of New Yorker

Liberty and discipline; living under elected tyranny until 1966 election. R. Moley. Newsweek 68:136 N 21 '66

LBJ, near great. W. V. Shannon. Commonweal 85:361-2 Ja 6 '67

Lyndon B. Johnson: the exercise of power. R. Evans and R. Novak. il Sat Eve Post 239:26-9+ S 24; 42-6+ O 8; 40-4+ O 22 '66

LBJ's balancing act: can it last; il U S News 60:31-2 F 28 '66

National affairs. See issues of Newsweek

New direction in the U.S: right? R. Kirk. il N Y Times Mag p20-1+ Ag 7 '66

New game begins. K. Crawford. Newsweek 68:32 D 5 '66

Next two years. New Repub 155:5-6 D 3 '66

Official information: how good is it? Nation 202:284 Mr 14 '66

Our government at work, 1966; symposium, ed. by D. Reische. il Sr Schol 88:2-22 F 18 '66

Anecdotes, facetiae, satire, etc.

Hit and miss parade; theatrical season in
Washington. Reporter 35:16 S 8 '66
Space parable. W. J. Coughlin. Tech W 19:
50 O 10 '66

Bibliography

Literature of American government. O. Gass.
bibliog f Commentary 41:67-72 Je '66

Popular culture

Age of the amateur. R. T. Reilly. America
115:255-6 S 10 '66
Bad dream. R. A. Schroth. America 114:699
My 14 '66
Church and camp. J. W. Goetz. Cath World
203:297-300 Ag '66
Cultural explosion; symposium. il Sr Schol
88:5-19 Ap 15 '66
Happenings in and out of school; interview,
ed. by D. W. Ecker. Sch Arts 65:23-8 Mr
'66
How big is the boom in culture? summary
of Performing arts: the economic dilemma.
W. J. Baumol and W. G. Bowen. il U S
News 61:14 N 28 '66
How culturally active are Americans? E.
Roper. Sat R 49:22-3 My 14 '66
In pursuit of culture; critical view of Amer-
ica's flourishing arts; symposium. il Holi-
day 39:10+ Mr '66
Instant culture. W. K. Zinsser. il Look 31:
14 Ja 24 '67
Notes and comment; Beatles more popular, or
more famous, than Jesus. New Yorker 42:
21-2 Ag 27 '66
Our creeping idiot savantism; maturity can
be magnificent; address, June 12, 1966. J.
Foxworth. Vital Speeches 32:596-9 Jl 15 '66
Pornography and the new expression. R.
Schechner. Atlan 219:74-8 Ja '67
Return of the (whoosh! there goes one!) su-
perhero! B. Rollin. il Look 30:113-14 Mr
22 '66
Status symbols of youth; with study-dis-
cussion program, by C. Smallenburg and
H. Smallenburg. E. J. Alpenfels. bibliog il
PTA Mag 60:4-6 Mr '66
Story of pop. P. Benchley. il Newsweek 67:
56-8+ Ap 25 '66
Whole country goes supermad. il Life 60:22-7
Mr 11 '66

Population

As family planning gains favor in U.S. il
U S News 62:48-50 Ja 9 '67
Effects of shift in population; census survey
report. il U S News 60:50-2 Mr 7 '66
Next shift in population: more young adults
with more to spend on themselves. il U S
News 60:73-4 Je 6 '66
Parks, or more people? W. H. Draper, jr.
il Nat Parks Mag 40:10-13 Ap '66
Population explosion: what it means for the
U.S. il Sr Schol 89:4-7+ N 4 '66
300,000,000 Americans would be wrong. D. E.
Lilienthal; discussion. N Y Times Mag
p75 Ja 30; 12+ F 20 '66
See also
Birth rate—United States
Cities and towns—United States
United States—Census

Post office department

Automated post office zips along, but slowly.
il Bsns W p38 Ja 29 '66
How to float on a sea of red ink. il News-
week 69:56-8 Ja 2 '67
Larry O'Brien: the pro takes on the post
office. D. R. Maxey. il Look 30:30-2 F 8
'66
More zip for the P.O. il Time 88:12-13 D
30 '66
U.S. mails; address, February 8, 1966. L. F.
O'Brien. Vital Speeches 32:290-1 Mr 1 '66
See also
Mail handling
Postal employees
Postal service—United States
Postmasters

UNITED STATES—*Continued*

President's advisory committee on labor-management policy

High-level help on economic guideposts; labor-management group to advise on how to maintain economic stability. il Bsns W p42-3 My 14 '66

Is LBJ looking for way to ease wage-price guideposts? U S News 60:100 My 9 '66

Washington desk. J. R. Slevin. Duns R 88:7 N '66

President's commission on heart disease, cancer and stroke

White House gifts said to trigger health law; multimillion dollar heart disease, cancer and stroke law. Sci N 90:136 Ag 27 '66

President's commission on law enforcement and administration of justice

Crime panel's next push. P. McBroom. Sci N 90:475 D 3 '66

Criminal justice; address, August 9, 1966. N. deB. Katzenbach. Vital Speeches 32:708-12 S 15 '66

High cost of imprisonment; preliminary report on findings of the National council on crime and delinquency. Nation 203:693 D 26 '66

Law to authorize federal eavesdropping? U S News 61:8 D 5 '66

Rethinking crime. P. McBroom. il Sci N 90:305-6 O 15 '66

President's commission on the assassination of President Kennedy

Allen Dulles answers Warren-report critics; excerpts from statement, December 4, 1966. A. Dulles. U S News 61:20 D 19 '66

Assassination: some serious exceptions to the Warren report. R. Butterfield. Harper 233:122+ O '66

Autopsy on the Warren commission; Time essay. Time 88:54-5 S 16 '66

Banned in Moscow: Warren commission report. Newsweek 68:40 S 12 '66

Confusion compounded. Nat R 18:1032-3 O 18 '66

Debate on who killed John Kennedy? comments by critics and defenders of the Warren commission findings. Sr Schol 89:21-2+ N 18 '66

Deep and growing doubts; questioning verdict of Warren commission. Newsweek 68:36+ O 10 '66

Doubts about Dallas. F. Russell. il Nat R 18:887-8+ S 6 '66

Enough is enough. W. V. Shannon. Commonweal 85:191-2 N 18 '66; Discussion. 85:331, 410-11 D 16 '66, Ja 13 '67

Failure of the Warren report. A. M. Bickel. Commentary 42:31-9 O '66

Fateful two hours without a president; excerpts from testimonies. il U S News 61:68-78 N 14 '66

Inquest: the Warren commission and the establishment of truth, by E. J. Epstein. Review

   Newsweek il 67:36-8 Je 13 '66
   Time il 88:86+ Jl 8 '66

JFK in Dallas; Warren report and its critics. A. L. Fein. il Sat R 49:36-8+ O 22 '66

Kennedy assassination. New Repub 155:8 N 12 '66

Kennedy assassination; with editorial comment. R. J. Whalen. il Sat Eve Post 240:19-25+, 74 Ja 14 '67

Lane says JFK death is still unsolved murder. Pub W 190:58 Ag 22 '66

New conflict over the assassination. il U S News 61:6+ D 5 '66

New wave of doubt; concerning Inquest. by E. J. Epstein. F. Knebel. il Look 30:66-72 Jl 12 '66

No conspiracy, but, two assassins, perhaps? H. Fairlie. il N Y Times Mag p52-5+ S 11 '66

Now U.S. gets JFK autopsy photos. il U S News 61:81 N 14 '66

Reexamining the Warren report. A. M. Bickel. New Repub 156:25-8 Ja 7 '67

Rush to judgment, by M. Lane. Review Newsweek 68:30-3 Ag 15 '66

Shadows of doubt. A. A. Gross. Christian Cent 83:1178 S 28 '66

Thinking the unthinkable: the Warren commission books. R. H. Smith. Pub W 190:55 O 10 '66

Those missing exhibits; photographs and X-rays turned over to National archives. Nation 203:500 N 14 '66

Truth about Kennedy assassination: was the Warren report written in haste to prove a theory? with interview with A. Specter. il U S News 61:44-50+ O 10 '66

Warren commission. O. Handlin. Atlan 218:117-18 Ag '66

Warren commission and the death of John F. Kennedy. il Sr Schol 89:14-20 N 18 '66

Warren commission report: some unanswered questions. F. J. Cook. il Nation 202:705-15 Je 13 '66

Warren commission report: testimony of the eyewitnesses. F. J. Cook. il Nation 202:737-46 Je 20 '66

Warren commission: the critics and the law; theories of E. J. Epstein and M. Lane. K. Goodall; A. L. Goodhart. il Reporter 35:44-8+ D 15 '66

Warren report is not enough; voices speaking in contradiction of report; call for new investigation. L. Wainwright. Life 61:38 O 7 '66

What did happen in Dallas? concerning H. Weisberg's and E .J. Epstein's theories on the Warren report. A. Campbell. New Repub 154:23-5 Je 25 '66

What the Warren report omits: vital documents. J. Cohen. il Nation 203:43-9 Jl 11 '66; Reply. F. J. Cook. 203:138+ Ag 22 '66

Who's afraid of the Warren report? E. J. Epstein. il Esquire 66:204+ D '66

President's commission on the patent system

U.S. patent system: Commission recommends reform to President. B. Nelson. Science 154:1629-30+ D 30 '66

President's committee on equal employment opportunity

See United States—President's equal employment opportunity commission

President's council on physical fitness

Dramatic gains in youth fitness. S. Musial. Parents Mag 41:30 Ag '66

Out of the cellar but not in the first division, America needs more than spring training. S. Musial. il Am Ed 2:28-30 S '66

President's equal employment opportunity commission

From the women: what about our job rights? il U S News 61:61-2 Jl 4 '66

Holcomb's trek; as permanent chairman of Equal opportunity commission. J. C. Evans. Christian Cent 83:956 Ag 3 '66

Job rights for Negroes: new pressure on employers. il U S News 60:84+ Ap 18 '66

Lost agency. Nation 203:660-1 D 19 '66

Now it's whites who are claiming their job rights. il U S News 60:86+ My 16 '66

Rules on hiring, promoting; questions answered. il U S News 60:93-6 F 21 '66

Where civil rights law is going wrong; reply. F. D. Roosevelt. Nations Bsns 53:10+ D '65

President's science advisory committee

Oceanography: PSAC panel calls for setting up new agency. D. S. Greenberg. Science 153:391-3 Jl 22 '66

Public health service

Are Americans too fat? results of a new survey. U S News 61:16 N 14 '66

Cleaning up the Nation's air. il Bsns W p88-92+ Jl 23 '66

New concepts in hospital laundry design; excerpts from The hospital laundry. il Arch Rec 140:219-24 O '66

Protecting human guinea pigs; PHS tightens rules. Bsns W p71 Jl 23 '66

Public health service: reorganizing the doctors. E. Langer. Science 152:1607-9 Je 17 '66

Uranium mystery in the Colorado basin; concerning special PHS report. New Repub 154:9 Mr 5 '66; Discussion. 154:36-7 Ap 16 '66

    See also
United States—National institutes of health

   Air pollution control division

Many angles on dirty air. il Sci N 90:529 D 24 '66

UNITED STATES—*Continued*

Public health service hospital, Lexington, Ky.

Visit to Narco. G. Samuels. il N Y Times Mag p32-3+ Ap 10 '66

Public land law review commission

Public lands under review. M. A. Pearl. Parks & Rec 1:416-18 My '66

Public roads, Bureau of

Sounding board. Am For 72:38-9 Ap '66

Race problems

Bridging the prejudice gap. K. D. Fishman. il N Y Times Mag p 114+ O 23 '66
See also
Church and race problems
Jews in the United States
Negroes in the United States

Reclamation, Bureau of
History
Politics of conservation, by F. E. Smith. Review
Sat R 50:90-2 Ja 14 '67. W. Stegner

Relations (diplomatic)
Catholic church
See Catholic church—Relations (diplomatic)—United States

Religious institutions and affairs

Are the churches in trouble? with excerpts from interview with J. A. Pike. il U S News 60:54-60 Ap 18 '66
Message from Bonhoeffer. J. C. Ridd. Christian Cent 83:827-9 Je 29 '66
World around us. Christian Cent 83:599-600 My 4 '66
See also
Baptists in the United States
Catholic church—Relations (diplomatic)—United States
Catholic church in the United States
Christian Science
Church and state
Jews in the United States
Mormons and Mormonism
Protestant churches—United States
Protestants in the United States
United States—Church history
also subhead Religious institutions and affairs under names of states, cities, e.g. Chicago—Religious institutions and affairs

Reserve forces
See United States—Armed forces—Reserves

Resources
See United States—Industries

Revenue

Plan for a tax transfusion; Heller plan. Life 61:6 D 9 '66
Sharing revenue: national taxes and local needs; W. Heller proposal to transfer federal revenue to individual states. R. A. Musgrave. Nation 204:78-80 Ja 16 '67
Unexpected receipts fill government's till; revenues higher than Treasury estimates. il Bsns W p66+ S 10 '66
See also
Taxation—United States

Riots

As Negro unrest continues to spread—. il U S News 61:30 Jl 25 '66
Can riots be stopped? the next move; with article by B. Shipp. il U S News 61:38-43 Ag 8 '66
Cities: summer riot fever in the black ghettos. il Newsweek 68:18-20 Ag 1 '66
Deterioration: anti-riot amendment to civil rights bill. Nation 203:138-9 Ag 22 '66
Goldwater advises LBJ: visit riot sites; excerpts from address. July 27, 1966. B. M. Goldwater. U S News 61:14 Ag 8 '66
Guerrilla warfare in U.S. streets, spreading and organized? il U S News 61:5 Ag 1 '66
Long, hot summer begins; racial violence. Bsns W p34 Jl 23 '66
Long, hot summer of race trouble ahead? with interview with F. B. McKissick. il U S News 60:34-8+ My 23 '66
Long summer; racial disturbances. il Time 88:22-3 S 9 '66

Making bad matters worse; HUAC inquiry into acts of violence. Christian Cent 83:1399-400 N 16 '66
Mounting concern over racial violence. U S News 61:6 Ag 22 '66
Now. more racial outbreaks in Midwest. il U S News 61:10 S 12 '66
Riots, battles, power marches; it's still a hot summer. il U S News 61:36-7 Ag 15 '66
Riots coming in thirty to forty more cities? U S News 61:10 Ag 29 '66
Simmering symptoms; racial disturbances. il Times 88:13 Ag 12 '66
Still hot; incidents in five communities across the Nation. il Newsweek 68:26-8 S 12 '66
Summer '66: cops on the spot. il Newsweek 67:22-6+ Je 27 '66
Violence in the city; ghetto riots. New Repub 155:5-6 Jl 30 '66
We have got to deliver nonviolent results; disorders across urban North. il Newsweek 68:58-9 Ag 22 '66
What Congress is doing to curb race rioting. U S News 61:12+ O 17 '66
Who is behind the race riots? P. A. McCombs. Nat R 18:934-5 S 20 '66
Why an antiriot law was asked. August 1966. W. C. Cramer. U S News 61:39 Ag 22 '66
See also subhead Riots under names of states, cities, e.g. Chicago—Riots

Rural electrification administration

Another co-op crutch; administration's plan for a federal bank for rural electric systems. R. Moley. Newsweek 67:98 My 30 '66
Giant step, by C. T. Ellis. Review
Sat R 49:35 Je 18 '66. T. C. Sorensen

Savings bonds
See Bonds. Government

School laws and legislation
See School laws and legislation—United States

Science and technology, Office of

LBJ and Hornig: close ties exist as science adviser starts third year. D. S. Greenberg. Science 151:431 Ja 28 '66

Seals

New law a first step to protect Great seal of the United States; statement, November 12, 1966. L. B. Johnson. Dept State Bul 55:924-5 D 19 '66

Secretary of state
See Secretaries of state (United States)

Securities and exchange commission

AT&T shareowners win a voice; protest FCC probe of the Bell system. Bsns W p 158+ O 22 '66
Can SEC police foreign concerns? enforcing law that American stockholders comply with U.S. securities regulations. Bsns W p 117-18+ S 3 '66
Cashing in on an inside tip; SEC vs. Texas Gulf sulphur company. M. Adams. New Repub 155:14-16 Jl 30 '66
Changes for Mutual funds: what government proposes. U S News 61:71 D 12 '66
Critical look at the stock market; interview. M. F. Cohen. U S News 60:36-40 My 30 '66
Crying on the inside; SEC insider regulations. Time 87:94 My 13 '66
Curb for Wall Street? il Newsweek 68:94-6 D 19 '66
Disclosure and insider investing; address. H. H. Budge. Duns R 87:21-2+ Ja '66
Heavy trading by institutions; summary of report. U S News 61:68 Jl 4 '66
Insider and the SEC. R. Phalon. il Duns R 88:38-40+ S '66
Keeping the sales pitch blurry; Mutual funds commercials severely restricted by SEC. il Bsns W p 129-30+ Je 4 '66
Laying down some rules for mutual funds. M. Rosenfeld. New Repub 156:13-14 Ja 7 '67
Mutual funds: the SEC cracks down. il Newsweek 68:81-2 D 12 '66
Mutual troubles; SEC advocates tough new laws. il Time 88:97 D 9 '66
On the side of the insiders; law professor H. G. Manne challenges SEC's condemnation of executives who use private information for personal stock trading. Bsns W p 160+ N 12 '66
Prosecutors and the judges. il Fortune 74:164-5+ D '66

UNITED STATES—Securities and exchange
commission—*Continued*
Relic of the 1920s returns; convertible partici-
pating preferred stock. il Bsns W p80+
Ag 13 '66
Savings for mutual investors? new proposals.
U S News 61:93-4 D 19 '66
SEC enters a period of persuasion. Bsns W
p94-6+ F 5 '66
SEC has a little list; with editorial comment.
C. J. Loomis. il Fortune 75:86, 110-15+ Ja
'67
SEC tackles Swiss fund. Bsns W p 128+
F 12 '66
SEC tells insiders to tell more; stocks held
by wives, children, and in-laws must be
disclosed. Bsns W p 142 My 7 '66
SEC vs. mutual funds: Congress will decide.
il Bsns W p 147-8+ D 10 '66
SEC watchmen prowl a new beat; investi-
gates Genesco and Georgia-Pacific cases.
il Bsns W p53-4+ My 7 '66
Where Manny Cohen is leading the SEC. C.
J. Loomis. Fortune 74:163-5+ D '66 (to
be cont)
Where the Texas Gulf ruling could lead;
court decision on insider trading case. il
Bsns W p 112+ Ag 27 '66

Small business administration

Facilities of the SBA; summary of address,
September 19, 1966. L. Gourlie. il Pub W
190:34-6 O 17 '66
Help for not-so-small; American motors and
eight tire companies eligible for favored
treatment. Bsns W p43 S 17 '66
Helping the poor to be boss; SBA's loans.
Time 88:90 D 16 '66
How big is small? SBA's new list. Newsweek
68:95 S 26 '66
Riding to the rescue of small businessmen;
Service corps of retired executives. il
Bsns W p 118+ F 12 '66
Small business loans. New Repub 155:9-10 S
24 '66

Social conditions

Common thread; address, May 3, 1966. H.
Ford, 2d. Vital Speeches 32:495-8 Je 1 '66
Down-to-earth look at a growing problem;
excerpts from letter. I. Palmer. U S News
61:53 Ag 22 '66
Empty society; excerpts from Massey lec-
tures. P. Goodman. Commentary 42:53-60 N
'66
National mood. W. V. Shannon. Common-
weal 84:603-4 S 23 '66
New class. D. T. Bazelon. Commentary 42:
48-53 Ag '66
Other U.S. S. Dedijer. Bul Atomic Sci 22:
28-30 F '66
Poverty areas of our major cities. J. R. Wetzel
and S. S. Holland. il Mo Labor R 89:1105-10
O '66
Profiles; E. Hoffer. C. Tomkins. New Yorker
42:34-6+ Ja 7 '67
Quiet summer afternoon. S. Lansdowne.
America 115:246 S 10 '66
Road to 1977. M. Ways. il Fortune 75:92-5+
Ja '67
This U.S.A. by B. J. Wattenburg and R. M.
Scammon. Review
Look 30:39-40 F 8 '66. R. L. Wilson
Thoughts of young radicals; series of per-
sonal statements (cont) New Repub 154:13-
15 F 5 '66
Welfare in affluence: the mirage of ra-
tionalism. R. McGee. il Nation 202:174-80
F 14 '66
See also
Cities and towns—United States
Crime and criminals—United States
Divorce—United States
Housing—United States
Labor and laboring classes—United States
Negroes in the United States
Poor—United States
United States—Population
Women—United States
Youth—United States

Bibliography

Home scene (cont) W. L. Lucey. America
114:661-2; 115:696+ My 7, N 26 '66

Social history

Anatomy of change 1939/1966. J. Brooks. il
Horizon 8:48-55 Aut '66
City and the road. A. Trachtenberg. Nation
202:526-8 My 2 '66
Great leap: the past twenty-five years in
America. by J. Brooks. Review
New Repub 155:18+ O 1 '66. S. Kauffmann
Newsweek 68:116+ S 26 '66

Informal history of love U.S.A. A. Schlesin-
ger, jr. il Sat Eve Post 239:30-2+ D 31 '66
My Adams uncles: Charles, Henry, Brooks.
A. A. Homans. Yale R 55:321-46 Mr '66
Protestantism and the American labor move-
ment; the Christian spirit in the gilded
age; excerpts from address, April 1965.
H. G. Gutman. bibliog f Am Hist R 72:74-
101 O '66
Proud tower, by B. W. Tuchman. Review
Commentary 41:89-92 My '66. J. Weight-
man
Harper 232:114-17 F '66. K. Epstein;
Reply with rejoinder. J. Barkham. 232:
6+ My '66
Nat R 18:117-19 F 8 '66. W. S. Schlamm
See also
Labor and laboring classes—United States—
History
Negroes in the United States—History
Slavery—United States

Social life and customs

Family of Levi Smith. B. Villet and G. Vil-
let. il Life 61:72-86+ N 25 '66
How America entertains. il Ladies Home J
83:85-112+ O '66
Levi Smith's bonus, fifteen grandchildren.
B. Villet and G. Villet. il Life 61:80-94 D 9
'66
Man talk; women are for weekends. D. New-
man and R. Benton. Mlle 63:46+ Je '66
Mr White and Mr Blue; notes on the new
middle class; excerpts from The great leap;
from the old world of 1939 to the new era.
J. Brooks. il Harper 232:88-91+ Je '66;
Reply. A. B. Bridges. 233:6 Ag '66
Nothing's too good for my daughter! B.
Davidson. il Sat Eve Post 239:28-35 Ag 13
'66
Polite Americans, by G. Carson. Review
Commonweal 84:579-81 S 16 '66. A. Pryce-
Jones
Sat R 49:42 Ap 16 '66. I. Haverstick
Three sons of Levi Smith. B. Villet and
G. Villet. il Life 61:68-82 D 2 '66
Why the Statue of Liberty looks to the east,
etc; excerpts from The third side of the
dollar. A. Laurinchukas. il N Y Times Mag
p8-9+ D 25 '66
Year our children discovered America; Amer-
ican children born in Egypt. E. W. Fernea.
il Redbook 128:12+ D '66
Youngest of the Smiths. B. Villet and G.
Villet. il Life 61:60-71 D 16 '66
See also
Christmas—United States
Colonial life and customs
also subhead Social life and customs
under names of cities, e.g. New York (city)
—Social life and customs

History

View of the water; American palaces by the
sea. J. T. Maher. il Holiday 40:48-53+
Jl '66

Social policy

Christian social relations; address, June 6,
1966. W. W. Wirtz. Vital Speeches 32:546-
50 Jl 1 '66
Dimming of the dream; Great society's im-
pact disappointingly slight. il Time 88:25-6
D 9 '66
For the record; excerpts from address. D.
Cater. Reporter 35:24-6 D 15 '66
Genesis of the Great society; how the Pres-
ident planned to develop program. W. E.
Leuchtenberg. il Reporter 34:36-9 Ap 21 '66
Great society and its future; a progress re-
port; with excerpts from statements by L.
B. Johnson. il U S News 61:32-5 D 19 '66
Great society; its impact of automation; ad-
dress, April 21, 1966. A. H. Raskin. Vital
Speeches 32:554-9 Jl 1 '66
Great society priorities; military budget and
Vietnam war funded at cost of social in-
vestments. S. Melman. Commonweal 84:
494-7 Ag 5 '66
Guaranteed $3,150? brand-new measures to
eliminate poverty. Newsweek 67:72 F 14 '66
Is brotherhood enough? proposals to improve
attitude towards Negroes. N. Wright. Cath
World 204:234-8 Ja '67
Is poverty a sin? Christian Cent 83:357 Mr
23 '66
Late, Great society program pullbacks to aid
Vietnam war. New Repub 154:5-6 Ap 9 '66;
Reply. C. White. 154:29-30 Ap 23 '66
Letter from Washington; concerning State of
the Union message. R. H. Rovere. New
Yorker 41:88+ Ja 22 '66

UNITED STATES—Social policy—*Continued*
News and views; the Great society myth. W. Stringfellow. Commonweal 85:188 N 18 '66

Now beginning; the cautious Congress; Great society programs, where they stand. U S News 62:27-8 Ja 16 '67

President Johnson's Great society. N. Thomas. Christian Cent 83:300-3 Mr 9 '66

Prime mover of Great society; Secretary of health, education & welfare, J. W. Gardner. il Bsns W p 130-2+ My 21 '66

Program for the social orphans: next step in social security. A. L. Schorr. il N Y Times Mag p32-3+ Mr 13 '66; Reply. D. Ferraro. p21+ My 1 '66

Reflections on the Great society. C. Malik. Sat R 49:12-15 Ag 6 '66

Republican answer to LBJ's program; interview. G. R. Ford. U S News 62:10 Ja 23 '67

State of the riposte; E. Dirksen and G. Ford criticize State of the Union message. il Newsweek 67:22 Ja 31 '66

State of the Union; address, January 17, 1966. G. R. Ford. Vital Speeches 32:259-61 F 15 '66

State of the Union; address, January 12, 1966. L. B. Johnson. Vital Speeches 32:226-30 F 1 '66; Excerpts. Dept State Bul 54:150-5 Ja 31 '66

Taking the Great society seriously. M. Harrington. Harper 233:43-9 D '66

Tensions and conservatism in American politics. O. Gass. bibliog f Commentary 42:63-70 N '66

War, taxes, Great society, Johnson's blueprint for '67; State-of-the-Union message, January 10, 1967. L. B. Johnson. il U S News 62:104-10 Ja 23 '67

Welfare in affluence: the mirage of rationalism. R. McGee. il Nation 202:174-80 F 14 '66

What tomorrow's political issues will be. il Nations Bsns 53:33-5+ D '65

What's Congress doing? the Great Society, and the Vietnam war. New Repub 154:7-8 My 7 '66

Where consensus breaks down; Great society. H. J. Morgenthau; discussion. New Repub 154:34+ F 19 '66

Where I stand. E. Brooke. Atlan 217:60-5 Mr '66

Who'll be helped, hurt by LBJ plans; concerning State-of-the-Union message. il U S News 62:27-30 Ja 23 '67

Social security administration
When you need to deal with the social security people. Changing T 20:19-20 Ap '66

Space nuclear propulsion office
Saturn nuclear stage seen possible in '75. H. M. David. il Tech W 19:118+ N 28 '66

Standards, National bureau of
Bureau of standards dedicates new headquarters near capital. W. S. Beller. il Tech W 19:18-19 N 21 '66

National bureau of standards. P. H. Abelson. Science 153:939 Ag 26 '66

STSers witness NBS move. il(p 161) Sci N 89:163 Mr 12 '66

Standards lab broadens its bailiwick; moves to Gaithersburg, Md. il Bsns W p96-8+ Je 18 '66
See also
United States—Institute for applied technology

State, Department of
Department announces plans for advisory panels; Department announcement, October 18, 1966. Dept State Bul 55:721-2 N 7 '66

Department to hold foreign policy conference for educators. Dept State Bul 54:897 Je 6 '66

Falsification of history; discrepancies between published and unpublished accounts of Franco-American relations. Nation 203:235 S 19 '66

Foreign policy conference to be held at Salt Lake City. Dept State Bul 54:116-17 Ja 24 '66

Four centers of U.S. foreign policy; government departments and the President's position. N. Cousins. Sat R 49:16-18 Jl 2 '66

Frances and the creeps; State department surveillance procedures. Newsweek 67:30 Ap 4 '66

National foreign policy conference for educators; Washington, D.C. June 16-17, 1966; with introd. by R. I. Phillips; symposium. Dept State Bul 55:71-109 Jl 18 '66

Publications. See issues of Department of state bulletin

Rise of the CIA; how foggy bottom lost its spies; excerpt from Anatomy of the State department. S. Simpson. Nation 204:38-42 Ja 9 '67

Room at the top. il Newsweek 67:30-1 My 23 '66

See here, Mr Ambassador; State department's regional foreign policy conference. M. Wall. il Am Ed 2:21-3 Jl '66

Senior scholastic interview. il Sr Schol 89:21 N 4 '66

Shaking up the jelly. il Newsweek 69:22-3 Ja 16 '67

State department travel bans: are they justified? pro and con discussion. il Sr Schol 88:15-16 F 25 '66

State moves up; Senior interdepartmental group. Newsweek 67:27 Mr 14 '66

Switching squads; changeover in foreign-policy establishment. Time 87:29-30 My 20 '66

Teach-in on Vietnam by: the President, Secretary of state, Secretary of defense and the Under Secretary of state. H. F. Graff. il N Y Times Mag p25+ Mr 20 '66

Theologians of the cold war; unflattering light on top personnel. Nation 202:506-7 My 2 '66
See also
Secretaries of state (United States)
United States—Foreign service
United States—Foreign service institute

Advisory committee on international business problems
Advisory group on international business problems meets. Dept State Bul 54:403-4 Mr 14 '66

African affairs, Bureau of
Two appointments; J. Palmer 2d succeeds G. M. Williams. New Repub 154:10 Mr 26 '66

East Asian and Pacific affairs, Bureau of
Advisory panel for East Asian and Pacific bureau named. Dept State Bul 55:868 D 5 '66

Department names advisory panel on China. Dept State Bul 55:966 D 26 '66

European affairs, Bureau of
Policy planning council, European affairs bureau advisers named. Dept State Bul 56:16-18 Ja 2 '67

Foreign scholarships, Board of
Board of foreign scholarships members sworn in. Dept State Bul. 54:627 Ap 18 '66

Members of Board of foreign scholarships announced. Dept State Bul 54:289 F 21 '66

International scientific and technological affairs, Office of
Science and state; dangers of not filling director's post. Nation 204:3-4 Ja 2 '67

Scientific advice in the State department. E. R. Skolnikoff. bibliog Science 154:980-5 N 25 '66

Passport division
All together now, Frances Knight is a bad woman. Nat R 18:351 Ap 19 '66

Inside look at a struggle over policy; excerpts from interview, ed. by V. Glaser. U S News 60:16 Mr '66

Keeping an eye on tourists; concerning F. Knight activities, FBI, and H. Hughes. D. Sanford. New Repub 154:9-10 Ap 9 '66

Passport please? Commonweal 84:67-8 Ap 8 '66

Truth about the Abba Schwartz case. G. Fritchey. Harper 232:33-4+ Je '66

Policy planning council
Policy planning council, European affairs bureau advisers named. Dept State Bul 56:16-18 Ja 2 '67

Refugee and migration affairs, Office of
Continuity of refugee and migration policies; address, March 22, 1966. W. J. Crockett. Dept State Bul 54:704-6 My 2 '66

Department transfers Office of refugee and migration affairs. Dept State Bul 55:725 N 7 '66

UNITED STATES—State, Department of—*Cont.*

Science adviser, Office of

See United States—State, Department of
—International scientific and technological
affairs, Office of

Security and consular affairs, Bureau of

Knifing of Abba Schwartz. New Repub 154:
12-13 Mr 19 '66
Quietly dropped; A. Schwartz to testify at
hearings. New Repub 154:8 My 28 '66
Role of the State department in the admin-
istration and enforcement of the new im-
migration law. A. P. Schwartz. bibliog f
Ann Am Acad 367:93-104 S '66
Storm at State; A. P. Schwartz's resigna-
tion. il Newsweek 67:2 Mr 21 '66
Truth about the Abba Schwartz case. C.
Fritchey. Harper 232:33-4+ Je '66

Statistics

Just average; comp. by H. Helfer. il N Y
Times Mag p32 My 1 '66
Seduction by statistics. E. M. Dirksen. Na-
tions Bsns 54:68-72 Jl '66
Sharpening the tools of decision-making; cen-
ter for coordinating government statistics. il
Bsns W p82+ N 19 '66
This U.S.A; an unexpected family portrait
of 194,067,296 Americans drawn from the
census, by B. J. Wattenberg and R. M.
Scammon. Review
Harper 232:149-51 Mr '66. D. J. Boorstin
See also
United States—Census

Supreme court

Cast of characters; forthcoming cases. News-
week 68:37 O 17 '66
Challenge from the South; South Carolina
v. N. deB. Katzenbach. il Time 87:18-19
Ja 28 '66
Choices and decisions. America 115:442-3 O 15
'66
Court is back in business; docket heavy with
antitrust and labor cases. Bsns W p 186+
O 8 '66
Expanding liberties, by M. R. Konvitz.
Review
Nation 203:289-90 S 26 '66. F. J. Donner
Hardly going out of business; new docket.
il Time 88:71-2 O 14 '66
High court's 20th century men; four younger
justices. il Bsns W p 190+ O 1 '66
Honorable Earl Warren. J. D. Weaver. il
Holiday 39:76-7+ Ap; 76-7+ My; 56-7+
Je '66
It is the Earl Warren court. F. Rodell. il
N Y Times Mag p30-1+ Mr 13 '66; Discus-
sion. p22+ Mr 27; 6 Apr 3 '66
Look at Supreme court Justice William O.
Douglas. P. Romero. Negro Hist Bul 29:
129-30+ Mr '66
May it please the Court; three cases of ob-
scenity. A. Kopkind; reply. D. Macdonald.
New Repub 154:37 Ja 29 '66
New look at the 14th. Time 88:76 S 23 '66
Petitioners, by L. Miller. Review
Nation 202:529-30 My 2 '66. E. H. Norton
Politics and the Warren court, by A. M.
Bickel. Review
Sat R 49:32-3 Ja 29 '66. M. Feldman
Supreme court and the Bill of rights. L.
Pfeffer. il Nation 203:315-18, 351-4, 385-8 O
3-17 '66
Supreme court; protector of rights; address,
March 1, 1966. C. L. Gowen. Vital Speeches
32:404-7 Ap 15 '66
Supreme court; the silent arm of govern-
ment. il Sr Schol 88:12-13 F 18 '66

Anecdotes, facetiae, satire, etc.

Day they killed the Constitution. D. W. Ryder. Nat R 18:838 Ag 23 '66

Decisions

Anchor in the past; antitrust cases. il Time
87:85 Je 24 '66
Antitrust: a tough new line; new ruling
overturns merger of two California supermarket chains. il Newsweek 67:81 Je 13 '66
Antitrust in a coonskin cap; merger between
Von's grocery co. and Shopping bag food
stores in Los Angeles declared illegal. Fortune 74:65-6 Jl 1 '66
Are supermarkets for autos next? selling
cars through franchised automobile dealers is being questioned. Bsns W p33 My 7
'66

Bad news for smut peddlers; Ginzburg, Mishkin and Fanny Hill. il Time 87:56+ Ap 1 '66
Bond's word; case of Julian Bond. Newsweek 68:27 D 19 '66
But can you do that? two decisions on free-
dom of speech and the press. H. F. Pilpel.
Pub W 189:70-1 Je 27 '66
Censorship and obscenity; what's happened to
taste? with press comments. D. Reische.
il Sr Schol 89:12-15 O 14 '66
Concern about confessions; Escobedo v. Il-
linois case. il Time 87:52-4+ Ap 29 '66
Confession debate continues. I. R. Kauf-
man. il N Y Times Mag p36-7+ O 2 '66
Confusion on obscenity. America 114:430 Ap
2 '66
Court stirs a hornet's nest; obscenity rulings.
Christian Cent 83:451-2 Ap 13 '66
Crime, confessions, and the Court; excerpt
from The crime war. R. M. Cipes. Atlan
218:51-8 S '66; Discussion. 218:46-8 D '66
Curb on protests. Sr Schol 89:27 D 9 '66
Day in Court; FBI and bugging installations.
Newsweek 68:22 Jl 25 '66
Decisions, decisions; major cases of 1965-
66 term. Newsweek 68:19-20 Jl 4 '66
Decisions, decisions: what's smut, what isn't?
opinions in Ginzburg case and Fanny Hill
case; excerpts. Newsweek 67:20 Ap 4 '66
Delicate balance; deciding major case against
Negro demonstrators. il Newsweek 68:29-
30 N 28 '66
Demeaning the Court; Ginzburg and other
obscenity cases. Nation 202:379 Ap 4 '66
Dialogue with Mrs O'Hair; interview, ed. by
N. C. Nielsen, jr. M. E. Murray. Chris-
tian Cent 83:615-18 My 11 '66
Dissent to the High court's harsh verdict;
R. Ginzburg case. L. Wainright. Life 60:
26 Ap 22 '66
Don't say a word, Mac. Nat R 18:606-8 Je
28 '66
Expanding liberties, by M. R. Konvitz. Re-
view
Commentary 42:91-2+ D '66. M. Harring-
ton
From songs to sedition; right to a reason-
able, orderly and limited protest against
unlawful segregation. Newsweek 67:27 Mr 7
'66
Ginzburg petitions for rehearing; urges fed-
eral censorship board. Library J 91:2440+
My 15 '66
Harassment for juries; expanded rights of
accused; jury prejudice. Time 88:38 D 23
'66
High court bars merger of rivals; in retail
grocery markets. Bsns W p36 Je 4 '66
High court's ruling against a state legislature; Julian Bond case and other actions.
U S News 61:8 D 19 '66
Hoffa decision; government informer issue.
Nation 204:5-6 Ja 2 '67
How Bert beat the bureaucrats; B. N. Adams
patent case. Time 87:61 Mr 4 '66
How not to read a dirty book. America 114:
614 Ap 30 '66
How Supreme court is making itself obsolete. F. Morley. il Nations Bsns 54:27-8 My
'66
How Supreme court overcame its racism;
excerpts from The petitioners. L. Miller.
il Ebony 21:57-62+ Mr '66
Implications of the Ginzburg affair; address,
April 20, 1966. K. Molz. il Wilson Lib Bul
40:941-7 Je '66
In Court: low score for unions. U S News 61:
105-6 N 21 '66
In the 13th year of the Warren revolution:
how Supreme court is changing U.S; with
criticisms by both law school professors
and justices. il U S News 60:48-53 Je 20
'66
Indecisive decision; controversy over Macon,
Ga.'s park willed for white people. il Time
87:40 Ja 28 '66
Is the Warren court too political? A. M.
Bickel. il N Y Times Mag p30-1+ S 25 '66;
Reply. F. Rodell. p22 O 16 '66
Let's have justice for non-criminals, too!
effect of decision on police authority and
safeguarding civil rights. E. H. Methvin.
Read Digest 89:53-60 D '66
More and more power for the trustbusters;
Brown shoe company case. U S News 60:15
Je 20 '66
More criminals to go free? effect of High
court's ruling; with excerpts from opinions
by Justices Warren, White and Harlan. il
U S News 60:32-6 Je 27 '66
Negro library protests upheld by Supreme
court; Clinton, Louisiana, public library.
Library J 91:1374 Mr 15 '66

UNITED STATES—Transportation, Department of—*Continued*
President urges the creation of a transportation department. Am City 81:123 Je '66
Pro for DOT. Time 88:33 N 18 '66
Quick approval of Boyd by Congress seen. Aviation W 85:40-1 N 14 '66
Road looks open for Johnson plan. Bsns W p 105 Mr 12 '66
Sanctity of pork. R. Harwood. New Repub 155:7-8 O 29 '66
They all want to call the shots; congressional committees and transportation industry. il Bsns W p78+ My 28 '66
Transportation dept. Commonweal 85:94-5 O 28 '66
Transportation tangle; President Johnson's request for cabinet-level Department of transportation. W. V. Shannon. Commonweal 83:574-5 F 18 '66; Reply with rejoinder. W. W. Belson. 84:245+ My 20 '66
Transport's rough road. Bsns W p38 S 3 '66
Untangling the nation's lifeline; A. S. Boyd, first Secretary of Transportation. il Bsns W p 111-12+ N 26 '66
Untangling traffic. Sr Schol 89:18-19 N 4 '66
What the President is proposing; new transportation dept. Bsns W p 158+ Ja 22 '66
White House: new traffic center? il Duns R 87:pt2 110-12+ My '66

Travel regulations
See Travel regulations

Travel service
America and the foreign visitor; symposium. il Sat R 49:49-52+ Mr 12 '66

Treasury department
Treasury department to control blocked foreign assets in U.S. Dept State Bul 54:945 Je 13 '66
U.S. Treasury hit by tight money. U S News 61:88 Ag 8 '66

Treaties
International defense commitments of the United States; statement, August 25, 1966. D. Rusk. Dept State Bul 55:377-81 S 12 '66
Treaty information. See issues of Department of state bulletin

Russia
Consular treaty, next bridge to Russia. Life 61:4 N 18 '66
Space treaty; a step forward. il Newsweek 68:21 D 19 '66

Togo
Treaty of amity and economic relations signed with Togo. Dept State Bul 54:367 Mr 7 '66

Weather bureau
Tornado season peak reached in spring; proposed natural disaster warning system. Sci N 89:205 Mr 26 '66

Work projects administration
For bread alone; art patronage. il Time 87:78 My 13 '66

Youth corps
First 50,000 Neighborhood youth corps enrollees. J. F. Tucker. il Mo Labor R 88:1442-4 D '65
Package deal in Suffolk; Youth corps program. W. W. Curley. il Library J 91:343-5 Ja 15 '66
Rhode Island's misspent youth; irregularities in youth corps projects. J. M. Berry. il Reporter 34:29+ Ja 27 '66

UNITED STATES air force academy, Colorado Springs
Air academy's cheating scandal; ed. by J. Shepherd. W. Snead, jr. Look 31:23-5 Ja 24 '67
Air force academy expansion involves not just additions, but alterations, to SOM's design. il Arch Rec 139:40 Ja '66
Bugle call for Negro cadets. il Ebony 21:73-4+ Je '66
U.S. air force chapel. il Sch Arts 65:38-40 Ja '66

UNITED STATES amateur championship. See Golf—Tournaments

UNITED STATES and Latin America; United States and Russia; etc. See Latin America and the United States; Russia and the United States; etc.

UNITED STATES army information school. See United States—Army—Defense information school

UNITED STATES Beltsville research center. See United States—Agricultural research center, Beltsville, Md.

UNITED STATES book exchange, incorporated
1965 disappointing at USBE; 554,968 items distributed; 18th annual meeting. Library J 91:2444 My 15 '66
USBE story: continued. A. D. Ball. il Library J 91:1349-53 Mr 15 '66

UNITED STATES book publishers association. See Authors

UNITED STATES camera (periodical)
1967 U.S. camera world annual; preview. il U S Camera 29:56-9 N '66

UNITED STATES-Canadian committee on trade and economic affairs. See Joint United States-Canadian committee on trade and economic affairs

UNITED STATES chess federation. See Chess

UNITED STATES coast guard academy
Coast guard academy to expand. il Motor B 118:123 S '66

UNITED STATES conference of mayors. See Mayors

UNITED STATES employment service. See United States—Employment service

UNITED STATES exploring expedition, 1838-1842
Ice ahead! R. K. Andrist. il Am Heritage 17:60-3+ Ag '66
Voyage to the bottom of the earth; Wilkes expedition. il Sr Schol 89:1 Ja 13 '67

UNITED STATES federal council for science and technology
U.S. lags in ocean plans. il Sci N 89:494 Je 18 '66

UNITED STATES foreign service. See United States—Foreign service

UNITED STATES forest service institute of forest genetics. See Institute of forest genetics

UNITED STATES gypsum company
Industry builds a showcase in the slums; experiment in Harlem. il Bsns W p40-1 F 26 '66
Private way; rehabilitation of a Manhattan east Harlem ghetto. il Time 87:89 Je 3 '66

UNITED STATES in art
Scenes of America by Bartlett and others; exhibition at Arnot art gallery, Elmira, N.Y. E. P. Birk. il Antiques 90:602+ N '66
See also
West in art

UNITED STATES information agency. See United States—Information agency

UNITED STATES information service. See United States—Information service

UNITED STATES-Japan committee on scientific cooperation. See Joint United States-Japan committee on scientific cooperation

UNITED STATES-Japan cooperative science program. See Science—International aspects

UNITED STATES junior chamber of commerce
America's ten outstanding young men of 1966. B. Baer. il Look 31:73-4 Ja 24 '67
Jaycees' good reading project. J. D. Burris. ALA Bul 60:635-6 Je '66

UNITED STATES marine band. See Bands (music)

UNITED STATES maritime authority. See Intergovernmental maritime consultative organization

UNITED STATES military academy, West Point
Bugle call for Negro cadets. il Ebony 21:73-4+ Je '66
Hilton on the Hudson. il Time 88:72 D 23 '66

UNITED STATES national arboretum. See Washington, D.C.—National arboretum

UNITED STATES national student association
Cc: IRS. Nat R 18:1205 N 29 '66
Crowded left. il Time 88:46 S 9 '66
Teen travel talk; International student identity card. il Seventeen 25:204 Mr '66

UNITED STATES naval academy, Annapolis
After a row over Naval academy grades. U S News 60:14-15 Ap 25 '66
Bugle call for Negro cadets. il Ebony 21:73-4+ Je '66
Flunk quota at Annapolis. il Time 87:50 Ap 22 '66
Trouble on the low C's. Newsweek 67:82 Ap 25 '66
U.S. naval academy; faculty unrest. L. J. Carter. Science 152:1043-5 My 20 '66

UNITED STATES naval oceanographic office, Suitland, Md.
Freak waves predictable. Sci N 90:132 Ag 27 '66
Navy plans increased funding of wide range of new projects. M. Getler. il Tech W 19:44+ S 26 '66

UNITED STATES of Central America (proposed) See Central America—Politics

UNITED STATES of Europe (proposed) See European federation

UNITED STATES office of education. See United States—Education, Office of

UNITED STATES Open golf championship. See Golf—Tournaments

UNITED STATES Operations Mission. See United States—Agency for international development

UNITED STATES power squadrons, incorporated

Under way with the USPS. See issues of Motor boating

USPS is 541 C. Schrage. Yachting 119:61+ Ja '66

With the power squadrons. C. Schrage. See issues of Yachting

You are invited to attend U.S. power squadrons free instruction classes in boat operation. H. M. Hutchings. Motor B 118:74-6 Ag '66

UNITED STATES-Russia air agreement. See Aviation—International aspects

UNITED STATES-South Africa leader exchange program, incorporated

New bridge of understanding and cooperation. F. S. Loescher. Sch & Soc 94:126-8 Mr 5 '66

UNITED STATES steel corporation

Big change at U.S. steel. T. J. Murray. il Duns R 87:36-9+ Mr '66

Big target; protests at segregated facilities. il Newsweek 67:93+ Je 20 '66

Steel giants face a blast on bias; NAACP blames USW. Bsns W p81-2 Je 11 '66

Toward the top at U.S. steel; E. H. Gott. Bsns W p52 S 10 '66

Without trumpet flares; charitable activities. L. L. L. Golden. Sat R 49:96 D 10 '66

UNITED STATES time corporation

Ticking at Timex. Newsweek 67:81 Mr 14 '66

UNITED STATES travel service. See United States—Travel service

UNITED steelworkers of America

Abel finds a broader role for the USW; unifying factor in AFL-CIO. il Bsns W p57-8+ My 28 '66

Peace pact opens way to merger; steelworkers may take over Mine, mill members. il Bsns W p 132 S 3 '66

Smelted; mutual assistance pact. Time 88:96 S 9 '66

Steel contract puts Abel on spot; dissatisfaction within union. Bsns W p97-8 Ja 22 '66

Steel men thrive on sabbaticals; thirteen weeks of paid vacation every five years. il Bsns W p 166-8 N 26 '66

Steelworkers seek a bigger voice; implications for future industry bargaining. il Bsns W p 160+ S 24 '66

UNITED technology center. See United aircraft corporation—United technology center

UNITED theological college of the West Indies. See Theological schools

UNITED world federalists

World federalists General assembly; Washington, D.C, June 16-19. H. Y. Williams. Christian Cent 83:941-2 Jl 27 '66

UNITS, Electric. See Electric units

UNIVAC computers. See Computers—Digital computers

UNIVERSAL city. See Moving picture studios

UNIVERSAL copyright convention. See Copyright

UNIVERSAL declaration of human rights

Recommendations for twentieth anniversary. UN Mo Chron 3:22-4 Mr '66

UNIVERSAL history. See World history

UNIVERSAL military training. See Military training

UNIVERSAL time. See Time measurements

UNIVERSE

Birth and life of the universe; observations through the Hale telescope at Palomar observatory. C. P. Gilmore. il N Y Times Mag p26-7+ Je 12 '66

Cosmology, 1966. B. Frisch. il Sci Digest 59: 66-72 My '66

Galaxies, quasars, and the expanding universe. T. D. Nicholson. il Natur Hist 76:36-9 Ja '67

Greatest explosion of them all; discoveries spark debate among astronomers over origin of universe. E. Ubell. Read Digest 88:123-7 F '66

Long look back to creation. M. Gunther. il Sat Eve Post 239:23-5 Mr 12 '66

Man on the mountain; M. Schmidt; quasars and theories of the universe. L. Jaroff. il Time 87:80-4 Mr 11 '66

See also
Cosmogony
Cosmology
Life on other planets
Milky way
Solar system

UNIVERSITIES. See Colleges and universities

UNIVERSITY administration. See Colleges and universities—Administration

UNIVERSITY athletics. See College athletics

UNIVERSITY bookstores. See College bookstores

UNIVERSITY college of Rhodesia, Salisbury. See Colleges and universities—Rhodesia

UNIVERSITY drama. See College and school drama

UNIVERSITY extension

Guidelines for library services to extension students; with report by N. E. Tanis. ALA Bul 61:50-5 Ja '67

Steelworkers on campus. H. J. Golatz. America 114:652-4 My 7 '66

UC extension keeps the pros up to date. il Bsns W p 196-8+ Mr 12 '66

Women moving ahead. A. Y. Scates. il Am Ed 2:1-4 Mr '66

See also
Colleges and universities—Off-campus centers
National university extension association

UNIVERSITY government. See Colleges and universities—Administration

UNIVERSITY librarians. See Librarians

UNIVERSITY libraries. See College libraries

UNIVERSITY lobbyists. See Lobbyists

UNIVERSITY microfilms, Ann Arbor, Mich.

Conference papers logjam; letter to the editor. Library J 91:3578 Ag '66

Legacy library; facsimiles of classic children's books. il Pub W 189:100-1 F 14 '66

University microfilms head resigns Michigan post. Pub W 189:47-8 Mr 28 '66

Weak arm of the law; case of E. B. Power. Nation 202:350 Mr 28 '66

Xerox: a new string to the bow; University microfilms enters children's book market. D. Dempsey. Sat R 49:39-40 F 19 '66

UNIVERSITY of Ghana. See Colleges and universities—Ghana

UNIVERSITY of Oklahoma ballet. See Ballet companies

UNIVERSITY of Sussex. See Colleges and universities—England

UNIVERSITY of Texas; University of Wisconsin; etc. See Texas. University; Wisconsin. University; etc.

UNIVERSITY of the Pacific, Stockton, Calif.

Learning in two languages; Elbert Covell college; Inter-American studies program. A. J. Cullen. il Américas 18:12-18 My '66

Schools make news; Callison college's projects. Sat R 49:63 My 21 '66

UNIVERSITY of the Seven Seas. See Colleges and universities, Traveling

UNIVERSITY presses

Attention foundations and university presses; here is a new way of getting those deletions back. D. Hall. Am Rec G 32:944-5+ Je '66

Check list of university press books; comp. by N. Sofian. Sat R 49:20 Je 11 '66

Elbowroom for the mind; with editorial comment. J. G. Lawler. America 116:28, 41-3 Ja 14 '67

Trade winds; news from various presses. D. B. Sutherland. il Sat R 49:16 Je 11 '66

University presses. il Pub W 190:66-9 Jl 4 '66

University presses study the problems of growth; summary of discussion at AAUP meeting. il Pub W 190:32-51 Jl 4 '66

University publishing and the pressures of growth. C. B. Grannis. Pub W 190:61 Jl 4 '66

What a way to grow; trend toward more popular books. D. Dempsey. Sat R 49:46 Je 11 '66

See also names of university presses, e.g. Rutgers university press

UNIVERSITY professors. See College professors and instructors
UNIVERSITY research. See Colleges and universities—Research
UNIVERSITY students. See College students
UNIVERSITY study tours. See Travel study courses
UNMARRIED men. See Single men
UNMARRIED mothers. See Mothers, Unmarried
UNMARRIED women. See Single women
UNRUH, Glenys G.
Parents can help their children succeed in school. NEA J 55:14-16 D '66
UNTERMEYER, Louis
Fates defied the muse. Sat R 49:32-3 N 5 '66
Person first, a poet second. Sat R 49:54+ D 3 '66
To each man his own metaphor. Sat R 49:45 F 19 '66
UPDIKE, John
Air show; poem. New Repub 155:25 D 17 '66
Amoeba; poem. New Repub 154:23 Je 25 '66
Bech in Rumania; story. New Yorker 42:54-63 O 8 '66
Books (cont) New Yorker 42:115-18+ F 26 '66
Harv is plowing now; story. New Yorker 42:46-8 Ap 23 '66
Marching through Boston; story. New Yorker 41:34-8 Ja 22 '66
Mastery of Miss Warner. New Repub 154:23-5 Mr 5 '66; Correction. 154:40 Mr 26 '66
Nabokov's look back: a national loss. Life 62:9+ Ja 13 '67
Pro; story. New Yorker 42:53-4 S 17 '66
Seal in nature; poem. New Repub 155:16 O 15 '66
Witnesses; story. New Yorker 42:27-9 Ag 13 '66
Your lover just called; story. Harper 234:48-51 Ja '67
about
Can a nice novelist finish first? J. Howard. il pors Life 61:74-74A+ N 4 '66
Domestic felicity? G. Hicks. Sat R 49:31 S 24 '66
John and Bruce. por Newsweek 68:116 S 26 '66
Language, myth and Mr Updike. A. Burgess. Commonweal 83:557-9 F 11 '66
Onward with Updike. S. Kauffmann. New Repub 155:15-17 S 24 '66
UPHOLSTERY
Care and safekeeping of upholstery. House & Gard 130:277-9 O '66
Providence cabinetmakers, chairmakers, upholsterers, and allied craftsmen, 1756-1838; a check list. W. D. Garrett. il Antiques 90:514-19 O '66
UPLAND college, Upland, Calif.
With a prayer, Upland goes on the block; sold to Salvation army. il Bsns W p 194-6+ N 5 '66
UPPER atmosphere. See Atmosphere, Upper
UPPER classes
In people discover, Acapulco. T. Meehan. il N Y Times Mag p38-9+ F 13 '66
New image of the socialite; Negro woman socialite. G. Major. il Ebony 21:63-4+ Ag '66
UPPER DARBY, Pa.
Upper Darby senior high builds a school in Africa. R. Hoopes. il Seventeen 25:98-9+ Ap '66
UPTON, Barna
Our first foreign war; letters, ed. with introd. by W. F. Goetzmann. Am Heritage 17:18-27+ Je '66
UPTON, Charles, and Upton, Helen
Living with antiques. Antiques 90:84-9 Jl '66
UPTON, Helen. See Upton, C. jt. auth.
UPTON, Lloyd G.
Try a croquet ball for hanging feeder. Audubon Mag 68:372 S '66
UPTON, T. Graydon
U.S.-Latin American relations; address, March 24, 1966. Vital Speeches 32:400-4 Ap 15 '66
UPWARD bound (program) See Socially handicapped children—Education
UR
Abraham, the friend of God. K. MacLeish. il Nat Geog Mag 130:739-89 D '66
URACIL
Addition radicals formed by hydroxyl radical bombardment of uracil. J. N. Herak and W. Gordy. bibliog il Science 153:1649-50 S 30 '66

Solution photochemistry of thymine and uracil. A. A. Lamola and J. P. Mittal. bibliog il Science 154:1560-1 D 23 '66
URANIUM
Canada goes shopping for tons of uranium. Sci N 90:246 O 1 '66
Distribution of uranium in some natural minerals. E. I. Hamilton. bibliog il Science 151:570-2 F 4 '66
Fusion of uranium atoms seen possible in future. Sci N 90:176 S 10 '66
Superconductivity of alpha-uranium and the role of 5f electrons. T. H. Geballe and others. bibliog il Science 152:755-7 My 6 '66
Superconductivity of beta-uranium. B. T. Matthias and others. bibliog il Science 151:985-6 F 25 '66
Superconductivity of beta-uranium. B. T. Matthias and others. bibliog il Science 151:985-6 F 25 '66; Reply with rejoinder. B. W. Howlett. 154:542-3 O 28 '66
Uranium prospectors invade German resort. Sci N 89:442 Je 4 '66
Isotopes
Uranium and lead isotopic stability in a metamict zircon under experimental hydrothermal conditions. R. T. Pidgeon and others. bibliog il Science 154:1538-40 D 23 '66
URANUS (planet)
Satellites
See Satellites
URATES. See Uric acid
URBAN America, incorporated
City's own pressure group; Urban America, champion of city interests. il Bsns W p 158+ O 1 '66
URBAN freeways. See Express highways
URBAN growth. See Cities and towns—Growth
URBAN league, National. See National urban league
URBAN redevelopment. See City planning; Urban renewal
URBAN renewal
Art judgment & social responsibility. J. J. Lovano and J. K. McFee. bibliog il Sch Arts 65:23-4 Ap '66
Boston's bristly Mr Logue; development program for the entire city. A. R. Talbot. Harper 233:18+ N '66
Chance for creative federalism; L. B. Johnson's program. Life 60:4 F 11 '66
City is the frontier, by C. Abrams. Review Commentary 41:93-5 Mr '66. E. C. Banfield; Reply with rejoinder. P. Goodman. 41:14+ My '66
Crisis in the cities: LBJ's plan of action. il U S News 60:55-7 F 7 '66
Do you understand your new clients? architects in city renewal; interview, ed. by E. Goble. W. L. Slayton. Arch Rec 140:9-10 Ag '66
Doing something about slums. H. J. Gans. Commonweal 83:688-93 Mr 18 '66
Dream of fair cities; beyond redemption? F. Getlein. Commonweal 85:366-8 Ja 6 '67
Fair chance against slums; H. S. Truman's federal welfare projects, 1949. il Sr Schol 89:2 Ja 6 '67
Fresh pattern for inner-city renewal; Louisville. il Am City 81:97+ F '66
Hope for the heart; HUD's responsibilities. il Time 87:29-33 Mr 4 '66
How much for rebirth? making U.S. big cities livable. il Bsns W p 106+ S 3 '66
Lady blocks the pork barrel; exemptions dropped from Housing and urban development bill. Life 61:6 S 23 '66
Mr Johnson's cut-rate revolution. il Arch Forum 124:29-31 Mr '66
New attack on city problems; how it is to work; federal grants for demonstration cities. U S News 61:47 O 31 '66
New frontiers of urban excellence? B. G. Lall. Bul Atomic Sci 22:37-40 Mr '66
Office building and urban renewal. il Arch Rec 140:177 N '66
Rebuilding the slums. J. Ridgeway. New Repub 156:22-5 Ja 7 '67
Room at the bottom: increased federal aid for community development. il Time 87:26-7 F 4 '66
Shapes of the new Southwest; Washington, D.C. P. Johnson-Marshall. il Arch Forum 125:60-7 Jl '66
Studying the urban revolution; urban universities. il Time 89:59 Ja 6 '67

URBAN renewal—*Continued*
Symbolic bells in Dixwell; New Haven. M. Hommann. il Arch Forum 125:54-9 Jl '66
Trillion dollars to save the cities? il U S News 61:73-6 O 3 '66
Unity and harmony at Rockefeller Center. D. Haskell. il Arch Forum 124:42-7 Ja '66
Urban planning with principles. R. Kirk. Nat R 18:221 Mr 8 '66
Urban renaissance, or boondoggle? Demonstration cities program. il Bsns W p 141-2 O 29 '66
Vision or television? hearings on the federal role in urban affairs. Reporter 35:8-9 D 29 '66
Weaver's trade; House approves Demonstration cities program. Newsweek 68:42+ O 24 '66
Where did Frank's building go? Nyack's renewal program. il Nations Bsns 54:36-7 Ja '66
        See also
City planning
Community organizations for the improvement of neighborhoods, incorporated
Urban America, incorporated

Anecdotes, facetiae, satire, etc.
Fable of the American cities; address, September 13, 1966. W. Owen. il U S News 61:77-8 O 3 '66
Grateful society; an urban fable. W. Owen. Arch Forum 125:92 O '66

URBAN-rural conflict. See City and country
URBAN sociology. See Sociology, Urban
URBAN universities. See Colleges and universities, Municipal
URBANISM. See Cities and towns
URBANIZATION
Discovering the role of art in a changing metropolitan environment; Baltimore high school summer program. G. F. Horn. il Sch Arts 65:36-8 Ap '66
        See also
Urban America, incorporated
URBANIZED areas. See Metropolitan areas
URDANG, Constance
Tree, lake, moon: and man. R. Roseliep. Poetry 108:56-7 Ap '66
UREA
Milk production of cows on protein-free feed. A. I. Virtanen. bibliog il Science 153:1603-14 S 30 '66
Rules for using urea in beef cattle rations. W. Woods. il Suc Farm 64:58 Ap '66
Urea synthesis in the lungfish: relative importance of purine and ornithine cycle pathways. R. P. Forster and L. Goldstein. bibliog il Science 153:1650-2 S 30 '66
Urease activity in blue-green algae. D. S. Berns and others. bibliog il Science 152:1077-8 My 20 '66
UREASE
Antiradiation vaccine. il Sci N 89:307 Ap 30 '66
URETERAL peristalsis. See Kidneys
URETZ, Robert B. See MacInnes, J. W. jt. auth.
UREY, Harold C.
Dust on the moon. bibliog Science 153:1419-20 S 16 '66
URIBURU, Ernesto C.
Fortresses of the past. Américas 18:33-6 My '66
URIC acid
Gout and greatness. il Newsweek 67:62 F 21 '66
Uric acid dihydrate: crystallography and identification. R. Shirley. bibliog il Science 152:1512-13 Je 10 '66
Uric acid, uric acid dihydrate, and urates in urinary calculi, ancient and modern. K. Lonsdale and P Mason. bibliog il Science 152:1511-12 Je 10 '66
URIC acid metabolism
Biting sickness; study findings on Nyhan's disease. Newsweek 68:52 S 5 '66
URICOLYTIC enzymes. See Enzymes
URINARY calculi. See Calculi, Urinary
URINARY organs
        See also
Bladder
URINE
        See also
Diuretics and diuresis

Incontinence
Bedwetting; a common problem. M. J. Gersh and S. Blumenfeld. il Parents Mag 41:44-5+ Ap '66

What parents need to know about bed-wetting. S. M. Linde. il Todays Health 44:50-1+ Ag '66
URLUS, Jacques
Historical records. A. Favia-Artsay. por Hobbies 71:38 My '66
UROFSKY, Melvin I.
Truth & power. New Repub 155:15-17 D 17 '66
URQUHART, Thomas
(ed) See Jones, G. Lady from Wales
URUGUAY
        See also
Education—Uruguay

Economic conditions
Country handcuffed by pure democracy. il U S News 61:64-6 S 12 '66
Snap jobs and cheap money; Uruguay's double inflation. R. O'Mara. il Nation 204:50-2 Ja 9 '67
Uruguay today. S. M. Socolow. Cur Hist 55:270-5 N '66

Economic policy
Disillusion in Utopia. Time 88:31 S 2 '66

Foreign relations
Enough was enough; order four Soviet embassy officers out of the country. Time 88:44 O 14 '66

Politics and government
Country handcuffed by pure democracy. il U S News 61:64-6 S 12 '66
Game of chance. Newsweek 68:61 D 12 '66
Peaceful revolution. Time 88:44 D 9 '66
Snap jobs and cheap money; Uruguay's double inflation. R. O'Mara. il Nation 204:50-2 Ja 9 '67
Uruguay today. S. M. Socolow. Cur Hist 55:270-5 N '66

Social policy
Uruguay: Utopia gone wild. J. Gunther. il Read Digest 88:187-8+ Ap '66

Treaties
Of law and the river; treaty defining the Uruguay-Argentine boundary. H. Martinez-Montero. il Américas 18:1-4 F '66
URUGUAY RIVER
Of law and the river; treaty defining the Uruguay-Argentina boundary. H. Martinez-Montero. il Américas 18:1-4 F '66
USE of time. See Time, Use of
USED automobiles; Used boats; etc. See Automobiles, Used; Boats, Used; etc.
USEEM, John
Work patterns of Americans in India. Ann Am Acad 368:146-56 N '66
USEEM, Ruth Hill
American family in India. Ann Am Acad 368:132-45 N '66
USSACHEVSKY, Vladimir
Musical events; demonstration of his electronic music at Bernard M. Baruch school of business and public administration. W. Sargeant. New Yorker 42:86+ My 28 '66
USTILAGO sphaerogena. See Fungi
USTINOV, Peter
Atlantic report. Atlan 218:16+ N '66
Politics and the arts; excerpt from address. por Atlan 218:44-8 Jl '66
Swiss watch; story. Atlan 218:84 O '66
        about
Polymorph. por Newsweek 68:99 O 10 '66
UTAH
        See also
Agriculture—Utah
Camping—Utah
Great Salt Lake
Great Salt Lake Desert
Hunting—Utah
Mines and mineral resources—Utah
Monument Valley, Utah and Arizona
Mormons and Mormonism
Natural Bridges National Monument
Radioactive fallout—Utah
Skis and skiing—Utah
Wilderness areas—Utah

Parks and reserves
        See also
Canyonlands National Park
UTAH symphony orchestra
Musical events; concert in Carnegie Hall. W. Sargeant. New Yorker 42:135-6 S 17 '66

UTAMARO (artist)
Ukiyo-ye prints. D. Powills. il Hobbies 71:120-1 S '66

UTERUS
Expectant mother: where the unborn baby grows; ed. by D. Meilach. E. A. Friedman. Redbook 127:35-6 S '66
Progesterone retards postpartum involution of the rabbit myometrium. F. R. Goodall. bibliog il Science 152:356-8 Ap 15 '66
See also
Cervix

UTERUS, Artificial
Womb with windows; surgery on monkey fetus at University of Nevada's laboratories of human development. il Life 61:65-6 Jl 29 '66

UTICA, N.Y.

Water supply

Granular lime takes bite out of water. J. H. Haberer. il Am City 81:183-4 My '66

UTILITY boats, Naval. See United States—Navy—Boats

UTILIZATION of waste. See Waste, Utilization of

UTOPIAS
Danger: utopia ahead. J. W. Krutch. Sat R 49:17-18+ Ag 20 '66
Pros and cons of paradise. C. Walsh. Sat R 49:36-7 Jl 30 '66
Saturnalia, satire, and utopia. R. C. Elliott. Yale R 55:521-36 Je '66

UTZON, Jørn
Utzon's position. Arch Forum 124:89 Ap '66

about

Breaking point in Sydney. R. Boyd. il Arch Forum 124:21-2 Ap '66
Dane's design rescued from the discards. D. Moser. il por Life 62:64+ Ja 6 '67

UZIELLI, Anne (Ford) See Ford, A.

UZIELLI, Giancarlo
Steering a different marriage. B. Walters. Ladies Home J 83:67 S '66

UZMAN, Betty G. See Morgan, R. S. jt. auth.

UZZLE, Warren
Out of the frying pan. il U S Camera 29:48-51+ Ag '66

V

VD. See Venereal diseases
VFW. See Veterans of foreign wars
VIS (Visitor information service) See United States—Forest service
VISTA. See Volunteers in service to America
VOA. See Voice of America (radio program)
VOM. See Voltohmmeters
VOR (visual omnirange) See Radio in aviation
V/STOL (vertical or short take-off and landing) See Airplanes, Vertical take-off and landing
VTOL. See Airplanes, Vertical take-off and landing
VACANCES pax; story. See Gallant, M.

VACATION houses
All the features a good vacation house should have. N. Seney. il Bet Hom & Gard 44:82-3 Mr '66
Building a different kind of tree house. il Sports Illus 25:56-9 O 17 '66
Expandable vacation home for families with children. R. Charles. il Parents Mag 41:65-8 F '66
Five fun-packed vacation homes; three-gable, A-frame weekender; three unique snow or sun hideaways; man-size Lincoln log kit. il Pop Mech 125:129-39 Ap '66
Gift for a lifetime, a vacation house. N. Seney. il Bet Hom & Gard 44:104-7 D '66
Holiday house built for fun. W. I. Fischman. il Pop Mech 125:90-7+ Ap '66
New shapes for vacations. il House & Gard 129:124-31 Je '66
Pavilions by the water; Slater vacation home in Boca Raton, Fla. il Life 60:84-7+ F 11 '66
Shingles, fanciful shapes for a carefree cottage. il Arch Rec 140:140-1 N '66

Weekend retreat. il Sunset 137:106-8 O '66
Year-round house for happy weekends. il House & Gard 129:108-9 F '66
Your vacation home. il Field & S 70:41-52 F '66
See also
Beach architecture
Summer homes

VACATION projects
See also
Libraries, Childrens—Projects

VACATION safety devices and measures. See Safety devices and measures

VACATION schools. See Summer schools

VACATION spending. See Vacations

VACATION villages
Low-cost high-old-time holiday; Club Méditerranée; with report by H. Moffett. il Life 60:74-86 F 25 '66
Producing vacations; Paris-based Club Méditerranée. il Time 87:94 My 27 '66
Revolution in the sun; sea-and-sun vacations at twenty-six sites of Club Méditerranée. L. Jonckheere. il Sr Schol 89:sup 12-13 Ja 13 '67

VACATIONS
Attractions for vacationers in national forests. il Good H 162:177 Je '66
Do-something-different vacations. N. Kuehnl. il Bet Hom & Gard 44:62-5 F '66
Get-away-from-it-all vacations; six regions described. P. Lindberg. il Bet Home & Gard 44:133-6+ Ap '66
Guide to winter sunshine vacations. il Bet Hom & Gard 44:121-2+ O '66
If you're thinking of a winter vacation. il U S News 62:54-7 Ja 16 '67
Made vacation plans yet? Changing T 20:6 Mr '66
Making the most of summer. J. W. Parks. Parents Mag 41:42-3+ Ag '66
More for your travel dollar (title varies) (cont) Bet Hom & Gard 44:28 Ag '66; 45:14 Ja '67
New & different vacations. il Changing T 20:35-8 My '66
Rent-free vacation by house-swapping. Sunset 138:45 Ja '67
Special feature on summer opportunities for teachers; symposium. il NEA J 55:28-38 My '66
Swap homes for a rent-free vacation. il Changing T 20:20 Ap '66
Their hearts are as big as their country; farm and ranch vacations for city children at McKay ranch, Ore. W. B. Morse. il Am For 72:30-1+ Ag '66
Vacation U.S.A., a Redbook guide to the national parks. R. Kirk. Redbook 126:43-50 Ap '66
Villa vacations; renting houses abroad, through agents in the U.S. C. Meyer. House & Gard 129:72+ My '66
Weekends for two on the town. G. G. Greer. il Bet Hom & Gard 44:135-6+ Mr '66
Where the beautiful people went this summer. Vogue 148:76-8 S 15 '66
Where to go fishing, vacationing, hunting. C. Fish. See issues of Outdoor life
See also
Camping
Teachers vacations

Anecdotes, facetiae, satire, etc.

Reflections in the East; a summer spent in Westport, Conn. and New York city. H. Sutton. Sat R 49:64+ O 15 '66
Vacation is going someplace without having to! reprint. H. Dunn. il Sr Schol 89:sup 14 S 16 '66

VACATIONS, Employee
Paid vacations and holidays in the United Kingdom. W. Gerber. Mo Labor R 89:272-3 Mr '66
See also
Leave of absence

VACCARIELLO, Barbara
Letter from Los Angeles. Nat R 18:270-1 Mr 22 '66
William H. Parker, RIP. Nat R 18:763 Ag 9 '66

VACCINATION
Conquering childhood diseases. W. H. Stewart. il Am Ed 2:30-2 Mr '66
Measles-smallpox vaccine jet-injected. il Sci N 90:67 Jl 30 '66
Smallpox vaccination blamed for stillbirth. Sci N 90:37 Jl 16 '66
Travel well: when getting your shots for foreign travel, shoot the works! E. N. Dye. Travel 125:67-8 Mr '66
See also
Immunity

VACCINES
Antiradiation vaccine. il Sci N 89:307 Ap 30 '66
New vaccine reduces respiratory illness. Sci N 89:348 My 7 '66
Strep throat vaccine here. Sci N 90:369 N 5 '66
Vaccines; achievements in 1966. J. L. Breeling. Todays Health 45:37-8 Ja '67
Vaccines, past to future. F Marley. il Sci N 89:512-13 Je 25 '66

VACCINIUM. See Blueberries

VACUUM
See also
Electric discharges through gases

VACUUM bottles. See Thermos containers

VACUUM cleaners
Make a vacuum cleaner for your car. J. McBride. il Pop Sci 188:143 Mr '66
Shopping center for vacuum cleaners. il Good H 162:220+ Mr '66
Vacuum cleaners. il Consumer Bul 49:30-5 Je '66

VACUUM technology
Vacuum freezing effects probed. J. F. Judge. il Miss & Roc 18:22-3 Mr 21 '66

VACUUM tubes
See also
Cathode ray tubes
Diodes

VACUUM welding. See Welding

VADIM, Roger
Blonde black panther. por Time 88:76 S 9 '66

VAERMAN, Jean Pierre, and Heremans, J. F.
Subclasses of human immunoglobulin A based on differences in the alpha polypeptide chains. bibliog Science 153:647-9 Ag 5 '66

VAGINAL smear tests. See Cancer—Diagnosis

VAGNOZZI, Egidio, abp
Inspector general. il por Newsweek 68:64+ O 31 '66

VAHANIAN, Gabriel
Dewart on belief. Commonweal 85:257-9 D 2 '66

VAIL-Ballou press, incorporated
Vail-Ballou has second plant in full operation. il Pub W 190:116+ O 3 '66

VAILE, Harvey, and Cornelison, Merle
Staggered starting hours. Am City 81:82-3 Je '66

VALACHI, Joseph
Government asks ban against Valachi memoirs. Pub W 189:56-7 My 23 '66
Whose thing? por Newsweek 67:93 My 23 '66

VALAITIS, Vytas
Eulogy: Vytas Valaitis. M. Orovan. il U S Camera 29:54-7+ Mr '66

VALANCES. See Curtains and draperies

VALCOUR ISLAND, Battle of. See United States—History—Revolution—Naval operations

VALDIVIA pottery. See Pottery, Ecuadorian

VALE, Michelle R.
Interstate library compact. Library J 91: 2419-22 My '66

VALEDICTORY; story. See Hutter, D.

VALENTE, Michael F.
Contraception: toward decision. Christian Cent 84:77-9 Ja 18 '67

VALENTI, Courtenay Lynda
When LBJ just can't say no. il pors Newsweek 67:19 My 2 '66

VALENTI, Jack
Macaulay and his critics. por Sat R 49:22-3 Ap 30 '66
Motion picture code and the new American culture. PTA Mag 61:16-19 D '66

about

Born hero-worshiper who serves his hero. P. Anderson. il pors N Y Times Mag p28-9+ F 20 '66
First 100 days. il por Time 88:38 S 2 '66
... Of Jack Valenti? il por Newsweek 68:84-5 Jl 4 '66
Revolving door at 1600. il por Newsweek 67:26-7 My 9 '66
Valedictory of Jack Valenti, or how to leave Lyndon. H. Sidey. por Life 60:46B My 6 '66

VALENTINE, Helen
Young wife's world. See issues of Good housekeeping

VALENTINE, Jean
Gabriel; poem. Commonweal 85:344 D 23 '66
Summer house; poem. Poetry 108:246-7 Jl '66

VALENTINE for Janie; story. See Turner, C. E.

VALENTINES day

Drama
Stolen heart. D. Newman. Plays 25:85-8, 96 F '66

Fiction
Golden fable for St Valentine's day. J. Wescott. Seventeen 25:28 F '66

VALENTRY, Duane
It's the poison. Sci Digest 60:66-8 D '66

VALÉRY, Paul
Polyphony in letters. V. Lange. New Repub 154:33-5 My 14 '66
Rose petals among the postscripts. L. LeSage. por Sat R 49:34-5 Ap 2 '66

VALIER, Louis A. jr
Owner's comments. Yachting 119:77+ Je '66

VÄLKKI, Anita
Northern lights; interview, ed. by M. W. Cushing. por Opera N 31:27 D 24 '66

VALLE, Antonio de la Cuesta. See Cuesta Valle, A. de la

VALLEY FORGE, Pa.
Valley Forge. P. James. il U S Camera 29: 64-5 Mr '66

VALLEY of the Redskins, France. See Amusement parks

VALLEY quail shooting. See Quail shooting

VALLEYS
See also
Rift valleys

VALTERS, Eric N.
Our shrinking planet; adaptation of U.N. radio programmes. UNESCO Courier 19:4-9 F '66

VALUATION
See also
Assessment

VALUE (psychology)
Is happy childhood the goal? with study-discussion program, by R. Strang. W. G. Hollister. bibliog il PTA Mag 60:10-12, 36 My '66
This younger generation; excerpts from address, August 1965. Sister Mary Dorothy Ann. Cath World 203:175-80 Je '66

VALUE added tax. See Taxation

VALUE of college education. See College education, Value of

VALUE of education. See Education, Value of

VALVERDE GARCÉS, Mario
Days of the round table. Américas 18:9-14 Mr '66

VALVES
See also
Automobile engines—Valves

VAN, George E.
Flying Buffalo wins Bayview classic. Yachting 120:48+ S '66

VAN, Tran-van-. See Tran-van-Van

VAN ALEN, Jimmy
Untroubled sport for those who play VAAGG. Sports Illus 25:48-50+ N 28 '66

about
Success for VASSS. por Time 87:61 Je 24 '66

VAN ALLEN, James A.
From outer space to basement workshop. por Pop Sci 189:98-100 N '66

VAN ALSTYNE, T. C. See McCafferty, P. jt. auth.

VAN ARK, Dorothy
Nobody cares about grandfather's clock but grandma. Read Digest 89:98-101 O '66

VAN AUSDALL, Clair W.
Frédéric Chopin: poet of the piano. Read Digest 89:269-72+ O '66

VAN BACKER, Lesley
Curl up and read. Seventeen 25:46 Ag '66

VAN BEAUMONT, W. and Bullard, R. W.
Sweating exercise stimulation during circulatory arrest. bibliog Science 152:1521-3 Je 10 '66

VAN BERG, Marion H.
Tradin' platers is Mr Van's game. J. Mann. il por Sports Illus 24:42-4+ Mr 21 '66

VAN BREDA KOLFF, Willem H.
Tiger in the Ivy. por Time 89:68 Ja 20 '67

VAN BUREN, Abigail, pseud.
Is there a snorer in the house? Read Digest 89:114-16 S '66

VAN BUREN, Martin
Furniture specifications and bidding documents. por Library J 91:5845-50 D 1 '66
Is carpet practical? por Library J 90:5152-6, 5322; 91:462+ D 1-15 '65, F 1 '66

VAN BUREN, Paul M.
Barth on Barth. Christian Cent 83:1512 D 7
'66
Secularization of Christianity, by E. L.
Mascall. Review
Nat R 18:370 Ap 19 '66. H. O. J. Brown
VANCE, Monk
Beef cows in drylot? il Suc Farm 64:60 Je
'66
He does assembly-line herd checks. il Suc
Farm 64:78 Ap '66
VAN CISE, Jerrold G.
Regulation, by business or government? bib-
liog f Harvard Bsns R 44:53-63 Mr '66
VAN CITTERS, Robert L. and others
Blood pressure responses of wild giraffes
studied by radio telemetry. bibliog Science
152:384-6 Ap 15 '66
VAN CLIBURN international quadrennial pi-
ano competition. See Music—Competitions
VANCOUVER, British Columbia

Description and travel
Here are treats many Vancouver visitors
miss. il Sunset 136:32+ Je '66
VANCOUVER film festival. See Moving pic-
ture festivals
VANCOUVER ISLAND, British Columbia
To Vancouver Island's Pacific coast. il Sun-
set 137:31-2+ S '66
VANCOUVER opera association
Vancouver; production of Cavalleria Rusti-
cana and Pagliacci. R. Sunter. il Opera N
31:32 D 24 '66
VANDAL; story. See Heinemann, A.
VANDALISM
Desecration in North Ireland. America 115:
475 O 22 '66
Disappearing seacoast. A. Bester. il Holiday
40:56-69+ Jl '66
Setting an example: Good outdoor manners
association. Time 87:66 Ap 15 '66
Speaking out; we need more slumlords. J.
Kahn. Sat Eve Post 239:8+ D 17 '66
When a vandal visited Capitol hill; damage
to historic paintings and statues in Capitol.
il U S News 61:16 D 19 '66
VAN DE GRAAFF accelerators. See Accelera-
tors (electrons, etc)
VAN DE GRAAFF generators. See Electric
generators, Electrostatic
VANDENBERGH, John G.
Rhesus monkey bands. Natur Hist 75:22-7
My '66
VAN DEN HAAG, Ernest
Vietnam: after all is said and done. Nat R
18:1210-12+ N 29 '66
VANDEN HEUVEL, Jean
Trance music of La Monte Young. Vogue
147:198+ My '66
VANDERBILT, Amy
Etiquette; questions and answers. See issues
of Ladies' home journal
VANDERBILT, Cornelius
Commodore left two sons. F. Clark. il por
Am Heritage 17:4-9+ Ap '66
VANDERBILT, Cornelius Jeremiah
Commodore left two sons. F. Clark. il pors
Am Heritage 17:4-9+ Ap '66
VANDERBILT, Gloria
Boogie man; poem. por McCalls 93:81 Je '66

about
Food at Faraway. il Vogue 147:192-5 F 1 '66
Private world: Connecticut house of Mr and
Mrs Wyatt Cooper. il pors Vogue 147:180-
91 F 1 '66
VANDERBILT, William Henry
Commodore left two sons. F. Clark. il pors
Am Heritage 17:4-9+ Ap '66
VANDERBILT family
Inheritors; Fruits of the legacy. il pors Am
Heritage 17:10-13 Ap '66
VANDERBILT national historic site
Vanderbilt mansion. Hobbies 71:111 N '66
VANDERHOEF, Ray W.
I'm a bookseller, not a bookkeeper. Pub W
190:42-4 O 3 '66
VAN DER KROEF, Justus M.
Peking's next target? Nat R 18:1165-6+ N
15 '66
VANDERLIPP, William T.
Where can a girl climb a tree? excerpts
from article. Recreation magazine, Sep-
tember 1945. Parks & Rec 1:355-6 Ap '66
VAN DINE, Alan C.
Those crazy questions kids ask. Parents Mag
41:30-1+ Jl '66

VANDOR, Augusto Timoteo
Another putsch in the Argentine? R. Peter.
Nat R 18:469 My 17 '66
Blood feud. Newsweek 67:55 My 30 '66
VAN DOREN, Irita
Irita Van Doren. Pub W 191:39 Ja 2 '67
Obituary
Nation 204:37 Ja 9 '67
Pub W por 190:63-4 D 26 '66
VAN DOREN, Ron
Missionaries in the classroom. Am Ed 3:10-
11+ D '66
VAN DYCK corporation
Where companies buy inventions. il Bsns W
p52-4 Jl 2 '66
VAN DYKE, Dick
Redbook readers talk; interview. pors Red-
book 128:57+ N '66

about
Good show quits while it's ahead. J. M.
Ferrer, 3d. Life 60:15 Je 3 '66
VAN DYKE, Vonda Kay
Promotional tour centers on Phoenix-area
teen market. il por Pub W 189:62-3 Mr 28
'66
VAN FOSSEN, Larry D.
How to build deep, narrow gutters for hog
houses. Suc Farm 64:54-5 F '66
VAN ITALLIE, Jean-Claude
America hurrah. Criticism
America 116:25 Ja 7 '67
Nation 203:587-8 N 28 '66
New Repub 155:31-3 D 3 '66
Newsweek 68:114 N 21 '66
Time il 88:79-80 N 18 '66
War. Criticism
Nation 202:404-5 Ap 4 '66
VANITIES (dressing tables) See Dressing tables
VAN LAWICK, Jane (Goodall) baroness
Are chimps really animals? D. Cohen. il pors
Sci Digest 59:58-64 F '66
VAN LEUVEN, Lauren
Prayer of the worm. Horn Bk 42:749 D '66
VAN MIDDLESWORTH, L. and others
Radium isotope accumulation in animal
thyroids. bibliog Science 151:453-4 Ja 28 '66
VAN OLPHEN, H.
Maya blue: a clay-organic pigment? Science
154:645-6 N 4 '66
VAN OVERBEEK, J.
Plant hormones and regulators. bibliog Sci-
ence 152:721-31 My 6 '66
VAN PATTEN, James J.
Neutrality's implications for education. bib-
liog f Sch & Soc 94:352-4 O 29 '66
VAN RENSSELAER, Susan
Banded creamware. Antiques 90:337-41 S '66
VAN ROO, William A.
Talk about God. America 114:691-4 My
14 '66
VAN SICKLE, Bernice L. See Freyman, L. jt.
auth.
VANSITTART, Sir Robert Gilbert
Professional touch. G. A. Craig. Reporter 34:
52+ Mr 10 '66
VAN SLYCK, Philip
Scholars face the future. Sat R 49:75-6 Je
11 '66
VAN TRUMP, James D.
History in houses: Hope lodge. Whitemarsh,
Pennsylvania. Antiques 89:542-5 Ap '66
VAN VALKENBURG, Samuel
Vietnam: its land and people. Cur Hist 50:
65-71+ F '66
VAN-van-Cua
Overworked mayor; arrest by American MPs.
Time 88:36 D 16 '66
VAN VEEN, Frederick
Measuring instruments for electronic com-
ponents. Electr World 76:36-8+ S '66
VAN WIJK, Uco
Obituary
Sky & Tel 32:198 O '66. G. S. Mumford
VANZETTI, Bartolomeo
See also
Sacco-Vanzetti case
VAPOR baths. See Baths, Vapor
VARACTOR diodes. See Diodes
VARAH, Chad
When listening means life. R. J. Levin. Sat
R 49:65 O 1 '66
VARAH, Edward Chad. See Varah, C.
VARDA, Agnès
Current cinema; woman movie director: Le
bonheur. B. Gill. New Yorker 42:113-14
My 28 '66

VARDYS, V. Stanley
How the Baltic republics fare in the Soviet Union. For Affairs 44:512-17 Ap '66
VARÈSE, Edgard
Scoring the D train. F. V. Grunfeld. il Reporter 34:47-8+ Ap 7 '66
VARGAS, Manuela
Manuela Vargas and company, ANTA theatre. D. Hering. Dance Mag 40:33 N '66
VARIABLE annuities. See Annuities
VARIABLE frequency oscillators. See Oscillators
VARIABLE hours system. See Hours of labor
VARIABLE stars. See Stars, Variable
VARIABLE sweep wings. See Airplane wings
VARIATION (biology) See Mutation (biology)
VARIATIONS; ballet. See Ballets—Criticisms
VARICOSE veins
Varied choice for varicose veins. il Time 88:61 N 4 '66
VARIETY (periodical)
Trade winds; tops in headline-writing. J. G. Fuller. Sat R 49:12+ Mr 19 '66
VARIETY programs. See Television broadcasting—Programs
VARNISH and varnishing
  See also
Shellac

Removal

  See Paint—Removal
VARNISH factories. See Paint and varnish factories
VARON, Charles
Kaleidoscope. il U S Camera 29:56-7 D '66
VARON, Myron L. and Cole, L. J.
Hemopoietic colony-forming units in regenerating mouse liver; suppression by anticoagulants. bibliog Science 153:643-4 Ag 5 '66
VARRIER, María Cristina. See Verrier, M. C.
VARSITY drive-in restaurant. See Atlanta—Hotels, restaurants, etc.
VÁSÁRY, Tamás
For Chopin, the voices of poets. H. Goldsmith. por Hi Fi 16:85 S '66
VASCULAR diseases
Increased cardiovascular reactivity to angiotensin caused by renin. G. M. C. Masson and others. bibliog il Science 153:1002-4 Ag 26 '66
VASCULAR surgery. See Blood vessels—Surgery
VAS DIAS, Robert
Greenness of the Burma jade world; Ceremony; poems. Poetry 107:306-7 F '66
VASES, Greek
Athenian vase painters; excerpt from Techniques of painted attic pottery. J. V. Noble. Am Artist 30:30-6+ F '66
VASILIEV, Vyacheslav
Vive le pub. il Time 87:69-70 F 25 '66
VASKA, L.
Reversible combination of carbon monoxide with a synthetic oxygen carrier complex. bibliog Science 152:769-71 My 6 '66
VASQUEZ, Esperanza del Valle
First artificial heart survivor. il por Sci Digest 60:37 N '66
VASSAMILLET, L. F. See Ashbee, K. H. G. jt. auth.
VASSAR college, Poughkeepsie, N.Y.
Eli Vassar? proposed Yale-Vassar marriage. il Newsweek 68:56-7 D 26 '66
New Haven, here we come; question of moving to New Haven. il Time 88:32 D 30 '66
Talk of Vassar, 1966; views of eight seniors, ed. by J. M. Russin. il Newsweek 67:74-5 Je 13 '66
VATICAN
To the celebration of princes; portfolio. Esquire 66:202-3 D '66
Vatican censor bureau said to be downgraded. Pub W 189:101-2 F 14 '66
VATICAN council, 1869-1870
Newman, Vatican I and II, and the church today. E. E. Kelly. Cath World 202:291-7 F '66
VATICAN council, 2d
After the noise: the hope of Vatican II. C. McCarthy. Christian Cent 83:167-70 F 9 '66

Aggiornamento. il Sr Schol 87:5 Ja 7 '66

America's survey of diocesan post-conciliar programs. America 114:825-7+; 115:28-30, 136-8, 343+ Je 11, Jl 9, Ag 6, S 24 '66
Boswell in St Peter's; D. Horton's Vatican diary. C. Northcott. Christian Cent 83:359 Mr 23 '66
Catholic layman confronts his changing church. D. Norton-Taylor. il Fortune 74:172-5+ D '66
Church in the modern world; concerning books on the council's teachings. G. A. Lindbeck. il Sat R 49:35-6 Jl 30 '66
Church to die in or to live in? M. P. Ryan. Cath World 203:17-21 Ap '66
Common goal. P. J. Hallinan. America 116:11-14 Ja 7 '67
Contraception and the council. J. T. Noonan, jr. Commonweal 83:657-62 Mr 11 '66
Council and the word; Constitution on divine revelation. America 114:283 F 26 '66
Council, one year later. A. C. Outler; R. M. Brown; S. I. Stuber. Commonweal 85:368-72 Ja 6 '67
Council, si. Commonweal 83:550 F 11 '66
Ecumenical symposium. A. P. Klausler. Christian Cent 83:376-8 Mr 23 '66
End to the Christian-Jewish dialogue. A. R. Eckardt. Christian Cent 83:360-3, 393-5 Mr 23-30 '66
Evolution in moral theology. G. H. Tavard. Cath World 203:29-32 Ap '66
Fruits of freedom; interpreting decrees and declarations. Commonweal 84:349-50 Je 17 '66
Impact of Vatican II on Protestantism; address. October 13, 1966. V. D. Rogers. Vital Speeches 33:91-4 N 15 '66
Laity lose their chains. J. B. Sheerin. Cath World 202:262-6 F '66
Letter from Vatican City. X. Rynne. New Yorker 42:140+ O 22 '66
Liberty within the Catholic church. P. Blanshard. Cath World 203:335-40 S '66
More on the council and contraception. J. C. Ford. America 114:553-7 Ap 16 '66
Newman, Vatican I and II, and the church today. E. E. Kelly. Cath World 202:291-7 F '66
Notre Dame conference; international conference on the theological issues of Vatican II. J. O'Gara. Commonweal 84:98 Ap 15 '66
On implementing the council. Commonweal 84:516 Ag 19 '66
Paul Blanshard on Vatican II, by P. Blanshard. Review
  Christian Cent 84:15 Ja 4 '67. G. A. Lindbeck
  Reporter 35:48-50 D 1 '66. J. Leo
  Sat R 49:55-6 N 12 '66. D. J. O'Hanlon
Peace, war and the Vatican council. T. M. Finn. Cath World 203:270-5 Ag '66
Protestantism at the Notre Dame conference. W. B. Blakemore. Christian Cent 83:506-10 Ap 20 '66
Reading the council documents. America 114:346-7 Mr 12 '66
Reflections of a council observer; interview, ed. by E. M. Gaffney. A. C. Outler. Cath World 203:353-60 S '66
Religious liberty: toward consensus. D. M. Kelley and C. D. Nelson. Christian Cent 83:651-3 My 18 '66
Religious value of the council; excerpt from address, December 6, 1965. Paul VI. Cath World 203:113-14 My '66
Rome, opponent or partner? by R. J. Ehrlich. Review
  Christian Cent 83:686-7 My 25 '66. S. I. Stuber
Statement on the Jews. J. L. Lichten. Cath World 202:357-63 Mr '66
Vatican II: anathema upon war. E. M. Borgese. il Nation 202:415-21 Ap 11 '66
Vatican II and Catholic education; interview, ed. by W. K. Richards. M. J. Hurley. Sr Schol 88:sup5 My 13 '66
Vatican II on social progress. B. L. Masse. America 114:776-8 My 28 '66
Vatican II was just the beginning. M. E. Marty. Christian Cent 83:455-7 Ap 13 '66
Vatican II: what does the future hold? R. M. Brown. Cath World 202:341-7 Mr '66
Vatican III? theologians congress to determine meaning of council documents. Newsweek 68:104 O 10 '66
War and peace and the American Catholic. W. V. O'Brien. Cath World 202:331-5 Mr '66

VATICAN council, 2d—*Continued*
What did the council say on contraception?
J. L. Thomas. America 114:294-6 F 26 '66
Will the bishops speed up renewal? J. B.
Sheerin. Cath World 204:132-3 D '66

4th session

Declaration on Christian education. Sch &
Soc 94:284-7 Sum '66
Fourth session, by X. Rynne. Review
America 115:346+ S 24 '66. D. R. Campion
New secular ecumenism. J. B. Sheerin. Cath
World 203:261-4 Ag '66
Note on schema fourteen. America 114:280
F 26 '66
See also
Religious liberty

Reports, records, etc.

Documents of Vatican II, ed. by W. M.
Abbott. Review
America 114:627 Ap 30 '66. V. A. Yzer-
mans
Ecumenical publishing falters briefly in
L.A; joint Protestant and Catholic pub-
lication of the Documents of Vatican II.
Pub W 189:81-2 Ap 25 '66
Romano, ma non troppo. J. R. Nelson. Chris-
tian Cent 83:825-6 Je 29 '66
Using council documents. R. M. Brown.
Commonweal 84:254-6 My 20 '66

VAUDABLE, Louis
Traveler, consider my Paris; ed. by R.
Joseph. pors Esquire 65:114-15+ Je '66

VAUDEVILLE
Burlesque returns, but the competition is
fierce. W. Markfield. il N Y Times Mag
p 10-11+ Je 26 '66
It's always warm here; Bobino music hall,
Paris. il Newsweek 69:69 Ja 9 '67
Ladies' day at the burleyque. M. Smith. il
Life 61:128-30+ S 16 '66

VAUDEVILLE of the elements (ballet) See
Ballets

VAUGHAN, Alden T.
Horrid and unnatural rebellion of Daniel
Shays. Am Heritage 17:50-3+ Je '66

VAUGHAN, Roger
It's a groovy thing to do. Life 60:119-20 My
20 '66

VAUGHAN WILLIAMS, Ralph
For the holidays: V. W.'s Hodie. J. Diether.
por Am Rec G 33:300-2 D '66

VAUGHN, Jack Hood
Peace corps highlights; excerpts from report. Dept State Bul 55:278-9 Ag 22 '66

about

School-to-school; a partnership in under-
standing. por Parents Mag 41:30+ Je '66
Yankee, don't go home! il por Time 87:16-17
Ja 28 '66

VAUGHN, LeRoy Franklin
Here comes Mr Parade. A. R. Roalman. il
pors Pop Mech 125:84-7+ Je '66

VAUGHN, Paula
Scientists discover secret of skin color. il por
Ebony 22:85-6+ Ja '67

VAULTING (sport)
Bittersweet taste of success; Seagren sets
record. il Time 87:72 Mr 18 '66
Champions of winter; J. Pennel. il Sports
Illus 24:12-13+ F 7 '66

VAWTER, Bruce
Books. Commonweal 83:674 Mr 11 '66
Churchly particularism and the Jews. Chris-
tian Cent 83:988 Ag 10 '66

VAYDIK, Frank
Merger, what now! por Parks & Rec 1:211
Mr '66

VEAL
See also
Cookery—Meat

VEALE, Frank
Two golf courses in record time. Parks &
Rec 1:410-12 My '66

VEATCH, Jeannette, and Hayes, Geneva
Some classroom-tested ideas. NEA J 55:38
N '66

VECTORCARDIOGRAPHY
Heart data distorted. Sci N 89:258 Ap 16 '66
Heart standards set for premature babies.
Sci N L 89:72 Ja 29 '66

VEDANTA
Book, by A. Watts. Review
Sat R 49:23+ D 31 '66. N. W. Ross

VEECK, Bill
Flawed diamond. J. Jacobs. Reporter 34:
57-8 Ja 27 '66

VEGA CARPIO, Lope Félix de
Bond honoured; adaptation. See Osborne, J.

VEGETABLE gardening
Are vegetables worth growing? F. C. Coulter.
Pop Gard 17:85 Ag '66
Ever tried your hand at tomatoes? il Bet
Hom & Gard 44:124 My '66
Fruits and vegetables. R. Gannon. il Horti-
culture 44:34-7+ My '66
Growing your own asparagus, artichokes,
rhubarb. il Sunset 138:134+ Ja '67
Plot to produce more. B. C. Kilvert, jr. il
Flower Grower 53:42-3 Mr '66
See also
Greenhouses
Herbs

VEGETABLE handling
See also
Motor trucks, Refrigerated

VEGETABLES
For 1966 the latest in vegetables. il Pop
Gard 17:84-5 Mr '66
Vegetables for shade. B. C. Kilvert, jr.
Flower Grower 53:28 Ap '66
See also
Cookery—Vegetables
Vegetable gardening
also names of vegetables, e.g. Asparagus

All America selections

See Plants—All America selections

Harvesting

See also
Harvesting machinery

Packing

See also
Containers

Storage

Carrots keep better using high humidity. Sci
N L 89:63 Ja 22 '66

VEGETABLES, Canned
Inside story on canned vegetables. il Bet
Hom & Gard 44:76-7 Ap '66

VEGETATION
Vegetation; identification of typal communities. R. Daubenmire. bibliog il Science 151:291-8 Ja 21 '66; Discussion. 152:
546-7 Ap 22 '66

VEGETATION meters. See Electronic apparatus and appliances

VEHICLES
Wheeler-dealers; Sotheby's antique vehicles
auction. il Newsweek 68:58-61 Jl 25 '66

VEHRENBERG, Hans
Some photographs by Hans Vehrenberg. il Sky
& Tel 32:88-91 Ag. '66

VEHSLAGE, Steve
Knockout of a champion. R. Lardner. il por
Sports Illus 24:30-2 F 7 '66

VEINS
See also
Varicose veins

VELDE, Paul
Sontag sensibility. Commonweal 84:390-2 Je
24 '66

VELEN, Elizabeth. See Velen, V. jt. auth.

VELEN, Victor, and Velen, Elizabeth
Florence: after the flood. Sat R 49:26-7+ D
24 '66

VELIE, Lester
Big business can help you be your own
boss. Read Digest 88:141-4 My '66
How the big strikes are settled. Read Digest
88:135-9 Je '66
How to go to college on nothing a year.
Read Digest 88:132-6 F '66
Our leaky pipeline to Vietnam. Read Digest
89:113-18 D '66
Riddle of the vanishing insurance companies.
Read Digest 89:109-13 S '66
Who's afraid of automation! Read Digest 88:
117-20 Ap '66

VELLMAN, Ruth
Library for the handicapped. bibliog por Library J 91:4200-4 S 15 '66

VELOCITY of light. See Light—Velocity

VELVET ants
Velvet ant's erratic path. il Sunset 136:83
My '66

VELVET worms. See Peripatus

VELZIAN, John
Very welcome redcoat. M. Kane. il por Sports
Illus 25:78-82 D 19 '66

VEMA (ship) See Ships, Research

VENABLES, Bernard
Postman. Esquire 66:20+ Jl '66

VENEREAL diseases
New venereal disease; vibrio fetus infections. Time 87:62 F 25 '66
Shall our schools teach about venereal disease? S. Podair. il Sat R 49:72-3+ Mr 19 '66
Truth can stop VD. P. Deutsch and R. Deutsch. Read Digest 90:55-9 Ja '67
VD: a national problem that can no longer be ignored. il Sr Schol 88:11-14 F 25 '66
Venereal disease books available in schools Sci N L 89:56 Ja 22 '66
VD menace alarming. P. McBroom. Sci N 90:402 N 12 '66
See also
Syphilis

VENETIAN architecture. See Architecture, Italian

VENEZUELA
Inside Venezuela. J. Gunther. il Read Digest 88:147-8+ Mr '66
See also
Colleges and universities—Venezuela
Communism—Venezuela
Guerrillas—Venezuela
Margarita Island
Music festivals—Venezuela
Natural resources—Venezuela
Petroleum industry and trade—Venezuela
Political parties—Venezuela
Tourist trade—Venezuela

Climate
Amateur scientist; study of the salty rain of Venezuela; periodic wind called alisio blows the calina fog away. G. Zuloaga. il Sci Am 215:136-8 D '66

Commerce
Venezuela broadens air freight exports. J. W. Carter. Aviation W 84:47+ Ap 11 '66

Description and travel
By car into Venezuela's high jungle. il Sunset 136:34+ Mr '66
Caracas's 400th: Bolivar and bulldozers. T. Moscoso. il Sat R 50:94+ Ja 7 '67
Personal business; new winter vacation spot. Bsns W p 171-2 N 12 '66
Picture portfolio: Venezuela. Travel 126:50-5 Jl '66

Economic conditions
Democracy for Venezuela? P. B. Taylor. jr. bibliog f Cur Hist 51:284-90+ N '66

Native races
See also
Indians of South America—Venezuela

Politics and government
Democracy for Venezuela? P. B. Taylor. jr. bibliog f Cur Hist 51:284-90+ N '66
Gone, the bold rebels; dwindling forces of the FALN. il Newsweek 67:42 F 7 '66
See also
Communism—Venezuela

VENEZUELA and the United States
U.S. Venezuela inaugurate undersea telephone cable; remarks, August 3, 1966. R. Leoni and L. B. Johnson. Dept State Bul 55:274-5 Ag 22 '66

VENEZUELAN cookery. See Cookery, Venezuelan

VENEZUELAN literature
See also
Authors, Venezuelan

VENICE

Architecture
Is Venice worth saving? R. Lynes. il Harper 233:26+ O '66
Queen of the Adriatic needs our help. B. Clark. il Read Digest 88:191-2+ F '66

Art
Disaster in Italy; damage done by flood. il Newsweek 68:110-11 N 21 '66
People and events. il Sr Schol 89:19 D 2 '66

City planning
Is Venice worth saving? R. Lynes. il Harper 233:26+ O '66

Description
Travel notes. R. Joseph. Esquire 65:66+ Ap '66
Traveler, consider my Venice; ed. by R. Joseph. G. Parise. il Esquire 65:150-2 Ap '66

Music
Venice. J. W. Freeman. Opera N 31:28 O 15 '66

VENICE biennale. See Art—Exhibitions

VENICE film festival. See Moving picture festivals

VENISON
See also
Cookery—Game

VENKATAVARADAN, V. S. See Lal, D. jt. auth.

VENOM
Cutting out snake bite. Time 89:53 Ja 13 '67
Pure venom saves victims; antigens against bees, wasps and other stinging insects. B. J. Culliton. il Sci N 90:323 O 22 '66
Snakebite accidents higher than believed. Sci N 89:212 Ap 2 '66
Treatment for snakebite. N. Laden. il Field & S 71:162-3+ S '66
See also
Rattlesnakes

Antidotes
See Antidotes

VENTILATION
See also subhead Heating and ventilation under various subjects, e.g. Apartment houses—Heating and ventilation

VENTURA COUNTY, Calif.
Ventura County: the barbarian conquest. D. Forbes. il Nation 202:128+ Ja 31 '66

VENTURES, Joint. See Joint adventures

VENTURI, Ken
Shakes in quake corner. por(cover) Sports Illus 24:56-66+ Je 13 '66

about
While the cats are away; wins Lucky international. il por Time 87:62 F 11 '66
Winning hands. Newsweek 67:84 F 14 '66

VENUS (planet)
Observations of the phase of Venus. il Sky & Tel 31:179 Mr '66
See also
Space flight to Venus

Atmosphere
Hospitable Venus? California Institute of technology conclusions after analysis of Mariner 2 signals. Newsweek 67:71 My 2 '66

Contamination
Venus' heat is lethal. Sci N 89:198 Mr 26 '66

VENUS probes. See Space probes

VENUS 3 probe. See Space probes, Russian

VENUS'S flytraps
Touch receptor of Venus flytrap, dionaea muscipula. J. R. DiPalma and others. bibliog il Science 152:539-40 Ap 22 '66

VERA foundation, incorporated
Train of clients; Manhattan summons project. H. Bowser. Sat R 49:26 Ap 16 '66

VERDI, Giuseppe
Aida. Criticism
New Yorker 42:229-30 N 19 '66
Opera N il 30:17-20 F 12 '66
Arias to fight by. por Time 87:65 Mr 18 '66
Catching up: Verdiana. C. J. Luten. Am Rec G 32:1080 Jl '66
Columbia's Falstaff. P. L. Miller. Am Rec G 33:202-3 N '66
Columbia's Falstaff: it goes at once to the windswept summit. C. L. Osborne. il Hi Fi 16:79-80 D '66
Falstaff. Criticism
Sat R 49:28 Mr 19 '66
Forum for Verdi. M. J. Marz. il Opera N 31:6-7 S 10 '66
London's Don Carlo. P. L. Miller. Am Rec G 32:680-2 Ap '66
Masked ball (Un ballo in maschera) Criticism
New Yorker 41:136+ F 19 '66
Opera N 30:18-20 F 26 '66
Opera N 30:24-5 F 26 '66
Middling Verdi. R. Gelatt. Reporter 34:39-40 Je 16 '66
Nabucco; first stereo edition. P. L. Miller. il Am Rec G 33:110-11 O '66
On records; Aida. Opera N 30:34 F 12 '66
On records; Requiem. Opera N 30:34 Ap 16 '66
On records: Un ballo in maschera. Opera N 30:34 F 26 '66
Records:
Nabucco. Opera N 31:32 O 15 '66
Records: Don Carlo. Opera N 31:34 S 10 '66

VERDI, Giuseppe—*Continued*
Rigoletto. Criticism
New Yorker 42:77-8 F 26 '66
Sat R 49:32 Mr 5 '66
Syracuse symphony presents Otello. L. C.
McGinn. il Opera N 30:23 My 7 '66
La Traviata. Criticism
Dance Mag 40:30-1 D '66
Hi Fi 16:MA14-15 D '66
New Yorker 42:209 O 1 '66
New Yorker 42:232 N 5 '66
Sat R 49:20+ O 8 '66
Verdi's Don Carlo. C. L. Osborne. Hi Fi
16:83-5 Ap '66
Verdi's real roots; forebears innkeepers, not
peasants. M. J. Matz. il Opera N 30:24-5
F 12 '66
VERDON, Gwen
Gwen Verdon all aglow; with report by T.
Thompson. il pors Life 60:99-100+ Mr 25
'66
VERDUN, Battle of, 1916
For the dead at Verdun, torches in memory
of the bloody battle that saved France.
il Life 60:40-1 Je 10 '66
Old marshal; Frenchmen commemorate bat-
tle. il Newsweek 67:60+ Je 13 '66
Verdun, the reason why. A. Horne. il N Y
Times Mag p36-7+ F 20 '66
VERMEER, Johannes
Letter from Paris; hundred-and-fiftieth an-
niversary exhibition at the Orangerie.
Genêt. New Yorker 42:149-51 O 8 '66
Phoenix by the Schie. il Time 88:78-81 S 9
'66
Vermeer painting. Am Artist 30:6 S '66
VERMILION, Ohio
Custom channelization tames an intersection.
H. Lechner. il Am City 81:120+ F '66
VERMONT
See also
Hunting—Vermont
Music festivals—Vermont
Skis and skiing—Vermont
Wilderness areas—Vermont
VERMOUTH. See Wine
VERNE, Jules
Black Indies; dramatization. See Olfson, L.
VERNON, James W.
Where the beaches go. il por Sci Digest 59:
38-9 Ap '66
VERNON, Walter, and Ulrich, Roger
Classical conditioning of pain-elicited ag-
gression. bibliog Science 152:668 Ap 29 '66
VERO BEACH, Fla.
Driftwood inn. M. Candee. il Travel 125:63
My '66
VERONA, Italy

Music
Verona. E. Davidson. Opera N 31:25-6 O
15 '66
VERONICA; drama. See White, J.
VERRAY parfit gentil knight; story. See Boles,
P. D.
VERRIER, Anthony
Guyana is free, to go where? N Y Times
Mag p54-5+ My 22 '66
VERRIER, Maria Cristina
Condor commandos. il por Newsweek 68:60
O 10 '66
Falkland caper. por Time 88:48 O 7 '66
VERSAILLES
Royal comeback; restoration of The grand
trianon. il Time 87:92-4 Je 17 '66
VERSAILLES, Palace of
Setting of the Sun King. L. Kronenberger.
il Atlan 219:58-61 Ja '67
VERSCHOTH, Anita
Time to remember: 3:51.3. Sports Illus 25:
10-13 Jl 25 '66
VERSIFICATION
Art of writing greeting cards. R. Galanoplos.
il Sat R 49:94-6 D 10 '66
See also
Poetics
VERTEBRATES
Inhibition in the central nervous system.
V. J. Wilson. il Sci Am 214:102-7+ bib-
liog (p 148) My '66
VERTICAL antennas. See Radio antennas
VERTICAL density currents. See Hydrome-
chanics
VERTOL division. See Boeing company—Vertol
division
VERUSCHKA
Veruschka. por Newsweek 68:74+ Ag 15 '66

VERVEEN, A. A. See Derksen, H. E. jt. auth.
VERWOERD, Hendrik Frensch
After assassination; future of white Africa.
il U S News 61:57-8 S 19 '66
Apartheid's symbol. il por Sr Schol 89:18-19
S 23 '66
Death of apartheid? New Repub 155:9 S 17
'66
Death of the architect. il por Time 88:38-40
S 16 '66
Great white laager. il por Time 88:18-22+ Ag
26 '66
Hendrik F. Verwoerd. America 115:272 S 17
'66
Hendrik Verwoerd, RIP. Nat R 18:920 S 20
'66
Laughter in Parliament. America 115:315 S 24
'66
Letter from Cape Town. E. J. Kahn, jr. New
Yorker 42:182+ N 5 '66
Man dies but not apartheid. il por News-
week 68:40-2+ S 19 '66
Mind of an assassin; Tsafendas jailed; in-
sane. Newsweek 68:56+ O 31 '66
Notes and comment. New Yorker 42:47 S 17
'66
Tapeworm murder; Tsafendas ruled insane.
Time 88:41 O 28 '66
U.S. expresses sympathy on death of Prime
Minister Verwoerd. L. B. Johnson; D.
Rusk. Dept State Bul 55:463 S 26 '66
Violent end for the apostle of apartheid; with
report by A. Sampson. il pors Life 61:40-3
S 16 '66
What now in South Africa? Christian Cent 83:
1136 S 21 '66
What Verwoerd's successor faces. por Bsns
W p48 S 10 '66
VERY high frequency radiophone. See Radio
telephone on ships, boats, etc.
VESICULAR stomatitis viruses. See Viruses
VESTAL, David
Great unknown photographer. il Pop Phot
59:114-17+ D '66
Its intense and total cowness. Pop Phot 59:
100-1 D '66
VETERANS. See Service men, Discharged
VETERANS home loans. See Service men,
Discharged—Benefits
VETERANS of foreign wars
Notes and comment; un-American to object
to din of parade at midnight. New Yorker
42:47 S 10 '66
VETERINARY medicine
Cattle bloat controlled by drug. il Sci N
89:224 Ap 2 '66
Keeping hogs healthy; interview. H. Helms.
Farm J 90:H15-16 N '66
Your pet's second best friend. D. J. Giese.
il Read Digest 89:177-80 Ag '66
VETLESEN prize
Dutch astronomer honored. G. S. Mumford.
Sky & Tel 32:333 D '66
VETRA, Vija
Vija Vetra, Carnegie recital hall. M. Marks.
Dance Mag 40:35 N '66
VETTER, Robert M.
Swiss and German pewter water cisterns
and lavabo sets. Antiques 89:690-4 My '66
VIBBER, Nene
Children's art 1966. Sch Arts 66:13 S '66
VIBRATION
Structures should have stiffness as well as
strength. H. S. Woodward. il Arch Rec
139:226-7 Ap '66
Vibration unit promises yield beyond initial
Saturn tasks; Wyle's Huntsville complex.
K. Voss. Tech W 19:37 N 7 '66
See also
Airplanes—Vibration

Measurement
Infrared study of the hydroxyl bands in
clinoamphiboles. R. G. Burns and R. G.
J. Strens. bibliog il Science 153:890-2 Ag
19 '66
VIBRATO
Simplified tremolo. W. R. Shippee. il Electr
World 76:88 O '66
VIBRATORS
See also
Multivibrators
VIBURNUMS
If you only know old snowball, meet the
other viburnums. il Sunset 137:233-4 N '66
VICARS. See Church of England—Clergy

VICE-PRESIDENTS

United States

Be it ever so humble; vice presidential mansion bill deferred. Newsweek 67:34 Mr 28 '66

Humphrey and 1972. W. V. Shannon. Commonweal 83:629-30 Mr 4 '66

Little White House for vice president? il U S News 60:58-9 Mr 28 '66

Mr Nixon advises Mr Kennedy. Nat R 18: 1146 N 15 '66

Undistinguished and unique: first and only vice-president to be elected by the U.S. Senate. il Sr Schol 88:5 F 4 '66

Vice presidency; H. Humphrey's and predecessors' duties. il Time 87:21-5 Ap 1 '66

VICENS, Luis

Build light-to-sound translator. Pop Electr 24:74-5+ Je '66

Impossible circuit. Pop Electr 25:72 O '66

VICHY, France

April in Vichy. A. Waugh. Nat R 18:577+ Je 14 '66

VICKERS, Harry Franklin

At Sperry Rand a conglomerate finally works to one purpose. il por Bsns W p 180-2+ Mr 19 '66

VICKY

Vicky. Nation 202:348 Mr 28 '66

VICTOR café. See Philadelphia—Hotels, restaurants, etc.

VICTOR talking machine company. See Radio corporation of America—RCA Victor division

VICTORIA, British Columbia

Description

Victoria. il Sunset 137:40-53 Ag '66

VICTORIAN architecture. See Architecture, Victorian

VICTORIAN furniture. See Furniture, Victorian

VICTORY number three; story. See Gilkey, L.

VIDEO records

For the record; possession of disk-TV denied by CBS. il Newsweek 67:67 Mr 14 '66

TV disc recorder. Electr World 75:85 My '66

Volume up for TV recording; disk and tape systems. il Bsns W p39-40 Mr 12 '66

VIDEO tape recorders and recording

Aircraft video system allows radar intercept ground replay. R. Lindsey. il Tech W 19: 45+ S 19 '66

Ampex home video recorder. J. Roizen. Electr World 75:52-4 My '66

Audio fidelity does it again; releases first audio-video tape; prerecorded video tape. Hi Fi 16:34 N '66

Directory of most popular, low-priced video tape recorders. il Electr World 76:36-7 N '66

Home video tape: is it ready now? N. Eisenberg. Mod Phot 30:41-2+ Mr '66

Home video tape recorder. il Consumer Rep 31:280 Je '66

Home video tape, the promise and the problems. N. Eisenberg. Hi Fi 16:53-4 Ag '66

How they do those magic TV tricks; using Videodisc. H. Shuldiner and R. M. Benrey. il Pop Sci 189:56-61 Ag '66

How to create your own TV show; many and various uses of video tape recorders. il Bsns W p 128-9 Ja 7 '67

How'd you like to sell/buy your home on TV? J. Neubauer. il Pop Phot 60:87 Ja '67

Instant video movies with Sony portable camera-recorder. H. V. Fondiller. il Pop Phot 59:80-1 N '66

More gear for home movie fans; television tape recorders. Bsns W p94 Jl 16 '66

Self-service TV; Sony's Videocorder. il Time 87:81 Ap 22 '66

Sight and sound with Sony's Videocorder. il Hi Fi 16:30+ Ag '66

Sony home video recorder. C. H. Fields and S. Oniki. il Electr World 75:42-4 My '66

Tape recorder guide. il Hi Fi 16:125-44 N '66

TV disc recorder. Electr World 75:85 My '66

TV shows when you want them. W. G. Salm. il Sci Digest 59:73-8 My '66

Three more VTRs unveiled. il Hi Fi 16:39 S '66

Video tape recorder for home use. E. Leman. il Electr World 75:49-52+ F '66

Video tape recorders. Mod Phot 30:114-15 N '66

Videotape recorders. il Pop Phot 59:145-6 O '66

Video tape recording methods. L. Wortman. il Electr World 75:32-4 My '66

VTR report, 1967: year of home color videotape. H. V. Fondiller. il Pop Phot 59:86 N '66

Volume up for TV recording; disk and tape systems. il Bsns W p39-40 Mr 12 '66

What's new that's good? L. Drukker. il Pop Phot 58:106+ Je '66

VIDEO tape recorders on airplanes. See Video tape recorders and recording

VIDEOCORDER. See Video tape recorders and recording

VIDICON. See Television cameras

VIEHMEYER, Glenn

Deciduous trees for the plains. Horticulture 44:48-9+ Mr '66

VIENNA

Description

Going places, finding things in Vienna. K. Bates. il House & Gard 129:18-19+ F '66

History

Vienna, by I. Barea. Review Newsweek il 68:70 Ag 29 '66

Hospitals

Morphinist; incident at Hospital of the city of Vienna, 1928. R. Berczeller. New Yorker 42:141-2+ Ap 16 '66

Music

Notes from our correspondents. W. Weaver. il Hi Fi 16:14+ Je '66

Ovations for Bernstein's Falstaff. W. Weaver. il Hi Fi 16:126-7 Je '66

Vienna. J. Wechsberg. il Opera N 30:32 Ap 9; 24 My 7; 31:28 N 19 '66

Stores

Keyhole shop. il Arch Forum 124:33-7 Je '66

VIENNA festival weeks. See Music festivals —Austria

VIENNA opera ballet. See Ballet—Austria

VIET rock; drama. See Terry, M.

VIETNAM

See also
Americans in Vietnam
Political parties—Vietnam
Rites and ceremonies—Vietnam

History

Issue is China. Christian Cent 83:355-7 Mr 23 '66; Discussion. 83:683-4 My 25 '66

Lost revolution, by R. Shaplen. Review Reporter 35:57-8 O 6 '66. J. Mecklin

Nation beyond Saigon. K. T. Young. Sat R 49:33-4 Jl 16 '66

Portent for the future: welfare imperialism in Vietnam. J. McDermott. il Nation 203: 76-88 Jl '25 '66

Profile of Viet Nam: divided nation that has divided the U.S. il Sr Schol 89:pt2 3 S 23 '66

So the war goes on; roots of present conflict. New Repub 154:5-7 F 12 '66

Toward perspective on Vietnam. H. S. Quigley. Christian Cent 83:104-6 Ja 26 '66

Two sides to the Dienbienphu story; concerning assessments by Bernard Fall and Vo Nguyen Giap. J. Mirsky. Nation 202: 781-4 Je 27 '66

Vietnam and southeast Asia; symposium. bibliog f il Cur Hist 50:65-97+ F '66

Viet-Nam witness 1953-66, by B. B. Fall. Review Sat R il 49:23-4 My 28 '66. D. Schoenbrun

What is owing to the Vietnamese? N. Cousins. Sat R 49:24 Mr 26 '66

Native races

See also
Montagnards

VIETNAM (Democratic Republic)

Corruption & defeatism; recent red articles and broadcasts. Time 88:36 D 16 '66

Other side of the 17th parallel; report on North Vietnam. B. B. Fall. il N Y Times Mag p4-5+ Jl 10 '66

Vietnam: its land and people. S. Van Valkenburg. il Cur Hist 50:65-71+ F '66

See also
Communism—Vietnam (Democratic Republic)

VIETNAM (Domocratic Republic)—See also
—*Continued*
Communist party (Vietnam [Democratic Republic])
Economic assistance in Vietnam (Democratic Republic)
Foreign visitors in Vietnam (Democratic Republic)
Haiphong
Hanoi
Russians in Vietnam
Technical assistance in Vietnam (Democratic Republic)

Army

Atlantic report; Vietnam war activities. Atlan 218:14+ O '66
Encouraging returns; highest ranking defector. Time 88:43 D 9 '66
Fresh from the North. Time 88:37 D 2 '66
Hugging the belt. Newsweek 68:49 N 7 '66
Is North Vietnam weakening? interviews with red prisoners; symposium. ed. by G. C. Troelstrup. U S News 61:52-4 D 12 '66
On the trail; supplies along the Sihanouk trail. F. Sully. il Newsweek 68:32 Jl 4 '66
Red Napoleon. il Time 87:32-6 Je 17 '66
Reporter at large; the enemy. S. Sheehan. New Yorker 42:62-6+ S 10 '66
Whose history? Rusk's testimony concerning North Vietnamese army in South Vietnam. New Repub 154:7 Mr 12 '66

Defenses

Deadly defense; air-defense system at Kep. Newsweek 68:40-1 O 17 '66
Has U.S. missed the boat in Vietnam? il U S News 60:38-9 Je 27 '66
North Vietnam may seek new SAM's. Tech W 19:15 Jl 4 '66
Soviet aid to Vietnam. A. Parry. il Reporter 36:28-33 Ja 12 '67
Wall of lead. Newsweek 68:64 Ag 22 '66

Foreign relations

Bad news for Uncle Ho. R. Hotz. Aviation W 85:21 N 14 '66
On the trail; Laotian and Cambodian routes used for Communist supply routes. F. Sully. il Newsweek 68:32 Jl 4 '66

Industries

Targets in Vietnam: vulnerable, and plenty of them. il U S News 60:30-1 F 7 '66

Politics and government

Dos & don'ts; Communist advice for beating imperialists. Time 87:32-3 Mr 11 '66
Faceless Viet Cong. G. A. Carver, jr. For Affairs 44:347-72 Ap '66
How strong is the NLF? D. Pike. il Reporter 34:20-4 F 24 '66
No room at the table; National liberation front of South Vietnam. il Newsweek 67:28 F 7 '66
Reporter at large; the enemy. S. Sheehan. New Yorker 42:62-6+ S 10 '66
Tough boss; Le Duan. il Newsweek 67:34 Ja 31 '66
Vietnam: between two truces, by J. Lacouture. Review
    Sat R 49:32-3 Ap 9 '66. W. J. Thorbecke

VIETNAM (Republic)
Big new base behind a dynamic strategy; Cam Ranh port. il Life 60:32-3 F 25 '66
Essayons! construction feats in Vietnam by U.S. army. il Time 87:25 F 11 '66
Long fear: fresh eyes on Viet Nam; the Delta. F. FitzGerald. Vogue 149:110-11+ Ja 1 '67
Mr Komer reports on progress in the other war in Viet-Nam; statement, November 7, 1966. R. W. Komer. Dept State Bul 55:892-4 D 12 '66
Vietnam: its land and people. S. Van Valkenburg. il Cur Hist 50:65-71+ F '66
Vietnam: U.S. digs in hard; with editorial comment. il Bsns W p51-4+. 156 Mr 5 '66
World of water; the delta. il Newsweek 68:55-6 D 19 '66
See also
Agriculture—Vietnam (Republic)
Americans in Vietnam
Children—Vietnam (Republic)
Cholon
Communism—Vietnam (Republic)
Crime and criminals—Vietnam (Republic)
Economic assistance in Vietnam (Republic)
Education—Vietnam (Republic)
Elections—Vietnam (Republic)
Foreign visitors in Vietnam (Republic)

Investments, Foreign (in Vietnam [Republic])
Journalism—Vietnam (Republic)
Labor and laboring classes—Vietnam (Republic)
Medical relief work—Vietnam (Republic)
Peasantry—Vietnam (Republic)
Public health—Vietnam (Republic)
Saigon
Shipping—Vietnam (Republic)
Strikes—Vietnam (Republic)
Technical assistance in Vietnam
Television broadcasting—Vietnam (Republic)
Tourist trade—Vietnam (Republic)
United Nations—Vietnam (Republic)
United States—Armed forces—Forces in Vietnam
United States—Foreign relations—Vietnam (Republic)
Women—Vietnam (Republic)
Youth—Vietnam (Republic)

Air force

VNAF emphasizing training, experience. C. M. Plattner. il Aviation W 84:74-5+ Ap 4 '66

Armed forces

Trouble at Danang; at the point of civil war. il Time 87:30 Ap 22 '66

Army

Bright spot in the Vietnamese war; Mekong Delta. il U S News 61:34-6 Jl 11 '66
General overhaul; General Quang removed from post. il Newsweek 68:36 N 28 '66
Hanging together; Popular forces; U.S. marines combined action program. il Newsweek 68:22+ Ag 29 '66
Ky question; ARVN role; General Chinh's grievances. Tran van Dinh. New Repub 156:21-2 Ja 21 '67
Shaping up; desertions. Time 88:36 S 9 '66

Cabinet

Cabinet crisis. Time 88:46+ O 21 '66
Maneuvers before Manila. Time 88:34-5 O 28 '66
North and South; reshuffle crisis. Newsweek 68:51-2 O 24 '66
Semifinals; background to crisis. il Newsweek 68:48 O 31 '66
Southern comfort. Time 88:38-9 N 25 '66

Economic conditions

Behind the battlefront: a search for stability. D. Warner. il Reporter 34:25-9 F 24 '66
Gut issue; inflation threatens entire social and economic system. Newsweek 67:43 Je 27 '66
Inflation is Saigon's other enemy. il Bsns W p54+ Mr 5 '66
Moving forward; R. Komer's report. il Time 88:23-4 S 23 '66
Pilot with a mission; Ky and his aims. il Time 87:26-31 F 18 '66
Saigon: a boomtown for U.S. businessmen. W. Tuohy. il Newsweek 67:70-2 Ja 31 '66
Saigon: drowning in dollars. D. Smith. il Nation 203:602-5 D 5 '66
Surprising assets of South Vietnam's economy; with editorial comment. E. K. Faltermayer. il Fortune 73:104+, 110-13+ Mr '66
With the quiet heroes of Vietnam; U.S. Operations Mission workers and projects. D. Reed. Read Digest 88:103-7 Mr '66

Foreign relations

Johnson's dilemma: alternatives now in Vietnam. H. J. Morgenthau. New Repub 154:12-16 My 28 '66
Question of survival; anti-government, anti-American demonstrations. il Newsweek 67:26-8 Ap 18 '66
Taste for tulips; Saigon's ambassador to Washington. Time 87:27 Ap 29 '66
Waiting game; Buddhist demonstrations against U.S. support of Ky's regime. il Newsweek 67:34 Je 6 '66

History

How the U.S. got there. il Sr Schol 89:10-15 O 28 '66

Moral conditions

How U.S. troops really behave in Vietnam. G. C. Troelstrup. il U S News 60:57-8+ My 23 '66
See also
Prostitution
Saigon—Moral conditions

Nationalism

Viet people favor VC. Sci N 90:200 S 17 '66

VIETNAM (Republic)—*Continued*

Navy

Johnson's choice. R. Walner. New Repub 154: 37-8 Mr 19 '66

Politics and government

Agreement or turmoil? il Sr Schol 88:13-14 Ap 29 '66

Ahead on points; political monks excluded from civilian junta. il Newsweek 67:57 Je 20 '66

And now, civil war. il Time 87:26 My 27 '66

Behind the battlefront: a search for stability. D. Warner. il Reporter 34:25-9 F 24 '66

Bitter Thi; Nguyen-chanh-Thi ousted. Newsweek 67:40 Mr 21 '66

Buddhists again; repercussions of Thi dismissal. Newsweek 67:40 Mr 28 '66

Buddhists score a point; election outcome prospects. il Newsweek 67:32-3 Ap 25 '66

Buddhists vs. the generals. il Sr Schol 88:11-12 Ap 22 '66

Capital of discontent. il Time 87:34 Ap 8 '66

Central figures in the struggle for leadership of Vietnam. il U S News 60:14 Mr 28 '66

Civil war within a war? Da Nang and Saigon demonstrations; with report by M. D. Perry. il Newsweek 67:38+ My 30 '66

Coppered bets; preparing for the elections. il Newsweek 67:39 My 9 '66

Decisive test. New Repub 154:4 Ap 23 '66

Declaration of Honolulu; text, February 7, 1966. Nguyen-van-Thieu and others. Cur Hist 50:238-9+ Ap '66

Depression in the Capitol; concerning forthcoming elections in Saigon. M. McGrory. America 114:688 My 14 '66

Dissent from the dissenters; why the U.S. is in Vietnam. A. de Borchgrave. Newsweek 67:32-3 Je 6 '66

Distaff delegate; Madame Xa. Time 88:42 O 14 '66

Divided Buddhists of South Vietnam. D. Warner. Reporter 34:22-4 Je 16 '66

Fiery rebellion: self immolations in South Vietnam. il Newsweek 67:48-9 Je 13 '66

For America, troubles grow in Vietnam. il U S News 60:8 Ap 11 '66

French eyes on Vietnam: America's colony in hell; concerning Robert Guillain's articles in Le Monde. A. Werth. Nation 202: 702-4 Je 13 '66

Gangrene of Vietnam; comment on Robert Guillain's articles in Le Monde. A. Werth. Nation 202:414-15 Ap 11 '66

How much power does Tri Quang want? background to March-April crisis. D. Warner. il Reporter 34:11-14 My 5 '66

How the U.S. got there. il Sr Schol 89:10-15 O 28 '66

In the eye of the storm. Time 87:21 Ap 15 '66

Incident at the pagoda; rebel fight against the Ky government. il Time 87:25 Je 3 '66

Insurrection inside the war. il Life 60:28-33 Ap 22 '66

Issue and goal in Viet-Nam; address, March 14, 1966. A. Johnson. Dept State Bul 54: 529-36 Ap 4 '66

Johnson's dilemma: alternatives now in Vietnam. H. J. Morgenthau. New Repub 154: 12-16 My 28 '66

Key test for Ky; anti-government demonstrations. Newsweek 67:42 Ap 11 '66

Ky makes it harder for U.S; prospects for civilian rule uncertain. il Bsns W p44 My 21 '66

Ky question; internal conflict between northerners and southerners. Tran van Dinh. New Repub 156:21-3 Ja 21 '67

Ky's crackdown. il Newsweek 68:28 Jl 4 '66

Ky's plan for final victory, invade North Vietnam; interview. Nguyen-cao-Ky. il U S News 61:22-4 Ag 1 '66

Letter from Saigon (cont) R. Shaplen. New Yorker 42:155-62+ Ap 16 '66

Letter from Saigon; situation confronting the newly elected Constituent assembly. R. Shaplen. New Yorker 42:191-2+ O 1 '66

Letter from South Vietnam. R. Shaplen. il New Yorker 42:58-60+ Mr 12; 142-4+ Je 4 '66

Letter from Vietnam. D. Finley. America 115: 380-1 O 1 '66

Letter from Washington. R. H. Rovere. New Yorker 42:180-5 Ap 23 '66

Loss of face; Ky's image. il Newsweek 67: 56+ My 16 '66

New crisis in Vietnam war. U S News 60: 33-4 Ap 18 '66

Object lesson in Saigon; Ta Vinh execution. il Life 60:36 Mr 25 '66

One more step. Time 88:17-18 D 30 '66

Opposition of the altar il Time 87:39 Je 17 '66

Other war in Vietnam: progress report; with text of letter of transmittal, September 13, 1966. R. W. Komer. Dept State Bul 55:549-67, 591-601 O 10-17 '66

Outlook now in Vietnam. il U S News 60: 35-7 Je 13 '66

Pilot with a mission; Ky and his aims. il Time 87:26-31 F 18 '66

Political climate; antigovernment protests. il Time 87:30 Ap 1 '66

Political war; question of what the U.S. would do if an elected civilian government negotiates with the Viet Cong. K. Crawford. Newsweek 67:30 Ap 25 '66

Politically, the tide begins to turn. il Bsns W p52-3 Mr 5 '66

Politician from the pagoda. il Time 87:25-6+ Ap 22 '66

Politicking begins; opening session of the National constituent assembly. il Time 88:41 O 7 '66

President comments on internal developments in Viet-Nam; statement. May 21, 1966. L. B. Johnson. Dept State Bul 54:888 Je 6 '66

Preventing the peace: report from an intermediary. P. Devillers. Nation 203:597-602 D 5 '66

Question of survival; anti-government, anti-American demonstrations. il Newsweek 67: 26-8 Ap 18 '66

Rebellion is shot down in Danang; Buddhist-led insurrection; with report by F. McCulloch. il Life 60:26-9 Je 3 '66

Reflections on Vietnam. R. N. Goodwin. il New Yorker 42:57-8+ Ap 16 '66

Saigon Thi party. Time 87:33 Mr 18 '66

Showdown in Danang. D. Warner. il Reporter 34:14-16 Je 2 '66

South Vietnam's political awakening. D. Warner. il Reporter 35:40-3 N 17 '66

Stake in stability. Time 87:34-5 Ap 29 '66

Storm breaks; war in the streets. il Time 87: 28-9 Ap 15 '66

Struggle for power. il Newsweek 69:35-6 Ja 16 '67

Success & a promise; Ky not to tolerate a Communist or neutralist regime. Time 87:34 My 13 '66

Surprise? Nation 202:634 My 30 '66

Taking stock on Viet Nam; with press comments. Sr Schol 88:6, 9 My 6 '66

Talk with Thich Tri Quang. Thich-tri-Quang. Time 87:27 Ap 22 '66

Tempest in a Thi-pot. il Newsweek 67:56 Ap 4 '66

Thich Tri Quang speaks out; interview, ed. by E. G. Martin. Thich-tri-Quang. Newsweek 67:33+ Ap 25 '66

Time for patience & resolve. Time 87:19 Ap 22 '66

Trouble at Danang; at the point of civil war. il Time 87:30 Ap 22 '66

Turmoil in Vietnam: war within a war? il Newsweek 67:24-5 Ap 18 '66

Turning point in Vietnam. W. Lippmann. Newsweek 67:17 Ap 25 '66

Two key men back of Vietnam's unrest. il U S News 60:21 Ap 18 '66

Uncle's head in the noose. Nation 202:113-14 Ja 31 '66

U.S. holds firm in wobbly Vietnam; Buddhist anti-government demonstrations and riots shake Saigon regime. il Bsns W p39-40 Ap 16 '66

Uses of power; Ky issues electoral laws. il Newsweek 68:36 Jl 11 '66

Vietcong as negotiators? J. B. Sheerin. Cath World 203:6-10 Ap '66

Vietcong, by D. Pike. Review New Repub 155:18-19 N 19 '66. S. Karnow

Vietnam: agonizing reappraisal begins; with report by G. C. Troelstrup. il U S News 60: 37-9 Ap 25 '66

Vietnam between riots and elections. Life 60: 4 My 6 '66

Vietnam: between two truces, by J. Lacouture. Review New Repub 154:27 Ap 16 '66. A. Campbell Sat R 49:32-3 Ap 9 '66. W. J. Thorbecke

Vietnam, from disorder to what? meeting with Thich Tam Chau and Thich Tri Quang. R. S. Browne. New Repub 154:11-12 Ap 23 '66

VIETNAM (Republic)—Politics and government
—Continued
Viet Nam in the balance. B. B. Fall. bibliog f
For Affairs 45:1-18 O '66
Vietnam must choose. New Repub 154:5-6
Ap 16 '66
Vietnam: questions old and new; new crisis
and U.S. reactions. il Newsweek 67:21-2 Ap
25 '66
Vietnam: real test is still to come. il U S
News 60:35-6 Je 6 '66
Vietnam: the quest for stability. B. B. Fall.
bibliog f il Cur Hist 52:8-15+ Ja '67
Vietnam: the week of wild uncertainty. D.
Moser. il Life 60:44-44C Ap 15 '66
Vietnamese elections. Commonweal 84:245-6
My 20 '66
Vietnam's Buddhists emerge as key power;
vital third force to determine war's course
and future U.S. presence. il Bsns W p38-
40 Ap 23 '66
Waiting game; Buddhist demonstrations
against U.S. suport of Ky's regime. il News-
week 67:34 Je 6 '66
War crisis; as General Thi sees it; inter-
view. Nguyen-chanh-Thi. U S News 60:22
Ap 25 '66
Way out in Vietnam. J. M. Burns. Harper
233:34-5 Ag '66
Way out there in Vietnam, he can't see 'em
or hear 'em; front that is so frustrating
to LBJ. H. Sidey. il Life 60:36B Je 3 '66
What comes next in Vietnam war? il U S
News 60:27-9 My 30 '66
Whole year. Time 87:40 Je 24 '66
Wider mandate; Constituent assembly. il
Time 88:24 D 23 '66
Young generals who run the country. F. Mc-
Culloch. il Life 60:52B+ F 25 '66
    See also
Vietnam (Republic)—Cabinet

Anecdotes, facetiae, satire, etc.
Theater of war; players and plot. G. Ace.
Sat R 49:14 Je 11 '66

Relief work
    See also
Medical relief work—Vietnam (Republic)

Religious institutions and affairs
Religious groups in South Vietnam. il U S
News 60:30 My 30 '66
Vietnam, from disorder to what? meeting
with Thich Tam Chau and Thich Tri
Quang. R. S. Browne. New Repub 154:11-12
Ap 23 '66
    See also
Buddha and Buddhism
Buddhists

Riots
Anniversary waltz; Saigon; Hué monks ac-
tivities. il Newsweek 67:43 Je 27 '66
Question of survival; anti-government, anti-
American demonstrations. il Newsweek 67:
26-8 Ap 18 '66
Vietnam: the week of wild uncertainty. D.
Moser. il Life 60:44-44C Ap 15 '66

Social conditions
Moving forward; R. Komer's report. il Time
88:23-4 S 23 '66
Other war in Vietnam; progress report; with
text of letter of transmittal, September 13,
1966. R. W. Komer. Dept State Bul 55:
549-67, 591-601 O 10-17 '66
Smoke, fire & welfare. il Time 87:24-5 Mr 25
'66
U.S. task force studies Viet-Nam health and
education needs. Dept State Bul 54:492 Mr
28 '66

Social policy
Adding social reform to Vietnam arsenal;
topics of Honolulu conference. il Bsns W
p27-8 F 12 '66
Building a better society, the main test in
Viet-Nam; excerpt from address, February
16, 1966. L. B. Johnson. Dept State Bul
54:363-4 Mr 7 '66
Greatest drama. il Time 87:19-20 Ap 1 '66
Letter from South Vietnam. R. Shaplen. il
New Yorker 42:58-60+ Mr 12 '66
New realism; Honolulu conference. il Time
87:19-21 F 18 '66
Now those Vietnamese are more than names;
summit meeting between U.S. and South
Vietnamese officials in Honolulu. R. B.
Stolley. il Life 60:32-32A F 18 '66

Pilot with a mission; Ky and his aims. il
Time 87:26-31 F 18 '66
Second front; U.S.-backed program of social,
economic and political reforms. il Newsweek 67:35-6 F 21 '66
Vietnam: the ordeal of pacification; Revolutionary development program. D. Warner.
il Reporter 35:24-8 D 1 '66

Treaties
So the war goes on; accords of the Geneva
agreements. New Repub 154:6-7 F 12 '66;
Discussion. 154:35-6 Mr 5 '66
VIETNAM (Republic) and the United States
Cam Ne fund. N. Cousins. Sat R 49:25 My
14 '66
Vietnam is like an oriental western. A. Car-
thew. il N Y Times Mag p8-9+ Ja 23 '66
    See also
United States—Foreign opinion—Vietnamese
VIETNAMESE
Life and death of the Vietnamese village. F.
Fitzgerald. il N Y Times Mag p4-5+ S 4
'66
Love and hate in the Mekong delta. S. Alsop.
il Sat Eve Post 239:12 D 31 '66
Nation beyond Saigon. K. T. Young. Sat R
49:33-4 Jl 16 '66
Not a dove, but no longer a hawk. N. Shee-
han. il N Y Times Mag p27+ O 9 '66;
Reply. Nation 203:404 O 24 '66
People on and behind the battle lines. il Sr
Schol 89:19-21 O 28 '66
Speaking out; we must colonize Vietnam. J.
Morris. Sat Eve Post 239:10+ Mr 26 '66
Thich Nhat Hanh; interview. Nhat Hanh.
New Yorker 42:21-3 Je 25 '66
Vietnam is like an oriental western. A. Car-
thew. il N Y Times Mag p8-9+ Ja 23 '66
Vietnam: its land and people. S. Van Valken-
burg. il Cur Hist 50:65-71+ F '66
War without guns, by G. K. Tanham. Review
Sat R 49:28-9 My 28 '66. K. T. Young
What is owing to the Vietnamese? N.
Cousins. Sat R 49:24 Mr 26 '66
    See also
Montagnards
Peasantry—Vietnam (Republic)
VIETNAMESE crisis, 1964
Congress and the undeclared war. Christian
Cent 83:195-6 F 16 '66
VIETNAMESE in France
Safe, unhappy exiles. Time 88:37 N 11 '66
VIETNAMESE in the United States
Other war in Vietnam; Vietnamese paraple-
gics and medical team rehabilitation train-
ing in U.S. H. A. Rusk. il Read Digest
89:108-12 Jl '66
Viet victory in America; saving paralyzed
Vietnamese soldiers and training doctors
and nurses. D. Chapman. il Look 30:28-31
Ap 19 '66
VIETNAMESE poetry
Prison diary, by Ho chi Minh. Review
Nation 202:302-3 Mr 14 '66. J. Mirsky
VIETNAMESE propaganda. See Propaganda,
Vietnamese
VIETNAMESE soldiers. See Vietnam (Republic)
—Army
VIETNAMESE students
Vietnam: whose war? opinion of student
leaders from Saigon university. S. Alsop.
Sat Eve Post 240:16 Ja 28 '67
VIETNAMESE war, 1957-
As simple as that; J. Steinbeck's reply to Y.
Yevtushenko. America 115:89 Jl 23 '66
Bigger war in the new year, and no end in
sight. il U S News 62:26-7 Ja 9 '67
Bomb something! test to take. il Esquire
66:59-61 Ag '66
Bombs fall again. America 114:219-20 F 12 '66
Burden of Vietnam. O. Handlin. Atlan 218:
140-3 Jl '66
Cardinal Spellman's holy war. Christian Cent
84:36 Ja 11 '67
Challenge came in Vietnam; address, Novem-
ber 15, 1966. E. G. Wheeler. Vital Speeches
33:130-3 D 15 '66
CB, entering wedge; Harvard professors
protest use of chemical-biological weapons
in Vietnam. Nation 204:68 Ja 16 '67
De-escalating the war. Commonweal 83:523-4
F 4 '66
End of the holiday. il Time 87:13-14 Ja 28
'66
Free world's stake in Viet-Nam; address,
October 19, 1966. D. MacArthur, 2d. Dept
State Bul 55:745-50 N 14 '66

VIETNAMESE war, 1957- —*Continued*

From America's top military leaders: a report on Vietnam; excerpts from testimony, February 15, 1966. il U S News 60:14 F 28 '66

From the field: new box score on the war in Vietnam. il U S News 61:37-9 Ag 29 '66

Gas and guerrillas, a word of caution. D. Savitz. New Repub 154:13-14 Mr 19 '66; Discussion. 154:35-6 Ap 2 '66

General Westmoreland reports on Vietnam war; interview. W. C. Westmoreland. il U S News 61:44-9 N 28 '66

Hard lines and guidelines; surrender to Washington; address, December 3, 1965. R. M. Nixon. Vital Speeches 32:194-7 Ja 15 '66

Hazards of war. Commonweal 84:272-3 My 27 '66

How the White House sees the war in Vietnam. U S News 61:25 Ag 22 '66

Ike; interview. D. D. Eisenhower. Nat R 18:1205 N 29 '66

Invade North Vietnam? Ky's plan sparks debate; concerning interview in August 1 issue of U.S. news & World report. il U S News 61:10 Ag 8 '66

Is end of Vietnam war in sight? il U S News 61:25-8 Jl 25 '66

Just ahead: more action, more casualties in the Vietnam war? il U S News 60:6 Ap 4 '66

Kremlin's move? J. Burnham. Nat R 18:822 Ag 23 '66

Ky's plan for final victory, invade North Vietnam; interview. Nguyen-cao-Ky. il U S News 61:22-4 Ag 1 '66

Letter from South Vietnam (cont) R. Shaplen. New Yorker 42:142-4+ Je 4 '66

Life and death of a Vietnamese village. F. Fitzgerald. il N Y Times Mag p4-5+ S 4 '66

Long fear: fresh eyes on Viet Nam; the Delta. F. FitzGerald. Vogue 149:110-11+ Ja 1 '67

Love and hate in the Mekong Delta. S. Alsop. il Sat Eve Post 239:12 D 31 '66

Missile myths exploding. R. Hotz. Aviation W 84:21 Ja 24 '66

My dear friend Genya; reply to Yevgeny Yevtushenko. J. Steinbeck. Read Digest 89:128 S '66

Nation beyond Saigon. K. T. Young. Sat R 49:33-4 Jl 16 '66

New side effects of Viet Nam fighting. F. Morley. il Nations Bsns 54:27-8 Ap '66

Not a dove, but no longer a hawk. N. Sheehan. il N Y Times Mag p27+ O 9 '66; Reply. Nation 203:404 O 24 '66

Offense is the worst defense. E. Rabinowitch. Bul Atomic Sci 22:32-4 O '66

Other side of the 17th parallel; report on North Vietnam. B. B. Fall. il N Y Times Mag p4-5+ Jl 10 '66

Our war, their peace; who wants what in South Vietnam? A. Campbell. New Repub 154:19-23 Mr 19 '66

Politically, the tide begins to turn. il Bsns W p52-3 Mr 5 '66

President and the New Year. H. Brandon. Sat R 49:9 D 31 '66

Russian dilemma. il Newsweek 67:40+ Je 20 '66

Secretary Rusk meets with Asian leaders; statements on various occasions during the trip, transcripts of news conferences; with texts of communiques. D. Rusk. Dept State Bul 55:169-75 Ag 1 '66

Secretary Rusk's news conference of May 17, 1966. D. Rusk. Dept State Bul 54:882-7 Je 6 '66

Semifinals. il Newsweek 68:48 O 31 '66

Spain and Vietnam; comparing two civil wars. W. C. McWilliams and D. Hale. Commonweal 84:575-7 S 16 '66

Sunday with Westmoreland; the general who runs our war in Vietnam. C. S. Wren. il Look 30:27-31 O 18 '66

Then and now, the difference; state of the Vietnamese war today. A. de Borchgrave. il Newsweek 67:40-2 Mr 14 '66

Top authority looks at Vietnam war and its future; interview. M. D. Taylor. U S News 60:38-42+ F 21 '66

Two sides to the Dienbienphu story; concerning assessments by Bernard Fall and Vo Nguyen Giap. J. Mirsky. Nation 202:781-4 Je 27 '66

Unfinished business: promise of last February's Honolulu conference. il Time 87:26 Je 3 '66

Vietnam between riots and elections. Life 60:4 My 6 '66

Vietnam: between two truces, by J. Lacouture. Review
 New Repub 154:27 Ap 16 '66. A. Campbell
 Sat R 49:32-3 Ap 8 '66. W. J. Thorbecke

Vietnam in perspective. R. C. Hottelet. il Reporter 35:20-7 N 3 '66

Viet Nam report. il Sr Schol 89:6 O 28 '66

Vietnam: the quest for stability. B. B. Fall. bibliog f il Cur Hist 52:8-15+ Ja '67

Vietnam: whose war? opinion of student leaders from Saigon university. S. Alsop. Sat Eve Post 240:16 Ja 28 '67

Viet-Nam witness 1953-66, by B. B. Fall. Review
 Sat R il 49:23-4 My 28 '66. D. Schoenbrun

War outlook: as McNamara sees it now. il U S News 61:26 O 24 '66

Why Ho keeps saying no; Time essay. Time 88:30-1 N 11 '66

Why our methods aren't working; Viet Cong proving they can provide a normal life for the people. A. C. Weed, 2d. New Repub 154:20 F 5 '66

Why Vietnam? F. N. Trager. Review
 Nat R 18:1329-30 D 27 '66. G. Niemeyer

See also
Vietnam (Democratic Republic)—Army
Vietnam (Democratic Republic)—Politics and government
Vietnam (Republic)—Politics and government

Aerial operations

Air raids, leftover puzzles: North Vietnamese reaction to raids on petroleum storage areas. B. B. Fall. il New Repub 155:7-8 Jl 16 '66

Air war: a turn for the worse? il U S News 61:39 Ag 29 '66

Air war heats up: action near Chinese border. Nation 202:572 My 16 '66

Air war in Vietnam, introd. by E. D. Muhlfeld. F. Harvey. il Flying 79:38-95 N '66

Air war in Vietnam: is it worth the price? il U S News 61:28-9 Ag 8 '66

Air war in Vietnam: it grows bigger and bigger. U S News 61:8 Jl 18 '66

Air war: less than a success. il Newsweek 68:21-2 Ag 29 '66

Air war; with photographs by L. Burrows and account by T. Flaherty. Life 61:44-57+ S 9 '66

Air, water, nuts & bolts. Time 87:36-7 My 20 '66

Airpower gives U.S. edge in Vietnam war. C. Brownlow. il Aviation W 86:16-21 Ja 9 '67

Another pilot's report from Vietnam; letter. N. Wilson. Aviation W 85:21+ O 24 '66; Excerpts. U S News 61:64 O 31 '66

As the air war heats up in Vietnam; with interview with J. P. McConnell. il U S News 60:27-9 My 9 '66

At Hanoi, the war's flaming new turn. il Life 61:20-5 Jl 15 '66

Atlantic alliance; southeast Asia; address, September 13, 1966. B. K. Holloway. Vital Speeches 33:11-14 O 15 '66

Back on the job. M. D. Perry; F. Sully. il Newsweek 67:21-2 F 14 '66

Back to the Valley of Death; Air Cav. Time 87:34-5 Ap 8 '66

Beneficence of American power. D. Lawrence. U S News 61:108 Jl 11 '66

Bigger bombing: where will it lead? with excerpts from news conference with R. S. McNamara. il U S News 61:31-3 Jl 11 '66

Blue bombs on the Panhandle. il Time 88:23 S 2 '66

Bomb shortages? an on-the-scene report. il U S News 60:10 My 2 '66

Bombing seen forcing Hanoi to disengage. E. H. Kolcum. Aviation W 85:29 Jl 18 '66

Bombing the North. New Repub 154:5-6 Ap 23 '66

Bombs in the North and the moral issue. America 116:32 Ja 14 '67

Brave men in frail planes; Forward air controllers. J. G. Hubbell. il Read Digest 88:76-80 Ap '66

Call it off. New Repub 156:9 Ja 21 '67

Chances of the game; unintended targets. il Newsweek 68:29 S 5 '66

VIETNAMESE war, 1957- —Aerial operations
—*Continued*
Civilians weren't the target, but: U.S. air raids in North Vietnam. il Newsweek 69:17-18 Ja 9 '67
Close Haiphong? what mines could do. il U S News 60:37 Mr 28 '66
Combat forces new limited war studies. C. Brownlow. il Aviation W 84:90-4 Mr 28 '66
Congress debates air war restrictions. G. C. Wilson. Aviation W 84:2-9 F 14 '66
Cost accounting; cutback in South; strikes in North; results. W. Cook. il Newsweek 67:25-6+ My 2 '66
Cost and results in the air war. il U S News 61:55 D 19 '66
Cost of pause; possibility of a Christmas truce. Time 88:32 N 25 '66
Craters within craters. Time 88:31 S 23 '66
Curtain of fire; North Viet Nam. il Time 87:34 Ap 29 '66
Decision of mind and experience, not of heart and hope; oil-dump bombings at Hanoi and Haiphong. H. Sidey. il Life 61:28B Jl 8 '66
Despite the uproar: does world really want U.S. to quit? il U S News 62:31-2 Ja 16 '67
Duels in the sun. il Time 87:28 My 6 '66
E-2A controls navy North Vietnam strikes. C. Brownlow. il Aviation W 85:57+ Ag 1 '66
End of the pause. il Sr Schol 88:14 F 11 '66
Eyes in the sky; air photographs of the 460th Tactical reconnaissance wing. il Time 88:20 Jl 29 '66
Facts in a propaganda war over U.S. bombing; civilian casualties. U S News 62:6+ Ja 9 '67
Feeling for freedom; airman twice shot down over North Viet Nam and twice rescued. Time 88:13 Jl 29 '66
Flak from Hanoi; U.S. bombing raids as reported by H. Salisbury. il Time 89:13-14 Ja 6 '67
Fliers in Vietnam say: it's a no-win half war. il U S News 61:24-6 D 26 '66
Great bomb flap; claims that Hanoi was bombed. il Time 88:23-4 D 23 '66
Helluva way to grow up fast; paratrooper at Ft Benning, Ga. C. S. Wren. il Look 30:73-7 S 20 '66
Hero lost; American plane losses. Time 88:27 Ag 19 '66
How accidents happen; air force drops napalm on the U.S. lines. Time 88:23 S 2 '66
How an ex-President views Vietnam now; excerpts from statement, January 31, 1966. D. D. Eisenhower. U S News 60:19 F 14 '66
Hurting; how North Vietnam is retaliating against U.S. raids. il Newsweek 68:28 Jl 18 '66
I thought I'd better shoot; dogfights. Time 88:29 S 30 '66
Is bombing the answer? excerpts from statements, January 21, 1966. S. Symington; R. S. McNamara. U S News 60:47-8 F 28 '66
It's great to be alive; daring rescue of D. W. Myers, by B. F. Fisher at Ashau. R. Armstrong. il Sat Eve Post 239:21-6 Je 4 '66; Same abr. with title Pilot is down! Read Digest 89:42-8 Ag '66
Major Viet Cong summer offensive seen. Aviation W 84:29 Ap 18 '66
Marine control of air tested in combat. C. M. Plattner. il Aviation W 84:90-1+ F 14 '66
Matter of opinion? Harrison Salisbury's reports of U.S. bombings of Namdinh. Reporter 36:20+ Ja 12 '67
Matter of probability; U.S. target errors. il Newsweek 68:64 Ag 22 '66
Memo from Haiphong, North Vietnam; under American bombs. N. Barrymaine. Look 30:62 N 29 '66; Same with title Bomb damage in North Vietnam described. il Aviation W 85:47+ D 26 '66
Modern air force; address, February 25, 1966. H. Brown. Vital Speeches 32:354-8 Ap 1 '66
Monsoons fail to stop Viet air support. Aviation W 84:80-1 Mr 14 '66
More effective airpower. R. Hotz. Aviation W 85:21 Jl 11 '66
Mouth of the dragon; attempts to knock down bridge at Thanh Hoa. Newsweek 69:24 Ja 2 '67
New bombings. Commonweal 83:548-9 F 11 '66
New tempo in the air war in Vietnam. U S News 60:8 My 2 '66

New U.S. strategy: hit North Vietnam where it hurts. il Life 61:28-28A Jl 8 '66
No sanctuary in Viet war? il Sr Schol 88:16 My 13 '66
North Vietnam air war; excerpts from comments. H. Brown. Aviation W 85:21 D 12 '66
Notice to the North; concerning air opposition. Time 88:17 D 30 '66
Now, heavier bombing of North Vietnam. il U S News 60:6 Je 13 '66
Of bombs and bruises; context in which Asians view the bombing. N. Cousins. Sat R 49:34 F 19 '66
Off at the elbow; U.S. aerial ambush. il Time 89:24 Ja 13 '67
Off limits to bombers; President's restriction of U.S. bomber fleet. il Newsweek 67:34 F 28 '66
Oil depot bombings mark new Viet phase. C. Brownlow. il Aviation W 85:20-3 Jl 4 '66
One allied leader speaking up for U.S; excerpts from address, February 9, 1966. H. Wilson. U S News 60:21 F 21 '66
One more rung; bombing of oil storage depots near Hanoi and Haiphong. Nat R 18:659-60 Jl 12 '66
Our fabulous choppers; eyewitness report. J. H. Winchester. il Pop Sci 188:80-3+ F '66
Our pilots call Hanoi Dodge City. S. Butz. il N Y Times Mag p30-1+ O 16 '66
Our war with red China; in Vietnam. A. Harrigan. il Nat R 18:204-6 Mr 8 '66
Pentagon answer to critics of bombing; controversy of civilian casualties; excerpts from letter. P. G. Goulding. U S News 62:16 Ja 16 '67
Phantom vs. MIG; growing air battle. il U S News 62:11-12 Ja 16 '67
Pilot report from Vietnam; letter. Aviation W 85:21+ S 19 '66; Discussion. 85:122 O 3; 130 O 24; 144 N 14; 142 N 21 '66; 86:106 Ja 9 '67
Plane for all seasons; Tiger squadron. il Time 88:38 N 25 '66
Pressure goes up; more bombing raids into North Vietnam; with editorial comment. il Bsns W p37-8, 168 Jl 9 '66
Publisher's memo; F. Harvey's six weeks in Vietnam. E. D. Muhlfeld. il Flying 79:6 S '66
Quick-reacting applications unit spurs development for Vietnam. il Aviation W 85:41 mid-D '66
Quiet no more; bombing off the demilitarized buffer zone. il Time 88:20 Ag 12 '66
Reasons of state; Hanoi-Haiphong raids condemned by Great Britain. Newsweek 68:40 Jl 11 '66
Refreshed by the pause. il Newsweek 67:32 Ja 31 '66
Report from Vietnam. W. J. Coughlin and M. Getler. il Miss & Roc 18:44-8+ Mr 28 '66
Resumption of Viet bombings; press comments. Sr Schol 88:24-5 F 18 '66
Ripping the sanctuary; bombing raids on Hanoi-Haiphong complex. il Time 88:11-17 Jl 8 '66; Same abr. with title Turning point in Vietnam? Read Digest 89:87-91 S '66
Rolling thunder. il Time 87:29 Ap 15 '66
Scenario for attack; step up expected. Newsweek 68:16 Jl 4 '66
Senate investigators urge TAC review. il Aviation W 85:86-9+ Ag 22 '66
Shocked senators; reactions to L. B. Johnson's decision to resume bombing. New Repub 154:4 F 12 '66
Sitting ducks of aerial war. il Ebony 22:58-60+ N '66
Step-up in the war, and its risks. il Newsweek 67:25-6 My 9 '66
Storm over Viet Nam bombings; civilian casualties, concerning dispatches to New York times by H. E. Salisbury. il Sr Schol 89:12-13 Ja 13 '67
Striking in the air. Time 87:30 Ap 22 '66
String runs out; U.S. pause to end; Congress reactions. il Time 87:21-6 F 4 '66
SAMS spur changes in combat tactics, new equipment. C. M. Plattner. il Aviation W 84:26-31 Ja 24 '66
Talking at a distance; summary of statement on Asian policy. L. B. Johnson. il Newsweek 68:39+ Jl 25 '66
Target: Hanoi; attacks on Hanoi-Haiphong oil tanks. il Newsweek 68:21-2 Jl 11 '66
That others may live; Aerospace rescue and recovery service. il Newsweek 67:58 Ap 4 '66

VIETNAMESE war, 1957- —American participation—*Continued*

Fifth anniversary of the Peace corps; remarks, March 1, 1966. L. B. Johnson. Dept State Bul 54:441-3 Mr 21 '66

Fooling the people. New Repub 155:5-7 Ag 13 '66

Foot-in-mouth syndrome; public statements of D. Eisenhower and Madame Chiang Kaishek. Christian Cent 83:1263 O 19 '66

Freedom is an indivisible word; U.S. aims; statement. L. B. Johnson. Time 87:26 Mr 4 '66

French eyes on Vietnam: America's colony in hell; concerning Robert Guillain's articles in Le Monde. A. Werth. Nation 202: 702-4 Je 13 '66

From a top senator: how Vietnam war grew, what to do now; excerpts from statement, January 27, 1966. J. C. Stennis. U S News 60:6 F 7 '66

From containment to isolation; excerpts from address. G. K. Kennan. Time 87:20 F 18 '66

From Ho, with love. J. Burnham. Nat R 18: 203 Mr 8 '66

Gray capital, gray debate. E. J. Hughes. Newsweek 67:23 F 21 '66

Has U.S. missed the boat in Vietnam? il U S News 60:38-9 Je 27 '66

Heart of the matter in Vietnam; G. F. Kennan before Senate foreign relations committee. America 114:282-3 F 26 '66

Heresy at Omaha; concerning L. B. Johnson's remarks about rights and duties. W. Lippmann. Newsweek 68:17 Jl 18 '66

Honolulu meeting, and after; with press comments. il Sr Schol 88:3-4 F 25 '66

Hopeful President joins the debate. il Newsweek 67:23 Mr 7 '66

Hot seat; public hearings. Newsweek 67:18 F 28 '66

How big the war in its next phase? il U S News 60:34-5 Je 20 '66

How firmness in Vietnam is paying off; interview. W. E. Griffith. Read Digest 88: 112-16 Ap '66

How it looks from Saigon; Richard Nixon states local military commanders propositions. Nat R 18:816+ Ag 23 '66

How much is enough? views of General Maxwell Taylor. New Repub 154:8 F 26 '66

How much power does Tri Quang want? background to March-April crisis. D. Warner. il Reporter 34:11-14 My 5 '66

How not to fight a war; downgrading our objectives in Vietnam. D. Lawrence. U S News 60:100 My 30 '66

How to win the war in South Vietnam; interview. U. S. G. Sharp. il U S News 60: 38-41 Mr 28 '66

How U.S. hopes to cut troop buildup in Asia. il Bsns W p38-9 D 3 '66

Hudson Valley teach-in on Vietnam; the host: Marist college, Poughkeepsie, N.Y. C. Austin. Christian Cent 83:503-5 Ap 20 '66

Humphrey's chickens; concerning reply to R. Kennedy's proposed coalition government for Saigon. K. Crawford. Newsweek 67:38 Mr 14 '66

Humphrey's role; selling a consensus. il U S News 60:20 Mr 7 '66

Idiot logic of escalation. Nation 203:170 S 5 '66

Ike sparks a new debate: how much force to use in Vietnam? statements. D. D. Eisenhower. U S News 61:23 O 17 '66

In Congress, crucial votes on Vietnam. U S News 60:12 Mr 14 '66

Is dissent traitorous? concerning President Johnson's Chicago address, My 17, 1966. Christian Cent 83:703 Je 1 '66

Is U.S. trapped in a hopeless war? M. L. Stone. il U S News 61:40-9 D 5 '66

It may be the year we start winning; outlook for '67. il Bsns W p21-2 D 31 '66

It's our war. Farm J 90:134 Mr '66

Johnson's dilemma: alternatives now in Vietnam. H. J. Morgenthau. New Repub 154: 12-16 My 28 '66

Keeping our commitment to peace; address, March 14, 1966. D. Rusk. Dept State Bul 54:514-21 Ap 4 '66

Kennan on Vietnam; statement; with questions and answers. G. F. Kennan. New Repub 154:19-30 F 26 '66

Legality of United States participation in the defense of Viet-Nam; legal memorandum submitted to the Senate committee on foreign relations, March 8, 1966. L. C. Meeker. bibliog f Dept State Bul 54:474-89 Mr 28 '66

Lessons of Vietnam. W. J. Coughlin. Miss & Roc 18:160 Mr 28 '66

Letter from Washington (cont) R. H. Rovere. New Yorker 42:167-72 Mr 19; 180-5 Ap 23 '66

Letter from Washington; concerning State of the Union message. R. H. Rovere. New Yorker 41:90+ Ja 22 '66

Life of a salesman; administration's Vietnam line. il Newsweek 67:25-6 Mr 7 '66

Lin Piao on deck. Nat R 18:868-9 S 6 '66

A look at the score card; President's aim and the public's desire to be informed. il Time 87:23 Je 17 '66

Looking for a war. H. Mitgang. il N Y Times Mag p28-9+ My 22 '66

LBJ in Hawaii: a look and a promise. il Newsweek 67:24-7 F 21 '66

McNamara's war; what the record shows. U S News 61:36-7 Jl 25 '66

Matter of understanding; L. B. Johnson defines policy. Reporter 35:8 Ag 11 '66

Middle way out of Vietnam. A. Schlesinger, jr. il N Y Times Mag p47-9+ S 18 '66; Discussion. p22+ O 9; 98 O 16; 139-40 O 30 '66

Military policy in Vietnam. R. Dudman. bibliog f Cur Hist 50:91-7+ F '66

Momentum of power; concerning Senator Fulbright's Arrogance of power speech. Nation 202:602 My 23 '66

More and more, an American war. U S News 60:10 Ap 25 '66

More light, less heat; justifying war in Viet Nam. il Time 87:27-8 My 20 '66

New crisis in Vietnam: what if U.S. gets out? questions and answers. S. W. Sanders. il U S News 60:34-7 Ap 18 '66

New light on why U.S. is in Vietnam; excerpts from television broadcast, January 17, 1966. J. Reston. il U S News 60:16 Ja 31 '66

New roadblocks on the way to peace. il U S News 60:35-7 F 14 '66

1954 and 1966: is U.S. repeating French mistakes in Vietnam? interview. M. Taylor. il U S News 60:36-7 F 28 '66

No cure in consensus; how U.S. is doing in Viet Nam. il Time 87:31-2 Je 10 '66

Not in the mood; Russian attack on the U.S. involvement. il Time 88:28 Jl 22 '66

On hawks and doves; D. Rusk's tasks. M. Ascoli. Reporter 34:24 Mr 24 '66

Opinion: on Vietnam. G. S. McGovern. il Mlle 62:66+ Mr '66

Our intentions in Vietnam. Commonweal 84: 453-4 Jl 22 '66

Our war with red China; in Vietnam. A. Harrigan. il Nat R 18:204-6 Mr 8 '66

Outlook now in Vietnam. il U S News 60: 35-7 Je 13 '66

Point beyond decency. O. Lattimore. Nation 202:212-13 F 21 '66

Politics. D. Macdonald. Esquire 67:26+ Ja '67

Presence of Marcos; reaping dividends from the American presence in Vietnam. Nat R 18:969-70 O 4 '66

President answers; character of U.S. participation. M. Ascoli. Reporter 35:12 Jl 14 '66

President answers congressional letter on Viet-Nam situation; text of letter, January 22, 1966. L. B. Johnson. Dept State Bul 54:253-4 F 14 '66

President Johnson and General Westmoreland discuss the situation in Viet-Nam. L. B. Johnson; W. C. Westmoreland. Dept State Bul 55:335-8 S 5 '66

President signs supplemental military authorization bill; remarks, March 15, 1966. L. B. Johnson. Dept State Bul 54:578-9 Ap 11 '66

Price of peace. Christian Cent 83:163-4 F 9 '66

Problems confronting us; address, December 3, 1965. M. D. Taylor. Vital Speeches 32: 264-8 F 15 '66

Prospect ahead. il Time 88:17-18 Ag 19 '66

Pull-out, all-out, or stand fast in Vietnam? M. B. Ridgway. Look 30:81-2+ Ap 5 '66

Pull out of Vietnam? what key senators say about next moves in the war; symposium. il U S News 62:40-5 Ja 23 '67

Question of intervention in the domestic affairs of states; statement, December 10, 1965. A. J. Goldberg. Dept State Bul 54: 124-8 Ja 24 '66

Questions on campus; summary of answers. A. de Borchgrave. il Newsweek 68:55-6 D 5 '66

Rate of dissent. T. C. Sorensen. Sat R 49: 26 Ap 2 '66

VIETNAMESE war, 1957- —American participation—*Continued*

Recurrent questions. E. J. Hughes. Newsweek
69:15 Ja 9 '67

Reflections on Vietnam. R. N. Goodwin. il
New Yorker 42:57-8+ Ap 16 '66

Reinhold Niebuhr discusses the war in Vietnam. R. Niebuhr. New Repub 154:15-16
Ja 29 '66

Role of the writer as critic. S. Sontag. il
Pub W 189:36-7 Mr 28 '66

Rusk doctrine. New Repub 154:5-7 Mr 5 '66

Rusk tells student leaders: why America is
in the Vietnam war; questions and excerpts
from answers. D. Rusk. U S News 62:16
Ja 16 '67

Rusk's problem in Europe: trying to explain
Vietnam. U S News 60:22 Je 13 '66

Scattering of doves. il Newsweek 67:26-7 Mr
14 '66

Secretary Rusk and Vietnamese premier
restate basic positions; joint communique,
January 16, 1966. D. Rusk and Nguyen-cao-
Ky Dept State Bul 54:155-6 Ja 31 '66

Secretary Rusk's news conference:
July 12, 1966. Dept State Bul 55:162-8 Ag
1 '66
August 5, 1966. Dept State Bul 55:258-
65 Ag 22 '66

Senate hearings; Foreign relations committee's public review of U.S. wartime policy.
Newsweek 67:27 F 21 '66

Senator Russell on Vietnam: go in and win,
or get out; interview. R. B. Russell. U S
News 60:56-7 My 2 '66

Sleepwalkers; President Johnson and U.N.
Secretary General on collision course. il
New Repub 155:1+ Jl 2 '66

Some answers to Vietnam quetions; address,
July 7, 1966. B. C. Clarke. Vital Speeches
32:741-6 O 1 '66

Special issue: the U.S. in Viet Nam; symposium, ed. by R. Hemming. il Sr Schol 89:
8-24 O 28 '66

Spotlight on Viet Nam; Senate foreign relations committee hearings. Sr Schol 88:11
Mr 4 '66

State of the Union; address, January 12,
1966. L. B. Johnson. Vital Speeches 32:
226-30 F 1 '66; Excerpts. Dept State Bul
54:150-5 Ja 31 '66

State of the Union: address, January 17, 1966.
E. M. Dirksen. Vital Speeches 32:258-9 F
15 '66

Still talking: defense of the American stand.
Time 87:27A-27B Mr 18 '66

Taking stock on Viet Nam; with press comments. Sr Schol 88:6, 9 My 6 '66

Talk-in on Vietnam; New York intellectuals
meet with Prof. Schlesinger. il N Y Times
Mag p 12-13+ F 6 '66

Teach-in on Vietnam by: the President, Secre-
tary of state, Secretary of defense and the
Under Secretary of state. H. F. Graff. il
N Y Times Mag p25+ Mr 20 '66

Ten ways out of the peace issue. A. Vorspan.
Christian Cent 83:1029-31 Ag 24 '66

Thin end of the wedge. W. Lippmann. Newsweek 67:15 F 14 '66

This month's feature: Congress and the war
in Vietnam. Cong Digest 45:99-128 Ap '66

Transition point. J. Burnham. Nat R 19:32
Ja 10 '67

Trial of LBJ: B. Russell's mock court to
try U.S. administration. Newsweek 68:42
Ag 15 '66

Turn for better seen in war's fortunes. il
U S News 60:31-3 Mr 7 '66

Two threats to peace: hunger and aggression;
address, June 30, 1966. L. B. Johnson. Dept
State Bul 55:114-19 Jl 25 '66; Same with
title Vietnam war. Vital Speeches 32:578-82
Jl 15 '66

U.S. and South Vietnamese leaders meet at
Honolulu; remarks, with text of joint communique and declaration of Honolulu. L. B.
Johnson; Nguyen-van-Thieu; H. H. Humphrey. Dept State Bul 54:302-9 F 28 '66

United States and the Far East: problems
and policies; address, February 18, 1966.
L. Unger. Dept State Bul 54:451-9 Mr 21
'66

U.S. commitment in Viet-Nam: fundamental
issues; statements, February 17, 18, 1966.
D. Rusk; M. D. Taylor. bibliog f Dept State
Bul 54:346-62 Mr 7 '66

U.S. policy in southeast Asia: what's ahead?
W. C. Johnstone. Cur Hist 50:106-11+ F '66

Unity? resumption of bombing North Vietnam. Nation 202:169-70 F 14 '66

Vice President Humphrey reports to Presi-
dent on Asian trip; text of memorandum;
March 6, 1966. H. H. Humphrey. Dept State
Bul 54:489-91 Mr 28 '66

Vietnam: after all is said and done. E. Van
Den Haag. Nat R 18:1210-12+ N 29 '66

Vietnam; agonizing reappraisal. C. Emmet.
America 114:349-52 Mr 12 '66

Vietnam: agonizing reappraisal begins; with
report by G. C. Troelstrup. il U S News
60:37-9 Ap 25 '66

Vietnam: America's war now. il U S News
61:41-2 O 17 '66

Vietnam and the crisis in war. D. Graham.
Yale R 55:391-402 Mr '66

Vietnam; cause of human freedom; address,
February 23, 1966. L. B. Johnson. Vital
Speeches 32:322-5 Mr 15 '66; Same with title
Vietnam: the struggle to be free. Dept State
Bul 54:390-6 Mr 14 '66; Excerpt. Cong
Digest 45:105-6 Ap '66

Vietnam: correcting the crucial error. E. G.
Martin. Newsweek 68:48-9 S 12 '66

Vietnam: dissent from dissent. P. Ramsey. il
Christian Cent 83:909-13 Jl 20 '66; Discussion. 83:1118+, 1150 S 14-21 '66

Vietnam: great miscalculation? S. Alsop. Sat
Eve Post 239:18 S 10 '66

Vietnam: how wrong was McNamara? S.
Alsop. il Sat Eve Post 239:14 Mr 12 '66

Viet Nam in the balance. B. B. Fall. bibliog f For Affairs 45:1-18 O '66

Vietnam not above campaign. J. N. Eller.
America 114:615 Ap 30 '66

Vietnam: questions old and new; new crisis
and U.S. reactions. il Newsweek 67:21-2 Ap
25 '66

Vietnam: real test is still to come. il U S
News 60:35-6 Je 6 '66

Viet-Nam: resumption of bombing and appeal to the United Nations; symposium.
Dept State Bul 54:222-46 F 14 '66

Vietnam: SNAFU. Nat R 18:397-8 My 3 '66

Vietnam: the Republican performance. F. S.
Meyer. Nat R 18:316 Ap 5 '66

Vietnam: the war is worth winning. H.
Donovan. il Life 60:27-31 F 25 '66

Vietnam, top marine's size up; excerpts
from news conference, January 17, 1966.
W. M. Greene, jr. U S News 60:15 Ja 31
'66

Vietnam: U.S. digs in hard; with editorial
comment. il Bsns W p51-4+, 156 Mr 5 '66

Vietnam war: as McNamara sees it; excerpts
from statements. R. S. McNamara. U S
News 60:21 Mr 14 '66

Vietnam: what should we do now? symposium, ed. by L. Rosten. il Look 30:24-6
Ag 9 '66; Reply. Nat R 18:757 Ag 9 '66

Viet-Nam witness 1953-66, by B. B. Fall.
Review
Sat R il 49:23-4 My 28 '66. D. Schoenbrun

Vietnam's Buddhists emerge as key power:
vital third force to determine war's course
and future U.S. presence. il Bsns W p38-40
Ap 23 '66

Voices of dissent: Gavin and Kennan; testimony before the Senate foreign relations
committee; excerpts. il Newsweek 67:28-9
F 21 '66

War fans; Affirmation Vietnam; rally, Atlanta. H. Zinn. Nation 202:227 F 28 '66

War in Vietnam (cont) C. M. Plattner. il
Aviation W 84:42-6 Ja 31 '66

War of ambush; anti-guerrilla and pacification mission in the Delta. E. Martin. il
Newsweek 69:23-4 Ja 2 '67

War, taxes, Great society. Johnson's blue-
print for '67; State-of-the-Union message,
January 10, 1967. L. B. Johnson. il U S
News 62:104-10 Ja 23 '67

War's turning point; which way next? il
U S News 60:25-6 Ja 31 '66

Way Congress sizes up the war: story a
survey tells. il U S News 60:28-31 Ja 31 '66

We cannot accept a Communist seizure of
Vietnam. R. A. Scalapino. il N Y Times
Mag p46-7+ D 11 '66; Reply. New Repub
155:5-7 D 24 '66

Welcome aboard; pressuring the President
through a No wider war committee. Nation 203:339-40 O 10 '66

What it will take to win the war. il U S
News 61:23-5 Ag 22 '66

What's wrong with the Republican party.
E. W. Brooke. il Pub W 189:38-9 Mr 28 '66

Where the Vietnam pipeline begins. Bsns W
p 188+ Ap 16 '66

Which way? il Time 88:31-2 O 14 '66

VIETNAMESE war, 1957- —American partici-
    pation—*Continued*
White sound of Richard Nixon. E. J. Hughes.
    Newsweek 68:19 Ag 22 '66
Why our foreign policy is failing; interview,
    ed. by E. Sevareid. J. W. Fulbright. il
    Look 30:23-31 My 3 '66
Why the U.S. fights: Rusk and Taylor; ex-
    cerpts from Fulbright committee hearings.
    D. Rusk; M. Taylor. Newsweek 67:19-20
    F 28 '66
Why Vietnam war worries U.S. allies. il U S
    News 60:38-9 Je 13 '66
Why we can win in Vietnam. J. Alsop. il Sat
    Eve Post 239:27-8+ Je 4 '66
Winding line of LBJ. Nat R 18:250-2 Mr
    22 '66
World of water; the delta. il Newsweek 68:
    55-6 D 19 '66
Yet another debate; critics of Mr Johnson.
    K. Crawford. Newsweek 67:32 F 28 '66
    See also
United States—Armed forces—Forces in Viet-
    nam

Anecdotes, facetiae, satire, etc.
King's X: dialogue for a White House ap-
    pointment. J. T. Hefley. Christian Cent
    83:1274-5 O 19 '66

Atrocities
Angle shots; Viet Cong's terror and brutality.
    il Time 87:29 My 6 '66
Atrocities in Vietnam; tortures by South Viet-
    namese. J. D. Frank. Sat R 49:31 Je 4 '66
Crime of silence; are we accomplices in mass-
    murder in Vietnam? G. C. Zahn. Common-
    weal 84:354-6 Je 17 '66; Discussion. 84:429+,
    485 Jl 8-22 '66
Death at prayers; killing of Ap Quang Nam's
    mayor and other incidents. il Time 87:31-2
    F 25 '66
Ngo Tuong, RIP. P. T. Duggan. Nat R 18:
    610 Je 28 '66
Speaking of killing civilians; look at what's
    happening to the South Vietnamese. il
    U S News 62:34-6 Ja 16 '67
Torture. Commonweal 83:684 Mr 18 '66
Vietnam; photographs we're never asked for;
    Vietcong atrocities. Nat R 18:1048-51 O 18
    '66

Australian participation
Australia votes to stay in Vietnam. D. War-
    ner. il Reporter 35:29-31 D 29 '66
End of a fiery campaign. M. Tatlow. Nat R
    18:1208 N 29 '66
Fighting first. il Newsweek 67:34-5 F 28 '66
Germs of violence; A. A. Calwell shot at
    over anti-involvement policy. il Newsweek
    68:41-2 Jl 4 '66
New man in Canberra; H. Holt's beliefs and
    policies. D. Warner. il Reporter 34:33-6 Ap
    21 '66
One for the diggers. Time 88:17 Ag 26 '66
Other guns. il Time 88:26-7 Jl 22 '66
Sinister word; conscripts; domestic reac-
    tions. il Newsweek 67:44+ My 16 '66
United States and Australia reaffirm common
    goals; exchange of greetings; exchange of
    toasts, June 29, 1966. L. B. Johnson; H. E.
    Holt. Dept State Bul 55:130-7 Jl 25 '66
Vital election; H. E. Holt's support of U.S.
    involvement in Vietnam. M. Tatlow. Nat R
    18:837+ Ag 23 '66
Why Australia backs U.S. in the Vietnam
    war; interview. H. Holt. U S News 62:58-61
    Ja 2 '67

Bibliography
Battle of words over the war. W. Henderson.
    Sat R 49:32-3 D 17 '66
Books on Vietnam. Pub W 191:82-3 Ja 16 '67
Four views of war. B. B. Fall. Sat R 49:101-3
    O 8 '66

Campaigns and battles
A Shau's aftermath; result of Nungs' panic.
    il Newsweek 67:42 Mr 28 '66
Afloat in the delta; Cai Cai operation. E. G.
    Martin. il Newsweek 68:52 O 24 '66
Alltime high for action. Time 87:27 My 27 '66
Alone at last; B-52 strike Mu Gia pass. il
    Newsweek 67:35-6 Ap 25 '66
American way of war; year of victory. il
    Newsweek 68:49-50+ D 5 '66
Americans at war; Operation Hastings. il
    Newsweek 68:28-32+ Ag 1 '66
And now the Delta. il Time 88:27 Ag 19 '66
As war spreads into neutral Cambodia. il
    U S News 60:11 My 16 '66
Attack at dawn; defeat of North Vietnamese
    regulars in battle near Tuy Hoa. il Time
    88:26+ Jl 1 '66

Barring the door; attack on observation post
    northwest of Chu Lai. Newsweek 67:42 Je
    27 '66
Battle for Hill 400; of Operation Prairie;
    Rockpile fight. A. de Borchgrave. il News-
    week 68:46-8 O 10 '66
Between two truces. il Time 89:24-5 Ja 6 '67
Birmingham, borderline case; operations
    Birmingham and Davy Crocket. il News-
    week 67:56 My 16 '66
Bitter bit; Minh Thanh battle. Newsweek 68:
    31 Jl 25 '66
Bloody checkerboard; PAVN ambush foiled.
    M. D. Perry. il Newsweek 67:64+ My
    23 '66
Buildup on the border. il Time 88:29 S 30 '66
Closing the trap; ground action in the south
    reaching new heights. il Newsweek 67:
    22-3 F 14 '66
Crazy Horse. il Newsweek 67:34+ Je 6 '66
Death in the Ia Drang Valley. J. P. Smith.
    il Sat Eve Post 240:80-5 Ja 28 '67
Disappearing act. Time 88:37-8 N 25 '66
Division from the North; Operation Hastings.
    il Time 88:21 Jl 29 '66
Down to the sea. il Time 88:41-2 O 14 '66
Evil-eye complex; Operation Texas. M. D.
    Perry and W. J. Cook. Newsweek 67:56+
    Ap 4 '66
Fall of a fortress; A Shau. il Time 87:32-3
    Mr 18 '66
Fight at Monkey; excerpt from Battles in the
    monsoon. S. L. A. Marshall. il Harper
    233:111-14+ N '66
Fresh from the North; mission in Ia Drang
    Valley. Time 88:37 D 2 '66
General salutes; Operation Hawthorne. il
    Newsweek 67:42 Je 27 '66
Giant spoiler; Operation Attleboro. il Time
    88:34 N 18 '66
Greeted by waves; assaults against the 4th
    division. Time 88:36 N 4 '66
Growing pressure. il Time 87:32 Mr 18 '66
Heroic battle in Vietnam, what it proved:
    Ashau. il U S News 60:13 Mr 21 '66
Iron triangle; Operation Cedar Falls. il
    Newsweek 69:38-9 Ja 23 '67
Just survivors; defeated enemy at Chau
    Nha; siege of A Shau. il Newsweek 67:38+
    Mr 21 '66
Magic Dragon; Puff mission near Da Nang.
    J. Berthelson. il Newsweek 68:48 O 31 '66
Making contact; Double Eagle and White
    Wing operations. il Time 87:31 F 25 '66
Man's best friend; attack on Tan Son Nhut
    airport. il Newsweek 68:55 D 19 '66
Marines blunt the invasion from the North;
    action in the DMZ; with report by M.
    Parker. il Life 61:30-9 O 28 '66
Men facing death; destruction of an Ameri-
    can platoon; Operation Crazy Horse; ex-
    cerpt from Battles in the monsoon. S. L.
    A. Marshall. il Harper 233:47-57 S '66
Men for all seasons; Operation Hawthorne.
    il Newsweek 67:52+ Je 20 '66
Military, we can win it; recent operations.
    il Newsweek 67:28-31 Ap 18 '66
Name of the game; operations code names.
    Newsweek 67:26 Mr 21 '66
New turn in the ground war in Vietnam;
    attack on Iron Triangle of Viet Cong. il
    U S News 62:8 Ja 23 '67
Noise in the North; Operation White Wing
    and five others. il Time 87:28-9 F 11 '66
On with the war and Operation Masher; and
    Operation Double Eagle; with photographs
    by H. Huet. Life 60:20-24E F 11 '66
Quickening pace; second week of Operation
    Hawthorne. Time 87:40 Je 24 '66
Rabbits and elephants; second phase of
    Operation Masher. A. de Borchgrave. il
    Newsweek 67:36 F 21 '66
Red Napoleon. il Time 87:32-6 Je 17 '66
Reporter at large; Operations Hastings and
    Prairie. R. Shaplen. New Yorker 42:129-
    30+ D 17 '66
Rockpile; marines capture the Razorback and
    Hill 400. il Time 88:40-1 O 7 '66
Roughest yet; Operation Hastings. il News-
    week 68:30 Ag 8 '66
Securing Saigon; Operation Cedar Falls. il
    Time 89:23 Ja 20 '67
Sharp end. Newsweek 68:36 N 28 '66
Slogging it out; Operation Paul Revere.
    Newsweek 68:34-5 Ag 15 '66
Smoke, fire & welfare; Hanoi's heat for
    battle. il Time 87:24-5 Mr 25 '66
Ticket to Vung Tau; Khanh Van pacifica-
    tion. A. de Borchgrave. il Newsweek 68:54
    O 3 '66

VIETNAMESE war, 1957- —Campaigns and
battles—*Continued*
Toughest enemy; Operation Attleboro. il
Newsweek 68:58 N 21 '66
Truth about the most publicized battle of
Vietnam; what really happened on Carpenter's mountain; excerpt from Battles in
the monsoon. S. L. A. Marshall. il Harper
234:67-70+ Ja '67
Two-edged sword; Viet Cong ambush foiled
along Route 13. il Newsweek 68:37 Jl 11 '66
Ugly war in Vietnam, and its heroes; chase
through the jungles of Kontum by 101st
Airborne division. U S News 60:8 Je 20
'66
Up one notch; escalating the war. Newsweek
67:42 Mr 14 '66
War on the river; Operation Game Warden.
il Newsweek 68:59 O 3 '66
We want you; 2nd battalion of the 7th
cavalry of the 1st cavalry division in an
enemy ambush. il Time 88:21 Ag 12 '66
We're better; U.S. and South Vietnamese
activities. il Newsweek 68:28+ Jl 4 '66
Young commander went looking for trouble;
Captain Carpenter's battle in the Dak Ta
Kan River Valley. A. Zich. il Life 61:60+
Jl 8 '66
Zero elevation; spectacular parachute jump
and savage hand-to-hand battles. il News-
week 69:26 Ja 9 '67

Caricatures and cartoons
1966: Mauldin on Vietnam. B. Mauldin. New
Repub 156:19-21 Ja 7 '67

Casualties
A Shau's aftermath; result of Nungs' panic.
il Newsweek 67:42 Mr 28 '66
As war goes on and costs soar. il U S News
62:17-19 Ja 2 '67
Break? concerning Harrison Salisbury's
reports on U.S. bombings of Hanoi. Nation
204:34 Ja 9 '67
Chances of the game; unintended targets. il
Newsweek 68:29 S 5 '66
Civilian bit. Nat R 19:11 Ja 10 '67
Civilians weren't the target, but. il News-
week 69:17-18 Ja 9 '67
Count the civilians; hypocrisy of the Pen-
tagon's figuring. Nation 202:763 Je 27 '66
Death of a navy pilot. S. Booker. il Ebony
22:25-8+ Ja '67
Different kind of war's casualties. Sr Schol
89:20 N 4 '66
Dust-off! Dust-off! lifeline home from Viet-
nam. J. H. Winchester. il Read Digest 88:
60-6 My '66
Facts in a propaganda war over U.S. bomb-
ing; civilian casualties. U S News 62:6+
Ja 9 '67
Flak from Hanoi; civilian deaths. il Time 89:
13-14 Ja 6 '67
Hanoi's humanitarianism; U.S. casualties.
Time 88:26 Ag 5 '66
Home is the soldier; mother of Negro Viet-
nam casualty refuses to have son buried
in a segregated cemetery. Newsweek 67:
31 Je 6 '66
Matter of probability; U.S. target errors. il
Newsweek 68:64 Ag 22 '66
Medic, calm and dedicated; T. Cole tends
the wounded; photographs. H. Huet. Life
60:24D-24E F 11 '66
New peak for U.S. casualties in Vietnam. il
U S News 60:8 Je 6 '66
Now, 4,440 U.S. deaths in Vietnam war. il
U S News 61:6 Ag 8 '66
Parents; reactions of bereaved families. Na-
tion 202:475-6 Ap 25 '66
Pentagon answer to critics of bombing; con-
troversy of civilian casualties; excerpts
from letter. P. G. Goulding. U S News 62:16
Ja 16 '67
Public relations of napalm; medical care for
child victims; U.S. refuses support *Terre
des hommes.* Nation 203:141-2 Ag 22 '66
Roughest yet; Operation Hastings. il News-
week 68:30 Ag 8 '66
Soldier is buried in Charleston. C. Brossard.
il Look 30:72-6 My 31 '66
Sorry 'bout that; paucity of official news on
civilian casualties. New Repub 156:7-9 Ja 7
'67
Storm over Viet Nam bombings; civilian
casualties, concerning dispatches to New
York times by H. E. Salisbury. il Sr Schol
89:12-13 Ja 13 '67
Suffer the little children. M. Gellhorn. il Ladies Home J 84:57+ Ja '67

Town's troubled mood as a war comes home;
death of Herm Wuertz. il Life 61:52-52A
Ag 12 '66
U.S. casualties in Vietnam; how high will
they go? il U S News 61:23 Jl 4 '66
Vietcong mortar shell inside a living soldier.
il Life 61:98A-98B+ O 14 '66
Vietnam casualties mount; how big now? il
U S News 60:42-3 Mr 21 '66
Vietnam: biggest week for U.S. casualties.
U S News 61:21 O 10 '66
Vietnam's wounded waifs; appeal by the
Swiss organization, Terre des hommes.
M. Hope. Christian Cent 83:1111-12 S 14
'66
Walk in ward 34; President visits the
wounded. Time 87:28 My 20 '66
When a GI becomes a casualty. il U S News
60:44-5 Ap 4 '66

Catholic church
See Vietnamese war, 1957- —Moral and
religious aspects

Causes
Preventing the peace; report from an inter-
mediary. P. Devillers. Nation 203:597-602
D 5 '66

Children and the war
See War and children

Compensation of non-combatants
How much for a life? civilians killed by
misdirected U.S. air attacks. Nation 203:
372 O 17 '66

Construction
See Vietnamese war, 1957- —Engineering
and construction

Damage to property
See Vietnamese war, 1957- —Destruction
and pillage

Destruction and pillage
Break? concerning Harrison Salisbury's reports on U.S. bombings of Hanoi. Nation
204:34 Ja 9 '67
Matter of opinion? Harrison Salisbury's reports of U.S. bombings of Namdinh. Reporter 36:20+ Ja 12 '67
Storm over Viet Nam bombings; civilian
casualties, concerning dispatches to New
York times by H. E. Salisbury. il Sr Schol
89:12-13 Ja 13 '67

Economic aspects
Aid to Vietnam; business corruption nur-
tured on US aid. New Repub 154:9 Je 18
'66
And if peace should come? effects on U.S.
economy. il Newsweek 68:73 Jl 18 '66
As war goes on and costs soar. il U S News
62:17-19 Ja 2 '67
Balance of forces. il Fortune 74:15-16+ Jl 1
'66
Behind the battlefront; a search for stability.
D. Warner. il Reporter 34:25-9 F 24 '66
Budget keeps climbing on Vietnam escalator;
defense spending for fiscal 1967 $67-billion.
il Bsns W p36-7 D 10 '66
Business and Vietnam. J. Perham. il Duns
R 87:40-2+ Ap '66
Business feels the spurs. il Bsns W p21-3
F 5 '66
Businessman's formula to head off inflation;
excerpts from address, February 19, 1966.
R. M. Blough. U S News 60:87-8 Mr 7 '66
Capital's last frontier; why the U.S. is fight-
ing. J. Henry. il Nation 202:480-3 Ap 25
'66
C'est la guerre; U.S. domestic troubles blamed
on war. K. Crawford. Newsweek 67:53 Ap
18 '66
Defense orders head for plateau. il Bsns W
p50-2 S 24 '66
Deficit of war. Newsweek 67:68 My 30 '66
Deflating the fears of a recession. il Bsns W
p 122-4+ O 22 '66
Dissent & defeat; Congress approves President Johnson's request for additional funds
for Viet Nam. il Time 87:24 Mr 11 '66
Dollars are draining faster; balance-of-payments deficit. Bsns W p28 My 7 '66
Economics of it. Nation 202:197-8 F 21 '66
Economics of war. P. A. Samuelson. Newsweek 68:107 N 21 '66
Experts turn against tax boosts; survey of
100 top men finds 60 per cent opposed. il
Bsns W p 154-5+ My 28 '66

VIETNAMESE war, 1957- —Economic aspects
—*Continued*
Fairy-tale figures on defense. il Bsns W p 182-4 O 29 '66
Fallout; Asia benefits from U.S. involvement. il Time 87:84+ Ap 1 '66
Fear of credit crisis dulls investors' spirits. il Bsns W p36-7 Mr 12 '66
Great society priorities; effect on U.S. social projects. S. Melman. Commonweal 84:494-7 Ag 5 '66
Growing burden of Vietnam. il Newsweek 67:67 My 30 '66
Growing cost of fighting a war. U S News 60:12 Ja 31 '66
Guns and butter, too; concerning State-of-the-Union message. D. Lawrence. U S News 62:112 Ja 23 '67
Guns or butter, or both for the U.S? il Sr Schol 88:8-10 Mr 4 '66
Gut issue; inflation threatens entire social and economic system in Vietnam. Newsweek 67:43 Je 27 '66
High cost of fighting. Nation 202:478 Ap 25 '66
How high is the cost of the Vietnam war? excerpts from television interview. J. Stennis. U S News 61:22 O 24 '66
How war spending is forcing a tax rise. il U S News 62:49-50 Ja 2 '67
I saw a farmers' war in Vietnam. C. P. Streeter. il Farm J 90:34-5+ Ap '66
Inflation: the elusive pickpocket. il Sr Schol 89:11-13 N 4 '66
Just right; prop of current United States prosperity. N. Cousins. Sat R 49:30 Mr 5 '66
Late, Great society; effect on U.S. domestic programs. New Repub 154:5-6 Ap 9 '66; Reply. C. White. 154:29-30 Ap 23 '66
Limited-war funding continues surge. H. Taylor. il Miss & Roc 18:143-5+ Mr 28 '66
Mounting cost of war. il Bsns W p 17-18 Jl 2 '66
Negroes tell Congress: poverty war on—. il U S News 61:31 D 19 '66
Painless war; escalation costs. W. Lippmann. Newsweek 67:27 My 23 '66
Plenty of zip for the economy; Wharton school's econometric model prediction; with editorial comment. il Bsns W p53-4+, 160 S 3 '66
Pressures of Viet Nam. il Time 88:101 O 7 '66
Price of Vietnam. Commonweal 83:651-2 Mr 11 '66
Remembered reckoning; burden of armaments. E. J. Hughes. Newsweek 68:17 Jl 11 '66
Saigon: at night, war flares and road checks; corruption and profiteering. S. Angeloff. il Life 60:47-52A F 25 '66
Saigon: stained pearl of the Orient. S Castan. il Look 30:70-4+ My 17 '66
Squeeze tightens; Pentagon orders accelerating, list of shortages growing longer. Bsns W p39 Je 11 '66
Surprising assets of South Vietnam's economy; with editorial comment. Fortune 73:104+, 110-13+ Mr '66
Tale of two problems. H. C. Wallich. Newsweek 67:94 Je 13 '66
Top secret: Vietnamese war cost. Nation 203:434-5 O 31 '66
Vietnam financing challenges industry. W. H. Gregory. il Aviation W 84:26-8 Ap 11 '66
Vietnam holds the key: economic outlook for next year. il Bsns W p33-4 D 17 '66
Vietnam needs cloud advanced projects; with table. C. Brownlow. Aviation W 84:16-21 Ja 31 '66
Vietnam vs. space. Nation 202:603 My 23 '66
Vietnam war: a cost accounting. W. Bowen. il Fortune 73:118-23+ Ap '66
Vietnam's economic lesson: peace can yield fatter profits than war. T. G. Harris. il Look 30:44+ My 31 '66
War costs blunt drive on payments deficit; outflow of dollars for Vietnam chief factor in worsening of U.S. trade balance. il Bsns W p50 My 21 '66
What the added billions for arms will buy. il U S News 60:47-8 F 21 '66
What the war in Vietnam will do to business now. il U S News 60:42-3 F 14 '66
Where dollars go for the weapons. il Bsns W p 130-2+ Ja 22 '66
Where our treasure is. Commonweal 84:191-2 My 6 '66
Where shortages are beginning to pinch. il U S News 60:49-50 Mr 14 '66

Who's nervous? Nation 202:666 Je 6 '66
See also
Inflation (finance)
Vietnamese war, 1957- —Equipment and supplies

Engineering and construction

Air force beachhead at Tuy Hoa; U.S. air force contract with Walter Kidde constructors, inc. Fortune 74:198 S '66
Building by the billion in Vietnam. J. Mecklin. il Fortune 74:112-17+ S '66

Equipment and supplies

Air cargo shows what it can do. il Bsns W p96-8+ Jl 16 '66
Another pilot's report from Vietnam; letter. N. Wilson. Aviation W 85:21+ O 24 '66
Army seeks to improve ground positioning; man-pack receiver version of Loran tactical radio navigation system. M. Getler. il Tech W 19:14-15 O 17 '66
Arsenal in action; American weaponry. il Time 88:34-9 N 18 '66
Battle to uncork supplies for Vietnam; construction of port facilities, air fields. il Bsns W p 102-4+ F 5 '66
Birmingham, borderline case; Viet Cong route cut off. il Newsweek 67:56 My 16 '66
Bloodless use of superior force. R. Moley. Read Digest 88:60-1 Mr '66
Bomb shortages? an on-the-scene report. il U S News 60:10 My 2 '66
Combat forces new limited war studies. C. Brownlow. il Aviation W 84:90-4 Mr 28 '66
Cost accounting; question of armament shortages. W. Cook. il Newsweek 67:25-6+ My 2 '66
Cupboard is bare; summary of article. H. W. Baldwin. Nat R 18:195 Mr 8 '66
Did the whiz kids flunk their arms test? with excerpts from testimony by R. S. McNamara. il U S News 60:40-2 Ap 25 '66
Dirksen-Ford rumpus: a split over war mismanagement? il U S News 60:15 My 2 '66
Getting guns, and butter. il Bsns W p94-8 Ap 30 '66
Goods of war pour out. C. Burck. il Fortune 73:114-21 Mr '66
Helping hand; U.S. probably bought steel manufactured in Communist China. Newsweek 69:30+ Ja 2 '67
ILA tries its hand at unclogging Saigon; effort to move supplies delayed by antiquated docks and working habits. il Bsns W p53+ F 19 '66
King of cumshaw; B. G. Feddersen. il Time 88:21-2 Jl 29 '66
Lessons of Vietnam. W. J. Coughlin. Miss & Roc 18:160 Mr 28; 50 Ap 4; 46 Ap 11; 46 18 '66
Limited war problems challenge industry; with editorial comment. C. Brownlow. il Aviation W 84:21, 26-9 Mr 14 '66
Military and industry response. il Miss & Roc 18:73-6+ Mr 28 '66
Mobility problems still vex army. W. S. Beller. il Miss & Roc 18:74-6 Mr 28 '66
New Viet shortage inquiries seen. C. Brownlow. Aviation W 85:26-7 O 24 '66
North Vietnam air war; excerpts from comments. H. Brown. Aviation W 85:21 D 12 '66
On the trail; supplies along the Sihanouk trail. F. Sully. il Newsweek 68:32 Jl 4 '66
On the waterfront: Saigon dock workers union on strike. il Time 89:25 Ja 6 '67
Pilot report from Vietnam; letter. Aviation W 85:21+ S 19 '66; Discussion. 85:122 O 3; 130 O 24 '66
Quick reaction speeds spares to Vietnam; army Red ball express and USAF STAR. C. M. Plattner. il Aviation W 84:72-3+ Ap 11 '66
Research for Vietnam; excerpts from testimony, 1966. J. S. Foster, jr. Aviation W 84:21 Mr 21 '66
Senate investigators urge TAC review. il Aviation W 85:86-9+ Ag 22 '66
Something for real; Air national guardsmen's missions. Newsweek 68:18-19 Jl 4 '66
Special report: Vietnam procurement. il Aviation W 85:15-39+ mid-D '66
Technology vs. the VC. il Newsweek 68:108+ D 19 '66
Unprecedented application of mobility. il **Life** 60:38-41 F 25 '66

VIETNAMESE war, 1957—Equipment and sup-
plies—*Continued*
Vietnam strike that hurt the U.S. war effort;
civilian longshoremen. il U S News 62:8
Ja 9 '67
War where U.S. supplies are getting to both
sides. il U S News 60:37-9 Je 6 '66
What McNamara learned in Vietnam. il U S
News 61:41-2 O 24 '66
What the added billions for arms will buy.
il U S News 60:47-8 F 21 '66
Why not blockade North Vietnam? H. W.
Baldwin. Read Digest 88:58-62 Mr '66
Wild new weapons for Vietnam. M. Schultz.
il Pop Mech 127:95-8+ Ja '67

Fiction

Vietnam: no place for people. D. Powers.
Sat R 49:41 Ap 2 '66

Foreign participation

China and Vietnam. E. Snow. New Repub
155:12-14 Jl 30 '66; Discussion. 155:37-8
Ag 27 '66
Chinese puzzle: if China enters the war.
H. Brandon. Sat R 49:18 Mr 5 '66
South Korea takes off: an Asian success story.
il U S News 61:42-3 O 31 '66
Step-up in the war, and its risks. il News-
week 67:25-6 My 9 '66
T.R.B. from Washington; vital support in
Vietnam. New Repub 154:4 Mr 5 '66
Talking at a distance; China and Russia. il
Newsweek 68:39+ Jl 25 '66
Toward peace in Indochina, twelve steps to
a long-range settlement. Avon. il Harper
233:36-43 Ag '66
U.S. allies: how much help? il U S News
61:26-7 Ag 8 '66
Vietnam war: how much bigger will it get?
il U S News 61:25-7 Ag 1 '66
What LBJ will find in Asia? Allies say: win
the war. il U S News 61:37-40 O 24 '66
What U.S. can expect from allies in Vietnam:
with chart. U S News 60:31-3 Mr 14 '66
When will China intervene? Nation 204:66 Ja
16 '67

Guerrillas

Alone at last; Viet Cong attack on Tan Son
Nhut. il Newsweek 67:35-6 Ap 25 '66
Armchair guide to guerrilla warfare. il Es-
quire 65:88-93 Mr '66
Beating reds at their own kind of war; with
interviews with red prisoners; ed. by G. C.
Troelstrup. W. S. Merick. il U S News 61:
50-4 D 12 '66
Braving the terror; attack on Binh Chanh
to frighten people from going to vote.
E. G. Martin. il Newsweek 68:60+ S 26
'66
Changing the rules of guerrilla war. il
Bsns W p67-8 Mr 5 '66
Deadly booby traps in a dirty war. E. Hym-
off. il Pop Mech 125:70-3+ Je '66
Does Vietnam need a supreme commander?
D. Warner. il Reporter 34:11-15 Je 30 '66
It would be idiotic to deal with the Viet
Cong; interview. R. L. Houston. U S News
61:44-5 O 17 '66
Just what is the Viet Cong? questions and
answers. U S News 60:38 F 28 '66
New plan for Vietnam war. il U S News
61:31-3 N 7 '66
Outlook now for the war in Vietnam; inter-
view. H. C. Lodge. U S News 61:66-8 N 21
'66
Rail splitters; Viet Cong target, incidents.
il Time 87:31 F 4 '66
Small, hard war in the delta. D. Warner. il
Reporter 35:27-8+ D 15 '66
Suburban warfare; Saigon area. F. Sully.
Newsweek 68:29 S 5 '66
Two-edged sword; Viet Cong ambush foiled
along Route 13. il Newsweek 68:37 Jl 11 '66
Under Viet Cong control. S. De Gramont.
il Sat Eve Post 239:27-33+ Ja 29 '66
Viet reds winning battle for rice. il U S
News 61:41 O 3 '66
War of ambush; anti-guerrilla and pacifica-
tion mission in the Delta. E. Martin. il
Newsweek 69:23-4 Ja 2 '67
World of water; the delta. il Newsweek 68:
55-6 D 19 '66

Korean participation

Other guns. il Time 88:26-7 Jl 22 '66
With the side of the hand; White Horse
division of South Korea. il Newsweek 68:
54+ S 19 '66

Medical and sanitary affairs

Angels of Saigon; two army nurses. il Ebony
21:44-6 Ag '66
Disneyland east; brothel quarter built ex-
clusively for American soldiers. il Time 87:
29-30 My 6 '66
Even an operating room lifted and flown
into battle. il Life 60:40-1 F 25 '66
Medic, calm and dedicated; T. Cole; photo-
graphs. H. Huet. Life 60:24D-24E F 11 '66
Other war in Vietnam; Vietnamese par-
aplegics and medical team rehabilitation
training in U.S. H. A. Rusk. il Read
Digest 89:108-12 Jl '66
Physician and Vietnam. W. G. Bronston. Bul
Atomic Sci 22:24 N '66
Plague and war, 1966. D. Lyle. il Esquire
66:158-63+ S '66
Plague on both houses; bubonic plague. Time
88:61 S 2 '66
Viet victory in America; saving paralyzed
Vietnamese soldiers and training doctors
and nurses. D. Chapman. il Look 30:28-31
Ap 19 '66
Vietcong mortar shell inside a living soldier.
il Life 61:98A-98B+ O 14 '66
Vietnam's wounded waifs; appeal by the
Swiss organization. Terre des hommes. M.
Hope. Christian Cent 83:1111-12 S 14 '66
When a GI becomes a casualty. il U S News
60:44-5 Ap 4 '66
Women; uniformed nurses; interviews, ed. by
F. Sully. il Newsweek 67:40-2 Mr 28 '66
Wounds in Vietnam. Sci N 91:40 Ja 14 '67
See also
Hospital ships
United States—Armed forces—Dental service

Moral and religious aspects

American bishops on modern war. J. Gal-
lagher. America 115:548-9 N 5 '66
Berrigan: co-chairman of Clergy concerned
about Vietnam. New Yorker 42:34-5 Ap 9
'66
Bishops and the Vietnam war; concerning
American Catholic bishops' statement. J.
B. Sheerin. Cath World 204:196-7 Ja '67
Bishops and Vietnam. Commonweal 84:93-4
Ap 15 '66
Bombs in the North and the moral issue.
America 116:32 Ja 14 '67
Cardinal on war; excerpts from L. J. She-
han's pastoral letter. J. O'Gara. Common-
weal 84:459 Jl 22 '66
Cardinal, Pope and war. Commonweal 85:
391-2 Ja 13 '67
Cardinal Spellman, Charles Davis. J. M.
Cameron. Commonweal 85:417-18 Ja 20 '67
Catholics and peace. J. O'Gara. Commonweal
85:158 N 11 '66
Christian realism in Vietnam. J. C. Ben-
nett. America 114:616-17 Ap 30 '66
Crime of silence; are we accomplices in
mass-murder in Vietnam? G. C. Zahn.
Commonweal 84:354-6 Je 17 '66; Discussion.
84:429+, 485 Jl 8-22 '66
Crop destruction in South Vietnam; mili-
tary measure practiced by United States
military forces. J. Mayer and V. W. Sidel.
Christian Cent 83:829-32 Je 29 '66
Crop destruction in Vietnam; letter. J. Mayer.
Science 152:291 Ap 15 '66
Farewell to Christian realism. P. Ramsey.
America 114:618-22 Ap 30 '66
Hero's courage on a nameless trail. L. Wain-
wright. Life 60:32 My 6 '66
Insurrection inside the war. il Life 60:28-33
Ap 22 '66
Laymen lay low. Nat R 19:11-12 Ja 10 '67
Moral reassessment of our war in Vietnam.
P. Wogaman. Christian Cent 84:7-9 Ja 4 '67
Morality of the Vietnam war. J. B. Sheerin.
Cath World 202:326-30 Mr '66; Discussion.
203:130-1 Je '66
Of bombs and bruises; context in which
Asians view the bombing. N. Cousins.
Sat R 49:34 F 19 '66
Peace and patriotism. America 115:50 Jl 16 '66
Religion and war. J. V. Schall. Commonweal
85:193-6 N 18 '66; Discussion. 85:303-4, 311+,
335+ D 9-23 '66
Some fallacies about the Vietnam war. J. W.
Clifford. Cath World 203:361-4 S '66
Strategy of the weak. W. Pfaff. Commonweal
84:456-7 Jl 22 '66
White House rebuttal to Vietnam critics; in-
terview, ed. by R. Pierpoint. B. Moyers.
Cath World 204:52-4 O '66
Who speaks for the church on Vietnam?
J. B. Sheerin. Cath World 204:72-6 N '66

VIETNAMESE war, 1957- —*Continued*

Naval operations

A's for the E; U.S.S. Enterprise. il Time 87: 27-8 Ap 29 '66

Big E at work; aerial missions off USS Enterprise. W. Tuohy. il Newsweek 67:42+ Ap 11 '66

Fliers in Vietnam say: it's a no-win half war. il U S News 61:24-6 D 26 '66

Guardians of the Viet Nam coastline. il Ebony 22:129-30+ D '66

How the navy helps fight a jungle war; Seventh fleet. G. C. Troelstrup. il U S News 61:44-6 S 12 '66

McCoy's navy; Inshore fire support division 93. il Time 88:26-7 Ag 5 '66

New job for old battleships? il U S News 62:12 Ja 23 '67

Policing the dragons; PBR; U.S. navy's newest weapon against Viet Cong smugglers. il Time 87:24 Ap 22 '66

River patrol boat for Viet Nam. B. Cobb, jr. il Yachting 120:65+ D '66

Shore bombardment target location still plagues navy. il Miss & Roc 18:98+ Mr 28 '66

Signs of a new turn in the Vietnam war. il U S News 61:13-14 N 14 '66

Skunk watchers; U.S.S. Conserver and Russian ship in Tonkin Gulf. il Time 88:43 O 14 '66

Stand by to launch aircraft; operations on USS Independence; excerpt from Vietnam; the confusing war. H. Mulligan. il Read Digest 90:84-8 Ja '67

War on the river; Operation Game Warden and U.S. river patrol activities in Vietnam waters. il Newsweek 68:59 O 3 '66

Water war in Viet Nam. G. L. Chapelle. il Nat Geog Mag 129:272-96 F '66

Negroes

Birdmen with black rifles; Screaming Eagle paratroopers. il Ebony 21:37-42 O '66

Guardians of the Viet Nam coastline. il Ebony 22:129-30+ D '66

How Negro Americans perform in Vietnam; with chart. il U S News 61:60-3 Ag 15 '66

Parachute troops

See United States—Army—Parachute troops

Peace and mediation

Acting Secretary Ball's news conference of July 6, 1966. G. W. Ball. Dept State Bul 55:121-8 Jl 25 '66

After the pause; motion or progress? il Newsweek 67:17-21 F 14 '66

Air raids, leftover puzzles. B. B. Fall. il New Repub 155:7-8 Jl 16 '66

All the talk of peace. il Newsweek 69:35 Ja 16 '67

Ambassador Harriman discusses his post-Manila trip; excerpts from press conference, November 11, 1966; with questions and answers. W. A. Harriman; L. B. Johnson. Dept State Bul 55:889-92 D 12 '66

Appeal to American citizens; statement issued by the Japanese fellowship of reconciliation, December 10, 1965. Christian Cent 83:114 Ja 26 '66

Appointment in Manila. Newsweek 68:36 O 10 '66

As Secretary Rusk looks ahead; excerpts from news conference, January 21, 1966. D. Rusk. U S News 60:8 Ja 31 '66

Asian summit, what to expect. U S News 61:35 O 10 '66

Atlantic report; M. Mansfield's proposal for summit conference of Asian nations. Atlan 217:6+ Je '66

Bobby on Vietnam; views of R. Kennedy. K. Crawford. Newsweek 67:33 Mr 7 '66

Bombing and fadeout. Commonweal 85:415-16 Ja 20 '67

Burden of Vietnam. O. Handlin. Atlan 218: 140-3 Jl '66

But there is no peace. Nat R 18:968-9 O 4 '66

Buying off Ho Chi Minh. America 114:190 F 5 '66; Discussion. 114:368, 536 Mr 19, Ap 16 '66

Cardinal's mistake; reactions to F. J. Spellman's view. Nation 204:69 Ja 16 '67

Christmas in Vietnam; Christmas cease-fire as a stage for ending the war. N. Cousins. Sat R 49:35 D 10 '66

Christmas truce; the U.S. dilemma. America 115:818 D 24 '66

Churches and Vietnam. G. Harkness. Christian Cent 83:111-13 Ja 26 '66

Clarifying U.S. role. Sr Schol 89:19 O 7 '66

Clergy concerned about Vietnam. Christian Cent 83:99-100 Ja 26 '66

Coonskin; consequence of Manila conference. New Repub 155:7 N 12 '66

Crooked road to peace. E. J. Hughes. Newsweek 68:23 N 14 '66

Daylight in the tunnel. H. Brandon. Sat R 49: 14+ Jl 30 '66

Deflating the dragon. il Time 87:16-17 Mr 25 '66

Eight-day truce in Vietnam; Christmas and New Year cease-fire. Christian Cent 83: 1528 D 14 '66

Elections in Vietnam; prelude to an honorable settlement? Tran-van-Dinh. New Repub 155:19-22 Jl 2 '66

Emerging victory in Asia. il Fortune 74:97-8 Ag '66

Establishing credibility; Administration's quest for peace. Commonweal 85:67-8 O 21 '66

Fact or, fancy? change in the behavior pattern of Soviet diplomats. Newsweek 68:51 S 19 '66

Fight RFK started; should we negotiate with the Viet Cong? U S News 60:20 Mr 7 '66

Four views of war. B. B. Fall. Sat R 49: 101-3 O 8 '66

Fox in a chicken coop; reactions to R. F. Kennedy statement on Viet Cong role. Time 87:26-7 Mr 4 '66

From top officials, optimism on Vietnam. U S News 61:19 Jl 18 '66

Getting out. Commonweal 85:335-6 D 23 '66; Discussion. 85:415+ Ja 20 '67

Goldberg proposals. New Repub 155:5-6 O 1 '66

Hard questions on Vietnam. il Sat Eve Post 239:98 Mr 12 '66

Holiday truce. Newsweek 68:24 D 12 '66

Holiday truce; the reason for concern. U S News 61:8 D 12 '66

Hope in Vietnam. H. Brandon. Sat R 49:12+ N 19 '66

Humphrey's chickens; concerning reply to R. Kennedy's proposed coalition government for Saigon. K. Crawford. Newsweek 67:38 Mr 14 '66

If he wants peace... D. Grant. Nation 203: 338-9 O 10 '66

Is end of Vietnam war in sight? il U S News 61:25-8 Jl 25 '66

Is peace naive? achievement methods. F. Kuh. Nation 203:69 Jl 25 '66

Issue (and some miscellaneous trimmings) C. Fritchey. Harper 232:32+ My '66

It would be idiotic to deal with the Viet Cong; interview. R. L. Houston. U S News 61:44-5 O 17 '66

Johnson's choice; reply. R. Walner. New Repub 154:37-8 Mr 19 '66

Kennedy caper. Newsweek 67:24-5 Mr 7 '66

Kennedy initiative. Nation 202:253 Mr 7 '66

Korea and Vietnam. Nation 203:435-6 O 31 '66

Lin Piao on deck. Nat R 18:868-9 S 6 '66

Looking for a way out; with press comments. il Sr Schol 87:17-19 Ja 14 '66

LBJ: in a dilemma, and no consensus. U S News 60:19 F 14 '66

LBJ moves out for peace; Asian trip plans. il Bsns W p37-9 O 15 '66

LBJ tells Hanoi: agree to peace talks, or face more bombing; excerpts from addresses, June 30, 1966. L. B. Johnson. il U S News 61:20 Jl 11 '66

Mansfield appeal, new road to Vietnam peace? summary of statement. M. Mansfield. U S News 60:16 My 2 '66

Marcos proposal. il Newsweek 68:20 O 3 '66

Mayor on Vietnam. Nat R 18:1254+ D 13 '66

Message to the churches; adopted by the National council of churches general board. Christian Cent 83:114-15 Ja 26 '66

Middle way out of Vietnam. A. Schlesinger, jr. il N Y Times Mag p47-9+ S 18 '66; Discussion. p22+ O 9; 98 O 16; 139-40 O 30 '66

Mrs Gandhi: peaceful, Kosygin: hostile. il U S News 61:20 Jl 25 '66

New moves & old intransigence. Time 88:40 O 7 '66

New moves for peace; Kosygin, others give clues. U S News 61:26 O 24 '66

New roadblocks on the way to peace. il U S News 60:35-7 F 14 '66

No court above you; Republican formulas. Nat R 18:1028 O 18 '66

No instant peace. Christian Cent 83:227-8 F 23 '66

No room at the table; National liberation front of South Vietnam. il Newsweek 67: 28 F 7 '66

VIETNAMESE war, 1957- —Peace and mediation—Continued

Official U.S. stand on dealing with the Viet Cong; excerpts from statement, January 23, 1966. D. Rusk. U S News 60:14 F 7 '66

On timetables; U.S. rejection of de Gaulle's initiative. Nation 203:234 S 19 '66

Open letter to the N.C.C. from the Japan Christian council for peace in Vietnam. Christian Cent 83:430 Ap 6 '66

Pacific mission; Johnson's proposed six-nation tour of Asia. il Time 88:32-3 O 14 '66

Peace and the Pentagon; Hanoi bombings and L. B. Johnson. Nation 204:2-3 Ja 2 '67

Peace hopes weaken as shooting resumes. il Bsns W p30-1 Ja 29 '66

Peace, peace. Nat R 18:1303 D 27 '66

Peace talks with Ho in the wind. U S News 60:16 Je 27 '66

Policemen without power; International control commission for Indochina. il Newsweek 68:30-1 S 5 '66

President's speech: State of the Union message. M. Ascoli. Reporter 34:22 Ja 27 '66

Preventing the peace: report from an intermediary. P. Devillers. Nation 203:597-602 D 5 '66

Public and private; views of Henry Cabot Lodge and U Thant. il Newsweek 69:38 Ja 23 '67

Quest for peace in Viet-Nam: address, January 17, 1966. A. J. Goldberg. Dept State Bul 54:197-201 F 7 '66

Re-election of U Thant. W. Lippmann. Newsweek 68:19 D 19 '66

Remarks to press on developments in Viet-Nam. Thant. UN Mo Chron 3:32 Ag '66

Rising pressures. Nation 202:254 Mr 7 '66

Russian equation; LBJ urges new spirit of common endeavor between Moscow and Washington. il Time 88:11-12 S 2 '66

Scenario for attack; Chester Ronning mission fails. Newsweek 68:16 Jl 4 '66

Secretary Rusk discusses Viet-Nam on Canadian TV program: interview, December 30, 1965. D. Rusk. Dept State Bul 54:86-9 Ja 17 '66

Secretary Rusk's news conference of January 21, 1966. D. Rusk. Dept State Bul 54:189-97 F 7 '66

Seeing things through; trying hard to extend lull into permanent cease-fire. il Time 88:9 D 30 '66

Sleepwalkers; President Johnson and U.N. Secretary General on collision course. il New Repub 155:1+ Jl 2 '66

So the war goes on. New Repub 154:5-7 F 12 '66

Somber words. il Newsweek 67:20 Ja 31 '66

Sound & reality. Time 88:18 Jl 15 '66

Speaking out: we must negotiate peace in Vietnam. J. W. Fulbright. Sat Eve Post 239:10+ Ap 9 '66

Static of distress; North Viet Nam trouble. il Time 89:11 Ja 13 '67

Step on the road to peace. Bsns W p202 O 15 '66

Stopper; alternatives to fighting. Nation 202:226 F 28 '66

Strange interlude: peace on earth. il Newsweek 69:15-16 Ja 2 '67

String runs out; Ho Chi Minh denounces U.S. effort. il Time 87:21-6 F 4 '66

Support Johnson's appeal to U.N. Christian Cent 84:36 Ja 11 '67

Tactics of a truce. J. D. Forbes. Nation 202:229-30 F 28 '66

Tale of three cities: hopeful words about peace talks. il Time 88:30 S 16 '66

Ten ways out of the peace issue. A. Vorspan. Christian Cent 83:1029-31 Ag 24 '66

To end the war, a new offer; U.S. proposal presented by A. Goldberg at UN. il Newsweek 68:19-20 O 3 '66

Topic A: U.N. discussions. il Newsweek 68:54 O 10 '66

Toward peace in Asia. J. M. Burns; Avon. il Harper 233:33-43 Ag '66

Truce can lead to peace in Vietnam. V. Zorza. il Look 30:22-3 D 27 '66

Truce try fails: war's next turn. il U S News 61:21-3 Jl 4 '66

U Thant's secret. Commonweal 85:311-12 D 16 '66

U.S. calls for peaceful settlement of Middle East disputes; urges U.S.S.R. to move for peace in Viet-Nam: texts of statements, July 29, August 3, 1966. J. J. Sisco. Dept State Bul 55:313-17 Ag 29 '66

U.S. commitment to political solution in Viet-Nam reaffirmed; statement, October 18, 1966. A. J. Goldberg. Dept State Bul 55:757-8 N 14 '66

U.S. peace efforts reported to members of U.N; letter, January 4, 1966. A. J. Goldberg. Dept State Bul 54:117 Ja 24 '66

U.S. withdrawal from Viet-Nam depends on halt of aggression; excerpt from remarks, September 5, 1966. L. B. Johnson. Dept State Bul 55:455 S 26 '66

Vice President Humphrey returns from Far East mission; remarks, January 3, 1966, with text of outline of U.S. position on Viet-Nam. H. H. Humphrey. Dept State Bul 54:114-16 Ja 24 '66

Vietcong as negotiators? J. B. Sheerin. Cath World 203:6-10 Ap '66

Vietnam debate. Commonweal 83:627-8 Mr 4 '66

[Vietnam debate] R. F. Kennedy; H. H. Humphrey; M. R. Laird. il U S News 60:68-72+ Mr 14 '66

Vietnam: dissent from dissent. P. Ramsey. il Christian Cent 83:909-13 Jl 20 '66; Discussion, 83:1118+, 1150 S 14-21 '66

Vietnam, garbled signals. New Repub 155:5-6 O 15 '66

Vietnam: importance of January. P. D. Scott. Nation 204:74-7 Ja 16 '67

Vietnam: peace on the 1954 terms? F. N. Trager. Nat R 18:778-81 Ag 9 '66

Vietnam potpourri; discussion. Nat R 18:235 Mr 18 '66

Vietnam: pro and con of Kennedy's peace plan: statement, February 19, 1966, with editorial from The Washington star, February 21. R. F. Kennedy. U S News 60:104-7 Mr 7 '66

Viet-Nam: resumption of bombing and appeal to the United Nations: symposium. Dept State Bul 54:222-46 F 14 '66

Vietnam: the U.S. tries harder; President Johnson accepts invitation of President Marcos to summit conference in Manila. il Bsns W p38-9 O 1 '66

War and peace; U.N. gets a role. il U S News 61:37-8 O 3 '66

War in Vietnam: which way now? il U S News 62:11 Ja 16 '67

War president; why North Vietnam and Viet Cong refuse to negotiate. New Repub 155:5-6 Jl 16 '66

War: the corner turned? il Sr Schol 89:20 O 21 '66

War's turning point; which way next? il U S News 60:25-6 Ja 31 '66

What LBJ is offering the Asians. il U S News 61:33-4 O 31 '66

What the U.S. wants; pleas, proposals, propaganda. il Time 88:19-20 S 30 '66

What was decided in Manila; new plan for peace. il U S News 61:33-4 N 7 '66

When free Asians get together. Life 61:6 O 14 '66

Where do we go from here? il Sr Schol 89:16-19 O 28 '66

Why Ho keeps saying no; Time essay. Time 88:30-1 N 11 '66

Why LBJ can't pull victory rabbit from Viet Nam hat. P. Lisagor. il Nations Bsns 54:23-4 O '66

Words and action; Thailand, Cambodia proposals. Newsweek 68:34 Ag 15 '66

Working for peace. Commonweal 83:491-2 Ja 28 '66

Would a truce end Vietnam war? il U S News 61:31-3 O 10 '66

See also

United Nations—Vietnam (Republic)

Personal narratives

AFP's man in Hanoi: account of J. Raeffaelli. il Newsweek 68:54 Ag 15 '66

Back from Vietnam. E. Taylor. il Reporter 34:23-6 Ja 27 '66

Battle for Hill 400; of Operation Prairie; Rockpile fight. A. de Borchgrave. il Newsweek 68:46-8 O 10 '66

Bob Hope on Viet Nam: interview. B. Hope. il Nations Bsns 54:44-6+ F '66

Combat pilot's plea: give us half a chance to win; excerpts from letter. N. Wilson. U S News 61:64 O 31 '66

Death in the Ia Drang Valley. J. P. Smith. il Sat Eve Post 240:80-5 Ja 28 '67

Diary of a soldier; ed. by F. Sully. Nguyenquang-Le. il Newsweek 67:36+ My 9 '66

Eyewitness in Vietnam: jungles and black markets, and terrific firepower. J. P. Sutherland. il U S News 60:41-3 Ap 4 '66

VIETNAMESE war, 1957- —Personal narratives
—*Continued*
Fight at Monkey; excerpt from Battles in the
monsoon. S. L. A. Marshall. il Harper
233:111-14+ N '66
Great to be alive. il Newsweek 68:65 S 26
'66
He's winning our war in Vietnam. S. L. A.
Marshall. il Look 31:57-9 Ja 10 '67
How Communists tortured an American. il
U S News 61:26 S 26 '66
I escaped from a red prison. D. Dengler. il
Sat Eve Post 239:27-33 D 3 '66
It almost makes one cry: what a doctor sees
in Vietnam; excerpts from diary. M. T.
Hoekenga. il U S News 61:74-6+ S 19 '66
It's great to be alive; daring rescue of
D. W. Myers, by B. F. Fisher at Ashau.
R. Armstrong. il Sat Eve Post 239:21-6
Je 4 '66; Same abr. with title Pilot is
down! Read Digest 89:42-8 Ag '66
M; account of one company of American sol-
diers. J. Sack. Esquire 66:79-86+ O '66
Marine comes home from Vietnam. C. S.
Wren. il Look 30:30-2+ Mr 8 '66
Men facing death; destruction of an Ameri-
can platoon; Operation Crazy Horse; ex-
cerpt from Battles in the monsoon. S. L.
A. Marshall. il Harper 233:47-57 S '66
My son in Vietnam. H. H. Martin. il Sat Eve
Post 239:34-8+ Jl 16 '66
Never before a war like this. L. Bergquist.
il Look 30:27-35 D 13 '66
Not a dove, but no longer a hawk. N. Shee-
han. il N Y Times Mag p27+ O 9 '66; Reply.
Nation 203:404 O 24 '66
Once & future hero; W. S. Carpenter. il
Time 87:24 Je 17 '66
Report from Vietnam. A. Beechy. Sat R 49:
26+ D 3 '66
Snakes & the angel; D. Dengler escapes. il
Time 88:32+ S 23 '66
To die in Vietnam. W. Eastlake. Nation 203:
418-19 O 24 '66
Truth about the most publicized battle of
Vietnam; Captain Carpenter's action; ex-
cerpt from Battles in the monsoon. S. L. A.
Marshall. il Harper 234:67-70+ Ja '67
U.S. navy flier's account of torture and
escape in Vietnam. il Life 61:42C S 23 '66
View of Vietnam. E. J. Hughes. Newsweek
67:22-3 My 30 '66
What it's like for the fighting man; excerpt
from Vietnam: the confusing war. H. Mul-
ligan. Read Digest 89:68-73 N '66
What U.S. bombs in North Vietnam; a navy
pilot's account; excerpt from statement,
December 28, 1966, ed. by J. Kestner. R. C.
Mandeville. U S News 62:13 Ja 9 '67
You can tell 'em, Buddy; report from Artil-
lery Plateau. B. B. Fall. New Repub 156:
17-20 Ja 14 '67
You never know who's in Vietnam; con-
versation with ex-soldiers. J. Higgins. New
Repub 154:12 Ag 16 '66
Young commander went looking for trouble;
Captain Carpenter's battle in the Dak Ta
Kan River Valley. A. Zich. il Life 61:60+ Jl
8 '66
Young Winston Churchill reports on Vietnam.
W. S. Churchill. il Look 30:59-60+ Jl 26 '66

Photography
Cameras record air force, navy strikes on
North Viet oil areas. il Aviation W 85:80-1
Jl 18 '66
Combat photographer. il U S Camera 29:48-9
O '66
Navy plans Vietnam exhibit. J. Neubauer. il
Pop Phot 59:42+ Jl '66
New war photographers. L. Barry. il Pop
Phot 58:60-1+ Mr '66
Photographs. S. Castan. Harper 233:56-7 S '66
Third war of Horst Faas. B. C. Brown.
il Pop Phot 58:58-9+ Mr '66
Unbowed Brit; T. Page. il Time 88:39-40
Ag 19 '66
Vietnam: photographs we're never asked for;
Vietcong atrocities. Nat R 18:1048-51 O 18
'66
Vietnam: unthinking the thinkable. Esquire
66:62-3 Ag '66
See also
Aerial reconnaissance

Poetry
Poetry of the read-in campaign. Nation 202:
635-5 My 30 '66
U.S. offers condolence and aid to Vietnamese
bombed in error. M. Hamburger. Nation
203:711 D 26 '66

What were they like? D. Levertov. Nation
202:781 Je 27 '66

Press reports and censorship
Information war in Saigon; weaknesses in
public-relations apparatus in Washington
and Vietnam. H. W. Baldwin. il Reporter
34:29-31 F 24 '66
Letter from Paris; news from Hanoi. Genêt.
New Yorker 42:140+ S 10 '66
Managed news from Vietnam? here's what
the Pentagon says; excerpts from testi-
mony, August 31, 1966. A. Sylvester. U S
News 61:104-5 S 12 '66
Propaganda junkets; subsidized visits of Eu-
ropean and Asian newsmen to Vietnam
for pro-America propaganda. Nation 203:
173 S 5 '66
Saigon follies? newsmen accuse USIS of
withholding news. Newsweek 68:54+ Ag 15
'66
Salinger tells how Kennedy tried to hide
Vietnam build-up; excerpts from With
Kennedy. P. Salinger. il U S News 61:103
S 12 '66
Snow job; Administration's news distortion
campaign. Nation 203:66-7 Jl 25 '66
View from abroad; differing opinions con-
cerning step-up of guerrilla warfare. Nation
203:204 S 12 '66
Voice of the Times, is not, *laus tibi domine*,
the voice of Asia; opinions in various news
sources on U.S. policy. Nat R 18:714-16 Jl 26
'66
Who's McGinty? Nation 203:236 S 19 '66
See also
Vietnamese war, 1957- —War correspondents

Prisoners and prisons
Charges dismissed; against G. E. Smith and
C. McClure. Newsweek 67:24 Ap 25 '66
Dangerous decision; captured American air-
men up for trial? il Newsweek 68:31 Jl 25
'66
Deplorable & repulsive; North Viet Nam plan
to prosecute captured U.S. pilots as war
criminals. Time 88:12-13 Jl 29 '66
Dissent. T. Blockley. Nat R 18:1089 N 1 '66
Great to be alive. il Newsweek 68:65 S 26
'66
Guests of the VC; escape of W. W. Eckes and
J. Dodson. il Newsweek 68:36-7 Jl 11 '66
Hanoi's humanitarianism; captured American
airmen. Time 88:26 Ag 5 '66
Hanoi's kind of escalation; American airmen.
il Time 88:17 Jl 22 '66
Hanoi's special weapons system; threatened
execution of captured American pilots as
war criminals. J. Burnham. Nat R 18:765
Ag 9 '66
How Communists tortured an American. !'
U S News 61:26 S 26 '66
I escaped from a red prison. D. Dengler. il
Sat Eve Post 239:27-33 D 3 '66
If North Vietnam convicts captured U.S.
fliers. il U S News 61:20-1 Ag 1 '66
Instructive episode; confusion over the
threatened trial of the American flyers held
by the North Vietnamese. Nation 203:108
Ag 8 '66
Is Hanoi preparing for war crimes trials? il
U S News 61:8 Jl 18 '66
Mr Harriman to supervise U.S. actions on
POW's in Viet-Nam; statement, May 18,
1966. R. J. McCloskey. Dept State Bul 54:
888 Je 6 '66
Prisoners of war; North's concern about
treatment towards captives in South's
camps. K. Crawford. Newsweek 68:32 Ag 15
'66
Snakes & the angel; D. Dengler escapes. il
Time 88:32+ S 23 '66
Tale of two prisoners; Dodson and Eckes.
Time 88:27 Jl 8 '66
Trial and error; U.S. pilot's escape and
rescue; Hanoi's handling of prisoner of war
issue. il Newsweek 68:35-6 Ag 1 '66
Two GI's in limbo; Smith-McClure case.
H. W. Ernst. il Nation 202:294-5 Mr 14 '66

Propaganda
Enemy lies backfire, help promote immuniza-
tion of South Viet children. il Todays
Health 44:10 Jl '66
Films from the Vietcong. P. Gessner. Na-
tion 202:110-11 Ja 24 '66
From Peking; like lips and teeth; com-
ments from Peking review, January 21.
Nat R 18:209 Mr 8 '66
Hanoi Harry; Radio stateside. il Newsweek
67:23 F 14 '66

VIETNAMESE war, 1957- —Propaganda—*Cont.*
How many did we zap today? concerning
    How to stay alive in Vietnam by Colonel
    Robert B. Rigg. Christian Cent 83:1291 O
    19 '66
Issue is China. Christian Cent 83:355-7 Mr 23
    '66; Discussion. 83:683-4 My 25 '66
Refreshed by the pause; U.S. and Saigon
    New Year's campaign. il Newsweek 67:32
    Ja 31 '66
Snow job: Administration's news distortion
    campaign. Nation 203:66-7 Jl 25 '66
South Viet Nam; political action teams and
    other propaganda troops. il Time 87:30 F
    18 '66
Straight talk. Nat R 18:1089 N 1 '66
There is no readiness for peace in that re-
    gime today; concerning General Giap's ar-
    ticle. il Life 60:24B-24C F 11 '66
This Granny Goose; influence peddlers. Sr
    Schol 88:5 F 25 '66

Protests, demonstrations, etc, against

Agit-prop pop opera; San Francisco's Romeo
    and Pagliacci. J. O'Connor. Nation 203:
    716-17 D 26 '66
Anti-Vietnam politics; peace candidates in
    Oregon, California. A. Kopkind. New Repub
    154:15-18 Je 4 '66; Discussion. 154:38 Je 25
    '66
Bankruptcy of the liberals; address, Novem-
    ber 27, 1965. C. Oglesby; discussion. Com-
    monweal 83:400-1, 547+ Ja 7, F 11 '66
Be ready; imbalance between intellectuals'
    protests and the President's pique. Nation
    202:636-7 My 30 '66
Berrigan; co-chairman of Clergy concerned
    about Vietnam. New Yorker 42:34-5 Ap 9
    '66
Bishop's hair shirt; C. O. Rice's activities.
    Nation 202:411 Ap 11 '66
Card is not for burning; concerning case of
    D. R. Miller. il Time 88:56 O 21 '66
Conduct unbecoming; lieutenant on the peace
    line; case of H. H. Howe. J. Rechy. il
    Nation 202:204-8 F 21 '66; Reply. J. L.
    Howe 202:346+ Mr 28 '66
Drafting of protectors challenged. Sr Schol
    87:16 Ja 21 '66
HUAC eyes the campus; ACLU urges resist-
    ance against intimidation. Nation 203:628-
    9 D 12 '66
HUAC: from pillory to farce; hostile wit-
    nesses disrupt hearing on bill to amend
    the Internal security act. F. J. Donner.
    Nation 203:174-6 S 5 '66
HUAC hellzapoppin. New Repub 155:5-6 Ag
    27 '66
Hullabaloo at HUAC; excerpt from hearings
    on J. Pool bill. il Newsweek 68:15-16 Ag 29
    '66
Immolations and consensus; the justification
    of innocence. A. Towne; discussion. Chris-
    tian Cent 83:276 Mr 2 '66
In the camp of the enemy; HUAC hearings. J.
    Burnham. Nat R 18:876 S 6 '66
Los Angeles: tower for peace. il Art N 65:25
    Ap '66
Meaning? US; new play directed against war.
    il Newsweek 68:98+ O 31 '66
Mob scene on Capitol hill; When a federal
    court challenged Congress. il U S News 61:
    12 Ag 29 '66
Moral question; protest preferred to indif-
    ference. Nation 203:594 D 5 '66
No news; SANE peace rally and the New
    York times. Nation 203:692 D 26 '66
Not *the* Dr Spock! R. K. Massie. il Sat Eve
    Post 239:80-2+ My 7 '66
Now the Germans. Nation 202:86-7 Ja 24 '66
One last fling; S. Lynd denounces U.S. in-
    volvement in Viet Nam on BBC TV. Time
    87:21 F 11 '66
Open season on dissenters; demonstrators in
    South Boston. Christian Cent 83:483-4 Ap 20
    '66
Patriotism of dissent. J. W. Fulbright. Red-
    book 128:44+ N '66
Peace; Catholic peace fellowship; interview.
    T. Cornell. New Yorker 42:23-5 D 24 '66
Poetry of the read-in campaign. Nation 202:
    653-5 My 30 '66
Potpourri of protest; Artists tower of protest.
    Los Angeles. il Newsweek 67:101 Mr 14 '66
Second session at the Monument; march on
    Washington for peace in Vietnam. L.
    Lorrinson. America 114:769 My 28 '66
Selective reprisal; sniping at dissent; inci-
    dents and retaliatory acts by U.S. govern-
    ment and private citizens. M. L. Wulf.
    il Nation 203:149-52 Ag 22 '66

Serious to-do about a silly law; trial of
    D. J. Miller. L. Wainwright. Life 60:17
    Mr 4 '66
Speaking out; we're unfair to draft-card
    burners. R. E. Rubenstein. Sat Eve Post
    239:10+ F 12 '66
Stop the killing; open letter from eleven
    Vietnamese priests; translation from
    French. Commonweal 84:48-9 Ap 1 '66
Summer madness; HUAC hearing. il Time 88:
    10-11 Ag 26 '66
T.R.B. from Washington; fellow-travelers.
    New Repub 155:4 Ag 27 '66
Tantrums; President Johnson shielded from
    anti-war pickets in Indianapolis. Nation
    203:141 Ag 22 '66
Tower against war; artists in Los Angeles
    and writers in New York to act. Nation
    202:143 F 7 '66
Unrest in U.S. churches. il U S News 62:68-71
    Ja 23 '67
Vietnam as viewed from the Philippines;
    statement by four churchmen. Christian
    Cent 83:717 Je 1 '66
Voices crying in the Vietnam wilderness.
    Christian Cent 83:608 My 11 '66
Voices of protest; antiwar plays. Time 88:
    61 O 21 '66
War comes to the campus; protests against
    selective service system and the war. il
    Newsweek 67:29-30 My 23 '66
What do you think we are here for? Read-in
    for peace in Vietnam at Town Hall. Nat R
    18:198 Mr 8 '66
When soldiers claim the war is illegal. U S
    News 61:10 S 19 '66
Wrong place; South Boston. il Time 87:28
    Ap 8 '66

Psychological aspects

Dos & don'ts; Communist advice for beating
    imperialists. Time 87:32-3 Mr 11 '66
Hurting; how North Vietnam is retaliating
    against U.S. raids. il Newsweek 68:28 Jl 18
    '66
On the couch; a psychiatrist and psychologist
    testify at hearing of Senate foreign rela-
    tions committee. Time 87:20-1 Je 3 '66
Psychoanalyzing Vietnam; doctors testify at
    Foreign relations committee hearing. News-
    week 67:25 Je 6 '66
U.S. may swallow hook. Sci N 89:447 Je 4
    '66
When psychiatrists look at the war. U S
    News 60:8 Je 6 '66

Public opinion

Agony, yes; arrogance, no; attack on U.S.
    foreign policy. America 114:767 My 28 '66
Americans view the war; to get the truth,
    I just don't know; views of citizens of
    Auburn, Wash. R. S. Johnson. il Nation
    203:502-5 N 14 '66
As others see it; some Catholic opinions. Com-
    monweal 84:631-5 S 30 '66
Awash; British opinion on U.S. policy in Viet
    Nam. il Time 88:32 Jl 15 '66
Blinkers. Nat R 18:713-14 Jl 26 '66
Boss Meany; AFL-CIO statement of policy
    on Vietnam. Nation 203:204-5 S 12 '66
British support on Vietnam? with statements.
    J. Fletcher. Nat R 18:356-8 Ap 19 '66
Changing climate; extreme opposition less
    raucous. il Time 88:12 S 2 '66
Conversations on the Red Riviera; everything
    comes back to; but what about Vietnam?
    P. Ben. New Repub 155:9 O 29 '66
Dangers of disbelief; Russian view of domes-
    tic ground swell against Mr Johnson's pol-
    icy. Newsweek 68:67-8 Ag 22 '66
Déjà vu; French reaction. E. Taylor. Re-
    porter 35:18 +O 6 '66
Dissent in wartime. Commonweal 84:269-70
    My 27 '66
Dissent; it questions and attacks U.S. in-
    volvement in Vietnam; interviews. D.
    Nevin. il Life 60:56B-60+ F 25 '66
D.O.V.E from U.N.C.L.E; Robert Vaughn's
    Washington mission. il Time 87:75-6 Ap 1
    '66
Doubts about Vietnam; letter to President
    Johnson from student leaders. Newsweek
    69:49 Ja 9 '67
Doubts of Europe. R. Steel. Commonweal 84:
    629-31 S 30 '66
East and west from Paris; U.S. bombing of
    North Vietnam. A. Werth. Nation 202:225-6
    F 28 '66
Every man for himself; war in Vietnam and
    the congressional campaigns. Newsweek 68:
    21 Jl 25 '66

VIETNAMESE war, 1957- —Public opinion—
Continued
For Mr Johnson to think about; Stanford-Chicago universities survey findings. Nation 202:347 Mr 28 '66
Ground slipping. J. Burnham. Nat R 18:509 My 31 '66
How Asians view the Vietnam war. il U S News 62:6 Ja 2 '67
How not to fight a war; downgrading our objectives in Vietnam. D. Lawrence. U S News 60:100 My 30 '66
I resign; W. James leaves Louisville Courier-journal. W. James. Time 87:63-4 Ap 22 '66
Is war in Vietnam to blame for the decline in LBJ's popularity? il U S News 60:22 Ap 11 '66
LBJ and the war; what polls show. il U S News 60:6 My 30 '66
Morality of the Vietnam war. J. B. Sheerin. Cath World 202:326-30 Mr '66; Discussion. 203:66-7 My '66
New poll on Vietnam; Stanford and Chicago universities' findings. New Repub 154:9 Mr 26 '66
No more myths. Commonweal 84:325 Je 10 '66
On and on it goes. Commonweal 84:625-6 S 30 '66
Painless war; American attitude. Nation 203:236-7 S 19 '66
Papa knows best; interpreting poll by social scientists at Stanford and Chicago universities. New Repub 154:6 Mr 26 '66
People, resigned; interviews with Vietnamese people, ed. by F. Sully. il Newsweek 67:33-4 Ap 18 '66
Polls and the war. W. Lippmann. Newsweek 68:13 Jl 4 '66
Price of peace. Christian Cent 83:163-4 F 9 '66
Rate of dissent. T. C. Sorensen. Sat R 49:26 Ap 2 '66
Russian summer; worried vacationists; Vietnamese war causing anxiety. A. Werth. Nation 203:176-9 S 5 '66
Sick of Vietnam; U.S. political reaction. New Repub 154:4 Je 25 '66
Small war for a great power; defeatism about war in Vietnam. S. Alsop. il Sat Eve Post 239:16 Ap 9 '66
Speaking out; McCarthyism is threatening us again. A. Schlesinger, jr. Sat Eve Post 239:10+ Ag 13 '66
Student support; petition of support from college and university students. Sr Schol 87:16 Ja 21 '66
Students for victory; VIVA, or, Victory in Vietnam association. R. Kirk. Nat R 18:535 My 31 '66
Support & concern; conversation at the annual Western governor's conference in Las Vegas. Time 87:21 My 6 '66
T.R.B. from Washington. New Repub 155:4 D 24 '66
Through European eyes; you're on your own. J. Blocker. Newsweek 68:34-5 O 31 '66
Thrust of policy; U.S. concern over L. B. Johnson's operational policy. Nation 202:314 Mr 21 '66
Town's troubled mood as a war comes home; Massillon, Ohio questions administration's position. il Life 61:50-7 Ag 12 '66
Vietnam; correcting the crucial error; apparent Vietnamese impassivity. E. G. Martin. Newsweek 68:48-9 S 12 '66
Vietnam; questions old and new; new crisis and U.S. reactions. il Newsweek 67:21-2 Ap 25 '66
Viet Nam shadows; U.S. elections. Sr Schol 88:6-7 My 6 '66
View from Germany; and western Europe. H. Brandon. Sat R 49:16 Ap 2 '66
View of Vietnam. E. J. Hughes. Newsweek 67:22-3 My 30 '66
Viewpoints; pros and cons of the U.S. role in Vietnam. Sr Schol 89:22-4 O 28 '66
What people want to do about Vietnam. U S News 60:12 Je 27 '66
Why the 4th of July means more this year. C. P. Streeter. Farm J 90:74 Jl '66
Why we will win in Viet Nam. W. M. Greene, jr. il Nations Bsns 54:36-9+ Ap '66
Wisdom of pessimism. Commonweal 84:302-3 Je 3 '66
Word from Zephyr; L. Harris survey. Newsweek 67:31 My 16 '66
Youth questions the war; excerpts from letter to President Johnson by student leaders. Time 89:22 Ja 6 '67

Refugees
As Ky bolsters his rule, an American ark sealifts a village; relocation of Ban Thach. S. Angeloff. il Life 60:30-3 Je 3 '66
Brief report on the Cam Ne fund; projects. Sat R 49:26 D 3 '66
Cam Ne fund; visit of Mrs Janet Stark. N. Cousins. Sat R 49:25 My 14 '66
Fresh look at Vietnam. E. M. Kennedy. il Look 30:21-3 F 8 '66
Reporter at large; self supporting thirteen-year-old orphan in Danang. S. Sheehan. New Yorker 42:137-8+ N 5 '66
Saigon; the impact of the refugees; national and international projects. E. B. Marks. il Reporter 36:33-6 Ja 12 '67

Relief work
Fresh look at Vietnam. E. M. Kennedy. il Look 30:21-3 F 8 '66
Mademoiselle Merit awards 1966; U.S. A.I.D. nurses; in Vietnam. il Mlle 64:47 Ja '67
Now that Vietnam has voted. il U S News 61:48 S 26 '66
Pacification in Vietnam; here's how it's to be done. il U S News 60:34-6 F 21 '66
Second front in Vietnam. N. Cousins. Sat R 49:22+ O 29 '66
War at the grass roots; pacification in Vietnam; AID, as the main civilian instrument. il U S News 61:50-2 S 26 '66

Songs and music
G-eye view of Vietnam. J. B. Treaster. il N Y Times Mag D 104+ O 30 '66
Hail to Green Berets; with report by D. Martin. il Life 60:93-4+ Mr 4 '66
Purple heart boogie; top tunes in Viet Nam. Time 87:41 Mr 4 '66
Senior scholastic interviews; balladeer of the Green Berets; ed. by J. Nickerson. B. Sadler. il Sr Schol 88:3+ Mr 4 '66

Statistics
Atlantic report. Atlan 218:14+ O '66

Strategy
Advisers who shaped the new Vietnam policy. il U S News 60:20 F 21 '66
After the pause; motion or progress? il Newsweek 67:17-21 F 14 '66
Ahead in Vietnam; a bloody stalemate? il U S News 60:36-7 Ap 11 '66
Appointment in Manila. Newsweek 68:36 O 10 '66
As Goldwater now sees the war in Vietnam; interview. B. M. Goldwater. U S News 60:44-6 Ap 25 '66
Atlantic report. Atlan 218:14+ O '66
Back from Vietnam. E. Taylor. il Reporter 34:23-6 Ja 27 '66
Bit-by-bit war. J. B. Burnham. Nat R 19:35-7 Ja 10 '67
Bomb pause causes major tactics shift. C. Brownlow. il Aviation W 84:26-8 F 14 '66
Brutality with a purpose; political weapon of the Viet Cong. Time 88:38 S 16 '66
Carrot and stick; Honolulu conference. Commonweal 83:599 F 25 '66
Communication on Vietnam; letter. J. M. Gavin. il Harper 232:16+ F '66; Discussion. 232:6+ Ap '66; Nat R 18:151, 246-7+ F 22, Mr 22 '66
D-day in the Delta; Delta patrol. il Time 88:42 D 9 '66
Deadly booby traps in a dirty war. E. Hymoff. il Pop Mech 125:70-3+ Je '66
Dilemmas and agonies for all. N. Cousins. Sat R 49:32 F 5 '66
Disputed views of General Gavin; excerpts from testimony, February 8, 1966. J. M. Gavin. U S News 60:21 F 21 '66
Does Vietnam need a supreme commander? D. Warner. il Reporter 34:11-15 Je 30 '66
Escalation; the back-room talk. il Newsweek 68:42+ S 12 '66
Exterminators; American scientists petition President Johnson about use of chemical weapons. New Repub 155:7 O 1 '66
Four against the red China lobby; symposium; ed. with introd. by T. Lit. il Nat R 18:513-28 My 31 '66; Correction. 18:598+ Je 28 '66
General LeMay tells how to win the war in Vietnam. C. E. LeMay. il U S News 61:36-8+ O 10 '66
General Taylor hits holding strategy, defends Vietnam policy; excerpts from address, February 3, 1966. M. D. Taylor. U S News 60:20 F 14 '66

VIETNAMESE war, 1957- —War aims—*Cont.*
Looking-glass war of words; quotations from both sides. comp. by. T. C. Sorensen. Sat R 49:19 Ag 20 '66
Mahan's long shadow. R. Moley. Newsweek 68:100 Jl 18 '66
Munich and Vietnam: a valid analogy? M. S. Fasteau. Bul Atomic Sci 22:22-5 S '66
New Viet targets, same U.S. aims. Life 61:4 Jl 15 '66
We cannot accept a Communist seizure of Vietnam. R. A. Scalapino. il N Y Times Mag p46-7+ D 11 '66

War correspondents

AFP's man in Hanoi. il Newsweek 68:54 Ag 15 '66
Basic flaw in Viet Nam. il Time 88:86 O 21 '66
Behind enemy lines; report of H. E. Salisbury. il Newsweek 69:61-2 Ja 9 '67
Covering Viet Nam; crud, fret & jeers. il Time 87:54+ Je 10 '66
Eye of the veteran; J. Steinbeck. il Time 88:41 D 30 '66
Femininity at the front. il Time 88:73 O 28 '66
Information war in Saigon; weaknesses in public-relations apparatus in Washington and Vietnam. H. W. Baldwin. il Reporter 34:29-31 F 24 '66
Invitation to Tinh Hoi pagoda; correspondents fired on. G. P. Hunt. il Life 60:3 Je 3 '66
It's a dirty war for correspondents, too. J. Raymond. il N Y Times Mag p32-3+ F 13 '66
Letter from Paris; New York times coverage of the war in Viet Nam attacked; text of letter; excerpts. F. E. Nolting, jr. Time 88:79 N 4 '66
Miserable night, par for the course. A. Zich. Life 61:3 Jl 8 '66
Pagoda picture; Buddhists fire on newsmen in Da Nang. il Newsweek 67:62 Je 6 '66
Rebuttal & reply; concerning S. L. A. Marshall's criticism of military coverage. Time 88:96 N 25 '66
Ride in the country; two French reporters. Newsweek 67:28 F 7 '66
Tear gas, a problem for photographers; Life's team. G. P. Hunt. il Life 60:3 Ap 22 '66
Three for AP. il Newsweek 67:92-3 My 16 '66
Vietnam witness; B. B. Fall awarded George Polk memorial award. il Newsweek 67:98 Ap 11 '66
What was a woman doing there? W. E. Garrett. il Nat Geog Mag 129:270-1 F '66

Women and the war

When crisis is a way of life. L. G. Martin. il Mlle 64:172-3+ N '66
Women of Vietnam. L. Bergquist. il Look 30:17-21 D 27 '66
VIETNAMESE war brides. See War marriages
VIEW finders
Shoot low with 35. C. W. Kennedy. il Pop Phot 58:68 Mr '66
VIEWER-projectors. See Projection apparatus
VIGILANCE committees
See also
Civil rights organizations
VIGUERS, Ruth Hill
Journal of Beatrix Potter from 1881 to 1897; review. Horn Bk 42:399-400 Ag '66
—and others
(comp) Booklist (title varies) See issues of Horn book magazine
VIKING Princess fire. See Ships—Fires and fire protection
VIKINGS
Map flap; skeptics suspect Vinland map may be fake. Newsweek 67:68 Ap 11 '66
Men before Columbus; excerpt from Westviking, the ancient Norse in Greenland and North America. F. Mowat. il Read Digest 89:200-2+ N '66
Vinland map and the Tartar relation; excerpts, with introd. by O. Jensen. R. Skelton and G. D. Painter; discussion. Am Heritage 17:100-1 F '66
VILLA, Francisco
Pancho to the pantheon. Time 88:47 N 25 '66
VILLA, Pancho. See Villa, F.
VILLA Sparta gardens. See Gardens—Italy
VILLAGE voice (newspaper)
Voice of the partially alienated. il Time 88:90+ N 11 '66

VILLAGES
Reshaping of Chinese society; facets of life in Liu Ling village. J. Myrdal. Bul Atomic Sci 22:76-9 Je '66
VILLAGES, Models of. See Models of cities, towns, etc.
VILLAGES, Restored
Movers and Shakers; Shaker community, Hancock, Mass. R. Lynes. il Harper 233:34+ D '66
Next in size to San Francisco; Barkerville, British Columbia. il Sunset 136:74+ Ap '66
Restoring the past puts life in the till; restaurants the biggest draws. il Bsns W p 190-2 S 24 '66
Traveling through history; living museums. M. Goodman. il Redbook 127:97+ S '66
VILLAINESSES in opera. See Characters in opera
VILLAINS in literature. See Characters in literature
VILLAR, Antonio Rodriguez. See Rodriguez Villar, A.
VILLEFRANCHE, France
Revisiting the Riviera. A. Waugh. Nat R 18:368+ Ap 19 '66
VILLELLA, Edward
Edward Villella talks; ed. by O. Maynard. pors Dance Mag 40:50-4+ My '66
VILLENA, Spain
Gypsy's treasure. B. Wason. il Horizon 9:102-4 Wint '67
VILLET, Barbara, and Villet, Grey
Family of Levi Smith. il Life 61:72-86+ N 25 '66
Levi Smith's bonus, fifteen grandchildren. il Life 61:80-94 D 9 '66
Three sons of Levi Smith. il Life 61:68-82 D 2 '66
Uncommon American family. il Life 61:68-82 D 2; 80-94 D 9; 60-71 D 16 '66
VILLET, Grey. See Villet, B. jt. auth.
VILLIARD, Paul
Information please. Read Digest 88:62-5 Je '66
VILLIERS, Alan
Alice in Australia's wonderland. Nat Geog Mag 129:230-57 F '66
VILLON, Raymond Duchamp-. See Duchamp-Villon, R.
VILSTRUP, Dick
Raising and selling dairy replacements. Suc Farm 64:54-5+ Mr '66
VINALHAVEN ISLAND
Rubber boot Bali Ha'i. L. Dietz. il Field & S 71:62-3+ My '66
VINAY, Ramon
Child of nature; interview. ed. by J. W. Freeman. por Opera N 30:32-3 Ap 2 '66
VINCENT-BARWOOD, Aileen
Awakening; story. Redbook 126:62-3 F '66
VINCENT Price collection of fine art. See Art—Private collections
VIND, Harold P.
Undersea air supply. bibliog Science 153:873-5 Ag 19 '66
VINE, F. J.
Spreading of the ocean floor; new evidence. bibliog Science 154:1405-15 D 16 '66
VINEBERG, Arthur M.
Increasing the blood flow. il Time 87:57-8 F 18 '66
New life for failing hearts. J. D. Ratcliff. il Read Digest 88:181-2+ F '66
VINES. See Climbing plants
VINIFERA grapes. See Grapes
VINLAND map. See America—Discovery and exploration—Maps
VINSON, Carlos
Alone with the squirrels. Outdoor Life 138:62-3+ O '66
VINTAGE sports car club of America. See Automobiles—Collectors and collecting
VIOBIN corporation
FPC; nearing approval? B. J. Culliton. il Sci N 90:474 D 3 '66
VIOLAS (flowers) See Violets
VIOLENCE
American amok; is the gun-ridden USA a violent nation? R. Coles. New Repub 155:12-15 Ag 27 '66
Are we a nation of hoods? P. Johnson. Read Digest 89:127-9 D '66
Call for courage in handling unrest; excerpts from address, July 25, 1966. H. W. Smith. U S News 61:14 Ag 8 '66

VIOLENCE—*Continued*
Crime wave, what can be done about it?
il U S News 61:46-51 Ag 1 '66
Making the violent scene. M. Lebowitz. Nation 204:57-9 Ja 9 '67
Myth of natural aggression. Nation 203:340 O 10 '66
On aggression, by K. Lorenz. Review
Time il 87:104+ Je 17 '66
On an LBJ tour, firm talk about civil-rights violence. U S News 61:8 Ag 29 '66
Patterns of violence; symposium, ed. by M. E. Wolfgang. bibliog f il Ann Am Acad 364: 1-157 Mr '66
Sign for Cain, by F. Wertham. Review
Sat R 49:40-1 N 19 '66. S. J. Fox
Time 88:106+ S 23 '66
Violence not surprising. Sci N 90:68 Jl 30 '66
What young men need: a substitute for violence. J. Fischer. Read Digest 88:82-5 Mr '66
See also
Terrorism

VIOLETS
Colorful cousins: violas and pansies. il Sunset 136:96-7 Mr '66

VIOLIN
Little wooden song box. il Time 88:40 D 30 '66
Simple confession: author's war with the inanimate. A. Gingrich. il Esquire 65:82-3+ Mr '66

Instruction and study
Simple confession: author's war with the inanimate. A. Gingrich. il Esquire 65:82-3+ Mr '66

VIOLIN music
Encyclopedia of the violin, by A. Bachmann. Review
Am Rec G 32:903-6 My '66. E. Belov
See also
Phonograph records—Violin music

VIOLIN playing
See also
Violin—Instruction and study

VIOLINISTS
See also
Concertmasters
Fuchs, J.
Harth, S.

VIOLONCELLO music
See also
Phonograph records—Violoncello music

VIORST, Milton
Could this Jew be president? Esquire 65:100-4+ Ap '66
De Gaulle among the Boswells. New Repub 155:28-31 Ag 13 '66
Honk, honk, the marigold. Esquire 66:116-19+ O '66
Politics of equivocation: two faces of the GOP. Nation 203:630-2 D 12 '66

VIRGIN Mary. See Mary, Virgin

VIRGIN ISLANDS
See also
St John Island
Tourist trade—Virgin Islands

Description and travel
Chartering in the Virgins. E. Horan; B. Robinson. il Yachting 120:42-4+ N '66
Other islands, other reefs. B. Thielen. il Holiday 40:60-7+ D '66
Picture islands. L. Barry. il Pop Phot 59: 94-8+ N '66
Virgin Islands: our Caribbean treasure. L. M. Rhodes. il Todays Health 44:44-9 D '66

VIRGIN ISLANDS, BRITISH. See British Virgin Islands

VIRGIN ISLANDS NATIONAL PARK
Beneath the surface. E. L. Rothfuss. il Parks & Rec 1:715-16+ S '66

VIRGINIA, Sister Marie. See Marie Virginia, Sister

VIRGINIA
See also
Architecture, Domestic—Virginia
Booksellers and bookselling—Virginia
Cumberland Gap
Education—Virginia
Fishing—Virginia
Hunting—Virginia
Justice, Administration of—Virginia
Monticello (historic house)
Prince Edward County

Antiquities
Mathews manor: preview of a major archeological discovery in Virginia. I. N. Hume. il Antiques 90:832-6 D '66

Historic houses, etc.
See also
Monticello (historic house)

History
Knights of the golden horseshoe. H. D. Crawford. il Am For 72:28-31+ N '66

Marriage law
See Marriage law—United States

Outdoor recreation study commission
Virginia outdoors plan. F. Bemiss. il Parks & Rec 1:964-5+ D '66

Politics and government
Double feature in Byrdland: candidates for senatorial primaries. J. I. Brooks. Reporter 34:25-7 Je 16 '66
New dominion. il Time 88:22 Jl 22 '66
Stillness at Berryville. J. Fletcher. Nat R 18: 781-3+ Ag 9 '66
Think about that; primary results; with analytical review by L. Harris. il Newsweek 68:23-4 Jl 25 '66

Race problems
They closed their schools, by B. Smith. Review
Nation 203:521-2 N 14 '66. K. Jackson, jr

VIRGINIA Frank child development center, Chicago. See Nursery schools

VIRGINIA military institute, Lexington
George C. Marshall oral history project. F. C. Pogue. il Wilson Lib Bul 40:606-8+ Mr '66

VIRGINIA museum of fine arts
Hogarth in Virginia. il Newsweek 69:82-3+ Ja 23 '67

VIRGINIA primary. See Primaries

VIRGINIA state college, Petersburg
Integration: Negro college hires an impatient Briton. L. J. Carter. il Science 152:481-5 Ap 22 '66

VIRGINITY
Meaning of virginity. E. M. Prevallet. America 115:93-5 Jl 23 '66; Discussion. 115:165 Ag 20 '66

VIRTANEN, Artturi I.
Milk production of cows on protein-free feed. bibliog Science 153:1603-14 S 30 '66

VIRTUE is her own reward; drama. See Hervey, M.

VIRUS diseases
See also
Cold (disease)
Virus research

VIRUS diseases in animals
See also
Cattle—Diseases and pests

VIRUS research
Possible virus-MS link. Sci N 89:507 Je 25 '66
Teen-age scientist, a college drop-out, reports on virus research. Todays Health 44:13 S '66
Virus enemy; with report by R. Campbell and N. Genet. il Life 60:56-69 F 18 '66

VIRUSES
Genetic control of the shape of a virus. E. Kellenberger. il Sci Am 215:32-9 bibliog (p 154) D '66
Interaction among virus, cell, and organism; address, December 11, 1965. A. Lwoff. Science 152:1216-20 My 27 '66
Lymphocystis virus: isolation and propagation in centrarchid fish cell lines. K. Wolf and others. bibliog il Science 151:1004-5 F 25 '66
Pentagonal aggregation of virus particles. G. Milman and others. bibliog il Science 152:1381-3 Je 3 '66
Reovirus-specific polyribosomes in infected L-cells. L. Prevec and A. F. Graham. bibliog il Science 154:522-3 O 28 '66
Simian virus 40: replication in the presence of specific antiserum and adenovirus 4. J. M. Easton and C. W. Hiatt. bibliog il Science 151:582-3 F 4 '66
Spontaneous mammary tumors: decrease of incidence in mice infected with an enzyme-elevating virus. V. Riley. bibliog il Science 153:1657-8 S 30 '66
Subacute sclerosing leukoencephalitis: ultrastructure of intranuclear and intracytoplasmic inclusions. I. Tellez-Nagel and D. H. Harter. bibliog il Science 154:899-901 N 18 '66

VIRUSES—*Continued*
Thing that's going around; ARD (acute respiratory disease) B. Davidson. il Sat Eve Post 239:88-90 My 7 '66
Vesicular stomatitis virus replication in human leukocyte cultures: enhancement by phytohemagglutinin. R. Edelman and E. F. Wheelock. bibliog il Science 154:1053-5 N 25 '66
Viruses cause epidemics. Sci N 90:215 S 17 '66
See also
Adenoviruses
Cold viruses
Coxsackie viruses
Microorganisms, Pathogenic
Virus research
also names of viruses, e.g. Herpes simplex virus

Resistance
Virus enemy; with report by R. Campbell and N. Genet. il Life 60:56-69 F 18 '66

VIRUSES, Plant
Cylindrical inclusions in the cytoplasm of leaf cells infected with tobacco etch virus. J. R. Edwardson. bibliog il Science 153:883-4 Ag 19 '66
Stylet-borne virus: active probing by aphids not required for acquisition. C. B. Barnett, jr. and T. P. Pirone. bibliog il Science 154:291 O 14 '66

VISAS. See Passports
VISCERAL reflex. See Reflexes
VISHNIAC, Roman
Child of affluence. W. Miller. Nation 202: 338-9 Mr 21 '66
VISIBLE surface; story. See Heinemann, A.
VISION. See Sight
VISIONS of sugar plums; drama. See Martens, A. C.
VISITATION; opera. See Schuller, G.
VISITATION; story. See Woiwode, L.
VISITING, Hospital. See Hospitals—Visitors
VISITING college professors and instructors. See College professors and instructors
VISITING housekeepers
Stand-in for mother. M. Albrecht. il Parents Mag 41:58-9+ Mr '66
VISITING nurses. See Nurses and nursing, Public health
VISITOR information service. See United States—Forest service
VISITORS. See Guests; Hospitals—Visitors
VISITORS, Interchange of. See Exchange of persons programs
VISOTACTOR. See Reading machines
VISSER 'T HOOFT, Willem Adolf
Lengthened shadow. B. Thompson. Christian Cent 83:610-11 My 11 '66
Mirroring the world. H. E. Fey. Christian Cent 83:978-9 Ag 10 '66
Unifying Dutchman. il por Time 88:91 D 9 '66
Visser 't Hooft: a tribute. E. C. Blake. Christian Cent 83:1467-9 N 30 '66
VISTA. See Volunteers in service to America
VISUAL adaptation. See Eye—Accommodation and refraction
VISUAL aids. See Audio-visual aids
VISUAL disappearances. See Optical illusions
VISUAL graphics corporation
New typefaces chosen in world-wide contests; first International type face design competition. il Pub W 190:120+ S 5 '66
VISUAL illusions. See Optical illusions
VISUAL images. See Images and imagery (psychology)
VISUAL instruction. See Audio-visual instruction
VISUAL language. See Communication
VISUAL perception. See Perception
VISUAL pigments. See Retina
VISUAL stimulus. See Stimulus and response
VITA, Luis Washington
Current trends in Brazilian philosophy. Américas 18:32-6 Ag '66
VITAL statistics
Don't tell it to the computer. V. Packard. il N Y Times Mag p44-5+ Ja 8 '67
VITAMIN deficiency. See Diet, Deficient
VITAMINS
Showdown on vitamins. R. L. Smith. il Nation 203:578-80 N 28 '66
Vitamin crackdown. il Time 88:48+ Jl 1 '66

Vitamin A
Vitamin A improves cows' fertility. Sci N 89:453 Je 4 '66

Vitamin B₃
See also
Niacin

Vitamin C
Vitamin C-induced increase of dermatan sulfate in cultured Hurler's fibroblasts. I. A. Schafer and others. bibliog il Science 153:1008-10 Ag 26 '66

Vitamin D
Too much vitamin D? Consumer Rep 31:52-4 F '66

Vitamin D₃
Vitamin D₃-induced calcium-binding protein in chick intestinal mucosa. R. H. Wasserman and A. N. Taylor. bibliog il Science 152:791-3 My 6 '66

Vitamin H
See Biotin

VITICULTURE
Farm union reaps first California victory; recognition by Schenley and Christian brothers vineyards. il Bsns W p 158+ Ap 16 '66
Schenley surrenders; migrant workers vs California grape growers. Christian Cent 83:515-16 Ap 27 '66

History
Search for good wine. M. A. Amerine. bibliog il Science 154:1621-8 D 30 '66

VITIS. See Grapes
VITT, Sam B.
In praise of memos. Nations Bsns 54:70 N '66
VITTI, Monica
Monica Vitti. E. Walter. il pors Vogue 147: 122-5+ F 15 '66
Monica Vitti: she's not that way at all. il pors Look 30:83-5 Je 14 '66
VIVA Vivaldi; ballet. See Ballets—Criticisms
VIVANTE, Arturo
Angels in the air; story. New Yorker 42:24-7 Je 25 '66
Little ark; story. New Yorker 42:61-3 N 19 '66
Mr Harty. New Yorker 41:81-7 Ja 22 '66
Room; story. New Yorker 42:24-5 Jl 30 '66
Secret; story. New Yorker 42:47-51 My 7 '66
VIVISECTION
Antivivisection and Congress. Sci Am 214: 55-6 Mr '66
Scientists vs. animal lovers. L. Eisenberg. il Harper 233:101-2+ N '66; Discussion. 234: 4+ Ja '67
VIZZARD, James L.
Grape strike. Commonweal 84:295-6 My 27 '66
VLACHOS, Helen
Helen of Athens. il por Time 87:58 My 20 '66
VLADIMIROV, Iuril
Two for tomorrow. il por Time 87:62 My 27 '66
VLAHOS, Charles, and Weis, B. G.
Build a hip squawk box. Pop Electr 25:97-8+ O '66
VLASTOVSKY, Vladimir
Our pint-size ancestors. UNESCO Courier 19:27-9 F '66
VO-nguyen-Giap
Red Napoleon. il Time 87:32-6 Je 17 '66
There is no readiness for peace in that regime today. il Life 60:24B-24C F 11 '66
Voice of the enemy; excerpts from magazine article. por Newsweek 67:19 F 14 '66
VOCABULARY
See also
Words
VOCABULARY tests
It pays to increase your word power. P. Funk. See issues of Reader's digest
VOCAL cord polyps. See Tumors
VOCAL cords, Artificial. See Larynx, Artificial
VOCAL organs. See Voice
VOCATION (in religion)
Deepening mystery; decrease in priestly and religious vocations. America 114:822-3 Je 11 '66; Discussion. 115:95-6 Jl 23 '66
McNally is in touch; priestly vocations. K. M. Reed. America 115:84 Jl 23 '66
Renewed priesthood. E. C. Bianchi. America 116:48-50+ Ja 14 '67
September vocations. America 115:409 O 8 '66

VOCATION, Religious. See Vocation (in religion)

VOCATIONAL agricultural training. See Agriculture—Study and teaching

VOCATIONAL counseling. See Vocational guidance

VOCATIONAL education
Coming revolution against boredom in the classroom. J. N. Miller. il PTA Mag 60:18-21 Ap '66; Same abr. with title New cure for boredom in the classroom. Read Digest 88:171-2+ My '66
Federal challenge and peril to the American school; adaptation of address, December 17, 1965. F. M. Cordasco. Sch & Soc 94:263-5 Sum '66
Vocational education: road to jobs. Sr Schol 88:sup4 Ap 29 '66
Working one's way through tomorrow. B. Michael and E. Weinstein. il Am Ed 2:29-32 D '65
See also
Agriculture—Study and teaching
Technical education
Trade schools

Federal aid
See Federal aid to education

VOCATIONAL guidance
Attitudes and realities; study of college students' career plans carried out by ACPA. M. Ricking. ALA Bul 60:667-9 Je '66
College and career; questions and answers. H. Zuckerman. See occasional issues of Senior scholastic
Help your child to a career. J. J. Cox. il Todays Health 44:29-31+ D '66
Manpower projections: some conceptual problems and research needs. S. Swerdloff. il Mo Labor R 89:138-43 F '66
Scientists were kids, too, once; need for the non-specialist. H. Downs. Sci Digest 60:90-3 Ag '66
See also
Occupations

VOCATIONAL high schools. See Trade schools

VOCATIONAL rehabilitation
Employment for the handicapped; observance of National employ the physically handicapped week; letter to the editor. R. S. Bray. Wilson Lib Bul 41:25 S '66
From relief rolls to rehabilitation; training program launched by Cook County department of public aid in association with Institute of technological training. il Am City 81:34+ Ag '66
Handicapped teachers. NEA J 55:39-40 My '66
His way of working. B. Roddey. il U S Camera 29:40+ D '66
Man can't afford to get soft! P. Friggens. il Farm J 90:26-7+ D '66; Same abr. Read Digest 90:127-31 Ja '67
Student nurse with heart: double amputee studying at Mercy hospital school of nursing in Charlotte, N.C. C. Brossard. il Look 30:M16-21 D 13 '66
3M's self-help plan; setting up physically handicapped in copying-service businesses. il Bsns W p62 D 3 '66
See also
Abilities, incorporated

VOCATIONAL schools. See Trade schools; Vocational education

VOCATIONAL-technical and adult school, Milwaukee. See Trade schools

VOCODER. See Sound—Apparatus

VODKA
Vodka spectrum. il Esquire 66:96-7 O '66

VOGEL, Robert M.
Respect and trust; address, September 14, 1966. Vital Speeches 33:46-9 N 1 '66

VOGT, Lesster H. Jr, and others
Crystal and molecular structure of a double complex of manganese with phthalocyanato and pyridine ligands. bibliog Science 151:569-70 F 4 '66

VOICE
Air; importance of voices on television. M. Arlen. New Yorker 42:140+ D 10 '66
Singing voice: first sounds. R. Rushmore. il Opera N 31:24-7 Ja 21 '67
Too much too soon. C. L. Osborne. Opera N 31:6-7 D 24 '66

VOICE of America (radio program)
America's voice swings a little. W. Rogers. il Look 30:46+ N 15 '66

Image; new program formula. New Repub 155:5 N 19 '66
Struggle for the world's airwaves and men's minds. il Sr Schol 87:7-9+ Ja 21 '66
Swinging voice. il Time 88:31 D 9 '66

VOICE prints. See Voiceprints

VOICEPRINTS
Now, the voiceprint. il Newsweek 67:30 Ap 25 '66
Voice from Watts; E. L. King arson charge after identification from TV interview. il Newsweek 67:68 Je 20 '66
Voiceprint introduced in court for first time. Sci N 89:293 Ap 23 '66

VOICES of spring; story. See Mitchell, D.

VOIT, W. J, rubber corporation
Automation scores in sports ball plant. il Bsns W p96-7 Ag 13 '66

VOLCANIC ash, tuff, etc.
Deep layer of sediments in Alpine Lake in the tropical mid-Pacific. A. H. Woodcock and others. bibliog il Science 154:647-8 N 4 '66

VOLCANIC rocks. See Rocks, Igneous

VOLCANOES
Hottest job on earth; volcanology. G. Kent. il Read Digest 90:184-6+ Ja '67
Mt Taal active again. il Sci N 89:310 Ap 30 '66
1965 eruption of Taal volcano. J. G. Moore and others. il Science 151:955-60 F 25 '66
Volcano that shaped the western world; Santorini eruption: theories of A. Galanopoulos. J. Lear. il Sat R 49:57-60+ N 5 '66; Discussion. 49:93-4 D 3 '66
Volcano watch proposed. il Sci N 89:311 Ap 30 '66
Volcanoes tell secrets in Hawaii. H. H. Waesche and D. L. Peck. il Natur Hist 75:20-9 Mr '66
See also
Craters
Etna, Mount
Krakatoa (island)
Mauna Kea
Mud volcanoes
Paricutin
Redoubt, Mount
Thera (island)

VOLCANOES in religion, folklore, etc.
See also
Kilauea (crater)

VOLIN, Larry K. See Bray, R. S. jt. ed.

VOLITION. See Will

VOLKSWAGEN. See Automobiles, Foreign

VOLKSWAGENWERKE, gmbh. See Automobile industry and trade—Germany (Federal Republic)

VOLLE, Robert L. See Pappano, A. J. jt. auth.

VOLLERT, Cyril
Evolution as revelation. Sat R 49:49-50 Je 4 '66

VOLLEYBALL
Another big Selznick production; G. Selznick's Sand & sea club dominated the national championships. J. Jares. il Sports Illus 24:72 My 23 '66

Anecdotes, facetiae, satire, etc.
Thank you Annette Funicello. A. Kopit. il Sat Eve Post 239:74-7 Jl 16 '66

VOLPE, E. Peter, and Gebhardt, B. M.
Evidence from cultured leucocytes of blood cell chimerism in ex-parabiotic frogs. bibliog Science 154:1197-9 D 2 '66

VOLSTEAD law. See Prohibition—United States

VOLTAGE calibrators. See Calibrators

VOLTAGE regulators
Build a zener regulated power supply. E. A. Morris. il Pop Mech 127:192-5+ Ja '67

VOLTMETERS
See also
Voltohmmeters

VOLTOHMMETERS
Effective use of the V.O.M. C. J. Diodati. il Electr World 75:82 Ap '66
VOM range splitter. J. Rossnick. il Pop Electr 26:70-1+ Ja '67

VOLUNTARY poverty. See Poverty, Voluntary

VOLUNTEER service
Awards for volunteers; Stockton, Calif. Parks & Rec 1:945 N '66
Dial Fish for help. il Time 88:70-1 O 21 '66
Expanded program of youth service? U S News 61:14 S 26 '66

VOLUNTEER service—*Continued*
First, brush off the cobwebs; college students help mentally retarded at Mansfield state training school, Conn. J. Steinberg. il Mlle 64:112-13+ D '66
Getting-involved-for-good club. H. T. Gott and M. L. Hurlburt. NEA J 55:15-16 S '66
Great free society; address, May 9, 1966. A. H. Motley. Vital Speeches 32:684-7 S 1 '66
New deal for an old problem. A. Grant. il Mlle 63:133-5+ Je '66
Our neighbors helped us rebuild out of the ashes; Negro family's house burned; ed. by L. Shecter. B. DeCausey. il Good H 162:98-9+ Je '66
Seminarians and service. R. P. Mohan. America 114:384-5 Mr 19 '66
Something more; student tutors. D. Mallery. il Sat R 49:70-1 Je 18 '66
Teen travel talk; gift of service on next summer's vacation. il Seventeen 25:140 D '66
Teenagers provide recreation for the mentally retarded. J. Lavker and N. Rosett. Parks & Rec 1:487 Je '66
Town that refused to go away. J. Bailey. il Arch Forum 125:78-81 O '66
Wanted: volunteers who mean it. P. Rifield. il Mlle 64:118-19+ D '66
Women who do things; assisting with public park and recreation programs. A. R. Kimsey. il Parks & Rec 1:836-8+ O '66
See also
Community service
English in action (organization)
Hospitals—Volunteer workers
National recreation and park association—Volunteer division
Social workers, Volunteer
Teachers aides
VOLUNTEER service, International
Exchange peace corps; foreign volunteers to help our society. T. E. Quigley. America 114:834-5 Je 11 '66
Limited response; foreign Peace corps. il Newsweek 67:46-7 F 14 '66
Peace corps; symposium. ed. by J. N. Parmer. bibliog f il Ann Am Acad 365:1-146 My '66
Reconciliation in Israel; Service of reconciliation. I. Halperin. Christian Cent 83:216-22 F 16 '66
Toward a draft without guns; universal voluntary service. H. Wofford. Sat R 49:19-21+ O 15 '66
Voluntary service for all youth; address, May 19, 1966. R. S. McNamara. Vital Speeches 32:484-8 Je 1 '66
Volunteer foreign aid: M.D.s' mission to Honduras; Florida medical association. J. L. Breeling. il Todays Health 44:20-4 Jl '66
See also
International voluntary workcamps
Laymen's overseas service (organization)
United States—Peace corps
VOLUNTEER social workers. See Social workers, Volunteer
VOLUNTEER workers in education
Learning by doing; Manhattan's antipoverty Mobilization for youth program. il Time 88:98+ O 21 '66
VOLUNTEERS in service to America
Case for a National service corps. M. K. Sanders. il N Y Times Mag p 16-17+ Ag 7 '66
Conversations parents never hear; VISTA worker. il Look 30:50 S 20 '66
Fighting the poverty war on all fronts. Parks & Rec 1:888 N '66
Judy Lewis reaches people. I. Mothner. il Look 30:68-72 D 27 '66
Of many things; training for priests. T. N. Davis. America 114:815 Je 11 '66
Schools make news; grants designed to encourage the reading and owning of pleasurable books by disadvantaged children and adults. Sat R 49:63 My 21 '66
Seminarians to the Peace corps? M. McGrory. America 114:167 Ja 29 '66
This month's feature: Congress & the Johnson poverty program. Cong Digest 45:72 Mr '66
VISTA, on a cloudy day. A. Kopkind. New Repub 154:17-18 Mr 19 '66
VOLUSIA COUNTY, Fla.
I guess we're just impatient: PRIDE projects. P. Mann. il Am Ed 2:5-7 Mr '66
VON ARX, William S.
Level-surface profiles across the Puerto Rico Trench. bibliog Science 154:1651-4 D 30 '66

VON BORSTEL, R. C.
Yeast genetics. Science 152:1287-8 My 27 '66
VON BRAUN, Wernher
Astronauts get a tool kit. por Pop Sci 189:146-7+ O '66
Beating the perils of manned space flight. Pop Sci 188:118-20 Ap '66
Bonanzas on the way to the moon. por Pop Sci 188:106-7+ Mr '66
For astronauts in trouble, this way out. por Pop Sci 188:72-4+ My '66
Lifeboats in space. por Pop Sci 189:96-7+ S '66
Living room in orbit. por Pop Sci 189:84-5+ Ag '66
Man on the moon in '68? interview. por U S News 61:62-7 D 12 '66
Photo spacecraft to circle moon. por Pop Sci 188:92-3+ Je '66
Practicing a moon landing on earth. Pop Sci 188:98-9+ F '66
These spacecraft say ouch! por Pop Sci 189:76-7+ Jl '66
What we'll do on the moon. por Pop Sci 189:90-2+ N '66
VONDERSCHMITT, B. V. and Sanquini, R. L.
Linear integrated circuits. Electr World 76:23-6+ N '66
VON DREELE, W. H.
Adam Clayton Powell; poem. Nat R 19:37 Ja 10 '67
Bird watching; poem. Nat R 18:1254 D 13 '66
Further signs of decline; poem. Nat R 18:713 Jl 26 '66
School days; poem. Nat R 18:1104 N 1 '66
Sea around us; Good times comin'; poems. Nat R 18:1205, 1217 N 29 '66
Season's greetings; poem. Nat R 18:1307 D 27 '66
Who's for open housing? poem. Nat R 19:12 Ja 10 '67
VON ECKARDT, Wolf
City as it is. New Repub 155:37-9+ N 5 '66
New York's trade center, world's tallest fiasco. Harper 232:94-8+ My '66
Shaper of things to come. Holiday 40:110+ Ag '66
VON HUENE, R. E. See Hamilton, E. L. jt. auth.
VON KRONENBERGER, G. R.
What to do when lightning strikes. Read Digest 89:169-70+ S '66
VON MISES, Ludwig
Wilhelm Roepke, RIP. Nat R 18:200 Mr 8 '66
VONNEGUT, Bernard, and Weyer, J. R.
Luminous phenomena in nocturnal tornadoes. bibliog Science 153:1213-20; 155:32 S 9 '66, Ja 6 '67
VONNEGUT, Kurt, 1922-
Kurt Vonnegut on target. C. D. B. Bryan. New Repub 155:21-2+ O 8 '66
VON NEUMANN, John
Thinker's dream; excerpts from Theory of self-producing automata. Sat R 49:56 S 3 '66
VON RECKLINGHAUSEN, Daniel R.
Automatic stereo multiplex demodulators. Electr World 76:32-3+ Jl '66
VON SCHLEGELL, David
Controlled: exhibition of Radio-controlled sculpture at the Whitney museum. New Yorker 42:42 Ap 16 '66
VON SCHMELING, B. and Kulka, Marshall
Systemic fungicidal activity of 1,4-oxathiin derivatives. Science 152:659-60 Ap 29 '66
VOODOO plant. See Sauromatum
VORIS, John R.
Give the elderly a chance to be useful! Christian Cent 83:1234 O 12 '66
VORSPAN, Albert
Ten ways out of the peace issue. Christian Cent 83:1029-31 Ag 24 '66
VORSTER, Balthazar Johannes
Story of race and progress in Africa's richest nation; interview. ed. by A. J. Meyers. por U S News 61:94-6+ N 14 '66
Vorster on Vorster, and race; interview. ed. by P. Webb. por Newsweek 68:55 O 17 '66
about
Balthazar Vorster; with excerpts from 1962 article by W. F. Buckley, jr. Nat R 18:971-2 O 4 '66
More of the same. il por Newsweek 68:56-7 S 26 '66
Security man. il por Time 88:34+ S 23 '66
South Africa gets a new warden. A. Delius. il Reporter 35:38-40 O 6 '66

VORSTER, Balthazar Johannes—about—*Cont.*
Tougher racial policy from a tough new leader? il por U S News 61:24 S 26 '66
What now in South Africa? Christian Cent 83:1136 S 21 '66
What Verwoerd's successor faces. Bsns W p48 S 10 '66

VOSBURGH, Frederick G.
To Gilbert Grosvenor: monthly monument twenty-five miles high. Nat Geog Mag 130: 445-87 O '66

VOSBURGH, Gilbert J. and Boylan, B. R.
Expectant mother. Redbook 127:40+ My '66

VOSKHOD (space vehicle) See Space vehicles, Russian

VOSPER, Robert G.
Library cooperation for reference and research: introduction. ALA Bul 60:1133-4 D '66
Library support; address, March 23, 1966. Vital Speeches 32:504-6 Je 1 '66

VOSS, Kurt
AF uprates satellite tracking center. Tech W 19:32-3 Jl 11 '66
Memo from the publisher. J. Claar. il por Miss & Roc 18:5 Ap 4 '66

VOSS, Virginia
Golden year for U.S. youth in Athens. Mlle 62:166-7+ F '66

VOTE, Labor. See Trade unions—Political activities

VOTERS. See Suffrage

VOTERS, Registration of
Bolstering the barriers in Connally's corral; Texas voter registration law. J. C. Evans. Christian Cent 33:487 Ap 20 '66
Is the Constitution being abolished? D. Lawrence. U S News 60:120+ Mr 21 '66
New Texas voters; Governor J. Connally's new law to avenge poll tax removal. Nation 202:381 Ap 4 '66
Some needed nudges; Supreme court upheld provisions of Voting rights act of 1965. Time 87:29-29A Mr 18 '66
Strange march through Mississippi. il U S News 60:48 Je 27 '66
Trap, not a test; Virginia asks Supreme court to outlaw voting tax. Time 87:27 F 4 '66
Vote: more people have it, how many will use it? il Sr Schol 89:14-15+ S 30 '66
Voting act upheld. Sr Schol 88:7-8 Mr 25 '66
Voting rights test; Supreme court discusses illiterate blacks. il Newsweek 67:24 Ja 31 '66

VOTING
Changing U.S. offers GOP hope. Newsweek 68:34-5 O 10 '66
New melting pot; Time essay. Time 88:30-1 D 2 '66
What can I do? D. Lawrence. U S News 61: 116 S 12 '66
What worries the voter. il Bsns W p33-4 O 29 '66
See also
Referendum
Suffrage—United States
United States—Congress—Voting
Voters, Registration of

Anecdotes, facetiae, satire, etc.
Notes and comment; advocating that polls be kept open the whole year round. New Yorker 42:47 N 19 '66

VOTING, Fraudulent. See Elections—Corrupt practices

VOTING age. See Suffrage—United States

VOULKOS, Peter H.
Ceramics, West coast; a discussion. pors Craft Horiz 26:25-8+ Je '66

VOYAGE to the stars; story. See Dorman, S.

VOYAGER (space vehicle) See Space vehicles

VOYAGER probe. See Space probes

VOYAGES
Across the western ocean, by W. T. Snaith. Review
Motor B 118:80 S '66. E. F. Haylock
Concrete of the city, the wispy dreams of the sea. M. Petersen. il Motor B 117:30-1+ My '66
Crossing the Atlantic in a 13-foot sailboat; excerpts from Tinkerbelle. R. Manry. il Harper 232:41-50 Je '66
Dalmatian coast on the cheap. S. Corbett. il Atlan 218:125-7 D '66
Final escape; David Johnstone and John Hoare missing in battle to cross Atlantic by rowboat. il Newsweek 68:54 O 31 '66

From Athens to Rome. J. Fairley. bibliog il Yachting 119:64-6+ F; 84-5+ Mr '66
Glacier ice for cocktails; passage to Newfoundland and return. M. Willey. il Yachting 120:44-5+ O '66
Heroes' reward; row from Cape Cod to Ireland's Aran Islands. Newsweek 68:56 S 19 '66
Nassau to New York, non-stop. R. E. Carter. il Yachting 119-98-100+ Ap '66
Once over heavily; passage from Newport, R.I. to Scotland aboard a motor cruiser. N. D. Hoyt. il Yachting 120:37-9+ Ag '66
Once over lightly; return passage from Europe. N. D. Hoyt. il Yachting 120:51-3+ S '66
Single-handed mania; solo voyagers. B. Robinson. il Yachting 119:73-6+ F '66
Singlehanded to Alaska. J. S. Letcher, jr. il Yachting 119:66-8+ Je '66
Stornoway progress report. M. Petersen. il Motor B 118:52+ Jl; 89+ Ag; 92-3+ S; 52+ O; 50+ N; 25+ D '66; 119:114+ Ja '67
Tinkerbelle; excerpt. R. Manry. il Read Digest 89:195-8+ Jl '66
Vacation: sailing alone to England in eleven-and-a-half-foot boat; interview. W. Willis. New Yorker 42:20-2 Jl 30 '66
We rowed across the North Atlantic; ed. by J. Atwater. J. Ridgway. il Sat Eve Post 239:30-6+ N 5 '66
We take a cruise to Bermuda. S. L. Seaton. il Motor B 117:26-7+ Je '66
With the moan of the wind and a barrel of beer; trip from England to Australia by F. Chichester. il Time 88:41 D 16 '66
See also
Cruising

VOYAGES around the world
Great white fleet, by R. A. Hart. Review
Am Heritage 17:66-7 F '66. B. Catton

VOYNICH, Wilfrid Michael
Roger Bacon and the Voynich manuscript. J. Ashbrook. il Sky & Tel 31:218-19 Ap '66

VOYNOW, Nancy K. See Bach, F. H. jt. auth.

VOZNESENSKII, Andrei
Autumn in Sigulda; poem, tr. by W. H. Auden. Sat R 49:17 My 21 '66
First frost: I am Goya; poems; tr. by S. Kunitz. New Repub 154:29 Ap 16 '66
Give me peace; poem, tr. by M. Hayward. Nation 203:162 Ag 22 '66
Her shoes; Of Stalin do not sing; poems; tr. by W. J. Smith. New Repub 154:28-9 Ap 16 '66
Last train to Malakhovka; poem, tr. by J. Garrigue. New Repub 154:26 Ap 30 '66
Laziness; poem; tr. by S. Moss. New Repub 154:29 Ap 16 '66
My Achilles heart; poem, tr. by W. H. Auden. por Newsweek 68:93 Jl 11 '66
My Achilles heart; Striptease; Ballad of the full stop; tr. by S. Kunitz. Life 60:72 Ap 1 '66
Party; poem; tr. by W. H. Auden. New Repub 154:28 Ap 16 '66
Six poems by Andrei Voznesensky; with introduction by R. Lowell. New Repub 154: 28-9 Ap 16 '66
Talk with Andrei Voznesensky; discussion. por Atlan 218:49+ Jl '66
Two poems; tr. by S. Kunitz. Atlan 218:50 Jl '66
about
Belligerent young bard. il por Time 88:70+ Jl 29 '66
Eloquent new voice in Russia. P. Young. il pors Life 60:69-71 Ap 1 '66
Step on the gas. Newsweek 68:93 Jl 11 '66
Voznesensky, and more Yevtushenko. Am Rec G 33:62 S '66

VRIES, Bernard de
Dadaists in politics. J. Lelyveld. il por N Y Times Mag p32-5+ O 2 '66

VROOM, Barbara
Hole. New Yorker 42:96-7 Ag 6 '66

VU-van-Thai
Taste for tulips. por Time 87:27 Ap 29 '66

VULGARITY
Bad dream. R. A. Schroth. America 114:699 My 14 '66
When good taste becomes bad taste. M. Mannes. McCalls 94:16+ Ja '67

VULTURES
Birds that throw stones. il Time 89:34 Ja 6 '67
See also
Condors

W

WABCO. See Westinghouse air brake company

WCAU (radio station) See Radio stations

W. E. B. DuBois clubs of America
Bunch of DuBois were whooping it up. Nat R 18:256 Mr 22 '66
DuBois clubs and the jungle. Amerca 114: 372 Mr 19 '66
Du Bois will be boys. il Newsweek 67:35 Mr 21 '66
Guilt by pronunciation; Nicholas Katzenbach's crusade against DuBois clubs. Nation 202:317 Mr 21 '66
Notes and comment; summary of statement. R. M. Nixon. New Yorker 42:41 Mr 19 '66
Subversive? Sr Schol 88:8 Mr 25 '66
Subversives list. Commonweal 84:45 Ap 1 '66
Warning to the unwary; proceedings to force W.E.B. DuBois clubs to register as a Communist front. Time 87:28 Mr 11 '66

WESCON. See Western electronics show and convention

WHO. See World health organization

W. J. Barrow research laboratory. See Barrow, W. J, research laboratory

W. J. Voit rubber corporation. See Voit. W. J. rubber corporation

WLBT, Jackson, Miss. See Television stations

WMCA (radio station) See Radio stations

WNBC (radio station) See Radio stations

WPA. See United States—Work projects administration

W. W. Norton and company, incorporated. See Norton, W. W. and company, incorporated

WABASH RIVER
Hush-a-bye, Indiana; changing of historical facts by local pride and press agentry. W. E. Wilson. il Am Heritage 18:68-71 D '66

WACKERLING, Lloyd R. See Henize, K. G. jt. auth.

WACO aircraft company
Call me a Waco. R. Weeghman. il Flying 79:40-5 D '66

WADDELL, John Henry, 1928-1966
Solar astronomer dies. G. S. Mumford. Sky & Tel 33:31 Ja '67

WADE, Ben F.
Text for tyros. Christian Cent 83:1243 O 12 '66

WADE, N. J. See Day, R. H. jt. auth.

WADE, Richard C.
Backlash in the Percy campaign. Reporter 36:37-40 Ja 12 '67

WADERS (boots) See Shoes, Rubber, plastic, etc.

WADING pools
Two toadstools and a wall of water; Montclair, Calif. S. E. Scholl. il Am City 81:94-5 Mr '66

WADING staff. See Fishing—Implements and appliances

WADSWORTH, Betty G.
Ideas from Parents' magazine's better homemaking center. See issues of Parents' magazine and better homemaking

WAESCHE, Hugh H. and Peck, D. L.
Volcanoes tell secrets in Hawaii. Natur Hist 75:20-9 Mr '66

WAETJEN, Walter B.
Prevention of failure. NEA J 55:37-40 Ap '66

WAFFLE irons
Combination waffle bakers and grills. il Consumer Bul 49:33-6 S '66

WAFFLES
After-game treat for your gang; with recipe. il Farm J 90:78 O '66
One answer is to have a waffle party. il Sunset 136:190+ Mr '66
Pancakes and waffles. il Bet Hom & Gard 44:103-4 Mr '66

WAGE differentials
Bargaining and wages in local cartage. V. J. Sheifer. il Mo Labor R 89:1076-84 O '66

WAGE payment plans
Technology and the guaranteed wage. A. M. Sullivan. Duns R 88:124 S '66
Wage calendar for 1967; with tables. C. Ward and W. Davis. Mo Labor R 89:1339-55 D '66

WAGE-price policy. See Price regulation by government—United States

WAGE stabilization. See Wages—Regulation

WAGENHEIM, Kal
Bridge to disenchantment. Nation 204:25-6 Ja 2 '67
Dominican Republic; burden of the past. Nation 203:541-4 N 21 '66
No David in sight. Nation 203:615-16 D 5 '66

WAGER, W. Warren
Roundheads and bluenoses. Nation 202:216-17 F 21 '66

WAGES
Foreign labor briefs. Mo Labor R 89:410-14, 528-31, 659-61, 774-5, 890-1, 1267-8 Ap-Ag, N '66
See also
Income
Labor cost
Non-wage payments
Overtime
Profit sharing
Salaries

Cost of living adjustments
Deferred increases and wage escalation. G. Ruben. il Mo Labor R 88:1438-41 D '65
Prevalence of escalator clauses and experience with them in the past twenty years. Mo Labor R 89:III-IV S '66
Wage calendar for 1967; with tables. C. Ward and W. Davis. Mo Labor R 89:1339-55 D '66

Economic aspects
Another look at the new economics. E. L. Dale, jr. il N Y Times Mag p50-1+ S 18 '66
Boom gives labor its '67 leverage; economists fear wage-price spiral; with editorial comment. il Bsns W p40-1, 200 My 14 '66
Guideposts. wages, and collective bargaining. J. T. Dunlop. Mo Labor R 89:630-3 Je '66
Lesser of the evils; tax boost better anti-inflation weapon than guideposts. il Bsns W p 160+ My 28 '66
Where we are and why. A. M. Ross. il Mo Labor R 89:624-9 Je '66

Regulation
AFL-CIO heads for Johnson clash. il Bsns W p57-8 F 26 '66
Desert guideposts. H. C. Wallich. Newsweek 68:82 Ag 22 '66
Flaw in the wage-price guideposts. C. A. Bliss. Harvard Bsns R 44:73-8 My '66
Game of guidelines. Nation 202:113 Ja 31 '66
Labor's political frustrations; gripes against the guideposts. A. H. Raskin. il Reporter 34:26-8+ Ap 7 '66
Soliloquy for the guideposts; interview. L. Keyserling. Duns R 88:32 S '66
Spiral cloud. il Time 87:91 F 25 '66
Taking the lid off wages? anti-guidelines opposition. il Newsweek 68:17-18 Ag 8 '66
Unions press harder against the guideposts. il Bsns W p 117-18 Mr 5 '66
Why there is talk about wage controls. il U S News 60:106+ Mr 14 '66
Year-round pay in construction? U S News 61:72 Jl 25 '66

Stabilization
See Wages—Regulation

Statistics
Footwear plant earnings in April 1965. G. L. Stelluto. il Mo Labor R 89:296-9 Mr '66
How profits could become losses. il Nations Bsns 54:37 My '66
Metropolitan area pay levels and trends in 1965. K. J. Hoffmann. il Mo Labor R 89: 22-8 Ja '66
See also
Wage differentials

Canada
Canada: the outlook for wages. U S News 61:88 O 3 '66
Wage parity with U.S. will be Canadian issue; equal pay for equal jobs big factor in bargaining. il Bsns W p 153-4+ Mr 19 '66

Europe, Western
Wages of prosperity. il Time 88:102 N 11 '66

Great Britain
How Britain is groping for a wage policy. U S News 61:116 O 24 '66
How Great Britain is trying to hold wage raises in line. U S News 60:90 My 16 '66

WAGES—Great Britain—*Continued*
Letter from Britain: inconsistency in applying incomes policy. R. Williams. Nation 203:18-19 Jl 4 '66
Letter from London. M. Panter-Downes. New Yorker 42:112+ Ag 20 '66
Paid vacations and holidays in the United Kingdom. W. Gerber. Mo Labor R 89:272-3 Mr '66
Voluntary controls on wages: what Europeans have learned. il U S News 60:78-9 Ja 31 '66
Wage freeze gets a cool reception; labor fears it will create unemployment. il Bsns W p 160+ O 15 '66
What happens when a country freezes wages. U S News 61:100+ D 12 '66

Netherlands
How the Dutch will curb wages. U S News 60:103 Je 6 '66
Voluntary controls on wages: what Europeans have learned. il U S News 60:78-9 Ja 31 '66

Russia
How Russia ranks. il Time 87:98 F 18 '66
U.S.S.R. worktime requirements for consumer purchases. E. Nash. il Mo Labor R 89:772-3 Jl '66

Southern states
Earnings and hours in southern metropolitan areas. June 1965. A. Bauman. il Mo Labor R 89:984-9 S '66

Sweden
Sweden's decision: inflation is better than strikes. il U S News 60:92+ Ap 25 '66

United States
Adaptation of labor resources to changing needs; excerpt from Manpower planning in a free society. R. A. Lester. Mo Labor R 89:245-9 Mr '66
Are limits off for pay raises? U S News 61:103 D 12 '66
Changing structure of compensation. A. Strasser. il Mo Labor R 89:953-8 S '66
Earnings and hours; tables. See issues of Monthly labor review
Getting more money now? here's what it's worth. il U S News 61:39-40+ Ag 1 '66
Gone guideposts. Time 88:65 Ag 12 '66
Is sky the limit on wage raises? il U S News 61:34-5 Ag 29 '66
Labor raises its sights on wages; consider the 3.2 per cent guideline defunct. Bsns W p64+ S 17 '66
Major collective bargaining settlements, 1965. L. M. David. il Mo Labor R 89:372-6 Ap '66
Mood is militant; union members press for wage increases. il Bsns W p47-9 S 24 '66
More—now! il Time 88:71 S 2 '66
New number to live by; General electric settlement with unions establishes 5 per cent as pattern for wage increases il Bsns W p37-8 O 22 '66
Now it's union vs. union in bids for biggest raises. il U S News 61:78-9 D 19 '66
Open door to inflation? A. H. Raskin. il Reporter 35:24-7 S 8 '66
Pay hikes due in '67. a record. U S News 61:67 D 26 '66
Payment by the hour? the week? the year? for life? A. H. Raskin. il N Y Times Mag p6-7+ S 4 '66
Pressure for big raises gets a new push. il U S News 61:118+ N 14 '66
Prices: a wage question. il Fortune 74:20+ Ag '66
Recommendation for periodic evaluation of guideposts. Mo Labor R 89:1122 O '66
Shift in unions' demands: back to living-cost raises. il U S News 60:92-3 Je 27 '66
Unions call 5 per cent a minimum for '67; win Wirtz's blessing. Bsns W p 163-4 N 26 '66
Wages in nonmetropolitan areas of two regions; Southern and North Central. A. Bauman. il Mo Labor R 89:1116-21 O '66
White House rebuff to unions; excerpts from address, October 26, 1966. G. Ackley. U S News 61:72 N 7 '66
See also
Government employees—Salaries. allowances, etc.
Minimum wage—United States
Wages—Cost of living adjustments
Wages—Regulation
Wages—Southern states
also subhead Wages and hours under names of industries. e.g. Automobile industry and trade—Wages and hours

WAGGONNER, Joe David, 1918-
Excerpt from debate. July 28. 1966. Cong Digest 45:279+ N '66
WAGMAN, Frederick H.
Wagman blasts Michigan student paper, defends Power against conflict charge; excerpts from letter. Library J 91:2296-7 My 1 '66
WAGNER, Alan
Master of style. Opera N 30:26-7 F 19 '66
WAGNER, Arthur
(ed) See Odets, C. How a playwright triumphs
WAGNER, Aubrey Joseph
Second spring stirs the TVA. il Bsns W p 112-15+ O 29 '66
WAGNER, Richard, 1813-1883
And this from Wagner's grandson! E. Helm. il por N Y Times Mag p68-9+ Je 5 '66
Completion of London's Ring; a Walküre to fulfill all promise. C. L. Osborne. Hi Fi 16:93-4+ N '66
First complete recording of a Wagner opera ever made in the U.S.A; Lohengrin. P. L. Miller. il Am Rec G 32:1104-6 Ag '66
Lohengrin. Criticism
New Yorker 42:195-6 D 17 '66
Opera N 31:6 Ja 21 '67
Opera N 31:18-20 Ja 21 '67
Sat R 49:30 D 24 '66
Sat R 50:26 Ja 7 '67
Time 88:58 D 23 '66
Lohengrin in its entirety, with the full forces of Boston. C. L. Osborne. il Hi Fi 16:83-4 S '66
Ludwig's world. H. Bailey. il Opera N 30:26-9 Mr 26 '66
Die Meistersinger von Nürnberg. Criticism
Opera N il 31:17-20 Ja 14 '67
Opera N 31:24-5 Ja 14 '67
Sat R 50:96 Ja 14 '67
New directions for the Ring. J. Culshaw. il Hi Fi 16:65-8 N '66
On records; Parsifal. Opera N 30:38 Ap 2 '66
Parsifal. Criticism
New Yorker 42:198+ Mr 19 '66
Opera N il 30:20-2 Ap 2 '66
Opera N il 30:26-7 Ap 2 '66
Sat R 49:51 Mr 26 '66
Phantom of the Festspielhaus; comp. by R. McMullen; with editorial comment. il Hi Fi 16:59-64 N '66
Records:
Lohengrin. il Opera N 31:30 N 5 '66
Tristan und Isolde. Opera N 31:34 Ja 21 '67
Die Walküre. Opera N 31:34 D 17 '66
Ring completed. R. Lawrence. Sat R 49:70-1+ O 29 '66
Strong beginning. T. H. Mulligan. il Opera N 30:24-5 Mr 26 '66
Tannhäuser. Criticism
New Yorker 42:176-7 Mr 26 '66
Opera N 30:24-5 Mr 26 '66
Opera N il 30:17-20 Mr 26 '66
Sat R 49:45 Ap 2 '66
Tristan und Isolde. Criticism
New Yorker 42:200-2 D 3 '66
Sat R 49:76 D 3 '66
Sat R 49:70 D 10 '66
Sat R 50:26 Ja 7 '67
Tristan und Isolde. C. J. Luten. il Am Rec G 33:284-8 D '66
Wagner operas on records; a discography. C. L. Osborne. Hi Fi 16:78-82+ N; 26+ D '66
Die Walküre. H. Glass. il Am Rec G 33:196-9 N '66
See also
Bayreuth festival
WAGNER, Richard, family
Family album; collection of Wagner family pictures. il Hi Fi 16:69-77 N '66
World of Wieland Wagner. E. Salzman. il Opera N 31:8-15 Ja 21 '67
WAGNER, Robert Ferdinand, 1910-
Wagner to head New York library for papers of the presidents. Library J 91:3140+ Je 15 '66
WAGNER, Victoria
Age of discovery. Parks & Rec 1:904-5 N '66
WAGNER, Wieland
And this from Wagner's grandson! E. Helm. il pors N Y Times Mag p68-9+ Je 5 '66
Obituary
Opera N por 31:28 N 19 '66
Period piece. il Time 88:58 D 23 '66
Phantom of the Festspielhaus; comp. by R. McMullen; with editorial comment. il Hi Fi 16:59-64 N '66

WAGNER, Wieland—_Continued_
Strauss vs. Wagner. A. M. Lingg. il Opera
N 31:6 D 10 '66
Wagner, legends and legacy. G. Movshon. il
Hi Fi 16:MA22-3+ O '66
World of Wieland Wagner. il pors Opera N
31:8-15 Ja 21 '67

WAGNER-Murray-Dingell bill. See Medical
service. State

WAGNERIANS; story. See Auchincloss, L.

WAGONER, David
At St Vincent de Paul's; poem. New Yorker
42:132 N 5 '66
Escape artist; poem. Sat R 49:40 Jl 9 '66
Learning to swim; poem. Sat R 49:39 S 24
'66
Night passage; poem. New Yorker 42:54 Mr
19 '66
One for the sun, one for the moon; poem.
Sat R 49:82 O 8 '66
Soles; poem. Sat R 49:102 My 7 '66
Tumbleweed; poem. Sat R 49:35 D 10 '66

WAGONER, Walter D.
Time, tide and seminary priorities. Christian Cent 83:519-21 Ap 27 '66

WAGONS
Ice wagon cometh. il Am Heritage 17:54-5
Je '66
Wagons ho! prairie schooner trips across
western Kansas. H. J. Samuels. il Travel
126:37-9+ Ag '66

WAGONS ho! (organization)
Wagons ho! prairie schooner trips across
western Kansas. H. J. Samuels. il Travel
126:37-9+ Ag '66

WAGRAIN, Austria
Christmas in Austria. H. Ehrlich. il Look
30:51-6 D 27 '66

WAHL, Arnold C.
Molecular orbital densities; pictorial studies.
bibliog Science 151:961-7 F 25 '66

WAHL, Paul
Hold still for sharper pictures. Pop Sci 189:
106-9 Ag '66
Secrets of using flash for better color pic-
tures. Pop Sci 188:140-3+ My '66
Sixty-second answers to Polaroid problems.
Pop Sci 189:144-7 Jl '66
Whose hue? PS guide to color films. Pop Sci
188:63-5+ Je '66

WAIN, John
Celtic strain. Commentary 41:89-93 Ap '66
Down our way; story. Reporter 34:34-7 Je
30 '66
Japanese modern. New Repub 155:25-8 Jl 30
'66
Lowry's subjective equipment. New Repub
154:23-4 Ja 15 '66; Correction. 154:37 F 5 '66
Mailer's America. New Repub 155:19-20 O 1
'66
Robert Penn Warren: the drama of the past.
New Repub 155:16-18 N 26 '66

WAINWRIGHT, Jonathan Mayhew
Fall of Corregidor; excerpts from Battles lost
and won; great campaigns of World war II.
H. W. Baldwin. il Am Heritage 17:19-23+
Ag '66

WAINWRIGHT, Loudon
View from here. See issues of Life
Who the gentle victims were. Life 61:18-27 Jl
29 '66

WAISMAN, Harry A. See Kerr, G. R. jt. auth.

WAIT a minim! revue. See Musical comedies,
revues, etc.—Criticisms, plots, etc.

WAIT until dark; drama. See Knott, F.

WAITERS and waitresses
Arms against Venus; topless waitresses. G.
Ace. Sat R 49:16 D 10 '66
Manhattan catches up; topless waitresses.
Newsweek 68:52 N 21 '66
Naked luncheon. G. Berriault. il Esquire 65:
96-7+ Mr '66
One man's meat; a British view of New
York waiters. A. Brien. Sat R 49:55 F 5 '66
West passes the topless test: San Francisco
scene. A. Levy. il Life 60:79-80+ Mr 11 '66

WAITRESSES. See Waiters and waitresses

WAKE, F. R.
Are parents the best sex educators? PTA Mag
61:8-10 bibliog(p35) N '66

WAKEFIELD, Dan
Confessions of a summer camper (lit'ry
division) N Y Times Mag p 10-11+ Jl
31; 22 Ag 28 '66
Incident in Jerusalem. Commentary 41:49-55
F '66
Personal voice and the impersonal eye. Atlan
217:86-90 Je '66
(ed) See Baez, J. I'm really a square

about
Free-lance. J. Epstein. Commentary 42:96-100
N '66
Tammany Hall, Spain, etc. S. Elmerl. Re-
porter 34:46-8 Je 16 '66

WAKEFIELD, George P.
Strands and stranding. Yachting 119:242-3 Mr
'66

WAKES (aerodynamics)
Gemini wake measurements may lead to
automatic docking. il Tech W 19:24-5 Jl 18
'66

WAKIN, Edward
Crisis at St John's. Sat R 49:93 Ap 16 '66
How Catholic is the Catholic college? Sat R
49:92-4+ Ap 16 '66
Religion and the schools. Sat R 49:85-6 Mr
19 '66

WAKNIN, Ben
Juliet on a ladder. Commonweal 84:96-7 Ap
15 '66

WALCOTT, Charles. See Michener, M. C. jt.
auth.

WALCOTT, Daniel H.
Good bad man. il Time 87:36 F 11 '66

WALD, George
George Wald; interview. New Yorker 42:42-
4 Ap 16 '66

about
Profess with a passion. il por Time 87:84 My
6 '66

WALDMAN, Diane
Samaras: reliquaries for St Sade. Art N 65:
44-6+ O '66
Thiebaud: eros in cafeteria. Art N 65:39-41+
Ap '66

WALDMAN, Eric
Book review. America 115:38 Jl 9 '66

WALDO LAKE
Waldo Lake. Liv Wildn 29:44 Wint '65

WALES, Jane
In my opinion. por Seventeen 25:154 Jl '66

WALES
See also
Aberfan
Coal mines and mining—Wales

WALESKI, Dorothy
Regulating student dress. NEA J 55:12-14
Ap '66

WALFORD, Roy L.
Increased incidence of lymphoma after injections of mice with cells differing at
weak histocompatibility loci. bibliog Science 152:78-80 Ap 1 '66

WALINSKY, Louis J.
Days between depression and war. Sat R 49:
37 Ap 2 '66
Keynes isn't enough. New Repub 154:14-16
Ap 16 '66

WALKER, Cora
Lady fights back. J. Horwitz. il por Look 30:
32+ O 4 '66

WALKER, Dorothea
Going places finding things: Europe's opera
houses. House & Gard 129:52-5+ Mr '66

WALKER, Franklin
To keep the pot boiling. Nation 202:105-7
Ja 24 '66

WALKER, Harry
Voice of the Pirates. J. Mann. il pors Sports
Illus 25:14-17 S 5 '66

WALKER, Iva L.
Geography as invention. Sr Schol 89:sup8 O
14 '66

WALKER, John
Celebration of masterpieces. Vogue 147:94-5+
Mr 15 '66
Washington's Byzantine empress: Mrs Robert
Bliss. Vogue 147:180-1+ F 1 '66

about
Throwing a party. por H. Brandon. Sat R
49:18+ Mr 19 '66

WALKER, Joseph A.
Best. il por Newsweek 67:38 Je 20 '66
Fall of the Valkyrie. il Time 87:29 Je 17 '66
Full story of the 2.8 seconds that killed the
XB70. K. Wheeler. il por Life 61:128-30+ N
11 '66

WALKER, Lewis Wayne. See Carr, W. H.

WALKER, Margaret
Soul-searching in Tennessee. Sat R 50:35 Ja
7 '67

WALKER, Michael J.
Lonely sentinels in dirty jobs. Sci N 90:499 D
10 '66
Seeing the unseen with infrared. Sci N 90:
273-4 O 8 '66

WALKER, Perry
Nightquest; poem. America 115:339 S 24 '66

WALKER, Robert Barney
High-stakes strategy of American tobacco. J. B. Weiner. il por Duns R 88:43-7+ N '66
WALKER, Ted
After fever; poem. New Yorker 42:62 O 15 '66
Homing pigeons; poem. New Yorker 42:54 Ap 16 '66
Lemons; poem. New Yorker 42:58 N 26 '66
On Scafell Pike; poem. New Yorker 42:36 Ag 13 '66
WALKER, Ted R. and Kiefer, J. E.
Ciliastatic components in the gas phase of cigarette smoke. bibliog Science 153:1248-50 S 9 '66
WALKER, Warren
Selecting the proper indicating light. Electr World 76:29-32+ Ag '66
WALKERS, Orthopedic
Cart made for walking: moonwalker vehicle. il Life 60:53-4 Je 17 '66
On limbs of steel; modified version of a moon walker. il Time 87:42 Je 3 '66
WALKING
Footpath in the wilderness: Mt Oglethorpe in Georgia to Mt Katahdin in Maine. D. Laker. il Travel 126:41-3 Ag '66
Hiking high; Tetons country, Wyo. F. A. Blackburn. il Liv Wildn 30:3-5 Sum '66
Togetherness on the trail; German tradition. il Time 87:32-3 F 4 '66
Trail camping. C. B. Colby. il Outdoor Life 138:96-7+ Jl '66
See also
Trails
WALKING happy; musical comedy. See Musical comedies, revues, etc.—Criticisms, plots, etc.
WALKING in sleep. See Somnambulism
WALKING sticks (insects). See Walkingsticks (insects)
WALKINGSTICKS (insects)
Nature note; walking sticks. Sci N 89:272 Ap 16 '66
WALKS (paths) See Garden walks
WALL, Carol
Foreign press in US libraries. por Library J 91:638-41 F 1 '66
WALL, E. H.
Tragic dilemma. Nat R 18:843-4 Ag 23 '66
WALL, James M.
Filmdom and demonology. Christian Cent 83:1416 N 16 '66
Movies (cont) Christian Cent 83:1474-5 N 30 '66
WALL, Marvin
See here, Mr Ambassador. Am Ed 2:21-3 Jl '66
WALL, Patrick D. and Sweet, W. H.
Temporary abolition of pain in man. bibliog Science 155:108-9 Ja 6 '67
WALL decoration. See Mural painting and decoration
WALL painting. See Mural painting and decoration
WALL paper. See Wallpaper
WALL paper, Photographic. See Photographic murals
WALL shelves. See Shelves
WALL Street Journal
Journal's daily dividend. Time 88:39 Ag 19 '66
WALL-to-wall carpeting. See Rugs and carpets
WALLABIES. See Kangaroos
WALLACE, Burt
Struck by Ford lightning. Sat R 49:86-7+ Ap 16 '66
WALLACE, DeMille L.
Religion and the public schools. Christian Cent 83:612-15 My 11 '66
WALLACE, George Corley
Alabama's Wallace: aiming at presidency? interview. por U S News 60:23 My 16 '66
Third party could be party of leverage; interview. por U S News 61:96 N 21 '66
about
Alabama's new era: the Negro votes. il por Newsweek 67:25-30 My 16 '66
Analyzing the vote and its lessons. il Newsweek 67:27 My 16 '66
Bonnet in the ring. Newsweek 67:30 F 28 '66
George's better half. por Time 87:28 Mr 4 '66
In first big test of the Negro vote. il por U S News 60:37-9 My 16 '66
In the governor's race, Lurleen sweeps on toward a Wallace dynasty. il pors Life 60:42-42A My 13 '66

Letting George do it. il por Sr Schol 88:6 My 20 '66
Mr & Mrs Wallace run for governor of Alabama. R. Jenkins. il pors N Y Times Mag p28-9+ Ap 24 '66
Pa and Ma Wallace as a dynasty. Life 60:4 Mr 11 '66
Race of the thousand clowns. H. H. Martin. il por Sat Eve Post 239:25-9 My 7 '66
Southern discomfort; satirical comment on presidential aims. G. Ace. Sat R 49:11 O 1 '66
Wallace's woes. New Repub 154:8 F 5 '66
What to expect of Wallaces now. por U S News 61:27 N 21 '66
WALLACE, Kenneth Dean
Mr Samuel and the Rockefeller premieres. Hi Fi 16:MA26+ Jl '66
New Mozart & twelve-tone captive maidens. Hi Fi 16:MA24-5 N '66
Spring opera 1966, triumph and trouble. Hi Fi 16:MA8+ Ag '66
20th-century innovations, more or less. Hi Fi 16:MA18-19+ O '66
WALLACE, Lurleen (Burns)
Alabama's new era: the Negro votes. il por Newsweek 67:25-30 My 16 '66
Analyzing the vote and its lessons. il Newsweek 67:27 My 16 '66
Best man's wife. J. Richardson. il por Esquire 66:68-71+ Jl '66
George's better half. por Time 87:28 Mr 4 '66
In first big test of the Negro vote. il por U S News 60:37-9 My 16 '66
In the governor's race, Lurleen sweeps on toward a Wallace dynasty. il pors Life 60:42-42A My 13 '66
Let George do it. por Time 87:24 My 13 '66
Letting George do it. il por Sr Schol 88:6 My 20 '66
Mr & Mrs Wallace run for governor of Alabama. R. Jenkins. il pors N Y Times Mag p28-9+ Ap 24 '66
On the lookout for Lurleen. S. Alexander. Life 61:19 Jl 22 '66
Pa and Ma Wallace as a dynasty. Life 60:4 Mr 11 '66
Race of the thousand clowns. T. H. Martin. il por Sat Eve Post 239:25-9 My 7 '66
Wallace-ism is what Alabama (white) wants. P. Watters. New Repub 154:7 My 14 '66
What to expect of Wallaces now. por U S News 61:27 N 21 '66
Which is the better half? Reporter 34:20 Mr 24 '66
Who's in charge here? il pors Newsweek 69:24 Ja 9 '67
Why I feel sorry for Lurleen Wallace and Alabama. L. I. Smylie. por Ladies Home J 83:64+ S '66
WALLACE, Mary
Brendan; story; excerpt. McCalls 93:74-7 F '66
Island; story. McCalls 93:88-9 Ag '66
Magic morning in Massachusetts. Sat R 49:47-9 Je 18 '66
WALLACE, Mary C.
Swans into Larks. H. Gilbert. il por Library J 91:2780-2 Je 1 '66
WALLACE, Robert
Down from the forked hill unsullied. Poetry 108:121-4 My '66
It; poem. Harper 232:53 My '66
Like the Achaean gift: full of murder; poem. Sat R 49:34 D 17 '66
Moving; poem. Reporter 35:59 N 17 '66
Ungainly things; poem. Reporter 35:56 O 6 '66
about
What we are, and are not. B. Cutler. Poetry 108:270-1 Jl '66
WALLACH, Lew
Face to face. por Seventeen 25:143 O '66
WALLANT, Edward Lewis
Prisoner of time. R. A. Schroth. America 115:98 Jl 23 '66
WALLBANK, Alfred M. and others
1-Adamantanamine hydrochloride: inhibition of rous and esh sarcoma viruses in cell culture. bibliog Science 152:1760-1 Je 24 '66
WALLBOARD
It's easier to install the new plasterboard; gypsum wallboard. H. Pfister. il Pop Sci 189:164-8 S '66
WALLENDA family. See Acrobats and acrobatism
WALLENSTEIN, Alfred Franz
Wallenstein's Beethoven. T. Heinitz. Sat R 50:107 Ja 14 '67

WALLER, Kim Kurt
College readiness program of east Harlem.
Sat R 49:90-1+ Ap 16 '66
WALLER, Thomas
Comic mask of Fats Waller. M. Williams.
il por Sat R 49:63 Mr 26 '66
WALLEYE fishing. See Perch fishing
WALLIS, Allen
Wallis on Lowry. Atlan 217:50 Mr '66
WALLOON language question. See Belgium—
Languages
WALLPAPER
Basic guide to wallpapering. il Good H 162:167
My '66
How to shop for wallpaper. Bet Hom & Gard
44:108-9 O '66
New ways with walls. R. Charles. il Parents
Mag 41:90-5+ Ag '66
News is in the papers; new designs. il
McCalls 94:62-7+ Ja '67
Paysage inconnu; scenic wallpaper in Cam-
bridge historical society of Cambridge, Mass.
il Antiques 90:694-5 N '66
Removable wall coverings. il House & Gard
129:58-9 Mr '66
Wallpaper; op art, pop art, paisley & chintz.
il Changing T 20:17-18 Ap '66
Wallpaper whizz-ardry. M. White. il Ladies
Home J 83:78-83 Ap '66
WALLS
Demand for bigger spans has brought back
the bearing wall and also led to practical
solutions for bold cable structures. il Arch
Rec 140:156-7 Jl '66
How materials react to solar energy. J. I.
Yellott. il Arch Rec 139:196-8 My '66
Masonry bearing wall for residential scale.
il Arch Rec 140:138-9 N '66
Two rooms from one. il Pop Mech 126:137-42+
D '66
See also
Paneling
Storage walls
Wallboard
WALLS (fortifications)
Humpty-dumpty fixation; walls in history.
P. W. Schmidtchen. il Hobbies 71:104-5+
Ja '67
WALLS, Concrete
Easy but elegant patio wall. il Pop Mech
126:128-9 Ag '66
WALLS, Glass
Cedar and glass build a dramatic house in the
Pacific Northwest. il House & Gard 130:
258-65+ N '66
WALNER, Robert
Johnson's choice. New Repub 154:37-8 Mr 19
'66
WALNUT Creek Leisure World, Calif. See
Aged—Housing
WALNUT trees
Gross $100 an acre from black walnut. Farm J
90:68J Mr '66
Money tree; black walnut trees. il Am For
72:33 O '66

Diseases and pests
This fly makes it harder to husk a walnut;
walnut husk fly. il Sunset 137:156 Jl '66
WALSH, Bryan O.
Cubans in Miami. America 114:286-9 F 26 '66
WALSH, Chad
Pros and cons of paradise. Sat R 49:36-7 Jl 30
'66
Spacechild's revery; poem. Cath World 204:
218 Ja '67
Walking with a young grandson; poem.
Reporter 34:48 Mr 24 '66
White on white; poem. America 114:262 F 19
'66
WALSH, F. J.
Planning for reliable electric power. Arch
Rec 139:187-92 F; 185-8 Mr '66
WALSH, James Edward, bp
Call for release of American prisoners held by
Communist China; address, May 7, 1966.
W. P. Bundy. Dept State Bul 54:866-9
My 30 '66
WALSH, Jim
Favorite pioneer recording artist. See issues
of Hobbies
WALSH, Joan
News and views; excerpts from Cosmopolitan
magazine article, What it's like to be a
Catholic girl. Commonweal 83:682 Mr 18 '66
WALSH, Moira
Films. See issues of America
WALSH, Richard
First congress of the poor. R. A. Cloward
and R. M. Elman. il Nation 202:150-1 F 7
'66

WALSH, William B.
Yanqui, come back! the voyage of the S.S.
Hope to Peru; condensation. Read Digest
89:237-40+ D '66
WALT, Lewis W.
Men who run the war. por Newsweek 68:53
D 5 '66
WALTER, Bruno
Living heritage of Bruno Walter. J. Lyons.
il por Am Rec G 32:1107 Ag '66
WALTER, Claire
Boston. U S Camera 29:60-1+ O '66
Mission. U S Camera 29:16-17 Mr '66
WALTER, Eugene
Monica Vitti. Vogue 147:122-5+ F 15 '66
WALTER, James Willis
House that Jim built. R. Levy. por Duns R
87:51-2 My '66
WALTER Kidde and company. See Kidde, Wal-
ter, and company
WALTERS, Barbara
How now, Princess Grace? por Ladies Home
J 83:65 N '66
Steering a Ford marriage. por Ladies Home J
83:67 S '66
(ed) See Javits. M. Will Marion Javits move
the White House to New York
about
Early to rise, wealthy and wise. il pors
Life 60:49-50+ F 18 '66
WALTERS, David R. and Williams, C. M.
Reaggregation of insect cells as studied by
a new method of tissue and organ culture.
bibliog Science 154:516-17 O 28 '66
WALTERS, Everett
Identifying the excellent. Sat R 49:75-6 Je
18 '66
WALTERS, R. W. Jr
How to keep the go-getters. Nations Bsns
54:47+ Je '66
WALTERS, Raymond, Jr
Nation's principles in practice. Sat R 49:35-
6 N 5 '66
WALTERS, Richard H.
Implications of laboratory studies of aggres-
sion for the control and regulation of
violence. bibliog f Ann Am Acad 364:60-72
Mr '66
WALTNER, E. J.
Doctor of spinning wheels. W. Waltner and
E. Waltner. il pors Pop Mech 125:110-12
Mr '66
WALTNER, Elma, and Waltner, Willard
500-hog setup for $7,500. Farm J 90:50N+
S '66
—See Waltner, W. jt. auth.
WALTNER, Willard, and Waltner, Elma
Doctor of spinning wheels. Pop Mech 125:
110-12 Mr '66
Three pull-apart pull toys. Pop Mech 126:
143-5 D '66
—See Waltner, E. jt. auth.
WALTON, Harry
Amazing new cone drive is clutch, transmis-
sion, differential. Pop Sci 188:59-62+ Je '66
They've thrown away the carb on new
Sears mower. Pop Sci 188:154-6 Je '66
—See Brown, R. L. jt. auth.
WALTON, Mae S. See Mendel, J. L. jt. auth.
WALTON, Richard Rhodes
Expert's blueprint for successful inventing;
interview, ed. by C. P. Gilmore. pors Pop
Mech 126:102-5+ D '66
WALTON, William
Parnassus on Potomac. Art N 65:36-9+ Mr
'66
Washington's unknown memorials; excerpts
from Evidence of Washington. Arch
Forum 125:60-5 N '66
about
Four score and seven hours ago. R. S. Gal-
lagher. il Horizon 8:38-9 Aut '66
WALTZ, Jon R.
Equality and the court. Sat R 49:40-1 Mr 12
'66
WAMSLEY, Howard
Archaist; poem. Poetry 107:303-5 F '66
Speeding hackney cabriolet. Poetry 109:185-
7 D '66
WANDRES, J.
Akihabara; Tokyo's radio row. Pop Electr
24:54-5 My '66
WANDRUS, Harry
Obituary
Hobbies 70:52 F '66
WANEBO, Harold J. and others
Paraproteinemia and reticulum cell sarcoma
in an inbred mouse strain. bibliog Science
154:901-3 N 18 '66

WANG, Ching-hsien
Two poems by Wang Ching-hsien: On the way home; Quemoy, winter 1963. Mlle 64: 118 N '66

WANG, H. H. and others
Periventricular cerebral impedance after intraventricular injection of calcium. bibliog Science 154:1183-5 D 2 '66

WANG, Yung-ching
Tiger in plastics. il por Fortune 74:44 Jl 1 '66

WANKEL engines. See Automobile engines; Gas and oil engines

WANNER, James F.
Visual binary Krüger 60. Sky & Tel 33:16-17 Ja '67

WAPITI hunting. See Elk hunting

WAR
Can we control the war in Vietnam? what history tells us about limited conflicts. H. S. Commager. Sat R 49:25-7 S 17 '66
Great wars as living history. R. F. Allen. Sr Schol 89:sup 14-15 N 18 '66
Peace and war, by R. Aron. Review
New Yorker 42:117-22 Ja 14 '67. G. Steiner
See also
Aggression (international law)
Atomic warfare
Chemical warfare
Conscientious objectors
Gases in warfare
Guerrilla warfare
International security
Military art and science
Military preparedness
Pacifism
Peace

Economic aspects
Bad business of war prosperity. il Bsns W p 144+ Ag 13 '66
If you are worried about war's cost. il U S News 61:46 S 26 '66

Moral aspects
Morality of war; Time essay. Time 89:40-1 Ja 20 '67
Navy chaplaincy: muzzled ministry; cooperation without compromise. N. MacFarlane. Christian Cent 83:1338-9 N 2 '66
Overriding moral issues of modern warfare; pastoral letter, June 28, 1966. L. J. Shehan. Cath World 203:365-7 S '66
Peace and modern war in the judgment of the church, by K. Hörmann. Review
Cath World 204:186-7 D '66. M. V. Gannon
Peace, war and the Vatican council. T. M. Finn. Cath World 203:270-5 Ag '66
Sincerity or sophistry? Commonweal 83:598-9 F 25 '66
So you don't remember Pearl Harbor? D. V. Gallery. il Pop Mech 126:84-6+ D '66
See also
Atomic warfare—Ethical aspects
Vietnamese war, 1957- —Moral and religious aspects
War, Ethics of

Psychological aspects
See also
Fighting (psychology)
Vietnamese war, 1957- — Psychological aspects

Social aspects
Vietnam and the crisis in war. D. Graham. Yale R 55:391-402 Mr '66

Terminology
Name of the game; operations code names. Newsweek 67:26 Mr 21 '66

WAR, Causes of
Tragic flaw; connections between cause and effect. N. Cousins. Sat R 49:22 F 12 '66
World politics and tension areas, by F. Gross. Review
Sat R 49:53 Je 11 '66. H. H. Ransom

WAR, Ethics of
Ethics and Vietnam. C. C. Richardson; R. K. Anderson; C. F. Hass. Christian Cent 83:1118+ S 14 '66

WAR aims
See also
Vietnamese war, 1957- —War aims

WAR and children
Crop destruction in Vietnam; letter. J. Mayer. Science 152:291 Ap 15 '66
Vietnam's wounded waifs; appeal by the Swiss organization, Terre des hommes. M. Hope. Christian Cent 83:1111-12 S 14 '66

WAR and economics. See War—Economic aspects

WAR and education
Revolution in peace education; Clark-Sohn plan and the World law fund. R. A. Falk. il Sat R 49:59-61+ My 21 '66

WAR and libraries. See Libraries and war

WAR and literature
Heroes' twilight, by B. Bergonzi. Review
Commonweal 84:443-4 Jl 8 '66. B. McCabe
New Repub 154:21-4 F 5 '66
Profiles. H. Arendt. New Yorker 42:68-70+ N 5 '66

WAR and morals. See War—Moral aspects

WAR and religion
Appeal to American citizens; statement issued by the Japanese fellowship of reconciliation, December 10, 1965. Christian Cent 83:114 Ja 26 '66
Chaplaincy vs. mission in a secular age. W. R. Miller. Christian Cent 83:1335-7 N 2 '66
Churches and Vietnam. G. Harkness. Christian Cent 83:111-13 Ja 26 '66
Escalation, seen from Japan. S. H. Franklin. Christian Cent 83:1409-10 N 16 '66; Discussion. 83:1543 D 14 '66
Korea, 1951; Vietnam, 1966; reprint, with painting. D. Lawrence. U S News 61:48-9 Ag 22 '66
Message to the churches; adopted by the National council of churches general board. Christian Cent 83:114-15 Ja 26 '66
Moral stance and political action. R. L. Holmes. Christian Cent 83:776-7 Je 15 '66
N.C.C. general board takes peace-oriented action. Christian Cent 83:293 Mr 9 '66
Open letter to the N.C.C. from the Japan Christian council for peace in Vietnam. Christian Cent 83:430 Ap 6 '66
Priority program on peace? of NCC. P. Peachey. Christian Cent 83:959-61 Ag 3 '66
Problems of peacemaking. W. V. Kennedy. America 114:855-7 Je 18 '66
Religion and war. J. V. Schall. Commonweal 85:193-6 N 18 '66; Discussion. 85:303-4, 311+ 335+ D 9-23 '66
Theology of nonresistance. V. Eller. Christian Cent 83:1534-7 D 14 '66; Discussion. 84:80-1 Ja 18 '67
Vatican II: anathema upon war; cases of Italian conscientious objectors. E. M. Borgese. il Nation 202:415-21 Ap 11 '66
War and peace and the American Catholic. W. V. O'Brien. Cath World 202:331-5 Mr '66
Wednesdays in Washington; churchmen to share with their congressmen concern about the war in Vietnam. Christian Cent 83:518 Ap 27 '66
W.C.C. central committee speaks out on Vietnam. Christian Cent 83:262 Mr 2 '66
See also
National emergency committee of clergy concerned about Vietnam
Vietnamese war, 1957- —Moral and religious aspects

WAR booty. See Booty

WAR correspondents
See also
Vietnamese war, 1957- —War correspondents

WAR crime trials. See Nuremberg trials

WAR damage compensation. See Vietnamese war, 1957- —Compensation of non-combatants

WAR debts. See Debts, Public

WAR; drama. See Van Itallie, J. C.

WAR films. See Moving pictures—War films

WAR finance

United States
See also
Taxation—United States

WAR games
Sensors developed in simulated war area; USAF's Project Underbrush. G. Alexander. il Aviation W 85:34-5 mid-D '66

WAR graves. See Service mens graves

WAR in fiction. See War in literature

WAR in literature
Separate peace; concerning J. Knowles' novel, A separate peace. R. A. Schroth. America 114:356 Mr 12 '66

WAR inventions. See Inventions

WAR marriages
Honorable estate; boom in U.S.-Vietnamese marriages. il Newsweek 68:31 Ag 8 '66

WAR materials
See also
Strategic materials
Vietnamese war, 1957- —Equipment and supplies
WAR memorials
To each his own; memorial on Guam. Newsweek 68:32 D 5 '66
Tribute garden. Mrs G. Smith. il Horticulture 44:49 O '66
WAR objectors. See Conscientious objectors
WAR on poverty (program) See Anti-poverty program, 1964-
WAR poetry
On Randall Jarrell. R. W. Flint. Commentary 41:79-81 F '66
See also
Vietnamese war, 1957- —Poetry
WAR profiteering. See Black markets
WAR propaganda. See Moving pictures—Propaganda films
WAR slang. See Slang
WAR songs
See also
Vietnamese war, 1957- —Songs and music
WAR supplies
See also
Vietnamese war, 1957- —Equipment and supplies
WAR surplus. See Surplus products
WAR tax (United States) See Taxation—United States
WAR taxation. See Taxation—United States
WAR toys. See Toys
WAR veterans. See Service men, Discharged
WARBLERS
Warbler of the jack pines. H. Titus. il Field & S 71:51+ My '66
WARBURG, Eric
Warburgs. il por Time 87:98 Ap 29 '66
WARBURG, S. G. and company. See London—Banks
WARBURG, Siegmund George
Profiles. J. Wechsberg. New Yorker 42:45-8+ Ap 9 '66
Warburgs. il por Time 87:98 Ap 29 '66
WARBURG family
Profiles. J. Wechsberg. New Yorker 42:45-8+ Ap 9 '66
WARD, A. Dudley
Creative venture in housing. Christian Cent 83:491-3 Ap 20 '66
WARD, Aileen
When two ships ruled the waves. Reporter 34:53-4 Mr 24 '66
WARD, Arthur Sarsfield. See Rohmer, S. pseud.
WARD, Barbara (Lady Jackson)
Stevenson memorial. Sat R 49:19 Jl 9 '66
WARD, Clark Gable
Houston's compassionate assistant DA. il pors Ebony 21:49-50+ Mr '66
WARD, Clint
Complete skiing boat. Motor B 118:25-6 Jl '66
WARD, Douglas Turner
Day of absence. Criticism
Commonweal 84:440 Jl 8 '66
Life 60:10 Ja 28 '66
Reporter 34:47-8 F 24 '66
Sat R 49:41 Je 25 '66
Happy ending. Criticism
Commonweal 84:440 Jl 8 '66
Life 60:10 Ja 28 '66
Reporter 34:47-8 F 24 '66
Sat R 49:41 Je 25 '66
WARD, Fred
Back of the car should have read, just photographed. il Pop Phot 59:88+ D '66
WARD, Lyla Blake
Youth hostile; poem. McCalls 93:149 Mr '66
WARD, Muriel
Mr Lazy man's family; drama. Plays 26:45-56, 96 Ja '67
WARD, Paul L.
History with spirit of inquiry; excerpts from address, November 1966. por Sr Schol 89:sup 14 D 9 '66
WARD, Ross J.
Great American West in miniatures. por Hobbies 71:122-3 S '66
WARD, William
Warm and the cool of it. il U S Camera 29:62-3 Mr '66
WARD, William J. Jr
Facelift for your front door. Pop Sci 188:156-64 Ap '66
WARD foods, incorporated
New baker adds yeast to Ward. il Bsns W p80-2+ Jl 16 '66

WARDENS, Game. See Game wardens
WARDROBES. See Closets
WARDWELL, Allen
One hundred years of American tankards. Antiques 90:80-3 Jl '66
WARE, Martha L. See Lillywhite, R. L. jt. auth.
WAREHOUSES
Full regional distribution is a hit at McGraw-Hill. il Pub W 191:22-7 Ja 2 '67
Warehouse for weekends; warehouse in Connecticut restored. B. Plumb. il N Y Times Mag p76-7+ Mr 13 '66
Warehouses and distribution centers. il Arch Rec 140:121-5 D '66
Wizard of the warehouse. R. Levy. il Duns R 87:49-50 My '66
WARFARE. See Military art and science
WARFARE, Mechanized. See Mechanization, Military
WARFARE, Submarine. See Submarine warfare
WARFIELD, Rebecca
Have you read any good legs lately? Vogue 148:98+ Jl '66
Strange rapture worth billions. Mlle 63:130-3+ O '66
WARGA, Wayne
I really didn't know much about evolution. Life 61:98 D 9 '66
WARHOL, Andy
Warhol: the silver tenement. D. Antin. il Art N 65:47-9+ Sum '66
WARHOL, Julia
Andy Warhol's mother. B. Weinraub. pors Esquire 66:99+ N '66
WARING, James
Reviews: production at East 74th street theatre. M. Marks. Dance Mag 40:23 F '66
WARING, Michael, and Britten, R. J.
Nucleotide sequence repetition: a rapidly reassociating fraction of mouse DNA. bibliog Science 154:791-4 N 11 '66
WARNCKE, Ruth
Careers in librarianship. ALA Bul 60:805-9 S '66
WARNER, Aaron W.
Future of maritime manpower. Mo Labor R 89:268-71 Mr '66
WARNER, Denis
Australia votes to stay in Vietnam. Reporter 35:29-31 D 29 '66
Behind the battlefront: a search for stability. Reporter 34:25-9 F 24 '66
Divided Buddhists of South Vietnam. Reporter 34:22-4 Je 16 '66
Does Vietnam need a supreme commander? Reporter 34:11-15 Je 30 '66
Ho Chi Minh trail and our Thai buildup. Reporter 34:26-8 Ja 27 '66
Indonesia's unfinished revolution. Reporter 35:28-9+ Jl 14 '66
New man in Canberra. Reporter 34:33-6 Ap 21 '66
President Marcos and the Huk resurgence. Reporter 35:28-31 N 3 '66
Showdown in Danang. Reporter 34:14-16 Je 2 '66
Singapore and Malaysia: a divorce of inconvenience. Reporter 34:44-6 Ap 7 '66
Small, hard war in the Delta. Reporter 35:27-8+ D 15 '66
South Vietnam's political awakening. Reporter 35:40-3 N 17 '66
Vietnam prepares for elections. Reporter 35:12-15 Ag 11 '66
Vietnam: the ordeal of pacification. Reporter 35:24-8 D 1 '66
WARNER, Donald T.
Structure of cell membranes at the molecular level. Science 153:324-6 Jl 15 '66
WARNER, Jack Leonard
Last tycoon. il por Newsweek 68:88 N 28 '66
WARNER, John
Terrifying immediacy. Sat R 49:100 Ap 16 '66
WARNER, Ken
Antique outboards too frisky to retire. Pop Mech 125:142-4+ Mr '66
Gardens for free. Pop Mech 125:104-6 Je '66
Sarasota mystery. Pop Electr 24:50-3 Mr; 48 Ap '66
Swinging fisherman. Pop Mech 125:110-11 Ap '66
Which type of home freezer for you? Pop Mech 125:140-1+ F '66
WARNER, Leslie Harry
Warner of General telephone & electronics. por Fortune 73:51 Je '66

WARNER, Sylvia Townsend
Candles; story. New Yorker 41:38-41 F 5 '66
Item, one empty house. New Yorker 42:131-2+ Mr 26 '66
Oxenhope; story. New Yorker 42:25-9 Jl 9 '66
Winding stair, a fox hunt, a fulfilling situation, some sycamores, and the church at Henning. New Yorker 42:38-41 F 26 '66

about

Mastery of Miss Warner. J. Updike. New Repub 154:23-5 Mr 5 '66; Correction. 154:40 Mr 26 '66

WARNER, Winthrop L.
Designer's comments. Yachting 119:76 Je '66

WARNER brothers pictures, Incorporated
Last tycoon; agreement in principle to sell stock to Seven arts productions, ltd. il Newsweek 68:88 N 28 '66

WARNER-Lambert pharmaceutical company
Contract that left the lawyers breathless; 1881 royalty agreement on Listerine mouthwash. il Bsns W p 122+ Ag 20 '66
Riches from royalties; royalty arrangement on Listerine antiseptic. il Time 88:92 D 16 '66
Suffering from seizure; Peritrate seizure by FDA. il Time 87:90 Mr 11 '66
Warner-Lambert's new math. R. Levy. Duns R 87:49-50 Ap '66

WARNICK, Dorothy Brant
Grounds for travel. Travel 126:46-9+ O '66

WARNING labels. See Labels

WARNKE, Frank J.
Voyages of Elizabeth Bishop. New Repub 154: 19-21 Ap 9 '66

WARNOCK, M. J.
Stretch of the imagination; address, December 7, 1965. Vital Speeches 32:234-7 F 1 '66

WARRANTY
Do you save home equipment warranties? Bet Hom & Gard 44:8 Jl '66
How warranties work. M. Lamm. Motor T 18:124 N '66
Personal business; 1967 car warranties. Bsns W p 165 O 8 '66
What are your rights under warranty? questions and answers. E. Rosen. il Motor T 18:33-4 My '66
Which guarantee do you use? FTC case against Montgomery Ward & co. Consumer Rep 31:472 O '66

WARREN, Albert
Coming cable TV war. Sat R 49:90+ Je 11; 58 Ag 13 '66

WARREN, Austin
New England saint. S. Paul. Nation 203:647-8 D 12 '66

WARREN, David B.
American decorative arts in Texas. Antiques 90:796-815 D '66

WARREN, Earl
Pro and con: here's what the justices said; excerpts from majority opinion. por U S News 60:34-6 Je 27 '66
World peace through law; address, March 12, 1966. Vital Speeches 32:387-90 Ap 15 '66

about

Honorable Earl Warren. J. D. Weaver. por Holiday 39:76-7+ Ap; 76-7+ My; 56-7+ Je '66
Is the Warren court too political? A. M. Bickel. il N Y Times Mag p30-1+ S 25 '66; Reply. F. Rodell. p22 O 16 '66
It is the Earl Warren court. F. Rodell. il pors N Y Times Mag p30-1+ Mr 13 '66; Discussion. p22+ Mr 27; 6 Ap 3 '66
Washington: ten of its most powerful men. por Vogue 148:151 N 15 '66

WARREN, Frank A. 3d
Liberalism: opportunity from impasse. Nation 202:238-41 F 28 '66

WARREN, James C. and Peterson, D. M.
Structure-disrupting ions: detection of qualitative change in an enzyme. bibliog Science 152:1245-6 My 27 '66

WARREN, Leonard
Lasting tribute: memorials to three great singers. il Opera N 31:30-1 O 15 '66

WARREN, Lesley Ann
[Mademoiselle's Merit award winner] por Mlle 62:49 Ja '66

WARREN, Robert Penn
Homage to Emerson, on a night flight to New York; poem. New Yorker 42:30-1 Jl 16 '66
Malcolm X: mission and meaning. Yale R 56: 161-71 D '66

Notes on a life to be lived; poem. New Yorker 41:30 F 12 '66
Patriotic tour and postulate of joy; poem. New Yorker 41:28 Ja 22 '66
Saul; poem. Yale R 55:481-7 Je '66
Three poems by Robert Penn Warren: Dream of a dream the small boy had; Two poems about suddenly and a rose; Love: two vignettes. Sat R 49:21 Ag 13 '66

about

Robert Penn Warren: the drama of the past. J. Wain. New Repub 155:16-18 N 26 '66

WARREN, Virginia
No lid on learning. Am Ed 3:25-6 D '66

WARREN, William
Most beautiful word in English? Bangkok says. progress. N Y Times Mag p 18-19+ Ag 7 '66

WARREN report. See United States— President's commission on the assassination of President Kennedy

WARSAW
Report from a surrealist capital. K. Botsford. il N Y Times Mag p58-9+ S 11 '66; Reply. A. N. Oakes. p 122 O 23 '66

Description

Encounter in Warsaw. F. Russell. Nat R 18: 430-2 My 3 '66

Intellectual life

Encounter in Warsaw. F. Russell. Nat R 18: 430-2 My 3 '66

Music

New house, old problems. P. Heyworth. Hi Fi 16:146 F '66
Notes from our correspondents. E. Helm. Hi Fi 16:20+ Ap '66

Theater

Warsaw. T. Andrew. il Dance Mag 40:62-3 Ap '66

WARSAW convention
United States and the Warsaw convention; statements, February 1, 14, 1966. A. F. Lowenfeld. il Dept State Bul 54:580-8 Ap 11 '66
U.S. to continue adherence to Warsaw convention; Department announcement; with text of United States note. Dept State Bul 54:955-7 Je 13 '66

WARSAW pact, 1955
Rumania rocks the boat; calls for changes in Warsaw treaty. il Newsweek 67:46+ My 30 '66
Show of unity; summit conference in Bucharest. il Newsweek 68:34+ Jl 18 '66
Tattered and torn. Newsweek 67:46-7 Je 27 '66

WARSHIPS

Electronic equipment

Radar/sonar monitor tested for ships. R. Pay. il Miss & Roc 18:39-40 Ap 4 '66

Great Britain

Annals of the sea: biggest battleship in the world: dreadnought Argincourt. R. Hough. il New Yorker 42:41-4+ Ag 20 '66

United States

Congressman opposes FY '68 funding for FDLS program; fast deployment logistics ships. H. M. David. Tech W 20:16-17 Ja 16 '67
Navy readies rfp's for new assault ship; LHA amphibious assault ship. il Tech W 19:14 D 5 '66
New job for old battleships? il U S News 62:12 Ja 23 '67
Proud new victory for navy destroyer; USS Taussig under command of Negro skipper. il Ebony 21:25-8+ Jl '66
Radar/sonar monitor tested for ships: ASW destroyer escorts. R. Pay. il Miss & Roc 18: 39-40 Ap 4 '66
Wide gains for shipbuilding seen in FDLS; fast deployment logistics ships. M. Getler. il Tech W 19:14-16 Ag 15 '66

WARSHIPS, Atomic powered
Atomic fleet: navy chief vs. McNamara. il U S News 60:20 Je 13 '66
Battle for a nuclear navy: will McNamara or Congress win? il U S News 60:44-6 Je 27 '66
Conferees drop bid to force building of nuclear frigates. Tech W 19:17 Jl 4 '66

WARSHIPS, Atomic powered—*Continued*
Creation of a nuclear navy; address. January 17, 1966. C. Holifield. Vital Speeches 32: 261-4 F 15 '66
Rickover vs. McNamara on a nuclear navy; excerpts from testimony. June 23, 1966. H. G. Rickover. U S News 61:10-11 Jl 4 '66
Times of crisis. W. J. Coughlin. Miss & Roc 18:54 My 9 '66
See also
Submarine boats, Atomic powered

WARSHOFSKY, Fred
Beware the deadly man-of-war! Read Digest 88:81-4 Je '66
Opposite of you is uoy. Esquire 66:82-3+ Ag '66
Pesticides: handle with care. Read Digest 88: 99-102 My '66
Science tackles the baldness problem. Read Digest 88:87-91 F '66

WARWICK, Dionne
Gospel girl; Philharmonic Hall concert. H. Saal. por Newsweek 68:101-2 O 10 '66

WARWICK electronics-Whirlpool merger. See Business consolidations and mergers

WASAWO, David P. S.
Developing the academic spirit in East Africa. Bul Atomic Sci 22:19-21 O '66

WASH basins. See Washbasins

WASH drawing. See Brush drawing

WASHBASINS
Swiss and German pewter water cisterns and lavabo sets. R. M. Vetter. il Antiques 89:690-4 My '66

WASHBORN family
Washbourne/Washborn. H. K. Eilers. il Hobbies 71:124-5 S '66

WASHBOURNE family
Washbourne/Washborn. H. K. Eilers. il Hobbies 71:124-5 S '66

WASHBURN, O. A.
Bargain jaguar. Field & S 71:50-2+ Ag '66

WASHING machines
Automatic clothes washers. il Consumer Rep 31:8-25 D '66
Automatic washing machines. il Consumer Rep 31:428-36 S '66
I am a washer. M. Davidson. il Ladies Home J 83:48+ F '66
Washing machine repairs. Consumer Rep 31: 143-5 Mr '66

WASHING of clothes. See Laundry

WASHINGTON, Bennetta B.
Books to make them proud. NEA J 55:20-2 My '66

WASHINGTON, Booker Taliaferro
Booker T. Washington and the white man's burden. L. R. Harlan. bibliog f Am Hist R 71:441-67 Ja '66
Innocent eye. H. Cohen. il Reporter 34:45-8 Mr 10 '66

WASHINGTON, Gene
Move over, chief. por Sports Illus 25:88 S 19 '66

WASHINGTON, George
Farewell with honor. Sr Schol 89:3 S 16 '66
French gentleman and the Washington portraits of 1776. C. C. Sellers. pors Antiques 89:248-55 F '66
French volunteer. M. Bishop. il Am Heritage 17:46-9+ Ag '66
They made our world. L. Rosten. por Look 30:74-5 Mr 8 '66

Statues, portraits, etc.
Son's tribute. D. G. Lowe. Am Heritage 17:16-21+ F '66

WASHINGTON, D.C.
Beacon of beauty; beautification projects. C. J. Smith. il Parks & Rec 1:636-7+ Ag '66
They build a bridge to Washington; top lawyers of the capital. il Bsns W p86-7+ Ap 23 '66
See also
Booksellers and bookselling—Washington, D.C.
Maryland-National capital park and planning commission
White House

Airports
Carriers improve Washington terminal. W. Wright. il Aviation W 85:39-40 Jl 11 '66
Clear and present danger. R. B. Parke. Flying 79:34 Ag '66
500-mi. leg limit proposed for National. Aviation W 85:34 Jl 4 '66
McKee yields on National airport, proposes hourly limit on flights. Aviation W 85:34 Ag 1 '66

Sorting out the mess at capital's airports; FAA orders flights held to forty an hour. il Bsns W p74-6 Ag 27 '66
Voluntary National airport limits achieved by fifty-eight-operation cutback. Aviation W 85:49 S 5 '66

Architecture
See also
Washington, D.C.—Public buildings

Churches
Washington national cathedral: our nation's spiritual landmark. C. E. Bryant. il Read Digest 88:147-8+ F '66

City planning
New grandeur for Washington; plan for Pennsylvania avenue. D. Haskell. il Harper 232:84-91 Ap '66
Renaissance of the grand Mall. T. S. Jett. il Parks & Rec 1:324-6 Ap '66
Shapes of the new Southwest. P. Johnson-Marshall. il Arch Forum 125:60-7 Jl '66
Washington: the lost colony. A. Kopkind and J. Ridgeway. New Repub 154:13-17 Ap 23 '66

Clubs
No-progress report; racial policies of Metropolitan club. Reporter 35:18+ S 22 '66
Pigskin club scores finest hour. il Ebony 21:103-6 F '66

Crime
More police leeway in quizzing suspects? U S News 62:8 Ja 9 '67
Surging crime, growing mob violence; reasons why. il U S News 61:14 O 3 '66

Description
Capital ideas. L. Dennis. il Travel 125:40-4 Mr '66
Welcome to Washington. G. B. Hartzog, jr. il Parks & Rec 1:687-8 S '66

Education
Dunbar story (1870-1955) Review
Negro Hist Bul 29:117 F '66. L. Langborne
See also
Americanization school

Galleries and museums
4,000 paintings and 1,500 sculptures; J. Hirshhorn's mine of modern art. V. Raynor. il N Y Times Mag p52-5+ N 27 '66
Summer without smoke. L. Lastra. il Américas 18:40-1 O '66
See also
Corcoran gallery of art
Freer gallery of art
National gallery of art
Smithsonian institution

Historic houses, etc.
Closets at Blair House. il House & Gard 129: 200-3 Ap '66

Hospitals
It's a miracle that we save any of them; remodeling plans. W. R. Young. il Life 61: 102-4+ D 2 '66
Who decides what is reasonable cost for hospital care? il U S News 60:44 Ap 11 '66

Housing
Washington: the lost colony. A. Kopkind and J. Ridgeway. New Repub 154:13-17 Ap 23 '66
See also
Community organizations for the improvement of neighborhoods, incorporated

Libraries
See also
Folger Shakespeare library
United States—Library of Congress

Metropolitan district
Research labs swarm to capital. il Bsns W p 144-6+ Ap 23 '66

Monuments, statues, etc.
Darts of stone. il Time 88:26 D 30 '66
FDR's memorial: a plan for stone darts. il U S News 62:8-9 Ja 2 '67
Two new statutes in Washington; commemoration of Winston Churchill and Robert Emmet. M. McGrory. America 114: 581 Ap 23 '66
Washington's unknown memorials; excerpts from Evidence of Washington; photographs by E. Hofer. W. Walton. Arch Forum 125: 60-5 N '66

WASHINGTON, D.C.—*Continued*

Music
See also
Opera society of Washington

National arboretum
Don't miss the National arboretum. J. C. S. Freeman. il Parks & Rec 1:566-7+ Jl '66

National zoological park
See National zoological park, Washington, D.C.

Negroes
Civil rights, or a form of blackmail? question of boycotting merchants. il U S News 60:23 Mr 21 '66

Negro stake in Washington home rule. M. F. Nolan. Reporter 35:18-21 Ag 11 '66

Right to riot? W. Raspberry. U S News 60: 128 Ap 25 '66

Washington: life in the lost colony. A. Kopkind and J. Ridgeway. il New Repub 154:19-22 Ap 30 '66; Reply. J. E. Mohbat. 154:39 My 21 '66

Parks and playgrounds
Dump in Nation's capital is transformed into neighborhood park; Watts branch park. il Nat Parks Mag 40:22 Jl '66

Renaissance of the grand Mall. T. S. Jett. il Parks & Rec 1:324-6 Ap '66

Two new projects expand the Riis ideas; Capper plaza and Buchanan school playground. il Arch Rec 140:136-7 D '66

Police
Assist for police: Congress tackles crime; new crime code. U S News 61:46 O 31 '66

Politics and government
Boycott for home rule. M. Phelps. America 114:408 Mr 26 '66

Negro stake in Washington home rule. M. F. Nolan. Reporter 35:18-21 Ag 11 '66

Washington: life in the lost colony; home rule activists. A. Kopkind and J. Ridgeway. il New Repub 154:19-22 Ap 30 '66

Prisons and reformatories
No room in the jail; District of Columbia jail. R. Goldfarb. New Repub 154:12-14 Mr 5 '66

Public buildings
Pedestrian on Capitol hill; Rayburn house office building. Fortune 74:102+ S '66

When Washington entertains in halls of government. il U S News 60:78-9 Je 27 '66
See also
United States—Capitol

Recreation
Creative leisure in the Nation's capital. N. L. Hunt. il Parks & Rec 1:564-5+ Jl '66
See also
League of federal recreation associations

Religious institutions and affairs
President's pastor; G. R. Davis of National city. Time 87:54 F 4 '66

Riots
After spring riots: are more on the way? il U S News 60:8+ Ap 25 '66

Negro-led study of a Negro mob in the Nation's capital. il U S News 60:12 My 16 '66

Right to riot? W. Raspberry. U S News 60: 128 Ap 25 '66

Social life and customs
Capital that has seceded from the Union. H. Sidey. il Life 60:32F My 27 '66

Capital where the caterer is king. il Bsns W p42-4 Je 11 '66

Here comes, there goes Barbara; interview, ed. by de Rosset Morrissey. il Life 61:48-50+ Jl 29 '66

It's inhabited by human beings after all. P. Lisagor. il Nations Bsns 54:23-4 D '66

Look what's going on in Washington. il U S News 60:56-7 My 30 '66

Lyndon's set. Nation 202:637 My 30 '66

Partying: Great society style; gyrating dances, peekaboo dresses; excerpts from address, May 10, 1966. H. R. Gross. il U S News 60:10 My 23 '66

Problems of the new Negro elite. C. T. Rowan. il Ebony 21:43-6+ F '66

Repulse of the swing set. C. Fritchey. Harper 233:38+ S '66

Scapegoat or sin city? J. N. Eller. America 114:824 Je 11 '66

Time to catch breaths and mend fences. P. Lisagor. il Nations Bsns 53:21-2 D '65

Washington's swinging scene: Kuwaiti; Moroccan; Algerian embassies' parties and people. il Newsweek 67:34-8 Je 20 '66

Will Marion Javits move the White House to New York? interview, ed. by B. Walters. M. Javits. Ladies Home J 83:40 Ag '66

Stores
Where the computers care, too; EDP in Washington's Woodward & Lothrop. il Bsns W p 140-2+ Mr 12 '66

Streets
Redeemer; plan to face-lift Pennsylvania avenue. il Newsweek 68:33 S 26 '66

Theater
[Theatre across America] J. Novick. Nation 203:27-8 Jl 4 '66

Where Lincoln was shot; Ford's theater restoration and reopening plans. il Newsweek 68:86 Jl 4 '66
See also
John F. Kennedy Center for the performing arts

Transportation
Minibus + 5-cent fare = transit success story. il Am City 81:53 Mr '66

Water supply
Bad year, this. Nat Parks Mag 40:21 O '66

WASHINGTON (state)
Design for Washington state; citizens go into action. il Parks & Rec 1:834-5 O '66
See also
Architecture, Domestic—Washington (state)
Cascade Range
Festivals—Washington (state)
Hunting—Washington (state)
Olympic National Park
Puget Sound
San Juan Islands
Wilderness areas—Washington (state)

Description and travel
Way along the lonely Snake. il Sunset 136: 73-4 My '66

Industries
Pugetopolis. il Time 87:90 My 27 '66

WASHINGTON (state) University, Seattle
Student dorms: a university tries variety. D. Lyndon. il Arch Forum 124:62-7 Mr '66

WASHINGTON (state) university bookstore.
See College bookstores

WASHINGTON biologists' field club
Island. E. J. Long. il Am For 72:22-4+ F '66

WASHINGTON correspondents. See Reporters and reporting

WASHINGTON COUNTY news. See Country newspapers

WASHINGTON national airport. See Washington, D.C.—Airports

WASHINGTON post and Times herald
Expansionist spree in Washington. il Time 88:87 O 21 '66

Muckraker; D. Pearson's Washington merry-go-round. il Newsweek 67:87 Je 27 '66

Paris herald-post. il Newsweek 68:56 Ag 15 '66

WASHINGTON Redskins (football club) See Football clubs

WASHINGTON Square press, Incorporated
Inventive illustration and design in new edition of The divine comedy. il Pub W 191: 84-5 Ja 2 '67

WASHINGTON university, St Louis, Mo.
By using nature as a lab. B. Commoner. Sat R 49:68-9 My 7 '66

Computer cycle; enthusiasm and despair; excerpts from annual report of library, School of medicine. Library J 91:4907 O 15 '66

How to grow a campus. P. Blake. il Arch Forum 124:62-7 Ap '66

WASON, Betty
Gourmet diet cook book. House & Gard 129: 149+ Je '66

Gypsy's treasure. Horizon 9:102-4 Wint '67

WASP venom. See Venom

WASPS
Accessory burrows of digger wasps; excerpts from Comparative ethology and evolution of the sand wasps. H. E. Evans. bibliog il Science 152:465-71 Ap 22 '66

Nature note; jewel wasp. Sci N 90:109 Ag 13 '66

WASPS—*Continued*
Wasp digs blind hole to confuse enemies.
Sci N 89:323 Ap 30 '66
Yellowjackets trapped. Sci N 90:214 S 17 '66

WASSERMAN, Aaron O.
It could be a froad; maybe a trog. il Natur Hist 75:18-23 Ap '66

WASSERMAN, Burt
Moiré pattern projections. Sch Arts 65:17-20 Je '66
To be a human being. Sch Arts 66:28-32 O '66

WASSERMAN, Joseph
Way to influence the environment. il Arch Rec 139:207-14 Ap '66

WASSERMAN, R. H. and Taylor, A. N.
Vitamin D₃-induced calcium-binding protein in chick intestinal mucosa. bibliog Science 152:791-3 My 6 '66

WASSERMAN, Seymour. See Oppenheim, A. jt. auth.

WASSERSUG, Joseph D.
Do hay fever shots really work? Sci Digest 60:57-62 Ag '66
I prescribe. . . . Sci Digest 60:55-60 O; 67-71 N; 79-83 D '66; 61:82-6 Ja '67
If you can't lose weight, what science says. Sci Digest 60:69-70+ Jl '66

WASSMER. See Airplane industry and trade—France

WASSON, Donald
(comp) Source material. See issues of Foreign affairs

WASSON, John T.
Butler, Missouri: an iron meteorite with extremely high germanium content. bibliog Science 153:976-8 Ag 26 '66

WASTE (economics)
In defense of waste; Time essay. Time 88: 56-7 N 18 '66

WASTE, Disposal of. See Refuse and refuse disposal; Sewage disposal

WASTE, Utilization of
Rocket research studies using manned vehicle waste for fuel; Monex W. il Tech W 20:30+ Ja 2 '67
Utilization: wood wastes find new uses. il Am For 72:38-40 Je '66

WASTE disposal plants. See Sewage disposal plants

WASTE in industry
See also
Efficiency, Industrial

WASTE land. See Reclamation of land

WASTE paper
Shredded secrets; Document disintegration, inc. Los Angeles. Newsweek 67:80 F 28 '66

WASTE products
See also
Refuse, Utilization of

WASTE water. See Trade waste

WATANABE, Akira, and others
Effects of tetrodotoxin on excitability of squid giant axons in sodium-free media. bibliog Science 155:95-7 Ja 6 '67

WATCH holders
Watch holders. M. E. Flower. il Antiques 89:862-6 Je '66

WATCH makers. See Clock and watch makers

WATCHES
Buying a man's wrist watch? il Consumer Bul 49:43+ O '66
Shape of time. il Seventeen 25:222 N '66
What makes a watch tick. il Bsns W p58-9 D 24 '66

History
Collecting old time-pieces; American watches. L. W. Slaughter. il Hobbies 71:46-7+ D '66; 46-7 Ja '67

WATCHMAKERS. See Clock and watch makers

WATER
Calcium and bromide contents of natural waters. R. J. Anderson and others. bibliog il Science 153:1637-8 S 30 '66; Reply with rejoinder. P. C. Mangelsdorf, jr. 154:1473 D 16 '66
H₂O, element of life. B. Tufty. il Sci N 90: 378-9 N 5 '66
Instant information on water needed; data from satellites and computers. Sci N 89:207 Mr 26 '66
Nature note; hydrological cycle. il Sci N 90: 256 O 1 '66
Old office standby freshens up its style. il Bsns W p68+ Jl 9 '66
Oxygen as a primary species in radiolysis of water. M. Daniels and E. Wigg. bibliog il Science 153:1533-4 S 23 '66

Photosensitizing compounds in extracts of drinking water. S. S. Epstein and F. B. Taylor. bibliog il Science 154:261-3 O 14 '66
Synthetic detergents: their influence upon iron-binding complexes of natural waters. F. Kent and F. F. Hooper. bibliog il Science 153:526-7 Jl 29 '66
See also
Ice

Analysis
Thermal properties of water: discontinuities questioned. M. Falk and G. S. Kell. bibliog il Science 154:1013-15 N 25 '66

Anecdotes, facetiae, satire, etc.
Waters one through four; a discourse on the waters of the Peoria Indians. W. Massee. Esquire 66:34 Ag '66

Pollution
See Water pollution

Purification
See Water purification

WATER, Distilled
Solving the water problem. P. Farber. U S Camera 29:24+ Je '66

WATER, Saline
See also
Sea water

WATER, Underground
Fresh water gushes from ocean floor. il Sci N 89:219 Ap 2 '66
Freshwater leaks spotted in Hawaii. Sci N 90:379 N 5 '66

WATER bird shooting. See Shooting

WATER birds
See also names of water birds, e.g. Terns

Accidents and hazards
See Birds—Accidents and hazards

WATER closets
Better john guide: where to go in New York, by J. Routh and S. Stewart. Review Newsweek il 67:119-21 My 23 '66
Instead of the bedpan; self-contained toilet. Time 88:72 Jl 22 '66

WATER color painting
Amateurs, Frakturs and elegant young ladies; Garbisch collection of American watercolors and pastels at the National gallery, Washington, D. C. W. P. Campbell. il Art N 65: 50-3+ O '66
AWS, 1866-1966; Metropolitan museum of art's 200 years of watercolor painting in America. il Am Artist 30:77 D '66
Paintings of Serene Flax. S. Flax. il Am Artist 31:44-9+ Ja '67
Segonzac's instant vision. H. La Farge. il Art N 65:43+ My '66
Two hundred years of water color painting in America; preview of an exhibition. S. P. Feld. il Antiques 90:840-5 D '66
Water color page. See issues of American artist
Water colors to grace the walls of the Metropolitan. E. P. Birk. il Antiques 90:754+ D '66
See also
American water color society

History
On watercolor; excerpts from A history of watercolor painting in America. A. T. Gardner. Am Artist 31:79-81 Ja '67

WATER conduits. See Flumes

WATER conservation
Don't waste, renovate and reuse. J. F. Malina, jr. il Am City 81:160+ Mr '66
Down the drain. R. M. Carleton. il Flower Grower 53:26-7 O '66
New methods urged for handling water. Sci N 90:104 Ag 13 '66
Sea salt kept from land; injection wells to preserve fresh water reserves in coastal regions. Sci N L 89:50 Ja 22 '66
Walls for wandering farms. A. Whitman. il Pop Mech 125:95-7+ Je '66
Water conservation. J. J. Hanan. il Horticulture 44:26-7 N '66
See also
National watershed congress

WATER coolers, Electric. See Electric water coolers

WATER departments
Electronics makes a better water system; Modesto, Calif. R. A. Hosegood. il Am City 81:137+ N '66

WATER distribution
Can the world slake its thirst? il Bsns W p
138+ Ag 13 '66
East-West water conflict. Am City 81:37+
Ag '66
WATER falls. See Waterfalls
WATER filters. See Filters and filtration
WATER filters in photography. See Photography
—Apparatus and supplies
WATER fleas. See Cladocera
WATER for peace conference. See International
conference on water for peace (proposed)
WATER gardens
New way to display water plants. il Pop
Gard 17:6 Ag '66
Sight and sound of water dripping over stone
is always refreshing. il Sunset 136:127-8
Ap '66
See also
Garden pools
Gardens, Bog
Waterfalls in gardens
WATER heaters
Static-free thermistorized aquarium heater.
A. E. Donkin. il Pop Electr 25:73-5+ S '66
WATER in rocks
Molecules crack rocks. il(p65) Sci N 90:69
Jl 30 '66
WATER in the body
Cutaneous water loss in reptiles. P. J. Bent-
ley and K. Schmidt-Nielsen. bibliog il
Science 151:1547-9 Mr 25 '66; Discussion.
152:1523 Je 10 '66
Desert tortoise gopherus agassizii: cutaneous
water loss. K. Schmidt-Nielsen and P. J.
Bentley. il Science 154:911 N 18 '66
WATER lilies
These are outstanding water lilies. Sunset
136:236 Mr '66
Water lilies really are easy to grow. il
Sunset 136:234-5 Mr '66
WATER meters
Good water-meter management; Minneapolis,
Minn. L. E. LaLonde. il Am City 81:167-8
My '66
Our customers like remote-reading meters;
West Allis, Wis. F. J. Groth. il Am City
81:78-9 Je '66

Repairing
Maintain your water meters; Memphis, Tenn.
J. Baker. il Am City 81:99-101+ N '66
WATER on the brain. See Hydrocephalus
WATER picks, Electric. See Toothpicks, Elec-
tric
WATER pipes
See also
Pipe laying
WATER plants. See Aquatic plants
WATER pollution
Aging Great Lakes. C. F. Powers and A.
Robertson. il Sci Am 215:94-100+ bibliog(p
160) N '66
Air and water; address, December 6, 1966.
M. A. Wright. Vital Speeches 33:173-6 Ja
1 '67
And not a drop to drink; quiz. J. Daugherty
and M. Daugherty. il Sci Digest 61:94-6 Ja
'67
Boatmen's paradox; consumers of the river.
W. Berry. il Nation 203:381-5 O 17 '66
Cleaning up the mess. il Newsweek 68:75 N 7
'66
Congress receives IJC report on pollution
of lakes. Dept State Bul 54:293-4 F 21 '66
Danger in swimming hole; leptospires in-
fected farm ponds. Sci N 89:362 My 14 '66
Dave Lee takes a poke at pollution. D. B.
Lee. Am City 81:101-4 S '66
Death of the sweet waters; excerpt. D. E.
Carr. Atlan 217:93-7+ My '66
Detergents may help determine water purity.
Sci N 89:480 Je 18 '66
Dirty water, dirty air: new facts on pollution.
U S News 61:24 N 14 '66
Dying lake. B. Tufty. il(p 1) Sci N 90:10-11
Jl 2 '66
Economics of pollution. Nation 203:4 Jl 4 '66
Environmental pollution; 133rd AAAS meet-
ing, Washington, D.C. H. B. Stewart, jr.
il Science 154:1056-7 N 25 '66
Great pollution pickle. R. Stone and J.
Napier. il Motor B 119:352-3+ Ja '67
H₂O, element of life. B. Tufty. il Sci N 90:
378-9 N 5 '66
Handy lab detects pollution. il Sci N 90:272
O 8 '66

House space committee urges systems ap-
proach to pollution. H. M. David. Tech W
19:20 O 31 '66
Hudson River clean-up: it can be clear, blue
and wonderful again. P. T. White. il N Y
Times Mag p8-9+ Jl 17 '66
Industry action to combat pollution. J. J.
Hanks and H. D. Kube. bibliog f il Har-
vard Bsns R 44:49-62 S '66
Industry joins battle to stem pollution tide.
il Bsns W p76-7 D 31 '66
Keeping Tahoe alive. il Time 88:46-7 Ag 12
'66
Lake Erie: test case in water-pollution bat-
tle. U S News 61:12 Jl 4 '66
Lake Tahoe: measured for pollution; letter.
E. S. Deevey, jr. Science 154:68 O 7 '66
On the side of the cities; excerpt from The
living end. R. Starr. il Horizon 8:66-71
Aut '66
Our air and water can be made clean. Life
61:4 Ag 12 '66
Our dying waters. J. Bird. il Sat Eve Post
239:29-35+ Ap 23 '66
Plea for partnership. W. C. Cramer. Todays
Health 44:64-5 Mr '66
Polipollutionists; movement for the survival
of pollution. J. K. Galbraith. Atlan 219:
52-4 Ja '67
Pollution abatement: President seeks river-
basin approach. L. J. Carter. il Science
151:1204-7 Mr 11 '66
Pollution and politics. New Repub 154:6 Mr
12 '66
Pollution: NAS report examines dual aspect
of the problem; with editorial comment.
J. Walsh. Science 152:297, 329-31 Ap 15 '66
Pollution of man's environment. E. R. Fos-
dick. il Nat Parks Mag 40:16-20 S '66
Pure water is basic. C. K. Fox. Esquire 66:
48+ O '66
Resourceful waste management; address,
June 7, 1966. A. Spilhaus. il Sci N 89:486-
8+ Je 18 '66
Rising tide of water pollution. R. Hazen. il
Duns R 87:pt2 138-40+ Mr '66
That dirty mess: water pollution. H. G.
Earl. il Todays Health 44:52-6 Mr '66
Three-ship navy fights Great Lakes pollu-
tion. Sci N 90:105 Ag 13 '66
Toward cleaner streams. P. H. Abelson. Sci-
ence 154:1401 D 16 '66
War on pollution. Sci N 89:236 Ap 9 '66
Washington muddies the water crisis. Na-
tions Bsns 53:74-6+ D '65
Water and the budget. Nat Parks Mag 40:
21-2 Mr '66
Water pollution. P. H. Abelson. Science
152:1015 My 20 '66; Reply. D. E. Elrick.
154:1275 D 9 '66
What a state can do to stop water pollution;
Connecticut's program. Am City 81:43 S '66
Would you throw trash in your bathtub?
J. T. Starr. il Am For 72:4-5+ Jl '66
Yachtsman's role in pollution prevention.
H. Williams. Yachting 119:78-9+ F '66
See also
Sewage disposal
Trade waste
United States—Federal water pollution con-
trol administration
Water purification
WATER pollution control administration. See
United States—Federal water pollution con-
trol administration
WATER power
See also
Hydroelectric power
Tide power
WATER power electric plants. See Hydroelec-
tric plants
WATER purification
Before you build that water filter; address,
1965. H. O. Hartung. il Am City 81:89-92
Ag; 105-8 S '66
Conservation's big one-two; excerpts from
addresses, February 23, 1966. L. B. John-
son; C. A. T. Johnson. il Am For 72:6-7+
Ap '66
Design, build, operate and train; water-treat-
ment plant at Saigon, South Viet Nam. W.
T. McPhee and J. F. Lenard. il Am City
81:100-3 O '66
Don't waste, renovate and reuse. J. F. Malina,
jr. il Am City 81:160+ Mr '66
Flocculation without filtration; cleans Hudson
River water scheduled for New York city
taps. il Am City 81:98-9 Je '66

WATER purification—_Continued_
Granular lime takes bite out of water; Utica, N.Y. J. H. Haberer. il Am City 81:183-4 My '66
How LBJ would clean up the water and air; summary of message, February 23, 1966. L. B. Johnson. U S News 60:14 Mr 7 '66
More federal billions to clean dirty water. il U S News 61:12 O 24 '66
Oases for the future; excerpts from address, August 1966. K. Hickman. bibliog Science 154:612-17 N 4 '66
People won't drink cedar water; Melbourne, Fla. R. McColgan. il Am City 81:103-5+ D '66
Remember Ray Goudey? Am City 81:8 My '66
Secondhand water? why not? J. Frye. il Todays Health 44:56-61 Mr '66
Waste water renovation; Waste water renovation and conservation research project at Pennsylvania state university. Nat Parks Mag 40:18 D '66
See also
Space vehicles—Water supply

Desalting
Fresh water from a brackish source; Mansfield, Tex. C. R. Johnson. il Am City 81: 122-3 Ap '66
See also
Sea water—Desalting

WATER purifiers, Domestic
Portable demineralizers. il Consumer Bul 49: 19-21 Ag '66
Water purifying devices. Consumer Bul 49: 18-19 Je; 16 O '66

WATER rates
Rate increase offered the best solution; San Antonio, Tex. Am City 81:148 N '66

WATER-repellent topcoats. See Coats

WATER repellents
New coating repels water. Sci N 90:295 O 15 '66

WATER requirements of plants. See Plants—Water requirements

WATER resources development
Potential freshwater reservoir in the New York area. R. D. Gerard. bibliog il Science 153:870-1 Ag 19 '66; Discussion. 154:215-16 O 14 '66
Satellites and computers may measure world's water; proposal to consider global water information system. D. Behrman. UNESCO Courier 19:31 Ap '66
Water resources development; inter-regional seminar held in Fergana, Uzbek SSR. UN Mo Chron 3:81 Ag '66

WATER skis and skiing
Cypress Gardens driver tells: how to rig your ski boat. E. Rehling. il Pop Mech 125:138-40 Mr '66
Kick up a spray this weekend; make your own skis or sled. H. Clark. il Pop Mech 126:136-7 Jl '66
Perfect boat for skiers; Field & stream interview. W. D. Clifford. il Field & S 71: 34-5+ Ja '67
Practice waterskiing indoors; Williamalane park and recreation district, Springfield, Ore. G. R. McGuire. il Parks & Rec 1:754-5 S '66
Ride the waves on skis. E. Hilligan and G. E. Maxwell. il Todays Health 44:40-5 Ag '66

Equipment
Complete skiing boat. C. Ward. il Motor B 118:25-6 Jl '66

WATER sleds. See Aquaplaning

WATER softeners
See also
Culligan, incorporated

WATER softening
How soft is soft water? F. K. Lindsay. Am City 81:148 Je '66

WATER sports. See Aquatic sports

WATER storage
Saving trout from drought; Lake Creek Water Yield Improvement project, Colo. R. Cantwell. il Sports Illus 25:66-7 O 24 '66
Water storage strives to become an art form. il Am City 81:100-1 Mr '66
See also
Water towers

WATER supply
H₂O, element of life. B. Tufty. il Sci N 90: 378-9 N 5 '66
Oases for the future; excerpts from address, August 1966. K. Hickman. bibliog Science 154:612-17 N 4 '66

Water for peace; excerpt from remarks, September 3, 1966. L. B. Johnson. Dept State Bul 55:456-7 S 26 '66
Water gap. Newsweek 68:66 S 19 '66
Water supply and treatment. See issues of American city
See also
Arid regions
Droughts
International conference on water for peace (proposed)
Plumbing
Water, Underground
Water pollution
Water storage

Fluoridation
Fluoridation: a meeting in Detroit raises some questions. D. S. Greenberg. Science 153: 1499-500 S 23 '66; Reply. A. W. Burgstahler. 154:590 N 4 '66
Fluoridation supported. F. Marley. Sci N L 89:133 F 26 '66
Get tough for fluoride Dental assembly urged. Sci N L 89:121 F 19 '66
Turn to fluoridation. Newsweek 67:62 F 21 '66

International aspects
International water cooperation; International conference on water for peace. Am City 81:46-7 D '66

Arizona
See also
Central Arizona project (proposed)

Canada
Canada guards its water against our big thirst. D. O'Leary. il Reporter 34:36-8 Ja 27 '66; Discussion. 34:13 F 24 '66

Egypt
See also
Nile River

Florida
Everglades & dollars; Everglades Park water problems. Nat Parks Mag 40:19-20 D '66
Florida: natural resources down the drain. il Newsweek 68:111-12+ O 24 '66
Interim in the Everglades. H. V. L. Bloomfield. il Am For 72:22-4+ Jl '66; Discussion. 72:5-7 S '66
Needless crisis in a great park. Life 60:4 Mr 25 '66
Unraveling the Everglades furor. E. Buckow. il Field & S 71:12-16+ O '66
Water and the Everglades. W. J. Schneider. il Natur Hist 75:32-41 N '66

Hawaii
Freshwater leaks spotted in Hawaii. Sci N 90: 379 N 5 '66
Infra-red divining rod; underground freshwater flows. il Time 88:88 N 11 '66

Hong Kong
Hong Kong a thirsty city. W. H. Owens. il UNESCO Courier 19:24-6 F '66

India
Touching America's untouchables; Action for food production project to develop resources. Christian Cent 83:855-6 Jl 6 '66

Israel
Ambassador Bunker to review Israel desalination proposals; excerpt from opening statement at news conference, October 13, 1966. L. B. Johnson. Dept State Bul 55:687 O 31 '66

Northeastern states
Northeast water drought, end not in sight. il Am For 71:30-1+ O '65
On the water front; no improvement. Newsweek 67:88 Je 6 '66

Northwestern states
30 million Americans fighting over a river. il U S News 61:70-3 S 19 '66

Southwestern states
Danger facing boom in the desert. il U S News 60:66-70 My 9 '66
Grand Canyon: Colorado dams debated. L. J. Carter. il Science 152:1600-5 Je 17 '66
How to save the Grand Canyon and water the desert, too; interview. B. M. Goldwater. il U S News 61:124-6 O 24 '66
Southwest gropes for new ways to end water shortage; with statement by D. Brower. il U S News 61:59-61 D 12 '66

WATER supply—Southwestern states—*Cont.*
30 million Americans fighting over a river. il U S News 61:70-3 S 19 '66
Water project that dried up; Colorado River project. il Bsns W p72+ S 3 '66

United States

Bold water planning urged. Sci N 90:187 S 10 '66
Can the world slake its thirst? il Bsns W p 138+ Ag 13 '66
Canada guards its water against our big thirst. D. O'Leary. il Reporter 34:36-8 Ja 27 '66; Discussion. 34:13 F 24 '66
Coming water crisis. Nation 203:205-6 S 12 '66
Crisis in water; its sources, pollution and depletion; symposium; discussion. Sat R 48: 29 N 27 '65; 49:71-2 F 5 '66
Death of the sweet waters; excerpt. D. E. Carr. Atlan 217:93-7+ My '66
Drawing water from wastes. J. R. Porter. Sat R 49 My 7 '66
East-West water conflict. Am City 81:37+ Ag '66
Experts look at water in the national parks; U.S. geological survey. W. J. Schneider. il Nat Parks Mag 40:20-1 Ag '66
New thinking needed in river basin planning. Nat Parks Mag 40:18 D '66
North American water colossus. T. E. Stimson. il Pop Mech 126:80-1+ Ag '66
Washington muddies the water crisis. Nations Bsns 53:74-6+ D '65
See also subhead Water supply under names of cities, e.g. Pompano Beach, Fla —Water supply

WATER tanks
Like a lighted fountain; Spokane, Wash. G. A. Yake. il Am City 81:147-8+ Ag '66
See also
Water towers

WATER towers
Designer and the water tower. il Design 67: 10-11 Mr '66

WATER transportation, Inland. See Inland water transportation

WATER tunnels
Tunnel: Richmond tunnel, aqueduct tunnel from Staten Island to Brooklyn; interview. M. J. Barkin. New Yorker 42:48-51 N 26 '66

WATER vapor
Role of the oceans. R. Revelle. il Sat R 49: 39-41 My 7 '66

WATER works. See Waterworks
WATERBURY, John W. See Praeger, R. Q. jt. auth.
WATERCOLOR painting. See Water color painting

WATERFALL, Richard
Hattersley class: variations on a theme. il Pop Phot 59:51-4 S '66

WATERFALLS
Concrete cascade in Portland, Ore. D. Lyndon. il Arch Forum 125:74-9 Jl '66
Land of tumbling waters; North Carolina's western mountains. M. J. Dunn, 3d. il Travel 126:37-42 O '66
See also
Horse Tail Falls

WATERFALLS in gardens
Waterfall for your back yard. E. Widdis. il Pop Sci 189:116-18 Ag '66

WATERFORD, Conn.
Youth: what they need is a place to go; dance club. il Life 61:41-3 Ag 19 '66

WATERHOUSE, Keith, and Hall, Willis
Help stamp out marriage! Criticism New Yorker 42:116+ O 8 '66
Sat R 49:63 O 15 '66

WATERING of gardens, lawns, etc.
Be lazy about lawn sprinkling. il Pop Mech 125:108-11 Je '66
How to irrigate your garden. il Suc Farm 64: 48F Jl '66
Little water goes a long way. il Pop Gard 17:86-7+ Ag '66
When to water? il Bet Hom & Gard 44:148 My '66

WATERING places. See Health resorts, watering places, etc.

WATERLOO, Iowa
Injun country nature area. L. T. Katoski. il Parks & Rec 1:251-3 Mr '66

WATERMAN, Alan T.
Federal support of science. Science 153:1359-61 S 16 '66

WATERMAN, Talbot H. and Horch, K. W.
Mechanism of polarized light perception. bibliog Science 154:467-75 O 28 '66

WATERPROOFING
Neoprene sheet for waterproofing structures. il Arch Rec 139:193-4 Mr '66
See also
Water repellents

WATERPROOFING of textiles
Waterproof proof; Scotchgard. C. Conley. il Field & S 71:93 Ag '66

WATERS, Harry F.
Disenchanted; girls in the city. N Y Times Mag p28-30+ F 6 '66

WATERS, J. Kevin
Records and risks. America 114:839-41 Je 11 '66

WATERS, John Knight
General tells how U.S. can win in Vietnam. por U S News 61:56-7 D 19 '66

WATERS, Mark
Man who wrote his own obituary. por Read Digest 89:81-3 Jl '66

WATERS, Odale D. Jr
New frontiers for the U.S; untold riches in the sea; interview. por U S News 61:66-9 Ag 22 '66

WATERS, Somerset R.
American tourist. Ann Am Acad 368:109-18 N '66

WATERWAYS
See also
Rivers

Canada
See also
Welland Ship Canal

China
See also
Canals—China

France
Meander down the Marne. P. R. Smyth. il Travel 126:31-6 Ag '66

Sweden
See also
Göta Canal

United States
Business booms on the waterways. R. S. Strother. il Read Digest 88:213-14+ F '66
National transportation policy; address, February 8, 1966. J. Miller. Vital Speeches 32:292-4 Mr 1 '66
See also
Canals—United States
Florida Ship Canal project

WATERWORKS
Chicago's new-fashioned waterworks; photographs. Fortune 73:159-61 Ap '66
Construct the critical units first; Fort Lauderdale, Fla. C. S. McKinney. il Am City 81:112-13 My '66
Fresh water from a brackish source; Mansfield, Tex. C. R. Johnson. il Am City 81: 122-3 Ap '66
Not just for hurricanes; auxiliary engine in the water plant. R. C. Mills. il Am City 81:97-9+ Ap '66
People won't drink cedar water; Melbourne, Fla. R. McColgan. il Am City 81:103-5+ D '66
Politics took second place; selection of a water-works control system, South Bend, Ind. H. R. Goodhew. il Am City 81:177+ S '66
Small town solves a big water problem; Saxton, Pa. P. S. Siebert, jr. il Am City 81: 83-5 N '66
Water supply and treatment. See issues of American city
We have the tools to do the job; Troy, N.Y. J. P. Buckley. il Am City 81:86-9 F '66
See also
Filter plants

WATKINS, Dorothy J.
Territorial for New Mexico. Library J 91: 5867-8 D 1 '66

WATKINS, Edward
Opera is like that; poem. Opera N 31:37 Ja 14 '67

WATKINS, Franklin
Painter's search for meaning; interview, ed. by E. P. Richardson. il por Atlan 218:80-6 Jl '66

WATKINS, Grace V.
Should you flee the weather? Todays Health 44:24-5+ N '66

WATKINS, John V.
Gardens of the West Indies. Horticulture 44: 18-21+ D '66
Hibiscus. Horticulture 44:24-5+ Je '66

WATKINS, Lura W.
Highfields and its heritage. Antiques 90:204-7 Ag '66

WATKINS, Vernon
Beaver's story; poem. New Yorker 42:198
O 15 '66
Cornfields; poem. New Yorker 42:65 D 24 '66
Digging the past; To a shell; poems. Poetry
107:312-17 F '66
Napkin and stone; poem. New Yorker 42:112
My 28 '66

WATKINS, Winifred M.
Blood-group substances. bibliog Science 152:
172-81 Ap 8 '66

WATKINS-Johnson company
System aids RF spectrum surveillance; identifying and analyzing unknown electromagnetic signals. il Aviation W 86:61+ Ja
9 '67

WATSON, Barbara Bellow
Late light; poem. New Yorker 41:36 F 12
'66

WATSON, Bryan
Boy on Bobby's back is back. G. Ronberg.
il por Sports Illus 25:71-3 N 28 '66

WATSON, Donald P.
Improving the garden club's image. Horticulture 44:14-15 D '66

WATSON, Ernest W.
Founder reflects. Am Artist 30:3+ My '66

WATSON, Harold M.
French authors and Roman indexers. America
114:79-83, 212 Ja 15, F 12 '66

WATSON, Robert
Two books of criticism. Poetry 107:332-3 F
'66

WATSON, Thomas J. 1914-
SR's businessman of the year. W. D. Patterson. por Sat R 50:74+ Ja 14 '67

WATSON, W. Marvin
Sorry, wrong number. por Newsweek 67:21
Ja 31 '66
White House at work; a mystery explained.
il por U S News 60:36-7 F 7 '66

WATSONVILLE, Calif.

Hospitals

Rural hospital is designed to grow outward
and upward; Watsonville community hospital. il Arch Rec 140:208-9 O '66

WATT, Douglas
Concert records (cont) New Yorker 42:235-7
N 5; 232+ N 19 '66
Popular records (cont) New Yorker 42:200-2+
Mr 19; 197-9 D 17 '66

WATT, Lois B.
Educational materials center. Am Ed 2:24-5
Jl '66

WATT, Reuben
Batman's backstage helper. il pors Ebony
21:40-2+ Ap '66

WATTEAU, Jean Antoine
Watteau's forbidden world: adaptation. J.
Canaday. il Horizon 8:60-79 Sum '66

WATTERS, Pat
Wallace-ism is what Alabama (white) wants.
New Repub 154:7 My 14 '66

WATTS, Alan
Redbook dialogue. por Redbook 127:52-3+ My
'66

WATTS, Andre
Musical events; recital in Philharmonic Hall.
W. Sargeant. New Yorker 42:234 N 5 '66

WATTS, Bill
Rich, full life of a bad guy. M. Cope. il pors
Sat Eve Post 239:88-91 F 12 '66

WATTS, Frances B.
Arthur Bones, the reading dog; drama. Plays
26:63-9 N '66
Barefoot trader; drama. Plays 26:79-85 N '66
Christmas eve in pine cone forest; drama.
Plays 26:75-9 D '66
Harvest moon supper; drama. Plays 26:75-80
O '66
Leprechaun shoemakers; drama. Plays 25:
43-8, 66 Mr '66

WATTS, Franklin
First trip to East Pakistan. Pub W 190:
40-2 O 10 '66
Meeting a crisis in prosperity. por Pub W
191:72+ Ja 2 '67

WATTS, Franklin, incorporated
Meeting a crisis in prosperity. F. Watts.
Pub W 191:72+ Ja 2 '67

WATTS, Raymond N. Jr
Roster of space activity. Sky & Tel 33:28-30
Ja '67
—and Ashbrook, J.
Results from Lunar Orbiter 2. Sky & Tel 33:
22-6 Ja '67

WATTS, Steve L.
Obituary
Pub W 189:105 Je 13 '66

WATTS, Calif. See Los Angeles
WATTS branch park. See Washington, D.C.—
Parks and playgrounds
WATTS riots. See Los Angeles—Riots

WATZEK, Peter F.
Doctor Verne L. Harper, first recipient of
Fernow award; remarks, September 6, 1965.
por Am For 71:7+ O '65

WAUGH, Alec
Captain's paradise. Nat R 18:272+ Mr 22 '66
Delectations. See issues of National review,
March 22, 1966-

WAUGH, Auberon
Christmas sermon. Nat R 18:1312-14+ D 27
'66

WAUGH, Dorothy
Meteoric career of Ed Emberley. Am Artist
30:54-61 N '66
Milton Glaser of push pin studios. Am Artist
30:56-61+ Je '66
Nonny Hogrogian: decorator of books for
children. Am Artist 30:52-7 O '66

WAUGH, Evelyn
Books. M. Muggeridge. Esquire 66:24+ Ag '66
Death of a craftsman. F. Clinton. Nat R 18:
416-17 My 3 '66
Evelyn Waugh faces Life and vice versa. J.
Osborne. Atlan 218:114-15 D '66
Evelyn Waugh: in memoriam. H. Kenner.
Nat R 18:418+ My 3 '66
Evelyn Waugh, R.I.P. J. M. Cameron. Commonweal 84:167-8 Ap 29 '66
In memoriam: Arthur Evelyn St John Waugh,
1903-1966. C. A. Brady. America 114:594-5
Ap 23 '66
Obituary
Nat R 18:400+ My 3 '66. W. F. Buckley,
jr
Newsweek il por 67:92 Ap 25 '66
Pub W 189:85 Ap 18 '66
Time 87:84 Ap 22 '66
Ordeal of Evelyn Waugh. J. Featherstone.
New Repub 155:21-3 Jl 16 '66
Waugh the artist. T. F. Staley. Commonweal
84:280-2 My 27 '66

WAUGH, Frederick Judd
Frederick Waugh, America's most popular
marine painter. G. R. Havens. il por Am
Artist 31:30-7+ Ja '67

WAUKEGAN, Ill.

Riots
Still hot. il Newsweek 68:27-8 S 12 '66

WAVEMETERS
Dual-sensitivity field strength and absorption
meter. R. N. Tellefson. il Pop Electr 24:
67-8 Ja '66

WAVES
Freak waves predictable; routing service of
the navy's oceanographic office. il(p 129)
Sci N 90:132 Ag 27 '66
See also
Vibration

WAVES, Brain. See Brain waves

WAWZONEK, Stanley
Synthetic electroorganic chemistry. bibliog
Science 155:39-44 Ja 6 '67

WAX figures
Letter from London; Mme Tussaud's exhibition. M. Panter-Downes. New Yorker
42:213 D 3 '66

WAXES
Low-down on floor wax. R. Martens. il Farm
J 90:97 Ap '66

WAY, James L. and others
Cyanide intoxication: protection with oxygen. bibliog Science 152:210-11 Ap 8 '66

WAY of the cross. See Stations of the cross

WAYS, Max
Antitrust in an era of radical change. Fortune 73:128-31+ Mr '66
Europe's new nationalism. Fortune 74:108-11+
S '66
Road to 1977. Fortune 75:92-5+ Ja '67
Tomorrow's management: a more adventurous life in a free-form corporation. Fortune
74:84-7+ Jl 1 '66

WAYS and means committee. See United
States—Congress—House of representatives
—Ways and means committee

WE had us some Christmas; story. See Owens,
W. A.

WE have always lived in the castle; drama.
See Jackson, S.

WEAD, George
Fear, games and Virginia Woolf. America
115:325-9 S 24 '66

WEATHER research—*Continued*
Swedish air force orders **weather system.**
Sci N 90:387 N 5 '66
World weather watch; 133rd AAAS annual
meeting, 26-31 December 1966, Washington,
D.C. T. F. Malone. il Science 154:678-9 N 4
'66
WEATHER stations. See Meteorological stations
WEATHERBY, W. J.
Lovers with different loyalties. E. M. Yoder,
jr. Sat R 49:35 My 21 '66
WEATHERFORD, John
On the grindstone (cont) Library J 91:646,
1182, 1790, 2290, 2784, 3366, 3664-5, 3886,
4588, 5346, 5906 F 1, Mr 1, Ap 1, My 1, Je 1,
Jl-S 1, O 1, N 1, D 1 '66
WEATHERING of wood. See Wood—Weathering
WEAVER, Al
Kansas' first deer hunt. Outdoor Life 138:
64-5+ N '66
WEAVER, Ellen C. and Chon, H. P.
Spin label studies in chlamydomonas. bibliog
Science 153:301-3 Jl 15 '66
WEAVER, John D.
Honorable Earl Warren. Holiday 39:76-7+ Ap;
76-7+ My; 56-7+ Je '66
WEAVER, Kenneth F.
Giant comet grazes the sun. Nat Geog Mag
129:258-61 F '66
Space rendezvous; milestone on the way
to the moon. Nat Geog Mag 129:538-53
Ap '66
WEAVER, Richard
Legacy of Richard Weaver. A. Lejeune. Nat
R 18:473-4 My 17 '66
WEAVER, Robert
Visible devils. Reporter 34:55-7 Mr 10 '66
WEAVER, Robert Clifton
Excerpt from testimony, March 25, 1965. Cong
Digest 45:14+ Ja '66
Housing and urban development; address,
August 1, 1966. Vital Speeches 32:674-8 S 1
'66
Urban development part of HUD; interview.
il pors Am City 81:87-9+ Jl '66
Ventilating the crowded city. Parks & Rec
1:893 N '66

about
Are cities livable? J. O'Gara. Commonweal
83:656 Mr 11 '66
First Negro Cabinet officer. por Sr Schol 88:19
F 4 '66
Great society's advance man. il por Bsns W
p51-2+ Ja 22 '66
Hope for the heart; biographical sketch. il
por Time 87:31-3 Mr 4 '66
Robert C. Weaver: quiet man wins spot in
Cabinet. S. Booker. il pors Ebony 21:82-4+
Ap '66
Robert Clifton Weaver; Secretary of housing
and urban development. F. Parker. bib-
liog por(p73) Negro Hist Bul 29:75-6 Ja '66
Weaver nominated for cabinet post. Chris-
tian Cent 83:101-2 Ja 26 '66
Weaver's HUD. New Repub 154:8 Ja 29 '66
WEAVER, Warren, 1894-
Confessions of a scientist-humanist. por Sat
R 49:12-15 My 28 '66
Good teaching. Science 151:1335 Mr 18 '66
Inner nature of science; excerpts from ad-
dress, October 14, 1965. UNESCO Courier
19:34 Ja '66
Moon race: is it worth it? excerpts from
interview. Read Digest 88:219-22 Ap '66
WEAVER, Warren, 1923-
Four hearties of the good ship G.O.P. N Y
Times Mag p50-1+ N 27 '66
Front runners for '72. N Y Times Mag p26-7+
My 22 '66
WEAVER, William
Afloat in a sea of troubles: Rome-Naples-
Florence. Hi Fi 16:144-5 Mr '66
Before the opera, Italy's busy fall. Hi Fi
16:MA25+ D '66
Caballé records her first complete opera.
Hi Fi 16:99-102 O '66
Menotti's superb new Pelléas. Hi Fi 16:MA23
S '66
Metastasio: librettist to a century. Hi Fi
16:53-5 Jl '66
New management for the Maggio. Hi Fi 16:
MA22+ Ag '66
Notes from our correspondents (cont) Hi
Fi 16:12+ F; 14+ Je '66

Ovations for Bernstein's Falstaff. Hi Fi 16:
126-7 Je '66
Prague report. Hi Fi 16:162-3 Ap '66
Summer's crop of star-strewn operas. Hi Fi
16:11-12+ O '66
TV Italian style. Opera N 31:14-15 D 31 '66
WEAVER, William J.
Sound advice. See occasional issues of Modern
photography
WEAVERS
Wizard of Plockropool; Harris tweed. V.
Thomas. il Atlan 217:124-6 Je '66
WEAVING
Creative weaving. B. A. Hadley. il Sch Arts
65:36-7 F '66
Weaver's high art; folk textiles of Latin
America, Mexico and southwestern United
States; reprint. P. Kelemen. il Américas
18:1-10 D '66
See also
Gobelin tapestry

History
Weaving of Crete. H. Pomerance. il Craft
Horiz 26:32-5+ S '66
WEBB, Aileen O.
Craft horizons: 25th anniversary. por Craft
Horiz 26:12 Je '66
WEBB, David
Golden web. il Vogue 147:202-3 My '66
WEBB, Eugene J. See Ray, M. L. jt. auth.
WEBB, James E.
Opportunities vast, budget confining. por
Tech W 19:44 N 28 '66
Webb's space warning. Aviation W 84:21 My
23 '66

about
Collier trophy award. B. Kocivar. il por Look
30:96+ N 1 '66
Test of time. W. J. Coughlin. Tech W 19:152
Jl 25 '66
WEBB, John A.
Plant physiology in Canada. Science 155:112+
Ja 6 '67
WEBB, Leland
Ballad of Tremble Dove; story. Redbook 127:
62-3 O '66
WEBB, R. K.
Social rebels and bandits. Nation 202:625-6 My
23 '66
WEBB, Taylor
Problems facing Mississippi; address, April
6, 1966. Vital Speeches 32:459-61 My 15 '66
WEBBER, George W.
MUST: project for urban service. D. M.
Lindsey. Christian Cent 83:1041-2 Ag 24 '66
WEBBER, Ross A.
Advertising responsibility. Cath World 204:
87-91 N '66
Automobile smashup. America 114:851-3 Je
18 '66
WEBER, Arnold R.
Program proposals for manpower policy. Mo
Labor R 89:130-1 F '66
Strategies for decentralization; excerpt from
paper presented at American assembly. Mo
Labor R 89:1386-7 D '66
WEBER, Dick
Dick Weber: king of the bowlers. W. J.
McKean. il pors Look 30:M12+ N 1 '66
WEBER, George
Enzyme regulation in mammalian tissues.
Science 151:479-81 Ja 28 '66
WEBER, George, and others
Feedback inhibition of key glycolytic
enzymes in liver; action of free fatty acids.
bibliog Science 154:1357-60 D 9 '66
WEBER, Jerome B. and Scott, D. C.
Availability of a cationic herbicide adsorbed
on clay minerals to cucumber seedlings.
Science 152:1400-2 Je 3 '66
WEBER, Jim E.
Better battery care means better boating.
Motor B 117:36-7+ Je '66
Cool counsel for sweltering skippers. Motor B
118:28-31+ S '66
Throwing a bowline. Motor B 118:38 Jl '66
WEBER, Karl Maria Friedrich Ernst, freiherr
von
Records; der Freischütz. Opera N 31:30 N 5
'66
WEBER, Neal A.
Fungus-growing ants. bibliog Science 153:
587-604 Ag 5 '66
WEBER, Rhoda
Autumn is that wide-eyed feeling. Farm J
90:71 O '66

WEBERN, Anton von
In quest of Webern. H. Moldenhauer. il Sat
R 49:47-9+ Ag 27 '66
Webern in perspective; excerpts from Anton
von Webern, by E. Krenek; E. Wellesz; C.
Bresgen. pors Sat R 49:47-9+ My 28 '66
WEBERN, Hermine von
In quest of Webern. H. Moldenhauer. il Sat
R 49:47-9+ Ag 27 '66
WEBS, Spiders. See Spider webs
WEBSTER, Daniel P.
Kidproofing the backyard pool. Todays Health
44:34-7 Je '66
WEBSTER, Sir David
No hard lines; interview, ed. by F. Merkling.
por Opera N 31:13 D 17 '66
WEBSTER, Lyle
Report from India; ed. by D. Hanson. Suc
Farm 64:6 Mr '66
WEBSTER, Noah
Noah's ark of words. P. W. Schmidtchen.
il por Hobbies 71:108-9+ My '66
WEBSTER college, Webster Groves, Mo.
Another nun defects. Time 89:66 Ja 20 '67
New vows. il Newsweek 69:63-4 Ja 23 '67
WECHSBERG, Joseph
Bridge that breathes. Holiday 41:124a-124e+
Ja '67
Gastronomy. Esquire 65:66-7 My '66
Is the ensemble dead? Opera N 30:10-12 F 12 '66
Letter from Berlin. New Yorker 42:149-50+
O 15 '66
Profiles (cont) New Yorker 41:42-6+ F 5;
42:45-8+ Ap 9; 52-4+ Ap 30; 65-6+ S 17 '66
WECHSLER, David
I.Q. is an intelligent test. N Y Times Mag
p 12-13+ Je 26; 2+ Jl 17 '66
WECHSLER adult intelligence scale. See In-
telligence tests
WEDDELL seals. See Seals (animals)
WEDDING cake. See Cake
WEDDING gift; story. See Evans, D.
WEDDING gifts
Flood of gifts for Pat and Luci. U S News
61:11 Ag 29 '66
Here's to the bride; wedding gifts $25 and
under. B. Plumb. il N Y Times Mag p46-7
My 29 '66
WEDDING invitations. See Invitations
WEDDING meals
Open season for entertaining; romantic
wedding receptions; with recipes. il McCalls
93:104-5+ My '66
WEDDINGS
Great American wedding; you are invited to
see how it was covered. J. Neubauer; B.
Brown; F. Ward. il Pop Phot 59:85-9+
D '66
It's wedding week at the White House. il
U. S. News 61:36-7 Ag 8 '66
Luci's White House wedding; review. M.
Simons and M. Kaytor. il Look 30:34-9
Ag 9 '66
Nothing's too good for my daughter! B.
Davidson. il Sat Eve Post 239:28-35 Ag 13
'66
Now, the miniwedding; J. Ormsby Gore-
M. Rainey. il Newsweek 68:56 O 10 '66
Orange blossoms; marriage of Princess Bea-
trix. il Time 87:51-2 Mr 18 '66
Splendor of Luci's wedding. il Life 61:20-7
Ag 19 '66
Your most cherished day. K. Davis. il Farm
J 90:47-8 Je '66
See also
Wedding gifts
Wedding meals
WEDDLE, Dick. See Althoff, S. jt. auth.
WEDDLE, Ferris
Cougar in our national parks and monuments.
Nat Parks Mag 40:4-7 My '66
WEDEL, Cynthia Clark
Church women and Christian unity. por Cath
World 202:278-82 F '66
WEDEMEYER, Gary
Dechlorination of DDT by aerobacter aero-
genes. bibliog Science 152:647 Ap 29 '66
WEDGE, Bryant
What the visitors really think. Sat R 49:98+
Mr 12 '66
WEDGWOOD, C. V.
300 years ago, fire! N Y Times Mag p6+
Ag 28 '66
WEED, A. C. 2d
Why our methods aren't working. New
Repub 154:20 F 5 '66

WEEDS
See also
Aquatic plants

Chemical control
Dozen common lawn weeds, and how to con-
trol them. il Pop Gard 17:56-9 My '66
Safe and accurate dilution of garden chemi-
cals. il Sunset 136:240 Je '66
They use chemical weed killers to boost
yields, cut costs, save work. il Suc Farm
64:90 Ap '66
Unroll your weed killer? C. E. Ball. il Farm
J 90:36J Ag '66
Weed and insect control guide. L. E. Zeman.
il Suc Farm 64:69+ Mr '66
Weeds in grain sorghum, how to control
them. O. C. Burnside. Suc Farm 64:112 Mr
'66
See also
Herbicides

Control
See also
Weeds—Chemical control
WEEGEE, pseud. See Fellig. A.
WEEKEND guests. See Guests
WEEKEND houses. See Vacation houses
WEEKEND vacations. See Vacations
WEEKLY newspapers. See Newspapers
WEEKS, Edward Augustus
Peripatetic reviewer. See issues of Atlantic

about
From the new editor. R. Manning. Atlan 217:
53 Ap '66
WEEMS, David B.
Build a long-tailed phase inverter. Pop Electr
25:69-72+ S '66
Four on the floor. Pop Electr 25:74-6 N '66
Put an air brake on your woofer. Pop Electr
24:60-3 Mr '66
Totem poles for stereo. Pop Electr 24:48-52+
Ja '66
WEERTMAN, W. L. and Lechner, R. J.
Hemi white paper; excerpts from address.
por Hot Rod 19:72-7+ Ag '66
WEESE, Harry
Informal wood frame campus buildings. Arch
Rec 139:184-8 My '66
WEHNER, Herbert
Bridge on the River Saale. il por Time 88:18-
19 D 30 '66
WEI, Tsing-sing Louis
Church in China; reprint. Commonweal 85:
222-5 N 25 '66
WEIDEN, Norman
Number 0001 at Merrill Lynch. il por Fortune
73:138-9 Ap '66
WEIDMAN, Charles
Charles Weidman and company, expression of
Two arts theatre. J. Anderson. Dance Mag
40:62 F '66
Turtle and the bee. E. Stodelle. il pors Dance
Mag 40:16-19 Mr '66
WEIDMAN, Jerome
Wife of the man who suddenly loved women;
story. Ladies Home J 83:72-3+ Je '66
WEIDNER, Edward W.
Professor abroad: twenty years of change.
Ann Am Acad 368:60-70 N '66
WEIDNER, Mary K.
Decatur: pioneer in data processing; reprint.
Wilson Lib Bul 41:409-10+ D '66
WEIGHT (physiology)
Advice to dieters from a formerly fat psy-
chiatrist; excerpts from The thin book.
T. I. Rubin. Todays Health 44:35+ Jl '66
If you can't lose weight, what science says.
J. D. Wassersug. Sci Digest 60:69-70+
Jl '66
Thin story; advice for the skinny. il Mlle
63:184 S '66
See also
Corpulence

Anecdotes, facetiae, satire, etc.
How I lost four ounces in three weeks.
J. L. Collier. il Read Digest 89:129-32 N '66
WEIGHT lifting
Looking for a lift; N. Schemansky. M.
Kram. il Sports Illus 25:128-30+ S 12 '66
WEIGHT reducing machines. See Exercising
equipment
WEIGHT reducing preparations
Those doctors who hand out diet pills. M. A.
Guitar. il Ladies Home J 83:79+ My '66;
Same abr. with title Diet pill menace. Read
Digest 89:55-8 Jl '66

WEIGHTLESSNESS
AS-205 experiment to define zero-G effects on middle ear. Tech W 19:41 O 10 '66
Douglas cites test rseults of simulated zero-G study. H. M. David. il Miss & Roc 18: 40-1+ My 16 '66
Gemini pilots cite EVA training needs. E. J. Bulban. Aviation W 85:30 O 3 '66
GE facility to study zero-G performance. K. Voss. il Tech W 20:17 Ja 2 '67
Li'l Atlas defies gravity. W. J. Price. il Pop Electr 24:67-70+ My '66

WEIGHTMAN, John G.
French literary scene. Commentary 41:57-62 F '66
Ionesco: the absurd and beyond. N Y Times Mag p24-5+ My 1 '66
Tidbit history. Commentary 41:89-92 My '66

WEIL, James L.
For sharing. Poetry 109:195-7 D '66
Runnymede: 14 May 1965; About roses; Like that; poems. Poetry 108:27-8 Ap '66

WEILER, Howard
How an expert rigs an outboard for rough water. J. Martenhoff. il pors Pop Sci 188: 124-8+ Mr '66

WEILL, David P.
Invisible chains. por Library J 91:4054-6 S 15 '66

WEILL-TUCKERMAN, Anne
Detente rides again. Nation 203:402-3 O 24 '66
Running hard to stand still. Nation 203:626-7 D 12 '66
Storm signals on the East River. Nation 203:298 O 3 '66
U Thant on war and peace. Nation 203:38-9 Jl 11 '66
Vietnam at the UN. Nation 202:169 F 14 '66

WEIMER, Arthur M.
Real estate decisions are different. Harvard Bsns R 44:105-12 N '66

WEIN, George
George Wein: jazz by the sea. M. J. Arlen. il por Holiday 40:91-2+ Jl '66

WEINBERG, Alvin M.
Can technology replace social engineering? address, 1966. Bul Atomic Sci 22:4-8 D '66
Samuel K. Allison, 1901-1965. Bul Atomic Sci 22:2 Ja '66
Science, choice, and human values; address, October 1965. Bul Atomic Sci 22:8-13 Ap '66

WEINBERG, Arthur, and Weinberg, Lila
Where are today's muckrakers? Sat R 49: 54-5 Jl 9 '66

WEINBERG, Elisworth A.
Coast guard auxiliary offers free boating courses. por Motor B 118:77 Ag '66

WEINBERG, Herman G.
Dream of Indians. Sat R 49:46-7 F 5 '66

WEINBERG, Lawrence
Big man. Criticism
New Yorker 42:79-80 My 28 '66
Duet for three. Criticism
New Yorker 42:79 My 28 '66

WEINBERG, Lila. See Weinberg, A. jt. auth.

WEINBERG, Sidney J.
Balancing ability with humility; interview. pors Nations Bsns 53:44-6+ D '65

WEINBERG, Stanley
Foto facts; Dialite. P. Farber. il U S Camera 29:34-5 N '66

WEINFELD, Edward
End to copping. Time 87:54 Je 24 '66

WEINGARTEN, Romain
L'été (Summer) Criticism
New Yorker 42:112 Ja 14 '67

WEINGARTEN, Violet
Man who saw through heaven; story. Atlan 218:103-6 S '66

WEINLAND, James D.
Take stock of yourself. Nations Bsns 54: 106-7 Ap '66

WEINRAUB, Bernard
Brilliancy of black. Esquire 67:130-5 Ja '67
Four ways to go: Tommy Rodd went to jail. Esquire 66:124+ S '66
Girl of the year, 1938. Esquire 66:72-5+ Jl '66
Happening called Hoving. N Y Times Mag p 10-11+ Jl 10 '66
Mothers. Esquire 66:96-101+ N '66
Not exactly a Jimmy Cagney cop. N Y Times Mag p28-9+ O 30 '66

WEINSTEIN, Brian
French community, does it exist? bibliog f Cur Hist 50:214-20+ Ap '66

WEINSTEIN, Emanuel. See Michael, B. jt. auth.

WEINSTOCK, Arnold
Tough taskmaster who got results. por Fortune 74:80 O '66

WEINSTOCK, Herbert
Caballé as Lucrezia Borgia. Sat R 49:54 D 31 '66
Lang's masterly Handel. Sat R 49:66 O 29 '66
Miracles on West 34th street. Sat R 49:74-5 N 26 '66
Mozart and opera seria. Sat R 49:67-8 Mr 26 '66
Music to my ears. Sat R 49:70 D 10 '66
Rossini's Moses. Sat R 49:62 Ja 29 '66
Two centuries of Messiah. Sat R 49:73 D 10 '66
Verdi's Nabucco revealed. Sat R 49:50 Ag 27 '66

WEINTRAUB, Ronald M. and others
Mouse complement: influence of sex hormones on its activity. bibliog Science 152:783-5 My 6 '66

WEINTRAUB, Stanley
From writing poetry to war. Sat R 49:39 S 17 '66
Old acquaintance. Sat R 49:28-9 Jl 9 '66
Spanish volunteers. New Repub 154:27-8 Mr 12 '66
To Dublin in a donkey cart. Sat R 49:47 Je 4 '66

WEIR, John M.
Unconquered plague. Bul Atomic Sci 22:46-8 O '66

WEIS, Earl A.
Milestone in religious publishing. America 115:586-7 N 12 '66

WEISBURD, Mel
Pollution: everybody's adversary. Todays Health 44:38-40 Mr '66

WEISBURGER, J. H. and others
Liver cancer: neonatal estrogen enhances induction by a carcinogen. bibliog Science 154:673-4 N 4 '66

WEISGALL, Hugo David
Music to my ears; Purgatory performed by Juilliard opera theater. I. Kolodin. Sat R 49:38 Je 4 '66

WEISKOPF, Herman
Baseball's week. See issues of Sports illustrated published during baseball season
College football. Sports Illus 25:63-4 O 3 '66
Diving. Sports Illus 24:85-7 Mr 21 '66
Gymnastics. Sports Illus 24:78+ My 16 '66

WEISKRANTZ, L. and Cowey, A.
Comparison of the effects of striate cortex and retinal lesions on visual acuity in the monkey. bibliog Science 155:104-6 Ja 6 '67

WEISMAN, Abner I.
Relics show their merits. F. Marley. il Sci N 90:396-7 N 12 '66

WEISMILLER, Edward
Conversation in the garden; poem. Sat R 49: 32 Mr 12 '66
Sunken forest; poem. New Yorker 42:48 Ap 30 '66

WEISS, Margaret R.
Big top's Mathew Brady. Sat R 49:146-7 Mr 12 '66
Brief exposures for holiday giving. Sat R 49:36-7 D 3 '66
Chim: shadow of violence. Sat R 50:128-9 Ja 14 '67
Encore at the Louvre: Henri Cartier-Bresson. Sat R 49:23-8 N 26 '66
Gentle persuasion. Sat R 49:76-7 S 10 '66
Place in the sun. Sat R 49:16-17 Ag 27 '66
Recording life-in-process. Sat R 49:50-1 Mr 5 '66
Riboud's camera covers China. Sat R 49:89-91 D 10 '66
Show of color. Sat R 49:45-52 S 24 '66
Speaking likeness. Sat R 49:96-7 Je 11 '66
Two for the title. Sat R 49:72-3 My 14 '66
World exposure. Sat R 50:90 Ja 7 '67

WEISS, Marian
New for amputees: instant limbs. A. T. Jordan. Todays Health 44:37-9+ D '66; Same abr. with title They walk again, at once. Read Digest 89:61-4 D '66

WEISS, Paul
Four possibilities of being. R. Abel. Sat R 49:35 Ja 29 '66

WEISS, Paul Alfred
Bringing the public to science; address, October 25, 1965. Vital Speeches 32:221-4 Ja 15 '66

WEISS, Penelope
Three poets. Poetry 108:57-64 Ap '66

WEISS, Peter
I come out of my hiding place; address,
April 25, 1966. Nation 202:652+ My 30 '66
about
Films. M. Goldman. Nation 202:222 F 21 '66
Investigation. Criticism
America 115:525 O 29 '66
Christian Cent 83:1540-1 D 14 '66
Commentary 42:75-6 D '66
Commonweal 85:139-41 N 4 '66
Life 61:8+ O 28 '66
Nation 203:395-6 O 17 '66
New Repub 155:42-4 N 26 '66
New Yorker 42:118 O 15 '66
Newsweek il 68:98 O 17 '66
Sat R 49:72 O 22 '66
Time il 88:93 O 14 '66
Vogue 148:99 N 15 '66
Marat/Sade. Criticism
America 114:181-2 Ja 29 '66
Cath World 203:63-4 Ap '66
Commentary 41:75-6 Mr '66
Commonweal 83:636-8 Mr 4 '66
Harper 232:124 Ap '66
Life 60:26B-27 Mr 11 '66
Look 30:106-10 F 22 '66
Newsweek 69:93 Ja 16 '67
Reporter 34:48-9 Ja 27 '66
Vogue 147:56 F 15 '66
Marat/Sade. S. Potter. il Am Rec G 32:
790-1+ My '66
People are talking about... il por Vogue
148:148-9 N 15 '66
Scourge of the world's theater; with report
by P. Dragadze. il pors Life 61:49-50+
O 28 '66
Weiss, propagandist and Weiss, playwright.
O. Clausen. il pors N Y Times Mag p28-9+
O 2 '66

WEISS, Theodore
Letter from the pygmies; poem. Sat R 49:65
F 19 '66
Sweet talk; poem. Nation 203:221 S 12 '66
Ultimate antientropy; poem. Nation 204:24 Ja
2 '67

WEISSBERG, Franklin R.
Beginning; interview. New Yorker 42:22-3
Ag 13 '66

WEISSLITZ, E. F.
Baldpate pond; poem. New Yorker 42:118
O 8 '66
Early games: three poems. Yale R 56:110-12
O '66

WEISSMANN, Ernest
Urban crisis, its meaning for development.
bibliog f UN Mo Chron 3:48-56 Ap '66

WEISSMANN, Gerald, and others
Staphylococcal alpha-toxin: effects on artificial lipid spherules. bibliog Science 154:772-
4 N 11 '66

WEISZ, Victor. See Vicky

WEITZ, Joe
Joe Weitz. il Pop Phot 58:74-7+ Mr '66

WEITZ, John
Men in fashion: two American designers. por
Esquire 65:104 Mr '66

WEITZEN, Hyman G.
Programmed child. Mlle 62:70-1+ Ja '66

WELCH, Claude E.
Shifting authority in West Africa. bibliog f
Cur Hist 50:153-8+ Mr '66

WELCH, Helen M.
Price indexes for 1966; US periodicals. Library J 91:3339-41 Jl '66

WELCH, Mary Scott
Redbook's guide to family pets. Redbook 127:
88-96 S '66
—See Nixon, R. E. jt. auth.

WELCH, Philip
Equipment-replacement plan. Am City 81:84-5
D '66

WELCH, Raquel
Mad about the girl. il por Time 87:80 Je
24 '66
On her way with zap and socko. il pors Life
61:65-6+ Ag 26 '66

WELCH, Robert Henry Winborne
Bedeviled Birchers. Time 88:25 S 9 '66
Birch tree grows. J. Freedman. il Library J
91:624-8 F 1 '66
Is Robert Welch's doctrine Christian? A.
Croce. Nat R 18:762 Ag 9 '66; Discussion.
18:910+ S 20 '66
Touched; concerning speech in Salt Lake
City. Time 87:25 Ap 15 '66

WELCHER, Irwin
Dorothea Lange and her printer. J. Deschin.
il Pop Phot 59:28+ Jl '66

WELDERS
Non-vacuum electron beam welder to get
Saturn tasks. il Tech W 19:18-20 Jl 4 '66

WELDING
Cold welding dangerous. Sci N 90:371 N 5 '66
Cold-welding experiments set for ORS-2. I.
Stone. il Aviation W 84:85-7 My 23 '66
Cold welding promises means to bond dis-
similar metals. J. F. Judge. il Miss & Roc
18:24 Ap 4 '66
Vacuum welding of olivine. P. R. Bell. bibliog
il Science 153:410-11 Jl 22 '66
See also
Electric welding

WELDING machines, Electric. See Electric
welding machines

WELDON, Don
Dropouts anonymous. Parents Mag 41:44-5+
My '66; Same abr. Read Digest 89:17-18+
Ag '66

WELDY, M. L.
Those critical five days. Suc Farm 64:53+
O '66

WELFARE, Public. See Public welfare

WELFARE legislation. See Social legislation

WELFARE state. See Social and economic security

WELFARE work. See Public welfare

WELL drilling. See Oil well drilling

WELLAND SHIP CANAL
Toll tempest on the Seaway; 10 per cent
boost in tolls proposed. il Bsns W p 120+
Jl 23 '66

WELLER, Lloyd W.
Kansas City's West side story. Am City 81:
108-11 F '66

WELLES, Chris
Accusers: Detroit botches its job. Life 60:
40+ Mr 25 '66
How it feels to live in total design. Life
60:59+ Ap 29 '66
Putting food to sleep. Life 60:71-2 F 18 '66
Tangled tower of CATV. Life 61:53-4+ N 18
'66
Variable sweep vs. the fixed Delta. Life 61:
79+ O 28 '66

WELLESLEY college, Wellesley, Mass.
New name on Wellesley's door. Time 87:70
Mr 25 '66

WELLESZ, Egon
Early days in Vienna; excerpt from Anton
von Webern. Sat R 49:49+ My 28 '66

WELLINGTON, C. Burleigh. See Wellington,
J. jt. auth.

WELLINGTON, Jean, and Wellington, C. B.
Should teachers see student records? NEA J
55:35-6 O '66

WELLINGTON management-Ivest merger. See
Business consolidations and mergers

WELLIVER, Neil
(ed) See Albers, J. Albers on Albers

WELLS, Anna Mary
And then the queen died. Writer 79:12-14
S '66

WELLS, Bill
Water in the gas. Motor B 117:66+ Mr '66

WELLS, George S.
Mexico's railroad in the sky. McCalls 93:
29-30+ F '66

WELLS, H. G.
Light in a thousand dark places. J. B.
Priestley. il por Horizon 8:32-7 Wint '66
Outline of H. G. Wells. G. Smith. il pors N Y
Times Mag p30-1+ Ag 21 '66
Wells and the cosmic despair. R. H. Costa.
Nation 203:222-4 S 12 '66

WELLS, Henry
Dominican search for stability. Cur Hist 51:
328-32+ D '66

WELLS, Herman B.
Branches for opportunity. por Am Ed 2:5-8
F '66

WELLS, Junior
Blues is how it is. il por Time 88:53 S 2 '66

WELLS, Martin J.
Invertebrate learning. Natur Hist 75:34-41
bibliog(p68) F '66

WELLS, Mary
Girl wonder. por Newsweek 67:80 Ap 18 '66
Madison avenue: see Mary run. il Newsweek
68:82-4 O 3 '66

WELLS, Philip V.
Late Pleistocene vegetation and degree of
pluvial climatic change in the Chihuahuan
Desert. bibliog Science 153:970-5 Ag 26 '66

WELLS, Rich, Greene, incorporated
Girl wonder. Newsweek 67:80 Ap 18 '66
Madison avenue: see Mary run. il Newsweek
68:82-4 O 3 '66
On lovable Madison avenue with Mary, Dick,
and Stew. P. Siekman. il Fortune 74:142-6+
Ag '66

WELLS, Roe E. and others
Blood flow in the microvasculature of the conjunctiva of man. Science 151:995-6 F 25 '66

WELLS, Samuel A. Jr, and others
Viral neoplastic transformation of hamster pineal cells in vitro: retention of enzymatic function. bibliog Science 154:278-9 O 14 '66

WELLS-Thorn house. See Deerfield, Mass.—Historic houses, etc.

WELLS
Leave well enough alone? R. Hendrickson. Flower Grower 53:31+ Ag '66
Sea salt kept from land; injection wells to preserve fresh water reserves in coastal regions. Sci N L 89:50 Ja 22 '66

WELS, Byron G.
Been printing on paper? now try. U S Camera 29:60-1+ My '66
—See Vlahos, C. jt auth.

WELSH, Christopher Norton
(ed) See Einem, G. von. Craftsman

WELSH, James
Higher education in Pennsylvania; a case of schizophrenia. Sat R 49:66-7+ Mr 19 '66

WELSH, James A.
Welcome gift. Negro Hist Bul 29:156+ Ap '66

WELSH, James F.
Ribicoff is a cautious crusader. N Y Times Mag p32-3+ Je 12 '66

WELSH, Peter C.
Trotter. Am Heritage 18:30-49 D '66

WELSH
We Welsh are all the same, we dig our roots deep. J. Hicks. il Life 62:24-7 Ja 6 '67

WELSHONS, Paul R.
Microfilm gives us 90 per cent more space. Am City 81:117 My '66

WELTE, Lou Ann
To an ant; poem. Horn Bk 42:92 F '66

WELTNER, Charles Longstreet
Pride and progress. Am Ed 2:23-5 O '66

about
Georgian quits in protest. por Sr Schol 89: 18 O 21 '66
Out of the battle. por Time 88:35 O 14 '66
Political triumph over racism. B. Galphin. Sat R 49:97-8 My 7 '66
Profile in courage. por Newsweek 68:30 O 17 '66
Refusal to go along with hate; with report by R. B. Stolley. il pors Life 61:109-10 O 14 '66
Weltner bill: clear and present danger. V. Countryman. il Nation 203:16-18 Jl 4 '66

WELTNER bill. See Communism—United States—Anti-Communist measures

WELTY, Eudora
Demonstrators; story. New Yorker 42:56-63 N 26 '66
English from the inside. por Am Ed 2:18-19 F '66
Interview with Eudora Welty. por Sr Schol 89:sup 18 D 9 '66

WENDEL, William Hall
Comeback at Carborundum. J. Berry. il pors Duns R 87:36-9+ Ap '66

WENDZEL, Douglas
How to catch the smartest trout of all. pors Outdoor Life 137:54-5+ Mr '66

WENHAM, Brian
How will Wilson get out of this one? New Repub 154:10-11 Je 18 '66
Mr Wilson under fire. New Repub 155:14 N 5 '66
Party will soon be over. New Repub 156: 14-15 Ja 7 '67
Sex and the lords. New Repub 154:9-10 F 12 '66
Wilson and the unions. New Repub 155:12 S 24 '66
Wilson, the juggler. New Repub 154:9-10 Ap 23 '66

WENK, Gladys
Maryland, my Maryland. Newsweek 68:41-2 O 10 '66

WENKHAM, Robert
Olulaau O Kauai (the forest of Kauai) il Audubon Mag 68:430-5 N '66

WENNERSTRÖM, Stig
Agent in place, by T. Whiteside. Review Newsweek il por 68:90 Ag 15 '66
Annals of espionage. T. Whiteside. New Yorker 42:58-60+ Mr 26; 51-2+ Ap 2; 92+ Ap 9 '66

WENSBERG, Erik
Lovely to look at, depressing to know. Reporter 34:55-6 My 19 '66

WENTWORTH, Mary
Happiness is bugs in the grass. il por Redbook 127:10+ O '66

WENTZ, Myron W. and others
Clostridium botulinum type F: seasonal inhibition by bacillus licheniformis. bibliog Science 155:89-90 Ja 6 '67

WENTZ, Richard E.
End of the Catholic era? Christian Cent 83: 716-17 Je 1 '66

WERDEGAR, Loraine
Papier-mâché animals. Sch Arts 65:5-9 Mr '66

WERNER, Alfred
Brilliance of light. Reporter 35:50+ N 3 '66
Conflagration in the soul. Reporter 34:47-8 Mr 24 '66
Golden age of Rembrandt. Reporter 35:34-6 D 29 '66
In the land of promise. Reporter 35:50-2 O 6 '66
Lautrec in stone. Reporter 34:52+ Ap 21 '66
Medieval splendors. Am Artist 30:38-42+ D '66
Poet as critic. Reporter 34:58+ F 24 '66
Village of painters. Reporter 35:49-50 S 8 '66

WERNER, M. R.
Harness racing. Sports Illus 25:69 N 7 '66

WERNER, Oskar
Dogs and mice can be movie stars; ed by E. Miller. pors Seventeen 25:112-13+ Je '66

about
Very phony profession. T. Armbrister. il pors Sat Eve Post 239:100-2+ O 8 '66

WERNICK, Robert
Perfect candidate. Life 60:41-2+ Je 3 '66
Wars of the instant Medicis. Life 61:102-3+ O 28 '66

WERSCH, L. van, and Suér, Henk
Celibacy in Holland; excerpts. Cath World 204:177-9 D '66

WERTH, Alexander
Akhmatova: tragic Queen Anna. Nation 203: 157-60 Ag 22 '66
Ben Barka is dead. Nation 202:350-2 Mr 28 '66
French eyes on Vietnam: America's colony in hell. Nation 202:702-4 Je 13 '66
Gangrene of Vietnam. Nation 202:414-15 Ap 11 '66
Kosygin in Paris: differences within amity. Nation 203:693-6 D 26 '66
Russian summer: worried vacationists. Nation 203:176-9 S 5 '66
Straws in the wind. Nation 202:442 Ap 18 '66
23rd congress: no more angry shouts? Nation 202:621-2 My 23 '66
Two sides of a miracle. Sat R 49:40-1 F 19 '66

WESCON electronics show. See Western electronics show and convention

WESCOTT, Jimmy
From a boy's point of view. See issues of Seventeen to December 1966
Golden fable for St Valentine's day; story. Seventeen 25:28 F '66

WESKER, Arnold
Chips with everything. Criticism
    Commonweal 84:473 Jl 22 '66
Kitchen. Criticism
    Life 61:17 Ag 12 '66
    Newsweek il 67:89 Je 27 '66
    Sat R 49:36 Jl 2 '66

WESLEY, Charles H.
Aspect of bibliography and research in Negro history; address, October 22, 1965. por Negro Hist Bul 29:51-2+ D '65
Foreword to the pictorial history of the American Negro; reprint. por Negro Hist Bul 29:105-6 F '66

WESLEY, Walt
Go Wesley young man! H. L. Masin. il por Sr Schol 88:20 F 25 '66

WESLEYAN university, Middletown, Conn.
From Amex to academe; new president. Time 88:53 Jl 22 '66

WESLEYAN university press
Wesleyan university press publishes its 100th title. il Pub W 190:36-7 N 28 '66

WESSEL, Morris A.
Babies are my business. Parents Mag 41:66-7+ N '66
How does a baby learn? Parents Mag 41:48-9+ Mr '66

WESSON, Jerry
Sound. See issues of U.S. camera & travel

WEST, Adam
Waves; poem. por McCalls 93:81 Je '66

about
Has TV gasp! gone Batty? J. Skow. il pors Sat Eve Post 239:93-7 My 7 '66

WEST, Allan M.
What is the professional services campaign?
NEA J 55:27-8 F '66

WEST, Anthony
Books. New Yorker 41:129-34 F 5; 42:88-9
Jl 9; 76+ Jl 30 '66
Mrs Barker; story. New Yorker 42:52-6 My
14 '66
Paintings one lives with brighten the house.
House & Gard 130:84-5+ Jl '66
Real Christmas. House & Gard 130:158-9+
D '66
Theatre. Vogue 147:95 Mr 1; 58 Mr 15; 109
Ap 1; 64 Ap 15; 145 My; 54 Je; 148:28 Jl;
150 N 1; 99 N 15 161 D '66

WEST, Carolyn
Island-hopping holiday. Motor B 119:88-9+
Ja '67
Revamping the older powerboat. il Yachting
119:92-4+ Ap '66
—and West, Jack
Robust, exciting; it's called California.
Motor B 117:22-6+ My '66

WEST, Chuck
Dioramas out of the deepfreeze. Pop Mech
125:126-9+ F '66

WEST, Daphene. See Sloan, W. jt. auth.

WEST, Jack. See West, C. jt. auth.

WEST, Jessamyn
Matter of time; story. Redbook 127:163 S;
165 O '66
Should this father raise his son? Ladies
Home J 83:88+ My '66

about

Gentle storyteller challenges death. W.
Schott. Life 61:8 O 21 '66

WEST, Mae
So I went up to see Mae West. P. Gowland.
il Pop Phot 59:32+ Jl '66

WEST, Paul
Two British chronicles. R. J. Mills, jr. Poetry
107:409 Mr '66

WEST, Mrs Paul
Housewife rebellion. il pors Life 61:57-8 N
4 '66

WEST, Dame Rebecca
Grave and reverend book. Harper 232:108+
F; 4 My '66
Specialist in traitors, spies and weeds; in-
terview, ed. by J. Hicks. pors Life 61:55-
6+ S 30 '66

WEST, Richard
Why Latin Americans say, go home, Yanqui.
N Y Times Mag p8-9+ My 29 '66

WEST, Robert D, family
Robert West's second life. K. Wheeler. il
pors Life 61:90-2+ D 16 '66

WEST, Ruth
(ed) See Masters, W. H. B, to keep men
vital

WEST
Pacific America. H. Gold; N. Morgan; A.
Swensson. il Sat R 49:51-2+ O 8 '66
See also
Art—Western states
Botany—Western states
Fishing—Western states
Frontier and pioneer life—United States
Hunting—Western states
Northwest

Description and travel

Frontierland frolic. L. M. Rhodes. il Travel
125:47-9 Ap '66
[Month] travel in and beyond the West. See
issues of Sunset
West coast wanderings. P. Noyes. See issues
of Travel
See also
Southwest—Description and travel

Discovery and exploration

Journals of Zebulon Montgomery Pike, with
letters and related documents, ed. by D.
Jackson. Review
Sat R 49:33 S 3 '66. J. A. Hawgood

History

See also
California—History
Lewis and Clark expedition

Industries

West coast electronics industry: a special
EW report. L. Zietsoff. il Electr World 75:
25-8+ Ap '66

Politics

Outlook in twenty-four states; little change.
U S News 61:38-40 O 17 '66
Victory in depth; election results. il Time 88:
32 N 18 '66

WEST and East. See East and West

WEST BERLIN. See Berlin (West Berlin)

WEST EUROPEAN aerospace industry association. See Eurospace

WEST Ford dipoles. See Dipole orbital belts in
space

WEST in art
Roundup time. il Time 88:56-8 Ag 12 '66
Russell gallery at Great Falls. J. Meyer. il
Am Artist 30:26-9+ N '66

WEST INDIAN cookery. See Cookery, West
Indian

WEST INDIES
See also
Antigua (island)
Barbados
Caribbean Region
Dominican Republic
Gardens—West Indies
Leeward Islands
Navassa (island)
St Martin (island)

WEST INDIES, BRITISH
See also
Young's Island

History

Slave society in the British Leeward Islands
at the end of the eighteenth century, by
E. V. Goveia. Review
Nation 202:754-5 Je 20 '66. O. H. Olsen

WEST POINT military academy. See United
States military academy, West Point

WEST RUTLAND, Vt.
Washington slipped here. il Nations Bsns
54:38-9+ Ag '66

WEST side of the island; story. See Buitrago,
F.

WEST VIRGINIA
See also
Hunting—West Virginia

Politics and government

Turncoat Rockefeller; John D. IV, to run for
House of delegates. C. Boiarsky. New Repub 154:9 F 26 '66

WEST VIRGINIA pulp and paper company
Seminars on book publishing topics; report
on panel discussion. il Pub W 190:70+ Ag
1: 96-7+ S 5 '66

**WEST VIRGINIA State college, Institute,
W.Va.**
For the fine arts and humanities; statement,
December 5, 1965. J. W. Davis. Negro Hist
Bul 29:57-8 D '65
Living laboratory of human relations. B.
Francois. il Sat R 49:64-5 My 21 '66

WESTBURY, N.Y.
Tape recorders insure accuracy at public
meetings. J. Sharkey. il Am City 81:36 Jl
'66

WESTBURY house garden. See Gardens—Long
Island

WESTCHESTER, Ill.
Tandem plowing clears snow curb-to-curb.
H. Witcher. il Am City 81:92-3 O '66

WESTCHESTER library system
YA's disclose favorite reading, library uses,
in Westchester survey. Library J 91:2184
Ap 15 '66

WESTCOTT, Cynthia
Fragrant roses are back in style. por Flower
Grower 53:32-3+ F '66
H&G's 1966 guide to plant protection. House
& Gard 129:94-7+ Ap '66

WESTEC corporation
Bankruptcy for Westec. Newsweek 68:95 O
10 '66
Broadsider. Time 88:96 S 9 '66
Trouble at Westec. Newsweek 68:78+ S 12 '66
Why Westec turned to chapter X; bank-
ruptcy petition, SEC continues investiga-
tion. Bsns W p44 O 1 '66

WESTERFIELD, Nancy G.
At Stonehenge; poem. Reporter 35:39 Ag 11
'66

**WESTERN amateur astronomers (organiza-
tion)**
Western amateurs convene in California.
J. W. Goodman. il Sky & Tel 32:188-90
O '66

WESTERN book exhibition. See Book exhibits

WESTERN Catholic reporter. See Catholic
press

WESTERN civilization. See Civilization

WESTERN electronics show and convention
Electronics tastes new riches; resulting from
military needs and demand for color TV
sets. il Bsns W p 144+ S 3 '66

WESTERN electronics show and convention
—*Continued*
Industry growth reflected at WESCON. il
Tech W 19:33-7 S 5 '66
Seaborg presses nuclear case at WESCON.
C. D. LaFond. Tech W 19:18-19 Ag 29 '66
WESTERN fence lizards. See Lizards
WESTERN GERMANY. See Germany (Federal
Republic)
WESTERN printing and lithographing company
Western's quality control features inspection unit. il Pub W 191:95 Ja 2 '67
WESTERN publishing company
S&S to sell its holdings in Western publishing co. Pub W 190:30 D 12 '66
**WESTERN RESERVE university, Cleveland,
Ohio**
U.S. seeks wider base for science; NSF's centers of excellence program in Case and
WRU. il Bsns W p60-2 S 3 '66
WESTERN states. See West
WESTERN stories
My stories of the wild West. E. S. Gardner.
il Atlan 218:60-2 Jl '66
WESTERN test range. See Proving grounds
WESTERN testing, incorporated
Clubs feed cattle, and the kitty. il Bsns W
p 132-3+ Je 25 '66
WESTERN theatre ballet (organization)
London's world of dance. M. Seif. il Sat R
49:67-8+ S 24 '66
WESTERN union telegraph company
FCC studies Western union bids for satellite
network. Aviation W 85:33 N 14 '66
WESTERN WASHINGTON state college, Bellingham
Project overcome. D. Connelly. il Parents
Mag 41:52-5+ Ag '66
WESTERNERS
See also
Texans
WESTGARDE, Edward
Invisible moose. pors Outdoor Life 137:32-5+
Je '66
WESTHEIMER, David
My sweet Charlie. Criticism
Christian Cent 84:86 Ja 18 '67
Nation 204:30 Ja 2 '67
New Yorker 42:117 D 17 '66
Newsweek 68:106 D 19 '66
Sat R 49:61 D 24 '66
Time 88:87 D 16 '66
WESTIN, Av
Victorygraph; interview. New Yorker 42:51-3
N 5 '66
WESTINGHOUSE air brake company
Pulling the big switch. il Bsns W p 182-4+
F 19 '66
WESTINGHOUSE electric corporation
How computers liven a management's ways.
il Bsns W p 112-14+ Je 25 '66
How to make money out of obsolescence;
replacement parts for obsolete electrical
apparatus. il Bsns W p80-2 F 5 '66
Spreading the message with tape. il Bsns W
p87 Jl 9 '66
Tempest in a coffee cup; concerning raised
prices in cafeterias in Westinghouse electric corp.'s Defense center at Maryland.
Newsweek 67:61 F 7 '66
WESTLEY, William A.
Escalation of violence through legitimation.
bibliog f Ann Am Acad 364:120-6 Mr '66
WESTMINSTER abbey. See London—Westminster abbey
WESTMINSTER kennel club show. See Dog
shows
WESTMORELAND, William Childs
General Westmoreland reports on Vietnam
war; interview. por U S News 61:44-9 N 28
'66
Gift of love. McCalls 94:73-4 D '66
President Johnson and General Westmoreland
discuss the situation in Viet-Nam; transcript of news conference, August 14, 1966.
Dept State Bul 55:336-8 S 5 '66

about
American way of war. il por Newsweek 68:
49-50+ D 5 '66
Day with Westmoreland. O. Elliott. il por
Newsweek 67:32 Ap 18 '66
Sunday with Westmoreland; the general
who runs our war in Vietnam. C. S.
Wren. il pors Look 30:27-31 O 18 '66
Westmoreland: the four-star eagle scout. D.
Moser. il pors Life 61:68-70+ N 11 '66
Why we can win in Vietnam. J. Alsop. il
por Sat Eve Post 239:27-8+ Je 4 '66
WESTOFF, Charles F. See Ryder, N. B. jt.
auth.

WESTON, Edward
Discovered: new Weston letter! Pop Phot 59:
16+ N '66
WESTON, Hugh
Letter from Australia. Nation 203:512-13 N
14 '66
WESTON, Ill.
For the Midwest, a scientific plum. il U S
News 61:6 D 26 '66
Near the tree; site for atom-smashing accelerator. Time 88:21 D 23 '66
WESTPORT, Conn.
Dewatering by wells; solution to high-watertable problem on a sewer-construction
project. J. E. Czel, jr. il Am City 81:80-1
Je '66
Hazards of Roseville road. G. C. Maurer. il
Pop Phot 58:60-2 Je '66
WESTREX division. See Litton industries, incorporated
WESTRUM, L. E. See Lund, R. D. jt. auth.
WESTRUM, Wes
Team that can make a man cry. J. Mann.
il Sports Illus 24:36-8+ Je 27 '66
WET storage. See Boats—Storage
WETLANDS for wildlife (proposed) See Wildlife sanctuaries
WETMORE, Reagh C.
Drownproofing keeps you afloat till help
comes. Pop Sci 189:58-9 Jl '66
WETZEL, Charles J.
Peace corps in our past. bibliog f Ann Am
Acad 365:1-11 My '66
WEXFORD festival. See Music festivals—Ireland
WEXLER, Sidney F.
Franco's peace: Spain thirty years after the
insurrection. Yale R 56:25-44 O '66
WEYBRIGHT, Victor
Weybright and Talley: new publishing firm.
il Pub W 190:36-7 D 5 '66
WEYBRIGHT and Talley, incorporated
Weybright and Talley: new publishing firm.
il Pub W 190:36-7 D 5 '66
WEYER, James R. See Vonnegut, B. jt. auth.
WEYERHAEUSER company
Weyerhaeuser division absorbs Crocker
Hamilton. Pub W 189:133-4 F 7 '66
WEYGOLDT, Peter
Spermatophore web formation in a pseudoscorpion. bibliog Science 153:1647-9 S 30 '66
WEYMAR, Caroline S. See Skibbins, G. J. jt.
auth.
WEYMOUTH, Mass.
2.0-mgd water plant built in 2½ months;
diatomaceus-earth filtration plant, address, April 14, 1966. R. M. Pope. il Am
City 81:82-3 Jl '66
WHALEN, George J.
Build the Modbox. Pop Electr 25:41-5+
Ag '66
WHALEN, Richard J.
Kennedy assassination. Sat Eve Post 240:
19-25+ Ja 14 '67
This Lindsay takes on that city. Fortune
73:126-9+ Je '66
WHALEN, Robert G.
Gout is in. N Y Times Mag p66+ My 1 '66
WHALEN, William Henry
Bizarre account of what Whalen says he did;
interview, ed. by S. McBee. pors Life 61:
24-7 Jl 22 '66

about
Carrot & careless George. por Time 88:23
Jl 22 '66
In the cold war, new charges of spying. il
U S News 61:12 Jl 25 '66
Red hot week for the spy business. il por
Life 61:20-1 Jl 22 '66
Way down. il por Newsweek 68:22-3 Jl 25 '66
WHALERS
Of trypots and topless windjammers; the
Charles W. Morgan, at Marine historical
association. Mystic, Conn. F. Rohr. il Motor B 119:98-100+ Ja '67
WHALES
Camera whaling has problems unknown to
Ahab; migration of the Pacific gray whale
along the California coast. W. Lane. il
Travel 126:68 D '66
Eviction of whales; threat to breeding ground
of the great gray whale. W. Marx. il
Atlan 217:91-5 Ap '66
Extinction for whales? Nat Parks Mag 40:26
Ag '66
Heavyweight high jump; Makapuu; performing whale at Hawaii's Sea life park. il Life
61:121-2+ N 25 '66

WHALES—*Continued*
Kindly killer whale. Sci Am 215:72+ N '66
Last of the great whales. S. McVay. il Sci
Am 215:13-21 bibliog(p 114) Ag '66
Making friends with a killer whale. E. I.
Griffin. il Nat Geog Mag 129:418-46 Mr '66
Whale of a mystery; suicides off Florida
Keys. il Newsweek 68:62 Ag 29 '66
Whales saved may be last of their kind.
Sci N 90:277 O 8 '66

WHALING
Last of the great whales. S. McVay. il Sci
Am 215:13-21 bibliog(p 114) Ag '66

History
Of trypots and topless windjammers. F.
Rohr. il Motor B 119:98-100+ Ja '67

WHALING ships. See Whalers

WHALL, Hugh
Boating (cont) Sports Illus 24:49-51 F 21;
56-7 Mr 28; 96-8 Ap 4; 25:48-9 Ag 15; 116-18
S 12; 110-11 S 19; 62-4 D 12 '66
High fashion model takes over. Sports Illus
25:38-42 Jl 4 '66

WHARTON, Don
Built-in press for your clothes. Read Digest
88:128-31 F '66
How soon will we wear paper clothes? Read
Digest 89:53-5 Ag '66
Look what's happened to ice cream. Read
Digest 88:101-3 Je '66
They're saving America's priceless seashore.
Read Digest 89:181+ Ag '66

WHARTON, Hazel
Telling the park story. Parks & Rec 1:622-4+
Ag '66

WHARTON, John F.
Causes of peace. Sat R 49:12-14+ Jl 2 '66
Does anyone know reality? por Sat R 49:21-3
D 3 '66

WHARTON school of finance and commerce.
See Pennsylvania. University—Wharton
school of finance and commerce

WHARVES

Fire and fire protection
Scuba-diving fire-eaters. B. Grant. il Pop
Mech 126:102-4 Ag '66

WHATMORE, Marvin C.
Private profit and public gain; address, June
6, 1966. Vital Speeches 32:571-3 Jl 1 '66

WHEAT, Joe Ben
Paleo-Indian bison kill; with biographical
sketch. Sci Am 216:21, 44-52 Ja '67

WHEAT
How to fertilize for high-yield, high-quality
wheat. F. W. Smith and L. E. Zeman. il
Suc Farm 64:52-3 S '66
1966 wheat-feed grain programs. F. Bailey,
jr. Suc Farm 64:50-1 F '66
Now it's a different wheat crisis that faces
U.S. il U S News 61:50-3 Jl 4 '66
Those extra wheat acres. Farm J 90:22+ S '66
Those extra wheat acres. C. W. Gifford. Farm
J 90:67 D '66
Wheat shortage is here. K. Hobson. Farm J
90:21+ Ag '66

History
Distribution of wild wheats and barley. J. R.
Harlan and D. Zohary. bibliog il Science
153:1074-80 S 2 '66

Hybrids
Hybrid wheat; here's a last-minute report.
G. Morgan. il Suc Farm 64:36-7 O'66

Prices
Wheat woes. Newsweek 67:90+ Je 13 '66

WHEATLEY, Phillis
Miss Wheatley's distinction. H. Cohen. Reporter 34:46+ Je 30 '66

WHEDON, Julia
It's magic time; story. Ladies Home J 84:
58-9 Ja '67

WHEELER, Bruce E.
Lincolniana in 1965. Hobbies 70:28-9+ F '66

WHEELER, Earle Gilmore
Challenge came in Vietnam; address, November 15, 1966. Vital Speeches 33:130-3 D
15 '66
Gavin plan will not work; excerpts from
testimony, January 22, 1966. por U S News
60:27-8 F 7 '66

WHEELER, Harry, and Hanchey, P. J.
Respiratory control: loss in mitochondria
from diseased plants. bibliog Science 154:
1569-71 D 23 '66

WHEELER, Harvey
Means, ends and human institutions. Nation
204:9-16 Ja 2 '67

WHEELER, Helen
Introducing the library through film. Wilson
Lib Bul 41:197-9 O '66
Twenty-seven tips for the new librarian.
Library J 91:6164-5 D 15 '66

WHEELER, John N.
Unforgettable Ring Lardner. Read Digest 89:
113-17 O '66

WHEELER, Joseph L.
Mezzanines: use & abuse. Library J 91:5851
D 1 '66

WHEELER, Judith
Electronic age. Sat R 49:21-2 Je 4 '66

WHEELER, Keith
Full story of the 2.8 seconds that killed the
XB70. Life 61:126-30+ N 11 '66
Integration vendetta in a northern town.
Life 60:94-6+ My 6 '66
Off-year election with a difference. Life 61:
61-4+ N 4 '66
Robert West's second life. Life 61:90-2+ D
16 '66
—and Lambert, William
Uneasy balance, ethics vs profits. Life 60:
86-8+ Je 24 '66

WHEELER, Monroe
Turner. Look 30:42-6 Ap 5 '66

WHEELER, Richard F.
Amateur scientist. Sci Am 214:120-4+ F '66

WHEELING, W.Va.

City planning
Cooperation built a market plaza. M. J.
Rody. il Am City 81:104-5 Ap '66

WHEELING steel and Crucible steel merger.
See Business consolidations and mergers

WHEELING steel corporation
Wheeling deals a new suit; charges Hanna
mining and Cleveland-Cliffs with price fixing. Bsns W p58 S 24 '66

WHEELIS, Allen
Sea-girls; story. Yale R 55:570-84 Je '66

WHEELOCK, E. Frederick. See Edelman, R.
jt. auth.

WHEELOCK, John Hall
Amagansett beach revisited; poem. New
Yorker 42:34 Je 18 '66
Random reflections on a summer evening;
poem. New Yorker 42:26-7 Jl 30 '66

WHEELS
See also
Airplanes—Wheels
Automobiles—Wheels
Motor trucks— Wheels
Motor vehicles—Wheels

WHEELS in art. See Art—Themes

WHERE early falls the dew; story. See Loeser,
K.

WHERE will all the bluebirds go? story. See
Amft, M. J.

WHERE'S Charley? musical comedy. See Musical comedies, revues, etc.—Criticisms,
plots, etc.

WHERE'S daddy? drama. See Inge, W.

WHETTEN, John T.
Sediments from the lower Columbia River
and origin of graywacke. bibliog Science
152:1057-8 My 20 '66

WHIG party (Great Britain) See Political parties—Great Britain

WHIPPED cream. See Cream

WHIPPING. See Corporal punishment

WHIPPLE, Fred L.
Chondrules: suggestion concerning the origin.
bibliog il Science 153:54-6 Jl 1 '66

WHIRLPOOL corporation
Whirlpool moves into living room; merger
with Warwick electronics, manufacturer
of home entertainment equipment for Sears.
Bsns W p33 Ag 20 '66

WHIRLWINDS
Dust devils produced. il Sci N 90:234 S 24
'66

WHISKERS. See Beards

WHISKERS, Metal. See Metal crystals

WHISKEY
Manner of speaking; calories in liquors. J.
Ciardi. Sat R 49:19 O 22 '66
Water of life. F. Allen. Horizon 9:120 Wint
'67

Anecdotes, facetiae, satire, etc.
Troubling of the waters; Quoylay whiskey.
G. M. Brown. Atlan 218:142 N '66

WHISTLERS (radio waves) See Radio waves

WHITAKER, Frederic
New dimension of Douglas Gorsline. Am
Artist 30:38-43+ My '66
Paintings of Franklin Jones. Am Artist 30:
24-9+ D '66

WHITAKER, Horace
Whitaker's forest. G. B. Larson. il Am For 72:22-5+ S '66

WHITAKER, Robert B.
Angling paradise of the Apaches. pors Outdoor Life 138:36-9+ S '66

WHITAKER'S forest. See Forests and forestry—California

WHITBREAD, Jane
Kids and money. Parents Mag 41:70-2+ D '66

WHITE, Al
Full story of the 2.8 seconds that killed the XB70. K. Wheeler. il pors Life 61:128-30+ N 11 '66

WHITE, Byron R.
Pro and con: here's what the justices said; excerpts from dissenting opinion. por U S News 60:36 Je 27 '66

WHITE, Dori
Woman's work; story. Redbook 127:66-7 Ag '66

WHITE, E. B.
Annals of birdwatching. New Yorker 42:42-6+ F 26 '66
Anne Carroll Moore urged withdrawal of Stuart Little. E. B. White reports; excerpts from article. Library J 91:2187 Ap 15 '66
Deserted nation; poem. New Yorker 42:53 O 8 '66
Following one's instincts. Writer 79:22-3 Jl '66

WHITE, Edna
Phenomenal career. F. Summerill. il por Hobbies 71:40 My; 40-1+ Je; 38+ Jl '66

WHITE, Edna M.
Soft blanket, tough nest. Audubon Mag 68:124 Mr '66

WHITE, Elgin
Enjoying the ancient Apalachicola. Motor B 118:34-6+ O '66

WHITE, Ellington
Fishing (cont) Sports Illus 25:60-2+ O 10 '66

WHITE, George Henry
George Henry White: a militant Negro congressman in the age of Booker T. Washington. W. Katz. bibliog Negro Hist Bul 29:125-6+ Mr '66

WHITE, Gilbert F. See Sewell, W. R. D. jt. auth.

WHITE, H. Lee
At the eye of the shipping storm. por Bsns W p 132+ Je 18 '66

WHITE, Jack G.
Small communities can have centralized purchasing. Am City 81:162 N '66

WHITE, Joan
Gibraltar revisited. Sat R 49:44-6 Jl 30 '66

WHITE, John
Bugs. Criticism
Life 60:10 Ja 28 '66
Reporter 34:47-8 F 24 '66
Veronica. Criticism
Life 60:10 Ja 28 '66
Reporter 34:47-8 F 24 '66

WHITE, John F.
ST interview; ed. by P. Dilts. por Sr Schol 88:sup 14 F 18 '66
about
1966: the year ETV comes of age. por Sr Schol 89:sup2 N 4 '66

WHITE, Katharine S.
Onward and upward in the garden (cont) New Yorker 42:149-50+ D 10 '66

WHITE, Lee C.
New power in the FPC. por Bsns W p27 Jl 30 '66

WHITE, Mary Alice
Speculations on the child's world of learning. NEA J 55:20-2 Mr '66

WHITE, Peter T.
Camera keeps watch on the world. N Y Times Mag p26-7+ Ap 3 '66
Hudson River clean-up: it can be clear, blue and wonderful again. N Y Times Mag p8-9+ Jl 17 '66

WHITE, Philip L.
(ed) Let's talk about food. See issues of Today's health

WHITE, Philip R.
Versatile perfusion chamber for living cells and organs. bibliog Science 152:1758-60 Je 24 '66

WHITE, Richard Crawford
New way to roll out the pork barrel. il pors Nations Bsns 54:38-9+ Je '66

WHITE, Robert M.
By simulating catastrophe. Sat R 49:62-4 My 7 '66

WHITE, Sheffield
What's the matter with the British businessman? Read Digest 88:207-8+ Ap '66

WHITE, Stanford
Splendid world of Stanford White; with photographs by T. Frissell and account by A. Saarinen. pors Life 61:87-101+ S 16 '66

WHITE, Tyner
Dismantling a Rhine barge; Loneliness of a sailor in Jersey City; poems. Atlan 218:92-3 S '66

WHITE, Vera Randal
Let's be friends; story. Seventeen 25:162-3 Ap '66
Natural immunity; story. McCalls 94:122-3 O '66

WHITE, W. L.
Rising risk of runaway inflation. Read Digest 89:128-32 Ag '66

WHITE, William V.
Safe mowing. Horticulture 44:32-3 Ag '66

WHITE alder. See Alder

WHITE BEAR LAKE, Minn.
First unit for a new Lutheran church; St Stephen Lutheran church. il Arch Rec 140:109 Ag '66

WHITE collar workers. See Office workers

WHITE footed mice. See Mice. White footed

WHITE House
Christmas in the White House. C. B. Luce. McCalls 94:48+ D '66
Crèche in the White House. il Ladies Home J 83:98-9 D '66
Death at White House: LBJ's favorite dog. il U S News 60:10 Je 27 '66
Entertaining people; planning, staging and presenting social fuctions. il McCalls 94:24+ N '66
Gadgetized White House pleases the POTUS. H. Sidey. il Life 61:33B Ag 26 '66
Living White House. L. Aikman. il Nat Geog Mag 130:593-643 N '66
Mrs Johnson talks about her love for the White House. R. F. Pomeroy. il Redbook 127:72-8+ Jl '66
Sorry, wrong number; W. M. Watson's critics. Newsweek 67:21 Ja 31 '66
Upstairs at the White House. il House & Gard 130:197-209 O '66
White House at work; a mystery explained. il U S News 60:36-7 F 7 '66
See also
Presidents—United States

Libraries
ABA's White House library presentation takes place. Pub W 189:153 F 21 '66
1965 ABA's presentation to the family library of the White House; with list of books. il Pub W 189:50-7 F 28 '66

WHITE House airplanes. See Airplanes, Government

WHITE House conference on civil rights, 1966
Civil rights: can any program satisfy everyone? il U S News 60:60-2 Je 13 '66
Civil rights conference stresses practical steps; To fulfill these rights. Sci N 89:458 Je 11 '66
Letter from Washington. R. H. Rovere. New Yorker 42:118+ Je 18 '66
Moderate vs. militant. Newsweek 67:38 Je 13 '66
More for Negroes? a price tag of billions. U S News 60:10 Je 6 '66
Moynihan report: Negro family, the case for national action; reply. H. L. Harrod. Christian Cent 83:180-2 F 9 '66
New battlefields; council's proposals. Newsweek 67:26 Je 6 '66
New drive to fulfill these rights; emphasis on local efforts by business, labor, and government. il Bsns W p38-40 My 28 '66
No fire this time. A. Kopkind. New Repub 154:15-16 Je 18 '66
No miracles. il Time 87:35 Je 10 '66
Protesting too much? Reporter 34:10 Je 16 '66
To fulfill these rights. America 114:823 Je 11 '66
Urgent new reach to be equal; conference preview. J. K. Jessup. il Life 60:88-90+ Je 3 '66
White House conference: bubble of unreality. R. G. Sherrill. il Nation 202:734-7 Je 20 '66

WHITE House conference on international cooperation. 1965
Blueprint for peace, by R. N. Gardner. Review
Sat R 50:42+ Ja 21 '67. G. N. Shuster

WHITE House conference on international co-
operation, 1965—*Continued*
ICY plus one: an inventory. R. N. Gardner.
Sat R 49:24-5+ N 5 '66
International cooperation at the White House.
B. G. Lall. Bul Atomic Sci 22:41-3 F '66
Senator Clark on the White House con-
ference. J. S. Clark. Bul Atomic Sci 22:30-3
Mr '66
Washington report. J. Lloyd. Sr Schol 87:
sup 10 Ja 21 '66
White House committee to review ICY con-
ference recommendations; White House an-
nouncement; with text of memorandum
from President. Dept State Bul 55:275-6 Ag
22 '66
White House ICY conference urges greater
world library cooperation. Library J 91:221
Ja 15 '66
WHITE House entertaining. See Government
entertaining
WHITE House fellows. See Scholarships and
fellowships
WHITE House receptions. See Government
entertaining
WHITE House staff. See Public officers
WHITE House youth conference on natural
beauty and conservation
If all you want is a penguin's egg . . ; ad-
dress, June 27, 1966. S. F. Francis. il Liv
Wildn 30:20-1 Sum '66
National youth conference; Washington, June
26-29. Liv Wildn 30:22-3 Sum '66
WHITE MOUNTAIN scenic railroad, Ariz. See
Railroads, Short line
WHITE MOUNTAINS
See also
Franconia Notch
WHITE PLAINS, N.Y.
Recreation
Into the wild blue yonder; Flying for
recreation program. B. Dille. il Parks &
Rec 1:332-3 Ap '66
WHITE rhinoceros. See Rhinoceros
WHITE sales. See Bargain sales
WHITE sharks. See Sharks
WHITE Sox (baseball) See Baseball clubs
WHITE sweater; story. See Oakes, T.
WHITE tailed deer hunting. See Deer hunt-
ing
WHITE-throated sparrows. See Sparrows
WHITE-winged pheasants. See Pheasants
WHITEBREAD, Thomas
Children's snow; poem. New Yorker 42:54
Mr 12 '66
WHITEHORN, Ethel. See McMahan, I. jt. auth.
WHITEMARSH, Pa.
Historic houses, etc.
History in houses: Hope lodge. Whitemarsh,
Pennsylvania. J. D. Van Trump. il Antiques
89:542-5 Ap '66
WHITESIDE, Robert J.
Desirable location: factories wanted. Amer-
ica 114:261 F 19 '66
WHITESIDE, Thomas
Annals of espionage. New Yorker 42:58-60+
Mr 26; 51-2+ Ap 2: 92+ Ap 9 '66
WHITFORD, A. E.
American pioneer in photoelectric astronomy.
Sky & Tel 31:268-9 My '66
New Santa Cruz headquarters for Lick ob-
servatory. Sky & Tel 32:328-32 D '66
WHITMAN, Alden
Mr Bad News. G. Talese. il por Esquire 65:
88-9+ F '66
WHITMAN, Ardis
God is dead debate. Redbook 127:62-3+ Je '66
Why husbands don't say what they really
think. McCalls 93:75+ S '66
WHITMAN, Arthur
Clinic for sick missiles. Pop Mech 125:120-4
F '66
Hunting with a cheetah! Pop Mech 125:96-9
F '66
Music goes round and round, and comes out
over yonder. Pop Mech 126:100-1 S '66
Our keenest ear tunes in on space. Pop Mech
127:130-3 Ja '67
Planning a war? see Sam! Pop Mech 125:
90-2+ My '66
Str-r-r-etch to a luxury limousine. Pop
Mech 125:116-19+ Je '66
Walls for wandering farms. Pop Mech 125:
95-7+ Je '66

WHITMAN, Charles Joseph
All-American boy. il pors Newsweek 68:24-6+
Ag 15 '66
American amok. R. Coles. New Repub 155:
12-15 Ag 27 '66
Can killers be predicted? P. McBroom. Sci N
90:117 Ag 20 '66
Madman in the tower. il por Time 88:14-19
Ag 12 '66
Mass murder on a campus. il por U S News
61:6 Ag 15 '66
Real story of Austin's mass killer. por U S
News 61:9 Ag 22 '66
Tumor found innocent. P. McBroom. Sci N
90:98 Ag 13 '66
Under the clock, a sniper with 31 minutes to
live; with report by D. Nevin. il Life 61:
24-31 Ag 12 '66
WHITMAN, Dana, Jr
Grass-roots facelifting. Am City 81:96-7 O '66
WHITMAN, Ruth
She doesn't want to bring the tides in any
more; poem. Nation 202:429 Ap 11 '66
(tr) See Singer, I. B. Parrot
WHITMAN, Walt
Idea of poetry. B. Duffey. Poetry 107:397-9
Mr '66
Walt Whitman. K. Rexroth. Sat R 49:43 S 3
'66
WHITMAN house. See Huntington, N.Y.—His-
toric houses, etc.
WHITMORE, G. F. and Gulyas, S.
Synchronization of mammalian cells with
tritiated thymidine. bibliog Science 151:
691-4 F 11 '66
WHITNEY, Dale
Sterile flies used to combat dacus. il Natur
Hist 75:30-5 Mr '66
WHITNEY, Frank L.
Impact of the total redevelopment of cities;
address. March 21, 1966. Vital Speeches
32:414-16 Ap 15 '66
WHITNEY, Gertrude (Vanderbilt)
Heiress who championed Americans. il pors
Life 61:100 O 7 '66
WHITNEY, John Hay
How a newspaper can be suppressed; state-
ment, April 22, 1966. por U S News 60:37
My 2 '66
about
Very special paper. il por Newsweek 68:90-1
Ag 22 '66
WHITNEY, Monroe
How the British score on us. Sat R 49:63+
Ag 20 '66
WHITNEY family
Whitney coat-of-arms. H. K. Eilers. il Hob-
bies 70:126-7 F '66
WHITNEY museum of American art, New
York
American art and the Whitney museum. L.
Goodrich. il Antiques 90:655-62 N '66
American classic art. H. Cohen. il Reporter
35:60-2 N 17 '66
Architecture. E. Galantay. Nation 203:292-4
S 26 '66
Art galleries. R. M. Coates. New Yorker 42:
192-5 O 8 '66
Art galleries: 1966 sculpture and prints an-
nual. R. M. Coates. New Yorker 42:84-6
Ja 7 '67
Cliffhanger on Madison avenue. il Time
88:88-91 O 7 '66
Movers and Shakers. R. Lynes. il Harper
233:33-4+ D '66
New Whitney. il Newsweek 68:98+ O 3 '66
New Whitney. F. Getlein. New Repub 155:
45-6 N 5 '66
New Whitney. P. P. Witonski. Nat R 18:1335-6
D 27 '66
People are talking about. . . il Vogue 148:
218-19 O 1 '66
Poetic emptiness; sculpture. il Time 88:51 D
23 '66
Splendid new Whitney. K. Kuh. il Sat R 49:
53-5 N 5 '66
Vale atque ave Whitney. T. B. Hess. Art N
65:29 O '66
Vernissage; exhibition: Art of the United
States: 1670-1966. New Yorker 42:48-9 O 8
'66
Whitney: big for its size. J. M. Dixon.
il Arch Forum 125:80-5 S '66
Whitney, jazz and folk. C. J. McNaspy.
America 115:465 O 15 '66
Ziggurat for Whitney's art. il Life 61:95-6+
O 7 '66

WIGS—*Continued*

Rise of the fall; Kenneth's and other creations. il Life 60:51-2 Je 3 '66

Switch on, switch off. L. D. Kirk. il Parents Mag 41:72 Jl '66

WIKLER, Elinor

Everybody has a Beatle. Read Digest 89: 72-5 O '66

WIKSTEN, Barry Frank

Living by the numbers. il pors Life 60:76A-78+ F 18 '66

WILBUR, Dwight L.

Wanted: 750,000 humanitarians. Todays Health 45:88+ Ja '67

WILBUR, Richard

Rillons, rillettes; poem. New Yorker 41:28 Ja 29 '66

Under cygnus; poem. Nation 203:675 D 19 '66

(tr) See Molière. J. B. P. Misanthrope

WILCOX, Eleanor Reindollar

1066, 1492, and student 49631; letter. NEA J 55:22-3 O '66

WILCOX, John M.

Solar and interplanetary magnetic fields. bibliog Science 152:161-6 Ap 8 '66

WILCOX, Robert

Leaf printing with textile paint. Design 68: 38-42 S '66

WILCOX, Wayne A.

Contemporary American influence in south and southeast Asia. bibliog f Ann Am Acad 366:108-16 Jl '66

WILD, George O.

Animals from the rough. il Natur Hist 75:54-7 My '66

WILD, William F.

Draft board head wants all to serve. por Life 61:48-9 D 9 '66

WILD animal pets. See Pets

WILD animals in art. See Animals in art

WILD dogs

Hounds of Hades; dogs lost, left, or loose; revert to wild state. C. Robinson. il Field & S 71:64-5+ D '66

WILD duck; drama. See Ibsen, H.

WILD flower gardens. See Gardens, Wild

WILD flowers

Flowers: reception celebrating publication of first volume of Wild flowers of the United States, held by New York botanical garden. New Yorker 42:49-50 O 8 '66

Mrs LBJ country; ed. by M. Simons. C. A. T. Johnson. il Look 30:35-41 Jl 12 '66

Wild flowers of the United States; comp. by H. W. Rickett. Review
New Yorker 42:149-50+ D 10 '66. K. S. White

WILD food. See Food

WILD fruits. See Fruit

WILD gardens. See Gardens, Wild

WILD geese. See Geese, Wild

WILD horses; story. See Boyle, K.

WILD orchids. See Orchids

WILD pig hunting. See Woods hog hunting

WILD turkeys. See Turkeys, Wild

WILD West shows. See Rodeos

WILDCAT hunting. See Bobcat hunting

WILDE, Alexander W.

Death of a rebel priest. Commonweal 83:693-6 Mr 18 '66

WILDE, Frazar B.

Changing directions in American education. Sat R 50:37 Ja 14 '67

WILDE, M. S.

Europe's expanding nuclear research center. UNESCO Courier 19:4-9+ Mr '66

WILDER, Billy

Billy, Willie, and Jack. H. Alpert. Sat R 49: 30 S 24 '66

Message in Billy Wilder's Fortune cookie: well, nobody's perfect. R. Lemon. il pors Sat Eve Post 239:30-4+ D 17 '66

WILDER, Thornton Niven

Happy journey to Trenton and Camden. Criticism
America 115:431 O 8 '66
Nation 203:334 O 3 '66
New Yorker 42:129 S 17 '66
Sat R 49:54 S 24 '66

Long Christmas dinner. Criticism
America 115:431 O 8 '66
Nation 203:334 O 3 '66
New Yorker 42:126 S 17 '66
Sat R 49:54 S 24 '66

Queens of France. Criticism
America 115:431 O 8 '66
Nation 203:334 O 3 '66
New Yorker 42:126+ S 17 '66
Sat R 49:54 S 24 '66

WILDERNESS areas

Approximate dates for wilderness hearings. Liv Wildn 29:47 Wint '65

Battle in the wilderness: benevolent wreckers. L. P . Hudson. il Nation 202:393-6 Ap 4 '66

Candidate areas for addition to the National wilderness preservation system on which review should be completed by September 3, 1967. Liv Wildn 30:52-3 Spr '66

Don't let the eagle lay an egg; Land and water conservation fund bill, administered by Bureau of outdoor recreation. G. H. Gillelan. Outdoor Life 138:24+ N '66

Great Smokies park and the wilderness act. il Liv Wildn 29:20-4 Aut '65

If all you want is a penguin's egg. . ; address, June 27, 1966. S. F. Francis. il Liv Wildn 30:20-1 Sum '66

Let us preserve its aged grandeur. H. Nash. il Parks & Rec 1:497-500 Je '66

Our wilderness rights are missing; excerpt from A wilderness bill of rights; ed. by R. D. Butcher. W. O. Douglas. il Audubon Mag 68:85 Mr '66

Rivers, recreation, and you; interview. F. Church. il Field & S 71:10-13+ Jl '66

Saylor bill offers real protection for America's remaining wilderness rivers. C. H. Callison. il Audubon Mag 68:226-7 Jl '66

Setting new patterns under a landmark law; adaptation of address. S. M. Brandborg. il Liv Wildn 30:40-51 Spr '66

Trail and campfire country; an editorial. A. W. Smith. Nat Parks Mag 40:2 S '66

Use for wilderness. R. C. Clement. il Audubon Mag 68:94-5 Mr '66

Why not plan big? A. W. Smith. Nat Parks Mag 40:2+ Je '66

Wilderness bill of rights, by W. O. Douglas. Review
Liv Wildn 29:29-30 Wint '65. P. H. Oehser
Nat Parks Mag il 40:18-19 Mr '66. G. S. Leisure

Wilderness hearings and reviews. Nat Parks Mag 40:23 My '66

Wilderness makes the Smokies; editorial. Liv Wildn 30:38 Spr '66

Wilderness trails. Natur Hist 75:75-6 O '66

With the national parks. Natur Hist 75:72+ O '66
See also
Forests, State
Trail riders of the wilderness

Arizona

Pine Mountain wilderness hearing date announced. Nat Parks Mag 40:20 N '66

California

For tramping and camping in May, look into the Sespe. il Sunset 136:42-5+ My '66

In California's lonely corner; South Warner wilderness. il Sunset 137:42+ S '66

Rock gardens of the wilderness. F. Morton. Nat Parks Mag 40:17 My '66

San Gorgonio. Liv Wildn 29:2 Aut '65

San Gorgonio belongs to all Americans. il Liv Wildn 29:33-4 Aut '65

Colorado

Battle in the wilderness: benevolent wreckers. threat to Flat Tops. L. P. Hudson. il Nation 202:393-6 Ap 4 '66

Idaho

Seesaw in the Sawtooth. V. Fischer. il Am For 72:36-9+ N '66

Maine

Allagash: a pattern emerges. J. B. Craig. il Am For 72:26-9+ Ag '66

Allagash victory appears near. il Audubon Mag 68:213 Jl '66

Saving the Allagash. L. Stuart. il Parks & Rec 1:852-4 O '66

Montana

Montana's drive-in wilderness. B. W. Dalrymple. il Field & S 70:122-4+ F '66

Now it's traffic jams on the last frontier; Beartooth primitive area. il U S News 61: 56-9 Ag 29 '66

New York (state)

Bob Marshall, Mount Marcy, and, the wilderness. P. Schaefer. il Liv Wildn 30:6-9 Sum '66

WILDERNESS areas—*Continued*

North Carolina

Handbook for Smokies wilderness; with the wilderness regulations of the Departments of agriculture and interior under the Wilderness act; symposium. il Liv Wildn 30:1+ Spr '66

Northwestern states

North Cascades, condensation of testimony at hearings of the Committee on interior and insular affairs, February 11 and 12, 1966. A. W. Smith. Nat Park Mag 40:2 Ap '66

Use of high country in Switzerland; North Cascades debate continues using Switzerland as yardstick. A. Netboy. il Am For 72:6-7+ O '66

See also
Wilderness areas—Washington (state)

Oregon

Forest wilderness hearings; October 26, Salem, Ore. Nat Parks Mag 40:20 O '66

Wilderness research, a start; studies on unmanned registration stations at Three Sisters wilderness area and the Mountain Lakes wild area. W. B. Morse. il Am For 72:32-3+ Je '66

Tennessee

Handbook for Smokies wilderness; with the wilderness regulations of the Departments of agriculture and interior under the wilderness act; symposium. il Liv Wildn 30:1+ Spr '66

Utah

Mike Frome; plight of the High Uintas of Utah. M. Frome. Am For 72:9+ D '66

Vermont

Wilderness in Vermont. Liv Wildn 30:31 Sum '66

Washington (state)

Cougar lakes excursion; report. H. Broome. Liv Wildn 29:34 Aut '65

Great Cascades debate. S. Raymond. il Field & S 71:10-12+ N '66

Wyoming

Hiking high; Tetons country, Wyo. F. A. Blackburn. il Liv Wildn 30:3-5 Sum '66

WILDERNESS nature centers. See Nature centers

WILDERNESS society
Notes from a diarist. B. MacKaye. il Liv Wildn 29:27-8 Wint '65

Thirty years. H. Broome. il Liv Wildn 29: 15-26 Wint '65

Wilderness council in Colorado; Conservation award to the Wilderness society. il Liv Wildn 29:30-3 Aut '65

WILDEY, Robert L.
Hot shadows of Jupiter (cont) Science 147: 1035-6; 153:1418-19 F 26 '65, S 16 '66

Measuring the shape of the moon. il Sky & Tel 31:147-50 Mr '66

WILDFLOWERS. See Wild flowers

WILDI, Ernst
Consider the audience. U S Camera 29:68-9+ Jl '66

Make your house move. Mod Phot 30:72-3+ Ag '66

Ten ways to better cuts. Mod Phot 31:78-80+ Ja '67

Voice in films. U S Camera 29:74-5+ O '66

WILDLIFE census
Wildlife census precedes drilling of oil wells; Australia's Barrow Island. Sci N 90:411 N 12 '66

WILDLIFE conservation
Alaska Dam would be resources disaster. A. S. Leopold and J. W. Leonard. il Audubon Mag 68:176-8 My '66

Extinction threatens; conservationists fighting to protect Australian wildlife. il Sci N 90:483 D 3 '66

Federal controls needed for kangaroo industry; protecting kangaroos and wallabies from indiscriminate slaughter. il Sci N 90:251 O 1 '66

Interior department asks new wildlife laws. Nat Parks Mag 40:25 Ag '66

Let's not kill ourselves; threat to hunting; insecticides' effect on wildlife. D. B. Peakall and B. East. il Outdoor Life 138:29-31+ S '66

Need reverses trend. B. Tufty. il Sci N 91:50-1 Ja 14 '67

Plight of the ice bear; with letter from E. L. Bartlett. F. Dufresne. il Audubon Mag 68: 418-25 N '66

Spirit of the mountain. S. A. Cain. il Américas 18:1-8 Mr '66

Wildlife conservation. F. Osborn. il Parks & Rec 1:646-7+ Ag '66

See also
Audubon nature centers
Bird sanctuaries
Fish protection
Wildlife sanctuaries

WILDLIFE photographs. See Animals—Photographs

WILDLIFE photography. See Photography of animals

WILDLIFE sanctuaries
City-side sanctuary; Rhode Island State Great swamp wildlife reservation. R. Mallan. il Travel 125:12 Je '66

Coto Doñana. O. S. Pettingill, jr. il Audubon Mag 68:304-306A S '66

Forest service special areas. Nat Parks Mag 40:20 Je '66

Horicon marsh, the firmament showeth His handiwork. A. Yaudes. il Am For 71:8-9+ O '65

Life along an Arctic river; excerpt from Downstream: a natural history of the river. J. Bardach. Liv Wildn 29:14-19 Aut '65

New NAS sanctuary; Rookery Bay wildlife sanctuary. C. W. Buchheister. Audubon Mag 68:212 Jl '66

Now, refuges for endangered species. C. H. Callison. il Audubon Mag 68:462 N '66

Paradise nearly lost. J. F. Shrawder. il Audubon Mag 68:228-9 Jl '66

Reporter at large; wild whooping cranes at Arkansas national wildlife refuge, Tex. F. McNulty. il New Yorker 42:31-6+ Ag 6 '66

Should wildlife refuges become public playgrounds? question for the Leopold committee. C. H. Callison. il Audubon Mag 68: 312-13 S '66

Those curious midgets; Florida Key deer. J. Browder. il Am For 72:12+ O '66

Wetlands; stepchild of land use. F. G. Ashbrook. il Nat Parks Mag 40:17-19 Ag '66

See also
Audubon nature centers
Bird sanctuaries
Game preserves
Kruger National Park

WILDLIFE service. See United States—Fish and wildlife service

WILDLIFE survival center. See New York zoological park

WILDMAN, S. G. See Tewari, K. K. jt. auth.

WILDMAN, Wesley A.
Conflict issues in negotiations; excerpt from address. Mo Labor R 89:617-20 Je '66

WILEY, Jack
Pogo shoes give you a lift. Pop Mech 125: 157 Je '66

WILEY, Marcia
Cabin talk. See issues of Yachting
Waterfront news. See issues of Yachting

WILEY, W. Bradford
ABPC annual meeting; the international role of the book; summary of address. por Pub W 189:80-1 Je 13 '66

WILHELM, Eugene J. Jr
Nahuel Huapi, Tiger Island of Argentina. il Nat Parks Mag 40:14-17 Mr '66

WILHELM, Robert C. and Ludlum, D. B.
Coding properties of 7-methylguanine. bibliog Science 153:1403-5 S 16 '66

WILHELM, Warren
There's plenty of promise in the underdeveloped land. Fortune 74:150-2 O '66

WILHELMSEN, Frederick D.
Chandelier of existence. Nat R 19:45-7 Ja 10 '67

Traditionalist right. Nat R 18:172-3 F 22 '66

WILKES, Charles
Ice ahead! R. K. Andrist. il por Am Heritage 17:60-3+ Ag '66

Voyage to the bottom of the earth. il por Sr Schol 89:1 Ja 13 '67

WILKES exploring expedition. See United States exploring expedition, 1838-1842

WILKINS, B. Hughel
Looking to the past for progress. Sat R 49: 37-8 F 12 '66

WILKINS, Mira
Businessman abroad. Ann Am Acad 368:83-94 N '66

WILKINS, Roy
NAACP head warns black power means black
death; excerpts from address. July 5, 1966.
U S News 61:34 Jl 18 '66
WILKINSON, Charles B.
Quality of fitness; excerpt from address. por
Parks & Rec 1:149-50 F '66
WILKINSON, J. F.
Deadly animal that adopts people. Todays
Health 45:8+ Ja '67
WILKINSON, Stephan
Automobile racing. Holiday 40:89-95 Ag '66
WILKINSON, Sylvia
[Mademoiselle Merit award winner] por Mlle
64:49 Ja '67
WILKINSON, William H. See Ziegenfelder,
R. F. jt. auth.
WILL, Frederic
Three from China: The scholar; Lo-Fu; In-
tercult talk; poems. Poetry 109:77-82 N '66
WILL
Ways of the will, by L. H. Farber. Review
New Repub 154:25-7 Je 25 '66. S. Ruben-
feld
Sat R 49:29-30 Ag 20 '66. R. J. Levin
WILLE, Lois
Woman's work. por Newsweek 68:82 Jl 11 '66
WILLEMS, Boniface A.
Death of God phenomenon. Cath World 204:
17-19 O '66
WILLETT, T. C.
Dangerous driving is no accident; concerning
report. Read Digest 88:98-100 F '66
WILLIAM I, the Conqueror, king of England
Norman conquest. K. M. Setton. il por Nat
Geog Mag 130:206-51 Ag '66
WILLIAM Doyle and company. See Glass in-
dustry
WILLIAM Edrington Scott theater. See Fort
Worth, Tex.—Theater
WILLIAM Morrow and company. See Morrow,
William, and company
WILLIAM Penn memorial museum. See Harris-
burg, Pa.—Galleries and museums
WILLIAM Rockhill Nelson gallery of art,
Kansas City, Mo.
Miniatures by John Smart: Starr collection.
D. Foskett. il Antiques 90:354-7 S '66
WILLIAM Underwood company. See Under-
wood, William, company
WILLIAMS, Alvida
Honey, will you go get... por Farm J 90:
51+ Ag '66
WILLIAMS, Andy
Andy Williams. A. Hano. il pors Good H
162:66+ Ap '66
WILLIAMS, Anthony
Music on Blue note. M. Williams. por Sat R
49:58 S 17 '66
WILLIAMS, C. K.
World's greatest tricycle rider; poem. New
Yorker 42:137 Ap 2 '66
WILLIAMS, Carroll M. See Spielman, A; Wal-
ters, D. R. jt. auths.
WILLIAMS, Charles
Patriot's gift. il por Time 88:14 Jl 1 '66
Posthumous career of Charles Williams. J.
Heath-Stubbs. New Repub 154:19-21 Je 11
'66
WILLIAMS, Christine
For long legs, a short lens. P. Gowland. por
Pop Phot 59:26+ S '66
WILLIAMS, Cleveland
Big cat and Clay. il Newsweek 68:64+ N 14
'66
Delayed payday for Cleve. E. Shrake and
M. Sharnik. il por Sports Illus 25:34-6 D 5
'66
Massacre. M. Kane. il pors Sports Illus 25:22-
5 N 21 '66
Skinning the Cat. il por Time 88:64 N 25 '66
Waiting for Cassius. il por Time 88:36 N 4
'66
You watch out, Ali! M. Kane. il por Sports
Illus 25:26-9 N 14 '66
WILLIAMS, Curtis A. Jr. See Hafleigh, A. S.
jt. auth.
WILLIAMS, Edward Bennett
Legal eagle and his boy scout. R. H. Boyle.
il pors Sports Illus 25:54-60 Jl 25 '66
WILLIAMS, Gene
Yellow brick road; story. New Yorker 42:
32-4 Je 4 '66
WILLIAMS, Gerhard Mennen
Crisis in Southern Rhodesia; address, January
28, 1966. Dept State Bul 54:265-70 F 21 '66
United States policy toward South Africa;
statement, March 1, 1966. Dept State Bul
54:430-40 Mr 21 '66

about
Ballad of the green bow tie. J. Ter Horst. il
Reporter 35:36-8 S 8 '66
Dubious dialogue. Nation 202:316 Mr 21 '66
In political spotlight again: Mennen Williams.
por U S News 61:10 Ag 15 '66
Return of the boy wonder. il por Time 88:12
Ag 12 '66
WILLIAMS, Gordon
Academic librarianship: the state of the art;
excerpts from address. por Library J 91:
2413-18 My 15 '66
Preservation of deteriorating books; excerpts
from report (cont) Library J 91:189-94 Ja
15 '66
WILLIAMS, Greer
Quality versus quantity in American medical
education. bibliog Science 153:956-61 Ag 26
'66
WILLIAMS, Harrison Arlington, 1919-
Excerpt from statement, July 1965. Cong
Digest 45:48+ F '66
WILLIAMS, Howard
Yachtman's role in pollution prevention.
Yachting 119:78-9+ F '66
WILLIAMS, J. F.
Computer programming, today's high-pay
career. Sci Digest 59:50-5 My '66
WILLIAMS, James R.
What every young father should know about
health insurance. Parents Mag 41:86+ N
'66
WILLIAMS, John A.
Black man in Europe. Holiday 41:8+ Ja '67
WILLIAMS, John Bell
Nation builder. Time 88:25 S 30 '66
WILLIAMS, John J.
How big is the Johnson deficit? excerpts
from address, January 17, 1966. por U S
News 60:73 Ja 31 '66
Reaction in the Senate; excerpt from ad-
dress, October 17, 1966. U S News 61:68
O 31 '66
about
Senator contends church maligned. Chris-
tian Cent 83:454, 1137 Ap 13, S 21 '66
WILLIAMS, Jonathan
Southern Appalachians. Craft Horiz 26:46-67
Je '66
WILLIAMS, Jonathan W.
Protect your orchids from pests and dis-
eases. Horticulture 44:22-3 D '66
WILLIAMS, Martin
Catching up with a colleague. Sat R 49:55
Je 25 '66
In memoriam. Bud Powell. Sat R 49:51 Ag
27 '66
More of the Ellington era. Sat R 49:53 Jl 30
'66
Mostly about pianists. Sat R 49:130 Mr 12 '66
Mostly modernists. Sat R 49:53 D 31 '66
Music on Blue note. Sat R 49:58 S 17 '66
Ornette Coleman in Stockholm. Sat R 49:83+
Je 11 '66
Problematic Mr Shepp. Sat R 49:90 N 12 '66
Where's the melody? Am Rec G 32:774-5+
My '66
WILLIAMS, Mary Frances
Our teenage cook. See issues of Good house-
keeping
Susan makes cartwheel tuna pie. Good H
162:206 Ap '66
WILLIAMS, Miller
So long at the fair; poem. Sat R 49:46 Jl 9 '66
WILLIAMS, Norman, Jr
(ed) Zoning and planning decisions. See
issues of American city
WILLIAMS, Philip M.
On the left. Commentary 42:102-3+ S '66
WILLIAMS, Ralph Vaughan. See Vaughan
Williams, R.
WILLIAMS, Raymond
Affluence after anger. Nation 203:676-7 D
19 '66
Letter from Britain. See issues of Nation to
September 1966
WILLIAMS, Robert
Saint-satan leader as a public speaker, the
crusader: Robert Williams. M. H. Boul-
ware. por Negro Hist Bul 29:81-2 Ja '66
WILLIAMS, Robert Edmond
Anatomy of the creative decision; address,
March 10, 1966. Vital Speeches 32:508-12
Je 1 '66
WILLIAMS, Robert H. See Porte, D. jr. jt.
auth.

WILSON, Edmund—*Continued*
Notes from a European diary: 1963-64. New Yorker 42:54-6+ My 21; 42-6+ My 28; 88+ Je 4 '66

about

Edmund Wilson; recipient of National medal for literature. Nation 202:733 Je 20 '66
Edmund Wilson, then and now. R. Gilman. New Repub 155:23-8 Jl 2 '66; Reply. H. A. Perluck. 155:35-7 Ag 13 '66
Edmund Wilson wins National literature medal. por Pub W 189:188-9 Je 6 '66
Laureate. por Newsweek 67:103 Je 6 '66
Literary vocation. D. Jacobson. Commentary 41:92+ My '66
Our greatest living man of letters. R. Kostelanetz. il Reporter 34:53-4 Ja 27 '66

WILSON, Edward C. 3d
Time scales & time measurements. Electr World 75:42-3 Ja; 23 My '66

WILSON, George
My son the quarterback. il por Time 88:86 N 4 '66

WILSON, George C.
Anti-missiles: new twist in the arms spiral. Nation 204:46-9 Ja 9 '67

WILSON, Gill Robb
First twenty-five years of CAP. M. W. Horowitz. il Flying 78:94-7 Ap '66
Gill Robb Wilson, 1893-1966; a tribute. il por Flying 79:54-5 D '66
In memoriam. por Flying 79:6 N '66
Legend of Gill Robb Wilson. R. Bach. pors Flying 79:56-7 D '66

WILSON, H. W, company
Lighthouse. See issues of Wilson library bulletin to June 1966
Third edition of serials list includes over 150,000 titles. Library J 91:649+ F 1 '66
Union list published: third and final edition. il Wilson Lib Bul 40:483-4 F '66

WILSON, Harold
Address in General assembly, December 16, 1965; summary. por UN Mo Chron 3:73-5 Ja '66
British economic situation; address, July 20, 1966. Vital Speeches 32:642-6 Ag 15 '66
One allied leader speaking up for U.S; excerpts from address, February 9, 1966. por U S News 60:21 F 21 '66
President Johnson confers with British Prime Minister; exchange of toasts, July 29, 1966. Dept State Bul 55:267-8 Ag 22 '66

about

Admission of failure. il por Time 88:35-6 D 16 '66
Atlantic report. Atlan 217:16+ F '66
Awash. il por Time 88:32 Jl 15 '66
Britain brings its woes to Washington. por U S News 61:25-6 Ag 8 '66
Britain: labor's chance to govern. il por Newsweek 67:46+ Ap 11 '66
Britain's Labor. Commonweal 84:96 Ap 15 '66
Dividing the critics. Time 87:35-6 Je 24 '66
Dramatic meeting between H. Wilson and I. Smith. Time 88:41-2 D 9 '66
England gambles for survival. H. Ehrlich. il pors Look 30:27-35 N 29 '66
Final fortnight. il por Time 87:26 Mr 25 '66
Footnote on Wilson. C. Brogan. Nat R 18:149 F 22 '66
For Wilson and labor, 150-seat gain? or fifty? por U S News 60:24 Mr 14 '66
Freeze & squeeze. por Time 88:19 Jl 29 '66
Keeping his counsel. Newsweek 67:52+ F 21 '66
Labor insider vs. the Tory outsider. A. Lewis. il por N Y Times Mag p27+ Mr 27 '66
Labor is the favorite. Bsns W p48-9 Mr 26 '66
Letter from London (cont) M. Panter-Downes. New Yorker 42:131-2+ Ap 16; 81-2+ Jl 9; 88+ Ag 6; 204+ D 3; 54-5 D 24 '66
Make or break year. por Newsweek 67:45 Mr 14 '66
Mr Wilson goes to Washington. il por Newsweek 68:32 Ag 8 '66
Mr Wilson sees it through. il por Newsweek 67:31-2 F 7 '66
Mr Wilson squeaks through. C. Sterling. Reporter 35:32-3 O 6 '66
Mr Wilson's nostrums. A. Lejeune. Nat R 18:879+ S 6 '66

No furs; trip to Moscow. il por Newsweek 67:48 Mr 7 '66
People of the week. por U S News 61:19 Jl 18 '66
Prime Minister stands his ground. J. L. Schecter. por Fortune 74:65-6 S '66
Rhodesia: the fight goes on. il por Newsweek 68:33+ D 19 '66
Riding the tiger; Wilson and Smith meet. Newsweek 68:54+ D 12 '66
Right extraordinary Harold Wilson wins his big victory. J. Hicks. il pors Life 60:44-44B+ Ap 8 '66
Seven days' humiliation; concerning Rhodesian debate at Commonwealth prime ministers' conference. E. Huxley. Nat R 18:989 O 4 '66
Severest controls in peacetime history. Time 88:40 O 14 '66
Socialist landslide in Britain, its meaning to U.S. por U S News 60:6 Ap 11 '66
Sticking to the issues. il Newsweek 67:47 Mr 28 '66
Storm signals on Rhodesia. A. Lejeune. Nat R 18:1309-10 D 27 '66
Veering toward a vote. il por Time 87:36 Mr 4 '66
Victory gives Wilson strong grip on future. por Bsns W p 119 Ap 9 '66
Vote where U.S. policy is the issue. por U S News 60:16 Mr 28 '66
Why Britain needs Wilson's recession. Life 61:4 Ag 5 '66
Wilson sounds the call for all British voters. por Bsns W p35-6 Mr 5 '66
Wilson under fire. Time 88:25 Ag 12 '66
Wilson's big chance. Life 60:6 Ap 15 '66
Wilson's mission: a test of U.S.-British partnership. il U S News 61:33-4 Ag 1 '66

WILSON, Helen Van Pelt
Easy to grow lilies. Flower Grower 53:26-7 Ag '66
Ivy geraniums. Flower Grower 53:34+ O '66
Perennials that stand up to summer. Flower Grower 53:46-7+ My '66
Regional pointers: North. See issues of Flower grower, the home garden
Trees that stay small. Flower Grower 53:46-7+ Mr '66
—See Bell, L. jt. auth.

WILSON, Hugh
En route to Christmas. Travel 126:30-2+ D '66

WILSON, Jerry Bryan
Coup de grâce and the complexity of decision. Christian Cent 84:82-3 Ja 18 '67

WILSON, John B.
Brook Farm; seedbed of education. bibliog f Sch & Soc 94:43-7 Ja 22 '66

WILSON, John S.
Jazz. See issues of High fidelity incorporating Musical America
Lighter side. See issues of High fidelity incorporating Musical America

WILSON, Johnny
Southward ho. See issues of Motor boating

WILSON, José
Going places, finding things in San Francisco. House & Gard 130:18+ Jl '66
Going places, finding things in seven Caribbean islands. House & Gard 131:16+ Ja '67

WILSON, Joseph Ruggles
Thomas Woodrow Wilson; excerpts; with reply by A. Dulles. S. Freud and W. C. Bullitt. il por Look 30:36-8+ D 13 '66; Discussion. 30:12 D 27 '66

WILSON, Juana. See Wilson, B. jt. auth.

WILSON, Kenneth M.
New Amelung tumbler. Antiques 90:334-6 S '66

WILSON, Lanford
Ludlow fair. Criticism
    New Yorker 42:124 Ap 2 '66
Madness of Lady Bright. Criticism
    Commonweal 84:178 Ap 29 '66
    New Yorker 42:124 Ap 2 '66
This is the rill speaking. Criticism
    Nation 202:403-4 Ap 4 '66

WILSON, Logan
Institutional priorities in higher education; address, March 9, 1965. Sch & Soc 94:92+ F 19 '66
Integrity of the private college; summary of address, June 1966. por Sch & Soc 94:436-8 D 10 '66

WILSON, Martha
Plain brown bird; story. Redbook 127:62-3
Ag '66
WILSON, Mary
After the bomb had fallen; poem. Time 88:32
Jl 15 '66
Off the record with the Supremes; ed. by E.
Miller. pors Seventeen 25:280-1+ Ag '66
WILSON, Mike
In Ceylon: the normal way to remove a
demon. Vogue 147:84+ Je '66
WILSON, Nancy
Nancy Wilson. il pors Ebony 21:140-2+ My
'66
Sweet Nancy. il pors Life 60:53-4+ Je 24 '66
WILSON, Norde
Another pilot's report from Vietnam; letter.
Aviation W 85:21+ O 24 '66; Excerpts
U S News 61:64 O 31 '66
WILSON, O. C.
Stellar chromospheres. bibliog Science 151:
1487-98 Mr 25 '66
WILSON, Orlando Winfield
Policeman looks at crime; interview. por U S
News 61:51-2 Ag 1 '66

about

Chicago's scholarly cop. H. Bruno. Reporter
34:30-3 Mr 24 '66
Crime-Stop stops crime. K. Detzer. il Read
Digest 89:133-6 O '66
WILSON, Peter
Wilson of Sotheby's interview. New Yorker
42:48-50 D 3 '66

about

World's fastest art market; with portfolio of
art objects. D. Norton-Taylor. il por Fortune
74:134-46+ S '66
WILSON, Peter A. G.
Light sense in nematodes. bibliog Science
151:337-8 Ja 21 '66
WILSON, Ralph C. Jr
Triple-threat entrepreneur. W. Berry. il por
Duns R 88:46+ S '66
WILSON, Richard L.
U.S. isn't as sick as we think. Look 30:39-40
F 8 '66
WILSON, Robert A.
Which hormone to take when. Vogue 147:
92-5+ Je '66

about

Can a woman be feminine forever? N. Som-
mers and J. Ridgeway. New Repub 154:15-
16 Mr 19 '66
Pills to keep women young. il por Time 87:
50+ Ap 1 '66
WILSON, Robley, Jr
Four poems: Lines for later anniversaries; A
woman; Certain stately structures; Sniper
in the tower. New Repub 156:31 Ja 14 '67
Great teachers; poem. Reporter 35:56 S 22 '66
Iceboxes; Iowa; poems. Reporter 35:52 Jl 14
'66
March; poem. Commonweal 83:666 Mr 11 '66
When we think of April; Flower gifts; poems.
Reporter 34:48 Ap 21 '66
WILSON, Rowland B.
Great fad crash. Esquire 66:104-5 N '66
WILSON, Ryder
Audio calibrator for transistor amplifiers.
Electr World 76:67 Ag '66
Build a stick-shift electric shaver. Pop Electr
25:90 O '66
WILSON, Sloan
Snob cure. Read Digest 88:185-8 Mr '66
WILSON, Theodore
Guardians of the Viet Nam coastline. il pors
Ebony 22:129-30+ D '66
WILSON, Victor J.
Inhibition in the central nervous system;
with biographical sketch. Sci Am 214:18,
102-7+ bibliog(p 148) My '66
—See Thomas, R. C. jt. auth.
WILSON, Wilbor O.
Poultry production; with biographical sketch.
Sci Am 215:15, 56-62+ bibliog(p 131) Jl '66
WILSON, William E.
Hush-a-bye, Indiana. Am Heritage 18:68-71
D '66
There I grew up. Am Heritage 17:30-1+
O '66
WILSON, Winston P.
If war brings a call-up of the reserves; inter-
view. por U S News 60:38-40 F 7 '66

WILSON, Woodrow
Papers of Woodrow Wilson. ed. by A. S.
Link and others. Review
New Repub 155:27-8 O 29 '66. J. Daniels
President's first politics. H. Hansen. Sat R
49:37-8 N 5 '66
Thomas Woodrow Wilson; excerpts; with re-
ply by A. Dulles. S. Freud and W. C. Bul-
litt. il pors Look 30:36-8+ D 13 '66; Dis-
cussion. 30:12 D 27 '66
WILSON library bulletin
Lighthouse. See issues of Wilson library
bulletin to June 1966
WILSON snipe. See Snipes
WILTSHIRE, England
Travel notes; Castle Combe. R. Joseph.
Esquire 65:34 Mr '66
WIMMER, Lynn
VOL I serves varied clientele in Chicago's
renovated Piper's alley. Pub W 189:72-4
My 9 '66
WINCHESTER, James H.
Alaska's Panhandle. Travel 125:38-41 Je '66
Blunderbuss doctors of early America. Todays
Health 44:26-9+ N '66
California's mission trail. Travel 126:37-9 D '66
Doctors of the new United States. Todays
Health 44:40-3 D '66
Dust-off! Dust-off! lifeline home from Viet-
nam. Read Digest 88:60-6 My '66
How science tricks your taste. Pop Sci 189:79-
81+ S '66
Iceland: a nation hurrying toward tomorrow.
Read Digest 88:197-200+ Je '66
Orange Blossom trail. Travel 125:35-8 F '66
Our fabulous choppers. Pop Sci 188:80-3+
F '66
Skim boats: our new weapon in Vietnam.
Pop Sci 189:122-5+ O '66
Viet Nam: U.S. doctors are there. Todays
Health 44:18-24+ Mr '66
WINCHESTER, John W. See Schilling. J. G.
jt. auth.
WINCHESTER rifles. See Rifles
WINCHESTER-Western division. See Olin
Mathieson chemical corporation—Winchest-
er-Western division
WIND, Herbert Warren
Sporting scene (cont) New Yorker 41:116+
F 12; 42:135-6+ Mr 12; 134+ Ap 30; 100+
Ag 13 '66
WIND machine; story. See Maddow. B.
WIND power
See also
Windmills
WIND tunnel models
Amateur scientist; how to build a wind
tunnel that achieves supersonic speeds with
a vacuum system. G. S. Settles. il Sci Am
215:120-4+ O '66
WIND tunnels
Amateur scientist; how to build a wind
tunnel that achieves supersonic speeds with
a vacuum system. G. S. Settles. il Sci
Am 215:120-4+ O '66
New wind tests devised; study of oscillatory
behavior of two skyscrapers for World
trade center. il Sci N L 89:86 F 5 '66
Super wind tunnel. Sci Digest 60:18 O '66
WINDGASSEN, Wolfgang
Wandering minstrel; interview. ed. by D.
Stevens. por Opera N 30:16 Mr 26 '66
WINDJAMMER cruises. See Cruising
WINDMILLS
India gets low-cost windmill for farmers.
Sci N 90:329 O 22 '66
WINDOW boxes. See Flower boxes, planters,
etc.
WINDOW displays. See Show windows
WINDOW gardening
Plant-worthy window. il House & Gard 130:
172-5 D '66
WINDOW sashes
Window springs for the window with a
broken sash cord. Consumer Bul 49:11 F '66
WINDOW shades
Keeping window shades like new. il Parents
Mag 41:66 Ag '66
Repairing window shades. P. McCafferty.
il Pop Sci 188:180-1 Mr '66
Shades of difference. il Bet Hom & Gard
44:132 My '66
WINDOWS
Windows: new ways of covering them. B.
Plumb. il Mlle 62:96-7 Ap '66

WINTER PARK, Fla.—*Continued*
Sanitary affairs
Big transfer trailer. R. G. Simmons. il Am City 81:108-9 O '66
WINTER photography. See Photography—Cold weather conditions
WINTER proofing. See Houses—Maintenance and repair
WINTER protection of plants. See Plants, Protection of
WINTER resorts
America's best ski runs. B. Ottum. il Sports Illus 25:52-69 N 14 '66
At Mammoth in the spring; California's Mammoth Mountain. il Sunset 136:86-95 Mr '66
Let's travel: to ski. il Mlle 64:191-2+ N '66
New ski town in the French Alps; Flaine, France. il Arch Rec 139:180-3 Ap '66
Ski report: excellent; Crystal Mountain, Washington. M. Frome. il Holiday 40:90-7+ D '66
Traveling with Mlle: skimanship; symposium. Mlle 64:185+ N '66
   See also
Sun Valley, Idaho
WINTER sleep. See Hibernation
WINTER sports
   See also
Curling
Skating
Skis and skiing
WINTER tires. See Tires, Automobile
WINTER travel. See Travel
WINTER vacations. See Vacations
WINTERBERRY
   See also
Alder
WINTERICH, John Tracy
Charles A. Madison's Book publishing in America. Pub W 190:49-51 O 31 '66
—and Glixon, D. M.
(ed) Your literary I.Q. See issues of Saturday review
WINTERNATIONALS, Pomona, Calif. See Automobile racing
WINTERS, Austin P.
Fully found marina. Motor B 118:26+ O '66
WINTERS, Glenn R.
What can be done about pettifoggery and legal delays? bibliog f Ann Am Acad 363: 52-9 Ja '66
WINTERS, Helen
ABC Bahamas Baedeker. Motor B 118:38+ O '66
From Boston to Boothbay and beyond. il Motor B 117:28-31+ Ap '66
WINTERS, Kay
Perk up your faculty meeting. NEA J 55:30-1 O '66
WINTERTHUR gardens. See Gardens—Delaware
WINTHROP, Henry
Skid row of academe. Sch & Soc 94:267-9 Sum '66
WINTHROP Rockefeller collection. See Automobile museums
WIRE fences. See Fences
WIRE tapping
Bugging. Nat R 18:1306-7 D 27 '66
Dirty business. Nation 203:690-1 D 26 '66
How to be alone; bug-proof conference room. S. V. Jones. il Sci Digest 59:20 Ap '66
Lawless lawmen; violations of eavesdropping prohibitions by FBI. A. Barth. New Repub 155:19-22 Jl 30 '66
Snooping electronic invasion of privacy; devices, systems, legal problems, FCC regulations; with report by J. Neary. il Life 60: 38-47 My 20 '66
Wiretap war: Kennedy, Johnson and the FBI. R. M. Cipes. New Repub 155:16-22 D 24 '66
WIRE walking. See Acrobats and acrobatism
WIRELESS microphones. See Microphones
WIRELESS museums. See Museums
WIRELESS telegraph. See Telegraph, Wireless
WIREMAN, Billy O.
Not by talent alone; address, January 18, 1966. Vital Speeches 32:370-2 Ap 1 '66
WIRETAPPING. See Wire tapping
WIRGES, Eugene Henry
Embattled crusader of Conway County. T. Armbrister. il pors Sat Eve Post 239:25-9+ N 19 '66
Trials of an editor. il por Newsweek 67:91-2 F 14 '66

WIRING, Electric. See Electric wire and wiring
WIRKOLA, Bjorn
Soaring week for the nervy Norse. B. Ottum. il Sports Illus 24:52-5 Mr 7 '66
WIRKUS, Denton
Build a swimming pool just for the fun of it. Pop Mech 125:152-5 Je '66
WIRSIG, Woodrow
Tomorrow's consumer; address, October 19, 1966. Vital Speeches 33:81-6 N 15 '66
WIRTH, Conrad L.
Foundation of a new era. por Parks & Rec 1:485-6 Je '66
Let's look ahead. por Parks & Rec 1:955 D '66
Mission called 66. por Nat Geog Mag 130: 6-47 Jl '66
WIRTH, F. Harold
Occlusal rehabilitation correlates dental treatment. Todays Health 44:30 Mr '66
WIRTZ, William Willard
Christian social relations; address, June 6, 1966. Vital Speeches 32:546-50 Jl 1 '66
Excerpt from testimony, May 25, 1965. Cong Digest 45:44+ F '66
Policy for youth; address, November 16, 1966. Vital Speeches 33:162-5 Ja 1 '67
   about
Apples of wrath; excerpts from daily notes, ed. by F. Russell. W. Doe. Nat R 18:932-3 S 20 '66
Hard sledding for full work year. por Bsns W p48+ Jl 16 '66
His goal is full employment. I. Ross. por Read Digest 89:119-23 S '66
Report on our migrant workers. America 114:346 Mr 12 '66
Stooping to conquer. Newsweek 67:61-2 F 7 '66
Strength through joy again? R. Kirk. Nat R 18:1328 D 27 '66
Two key figures in the LBJ-labor split. por U S News 60:24 Mr 14 '66
Unions call 5 per cent a minimum for '67. por Bsns W p 163-4 N 26 '66
WISCONSIN
   See also
Architecture, Domestic—Wisconsin
Booksellers and bookselling—Wisconsin
Fishing—Wisconsin
WISCONSIN. University, Madison
Action for fraternity non-discrimination. Sch & Soc 94:258 Sum '66
WISDOM, Norman
Norman Wisdom; interview. New Yorker 42: 44-7 D 17 '66
WISDOM teeth. See Teeth
WISE, Bill
Of 10,147 flying saucer sightings, there are rational explanations for all but 646. Life 60:30-1 Ap 1 '66
Pop music and discipline. Life 61:68 N 25 '66
WISE, Isaac Mayer
When reform was young. L. S. Dawidowicz. Commentary 42:63-7 Jl '66
WISE, Robert
Typhoons and taxes. il Newsweek 67:98+ My 9 '66
WISE, T. A.
I.B.M.'s $5,000,000,000 gamble. Fortune 74: 118-23+ S; 139+ O '66
Very private world of Peat, Marwick, Mitchell. Fortune 74:88-91+ Jl 1 '66
WISE people of Gotham; drama. See Leuser, E.
WISEMAN, Richard D.
Sneeze sleuth discovers allergy begins in your home. R. Gannon. il Pop Sci 189:74-6+ Ag '66
WISER, Forwood Cloud, 1921-
Wiser presses improvements to Northeast. W. Wright. Aviation W 84:41-2 My 23 '66
WISHNETSKY, Richard
Last testament. Newsweek 67:32 F 28 '66
Murder of Rabbi Adler. T. V. LoCicero. Commentary 41:49-53 Je '66; Discussion. 42:24+ O '66
WISNER, Bill
Always on Sunday. Motor B 117:40-3+ Je '66
WIT and humor. See Humor
WITCH hazel
Color when you least expect it. R. D. Roe. il Flower Grower 53:44-5 Mr '66
Witch hazel. R. C. Hands. il Horticulture 45: 28-9 Ja '67

WITCHCRAFT
How to hex, unhex. Sci Digest 60:21-2 S '66
Out for a night at the local caldron; British witches. J. Kobler. il Sat Eve Post 239: 76-8 N 5 '66
Witches of 1966. V. Thomas. il Atlan 218:119-25 S '66
Without broomsticks. B. Cook. Cath World 204:92-7 N '66

WITCHER, Harry
Tandem plowing clears snow curb-to-curb. Am City 81:92-3 O '66

WITCOVER, Jules
Availability of Richard Nixon. Reporter 35: 27-9 Ag 11 '66
Beware state police bearing protection. New Repub 154:11-12 Je 25 '66
Robert Kennedy on tour. New Repub 155:9-10 O 1 '66

WITHHOLDING tax
Personal business. il Bsns W p 173-4 Mr 19 '66
Tax plan in Congress: what the changes mean to you. il U S News 60:97-8 F 21 '66
Taxes' new bite: what it will be like. il U S News 60:105-8 Mr 21 '66
What if they don't withhold enough income tax? Bet Hom & Gard 44:6 F '66

WITKIN, Evelyn M.
Radiation-induced mutations and their repair. bibliog Science 152:1345-53 Je 3 '66

WITNESSES
Hoffa decision: government informer issue. Nation 204:5-6 Ja 2 '67

WITNESSES; story. See Updike. J.

WITNEY, Fred
Labor and the Spanish syndical system; excerpt from Labor policy and practices in Spain. Mo Labor R 89:867-70 Ag '66

WITONSKI, Peter P.
General Bor. RIP. Nat R 18:921 S 20 '66
Letter from Alabama. Nat R 18:1040+ O 18 '66
New Whitney. Nat R 18:1335-6 D 27 '66

WITT, Harold
Home movies at Newport; poem. Reporter 34:50 F 24 '66
Leslie Aumaire; poem. Sat R 49:39 N 19 '66
Without its meanings, language is a noise; poem. Sat R 49:44 F 19 '66
Yellow jackets; poem. Sat R 49:54 D 31 '66

WITTEN, Alfred H. and Daigler, G. W.
Tips for college-bound youngsters. Parents Mag 41:50-1+ Mr '66

WITTES, Robert E. See Goldberg, A. L. jt. auth.

WITTHOLZ, Charles W.
Other man's boat. Yachting 119:80-1 My '66

WITTIG, Monique
Child's world without wonder. A. Balakian. por Sat R 49:33 Jl 2 '66

WITTMAN, Martha
Reviews; production at East 74th street theatre. M. Marks. Dance Mag 40:24 F '66

WITTMANN, Otto
What it takes to put on a $50-million art exhibit. il pors Bsns W p 112-14+ D 10 '66

WITTREICH, Warren J.
How to buy, sell professional services. Harvard Bsns R 44:127-34+ Mr '66

WITTY, Helen S.
Grow sweet basil for flavor and fragrance. Flower Grower 53:65 Mr '66
Magic of mushrooms. il Flower Grower 53:39 F '66
Midsummer feast. Flower Grower 53:36+ Ag '66
Season's fare. See issues of Flower grower, the home garden

WIVES
Adventure of being a wife. R. S. Peale. Read Digest 88:71-4 Je '66
American family in India. R. H. Useem. Ann Am Acad 368:132-45 N '66
Big men and the woman behind them. M. Simons. il Look 31:68-9 Ja 10 '67
Five years that taught me how to live: husband with fatal heart disease. M. H. Clark. il Redbook 128:10+ N '66
How to be a good mother without neglecting your husband. E. Desmond. il Parents Mag 41:32-3+ Jl '66
How young wives can help their husbands succeed. S. Blum and S. C. Soman. Redbook 127:47+ My '66
I don't know where to look for me. A. Taylor; discussion. Redbook 127:43+ Ag '66

Never underestimate her power; executives' wives. il Newsweek 68:64-6 D 26 '66
That glittering overseas investment, the executive's lady. il Fortune 73:132-9 Je '66
Unpaid, uncomplaining, but not unappreciated: a wife, the best photo assistant of them all. A. Bosworth. il U S Camera 29:40+ Ag '66
What every husband ought to know. H. Boyle. il Read Digest 89:40 Jl '66
What, if anything, is wrong with American wives? J. J. Osten. Mlle 63:175+ My '66
When can infidelity be justified or forgiven? results of McCall's questioning 1,112 men and women. S. Blum. il McCalls 93:73+ My '66
Young wife's world. H. Valentine. See issues of Good housekeeping
    See also
College professors and instructors—Wives
Domestic relations
Governors wives
Housewives
Mothers
Widows

WOBECK, Earl
Build this beach dolly for your boat. Pop Sci 189:100-1 Jl '66

WOBURN abbey. See Country estates—England

WOEHRLIN, Molly
Mother who learned to fight. A. Lake. il por Redbook 128:62-3+ N '66

WOELFEL, James W.
Love, faith, hope: three attitudes in contemporary theology. Christian Cent 83:1570-3 D 21 '66

WOELL, James Fred
Adventure in art: plastic. Sch Arts 65:10-12 Mr '66

WOFFORD, Harris
Future of the Peace corps. bibliog f Ann Am Acad 365:129-46 My '66
Toward a draft without guns. Sat R 49:19-21+ O 15 '66

WOGAMAN, Philip
Moral reassessment of our war in Vietnam. Christian Cent 84:7-9 Ja 4 '67

WOHLERS, H. C.
Air-pollution credo. Am City 81:187+ S '66

WOHLSTETTER, Roberta
What really happend at Pearl Harbor; summary of Pearl Harbor: warning and decision. U S News 61:46-7 D 12 '66

WOIWODE, L.
Beyond the bedroom wall; story. New Yorker 42:38-41 Mr 5 '66
Brothers; story. New Yorker 42:43 My 21 '66
Crystals from North Dakota; poem. New Yorker 42:34 Je 4 '66
Near the Straits of Mackinac; story. New Yorker 42:40-4 Ap 9 '66
Visitation; story. New Yorker 42:56-61 S 10 '66

WOJTAS, Edward J.
Narrow gauge to Ozumba. Travel 126:46-9 N '66
Possum trot! Travel 126:48-9 D '66

WOLBARST, John
1966 film-developer roundup; ed. by T. Hill. Mod Phot 30:62-7+ Mr '66

WOLCOTT, Jean
Ancient art revived. Parks & Rec 1:168-9 F '66

WOLCOTT, Conn.
Mercuries mean more light for less money. E. Bagley, jr. il Am City 81:114 Jl '66

WOLDRING, Sabbo, and others
Blood gases: continuous in vivo recording of partial pressures by mass pectrography. bibliog Science 153:885-7 Ag 19 '66

WOLF, Charles, jr
Insurgency and counterinsurgency: new myths and old realities. Yale R 56:225-41 D '66

WOLF, Edwin, 2d
Book for an early American bookcase. Antiques 90:211-13 Ag '66

WOLF, H. R.
Anthology of nothings. Nation 204:26-7 Ja 2 '67

WOLF, Henry
Photography for inept sophisticates. Mod Phot 30:54-5+ Jl '66

WOLF, Howlin'
Mean old blues. il por Newsweek 67:91A F 21 '66

WOLF, Hugo
Records:
    Eighteen songs. Opera N 31:34 D 24 '66

WOLF, Jerome
Church and Delano. Commonweal 84:168-9 Ap 29 '66
WOLF, John R.
Stamford's attempt to integrate suburbia. Reporter 35:20+ D 29 '66
WOLF, Ken, and others
Lymphocystis virus: isolation and propagation in centrarchid fish cell lines. bibliog Science 151:1004-5 F 25 '66
WOLF, Leonard
Dervish and the horse; poem. Commonweal 84:311 Je 3 '66
WOLF, Manfred
Angry young Dutchman. Reporter 34:56 Ap 7 '66
WOLF, Marguerite
Day camp with a difference. Parents Mag 41: 50-1+ My '66
WOLF, William
Get with the action. il U S Camera 30:16 Ja '67
WOLF hunting
Trophy you'll never get. R. W. Young. il Field & S 71:42-3+ Ag '66
WOLF spiders. See Spiders
WOLF traps. See Traps
WOLFE, Bernard
Thirty years after Stalin's great purge. N Y Times Mag p66-7+ S 18 '66
WOLFE, Donald
Trouble with maple. Am For 72:18-21+ Je '66
WOLFE, Evelyn
Visit to Joan Miró. Sr Schol 88:sup26 Ap 15 '66
WOLFE, Henry C.
Progress East of the Berlin wall. Sat R 49:35 6 S 17 '66
Worried look at West Germany. Sat R 49:22-3+ Mr 26 '66
WOLFE, John H.
How persuasive are you? with test questions and answers. Read Digest 89:37-8+ D '66
WOLFE, Michael
Statue of Eve; poem. Atlan 217:64 My '66
WOLFE, Thomas K.
Speaking out. por Sat Eve Post 239:10+ D 3 '66
about
Big bad Wolfe? por Newsweek 67:60 Ja 31 '66
Tom Wolfe . . . but exactly, yes! E. Dundy. por Vogue 147:124-5+ Ap 15 '66
WOLFE, Thomas W.
Levels of nuclear strategy. Reporter 36:63-4 Ja 12 '67
WOLFE, Tom. See Wolfe, T. K.
WOLFE, Winifred
Some of the nicest people are superstitious. Good H 162:100-1+ Mr '66
WOLFENSBERGER, Wolf
Ethical issues in research with human subjects. bibliog Science 155:47-51 Ja 6 '67
WOLFF, Geoffrey A.
Exemplary novelists. New Repub 155:35-6 N 26 '66
WOLFF, George L. See Bartke, A. jt. auth.
WOLFF, Ivan A.
Seed lipids. bibliog Science 154:1140-9 D 2 '66
WOLFF, Max
Case for educational parks. Arch Rec 139: 180-1 F '66
WOLFGANG, Marvin E.
(ed) Patterns of violence. bibliog f Ann Am Acad 364:1-157 Mr '66
Preface to violence. bibliog f Ann Am Acad 364:1-7 Mr '66
WOLFMAN, Augustus
Wolfman on printing. See issues of Modern photography
WOLFSON, Bernice J.
Individualizing instruction. NEA J 55:31-3 N '66
WOLFSON, Louis Elwood
Woes of Wolfson. il por Time 88:106+ S 30 '66
Wolfson at bay. Newsweek 68:89 O 3 '66
WOLFSON, Victor
Human side of a hero. Sat R 49:32-3 F 26 '66
WOLFYS, Noel
Princess and the dragon; drama. Plays 25: 81-5 Mr '66
WOLITZER, Hilma
Today, a woman went mad in the supermarket; story. Sat Eve Post 239:50-2 Mr 12 '66
WOLMAN, Benjamin B.
Creativity and mental health: are they related? Dance Mag 40:42-4 Mr '66

WOLPE, Stefan
From Folkways, Brecht by Bentley; and the Wolpe music. R. Franceschini. il Am Rec G 32:747 Ap '66
WOLPERT, Arnold W.
Response from the NEA. Mo Labor R 89:621-2 Je '66
WOLSTENCROFT, J. H. See Gwyn, D. G. jt. auth.
WOLVERINE shoe and tanning corporation
Management's rule-breakers: the ways of the winners. J. Weiner. Duns R 87:83-4 Ja '66
WOLVERINES
Much maligned wolverine. A. Russell. il Field & S 71:74+ N '66
WOLVES
Archaic bounty system. Nat Parks Mag 40: 21 F '66
Enjoying nature; on an Algonquin howllalong. B. McMaster. il Audubon Mag 68:472-5 N '66
North American wolves. S. Young. il Am For 72:8-9+ O '66
Wolf; North American predator on the verge of extinction. R. J. Aulerich. il Nat Parks Mag 40:10-13 N '66
Wolves ain't so smart. W. Page. il Field & S 70:65-7+ Mr '66
Wolves social as dogs. P. McBroom. il Sci N 90:174-5 S 10 '66
WOLVES in the attic; story. See Klein, D. M.
WOMAN
Beauty and heart. L. Barzini. Vogue 148:183-4+ O 1 '66
David Bailey talks of women, beauty, marriage; interview, ed. by P. Devlin. D. Bailey. il Vogue 148:166-72+ N 15 '66
Henry Miller's real woman; conversation, ed. by D. Dury. H. Miller. Mlle 64:90-1+ D '66
On being a woman. J. Brothers. See issues of Good housekeeping
Thoughts to remember. H. Golden. Good H 162:246 Je '66
Trouble with starlets. J. Fowles. il Holiday 39-12+ Je '66
Why woman act that way; reprint. J. Churchill. il Read Digest 90:68-9 Ja '67
See also
Beauty, Personal
Education of women
Housewives
Inter-American commission of women
Love
Mothers
Sex differences
Single women
Widows
Wives
Women in church work
Young women

Biography
Longer view of the educated woman; excerpt from Educated American women: self-portraits. E. Ginzberg and A. M. Yohalem. Sch & Soc 94:391-2+ N 12 '66

Crime
History
Delaware's amazon outlaw. M. B. Duda. il Negro Hist Bul 29:153-4 Ap '66

Defense
See Self defense for women

Diseases
Parasite effect studied. Sci N 90:503 D 10 '66

Dress
See Clothing and dress

Education
See Education of women

Employment
Good man is hard to find, so they hire women. il Time 88:92-3 N 4 '66
Unless we begin now; address, July 25, 1966. J. W. Macy, jr. Vital Speeches 32:678-82 S 1 '66
What educated women want; report: views of Vassar seniors, ed. by J. M. Russin. il Newsweek 67:68-72+ Je 13 '66
See also
Business and professional women
Married women—Employment
Negro women—Employment
Woman—Equal rights

WOMAN—*Continued*

Equal rights

Better half. by A. Sinclair. Review
Commentary 41:100-2+ Ap '66. C. Lasch
Nation 203:490-2 N 7 '66. N. Reeves
Elimination of discrimination against women;
report on 19th session of the U.N. Commission on the status of women. G. A. Tillett. Dept State Bul 55:284-8 Ag 22 '66
From the women: what about our job rights?
complaints to Equal employment opportunity commission. il U S News 61:61-2
Jl 4 '66
See also
United Nations—Commission on the status of
women

Health and hygiene

She's a very pretty girl, but. Seventeen 25:
128-9 F '66
See also
Beauty, Personal
Menopause
Pregnancy

History

Women of India. K. Singh. il N Y Times
Mag p24-5+ Mr 13 '66

Legal status, laws, etc.

Legal rights of working wives. il Good H
162:180 Mr '66

Occupations

See also
Business and professional women
Secretaries
Woman—Employment
Women as authors

Psychology

Deadlier than the male. M. Mannes. McCalls
94:30 N '66
Man talk; sense and sensibility. D. Newman
and R. Benton. il Mlle 63:104 My '66
On being a woman. J. Brothers. See issues
of Good housekeeping
Psychology of modern women. F. R. Schreiber
and M. Herman. il Sci Digest 60:16-21
Ag '66
Skeptical report on the experts who tell
women how to be women. E. Janeway. il
McCalls 93:94-5+ Ap '66
Sleeping beauty; problem of the unawakened
woman. R. May and R. J. Levin. il Redbook 127:62-3+ S '66
Turning points of life. G. Caplan and V. Cadden. McCalls 94:114-15+ O '66; Same abr.
with title How to deal with a crisis. Read
Digest 90:80-3 Ja '67
What every girl should know. M. Mannes.
Mlle 62:83+ Ja '66
Why woman act that way; reprint. J. Churchill. il Read Digest 90:68-9 Ja '67

Religious life

See also
Women and religion

Rights of women

See Woman—Equal rights

Social and moral questions

Speaking out; why do they treat women like
guinea pigs? E. Kendall. il Sat Eve Post
239:10+ Jl 16 '66
What every girl should know. M. Mannes.
Mlle 62:83+ Ja '66
See also
Alcoholism

WOMAN suffrage

United States

Better half. by A. Sinclair. Review
Nation 203:490-2 N 7 '66. N. Reeves
WOMAN without a shadow; opera. See Strauss,
R.
WOMAN'S work; story. See White, D.
WOMB. See Uterus
WOMB, Artificial. See Uterus, Artificial
WOMEN

Asia

New angles; visit to plastic-surgery clinics.
il Time 88:24-5 D 23 '66

Brazil

Breaking the padlock. il Newsweek 67:60 My
16 '66

England

Mothers & daughters. C. MacInnes. Mlle 62:
186-7+ Mr '66
Ready, steady, go! career girls; London. A.
Grant. il Mlle 62:188-90 Mr '66

India

On the role of women. G. D. Berreman. Bul
Atomic Sci 22:26-8 N '66
Women of India. K. Singh. il N Y Times
Mag p24-5+ Mr 13 '66

Japan

Three cheers of *banzai*; Housewives association fights dry cleaners' lobby. il Time 87:
41 Je 24 '66
Woman's world. Newsweek 67:40-1 F 21 '66

Tunisia

Shudder at the knees; banning the miniskirt.
il Time 88:26+ Ag 26 '66

Turkey

Alla Turca; life once lived within the sultan's palace. L. Blanch. Vogue 148:266-7+
D '66

United States

Art Buchwald's ladies of choice; ten most
beautiful women in Washington. il Newsweek 67:26-7 Je 6 '66
Boring American beauty. M. Mannes. McCalls 93:45+ Mr '66
Crumbling cliché of the too-bright girl; concerning Eli Ginzberg's study. Life 60:4 My
6 '66
How America looks; a 20th reunion in
Dallas. il Ladies Home J 83:71-9+ S '66
How women's role in U.S. is changing. il
U S News 60:58-60 My 30 '66
Mademoiselle Merit awards, 1966. il Mlle 64:
47-51 Ja '67
Mademoiselle's annual Merit awards, 1965.
il Mlle 62:45-9 Ja '66
On the role of women. G. D. Berreman. Bul
Atomic Sci 22:26-8 N '66
Portfolio of American mothers and daughters.
il McCalls 93:47-55 Jl '66
Pretty, lascivious, undignified; individuality
of women. J. Mitford. Vogue 147:92-3 Mr
15 '66
Trouble with starlets. J. Fowles. il Holiday
39:12+ Je '66
We wonder what will happen. America 115:
822 D 24 '66
See also
Divorce—United States
Education of women—United States
General federation of women's clubs
Negro women
Woman—Employment
Woman—Equal rights
Woman suffrage—United States

Vietnam (Republic)

When crisis is a way of life. L. G. Martin.
il Mlle 64:172-3+ N '66
Women of Vietnam. L. Bergquist. il Look
30:17-21 D 27 '66
WOMEN, Famous
Portfolio of American mothers and daughters.
il McCalls 93:47-55 Jl '66
Romantic way. by V. Cronin. Review
Sat R 49:33-4 F 26 '66. M. Laski
Unknockables. il Esquire 65:84-5 Je '66
See also
Celebrities

Anecdotes, facetiae, satire, etc.

Freeman's guide to unsatisfactory people.
N. B. Freeman. il Nat R 18:924-5 S 20 '66
WOMEN, Negro. See Negro women
WOMEN and men
Deadlier than the male. M. Mannes. McCalls
94:30 N '66
Love and the battle of the sexes. J. Brothers.
Good H 162:40+ F '66
Outwitting the custodial spouse. R. Starnes.
Field & S 71:16+ D '66
Personal fulfillment in man and woman; excerpt from Man and woman. M. O'Keefe
and J. J. Evoy. America 115:582-6 N 12 '66
Pride and prejudice. D. Newman and R.
Benton. Mlle 62:44+ F '66
Total gift. J. T. Culliton. America 115:770-3
D 10 '66
Trouble with starlets. J. Fowles. il Holiday
39:12+ Je '66

WOMEN and men—*Continued*
Violence and the masculine ideal: some qualitative data; with excerpts from a tape-recorded interview with an imprisoned armed robber. J. Toby. bibliog f Ann Am Acad 364:19-27 Mr '66
What entertains a man entertains a woman. il Vogue 148:113+ N 15 '66
Who says he's a flop? C. Brossard. Look 31: 23-4 Ja 10 '67

WOMEN and politics
Negro woman in politics. il Ebony 21:96-100 Ag '66
Nun for Congress. W. More. America 115:797 D 17 '66
    See also
Congresswomen
League of women voters of the United States
Women as governors

WOMEN and religion
Woman's role in the church. M.-A. Harper. America 115:91-3 Jl 23 '66; Discussion. 115: 195-6, 436 Ag 27, O 15 '66

WOMEN and the church
Church women and Christian unity. C. C. Wedel. Cath World 202:278-82 F '66
Putting sisters in their place. S. Kelly; discussion. America 114:329-30 Mr 5 '66

WOMEN and war
    See also
Vietnamese war, 1957- —Women and the war

WOMEN as air pilots
Last weekend I learned to fly. J. Bryant. il Sci Digest 61:61-4 Ja '67
Nuts to fashion. P. Shamburger. il Flying 79:88 O '66
Skirts flying. S. Buegeleisen. See issues of Flying
Skirts flying; Michigan Smallrace. S. Buegeleissen. il Flying 80:74 Ja '67
Weekend fling. M. Kvaka. il Flying 79:62-4 S '66

WOMEN as architects
Battleground of the spirit. E. R. Kohlberg. il Mlle 63:162-3+ My '66

WOMEN as athletes
Are girl athletes really girls? sex inspections stir international furor. il Life 61:63-6 O 7 '66
Brown baby Olympic hopeful from Japan. il Ebony 21:58-60 O '66
Found: a pretty Penny; performance of U.S. girls at World ski championships. Portillo, Chile. B. Ottum. il Sports Illus 25:12-15 Ag 15 '66
Game girl in a man's game; R. G. Bingay of Boston. G. S. Brown. il Sports Illus 24:67-8+ My 2 '66
Girl on the varsity. il Ebony 21:71-2+ My '66
In defense of womanhood. Sports Illus 25: 24 S 12 '66
Preserving la différence; physical examination to prove sex. il Time 88:70 S 16 '66

WOMEN as authors
Cherchez l'homme: seven best librarian-authors all women! J. Shera. Wilson Lib Bul 41:423+ D '66

WOMEN as automobile drivers. See Automobile drivers

WOMEN as college professors and instructors
My first sixty years, by L. B. Morton. Review
    Negro Hist Bul 29:41 N '65. E. Menard

WOMEN as criminals. See Woman—Crime

WOMEN as executives
Lady shows them how it's done; Mrs S. Boltz, president and treasurer of Goddard & Goddard co. il Bsns W D 134-6+ O 15 '66
Prettiest veep: P. Kaniclides. Newsweek 67: 69 F 7 '66
Women at the top. il Newsweek 67:76-8 Je 27 '66
Women, industry's newest challenge; with editorial comment. J. Perham. il Duns R 88:23. 36-7+ Ag '66

WOMEN as farmers
So your daughter wants to take ag? C. Eckhardt; discussion. Farm J 90:66R Ap '66

WOMEN as foreign service employees
Protocol in practice. B. Angelo. il Mlle 62: 168-9+ F '66

WOMEN as governors
Me for ma, and I ain't got a dern thing against pa. R. S. Gallagher. il Am Heritage 17:46-7+ O '66
Pa and Ma Wallace as a dynasty. Life 60:4 Mr 11 '66

WOMEN as lawyers
Mission of Marian Wright. P. Pierce. il Ebony 21:94-7+ Je '66

WOMEN as members of Congress. See Congresswomen

WOMEN as ministers
Big event at Wheeling; interim report from a special committee appointed to study the role of women in the ministry. Christian Cent 83:1529 D 14 '66
Union agreement must include women ministers; United church of Canada and Anglican church of Canada. Christian Cent 83:609 My 11 '66
    See also
Women as priests

WOMEN as musicians
Ladies' day; orchestras. il Time 88:94-5 D 9 '66

WOMEN as photographers
Photographed by: Susanne Singer. M. P. R. Thomas. il U S Camera 29:50-3 D '66
Woman's role in photography. P. Stackpole. U S Camera 29:14+ Mr '66
    See also
Frampton, M.

WOMEN as priests
Male church. A. Swidler. Commonweal 83: 387-9 Je 24 '66
Woman's role in the church. M.-A. Harper. America 115:91-3 Jl 23 '66; Discussion. 115: 195-6, 436 Ag 27, O 15 '66
Women clergy for Rome? Holy Spirit answering affirmatively. R. Lauer. Christian Cent 83:1107-10 S 14 '66

WOMEN as public officers
Kiss of the muse; K. Louchheim's State appointment. Newsweek 68:32 O 17 '66

WOMEN as reporters
Femininity at the front; Viet Nam's female press corps. il Time 88:73 O 28 '66
    See also
Higgins, M.

WOMEN as scientists
Pair of lubbers takes to the sea; women oceanographers. il Ebony 21:112-14+ Ap '66

WOMEN as teachers
Teaching sisters. America 116:76-7 Ja 21 '67

WOMEN as wrestlers. See Wrestling

WOMEN college graduates. See College graduates, Women

WOMEN college students. See College students, Women

WOMEN come and go; story. See Hecht, F.

WOMEN golf players. See Golfers

WOMEN in boating
Boat-wife handling. W. S. Kals. il Motor B 117:90-1 Ja '66
Cabin talk. M. Wiley. See issues of Yachting
Closeup: Barbara Holt, fisherman. J. Mazurki. il Motor B 117:48-9+ My '66
Concrete of the city, the wispy dreams of the sea. M. Petersen. il Motor B 117: 30-1+ My '66
Glacier ice for cocktails; passage to Newfoundland and return. M. Wiley. il Yachting 120:44-5+ O '66
Ladies day at sea. N. Brower. il Motor B 119:76-9+ Ja '67
Marriage sailboat style. M. Badham. il Motor B 117:32-4+ F '66

Anecdotes, facetiae, satire, etc.

Little boat that grew. H. Bottel. il Motor B 117:126+ F '66

WOMEN in business. See Business and professional women

WOMEN in church work
Methodist women in quadrennial assembly. B. Thompson. Christian Cent 83:784-6 Je 15 '66

WOMEN in fishing. See Fishing

WOMEN in motor boat racing. See Motor boat racing

WOMEN in politics. See Women and politics

WOMEN in the armed forces. See United States —Armed forces—Womens services

WOMEN'S clothes. See Clothing and dress

WOMENS clubs and societies
How to tell an Elk from an Eagle; a field guide to clubs and lodges. il Changing T 20:13-15 S '66
    See also
General federation of women's clubs

WOMENS electric shavers. See Razors

WOODSTOCK, N.Y.
Woodstock, N.Y. Turnau opera players. R.
D. Daniels. Opera N 31:28 S 10 '66

WOODWARD, Bliss
Under the blue ensign. See issues of Motor
boating

WOODWARD, C. Vann
What happened to the civil rights movement?
Harper 234:29-37 Ja '67

WOODWARD, Harold S.
Structures should have stiffness as well as
strength. Arch Rec 139:226-7 Ap '66

WOODWARD, Kenneth L.
Comment. Commonweal 85:393-4 Ja 13 '67

WOODWARD, O. J.
City that puts people first. B. Taper. McCalls
93:186 Ap '66

WOODWARD, Robert Burns
Recent advances in the chemistry of natural
products; address, December 11, 1965. bibliog Science 153:487-93 Jl 29 '66

WOODWARD and Lothrop (store) See Washington, D.C.—Stores

WOODWARD stakes. See Horse racing

WOODWELL, George M. and Dykeman, W. R.
Respiration of a forest measured by carbon
dioxide accumulation during temperature
inversions. bibliog Science 154:1031-4 N 25
'66

WOODWORKING
From outer space to basement workshop.
J. A. Van Allen. il Pop Sci 189:98-100 N '66
How to use the drinking-cup trick in wood-
working. R. J. De Cristoforo. il Pop Sci
189:116-20 Jl '66
Woodworking tricks that make you a whiz!
W. C. Leckey. il Pop Mech 126:162-5 D '66
    See also
Sanding

Projects

Chain saw speeds rustic log projects. il Pop
Mech 125:150-3 Ap '66
It's easier now to build good furniture. L. D.
Kreitz. il Pop Sci 189:164-6 O '66
Reproduce this prized antique on your lathe;
ed. by A. W. Lees. E. R. Haan. il Pop
Mech 125:176-81+ Mr '66
Winter workshop projects. il Pop Gard 17:38-
43 D '66
Wordless workshop. R. Doty. See issues of
Popular science monthly
    See also
Chopping blocks
Furniture, Outdoor
Stools

WOODWORKING machinery
    See also
Routing machines
Shapers

WOODWORTH, Laurence N.
Where tax bills run the gauntlet. il pors
Bsns W p 106+ Je 11 '66

WOOFER speakers. See Loud speaking apparatus

WOOL, Harold
Military and civilian occupational structures;
excerpt from Military specialist: specialized
manpower requirements and resources of
the armed forces. Mo Labor R 89:29-33 Ja '66

WOOL, Ira G. See Stirewalt, W. S. jt. auth.

WOOLDRIDGE, William O.
Noncom sir. il por Time 88:24 Jl 22 '66

WOOLEDGE, John
Investing takes up the slack. por Bsns W
p80 F 26 '66

WOOLEN and worsted fabrics
At last: woolens you can wash by machine.
J. A. Morris. Read Digest 89:233-7 O '66
    See also
Cashmere
Tweed

WOOLF, Neville J.
James Croll and solar evolution. Sky & Tel
31:150-1 Mr '66

WOOLF, Virginia (Stephen)
Virginia Woolf and her works, by J. Guiguet.
Review
    Commonweal 85:57-9 O 14 '66. J. R.
    Mellow

WOOLMAN, Collett Everman
Final flight. por Time 88:91-2 S 23 '66

WOOLWICH, John Arthur Thomas Robinson,
bp of. See Robinson, J. A. T.

WOOTEN, Mary Lee
Creative art in the classroom curriculum.
Sch Arts 66:4-8 D '66

WORCESTER, Donald E.
(comp) Articles and other books received;
Latin America. See issues of American
historical review

WORCESTER art museum, Worcester, Mass.
Worcester art museum. D. C. Rich and L.
Dresser. il Antiques 90:647-54 N '66

WORD, Buford, and Boylan, B. R.
Expectant mother. Redbook 127:20+ O '66

WORD blindness
Some Johnnies just can't; dyslexia. il Time
87:56+ My 13 '66
Teaching the dyslexic child: new hope for
non-readers; McGlannan school method. C.
Ellingson and J. Cass. il Sat R 49:82-5+
Ap 16 '66

WORD games
Trade winds. J. G. Fuller. il Sat R 49:16+
F 19 '66
    See also
Crossword puzzles

WORD maze. See Teaching—Aids and devices

WORD-of-mouth advertising. See Advertising
mediums

WORD tests. See Vocabulary tests

WORDS
Brief and to the point. D. M. Titler. Writer
79:28 Jl '66
In my opinion; wonderful is worth saving.
E. House. Seventeen 25:184 Je '66
Manner of speaking; mumpsimus; definition.
J. Ciardi. Sat R 49:22+ My 7 '66
Pleasant land of counterpane. C. Lewis. il
Horn Bk 42:542-7 O '66
    See also
Semantics

WORDS and thought. See Thought and
language

WORK benches
Build your own home hobby center. C. E.
Rhine. il Pop Sci 188:158-60 F '66
Foldaway workbench for a garage. il Pop
Sci 189:149 S '66
Put your shop in order with this rugged
bench. D. Jordan. il Bet Hom & Gard 44:
67 O '66

WORK camps, International voluntary. See
International voluntary workcamps

WORK furlough programs. See Prisoners—Rehabilitation

WORK measurement
Deterioration of work standards. C. W.
Graves. il Harvard Bsns R 44:117-22+ S
'66

WORK performance standards. See Performance standards

WORK projects administration. See United
States—Work projects administration

WORK satisfaction. See Job satisfaction

WORK stoppages. See Strikes

WORK-study plan. See Education. Cooperative

WORK tables
Woodworking champ of any shop. R. J. De
Cristoforo. il Pop Sci 188:166-71+ F '66

WORKBENCHES. See Work benches

WORKER (newspaper)
More dead than read. il Newsweek 68:100+
D 5 '66

WORKER priests
Working priests in France. R. Rouquette.
Cath World 203:161-4 Je '66

WORKERS education. See Labor and laboring
classes—Education

WORKING day. See Hours of labor

WORKING girls and women
    See also
Business and professional women

WORKING mothers. See Married women—
Employment

WORKING week. See Hours of labor

WORKS progress administration. See United
States—Work projects administration

WORKSHOPS
Coming events. Parks & Rec 1:483 Je '66
From outer space to basement workshop. J.
A. Van Allen. il Pop Sci 189:98-100 N '66
How to fit a workshop into a small place.
il Bet Hom & Gard 44:126 Mr '66
How to set up a home print shop. J.
Burroughs. il Pop Sci 189:124-8+ Jl '66

Equipment

Ideas you can use in a good farm shop. il
Suc Farm 64:58 F '66

WORKSHOPS, Dance. See Dance institutes
and workshops

WORKSHOPS, Library. See Library institutes
and workshops

WORLD almanac and book of facts
Little book that knows everything. il Changing T 21:45-6 Ja '67

WORLD bank. See International bank for reconstruction and development

WORLD book encyclopedia
5000 attend World book's 50th-year sales convention. Pub W 190:28 O 24 '66

WORLD bridge championship. See Bridge tournaments

WORLD church (sect) See Sects

WORLD citizenship, Education for. See International education

WORLD conference on church and society. See
World council of churches

WORLD congress for the lay apostolate
Distaff meeting in Rome. America 116:7 Ja 7
'67

WORLD congress of writers. See PEN club

WORLD congress on evangelism. See Religious
conferences

WORLD contract bridge team championship.
See Bridge tournaments

WORLD council of churches
American in Geneva; General Secretary, E.
C. Blake. il Time 87:80 F 18 '66
Blake elected W.C.C. General Secretary.
Christian Cent 83:229 F 23 '66
Churchmen at Geneva; World conference on
church and society. America 115:147 Ag
13 '66
Demonstrating the Gospel; World conference
on church and society. Christian Cent 83:
927-8 Jl 27 '66
Fact-facing Christians. Christian Cent 83:671-
2 My 25 '66
Geneva, 1966; World conference on church
and society. H. Cox. Commonweal 84:
525-8 Ag 19 '66
Inescapably political; World conference on
church and society in Geneva. H. E. Fey.
Christian Cent 83:954-5 Ag 3 '66
Lengthened shadow; farewell dinner for WCC
retiring general secretary W. A. Visser 't
Hooft. B. Thompson. Christian Cent 83:610-
11 My 11 '66
Man for all churches; Protestant pope. il
Newsweek 67:92 F 21 '66
Mirroring the world; World conference on
church and society. H. E. Fey. Christian
Cent 83:978-9 Ag 10 '66
New era begins in Geneva. America 114:
283-4 F 26 '66
Race tension worldwide; thoughts from
Geneva. D. Kitagawa. Christian Cent 83:
1220-3 O 5 '66
Radical new voice; report on Geneva con-
ference on church and society. il Time 88:
69-70 Ag 5 '66
Trade and the war on world poverty. R. M.
Fagley. Christian Cent 83:745-8 Je 8 '66
Unifying Dutchman; Visser 't Hooft. il Time
88:91 D 9 '66
World council: candor and hope; Central
committee meets in Geneva. C. North-
cott. Christian Cent 83:263-4 Mr 2 '66
World council of churches. G. Murray. Christ-
ian Cent 83:1357-9 N 2 '66
W.C.C. central committee speaks out on
Vietnam. Christian Cent 83:262 Mr 2 '66
WCC on church and society; meeting of
World conference on church and society.
Geneva, July 12-26, 1966. America 115:199
Ag 27 '66

WORLD council of peace. See World peace
council

WORLD court. See International court of
justice, The Hague

WORLD crafts council
Montreux; World crafts council. il Craft
Horiz 26:16-19+ S '66

WORLD economics. See Economic conditions

WORLD fairs. See Exhibitions

WORLD federation of the United Nations associations
WFUNA appointment; commissioner-general
of EXPO '67. UN Mo Chron 3:123 O '66

WORLD festival of Negro arts. See Festivals—
Senegal

WORLD flights. See Aviation—World flights

WORLD food program. See Food supply

WORLD food supply. See Food supply

WORLD forestry congress
Forestry needs friends; congress held at
Madrid. J. B. Craig. Am For 72:13 Jl '66

Letter from Madrid: wood in the world; sixth
congress. J. B. Craig. il Am For 72:10-17+
Ag '66
Seattle's trees for peace. International
friendship grove; photographs. Am For 72:
34-7 Je '66

WORLD government. See International organization

WORLD health. See Public health

WORLD health organization
World health organization. il UN Mo Chron
3:80 Je '66

WORLD history
Bibliography
New books for teaching world history. F. S.
Gross; H. M. Long. Sr Schol 89:sup20-2 N
18 '66
[New books on world history] H. L. Hur-
witz. Sr Schol 88:sup 10-11 Mr 11 '66

WORLD Jewish congress
Germans and Jews. Newsweek 68:72+ Ag 15
'66

WORLD journal tribune
Hello Dolly! Newsweek 68:102 S 19 '66
New daily for New York. il Time 88:100+
S 16 '66
Paper that actually came out. Time 88:82+
S 23 '66
Putting pop in the WJT. il Newsweek 69:81
Ja 16 '67
WJT. il Newsweek 68:75 S 26 '66

WORLD land reform conference
Land reform and the world food crisis; sum-
mary of conference. UN Mo Chron 3:45-8
Jl '66
Land reform conference. UN Mo Chron 3:
35-6 Jl '66
World land reform conference. UN Mo Chron
3:45 Ag '66

WORLD language. See Language, Universal

WORLD law. See International law

WORLD law fund
Revolution in peace education. R. A. Falk.
il Sat R 49:60-1+ My 21 '66

WORLD maps
Dilemmas, problems, troubles; publishing of
Hammond's new atlases. D. Dempsey. Sat
R 49:39 N 12 '66
Economic map of the world. Sr Schol 89:pt2
16-17 S 23 '66

WORLD medical association
Are human tests ethical? Helsinki declaration. F. Marley. Sci N 90:115 Ag 20 '66

WORLD meteorological organization
World meteorological day; statement, March
23, 1966. L. B. Johnson. Dept State Bul
54:618-19 Ap 18 '66

WORLD Methodist conference. See Methodist
world conference

WORLD monetary and economic conference.
See Monetary and economic conference,
London, 1933

WORLD of apples; story. See Cheever, J.

WORLD of Günter Grass (dramatic reading)
See Grass, G.

WORLD of strangers; story. See Davis, M.

WORLD opinion. See Public opinion

WORLD organization. See International organization

WORLD peace council
World peace council: worn record. J. M.
Swomley. Christian Cent 83:945-6 Jl 27 '66

WORLD politics
Democracy and peace; address, May 24, 1966.
Thant. UN Mo Chron 3:61-70 Je '66
Shape of events from one year to next; re-
view of 1966. Life 62:4 Ja 6 '67
Vanishing ideologues. E. J. Hughes. News-
week 67:22 Ap 18 '66
World politics of responsibility. O. Gass;
discussion. Commentary 41:12+ Ap '66
See also
Balance of power
Current events
International relations

WORLD politics, 1945-
Beginnings of the cold war. by M. F. Herz.
Review
Sat R 49:42 Ap 2 '66. F. Altschul
Communism 1966; success or failure? V. C.
Ferkiss. Cath World 204:11-16 O '66
Confronting the dream world; cold war.
Pyrrho. il Nat R 18:274-5 Mr 22 '66
Current documents. See Issues of Current
history

WORLD politics, 1945- —*Continued*
Goals for American power. R. D. Masters. Yale R 55:365-88 Mr '66
Hints of a changing equation. il Time 87:25 Mr 4 '66
How U.S. leaders see today's world. il U S News 61:28-31 D 26 '66
Limits of military aid. N. A. Graebner. Cur Hist 50:353-7+ Je '66
Lin Piao in the people's war; excerpts from article. P. Lin. Cur Hist 51:172-4+ S '66
Plenty afoot all over. il Life 61:32-3 S 9 '66
Political influence in the General assembly. R. O. Keohane. bibliog f il Int Council 557:5-64 Mr '66
Restoration Europe and world politics. R. Strausz-Hupé. Yale R 55:488-99 Je '66
U.S. and world affairs annual; ed. by R. Hemming and others. il Sr Schol 89:pt2 1-31 S 23 '66
Worldgram: from the capitals of the world. See issues of U.S. news & World report
See also
Atomic power—International control
WORLD population. See Population
WORLD population conference, Belgrade, 1965
Our shrinking planet; adaptation of U.N. radio programmes. E. N. Valters. UNESCO Courier 19:4-9 F '66
WORLD press Institute. See Macalester college, St Paul, Minn.
WORLD publishing company
Sheppard book available one week after acquittal. il Pub W 191:94 Ja 2 '67
WORLD records
Good or bad, it's a record. H. A. Smith. il Holiday 40:28+ D '66
WORLD satellite terminals, limited
U.K. company bids on satellite terminals. il Aviation W 85:93 N 28 '66
WORLD security. See International security
WORLD series (baseball)
But Mahoney stood outside; how the Orioles won the world series. G. W. Johnson. New Repub 155:8 O 22 '66
Goose eggs from the Orioles. il Time 88:79 O 14 '66
I've been living with it a long time; flubbing a third strike and becoming 1941 world series goat. W. C. Heinz. il Sat Eve Post 239:112-17 O 8 '66
Reasons why the Orioles won; Dodgers can't hit fast balls. W. Leggett. il Sports Illus 25:64-5 O 24 '66
Sporting scene. R. Angell. New Yorker 42:184+ O 29 '66
Those happy Birds! J. Mann. il Sports Illus 25:30-7 O 17 '66
WORLD series of golf. See Golf—Tournaments
WORLD shooting championship. See Shooting—Competitions
WORLD ski championship. See Skis and skiing
WORLD tariffs. See Tariff
WORLD tours
Notes from a world tour: questions asked abroad. T. C. Sorensen. Sat R 49:31 O 1 '66
WORLD trade. See Commerce
WORLD trade center. See New York (city)—World trade center (proposed)
WORLD trade corporation. See International business machines corporation
WORLD trade week
World trade week, 1966 proclamation, April 29, 1966. L. B. Johnson. il Dept State Bul 54:837 My 30 '66
WORLD travel. See Travel
WORLD unity. See International organization; International relations
WORLD war, 1939-1945
Götterdämmerung, with beer and pretzels. E. Grossman. Harper 232:106-8 My '66
How Germany was partitioned. C. Ryan. Pub W 189:39 Mr 28 '66
Last 100 days, by J. Toland. Review
New Yorker 42:124-6 Ag 27 '66. N. Bliven
Newsweek il 67:101-101A+ Mr 7 '66
Sat R il 49:42 Mr 12 '66. T. Taylor

Aerial operations
I shot down Yamamoto. T. G. Lanphier, jr. il Read Digest 89:82-7 D '66
See also
Berlin—Air raids

Armistices
Secret surrender, by A. Dulles. Review
Time 88:124+ O 21 '66
Secret surrender; excerpts. A. W. Dulles. il Harper 233:37-48 Jl; 61-4+ Ag '66

Art and the war
Expensive stew; H. Deutsch and the Hatvany collection. Newsweek 67:49-50 My 16 '66
$1,000,000 in Dürers found in Brooklyn; E. Elicofon acquisitions stolen from Weimar collection. il Life 60:34-5 Je 3 '66

Atrocities
Dina Mironovna Pronichev remembers Babi Yar; excerpt from novel, Babi Yar. A. Kuznetsov. N Y Times Mag p45+ D 11 '66
Investigation; theme of P. Weiss's play. R. J. Schroeder. Commonweal 85:139-41 N 4 '66
Memories make the future. J. J. Navone. Cath World 204:149-53 D '66
Was silence the only solution? G. Lewy. Sat R 49:26-7 My 21 '66
Worst that ever happened; with editorial comment. S. Bedford. il Sat Eve Post 239:29-33+, 112 O 22 '66

Campaigns and battles
Battles lost and won: great campaigns of World war II, by H. W. Baldwin. Review
Nat R 18:1277-8 D 13 '66. G. F. Eliot

Pacific
See also
Guadalcanal, Battle of, 1942-1943
Pearl Harbor, Attack on, 1941
World war, 1939-1945—Philippines

Russia
Day Hitler attacked Russia. A. Clark. il N Y Times Mag p 12-13+ Je 19 '66

Western front
See also
Berlin, Battle of, 1945

Catholic church
One pope, 860,000 Jews; Pinhaus Lapide credits Pius. Newsweek 67:68 My 9 '66
Pius' silence. il Time 87:63 Je 3 '66
Pius XII and the Third Reich; excerpts, ed. by R. Leiber. S. Friedländer. il Look 30:36-8+ My 17 '66
Was silence the only solution? G. Lewy. Sat R 49:26-7 My 21 '66

Children
We came as children, ed. by K. Gershon. Review
New Repub 155:20-4 N 26 '66. L. Segal

Confiscation of art treasures, etc.
See World war, 1939-1945—Art and the war

Destruction and pillage
See also
Berlin—Air raids

Diplomatic history
Diplomacy of victory in Europe. F. Calhoun. Sat R 49:29 D 31 '66
See also
World war, 1939-1945—Peace and mediation

Jews
Belsen remembered. L. S. Dawidowicz. Commentary 41:82-5 Mr '66
Case against Eichmann continues. A. L. Fein. Sat R 49:27+ Jl 2 '66
Denmark's heroic week. il Sr Schol 89:3 O 7 '66
Lingering shadow of nazism. il Sr Schol 89:10-11 O 14 '66
Tragic dilemma. E. H. Wall. Nat R 18:843-4 Ag 23 '66

Memorials and monuments
See War memorials

Moral and religious aspects
See also
World war, 1939-1945—Catholic church

Naval operations
Battle off Samar. W. P. Deac. il Am Heritage 18:20-3+ D '66
Yamamoto: the man who menaced America, by J. D. Potter. Review
Am Heritage 17:67-8 F '66. B. Catton
See also
Guadalcanal, Battle of, 1942-1943

Negroes
Brief history of the 761st tank battalion in World war II. W. Lewis. Negro Hist Bul 29:46-7 N '65

WORLD war, 1939-1945—*Continued*

Peace and mediation

Secret surrender, by A. Dulles. Review
Newsweek il 68:122+ O 24 '66. S. K.
Oberbeck

Personal narratives

Coastwatcher's diary: Guadalcanal; with introd. by S. W. Sears. M. Clemens. Am Heritage 17:104-10 F '66
God, please get us out of this; experience of being trapped at the bottom of Pearl Harbor. S. B. Young. il Am Heritage 17:48-51+ Ap '66
I shot down Yamamoto. T. G. Lanphier, jr. il Read Digest 89:82-7 D '66
Years between, by C. Beaton. Review
New Yorker 41:102+ Ja 22 '66. N. Bliven

Secret service

Secret surrender, by A. Dulles. Review
Newsweek il 68:122+ O 24 '66. S. K.
Oberbeck
Secret surrender; excerpts. A. W. Dulles. il Harper 233:37-48 Jl; 61-4+ Ag '66

War criminals

Criminal state and German responsibility: a dialogue; tr. by W. J. Dannhauser. K. Jaspers; R. Augstein. Commentary 41:33-9 F '66
Last prisoner of Spandau; R. Hess. P. Shabecoff. il N Y Times Mag p28-9+ Ag 28 '66
See also
Nuremberg trials

France

No laurels for de Gaulle; an appraisal of the London years, by R. Mengin. Review
New Yorker 42:242-7 O 22 '66. N. Bliven

Germany

Hitler and Russia, by T. Higgins. Review
Newsweek il 68:114+ S 19 '66

Great Britain

Battle of Britain. J. M. Flagler. il Look 30:44-51+ F 22 '66
Eagle day, by R. Collier. Review
Atlan 218:134 Jl '66. E. Weeks
Sat R 49:48 Jl 23 '66. T. Taylor
No laurels for de Gaulle; an appraisal of the London years, by R. Mengin. Review
New Yorker 42:242-7 O 22 '66. N. Bliven

Italy

Diplomacy of victory in Europe. F. Calhoun.
Sat R 49:29 D 31 '66

Japan

Pearl Harbor and the bomb. il U S News 61:47 D 12 '66
Return of the Samurai; war reunion of one of the Kamikaze special attack corps. il Time 88:34 Ag 19 '66
See also
Pearl Harbor, Attack on. 1941
World war, 1939-1945—Philippines

Philippines

Fall of Corregidor; excerpts from Battles lost and won: great campaigns of World war II. H. W. Baldwin. il Am Heritage 17:16-23+ Ag '66

Russia

Hitler and Russia, by T. Higgins. Review
Newsweek il 68:114+ S 19 '66
Stalin at war. Newsweek 68:58 S 26 '66

United States

That unforgettable month: December 1941. S. A. Mix. il Todays Health 44:12-15 D '66
WORLD war I debts. See Debts, Public
WORLD weather watch. See Weather forecasts
WORLDS, Plurality of. See Life on other planets
WORLDS fair, Montreal. See Montreal—Worlds fair. 1967
WORLDS fair, Seattle. See Seattle—Century 21 exposition, 1962
WORLEY, James
Plea; poem. Christian Cent 83:106 Ja 26 '66
Thoughts while returning from Samarra; poem. Christian Cent 83:361 Jl 6 '66

WORM runner's digest
Worm runners on the run. il Time 88:56 N 4 '66
WORMAN, Charles G.
Colt model of 1911. Hobbies 71:122-3 Je '66
Firearms. See issues of Hobbies
Model 1866 Winchester. Hobbies 71:124-5 My '66
WORMS
See also
Earthworms
Nematodes
WORMS, intestinal and parasitic
Beware of the dog and cat? Sci Am 215:104+ S '66
Devil within. D. M. Duffey. il Outdoor Life 137:138-40+ My '66
Intestinal parasites: the enemy within. M. J. E. Senn. McCalls 93:46+ Je '66
WORRELL, Eric
Our far-flung correspondents. A. Moorehead.
New Yorker 42:186-91 N 19 '66
WORRY
See also
Anxiety
WORSHIP
Minister at mass; Lutheran clergyman worships in a Catholic church. W. Bockelman.
America 115:832-3 D 24 '66
To genuflect or not to genuflect? distinctions between Roman Catholic and Protestant worship as expressions of churches' growth toward unity. il Time 87:95-6 My 20 '66
Worship in the city of God. C. J. McNaspy.
America 115:176-7 Ag 20 '66
See also
Church services
Sacraments
WORSTHORNE, Peregrine
Bobby Kennedy's tactics; a view from abroad; excerpts from report. U S News 61:10 S 19 '66
WORTH, Edith
Edith Worth exhibit; photographs. Dance Mag 41:47-9 Ja '67
WORTH, Marielle
Young, surprised, and hungry in Warsaw.
Vogue 148:162 S 1 '66
WORTHAM, Buel Ray
Expensive caper. il por Newsweek 69:28 Ja 2 '67
Want to change dollars? il por Time 88:22 D 30 '66
What it costs to break rules in Russia. il por U S News 62:12 Ja 2 '67
WORTHINGTON, Leslie B.
Come and get it! address, October 21, 1966.
Vital Speeches 33:78-81 N 15 '66
WORTMAN, Leon A.
Video tape recording methods. Electr World 75:32-4 My '66
WOULFE, William
(ed) See Long, F. Library and the functionally illiterate in Cleveland
WOUNDED, Vietnamese war. See Vietnamese war, 1957- —Casualties
WOUNDS
See also
Bruises
WOYZECK; drama. See Buechner, G.
WRAIGHT, Robert
What is art coming to? Horizon 8:4-11 Spr '66
WRAPPING of packages
Buckets of love; cardboard paint buckets into gift wraps. il Seventeen 25:114-15 D '66
Christmas-wrap zoo. M. White. il Ladies Home J 83:84-5+ D '66
Gay crop of Christmas wrappings. il House & Gard 130:156-7 D '66
Packages can be people or animals or cars or things. il Sunset 137:100 D '66
Packing sea-shells for mailing. A. G. Melvin.
il Hobbies 71:130 My '66
Redbook's Christmas cookbook; ways to wrap them all for Christmas giving. il Redbook 128:79-106 D '66
See also
Packing for shipment
WRAY-MCCANN, Hugh
Fatherhood in deep freeze. Sci Digest 60:12-14 Jl '66
WREATHS, Christmas. See Christmas decorations; Christmas greens
WRECKING
Closing a hotel, at a profit; British commercial property administration sells furnishings of Sheraton East hotel. il Bsns W p64-6 Jl 23 '66
See also
Automobiles—Wrecking

WREDE, Burton L.
Hot-flooded ice rinks. Parks & Rec 1:760+ S '66

WREN aircraft corporation
Wren pushing for zero-zero certification; Wren 460 STOL aircraft. il Aviation W 84:115+ Je 13 '66

WRESTLING
How to lose six pounds in sixty minutes; wrestling squad at the New York athletic club. H. Ehrlich. il Look 30:M16-20 N 15 '66

My father the Thing. J. Jares. il Sports Illus 24:92-6+ Mr 21 '66

Rich, full life of a bad guy. M. Cope. il Sat Eve Post 239:88-91 F 12 '66

Woman's place is on the mat. R. Drexler. il Esquire 65:79-81+ F '66

WRIGHT, Alfred
Golf. Sports Illus 24:40-1 Ja 31; 25:74-6 O 17 '66

Motor sports. Sports Illus 25:76+ O 3 '66

WRIGHT, Alma
Episcias. Horticulture 44:14-15+ Jl '66

WRIGHT, Arthur W.
Soviet economy. bibliog f Cur Hist 51:218-25+ O '66

WRIGHT, Barbara E.
Multiple causes and controls in differentiation. bibliog Science 153:830-7 Ag 19 '66

WRIGHT, C. P. and Hanly, E. W.
Pteridines in the fat body of a mutant of drosophila melanogaster. bibliog Science 152:533-5 Ap 22 '66

WRIGHT, Carolyn Callander
Rear-view mirror; poem. McCalls 94:195 O '66

WRIGHT, Charles
Homecoming; poem. New Yorker 42:108 Ag 27 '66

Night watch; poem. Nation 202:593 My 16 '66

WRIGHT, Donald E.
Reaching out with books. Library J 91:3648-9 Ag '66

WRIGHT, Francis S. See Bradley, W. E. jt. auth.

WRIGHT, Ian Michael, and Kerfoot, Oliver
African baobab, object of awe. Natur Hist 75:50-3 My '66

WRIGHT, J. Skelly
Should Negro children be bused to suburban schools? statements. por U S News 61:28 O 24 '66

WRIGHT, James P. See Phipps, D. jt. auth.

WRIGHT, Jesse
Wisdom gained in gardens in the evening; poem. America 114:808 Je 4 '66

WRIGHT, John J. bp
Bishop speaks out. America 114:718 My 21 '66

Bishop Wright's challenge. America 115:310 S 24 '66

WRIGHT, K. O.
Michigan stellar spectroscopist. Sky & Tel 31:91 F '66

WRIGHT, Margaret A. See Gamage, G. K. jt. auth.

WRIGHT, Marian Elizabeth
[Mademoiselle's Merit award winner] por Mlle 62:48 Ja '66

Mission of Marian Wright. P. Pierce. il pors Ebony 21:94-7+ Je '66

WRIGHT, Mary Kathryn
Mickey finds a game she likes. P. Ryan. por Sports Illus 24:78+ Ap 11 '66

Money is a girl's best friend. P. Ryan. il por Sports Illus 25:36-9+ S 12 '66

WRIGHT, Mickey. See Wright, M. K.

WRIGHT, Myron Arnold
Air and water; address, December 6, 1966. Vital Speeches 33:173-6 Ja 1 '67

Solving problems by organized action; interview. pors Nations Bsns 54:44-5+ My '66

Trouble with antitrust; excerpts from address. Duns R 88:50-1+ N '66

WRIGHT, Nathan, jr
Black power. Cath World 204:46-51 O '66

Is brotherhood enough? Cath World 204:234-8 Ja '67

WRIGHT, Percy H.
Lack of hardiness from too rapid growth. Horticulture 45:15 Ja '67

WRIGHT, Phyllis M.
Medicine today; ed. by V. Cohn. See issues of Ladies' home journal

Tell me where it hurts. Ladies Home J 83: 165 Mr '66

What really matters when you're in the maternity ward. Ladies Home J 83:48+ Ag '66

WRIGHT, Thomas L. See Sato, M. jt. auth.

WRIGHTSMAN, Charles Bierer
Mrs Charles Wrightsman: collector's pursuit of art and perfection; with account by B. Robertson. il por Vogue 148:236-41+ O 1 '66

WRIGHTSMAN, Jayne (Larkin)
Mrs Charles Wrightsman: collector's pursuit of art and perfection; with account by B. Robertson. il pors Vogue 148:236-41+ O 1 '66

WRIST fractures. See Fractures

WRIST watches. See Watches

WRISTON, John C. jr. See Yellin, T O. jt. auth.

WRITERS. See Authors

WRITERS, World congress of. See PEN club

WRITERS colonies. See Authors colonies

WRITERS conferences. See Authors conferences

WRITERS workshops. See Educational workshops

WRITING
See also
Authorship
Typewriting

Materials and instruments
See also
Pens

WRITING (authorship) See Authorship

WRITING (composition) See English language —Composition

WRITING paper. See Stationery

WROCLAW, Poland
Breslau revisited. F. Russell. il Horizon 9: 46-56 Wint '67

WU, Yuan-li
Third five-year plan: an economic dilemma. bibliog f Cur Hist 51:159-64 S '66

WUJEK, Joseph H. jr
Magnetic measurements in space. Electr World 75:36-7+ Ja '66

Radiation measurements in space. Electr World 76:19-21+ Ag '66

WULF, Melvin L.
Prudent jurist. Commentary 41:106+ Ap; 42:18-20 Jl '66

Selective reprisal; sniping at dissent. Nation 203:149-52 Ag 22 '66

WULFF, Lee
Fly rod over the deep blue. pors Esquire 66: 253-5+ D '66

WUNDERLICH, Bernhard, and Melillo, Louis
Surface recrystallization of polyethylene extended-chain crystals. bibliog Science 154:1329-30 D 9 '66

WUNDERLICH, Fritz
Beautiful singing, lieder by Fritz Wunderlich. H. Glass. por Am Rec G 33:106-7 O '66

Obituary
Opera N por 31:34 O 15 '66. E. Davidson

WURF, Jerry
Coming: unionized government; interview. pors U S News 61:96-9 S 26 '66

about

Young militant out to unionize city and county employes. il pors Life 61:36-36B Ag 26 '66

WURLITZER, Rudolph
Boiler room; story. Atlan 217:127-32 Mr '66

WURTELE, M. G.
Where the air is unclear. Nation 203:359-60 O 10 '66

WURTMAN, Richard J.
Latin American symposium on catecholamines. Science 154:680-1 N 4 '66

WYANT, Rowena
Business failures. See issues of Dun's review and modern industry

WYCHERLEY, William
Country wife. Criticism
Vogue 147:99 F 1 '66

WYER, Malcolm Glenn
Malcolm Glenn Wyer. M. W. Killinger. por ALA Bul 60:383-4 Ap '66

WYETH, Andrew
Cover. il por Am Artist 30:4 O '66

Preservationist. il por Time 88:88-9 O 21 '66

Wyeth's world. H. Cohen. Reporter 35:56-8+ D 15 '66

X

Y

YABERG, Forrest L. and Kenmir, R. C.
Water program cuts fire-insurance rates. Am City 81:110-11 O '66

YABLONSKY, Lewis
Ivy league rebels. New Repub 154:29-32 Je 4 '66
Stoned on methadone; with excerpts from interview with Synanon staff. New Repub 155:14-16 Ag 13 '66

YACHT clubs
Always on Sunday; Tri club yacht racing association. B. Wisner. il Motor B 117:40-3+ Je '66
Hundredth for the Boston yacht club. B. Harris. il Motor B 118:46-7+ S '66
Personal business. Bsns W p 169-70 Je 18 '66
Transatlantic skippers toast the centenary of the Royal Danish yacht club. il Motor B 118:78-9 D '66
Where sailing is all; Noroton yacht club. W. Roberts. il Yachting 119:70-2+ F '66

YACHT racing
Across the past to Manila; Columbine on third biennial yacht race across the China Sea from Hong Kong to Manila. A. Zich. il Sports Illus 24:46-8 Ap 18 '66
Aegean rally. B. Robinson. il Yachting 120: 40+ S '66
America's cup news. il Yachting 120:174-5 N; 146-7 D '66
America's cup; portents and progress for the '67 match. F. Rohr. il Motor B 119:90-3+ Ja '67
Aussies are coming; America's cup challengers. il Newsweek 68:63 S 5 '66
Bermuda race preview; symposium. il Yachting 119:92-8+ Je '66
Bermuda race reports. il Yachting 120:31-6+ Ag '66
Blitzen leads fleet from Chicago. F. C. Heyes. il Yachting 120:49+ S '66
Blue-water racers; Newport-to-Bermuda; contenders. il Newsweek 67:82-3 Je 27 '66
Boatman's year, '65. il Motor B 117:62-77 Ja '66
Comments and asides on ocean racing. B. Snaith. il Yachting 119:69-71+ My '66
Courtly confusion at Copenhagen; Royal yacht club birthday party. H. Whall. il Sports Illus 25:48-9 Ag 15 '66
Deep water racing. B. D. Barker, 3d. See issues of Yachting
Elena vs. Atlantic, 1928. G. Bradford. il Yachting 119:190 F '66
Fast dame on the make; America's cup. il Time 88:72 N 11 '66
Flying Buffalo wins Bayview classic. G. E. Van. il Yachting 120:48+ S '66
Knockdown for a dowager; Idem, the one-design racing sloop. J. Gould. il Sports Illus 25:66+ S 26 '66
Legislative status for a victory at sea; Congressional cup. H. Whall. il Sports Illus 24: 49-51 F 21 '66
Mexican scalp for Ondine; San Diego-Acapulco race. A. Lockabey. il Yachting 119: 102-3+ Ag '66
Month in yachting. See issues of Yachting
New concepts for Bermuda racers. W. S. Cox. Motor B 117:22-3 Je '66
On the racing circuit. See issues of Motor boating
One ton cup. il Yachting 120:39+ S '66
Preparation for offshore racing. W. D. Teague. il Yachting 119:84-6+ Ap '66
Regatta results. See issues of Yachting
Report from a racing sailor. K. Lamott. il Holiday 40:8+ Jl '66
Rough-and-tumble honeymoon for Guinevere; transatlantic yacht race. N. D. Hoyt. Sports Illus 25:48-9 Ag 8 '66
San Quintin: the forgotten harbor; Cinco de mayo classic. L. Parsons. il Motor B 117:156-7+ My '66
They couldn't beat Bluenose. D. MacDonald. il Read Digest 89:118-22 O '66
Thunderbird soars to Bermuda win. F. Rohr. il Motor B 118:82-3+ Ag '66
Transatlantic race. B. Robinson; R. Robinson. il Yachting 120:36-8+ S '66
Transatlantic triumph for Ondine. E. F. Haylock. il Motor B 118:129-30 S '66
Vamp X, new victor on southern seas. F. Rohr. il Motor B 117:174-9 My '66
Vindication in the Mallory; Bill Cox wins the Mallory cup. H. Whall. il Sports Illus 25:116-18 S 12 '66

Wanted: wholesome boats for the America's cup; reprint from Yachting's first issue, 1907. T. Lipton. il Yachting 120:43+ D '66
Wet wondrous way to joy. Sports Illus 25: 32-3 Jl 4 '66
Wildwind sweeps multihull championships. il Motor B 118:88-91 N '66
Will the real Huey Long please stand up. S. M. Fertitta. il Motor B 118:88+ Ag '66
With the racing classes. B. Robinson. See issues of Yachting
See also
Catamaran racing

History
Bermuda race past and present. A. F. Loomis. il Yachting 119:92-3+ Je '66
Great ocean race of 1866. A. F. Loomis. il Yachting 120:60-1+ D '66
Then and now, yachting on the Chesapeake. W. L. Henderson. il Yachting 119:66-7+ Mr '66

YACHT safety bureau
Yacht safety bureau. C. F. Kelley. il Yachting 119:87-9+ Ap '66

YACHTING (periodical)
Sixty years of Yachting; symposium. il Yachting 120:42-7+ D '66

History
That was the year that was. B. Robinson. il Yachting 120:44+ D '66

YACHTS
Highlights for '66; symposium. il Pop Sci 188:132-51 F '66

Chartering
On a bare-boat basis; chartering in the Virgins. B. Robinson. il Yachting 120:43+ N '66
With a professional crew; chartering in the Virgins. E. Horan. il Yachting 120:42+ N '66

History
Crazy capers of the Caribbean charter fleet. D. M. Street, jr. il Yachting 120:50-1+ N '66

Design
Boats we meet: Meander. J. Emmett. il Yachting 120:47-9 Ag '66
Designs. W. H. DeFontaine. il Yachting 119: 120-6+ Ja '66
From dream to reality. E. L. Parks. il Motor B 119:94-7+ Ja '67 (to be cont)
Great American sailboats; Finisterre; ed. by R. Stephens. C. Mitchell. il Motor B 117: 24-5+ Je '66
Henry S. Morgan's 62-foot motorsailer Djinn. B. D. Barker, 3d. il Yachting 120:46-7+ O '66
High fashion model takes over; Conquistador. H. Whall. il Sports Illus 25:38-42 Jl 4 '66
Offshore cruiser. E. Monk. il Yachting 119: 74-6+ Mr '66
Old New York yacht, launch & engine co. G. A. Taylor. il Motor B 118:36-7+ D '66
Once over lightly; return passage from Europe. N. D. Hoyt. il Yachting 120:51-3+ S '66
Other man's boat; cruising tug Maleo. C. W. Wittholz. il Yachting 119:80-1 My '66
Other man's boat; Puffin. K. L. Smith; G. C. Rand. il Yachting 120:68-9+ Jl '66
Other man's boat; Sunkist Lady. G. Dunham; E. E. Eldredge. il Yachting 120:72-3+ N '66
Other man's boat; Sweet and low. R. H. Wiley. il Yachting 119:86-7+ F '66
Other man's boat; Tere. W. L. Warner; L. A. Valier, jr. il Yachting 119:76-7+ Je '66
Plans from long ago. W. H. de Fontaine. il Yachting 120:46+ D '66
37' practical motor-sailer, Summer Place. J. Atkin. il Motor B 117:98-101+ Ja '66
Thunderbird, computer or no. B. Robinson. il Yachting 120:31+ Ag '66
U.S. entries for the IYRU trials. E. W. Etchells; B. Chance, jr. il Yachting 120:44-5 S '66
Yachts of the year '65. il Motor B 117:102-11 Ja '66

Electronic equipment
Electronics, 1966. il Motor B 117:168-73+ Ja '66

Equipment
Preparation for offshore racing. W. D. Teague. il Yachting 119:84-6+ Ap '66

YASUMURA, Yoshihiro, and others
Establishment of four functional, clonal strains of animal cells in culture. bibliog Science 154:1186-9 D 2 '66

YATES, Donald A.
Authors in search of identity. Sat R 49:27-8 Ag 27 '66

YATES, Peter
Festival small but powerful. Hi Fi 16:MA15 Ag '66
Sun treader, the work of an American radical, in its first American hearing. Hi Fi 16:85-6 Ap '66
That frustrating flourishing art. Holiday 39: 152+ Mr '66

YATES, Ted. See Rogers, R. jt. auth.

YATVIN, Milton B.
Hypophyseal control of genetic expression during chick feather and skin differentiation. bibliog Science 153:184-5 Jl 8 '66
Polysome morphology: evidence for endocrine control during chick embryogenesis. bibliog Science 151:1001-3 F 25 '66

YAUDES, Addie
Horicon marsh, the firmament showeth His handiwork. Am For 71:8-9+ O '65

YEAR
See also
Calendar

YEAR round schools. See School year

YEARBOOKS, High school. See High school annuals

YEARY, William Houston
World's oldest Chevy driver? 103 skiddoo! F. X. Tolbert. il por Motor T 18:93 Mr '66

YEASTS
Nucleotide sequence of a yeast tyrosine transfer RNA. J. T. Madison and others. bibliog il Science 153:531-4 Jl 29 '66
Yeast genetics; report on conference. R. C. Von Borstel. Science 152:1287-8 My 27 '66

YEGORYCHEV, Nikolaĭ Grigorievich. See Egorychev, N. G.

YEHUDI Menuhin festival. See Music festivals —Switzerland

YELLIN, Tobias O. and Wriston, J. C. Jr
Antagonism of purified asparaginase from guinea pig serum toward lymphoma. bibliog Science 151:998-9 F 25 '66

YELLOTT, John I.
How materials react to solar energy. Arch Rec 139:196-8 My; 197-8 Je '66

YELLOW brick road; story. See Williams, G.

YELLOW perch. See Perch

YELLOW SPRINGS, Ohio
Negro in the village of Yellow Springs, Ohio. W. Robinson. Negro Hist Bul 29:103-4+ F '66

YELLOWJACKETS. See Wasps

YELLOWSTONE LAKE. See Yellowstone National Park

YELLOWSTONE NATIONAL PARK
Summer among the savages; college students' summer jobs. il Seventeen 25:96-7 Je '66
Up on Yellowstone Lake. J. P. Jackson. il Am For 72:14-17+ N '66

YEMEN
In the old style; death for those involved in anti-Nasser opposition. Time 88:42 N 4 '66

YEN, Chia-kan
Problems of age. Time 87:33 Ap 1 '66

YERBY, Frank Garvin
Famous writer faces a challenge. H. W. Fuller. il pors Ebony 21:188-90+ Je '66

YERMA; drama. See García Lorca, F.

YESUFU, Segun Babatunde
Turmoil in an African university. America 114:200-3 F 5 '66

YEVTUSHENKO, Yevgeny Aleksandrovich. See Evtushenko, E. A.

YEZO. See Hokkaido (island)

YGLESIAS, José
Letter from Prague. Nation 204:59-61 Ja 9 '67
Pablo Neruda: the poet in New York. Nation 203:52-5 Jl 11 '66
Writers confer: good show at the Paramount. Nation 202:460-2 Ap 18 '66

YIDDISH literature
Other Singer; concerning brothers I. J. and I. B. Singer. Commentary 41:78+ Mr '66

YOAKUM, Robert
Medicine men and public health. New Repub 156:35-6 Ja 21 '67
To corrupt absolutely. New Repub 154:29+ Ap 2 '66

YOB, Parry C.
Homemade spot puts glamour in your pictures. Pop Mech 126:188-9+ N '66

YOCOM, Thomas R.
Headlights-on alarm. Pop Electr 24:81 Ja '66

YOCUM, Harrison G.
Magnificent palms. il Horticulture 44:22-3+ Ap '66

YODER, Edwin M. Jr
His own way to fame. Sat R 49:40+ N 12 '66
In the best Tory tradition. Sat R 49:99-100 O 8 '66
Lovers with different loyalties. Sat R 49: 35 My 21 '66
No catch for the hawk. Sat R 49:40 F 12 '66

YOFFE, Lydia
Lopukhov dynasty. Dance Mag 41:35-9+ Ja '67

YOGA
Taking the waters; Rao's water walk fails. il Newsweek 67:48 Je 27 '66

YOGURT
See also
Cookery—Yogurt

YOHALEM, Alice M. See Ginzberg, E. jt. auth.

YOLLES, Stanley F.
Mystery gland. Todays Health 44:76-9 Mr '66
Parent and child. N Y Times Mag p91+ Ap 17 '66
What you don't know about mothering. Ladies Home J 83:50 Ag '66

YOMIURI country club course. See Golf courses

YORK, Marjorie Ann
Treasure Island; dramatization of novel by R. L. Stevenson. Plays 25:87-94 Mr '66

YORK festival. See Music festivals—England

YORTY, Samuel William
Urban brawl; summary of testimony at Ribicoff hearings. por Newsweek 68:19 S 5 '66

about
Magnet in the West. il por Time 88:14-19 S 2 '66
Two's a crowd. Time 87:29A-29B Mr 18 '66

YOSEMITE NATIONAL PARK
Books in review; California's high country. W. H. Carr and L. W. Walker. Natur Hist 75:54-65 Je '66
Fatal affection; crowding of Yosemite Valley campgrounds. Nat Parks Mag 40:21-2 N '66
Overnight above Yosemite Valley; Mountain house. il Sunset 137:55 O '66
Parkscape U.S.A. il Audubon Mag 68:416-17 N '66

YOSEMITE VALLEY
California: climb beyond the possible; ascent of sheer rock. C. S. Wren. il Look 30:70-2 Je 28 '66
In the track of Yosemite's glaciers. il Sunset 137:35-6 Jl '66

YOSHIDA, Akira, and others
Negro variant of glucose-6-phosphate dehydrogenase deficiency (A-) in man. bibliog Science 155:97-9 Ja 6 '67

YOSHIDA, M. and Ohtsuki, H.
Compound ocellus of a starfish: its function. bibliog Science 153:197 Jl 8 '66

YOSHITSUNE
Chronicle of Yoshitsune; tr. by H. Craig. Review
Sat R 49:58 Je 11 '66. E. Miner

YOST, Charles W.
United Nations: crisis of confidence and will. For Affairs 45:19-35 O '66

YOSTIE; story. See O'Hara, J.

YOU take the easy road to success in writing; story. See Leggett, J.

YOUNG, A. P.
Nickel orthouronate: high-pressure synthesis. bibliog Science 153:1380-1 S 16 '66

YOUNG, Allen
Mozart and Elliott Carter in Colorado. Hi Fi 16:MA20-1 O '66
University of Colorado: the musical panorama. Hi Fi 16:123+ Je '66

YOUNG, Anne
Deep sea; poem. Commonweal 85:326 D 16 '66

YOUNG, Donald
Everyman's aristocrat. Sat R 49:100-1 O 8 '66
Reminiscence of a braintruster. Sat R 49: 49-51+ D 24 '66
Review of the Presidential record. Sat R 49: 54-6 O 22 '66

YOUNG, E. Gordon. See Conway, E. jt. auth.

YOUTH—*Continued*
To all young people twenty years old. R.
Maheu. il UNESCO Courier 19:30 F '66
Uni-sex; neuter look of teen-agers. il News-
week 67:59-60 F 14 '66
U.N. charter for youth; with text of prin-
ciples. UNESCO Courier 19:31 F '66
We are not interested. America 115:129 Ag
6 '66
What's happening, baby? a look at today's
teen-ager; address, June 21, 1966. P. C.
Harper, jr. Vital Speeches 33:57-61 N 1 '66
    See also
Adolescence
Boys
Discipline
Girls
High school students
Young men
Young women

Adjustment
    See Adjustment, Social

Employment
Case for a National service corps. M. K.
Sanders. il N Y Times Mag p 16-17+ Ag 7
'66
Employment lab for teenagers in trouble;
Youth and work project, New York. S. L.
Horwitz. il Parents Mag 41:64-7+ D '66
Employment of high school graduates and
dropouts in 1965. H. R. Hamel. il Mo Labor
R 89:643-9 Je '66
Employment of school age youth, October
1965. F. A. Bogan. il Mo Labor R 89:739-
43 Jl '66
First 50,000 Neighborhood youth corps en-
rollees. J. F. Tucker. il Mo Labor R 88:
1442-4 D '65
Forecast for high schoolers. A. M. Ross. il
PTA Mag 60:18-19 My '66
It's a most unseasonal summer. il Newsweek
68:67 Jl 25 '66
No room at the bottom; plight of those who
don't make the first rung of the ladder of
success. R. L. Heilbroner. Sat R 49:29-32
F 19 '66
Out-of-school youth two years later; resurvey
of graduates and dropouts. V. C. Perrella
and E. Waldman. il Mo Labor R 89:860-6
Ag '66
Policy for youth; address, November 16, 1966.
W. W. Wirtz. Vital Speeches 33:162-5 Ja
1 '67
Strength through joy again? R. Kirk. Nat R
18:1328 D 27 '66
They wouldn't cry uncle; teen-agers in
Washington, D.C. busy making money. il
Nations Bsns 54:52-4+ Mr '66
    See also
Student employment
United States—Job corps
Youthpower, incorporated

Health and hygiene
Health problems of adolescents; with study-
discussion program, by C. Smallenburg
and H. Smallenburg. M. Clark. bibliog il
PTA Mag 60:4-7, 33-4 Ap '66
Medical problems of adolescents. M. J. E.
Senn. McCalls 94:64+ N '66
Teenagers: fitness report: good; Newsweek
survey of U.S. teenagers. M. Clark. il
Newsweek 67:63-4 Mr 21 '66
What doctors can do for teen-agers today;
symposium, ed. by L. R. Chevalier. il Ladies
Home J 84:32+ Ja '67

Management and training
Heading for trouble; teenager needs a
mother to say no. il Good H 162:12+ Ap '66
Our children, our problem; parents groups
for solving problem of rebellious children.
W. Abraham. il Todays Health 44:58-64
F '66
Regulating student dress. D. Waleski. il
NEA J 55:12-14 Ap '66
Truth about teenage rebellion. J. G. Delano
and E. G. Neisser. il Parents Mag 41:42-4+
Jl '66
Which teen-agers are really in trouble, and
which aren't? J. Donnelly. Ladies Home J
84:34+ Ja '67

Political activities
Extremism: danger to our schools; address,
June 30, 1966. E. H. Methvin. Vital
Speeches 32:694-700 S 1 '66
Face to face with a successful political
writer; ed. by C. Schwalberg. S. Kelman.
Seventeen 25:169 D '66

In my opinion; experience of a teen-age
volunteer worker. S. Sponzilli. Seventeen
25:246 N '66

Quotations, maxims, etc.
Accent on youth; comp. by E. F. Murphy.
N Y Times Mag p 132 Ap 3 '66

Reading
    See Books and reading; Reading lists

Religion
Faith of the young: an emerging problem;
American Catholic youth. America 115:54
Jl 16 '66; Discussion. 115:215 S 3 '66
Today's rebellious generation. America 115:271
S 17 '66; Discussion. 115:684-7, 828-30 N 26,
D 24 '66

Social life and customs
Happenings and happiness. E. Lester. Com-
monweal 84:466+ Jl 22 '66
    See also
Argentina
Argentine students

Communist countries
Uninfected. Time 87:54+ Ap 8 '66

Dominican Republic
Lessons of dictatorship; report of talks with
Dominican youth. R. S. Arnon. Mlle 62:
180-1+ Ap '66

England
    See Youth—Great Britain

France
Baedeker of Beatnik territory. H. R. Lottman. il N Y Times Mag p40-1+ Ag 7 '66
Elite proletarians all; students in France go
Communist. K. Botsford. il N Y Times Mag
p54-5+ N 13 '66
There is a difference; comparison of French
and American girls. C. McConnell. Seventeen
26:98 Ja '67

Germany (Federal Republic)
Lively arts; interview, ed. by R. Hemming.
H. Jankowski. Sr Schol 89:22 O 14 '66
Reconciliation in Israel; Service of reconcilia-
tion. I. Halperin. Christian Cent 83:216-22
F 16 '66

Great Britain
London: the cutting edge. G. Zimmermann. il
Look 30:82-4 S 20 '66
Policy for youth; address, November 16, 1966.
W. W. Wirtz. Vital Speeches 33:162-5 Ja
1 '67
Where have all the nice English girls gone?
P. H. Johnson. McCalls 94:28+ D '66

Indonesia
    See also
Indonesian students

Japan
Japan joins the hipster international; League
of criminals movement. H. Passin. il Reporter 34:45-7 Ja 27 '66
Rise of the Japanese teen-ager. B. C. Duke.
il Seventeen 25:406-7 Ag '66

Netherlands
Dadaists in politics; zany protest movement,
the Provos. J. Lelyveld. il N Y Times Mag
p32-5+ O 2 '66

Russia
Cool Communists. L. Gross. il Look 30:96-100
S 20 '66
Man from S.M.O.G. (boldness, thought,
image, profundity) D. Brown. il N Y Times
Mag p28-9+ Mr 20 '66
USSR delinquents bored. Sci N 90:208 S 17 '66

Scandinavia
Scandinavian youth. D. S. Connery. il Holiday 40:76-7+ N '66

United States
Are U.S. teenagers spoiled? pro and con dis-
cussion. Sr Schol 88:10-11 F 4 '66
Disenchanted: girls in the city. H. F. Waters.
il N Y Times Mag p28-30+ F 6 '66
Farewell to the new breed. A. M. Greeley.
America 114:801-4 Je 4 '66
Forgotten youth in today's America: the
"just average" majority. il U S News 60:
52-4+ F 21 '66

YUCATAN
  See also
Cozumel Island

Description and travel
Yucatan. J. Faber. il U S Camera 30:64-5+
  Ja '67
YUGOSLAV artists. See Artists, Yugoslav
YUGOSLAV painting. See Painting, Yugoslav
YUGOSLAVIA
  Beyond dictatorship. il Time 89:32 Ja 20 '67
  See also
  Art—Yugoslavia
  Censorship—Yugoslavia
  Communism—Yugoslavia
  Communist party (Yugoslavia)
  Food relief—Yugoslavia
  Hiebine
  Investments, Foreign (in Yugoslavia)
  Labor and laboring classes—Yugoslavia
  Newspapers—Yugoslavia
  Periodicals—Yugoslavia
  Secret service—Yugoslavia
  Skoplje
  Socialism—Yugoslavia
  Tourist trade—Yugoslavia
  Trials—Yugoslavia

Description and travel
Dalmatian coast on the cheap.   S. Corbett.
  il Atlan 218:125-7 D '66
Travel. D. Messinesi. Vogue 147:68+ My '66
Yugoslavia; with report by M. Leatherbee.
  il Life 60:52-63 My 27 '66

Economic conditions
Belgrade report: keeping up with the
  Jovanovics. D. Binder. il N Y Times Mag
  p24-5+ Ap 3 '66
Economics of socialism in a developed country. R. Bićanić. For Affairs 44:633-50 Jl '66
Tito's Yugoslavia: is it communism? with
  report by F. Y. Blumenfeld. il Newsweek
  68:49-54 O 17 '66

Economic policy
Economics of socialism in a developed coun-
  try. R. Bićanić. For Affairs 44:633-50 Jl '66
When it's your own money. S. G. Slappey. il
  Nations Bsns 54:72-6+ N '66
Where the lure of the auto is killing com-
  munism. K. Lachmann. il U S News 60:
  76-8 Je 20 '66

Economic relations
Yugoslavia: a red carpet for foreign capital?
  Bsns W p 118 D 3 '66

Industries
  See also
Automobile industry and trade—Yugoslavia

Politics and government
Beyond the halfway house. il Time 88:28+
  Jl 15 '66
Limits to liberalization; Mihajlov's demand
  for multiparty system. il Time 88:46 S 30
  '66
Permanent revolution; Tito's reforms. News-
  week 68:42+ Jl 11 '66
Tito's Yugoslavia: is it communism? with
  report by F. Y. Blumenfeld. il Newsweek
  68:49-54 O 17 '66
Unmeritorious pardon. Time 88:42 D 16 '66
  See also
Communist party (Yugoslavia)

Religious institutions and affairs
Yugoslavia: religious freedom not unknown.
  M. Bourdeaux. Christian Cent 84:21-2+ Ja
  4 '67

Social conditions
Socialism of sorts. il Time 87:42+ Je 10
  '66
YUKON
Description and travel
Ten days in the ice age. J. Dos Passos.
  il Holiday 39:70-5+ Ap '66
YUKON FLATS
  Alaska Dam would be resources disaster.
  A. S. Leopold and J. W. Leonard. il Au-
  dubon Mag 68:176-8 My '66
YUKON RIVER
  Rampart Dam: a costly gamble. S. H. Spurr.
  il Audubon Mag 68:172-5+ My '66
YULE logs
  Yule logs to make as gifts. il Sunset 137:90
  D '66

YULETIDE. See Christmas
YUNG, Bob
  Focus on Bob Yung. H. V. Fondiller. il
  pors Pop Phot 58:100-3+ F '66
YUNICK, Henry. See Yunick, S.
YUNICK, Smokey
  Say, Smokey; questions and answers. See
  issues of Popular science monthly
YURCHENCO, Henrietta
  Folk music. See issues of American record
  guide
  George Korson: a folk-music classic revisited.
  Am Rec G 32:475-7 Ja '66
  Taping history in Mexico. Am Rec G 33:4-
  7+ S '66
YURICK, Sol
  Sob-sister gothic. Nation 202:158-60 F 7 '66
YURIKO
  Yuriko and dance company. 92nd street Y.
  J. Maskey. Dance Mag 40:64 Mr '66
YZERMANS, Vincent A.
  Book review. America 114:627 Ap 30 '66

Z

ZIP (zoning improvement plan) See Postal
  service—United States
ZABIN, Irving. See Fowler, A. V. jt. auth.
ZABLOCKI, Clement John
  Excerpt from debate, July 13, 1966. Cong
  Digest 45:221+ Ag '66
ZACHARIAS, Jerrold Reinach
  Curriculum molder. il por Time 88:110+ D 16
  '66
ZACHARY, Jane
  Cover girl grows up. il pors Good H 162:
  10+ Je '66
ZACHRY, William
  Computers occupy the royal suite. Am City
  81:107 O '66
ZACKS, Robert
  Coming: fantastic devices to end riots. Na-
  tions Bsns 54:62-4 Jl '66
ZADIG, Ernest A.
  How I air-conditioned my car for $24.74. Pop
  Sci 188:126-30 Je '66
ZAGAROLO, Italy
  Zagarolo. P. Dallas. Atlan 218:145-7 N '66
ZAGOREN, Ruby
  Where children are; poem. Farm J 90:106
  My '66
ZAGORIA, Donald S.
  China's crisis of foreign policy. N Y Times
  Mag p22-3+ My 1 '66
ZAHALSKY, Arthur C. See Malkin, M. F. jt.
  auth.
ZAHN, Gordon C.
  Crime of silence. Commonweal 84:354-6 Je
  17 '66
ZAHNISER, Jay
  Action painting in the classroom. Sch Arts
  65:27-8 My '66
ZAIDAN, Abe S.
  Wonderful world of Governor Rhodes. Re-
  porter 35:44-6 O 6 '66
ZAKIA, Richard D. See Todd, H. N. jt. auth.
ZAMBIA
  Africa's good guy under pressure. L. Gar-
  rison. il N Y Times Mag p 14-15+ Ag 7 '66
  Will the lion bite? outburst in Lusaka pre-
  cedes exploratory talks with Britain. News-
  week 67:50+ My 16 '66
  Zambia. N. Gordimer. il Holiday 39:38-47+
  Je '66
  See also
  Copper industry and trade—Zambia
  Petroleum industry and trade—Zambia
  Petroleum supply—Zambia

Industries
  See also
Copper industry and trade—Zambia

Politics and government
New foe emerging; Commonwealth departure
  threat; reasons. Newsweek 68:47-8 Ag 1 '66
ZAMCHICK, David
  Drama: from page to stage. Sr Schol 89:sup
  10-11 S 16 '66
ZAMENHOF, Stephen, and others
  Stimulation of the proliferation of cortical
  neurons by prenatal treatment with growth
  hormone. bibliog Science 152:1396-7 Je 3 '66

ZIMPEL, Lloyd
Surprise in the wings. Nation 202:276-8 Mr 7 '66
ZINC
Zinc and cobalt: effect on the iron metabolism of ustilago sphaerogena. H. Komai and J. B. Neilands. bibliog il Science 153:721-2 Ag 12 '66
ZINC in the body
Pancreatic carboxypeptidases: activities in zinc-deficient rats. J. M. Hsu and others. bibliog il Science 153:882-3 Ag 19 '66
ZINC selenate
Quenchable high-pressure polymorph of zinc selenate. C. W. F. T. Pistorius. bibliog il Science 151:1003 F 25 '66
ZINC sulfide
Thermal recrystallization of precipitated zinc sulfide. L. J. Bodi and C. F. Tufts. il Science 153:872-3 Ag 19 '66
ZINDER, Norton D. See Lodish, H. F. jt. auth
ZINKIN, Sheila, and Miller, A. J.
Recovery of memory after amnesia induced by electroconvulsive shock. bibliog Science 155:102-4 Ja 6 '67
ZINN, Howard
Negroes and Vietnam. Commonweal 83:579-80 F 18 '66
New direction for Negro colleges. Harper 232:75-81 My '66
Old left & the new: emancipation from dogma. Nation 202:385-9 Ap 4 '66
Should Harlem secede? Nation 203:189-91 S 5 '66
War fans. Nation 202:227 F 28 '66
ZINNES, Harriet
Turquoise; poem. Mlle 62:158 Ap '66
ZINO, Betty
Whaling in Old Mystic. Sch Arts 65:33-5 Ap '66
ZINSSER, William K.
American humor, 1966. Horizon 8:116-20 Spr '66
Ben Casey at the bat. Sat Eve Post 239:20 Mr 26 '66
Lady be good (and so will I) Sat Eve Post 239:20 S 24 '66
Looking around with Zinsser. Look 31:14 Ja 24 '67
Mother ship will take care of you. Horizon 8:105-9 Aut '66
Please don't feed the fun furs. Horizon 9:118-19 Wint '67
This year give baby an ego-expander. Life 61:10 D 16 '66
ZIOLKOWSKI, Korczak
Dream as big as a mountain. H. Jones. il por Sat Eve Post 239:30-1 S 10 '66
Largest; figure of Crazy Horse. Am Artist 30:6 S '66
ZIONISM
See also
Israel
ZIPPERS
Zipper that is almost undetectable; Lily hideaway. il Consumer Bul 49:40 Je '66
ZIPPO manufacturing company
Mark of Zippo. R. Levy. il Duns R 88:53-4+ O '66
ZIRCON
Uranium and lead isotopic stability in a metamict zircon under experimental hydrothermal conditions. R. T. Pidgeon and others. bibliog il Science 154:1538-40 D 23 '66
ZIRIN, James D.
Blackstone on gutbucket. Reporter 35:48-9 O 6 '66
ZISK, Stanley H.
Brightness distributions of radio sources at 2-centimeter wavelength. bibliog Science 153:1107-9 S 2 '66
ZNAMIEROWSKI, Nell
Craftsmen USA '66; Southeast Region. Craft Horiz 26:78-81+ Je '66
ZOHARY, Daniel. See Harlan, J. R. jt. auth.
ZOLL, Stephen
To and from babel. Nation 202:398-9+ Ap 4 '66
Too good for others. Nation 202:753-4 Je 20 '66
ZOLLINGER, Marian
Speech is English too. Sr Schol 89:sup52 S 23 '66
ZOLOTOW, Maurice
Through darkest Britain by car. Sat R 49:64-6 Jl 23 '66

ZOLOVICK, A. J. and others
Monoamine oxidase activity in various parts of the rat brain during the estrous cycle. bibliog Science 154:649 N 4 '66
ZONAL centrifuges. See Centrifuges
ZONE mail system. See Postal service—United States
ZONING
Invitation to bribery; corruption among zoning officials. A. Balk. Harper 233:18+ O '66
Structure that meets two different needs; piers for parking needs and zoning requirements. il Arch Rec 140:174-5 N '66
Zoning and planning decisions; ed. by N. Williams, jr. See issues of American city
ZONING improvement plan. See Postal service—United States
ZONING law
See also
Building laws and regulations
ZOOLOGICAL gardens
How to start a children's zoo; zoo fever sweeps Lincoln, Neb. A. R. Folsom. il Parks & Rec 1:430-2 My '66
Inbreeding of zoo animals. R. Bogart. bibliog il Parks & Rec 1:254-7 Mr '66
Jerusalem's biblical zoo. P. E. Lapide. Christian Cent 84:17-18 Ja 4 '67
Of gerenuks and dibatags. il Sci N 90:359 O 29 '66
What's new at San Francisco's children's zoo. il Sunset 136:76 Mr '66
Where animals welcome the children; Knowland state park. il Sunset 137:56-7 O '66
Why have a zoo? W. G. Conway. il Parks & Rec 1:488-90 Je '66
Zoo babies numerous. B. Tufty. il Sci N 89:440-1+ Je 4 '66
See also
National zoological park, Washington, D.C.
New York zoological park

Anecdotes, facetiae, satire, etc.
Safari; afternoon at the zoo. W. M. Gibb. il Atlan 218:140-1 N '66
ZOOLOGICAL research
See also
Fishery research
ZOOLOGICAL specimens

Collection and preservation
See also
Insects—Collection and preservation
Taxidermy
ZOOLOGY
See also
Cave fauna and flora

Classification
Numerical taxonomy. R. R. Sokal. il Sci Am 215:106-16 bibliog(p 155) D '66
Zoological classification system of a primitive people. J. M. Diamond. bibliog Science 151:1102-4 Mr 4 '66

Africa
Of gerenuks and dibatags. il Sci N 90:359 O 29 '66

Africa, East
Immersion in life: journey to East Africa. A. M. Lindbergh. il Life 61:88-90+ O 21 '66; Same abr. with title Discovery and renewal. Read Digest 90:37-43 Ja '67

Arctic Regions
See also
Musk oxen

Australia
Bush mammalogist; interview. W. H. Butler. New Yorker 42:18-20 Ag 6 '66
Nightmare on wings; giant flying foxes of Australia. il Sci N 90:373-4 N 5 '66
Our far-flung correspondents; snake farm at Gosford, north of Sydney. A. Moorehead. New Yorker 42:186-91 N 19 '66
Overbreeding Down Under; wild rabbits. il Time 88:120+ N 18 '66
Wildlife census precedes drilling of oil wells. Sci N 90:411 N 12 '66
See also
Kangaroos

Colombia
Capturing strange creatures in Colombia. M. Latham. il Nat Geog Mag 129:682-93 My '66

ZOOLOGY—*Continued*

India

Tiger and its prey. G. B. Schaller. il Natur Hist 75:30-7 O '66

Malaya

Two in the bush; animal adventures in Malaya. G. Durrell. il Harper 233:98+ O '66

Montana

Summer of riches; Montana's Mission Valley. H. Cruickshank. il Audubon Mag 68:86-91 Mr '66

New Zealand

New Zealand at the crossroads. F. C. Hibben. il Field & S 71:12-13+ Ag '66
Two in the bush. G. Durrell. il Harper 233:96-8 O '66

Norway

Herds of Hardangervidda. W. Page. il Field & S 71:38-41 Ag '66

Rhodesia

Wildlife and the tsetse fly in Rhodesia. A. S. Mossman. il Nat Parks Mag 40:10-15 S '66

ZOOM lenses
Matzkin on movies; power zooming. M. A. Matzkin. il Mod Phot 30:88 N '66
Matzkin on movies; zoom lenses for super 8 cameras. M. A. Matzkin. Mod Phot 30:30+ O '66
When you zoom, stop at wide-angle. M. A. Matzkin. il Mod Phot 30:84 Ap '66
Zooms for skeptics. C. W. Kennedy. il Pop Phot 59:118-21+ D '66

ZOOS. See Zoological gardens

ZOROASTRIANISM
India's prosperous Parsis. il Time 88:84 S 9 '66
Seven commandments of Zoroaster. A. S. Mehdevi. il N Y Times Mag p32-3+ Mr 27 '66

ZORZA, Victor
Arms and the Soviet Union. New Repub 156:13-15 Ja 14 '67
China: has a succession struggle begun? New Repub 154:10-11 My 28 '66
Hidden battle for power in red China. Look 30:25-8 Ag 23 '66
Rumania and Russia. New Repub 154:10-11 Je 4 '66
Truce can lead to peace in Vietnam. Look 30:22-3 D 27 '66
Why the Red guards? New Repub 155:14-15 O 8 '66

ZOYSIA grass. See Grasses

ZUCKER, Harvey
Super 35, coming soon? Pop Phot 59:40+ S '66

ZUCKERMAN, Art
Get the microphone that's right for you. Pop Mech 125:196-200+ F '66

ZUCKERMAN, Harold
College and career; questions and answers. See occasional issues of Senior scholastic

ZUCKERT, Eugene M.
Service secretary: has he a useful role? For Affairs 44:458-79 Ap '66

ZUKOFSKY, Louis
A-15; poem. Poetry 108:357-75 S '66
ZUKOWSKI, Eduard
How not to clean a painting. Am Artist 30:8 Ap '66
ZULOAGA, Guillermo
Amateur scientist; study of the salty rain of Venezuela. Sci Am 215:136-8 D '66
ZULU war, 1879
Washing of the spears, by D. R. Morris. Review
New Yorker 41:129-34 F 5 '66. A. West
ZULUS. See Africa—Native races
ZUMSTEIN, John
Reindeer find a Santa Claus. V. Kraft. il por Sports Illus 25:40-2+ D 12 '66
ZUNKEL, C. Wayne
Reply from the hills. Christian Cent 83:1010 Ag 17 '66
ZUNKER, Don. See Raeburn, G. jt. auth.
ZUPPA inglese. See Cookery, Italian
ZURAKOWSKI, Jan
Zurabatic cartwheel. P. R. Cope. il Flying 78:69 My '66
ZURICH, Switzerland

Banks

Where money talks in a hush. il Newsweek 69:54-6 Ja 9 '67

Music

Zurich. E. V. Epstein. il Opera N 30:32 Mr 26 '66
Zurich; Traviata at the Zurich opera. E. V. Epstein. il Opera N 31:30 D 17 '66
ZWAIG, N. and Lin, E. C. C.
Feedback inhibition of glycerol kinase, a catabolic enzyme in escherichia coli. bibliog Science 153: 755-7 Ag 12 '66
ZWART, Elizabeth Clarkson
Smart cook. Bet Hom & Gard 44:79 Jl '66
ZWASS, Sam
Inductor industry. Electr World 76:37 O '66
Testing and measuring inductors. Electr World 76:30-2+ S '66
Toroidal inductors. Electr World 76:38-41 O '66
ZWEIG, Ferdynand
Mass of floating anxiety. Nation 202:245-6 F 28 '66
ZWEIG, Paul
American outsider. Nation 203:517-19 N 14 '66
Gifts for the silent boy; Walking over Brooklyn; poems. Poetry 109:12-13 O '66
Pain; poem. Nation 203:330 O 3 '66
Paris falls again, into this world. Nation 202:557-9 My 9 '66
Upon seeing a frieze of Greek marbles; poem. Nation 203:652 D 12 '66

about

Land came to an end; poem. Nation 202:370 Mr 28 '66
ZWICKY, F.
Pygmy stars; first pair. bibliog Science 153:53-4 Jl 1 '66
ZYGMUND, George
Camera from Shanghai. U S Camera 29:16+ Ap '66

Gary Library - Union Inst & Univ

VERMONT COLLEGE
MONTPELIER, VT.

WITHDRAWN